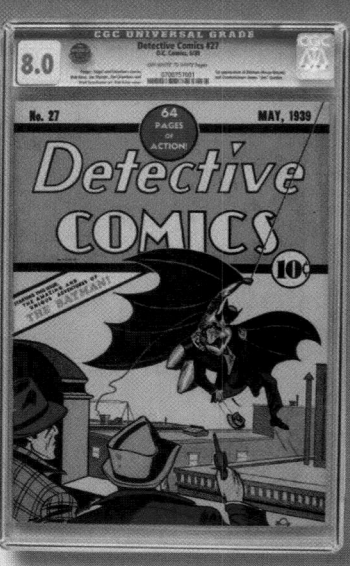

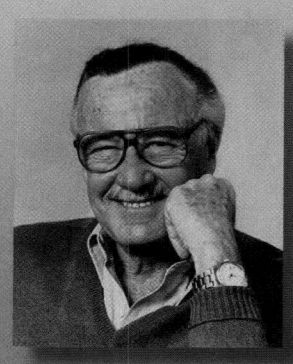

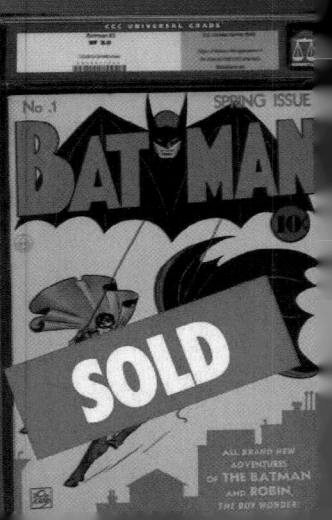

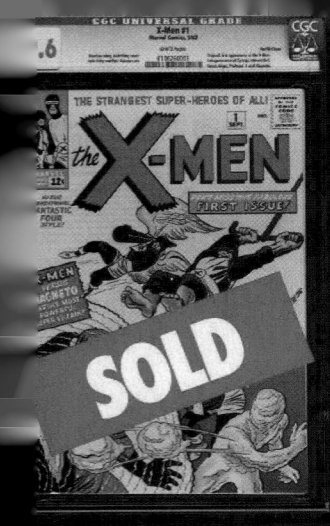

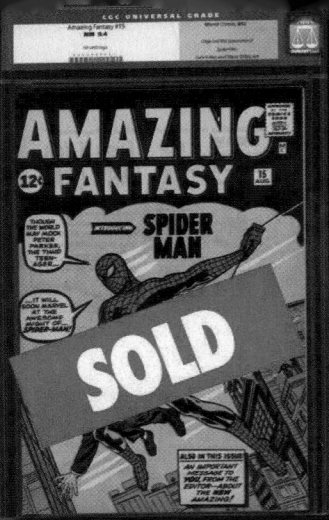

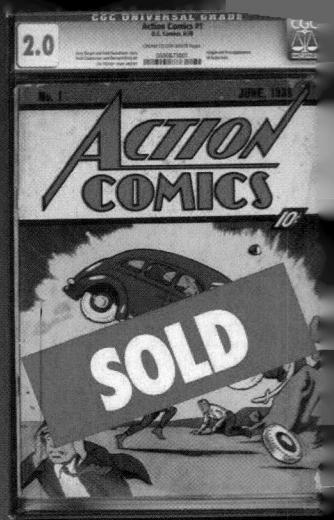

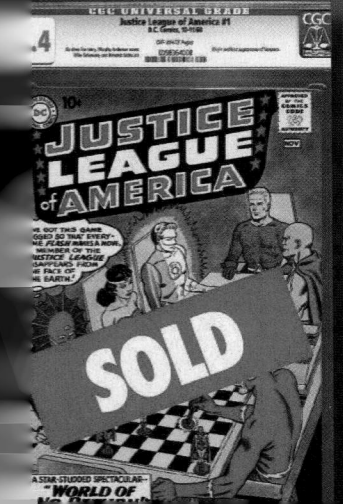

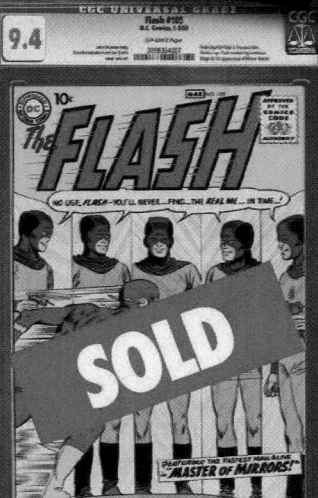

THE OVERSTREET® COMIC BOOK PRICE GUIDE

40th Anniversary Edition

COMICS FROM THE 1500s-PRESENT INCLUDED
FULLY ILLUSTRATED CATALOGUE & EVALUATION GUIDE

by ROBERT M. OVERSTREET

GEMSTONE PUBLISHING

J.C. Vaughn, Executive Editor & Associate Publisher
Mark Huesman, Creative Director & Production Coordinator
Heather Winter, Office Manager

SPECIAL CONTRIBUTORS TO THIS EDITION

Robert Beerbohm • Dr. Arnold T. Blumburg • Steve Geppi • Gene Gonzales
Jon McClure • Richard D. Olson, Ph.D. • Jim Shooter • J.C. Vaughn • Richard Samuel West

SPECIAL ADVISORS TO THIS EDITION

Grant Adey • Bill Alexander • David Alexander • Tyler Alexander • Lon Allen • David J. Anderson, DDS
Matt Ballesteros • Stephen Barrington • L.E. Becker • Robert L. Beerbohm • Dr. Arnold T. Blumberg
Steve Borock • Frank Cwiklik • Gary Dolgoff • Walter Durajlija • Ken Dyber • Bruce Ellsworth
Richard Evans • D'Arcy Farrell • Dan Fogel • Steven Gentner • Steve Geppi • Eric Groves
John Haines • Mark Haspel • Dennis Keum • Paul Litch • Keith Marlow • Dave Matteini • Jon McClure
Todd McDevitt • Steve Mortensen • Jamie Newbold • Richard D. Olson, Ph.D. • Terry O'Neill
Jim Pitts • Bill Ponseti • Mick Rabin • Greg Reece • Rob Reynolds • Dave Robie • Barry Sandoval
Matt Schiffman • Doug Schmell • Doug Simpson • Ben Smith • Mark Squirek • Al Stoltz
Doug Sulipa • Chris Swartz • Michael Tierney • Frank Verzyl • John Verzyl • Rose Verzyl
Rick Whitelock • Mike Wilbur • Harley Yee • Mark Zaid • Vincent Zurzolo, Jr.

See a full list of Overstreet Advisors on pages 1104-1107

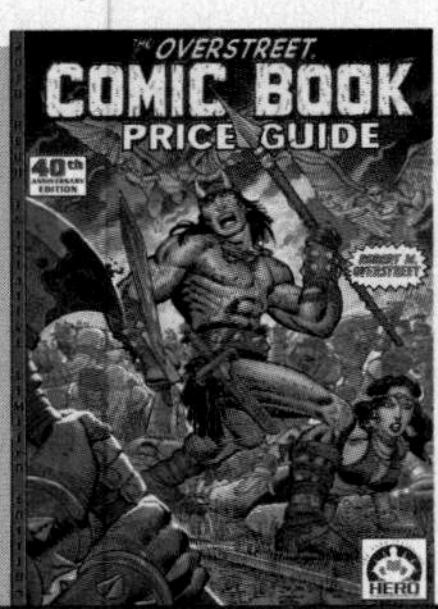

Batman Hardcover Edition ISBN: 978-1-60360-119-1
Batman Soft Cover Edition ISBN: 978-1-60360-120-7

Captain America Hardcover Edition ISBN: 978-1-60360-121-4
Captain America Soft Cover Edition ISBN: 978-1-60360-122-1

Conan the Barbarian Hardcover Edition ISBN: 978-1-60360-125-2

Printed in the United States of America

10 9 8 7 6 5 4 3 2 1

Fortieth Edition: July 2010

TABLE OF CONTENTS

ACKNOWLEDGEMENTS

Thanks to my wife, Caroline, for sharing in this landmark edition of *The Overstreet Comic Book Price Guide*.

For kicking off this 40th anniversary edition in such incredible style, I would also like to thank Mark Chiarello for his fantastic Batman cover, Darwyn Cooke for his tremendous Captain America cover, and John Romita, Jr., Klaus Janson and Dean White for their wonderful celebration of another 40th anniversary, *Conan The Barbarian* #1, which also debuted in 1970.

After a year that saw a lot of ups and downs, Mark Huesman and J.C. Vaughn worked tirelessly to make sure that the *Guide* not only came out on time, but that this anniversary year was widely recognized. Not only did they work with our various contributors, advisors, and advertisers, but they developed and executed our Free Comic Book Day publication and coordinated the promotional efforts for the *Guide* and worked with the Hero Initiative's Jim McLauchlin to facilitate the Conan cover edition.

The articles and Hall of Fame entries for this special edition were contributed by longtime dealer and historian Robert Beerbohm, our former Editor (now Curator of Geppi's Entertainment Museum) Dr. Arnold T. Blumberg, noted historian and longtime Overstreet Advisor Richard Olson, PhD, Gemstone Publishing's President and CEO (and another longtime Overstreet Advisor) Steve Geppi, historian and writer Jon McClure, frequent contributor Charles S. Novinskie, former Marvel Comics Editor-in-Chief and Overstreet Hall of Fame member Jim Shooter, J.C. Vaughn, and the "About This Book" section was once again illustrated by the fabulous Gene Gonzales.

Special Thanks to the Overstreet Advisors who contributed to this edition, including Grant Adey, Bill Alexander, David Alexander, Tyler Alexander, Lon Allen, David J. Anderson, DDS, Matt Ballesteros, Stephen Barrington, L.E. Becker, Robert L. Beerbohm, Dr. Arnold T. Blumberg, Steve Borock, Frank Cwiklik, Gary Dolgoff, Walter Durajlija, Ken Dyber, Bruce Ellsworth, Richard Evans, D'Arcy Farrell, Dan Fogel, Steven Gentner, Steve Geppi, Eric Groves, John Haines, Jim Halperin, Mark Haspel, Dennis Keum, Paul Litch, Keith Marlow, Dave Matteini, Jon McClure, Todd McDevitt, Steve Mortensen, Jamie Newbold, Richard D. Olson, Ph.D., Terry O'Neill, Jim Pitts, Bill Ponseti, Mick Rabin, Greg Reece, Rob Reynolds, Dave Robie, Barry Sandoval, Matt Schiffman, Doug Schmell, Marc Sims, Doug Simpson, Ben Smith, Mark Squirek, Al Stoltz, Doug Sulipa, Chris Swartz, Michael Tierney, Frank Verzyl, John Verzyl, Rose Verzyl, Eddie Wendt, Rick Whitelock, Mike Wilbur, Harley Yee, Mark Zaid and Vincent Zurzolo, Jr., as well as to our additional contributors, including Mark Arnold, Stephen Baer, Jonathan Bennett, Tim Berger, Jon Bevans, Jonathan Calure, Anthony Caputo, Don French, Matthew Hawes, Paul Howley, Alan Hutchinson, Mike Janis, Ben Labonog, Jason Lohr, Boyd Magers, Rod Matlack, Bill Parker, James Pender, Dennis Petilli, Lynn Potter, Patrick Simpson, Tom Trombley and Neil Young. Without their active participation, this project would not have been possible.

Additionally, I would like to personally extend my thanks to all of those who encouraged and supported first the creation of and then subsequently the expansion of the *Guide* over the past four decades. While it's impossible in this brief space to individually acknowledge every individual, mention is certainly due to Lon Allen (Golden Age data); Mark Arnold (Harvey data); Larry Bigman (Frazetta-Williamson data); Bill Blackbeard (Platinum Age cover photos); Steve Borock and Mark Haspel (Grading); Glenn Bray (Kurtzman data); Gary Carter (DC data); J. B. Clifford Jr. (EC data); Gary Coddington (Superman data); Gary Colabuono (Golden Age ashcan data); Wilt Conine (Fawcett data); Chris Cormier (Miracleman data); Dr. S. M. Davidson (Cupples & Leon data); Al Dellinges (Kubert data); Stephen Fishler (10-Point Grading system); Chris Friesen (Glossary additions); David Gerstein (Walt Disney Comics data); Gene Gonzales (introduction illustrations); Kevin Hancer (Tarzan data); Charles Heffelfinger and Jim Ivey (March of Comics listing); R. C. Holland and Ron Pussell (Seduction and Parade of Pleasure data); Grant Irwin (Quality data); Richard Kravitz (Kelly data); Phil Levine (giveaway data); Paul Litch (Copper & Modern Age data); Dan Malan & Charles Heffelfinger (Classic Comics data); Jon McClure (Whitman data); Fred Nardelli (Frazetta data); Michelle Nolan (Love comics); Mike Nolan (MLJ, Timely, Nedor data); George Olshevsky (Timely data); Dr. Richard Olson (Grading and Yellow Kid info); Chris Pedrin (DC War data); Scott Pell ('50s data); Greg Robertson (National data); Don Rosa (Late 1940s to 1950s data); Matt Schiffman (Bronze Age data); Frank Scigliano (Little Lulu data); Gene Seger (Buck Rogers data); Rick Sloane (Archie data); David R. Smith, Archivist, Walt Disney Productions (Disney data); Bill Spicer and Zetta DeVoe (Western Publishing Co. data); Tony Starks (Silver and Bronze Age data); Al Stoltz (Golden Age & Promo data); Doug Sulipa (Bronze Age data); Don and Maggie Thompson (Four Color listing); Mike Tiefenbacher & Jerry Sinkovec (Atlas and National data); Raymond True & Philip J. Gaudino (Classic Comics data); Jim Vadeboncoeur Jr. (Williamson and Atlas data); Richard Samuel West (Victorian Age and Platinum Age data); Kim Weston (Disney and Barks data); Cat Yronwode (Spirit data); Andrew Zerbe and Gary Behymer (M. E. data).

Finally, thanks, as always, to our advertisers, whose support makes this project possible, and to all of you who have purchased this edition.

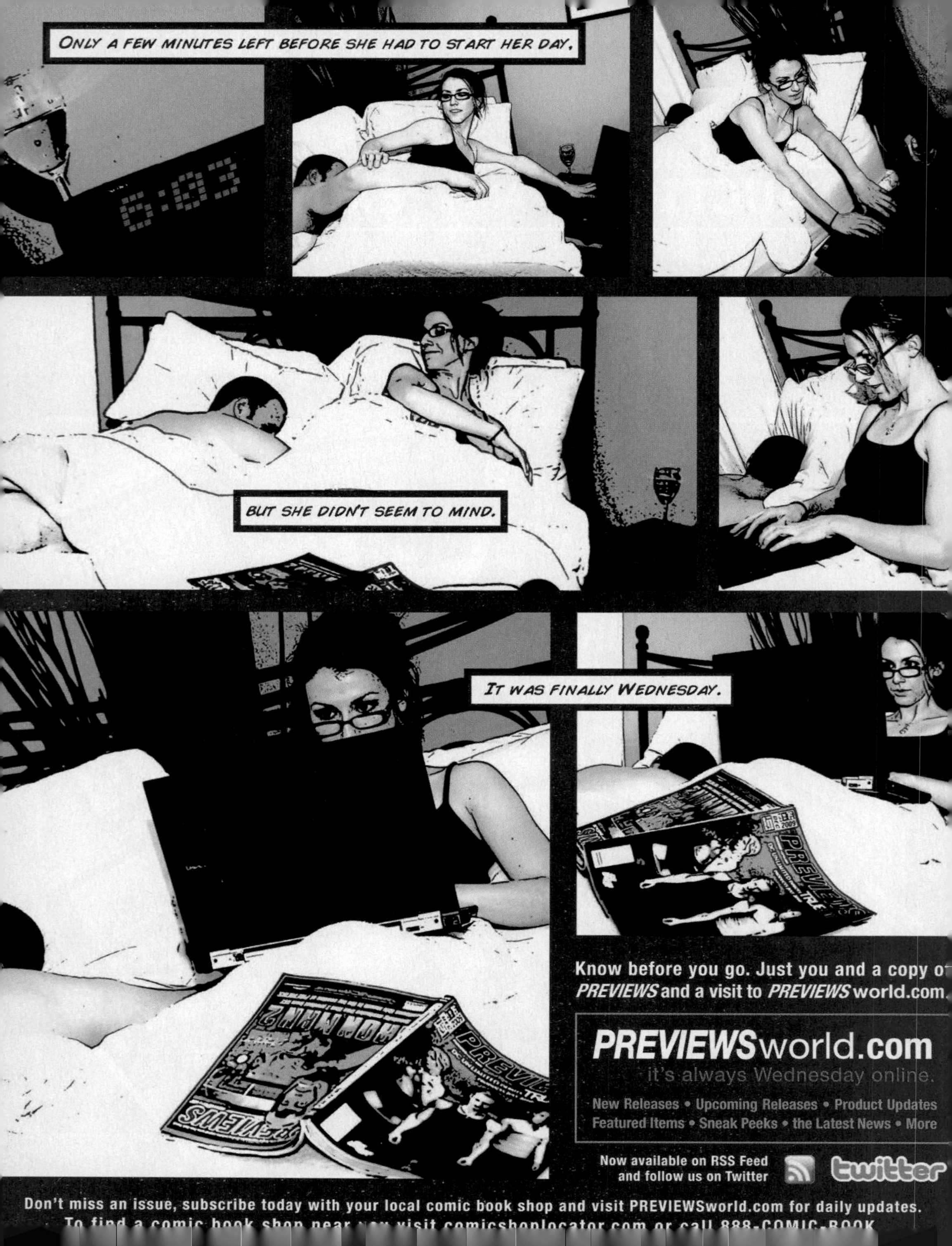

ONLY A FEW MINUTES LEFT BEFORE SHE HAD TO START HER DAY.

6:03

BUT SHE DIDN'T SEEM TO MIND.

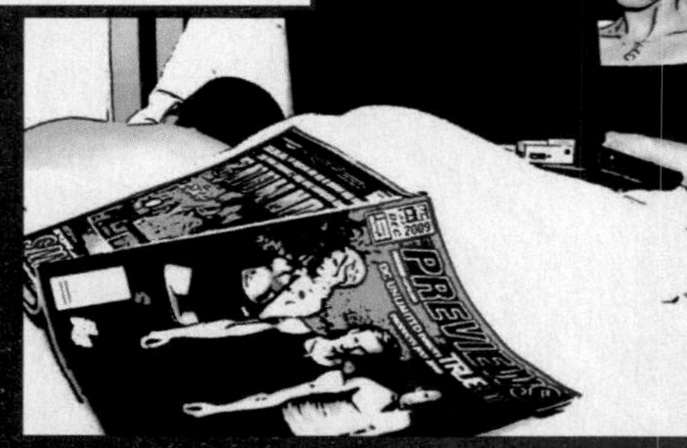

TOY STORY 3 OPENS JUNE 18, 2010!

TOY STORY: MYSTERIOUS STRANGER
SC $9.99 ISBN 9781934506912
HC $24.99 ISBN 9781608865239

TOY STORY: THE RETURN OF BUZZ LIGHTYEAR
SC $9.99 ISBN 9781608865574
HC $24.99 ISBN 9781608865581

FINDING NEMO: REEF RESCUE
SC $9.99 ISBN 9781934506882
HC $24.99 ISBN 9781608865246

THE INCREDIBLES: FAMILY MATTERS
SC $9.99 ISBN 9781934506837
HC $24.99 ISBN 9781608865253

THE MUPPET SHOW COMIC BOOK: MEET THE MUPPETS
SC $9.99 ISBN 9781934506851
HC $24.99 ISBN 9781608865277

CARS: THE ROOKIE
SC $9.99 ISBN 9781934506844
HC $24.99 ISBN 9781608865222

MUPPET ROBIN HOOD
SC $9.99 ISBN 9781934506790
HC $24.99 ISBN 9781608865260

THE LIFE AND TIMES OF SCROOGE MCDUCK VOL. 1
VOLUME 1 OF 2
HC $24.99 ISBN 9781608865383

CASH BUYER!!!

hey, you got that new $40 trade....?

I wish I sold some of this stuff to Neat Stuff, then I could find it.

Don't let the unsold clutter hurt your business!

Buying Store Backstock!

- New Comics and Toys
- Vintage Comics and Toys
- Corporate Overstocks
- Personal Collections, Original Art, Sports and Movie Stuff, ALL COLLECTIBLES !

We make it easy for you to make money!

- Big $$$ on hand for any size purchase!
- We travel to your warehouse or home
- We remove and buy everything you have
- References from dozens of large dealers available

MAKE MORE MONEY, LET ME PAY YOUR RENT!
FINDERS FEE $$$ paid for ANY referrals -
If collectors call you to sell, call me!

CALL BRIAN NOW
1-800-730-3954

Email Address : buyingeverything@yahoo.com
TEXT MESSAGE at 201-923-1230

704 76th Street, North Bergen NJ 07047

Phil Hester • Michael Broussard
THE DARKNESS: ACCURSED VOLUME 1

Ron Marz • Mike Choi
WITCHBLADE VOLUME 1

Join the Top Cow Universe with these introductory priced trades.

$4.99 Trades

Let Us Win YOU Over!

www.topcow.com

BY CROM!
ET THEE ONE!

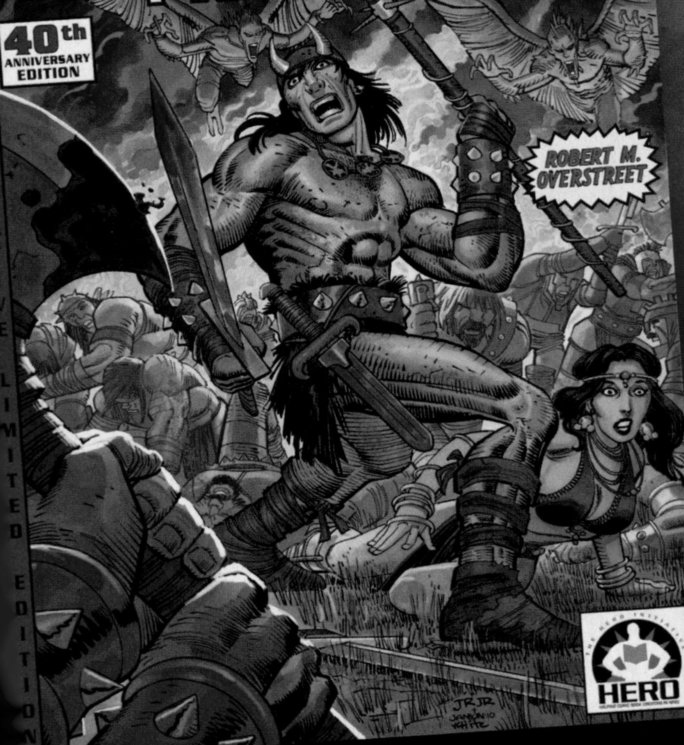

$35

OVERSTREET® COMIC
OK PRICE GUIDE #40

ro Initiative exclusive limited edition, **500 hardcover copies ONLY**
m the Hero Initiative at Comic-Con International: San Diego July 21, 2010
niversary Conan cover art by John Romita Jr., Klaus Janson, and Dean White

For the next generation of Radical content visit...
WWW.RADICALPUBLISHING.COM

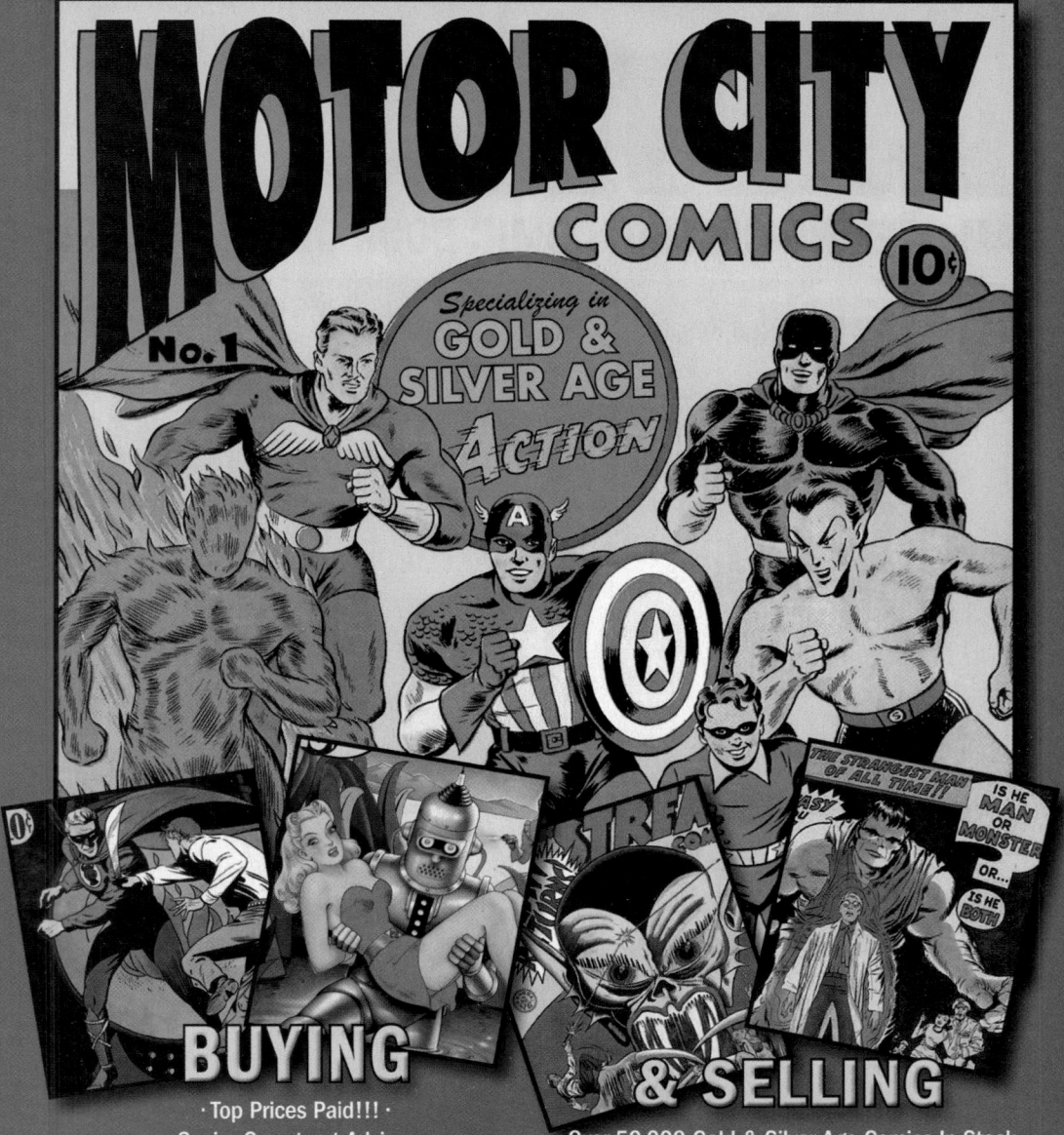

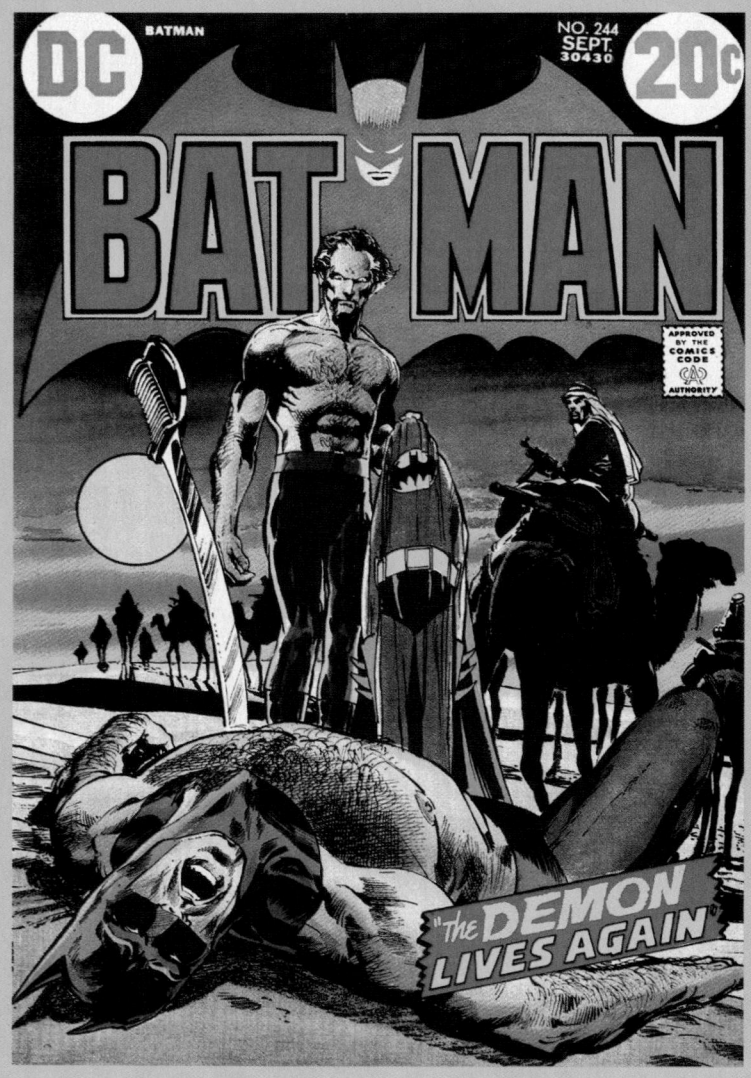

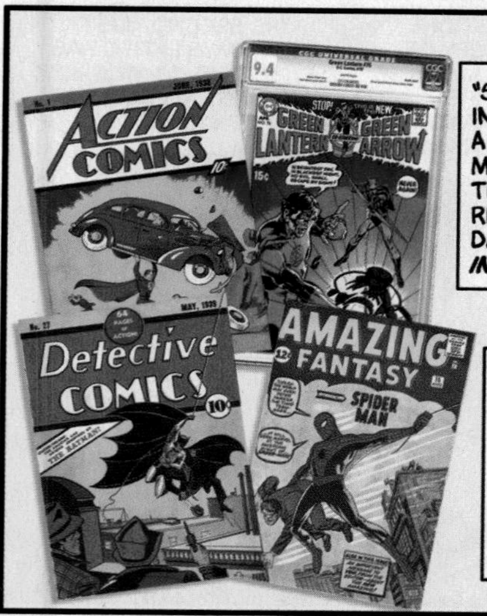

"SINCE THE *GUIDE*'S DEBUT IN 1970, THERE HAVE BEEN A LOT OF CHANGES IN THE MARKETPLACE. FOR INSTANCE, THERE HAVE ALWAYS BEEN RECORD PRICES, BUT THESE DAYS THEY CAN MAKE ***INTERNATIONAL NEWS...***"

"WHEN YOU KEEP UP WITH ***RECORD PRICES***, WHAT'S ***SELLING***, WHAT'S ***NOT*** SELLING, AND WHAT'S SUDDENLY ***IN DEMAND***, IT HELPS YOU KNOW WHAT YOU SHOULD BE WILLING TO PAY OR WHEN TO SELL."

ONE OF THE COOL THINGS ABOUT COMIC BOOKS IS THAT THERE ARE LOTS OF NEW ONES TO DISCOVER...

AND THERE ARE LITERALLY HUNDREDS OF THOUSANDS OF DIFFERENT BACK ISSUES, TOO!

BACK ISSUE COMICS RANGE FROM LESS THAN COVER PRICE TO **$1,000,000.**
A COMIC BOOK FOR, ***$1 MILLION?*** HARD TO BELIEVE, HUH?

THE FIRST ONE WAS A COPY OF ***ACTION COMICS #1,*** THE FIRST APPEARANCE OF ***SUPERMAN.***
THE SECOND, JUST A FEW DAYS LATER, WAS ***DETECTIVE COMICS #27,*** THE FIRST APPEARANCE OF ***BATMAN.***

MANY OTHERS HAVE SOLD FOR RECORD PRICES IN THE LAST YEAR OR SO, EVEN WITH THE TOUGH ECONOMY NATIONALLY.

BE SURE TO CHECK OUT OUR MARKET REPORTS FOR OBSERVATIONS FROM OUR OVERSTREET ADVISORS.

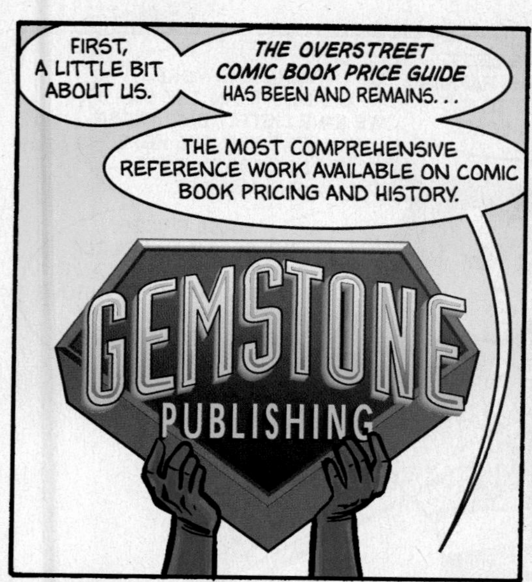

FIRST, A LITTLE BIT ABOUT US.
THE OVERSTREET COMIC BOOK PRICE GUIDE HAS BEEN AND REMAINS. . .
THE MOST COMPREHENSIVE REFERENCE WORK AVAILABLE ON COMIC BOOK PRICING AND HISTORY.
GEMSTONE PUBLISHING

IT'S RESPECTED AND USED BY DEALERS AND COLLECTORS EVERYWHERE.
OVERSTREET PRICING AND GRADING STANDARDS ARE THE ACCEPTED FOUNDATIONS OF THE COMIC BOOK MARKETPLACE AROUND THE WORLD.
THROUGH HARD WORK, DILIGENCE AND CONSTANT CONTACT WITH THE MARKET FOR DECADES, OVERSTREET HAS BECOME THE MOST TRUSTED NAME IN COMICS.

OUR BOOK IS A DETAILED ALPHABETICAL LIST OF COMIC BOOKS AND THEIR MARKET VALUES.

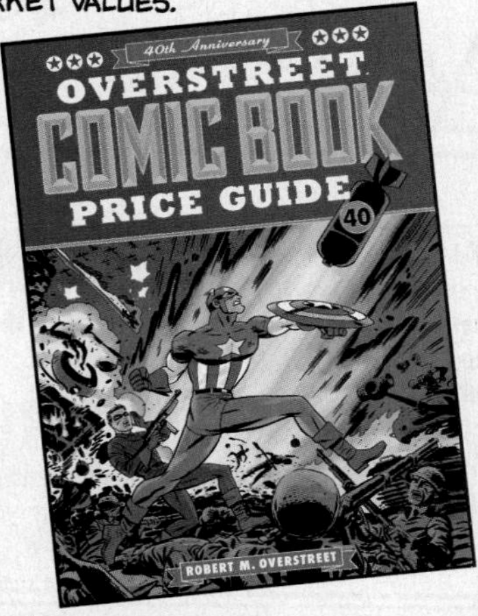

COMIC BOOKS ARE LISTED BY TITLE.
YOU KNOW. . .
ALPHABETICALLY, REGARDLESS OF PUBLISHER.
A
B
C

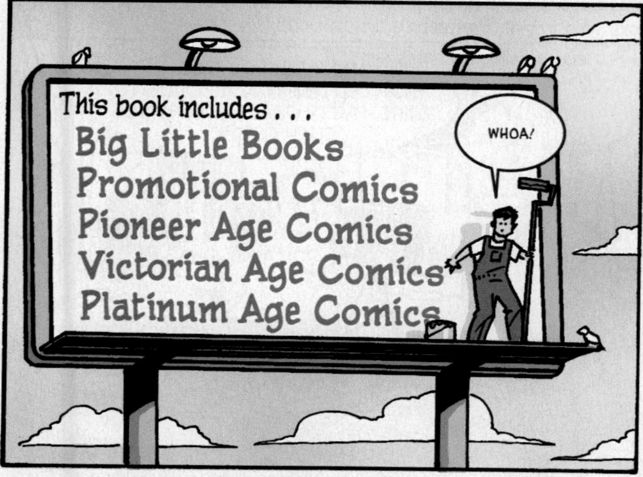

This book includes . . .
Big Little Books
Promotional Comics
Pioneer Age Comics
Victorian Age Comics
Platinum Age Comics
WHOA!

THE MAIN PRICING SECTION FEATURES COMICS FROM 1938 THROUGH THE PRESENT!

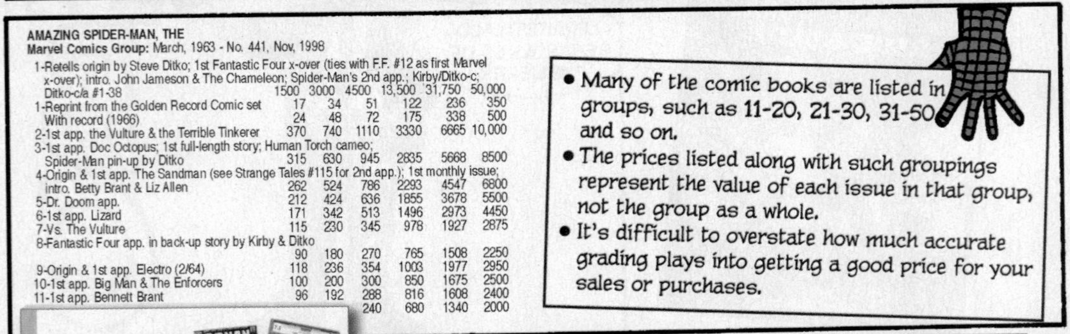

9.2
9.0
8.5
8.0
7.5
7.0
6.5
6.0
5.5
5.0
4.5
4.0
3.5
3.0
2.5
2.0

PRICES ARE LISTED IN SIX GRADES, RANGING FROM 2.0 TO 9.2 ON A 10.0 SCALE.

THERE ARE MORE GRADES THAN THE SIX WE HAVE LISTED, BUT THESE WILL GIVE YOU THE KEYS TO UNDERSTANDING THE MARKET.

WHILE PRICES BELOW 9.2 ARE FAIRLY STEADY, IT'S IMPORTANT TO NOTE THAT PRICES ABOVE 9.2 ARE FREQUENTLY CONSIDERED EXTREMELY VOLATILE.

AMAZING SPIDER-MAN, THE
Marvel Comics Group: March, 1963 - No. 441, Nov, 1998

1-Retells origin by Steve Ditko; 1st Fantastic Four x-over (ties with F.F. #12 as first Marvel x-over); intro. John Jameson & The Chameleon; Spider-Man's 2nd app.; Kirby/Ditko-c; Ditko-c/a #1-38	1500	3000	4500	13,500	31,750	50,000
1-Reprint from the Golden Record Comic set	17	34	51	122	236	350
With record (1966)	24	48	72	175	338	500
2-1st app. the Vulture & the Terrible Tinkerer	370	740	1110	3330	6665	10,000
3-1st app. Doc Octopus; 1st full-length story; Human Torch cameo; Spider-Man pin-up by Ditko	315	630	945	2835	5668	8500
4-Origin & 1st app. The Sandman (see Strange Tales #115 for 2nd app.); 1st monthly issue; intro. Betty Brant & Liz Allen	262	524	786	2293	4547	6800
5-Dr. Doom app.	212	424	636	1855	3678	5500
6-1st app. Lizard	171	342	513	1496	2973	4450
7-Vs. The Vulture	115	230	345	978	1927	2875
8-Fantastic Four app. in back-up story by Kirby & Ditko	90	180	270	765	1508	2250
9-Origin & 1st app. Electro (2/64)	118	236	354	1003	1977	2950
10-1st app. Big Man & The Enforcers	100	200	300	850	1675	2500
11-1st app. Bennett Brant	96	192	288	816	1608	2400
			240	680	1340	2000

- Many of the comic books are listed in groups, such as 11-20, 21-30, 31-50 and so on.
- The prices listed along with such groupings represent the value of each issue in that group, not the group as a whole.
- It's difficult to overstate how much accurate grading plays into getting a good price for your sales or purchases.

THE DEFINITIVE GUIDE TO GRADING COMIC BOOKS!
OFFICIAL
OVERSTREET® COMIC BOOK GRADING GUIDE
THIRD EDITION
FEATURING THE 10 POINT GRADING SYSTEM!
ROBERT M. OVERSTREET AND DR. ARNOLD T. BLUMBERG
HOUSE OF COLLECTIBLES

It's a good practice to develop relationships with dealers and other collectors who prove themselves trustworthy.

MANY PEOPLE HAVE STARTED USING INDEPENDENT, THIRD-PARTY GRADING SERVICES, SUCH AS CGC.

HEY, SOMEONE TOOK A BITE OUT OF THIS COMIC!

WHAT'S THE FIRST APPEARANCE OF WOLVERINE?
I THINK IT WAS INCREDIBLE HULK #181, BUT LET'S LOOK IT UP IN OVERSTREET.
COMIC BOOK

DID BRIAN BENDIS OR GEOFF JOHNS WRITE IT?
NO, THAT WAS BEFORE THEY WROTE EVERYTHING.
HERE IT IS. WOLVERINE HAD A BRIEF APPEARANCE AT THE END OF #180 AND SHOWED UP FOR REAL IN #181.

MANY FIRST APPEARANCES AND OTHER IMPORTANT ISSUES ARE NOTED.
Detective COMICS
CONAN THE BARBARIAN
PEP COMICS

WHAT ABOUT THE 34TH APPEARANCE OF GOAT RIDER?
UH, NO.
COMIC BOOK

IT IS IMPORTANT TO UNDERSTAND THAT VALUES LISTED IN THIS BOOK ARE APPROXIMATIONS OR GUIDELINES, PRESENTING AN AVERAGE RANGE OF WHAT ONE MIGHT EXPECT TO PAY FOR THE CORRESPONDING ITEMS.

THAT'S A COMPLICATED WAY OF SAYING "IT'S A GUIDE, NOT A PRICE LIST." IN THE MARKETPLACE, BUYERS AND SELLERS DETERMINE PRICES ASKED AND PRICES PAID.

WITH INPUT FROM A NETWORK OF EXPERIENCED ADVISORS INCLUDING WELL ESTABLISHED COLLECTORS, DEALERS AND HISTORIANS OF POPULAR CULTURE, WE HAVE UNDERTAKEN SIGNIFICANT EFFORT TO ASSEMBLE THIS PRICING INFORMATION.

THE RESULTING LISTINGS COME THROUGH THE OBSERVATION AND DOCUMENTATION OF PRICES REALIZED THROUGH HOBBY AND TRADE SHOWS, CATALOG SALES, RETAIL SALES, AND INTERNET, LIVE AND MAIL-IN AUCTIONS. DOCUMENTED PERSONAL SALES MAY ALSO BE INCLUDED.

WE HAVE EARNED OUR REPUTATION FOR OUR CAUTIOUS, CONSERVATIVE APPROACH TO PRICING.

WE ACTIVELY ENCOURAGE READERS WHO BELIEVE THEY HAVE DISCOVERED AN ERROR TO MAIL RELATED INFORMATION TO THE AUTHOR.
WRITE TO: ROBERT M. OVERSTREET GEMSTONE PUBLISHING, INC. 1966 GREENSPRING DRIVE TIMONIUM, MD 21093
OR EMAIL FEEDBACK@GEMSTONEPUB.COM
VERIFIED CORRECTIONS WILL BE INCORPORATED INTO FUTURE EDITIONS OF THIS BOOK.
Editor's note: For more updates, visit *Scoop* at http://scoop.diamondgalleries.com.

BAD ECONOMY, RESILIENT COMIC MARKET?
STORMS OF 2009 SET UP RECORD-BREAKING 2010

by Robert M. Overstreet

On February 22, 2010, the first $1 million comic was sold, an 8.0 ***Action Comics*** *#1.*
It was followed by an 8.0 ***Detective Comics*** *#27 ($1,075,500) and on March 30 by an 8.5* ***Action Comics*** *#1 ($1,500,000).*
In that same period a 9.6 copy of ***Flash Comics*** *#1 hit $450,000.*

The Financial crisis of 2008-2009 changed forever the banking structure of this country. Lehman Brothers went out of business, Merrill Lynch and Bear Stearns were sold at liquidation prices and Fannie Mae and Freddy Mac were placed into conservatorship by the U.S. government in September 2008. Also the insurance giant AIG, who insured many of the failed banks toxic loans, defaulted and was taken over by the federal government that same month.

Furthermore, with the steep decline in the economy during this time and millions of workers being laid off, the car industry imploded with the U.S. government becoming shareholders of General Motors, and forcing the sale of Chrysler to Fiat at a salvage price. Hundreds of car dealerships across the country went out of business.

This 2008-2009 faltering of the U.S. economy spread all over the world and has been dubbed by the President "the worst crash since 1929." The unemployment rate reached double-digits (higher than 17% when we count the people who have simply stopped looking for work) while the U.S. government kept spending and dumping cash into the economic system in an attempt to soften or slow down its decline.

With all the bad economic news permeating the media outlets month after month, one might think the comics market would have suffered a dramatic decline as well, but this is not the case. As noted by one of our advisors Eric Groves, "Despite the turmoil of the times, we perceive no loss of passion in the comic collecting community. The spirit is willing, though the wallet may be weak." Other advisors such as Walter Durajlija and Marc Sims of Big B Comics write, "The retail comic book market and the collectible comic book market both showed tremendous resiliency in 2009." Terry O'Neill of Terry's Comics writes, "Sales from 2008 to 2009 have been mixed but not too bad, despite the economic slowdown."

$1 Million Babies: During the last year, there has been no shortage of record prices set. The last week of February 2010 saw two comics break the mythic $1 million barrier.

First, on Monday, February 22, ComicConnect.com sold an CGC-certified 8.0 copy of *Action Comics* #1 for $1,000,000. Then, on Thursday, February 25, a CGC-certified 8.0 copy of *Detective Comics* #27 offered by Heritage Auction Galleries closed at $1,075,500.

These prices are amazing, and they certainly garnered much attention from the mainstream media, but the foundation has long been in place for rare, high-grade, vintage comics to reach this level.

So, perhaps it's not surprising then that a CGC-certified 8.5 copy of *Action Comics* #1 was sold a little more than a month later for a reported $1.5 million by ComicConnect. It has likewise been reported that the owner of the Mile High copy of this issue, which to date has not been certified by CGC, passed on an offer of double the price of the 8.5 (it has been speculated that Mile High copy would grade 9.2 or 9.4, but of course this is precisely that, speculation).

High-grade copies of such comics as *Amazing Fantasy* #15, *Detective Comics* #27, *Batman* #1, *Superman* #1, and other copies of *Action Comics* #1 first broke and then sustained six-figure prices over a period of years. *Incredible Hulk* #1 joined that group late last year. In March 2010, a 9.6 copy of *Flash Comics* #1 sold through Heritage for $450,000 (the same copy sold in January 2006 for $273,125) and there are others waiting in the wings. In all of these cases, of course, condition was very important in determining the price realized.

In the case of *Action Comics* #1, most industry experts agree that there are about 100 copies of this issue. If we're wrong and there turn out to be 200 copies, this would still be an amazing purchase. We live in a nation of more than 300 million people and Superman is the most recognized character in the world. *Action Comics* #1 will always be in high demand, particularly the better the grade.

Likewise, the first appearance of Batman in *Detective Comics* #27 is an appealing purchase as well. With the strong box office performance of *Batman Begins* (2005) and phenomenal success of *The Dark Knight* (2008), it seems safe to suggest that more people than ever are at least aware of Batman, and that if even a small percentage of those people are interested in acquiring the character's first appearance this will also turn out to be a smart investment.

If these sales stand the test of time – and it seems likely they will – someday, in the not-too-distant future, it may be difficult for high end collectors and investors to remember what a watershed moment this week was for collecting. To break the $1 million threshold and to do so twice in a span of four days sends a definite signal. The strength and liquidity of rare, vintage, collectible comic books is clearly accepted even in otherwise bleak economic times.

Other Record-Breakers: Those record-breaking purchases did not happen in a vacuum. As mentioned earlier, comic books have been selling for record prices: the large Heritage comic book and original art auction held in November 2008 produced record sales with top prices being paid for key books. In this auction, a *Batman* #1 in CGC 3.0 sold for $19,120; an *Archie Comics* #1 in CGC 7.0 brought $38,837; in 4.0 sold for $8,962. Barry Sandoval of Heritage Auction Galleries wrote "we have clients lined up to bid on any other copies that might surface. And the same is true for #2-10." A *Mickey Mouse Four Color* #16 in CGC 9.2 fetched $65,725; a *Donald Duck Four Color* #9 in CGC 9.4 for $31,070; a *Donald Duck Four Color* #29 in CGC 9.0 for $17,925; a *Walt Disney's Comics & Stories* #1 in CGC 9.4 brought a record $116,512! Silver Age books sold include *Amazing Fantasy* #15, CGC 6.0 for $13,145, *Amazing Spider-Man* #1 in CGC 9.4 for $83,650; #5 in CGC 9.4 for $19,250, *Avengers* #4 in CGC 9.6 for $64,000, a #1 in CGC 8.0 for $11,352! In February 2009, Pedigree Comics sold an *Amazing Fantasy* #15, CGC 9.2 for a record $190,000.

The trend of record prices included an *Action Comics* #1 in CGC 6.0 sold for a record $317,200 in ComicConnect's March 2009 auction. Until the $1 million mark was reached, this stood for 11 months as the top price paid for a comic book. The sale was covered in the prestigious *Forbes Magazine*, on Yahoo, CNN, Google News, MSNBC, Fox News and many other media outlets, and a CGC 2.5 copy in a separate auction brought $121,000. Obviously this sort of media focus continued for the two issues that topped $1 million. The company's Rob Reynolds also reported, "a CGC 1.8 GD- hammered for a record $94,001. *Action* #7 (the second Superman cover) is becoming much sought after with a copy in CGC 7.0 bringing a record $47,800!

Other key books continued to set records: A *Captain Marvel Adventures* #1 in CGC 4.0 for $11,352, in CGC 7.0 for $4,780, a *Detective* #27 in CGC 1.5 sold for $83,650. The *Marvel Comics* #1 (Denver copy) in CGC 8.5 sold for $155,350 in February 2009, but previously sold for $172,500 in 2005. *Marvel Mystery* #9 in 9.4 for $107,550, #10 in 9.4 for $31,070; *Incredible Hulk* #1 in CGC 8.5 for $36,000, #181 in CGC 9.8 for $26,290, *Showcase* #4 in CGC 9.6 brings an unbelievable $179,250 and *Tales Of Suspense* #39 in CGC 9.2 fetched $31,000 and in CGC 8.5 for $16,757, *Tales To Astonish* #27 in CGC 9.2 for $32,500.

The Heritage November 2009 auction was their fourth best ever, taking in $4.8 million. Golden Age sales in this and other auctions were mixed depending on title and grade. Although some books brought less than expected, there were record sales that occurred as follows: *Action Comics* #17 in CGC 6.5 for $5,078; *Amazing Fantasy* #15 in CGC 8.5 for $104,562, in 8.0 for $52,281, in 7.0 for $28,680, in 6.5 for $20,315; *Amazing Spider-Man* #1 in CGC 9.4 for $104,200. *Archie Comics* #4 in CGC 7.5 for $6,572; *Captain Marvel* #1 in CGC 5.0 for $10,157; *Detective* #31 (Crippen "D" copy) in CGC 5.5 for $26,290; *Donald Duck Four Color* #4 in CGC 8.0 for $19,120; *Human Torch* #2(#1) in CGC 9.4 for $92,612; *Incredible Hulk* #1 in CGC 9.2 for $125,475, in 9.0 for $100,000; *Jackpot* #4 in CGC 9.2 for $11,950; *Mickey Mouse Four Color* #16 in CGC 9.2 for $50,787; *More Fun* #67 in CGC 9.4 for $26,290; *Police Comics* #1 in CGC 9.4 for $31,070; *Showcase* #22 in CGC 9.0 for $59,750; *Superman* #14 in CGC 7.5 for $8,365; *Uncle Scrooge Four Color* #386 in CGC 9.4 for $23,900.

Rob Reynolds of ComicConnect reported, "The Silver Age and Bronze Age of comic books saw plenty of records fall in the Event Auctions as well. The *Green Lantern* #76 CGC 9.6 NM+ sold at $30,500 and sent a strong message to collectors and dealers alike that the Bronze Age market had come into its own."

Douglas Schmell, whose Pedigree Comics specializes in CGC-certified 1960s and 1970s comics, wrote, "On rare, highest graded material, particularly from the Silver Age, we have seen an incredible number of new, record-breaking sales here. This is where the auction format works at its best, as all you need are at

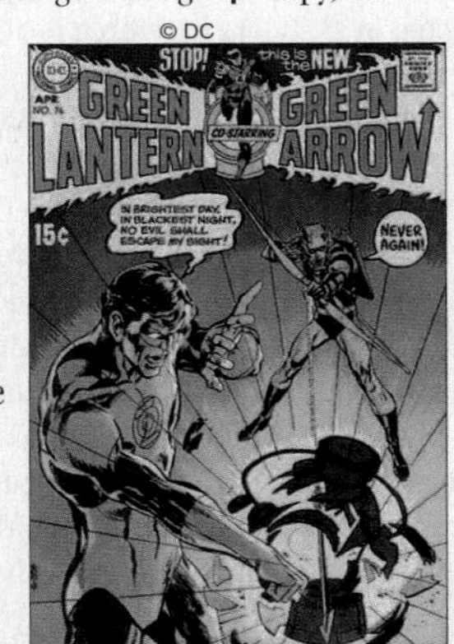

The sale of a **Green Lantern** #76 CGC-certified 9.6 for $30,500 - more proof that the Bronze Age market had come into its own.

least two bidders aggressively interested and bidding on the same book, and the end result is an often times astonishing final bid. We have run four Grand Auctions in 2009 with total sales well over $3 million."

Key issues from all periods continue to be bought and sold as well as books from the top pedigree collections such as Gaines, Mile High, River City, Larson, San Francisco, Northford, and others.

eBay: All of this success with rare, high-grade, vintage issues has not been seen across the board, though. Many Overstreet Advisors and other dealers have reported that they have had to work very hard to move mid-grade comics, particularly through venues like eBay.

As reported by Al Stoltz, "...we have almost 7,000 items listed in it for sale, but sales have not regained the strength they had a little over a year ago before the economic collapse." Ken Dyber of Cloud Nine Comics wrote, "Most books (on eBay) unless they are high-grade Silver Age books are not only selling below *Guide*, but often well below." Todd McDevitt noted, "It seems eBay buyers are almost always bargain hunters."

Silver Age keys like **Incredible Hulk #1** brought record prices in 2009. A CGC-certified 9.2 sold for $125,475

Comic Conventions: The convention season is longer than ever! 2009 began with the New York Comic Con and the Orlando, FL MegaCon in February, which were both well attended and sales were brisk. Then San Francisco WonderCon in February-March followed by the Pittsburgh Comicon in April. In June the Wizard World East in Philadelphia, PA was held. In July, the giant Comic-Con International: San Diego with over 126,000 attendees was held. Wizard World Chicago, GenCon in Indianapolis and the Canadian National Comic Book Expo of Toronto were held in August. September brought DragonCon in Atlanta. They were followed by the Baltimore Comic-Con, Boston Comic Con and New York Big Apple Con. In November, the long-running Virginia Comic-Con expanded to its first two-day show in Richmond.

When attending conventions, the collector has the opportunity to actually see and handle those books sought before buying, as well as being able to compare prices before committing and finally negotiating a better price, especially if multiple copies of the same book are available on the floor. This year brought the addition of the new Chicago show, known as C2E2, from Reed Exhibitions, the company who has had the New York Comic Con, one of the largest events in the Big Apple. According to Crain's, it already has outdrawn the New York Marathon. Additionally, with Wizard's Gareb Shamus lining up a whole slate of new conventions, it will be interesting to see the impact on convention-goers, dealers and the marketplace as a whole.

Movies: One of our advisors, Chris Swartz wrote, "The trend for strong comics sales in conjunction with movie releases will continue. They remain highly desired by collectors as the dates for those movies releases grow close. Comics related to *Iron Man 2*, *Captain America*, *The Avengers*, *Jonah Hex*, and *Green Lantern* are sought out by buyers. Key appearances will always be the most sought after." We have already had reports of some consignors holding back early *Journey Into Mystery* issues in anticipation of the *Thor* feature film.

Summary: The 2009 comic market showed thousands of books sold, some with record prices, others at or below *Guide* list. It is becoming more obvious that demand for the top key Golden Age and Silver Age books in all grades has been solid. *Action Comics* #1, complete, in any grade was selling for well over *Guide*. The same for *All-American Comics* #16, *Detective Comics* #27, *Batman* #1 and *Superman* #1. Top Silver Age keys such as *Amazing Fantasy* #15, *Amazing Spider-Man* #1, *Fantastic Four* #1, *Incredible Hulk* #1, *Avengers* #1, *Tales of Suspense* #39 also broke records. Late in the year, mixed issues of *Tales of Suspense* #40-up from the White Mountain collection in 9.0 and higher sold for high multiples over *Guide*, Examples were #58 in CGC 9.4 for $5975 and #63 in CGC 9.6 for $10,755. DC Silver Age titles which have always been rare in high grade, such as *The Flash*, *Brave and the Bold*, *Green Lantern*, *Justice League* and *Showcase* sold for multiples of *Guide* list in 9.0 and above grades.

As Steve Mortensen of Colossus Comics pointed out, "2010 looks as if it will be another impressive year," and Al Stoltz of Basement Comics wrote, "The economy is slowly climbing back up and orders for comics in mid-November and December carry onto 2010...and keep comics rolling for another 40 years." Terry O'Neill wrote, "In summary, despite the worst recession of my lifetime this past year, we have managed to maintain generally good sales." Dave Anderson reported, "The bottom line is that desirable, high demand titles will continue to sell well and for strong above *Guide* prices, whereas commonly seen, lower grade, less desirable comics will sell below *Guide*." Harley Yee said, "I think that 2010 will continue the trends of 2009 with high grade CGC or non-CGC Silver Age DCs and Marvels, Golden Age DCs, Timelys, early Archies, early Disneys and ECs staying hot." He continued, "I do a lot of conventions all over the country and sales were generally up..." Matt Schiffman added, "Overall the strength of the comic hobby is as strong as ever."

2009 again showed thousands of price changes, mostly positive, reflected in this edition. Please refer to individual listings which include these changes.

The following market reports were submitted from some of our many advisors and are published here for your information only. The opinions in these reports belong to each contributor and do not necessarily reflect the views of the publisher or the staff of *The Overstreet Comic Book Price Guide* or Gemstone Publishing.

See you next time!

PRICES: 1970 vs. TODAY

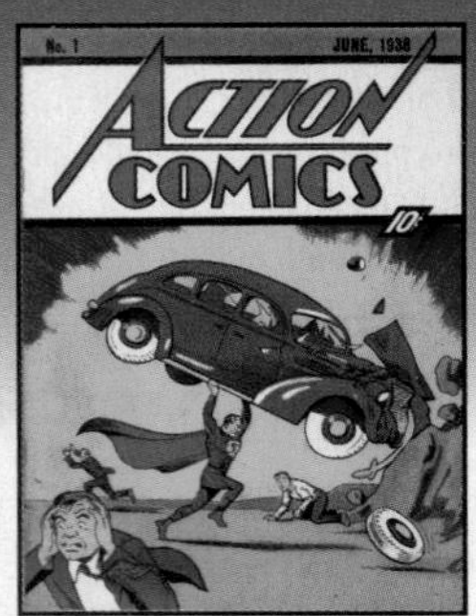

Action Comics #1
First appearance of Superman
1970 Mint Price: $300
2010 NM– Price: $1,200,000

Detective Comics #27
First appearance of Batman
1970 Mint Price: $275
2010 NM– Price: $1,050,000

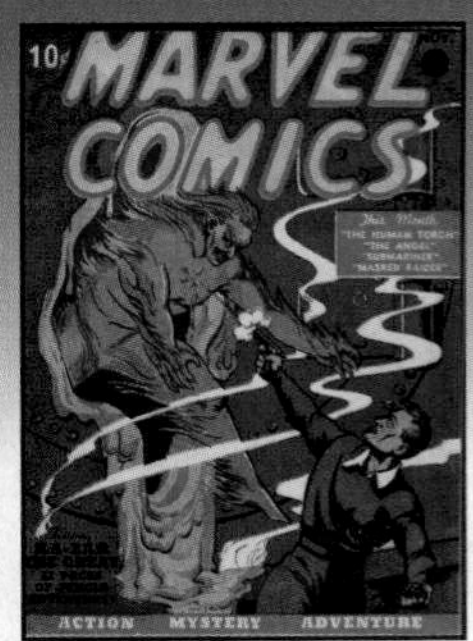

Marvel Comics #1
First Sub-Mariner and Human Torch
1970 Mint Price: $250
2010 NM– Price: $450,000

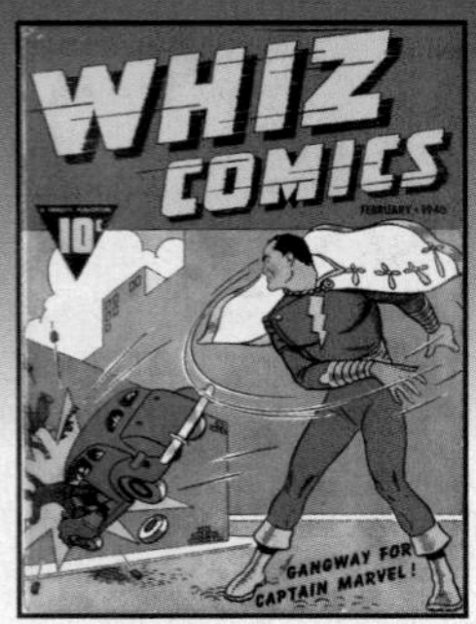

Whiz Comics #1 (#2)
First appearance of Captain Marvel
1970 Mint Price: $235
2010 NM– Price: $95,000

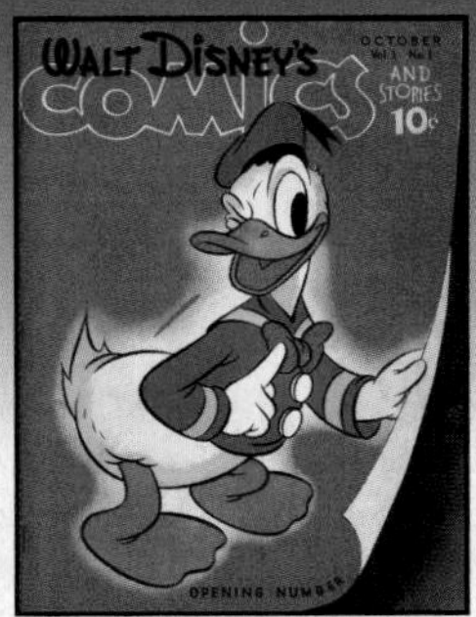

Walt Disney's Comics & Stories #1
Donald Duck, Mickey Mouse reprints
1970 Mint Price: $115
2010 NM– Price: $40,000

All Star Comics #3
First Justice Society of America
1970 Mint Price: $135
2010 NM– Price: $85,000

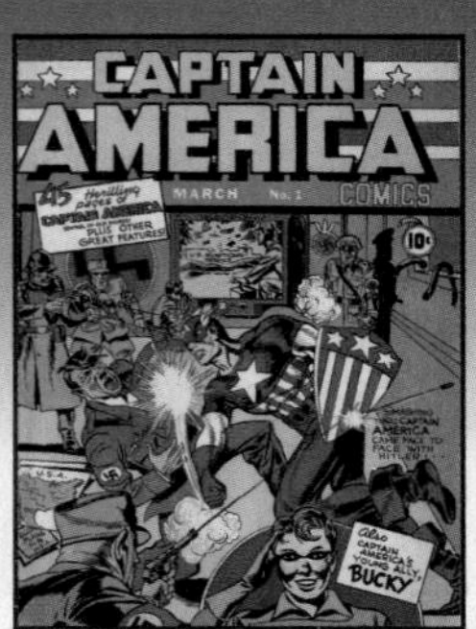

Captain America Comics #1
First appearance of Captain America
1970 Mint Price: $150
2010 NM– Price: $215,000

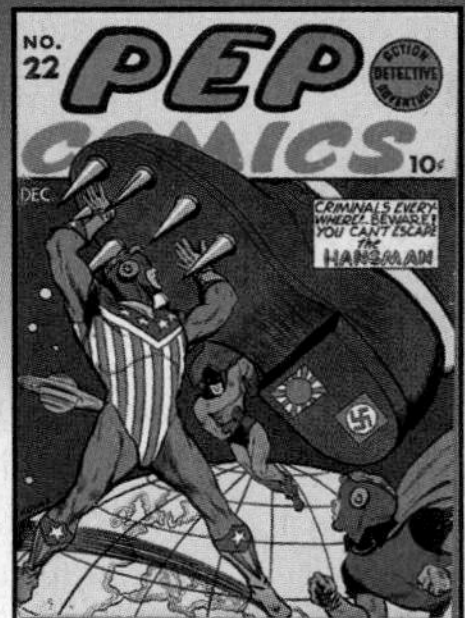

Pep Comics #22
First appearance of Archie
1970 Mint Price: $10
2010 NM– Price: $50,000

Showcase #4
First appearance of Silver Age Flash
1970 Mint Price: $12
2010 NM– Price: $54,000

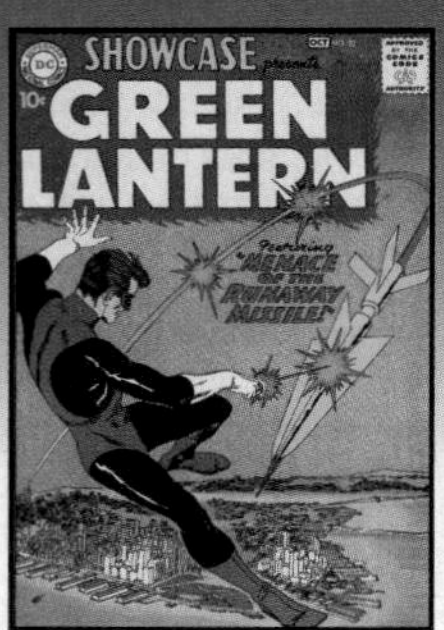

Showcase #22
First Silver Age Green Lantern
1970 Mint Price: $6
2010 NM– Price: $12,500

Brave and the Bold #28
First Justice League of America
1970 Mint Price: $5
2010 NM– Price: $16,000

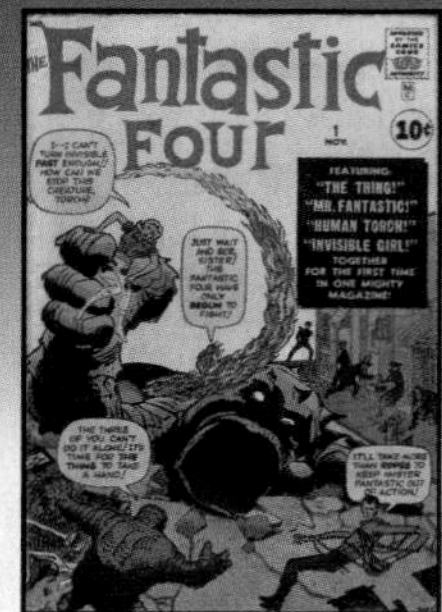

Fantastic Four #1
First appearance of the Fantastic Four
1970 Mint Price: $12
2010 NM– Price: $70,000

Incredible Hulk #1
First appearance of the Hulk
1970 Mint Price: $14
2010 NM– Price: $65,000

Amazing Fantasy #15
First appearance of Spider-Man
1970 Mint Price: $16
2010 NM– Price: $100,000

Journey Into Mystery #83
First appearance of Thor
1970 Mint Price: $10
2010 NM– Price: $24,000

Tales of Suspense #39
First appearance of Iron Man
1970 Mint Price: $6
2010 NM– Price: $20,000

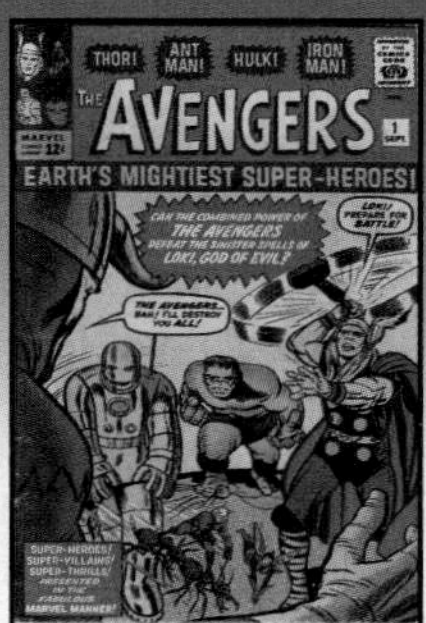

The Avengers #1
First appearance of the Avengers
1970 Mint Price: $6
2010 NM– Price: $12,500

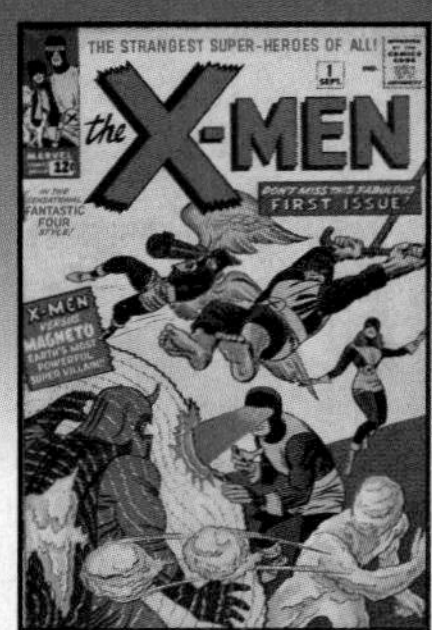

X-Men #1
First appearance of the X-Men
1970 Mint Price: $6
2010 NM– Price: $26,000

When the first edition of *The Overstreet Comic Book Price Guide* was released in 1970, some collectors and dealers actually complained the prices listed in the book were too high!

Bill D. Alexander Collector/Dealer

We all are aware a recession has hit us here in the USA and even the comic market felt its effect in one way or another. I noticed a big drop in sale prices realized on many books listed at online auction sites, especially on mainstream Silver and Bronze Age books that were not Key books. Key Silver and Bronze Age Marvel and DC books in CGC 9.6 and 9.8 continue to set record high sales at online auction sites and show no signs of slowing down soon. As many may already be aware, there have been three amazing Bronze Age high end sales realized lately and they are *Green Lantern* #76 CGC 9.6 $30,500.00, #76 CGC 9.6 $22,000.00, *Star Wars* #1 35¢ Variant CGC 9.6 $26,250.00. Also a Silver Age high end sale occured with the *Amazing Spider-Man* #5 CGC 9.8 going for $97,000.00 at auction.

Being the big Marvel magazine collector I am, I would like to point out what I call the "elusive five" Marvel magazine issues of the early 70s that are beyond hard-to-find in CGC 9.4 grade or better. Consider trying to find a *Dracula Lives* #2, *Tales of the Zombie* #1, #10, *Monsters Unleashed* #2, or a *Monsters of the Movies* #1 in better than a CGC 9.4 grade in regard to the just one or couple of copies that have been found in that grade and good luck to one in trying. After 7 years of CGC grading Marvel magazines, those books have a census high of only one CGC 9.4 copy graded except for *Tales of the Zombie* #1. One might also note that the premiere issues of Skywald magazines of the early 70s like *Nightmare* #1, *Psycho* #1 and *Scream* #1 are very hard to come by in high grade 9.4 or better and are still very undervalued in my opinion.

Many new discoveries in comics have been made lately that I believe will excite collectors new and old. Check out the article on variant comics and publisher experimentation featured in this edition of the *Guide*.

I hope everyone fills the holes in their comic collections, and I feel the year 2010 will be a good one for the hobby. Happy collecting to all.

David T. Alexander, Tyler Alexander and Eddie Wendt DTACollectibles.com

Crisis and trauma have been evident in the financial sectors this year. During our 41 years in the paper collectibles business, we have seen many market fluctuations and financial roller coasters. None of the past tough times have ever had much of an effect on our operations. This year has been different and radically so. By mid-year many collectors had been affected by the downturn and had to cut back on active collecting. On the positive side, collector enthusiasm is still a powerful and driving force and is a stronger influence than the negative economic news. Collectors still want those comic books and have inspirational ways to keep the collections growing. At mid-year we had more trade deals going than at any previous time and we also paid many generous finders fees to collectors who directed us to deals that we were able to close. Summer is typically slow for mail order sales and we decided to stimulate website sales by presenting several 20% discount sales to those on our email list. These events were well received and we had several dealers sign up for our list in order to take advantage of the discount opportunity. Maybe the cold weather had an influence on collecting but by late Fall and early Winter things were beginning to heat up again. Either the economy was rebounding or collectors were determined to limit their deprivation. Sales activity was HOT in November and December.

Golden Age Comics: We have had loads of activity with Golden Age comic books. The DC superhero titles were the hottest sellers. *Batman*, *Detective*, *Action*, *All-American*, *Superman*, *Adventure*, *Superboy*, *Sensation*, *Wonder Woman* and *More Fun* were the most requested titles in order of demand. *Flash* and *World's Finest* also were sought after but not as heavily as the top tier titles. The pre-hero DC issues still have a lot of interest and we have great difficulty filling requests. We have been researching the pre-hero DC comics for a long time and after considerable discussions with *Price Guide* advisors, historians and advanced collectors, we feel that the first contemporary super hero comic cover appearance was Dr. Occult on *New Book of Comics* #2. This was a Giant Size edition published in 1938 prior to the appearance of *Action* #1 which featured Superman. Dr. Occult is only on a small panel on this cover, but he is there, 1st time ever!

1950s DC War, Western and Romance titles were very popular with the Romance issues having about 3 times the requests as the Western issues. Early DC War comics are always consistent sellers. Timely comics are always popular but we had fewer requests for superhero titles this year. Is it possible that many collectors are changing the focus of their want lists to look for comic book sets that can conceivably be completed? The Timelys that were hot this year were the Good Girl Art, Teen Age and Funny Animal titles. *Patsy Walker*, *Jeanie*, *Tessie*, *Hedy*, *Frankie*, *Annie Oakley*, *Margie*, *Oscar*, *Super Rabbit*, *Joker* and related series were the basis of many sales. We had many multiple orders for these and similar titles. Harvey Kurtzman & Basil Wolverton appeared in many issues and there are some outrageous covers and stories hidden among these often undiscovered treasures. Prices are relatively low but don't expect that

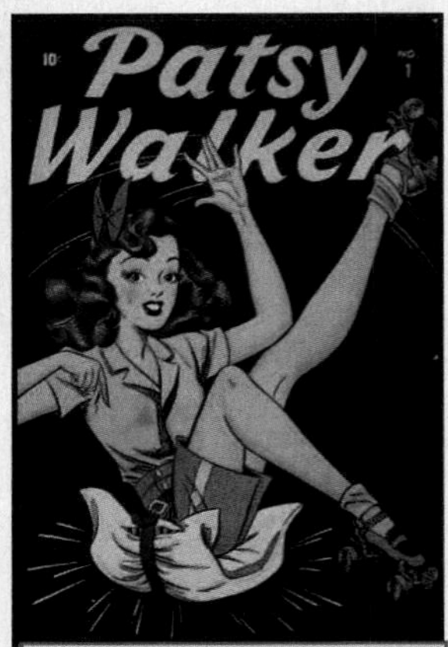

***Patsy Walker** #1 and other Good Girl Art comics were among the Hot Timelys in 2009.*

trend to continue. Fawcett superhero comics are not spectacular in sales terms but they are constant movers. We are always happy to get them in and we always seem to have fewer in stock than we thought we had. The most popular sellers are *Captain Marvel Adventures*, *Captain Marvel Jr*, *Mary Marvel*, *Wow*, *Marvel Family* and *Whiz*. Fiction House titles are constant sellers in all grades. People want them all from Poor to Mint. Let's face it, they are great books and a dozen or so issues can provide a weekend of fun.

MLJ and Archie titles with superheroes went like a wild fire. The Archie characters are constant movers but the superhero issues are tops. Centaur titles still have a small but energetic following. We actually took in about a dozen issues, which is a lot for us, and they are all gone.

We have seen renewed interest in Walt Disney titles and have been shipping tons of Carl Barks art issues to Europe. Tyler Alexander is still operating our Foreign Sales Division in Hannover, Germany and we hope at some point he has a chance to buy some of these books back. When we ship to Europe now we don't feel like those books are gone forever. For those who are interested in European sales and purchases, Tyler can still be reached at talexander@cultureandthrills.com.

Silver Age Comics: There is lots of information about Silver Age available here and it is positive. Everyone loves Silver, the books are fun to read and collect. We have seen a surge in interest for these titles: *Journey Into Mystery*, *Strange Tales*, *Tales of Suspense*, *Tales to Astonish*, *Justice League of America*, *Mystery in Space* and *Hawkman*. Is it possible that increased demand for these titles was due to collectors seeking less expensive issues during the economic downturn? The mainstream titles like *Amazing Spider-Man*, *Batman*, *Detective* and *X-Men* are still popular sellers but we did not feel that there were significant price pushes for these issues. *Fantastic Four* was actually down in demand. High grade copies were the exception and they sold at ever increasing prices throughout the year. CGC copies show no lack of interest. As you know there are not that many copies of any early Silver Age issues in CGC 9.4 or higher and there are clearly not enough copies to meet current demand. We project that this trend will continue. The Silver Age sleeper of the year is Charlton. Many early Silver Age and prior issues are priced low in the *Guide* and actually bring multiples of *Guide* values, some actually go for 20 times *Guide*.

Newly Discovered Titles and Variants: We were able to unearth several previously undocumented titles and cover variants in 2009. Probably the most amazing discovery was a copy of *Amazing Spider-Man Giant Comics To Color*, published in 1976. It appears to be a one-shot oversize edition that was not sold at the traditional comic book outlets. At 10 3/4" x 15" it is larger than a standard Treasury Edition and carries a cover price of 69 cents. This comic was licensed by Whitman from Marvel Publications. It is absolutely a comic book and has a book length 48 page story. The inside covers are blank and the back cover is a Spider-Man mask that was surely cut out by many of the original owners of this book. It is easy to see why collectors have overlooked this issue as its awkward size and unconventional price almost assures that it would not be seen by most collectors. We know of several people who claim to have complete Spider-Man collections. We wonder if they have copies of this issue.

A.G. Spalding published baseball and football yearbooks, commonly called guides, from 1876 up into the early 1940s. They also manufactured equipment for those sports and eventually devoted their efforts solely to that endeavor. In 1947 they produced two films, one devoted to baseball and the other to football. They also took another shot at publishing and did two promotional comic books to publicize the two films. We have been fortunate to obtain a copy of each book. The baseball comic book *Circling the Bases* has a New York Yankees cover and art by Willard Mullin on the back cover. The football comic says *Spalding Official Sports Series* #2 on the cover and is titled "Inside Football". It features Sid Luckman, Sammy Baugh, Ken Strong and Grantland Rice. We have had interest in these items from comic book, sports and movie collectors. They are great crossover items.

© MAR

Amazing Spider-Man Giant Comics to Color and **Blade Sins of the Father** *may not be known to most collectors.*

A previous movie theater manager contacted us to sell his movie memorabilia collection. We got tons of posters and a lot of interesting promotional material. The thing that really caught our attention was a Marvel comic book. *Blade Sins of the Father Theatrical Preview* issue #1 August 1996. This is a 24 page issue with a paper cover and no cover price. The top of the cover says "Exclusive Theater Edition". We have presented this to several *Price Guide* advisors and advanced collectors and none had ever seen a copy or were aware of its existence. The manager told us that this was limited to 2000 copies - one copy per theater, but he also told us a lot of wacky film related stories, so we can't really know how factual he was being.

Cover price variants have become a popular area for discussions, collecting and speculation. We have discovered two issues that appear to have been undocumented. *Walt Disney's Zorro, Dell Four Color* #933 is a cool comic featuring a Guy Williams TV series photo cover and action packed Alex Toth art. We have had numerous copies over the years and all had the standard 10 cent cover price. We recently discovered a variant edition that has "10 cents NOW" on the cover. We think this is unique to have cover price variants that both have the same price on the cover! Copies of *Tom and Jerry's Toy Fair* #1, a 1958 Dell Giant, came into our hands with both 25 and 30 cent cover prices. These books are identical except for the cover prices, and we were intrigued that the cents symbol was different on each of them. The higher priced copy was probably printed for Canadian distribution.

Format variations are another area that we look for and we were able to find a couple of significant items this year. In the mid 1950s EC began to reprint some of the best *Mad* comics in paperback book format. Controversy over the newly adopted Comics Code kept William Gaines from publishing the horror and sci-fi titles in a similar format. Ten years later the dust had settled on the Comics Code issue and several paperback books came out that reprinted some of the best horror and sci-fi comic stories. They had original covers by Frank Frazetta and are well worth owning today. These popular titles include: *Tales From the Crypt*, *The Autumn People*, *Vault of Horror*, *Tomorrow Midnight* and *Tales of the Incredible*. Warren Publications also did a paperback reprinting stories by Frazetta, Toth, Ditko and others. It was titled *Best of Creepy* and had several printings and is highly sought after in the current marketplace. What really caught our attention were two paperback books with new, non reprint comic book stories. The first is *Dracula*, Ballantine Books #U2271 published in 1966, which contains a 159 page horror story with art by Al McWilliams. In addition, we located a copy of *Christopher Lee's Treasury of Terror*, Pyramid Books #R-1498 published in 1966. Although it looks like it would contain standard text stories, we were surprised to see that it was filled with comic book stories. Horror stories by H.P. Lovecraft and Bram Stoker had been adapted into comic books by top artists: Johnny Craig, Frank Bolle and Al McWilliams. These are not reprints, and contain original material.

Comeback Title of the Year: It was first published in 1977 and featured a variety of top international artists such as Moebius, Druillet, Bodé and Richard Corben. *Heavy Metal* caused quite a stir when it first came out and was aimed at an adult audience. This magazine format comic book had a cover price of $1.50 when most comic books were selling for 30 cents. That fact alone caused it to grab more adult readers. The series was in vogue for several years and as cover prices rose it began to languish on retailers racks and disappeared from want lists. During the last 30 years the title has been dormant as a collectors item. We were fortunate to obtain a small group of high grade early issues and were surprised to realize that after almost 30 years of obscurity the title has renewed interest and we had strong sales on the available copies. Only the high grade copies are in demand and we recently saw a CGC 9.8 at $500.

Pulp Magazines and Edgar Rice Burroughs: As always, pulp magazines, the forerunners to comic books, were big sellers for us. The most popular title this year was *Black Mask*. The hard-boiled detective concept first appeared in this title and was made popular by authors such as Raymond Chandler and Dashiell Hammett. Top authors appeared in this title that ran from 1921 to 1951. A large number of stories were turned into movies and TV series, and several comic book writers found plots and storylines in the pages of *Black Mask*. *Doc Savage* was again the most popular pulp hero series and the Man of Bronze left the Shadow and the Spider in his wake. Science Fiction pulps maintained their popularity and overall had a slight price increase. Tarzan and Edgar Rice Burroughs material did very well. The early pulp appearances began in 1910 and generally appeared before the story was available as a hardcover making them the true first editions. Our biggest Burroughs thrill of the year was the discovery of TWO copies of *Adventure Library* #1. Tarzan the Mighty is featured in the first issue of *Adventure Library*, Oct, 1928. This rare silent movie give-away item has 8 pages, is printed on pulp style newsprint, and is 6" x 9". It features photos from the movie serial and three chapters of the film story. We have spoken to several Burroughs historians and collectors and not one of them was aware of this rare item. From the looks of this item the feeling was that it had a very limited distribution and was probably given away in only a handful of theaters. Could many copies have survived the last 80 years? We offered one copy for sale and it went like a gunshot. More information about it is available on our website. Sadly the ERB and pulp collecting community was shocked at mid-year to learn of the tragic death of Danton Burroughs, grandson of Edgar Rice Burroughs. Danton, who had been a close friend since 1972, when he sold me his grandfather's copies of *Marvel Comics/Marvel Mystery* #1-10, maintained what was actually a museum for ERB memorabilia and artifacts in his Tarzana, CA home. In mid-summer the home caught on fire and the structure and contents suffered heavy damage. He was told to stay in a hotel, but after the fire department left, he stayed in the damaged house. Danton's heart stopped the next day, which ironically, was the same day he was to take the position of President of Edgar Rice Burroughs, Inc. We shared a

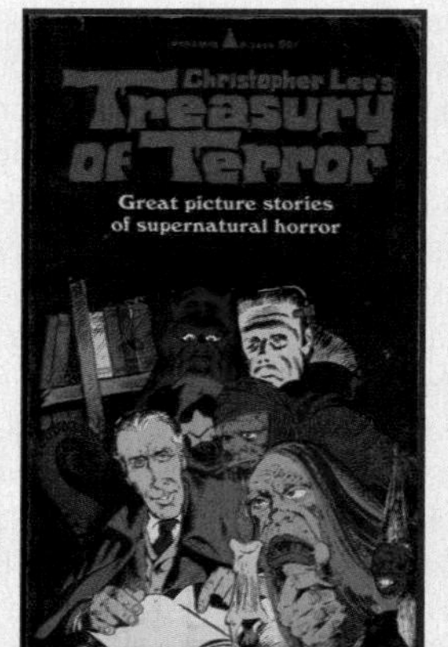

Comic book stories can even turn up in paperback books like ***Christopher Lee's Treasury of Terror*** *from 1966.*

tremendous love for Tarzan and everything that Edgar Rice Burroughs created and stood for. RIP, my friend.

Acquisitions: Maybe it was due to the economy or maybe it was due to the publicity that collecting has recently received, but whatever caused it, we are happy about the loads of collections that were offered to us. Again, we kept our record perfect, we did not turn anything down. We have not had time to determine the quantity of issues that came in during the last year, but we did have to add a couple thousand feet of additional shelving space. Please keep it coming, and U-Haul, do we qualify for the volume discount yet?

Dave Anderson, DDS
Collector

As the U.S. economy began the slow process of recovery in 2009, the comic collecting community cautiously watched to see how it would be affected. The combination of a bad economy, unemployment and an abundance of material for sale resulted in slightly lower prices realized for 75% of the material offered. Since so much of the comic market's activity is auction-fueled, savvy bidders held back their bids somewhat, recognizing that yet another auction was right around the corner with many more items to bid on if they were unsuccessful in the current auction. Some good news however is that a large percentage of auction activity is dealer bidding, so after the auctions, items won are subsequently resold for more money. The other good news is that the other 25% of the material offered during the year consisted of higher quality items that brought consistently high prices. You can generally throw out the *Guide* price when it comes to high grade early Marvels, unrestored key Golden Age comics, high grade Disneys, and less commonly seen titles. The bottom line is that desirable, high demand titles will continue to sell well and for strong above *Guide* prices, whereas commonly seen, lower grade, less desirable comics will sell below *Guide*. These trends can be expected to remain, independent of the state of the economy.

Stephen Barrington
with Ronnie Hayes
Flea Market Comics

While the back-issue market was slow for 2009, it was the new comics sales that had our accountant smiling. DC led the way with its blockbuster Blackest Night series and crossovers. Marvel's Dark Reign line also enjoyed healthy sales.

Green Lantern is one of the hottest commodities around along with the relaunch of *Adventure Comics*. *Amazing Spider-Man*, despite coming out several times a month, still enjoys strong sales. However, Marvel has too many X-titles out there, diluting the new comic market. *X-Men Legacy* and *Uncanny X-Men* were the top sellers for Marvel along with the *New Avengers*.

But in the midst for these popular storylines, Superman sales have dipped as has *Detective Comics* as well as some of DC's lower tier comics. Daredevil and Punisher, two perennials for Marvel as well as their lesser characters are bordering on stagnant mediocrity. The Vertigo and Max titles along with the Stephen King titles are poor sellers while Dark Horse's *Star Wars* titles are suffering badly. Image, with the exception of *Spawn*, *Invincible* and *Walking Dead* are so-so sellers while the rest of their line is barely being requested. A note on some of Marvel's Max issues: This line borders on soft pornography with little or no redeeming qualities.

While new comics provide a nice profit margin, it's the steady price increases that are causing some collectors to balk at buying numerous titles. These price increases by the main publishers are squeezing out the smaller companies. DC and Marvel are the top companies while Dark Horse, Dynamite, Image and others are suffering a slow death.

The overall market for comic shops in the Greater Mobile, Alabama area is still weak with our shop (a part-time one at that) still the only source for a full-line comic business. The nearest shops are in Mississippi and Florida, just far enough to keep our business strong. Greater Mobile has a population of over 400,000.

Sales of comic collecting supplies are extremely strong.

The Golden Age market, as in years past, is almost nonexistent. Comics from this period rarely show up and for the most part are difficult to sell due to the high prices on the popular characters. Batman seems to be the exception, though.

CGC books don't sell. As a CGC agent, it's only once in a blue moon that someone wants to use our services in sending their issues off to be graded. CGC books never come in for collectors to sell. Another sore point is that too many brand new comics are being graded, flooding the market and depressing prices.

Popular Silver Age titles are *Batman* and *Amazing Spider-Man* while *Superman* and *Fantastic Four* are only so-so. *Justice League of America*, *World's Finest*, *Tales Of Suspense*, *Strange Tales*, *Thor* and *Tales To Astonish* barely create a ripple for the 1960s market.

Bronze Age comics sales are fair, because the prices are more affordable. The same holds true for Copper Age comics.

The dollar and quarter comics move briskly with a lot of readers looking for that bargain. The top dollar sellers are Wolverine, Superman and Spider-Man while various DC and Marvel titles lead the way in the 25-cent boxes. Other popular dollar comics are Archie, Disney and Harvey titles. These are hard to keep in stock.

The sluggish economy has brought in a lot of Silver Age comics into the shop but not in high grade. Bronze and Copper Age comics suffer the same fate condition-wise. Former collectors are selling their comics because they are unemployed and need the money. On the flip side, we see a lot of junk coming in from the 1990's but we try to be tactful when we decline to buy them.

Our eBay sales are good but most issues only command 25 to 30 percent of *Guide*. Comic lots do well, though. Some sticking points are that too many eBay stores have their prices way too high. Another bugaboo are the grading skills, or lack thereof, of many sellers. Just because a comic is old doesn't make it valuable. Thank goodness for scans!

Dell Comics sales from the 1950s are comatose and this includes all titles. War comics from this period do OK as well as pre-code Horror issues. *Classics Illustrated* do well in spurts and can be hard to replenish.

Chicago Wizard World: The 2009 Chicago convention was amazing with many dealers offering fantastic deals throughout the show. Moving the convention back to two weeks after San Diego ComicCon didn't appear to hurt the attendance. Bedrock City, Comic Heaven (John Verzyl is a character), Graham Crackers, JHV Associates, Metropolis, Superworld, Terry's Comics, and Harley Yee had some of the best comics at the show.

L.E. Becker
WARP 9 Comics

I was reading my market overview from last year to prepare myself for writing this one. Last year I mentioned that the economy was playing a factor into what people were purchasing and collecting. Now, here we are in 2009, and, at least here in Michigan, it ain't getting better. The entertainment industry (which obviously includes comic books) has been taking a hit in almost every aspect. Movie sales are down (along with DVD sales/rentals), many magazine circulations have dropped by as much as 30%, and many genre mags have been canceled (ie: *Modern Bride*), and even the almighty video game industry has been floundering. So what does this mean for the comic industry? Are we doomed into extinction like the already fading newspapers? Will comic books lose the printing aspect and be deligated to nothing more that an iPhone application?

Yes and no. Marvel has already started with online motion comics, and, although far behind the curve, DC has their Zuda line of online comics. The print aspect of publishing seems very close to extinction. Except that you can't collect an iPhone app.

Comic books will always (fortunately or unfortunately, depending on your point of view) be a collectible. Collectors will ALWAYS want to have a physical copy of a comic in their hand, to read, bag and board, to COLLECT. People like it when they buy a comic (whether casual reader or hardcore collector) and after a few months (or even a few hours) the comic is "hot" and goes for many times over the cover price. Disagree? Then look no further than... *Amazing Spider-Man* #583 Obama Variant! Like or hate him, agree or disagree with him, Obama becoming President was history in the making. Marvel capitalizing on Obama's popularity was pure genius. Shops that were smart enough (and qualifed for the variant) received their "stimulus package" early that year. First printings were sold here for $20.00 IF you pre-ordered it, $40.00 the day it came out, and within 3 weeks (or by the 4th print), $160.00!!! I doubt the "i-comic" equivalent would be as popular.

The other "Obama Appearances" from Marvel were great sellers also. *Thunderbolts* #128 & 129 which weren't solicitated as an Obama appearance were hot right out of the gate. #128 reached a high of $25.00 online within the first week. #129 was a solid $9.99. Obviously everything has cooled off now, but the ride was great while it lasted!

Too bad almost everything else with Marvel this year hasn't been as hot. The only new title that Marvel released this year that had steady increases in orders is *Dark Avengers*. Everything else has had lower than average numbers. This is due in part to: 1) Higher cover prices (a $1.00 jump will hurt ANY magazine sales) 2) Too many titles (Marvel still produces 120-150 titles per month), 3) A weak economy.

Marvel's main reason for the price increase was said to be to help some of the lower performing titles survive. The strong in essence will carry the weak. The problem with that is if a product is too weak to support itself, then most likely, it needs to die. It's just simple business logic. Warren Ellis's *New Wave* comic was a great read to me, and I was very disappointed when it ended a few years ago. However, the title was not supporting iteslf, so it had to go. "The needs of the many outweigh the needs of the few", or some such rhetoric aside, it's better to cut the losses rather than making a few dozen people happy in the wake of thousands.

DC Comics: Finally starting to pick up steam! Blackest Night is the talk of the shops! Our sell through on this series has been better than the last few Marvel major crossovers. The variants of these books haven't hurt either. The 1:25 variants go for $20-25 each, and the sketch variants have done well too (#1 sold for a high of $200). The crossovers have done well too. The ring promotion which just started for us, has done exceedingly well, as the titles have sold out for us (ie: *Doom Patrol* #4, *Booster Gold* #26).

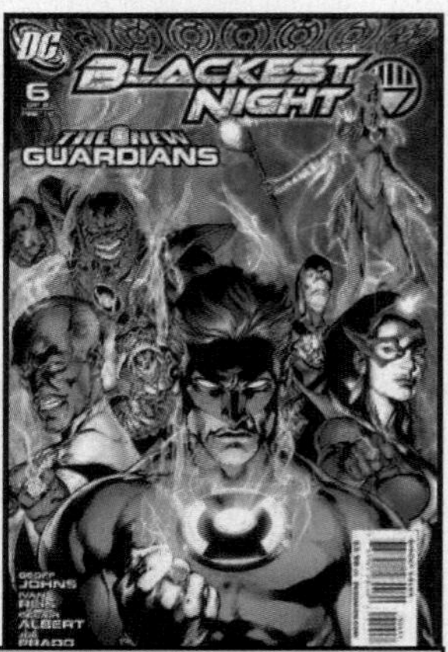

© DC

DC's **Blackest Night** crossover (#6 shown) is the talk of the shops.

Batman & Robin is our highest ordered regular DC title right now. It seems as if everyone has forgotten/forgiven the Batman R.I.P. and *Final Crisis* debacles, and has given this title a well deserved chance. Some of the other Batman related titles have grown in sales and popularity also. *Red Robin* sells 1-1/2 times better than the regular *Robin* series did, and *Gotham Sirens* has found a following.

Now if DC could just do something with the Superman titles. Here's a little tip to DC...If you put out a book called "*Superman*", you might want to keep the main character (Superman) inside the book. Sales for all of the related Superman titles have plummeted to a level I haven't seen since we opened up 10 years ago...(ugh).

DC's Vertigo line has taken a hit also. None of the titles out right now have peaked much curiosity OR sales, with the exception of *Unwritten*. Great concept, and it could totally be adapted for film or TV, but almost everything else from this line has created nothing but lethargic looks and the occasional yawn. I will say though that Vertigo's $1.00 price point for new releases was a very good idea. It made people pick up the 1st issue (ie: *Sweet Tooth*, *Greek Street*, etc), but with the exception of *Unwritten*, it didn't make any lasting impressions on anyone after the 1st issue.

On a related note, *Watchmen* came out touted as THE movie of the year, and lasted maybe one month in the top 10 theatre releases. Back issues of *Watchmen* were very hot, as #1 sold regularly at $25.00 and #10 (the hardest one to find) sold for $35.00. People who I talked to who saw the movie AFTER reading the comic were slightly disapointed with it.

Independents: Image's *Chew* was the biggest hit this year. An ingenious concept and nicely paced story made this one of the must-have comics of the year. *Chew* #1 1st prints have sold as high as $100.00. There was a low publicized Larry's Comics sketch variant (limited to 1000 copies) which fetches $30-40.00 also. Robert Kirkman brought back Todd McFarlane to help plot *Haunt*. As of this writing, #1 has gone into a 3rd print, and #2 is going back for a 2nd. The variants of this book were the hottest thing on eBay, with a master set of #1 regular, plus the 1:10, 1:25, 1:50, 1:100 variants going for $200+!

IDW's hottest hit was *Star Trek: Countdown*. This movie prequel series was highly underordered, and with the fury of the new *Star Trek* movie buzz, this series shot up in price quickly overnight. #1=$25.00, #2=$15.00. Unfortunately, once the hype died down after the movie, so did the sales. The GI Joe and Transformers titles didn't fare any better in sales, even with the release of each respective movie.

Boom! Studios is the newest company on the rise, picking up licenses no one would have bothered with. Although not a great seller, *Die Hard Year One* did better than expected, and *Do Androids Dream of Electric Sheep* (the novel off which *Blade Runner* was based) did very well, with #1 selling for $10.00 anytime we have a copy in stock. *Farscape* was the company's breakout hit when it was initialy released ($15.00 for the 1st issue), but has cooled off a bit. Boom's kids line has been doing very well with both kids and adults. Looks like Boom! has a hit with *Muppet Show* and *WALL*E*.

The Stuff of Legends is this year's *Mouse Guard*. A great story with interesting art by the publishers at Th3rdworld Studios (not a typo) that we have recommended to people who like DC's *Fables*. Although only a 2 issue series (with more 2 issue series coming), the 1st print of #1 goes for a solid $25.00, and the Baltimore Comic Con exclusive (limited to a mere 100...that's ONE HUNDRED copies) at $100.00!!!

Steve Borock
Steve Borock Collectibles
Heritage Auctions

Hello and welcome to the 40th edition of the *OCBPG*! Congratulations to Bob Overstreet, the man who helped shape my (and many, many others) life, hobby, and profession for 40 years! Without Bob keeping a careful and impartial eye on comic prices over the years, I truly believe that the market and our hobby would not be as stable as it is today! It has been an honor to help work on the price guides over the years and an even bigger honor to be friends with Bob and to get the advice he has given me over the years. BOB, THANKS FOR 40 WONDERFUL YEARS!

Speaking of the market, Heritage Auctions is now the world's leading collectibles auction house as well as the world's third largest auction house. Heritage's online and live auctions are the strongest in our hobby! Not just that, but Heritage has just sold the only comic book, *Detective Comics* #27 CGC 8.0, to ever sell in a public auction for over one million dollars! Did you catch that? A comic book sold for over one million dollars! I still can't believe it!

I have been working with Heritage for about a year now and am having a blast! What I like best about working with a major auction house is that it's a win-win situation for all involved. If a consigner does not make money, the auction house does not make enough money to be worth their costs, so it behooves the auction house to get consigners top dollar for their comic books and original comic art. Heritage spends more money on producing top quality full color catalogs, maintaining all past auction sales (a great tool for anyone, novice and veteran collector alike, wanting to watch trends and prices over the last nine years), massive advertising campaigns, and much more, all to help consigners reach the largest audience and get the best prices possible.

Moving on, let's talk about modern "hot" books: BE CAREFUL! If a comic book comes out and you can't find it that week or that month, have some patience. If you are looking for a reading copy, most will be available as a trade within six months to a year. If you are looking to put a high grade copy in your collection, most of the time, when the "hype" dies down, you will find it at a much lower price as well. I personally believe that most modern comics will not be a good place to put your hard earned money as an investment. In my opinion, if you are going to invest money in comic books, you are better off putting your money into pre-1968 comic books.

Speaking of places to put your money.........please check out the Hero Initiative (www.heroinitiative.org). This is the one place that we can really help the people who bring and have brought us the many, many hours we have enjoyed these comics. To quote the website: "The Hero Initiative creates a financial safety net for comic creators who may need emergency medical aid, financial support for essentials of life, and an avenue back into paying work. Since inception, the Hero Initiative has been fortunate enough to benefit over 40 creators and their families with over $400,000 worth of much-needed aid, fueled by your contributions! It's a chance for all of us to give back something to the people who have given us so much enjoyment." If you would accept help, you should also give it, fair is fair. Let's hope most of us never need help, but let's help those that do.

As for the comic book market itself, everything looks pretty darn good. Others in their market report here will give you all the figures of prices they have sold comics for, so I will let you read those reports. The last thing you need to hear from me is more "top" prices. Please remember, while you are seeing these "highest" prices, there is always a chance that on many occasions, you can find that same book in the same grade for less than reported here.

Don't forget to check out the CGC message boards! They are a wealth of information and, more importantly, fun. (www.cgccomics.com)

I will end my report the same way I did last year: Even though I believe in this market, there is no "free lunch". If you are going to invest in comic books, you had better love what you buy. If the economy ever gets really bad, just like if you own stocks, you will not be able to sell them for a really high price quickly and you can certainly not use them to house or feed yourself or your family. The best advice I can give anyone, and have been doing so since I can remember, is: "Buy what you love and can afford." It really is that simple. Enjoy collecting and reading comic books, enjoy the friendships we make in this wonderful hobby, look at and enjoy all the cool stuff around us, from original comic art to movies based on our favorite comics to comic book memorabilia, and it will all seem worthwhile in the end.

Thank you for taking the time to read this and HAPPY COLLECTING!

Comic Book Collecting Association www.comiccollecting.org

In February 2010, the Comic Book Collecting Association (CBCA) announced its launch and website at www.comiccollecting.org. Guided by the principles of Fellowship, Education and Ethics, the CBCA is a nonprofit international organization made up of comic book enthusiasts who share an appreciation for the history, artistic merit, and significance of the comic book medium as an important element of popular culture. Our Mission Statement reads:

"The mission of the CBCA is to promote the comic book art form and hobby of comic book collecting for people of all ages by encouraging fellowship among comic book enthusiasts, providing information and education to the public, and helping to facilitate the buying, selling, and trading of comic books and related material in an environment of trustworthiness and integrity."

The CBCA is modeled after prominent organizations from other hobby communities such as the American Philatelic Society and the Universal Autograph Collectors Club. The CBCA Code of Ethics is patterned after industry best practices while being tailored to the hobby of comic collecting. Our complete Code of Ethics can be read at www.comiccollecting.org.

The CBCA's mission includes education and fellowship, as well as the goal to be an association inclusive of collectors and dealers. And much like its predecessor, the Network of Disclosure, the CBCA promotes the practice of proactive disclosure. Thus our Code of Ethics states, "A CBCA member shall be responsible, to the best of their knowledge, for the accurate description of all comic book and comic-related material offered for sale. All conservation, restoration, enhancements and significant defects should be clearly noted and made known to those to whom the material is offered or sold."

We were pleased to announce the creation of our initial Board of Advisors, which features some of the most prominent members of our community. We are ecstatic that they have chosen to lend their names in support of the CBCA's efforts, and we look forward to soliciting their advice on topics of interest to our hobby.

The Advisory Board, at the time of printing, includes: Dan Cusimano (Flying Donut Trading Co.); Steve Eichenbaum (CEO - Certified Collectibles Group/CGC); Danny Fingeroth (former Marvel editor, comic writer); Jamie Graham (Graham Cracker Comics); Tracey Heft (Eclipse Paper - Restoration Expert); Dave Kapelka (North Coast Nostalgia); John Jackson Miller (Comic book writer/commentator); Josh Nathanson (Comiclink); Brian Peets (A-1 Comics); Dave Reynolds (Dave's American Comics); Wayne Smith (VP, Warner Bros. Entertainment Inc.); John Snyder Jr. (Past President, Geppi's Entertainment, Inc.); Doug Sulipa (Comic World); Bob Storms (High Grade Comics); Joe Vereneault (JHV Associates) and Vincent Zurzolo (Metropolis Collectibles).

We were also honored to announce that the first new member of the CBCA is George Pantela of GPAnalysis (comics.gpanalysis.com), the leading analysis and reporting service for online auction and dealer comic book sales.

We plan to offer many exciting and new educational programs and services to the broad collecting community through our website, message board, Comic Book Quarterly newsletter, seminars at conventions and other initiatives. Please visit www.comiccollecting.org for more information.

Our success depends on comic collectors and dealers like you supporting this initiative with membership and ideas. We look forward to your feedback and participation in this exciting effort!

Gary Dolgoff
Gary Dolgoff Comics

2009... Comics "lead...the economy"! Yes, I know that, in many ways these are tough times, and yet comic books, original comic art, etc. still defy this trend! In fact, the "good stuff" is selling BETTER THAN EVER!

This year (2009), I managed to spend $90,000 in about 5 weeks. I bought a collection of 1940s and 1950s *Action* and *Superman* comics (mostly in my clean VG to FN+ with some better!) for about 70% of *Guide* from a long-time collector, spending $40,500 total. I found the deal to be worthwhile even though I gave the fella who found me the deal a $5,500 finder's fee! It was wonderful pouring over all of these early Superman comics... and even the restored issues sold well! Nicely restored comics can often sell at *Guide* GD/VG to VG.

A few weeks after that "lovely and lively purchase", a fella from upstate NY called me. It seems he was going to sell his collection (at age 69, he felt like this was the time to do that), and he liked the "sound" of my *Overstreet* ads. When someone is "ready to sell", I don't believe in "hammering the seller", preferring instead to just offer a "hearty yet fair price" that is worthwhile for both parties. So I drove up to his house the next day and upon looking at his collection, I "got a kick" out of the variety of his collection - as he had Golden Age DCs (including *Batman* #5,9; *All Star* #9, 18, etc.) a "boatload" of early to mid 1940s Disneys (*Comics & Stories* from #6 up, including 3 copies of #31, the 1st Carl Barks *C&S* issue) *Donald Duck Four Color* #9, 29, 62, etc.- and much, much more... like "minor multiples" of 1940s – early 1950s Baseball comics (*Roy Campanella, Eddie Stanky*, etc.) The only thing is, he didn't seem to realize that a number of his better books had restoration done to them (which significantly reduces their value compared with similar looking non-restored comics.) He was calling his restored *Batman* #5, for instance, a Very Fine! (I realistically sold it for *Guide* GVG, plus a little.) Despite this, the fella selling the books realized that the "restoration was real" in those comics, once I pointed out the restoration to him. In the end, I paid him approximately 60% of *Guide* for his collection.

You can find "totally beautiful and compelling covers" on **Mystery Men Comics.** (#12 shown, cover by Joe Simon)

Golden Age: I've found a lot more of these "Golden Oldies" than I had in recent years. (It could be because more folks "in the industry" and so forth are seeing me paying 60%-80%+ for the stuff.) Timely comics "sell like hot-cakes" for *Guide* and more. I especially love to buy Golden Age *Captain America*, and I usually "keep 'em when I get 'em".

1930s-early 1950s superhero DCs are solid sellers. This year, I sold a load of old *Actions*, for an average of "*Guide* and more". I haven't gotten in lately my favorite Golden Age DC title... *More Fun Comics* with the Spectre! I love those awesome-covers.

Early-mid 1940s Disneys in nice VG-/VG and better sell moderately well(though superhero stuff, generally speaking, is King.) Comics from Centaur Publishing, (*Amazing Man*, etc.) sell great. *Mystery Men* and *Wonderworld* (Fox) have, "totally beautiful and compelling covers", and sell quite well... and I really dig getting in those elusive Hangman comics! *Phantom Lady* (and some later *Blue Beetle* Good Girl comics) sell well. Unfortunately, a number of later 1940s comics don't sell quite as well as they used to (later *Police Comics, Blackhawk, Captain Marvel Advs., Modern* and others). However, the early counterparts of many of these titles still sell well. I sold a *Captain Marvel Adventures* #1 with the covers separated from each other for 80% of the GD price. In fact, most early 1940s (and late 1930s) superhero comics still hold sway sales-wise, if properly graded. I recently paid 65% of *Guide* for a group of assorted early 1940s #1s (including *All Star* #1, *Comic Cavalcade* #1, *Leading* #1, *Tough Kid Squad* #1, etc.) I sold them all, pretty quickly, at "*Guide* by my grading".

Crime comics don't seem as hot as they were a few years ago. DCs like *Gangbusters*, and especially *Mr. District Attorney*, are slow sellers. Funny Animal comics (including DCs) don't move out, despite their coolness and charm. Most ECs, however, still sell great - especially Horror (*Haunt of Fear*, *Tales from the Crypt*, *Vault of Horror*) and for the most part, pre-code Horror comics from the early 1950s' miscellaneous publishers are solid sellers. Most Funny Animal Dells from the 1950s are terrible sellers, even at 25% to 50% off of *Guide*. They're very common. Western comics sales have slowed down.

Silver Age: I enjoy buying and accumulating books from this era, though I have over 50,000 comics from the Silver Age (but I...want...more!) Silver Age is, to my mind, the "bread and butter" of the comics' industry. I have, for instance, an overseas buyer who purchases runs of 1960s and 1970s comics (about 20,000 pieces a year) and then sells them to his customers throughout the year. This year, I have gotten in a number of Marvel runs (*Fantastic Four* #1-150, *Daredevil* #1-100, *Journey into Mystery* #83-125, *Incredible Hulk* #1-6, 102-200, *Amazing Spider-Man* #1-150, *Avengers* #1-150, etc.) and paying 50%-70% *Guide* for

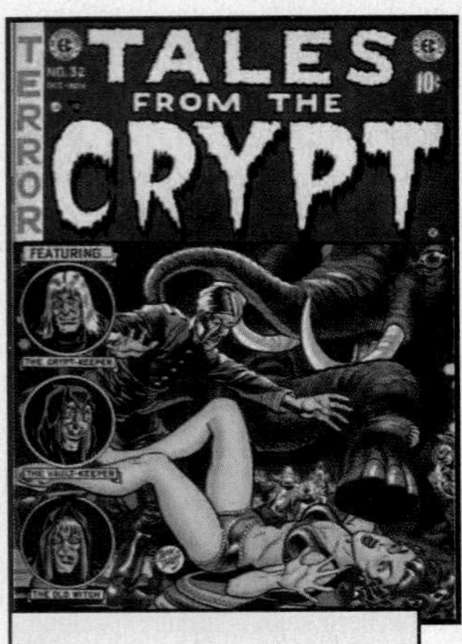

*Most ECs still sell great, especially Horror. (**Tales From the Crypt** #32 shown)*

them. When I sell them as sets, they move quite well. These days are truly the "Marvel Age of Comics" in many ways. Early 1960s Marvels sell well individually as well. The main titles sell well, all the way through the 1960s and early to mid 1970s.

In the "DC realm", Batmans generally do particularly well, as do "nice-shaped" 1950s and 1960s DCs for sure. I have found, however, in more recent times that I must often discount my lower-grade (FAIR/POOR to GD/VG) 2nd tier titles (especially in package-deals or group-deals) in order to keep them moving. These books get discounted from me by 20%-40%...yes, sometimes even 50%! However, almost all 1960s-'71 books sell well, in "sharp-shape". Examples of 2nd tier 1960s books: later issues of *Strange Tales*, *Tales of Suspense*, *Tales to Astonish*; non-superhero Marvels (War, Western, Romance); DC titles such as *Aquaman*, *Atom*, *Hawkman*, *Hawk & Dove*, *Superboy*, *Jimmy Olsen*, *Lois Lane*, etc; non-Marvel and DC titles such as *The Fly*, *Jaguar*, most Charltons, Archies, Dell/Gold Key Funny Animal etc. Once I do discount them, people enjoy buying them, as they are cool books.

Bronze Age (1970's-1981; 20¢-40¢ cover-price): These are the "newer heroes" of the comics' industry, sales-wise. I've found that comics from the 1970s (and to a certain extent, some books from the earlier 1980s) are "moving on out" better than ever as more and more folks (who bought them new when they first came out) are realizing that comics from this era are cool, affordable, and fun to own! And it's a good thing that I own 150,000-200,000+ comics from this era. Some of these books I've "stocked on shelves" in my warehouse for 10-20+ years. Also, I've lately been buying up "loads" of 1970s collections, many of them in real nice shape! I bought one of them (primarily 1970s with some 1960s included and a lot of '70s keys.) For $17,000, I acquired this collection of 5,000+ comics.

In general, the best-sellers from this era are:

(A) Nice-condition Bronze. I recently got an 8-box want list from a long-term, reliable customer for '70s-early '80s. As long as they're in nice shape and strictly graded, he wants up to "three of an issue number"!

(B) The mainline titles (especially through the mid-1970s): *Amazing Spider-Man*, *Avengers*, *Batman*, *Incredible Hulk*, *Iron Man*, *Justice League of America*, *X-Men*, etc., in most any shape.

(C) 1970s keys and "special issues" - explosive sellers: *Amazing Adventures* #11; *Amazing Spider-Man* #121, 122, 129; *Incredible Hulk* #180, 181; *Giant-Size X-Men* #1; Neal Adams' Batmans; *Marvel Spotlight* #5; *Ghost Rider* '73 #1; *Iron Man* #55; *Werewolf By Night* #32; etc, etc. Many of these keys from the 1970s sell for somewhat above *Guide*!

(D) 1970s - early 80s lots that I sell by the box for 50¢ each.

Late 1980s - 2000s: A market that I admit, I've been largely underestimating. As long as I sell them for 1/3-1/2 of *Guide*, they seem to move okay to pretty well (and then, when I have too many pallets of them, I "bulk 'em out" by the pallet for 8¢-12¢ a book!) In my newly revamped web-site, I plan to list thousands of late 80s - 2000s comics, individually for 50¢-75¢ each in nice shape.

Original Art: I've been getting into buying art, and the result is "more cool original stuff"! I bought an unpublished late 1930s Wolverton page for $6,500 and then sold that. I've also been buying collections of art from the 1970s to present: superhero, Archie, Millie the Model, and so forth. I plan to buy a lot more original comic art this year and onwards. I like it from all years, early 1900s to the present. It is wonderful to own. I like to keep covers, splashes, and other cool stuff. I love the idea that it is one-of-a-kind stuff, that the "artist drew with his own hand."

A Special Note to Potential Sellers: When evaluating your collection (or inheritance) please note:

1) Most comics from the 1930s - 1960s are in Good to Fine condition (the 1st three lower-priced columns in this *Guide*). In order to be Very Fine or better, they have to essentially look like they just came off the stands: very sharp! Keep in mind please, that a couple/few "relatively small flaws" can reduce the book from high-grade to 'Fine or less'. The top three prices for each (old) book are expensive because less than 10% (or so) of a given book is in Very Fine to Near Mint. The other 90%-99% of copies that exist are in Fair to Fine because they've been read, with general wear and just general handling of the comics.

2) Sometimes a seller will say, "I've seen this book for "over a thousand" on the internet!" True, but is your copy of this book as nice as that internet copy? Also, did that copy actually sell for that price, and if so, was it legitimate? Remember please, folks... the GRADE of a given book determines its VALUE! Although, if your books (or some of them) are in Very Fine or better condition, then you deserve an offer on them that reflects that condition. And finally, on older comics, even if the condition of the books is less than stellar and depending upon what you have, your collection could still be worth many thousands, or even tens of thousands or more in value!

So in closing, I say, "Have a Great Comic Book Summer and Year!" - Gary D.

Walter Durajlija and Marc Sims
Big B Comics

The retail comic book market and the collectible comic book market both showed tremendous resiliency in 2009. The doom and gloom that everyone thought the year would bring just didn't materialize, at least not here in Southern Ontario. In collectible comics this was actually a banner year with record setting prices being set online every month. It seems that some new blood has entered the market, perhaps getting out of the volatile stock market and choosing comics as a blue chip investment.

We were honored to be nominated for the Eisner Spirit of Retailing Award this past year. Congratulations to Tate's Comics of Lauderhill, Florida on their well deserved win. Our stores (Big B Comics in Hamilton, Ontario and Blue Beetle Comics in Barrie, Ontario) actually showed a small overall sales gain compared to 2008, but we did see a bit of a drop in the number of customers through the door year over year. This means that fewer people were coming in but actually spending more per transaction. A $1.00 price increase on many new comics and a glut of new product from Marvel and DC are mostly to blame for this. This is a troubling trend, but all things considered, we had a solid year and look to continue to grow in 2010.

Back issue comics sold well all year long, especially key issues and issues in high grade. This is nothing new of course - the gap is just really increasing in terms of what sells and what does not. Good books continue to get good money, really good books (CGC 9.6 Silver Age for example) get stupid money, and common/low demand books continue to plummet in value. This is a trend that has been ongoing for the last 6-7 years and I see no signs of it stopping. For buyers, especially reader-collectors, it's great. A lot of fun books in mid-grade are affordable and can be routinely acquired for 40-50% *Guide*, if not less. For dealers, it just means we have to adjust our buying practices to reflect the changes in the market. For collectors who have been sitting on runs of mid-grade *Aquaman*s and *Thor*s thinking that they will cash in some day, reality is starting to set in rather harshly.

This is somewhat reflected in the fact that our expenditures for the year were a bit off from the year before, simply because we could not source many large collections. Part of this is simply a lack of leads coming in, but we have also had to refuse many collections of more common books. For example, a local collector wanted to sell his complete mid-grade run of *Daredevil* #1-200 to us, but we could not justify paying him more than 10% *Guide* for everything except a handful of the issues. We were willing to pay him good money for the #1-10, 131, 158, & 168, but he almost would have had to pay us to take the rest. We did purchase one large collection in the spring of 2009, but the balance of our buying activity was opportunistic. A few books here, a good one there, a small collection here, an incomplete Spidey run there etc. Where we could, we continued to buy aggressively and found ourselves paying much higher percentages of *Guide* just to have good comics. All the eras were well represented in our acquisitions allowing us to comment on each.

Golden Age: Quality Golden Age sold as soon as we got it. A *Batman* #62 I graded a GD/VG sold for $250, *All-American Comics* #61 CGC 4.0 sold for $2000.00, *Tip Top Comics* #1 CGC 4.0 sold for $2400. Other quick sales included the first two *Four Color* Tarzans. Not all Golden Age moved briskly though. We had several CGC'd later *All-American* run books that had to be priced at about 70% of *Guide* to move. I'm looking for the Golden Age to have a great 2010. Collectors being priced out of the high end Silver Age market will discover a lot of quality from the Golden Age still remains undervalued.

Silver Age: Is there no end to the incredible run up in value that high quality Silver Age books are experiencing? It seems like every week we read about new record prices being set. Our Silver Age sales included a restored *Amazing Fantasy* #15 I graded at an App 3.5 for $2700, *Fantastic Four* #5 CGC 5.0 for $1000, *X-Men* #1 CGC 4.0 for $1500.00, *Tales to Astonish* #27 I graded at VG- for $800, *Avengers* #1 CGC 3.0 for $900, and an *Adventure Comics* #247 I graded at VG- for $1100. We were always able to sell lower and mid-grade semi-key issues at around *Guide*. Mid-grade copies of *Amazing Spider-Man* #14,15,39,40 and 50, *Avengers* #5, *Batman* #171 and 181, *Tales of Suspense* #58, *Tales to Astonish* #59 and *X-Men* #12 all sold for us at around *Guide*. DC War is also extremely popular and always sells briskly.

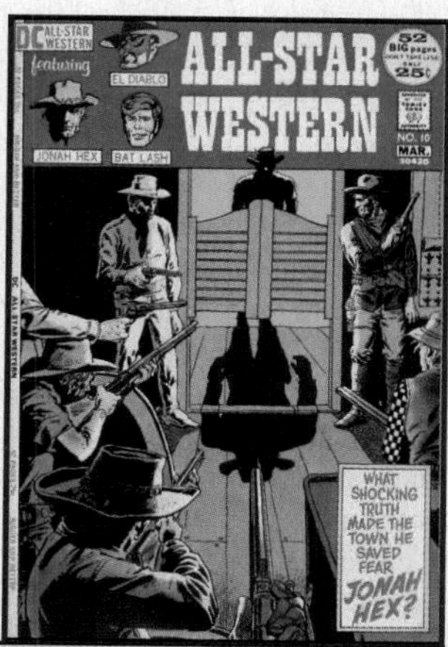

Anticipation for the **Jonah Hex** movie made **All-Star Western #10** a very hot book in 2009.

I honestly don't know where this high grade Silver Age Market will stop. I do wish it would slow a bit though. We need steady long term growth in value. We do not need a speculative gold rush.

Bronze Age: Although it has definitely been pushed to the sidelines by all the Silver Age activity, the Bronze Age is still strong, with the usual suspects holding their ground fairly well. Over the year we sold at least 10 copies of *Amazing Spider-Man* #129. This book sells for *Guide* in all grades and it sells fast. Other notables include a 9.4 copy of *All-Star Western* #10 for which we got $1800 (this book is very hot) and *Batman* #227 that I graded at VF/NM for $275. As hard as I tried, I could not buy a copy of *Green Lantern* #76. All the ones I looked at seemed too pricey for me to actually resell for a profit. In hindsight I could have made money on all of them. Slow books include *Giant-Size X-Men* #1 and *X-Men* #94. They do not get *Guide*, even in very high grade. *Incredible Hulk* #181 has cooled a bit but still sells fairly quickly at 90-100% *Guide*. Aside from *Batman*, *Detective* and various Neal Adams books, Marvel rules the roost in the Bronze Age. All Marvels sell immediately in true high grade, while many DC titles will sit, even when priced affordably. Non superhero books are very difficult to sell for anything other than $2-3.

Copper/Modern Age: The only sale of note for us was a *Cerebus* #1 that I graded a GD/VG for $100. Every year we're able to sell multiple copies of comics like *Amazing Spider-Man* #238,252,300, *Uncanny X-Men* #266, *New Mutants* #98 and a small list of others. These comics get decent prices. The rest of the comics from this era are tough sells and most find their way into our bargain basement. We are even tossing in high grade copies of books that *Guide* at $20. I'm looking at you *Wolverine* (ongoing) #1, *X-Men* #244, *Spawn* #1, and friends. Anyone trying to get *Guide* for those is fooling himself. The good news is that there are lots of people buying these issues at the $2 price point. They are buying because they read and collect.

CGC grading of Moderns and Coppers is not a new phenomenon at all, but there were some interesting new trends this year. A lot of books from this era that were once hot and selling for big bucks in CGC 9.8 (*New Mutants* #98, *Harbinger* #1, *G.I. Joe* #21, etc) have cooled off considerably. I guess that people have finally figured out that books from this era are not scarce at all in high grades and thankfully the market is starting to correct itself. For the people that are chasing 9.9s and 10s, or slabbing comics that routinely sell for 25 cents (*Action Comics Weekly*?!?), all I can say there is you're playing with fire and it will only end poorly. It reminds me of the speculator boom in the early 90s, and we all know what happened there.

I write a weekly column called Auction Highlights for the comic news website *comicbookdaily.com*. I basically follow the results of eBay and all the other comic auction sites and report and comment on interesting results. One thing I've noticed is the sporadic pricing realized by comics that are grouped in the same run and even within the same *Guide* price structure. For example, a run within the *Fantastic Four* title could all *Guide* at $200 at the 9.2 grade yet a few issues will sell for multiples of *Guide* while a few will sell at *Guide* or just below. Why the discrepancy? One piece of information that has emerged as an important determinant of price is the CGC Census. The CGC grading company keeps a census of all graded comics and this information is available to all on their website. If I put up for auction a *Fantastic Four* #33 and a *Fantastic Four* #34 both graded at CGC 9.4, I may get very different prices depending how each of the comics show on the census. Issue #33 may show 3 graded at 9.4 and only 1 at 9.6 while issue #34 may show 11 at 9.4 and 3 at 9.6. In this case, issue #33 will realize a much higher price (perhaps even a multiple) than issue #34. This census driven market is even more evident when looking at comics with no high grades. I'll use *Star Spangled War Stories* #84 (1st appearance Mme. Marie) as an actual example. The four highest grades on the CGC Census at one point last year were 7.5, 7.0, 6.5 and 6.5. The CGC 6.5 copy sold for $477.00 which was about 7 times *Guide* at the time. A mid-grade comic book should not be getting 7 times *Guide* except of course when it happens to be the second highest graded copy in existence (the 7.0 came on the census after this sale).

The CGC Census has turned into a reference guide much like the old Gerber scarcity guide. The Gerber actually did a great job in noting the number of copies in existence of certain comics. Gerber's number system for scarcity is well known to seasoned collectors. The CGC Census actually comes up short against the Gerber since it only tracks how many copies have been graded. The Gerber comes up short against the CGC Census since it cannot give a breakdown for grade scarcity. Since it's all about scarcity I'd also make a quick Gerber reference before plopping down the big money for a comic advertised as "only 3 graded better" etc. There's never a guarantee but at least you could play the odds better. Nobody can ever account for new collections, warehouse finds and file copy discoveries.

Crazy money for comics that are good but not necessarily great is a phenomenon that is only a few years old. There are a lot of collections still out there where perhaps the 1st issue of a strong title has been graded but since costs are prohibitive many of the other issues are not graded. When common run issues in high grade start realizing crazy money we'll see a lot more of these being CGC graded. What looks scarce today may not look so scarce 4 years from now. We'll need a decade at least to populate the census enough to consider it at least semi-accurate. Until then, people need to be very wary of paying record setting prices for highest graded copies. The reality is there are other copies out there that could grade just as high, if not higher. Suddenly your registry set of highest graded comics that you shelled out big bucks for isn't worth half of what you paid for it, and no one wants to experience that. Be smart in your acquisitions, think long term, buy what you love, and most importantly, have fun! That's what comics are all about.

Marc and I wish to thank everyone at Big B Comics and Blue Beetle Comics for all their hard work and enthusiasm.

Ken Dyber
Cloud Nine Comics

Greetings, I am a collector/dealer of 25 years specializing in Bronze and Copper Age keys, with a growing interest in Gold and Silver Age books, especially Horror, ECs, Fiction House, Avon One Shots, Nedors, and most recently magazines. I have also spent quite a bit of time researching CGC sales on GPAnalysis, analyzing comparative sales between *Guide* pricing and sales of slabbed and unslabbed books.

This year I was able to travel to the Midwest and east coast to shop, and can also offer some input on sales/availability across the country. Feel free to visit my website: www.cloudninecomics.com or email at info@cloudninecomics.com .

First off, I would not call 2009 "Another Banner Year" as it seems is heralded by many dealers in this *Guide* year after year. Global economic problems, a continued collapse in the housing market, and high unemployment are putting strains on everyone regardless of their income level. Heck even *Amazing Spider-Man* isn't invincible. In August, a CGC 9.4 sold for $83,650, down $20,000 from its previous sale. Ebay still continues to move huge amounts of books, and represents a pretty good market value. Most books, unless they are high grade, keys, or scarce books are not only selling below *Guide*, but often well below. I've actually purchased some great high grade Silver Age books on eBay this year at well below *Guide*, so.... if you have money, now is a GREAT time to buy! I'm also noticing an increasing trend of more people entering the hobby due to our beloved books hitting the big screen. Yes, books often soar in value 2 years to six months before the film is released, then the bottom falls out of those books (*300*, *Watchmen*, etc..), or the movies do little to increase sales (*Spider-Man 3*, *Transformers 2*, etc.). What I am noticing though, is that these movies are creating an overall resurgence in people returning to collecting. Many of my customers are in their mid 30s, and have children 1-5 years old, and are now buying cheap 50¢ books for their kids to read. This is easing my worries about new comics disappearing (say like our newspapers) or if there will be a "next generation" of collectors. I was also worried that comics could suffer the same fate as the music industry where teenagers have all but abandoned purchasing CDs or LPs, and are just purchasing mp3s/downloads. Will today's pre-teens purchase paper comics and not DVDs in the future? My current thoughts are, "Yes."

Golden Age: Record sales this year include *Action Comics* #1 CGC 6.0 $317,200 (at the time the highest unrestored, certified copy to sell on the open market with only 4 certified higher, the highest being an 8.5), *Walt Disney's Comics & Stories* #1 CGC 9.4 $116,513, *Detective Comics* #27 CGC 1.5 $83,650, *Action Comics* #1 CGC 1.8 $94,001, and a *Captain America Comics* #2 CGC 9.2 $103,099. In general I saw less Golden Age books at shows, on the web and in shops this past year. Books that have sat in our local shops for the last few years are now gone. On a regional level I attribute this to a few things: more collectors in the Northwest entering this market and the market catching up to the prices on these books as they continue to look like better values compared with modern $4.00 cover prices. People who might have spent $20 on a hot new variant are now purchasing older books. In demand: Timely, Nedor, DC, Fiction House, Dell, MLJ. Not in demand: *Classics Illustrated*, *Boy Comics*, *True Comics*.

Atomic Age: An often overlooked and still very affordable portion of the market from the end of WW2 presents tons of great artwork and stories that are not that common. ECs, Star, St. John, Allen Hardy, Avon One Shots, the boom of Romance books (which are less common then most think, especially in grade), Good Girl artwork, War Titles, Charlton's numerous titles, the list goes on. This period to me parallels the Bronze Age where publishers were trying many things with crazy stories and pushing the (pre-code) boundaries. Tons of great artwork from Baker, Feldstein, Ditko, L.B. Cole, Wolverton and many others. L.B.'s Romance books in this period are awesome! Prices across the board here are affordable with many titles and keys within reach of those without deep pockets. In demand: High grade, Horror, Romance, and artwork from key artists. Not in demand: Funny Animals.

Silver Age: *Amazing Fantasy* #15 continues to be the best book to invest in. It is more affordable and available than the Golden Age keys and shows large returns in short periods of time. A CGC 8.0 sold for $70,500! The only Golden Age books at 8.0 or lower to sell for this value are: *Action* #1, *Detective* #27, *Batman* #1, and *Marvel Comics* #1. This book sold at an average of $1,200 in 2002 in CGC 2.0 and now, 8 years later, sells at an average of $3,200 at CGC 2.0. That's doubling at the Good listing every 3 years! Some of my sales include: *Amazing Spider-Man* #19 (4.0) $42, *Avengers* #1 (5.0)(r) $335, *Batman* #181 (7.0) $80, *Daredevil* #37 (9.2) $75, *Fantastic Four* #52 (8.5) $85, #75 (9.0) $110, *Iron Man* # 1 (8.0)(r) $100, and *World's Finest* #176 (8.0) $30. I'm seeing increased action in DCs like *Green Lantern*, *Flash*, *Wonder Woman*. High grades of these books are scarce and sell above guide almost always with little resistance. *Green Lantern* #7 (origin/1st Sinestro) I think is going to explode as this book is scarce in any grade. I looked on eBay, Comiclink, Mile High, and Metropolis' websites for this book, and there was only 1 copy for sale, a VG on eBay, with heavy bidding, selling well above *Guide*. I'm also seeing increased interest in *Mystery In Space*, *Hawkman*, *Aquaman*, *Showcase*, *Teen Titans*, and *Brave and the Bold*. Finding these in VF or higher is difficult, and forget NM- or higher. On the Marvel side, *Avengers* prices have skyrocketed with the movie in the works. *Avengers* #1 is pretty common compared with *Incredible Hulk* #1, but is selling above *Guide* in all grades. *Tales of Suspense* Iron Man appearances are moving steady in all grades and Thor's *Journey Into Mystery* issues are hard to find anywhere in VF or higher. Although *Amazing Spider-Man* outpaces all other titles in sales by a large percentage, sales on many books have been flat or need to be discounted a little to move unless they are true NM- or higher. Also, *Detective Comics* #378 has an ad for Angel and The Ape in it which predates their first appearance in *Showcase* by a month. I know this makes a difference for the TMNT in the Modern Age, should it for other periods/titles/characters? In demand: High Grade Marvel & DC, Marvels starting at VF/NM 9.0 and DCs starting at VF 8.0, early Horror magazines like *Creepy* and *Vampirella* #1. *Avengers* 12¢ issues are very hot, as are 9.4 *Green Lanterns*. Not in demand: VG-VF on non keys.

Bronze Age: My favorite period due to its diversity of genres, it's still a great time for investment, but time is running out, as more people begin to realize this, and are cleaning out shops of books that have sat for years. Some of my sales include: *Amazing Spider-Man* #101 (3.0) $14, #129 (9.0) $400, #135 (9.0) $70, #194 (9.2) $60, *Beyond the Grave* #1 (9.2) $30, *Champions* #1 (8.5) $20, *Daredevil* #168 (9.4) $175 & (9.0) $75, *Ghost Rider* #1 (7.5) $62, *Inhumans* #1 (9.4) $30, *Spider-Woman* #1 (9.2) $20, and *Uncanny X-Men* #136 (9.4) $55. Great titles include: *Werewolf By Night*, *Luke Cage*, *Conan*, *Night Nurse* (yes, *Night Nurse*!), *Tomb of Dracula*, *New Gods*, *Iron Fist*, Byrne *X-Men*, Neal Adams' *Green Lantern*, *Batman*, *Cerebus The Aardvark*, *Astonishing Tales*, *House of Secrets*, *Ghost Rider*, *Forever People*, *Shade The Changing Man*, *Firestorm*, and the list goes on and on. Some crazy sales occurred this year including *Green Lantern* #76 (9.6) $30,500, *Incredible Hulk* #181 (9.8, sig. series) $32,001, *Batman* #227 (9.8) $13,000, *Cerebus* #1 (9.4, sig. series) $7,754, *Night Nurse* #1 (9.8) $3,850, and *Marvel Spotlight* #2 (9.6) $3,000. Many books in this period have doubled in only 5 years or close to that. *Tomb of Dracula* #10 (1st Blade) went from $175 to $350, *Marvel Spotlight* #5 (1st Ghost Rider) from $220 to $450, *Marvel Spotlight* #2 (1st Werewolf By Night) from $230 to $375, *Wonder Woman* #179 (1st issue without costume) from $65 to $115, *Green Lantern* #76 from $500 to $1200 (and may I add, selling well above this presently!), *Conan* #1 from $270 to $400 & #23 (1st Red Sonja) from $40 to $80. Then you've got the price variants like *Iron Fist* #14 (35¢-c) which went from $400 to $1200 (selling well above this), and *Star Wars* #1 $(35¢-c variant) which just finally got a line listing in the *Guide* and had a CGC 9.0 sell this year for $3,000 (2x *Guide*). Many non-keys though are also going up faster percent wise than other time periods such as *Werewolf By Night*, which has increased about 60% as a title in 5 years, same as Byrne's *X-Men* run. Try finding high grade 9.6 or higher copes of *Firestorm* #1 or *Shade The Changing Man* #1. Try finding a *Ghosts* #1 in 9.2 or higher. I haven't even seen that book in Portland in the six years I've lived here (in any grade!). Tough books like *Batman* #227 are selling for crazy multiples above *Guide* in 9.6 or 9.8's. In demand: High grade of almost any title/publisher and Good copies for $.50 to read. Not in demand VG-VF unless in the $.50-$1 range.

Copper/Modern Age: There are many opportunities to find key issues here, but large print runs and plenty of high grades still floating around keep prices down. Some of my sales include: *Amazing Spider-Man* #225 (9.6) $33, #238 (9.6) $125, #245 (9.8) $38, #252 (9.0) $40, *Fables* #1 (9.4) $45, *John Byrne's Next Men* #22 (9.4) $45 & $35, *Ms. Marvel* #17 (9.4) $40, *New Mutants* #1 (PGX 9.9) $120, #98 (9.4) $62(2 sales), *Preacher* #1 (9.2) $25, *Sandman* #1 (9.4) $45, and Transformers #1 (9.2) $25. I've noticed an increase in demand for 50¢ and 75¢ cover price books. *Moon Knight* #1 50¢ cover is getting harder to find in NM-, as is *New Mutants* #1, and *Alpha Flight* #1. *Ghost Rider* ('92 series) is in demand again, as are Valiants, especially *Solar Man of the Atom*, *Rai*, and *Harbinger*. Now is the time to put complete runs together of 9.6/9.8s of these books while they are cheap, because these books that are $6 in *Guide* will be $15 in *Guide* probably sooner then you realize. *Solar Man of the Atom* #10 CGC 9.8 sells around $500, but watch for 9.8s of issues #4 & 5, both tough to find in grade.

© Robert Kirkman

One of the most valuable Modern Age books is ***The Walking Dead*** *#1.*

The new *House of Mystery* series is a great read and has awesome mini-stories within most issues by some great upcoming writers & artists. *Mouse Guard* first printings are hard to find and a great read/investment. *Buffy The Vampire Slayer* season 8 sells well, although the story is beginning to drag. *Walking Dead* #1 CGC 9.2s & unslabbed NM- books are selling between $100-$150, which makes it one of the most valuable Modern Age books (could someone tell me why?). I know Kirkman is doing good work, but why this series and not *Invincible* or *Marvel Zombies*? Buy all three of these though, all great reads/artwork and valuable books.

Miracleman continues to sell well in all issues with later issues scarce in grade. Trying finding a 9.8 of issue #23 or 24! There is only 1 recorded sale of a Miracleman #23 CGC 9.8, which happened in 2008 for $823, where issue #15 sells every year in this grade for less. NYX #3 has cooled a bit, but I think over the long run is going to be an important modern key book as this character develops. The entire 7 issue series is a great read with awesome artwork. Small indies are available all over the place, many not in the *Guide*, such as *Continum* and *Panda Khan*.

Vertigo, Dark Horse, and Image seem to be paving the way on the modern front with great stories/artwork, and Marvel/DC seem to be more and more predictable. Older Vertigo #1s are high in demand and sell at or above *Guide* consistently. *New Mutants* #87 & 98 are very much in demand. *Fables* #1 is a hot book and the entire series sells well, as does *Grimm's Fairy Tales*. Transformers and GI Joe titles are both selling well and good investments. In demand: Vertigo #1s, Kirkman (*Invincible*, *Walking Dead*, *Marvel Zombies*), *Kick-Ass*, *Chew*, *New Mutants* #1, 87, 98, *Green Lantern*, and *Buffy* season eight. Not in demand: $3 back issues & $4 cover prices!

Bruce Ellsworth with Grant Adey
Fats Comics - Australia

Hello from down under from Bruce Ellsworth. Somebody send me 20 *Spider-Man* ones and good. Just joking (not). It has been a rough year for me. I have been through a kidney transplant and a toe amputation.

The only American books that sell are Marvel, older key issues or high grade Silver Age in 9.4 or better. Of course Phantom is the King, any issues below #500 sell immediately. Toys seem to be on the rise especially 50's and 60's toys with boxes.

Enjoy our market report and see you next year.

Frew Phanotm Comics: Frew began publishing Lee Falk's *The Phantom* in 1948 and still continues to publish today. What I believe to be one of the longest running single title comics in the world. Starting with #1 in 1948 til today #1565 never missing a beat in 61 years. A credit to the company.

Frew Phantom comics continue to increase in popularity with Australian collectors, with record prices being paid both by auction and retail sales. The worldwide trend for high grade comics is most certainly true for the Australian market, some Phantoms have reached 8 times guide at auction. Within 6 months of the new *Johnson's Phantom Price Guide* being released, collector lust had blown away all NM prices. Near Mint Frew Phantoms are incredibly scarce due to their newsprint cover and Australian climate conditions less than favourable to newsprint paper. Early numbers from the late 1940s and 1950s hardly ever turn up in true NM condition, most being Fine at best. Metropolis Comics in NYC recently sold a Frew *Phantom* #1 in Good+ for a record $7,500 US, roughly $11,500 aud. The comic was sold in less than 2 weeks of it being listed on their site.

Australian Six-penny Comics (6d): They've laid dormant for many years, only picking up the pace in the last 5 years. Australia had a massive comic industry during the '40s/'50s and into the early '60s. The arrival of television changed that. It was a new addition to the household here in the '60s. I can remeber inviting my 3rd grade friends to my house to watch Neil Armstrong walk on the Moon. In 1969, very few people had a television set. The hey day of 6d comics had such titles as *Ginger Megs*, *Fatty Finn*, *Pirates of the South Seas*, and *Crimson Comet*. Prices for these vary a lot. To my dismay, a 1940s Sunbeam's comic of *Ginger Megs* in very fine can be bought for as little as $20 on the internet.

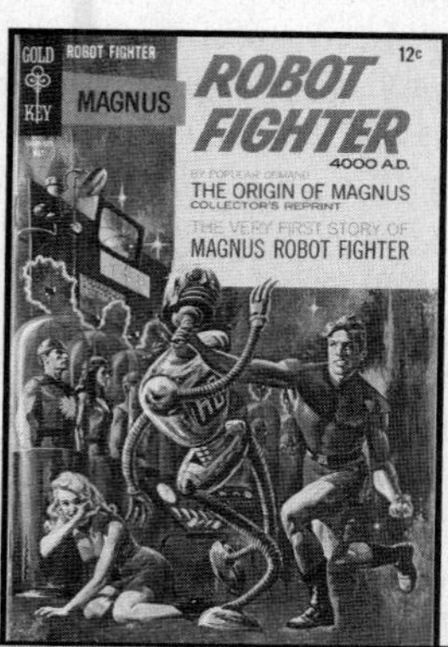

Gold Key comics with painted covers are selling well. (**Magnus Robot Fighter** #22 shown)

Silver Age Comic Sales: Silver Age comics in Fine/Very Fine are selling well. Collectors are finding that hole in the market which supplies a very nice looking comic at a reasonable price. Most collectors still want to complete a run rather than focus on just keys in high grade. *Amazing Spider-Man*, *X-Men*, *Iron Man* ride high on the back of the recent movies. The '60s comics in low grade sell well to the reader market when priced under $20. Here are some of the yearly sales:

Amazing Fantasy #15 (GD+) $3500, *Captain America* #100 (VG) $30, and *Incredible Hulk* #3 (VG-) $320. A big surprise is that Gold Key comics are starting to move and move well. Photo and painted covers are selling well over *Guide*, with high grade up to 3 times *Guide*.

Modern and New Issues: With 2009 drawing to a close, the bursting of the multi-part crossover bubble from Marvel and DC still hasn't burst. Readers are still buying into Marvel's Dark Reign crossover, and even moreso into DC's Blackest Night. That said, surely growing discontent with readers cannot allow this habit to continue indefinitely, with both companies seeking to soften the eventual fall with self-contained, out of continuity projects like DC's *Wednesday Comics* and Marvel's somewhat less ambitious line of Noir miniseries.

The prevalence of trade paperback collections from the "big two" should continue to undermine the demand for rare single back issues among casual readers, who are able to find reprints of the stories they are after with less effort and expense than scouring back issue bins.

Amongst the second-tier publishers, there has been a great deal of growth in companies such as IDW, Dynamite Entertainment and Boom! Studios, who are experiencing a great deal of success (as Dark Horse did in the 1990s) with licensed properties. Whether this success will be able to be maintained, especially for Boom! Studios who are increasingly producing work designed to be optioned in other media, is yet to be seen. Dark Horse, meanwhile, seems content to hold their position in terms of comics production, while increasingly dedicating their resources to producing collectibles and merchandise.

As for recent trends, manga continues to sell well, though there is evidence that this cannot continue at the same pace as it has previously, with fewer licensable properties available to support its previous manic growth. This can be seen in the uncertain fate of publisher Tokyopop, who overextended themselves dramatically and seemed unprepared for the sudden drop in interest. That said, it should continue to thrive, as long as publishers maintain a more even, deliberate pace in terms of releases, distribution and marketing.

Similarly, attempts to capture the audiences of creators outside the comics field such Joss Whedon, Laurel K. Hamilton and Stephen King have yielded well initially, and though interest has waned somewhat after the initial "feeding frenzy", the simple fact is that many popular authors and television creators are using similar tropes and structures to those used in comics and vice versa. There will always be dedicated fans who will appreciate these similarities if they can be executed to the exacting demands of the fan. The thing to watch out for here is the degree to which Stephanie Meyer's *Twilight* series can be adapted.

Of course, 2009's big news was the purchase of Marvel Comics by the Walt Disney Corporation. In the main, this means that Marvel Comics will now have the backing DC has been receiving from parent company Warner Brothers. If Marvel, through media savvy publisher Avi Arad, can translate this into an increased successful presence in cinemas, it represents a real potential in terms of growth and audience recognition for the company and its properties.

Many thanks to Paul Russell, Ace Comics and collector Mike Clark for their invaluable help putting this report together.

Hang Ten. - Bruce and Grant

D'Arcy Farrell
Pendragon Comics

2009 Overview: This year, I decided to concentrate on the new comic sales in my review. It is of the utmost importance (to me) to help readers old and new alike to see trends in both good and bad books. Teaching the fanbase the value of money as well as suggesting good reading material, will keep publishers on their toes and avoid another fiasco like we saw in the 1990s – i.e. it sparkles a lot, it's got a variant cover and who cares about the story, we'll rehash it over and over again by recounting the origin over and over again and overpopulate the stands with too much in quantity and not enough in quality. So my objective is simply to inform the fans and open their eyes to good stories they may have missed out on. Whether you buy back issues or trades, my lists below should have some appeal to everyone.

One nice thing I noticed this year is that finally a company is doing great things for young readers. That would be BOOM! Studios. They are doing some great Disney books for all ages. I hope they make some affordable trades for the mini-series that they have coming out. Disney's purchase of Marvel can be good or bad. It may lead to additions to their theme parks or it may also lead to censorship and mismanagement. Time will tell.

Hands off would be my approach. Add more kid friendly books. But they will have to walk a fine line between growth of their brands and the growth of the general market.

Unfortunately, I really see nothing I can recommend to the tweens except manga. This is a tough market to sell to as their tastes change faster than the weather. Obviously I can't sell a 10 year old child something like *The Walking Dead*, *Blackest Night* or even *Wolverine*. Maybe *Superman*? But they can't be bothered with *Nemo* by BOOM! either. All I can see is selling them reader copies of superhero comics from the 1970s and 1980s. Perhaps new comics are too mature? Too realistic? Remember Wolverine's relaunch a few years back? He dealt with pimps, hookers, bike gangs and drugs. Not proper reading for that age group.

Sales overall in new books expanded very well. Year to year shows a huge gain in sales and number of fans. There is a growth in the marketplace, for new and vintage comics, that has not been seen in a long time.

The various movies helped somewhat, but *Transformers* and *G.I. Joe* were not big sellers for us. *Star Trek* was great as a movie, and gave some growth to that license. *Wolverine* was mediocre at best. The biggest thing for movies affecting our business are the expected movies. The biggest movies would be the Avengers line (*Avengers*, *Thor*, *Captain America*, *Iron Man 2*), followed by the potential in the JLA line. *X-Men* is going to be redone sometime. Let us hope this time it is done better.

New Comic Sales - DC Comics: DC has been going strong with their mop up of the "Final Crisis" storyline and the tragic supposed "death" of Batman. The 2-part Neil Gaiman story was a great shift in perspective, followed by "Battle for the Cowl" and "Batman Reborn". Everything Batman has been excellent this year, including the new title *Batman and Robin* which has been doing exceptionally well thanks to the award-winning team of writer Morrison/artist Quitely. *Red Robin* is an awesome comic as well. Everyone likes Drake. Timothy has hit rock bottom, losing his parents as well as Bruce (again supposedly) and then losing Robin status to Damien. Timothy is also the only one looking for Bruce!

The second half of the year brought us Blackest Night, the explosive storyline 15+ years in the making. The crossover is concise enough to be manageable and thus far has been very engaging, foreshadowing definite changes in the DC universe by the time it is finally over. Parallax is expected back in *Green Lantern* #50 (already out by the time you read this) and is going to be a top seller for sure. Oh, and everyone loves the new Lantern rings! I'm already calling Hal the "Rainbow Lantern".

The Kingdom Come "sequel" in *Justice Society* was a bit of a let down. The original was great, but the sequel seemed to be written simply to bring Gog and Magog into the current timeline. Best thing about it was the low cost compared to a prestige format. Incorporating that story into the ongoing *Justice Society* title was the fair thing to do, and helped with sales of that title. Unfortunately, it was just too drawn out.

Superman's "World of New Krypton" story arc has hit a low, possibly because of the lack of focus in the story. Earlier in the year, "Faces of Evil" was a nice focus on the villains of DC, with lots of great variants, and we hope to see more theme-inspired events like this in DC.

Vertigo is strong as always, with the dramatic conclusion of the *100 Bullets* series this year, but hopefully has more great stories to come.

Ex Machina (Vaughan/Harris): Although it will be over by the time you read this, try to get it in trade if you can. A well thought out and crafted story that doesn't dwell on the powers of the hero, rather it focuses on the interactions of the characters. Generally positive feed back from customers for this title.

The *Watchmen* movie was very well done, though *The*

Spirit fell way short of expectations.

Hopefully DC will keep on trying until they get it just right! We're looking forward to the upcoming *Green Lantern* movie.

New Comic Sales - Marvel Comics, The Good: With the overlong, repetitive "Secret Invasion" crossover finally behind us, "Dark Reign" has definitely made an impact. Norman Osborn's return has brought about the formation of the *Dark Avengers*, which has been a hot seller from day one. Runner up is *Dark Reign - The List*. It is unusual for this crossover not to have a main title, like so many other crossovers, and this makes it more difficult to follow and definitely harder for the readers who just want to get the main points without having to spend a fortune.

X-Men titles are going strong as always, with the X-Force "mini-crossovers" being a fan favourite (Bishop vs. Cable with Hope). Perhaps in the crossover world, less is more?

Also, there is the rapidly rising popularity of Deadpool comics. Fans love this guy! Lots of action and humour, which is definitely a good combination.

We do hope to see more "What If?" material from Marvel in the upcoming year.

Stephen King graphic novels have been very popular this year, with the main benefit of these great stories being that they introduce new readers to the comic book genre and increase the range and variety of material available.

Captain America: Reborn is approaching the end and sales have waned a bit but are still strong. The most popular storylines this year for Marvel were the *Wolverine* "Old Man Logan" storyline and *Kick-Ass*, which was just "kick-ass." These ones just flew off the racks! Fans loved them, we loved them, and we'd like more please!! If you missed those, pick up the trade or hardcover.

Criminal and *Incognito* (Brubaker/Phillips) are hard edged, film noir type of stories which don't come to a comfortable resolution. Very positive feedback on these stories.

Marvel Comics, The Bad: We had to add this extra for Marvel as there was as much bad as there was good! As mentioned above, "Secret Invasion". Too long, too repetitive, too boring. Marvel almost always ruins a year with something along those lines. But that is not the worst: Spider-Man!!!

"One More Day/Brand New Day" for Spider-Man has to be the biggest slap in the face to loyal Spider-Man fans. 25 years of continuity just wiped out. The sad part is that it's not even a consistent wipe. Harry Osborn never died? But Kraven remains dead? And no one notices? What about Ned Leeds? Everyone's memory of Peter Parker is wiped out, and that somehow prevents Harry from dying. Since when did Mephisto have that kind of power? And just how many goblin variants do we need? I have fans who've collected *ASM* for 20+ years, and they have had it. I have numerous cancellations by reserve members. This may have started with the Hudlin storyline with Wakanda a couple years back, but the Mephisto story is the nail on the coffin.

Marvel's 70th anniversary. Such potential wasted. Variant covers? That's it? Oh wait, a couple of small reprints. The Ultimate Comics line is seeing a huge decrease in popularity with the relaunch. It seems like Marvel didn't learn from Image's mistakes in the 1990s. *March on Ultimatum* was extremely disappointing. Jeph Loeb has gone from a decent writer to "let's tear everything down for the sake of destroying it". The "manga" style of art in *Ultimate Comics: Spider-Man* is terrible.

Red Hulk - disappointing. Oh, wait. It's Jeph Loeb. Churchill's art is noticeably going downhill as well. Every Red Hulk cover has him spitting or drooling. A far cry from Churchill's DC days.

As mentioned in the "good" section, the Wolverine: Old Man Logan story line was fantastic. Too bad the rest of the Wolverine storyline has been so hit and miss. *Dark Wolverine* is terrible. *Weapon X* is terrible. *Origins* is okay, but barely. At least it has a more or less consistent storyline.

Marvel has attempted to do the "Noir" style with their main titles, but it seemed to be a photocopy of a photocopy; not very satisfying whereas the originals are very much so.

New Comic Sales - Independent Comics: Too many companies think that selling mini-series is better for sales than an ongoing series. If possible, some of the better independents should look at taking a cue from DC or Marvel. Develop a character that will resonate with the fans and grow that character. Batman has not ended since it's inception, has many miniseries, spin-offs, one-shots and the like.

My advice for all indies would be to put your best into an ongoing series and keep it fresh, support it with miniseries, one-shots, crossovers, and jumping on points, and you will see success. If you find you must constantly restart, relaunch and then stop again, or if you are unable to make your deadlines and only do only mini-series, you will not see a strong fan base. Chaos is a good example. Those books were overpriced and had many random mini-series that caused nothing but confusion to fans. Where is that company now?

I wish for the days of Valiant, a shining light for independents of the 1990s. Valiant died as well, but for other reasons.

Image Comics: *Haunt* is fair on sales, but it's just another McFarlane creation in a black suit with white markings. Though it's a bit too early to say just how well it will do, I believe it will be a slow death even with Kirkman doing the writing. *Walking Dead* is still going very strong and the new series *Chew* has been doing remarkably well.

We can't seem to keep any in stock. The *Chew* (Layman/Guillory) story is, suffice to say, a very original and enjoyable concept and has struck a chord with fans. *Walking Dead* (Kirkman/Adlard): buy it! Although "enjoyable" would not be an adjective most of the customers use. "Disturbing" and "unsettling, but compelling" are the most common ones. The 48-issue compendium at $60 is an amazing buy.

The apocalyptic "Image United" crossover looms on the horizon, and it most likely will flop. Only the true independents of Image seem to do well (like *Chew*, *Walking Dead*, *Invincible*). *Spawn* sales, for example, are at an all-time low. That does not bode well for Image or it's future.

I also must mention that the Luna Brothers continue to produce good work with *The Sword*, a re-imagining of mythology to include gods who still live among us. Good story, and the art, which is best described as uncluttered, suits it. Also take a look at *Girls*, which has a unique take on an alien invasion in a small town.

I would also like to mention *Fell* (by Image) but that appears to have fallen by the wayside; however, for 9 issues it was a very good read with each issue a self contained story.

IDW Publishing: Not much out of the ordinary here. Transformers, Star Trek and G.I. Joe will stay fan favorites forever.

We're happy to see a new *Transformers* ongoing series. It's a shame that the *Transformers* and *G.I. Joe* movies fell so short of expectations, missing the opportunity to attract some new fans to the titles. *Star Trek* is still riding on the success of the last film, and the fans are ready for another! *Angel* is still popular, though now that it has turned into a series of miniseries, the popularity has decreased somewhat.

Locke & Key (Hill/Rodriguez). By now everybody should be aware of how good this story is so I don't think I have to dwell on the details, but note that Joe Hill was nominated for best writer and the book for best series. Gabriel Rodriguez has won the 2009 Walt Whitman Award for his art, and the *Locke and Key* series has won the British Fantasy Society Award for Best Comic/Graphic Novel. It would be worth your time to get the trade if you are unable to score the first series.

Dark Horse: *Buffy* and *Star Wars* still headline the sales with *Hellboy* and *Conan* not far behind. The Dark Horse one-shots have been doing fairly well, though they are usually bought based on the writer/artist team-up. *Aliens* and *Predator* saw a brief appearance in the two mini-series this year, but overall there is not much unusual with Dark Horse, but maybe we've missed something due to a shortage of *Star Wars* fans in our clientele.

© DIS/Pixar

BOOM! Studios is bringing to comics the characters kids already know and love. (**Toy Story** #1 shown)

BOOM! Studios: Boom! has really gone explosive this year. Where to begin? The minis: numerous quality miniseries over the course of the year and more to come. We hope they stay consistent.

Farscape: old fans and new rejoice not only at the numerous stories published but also to the new ongoing monthly coming at the end of the year.

Most importantly perhaps is BOOM! Kids, as no other publisher currently makes so many comics for children. The deal with Disney-Pixar really allows Boom! to make comics based on characters kids already know and love, giving fans more of what they want and there's nothing wrong with that. The only problem might be Disney's acquisition of Marvel. It would be a shame to see the Pixar comics disappear from print in favour of a new deal. We are very pleased to see more kids books out there (as are our little fans) and it's nice to see. DC and Marvel making a little bit of effort in that same direction (*Tiny Titans*, *Superhero Squad*, etc.).

Irredeemable (Waid/Krause) is a story of what happens when a good superhero goes bad. Since the first couple of issues sold out, I think we can say it has struck a chord with the customers. Good story and as it progresses, not as simple as it seems at first glance.

Unknown (Waid/Oosterveer) is a story that revolves around a terminally ill detective trying to see beyond the veil before she dies, so she only takes cases which have some aspect of the supernatural. So far there are two mini-series and both are good reads.

Dynamite Entertainment: Lots happening at D.E. as usual. *Project: Superpowers* though, declined in popularity since the 1st volume. *Red Sonja*, *Zorro* and *Jungle Girl* remain favourites for many fans who are happy to read new stories and the new *Robocop* ongoing series is generating a bit of excitement before its arrival. More regular monthly titles is something that D.E. definitely needs as it is currently tough for the readers to keep track of the numerous minis of the same characters. The various *Battlestar Galactica* minis were an exception to this, as it was not necessary to read them in any particular order.

The Boys (Ennis/Robertson). What can you say about a group of individuals who kick superhero ass? This is one of the best irreverent takes on the superhero genre. Only *The Pro*, which is by the same writer, is better. Buy it if you are just a little bit tired of the spandex crowd. *Herogasm*, the spinoff, sells quite well also!

Avatar: Avatar has seen quite a bit of activity this past year with many wonderful limited series like *Anna Mercury*, *Blackgas*, *Black Summer* and many others. *Supergod* was amazing in sales but it is too early to see if it maintains the #1 sales spot. Ellis is always entertaining and we will always recommend his stories! *Crossed* (Ennis/Burrows) is a very, very dark horror story. Definitely not to all tastes. The story revolves around a group of survivors trying to stay alive amid total carnage after a virus turns most of the population into murdering maniacs. Customers have been very positive about this but confirmed that is not for the squeamish. A great trade in the making as it is a 9-part mini. At this point I have to restate that anything by Warren Ellis is worth the money and time. Look at this list: *No Hero*, *Doktor Sleepless*, *Anna Mercury* (1 & 2), *Black Summer* or *Gravel*.

Radical Press: For such a small imprint, they have great stories, superb production, and all at a great price. Could be one of the best lines out there in the future, there just are not enough titles yet! *Shrapnel: Artesia Rising* was especially good. *FVZA: The Federal Vampire and Zombie Agency* looks interesting as well. Decent art, prestige format and good stories for $3.99 cannot be ignored. *City of Dust* and *Hercules* are also enjoyable reads. To be blunt, very good value for the money. Take a look at the number of pages you get in *FVZA* versus some of the other books at the same price; plus the story is superior to some of the other product out there. Try them out!

***Glamourpuss* (Dave Sim):** Not your standard linear story line but rather a parody of fashion magazines with a history of photo-realism thrown in. There is no middle ground; people like it a lot or hate it. If imitation is the most sincere form of flattery, then Marvel must like Mr. Sim's work because they have come out with *Models* which bears a striking resemblance to the *Glamourpuss* style. But maybe it is a coincidence.

***Echo* (Terry Moore):** What do you do when a piece of high tech military hardware bonds to you? This series attempts to answer that question. This has a solid story and deceivingly simple art which conveys myriad details in a few lines. Yes it is in black and white, but also awesome and fitting.

***Atomika* (Abbinanti):** Again the initial 12-issue run should be completed by the time this goes out, but take some time and get the back issues, or if a trade comes out, get it. This is a very good modern mythology written for the atomic age. It helps if you're familiar with some of the Russian mythology. It is rather unfortunate it took 4 years to get the complete first story line out. Customers who were patient enough to wait will, hopefully, be rewarded with a satisfying conclusion.

Archaia Studio Press: *The Killer* (Jacamon/Matz) is one of the best crime stories to come out in years. The combination of text and image tells a complex story in a mere ten issues. Essentially it is focused on an amoral assassin and the relationships he develops while plying his trade. Get the trade if you can't get the back issues. It is simply one of the best crime stories (with apologies to Mr. Brubaker's *Criminal*). Top choice!!!

Back Issue Sales: Although my review this year focuses on current books, I would be remiss if I didn't at least touch on the foundation of our hobby: the back issues.

Modern 1984-2009: We are selling a lot more complete sets and runs than single back issues. Overall, this is due to the increased amount of trades available. Collectors desire the individual issues and love the ability to buy a complete story arc at once, while casual readers love the affordability of the trades. Also, when buying complete sets,usually it is far cheaper than buying separately. Mostly DC and Marvel sell, as the only major force in independents are by Image, and really, who wants those books? Those are dead, dead, dead! So sales on single books are low, but the sets and runs are higher than last year.

Copper - Late Bronze Age Back Issues (1976-1984): I'm still seeing demand for the cheaper low print runs of the DCs from the early 1980s. Of course they must be top shape, but there are still plenty around. People are rushing to fill their holes before prices go up. We are nearing the 30 year mark for the 1980s, and with more fans backtracking, it will begin to dry up eventually. Prices will soar within 5 years! Sales are better than last year.

Early Bronze Age Back Issues (1970-1975): Well, prices have climbed so much that you may as well go into the 1960s and start collecting there. That's what I've noticed. The low prices for this group are all but gone. I still love DC's War and Horror stuff at this time, and Marvel's Westerns and new superheroes, but price point makes the end of the 1960s close, so I've seen people shift that way. Sales are okay, but not as good as last year.

1960s Marvel: This is old news. Marvel always sells in this time. For example, we just sold 2 runs of *X-Men* from #1 up within 2 weeks! *Amazing Spider-Man*, *X-Men*, *Fantastic Four* and especially *The Avengers* are always going nuts. I still believe *Fantastic Four* #25 is undervalued and *Fantastic Four* #26 is overvalued. Other overvalued books to me are: *Captain America* #100, *Incredible Hulk* #102, *Iron Man* #1 and similar titles. These are not the 1st appearances. The one-shot with Iron-Man/Sub-Mariner which, predates both *Iron Man* #1 and *Sub-Mariner* #1, is more significant. *Tales Of Suspense* #58-66 (early Captain America, Red Skull, Cosmic Cube) is another example. These are undervalued and a better buy.

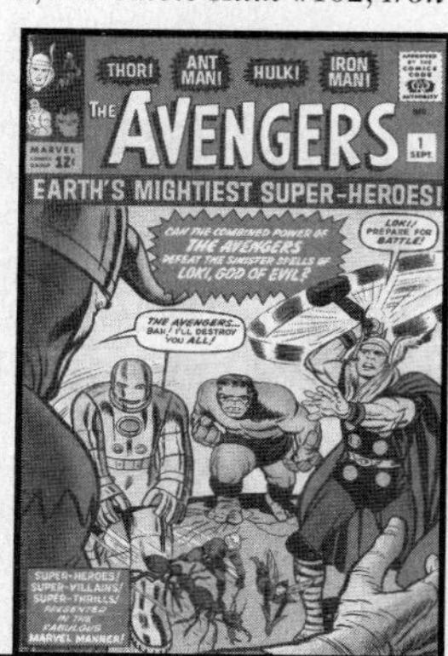

***Avengers* #1** *is one of those 1960s Marvels whose sales are always going nuts.*

1960s DC: Batman and Neal Adams are always the hottest and in the most demand. I believe a surge in *JLA* is coming, so watch out. *Green Lantern* is selling extremely well. Superman slowed, except for the Neal Adams cover issues, like *Superman* #233. Sgt. Rock is also super hot (*Our Army at War*).

1960s Other: Gold Key is my best in sales of all the Horror titles. Watch out for the *Dark Shadows* movie with Depp as Barnabas!

High grade low value books sell great. It doesn't matter the title. I've sold tons of Harveys and Charltons, ACG, and even Archies that fall under $50, but they are in top shape. Nothing really flat except the Classics Illustrated and the various Romance titles.

Golden Age - Atomic Age (1939-1955): Horror rules right now. Too much cool stuff. Not the EC fair, but all the rest. I find EC is too expensive and people prefer *Eerie* and the like. Of course anything by DC in this era sells, especially *Action* and *Detective*.

Toronto Conventions 2009: The big end-of-summer blast in August 2009 for Hobbystar drew 60,000 fans. This show gets bigger all the time. Reports had good sales all around. Everything sold from cheap bin books to bigger vintage items. We personally sold some early *Fantastic Four*, a couple Timely's and about 6 *Supermans* under #100. I noticed more money overall spread over our vintage books and new trades. Moderns really only sell well if very current. The older moderns tend to be sold at half price or less. The November one-day show was the best Fall show I ever had. I actually sold some better vintage items, mostly DC titles like *Action*. It was a big crowd for the one-day show. Wizard will have done a March 2010 show by the time you read this, as well as the big Hobbystar Con in June 2010. I cannot foretell what will occur, but I'll report on it next review. Toronto is a huge marketplace and rivals many big cities in the U.S. for quantity of stores and fans. If you are coming up here, try to visit the August Hobbystar show, especially if you have time for all 3 days.

Conclusion: For vintage books, Timelys are still impossible to find, especially *Caps*. *Action* and *Detective* under #100 are also hard to find whereas *Superman* and *Batman* are much more common. Big early Marvels are on the move again, especially *Avengers* #1-4 and *Tales Of Suspense* #39. New comic sales have hit record highs at our stores with many older fans coming back into the fold. I have also seen new young fans, thanks to BOOM! Kids. I have also seen once-retired fans rekindle their passion with vintage collecting, leading to a rise unseen by me in vintage sales. There is, as always, still room to grow. The publishers are on the right track with all-ages books, but these fall way too short for the young teen/tween readers between 9-13 years of age.

The best thing about this past decade is not even Marvel's resurgence; it would be the growth and strength of the real independent companies like Radical, Zenescope, BOOM, Avatar and Dynamite. We have never seen such a great pool of independent publishers. It's not about quantity, or flashy sparkly variants, nor whether it is published in only black & white. It's always about quality storytelling and consistency. Remember *Fell*? *Fell* was black and white. It was a great story. Yet, it FELL short by not being consistent nor even finishing. A shame really. It came close. There is always some backroom reason only the publisher or writer/artist knows about, and perhaps it is a good one, but eventually the fans suffer, and then so does our industry as a whole. Remember the huge delay in *Ultimate Wolverine Vs. Hulk*? At least, even though it took 2-3 years, it was completed.

Dan Fogel
Hippy Comix Inc.

Despite a tumultuous and uncertain economic climate, the past year has seen amazing volume and record high-end sales in the comics and collectibles market! What does this mean beyond objective financial gains? That we're essentially a commodities market that holds its values better than pork bellies and sorghum? Well, yes, but people feel safe investing in what they love with a record of realized sales easily trackable on the Internet. Like the stock market, but without the extreme volatility.

Current titles that were hot in 2009 included the Green Lantern-driven *Blackest Night* cross-over event and the new *Batman and Robin* Grant Morrison-Frank Quitely produced series from DC. *Captain America: Reborn* and *Dark Avengers* were among Marvel's successes, while Archie Comics brought us multiple redheaded nuptials!

My annual negative summary of 99% of 1980s and 90s books returns again like a Latverian despot! Over-printed, most of dubious quality, this unloved stepchild of an era generally sells at steep discounts. Truly high-grade slabbed keys, quality variants, and smaller press runs like *Teenage Mutant Ninja Turtles* and *Cerebus* are among the exceptions.

Bronze Age titles were stronger than ever! The ultra-high grade, almost invariably slabbed specimens achieved record sales repeatedly. Key issues were joined by highest-graded copies in the winner's circle, due to competing completists. Low and mid-grade books were very soft in comparison.

Silver Age superhero keys in all grades were in strong demand with record sales. High-grade copies of non-keys were popular as well, like their Bronze-Aged brethren, especially previously undervalued later Silver Age titles.

EC ruled the Atom Age in 2009, as EC Post-Trend, Annuals, 3D & magazine titles started picking up and the New Trend stayed strong. Charlton collectors and completists especially enjoyed the plentiful titles from this era.

Timelys, Superman, Batman and JSA-member titles remained Golden Age royalty. Fawcett and Quality devotees were vocal with their dollars, despite their fewer numbers.

Platinum books are nice to have, but so few people buy or collect them that it's a true shame! Big Little Books and related items do have their admirers, but usually only for the truly scarce editions in decent or better grade.

Insert here my annual shameless plug for *Fogel's Underground Comix Price Guide* and the new Supplement, which added mini-comix and UK titles to the mix, along with price increases and record sales reports. My fellow Overstreet advisors and other retailers and collectors have been gradually sampling the non-mainstream market. Look for fanzines to be the next esoteric collecting frontier!

Perennial thanks and props to Bob Overstreet, Steve Geppi, J.C. Vaughn, and Mark Huesman of Gemstone Publishing for their ongoing hard work maintaining this *Guide*'s accuracy and integrity into its 40th year! And a big shout-out to all the past, present, and future friends in comics who read my market reports and give me positive feedback between *Overstreet* editions!

Stephen Gentner
Collector

I feel that in light of the Stock Market, job market and the economy in general, the comic book market is in remarkably good shape! I have spoken before about the "love of books" with a healthy regard for monetary appreciation. This year, on a purely economic note, stock portfolios have not performed as well, nor held their value as have comic books.

High grade slabbed Marvel Silver Age keys are still performing well, and certain books like *The Avengers* #1 and #4 are jumping up in anticipation of the movies featuring the team. *Showcase* #22 over on the DC side should also benefit upwards as the *Green Lantern* movie sets for release. It is true there is speculation on these and other Silver Keys, but a smash movie kindles a strong flame under these books especially. We can hope that *The Avengers*, *Captain America*, *Green Lantern* and even the *Green Hornet* productions live up to hopes and expectations. I am uncertain how the Golden Age books of Captain America, Green Lantern or Green Hornet will react in relation to their Silver Age counterparts. Golden Age Captain America titles including *Captain America Comics*, *USA Comics*, *All Select*, etc. are already very sought after and valuable books. The movies, if good, will bolster them. If the movies fall short, these Golden Age titles will continue their strong showings anyway.

I would assume that Golden Age *Green Lantern* and *All-American Comics* will benefit from the movie, albeit Alan Scott isn't the star "Lantern" coming to theaters. My opinion about the Green Hornet is that where the 1960s *Batman* series helped the Batman comic titles enormously, the Green Hornet's TV show did little for the comics bearing his name. There are some really cool Alex Schomburg *Green Hornet* covers in the Golden Age title, but I feel that it was and is Schomburg's covers driving their increased popularity over the TV show's influence.

Increased interest from movie exposure to these characters helps the whole tide of cool, valuable Gold and especially Silver Age keys. Savvy collectors will try to secure copies of their favorites before catastrophic jumps in value put them out of reach. Another illustration of popular movie influence HAS to be that of Iron Man. *Tales of Suspense* #39 has become a true blue-chip Silver Age investment. The next *Iron Man* movie, along with the *Avengers* connection, will help further *Tales of Suspense* #39's strength. I don't think the second *Hulk* movie, although better than the first attempt, has pushed the Hulk titles as much as *Iron Man*. If the *Avengers* movie can properly advance the Hulk's character, this will change, to say nothing about Thor and Ant Man.

I am not a dealer, but I have watched the market keenly as our market/hobby has weathered the economic storm. I have seen jokes and heard investors kid about how they wished their portfolios were performing as well as their son's comic book collection! I sincerely hope our country's leadership can help "right the ship" of our economy for all Americans.

I have been pursuing *Adventure Comics* featuring the Legion of Super-Heroes this year. When I was growing up, *Adventure* and the Legion were the hottest comics and characters in my neighborhood. Later on, Marvel would assert itself, but in 1959-63, the Legion was my favorite. I had been avoiding putting together a run in favor of *Flash*, *Dr. Strange*, *Tales Of Suspense*, *Tales To Astonish* and Schomburg Golden Age books. But now I have come full circle. The charm of the Legion in *Adventure* still moves me. The concept of a superhero team comic and how popular they could be was demonstrated by *All Star*, *Leading*, *Justice League of America*, etc. Taking teenage superheroes from different planets and having them team up with Superboy was a good idea! New heroes would join along the way, changing and enhancing the relationships between the "Legionaires," and various members would be featured in story arcs; Lightning Lad dying, coming back, losing his arm, getting it back, etc. I have found that finding nicer grade copies of many Legion books is remarkably hard. Prices for these books in *Guide* are very reasonable. In the higher grades, $100 to $400 each seems to be enough... but the problem is finding them. I had thought that chasing down the Adam Strange appearances in *Mystery in Space* was hard... this is harder. Whether the Legion catches fire or not, I love the stories, art and the charm.

Just one more thought on *Adventure* with the Legion: so many of the stories revolved around super teenagers trying to join the Legion. Lots of heroes with lame powers tried to join. What was odd was how totally cruel the Legionaires were in rejecting them, especially Saturn Girl. For as "white bread" as DC was back then, the Legionaires "ripped the rejects a new one!" Even at the time, I thought how cold they were to the prospective members. Incidently, the rejects which the editors liked became the Legion of Substitute Heroes, joining the Legion mythos alongside the Legion of Super-Pets, Legion of Super-Villains and more.

Good luck in the coming year collecting!

Eric Groves
The Comic Art Foundation

The worst economic decline since the Great Depression depleted disposable income and diminished consumer confidence in 2009. Accordingly, we observed modestly slower sales and in some instances, a reduction in prices. On the other hand, we also saw a "flight to quality" as those with money to spend did not hesitate to invest in blue chip titles. Despite the turmoil of these times, we perceive no loss of passion in the comic collecting community. The spirit is willing, though the wallet may be weak.

For those interested in comics strictly as an investment or for speculation, high grade Silver Age Marvels, especially keys, are in the driver's seat. No doubt Marvel's largely successful exploitation of its characters in motion pictures plays a role in this phenomenon. One assumes Disney's acquisition of Marvel will not alter this business model. On the DC side, nothing Marvel has done can tarnish the astounding impact of *The Dark Knight* as enhancing the iconic status of Batman and the consequent healthy sales of that title.

The Golden Age Market: The most remarkable aspect of Golden Age comics is that just about everything sells sooner or later, even in mid to lower grade. At the VG level, there are numerous bargains to be found. This is especially true with Timelys, the imprint that continues to dominate year after year. Some collectors just want to own a few of them, even if they can never afford to complete an entire run. *Captain America Comics*, *Human Torch*, *Sub-Mariner*, *Marvel Mystery*, and *Young Allies* never have trouble finding a new home.

Close on the heels of Timely books are DCs, particularly *Batman*, *Detective* and *Superman*. We also see high demand for *All-American*, *Green Lantern*, any *Adventure* with Simon & Kirby art, early *Action* issues, *More Fun*, *Sensation*, *Wonder Woman* and even *Star Spangled*. Some of the lower numbers of these titles are turning up less frequently, but the thirst for them is evident.

Other GA comics continue to move for us as well because prices for mid-grade copies are quite reasonable. Quality titles such as earlier *Military* issues are excellent comics and, comparatively, a real value. We also receive requests for lower numbers of *National*, *Smash*, *Crack* and *Plastic Man*. Fawcetts, too, are good deals in mid-grade. *Captain Marvel Adventures*, *Captain Marvel, Jr.* (with Raboy art), early *Whiz*, *Marvel Family* and *Mary Marvel* are reliable, steady sellers.

There is continued collector interest in obtaining MLJ titles as well, although they are increasingly harder to turn up. Lev Gleason's *Boy* and *Daredevil* comics will sell, too, mostly the early numbers with World War II covers. The Fox imprint is also attractive, depending to some extent on the contributing artists. The same is largely true of Centaur comics. Early issues of Fiction House titles such as *Jumbo*, *Planet* and *Wings* are becoming tough to find, but collectors want them. Later Fiction House comics sell more slowly, but steadily.

©DC

With DC War, the low numbers go quickly, even in mid-grade. ***(Star Spangled War Stories** #62 shown)*

Somewhat overlooked in the Golden Age era are early Dell *Four Colors*. Granted, many are reprints of comic strips, but their eye appeal can be astounding, especially in high grade. Also, although higher numbers of *Walt Disney's Comics and Stories* and *Looney Tunes* are plentiful, the issues under, say, number 20, are difficult to locate. We could sell these comics for very respectable prices if we had them.

The Atomic Age Market: Collector interest in this era is undiminished, and in some cases, has increased. Students of the art form are increasingly cognizant of this period as spawning the greatest proliferation of titles in history. It was during this time that the Romance, Crime, Horror and War genres were created and, some might say, perfected. Notably, the Atomic Age came to an end with the imposition of the Comics Code Authority, the manifestation of a very nasty censorship movement.

Demand is solid for early Romance comics with Simon & Kirby art, as well as other artists who honed their skills in the titles of that time. There is increased interest in pre-Code War comics, some of them with excellent art and stories, including Atlas and Harvey Titles. Pre-Code Horror comics sell steadily, often as examples of sensationalism which drew the ire of the do-gooders. Crime comics, not so much, but some of the gory titles do well. L.B. Cole covers in all genres are sought after.

As always, the so-called "teen-age" comics of the postwar era continue to attract fans. Pre-1950 Archie comics are solid. Likewise with Timely or Marvel titles such as *Millie*, *Tessie*, *Gay*, *Comedy* and *Patsy Walker*. The first to go, when we have them, are Matt Baker comics such as *Teen Age Temptations*.

Finally, there is the gold standard of the Atomic Age: EC Despite the multitude of reprints, there are nonetheless collectors who want to own the originals. After all, no one has ever surpassed the talent Bill Gaines assembled for the EC bullpen. Leading the way are the Horror titles, *Vault of Horror* and *Tales From the Crypt*, followed by the Science Fiction comics *Weird Fantasy* and *Weird Science*. The War comics, *Frontline Combat* and *Two-Fisted Tales*, easily the best ever done, are somewhat slower, as are the crime titles. *Mad* comics are desirable, too, but not as much. The "New Direction" titles, as well executed as they were, are moderate but steady sellers.

The Silver Age Market: What can we say that will not be said by others? Silver Age Marvels are hot, especially keys, but condition is critical. *Amazing Spider-Man*, *X-Men*, *Hulk* and *Fantastic Four* are widely collected, even though much of their content has been reprinted. Earlier issues of *Tales of Suspense* are in demand, for obvious reasons.

Silver Age DCs are no slackers in the marketplace, but we do not see the obsession with condition that we observe with Marvel fans. *Batman*, *Superman* and *Detective* are as solid as ever. One current trend is long overdue attention to DC War titles: *All-American Men of War*, *Our Army at War*, *Our Fighting Forces* and *Star Spangled War Stories*. They sell steadily and the low numbers go very quickly, even in mid-grade.

One caveat about Silver Age Marvels: too much speculation in 9.4 or 9.6 CGC copies can lead to trouble in the hobby in much the same way as over-inflated real estate values nearly cratered the national economy. Pushing prices beyond reasonable limits merely conjures up illusory wealth. When the holders of these items decide to sell, and the market has neither the resources nor the will to buy them, the imaginary value vanishes and the price plummets.

The Convention Scene: We have often touted conventions as the best venue to buy and sell comic books, superior to impersonal eBay or the bidding fever of auctions. The opportunity to inspect raw books and haggle face-to-face with other dealers or collectors often results in deals mutually beneficial to both parties.

Our unscientific survey of other dealers and fans around the country reveals, unfortunately, a palpable level of discontent with the two largest conventions: San Diego and Chicago. Both shows can be enjoyed for what they are and good items turn up at them. But San Diego is now devoted largely to motion pictures. Comics are a subsidiary interest and the cost of setting up is very nearly prohibitive. Chicago, on the other hand, is best characterized as a scene for fans of a variety of popular cultural activities, such as professional wrestling. The number of actual comic dealers is decreasing and so is the number of serious collectors with money to spend on comics. We will not be attending either show in the future. We think other regional conventions have more to offer for dealers and fans alike.

Finally: although we are all in the great treasure hunt, we should be ever mindful of a larger mission: to inspire an appreciation of comic art for this and future generations. More than anything else, this will ensure that the artifacts we have accumulated will maintain their value in the years to come.

John Haines
John Haines Rare Comics

Hello from Ohio! Sales in this area of the country are slow slow slow. Sales on a national level are fast fast fast. Our online sales have been steadily growing even during the down economy and our convention sales have held firm. What are they asking for? Marvels. Yep, pre-1965 copies of Marvel superhero issues cannot be kept in stock at *Guide* prices. Ditto the mid-1970 and up Marvels, especially key issues and first appearances. Even *Tales to Astonish* Ant-Man issues are moving now, however *Strange Tales* is a little slower than the other titles. Those first six *Hulk*s sell the fastest.

Marvel Bronze Age continues to be our biggest selling area by volume. What else? We were fortunate to be able to acquire two decent collections (around 80 issues each) of Silver Age DC War titles this year - almost all are gone now. It has seemed to us that most dealers are passing on Disney material as well as Movie/TV comics. We have been fairly aggressive in our buying in these genres and have been mildly rewarded.

There is solid demand for Movie/TV issues (more for TV) as long as they look good – no creases or stains allowed. Photo cover or drawn cover seems to make no difference – collectors want both, with the most requests for *The Monkees* title.

Disney has slowed somewhat this year, mainly because there is so darn much of it – however we have had good success with the *Four Color* line.

On the Golden Age front, it is all selling, and I mean all. EC – sells. DC – sells. Timely - sells. Dell – sells, Fox – sells, MLJ – sells (instantly!), Fiction House – sells, St. John – sells, Nedor – sells, Centaur – sells (if you can ever find any), Fawcett – sells, Harvey – sells (try those early *Speed*, *Champ*, or *Green Hornet* issues), Quality – sells, Hillman – sells, Gleason – well…. not so much… but it does eventually sell.

On a final note, we purchased a large collection consisting of 1950s superhero comics from the estate of the original owner. All were nice, clean copies, and we had a great time looking at comics from an era that is seldom seen. We handled issue after issue of main DC titles like *Batman* and *Action* that we had not seen before as well as all but two of Atlas' superhero output. The collection was debuted at the 2009 Baltimore Comicon and received a great reception from Golden Age buyers there. We had a great 2009 and are really looking forward to 2010.

Dennis Keum
Fantasy-Comics

Despite continued weakness in the U.S. economy, our sales have held steady this past year with most of the past trends continuing in the same direction. High end Golden and Silver Age prices continue to escalate, with low to mid grade Silver and Bronze Age books selling at *Guide* prices, and Modern books showing price fluctuation but continuing to be solid sellers. While overall demand was steady, CGC graded Modern and late Bronze books showed dramatic price decreases starting from the early part of this year. There were instances in our sales where certain raw modern books were selling at above the same GPA-listed CGC graded price. While there was notable price weakness in CGC graded Modern books, prices appear to have bottomed out and we should expect it to come back in the upcoming years.

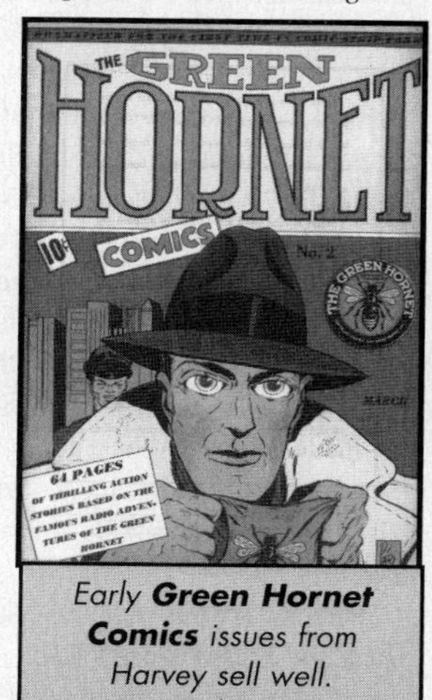

Early ***Green Hornet Comics*** *issues from Harvey sell well. (#2 shown)*

While overall comic book prices have held up for the most part, there were many reports of slowdowns at conventions sales and online price discounting of common issues by most major comic retailers. For the most part, we held our pricing at *Guide* and our sales grew proportionally to the number of items posted on our online inventory. Any slack in domestic sales was more than made up for in ever-increasing sales to our international customers.

On the buying side, we purchased many original owner Silver and Bronze Age collections this past year, adding to our stockpile of books that are pending grading and pricing. We are excited about bringing these books to the market over the upcoming years. Look for us to post more items on our eBay store, expand our website inventory, and attend more shows in the upcoming year. We are especially looking forward to setting up at the major shows and getting to meet many of our customers we have dealt with over the years.

Dave Matteini
Collector

Greetings comic collectors! What a crazy year 2009 has been for comics. Let's jump right in.

I feel like this gets to be cliché, but wasn't this really the year of record sales? The list is long and numerous examples are highlighted elsewhere in this book, but in particular I would like to address the *Action Comics* #1 CGC 6.0 sold on ComicConnect.com in early March 2009. This was an important sale for several reasons. First, the $317,000 sale was the highest all-cash sale ever publicly reported at that time, and even the more impressive given the economic condition at the time (the S&P bottomed out shortly thereafter and the credit crisis was still in full swing). The sale also generated solid publicity furthering awareness and interest in the hobby on a mainstream level.

Perhaps most importantly, this book showed that people view comics as a viable investment alongside such traditional investments as stocks and bonds. While *Action* #1s are rare and hard to come across, there have been numerous six figure sales in comics in both the Golden Age and the Silver Age. Is this a good or bad thing? Like everything, there are pros and cons. It is certainly a benefit to collectors to have a relatively liquid market to monetize their collection. The biggest drawback is that investors put their money where they feel they can have the highest expected return – whether it be funny books or otherwise. Having a hobby dominated by investors is certain to create excessive volatility and heighten collectors and investors monetary risk.

While 2009 saw several record sales, the comic market seems to be more and more a tale of two cities – the investment-grade collectible and everything else. Books such as the *Action* #1 or the high grade Silver Age Marvel key continue to push the envelope and set new records, but the lower high grade (anything 8.0 and below, from the late Silver Age on) just wallows in inventory or sells at bargain levels.

Personally, I was very active this year on eBay as both a buyer and a seller. I can tell you that eBay is still a great place to buy and sell comics, but eBay has its unique challenges. I have found that the mid-grade Silver Age books sell cheaply while the lower grade Silver Age books sell for pennies on the dollar. In the Copper and Modern eras, if it isn't today's hot book, it has a hard time moving.

I have found great deals on eBay buying lots of books of what would be otherwise complete runs except for one or two missing issues. I recently bought a run of *Harbinger* from #0 to #41 missing no more than five issues including #1, and a few of the later issues (although #41 was included) for the opening bid of $0.99. I also picked up a full run of *Batman: Legends of the Dark Knight* for $100 delivered with only two missing issues. Deals like this make it a great time to be a collector!

I have noticed more availability of books on eBay than in the past few years. I believe a lot of this increase in supply was due to eBay's recent decision to allow five free monthly listings. Under this new program, sellers can list up to five items every 30 days for free and only pay a final value fee and associated PayPal fees. This free option to list things has tempted me to put several items up for sale and seems to have had a similar impact on others.

More generally, if you have a want list, this was the year to fill it. Not only on eBay, but some of the best material hit the markets in droves. Similar to the *Action* #1 mentioned earlier, there have been tons of hard to find, high grade books that have come to market. In almost all cases, the prices have been exceptional. Happy Collecting!

Jon McClure
Comics Historian

I expect 2009 will be remembered for many record sales of high grade books, such as *Green Lantern* #76 in CGC 9.6 for $30,500 and another copy later in the same grade for $22,000. On 10/18/09 a copy of *Star Wars* #1 35¢-c variant in CGC 9.6 sold for $26,250. The 30¢ and 35¢ Marvel Price Variants continue to grow in demand as collectors follow the age old rule of pursuing what the other guy can't find or doesn't have, a rule otherwise known as "scarcity and demand."

This year was good for me selling low-grade keys over *Guide*, with solid sales of Charlton, DC, Gold Key, and Marvels leading the way, and even minor keys sold well when priced under $100. *All-Star Western* #10-11, *Weird Western Tales* #12-38, and *Jonah Hex* #1-20 were impossible to keep in stock even at 50% over *Guide*, because they are great reads and no doubt because of the upcoming movie. With contemporary books averaging $4 each, common stock of older books (mid 1950s to mid 1970s) in lower grade sold well in the $5 to $15 range of decent and obscure titles, and I've heard from other dealers that a lot of 1980s to 1990s "junk" moves well in the $1.50 to $2 range for decent titles. The low grade older books sell to mostly middle aged folks looking for "memory triggers" from their childhood, and anything pre-1980 that is inexpensive and looks fun sells well in the $4-6 range, often because parents are trying to share their interest with younger children and want material that is more wholesome and less violent and sexual. My favorite comic has been *The Walking Dead* for some years now, but it is not a first choice for young readers with thoughtful parents, and neither are many other contemporary comics, when you can buy a 30 to 40 year old comic for the same price. Even in a sluggish economy, items that are fairly priced and reasonable discounts for quantity moves average material.

Todd McDevitt
New Dimension Comics

I always think some background info on those writing these market reports is helpful, so here's a little about me. I started New Dimension Comics in 1986 while still in high school in my hometown. I have made comic books my life. The business has grown to 5 stores surrounding the Pittsburgh, PA area. Many fortunate things have happened to me to get me this far. When I started, I thought I'd be one guy in my one store doing what I love and making enough money somedays to eat steak, and others to get by with ramen noodles. I never expected to grow to this level. One of my rules has always been to buy everything I can. I think keeping a fresh and relentless flow of new material through my stores has been a huge component to my success. With the purchase of a giant warehouse a few years ago, nothing holds me back from taking on loads of comics 100s of thousands at a time. So... I guess handling all these comics has brought me some insight to share here.

Golden Age: It still happens. I bought some great collections this past year of "attic finds". Just when you start to think there aren't any more raw comics to be found, they roll in. I even paid over *Guide* price for a great find, *Detective Comics* #16 in 8.0. I do my best to get awesome books. And it's also nice to see that the demand for these books is as strong as ever. I sold many of these great finds, within a week of owning them, to my regular clients. Some sample sales include: *Sub-Mariner* #21 FN $400, #26 VG $275, #32 GD/VG $500, *Green Lantern* #9 FN $650, #16 VG $350, #18 FN $500, *Sensation Comics* #16 FN+ $450, #17 GD $120, #18 VG/FN $300, #39 VF- $350, #50 VG+ $150, *Wonder Woman* #6 VG+/FN $400, #9 FN/VF $900, *Superman* #26 FN/VF $1200, #37 FN+ $375, *Detective* #80 VG+ $250, #101 FN $300, *All-Flash* #17 VF $500, *Action* #64 FN- $400, *Flash* #63 VG/FN $200, #62 FN- $320, #40 VG/FN $300, *All Winners* #12 VG+ $450, #21 VG+ $1200, *Human Torch* #11 VG $500, *USA Comics* #14 VG+ $380.

Silver Age: Comics from this era are great, but they seem to be polarizing in price. Desirable key books command top dollar and get it while more common, filler issues are tough to sell for full *Guide* price. I maintain a Silver Age inventory that is one of each of all that I acquire. Spares beyond that, unless fairly desirable, I bump into a $5, $3, or $1 sale stock. This often goes with me to conventions since folks there like 2 things: A deal and the thrill of the hunt! But even great books that are "*Guide*" at $8-15 put out for $3 each don't fly out the door.

Modern Age: Another regional point worth mentioning is the doom and gloom of the economy. Well, it hasn't affected us much at all. In fact, new comic sales are very strong. There has been some hesitation with the increased cover price costs, but only slightly. Fans might have to pick and choose a little more to afford what they can spend, but they are still sticking with their hobby. I get a sense that being involved with the comic hobby is cooler than ever. Being part of the secret society where trends are seeded adds to the appeal of the hobby. It's like liking that unknown rock band for years, and then suddenly they hit it big. "I liked them before they were cool" kind of mentality.

Miracleman is still hot, and will likely only get hotter as Marvel proceeds with plans for it. We are still selling the foil editions well, many for $200-250 each with limited print runs of 25-250. Variants have flowed even freer than last year, but still have some life in them although I'm seeing some it start to fade a bit.

Mark Jewelers Ad Books: As collectors, more importantly completists, continue to quest for something new add to their stash, I see these books becoming more sought after. I compare them to the price variations that are chased down now. For those who don't know, some comics were released in certain regions, particularly near military bases, with an ad insert in the center for Mark Jewelers. These are especially rare in high grade due to the life they had after being bought by a serviceman who jammed them in barracks and often didn't bother to drag them home. I sold a *Hulk* #181 in Fine for $800 with this insert. Another variation worth mentioning are the National Book Store reprints. I have seen 2 recently from 1972 (*Tarzan* #211 and *Korak* #48) which I have sold quickly for $25 each. These reprints have custom ads for National Book Store Inc. inside the front and back covers. Very unusual.

Online Sales: With the rise in fees and more so aggravation of eBay, we have turned much more to just posting items into an eBay store and letting them sit until that special customer connects with them. You can see our thousands of listings at eBay user ID ndcauctions. Sales there are very steady, but nothing to get excited about. It's a sideline and is usually where we post items too obscure for our local customers. Even CGC books have dipped there. It seems eBay buyers are almost always bargain hunters. Some highlights include: *Journey Into Mystery* #92 in 9.0 $1000, #103 in 8.5 $436, *Batman* #366 (great Joker cover) in 9.8 $159, *Amazing Spider-Man* #68 in 9.6 $925, #129 in 9.2 $820, #238 in 9.8 $375, *Defenders* #10 in 9.4 $199, *Swamp Thing* #37 in 9.8 $250, *Jonah Hex* #92 in 9.8 $184.

Steve Mortensen
Collector

2008 and 2009 were good years for comics. Many high grade Bronze/Silver/Golden Age issues saw record prices at auction. Last year I closed my business Colossus Comics and became a full-time collector again. I have enjoyed following the hobby and adding to my collection. I still buy and sell CGC modern books and track the modern market in my column "I've Been Slabbed," which I write for *Comic Buyer's Guide*. The current market for new comics in CGC 9.8 has continued to be flat. It's still fun to add graded books to an ongoing series as a collector, but it's hard to be a speculator with Moderns – especially since many books sell for less than the cost of grading. The 9.9/10.0 market continues to be strong, although submitting books hoping to receive a 9.9 or 10.0 is a set-up for disappointment. I continue to encourage collectors to take advantage of CGC's prescreening service for their Modern books. That way they're not stuck with 9.6s or below, which for Moderns are basically impossible to sell.

The market has been tough for sellers selling CGC 9.8 Moderns. One friend once told me that he was happy to make $1 on each CGC 9.8 current comic he sold. Subsequently, he's no longer in business.

The Year in Review

In November 2008, *Y: The Last Man* was added to the ever-growing list of comics that are being made into movies. Also, *Thor* #600 came out, bringing more attention to Marvel's new movie slated for 2011.

In December 2008 it was announced that *Ultimate Wolverine vs. Hulk* was finally going to complete its run. Sales of the #1 sketch cover sold for as much as $350 in CGC 9.8, although prices dropped almost in half since the book first came out. Prices for the #1 sketch cover in CGC 9.8 currently sell for about $200.

© MAR

The market was stunned by the sales of **Amazing Spider-Man** #583 and other comics featuring President Obama.

In January 2009, with the *GI Joe* movie coming later in the year, back issues of the Marvel series from the '80s were hot in CGC 9.8. Many common issues were selling for $80-100 where more rare issues like #150-155 were selling in the $400-800 range. Also at the beginning of 2009, *Watchmen* issues did very well in CGC 9.8 – some as high as $400 each. In November 2009, however, prices dropped drastically, as is frequent when the hype of a movie has passed. #1 in CGC 9.8 last sold in November 2009 for $58. It sold for a high of $1,050 in 2007. Ouch!

In February 2009, Barack Obama stunned the comic market with his appearances in *Amazing Spider-Man*, *Savage Dragon* and *Thunderbolts*. *Amazing Spider-Man* #583 variant cover led the way with prices as high $400 in CGC 9.8. By November 2009, prices settled into the $100 range for CGC 9.8 copies.

The *Jonah Hex* movie was announced in March 2009 and sales of *All-Star Western* #10 (1st appearance) have done very well since then. One of two known copies in CGC 9.8 sold in September 2009 for $10,400 (14 times *Guide*). CGC 9.4 copies have been selling in the $1200-1500 range (about 2 times *Guide*). *Jonah Hex* #1 in CGC 9.8 is selling for around $400 (more than 3 times *Guide*).

In April 2009, ComicConnect made headlines with their sale of *Action Comics* #1 CGC 6.0 for $317,000. Mainstream media announced the auction and sale and it showed how high grade comic books were weathering the economic storm just fine. *Amazing Fantasy* #15 CGC 8.5 sold for a whopping $118,977 and other beautiful Silver Age comics in CGC 9.6 and CGC 9.8 have been selling for record prices. Also, at about this time there was a shift by sellers and buyers who moved from eBay to ComicLink and ComicConnect to exclusively purchase and sell their high grade Bronze/Silver/ Golden Age books. eBay has tainted its own market with unpopular policies and higher fees, and as a result, the big sales are now found elsewhere.

In May 2009, comic book collectors wanted to know what happened to Bruce Wayne. At the end of *Final Crisis* #6, Bruce Wayne is apparently killed but afterwards he appears alive back in the Stone Age. As you know, Dick Grayson is now Batman, but collectors haven't embraced that as an ongoing concept. I think most collectors believe that we haven't seen the last of Bruce Wayne as Batman. Prices for *Final Crisis* #6 in CGC 9.8 never reached prices above $100 and by November 2009 the prices settled in the $50 range – a fairly small sum for what may be a key issue moving forward.

Later in June 2009, Dick Grayson and Damian Wayne began their new series by Grant Morrison and Frank Quietly. Pre-sells for this book in CGC 9.8 were around $40, which is a solid price for a current comic. Ungraded comics of the sketch cover (1 in 250) were selling for as high as $170. Graded copies of *Batman* #657 may someday gain ground. It's the first appearance of Damian in Robin's costume. In August 2009 the book only sold for $20 in CGC 9.8.

In July 2009, the recent death of Michael Jackson had affected the comics market with the sale of *Moonwalker 3-D* #1 CGC 9.6, which sold for $735. It was a relatively unknown comic that suddenly sold for an amazing price.

San Diego Comic Con was fun for me to attend this year, but it was dominated by media and non-comic dealers. From what I hear from my dealer friends, it was a difficult year to make money. Lots of people came to the Con, but they didn't bring money to spend (many came for the freebies and the signings). Some dealers said they made less than half of what they made on Friday and the rest of the weekend was a big disappointment. I'm sure that the economy had something to do with it. I know I brought less cash than usual.

This year Stan Sakai celebrated 25 years of creating stories around Usagi Yojimbo. *Albedo* #2 is still an elusive book in CGC 9.8, selling well above $1,000. At the SDCC, Stan was readily available for sketches and signings and was very courteous to his fans.

Also in the summer, Todd McFarlane and Robert Kirkman announced their partnership in a new series called *Haunt*, one that has been well-received as of this writing.

In September 2009, Disney bought Marvel. At this point it's hard to tell how this will affect the comic market. The Image comic book *Chew* built up a huge following of collectors just after it came out. #1 sold in CGC 9.8 for as high as $290. It settled back down into the $100 range as of November 2009. Another popular series has been the retelling of the *Wonderful Wizard of Oz* by Eric Shanower and Skottie Young. In San Diego, an ungraded copy of #1 was selling for $15-20. CGC 9.8 copies have sold for $50-$80. In September, they also announced a new series based around L. Frank Baum's second novel, *Marvelous Land of Oz*.

Many Golden and Silver Age comics are reaching almost 50 times *Guide* as in the case of *Amazing Spider-Man* #37, (intro. of Norman Osborn) which sold in May 2009 for $21,111 in CGC 9.6. The *Overstreet* price for the book is $450 in NM- condition. The same book in March 2009 sold for $478 in CGC 9.2.

In November 2009, I began looking to add low grade copies of key Silver Age books to my own collection, but I keep getting outbid! *Journey Into Mystery* #83 has been selling well in all grades, especially because of the *Thor* movie coming up. A CGC 4.0 copy will cost you about $1,800, which is 50% over *Guide* - not too bad for those looking to pick up an affordable copy. This shows a strong market for low-grade key Marvel issues from the '60s.

In conclusion, 2010 looks as if it will be another impressive year for comics. As Hollywood continues to produce films with comic characters, the back issue market should stay pretty solid. For modern CGC collectors, '80s titles (Copper age) look to be the next boom. Copies of *Teenage Mutant Ninja Turtles* #1, *Albedo* #2, *Amazing Spider-Man* #238, 252 & 300, *Cerebus* #1, *Transformers*, *GI Joe*, and *Bone* #1 are some of the great titles and issues to look for in high grades. Note how many are independents! Hmmm... interesting.

Jamie Newbold
Southern California Comics

Greetings readers. It's October and San Diego is experiencing yet another dry spell. There is also a continuing "dry spell" in the comic book sales arena. I'm speaking about two years of recessive sales nationwide finally catching up to "new comics" sales (more later). Capitalism is still reeling under the weight of mortgage defaults, stalled loans, unemployment, and bailout fallout. But, one collectible continues to hold its own in battle - the old comic book.

Capitalism is capital-schism in my world! Our 2009 economic reality split from much of the sadness in other parts of the business world. The average Gold, Silver, and Bronze comics remained popular purchases. They consistently sold well worldwide at the same basic pricing points as they did in 2006. While other markets either feel the pinch of current economic woes or are returning to normal, comic book back issues flourish as though the state of America's retail business was bi-polar!

Beginning with the tragedy of 9-11, our business has survived potential sales droughts as the economy reshuffles itself. After the recession began this time around I expected to see horrible sales figures, books go unwanted, and money not made. Instead, as with 9-11's impact on the U.S. economy, our current economic insecurities have reduced back issue sales very little.

Our sales are not huge, not even big, but they are consistent. Back issue sales from ages past to the present rarely slowed down throughout the year. Prices achieved reflect a market savvier from sacrifices made by businesses to stay alive and attract customers.

Sure, some people have stopped buying new comics. We've seen it and continue to witness the slow departure of customers that we depended on for new comics sales. We've seen stores apply ridiculous discounts to retain customers. The selling of new comics to make a living is truly an art.

However, older comics continue to keep moving. Why? Older comics are just so darn appealing and the prices are right. Many customers choose comic books that are priced to their liking because old comics often stay the same price. There usually is no fluctuation with these books, unlike purchasing food or gas. At the very least, you can negotiate a comic book sale. Try negotiating your gas price at Chevron or the cost of milk at a 7-11!

Selective discounting at the retail store level helps move books that would sit at full price for years. We found that round-filing lower graded pre-1980s books into $5 and $10 price tags have better turn out. By ignoring established prices and buying and selling at cheaper rates, this strategy works for everyone (except those determined to get more). There are plenty of buyers at our end of the state making it worth our while to carry them.

Customers of eBay set the standards years ago and the recession has reinforced those pricing standards. There is no need to try and sell a VG copy of *Strange Tales* #163 for $12.00. Better to slap $5 on it and the buyer will eventually arrive to collect it. Wholesalers and collection owners offering these kinds of books to us see the same reality. We are getting opportunities to buy older collections with less resistance to lower offers. Those same eBay standards are seen by everyone.

Store Sales: Comic book buyers love a store that sells new and old comics. At our store, the "hands-on" ability to hold comics before making a purchase breeds trust and loyalty. I cannot emphasize enough how easy it is to sell a comic book if the buyer can see it in three dimensions first. The tactile sale and the fact that there are not many stores left with exotic comics in quantities give us a huge advantage over eBay.

The past two years of economic headaches created our dependency on greater numbers of out-of-town buyers for older back issues. San Diego's transitory-resident nature drove out a few customers through the year due to both financial and career related reasons. Unfortunately, these were the same people that frequented our back issues on regular basis. Although the drop was relatively minor, we were able to bounce back with the amount of tourists visiting the area. Many of these visitors came in to the store inspired by on-line reviews, *Overstreet*, prior contacts, or internet sales activity. Often, they would share stories of other dealers and collectors with me. These discussions provided different perspectives of pricing/collecting and also allowed for informative feedback. Plus, you get a real good feel of the nationwide market scheme through the visitors.

New Comics: 2008 brought about a 20-30% loss in business. Retail numbers steadily began a return right after Christmas. It was as though everybody took a collective sigh of relief and returned to old habits. 2009 proved to be different in that summertime brought positive growth and spending with some help from Comic-Con attendees. However, college tuition hikes, labor shortages, and recurrent fuel increases spelled trouble just on the horizon. California's sales tax increase also hampered sales of new comics. These unfortunate events produced the next round of disappearances that affected the sale of new comics.

I ended up in a new round of cutting quantities of pre-ordered monthly comics. Diamond Comic Distributor's F.O.C. (Final Order Cutoff) feature became a steady function every Wednesday (adjusting ordering numbers--downward). Now, in the fall of 2009, we are still regularly reducing the quantity of title orders. This has slowed down a market we enjoyed for the first 8 months.

Marvel's general cover price increase to $3.99 across a majority of their titles did not impact us immediately. We initially saw increased daily sales figures as our customers segued into new cover prices. Slowly, customer complaints about the extra dollar per book, the constant one-shots, tie-ins, and limited stories against their tightened budgets abounded. Two common complaints we have heard centered on substandard story arcs and late titles. Even fan favorites, like *Kick-Ass* and *Captain America: Reborn,* got sales-slammed. Similarly, DC presented $3.99 issues. If DC had retained $2.99 prices universally, I could have countered Marvel sales decline with DC titles as affordable reading alternatives for Marvel fans. Raising cover prices in a recession, for easily dropped comic books--NO!

Cover prices, delays, and a bad economy forced some of my die-hard, big pull customers to consider which titles they absolutely must have. Whether the page count was 32 or 48, the $3.99 cover price continued to hurt business as I stacked unsold copies in hopes that buyers would still pick them up. To alleviate money problems, many of our regular pull-list customers deleted Marvel titles from the subscriptions all together.

I must add that the current theme of DC and Marvel's constant story events seem to be losing gas each time they come out. Dark Reign and Blackest Night story lines started off strong. Then, too many comics sharing the same storylines (with convoluted continuities -- Spider-Man!) and no end in sight created buyer backlash in hard times. These problems stopped buyers from purchasing them, even if the story line was good. It was done to save money at a time where comics' creators need to compensate for this phenomenon.

On a brighter note, trade paperback book sales have continued to rise in quantity. My customers have a combative nature when it comes to overpaying for comics. They see that some small publishers cover price their books at $9.00 across the board. My customers pursue those comics in very small quantities as though they were luxuries. They require Marvel and DC to toe the line at lower prices to remain active readers. Their frequency of TPB purchases against buying single issues indicates:

1) Customer's reluctance to experience $3.99 cover prices
2) Their patience to await a full stories' release in book form months after the comics were released
3) A way to send a message to the publishers that pricing should be a serious consideration.

*Dealers are selling generous helpings of current Marvels thanks to the continued quality of the stories. (**Thor** #600 shown)*

Marvel Comics: The Dark Reign event is entertaining. I like what's been played out so far in the storylines. I think *Dark Avengers*, *Wolverine*, and *Invincible Iron Man* have been both well drawn and written. Although these series were enjoyable, some of the limited Dark Reign series and one-shots alternated between necessary and wastes of money. Spider-Man was retooled and continued to succeed even though I lost track of exactly who knows what about Peter Parker/Spider-Man. I was surprised with the return of the clone legend. That old chestnut bore Marvel shame in the '90s. Now, it's back for reasons unknown and without much fan desire at my store.

Marvel's concern for its standard bearer titles reflected in the overall quality of art and writing. I sold generous helpings of titles like *The Avengers*, *Hulk*, *Thor*, *Daredevil* and more because they continue to be that good. Brilliant titles like *The Torch*, *The Marvels Project*, *Doctor Voodoo*, and Icon's *Incognito* rocked! Marvel's "Noir" titles sold in small numbers contrary to their potent entertainment value. It's just hard to push variety onto a money-tight clientele.

Disappointing fans with delivery delays and high cover prices slowed the momentum on heavily publicized series like *Captain America: Reborn*, *The Twelve*, and movie phenomenon *Kick-Ass*. *Captain America: Reborn* ran out of steam so fast that it literally chopped the sales of the regular title in half.

The "War of Kings" story event was surprisingly entertaining for me. I'd long since lost touch with the back stories of many of Marvel's space-based heroes and villains. Bashing Inhumans into the Kree and others was fun. With the Skrull invasion all but forgotten, the War of Kings stories were briefly entertaining and offered suitable space opera replacements.

Marvel trade paperback book sales increased and continue to generate steady revenue through the year.

Marvel's success formula for Wolverine in 2009 = "Old Man Logan". Formula for a successful Wolverine story in 2010 = repeat the same as above!

Marvel continues to dominate back issue sales. 1960s Marvels remain on many buyers' fantasy purchase lists. Conversely, new Marvel comics can be just as difficult to obtain after a sell-through as they were when Marvel began its "no over-ship" policy years ago.

DC Comics: DC titles showed surprising resiliency in an unsteady market. I found a handful of their comics held their own sales weight against Marvel in numbers I don't usually see. The "Blackest Night" story arc overwhelmed anything Marvel had. Blackest Night had the luxury of promotion at San Diego's Comic Con and the wealth of Green Lantern merchandising in '09. Blackest Night sales began shortly before that show and caught fire with its inception.

I've enjoyed the new characters inhabiting the roles of Batman and Robin. The sales figures on the Bat titles remained consistent and I received favorable feedback from my customers. DC failed to produce much splash with the overworked Superman family. Flash and other frontline DC characters waded in shipping delays or uninteresting stories.

Vertigo usually produces several interesting titles each year, one or two which resonate strongly with my readers. *Sweet Tooth*, *Haunted Tank*, and *Unknown Soldier* were tremendously entertaining. The emergence of Sgt. Rock in the hands of Billy Tucci was a supreme attempt at blending DC fiction with World War Two fact. Ongoing series such as *Northlanders* have sold steadily while former strong sellers (*Y, The Last Man*, *Preacher*, *100 Bullets*, and *Fables*) continue to dominate at trade paperback sales levels.

WildStorm's *Ex Machina* continues to be a strong trade paperback seller. *Gen13* and *The Authority* were best sellers in my store. At last, the final issue of *Planetary* arrived. However, their video game-based monthly titles have done less than I anticipated. They have a strong talent pool and many tradesmen to draw from. I'm anticipating that they must have something heavy waiting just behind the curtains.

IDW, Image, Dark Horse and everyone else: IDW works hard to find new subject matter and talent to bring to market. IDW is a company that works hard at their craft and keeps trying new things. It's always fun to see what they produce next.

Retooled *Transformers* and *GI Joe* comics spotlighted IDW's licensed titles. Their sales numbers plateaued after this year's movie releases. A promising *The Ghoul* from Niles and Wrightson looks like fun. The *Angel* TV show comics continue to do real well. Joe Hill's *Locke & Key* title has also been a store favorite with customers eagerly anticipating the upcoming third series.

Image Comics delivered with *Chew* this past summer. The first 5-issue storyline was great fun and sold extremely well. In fact, it met *Walking Dead* sales numbers quickly! *Walking Dead* is the king of trade paperback sales and sells constantly. *Back To Brooklyn* is a violent, tough-gangster 5-issue story. Garth Ennis and Jimmy Palmiotti captured a lifestyle that comics rarely engage at that depth (unless you read any Garth Ennis Punisher story!). *Haunt* with McFarlane's cover art started well and with Kirkman's writing, it proves to be a big hit with the customers.

Dark Horse has entertaining comics but customers are not purchasing them. Conan's re-launch as *Conan The Cimmerian* is a great read and should sell better. *Kull* was exciting, well-done, and should have brought more attention. Even the *Star Wars* titles have left more unsold copies behind than in the past. *Aliens* and *Predator* were relaunched with little fanfare. I liked both but the franchises as comic books have slowed way down over the years.

Conan's relaunch as **Conan the Cimmerian** *is a great read. (#1 shown)*

Avatar's *Crossed*, *Chronicles of Wormwood* and *Ignition City* should be avoided unless you really want to be highly entertained!

In my opinion, these companies and other independent publishers have suffered from uneven sales in 2009. It's clear from a drop in our new comics sales that my customers have sacrificed almost everything to satisfy their Marvel and DC demands. That is a shame. Dynamite Entertainment (*The Boys*, *The Boys: Herogasm*, and Garth Ennis' *Battlefields*), Boom! Studios (various Disney/Muppet titles and *Irredeemable*) and Zenescope (anything from the *Grimm Fairy Tales* series) make good reads and deserve to sell more copies than I'm currently able to sell.

Website Sales: Slow, steady. Our new website produced a few more customers and made navigation easier. The fan site Yelp was added as a link to our site. Favorable comments left on Yelp by customers have snowballed into more new customers. The guise off the comments when they check sites like Yelp to shop for the stores they consider the best. It's important to respect the power Yelp, Google and others generate. We see more customers land at our store purely off what they read online and not through the Yellow Pages.

We don't pay for much online advertising and rely on the whims of internet exploration to match up with customers. Previous local ads to draw people into our store have produced limited results. The randomness of existence in the ether of the internet does provide some exposure. But often the cost of an ad is not exponential to the advantage of paying for nothing. Yelp provides plenty of exposure for those that do "search for comic book stores" entries. They post reviews that tell everyone if a store is worth visiting and are easily directed to our website. The next step up from free listings is an ad that cost about $350. The Yelp! sales people promise more site exposure for your money. For a small business I'd rather take my chances with the free aspect. Many internet advertisers set ad costs above what a store my size can justify. To put that in perspective we pay $270 monthly for five AT&T Yellow Page directories servicing all two million-plus people here in San Diego.

eBay/Auction Sales: Ahhh, eBay, why have you forsaken me? Buyer friendlier but little improvement for small sellers. We run a set number of comic book auctions each week. We've been doing it with relative sameness each time. This year, there's been a disruption in the successful number of sales. Fewer sold items (at steeply discounted minimums) and fewer return buyers (we still maintain 100% positives so it ain't us!). I've noticed regular buyers have disappeared, people that bid and won consistently for years. They've been replaced or subdued by new bidders that come and go. We continue to collect their positive feedbacks but we don't see the same amount of return buyers as from past years. One theory, based on the wide array of items won is that the buyers were simply buying for resale. The sales never panned out for them so they stopped buying from us. There's always somebody on eBay selling the same thing for less (with more risk to the bidders!).

We sell mostly comics on eBay. Most of the comics we sell are commons. I have choicer stuff I prefer to display at my store but when times are tough eBay continues to furnish badly needed income. I take a price hit against *Overstreet* pricing when I sell common comic books on eBay. I constantly get buying opportunities for collections of old comics at my store. I scale my purchase prices against an inevitable sale on eBay. eBay governs many of my bottom-line business decisions in the back issue market.

CGC Comics: Fees went up and buyer confidence remains about the same. CGC copies sell like always. The concerns over pressing and re-slabbing have not disappeared. I know collectors who still favor disclosure of pressed books to CGC as a rule. I know if I bought a CGC'd copy of anything I'd want to know its history—all of its history!

Golden Age: It's tough to talk about Golden Age if you don't have it to sell. Opportunities to buy for resale are scarce at our store. Options at conventions often depend on other dealers. Our show, Comic-Con International sees fewer dealers each year and less buying for Gold. We do see collections come into the store that contain random GA books. Past lessons for retailing much of what we see still apply.

Gemstone began publishing EC reprints in a new form two-three years ago. The books did not sell well for us. They came along too late to attract a decreased reader interest in ECs. Original EC comics are the best. But the market seems much smaller than ever. We've picked up quite a few ECs in the past 18 months. Comics I've always loved only to find market resistance at anything close to *Overstreet* prices for low grade all the way up to VF. Getting 1/2 *Guide* is even hit-and-miss. Changing times and changing collectors.

We experiment with CGC'd GA books to see what will happen. Usually the book chosen to go to CGC will be one many people will want or have a value well above the submission costs. Because of the wide variety of GA books I can only attest to a few sales trends. On average, we get about 60-75% of *Overstreet* for CGC'd DC commons or semi-keys. Our best stuff, high-grade copies do closer to 75%.

Most of our better Golden Age sales stories surround Comic-Con or auctions online. Some examples: *Mad* #2 CGC 7.5 $775.00; *Donald Duck Four Color* #108 CGC 9.2 $9,400 (thanks ComicLink); *Top Notch* #13 CGC 9.2 $1,500; *Walt Disney's Comics and Stories* #46 VF+ $400; *Jumbo Comics* #154 CGC 9.2 Mile High copy $450; and *Batman* #18 CGC 4.0 $575

Silver Age: Collections come and collections go. Some stand out and the purchase of *Batman* #101-230 created a bit of a sensation this year. That was one of the more singular collections we've seen in awhile. (Yep, same collector that sold us #1-100 in the past).

We saw a frequency of smaller Silver Age collections come into our store throughout the year. One old-time comic collector contacted us and sold a large selection of less-common Gold and Silver Age books. Fun to go through the stuff and grade things we rarely ever get to see. 1950s Atlas war comics, 1960s Dell and Gold Key TV/movie comics that I never get to see. Miscellaneous '50s titles that just look cool and rarely turn up in collections.

Still, opportunities abound when you own a store. Coaxing owners to take my money is not so easy. This year we let a couple of varied comic collections go. Average stuff like '50s and '60s Funny Animal comics, 1960s commons, Dells and Gold Keys. The owners in each case wanted more than I could justify. Owners steeped in information gathered from eBay without corresponding knowledge of grading and issue differences refused to sell to me. They felt they could do better. Pretty standard behavior for comic book owners swept up in the hype of comics' values but no experience on which comics got there and how.

I enjoyed the variety of collections that came in and the singles that went out. To this day I'm amazed how few '60s and '70s DC comics enter our shop in comparison to the much greater volume of Marvels. The *Batman* run was not only significant for its consecutive issue count but also for its singularity as all-DC in one collection. I've had plenty of Silver Age Marvel collections make their way to this store for years. Usually they're spotted with DCs but it's never the other way around! Our inventory reflects the proportion of Marvels to DCs. Our Marvel selection is often deep from the earliest issues right up through the Bronze Age stuff. With DC we are lucky to have one or two of anything from the 1960s. Three or more of any one issue in quantity is unheard of!

DCs are popular but without frequent DC collections popping up for purchase I might as well be trying to buy Golden Age.

Amazing Fantasy #15 CGC 4.5 $6,600.00
Amazing Fantasy #15 CGC 1.8 $2,250.00
Amazing Spider-Man #1 GD+ $1,800.00
Amazing Spider-Man #1 CGC 6.5 $5,500.00
Amazing Spider-Man #14 CGC 7.0 $850.00
Amazing Spider-Man #47 CGC 9.6 $1,800.00
Amazing Spider-Man #50 CGC 7.5 $450.00
Avengers #1 CGC 4.5 $900.00
Avengers #46 CGC 9.6 $540.00
Daredevil #14 CGC 9.6 $1,125.00
Daredevil #18 CGC 9.6 $1,125.00
Journey Into Mystery #124 CGC 9.4 $500.00
Showcase #56 CGC 9.6 $500.00
Tales Of Suspense #29 CGC 8.5 $350.00
Tales To Astonish #93 CGC 9.4 $900.00
Thor #137 CGC 9.8 $1,100.00
Thor #139 CGC 9.6 $315.00
X-Men #1 GD $700.00
X-Men #4 CGC 7.0 $489.00
X-Men #17 CGC 9.6 $2,000.00
X-Men #25 CGC 9.4 $540.00

Bronze Age: Marvel keys retain the same demand. Marvel commons from all titles just sit unless they are lot-priced or sold cheap. CGCing them is an option but the fine line between a 9.6 anything and a more profitable 9.8 makes submission selection tricky.

1970s DCs including all the Kirby Fourth World stuff, issues of *Swamp Thing*, *The Shadow*, and *Shazam!* linger at the "tough to sell" category. The #1s are in great abundance and in high grade almost every time I get one. But who is buying them at *Overstreet* prices?

I remember working at Richard Alf's Comic Kingdom in the mid 1970s and purchasing stacks of these things, along with *Dr. Strange* #1, *Howard the Duck* #1 and others from distribution. The beginning stages of speculation - when the resale on new, "hot" comics was being exploited by store owners, employees and insiders.

Now, all those copies I sold back then are coming back to haunt me! Some significant sales:

Amazing Spider-Man #129 NM- $800.00
Defenders #1 CGC 9.6 $425.00
Giant-Size X-Men #1 CGC 9.0 $1,100.00
Incredible Hulk #181 VF/NM $1,200.00
(Copper Age) *Amazing Spider-Man* #300 9.8 $1,200.00

Prices Up or Down?: This is always the conflicting issue with the *Price Guide* as a tool. Should any prices in *Overstreet* be raised? Is the 9.2 category relevant for price increases on anything other than high-demand books? The construction of the book makes it difficult to follow market trends for high-grade (9.4 and higher) comics. With 9.2 as the ceiling I go elsewhere for pricier numbers. It's clear some books have surpassed last year's *Price Guide* standards. For our purposes those successful books continue to be key books.

I don't collect and collate stats. I keep that information at my fingertips when I need references. GPAnalysis, the big auction house sales stats and studious internet watchers keep me informed.

I can attest to certain trends based upon the frequency and qualities of my sales. Key Marvels, key Silver Age DCs (which ones are popular enough to be hot books in this decade is debatable) and key Bronze Age books continue to set new sales prices. *Overstreet* can continue to match those prices in print.

Golden Age books will sell frequently at half price regardless of what they are. Buying GA comics is problematic when the owners are aware of posted *Overstreet* prices. Offering to buy them at 1/4 of *Guide* so I can sell them at 1/2 *Guide* can be a struggle. Owners don't understand my reality and only believe what they see in print. *Overstreet* may want to consider dropping GA prices on commons about 10% this year. The difference in two years of *Guide* prices pointing downward provides a demonstration model. I can show collection owners the down trend and the logic of my offers will be undeniable. Hopefully, my fellow dealers recognize the inevitability in price reduction. The reality is, they're going to sell that low, anyway.

I understand that perspective buyers will see the price reductions and slant their bottom line to match, to offer even less money. What else can you do?

Raw Silver Age Marvels routinely sell for me at about 1/3 of *Guide*. Whether it's eBay, my website or my store, 1/3 is the base price to guarantee an eventual sale for just about any 1960s book. Fortunately, many DCs and Marvels will sell at close to full retail. It just takes longer and requires the right shopper. 1960s DCs slip a little further in the percentages. 1/4 of *Overstreet* is too often the best I can get for all but the most desirable issues.

Can *Overstreet* reduce the prices on low and mid-grade Silver Age books? Market corrections have already been made. *Overstreet* has reduced prices in many categories. I respect the interest in lining up with new market standards. But, the average prices for '60s commons in mid-grade are still too high, by far. I don't know if *Overstreet* can go much lower without identifying the truth of the current market--that many copies are now only good enough to read and not good enough to spend more than a couple of bucks.

Convention Sales: On a convention level, my main show presence is at the San Diego Comic Con International. I also attend one or two other shows during the year. I gather gossip and stories from other dealers (including other Overstreet advisors).

Patterns develop each year and I'm privy to the information that explains those patterns. One pattern that escaped my best prediction was the lack of sales at the 2009 San Diego Con.

2008 was a banner year for us in that the convention was just a good, easy show all the way around. However, in 2009, the show was set squarely in the second year of our country's economic recession. In contrast to the previous show, I felt the reluctance of buyers spending money this year. Factors included an overcrowded dealer's room, freebie frenzy by attendees, a lack of back-issue buyers (the common feeling was that many held off until Sunday to make their purchases) and the Hollywood distraction. I commiserated with many fellow dealers and learned it wasn't just me who experienced low sales. No one changed seller styles or offered different products...which generally stay the same each year. The fact is that we didn't change--the Con changed. One major difference that many have seen is that the Gold and Silver Age sellers have reduced in numbers but attendance has increased.

Where and why have all the buyers gone? One dire consequence of dealer placement and large crowds are the throngs of people blocking access to one booth to get freebies or signings at another. Small press and publishers have been crammed into the same, tight area we occupy. They run promotions that generate huge lines of people and block aisles. Back issue guys don't draw large crowds so we can't fight back. The Con managers do little or nothing to alleviate the stress. What a zoo. The sheer volume of people at our end of the room makes access to our booths a struggle. I'd like to see the show authorities fix that.

Adventure Comics (#67 shown) is a Golden Age DC title in high demand in Very Good to Fine condition.

One irksome, logistical nightmare that Comic Con presents is their feedback period. Dealers with issues relating to convention problems are welcome to present them on the last day of the show. As a veteran of many Cons, I've gathered plenty of complaints, but I never get to air them. Why? The main reason is that the forum is held for one hour late in the afternoon on the last day when business and theft are especially heavy. At a time when we are all busy standing in long pre-registration lines for next year's show. When the crush to leave the dealer's room is at its greatest, I'm stuck at my booth working. In fifteen years I've never had a problem-free show and never been able to make it to the forum. COME ON!

I give kudos to the fledgling Long Beach Comic Con. Wizard World LA left a gap when it disappeared. The Long Beach people happily filled that gap. I thought the little show had heart. Now, go see it and spend some money when it returns!

Terry's Comics runs its own annual show in Orange County. It's dominated by Terry's desire to honor the traditions of shows of yesteryear where back issues were the draw. Support Terry and all of us Gold/Silver/Bronze guys and show up.

Terry O'Neill
Terry's Comics
CalComicCon

Sales from 2008 to 2009 have been mixed but not too bad, despite the economic slowdown. All comic book conventions appeared to have record attendance, while all of my West Coast shows, except Seattle, have had sales decreases. I also had my best show ever in Chicago. Shows in other places have had mixed sales. Catalog orders have been steady, but some customers are choosing to suspend their collecting or just outright sell their collections. As a result, we have been able to acquire more great comics than in years past. We continue to pay higher percentages on Marvel and DC keys, and many Atomic Age comics.

Golden Age: Sales of these comics are steady, but only certain titles are in demand. As always, *Action*, *Adventure*, *Batman*, *Detective* & *Superman* titles in Very Good-to-Fine copies are in high demand and many sell well at above *Guide*. Fawcett's Marvel Family titles, (*Captain Marvel Adv.*, *Captain Marvel Jr.*, *Master*, *Marvel Family*, *Mary Marvel*, *Whiz* and *Wow*) are steady sellers at around *Guide*. Many Golden Age keys are slow sellers due to their inflated prices in low-to-middle grade. Timely titles mostly sell over *Guide*, but are also hard to get unless you want to purchase them for top dollar. Early *Walt Disney's Comics and Stories*, and *Looney Tunes* are easy to sell at around *Guide*. Other titles with L.B. Cole, Schomburg, Crandall, Lou Fine and other good artist covers are also being sought out. Lower grade comics at less than $50 seem to always sell fast, regardless of title, if priced and discounted right.

Atom Age: Atlas (Marvel) comics from this era are selling very well with Horror (*Mystery Tales*), Western (*Two Gun Kid*), War (*Battlefield*) and Jungle (*Jann of the Jungle*) titles selling best. We have a large selection of over 2000 different issues to choose from, so we can gauge this group pretty well. Teen and Romance titles were also selling well. DC titles from this era that were selling well were the Big 5 War titles (*Our Army at War* and *G.I. Combat*) and most Superman titles (*Lois Lane*, *Superboy* and *Jimmy Olsen*) due to their relative scarcity. DC Humor titles such as *Dean Martin and Jerry Lewis*, *Bob Hope*, *Jackie Gleason* and *Sgt. Bilko* were selling well. Other publishers that were selling well were Fawcett and Dell westerns like *Rocky Lane* and *Roy Rogers*. Non-Atlas Romance, Crime and Funny Animal titles were all slow, except Disney titles. We haven't purchased many ECs recently, but we get many requests for them at conventions.

Silver Age: One area where sales continue to surprise us is high grade Silver Age Marvels. We purchased a couple of original-owner collections of mostly Marvel comics and did very well selling high grade slabbed and un-slabbed comics.

As always, *Amazing Spider-Man* was the most popular but there was also strong demand for *Avengers* and their group member titles such as *Incredible Hulk*, *Iron Man*, and *Thor*. Most Marvel keys are still able to sell above *Guide*, especially *Amazing Fantasy* #15, *Fantastic Four* #1 and *Incredible Hulk* #1. Issues like *Captain America* #100, *Incredible Hulk* #102 and *Iron Man* #1 that were once plentiful now sell fast. DC Silver, while much rarer in high grade, is still harder to sell even at *Guide*. This may be because there are just fewer collectors for this material. The exception is DC War in high grade (especially gray tone covers) and *Green Lantern*, with #76 and *Showcase* #22 being very hot. Batman and Superman titles both sell okay in mid-to-lower grade but they are usually discounted below to make sales. Archie titles are selling well but mostly for less than $10. TV and Movie titles have cooled off a little except the Western titles like *Bonanza* and *Maverick*, but Charlton superheroes, like *Blue Beetle* and fantasy titles like *Konga* and *Gorgo* are requested more than usual.

Bronze Age: High grade Marvel Superheroes are selling extremely well followed closely by high grade DC Mystery titles like *House of Secrets*, *Phantom Stranger* and *Witches Tales*. Some of the better selling Superheroes titles are *Avengers*, *Captain America*, *Conan*, *Batman*, *Detective* and *Green Lantern*. *Marvel Team-Up*, *Defenders* and *Champions* are finally getting some respect. *Incredible Hulk* #181 and *Amazing Spider-Man* #129 continue to be the two best selling books from this era. Marvel Monster books such as *Werewolf by Night*, *Tomb of Dracula* and *Frankenstein* have cooled a little from previous years, as have the mystery reprint books and X-Men titles. Humor, Funny Animal and TV/movie comics (*Pink Panther*, *Scooby Doo*, *Donald Duck* and *Star Trek*) from this era are a little harder to find and usually sell fast if you price them at *Guide*.

Magazines: Where are all those Comic Magazine collections? Sales of this material were weak, but again, we have not been able to acquire much of this material. Some titles that were selling were *Creepy*, *Eerie*, *Famous Monsters*, *Mad*, *1984*, *Elfquest* and *Savage Sword of Conan*. Some sales of note were *Creepy* #9 in 8.0 for $60, *Blazing Combat* #4 in 8.0 for $45 and *Web of Horror* #1 in 8.0 for $50. We have had a lot of requests for high grade magazines, early Warrens and comic-related Fanzines. Also those Eerie Publications magazines like *Weird*, *Terror Tales* and *Tales of Voodoo* are being sought out.

Modern Age & Independents: *Watchmen* was a big hit and we sold every issue we had accumulated over the years. *Wolverine* miniseries #1-4 were also selling better than usual, thanks to the *Origins* movie. We had many very high grade Marvel titles like *Avengers*, *Spider-Man* and *X-Men* from a large original-owner collection we purchased; they all sold very well at above *Guide*. The guests at the CalComicCon this year were Bruce Jones and Berni Wrightson, so we were able to sell quite a few PC titles like *Berni Wrightson, Master of the Macabre* and *Bruce Jones Twisted Tales*. Both of these guys are professionals of the highest caliber and would sign anything that was put before them. I watched Berni sign a stack of comics from the floor to the top of the table for one person. Some sales of note were *Wolverine* V1#1 CGC 9.6 for $150, *Sgt. Rock* #303 CGC 9.6 for $100 and *Daredevil* #181 CGC 9.8 for $100.

Graded books: I am convinced that this is the best way to sell pre-1975 comics in very high grade. The only drawback is the cost of getting books graded; this will often be recovered when you sell the comic. It is a wonderful way to keep really nice comics from getting damaged and to tell if any repairs or restoration have been done. With most stocks losing up to half their value almost overnight, many people are investing in graded comics. Some sales of note were *Iron Man* #1 CGC 9.4 for $1800, *Incredible Hulk* #1 CGC 4.5 (restored) for $1800, *Amazing Fantasy* #15 CGC 1.5 for $1924, *Detective* #225 CGC 5.0 for $1300 and *Tales of Suspense* #39 CGC 4.5 for $1800.

Internet Sales: Most of our internet sales have been through our eBay store, even though we have two websites with over 40,000 items listed. We usually sell only CGC graded books on eBay, but we list our entire inventory at www.Terryscomics.com and www.NationwideKomics.com.

In summary, despite the worst recession of my lifetime this past year, we have managed to maintain generally good sales. I attribute this to two things. First there's nostalgia, a desire for better times that comics bring to us, if only in our minds. The second is with all the uncertainty in financial markets, collectibles and particularly comics, seem to be a good place to spend our money.

Jim Pitts
Surf City Comix

A crazy year of ups and downs. While books that are the "Best of the Best" bring incredible multiples of *Guide*, you have to ask yourself, "At what point do I want to spend as much money on "The Best" *Amazing Spider-Man* #66 as you could on an "unslabbed" VG early Timely?" So here's what I had, and sold, this year!

Pulps: Almost anything that is 1910 or back has interest right now. Soft prices in pulps by comparison to Golden Age, when you consider surviving numbers. Horror, Sci-Fi, and violent Western Covers are my best sellers. Low grade "bondage" and "needle" covers from the late '30s to mid '50s still fetch $30 to $50. More "generic" covers tend to sit at $15 to $20 in lower grade. Alex Schomburg covers, Kelly Freas covers, and Vaughn Bodé covers tend to be my best movers in the late '50 to late '60s pulps. Their covers move easily at $15 to $25, but "generic" issues tend to sit at $5.

Big Little Books: I wasn't offered a lot that fit my "tight criteria" of being complete this year. The few I sold included, *Blondie and Dagwood in Hot Water* (1946) VF $75, *Donald Forgets to Duck* (1939) FN $100, *Shadow and the Master of Evil* (1941) FN- $150.

Golden Age: A tough year for me "buying wise". Even with the economy, demand outstripped supply. Early Richie Rich and Archie issues sold quickly in almost any grade for me. Low grade early issues of Barks' Duck books still move well for me, as do early *WDCS*. My best sellers, in any grade, were Fawcetts. Their bright covers make the superhero books the top of the heap for me. My overall Golden Age sales included the following: *Action Comics* #57 (2nd Lois Lane cover) VG+ $360, #100 GD $140, *Adventure Comics* #214 (2nd Krypto) FN- $200, *America's Greatest Comics* #1 GD $400, *Archie's Girls Betty and Veronica* #2 VG/FN $275, *Archie's Pal Jughead* #2 VG $165, *Batman* #85 VG $140, *Detective Comics* #70 $500, *Fawcett's Funny Animals* #14 (Crowley) VF+ $100, *Four Color* #16 (Porky Pig #1) FN $300, *Human Torch* #20 VG+ $350, *National Comics* #9 VG $275, #21 FN $250, #24 FN $250, *Plastic Man* #2 GD- $200, *The Spirit* #1 FN $350, *Spy Smasher* #2 VG $350.

Silver Age: Here the key is "keys". If you have the "key" book of the title, or the hot book of the moment, you can't keep them in stock. The other issues need discounts to move, unless it's the "highest graded copy" or something zany like that. DC Silver Age actually seemed to be my biggest mover this last year. People scooped up stacks of low grade *Superboy*, *Adventure*, *World's Finest*, and *Detective* as quick as I could price them. On the Marvel side of the fence, people were really buying up *Sgt. Fury*, *Strange Tales*, *Tales to Astonish*, *Tales of Suspense*. *Spider-Man* and the *FF* seem to have cooled off some for me, unless I had that #1 issue. Dell, Harvey, and Archie all have people looking for them. A few sales worth noting included: *Adventure Comics* #267 GD $110, #300 FN+ $160, *Batman* #136 VF $225, *Classics Ill.* #169 (last issue, 1st print) VF/NM $175, *Incredible Hulk* #3 VG $350, #5 GD+ $180, *Tales of Suspense* #40 GD+ $200, *Tales of the Unexpected* #1 GD $120.

Bronze Age: Since I don't sell "slabbed" books I don't have any monster sales to report from this era. But what sells the best for me out the Bronze stuff I pick up? Marvel and DC Horror and War sell really well, as does *Conan*. Also, Marvel reprint books, Gold Key Sci-Fi titles, low grade Archie titles, and Treasury Editions are what seem to do best for me.

Modern Age: Since I don't sell "slabbed" books, most items in this area are sold at a discount. Items that sell for me without discounting include: *TMNT* first prints of the first four issues, Marvel and Gold Key/Whitman Price Variants, last issues of many of the Whitman titles, any of the comic book appearances of KISS.

Magazines: Slowed down a bit this year. Warren mags are still the most asked for thanks to *Vampirella*. Skywald stuff seems to have slowed after the price surge they had over the past few years. Marvel mags still sell well, with *Conan* at the top of the heap. *MAD*s still sell well in almost any shape up to about #120. After that, collectors seem to only really want ones without the fold-ins done.

Undergrounds: Sold well for me all year long. While most sales are of the smaller variety, the following did well for me: Robert Crumb titles in off grade (vintage Crumb at around $10 to $20 just flies), Rick Griffin titles (I sold several *Tales from the Tube* at $50 to $150 and 6 copies of *Man From Utopia* at $80 each), Freak Brothers anything (the "best sellers" in Underground history), early Art Spiegelman stuff (his new work created interest in his old work), Larry Welz titles, Larry Todd titles, Vaughn Bodé titles, Yellow Dog tabloid Second Prints (they stayed too cheap for something 35+ years old).

Hopefully this year looks up for all of us! See you in the funny papers!

Bill Ponseti
Collector

2009 was a tough year in terms of the economic impact felt by a large portion of people across America, and certainly the comic market was not immune to this severe downturn. Or was it? I guess it depends on the level at which you play.

From my perspective it seems that for those who play at the very top of the market, high grade – high dollar books, they were apparently insulated from the negative impact of the recession on their ability to spend as a group. The disparity between those who can, and do, spend what would seem to be "crazy money" in pursuit of comic book grading perfection and those who are simply trying to complete runs or sets, has never been greater. I've been around this hobby for over 35 years and have often been wrong in my prognostications about what comics will sell for, and when prices will stabilize, so I gave up making those sorts of predictions a long time ago. Just when I think a book or segment of books has topped out, boom, another record shattering price is realized!

More so than I can ever remember before though, non-key, relatively common books in extreme high grade are selling for astounding amounts of money. Five figure sales for these types of books in 9.8 are becoming the norm. So some real thought needs to go into the spread this year to accurately reflect how the market behaves. How do we properly create a pricing spread when a comic lists for $29 in 2.0 *Guide* and a 9.6 sells for $4500? And this is nowhere near an extreme example of the disparity in sales by grade.

I guess the good news for this kind of market is that the "bottom feeders" have been able to take advantage of the high grade feeding frenzy and scoop up lots of low grade books at much lower than *Guide* prices. I've seen

© Harris

Warren magazines lead in buyers' demand, thanks to **Vampirella**. (#85 shown)

this across the board; even the much hallowed halls of Timely Golden Age have been affected. But the downside is that if you would like to collect some higher grade books that don't *Guide* for much at the top, that ship has sailed. So those collectors are faced with the prospect of changing what they collect or not collecting at all. For me, I've had to dramatically change the focus of what I collect to be able to keep collecting within my ever shrinking comic budget. However, there are tons of great comics to be had at nice prices so I am still a happy collector! There is one last negative to this though, more competition for the stuff that I want than ever before. I used to be one of only a handful of people collecting Dick Tracy comics, now they seem to get scooped up at auctions for more than I really want to pay for them sometimes. This phenomenon has crept into a few other historically slow titles that I collect as well. *Famous Funnies* is another title that I've experienced increased competition on. The mainstream titles that I chase have simply become too expensive for me, even in mid-grade, to collect anymore. I simply won't pay $500 or more for mid-grade mid-run Golden Age issues. So, like many others, I have started chasing lower grades than I would normally have went for.

Page quality has always been important to me and most collectors, but now, at both ends of the market, it is more important than ever before. Super high-grade books with white pages do much better than their counterparts with off-white or lower quality pages. Cream to off-white can seriously damage a very high-graded book's sales potential. This goes to the argument that I've made for years that page quality should be a factor of the grade, not simply just a notation to the grade, as it is now. In my view, two comics with equal structural grades but different page quality are different grades. Are we not, after all, grading the total state of preservation from Mint for a comic when we grade it? At the bottom of the market, page quality is key as well. If those of us who have been forced down the ladder of grade by price are going to enjoy this new found situation as best we can, then we want pages to be as white as we can find them. I am much happier with a 2.0 book when the pages are as white as snow. I'll often pass on one with cream or worse page quality.

Ok, so now onto prices. Here are some notable sales for me this year: *Fantastic Comics* #3 (1.0)(EA) for $1950, *Four Color* #16 (4.0)(MP) for $1575, *Jungle Comics* #1 (5.5)(Rockford) for $1100, *Detective Comics* #225 (1.5) for $275, *Phantom Lady* #13 (4.5) for $750, *Batman* #11 (5.5) for $1900, *Planet Comics* #1 (4.0)(EA) for $1000, *Amazing Spider-Man* #14 (8.5) for $1700, *Sub-Mariner Comics* #1 (1.0) for $1500, *Fantastic Comics* #1 (8.0) for $2250, *All Star Comics* #3 (1.5) for $2000, *Fantastic Comics* #6 (9.0)(SF) + *Pep Comics* #17 (7.5) + *Single Series* #20 (8.5) in a package deal for $6750, and *All Star Comics* #3 (5.5) for $8000.

Here are some notable purchases for me this year: *Blue Beetle* #1 (4.5)(SP)(Larson) for $1700, *Exciting Comics* #9 (2.0) for $1200, *Startling Comics* #10 (3.0) for $450, *Black Cat Comics* #26 (9.0) for $175, *Avengers* #1 (3.5) for $700, *Pep Comics* #17 (7.5) for $2200, *Fantastic Comics* #8 (7.0)(SF) for $1500, *Marvel Mystery Comics* #7 (2.0) for $1250.

By and large it was an excellent year for the hobby as lots and lots of comics, and money, changed hands in 2009. My personal collecting has slowed down over 50% from 2008 and will probably take another 25% reduction for 2010 unless something unforeseen happens. As with previous years, low and mid-grade Gold and Silver sell for a fairly large discount from *Guide*, at least 20% or more for Gold and 50% or more for Silver. High grades are quite unpredictable, but mostly go for way over *Guide*. A new area of collecting for me has been Copper Age comics. When I was a comic shop owner we had tons of this era, but I never really paid that much attention to it. I've been buying quite a bit of it this year. It's nice and cheap. You can buy it by the box load and enjoy reading them without fear of losing thousands on a small crease or bend. Hopefully 2010 will be huge year for comics and comic movies! See ya next year!

Greg Reece
Greg Reece's Rare Comics

First and foremost, thanks to all of my customers who let me live the dream. 2009 was another banner year for Gold, Silver and Bronze Age comics. There are tons of great reports in this *Guide* about how 2009 went, and I'll share some thoughts as well, but my focus is on trying to figure out where we're going (I know, good luck, right?) The old staple, "buy what you like" is always true but if you're also looking at comics as an investment, read on. Hottest book on the planet? *Showcase* #22 for sure. I purchased 4 copies all at once, (paying well over *Guide* to get them) and owned them for less than 120 days. While any book that gets this hot ultimately cools off (even by the time you are reading this maybe?), I still believe this will turn out to be a solid investment. The anticipated release of the *Green Lantern* movie underscores just how elusive this issue is (in any grade), but particularily in grade 6.0 or better. While demand may cool, I do not expect prices to ease. In fact, I see a steady climb from here as it was unrecognized just how tough this book really is. The 2nd hottest book? *Avengers* #4. A tale of two cities here though as copies graded 6.0 and below are readily available. As with many issues, I expect high grade copies to continue to move up but copies graded 5.5 and below to lag. I saw a nice mix of collectors looking to fill runs and the key/high grade collector and I expect this trend to continue. Despite the many dire predictions for our industry, I see many in the 35 and under crowd collecting, and this bodes extremely well for the future of the hobby.

I could not keep an *Amazing Fantasy* #15 in stock. While not particularily tough, this is one of the blue chips of comic book investing. You cannot lose if you buy and hold.

Even though there have continued to be seemingly endless explosions in price difference between 9.4, 9.6 and 9.8s, I think that trend continues. There is always the notable exception where someone can overpay of course, but overall I think our hobby is still just beginning to appreciate how rare über-high grade books are. If book XYZ has 6 copies in 9.4 and only one stand-alone in 9.6, then simple math tells us the 9.6 is worth 6X the 9.4s. But that's assuming a demand that's equally divided among the 9.4s and the 9.6s, which of course, isn't true. Yet you can find many real life examples where a 9.4 (of which there are multiple copies) goes for $300 and the 9.6 can be had for $700- $800. 9.8s are rarer still and will not magically appear out of the woodwork. From an investment standpoint, buy the best you can afford, you will not regret it.

There are a few books that I think are undervalued and could turn out to be great investments in high grade. Please remember many of these books are not rare in lower grades but are nearly impossible in 9.0 or better: *Strange Tales* #115, #135, *Showcase* #4 (Can a *Flash* movie be too far in the distant future?), *Journey Into Mystery* #83-100, *Brave and The Bold* #28, *Justice League of America* #1, *Adventure Comics* #247, *Action Comics* #252, *Showcase* #9, *Lois Lane* #1-20, *Jimmy Olsen* #1-20, *Green Lantern* #76, virtually all Timely superheroes. I am not a big believer in the Bronze Age in the near term as I think prices have already gotten there, while supply of very high grade books will continue to find their way to the market. That's not to say certain Bronze books won't appreciate, but there are better opportunities out there. Also, I would recommend staying with titles that continue to be published (*Superman*, *Amazing Spider-Man*, *Iron Man*, *Batman*, etc) and stay away from now long dormant titles (*Phantom Stranger*, *The Shadow*, *Plastic Man*, etc).

In closing, I look forward to seeing many of you on the 2010 circuit, I wish you and your families good health and I hope you find that *Action Comics* #1 at the local garage sale (and of course, call me if you do.)

Dave Robie
BigScoreCollectibles.com

A lot of Big Little Books came on the market in 2009 with a big group from Diamond International Galleries, and Heritage Galleries selling off many from the Don Vernon Collection. As a result of this, and many books coming out of attics and hitting eBay, the market for low to mid-grade books is stagnant, or a little down. The market for very high grade books in unrestored condition is strong.

Big Little Books with crossover appeal continue to be in demand with notables like Popeye, Betty Boop, Dick Tracy, Smokey Stover, Shadow, Phantom, Sci-Fi, Westerns, etc. Any super rare pieces like the Mickey Mouse and Famous Comics sets that came in boxes with crayons are bringing top prices, since only a handful in any condition are known. Over the last 5-10 years eBay has brought so many Big Little Book collectibles out that we now know which are the truly rarest.

Big Little Book cards continue to garner high demand with many bringing in the hundreds of dollars. It is common knowledge among non-sports card collectors that the 224 Big Little Book promotional card set is one of the hardest sets to complete . . . if ever.

Highly sought-after premiums include the two Pan Am *Tarzans*, the *King of the Royal Mounted/Far North Buddy Book*, and the two Mickey Mouse Macys. Fast Action books are on the slow side in any grade. There is more demand for the superhero Dime Action books. The Thornton Burgess *Wee Little Book* sets in their boxes are always hot.

There are now three known copies of the ultra rare *Mickey Mouse Mail Pilot* variation with the Mickey cover. Only a few true Near Mint copies (no restoration) are known of the first Big Little Book – *The Adventures of Dick Tracy*, so check closely when spending the thousands of dollars required to buy one.

Heritage sold Don Vernon's grouping of Better Little Book original artwork covers which brought multiple thousands of dollars – far above estimates (e.g. Popeye-$19k, Red Ryder-$11k, Bugs Bunny-$17k). A number of 2000 series original artwork covers from the Whitman archives were sold on eBay in the mid to upper hundreds of dollars.

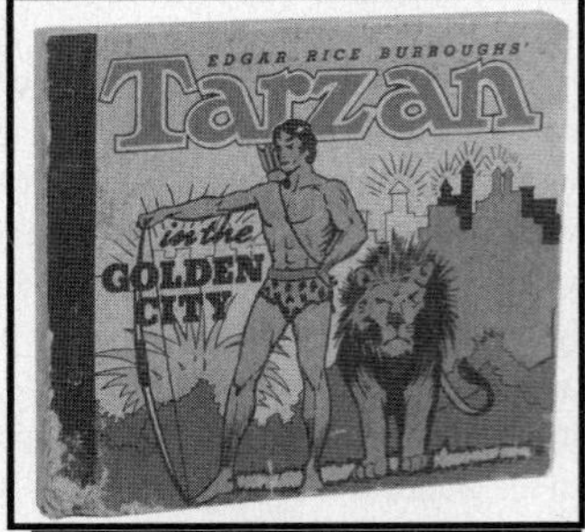

© ERB

*The Pan-Am version of **Tarzan in the Golden City** is a sought-after premium in the Big Little Book category.*

Many collectors ask me what I think are the rarest in the Big Little Book category. I would have to say the softcover variations of the Engle Van Weisman books, the *Mickey Mouse Mail Pilot* variation and two Macys premiums, the Pan Am *Tarzan in the Golden City* and *A Visit to Santa Claus by Snow Plane*, and the English "Dean" *Mickey Mouse Mail Pilot*. Almost all Big Little Books are around, but some of the harder to find in any condition are the *Big Little Paint* books, the original 320 page Big Little Books with their spines complete and unrestored, some of the 3-color variations, and the *Big Chief Wahoo* books.

I am told by general antique dealers that selling a few Big Little Books is tough. Those that specialize in collectibles or Big Little Books alone continue to do the best. These dealers become sought after just as with comics. Many comic collectors are also collecting Big Little Books. I believe the market would see a big jump if Big Little books could ever be slabbed like comics are with CGC. As always, restoration, insect damage, missing pages, writing on covers, and colored pages greatly lower the value of a book.

The Big Little Book Club and its bi-monthly news pamphlet, *The Big Little Times*, are now entering their 29th year. It's sad to hear that its President, Larry Lowery, will be ending the Club and *Times* at the end of 2011 due to eyesight and age. Anyone interested in continuing it can contact him at www.biglittlebooks.com.

Barry Sandoval Heritage Auction Galleries (HA.com)

Fortunately for all of us, the suspicion that "all of the good Golden Age has already been discovered" was put to the lie once again in the past year when we had the privilege to offer the original-owner collection of Ralph Chicorel. His auction total was more than $620,000 for only about 150 comics! That's because these were choice superhero books from 1939-1947, led by a *Marvel Mystery* #9 that CGC graded 9.4. It sold at auction for $107,550. We are always eager to grab the phones, hoping that another collection like Ralph's will come along!

Of course, there are plenty of other outstanding collections that were not original-owner hoards but were put together in the 1960s and 1970s when spending $50 or $100 on one comic was considered "insane" in most quarters. Those amounts would have bought you *All-American* #16 and *More Fun* #52 (respectively) in Mint condition if you had found Mint copies offered at the *Guide* price in 1970. Not that it was easy to find these books, but patient collectors who gladly paid the going rate at the time are being rewarded when they sell the books at auction now.

Below are some notable trends and results from the past year (you can find any of the items mentioned in our free auction archives at HA.com/Comics).

Early (1942-44) Archies: One auction result that got a lot of press this year was $38,837 for an *Archie Comics* #1, CGC-graded FN/VF 7.0. This book was only at #37 in the Top Golden Age Books list in last year's *Guide*. We assume it will have moved way up in the volume you are holding, and we have clients lined up to bid on any other copies that might surface. And the same is really true for #2-10 of the main series. Incidentally, #2 should definitely be called "scarce" in the *Guide* just as #1 and #3 already are. We've only seen one copy of #2 ever, and it was a FR/GD at that.

The book that would really set off a bidding frenzy would be *Pep Comics* #22 (Archie's first appearance). It's been a long time since we've seen one of these change hands in any venue.

Undergrounds: While these are not covered by the *Guide*, it's worth noting that we sold a pristine first printing of *Zap Comix* #1 for $13,145.

Scarce Comics: With each passing year we get a better and better feel for which books are truly scarce and which aren't. The following books deserve Bob Overstreet's "scarce" designation in our estimation:

- *Fight Comics* #15 We've only seen one and that was beat-up. First appearance of the Super-American.
- *Master Comics* #23 is tough, unusual for a 1941 Fawcett. Probably a case of nobody wanting to part with this striking Captain Marvel Jr. cover.
- *Thrilling Comics* #19 (first American Crusader, Schomburg cover). We haven't seen a copy in seven years, and CGC has only graded two.
- *USA Comics* #11 (bondage cover). Several issues of the middle part of the *U.S.A.* run have proven very tough to find. We're not sure why these turn up so much less often than other Timely books.
- *Wonder Comics* #1 (from the Nedor series) We haven't seen a copy in six years.
- *Wonderworld Comics* #28. Very cool bondage/monster cover, we last glimpsed one in 2002.

Comics That Are Not Rare:

- *Star Trek* #1 "rare variation with photo back cover." Most collectors have probably never seen a copy that didn't have the photo back cover, nor have we ever sold one!
- *Gene Autry Comics* #1 (Fawcett). CGC has certified 20 copies, and we auction copies of this book fairly frequently.

Does it exist?: Bob Overstreet & Co. have done a great job winnowing out the comics that don't really exist over the years, but one we are wondering about is the supposed 1953 Flying Saucers... we have never seen this one.

Original Comic Art: A few trends are worthy of note here: It hardly even makes news when we sell a big Silver Age cover or panel page for an amount well into five figures, and the work of the Jack Kirbys and John Buscemas of the world powers our auctions to a great degree. But what the past year's results underscored is that more recent pieces are achieving these prices with more and more regularity if they are exceptional pieces with all of the key elements in place. For example Dave Cockrum's *X-Men* #102 original cover art (Colossus vs. the Juggernaut from 1976) sold for $65,725.

We have also seen a few pieces not drawn for mainstream comic books achieve previously unheard-of prices. A Steve Ditko piece drawn for the fanzine *Comic Crusader* sold for $38,837, with bidders responding to the way it perfectly embodied Ditko's unique style. Also, while Todd McFarlane has obviously been a high-demand artist all along, his cover art featuring Spider-Man and other Marvel characters sold for $26,290 despite being drawn for an *Amazing Heroes Special*, not a newsstand Marvel comic.

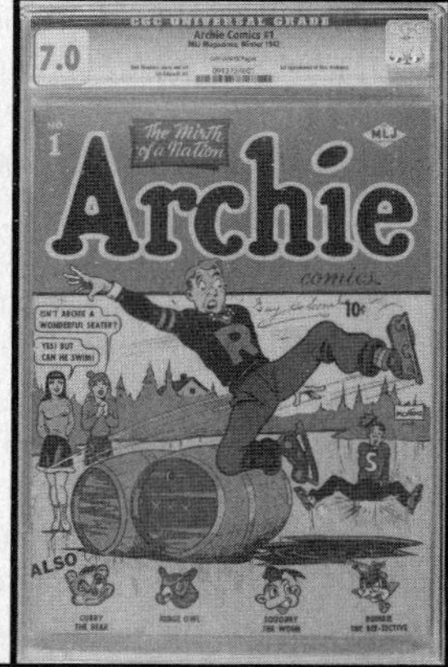

The sale of a CGC-certified 7.0 copy of **Archie Comics** #1 for $38,837 got a lot of press.

© AP

Another trend is that pieces that have been offered for public sale on a number of occasions are clearly taking a backseat to art that is "fresh," that is to say has been in someone's private collection for 20 years or more. There was a lot of excitement when Joe Kubert entrusted us with auctioning pieces from his archives for precisely this reason.

We look forward to helping more collectors maximize the value of their four-color treasures in the coming year.

Matt Schiffman
Collector

2009 held many surprises and most were pleasant for buyers and sellers. As auction records continued to be set at new highs, those great prices brought out some material that had not seen the light of day for quite some time. Mile High books that were assumed to be long buried in collectors' vaults were brought to market for some spectacular prices that reinvigorated the high-end Golden Age market. Silver Age, especially Marvel, continued its upward march and even the second and third level keys moved into the five figure range. The Bronze Age shifted its focus to new keys, but pushed those prices up and past the old level keys. Copper continued to stun the market as collectors realized, again, that many of these books either were not published in any traditional volume, nor were many of them stored particularly well. The downside of the market continued to be the lower grade material finding a home at any reasonable prices. Volumes of books from 1983 to present falling below 9.2 grade are sold for a dime a book. This trend does not show much sign of changing in the near future, but one can hope. To a lesser extent this trend extends into books from the Golden Age to Bronze. For example, *Tales of Suspense* #82 in Good. This book repeatedly sold during all of 2009 for 99¢ on eBay. Golden Age in GD to VG sells for mere fractions of the *Guide* or traditional levels. Is this good for the hobby? We'll just have to see if it brings collectors back into purchasing reading copies, or if the sheer volume to previous understood "rare" books will languish for the near future. The other very interesting shift is in the CGC race to the top. As books reach higher into the 9.6 and 9.8 grades, prices have fallen drastically with the 9.0 to 9.2 books, and even 9.4/9.6 in books from 1975 to present. Many of these books have fallen below the cost to have the book graded, shipped, insured and purchased raw. What happens next with this imbalance depends? 2010 will be telling.

The overall health of the market remained strong, even in the face of the economic setback. Unfortunately many retail stores did suffer and continue to struggle to find their way through lowest point we've seen in the hobby over the past 30 years. There is still no replacement for the smell of aging paper, the careful flipping through a dusty comic box, or the chance to talk shop with fellow collectors while surrounded by thousands of comics. Just looking at the convention attendance numbers from 2008 and 2009 proves this point.

Platinum Age: Overall the market stabilized and a renewed interest in lower grade and commonly found issues increased. The health of the market definitely improved, even if there was some pullback on the high end.

Golden Age: Auction prices were very impressive for the high-end books and there seemed to be no shortage of great material coming onto the market. All the traditional players held strong - Timely, Batman, Superman, Fiction House, Fox, and Wonder Woman. If there is no shortage of material available, there is a lack of collectors to snap up the majority of these great books in FN- to GD. The focus on keys and only keys has captured the majority of the attention of GA collectors and many great books are sitting around at a fraction of the *Guide* prices. Not many new collectors are looking to put together a "run" of a title, when many long time collectors are placing their complete "run" onto the market. It will take a bit of time for this to sort itself out.

Atomic Age: Probably the only area where new and vast collections have not surfaced in the past year, which was great for sales. Horror, Romance, DC and Marvel titles remained strong. Sci-Fi books saw a resurgence from outside interests and made for strong price appreciation. The strong interest in Matt Baker Romance moved into other Romance titles with collectors realizing that these books are very difficult to find in higher grade.

Silver Age: Silver Age keys are the new modern currency of collectibles. Liquidity is no problem. Multiples of *Guide* is not a problem. Finding them is a problem. The lean still goes to Marvel, but the high grade DC issues continue to climb in value/multiples of *Guide*. The continuing trend of multiples of *Guide* for Marvel keys continues to dip into the 6.0 and 7.0 range. The rest of the field does languish a bit and lower grade books are bringing only a fraction of *Guide*. Again, finding the collector that is looking to obtain the entire run is rare, but still exists.

Bronze Age: The have and the have nots. IF you have the correct issue, in the correct grade, then well done. For the rest of us, we are seeing our lower grade issues drop in value. The good news is that more and more collectors that are new to our hobby are jumping into the Bronze market. Strictly Silver and Gold collectors are also finding their way into the genre and that does keep volume alive. Records set here were so impressive in 2009, that the overall health of this market is strong and will continue to remain so through 2010. The Bronze market is faced with an exacerbated price spread, just like the GA and SA, but to the extreme. *Avengers* #93 can sell in high grade for over $6,000 and then sell for $5.00 in Good. Many others selling for hundreds of dollars in 9.4 or above, will languish at $1.00 in Good. What does this bode for this segment? We'll just have to wait and watch.

Copper Age/Modern Age: For many long time collectors, using the word scarce in the same sense as Copper or Modern Age is not working with the same definition. Yes, there are a few books that are just not readily found at all. *Albedo* #2, *Gobbledygook*, and the *Miracleman* colored editions. But many others are very, very difficult to find and cannot even come close to meeting market demand, and in the grade requested. That drives the market and has created a very healthy market indeed for these tougher books. Some previous keys have fallen in price with volume meeting demand, but they still show very strong staying power. *GI Joe* #21, and the end of run issues, as well as the end of run issues of *Vampirella, Transformers, Wonder Woman, World's Finest* and many other final issues of a popular title, we now can see that print runs were dropped drastically. Collectors are having a ball mining this genre and unearthing new and hidden gems. No other segment of our market offers the undiscovered, undocumented and reward that 1983 to 2000 can. Most of the hobby still does not know the end issue on a vast number of titles published, let alone that some even do exist. Printed volume was so low, out of norm sizes, and low print quality offers excitement for relatively low pricing.

Limited Edition and specialty books 1970 - 2000: There has always been the niche field of limited edition, collected works, hardcover editions, and specialty books. Yet over the past two years the market has recognized the importance and rarity of these books and prices have reflected this. In hindsight, Graphitti Press did the field of collecting an incredible favor for putting out some of the most gorgeous and collectible hardcover and limited edition books, that we all owe them a well overdue round of applause. The king of all being the collected *Dark Knight Returns* limited hardcover. I fell so in love with this book, the price I paid in 1986 has still yet to reach current market prices - and I don't regret it for an instance. This is arguably one of the most important collected works over the past 40 years. They even issued collected and signed works from First publishing, works by Moebius, Akira, Alan Moore, Frank Miller, Marvel and DC and some of the most important creators. Ever. Firesides are very much alive as well in hardcover and soft. Hardcover Treasury Editions are always rare, and the signed editions even more so. The *Watchmen* collected works in any limited form remain strong, as well as the first Hardcover print of *V for Vendetta*. Even with the re-issue, this 1990 HC is hard to find. The excitement of Graphic Novels continues to find a welcome audience in the mainstream. If the *New York Times* publishes the top 10 in various categories, you know they have arrived. Often with low print runs, low quality production, and varied distribution, this segment is alive with possibilities.

Overall the strength of the Comic Hobby is as strong as ever. We've not taken the hits that other collectible and antique fields have. The collectors with passion to read, preserve and document still outweigh the investors. That the mainstream still shows a very strong interest in the hobby and the world continues to be fascinated by comic books does show that a tactile medium can survive and thrive. We'll see many more twists and turns with technology, printing processes and delivery systems. But until they can replicate the feel and smell a comic book, we'll have the edge over most others. Best of luck with your collecting in '10 and '11.

Doug Schmell
Pedigree Comics, Inc.

Hello to everyone from South Florida. For those of you unfamiliar with us, Pedigree Comics is an internet based company dealing exclusively in CGC certified comics and magazines. We specialize in ultra high grade (9.4 and higher) and investment quality books from the Silver and Bronze Ages (Marvel and DC), but we are more known for our expertise in CGC graded 1960s and 1970s Marvel comics. It is the Thanksgiving weekend as I prepare this report and we are about to end perhaps the busiest and most unprecedented month in the history of our great hobby. The reason I say this is due to the fact that there have been no less than seven live auctions from various known websites this month alone, all offering a wide selection of high grade raw and CGC certified comics. The month began with the 2-day Mound City Auction in St. Louis and Pedigree Comics' 6th ever Grand Auction and ended with the Heritage auction. Never before in the comic book industry have so many great CGC graded books been offered for sale at the same time, as supply seems to have outweighed demand. The anticipated effect is a reduction in prices being offered, and eventually paid, for many high grade and ultra high grade issues. I have seen this for a few months now but it culminated in November, 2009.

© MAR

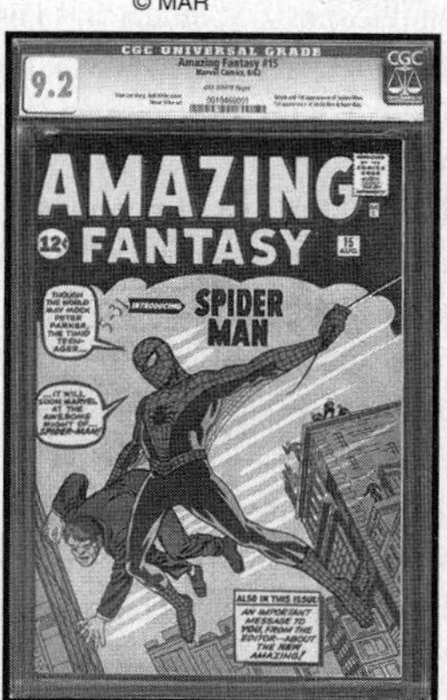

*2009 had the significant sale of an **Amazing Fantasy** #15 in CGC 9.2 for $190,000.*

This is not necessarily a bad thing, as any market will suffer a downturn when supply is greater than demand, and the prices we are still seeing paid for CGC certified comics is consistently high, but it does seem easier now for most collectors to find an issue they need and not pay a ridiculous multiple of *Guide*.

More and more collectors, who were once priced out of the high grade certified market, have and will continue to come back in earnest and participate in live and online auctions and this is good for the hobby. Many of these collectors are looking to upgrade on existing issues they own (for example, from a 9.4 to a 9.6) or on page quality (from off-white or off-white/white to white) and this type of linear activity will ensure that more and more books become available. Once the 9.6 copy is obtained, the 9.4 is put in the market, keeping the supply steady, and I see this happening now more than ever. Gone are the days when collectors would keep an "under copy" or even a copy they thought was as nice as the primary one in their collection because of CGC certification, which has helped eliminate guesswork and speculation.

The exception to the supply exceeds demand = lower

prices paid route is with rare, highest graded material, particulary from the Silver Age. The demand is significantly higher than the supply in this investment grade area, and we have seen an incredible number of new, record-breaking sales here. This is where the auction format works at its best, as all you need are at least two bidders aggressively interested and bidding on the same book, and the end result is an often-times astonishing final bid. I have seen this time and time again in my Grand Auctions, and I do not anticipate this trend to end any time soon. In fact, I predict the future of the high end, highest graded market (think CGC certified 9.6 to 9.9 with some exceptions in 9.4) to be mostly in "live" online auctions, as it just does not seem prudent as a seller or consignor to set a list price on a website when there is no telling what the book is actually worth under the auction bidding format. Sometimes it is due to the issue itself (*Fantastic Four* #25 or *Incredible Hulk* #181) but for the most part it is the grade (9.6 or 9.8) that spurs the frenzied bidding.

I learned this pretty quickly when I started utilizing the Grand Auction for the first time in July, 2008. I was quite amazed at some of the prices we were getting and at that point realized that the online auction is the direction of this hobby, specifically with investment quality books. We have run four Grand Auctions in 2009 (in February, May, August and November) with total sales well over 3 Million dollars. When you factor in the many post-auction deals that get done, the number is ever higher. When I looked back in our database to verify the actual numbers for this report, I could not believe some of the individual prices realized. Yes, a lot of "common" books did well in these online bidding events, but the in-demand ultra high grade Silver and Bronze Age Marvel comics went through the roof. The Silver Age stuff is older, scarcer and more sought after by my customers and most high-end collectors and investors, but the Bronze Age material (specifically 1970s Marvel keys in 9.8) did incredibly well too. The usual titles and issues sold at many multiples of *Guide*, with many notable results. The following is a list of some of the significant and record setting Grand Auction sales of 2009:

Amazing Fantasy #15 (9.2)	$190,000
Amazing Spider-Man #1 (9.0)	$41,000
Atom #1 (9.6)	$21,000
Avengers #4 (9.6)	$64,000
Captain America #100 (9.8)	$8,255 (Boston)
Conan the Barbarian #1 (9.8)	$8,300
Daredevil #1 (9.4)	$23,251
Daredevil #1 (9.4)	$20,750
Fantastic Four #1 (8.5)	$75,100
Fantastic Four #1 (8.0)	$50,400
Fantastic Four #50 (9.4)	$16,000 (Valparaiso)
Green Lantern #76 (9.6)	$22,750
Incredible Hulk #181 (9.8)	$32,001 (CGC Sig. Series)
Incredible Hulk #181 (9.8)	$26,501 (Valparaiso)
Iron Man #1 (9.8)	$18,500 (CGC Sig. Series)
New Mutants #98 (9.9)	$12,250
Nick Fury #1 (9.8)	$2,850
Night Nurse #1 (9.8)	$3,850
Silver Surfer #10 (9.8)	$10,009
Swamp Thing #1 (9.8)	$6,766 (CGC Sig. Series)
Tales of Suspense #39 (9.4)	$114,990
Tales of Suspense #39 (8.5)	$16,757
Teenage Mutant Ninja Turtles #1 (9.6)	$11,500
Werewolf By Night #32 (9.6)	$3,479
X-Men #1 (9.0)	$33,333
X-Men #94 (9.8)	$27,779

We have also had numerous significant sales off the main site (*Avengers* #1 9.0 for $25,500; *Avengers* #4 9.4 for $25,000; *Avengers* #2 9.8 for $70,000; *Avengers* #2 9.4 for $13,500; *Fantastic Four* #37 9.6 for $10,000; *Incredible Hulk* #1 9.0 for $100,000, *Tales of Suspense* #39 8.5 for $17,000; *Tales to Astonish* #27 9.2 for $32,500; *X-Men* #2 9.6 for $25,000, etc.), but the predominance of our record breaking sales (and those of our competitors) are, and will continue to be, from the auction setting. You would not believe how many times I have had to shake my head at an unprecedented sale after the bidding has ended, looking at the final, winning bid price with sheer amazement. Indeed, the format of a "live" bidding atmosphere causes this kind of frenzy and fuels the "Gotta have this book" mentality when two (or more) people are bidding against one another. A bidder has invested so much time, effort and sheer will in the bidding process that it does not make sense to "lose" the item when the auction ends.

In my opinion, as both a high end/investment grade dealer and collector, there are other factors that drive this top CGC certified market. Ego is one, as many collectors want to own the best existing and single highest CGC graded copy. There is nothing quite like owning the best of the best. Upgrading an inferior copy, as mentioned above, is also a factor. As collectors finally fill enough holes in their want lists and complete their runs, the next logical step is in replacing a 9.2 with a 9.4, a 9.4 with a 9.6 or a 9.6 with a 9.8. The collecting bug in all of us searches for the best conditioned copy we can find. The advent of pressing is another. As more and more buyers and investors become educated about pressing and the possibilities of upgrading a particular copy, they see the money that can be made in the value difference between what the book is currently graded and what it might be after pressing. Pressing is more prevalent now than it has ever been and most of the participants in our hobby realize it is quite safe and is not considered restoration. It goes without saying that the CGC is a huge factor, as without certification none of the above would be possible. I amplified this point in a previous market report but cannot overstate how important certification has been to the growth and popularity of the entire comic book hobby.

Perhaps the most underestimated factor in driving this market is the CGC Collectors Society and Comics Registry. What began in the early 2000s with a few collectors registering a couple of popular sets (*Amazing Spider-Man* #1-#100, *Fantastic Four* #1-#102, *Flash* #105-#350, etc.) has evolved into an incredbly competitive and important arena with thousands of registrants and hundreds of sets (and many more of both on the way). It is now more and more often that I will hear from a particular collector: "I just reached 500,000 points on the Registry" or "I own the best Wonder Woman set" or "I just cracked the top 10 in total Registry points." This type of competitive collecting was unheard of only 8 years ago, but now is very common in our hobby, probably more so than any other hobby in the world. Whereas CGC certification has brought many sick-of-getting-ripped-off collectors back into the hobby, the CGC Registry has kept them here and added a lot of fun to the equation. When I first began registering my books back in November 2003 (exactly 6 years ago as it was also Thanksgiving weekend), I just couldn't believe how cool and fun it was. Even going through the registration process and choosing a nickname to use is exciting, but nothing beats seeing your own books up there in a competitive set, watching how many points you accumulate with each book listed, matched against some of the best collections in the world. It has really opened up an entirely new level to collecting, and the entire comic book industry is in debt to the Comics Guaranty Corporation for implementing the Comics Registry, maintaining it and helping it grow.

2009 has been another incredible year for the comic book industry and for Pedigree Comics in particular. Due to the Grand Auction sales and the consistent sales of our regular inventory we have experienced our best year yet. We expect more of the same in 2010 and want to thank all of our friends, consignors, customers, collectors, CGC forum-ites, CGC Registrants and fellow dealers for making this possible.

Doug Simpson
Paradise Comics

What can be said about 2009, except that it was a challenging year, for not only the global economy but also Paradise Comics. Despite all the issues involving retailers, our sales continued to show a modest growth at around 6%; thanks in no small part to our growing customer base. Our Internet sales also continued to grow and our website contributed to an 8% increase in sales over last year.

The greatest area of growth in-store remains our sale of graphic novels. I have stated before that this format is definitely the direction the hobby is going and the major companies have started to take notice. Most of our new customers are coming to pick up graphic novels instead of regular monthly issues.

High grade Key issues from the Silver and Bronze Age are selling consistently well and demand continued to be high. I simply couldn't keep up with the demand for high grade Silver and Bronze Age books.

The usual suspects were in great demand: *Amazing Fantasy* #15, *Fantastic Four* #1, *Daredevil* #1, *Giant Size X-Men* #1, *Incredible Hulk* #181, *X-Men* #94, *Incredible Hulk* #1, *Tales of Suspense* #39, and *Avengers* #4, were all highly requested along with a few other surprises: *Amazing Spider-Man* #100, *Iron Fist* #14, *Wonder Woman* #199 and *Cerebus* #1 are just a few examples.

Golden Age sales are still very sluggish and only Timely and early *Detective Comics* are a guaranteed sale. There is always a market for standard Golden Age hero comics, but never at *Guide*, and usually well below. However, we were very lucky that we found an early Disney collection with many issues featuring Carl Barks art, and they disappeared immediately.

Silver Age sales continued to be the bulk of our back issue market, with any high-grade copies selling out as fast as I can get them in.

For DC Silver Age, the greatest demand rests once again with the iconic characters Batman, Superman, Flash, and Green Lantern. Most other titles have been slow sellers. The one book that continued to be high on everyone's wish list was *Green Lantern* #7, the first Sinestro appearance.

Marvel Silver Age is selling very well, with *Amazing Spider-Man* and *X-Men* leading the way, and demand for secondary titles like *Avengers* and *Iron Man* is increasing. The Marvel Silver Age market is always strong and doesn't look to be slowing down anytime soon.

Bronze Age comic sales continued to rise but only for books in high grade, while demand for mid-grade copies has decreased sharply.

Marvel leads the way in this category, with John Byrne *X-Men* (#107-143) and all *Amazing Spider-Man* issues between #100 and #200 leading the way. These issues are on almost everyone's list and if I had an entire box of each, they would be gone within a week. I have also noticed an increase in demand for *Avengers* and *Iron Man*. It goes without saying that *Incredible Hulk* #181 is the most in-demand Bronze age book out there today.

DC titles, including *Batman*, *Justice League of America* and *Flash*, are always in high demand, and *Green Lantern* is still seeing incredible growth thanks to the Blackest Night storyline.

Modern book sales have continued to fall in 2009, with the only bright spots being DC's Blackest Night and Marvel's Dark Reign mega-events.

Surprisingly, with all the controversy over the most recent *Amazing Spider-Man* stories, the sales continue to be high. I feel that the future of the medium is with the graphic novel and the increased output by all publishers will continue this trend.

As mentioned above, our on-line sales were a real surprise to us and continued to grow all year – our eBay store has continued to be a great addition to our business. Our website will continue to provide a consistent source of Silver Age and graphic novels in 2010. (www.paradisecomics.com)

CGC continues to be the standard in independent third-party grading. I would like to mention that CGC is the exclusive grading company for Paradise Comics.

Some recent CGC sales include:

Amazing Spider-Man #1 (2.5) $2,000.00
Amazing Spider-Man #2 (6.5) $2,200.00

Amazing Spider-Man #129 (9.6) $2,100.00
Avengers #57 (9.2) $980.00
Giant-Size X-Men #1 (9.6) $2,310.00
Incredible Hulk #181 (9.6) $5,500.00
X-Men #1 (4.0) $1,450.00
X-Men #3 (9.0) $1,600.00
X-Men #4 (8.0) $1,200.00
CGC Signature Series *Amazing Spider-Man* #5 (4.5) $750.00
CGC Signature Series *Nick Fury* #1 (7.5) $250.00
CGC Signature Series *Incredible Hulk* #181 (8.0) $1,200.00
CGC Signature Series *Incredible Hulk* #162 (9.6) $950.00
CGC Signature Series *Giant-Size X-Men* #1 (5.5) $400.00

I would like to finish by mentioning the biggest happening for Paradise Comics in 2009. We have sold the Toronto Comicon. Gareb Shamus, CEO of New York-based Wizard Entertainment, announced today that he has purchased the Toronto Comicon, a show that has been consistently awarded The Best International Comic Book Convention (non-USA) by ComicBookConventions.com, for the last 5 years.

© MAR

Bronze Age sales continue to rise for high grade only. (**X-Men** #141 shown)

"We've always had a strong following in Canada, so buying the Toronto Comicon is something that allows me to give back to our fans. These attendees are known to be serious collectors and comic industry followers," said Shamus. "I am thrilled to offer the guests, celebrities, artists, dealers and exhibitors to our Canadian audience for the very first time."

Peter Dixon, owner of Paradise Conventions and former owner of the Toronto Comicon, will still be intimately involved in the show production, his friendly manner ensuring the continuation of the trademarked relaxed atmosphere of the show.

Al Stoltz
Basement Comics

Well the 2009 business year is winding down and the racks and hand trucks and show inventory is back in our building well worn from a year of traveling all over the USA. With the economy always in discussion in the news and on everyone's minds I had to wonder if this year would be a lot tougher to dig money out of show attendees than the great year I had in 2008. It really does seem that when fear of recessions or worse economic conditions creep up on the television sets and in a constant barrage from other media sources, people seem to buy what they like and can hold and speculate on for future economic upswings. Comic books seem to be one of those collectible items that people gravitate to and seek to invest in. While CGC graded items were bought from us in record numbers this year, plenty of raw material was sold as well. We have focused on finding those items that are very low in the CGC census or that have no graded copies at all. While this is getting harder to do as the census seems to just completely fill in, we search and find those items that could be unique and have them graded. While superhero items usually are the leaders in sales we tend to focus on scarce and unusual items and have maintained a loyal following that buys the odd-ball items that we accumulate through out the year.

Shows: All initial fears of a slow show season were put to rest after setting up at NY Comic Con the Reed Show in February. Great lucky weather and a chance to start the year off at what is quickly becoming a monster show to attend on the East Coast. Expanded to two booths for this show and the expense was justified! Super crowded show and people were happy to come out of the cold and purchase that comic that they just had to have. Lots of high end and rare items were sold and customers did not seem to haggle at all over prices.

Mega Con in Florida was decent as well in spite of only setting up in one corner booth, I had a fantastic show and even managed to buy some fun new material for later sales! Also hanging out looking at comics in 70+ degree weather while Maryland is nice and freezing is not a bad thing at all!! Lots of CGC graded 9.8 Bronze comics sold along with lots of our $10.00 special Silver Age markdown boxes.

Wizard Con Philly and Chicago were both pretty decent and while customers were a little thin at the Philadelphia show, they were out on force for the Chicago event and we had great success with the new High Grade Dell/Gold Key collection we bought a few weeks prior to the show. The usual hunt for high grade comics from buyers at a bigger show makes me usually crazy but we had a good amount in stock and I know this will be a stunner.......but people actually bought comics NOT in high grade to add to their collections and to read...I know that is a crazy thing to happen.

San Diego Comic-Con is officially off my list of shows to set up at starting in 2009 but I will attend the show to buy and sell and to enjoy the fantastic San Diego weather and sites to see. My wife and I flew out this year and I stuffed a backpack and some luggage with some CGC graded comics and higher end key books to try and sell. I shopped the show and then for a day and a half I managed to sell many of the items I brought and did not have the horrible task of being tied to a booth or the expenses associated with that. I had more fun walking and selling and chatting with retailers I would have never had the chance to speak to if I was set up at the show. This show is slowly becoming less of a comic show, and the costs of setting up eventually will make the most die-hard comic vendor think twice about traveling to this location. Not to mention I heard it was one of the slowest years yet for comic sales to the public, I guess I picked a great year to bail out on this one !

Pittsburgh Comic Con was a joy to set up at this year!! New building that made load in and out as simple as it can possibly be and the smell of the new paint made the customers eager to spend and buy some top end material. Renee George had Stan Lee as her guest of honor and people were piled in on Saturday to meet Stan "The Man" Lee. Not only was this show decent for selling but we did buy a large amount of material and some original art that is now hanging in my office. One of the smaller shows I do for the year but always a fun event and the charity auction is usually a high light of the weekend.

Baltimore Comic Con had its TENTH anniversary and expanded its size a good bit for this show. Marc Nathan, the promoter of the show did another outstanding job and the crowd poured in, in spite of a Baltimore Ravens home game and the Baltimore Marathon competing for the parking spots needed by our buyers. Now I just have to love this show since it is a whole thirty five minutes from my house...finally an easy event to do! This is the only show for the year where we have three full booths of material and try and bring everything we can out to show and maybe even get rid of. While sales were not as maniacal as last year's, we did manage to sell great books to a very solid core of Golden Age buyers and rare material seekers.

New York Comic Con Wizard/Carbonaro was the last large show of the year for us and it was a week after the Baltimore Comic Con this year, that means no rest for the weary and only good news was that the van was already loaded for the trip. Load in was provided for free by Mike Carbonaro and it was the easiest load in ever! Two full vans of material were inside the building and out of the light drizzle that was falling in less than twenty minutes, you just have to love that! The building for the event was on the water near the cruise ship areas and it was as cold inside as the scenes from Rocky when he was punching the beef. Huge space but never seemed to get overwhelmed with questions or people wanting to look at comics. A decent first try at a show of this scale in NY City and in the end we managed to do okay, not great but okay.

eBay: eBay has fallen on hard times it seems and unless they can make significant changes at the CEO level it will continue to spin out of control. Now, that being said we still have an online eBay store BASEMENTCOMICS and do have almost 7,000 items listed in it for sale as of this report being typed. BUT, sales have not regained the strength they had a little over a year ago before the economic collapse and the very strange changes that Upper Management decided to impose on the very sellers that helped make eBay as great as it was. Sales of CGC graded material is still very strong on this site and lower grade DC and Marvel Silver Age comics sell briskly if priced at a bargain level for these buyers. We are always working hard to make sure we have a good blend of comics, magazines, Monster material, Fanzines and strip reprint items on and are moving away from items that are $5.00 or less being listed, as the profits are not meeting the labor in listing them. Still a nice market to survive off of during the lean Winter months, but I can see a massive change coming eventually from the once giant auction company and it may not be great for comic sellers.

Yeah Yeah Yeah, what books were sold during the year? Let's see if we can at least rattle off some decent sales that are scribbled on paper or in my memory. *Feature Book* nn *Popeye* FN+ $3,000, *Suspense* #4 FN+ $2,000, *Speed Comics* #28 VG+ $800.00, *Donald Duck Linen Book* VG+ $325.00, *Amazing Spider-Man* #14 CGC 8.0 $1600.00, *All Winners* #12 VG/FN $680.00, *Black Cat* #50 GD $400.00, *Green Lantern* #76 GD/VG $175.00, *Looney Tunes* #12 CGC 9.4 $1300.00. Sold in a group in large purchase were *Four Color* #12 CGC 9.2, *Four Color* #15 CGC 9.2, *Four Color* #43 CGC 9.0, *Four Color* #131 CGC 9.4, *America's Best Comics* #6 GD+ $250.00, *Little Lulu* #6, #25 & #26 File Copies for $600.00, *Journey Into Mystery* #107 CGC 9.2, *Sgt. Fury* #1 VF- $1600.00, *Journey Into Mystery* #83 GD- $600.00, *Cracked Magazine* #1 VG $45.00, *Witches Tales* #2 FN+ Double Cover $200.00. Now lots of material came and went during the year and maybe one of these years I will be organized enough to have a better list of the year's sales, but that is a pretty good list to start off with.

HAPPY 40TH BIRTHDAY OVERSTREET GUIDE !!! I have now been buying and peeling through the pages of an *Overstreet Comic Guide* since issue FOUR !! I still have my super tattered copy and that is one of my favorite covers of all time. As an twelve year old capitalist I was amazed that money could be made off of the buying and selling of comics and in the same year I met Bob Cook, Gene Carpenter, Dave Wiemer, John Knight, Redbeard Ron Pussell himself, Steve Geppi and many more guys that were the first wave of buyers and sellers that helped to shape my ideas and knowledge about the books I still chase after. I was far younger than all of these guys but I could hold my own with crazy facts and info about items in comics thanks to the zillion hours I poured into the *Overstreet Guide* to learn every odd fact that could be an asset to me as far as buying and selling. I now have a complete set of the *Overstreet Guides* and every now and then glance back and wince at the prices of time gone past and I am amazed at how recognized and mainstream the hobby is today. A solid pricing tool that helped establish at least a starting place for bargaining for or selling comics was essential in those early years and made everything legitimate. Very glad that later in years that I was added to the cast of people that could contribute to this invaluable tool in our hobby.

Looking Forward To 2010: The economy is slowly climbing back up and orders for comics in mid-November (and I hope December) carry onto 2010. With a few new shows added this year, it will bring more of the public into our hobby and keep comics rolling along for another 40 years.....Lord knows I never want to work doing anything else.

Doug Sulipa
Doug Sulipa's Comic World

The worldwide economy, along with home values and jobs took a big plunge into recession in late 2008 and through all of 2009. My sales took a big dip in 10-11/2008, but by 12/2008, they were already recovering. My American buyer sales dropped by about 40% in 10-11/2008, but returned to about 85% of the previous year's levels for the rest of 2009. My Canadian and overseas buyer sales dropped by about 20% in 10-11/2008, but returned to previous years' levels by 12/2008 and through to the present. American comics are valued worldwide in U.S. funds, but because the U.S. dollar was devalued this year, its buying power value as an investment in the worldwide market has also fallen. This year many saw their lifetime investments take large decreases in value, while comics at least held steady in the U.S. dollars market value. The main change I have noted in the market is less demand for high grade and higher priced items in general. I have seen virtually zero change in the buying habits of the zillions of collectors that mainly buy GD, VG and FN graded comics. Many of our High Grade (and other) collectors have started Key issue collecting (high demand and easy-to-resell issues) and are actively buying GD thru FN/VF graded comics (more affordable & plentiful). You can typically buy multiple copies of Key issues in GD-FN for the price of one High Grade example. I still have a huge selection of 20,000+ raw comics (90% from 1975-1987 era) in High Grades on my website (most from the Manitoba collection) graded in 9.0-9.8, and they again were among my best-sellers, but with resistance to most items priced at over $100, and with $10-20 High Grade items being the fast movers. If I single out the "Trend of the Year" for us, it would be that customers are seeking out anything that is hard to find, with condition being the less important factor. For the last 30+ years, I have directed my focus on going out of my way to keep in stock items that everyone else does not bother with. We have in stock literally thousands of comics, books, magazines, records, movies, posters, that no other dealer on the internet has in stock. Most of these items are not of high value, but are very often extremely elusive, so we get daily requests from buyers who are very happy to have located their long lost treasures.

I started as a comics reader and collector in 1965. By 1970, I had 5000 comics and was already selling locally out of my parents basement at age 13-14. In February 2010, I will have hit the FORTY YEARS mark of selling back issue comics. Within a year, by 1971, I was already a mail order dealer with ads in the *RBCC*, then later in the *CBG*. By February 1974 I had opened my first all-comics store after school, 160 square feet on a 2nd floor location in downtown Winnipeg (one of the first in Canada). I estimate I have bought over 6 million comics over those 40 years, and sold around 5 million of them, with a current inventory of approximately 1,300,000 comics and related items in stock. The face of comics collecting has had drastic chances every decade or so through all those years. In the 1960s, back issues were often near impossible to find, even 5-10 year old ones. We had to depend on second-hand stores and other collectors (flea markets and garage sales were near non-existent in our city of 500,000+ in that period). The release of the first *Overstreet Guide* started out as a quiet event, but kept gaining momentum through the 1970s, and within a decade it was the undisputed main catalyst and driving force for the hobby. In those early days, condition was not much of a factor in collecting, with many dealers catalogues proclaiming "everything in GOOD or Better condition, unless otherwise stated". Grading was not yet considered a necessity, other than separating comics with covers and without. Some dealers claimed that they did NOT consider tape to be a defect. In the early 1970s, very few comics actually sold for over $100. Until this time in collecting, finding the wanted comics was the only real concern. Most fans still bought almost exclusively their favorite characters, with no regard to investment. Condition, price and investment potential were all lesser concerns. As fans found fanzines and mail order dealers, things started to change. Fan/pro articles (in *RBCC*, *CBG*, etc.) and advance comics news (*Comic Reader*, etc.) started a drive to collect what was "Hot". Stampedes to collect, hoard and invest in new comics began, and still continue through to today. In the 1970s, the hot titles included: *Conan*, *Shazam!*, Jack Kirby, Marvel Horror comics, new *X-Men*, *Howard the Duck*, Marvel and DC #1-10s, etc. Most of those hot '70s titles are still among the most plentiful comics of the period today and are only uncommon in VF/NM, while all the "Lesser" titles are a lot scarcer in strict high grades. By the mid-1970s, a high grade *Action Comics* #1 sold for an astounding $1800, and this was worldwide news. By the late 1970s, the high grade Edgar Church Mile High comics hit the marketplace. Suddenly condition was becoming a very important factor. What many dealers called Mint in the late 1970s would grade about a FN average today. What most called NM in the late 1980s would grade about a VF average today. Items that are scarce in any grade have always been good sellers for me, as I have always offered a huge selection. Many collectors wanted their favorite titles and characters to be scarce and valuable, but this was not the case for most of the 1970s-1990s. With the advent of CGC grading, for many collectors, condition became the most important factor in their

It was worldwide news in the mid-1970s when a high grade **Action Comics** #1 sold for an astounding $1800.

buying habits. Suddenly common and uncommon items could be considered scarce to rare, in certain high grades, so especially the Marvel comics market went through the roof (with DC not far behind) in value in the last decade or so.

Strangely enough, the (post-1960) items that are truly Scarce to Rare in high grade (Cartoon, Teen, Western, Love, War, etc.) are only of low interest to investors. The high multiples for high grade, are mainly focused on Marvel and DC comics (especially superhero), typically many of the most plentiful comics of each given time period. On the flip side, low grade obscure collectible items that are scarce in any grade change hands daily worldwide via retail sales and auctions at high multiples of established values, completely under the radar of the vast majority of collectors and dealers. These obscure and scarce items are the backbone of my inventory, have held a huge fascination for me for decades, and provide an endless stream of recession proof buyers (collectors, investors, researchers, readers, as well as creators and their family, friends and decendants). The internet has connected buyers and sellers in an historically unparalleled way. Dealers and collectors looking for a way to expand their horizons, take heed as this is one of the most exciting areas of collecting, but beware as it can easily become an obsession.

Archie Comics: The Marriage of Archie and Veronica was the news event of the year for this publisher, but it lost some steam once he then married Betty. They will still be in high demand as back issues for years to come, as Archie does not have a lot of Key issues. Archie Digests are sold in more locations than perhaps any other type of new comics, as they target sales to the general public in places such as supermarket checkout stands. It is suprising that the Marriage Event took place in the standard size *Archie Comics* series #600-605. Archie and his friends first appeared in *Pep* #22 (Dec. 1941) and their 70th Anniversary approaches, making them among the Top-10 most enduring and long-lasting characters. All comics with Archie and his gang are highly collected, but are out of the mainstream, going unnoticed by the great majority of dealers and collectors. In general, most collectors are satisfied with decent middle grade copies, so most are affordable and not high profile items. I also sell a large volume to the fans who just want low grade, complete affordable copies. My inventory is the world biggest, with 35,000+ Archie comics and 10,000+ digests in stock. I sell a better percentage of my total inventory of this publisher each year, than virtually anything else. Even the sellers who do keep a good size inventory of Archie back issues normally tend to be sold out on 50-75% of everything printed. Collectors need to do a lot of hunting to fill in the sets. Luckily for them it happens to be one of our specialties.

There is a huge shortage of 1941-1950 Archie titles, with most that do surface being in GD/VG or lower grades, thus even VG or better runs are very difficult to assemble. Most sell swiftly at 125%-150% *Guide* in any grade. These classic 1940s issues have the big appeal of the more realistic early look, often with Good Girl Art. *Archie's Girls Betty & Veronica* is not the most valuable set, but is the the most collected title by this publisher. Beginning with issue #4, Dan DeCarlo started changing the look of the characters, a look that would last for over 50 years, making this one of the most overlooked major Key issues in comics history, still with zero premium value in *Guide*. Just try to find one in ANY grade.

All Archies from 1951-1964 are strong steady sellers, in low supply, with many collectors attempting to complete all their runs. These are difficult to restock once sold. Most GD-FN copies we sell go at 120-140% *Guide*. These did not change much through this period, and are all highly collectible and still affordable, and there are many still undiscovered minor key issues. Among the most prized collectible issues of the period are all the Horror/Sci-Fi cover issues. All the early Girl titles are in even good demand, including *Ginger*, *Katy Keene*, and *Suzie*. Overgraded copies of hard-to-find issues often sell at 200% to 400% *Guide* on eBay, especially on lower graded copies as fans don't want to miss them.

By the early 1960s, Archie began to expand its titles, with the most collectible today being Sabrina issues of *Mad House*, and *Josie* (Dan DeCarlo's classic new creation). Neal Adams' first published comics work appeared in *Archie Joke Book* #44-48 and are not major Key issues. Archie's Silver Age experimentation continued with the superhero characters (Pureheart the Powerful, Super Teen, Evil Heart, etc), Mystery stories (*Life with Archie*), Secret Agent stories (Man and Girl from R.I.V.E.R.D.A.L.E., etc), Musical Bands (the Archies, *Josie & the Pussycats* - which became TV cartoons), Cavemen Archie Gang stories, loads of great Squarebound Giant issues, return of the classic Golden Age MLJ superheroes (including back-up stories in *Laugh* and *Pep*), *That Wilkin Boy* (with the Bingoes; #50-52 are undervalued and scarcer), *Cosmo the Merry Martian* and more. You never know for sure what you will discover in these Silver Age issues. They are fun to collect and good steady sellers at 115-135% *Guide*.

The Bronze Age issues from 1970-1984 are typically considered the most plentiful of the Archie Comics, but actually it was mainly the 1970-1980 issues. Through most of the 1970s, there were very few notable changes for the Archie Gang characters. I suppose they chose to rest on their laurels, thus these tended to be a bit slower than other eras. But they did usher in their Red Circle line of comics, beginning with the Horror titles *Chilling Adventures in Sorcery* #1-11, *Mad House* #95-97 and the one-shot *Super Cops*, all of which are highly collected and scarce in High Grade. In 1983 the Red Circle Line was revived this time with the return of the MLJ and other superheroes. These were well done, but short lived. In 1984, half of these titles were cancelled, the Red Circle logo was dropped and they began the Archie Adventure Series logo. These were all low print and scarcer (now bringing 150% *Guide*). The 1981-1984 issues are in much lower supply. In addition to the cancellation of half their titles, they also cut back others from monthly to bi-monthly or quarterly. In the 37-month period from 10/79 through 10/82, only 7 issues of *Josie & the Pussycats* were published (#100-106). All are low print run and scarcer, bringing 150-200% *Guide*. *Sabrina the Teen-Age Witch* #71-77 are also Low Print (bringing 150% *Guide*). Four highly collectible titles: *Mad House*, *Sabrina*, *Josie* and *Little Archie* (with Little Sabrina) saw cancellation in this implosion era. But the most important new character of the Bronze Age era of Archie did not appear until October 1982 when Cheryl Blossom was first introduced in *Archie's Girls Betty and Veronica* #320 (and the same month in the very overlooked and undervalued *Jughead* #325). Both issues appeared in this Low Print era, are major Key issues, are tough to find and are fast sellers at 200% *Guide* in any grade. Canadian Newsstand Variant Cover Price editions exist for both, bringing 250-300% *Guide*. (See Variants further down in this report). All 1982-1985 early appearances of Cheryl Blossom are in very high demand and low supply (bringing 150%+ of *Guide*). All pre-11/1994 appearances of Cheryl Blossom are also in strong demand, when identified as such. *Archie Comics* #429(11/1994) featured the "Love Showdown" part 1, which began the famous storyline in which Archie chooses Cheryl Blossom over both Betty and Veronica, a turning point that made her forevermore a major character in the Archie Saga. Fans scrambled through back issues to find her first and early appearances, but they were near impossible to find in the short print era stacks, thus the prices began their meteoric rise, outpricing most Marvel and DC Key comics of the era.

Early 1960s Archies are good steady sellers and are fun to collect. (**Archie's Mad House** #27 shown)

By the mid-1980s digests started to rival and then surpass the sales of the standard comics. The comics have always had the items that appealed to collectors, but also supplied new material that could one day be reprinted in the popular digests.

The "Low Sales and Low Print Era" continued into the 1987-1992 era as 12 major titles were cancelled, the last issues including: *Archie and Me* #161 (2/87), *Archie at Riverdale High* #113 (2/87), *Archie Giant Series* #632 (7/92), *Archie's Girls B&V* #347 (4/87), *Archie's Pals N Gals* #224 (9/91), *Archie's TV Laugh-Out* #105 (2/86), *Betty and Me* #200 (8/92), *Everything's Archie* #157 (9/91), *Jughead* #352 (6/87), *Laugh* #400 (4/87), *Life with Archie* #286 (9/91), *Pep* #411(3/87). All these 12 last issues are now highly sought Key issues by collectors, are tough to find and bring 150-200% *Guide*. In addition, it should be noted that the last 10-12 issues of all these titles had low print runs and are also hard to complete, bringing 150% *Guide*. In the late '80s through early '90s, Archie used the Marvel formula and rebooted many of their titles by starting again fresh with many new series starting again at #1. This revitalized the publisher and got more collectors interested once again. The new wave of Modern titles included the highly successful *Teenage Mutant Ninja Turtles Adventures*. This is the TMNT title that the general public and toy-buying crowd identifies with and are by far the most requested TMNT back issues. *TMNT Advs.* #50-72, *Special* #6-10, *Sourcebook* #1-2, Digests, and *Mighty Mutant Animals* #5-9, are low print items, selling at 200-400% *Guide*, if you can find them. *Sonic the Hedgehog* turned out to be a high successful title for the publisher, already passing issue #200 with early issues coveted and among the most valuable comics of the 1990s. The 1990s Hanna-Barbera titles were largely ignored by collectors and were then already hard to find. The #1-5 issues are uncommon, with most #6-up issues being scarcer. These are undervalued, and sell at around 200% *Guide*.

Archie began a series of Specials (Super Teens, Spring Break, Vacation, etc), that happened to include three Cheryl Blossom 3-issue mini-series from 1995-1997, plus the 4 issues Special series. This finally led to "Bad Girl" Cheryl Blossom being awarded her own series, which lasted 37 issues and is already collectible. In the post-2000 era, Archie has once again started to experiment, with TV Cartoons, Weird Mysteries, the return of Katy Keene, the manga look in *Sabrina*, realistic looking stories in Digests, and the Marriage limited series and more. These are the future collectibles. It is amazing that this rich history of collectibles is completely missed by many mainstream collectors.

Atlas/Marvel: These have become one of our bestsellers, with a high turnover rate, and they sell in any complete grade. This year the Western titles were the most requested, especially all titles that eventually became post-1962 Marvel titles (at 120-135% *Guide*). Second most popular were all the Teen titles (at 120-135% *Guide*). *Millie the Model* #18-93 by Dan DeCarlo were on many want lists, but are now very hard to find (GD-FN copies bring 150-200% *Guide*; VF-NM copies at 125-150% *Guide*). The Humor, Cartoon and Parody titles were great sellers (at 120-135% *Guide*). The War titles were moderate sellers (at 120-135% *Guide*). All of the above had a good number of collectors attempting to find missing issues and complete sets within all those genres. Crime/Mystery, Funny Animal, Romance, Sports, and Spy titles were slower but still decent sellers. They are uncommon and all eventually move (selling at 110-120% *Guide*). The Horror and SF titles are always steady sellers, but as they are more expensive, tend to have less completionists. The hot 1970s Marvel Horror reprints continue to fuel demand for these, as collectors seek specific reprinted stories in their original incarnation. Fin Fang Foom's debut in *Strange*

Tales #89 is now widely considered to be a Key issue, as are all the hot prototype issues and issues with Kirby and Ditko art. Finally of note, there is an eternal appeal to sample Pre-Code Horror issues.

Canadian Comics: The rare Golden Age Original Material "Canadian White" comics were basically non-existent on the market this year and in huge demand. When they do appear, the average current value for a non-Key issue is: (FN=$150; VG=$100; and GD=$65). The pre-1947 Canadian Whites of Fawcett (*Capt. Marvel*, *Grand Slam*, *Three Aces*, *Wow*, etc.) although re-drawn by Canadian artists, are still in high demand. Average value for non-Key issues is: FN=$100; VG=$75; and GD=$50. *Triumph* (Nelvana of the Northern Lights), and *Dime* comics (Johnny Canuck), Doc Stearne/Mr. Monster, and Men of the Mounted issues bring 200% or more of the above prices, with Key issues even higher. Vintage Canadian Variant Editions of the 1940s and early 1950s U.S. comics are 10-50 times scarcer than the U.S. editions. Issues with same page counts bring 80-100% of the value of U.S. editions. Those with less pages than their U.S. counterparts sell for about 60% of their U.S. equivalents. Canadian Variants (mostly 1946-1954) include these publishers: Archie, Atlas, Avon, Classics, DC, Dell, EC, Fawcett, Fiction House, Lev Gleason, Quality, Timely, Toby, and others. The Canadian *Classics Illustrated* Variants are the most collected and bring the biggest premiums, at 150-300% *Guide*. *Classics* #17-20 with blank inside covers are Canadian Editions and are perhaps the rarest of all the Variants. (VG copies are worth in the $100-200 each range). The Canadian EC Comics bring about 60% of U.S. values, due to poor printing. The rare EC Variant *Weird SuspenStories* copies in FN bring $1000+ each. I once owned a *Captain America* Annual (1942) that was a Canadian Printing. If it surfaced again, it would likely be the single most valuable Canadian comic (estimated at $15,000+ in VG).

I have 3000 Canadian French language comics in stock (Archie, DC and Marvel from the late 1966-1990). They had small print runs of 2000-10,000 each, and smaller survival rates, making these desirable and collectible (most at $3-$10 each). The new material French language comic digests (1950-1970s, Adventure, Jungle, Romance, Western, War) sell at $3-$7 each. The well-known-character titles bring $5-$12 each. The 1970-1982 era French Horror comic digests (Italian reprints and new French material) are rare and are the best sellers of them all at $10-$25 each. These are full of nudity, violence, bondage, torture and more, and most have great covers. *Existing Earth* #1 is a consistant seller (1987, 1500 copies printed, art by Brent L. Butt of Canadian TV's #1 comedy - *Corner Gas.*) Canadian artist Owen McCarron is a Cult figure among collectors (Puzzle Books; Marvel Fun and Games comic, Fireside Marvel Fun and Game Books, Marvel Tempo puzzles books, *Binkly and Doinkel*, *Spidey Super Stories* #29,42,43, *Ghost Rider* #28 and *Super Villian Team-Up* #8). There are a growing number of Canadian Comic Completionists interested in getting one each of everything printed from 1961-2010. Perhaps 40% or more of what exists in this Era were Giveaways and another 50% were Small Print Run independents.

Captain Canuck: All the main Captain Canuck titles were distributed in the U.S., thus the listing in the *Guide*. This is by far Canada's most famous title. We again sold over 20 sets of the Original series of #1-14 and Special #1 (1975-1981). They remain scarcer in the U.S. due to lower sales. The 1975-1981 issues are getting scarcer in strict VF/NM or better. *Captain Canuck* #1(7/75) has one CGC graded copy in 10.0 and one in 9.9. The seller of the 10.0 is asking a staggering $5000. I sold several copies of the original oversized #4 (2/77; 1st Print) in the VG-VF range at $50-$100 each. The second printing of #4 (2/77) is one of the rarest comics of the entire Bronze Age, with 100 times the demand as compared to supply, and sells at 400-800% *Guide* on the rare occasion that one surfaces. Captain Canuck has appeared twice on the cover of *Time* magazine ($10-15 ea). Comely confirmed small print runs for *Captain Canuck Re-Born* (1993/1994); #0(English = 90,000 Copies), #0(French = 6000), #1(47,000 Newsstand green-c); #1(40,000 bagged gold-c); #1(French = 6000); #2(30,000), #3(8,000 copies = $25+). All are in big demand and very hard to restock. 99% of all Capt. Canuck 1975-81 original art was donated to Canada's National Archives, thus the few left command high prices. *Captain Canuck* #15 (150 copies) is virtually impossible to find and brings $75-125. *Captain Canuck Legacy* #1(9-10/2006), and *Legacy* Special Edition #1(limted to 1000 Copies) were issued for the 30th Anniversary. The Canada - Superheroes official Postage Stamps Sets, one of the most popular Canadian Collectible stamp sets of all-time, are fast sellers at $15+ per set. Early 1990s includes Superman by Canadian Joe Shuster, Johhny Canuck by Leo Bachle/Les Barker, Nelvana of the Northern Lights by Adrian Dingle, Fleur de Lys by Mark Shainblum, Captain Canuck by Richard Comely, illustration by George Freeman. Comely's *Star Rider and the Peace Machine* #1-2 (1982) are getting scarcer too. All memorabila and promo items are fast sellers.

Charlton Comics: If you like oddball comics, this is the ultimate publisher to collect. They had more genres than any other publisher, and quality varied from "crude" to "superior". Distribution was poor, most comic shops did not bother to carry them, and the print runs range from moderate to low. Most copies were in the hands of the general public, with many damaged and discarded, thus a low survival rate. Under only minor editorial control, many creators thrived under this publisher. We have about 35,000 Charlton comics in stock, including 95% of 1960-1986 issues and about 50% of the 1940s through 1959 issues. The Horror titles were easily the strongest selling titles, with hundreds of copies in the GD-FN ranges, helping many collectors fill in dozens of sets. These were published with Cereal Box type covers (thicker than normal, stiff, low quality paper) on many issues, with interior pages often misaligned and miscut, and a host of other printing problems making these tough to find in strict VF or better (with VF/NM or better copies scarce to rare). Investors like VF/NM or better copies, as there are very few CGC graded copies, thus we sold nearly 100 of them this year (mainly from the Manitoba collection).

One fan recently said to us, "If people talk about Horror comics and fail to mention Tom Sutton, well then they are not really talking about Horror comics at all". Because Charlton is viewed as a marginal company by many, they missed some of the best artwork ever produced by Aparo, Boyette, Glanzman, Himes, Wayne Howard, Sanho Kim, Larson, Morisi, Don Newton, Staton, Tom Sutton, Wildman, and Mike Zeck. In addition, you can find great art by Buscema, John Byrne, Ditko, Giordano, Mastroserio, Severin, Williamson, and Wood. The 1945-1950 issues are all very scarce, with most 1951-1957 issues also scarce, all being in high demand with a growing number of completionists who gladly buy them in any grade (at 120-150% *Guide*). The 1958-1969 Silver Age issues are uncommon to scarce, but with some legwork, most sets are possible to complete in a reasonable amount of time. These are in moderate demand (at 115-125% *Guide*). The 1970-1986 Bronze Age issues are uncommon, with most of the 1984-1986 being lower print and scarcer issues. These are in above-average demand (at 120-135% *Guide*).

There is a large following for Hanna Barbera comics from all publishers (one of our speciaties) and many of these are scarcer than most of the Dell and Gold Key issues. The pre-1962 Western comics are up in demand, and the 1960s issues' new backup series are also in higher demand, including: *Billy the Kid* (Bounty Hunter series), *Cheyenne Kid* #66-87 (classic Wander Sci-Fi/ Western backup by Jim Aparo), *Cheyenne Kid* #88-up (Apache Red series begins by Fred Himes); *Outlaws of the West* (Capt. Doom, Kid Montana, Sharp Shooter), *Six Gun Heroes* (Gun Master). Most of the 1950s and 1960s War comics are above average sellers. Fans especially like the Glanzman art issues. The 1960s issues new backup series are also in higher demand, including: *Army War Heroes* (Iron Corporal) and *Fightin Army* (Lonely War of Willie Schultz).

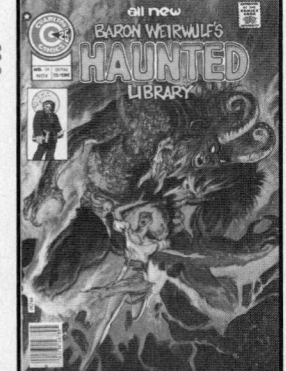

Charlton Horror features some of the best artwork ever, including Tom Sutton's ***Haunted*** *#24 cover.*

All the other genres are solid steady sellers (at 115-125% *Guide*) including: Adult Cartoons, Cartoon, Crime, Funny Animals, History, Humor/Parody, Licensed Characters, Movie, Hot Rod, Jungle, Martial Arts, Mythology, Mystery, Newspaper Comic Strip, Pirates, Pop Music Stars, Radio, Romance, Science, SF, Soap Opera, Superhero, Teenage, TV). The scarcer items include: Digests, Comic Magazines, Horror Mags and Non-Comic mags (Adult Cartoon, Crossword and Puzzle mags, Horror Film mags, Kung-Fu and Karate mags, *Sick* mag, True Romance mags, True Western mags). These fascinate many collectors and are above average sellers.

Comic Digests: I have the world's biggest inventory of comic digests (10,000 Archie digests and 5,000 other comics digests), so I always do well with them. This year the Archie digest saw the most activity, with about 85% of the requests being for GD-FN copies to fill in "reading copy" to "presentable condition" sets (at 120-150% *Guide*). There was only moderate demand for high grade copies, but as pre-1985 copies are scarce to rare in VF/NM or better, we still ended up selling about 1/3 of our high grade inventory. The 1974-1975 early issues are getting harder to find and are easily the most sought issues (bringing 150-200% *Guide*). Next best selling are all issue #1-10s (at 120-150% *Guide*).

The Gold Key digests are the ones that started the trend way back in 1968. All are uncommon to scarce in any grade (with strict VF or better copies scarce to Rare). *Mystery Comics Digest* (only 1 Gold Key issue CGC graded), *Golden Comics Digest* (only 16 CGC graded), *Walt Disney Comics Digest* (only 7 CGC graded), Story Digests (*Boris Karloff, Dark Shadows, Ripley's, Tarzan* = only 7 CGC graded in total). *Golden Comics Digest* #2,7,11 are the most requested (bringing 150-200% *Guide* in any grade). The three main titles issue #1-10 are in low supply and high demand (150% *Guide* in any grade), with #11-up in good demand (at 125% *Guide*). *Dennis the Menace Pocket Full of Fun Digest* #1-20 are in low supply and high demand (bringing 150-200% *Guide* in any grade), with #11-up in good demand (at 150% *Guide*) and no examples yet graded by CGC.

The Harvey digests are on many completionist lists. The 1977-1985 issues are uncommon, selling at 120-135% *Guide*, and 1986-1993 are 2-10 times scarcer than the earlier issues, bringing 150-600% *Guide*. These are amazingly tough sets to complete, as all major dealers are sold out of the later issues of the 1990s. *Shocking Tales Digest* #1 (Powell, Kirby and Nostrand-a) is an uncommon one-shot title, but in constant demand (at 135% *Guide*). The scarce issues (bringing 200% *Guide*) include: *Casper Adventure Digest* #6-8, *Casper Digest* (10/86-91) #11-18, *Casper Digest* (V2; 9/91-11/94) #6-14, *Casper Enchanted Tales* #6-10, *Harvey Wiseguys* #3,4, *Hot Stuff Digest* #2-5, *Million Dollar Digest*(11/86-11/94) #11-20, *New Kids on the Block* Digest #1-5, *Richie Rich Adventure Digest* #4-7, *Richie Rich Digest* (10/86-10/94) #11-20, *Richie Rich Digest Stories* #11-17, *Richie Rich Digest Winners* #11-16, *Richie Rich Gold Nuggets* #1-4, *Richie Rich Million Dollar Digest* #6-10, *Richie Rich Money World Digest* #1-8, *Richie Rich Digest* (11/77-8/82) #7-9, *Wendy Digest* #2-5. The very scarce issues that everyone needs (bringing 300-500% *Guide*) include: *Richie Rich Million Dollar Digest*(11/86-11/94) #21-34 and *Richie Rich Digest* (10/86-10/94) #21-42.

High grade pre-1990 DC and Marvel comic digests in VF to VF/NM are uncommon to scarce, with 9.2 to 9.6 copies being rare. These are by far the most sought in high grades. Only low quantities have so far been graded by CGC, considering the highly collectible status of these titles. The War and Horror titles are the bestsellers. *DC Special Blue Ribbon Digest* #20(Dark Mansion) is the tough major Key that everyone desires (bringing 150% *Guide*). The 4 Digest issues of *DC Special Series* #18,19,23,24 are top sellers as many collectors are trying to complete sets. *Best of DC* #41-71 are all low print and scarce, making it a tough set to complete. The Jonah Hex digests have been up in demand since the announcement of the movie. The Atari promo/give-away mini-comics (*Atari Force*, *Centipede* and *Swordquest*) are in high demand, with only issue #1's being easier to find. The Marvel digests (*Alf*, *Dennis the Menace*, *G.I. Joe*, *Haunt of Horror*, *Spider-Man*, *Star* and *Transformers*) are already uncommon in any grade and scarce in strict VF/NM or better (bringing 150% *Guide* in any grade).

The 1970s Charlton/Xerox/Now Age comic digests are all low print, and scarce to rare, including: *Barney & Betty*, *Bugs Bunny*, *Dino*, *Dr. Graves*, *Flintstones*, *Jetsons*, *Pebbles & Bamm-Bamm*, *Road Runner*, *Scooby Doo*, *Space: 1999*, *Tweety & Sylvester*, *Woody Woodpecker* and *Yogi Bear* (bringing 200-300% *Guide* in any grade). These are tough to find in even Fine, much less high grade, thus no copies have yet been graded by CGC. *Fiction Illustrated* digests #1-2 are in good demand (at 120% *Guide*), with #3 (Chandler by Steranko) rating as hot and hard to keep in stock (at 200% *Guide*). The TPB versions of #3, 4 are scarce and good sellers (at 150% *Guide*).

Comic & Cartoon Mass Market Paperbacks: I have in stock over 6000 Cartoon and Newspaper Comic Strip Mass Market Paperbacks, with perhaps the world's biggest selection of different cartoon books. I usually sell about 300-500 of these in a year. The majority sell to readers (who are not otherwise comic collectors) in the $2 to $5 each range. In almost all cases, the later titles had just one printing with smaller print runs and are scarcer. For example, most late 1980s *Peanuts* books are 10-30 times scarcer than 1950s-1960s titles. The popular characters typically have 20 to 100 titles each, with about 50% being common, 25% uncommon, and 25% scarce to rare. The scarce titles often bring $10-$25, and rare titles can sell for $25-$50 each. Comic collectors who cross over into this area of the hobby often want the scarcest titles and often in the highest grades (presumably because they already have the common titles).

Some of the scarcer and more valuable series and titles (at $10-50 each) include: *Archie at Riverdale High* series, *Autumn People* by Ray Bradbury, *Beetle Bailey* (Giant Size titles), *Berenstains*, *Best of Creepy*, *Conchy*, *Cracked*, *Dick Tracy*, *Dracula* (Russ Jones), *Famous Monsters of Filmland* ($50-100 each), *Funky Winkerbean*, *Hagar* (later titles can be rare), Harvey Kurtzman (*Help*, *Humbug*, *Jungle Book*, etc.), *High-Camp Super-Heroes*, *Hocus-Focus*, Jimmy Hatlo, (*Hatlo's Inferno* at $35-50), *Lockhorns*, *Luann*, *Richie Rich*, *Rose is Rose*, *Scooby Doo*, *Scroogie*, *Sick*, *Spirit*, *Tales From the Crypt*, *Tales of the Incredible*, *There Outta be a Law*, *THUNDER Agents*, *Tomorrow Midnight* by Ray Bradbury, *U.S./Acres* by Jim Davis, *Vampirella* (USA and UK), and *Vault of Horror*. The Tempo Puzzle Books for both Marvel and DC circa 1977 are all scarce, especially un-marked and bring $10-$25 each.

Over 100 Marvel and DC related Mass Market Comic paperbacks in the 1966-1988 era exist. These are by far the most sought paperbacks by comic collectors. The 1960s titles are scarce in FN or better and sell at: (GD=$6-12; VG=$10-$20; VF=$25-$50). The 1975-1985 titles are scarce in VF or better and sell at: (VF/NM=$15-$35; VF=$10-$20; VG=$5-10). The Marvel and DC titles are the most requested in high grade investment quality copies. We got in a nice batch of 9.0-9.6 copies from the Manitoba collection and about 50% of them sold at 25-100% premiums. But the standard GD-FN copies of the Marvel and DC paperbacks remained the bestsellers.

DC Comics: Many collectors have not yet tried to complete their 1980s series, assuming they will be easy to pick up any time they want them. But take note, that dealer inventories have shrunken greatly on a lot of these titles, because *Guide* value remain so low. High grade collectors should take special note that most of these books are already scarce in strict VF/NM or better in dealer inventories. As they are low value, most sellers have not gone the extra mile to preserve high grade copies. Average dealer inventory copies that are graded or assumed to be in NM are more like FN/VF to VF average, if submitted to CGC. I have sold a good quantity of high grade copies to speculators who can only see the upside on these.

These issue numbers have the lowest print runs in the history of the pre-1999 era of each title (only 50,000 to 99,000 copies per month, whereas most had double the print runs or higher on issues that are a decade older). *Batman* #357-402, *Brave and the Bold* #170-200, *Detective Comics* #482-569, *Flash* #293-350, *Green Lantern* #113-224, *Justice League* #234-261, *Sgt. Rock* #372-422, *Superman* #401-423, *Wonder Woman* #263-329, and *World's Finest* #248-323. If the print runs are so small on all these major titles, imagine how small they are on a lot of the lesser titles.

Batman titles are the most consistantly demanded of all DC titles from the last 60 years. All key issues, better artist issues and major villain issues, as well as Bronze Age Giant issues are in extra high demand, and do not currently have enough of a premium added in the *Guide*. This year I have seen a nearly 50% increase in demand for *Detective Comics* in the #250-600 number range. Collectors have noted they are less common and cheaper than *Batman* comics of the same vintage, with less CGC graded copies too. *Batmans* with Neal Adams covers and art are the most requested.

1950s DC sold moderately well this year, but I have noted that 1960s issues were slower in general, likely due to the economy. But almost everything from the more affordable

1970 Bronze Age through to the 1985 Crisis era was selling consistantly well. *Green Lantern* #76-89 are hot sellers, with #76 continuing to set record prices in VF or better. All Neal Adams DC comics are in high demand, but especially those with Adams covers, as most carry no premiums over surrounding vintage issues (many should list at 25-50% higher than current levels). *Aquaman* #53(10/1970), 54, 55, 56(4/1971) are extremely under-valued. These should list in the $35-$50 range.

All 52, 68, and 100 Page Giants are considered to be key issues by fans and sold about 200% better than surrounding regular sized issues, and most remained elusive in higher grades. The "Dollar" Giants of the late 1970s were round-bound with 2 staples (as opposed to squarebound) and are a very tough set to put together in high grade and thus are a good long term investment in high grade. Many factors tended to lower the grades of these Dollar comics including: (1) weight of the book pulled at the staples, (2) they are slightly taller than other DCs of the period and got crushed as they stuck out of stacks and in dealer long boxes, (3) they were thicker and did not cut well at the presses thus most have splits to the covers at top and bottom of the spine. The Bronze Age bestsellers for us this year (at 120% to 150% *Guide*) included: all Treasury editions, all Digests, All Big-5 War comics, all Batman and Superman titles, all Teenage, Romance, Cartoon and Obscure titles, all Horror titles, all 52, 68, and 100 Page Giants, *Teen Titans*, *Flash*, *Green Lantern*, *Tarzan*, *V for Vendetta*, *Watchmen*, *Warlord*, and *Wonder Woman*. In the last year, I sold about 700+ raw high grade and Manitoba collection DC comics of all types in the 9.0 to 9.8 range, mainly from the 1974-1987 era at 125% to 300% *Guide*.

The *Jonah Hex* movie starring Josh Brolin is due in theaters June 2010, with Voodoo and Army of the Undead. It might be a hit and collectors have already started to show increased interest. Many fans consider it to be the best Western comic series of all time, and *All-Star Western* #10 is already one of the most valuable of all Bronze Age comics. *Jonah Hex* #81-92 had a low print run and most dealers are perpetually sold out on them. They should *Guide* about 50% higher than current levels. The *Hex* (1985-87) #1-18 were near universally hated by fans and I think DC wants to forget they exist, but they are part of the saga and most completionists buy them, with #11-18 a bit tougher to find. Most *Jonah Hex* #21-91 issues have only 5-10 copies each so far graded and are scarcer in high grade than most collectors would think. *DC Special Series* #16 the "Death of Jonah Hex" story is a Bronze classic and is a recommended must buy.

The DC Big-5 War Comics (all issues 1950s through 1988; *All-American Men of War*, *G.I. Combat*, *Our Army at War/Sgt Rock*, *Our Fighting Forces* and *Star Spangled War Stories/Unknown Soldier*) and all DC Horror/SF comics (of the 1968-1985 era) were consistantly our best selling DC Bronze Age sellers in any grade, outselling all superhero titles with the exception of *Batman* and *Detective*. *Weird War* combines elements of both Horror and War, thus appealing to both type fans, with #37-123 quite undervalued in the *Guide*, perhaps due for a 35-50% price increases (and #64,68,93,94,100,101,124 even higher increases). *Weird War* #64 and 68 are the hottest issues and sell instantly at 150-200% *Guide*. Low grades appeal to readers, who tend to buy in larger quantities. Medium grades appeal to collectors who want them, but have opted to go after affordable presentable examples. Many investors view these as scarce in high grade among DC's strongest demand titles and thus a good long term investment. *Our Army at War* #83-130 are near impossible to keep in stock in any grade and are the only Silver Age comics that outsell *Batman*. *OAAW* #81-82 are now seen as overpriced Sgt. Rock prototypes and are slow selling, perhaps due for a drop in price. Meanwhile *G.I. Combat* #68 and *OOAW* #83 in huge demand, but impossible to find, and easily worth 150-200% current *Guide* values. *Sgt. Rock* #400-422 had low print runs and sold out in most dealer inventories, selling well at 150-175% *Guide*. All appearances of Haunted Tank, Enemy Ace and Unknown Soldier are top sellers, most are scarce in high grade. The early Haunted Tank issues in *G.I. Combat* #87-114 and War that Time Forgot/Dinosaur issues of *Star Spangled War* #90-100 are in very low supply and high demand, in any grade.

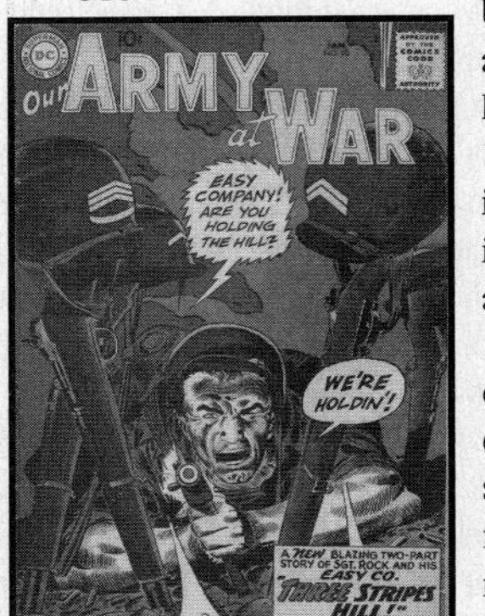

Our Army at War issues are the only Silver Age comics that outsell **Batman** of that era. (#90 shown)

1950s through 1962 DC Horror comics are in moderate but consistant demand. The 1963-1967 issues are slow sellers, but the 1968-1985 issues have remained among bestsellers for a decade now. The 1968-1974 Horror issues are especially tough in high grades, many fans still want them badly, thus are now happy with a nice VF, or even a FN/VF. Neal Adams and Wrightson issues, including all covers only and one page art issues are all in the highest demand, at 125-150% *Guide*. DC Horror are among our most requested titles in low grade reading copies. *Swamp Thing* #20-64 classics by Alan Moore are highly collected, undervalued and a good investment in strict VF/NM or better. 1975-1988 DC Horror & War issues in strict VF/NM are still among our Top selling DCs, as most copies in the marketplace are in the VG to FN/VF range.

Dell Comics: Dell comics have been strong and steady sellers for nearly 40 solid years for me, thus I always strive to carry a large inventory of them. They have worldwide appeal, with virtually everything they published always being sought by someone somewhere out there, both within the comics collecting hobby, but also by non-collectors who are nostalgic about the characters and just want a few examples. Price seems to be the most important factor to most of the majority of buyers, with over 90% of what actually sells in the FA/GD to FN condition range. Most FN/VF, VF, VF/NM copies see price resistance and are slow sellers (often only selling if I do not have a more affordable copy in stock). The exceptions that are still in demand in high grades include: Carl Barks comics, key and first issues, *Tarzan*, *Turok*, better Hanna-Barbera, better cartoon and popular TV and Movie comics. Dell comics in CGC graded VF/NM 9.0, NM- 9.2 and NM 9.4 have among the lowest multiples of *Guide* among all older comics, with many non-key issues regularily selling below *Guide* at auctions (not to mention the $25+ cost lost to slabbing fees). What this tells me is clear: most Dell comics in GD-FN are under-valued in the *Guide*, while many VF-NM Dells are overvalued in the *Guide*. This was caused by using the same Price-to-Condition spreads for Dell as wide as for Superhero comics while that is not the reality of the marketplace.

The bestselling titles (GD-FN = 120-140% *Guide*; FN/VF-VF/NM= 100-115% *Guide*) included: *Adventures of Mighty Mouse*, *Air War*, *Andy Panda* #35-56 (Chilly Willy backup-s issues), *Annie Oakley*, *Bat Masterson*, *Beetle Bailey*, *Beep Beep Road Runner, Ben Bowie, Beverly Hillbillies, Bewitched, Big Valley, Brave Eagle, Bugs Bunny, Bullwinkle, Cheyenne, Chilly Willy, Cisco Kid, Colt 45, Combat, Creature*, Dell Giants (Bugs Bunny, Lone Ranger, Little Lulu, Nancy, Tarzan, Western Roundup, Yogi Bear, etc.), *Dracula* #1, *Dunc & Loo, Felix the Cat, Flintstones, Flying Nun, Flying Saucers, Four Color* (over 100 hot issues, over 300 issues in high demand, about 700 are moderate sellers, with only about 200 being slower sellers), *Frankenstein* #1, *Fritzi Ritz* (with Peanuts), *F-Troop, Gene Autry* #101-121, *Get Smart, Ghost Stories, Gidget, Have Gun Will Travel, Hogan's Heroes, Howdy Doody, Huckleberry Hound, I Dream of Jeannie, I Love Lucy, Indian Chief, Jetsons, John Carter of Mars, John Wayne* (all), *Jungle War, King of Royal Mounted, Kona, Laramie, Lawman, Leave it to Beaver, Little Lulu, Lone Ranger* #1-10, 112-145, *Looney Tunes* #1-50, 201-246, *March of Comics* (50% of this Promo giveaway series are above average sellers), *Maverick, McHale's Navy, Melvin Monster, Monkees*, Movie Classics (Western, SF and Horror), *Mummy, Nancy* (Peanuts-s, Oona-s, Stanley-a), *New Funnies* #65-120, 241-288, *Outer Limits, Peanuts, Pogo, Ponytail, Popeye, Quick Draw McGraw, Rawhide, Real McCoys, Red Ryder* #1-118, *Ricky Nelson, Rifleman, Rin Tin Tin* #18-38(TV's Rusty and the Cavalry of Fort Apache issues), *Rocky & Friends, Roy Rogers* #119-145, *Sgt. Preston, Smokey Stover, Tales of Wells Fargo, Tarzan* #1-30, 80-131, *Thirteen, Tip Top* #211-225(with Nancy and Peanuts), *Tom & Jerry* #60-100, *Tonto, Top Cat, Turok, Twilight Zone, Voyage to the Bottom of the Sea, Wolfman, Woody Woodpecker, Wyatt Earp, Yak Yak, Yogi Bear and Zorro.*

Gold Key Comics: I have 35,000 Gold Key comics in stock, with about 95% of their entire output always in stock. We had above average sales on GD-FN copies this year for many dozens of collectors looking to fill in their sets. Many dealers have a good stock of the Horror, SF, Hero and Adventure titles, but we always have about 99% of them, thus many buyers ask for bulk prices on bigger batches of these when they want to start a new title, and naturally we are accommodating. Most dealers do not bother with Cartoon titles, while many others have only 25-50% of all the existing issues in stock. We typically have 90-95% in stock, even with choice of grade on most, thus we are probably the #1 destination for collectors wanting to finally finish completing these titles. The Hanna-Barbera titles are all highly collected and are one of our specialties.

© 20th Century Fox

***Land of the Giants** was a Gold Key best seller in 2009. (#1 shown)*

Awareness of Whitman Variants of the Gold Key comics and Canadian Newsstand Variant cover price issues has risen and thus demand nearly doubled this year (see Variants for more info).

Demand for high grade copies was down about 25% this year, due to tighter money in the economy, but still in strong demand if you have the titles that investors wanted. Raw copies (mainly from the Manitoba collection) in demand in high grade (sold at VF to VF/NM =120-135% *Guide*; 9.2= 150% *Guide*) included: *Atom Ant, Astro Boy, Auggie Doggie, Avengers* (TV) #1(photo back-c), *Beatles Yellow Submarine, Beneath Planet of Apes, Boris Karloff, Dark Shadows, Doc Savage, Dr. Solar, Fantastic Voyage* #2 (12/69; "Civilian Miniaturized Defense Force" variant), *Grimm's Ghost*, Hanna-Barbera (all #1 and key issues), *Hanna-Barbera Super TV Heroes, Honey West, Korak, John Carter, Jonny Quest, Marge's Little Lulu* #165-206, *Magnus Robot Fighter, Mars Patrol, Mighty Samson, Munsters, Occult Files of Dr. Spector, Peanuts, Phantom, Popeye, Ripley's Believe it or Not, Scooby Doo, Secret Squirrel, Space Family Robinson, Space Ghost, Spine Tingling Tales, Star Stream, Star Trek* #1-9, *Tarzan, Tasmanian Devil* #1, *Turok* and *Twilight Zone*, all variants (see Variant Comics in this report), *Wild Wild West* and *Yakkey Doodle*.

The bestsellers this year (at VF-NM= 110-120% *Guide*; GD-FN=120-140% *Guide*) included: *Addams Family, Amazing Chan, Bamm Bamm, Banana Splits, Battle of the Planets, Beep Beep* #1-10, *Beetle Bailey, Bugs Bunny* #86-100, *Bullwinkle, Cave Kids, Close Shaves of Pauline Peril, Daffy Duck* #31-50, *Dagar*, Dan Curtis (Giveaways) #1-9, *Daniel Boone, Family Affair, Fat Albert, Flash Gordon, Flintstones, Frankenstein Jr., Fun-In, Funky Phantom, George of the Jungle, Gold Key Spotlight, Gomer Pyle, Hair*

Bear Bunch, Hanna-Barbera Bandwagon, Happy Days, H.R. Pufnstuf, Huckleberry Hound, Inspector, Jetsons, Krofft Supershow, Lancelot Link, Land of Giants, Laredo, Lidsville, Little Lulu #207 up, *Little Monsters, Lone Ranger, Looney Tunes* #1-10, *Lucy Show, Magilla Gorilla, Mighty Hercules, Mighty Mouse, Milton Monster, Mr. Ed, Mr. & Mrs. J Evil Scientist, My Favorite Martian, Nancy & Sluggo, Peter Potomus, Pink Panther, Quick Draw McGraw, Rifleman, Rocky & Fiendish Friends, Snagglepuss, Snooper & Blabber, Space Mouse, Supercar, Three Stooges, Time Tunnel, Top Cat, UFO Flying Saucers, Underdog, Wacky Races, Wacky Witch, Wagon Train, Woody Woodpecker* #75-100, and *Zody the Mod Rob*.

Harvey Comics: All 1950-1975 Cartoon titles were in above-average demand, in FA/GD through FN grades. Most 1976-1990 were in moderate demand (mostly in VG to VF grades). Most 1991-1994 titles were in low supply and good demand, in any grades.

Bestselling titles (9.2=150%; VF-VF/NM=120-130% *Guide*; GD-FN=125-150% *Guide*) include: all 35¢-cover variants of squarebound Giants, *Baby Huey* #1-10, *Blondie* (undervalued), *Casper's Ghostland, Casper & Nightmare, Dagwood, Devil Kids, Family Funnies, Flintstones, Fruitman, Hanna-Barbera Giant Size, Harvey Hits* #1-75, *Harvey Pop, Hot Stuff the Little Devil, Jetsons, Little Dot, Little Dot's Uncles & Aunts, Little Lotta, Playful Little Audrey, Pebbles & Bamm-Bamm,* Richie Rich (all 1960-1974), Sad Sack (all pre-1965), *Scooby Doo, Spooky, Stumbo Tinytown, Tuff Ghosts, TV Casper & Co., Underdog, Unearthly Spectacular, Wendy*, and *Yogi Bear*.

Other great sellers (VF-VF/NM=110-120% *Guide*; GD-FN=120-140% *Guide*) include: all 25¢-cover squarebound Giants, *Alarming Tales, Alarming Advs., Alvin, Astro Comics* (giveaway with 15+ variations), *Baby Huey* #11-up, *Black Cat, Blast-Off, Bunny, Casper the Friendy Ghost* #1-20, Casper (assorted titles 1961-1974), *Chamber of Chills, Dotty Dribble, Felix the Cat, First Love, First Romance, Friendly Ghost Casper, Harvey Collectors' Comics, Harvey Hits* #76-122, *Joe Palooka*, Little Audrey (all titles), *Little Max, Man in Black, Mazie, Mutt & Jeff,* Richie Rich (all 1976-1994), Sad Sack (all 1965-up), *Tastee-Freez, Thrill-O-Rama, Tomb of Terror, Warfront, Witches Tales* and *Woody Woodpecker*.

IW & Super Reprint Comics (1958-1964): These 46-52 year old vintage comics have low *Guide* values and thus are highly sought by collectors. Most reading copies are only in the $5-$10 range. Many have Pre-Code reprints at much lower prices than the slightly earlier vintage original, but at a fraction of the price. None of these comics carry the Comic Code in a time period when all comics should have had them. There was a wide variety of genres published, with the Horror/SF, Western and War titles being the bestsellers. The Superhero, Jungle, Teenage, Humor and Romance titles are all moderate sellers. Funny Animal and Cartoon titles are generally the slowest. Many issues contain top artists including: Powell, DeCarlo, Frazetta, Wood, Kirby, Crandall, Ward, Kinstler, Lou Fine, Severin, Cole, Krigstein, Davis, and Heath. About 340 different issues exist and many completionists are attempting to gather them all. The *Guide* lists far too many under $20 with many as low as $12-14 in NM-. I believe this needs to change so that none list under $20. They are quite scarce in VF/NM or better and even $25 seems very low for the minimum price for a NM- in *Guide*. If they listed higher, perhaps more would come out of hiding and hit the marketplace. Those who like old cheap books usually buy reading copies. The completionist generally prefers the higher graded copies. The scarcer titles tend to sell instantly when listed, as they are extremely undervalued in the *Guide* and due for a big upward price adjustment. About 1/3 are common, another 1/3 are uncommon, with 1/3 being scarce to rare. I sell these for minimum prices of: GD=$4; VG=$7; FN=$10; VF=$18, VF/NM=$24, with the more collectible titles selling for about 50-100% higher.

Marvel Comics: The Marvel movies continue to fuel demand for these classic back issues. Slated for eventual release as movies (and characters to buy now) include: *Ant-Man, Avengers, Black Panther, Captain America, Iron Man 2, Luke Cage, Planet Hulk* and *Thor* (with a Punisher app.). It was big news when Disney Studios purchased Marvel Entertainment. I expect we haven't even seen the beginning of merchandising Marvel, as this is Disney's cash cow. The TV cartoons *Super-Hero Squad, Iron Man Adventures* and *Black Panther*, plus the animated DVDs, are getting the younger non-comics reading crowd more interested in these characters. Although Marvel comics are typically the most plentiful, they also have had the highest demand for back issues over the last 45 years, with no end in site. For the majority of dealers worldwide, Marvel is the backbone of the back issue industry, many dealers having over 2/3 of their inventory as Marvel comics. Many mistakenly think they are the only comics worth investing in.

Low print run Marvels of the late Bronze Age into the Copper Age have picked up in sales and are good long term investments, especially in high grades. Dealer inventories are low on a lot of these titles, as *Guide* values are still low. Strict high grade investment quality copies are a lot scarcer than you would think, as there are a lot less copies around to choose from. These issue numbers are the lowest print runs in the history of the pre-1999 era of each title (only 100,000 to 150,000 copies per month, whereas most had 50-100% higher print runs only a decade earlier): *Avengers* #382-402, *Capt. America* #206-228, 286-294, 313-336, *Conan the Barbarian* #190-275, *Daredevil* #129-177, *Ghost Rider* #36-81, *Incredible Hulk* #423-474; *Iron Man* #297-332, *Spectacular Spider-Man* #235-263, *Thor* #328-338,469-502 and *X-Men* #81-116. Since print runs are small on all these major titles, many lesser titles often had print runs of half these low levels.

We sold a lot of "oddball" comics and other format items (Marvel fanzines, giveaway/promo items, memorabilia, posters, Slurpee cups, calendars, portfolios, digests, Treasury editions, paperbacks and magazines, etc,) because of our huge selection. The TNC (Traditionally Non-Collected) genres of comics (Cartoon, Humor and Parody, TV/Movie, Romance, Teenage, Toy-Related, TV, War, and Western) sold steady as always, at 125-200% *Guide*, with GD-FN the most requested. These are especially popular among completionists and those who like items that are scarce in any condition. The rare "*Pow Biff Pops*" is a 1977 Promo comic for the Boston Pops, Orchestra (with Spider-Man, Captain America, Batman and Superman) which had only 250 printed. The unsold copies were destroyed and only about 10 copies exist. It rarely surfaces and is worth approximately $1000-$2000.

All the Marvel 1970s Horror reprint titles were top sellers in all grades all through the year. It seems everyone was scrambling to complete all these sets and dealers inventories are at an all-time low. To keep them in stock, we pay more and we sell most at 125-150% *Guide* ranges. All these issues are hot sellers: *Beware* #1-8, *Chamber of Chills* #1-25, *Chamber of Darkness* #1-8 and Special #1, *Creatures on the Loose* #11-15, *Crypt of Shadows* #1-21, *Dead of Night* #1-11, *Fear* #1-9, *Giant-Size Chillers* (1975; 2nd series) #1-3, *Journey into Mystery* (2nd series) #1-19, *Tomb of Darkness* #9-23, *Tower of Shadows* #1-9 and Special #1, *Uncanny Tales* (2nd series) #1-12, *Vault of Evil* #1-23, *Weird Wonder Tales* #1-22, *Where Creatures Roam* #1-8 and *Where Monsters Dwell* #1-38. The three 1990s titles all had low print runs and are already hard to find (with the exception of the semi-common issue #1s) and all are great sellers: *Book of the Dead* #1-4, *Curse of the Weird* #1-4 and *Monster Menace* #1-4. The "New Material" Horror titles (color comics and B&W mags) *Dracula*, *Fear* #10-31, *Frankenstein*, *Ghost Rider*, *Man-Thing*, *Monsters Unleashed*, *Scarecrow*, *Supernatural Thrillers*, *Tales of the Zombie*, *War is Hell* #9-15, and *Werewolf* are all in strong demand in all grades.

1961-1964 Marvel Superhero comics were still in big demand in every grade. 1965-1969 Marvel Superheroes were slower sellers, but all other genres of the 1961-1969 era had steady sales. 1970 through 1987 Bronze to Copper Age comics were in high demand in all grades. GD-FN copies of 1965-1974 Marvels sold about twice as fast as VF or better copies, mainly because buyers were more careful with spending in the current economy. The more affordable 1975-1987 Marvels sold about equally well in lower vs. higher grades. *Dazzler* #33 (Michael Jackson *Thriller*-c/s) was the surprise Marvel sell-out of the year (at 600% *Guide* in any grade), due to the hysteria of Michael Jackson's passing. 1988-1995 are still the slowest selling Marvels, but actually sold quite well as "Overstocked Clearance Sets" at 40-70% off *Guide*, especially the strong character titles. Modern 1996-2009 Marvels have small print runs (40,000 to 100,000 copies) and most dealers have small inventories of these years. Even a slight spike in demand can cause a large rise in back issue prices. *New Mutants* #98 (first app. of Deadpool) is one of the hottest Modern Marvel comics, with almost all dealers sold out, and it should list higher than the slow selling #87. VF to NM raw/unslabbed copies are selling for $35 to $75 each range on eBay (a CGC 9.9 of #98 sold for $12,250 in 11/2009). All other Deadpool titles and issues are also hot, with many dealers asking $5 to $10 each or more for ordinary issues of the main series and all the smaller titles too. There has been a decline in demand and prices for CGC-graded Marvel comics on much of the more average and lower graded comics.

Meanwhile, the scarce high grade comics, as well as the highest graded copies seem to be doing better, with some record prices still being set. I have a large selection of about 20,000 raw/unslabbed high grade comics listed on my website (approx 2/3 are from the Manitoba Collection), and have noted that pre-1975 sales have slowed by about 15-25% over the previous year, but with 1976-up issues holding steady and about even with last year's sales. Many collectors have resorted to collecting only key issues and high demand titles, perhaps as a buffer against investment in the hobby. The 1975-1984 era Bronze Age key issues are in high demand in all grades, but virtually all are currently undervalued in the *Guide* in GD, VG and FN grades, due to overly wide "Price-to-Condition" spreads in the *Guide*. These keys are way up in demand, with many collectors (some probably part time dealers) buying multiple copies, with many selling well at 125-150% *Guide* (in GD-FN) and with the hottest issues at 150-200% *Guide*.

National Lampoon: National Lampoon has cried out to be listed in the *Guide* for years. These classic mags are loaded with great material that is unknown or forgotten. In the 1950s and 1960s, *Mad* was arguably the greatest Parody magazine of them all, but in the 1970s, National Lampoon took that position. With their superb roster of artists, one would think many more would be slabbed. Included in the series is great art by: Adams, Bodé, Frazetta, Jeff Jones, Kaluta, Morrow, Romita, Arnold Roth, Barry Windsor-Smith, Gahan Wilson, Berni Wrightson and many others.

Price ranges: *National Lampoon* #1($50-$200), #2-10(1970 at $30-$75 each); #10-21(1971 sell for $20-$50); #22-33(1972 sell for $12-30); 1973-1990 sell at $4 to $20 each price range. The 9 different issues published in 1993-1997 had very small print runs and rarely show up even on eBay. They bring $15-$30+ each if you can find them at all. The last issue (11/98) is incredibly hard to find and can sell for $50-$100 to completionists. 90% of the issues we sell are in the GD-FN range.

Religious Comics: I have specialized in carrying all Religious comics for over 25 years, and I have about the best selection around, thus consistantly selling many each year. The Spire titles are by far the most collected and are perhaps 35-40% of our entire yearly sales. There are 19 Archie titles and they are always in the highest demand at 125-150% *Guide*. The scarce Archie Spires titles (bringing 200-250% *Guide*) include: *Archie & Mr. Weatherbee*, *Archie's Circus*, *Archie's Date Book*, *Archie's Festival*, *Archie's Roller Coaster*, *Archie's Sports Scene* and *Christmas with Archie*. There are about 38 non-Archie Spire titles and many completionists want them all (we sell them at 125-150% *Guide*). Spire comics are typically found in GD or VG condition, with FN copies being uncommon and VF or better copies being scarce. Easily the bestsellers (at 150-200% *Guide*) are: *Hansi the Girl Who Loved the Swastika, Hello I'm Johnny Cash*, and *Tom Landry and the Dallas Cowboys*. The Barney Bear Series (9 diff.) is actually quite hard to put together;

Sunday Pix (David C. Cook) are good sellers, with most being uncommon to scarcer, and low prices making them sell fast. Most dealers have less than a handful of copies in stock and many have never heard of the title. The 1949-1955 issues are all scarce to rare, with over 700 issues in this series (one of the biggest titles in comics history), the set is nearly impossible to complete. Most buyers seem to try to collect certain storylines (Tullas, H.G. Wells, John Glenn Astronaut etc.). The David C. Cook Mass Market Paperback series (1973-1977) are always in demand (at $4-$12 each) including: *The Picture Bible for All Ages, Jesus and the Early Church, Christian Family Classics*, and *Tullus in the Ancient Roman Empire*. *Topix* (Catechetical Guild, thus related to *Classics*) had over 150 different issues, yet there are almost zero copies for sale on the market. *Topix* are among the most requested of all Religious comics and among the hardest to find in any grade. I know several buyers who have been trying to complete the set for over a decade and are having a hard time getting past the half way point.

© MAR

Captain America's Bicentennial Battles #1 *was a popular Treasury Edition in 2009.*

Boy's Life Magazine has both Boy Scout and Christian themes and includes comics. The 5-issue Gilberton Pub. series *Best from Boy's Life* collects some of these stories. Thus the magazine is both *Classics Illustrated* and Christian comic-related and are collectible. *Crusaders* #1-17 which feature superb art by Jack T. Chic along with in-your-face "fire and brimstone" type messages, are loaded with religious propaganda, and thus are recommended just for being over-the-top.

Life of Pope John Paul II #1 is still the bestselling of all Christian comics at 200-300% *Guide*. Other consistent DC and Marvel sellers include *Easter Story, Francis Brother of the Universe* #1, *Life of Christ, Limited Collectors' Edition* C-36 (Bible), *Mother Teresa and Life of Christ, Pilgrims Progress*, and *Screwtape Letters*. With over 500 issues in the series, *Treasure Chest* is also one of the biggest titles in comics history. We have about 2000 in stock, so many fans come to us to fill holes in their sets. Most of what we sell are GD-FN copies, with little demand for higher graded copies. Volume 1-10 (1946-1955) and Volume 26-27(1971-1972) are the best sellers at 125-150% *Guide*, with the other issues being more common and selling at 110-125% *Guide*. A good number of fans are trying to complete their favorite serialized stories and we often flip through issues to find where stories start and end, as long as they can identify at least one issue in the series.

The Jack T. Chic "*Tracks*" mini comics (over 215 different, not including variants and multiple printings, not listed in the *Guide*) are quite collectible with most selling at $1-$5 each, but scarce to rare titles at $10-25+. These have the "fire and brimstone" type religious propaganda, with a different message in each title. With over 500 million sold worldwide in about 100 languages, this is the best-selling comics series of all-time (sold in Christian book stores, by mail order and given out at churches, schools, etc.). The 30-40 year old first printings are scarce, especially in higher grades. Virtually none of the major comic dealers carry these in their inventories, so collectors tend to hunt them down on eBay. I have carried a good stock of these for over a decade and typically sell over 100 of these in a given year.

Treasury Editions: These were traditionally not widely collected, most were not stored well, not bagged and over handled, and thus the majority of the copies in the market fall into the GD/VG to Fine condition ranges. Luckily they are very popular in lower graded cheaper copies.

Strict VF copies are uncommon, and most are scarce in strict VF/NM 9.0 or better grades. I usually have about 95% of these titles in stock. The bestsellers of the year (selling at: GD-FN=120-140% *Guide*; FN/VF-VF+=110-120% *Guide*; VF/NM to NM at 135-200% *Guide*) included: *All-New Collectors' Edition* C-54 (Superman vs. Wonder Woman), C-55(Legion marriage issue), C-56 (Superman vs. Muhammad Ali), *Captain America's Bicentennial Battles* #1(Kirby/Smith-a), *DC Special Series* #27(Batman vs. Hulk), *Giant Superhero Holiday Grab-Bag* #1(1974), *Limited Collector's Edition* C-23 (*House of Mystery*), C-25, C-37, C-44, C-51(all Batman), C-32(Ghosts), C-39, C-45 (Super Villains), C-41(*Super Friends*), C-43(Superhero Xmas), C-46(JLA), C-48(Superman vs. Flash), C-49(Legion), C-59(Batman's Strangest Cases), *Marvel Special Edition featuring Spectacular Spider-Man* #1(1975), *Marvel Treasury* #1-5, 7,14,15,17-28, *Savage Fists of Kung Fu* #1(Adams and Starlin-a), *Star Wars* #1-3, *Superman vs Spider-Man* #1. *Captain E-O 3-D* #1(Michael Jackson-c/s) was the surprise Treasury sell-out of the year (at 400% *Guide* in any grade), due to the hysteria of MJ's passing.

UK / British Comics: The Horror comics by Alan Class, Miller and others, are among our bestsellers. They are B&W squarebound giants (60-100 pages featuring vintage U.S. Horror and SF titles from Atlas/Marvel, Archie, ACG, Charlton, DC, etc.). Alan Class 1950s-1980s sell for $7-$12, with early issues higher. Miller issues from 1960s sell at

$12-$30 each. The British hardcover annuals of 1950s through 1990s are scarce in the U.S., with only later issues seeing some U.S. Direct Only distribution. They have many major characters of the period, including those from Marvel, DC, Cartoons, Hanna-Barbera, Walt Disney, TV series, Cowboys and Westerns, Music Stars. They are packed with great covers, comics, art, text stories, photos, puzzles and games. Much of it is new material not seen in U.S. Issues from 1950-1975 sell at $20-$50 each, and those from 1976-1990+ sell at $12-$25 each. The 1950s DC and Superman annuals are scarce to rare and can command $50 to $200+.

I sold about 250+ UK War comic digests (*Battle Picture Library*, *Commando*, *War Picture Library*, etc.) containing all original UK material (excellent reading and art for War comic fans, including many True War based campaigns and stories) at (1950s/60s = $6-$20 and 1970s-1980s = $2-$6 each). The vintage all-British new material weekly comics (*Beano*, *Dandy*, etc.) of the 1937-1950s, are totally alien products to Americans, yet they set World Record prices each year in the UK (with #1s often over $5000+ each).

I have one of the world's biggest selections of UK Marvel, with over 10,000 in stock (1966-1990; $3-$12 ea) plus we have about 1000 Marvel "Pocket Book" comics digests from the 1980-1982 era ($5-$12 ea). We have 1000+ British DC related comics. The bestselling characters and artists include: *Action Force* (G.I. Joe), Avengers, Batman, Captain Britain, Dr. Who, Hulk, *Planet of the Apes*, Silver Surfer, Spider-Man, *Star Wars*, Superman, *Transformers*, Wonder Woman, X-Men, Adams, Bolland, Byrne, Grant, Kirby, Miller, Alan Moore, Pérez, Starlin, Bryan Talbot and others. Terry Austin, Alan Moore, Barry Windsor-Smith, and Jim Starlin did original work in the 1970's UK Marvel never published in the U.S.

Variant Edition Comics: I spent about 40-50 hours assisting Jon McClure in identifying and verifying variants for his large article in this edition of the *Guide*. I have discovered and actively been selling thousands of these variants for about a decade now. The Marvels 30¢-c and 35¢-c variants are now among the hottest of all Bronze Age comics, but we do not see many of these up in Canada. Here they're always selling at above *Guide* prices in all grades. *Star Wars* #1(35¢-c variant) is legendary and still brings the top premiums, although it is one of the most common of these 35¢-c variants, it has gone unfilled on hundreds of Marvel want lists for up to 30 years (yet regular printings of *Star Wars* #1 are slow to DEAD sellers). If all the 35¢-c variants had been listed in the *Guide* for the last 30 years (rather than 10 or so years), *Iron Fist* #14 would easily be the #1 most valuable Bronze Age comic. The *Star Wars* #1 variant lists at 24 times the price of the regular edition, yet the much scarcer *Iron Fist* #14 lists at only 5 times.

The 35¢ cover variant of **Star Wars #1** has gone unfilled on hundreds of Marvel want lists.

Canadian Newsstand cover price variant editions were our bestselling variants of the year. These are not broken out and listed in the *Guide* because there are far too many of them (over 5000?). I sell these variants at 125-150% *Guide* for most, then more for high grade copies. I am often asked how many of these exist, or how scarce they are. Canadian print runs are 10% or less of American issue quantities, thus of 200,000 printed, about 20,000 would be Canadian. Of those 50% would have been Direct and 50% Newsstand. Approximately 75% of Direct editions still exist today in collections and comic dealer inventories, but the survival rate of Newsstand copies is about 25% of the original print runs (because they were sold to non-collectors). As a result, Canadian editions are about 50-100 times scarcer than a U.S. Direct Edition printings. Because newsstand copies were sold to non-collectors, perhaps 90%, are lower grades (GD through FN). Only a handful of these variants have even been graded by CGC, perhaps because they have not yet realized some of them are variants yet.

Limited Edition Modern variants (mainly 1990-2010) including Gold Editions, Multiple Cover Variants, Convention Editions, Dynamic Forces, Signed Copies, Hologram covers, Platinum covers, Polybagged specials, and Signed and Numbered are often red hot upon release, but most have not performed well once 1-10 years old. It seems as soon as the newest "Hot" Limited Edition Variant gets released, the previous ones tend to get forgotten. Unfortunately this is what happened to Limited Edition Sports Cards. One can always make more new limited editions and the old ones get more and more diluted in value. The ones that seem to hold value and demand are those in which there is constant demand for the Regular editions. I actually have a big selection of about 1000 different variants, yet rarely seem to have the issues requested on want lists. These tend to be our slowest selling variants, possibly as most are modern as opposed to older vintages. I buy low and sell high on these, to make them worthwhile. Given another 10-20 years, they should actually turn out to be a better long-term investment, especially if you can buy them up at clearance sale prices. Giveaway and Ashcan variants on the other hand, seem to be much better sellers and sell propotionately about twice as well as the current popularity of the titles, as there are many collectors who specialize in these type of variants.

Scarce 2nd, 3rd and beyond variant printings (mostly from Marvel and DC comics in the 1980s to early 1990s) are becoming more and more sought items. *Batman: The Killing Joke* (1988) has at least 11 printings, with only the 1st printings being commom and a complete set near impossible to assemble. Typically 65-90% of the copies on the market are First Printings, because dealers did not stock up on reprints. *Batman* #397-399, 401-403, 408-416, 421-425, 430-432 all had at least 2 printings each, some with 6 or more printings. About 50% have the printings noted in the indicia inside. The other printings, one can only tell apart by comparing the ads on the back cover. Approximately 75-100 different printings exist for these 23 different issues - an extremely difficult set to assemble. Other early 1990s and older second printings include: *Uncanny X-Men* #248,270,275,282, *New Mutants* #87, 100, *New Warriors* #1, *G.I. Joe* #2-64, *Amazing Spider-Man* #361,256,270, *Silver Surfer* #34, *Star Wars* #1-6, *Transformers* #7-9, and many assorted other Marvel and DC comics. Variant collectors are usually happy to pay multiples to complete these sets because most still have low *Guide* values in the $2-$5 price range. The 2nd/3rd Printings of *G.I. Joe* #2-64 are sure to gain value as awareness spreads, as only a few are common (mostly #2-10) while the later issues are uncommon to scarce, a very tough variant set to assemble in any grade.

Walt Disney Comics: We have about 20,000 Walt Disney comics in stock (all publishers). The Live Action TV Series and Movie Classics comics were in steady demand, especially if they had photo covers (with the exception of Nature/Science titles). Good artists (Toth, Manning, Buscema, etc.) had even more demand. *Scarecrow of Romney Marsh* #1-3 were the most requested Disney issues of the year and near impossible to keep in stock (bringing 150% *Guide* in any grade). The rare *Black Hole* #4 is in constant demand (at 300% *Guide*). All 1940-1949 Disney titles were in above average demand, in FA/GD through FN grades. Most 1950-1962 Dell and 1970-1980 Gold Key Disney comics were in moderate demand (mostly in VG to VF grades). Most 1963-1969 and 1980-1984 Whitman Disney titles were in above average demand in all grades.

Carl Barks is considered by many to be the greatest writer/artist/creator in comics history (just check out the value of his original art), thus the multiple printings of his finite output. All these reprints have held back the value and salability of the originals for many years, but that started to change, as they are up in demand again in all grades. In fact, high grade 9.0 or better CGC copies of pre-1965 Carl Barks original (non-reprint) comics are among the only Dell comics that bring strong multiples of *Guide*. For the average Dell comic, about 15% of what we sell ships overseas (Marvel and DC are at about 10%), but for Walt Disney comics it is closer to 25%. Several copies of *Uncle Scrooge* #310 sold on eBay this year, and all at over $100, easily the hottest modern Disney comic. The bestselling titles (GD-FN= 120-140% *Guide*; FN/VF-VF/NM= 100-115% *Guide*) included: *Annette, Aristokittens, Black Hole, Chip N' Dale* (GK) #1-20, *Beagle Boys* #1-10, *Davy Crockett* FC, *Donald Duck* all FC, and #81-120, 221-245, *Donald in Mathmagic Land, Four Color* (over 50% of the existing titles), Dynabrite titles, *Goofy* FC, *Gyro Gearloose* FC, *Hardy Boys, Huey Dewey Louie Junior Woodchucks* #1-20, *Jungle Book* treasury, *Mickey Mouse* FC, and #71-120, 205-218, and Dell Giants, *Mickey Mouse in Magic Land, Moby Duck, Movie Classics* (most pre-1970 Cartoon and popular Live-Action), *Scamp* (GK) #1-20, *Spin & Marty, Super Goof* #1-20, 58-74, *Tinker Bell* FC, *Uncle Scrooge* #1-10, 39-70, 285-320, all variants (see Variant Comics in this report), *Walt Disney's Comics & Stories* #31-100, 250-300, 474-510, *WD Paint Books* , *WD Presents, WD Showcase, Winnie the Pooh* and *Zorro*.

Warren, Skywald & Misc. Horror Comic Magazines: *Creepy*, *Eerie* and *Vampirella* account for 90% of Warren sales, yet represent less than 1/2 their total output. These 3 titles are among our highest turnover series out of all back issue comics. *Creepy* has emerged as the bestselling title. *Vampirella* sales were hampered slightly this year, as they are the most expensive of the main 3 comic titles. *Famous Monsters of Filmland* is the highest valued set (about $15,000 in VF), but is a photo/article magazine, and thus not in the *Guide*.

Demand for high grade *Vampirella* was down about 1/3 this year, probably due to higher prices. *Creepy* and *Eerie* #41-80 were the most requested issues in high grades (probably because there are less copies on the market than the #40 and lower number issues.)

The Horror mags by Eerie Publ, Globe, Hamilton, Major, Modern Day, Stanley, Tempest Pub, and World Famous are in steady demand, with affordable reading copies outselling FN/VF through VF+ copies by about 6 to 1. There are a growing number of collectors starting to assemble sets in VF/NM or better. It is the over-the-top shocking gruesome colorful covers that are the biggest appeal in these. The interiors also include blood and gore, bloody stake through the heart, bondage, decapitations, severed heads and limbs, skeletons, torture, vampires, werewolfs and more. Stanley Publ. mags have a lot of pre-code horror reprints, thus added appeal. The 1966-1970 issues and the low print 1980-1983 issues are the scarcest and are in constant demand in any grade. All first issues have double the demand.

Nightmare, *Psycho* and *Scream* (from Skywald) are often compared to Warren mags, but they did not have a big inventory of back issues upon folding, as did Warren, thus they are 3-6 times harder to find than Warren mags of the same time period. Very few dealers can manage to keep these in stock and in fact most are typically sold out of 75-90% or more of all issues. There is an endless stream of collectors seeking to complete all sets, thus they sell in all grades (at 135-160% *Guide*).

Whitman: The Whitman variants of DC comics are still in high demand by variant collectors. Approximately 160 are confirmed to exist and many are striving to complete the set. About 75% of the issues are uncommon, but the last 25% are scarcer and a bit of a challenge to complete in any grade. As these were sold mainly in chain stores direct to the general public, survival rate is low. They are about 20-50 times scarcer than standard DC printings, and most are tough to find in even a strict VF or better. High grade VF/NM or better copies are fast sellers (at 150-200% *Guide*) as only a low quantity have so far been graded by CGC. Marvel Whitman variants DO NOT exist, but are in fact lower print run early Direct Market variant editions from the 1977-1979 era. (See Jon McClure's Variant article).

The "pre-pack only" Whitman comics from 8-12/80 issues are now well known as scarce (bring 150-300% *Guide*), with 1983-1984 issues are uncommon (120-200% *Guide*).

About 69% of all Gold Key comics published from 11/1971 through 2/1980 are now proven to exist as Whitman Variant Editions (over 1600 variants, not all listed in the *Guide*). These are uncommon to scarce, with some rare. On average, these are 5-50 times scarcer than regular Gold Key printings with a complete set being near impossible to collect. What even exists had not yet been known before this point in time. See Jon McClure's Variants article for the near complete list of known issues.

Chris Swartz
Collector

Well, here is my first attempt at being an advisor for the *Overstreet Guide*. I will try to keep it short and simple, while hopefully providing what insight I can on the status of the comic book market in 2009.

First off, while the overall economy has been horrendous this past year, the comic book market has remained strong, with some exceptions. These exceptions are the majority of current comics being published and CGC high grade copies (9.4 & above) of common Silver and Bronze Age books. With unemployment at an all-time high, is it really a smart decision to raise comic prices to $3.99 per monthly book being published? I myself along with other collectors have stopped buying monthly books altogether and have decided it is a better choice to just purchase collected trades of comic book storylines. This way it's cheaper than buying the books monthly, and you can read a storyline straight through without having to wait a full year for the conclusion (and that is without publishing delays).

I have noticed that all of the people who have paid ridiculous prices for CGC 9.4 or higher on common issues of Silver/Bronze Age books these past couple of years have finally realized that a copy of *Amazing Spider-Man* #66 graded CGC 9.6 is not worth $1,500 (10x *Guide*). It is a safer bet to go ahead and spend the hundred bucks on a VF/NM 9.0 copy of the book. However, high grade CGC copies of key issues have continued to sell way above *Guide* value and don't seem to being cooling off anytime soon.

The trend for strong comics sales in conjunction with movie releases will continue. They remain highly desired by collectors as the dates for those movies releases grow close. Comics related to *Iron Man 2*, *Captain America*, *The Avengers*, *Jonah Hex*, *Green Lantern* and *Spider-Man 4* are sought out by buyers. Key appearances will always be the most sought after.

Some changes that I would like to see reflected in the price guide in the future would be to have the prices for trade paperbacks, such as *Marvel Essential* and *DC Showcase Presents* not included in the price guide. They are all just worth cover price, so there is no point in having them in the price guide at all. In the same reference, I really do not see the need in listing lower grade prices for common Silver and Bronze Age books. Do we really need to know what *Sub-Mariner* #21 goes for in GD condition; no one is going to pay more then a buck for it. Also, listing the prices for most Copper and Modern Age books (except Keys) just takes up space. The vast majority of Modern Age books are just worth cover price, and most of them can not even sell for that. An example of how I think the price guide should list Modern Age prices is: (*Spawn* #5-195) all worth cover price. As for changes in the increasing or decreasing of comic book values for 2009, I believe that the only books that should increase in price this year are key Golden through Bronze Age books. All other books just have not been selling at or over *Guide* value during the past year and do not warrant having a price increase in any grade. If anything, most common books through any Age have decreased in value. This is most likely due to the current state of our economy, but only time will tell.

Golden Age:

DC: No surprise here with *Action Comics* #1-25, *Detective Comics* #27-50,58,66,140, *Batman* #1-11,47,59, *Superman* #1-20, *All-American* #16-25,61, *Wonder Woman* #1-20, *All Star Comics* #8, and *More Fun Comics* #52-73 selling well in all grades. Pre-Robin *Detective* #(28-37) are guaranteed to sell above *Guide* in any grade, along with early Superman *Action* covers (#7,10,13,15) and Spectre *More Fun* covers (#52-54,55,57-60,62-67). Restored key books have become more desirable with collectors the past few years with recent prices reflecting this trend. A restored *All-American Comics* #16 CGC 8.0 sold for $17,925 in May 2009. The stigma associated in the past with restored books has changed. Collectors have realized that the likelihood of them finding and affording a key unrestored book, such as *All-American Comics* #16, without selling their souls is damn near impossible. Some have sold their souls and still own these wonderful books!

Timely/Marvel: *Captain America Comics* #1-15,74 has been steadily selling whenever offered, especially with the *Captain America* movie coming up. Also, I suppose it doesn't hurt to have some of the coolest covers of that timeframe. *Marvel Mystery Comics* #2-20, *Human Torch* #1-10, *Sub-Mariner* #1-10, *All-Select* #1-9 are all in high demand. The past year has had many copies of *Marvel Comics* #1 offered for sale with an unrestored CGC 8.5 Denver Pedigree copy selling for $155,350 in February 2009. The one Timely that is very underrated in the *Guide* is *Motion Pictures Funnies Weekly* #1. Try finding someone with a copy of this book that will let it go for less than your first newborn son.

All Other Golden Age: With some of the more obscure Golden Age characters receiving a revitalization in the past few years, their first appearances have been selling quite well. *Exciting Comics* #9 (1st Black Terror), and *Silver Streak* #6 (1st Daredevil) have both benefited from Dynamite Entertainment's *Project Super Powers* comic book series. *Blue Beetle* #49-55, *Police Comics* #1,11, *Phantom Lady* #13-19, *Mystery Men* #1, and *Whiz Comics* #1-10,25 are also in demand. Good Girl cover art books sell especially well, such as *Blue Beetle* #54 and *Phantom Lady* #17.

Silver Age:

Marvel: *Amazing Fantasy* #15 leads the way here, selling above *Guide* value in all conditions, with lowered graded copies selling without a problem whenever offered. *Amazing Spider-Man* #1-50, *Journey Into Mystery* #83-86, *Fantastic Four* #1-20, *Tales of Suspense* #39-52, *The Avengers* #1-4, and *Incredible Hulk* #1-6 are always in demand. Copies of *X-Men* #1 have been selling below *Guide* value in mid to low grade. I realized that collectors are more willing to spend 20-50% above *Guide* value on lower graded key books, such as *Amazing Fantasy* #15, *Fantastic Four* #1, and *Incredible Hulk* #1, more so than spending the extra $5,000-$10,000 on a mid-grade copy of the same book. Most collectors just want to own a first appearance of their favorite character without having to tell their kids that college is out of the question because Daddy spent $30,000 on a comic book.

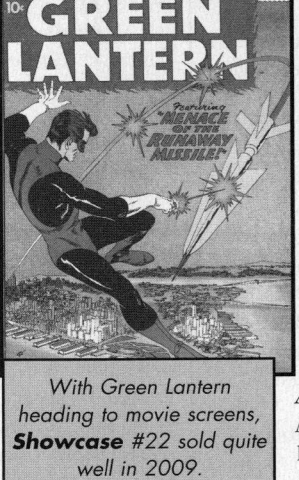

©DC

With Green Lantern heading to movie screens, **Showcase** #22 sold quite well in 2009.

DC: *Green Lantern* #1-59 and *The Flash* #105-150 are the two hottest series to collect from 2009. This is due to the excellent storylines involving them the past year (*Blackest Night* and *Flash: Reborn*). *Showcase* #4, 22, *Brave and the Bold* #28, *Adventure Comics* #247, *Justice League* #1-22, and *Batman* #121,155,171,181-200 have been in demand. *Showcase* #22 has sold quite well in 2009 with almost all copies selling multiple times *Guide* value.

Bronze Age:

Marvel: *Incredible Hulk* #181 is still in the king of this era, even though there are plenty of copies of this book available. High grade CGC copies of this book still sell quite well, but I have noticed some stabilization in regards to 9.4 and 9.6 copies being sold in the past year. Other notable Marvel books including *Iron Fist* #14, *Giant-Size X-Men* #1, *Amazing Spider-Man* #129, *Hero For Hire* #1, *Marvel Spotlight* #5, *Daredevil* #131, and *Iron Man* #55 sell well in mid-high grade. Horror books, such as *Werewolf By Night* and *Tomb of Dracula* are also strong sellers.

DC: If you don't already own a copy of *Green Lantern* #76 in 9.0 or above it is too late for you to get one under $1,000. High grade copies of this book are becoming very scarce and even mid-grade copies have been selling steadily. Other DC keys in high demand include: *All Star Western* #10, *Batman* #232-251, *Detective* #400, and *Green Lantern* #77-89.

San Diego Comic-Con: This past Comic-Con did not lead to any sufficient acquisitions of comic books on my part. I ended up purchasing more original art than comic books at the San Diego Comic-Con just like the past three years. This is due to the fact that most of the dealers hike up the prices on key Golden and Silver Age books for Comic-Con. While this may have worked in the past (pre-internet), collectors are not going to pay five times *Guide* value for a book just because it is being offered at Comic-Con. With fewer back issue dealers appearing at the show there did not seem to be much discounting. Much of the Gold/Silver activity at the Con seemed to be between dealers. There were plenty of opportunities to acquire lower grade Silver and Bronze Age books for a decent price.

Here are some notable books that I have purchased or sold within 2009:

Detective Comics #36 CGC 4.0 (Moderate Professional Restoration) $1,700
Detective Comics #36 CGC 3.0 $2,150
Detective Comics #66 CGC 6.5 (Moderate Professional Restoration) $912
Detective Comics #58 CGC 1.8 $410
Batman #11 CGC 1.0 $325
Batman #121 CGC 4.5 $290
Showcase #22 CGC 3.0 $950
Showcase #22 CGC 4.0 $1,200
Fantastic Four #4 CGC 3.5 $400
Fantastic Four #5 CGC 4.0 $700
Amazing Fantasy #15 CGC 1.8 (Signature Series Stan Lee) $2,150
Incredible Hulk #1 CGC 1.5 $960
Incredible Hulk #181 CGC 8.0 $725
Tales of Suspense #39 CGC 6.0 $2,500
Tales of Suspense #39 CGC 2.5 $850
Detective Comics #140 CGC 6.0 $2,100
Amazing Fantasy #15 CGC 3.5 $5,000
More Fun Comics #73 CGC 7.5 (Moderate Professional Restoration) $3,100
More Fun Comics #60 CGC 2.0 $500
World's Finest #3 CGC 3.0 $405

The best advice I can give to collectors/investors is to buy books that you personally enjoy and want to own for numerous years. If your sole concern is to make a profit on the book, then you should probably rethink your purchasing criteria. Good luck with your comic book collecting and always remember that *Rom: Space Knight* is never going to be cool.

Michael Tierney
Collector's Edition/ The Comic Book Store

I've often said that "whatever sells new determines what sells old." That was never truer than in 2009. When I opened my first store back in 1982, the hottest back issues were Silver Age Marvels, and DCs were very difficult to move.

That is no longer the pattern, as the demand for Marvel has plummeted in my marketplace, while Silver and Golden Age DCs have steadily gotten hotter. A lot has happened during the last 27 years to create this change.

Back in the Eighties, Marvel was dominant in both new and old comic sales. Books always shipped on time, and ease of access for new readers was a strong component of every issue. The era of Jim Shooter had Marvel accounting for nearly two-thirds of my total new comic sales. The joke back then was that if Marvel sneezed, the entire industry caught a cold. This turned out to be prophetic as Marvel went through several management changes, went public on the stock market, and was then bankrupted. They basically slipped into a coma. It was during this time that thousands of comic retailers went out of business. Some published estimates have put the number of failed comic book stores as high as 12,000 during a 10 year period from the late Nineties to the New Millennium.

Then, the huge success of the first *Spider-Man* movie came along and put Marvel back in the black. But they have never reclaimed their once overwhelming dominance. New Marvels today now sell in print runs so tiny, that 10 or 20 years ago they'd have been canceled. To compensate, many cover prices have escalated to a new height of $3.99, which in turn drove sales even lower. In 2009, Marvel saw new comic sales decline in excess of 40% when compared to the previous year.

DC has not been immune to declining sales, either. But they did have the hottest titles of the year with *Blackest Night*. These tales of the reanimated dead, which DC insists are not "zombies", had DC topping of the sales charts with a domination that hadn't happened since the Sixties. The rest of the DC line struggled with low print runs, but their back issue demand has grown, with Golden Age DCs being the hottest books moving over the last year.

What happened to cause new comics to sell so poorly? Judging by my market, it's been the loss of entry points for new and young readers. When *Watchmen* and *The Dark Knight Returns* debuted in the Eighties, it was discovered that the mature reader market was being under-served. From that point on, the market pendulum swung from targeting youth to aiming for mature readers. At first this was good, because that was an untapped market. New and old comic sales boomed.

Unfortunately, the pendulum swung completely to the other side and the youth market was left largely forgotten. The next generation of readers was not cultivated. Now, a couple of decades later, we're paying the price with the lowest average print runs in industry history. It's a problem with an obvious solution. While the mature reader market should not be abandoned, the youth market needs to be readdressed. New publishers like Boom! have found success over the last year by doing exactly that, releasing new Disney comics and Pixar titles like *Cars*, *Finding Nemo*, and *The Incredibles*. Their top selling line was the Muppets.

At the time of this writing, it looks like Disney will buy Marvel, which should bode well for widening their market appeal. If this deal should fall through, my next best hope would be that a cigarette manufacturer takes over Marvel and redraws Wolverine's face to look like that of a camel. Cigarette manufacturers, to their great discredit, certainly know the importance of growing a market by appealing to youth.

As far as the influence of movies on the industry, this is no longer a guarantee of success. Back in 1989, the Michael Keaton *Batman* movie exploded sales on all Batman comics. But the movies released in 2009 had no such effect. In fact, I saw only declines in titles with movie launches. IDW had the most movie-connected comics, releasing multiple titles for all of the G.I. Joe, Star Trek, and Transformers franchises. But sales on these titles saw drastic declines once the movies hit theaters.

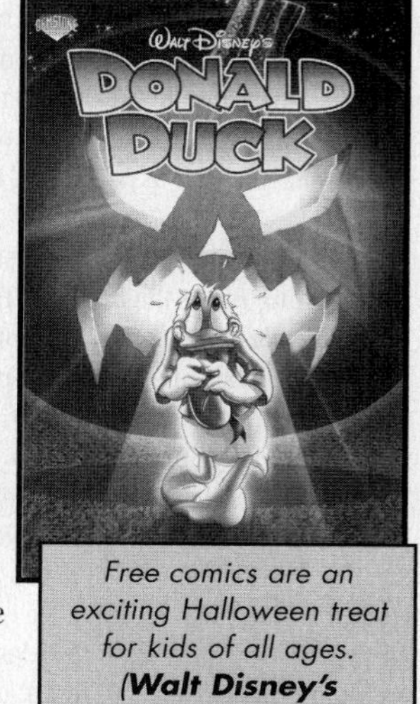

© DIS

Free comics are an exciting Halloween treat for kids of all ages. ***(Walt Disney's Donald Duck** 2008 giveaway shown)*

Some might infer that younger readers no longer have an interest in comics. Nothing could be farther from the truth. Every year at Halloween, my North Little Rock store, Collector's Edition, gives away thousands of free comics to excited trick-or-treaters, who often make repeat visits, while their parents lean in and ask for a copy for themselves. Even CBS's *Big Bang Theory* television show has brought younger readers in, who want to discover the fun of the 'Comic Book Store" experience. Comics are now considered more socially acceptable than they've ever been before. There is no reason for print runs to be so low, except for misjudging the market.

Making more comics accessible to readers of all ages is the key to growth in my market. A universal rating system, similar to those used by the Movie and Television industries would likewise be a huge boon.

A difficult economy with local unemployment in the double digits doesn't help the comics market. And there are other problems hurting new comic sales. 'Event' storylines that run across entire lines make stand-alone stories a rarity, which closes off entry points for new readers. Worse, sometimes plot resolutions and the rebirth of dead characters now happen so slowly, that they often exceed the expiration of customer expectations. That's what happened when the Red Hulk storyline loss all of its fizz. And by the time that Captain America's return was hinted at in #600, fans had already moved on. Late shipping is culpable in this problem, as happened in *Wolverine*'s Old Man Logan story, which caused the series to be published out of sequence. Tardiness seems to be a plague that won't go away.

A new problem emerged in 2009, when Marvel developed the self-destructive habit of massive product-dumping at the end of each month. Customers fashioned their budgets based on the early light weeks, and then made difficult choices during the heavy weeks. This drove my orders way down on any titles shipping within that time frame. Books like *Wolverine: Weapon X*, which debuted to strong sales, quickly withered on the shelves. Basically, Marvel did a worse job of satisfying their fans over the last year than did DC, causing the shift in popularity. But, all of this is nothing new.

The history of the comics industry has been filled with market shifts across the decades. The witch hunts of the Fifties devastated EC comics and turned the industry upside down. For a while afterwards, the majority of comic readers were women, which is why the *Price Guide* is filled with so many Romance comics, that see so little activity today. Western comics managed to survive for a while, but now only the ones with John Wayne covers still move in my market. The Duke does still sell with a quick turnaround. Then came the Super-Hero resurgence of the Sixties, which targeted youth for the next three decades. This is where today's customers came from, and this audience is reflected in my key sales.

DC's Silver Age science-fiction comics sold well, drawing above *Guide* activity on *Mystery in Space*, *Strange Adventures* and *Tales of the Unexpected*. But it was Batman and Superman who made up my best sales. My biggest *Batman* sale was issue #37, which features a Joker cover and story, and sold for $400 in Fine. One other note on this key book is that Batman's face on the logo was actually printed in blue. I've seen many online sellers who errantly thought his face to be colored in by a previous owner. *World's Finest* #59 was close behind, going for $310 in FN. Superboy did well, with *Adventure Comics* #140 selling for $250 in FN+, #167 for $200 in FN+, and #171 for $140 in VF+. *Superboy* #36 went for $77 in FN+. *Superman* #24, with the classic Flag cover, sold for $200 in GD-, #42 with a Lois Lane cover went for $125 in VG-, #43 for $350 in VF-, and #64 for $80 in GD+.

Fawcett's Captain Marvel still commands strong demand. *Captain Marvel Adventures* #18, featuring the origin and 1st appearance of Mary Marvel and the Marvel Family, sold in VG for $400. *Captain Marvel Adventures* #53 went for $75 in VF. *America's Greatest Comics* #2 sold in GD- for $100. *Master Comics* #72, with Captain Marvel Jr., sold in FN for $40.

My best Marvel sale was *Avengers* #4, featuring the 1st S.A. appearance of Captain America, in VG- for $200. Sold a fair amount of early *Amazing Spider-Man*, with the best being #23, featuring the 3rd app. of the Green Goblin, for $45 in GD+, #35 in VG+ for $67, and a couple of #100s for $25 and $35 in GD and VG+, respectively. *Journey Into Mystery* #87, with an early Thor appearance, sold for $70 in GD+. *Incredible Hulk* #181, featuring the 1st full appearance of Wolverine, went for $60 in GD. At one time the hottest selling of all back issues, *X-Men* #94, was slow to move in FN+ at $95.

The best Modern Age Marvel back issue was 2009's limited variant of *Amazing Spider-Man* #683, with the Obama cover, that sold in NM for $45 throughout the year.

I sold several nice Dell *Four Color* comics. *Four Color* #161 featured an early Tarzan appearance in VG- for $85. *Four Color* #223, featuring Donald Duck, sold for $90 in VG. *Four Color* #1060, featuring the movie adaptation of the *Journey to the Center of the Earth*, went for $30 in VG+. *Four Color* #1083, with Murphy Anderson's Men In Space was $35 in FN+. Other non-super hero sales were *Classics Illustrated* #63, 1st Printing of *The Man Without a Country*, for $56 in VF+, and *Lancelot Link* #1 went for $15 in FN-.

Finally, the biggest back issue activity was on Eighties comics. Most of them are Comics Code Approved for All Ages, making easy choices for parents, and priced for less than a new comic. I moved countless big stacks of these. Even saw some rare activity from the Nineties comics, as I sold many large Valiant runs.

Rick Whitelock
New Force Comics

Greetings from the almost always sunny Florida (as long as you don't count the daily summer rains!) 2009 saw an incredible depth of comic books coming to the marketplace, both via public auction and private sales, and a very busy convention season. The comic book market was highlighted by some incredible books being bought and sold, ranging from *Action* #1 to *Zip* #47.

Having closely followed the vintage market for the past 5 years and being a comic collector for almost 25 years now (predominantly Golden Age, but I pay attention to the Silver Age market as well), I can confirm the following opinion: Key books and ultra high grade in-demand books continue to push upward price wise, many times with new pricing records established. On the flip side, lower to mid-grade books, even in the Superhero genre, and many former "hot" books, have seen realized prices becoming flat and in some cases, moving downward...sometimes significantly, sometimes more moderately.

Let me start with the Golden Age. Man oh man, where is my money tree? I have never seen so many "bargains" available...and we are not just talking about lower grade ECs either! We are talking mainstream Superhero here! When an ext. restored 8.0 *All-American* #16 sells for $8600 (Heritage Nov.), I almost wonder if we should start screaming "the sky is falling" (just kidding of course). That book is the extreme, but savvy Golden Age collectors have no doubt noticed the trend. *Captain America Comics* #8, in my opinion is the toughest issue from #1-10 to find in nice unrestored condition, typically selling for a minimum of 1.5 to 2x *Guide*. In a 2009 Clink auction, the Rockford copy (CGC 7.0) sold for $2129, slightly

UNDER *Guide*! The good news is that a plethora of great books are coming to the market. The great news for buyers is that the majority are selling lower than they previous have or might have (given stronger economic conditions.) The bad news is really for someone that "has" to sell right now, because unless you have a very rare or very high grade copy, you are likely not to realize as strong of a price today as you might have previously (or might again going forward).

Outside of the big 2 publishers (DC and Timely) some titles that I have noticed increased attention (and even some moderate price moves up) are: *Planet*, *Startling* (both early Nedor and later Xela/Schomburg covers), *Exciting* (the Xela covers seem to be in strong demand at the moment) and WW2 covers, especially those featuring Hitler (*Headline* #8, *Speed* #31 and the likes).

On the DC front, early issues of *Action* (#1-15) as well as mid-numbered WW2 *Action* (#40-60 or so) have more demand than supply and prices are strong. *Action* #23 is a great issue as well, though prices seemed to have pulled back a bit of late. An example was a 6.0 copy selling for $6600 in late summer that was later auctioned in November and closed about $2000 less! *Action* #7, #10 and #13 continue to be in high demand, with virtually no copies coming to market to even begin to meet demand (outside of *Action* #1, those 3 are the most requested *Action* issues I get). We were very fortunate to be able to purchase at least one copy of each *Action Comics* issue from #1-15 in 2009, but prices were well above *Guide*.

Detective Comics #27-38 always seem to be in demand, with multiples of each issue changing hands in 2009. That really added some excitement for buyers! We sold several copies of *Detective* #27 (a CGC 7.0 ext for $55,000 and a CGC 2.5 universal for $95,000). Every issue, in unrestored condition from #28-38 has had a least 2-3 copies available, and each time they sell higher than before! *Batman* #1 is "hotter" than ever, with new price highs being reached on unrestored copies in all grades ($100,000 for an 8.0 that only 2 years ago sold for $63,000). Let us not forget Superman! *Superman* #14 still has far more demand than supply, but pricing has been "reaching" a bit of late, with available copies being priced about 10-20% too high (in my opinion). Other DC Superhero titles sell well, when priced at current fair market value!

Prices for **Marvel Comics #1** have softened as supply has exceeded demant of late.

Onto Timely: *Captain America* key issues are selling and experience HUGE demand. Naturally the first issue, but very popular and "name your price" type issues currently seem to be #3, #13, #16 and the holocaust cover #46. Just too much demand, and not enough supply for those issues, while surrounding issues are actually selling slightly to moderately off past norms. *Marvel Mystery Comics* will continue to sell, when priced right (again, not at the extreme multiples of past, but generally still over *Guide*.) *Marvel Comics* #1 has seen supply exceed demand of late, and prices have softened across both restored and unrestored copies. Now might be your best time/chance to pick up a copy! Other Timely titles, where demand exceeds supply (*Mystic* #6-10, *USA* #5-11, etc.) still sell briskly and at or above recent prices, while a former stalwart, *All Select* #1, has recently seen a downward movement in pricing (both restored and unrestored).

My Golden advice, unless you are trying to buy an *Action* #7 or *Detective* #31, is to keep searching for those great deals and watch your collection grow! There are some wonderful books out there right now, especially those outside of the DC and Timely runs. Check out the other publishers and start a run today!

Let us move onto the Silver Age. *Amazing Fantasy* #15 was scorching hot through most of 2008, with an upswing in pricing sometimes 100% over previous highs in a relatively short period of time. Early 2009 had seen a gradual cooling off, but now an almost brisk retraction is in place (end of 2009). When 8.0 graded copies sold for as much as $85,000 a year ago, and then similarly graded copies top out at $58,800 a year later, the market is definitely price correcting. Demand still remains high, but pricing has not kept pace.

Showcase #22 was another book that skyrocketed in value during the spring/summer of 2009, but in the last 3 months, sale prices seem to have retracted, sometimes in double digits percentages. We sold 14 copies of *Showcase* #22 last year, with the first sale occurring in early summer (a CGC 5.0 for $1250!). By the San Diego Comic Con, we were getting $1250 for CGC 4.0 copies and almost $2500 for CGC 5.0. In September, we sold a CGC 7.5 copy for over $10,000 and then sold a CGC 6.5 copy for almost $6,000. Demand for this book was increasing at a feverish pace all through the fall, with supply of copies above 5.0 (and with off-white or better pages) extremely limited. Even lower grade copies (2.0 to 3.5) that had sold for $100-300 just 6 months earlier were breaking the $1000 mark! However, as more and more copies changed hands, prices started to cool off on the lower end. 2010 will be a tell-tale year for pricing stabilization on this issue, and it should be fun!

I think these 2 examples are more an indication of price correction and market emphasis, than economically driven. But what about other Key or former highly sought after Silver Age books. I sold a copy of *Showcase* #13 in (8.5) for approximately $6000 this past summer (almost 10% drop from previous sale price). Then in early winter on eBay, I noticed the book was resold by the current owner at $4500 or so, a HUGE price drop. If you followed the Silver Age offerings in all the recent auctions, I think this is a trend most noticed...a somewhat significant price drop, relative to previously and similarly graded copies. Naturally, there are a few exceptions, like an *X-Men* #1 (9.4) topping the $100K mark, but the general rule of thumb seems to be that most Silver Age books, and Keys in lower to mid-grade, can be had at slightly to moderately lower prices now, than just a year ago (*Incredible Hulk* #1 in CGC 4.5 sold for $4022 last year, then sold for $3250 in the last month. An *Amazing Spider-Man* #1 in CGC 7.0 that we sold for $9900 earlier this year on eBay resold for $8100 just this month). On the flip side, a Silver Age book that seems to be garnering some steam is *Brave and the Bold* #28, with several recent sales higher than previous prices realized. You might want to check your doubles box for a copy!

Harley Yee
Harley Yee Comics

After a record 2008, and the equally positive previous eight years, 2009 may prove to be even better. I have not totaled the year up yet, but based on my impressions, the old adage that comic books have always been recession proof continues to be true.

I do a lot of conventions all over the country and sales were generally up around the country. This was true at the northeast, south, southwest while sales were steady in the midwest and west. At the shows, I do well with mid to low grade Golden Age DCs, attractive high grade Silver Age DCs and Marvels, ultra high grade Bronze Marvels, ECs, Westerns, Classics, Archies and Timelys.

My internet sales are not where they should be, so look out for a new website by the time this book is published. In the meantime, most of my internet sales are done with my eBay store. With the internet, ultra high grade CGC and non-CGC Silver Age DCs and Marvels have always been strong. Recent Golden Age sales have also been strong. Seems to me that more of the younger collectors are moving into Golden Age, which is a good trend. The Golden Age offers many classic artists from a wide range of publishers with much to offer that will expand any collector's horizons.

To sum up, I think that 2010 will continue the trends of 2009 with high grade CGC or non-CGC Silver Age DCs and Marvels, Golden Age DC, Timelys, early Archies, early Disneys and ECs staying hot.

Mark S. Zaid, Esq.
Esquire Comics

As the U.S. recession starts to wane and the economy begins its slow recovery, the question on everyone's mind is what impact will we see on the comic book market and when? In my opinion, the downward trend hit the comic book market late, at least when compared to other areas of the economy. February 2009 was when I truly noticed the recession had hit home in our community. But one person's misfortune is another person's fortune. The last year has been a bountiful one for the purchase of comics at prices truly so low it felt criminal at times to do so. Many major collectors chose, for reasons that no doubt varied, to sell off significant high-end collections, primarily though the major auction houses. At times it was like fishing in a barrel. This will likely continue in the short term throughout most if not all of 2010, and possibly into 2011. But it is an impact that I believe will not last and the trend will crest yet again.

Even the most precious and desirable of collectible comics – Edgar Church/Mile High copies – have finally reached the day when their multiples are no longer automatic. Once reaching a predictable 3x -5x *Guide*, and even sometimes as much as 10x *Guide*, many Church books can now be found, particularly the lesser non-superhero covers and those below 9.0 grade, at barely 2x *Guide*. And they are breaking into the marketplace at astounding rates. Indeed, sometimes I miraculously even stumble upon a Church book that is below *Guide*! These books are real steals because they typically present beautifully but have some sort of significant structural defect that is often difficult to discern, particularly in a CGC holder.

While now is the time to buy, it obviously needs to be done intelligently. Predicting comic trends is somewhat akin to the stock market; few know what will rise or fall at any given time! But if you have disposable cash you should explore taking some and investing in the comic market, particularly with high end superhero Golden and Silver Age. Much in the same way that even the best Fortune 500 Company will be negatively impacted when the entire market declines, comics do the same. When the market returns, those that were strong before often recapture their vitality if not become stronger.

Marvel and DC are feverishly trying to move their characters, like Captain America, to the big screen. (**Capt. America** #100 shown)

I do have my doubts, however, whether many books published after 1975, and even some key Silver Age books, will recover to 2003-2006 levels as the CGC census becomes more of a key factor in how collectors view "rarity". Although Golden (and some Silver) Age books are slowing in their submissions to CGC, the census is starting to reflect just how many über high-grade (9.6 – 10.0) copies actually exist from the Bronze and Copper Ages. As more copies surface, the question must be asked as to whether the community can sustain the demand. It is not uncommon even now to be able to purchase CGC 9.8 books from the late 1970s or early 1980s for less than what the submitter likely paid for the encapsulation.

To be sure there are individual comics and titles, if not entire themes, that clearly have suffered in the last few years. The sales value of many books really fell, but I would postulate that for many comics the low prices were not reflective of the true value of the book but simply illustrative of the economic environment and the seller's need for immediate cash due to other financial stresses. That is, it is a temporary measure.

Of course, there will always be issues or titles that will become hot because of external forces such as marketing, movies, toys or just a craze. Right now it is a mad rush for Marvel and DC to feverishly move as many of its characters to the big screen as possible. The money is in film not comics but fortunately the latter benefits as a result of the renewed interest in oftentimes old characters. These prices always adjust themselves over time, but what is really occurring now, and which I believe is overshadowing the economic plight, is a marked generational shift. The baby boomers, who read Platinum and early Golden Age books, are entering retirement and disposing of their material goods, so their children, who relished the exploits of the Silver and Bronze Ages, have taken over. The interests are significantly different.

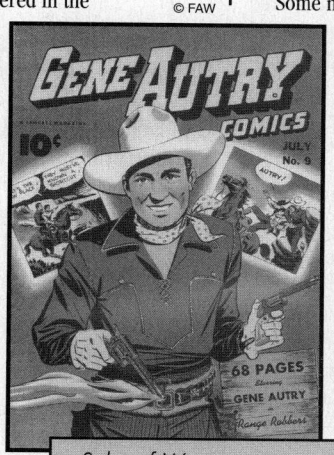

Sales of Western comics are victims of a generational shift. (**Gene Autry Comics** #9 shown)

For example, Western comics from the 1950s are on a total downward slide. Even high-grade gorgeous photo covers, such as published by Fawcett, can be found from 50% - 70% of *Guide* at times. The market for Western books has dwindled, but I doubt the economy played a significant role in that trend. Instead, it is factor of aging and social interests. Those baby boomers who grew up on Westerns simply do not have the interest any longer and the best of the West with such characters as Gene Autry, Hopalong Cassidy, Tom Mix and even the Lone Ranger are simply not as known any longer to the current more youthful generations. Roy Rogers has more in common now with McDonald's than he does with a six gun and a horse!

Other "victims" of the generational shift include numerous ECs, even high grade copies, many Harvey and Fawcett titles (including superheroes) and Walt Disney books (especially non-keys). Platinum books, too, are, sadly in my mind, another obvious victim of the aging baby boomer generation. There is less and less interest for the books that created our modern day comic book community. Prices continue to fall way below *Guide* in every condition, which of course is great if you are a collector as I am, but terrible if you are trying to sell any! I do believe, and perhaps this is idealistic, that Platinum books will rise again in price, particularly when collectors realize how incredible it is to own what is literally a piece of history. These books are, in fact, antiques.

Some notable sales/purchases during the last year: CGC: *More Fun Comics* #56 CGC 9.2 (Edgar Church) - $30,000.00; *Motion Picture Funnies Weekly* #1 CGC 5.5 - $20,315.00; *More Fun Comics* #56 CGC 8.0 - $11,000.00; *Detective* #38 CGC 4.5 - $8,500.00; *Famous Funnies* #1 (Series 2) CGC 4.0 - $5,000.00; *Detective Comics* #97 CGC 9.4 (Crowley/File) - $2,500.00; *New Book of Comics* #1 CGC 2.0 - $2,000.00; *Target Comics* v3 #3 CGC 9.2 (Edgar Church) - $726.00; *Captain Midnight* #31 CGC 9.4 (Crowley/File) - $440.00; *Tarzan* #1 CGC 6.5 - $400.00; *King Comics* #32 CGC 9.0 (Edgar Church) - $385; *Strange As It Seems (John Hix)* #2 CGC 7.0 (Larson) - $210.

Non-CGC: *Radio Funnies* nn, GD/VG (Ashcan, 1939) - $4,481.25; *X-Men* #1, 4.5 - $1,650.00; *Spotlight Comics* nn, NM (Ashcan, 1940) - $1,015.75; *Tales to Astonish* #27, 4.5 - $720.00; *Four Color* #386, 5.0/5.5 - $360.00; *Avengers* #3, 6.5/7.0 - $325.

I encourage anyone who has an interest in rare and unusual comics to check out my website's "Special Collections" section (www.EsquireComics.com) which features hundreds of fascinating books from my personal collection. Here you will find numerous examples of comics that have achieved the illustrious, though possibly deceiving, Gerber 8, 9 or 10 scarcity rating. Or you can closely examine esoteric examples of little known anti-Communism books designed to sway public opinion and published during the height of the Cold War.

Unfortunately during 2009 my day job as an attorney kept me far busier than I had hoped and EsquireComics.com had to take somewhat of a back seat. But I never stopped watching what the market was doing and always kept my hands in the till. Of course, every year there are examples of opportunities for me to combine my two career paths, usually to help combat fraudulent activity in the marketplace. As a practicing attorney I am often contacted and retained by collectors and dealers who have suffered losses due to questionable and sometimes criminal activity. I will not hesitate to assist, as best I can, any individual who has become a victim of fraudulent behavior stemming from a comic book transaction. Those who potentially require assistance can contact me at EsquireComics@aol.com. I am also available to offer expert estate valuations for charitable tax purposes.

I am a big believer in fostering education in our community and researching the history of the origins of comics. As such, I strive every year to create and present educational lectures. During 2009 I started presenting a 1-2 hour lecture entitled "From Cave Art to Superheros: Comic Books & Social Commentary" which features an interactive visual arts presentation tracing the historical creation and development of comic books and their characters, and particularly how comics addressed social issues of the day (including such topics as war, sex, civil rights, women's liberation, politics, censorship, violence, and terrorism). The lecture I delivered at the 2009 San Diego Comic Con can be watched online at http://vimeo.com/6690892. I welcome any feedback or constructive criticism which can be sent to me at EsquireComics@aol.com.

I was also pleased to continue my trend in helping contribute interesting comic items for display or publication so that others can enjoy them as much as I do. In 2009 I had some Batman related collectibles published in *The Batman Vault: A Museum-in-a-Book Featuring Rare Collectibles From the Batcave* (Running Press, 2009) and I helped shape a fantastic comic book exhibit on The Drawn-Out History of Comic Books at the Elmhurst Historical Museum in Elmhurst, Illinois which ran from June 16 - September 6, 2009. I am currently working with an Ivy League Law School to create an exhibition on the law and comic books tentatively scheduled to open in Fall 2010.

I am most pleased and excited that in February 2010, the Comic Book Collecting Association (CBCA), a nonprofit international organization made up of comic book enthusiasts who share an appreciation for the history, artistic merit, and significance of the comic book medium as an important element of popular culture, announced its public launch. Formerly known as the Network of Disclosure, which I helped create in 2006, CBCA is the culmination of years of work to establish a broader organization similar to that found in some of our sister hobbies such as the American Philatelic Society and the Universal Autograph Collectors Club. I took great pleasure in helping to recruit some of the leaders within our hobby to serve on the CBCA's initial Board of Advisors in order to help steer our direction in a way most beneficial to the community. The mission of the CBCA is to "promote the comic book art form and hobby of comic book collecting for people of all ages by encouraging fellowship among comic book enthusiasts, providing information and education to the public, and helping to facilitate the buying, selling, and trading of comic books and related material in an environment of trustworthiness and integrity." A Code of Ethics was adopted that was patterned after industry best practices while being tailored to the hobby of comic collecting. When collectors and dealers think of the CBCA, it is envisioned that three words will come to mind: Fellowship, Education and Ethics. More information can be found at www.comiccollecting.org and I encourage those who share our principles to consider joining.

Finally, I also continue to freely supply market data to www.GPAnalysis.com, a fantastic internet resource operated from Australia that tracks actual CGC sales data. This subscription based service is a must for buyers and sellers alike to use when negotiating sales and purchases. The proprietors are incredibly tech-savvy and ensure the latest features are available for the iPhone or Blackberry. I am also pleased as well to continue to serve as a CGC member dealer.

I hope 2010-11 proves to be a fantastic year for the comic book collecting and dealing community, and I look forward to hearing from fellow hobbyists on any of the topics above.

Vincent Zurzolo, Frank Cwiklik & Rob Reynolds Metropolis/ComicConnect.com

Vincent Zurzolo - Metropolis Comics

2009... It was the worst of times, it was the best of times. 2008 was a very strong year for Metropolis but it was unclear how 2009 would work out. With a recession hanging over our heads it was decided that through a continuing strategy of innovation and greater flexibility Metropolis would forge ahead with the goal of not maintaining the status quo but increasing sales. Did we succeed? Read on True Believer!

Sales for 2009 have been robust and have exceeded sales of 2008. I attribute this to increased customer confidence in the viability of comics as an investment vehicle. Simply put, most of us are making nothing in our savings or money market accounts, the real estate market is in the toilet and the stock market is volatile at best. Vintage comics have been and continue to be a stable place to put your money in hopes for good returns. Is it a fool-proof way of making money? No. Nothing is, there is always a chance to break-even or lose. But it is not very difficult to watch trends and get on the bandwagon early. Other reasons for strong sales were increasing our web presence, providing interest-free time payment plans, being more negotiable on prices and seeking out want list comic books for customers.

We have all been watching it happen with Green Lantern, Avengers and Captain America. Prices for *All-American* #16, *Showcase* #22 and *Green Lantern* #1, *Avengers* #1 as well as *Avengers* #4, *Captain America Comics* #1 and *Captain America* #100 have increased on average 25-150% in the last year. As we haven't seen a trailer for any of these movies (at the time of writing this market report) I can only imagine there is more room for growth, as long as the trailers look good.

Due to the ever-increasing popularity of Iron Man, we made a record-breaking sale with *Tales of Suspense* #39 CGC 9.4 off white/to white pages at $118,000.00! In 2009 we sold more *Detective* #27s than any other dealer, auction house or consignment site in the comic book business. *Detective* #27 CGC 4.0 off white pages sold for $115,000.00, *Detective* #27 CGC 7.5 with slight professional restoration sold for $100,000.00 and *Detective* #27 CGC 7.0 with moderate professional restoration sold for $50,000.00. As stated in the previous paragraph Green Lantern is hot! *All-American* #16 3.5 sold for $26,500.00, another copy, a CGC graded 4.5 sold for $42,500 and a Golden Age *Green Lantern* #1 in CGC 7.0 sold for $11,000.

Amazing Fantasy #15 has been the shining example for the last 5-10 years of how much a comic can appreciate in value. Early in 2009 the book continued to climb in value but has hit a slight plateau toward the end of 2009. Sales include a CGC 6.0 at $21,000 and several copies in 5.0 at $10,000.00. Other notable *Amazing Spider-Man* sales include a #1 CGC 6.5 for $6,500, #3 CGC 9.4 for $25,500, a #10 CGC 9.4 for $5,675.

Comic books like *Funnies on Parade* from 1933 in 8.0 condition sold for $18,000 proved interest in early Golden Age was strong. The Mile High copy of *Great Comics* #3 with the classic Hitler story sold for $16,000 in 9.0. *Wonder Woman* #1 sales have increased dramatically with sales of a CGC 7.0 at $13,500 and a CGC 7.5 for $16,000. *Suspense* #3 in a CGC 6.5 sold for $15,850 as well.

© MAR

Some younger collectors consider a mid-grade **Iron Fist** #14 to be one of their "bragging books."

Other trends to note include restored early and key Golden Age selling more quickly and for higher prices and Bronze Age in general continuing to sell well though as more books enter the CGC population reports prices may decrease.

In closing I'd like to thank all of you for making this a great year. I am very proud of the relationships we have built over the years with our customers. The continued business we do as well as personal friendships we have made are a testament to the passion we share for comic books!

Frank Cwiklik - Metropolis Collectibles

This year's market reports may be top-heavy with gloomy assessments of the current world economy. I'm sure anyone who reads these reports also keeps up with current events, whether online or in the papers so I'm not going to bore you with yet another recap. What I do find interesting is the ways in which this economy has affected some sectors of the collectibles business, while others seem virtually untouched, or conversely, stronger.

The strongest part of the market remains the high-end keys and rarities. Looking at the past year's sales, you wouldn't think we were necessarily in a downturn, as the results boast an impressive array of keys and high-ticket grail books, with all the usual suspects represented. *Amazing Fantasy* #15 copies were in demand as always; the Iron Man streak continued with *Tales of Suspense* #39 selling well, including a beautiful unrestored 9.4 CGC copy; early Batman, especially *Detective* #27 and *Batman* #1, remained in high demand and sold almost as quickly as we could obtain them. The announcement of the upcoming Green Hornet and Green Lantern movies caused the key issues for those previously moribund titles to suddenly explode in popularity. In fact, we sold more copies of *Showcase* #22 at San Diego this year than we did of *Amazing Fantasy* #15, which took us by surprise.

Collectors who in the past had larger budgets with which to pursue their collecting grails still, for the most part, have the disposable income to spend freely. This accounts for the continued strength, and even growth, of high-grade and high-demand vintage comic books. While they may be a little more hesitant to part with their money, and they may be looking for more discounts than in the past, they are still aggressively and happily buying up better books. Savvy collectors have been doing very well, as we have seen in our dealings this past year. It just takes a little more time, work, and persistence than it may have in recent years.

The mid-priced and low to mid-grade comic books remain surprisingly strong and reliable sellers. Most of the customers we have who buy lower-grade or more obscure reader material tend to be either stable-income collectors who have long since worked out their budget for collectibles or younger clientele who are just starting to come into their own financially and build their collection. These younger collectors are just getting started, and for them a mid-grade *Incredible Hulk* #181 or *Iron Fist* #14 is their bragging book, which is very cool. These collectors may only buy a few times a year, but they are serious collectors nonetheless.

Tough times can prove to be a boon for savvy buyers although tough on sellers. Several longtime collectors have either chosen or unfortunately have had to sell their collections. In several cases, this resulted in hard-to-find "black hole" books finally coming back to market and into the hands of grateful buyers.

Obscure Golden Age series, tough keys, unusual and scarce pre-hero Atlas books, genre comics (War, Western, Horror), and other rarities have been made available to us over the past year and have done very well. This has caused a continued trend that I noticed in last year's report, which is a shift in the buying trends away from constant sales on the same two or three books or genres, and toward a more diversified market. Many days we may not sell any major Marvel or DC key issues at all, but have a healthy slate of invoices chock full of Charlton hero books, mid-grade Disney, Western comics, Funny Animal books or Crime comics. This has been tremendous for selling stock that might have gathered dust just a couple of years ago.

Even at conventions, sales can be erratic, if not downright baffling. While we have enjoyed healthy sales at shows over the past year, there's no denying that customers are more careful with their purchases. However, the strength of

Showcase #22 and *Green Lantern* #1; the usual Marvel standbys, especially *Hulk* #181 and *Tales of Suspense* #39; and the influx of new buying blood from people who are excited by the ongoing Hollywood wave of superhero films have kept our booths busy. The sales results from each show also display a trend toward less homogenized buying patterns, as Fawcett, pre-code horror, and novelty comics like *Hansi* (look it up, you won't believe it) capture attention and buyers' wallets.

As for trends, I notice that high-grade Bronze is still a growing market, and we're doing quite well moving these relatively inexpensive, but still high demand books, especially Bronze Marvel, Neal Adams covers, and DC Horror titles. The most interesting trend I've noticed is toward Wonder Woman. We've sold at least one or two keys or high-grade *Wonder Woman* or *Sensation* issues at almost every convention this year, and have sold a staggering 8 copies of *Wonder Woman* #1 alone over the past 12 months. Perhaps it is the rumblings of a Wonder Woman movie being made but whatever the reason, both her solo title and *Sensation* are selling like crazy again. As a Wonder Woman collector I find this both exciting and frustrating. On the one hand, I'm very glad to see this character finally getting her due, both with the renewed commitment DC has shown to this iconic figure with the terrific new series by Gail Simone and Aaron Lopresti (which I can't recommend enough), and from the collecting community itself. Golden Age *Wonder Woman* and *Sensation* are some of the toughest, rarest, and most undervalued of all major comic series and it is good that more and more people are starting to realize their value. On the other hand, I'm still trying to finish my runs of these extremely tough books, and now I'm competing with even more buyers than before!

High grade early issues of **Wonder Woman** and **Sensation Comics** (#4 shown) are selling like crazy again.

In conclusion, there are great sales and great deals out there for those buyers and sellers willing to do the legwork and put in the hours, but you really have to be more aggressive than in the past. I strongly feel that as the economy continues to come around there will be a new and even more eager collector and investor base ready to enter the market. Collectors and investors who stay on top of the market and are ready to buy and sell over the next few years will be uniquely positioned to take advantage of the market.

Rob Reynolds - ComicConnect.com

ComicConnect.com's 2009 can be summed up by one single comic, *Action Comics* #1, and one simple word, momentum. With a total of eight sales of the historic grail comic and holiest of holies, we set a precedent that may never be matched. In March 2009, we made a big splash with the sale of an unrestored CGC 6.0 FN that at the time, set the world record for the highest price ever paid for a comic book at auction, hammering at $317,200. The news of the sale of this single comic landed on the home pages of Yahoo!, AOL, MSN, Google News, CNN, and Fox News among thousands of global media sites. The auction led to interviews that aired on dozens of television networks and radio programs around the world.

The sale and subsequent media attention led to a cascade of demand where it seemed ComicConnect.com was the only auction house with the ability to tap-in to the short supply. Our year culminated with the distinction of selling the first comic to breach the million dollar barrier with the Kansas City copy CGC-rated 8.0 VF. We followed that a month later with a $1.5 million dollar sale of the highest graded *Action Comics* #1 in existence, rated 8.5 VF+ by CGC, which is, to date, the most expensive comic ever sold.

Comics of note sold through ComicConnect.com from the Golden Age include:

Action Comics #60 CGC 9.8 $15,800
All Negro Comics #1 CGC 7.5 VF- $10,600
All Star Comics #3 CGC 6.0 FN $10,000
Batman #1 CGC 5.0 VG/F $46,200
Batman #1 CGC 3.5 VG- #30,601
Batman #1 CGC 2.5 G+ $18,200
Batman #1 CGC 7.5 VF- (R) $16,395
Batman #1 CGC 6.0 FN (R) $10,300
Batman #3 CGC 9.0 VF/NM $15,755
Batman #17 CGC 9.4 NM $11,311
Captain America Comics #1 CGC 6.5 FN+ $28,400
Captain America Comics #1 CGC 3.5 VG- $13,900
Captain America Comics #8 CGC 9.2 NM- $22,001
Detective Comics #1 CGC 3.0 G/VG $17205
Detective Comics #28 CGC 3.5 VG- $15,600
Detective Comics #29 CGC 5.0 VG/F $22,200
Detective Comics #35 CGC 3.5 VG- $11,813
Flash Comics #1 CGC 4.0 VG $14,400
Green Lantern #1 CGC 7.5 VF- $10,289
Marvel Comics #1 CGC 2.0 G $21,500
Superman #1 CGC 1.0 FA $18,000
Superman #1 PGX 5.0 VG/F (R) $16,755
Superman #1 PR $13,400
Superman #3 CGC 8.5 VF+ $11,000
Thrill Comics #1 CGC 8.0 VF $12,999
Uncle Scrooge #1 (*Four Color* #386) CGC 9.4 $22,500
Whiz Comics #1 CGC 2.5 G+ $10,852
Young Allies #1 CGC 9.6 NM+ $45,500

ComicConnect.com didn't just spend 2009 auctioning off an unprecedented number of *Action Comics* #1's. The Silver Age and Bronze Age of comic books saw plenty of records fall in the Event Auctions as well. We were very pleased for our consignor at the performance of the *Green Lantern* #76 CGC 9.6 NM+. This highest graded comic set the record for the most expensive Bronze Age comic ever sold at $30,500 and sent a strong message to collectors and dealers alike that the Bronze Age market had come into its own. Other Bronze Age record setters were the *Detective Comics* #400 CGC 9.8 NM/MT that closed at an astounding $13,534 and *Batman* #232 CGC 9.8 NM/MT that sold for $3955.

Even with all of the talk of the *Action Comics* #1s at ComicConnect.com, we experienced the most growth this year in the Silver Age market. Collectors and consignors have known us since inception to be the standard of auctioneers for the Golden Age market. This year, dealers and collectors had to stand up and take notice of the quality and quantity of Silver Age gems that found their way to the auction block through ComicConnect.com. Spider-Man proved to be a lasting investment as *Amazing Fantasy* #15 and *Amazing Spider-Man* #1 cemented their positions as the blue chip Marvel comics of the Silver Age. An *Amazing Spider-Man* #1 CGC 9.4 NM set the record at $104,200 while a *Spidey* #14 CGC 9.6 NM+ also set a new record at $53,195. The 1960s weren't all about "ol' Web-Head". Marvel's favorite family the Fantastic Four scored a record with issue #72 CGC 9.8 NM/MT, featuring the Silver Surfer, which hammered at a jaw-dropping $25,389. Other sales of note include: *Amazing Spider-Man* #68 CGC 9.8 NM/MT $4,003 (Record-Setting Price), *Avengers* #1 CGC 7.5 VF- $8,100 (Record-Setting Price), *Fantastic Four* #12 CGC 9.2 NM- $21,400, *Fantastic Four* #100 CGC 9.8 NM/MT $2,215 (Record-Setting Price), *Journey into Mystery* #83 CGC 9.0 VF/NM $27,800 (Record-Setting Price).

© DC

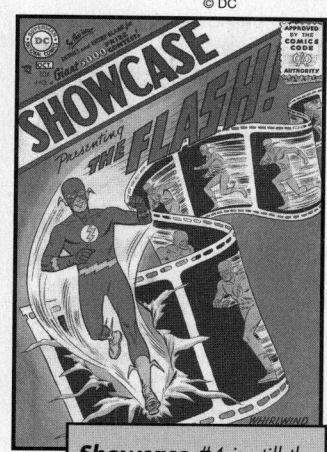

Showcase #4 is still the "Holy Grail" for many Silver Age collectors.

Marvel wasn't the only publisher of comics in the Silver Age setting records in the Event Auctions. DC Comics at ComicConnect.com turned to gold for our consignors in 2009. The "Holy Grail" for Silver Age DC Comic collectors, *Showcase* #4 CGC 9.4 NM hammered at $160,200 (Record-Setting Price). A *Green Lantern* #1 CGC 8.5 VF+ shattered the previous record at $9,500, a *Flash* #175 CGC 9.8 NM/MT streaked to a $7,577 finish. *Green Lantern* #1 and *Showcase* #22 featuring the first Silver Age Green Lantern were the major gainers this year as prospectors snapped up comics in anticipation of higher demand from the upcoming movie. Notable sales: *Action Comics* #347 CGC 9.8 NM/MT $2,655, *Batman* #213 CGC 9.8 NM/MT $2,655, and *World's Finest* #198 CGC 9.8 NM/MT $3,088.

Noteworthy Silver and Bronze Age Sales include:

Adventure Comics #247 CGC 9.2 NM- $17,777
Amazing Fantasy #15 CGC 7.0 F/VF $30,000
Amazing Fantasy #15 CGC 6.0 FN $18,200
Amazing Fantasy #15 CGC 5.5 FN- $13,200
Amazing Spider-Man #1 CGC 8.5 VF+ $23,500
Amazing Spider-Man #2 CGC 9.2 NM- $11,200
Amazing Spider-Man #17 CGC 9.6 NM+ $13,195
Amazing Spider-Man #19 CGC 9.9 MT $29,000
Amazing Spider-Man #24 CGC 9.6 NM+ $20,195
Amazing Spider-Man Annual #1 CGC 9.6 NM+ $15,200
Batman #227 CGC 9.8 NM/MT $13,000
Fantastic Four #2 CGC 9.2 NM- $10,199
Fantastic Four #12 CGC 9.2 NM- $21,400
Incredible Hulk #181 CGC 9.8 $15,601
Journey into Mystery #83 CGC 9.0 VF/NM $27,800
Tales of Suspense #39 CGC 9.2 NM- $30,650

ComicConnect.com Event Auctions featured original art for the first time in June with a modest initial offering and performed so well that by the November auction, over 100 original art lots were up for grabs. Our consignors showed their appreciation for our policy of no buyer's premium and only a 10% commission by sending us some top-notch lots. Notable art sales include a Jack Kirby page from *Avengers* #3 at $13,601, a page from *Fantastic Four* #19 that went for $13,200, the complete 24 page story to *Angel & the Ape* #1 by Bob Oksner for $4,450, a page by John Byrne and Terry Austin from *X-Men* #120 went for $3,951, and a page by Frank Miller and Klaus Janson from *Daredevil* #190 sold for $4,560.

As the new Director of Consignments, I couldn't be more pleased with or proud of the staff at ComicConnect.com and the effort they put into the record setting 2009 Event Auctions. I would also like to thank all of the customers and consignors that made this year such an amazing success. ComicConnect.com only charges a 10% seller's premium, and never any buyer's premiums. That means 90% of the price realized for the sale of your comics goes back to the place it rightfully belongs – in your pocket. Our automated and proprietary payment system also makes sure you get paid quickly for the sales of your consignments -- making waiting a thing of the past! Free scanning is available for all CGC & PGX graded comics shipped to ComicConnect.com for auction at $1 start & no reserve! We are also able to offer generous cash advances up to $1 million dollars on top notch consignments. If you're planning to sell comics or original art this year, please contact me at support@comicconnect.com or call me at 212.895.3999 for a free consultation. It will be my pleasure to discuss your collection and work with you on a selling strategy to help you realize the most money for your comics.

THE WAR REPORT

by Matt Ballesteros

with Richard Evans, Keith Marlow and Mick Rabin & the War Correspondents

Hello! You are reading the second War Correspondent Report, which is a report dedicated to the propagation of the War comic collecting pastime. This report was developed by a group of enthusiasts who have a broad knowledge of the War comic genre and have been collecting, reading and revering War books for quite a long time. This year's team of War Correspondents (just like last year's inaugural crew) consists of some well-known names in the (War) comic collector market. So, I would like to open by thanking Richard Evans, Keith Marlow and Mick Rabin for their time, dedication and contributions. This report would be sorely lacking without their keen perspective and insight.

Last year's main objective was to create a definitive ranking for the top 10 or 20 War comic books in the genre. Through what we found to be a painstaking yet fulfilling process, we were able to develop what we hope is a sound ranking for the category.

In this year's report, you will find that we have made a couple of small modifications to our rankings that were developed and published in *The Overstreet Comic Book Price Guide* #39 and we are furnishing that updated information here. We are including a glimpse at some (subsequent) ranking results that we did not present last year, we have also expressly delved into and scrutinized some non-DC War books and generated a corresponding rank for these. In addition, we attempted to tackle subject matter on common queries as they relate to the market and did our best to address those here. I hope you enjoy our offerings, but, more importantly, I hope that you gain a better understanding of the War comic hobby with each report.

Definition of a "War Book" revisited

If you had the opportunity to read last year's report, you may recall how we developed a laborious categorization methodology in order to catalog, define, refine and classify War comics individually and as a whole. Without elaborating on all the details here, the following is a summary of our approach.

We combed through *The Overstreet Comic Book Price Guide* and other resources to identify and record every possible instance of a title or issue that was either a War comic, or that had War subject matter, or that contained the appearance of a War-related character or, simply, just smacked of War. We found almost 2,000 of them (yet we no doubt still managed to have *missed* characters, issues and even entire title runs that may have qualified as War material). We defined War itself as it related to the comic book genre. We set parameters that narrowed the field by characterizing War comics as "stories centered on the military, which is involved in armed conflicts" and, as such, needed to be relegated to those wars "categorized as a major conflict". (No Cold War, police actions, spy stories etc.)

We eliminated war stories with super-heroes (by employing the notion that "any War story blended with a super-hero is by definition a 'fantasy' story and would not be a War story). Sorry Schomburg!

We defined and developed a classification for specific War themes: War Battle Tales (Stories that were predominantly centered on characters engulfed in battle).
We picked this one.
Others included – Military Life, War Adventure, War Propaganda, Tragedy in Wartime and more.......
We categorized two main comic book ages:

- The Golden Age
- The Atom/Silver Age

Of course other ages exist, – but 99% of all current key War titles live in those two categories

News from the Front - A Market Report

One thing can be said for sure. War comics have gained some serious momentum in 2009! The War comic market this last year has been propelled both by steadfast fans of the genre and incoming collectors who have truly begun to appreciate this specific niche of the comic collecting hobby.

One obvious driver for the war market as a whole is the mounting and avaricious zeal for DC War comics that is apparently influencing the comic book marketplace. Key appearances, great covers, scarceness and the pursuit of the highest grade are some of the catalysts for new record prices across the board in this genre. Although long time War book collectors have been keeping the genre healthy for the last decade, the last two years have witnessed a demonstrable spike, with noticeably more interest and many newly recruited enthusiasts.

Taking note of the remarkable change in the market, we

would like to contend, once again for prosperity's sake, that there was a defined moment in recent time when this sector began to surge (noted in our last report). Specifically, several of us credit this recent spark in War-comic fervor as having been ignited by a series of key sales between August and November of 2007. Among other notable transactions in that time frame, the market saw the sale/auction of *G.I. Combat* #44 CGC 9.0, *G.I. Combat* #68 CGC 7.5, and *Our Army at War* #1 CGC 8.0—each of which sold for around $3,000.

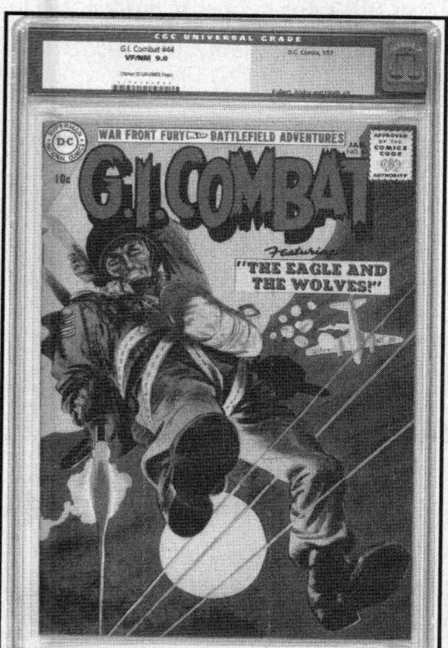

Despite the image of the parachutist, prices for ***G.I. Combat #44*** *are definitely not plummeting.*

It is not that key War sales hadn't occurred before, but what makes this time period stand out was the sheer volume of key books that moved in that specific time span. Furthermore, these sales primarily took place in auction settings that were highly publicized, such as Keith Marlow's first publicized auction of his original War book collection (which we have also mentioned in our previous report). We again note this uptick in the market, not to belabor the point, but simply to remind ourselves of the duration of the current War-book auctioning and acquisition fervency. This is something to keep in mind as markets fluctuate over time.

Accordingly, while high grade War comics have always been difficult to come by, now the War comic prices are competing with, and in many cases, surpassing their superhero counterparts from the same publishers and time periods. This can be partly explained by the fact that the reason that many War collectors (some of us included) originally became interested in DC War was because it featured such extraordinary characters, stories, art, and covers—and advantageously, back issues could be acquired for a fraction of the price of the superhero comics.

This remains basically true for lower-grade issues, but now CGC 8.5 through 9.2 non-key War books with covers that are *not* in the "knock-your-socks-off" category are still commanding prices in excess of a $1,000. You can buy a *lot* of semi-key Silver Age and even Golden Age super-hero comics for that kind of change. However, before you go sell away all your spandex-wearing hero-books in the hopes of cashing-in on the new burgeoning War comic market, you may want to test the waters with mid-grade acquisitions and/or pursue high-grade books that aren't currently scorching price benchmarks. How about buying reader copies to... dare we say...to "read and enjoy the comics" and gain some perspective on what the fuss is all about? Our reasoning for this conservative recommendation is simple. Although the market has definitely shifted to an entirely new and higher gear, some of the recent prices may reflect a "frenzy" mentality and aren't necessarily indicative of the market that is made up of people who are long-term War comic collectors. In some cases, comics that were bought at high auction prices were later unloaded for a bit less and without the auction buyer's premium or other expenses associated with the higher-end auction houses that the sellers then had to absorb. It's a matter of supply and demand, of course, combined with the fear that no other copy of a particular War book exists in a certain grade or higher. Obviously time will tell.

As we are in the midst of a shake-out (that is, a cycle where a certain amount of books are assumed to exist; yet, with this new notoriety and demand, dealers and collectors are shaking out of the woodwork a number of previously unrecorded copies), so it is difficult to gauge how many more hidden gems will suddenly come to light and influence the market. OK, we are *not* saying that the key War books are appearing at a record rate or that super high-grade copies are falling out of the sky (that is not the case!). However, we strongly suggest that collectors should purchase carefully, watch the market, check the census, use this price guide, chat on forums and get a sense to what is reasonable and what is not. Prices may settle after the shake-out (though, we anticipate, not too much).

Yet, if...If the War comic collector demographic continues to grow the way it has, the War comic marketplace just may maintain or outpace current sales records to date. Our advice is painfully simple: just pay attention and don't get caught off guard whichever way the market goes.

Notwithstanding the aforementioned, here are some factors that we are certain of: dealers have definitely started either stocking War comics whenever possible or seeking them out on a more aggressive level. Auction houses are now featuring more and more War books in each of their auctions; prices as a whole generally continue to escalate on high-grade or scarce DC War issues as evidenced by recent sales (there are very, very few early key DC War books in the market that grade higher than a 9.0). You should know that a small, avid group of collectors are fighting over not only a limited number of DC War, but EC and key Golden Age War as well. All of these factors push prices ever higher in all War categories (and there are even fewer key Golden Age War books available in 8.0 or better).

There is an unprecedented halo-effect as a consequence of the heavy interest in DC, EC and Golden Age War books, evidenced by the obvious growing demand for a myriad of War titles across the entirety of the genre. Significant books in Atlas, Charlton, Dell, etc. are also gaining notoriety and achieving some higher price momentum. We see all of these trends continuing.

One of our Own

Not to yet again spotlight one of the contributors to this report, but the rest of the War Correspondents would like to point out that Keith Marlow once again sold a large batch of high-grade Silver Age DC War books in 2009 in a high-profile auction setting that realized some astronomical prices due to pent up demand.

Hollywood on the Loose

The *Sgt. Rock* movie development seems to be gaining momentum... Unfortunately, as of this report, we have learned that the producers seem to think that the WWII era has played itself out, and that it would be better to set his film in the future. Oh no! We realize that perhaps there have been a ton of WWII period pieces in the last decade, so strategically we understand the draw to create a new environment. But, you are talking about a character that was specifically sewn from the fabric of that conflict and was created by artists who had a clearer understanding of that generation, that war, and what moved and influenced them. Rock himself is the representation of everything that was the grit of WWII for a generation of readers, fans and even to the pop culture movement. It would be like making the *Pride of the Yankees* a movie about an extraordinary flutist from New York who is beloved by his quartet but has to retire because of lip cancer. Or if they were to have Peter Parker stung by a radioactive bee instead, yet still refer to him as Spider-Man. Similar constructions, totally different theme and impact! Hope they reconsider . . . .

Speaking of an American Icon...

2009 was the 50th anniversary of the first appearance of Sgt. Rock in *Our Army At War* #83, dated June 1959.

GAINING RANK

TOP 20 ATOM AND SILVER AGE WAR COMICS

ISSUE	2010 RANK	2009 RANK
Our Army at War #83	1	1
G.I. Combat #87	2	2
G.I. Combat #68	3	3
Our Army at War #81	4	4
Our Army at War #82	5	5
Our Army at War #1	6	6
Two Fisted Tales #18	7	7
Frontline Combat #1	8	8
Our Army at War #90	9	9
Sgt. Fury #1	10	10
G.I. Combat #44	11	11
Our Army at War #88	12	12
Our Fighting Forces #1	13	13
Our Fighting Forces #45	14	14
Our Army at War #91	15	15
Star Spangled War Stories #131	16	17
All-American Men of War #127	17	18
All-American Men of War #28	18	16
Our Army at War #151	19	19
Star Spangled War Stories #84	20	20

© DC

Our Army at War #83

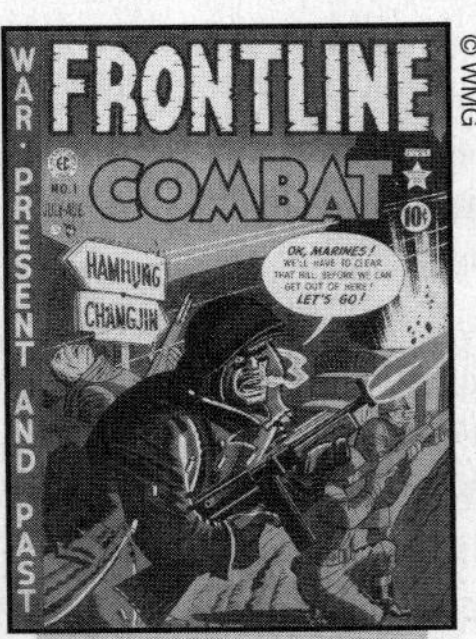

© WMG

Frontline Combat #1

TOP 10 GOLDEN AGE WAR COMICS

ISSUE	2010 RANK	2009 RANK
Wings Comics #1	1	1
War Comics #1	2	2
Real Life Comics #3	3	3
Contact Comics #1	4	4
Real Life Comics #1	5	5
Bill Barnes Comics #1	6	7
Wings Comics #2	7	6
Rangers Comics #8	8	8
Remember Pearl Harbor nn	9	9
United States Marines	10	10

© FH

Wings Comics #1

© S&S

Remember Pearl Harbor

Other Notable Golden Age War Comics:

Don Winslow of the Navy V1 #1
– Early app. of Don Winslow

American Library nn (#1) Thirty Seconds over Tokyo
– Classic title and cover

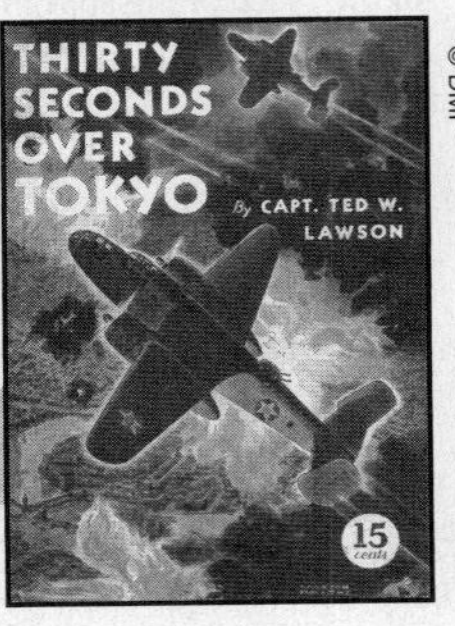

© DMP

THE NEXT 10 BEST ATOM & SILVER AGE WAR BOOKS THAT YOU DID NOT SEE FROM OUR POLL IN 2009 FOR OVERSTREET #39 (UPDATED FOR OVERSTREET #40)

ISSUE	RANK
Two Fisted Annual #1	21
G.I. Combat #1	22
Our Army At War #112	23
Our Army At War #85	24
Our Army At War #84	25
All American Men of War #67	26
Our Army At War #86	27
Blazing Combat #1	28
Fightin' Marines #15(#1)	29
All American Men of War #82	30

© WMG

Other Notable Atom/Silver Age War Books:

Foxhole #1 – Classic autobiographical Kirby war cover

Star Spangled War Stories #151 – 1st solo appearance of the Unknown Soldier

NEW RECRUITS

A Ranking of the Top 5 Atlas and Charlton War Books

Utilizing our resource database developed last year and employing our methodologies for classification and voting established over that time period, we have tackled yet another category: creating a rank list of the top Atlas and Charlton War comics. Although we are confident enough to publish our conclusions, by no means do we feel that this is the final definitive list for this category. However, we place it here for your consideration and anticipate either garnering your approbation or potentially having you challenge the findings. Preferentially, we want this list to solidify over the course of the next few years, based on feedback, new data and market movement. Use these lists to your advantage but with discretion. Enjoy!

TOP 5 ATLAS WAR BOOKS

ISSUE	RANK
Combat #1	1
War Comics #1	2
War Action #1	3
Battleground #1	4
Navy Action #1	5

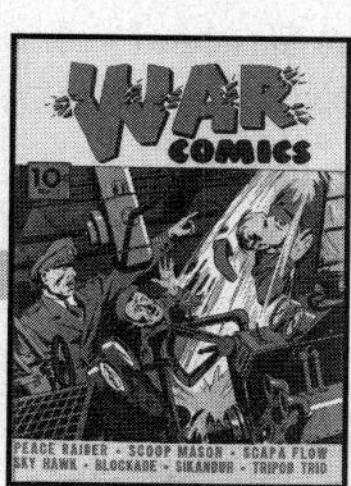

© MAR

TOP 5 CHARLTON WAR BOOKS

ISSUE	RANK
Fightin' Marines #15(#1)	1
Soldier & Marine Comics #1	2
Attack #54	3
U.S. Air Force Comics #1	4
Fightin' Air Force #3	5

© CC

FIELD REPORT

A little information on the above books so that there is a bit of perspective versus just price guide values: With Atlas there were continuing characters that preceded Sgt. Rock. Battle Brady, Combat Kelly, and Combat Casey were the most prominent, but none of them maintained the continuity that would make the DC characters notable. Like DC, some incredible artists contributed fine work in hundreds of different issues, but there are few titles that featured uninterrupted runs comparable to *G.I. Combat* or *Our Army at War*. This was mainly because there are so many different titles, and the titles did not carry a viable continuous character of note. There are great deal of covers that are widely acknowledged as outstanding, but few are broken out in the *Overstreet Guide* with the notable exception of *War Comics* #11.

Charlton had myriad titles that had good runs as well, but also lacked deep character development; therefore, it too did not develop a fan base following of the more prominent War comic pedigrees. There was obviously some stand out title runs in that publishing line and a few significant stories or characters of note, specifically issues like *Fightin' Army* #76 which launched the "Lonely War of Willy Schultz" storyline and *Army War Heroes* # 22 which introduced the semi-ferrous Iron Corporal (seven years before Wolverine showed up... Okay, it was only his ribs, – but he did predate the mutant).

Intel from the War Correspondents

In this section of our report we wanted to provide whatever useful and helpful information that might aid you in the pursuit of the War comic book collecting hobby. We considered some key questions that we typically discuss amongst ourselves and proceeded to document our deliberations in summary. Some of the information provided might actually shed light on how certain titles or issues work their way up on to our top War lists. Here are some of the questions and notions we contemplated followed by the War Correspondents' subsequent elucidations:

Name some War books that are underrated or underappreciated and why:

Our Army at War #90: "3 Stripes Hill" is the first explanation of how Rock became a Sergeant, amounting to the earliest origin issue in the Sgt. Rock storyline. It was a mere seven issues from his first definitive appearance in *Our Army at War* #83. OK, before you start waving your arms... Issue #128 is also an origin issue – and has the distinction of being the first book to recall Sgt. Rock's time in boot camp. But issue #90 is the first book to explain how Rock became *Sergeant* Rock. So, *Our Army at War* #90 – Sgt. Rock's earliest origin issue. Let's see what kind of reaction we get from this statement of ours.

Our Army at War #109: This is also an unaccredited Sgt. Rock near-origin issue that distinctively tells the story of

Rock's very first engagement in battle. The story line is not unlike the origin tale of how Sgt. Rock got his stripes in the story "3 Stripes Hill" in issue #90 (above), however, the story "Roll Call of Heroes" in #109 specifically calls out his first encounter with the enemy in "North Africa" which would actually predate the origin story in issue #90. Of course, both issue #90 and issue #128 are still origin issues of the character Sgt. Rock, but #109 tells the tale of his very first skirmish in WWII. So, *Our Army at War* #109 – Tale of Sgt. Rock's very first battle.

Our Army at War #112: Deserves much more notoriety outside of avid war collectors. It reminds you that Easy Co. is the backbone of Sgt. Rock. Plus who can argue that it isn't one of the coolest covers from *Our Army at War* #84 through #128. Couple that with the fact that (i) there are barely a dozen of those books slabbed, (ii) none cresting over the single 8.5 book on census (as of this report), and (iii) said copy recently garnered nearly $5,000 in an auction and you have a book you simply can't ignore. So, as far as we see it, *Our Army at War* #112 should get even more respect and command even higher dollar figures.

We did not intend to merely focus all our attention on *Our Army at War* and Rock in this recent debate... But, let's face it, that title is hot right now!

Name some War books to look out for in 2010-2011:

Don Winslow: His early books may gain momentum as the character's historic significance continues to grow.

Fight Comics #22 (and various through #20s and #30s): these may also garner some more interest in the next year or two.

G.I. Combat #75 through #86+: The buzz these covers continue to get will only make high grade copies harder and harder to get.

Our Army at War #100: It's a beautiful cover and a great story. If you can find one, grab it.

Star Spangled War Stories #84 through #89: Appearances of Mademoiselle Marie. Her importance to the DC War mythos is starting to come to light. Snap this up before prices get out of control. Hmmm... may be too late.

Name War books that are perhaps overrated:

Star Spangled War Stories #90 and the Dinosaur storyline: Although the fantasy premise is fairly interesting and it certainly has a strong fan base, the prices seem a bit steep for its significance in the DC War mythos. Dinosaur books also seem to be abundantly available. However, some (including #90) are very difficult to find in high grade... So, don't pass up on a high quality copy – just haggle on the price if you can.

Super early issues of *All American Men of War*, *Our Army at War*, and *Star Spangled War Stories*: They are genuinely difficult to find, but except for "completists" (those collectors seeking to complete the acquisition of the entire series), few collectors are interested in paying the prices these are commanding because there isn't anything terribly interesting in the interiors and there are certainly better covers as each of these titles mature.

Name which War books have been easiest to find in 2008-2009:

Weird War Tales #1: All the way up to 9.2's. Seem to be all over the place.

In lower grades, there are *many* copies of *Our Army at War* #81 and *G.I. Combat* # 87. They may be overrepresented since they are keys, but they are certainly in abundance. Good luck finding either in 7.5 or better, though.

Wings #1: While important, seems relatively common in mid to high grade

Name War books that are overabundant:

Our Army at War #151 (in mid & low grades), *Sgt. Fury* #1, *Sgt. Fury* #13, and *Showcase* #45 (in mid and low grades)

Name which War books have been the hardest to find in 2008-2009:

Fightin' Marines #1 and #2: If you find these in mid grade or better, snap 'em up.

American Library nn (#1) (Thirty Seconds Over Tokyo): There are nice copies out there, they just don't pop up all the time.

G.I. Combat #88, *Our Army at War* #108 and *Our Fighting Forces* #10: They just do not seem to surface in anything above 6.5.

In general for DC War — 10¢ers in 8.5 or better

NOTE: There appear to be fewer and fewer high-grade raw issues offered for sale – many have been slabbed. So trying to find that hidden jewel that has not been graded by a third party is becoming an incredibly difficult thing to find.

Name War books that are out there, but are known to be scarce: (alphabetically)

All American Men of War #4, *Contact Comics* #1, *Foxhole* #1, *Our Army at War* #5, *Our Fighting Forces* #49, *Rangers Comics* #18, *Two- Fisted Tales* #20 and *Wings* #7

Name featured key sales in 2009 and why they were important?

The Mound City Collection is the only original owner collection that we were aware of that features copies of ANY of the "perty-thirty" washtones (*GIC* #'s75 -104) and it also had a formidable supply of early Sgt. Rocks that were in the CGC 8.0 and above range (something no other original owner collection could claim). Some jaw-dropping prices were realized for many issues, but a couple of highlights were the *OAAW* #112 CGC 8.5 that went for more than 11x the 9.2 *Guide* value, a CGC 9.4 *OAAW* #116 that went for nearly 11x the 9.2 *Guide* value, and a CGC 8.0 *GIC* # 80 that went for nearly 4x the 9.2 *Guide* value.

Name key individual sales in 2009:

The Novia Scotia *AAMOW* #1 CGC 8.5 sold for $4675.

Bulldozer's entry into Easy Co. in *OAAW* # 95 CGC 9.0 went for $4600.

The classic cover gem *GIC* #83 CGC 9.2 racked up $4000.

Sgt Rock's "first battle" origin book *OAAW* #109 CGC 9.0 swept in $3450.

Unknown Soldier's first solo foray in *SSWS* #151 CGC 9.8 garnered $2629 for this super high-grade copy.

EC's classic *Two- Fisted Tales* #19 CGC 9.8 whipped up $2000 for this current its highest grade.

Not a key book in the run, but coveted because it is an 80-Page Giant, *OAAW* #190 CGC 9.6 sold for $1877.

A copy of the Golden Age War vintage *Wings* #1 CGC 8.5 was picked up for $1800.

The very difficult to find in any mid to high grade *United States Marines* #2 CGC 9.0 brought in $1775.

The early issue *OFF* #21 CGC 9.2 captured $1,125.

Highlighting the emergence of Bronze Age war books, *War is Hell* #1 CGC 9.8 took in $900.

Some lucky and shrewd schmo snapped up *True War Experience* #2 CGC 9.2 for under $100. Nice one.

Name a Copper thru Modern Age War book worth getting your hands on:

Unknown Soldier: Mick pointed out that the *Unknown Soldier* issues that featured Enemy Ace (#'s 251-253, 260, 261, and 265-267) drawn by John Severin were truly spectacular. One of Severin's (many) fortes is his penchant for detail coupled with a photorealistic style. "They're as good (gulp) as the Joe Kubert stuff that everybody acknowledges as outstanding." The *Unknown Soldier* issues can still be had in nice shape for a fraction of the 9.2 value. You should comb for those in the low-priced boxes, because one of these days, collectors will discover how wonderful they are.

Sgt. Rock: The Lost Batallion: Keith mentioned that the 2009 six-issue series written and drawn by Billy Tucci "should be read and appreciated for all the effort that went into it." You can get your hands on those without any trouble right now... so pick 'em up.

The Vietnam War: It goes without saying that both *The 'Nam* and the *Vietnam Journal* produced some good stories throughout their runs. So, Richard identified "*The 'Nam* #68 through #84 and any of the early issues of *Vietnam Journal*, Apple's' venture into the Vietnam conflict" as good books to go back and snap up.

War Story: If you have not picked up Garth Ennis' "War Story" one-shots, then, as far I am concerned, you are missing out on some of the better War comic storytelling of recent note. Not to mention missing out on the contributions by the cadre of talented illustrators who take turns making each individual story come to life.

Name this year's choice for best DC War Cover (an exercise drill):

There has been a good deal of online discussion and surveying around this topic. Recently, war comic connoisseur Andy Greenham polled a large group on the CGC Board to shed some light on that question. The online community of enthusiasts viewed more than a hundred nominated submissions for best DC War cover, and, through a controlled voting process, whittled it down to a short list. The result: *G.I. Combat* #80 won the distinction of being best DC War cover not once, but twice in a series of heated voting. You'll also be interested to know that the runners-up to that title-holder were *All American Men of War* #94 and *G.I. Combat* # 91.

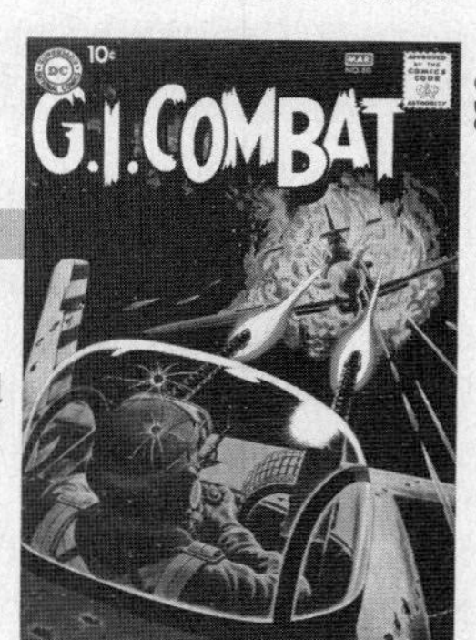

Here are other issues that received top votes from that poll: *All American Men of War* #9, *G.I. Combat* #44, 78, 83, 88, *Our Fighting Forces* #71 and *Weird War Tales* #15.

A Great Reference Guide

If you have not bought it yet, pick up a copy of Mike Conroy's *"War Stories – A Graphic History"*. His chronicling of the War comic genre is especially well done, thorough and a very smooth read. He has clearly done exhaustive research (which he shares with you) – yet he does not mire you in every detail. His book manages to capture both domestic and international titles, publishers and artists and he examines and presents a fairly comprehensive cross section of all the main War comic categories; so, it's a great buy for those of you who are interested in broadening your War book collecting horizons. Buy it today.

Over and Out

Okay, that's it for this year. We hope you found this report useful and entertaining. If you would like to hear more, would like us to cover a certain topic, would like to support or challenge our deliberations, *or* would like to *contribute* to next year's report, please do not hesitate to contact the War Correspondents themselves at theboyz@warcomic.com .

The War Correspondents would like to thank Bob Overstreet and the *Guide*'s J.C. Vaughn and Mark Huesman for allowing to us to pontificate ad nauseam. We would also like to pay heed to our fellow cohorts Andy Greenham and Alan Bartholomew ...thanks for making war comic collecting much more fun that it should be.

I would like to personally close by once again thanking my counterparts, Richard, Keith and Mick, for without their participation and contributions, this report would surely be deficient in lack any substance.

KEY SALES FROM 2009-2010

The following lists of sales were reported to Gemstone during the year and represent only a small portion of the total amount of important books that have sold.

PLATINUM AGE SALES

Bringing Up Father #4 VG+ $65.73
Bringing Up Father #16 FR $18
Charlie Chaplin At the Movies #316 FN/VF $507.88
Comic Monthly #1 Polly and Her Pals VG $388.38
Comic Monthly #7 Little Jimmy FN $240.20
Comic Monthly #10 Foolish Questions VG/FN $203.15
Gumps, The #6 VG $27
Katzenjammer Kids 1902 GD $507.88
Keeping Up With the Joneses #1 VG/FN $45
Lady Bountiful nn(1917) GD $44
Little Orphan Annie #2 VG/FN $59
Mickey Mouse Book (1st printing) VG/FN $2,151
Moon Mullins Series 7 FN $107.55
Mutt and Jeff Book 8 FN/VF $143.40
Mutt and Jeff Book 12 VG/FN $60.95
Reg'lar Fellers #1 VG+ $48
Robert Bean, R.G. #1 GD $26
Toonerville Trolley #1 VG/FN $179.25

GOLDEN AGE - ATOM AGE SALES

Action Comics #20 GD+ $750
Action Comics #23 VF/NM $2,300 (restored)
Action Comics #92 GD+ $135
Adventure Comics #140 FN+ $250
Adventure Comics #167 FN+ $200
Adventure Comics #171 VF- $140
Adventure Comics #194 VG+ $80
Adventure Comics #216 FN- $65
Advs. Of Dean Martin & Jerry Lewis #12 VG $20
All-American Comics #95 VG+ $270
All Star Comics #8 VG+ $7,000
All Star Comics #33 GD/VG $347.75
Amazing Adventures #1 FN $119.50
America's Greatest Comics #2 GD- $100
Archie Comics #7 GD- $175
Archie's Girls Betty & Veronica #20 GD- $25
Astonishing #62 GD $12
Batman #1 FN $19,000 (restored)
Batman #37 FN $400
Batman #68 FN $275
Blue Bolt #106 GD- $19.50
Captain America Comics #1 FN+ $19,000 (restored)
Captain America Comics #1 FN $9,800
Captain America Comics #69 FN $478
Captain Marvel Adventures #18 VG $400
Captain Marvel Adventures #53 VF $75
Classics Illustrated #63 VF+ $56.25
Crime Does Not Pay #49 FN- $18
Detective Comics #18 VG+ $1,700
Detective Comics #33 FR/GD $6,000
Detective Comics #37 FN $2,150
Detective Comics #140 FN+ $1,750
Detective Comics #168 VG $388.38
Donald Duck Four Color #223 VG- $90
Human Torch #8 GD/VG $950
Madhouse #1 FN/VF $155.35
Marge's Little Lulu #56 VG- $12
Master Comics #27 FN $203.15
Master Comics #72 FN $40
Mystery in Space #1 VG+ $418.25
Phantom Lady #14 GD/VG $334.60
Police Comics #1 GD+ $567.63
Popeye #59 VG- $12
Superboy #36 FN+ $77
Superman #1 PR $13,400
Superman #14 VG- $785
Superman #24 GD- $200
Superman #41 VG+ $230
Superman #42 VG- $125
Superman #43 VF- $350
Superman #64 GD+ $80
Tarzan Four Color #161 VG- $85
Terry and the Pirates Four Color #9 FN $143.40
Two-Fisted Tales #29 VG- $29
USA Comics #8 GD/VG $250
USA Comics #14 VG/FN $800
USA Comics #15 GD/VG $315
Valor #1 VF+ $107.55
Walt Disney's Comics & Stories #50 VF $364.48
Wonder Comics #1 FR/GD $250
World's Finest Comics #59 FN $310
World's Finest Comics #97 VG+ $45

SILVER AGE SALES

Action Comics #271 VG+ $30
Amazing Fantasy #15 VG/FN $6,000
Amazing Spider-Man #1 VG $2,750
Amazing Spider-Man #1 GD+ $1,800
Amazing Spider-Man #1 FR $700
Amazing Spider-Man #2 VF+ $2,076
Amazing Spider-Man #7 FN+ $503
Amazing Spider-Man #8 FN $306
Amazing Spider-Man #9 FN+ $679
Amazing Spider-Man #14 VG/FN $420
Amazing Spider-Man #23 GD+ $45
Amazing Spider-Man #35 VG+ $67.50
Amazing Spider-Man #36 VG $25
Amazing Spider-Man #56 GD+ $12
Amazing Spider-Man #67 VG- $17.75
Amazing Spider-Man Annual #2 VG+ $44.25
Archie Giant Series #6 FN+ $119.50
Avengers #4 FN+ $200
Avengers #4 VG- $203.15
Avengers #14 VG+ $33.75
Batman #127 FN+ $84
Batman #128 FN+ $58
Batman #134 VG+ $65
Batman #135 FN- $56.25
Batman #137 VF $45
Batman #138 FN+ $54
Batman #155 VF- $56
Batman #161 VG+ $22
Batman Annual #3 VG+ $65
Captain America #100 VF $191.20
Detective Comics #259 VG $35
Detective Comics #313 VG $18
Detective Comics #317 VF $25.75
Detective Comics #319 VG+ $19.50
Fantastic Four #4 GD- $26.25
Fantastic Four #12 VG/FN $564
Fantastic Four #48 FN+ $285
Fantastic Four #50 FN $95.60
Fantastic Four #51 GD+ $12.50
Fantastic Four #55 VF- $107
Flash #175 FN- $17.50
Flash #180 VG- $12
Flash Annual #1 FN/VF $84
Forbidden Worlds #90 VG+ $12
G.I. Combat #136 FN- $19
Green Lantern #11 VG+ $27
Green Lantern #29 FN+ $49
Green Lantern #33 VF+ $30
Green Lantern #37 VG+ $22
Green Lantern #45 FN+ $26
House of Mystery #58 VG $21
House of Secrets #26 GD- $22.50
Incredible Hulk #1 VF+ $28,000
Iron Man #1 VF $240
Journey Into Mystery #74 VG $17
Journey Into Mystery #83 G+ $115
Journey Into Mystery #87 GD+ $70
Justice League of America #65 FN $18
Mad Magazine #132 VF- $14.50
Men Into Space (Four Color) #1083 FN+ $35.50
Midnight Mystery #6 VF $19.50
Mystery in Space #68 GD $13.50
Mystical Tales #5 GD+ $27
Nick Fury, Agent of SHIELD #2 FN+ $12.25
Nick Fury, Agent of SHIELD #15 FN- $19
Phantom #1 VF- $84
Sgt. Fury Annual #1 GD+ $15
Showcase #13 GD $167.30
Showcase #14 GD/VG $191.20
Showcase #23 VG $143.40
Showcase #64 VG- $29.75
Showcase #73 VG- $19.75
Showcase #74 NM- $89.63
Silver Surfer #1 FN $84
Spooky #7 VF+ $11
Star Trek (GK) #1 GD- $12.50
Strange Adventures #81 FN- $22
Strange Adventures #106 FN $15
Strange Adventures #142 GD+ $12
Strange Adventures #149 VG+ $11
Strange Tales #110 VG- $191.20
Sub-Mariner #1 VG- $22
Sub-Mariner #6 FN- $11.50
Superman #202 VF $16.50
Tales of the Unexpected #66 VG $23.50
Tales to Astonish #44 GD- $27.50
Tarzan #117 FN+ $11
Tarzan #126 VF $12.50
Thor #141 VG+ $12.50
Three Stooges #33 VG+ $15
Three Stooges #36 VG+ $12
Uncle Scrooge #26 GD+ $15
World's Finest Comics #111 FN $28
World's Finest Comics #129 FN+ $35
World's Finest Comics #139 VF+ $29
X-Men #1 GD+ $968
X-Men #1 GD $700
X-Men #5 FN- $95.60
X-Men #51 VG- $12.75
X-Men #56 GD $11

BRONZE AGE TO MODERN AGE SALES

Bronze Age Sales:

Amazing Spider-Man #100 VG+ $35
Amazing Spider-Man #100 GD $25
Amazing Spider-Man #107 VG+ $14.25
Amazing Spider-Man #122 VF- $95.60
Amazing Spider-Man #129 NM- $800
Amazing Spider-Man #129 VG+ $95.60
Amazing Spider-Man #150 FN+ $11.50
Amazing Spider-Man #175 VF+ $12
Casper & Wendy #8 VF+ $11
Conan the Barbarian #1 FN- $79
Dark Shadows #14 VG $29
Detective Comics #408 VF+ $42
Detective Comics #419 FN+ $15
Fantastic Four #103 NM $190
Fantastic Four #112 VF+ $101.58
Fantastic Four #115 NM- $100
Ghost Rider #1 VF+ $107.55
Green Lantern #76 VG+ $95.60
House of Secrets #92 VG+ $79
Incredible Hulk #181 VF/NM $1,200
Incredible Hulk #181 FN+ $310.70
Incredible Hulk #181 GD- $60
Iron Man #128 VF+ $17
Lancelot Link #1 FN- $15
Marvel Spotlight #5 VF- $107.55
Swamp Thing #1 VF/NM $84
Uncanny X-Men at the State Fair of Texas #1 FN- $15
Weird War Tales #1 GD+ $26.50
Werewolf By Night #1 VF/NM $56
X-Men #94 FN+ $95
X-Men #101 VF $47
X-Men #129 FN- $14
X-Men #130 FN $12.50
X-Men #131 NM- $28.50
X-Men #143 VG+ $12

Copper Age Sales:

Batman #404 VF+ $19.50
Spider-Man vs. Wolverine #1 VF+ $11
Watchmen #2 VF+ $12
Watchmen #4 MT $12
Watchmen #11 VF+ $12
Wolverine (v1) #1 VF+ $28.50

Modern Age Sales:

Amazing Spider-Man #361 VG- $12
Amazing Spider-Man #529 NM $20
Amazing Spider-Man #683 NM $45 (1st Print Obama variant)
Captain America #25 ('07) Epting-c NM $20
Daredevil (v2) #1 NM- $12
Hybrids Deathwatch 2000 #0 VF- $15
Superman (v2) #75 NM $20 (Black bagged ed)
Walking Dead #1 MT $393.68
Walking Dead #1 NM $335
Wolverine: The Origin #1 NM $25
Wolverine: The Origin #3 NM+ $10

GOLDEN AGE - SALES OF CGC-CERTIFIED COMICS

Action Comics #1 VF+ (8.5) $1,500,000
Action Comics #1 VF (8.0) $1,000,000
Action Comics #1 FN (6.0) $317,200
Action Comics #1 VG/FN (5.0) $80,000 (restored)
Action Comics #1 GD/VG (3.0) $300,000
Action Comics #2 FN- (5.5) $18,500 Rockford
Action Comics #8 GD+ (2.5) $2,905
Action Comics #9 VG- (3.5) $3,201
Action Comics #13 VG/FN (5.0) $4,550 (restored)
Action Comics #17 FN+ (6.5) $5,078
Action Comics #23 FN (6.0) $6,649
Action Comics #23 VG- (3.5) $2,250
Action Comics #23 GD+ (2.5) $3,000
Action Comics #60 NM/MT (9.8) $15,800
Adventure Comics #72 NM/MT (9.8) $27,485 Mile High
All-American Comics #16 VF (8.0) $17,925
All-American Comics #16 VG- (3.5) $26,500
All-American Comics #16 VG+ (4.5) $42,500
All-Flash #1 VF (8.0) $5,604
All-Negro Comics #1 FN (6.0) $10,200
All Select Comics #1 NM- (9.2) $31,070 Pennsylvania
All-Star Comics #3 FN (6.0) $10,000
All Winners Comics #1 NM- (9.2) $22,705
All Winners Comics #1 VG+ (4.5) $3,000
Amazing Mystery Funnies V2 #7 VG+ (4.5) $200 (restored)
Archie Comics #1 FN/VF (7.0) $38,837
Archie Comics #4 VF- (7.5) $6,572
Batman #1 VF- (7.5) $16,395 (restored)
Batman #1 FN/VF (7.0) $98,500
Batman #1 FN (6.0) $10,300 (restored)
Batman #1 VG/FN (5.0) $46,200
Batman #1 VG- (3.5) $30,601
Batman #1 GD+ (2.5) $18,200
Batman #3 VF/NM (9.0) $15,755

Batman #17 NM (9.4) $11,311
Batman #17 VF- (7.5) $935
Batman #42 FN/VF (7.0) $750
Batman #47 VF+ (8.5) $6,507
Batman #47 FN/VF (7.0) $3000
Batman #50 VG+ (4.5) $225
Brenda Starr #13 FN+ (6.5) $250
Canteen Kate #2 VF (8.0) $370
Captain America Comics #1 VF+ (8.5) $95,600
Captain America Comics #1 FN+ (6.5) $28,400
Captain America Comics #1 VG/FN (5.0) $16,730
Captain America Comics #1 VG- (3.5) $13,900
Captain America Comics #1 VG- (3.5) $16,800
Captain America Comics #2 VG (4.0) $3,850
Captain America Comics #3 VG/FN (5.0) $4,500
Captain America Comics #3 VG/FN (5.0) $5,000
Captain America Comics #8 NM- (9.2) $22,001
Captain America Comics #18 VG/FN (5.0) $1,600
Captain America Comics #28 GD/VG (3.0) $750
Captain America Comics #64 GD (2.0) $350
Captain America Comics #74 GD/VG (3.0) $2,550
Captain America Comics #75 VG/FN (5.0) $700
Captain Marvel Adventures #1 FN/VF (7.0) $4,780
Captain Marvel Adventures #1 FN- (5.5) $2,910
Captain Marvel Adventures #1 VG (4.0) $11,352
Captain Marvel Adventures #1 VG/FN (5.0) $10,157
Captain Marvel Jr. #1 VG- (3.5) $750
Catman Comics V2 #7 GD/VG (3.0) $1,800
Crackajack Funnies #1 NM (9.4) $2,868 Denver
Daredevil Comics #1 NM (9.4) $16,730
Daredevil Comics #2 FR (1.0) $135
Daring Mystery Comics #2 VF/NM (9.0) $13,145 Larson
Detective Comics #1 GD/VG (3.0) $17,205
Detective Comics #8 FR/GD (1.5) $1,900
Detective Comics #27 VF (8.0) $1,075,500
Detective Comics #27 VF- (7.5) $100,000 (slight rest.)
Detective Comics #27 FN/VF (7.0) $50,000 (moderate rest.)
Detective Comics #27 FN (6.0) $575,000
Detective Comics #27 VG (4.0) $115,000
Detective Comics #27 GD+ (2.5) $95,000
Detective Comics #27 FR/GD (1.5) $83,650
Detective Comics #28 VG- (3.5) $15,600
Detective Comics #29 VG/FN (5.0) $22,200
Detective Comics #29 FR/GD (1.5) $7,000
Detective Comics #31 FN- (5.5) $26,290 Crippen
Detective Comics #31 PR (0.5) $5,000
Detective Comics #31 VG/FN (5.0) $20,000
Detective Comics #33 VG+ (4.5) $13,000
Detective Comics #35 FN (6.0) $25,000 Rockford
Detective Comics #35 VG- (3.5) $11,813
Detective Comics #114 NM/MT (9.8) $23,900 Mile High
Detective Comics #118 VF- (7.5) $651
Detective Comics #123 VF+ (8.5) $500
Detective Eye #1 FN/VF (7.0) $750
Dick Tracy Four Color #8 VG/FN (5.0) $250
Donald Duck Four Color #4 VF (8.0) $19,120
Durango Kid #1 NM+ (9.6) $1,135.25
Dynamic Comics #1 NM- (9.2) $5,377.50 Mile High
Flash Comics #1 NM+ (9.6) $273,125 Mile High
Flash Comics #1 VG (4.0) $14,400
Flash Comics #7 NM (9.4) $20,315
Flash Comics #92 NM- (9.2) $11,352.50 Mile High
Green Lantern #1 VF/NM (9.0) $29,875
Green Lantern #1 VF- (7.5) $10,289
Green Lantern #1 FN/VF (7.0) $11,000
Green Mask #10 VF- (7.5) $200 Crippen
Hopalong Cassidy #1 VF/NM (9.0) $5,676.25 Denver
Human Torch #2(#1) NM (9.4) $92,612.50
Human Torch #8 VG+ (4.5) $1,975
Human Torch #8 VG (4.0) $1,225
Ideal Comics #1 VF- (7.5) $110
Jackpot #4 NM- (9.2) $11,950
Mad #2 NM/MT (9.8) $3,107 Gaines File
March of Comics #4 NM+ (9.6) $26,290
Marvel Comics #1 VF/NM (9.0) $227,050 Pay Copy
Marvel Comics #1 VF+ (8.5) $155,350 Denver
Marvel Comics #1 VF (8.0) $89,625 Larson
Marvel Comics #1 FN/VF (7.0) $83,650
Marvel Comics #1 VG+ (4.5) $33,460
Marvel Comics #1 GD (2.0) $21,500
Marvel Mystery Comics #2 VF/NM (9.0) $38,837.50 Larson
Marvel Mystery Comics #5 VG+ (4.5) $6,800
Marvel Mystery Comics #9 NM (9.4) $107,550
Marvel Mystery Comics #9 GD/VG (3.0) $13,000
Marvel Mystery Comics #10 NM (9.4) $31,070
Marvel Mystery Comics #43 GD/VG (3.0) $400
Marvel Mystery Comics #57 VF- (7.5) $1,500
Marvel Mystery Comics #66 FN+ (6.5) $750
Masked Marvel #1 FN (6.0) $200 (restored)
Mickey Mouse Four Color #16 NM- (9.2) $50,787.50
Moon Girl And The Prince #1 VF- (7.5) $500
More Fun Comics #52 NM- (9.2) $89,625 Larson
More Fun Comics #53 VF+ (8.5) $4,500
More Fun Comics #63 FN+ (6.5) $1,000 (restored)
More Fun Comics #67 NM (9.4) $26,290 Mile High
More Fun Comics #73 NM (9.4) $38,837.50 Mile High
Mystery Men Comics #6 VG- (3.5) $221
Mystery Tales #2 FN/VF (7.0) $500
Mystic Comics #1 VF+ (8.5) $7,767.50
Nickel Comics #1 NM (9.4) $8,962.50 Mile High
Our Gang Comics #1 VF+ (8.5) $1,195 Carson City

Pep Comics #1 NM- (9.2) $10,157
Pep Comics #89 NM- (9.2) $200
Phantom Lady #15 VF+ (8.5) $1,000
Planet Comics #1 GD/VG (3.0) $1,400
Planet Comics #69 VF- (7.5) $350
Police Comics #1 NM (9.4) $31,070 Mile High
Rangers Comics #27 VF (8.0) $300
Reform School Girl # GD+ (2.5) $595
Sensation Comics #1 NM (9.4) $83,650
Sensation Comics #17 VF (8.0) $740 Rockford
Sensation Comics #63 VG+ (4.5) $175
Sensation Comics #78 GD/VG (3.0) $72
Sensation Comics #79 VG- (3.5) $115
Sensation Comics #90 FN+ (6.5) $185
Sensation Comics #99 FN- (5.5) $148
Shadow Comics #1 VF/NM (9.0) $14,340 Mile High
Sheena, Queen of the Jungle #1 FN/VF (7.0) $1,314.50
Single Series #20 Tarzan VF+ (8.5) $2,629
Star Spangled Comics #47 FN (6.0) $250
Sub-Mariner Comics #28 VG/FN (5.0) $700
Superboy #9 VF- (7.5) $550
Superman #1 VG/FN (5.0) $16,730
Superman #1 GD/VG (3.0) $40,331.25
Superman #1 FR (1.0) $18,000
Superman #3 VF+ (8.5) $12,547
Superman #3 VF+ (8.5) $11,000
Superman #14 VF (8.0) $9,000
Superman #14 VF- (7.5) $8,365
Superman #14 FN/VF (7.0) $5,150
Superman #14 FN+ (6.5) $3,250
Superman #14 VG (4.0) $1,050
Superman #15 FN+ (6.5) $1,000
Superman #58 VF (8.0) $500
Superman #100 GD/VG (3.0) $148
Suspense Comics #1 VF+ (8.5) $5,078.75 Mile High
Tales From the Crypt #29 NM (9.4) $1,195 Gaines File
Target Comics V1 #7 GD- (1.8) $600
Thrill Comics #1 VF (8.0) $12,999
Uncle Scrooge Four Color #386 NM (9.4) $23,900
USA Comics #7 VG- (3.5) $2,000
Vault of Horror #18 NM+ (9.6) $1,912 Gaines File
Whiz Comics #2(#1) GD+ (2.5) $10,852
Whiz Comics #3(#2) FN+ (6.5) $4,182.50
Wings Comics #89 VF (8.0) $492.50
Wonder Woman #1 VF+ (8.5) $53,775 Crowley
Wonder Woman #1 GD/VG (3.0) $3,400
World's Finest Comics #52 GD (2.0) $100
World's Finest Comics #86 FN/VF (7.0) $108
Young Allies Comics #1 NM+ (9.6) $45,500
Young Allies Comics #1 VF/NM (9.0) $10,157.50

SILVER AGE - SALES OF CGC-CERTIFIED COMICS

Adventure Comics #247 NM- (9.2) $17,777
Adventures Into The Unknown #169 NM (9.4) $112
Amazing Fantasy #15 NM- (9.2) $190,000
Amazing Fantasy #15 VF+ (8.5) $118,977
Amazing Fantasy #15 VF+ (8.5) $104,562.50
Amazing Fantasy #15 VF (8.0) $52,281.25
Amazing Fantasy #15 FN/VF (7.0) $30,000
Amazing Fantasy #15 FN/VF (7.0) $28,680
Amazing Fantasy #15 FN+ (6.5) $20,315
Amazing Fantasy #15 FN (6.0) $18,200
Amazing Fantasy #15 FN- (5.5) $13,200
Amazing Fantasy #15 VG/FN (5.0) $10,000
Amazing Fantasy #15 VG+ (4.5) $6,600
Amazing Fantasy #15 VG (4.0) $6,800
Amazing Fantasy #15 GD-(1.8) $2,250
Amazing Fantasy #15 FR/GD (1.5) $1,924
Amazing Spider-Man #1 NM (9.4) $104,200
Amazing Spider-Man #1 NM (9.4) $83,650
Amazing Spider-Man #1 VF/NM (9.0) $41,000
Amazing Spider-Man #1 VF+ (8.5) $23,500
Amazing Spider-Man #1 VF- (7.5) $15,000
Amazing Spider-Man #1 FN+(6.5) $5,500
Amazing Spider-Man #1 GD+ (2.5) $2,000
Amazing Spider-Man #2 NM- (9.2) $11,200
Amazing Spider-Man #2 FN+ (6.5) $2,200
Amazing Spider-Man #2 GD+ (2.5) $330.01
Amazing Spider-Man #3 NM- (9.2) $11,100
Amazing Spider-Man #4 VF/NM (9.0) $225
Amazing Spider-Man #5 NM (9.4) $19,250
Amazing Spider-Man #5 FN- (5.5) $550
Amazing Spider-Man #5 VG+ (4.5) $750
CGC Signature Series
Amazing Spider-Man #6 VF (8.0) $1,500
Amazing Spider-Man #6 FN+ (6.5) $600
Amazing Spider-Man #7 FN+ (6.5) $500
Amazing Spider-Man #9 FN/VF (7.0) $600
Amazing Spider-Man #11 VF/NM (9.0) $730
Amazing Spider-Man #12 NM (9.4) $7,100
Amazing Spider-Man #14 NM+ (9.6) $53,195
Amazing Spider-Man #14 NM+ (9.6) $53,000
Amazing Spider-Man #14 NM (9.4) $9,995
Amazing Spider-Man #14 FN/VF(7.0) $850
Amazing Spider-Man #17 NM+ (9.6) $13,195
Amazing Spider-Man #19 MT (9.9) $29,000
Amazing Spider-Man #24 NM+ (9.6) $20,195
Amazing Spider-Man #28 VF (8.0) $850
Amazing Spider-Man #28 FN/VF (7.0) $225
Amazing Spider-Man #29 NM+ (9.6) $5,100

Amazing Spider-Man #34 NM/MT (9.8) $25,250
Amazing Spider-Man #34 VF/NM (9.0) $359.50
Amazing Spider-Man #37 NM+ (9.6) $21,111
Amazing Spider-Man #38 NM- (9.2) $670
Amazing Spider-Man #39 NM (9.4) $4,350
Amazing Spider-Man #39 VF/NM (9.0) $600
Amazing Spider-Man #39 VF- (7.5) $188.88
Amazing Spider-Man #40 NM- (9.2) $800
Amazing Spider-Man #43 NM+ (9.6) $6,729
Amazing Spider-Man #45 NM+ (9.6) $3,800 Valparaiso
Amazing Spider-Man #46 VF/NM (9.0) $300
Amazing Spider-Man #47 NM+ (9.6) $1,800
Amazing Spider-Man #47 NM (9.4) $500
Amazing Spider-Man #50 NM+ (9.6) $20,500
Amazing Spider-Man #66 NM/MT (9.8) $5,500 Rocky Mountain
Amazing Spider-Man #68 NM- (9.2) $150
Amazing Spider-Man #75 NM (9.4) $425
Amazing Spider-Man Ann. #1 NM+ (9.6) $15,200
Atom #1 NM+ (9.6) $21,000
Avengers #1 VG/FN (5.0) $800
Avengers #1 VG/FN (5.0) $335 (restored)
Avengers #1 VG+(4.5) $900
Avengers #1 GD+ (2.5) $370
Avengers #2 NM (9.4) $13,500
Avengers #2 NM- (9.2) $1,700
Avengers #2 VG/FN (5.0) $150
Avengers #4 NM+ (9.6) $64,000
Avengers #4 VF/NM (9.0) $3,400
Avengers #4 FN (6.0) $600
Avengers #5 NM- (9.2) $3,800
Avengers #9 NM- (9.2) $6,099 White Mountain
Avengers #12 NM+ (9.6) $10,000
Avengers #12 NM+ (9.6) $9,089 Northland
Avengers #19 NM+ (9.6) $4,100
Avengers #46 NM+ (9.6) $540
Avengers #70 NM/MT (9.8) $3,000
Batman #181 FN/VF (7.0) $80
Brave And The Bold #28 VG (4.0) $700
Brave And The Bold #54 VF- (7.5) $242
Captain America #100 NM/MT (9.8) $8,255 Boston
Captain America #104 NM/MT (9.8) $3,877 Boston
Captain America #107 NM (9.4) $230
Daredevil #1 NM (9.4) $23,251
Daredevil #1 NM (9.4) $20,750
Daredevil #1 VG (4.0) $510
Daredevil #1 GD/VG (3.0) $316
Daredevil #2 NM+ (9.6) $8,600
Daredevil #2 NM- (9.2) $1,700
Daredevil #14 NM+ (9.6) $1,125
Daredevil #17 NM (9.4) $650
Daredevil #18 NM+ (9.6) $1,125
Daredevil #18 VF/NM (9.0) $125
Detective Comics #225 VG/FN (5.0) $1,300
Doctor Strange #179 NM+ (9.6) $250
Dynamo #4 NM (9.4) $101
Fantastic Four #1 VF+ (8.5) $75,100
Fantastic Four #1 VF (8.0) $50,400
Fantastic Four #2 NM- (9.2) $10,199
Fantastic Four #9 NM+ (9.6) $23,250
Fantastic Four #10 NM+ (9.6) $27,999
Fantastic Four #11 NM (9.4) $17,010
Fantastic Four #12 NM (9.4) $35,000
Fantastic Four #12 NM- (9.2) $21,400
Fantastic Four #14 NM+ (9.6) $13,905
Fantastic Four #17 NM (9.4) $7,877 Northland
Fantastic Four #19 NM (9.4) $8,600
Fantastic Four #20 NM+ (9.6) $15,950
Fantastic Four #28 NM+ (9.6) $16,251
Fantastic Four #29 NM+ (9.6) $24,200
Fantastic Four #40 NM+ (9.6) $14,750
Fantastic Four #50 NM (9.4) $16,000 Valparaiso
Fantastic Four #50 NM (9.4) $10,000
Fantastic Four #52 FN+ (6.5) $85
Fantastic Four Annual #1 NM+ (9.6) $15,250
Flash #105 NM- (9.2) $19,120
Flash #123 NM (9.4) $16,730
Green Lantern #1 FN+ (6.5) $1,050
Green Lantern #7 FN (6.0) $110
Green Lantern #41 NM+ (9.6) $938
Hawkman #1 NM- (9.2) $665 (restored)
I Love You #26 VF+ (8.5) $25
Incredible Hulk #1 NM- (9.2) $125,475
Incredible Hulk #1 VF+ (8.5) $36,000
Incredible Hulk #1 GD/VG (3.0) $2,250
Incredible Hulk #1 GD/VG (3.0) $2,000
Incredible Hulk #1 VG+ (4.5) $1,800 (restored)
Incredible Hulk #2 FN/VF (7.0) $1,400
Iron Man #1 NM/MT (9.8) $18,500 CGC Signature Series
Iron Man #1 NM (9.4) $1,800
Iron Man #1 NM (9.4) $1,600
Iron Man #1 VF/NM (9.0) $1,000
Iron Man #1 VF (8.0) $100 (restored)
Journey Into Mystery #73 FN/VF (7.0) $300
Journey Into Mystery #83 VG+ (4.5) $2,250
Journey into Mystery #83 VF/NM (9.0) $27,800
Journey Into Mystery #83 VG/FN (5.0) $2,000
Journey Into Mystery #83 GD+ (2.5) $1,300
Journey Into Mystery #105 NM+ (9.6) $6,766
Journey Into Mystery #124 NM (9.4) $500
Journey Into Mystery Ann #1 NM+ (9.6) $7,100
Justice League Of America #1 FN- (5.5) $901
Justice League Of America #1 VG+ (4.5) $630
Marvel Tales #1 VF (8.0) $215

Metal Men #1 FN (6.0) $91
Nick Fury, Agent of SHIELD #1 NM/MT (9.8) $2,850
Plastic Man #2 NM (9.4) $112
Plastic Man #10 NM (9.4) $112
Showcase #4 NM+ (9.6) $179,250
Showcase #8 VF (8.0) $8,000
Showcase #22 VF/NM (9.0) $59,750
Showcase #22 GD/VG (3.0) $1,350
Showcase #22 GD+ (2.5) $1,050
Showcase #22 VG/FN (5.0) $900
Showcase #22 GD (2.0) $900
Showcase #23 FN- (5.5) $500
Silver Surfer #1 VF/NM (9.0) $375
Silver Surfer #10 NM/MT (9.8) $10,009
Strange Tales #110 NM (9.4) $17,500 Northland
Strange Tales #110 NM (9.4) $15,249
Sub-Mariner #1 NM/MT (9.8) $8,775 Western Penn
Superman #180 NM- (9.2) $101
Superman's Girlfriend Lois Lane #1 VG/FN (5.0) $1,000
Superman's Girlfriend Lois Lane #70 NM (9.4) $1,800
Tales Of Suspense #29 VF+ (8.5) $350
Tales Of Suspense #39 NM (9.4) $118,000
Tales Of Suspense #39 NM (9.4) $114,990
Tales Of Suspense #39 NM- (9.2) $31,000
Tales Of Suspense #39 VF+ (8.5) $16,757
Tales Of Suspense #39 VG/FN (5.0) $2,200
Tales Of Suspense #39 VG+ (4.5) $1,800
Tales Of Suspense #48 NM+ (9.6) $8,077
Tales Of Suspense #58 NM (9.4) $12,755
Tales Of Suspense #63 NM+ (9.6) $8,255
Tales To Astonish #27 NM- (9.2) $32,500
Tales To Astonish #27 GD/VG (3.0) $500
Tales To Astonish #59 NM+ (9.6) $4,500
Tales To Astonish #93 NM (9.4) $900
Teen Titans #1 FN (6.0) $64
Thor #137 NM/MT (9.8) $1,100
Thor #139 NM+ (9.6) $315
Uncle Scrooge #14 NM/MT (9.8) $4,600
X-Men #1 VF/NM (9.0) $33,333
X-Men #1 VF (8.0) $14,340
X-Men #1 VG (4.0) $1,450
X-Men #1 GD- (1.8) $725
X-Men #3 VF/NM (9.0) $1,600
X-Men #4 VF (8.0) $1,200
X-Men #4 FN/VF (7.0) $489
X-Men #11 NM (9.4) $6,666 Northland
X-Men #17 NM+ (9.6) $2,000

BRONZE AGE - SALES OF CGC-CERTIFIED COMICS

Amazing Spider-Man #98 NM+ (9.6) $461
Amazing Spider-Man #99 VF/NM (9.0) $100
Amazing Spider-Man #100 NM+ (9.6) $800
Amazing Spider-Man #122 NM+ (9.6) $1,200
Amazing Spider-Man #129 NM+ (9.6) $2,100
Amazing Spider-Man #129 NM+ (9.6) $2,000
Amazing Spider-Man #129 VF/NM (9.0) $400
Amazing Spider-Man #174 NM+ (9.6) $100
Amazing Spider-Man #194 MT (9.9) $3,625
Amazing Spider-Man #194 MT (9.9) $4,331.88
Amazing Spider-Man #194 NM- (9.2) $62.50
Amazing Spider-Man #238 NM+ (9.6) $125
Avengers #100 VF+ (8.5) $100
Batman #227 NM/MT (9.8) $13,000
Batman #227 NM+ (9.6) $3,226.50
Batman #232 NM+ (9.6) $1,000
Batman #234 VF+ (8.5) $175
Batman #366 NM/MT (9.8) $120
Batman #368 NM/MT (9.8) $100
Beyond the Grave #1 NM (9.4) $30
Champions #1 VF/NM (9.0) $20
Conan the Barbarian #1 NM/MT (9.8) $8,300
Conan The Barbarian #1 NM+ (9.6) $1,300
Conan The Barbarian #1 NM+ (9.6) $1,434
Conan The Barbarian #1 VF/NM (9.0) $180.49
Daredevil #168 NM- (9.2) $175
Daredevil #181 NM/MT (9.8) $100
Defenders #1 NM+ (9.6) $425
Defenders #10 NM- (9.2) $175
Fantastic Four #100 NM (9.4) $300
Fantastic Four #112 NM+ (9.6) $24,017
Forever People #1 NM/MT (9.8) $448.13
Ghost Rider #1 NM/MT (9.8) $7,100
Ghost Rider #1 VF- (7.5) $65
Giant-Size X-Men #1 NM+ (9.6) $2,310
Giant-Size X-Men #1 NM (9.4) $1,553.50
Giant-Size X-Men #1 VF- (7.5) $450
Giant-Size X-Men #1 FN- (5.5) $400 CGC Signature Series
Green Lantern #76 NM- (9.2) $2,750
Green Lantern #76 NM+ (9.6) $22,750
Green Lantern #76 NM+ (9.6) $30,500
Green Lantern #76 VF (8.0) $450.01
Green Lantern #76 VF/NM (9.0) $2,031.50
Green Lantern #85 NM (9.4) $250
Green Lantern #85 NM/MT (9.8) $3,585
Hero For Hire #1 VF+ (8.5) $188
House Of Mystery #257 NM+ (9.6) $102
Incredible Hulk #141 NM/MT (9.8) $1,912
Incredible Hulk #162 NM+ (9.6) $950

CGC Signature Series
Incredible Hulk #181 NM/MT (9.8) $32,001
CGC Signature Series
Incredible Hulk #181 NM/MT (9.8) $26,501
Valparaiso
Incredible Hulk #181 NM/MT (9.8) $26,290
Incredible Hulk #181 NM/MT (9.8) $15,535
Incredible Hulk #181 NM+ (9.6) $5,500
Incredible Hulk #181 NM (9.4) $3,107
Incredible Hulk #181 VF/NM (9.0) $600
(restored)
Incredible Hulk #181 VF (8.0) $1,200
CGC Signature Series
Inhumans #1 NM (9.4) $30
Iron Fist 35¢ #14 GD+ (2.5) $575
Iron Man #128 NM/MT (9.8) $657.25
Iron Man #26 NM (9.4) $100
Iron Man #55 NM (9.4) $550
Iron Man #55 VF/NM (9.0) $300
Jonah Hex #11 NM+ (9.6) $100
Marvel Feature #3 NM (9.4) $112
Marvel Spotlight #5 NM+ (9.6) $2,390
Marvel Spotlight #5 FN+ (6.5) $135
Ms. Marvel #17 NM (9.4) $40
New Gods #2 NM+ (9.6) $157
New Mutants #1 PGX 9.9 $125
Night Nurse #1 NM/MT (9.8) $3,850
Sgt Rock #302 NM+ (9.6) $160
Sgt Rock #303 NM+ (9.6) $100
Spider-Woman #1 NM- (9.2) $20
Star Wars #1 (35¢-c) NM+ (9.6) $26,250
Sub-Mariner #56 NM+ (9.6) $120
Superman's Pal Jimmy Olsen #133 NM (9.4) $112
Superman's Pal Jimmy Olsen #136 NM+ (9.6) $135
Swamp Thing #1 NM/MT (9.8) $6,766
CGC Signature Series
Thor #165 NM+ (9.6) $3,005
Tomb of Dracula #1 NM+ (9.6) $675
Weird War Tales #2 NM (9.4) $202
Weird War Tales #8 NM (9.4) $157
Werewolf By Night #32 NM+ (9.6) $3,479
Witching Hour #12 NM (9.4) $101
Wolverine (mini) #1 GM (10.0) $15,535
X-Men #94 NM/MT (9.8) $27,779
X-Men #94 NM/MT (9.8) $28,000
X-Men #101 NM- (9.2) $185
X-Men #114 NM/MT (9.8) $1,792.50
X-Men #122 NM- (9.2) $47
X-Men #136 NM (9.4) $55
X-Men #141 MT (9.9) $11,950

COPPER AGE - SALES OF CGC-CERTIFIED COMICS

Albedo #4 NM+ (9.6) $125
Amazing Spider-Man #300 NM/MT (9.8) $1,200
Amazing Spider-Man #300 NM+ (9.6) $275
Signed by McFarlane
Blackthorne 3-D-Moonwalker #75 NM+ (9.6) $735
G.I. Joe, A Real American Hero #21 NM+ (9.6)
$155.35
Marvel Super Heroes Secret Wars #8 MT (9.9)
$657.25
Saga of the Swamp Thing #21 NM/MT (9.8) $84
Sandman #1 NM (9.4) $45
Star Wars #107 NM/MT (9.8) $657.25
Teenage Mutant Ninja Turtles #1 NM+ (9.6) $11,500
Transformers #1 NM- (9.2) $25
Web of Spider-Man #1 MT (9.9) $776.75
Wolverine (1988) #1 NM+ (9.6) $150
Wonder Woman #1 NM/MT (9.8) $69
X-Men #212 MT (9.9) $1,912

MODERN AGE - SALES OF CGC-CERTIFIED COMICS

All Star Batman and Robin #10 NM/MT (9.8) $200
(recalled edition, Quitely variant cover)
Amazing Spider-Man V2 #36 NM+ (9.6) $42
Batman #492 Platinum Ed. NM/MT (9.8) $224.99
Captain America #25 ('07) Epting-c NM/MT (9.8) $42
Chew #1 NM/MT (9.8) $290
Fables #1 NM (9.4) $45
G.I. Joe, A Real American Hero #155 NM/MT (9.8)
$507.88
Harbinger #1 NM (9.4) $23
Identity Crisis #1 NM/MT (9.8) $26
John Byrne's Next Men #21 NM (9.4) $45
John Byrne's Next Men #21 NM (9.4) $35
Kick-Ass #1 NM/MT (9.8) $76
New Mutants #98 MT (9.9) $12,250
New Mutants #98 NM (9.4) $62
New Mutants #98 NM- (9.2) $56
Preacher #1 NM (9.4) $25
Spawn #1 NM/MT (9.8) $90
Ultimate Spider-Man #1 NM/MT (9.8) $375
Ultimate Spider-Man #1 White-c NM/MT (9.8) $565
Venom: Lethal Protector #1 Black-c GM (10.0)
$3,585
Walking Dead #1 NM/MT (9.8) $540

TOP BOOKS

The following tables denote the rate of appreciation of the top Golden Age, Platinum Age, Silver Age and Bronze Age books, as well as selected genres over the past year. The retail value for a Near Mint- copy of each book (or VF where a Near Mint- copy is not known to exist) in 2010 is compared to its Near Mint- value in 2009. The rate of return for 2010 over 2009 is given. The place in rank is given for each comic by year, with its corresponding value in highest known grade. These tables can be very useful in forecasting trends in the market place. For instance, the investor might want to know which book is yielding the best dividend from one year to the next, or one might just be interested in seeing how the popularity of books changes from year to year. For instance, *Action Comics* #7 was in 17th place in 2009 and has increased to 10th place in 2010. Premium books are also included in these tables and are denoted with an asterisk(*).

The following tables are meant as a guide to the investor. However, it should be pointed out that trends may change at anytime and that some books can meet market resistance with a slowdown in price increases, while others can develop into real comers from a presently dormant state. In the long run, if the investor sticks to the books that are appreciating steadily each year, he shouldn't go very far wrong.

TOP 100 GOLDEN AGE BOOKS

TITLE/ISSUE#	2010 RANK	2010 NM- PRICE	2009 RANK	2009 NM- PRICE	$ INCR.	% INCR.
Action Comics #1	1	$1,200,000	1	$750,000	$450,000	60%
Detective Comics #27	2	$1,050,000	2	$575,000	$475,000	83%
Superman #1	3	$500,000	4	$440,000	$60,000	14%
Marvel Comics #1	4	$450,000	3	$460,000	-$10,000	-2%
All-American Comics #16	5	$350,000	5	$280,000	$70,000	25%
Batman #1	6	$250,000	6	$215,000	$35,000	16%
Captain America Comics #1	7	$215,000	7	$190,000	$25,000	13%
Flash Comics #1	8	$145,000	8	$135,000	$10,000	7%
More Fun Comics #52	9	$135,000	9	$125,000	$10,000	8%
Adventure Comics #40	10	$115,000	10	$105,000	$10,000	10%
Action Comics #7	11	$100,000	17	$72,000	$28,000	39%
Whiz Comics #2 (#1)	12	$95,000	11	$95,000	$0	0%
Detective Comics #33	13	$92,000	12	$85,000	$7,000	8%
Detective Comics #31	14	$90,000	15	$78,000	$12,000	15%
All Star Comics #3	15	$85,000	13	$80,000	$5,000	6%
Detective Comics #38	15	$85,000	13	$80,000	$5,000	6%
Action Comics #2	17	$84,000	16	$75,000	$9,000	12%
Detective Comics #29	18	$80,000	17	$72,000	$8,000	11%
Detective Comics #1	19	VF $77,000	19	VF $70,000	$7,000	10%
All Star Comics #8	20	$70,000	20	$65,000	$5,000	8%
Marvel Mystery Comics #9	20	$70,000	27	$58,000	$12,000	21%
More Fun Comics #53	20	$70,000	20	$65,000	$5,000	8%
Marvel Mystery Comics #2	23	$65,000	26	$60,000	$5,000	8%
Human Torch #2 (#1)	24	$64,000	23	$62,000	$2,000	3%
Sub-Mariner Comics #1	24	$64,000	23	$62,000	$2,000	3%
Green Lantern #1	26	$62,000	25	$61,000	$1,000	2%
Sensation Comics #1	27	$60,000	20	$65,000	-$5,000	-8%
Action Comics #10	28	$55,000	35	$42,000	$13,000	31%
Captain Marvel Adventures #1	28	$55,000	28	$51,000	$4,000	8%
Action Comics #3	30	$54,000	33	$48,000	$6,000	13%
Marvel Mystery Comics #5	30	$54,000	29	$50,000	$4,000	8%
Adventure Comics #48	32	$52,000	29	$50,000	$2,000	4%
Wonder Woman #1	32	$52,000	29	$50,000	$2,000	4%
New Fun Comics #1	34	VF $51,000	29	VF $50,000	$1,000	2%
Archie Comics #1	35	$50,000	37	$38,000	$12,000	32%
Detective Comics #28	35	$50,000	34	$44,000	$6,000	14%
Pep Comics #22	35	$50,000	37	$38,000	$12,000	32%
Suspense Comics #3	38	$45,000	40	$36,000	$9,000	25%
Detective Comics #35	39	$40,000	46	$30,000	$10,000	33%
Walt Disney's Comics & Stories #1	39	$40,000	40	$36,000	$4,000	11%

TITLE/ISSUE#	2010 RANK	2010 NM- PRICE	2009 RANK	2009 NM- PRICE	$ INCR.	% INCR.
All Winners Comics #1	41	$38,000	36	$40,000	-$2,000	-5%
Daring Mystery Comics #1	41	$38,000	39	$37,000	$1,000	3%
All-American Comics #19	43	$37,000	42	$34,000	$3,000	9%
Marvel Mystery Comics #3	44	$36,000	43	$33,000	$3,000	9%
*Marvel Mystery Comics 132 pg.	44	VF $36,000	44	VF $32,000	$4,000	13%
Captain America Comics #2	46	$35,000	51	$29,000	$6,000	21%
Superman #2	46	$35,000	45	$31,000	$4,000	13%
Captain America Comics 132 pg.	48	VF $33,000	46	VF $30,000	$3,000	10%
Batman #2	49	$32,000	46	$30,000	$2,000	7%
More Fun Comics #54	49	$32,000	51	$29,000	$3,000	10%
*Motion Picture Funnies Wkly #1	49	$32,000	46	$30,000	$2,000	7%
Action Comics #4	52	$31,000	56	$28,000	$3,000	11%
Action Comics #5	52	$31,000	56	$28,000	$3,000	11%
Action Comics #6	52	$31,000	56	$28,000	$3,000	11%
More Fun Comics #55	52	$31,000	51	$29,000	$2,000	7%
Famous Funnies-Series 1	56	VF $30,000	51	VF $29,000	$1,000	3%
More Fun Comics #73	56	$30,000	56	$28,000	$2,000	7%
New Book of Comics #1	56	VF $30,000	46	VF $30,000	$0	0%
Amazing Man Comics #5	59	$29,000	56	$28,000	$1,000	4%
Marvel Mystery Comics #4	59	$29,000	65	$26,000	$3,000	12%
New York World's Fair 1939	59	VF/NM $29,000	51	VF/NM $29,000	$0	0%
All-Select Comics #1	62	$28,000	65	$26,000	$2,000	8%
All Flash #1	63	$27,500	62	$27,000	$500	2%
Wonder Comics #1	63	$27,500	62	$27,000	$500	2%
Captain America Comics #3	65	$27,000	73	$24,000	$3,000	13%
Mystic Comics #1	65	$27,000	65	$26,000	$1,000	4%
Wow Comics (FAW) #1	65	$27,000	62	$27,000	$0	0%
Silver Streak Comics #6	68	$26,000	69	$25,000	$1,000	4%
Young Allies Comics #1	69	$25,500	65	$26,000	-$500	-2%
Action Comics #13	70	$25,000	88	$20,000	$5,000	25%
Adventure Comics #73	70	$25,000	72	$24,500	$500	2%
Marvel Mystery Comics #8	70	$25,000	82	$22,000	$3,000	14%
World's Best Comics #1	70	$25,000	69	$25,000	$0	0%
Adventure Comics #61	74	$24,000	75	$23,000	$1,000	4%
Four Color Ser. 1 (Donald Duck) #4	74	$24,000	75	$23,000	$1,000	4%
New Fun Comics #6	74	VF $24,000	74	VF $23,500	$500	2%
Planet Comics #1	74	$24,000	75	$23,000	$1,000	4%
Red Raven Comics #1	78	$23,500	80	$22,500	$1,000	4%
All Star Comics #1	79	$23,000	78	$22,500	$500	2%
Daredevil #1	79	$23,000	78	$22,500	$500	2%
Famous Funnies #1	81	VF $22,500	82	VF $22,000	$500	2%
All-American Comics #18	82	$22,000	88	$20,000	$2,000	10%
Detective Comics #2	82	VF $22,000	88	VF $20,000	$2,000	10%
Green Giant Comics #1	82	$22,000	86	$21,000	$1,000	5%
Looney Tunes and Merrie Melodies #1	82	$22,000	86	$21,000	$1,000	5%
New Fun Comics #2	82	VF $22,000	84	VF $21,500	$500	2%
Jumbo Comics #1	87	VF $21,500	84	VF $21,500	$0	0%
All-American Comics #25	88	$21,000	93	$19,000	$2,000	11%
Daring Mystery Comics #2	89	$20,000	93	$19,000	$1,000	5%
Double Action Comics #2	89	$20,000	91	$19,500	$500	3%
New Comics #1	89	VF $20,000	91	VF $19,500	$500	3%
Superman #3	89	$20,000		$17,000	$3,000	18%
USA Comics #1	89	$20,000	80	$22,500	-$2,500	-11%
All-American Comics #17	94	$19,900	61	$27,500	-$8,500	-31%
*Century of Comics	94	VF $19,000	69	VF $25,000	-$6,000	-24%
Comics Magazine #1	94	VF $19,000	98	VF $18,000	$1,000	6%
Dick Tracy Feature Book nn (#1)	94	$19,000		$17,500	$1,500	9%
Exciting Comics #9	94	$19,000		$17,500	$1,500	9%
Four Color Ser. 2 (Donald Duck) #9	94	$19,000	98	$18,000	$1,000	6%
Mickey Mouse Magazine - 1935 #1	94	VF/NM $19,000	96	VF/NM $18,500	$500	3%
Silver Streak Comics #1	94	$19,000	96	$18,500	$500	3%

TOP 20 SILVER AGE BOOKS

TITLE/ISSUE#	2010 RANK	2010 NM- PRICE	2009 RANK	2009 NM- PRICE	$ INCR.	% INCR.
Amazing Fantasy #15	1	$100,000	1	$65,000	$35,000	54%
Fantastic Four #1	2	$70,000	2	$52,000	$18,000	35%
Incredible Hulk #1	3	$65,000	5	$40,000	$25,000	63%
Showcase #4 (The Flash)	4	$54,000	3	$48,000	$6,000	13%
Amazing Spider-Man #1	5	$50,000	4	$44,000	$6,000	14%
X-Men #1	6	$26,000	6	$22,000	$4,000	18%
Journey Into Mystery #83 (Thor)	7	$24,000	7	$18,000	$6,000	33%
Tales of Suspense #39 (Iron Man)	8	$20,000	9	$15,000	$5,000	33%
Showcase #8 (The Flash)	9	$18,500	7	$18,000	$500	3%
Brave and the Bold #28	10	$16,000	12	$13,000	$3,000	23%
The Flash #105	10	$16,000	10	$14,000	$2,000	14%
Justice League of America #1	12	$14,000	13	$12,000	$2,000	17%
Showcase #9 (Lois Lane)	12	$14,000	11	$13,500	$500	4%
Adventure Comics #247 (Legion)	14	$13,500	13	$12,000	$1,500	13%
Fantastic Four #5	15	$13,000	15	$10,000	$3,000	30%
Tales To Astonish #27 (Ant-Man)	15	$13,000	15	$10,000	$3,000	30%
Avengers #1	17	$12,500	20	$9,200	$3,300	36%
Showcase #22 (Green Lantern)	17	$12,500	15	$10,000	$2,500	25%
Green Lantern #1	19	$11,000	18	$9,500	$1,500	16%
Fantastic Four #2	20	$10,500	18	$9,500	$1,000	11%

TOP 10 BRONZE AGE BOOKS

TITLE/ISSUE#	2010 RANK	2010 NM- PRICE	2009 RANK	2009 NM- PRICE	$ INCR.	% INCR.
Star Wars #1 (35¢ price variant)	1	$2,500	1	$2,300	$200	9%
Green Lantern #76	2	$2,000	5	$1,200	$800	67%
Incredible Hulk #181	3	$1,650	3	$1,550	$100	6%
Iron Fist #14 (35¢ price variant)	4	$1,600	2	$1,600	$0	0%
Giant-Size X-Men #1	5	$1,300	4	$1,250	$50	4%
X-Men #94	6	$1,200	6	$1,150	$50	4%
Cerebus #1	7	$1,100	8	$1,000	$100	10%
House of Secrets #92	7	$1,100	7	$1,050	$50	5%
DC 100 Page Super Spectacular #5	9	$1,050	9	$975	$75	8%
Amazing Spider-Man #129	10	$900	10	$800	$100	13%

TOP 10 COPPER AGE BOOKS

TITLE/ISSUE#	2010 RANK	2010 NM- PRICE	2009 RANK	2009 NM- PRICE	$ INCR.	% INCR.
Miracleman #1 Gold Edition	1	$1,500	1	$1,500	$0	0%
Gobbledygook #1	2	$1,200	2	$1,100	$100	9%
Miracleman #1 Blue Edition	3	$800	3	$800	$0	0%
Gobbledygook #2	4	$750	4	$700	$50	7%
Albedo #2	5	$700	5	$650	$50	8%
Vampirella #113	6	$535	6	$510	$25	5%
Grendel #1	7	$190	7	$180	$10	6%
Primer #2	8	$150	8	$140	$10	7%
Spider-Man #1 (Platinum)	9	$130	9	$130	$0	0%
Spider-Man #1 (2nd pr. w/Gold UPC)	10	$120	10	$120	$0	0%

*__Teenage Mutant Ninja Turtles #1__ - Recent sales of this book include a CGC 9.6 for $11,500

TOP 20 BIG LITTLE BOOKS

BOOK #	TITLE	2010 RANK	2010 VF/NM PRICE	2009 RANK	2009 VF/NM PRICE	$ INCR.	% INCR.
731	**Mickey Mouse the Mail Pilot** (variant version of Mickey Mouse #717) (Fine copy sold at auction for $5,090)						
nn	**Mickey Mouse and Minnie Mouse at Macy's**	2	$3,500	2	$3,500	$0	0%
717	**Mickey Mouse** (skinny Mickey on-c)	3	$3,135	3	$3,135	$0	0%
nn	**Mickey Mouse and Minnie March to Macy's**	4	$2,400	4	$2,400	$0	0%
W-707	**Dick Tracy The Detective**	5	$2,310	5	$2,310	$0	0%
725	**Big Little Mother Goose** HC	6	$2,200	6	$2,035	$165	8%
717	**Mickey Mouse** (reg. Mickey on-c)	7	$1,650	7	$1,650	$0	0%
4063	**Popeye Thimble Theater Starring...** (2nd printing)	8	$1,620	8	$1,620	$0	0%
721	**Big Little Paint Book** (336 pg.)	9	$1,500	9	$1,540	-$40	-3%
725	**Big Little Mother Goose** SC	9	$1,500	10	$1,495	$5	1%
4062	**Mickey Mouse and the Smugglers**	11	$1,430	12	$1,430	$0	0%
nn	**Mickey Mouse** (Great Big Midget Book)	12	$1,400	10	$1,485	-$85	-6%
nn	**Mickey Mouse the Mail Pilot** (Great Big Midget Book)	12	$1,400	-	-	-	-
4063	**Popeye Thimble Theater Starring...**(1st pr.)	14	$1,385	14	$1,385	$0	0%
nn	**Buck Rogers**	15	$1,320	15	$1,320	$0	0%
nn	**Mickey Mouse Silly Symphonies**	15	$1,320	15	$1,320	$0	0%
4062	**Mickey Mouse, The Story of...**	17	$1,210	17	$1,210	$0	0%
721	**Big Little Paint Book** (330 pg.)	18	$1,200	-	-	-	-
nn	**Mickey Mouse Sails For Treasure Island** (Great Big Midget Book)	18	$1,200	18	$1,150	$50	4%
nn	**Mickey Mouse and the Magic Carpet**	20	$1,050	19	$1,050	$0	0%

TOP 10 PLATINUM AGE BOOKS

TITLE/ISSUE#	2010 RANK	2010 PRICE	2009 RANK	2009 PRICE	$ INCR.	% INCR.
Yellow Kid in McFadden Flats	1	FN $14,000	1	FN $14,000	$0	0%
Mickey Mouse Book (2nd printing)-variant	2	FN $12,000	2	FN $12,000	$0	0%
Mickey Mouse Book (1st printing)	2	VF $12,000	2	VF $12,000	$0	0%
Mickey Mouse Book (2nd printing)	4	VF $10,000	4	VF $10,000	$0	0%
Little Sammy Sneeze	5	FN $6,000	5	FN $6,000	$0	0%
Pore Li'l Mose	6	FN $5,775	6	FN $5,775	$0	0%
Buster Brown and His Resolutions 1903	7	FN $5,500	7	FN $5,500	$0	0%
Little Nemo 1906	8	FN $5,000	8	FN $5,000	$0	0%
Little Nemo 1909	9	FN $4,000	9	FN $4,000	$0	0%
Yellow Kid #1	10	FN $3,500	10	FN $3,500	$0	0%

TOP 10 CRIME BOOKS

TITLE/ISSUE#	2010 RANK	2010 NM- PRICE	2009 RANK	2009 NM- PRICE	$ INCR.	% INCR.
Crime Does Not Pay #22	1	$7,500	1	$4,800	$2,700	56%
Crime Does Not Pay #24	2	$4,500	3	$2,500	$2,000	80%
Crime Does Not Pay #23	3	$3,000	2	$2,600	$400	15%
True Crime Comics #2	4	$2,500	4	$2,400	$100	4%
Crimes By Women #1	5	$1,900	5	$1,825	$75	4%
The Killers #1	6	$1,850	6	$1,750	$100	6%
True Crime Comics #3	7	$1,800	7	$1,725	$75	4%
True Crime Comics #4	8	$1,525	8	$1,475	$50	3%
The Killers #2	9	$1,500	9	$1,425	$75	5%
True Crime Comics V2 #1	10	$1,400	10	$1,350	$50	4%

TOP 10 HORROR BOOKS

TITLE/ISSUE#	2010 RANK	2010 NM- PRICE	2009 RANK	2009 NM- PRICE	$ INCR.	% INCR.
Vault of Horror #12	1	$8,500	1	$8,300	$200	2%
Eerie #1	2	$8,200	2	$7,800	$400	5%
Tales of Terror Annual #1	3	VF $6,400	3	VF $6,000	$400	7%
Journey into Mystery #1	4	$5,500	4	$5,300	$200	4%
Strange Tales #1	5	$5,300	5	$5,100	$200	4%
Crypt of Terror #17	6	$5,100	6	$5,000	$100	2%
Haunt of Fear #15	6	$5,100	6	$5,000	$100	2%
Crime Patrol #15	8	$4,700	8	$4,600	$100	2%
Tales to Astonish #1	9	$4,000	10	$3,600	$400	11%
House of Mystery #1	10	$3,800	9	$3,650	$150	4%

TOP 10 ROMANCE BOOKS

TITLE/ISSUE#	2010 RANK	2010 NM- PRICE	2009 RANK	2009 NM- PRICE	$ INCR.	% INCR.
Giant Comics Edition #12	1	$4,000	1	$2,800	$1,200	43%
Negro Romance #1	2	$2,000	2	$1,850	$150	8%
Negro Romance #2	3	$1,600	3	$1,450	$150	9%
Negro Romance #3	3	$1,600	3	$1,450	$150	9%
Intimate Confessions #1	5	$1,400	5	$1,300	$100	8%
Giant Comics Edition #9	6	$1,250	10	$1,000	$250	25%
Modern Love #1	6	$1,250	6	$1,175	$75	6%
A Moon, A Girl...Romance #9	6	$1,250	6	$1,175	$75	6%
A Moon, A Girl...Romance #12	6	$1,250	6	$1,175	$75	6%
Forbidden Love #11	10	$1,175	9	$1,140	$35	3%

TOP 10 SCI-FI BOOKS

TITLE/ISSUE#	2010 RANK	2010 NM- PRICE	2009 RANK	2009 NM- PRICE	$ INCR.	% INCR.
Mystery In Space #1	1	$6,300	1	$6,000	$300	5%
Strange Adventures #1	2	$5,900	2	$5,700	$200	4%
Showcase #17 (Adam Strange)	3	$5,000	3	$4,700	$300	6%
Weird Science-Fantasy Annual 1952	4	$4,200	4	$4,000	$200	5%
Journey Into Unknown Worlds #36	5	$4,000	5	$3,850	$150	4%
Showcase #15 (Space Ranger)	6	$4,000	6	$3,750	$250	7%
Fawcett Movie #15 (Man From Planet X)	7	$3,800	7	$3,600	$200	6%
Strange Adventures #9	8	$3,550	10	$3,400	$150	4%
Weird Fantasy #13 (#1)	9	$3,500	8	$3,500	$0	0%
Weird Science #12 (#1)	9	$3,500	8	$3,500	$0	0%

TOP 10 WESTERN BOOKS

TITLE/ISSUE#	2010 RANK	2010 NM- PRICE	2009 RANK	2009 NM- PRICE	$ INCR.	% INCR.
Gene Autry Comics #1	1	$10,000	1	$11,000	-$1,000	-9%
Hopalong Cassidy #1	2	$7,500	2	$8,400	-$900	-11%
*Lone Ranger Ice Cream 1939 2nd	3	VF $6,000	3	VF $6,500	-$500	-8%
*Lone Ranger Ice Cream 1939	4	VF $4,200	4	VF $6,000	-$1,800	-30%
*Red Ryder Victory Patrol '42	5	$4,000	5	$4,500	-$500	-11%
Roy Rogers Four Color #38	5	$4,000	6	$4,000	$0	0%
Red Ryder Comics #1	7	$3,800	6	$4,000	-$200	5%
*Tom Mix Ralston #1	8	$3,600	10	$3,800	-$200	-5%
*Red Ryder Victory Patrol '43	9	$3,500	6	$4,000	-$500	-13%
*Red Ryder Victory Patrol '44	9	$3,500	6	$4,000	-$500	-13%

GRADING DEFINITIONS

10.0 GEM MINT (GM): This is an exceptional example of a given book - the best ever seen. The slightest bindery defects and/or printing flaws may be seen only upon very close inspection. The overall look is "as if it has never been handled or released for purchase." Only the slightest bindery or printing defects are allowed, and these would be imperceptible on first viewing. No bindery tears. Cover is flat with no surface wear. Inks are bright with high reflectivity. Well centered and firmly secured to interior pages. Corners are cut square and sharp. No creases. No dates or stamped markings allowed. No soiling, staining or other discoloration. Spine is tight and flat. No spine roll or split allowed. Staples must be original, centered and clean with no rust. No staple tears or stress lines. Paper is white, supple and fresh. No hint of acidity in the odor of the newsprint. No interior autographs or owner signatures. Centerfold is firmly secure. No interior tears.

9.9 MINT (MT): Near perfect in every way. Only subtle bindery or printing defects are allowed. No bindery tears. Cover is flat with no surface wear. Inks are bright with high reflectivity. Generally well centered and firmly secured to interior pages. Corners are cut square and sharp. No creases. Small, inconspicuous, lightly penciled, stamped or inked arrival dates are acceptable as long as they are in an unobtrusive location. No soiling, staining or other discoloration. Spine is tight and flat. No spine roll or split allowed. Staples must be original, generally centered and clean with no rust. No staple tears or stress lines. Paper is white, supple and fresh. No hint of acidity in the odor of the newsprint. Centerfold is firmly secure. No interior tears.

9.8 NEAR MINT/MINT (NM/MT): Nearly perfect in every way with only minor imperfections that keep it from the next higher grade. Only subtle bindery or printing defects are allowed. No bindery tears. Cover is flat with no surface wear. Inks are bright with high reflectivity. Generally well centered and firmly secured to interior pages. Corners are cut square and sharp. No creases. Small, inconspicuous, lightly penciled, stamped or inked arrival dates are acceptable as long as they are in an unobtrusive location. No soiling, staining or other discoloration. Spine is tight and flat. No spine roll or split allowed. Staples must be original, generally centered and clean with no rust. No staple tears or stress lines. Paper is off-white to white, supple and fresh. No hint of acidity in the odor of the newsprint. Centerfold is firmly secure. Only the slightest interior tears are allowed.

9.6 NEAR MINT+ (NM+): Nearly perfect with a minor additional virtue or virtues that raise it from Near Mint. The overall look is "as if it was just purchased and read once or twice." Only subtle bindery or printing defects are allowed. No bindery tears are allowed, although on Golden Age books bindery tears of up to 1/8" have been noted. Cover is flat with no surface wear. Inks are bright with high reflectivity. Well centered and firmly secured to interior pages. One corner may be almost imperceptibly blunted, but still almost sharp and cut square. Almost imperceptible indentations are permissible, but no creases, bends, or color break. Small, inconspicuous, lightly penciled, stamped or inked arrival dates are acceptable as long as they are in an unobtrusive location. No soiling, staining or other discoloration. Spine is tight and flat. No spine roll or split allowed. Staples must be original, generally centered, with only the slightest discoloration. No staple tears, stress lines, or rust migration. Paper is off-white, supple and fresh. No hint of acidity in the odor of the newsprint. Centerfold is firmly secure. Only the slightest interior tears are allowed.

9.4 NEAR MINT (NM): Nearly perfect with only minor imperfections that keep it from the next higher grade. The overall look is "as if it was just purchased and read once or twice." Subtle bindery defects are allowed. Bindery tears must be less than 1/16" on Silver Age and later books, although on Golden Age books bindery tears of up to 1/4" have been noted. Cover is flat with no surface wear. Inks are bright with high reflectivity. Generally well centered and secured to interior pages. Corners are cut square and sharp with ever-so-slight blunting permitted. A 1/16" bend is permitted with no color break. No creases. Small, inconspicuous, lightly penciled, stamped or inked arrival dates are acceptable as long as they are in an unobtrusive location. No soiling, staining or other discoloration apart from slight foxing. Spine is tight and flat. No spine roll or split allowed. Staples are generally centered; may have slight discoloration. No staple tears are allowed; almost no stress lines. No rust migration. In rare cases, a comic was not stapled at the bindery and therefore has a missing staple; this is not considered a defect. Any staple can be replaced on books up to Fine, but only vintage staples can be used on books from Very Fine to Near Mint. Mint books must have original staples. Paper is cream to off-white, supple and fresh. No hint of acidity in the odor of the newsprint. Centerfold is secure. Slight interior tears are allowed.

9.2 NEAR MINT– (NM–): Nearly perfect with only a minor additional defect or defects that keep it from Near Mint. A limited number of minor bindery defects are allowed. Cover is flat with no surface wear. Inks are bright with only the slightest dimming of reflectivity. Generally well centered and secured to interior pages. Corners are cut square and sharp with ever-so-slight blunting permitted. A 1/16"-1/8" bend is permitted with no color break. No creases. Small, inconspicuous, lightly penciled, stamped or inked arrival dates are acceptable as long as they are in an unobtrusive location. No soiling, staining or other discoloration apart from slight foxing. Spine is tight and flat. No spine roll or split allowed. Staples may show some discoloration. No staple tears are allowed; almost no stress lines. No rust migration. In rare cases, a comic was not stapled at the bindery and therefore has a missing staple; this is not considered a defect. Any staple can be replaced on books up to Fine, but only vintage staples can be used on books from Very Fine to Near Mint. Mint books must have original staples. Paper is cream to off-white, supple and fresh. No hint of acidity in the odor of the newsprint. Centerfold is secure. Slight interior tears are allowed.

9.0 VERY FINE/NEAR MINT (VF/NM): Nearly perfect with outstanding eye appeal. A limited number of bindery defects are allowed. Almost flat cover with almost imperceptible wear. Inks are bright with slightly diminished reflectivity. An 1/8" bend is allowed if color is not broken. Corners are cut square and sharp with ever-so-slight blunting permitted but no creases. Several lightly penciled, stamped or inked arrival dates are acceptable. No obvious soiling, staining or other discoloration, except for very minor foxing. Spine is tight and flat. No spine roll or split allowed. Staples may show some discoloration. Only the slightest staple tears are allowed. A very minor accumulation of stress lines may be present if they are nearly imperceptible. No rust migration. In rare cases, a comic was not stapled at the bindery and therefore has a missing staple; this is not considered a defect. Any staple can be replaced on books up to Fine, but only vintage staples can be used on books from Very Fine to Near Mint. Mint books must have original staples. Paper is cream to off-white and supple. No hint of acidity in the odor of the newsprint. Centerfold is secure. Very minor interior tears may be present.

8.5 VERY FINE+ (VF+): Fits the criteria for Very Fine but with an additional virtue or small accumulation of virtues that improves the book's appearance by a perceptible amount.

8.0 VERY FINE (VF): An excellent copy with outstanding eye appeal. Sharp, bright and clean with supple pages. A comic book in this grade has the appearance of having been carefully handled. A limited accumulation of minor bindery defects is allowed. Cover is relatively flat with minimal surface wear beginning to show, possibly including some minute wear at corners. Inks are generally bright with moderate to high reflectivity. A 1/4" crease is acceptable if color is not broken. Stamped or inked arrival dates may be present. No obvious soiling, staining or other discoloration, except for minor foxing. Spine is almost flat with no roll. Possible minor color break allowed. Staples may show some discoloration. Very slight staple tears and a few almost very minor to minor stress lines may be present. No rust migration. In rare cases, a comic was not stapled at the bindery and therefore has a missing staple; this is not considered a defect. Any staple can be replaced on books up to Fine, but only vintage staples can be used on books from Very Fine to Near Mint. Mint books must have original staples. Paper is tan to cream and supple. No hint of acidity in the odor of the newsprint. Centerfold is mostly secure. Minor interior tears at the margin may be present.

7.5 VERY FINE– (VF–): Fits the criteria for Very Fine but with an additional defect or small accumulation of defects that detracts from the book's appearance by a perceptible amount.

7.0 FINE/VERY FINE (FN/VF): An above-average copy that shows minor wear but is still relatively flat and clean with outstanding eye appeal. A small accumulation of minor bindery defects is allowed. Minor cover wear beginning to show with interior yellowing or tanning allowed, possibly including minor creases. Corners may be blunted or abraded. Inks are generally bright with a moderate reduction in reflectivity. Stamped or inked arrival dates may be present. No obvious soiling, staining or other discoloration, except for minor foxing. The slightest spine roll may be present, as well as a possible moderate color break. Staples may show some discoloration. Slight staple tears and a slight accumulation of light stress lines may be present. Slight rust migration. In rare cases, a comic was not stapled at the bindery and therefore has a missing staple; this is not considered a defect. Any staple can be replaced on books up to Fine, but only vintage staples can be used on books from Very Fine to Near Mint. Mint books must have original staples. Paper is tan to cream, but not brown. No hint of acidity in the odor of the newsprint. Centerfold is mostly secure. Minor interior tears at the margin may be present.

6.5 FINE+ (FN+): Fits the criteria for Fine but with an additional virtue or small accumulation of virtues that improves the book's appearance by a perceptible amount.

6.0 FINE (FN): An above-average copy that shows minor wear but is still relatively flat and clean with no significant creasing or other serious defects. Eye appeal is somewhat reduced because of slight surface wear and the accumulation of small defects, especially on the spine and edges. A FINE condition comic book appears to have been read a few times and has been handled with moderate care. Some accumulation of minor bindery defects is allowed. Minor cover wear apparent, with minor to moderate creases. Inks show a major reduction in reflectivity. Blunted or abraded corners are more common, as is minor staining, soiling, discoloration, and/or foxing. Stamped or inked arrival dates may be present. A minor spine roll is allowed. There can also be a 1/4" spine split or severe color break. Staples show minor discoloration. Minor staple tears and an accumulation of stress lines may be present, as well as minor rust migration. In rare cases, a comic was not stapled at the bindery and therefore has a missing staple; this is not considered a defect. Any staple can be replaced on books up to Fine, but only vintage staples can be used on books from Very Fine to Near Mint. Mint books must have original staples. Paper is brown to tan and fairly supple with no signs of brittleness. No hint of acidity in the odor of the newsprint. Minor interior tears at the margin may be present. Centerfold may be loose but not detached.

5.5 FINE– (FN–): Fits the criteria for Fine but with an additional defect or small accumulation of defects that detracts from the book's appearance by a perceptible amount.

5.0 VERY GOOD/FINE (VG/FN): An above-average but well-used comic book. A comic in this grade shows some moderate wear; eye appeal is somewhat reduced because of the accumulation of defects. Still a desirable copy that has been handled with some care. An accumulation of bindery defects is allowed. Minor to moderate cover wear apparent, with minor to moderate creases and/or dimples. Inks have major to extreme reduction in reflectivity. Blunted or abraded corners are increasingly common, as is minor to moderate staining, discoloration, and/or foxing. Stamped or inked arrival dates may be present. A minor to moderate spine roll is allowed. A spine split of up to 1/2" may be present. Staples show minor discoloration. A slight accumulation of minor staple tears and an accumulation of minor stress lines may also be present, as well as minor rust migration. In rare cases, a comic was not stapled at the bindery and therefore has a missing staple; this is not considered a defect. Any staple can be replaced on books up to Fine, but only vintage staples can be used on books from Very Fine to Near Mint. Mint books must have original staples. Paper is brown to tan with no signs of brittleness. May have the faintest trace of an acidic odor. Centerfold may be loose but not detached. Minor tears may also be present.

4.5 VERY GOOD+ (VG+): Fits the criteria for Very Good but with an additional virtue or small accumulation of virtues that improves the book's appearance by a perceptible amount.

4.0 VERY GOOD (VG): The average used comic book. A comic in this grade shows some significant moderate wear, but still has not accumulated enough total defects to reduce eye appeal to the point that it is not a desirable copy. Cover shows moderate to significant wear, and may be loose but not completely detached. Moderate to extreme reduction in reflectivity. Can have an accumulation of creases or dimples. Corners may be blunted or abraded. Store stamps, name stamps, arrival dates, initials, etc. have no effect on this grade. Some discoloration, fading, foxing, and even minor soiling is allowed. As much as a 1/4" triangle can be missing out of the corner or edge; a missing 1/8" square is also acceptable. Only minor unobtrusive tape and other amateur repair allowed on otherwise high grade copies. Moderate spine roll may be present and/or a 1" spine split. Staples discolored. Minor to moderate staple tears and stress lines may be present, as well as some rust migration. Paper is brown but not brittle. A minor acidic odor can be detectable. Minor to moderate tears may be present. Centerfold may be loose or detached at one staple.

3.5 VERY GOOD– (VG–): Fits the criteria for Very Good but with an additional defect or small accumulation of defects that detracts from the book's appearance by a perceptible amount.

3.0 GOOD/VERY GOOD (GD/VG): A used comic book showing some substantial wear. Cover shows significant wear, and may be loose or even detached at one staple. Cover reflectivity is very low. Can have a book-length crease and/or dimples. Corners may be blunted or even rounded. Discoloration, fading, foxing, and even minor to moderate soiling is allowed. A triangle from 1/4" to 1/2" can be missing out of the corner or edge; a missing 1/8" to 1/4" square is also acceptable. Tape and other amateur repair may be present. Moderate spine roll likely. May have a spine split of anywhere from 1" to 1-1/2". Staples may be rusted or replaced. Minor to moderate staple tears and moderate stress lines may be present, as well as some rust migration. Paper is brown but not brittle. Centerfold may be loose or detached at one staple. Minor to moderate interior tears may be present.

2.5 GOOD+ (GD+): Fits the criteria for Good but with an additional virtue or small accumulation of virtues that improves the book's appearance by a perceptible amount.

2.0 GOOD (GD): Shows substantial wear; often considered a "reading copy." Cover shows significant wear and may even be detached. Cover reflectivity is low and in some cases completely absent. Book-length creases and dimples may be present. Rounded corners are more common. Moderate soiling, staining, discoloration and foxing may be present. The largest piece allowed missing from the front or back cover is usually a 1/2" triangle or a 1/4" square, although some Silver Age books such as 1960s Marvels have had the price corner box clipped from the top left front cover and may be considered Good if they would otherwise have graded higher. Tape and other forms of amateur repair are common in Silver Age and older books. Spine roll is likely. May have up to a 2" spine split. Staples may be degraded, replaced or missing. Moderate staple tears and stress lines may be present, as well as rust migration. Paper is brown but not brittle. Centerfold may be loose or detached. Moderate interior tears may be present.

1.8 GOOD– (GD–): Fits the criteria for Good but with an additional defect or small accumulation of defects that detracts from the book's appearance by a perceptible amount.

1.5 FAIR/GOOD (FR/GD): A comic showing substantial to heavy wear. A copy in this grade still has all pages and covers, although there may be pieces missing. Books in this grade are commonly creased, scuffed, abraded, soiled, and possibly unattractive, but still generally readable. Cover shows considerable wear and may be detached. Nearly no reflectivity to no reflectivity remaining. Store stamp, name stamp, arrival date and initials are permitted. Book-length creases, tears and folds may be present. Rounded corners are increasingly common. Soiling, staining, discoloration and foxing is generally present. Up to 1/10 of the back cover may be missing. Tape and other forms of amateur repair are increasingly common in Silver Age and older books. Spine roll is common. May have a spine split between 2" and 2/3 the length of the book. Staples may be degraded, replaced or missing. Staple tears and stress lines are common, as well as rust migration. Paper is brown and may show brittleness around the edges. Acidic odor may be present. Centerfold may be loose or detached. Interior tears are common.

1.0 FAIR (FR): A copy in this grade shows heavy wear. Some collectors consider this the lowest collectible grade because comic books in lesser condition are usually incomplete and/or brittle. Comics in this grade are usually soiled, faded, ragged and possibly unattractive. This is the last grade in which a comic remains generally readable. Cover may be detached, and inks have lost all reflectivity. Creases, tears and/or folds are prevalent. Corners are commonly rounded or absent. Soiling and staining is present. Books in this condition generally have all pages and most of the covers, although there may be up to 1/4 of the front cover missing or no back cover, but not both. Tape and other forms of amateur repair are more common. Spine roll is more common; spine split can extend up to 2/3 the length of the book. Staples may be missing or show rust and discoloration. An accumulation of staple tears and stress lines may be present, as well as rust migration. Paper is brown and may show brittleness around the edges but not in the central portion of the pages. Acidic odor may be present. Accumulation of interior tears. Chunks may be missing. The centerfold may be missing if readability is generally preserved (although there may be difficulty). Coupons may be cut.

0.5 POOR (PR): Most comic books in this grade have been sufficiently degraded to the point where there is little or no collector value; they are easily identified by a complete absence of eye appeal. Comics in this grade are brittle almost to the point of turning to dust with a touch, and are usually incomplete. Extreme cover fading may render the cover almost indiscernible. May have extremely severe stains, mildew or heavy cover abrasion to the point that some cover inks are indistinct/absent. Covers may be detached with large chunks missing. Can have extremely ragged edges and extensive creasing. Corners are rounded or virtually absent. Covers may have been defaced with paints, varnishes, glues, oil, indelible markers or dyes, and may have suffered heavy water damage. Can also have extensive amateur repairs such as laminated covers. Extreme spine roll present; can have extremely ragged spines or a complete, book-length split. Staples can be missing or show extreme rust and discoloration. Extensive staple tears and stress lines may be present, as well as extreme rust migration. Paper exhibits moderate to severe brittleness (where the comic book literally falls apart when examined). Extreme acidic odor may be present. Extensive interior tears. Multiple pages, including the centerfold, may be missing that affect readability. Coupons may be cut.

PUBLISHERS' CODES

The following abbreviations are used with cover reproductions throughout the book for copyright purposes:

ABC-America's Best Comics
AC-AC Comics
ACE-Ace Periodicals
ACG-American Comics Group
AJAX-Ajax-Farrell
AP-Archie Publications
ATLAS-Atlas Comics (see below)
AVON-Avon Periodicals
BP-Better Publications
C & L-Cupples & Leon
CC-Charlton Comics
CEN-Centaur Publications
CCG-Columbia Comics Group
CG-Catechetical Guild
CHES-Harry 'A' Chesler
CLDS-Classic Det. Stories
CM-Comics Magazine
CN-Cartoon Network
CPI-Conan Properties Inc.
DC-DC Comics, Inc.
DELL-Dell Publishing Co.
DH-Dark Horse
DIS-Disney Enterprises, Inc.
DMP-David McKay Publishing
DS-D. S. Publishing Co.
EAS-Eastern Color Printing Co.
EC-E. C. Comics
ECL-Eclipse Comics
ENWIL-Enwil Associates
EP-Elliott Publications
ERB-Edgar Rice Burroughs
FAW-Fawcett Publications
FC-First Comics
FF-Famous Funnies
FH-Fiction House Magazines
FOX-Fox Features Syndicate
GIL-Gilberton
GK-Gold Key
GP-Great Publications
HARV-Harvey Publications
H-B-Hanna-Barbera
HILL-Hillman Periodicals
HOKE-Holyoke Publishing Co.
IM-Image Comics
KING-King Features Syndicate
LEV-Lev Gleason Publications
MAL-Malibu Comics
MAR-Marvel Characters, Inc.
ME-Magazine Enterprises
MLJ-MLJ Magazines
MS-Mirage Studios
NOVP-Novelty Press
NYNS-New York News Syndicate
PG-Premier Group
PINE-Pines
PMI-Parents' Magazine Institute
PRIZE-Prize Publications
QUA-Quality Comics Group
REAL-Realistic Comics
RH-Rural Home
S & S-Street and Smith Publishers
SKY-Skywald Publications
STAR-Star Publications
STD-Standard Comics
STJ-St. John Publishing Co.
SUPR-Superior Comics
TC-Tower Comics
TM-Trojan Magazines
TMP-Todd McFarlane Prods.
TOBY-Toby Press
TOPS-Tops Comics
UFS-United Features Syndicate
VAL-Valiant
VITL-Vital Publications
WB-Warner Brothers.
WEST-Western Publishing Co.
WHIT-Whitman Publishing Co.
WHW-William H. Wise
WMG-William M. Gaines (E. C.)
WP-Warren Publishing Co.
YM-Youthful Magazines
Z-D-Ziff-Davis Publishing Co.

OVERSTREET ADVISORS

Even before the first edition of *The Overstreet Comic Book Price Guide* was printed, author Robert M. Overstreet solicited pricing data, historical notations, and general information from a variety of sources. What was initially an informal group offering input quickly became an organized field of comic book collectors, dealers and historians whose opinions are actively solicited in advance of each edition of this book. Some of these Overstreet Advisors are specialists who deal in particular niches within the comic book world, while others are generalists who are interested in commenting on the broader marketplace. Each advisor provides information from their respective areas of interest and expertise, spanning the history of American comics.

While some choose to offer pricing and historical information in the form of annotated sales catalogs, auction catalogs, or documented private sales, assistance from others comes in the form of the market reports such as those beginning on page 70 in this book. In addition to those who have served as Overstreet Advisors almost since *The Guide*'s inception, each year new contributors are sought.

With that in mind, we are pleased to present our newest Overstreet Advisors:

THE CLASS OF 2010

GRANT ADEY
Fats Comics
Brisbane, QLD, Australia

ANDREW COOKE
Writer/Director
New York City, NY

JON B. COOKE
Editor - *Comic Book Artist* Magazine
West Kingston, RI

KEN DYBER
Collector
Portland, OR

BRENT MOESHLIN
Quality Comix
Montgomery, AL

GREG REECE
Greg Reece's Rare Comics
Ijamsville, MD

MARK SQUIREK
Diamond International Galleries
Timonium, MD

CHRIS SWARTZ
Collector
San Diego, CA

MIKE WILBUR
Diamond International Galleries
Timonium, MD

A complete listing of our Overstreet Advisors can be found on our title page and beginning on page 1104.

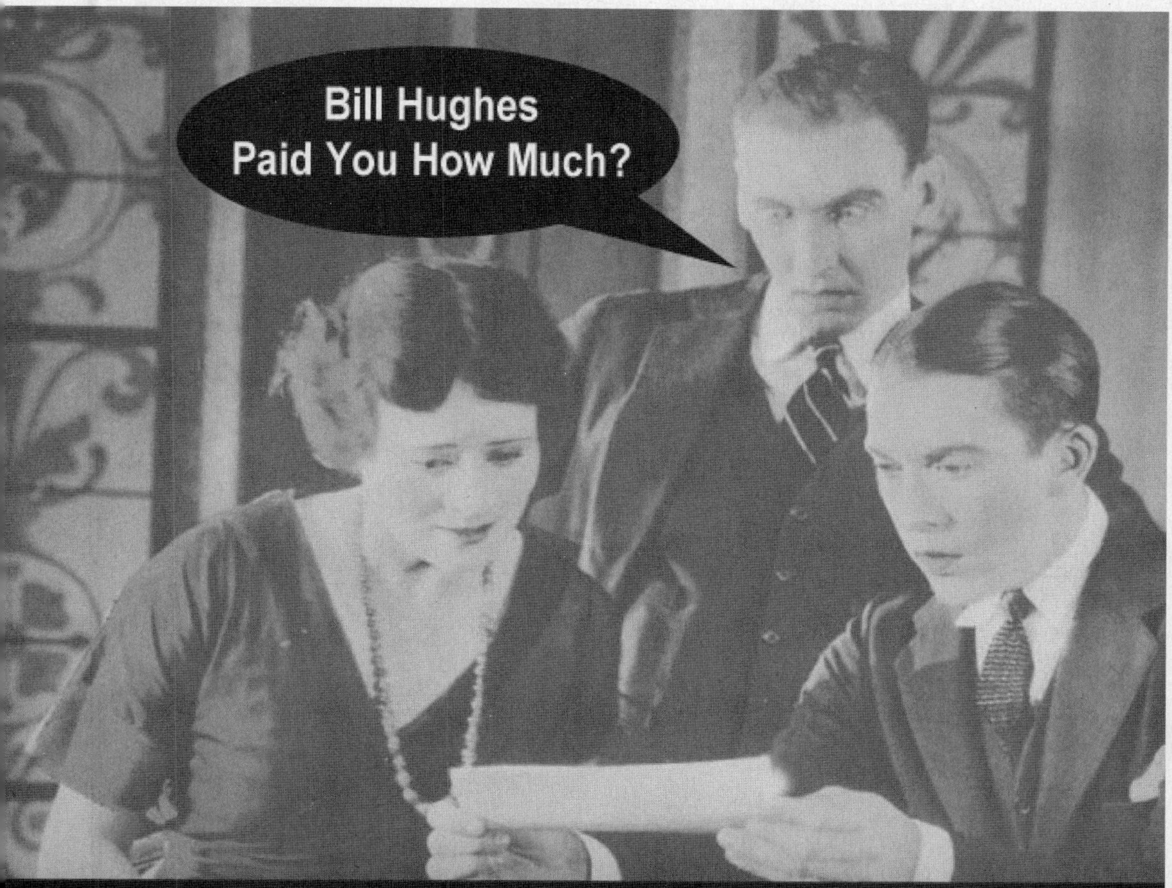

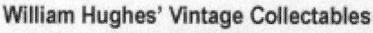

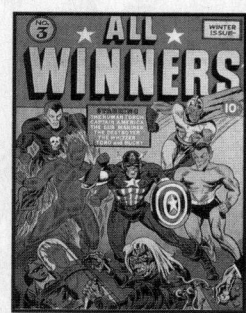

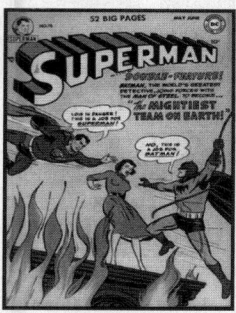

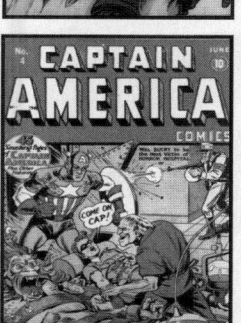

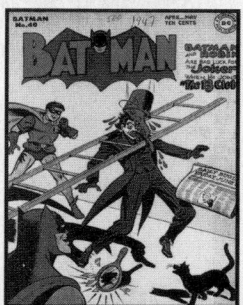

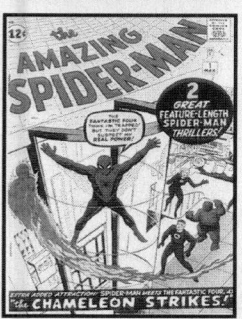

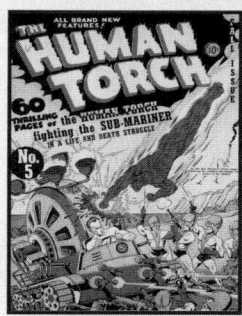

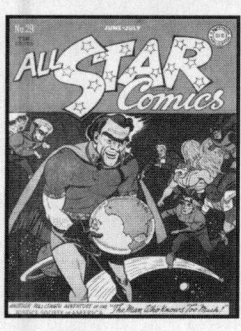

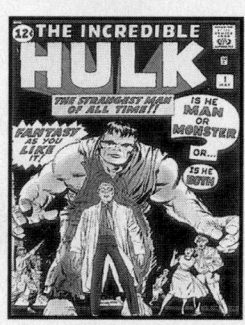

DISCOVER...
Senior Advisor
Overstreet
Price Guide

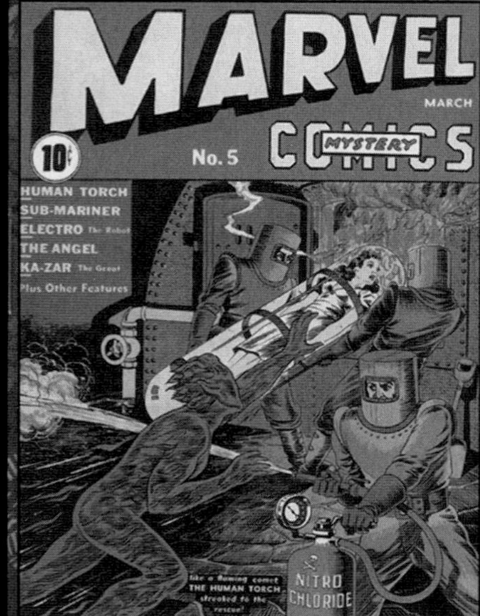

MARVEL
MARCH
10¢
No. 5
MYSTERY COMICS
HUMAN TORCH
SUB-MARINER
ELECTRO The Robot
THE ANGEL
KA-ZAR The Great
Plus Other Features
NITRO CHLORIDE
Like a flaming comet THE HUMAN TORCH streaked to the rescue!

12¢
the AMAZING SPIDER-MAN
APPROVED BY THE COMICS CODE AUTHORITY
1 MAR.
THE FANTASTIC FOUR THINK I'M TRAPPED! BUT THEY DON'T SUSPECT MY REAL POWER!
2 GREAT FEATURE-LENGTH SPIDER-MAN THRILLERS!
EXTRA ADDED ATTRACTION: SPIDER-MAN MEETS THE FANTASTIC FOUR, AS
"the CHAMELEON STRIKES!"

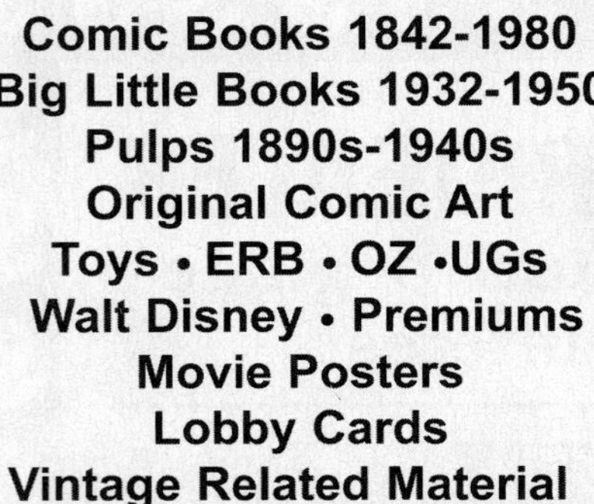

BLB
COMICS

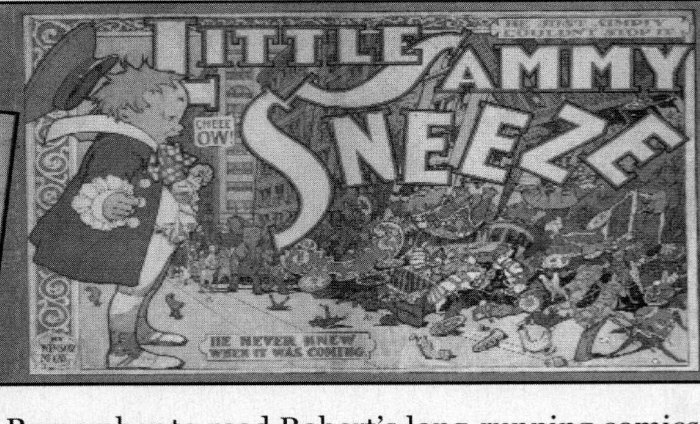

LITTLE SAMMY SNEEZE
HE NEVER KNEW WHEN IT WAS COMING

WHY?

Yes, this is what we ask ourselves when a collection has sold for less than what we would pay. You have everything to gain by contacting us.

Here are some of the major collections we have purchased by outbidding our competition:

THE DENVER COLLECTION

THE LOS GATOS COLLECTION

THE CALIFORNIA COLLECTION

THE ALLENTOWN COLLECTION

THE NOVA SCOTIA COLLECTION

THE TEXAS COLLECTION

Why did these collectors sell to us? Quite honestly we paid more than anyone else. These collectors made the right choice by contacting us. Shouldn't you find out what we have to say? For immediate payment, honesty, integrity, and a respect for your needs call or email us today.

Give us the opportunity to pay you your best price!
Call 603-869-2097 today!

JAMES PAYETTE
Rare Books & Comics
P.O. Box 750 • Bethlehem, NH 03574
Tel (603) 869-2097 • Fax (603) 869-3475
www.jamespayettecomics.com
jimpayette@msn.com

CREDENTIALS

Special Advisor to Overstreet Guide	1985–present
Member AACBC	1990–present
Sotheby's Authenticating, Certification, and Grading committee	1991–2002
Experience as a Dealer/Collector	since 1975
CBG Customer Service Award Winner for many years	

PLEASE SEE OUR OTHER ADS FOR FURTHER REFERENCE

We are paying 65% of Guide for the following:

Action 16-200
Adventure 32–100
All American
All Flash
All Top 8–18
Blonde Phantom
Blue Beetle 47–57
Brenda Starr 1–12
Crash
Daring Mystery
Fantastic
Flash (1st)
Hit 1–20
John Wayne
JO-JO 7–29
Kid Komics
Miss Fury
More Fun 52–107
Mysterious Adventure
Mystic (1st)
National 1–23
New Book of Comics
Pep 1–21
Phantom Lady
Phantom Stranger
Rangers 1-20
Rulah
Science (Fox)
Sensation
Silver Streak 1-17
Smash
Speed 1-20
Strange Tales 1–100
U.S.A. 1-5
Weird Comics
Zoot 7–16

We are paying 60% of Guide for the following:

Adventure 101–200
Adv. of Bob Hope 1–50
Adv. of Jerry Lewis 1-50
Adv. of Ozzie & Harriet
Air Fighters
All Star
Amazing Spiderman 3–10
America's Greatest
Batman 2-100
Blue Ribbon 2-20
Brave & the Bold 1–20
Bulletman
Captain Marvel
Captain Marvel Jr.
Captain Midnight
Challengers 1–10
Comic Cavalcade 1–29
Daredevil 1st 1–20
Detective 28-100
Dollman
Fantastic Four 3–10
Fight 1–30
Frontier Fighters
Green Hornet 1–20
Green Lantern (1st)
House of Mystery 1–50
House of Secrets 1–25
Ibis
Journey Into Mystery 1–115
Jumbo 11–50
Jungle 1–50
Lash Larue 1–46
Leading 1–14
Legend of D. Boone
Marvel Family
Mary Marvel
Master
Military
Modern
Movie Comics (D.C.)
My Greatest Adv. 1–50
Mystery in Space 1–50
Nickel
Planet
Police 1–20
Red Ryder 1-100
Saint
Shadow (1st)
Showcase 1–3, 5-20
Shield Wizard
Spy Smasher
Star Spangled
Superman 2–125
Superman's Pal 2–30
Strange Adventure 1–120
Superboy 1–50
Top-Notch
W.D. Comics & Stories 1–40
Whiz
World's Finest 1–110
Zip 1–39

We are also paying 50-100% of Guide for many other titles. Comics must be properly graded and complete. Please send your listing of comics for sale or a list of comics you wish to purchase. We are dealing in Marvels, D.C.'s, Timelys, Nedors, Western, Funny Material and much more! Please check our web site or send for our 100-page catalog. We will travel for large collections or, if you're passing through the area, call for an appointment.

JAMES PAYETTE
Rare Books & Comics
P.O. Box 750 • Bethlehem, NH 03574
Tel (603) 869-2097 • Fax (603) 869-3475
www.jamespayettecomics.com
jimpayette@msn.com

CREDENTIALS

Special Advisor to Overstreet Guide	1985–present
Member AACBC	1990–present
Sotheby's Authenticating, Certification, and Grading committee	1991–2002
Experience as a Dealer/Collector	since 1975
CBG Customer Service Award Winner for many years	

PLEASE SEE OUR OTHER ADS FOR FURTHER REFERENCE

DON'T BUY OR SELL ANOTHER

This X-men #66 had previously graded CGC 9.2. Utilizing the **pressing service**, the book obtained a CGC 9.6 grade upon resubmission. Cost for pressing: $25.

A Batman #1 with an ugly sticker on the front cover, dying to be removed using the **conservation service**. Cost for conservation: $125.

WHAT WE DO

For over a decade, Classics Incorporated has been helping collectors preserve their treasures. Given the advanced state of the hobby these days, it's imperative that you make the right decisions whether you're buying or selling one comic, or an entire collection. Classics Incorporated is an expert in all aspects of the marketplace, from third-party grading and auctions, to pedigreed comics, restoration, and investment consulting. Our accuracy in CGC grading, pressing and valuation is unparalleled. Using our unique combination of services and advice will ensure that you make the best decision for your comics.

The process is easy. Our website classicsincorporated.com will answer any questions you have about our services, and guide you through the easy process of submission. In addition, the website offers many insights into the marketplace, including published articles, comic valuation tables, before and after pictures of our work, and links to helpful sites that delve deeper into the nuances of comic collecting. You will not find such a complete accumulation of crucial information anywhere else.

A quick look at a few of the many services we offer:

PRESSING

One of the most popular services used by our clients today, pressing is best utilized for **high grade, unrestored comics**. Pressing is not considered restoration, and is used to remove light defects to make a high grade even higher (for example, pressing a Spider-man #20 from CGC 9.0 to 9.2). The age of the comic does not matter, and because of the low cost of pressing (as low as $12 per book), the comic's value does not have to be high for the service to be beneficial. But it takes practice to find the right candidates for pressing. Many factors must be considered for each book, such as how to spot "bad" and "good" defects. Guidelines are set forth on classicsincorporated.com so you can make informed decisions before sending us your books for review.

CONSERVATION

Another low-cost service, conservation best suits **lower to mid grade comics in the GD to VF range**. Its main goal is to rid a comic book of harmful agents (tape, glue, stains, mold), and/or improve the appearance and

(972) 980-8040 • 1440 Halsey Way, Suite 114 • Carrollton, TX 75007 • www.classicsincorporated.com

desirability through light restorative techniques. Comics older than 1964 are the best candidates for conservation, although there are exceptions. Value is not a significant factor due to the low cost of conservation, which starts at $30. Conservation can include water, dry, and solvent cleaning, tear seals, support, staple cleaning/replacement and pressing. A breakdown of costs can be found on classicsincorporated.com.

This Amazing Fantasy #15 is a prime **restoration** candidate. Other than the torn off logo area, the book is in VF. Current value is $750.

RESTORATION

The eldest of the services offered, restoration targets **low grade comics in the FA to GD+ range**. It utilizes every weapon in our arsenal to maximize the grade of a comic, including piece replacement, grafting and color matching. The best candidates for restoration are pre-1960 comics with a current value of $1000 or more. The truth is as many as 50% of comics submitted to us for restoration are turned down because the work is either unnecessary or detrimental to its value. But restoring the right candidates can produce eye-popping results. Classicsincorporated.com offers guidelines that will aid you in finding the right books for this service. We also offer free appraisals on emailed scans and online auctions.

RE-CREATION

This service is strictly for coverless comics, particularly the key issues like Spider-man #1, Superman #1, and Marvel Comics #1. We attach exact replicas of covers onto these **coverless comics**, each cut to fit the comic perfectly. Many collectors purchase coverless key issues because of their affordability. This service allows the comic to appear complete without the collector having to pay thousands of dollars more for a real cover. Cost is $150 per cover, and includes any necessary interior support, tear seals, assembly and pressing. Check classicsincorporated.com for more information and a complete list of available covers.

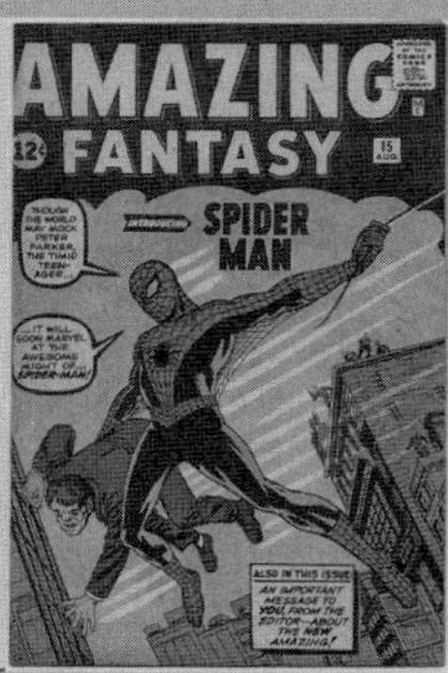

The same Amazing Fantasy #15 after restoration. Its new grade is VF, with a value of $2000. Cost of restoration: $650

RESTORATION REMOVAL

On occasion, you may find minor unnecessary restoration on one of your books. Is removal feasible? Minor professional restoration, such as tear seals and support using rice paper and water-soluble adhesive, and acrylic and water-based color touch are the safest to remove. In some cases a book's value can significantly increase with this service, but great care must be taken in choosing the right candidates. Check classicsincorporated.com if you think you have a book that can benefit from restoration removal.

COMICS TO ASTONISH
WE SELL!
-COMICS OLD AND NEW!
-MAGIC THE GATHERING!
-WIZKIDS!
-NON SPORT CARDS!
-GRADED COMICS!
-STATUES!
-ACTION FIGURES!
-TPB'S!
-MANGA AND ANIME!
-DC DIRECT!
-COMIC SUPPLIES!
9400 SNOWDEN RIVER PKWY
COLUMBIA, MD 21045
MONDAY-SATURDAY 12-8PM
410-381-2732
Check out our new website w/h tons of CGC books
CONTACT:
KEEGAN F. CONRAD
410-381-2732
COMICS2U@AOL.COM
VBBB
WE BUY!
-ALL COMICS 30'S TO 80'S!
-ENTIRE COLLECTIONS!
-BRONZE TO GOLDEN AGE!
-GRADED BOOKS!
WE HAVE OVER 80,000 BACK ISSUES!
X-Men ©2010 Marvel Characters, Inc. All rights reserved.
WWW.COMICSTOASTONISH.COM

Hear what Collectors are saying about CGC.

"CGC is a GREAT organization and the staff and company are simply the best out there. I believe that CGC is going to stay the industry leader of which the other small timers will try to strive for, but never even come close to reaching."
Michael Gray • Collector

"I want to say that the level of service that your company has provided so far has been first rate. On my family's vacation to Florida in August, Scott agreed on short notice to accept my books for grading in person. What a terrific experience. Friendly reception, great communication and consistent grading among all of my books. You guys do a terrific job. Despite the heated discussions going around regarding grading consistency (I suppose everyone thinks their books are NM!!) I understand your position and the pressure involved to perform. I commend you on your ability to remain consistent, as far as I can see, in your grading standards."
Roy Delic • Collector

"Thanks for the excellent service I consistently receive from you! I have been in this field for over 40 years, and appreciate the important role that third party grading can have in facilitating the wonderful world of rare comic books. Over time I have personally developed a tremendous respect for all of the effort that CGC puts into its operation. There are very few people I will let handle my best comics, but I have met CGC's Mark Haspel and the CGC grading team and trust them with my books. Doing business with CGC has been a real pleasure. Thanks CGC!"
Charles Wooley • Collector and Dealer

"Thank you for your professional service during my visit to your operations. I am now more confident your abilities to be the best grading service in comics for the collector, investor or dealer. After seeing every aspect of the operation, one could see that CGC will be the main player in securing high grade comics for all of us!"
Dan Davis • Collector

"The CGC grading team are real professionals. The service you provide fills the credibility gap in comic book collection which private collectors (like me) have been searching for. Your service has further legitimized this collectible."
Michael Katz • Collector

"I recently sold a several hundred comic book collection book by book for $12,000 on eBay. Unfortunately, I only submitted a few books to CGC. What a mistake! Were I to do it again, I would have submitted everything. The graded books went at guide or much better every time. The ungraded books went at a discount to guide, simply because one person's grading standards vary from another. The CGC grade was one that everyone trusted."
Mike Finn • Collector

"I've been a collector since 1974...I have certainly seen this hobby mature through the years. I truly feel that CGC has been the catalyst to finally bring a standard structure to our hobby — no small feat! CGC has carried our hobby to a new level of integrity and safety that was much needed. All while providing outstanding professionalism, quality and customer service. THANKS!!!"
Jon Lindstrom • Collector

"CGC has taken the guessing game out of the comic business for me. I can't imagine going back to the days of overgrazed comics and undisclosed restoration. CGC has set a standard of grading in the hobby that has taken everyone's grading to another level. I think what I appreciate most about the CGC staff is their courtesy and professionalism. They follow through with what they say and treat the customer with respect. My hats off to Scott and Korey."
Jeff Williams • Collector

"CGC has added real value to collections. I am very excited that Overstreet has recognized CGC's expertise and I hope that the result will be a new price guide which reflects the true marketplace."
Scott Collins • Collector

"My opinion of CGC's grading has been verified. I want to thank you and the CGC grading team for your honesty and your accuracy and look forward to many many years of future grading."
Kennith M. Basteiro • Collector

"I have been happily following CGC's impact on the marketplace. Speaking as a collector that has been into comics for over 30 years, and the founder of the Western PA collection, I believe such a service is long overdue in this hobby."
Michael Friedlander • Collector

"I have been a part of comic fandom since 1963. Since having my first comics graded in 2002, I have had nothing but good things to say about my experience with CGC. The CGC grading team has been consistent with their grading and turn around times. I know I am one of the few "underground" comics collectors around and I really appreciate the extra time and effort Mark Haspel has put into the analysis of each book to verify its proper printing and grade."
Howard Gerber • Collector

"If it wasn't for the advice and help of the CGC grading team, I wouldn't have known about the alterations to the book. I can only imagine the horror and disappointment in finding out later. I really appreciate all your extra efforts and taking the time to help me. You've been great. CGC provides an invaluable resource to collectors. I'm glad you guys are around to make a new era of collecting a better place."
Rob Gonzalez • Collector

Showcase and protect your comics with the only expert, impartial 3rd party grading company in the hobby. Call 1-877-NM-COMIC or visit www.CGCcomics.com for information on submitting your comic books to CGC.

P.O. Box 4738 | Sarasota, Florida 34230 | 1-877-NM-COMIC (662-6642) | www.CGCcomics.com

An Independent Member of the Certified Collectibles Group

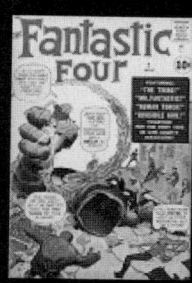

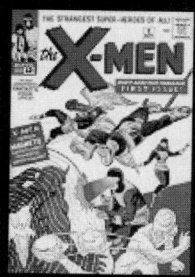

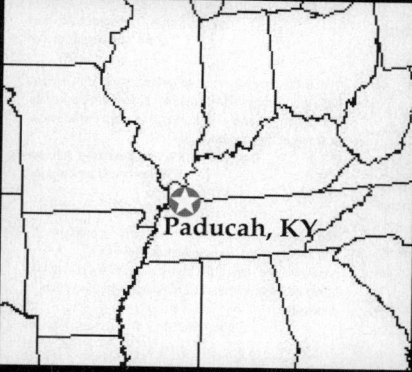

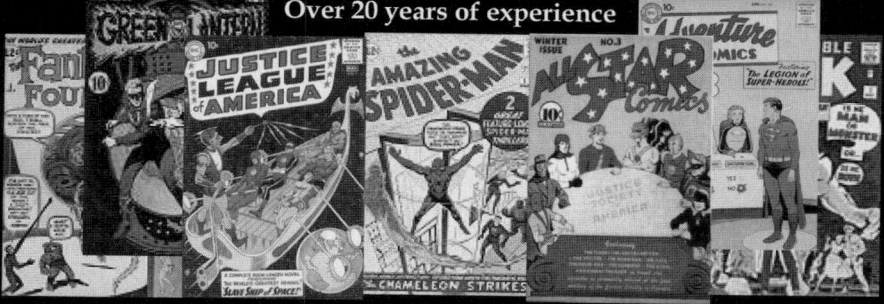

FAN
FANDOM ADVISORY NETWORK™

UNBEATABLE!

RECORD SALES!

A Million+ Reasons to consign with Pedigree Comics and sell in their GRAND AUCTIONS!...

PEDIGREE COMICS SALES:

Comic	Grade	Note	Price	Year
INCREDIBLE HULK 1	CGC 9.0		$100,000	2009
TALES TO ASTONISH 27	CGC 9.4		$75,000	2009
AVENGERS 1	CGC 9.0		$25,500	2009
AVENGERS 2	CGC 9.8		$70,000	2009
AVENGERS 4	CGC 9.4		$25,000	2009
FANTASTIC FOUR 1	CGC 9.6		$175,00 (PLUS TRADE)	2008
TALES OF SUSPENSE 39	CGC 9.2		$35,000	2008
INCREDIBLE HULK 1	CGC 8.5		$32,500	2008
AMAZING FANTASY 15	CGC 9.0	CURATOR	$60,000	2007
AMAZING SPIDER-MAN 1	CGC 9.0		$34,000	2007
AMAZING SPIDER-MAN 12	CGC 9.6	PACIFIC COAST	$16,500	2007
FANTASTIC FOUR 1	CGC 8.5		$50,000	2007
INCREDIBLE HULK 181	CGC 9.8		$18,000	2007
STRANGE TALES 101	CGC 9.4		$10,000	2007
STRANGE TALES ANNUAL 2	CGC 9.8	PACIFIC COAST	$25,000	2007
TALES TO ASTONISH 27	CGC 9.2		$17,000	2007
FANTASTIC FOUR 4	CGC 9.4		$18,000	2006
FANTASTIC FOUR 5	CGC 9.2		$21,000	2006
JOURNEY INTO MYSTERY 112	CGC 9.6	MASSACHUSETTS	$14,500	2006
X-MEN 94	CGC 9.8		$25,000	2006
AMAZING SPIDER-MAN 1	CGC 9.6	WHITE MOUNTAIN	$110,000	2005
AMAZING SPIDER-MAN 14	CGC 9.6	PACIFIC COAST	$24,500	2005
GIANT-SIZE X-MEN 1	CGC 9.8		$12,750	2005
AMAZING FANTASY 15	CGC 9.4	WHITE MOUNTAIN	$150,000	2004
INCREDIBLE HULK 1	CGC 9.2	NORTHLAND	$75,000	2004
INCREDIBLE HULK 4	CGC 9.6		$20,000	2004
X-MEN 1	CGC 9.6	PACIFIC COAST	$100,000	2004

2009/2010 GRAND AUCTION RESULTS:

Comic	Grade	Note	Price
AMAZING FANTASY 15	CGC 9.2		$190,000
FANTASTIC FOUR 1	CGC 9.2		$143,000
TALES OF SUSPENSE 39	CGC 9.4		$114,990
FANTASTIC FOUR 1	CGC 8.5		$75,100
AVENGERS 4	CGC 9.6		$64,000
DAREDEVIL 1	CGC 9.6		$62,000
X-MEN 1	CGC 9.2		$55,000
FANTASTIC FOUR 1	CGC 8.0		$50,400
X-MEN 1	CGC 9.0		$33,333
INCREDIBLE HULK 181	CGC 9.8	CGC SIGNATURE SERIES	$32,001
X-MEN 94	CGC 9.8		$29,589
FANTASTIC FOUR 10	CGC 9.6		$27,999
AMAZING SPIDER-MAN 34	CGC 9.8		$25,250
FANTASTIC FOUR 26	CGC 9.6		$24,200
FANTASTIC FOUR 112	CGC 9.8		$24,017
ATOM 1	CGC 9.6		$21,000
AMAZING SPIDER-MAN 5	CGC 9.4		$19,250
AVENGERS 2	CGC 9.4		$13,500
TALES OF SUSPENSE 58	CGC 9.4		$12,755
NEW MUTANTS 98	CGC 9.9		$12,250

Charter Member Dealer

Pedigree Comics, Inc. • 12541 Equine Lane • Wellington, Florida 33414
www.PedigreeComics.com • email: DougSchmell@pedigreecomics.com
Toll Free: (877) 6-COMICS [626-6427] • Cell: (561) 596-9111 • Fax: (561) 422-1120

Sale Reporting Partner
GPAnalysis

FROM OUR STORE TO
MIDTOWN COMICS NYC
NYC #1
MIDTOWN COMICS.COM
BACK ISSUES ONLINE!
NO GIMMICKS, JUST GREAT PRICES!
THOUSANDS OF ITEMS ADDED DAILY!
FASTEST DELIVERY IN THE INDUSTRY!
SUBSCRIBE ONLINE! NEVER MISS AN ISSUE!
SPECIAL SAVINGS!
SUBSCRIBE TO MIDTOWN'S NEWSLETTER FOR EXCITING WEEKLY CODEWORD SALES!
MIDTOWN COMICS® NYC
TIMES SQUARE - 200 W. 40TH ST.
GRAND CENTRAL - 459 LEXINGTON AVE.

MUST VISIT WHILE IN
NOIS
FREE PULL & HOLD SERVICE!
OUT OF STATE? VISIT OUR WEBSITE!
GOLD/SILVER/MODERN!
EXCLUSIVE COVERS!
AMAZING SELECTION!
WE ALSO BUY COMICS!!
CALL BRIAN
(815) 254-3410
to set up an appointment!
CRACKERS.COM

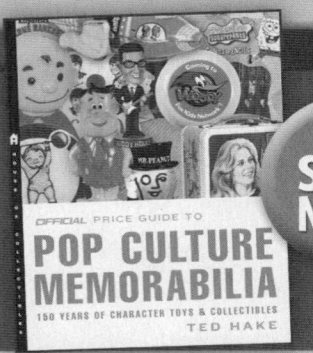

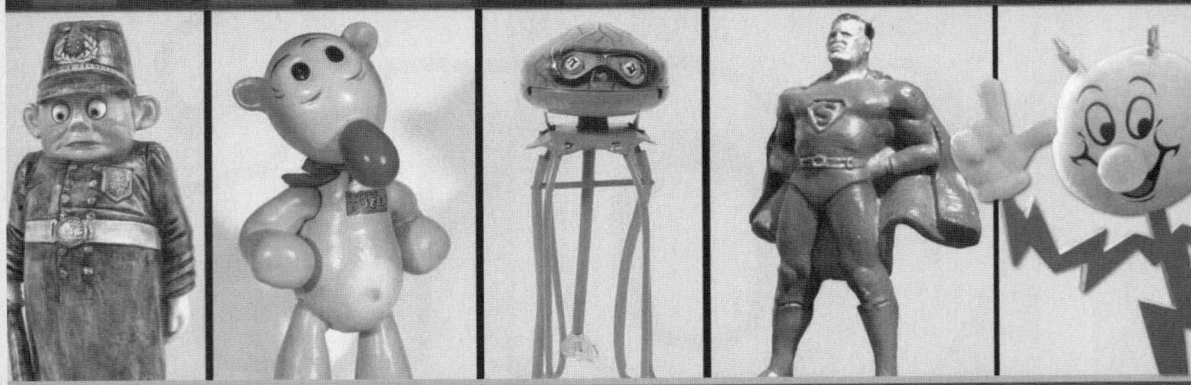

COMICS TO ASTONISH
9400 SNOWDEN RIVER PKWY
COLUMBIA, MD 21045
MONDAY-SATURDAY 12-8PM
410-381-2732
WE BUY!
- ALL COMICS 30'S TO 80'S!
- ENTIRE COLLECTIONS!
- BRONZE TO GOLDEN AGE!
- GRADED BOOKS!
CONTACT:
KEEGAN F. CONRAD
410-381-2732
COMICS2U@AOL.COM
WE HAVE OVER
80,000
BACK ISSUES!
NOVA
ROCKS!
Check out our
new website w/h
tons of CGC books
CHECK OUT OUR WEB COMIC AT:
WWW.FATGUYBLACKGUYBALDGUY.COM
WWW.COMICSTOASTONISH.COM

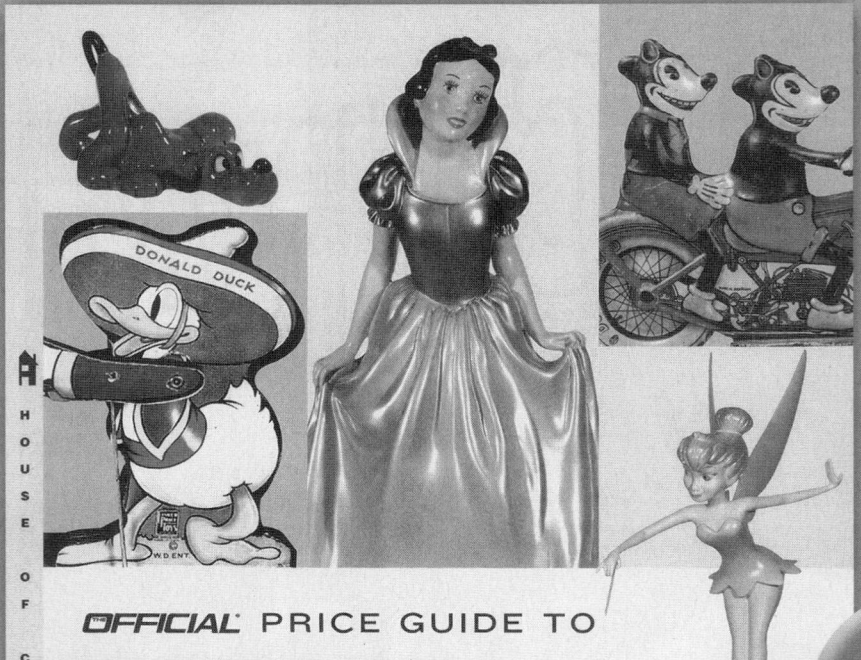

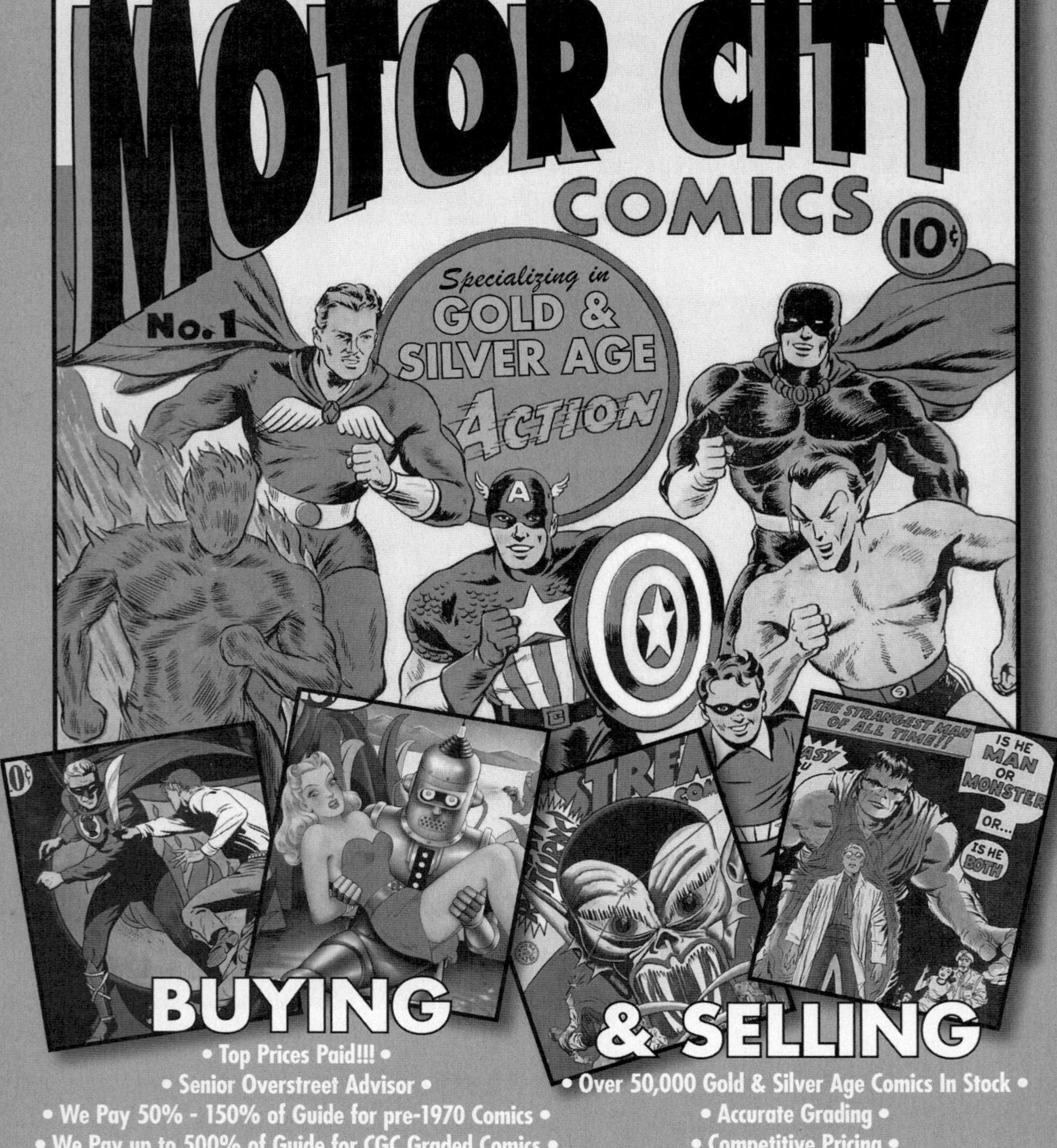
MOTOR CITY
COMICS
10¢
No. 1
Specializing in
GOLD &
SILVER AGE
ACTION
THE STRANGEST MAN OF ALL TIME!!
IS HE MAN OR MONSTER
OR...
IS HE BOTH
BUYING
& SELLING

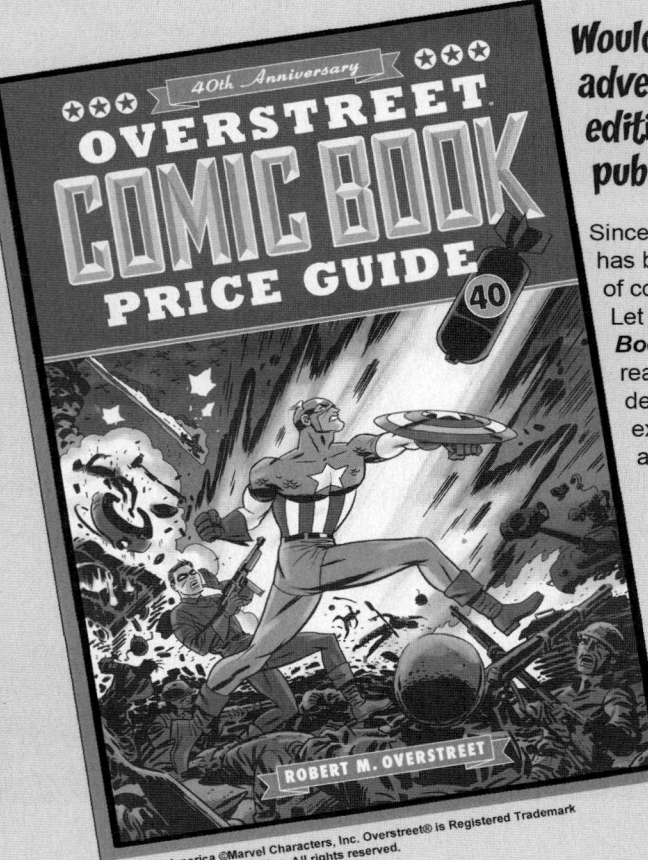

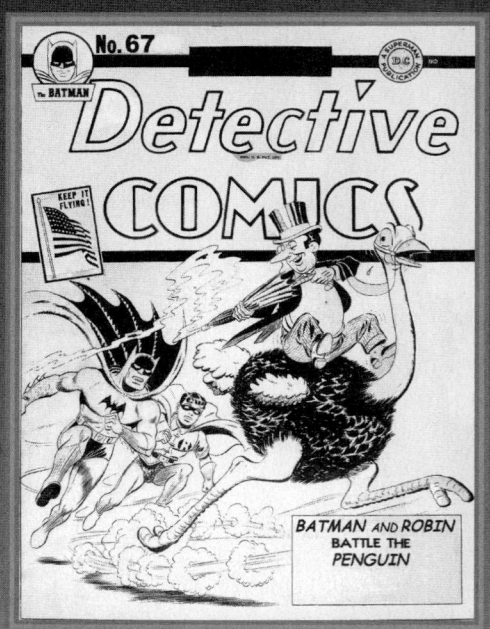

SPIDER-MAN
15¢ 87 AUG
MARVEL COMICS GROUP
the AMAZING BEST COMICS
EST. 1991
INTERNATIONAL
I MADE THE MISTAKE OF TRADING WITH SOMEONE ELSE!
WE BUY AND SELL ORIGINAL ART AND PRINTS!
WE ACCEPT ALL FOREIGN AND DOMESTIC ORDERS!!
PETER!! WHAT A MISTAKE!
YOU SHOULDN'T HAVE!!
IF YOU VISIT ONE STORE IT SHOULD BE... BEST COMICS!!
HOW COULD YOU!?
I TOLD YOU TO USE TOMMY!!
ROMITA
WE HAVE ALL OF THE OLD COMICS YOUR MOTHER THREW OUT!!
NEW COMICS AND STATUES EVERY WEEK!
BESTCOMICS.COM
CGC AND RAW BOOKS AVAILABLE!
1300 JERICHO TURNPIKE
NEW HYDE PARK, NY. 11040
516-328-1900
WE BUY GOLDEN, SILVER, AND BRONZE AGE COMICS, TOYS, AND STATUES.
TOMMYBEST@AOL.COM
all characters copyright Marvel Comics all rights reserved 2010

COMIC

- **Timelys**
- **MLJs**
- **Golden Age DCs**
- **"Mile High" Copies (Church Collection)**
- **"San Francisco," "Bethlehem" and "Chicago" Copies**
- **1950s Horror and Sci-Fi Comics**
- **Fox/Quality/ECs**
- **Silver Age Marvels and DCs**
- **Most other brands and titles from the Golden and Silver Age**

Specializing In Large Silver And Golden Age Collections

HEAVEN

I N G

JOHN VERZYL AND DAUGHTER ROSE, "HARD AT WORK."

John Verzyl started collecting comic books in 1965, and within ten years he had amassed thousands of Golden and Silver Age comic books. In 1979, with his wife Nanette, he opened "COMIC HEAVEN," a retail store devoted entirely to the buying and selling of comic books.

Over the years, John Verzyl has come to be recognized as an authority in the field of comic books. He has served as a special advisor to the "Overstreet Comic Book Price Guide" for the last 25 years. Thousands of his "mint" comics were photographed for Ernst Gerber's "Photo-Journal Guide to Comic Books." His tables and displays at the annual San Diego Comic Convention and the Chicago Comic Convention draw customers from all over the country.

The first COMIC HEAVEN AUCTION was held in 1987, and today his Auction Catalogs are mailed out to more than ten thousand interested collectors and dealers.

Comic Heaven
John and Nanette Verzyl
P.O. Box 900
Big Sandy, TX 75755
www.comicheaven.net
1-903-636-5555

THESE DIDN'T HAPPEN WITHOUT YOUR HELP.

The Overstreet Comic Book Price Guide doesn't happen by magic. A network of advisors – made up of experienced dealers, collectors and comics historians – gives us input for every edition we publish. If you spot an error or omission in this edition or any of our publications, let us know!

Write to us at Gemstone Publishing Inc., 1966 Greenspring Dr., Timonium, MD 21093. Or e-mail **feedback@gemstonepub.com**.

We want your help!

BIG LITTLE BOOKS

INTRODUCTION

In 1932, at the depths of the Great Depression, comic books were not selling despite their successes in the previous two decades. Desperate publishers had already reduced prices to 25¢, but this was still too much for many people to spend on entertainment.

Comic books quickly evolved into two newer formats, the comics magazine and the Big Little Book. Both types retailed for 10¢.

Big Little Books began by reprinting the art (and adapting the stories) from newspaper comics. As their success grew and publishers began commissioning original material, movie adaptations and other entertainment-derived stories became commonplace.

GRADING

Before a Big Little Book's value can be assessed, its condition or state of preservation must be determined. A book in **Near Mint** condition will bring many times the price of the same book in **Poor** condition. Many variables influence the grading of a Big Little Book and all must be considered in the final evaluation. Due to the way they are constructed, damage occurs with very little use - usually to the spine, book edges and binding. More important defects that affect grading are: Split spines, pages missing, page browning or brittleness, writing, crayoning, loose pages, color fading, chunks missing, and rolling or out of square. The following grading guide is given to aid the novice:

9.4 Near Mint: The overall look is as if it was just purchased and maybe opened once; only subtle defects are allowed; paper is cream to off-white, supple and fresh; cover is flat with no surface wear or creases; inks and colors are bright; small penciled or inked arrival dates are acceptable; very slight blunting of corners at top and bottom of spine are common; outside corners are cut square and sharp. Books in this grade could bring prices of guide and a half or more.

9.0 Very Fine/Near Mint: Limited number of defects; full cover gloss with only very slight wear on book corners and edges; very minor foxing; very minor tears allowed, binding still square and tight with no pages missing; paper quality still fresh from cream to off-white. Dates, stamps or initials allowed on cover or inside.

8.0 Very Fine: Most of the cover gloss retained with minor wear appearing at corners and around edges; spine tight with no pages missing; cream/tan paper allowed if still supple; up to 1/4" bend allowed on covers with no color break; cover relatively flat; minor tears allowed.

6.0 Fine: Slight wear beginning to show; cover gloss reduced but still clean, pages tan/brown but still supple (not brittle); up to 1/4" split or color break allowed; minor discoloration and/or foxing allowed.

4.0 Very Good: Obviously a read copy with original printing luster almost gone; some fading and discoloration, but not soiled; some signs of wear such as corner splits and spine rolling; paper can be brown but not brittle; a few pages can be loose but not missing; no chunks missing; blunted corners acceptable.

2.0 Good: An average used copy complete with only minor pieces missing from the spine, which may be partially split; slightly soiled or marked with spine rolling; color flaking and wear around edges, but perfectly sound and legible; could have minor tape repairs but otherwise complete.

1.0 Fair: Very heavily read and soiled with small chunks missing from cover; most or all of spine could be missing; multiple splits in spine and loose pages, but still sound and legible, bringing 50 to 70 percent of good price.

0.5 Poor: Damaged, heavily weathered, soiled or otherwise unsuited for collecting purposes.

IMPORTANT

Most BLBs on the market today will fall in the **Good** to **Fine** grade category. When **Very Fine** to **Near Mint** BLBs are offered for sale, they usually bring premium prices.

A WORD ON PRICING

The prices are given for **Good**, **Fine** and **Very Fine/ Near Mint** condition. A book in **Fair** would be 50-70% of the **Good** price. **Very Good** would be halfway between the **Good** and **Fine** price, and **Very Fine** would be halfway between the **Fine** and **Very Fine/**

Near Mint price. The prices listed were averaged from convention sales, dealers' lists, adzines, auctions, and by special contact with dealers and collectors from coast to coast. The prices and the spreads were determined from sales of copies in available condition or the highest grade known. Since most available copies are in the **Good** to **Fine** range, neither dealers nor collectors should let the **Very Fine/Near Mint** column influence the prices they are willing to charge or pay for books in less than near perfect condition.

The prices listed reflect a six times spread from **Good** to **Very Fine/ Near Mint** (1 - 3 - 6). We feel this spread accurately reflects the current market, especially when you consider the scarcity of books in **Very Fine/Near Mint** condition. When one or both end sheets are missing, the book's value would drop about a half grade.

Books with movie scenes are of double importance due to the high crossover demand by movie collectors.

Abbreviations: a-art; c-cover; nn-no number; p-pages; r-reprint.

Publisher Codes: BRP-Blue Ribbon Press; **ERB**-Edgar Rice Burroughs; **EVW**-Engel van Wiseman; **FAW**-Fawcett Publishing Co.; **Gold**-Goldsmith Publishing Co.; **Lynn**-Lynn Publishing Co.; **McKay**-David McKay Co.; **Whit**-Whitman Publishing Co.; **World**-World Syndicate Publishing Co.

Terminology: *All Pictures Comics*-no text, all drawings; *Fast-Action*-A special series of Dell books highly collected; *Flip Pictures*-upper right corner of interior pages contain drawings that are put into motion when rifled; *Movie Scenes*-book illustrated with scenes from the movie. *Soft Cover*-A thin single sheet of cardboard used in binding most of the giveaway versions.

"Big Little Book" and "Better Little Book" are registered trademarks of Whitman Publishing Co. "Little Big Book" is a registered trademark of the Saalfield Publishing Co.

"Pop-Up" is a registered trademark of Blue Ribbon Press. "Little Big Book" is a registered trademark of the Saalfield Co.

Top 20 Big Little Books and related size books*

Issue#	Rank	Title	Price
731	1	Mickey Mouse the Mail Pilot (variant version of Mickey Mouse #717) (Fine copy sold at auction for $5,090)	
nn	2	Mickey Mouse and Minnie Mouse at Macy's	$3,500
717	3	Mickey Mouse (skinny Mickey on-c)	$3,135
nn	4	Mickey Mouse and Minnie March to Macy's	$2,400
W-707	5	Dick Tracy The Detective	$2,310
725	6	Big Little Mother Goose HC	$2,200
717	7	Mickey Mouse (reg. Mickey on-c)	$1,650
4063	8	Popeye Thimble Theater Starring... (2nd printing)	$1,620
721	9	Big Little Paint Book (336 pg.)	$1,500
725	9	Big Little Mother Goose SC	$1,500
4062	11	Mickey Mouse and the Smugglers	$1,430
nn	12	Mickey Mouse (Great Big Midget Book)	$1,400
nn	12	Mickey Mouse Mail Pilot (Great Big Midget Book)	$1,400
4063	14	Popeye Thimble Theater Starring... (1st printing)	$1,385
nn	15	Buck Rogers	$1,320
nn	15	Mickey Mouse Silly Symphonies	$1,320
4062	17	Mickey Mouse, The Story of...	$1,210
721	18	Big Little Paint Book (320 pg.)	$1,200
nn	18	Mickey Mouse Sails For Treasure Island (Great Big Midget Book)	$1,200
nn	20	Mickey Mouse and the Magic Carpet	$1,050

*Includes only the various sized BLBs; no premiums, giveaways or other divergent forms are included.

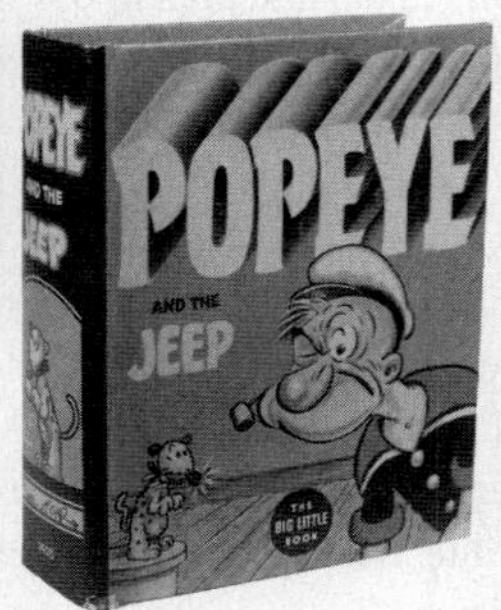

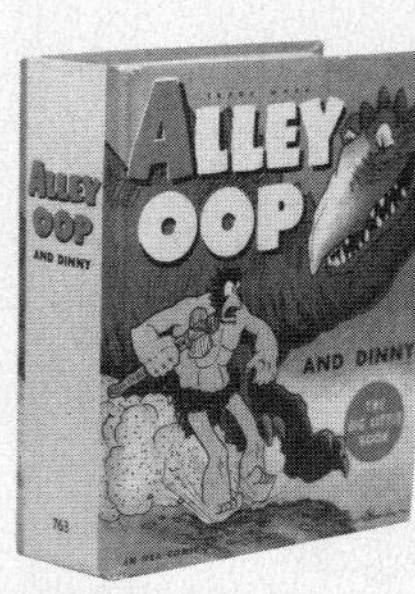

763 - Alley Oop and Dinny © WHIT

1083 - Barney Google © Saalfield

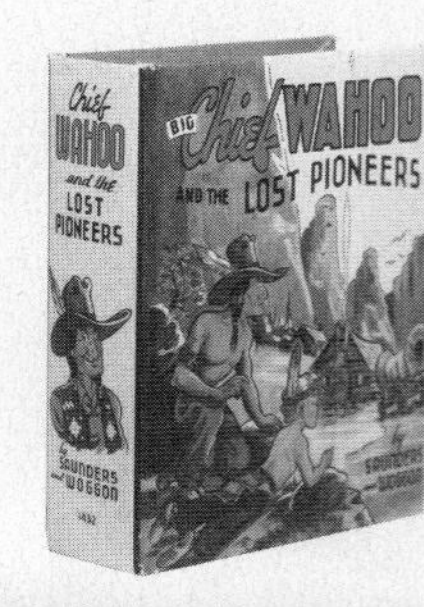

1432 - Big Chief Wahoo and the Lost Pioneers © WHIT

	GD	FN	VF/NM
1175-0- Abbie an' Slats, 1940, Saalfield, 400 pgs.	12.00	30.00	80.00
1182- Abbie an' Slats-and Becky, 1940, Saalfield, 400 pgs.	12.00	30.00	80.00
1177- Ace Drummond, 1935, Whitman, 432 pgs.	12.00	30.00	85.00
Admiral Byrd (See Paramount Newsreel ...)			
nn- Adventures of Charlie McCarthy and Edgar Bergen, The, 1938, Dell, 194 pgs., Fast-Action Story, soft-c	26.00	65.00	185.00
1422- Adventures of Huckleberry Finn, The, 1939, Whitman, 432 pgs., Henry E. Vallely-a	12.00	30.00	75.00
1648- Adventures of Jim Bowie (TV Series), 1958, Whitman, 280 pgs.	5.00	12.50	33.00
1056- Adventures of Krazy Kat and Ignatz Mouse in Koko Land, 1934, Saalfield, 160 pgs., oblong size, hard-c, Herriman-c/a	72.00	180.00	505.00
1306- Adventures of Krazy Kat and Ignatz Mouse in Koko Land, 1934, Saalfield, 164 pgs., oblong size, soft-c, Herriman-c/a	79.00	237.00	550.00
1082- Adventures of Pete the Tramp, The, 1935, Saalfield, hard-c, by C. D. Russell	12.00	30.00	75.00
1312- Adventures of Pete the Tramp, The, 1935, Saalfield, soft-c, by C. D. Russell	12.00	30.00	75.00
1053- Adventures of Tim Tyler, 1934, Saalfield, hard-c, oblong size, by Lyman Young	26.00	65.00	180.00
1303- Adventures of Tim Tyler, 1934, Saalfield, soft-c, oblong size, by Lyman Young	26.00	65.00	180.00
1058- Adventures of Tom Sawyer, The, 1934, Saalfield, 160 pgs., hard-c, Park Sumner-a	12.00	30.00	75.00
1308- Adventures of Tom Sawyer, The, 1934, Saalfield, 160 pgs., soft-c, Park Sumner-a	12.00	30.00	75.00
1448- Air Fighters of America, 1941, Whitman, 432 pgs., flip picture	12.00	30.00	85.00
Alexander Smart, ESQ. (See Top Line Comics)			
759- Alice in Wonderland, 1933, Whitman, 160 pgs., hard-c, photo-c, movie scenes	43.00	129.00	300.00
1481- Allen Pike of the Parachute Squad U.S.A., 1941, Whitman, 432 pgs.	12.00	30.00	85.00
763- Alley Oop and Dinny, 1935, Whitman, 384 pgs., V. T. Hamlin-a	21.00	52.50	145.00
1473- Alley Oop and Dinny in the Jungles of Moo, 1938, Whitman, 432 pgs., V. T. Hamlin-a	21.00	52.50	145.00
nn- Alley Oop and the Missing King of Moo, 1938, Whitman, 36 pgs., 2 1/2" x 3 1/2", Penny Book	12.00	30.00	85.00
nn- Alley Oop in the Kingdom of Foo, 1938, Whitman, 68 pgs., 3 1/4" x 3 1/2", Pan-Am premium	29.00	73.00	200.00
nn- "Alley Oop the Invasion of Moo," 1935, Whitman, 260 pgs., Cocomalt premium, soft-c; V. T. Hamlin-a	22.00	52.50	155.00
Andy Burnette (See Walt Disney's...)			
Andy Panda (Also see Walter Lantz ...)			
531- Andy Panda, 1943, Whitman, 3 3/4x8 3/4", Tall Comic Book, All Pictures Comics	26.00	65.00	180.00
1425- Andy Panda and Tiny Tom, 1944, Whitman, All Pictures Comics	12.00	30.00	85.00
1431- Andy Panda and the Mad Dog Mystery, 1947, Whitman, 288 pgs., by Walter Lantz	12.00	30.00	80.00
1441- Andy Panda in the City of Ice, 1948, Whitman, All Picture Comics, by Walter Lantz	12.00	30.00	85.00
1459- Andy Panda and the Pirate Ghosts, 1949, Whitman, 88 pgs., by Walter Lantz	12.00	30.00	80.00
1485- Andy Panda's Vacation, 1946, Whitman, All Pictures Comics, by Walter Lantz	12.00	30.00	85.00
15- Andy Panda (The Adventures of), 1942, Dell, Fast-Action Story	26.00	65.00	180.00
707-10 - Andy Panda and Presto the Pup, 1949, Whitman	12.00	30.00	80.00
1130- Apple Mary and Dennie Foil the Swindlers, 1936, Whitman, 432 pgs. (Forerunner to Mary Worth)	12.00	30.00	80.00
1403- Apple Mary and Dennie's Lucky Apples, 1939, Whitman, 432 pgs.	12.00	30.00	80.00
2017- (#17)-Aquaman-Scourge of the Sea, 1968, Whitman, 260 pgs., 39 cents, hard-c, color illos	4.00	10.00	27.00

	GD	FN	VF/NM
1192- Arizona Kid on the Bandit Trail, The, 1936, Whitman, 432 pgs.	11.00	27.50	70.00
1469- Bambi (Walt Disney's), 1942, Whitman, 432 pgs.	26.00	65.00	180.00
1497- Bambi's Children (Disney), 1943, Whitman, 432 pgs., Disney Studios-a	26.00	65.00	180.00
1138- Bandits at Bay, 1938, Saalfield, 400 pgs.	10.00	25.00	65.00
1459- Barney Baxter in the Air with the Eagle Squadron, 1938, Whitman, 432 pgs.	12.00	30.00	80.00
1083- Barney Google, 1935, Saalfield, hard-c	21.00	52.50	145.00
1313- Barney Google, 1935, Saalfield, soft-c	21.00	52.50	145.00
2031-(#31)- Batman and Robin in the Cheetah Caper, 1969, Whitman, 258 pgs.	4.00	10.00	27.00
5771- Batman and Robin in the Cheetah Caper, 1974, Whitman, 258 pgs., 49 cents	2.00	5.00	11.00
5771-1- Batman and Robin in the Cheetah Caper, 1974, Whitman, 258 pgs., 69 cents	2.00	5.00	11.00
5771-2- Batman and Robin in the Cheetah Caper, 1975?, Whitman, 258 pgs.	2.00	5.00	11.00
nn- Beauty and the Beast, nd (1930s), np (Whitman), 36 pgs., 3" x 3 1/2" Penny Book	4.00	10.00	27.00
760- Believe It or Not!, 1933, Whitman, 160 pgs., by Ripley (c. 1931)	12.00	30.00	80.00
Betty Bear's Lesson (See Wee Little Books)			
1119- Betty Boop in Snow White, 1934, Whitman, 240 pgs., hard-c; adapted from Max Fleischer Paramount Talkartoon	79.00	237.00	550.00
1119- Betty Boop in Snow White, 1934, Whitman, 240 pgs., soft-c; same contents as hard-c (Rare)	114.00	342.00	800.00
1158- Betty Boop in "Miss Gullivers Travels," 1935, Whitman, 288 pgs., hard-c (Scarce)	86.00	258.00	600.00
2070- Big Big Paint Book, 1936, Whitman, 432 pgs., 8 1/2" x 11 3/8", B&W pages to color	29.00	87.00	200.00
1432- Big Chief Wahoo and the Lost Pioneers, 1942, Whitman, 432 pgs., Elmer Woggon-a	12.00	30.00	80.00
1443- Big Chief Wahoo and the Great Gusto, 1938, Whitman, 432 pgs., Elmer Woggon-a	12.00	30.00	80.00
1483- Big Chief Wahoo and the Magic Lamp, 1940, Whitman, 432 pgs., flip pictures, Woggon-c/a	12.00	30.00	80.00
725- Big Little Mother Goose, The, 1934, Whitman, 580 pgs. (Rare) Hardcover	275.00	825.00	2200.00
725- Big Little Mother Goose, The, 1934, Whitman, 580 pgs. (Rare) Softcover	188.00	564.00	1500.00
1005- Big Little Nickel Book, 1935, Whitman, 144 pgs., Blackie Bear stories and Donna the Donkey	11.00	27.50	70.00
1006- Big Little Nickel Book, 1935, Whitman, 144 pgs., Blackie Bear stories, folk tales in primer style	11.00	27.50	70.00
1007- Big Little Nickel Book, 1935, Whitman, 144 pgs., Peter Rabbit, etc.	11.00	27.50	70.00
1008- Big Little Nickel Book, 1935, Whitman, 144 pgs., Wee Wee Woman, etc.	11.00	27.50	70.00
721- Big Little Paint Book, The, 1933, Whitman, 320 pgs., 3 3/4" x 8 1/2", for crayoning; first printing has green page ends; second printing has purple page ends (both are rare)	150.00	450.00	1200.00
721- Big Little Paint Book, The, 1933, Whitman, 336 pgs., 3 3/4" x 8 1/2", for crayoning; first printing has green page ends; second printing has purple page ends (both are rare)	188.00	564.00	1500.00
1178- Billy of Bar-Zero, 1940, Saalfield, 400 pgs.	11.00	27.50	70.00
773- Billy the Kid, 1935, Whitman, 432 pgs., Hal Arbo-a	12.00	30.00	80.00
1159- Billy the Kid on Tall Butte, 1939, Saalfield, 400 pgs.	11.00	27.50	70.00
1174- Billy the Kid's Pledge, 1940, Saalfield, 400 pgs.	11.00	27.50	70.00
nn- Billy the Kid, Western Outlaw, 1935, Whitman, 260 pgs., Cocomalt premium, Hal Arbo-a, soft-c	12.00	30.00	85.00
1057- Black Beauty, 1934, Saalfield, hard-c	10.00	25.00	65.00
1307- Black Beauty, 1934, Saalfield, soft-c	10.00	25.00	65.00
1414- Black Silver and His Pirate Crew, 1937, Whitman, 300 pgs.	12.00	30.00	75.00

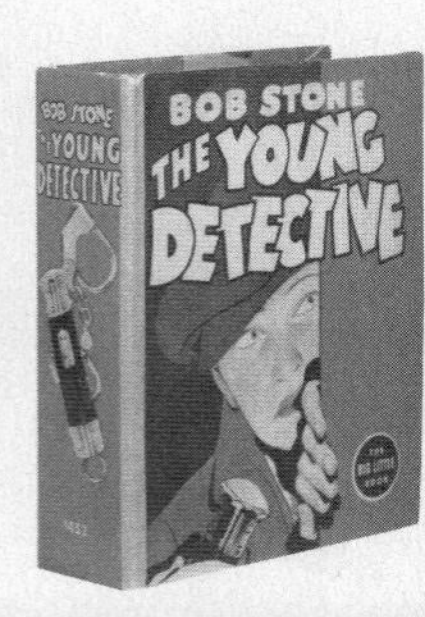

1432 - Bob Stone the Young Detective © WHIT

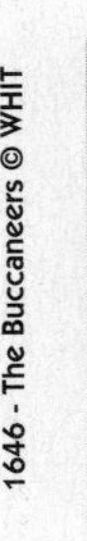
1646 - The Buccaneers © WHIT

1169 - Buck Rogers and the Depth Men of Jupiter © KING

No.	Title	GD	FN	VF/NM
1447-	**Blaze Brandon with the Foreign Legion**, 1938, Whitman, 432 pgs.	12.00	30.00	75.00
1410-	**Blondie and Dagwood in Hot Water**, 1946, Whitman, 352 pgs., by Chic Young	12.00	30.00	80.00
1415-	**Blondie and Baby Dumpling**, 1937, Whitman, 432 pgs., by Chic Young	12.00	30.00	85.00
1419-	**Oh, Blondie the Bumsteads Carry On**, 1941, Whitman, 432 pgs., flip pictures, by Chic Young	12.00	30.00	85.00
1423-	**Blondie Who's Boss?**, 1942, Whitman, 432 pgs., flip pictures, by Chic Young	12.00	30.00	85.00
1429-	**Blondie with Baby Dumpling and Daisy**, 1939, Whitman, 432 pgs., by Chic Young	12.00	30.00	85.00
1430-	**Blondie Count Cookie in Too!**, 1947, Whitman, 288 pgs., by Chic Young	12.00	30.00	80.00
1438-	**Blondie and Dagwood Everybody's Happy**, 1948, Whitman, 288 pgs., by Chic Young	12.00	30.00	80.00
1450-	**Blondie No Dull Moments**, 1948, Whitman, 288 pgs., by Chic Young	12.00	30.00	80.00
1463-	**Blondie Fun For All**, 1949, Whitman, 288 pgs., by Chic Young	12.00	30.00	80.00
1466-	**Blondie or Life Among the Bumsteads**, 1944, Whitman, 352 pgs., by Chic Young	12.00	30.00	85.00
1476-	**Blondie and Bouncing Baby Dumpling**, 1940, Whitman, 432 pgs., by Chic Young	12.00	30.00	85.00
1487-	**Blondie Baby Dumpling and All!**, 1941, Whitman, 432 pgs. flip pictures, by Chic Young	12.00	30.00	85.00
1490-	**Blondie Papa Knows Best**, 1945, Whitman, 352 pgs., by Chic Young	12.00	30.00	80.00
1491-	**Blondie-Cookie and Daisy's Pups**, 1943, Whitman, 1st printing, 432 pgs.	12.00	30.00	85.00
1491-	**Blondie-Cookie and Daisy's Pups**, 1943, Whitman,. 2nd printing with different back-c & 352 pgs.	12.00	30.00	75.00
703-10-	**Blondie and Dagwood Some Fun!**, 1949, Whitman, by Chic Young	10.00	25.00	65.00
21-	**Blondie and Dagwood**, 1936, Lynn, by Chic Young	21.00	52.50	145.00
1108-	**Bobby Benson on the H-Bar-O Ranch**, 1934, Whitman, 300 pgs., based on radio serial	13.00	32.50	90.00
	Bobby Thatcher and the Samarang Emerald (See Top-Line Comics)			
1432-	**Bob Stone the Young Detective**, 1937, Whitman, 240 pgs., movie scenes	12.00	30.00	85.00
2002-	**(#2)-Bonanza-The Bubble Gum Kid**, 1967, Whitman, 260 pgs., 39 cents, hard-c, color illos	4.00	10.00	27.00
1139-	**Border Eagle, The**, 1938, Saalfield, 400 pgs.	10.00	25.00	65.00
1153-	**Boss of the Chisholm Trail**, 1939, Saalfield, 400 pgs.	10.00	25.00	65.00
1425-	**Brad Turner in Transatlantic Flight**, 1939, Whitman, 432 pgs.	11.00	27.50	70.00
1058-	**Brave Little Tailor, The** (Disney), 1939, Whitman, 5" x 5 1/2", 68 pgs., hard-c (Mickey Mouse)	16.00	40.00	115.00
1427-	**Brenda Starr and the Masked Impostor**, 1943, Whitman, 352 pgs., Dale Messick-a	15.00	37.50	105.00
1426-	**Brer Rabbit** (Walt Disney's ...), 1947, Whitman, All Picture Comics, from "Song Of The South" movie	22.00	52.50	155.00
704-10-	**Brer Rabbit**, 1949, Whitman	19.00	47.50	135.00
1059-	**Brick Bradford in the City Beneath the Sea**, 1934, Saalfield, hard-c, by William Ritt & Clarence Gray	18.00	45.00	125.00
1309-	**Brick Bradford in the City Beneath the Sea**, 1934, Saalfield, soft-c, by Ritt & Gray	18.00	45.00	125.00
1468-	**Brick Bradford with Brocco the Modern Buccaneer**, 1938, Whitman, 432 pgs., by Wrn. Ritt & Clarence Gray	12.00	30.00	80.00
1133-	**Bringing Up Father**, 1936, Whitman, 432 pgs., by George McManus	16.00	40.00	115.00
1100-	**Broadway Bill**, 1935, Saalfield, photo-c, 4 1/2" x 5 1/4", movie scenes (Columbia Pictures, horse racing)	12.00	30.00	85.00
1580-	**Broadway Bill**, 1935, Saalfield, soft-c, photo-c, movie scenes	12.00	30.00	85.00
1181-	**Broncho Bill**, 1940, Saalfield, 400 pgs.	11.00	27.50	70.00
nn-	**Broncho Bill**, 1935, Whitman, 148 pgs., 3 1/2" x 4", Tarzan Ice Cream cup lid premium	36.00	90.00	255.00
nn-	**Broncho Bill in Suicide Canyon** (See Top-Line Comics)			
1417-	**Bronc Peeler the Lone Cowboy**, 1937, Whitman, 432 pgs., by Fred Harman, forerunner of Red Ryder (also see Red Death on the Range)	12.00	30.00	80.00
nn-	**Brownies' Merry Adventures, The**, 1993, Barefoot Books, 202 pgs., reprints from Palmer Cox's late 1800s books	3.00	7.50	18.00
1470-	**Buccaneer, The**, 1938, Whitman, 240 pgs., photo-c, movie scenes	13.00	32.50	90.00
1646-	**Buccaneers, The** (TV Series), 1958, Whitman, 4 1/2" x 5 1/4", 280 pgs., Russ Manning-a	5.00	12.50	33.00
1104-	**Buck Jones in the Fighting Code**, 1934, Whitman, 160 pgs., hard-c, movie scenes	19.00	47.50	135.00
1116-	**Buck Jones in Ride 'Em Cowboy** (Universal Presents), 1935, Whitman, 240 pgs., photo-c, movie scenes	19.00	47.50	135.00
1174-	**Buck Jones in the Roaring West** (Universal Presents), 1935, Whitman, 240 pgs., movie scenes	19.00	47.50	135.00
1188-	**Buck Jones in the Fighting Rangers** (Universal Presents), 1936, Whitman, 240 pgs., photo-c, movie scenes	19.00	47.50	135.00
1404-	**Buck Jones and the Two-Gun Kid**, 1937, Whitman, 432 pgs.	13.00	32.50	90.00
1451-	**Buck Jones and the Killers of Crooked Butte**, 1940, Whitman, 432 pgs.	13.00	32.50	90.00
1461-	**Buck Jones and the Rock Creek Cattle War**, 1938, Whitman, 432 pgs.	13.00	32.50	90.00
1486-	**Buck Jones and the Rough Riders in Forbidden Trails**, 1943, Whitman, flip pictures, based on movie; Tim McCoy app.	18.00	45.00	125.00
3-	**Buck Jones in the Red Rider**, 1934, EVW, 160 pgs., movie scenes	36.00	108.00	250.00
8-	**Buck Jones Cowboy Masquerade**, 1938, Whitman, 132 pgs., soft-c, 3 3/4" x 3 1/2", Buddy Book premium	43.00	108.00	300.00
15-	**Buck Jones in Rocky Rhodes**, 1935, EVW, 160 pgs., photo-c, movie scenes	43.00	129.00	300.00
4069-	**Buck Jones and the Night Riders**, 1937, Whitman, 7" x 9", 320 pgs., Big Big Book	79.00	198.00	550.00
nn-	**Buck Jones on the Six-Gun Trail**, 1939, Whitman, 36 pgs., 2 1/2" x 3 1/2", Penny Book	12.00	30.00	80.00
nn-	**Buck Jones Big Thrill Chewing Gum**, 1934, Whitman, 8 pgs., 2 1/2" x 3 1/2" (6 diff.) each...	20.00	50.00	140.00
742-	**Buck Rogers in the 25th Century A.D.**, 1933, Whitman, 320 pgs., Dick Calkins-a	47.00	118.00	330.00
nn-	**Buck Rogers in the 25th Century A.D.**, 1933, Whitman, 204 pgs.,Cocomalt premium, Calkins-a	30.00	75.00	210.00
765-	**Buck Rogers in the City Below the Sea**, 1934, Whitman, 320 pgs., Dick Calkins-a	36.00	90.00	255.00
765-	**Buck Rogers in the City Below the Sea**, 1934, Whitman, 324 pgs., soft-c, Dick Calkins-c/a (Rare)	79.00	237.00	550.00
1143-	**Buck Rogers on the Moons of Saturn**, 1934, Whitman, 320 pgs., Dick Calkins-a	38.00	95.00	255.00
nn-	**Buck Rogers on the Moons of Saturn**, 1934, Whitman, 324 pgs., premium w/no ads, soft 3-color-c, Dick Calkins-a	64.00	160.00	450.00
1169-	**Buck Rogers and the Depth Men of Jupiter**, 1935, Whitman, 432 pgs., Calkins-a	36.00	90.00	255.00
1178-	**Buck Rogers and the Doom Comet**, 1935, Whitman, 432 pgs., Calkins-a	34.00	85.00	240.00
1197-	**Buck Rogers and the Planetoid Plot**, 1936, Whitman, 432 pgs., Calkins-a	34.00	85.00	240.00
1409-	**Buck Rogers Vs. the Fiend of Space**, 1940, Whitman, 432 pgs., Calkins-a	45.00	113.00	315.00
1437-	**Buck Rogers in the War with the Planet Venus**, 1938, Whitman, 432 pgs., Calkins-a	34.00	85.00	240.00
1474-	**Buck Rogers and the Overturned World**, 1941, Whitman, 432 pgs., flip pictures, Calkins-a	36.00	90.00	250.00
1490-	**Buck Rogers and the Super-Dwarf of Space**, 1943, Whitman, 11 Pictures Comics, Calkins-a	34.00	85.00	240.00
4057-	**Buck Rogers, The Adventures of**, 1934, Whitman, 7" x 9 1/2", 320 pgs., Big Big Book, "The Story of Buck Rogers on the Planet Eros," Calkins-c/a	130.00	327.00	1045.00

1465 - Bugs Bunny The Masked Marvel © WB

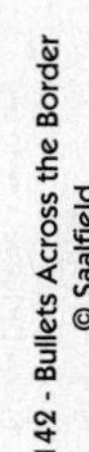
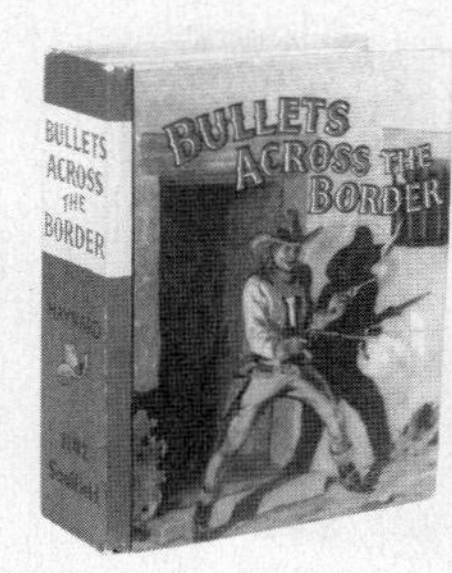

1142 - Bullets Across the Border © Saalfield

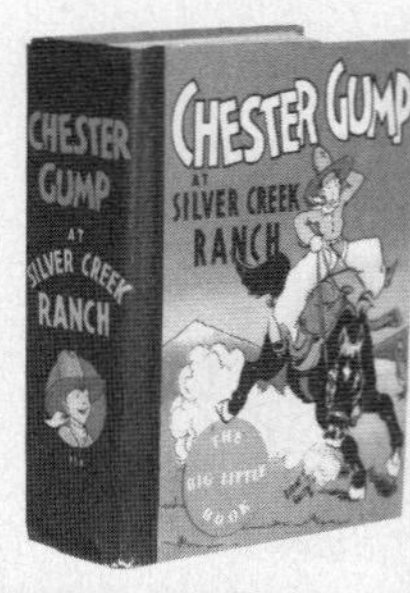

734 - Chester Gump at Silver Creek Ranch © WHIT

GD FN VF/NM

nn- **Buck Rogers**, 1935, Whitman, 4" x 3 1/2", Tarzan Ice Cream cup premium (Rare) 165.00 412.00 1320.00
nn- **Buck Rogers in the City of Floating Globes**, 1935, Whitman, 258 pgs., Cocomalt premium, soft-c, Dick Calkins-a 115.00 287.00 810.00
nn- **Buck Rogers Big Thrill Chewing Gum**, 1934, Whitman, 8 pgs., 2 1/2" x 3 " (6 diff.) each... 29.00 73.00 200.00
1135- **Buckskin and Bullets**, 1938, Saalfield, 400 pgs. 11.00 27.50 70.00
Buffalo Bill (See Wild West Adventures of ...)
nn- **Buffalo Bill**, 1934, World Syndicate, All pictures, by J. Carroll Mansfield 11.00 27.50 70.00
713- **Buffalo Bill and the Pony Express**, 1934, Whitman, hard-c, 384 pgs., Hal Arbo-a 12.00 30.00 80.00
nn- **Buffalo Bill and the Pony Express**, 1934, Whitman, soft-c, 384 pgs., Hal Arbo-a; three-color premium (Rare) 64.00 192.00 450.00
1194- **Buffalo Bill Plays a Lone Hand**, 1936, Whitman, 432 pgs., Hal Arbo-a 11.00 27.50 70.00
530- **Bugs Bunny**, 1943, Whitman, All Pictures Comics, Tall Comic Book, 3 1/4" x 8 1/4", reprints/Looney Tunes 1 & 5 31.00 78.00 215.00
1403- **Bugs Bunny and the Pirate Loot**, 1947, Whitman, All Pictures Comics 12.00 30.00 80.00
1435- **Bugs Bunny**, 1944, Whitman, All Pictures Comics 12.00 30.00 85.00
1440- **Bugs Bunny in Risky Business**, 1948, Whitman, All Pictures & Comics 12.00 30.00 80.00
1455- **Bugs Bunny and Klondike Gold**, 1948, Whitman, 288 pgs. 12.00 30.00 80.00
1465- **Bugs Bunny The Masked Marvel**, 1949, Whitman, 288 pgs. 12.00 30.00 80.00
1496- **Bugs Bunny and His Pals**, 1945, Whitman, All Pictures Comics; r/Four Color Comics #33 12.00 30.00 80.00
13- **Bugs Bunny and the Secret of Storm Island**, 1942, Dell,194 pgs., Fast-Action Story 36.00 90.00 255.00
706-10- **Bugs Bunny and the Giant Brothers**, 1949, Whitman 11.00 27.50 70.00
2007- **(#7)-Bugs Bunny-Double Trouble on Diamond Island**, 1967, Whitman, 260 pgs., 39 cents, hard-c, color illos 5.00 12.50 33.00
2029-**(#29)- Bugs Bunny, Accidental Adventure**, 1969, Whitman, 256 pgs., hard-c, color illos. 4.00 10.00 22.00
2952- **Bugs Bunny's Mistake**, 1949, Whitman, 3 1/4" x 4", 24 pgs., Tiny Tales, full color (5 cents) (1030-5 on back-c) 11.00 27.50 70.00
5757-2- **Bugs Bunny in Double Trouble on Diamond Island**,1967, (1980-reprints #2007), Whitman, 260 pgs., soft-c, 79 cents, B&W 2.00 5.00 12.00
5758- **Bugs Bunny, Accidental Adventure**, 1973, Whitman, 256 pgs., soft-c, B&W illos. 2.00 5.00 12.00
5758-1- **Bugs Bunny, Accidental Adventure**, 1973, Whitman, 256 pgs., soft-c, B&W illos. 2.00 5.00 12.00
5772- **Bugs Bunny the Last Crusader**, 1975, Whitman, 49 cents, flip-it book 2.00 5.00 12.00
5772-2- **Bugs Bunny the Last Crusader**, 1975, Whitman, $1.50, flip-it book 1.00 2.50 6.00
1169- **Bullet Benton**, 1939, Saalfield, 400 pgs. 11.00 27.50 70.00
nn- **Bulletman and the Return of Mr. Murder**, 1941, Fawcett, 196 pgs., Dime Action Book 54.00 135.00 375.00
1142- **Bullets Across the Border** (A Billy The Kid story), 1938, Saalfield, 400 pgs. 11.00 27.50 70.00
Bunky (See Top-Line Comics)
837- **Bunty** (Punch and Judy), 1935, Whitman, 28 pgs., Magic-Action with 3 pop-ups 16.00 40.00 115.00
1091- **Burn 'Em Up Barnes**, 1935, Saalfield, hard-c, movie scenes 15.00 37.50 105.00
1321- **Burn 'Em Up Barnes**, 1935, Saalfield, soft-c, movie scenes 15.00 37.50 105.00
1415- **Buz Sawyer and Bomber 13**,1946, Whitman, 352 pgs., Roy Crane-a 15.00 37.50 105.00
1412- **Calling W-1-X-Y-Z, Jimmy Kean and the Radio Spies**, 1939, Whitman, 300 pgs. 12.00 30.00 80.00

GD FN VF/NM

Call of the Wild (See Jack London's...)
1107- **Camels are Coming**, 1935, Saalfield, movie scenes 12.00 30.00 75.00
1587- **Camels are Coming**, 1935, Saalfield, movie scenes 12.00 30.00 75.00
nn- **Captain and the Kids, Boys Vill Be Boys, The**, 1938, 68 pgs., Pan-Am Oil premium, soft-c 15.00 37.50 105.00
1128- **Captain Easy Soldier of Fortune**, 1934, Whitman, 432 pgs., Roy Crane-a 15.00 37.50 105.00
nn- **Captain Easy Soldier of Fortune**, 1934, Whitman, 436 pgs., Premium, no ads, soft 3-color-c, Roy Crane-a 26.00 65.00 180.00
1474- **Captain Easy Behind Enemy Lines**, 1943, Whitman, 352 pgs., Roy Crane-a 13.00 32.50 90.00
nn- **Captain Easy and Wash Tubbs**, 1935, 260 pgs., Cocomalt premium, Roy Crane-a 13.00 32.50 90.00
1444- **Captain Frank Hawks Air Ace and the League of Twelve**, 1938, Whitman, 432 pgs. 12.00 30.00 80.00
nn- **Captain Marvel**, 1941, Fawcett, 196 pgs., Dime Action Book 65.00 163.00 460.00
1402- **Captain Midnight and Sheik Jomak Khan**, 1946, Whitman, 352 pgs. 26.00 65.00 180.00
1452- **Captain Midnight and the Moon Woman**, 1943, Whitman, 352 pgs. 28.00 70.00 195.00
1458- **Captain Midnight Vs. The Terror of the Orient**, 1942, Whitman, 432 pgs., flip pictures, Hess-a 28.00 70.00 195.00
1488- **Captain Midnight and the Secret Squadron**, 1941, Whitman, 432 pgs. 28.00 70.00 195.00
Captain Robb of.. (See Dirigible ZR90 ...)
nn- **Cauliflower Catnip Pearls of Peril**, 1981, Teacup Tales, 290 pgs., Joe Wehrle Jr.-s/a; deliberately printed on aged-looking paper to look like an old BLB 4.00 10.00 27.00
20- **Ceiling Zero**, 1936, Lynn, 128 pgs., 7 1/2" x 5", hard-c, James Cagney, Pat O'Brien photos on-c, movie scenes, Warner Bros. Pictures 12.00 30.00 80.00
1093- **Chandu the Magician**, 1935, Saalfield, 5" x 5 1/4", 160 pgs., hard-c, Bela Lugosi photo-c, movie scenes 16.00 40.00 115.00
1323- **Chandu the Magician**, 1935, Saalfield, 5" x 5 1/4", 160 pgs., soft-c, Bela Lugosi photo-c 18.00 45.00 125.00
Charlie Chan (See Inspector ...)
1459- **Charlie Chan Solves a New Mystery** (See Inspector..), 1940, Whitman, 432 pgs., Alfred Andriola-a 16.00 40.00 110.00
1478- **Charlie Chan of the Honolulu Police, Inspector**, 1939, Whitman, 432 pgs., Andriola-a 16.00 40.00 110.00
Charlie McCarthy (See Story Of ...)
734- **Chester Gump at Silver Creek Ranch**, 1933, Whitman, 320 pgs., Sidney Smith-a 15.00 37.50 105.00
nn- **Chester Gump at Silver Creek Ranch**, 1933, Whitman, 204 pgs., Cocomalt premium, soft-c, Sidney Smith-a 18.00 45.00 125.00
nn- **Chester Gump at Silver Creek Ranch**, 1933, Whitman, 52 pgs., 4" x 5 1/2", premium-no ads, soft-c, Sidney Smith-a 26.00 65.00 180.00
766- **Chester Gump Finds the Hidden Treasure**, 1934, Whitman, 320 pgs., Sidney Smith-a 15.00 37.50 105.00
nn- **Chester Gump Finds the Hidden Treasure**, 1934, Whitman, 52 pgs., 3 1/2" x 5 3/4", premium-no ads, soft-c, Sidney Smith-a 26.00 65.00 180.00
nn- **Chester Gump Finds the Hidden Treasure**, 1934, Whitman, 52 pgs., 4" x 5 1/2", premium-no ads, Sidney Smith-a 26.00 65.00 180.00
1146- **Chester Gump in the City Of Gold**, 1935, Whitman, 432 pgs., Sidney Smith-a 15.00 37.50 105.00
nn- **Chester Gump in the City Of Gold**, 1935, Whitman, 436 pgs., premium-no ads, 3-color, soft-c, Sidney Smith-a 30.00 75.00 210.00
1402- **Chester Gump in the Pole to Pole Flight**, 1937, Whitman, 432 pgs. 13.00 32.50 90.00
5- **Chester Gump and His Friends,** 1934, Whitman, 132 pgs., 3 1/2" x 3 1/2", soft-c, Tarzan Ice Cream cup lid premium 29.00 73.00 200.00
nn- **Chester Gump at the North Pole**, 1938, Whitman, 68 pgs.

1 - Count of Monte Cristo © EVW

2018 - Daktari - Night of Terror © WHIT

1124 - Dickie Moore in the Little Red School House © WHIT

	GD	FN	VF/NM
soft-c, 3 3/4" x 3 1/2", Pan-Am giveaway	29.00	73.00	200.00
nn- **Chicken Greedy**, nd(1930s), np (Whitman), 36 pgs., 3" x 2 1/2", Penny Book	4.00	10.00	22.00
nn- **Chicken Licken**, nd (1930s), np (Whitman), 36 pgs., 3" x 2 1/2", Penny Book	4.00	10.00	22.00
1101- **Chief of the Rangers**, 1935, Saalfield, hard-c, Tom Mix photo-c, movie scenes from "The Miracle Rider"	21.00	52.50	145.00
1581- **Chief of the Rangers**, 1935, Saalfield, soft-c, Tom Mix photo-c, movie scenes	21.00	52.50	145.00
Child's Garden of Verses (See Wee Little Books)			
L14- **Chip Collins' Adventures on Bat Island**, 1935, Lynn, 192 pgs.	12.00	30.00	85.00
2025- **Chitty Chitty Bang Bang**, 1968, Whitman, movie photos	4.00	10.00	27.00
Chubby Little Books, 1935, Whitman, 3" x 2 1/2", 200 pgs.			
W803- **Golden Hours Story Book, The**	7.00	17.50	40.00
W803- **Story Hours Story Book, The**	7.00	17.50	40.00
W804- **Gay Book of Little Stories, The**	7.00	17.50	40.00
W804- **Glad Book of Little Stories, The**	7.00	17.50	40.00
W804- **Joy Book of Little Stories, The**	7.00	17.50	40.00
W804- **Sunny Book of Little Stories, The**	7.00	17.50	40.00
1453- **Chuck Malloy Railroad Detective on the Streamliner**, 1938, Whitman, 300 pgs.	12.00	30.00	75.00
Cinderella (See Walt Disney's...)			
Clyde Beatty (See The Steel Arena)			
1410- **Clyde Beatty Daredevil Lion and Tiger Tamer**, 1939, Whitman, 300 pgs.	14.00	35.00	95.00
1480- **Coach Bernie Bierman's Brick Barton and the Winning Eleven**, 1938, 300 pgs.	11.00	27.50	70.00
1446- **Convoy Patrol** (A Thrilling U.S. Navy Story), 1942, Whitman, 432 pgs., flip pictures	11.00	27.50	70.00
1127- **Corley of the Wilderness Trail**, 1937, Saalfield, hard-c	11.00	27.50	70.00
1607- **Corley of the Wilderness Trail**, 1937, Saalfield, soft-c	11.00	27.50	70.00
1- **Count of Monte Cristo**, 1934, EVW, 160 pgs., (Five Star Library), movie scenes, hard-c (Rare)	36.00	108.00	250.00
1457- **Cowboy Lingo Boys' Book of Western Facts**, 1938, Whitman, 300 pgs., Fred Harman-a	12.00	30.00	75.00
1171- **Cowboy Malloy**, 1940, Saalfield, 400 pgs.	10.00	25.00	65.00
1106- **Cowboy Millionaire**, 1935, Saalfield, movie scenes with George O'Brien, photo-c, hard-c	15.00	37.50	105.00
1586- **Cowboy Millionaire**, 1935, Saalfield, movie scenes with George O'Brien, photo-c, soft-c	15.00	37.50	105.00
724- **Cowboy Stories**, 1933, Whitman, 300 pgs., Hal Arbo-a	12.00	30.00	85.00
nn- **Cowboy Stories**, 1933, Whitman, 52 pgs., soft-c, premium-no ads, 4" x 5 1/2" Hal Arbo-a	15.00	37.50	105.00
1161- **Crimson Cloak, The**, 1939, Saalfield, 400 pgs.	11.00	27.50	70.00
L19- **Curley Harper at Lakespur**, 1935, Lynn, 192 pgs.	11.00	27.50	70.00
5785-2- **Daffy Duck in Twice the Trouble**, 1980, Whitman, 260 pgs., 79 cents soft-c	1.00	2.50	6.00
2018-(#18)-**Daktari-Night of Terror**, 1968, Whitman, 260 pgs., 39 cents, hard-c, color illos	4.00	10.00	27.00
1010- **Dan Dunn And The Gangsters' Frame-Up**, 1937, Whitman, 7 1/4" x 5 1/2", 64 pgs., Nickel Book	45.00	114.00	320.00
1116- **Dan Dunn "Crime Never Pays,"** 1934, Whitman, 320 pgs., by Norman Marsh	14.00	35.00	95.00
1125- **Dan Dunn on the Trail of the Counterfeiters**, 1936, Whitman, 432 pgs., by Norman Marsh	14.00	35.00	95.00
1171- **Dan Dunn and the Crime Master**, 1937, Whitman, 432 pgs., by Norman Marsh	14.00	35.00	95.00
1417- **Dan Dunn and the Underworld Gorillas**, 1941, Whitman, All Pictures Comics, flip pictures, by Norman Marsh	14.00	35.00	95.00
1454- **Dan Dunn on the Trail of Wu Fang**, 1938, Whitman, 432 pgs., by Norman Marsh	16.00	40.00	115.00
1481- **Dan Dunn and the Border Smugglers**, 1938, Whitman, 432 pgs., by Norman Marsh	13.00	32.50	90.00
1492- **Dan Dunn and the Dope Ring**, 1940, Whitman, 432 pgs., by Norman Marsh	12.00	30.00	85.00
nn- **Dan Dunn and the Bank Hold-Up**, 1938, Whitman, 36 pgs., 2 1/2" x 3 1/2", Penny Book	11.00	27.50	70.00
nn- **Dan Dunn and the Zeppelin Of Doom**, 1938, Dell, 196 pgs., Fast-Action Story, soft-c	33.00	83.00	230.00
nn- **Dan Dunn Meets Chang Loo**, 1938, Whitman, 66 pgs., Pan-Am premium, by Norman Marsh	29.00	73.00	200.00
nn- **Dan Dunn Plays a Lone Hand**, 1938, Whitman, 36 pgs., 2 1/2" x 3 1/2", Penny Book	11.00	27.50	70.00
3 3/4" x 3 1/2", Buddy book	39.00	98.00	275.00
6- **Dan Dunn Secret Operative 48 and the Counterfeiter Ring**, 1938, Whitman, 132 pgs., soft-c, 3 3/4" x 3 1/2", Buddy Book premium	39.00	98.00	275.00
9- **Dan Dunn's Mysterious Ruse**, 1936, Whitman, 132 pgs., soft-c, 3 1/2" x 3 1/2", Tarzan Ice Cream cup lid premium	39.00	98.00	275.00
1177- **Danger Trail North**, 1940, Saalfield, 400 pgs.	11.00	27.50	70.00
1151- **Danger Trails in Africa**, 1935, Whitman, 432 pgs.	18.00	45.00	125.00
nn- **Daniel Boone**, 1934, World Syndicate, High Lights of History Series, hard-c, All in Pictures	11.00	27.50	70.00
1160- **Dan of the Lazy L**, 1939, Saalfield, 400 pgs.	11.00	27.50	70.00
1148- **David Copperfield**, 1934, Whitman, hard-c, 160 pgs., photo-c, movie scenes (W. C. Fields)	20.00	50.00	140.00
nn- **David Copperfield**, 1934, Whitman, soft-c, 164 pgs., movie scenes	20.00	50.00	140.00
1151- **Death by Short Wave**, 1938, Saalfield	12.00	30.00	75.00
1156- **Denny the Ace Detective**, 1938, Saalfield, 400 pgs.	10.00	25.00	65.00
1431- **Desert Eagle and the Hidden Fortress, The**, 1941, Whitman, 432 pgs., flip pictures	12.00	30.00	75.00
1458- **Desert Eagle Rides Again, The**, 1939, Whitman, 300 pgs.	12.00	30.00	75.00
1136- **Desert Justice**, 1938, Saalfield, 400 pgs.	10.00	25.00	65.00
1484- **Detective Higgins of the Racket Squad**, 1938, Whitman, 432 pgs.	12.00	30.00	75.00
1124- **Dickie Moore in the Little Red School House**, 1936, Whitman, 240 pgs., photo-c, movie scenes (Chesterfield Motion Picts. Corp)	13.00	32.50	90.00
W-707- **Dick Tracy the Detective, The Adventures of**, 1933, Whitman, 320 pgs. (The 1st Big Little Book), by Chester Gould (Scarce)	289.00	722.00	2310.00
nn- **Dick Tracy Detective, The Adventures of**, 1933, Whitman, 52 pgs., 4" x 5 1/2", premium-no ads, soft-c, by Chester Gould	100.00	250.00	695.00
nn- **Dick Tracy Detective, The Adventures of**, 1933, Whitman, 52 pgs., 4" x 5 1/2", inside back-c & back-c ads for Sundial Shoes, soft-c, by Chester Gould	107.00	268.00	750.00
710- **Dick Tracy and Dick Tracy, Jr.** (The Advs. of ...), 1933, Whitman, 320 pgs., by Chester Gould	79.00	198.00	550.00
nn- **Dick Tracy and Dick Tracy, Jr.** (The Advs. of ...), 1933, Whitman, 52 pgs., premium-no ads, soft-c, 4" x 5 1/2", by Chester Gould	79.00	198.00	550.00
nn- **Dick Tracy the Detective and Dick Tracy, Jr.**, 1933, Whitman, 52 pgs., premium-no ads, 3 1/2"x 5 1/4", soft-c, by Chester Gould	79.00	198.00	550.00
723- **Dick Tracy Out West**, 1933, Whitman, 300 pgs., by Chester Gould	49.00	122.00	345.00
749- **Dick Tracy from Colorado to Nova Scotia**, 1933, Whitman, 320 pgs., by Chester Gould	45.00	113.00	315.00
nn- **Dick Tracy from Colorado to Nova Scotia**, 1933, Whitman, 204 pgs., premium-no ads, soft-c, by Chester Gould	49.00	122.00	345.00
1105- **Dick Tracy and the Stolen Bonds**, 1934, Whitman, 320 pgs., by Chester Gould	26.00	65.00	185.00
1112- **Dick Tracy and the Racketeer Gang**, 1936, Whitman, 432 pgs., by Chester Gould	21.00	52.50	145.00
1137- **Dick Tracy Solves the Penfield Mystery**, 1934, Whitman, 320 pgs., by Chester Gould	26.00	65.00	185.00

1436 - Dick Tracy and the Mad Killer
© NYNS

1114 - Dog Stars of Hollywood
© Saalfield

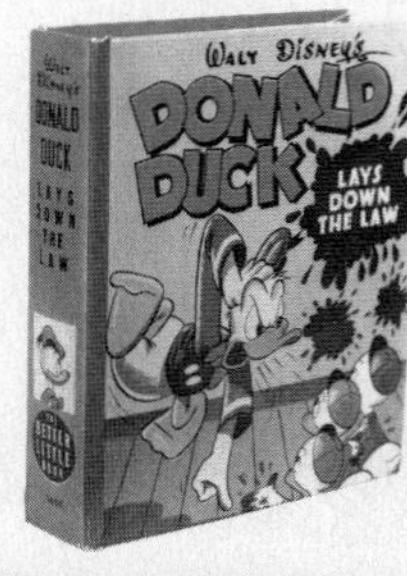

1449 - Donald Duck Lays Down the Law
© DIS

GD FN VF/NM

nn- Dick Tracy Solves the Penfield Mystery, 1934, Whitman, 324 pgs., premium-no ads, 3-color, soft-c, by Chester Gould 54.00 135.00 375.00

1163- Dick Tracy and the Boris Arson Gang, 1935, Whitman, 432 pgs., by Chester Gould 24.00 60.00 165.00

1170- Dick Tracy on the Trail of Larceny Lu, 1935, Whitman, 432 pgs., by Chester Gould 21.00 52.50 145.00

1185- Dick Tracy in Chains of Crime, 1936, Whitman, 432 pgs., by Chester Gould 24.00 60.00 165.00

1412- Dick Tracy and Yogee Yamma, 1946, Whitman, 352 pgs., by Chester Gould 21.00 52.50 145.00

1420- Dick Tracy and the Hotel Murders, 1937, Whitman, 432 pgs., by Chester Gould 24.00 60.00 165.00

1434- Dick Tracy and the Phantom Ship, 1940, Whitman, 432 pgs., by Chester Gould 24.00 60.00 165.00

1436- Dick Tracy and the Mad Killer, 1947, Whitman, 288 pgs., by Chester Gould 18.00 45.00 125.00

1439- Dick Tracy and His G-Men, 1941, Whitman, 432 pgs., flip pictures, by Chester Gould 24.00 60.00 165.00

1445- Dick Tracy and the Bicycle Gang, 1948, Whitman, 288 pgs., by Chester Gould 18.00 45.00 125.00

1446- Detective Dick Tracy and the Spider Gang, 1937, Whitman, 240 pgs., movie scenes from "Adventures of Dick Tracy" (Republic serial) 29.00 73.00 200.00

1449- Dick Tracy Special F.B.I. Operative, 1943, Whitman, 432 pgs. by Chester Gould 24.00 60.00 165.00

1454- Dick Tracy on the High Seas, 1939, Whitman, 432 pgs., by Chester Gould 24.00 60.00 165.00

1460- Dick Tracy and the Tiger Lilly Gang, 1949, Whitman, 288 pgs., by Chester Gould 18.00 45.00 125.00

1478- Dick Tracy on Voodoo Island, 1944, Whitman, 352 pgs., by Chester Gould 18.00 45.00 125.00

1479- Detective Dick Tracy Vs. Crooks in Disguise, 1939, Whitman, 432 pgs., flip pictures, by Chester Gould 24.00 60.00 165.00

1482- Dick Tracy and the Wreath Kidnapping Case, 1945, Whitman, 352 pgs. 20.00 50.00 140.00

1488- Dick Tracy the Super-Detective, 1939, Whitman, 432 pgs., by Chester Gould 24.00 60.00 165.00

1491- Dick Tracy the Man with No Face, 1938, Whitman, 432 pgs. 24.00 60.00 165.00

1495- Dick Tracy Returns, 1939, Whitman, 432 pgs., based on Republic Motion Picture serial, Chester Gould-a 24.00 60.00 165.00

2001- (#1)-Dick Tracy-Encounters Facey, 1967, Whitman, 260 pgs., 39 cents, hard-c, color illos 4.00 10.00 27.00

4055- Dick Tracy, The Adventures of, 1934, Whitman, 7" x 9 1/2", 320 pgs., Big Big Book, by Chester Gould 107.00 268.00 750.00

4071- Dick Tracy and the Mystery of the Purple Cross, 1938, 7" x 9 1/2", 320 pgs., Big Big Book, by Chester Gould (Scarce) 130.00 327.00 1045.00

nn- Dick Tracy and the Invisible Man, 1939, Whitman, 3 1/4" x 3 3/4", 132 pgs., stapled, soft-c, Quaker Oats premium; NBC radio play script, Chester Gould-a 41.00 103.00 285.00

Vol. 2- Dick Tracy's Ghost Ship, 1939, Whitman, 3 1/2" x 3 1/2", 132 pgs., soft-c, stapled, Quaker Oats premium; NBC radio play script episode from actual radio show; Gould-a 41.00 103.00 285.00

3- Dick Tracy Meets a New Gang, 1934, Whitman, 3" x 3 1/2", 132 pgs., soft-c, Tarzan Ice Cream cup lid premium 70.00 175.00 490.00

11- Dick Tracy in Smashing the Famon Racket, 1938, Whitman, 3 3/4" x 3 1/2", Buddy Book-ice cream premium, by Chester Gould 70.00 175.00 490.00

nn- Dick Tracy Gets His Man, 1938, Whitman, 36 pgs., 2 1/2" x 3 1/2", Penny Book 12.00 30.00 75.00

nn- Dick Tracy the Detective, 1938, Whitman, 36 pgs., 2 1/2" x 3 1/2", Penny Book 12.00 30.00 75.00

9- Dick Tracy and the Frozen Bullet Murders, 1941, Dell, 196 pgs., Fast-Action Story, soft-c, by Gould 41.00 103.00 285.00

6833- Dick Tracy Detective and Federal Agent, 1936, Dell, 244 pgs., Cartoon Story Books, hard-c, by Gould 49.00 122.00 345.00

nn- Dick Tracy Detective and Federal Agent, 1936, Dell, 244 pgs., Fast-Action Story, soft-c, by Gould 46.00 115.00 320.00

GD FN VF/NM

nn- Dick Tracy and the Blackmailers, 1939, Dell, 196 pgs., Fast-Action Story, soft-c, by Gould 46.00 115.00 320.00

nn- Dick Tracy and the Chain of Evidence, Detective, 1938, Dell, 196 pgs., Fast-Action Story, soft-c, by Chester Gould 46.00 115.00 320.00

nn- Dick Tracy and the Crook Without a Face, 1938, Whitman, 68 pgs., 3 1/4" x 3 1/2", Pan-Am giveaway, Gould-c/a 49.00 122.00 345.00

nn- Dick Tracy and the Maroon Mask Gang, 1938, Dell, 196 pgs., Fast-Action Story, soft-c, by Gould 46.00 115.00 320.00

nn- Dick Tracy Cross-Country Race, 1934, Whitman, 8 pgs., 2 1/2" x 3", Big Thrill chewing gum premium (6 diff.) 18.00 45.00 125.00

nn- Dick Whittington and his Cat, nd(1930s), np(Whitman), 36 pgs., Penny Book 5.00 12.50 33.00

Dinglehoofer and His Dog Adolph (See Top-Line Comics)

Dinky (See Jackie Cooper in ...)

1464- Dirigible ZR90 and the Disappearing Zeppelin (Captain Robb of ...), 1941, Whitman, 300 pgs., Al Lewin-a 20.00 50.00 140.00

1167- Dixie Dugan Among the Cowboys, 1939, Saalfield, 400 pgs. 12.00 30.00 85.00

1188- Dixie Dugan and Cuddles, 1940, Saalfield, 400 pgs., by Striebel & McEvoy 12.00 30.00 85.00

Doctor Doom (See Foreign Spies... & International Spy...)

Dog of Flanders, A (See Frankie Thomas in ...)

1114- Dog Stars of Hollywood, 1936, Saalfield, photo-c, photo-illos 16.00 40.00 115.00

1594- Dog Stars of Hollywood, 1936, Saalfield, photo-c, soft-c, photo-illos 16.00 40.00 115.00

Donald Duck (See Silly Symphony... & Walt Disney's ...)

800- Donald Duck in Bringing Up the Boys, 1948, Whitman, hard-c, Story Hour series 12.00 30.00 85.00

1404- Donald Duck (Says Such a Life) (Disney), 1939, Whitman, 432 pgs., Taliaferro-a 31.00 78.00 220.00

1411- Donald Duck and Ghost Morgan's Treasure (Disney), 1946, Whitman, All Pictures Comics, Barks-a; reprints Four Color #9 38.00 95.00 255.00

1422- Donald Duck Sees Stars (Disney), 1941, Whitman, 432 pgs., flip pictures, Taliaferro-a 31.00 78.00 215.00

1424- Donald Duck Says Such Luck (Disney), 1941, Whitman, 432 pgs., flip pictures, Taliaferro-a 31.00 78.00 215.00

1430- Donald Duck Headed For Trouble (Disney), 1942, Whitman, 432 pgs., flip pictures, Taliaferro-a 31.00 78.00 215.00

1432- Donald Duck and the Green Serpent (Disney), 1947, Whitman, All Pictures Comics, Barks-a; reprints Four Color #108 34.00 85.00 240.00

1434- Donald Duck Forgets To Duck (Disney), 1939, Whitman, 432 pgs., Taliaferro-a 31.00 78.00 215.00

1438- Donald Duck Off the Beam (Disney), 1943, Whitman, 352 pgs., flip pictures, Taliaferro-a 31.00 78.00 215.00

1438- Donald Duck Off the Beam (Disney), 1943, Whitman, 432 pgs., flip pictures, Taliaferro-a 31.00 78.00 215.00

1449- Donald Duck Lays Down the Law, 1948, Whitman, 288 pgs., 31.00 78.00 215.00

1457- Donald Duck in Volcano Valley (Disney), 1949, Whitman, 288 pgs., Barks-a 31.00 78.00 215.00

1462- Donald Duck Gets Fed Up (Disney), 1940, Whitman, 432 pgs.,Taliaferro-a 31.00 78.00 215.00

1478- Donald Duck-Hunting For Trouble (Disney), 1938, Whitman, 432 pgs., Taliaferro-a 31.00 78.00 215.00

1484- Donald Duck is Here Again!, 1944, Whitman, All Pictures Comics, Taliaferro-a 31.00 78.00 215.00

1486- Donald Duck Up in the Air (Disney), 1945, Whitman, 352 pgs., Barks-a 34.00 85.00 240.00

705-10- Donald Duck and the Mystery of the Double X, (Disney), 1949, Whitman, Barks-a 16.00 40.00 115.00

2033-(#33)- Donald Duck, Luck of the Ducks, 1969, Whitman, 256 pgs., hard-c, 39 cents, color illos. 4.00 10.00 22.00

2009-(#9)-Donald Duck-The Fabulous Diamond Fountain, (Walt Disney), 1967, Whitman, 260 pgs., 39 cents, hard-c, color illos 4.00 10.00 27.00

5756- Donald Duck-The Fabulous Diamond Fountain,

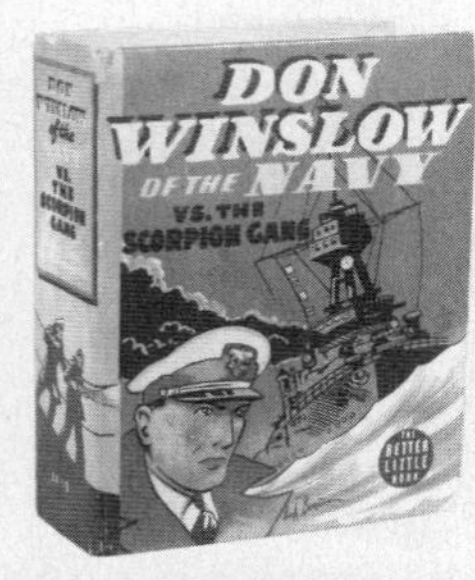

1419 - Don Winslow of the Navy Vs. the Scorpion Gang © WHIT

Ella Cinders Solves a Mystery © WHIT

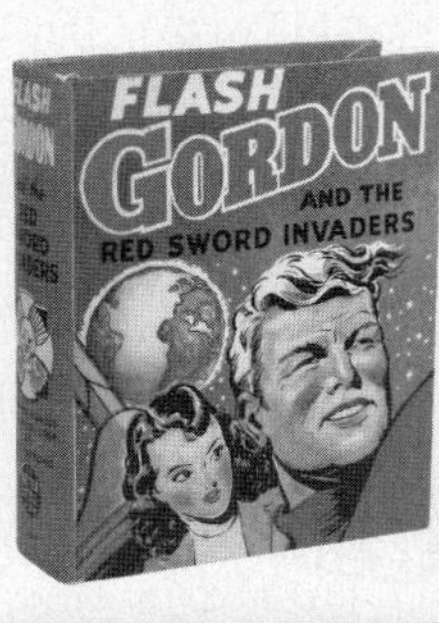

1479 - Flash Gordon and the Red Sword Invaders © KING

GD FN VF/NM

(Walt Disney), 1973, Whitman, 260 pgs., 79 cents, soft-c, color illos 3.00 7.50 20.00

5756-1- Donald Duck-The Fabulous Diamond Fountain, (Walt Disney), 1973, Whitman, 260 pgs., 79 cents, soft-c, color illos 3.00 7.50 20.00

5756-2- Donald Duck-The Fabulous Diamond Fountain, (Walt Disney), 1973, Whitman, 260 pgs., 79 cents, soft-c, color illos 3.00 7.50 20.00

5760- Donald Duck in Volcano Valley (Disney), 1973, Whitman, 39 cents, flip-it book 3.00 7.50 20.00

5760-2- Donald Duck in Volcano Valley (Disney), 1973, Whitman, 79 cents, flip-it book 2.00 5.00 14.00

5764- Donald Duck, Luck of the Ducks, 1969, Whitman, 256 pgs., soft-c, 49 cents, color illos. 3.00 7.50 20.00

5773- Donald Duck - The Lost Jungle City, 1975, Whitman, 49 cents, flip-it book; 6 printings through 1980 2.00 5.00 14.00

nn- Donald Duck and the Ducklings, 1938, Dell, 194 pgs., Fast-Action Story, soft-c, Taliaferro-a 58.00 146.00 410.00

nn- Donald Duck Out of Luck (Disney), 1940, Dell, 196 pgs., Fast-Action Story, has Four Color #4 on back-c, Taliaferro-a 58.00 146.00 410.00

8- Donald Duck Takes It on the Chin (Disney), 1941, Dell, 196 pgs., Fast-Action Story, soft-c, Taliaferro-a 58.00 146.00 410.00

L13- Donnie and the Pirates, 1935, Lynn, 192 pgs. 12.00 30.00 85.00

1438- Don O'Dare Finds War, 1940, Whitman, 432 pgs. 11.00 27.50 70.00

1107- Don Winslow, U.S.N., 1935, Whitman, 432 pgs. 20.00 50.00 140.00

nn- Don Winslow, U.S.N., 1935, Whitman, 436 pgs., premium-no ads, 3-color, soft-c 31.00 78.00 220.00

1408- Don Winslow and the Giant Girl Spy, 1946, Whitman, 352 pgs. 13.00 32.50 90.00

1418- Don Winslow Navy Intelligence Ace, 1942, Whitman, 432 pgs., flip pictures 18.00 45.00 125.00

1419- Don Winslow of the Navy Vs. the Scorpion Gang, 1938, Whitman, 432 pgs. 18.00 45.00 125.00

1453- Don Winslow of the Navy and the Secret Enemy Base, 1943, Whitman, 352 pgs. 18.00 45.00 125.00

1489- Don Winslow of the Navy and the Great War Plot, 1940, Whitman, 432 pgs. 18.00 45.00 125.00

nn- Don Winslow U.S. Navy and the Missing Admiral, 1938, Whitman, 36 pgs., 2 1/2" x 3 1/2", Penny Book 11.00 27.50 70.00

1137- Doomed To Die, 1938, Saalfield, 400 pgs. 11.00 27.50 70.00

1140- Down Cartridge Creek, 1938, Saalfield, 400 pgs. 11.00 27.50 70.00

1416- Draftie of the U.S. Army, 1943, Whitman, All Pictures Comics 12.00 30.00 75.00

1100B- Dreams (Your dreams & what they mean), 1938, Whitman, 36 pgs., 2 1/2" x 3 1/2", Penny Book 4.00 10.00 27.00

24- Dumb Dora and Bing Brown, 1936, Lynn 14.00 35.00 95.00

1400- Dumbo, of the Circus - Only His Ears Grew! (Disney), 1941, Whitman, 432 pgs., based on Disney movie 28.00 70.00 195.00

10- Dumbo the Flying Elephant (Disney), 1944, Dell, 194 pgs., Fast-Action Story, soft-c 46.00 115.00 320.00

nn- East O' the Sun and West O' the Moon, nd (1930s), np (Whitman), 36 pgs., 3" x 2 1/2", Penny Book 4.00 10.00 27.00

774- Eddie Cantor in an Hour with You, 1934, Whitman, 154 pgs., 4 1/4" x 5 1/4", photo-c, movie scenes 16.00 40.00 115.00

nn- Eddie Cantor in Laughland, 1934, Goldsmith, 132 pgs., soft-c, photo-c, Vallely-a 16.00 40.00 115.00

1106- Ella Cinders and the Mysterious House, 1934, Whitman, 432 pgs. 15.00 37.50 105.00

nn- Ella Cinders and the Mysterious House, 1934, Whitman, 52 pgs., premium-no ads, soft-c, 3 1/2" x 5 3/4" 22.00 52.50 155.00

nn- Ella Cinders, 1935, Whitman, 148 pgs., 3 1/4" x 4", Tarzan Ice Cream cup lid premium 36.00 90.00 255.00

nn- Ella Cinders Plays Duchess, 1938, Whitman, 68 pgs., 3 3/4" x 3 1/2", Pan-Am Oil premium 16.00 40.00 115.00

nn- Ella Cinders Solves a Mystery, 1938, Whitman, 68 pgs., Pan-Am Oil premium, soft-c 16.00 40.00 115.00

11- Ella Cinders' Exciting Experience, 1934, Whitman, 3 1/2" x 3 1/2", 132 pgs., Tarzan Ice Cream cup lid giveaway 36.00 90.00 255.00

1406- Ellery Queen the Adventure of the Last Man Club, 1940, Whitman, 432 pgs. 15.00 37.50 105.00

1472- Ellery Queen the Master Detective, 1942, Whitman, 432 pgs., flip pictures 15.00 37.50 105.00

1081- Elmer and his Dog Spot, 1935, Saalfield, hard-c 11.00 27.50 70.00

1311- Elmer and his Dog Spot, 1935, Saalfield, soft-c 11.00 27.50 70.00

722- Erik Noble and the Forty-Niners, 1934, Whitman, 384 pgs. 11.00 27.50 70.00

nn- Erik Noble and the Forty-Niners, 1934, Whitman, 386 pgs., 3-color, soft-c (Rare) 64.00 192.00 450.00

2019-(#19)- Fantastic Four in the House of Horrors, 1968, Whitman, 256 pgs., hard-c, color illos. 4.00 10.00 27.00

5775 - Fantastic Four in the House of Horrors, 1976, Whitman, 256 pgs., soft-c, color illos. 3.00 7.50 20.00

5775-1 - Fantastic Four in the House of Horrors, 1976, Whitman, 256 pgs., soft-c, color illos. 3.00 7.50 20.00

1058- Farmyard Symphony, The (Disney), 1939, 5" X 5 1/2", 68 pgs., hard-c 15.00 37.50 105.00

1129- Felix the Cat, 1936, Whitman, 432 pgs., Messmer-a 33.00 83.00 230.00

1439- Felix the Cat, 1943, Whitman, All Pictures Comics, Messmer-a 28.00 70.00 195.00

1465- Felix the Cat, 1945, Whitman, All Pictures Comics, Messmer-a 24.00 60.00 165.00

nn- Felix (Flip book), 1967, World Retrospective of Animation Cinema, 188 pgs., 2 1/2" x 4" by Otto Messmer 4.00 10.00 27.00

nn- Fighting Cowboy of Nugget Gulch, The, 1939, Whitman, 2 1/2" x 3 1/2", Penny Book 7.00 17.50 45.00

1401- Fighting Heroes Battle for Freedom, 1943, Whitman, All Pictures Comics, from "Heroes of Democracy" strip, by Stookie Allen 11.00 27.50 70.00

6- Fighting President, The, 1934, EVW (Five Star Library), 160 pgs., photo-c, photo ill., F. D. Roosevelt 12.00 30.00 85.00

nn- Fire Chief Ed Wynn and "His Old Fire Horse," 1934, Goldsmith, 132 pgs., H. Vallely-a, photo, soft-c 12.00 30.00 85.00

1464- Flame Boy and the Indians' Secret, 1938, Whitman, 300 pgs., Sekakuku-a (Hopi Indian) 11.00 27.50 70.00

22- Flaming Guns, 1935, EVW, with Tom Mix, movie scenes 71.00 213.00 500.00

1110- Flash Gordon on the Planet Mongo, 1934, Whitman, 320 pgs., by Alex Raymond 49.00 122.00 345.00

1166- Flash Gordon and the Monsters of Mongo, 1935, Whitman, 432 pgs., by Alex Raymond 41.00 103.00 290.00

nn- Flash Gordon and the Monsters of Mongo, 1935, Whitman, 436 pgs., premium-no ads, 3-color, soft-c, by Alex Raymond 61.00 153.00 430.00

1171- Flash Gordon and the Tournaments of Mongo, 1935, Whitman, 432 pgs., by Alex Raymond 43.00 108.00 300.00

1190- Flash Gordon and the Witch Queen of Mongo, 1936, Whitman, 432 pgs., by Alex Raymond 43.00 108.00 300.00

1407- Flash Gordon in the Water World of Mongo, 1937, Whitman, 432 pgs., by Alex Raymond 38.00 95.00 255.00

1423- Flash Gordon and the Perils of Mongo, 1940, Whitman, 432 pgs., by Alex Raymond 33.00 83.00 230.00

1424- Flash Gordon in the Jungles of Mongo, 1947, Whitman, 352 pgs., by Alex Raymond 24.00 60.00 170.00

1443- Flash Gordon in the Ice World of Mongo, 1942, Whitman, 432 pgs., flip pictures, by Alex Raymond 36.00 90.00 250.00

1447- Flash Gordon and the Fiery Desert of Mongo, 1948, Whitman, 288 pgs., Raymond-a 24.00 60.00 170.00

1469- Flash Gordon and the Power Men of Mongo, 1943, Whitman, 352 pgs., by Alex Raymond 36.00 90.00 250.00

1479- Flash Gordon and the Red Sword Invaders, 1945, Whitman, 352 pgs., by Alex Raymond 34.00 85.00 240.00

1467 - Flint Roper and the Six-Gun Showdown © WHIT

1164 - Freckles and the Lost Diamond Mine © WHIT

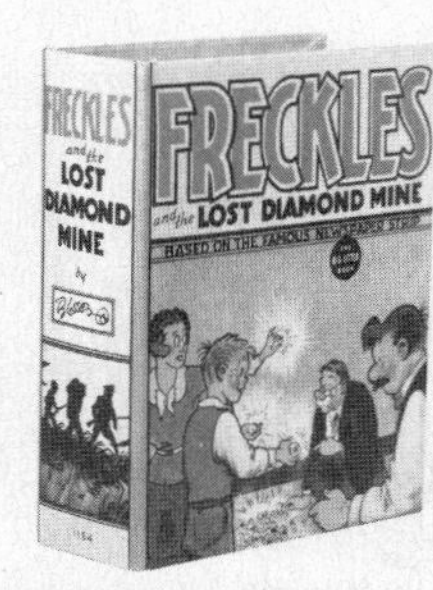

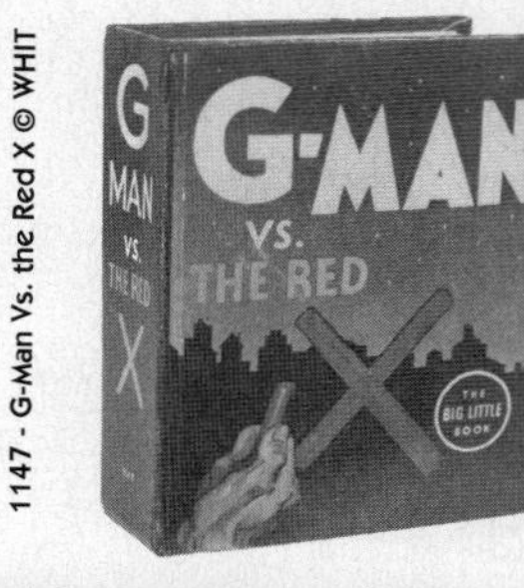
1147 - G-Man Vs. the Red X © WHIT

GD FN VF/NM

1484- Flash Gordon and the Tyrant of Mongo, 1941, Whitman, 432 pgs., flip pictures, by Alex Raymond 36.00 90.00 250.00

1492- Flash Gordon in the Forest Kingdom of Mongo, 1938, Whitman, 432 pgs., by Alex Raymond 46.00 115.00 320.00

12- Flash Gordon and the Ape Men of Mor, 1942, Dell, 196 pgs., Fast-Action Story, by Alex Raymond 64.00 160.00 450.00

6833- Flash Gordon Vs. the Emperor of Mongo, 1936, Dell, 244 pgs., Cartoon Story Books, hard-c, Alex Raymond-c/a 79.00 198.00 550.00

nn- Flash Gordon Vs. the Emperor of Mongo, 1936, Dell, 244 pgs., Fast-Action Story, soft-c, Alex Raymond-c/a 62.00 155.00 440.00

1467- Flint Roper and the Six-Gun Showdown, 1941, Whitman, 300 pgs. 11.00 27.50 70.00

2014-(#14)- Flintstones-The Case of the Many Missing Things, 1968, Whitman, 260 pgs., 39 cents, hard-c, color illos 4.00 10.00 27.00

nn- Flintstones: A Friend From the Past, 1977, Modern Promotions, 244 pgs., 49 cents, soft-c, flip pictures 2.00 5.00 11.00

nn- Flintstones: It's About Time, 1977, Modern Promotions, 244 pgs., 49 cents, soft-c, flip pictures 2.00 5.00 11.00

nn- Flintstones: Pebbles & Bamm-Bamm Meet Santa Claus, 1977, Modern Promotions, 244 pgs., 49 cents, soft-c, flip pictures 2.00 5.00 11.00

nn- Flintstones: The Great Balloon Race, 1977, Modern Promotions, 244 pgs., 49 cents, soft-c, flip pictures 2.00 5.00 11.00

nn- Flintstones: The Mystery of the Many Missing Things, 1977, Modern Promotions, 244 pgs., 49 cents, soft-c, flip pictures 2.00 5.00 11.00

2003-(#3)- Flipper-Killer Whale Trouble, 1967, Whitman, 260 pgs., hard-c, 39 cents, color illos 3.00 7.50 20.00

2032-(#32)- Flipper, Deep-Sea Photographer, 1969, Whitman, 256 pgs., hard-c, color illos. 3.00 7.50 20.00

1108- Flying the Sky Clipper with Winsie Atkins, 1936, Whitman, 432 pgs. 11.00 27.50 70.00

1460- Foreign Spies Doctor Doom and the Ghost Submarine, 1939, Whitman, 432 pgs., Al McWilliams-a 13.00 32.50 90.00

1100B- Fortune Teller, 1938, Whitman, 36 pgs., 2 1/2" x 3 1/2", Penny Book 5.00 12.50 33.00

1175- Frank Buck Presents Ted Towers Animal Master, 1935, Whitman, 432 pgs. 12.00 30.00 80.00

2015-(#15)-Frankenstein, Jr. - The Menace of the Heartless Monster, 1968, Whitman, 260 pgs., 39 cents, hard-c, color illos. 4.00 10.00 27.00

16- Frankie Thomas in A Dog of Flanders, 1935, EVW, movie scenes 15.00 37.50 105.00

1121- Frank Merriwell at Yale, 1935, 432 pgs. 11.00 27.50 70.00

Freckles and His Friends in the North Woods (See Top-Line Comics)

nn- Freckles and His Friends Stage a Play, 1938, Whitman, 36 pgs., 2 1/2" x 3 1/2", Penny Book 11.00 27.50 70.00

1164- Freckles and the Lost Diamond Mine, 1937, Whitman, 432 pgs., Merrill Blosser-a 12.00 30.00 85.00

nn- Freckles and the Mystery Ship, 1935, Whitman, 66 pgs., Pan-Am premium 16.00 40.00 115.00

1100B- Fun, Puzzles, Riddles, 1938, Whitman, 36 pgs., 2 1/2" x 3 1/2", Penny Book 4.00 10.00 27.00

1433- Gang Busters Step In, 1939, Whitman, 432 pgs., Henry E. Vallely-a 13.00 32.50 90.00

1437- Gang Busters Smash Through, 1942, Whitman, 432 pgs. 13.00 32.50 90.00

1451- Gang Busters in Action!, 1938, Whitman, 432 pgs. 13.00 32.50 90.00

nn- Gang Busters and Guns of the Law, 1940, Dell, 4" x 5", 194 pgs., Fast-Action Story, soft-c 41.00 103.00 285.00

nn- Gang Busters and the Radio Clues, 1938, Whitman, 36 pgs., 2 1/2" x 3 1/2", Penny Book 11.00 27.50 70.00

1409- Gene Autry and Raiders of the Range, 1946, Whitman, 352 pgs. 15.00 37.50 105.00

1425- Gene Autry and the Mystery of Paint Rock Canyon, 1947, Whitman, 288 pgs. 15.00 37.50 105.00

1428- Gene Autry Special Ranger, 1941, Whitman, 432 pgs., Erwin Hess-a 20.00 50.00 140.00

GD FN VF/NM

1433- Gene Autry in Public Cowboy No. 1, 1938, Whitman, 240 pgs., photo-c, movie scenes (1st Autry BLB) 38.00 95.00 255.00

1434- Gene Autry and the Gun-Smoke Reckoning, 1943, Whitman, 352 pgs. 19.00 47.50 135.00

1439- Gene Autry and the Land Grab Mystery, 1948, Whitman, 290 pgs. 14.00 35.00 95.00

1456- Gene Autry in Special Ranger Rule, 1945, Whitman, 352 pgs., Henry E. Vallely-a 19.00 47.50 135.00

1461- Gene Autry and the Red Bandit's Ghost, 1949, Whitman, 288 pgs. 13.00 32.50 90.00

1483- Gene Autry in Law of the Range, 1939, Whitman, 432 pgs. 19.00 47.50 135.00

1493- Gene Autry and the Hawk of the Hills, 1942, Whitman, 428 pgs., flip pictures, Vallely-a 19.00 47.50 135.00

1494- Gene Autry Cowboy Detective, 1940, Whitman, 432 pgs., Erwin Hess-a 19.00 47.50 135.00

700-10- Gene Autry and the Bandits of Silver Tip, 1949, Whitman 12.00 30.00 80.00

714-10- Gene Autry and the Range War, 1950, Whitman 12.00 30.00 80.00

nn- Gene Autry in Gun-Smoke, 1938, Dell, 196 pgs., Fast-Action story, soft-c 46.00 115.00 320.00

2035-(#35)- Gentle Ben, Mystery of the Everglades, 1969, Whitman, 256 pgs., hard-c, color illos. 3.00 7.50 20.00

1176- Gentleman Joe Palooka, 1940, Saalfield, 400 pgs. 16.00 40.00 115.00

George O'Brien (See The Cowboy Millionaire)

1101- George O'Brien and the Arizona Badman, 1936?, Whitman 15.00 37.50 105.00

1418- George O'Brien in Gun Law, 1938, Whitman, 240 pgs., photo-c, movie scenes, RKO Radio Pictures 15.00 37.50 105.00

1457- George O'Brien and the Hooded Riders, 1940, Whitman, 432 pgs., Erwin Hess-a 11.00 27.50 70.00

nn- George O'Brien and the Arizona Bad Man, 1939, Whitman, 36 pgs., 2 1/2" x 3 1/2", Penny Book 11.00 27.50 70.00

1462- Ghost Avenger, 1943, Whitman, 432 pgs., flip pictures, Henry Vallely-a 11.00 27.50 70.00

nn- Ghost Gun Gang Meet Their Match, The, 1939. Whitman, 2 1/2" x 3 1/2", Penny Book 10.00 25.00 65.00

nn- Gingerbread Boy, The, nd(1930s), np(Whitman), 36 pgs., Penny Book 4.00 10.00 22.00

1118- G-Man on the Crime Trail, 1936, Whitman, 432 pgs. 12.00 30.00 80.00

1147- G-Man Vs. the Red X, 1936, Whitman, 432 pgs. 14.00 35.00 95.00

1162- G-Man Allen, 1939, Saalfield, 400 pgs. 11.00 27.50 70.00

1173- G-Man in Action, A, 1940, Saalfield, 400 pgs., J.R. White-a 11.00 27.50 70.00

1434- G-Man and the Radio Bank Robberies, 1937, Whitman, 432 pgs. 13.00 32.50 90.00

1469- G-Man and the Gun Runners, The, 1940, Whitman, 432 pgs. 13.00 32.50 90.00

1470- G-Man vs. the Fifth Column, 1941, Whitman, 432 pgs., flip pictures 13.00 32.50 90.00

1493- G-Man Breaking the Gambling Ring, 1938, Whitman, 432 pgs., James Gary-a 13.00 32.50 90.00

nn- G-Man on Lightning Island, 1936, Dell, 244 pgs., Fast-Action Story, soft-c, Henry E. Vallely-a 33.00 83.00 230.00

nn- G-Man, Underworld Chief, 1938, Whitman, Buddy Book premium, 43.00 129.00 300.00

6833- G-Man on Lightning Island, 1936, Dell, 244 pgs., Cartoon Story Book, hard-c, Henry E. Vallely-a 29.00 73.00 200.00

4- G-Men Foil the Kidnappers, 1936, Whitman, 132 pgs., 3 1/2" x 3 1/2", soft-c, Tarzan Ice Cream cup lid premium 36.00 90.00 255.00

1157- G-Men on the Trail, 1938, Saalfield, 400 pgs. 11.00 27.50 70.00

1168- G Men on the Job, 1935, Whitman, 432 pgs. 12.00 30.00 85.00

nn- G-Men on the Job Again, 1938, Whitman, 36 pgs., 2 1/2" x 3 1/2", Penny Book 11.00 27.50 70.00

nn- G-Men and Kidnap Justice, 1938, Whitman, 68 pgs., Pan-Am premium, soft-c 12.00 30.00 85.00

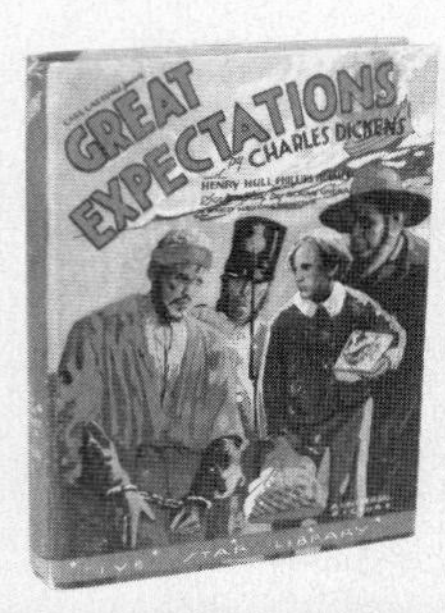

8 - Great Expectations © EVW

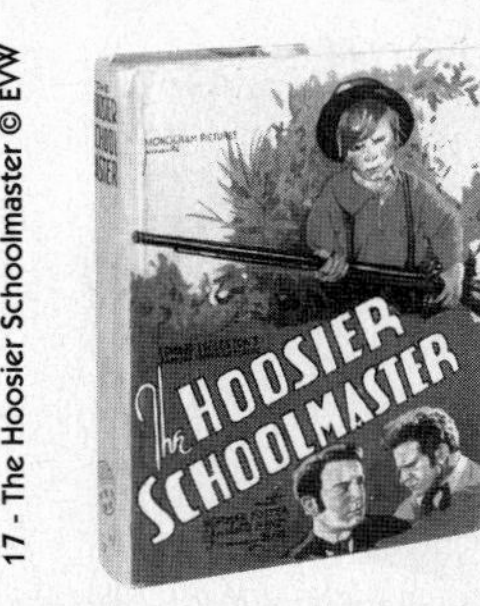

17 - The Hoosier Schoolmaster © EVW

1435 - Jack Armstrong and the Ivory Treasure © WHIT

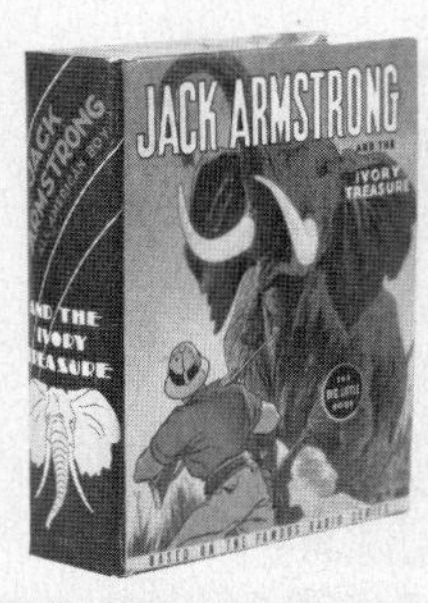

GD FN VF/NM

nn- G-Men and the Missing Clues, 1938, Whitman, 36 pgs., 2 1/2"x 3 1/2", Penny Book 11.00 27.50 70.00

1097- Go Into Your Dance, 1935, Saalfield, 160 pgs.. photo-c, movie scenes with Al Jolson & Ruby Keeler 15.00 37.50 105.00

1577- Go Into Your Dance, 1935, Saalfield, 160 pgs., photo-c, movie scenes, soft-c 15.00 37.50 105.00

2021- Goofy in Giant Trouble (Walt Disney's ...), 1968, Whitman, hard-c, 260 pgs., 39 cents, color illos. 3.00 7.50 20.00

5751- Goofy in Giant Trouble (Walt Disney's ...), 1968, Whitman, soft-c, 260 pgs., 39 cents, color illos. 3.00 7.50 20.00

5751-2- Goofy in Giant Trouble, 1968 (1980-reprint of '67 version), Whitman, soft-c, 260 pgs., 79 cents, B&W 1.00 2.50 6.00

8- Great Expectations, 1934, EVW, (Five Star Library), 160 pgs., photo-c, movie scenes 20.00 50.00 140.00

1453- Green Hornet Strikes!, The, 1940, Whitman, 432 pgs., Robert Weisman-a 49.00 122.00 345.00

1480- Green Hornet Cracks Down, The, 1942, Whitman, 432 pgs., flip pictures, Henry Vallely-a 46.00 115.00 320.00

1496- Green Hornet Returns, The, 1941, Whitman, 432 pgs., flip pictures 49.00 122.00 345.00

5778- Grimm's Ghost Stories, 1976, Whitman, 256 pgs., Laura French-s adapted from fairy tales; blue spine & back-c 2.00 5.00 13.00

5778-1- Grimm's Ghost Stories, 1976, Whitman, 256 pgs., reprint of #5778; yellow spine & back-c 2.00 5.00 13.00

1172- Gullivers' Travels, 1939, Saalfield, 320 pgs., adapted from Paramount Pict. Cartoons (Rare) 50.00 150.00 350.00

nn- Gumps In Radio Land, The (Andy Gump and the Chest of Gold), 1937, Lehn & Fink Prod. Corp., 100 pgs., 3 1/4" x 5 1/2", Pebeco Tooth Paste giveaway, by Gus Edson 24.00 60.00 165.00

nn- Gunmen of Rustlers' Gulch, The, 1939, Whitman, 36 pgs., 2 1/2" x 3 1/2", Penny Book 11.00 27.50 70.00

1426- Guns in the Roaring West, 1937, Whitman, 300 pgs. 11.00 27.50 70.00

1647- Gunsmoke (TV Series), 1958, Whitman, 280 pgs., 4 1/2" x 5 3/4" 7.00 17.50 44.00

1101- Hairbreath Harry in Department QT, 1935, Whitman, 384 pgs., by J. M. Alexander 12.00 30.00 85.00

1413- Hal Hardy in the Lost Land of Giants, 1938, Whitman, 300 pgs., "The World 1,000,000 Years Ago" 12.00 30.00 85.00

1159- Hall of Fame of the Air, 1936, Whitman, 432 pgs., by Capt. Eddie Rickenbacker 11.00 27.50 70.00

nn- Hansel and Grethel, The Story of, nd (1930s), no publ., 36 pgs., Penny Book 4.00 10.00 22.00

1145- Hap Lee's Selection of Movie Gags, 1935, Whitman, 160 pgs., photos of stars 15.00 37.50 105.00

Happy Prince, The (See Wee Little Books)

1111- Hard Rock Harrigan-A Story of Boulder Dam, 1935, Saalfield, hard-c, photo-c, photo illos. 11.00 27.50 70.00

1591- Hard Rock Harrigan-A Story of Boulder Dam, 1935, Saalfield, soft-c, photo-c, photo illos. 11.00 27.50 70.00

1418- Harold Teen Swinging at the Sugar Bowl, 1939, Whitman, 432 pgs., by Carl Ed 12.00 30.00 80.00

nn- Hercules - The Legendary Journeys, 1998, Chronicle Books, 310 pgs., based on TV series, 1-color (brown) illos 1.00 2.50 9.00

1100B- Hobbies, 1938, Whitman, 36 pgs., 2 1/2" x 3 1/2", Penny Book 4.00 10.00 22.00

1125- Hockey Spare, The, 1937, Saalfield, sports book 8.00 20.00 50.00

1605- Hockey Spare, The, 1937, Saalfield, soft-c 8.00 20.00 50.00

728- Homeless Homer, 1934, Whitman, by Dee Dobbin, for young kids 5.00 12.50 33.00

17- Hoosier Schoolmaster, The, 1935, EVW, movie scenes 15.00 37.50 105.00

715- Houdini's Big Little Book of Magic, 1927 (1933), 300 pgs. 16.00 40.00 115.00

nn- Houdini's Big Little Book of Magic, 1927 (1933), 196 pgs., American Oil Co. premium, soft-c 16.00 40.00 115.00

nn- Houdini's Big Little Book of Magic, 1927 (1933), 204 pgs., Cocomalt premium, soft-c 16.00 40.00 115.00

Huckleberry Finn (See The Adventures of...)

GD FN VF/NM

nn- Huckleberry Hound Newspaper Reporter, 1977, Modern Promotions, 244 pgs., 49 cents, soft-c, flip pictures 2.00 5.00 13.00

1644- Hugh O'Brian TV's Wyatt Earp (TV Series), 1958, Whitman, 280 pgs. 7.00 17.50 44.00

5782-2- Incredible Hulk Lost in Time, 1980, 260 pgs., 79¢-c, soft-c, B&W 2.00 5.00 10.00

1424- Inspector Charlie Chan Villainy on the High Seas, 1942, Whitman, 432 pgs., flip pictures 16.00 40.00 115.00

1186- Inspector Wade of Scotland Yard, 1940, Saalfield, 400 pgs. 11.00 27.50 70.00

1194- Inspector Wade and The Feathered Serpent, 1939, Saalfield, 400 pgs. 11.00 27.50 70.00

1448- Inspector Wade Solves the Mystery of the Red Aces, 1937, Whitman, 432 pgs. 11.00 27.50 70.00

1148- International Spy Doctor Doom Faces Death at Dawn, 1937, Whitman, 432 pgs., Arbo-a 12.00 30.00 85.00

1155- In the Name of the Law, 1937, Whitman, 432 pgs., Henry E. Vallely-a 11.00 27.50 70.00

2012-(#12)-Invaders, The-Alien Missile Threat (TV Series), 1967, Whitman, 260 pgs., hard-c, 39 cents, color illos. 4.00 10.00 27.00

1403- Invisible Scarlet O'Neil, 1942, Whitman, All Pictures Comics, flip pictures 12.00 30.00 85.00

1406- Invisible Scarlet O'Neil Versus the King of the Slums, 1946, Whitman, 352 pgs. 11.00 27.50 70.00

1098- It Happened One Night, 1935, Saalfield, 160 pgs., Little Big Book, Clark Gable, Claudette Colbert photo-c, movie scenes from Academy Award winner 21.00 52.50 145.00

1578- It Happened One Night, 1935, Saalfield, 160 pgs., soft-c 21.00 52.50 145.00

Jack and Jill (See Wee Little Books)

1432- Jack Armstrong and the Mystery of the Iron Key, 1939, Whitman, 432 pgs., Henry E. Vallely-a 12.00 30.00 85.00

1435- Jack Armstrong and the Ivory Treasure, 1937, Whitman, 432 pgs., Henry Vallely-a 12.00 30.00 85.00

Jackie Cooper (See Story Of..)

1084- Jackie Cooper in Peck's Bad Boy, 1934, Saalfield, 160 pgs., hard, photo-c, movie scenes 15.00 37.50 105.00

1314- Jackie Cooper in Peck's Bad Boy, 1934, Saalfield, 160 pgs., soft, photo-c, movie scenes 15.00 37.50 105.00

1402- Jackie Cooper in "Gangster's Boy," 1939, Whitman, 240 pgs., photo-c, movie scenes 15.00 37.50 105.00

13- Jackie Cooper in Dinky, 1935, EVW, 160 pgs., movie scenes 15.00 37.50 105.00

nn- Jack King of the Secret Service and the Counterfeiters, 1939, Whitman, 36 pgs., 2 1/2" x 3 1/2", Penny Book, by John G. Gray 11.00 27.50 70.00

L11- Jack London's Call of the Wild, 1935, Lynn, 20th Cent. Pic., movie scenes with Clark Gable 15.00 37.50 105.00

nn- Jack Pearl as Detective Baron Munchausen, 1934, Goldsmith, 132 pgs., soft-c 12.00 30.00 85.00

1102- Jack Swift and His Rocket Ship, 1934, Whitman, 320 pgs. 24.00 60.00 165.00

1498- Jane Arden the Vanished Princess, Whitman, 300 pgs. 11.00 27.50 70.00

1179- Jane Withers in This is the Life (20th Century-Fox Presents...), 1935, Whitman, 240 pgs., photo-c, movie scenes 15.00 37.50 105.00

1463- Jane Withers in Keep Smiling, 1938, Whitman, 240 pgs., photo-c, movie scenes 15.00 37.50 105.00

Jaragu of the Jungle (See Rex Beach's ...)

1447- Jerry Parker Police Reporter and the Candid Camera Clue, 1941, Whitman, 300 pgs. 11.00 27.50 70.00

Jim Bowie (See Adventures of ...)

nn- Jim Brant of the Highway Patrol and the Mysterious Accident, 1939, Whitman, 36 pgs., 2 1/2" x 3 1/2", Penny Book 10.00 25.00 65.00

1466- Jim Craig State Trooper and the Kidnapped Governor, 1938, Whitman, 432 pgs. 11.00 27.50 70.00

nn- Jim Doyle Private Detective and the Train Hold-Up, 1939, Whitman, 36 pgs., 2 1/2" x 3 1/2", Penny Book 12.00 30.00 75.00

1180- Jim Hardy Ace Reporter, 1940, Saalfield, 400 pgs., Dick Moores-a

1164 - Johnny Forty-Five © Saalfield

1442 - Ken Maynard and the Gun Wolves of the Gila © WHIT

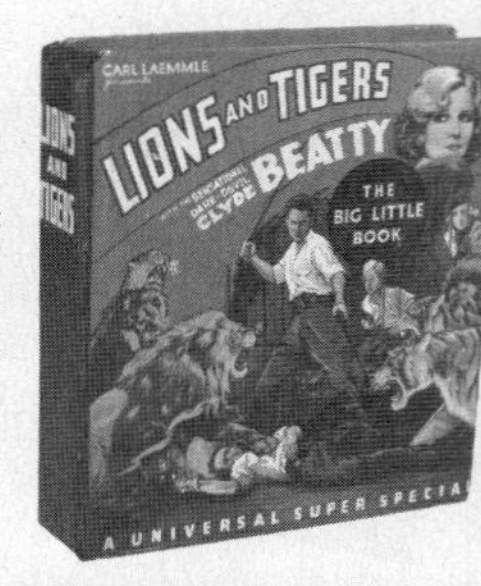

653 - Lions and Tigers (With Clyde Beatty) © WHIT

GD FN VF/NM

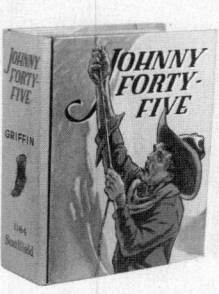

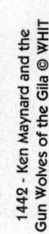

12.00 30.00 75.00
1143- **Jimmy Allen in the Air Mail Robbery**, 1936, Whitman, 432 pgs.
12.00 30.00 75.00
27- **Jimmy Allen in The Sky Parade**, 1936, Lynn, 130 pgs., 5 x 7 1/2", Paramount Pictures, movie scenes 13.00 32.50 90.00
L15- **Jimmy and the Tiger**, 1935, Lynn, 192 pgs. 12.00 30.00 75.00
1428- **Jim Starr of the Border Patrol**, 1937, Whitman, 432 pgs.
12.00 30.00 75.00
Joan of Arc (See Wee Little Books)
1105- **Joe Louis the Brown Bomber**, 1936, Whitman, 240 pgs., photo-c, photo-illos. 24.00 60.00 170.00
Joe Palooka (See Gentleman ...)
1123- **Joe Palooka the Heavyweight Boxing Champ**, 1934, Whitman, 320 pgs., Ham Fisher-a 22.00 52.50 155.00
1168- **Joe Palooka's Great Adventure**, 1939, Saalfield
18.00 45.00 125.00
nn- **Joe Penner's Duck Farm**, 1935, Goldsmith, Henry Vallely-a
12.00 30.00 85.00
1402- **John Carter of Mars**, 1940, Whitman, 432 pgs., John Coleman Burroughs-a 86.00 258.00 600.00
nn- **John Carter of Mars**, 1940, Dell, 194 pgs., Fast-Action Story, soft-c 100.00 300.00 700.00
1164- **Johnny Forty Five**, 1938, Saalfield, 400 pgs. 11.00 27.50 70.00
John Wayne (See Westward Ho!)
1100B- **Jokes** (A book of laughs galore), 1938, Whitman, 36 pgs., 2 1/2" x 3 1/2", Penny Book, laughing guy-c 4.00 10.00 22.00
1100B- **Jokes** (A book of side-splitting funny stories), 1938, Whitman, 36 pgs., 2 1/2" x 3 1/2", Penny Book, clowns on-c 4.00 10.00 22.00
2026-(#26)- **Journey to the Center of the Earth, The Fiery Foe**, 1968, Whitman 4.00 10.00 27.00
Jungle Jim (See Top-Line Comics)
1138- **Jungle Jim**, 1936, Whitman, 432 pgs., Alex Raymond-a
22.00 52.50 155.00
1139- **Jungle Jim and the Vampire Woman**, 1937, Whitman, 432 pgs., Alex Raymond-a 22.00 52.50 155.00
1442- **Junior G-Men**, 1937, Whitman, 432 pgs., Henry E. Vallely-a
12.00 30.00 80.00
nn- **Junior G-Men Solve a Crime**, 1939, Whitman, 36 pgs., 2 1/2" x 3 1/2", Penny Book 12.00 30.00 80.00
1422- **Junior Nebb on the Diamond Bar Ranch**, 1938, Whitman, 300 pgs., by Sol Hess 12.00 30.00 80.00
1470- **Junior Nebb Joins the Circus**, 1939, Whitman, 300 pgs. by Sol Hess 12.00 30.00 80.00
nn- **Junior Nebb Elephant Trainer**, 1939, Whitman, 68 pgs., Pan-Am Oil premium, soft-c 15.00 37.50 105.00
1052- **"Just Kids"** (Adventures of ...), 1934, Saalfield, oblong size, by Ad Carter 22.00 52.50 155.00
1094- **Just Kids and the Mysterious Stranger**, 1935, Saalfield, 160 pgs., by Ad Carter 15.00 37.50 105.00
1184- **Just Kids and Deep-Sea Dan**, 1940, Saalfield, 400 pgs., by Ad Carter
12.00 30.00 85.00
1302- **Just Kids, The Adventures of**, 1934, Saalfield, oblong size, soft-c, by Ad Carter 22.00 52.50 155.00
1324- **Just Kids and the Mysterious Stranger**, 1935, Saalfield, 160 pgs., soft-c, by Ad Carter , 15.00 37.50 105.00
1401- **Just Kids**, 1937, Whitman, 432 pgs., by Ad Carter
15.00 37.50 105.00
1055- **Katzenjammer Kids in the Mountains**, 1934, Saalfield, hard-c, oblong, H. H. Knerr-a 21.00 52.50 145.00
1305- **Katzenjammer Kids in the Mountains**, 1934, Saalfield, soft-c, oblong, H. H. Knerr-a 21.00 52.50 145.00
14- **Katzenjammer Kids, The**, 1942, Dell, 194 pgs., Fast-Action Story, H. H. Knerr-a 24.00 60.00 165.00
1411- **Kay Darcy and the Mystery Hideout**, 1937, Whitman, 300 pgs., Charles Mueller-a 13.00 32.50 90.00
1180- **Kayo in the Land of Sunshine** (With Moon Mullins), 1937, Whitman, 432 pgs., by Willard 15.00 37.50 105.00
1415- **Kayo and Moon Mullins and the One Man Gang**, 1939, Whitman, 432 pgs., by Frank Willard 12.00 30.00 85.00
7- **Kayo and Moon Mullins 'Way Down South**, 1938, Whitman,

GD FN VF/NM

132 pgs., 3 1/2" x 3 1/2", Buddy Book 31.00 78.00 220.00
1105- **Kazan in Revenge of the North** (James Oliver Curwood's...), 1937, Whitman, 432 pgs., Henry E. Vallely-a 11.00 27.50 70.00
1471- **Kazan, King of the Pack** (James Oliver Curwood's...), 1940, Whitman, 432 pgs. 10.00 25.00 65.00
1420- **Keep 'Em Flying! U.S.A. for America's Defense**, 1943, Whitman, 432 pgs., Henry E. Vallely-a, flip pictures 11.00 27.50 70.00
1133- **Kelly King at Yale Hall**, 1937, Saalfield 10.00 25.00 65.00
Ken Maynard (See Strawberry Roan, Western Frontier & Wheels of Destiny)
776- **Ken Maynard in "Gun Justice,"** 1934, Whitman, 160 pgs., hard-c, movie scenes (Universal Pic.) 21.00 52.50 145.00
776- **Ken Maynard in "Gun Justice,"** 1934, Whitman, 160 pgs., soft-c, movie scenes (Universal Pic.) 21.00 52.50 145.00
1430- **Ken Maynard in Western Justice**, 1938, Whitman, 432 pgs., Irwin Myers-a
12.00 30.00 85.00
1442- **Ken Maynard and the Gun Wolves of the Gila**, 1939, Whitman, 432 pgs. 12.00 30.00 85.00
nn- **Ken Maynard in Six-Gun Law**, 1938, Whitman, 36 pgs., 2 1/2" x 3 1/2", Penny Book 10.00 25.00 65.00
1134- **King of Crime**, 1938, Saalfield, 400 pgs. 11.00 27.50 70.00
King of the Royal Mounted (See Zane Grey)
nn- **Kit Carson**, 1933, World Syndicate, by J. Carroll Mansfield, High Lights Of History Series, hard-c 11.00 27.50 70.00
nn- **Kit Carson**, 1933, World Syndicate, same as hard-c above but with a black cloth-c 11.00 27.50 70.00
1105- **Kit Carson and the Mystery Riders**, 1935, Saalfield, hard-c, Johnny Mack Brown photo-c, movie scenes 18.00 45.00 125.00
1585- **Kit Carson and the Mystery Riders**, 1935, Saalfield, soft-c, Johnny Mack Brown photo-c, movie scenes 18.00 45.00 125.00
Krazy Kat (See Adventures of...)
2004- **(#4)-Lassie-Adventure in Alaska** (TV Series), 1967, Whitman, hard-c, 260 pgs., 39 cents, color illos 4.00 10.00 27.00
5754- **Lassie-Adventure in Alaska** (TV Series), 1973, Whitman, soft-c, 260 pgs., 49 cents, color illos 2.00 5.00 13.00
2027- **Lassie and the Shabby Sheik** (TV Series), 1968, Whitman, hard-c, 260 pgs., 39 cents 4.00 10.00 25.00
5762- **Lassie and the Shabby Sheik** (TV Series), 1972, Whitman, soft-c, 260 pgs., 39 cents 2.00 5.00 13.00
5769- **Lassie, Old One-Eye** (TV Series), 1975, Whitman, soft-c, 260 pgs., 49 cents, three printings 2.00 5.00 13.00
1132- **Last Days of Pompeii, The**, 1935, Whitman, 5 1/4" x 6 1/4", 260 pgs., photo-c, movie scenes 15.00 37.50 105.00
1128- **Last Man Out** (Baseball), 1937, Saalfield, hard-c
11.00 27.50 70.00
L30- **Last of the Mohicans, The**, 1936, Lynn, 192 pgs., movie scenes with Randolph Scott, United Artists Pictures 16.00 40.00 115.00
1126- **Laughing Dragon of Oz, The**, 1934, Whitman 432 pgs., by Frank Baum (scarce) 114.00 342.00 800.00
1086- **Laurel and Hardy**, 1934, Saalfield, 160 pgs., hard-c, photo-c, movie scenes 21.00 52.50 145.00
1316- **Laurel and Hardy**, 1934, Saalfield, 160 pgs. soft-c, photo-c, movie scenes 21.00 52.50 145.00
1092- **Law of the Wild, The**, 1935, Saalfield, 160 pgs., photo-c, movie scenes of Rex, The Wild Horse & Rin-Tin-Tin Jr. 12.00 30.00 85.00
1322- **Law of the Wild, The**, 1935, Saalfield, 160 pgs., photo-c, movie scenes, soft-c 12.00 30.00 85.00
1100B- **Learn to be a Ventriloquist**, 1938, Whitman, 36 pgs. 2 1/2" x 3 1/2", Penny Book 4.00 10.00 22.00
1149- **Lee Brady Range Detective**, 1938, Saalfield, 400 pgs.
10.00 25.00 65.00
L10- **Les Miserables** (Victor Hugo's ...), 1935, Lynn, 192 pgs., movie scenes 15.00 37.50 105.00
1441- **Lightning Jim U.S. Marshal Brings Law to the West**, 1940, Whitman, 432 pgs., based on radio program 12.00 30.00 85.00
nn- **Lightning Jim Whipple U.S. Marshal in Indian Territory**, 1939, Whitman, 36 pgs., 2 1/2" x 3 1/2", Penny Book 11.00 27.50 70.00
653- **Lions and Tigers** (With Clyde Beatty), 1934, Whitman, 160 pgs., photo-c movie scenes 15.00 37.50 105.00
1187- **Li'l Abner and the Ratfields**, 1940, Saalfield, 400 pgs., by Al Capp
19.00 47.50 135.00

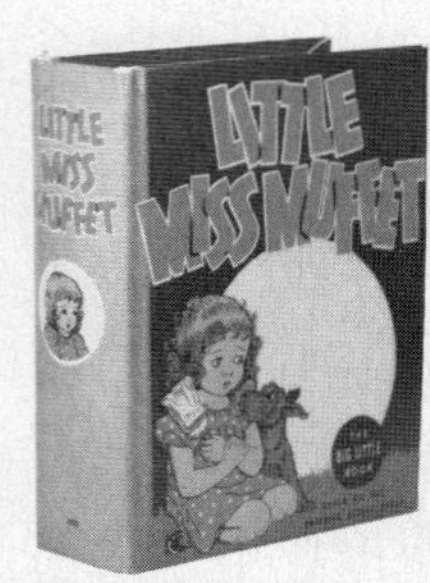
1120 - Little Miss Muffet © WHIT

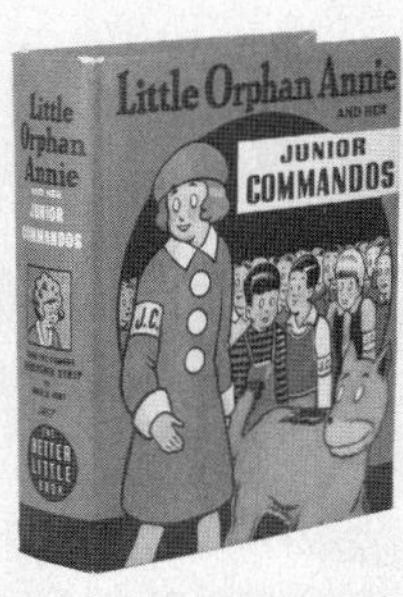
1457 - Little Orphan Annie and Her Junior Commandos © WHIT

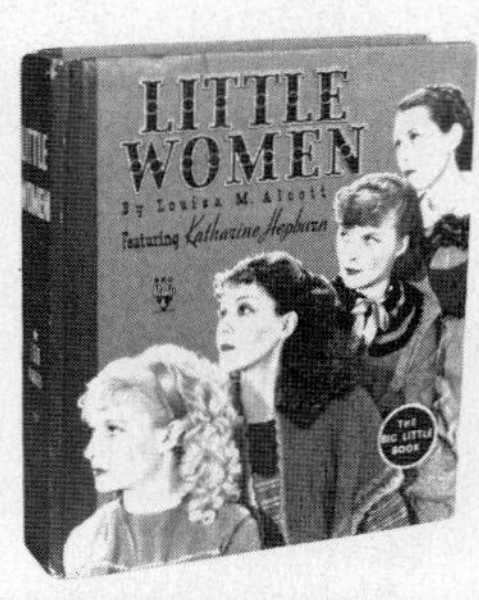
757 - Little Women © WHIT

GD FN VF/NM

1193- Li'l Abner and Sadie Hawkins Day, 1940, Saalfield, 400 pgs., by Al Capp 19.00 47.50 135.00

1198- Li'l Abner in New York, 1936, Whitman, 432 pgs., by Al Capp 21.00 52.50 145.00

1401- Li'l Abner Among the Millionaires, 1939, Whitman, 432 pgs., by Al Capp 21.00 52.50 145.00

1054- Little Annie Rooney, 1934, Saalfield, oblong - 4" x 8", All Pictures Comics, hard-c 20.00 50.00 140.00

1304- Little Annie Rooney, 1934, Saalfield, oblong - 4" x 8", All Pictures, soft-c 20.00 50.00 140.00

1117- Little Annie Rooney and the Orphan House, 1936, Whitman, 432 pgs. 12.00 30.00 80.00

1406- Little Annie Rooney on the Highway to Adventure, 1938, Whitman, 432 pgs. 12.00 30.00 80.00

1149- Little Big Shot (With Sybil Jason), 1935, Whitman, 240 pgs., photo-c, movie scenes 15.00 37.50 105.00

nn- Little Black Sambo, nd (1930s), np (Whitman), 36 pgs., 3" x 2 1/2", Penny Book 12.00 30.00 85.00

Little Bo-Peep (See Wee Little Books)

Little Colonel, The (See Shirley Temple)

1148- Little Green Door, The, 1938, Saalfield, 400 pgs. 11.00 27.50 70.00

1112- Little Hollywood Stars, 1935, Saalfield, movie scenes (Little Rascals, etc.), hard-c 15.00 37.50 105.00

1592- Little Hollywood Stars, 1935, Saalfield, movie scenes, soft-c 15.00 37.50 105.00

1087- Little Jimmy's Gold Hunt, 1935, Saalfield, 160 pgs., hard-c, Little Big Book, by Swinnerton 20.00 50.00 140.00

1317- Little Jimmy's Gold Hunt, 1935, Saalfield, 160 pgs., 4 1/4" x 5 3/4", soft-c, by Swinnerton 20.00 50.00 140.00

Little Joe and the City Gangsters (See Top-Line Comics)

Little Joe Otter's Slide (See Wee Little Books)

1118- Little Lord Fauntleroy, 1936, Saalfield, movie scenes, photo-c, 4 1/2" x 5 1/4", starring Mickey Rooney & Freddie Bartholomew, hard-c 12.00 30.00 85.00

1598- Little Lord Fauntleroy, 1936, Saalfield, photo-c, movie scenes, soft-c 12.00 30.00 85.00

1192- Little Mary Mixup and the Grocery Robberies, 1940, Saalfield 11.00 27.50 70.00

8- Little Mary Mixup Wins A Prize, 1936, Whitman, 132 pgs., 3 1/2" x 3 1/2", soft-c, Tarzan Ice Cream cup lid premium 36.00 90.00 255.00

1150- Little Men, 1934, Whitman, 4 3/4" x 5 1/4", movie scenes (Mascot Prod.), photo-c, hard-c 12.00 30.00 80.00

9- Little Minister, The,-Katharine Hepburn, 1935, 160 pgs., 4 1/4" x 5 1/2", EVW (Five Star Library), movie scenes (RKO) 16.00 40.00 115.00

1120- Little Miss Muffet, 1936, Whitman, 432 pgs., by Fanny Y. Cory 12.00 30.00 80.00

708- Little Orphan Annie, 1933, Whitman, 320 pgs., by Harold Gray, the 2nd Big Little Book 70.00 175.00 495.00

nn- Little Orphan Annie, 1928('33), Whitman, 52 pgs., 4" x 5 1/2", premium-no ads, soft-c, by Harold Gray 39.00 98.00 275.00

716- Little Orphan Annie and Sandy, 1933, Whitman, 320 pgs., by Harold Gray 33.00 83.00 230.00

716- Little Orphan Annie and Sandy, 1933, Whitman, 300 pgs., by Harold Gray 33.00 83.00 230.00

nn- Little Orphan Annie and Sandy, 1933, Whitman, 52 pgs., premium-no ads, 4" x 5 1/2", soft-c by Harold Gray 39.00 98.00 275.00

748- Little Orphan Annie and Chizzler, 1933, Whitman, 320 pgs., by Harold Gray 26.00 65.00 185.00

1010- Little Orphan Annie and the Big Town Gunmen, 1937, 7 1/4" x 5 1/2", 64 pgs., Nickel Book 15.00 37.50 105.00

nn- Little Orphan Annie with the Circus, 1934, Whitman, 320 pgs., same cover as L.O.A. 708 but with blue background, Ovaltine giveaway stamp inside front-c, by Harold Gray 58.00 146.00 410.00

1140- Little Orphan Annie and the Big Train Robbery, 1934, Whitman, 300 pgs., by Gray 20.00 50.00 140.00

GD FN VF/NM

1140- Little Orphan Annie and the Big Train Robbery, 1934, Whitman, 300 pgs., premium-no ads, soft-c, by Harold Gray 36.00 90.00 255.00

1154- Little Orphan Annie and the Ghost Gang, 1935, Whitman, 432 pgs. by Harold Gray 20.00 50.00 140.00

nn- Little Orphan Annie and the Ghost Gang, 1935, Whitman, 436 pgs., premium-no ads, 3-color, soft-c, by Harold Gray 36.00 90.00 255.00

1162- Little Orphan Annie and Punjab the Wizard, 1935, Whitman, 432 pgs., by Harold Gray 20.00 50.00 140.00

1186- Little Orphan Annie and the $1,000,000 Formula, 1936, Whitman, 432 pgs., by Gray 18.00 45.00 125.00

1414- Little Orphan Annie and the Ancient Treasure of Am, 1939, Whitman, 432 pgs., by Gray 16.00 40.00 115.00

1416- Little Orphan Annie in the Movies, 1937, Whitman, 432 pgs., by Harold Gray 16.00 40.00 115.00

1417- Little Orphan Annie and the Secret of the Well, 1947,Whitman, 352 pgs., by Gray 12.00 30.00 85.00

1435- Little Orphan Annie and the Gooneyville Mystery, 1947, Whitman, 288 pgs., by Gray 13.00 32.50 90.00

1446- Little Orphan Annie in the Thieves' Den, 1949, Whitman, 288 pgs., by Harold Gray 13.00 32.50 90.00

1449- Little Orphan Annie and the Mysterious Shoemaker, 1938, Whitman, 432 pgs., by Harold Gray 15.00 37.50 105.00

1457- Little Orphan Annie and Her Junior Commandos, 1943, Whitman, 352 pgs., by H. Gray 12.00 30.00 85.00

1461- Little Orphan Annie and the Underground Hide-Out, 1945, Whitman, 352 pgs., by Gray 12.00 30.00 85.00

1468- Little Orphan Annie and the Ancient Treasure of Am, 1949 (Misdated 1939), 288 pgs., by Gray 12.00 30.00 85.00

1482- Little Orphan Annie and the Haunted Mansion, 1941, Whitman, 432 pgs., flip pictures, by Harold Gray 16.00 40.00 115.00

3048- Little Orphan Annie and Her Big Little Kit, 1937, Whitman, 384 pgs., 4 1/2" x 6 1/2" box, includes miniature box of 4 crayons-red, yellow, blue and green 94.00 235.00 660.00

4054- Little Orphan Annie, The Story of, 1934, Whitman, 7" x 9 1/2", 320 pgs., Big Big Book, Harold Gray-c/a 102.00 255.00 715.00

nn- Little Orphan Annie Gets into Trouble, 1938, Whitman, 36 pgs., 2 1/2" x 3 1/2", Penny Book 11.00 27.50 70.00

nn- Little Orphan Annie in Hollywood, 1937, Whitman, 3 1/2" x 3 1/4", Pan-Am premium, soft-c 29.00 73.00 200.00

nn- Little Orphan Annie in Rags to Riches, 1939, Dell, 194 pgs., Fast-Action Story, soft-c 39.00 98.00 275.00

nn- Little Orphan Annie Saves Sandy, 1938, Whitman, 36 pgs., 2 1/2" x 3 1/2", Penny Book 11.00 27.50 70.00

nn- Little Orphan Annie Under the Big Top, 1938, Dell, 194 pgs., Fast-Action Story, soft-c 39.00 98.00 270.00

nn- Little Orphan Annie Wee Little Books (In open box)
nn, 1934, Whitman, 44 pgs., by H. Gray

	GD	FN	VF/NM
L.O.A. And Daddy Warbucks	9.00	22.50	55.00
L.O.A. And Her Dog Sandy	9.00	22.50	55.00
L.O.A. And The Lucky Knife	9.00	22.50	55.00
L.O.A. And The Pinch-Pennys	9.00	22.50	55.00
L.O.A. At Happy Home	9.00	22.50	55.00
L.O.A. Finds Mickey	9.00	22.50	55.00
Complete set with box	57.00	143.00	400.00

nn- Little Polly Flinders, The Story of, nd (1930s), no publ., 36 pgs., 2 1/2" x 3", Penny Book 4.00 10.00 22.00

nn- Little Red Hen, The, nd(1930s), np(Whitman), 36 pgs., Penny Book 4.00 10.00 22.00

nn- Little Red Riding Hood, nd(1930s), np(Whitman), 36 pgs., 3" x 2 1/2", Penny Book 4.00 10.00 22.00

nn- Little Red Riding Hood and the Big Bad Wolf (Disney), 1934, McKay, 36 pgs., stiff-c, Disney Studio-a 33.00 83.00 230.00

757- Little Women, 1934, Whitman, 4 3/4" x 5 1/4", 160 pgs., photo-c, movie scenes, starring Katharine Hepburn 21.00 52.50 145.00

Littlest Rebel, The (See Shirley Temple)

1181- Lone Ranger and his Horse Silver, 1935, Whitman, 432 pgs., Hal Arbo-a 29.00 73.00 200.00

5774 - The Lone Ranger Outwits Crazy Cougar © Lone Ranger Inc.

1438 - Mary Lee and the Mystery of the Indian Beads © WHIT

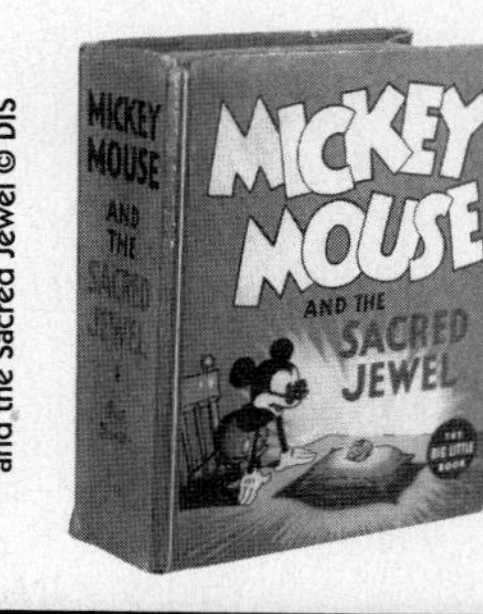

1187 - Mickey Mouse and the Sacred Jewel © DIS

GD FN VF/NM

1196- Lone Ranger and the Vanishing Herd, 1936, Whitman, 432 pgs. 24.00 60.00 165.00
1407- Lone Ranger and Dead Men's Mine, The, 1939, Whitman, 432 pgs. 22.00 52.50 155.00
1421- Lone Ranger on the Barbary Coast, The, 1944, Whitman, 352 pgs., Henry Vallely-a 19.00 47.50 135.00
1428- Lone Ranger and the Secret Weapon, The, 1943, Whitman, 19.00 47.50 135.00
1431- Lone Ranger and the Secret Killer, The, 1937, Whitman 432 pgs., H. Anderson-a 24.00 60.00 165.00
1450- Lone Ranger and the Black Shirt Highwayman, The, 1939, Whitman, 432 pgs. 22.00 52.50 155.00
1465- Lone Ranger and the Menace of Murder Valley, The, 1938, Whitman, 432 pgs., Robert Wiseman-a 21.00 52.50 145.00
1468- Lone Ranger Follows Through, The, 1941, Whitman, 432 pgs., H.E. Vallely-a 21.00 52.50 145.00
1477- Lone Ranger and the Great Western Span, The, 1942, Whitman, 424 pgs., H. E. Vallely-a 19.00 47.50 135.00
1489- Lone Ranger and the Red Renegades, The, 1939, Whitman, 432 pgs. 24.00 60.00 165.00
1498- Lone Ranger and the Silver Bullets, 1946, Whitman, 352 pgs., Henry E. Vallely-a 19.00 47.50 135.00
712-10- Lone Ranger and the Secret of Somber Cavern, The, 1950, Whitman 12.00 30.00 80.00
2013- (#13)-Lone Ranger Outwits Crazy Cougar, The, 1968, Whitman, 260 pgs., 39 cents, hard-c, color illos 4.00 10.00 27.00
5774- Lone Ranger Outwits Crazy Cougar, The, 1976, Whitman, 260 pgs., 49 cents, soft-c, color illos 4.00 10.00 22.00
5774-1- Lone Ranger Outwits Crazy Cougar, The, 1979, Whitman, 260 pgs., 69 cents, soft-c, color illos 4.00 10.00 22.00
nn- Lone Ranger and the Lost Valley, The, 1938, Dell, 196 pgs., Fast-Action Story, soft-c 43.00 108.00 300.00
1405- Lone Star Martin of the Texas Rangers, 1939, Whitman, 432 pgs. 18.00 45.00 125.00
19- Lost City, The, 1935, EVW, movie scenes 16.00 40.00 115.00
1103- Lost Jungle, The (With Clyde Beatty), 1936, Saalfield, movie scenes, hard-c 16.00 40.00 115.00
1583- Lost Jungle, The (With Clyde Beatty), 1936, Saalfield, movie scenes, soft -c 13.00 32.50 90.00
753- Lost Patrol, The, 1934, Whitman, 160 pgs., photo-c, movie scenes with Boris Karloff 15.00 37.50 105.00
nn- Lost World, The - Jurassic Park 2, 1997, Chronicle Books, 312 pgs., adapts movie, 1-color (green) illos 3.00 7.50 20.00
1189- Mac of the Marines in Africa, 1936, Whitman, 432 pgs. 12.00 30.00 80.00
1400- Mac of the Marines in China, 1938, Whitman, 432 pgs. 12.00 30.00 80.00
1100B- Magic Tricks (With explanations), 1938, Whitman, 36 pgs., 2 1/2" x 3 1/2", Penny Book, rabbit in hat-c 4.00 10.00 22.00
1100B- Magic Tricks (How to do them), 1938, Whitman, 36 pgs., 2 1/2" x 3 1/2", Penny Book, genie-c 4.00 10.00 22.00
Major Hoople (See Our Boarding House)
2022-(#22)- Major Matt Mason, Moon Mission, 1968, Whitman, 256 pgs., hard-c, color illos. 4.00 10.00 27.00
1167- Mandrake the Magician, 1935, Whitman, 432 pgs., by Lee Falk & Phil Davis 24.00 60.00 170.00
1418- Mandrake the Magician and the Flame Pearls, 1946, Whitman, 352 pgs., by Lee Falk & Phil Davis 15.00 37.50 105.00
1431- Mandrake the Magician and the Midnight Monster, 1939, Whitman, 432 pgs., by Lee Falk & Phil Davis 16.00 40.00 115.00
1454- Mandrake the Magician Mighty Solver of Mysteries, 1941, Whitman, 432 pgs., by Lee Falk & Phil Davis, flip pictures 16.00 40.00 115.00
2011-(#11)-Man From U.N.C.L.E., The-The Calcutta Affair (TV Series), 1967, Whitman, 260 pgs., 39 cents, hard-c, color illos 4.00 10.00 27.00
1429- Marge's Little Lulu Alvin and Tubby, 1947, Whitman, All Pictures Comics, Stanley-a 31.00 78.00 215.00
1438- Mary Lee and the Mystery of the Indian Beads, 1937, Whitman, 300 pgs. 11.00 27.50 70.00

GD FN VF/NM

1165- Masked Man of the Mesa, The, 1939, Saalfield, 400 pgs. 10.00 25.00 65.00
nn- Mask of Zorro, The, 1998, Chronicle Books, 312 pgs., adapts movie, 1-color (yellow-green) illos 1.00 2.50 9.00
1436- Maximo the Amazing Superman, 1940, Whitman, 432 pgs., Henry E. Vallely-a 15.00 37.50 105.00
1444- Maximo the Amazing Superman and the Crystals of Doom, 1941, Whitman,432 pgs., Henry E. Vallely-a 15.00 37.50 105.00
1445- Maximo the Amazing Superman and the Supermachine, 1941, Whitman, 432 pgs. 15.00 37.50 105.00
755- Men of the Mounted, 1934, Whitman, 320 pgs. 15.00 37.50 105.00
nn- Men of the Mounted, 1933, Whitman, 52 pgs., 3 1/2" x 5 3/4", premium-no ads; other versions with Poll Parrot & Perkins ad; soft-c 21.00 52.50 145.00
nn- Men of the Mounted, 1934, Whitman, Cocomalt premium, soft-c, by Ted McCall 12.00 30.00 85.00
1475- Men With Wings, 1938, Whitman, 240 pgs., photo-c, movie scenes (Paramount Pics.) 12.00 30.00 85.00
1170- Mickey Finn, 1940, Saalfield, 400 pgs., by Frank Leonard 12.00 30.00 85.00
717- Mickey Mouse (Disney), (1st printing) 1933, Whitman, 320 pgs., Gottfredson-a, skinny Mickey on cover 392.00 980.00 3135.00
717- Mickey Mouse (Disney), (2nd printing)1933, Whitman, 320 pgs., Gottfredson-a, regular Mickey on cover 206.00 515.00 1650.00
nn- Mickey Mouse (Disney), 1933, Dean & Son, Great Big Midget Book, 320 pgs. 186.00 464.00 1485.00
731- Mickey Mouse the Mail Pilot (Disney), 1933, Whitman, (This is the same book as the 1st Mickey Mouse BLB #717(2nd printing) but with "The Mail Pilot" printed on the front. Lower left of back cover has a small box printed over the existing "No. 717." "No. 731" is printed next to it.) (sold at auction in 2001 in Fine condition for $5,090)
726- Mickey Mouse in Blaggard Castle (Disney), 1934, Whitman, 320 pgs., Gottfredson-a 47.00 118.00 330.00
731- Mickey Mouse the Mail Pilot (Disney), 1933, Whitman, 300 pgs., Gottfredson-a 47.00 118.00 330.00
731- Mickey Mouse the Mail Pilot (Disney), 1933, Whitman, 300 pgs., soft cover; Gottfredson-a (Rare) 79.00 237.00 550.00
nn- Mickey Mouse the Mail Pilot (Disney), 1933, Whitman, 292 pgs., American Oil Co. premium, soft-c, Gottfredson-a; another version 3 1/2" x 4 3/4" 47.00 118.00 330.00
nn- Mickey Mouse the Mail Pilot (Disney), 1933, Dean & Son, Great Big Midget Book (Rare) 175.00 525.00 1400.00
750- Mickey Mouse Sails for Treasure Island (Disney), 1933, Whitman, 320 pgs., Gottfredson-a 47.00 118.00 330.00
nn- Mickey Mouse Sails for Treasure Island (Disney), 1935, Whitman, 196 pgs., premium-no ads, soft-c, Gottfredson-a (Scarce) 56.00 140.00 395.00
nn- Mickey Mouse Sails for Treasure Island (Disney), 1935, Whitman, 196 pgs., Kolynos Dental Cream premium (Scarce) 56.00 140.00 395.00
nn- Mickey Mouse Sails for Treasure Island (Disney), 1933, Dean & Son, Great Big Midget Book, 320 pgs. 150.00 450.00 1200.00
756- Mickey Mouse Presents a Walt Disney Silly Symphony (Disney), 1934, Whitman, 240 pgs., Bucky Bug app. 43.00 108.00 300.00
801- Mickey Mouse's Summer Vacation, 1948, Whitman, hard-c, Story Hour series 12.00 30.00 85.00
1111- Mickey Mouse Presents Walt Disney's Silly Symphonies Stories, 1936, Whitman, 432 pgs., Donald Duck app. 43.00 108.00 300.00
1128- Mickey Mouse and Pluto the Racer (Disney), 1936, Whitman, 432 pgs., Gottfredson-a 38.00 95.00 255.00
1139- Mickey Mouse the Detective (Disney), 1934, Whitman, 300 pgs., Gottfredson-a 43.00 108.00 300.00
1139- Mickey Mouse the Detective (Disney), 1934, Whitman, 304 pgs., premium-no ads, soft-c, Gottfredson-a (Scarce) 64.00 160.00 450.00
1153- Mickey Mouse and the Bat Bandit (Disney), 1935, Whitman, 432 pgs., Gottfredson-a 39.00 98.00 275.00
nn- Mickey Mouse and the Bat Bandit (Disney), 1935, Whitman, 436 pgs., premium-no ads, 3-color, soft-c, Gottfredson-a (Scarce)

1471 - Mickey Mouse and the Dude Ranch Bandit © DIS

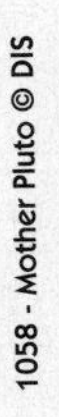

1058 - Mother Pluto © DIS

1179 - Ned Brant Adventure Bound © Saalfield

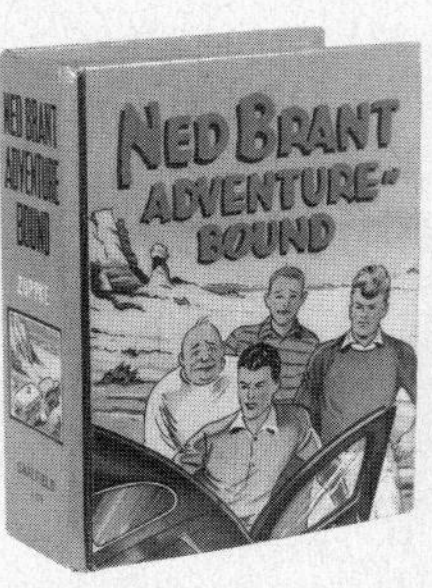

GD FN VF/NM

64.00 160.00 450.00

1160- Mickey Mouse and Bobo the Elephant (Disney), 1935, Whitman, 432 pgs., Gottfredson-a 39.00 98.00 275.00

1187- Mickey Mouse and the Sacred Jewel (Disney), 1936, Whitman, 432 pgs., Gottfredson-a 36.00 90.00 255.00

1401- Mickey Mouse in the Treasure Hunt (Disney), 1941, Whitman, 430 pgs., flip pictures of Pluto, Gottfredson-a 34.00 85.00 240.00

1409- Mickey Mouse Runs His Own Newspaper (Disney), 1937, Whitman, 432 pgs., Gottfredson-a 34.00 85.00 240.00

1413- Mickey Mouse and the 'Lectro Box (Disney), 1946, Whitman, 352 pgs., Gottfredson-a 24.00 60.00 165.00

1417- Mickey Mouse on Sky Island (Disney), 1941, Whitman, 432 pgs., flip pictures, Gottfredson-a; considered by Gottfredson to be his best Mickey story 34.00 85.00 240.00

1428- Mickey Mouse in the Foreign Legion (Disney), 1940, Whitman, 432 pgs., Gottfredson-a 34.00 85.00 240.00

1429- Mickey Mouse and the Magic Lamp (Disney), 1942, Whitman, 432 pgs., flip pictures 34.00 85.00 240.00

1433- Mickey Mouse and the Lazy Daisy Mystery (Disney), 1947, Whitman, 288 pgs. 24.00 60.00 165.00

1444- Mickey Mouse in the World of Tomorrow (Disney), 1948, Whitman, 288 pgs., Gottfredson-a 36.00 90.00 255.00

1451- Mickey Mouse and the Desert Palace (Disney), 1948, Whitman, 288 pgs. 24.00 60.00 165.00

1463- Mickey Mouse and the Pirate Submarine (Disney), 1939, Whitman, 432 pgs., Gottfredson-a 34.00 85.00 240.00

1464- Mickey Mouse and the Stolen Jewels (Disney), 1949, Whitman, 288 pgs. 33.00 83.00 230.00

1471- Mickey Mouse and the Dude Ranch Bandit (Disney), 1943, Whitman, 432 pgs., flip pictures 34.00 85.00 240.00

1475- Mickey Mouse and the 7 Ghosts (Disney), 1940, Whitman, 432 pgs., Gottfredson-a 34.00 85.00 240.00

1476- Mickey Mouse in the Race for Riches (Disney), 1938, Whitman, 432 pgs., Gottfredson-a 34.00 85.00 240.00

1483- Mickey Mouse Bell Boy Detective (Disney), 1945, Whitman, 352 pgs. 33.00 83.00 230.00

1499- Mickey Mouse on the Cave-Man Island (Disney), 1944, Whitman, 352 pgs. 33.00 83.00 230.00

2004- Mickey Mouse, Here Comes (Disney), 1936, Whitman, (Very Rare), 224 pgs., 12" x 8 1/4" box, with red, yellow and blue crayons, contains 224 loose pages to color, reprinted from early Mickey Mouse related movie and strip reprints
475.00 1187.00 3800.00

2020-(#20)- Mickey Mouse, Adventure in Outer Space, 1968, Whitman, 256 pgs.,hard-c, color illos. 4.00 10.00 27.00

5750- Mickey Mouse, Adventure in Outer Space, 1973, Whitman, 256 pgs.,soft-c, 39 cents, color illos. 2.00 5.00 13.00

3049- Mickey Mouse and His Big Little Kit (Disney), 1937, Whitman, 384 pgs., 4 1/2" x 6 1/2" box, includes miniature box of 4 crayons-red, yellow, blue and green 150.00 375.00 1210.00

3061- Mickey Mouse to Draw and Color (The Big Little Set), nd (early 1930s), Whitman, with crayons; box contains 320 loose pages to color, reprinted from early Mickey Mouse BLBs
123.00 308.00 880.00

4062- Mickey Mouse, The Story Of, 1935, Whitman, 7" x 9 1/2", 320 pgs., Big Big Book, Gottfredson-a 150.00 375.00 1210.00

4062- Mickey Mouse and the Smugglers, The Story Of, 1935, Whitman, (Scarce), 7" x 9 1/2", 320 pgs., Big Big Book, same contents as above version; Gottfredson-a 179.00 447.00 1430.00

708-10- Mickey Mouse on the Haunted Island (Disney), 1950, Whitman, Gottfredson-a 15.00 37.50 105.00

nn- Mickey Mouse and Minnie at Macy's, 1934 Whitman, 148 pgs., 3 1/4" x 3 1/2", soft-c, R. H. Macy & Co. Christmas giveaway (Rare, less than 20 known copies) 438.00 1095.00 3500.00

nn- Mickey Mouse and Minnie March to Macy's, 1935, Whitman, 148 pgs., 3 1/2" x 3 1/2", soft-c, R. H. Macy & Co. Christmas giveaway (scarce) 300.00 750.00 2400.00

nn- Mickey Mouse and the Magic Carpet, 1935, Whitman, 148 pgs., 3 1/2"x 4", soft-c, giveaway, Gottfredson-a, Donald Duck app.
131.00 328.00 1050.00

GD FN VF/NM

nn- Mickey Mouse Silly Symphonies, 1934, Dean & Son, Ltd (England), 48 pgs., with 4 pop-ups, Babes In The Woods, King Neptune
With dust jacket 165.00 412.00 1320.00
Without dust jacket 119.00 298.00 835.00

nn- Mickey Mouse the Sheriff of Nugget Gulch (Disney) 1938, Dell, 196 pgs., Fast-Action Story, soft-c, Gottfredson-a 56.00 140.00 395.00

nn- Mickey Mouse Waddle Book, 1934, BRP, 20 pgs., 7 1/2" x 10", forerunner of the Blue Ribbon Pop-Up books; with 4 removable articulated cardboard characters Book Only 100.00 200.00 500.00
Near Mint Complete $19,000

nn- Mickey Mouse with Goofy and Mickey's Nephews, 1938, Dell, Fast-Action Story, Gottfredson-a 56.00 140.00 395.00

16- Mickey Mouse and Pluto (Disney), 1942, Dell, 196 pgs., Fast-Action story 56.00 140.00 395.00

512- Mickey Mouse Wee Little Books (In open box), nn, 1934, Whitman, 44 pgs., small size, soft-c
Mickey Mouse and Tanglefoot 13.00 32.50 90.00
Mickey Mouse at the Carnival 13.00 32.50 90.00
Mickey Mouse Will Not Quit! 13.00 32.50 90.00
Mickey Mouse Wins the Race! 13.00 32.50 90.00
Mickey Mouse's Misfortune 13.00 32.50 90.00
Mickey Mouse's Uphill Fight 13.00 32.50 90.00
Complete set with box 93.00 233.00 650.00

1493- Mickey Rooney and Judy Garland and How They Got into the Movies, 1941, Whitman, 432 pgs., photo-c 15.00 37.50 105.00

1427- Mickey Rooney Himself, 1939, Whitman, 240 pgs., photo-c, movie scenes, life story 15.00 37.50 105.00

532- Mickey's Dog Pluto (Disney), 1943, Whitman, All Picture Comics, A Tall Comic Book , 3 3/4" x 8 3/4" 41.00 103.00 285.00

284- Midget Jumbo Coloring Book, 1935, Saalfield
64.00 192.00 450.00

2113- Midget Jumbo Coloring Book, 1935, Saalfield, 240 pgs.
64.00 192.00 450.00

21- Midsummer Night's Dream, 1935, EVW, movie scenes
15.00 37.50 105.00

nn- Minute-Man (Mystery of the Spy Ring), 1941, Fawcett, Dime Action Book 57.00 143.00 400.00

710- Moby Dick the Great White Whale, The Story of, 1934, Whitman, 160 pgs., photo-c, movie scenes from "The Sea Beast" 15.00 37.50 105.00

746- Moon Mullins and Kayo (Kayo and Moon Mullins-inside), 1933, Whitman, 320 pgs., Frank Willard-c/a 16.00 40.00 115.00

nn- Moon Mullins and Kayo, 1933, Whitman, Cocomalt premium, soft-c, by Willard 16.00 40.00 115.00

1134- Moon Mullins and the Plushbottom Twins, 1935, Whitman, 432 pgs., Willard-c/a 16.00 40.00 115.00

nn- Moon Mullins and the Plushbottom Twins, 1935, Whitman, 436 pgs., premium-no ads, 3-color, soft-c, by Willard 29.00 73.00 200.00

1058- Mother Pluto (Disney), 1939, Whitman, 68 pgs., hard-c
13.00 32.50 90.00

1100B- Movie Jokes (From the talkies), 1938, Whitman, 36 pgs., 2 1/2" x 3 1/2", Penny Book 4.00 10.00 22.00

1408- Mr. District Attorney on the Job, 1941, Whitman, 432 pgs., flip pictures 12.00 30.00 75.00

nn- Musicians of Bremen, The, nd (1930s), np (Whitman), 36 pgs., 3" x 2 1/2", Penny Book 4.00 10.00 22.00

1113- Mutt and Jeff, 1936, Whitman, 300 pgs., by Bud Fisher
26.00 65.00 180.00

1116- My Life and Times (By Shirley Temple), 1936, Saalfield, Little Big Book, hard-c, photo-c/illos 16.00 40.00 115.00

1596- My Life and Times (By Shirley Temple), 1936, Saalfield, Little Big Book, soft-c, photo-c/illos 16.00 40.00 115.00

1497- Myra North Special Nurse and Foreign Spies, 1938, Whitman, 432 pgs. 12.00 30.00 85.00

1400- Nancy and Sluggo, 1946, Whitman, All Pictures Comics, Ernie Bushmiller-a 13.00 32.50 90.00

1487- Nancy Has Fun, 1946, Whitman, All Pictures Comics
13.00 32.50 90.00

1150- Napoleon and Uncle Elby, 1938, Saalfield, 400 pgs., by Clifford McBride 12.00 30.00 85.00

1403 - Oswald Rabbit Plays G-Man © DIS

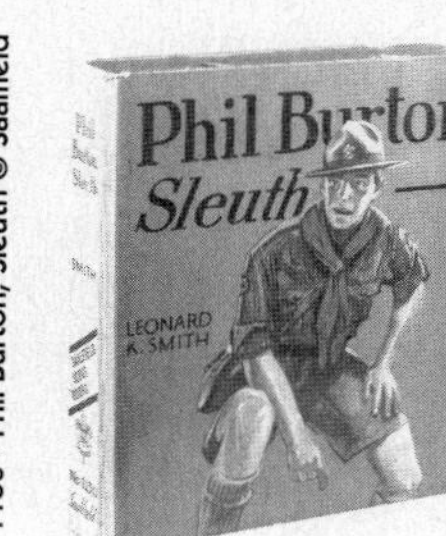

1130 - Phil Burton, Sleuth © Saalfield

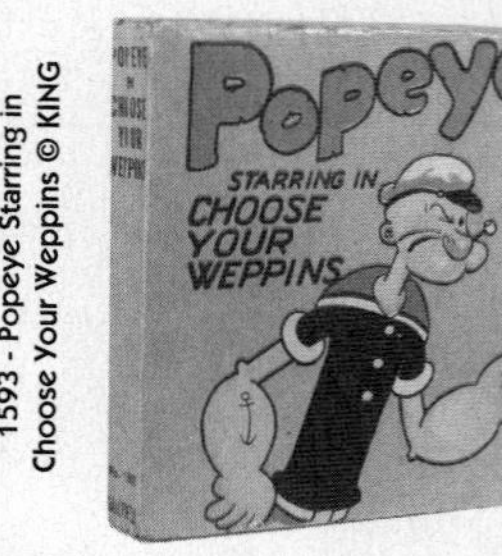
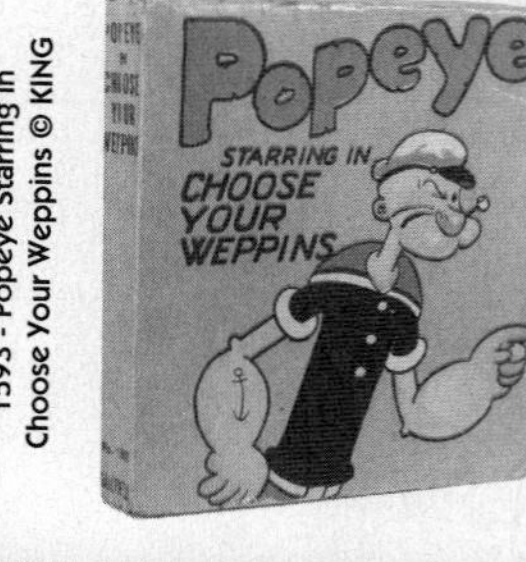

1593 - Popeye Starring in Choose Your Weppins © KING

	GD	FN	VF/NM
1166- Napoleon Uncle Elby And Little Mary, 1939, Saalfield, 400 pgs., by Clifford McBride	12.00	30.00	85.00
1179- Ned Brant Adventure Bound, 1940, Saalfield, 400 pgs.	11.00	27.50	70.00
1146- Nevada Rides The Danger Trail, 1938, Saalfield, 400 pgs., J.R. White-a	11.00	27.50	70.00
1147- Nevada Whalen, Avenger, 1938, Saalfield, 400 pgs.	11.00	27.50	70.00
Nicodemus O'Malley (See Top-Line Comics)			
1115- Og Son of Fire, 1936, Whitman, 432 pgs.	16.00	40.00	115.00
1419- Oh, Blondie the Bumsteads (See Blondie)			
11- Oliver Twist, 1935, EVW (Five Star Library), movie scenes, starring Dickie Moore (Monogram Pictures)	15.00	37.50	105.00
718- Once Upon a Time, 1933, Whitman, 364 pgs., soft-c	15.00	37.50	105.00
712- 100 Fairy Tales for Children, The, 1933, Whitman, 288 pgs., Circle Library	11.00	27.50	70.00
1099- One Night of Love, 1935, Saalfield, 160 pgs., hard-c, photo-c, movie scenes, Columbia Pictures, starring Grace Moore	15.00	37.50	105.00
1579- One Night of Love, 1935, Sat, 160 pgs., soft-c, photo-c, movie scenes, Columbia Pictures, starring Grace Moore	15.00	37.50	105.00
1155- $1000 Reward, 1938, Saalfield, 400 pgs.	11.00	27.50	70.00
Orphan Annie (See Little Orphan ...)			
L17- O'Shaughnessy's Boy, 1935, Lynn, 192 pgs., movie scenes, w/Wallace Beery & Jackie Cooper (Metro-Goldwyn-Mayer)	12.00	30.00	85.00
1109- Oswald the Lucky Rabbit, 1934, Whitman, 288 pgs.	21.00	52.50	145.00
1403- Oswald Rabbit Plays G-Man, 1937, Whitman, 240 pgs., movie scenes by Walter Lantz	22.00	52.50	155.00
1190- Our Boarding House, Major Hoople and his Horse, 1940, Saalfield, 400 pgs.	12.00	30.00	85.00
1085- Our Gang, 1934, Saalfield, 160 pgs., photo-c, movie scenes, hard-c	15.00	37.50	105.00
1315- Our Gang, 1934, Saalfield, 160 pgs., photo-c, movie scenes, soft-c	15.00	37.50	105.00
1451- "Our Gang" on the March, 1942, Whitman, 432 pgs., flip pictures, Vallely-a	15.00	37.50	105.00
1456- Our Gang Adventures, 1948, Whitman, 288 pgs.	12.00	30.00	85.00
nn- Paramount Newsreel Men with Admiral Byrd in Little America, 1934, Whitman, 96 pgs., 6 1/4" x 6 1/4", photo-c, photo ill.	16.00	40.00	115.00
nn- Patch, nd (1930s), np (Whitman), 36 pgs., 3" x 2 1/2", Penny Book	4.00	10.00	22.00
1445- Pat Nelson Ace of Test Pilots, 1937, Whitman, 432 pgs.	11.00	27.50	70.00
1411- Peggy Brown and the Mystery Basket, 1941, Whitman, 432 pgs., flip pictures, Henry E. Vallely-a	12.00	30.00	75.00
1423- Peggy Brown and the Secret Treasure, 1947, Whitman, 288 pgs., Henry E. Vallely-a	12.00	30.00	75.00
1427- Peggy Brown and the Runaway Auto Trailer, 1937, Whitman, 300 pgs., Henry E. Vallely-a	12.00	30.00	75.00
1463- Peggy Brown and the Jewel of Fire, 1943, Whitman, 352 pgs., Henry E. Vallely-a	12.00	30.00	75.00
1491- Peggy Brown in the Big Haunted House, 1940, Whitman, 432 pgs., Vallely-a	12.00	30.00	75.00
1143- Peril Afloat, 1938, Saalfield, 400 pgs.	11.00	27.50	70.00
1199- Perry Winkle and the Rinkeydinks, 1937, Whitman, 432 pgs., by Martin Branner	15.00	37.50	105.00
1487- Perry Winkle and the Rinkeydinks get a Horse, 1938, Whitman, 432 pgs., by Martin Branner	15.00	37.50	105.00
Peter Pan (See Wee Little Books)			
nn- Peter Rabbit, nd(1930s), np(Whitman), 36 pgs., Penny Book, 3" x 2 1/2"	5.00	12.50	33.00
Peter Rabbit's Carrots (See Wee Little Books)			
1100- Phantom, The, 1936, Whitman, 432 pgs., by Lee Falk & Ray Moore	47.00	118.00	330.00
1416- Phantom and the Girl of Mystery, The, 1947, Whitman, 352 pgs. by Falk & Moore	21.00	52.50	145.00
1421- Phantom and Desert Justice, The, 1941, Whitman, 432 pgs., flip pictures, by Falk & Moore	28.00	70.00	195.00
1468- Phantom and the Sky Pirates, The, 1945, Whitman, 352 pgs., by Falk & Moore	24.00	60.00	170.00
1474- Phantom and the Sign of the Skull, The, 1939, Whitman, 432 pgs., by Falk & Moore	29.00	73.00	205.00
1489- Phantom, Return of the..., 1942, Whitman, 432 pgs., flip pictures, by Falk & Moore	28.00	70.00	195.00
1130- Phil Burton, Sleuth (Scout Book), 1937, Saalfield, hard-c	9.00	22.50	55.00
Pied Piper of Hamlin (See Wee Little Books)			
1466- Pilot Pete Dive Bomber, 1941, Whitman, 432 pgs., flip pictures	11.00	27.50	70.00
5776- Pink Panther Adventures in Z-Land, The, 1976, Whitman, 260 pgs., soft-c, 49 cents, B&W	1.00	2.50	8.00
5776-2- Pink Panther Adventures in Z-Land, The, 1980, Whitman, 260 pgs., soft-c, 79 cents, B&W	1.00	2.50	8.00
5783-2- Pink Panther at Castle Kreep, The, 1980, Whitman, 260 pgs., soft-c, 79 cents, B&W	1.00	2.50	8.00
Pinocchio and Jiminy Cricket (See Walt Disney's ...)			
nn- Pioneers of the Wild West (Blue-c), 1933, World Syndicate, High Lights of History Series	10.00	25.00	65.00
With dustjacket	50.00	150.00	350.00
nn- Pioneers of the Wild West (Red-c), 1933, World Syndicate, High Lights of History Series	10.00	25.00	65.00
1123- Plainsman, The, 1936, Whitman, 240 pgs., photo-c, movie scenes with Gary Cooper (Paramount Pics.)	26.00	65.00	180.00
Pluto (See Mickey's Dog ... & Walt Disney's ...)			
2114- Pocket Coloring Book, 1935, Saalfield	39.00	98.00	270.00
1060- Polly and Her Pals on the Farm, 1934, Saalfield, 164 pgs., hard-c, by Cliff Sterrett	15.00	37.50	105.00
1310- Polly and Her Pals on the Farm, 1934, Saalfield, soft-c	15.00	37.50	105.00
1051- Popeye, Adventures of..., 1934, Saalfield, oblong-size, E.C. Segar-a, hard-c	58.00	146.00	410.00
1088- Popeye in Puddleburg, 1934, Saalfield, 160 pgs., hard-c, E. C. Segar-a	22.00	52.50	155.00
1113- Popeye Starring in Choose Your Weppins, 1936, Saalfield, 160 pgs., hard-c, Segar-a	46.00	115.00	320.00
1117- Popeye's Ark, 1936, Saalfield, 4 1/2" x 5 1/2", hard-c, Segar-a	24.00	60.00	165.00
1163- Popeye Sees the Sea, 1936, Whitman, 432 pgs., Segar-a	24.00	60.00	170.00
1301- Popeye, Adventures of..., 1934, Saalfield, oblong-size, Segar-a	58.00	146.00	410.00
1318- Popeye in Puddleburg, 1934, Saalfield, 160 pgs., soft-c, Segar-a	24.00	60.00	165.00
1405- Popeye and the Jeep, 1937, Whitman, 432 pgs., Segar-a	24.00	60.00	170.00
1406- Popeye the Super-Fighter, 1939, Whitman, All Pictures Comics, flip pictures, Segar-a	24.00	60.00	165.00
1422- Popeye the Sailor Man, 1947, Whitman, All Pictures Comics	16.00	40.00	115.00
1450- Popeye in Quest of His Poopdeck Pappy, 1937, Whitman, 432 pgs., Segar-c/a	24.00	60.00	170.00
1458- Popeye and Queen Olive Oyl, 1949, Whitman, 288 pgs., Sagendorf-a	16.00	40.00	115.00
1459- Popeye and the Quest for the Rainbird, 1943, Whitman, Winner & Zaboly-a	18.00	45.00	125.00
1480- Popeye the Spinach Eater, 1945, Whitman, All Pictures Comics	16.00	40.00	115.00
1485- Popeye in a Sock for Susan's Sake, 1940, Whitman, 432 pgs., flip pictures	18.00	45.00	125.00
1497- Popeye and Caster Oyl the Detective, 1941, Whitman, 432 pgs. flip pictures, Segar-a	21.00	52.50	145.00
1499- Popeye and the Deep Sea Mystery, 1939, Whitman, 432 pgs., Segar-c/a	21.00	52.50	145.00
1593- Popeye Starring in Choose Your Weppins, 1936, Saalfield, 160 pgs., soft-c, Segar-a	21.00	52.50	145.00

5761 - Popeye and Queen Olive Oyl © KING

101 - "Pop-Up" Mickey Mouse in "Ye Olden Days" © DIS

1447 - Ray Land of the Tank Corps, U.S.A. © WHIT

GD FN VF/NM

1597- Popeye's Ark, 1936, Saalfield, 4 1/2" x 5 1/2", soft-c, Segar-a 21.00 52.50 145.00

2008-(#8)- Popeye-Ghost Ship to Treasure Island, 1967, Whitman, 260 pgs., 39 cents, hard-c, color illos 4.00 10.00 27.00

5755- Popeye-Ghost Ship to Treasure Island, 1973, Whitman, 260 pgs., soft-c, color illos 2.00 5.00 11.00

2034-(#34)- Popeye, Danger Ahoy!, 1969, Whitman, 256 pgs., hard-c, color illos. 4.00 10.00 25.00

5768- Popeye, Danger Ahoy!, 1975, Whitman, 256 pgs., soft-c, color illos. 2.00 5.00 11.00

4063- Popeye, Thimble Theatre Starring, 1935, Whitman, 7" x 9 1/2", 320 pgs., Big Big Book, Segar-c/a; (Cactus cover w/yellow logo) 173.00 433.00 1385.00

4063- Popeye, Thimble Theatre Starring, 1935, Whitman, 7" x 9 1/2", 320 pgs., Big Big Book, Segar-c/a; (Big Balloon-c with red logo), (2nd printing w/same contents as above) 202.00 506.00 1620.00

5761- Popeye and Queen Olive Oyl, 1973, 260 pgs., B&W, soft-c 4.00 10.00 27.00

5761-2- Popeye and Queen Olive Oyl, 1973 (1980-reprint of 1973 version), 260 pgs., 79 cents, B&W, soft-c 2.00 5.00 11.00

103- "Pop-Up" Buck Rogers in the Dangerous Mission (with Pop-Up picture), 1934, BRP, 62 pgs., The Midget Pop-Up Book w/Pop-Up in center of book, Calkins-a 173.00 433.00 1385.00

206- "Pop-Up" Buck Rogers - Strange Adventures in the Spider Ship, The, 1935, BRP, 24 pgs., 8" x 9", 3 Pop-Ups, hard-c, by Dick Calkins 173.00 433.00 1385.00

nn- "Pop-Up" Cinderella, 1933, BRP, 7 1/2" x 9 3/4", 4 Pop-Ups, hard-c
With dustjacket ($2.00) 118.00 295.00 825.00
Without dustjacket 90.00 225.00 630.00

207- "Pop-Up" Dick Tracy-Capture of Boris Arson, 1935, BRP, 24 pgs., 8" x 9", 3 Pop-Ups, hard-c, by Gould 116.00 290.00 810.00

210- "Pop-Up" Flash Gordon Tournament of Death, The, 1935, BRP, 24 pgs., 8" x 9", 3 Pop-Ups, hard-c, by Alex Raymond 173.00 433.00 1385.00

202- "Pop-Up" Goldilocks and the Three Bears, The, 1934, BRP, 24 pgs., 8" x 9", 3 Pop-Ups, hard-c 45.00 113.00 315.00

nn- "Pop-Up" Jack and the Beanstalk, 1933, BRP, hard-c (50 cents), 1 Pop-Up 45.00 113.00 315.00

nn- "Pop-Up" Jack the Giant Killer, 1933, BRP, hard-c (50 cents), 1 Pop-Up 45.00 113.00 315.00

nn- "Pop-Up" Jack the Giant Killer, 1933, BRP, 4 Pop-Ups, hard-c
With dustjacket ($2.00) 118.00 295.00 825.00
Without dust jacket 90.00 225.00 630.00

nn- "Pop-Up" Little Black Sambo, (with Pop-Up picture), 1934, BRP, 62 pgs., The Midget Pop-Up Book, one Pop-Up in center of book 73.00 182.00 515.00

208- "Pop-Up" Little Orphan Annie and Jumbo the Circus Elephant, 1935, BRP, 24 pgs., 8" x 9 1/2", 3 Pop-Ups, hard-c, by H. Gray 119.00 298.00 835.00

nn- "Pop-Up" Little Red Ridinghood, 1933, BRP, hard-c (50 cents), 1 Pop-Up 57.00 143.00 400.00

nn- "Pop-Up" Mickey Mouse, The, 1933, BRP, 34 pgs., 6 1/2" x 9", 3 Pop-Ups, hard-c, Gottfredson-a (75 cents) 110.00 275.00 775.00

nn- "Pop-Up" Mickey Mouse in King Arthur's Court, The,1933, BRP, 56 pgs., 7 1/2" x 9 1/4", 4 Pop-Ups, hard-c, Gottfredson-a
With dust jacket ($2.00) 302.00 756.00 2420.00
Without dustjacket 188.00 470.00 1500.00

101- "Pop-Up" Mickey Mouse in "Ye Olden Days" (with Pop-Up picture), 1934, 62 pgs., BRP, The Midget Pop-Up Book, one Pop-Up in center of book, Gottfredson-a 130.00 327.00 1045.00

nn- "Pop-Up" Minnie Mouse, The, 1933, BRP, 36 pgs., 6 1/2" x 9", 3 Pop-Ups, hard-c (75 cents), Gottfredson-a 110.00 275.00 775.00

203- "Pop-Up" Mother Goose, The, 1934, BRP, 24 pgs., 8" x 9 1/4", 3 Pop-Ups, hard-c 79.00 198.00 550.00

nn- "Pop-Up" Mother Goose Rhymes, The, 1933, BRP, 96 pgs., 7 1/2" x 9 1/4", 4 Pop-Ups, hard-c
With dustjacket ($2.00) 107.00 268.00 750.00
Without dustjacket 84.00 210.00 580.00

209- "Pop-Up" New Adventures of Tarzan, 1935, BRP, 24 pgs., 8" x 9", 3 Pop-Ups, hard-c 130.00 327.00 1045.00

104- "Pop-Up" Peter Rabbit, The (with Pop-Up picture), 1934, BRP, 62 pgs., The Midget Pop-Up Book, one Pop-Up in center of book 73.00 182.00 515.00

nn- "Pop-Up" Pinocchio, 1933, BRP, 7 1/2" x 9 3/4", 4 Pop-Ups, hard-c
With dustjacket ($2.00) 118.00 295.00 825.00
Without dust jacket 90.00 225.00 630.00

102- "Pop-Up" Popeye among the White Savages (with Pop-Up picture), 1934, BRP, 62 pgs., The Midget Pop-Up Book, one Pop-Up in center of book, E. C. Segar-a 116.00 290.00 810.00

205- "Pop-Up" Popeye with the Hag of the Seven Seas, The, 1935, BRP, 24 pgs., 8" x 9", 3 Pop-Ups, hard-c, Segar-a 124.00 310.00 955.00

201- "Pop-Up" Puss In Boots, The, 1934, BRP, 24 pgs., 3 Pop-Ups, hard-c 46.00 115.00 320.00

nn- "Pop-Up" Silly Symphonies, The (Mickey Mouse Presents His ...), 1933, BRP, 56 pgs., 9 3/4" x 7 1/2", 4 Pop-Ups, hard-c
With dust jacket ($2.00) 172.00 430.00 1375.00
Without dust jacket 121.00 304.00 865.00

nn- "Pop-Up" Sleeping Beauty, 1933, BRP, hard-c, (50 cents), 1 Pop-up 53.00 132.00 370.00

212- "Pop-Up" Terry and the Pirates in Shipwrecked, The, 1935, BRP, 24 pgs., 8" x 9", 3 Pop-Ups, hard-c 110.00 275.00 775.00

211- "Pop-Up" Tim Tyler in the Jungle, The, 1935, BRP, 24 pgs., 8" x 9", 3 Pop-Ups, hard-c 84.00 210.00 580.00

1404- Porky Pig and His Gang, 1946, Whitman, All Pictures Comics, Barks-a, reprints Four Color #48 24.00 60.00 165.00

1408- Porky Pig and Petunia, 1942, Whitman, All Pictures Comics, flip pictures, reprints Four Color #16 & Famous Gang Book of Comics 16.00 40.00 115.00

1176- Powder Smoke Range, 1935, Whitman, 240 pgs., photo-c, movie scenes, Hoot Gibson, Harey Carey app. (RKO Radio Pict.) 14.00 35.00 95.00

1058- Practical Pig!, The (Disney), 1939, Whitman, 68 pgs., 5" x 5 1/2", hard-c 12.00 30.00 85.00

758- Prairie Bill and the Covered Wagon, 1934, Whitman, 384 pgs., Hal Arbo-a 12.00 30.00 85.00

nn- Prairie Bill and the Covered Wagon, 1934, Whitman, 390 pgs., premium-no ads, 3-color, soft-c, Hal Arbo-a 18.00 45.00 125.00

1440- Punch Davis of the U.S. Aircraft Carrier, 1945, Whitman, 352 pgs. 10.00 25.00 65.00

nn- Puss in Boots, nd(1930s), np(Whitman), 36 pgs., Penny Book 4.00 10.00 22.00

1100B- Puzzle Book, 1938, Whitman, 36 pgs., 2 1/2" x 3 1/2", Penny Book 4.00 10.00 27.00

1100B- Puzzles, 1938, Whitman, 36 pgs., 2 1/2" x 3 1/2", Penny Book 4.00 10.00 27.00

1100B- Quiz Book, The, 1938, Whitman, 36 pgs., 2 1/2" x 3 1/2", Penny Book 4.00 10.00 27.00

1142- Radio Patrol, 1935, Whitman, 432 pgs., by Eddie Sullivan & Charlie Schmidt (#1) 12.00 30.00 85.00

1173- Radio Patrol Trailing the Safeblowers, 1937, Whitman, 432 pgs. 11.00 27.50 70.00

1496- Radio Patrol Outwitting the Gang Chief, 1939, Whitman, 432 pgs. 11.00 27.50 70.00

1498- Radio Patrol and Big Dan's Mobsters, 1937, Whitman, 432 pgs. 11.00 27.50 70.00

nn- Raiders of the Lost Ark, 1998, Chronicle Books, 304 pgs., adapts movie, 1-color (green) illos 4.00 10.00 22.00

1441- Range Busters, The, 1942, Whitman, 432 pgs., Henry E. Vallely-a 11.00 27.50 70.00

1163- Ranger and the Cowboy, The, 1939, Saalfield, 400 pgs. 11.00 27.50 70.00

1154- Rangers on the Rio Grande, 1938, Saalfield, 400 pgs. 11.00 27.50 70.00

1447- Ray Land of the Tank Corps, U.S.A., 1942, Whitman, 432 pgs., flip pictures, Hess-a 11.00 27.50 70.00

1157- Red Barry Ace-Detective, 1935, Whitman, 432 pgs., by Will Gould 15.00 37.50 105.00

1426- Red Barry Undercover Man, 1939, Whitman, 432 pgs., by Will Gould 13.00 32.50 90.00

20- Red Davis, 1935, EVW, 160 pgs. 12.00 30.00 85.00

1427 - Red Ryder and the Code of the West © WHIT

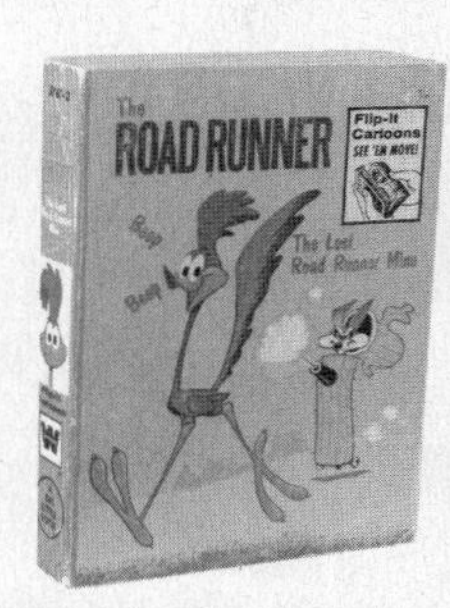
5767-2 - Road Runner, The Lost Road Runner Mine © WB

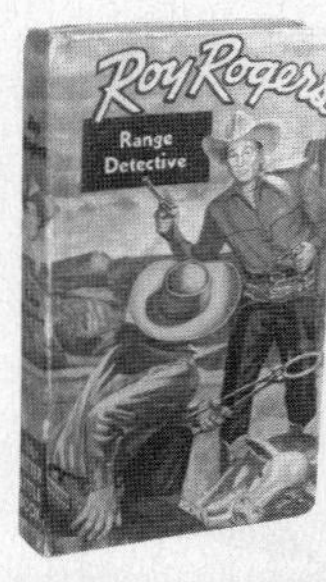
715-10 - Roy Rogers Range Detective © Roy Rogers

	GD	FN	VF/NM
1449- Red Death on the Range, The, 1940, Whitman, 432 pgs., Fred Harman-a (Bronc Peeler)	12.00	30.00	85.00
nn- Red Falcon Adventures, The, 1937, Seal Right Ice Cream, 8 pgs., set of 50 books, circular in shape			
Issue #1	87.00	218.00	605.00
Issue #2-5	60.00	150.00	420.00
Issue #6-10	49.00	122.00	345.00
Issue #11-50	31.00	78.00	220.00
nn- Red Hen and the Fox, The, nd(1930s), np(Whitman), 36 pgs., 3" x 2 1/2", Penny Book	4.00	10.00	22.00
1145- Red-Hot Holsters, 1938, Saalfield, 400 pgs.	11.00	27.50	70.00
1400- Red Ryder and Little Beaver on Hoofs of Thunder, 1939, Whitman, 432 pgs., Harman-c/a	20.00	50.00	140.00
1414- Red Ryder and the Squaw-Tooth Rustlers, 1946, Whitman, 352 pgs., Fred Harman-a	15.00	37.50	105.00
1427- Red Ryder and the Code of the West, 1941, Whitman, 432 pgs., flip pictures, by Harman	19.00	47.50	135.00
1440- Red Ryder the Fighting Westerner, 1940, Whitman, Harman-a	19.00	47.50	135.00
1443- Red Ryder and the Rimrock Killer, 1948, Whitman, 288 pgs., Harman-a	14.00	35.00	95.00
1450- Red Ryder and Western Border Guns, 1942, Whitman, 432 pgs., flip pictures, by Harman	19.00	47.50	135.00
1454- Red Ryder and the Secret Canyon, 1948, Whitman, 288 pgs., Harman-a	14.00	35.00	95.00
1466- Red Ryder and Circus Luck, 1947, Whitman, 288 pgs., by Fred Harman	14.00	35.00	95.00
1473- Red Ryder in War on the Range, 1945, Whitman, 352 pgs., by Fred Harman	15.00	37.50	105.00
1475- Red Ryder and the Outlaw of Painted Valley, 1943, Whitman, 352 pgs., by Harman	14.00	35.00	95.00
702-10- Red Ryder Acting Sheriff, 1949, Whitman, by Fred Hannan	12.00	30.00	85.00
nn- Red Ryder Brings Law to Devil's Hole, 1939, Dell, 196 pgs., Fast-Action Story, Harman-c/a	44.00	110.00	310.00
nn- Red Ryder and the Highway Robbers, 1938, Whitman, 36 pgs., 2 1/2" x 3 1/2", Penny Book	12.00	30.00	85.00
754- Reg'lar Fellers, 1933, Whitman, 320 pgs., by Gene Byrnes	13.00	32.50	90.00
nn- Reg'lar Fellers, 1933, Whitman, 202 pgs., Cocomalt premium, by Gene Byrnes	13.00	32.50	90.00
1424- Rex Beach's Jaragu of the Jungle, 1937, Whitman, 432 pgs.	11.00	27.50	70.00
12- Rex, King of Wild Horses in "Stampede," 1935, EVW, 160 pgs., movie scenes, Columbia Pictures	12.00	30.00	75.00
1100B- Riddles for Fun, 1938, Whitman, 36 pgs., 2 1/2" x 3 1/2", Penny Book	4.00	10.00	27.00
1100B- Riddles to Guess, 1938, Whitman, 36 pgs., 2 1/2" x 3 1/2", Penny Book	4.00	10.00	27.00
1425- Riders of Lone Trails, 1937, Whitman, 300 pgs.	12.00	30.00	75.00
1141- Rio Raiders (A Billy The Kid Story), 1938, Saalfield, 400 pgs.	12.00	30.00	75.00
2023-(#23)- The Road Runner, The Super Beep Catcher, 1968, Whitman, 256 pgs., hard-c, color illos.	1.00	2.50	9.00
5759- The Road Runner, The Super Beep Catcher, 1973, Whitman, 256 pgs., soft-c, 39 cents, B&W illos., and flip pictures	1.00	2.50	6.00
5767-2- Road Runner, The Lost Road Runner Mine, The, 1974 (1980), 260 pgs., 79 cents, B&W, soft-c	1.00	2.50	6.00
5784- The Road Runner and the Unidentified Coyote, 1974, Whitman, 260 pgs., soft-c, flip pictures	1.00	2.50	6.00
5784-2- The Road Runner and the Unidentified Coyote, 1980, Whitman, 260 pgs., soft-c, flip pictures	1.00	2.50	6.00
nn- Road To Perdition, 2002, Dreamworks, screenplay from movie, hard-c (Dreamworks and 20th Century Fox)	1.00	2.50	9.00
Robin Hood (See Wee Little Books)			
10- Robin Hood, 1935, EVW, 160 pgs., movie scenes w/Douglas Fairbanks (United Artists), hard-c	18.00	45.00	125.00
719- Robinson Crusoe (The Story of...), nd (1933), Whitman, 364 pgs., soft-c	13.00	32.50	90.00

	GD	FN	VF/NM
1421- Roy Rogers and the Dwarf-Cattle Ranch, 1947, Whitman, 352 pgs., Henry E. Vallely-a	18.00	45.00	125.00
1437- Roy Rogers and the Deadly Treasure, 1947, Whitman, 288 pgs.	18.00	45.00	125.00
1448- Roy Rogers and the Mystery of the Howling Mesa, 1948, Whitman, 288 pgs.	18.00	45.00	125.00
1452- Roy Rogers in Robbers' Roost, 1948, Whitman, 288 pgs.	18.00	45.00	125.00
1460- Roy Rogers Robinhood of the Range, 1942, Whitman, 432 pgs., Hess-a (1st)	21.00	52.50	145.00
1462- Roy Rogers and the Mystery of the Lazy M, 1949, Whitman	15.00	37.50	105.00
1476- Roy Rogers King of the Cowboys, 1943, Whitman, 352 pgs., Irwin Myers-a, based on movie	22.00	52.50	155.00
1494- Roy Rogers at Crossed Feathers Ranch, 1945, Whitman, 320 pgs., Erwin Hess-a , 3 1/4" x 5 1/2"	18.00	45.00	125.00
701-10- Roy Rogers and the Snowbound Outlaws, 1949, 3 1/4" x 5 1/2"	12.00	30.00	85.00
715-10- Roy Rogers Range Detective, 1950, Whitman, 2 1/2" x 5"	12.00	30.00	85.00
nn- Sandy Gregg Federal Agent on Special Assignment, 1939, Whitman, 36 pgs., 2 1/2" x 3 1/2", Penny Book	11.00	27.50	70.00
Sappo (See Top-Line Comics)			
1122- Scrappy, 1934, Whitman, 288 pgs.	20.00	50.00	140.00
L12- Scrappy (The Adventures of...), 1935, Lynn, 192 pgs., movie scenes	20.00	50.00	140.00
1191- Secret Agent K-7,1940, Saalfield, 400 pgs., based on radio show	11.00	27.50	70.00
1144- Secret Agent X-9, 1936, Whitman, 432 pgs., Charles Flanders-a	15.00	37.50	105.00
1472- Secret Agent X-9 and the Mad Assassin, 1938, Whitman, 432 pgs., Charles Flanders-a	15.00	37.50	105.00
1161- Sequoia, 1935, Whitman, 160 pgs., photo-c, movie scenes	12.00	30.00	85.00
1430- Shadow and the Living Death, The, 1940, Whitman, 432 pgs., Erwin Hess-a	65.00	163.00	460.00
1443- Shadow and the Master of Evil, The, 1941, Whitman, 432 pgs., flip pictures, Hess-a	65.00	163.00	460.00
1495- Shadow and the Ghost Makers, The, 1942, Whitman, 432 pgs., John Coleman Burroughs-c	65.00	163.00	460.00
2024- Shazzan, The Glass Princess, 1968, Whitman, Hanna-Barbera	4.00	10.00	27.00
Shirley Temple (See My Life and Times & Story of..)			
1095- Shirley Temple and Lionel Barrymore Starring In "The Little Colonel," 1935, Saalfield, photo hard-c, movie scenes	20.00	50.00	140.00
1115- Shirley Temple in "The Littlest Rebel," 1935, Saalfield, photo-c, movie scenes, hard-c	20.00	50.00	140.00
1575- Shirley Temple and Lionel Barrymore Starring In "The Little Colonel," 1935, Saalfield, photo soft-c, movie scenes	20.00	50.00	140.00
1595- Shirley Temple in "The Littlest Rebel," 1935, Saalfield, photo-c, movie scenes, soft-c	20.00	50.00	140.00
1195- Shooting Sheriffs of the Wild West, 1936, Whitman, 432 pgs.	11.00	27.50	70.00
1169- Silly Symphony Featuring Donald Duck (Disney), 1937, Whitman, 432 pgs., Taliaferro-a	38.00	95.00	255.00
1441- Silly Symphony Featuring Donald Duck and His (MIS) Adventures (Disney), 1937, Whitman, 432 pgs., Taliaferro-a	38.00	95.00	255.00
1155- Silver Streak, The, 1935, Whitman, 160 pgs., photo-c, movie scenes (RKO Radio Pict.)	12.00	30.00	75.00
Simple Simon (See Wee Little Books)			
1649- Sir Lancelot (TV Series), 1958, Whitman, 280 pgs.	7.00	17.50	44.00
1112- Skeezix in Africa, 1934, Whitman, 300 pgs., Frank King-a	14.00	35.00	95.00
1408- Skeezix at the Military Academy, 1938, Whitman, 432 pgs., Frank King-a	14.00	35.00	95.00
1414- Skeezix Goes to War, 1944, Whitman, 352 pgs., Frank King-a	14.00	35.00	95.00
1419- Skeezix on His Own in the Big City, 1941, Whitman, All Pictures			

1412 - Smilin' Jack Flying High with "Downwind" © WHIT

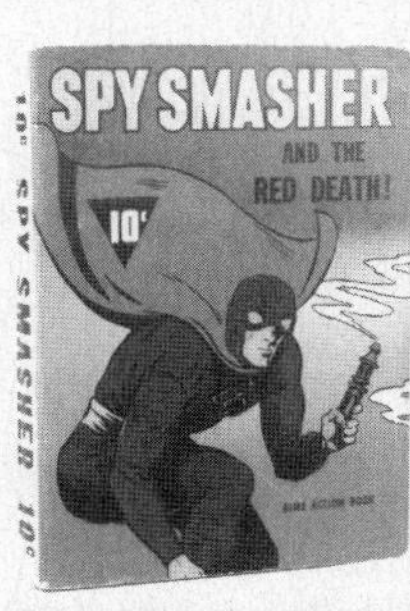

Spy Smasher and the Red Death © FAW

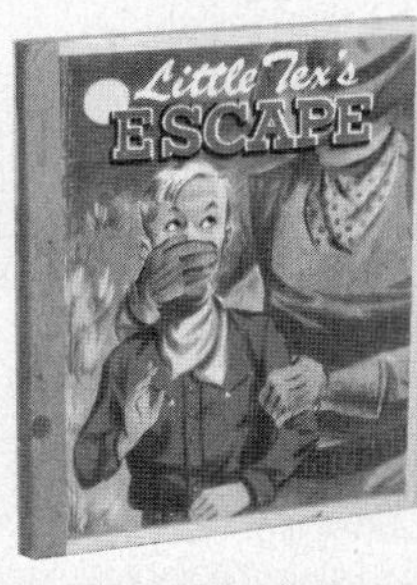

582 - "Swap It" Book
Little Tex in the Midst of Trouble
© Samuel Lowe Co.

	GD	FN	VF/NM
Comics, flip pictures, Frank King-a	14.00	35.00	95.00
761- **Skippy**, 1934, Whitman, 320 pgs., by Percy Crosby	14.00	35.00	95.00
4056- **Skippy, The Story of**, 1934, Whitman, 320 pgs., 7" x 9 1/2", Big Big Book, Percy Crosby-a	70.00	175.00	490.00
nn- **Skippy, The Story of**, 1934, Whitman, Phillips Dental Magnesia premium, soft-c, by Percy Crosby	14.00	35.00	95.00
1439- **Skyroads with Clipper Williams of the Flying Legion**, 1938, Whitman, 432 pgs., by Lt. Dick Calkins, Russell Keaton-a	12.00	30.00	85.00
1127- **Skyroads with Hurricane Hawk**, 1936, Whitman, 432 pgs., by Lt. Dick Calkins, Russell Keaton-a	12.00	30.00	80.00
Smilin' Jack and his Flivver Plane (See Top-Line Comics)			
1152- **Smilin' Jack and the Stratosphere Ascent**, 1937, Whitman, 432 pgs., Zack Mosley-a	16.00	40.00	115.00
1412- **Smilin' Jack Flying High with "Downwind,"** 1942, Whitman, 432 pgs., Zack Mosley-a	15.00	37.50	105.00
1416- **Smilin' Jack in Wings over the Pacific**, 1939, Whitman, 432 pgs., Zack Mosley-a	15.00	37.50	105.00
1419- **Smilin' Jack and the Jungle Pipe Line**, 1947, Whitman, 352 pgs., Zack Mosley-a	12.00	30.00	85.00
1445- **Smilin' Jack and the Escape from Death Rock**, 1943, Whitman, 352 pgs., Mosley-a	12.00	30.00	85.00
1464- **Smilin' Jack and the Coral Princess**, 1945, Whitman, 352 pgs., Zack Mosley-a	12.00	30.00	85.00
1473- **Smilin' Jack Speed Pilot**, 1941, Whitman, 432 pgs., Zack Mosley-a	16.00	40.00	115.00
2- **Smilin' Jack and his Stratosphere Plane**, 1938, Whitman, 132 pgs., Buddy Book, soft-c, Zack Mosley-a	39.00	98.00	275.00
nn- **Smilin' Jack Grounded on a Tropical Shore**, 1938, Whitman, 36 pgs., 2 1/2" x 3 1/2", Penny Book	11.00	27.50	70.00
11- **Smilin' Jack and the Border Bandits**, 1941, Dell, 196 pgs., Fast-Action Story, soft-c, Zack Mosley-a	36.00	90.00	255.00
745- **Smitty Golden Gloves Tournament**, 1934, Whitman, 320 pgs., Walter Berndt-a	15.00	37.50	105.00
nn- **Smitty Golden Gloves Tournament**, 1934, Whitman, 204 pgs., Cocomalt premium, soft-c, Walter Berndt-a	16.00	40.00	115.00
1404- **Smitty and Herby Lost Among the Indians**, 1941, Whitman, All Pictures Comics	11.00	27.50	70.00
1477- **Smitty in Going Native**, 1938, Whitman, 300 pgs., Walter Berndt-a	11.00	27.50	70.00
2- **Smitty and Herby**, 1936, Whitman, 132 pgs., 3 1/2" x 3 1/2", soft-c, Tarzan Ice Cream cup lid premium	36.00	90.00	255.00
9- **Smitty's Brother Herby and the Police Horse**, 1938, Whitman, 132 pgs., 3 1/4" x 3 1/2", Buddy Book-ice cream premium, by Walter Berndt	36.00	90.00	255.00
1010- **Smokey Stover Firefighter of Foo**, 1937, Whitman, 7 1/4" x 5 1/2", 64 pgs., Nickel Book, Bill Holman-a	16.00	40.00	115.00
1413- **Smokey Stover**, 1942, Whitman, All Pictures Comics, flip pictures, Bill Holman-a	14.00	35.00	95.00
1421- **Smokey Stover the Foo Fighter**, 1938, Whitman, 432 pgs., Bill Holman-a	14.00	35.00	95.00
1481- **Smokey Stover the Foolish Foo Fighter**, 1942, Whitman, All Pictures Comics	14.00	35.00	95.00
1- **Smokey Stover the Fireman of Foo**, 1938, Whitman, 3 3/4" x 3 1/2", 132 pgs., Buddy Book-ice cream premium, by Bill Holman	41.00	103.00	285.00
1100A- **Smokey Stover**, 1938, Whitman, 36 pgs., 2 1/2" x 3 1/2", Penny Book	12.00	30.00	80.00
nn- **Smokey Stover and the Fire Chief of Foo**, 1938, Whitman, 36 pgs., 2 1/2" x 3 1/2", Penny Book, yellow shirt on-c	12.00	30.00	80.00
nn- **Smokey Stover and the Fire Chief of Foo**, 1938, Whitman, 36 pgs., Penny Book, green shirt on-c	12.00	30.00	80.00
1460- **Snow White and the Seven Dwarfs** (The Story of Walt Disney's ...), 1938, Whitman, 288 pgs.	29.00	73.00	200.00
1136- **Sombrero Pete**, 1936, Whitman, 432 pgs.	11.00	27.50	70.00
1152- **Son of Mystery**, 1939, Saalfield, 400 pgs.	11.00	27.50	70.00
1191- **SOS Coast Guard**, 1936, Whitman, 432 pgs., Henry E. Vallely-a	12.00	30.00	75.00
2016-(#16)-**Space Ghost-The Sorceress of Cyba-3** (TV Cartoon), 1968, Whitman, 260 pgs., 39¢-c, hard-c, color illos	10.00	25.00	60.00
1455- **Speed Douglas and the Mole Gang-The Great Sabotage Plot**, 1941, Whitman, 432 pgs., flip pictures	11.00	27.50	70.00
5779- **Spider-Man Zaps Mr. Zodiac**, 1976, 260 pgs., soft-c, B&W	1.00	2.50	9.00
5779-2- **Spider-Man Zaps Mr. Zodiac**, 1980, 260 pgs., 79¢-c, soft-c, B&W	1.00	2.50	6.00
1467- **Spike Kelly of the Commandos**, 1943, Whitman, 352 pgs.	11.00	27.50	70.00
1144- **Spook Riders on the Overland**, 1938, Saalfield, 400 pgs.	11.00	27.50	70.00
768- **Spy, The**, 1936, Whitman, 300 pgs.	13.00	32.50	90.00
nn- **Spy Smasher and the Red Death**, 1941, Fawcett, 4" x 5 1/2", Dime Action Book	58.00	146.00	410.00
1120- **Stan Kent Freshman Fullback**, 1936, Saalfield, 148 pgs., hard-c	9.00	22.50	55.00
1132- **Stan Kent, Captain**, 1937, Saalfield	9.00	22.50	55.00
1600- **Stan Kent Freshman Fullback**, 1936, Saalfield, 148 pgs., soft-c	9.00	22.50	55.00
1123- **Stan Kent Varsity Man**, 1936, Saalfield, 160 pgs., hard-c	9.00	22.50	55.00
1603- **Stan Kent Varsity Man**, 1936, Saalfield, 160 pgs., soft-c	9.00	22.50	55.00
nn- **Star Wars - A New Hope**, 1997, Chronicle Books, 320 pgs., adapts movie, 1-color (blue) illos	3.00	7.50	20.00
nn- **Star Wars - Empire Strikes Back, The**, 1997, Chronicle Books, 296 pgs., adapts movie, 1-color (blue) illos	3.00	7.50	20.00
nn- **Star Wars - Episode 1 - The Phantom Menace**, 1999, Chronicle Books, 344 pgs., adapts movie, 1-color (blue) illos	1.00	2.50	9.00
nn- **Star Wars - Episode 2 - Attack of the Clones**, 2002, Chronicle Books, 340 pgs., adapts movie, 1-color (blue) illos	1.00	2.50	9.00
nn- **Star Wars - Return of the Jedi**, 1997, Chronicle Books, 312 pgs., adapts movie, 1-color (blue) illos	3.00	7.50	20.00
1104- **Steel Arena, The** (With Clyde Beatty), 1936, Saalfield, hard-c, movie scenes adapted from "The Lost Jungle"	12.00	30.00	85.00
1584- **Steel Arena, The** (With Clyde Beatty), 1936, Saalfield, soft-c, movie scenes	12.00	30.00	85.00
1426- **Steve Hunter of the U.S. Coast Guard Under Secret Orders**, 1942, Whitman, 432 pgs.	11.00	27.50	70.00
1456- **Story of Charlie McCarthy and Edgar Bergen, The**, 1938, Whitman, 288 pgs.	15.00	37.50	105.00
Story of Daniel, The (See Wee Little Books)			
Story of David, The (See Wee Little Books)			
1110- **Story of Freddie Bartholomew, The**, 1935, Saalfield, 4 1/2" x 5 1/4", hard-c, movie scenes (MGM)	12.00	30.00	75.00
1590- **Story of Freddie Bartholomew, The**, 1935, Saalfield, 4 1/2" x 5 1/4", soft-c, movie scenes (MGM)	12.00	30.00	75.00
Story of Gideon, The (See Wee Little Books)			
W714- **Story of Jackie Cooper, The**, 1933, Whitman, 240 pgs., photo-c, movie scenes, "Skippy" & "Sooky" movie	15.00	37.50	105.00
Story of Joseph, The (See Wee Little Books)			
Story of Moses, The (See Wee Little Books)			
Story of Ruth and Naomi (See Wee Little Books)			
1089- **Story of Shirley Temple, The**, 1934, Saalfield, 160 pgs., hard-c, photo-c, movie scenes	13.00	32.50	90.00
1319- **Story of Shirley Temple, The**, 1934, Saalfield, 160 pgs., soft-c, photo-c, movie scenes	13.00	32.50	90.00
1090- **Strawberry-Roan**, 1934, Saalfield, 160 pgs., hard-c, Ken Maynard photo-c, movie scenes	13.00	32.50	90.00
1320- **Strawberry-Roan**, 1934, Saalfield, 160 pgs., soft-c, Ken Maynard photo-c, movie scenes	13.00	32.50	90.00
Streaky and the Football Signals (See Top-Line Comics)			
5780-2- **Superman in the Phantom Zone Connection**, 1980, 260 pgs., 79¢-c, soft-c, B&W	1.00	2.50	9.00
582- **"Swap It" Book, The**, 1949, Samuel Lowe Co., 260 pgs., 3 1/2" x 4 1/2"			
1. Little Tex in the Midst of Trouble	7.00	17.50	44.00
2. Little Tex's Escape	7.00	17.50	44.00
3. Little Tex Comes to the XY Ranch	7.00	17.50	44.00
4. Get Them Cowboy	7.00	17.50	44.00
5. The Mail Must Go Through! A Story of the Pony Express			

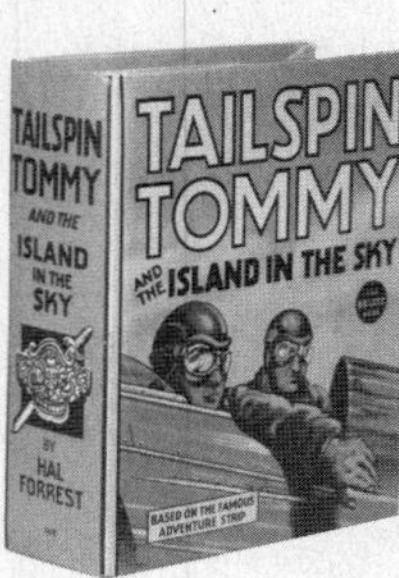
1110 - Tailspin Tommy and the Island in the Sky © WHIT

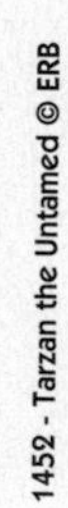
1452 - Tarzan the Untamed © ERB

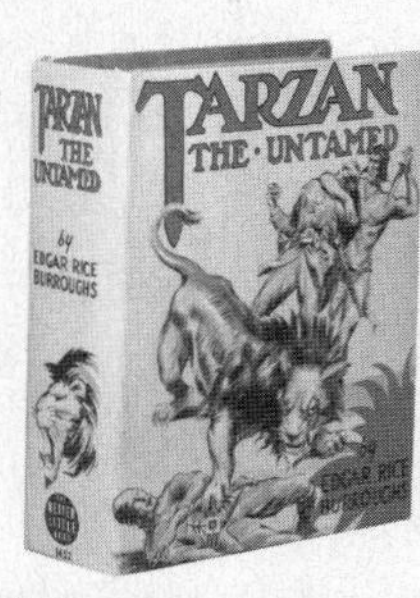

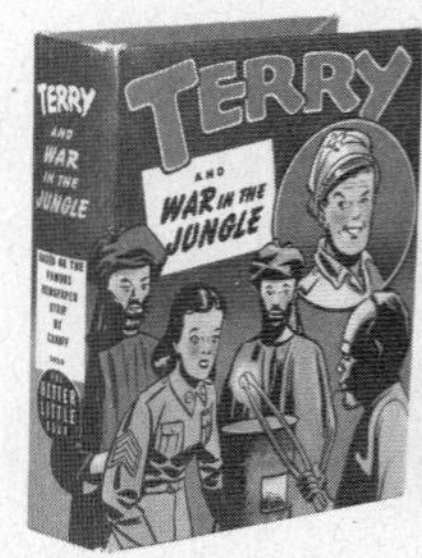
1420 - Terry and War in the Jungle © WHIT

GD FN VF/NM

7.00 17.50 44.00
6. Nevada Jones, Trouble Shooter 7.00 17.50 44.00
7. Danny Meets the Cowboys 7.00 17.50 44.00
8. Flint Adams and the Stage Coach 7.00 17.50 44.00
9. Bud Shinners and the Oregon Trail 7.00 17.50 44.00
10. The Outlaws' Last Ride 7.00 17.50 44.00

Sybil Jason (See Little Big Shot)

747- Tailspin Tommy in the Famous Pay-Roll Mystery, 1933, Whitman, hard-c, 320 pgs., Hal Forrest-a (# 1) 15.00 37.50 105.00

747- Tailspin Tommy in the Famous Pay-Roll Mystery, 1933, Whitman, soft-c, 320 pgs., Hal Forrest-a (# 1) 15.00 37.50 105.00

nn- Tailspin Tommy the Pay-Roll Mystery, 1934, Whitman, 52 pgs., 3 1/2" x 5 1/4", premium-no ads, soft-c; another version with Perkins ad, Hal Forrest-a 26.00 65.00 185.00

1110- Tailspin Tommy and the Island in the Sky, 1936, Whitman, 432 pgs., Hal Forrest-a 13.00 32.50 90.00

1124- Tailspin Tommy the Dirigible Flight to the North Pole, 1934, Whitman, 432 pgs., H. Forrest-a 15.00 37.50 105.00

nn- Tailspin Tommy the Dirigible Flight to the North Pole, 1934, Whitman, 436 pgs., 3-color, soft-c, premium-no ads, Hal Forrest-a 36.00 90.00 255.00

1172- Tailspin Tommy Hunting for Pirate Gold, 1935, Whitman, 432 pgs., Hal Forrest-a 13.00 32.50 90.00

1183- Tailspin Tommy Air Racer, 1940, Saalfield, 400 pgs., hard-c 13.00 32.50 90.00

1184- Tailspin Tommy in the Great Air Mystery, 1936, Whitman, 240 pgs., photo-c, movie scenes 15.00 37.50 105.00

1410- Tailspin Tommy the Weasel and His "Skywaymen," 1941, Whitman, All Pictures Comics, flip pictures 12.00 30.00 80.00

1413- Tailspin Tommy and the Lost Transport, 1940, Whitman, 432 pgs., Hal Forrest-a 12.00 30.00 80.00

1423- Tailspin Tommy and the Hooded Flyer, 1937, Whitman, 432 pgs., Hal Forrest-a 13.00 32.50 90.00

1494- Tailspin Tommy and the Sky Bandits, 1938, Whitman 432 pgs., Hal Forrest-a 13.00 32.50 90.00

nn- Tailspin Tommy and the Airliner Mystery, 1938, Dell, 196 pgs., Fast-Action Story, soft-c, Hal Forrest-a 47.00 118.00 330.00

nn- Tailspin Tommy in Flying Aces, 1938, Dell, 196 pgs., Fast-Action Story, soft-c, Hal Forrest-a 47.00 118.00 330.00

nn- Tailspin Tommy in Wings Over the Arctic, 1934, Whitman, Cocomalt premium, Forrest-a 20.00 50.00 140.00

nn- Tailspin Tommy Big Thrill Chewing Gum, 1934, Whitman, 8 pgs., 2 1/2" x 3 " (6 diff.) each.. 13.00 32.50 90.00

3- Tailspin Tommy on the Mountain of Human Sacrifice, 1938, Whitman, soft-c, Buddy Book 43.00 108.00 300.00

7- Tailspin Tommy's Perilous Adventure, 1934, Whitman, 132 pgs., 3 1/2" x 3 1/2" soft-c, Tarzan Ice Cream cup premium 43.00 108.00 300.00

nn- Tailspin Tommy, 1935, Whitman, 148 pgs., 3 1/2" x 4", Tarzan Ice Cream cup premium 54.00 135.00 385.00

L16- Tale of Two Cities, A, 1935, Lynn, movie scenes 15.00 37.50 105.00

744- Tarzan of the Apes, 1933, Whitman, 320 pgs., by Edgar Rice Burroughs (1st) 46.00 115.00 325.00

nn- Tarzan of the Apes, 1935, Whitman, 52 pgs., 3 1/2" x 5 1/4", soft-c, stapled, premium, no ad; another version with a Perkins ad 58.00 146.00 410.00

769- Tarzan the Fearless, 1934, Whitman, 240 pgs., Buster Crabbe photo-c, movie scenes, ERB 33.00 83.00 230.00

770- Tarzan Twins, The, 1934, Whitman, 432 pgs., ERB 118.00 295.00 825.00

770- Tarzan Twins, The, 1935, Whitman, 432 pgs., ERB 58.00 146.00 410.00

nn- Tarzan Twins, The, 1935, Whitman, 52 pgs., 3 1/2" x 5 3/4", premium-no ads, soft-c, ERB 79.00 198.00 550.00

nn- Tarzan Twins, The, 1935, Whitman, 436 pgs., 3-color, soft-c, premium-no ads, ERB 84.00 210.00 580.00

778- Tarzan of the Screen (The Story of Johnny Weissmuller), 1934, Whitman, 240 pgs., photo-c, movie scenes, ERB 34.00 85.00 240.00

GD FN VF/NM

1102- Tarzan, The Return of, 1936, Whitman, 432 pgs., Edgar Rice Burroughs 24.00 60.00 170.00

1180- Tarzan, The New Adventures of, 1935, Whitman, 160 pgs., Herman Brix photo-c, movie scenes, ERB 28.00 70.00 195.00

1182- Tarzan Escapes, 1936, Whitman, 240 pgs., Johnny Weissmuller photo-c, movie scenes, ERB 34.00 85.00 240.00

1407- Tarzan Lord of the Jungle, 1946, Whitman, 352 pgs., ERB 18.00 45.00 125.00

1410- Tarzan, The Beasts of, 1937, Whitman, 432 pgs., Edgar Rice Burroughs 21.00 52.50 145.00

1442- Tarzan and the Lost Empire, 1948, Whitman, 288 pgs., ERB 18.00 45.00 125.00

1444- Tarzan and the Ant Men, 1945, Whitman, 352 pgs., ERB 18.00 45.00 125.00

1448- Tarzan and the Golden Lion, 1943, Whitman, 432 pgs., ERB 22.00 52.50 155.00

1452- Tarzan the Untamed, 1941, Whitman, 432 pgs., flip pictures, ERB 22.00 52.50 155.00

1453- Tarzan the Terrible, 1942, Whitman, 432 pgs., flip pictures, ERB 22.00 52.50 155.00

1467- Tarzan in the Land of the Giant Apes, 1949, Whitman, ERB 18.00 45.00 125.00

1477- Tarzan, The Son of, 1939, Whitman, 432 pgs., ERB 22.00 52.50 155.00

1488- Tarzan's Revenge, 1938, Whitman, 432 pgs., ERB 22.00 52.50 155.00

1495- Tarzan and the Jewels of Opar, 1940, Whitman, 432 pgs. 22.00 52.50 155.00

4056- Tarzan and the Tarzan Twins with Jad-Bal-Ja the Golden Lion, 1936, Whitman, 7" x 9 1/2", 320 pgs., Big Big Book 115.00 288.00 810.00

709-10- Tarzan and the Journey of Terror, 1950, Whitman, 2 1/2" x 5", ERB, Marsh-a 12.00 30.00 75.00

2005- (#5)-Tarzan: The Mark of the Red Hyena, 1967, Whitman, 260 pgs., 39 cents, hard-c, color illos 4.00 10.00 27.00

nn- Tarzan, 1935, Whitman, 148 pgs., soft-c, 3 1/2" x 4", Tarzan Ice Cream cup premium, ERB (scarce) 130.00 327.00 1045.00

nn- Tarzan and a Daring Rescue, 1938, Whitman, 68 pgs., Pan-Am premium, soft-c, ERB (blank back-c version also exists) 64.00 192.00 450.00

nn- Tarzan and his Jungle Friends, 1936, Whitman, 132 pgs., soft-c, 3 1/2" x 3 1/2", Tarzan Ice Cream cup premium, ERB (scarce) 112.00 280.00 785.00

nn- Tarzan in the Golden City, 1938, Whitman, 68 pgs., Pan-Am premium, soft-c, ERB 71.00 213.00 500.00

nn- Tarzan The Avenger, 1939, Dell, 194 pgs., Fast-Action Story, ERB, soft-c 47.00 118.00 330.00

nn- Tarzan with the Tarzan Twins in the Jungle, 1938, Dell, 194 pgs., Fast-Action Story, ERB 47.00 118.00 330.00

1100B- Tell Your Fortune, 1938, Whitman, 36 pgs., 2 1/2" x 3 1/2", Penny Book 5.00 12.50 33.00

nn- Terminator 2: Judgment Day, 1998, Chronicle Books, 310 pgs., adapts movie, 1-color (blue-gray) illos 1.00 2.50 9.00

1156- Terry and the Pirates, 1935, Whitman, 432 pgs., Milton Caniff-a (#1) 18.00 45.00 125.00

nn- Terry and the Pirates, 1935, Whitman, 52 pgs., 3 1/2" x 5 1/4", soft-c, premium, Milton Caniff-a; 3 versions: No ad, Sears ad & Perkins ad 31.00 78.00 220.00

1412- Terry and the Pirates Shipwrecked on a Desert Island, 1938, Whitman, 432 pgs., Milton Caniff-a 15.00 37.50 105.00

1420- Terry and War in the Jungle, 1946, Whitman, 352 pgs., Milton Caniff-a 13.00 32.50 90.00

1436- Terry and the Pirates The Plantation Mystery, 1942, Whitman, 432 pgs., flip pictures, Milton Caniff-a 15.00 37.50 105.00

1446- Terry and the Pirates and the Giant's Vengeance, 1939, Whitman, 432 pgs., Caniff-a 15.00 37.50 105.00

1499- Terry and the Pirates in the Mountain Stronghold, 1941, Whitman, 432 pgs., Caniff-a 15.00 37.50 105.00

4073- Terry and the Pirates, The Adventures of, 1938, Whitman, 7" x 9 1/2", 320 pgs., Big Big Book, Milton Caniff-a 87.00 218.00 605.00

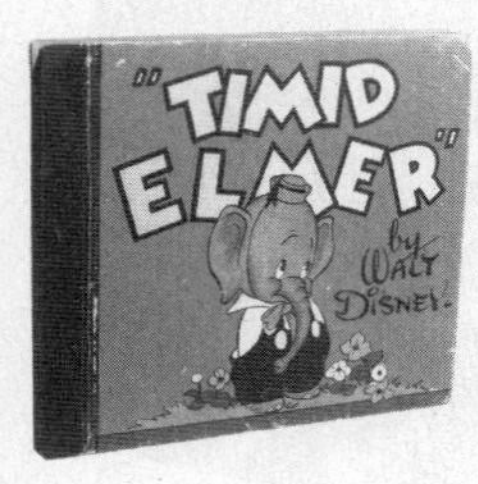

1058 - "Timid Elmer" © DIS

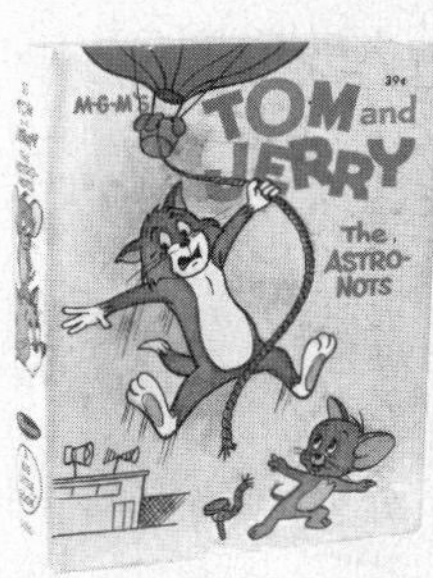

2030 - Tom and Jerry, The Astro-Nots © MGM

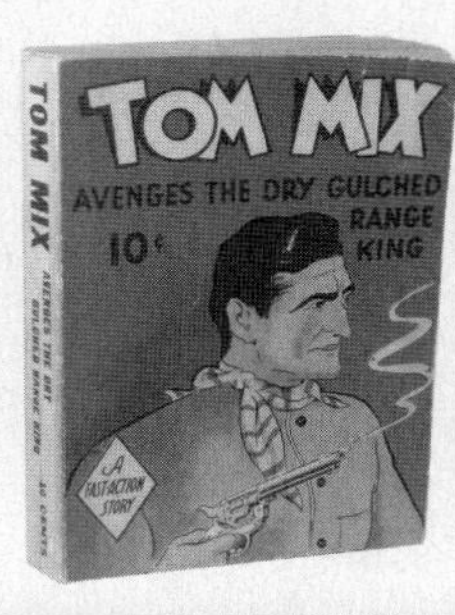

Tom Mix Avenges the Dry Gulched Range King © DELL

GD FN VF/NM

4- Terry and the Pirates Ashore in Singapore, 1938, Whitman, 132 pgs., 3 1/2" x 3 3/4", soft-c, Buddy Book premium 38.00 95.00 255.00
10- Terry and the Pirates Meet Again, 1936, Whitman, 132 pgs., 3 1/2" x 3 1/2", soft-c, Tarzan Ice Cream cup lid premium 58.00 146.00 410.00
nn- Terry and the Pirates, Adventures of, 1938, 36 pgs., 2 1/2" x 3 1/2", Penny Book, Caniff-a 11.00 27.50 70.00
nn- Terry and the Pirates and the Island Rescue, 1938, Whitman, 68 pgs., 3 1/4" x 3 1/2", Pan-Am premium 29.00 73.00 200.00
nn- Terry and the Pirates on Their Travels, 1938, 36 pgs., 2 1/2" x 3 1/2", Penny Book, Caniff-a 11.00 27.50 70.00
nn- Terry and the Pirates and the Mystery Ship, 1938, Dell, 194 pgs., Fast-Action Story, soft-c 39.00 98.00 275.00
1492- Terry Lee Flight Officer U.S.A., 1944, Whitman, 352 pgs., Milton Caniff-a 12.00 30.00 85.00
7- Texas Bad Man, The (Tom Mix), 1934, EVW, 160 pgs., (Five Star Library), movie scenes 24.00 60.00 165.00
1429- Texas Kid, The, 1937, Whitman, 432 pgs. 11.00 27.50 70.00
1135- Texas Ranger, The, 1936, Whitman, 432 pgs., Hal Arbo-a 11.00 27.50 70.00
nn- Texas Ranger, The, 1935, Whitman, 260 pgs., Cocomalt premium, soft-c, Hal Arbo-a 12.00 30.00 85.00
nn- Texas Ranger and the Rustler Gang, The, 1936, Whitman, Pan-Am giveaway 29.00 73.00 200.00
nn- Texas Ranger in the West, The, 1938, Whitman, 36 pgs., 2 1/2" x 3 1/2", Penny Book 10.00 25.00 65.00
nn- Texas Ranger to the Rescue, The, 1938, Whitman, 36 pgs., 2 1/2" x 3 1/2", Penny Book 10.00 25.00 65.00
12- Texas Ranger in Rustler Strategy, The, 1936, Whitman, 132 pgs., 3 1/2" x 3 1/2", soft-c, Tarzan Ice Cream cup lid premium 36.00 90.00 255.00
Tex Thorne (See Zane Grey)
Thimble Theatre (See Popeye)
26- 13 Hours By Air, 1936, Lynn, 128 pgs., 5" x 7 1/2", photo-c, movie scenes (Paramount Pictures) 14.00 35.00 95.00
nn- Three Bears, The, nd (1930s), np (Whitman), 36 pgs., 3" x 2 1/2", Penny Book 4.00 10.00 22.00
1129- Three Finger Joe (Baseball), 1937, Saalfield, Robert A. Graef-a 10.00 25.00 65.00
nn- Three Little Pigs, The, nd (1930s), np (Whitman), 36 pgs., 3" x 2 1/2", Penny Book 4.00 10.00 22.00
1131- Three Musketeers, 1935, Whitman, 182 pgs., 5 1/4" x 6 1/4", photo-c, movie scenes 18.00 45.00 125.00
1409- Thumper and the Seven Dwarfs (Disney), 1944, Whitman, All Pictures Comics 24.00 60.00 165.00
1108- Tiger Lady, The (The life of Mabel Stark, animal trainer), 1935, Saalfield, photo-c, movie scenes, hard-c 11.00 27.50 70.00
1588- Tiger Lady, The, 1935, Saalfield, photo-c, movie scenes, soft-c 11.00 27.50 70.00
1442- Tillie the Toiler and the Wild Man of Desert Island, 1941, Whitman, 432 pgs., Russ Westover-a 12.00 30.00 85.00
1058- "Timid Elmer" (Disney), 1939, Whitman, 5" x 5 1/2", 68 pgs., hard-c 12.00 30.00 85.00
1152- Tim McCoy in the Prescott Kid, 1935, Whitman, 160 pgs., hard-c, photo-c, movie scenes 20.00 50.00 140.00
1193- Tim McCoy in the Westerner, 1936, Whitman, 240 pgs., photo-c, movie scenes 18.00 45.00 125.00
1436- Tim McCoy on the Tomahawk Trail, 1937, Whitman, 432 pgs., Robert Weisman-a 12.00 30.00 85.00
1490- Tim McCoy and the Sandy Gulch Stampede, 1939, Whitman, 424 pgs. 12.00 30.00 75.00
2- Tim McCoy in Beyond the Law, 1934, EVW, Five Star Library, photo-c, movie scenes (Columbia Pictures) (Rare) 50.00 150.00 350.00
10- Tim McCoy in Fighting the Redskins, 1938, Whitman, 130 pgs., Buddy Book, soft-c 34.00 85.00 240.00
14- Tim McCoy in Speedwings, 1935, EVW, Five Star Library, 160 pgs., photo-c, movie scenes (Columbia Pictures) 24.00 60.00 165.00
nn- Tim the Builder, nd (1930s), np (Whitman), 36 pgs., 3" x 2 1/2", Penny Book 4.00 10.00 22.00
Tim Tyler (Also see Adventures of ...)

GD FN VF/NM

1140- Tim Tyler's Luck Adventures in the Ivory Patrol, 1937, Whitman, 432 pgs., by Lyman Young 13.00 32.50 90.00
1479- Tim Tyler's Luck and the Plot of the Exiled King, 1939, Whitman, 432 pgs., by Lyman Young 12.00 30.00 80.00
767- Tiny Tim, The Adventures of, 1935, Whitman, 384 pgs., by Stanley Link 15.00 37.50 105.00
1172- Tiny Tim and the Mechanical Men, 1937, Whitman, 432 pgs., by Stanley Link 13.00 32.50 90.00
1472- Tiny Tim in the Big, Big World, 1945, Whitman, 352 pgs., by Stanley Link 13.00 32.50 90.00
2006- (#6)-Tom and Jerry Meet Mr. Fingers, 1967, Whitman, 39¢-c 260 pgs., hard-c, color illos. 4.00 10.00 27.00
5752- Tom and Jerry Meet Mr. Fingers, 1973, Whitman, 39¢-c 260 pgs., soft-c, color illos., 5 printings 2.00 5.00 11.00
2030-(#30)- Tom and Jerry, The Astro-Nots, 1969, Whitman, 256 pgs., hard-c, color illos. 3.00 7.50 20.00
5765- Tom and Jerry, The Astro-Nots, 1974, Whitman, 256 pgs., soft-c, color illos. 2.00 5.00 11.00
5787-2- Tom and Jerry Under the Big Top, 1980, Whitman, 79¢-c, 260 pgs., soft-c, B&W 2.00 5.00 11.00
723- Tom Beatty Ace of the Service, 1934, Whitman, 256 pgs., George Taylor-a 13.00 32.50 90.00
nn- Tom Beatty Ace of the Service, 1934, Whitman, 260 pgs., soft-c 13.00 32.50 90.00
1165- Tom Beatty Ace of the Service Scores Again, 1937, Whitman, 432 pgs., Weisman-a 12.00 30.00 80.00
1420- Tom Beatty Ace of the Service and the Big Brain Gang, 1939, Whitman, 432 pgs. 12.00 30.00 80.00
nn- Tom Beatty Ace Detective and the Gorgon Gang, 1938?, Whitman, 36 pgs., 2 1/2" x 3 1/2", Penny Book 11.00 27.50 70.00
nn- Tom Beatty Ace of the Service and the Kidnapers, 1938?, Whitman, 36 pgs., 2 1/2" x 3 1/2", Penny Book 11.00 27.50 70.00
1102- Tom Mason on Top, 1935, Saalfield, 160 pgs., Tom Mix photo-c, from Mascot serial "The Miracle Rider," movie scenes, hard-c 20.00 50.00 140.00
1582- Tom Mason on Top, 1935, Saalfield, 160 pgs., Tom Mix photo-c, movie scenes, soft-c 20.00 50.00 140.00
Tom Mix (See Chief of the Rangers, Flaming Guns & Texas Bad Man)
762- Tom Mix and Tony Jr. in "Terror Trail," 1934, Whitman, 160 pgs., movie scenes 20.00 50.00 140.00
1144- Tom Mix in the Fighting Cowboy, 1935, Whitman, 432 pgs., Hal Arbo-a 15.00 37.50 105.00
nn- Tom Mix in the Fighting Cowboy, 1935, Whitman, 436 pgs., premium-no ads, 3 color, soft-c, Hal Arbo-a 29.00 73.00 200.00
1166- Tom Mix in the Range War, 1937, Whitman, 432 pgs., Hal Arbo-a 12.00 30.00 85.00
1173- Tom Mix Plays a Lone Hand, 1935, Whitman, 288 pgs., hard-c, Hal Arbo-a 12.00 30.00 85.00
1183- Tom Mix and the Stranger from the South, 1936, Whitman, 432 pgs. 12.00 30.00 85.00
1462- Tom Mix and the Hoard of Montezuma, 1937, Whitman, H. E. Vallely-a 12.00 30.00 85.00
1482- Tom Mix and His Circus on the Barbary Coast, 1940, Whitman, 432 pgs., James Gary-a 12.00 30.00 85.00
3047- Tom Mix and His Big Little Kit, 1937, Whitman, 384 pgs., 4 1/2" x 6 1/2" box, includes miniature box of 4 crayons-red, yellow, blue and green 100.00 250.00 700.00
4068- Tom Mix and the Scourge of Paradise Valley, 1937, Whitman, 7" x 9 1/2", 320 pgs., Big Big Book, Vallely-a 70.00 175.00 490.00
6833- Tom Mix in the Riding Avenger, 1936, Dell, 244 pgs., Cartoon Story Book, hard-c 31.00 78.00 220.00
nn- Tom Mix Rides to the Rescue, 1939, 36 pgs., 2 1/2" x 3", Penny Book 11.00 27.50 70.00
nn- Tom Mix Avenges the Dry Gulched Range King, 1939, Dell, 196 pgs., Fast-Action Story, soft-c 33.00 83.00 230.00
nn- Tom Mix in the Riding Avenger, 1936, Dell, 244 pgs., Fast-Action Story 33.00 83.00 230.00
nn- Tom Mix the Trail of the Terrible 6, 1935, Ralston Purina Co., 84 pgs., 3" x 3 1/2", premium 24.00 60.00 170.00
4- Tom Mix and Tony in the Rider of Death Valley,

540 - Top-Line Comics
Broncho Bill in Suicide Canyon © WHIT

1104 - Two-Gun Montana © WHIT

1066 - Walt Disney's Story of Pluto the Pup © DIS

GD FN VF/NM

1934, EVW, Five Star Library, 160 pgs., movie scenes (Universal Pictures), hard-c 24.00 60.00 165.00

4- Tom Mix and Tony in the Rider of Death Valley, 1934, EVW, Five Star Library, 160 pgs., movie scenes (Universal Pictures), soft-c (Rare) 50.00 150.00 350.00

7- Tom Mix in the Texas Bad Man, 1934, EVW, Five Star Library, 160 pgs., movie scenes, hard-c 24.00 60.00 165.00

7- Tom Mix in the Texas Bad Man, 1934, EVW, Five Star Library, 160 pgs., movie scenes; soft-c (Rare) 50.00 150.00 350.00

10- Tom Mix in the Tepee Ranch Mystery, 1938, Whitman, 132 pgs., Buddy Book, soft-c 34.00 85.00 240.00

1126- Tommy of Troop Six (Scout Book), 1937, Saalfield, hard-c 10.00 25.00 65.00

1606- Tommy of Troop Six (Scout Book), 1937, Saalfield, soft-c 10.00 25.00 65.00

Tom Sawyer (See Adventures of ...)

1437- Tom Swift and His Magnetic Silencer, 1941, Whitman, 432 pgs., flip pictures 50.00 150.00 350.00

1485- Tom Swift and His Giant Telescope, 1939, Whitman, 432 pgs., James Gary-a 36.00 108.00 250.00

540- Top-Line Comics (In Open Box), 1935, Whitman, 164 pgs., 3 1/2" x 3 1/2", 3 books in set, all soft-c:
Bobby Thatcher and the Samarang Emerald 18.00 45.00 125.00
Broncho Bill in Suicide Canyon 18.00 45.00 125.00
Freckles and His Friends in the North Woods 18.00 45.00 125.00
Complete set with box 62.00 155.00 440.00

541- Top-Line Comics (In Open Box), 1935, Whitman, 164 pgs., 3 1/2" x 3 1/2", 3 books in set; all soft-c:
Little Joe and the City Gangsters 18.00 45.00 125.00
Smilin' Jack and His Flivver Plane 18.00 45.00 125.00
Streaky and the Football Signals 18.00 45.00 125.00
Complete set with box 62.00 155.00 440.00

542- Top-Line Comics (In Open Box), 1935, Whitman, 164 pgs., 3 1/2" x 3 1/2", 3 books in set; all soft-c:
Dinglehoofer Und His Dog Adolph by Knerr 18.00 45.00 125.00
Jungle Jim by Alex Raymond 22.00 52.50 155.00
Sappo by Segar 22.00 52.50 155.00
Complete set with box 79.00 198.00 550.00

543- Top-Line Comics (In Open Box), 1935, Whitman, 164 pgs., 3 1/2" x 3 1/2", 3 books in set; all soft-c:
Alexander Smart, ESQ by Winner 18.00 45.00 125.00
Bunky by Billy de Beck 18.00 45.00 125.00
Nicodemus O'Malley by Carter 18.00 45.00 125.00
Complete set with box 62.00 155.00 440.00

1158- Tracked by a G-Man, 1939, Saalfield, 400 pgs. 10.00 25.00 65.00

25- Trail of the Lonesome Pine, The, 1936, Lynn, movie scenes 16.00 40.00 115.00

nn- Trail of the Terrible 6 (See Tom Mix ...)

1185- Trail to Squaw Gulch, The, 1940, Saalfield, 400 pgs. 11.00 27.50 70.00

720- Treasure Island, 1933, Whitman, 362 pgs. 21.00 52.50 145.00

1141- Treasure Island, 1934, Whitman, 164 pgs., hard-c, 4 1/4" x 5 1/4", Jackie Cooper photo-c, movie scenes 16.00 40.00 115.00

1141- Treasure Island, 1934, Whitman, 164 pgs., soft-c, 4 1/4" x 5 1/4", Jackie Cooper photo-c, movie scenes 16.00 40.00 115.00

1018- Trick and Puzzle Book, 1939, Whitman, 100 pgs., soft-c 4.00 10.00 22.00

1100B- Tricks Easy to Do (Slight of hand & magic), 1938, Whitman, 36 pgs., 2 1/2" x 3 1/2", Penny Book 4.00 10.00 22.00

1100B- Tricks You Can Do, 1938, Whitman, 36 pgs., 2 1/2" x 3 1/2", Penny Book 4.00 10.00 22.00

5777- Tweety and Sylvester, The Magic Voice, 1976, Whitman, 260 pgs., soft-c, flip-it feature; 5 printings 2.00 5.00 11.00

1104- Two-Gun Montana, 1936, Whitman, 432 pgs., Henry E. Vallely-a 11.00 27.50 70.00

nn- Two-Gun Montana Shoots it Out, 1939, Whitman, 36 pgs., 2 1/2" x 3 1/2", Penny Book 11.00 27.50 70.00

1058- Ugly Duckling, The (Disney), 1939, Whitman, 68 pgs., 5" x 5 1/2", hard-c 14.00 35.00 95.00

GD FN VF/NM

nn- Ugly Duckling, The, nd (1930s), np (Whitman), 36 pgs., 3" x 2 1/2", Penny Book 4.00 10.00 22.00

Unc' Billy Gets Even (See Wee Little Books)

1114- Uncle Don's Strange Adventures, 1935, Whitman, 300 pgs., radio star-Uncle Don Carney 12.00 30.00 75.00

722- Uncle Ray's Story of the United States, 1934, Whitman, 300 pgs. 12.00 30.00 75.00

1461- Uncle Sam's Sky Defenders, 1941, Whitman, 432 pgs., flip pictures 11.00 27.50 70.00

1405- Uncle Wiggily's Adventures, 1946, Whitman, All Pictures Comics 16.00 40.00 115.00

1411- Union Pacific, 1939, Whitman, 240 pgs., photo-c, movie scenes 12.00 30.00 85.00
With Union Pacific letter 50.00 150.00 350.00

1189- Up Dead Horse Canyon, 1940, Saalfield, 400 pgs. 10.00 25.00 65.00

1455- Vic Sands of the U.S. Flying Fortress Bomber Squadron, 1944, Whitman, 352 pgs. 12.00 30.00 85.00

1645- Walt Disney's Andy Burnett on the Trail (TV Series), 1958, Whitman, 280 pgs. 4.00 10.00 27.00

803- Walt Disney's Bongo, 1948, Whitman, hard-c, Story Hour Series 12.00 30.00 85.00

711-10-Walt Disney's Cinderella and the Magic Wand, 1950, Whitman, 2 1/2" x 5", based on Disney movie 12.00 30.00 75.00

845- Walt Disney's Donald Duck and his Cat Troubles (Disney), 1948, Whitman, 100 pgs., 5" x 5 1/2", hard-c 12.00 30.00 85.00

845- Walt Disney's Donald Duck and the Boys, 1948, Whitman, 100 pgs., 5" x 5 1/2", hard-c, Barks-a 28.00 70.00 195.00

2952- Walt Disney's Donald Duck in the Great Kite Maker, 1949, Whitman, 24 pgs., 3 1/4" x 4", Tiny Tales, full color (5 cents) 11.00 27.50 70.00

804- Walt Disney's Mickey and the Beanstalk, 1948, Whitman, hard-c, Story Hour Series 12.00 30.00 85.00

845- Walt Disney's Mickey Mouse and the Boy Thursday, 194 pgs., Whitman, 5" x 5 1/2", 100 pgs. 12.00 30.00 85.00

845- Walt Disney's Mickey Mouse the Miracle Maker, 1948, Whitman, 5" x 5 1/2", 100 pgs. 12.00 30.00 85.00

2952- Walt Disney's Mickey Mouse and the Night Prowlers, Whitman, 1949, 24 pgs., 3 1/4" x 4", Tiny Tales, full color (5 ¢) 11.00 27.50 70.00

5770- Walt Disney's Mickey Mouse - Mystery at Disneyland, Whitman, 1975, 260 pgs., four printings 2.00 5.00 13.00

5781-2- Walt Disney's Mickey Mouse - Mystery at Dead Man's Cove, Whitman, 1980, 260 pgs., two printings 2.00 5.00 11.00

845- Walt Disney's Minnie Mouse and the Antique Chair, 1948, Whitman, 5" x 5 1/2", 100 pgs. 12.00 30.00 85.00

1435- Walt Disney's Pinocchio and Jiminy Cricket, 1940, Whitman, 432 pgs. 21.00 52.50 145.00

845- Walt Disney's Poor Pluto, 1948, Whitman, 5" x 5 1/2", 100 pgs., hard-c 12.00 30.00 85.00

1467- Walt Disney's Pluto the Pup (Disney), 1938, Whitman, 432 pgs., Gottfredson-a 18.00 45.00 125.00

1066- Walt Disney's Story of Clarabelle Cow (Disney), 1938, Whitman, 100 pgs. 12.00 30.00 85.00

66- Walt Disney's Story of Dippy the Goof (Disney), 1938, Whitman, 100 pgs. 12.00 30.00 85.00

1066- Walt Disney's Story of Donald Duck (Disney), 1938, Whitman, 100 pgs., hard-c, Taliaferro-a 12.00 30.00 85.00

1066- Walt Disney's Story of Mickey Mouse (Disney), 1938, Whitman, 100 pgs., hard-c, Gottfredson-a, Donald Duck app. 12.00 30.00 85.00

1066- Walt Disney's Story of Minnie Mouse (Disney), 1938, Whitman, 100 pgs., hard-c 12.00 30.00 85.00

1066- Walt Disney's Story of Pluto the Pup, (Disney), 1938, Whitman, 100 pgs., hard-c 12.00 30.00 85.00

2952- Walter Lantz Presents Andy Panda's Rescue, 1949, Whitman, Tiny Tales, full color (5 cents) (1030-5 on back-c) 11.00 27.50 70.00

751- Wash Tubbs in Pandemonia, 1934, Whitman, 320 pgs., Roy Crane-a 12.00 30.00 85.00

nn- Wash Tubbs in Pandemonia, 1934, Whitman, 52 pgs., 4" x 5 1/2", premium-no ads, soft-c, Roy Crane-a 20.00 50.00 140.00

518 - Wee Little Books © WHIT

1458 - Wimpy the Hamburger Eater © KING

5 - Zane Grey's King of the Royal Mounted in the Far North © WHIT

	GD	FN	VF/NM
1455- Wash Tubbs and Captain Easy Hunting For Whales, 1938, Whitman, 432 pgs., Roy Crane-a	12.00	30.00	85.00
6- Wash Tubbs in Foreign Travel, 1934, Whitman, soft-c, 3 1/2" x 3 1/2", Tarzan Ice Cream cup premium	34.00	85.00	240.00
513- Wee Little Books (In Open Box), 1934, Whitman, 44 pgs., small size, 6 books in set			
Child's Garden of Verses	5.00	12.50	30.00
The Happy Prince (The Story of)	5.00	12.50	30.00
Joan of Arc (The Story of)	5.00	12.50	30.00
Peter Pan (The Story of)	5.00	12.50	30.00
Pied Piper Of Hamlin	5.00	12.50	30.00
Robin Hood (A Story of...)	5.00	12.50	30.00
Complete set with box	31.00	78.00	220.00
514- Wee Little Books (In Open Box), 1934, Whitman, 44 pgs., small size, 6 books in set			
Jack And Jill	5.00	12.50	30.00
Little Bo-Peep	5.00	12.50	30.00
Little Tommy Tucker	5.00	12.50	30.00
Mother Goose	5.00	12.50	30.00
Old King Cole	5.00	12.50	30.00
Simple Simon	5.00	12.50	30.00
Complete set with box	33.00	83.00	230.00
518- Wee Little Books (In Open Box), 1933, Whitman, 44 pgs., small size, 6 books in set, written by Thornton Burgess			
Betty Bear's Lesson-1930	5.00	12.50	30.00
Jimmy Skunk's Justice-1933	5.00	12.50	30.00
Little Joe Otter's Slide-1929	5.00	12.50	30.00
Peter Rabbit's Carrots-1933	5.00	12.50	30.00
Unc' Billy Gets Even-1930	5.00	12.50	30.00
Whitefoot's Secret-1933	5.00	12.50	30.00
Complete set with box	33.00	83.00	230.00
519- Wee Little Books (In Open Box) (Bible Stories), 1934, Whitman, 44 pgs., small size, 6 books in set, Helen Janes-a			
The Story of David	5.00	12.50	30.00
The Story of Gideon	5.00	12.50	30.00
The Story of Daniel	5.00	12.50	30.00
The Story of Joseph	5.00	12.50	30.00
The Story of Ruth and Naomi	5.00	12.50	30.00
The Story of Moses	5.00	12.50	30.00
Complete set with box	33.00	83.00	230.00
1471- Wells Fargo, 1938, Whitman, 240 pgs., photo-c, movie scenes	14.00	35.00	95.00
L18- Western Frontier, 1935, Lynn, 192 pgs., starring Ken Maynard, movie scenes	21.00	52.50	145.00
1121- West Pointers on the Gridiron, 1936, Saalfield, 148 pgs., hard-c, sports book	10.00	25.00	65.00
1601- West Pointers on the Gridiron, 1936, Saalfield, 148 pgs., soft-c, sports book	10.00	25.00	65.00
1124- West Point Five, The, 1937, Saalfield, 4 3/4" x 5 1/4", sports book, hard-c	10.00	25.00	65.00
1604- West Point Five, The, 1937, Saalfield, 4 1/4" x 5 1/4", sports book, soft-c	10.00	25.00	65.00
1164- West Point of the Air, 1935, Whitman, 160 pgs., photo-c, movie scenes	12.00	30.00	85.00
18- Westward Ho!, 1935, EVW, 160 pgs., movie scenes, starring John Wayne (Scarce)	71.00	213.00	500.00
1109- We Three, 1935, Saalfield, 160 pgs., photo-c, movie scenes, by John Barrymore, hard-c	11.00	27.50	70.00
1589- We Three, 1935, Saalfield, 160 pgs., photo-c, movie scenes, by John Barrymore, soft-c	11.00	27.50	70.00
5- Wheels of Destiny, 1934, EVW, 160 pgs., movie scenes, starring Ken Maynard	21.00	52.50	145.00
Whitefoot's Secret (See Wee Little Books)			
nn- Who's Afraid of the Big Bad Wolf, "Three Little Pigs" (Disney), 1933, McKay, 36 pgs., 6" x 8 1/2", stiff-c, Disney studio-a	39.00	98.00	275.00
nn- Wild West Adventures of Buffalo Bill, 1935, Whitman, 260 pgs., Cocomalt premium, soft-c, Hal Arbo-a	15.00	37.50	105.00
1096- Will Rogers, The Story of, 1935, Saalfield, photo-hard-c	12.00	30.00	75.00
1576- Will Rogers, The Story of, 1935, Saalfield, photo-soft-c	12.00	30.00	75.00
1458- Wimpy the Hamburger Eater, 1938, Whitman, 432 pgs., E.C. Segar-a	24.00	60.00	165.00
1433- Windy Wayne and His Flying Wing, 1942, Whitman, 432 pgs., flip pictures	11.00	27.50	70.00
1131- Winged Four, The, 1937, Saalfield, sports book, hard-c	11.00	27.50	70.00
1407- Wings of the U.S.A., 1940, Whitman, 432 pgs., Thomas Hickey-a	11.00	27.50	70.00
nn- Winning of the Old Northwest, The, 1934, World Syndicate, High Lights of History Series, full color-c	11.00	27.50	70.00
nn- Winning of the Old Northwest, The, 1934, World Syndicate, High Lights of History Series; red & silver-c	11.00	27.50	70.00
1122- Winning Point, The, 1936, Saalfield, (Football), hard-c	9.00	22.50	58.00
1602- Winning Point, The, 1936, Saalfield, soft-c	9.00	22.50	58.00
nn- Wizard of Oz Waddle Book, 1934, BRP, 20 pgs., 7 1/2" x 10", forerunner of the Blue Ribbon Pop-Up books; with 6 removable articulated cardboard characters. Book only	54.00	135.00	375.00
Dust jacket only	61.00	153.00	490.00
Near Mint Complete - $12,500			
710-10-Woody Woodpecker Big Game Hunter, 1950, Whitman, by Walter Lantz	10.00	25.00	65.00
2010-(#10)-Woody Woodpecker-The Meteor Menace, 1967, Whitman, 260 pgs., 39¢-c, hard-c, color illos.	4.00	10.00	27.00
5753- Woody Woodpecker-The Meteor Menace, 1973, Whitman, 260 pgs., no price, soft-c, color illos.	1.00	2.50	6.00
2028- Woody Woodpecker-The Sinister Signal, 1969, Whitman	4.00	10.00	22.00
5763- Woody Woodpecker-The Sinister Signal, 1974, Whitman, 1st printing-no price; 2nd printing-39¢-c	1.00	2.50	6.00
23- World of Monsters, The, 1935, EVW, Five Star Library, movie scenes	16.00	40.00	115.00
779- World War in Photographs, The, 1934, Whitman, photo-c, photo illus.	11.00	27.50	70.00
Wyatt Earp (See Hugh O'Brian ...)			
nn- Xena - Warrior Princess, 1998, Chronicle Books, 310 pgs., based on TV series, 1-color (purple) illos	1.00	2.50	9.00
nn- Yogi Bear Goes Country & Western, 1977, Modern Promotions, 244 pgs., 49 cents, soft-c, flip pictures	2.00	5.00	13.00
nn- Yogi Bear Saves Jellystone Park, 1977, Modern Promotions, 244 pgs., 49 cents, soft-c, flip pictures	2.00	5.00	13.00
nn- Zane Grey's Cowboys of the West, 1935, Whitman, 148 pgs., 3 3/4" x 4", Tarzan Ice Cream Cup premium, soft-c, Arbo-a	39.00	98.00	275.00
Zane Grey's King of the Royal Mounted (See Men of the Mounted)			
1010- Zane Grey's King of the Royal Mounted in Arctic Law, 1937, Whitman, 7 1/4" x 5 1/2", 64 pgs., Nickel Book	15.00	37.50	105.00
1103- Zane Grey's King of the Royal Mounted, 1936, Whitman, 432 pgs.	14.00	35.00	95.00
nn- Zane Grey's King of the Royal Mounted, 1935, Whitman, 260 pgs., Cocomalt premium, soft-c	18.00	45.00	125.00
1179- Zane Grey's King of the Royal Mounted and the Northern Treasure, 1937, Whitman, 432 pgs.	14.00	35.00	95.00
1405- Zane Grey's King of the Royal Mounted the Long Arm of the Law, 1942, Whitman, All Pictures Comics	14.00	35.00	95.00
1452- Zane Grey's King of the Royal Mounted Gets His Man, 1938, Whitman, 432 pgs.	14.00	35.00	95.00
1486- Zane Grey's King of the Royal Mounted and the Great Jewel Mystery, 1939, Whitman, 432 pgs.	14.00	35.00	95.00
5- Zane Grey's King of the Royal Mounted in the Far North, 1938, Whitman, 132 pgs., Buddy Book, soft-c (Rare)	50.00	150.00	350.00
nn- Zane Grey's King of the Royal Mounted in Law of the North, 1939, Whitman, 36 pgs., 2 1/2" x 3 1/2", Penny Book	9.00	22.50	58.00
nn- Zane Grey's King of the Royal Mounted Policing the Frozen North, 1938, Dell, 196 pgs., Fast-Action Story, soft-c	26.00	65.00	180.00
1440- Zane Grey's Tex Thorne Comes Out of the West, 1937, Whitman, 432 pgs.	11.00	27.50	70.00
1465- Zip Saunders King of the Speedway, 1939, 432 pgs., Weisman-a	11.00	27.50	70.00

PROMOTIONAL COMICS

THE MARKETING OF A MEDIUM

by Dr. Arnold T. Blumberg, DCD

with new material and additional research by Sol M. Davidson, PhD, and Robert L. Beerbohm

Everyone wants something for free. It's in our nature to look for the quick fix, the good deal, the complimentary gift. We long to hit the lottery and quit our job, to win the trip around the world, or find that pot of gold at the end of the proverbial rainbow. Collectors in particular are certainly built to appreciate the notion of the "free gift," since it not only means a new item to collect and enjoy, but no risk or obligation in order to acquire it.

Ah, but there's the rub. Because things are not always what they seem, and "free gifts" usually come with a price. As the saying goes, "there's no such thing as a free lunch," so if it seems too good to be true, it probably is. This is the case even in the world of comics, where premiums and giveaways have a familiar agenda hidden behind the bright colors and fanciful stories. But where did it all begin?

Some of the earliest characters that were used as successful tools in promotional comics were Palmer Cox's creation "The Brownies." The illustration shown here showcases them drinking and endorsing Seal Brand Coffee.

EXTRA EXTRA

As we learn more about the early history of the comic book industry through continual investigation and the publishing of articles like those regularly featured in this book, we gain a much greater understanding of the financial and creative forces at work in shaping the medium, but perhaps one of the most intriguing and least recognized factors that influenced the dawn of comics is the concept of the premium or giveaway. (Note: Some of the historical information referenced in this article is derived from material also presented in Robert L. Beerbohm's introductory articles to the Platinum Age and Modern Age sections.)

The birth of the comic book as we know it today is intimately connected with the development of the comic strip in American newspapers and their use as an advertising and marketing tool for staple products such as bread, milk, and cereal. From the very beginning, comic characters have played several roles in pop culture, entertaining the youth of the country while also (sometimes none too subtly) acting as hucksters for whatever corporation foots the bill. From important staples to frivolous material produced simply to make a buck, these products have utilized the comics medium to sell, sell, sell. And what better way to hook a prospective customer than to give them "something for nothing?"

Starting in the 1850s, comics were being used in free almanacs such as **Elton's**, **Hostetter's** and **Wright's** to lure readers for the little booklets to sell patent medicine, farm products, tobacco, shoe polish, etc. Most of these are exceedingly rare today, hence it is difficult to compile an accurate history. More mention of these early precursors can be found in the Victorian Comics Era essay following this one. But although comic characters themselves were already being aggressively merchandised all around the world by the mid-1890s--as with, for example, Palmer Cox's **The Brownies**--the real starting point for the success of comics as a giveaway marketing mechanism can be traced to the introduction of **The Yellow Kid**, Richard Outcault's now legendary newspaper strip.

Newspaper publishers had already recognized that comic strips could boost circulation as well as please sponsors and advertisers by drawing more eyes to the page, so Sunday "supplements" were introduced to entice fans. Outcault's creation cemented the theory with proof of comic characters' marketing and merchandising power.

This unused cover was designed as the second cover for "Motion Picture Funnies Weekly." While the concept for this promotional comic title never caught on, the inaugural issue did feature the origin and first printed appearance of the Sub-Mariner.

Soon after, Outcault (who had most likely been inspired by Cox's merchandising success with **The Brownies** in the first place) caught lightning in a bottle once more with **Buster Brown**, who has the distinction of being America's first nationally licensed comic strip character. Soon, comic strips proliferated throughout the nation's newspapers as tycoons like Hearst and Pulitzer recognized the drawing power of the new medium and fought circulation wars to capture the pennies of the nouveau readership. They paid exorbitant salaries to comic strip artists such as Rudolph Dirks (**Katzenjammer Kids**), and used the funnies as newspaper supplements and as premiums to attract readers. Corporations soon had the chance to license recognizable personas as their own personal pitchmen (or women or animals...). Comic character merchandise wasn't far behind, resulting in a boom of future collectibles now catalogued in volumes like **Hake's Price Guide to Character Toys**.

TWO BIRTHS FOR THE PRICE OF ONE

Comic books themselves were at the heart of this movement, and giveaway and premium collections of comic strips not only appealed to children and adults alike, but provided the impetus for the birth of the modern comic book format itself. It could be said that without the concept of the giveaway comic or the marketing push behind it, there would be no comic book industry as we have it today. Well-known now is the story of how in spring 1933 Harry Wildenberg of Eastern Color Printing Company convinced Proctor & Gamble to sponsor the first modern comic book, **Funnies on Parade**, as a premium. Its success led to the first continuing comic book, **Famous Funnies**, and the rest, as they say, is history.

In 1935, while working on the printing presses of Eastern Color developing how modern comic books get printed, Juliun J. Proskauer came up with an idea for printing "Comic-Books-For-Industry." In July 1936 he made his first sale through his newly formed William C. Popper & Co. to David M. Davies, then advertising manager for Seagram's Distillers Corp. for three million copies of **Seagram's Merrymakers** in time for the 1936-37 Christmas season. "Thus was a new industry born," wrote **Printing News** in August 1945.

Even a casual perusal of the listings in this section of the Guide will dazzle the reader with the endless variety of purposes that this medium has served. Yes, promos have been used to hawk products from athletic equipment to zithers and zip codes, but comics are too versatile an art form to be confined to a few uses. They've swayed elections in cities (**The O'Dwyer Story**, 1949), in states (**Giant for a Day**: Jacob Javits, 1946) and nationwide (**The Story of Harry Truman**, 1948); solicited for charities (**Donald Duck and the Red Feather**, 1948); addressed health issues (**Blondie**, 1949, mental hygiene); discouraged kids from smoking (**Captain America Meets the Asthma Monster**, 1987); coached youngsters in sports skills (**Circling the Bases**, 1947, A.G. Spaulding); explained scientific complexities (**Adventures in Science**, 1946-61, GE); pleaded for social justice (**Consumer Comics**, 1975); espoused religious causes (**Oral Roberts' True Stories**, 1950s); protected the environment (**Our Spaceship Earth**, 1947); encouraged tourism (**Wyoming, The Cowboy State**, 1954); conveyed a sense of history (**Louisiana Purchase**, 1953); taught about computers (**Superman Radio Shack Giveaway**, 1980); trained employees (**Dial Finance Dialogues**, 1961-70) and executives (**Beneficial Finance System, Managing New Employees**, 1950s); cautioned safety (**Willy Wing Flap**, 1944(?)); announced corporate annual results (**Motorola Annual Report**, 1952); defended free enterprise (**Steve Merritt**, 1949); hammered communism (**How Stalin Hopes to Destroy America**, 1951); fought discrimination (**Mammy Yokum & the Great Dogpatch Mystery**, 1956, B'nai Brith); aided young workers in job-hunting (**The Job Scene**, 1969); battled the scourge of sickle cell anemia (**Where's Herbie**, 1972, U.S. H.E.W.); inspired the overcoming of adversity (**Al Capp by Li'l Abner**, 1946); fostered reading (**Linus Gets a Library Card**, 1960); recruited for the armed forces (**Li'l Abner Joins the Navy**, 1950); beguiled readers into

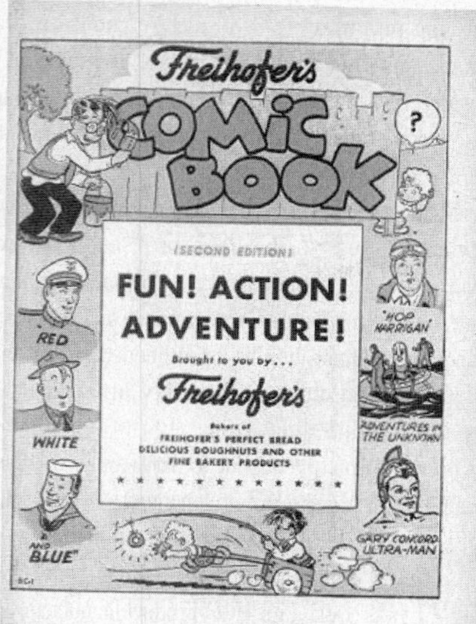

Every market and product has been on the promotional comic book bandwagon. Freihofer's Baking Company distributed a comic in the 1940s that featured reprinted pages from "All-American Comics."

learning languages (**Blondie**, 1949, Philadelphia public schools); and even instructed in such delicate matters as birth control (**Escape from Fear**, 1950 (revised 1959, etc.), for Planned Parenthood).

READ ALL ABOUT IT

The impact of this new approach to advertising was not lost on the business world. Contrary to modern belief, comic books were hardly discounted by the adults of the time...at least not those who had the marketing savvy to recognize an opportunity - or a threat - when they saw one. In the April 1933 issue of **Fortune** magazine, an article titled "The Funny Papers" trumpeted the arrival of comics as a force to be reckoned with in the world of advertising and business, and what's more, a force to fear as well. At first providing a brief survey of the newspaper comic strip business (which for many of the magazine's readers must have seemed a foreign topic for serious discussion), the article goes on to examine the incredible financial draw of comics and their characters:

"Between 70 and 75 per cent {sic} of the readers of any newspaper follow its comic sections regularly...Even the advertiser has succumbed to the comic, and in 1932 spent well over $1,000,000 for comic-paper space."

"**Comic Weekly** is the comic section of seventeen Hearst Sunday papers...Advertisers who market their wares through balloon-speaking manikins {sic} may enjoy the proximity of Jiggs, Maggie, Barney Google, and other funny Hearst headliners."

Although the article continues to cast the notion of relying on comic strip material to sell product in a negative light, actually suggesting that advertisers who utilize comics are violating unspoken rules of "advertising decorum" and bringing themselves "down to the level" of comics (and since when have advertisers been stalwart preservers of good taste and high moral standards), there is no doubt that they are viewing comics in a new light. The comic characters have arrived by 1933...and they're ready to help sell your merchandise too.

Fortune wasn't the only one to take notice as World War II came and went. In 1948, Louis P. Birk, the head of Brevity, Inc., an important promotional comics publisher said, "Comics are serious business." In an article in **Printers' Ink** magazine, he estimated that more than 80 different "comic booklets" had been produced and more than 45,000,000 million copies distributed in the five years before 1948. But of course, comics were serious business long before businessman/historian Birk noted the fact for posterity.

THE MARCH OF WAR AND BEYOND

Through the relentless currents of time, comic strips, books, and the characters that starred in them became more and more an intrinsic part of American culture. During the turmoil of the Great Depression and World War II, comic characters in print and celluloid form entertained while informing and selling at the same time, and premium and giveaway comics came well and truly into their own, pushing everything from loaves of bread to war bonds.

In the 1950s and '60s, there was a shift in focus as the power of giveaway and premium comics was applied to more altruistic endeavors than simply selling something. Comic book format pamphlets, fully illustrated and often inventively written, taught children about banking, money, the dangers of poison and other household products, and even chronicled moments in

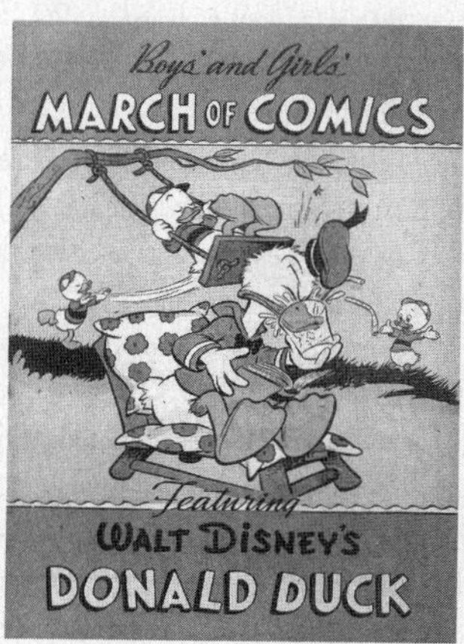

The promotional title "March of Comics" was a prolific comic that ran for 36 years and 488 issues featuring a variety of subjects and characters. (#20 shown)

American history. The comic book as giveaway was now not only a marketing gimmick--it was a tool for educating as well.

The 1970s and '80s saw another boom in premium and giveaway comics. Every product imaginable seemed to have a licensing deal with a comic book character, usually one of the prominent flag bearers of the Big Two, Marvel or DC. Spider-Man fought bravely against the Beetle for the benefit of All Detergent; Captain America allied himself with the Campbell Kids; and Superman helped a class of computer students beat a disaster-conjuring foe at his own game with the help of Radio Shack Tandy computers.

Newspapers rediscovered the power of comics, not just with enlarged strip supplements but with actual comic books. Spider-Man, the Hulk, and others turned up as giveaway comic extras in various American newspapers (including Chicago and Dallas publications), while a whole series of public information comics like those produced decades earlier used superheroes to caution children about the dangers of smoking, drugs, and child abuse.

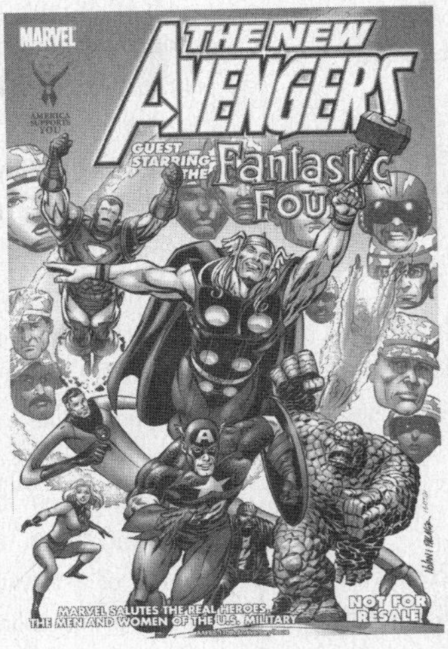

Comics also turned up in a plethora of other toy products as the 1980s introduced kids to the joy of electronic games and action figures. Supplementary comics provided "free" with action figure and video game packages told the backstory about the product, adding depth to the play experience while providing an extra incentive to buy. Comics became an intrinsic part of the Atari line of video cartridges, for example, eventually spawning its own full-blown newsstand series as well.

As the twentieth century gave way to the twenty-first, giveaway comics were still being produced for inclusion in action figure and video game packages, as well as in conjunction with countless consumer items and corporations. It seems that the medium still has a lot to offer for all those companies desperate to make the most of their market share.

Today, promotional comics continue to be used as a marketing tool to reach both children and adults alike. This 2005 comic was produced by Marvel Comics as a salute to the men and women of the armed forces.

A COMIC BY ANY OTHER NAME

One of the earliest names for promotional comics was "special purpose comics." In their pursuit of superheroes, collectors have allowed promotional comics to lie fallow - underappreciated and uncollected. Without a legitimate name, these products were given sundry other appellations - industrial comics, promos, giveaways, premiums, promics - each accurate but only for a small segment of the unorganized but lusty and lively medium. Perhaps no one name can cover all the variations and purposes of this branch of comic art, but for practical reasons if we accept the general premise that these comics were created to promote an idea, a product or a person, then "Promotional Comics" is probably as convenient a catch-all title as we can come up with.

We used the phrase "for practical reasons" because the word "practical" goes to the heart of promotional comics more than it does for any other comics product. What greater testimony is there to the medium's impact on American culture than to note their use by hard-headed, profit-minded business people and corporations? They invest their money and they expect results.

Today, premium comics continue to thrive and are still utilized as a valuable marketing and promotional tool. "Free" comics are still packaged with action figures and video games, and offered as mail-away premiums from a variety of product manufacturers. The comic industry itself has expanded its use of giveaway comics to self-promote as well, with "ashcan" and other giveaway editions turning up at conventions and comic shops to advertise upcoming series and special events. Many of these function as old-fashioned premiums, with a coupon or other response required from the reader to receive the comic.

As for the supplements and giveaways printed all those years ago, they have spawned a collectible fervor all their own, thanks to their atypical distribution and frequent rarity. For that and the desire to delve deeper into comics history, we hope that by focusing more directly on this genre, we can enhance our understanding of this vital component in the development and history of the modern comic book.

Whether you're a collector or not, we're all motivated by that desire to get something for nothing. For as long as consumers are enticed by the notion of the "free gift," promotional comics will remain a vital marketing component in many business models, but they will also continue to fight the stigma that has long been associated with the industry as a whole. "Respectable" sources like **Fortune** may have taken notice of the power of comic-related advertising 71 years ago, but after all this time comics still fight an uphill battle to establish some measure of dignity for the medium. Perhaps the higher visibility of promotional comics will eventually prove to be a deciding factor in that intellectual war.

See ya in the funny papers.

Adventures of Big Boy #1
© Shoney's

Alice in Blunderland
© Industrial Servces

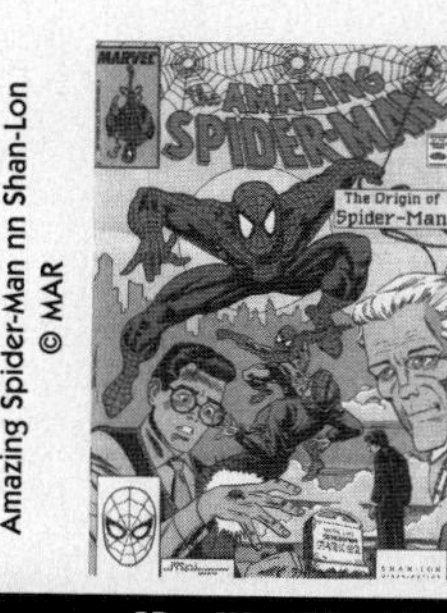

Amazing Spider-Man nn Shan-Lon
© MAR

GD 2.0 | VG 4.0 | FN 6.0 | VF 8.0 | VF/NM 9.0 | NM- 9.2

ACTION COMICS
DC Comics: 1947 - 1998 (Giveaway)
1 (1976) paper cover w/10¢ price, 16 pgs. in color; reprints complete Superman story from #1 ('38) 3 6 9 20 30 40
1 (1976) Safeguard Giveaway; paper cover w/"free", 16 pgs. in color; reprints complete Superman story from #1 ('38) 3 6 9 20 30 40
1 (1983) paper cover w/10¢ price, 16 pgs. in color; reprints complete Superman story from #1 ('38) 3 6 9 14 20 25
1 (1987 Nestle Quik; 1988, 50¢) 1 2 3 5 7 9
1 (1993)-Came w/Reign of Superman packs 4.00
1 (1998 U.S. Postal Service, $7.95) Reprints entire issue; extra outer half-cover contains First Day Issuance of 32¢ Superman stamp with Sept. 10, 1998 Cleveland, OH postmark 1 2 3 5 6 8
Theater (1947, 32 pgs., 5" x 7", nn)-Vigilante story based on Columbia Vigilante serial; no Superman-c or story 63 126 189 400 688 975

ACTION ZONE
CBS Television: 1994 (Promotes CBS Saturday morning cartoons)
1-WildC.A.T.s, T.M.N.Turtles, Skeleton Warriors stories; Jim Lee-c 4.00

ADVENTURE COMICS
IGA: No date (early 1940s) (Paper-c, 32 pgs.)
Two diff. issues; Super-Mystery-r from 1941 21 42 63 123 204 285

ADVENTURE IN DISNEYLAND
Walt Disney Productions (Dist. by Richfield Oil): May, 1955 (Giveaway, soft-c., 16 pgs)
nn 10 20 30 56 76 95

ADVENTURES @ EBAY
eBay: 2000 (6 3/4" x 4 1/2", 16 pgs.)
1-Judd Winick-a/Rucka & Van Meter-s; intro to eBay comic buying 2.50

ADVENTURES OF BARRY WEEN, BOY GENIUS, THE
Oni Press: July, 2004 (Free Comic Book Day giveaway)
...: Secret Crisis Origin Files -Judd Winick-s/a 2.50

ADVENTURES OF BIG BOY (Also titled Adventures of the Big Boy)
Timely Comics/Webs Adv. Corp./Illus. Features: 1956 - Present (Giveaway) (East & West editions of early issues)
1-Everett-c/a 103 206 309 654 1127 1600
2-Everett-c/a 37 74 111 222 361 500
3-5: 4-Robot-c 19 38 57 110 175 240
6-10: 6-Sci/fic issue 10 20 30 73 129 185
11-20: 11,13-DeCarlo-a 7 14 21 45 73 100
21-30 4 8 12 26 41 55
31-50 3 6 9 17 25 32
51-100 2 4 6 9 13 16
101-150 2 4 6 8 10 12
151-240 1 2 3 5 7 9
241-265,267-269,271-300: 6.00
266-Superman x-over 3 6 9 18 27 35
270-TV's Buck Rogers-c/s 3 6 9 14 20 25
301-400 4.00
401-500 3.00
1-(2nd series - '76-'84,Paragon Prod.) (...Shoney's Big Boy) 1 3 4 6 8 10
2-20 5.00
21-50 3.00
Summer, 1959 issue, large size 7 14 21 50 83 115

ADVENTURES OF G. I. JOE
1969 (3-1/4x7") (20 & 16 pgs.)
First Series: 1-Danger of the Depths. 2-Perilous Rescue. 3-Secret Mission to Spy Island. 4-Mysterious Explosion. 5-Fantastic Free Fall. 6-Eight Ropes of Danger. 7-Mouth of Doom. 8-Hidden Missile Discovery. 9-Space Walk Mystery. 10-Fight for Survival. 11-The Shark's Surprise.
Second Series: 2-Flying Space Adventure. 4-White Tiger Hunt. 7-Capture of the Pygmy Gorilla. 12-Secret of the Mummy's Tomb.
Third Series: Reprinted surviving titles of First Series. **Fourth Series:** 13-Adventure Team Headquarters. 14-Search For the Stolen Idol.
each.... 3 6 9 18 27 35

ADVENTURES OF JELL-O MAN AND WOBBLY, THE
Welsh Publishing Group: 1991 ($1.25)
1 4.00

ADVENTURES OF KOOL-AID MAN
Marvel Comics: 1983 - No. 3, 1985 (Mail order giveaway)
Archie Comics: No. 4, 1987 - No. 8, 1989
1-8: 4-8-Dan DeCarlo-a/c 1 2 3 5 7 9

ADVENTURES OF MARGARET O'BRIEN, THE
Bambury Fashions (Clothes): 1947 (20 pgs. in color, slick-c, regular size) (Premium)
In "The Big City" movie adaptation (scarce) 19 38 57 112 181 250

ADVENTURES OF QUIK BUNNY
Nestle's Quik: 1984 (Giveaway, 32 pgs.)
nn-Spider-Man app. 2 4 6 9 113 16

ADVENTURES OF STUBBY, SANTA'S SMALLEST REINDEER, THE
W. T. Grant Co.: nd (early 1940s) (Giveaway, 12 pgs.)
nn 7 14 21 37 46 55

ADVENTURES OF VOTEMAN, THE
Foundation For Citizen Education Inc.: 1968
nn 4 8 12 28 44 60

ADVENTURES WITH SANTA CLAUS
Promotional Publ. Co. (Murphy's Store): No date (early 50's) (9-3/4x 6-3/4", 24 pgs., giveaway, paper-c)
nn-Contains 8 pgs. ads 6 12 18 29 36 42
16 pg. version 6 12 18 33 41 48

ADVENTURES WITH THE DC SUPER HEROES (Interior also inserted into some DC issues)
DC Comics/Geppi's Entertainment Museum: 2007 Free Comic Book Day giveaway
"The Batman and Cal Ripken, Jr. Hall of Fame Edition "A Rare Catch" " in indicia 2.25

AIR POWER (CBS TV & the U.S. Air Force Presents)
Prudential Insurance Co.: 1956 (5-1/4x7-1/4", 32 pgs., giveaway, soft-c)
nn-Toth-a? Based on 'You Are There' TV program by Walter Cronkite 10 20 30 56 76 95

ALASKA BUSH PILOT
Jan Enterprises: 1959 (Paper cover)
1-Promotes Bush Pilot Club (Value will be based on sale)
NOTE: *A CGC certified 9.9 Mint sold for $632.50 in 2005.*

ALICE IN BLUNDERLAND
Industrial Services: 1952 (Paper cover, 16 pgs. in color)
nn-Facts about government waste and inefficiency 14 28 42 76 108 140

ALICE IN WONDERLAND
Western Printing Company/Whitman Publ. Co.: 1965; 1969; 1982
Meets Santa Claus(1950s), nd, 16 pgs. 6 12 18 28 34 40
Rexall Giveaway(1965, 16 pgs., 5x7-1/4) Western Printing (TV, Hanna-Barbera) 3 6 9 16 23 30
Wonder Bakery Giveaway(1969, 16 pgs, color, nn, nd) (Continental Baking Company) 3 6 9 16 22 28

ALICE IN WONDERLAND MEETS SANTA
No publisher: nd (6-5/8x9-11/16", 16 pgs., giveaway, paper-c)
nn 9 18 27 50 65 80

ALL ABOARD, MR. LINCOLN
Assoc. of American Railroads: Jan, 1959 (16 pgs.)
nn-Abraham Lincoln and the Railroads 6 12 18 28 34 40

ALL NEW COMICS
Harvey Comics: Oct, 1993 (Giveaway, no cover price, 16 pgs.)(Hanna-Barbera)
1-Flintstones, Scooby Doo, Jetsons, Yogi Bear & Wacky Races previews for upcoming Harvey's new Hanna-Barbera line-up 1 2 3 4 5 7
NOTE: *Material previewed in Harvey giveaway was eventually published by Archie.*

ALL-STAR SUPERMAN
DC Comics: June, 2008 (Free Comic Book Day giveaway)
1-Grant Morrison-s/Frank Quitely-a/c 2.00

AMAZING SPIDER-MAN, THE
Marvel Comics Group
Acme & Dingo Children's Boots (1980)-Spider-Woman app. 2 4 6 11 16 20
Adventures in Reading Starring... (1990,1991) Bogdanove & Romita-c/a 5.00
Aim Toothpaste Giveaway (36 pgs., reg. size)-1 pg. origin recap; Green Goblin-c/story 2 4 6 9 13 16
Aim Toothpaste Giveaway (16 pgs., reg. size)-Dr. Octopus app. 2 4 6 9 13 16
All Detergent Giveaway (1979, 36 pgs.), nn-Origin-r 2 4 6 9 13 16
Amazing Fantasy #15 (8/02) reprint included in Spider-Man DVD Collector's Gift Set 5.00
Amazing Fantasy #15 (2006) News America Marketing newspaper giveaway 4.00
Amazing Spider-Man nn (1990, 6-1/8x9", 28 pgs.)-Shan-Lon giveaway; retells origin of Spider-Man; Bagley-a/Saviuk-c 2 4 6 8 10 12
Amazing Spider-Man nn (1990, 6-1/8x9", 28 pgs.)-Shan-Lon giveaway; reprints Amazing Spider-Man #303 w/McFarlane-c/a 2 4 6 8 10 12
Amazing Spider-Man #1 Reprint (1990, 4-1/4x6-1/4", 28 pgs.)-Packaged with the book "Start Collecting Comic Books" from Running Press 4.00

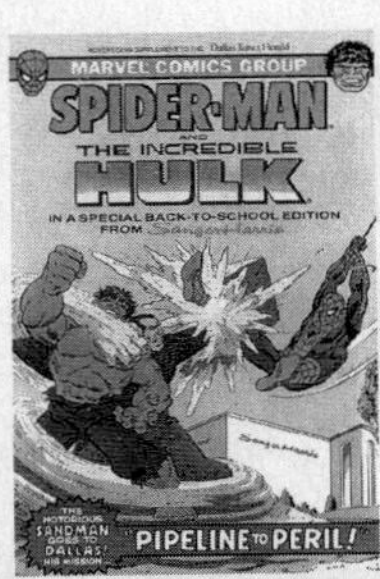

Amazing Spider-Man & The Incredible Hulk © MAR

Archie's Weird Mysteries © AP

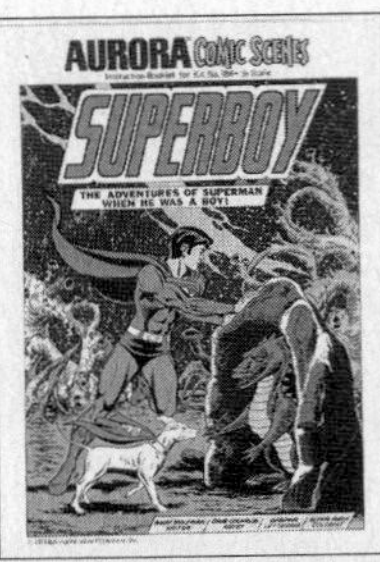

Aurora Comic Series 186-140 © DC

GD 2.0 | VG 4.0 | FN 6.0 | VF 8.0 | VF/NM 9.0 | NM- 9.2

Amazing Spider-Man #3 Reprint (2004)-Best Buy/Sony giveaway 2.50
Amazing Spider-Man #50 (Sony Pictures Edition) (8/04)-mini-comic included in Spider-Man 2 movie DVD Collector's Gift Set; r/#50 & various ASM covers with Dr. Octopus 2.50
Amazing Spider-Man #129 (Lion Gate Films) (6/04)-promotional comic given away at movie theaters on opening night for The Punisher 2.50
...& Power Pack (1984, nn)(Nat'l Committee for Prevention of Child Abuse) (two versions, mail offer & store giveaway)-Mooney-a; Byrne-c
Mail offer 2 4 6 9 11 14
Store giveaway 5.00
...& The Hulk (Special Edition)(6/8/80; 20 pgs.)-Supplement to Chicago Tribune
2 4 6 9 13 16
...& The Incredible Hulk (1981, 1982; 36 pgs.)-Sanger Harris or May D&F supplement to Dallas Times, Dallas Herald, Denver Post, Kansas City Star, Tulsa World; Foley's supplement to Houston Chronicle (1982, 16 pgs.)- "Great Rodeo Robbery"; The Jones Store-giveaway (1983, 16 pgs.) 2 4 6 13 18 22
...and the New Mutants Featuring Skids nn (National Committee for Prevention of Child Abuse/K-Mart giveaway)-Williams-c(i) 5.00
... Battles Ignorance (1992)(Sylvan Learning Systems) giveaway; Mad Thinker app. Kupperberg-a 1 2 3 5 7 9
...Captain America, The Incredible Hulk, & Spider-Woman (1981) (7-11 Stores giveaway; 36 pgs.) 2 4 6 10 14 18
...: Christmas in Dallas (1983) (Supplement to Dallas Times Herald) giveaway 2 4 6 10 14 18
...: Danger in Dallas (1983) (Supplement to Dallas Times Herald) giveaway 2 4 6 10 14 18
...: Danger in Denver (1983) (Supplement to Denver Post) giveaway for May D&F stores 2 4 6 10 14 18
..., Fire-Star, And Ice-Man at the Dallas Ballet Nutcracker (1983; supplement to Dallas Times Herald)-Mooney-p 2 4 6 10 14 18
Giveaway-Esquire Magazine (2/69)-Miniature-Still attached (scarce)
13 26 39 93 172 250
Giveaway-Eye Magazine (2/69)-Miniature-Still attached
9 18 27 65 113 160
...: Riot at Robotworld (1991; 16 pgs.)(National Action Council for Minorities in Engineering, Inc.) giveaway; Saviuk-c 1 2 3 5 6 8
..., Storm & Powerman (1982; 20 pgs.)(American Cancer Society) giveaway; also a 1991 2nd printing and a 1994 printing 1 2 3 5 6 8
...: Swing Shift (2007 FCBD Edition) Jimenez-c/a; Slott-s 2.25
...Vs. The Hulk (Special Edition; 1979, 20 pgs.)(Supplement to Columbus Dispatch)
2 4 6 13 18 22
...Vs. The Prodigy (Giveaway, 16 pgs. in color (1976, 5x6-1/2")-Sex education; (1 million printed; 35-50¢) 2 4 6 10 14 18
Spidey & The Mini-Marvels Halloween 2003 Ashcan (12/03, 8 1/2"x 5 1/2") Giarusso-s/a; Venom and Green Goblin app. 2.00

AMERICA MENACED!
Vital Publications: 1950 (Paper-c)
nn-Anti-communism 33 66 99 198 324 450

AMERICAN COMICS
Theatre Giveaways (Liberty Theatre, Grand Rapids, Mich. known): 1940's
Many possible combinations. "Golden Age" superhero comics with new cover added and given away at theaters. Following known: Superman #59, Capt. Marvel #20, Capt. Marvel Jr. #5, Action #33, Classics Comics #8, Whiz #39. Value would vary with book and should be 70-80 percent of the original.

ANDY HARDY COMICS
Western Printing Co.:
...& the New Automatic Gas Clothes Dryer (1952, 5x7-1/4", 16 pgs.) Bendix Giveaway (soft-c) 6 12 18 31 38 45

ANIMANIACS EMERGENCY WORLD
DC Comics: 1995
nn-American Red Cross 4.00

APACHE HUNTER
Creative Pictorials: 1954 (18 pgs. in color) (promo copy) (saddle stitched)
nn-Severin, Heath stories 15 30 45 85 130 175

AQUATEERS MEET THE SUPER FRIENDS
DC Comics: 1979
nn 2 4 6 10 14 18

ARCHIE AND HIS GANG (Zeta Beta Tau Presents...)
Archie Publications: Dec. 1950 (St. Louis National Convention giveaway)
nn-Contains new cover stapled over Archie Comics #47 (11-12/50) on inside; produced for Zeta Beta Tau 15 30 45 88 137 185

ARCHIE COMICS (Also see Sabrina)
Archie Publications
... And Friends and the Shield (10/02, 8 1/2"x 5 1/2") Diamond Comic Dist. 4.00
... And Friends - A Halloween Tale (10/98, 8 1/2"x 5 1/2") Diamond Comic Dist.; Sabrina and Sonic app.; Dan DeCarlo-a 4.00
... And Friends - A Timely Tale (10/01, 8 1/2"x 5 1/2") Diamond Comic Dist. 4.00
... And Friends Monster Bash 2003 (8 1/2"x 5 1/2") Diamond Comic Dist. Halloween 4.00
...And His Friends Help Raise Literacy Awareness In Mississippi nn (3/94)
1 2 3 5 6 8
...And His Friends Vs. The Household Toxic Wastes nn (1993, 16 pgs.) produced for the San Diego Regional Household Hazardous Materials Program
1 2 3 5 6 8
...And His Pals in the Peer Helping Program nn (2/91, 7"x4 1/2") produced by the FBI
1 2 3 5 6 8
...And the History of Electronics nn (5/90, 36 pgs.)-Radio Shack giveaway; Bender-c/a
1 2 3 5 6 8
Fairmont Potato Chips Giveaway-Mini comics 1970 (6 issues-nn's.,6 7/8" x 2 1/4", 8 pgs. each)
3 6 9 18 27 35
Fairmont Potato Chips Giveaway-Mini comics 1971 (4 issues-nn's.,6 7/8" x 5", 8 pgs. each)
3 6 9 18 27 35
... Free Comic Book Day Edition 1,2: 1-(7/03). 2-(9/04) 3.00
Little Archie, The House That Wouldn't Move ('07, 8-1/2" x 5-3/8" Halloween mini-comic) 2.00
Little Archie "The Legend of the Lost Lagoon" FCBD Edition (5/07) Bolling-s/a 3.00
Official Boy Scout Outfitter (1946, 9-1/2x6-1/2, 16 pgs.)-B. R. Baker Co.
(Scarce) 47 92 141 296 498 700
... Presents the Mighty Archie Art Players ('09) Free Comic Book Day giveaway 3.00
...'s Ham Radio Adventure (1997) Morse code instruction; Goldberg-a 6.00
...'s 65th Anniversary Bash ('06) Free Comic Book Day giveaway 3.00
...'s Summer Splash FCBD Edition (5/10) Parent-a; Cheryl Blossom app. 2.50
...'s Weird Mysteries (9/99, 8 1/2"x 5 1/2") Diamond Comic Dist. Halloween giveaway 3.00
Tales From Riverdale (2006, 8 1/2"x 5 1/2") Diamond Comic Dist. Halloween giveaway 3.00
...: The Mystery of the Museum Sleep-In ('08, 8-1/2" x 5-3/8" Halloween mini-comic) 2.50

ARCHIE SHOE-STORE GIVEAWAY
Archie Publications: 1944-50 (12-15 pgs. of games, puzzles, stories like Superman-Tim books, No nos. - came out monthly)

	GD 2.0	VG 4.0	FN 6.0	VF 8.0	VF/NM 9.0	NM- 9.2
(1944-47)-issues	15	30	45	94	147	200
2/48-Peggy Lee photo-c	15	30	45	94	147	200
3/48-Marylee Robb photo-c	15	30	45	85	130	175
4/48-Gloria De Haven photo-c	15	30	45	94	147	200
5/48,6/48,7/48	15	30	45	85	130	175
8/48-Story on Shirley Temple	17	34	51	98	154	210
10/48-Archie as Wolf on cover	15	30	45	88	137	185
5/49-Kathleen Hughes photo-c	14	28	42	82	121	160
7/49	14	28	42	80	115	150
8/49-Archie photo-c from radio show	19	38	57	112	181	250
10/49-Gloria Mann photo-c from radio show	15	30	45	88	137	185
11/49,12/49, 2/50, 3/50	14	28	42	80	115	150

ARCHIE'S JOKE BOOK MAGAZINE (See Joke Book ...)
Archie Publications
Drug Store Giveaway (No. 39 w/new-c) 7 14 21 35 43 50

ARCHIE'S TEN ISSUE COLLECTOR'S SET (Title inside of cover only)
Archie Publications: June, 1997 - No. 10, June, 1997 ($1.50, 20 pgs.)
1-10: 1,7-Archie. 2,8-Betty & Veronica. 3,9-Veronica. 4-Betty. 5-World of Archie. 6-Jughead. 10-Archie and Friends each... 5.00

ASTRO COMICS
American Airlines (Harvey): 1968 - 1979 (Giveaway)(Reprints of Harvey comics)
1968-Richie Rich, Hot Stuff, Casper, Wendy on-c only; Spooky and Nightmare app. inside
4 8 12 24 37 50
1970-Casper, Spooky, Hot Stuff, Stumbo the Giant, Little Audrey, Little Lotta, & Richie Rich reprints. Five different versions 3 6 9 20 30 40
1973,1975,1976: 1973-Three different versions 3 6 9 17 25 32
1977-r/Richie Rich & Casper #20. 1978-r/Richie Rich & Casper #25. 1979-r/Richie Rich & Casper #30 (scarce) 3 6 9 16 23 30

ATARI FORCE
DC Comics: 1982 - No. 5, 1983
1-3 (1982, 5X7", 52 pgs.)-Given away with Atari games
1 2 3 5 6 8
4,5 (1982-1983, 52 pgs.)-Given away with Atari games (scarcer)
2 4 6 9 12 15

AURORA COMIC SCENES INSTRUCTION BOOKLET (Included with superhero model kits)
Aurora Plastics Co.: 1974 (6-1/4x9-3/4," 8 pgs., slick paper)
181-140-Tarzan; Neal Adams-a 3 6 9 18 27 36
182-140-Spider-Man. 4 8 12 24 37 50
183-140-Tonto(Gil Kane art). 184-140-Hulk. 185-140-Superman. 186-140-Superboy. 187-140-Batman. 188-140-The Lone Ranger(1974-by Gil Kane). 192-140-Captain America(1975). 193-140-Robin 3 6 9 16 23 30

AVENGERS (Free Comic Book Day giveaway)
Marvel Comics: May, 2009

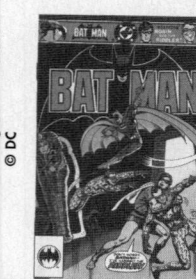

Batman #279 Monogram mini-comic © DC

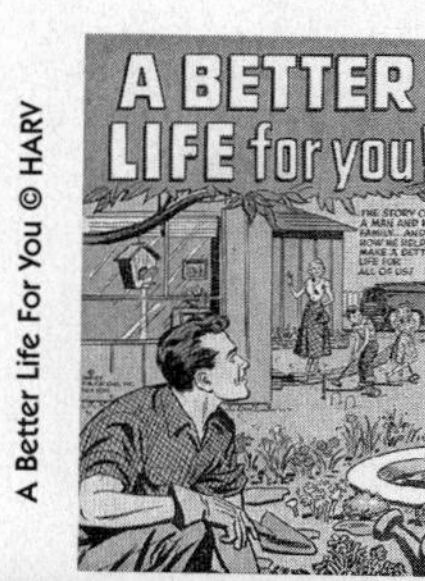

A Better Life For You © HARV

The Blazing Forest © WEST

GD 2.0 | VG 4.0 | FN 6.0 | VF 8.0 | VF/NM 9.0 | NM- 9.2

1-New Avengers 1st battle vs. Dark Avengers; Bendis-s/Cheung-a/c 3.00

BACK TO THE FUTURE
Harvey Comics
Special nn (1991, 20 pgs.)-Brunner-c; given away at Universal Studios in Florida 6.00

BALTIMORE COLTS
American Visuals Corp.: 1950 (Giveaway)
nn-Eisner-c 43 86 129 271 461 650

BAMBI (Disney)
K. K. Publications (Giveaways): 1941, 1942
1941-Horlick's Malted Milk & various toy stores; text & pictures; most copies mailed out with store stickers on-c 40 80 120 252 426 600
1942-Same as 4-Color #12, but no price (Same as '41 issue?) (Scarce) 77 154 231 489 845 1200

BATMAN
DC Comics: 1966 - Present
Act II Popcorn mini-comic(1998) 4.00
Batman #121 Toys R Us edition (1997) r/1st Mr. Freeze 4.00
Batman #279 Mini-comic with Monogram Model kit (1995) 4.00
Batman #362 Mervyn's edition (1989) 5.00
Batman #608 New York Post edition (2002) 4.00
Batman Adventures #1 Free Comic Book Day edition (6/03) Timm-c 4.00
Batman Adventures #25 Best Western edition (1997) 4.00
Batman and Other DC Classics 1 (1989, giveaway)-DC Comics/Diamond Comic Distributors; Batman origin-r/Batman #47, Camelot 3000-r, Justice League-r('87), New Teen Titans-r 5.00
Batman and Robin movie preview (1997, 8 pgs.) Kellogg's Cereal promo 3.00
Batman Beyond Six Flags edition 1 2 3 5 6 8
Batman: Canadian Multiculturalism Custom (1992) 5.00
Batman Claritan edition (1999) 3.00
Kellogg's Poptarts comics (1966, Set of 6, 16 pgs.); All were folded and placed in Poptarts boxes. Infantino art on Catwoman and Joker issues.
"The Man in the Iron Mask", "The Penguin's Fowl Play", "The Joker's Happy Victims", "The Catwoman's Catnapping Caper", "The Mad Hatter's Hat Crimes", "The Case of the Batman II"
each.... 5 10 15 30 48 65
Mask of the Phantasm (1993) Mini-comic released w/video 1 2 3 5 7 9
Onstar - Auto Show Special Edition (OnStar Corp., 2001, 8 pgs.) Riddler app. 3.00
Pizza Hut giveaway (12/77)-exact-r of #122,123; Joker-c/story 2 4 6 8 11 14
Prell Shampoo giveaway (1966, 16 pgs.)- "The Joker's Practical Jokes" (6-7/8x3-3/8") 7 14 21 45 73 100
Revell in pack (1995) 4.00
The Batman Strikes #1 Free Comic Book Day edition (6/05) Penguin app. 3.00
...: The 10-Cent Adventure (3/02, 10¢) intro. to the "Bruce Wayne: Murderer" x-over; Rucka-s/Burchett & Janson-a/Dave Johnson-c; these are alternate copies with special outer half-covers (at least 10 different) promoting comics, toys and games shops 3.00

BATMAN RECORD COMIC
National Periodical Publications: 1966 (one-shot)
1-With record (still sealed) 13 26 39 93 177 260
Comic only 8 16 24 58 97 135

BATTLESTAR GALACTICA SEASON ZERO/THE LONE RANGER #0
Dynamite Entertainment: 2007 Free Comic Book Day Edition
nn-Flip book with Cassaday Lone Ranger-c 2.25

BEETLE BAILEY
Charlton Comics: 1969-1970 (Giveaways)
Armed Forces ('69)-same as regular issue (#68) 2 4 6 10 14 18
Bold Detergent ('69)-same as regular issue (#67) 2 4 6 10 14 18
Cerebral Palsy Assn. V2#71('69) - V2#73(#1,1/70) 5.00
Red Cross (1969, 5x7", 16 pgs., paper-c) 2 4 6 10 14 18

BELLAIRE BICYCLE CO.
Bellaire Bicycle Co.: 1940 (promotional comic)
nn-Contains Wonderworld #12 w/new-c. Contents can vary w/diff. 1940's books 24 48 72 140 230 320

BEST WESTERN GIVEAWAY
DC Comics: 1999
nn-Best Western hotels 2.50

BETTER LIFE FOR YOU, A
Harvey Publications Inc.: (16 pgs., paper cover)
nn-Better living through higher productivity 3 6 9 16 22 28

BETTY AND VERONICA
Archie Comic Publications: 2005
... Free Comic Book Day Edition #1 (6/05) Katy Keene-c/app.; Cheryl Blossom app. 2.50

GD 2.0 | VG 4.0 | FN 6.0 | VF 8.0 | VF/NM 9.0 | NM- 9.2

BEWARE THE BOOBY TRAP
Malcolm Alter: 1970 (5" x 7")
nn-Deals with drug abuse 4 8 12 24 37 50

B-FORCE (Milwaukee Brewers and Wisconsin Dental Asso.)
Dark Horse Comics: 2001 (School and stadium giveaway)
nn-Brewers players combat the evils of smokeless tobacco 3.00

BIG BOY (see Adventures of...)

BIG JIM'S P.A.C.K.
Mattel, Inc. (Marvel Comics): No date (1975) (16 pgs.)
nn-Giveaway with Big Jim doll; Buscema/Sinnott-c/a 4 8 12 24 37 50

"BILL AND TED'S EXCELLENT ADVENTURE" MOVIE ADAPTATION
DC Comics: 1989 (No cover price)
nn-Torres-a 4.00

BIONICLE (LEGO robot toys)
DC Comics: Jun, 2001 - No. 27, Nov, 2005 ($2.25/$3.25, 16 pages, available to LEGO club members)
1 1 2 3 5 6 8
2-5 6.00
6-13 4.00
14-27 3.00
The Legend of Bionicle (McDonald's Mini-comic, 4-1/4 x 7") 4.00
Special Edition #0 (Six Heroes...One Destiny) '03 San Diego Comic Con; Ashley Wood-c 6.00

BLACK GOLD
Esso Service Station (Giveaway): 1945? (8 pgs. in color)
nn-Reprints from True Comics 6 12 18 27 33 38

BLADE SINS OF THE FATHER
Marvel Comics: Aug, 1996 (24 pgs. with paper cover)
1-Theatrical preview; possibly limited to 2000 copies (Value will be based on sale)

BLAZING FOREST, THE (See Forest Fire and Smokey Bear)
Western Printing: 1962 (20 pgs., 5x7", slick-c)
nn-Smokey The Bear fire prevention 3 6 9 14 19 24

BLESSED PIUS X
Catechetical Guild (Giveaway): No date (Text/comics, 32 pgs., paper-c)
nn 6 12 18 31 38 45

BLIND JUSTICE (Also see Batman: Blind Justice)
DC Comics/Diamond Comic Distributors: 1989 (Giveaway, squarebound)
nn-Contains Detective #598-600 by Batman movie writer Sam Hamm, w/covers; published same time as originals? 6.00

BLONDIE COMICS
Harvey Publications: 1950-1964
1950 Giveaway 8 16 24 40 50 60
1962,1964 Giveaway 3 6 9 16 23 30
N. Y. State Dept. of Mental Hygiene Giveaway-(1950) Regular size; 16 pgs.; no # 4 8 12 24 37 50
N. Y. State Dept. of Mental Hygiene Giveaway-(1956) Regular size; 16 pgs.; no # 3 6 9 17 25 32
N. Y. State Dept. of Mental Hygiene Giveaway-(1961) Regular size; 16 pgs.; no # 3 6 9 16 22 28

BLOOD IS THE HARVEST
Catechetical Guild: 1950 (32 pgs., paper-c)
(Scarce)-Anti-communism (13 known copies) 168 336 504 1067 1834 2600
Black & white version (5 known copies), saddle stitched 87 174 261 552 951 1350
Untrimmed version (only one known copy); estimated value - $1000
NOTE: *In 1979 nine copies of the color version surfaced from the old Guild's files plus the five black & white copies.*

BLUE BIRD CHILDREN'S MAGAZINE, THE
Graphic Information Service: V1#2, 1957 - No. 10 1958 (16 pgs., soft-c, regular size)
V1#2-10: Pat, Pete & Blue Bird app. 2 4 6 8 11 14

BLUE BIRD COMICS
Various Shoe Stores/Charlton Comics: Late 1940's - 1964 (Giveaway)
nn(1947-50)(36 pgs.)-Several issues; Human Torch, Sub-Mariner app. in some 18 36 54 103 162 220
1959-Li'l Genius, Timmy the Timid Ghost, Wild Bill Hickok (All #1) 3 6 9 15 21 26
1959-(6 titles; all #2) Black Fury #1,4,5, Freddy #4, Li'l Genius, Timmy the Timid Ghost #4, Masked Raider #4, Wild Bill Hickok (Charlton) 3 6 9 14 20 25
1959-(#5) Masked Raider #21 3 6 9 16 22 28
1960-(6 titles)(All #4) Black Fury #6,8,9, Masked Raider #6, Freddy #8,9, Timmy the Timid

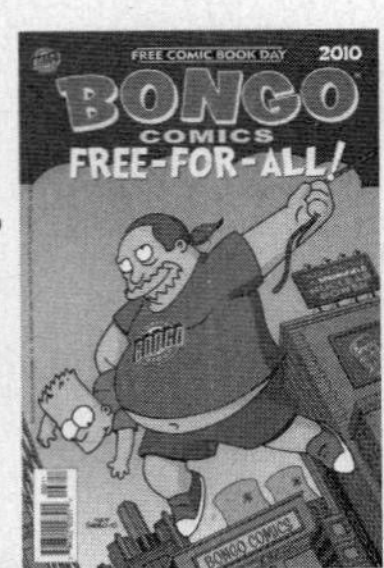

Bongo Comics Free-For-All 2010 © Bongo

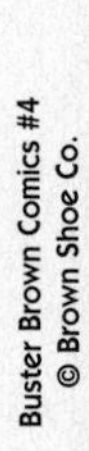
Buster Brown Comics #4 © Brown Shoe Co.

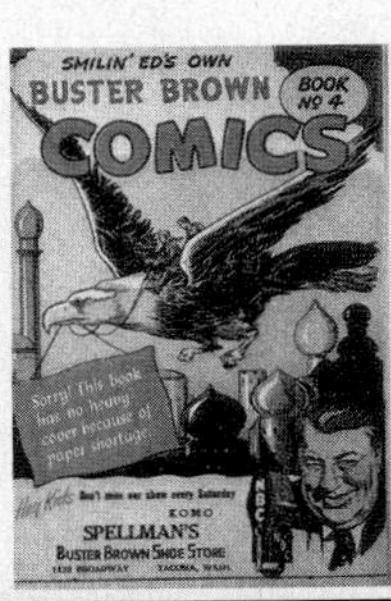

Captain America Goes to War Against Drugs © MAR

	GD 2.0	VG 4.0	FN 6.0	VF 8.0	VF/NM 9.0	NM- 9.2

Ghost #6,9, Li'l Genius #7,9 (Charlt.) 3 6 9 14 19 24
1961,1962-(All #10's) Atomic Mouse #12,13,16, Black Fury #11,12, Freddy, Li'l Genius, Masked Raider, Six Gun Heroes, Texas Rangers in Action, Timmy the Ghost, Wild Bill Hickok, Wyatt Earp #3,11-13,16-18 (Charlton) 2 4 6 13 18 22
1963-Texas Rangers #17 (Charlton) 2 4 6 9 13 16
1964-Mysteries of Unexplored Worlds #18, Teenage Hotrodders #18, War Heroes #18 (Charlton) 2 4 6 9 13 16
1965-War Heroes #18 2 4 6 8 10 12
NOTE: *More than one issue of each character could have been published each year. Numbering is sporadic.*

BOB & BETTY & SANTA'S WISHING WHISTLE
Sears Roebuck & Co.: 1941 (Christmas giveaway, 12 pgs.)
nn 13 26 39 72 101 130

BOBBY BENSON'S B-BAR-B RIDERS (Radio)
Magazine Enterprises/AC Comics
...in the Tunnel of Gold-(1936, 5-1/4x8"; 100 pgs.) Radio giveaway by Hecker-H.O. Company (H.O. Oats); contains 22 color pgs. of comics, rest in novel form 11 22 33 64 90 115
...And The Lost Herd-same as above 11 22 33 64 90 115

BOBBY SHELBY COMICS
Shelby Cycle Co./Harvey Publications: 1949
nn 5 10 14 20 24 28

BONE
Cartoon Books: Halloween, 2008 (8-1/2" x 5-3/8" mini-comic giveaway)
nn-Jeff Smith-s/a 2.00

BONGO COMICS ...
Bongo Comics: 2005 - 2010 (Free Comic Book Day giveaways)
Gimme Gimme Giveaway! (2005) - Short stories from Simpsons Comics, Futurama Comics and Radioactive Man 2.50
Free-For-All! (2006, 2007, 2008, 2009,2010) - Short stories in each 2.50

BOY SCOUT ADVENTURE
Boy Scouts of America: 1954 (16 pgs., paper cover)
nn 5 10 14 20 24 28

BOYS' RANCH
Harvey Publications: 1951
Shoe Store Giveaway #5,6 (Identical to regular issues except Simon & Kirby centerfold replaced with ad) 14 28 42 76 108 140

BOZO THE CLOWN (TV)
Dell Publishing Co.: 1961
Giveaway-1961, 16 pgs., 3-1/2x7-1/4", Apsco Products 5 10 15 32 51 70

BRER RABBIT IN "ICE CREAM FOR THE PARTY"
American Dairy Association: 1955 (5x7-1/4", 16 pgs., soft-c) (Walt Disney) (Premium)
nn-(Scarce) 37 74 111 222 361 500

BUCK ROGERS (In the 25th Century)
Kelloggs Corn Flakes Giveaway: 1933 (6x8", 36 pgs)
370A-By Phil Nowlan & Dick Calkins; 1st Buck Rogers radio premium & 1st app. in comics (tells origin) (Reissued in 1995) 88 176 264 650 - -
with envelope 108 216 324 800 - -

BUGS BUNNY (Puffed Rice Giveaway)
Quaker Cereals: 1949 (32 pgs. each, 3-1/8x6-7/8")
A1-Traps the Counterfeiters, A2-Aboard Mystery Submarine, A3- Rocket to the Moon, A4-Lion Tamer, A5-Rescues the Beautiful Princess, B1-Buried Treasure, B2-Outwits the Smugglers, B3-Joins the Marines, B4-Meets the Dwarf Ghost, B5-Finds Aladdin's Lamp, C1-Lost in the Frozen North, C2-Secret Agent, C3-Captured by Cannibals, C4-Fights the Man from Mars, C5-And the Haunted Cave
each.... 9 18 27 52 69 85
Mailing Envelope (has illo of Bugs on front)(Each envelope designates what set it contains, A,B or C on front) 9 18 27 52 69 85

BUGS BUNNY (3-D)
Cheerios Giveaway: 1953 (Pocket size) (15 titles)
each.... 11 22 33 62 86 110
Mailing Envelope (has Bugs drawn on front) 11 22 33 62 86 110

BUGS BUNNY
DC Comics: May, 1997 ($4.95, 24 pgs., comic-sized)
1-Numbered ed. of 100,000; "1st Day of Issue" stamp cancellation on-c 6.00

BUGS BUNNY POSTAL COMIC
DC Comics: 1997 (64 pgs., 7.5" x 5")
nn -Mail Fan; Daffy Duck app. 4.50

BULLETMAN
Fawcett Publications
Well Known Comics (1942)-Paper-c, glued binding; printed in red (Bestmaid/Samuel Lowe giveaway) 15 30 45 85 130 175

BULLS-EYE (Cody of The Pony Express No. 8 on)
Charlton: 1955
Great Scott Shoe Store giveaway-Reprints #2 with new cover 18 36 54 103 162 220

BUSTER BROWN COMICS (Radio)(Also see My Dog Tige in Promotional sec.)
Brown Shoe Co.: 1945 - No. 43, 1959 (No. 5: paper-c)
nn, nd (#1,scarce)-Featuring Smilin' Ed McConnell & the Buster Brown gang "Midnight" the cat, "Squeaky" the mouse & "Froggy" the Gremlin; covers mention diff. shoe stores. Contains adventure stories 60 120 180 381 653 925
2 19 38 57 111 178 245
3,5-10 13 26 39 74 105 135
4 (Rare)-Low print run due to paper shortage 17 34 51 98 154 210
11-20 9 18 27 47 61 75
21-24,26-28 6 12 18 31 38 45
25,33-37,40,41-Crandall-a in all 10 20 30 56 76 95
29-32-"Interplanetary Police Vs. the Space Siren" by Crandall (pencils only #29) 10 20 30 58 79 100
38,39,42,43 6 12 18 31 38 45

BUSTER BROWN COMICS (Radio)
Brown Shoe Co: 1950s
...Goes to Mars (2/58-Western Printing), slick-c, 20 pgs., reg. size 12 24 36 69 97 125
...In "Buster Makes the Team!" (1959-Custom Comics) 8 16 24 44 57 70
...In The Jet Age ('50s), slick-c, 20 pgs., 5x7-1/4" 10 20 30 58 79 100
...Of the Safety Patrol ('60-Custom Comics) 3 6 9 18 27 35
...Out of This World ('59-Custom Comics) 7 14 21 35 43 50
...Safety Coloring Book ('58, 16 pgs.)-Slick paper 7 14 21 35 43 50

CALL FROM CHRIST
Catechetical Educational Society: 1952 (Giveaway, 36 pgs.)
nn 6 12 18 31 38 45

CANCELLED COMIC CAVALCADE
DC Comics, Inc.: Summer, 1978 - No. 2, Fall, 1978 (8-1/2x11", B&W)
(Xeroxed pgs. on one side only w/blue cover and taped spine)(Only 35 sets produced)
1-(412 pgs.) Contains xeroxed copies of art for: Black Lightning #12, cover to #13; Claw #13,14; The Deserter #1; Doorway to Nightmare #6; Firestorm #6; The Green Team #2,3.
2-(532 pgs.) Contains xeroxed copies of art for: Kamandi #60 (including Omac), #61; Prez #5; Shade #9 (including The Odd Man); Showcase #105 (Deadman), 106 (The Creeper); Secret Society of Super Villains #16 & 17; The Vixen #1; and covers to Army at War #2, Battle Classics #3, Demand Classics #1 & 2, Dynamic Classics #3, Mr. Miracle #26, Ragman #6, Weird Mystery #25 & 26, & Western Classics #1 & 2.
(A FN set of Number 1 & 2 was sold in 2005 for $3680; a VG set sold in 2007 for $2629)
NOTE: *In June, 1978, DC cancelled several of their titles. For copyright purposes, the unpublished original art for these titles was xeroxed, bound in the above books, published and distributed. Only 35 copies were made. Beware of bootleg copies.*

CAP'N CRUNCH COMICS (See Quaker Oats)
Quaker Oats Co.: 1963; 1965 (16 pgs.; miniature giveaways; 2-1/2x6-1/2")
(1963 titles)- "The Picture Pirates", "The Fountain of Youth", "I'm Dreaming of a Wide Isthmus". (1965 titles)- "Bewitched, Betwitched, & Betweaked", "Seadog Meets the Witch Doctor", "A Witch in Time" 5 10 15 34 55 75

CAPTAIN ACTION (Toy)
National Periodical Publications
...& Action Boy('67)-Ideal Toy Co. giveaway (1st app. Captain Action) 12 24 36 84 150 215

CAPTAIN AMERICA
Marvel Comics Group
...& The Campbell Kids (1980, 36pg. giveaway, Campbell's Soup/U.S. Dept. of Energy) 2 4 6 9 13 16
...Goes To War Against Drugs(1990, no #, giveaway)-Distributed to direct sales shops; 2nd printing exists 1 2 3 5 6 8
...Meets The Asthma Monster (1987, no #, giveaway, Your Physician and Glaxo, Inc.) 1 2 3 5 6 8
Return of The Asthma Monster Vol. 1 #2 (1992, giveaway, Your Physician & Allen & Hanbury's) 1 2 3 5 6 8
...Vs. Asthma Monster (1990, no #, giveaway, Your Physician & Allen & Hanbury's) 1 2 3 5 6 8

CAPTAIN AMERICA COMICS
Timely/Marvel Comics: 1954
Shoestore Giveaway #77 74 148 222 470 810 1150

CAPTAIN ATOM

Captain Marvel Adventures Well Known Comics © FAW

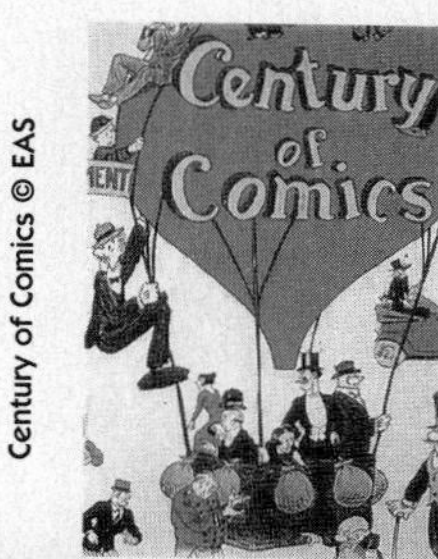

Century of Comics © EAS

Cheerios Premiums Z2 © DIS

	GD 2.0	VG 4.0	FN 6.0	VF 8.0	VF/NM 9.0	NM- 9.2

Nationwide Publishers
...- Secret of the Columbian Jungle (16 pgs. in color, paper-c, 3-3/4x5-1/8")-
Fireside Marshmallow giveaway 6 12 18 28 34 40

CAPTAIN BEN DIX
Bendix Aviation Corporation: 1943 (Small size)
nn 8 16 24 42 54 65

CAPTAIN BEN DIX IN ACTION WITH THE INVISIBLE CREW
Bendix Aviation Corp.: 1940s (nd), (20 pgs, 8-1/4"x11", heavy paper)
nn-WWII bomber-c; Japanese app. 7 14 21 35 43 50

CAPTAIN BEN DIX IN SECRETS OF THE INVISIBLE CREW
Bendix Aviation Corp.: 1940s (nd), (32 pgs, soft-c)
nn 6 12 18 31 38 45

CAPTAIN FORTUNE PRESENTS
Vital Publications: 1955 - 1959 (Giveaway, 3-1/4x6-7/8", 16 pgs.)
"Davy Crockett in Episodes of the Creek War", "Davy Crockett at the Alamo", "In Sherwood Forest Tells Strange Tales of Robin Hood" ('57), "Meets Bolivar the Liberator" ('59), "Tells How Buffalo Bill Fights the Dog Soldiers" ('57), "Young Davy Crockett"
4 7 9 14 17 20

CAPTAIN GALLANT (...of the Foreign Legion) (TV)
Charlton Comics
Heinz Foods Premium (#1?)(1955; regular size)-U.S. Pictorial; contains Buster Crabbe photos; Don Heck-a 1 3 4 6 8 10
Mailing Envelope 20.00

CAPTAIN JOLLY ADVENTURES
Johnston and Cushing: 1950's, nd (Post Corn Fetti cereal giveaway) (5-1/4" x 4-1/2")
1-3: 1-Captain Jolly Advs. 2-Captain Jolly and His Pirate Crew in Off To Treasure Island. 3-C.J. & His Pirate Crew in The Terror Of The Deep
2 4 5 7 8 10

CAPTAIN MARVEL ADVENTURES
Fawcett Publications
Bond Bread Giveaways-(24 pgs.; pocket size-7-1/4x3-1/2"; paper cover): "...& the Stolen City" ('48), "The Boy Who Never Heard of Capt. Marvel", "Meets the Weatherman" (1950) (reprint) each.... 21 42 63 126 208 290
...Well Known Comics (1944; 12 pgs.; 8-1/2x10-1/2")-printed in red & in blue; soft-c; glued binding - (Bestmaid/Samuel Lowe Co. giveaway) 15 30 45 94 147 200

CAPTAIN MARVEL ADVENTURES (Also see Flash and Funny Stuff)
Fawcett Publications (Wheaties Giveaway): 1945 (6x8", full color, paper-c)
nn- "Captain Marvel & the Threads of Life" plus 2 other stories (32 pgs.)
93 186 419 700 - -

NOTE: *All copies were taped at each corner to a box of Wheaties and are never found in Fine or Mint condition. Prices listed for each grade include tape.*

CAPTAIN MARVEL AND THE LTS. OF SAFETY
Ebasco Services/Fawcett Publications: 1950 - 1951 (3 issues - no No.'s)
nn (#1) "Danger Flies a Kite" ('50, scarce), 77 154 231 493 847 1200
nn (#2)"Danger Takes to Climbing" ('50), 58 116 174 371 636 900
nn (#3)"Danger Smashes Street Lights" ('51) 58 116 174 371 636 900

CAPTAIN MARVEL, JR.
Fawcett Publications: (1944; 12 pgs.; 8-1/2x10-1/2")
...Well Known Comics (Printed in blue; paper-c, glued binding)-Bestmaid/Samuel Lowe Co. giveaway 14 28 42 76 108 140

CARDINAL MINDSZENTY (The Truth Behind the Trial of...)
Catechetical Guild Education Society: 1949 (24 pgs., paper cover)
nn-Anti-communism 10 20 30 56 76 95
Press Proof-(Very Rare)-(Full color, 7-1/2x11-3/4", untrimmed)
Only two known copies 290.00
Preview Copy (B&W, stapled), 18 pgs.; contains first 13 pgs. of Cardinal Mindszenty and was sent out as an advance promotion. Only one known copy 300.00 - 400.00

NOTE: *Regular edition also printed in French. There was also a movie released in 1949 called "Guilty of Treason" which is a fact-based account of the trial and imprisonment of Cardinal Mindszenty by the Communist regime in Hungary.*

CARNIVAL OF COMICS
Fleet-Air Shoes: 1954 (Giveaway)
nn-Contains a comic bound with new cover; several combinations possible; Charlton's Eh! known 5 10 15 24 30 35

CARS, WORLD OF (Free Comic Book Day giveaway)
BOOM Kids!: May, 2009
1-Based on the Disney/Pixar movie 2.50

CARTOON NETWORK
DC Comics: 1997 (Giveaway)
nn-reprints Cow and Chicken, Scooby-Doo, & Flintstones stories 4.00

CARVEL COMICS (Amazing Advs. of Capt. Carvel)
Carvel Corp. (Ice Cream): 1975 - No. 5, 1976 (25¢; #3-5: 35¢) (#4,5: 3-1/4x5")
1-3 1 2 3 5 6 8
4,5(1976)-Baseball theme 2 4 6 8 10 12

CASE OF THE WASTED WATER, THE
Rheem Water Heating: 1972? (Giveaway)
nn-Neal Adams-a 4 8 12 28 44 60

CASPER SPECIAL
Target Stores (Harvey): nd (Dec, 1990) (Giveaway with $1.00 cover)
Three issues-Given away with Casper video 6.00

CASPER, THE FRIENDLY GHOST (Paramount Picture Star...)(2nd Series)
Harvey Publications
American Dental Association (Giveaways):
...'s Dental Health Activity Book-1977 2 4 6 8 11 14
...Presents Space Age Dentistry-1972 2 4 6 9 13 16
..., His Den, & Their Dentist Fight the Tooth Demons-1974
2 4 6 9 13 16
Casper Rides the School Bus (1960, 7x3.5", 16 pgs.) 2 4 6 9 13 16

CELEBRATE THE CENTURY SUPERHEROES STAMP ALBUM
DC Comics: 1998 - No. 5, 2000 (32 pgs.)
1-5: Historical stories hosted by DC heroes 4.00

CENTIPEDE
DC Comics: 1983
1-Based on Atari video game 2 4 6 8 11 14

CENTURY OF COMICS
Eastern Color Printing Co.: 1933 (100 pgs.)
Bought by Wheatena, Malt-O-Milk, John Wanamaker, Kinney Shoe Stores, & others to be used as premiums and radio giveaways. No publisher listed.
nn-Mutt & Jeff, Joe Palooka, etc. reprints 2500 5000 7500 19,000 - -

CHEERIOS PREMIUMS (Disney)
Walt Disney Productions: 1947 (16 titles, pocket size, 32 pgs.)
Mailing Envelope for each set "W,X,Y & Z" (has Mickey illo on front)(each envelope designates the set it contains on the front) 11 22 33 60 83 105
Set "W"
W1-Donald Duck & the Pirates 11 22 33 60 83 105
W2-Bucky Bug & the Cannibal King 7 14 21 37 46 55
W3-Pluto Joins the F.B.I. 7 14 21 37 46 55
W4-Mickey Mouse & the Haunted House 8 16 24 42 54 65
Set "X"
X1-Donald Duck, Counter Spy 11 22 33 60 83 105
X2-Goofy Lost in the Desert 7 14 21 37 46 55
X3-Br'er Rabbit Outwits Br'er Fox 7 14 21 37 46 55
X4-Mickey Mouse at the Rodeo 8 16 24 42 54 65
Set "Y"
Y1-Donald Duck's Atom Bomb by Carl Barks. Disney has banned reprinting this book
76 152 228 483 829 1175
Y2-Br'er Rabbit's Secret 7 14 21 37 46 55
Y3-Dumbo & the Circus Mystery 7 14 21 37 46 55
Y4-Mickey Mouse Meets the Wizard 8 16 24 42 54 65
Set "Z"
Z1-Donald Duck Pilots a Jet Plane (not by Barks) 11 22 33 60 83 105
Z2-Pluto Turns Sleuth Hound 7 14 21 37 46 55
Z3-The Seven Dwarfs & the Enchanted Mtn. 8 16 24 42 54 65
Z4-Mickey Mouse's Secret Room 8 16 24 42 54 65

CHEERIOS 3-D GIVEAWAYS (Disney)
Walt Disney Productions: 1954 (24 titles, pocket size) (Glasses came in envelopes)
Glasses only... 8 16 24 40 50 60
Mailing Envelope (no art on front) 9 18 27 47 61 75
(Set 1)
1-Donald Duck & Uncle Scrooge, the Firefighters 9 18 27 52 69 85
2-Mickey Mouse & Goofy, Pirate Plunder 9 18 27 47 61 75
3-Donald Duck's Nephews, the Fabulous Inventors 9 18 27 52 69 85
4-Mickey Mouse, Secret of the Ming Vase 9 18 27 47 61 75
5-Donald Duck with Huey, Dewey, & Louie; ...the Seafarers (title on 2nd page)
9 18 27 52 69 85
6-Mickey Mouse, Moaning Mountain 9 18 27 47 61 75
7-Donald Duck, Apache Gold 9 18 27 52 69 85
8-Mickey Mouse, Flight to Nowhere 9 18 27 47 61 75
(Set 2)
1-Donald Duck, Treasure of Timbuktu 9 18 27 52 69 85
2-Mickey Mouse & Pluto, Operation China 9 18 27 47 61 75

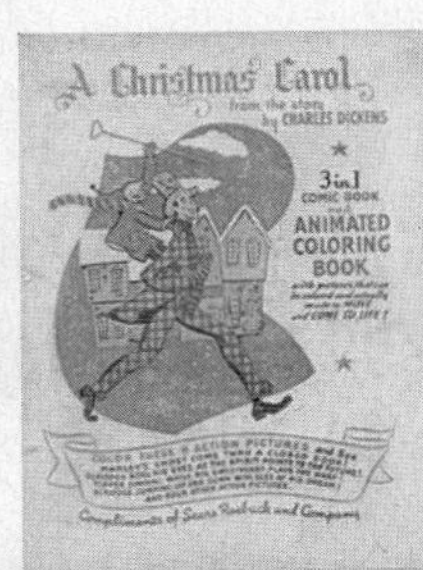

A Christmas Carol © Sears

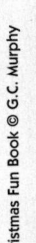

Christmas Fun Book © G.C. Murphy

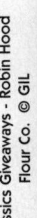

Classics Giveaways - Robin Hood Flour Co. © GIL

	GD 2.0	VG 4.0	FN 6.0	VF 8.0	VF/NM 9.0	NM- 9.2
3-Donald Duck and the Magic Cows	9	18	27	52	69	85
4-Mickey Mouse & Goofy, Kid Kokonut	9	18	27	47	61	75
5-Donald Duck, Mystery Ship	9	18	27	52	69	85
6-Mickey Mouse, Phantom Sheriff	9	18	27	47	61	75
7-Donald Duck, Circus Adventures	9	18	27	52	69	85
8-Mickey Mouse, Arctic Explorers	9	18	27	47	61	75
(Set 3)						
1-Donald Duck & Witch Hazel	9	18	27	52	69	85
2-Mickey Mouse in Darkest Africa	9	18	27	47	61	75
3-Donald Duck & Uncle Scrooge, Timber Trouble	9	18	27	52	69	85
4-Mickey Mouse, Rajah's Rescue	9	18	27	47	61	75
5-Donald Duck in Robot Reporter	9	18	27	52	69	85
6-Mickey Mouse, Slumbering Sleuth	9	18	27	47	61	75
7-Donald Duck in the Foreign Legion	9	18	27	52	69	85
8-Mickey Mouse, Airwalking Wonder	9	18	27	47	61	75

CHESTY AND COPTIE (Disney)
Los Angeles Community Chest: 1946 (Giveaway, 4pgs.)

	GD	VG	FN	VF	VF/NM	NM-
nn-(One known copy) by Floyd Gottfredson	77	154	231	489	845	1200

CHESTY AND HIS HELPERS (Disney)
Los Angeles War Chest: 1943 (Giveaway, 12 pgs., 5-1/2x7-1/4")

	GD	VG	FN	VF	VF/NM	NM-
nn-Chesty & Coptie	50	100	150	315	533	750

CHOCOLATE THE FLAVOR OF FRIENDSHIP AROUND THE WORLD
The Nestle Company: 1955

	GD	VG	FN	VF	VF/NM	NM-
nn	6	12	18	28	34	40

CHRISTMAS ADVENTURE, THE
S. Rose (H. L. Green Giveaway): 1963 (16 pgs.)

	GD	VG	FN	VF	VF/NM	NM-
nn	2	4	6	9	13	16

CHRISTMAS ADVENTURES WITH ELMER THE ELF
1949 (paper-c)

	GD	VG	FN	VF	VF/NM	NM-
nn	4	7	10	14	17	20

CHRISTMAS AT THE ROTUNDA (Titled Ford Rotunda Christmas Book 1957 on) (Regular size)
Ford Motor Co. (Western Printing): 1954 - 1961 (Given away every Christmas at one location)

	GD	VG	FN	VF	VF/NM	NM-
1954-56 issues (nn's)	7	14	21	37	46	55
1957-61 issues (nn's)	6	12	18	31	38	45

CHRISTMAS CAROL, A
Sears Roebuck & Co.: No date (1942-43) (Giveaway, 32 pgs., 8-1/4x10-3/4", paper cover)

	GD	VG	FN	VF	VF/NM	NM-
nn-Comics & coloring book	18	36	54	105	165	225

CHRISTMAS CAROL, A
Sears Roebuck & Co.: 1940s ? (Christmas giveaway, 20 pgs.)

	GD	VG	FN	VF	VF/NM	NM-
nn-Comic book & animated coloring book	17	34	51	100	158	215

CHRISTMAS CAROLS
Hot Shoppes Giveaway: 1959? (16 pgs.)

	GD	VG	FN	VF	VF/NM	NM-
nn	4	8	11	16	19	22

CHRISTMAS COLORING FUN
H. Burnside: 1964 (20 pgs., slick-c, B&W)

	GD	VG	FN	VF	VF/NM	NM-
nn	2	4	6	11	16	20

CHRISTMAS DREAM, A
Promotional Publishing Co.: 1950 (Kinney Shoe Store Giveaway, 16 pgs.)

	GD	VG	FN	VF	VF/NM	NM-
nn	5	10	15	23	28	32

CHRISTMAS DREAM, A
J. J. Newberry Co.: 1952? (Giveaway, paper cover, 16 pgs.)

	GD	VG	FN	VF	VF/NM	NM-
nn	4	8	12	18	22	25

CHRISTMAS DREAM, A
Promotional Publ. Co.: 1952 (Giveaway, 16 pgs., paper cover)

	GD	VG	FN	VF	VF/NM	NM-
nn	4	8	12	18	22	25

CHRISTMAS FUN AROUND THE WORLD
No publisher: No date (early 50's) (16 pgs., paper cover)

	GD	VG	FN	VF	VF/NM	NM-
nn	5	10	15	22	26	30

CHRISTMAS FUN BOOK
G. C. Murphy Co.: 1950 (Giveaway, paper cover)

	GD	VG	FN	VF	VF/NM	NM-
nn-Contains paper dolls	6	12	18	28	34	40

CHRISTMAS IS COMING!
No publisher: No date (early 50's?) (Store giveaway, 16 pgs.)

	GD	VG	FN	VF	VF/NM	NM-
nn	4	8	12	18	22	25

CHRISTMAS JOURNEY THROUGH SPACE
Promotional Publishing Co.: 1960

	GD	VG	FN	VF	VF/NM	NM-
nn-Reprints 1954 issue Jolly Christmas Book with new slick cover	3	6	9	16	23	30

CHRISTMAS ON THE MOON
W. T. Grant Co.: 1958 (Giveaway, 20 pgs., slick cover)

	GD	VG	FN	VF	VF/NM	NM-
nn	8	16	24	44	57	70

CHRISTMAS PLAY BOOK
Gould-Stoner Co.: 1946 (Giveaway, 16 pgs., paper cover)

	GD	VG	FN	VF	VF/NM	NM-
nn	8	16	24	44	57	70

CHRISTMAS ROUNDUP
Promotional Publishing Co.: 1960

	GD	VG	FN	VF	VF/NM	NM-
nn-Marv Levy-c/a	2	4	6	9	13	16

CHRISTMAS STORY CUT-OUT BOOK, THE
Catechetical Guild: No. 393, 1951 (15¢, 36 pgs.)

	GD	VG	FN	VF	VF/NM	NM-
393-Half text & half comics	8	16	24	42	54	65

CHRISTMAS USA (Through 300 Years) (Also see Uncle Sam's...)
Promotional Publ. Co.: 1956 (Giveaway)

	GD	VG	FN	VF	VF/NM	NM-
nn-Marv Levy-c/a	4	7	9	14	16	18

CHRISTMAS WITH SNOW WHITE AND THE SEVEN DWARFS
Kobackers Giftstore of Buffalo, N.Y.: 1953 (16 pgs., paper-c)

	GD	VG	FN	VF	VF/NM	NM-
nn	8	16	24	42	54	65

CHRISTOPHERS, THE
Catechetical Guild: 1951 (Giveaway, 36 pgs.) (Some copies have 15¢ sticker)

	GD	VG	FN	VF	VF/NM	NM-
nn-Stalin as Satan in Hell	21	42	63	121	201	280

CINDERELLA IN "FAIREST OF THE FAIR" (Walt Disney)
American Dairy Association (Premium): 1955 (5x7-1/4", 16 pgs., soft-c)

	GD	VG	FN	VF	VF/NM	NM-
nn	10	20	30	56	76	95

CINEMA COMICS HERALD
Paramount Pictures/Universal/RKO/20th Century Fox/Republic:
1941 - 1943 (4-pg. movie "trailers", paper-c, 7-1/2x10-1/2")(Giveaway)

	GD	VG	FN	VF	VF/NM	NM-
"Mr. Bug Goes to Town" (1941)	15	30	45	90	140	190
"Bedtime Story"	11	22	33	64	90	115
"Lady For A Night", John Wayne, Joan Blondell ('42)	18	36	54	107	169	230
"Reap The Wild Wind" (1942)	12	24	36	69	97	125
"Thunder Birds" (1942)	11	22	33	64	90	115
"They All Kissed the Bride"	11	22	33	64	90	115
"Arabian Nights" (nd)	12	24	36	69	97	125
"Bombardie" (1943)	11	22	33	64	90	115
"Crash Dive" (1943)-Tyrone Power	12	24	36	69	97	125

NOTE: *The 1941-42 issues contain line art with color photos. 1943 issues are line art.*

CLASSICS GIVEAWAYS (Classic Comics reprints)

	GD	VG	FN	VF	VF/NM	NM-
12/41–Walter Theatre Enterprises (Huntington, WV) giveaway containing #2 (orig.) w/new generic-c (only 1 known copy)	84	168	252	533	917	1300
1942–Double Comics containing CC#1 (orig.) (diff. cover) (not actually a giveaway) (very rare) (also see Double Comics) (only one known copy)	148	296	444	940	1620	2300
12/42–Saks 34th St. Giveaway containing CC#7 (orig.) (diff. cover) (very rare; only 6 known copies)	300	600	900	2011	3506	5000
2/43–American Comics containing CC#8 (orig.) (Liberty Theatre giveaway) (different cover) (only one known copy) (see American Comics)	97	194	291	616	1058	1500
12/44–Robin Hood Flour Co. Giveaway - #7-CC(R) (diff. cover) (rare) (edition probably 5 [22])	155	310	465	984	1692	2400

NOTE: How are above editions determined without CC covers? 1942 is dated 1942, and CC#1-first reprint did not come out until 5/43. 12/42 and 2/43 are determined by blue note at bottom of first text page only in original edition. 12/44 is estimated from page width each reprint edition had progressively slightly smaller page width.

	GD	VG	FN	VF	VF/NM	NM-
1951–Shelter Thru the Ages (C.I. Educational Series) (actually Giveaway by the Ruberoid Co.) (16 pgs.) (contains original artwork by H. C. Kiefer) (there are 5 diff. back cover ad variations: "Ranch" house ad, "Igloo" ad, "Doll House" ad, "Tree House" ad & blank) (scarce)	52	104	156	330	565	800
1952–George Daynor Biography Giveaway (CC logo) (partly comic book/pictures/newspaper articles) (story of man who built Palace Depression out of junkyard swamp in NJ) (64 pgs.) (very rare; only 3 known copies, one missing back-c)	360	720	1080	2556	4428	6300
1953–Westinghouse/Dreams of a Man (C.I. Educational Series) (Westinghousebio./ Westinghouse Co. giveaway) (contains original artwork by H. C. Kiefer) (16 pgs.) (also French/Spanish/Italian versions) (scarce)	47	94	141	296	498	700
NOTE: Reproductions of 1951, 1952, and 1953 exist with color photocopy covers and black & white photocopy interior ("W.C.N. Reprint")	2	4	5	7	8	10
1951-53–Coward Shoe Giveaways (all editions very rare); 2 variations of back-c ad exist: With back-c photo ad: 5 (87), 12 (89), 22 (85), 32 (85), 49 (85), 69 (87), 72 (no HRN), 80 (0), 91 (0), 92 (0), 96 (0), 98 (0), 100 (0), 101 (0), 103-105 (all Os)	29	58	87	170	278	385

With back-c cartoon ad: 106-109 (all 0s), 110 (111), 112 (0)

Classic Giveaways - Ben Franklin 5-10 © GIL

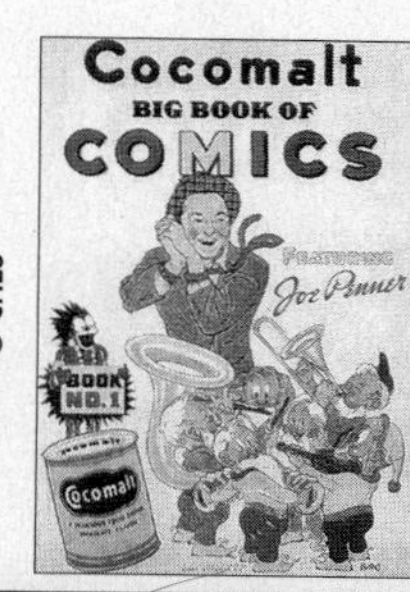

Cocomalt Big Book of Comics © CHES

Dan Curtis Giveaways Star Trek © Paramount

	GD 2.0	VG 4.0	FN 6.0	VF 8.0	VF/NM 9.0	NM- 9.2
	31	62	93	184	302	420
1956–Ben Franklin 5-10 Store Giveaway (#65-PC with back cover ad) (scarce)	24	48	72	142	234	325
1956–Ben Franklin Insurance Co. Giveaway (#65-PC with diff. back cover ad) (very rare)	47	94	141	296	498	700
11/56–Sealtest Co. Edition - #4 (135) (identical to regular edition except for Sealtest logo printed, not stamped, on front cover) (only two copies known to exist)	28	56	84	165	270	375
1958–Get-Well Giveaway containing #15-CI (new cartoon-type cover) (Pressman Pharmacy) (only one copy known to exist)	27	54	81	162	266	370
1967-68–Twin Circle Giveaway Editions - all HRN 166, with back cover ad for National Catholic Press.						
2(R68), 4(R67), 10(R68), 13(R68)	3	6	9	21	32	42
48(R67), 128(R68), 535(576-R68)	4	8	12	22	34	45
16(R68), 68(R67)	5	10	15	30	48	65
12/69–Christmas Giveaway ("A Christmas Adventure") (reprints Picture Parade #4-1953, new cover) (4 ad variations)						
Stacey's Dept. Store	3	6	9	21	32	42
Anne & Hope Store	5	10	15	32	51	70
Gibson's Dept. Store (rare)	5	10	15	32	51	70
"Merry Christmas" & blank ad space	3	6	9	21	32	42

CLEAR THE TRACK!
Association of American Railroads: 1954 (paper-c, 16 pgs.)

nn	5	10	15	22	26	30

CLIFF MERRITT SETS THE RECORD STRAIGHT
Brotherhood of Railroad Trainsmen: Giveaway (2 different issues)

...and the Very Candid Candidate by Al Williamson	1	3	4	6	8	10
...Sets the Record Straight by Al Williamson (2 different-c: one by Williamson, the other by McWilliams)	1	3	4	6	8	10

CLYDE BEATTY COMICS (Also see Crackajack Funnies)
Commodore Productions & Artists, Inc.

...African Jungle Book('56)-Richfield Oil Co. 16 pg. giveaway, soft-c	10	20	30	54	72	90

C-M-O COMICS
Chicago Mail Order Co.(Centaur): 1942 - No. 2, 1942 (68 pgs., full color)

1-Invisible Terror, Super Ann, & Plymo the Rubber Man app. (all Centaur costume heroes)	87	174	261	552	951	1350
2-Invisible Terror, Super Ann app.	52	104	156	322	549	775

COCOMALT BIG BOOK OF COMICS
Harry 'A' Chesler (Cocomalt Premium): 1938 (Reg. size, full color, 52 pgs.)

1-(Scarce)-Biro-c/a; Little Nemo by Winsor McCay Jr., Dan Hastings; Jack Cole, Guardineer, Gustavson, Bob Wood-a	207	414	621	1315	2258	3200

COMIC BOOK (Also see Comics From Weatherbird)
American Juniors Shoe: 1954 (Giveaway)
Contains a comic rebound with new cover. Several combinations possible. Contents determine price.

COMIC BOOK MAGAZINE
Chicago Tribune & other newspapers: 1940 - 1943 (Similar to Spirit sections) (7-3/4x10-3/4"; full color; 16-24 pgs. ea.)

1940 issues	7	14	21	37	46	55
1941, 1942 issues	6	12	18	28	34	40
1943 issues	5	10	15	24	30	35

NOTE: *Published weekly. Texas Slim, Kit Carson, Spooky, Josie, Nuts & Jolts, Lew Loyal, Brenda Starr, Daniel Boone, Captain Storm, Rocky, Smokey Stover, Tiny Tim, Little Joe, Fu Manchu appear among others. Early issues had photo stories with pictures from the movies; later issues had comic art.*

COMIC BOOKS (Series 1)
Metropolitan Printing Co. (Giveaway): 1950 (16 pgs.; 5-1/4x8-1/2"; full color; bound at top; paper cover)

1-Boots and Saddles; intro The Masked Marshal	6	12	18	28	34	40
1-The Green Jet; Green Lama by Raboy	19	38	57	112	181	250
1-My Pal Dizzy (Teen-age)	4	8	12	18	22	25
1-New World; origin Atomaster (costumed hero)	9	18	27	52	69	85
1-Talullah (Teen-age)	4	8	12	18	22	25

COMIC CAVALCADE
All-American/National Periodical Publications

Giveaway (1944, 8 pgs., paper-c, in color)-One Hundred Years of Co-operation-r/Comic Cavalcade #9	50	100	150	315	533	750
Giveaway (1945, 16 pgs., paper-c, in color)-Movie "Tomorrow The World" (Nazi theme); r/Comic Cavalcade #10	65	130	195	413	707	1000
Giveaway (c. 1944-45; 8 pgs, paper-c, in color)-The Twain Shall Meet-r/Comic Cavalcade #8	50	100	150	315	533	750

COMIC SELECTIONS (Shoe store giveaway)
Parents' Magazine Press: 1944-46 (Reprints from Calling All Girls, True Comics, True Aviation, & Real Heroes)

	GD 2.0	VG 4.0	FN 6.0	VF 8.0	VF/NM 9.0	NM- 9.2
1	5	10	15	22	26	30
2-6	4	8	11	16	19	22

COMICS FROM WEATHER BIRD (Also see Comic Book, Edward's Shoes, Free Comics to You & Weather Bird)
Weather Bird Shoes: 1954 - 1957 (Giveaway)
Contains a comic bound with new cover. Many combinations possible. Contents would determine price. Some issues do not contain complete comics, but only parts of comics. Value equals 40 to 60 percent of contents.

COMICS READING LIBRARIES (Educational Series)
King Features (Charlton Publ.): 1973, 1977, 1979 (36 pgs. in color) (Giveaways)

R-01-Tiger, Quincy	2	4	6	8	11	14
R-02-Beetle Bailey, Blondie & Popeye	2	4	6	10	14	18
R-03-Blondie, Beetle Bailey	2	4	6	8	11	14
R-04-Tim Tyler's Luck, Felix the Cat	3	6	9	16	23	30
R-05-Quincy, Henry	2	4	6	8	11	14
R-06-The Phantom, Mandrake	3	6	9	16	23	30
1977 reprint(R-04)	2	4	6	9	13	16
R-07-Popeye, Little King	2	4	6	13	18	22
R-08-Prince Valiant (Foster), Flash Gordon	3	6	9	18	27	36
1977 reprint	2	4	6	11	16	20
R-09-Hagar the Horrible, Boner's Ark	2	4	6	10	14	18
R-10-Redeye, Tiger	2	4	6	8	11	14
R-11-Blondie, Hi & Lois	2	4	6	8	11	14
R-12-Popeye-Swee'pea, Brutus	2	4	6	13	18	22
R-13-Beetle Bailey, Little King	2	4	6	8	11	14
R-14-Quincy-Hamlet	2	4	6	8	11	14
R-15-The Phantom, The Genius	2	4	6	13	18	22
R-16-Flash Gordon, Mandrake	3	6	9	18	27	36
1977 reprint	2	4	6	10	14	18
Other 1977 editions....	2	4	6	8	10	12
1979 editions (68 pgs.)	2	4	6	8	10	12

NOTE: *Above giveaways available with purchase of $45.00 in merchandise. Used as a reading skills aid for small children.*

COMMANDMENTS OF GOD
Catechetical Guild: 1954, 1958

300-Same contents in both editions; diff-c	5	10	15	24	29	34

COMPLIMENTARY COMICS
Sales Promotion Publ.: No date (1950's) (Giveaway)

1-Strongman by Powell, 3 stories	8	16	24	40	50	60

CONAN
Dark Horse Comics: May, 2006 (Free Comic Book Day giveaway)

...: FCBD 2006 Special (5/06) Paul Lee-a; flip book with Star Wars FCBD 2006 Special 2.50

COURTNEY CRUMRIN & THE NIGHT THINGS
Oni Press: 2003

Free Comic Book Day Edition (5/03) Naifeh-s/a 2.50

CRACKAJACK FUNNIES (Giveaway)
Malto-Meal: 1937 (Full size, soft-c, full color, 32 pgs.)(Before No. 1?)

nn-Features Dan Dunn, G-Man, Speed Bolton, Buck Jones, The Nebbs, Clyde Beatty, Freckles, Major Hoople, Wash Tubbs	74	148	222	470	810	1150

CROSLEY'S HOUSE OF FUN (Also see Tee and Vee Crosley...)
Crosley Div. AVCO Mfg. Corp.: 1950 (Giveaway, paper cover, 32 pgs.)

nn-Strips revolve around Crosley appliances	5	10	15	22	26	30

CSI: CRIME SCENE INVESTIGATION
IDW Publishing: July, 2004 (Free Comic Book Day edition)

Previews CSI: Bad Rap; The Shield: Spotlight; 24: One Shot; and 30 Days of Night 2.50

DAGWOOD SPLITS THE ATOM (Also see Topix V8#4)
King Features Syndicate: 1949 (Science comic with King Features characters) (Giveaway)

nn-Half comic, half text; Popeye, Olive Oyl, Henry, Mandrake, Little King, Katzenjammer Kids app.	9	18	27	52	69	85

DAISY COMICS (Daisy Air Rifles)
Eastern Color Printing Co.: Dec, 1936 (5-1/4x7-1/2")

nn-Joe Palooka, Buck Rogers (2 pgs. from Famous Funnies No. 18, 1st full cover app.), Napoleon Flying to Fame, Butty & Fally	31	62	93	186	301	425

DAISY LOW OF THE GIRL SCOUTS
Girl Scouts of America: 1954, 1965 (16 pgs., paper-c)

1954-Story of Juliette Gordon Low	5	10	15	22	26	30
1965	2	4	6	9	12	15

DAN CURTIS GIVEAWAYS
Western Publishing Co.: 1974 (3x6", 24 pgs., reprints)

1-Dark Shadows	3	6	9	16	23	30
2,6-Star Trek	3	6	9	16	23	30

3,4,7-9: 3-The Twilight Zone. 4-Ripley's Believe It or Not! 7-The Occult Files of Dr. Spektor.

DC Comics Mega Sampler 2010 © DC

Dick Tracy's Hatful of Fun © NYNS

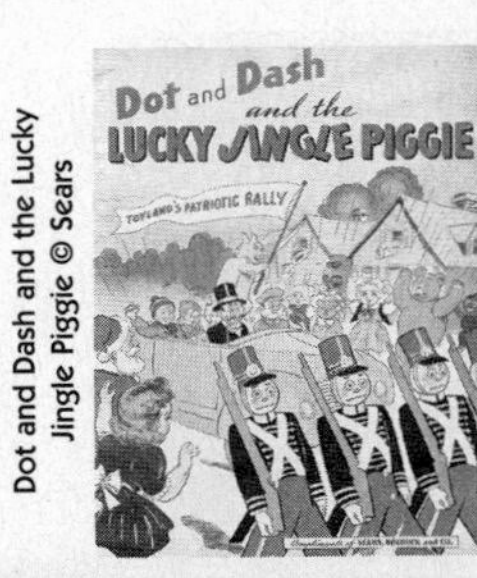

Dot and Dash and the Lucky Jingle Piggie © Sears

	GD 2.0	VG 4.0	FN 6.0	VF 8.0	VF/NM 9.0	NM- 9.2
8-Dagar the Invincible. 9-Grimm's Ghost Stories	2	4	6	11	16	20
5-Turok, Son of Stone (partial-r/Turok #78)	3	6	9	16	23	30

DANNY KAYE'S BAND FUN BOOK
H & A Selmer: 1959 (Giveaway)

nn	7	14	21	35	43	50

DAREDEVIL
Marvel Comics Group: 1993

...Vs. Vapora 1 (Engineering Show Giveaway, 16 pg.) - Intro Vapora 6.00

DAVY CROCKETT (TV)
Dell Publishing Co.

...Christmas Book (no date, 16 pgs., paper-c)-Sears giveaway	6	12	18	31	38	45
...Safety Trails (1955, 16pgs, 3-1/4x7")-Cities Service giveaway	8	16	24	40	50	60

DAVY CROCKETT
Charlton Comics

Hunting With... nn ('55, 16 pgs.)-Ben Franklin Store giveaway (Publ.-S. Rose)	5	10	15	24	30	35

DAVY CROCKETT
Walt Disney Prod.: (1955, 16 pgs., 5x7-1/4", slick, photo-c)

...In the Raid at Piney Creek-American Motors giveaway	8	16	24	40	50	60

DC SAMPLER
DC Comics: nn (#1) 1983 - No. 3, 1984 (36 pgs.; 6 1/2" x 10", giveaway)

nn(#1) -3: nn-Wraparound-c, previews upcoming issues. 3-Kirby-a	1	2	3	4	5	7

DC COMICS MEGA SAMPLER
DC Comics: 2009; Jul, 2010 (6-1/4" x 9-1/2", FCBD giveaways)

1, 2010- Short stories of kid-friendly titles; Tiny Titans, Billy Batson, Super Friends app. 2.50

DC SPOTLIGHT
DC Comics: 1985 (50th anniversary special) (giveaway)

1-Includes profiles on Batman:The Dark Knight & Watchmen 6.00

DEATH JR. HALLOWEEN SPECIAL
Image Comics: Oct, 2006 (8-1/2"x 5-1/2", Halloween giveaway)

nn-Guy Davis-a/Joe Morrisey-s; wraparound-c 2.50

DENNIS THE MENACE
Hallden (Fawcett)

...& Dirt ('59)-Soil Conservation giveaway; r-# 36; Wiseman-c/a	3	6	9	14	20	26
...& Dirt ('68)-reprints '59 edition	2	4	6	8	11	14
...Away We Go('70)-Caladryl giveaway	2	4	6	8	10	12
...Coping with Family Stress-giveaway	2	4	6	8	10	12
...Takes a Poke at Poison('61)-Food & Drug Admin. giveaway; Wiseman-c/a	2	4	6	8	10	12
...Takes a Poke at Poison-Revised 1/66, 11/70	1	2	3	5	6	8
...Takes a Poke at Poison-Revised 1972, 1974, 1977, 1981	1	2	3	4	5	7

DESERT DAWN
E.C./American Museum of Natural History: 1935 (paper-c)

nn-Johnny Jackrabbit stars. Three known copies: A Fair copy (brittle) sold for $657 in 2007. A GD+ copy (brittle) sold for $2300 in 2005. Another Fair copy (brittle) sold for $690 in 2004

DETECTIVE COMICS (Also see other Batman titles)
National Periodical Publications/DC Comics

27 (1984)-Oreo Cookies giveaway (32 pgs., paper-c) r-/Det. #27,#38 & Batman #1 (1st Joker)	5	10	15	32	51	70

38 (1995) Blockbuster Video edition; reprints 1st Robin app. 3.00
38 (1997) Toys R Us edition 3.00
359 (1997) Toys R Us edition; reprints 1st Batgirl app. 3.00
373 (1997, 6 1/4" x 4") Warner Brothers Home Video 3.00

DEVIL'S DUE FREE COMIC BOOK DAY
Devil's Due Publ.: May, 2005 (Free Comic Book Day giveaway)

nn-Short stories of G.I. Joe, Defex and Darkstalkers; Darkstalkers flip cover 2.50

DICK TRACY GIVEAWAYS
1939 - 1958; 1990

Buster Brown Shoes Giveaway (1940s?, 36 pgs. in color); 1938-39-r by Gould	29	58	87	170	278	385

Gillmore Giveaway (See Superbook)

...Hatful of Fun (No date, 1950-52, 32pgs.; 8-1/2x10")-Dick Tracy hat promotion; Dick Tracy games, magic tricks. Miller Bros. premium	15	30	45	90	140	190
Motorola Giveaway (1953)-Reprints Harvey Comics Library #2; "The Case of the Sparkle Plenty TV Mystery"	7	14	21	37	46	55
Original Dick Tracy by Chester Gould, The (Aug, 1990, 16 pgs., 5-1/2x8-1/2")-Gladstone Publ.; Bread Giveaway	1	3	4	6	8	10
Popped Wheat Giveaway (1947, 16 pgs. in color)-1940-r; Sig Feuchtwanger Publ.; Gould-a	4	8	12	18	22	25
...Presents the Family Fun Book; Tip Top Bread Giveaway, no date or number (1940, Fawcett Publ., 16 pgs. in color)-Spy Smasher, Ibis, Lance O'Casey app.	43	86	129	271	461	650
Same as above but without app. of heroes & Dick Tracy on cover only	14	28	42	82	121	160
Service Station Giveaway (1958, 16 pgs. in color)(regular size, slick cover)-Harvey Info. Press	5	10	14	20	24	28
Shoe Store Giveaway (Weatherbird and Triangle Stores)(1939, 16 pgs.)-Gould-a	14	28	42	76	108	140

DICK TRACY SHEDS LIGHT ON THE MOLE
Western Printing Co.: 1949 (16 pgs.) (Ray-O-Vac Flashlights giveaway)

nn-Not by Gould	8	16	24	42	54	65

DICK WINGATE OF THE U.S. NAVY
Superior Publ./Toby Press: 1951; 1953 (no month)

nn-U.S. Navy giveaway	5	10	15	24	30	35
1(1953, Toby)-Reprints nn issue? (same-c)	5	10	14	20	24	28

DIG 'EM
Kellogg's Sugar Smacks Giveaway: 1973 (2-3/8x6", 16 pgs.)

nn-4 different issues	1	3	4	6	8	10

DOC CARTER VD COMICS
Health Publications Institute, Raleigh, N. C. (Giveaway): 1949 (16 pgs. in color) (Paper-c)

nn	19	38	57	110	175	240

DONALD AND MICKEY MERRY CHRISTMAS (Formerly Famous Gang Book Of Comics)
K. K. Publ./Firestone Tire & Rubber Co.: 1943 - 1949 (Giveaway, 20 pgs.)
Put out each Christmas; 1943 issue titled "Firestone Presents Comics" (Disney)

1943-Donald Duck-r/WDC&S #32 by Carl Barks	71	142	213	451	776	1100
1944-Donald Duck-r/WDC&S #35 by Barks	68	136	204	432	741	1050
1945- "Donald Duck's Best Christmas", 8 pgs. Carl Barks; intro. & 1st app. Grandma Duck in comic books	100	200	300	635	1093	1550
1946-Donald Duck in "Santa's Stormy Visit", 8 pgs. Carl Barks	69	138	207	438	757	1075
1947-Donald Duck in "Three Good Little Ducks", 8 pgs. Carl Barks	69	138	207	438	757	1075
1948-Donald Duck in "Toyland", 8 pgs. Carl Barks	69	138	207	438	757	1075
1949-Donald Duck in "New Toys", 8 pgs. Barks	65	130	195	413	707	1000

DONALD DUCK
K. K. Publications: 1944 (Christmas giveaway, paper-c, 16 pgs.)(2 versions)

nn-Kelly cover reprint	92	184	276	584	1005	1425

DONALD DUCK AND THE RED FEATHER
Red Feather Giveaway: 1948 (8-1/2x11", 4 pgs., B&W)

nn	19	38	57	112	181	250

DONALD DUCK IN "THE LITTERBUG"
Keep America Beautiful: 1963 (5x7-1/4", 16 pgs., soft-c) (Disney giveaway)

nn	5	10	15	34	55	75

DONALD DUCK "PLOTTING PICNICKERS" (See Frito-Lay Giveaway)

DONALD DUCK'S SURPRISE PARTY
Walt Disney Productions: 1948 (16 pgs.) (Giveaway for Icy Frost Twins Ice Cream Bars)

nn-(Rare)-Kelly-c/a	232	464	696	1485	2543	3600

DOT AND DASH AND THE LUCKY JINGLE PIGGIE
Sears Roebuck Co.: 1942 (Christmas giveaway, 12 pgs.)

nn-Contains a war stamp album and a punch out Jingle Piggie bank	12	24	36	67	94	120

DOUBLE TALK (Also see Two-Faces)
Feature Publications: No date (1962?) (32 pgs., full color, slick-c)
Christian Anti-Communism Crusade (Giveaway)

nn-Sickle with blood-c	15	30	45	90	140	190

DRUMMER BOY AT GETTYSBURG
Eastern National Park & Monument Association: 1976

nn-Fred Ray-a	3	6	9	14	20	25

DUMBO (Walt Disney's..., The Flying Elephant)
Weatherbird Shoes/Ernest Kern Co.(Detroit)/ Wieboldt's (Chicago): 1941
(K.K. Publ. Giveaway)

nn-16 pgs., 9x10" (Rare)	42	84	126	265	445	625

nn-52 pgs., 5-1/2x8-1/2", slick cover in color; B&W interior; half text, half

Eat Right To Work and Win © Swift

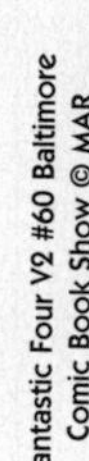

Fantastic Four V2 #60 Baltimore Comic Book Show © MAR

Forest Fire © AFA

	GD 2.0	VG 4.0	FN 6.0	VF 8.0	VF/NM 9.0	NM- 9.2
reprints 4-Color No. 17 (Dept. store)	22	44	66	131	216	300

DUMBO WEEKLY
Walt Disney Prod.: 1942 (Premium supplied by Diamond D-X Gas Stations)

	GD	VG	FN	VF	VF/NM	NM-
1	43	86	129	271	461	650
2-16	15	30	45	84	127	170
Binder only						250

NOTE: *A cover and binder came separate at gas stations. Came with membership card.*

EAT RIGHT TO WORK AND WIN
Swift & Company: 1942 (16 pgs.) (Giveaway)

Blondie, Henry, Flash Gordon by Alex Raymond, Toots & Casper, Thimble Theatre(Popeye), Tillie the Toiler, The Phantom, The Little King, & Bringing up Father - original strips just for this book -(in daily strip form which shows what foods we should eat and why)
31 62 93 186 301 425

EC SAMPLER - FREE COMIC BOOK DAY
Gemstone Publishing: May, 2008

Reprinted stories with restored color from Weird Science #6, Two-Fisted Tales #22, Crypt of Terror #17, Shock Suspenstories #6 — 2.50

EDWARD'S SHOES GIVEAWAY
Edward's Shoe Store: 1954 (Has clown on cover)

Contains comic with new cover. Many combinations possible. Contents determines price, 50-60 percent of original. (Similar to Comics From Weatherbird & Free Comics to You)

ELSIE THE COW
D. S. Publishing Co.

	GD	VG	FN	VF	VF/NM	NM-
Borden's cheese comic picture bk ("40, giveaway)	19	38	57	112	181	250
Borden Milk Giveaway-(16 pgs., nn) (3 ishs, 1957)	14	28	42	81	118	155
Elsie's Fun Book(1950; Borden Milk)	14	28	42	81	118	155
Everyday Birthday Fun With... (1957; 20 pgs.)(100th Anniversary); Kubert-a	14	28	42	81	118	155

ESCAPE FROM FEAR
Planned Parenthood of America: 1956, 1962, 1969 (Giveaway, 8 pgs., color) (On birth control)

	GD	VG	FN	VF	VF/NM	NM-
1956 edition	11	22	33	60	83	105
1962 edition	4	8	12	24	37	50
1969 edition	3	6	9	14	20	25

EVEL KNIEVEL
Marvel Comics Group (Ideal Toy Corp.): 1974 (Giveaway, 20 pgs.)

	GD	VG	FN	VF	VF/NM	NM-
nn-Contains photo on inside back-c	4	8	12	28	44	60

FAMOUS COMICS (Also see Favorite Comics)
Zain-Eppy/United Features Syndicate: No date; Mid 1930's (24 pgs., paper-c)

	GD	VG	FN	VF	VF/NM	NM-
nn-Reprinted from 1933 & 1934 newspaper strips in color; Joe Palooka, Hairbreadth Harry, Napoleon, The Nebbs, etc. (Many different versions known)	61	122	183	387	669	950

FAMOUS FAIRY TALES
K. K. Publ. Co.: 1942; 1943 (32 pgs.); 1944 (16 pgs.) (Giveaway, soft-c)

	GD	VG	FN	VF	VF/NM	NM-
1942-Kelly-a	39	78	117	236	388	540
1943-r-/Fairy Tale Parade No. 2,3; Kelly-a	25	50	75	150	245	340
1944-Kelly-a	22	44	66	131	216	300

FAMOUS FUNNIES -A CARNIVAL OF COMICS
Eastern Color: 1933

36 pgs., no date given, no publisher, no number; contains strip reprints of The Bungle Family, Dixie Dugan, Hairbreadth Harry, Joe Palooka, Keeping Up With the Jones, Mutt & Jeff, Reg'lar Fellers, S'Matter Pop, Strange As It Seems, and others. This book was sold by M. C. Gaines to Wheatena, Malt-O-Milk, John Wanamaker, Kinney Shoe Stores, & others to be given away as premiums and radio giveaways (1933). Originally came with a mailing envelope.
541 1082 1623 3950 6975 10,000

FAMOUS GANG BOOK OF COMICS (Becomes Donald & Mickey Merry Christmas 1943 on)
Firestone Tire & Rubber Co.: Dec, 1942 (Christmas giveaway, 32 pgs., paper-c)

	GD	VG	FN	VF	VF/NM	NM-
nn-(Rare)-Porky Pig, Bugs Bunny, Mary Jane & Sniffles, Elmer Fudd; r/Looney Tunes	68	136	204	432	741	1050

FANTASTIC FOUR
Marvel Comics

	GD	VG	FN	VF	VF/NM	NM-
nn (1981, 32 pgs.) Young Model Builders Club	2	4	6	9	12	15
Vol. 3 #60 Baltimore Comic Book Show (10/02, newspaper supplement) 200,000 copies were distributed to Baltimore Sun home subscribers to promote Baltimore Comic Con						4.00

FATHER OF CHARITY
Catechetical Guild Giveaway: No date (32 pgs.; paper cover)

	GD	VG	FN	VF	VF/NM	NM-
nn	5	10	15	24	29	34

FAVORITE COMICS (Also see Famous Comics)
Grocery Store Giveaway (Diff. Corp.) (detergent): 1934 (36 pgs.)

	GD	VG	FN	VF	VF/NM	NM-
Book 1-The Nebbs, Strange As It Seems, Napoleon, Joe Palooka, Dixie Dugan, S'Matter Pop, Hairbreadth Harry, etc. reprints	100	200	300	635	1093	1550
Book 2,3	61	122	183	387	664	940

FAWCETT MINIATURES (See Mighty Midget)
Fawcett Publications: 1946 (3-3/4x5", 12-24 pgs.) (Wheaties giveaways)

	GD	VG	FN	VF	VF/NM	NM-
Captain Marvel "And the Horn of Plenty"; Bulletman story	16	32	48	94	147	200
Captain Marvel "& the Raiders From Space"; Golden Arrow story	16	32	48	94	147	200
Captain Marvel Jr. "The Case of the Poison Press!" Bulletman story	16	32	48	94	147	200
Delecta of the Planets; C. C. Beck art; B&W inside; 12 pgs.; 3 printing variations (coloring) exist	20	40	60	120	198	275

FEARLESS FOSDICK
Capp Enterprises Inc.: 1951

	GD	VG	FN	VF	VF/NM	NM-
...& The Case of The Red Feather	6	12	18	27	33	38

FIGHT FOR FREEDOM
National Assoc. of Mfgrs./General Comics: 1949, 1951 (Giveaway, 16 pgs.)

	GD	VG	FN	VF	VF/NM	NM-
nn-Dan Barry-c/a; used in **POP**, pg. 102	6	12	18	31	38	45

FIRE AND BLAST
National Fire Protection Assoc.: 1952 (Giveaway, 16 pgs., paper-c)

	GD	VG	FN	VF	VF/NM	NM-
nn-Mart Baily A-Bomb-c; about fire prevention	15	30	45	85	130	175

FIRE CHIEF AND THE SAFE OL' FIREFLY, THE
National Board of Fire Underwriters: 1952 (16 pgs.) (Safety brochure given away at schools) (produced by American Visuals Corp.)(Eisner)

	GD	VG	FN	VF	VF/NM	NM-
nn-(Rare) Eisner-c/a	40	80	120	252	426	600

FLASH, THE
DC Comics

	GD	VG	FN	VF	VF/NM	NM-
nn-(1990) Brochure for CBS TV series						4.00
The Flash Comes to a Standstill (1981, General Foods giveaway, 8 pages, 3-1/2 x 6-3/4", oblong)	2	4	6	10	14	18

FLASH COMICS (Also see Captain Marvel and Funny Stuff)
National Periodical Publications: 1946 (6-1/2x8-1/4", 32 pgs.) (Wheaties Giveaway)

	GD	VG	FN	VF	VF/NM	NM-
nn-Johnny Thunder, Ghost Patrol, The Flash & Kubert Hawkman app.; Irwin Hasen-c/a	215	430	1000	-	-	-

NOTE: *All known copies were taped to Wheaties boxes and are never found in mint condition. Copies with light tape residue bring the listed prices in all grades*

FLASH FORCE 2000
DC Comics: 1984

	GD	VG	FN	VF	VF/NM	NM-
1-5						6.00

FLASH GORDON
Dell Publishing Co.: 1943 (20 pgs.)

	GD	VG	FN	VF	VF/NM	NM-
Macy's Giveaway-(Rare); not by Raymond	58	116	174	368	634	900

FLASH GORDON
Harvey Comics: 1951 (16 pgs. in color, regular size, paper-c) (Gordon Bread giveaway)

	GD	VG	FN	VF	VF/NM	NM-
1,2: 1-r/strips 10/24/37 - 2/6/38. 2-r/strips 7/14/40 - 10/6/40; Reprints by Raymond each....	2	4	6	10	14	18

NOTE: *Most copies have brittle edges.*

FLOOD RELIEF
Malibu Comics (Ultraverse): Jan, 1994 (36 pgs.)(Ordered thru mail w/$5.00 to Red Cross)

	GD	VG	FN	VF	VF/NM	NM-
1-Hardcase, Prime & Prototype app.						6.00

FOREST FIRE (Also see The Blazing Forest and Smokey Bear)
American Forestry Assn.(Commerical Comics): 1949 (dated-1950) (16 pgs., paper-c)

	GD	VG	FN	VF	VF/NM	NM-
nn-Intro/1st app. Smokey The Forest Fire Preventing Bear; created by Rudy Wendelein; Wendelein/Sparling-a; 'Carter Oil Co.' on back-c of original	18	36	54	103	162	220

FOREST RANGER HANDBOOK
Wrather Corp.: 1967 (5x7", 20 pgs., slick-c)

	GD	VG	FN	VF	VF/NM	NM-
nn-WIth Corey Stuart & Lassie photo-c	2	4	6	13	18	22

FORGOTTEN STORY BEHIND NORTH BEACH, THE
Catechetical Guild: No date (8 pgs., paper-c)

	GD	VG	FN	VF	VF/NM	NM-
nn	5	10	15	23	28	32

FORK IN THE ROAD
U.S. Army Recruiting Service: 1961 (16 pgs., paper-c)

	GD	VG	FN	VF	VF/NM	NM-
nn	2	4	6	11	16	20

48 FAMOUS AMERICANS
J. C. Penney Co. (Cpr. Edwin H. Stroh): 1947 (Giveaway) (Half-size in color)

	GD	VG	FN	VF	VF/NM	NM-
nn - Simon & Kirby-a	10	20	30	54	72	90

FOXHOLE ON YOUR LAWN
No Publisher: No date

Freedom Train © Condé Nast

Frito-Lay Giveaways © DIS

Gulf Funny Weekly #370 © Gulf

	GD 2.0	VG 4.0	FN 6.0	VF 8.0	VF/NM 9.0	NM- 9.2

nn-Charles Biro art 4 7 10 14 17 20

FRANKIE LUER'S SPACE ADVENTURES
Luer Packing Co.: 1955 (5x7", 36 pgs., slick-c)
nn - With Davey Rocket 4 8 12 17 21 24

FREDDY
Charlton Comics
Schiff's Shoes Presents... #1 (1959)-Giveaway 4 8 11 16 19 22

FREE COMICS TO YOU FROM... (name of shoe store) (Has clown on cover & another with a rabbit) (Like comics from Weather Bird & Edward's Shoes)
Shoe Store Giveaway: Circa 1956, 1960-61
Contains a comic bound with new cover - several combinations possible; some Harvey titles known. Contents determine price.

FREEDOM TRAIN
Street & Smith Publications: 1948 (Giveaway)
nn-Powell-c w/mailer 18 36 54 103 162 220

FREIHOFER'S COMIC BOOK
All-American Comics: 1940s (7 1/2 x 10 1/4")
2nd edition-(Scarce) Cover features All-American Comics characters Ultra-Man, Hop Harrigan, Red, White and Blue and others 57 114 171 362 619 875

FRIENDLY GHOST, CASPER, THE
Harvey Publications: 1967 (16 pgs.)
American Dental Assoc. giveaway-Small size 3 6 9 17 25 32

FRITO-LAY GIVEAWAY
Frito-Lay: 1962 (3-1/4x7", soft-c, 16 pgs.) (Disney)
nn-Donald Duck "Plotting Picnickers" 5 10 15 32 51 70
nn-Ludwig Von Drake "Fish Stampede" 3 6 9 20 30 40
nn- Mickey Mouse & Goofy "Bicep Bungle" 4 8 12 22 34 45

FRONTIER DAYS
Robin Hood Shoe Store (Brown Shoe): 1956 (Giveaway)
1 4 7 10 14 17 20

FRONTIERS OF FREEDOM
Institute of Life Insurance: 1950 (Giveaway, paper cover)
nn-Dan Barry-a 8 16 24 44 57 70

FUNNIES ON PARADE (Premium)(See Toy World Funnies)
Eastern Color Printing Co.: 1933 (36 pgs., slick cover)
No date or publisher listed
nn-Contains Sunday page reprints of Mutt & Jeff, Joe Palooka, Hairbreadth Harry, Reg'lar Fellers, Skippy, & others (10,000 print run). This book was printed for Proctor & Gamble to be given away & came out before Famous Funnies or Century of Comics. 1000 2000 3000 6000 10,500 15,000

FUNNY PICTURE STORIES
Comics Magazine Co./Centaur Publications: 1930s (Giveaway, 16-20 pgs., slick-c)
Promotes diff. laundries; has box on cover where "your Laundry Name" is printed 31 62 93 186 301 425

FUNNY STUFF (Also see Captain Marvel & Flash Comics)
National Periodical Publications (Wheaties Giveaway): 1946 (6-1/2x8-1/4")
nn-(Scarce)-Dodo & the Frog, Three Mouseketeers, etc.; came taped to Wheaties box; never found in better than fine 170 340 520 – – –

FUTURE COP: L.A.P.D. (Electronic Arts video game)
DC Comics (WildStorm): 1998
nn-Ron Lim-a/Dave Johnson-c 2.50

FUTURE SHOCK
Image Comics: 2006 (Free Comic Book Day giveaway)
...: FCBD 2006 Edition; Spawn, Invincible, Savage Dragon & others short stories 2.50

GABBY HAYES WESTERN (Movie star)
Fawcett Publications
Quaker Oats Giveaway nn's(#1-5, 1951, 2-1/2x7") (Kagran Corp.)-...In Tracks of Guilt, ...In the Fence Post Mystery, ...In the Accidental Sherlock, ...In the Frame-Up, ...In the Double Cross Brand known 10 20 30 54 72 90
Mailing Envelope (has illo of Gabby on front) 10 20 30 54 72 90

GARY GIBSON COMICS (Donut club membership)
National Dunking Association: 1950 (Included in donut box with pin and card)
1-Western soft-c, 16 pgs.; folded into the box 5 10 14 20 24 28

GENE AUTRY COMICS
Dell Publishing Co.
...Adventure Comics And Play-Fun Book ('47)-32 pgs., 8x6-1/2"; games, comics, magic (Pillsbury premium) 26 52 78 154 252 350
Quaker Oats Giveaway(1950)-2-1/2x6-3/4"; 5 different versions; "Death Card Gang", "Phantoms of the Cave", "Riddle of Laughing Mtn.", "Secret of Lost Valley", "Bond of the Broken Arrow" (came in wrapper) each... 12 24 36 67 94 120
Mailing Envelope (has illo. of Gene on front) 12 24 36 67 94 120
3-D Giveaway(1953)-Pocket-size; 5 different 12 24 36 67 94 120
Mailing Envelope (no art on front) 9 18 27 50 650 80

GENE AUTRY TIM (Formerly Tim) (Becomes Tim in Space)
Tim Stores: 1950 (Half-size) (B&W Giveaway)
nn-Several issues (All Scarce) 19 38 57 109 172 235

GENERAL FOODS SUPER-HEROES
DC Comics: 1979, 1980
1-4 (1979), 1-4 (1980) each... 12.00

G. I. COMICS (Also see Jeep & Overseas Comics)
Giveaways: 1945 - No. 73?, 1946 (Distributed to U. S. Armed Forces)
1-73-Contains Prince Valiant by Foster, Blondie, Smilin' Jack, Mickey Finn, Terry & the Pirates, Donald Duck, Alley Oop, Moon Mullins & Capt. Easy strip reprints (at least 73 issues known to exist) 8 16 24 42 54 65

GOLDEN ARROW
Fawcett Publications
...Well Known Comics (1944; 12 pgs.; 8-1/2x10-1/2"; paper-c; glued binding)- Bestmaid/ Samuel Lowe giveaway; printed in green 10 20 30 54 72 90

GOLDILOCKS & THE THREE BEARS
K. K. Publications: 1943 (Giveaway)
nn 13 26 39 74 105 135

GREAT PEOPLE OF GENESIS, THE
David C. Cook Publ. Co.: No date (Religious giveaway, 64 pgs.)
nn-Reprint/Sunday Pix Weekly 5 10 15 23 28 32

GREAT SACRAMENT, THE
Catechetical Guild: 1953 (Giveaway, 36 pgs.)
nn 5 10 15 22 26 30

GREEN HORNET
Dynamite Entertainment: 2010 (Free Comic Book Day giveaway)
1 - FCBD Edition; 5 previews of various new Green Hornet series; Cassaday-c 2.50

GREEN JET COMICS, THE (See Comic Books, Series 1)

GRENADA
Commercial Comics Co.: 1983 (Giveaway produced by the CIA)
1-Air dropped over Grenada during the 1983 invasion 30.00

GRIT (YOU'VE GOT TO HAVE...)
GRIT Publishing Co.: 1959
nn-GRIT newspaper sales recruitment comic; Schaffenberger-a. Later version has altered artwork 5 10 15 22 26 30

GULF FUNNY WEEKLY (Gulf Comic Weekly No. 1-4)(See Standard Oil Comics)
Gulf Oil Company (Giveaway): 1933 - No. 422, 5/23/41 (in full color; 4 pgs.; tabloid size to 2/3/39; 2/10/39 on, regular comic book size)(early issues undated)
1 61 122 183 387 669 950
2-5 28 56 84 165 270 375
6-30 18 36 54 105 165 225
31-100 14 28 42 80 115 150
101-196 10 20 30 54 72 90
197-Wings Winfair begins(1/29/37); by Fred Meagher beginning in 1938 22 44 66 129 212 295
198-300 (Last tabloid size) 14 28 42 81 118 155
301-350 (Regular size) 9 18 27 52 69 85
351-422 8 16 24 42 54 65

GULLIVER'S TRAVELS
Macy's Department Store: 1939, small size
nn-Christmas giveaway 14 28 42 76 108 140

GUN THAT WON THE WEST, THE
Winchester-Western Division & Olin Mathieson Chemical Corp.: 1956 (Giveaway, 24 pgs.)
nn-Painted-c 5 10 15 24 30 35

HAPPINESS AND HEALING FOR YOU (Also see Oral Roberts'...)
Commercial Comics: 1955 (36 pgs., slick cover) (Oral Roberts Giveaway)
nn 9 18 27 52 69 85
NOTE: *The success of this book prompted Oral Roberts to go into the publishing business himself to produce his own material.*

HAPPY TOOTH
DC Comics: 1996
1 3.00

HARLEM YOUTH REPORT (Also see All-Negro Comics and Negro Romances)

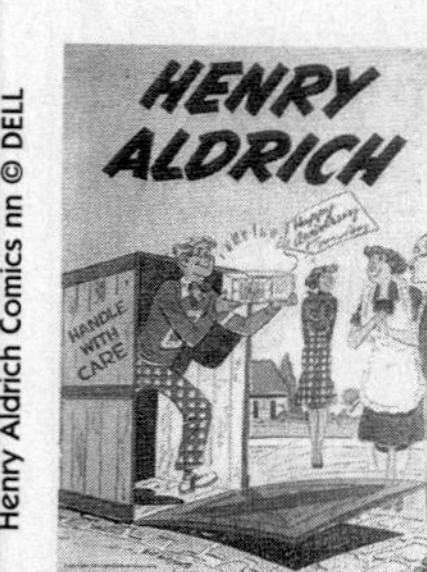

Henry Aldrich Comics nn © DELL

Iron Man/Thor 2010 FCBD Ed. © MAR

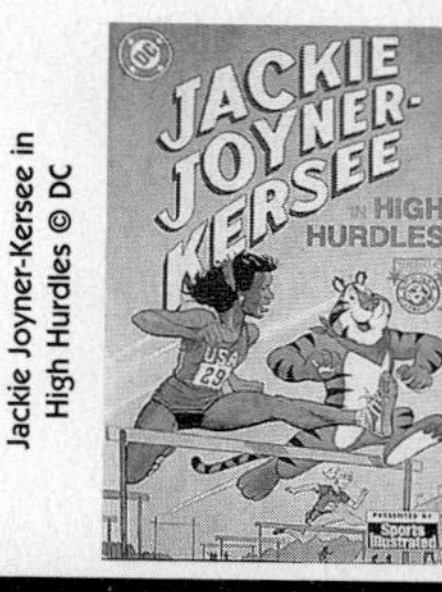

Jackie Joyner-Kersee in High Hurdles © DC

GD 2.0 | VG 4.0 | FN 6.0 | VF 8.0 | VF/NM 9.0 | NM- 9.2

Custom Comics, Inc.: 1964 (Giveaway)(No #1-4)
5-"Youth in the Ghetto" and "The Blueprint For Change"; distr. in Harlem only; has map of central Harlem on back-c (scarce) 100 200 300 635 1093 1550

HAWKMAN - THE SKY'S THE LIMIT
DC Comics: 1981 (General Foods giveaway, 8 pages, 3-1/2 x 6-3/4", oblong)
nn 2 4 6 10 14 18

HAWTHORN-MELODY FARMS DAIRY COMICS
Everybody's Publishing Co.: No date (1950's) (Giveaway)
nn-Cheerie Chick, Tuffy Turtle, Robin Koo Koo, Donald & Longhorn Legends 2 4 6 8 11 14

HELLBOY
Dark Horse Comics: Apr, 2008
... : Free Comic Book Day; Three short stories; Mignola-c; art by Fegredo, Davis, Azaceta 2.50

HENRY ALDRICH COMICS (TV)
Dell Publishing Co.
Giveaway (16 pgs., soft-c, 1951)-Capehart radio 3 6 9 17 25 32

HERE IS SANTA CLAUS
Goldsmith Publishing Co. (Kann's in Washington, D.C.): 1930s (16 pgs., 8 in color) (stiff paper covers)
nn 13 26 39 72 101 130

HERE'S HOW AMERICA'S CARTOONISTS HELP TO SELL U.S. SAVINGS BONDS
Harvey Comics: 1950? (16 pgs., giveaway, paper cover)
Contains: Joe Palooka, Donald Duck, Archie, Kerry Drake, Red Ryder, Blondie & Steve Canyon 19 38 57 112 181 250

HISTORY OF GAS
American Gas Assoc.: Mar, 1947 (Giveaway, 16 pgs.)
nn-Miss Flame narrates 6 12 18 29 36 42

HOME DEPOT, SAFETY HEROES
Marvel Comics.: Oct, 2005 (Giveaway)
nn-Spider-Man and the Fantastic Four on the cover; Olliffe-a/c; Roseman-s 2.50

HONEYBEE BIRDWHISTLE AND HER PET PEPI (Introducing...)
Newspaper Enterprise Assoc.: 1969 (Giveaway, 24 pgs., B&W, slick cover)
nn-Contains Freckles newspaper strips with a short biography of Henry Fornhals (artist) & Fred Fox (writer) of the strip 4 8 12 28 44 60

HOODS UP
Fram Corp.: 1953 (15¢, distributed to service station owners, 16 pgs.)
1-(Very Rare; only 2 known); Eisner-c/a in all (a CGC 9.0 copy sold for $1840 in 2006)
2-6-(Very Rare; only 1 known of #3, 2 known of #2,4) 48 96 144 302 514 725
NOTE: *Convertible Connie gives tips for service stations, selling Fram oil filters.*

HOPALONG CASSIDY
Fawcett Publications
Grape Nuts Flakes giveaway (1950,9x6") 14 28 42 80 115 150
...& the Mad Barber (1951 Bond Bread giveaway)-7x5"; used in **SOTI**, pgs. 308,309 18 36 54 107 169 230
...Meets the Brend Brothers Bandits (1951 Bond Bread giveaway, color, paper-c, 16 pgs., 3-1/2x7")- Fawcett Publ. 9 18 27 50 65 80
...Strange Legacy (1951 Bond Bread giveaway) 9 18 27 50 65 80
White Tower Giveaway (1946, 16pgs., paper-c) 10 20 30 56 76 90

HOPELESS SAVAGES
Oni Press: May, 2002 (B&W)
Free Comic Book Day giveaway-Reprints #1 with "Free Comic Book Day" banner on-c 2.50

HOPPY THE MARVEL BUNNY (WELL KNOWN COMICS)
Fawcett Publications: 1944 (8-1/2x10-1/2", paper-c)
Bestmaid/Samuel Lowe (printed in red or blue) 10 20 30 56 76 95

HOT STUFF, THE LITTLE DEVIL
Harvey Publications (Illustrated Humor):1963
Shoestore Giveaway 4 8 12 22 34 45

HOW KIDS ENJOY NEW YORK
American Airlines: 1966 (Giveaway, 40 pgs., 4x9")
nn-Includes 8 color pages by Bob Kane featuring a tour of New York and his studio (a VG copy sold for $180 and a FN+ sold for $250 in 2004)

HOW STALIN HOPES WE WILL DESTROY AMERICA
Joe Lowe Co. (Pictorial Media): 1951 (Giveaway, 16 pgs.)
nn 43 86 129 271 461 650

HURRICANE KIDS, THE (Also See Magic Morro, The Owl, Popular Comics #45)
R.S. Callender: 1941 (Giveaway, 7-1/2x5-1/4", soft-c)
nn-Will Ely-a. 9 18 27 47 61 75

IF THE DEVIL WOULD TALK
Roman Catholic Catechetical Guild/Impact Publ.: 1950; 1958 (32 pgs.; paper cover; in full color)
nn-(Scarce)-About secularism (20-30 copies known to exist); very low distribution 80 160 240 508 874 1240
1958 Edition-(Impact Publ.); art & script changed to meet church criticism of earlier edition; 80 plus copies known to exist 26 52 78 154 252 350
Black & White version of nn edition; small size; only 4 known copies exist 32 64 96 189 310 430
NOTE: *The original edition of this book was printed and killed by the Guild's board of directors. It is believed that a very limited number of copies were distributed. The 1958 version was a complete bomb with very limited, if any, circulation. In 1979, 11 original, 4 1958 reprints, and 4 B&W's surfaced from the Guild's old files in St. Paul, Minnesota.*

IMAGE COMICS SUMMER SPECIAL
Image Comics: July, 2004 (Free Comic Book Day giveaway)
1-New short stories of Spawn, Invincible, Savage Dragon and Witchblade 2.50

IN LOVE WITH JESUS
Catechetical Educational Society: 1952 (Giveaway, 36 pgs.)
nn 7 14 21 37 46 55

INTERSTATE THEATRES' FUN CLUB COMICS
Interstate Theatres: Mid 1940's (10¢ on cover) (B&W cover) (Premium)
Cover features MLJ characters looking at a copy of Top-Notch Comics, but contains an early Detective Comic on inside; many combinations possible 11 22 33 60 83 105

IN THE GOOD HANDS OF THE ROCKEFELLER TEAM
Country Art Studios: No date (paper cover, 8 pgs.)
nn-Joe Simon-a 8 16 24 42 54 65

IRON GIANT
DC Comics: 1999 (4 pages, theater giveaway)
1-Previews movie 3.00

IRON HORSE GOES TO WAR, THE
Association of American Railroads: 1960 (Giveaway, 16 pgs.)
nn-Civil War & railroads 3 6 9 14 20 25

IRON MAN
Marvel Comics
Marvel Halloween Ashcan 2007 (8-1/2" x 5-3/8") updated origin; Michael Golden-c 2.00
Free Comic Book Day 2010 (Iron Man: Supernova) #1 (5/10, 9-1/2" x 6-1/4") Nova app. 2.00
Free Comic Book Day 2010 (Iron Man/Thor) #1 (5/10, 9-1/2" x 6-1/4") Romita Jr.-a/c 2.00

IS THIS TOMORROW?
Catechetical Guild: 1947 (One Shot) (3 editions) (52 pgs.)
1-Theme of communists taking over the USA; (no price on cover) Used in **POP**, pg. 102 22 44 66 131 216 300
1-(10¢ on cover) 26 52 78 154 252 350
1-Has blank circle with no price on cover 28 56 84 165 270 375
Black & White advance copy titled "Confidential" (52 pgs.)-Contains script and art edited out of the color edition, including one page of extreme violence showing mob nailing a Cardinal to a door; (only two known copies). A VF+ sold in 2/08 for $3346. A NM 9.6 sold in 1/07 for $5975
NOTE: *The original color version first sold for 10 cents. Since sales were good, it was later printed as a giveaway. Approximately four million in total were printed. The two black and white copies listed plus two other versions as well as a full color untrimmed version surfaced in 1979 from the Guild's old files in St. Paul, Minnesota.*

IT'S FUN TO STAY ALIVE
National Automobile Dealers Association: 1948 (Giveaway, 16 pgs., heavy stock paper)
Featuring: Bugs Bunny, The Berrys, Dixie Dugan, Elmer, Henry, Tim Tyler, Bruce Gentry, Abbie & Slats, Joe Jinks, The Toodles, & Cokey; all art copyright 1946-48 drawn especially for this book 15 30 45 90 140 190

JACK & JILL VISIT TOYTOWN WITH ELMER THE ELF
Butler Brothers (Toytown Stores): 1949 (Giveaway, 16 pgs., paper cover)
nn 5 10 15 22 26 30

JACK ARMSTRONG (Radio)(See True Comics)
Parents' Institute: 1949
12-Premium version (distr. in Chicago only); Free printed on upper right-c; no price (Rare) 18 36 54 107 169 230

JACKIE JOYNER KERSEE IN HIGH HURDLES (Kellogg's Tony's Sports Comics)
DC Comics: 1992 (Sports Illustrated)
nn 5.00

JACKPOT OF FUN COMIC BOOK
DCA Food Ind.: 1957, giveaway
nn-Features Howdy Doody 11 22 33 64 90 115

JEEP COMICS

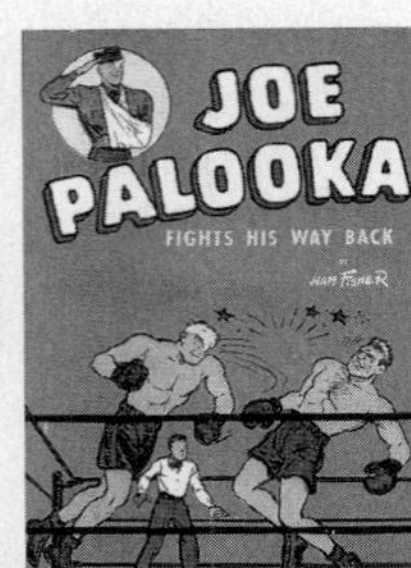

Joe Palooka Fights His Way Back © HARV

King James The King of Basketball © DC

Kite Fun Book 1963 © Jay Ward

	GD 2.0	VG 4.0	FN 6.0	VF 8.0	VF/NM 9.0	NM- 9.2

GD 2.0 VG 4.0 FN 6.0 VF 8.0 VF/NM 9.0 NM- 9.2

R. B. Leffingwell & Co.: 1945 - 1946

1-46 (Giveaways)-Strip reprints in all; Tarzan, Flash Gordon, Blondie, The Nebbs, Little Iodine, Red Ryder, Don Winslow, The Phantom, Johnny Hazard, Katzenjammer Kids; distr. to U.S. Armed Forces from 1945-1946 — 6 12 18 31 38 45

JINGLE BELLS CHRISTMAS BOOK
Montgomery Ward (Giveaway): 1971 (20 pgs., B&W inside, slick-c)

nn — 6.00

JOAN OF ARC
Catechetical Guild (Topix) (Giveaway): No date (28 pgs., blank back-c)

nn-Ingrid Bergman photo-c; Addison Burbank-a — 12 24 36 69 97 125

NOTE: *Unpublished version exists which came from the Guild's files.*

JOE PALOOKA (2nd Series)
Harvey Publications

...Body Building Instruction Book (1958 B&M Sports Toy giveaway, 16pgs., 5-1/4x7")-Origin — 9 18 27 47 61 75

...Fights His Way Back (1945 Giveaway, 24 pgs.) Family Comics — 15 30 45 85 130 175

...in Hi There! (1949 Red Cross giveaway, 12 pgs., 4-3/4x6") — 9 18 27 50 65 80

...in It's All in the Family (1945 Red Cross giveaway, 16 pgs., regular size) — 11 22 33 60 83 105

JOE THE GENIE OF STEEL
U.S. Steel Corp., Pittsburgh, PA: 1950 (16 pgs.)

nn — 5 10 15 22 26 30

JOHNNY JINGLE'S LUCKY DAY
American Dairy Assoc.: 1956 (16 pgs.; 7-1/4x5-1/8") (Giveaway) (Disney)

nn — 5 10 15 24 30 35

JO-JOY (The Adventures of...)
W. T. Grant Dept. Stores: 1945 - 1953 (Christmas gift comic, 16 pgs., 7-1/16x10-1/4")

1945-53 issues — 6 12 18 29 36 42

JOLLY CHRISTMAS BOOK (See Christmas Journey Through Space)
Promotional Publ. Co.: 1951; 1954; 1955 (36 pgs.; 24 pgs.)

1951-(Woolworth giveaway)-slightly oversized; no slick cover; Marv Levy-c/a — 7 14 21 37 46 55

1954-(Hot Shoppes giveaway)-regular size-reprints 1951 issue; slick cover added; 24 pgs.; no ads — 6 12 18 31 38 45

1955-(J. M. McDonald Co. giveaway)-reg. size — 6 12 18 28 34 40

JOURNEY OF DISCOVERY WITH MARK STEEL (See Mark Steel)

JUGHEAD COMICS. NIGHT AT GEPPI'S ENTERTAINMENT MUSEUM
Archie Comic Publ. Inc: 2008

Free Comic Book Day giveaway - New story; Archie gang visits GEM; Steve Geppi app. — 2.50

JUMPING JACKS PRESENTS THE WHIZ KIDS
Jumping Jacks Stores giveaway: 1978 (In 3-D) with glasses (4 pgs.)

nn — 6.00

JUNGLE BOOK FUN BOOK, THE (Disney)
Baskin Robbins: 1978

nn-Ice Cream giveaway — 2 4 6 9 12 15

JUSTICE LEAGUE ADVENTURES (Based on Cartoon Network series)
DC Comics: May, 2002

Free Comic Book Day giveaway-Reprints #1 with "Free Comic Book Day" banner on-c — 4.00

JUSTICE LEAGUE OF AMERICA
DC Comics: 1999 (included in Justice League of America Monopoly game); 2007

nn - Reprints 1st app. in Brave and the Bold #28 — 2.50

Free Comic Book Day giveaway-Reprints #0 with "Free Comic Book Day" banner on-c — 2.50

JUSTICE LEAGUE UNLIMITED (Based on Cartoon Network series)
DC Comics: May, 2006

Free Comic Book Day giveaway-Reprints #1 with "Free Comic Book Day" banner on-c — 2.25

KASCO KOMICS
Kasko Grainfeed (Giveaway): 1945; No. 2, 1949 (Regular size, paper-c)

1(1945)-Similar to Katy Keene; Bill Woggon-a; 28 pgs.; 6-7/8x9-7/8" — 17 34 51 100 158 215

2(1949)-Woggon-c/a — 13 26 39 74 105 135

KATY AND KEN VISIT SANTA WITH MISTER WISH
S. S. Kresge Co. : 1948 (Giveaway, 16 pgs., paper-c)

nn — 6 12 18 29 36 42

KELLOGG'S CINNAMON MINI-BUNS SUPER-HEROES
DC Comics: 1993 (4 1/4" x 2 3/4")

4 editions: Flash, Justice League America, Superman, Wonder Woman and the Star Riders each..... — 4.00

KERRY DRAKE DETECTIVE CASES
Publisher's Syndicate

...in the Case of the Sleeping City-(1951)-16 pg. giveaway for armed forces; paper cover — 6 12 18 29 36 42

KEY COMICS
Key Clothing Co./Peterson Clothing: 1951 - 1956 (32 pgs.) (Giveaway)

Contains a comic from different publishers bound with new cover. Cover changed each year. Many combinations possible. Distributed in Nebraska, Iowa, & Kansas. Contents would determine price, 40-60 percent of original.

KING JAMES "THE KING OF BASKETBALL"
DC Comics: 2004 (Promo comic for LeBron James and Powerade Flava23 sports drink)

nn - Ten different covers by various artists; 4 covers for retail, 4 for mail-in, 1 for military commissaries, and 1 general market; Damion Scott-a/Gary Phillips-s — 2.50

KIRBY'S SHOES COMICS
Kirby's Shoes: 1959 (8 pgs., soft-c)

nn-Features Kirby the Golden Bear — 3 5 7 10 12 14

KITE FUN BOOK
Pacific, Gas & Electric/Sou. California Edison/Florida Power & Light/ Missouri Public Service Co.: 1952 - 1998 (16 pgs, 5x7-1/4", soft-c)

	GD 2.0	VG 4.0	FN 6.0	VF 8.0	VF/NM 9.0	NM- 9.2
1952-Having Fun With Kites (P.G.&E.)	12	24	36	69	97	125
1953-Pinocchio Learns About Kites (Disney)	43	86	129	271	461	650
1954-Donald Duck Tells About Kites-Fla. Power, S.C.E. & version with label issues -Barks pencils-8 pgs.; inks-7 pgs. (Rare)	284	568	852	1803	3102	4400
1954-Donald Duck Tells About Kites-P.G.&E. issue -7th page redrawn changing middle 3 panels to show P.G.&E. in story line; (All Barks-a) Scarce	232	464	696	1473	2537	3600
1955-Brer Rabbit in "A Kite Tail" (Disney)	29	58	87	170	278	385
1956-Woody Woodpecker (Lantz)	14	28	42	80	115	150
1957-Ruff and Reddy (exist?)						
1958-Tom And Jerry (M.G.M.)	10	20	30	54	72	90
1959-Bugs Bunny (Warner Bros.)	5	10	15	30	48	65
1960-Porky Pig (Warner Bros.)	5	10	15	32	51	70
1960-Bugs Bunny (Warner Bros.)	5	10	15	32	51	70
1961-Huckleberry Hound (Hanna-Barbera)	6	12	18	37	59	80
1962-Yogi Bear (Hanna-Barbera)	4	8	12	28	44	60
1963-Rocky and Bullwinkle (TV)(Jay Ward)	7	14	21	49	80	110
1963-Top Cat (TV)(Hanna-Barbera)	4	8	12	24	37	50
1964-Magilla Gorilla (TV)(Hanna-Barbera)	4	8	12	22	34	45
1965-Jinks, Pixie and Dixie (TV)(Hanna-Barbera)	3	6	9	18	27	35
1965-Tweety and Sylvester (Warner); S.C.E. version with Reddy Kilowatt app.	2	4	6	11	16	20
1966-Secret Squirrel (Hanna-Barbera); S.C.E. version with Reddy Kilowatt app.	6	12	18	37	59	80
1967-Beep! Beep! The Road Runner (TV)(Warner)	3	6	9	14	20	25
1968-Bugs Bunny (Warner Bros.)	3	6	9	16	22	28
1969-Dastardly and Muttley (TV)(Hanna-Barbera)	4	8	12	24	37	50
1970-Rocky and Bullwinkle (TV)(Jay Ward)	5	10	15	32	51	70
1971-Beep! Beep! The Road Runner (TV)(Warner)	3	6	9	14	20	25
1972-The Pink Panther (TV)	2	4	6	13	18	22
1973-Lassie (TV)	3	6	9	18	27	35
1974-Underdog (TV)	3	6	9	14	20	25
1975-Ben Franklin	2	4	6	9	13	16
1976-The Brady Bunch (TV)	3	6	9	18	27	35
1977-Ben Franklin (exist?)	2	4	6	9	13	16
1977-Popeye	2	4	6	11	16	20
1978-Happy Days (TV)	3	6	9	14	20	25
1979-Eight is Enough (TV)	2	4	6	11	16	20
1980-The Waltons (TV, released in 1981)	2	4	6	11	16	20
1982-Tweety and Sylvester	2	4	6	10	14	18
1984-Smokey Bear	2	4	6	8	11	14
1986-Road Runner	2	4	6	8	10	12
1997-Thomas Edison						4.00
1998-Edison Field (Anaheim Stadium)						3.00

KNOW YOUR MASS
Catechetical Guild: No. 303, 1958 (35¢, 100 Pg. Giant) (Square binding)

303-In color — 7 14 21 35 43 50

KOLYNOS PRESENTS THE WHITE GUARD
Whitehall Pharmacal Co.: 1949 (paper cover, 8 pgs.)

nn — 6 12 18 27 33 38

K. O. PUNCH, THE (Also see Lucky Fights It Through & Sidewalk Romance)
E. C. Comics: 1948 (VD Educational giveaway)

nn-Feldstein-splash; Kamen-a — 83 166 249 527 906 1285

Little Abner & the Creatures From Drop-Outer Space © HARV

Loaded #1 © Gremlin

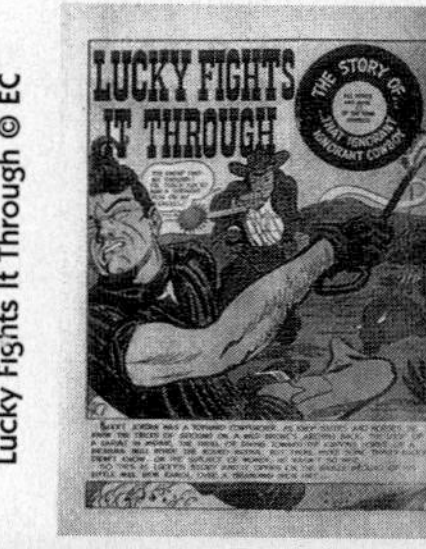
Lucky Fights It Through © EC

GD VG FN VF VF/NM NM-
2.0 4.0 6.0 8.0 9.0 9.2

KOREA MY HOME (Also see Yalta to Korea)
Johnstone and Cushing: nd (1950s)
nn-Anti-communist; Korean War 20 40 60 116 191 265

KRIM-KO KOMICS
Krim-ko Chocolate Drink: 5/18/35 - No. 6, 6/22/35; 1936 - 1939 (weekly)
1-(16 pgs., soft-c, Dairy giveaways)-Tom, Mary & Sparky Advs. by Russell Keaton, Jim Hawkins by Dick Moores, Mystery Island! by Rick Yager begin
14 28 42 76 108 140
2-6 (6/22/35) 10 20 30 56 76 95
Lola, Secret Agent; 184 issues, 4 pg. giveaways - all original stories each.... 7 14 21 37 46 55

LABOR IS A PARTNER
Catechetical Guild Educational Society: 1949 (32 pgs., paper-c)
nn-Anti-communism 20 40 60 116 191 265
Confidential Preview-(8-1/2x11", B&W, saddle stitched)-only one known copy; text varies from color version, advertises next book on secularism (If the Devil Would Talk)
24 48 72 142 234 325

LADY AND THE TRAMP IN "BUTTER LATE THAN NEVER"
American Dairy Assoc. (Premium): 1955 (16 pgs., 5x7-1/4", soft-c) (Disney)
nn 8 16 24 44 57 70

LASSIE (TV)
Dell Publ. Co
The Adventures of... nn-(Red Heart Dog Food giveaway, 1949)-16 pgs, soft-c; 1st app. Lassie in comics 31 62 93 184 302 420

LEAVE IT TO CHANCE
Image Comics: 2003
Free Comic Book Day Edition - James Robinson-s/Paul Smith-a 2.50

LEGION OF SUPER-HEROES IN THE 31ST CENTURY
DC Comics: June, 2007 (Free Comic Book Day giveaway)
1-Reprints #1 2.50

LIFE OF THE BLESSED VIRGIN
Catechetical Guild (Giveaway): 1950 (68pgs.) (square binding)
nn-Contains "The Woman of the Promise" & "Mother of Us All" rebound
7 14 21 35 43 50

LIGHTNING RACERS
DC Comics: 1989
1 4.50

LI'L ABNER (Al Capp's) (Also see Natural Disasters!)
Harvey Publ./Toby Press
...& the Creatures from Drop-Outer Space-nn (Job Corps giveaway; 36 pgs., in color) (entire book by Frank Frazetta) 21 42 63 121 201 280
...Joins the Navy (1950) (Toby Press Premium) 11 22 33 62 86 110
Al Capp by Li'l Abner (Circa 1946, nd, giveaway) Al Capp bio and his life as an amputee
11 22 33 62 86 110

LITTLE ALONZO
Macy's Dept. Store: 1938 (B&W, 5-1/2x8-1/2")(Christmas giveaway)
nn-By Ferdinand the Bull's Munro Leaf 9 18 27 50 65 80

LITTLE ARCHIE (See Archie Comics)

LITTLE DOT
Harvey Publications
Shoe store giveaway 2 4 8 12 28 44 60

LITTLE FIR TREE, THE
W. T. Grant Co. : nd (1942) (8-1/2x11") (12 pgs. with cover, color & B&W, heavy paper) (Christmas giveaway)
nn-Story by Hans Christian Anderson; 8 pg. Kelly-r/Santa Claus Funnies (not signed); X-Mas-c
87 174 261 552 951 1350

LITTLE KLINKER
Little Klinker Ventures: Nov, 1960 (20 pgs.) (slick cover) (Montgomery Ward Giveaway)
nn 2 4 6 9 13 16

LITTLE MISS SUNBEAM COMICS
Magazine Enterprises/Quality Bakers of America
Bread Giveaway 1-4(Quality Bakers, 1949-50)-14 pgs. each
6 12 18 31 38 45
Bread Giveaway (1957,61; 16pgs, reg. size) 5 10 15 24 30 35

LITTLE ORPHAN ANNIE
David McKay Publ./Dell Publishing Co.
Junior Commandos Giveaway (same-c as 4-Color #18, K.K. Publ.)(Big Shoe Store); same back cover as '47 Popped Wheat giveaway; 16 pgs; flag-c; r/strips 9/7/42-10/10/42 26 52 78 154 252 350
Popped Wheat Giveaway ('47)-16 pgs. full color; reprints strips from 5/3/40 to 6/20/40
4 8 12 18 22 25
Quaker Sparkies Giveaway (1940) 18 36 54 103 162 220
Quaker Sparkies Giveaway (1941, full color, 20 pgs.); "LOA and the Rescue"; r/strips 4/13/39-6/21/39 & 7/6/39-7/17/39. "LOA and the Kidnappers"; r/strips 11/28/38-1/28/39 15 30 45 94 147 200
Quaker Sparkies Giveaway (1942, full color, 20 pgs.); "LOA and Mr. Gudge"; r/strips 2/13/38-3/21/38 & 4/18/37-5/30/37. "LOA and the Great Am"
15 30 45 88 137 185

LITTLE TREE THAT WASN'T WANTED, THE
W. T. Grant Co. (Giveaway): 1960, (Color, 28 pgs.)
nn-Christmas story, puzzles and games 4 8 12 22 34 45

LOADED (Also see Re-Loaded)
DC Comics: 1995 (Interplay Productions)
1-Garth Ennis-s; promotes video game 4.00

LONE RANGER, THE
Dell Publishing Co.
Cheerios Giveaways (1954, 16 pgs., 2-1/2x7", soft-c) #1- "The Lone Ranger, His Mask & How He Met Tonto". #2- "The Lone Ranger & the Story of Silver"
each.... 15 30 45 85 130 175
Doll Giveaways (Gabriel Ind.)(1973, 3-1/4x5")- "The Story of The Lone Ranger," "The Carson City Bank Robbery" & "The Apache Buffalo Hunt"
2 4 6 12 16 20
How the Lone Ranger Captured Silver Book(1936)-Silvercup Bread giveaway
55 110 165 349 600 850
...In Milk for Big Mike (1955, Dairy Association giveaway), soft-c; 5x7-1/4", 16 pgs. 14 28 42 80 115 150
Legend of The Lone Ranger (1969, 16 pgs., giveaway)-Origin The Lone Ranger
4 8 12 22 34 45
Merita Bread giveaway (1954, 16 pgs., 5x7-1/4")- "How to Be a Lone Ranger Health & Safety Scout" 18 36 54 103 162 220

LONE RANGER COMICS, THE
Lone Ranger, Inc. : Book 1, 1939(inside) (shows 1938 on-c) (52 pgs. in color; regular size) (Ice cream mail order)
Book 1-(Scarce)-The first western comic devoted to a single character; not by Vallely 600 1200 1800 4200 - -
2nd version w/large full color promo poster pasted over centerfold & a smaller poster pasted over back cover; includes new additional premiums not originally offered (Rare) 857 1714 2571 6000 - -

LOONEY TUNES
DC Comics: 1991, 1998
Claritin promotional issue (1998) 3.00
Colgate mini-comic (1998) 3.00
Tyson's 1-10 (1991) 4.00

LOVE FIGHTS
Oni Press: July, 2004 (Free Comic Book Day giveaway)
1-Flip book with r/Love Fights #1 and preview of Everest Facing the Goddess 2.50

LUCKY FIGHTS IT THROUGH (Also see The K. O. Punch & Sidewalk Romance)
Educational Comics: 1949 (Giveaway, 16 pgs. in color, paper-c)
nn-(Very Rare)-1st Kurtzman work for E. C.; V.D. prevention
123 246 369 781 1341 1900
nn-Reprint in color (1977) 7.00
NOTE: *Subtitled "The Story of That Ignorant, Ignorant Cowboy". Prepared for Communications Materials Center, Columbia University.*

LUDWIG VON DRAKE (See Frito-Lay Giveaway)

MACO TOYS COMIC
Maco Toys/Charlton Comics: 1959 (Giveaway, 36 pgs.)
1-All military stories featuring Maco Toys 3 6 9 14 19 24

MAD MAGAZINE
DC Comics: 1997, 1999, 2008
Special Edition (1997, Tang giveaway) 3.00
Stocking Stuffer (1999) 3.00
San Diego Comic-Con Edition (2008) Watchmen parody with Fabry-a; Aragonés cartoons 3.00

MAGAZINELAND
DC Comics: 1977
nn-Kubert-c/a 3 6 9 16 22 28

MAGIC MORRO (Also see Super Comics #21, The Owl, & The Hurricane Kids)
K. K. Publications: 1941 (7-1/2 x 5-1/4", giveaway, soft-c)
nn-Ken Ernst-a. 10 20 30 54 72 90

MAGIC OF CHRISTMAS AT NEWBERRYS, THE

March of Comics #36 © KING

March of Comics #41 © DIS

March of Comics #90 © Gene Autry

E. S. London: 1967 (Giveaway) (B&W, slick-c, 20 pgs.)

	GD 2.0	VG 4.0	FN 6.0	VF 8.0	VF/NM 9.0	NM- 9.2
nn	1	3	4	6	8	10

MAJOR INAPAK THE SPACE ACE
Magazine Enterprises (Inapac Foods): 1951 (20 pgs.) (Giveaway)

	GD 2.0	VG 4.0	FN 6.0	VF 8.0	VF/NM 9.0	NM- 9.2
1-Bob Powell-c/a						6.00

NOTE: *Many warehouse copies surfaced in 1973.*

MAMMY YOKUM & THE GREAT DOGPATCH MYSTERY
Toby Press: 1951 (Giveaway)

	GD 2.0	VG 4.0	FN 6.0	VF 8.0	VF/NM 9.0	NM- 9.2
nn-Li'l Abner	15	30	45	88	137	185
nn-Reprint (1956)	5	10	15	22	26	30

MAN NAMED STEVENSON, A
Democratic National Committee: 1952 (20 pgs., 5 1/4 x 7")

	GD 2.0	VG 4.0	FN 6.0	VF 8.0	VF/NM 9.0	NM- 9.2
nn	9	18	27	47	61	75

MAN OF PEACE, POPE PIUS XII
Catechetical Guild: 1950 (See Pope Pius XII... & To V2#8)

	GD 2.0	VG 4.0	FN 6.0	VF 8.0	VF/NM 9.0	NM- 9.2
nn-All Powell-a	7	14	21	35	43	50

MAN OF STEEL BEST WESTERN
DC Comics: 1997 (Best Western hotels promo)

	GD 2.0	VG 4.0	FN 6.0	VF 8.0	VF/NM 9.0	NM- 9.2
3-Reprints Superman's first post-Crisis meeting with Batman						4.00

MAN WHO RUNS INTERFERENCE
General Comics, Inc./Institute of Life Insurance: 1946 (Paper-c)

	GD 2.0	VG 4.0	FN 6.0	VF 8.0	VF/NM 9.0	NM- 9.2
nn-Football premium	5	10	15	22	26	30

MAN WHO WOULDN'T QUIT, THE
Harvey Publications Inc.: 1952 (16 pgs., paper cover)

	GD 2.0	VG 4.0	FN 6.0	VF 8.0	VF/NM 9.0	NM- 9.2
nn-The value of voting	4	8	12	18	22	25

MARCH OF COMICS (Boys' and Girls'...#3-353)
K. K. Publications/Western Publishing Co.: 1946 - No. 488, April, 1982 (#1-4 are not numbered) (K.K. Giveaway) (Founded by Sig Feuchtwanger)

Early issues were full size, 32 pages, and were printed with and without an extra cover of slick stock, just for the advertiser. The binding was stapled if the slick cover was added; otherwise, the pages were glued together at the spine. Most 1948 - 1951 issues were full size,24 pages, pulp covers. Starting in 1952 they were half-size (with a few exceptions) and 32 pages with slick covers.1959 and later issues had only 16 pages plus covers. 1952 -1959 issues read oblong; 1960 and later issues read upright. All have new stories except where noted.

	GD 2.0	VG 4.0	FN 6.0	VF 8.0	VF/NM 9.0	NM- 9.2
nn (#1, 1946)-Goldilocks; Kelly back-c (16 pgs., stapled)	50	100	150	315	533	750
nn (#2, 1946)-How Santa Got His Red Suit; Kelly-a (11 pgs., r/4-Color #61 from 1944) (16pgs., stapled)	31	62	93	186	301	425
nn (#3, 1947)-Our Gang (Walt Kelly)	39	78	117	238	394	550
nn (#4)-Donald Duck by Carl Barks, "Maharajah Donald", 28 pgs.; Kelly-c? (Disney)	757	1514	2271	5602	9801	14,000
5-Andy Panda (Walter Lantz)	20	40	60	116	191	265
6-Popular Fairy Tales; Kelly-c; Noonan-a(2)	22	44	66	129	212	295
7-Oswald the Rabbit	20	40	60	120	198	275
8-Mickey Mouse, 32 pgs. (Disney)	47	94	141	296	498	700
9(nn)-The Story of the Gloomy Bunny	14	28	42	80	115	150
10-Out of Santa's Bag	14	28	42	76	108	140
11-Fun With Santa Claus	12	24	36	67	94	120
12-Santa's Toys	12	24	36	67	94	120
13-Santa's Surprise	12	24	36	67	94	120
14-Santa's Candy Kitchen	12	24	36	67	94	120
15-Hip-It-Ty Hop & the Big Bass Viol	11	22	33	62	86	110
16-Woody Woodpecker (1947)(Walter Lantz)	15	30	45	84	127	170
17-Roy Rogers (1948)	24	48	72	142	234	325
18-Popular Fairy Tales	14	28	42	78	112	145
19-Uncle Wiggily	12	24	36	69	97	125
20-Donald Duck by Carl Barks, "Darkest Africa", 22 pgs.; Kelly-c (Disney)	309	618	927	2194	3797	5400
21-Tom and Jerry	13	26	39	74	105	135
22-Andy Panda (Lantz)	12	24	36	67	94	120
23-Raggedy Ann & Andy; Kerr-a	14	28	42	82	121	160
24-Felix the Cat, 1932 daily strip reprints by Otto Messmer	20	40	60	118	194	270
25-Gene Autry	20	40	60	116	191	265
26-Our Gang; Walt Kelly	19	38	57	111	178	245
27-Mickey Mouse; r/in M. M. #240 (Disney)	35	70	105	207	339	470
28-Gene Autry	19	38	57	113	184	255
29-Easter Bonnet Shop	9	18	27	47	61	75
30-Here Comes Santa	8	16	24	44	57	70
31-Santa's Busy Corner	8	16	24	44	57	70
32-No book produced						
33-A Christmas Carol (12/48)	9	18	27	47	61	75
34-Woody Woodpecker	13	26	39	74	105	135
35-Roy Rogers (1948)	21	42	63	123	204	285
36-Felix the Cat(1949); by Messmer; '34 strip-r	18	36	54	105	165	225
37-Popeye	15	30	45	85	130	175
38-Oswald the Rabbit	10	20	30	58	79	100
39-Gene Autry	19	38	57	112	181	250
40-Andy and Woody	10	20	30	58	79	100
41-Donald Duck by Carl Barks, "Race to the South Seas", 22 pgs.; Kelly-c	300	600	900	2130	3665	5200
42-Porky Pig	11	22	33	60	83	105
43-Henry	10	20	30	56	76	95
44-Bugs Bunny	11	22	33	64	90	115
45-Mickey Mouse (Disney)	27	54	81	158	259	360
46-Tom and Jerry	11	22	33	64	90	115
47-Roy Rogers	19	38	57	110	175	240
48-Greetings from Santa	6	12	18	31	38	45
49-Santa Is Here	6	12	18	31	38	45
50-Santa Claus' Workshop (1949)	6	12	18	31	38	45
51-Felix the Cat (1950) by Messmer	15	30	45	94	147	200
52-Popeye	14	28	42	76	108	140
53-Oswald the Rabbit	10	20	30	54	72	90
54-Gene Autry	17	34	51	100	158	215
55-Andy and Woody	9	18	27	52	69	85
56-Donald Duck; not by Barks; Barks art on back-c (Disney)	28	56	84	165	270	375
57-Porky Pig	10	20	30	54	72	90
58-Henry	8	16	24	44	57	70
59-Bugs Bunny	10	20	30	58	79	100
60-Mickey Mouse (Disney)	25	50	75	150	245	340
61-Tom and Jerry	10	20	30	54	72	90
62-Roy Rogers	19	38	57	109	172	235
63-Welcome Santa (1/2-size, oblong)	6	12	18	31	38	45
64(nn)-Santa's Helpers (1/2-size, oblong)	6	12	18	31	38	45
65(nn)-Jingle Bells (1950) (1/2-size, oblong)	6	12	18	31	38	45
66-Popeye (1951)	12	24	36	69	97	125
67-Oswald the Rabbit	9	18	27	52	69	85
68-Roy Rogers	18	36	54	105	165	225
69-Donald Duck; Barks-a on back-c (Disney)	24	48	72	142	234	325
70-Tom and Jerry	9	18	27	50	65	80
71-Porky Pig	9	18	27	52	69	85
72-Krazy Kat	10	20	30	58	79	100
73-Roy Rogers	16	32	48	96	151	205
74-Mickey Mouse (1951)(Disney)	19	38	57	114	187	260
75-Bugs Bunny	9	18	27	52	69	85
76-Andy and Woody	9	18	27	50	65	80
77-Roy Rogers	15	30	45	90	140	190
78-Gene Autry (1951); last regular size issue	15	30	45	86	133	180

Note: All pre #79 issues came with or without a slick protective wrap-around cover over the regular cover which advertised Poll Parrot Shoes, Sears, etc. This outer cover protects the inside pages making them in nicer condition.
Issues with the outer cover are worth 15-25% more

	GD 2.0	VG 4.0	FN 6.0	VF 8.0	VF/NM 9.0	NM- 9.2
79-Andy Panda (1952, 5x7" size)	7	14	21	35	43	50
80-Popeye	10	20	30	58	79	100
81-Oswald the Rabbit	6	12	18	29	36	42
82-Tarzan; Lex Barker photo-c	15	30	45	90	140	190
83-Bugs Bunny	7	14	21	37	46	55
84-Henry	6	12	18	29	36	42
85-Woody Woodpecker	6	12	18	29	36	42
86-Roy Rogers	14	28	42	76	108	140
87-Krazy Kat	8	16	24	44	57	70
88-Tom and Jerry	6	12	18	31	38	45
89-Porky Pig	6	12	18	29	36	42
90-Gene Autry	12	24	36	69	97	125
91-Roy Rogers & Santa	13	26	39	74	105	135
92-Christmas with Santa	5	10	15	24	30	35
93-Woody Woodpecker (1953)	5	10	15	23	28	32
94-Indian Chief	10	20	30	54	72	90
95-Oswald the Rabbit	5	10	15	23	28	32
96-Popeye	10	20	30	54	72	90
97-Bugs Bunny	7	14	21	35	43	50
98-Tarzan; Lex Barker photo-c	15	30	45	86	133	180
99-Porky Pig	5	10	15	23	28	32
100-Roy Rogers	11	22	33	62	86	110
101-Henry	5	10	15	22	26	30
102-Tom Corbett (TV)('53, early app).; painted-c	14	28	42	76	108	140
103-Tom and Jerry	5	10	15	23	28	32
104-Gene Autry	11	22	33	60	83	105
105-Roy Rogers	11	22	33	60	83	105
106-Santa's Helpers	5	10	15	24	30	35
107-Santa's Christmas Book - not published						

March of Comics #112 © KING

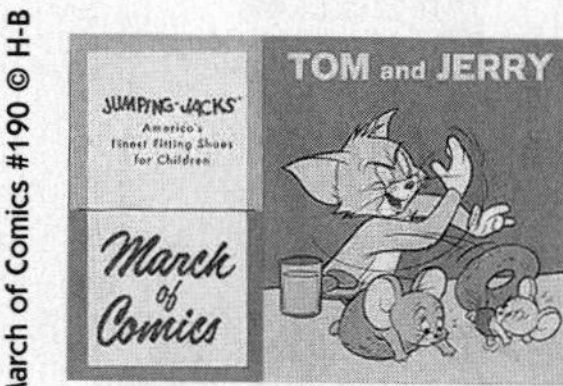

March of Comics #190 © H-B

March of Comics #233 © Jay Ward

	GD 2.0	VG 4.0	FN 6.0	VF 8.0	VF/NM 9.0	NM- 9.2
108-Fun with Santa (1953)	5	10	15	24	30	35
109-Woody Woodpecker (1954)	5	10	15	24	30	35
110-Indian Chief	6	12	18	31	38	45
111-Oswald the Rabbit	5	10	15	22	26	30
112-Henry	4	9	13	18	22	26
113-Porky Pig	5	10	15	22	26	30
114-Tarzan; Russ Manning-a	15	30	45	86	133	180
115-Bugs Bunny	6	12	18	27	33	38
116-Roy Rogers	11	22	33	60	83	105
117-Popeye	10	20	30	54	72	90
118-Flash Gordon; painted-c	12	24	36	67	94	120
119-Tom and Jerry	5	10	15	22	26	30
120-Gene Autry	11	22	33	60	83	105
121-Roy Rogers	11	22	33	60	83	105
122-Santa's Surprise (1954)	5	10	15	22	26	30
123-Santa's Christmas Book	5	10	15	22	26	30
124-Woody Woodpecker (1955)	4	9	13	18	22	26
125-Tarzan; Lex Barker photo-c	15	30	45	83	124	165
126-Oswald the Rabbit	4	9	13	18	22	26
127-Indian Chief	7	14	21	35	43	50
128-Tom and Jerry	4	9	13	18	22	26
129-Henry	4	8	12	17	21	24
130-Porky Pig	4	9	13	18	22	26
131-Roy Rogers	11	22	33	60	83	105
132-Bugs Bunny	5	10	15	23	28	32
133-Flash Gordon; painted-c	11	22	33	60	83	105
134-Popeye	8	16	24	42	54	65
135-Gene Autry	10	20	30	56	76	95
136-Roy Rogers	10	20	30	56	76	95
137-Gifts from Santa	4	7	10	14	17	20
138-Fun at Christmas (1955)	4	7	10	14	17	20
139-Woody Woodpecker (1956)	4	9	13	18	22	26
140-Indian Chief	7	14	21	35	43	50
141-Oswald the Rabbit	4	9	13	18	22	26
142-Flash Gordon	11	22	33	60	83	105
143-Porky Pig	4	9	13	18	22	26
144-Tarzan; Russ Manning-a; painted-c	14	28	42	80	115	150
145-Tom and Jerry	4	9	13	18	22	26
146-Roy Rogers; photo-c	10	20	30	56	76	95
147-Henry	4	8	11	16	19	22
148-Popeye	8	16	24	42	54	65
149-Bugs Bunny	5	10	15	22	26	30
150-Gene Autry	10	20	30	56	76	95
151-Roy Rogers	10	20	30	56	76	95
152-The Night Before Christmas	4	8	11	16	19	22
153-Merry Christmas (1956)	4	9	13	18	22	26
154-Tom and Jerry (1957)	4	9	13	18	22	26
155-Tarzan; photo-c	14	28	42	78	112	145
156-Oswald the Rabbit	4	9	13	18	22	26
157-Popeye	7	14	21	35	43	50
158-Woody Woodpecker	4	9	13	18	22	26
159-Indian Chief	7	14	21	35	43	50
160-Bugs Bunny	5	10	15	22	26	30
161-Roy Rogers	9	18	27	52	69	85
162-Henry	4	8	11	16	19	22
163-Rin Tin Tin (TV)	8	16	24	42	54	65
164-Porky Pig	4	9	13	18	22	26
165-The Lone Ranger	10	20	30	54	72	90
166-Santa and His Reindeer	4	7	10	14	17	20
167-Roy Rogers and Santa	9	18	27	52	69	85
168-Santa Claus' Workshop (1957, full size)	4	8	11	16	19	22
169-Popeye (1958)	7	14	21	35	43	50
170-Indian Chief	7	14	21	35	43	50
171-Oswald the Rabbit	4	8	12	17	21	24
172-Tarzan	11	22	33	64	90	115
173-Tom and Jerry	4	8	12	17	21	24
174-The Lone Ranger	10	20	30	54	72	90
175-Porky Pig	4	8	12	17	21	24
176-Roy Rogers	9	18	27	47	61	75
177-Woody Woodpecker	4	8	12	17	21	24
178-Henry	4	8	11	16	19	22
179-Bugs Bunny	4	8	12	17	21	24
180-Rin Tin Tin (TV)	7	14	21	37	46	55
181-Happy Holiday	4	7	9	14	16	18
182-Happi Tim	4	8	11	16	19	22
183-Welcome Santa (1958, full size)	4	7	9	14	16	18
184-Woody Woodpecker (1959)	4	8	11	16	19	22
185-Tarzan; photo-c	11	22	33	60	83	110

	GD 2.0	VG 4.0	FN 6.0	VF 8.0	VF/NM 9.0	NM- 9.2
186-Oswald the Rabbit	4	8	11	16	19	22
187-Indian Chief	6	12	18	28	34	40
188-Bugs Bunny	4	8	11	16	19	22
189-Henry	4	7	10	14	17	20
190-Tom and Jerry	4	8	11	16	19	22
191-Roy Rogers	8	16	24	44	57	70
192-Porky Pig	4	8	11	16	19	22
193-The Lone Ranger	9	18	27	52	69	85
194-Popeye	6	12	18	31	38	45
195-Rin Tin Tin (TV)	7	14	21	35	43	50
196-Sears Special - not published						
197-Santa Is Coming	4	7	10	14	17	20
198-Santa's Helpers (1959)	4	7	10	14	17	20
199-Huckleberry Hound (TV)(1960, early app.)	8	16	24	42	54	65
200-Fury (TV)	6	12	18	28	34	40
201-Bugs Bunny	4	8	11	16	19	22
202-Space Explorer	8	16	24	42	54	65
203-Woody Woodpecker	4	7	10	14	17	20
204-Tarzan	9	18	27	52	69	85
205-Mighty Mouse	6	12	18	33	41	48
206-Roy Rogers; photo-c	8	16	24	42	54	65
207-Tom and Jerry	4	7	10	14	17	20
208-The Lone Ranger; Clayton Moore photo-c	11	22	33	62	86	110
209-Porky Pig	4	7	10	14	17	20
210-Lassie (TV)	6	12	18	33	41	48
211-Sears Special - not published						
212-Christmas Eve	4	7	10	14	17	20
213-Here Comes Santa (1960)	4	7	10	14	17	20
214-Huckleberry Hound (TV)(1961)	7	14	21	35	43	50
215-Hi Yo Silver	8	16	24	40	50	60
216-Rocky & His Friends (TV)(1961); predates Rocky and His Fiendish Friends #1 (see Four Color #1128)	10	20	30	58	79	100
217-Lassie (TV)	6	12	18	31	38	45
218-Porky Pig	4	7	10	14	17	20
219-Journey to the Sun	5	10	15	24	30	35
220-Bugs Bunny	4	8	11	16	19	22
221-Roy and Dale; photo-c	8	16	24	42	54	65
222-Woody Woodpecker	4	7	10	14	17	20
223-Tarzan	9	18	27	52	69	85
224-Tom and Jerry	4	7	10	14	17	20
225-The Lone Ranger	8	16	24	40	50	60
226-Christmas Treasury (1961)	4	7	10	14	17	20
227-Letters to Santa (1961)	4	7	10	14	17	20
228-Sears Special - not published?						
229-The Flintstones (TV)(1962); early app.; predates 1st Flintstones Gold Key issue (#7)	11	22	33	60	83	105
230-Lassie (TV)	6	12	18	27	33	38
231-Bugs Bunny	4	8	11	16	19	22
232-The Three Stooges	10	20	30	54	72	90
233-Bullwinkle (TV) (1962, very early app.)	10	20	30	58	79	100
234-Smokey the Bear	5	10	15	23	28	32
235-Huckleberry Hound (TV)	7	14	21	35	43	50
236-Roy and Dale	7	14	21	35	43	50
237-Mighty Mouse	6	12	18	27	33	38
238-The Lone Ranger	8	16	24	40	50	60
239-Woody Woodpecker	4	7	10	14	17	20
240-Tarzan	8	16	24	44	57	70
241-Santa Claus Around the World	4	7	9	14	16	18
242-Santa's Toyland (1962)	4	7	9	14	16	18
243-The Flintstones (TV)(1963)	8	16	24	44	57	70
244-Mister Ed (TV); early app.; photo-c	7	14	21	35	43	50
245-Bugs Bunny	4	8	11	16	19	22
246-Popeye	6	12	18	27	33	38
247-Mighty Mouse	6	12	18	27	33	38
248-The Three Stooges	10	20	30	54	72	90
249-Woody Woodpecker	4	7	10	14	17	20
250-Roy and Dale	7	14	21	35	43	50
251-Little Lulu & Witch Hazel	12	24	36	67	94	120
252-Tarzan; painted-c	8	16	24	42	54	65
253-Yogi Bear (TV)	8	16	24	40	50	60
254-Lassie (TV)	6	12	18	27	33	38
255-Santa's Christmas List	4	7	10	14	17	20
256-Christmas Party (1963)	4	7	10	14	17	20
257-Mighty Mouse	6	12	18	27	33	38
258-The Sword in the Stone (Disney)	8	16	24	42	54	65
259-Bugs Bunny	4	8	11	16	19	22
260-Mister Ed (TV)	6	12	18	31	38	45
261-Woody Woodpecker	4	7	10	14	17	20

March of Comics #294 © KING

March of Comics #350 © Lone Ranger Inc.

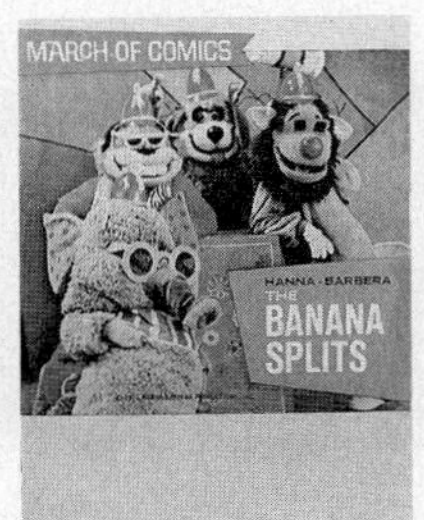

March of Comics #364 © H-B

	GD 2.0	VG 4.0	FN 6.0	VF 8.0	VF/NM 9.0	NM- 9.2
262-Tarzan	8	16	24	40	50	60
263-Donald Duck; not by Barks (Disney)	9	18	27	52	69	85
264-Popeye	6	12	18	27	33	38
265-Yogi Bear (TV)	6	12	18	31	38	45
266-Lassie (TV)	5	10	15	23	28	32
267-Little Lulu; Irving Tripp-a	10	20	30	56	76	95
268-The Three Stooges	9	18	27	47	61	75
269-A Jolly Christmas	3	6	8	12	14	16
270-Santa's Little Helpers	3	6	8	12	14	16
271-The Flintstones (TV)(1965)	8	16	24	44	57	70
272-Tarzan	8	16	24	40	50	60
273-Bugs Bunny	4	8	11	16	19	22
274-Popeye	6	12	18	27	33	38
275-Little Lulu; Irving Tripp-a	9	18	27	50	65	80
276-The Jetsons (TV)	14	28	42	76	108	140
277-Daffy Duck	4	8	11	16	19	22
278-Lassie (TV)	5	10	15	23	28	32
279-Yogi Bear (TV)	6	12	18	31	38	45
280-The Three Stooges; photo-c	9	18	27	47	61	75
281-Tom and Jerry	4	7	9	14	16	18
282-Mister Ed (TV)	6	12	18	31	38	45
283-Santa's Visit	4	7	9	14	16	18
284-Christmas Parade (1965)	4	7	9	14	16	18
285-Astro Boy (TV); 2nd app. Astro Boy	28	56	84	165	270	375
286-Tarzan	7	14	21	37	46	55
287-Bugs Bunny	4	8	11	16	19	22
288-Daffy Duck	4	7	10	14	17	20
289-The Flintstones (TV)	8	16	24	44	57	70
290-Mister Ed (TV); photo-c	5	10	15	24	30	35
291-Yogi Bear (TV)	6	12	18	27	33	38
292-The Three Stooges; photo-c	9	18	27	47	61	75
293-Little Lulu; Irving Tripp-a	8	16	24	42	54	65
294-Popeye	5	10	15	24	30	35
295-Tom and Jerry	4	7	9	14	16	18
296-Lassie (TV); photo-c	5	10	15	22	26	30
297-Christmas Bells	3	6	8	12	14	16
298-Santa's Sleigh (1966)	3	6	8	12	14	16
299-The Flintstones (TV)(1967)	8	16	24	44	57	70
300-Tarzan	7	14	21	37	46	55
301-Bugs Bunny	4	7	10	14	17	20
302-Laurel and Hardy (TV); photo-c	6	12	18	28	34	40
303-Daffy Duck	3	6	8	12	14	16
304-The Three Stooges; photo-c	8	16	24	44	57	70
305-Tom and Jerry	3	6	8	12	14	16
306-Daniel Boone (TV); Fess Parker photo-c	7	14	21	35	43	50
307-Little Lulu; Irving Tripp-a	7	14	21	37	46	55
308-Lassie (TV); photo-c	5	10	15	22	26	30
309-Yogi Bear (TV)	5	10	15	24	30	35
310-The Lone Ranger; Clayton Moore photo-c	11	22	33	62	86	110
311-Santa's Show	4	7	9	14	16	18
312-Christmas Album (1967)	4	7	9	14	16	18
313-Daffy Duck (1968)	3	6	8	12	14	16
314-Laurel and Hardy (TV)	6	12	18	27	33	38
315-Bugs Bunny	4	7	10	14	17	20
316-The Three Stooges	8	16	24	40	50	60
317-The Flintstones (TV)	8	16	24	42	54	65
318-Tarzan	7	14	21	35	43	50
319-Yogi Bear (TV)	5	10	15	24	30	35
320-Space Family Robinson (TV); Spiegle-a	12	24	36	69	97	125
321-Tom and Jerry	3	6	8	12	14	16
322-The Lone Ranger	7	14	21	37	46	55
323-Little Lulu; not by Stanley	5	10	15	24	30	35
324-Lassie (TV); photo-c	5	10	15	22	26	30
325-Fun with Santa	4	7	9	14	16	18
326-Christmas Story (1968)	4	7	9	14	16	18
327-The Flintstones (TV)(1969)	8	16	24	42	54	65
328-Space Family Robinson (TV); Spiegle-a	12	24	36	69	97	125
329-Bugs Bunny	4	7	10	14	17	20
330-The Jetsons (TV)	10	20	30	56	76	95
331-Daffy Duck	3	6	8	12	14	16
332-Tarzan	6	12	18	28	34	40
333-Tom and Jerry	3	6	8	12	14	16
334-Lassie (TV)	4	9	13	18	22	26
335-Little Lulu	5	10	15	24	30	35
336-The Three Stooges	8	16	24	40	50	60
337-Yogi Bear (TV)	5	10	15	24	30	35
338-The Lone Ranger	7	14	21	37	46	55
339-(Was not published)						

	GD 2.0	VG 4.0	FN 6.0	VF 8.0	VF/NM 9.0	NM- 9.2
340-Here Comes Santa (1969)	3	6	8	12	14	16
341-The Flintstones (TV)	8	16	24	42	54	65
342-Tarzan	3	6	9	20	30	40
343-Bugs Bunny	2	4	6	10	14	18
344-Yogi Bear (TV)	3	6	9	16	23	30
345-Tom and Jerry	2	4	6	9	13	16
346-Lassie (TV)	3	6	9	15	21	26
347-Daffy Duck	2	4	6	9	13	16
348-The Jetsons (TV)	6	12	18	39	62	85
349-Little Lulu; not by Stanley	3	6	9	16	23	30
350-The Lone Ranger	3	6	9	18	27	35
351-Beep-Beep, the Road Runner (TV)	2	4	6	11	16	20
352-Space Family Robinson (TV); Spiegle-a	8	16	24	54	90	125
353-Beep-Beep, the Road Runner (1971) (TV)	2	4	6	11	16	20
354-Tarzan (1971)	3	6	9	18	27	35
355-Little Lulu; not by Stanley	3	6	9	16	23	30
356-Scooby Doo, Where Are You? (TV)	6	12	18	43	69	95
357-Daffy Duck & Porky Pig	2	4	6	8	11	14
358-Lassie (TV)	3	6	9	14	19	24
359-Baby Snoots	2	4	6	10	14	18
360-H. R. Pufnstuf (TV); photo-c	6	12	18	43	69	95
361-Tom and Jerry	2	4	6	8	11	14
362-Smokey Bear (TV)	2	4	6	8	11	14
363-Bugs Bunny & Yosemite Sam	2	4	6	9	13	16
364-The Banana Splits (TV); photo-c	6	12	18	37	59	80
365-Tom and Jerry (1972)	2	4	6	8	11	14
366-Tarzan	3	6	9	18	27	35
367-Bugs Bunny & Porky Pig	2	4	6	9	13	16
368-Scooby Doo (TV)(4/72)	6	12	18	37	59	80
369-Little Lulu; not by Stanley	3	6	9	14	19	24
370-Lassie (TV); photo-c	3	6	9	14	19	24
371-Baby Snoots	2	4	6	9	13	16
372-Smokey the Bear (TV)	2	4	6	8	11	14
373-The Three Stooges	4	8	12	24	37	50
374-Wacky Witch	2	4	6	8	11	14
375-Beep-Beep & Daffy Duck (TV)	2	4	6	8	11	14
376-The Pink Panther (1972) (TV)	2	4	6	10	14	18
377-Baby Snoots (1973)	2	4	6	9	13	16
378-Turok, Son of Stone; new-a	8	16	24	56	93	130
379-Heckle & Jeckle New Terrytoons (TV)	2	4	6	8	11	14
380-Bugs Bunny & Yosemite Sam	2	4	6	8	11	14
381-Lassie (TV)	2	4	6	11	16	20
382-Scooby Doo, Where Are You? (TV)	5	10	15	32	51	70
383-Smokey the Bear (TV)	2	4	6	8	11	14
384-Pink Panther (TV)	2	4	6	8	11	14
385-Little Lulu	2	4	6	13	18	22
386-Wacky Witch	2	4	6	8	11	14
387-Beep-Beep & Daffy Duck (TV)	2	4	6	8	11	14
388-Tom and Jerry (1973)	2	4	6	8	11	14
389-Little Lulu; not by Stanley	2	4	6	13	18	22
390-Pink Panther (TV)	2	4	6	8	11	14
391-Scooby Doo (TV)	4	8	12	26	41	55
392-Bugs Bunny & Yosemite Sam	2	4	6	8	10	12
393-New Terrytoons (Heckle & Jeckle) (TV)	2	4	6	8	10	12
394-Lassie (TV)	2	4	6	9	13	16
395-Woodsy Owl	2	4	6	8	10	12
396-Baby Snoots	2	4	6	8	11	14
397-Beep-Beep & Daffy Duck (TV)	2	4	6	8	10	12
398-Wacky Witch	2	4	6	8	10	12
399-Turok, Son of Stone; new-a	7	14	21	50	83	115
400-Tom and Jerry	2	4	6	8	10	12
401-Baby Snoots (1975) (r/#371)	2	4	6	8	11	14
402-Daffy Duck (r/#313)	1	3	4	6	8	10
403-Bugs Bunny (r/#343)	2	4	6	8	10	12
404-Space Family Robinson (TV)(r/#328)	6	12	18	41	66	90
405-Cracky	1	3	4	6	8	10
406-Little Lulu (r/#355)	2	4	6	10	14	18
407-Smokey the Bear (TV)(r/#362)	2	4	6	8	10	12
408-Turok, Son of Stone; c-r/Turok #20 w/changes; new-a	6	12	18	39	62	85
409-Pink Panther (TV)	1	3	4	6	8	10
410-Wacky Witch	1	2	3	5	6	8
411-Lassie (TV)(r/#324)	2	4	6	9	13	16
412-New Terrytoons (1975) (TV)	1	2	3	5	6	8
413-Daffy Duck (1976)(r/#331)	1	2	3	5	6	8
414-Space Family Robinson (r/#328)	6	12	18	39	62	85
415-Bugs Bunny (r/#329)	1	2	3	5	6	8
416-Beep-Beep, the Road Runner (r/#353)(TV)	1	2	3	5	6	8

March of Comics #439 © WEST

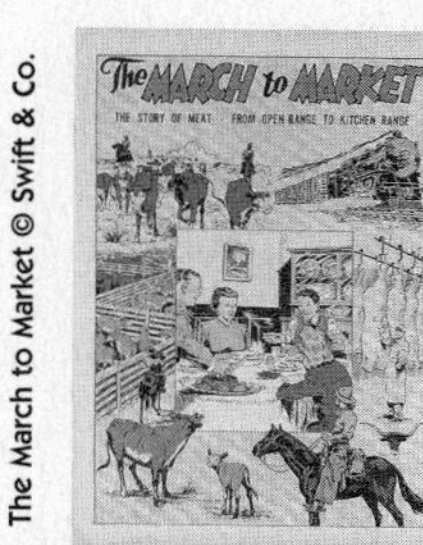

The March to Market © Swift & Co.

Marvel Guide to Collecting Comics © MAR

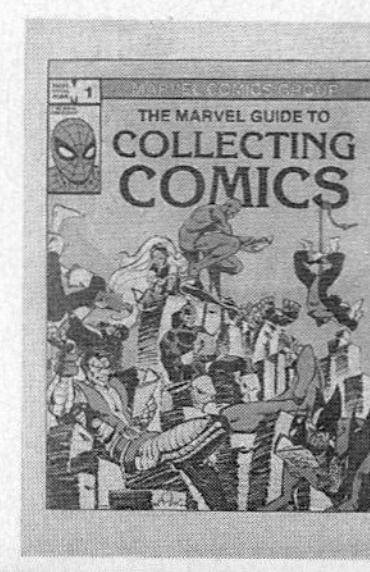

GD 2.0 | VG 4.0 | FN 6.0 | VF 8.0 | VF/NM 9.0 | NM- 9.2

417-Little Lulu (r/#323) 2 4 6 10 14 18
418-Pink Panther (r/#384) (TV) 1 2 3 5 6 8
419-Baby Snoots (r/#377) 1 3 4 6 8 10
420-Woody Woodpecker 1 2 3 5 6 8
421-Tweety & Sylvester 1 2 3 5 6 8
422-Wacky Witch (r/#386) 1 2 3 5 6 8
423-Little Monsters 1 3 4 6 8 10
424-Cracky (12/76) 1 2 3 5 6 8
425-Daffy Duck 1 2 3 5 6 8
426-Underdog (TV) 4 8 12 22 34 45
427-Little Lulu (r/#335) 2 4 6 8 11 14
428-Bugs Bunny 1 2 3 4 5 7
429-The Pink Panther (TV) 1 2 3 4 5 7
430-Beep-Beep, the Road Runner (TV) 1 2 3 4 5 7
431-Baby Snoots 1 2 3 5 6 8
432-Lassie (TV) 2 4 6 8 10 12
433-437: 433-Tweety & Sylvester. 434-Wacky Witch. 435-New Terrytoons (TV). 436-Wacky Advs. of Cracky. 437-Daffy Duck 1 2 3 4 5 7
438-Underdog (TV) 3 6 9 20 30 40
439-Little Lulu (r/#349) 2 4 6 8 11 14
440-442,444-446: 440-Bugs Bunny. 441-The Pink Panther (TV). 442-Beep-Beep, the Road Runner (TV). 444-Tom and Jerry. 445-Tweety and Sylvester. 446-Wacky Witch
1 2 3 5 6 8
443-Baby Snoots 1 2 3 5 6 8
447-Mighty Mouse 2 4 6 8 10 12
448-455,457,458: 448-Cracky. 449-Pink Panther (TV). 450-Baby Snoots. 451-Tom and Jerry. 452-Bugs Bunny. 453-Popeye. 454-Woody Woodpecker. 455-Beep-Beep, the Road Runner (TV). 457-Tweety & Sylvester. 458-Wacky Witch 1 2 3 5 6 8
456-Little Lulu (r/#369) 2 4 6 8 10 12
459-Mighty Mouse 2 4 6 8 10 12
460-466: 460-Daffy Duck. 461-The Pink Panther (TV). 462-Baby Snoots. 463-Tom and Jerry. 464-Bugs Bunny. 465-Popeye. 466-Woody Woodpecker
1 2 3 5 6 8
467-Underdog (TV) 3 6 9 18 27 35
468-Little Lulu (r/#385) 1 2 3 5 6 8
469-Tweety & Sylvester 1 2 3 5 6 8
470-Wacky Witch 1 2 3 5 6 8
471-Mighty Mouse 1 3 4 6 8 10
472-474,476-478: 472-Heckle & Jeckle(12/80). 473-Pink Panther(1/81)(TV). 474-Baby Snoots. 476-Bugs Bunny. 477-Popeye. 478-Woody Woodpecker
1 2 3 5 6 8
475-Little Lulu (r/#323) 1 3 4 6 8 10
479-Underdog (TV) 3 6 9 16 23 30
480-482: 480-Tom and Jerry. 481-Tweety and Sylvester. 482-Wacky Witch
1 2 3 4 5 8
483-Mighty Mouse 1 3 4 6 8 10
484-487: 484-Heckle & Jeckle. 485-Baby Snoots. 486-The Pink Panther (TV). 487-Bugs Bunny 1 2 3 4 5 8
488-Little Lulu (4/82) (r/#335) (Last issue) 2 4 6 10 14 18

MARCH TO MARKET, THE
Swift & Co.: 1950 (Giveaway)
nn-The story of meat 3 6 8 11 13 15

MARGARET O'BRIEN (See The Adventures of...)

MARK STEEL
American Iron & Steel Institute: 1967, 1968, 1972 (Giveaway) (24 pgs.)
1967,1968- "Journey of Discovery with..."; Neal Adams art
4 8 12 26 41 55
1972- "...Fights Pollution"; N. Adams-a 2 4 6 11 16 20

MARTIN LUTHER KING AND THE MONTGOMERY STORY
Fellowship Reconciliation: 1956 (Giveaway, 16 pgs.) (A Spanish edition also exists)
nn-In color with paper-c (a CGC 9.2 copy sold for $350 and a FN+ sold for $200 in 2004)

MARVEL ADVENTURES...
Marvel Comics: 2007, 2008 (Free Comic Book Day giveaway)
... Free Comic Book Day 2008 - Iron Man, Hulk, Ant-Man and Spider-Man app. 2.50
... Three-In-One (2007) 1-Iron Man, Incredible Hulk and Franklin Richards app. 2.50

MARVEL AGE SPIDER-MAN
Marvel Comics: Aug, 2004 (Free Comic Book Day giveaway)
1-Spider-Man vs. The Vulture; Brooks-a 2.50

MARVEL AGE SPIDER-MAN TEAM-UP (Marvel Adventures on cover)
Marvel Comics: June, 2005 (Free Comic Book Day giveaway)
1-Spider-Man meets the Fantastic Four 2.50

MARVEL COLLECTOR'S EDITION: X-MEN
Marvel Comics: 1993 (3-3/4x6-1/2")
1-4-Pizza Hut giveaways 5.00

MARVEL COMICS PRESENTS
Marvel Comics: 1987, 1988 (4 1/4 x 6 1/4, 20 pgs.)
...Mini Comic Giveaway
nn-(1988) Alf 1 2 3 5 6 8
nn-(1987) Captain America r/ #250 1 2 3 4 5 7
nn-(1987) Care Bears (Star Comics...) 1 2 3 4 5 7
nn-(1988) Flintstone Kids 1 2 3 5 6 8
nn-(1987) Heathcliffe (Star Comics...) 1 2 3 4 5 7
nn-(1987) Spider-Man-r/Spect. Spider-Man #21 1 2 3 4 5 7
nn-(1988) Spider-Man-r/Amazing Spider-Man #1 1 2 3 4 5 7
nn-(1988) X-Men-reprints X-Men #53; B. Smith-a 1 2 3 4 5 7

MARVEL GUIDE TO COLLECTING COMICS, THE
Marvel Comics: 1982 (16 pgs., newsprint pages and cover)
1-Simonson-c 1 2 3 4 5 7

MARVEL HALLOWEEN ASHCAN 2006
Marvel Comics: 2006 (8-1/2"x 5-1/2", Halloween giveaway)
nn-r/Marvel Adventures The Avengers #1 2.00

MARVEL MINI-BOOKS
Marvel Comics Group: 1966 (50 pgs., B&W; 5/8x7/8") (6 different issues) (Smallest comics ever published) (Marvel Mania Giveaways)
Captain America, Millie the Model, Sgt. Fury, Hulk, Thor
each... 3 6 9 14 20 25
Spider-Man 3 6 9 16 23 30
NOTE: *Each came from gum machines in six different color covers, usually one color: Pink, yellow, green, etc.*

MARVEL SUPER-HERO ISLAND ADVENTURES
Marvel Comics: 1999 (Sold at the park polybagged with Captain America V3 #19, one other comic, 5 trading cards and a cloisonnè pin)
1-Promotes Universal Studios Islands of Adventures theme park 4.00

MARY'S GREATEST APOSTLE (St. Louis Grignion de Montfort)
Catechetical Guild (Topix) (Giveaway): No date (16 pgs.; paper cover)
nn 5 10 15 23 28 32

MASK
DC Comics: 1985
1-3 6.00

MASKED PILOT, THE (See Popular Comics #43)
R.S. Callender: 1939 (7-1/2x5-1/4", 16 pgs., premium, non-slick-c)
nn-Bob Jenney-a 8 16 24 44 57 70

MASTERS OF THE UNIVERSE (He-Man)
DC Comics: 1982 (giveaways with action figures, at least 35 different issues, unnumbered)
nn 2 4 6 8 10 12

MATRIX, THE (1999 movie)
Warner Brothers: 1999 (Recalled by Warner Bros. over questionable content)
nn-Paul Chadwick-s/a (16 pgs.); Geof Darrow-c 1 2 3 5 6 8

McCRORY'S CHRISTMAS BOOK
Western Printing Co: 1955 (36 pgs., slick-c) (McCrory Stores Corp. giveaway)
nn-Painted-c 4 8 12 18 22 25

McCRORY'S TOYLAND BRINGS YOU SANTA'S PRIVATE EYES
Promotional Publ. Co.: 1956 (16 pgs.) (Giveaway)
nn-Has 9 pg. story plus 7 pgs. toy ads 4 8 11 16 19 22

McCRORY'S WONDERFUL CHRISTMAS
Promotional Publ. Co.: 1954 (20 pgs., slick-c) (Giveaway)
nn 4 8 12 18 22 25

McDONALDS COMMANDRONS
DC Comics: 1985
nn-Four editions 5.00

MEDAL FOR BOWZER, A (Giveaway)
American Visuals Corp.: 1966 (8 pgs.)
nn-Eisner-c/script; Bowzer (a dog) survives untried pneumonia cure and earns his medal; (medical experimentation on animals) 26 52 78 154 252 350

MEET HIYA A FRIEND OF SANTA CLAUS
Julian J. Proskauer/Sundial Shoe Stores, etc.: 1949 (18 pgs.?, paper-c)(Giveaway)
nn 6 12 18 31 38 45

MEET THE NEW POST-GAZETTE SUNDAY FUNNIES
Pittsburgh Post Gazette: 3/12/49 (7-1/4x10-1/4", 16 pgs., paper-c)
Commercial Comics (insert in newspaper) (Rare)
Dick Tracy by Gould, Gasoline Alley, Terry & the Pirates, Brenda Starr, Buck Rogers by Yager, The Gumps, Peter Rabbit by Fago, Superman, Funnyman by Siegel & Shuster, The Saint, Archie, & others done especially for

Mickey Mouse Magazine V2 #2 © DIS

Motion Picture Funnies Weekly #2 cover © First Funnies

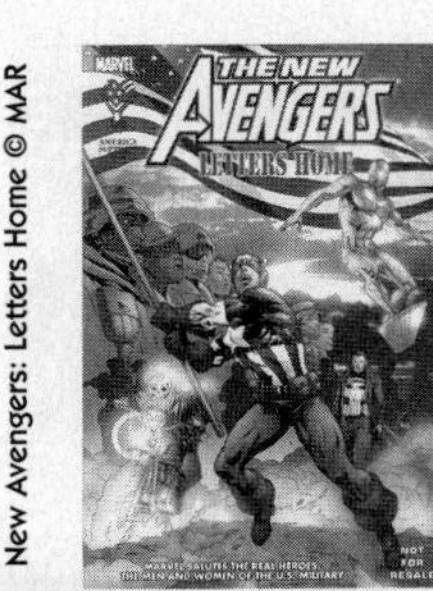

New Avengers: Letters Home © MAR

	GD	VG	FN	VF	VF/NM	NM-
	2.0	4.0	6.0	8.0	9.0	9.2

	GD	VG	FN	VF	VF/NM	NM-
	2.0	4.0	6.0	8.0	9.0	9.2

this book. A fine copy sold at auction in 1985 for $276.00.
300 600 900 1950 - -

MEN OF COURAGE
Catechetical Guild: 1949
Bound Topix comics-V7#2,4,6,8,10,16,18,20 6 12 18 31 38 45

MEN WHO MOVE THE NATION
Publisher unknown: (Giveaway) (B&W)
nn-Neal Adams-a 6 12 18 31 38 45

MERRY CHRISTMAS, A
K. K. Publications (Child Life Shoes): 1948 (Giveaway)
nn 6 12 18 33 41 48

MERRY CHRISTMAS
K. K. Publications (Blue Bird Shoes Giveaway): 1956 (7-1/4x5-1/4")
nn 4 8 12 18 22 25

MERRY CHRISTMAS FROM MICKEY MOUSE
K. K. Publications: 1939 (16 pgs.) (Color & B&W) (Shoe store giveaway)
nn-Donald Duck & Pluto app.; text with art (Rare); c-reprint/Mickey Mouse
Mag. V3#3 (12/37)(Rare) 245 490 735 1556 2678 3800

MERRY CHRISTMAS FROM SEARS TOYLAND (See Santa's Christmas Comic)
Sears Roebuck Giveaway: 1939 (16 pgs.) (Color)
nn-Dick Tracy, Little Orphan Annie, The Gumps, Terry & the Pirates
103 206 309 654 1127 1600

MICKEY MOUSE (Also see Frito-Lay Giveaway)
Dell Publ. Co
...& Goofy Explore Business(1978) 2 4 6 8 10 12
...& Goofy Explore Energy(1976-1978, 36 pgs.); Exxon giveaway in color;
regular size 2 4 6 8 10 12
...& Goofy Explore Energy Conservation(1976-1978)-Exxon
2 4 6 8 10 12
...& Goofy Explore The Universe of Energy(1985, 20 pgs.); Exxon giveaway in
color; regular size 1 2 3 5 7 9
The Perils of Mickey nn (1993, 5-1/4x7-1/4", 16 pgs.)-Nabisco giveaway w/
games, Nabisco coupons & 6 pgs. of stories; Phantom Blot app. 6.00

MICKEY MOUSE MAGAZINE
Walt Disney Productions: V1#1, Jan, 1933 - V1#9, Sept, 1933 (5-1/4x7-1/4")
No. 1-3 published by Kamen-Blair (Kay Kamen, Inc.)
(Scarce)-Distributed by dairies and leading stores through their local theatres.
First few issues had 5¢ listed on cover, later ones had no price.
V1#1 540 1080 2160 6500 - -
2-4 225 450 900 1750 - -
5-9 175 350 700 1350 - -

MICKEY MOUSE MAGAZINE
Walt Disney Productions: V1#1, 11/33 - V2#12, 10/35 (Mills giveaways issued by different dairies)
V1#1 155 310 465 992 1696 2400
2-12: 2-X-Mas issue 48 96 144 302 514 725
V2#1-4,6-12: 2-X-Mas issue. 4-St. Valentine-c 37 74 111 222 361 500
V2#5 (3/35) 1st app. Donald Duck in sailor outfit on-c 87 174 261 553 952 1350

MICKEY MOUSE MAGAZINE
K.K. Publications: V4#1, Oct, 1938 (Giveaway)
V4#1 40 80 120 252 426 600

MIGHTY ATOM, THE
Whitman
Giveaway (1959, '63, Whitman)-Evans-a 3 6 9 16 23 30
Giveaway ('64r, '65r, '66r, '67r, '68r)-Evans-r? 2 4 6 10 14 18
Giveaway ('73r, '76r) 2 4 6 8 11 14

MILES THE MONSTER (Initially sold only at the Dover Speedway track)
Dover International Speedway, Inc.: 2006 ($3.00)
1,2-Allan Gross & Mark Wheatley-s/Wheatley-a 3.00

MILITARY COURTESY
Harvey Publications: (16 pgs.)
nn-Regulations and saluting instructions 5 10 14 20 24 28

MINUTE MAN
Sovereign Service Station giveaway: No date (16 pgs., B&W, paper-c blue & red)
nn-American history 3 6 8 12 14 16

MINUTE MAN ANSWERS THE CALL, THE
By M. C. Gaines: 1942,1943,1944,1945 (4 pgs.) (Giveaway inserted in Jr. JSA Membership Kit)
nn-Sheldon Moldoff-a 21 42 63 121 201 280

MIRACLE ON BROADWAY
Broadway Comics: Dec, 1995 (Giveaway)
1-Ernie Colon-c/a; Jim Shooter & Co. story; 1st known digitally printed comic book;
1st app. Spire & Knights on Broadway (1150 print run) 20.00
NOTE: *Miracle on Broadway was a limited edition comic given to 1100 VIPs in the entertainment industry for the 1995 Holiday Season.*

MISS SUNBEAM (See Little Miss Sunbeam Comics)

MR. BUG GOES TO TOWN (See Cinema Comics Herald)
K.K. Publications: 1941 (Giveaway, 52 pgs.)
nn-Cartoon movie (scarce) 68 136 204 432 741 1050

MR. PEANUT, THE PERSONAL STORY OF
Planters Nut & Chocolate Co.: 1956
nn 4 8 12 22 34 45

MOTH, THE
Rude Dude Productions: May 2008 (Free Comic Book Day giveaway)
... Special Edition - Steve Rude-s/a; sketch pages 2.50

MOTHER OF US ALL
Catechetical Guild Giveaway: 1950? (32 pgs.)
nn 5 10 15 23 28 32

MOTION PICTURE FUNNIES WEEKLY (Amazing Man #5 on?)
First Funnies, Inc.: 1939 (Giveaway)(B&W, 36 pgs.) No month given; last panel in Sub-Mariner story dated 4/39 (Also see Colossus, Green Giant & Invaders No. 20)
1-Origin & 1st printed app. Sub-Mariner by Bill Everett (8 pgs.); Fred Schwab-c; reprinted in Marvel Mystery #1 with color added over the craft tint which was used to shade the black & white version; Spy Ring, American Ace (reprinted in Marvel Mystery #3) app.
(Rare)-only eight known copies, one near mint with white pages, the rest with brown pages.
4500 9000 13,500 18,450 32,000 -
Covers only to #2-4 (set) 900
NOTE: Eight copies (plus one coverless) were discovered in 1974 in the estate of the deceased publisher. Covers only to issues No. 2-4 were also found which evidently were printed in advance along with #1. #1 was to be distributed only through motion picture movie houses. However, it is believed that only advanced copies were sent out and the motion picture houses not going for the idea. Possible distribution at local theaters in Boston suspected. The "pay" copy (graded at 9.0) was discovered after 1974, bringing the total known to nine. The last panel of Sub-Mariner contains a rectangular box with "Continued Next Week" printed in it. When reprinted in Marvel Mystery, the box was left in with lettering omitted.

MY DOG TIGE (Buster Brown's Dog)
Buster Brown Shoes: 1957 (Giveaway)
nn 5 10 15 24 30 35

MY GREATEST THRILLS IN BASEBALL
Mission of California: Date? (16 pg. Giveaway)
nn-By Mickey Mantle 53 106 159 337 581 825

MYSTERIOUS ADVENTURES WITH SANTA CLAUS
Lansburgh's: 1948 (paper cover)
nn 13 26 39 72 101 130

NAKED FORCE!
Commercial Comics: 1958 (Small size)
nn 3 6 8 11 13 15

NASCAR HEROES
Starbridge Media Group: 2008 (Free Comic Book Day giveaway)
nn-The Mystery of Driver Z 2.50

NATURAL DISASTERS!
Graphic Information Service/ Civil Defense: 1956 (16 pgs., soft-c)
nn-Al Capp Li'l Abner-c; Li'l Abner cameo (1 panel); narrated by Mr. Civil Defense
10 20 30 54 72 90

NAVY: HISTORY & TRADITION
Stokes Walesby Co./Dept. of Navy: 1958 - 1961 (nn) (Giveaway)
1772-1778, 1778-1782, 1782-1817, 1817-1865, 1865-1936, 1940-1945:
1772-1778-16 pg. in color 5 10 15 22 26 30
1861: Naval Actions of the Civil War: 1865-36 pg. in color; flag-c
5 10 15 22 26 30

NEW ADVENTURE OF WALT DISNEY'S SNOW WHITE AND THE SEVEN DWARFS, A
(See Snow White Bendix Giveaway)

NEW ADVENTURES OF PETER PAN (Disney)
Western Publishing Co.: 1953 (5x7-1/4", 36 pgs.) (Admiral giveaway)
nn 14 28 42 76 108 140

NEW AVENGERS... (Giveaway for U.S Military personnel)
Marvel Comics: 2005 - Present (Distributed by Army & Air Force Exchange Service)
... Guest Starring the Fantastic Four (4/05) Bendis-s/Jurgens-a/c 4.00
...: Pot of Gold (AAFES 110th Anniversary Issue) (10/05) Jenkins-s/Nolan-a/c 4.00
(#3) ...: Avengers & X-Men Time Trouble (4/06) Kirkman-s 4.00

New Teen Titans nn © DC

Oxydol-Dreft #5 © AP

Porky's Book of Tricks © WB

GD 2.0 | VG 4.0 | FN 6.0 | VF 8.0 | VF/NM 9.0 | NM- 9.2

(#4) ...: Letters Home (12/06) Capt. America, Punisher, Silver Surfer, Ghost Rider on-c 4.00
5-The Spirit of America (10/05) Captain America app. 4.00
6-Fireline (8/08) Spider-Man, Iron Man & Hulk app. Richards-a/Dave Ross-c 4.00
7-An Army of One (2009) Frank Cho pin-up on back-c 4.00
8-The Promise (12/09) Captain America (Bucky) app. 4.00

NEW FRONTIERS
Harvey Information Press (United States Steel Corp.) : 1958 (16 pgs., paper-c)
nn-History of barbed wire 3 6 9 14 19 24

NEW TEEN TITANS, THE
DC Comics: Nov. 1983
nn(11/83-Keebler Co. Giveaway)-In cooperation with "The President's Drug Awareness Campaign"; came in Presidential envelope w/letter from White House (Nancy Reagan) 1 2 3 4 5 7
nn-(re-issue of Mando paper for direct sales market); American Soft Drink Industry version; I.B.M. Corp. version 5.00

NOLAN RYAN IN THE WINNING PITCH (Kellogg's Tony's Sports Comics)
DC Comics: 1992 (Sports Illustrated)
nn 5.00

OLD GLORY COMICS
Chesapeake & Ohio Railway: 1944 (Giveaway)
nn-Capt. Fearless reprint 8 16 24 40 50 60

ON THE AIR
NBC Network Comic: 1947 (Giveaway, paper-c)
nn-(Rare) 18 36 54 105 165 225

OUT OF THE PAST A CLUE TO THE FUTURE
E. C. Comics (Public Affairs Comm.): 1946? (16 pgs.) (paper cover)
nn-Based on public affairs pamphlet "What Foreign Trade Means to You" 20 40 60 116 191 265

OUTSTANDING AMERICAN WAR HEROES
The Parents' Institute: 1944 (16 pgs., paper-c)
nn-Reprints from True Comics 5 10 15 22 26 30

OVERSEAS COMICS (Also see G.I. Comics & Jeep Comics)
Giveaway (Distributed to U.S. Armed Forces): 1944 - No. 105?, 1946 (7-1/4x10-1/4"; 16 pgs. in color)
23-105-Bringing Up Father (by McManus), Popeye, Joe Palooka, Dick Tracy, Superman, Gasoline Alley, Buz Sawyer, Li'l Abner, Blondie, Terry & the Pirates, Out Our Way 7 14 21 35 43 50

OWL, THE (See Crackajack Funnies #25 & Popular Comics #72)(Also see The Hurricane Kids & Magic Morro
Western Pub. Co./R.S. Callender: 1940 (Giveaway)(7-1/2x5-1/4")(Soft-c, color)
nn-Frank Thomas-a 15 30 45 90 140 190

OXYDOL-DREFT
Toby Press: 1950 (Set of 6 pocket-size giveaways; distributed through the mail as a set) (Scarce)
1-3: 1-Li'l Abner. 2-Daisy Mae. 3-Shmoo 10 20 30 54 72 90
4-John Wayne; Williamson/Frazetta-c from John Wayne #3 14 28 42 76 108 140
5-Archie 13 26 39 72 101 130
6-Terrytoons Mighty Mouse 10 20 30 54 72 90
Mailing Envelope (has All Capp's Shmoo on front) 10 20 30 58 79 100

OZZIE SMITH IN THE KID WHO COULD (Kellogg's Tony's Sports Comics)
DC Comics: 1992 (Sports Illustrated)
nn-Ozzie Smith app. 5.00

PADRE OF THE POOR
Catechetical Guild: nd (Giveaway) (16 pgs., paper-c)
nn 5 10 15 24 30 35

PAUL TERRY'S HOW TO DRAW FUNNY CARTOONS
Terrytoons, Inc. (Giveaway): 1940's (14 pgs.) (Black & White)
nn-Heckle & Jeckle, Mighty Mouse, etc. 13 26 39 72 101 130

PEANUTS HALLOWEEN
Fantagraphics Books: Sept, 2008 (8-1/2" x 5-3/8" ashcan giveaway)
nn-Halloween themed reprints in color and B&W 2.00

PETER PAN (See New Adventures of Peter Pan)

PETER PENNY AND HIS MAGIC DOLLAR
American Bankers Association, N. Y. (Giveaway): 1947 (16 pgs.; paper-c; regular size)
nn-(Scarce)-Used in **SOTI**, pg. 310, 311 15 30 45 88 137 185
Diff. version (7-1/4x11")-redrawn, 16 pgs., paper-c 10 20 30 56 76 95

PETER WHEAT (The Adventures of...)
Bakers Associates Giveaway: 1948 - 1957? (16 pgs. in color) (paper covers)
nn(No.1)-States on last page, end of 1st Adventure of...; Kelly-a 26 52 78 154 252 350
nn(4 issues)-Kelly-a 14 28 42 82 121 160
6-10-All Kelly-a 10 20 30 54 72 90
11-20-All Kelly-a 9 18 27 50 65 80
21-35-All Kelly-a 8 16 24 40 50 60
36-66 6 12 18 28 34 40
...Artist's Workbook ('54, digest size) 6 12 18 28 34 40
...Four-In-One Fun Pack (Vol. 2, '54), oblong, comics w/puzzles 7 14 21 35 43 50
...Fun Book ('52, 32 pgs., paper-c, B&W & color, 8-1/2x10-3/4")-Contains cut-outs, puzzles, games, magic & pages to color 8 16 24 44 57 70
NOTE: *Al Hubbard art #36 on; written by Del Connell.*

PETER WHEAT NEWS
Bakers Associates: 1948 - No. 30, 1950 (4 pgs. in color)
Vol. 1-All have 2 pgs. Peter Wheat by Kelly 21 42 63 123 204 285
2-10 13 26 39 72 101 130
11-20 8 16 24 40 50 60
21-30 6 12 18 28 34 40
NOTE: *Early issues have no date & **Kelly** art.*

PINOCCHIO
Cocomalt/Montgomery Ward Co.: 1940 (10 pgs.; giveaway, linen-like paper)
nn-Cocomalt edition 43 86 129 271 456 640
nn-store edition 36 72 108 215 350 485

PIUS XII MAN OF PEACE
Catechetical Guild: No date (12 pgs.; 5-1/2x8-1/2") (B&W)
nn-Catechetical Guild Giveaway 6 12 18 31 38 45

PLOT TO STEAL THE WORLD, THE
Work & Unity Group: 1948, 16pgs., paper-c
nn-Anti commumism 18 36 54 103 162 220

POCAHONTAS
Pocahontas Fuel Company (Coal): 1941 - No. 2, 1942
nn(#1), 2-Feat. life story of Indian princess Pocahontas & facts about Pocahontas coal, Pocahontas, VA. 15 30 45 85 130 175

POLL PARROT
Poll Parrot Shoe Store/International Shoe
K. K. Publications (Giveaway): 1950 - No. 4, 1951; No. 2, 1959 - No. 16, 1962
1 ('50)-Howdy Doody; small size 18 36 54 107 169 230
2-4('51)-Howdy Doody 15 30 45 88 137 185
2('59)-16('62): 2-The Secret of Crumbley Castle. 5-Bandit Busters. 7-The Make-Believe Mummy. 8-Mixed Up Mission('60). 10-The Frightful Flight. 11-Showdown at Sunup. 12-Maniac at Mubu Island. 13-...and the Runaway Genie. 14-Bully for You. 15-Trapped In Tall Timber. 16-...& the Rajah's Ruby('62) 3 6 9 16 23 30

POPEYE
Whitman
Bold Detergent giveaway (Same as regular issue #94) 2 4 6 9 13 16
Quaker Cereal premium (1989, 16pp, small size,4 diff.)(Popeye & the Time Machine, --On Safari, --& Big Foot, --vs. Bluto) 2 4 6 8 10 12

POPEYE
Charlton (King Features) (Giveaway): 1972 - 1974 (36 pgs. in color)
E-1 to E-15 (Educational comics) 2 4 6 9 13 16
nn-Popeye Gettin' Better Grades-4 pgs. used as intro. to above giveaways (in color) 2 4 6 9 13 16

POPSICLE PETE FUN BOOK (See All-American Comics #6)
Joe Lowe Corp.: 1947, 1948
nn-36 pgs. in color; Sammy 'n' Claras, The King Who Couldn't Sleep & Popsicle Pete stories, games, cut-outs 11 22 33 64 90 115
Adventure Book ('48)-Has Classics ad with checklist to HRN #343 (Great Expectations #43) 10 20 30 56 76 95

PORKY'S BOOK OF TRICKS
K. K. Publications (Giveaway): 1942 (8-1/2x5-1/2", 48 pgs.)
nn-7 pg. comic story, text stories, plus games & puzzles 45 90 135 284 480 675

POST GAZETTE (See Meet the New...)

PUNISHER: COUNTDOWN (Movie)
Marvel Comics: 2004 (7 1/4" X 4 3/4" mini-comic packaged with Punisher DVD)
nn-Prequel to 2004 movie; Ennis-s/Dillon-a/Bradstreet-c 2.50

PURE OIL COMICS (Also see Salerno Carnival of Comics, 24 Pages of Comics, & Vicks Comics)
Pure Oil Giveaway: Late 1930's (24 pgs., regular size, paper-c)

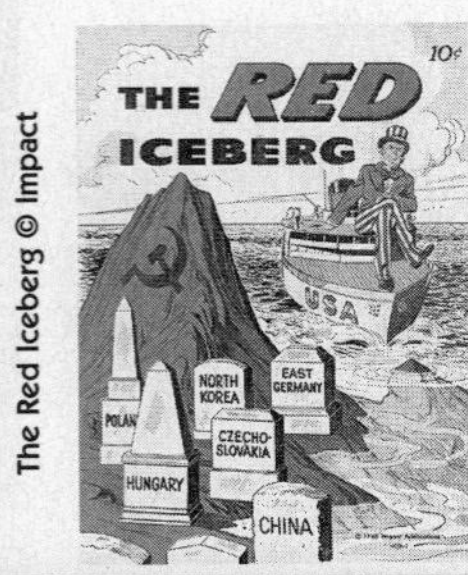

The Red Iceberg © Impact

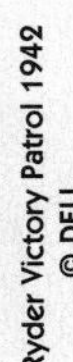
Red Ryder Victory Patrol 1942 © DELL

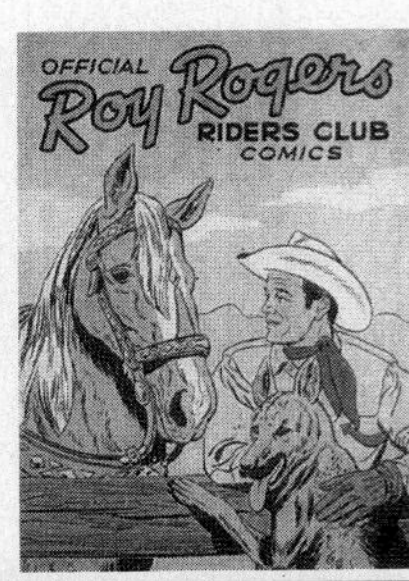

Roy Rogers Riders Club Comics © Roy Rogers

GD VG FN VF VF/NM NM-
2.0 4.0 6.0 8.0 9.0 9.2

nn-Contains 1-2 pg. strips; i.e., Hairbreadth Harry, Skyroads, Buck Rogers by Calkins & Yager, Olly of the Movies, Napoleon, S'Matter Pop, etc. Also a 16 pg. 1938 giveaway with Buck Rogers 34 68 102 204 332 460

QUAKER OATS (Also see Cap'n Crunch)
Quaker Oats Co.: 1965 (Giveaway) (2-1/2x5-1/2") (16 pgs.)

"Plenty of Glutton", starring Quake & Quisp; 3 6 9 14 19 24
"Lava Come-Back", "Kite Tale" 1 3 4 6 8 10

RAILROADS DELIVER THE GOODS!
Assoc. of American Railroads: Dec, 1954; Sept, 1957 (16 pgs.)

nn-The story of railway freight 5 10 15 24 30 35

RAILS ACROSS AMERICA!
Assoc. of American Railroads: nd (16 pgs.)

nn 5 10 15 24 30 35

REAL FUN OF DRIVING!!, THE
Chrysler Corp.: 1965, 1966, 1967 (Regular size, 16 pgs.)

nn-Schaffenberger-a (12 pgs.) 1 2 3 5 6 8

REAL HIT
Fox Features Publications: 1944 (Savings Bond premium)

1-Blue Beetle-r; Blue Beetle on-c 15 30 45 90 140 190

NOTE: *Two versions exist, with and without covers. The coverless version has the title, No. 1 and price printed at top of splash page.*

RED BALL COMIC BOOK
Parents' Magazine Institute: 1947 (Red Ball Shoes giveaway)

nn-Reprints from True Comics 4 8 11 16 19 22

REDDY GOOSE
International Shoe Co. (Western Printing): No number, 1958?; No. 2, Jan, 1959 - No. 16, July, 1962 (Giveaway)

nn (#1) 5 10 15 30 48 65
2-16 3 6 9 18 27 35

REDDY KILOWATT (5¢) (Also see Story of Edison)
Educational Comics (E. C.): 1946 - No. 2, 1947; 1956 - 1965 (no month) (16 pgs., paper-c)

nn-A Visit With Reddy (1948-1954?) 9 18 27 50 65 80
nn-Reddy Made Magic (1946, 5¢) 13 26 39 72 101 130
nn-Reddy Made Magic (1958) 9 18 27 50 65 80
2-Edison, the Man Who Changed the World (3/4" smaller than #1) (1947, 5¢) 13 26 39 72 101 130
...Comic Book 2 (1954)- "Light's Diamond Jubilee" 9 18 27 54 72 90
...Comic Book 2 (1958, 16 pgs.)- "Wizard of Light" 9 18 27 50 65 78
...Comic Book 2 (1965, 16 pgs.)- "Wizard of Light" 4 8 12 28 44 60
...Comic Book 3 (1956, 8 pgs.)- "The Space Kite"; Orlando story; regular size 9 18 27 47 61 75
...Comic Book 3 (1960, 8 pgs.)- "The Space Kite"; Orlando story; regular size 4 8 12 28 44 60

NOTE: *Several copies surfaced in 1979.*

REDDY MADE MAGIC
Educational Comics (E. C.): 1956, 1958 (16 pgs., paper-c)

1-Reddy Kilowatt-r (splash panel changed) 11 22 33 60 83 105
1 (1958 edition) 6 12 18 31 38 45

RED ICEBERG, THE
Impact Publ. (Catechetical Guild): 1960 (10¢, 16 pgs., Communist propaganda)

nn-(Rare)- "We The People" back-c 29 58 87 203 402 600
2nd version- "Impact Press" back-c 24 48 72 175 338 500
3rd version- "Explains comic" back-c 24 48 72 175 338 500
4th version- "Impact Press w/World Wide Secret Heart Program ad" 24 48 72 175 338 500
5th version- "Chicago Inter-Student Catholic Action" back-c 24 48 72 175 338 500

NOTE: *This book was the Guild's last anti-communist propaganda book and had very limited circulation. 3 - 4 copies surfaced in 1979 from the defunct publisher's files. Other copies do turn up.*

RED RYDER COMICS
Dell Publ. Co.

Buster Brown Shoes Giveaway (1941, color, soft-c, 32 pgs.) 20 40 60 120 198 275
Red Ryder Super Book of Comics (1944, paper-c, 32 pgs.; blank back-c) Magic Morro app. 22 44 66 131 216 300
Red Ryder Victory Patrol-nn(1942, 32 pgs.)(Langendorf bread; includes cut-out membership card and certificate, order blank and "Slide-Up" decoder, and a Super Book of Comics in color (same content as Super Book #4 w/diff. cover (Pan-Am)) (Rare) 258 516 774 1638 2819 4000
Red Ryder Victory Patrol-nn(1943, 32 pgs.)(Langendorf bread; includes cut-out "Rodeomatic" radio decoder, order coupon for "Magic V-Badge", cut-out membership card and certificate and a full color Super Book of comics comic book) (Rare) 226 452 678 1435 2468 3500
Red Ryder Victory Patrol-nn(1944, 32 pgs.)-r-/#43,44; comic has a paper-c & is stapled inside a triple cardboard fold-out-c; contains membership card, decoder, map of R.R. home range, etc. Herky app. (Langendorf Bread giveaway; sub-titled 'Super Book of Comics') (Rare) 226 452 678 1435 2468 3500
Wells Lamont Corp. giveaway (1950)-16 pgs. in color; regular size; paper-c; 1941-r 15 30 45 86 133 180

GD VG FN VF VF/NM NM-
2.0 4.0 6.0 8.0 9.0 9.2

RICHIE RICH, CASPER & WENDY NATIONAL LEAGUE
Harvey Publications: June, 1976 (52 pgs.) (newsstand edition also exists)

1 (Released-3/76 with 6/76 date) 3 6 9 16 22 28
1 (6/76)-2nd version w/San Francisco Giants & KTVU 2 logos; has "Compliments of Giants and Straw Hat Pizza" on-c 3 6 9 16 22 28
1-Variants for other 11 NL teams, similar to Giants version but with different ad on inside front-c 3 6 9 16 22 28

RIDE THE HIGH IRON!
Assoc. of American Railroads: Jan, 1957 (16 pgs.)

nn-The Story of modern passenger trains 5 10 15 24 30 35

RIPLEY'S BELIEVE IT OR NOT!
Harvey Publications

J. C. Penney giveaway (1948) 9 18 27 50 65 80

ROBIN HOOD (New Adventures of...)
Walt Disney Productions: 1952 (Flour giveaways, 5x7-1/4", 36 pgs.)

"New Adventures of Robin Hood", "Ghosts of Waylea Castle", & "The Miller's Ransom" each.... 5 10 15 22 26 30

ROBIN HOOD'S FRONTIER DAYS (...Western Tales, Adventures of... #1)
Shoe Store Giveaway (Robin Hood Stores): 1956 (20 pgs., slick-c)(7 issues?)

nn 5 10 15 25 31 36
nn-Issues with Crandall-a 8 16 24 40 50 60

ROBOCOP (FRANK MILLER'S...)
Avatar Press: Apr, 2003

Free Comic Book Day Edition - Previews Robocop & Stargate SG•1; Busch-c 2.50

ROCKET COMICS: IGNITE
Dark Horse Comics: Apr, 2003 (Free Comic Book Day giveaway)

1-Previews Dark Horse series Syn, Lone, and Go Boy 7 2.50

ROCKETS AND RANGE RIDERS
Richfield Oil Corp.: May, 1957 (Giveaway, 16 pgs., soft-c)

nn-Toth-a 14 28 42 82 121 160

ROUND THE WORLD GIFT
National War Fund (Giveaway): No date (mid 1940's) (4 pgs.)

nn 11 22 33 64 90 115

ROY ROGERS COMICS
Dell Publishing Co.

...& the Man From Dodge City (Dodge giveaway, 16 pgs., 1954)-Frontier, Inc. (5x7-1/4") 13 26 39 72 101 130
Official Roy Rogers Riders Club Comics (1952; 16 pgs., reg. size, paper-c) 22 44 66 131 216 300

RUDOLPH, THE RED-NOSED REINDEER
Montgomery Ward: 1939 (2,400,000 copies printed); Dec, 1951 (Giveaway)

Paper cover-1st app. in print; written by Robert May; ill. by Denver Gillen 15 30 45 83 124 165
Hardcover version 19 38 57 109 172 235
1951 Edition (Has 1939 date)-36 pgs., slick-c printed in red & brown; pulp interior printed in four mixed-ink colors: red, green, blue & brown 11 22 33 62 86 110
1951 Edition with red-spiral promotional booklet printed on high quality stock, 8-1/2"x11", in red & brown, 25 pages composed of 4 fold outs, single sheets and the Rudolph comic book inserted (rare) 46 92 138 290 490 690

SABRINA THE TEENAGE WITCH
Archie Comic Publications: (8 1/2"x 5 1/2", Diamond Comic Dist. Halloween giveaway)

... And The Archies (2004)-Tania Del Rio-s/a; manga-style; Josie and the Pussycats app. 2.50

SAD CASE OF WAITING ROOM WILLIE, THE
American Visuals Corp. (For Baltimore Medical Society): (nd, 1950?) (14 pgs. in color; paper covers; regular size)

nn-By Will Eisner (Rare) 43 86 129 271 461 650

SAD SACK COMICS
Harvey Publications: 1957-1962

Armed Forces Complimentary copies, HD #1-40 (1957-1962) 3 6 9 16 22 28

SALERNO CARNIVAL OF COMICS (Also see Pure Oil Comics, 24 Pages of Comics, & Vicks Comics)

Salute to the Boy Scouts © AAR

Santa Takes a Trip to Mars © B-D

Smokey Bear, True Story of... © DELL

	GD 2.0	VG 4.0	FN 6.0	VF 8.0	VF/NM 9.0	NM- 9.2
Salerno Cookie Co.: Late 1930s (Giveaway, 16 pgs, paper-c)						
nn-Color reprints of Calkins' Buck Rogers & Skyroads, plus other strips from Famous Funnies	42	84	126	265	445	625
SALUTE TO THE BOY SCOUTS						
Association of American Railroads: 1960 (16 pgs.)						
nn-History of scouting and the railroad	3	6	9	14	19	24
SANTA AND POLLYANNA PLAY THE GLAD GAME						
Sales Promotion: Aug, 1960 (16 pgs.) (Disney giveaway)						
nn	2	4	6	13	18	22
SANTA & THE BUCCANEERS						
Promotional Publ. Co.: 1959 (Giveaway)						
nn-Reprints 1952 Santa & the Pirates	2	4	6	11	16	20
SANTA & THE CHRISTMAS CHICKADEE						
Murphy's: 1974 (Giveaway, 20 pgs.)						
nn	2	4	6	8	10	12
SANTA & THE PIRATES						
Promotional Publ. Co.: 1952 (Giveaway)						
nn-Marv Levy-c/a	4	8	11	16	19	22
SANTA CLAUS FUNNIES (Also see The Little Fir Tree)						
W. T. Grant Co./Whitman Publishing: nd; 1940 (Giveaway, 8x10"; 12 pgs., color & B&W, heavy paper)						
nn-(2 versions- no date and 1940)	14	28	42	76	108	140
SANTA ON THE JOLLY ROGER						
Promotional Publ. Co. (Giveaway): 1965						
nn-Marv Levy-c/a	2	4	6	8	10	12
SANTA! SANTA!						
R. Jackson: 1974 (20 pgs.) (Montgomery Ward giveaway)						
nn	1	3	4	6	8	10
SANTA'S BUNDLE OF FUN						
Gimbels: 1969 (Giveaway, B&W, 20 pgs.)						
nn-Coloring book & games	2	4	6	8	10	12
SANTA'S CHRISTMAS COMIC VARIETY SHOW (See Merry Christmas From Sears Toyland)						
Sears Roebuck & Co.: 1943 (24 pgs.)						
Contains puzzles & new comics of Dick Tracy, Little Orphan Annie, Moon Mullins, Terry & the Pirates, etc.	52	104	156	325	555	785
SANTA'S CHRISTMAS TIME STORIES						
Premium Sales, Inc.: nd (Late 1940s) (16 pgs., paper-c) (Giveaway)						
nn	6	12	18	31	38	45
SANTA'S CIRCUS						
Promotional Publ. Co.: 1964 (Giveaway, half-size)						
nn-Marv Levy-c/a	2	4	6	8	11	14
SANTA'S FUN BOOK						
Promotional Publ. Co.: 1951, 1952 (Regular size, 16 pgs., paper-c) (Murphy's giveaway)						
nn	5	10	15	23	28	32
SANTA'S GIFT BOOK						
No Publisher: No date (16 pgs.)						
nn-Puzzles, games only	4	8	11	16	19	22
SANTA'S NEW STORY BOOK						
Wallace Hamilton Campbell: 1949 (16 pgs., paper-c) (Giveaway)						
nn	6	12	18	31	38	45
SANTA'S REAL STORY BOOK						
Wallace Hamilton Campbell/W. W. Orris: 1948, 1952 (Giveaway, 16 pgs.)						
nn	6	12	18	31	38	45
SANTA'S RIDE						
W. T. Grant Co.: 1959 (Giveaway)						
nn	3	6	9	14	19	24
SANTA'S RODEO						
Promotional Publ. Co.: 1964 (Giveaway, half-size)						
nn-Marv Levy-a	2	4	6	8	11	14
SANTA'S SECRET CAVE						
W.T. Grant Co.: 1960 (Giveaway, half-size)						
nn	2	4	6	11	16	20
SANTA'S SECRETS						
Sam B. Anson Christmas giveaway: 1951, 1952? (16 pgs., paper-c)						
nn-Has games, stories & pictures to color	4	8	12	17	21	24

	GD 2.0	VG 4.0	FN 6.0	VF 8.0	VF/NM 9.0	NM- 9.2
SANTA'S STORIES						
K. K. Publications (Klines Dept. Store): 1953 (Regular size, paper-c)						
nn-Kelly-a	15	30	45	88	137	185
nn-Another version (1953, glossy-c, half-size, 7-1/4x5-1/4")-Kelly-a	11	22	33	62	86	110
SANTA'S SURPRISE						
K. K. Publications: 1947 (Giveaway, 36 pgs., slick-c)						
nn	8	16	24	40	50	60
SANTA'S TOYTOWN FUN BOOK						
Promotional Publ. Co.: 1953 (Giveaway)						
nn-Marv Levy-c	4	8	11	16	19	22
SANTA TAKES A TRIP TO MARS						
Bradshaw-Diehl Co., Huntington, W.VA.: 1950s (nd) (Giveaway, 16 pgs.)						
nn	4	8	11	16	19	22
SCIENCE FAIR STORY OF ELECTRONICS						
Radio Shack/Tandy Corp.: 1975 - 1987 (Giveaway)						
11 different issues (approx. 1 per year) each....						3.00
SCOOBY-DOO!						
DC Comics.: 2002 (Burger King/Cartoon Network giveaway)						
1						2.50
SERGEANT PRESTON OF THE YUKON						
Quaker Cereals: 1956 (4 comic booklets) (Soft-c, 16 pgs., 7x2-1/2" & 5x2-1/2") Giveaways						
"How He Found Yukon King", "The Case That Made Him A Sergeant", "How Yukon King Saved Him From The Wolves", "How He Became A Mountie" each...	9	18	27	47	61	75
SHAZAM! (Visits Portland Oregon in 1943)						
DC Comics: 1989 (69¢ cover)						
nn-Promotes Super-Heroes exhibit at Oregon Museum of Science and Industry; reprints Golden Age Captain Marvel story	2	4	6	8	11	14
SHERIFF OF COCHISE, THE (TV)						
Mobil: 1957 (16 pgs.) Giveaway						
nn-Schaffenberger-a	4	9	13	18	22	26
SIDEWALK ROMANCE (Also see The K. O. Punch & Lucky Fights It Through)						
Health Publications: 1950						
nn-VD educational giveaway	30	60	90	176	288	400
SILLY PUTTY MAN						
DC Comics: 1978						
1	2	4	6	10	14	18
SKATING SKILLS						
Custom Comics, Inc./Chicago Roller Skates: 1957 (36 & 12 pgs.; 5x7", two versions) (10¢)						
nn-Resembles old ACG cover plus interior art	4	7	10	14	17	20
SKIPPY'S OWN BOOK OF COMICS (See Popular Comics)						
No publisher listed: 1934 (Giveaway, 52 pgs., strip reprints)						
nn-(Scarce)-By Percy Crosby	366	732	1098	2600	4500	6400
Published by Max C. Gaines for Phillip's Dental Magnesia to be advertised on the Skippy Radio Show and given away with the purchase of a tube of Phillip's Tooth Paste. This is the first four-color comic book of reprints about one character.						
SKY KING "RUNAWAY TRAIN" (TV)						
National Biscuit Co.: 1964 (Regular size, 16 pgs.)						
nn	6	12	18	41	66	90
SLAM BANG COMICS						
Post Cereal Giveaway: No. 9, No date						
9-Dynamic Man, Echo, Mr. E, Yankee Boy app.	9	18	27	50	65	80
SLAVE LABOR STORIES						
SLG Publishing: May, 2003 (Giveaway, B&W)						
1-Free Comic Book Day Edition; short stories by various; Dorkin Milk & Cheese-c						2.50
SMILIN' JACK						
Dell Publishing Co.						
Popped Wheat Giveaway (1947)-1938 strip reprints; 16 pgs. in full color	2	4	6	8	11	14
Shoe Store Giveaway-1938 strip reprints; 16 pgs.	5	10	15	24	30	35
Sparked Wheat Giveaway (1942)-16 pgs. in full color	5	10	15	24	30	35
SMOKEY BEAR (See Forest Fire for 1st app.)						
Dell Publ. Co.: 1959,1960						
True Story of..., The -U.S. Forest Service giveaway-Publ. by Western Printing Co.; reprints 1st 16 pgs. of Four Color #932. Inside front-c differs slightly in 1959 & 1960 editions						

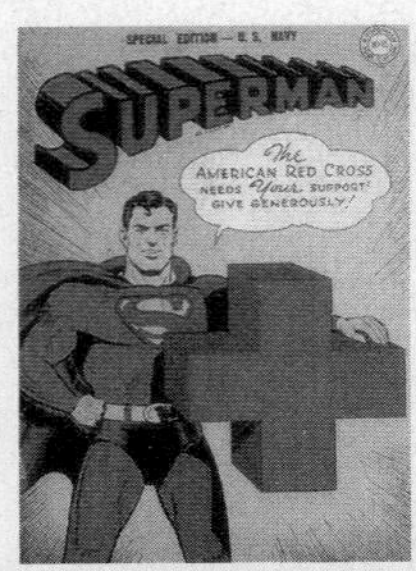

Special Edition #5 © DC

The Spirit (8/04/40) © Will Eisner

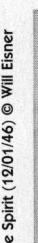

The Spirit (12/01/46) © Will Eisner

	GD 2.0	VG 4.0	FN 6.0	VF 8.0	VF/NM 9.0	NM- 9.2
	6	12	18	28	34	40
1964,1969 reprints	3	6	9	14	19	24

SMOKEY STOVER
Dell Publishing Co.

	GD	VG	FN	VF	VF/NM	NM-
General Motors giveaway (1953)	8	16	24	42	54	65
National Fire Protection giveaway(1953 & 1954)-16 pgs., paper-c	8	16	24	42	54	65

SNOW FOR CHRISTMAS
W. T. Grant Co.: 1957 (16 pgs.) (Giveaway)

	GD	VG	FN	VF	VF/NM	NM-
nn	4	8	12	18	22	25

SNOW WHITE AND THE SEVEN DWARFS
Bendix Washing Machines: 1952 (32 pgs., 5x7-1/4", soft-c) (Disney)

	GD	VG	FN	VF	VF/NM	NM-
nn	11	22	33	62	86	110

SNOW WHITE AND THE SEVEN DWARFS
Promotional Publ. Co.: 1957 (Small size)

	GD	VG	FN	VF	VF/NM	NM-
nn	6	12	18	28	34	40

SNOW WHITE AND THE SEVEN DWARFS
Western Printing Co.: 1958 (16 pgs, 5x7-1/4", soft-c) (Disney premium)

	GD	VG	FN	VF	VF/NM	NM-
nn- "Mystery of the Missing Magic"	6	12	18	31	38	45

SNOW WHITE AND THE 7 DWARFS IN "MILKY WAY"
American Dairy Assoc.: 1955 (16 pgs., soft-c, 5x7-1/4") (Disney premium)

	GD	VG	FN	VF	VF/NM	NM-
nn	7	14	21	35	43	50

SONIC THE HEDGEHOG
Archie Comic Publications: 2008 (Free Comic Book Day giveaway)

	GD	VG	FN	VF	VF/NM	NM-
Free Comic Book Day Edition 1 - Reprints Sonic the Hedgehog #1 from July 1993						4.00

SPACE GHOST COAST TO COAST
Cartoon Network: Apr, 1994 (giveaway to Turner Broadcasting employees)

	GD	VG	FN	VF	VF/NM	NM-
1-(8 pgs.); origin of Space Ghost						6.00

SPACE PATROL (TV)
Ziff-Davis Publishing Co. (Approved Comics)

	GD	VG	FN	VF	VF/NM	NM-
...'s Special Mission (8 pgs., B&W, Giveaway)	45	90	135	284	480	675

SPECIAL AGENT
Assoc. of American Railroads: Oct, 1959 (16 pgs.)

	GD	VG	FN	VF	VF/NM	NM-
nn-The Story of the railroad police	6	12	18	28	34	40

SPECIAL DELIVERY
Post Hall Synd.: 1951 (32 pgs.; B&W) (Giveaway)

nn-Origin of Pogo, Swamp, etc.; 2 pg. biog. on Walt Kelly
(One copy sold in 1980 for $150.00)

SPECIAL EDITION (U. S. Navy Giveaways)
National Periodical Publications: 1944 - 1945 (Regular comic format with wording simplified, 52 pgs.)

	GD	VG	FN	VF	VF/NM	NM-
1-Action (1944)-Reprints Action #80	52	104	156	330	565	800
2-Action (1944)-Reprints Action #81	52	104	156	330	565	800
3-Superman (1944)-Reprints Superman #33	52	104	156	330	565	800
4-Detective (1944)-Reprints Detective #97	52	104	156	330	565	800
5-Superman (1945)-Reprints Superman #34	52	104	156	330	565	800
6-Action (1945)-Reprints Action #84	52	104	156	330	565	800

NOTE: ***Wayne Boring** c-1, 2, 6. **Dick Sprang** c-4.*

SPIDER-MAN (See Amazing Spider-Man, The)

SPIRIT, THE (Weekly Comic Book)
Will Eisner: 6/2/40 - 10/5/52 (16 pgs.; 8 pgs.) (no cover) (in color)
(Distributed through various newspapers and other sources)
NOTE: **Eisner** script, pencils/inks for the most part from 6/2/40-4/26/42; a few stories assisted by Jack Cole, Fine, Powell and Kotsky.

	GD	VG	FN	VF	VF/NM	NM-
6/2/40(#1)-Origin/1st app. The Spirit; reprinted in Police #11; Lady Luck (Brenda Banks) (1st app.) by Chuck Mazoujian & Mr. Mystic (1st. app.) by S. R. (Bob) Powell begin (rare)	174	348	522	1105	1903	2700
6/9/40(#2)	40	80	120	245	410	575
6/16/40(#3)-Black Queen app. in Spirit	28	56	84	165	270	375
6/23/40(#4)-Mr. Mystic receives magical necklace	21	42	63	123	204	285
6/30/40(#5)	21	42	63	123	204	285
7/7/40(#6)-1st app. Spirit carplane; Black Queen app. in Spirit	22	44	66	131	216	300
7/14/40(#7)-8/4/40(#10): 7/21/40-Spirit becomes fugitive wanted for murder	19	38	57	112	181	250
8/11/40-9/22/40	18	36	54	105	165	225
9/29/40-Ellen drops engagement with Homer Creep	17	34	51	98	154	210
10/6/40-11/3/40	17	34	51	98	154	210
11/10/40-The Black Queen app.	17	34	51	98	154	210
11/17/40, 11/24/40	17	34	51	98	154	210
12/1/40-Ellen spanking by Spirit on cover & inside; Eisner-1st 3 pgs., J. Cole rest	20	40	60	120	198	275
12/8/40-3/9/41	15	30	45	85	130	175
3/16/41-Intro. & 1st app. Silk Satin	19	38	57	110	175	240
3/23/41-6/1/41: 5/11/41-Last Lady Luck by Mazoujian; 5/18/41-Lady Luck by Nick Viscardi begins, ends 2/22/42	15	30	45	83	124	165
6/8/41-2nd app. Satin; Spirit learns Satin is also a British agent	15	30	45	90	140	190
6/15/41-1st app. Twilight	15	30	45	86	133	180
6/22/41-Hitler app. in Spirit	15	30	45	86	133	180
6/29/41-1/25/42,2/8/42	14	28	42	78	112	145
2/1/42-1st app. Duchess	15	30	45	86	133	180
2/15/42-4/26/42-Lady Luck by Klaus Nordling begins 3/1/42	14	28	42	82	121	160
5/3/42-8/16/42-Eisner/Fine/Quality staff assists on Spirit	12	24	36	67	94	120
8/23/42-Satin cover splash; Spirit by Eisner/Fine although signed by Fine	15	30	45	94	147	200
8/30/42,9/27/42-10/11/42,10/25/42-11/8/42-Eisner/Fine/Quality staff assists on Spirit	11	22	33	64	90	115
9/6/42-9/20/42,10/18/42-Fine/Belfi art on Spirit; scripts by Manly Wade Wellman	9	18	27	47	61	75
11/15/42-12/6/42,12/20/42,12/27/42,1/17/43-4/18/43,5/9/43-8/8/43-Wellman/ Woolfolk scripts, Fine pencils, Quality staff inks	9	18	27	47	61	75
12/13/42,1/3/43,1/10/43,4/25/43,5/2/43-Eisner scripts/layouts; Fine pencils, Quality staff inks	9	18	27	52	69	85
8/15/43-Eisner script/layout; pencils/inks by Quality staff; Jack Cole-a	8	16	24	42	54	65
8/22/43-12/12/43-Wellman/Woolfolk scripts, Fine pencils, Quality staff inks; Mr. Mystic by Guardineer-10/10/43-10/24/43	8	16	24	42	54	65
12/19/43-8/13/44-Wellman/Woolfolk/Jack Cole scripts; Cole, Fine & Robin King-a; Last Mr. Mystic-5/14/44	8	16	24	40	50	60
8/20/44-12/16/45-Wellman/Woolfolk scripts; Fine art with unknown staff assists	8	16	24	40	50	60

NOTE: *Scripts/layouts by Eisner, or Eisner/Nordling, Eisner/Mercer or Spranger/Eisner; inks by Eisner or Eisner/Spranger in issues 12/23/45-2/2/47.*

	GD	VG	FN	VF	VF/NM	NM-
12/23/45-1/6/46: 12/23/45-Christmas-c	9	18	27	50	65	80
1/13/46-Origin Spirit retold	12	24	36	69	97	125
1/20/46-1st postwar Satin app.	11	22	33	62	86	110
1/27/46-3/10/46: 3/3/46-Last Lady Luck by Nordling	9	18	27	50	65	80
3/17/46-Intro. & 1st app. Nylon	11	22	33	62	86	110
3/24/46,3/31/46,4/14/46	9	18	27	50	65	80
4/7/46-2nd app. Nylon	10	20	30	54	72	90
4/21/46-Intro. & 1st app. Mr. Carrion & His Pet Buzzard Julia	12	24	36	69	97	125
4/28/46-5/12/46,5/26/46-6/30/46: Lady Luck by Fred Schwab in issues 5/5/46-11/3/46	9	18	27	50	65	80
5/19/46-2nd app. Mr. Carrion	10	20	30	54	72	90
7/7/46-Intro. & 1st app. Dulcet Tone & Skinny	11	22	33	62	86	110
7/14/46-9/29/46	9	18	27	50	65	80
10/6/46-Intro. & 1st app. P'Gell	13	26	39	72	101	130
10/13/46-11/3/46,11/16/46-11/24/46	9	18	27	50	65	80
11/10/46-2nd app. P'Gell	11	22	33	60	83	105
12/1/46-3rd app. P'Gell	9	18	27	52	69	85
12/8/46-2/2/47	9	18	27	47	61	75

NOTE: *Scripts, pencils/inks by Eisner except where noted in issues 2/9/47-12/19/48.*

	GD	VG	FN	VF	VF/NM	NM-
2/9/47-7/6/47: 6/8/47-Eisner self satire	9	18	27	47	61	75
7/13/47- "Hansel & Gretel" fairy tales	11	22	33	62	86	110
7/20/47-Li'L Abner, Daddy Warbucks, Dick Tracy, Fearless Fosdick parody; A-Bomb blast-c	12	24	36	69	97	125
7/27/47-9/14/47	9	18	27	47	61	75
9/21/47-Pearl Harbor flashback	10	20	30	54	72	90
9/28/47-1st mention of Flying Saucers in comics-3 months after 1st sighting in Idaho on 6/25/47	15	30	45	94	147	200
10/5/47- "Cinderella" fairy tales	11	22	33	62	86	110
10/12/47-11/30/47	9	18	27	47	61	75
12/7/47-Intro. & 1st app. Powder Pouf	12	24	36	69	97	125
12/14/47-12/28/47	9	18	27	47	61	75
1/4/48-2nd app. Powder Pouf	9	18	27	52	69	85
1/11/48-1st app. Sparrow Fallon; Powder Pouf app.	9	18	27	52	69	85
1/18/48-He-Man ad cover; satire issue	9	18	27	52	69	85
1/25/48-Intro. & 1st app. Castanet	12	24	36	69	97	125
2/1/48-2nd app. Castanet	9	18	27	50	65	80
2/8/48-3/7/48	9	18	27	47	61	75
3/14/48-Only app. Kretchma	9	18	27	50	65	80
3/21/48,3/28/48,4/11/48-4/25/48	9	18	27	47	61	75
4/4/48-Only app. Wild Rice	9	18	27	50	65	80
5/2/48-2nd app. Sparrow	9	18	27	47	61	75
5/9/48-6/27/48,7/11/48,7/18/48: 6/13/48-TV issue	9	18	27	47	61	75

The Spirit (2/19/50) © Will Eisner

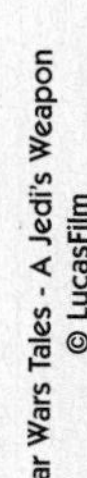

Star Wars Tales - A Jedi's Weapon © LucasFilm

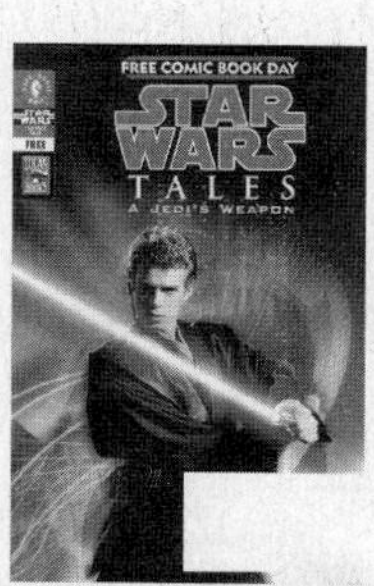

Steve Canyon - Strictly For the Smart Birds © HARV

	GD 2.0	VG 4.0	FN 6.0	VF 8.0	VF/NM 9.0	NM- 9.2
7/4/48-Spirit by Andre Le Blanc	8	16	24	40	50	60
7/25/48-Ambrose Bierce's "The Thing" adaptation classic by Eisner/Grandenetti	15	30	45	86	133	180
8/1/48-8/15/48,8/29/48-9/12/48	9	18	27	47	61	75
8/22/48-Poe's "Fall of the House of Usher" classic by Eisner/Grandenetti	15	30	45	86	133	180
9/19/48-Only app. Lorelei	9	18	27	52	69	85
9/26/48-10/31/48	9	18	27	47	61	75
11/7/48-Only app. Plaster of Paris	11	22	33	62	86	110
11/14/48-12/19/48	9	18	27	47	61	75

NOTE: *Scripts by Eisner or Feiffer or Eisner/Feiffer or Nordling. Art by Eisner with backgrounds by Eisner, Grandenetti, Le Blanc, Stallman, Nordling, Dixon and/or others in issues 12/26/48-4/1/51 except where noted.*

	GD 2.0	VG 4.0	FN 6.0	VF 8.0	VF/NM 9.0	NM- 9.2
12/26/48-Reprints some covers of 1948 with flashbacks	9	18	27	47	61	75
1/2/49-1/16/49	9	18	27	47	61	75
1/23/49,1/30/49-1st & 2nd app. Thorne	9	18	27	52	69	85
2/6/49-8/14/49	9	18	27	47	61	75
8/21/49,8/28/49-1st & 2nd app. Monica Veto	9	18	27	52	69	85
9/4/49,9/11/49	9	18	27	47	61	75
9/18/49-Love comic cover; has gag love comic ads on inside	9	18	27	52	69	85
9/25/49-Only app. Ice	9	18	27	50	65	80
10/2/49,10/9/49-Autumn News appears & dies in 10/9 issue	9	18	27	50	65	80
10/16/49-11/27/49,12/18/49,12/25/49	9	18	27	47	61	75
12/4/49,12/11/49-1st & 2nd app. Flaxen	9	18	27	50	65	80
1/1/50-Flashbacks to all of the Spirit girls-Thorne, Ellen, Satin, & Monica	13	26	39	74	105	135
1/8/50-Intro. & 1st app. Sand Saref	15	30	45	84	127	170
1/15/50-2nd app. Saref	12	24	36	69	97	125
1/22/50-2/5/50	9	18	27	47	61	75
2/12/50-Roller Derby issue	9	18	27	52	69	85
2/19/50-Half Dead Mr. Lox - Classic horror	11	22	33	62	86	110
2/26/50-4/23/50,5/14/50,5/28/50,7/23/50-9/3/50	9	18	27	47	61	75
4/30/50-Script/art by Le Blanc with Eisner framing	7	14	21	37	46	55
5/7/50,6/4/50-7/16/50-Abe Kanegson-a	7	14	21	37	46	55
5/21/50-Script by Feiffer/Eisner, art by Blaisdell, Eisner framing	7	14	21	37	46	55
9/10/50-P'Gell returns	9	18	27	52	69	85
9/17/50-1/7/51	9	18	27	47	61	75
1/14/51-Life Magazine cover; brief biography of Comm. Dolan, Sand Saref, Silk Satin, P'Gell, Sammy & Willum, Darling O'Shea, & Mr. Carrion & His Pet Buzzard Julia, with pin-ups by Eisner	11	22	33	62	86	110
1/21/51,2/4/51-4/1/51	9	18	27	47	61	75
1/28/51- "The Meanest Man in the World" by Eisner	11	22	33	62	86	110
4/8/51-7/29/51,8/12/51-Last Eisner issue	9	18	27	47	61	75
8/5/51,8/19/51-7/20/52-Not Eisner	7	14	21	37	46	55
7/27/52-(Rare)-Denny Colt in Outer Space by Wally Wood; 7 pg. S/F story of E.C. vintage	39	78	117	234	380	525
8/3/52-(Rare)- "Mission…The Moon" by Wood	39	78	117	234	380	525
8/10/52-(Rare)- "A DP On The Moon" by Wood	39	78	117	234	380	525
8/17/52-(Rare)- "Heart" by Wood/Eisner	33	66	99	198	324	450
8/24/52-(Rare)- "Rescue" by Wood	39	78	117	234	380	525
8/31/52-(Rare)- "The Last Man" by Wood	39	78	117	234	380	525
9/7/52-(Rare)- "The Man in The Moon" by Wood	39	78	117	234	380	525
9/14/52-(Rare)-Eisner/Wenzel-a	19	38	57	110	175	240
9/21/52-(Rare)- "Denny Colt, Alias The Spirit/Space Report" by Eisner/Wenzel	19	38	57	114	187	260
9/28/52-(Rare)- "Return From The Moon" by Wood	37	74	111	222	361	500
10/5/52-(Rare)- "The Last Story" by Eisner	18	36	54	103	162	220

Large Tabloid pages from 1946 on (Eisner) - Price 200 percent over listed prices.
NOTE: *Spirit sections came out in both large and small format. Some newspapers went to the 8-pg. format months before others. Some printed the pages so they cannot be folded into a small comic book section; these are worth less. (Also see Three Comics & Spiritman).*

SPY SMASHER
Fawcett Publications

	GD 2.0	VG 4.0	FN 6.0	VF 8.0	VF/NM 9.0	NM- 9.2
Well Known Comics (1944, 12 pgs., 8-1/2x10-1/2"), paper-c, glued binding, printed in green; Bestmaid/Samuel Lowe giveaway	15	30	45	83	124	165

STANDARD OIL COMICS (Also see Gulf Funny Weekly)
Standard Oil Co.: 1932-1934 (Giveaway, tabloid size, 4 pgs. in color)

	GD 2.0	VG 4.0	FN 6.0	VF 8.0	VF/NM 9.0	NM- 9.2
nn (Dec. 1932)	52	104	156	330	565	800
1-Series has original art	45	90	135	284	480	675
2-5	20	40	60	116	191	265
6-14: 14-Fred Opper strip, 1 pg.	14	28	42	76	108	140
1A (Jan 1933)	47	94	141	296	498	700
2A-14A (1933)	30	60	90	176	288	400
1B (1934)	37	74	111	222	361	500
2B-?B (1934)	30	60	90	176	288	400

NOTE: *Series A contains Frederick Opper's Si & Mirandi; Series B contains Goofus: He's From The Big City; McVittie by Walter O'Ehrle; interior strips include Pesty And His Pop & Smiling Slim by Sid Hicks.*

STAR TEAM
Marvel Comics Group: 1977 (6-1/2x5", 20 pgs.) (Ideal Toy Giveaway)

	GD 2.0	VG 4.0	FN 6.0	VF 8.0	VF/NM 9.0	NM- 9.2
nn	3	6	9	14	19	24

STAR WARS
Dark Horse Comics (Free Comic Book Day giveaways)

	NM- 9.2
...: Clone Wars #0 (5/09) flip book with short stories of Usagi Yojimbo, Emily the Strange	2.50
...: Clone Wars Adventures (7/04) based on Cartoon Network series; Fillbach Bros. -a	2.50
...: FCBD 2005 Special (5/05) Anakin & Obi-Wan during Clone Wars	2.50
...: FCBD 2006 Special (5/06) Clone Wars story; flip book with Conan FCBD Special	2.50
...: Tales - A Jedi's Weapon (5/02, 16 pgs.) Anakin Skywalker Episode 2 photo-c	2.50

STEVE CANYON COMICS
Harvey Publications

	GD 2.0	VG 4.0	FN 6.0	VF 8.0	VF/NM 9.0	NM- 9.2
Dept. Store giveaway #3(6/48, 36pp)	10	20	30	54	72	90
...'s Secret Mission (1951, 16 pgs., Armed Forces giveaway); Caniff-a	9	18	27	47	61	75
Strictly for the Smart Birds (1951, 16 pgs.)-Information Comics Div. (Harvey) Premium	8	16	24	40	50	60

STORIES OF CHRISTMAS
K. K. Publications: 1942 (Giveaway, 32 pgs., paper cover)

	GD 2.0	VG 4.0	FN 6.0	VF 8.0	VF/NM 9.0	NM- 9.2
nn-Adaptation of "A Christmas Carol"; Kelly story "The Fir Tree"; Infinity-c	29	58	87	172	281	390

STORY HOUR SERIES (Disney)
Whitman Publ. Co.: 1948, 1949; 1951-1953 (36 pgs., paper-c) (4-3/4x6-1/2")
Given away with subscription to Walt Disney's Comics & Stories

	GD 2.0	VG 4.0	FN 6.0	VF 8.0	VF/NM 9.0	NM- 9.2
nn(1948)-Mickey Mouse and the Boy Thursday	12	24	36	67	94	120
nn(1948)-Mickey Mouse the Miracle Master	12	24	36	67	94	120
nn(1948)-Minnie Mouse and Antique Chair	12	24	36	67	94	120
nn(1949)-The Three Orphan Kittens(B&W & color)	9	18	27	47	61	75
nn(1949)-Danny-The Little Black Lamb	9	18	27	47	61	75
800(1948)-Donald Duck in "Bringing Up the Boys"	15	30	45	88	137	185
1953 edition	11	22	33	64	90	115
801(1948)-Mickey Mouse's Summer Vacation	10	20	30	56	76	95
1951, 1952 editions	7	14	21	35	43	50
802(1948)-Bugs Bunny's Adventures	9	18	27	50	65	80
803(1948)-Bongo	8	16	24	40	50	60
804(1948)-Mickey and the Beanstalk	9	18	27	47	61	75
805-15(1949)-Andy Panda and His Friends	8	16	24	40	50	60
806-15(1949)-Tom and Jerry	8	16	24	44	57	70
808-15(1949)-Johnny Appleseed	8	16	24	40	50	60

1948, 1949 Hard Cover Edition of each....30% - 40% more.

STORY OF EDISON, THE
Educational Comics: 1956 (16 pgs.) (Reddy Killowatt)

	GD 2.0	VG 4.0	FN 6.0	VF 8.0	VF/NM 9.0	NM- 9.2
nn-Reprint of Reddy Kilowatt #2(1947)	7	14	21	35	43	50

STORY OF HARRY S. TRUMAN, THE
Democratic National Committee: 1948 (Giveaway, regular size, soft-c, 16 pg.)

	GD 2.0	VG 4.0	FN 6.0	VF 8.0	VF/NM 9.0	NM- 9.2
nn-Gives biography on career of Truman; used in **SOTI**, pg. 311	14	28	42	76	108	140

STORY OF THE BALLET, THE
Selva and Sons, Inc.: 1954 (16 pgs., paper cover)

	GD 2.0	VG 4.0	FN 6.0	VF 8.0	VF/NM 9.0	NM- 9.2
nn	4	8	11	16	19	22

STRANGE AS IT SEEMS
McNaught Syndicate: 1936 (B&W, 5" x 7", 24 pgs.)

	GD 2.0	VG 4.0	FN 6.0	VF 8.0	VF/NM 9.0	NM- 9.2
nn-Ex-Lax giveaway	8	16	24	44	57	70

STRAY
Dark Horse Comics: 2004 (8 1/2"x 5 1/2", Diamond Comic Dist. Halloween giveaway)

	NM- 9.2
nn-Reprint from The Dark Horse Book of Hauntings; Evan Dorkin-s/Jill Thompson-a	2.50

STRAY BULLETS
El Capitan Books: May, 2002 (48 pgs., B&W, flip book)

	NM- 9.2
Free Comic Book Day giveaway-Reprints #2 with "Free Comic Book Day" banner on-c; flip book with The Matrix (printing of internet comic)	2.50

SUGAR BEAR
Post Cereal Giveaway: No date, circa 1975? (2 1/2" x 4 1/2", 16 pgs.)

	GD 2.0	VG 4.0	FN 6.0	VF 8.0	VF/NM 9.0	NM- 9.2
"The Almost Take Over of the Post Office", "The Race Across the Atlantic", "The Zoo Goes Wild" each...	1	2	3	5	6	8

SUNDAY WORLD'S EASTER EGG FULL OF EASTER MEAT FOR LITTLE PEOPLE
Supplement to the New York World: 3/27/1898 (soft-c, 16pg, 4"x8" approx., opens at top, color & B&W)(Giveaway)(shaped like an Easter egg)

	GD 2.0	VG 4.0	FN 6.0	VF 8.0	VF/NM 9.0	NM- 9.2
nn-By R.F. Outcault	18	36	54	103	162	220

Super-Book of Comics #13 © NYNS

Super-Book of Comics (Omar) #23 © KING

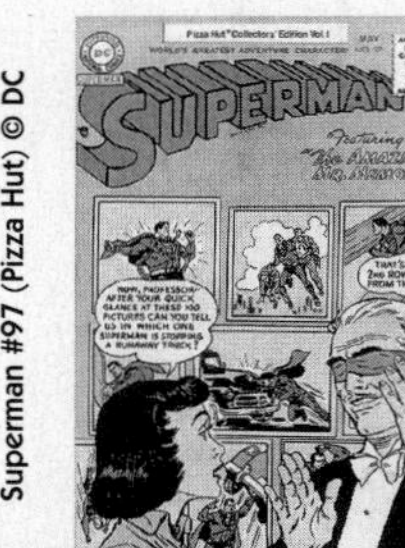

Superman #97 (Pizza Hut) © DC

	GD 2.0	VG 4.0	FN 6.0	VF 8.0	VF/NM 9.0	NM- 9.2

SUPER BOOK OF COMICS
Western Publishing Co.: nd (1942-1943?) (Soft-c, 32 pgs.) (Pan-Am/Gilmore Oil/Kelloggs premiums)

	GD 2.0	VG 4.0	FN 6.0	VF 8.0	VF/NM 9.0	NM- 9.2
nn-Dick Tracy (Gilmore)-Magic Morro app. (2 versions: Dick Tracy Jr. on cover and a filing cabinet cover)	31	62	93	184	302	420
1-Dick Tracy & The Smuggling Ring; Stratosphere Jim app. (Rare) (Pan-Am)	31	62	93	184	302	420
1-Smilin' Jack, Magic Morro (Pan-Am)	13	26	39	74	105	135
2-Smilin' Jack, Stratosphere Jim (Pan-Am)	13	26	39	74	105	135
2-Smitty, Magic Morro (Pan-Am)	13	26	39	74	105	135
3-Captain Midnight, Magic Morro (Pan-Am)	22	44	66	131	216	300
3-Moon Mullins?	13	26	39	74	105	135
4-Red Ryder, Magic Morro (Pan-Am). Same content as Red Ryder Victory Patrol comic w/diff. cover	15	30	45	85	130	175
4-Smitty, Stratosphere Jim (Pan-Am)	13	26	39	74	105	135
5-Don Winslow, Magic Morro (Gilmore)	15	30	45	85	130	175
5-Don Winslow, Stratosphere Jim (Pan-Am)	15	30	45	85	130	175
5-Terry & the Pirates	17	34	51	98	154	210
6-Don Winslow, Stratosphere Jim (Pan-Am)-McWilliams-a	15	30	45	85	130	175
6-King of the Royal Mounted, Magic Morro (Pan-Am)	15	30	45	85	130	175
7-Dick Tracy, Magic Morro (Pan-Am)	19	38	57	111	178	245
7-Little Orphan Annie	11	22	33	64	90	115
8-Dick Tracy, Stratosphere Jim (Pan-Am)	17	34	51	98	154	210
8-Dan Dunn, Magic Morro (Pan-Am)	11	22	33	64	90	115
9-Terry & the Pirates, Magic Morro (Pan-Am)	17	34	51	98	154	210
10-Red Ryder, Magic Morro (Pan-Am)	15	30	45	85	130	175

SUPER-BOOK OF COMICS
Western Publishing Co.: (Omar Bread & Hancock Oil Co. giveaways) 1944 - No. 30, 1947 (Omar); 1947 - 1948 (Hancock) (16 pgs.)

NOTE: The Hancock issues are all exact reprints of the earlier Omar issues. The issue numbers were removed in some of the reprints.

	GD 2.0	VG 4.0	FN 6.0	VF 8.0	VF/NM 9.0	NM- 9.2
1-Dick Tracy (Omar, 1944)	15	30	45	94	147	200
1-Dick Tracy (Hancock, 1947)	14	28	42	78	112	145
2-Bugs Bunny (Omar, 1944)	8	16	24	40	50	60
2-Bugs Bunny (Hancock, 1947)	6	12	18	32	39	46
3-Terry & the Pirates (Omar, 1944)	11	22	33	60	83	105
3-Terry & the Pirates (Hancock, 1947)	10	20	30	54	72	90
4-Andy Panda (Omar, 1944)	8	16	24	40	50	60
4-Andy Panda (Hancock, 1947)	6	12	18	32	39	46
5-Smokey Stover (Omar, 1945)	6	12	18	32	39	46
5-Smokey Stover (Hancock, 1947)	5	10	15	24	30	35
6-Porky Pig (Omar, 1945)	8	16	24	40	50	60
6-Porky Pig (Hancock, 1947)	6	12	18	32	39	46
7-Smilin' Jack (Omar, 1945)	8	16	24	40	50	60
7-Smilin' Jack (Hancock, 1947)	6	12	18	32	39	46
8-Oswald the Rabbit (Omar, 1945)	6	12	18	32	39	46
8-Oswald the Rabbit (Hancock, 1947)	5	10	15	24	30	35
9-Alley Oop (Omar, 1945)	11	22	33	64	90	115
9-Alley Oop (Hancock, 1947)	11	22	33	60	83	105
10-Elmer Fudd (Omar, 1945)	6	12	18	32	39	46
10-Elmer Fudd (Hancock, 1947)	5	10	15	24	30	35
11-Little Orphan Annie (Omar, 1945)	8	16	24	42	53	64
11-Little Orphan Annie (Hancock, 1947)	7	14	21	36	45	54
12-Woody Woodpecker (Omar, 1945)	6	12	18	32	39	46
12-Woody Woodpecker (Hancock, 1947)	5	10	15	24	30	35
13-Dick Tracy (Omar, 1945)	11	22	33	64	90	115
13-Dick Tracy (Hancock, 1947)	11	22	33	60	83	105
14-Bugs Bunny (Omar, 1945)	6	12	18	32	39	46
14-Bugs Bunny (Hancock, 1947)	5	10	15	24	30	35
15-Andy Panda (Omar, 1945)	6	12	18	28	34	40
15-Andy Panda (Hancock, 1947)	5	10	15	24	30	35
16-Terry & the Pirates (Omar, 1945)	11	22	33	60	83	105
16-Terry & the Pirates (Hancock, 1947)	9	18	27	47	61	75
17-Smokey Stover (Omar, 1946)	6	12	18	32	39	46
17-Smokey Stover (Hancock, 1948?)	5	10	15	24	30	35
18-Porky Pig (Omar, 1946)	6	12	18	28	34	40
18-Porky Pig (Hancock, 1948?)	5	10	15	24	30	35
19-Smilin' Jack (Omar, 1946)	6	12	18	32	39	46
nn-Smilin' Jack (Hancock, 1948)	5	10	15	24	30	35
20-Oswald the Rabbit (Omar, 1946)	6	12	18	28	34	40
nn-Oswald the Rabbit (Hancock, 1948)	5	10	15	24	30	35
21-Gasoline Alley (Omar, 1946)	8	16	24	42	53	64
nn-Gasoline Alley (Hancock, 1948)	7	14	21	36	45	54
22-Elmer Fudd (Omar, 1946)	6	12	18	28	34	40
nn-Elmer Fudd (Hancock, 1948)	5	10	15	24	30	35
23-Little Orphan Annie (Omar, 1946)	8	16	24	40	50	60
nn-Little Orphan Annie (Hancock, 1948)	6	12	18	32	39	46
24-Woody Woodpecker (Omar, 1946)	6	12	18	28	34	40
nn-Woody Woodpecker (Hancock, 1948)	5	10	15	24	30	35
25-Dick Tracy (Omar, 1946)	11	22	33	60	83	105
nn-Dick Tracy (Hancock, 1948)	9	18	27	50	65	80
26-Bugs Bunny (Omar, 1946))	6	12	18	28	34	40
nn-Bugs Bunny (Hancock, 1948)	5	10	15	24	30	35
27-Andy Panda (Omar, 1946)	6	12	18	28	34	40
27-Andy Panda (Hancock, 1948)	5	10	15	24	30	35
28-Terry & the Pirates (Omar, 1946)	11	22	33	60	83	105
28-Terry & the Pirates (Hancock, 1948)	9	18	27	47	61	75
29-Smokey Stover (Omar, 1947)	6	12	18	28	34	40
29-Smokey Stover (Hancock, 1948)	5	10	15	24	30	35
30-Porky Pig (Omar, 1947)	6	12	18	28	34	40
30-Porky Pig (Hancock, 1948)	5	10	15	24	30	35
nn-Bugs Bunny (Hancock, 1948)-Does not match any Omar book	6	12	18	28	34	40

SUPER CIRCUS (TV)
Cross Publishing Co.

	GD 2.0	VG 4.0	FN 6.0	VF 8.0	VF/NM 9.0	NM- 9.2
1-(1951, Weather Bird Shoes giveaway)	8	16	24	40	50	60

SUPER FRIENDS
DC Comics: 1981 (Giveaway, no ads, no code or price)

	GD 2.0	VG 4.0	FN 6.0	VF 8.0	VF/NM 9.0	NM- 9.2
...Special 1 -r/Super Friends #19 & 36	2	4	6	9	12	15

SUPERGEAR COMICS
Jacobs Corp.: 1976 (Giveaway, 4 pgs. in color, slick paper)

	GD 2.0	VG 4.0	FN 6.0	VF 8.0	VF/NM 9.0	NM- 9.2
nn-(Rare)-Superman, Lois Lane; Steve Lombard app. (500 copies printed, over half destroyed?)	21	42	63	148	287	425

SUPERGIRL
DC Comics: 1984, 1986 (Giveaway, Baxter paper)

	GD 2.0	VG 4.0	FN 6.0	VF 8.0	VF/NM 9.0	NM- 9.2
nn-(American Honda/U.S. Dept. Transportation) Torres-c/a	2	4	6	8	11	14

SUPER HEROES PUZZLES AND GAMES
General Mills Giveaway (Marvel Comics Group): 1979 (32 pgs., regular size)

	GD 2.0	VG 4.0	FN 6.0	VF 8.0	VF/NM 9.0	NM- 9.2
nn-Four 2-pg. origin stories of Spider-Man, Captain America, The Hulk, & Spider-Woman	3	6	9	14	20	26

SUPERMAN
National Periodical Publ./DC Comics

	GD 2.0	VG 4.0	FN 6.0	VF 8.0	VF/NM 9.0	NM- 9.2
72-Giveaway(9-10/51)-(Rare)-Price blackened out; came with banner wrapped around book; without banner	71	142	213	451	776	1100
72-Giveaway with banner	110	220	330	699	1200	1700
Bradman birthday custom (1988)(extremely limited distribution) - no reported sales for 2008						
... For the Animals (2000, Doris Day Animal Foundation, 30 pgs.) polybagged with Gotham Adventures #22, Hourman #12, Impulse #58, Looney Tunes #62, Stars and S.T.R.I.P.E. #8 and Superman Adventures #41						2.50
Kelloggs Giveaway-(2/3 normal size, 1954)-r-two stories/Superman #55	28	56	84	165	270	375
Kenner: Man of Steel (Doomsday is Coming) (1995, 16 pgs.) packaged with set of Superman and Doomsday action figures						4.00
...Meets the Quik Bunny (1987, Nestles Quik premium, 36 pgs.)	1	2	3	5	6	8
Pizza Hut Premiums (12/77)-Exact reprints of 1950s comics except for paid ads (set of 6 exist?); Vol. 1-r#97 (#113-r also known)	1	3	4	6	8	10
Radio Shack Giveaway-36 pgs. (7/80) "The Computers That Saved Metropolis", Starlin/Giordano-a; advertising insert in Action #509, New Advs. of Superboy #7, Legion of Super-Heroes #265, & House of Mystery #282. (All comics were 68 pgs.) Cover of inserts printed on newsprint. Giveaway contains 4 extra pgs. of Radio Shack advertising that inserts do not have	1	2	3	5	6	8
Radio Shack Giveaway-(7/81) "Victory by Computer"	1	2	3	5	6	8
Radio Shack Giveaway-(7/82) "Computer Masters of Metropolis"	1	2	3	5	6	8

SUPERMAN ADVENTURES, THE (TV)
DC Comics: 1996 (Based on animated series)

	GD 2.0	VG 4.0	FN 6.0	VF 8.0	VF/NM 9.0	NM- 9.2
1-(1996) Preview issue distributed at Warner Bros. stores						4.00
Titus Game Edition (1998)						2.50

SUPERMAN AND THE GREAT CLEVELAND FIRE
National Periodical Publ.: 1948 (Giveaway, 4 pgs., no cover) (Hospital Fund)

	GD 2.0	VG 4.0	FN 6.0	VF 8.0	VF/NM 9.0	NM- 9.2
nn-In full color	63	126	189	400	688	975

SUPERMAN AT THE GILBERT HALL OF SCIENCE
National Periodical Publ.: 1948 (Giveaway) (Gilbert Chemistry Sets / A.C. Gilbert Co.)

	GD 2.0	VG 4.0	FN 6.0	VF 8.0	VF/NM 9.0	NM- 9.2
nn	31	62	93	186	301	425

SUPERMAN/BATMAN

Superman-Tim 7/43 © DC

Tastee-Freez Comics #2 © HARV

Terry and the Pirates Popped Wheat © DELL

GD VG FN VF VF/NM NM-
2.0 4.0 6.0 8.0 9.0 9.2

DC Comics: June, 2006 (Free Comic Book Day giveaway)
1-Reprints #1 2.50

SUPERMAN (Miniature)
National Periodical Publ.: 1942; 1955 - 1956 (3 issues, no #'s, 32 pgs.)
The pages are numbered in the 1st issue: 1-32; 2nd: 1A-32A, and 3rd: 1B-32B
No date-Py-Co-Pay Tooth Powder giveaway (8 pgs.; circa 1942)
43 86 129 271 461 650
1-The Superman Time Capsule (Kellogg's Sugar Smacks)(1955)
24 48 72 142 234 325
1A-Duel in Space (1955) 22 44 66 131 216 300
1B-The Super Show of Metropolis (also #1-32, no B)(1955)
22 44 66 131 216 300
NOTE: *Numbering variations exist. Each title could have any combination-#1, 1A, or 1B.*

SUPERMAN RECORD COMIC
National Periodical Publications: 1966 (Golden Records)
(With record)-Record reads origin of Superman from comic; came with iron-on patch, decoder, membership card & button; comic-r/Superman #125,146
13 26 39 91 171 250
Comic only 7 14 21 45 73 100

SUPERMAN'S BUDDY (Costume Comic)
National Periodical Publications: 1954 (4 pgs., slick paper-c; one-shot) (Came in box w/costume)
1-With box & costume 123 246 369 781 1341 1900
Comic only 55 110 165 349 600 850
1-(1958 edition)-Printed in 2 colors 17 34 51 98 154 210

SUPERMAN'S CHRISTMAS ADVENTURE
National Periodical Publications: 1940, 1944 (Giveaway, 16 pgs.)
Distributed by Nehi drinks, Bailey Store, Ivey-Keith Co., Kennedy's Boys Shop, Macy's Store, Boston Store
1(1940)-Burnley-a; F. Ray-c/r from Superman #6 (Scarce)-Superman saves Santa Claus. Santa makes real Superman Toys offered in 1940. 1st merchandising story; versions with Royal Crown Cola ad on front-c & Boston Store ad on front-c; cover art on each has the same layout but different art 360 720 1080 2556 4428 6300
nn(1944) w/Santa Claus & X-mas tree-c 97 194 291 616 1058 1500
nn(1944) w/Candy cane & Superman-c 90 180 270 572 986 1400

SUPERMAN-TIM (Becomes Tim)
Superman-Tim Stores/National Periodical Publ.: Aug, 1942 - May, 1950 (Half size) (B&W Giveaway w/2 color covers) (Publ. monthly 2/43 on)
8/42 (#1)-All have Superman illos. 113 226 339 718 1234 1750
1/43 (#2) 39 78 117 234 380 525
2/43 (#3) 37 74 111 222 361 500
3/43 (#4) 37 74 111 222 361 500
4/43, 5/43, 6/43, 7/43, 8/43 33 66 99 198 324 450
9/43, 10/43, 11/43, 12/43 28 56 84 165 270 375
1/44-12/44 24 48 72 140 230 320
1/45-5/45, 10-12/45, 1/46-8/46 21 42 63 126 208 290
6/45-Classic Superman-c 23 46 69 138 227 315
7/45-Classic Superman flag-c 23 46 69 138 227 315
9/45-1st stamp album issue 48 96 114 302 509 715
9/46-2nd stamp album issue 40 80 120 252 426 600
10/46-1st Superman story 29 58 87 170 278 385
11/46, 12/46, 1/47-8/47 issues-Superman story in each; 2/47-Infinity-c.
All 36 pgs. 29 58 87 170 278 385
9/47-Stamp album issue & Superman story 40 80 120 245 410 575
10/47, 11/47, 12/47-Superman stories (24 pgs.) 29 58 87 170 278 385
1/48-7/48,10/48, 11/48, 2/49, 4/49-11/49 23 46 69 138 227 315
8/48-Contains full page ad for Superman-Tim watch giveaway
23 46 69 138 227 315
9/48-Stamp album issue 31 62 93 186 301 425
1/49-Full page Superman bank cut-out 23 46 69 138 227 315
3/49-Full page Superman boxing game cut-out 23 46 69 138 227 315
12/49-3/50, 5/50-Superman stories 25 50 75 150 245 340
4/50-Superman story, baseball stories; photo-c without Superman
29 58 87 170 278 385
NOTE: *All issues have Superman illustrations throughout. The page count varies depending on whether a Superman-Tim comic story is inserted. If it is, the page count is either 36 or 24 pages. Otherwise all issues are 16 pages. Each issue has a special place for inserting a full color Superman stamp. The stamp album issues had spaces for the stamps given away the past year. The books were mailed as a subscription premium. The stamps were given away free (or when you made a purchase) only when you physically came into the store.*

SUPER SEAMAN SLOPPY
Allied Pristine Union Council, Buffalo, NY: 1940s, 8pg., reg. size (Soft-c)
nn 4 8 12 17 21 24

SWAMP FOX, THE
Walt Disney Productions: 1960 (14 pgs, small size) (Canada Dry Premiums)
Titles: (A)-Tory Masquerade, (B)-Turnabout Tactics, (C)-Rindau Rampage; each came in paper sleeve, books 1,2 & 3;
Set with sleeves 5 10 15 34 55 75
Comic only 2 4 6 13 18 22

SWORDQUEST
DC Comics/Atari Pub.: 1982, 52pg., 5"x7" (Giveaway with video games)
1,2-Roy Thomas & Gerry Conway-s; George Pérez & Dick Giordano-c/a in all
2 4 6 10 14 18
3-Low print 3 6 9 16 22 28

SYNDICATE FEATURES (Sci/fi)
Harry A. Chesler Syndicate: V1#3, 11/15/37 (Tabloid size, 3 colors, 4 pgs.) (Editors premium) (Came folded)
V1#3-Dan Hastings daily strips-Guardineer-a 155 310 465 984 1692 2400

TALES FROM RIVERDALE (See Archie Comics)

TASTEE-FREEZ COMICS (Also see Harvey Hits and Richie Rich)
Harvey Comics: 1957 (10¢, 36 pgs.)(6 different issues given away)
1-Little Dot on cover; Richie Rich "Ride 'Em Cowboy" story published one year prior to being printed in Harvey Hits #9. 18 36 54 129 252 375
2,4,5: 2-Rags Rabbit. 4-Sad Sack. 5-Mazie 4 8 12 26 41 55
3-Casper 5 10 15 34 55 75
6-Dick Tracy 5 10 15 34 55 75

TAYLOR'S CHRISTMAS TABLOID
Dept. Store Giveaway: Mid 1930s, Cleveland, Ohio (Tabloid size; in color)
nn-(Very Rare)-Among the earliest pro work of Siegel & Shuster; one full color page called "The Battle in the Stratosphere", with a pre-Superman look; Shuster art thoughout.
(Only 1 known copy) Estimated value... 4000.00

TAZ'S 40TH BIRTHDAY BLOWOUT
DC Comics: 1994 (K-Mart giveaway, 16 pgs.)
nn-Six pg. story, games and puzzles 4.00

TEE AND VEE CROSLEY IN TELEVISION LAND COMICS (Also see Crosley's House of Fun)
Crosley Division, Avco Mfg. Corp. : 1951 (52 pgs.; 8x11"; paper cover; in color) (Giveaway)
Many stories, puzzles, cut-outs, games, etc. 7 14 21 35 43 50

TEEN-AGE BOOBY TRAP
Commercial Comics: 1970 (Small size)
nn 4 7 10 14 17 20

TEEN TITANS GO!
DC Comics: Sept, 2004 (Free Comic Book Day giveaway)
1-Reprints Teen Titans Go! #1; 2 bound-in Wacky Packages stickers 4.00

TENNESSEE JED (Radio)
Fox Syndicate? (Wm. C. Popper & Co.): nd (1945) (16 pgs.; paper-c; reg. size; giveaway)
nn 19 38 57 111 178 245

TENNIS (...For Speed, Stamina, Strength, Skill)
Tennis Educational Foundation: 1956 (16 pgs.; soft cover; 10¢)
Book 1-Endorsed by Gene Tunney, Ralph Kiner, etc. showing how tennis has helped them
6 12 18 28 34 40

TERRY AND THE PIRATES
Dell Publishing Co.: 1939 - 1953 (By Milton Caniff)
Buster Brown Shoes giveaway(1938)-32 pgs.; in color
19 38 57 112 181 250
Canada Dry Premiums-Books #1-3(1953, 36 pgs.; 2x5")-Harvey; #1-Hot Shot Charlie Flies Again; 2-In Forced Landing; 3-Dragon Lady in Distress)
14 28 42 78 112 145
Gambles Giveaway (1938, 16 pgs.) 9 18 27 50 65 80
Gillmore Giveaway (1938, 24 pgs.) 9 18 27 52 69 85
Popped Wheat Giveaway(1938)-Strip reprints in full color; Caniff-a
2 4 6 8 10 12
Shoe Store giveaway (Weatherbird & Poll-Parrot)(1938, 16 pgs., soft-c)(2-diff.)
9 18 27 52 69 85
Sparked Wheat Giveaway(1942, 16 pgs.)-In color 9 18 27 52 69 85

TERRY AND THE PIRATES
Libby's Radio Premium: 1941 (16 pgs.; reg. size)(shipped folded in the mail)
"Adventure of the Ruby of Genghis Khan" - Each pg. is a puzzle that must be completed to read the story 400 800 1200 2600 - -

THAT THE WORLD MAY BELIEVE
Catechetical Guild Giveaway: No date (16 pgs.) (Graymoor Friars distr.)
nn 4 8 12 18 22 25

30 DAYS OF NIGHT
IDW Publishing: July, 2004 (Free Comic Book Day edition)
Previews CSI: Bad Rap; The Shield: Spotlight; 24: One Shot; and 30 Days of Night 2.50

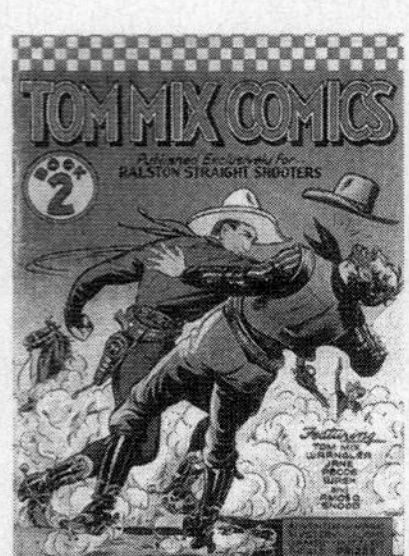

Tom Mix Comics #2 © FAW

Toy World Funnies © EAS

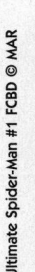

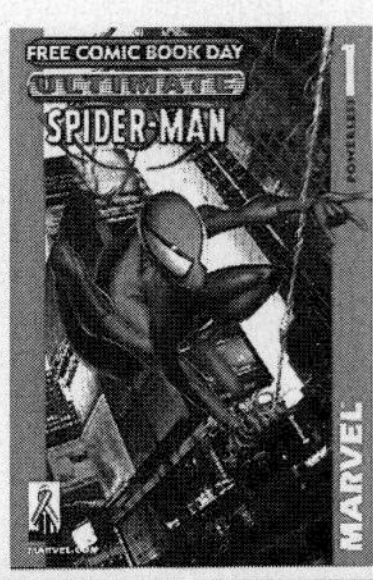

Ultimate Spider-Man #1 FCBD © MAR

	GD	VG	FN	VF	VF/NM	NM-
	2.0	4.0	6.0	8.0	9.0	9.2

3-D COLOR CLASSICS (Wendy's Kid's Club)
Wendy's Int'l Inc.: 1995 (5 1/2" x 8", comes with 3-D glasses)
The Elephant's Child, Gulliver's Travels, Peter Pan, The Time Machine, 20,000 Leagues Under the Sea: Neal Adams-a in all each.... 3.50

350 YEARS OF AMERICAN DAIRY FOODS
American Dairy Assoc.: 1957 (5x7", 16 pgs.)
nn-History of milk 3 6 8 12 14 16

THUMPER (Disney)
Grosset & Dunlap: 1942 (50¢, 32pgs., hardcover book, 7"x8-1/2" w/dust jacket)
nn-Given away (along with a copy of Bambi) for a $2.00, 2-year subscription to WDC&S in 1942. (Xmas offer). Book only 15 30 45 90 140 190
Dust jacket only 10 20 30 56 76 95

TICK, THE
New England Comics Press: May, 2010 (Free Comic Book Day edition)
FCBD Special Edition - reprints debut from 1988; Ben Edlund-s/a 2.00

TILLY AND TED-TINKERTOTLAND
W. T. Grant Co.: 1945 (Giveaway, 20 pgs.)
nn-Christmas comic 7 14 21 37 46 55

TIM (Formerly Superman-Tim; becomes Gene Autry-Tim)
Tim Stores: June, 1950 - Oct, 1950 (B&W, half-size)
4 issues; 6/50, 9/50, 10/50 known 17 34 51 98 154 210

TIM AND SALLY'S ADVENTURES AT MARINELAND
Marineland Restaurant & Bar, Marineland, CA: 1957 (5x7", 16 pgs., soft-c)
nn-copyright Oceanarium, Inc. 2 4 6 8 11 14

TIME MACHINE, THE
DC Comics: 2002 (10 pgs.)
nn-Promotes the 2002 DreamWorks movie 6.00

TIME OF DECISION
Harvey Publications Inc.: (16 pgs., paper cover)
nn-ROTC recruitment 4 7 10 14 17 20

TIM IN SPACE (Formerly Gene Autry Tim; becomes Tim Tomorrow)
Tim Stores: 1950 (1/2 size giveaway) (B&W)
nn 14 28 42 78 112 145

TIM TOMORROW (Formerly Tim In Space)
Tim Stores: 8/51, 9/51, 10/51, Christmas, 1951 (5x7-3/4")
nn-Prof. Fumble & Captain Kit Comet in all 14 28 42 78 112 145

TINY TITANS (All ages stories of Teen Titans in Elementary school)
DC Comics: June, 2008 (Free Comic Book Day giveaway)
1-Reprints Tiny Titans #1; Baltazar & Franco-s/a 2.25

TITANS BEAT (Teen Titans)
DC Comics: Aug, 1996 (16 pgs., paper-c)
1-Intro./preview new Teen Titans members; Pérez-a 4.00

TOMB RAIDER: THE SERIES (Also see Witchblade/Tomb Raider)
Image Comics (Top Cow Prod.): May, 2002
Free Comic Book Day giveaway-Reprints #1 with "Free Comic Book Day" banner on-c 2.50

TOM MIX (...Commandos Comics #10-12)
Ralston-Purina Co.: Sept, 1940 - No. 12, Nov, 1942 (36 pgs.); 1983 (one-shot)
Given away for two Ralston box-tops; 1983 came in cereal box
1-Origin (life) Tom Mix; Fred Meagher-a 232 464 696 1473 2537 3600
2 52 104 156 330 565 800
3-9 40 80 120 252 426 600
10-12: 10-Origin Tom Mix Commando Unit; Speed O'Dare begins; Japanese sub-c. 12-Sci/fi-c 37 74 111 222 361 500
1983- "Taking of Grizzly Grebb", Toth-a; 16 pg. miniature 2 4 6 9 12 15

TOM SAWYER COMICS
Giveaway: 1951? (Paper cover)
nn-Contains a coverless Hopalong Cassidy from 1951; other combinations known 3 6 9 14 20 25

TOP-NOTCH COMICS
MLJ Magazines/Rex Theater: 1940s (theater giveaway)
1-Black Hood-c; content & covers can vary 40 80 120 245 410 575

TOPPS COMICS PRESENTS
Topps Comics: No. 0, 1993 (Giveaway, B&W, 36 pgs.)
0-Dracula vs. Zorro, Teenagents, Silver Star, & Bill the Galactic Hero 2.50

TOWN THAT FORGOT SANTA, THE
W. T. Grant Co.: 1961 (Giveaway, 24 pgs.)
nn 3 6 9 16 23 30

TOY LAND FUNNIES (See Funnies On Parade)
Eastern Color Printing Co.: 1934 (32 pgs., Hecht Co. store giveaway)
nn-Reprints Buck Rogers Sunday pages #199-201 from Famous Funnies #5. A rare variation of Funnies On Parade; same format, similar contents, same cover except for large Santa placed in center (value will be based on sale)

TOY STORY
BOOM Kids!: May, 2010 (Free Comic Book Day giveaway)
FCBD Edition - reprints Toy Story #0 (11/09) The Return of Buzz Lightyear 2.00

TOY WORLD FUNNIES (See Funnies On Parade)
Eastern Color Printing Co.: 1933 (36 pgs., slick cover, Golden Eagle and Wanamaker giveaway)
nn-Contains contents from Funnies On Parade/Century Of Comics. A rare variation of Funnies On Parade; same format, similar contents, same cover except for large Santa placed in center (value will be based on sale)

TRANSFORMERS
Dreamwave Productions/IDW Publishing
... Animated (IDW, 5/08) Free Comic Book Day Edition; from the Cartoon Network series 2.00
... Armada (Dreamwave Prods., 5/03) Free Comic Book Day Edition 3.00
.../Beast Wars Special (IDW, 2006) Free Comic Book Day Edition; flip book 3.00
.../G.I. Joe (IDW, 2009) Free Comic Book Day Edition; flip book 2.00
... Movie Prequel (IDW, 5/07) Free Comic Book Day Edition; Figueroa-c 3.00

TRAPPED
Harvey Publications (Columbia Univ. Press): 1951 (Giveaway, soft-c, 16 pgs)
nn-Drug education comic (30,000 printed?) distributed to schools.; mentioned in **SOTI**, pgs. 256,350 2 4 6 8 10 12
NOTE: *Many copies surfaced in 1979 causing a setback in price; beware of trimmed edges, because many copies have a brittle edge.*

TRIPLE-A BASEBALL HEROES
Marvel Comics: 2007 (Minor league baseball stadium giveaway)
1-Special John Watson painted-c for Memphis, Durham and Buffalo; generic cover with team logos for each of the other 27 teams; Spider-Man, Iron Man, FF app. 3.00

TRIP TO OUTER SPACE WITH SANTA
Sales Promotions, Inc/Peoria Dry Goods: 1950s (paper-c)
nn-Comics, games & puzzles 5 10 15 22 26 30

TRIP WITH SANTA ON CHRISTMAS EVE, A
Rockford Dry Goods Co.: No date (Early 1950s) (Giveaway, 16 pgs., paper-c)
nn 5 10 15 22 26 30

TRUE BLOOD: THE GREAT REVELATION (Prequel to the 2008 HBO vampire series)
HBO/Top Cow: July, 2008 (no cover price, one shot continued on HBO website)
1-David Wohl-s/Jason Badower-a/c 2.25

TRUTH BEHIND THE TRIAL OF CARDINAL MINDSZENTY, THE (See Cardinal Mindszenty)

24 PAGES OF COMICS (No title) (Also see Pure Oil Comics, Salerno Carnival of Comics, & Vicks Comics)
Giveaway by various outlets including Sears: Late 1930s
nn-Contains strip reprints-Buck Rogers, Napoleon, Sky Roads, War on Crime 31 62 93 184 302 420

TWISTED METAL (Video game)
DC Comics: 1996
nn 3.00

TWO FACES OF COMMUNISM (Also see Double Talk)
Christian Anti-Communism Crusade, Houston, Texas: 1961 (Giveaway, paper-c, 36 pgs.)
nn 15 30 45 88 137 185

2001, A SPACE ODYSSEY (Movie)
Marvel Comics Group
Howard Johnson giveaway (1968, 8pp); 6 pg. movie adaptation, 2 pg. games, puzzles; McWilliams-a 2 4 6 9 12 15

ULTIMATE SPIDER-MAN
Marvel Comics: May, 2002
Free Comic Book Day giveaway - reprints #1 with "Free Comic Book Day" banner on-c 2.50
1-Kay Bee Toys variant edition 2 4 6 9 12 15

ULTIMATE X-MEN
Marvel Comics: July, 2003
1-Free Comic Book Day Edition - reprints #1 with "Free Comic Book Day" banner on-c 2.50

UMBRELLA ACADEMY (Zero Killer & Pantheon City on back-c)
Dark Horse Comics: Apr, 2007
1-Free Comic Book Day Edition - previews of the upcoming series; James Jean-c 10.00

UNCLE SAM'S CHRISTMAS STORY
Promotional Publ. Co.: 1958 (Giveaway)

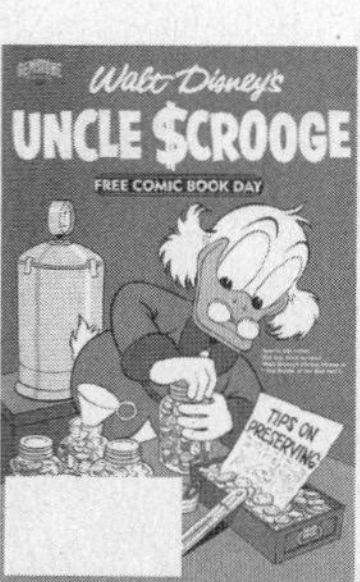

Walt Disney's Mickey Mouse & Uncle Scrooge FCBD 2004 © DIS

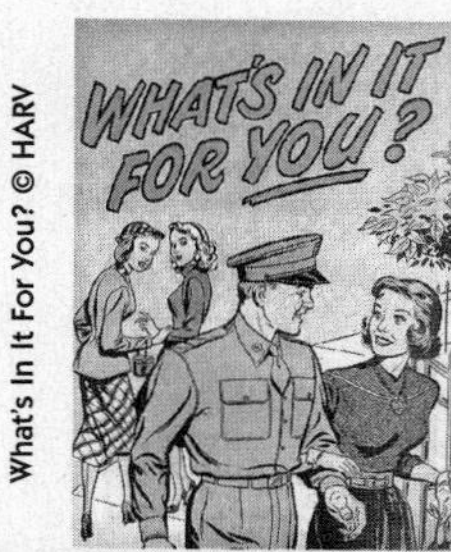

What's In It For You? © HARV

Wheaties A-7 © DIS

	GD 2.0	VG 4.0	FN 6.0	VF 8.0	VF/NM 9.0	NM- 9.2

nn-Reprints 1956 Christmas USA 2 4 6 10 13 16

UNCLE WIGGILY COMICS
Herberger's Clothing Store: 1942 (32 pgs., paper cover)
nn-Comic panels with 6 pages of puzzles 12 24 36 69 97 125

UNKEPT PROMISE
Legion of Truth: 1949 (Giveaway, 24 pgs.)
nn-Anti-alcohol 10 20 30 58 79 100

UNTOLD LEGEND OF THE BATMAN, THE
DC Comics: 1989 (28 pgs., 6X9", limited series of cereal premiums)
1-1st & 2nd printings known; Byrne-a 2 3 4 6 8 10
2,3: 1st & 2nd printings known 1 2 3 5 6 8

UNTOUCHABLES, THE (TV)
Leaf Brands, Inc.
Topps Bubblegum premiums produced by Leaf Brands, Inc.-2-1/2x4-1/2", 8 pgs. (3 diff. issues) "The Organization, Jamaica Ginger, The Otto Frick Story (drug), 3000 Suspects, The Antidote, Mexican Stakeout, Little Egypt, Purple Gang, Bugs Moran Story, & Lily Dallas Story" 3 6 9 16 23 30

VICKS COMICS (See Pure Oil Comics, Salerno Carnival of Comics & 24 Pages of Comics)
Eastern Color Printing Co. (Vicks Chemical Co.): nd (circa 1938) (Giveaway, 68 pgs. in color)
nn-Famous Funnies-r (before #40); contains 5 pgs. Buck Rogers (4 pgs. from F.F. #15, & 1 pg. from #16) Joe Palooka, Napoleon, etc. app. 54 108 162 343 592 840
nn-16 loose, untrimmed page giveaway; paper-c; r/Famous Funnies #14; Buck Rogers, Joe Palooka app. Has either "Vicks Comics" printed on cover or only a local store name as the logo. 22 44 66 131 216 300

WALT DISNEY'S COMICS & STORIES
K.K. Publications: 1942-1963 known (7-1/3"x10-1/4", 4 pgs. in color, slick paper) (folded horizontally once or twice as mailers) (Xmas subscription offer)
1942 mailer-r/Kelly cover to WDC&S 25; 2-year subscription + two Grosset & Dunlap hardcover books (32-pages each), of Bambi and of Thumper, offered for $2.00; came in an illustrated C&S envelope with an enclosed postage paid envelope
(Rare) Mailer only 21 42 63 123 204 285
with envelopes 27 54 81 158 259 360
1947,1948 mailer 17 34 51 98 154 210
1949 mailer-A rare Barks item: Same WDC&S cover as 1942 mailer, but with art changed so that nephew is handing teacher Donald a comic book rather than an apple, as originally drawn by Kelly. The tiny, 7/8"x1-1/4" cover shown was a rejected cover by Barks that was intended for C&S 110, but was redrawn by Kelly for C&S 111. The original art has been lost and this is its only app. (Rare) 39 78 117 233 377 520
1950 mailer-P.1 r/Kelly cover to Dell Xmas Parade 1 (without title); p.2 r/Kelly cover to C&S 101 (w/o title), but with the art altered to show Donald reading C&S 122 (by Kelly); hardcover book, "Donald Duck in Bringing Up the Boys" given with a $1.00 one-year subscription; P.4 r/full Kelly Xmas cover to C&S 99 (Rare) 17 34 51 98 154 210
1952 mailer-P1 r/cover WDC&S #88 14 28 42 80 115 150
1953 mailer-P.1 r/cover Dell Xmas Parade 4 (w/o title); insides offer "Donald Duck Full Speed Ahead," a 28-page, color, 5-5/8"x6-5/8" book, not of the Story Hour series; P.4 r/full Barks C&S 148 cover (Rare) 14 28 42 80 115 150
1963 mailer-Pgs. 1,2 & 4 r/GK Xmas art; P.3 r/a 1963 C&S cover (Scarce) 11 22 33 60 83 105
NOTE: *It is assumed a different mailer was printed each Xmas for at least twenty years.*

WALT DISNEY'S COMICS & STORIES
Walt Disney Productions: 1943 (36 pgs.) (Dept. store Xmas giveaway)
nn-X-Mas-c with Donald & the Boys; Donald Duck by Jack Hannah; Thumper by Ken Hultgren 43 86 129 271 461 650

WALT DISNEY'S DONALD DUCK
Gemstone Publishing: 2006
... Free Comic Book Day (5/06) r/WDC&S #531; Rosa-s/a; P&S. Block-s/a; Van Horn-s/a 2.50
nn-(8-1/2"x 5-1/2", Halloween giveaway) r/"A Prank Above" -Barks-s/a; Rosa-s/a 2.50
nn-(2008, 8-1/2"x 5-1/2", Halloween giveaway) "The Halloween Huckster"; Rota-s/a 2.50

WALT DISNEY'S DONALD DUCK ADVENTURES
Gemstone Publishing: May, 2003 (giveaway promoting 2003 return of Disney Comics)
...Free Comic Book Day Edition - cover logo on red background; reprints "Maharajah Donald" & "The Peaceful Hills" from March of Comics #4; Barks-s/a; Kelly original-c on back-c 2.50
...San Diego Comic-Con 2003 Edition - cover logo on gold background 2.50
...ANA World's Fair of Money Baltimore Edition - cover logo on green background 2.50
...WizardWorld Chicago 2003 Edition - cover logo on blue background 2.50

WALT DISNEY'S GYRO GEARLOOSE
Gemstone Publishing: May, 2008
... Free Comic Book Day (5/08) short stories by Barks, Rosa, Van Horn, Gerstein 2.50

WALT DISNEY'S MICKEY MOUSE
Gemstone Publishing: May, 2007
... Free Comic Book Day (5/07) Floyd Gottfredson-s/a 2.50

WALT DISNEY'S MICKEY MOUSE AND UNCLE SCROOGE
Gemstone Publishing: June, 2004 (Free Comic Book Day giveaway)
nn-Flip book with r/Uncle Scrooge #15 and r/Mickey Mouse Four Color #79 (only Barks drawn Mickey Mouse story) 2.50

WALT DISNEY'S UNCLE SCROOGE
Gemstone Publishing
nn-(5/07, FCBD) Reprints Uncle Scrooge's debut in Four Color Comics #386; Barks-s/a 2.50
nn-(2007, 8-1/2"x 5-1/2", Halloween giveaway) Hound of the Whiskevilles; Barks-s/a 2.50

WARLORD
DC Comics: (Remco Toy giveaway, 2-3/4x4")
nn 5.00

WATCH OUT FOR BIG TALK
Giveaway: 1950
nn-Dan Barry-a; about crooked politicians 7 14 21 37 46 55

WEATHER-BIRD (See Comics From..., Dick Tracy, Free Comics to You..., Super Circus & Terry and the Pirates)
International Shoe Co./Western Printing Co.: 1958 - No. 16, July, 1962 (Shoe store giveaway)
1 4 8 12 25 39 52
2-16 3 6 9 14 19 24
NOTE: *The numbers are located in the lower bottom panel, pg. 1. All feature a character called Weather-Bird.*

WEATHER BIRD COMICS (See Comics From Weather Bird)
Weather Bird Shoes: 1957 (Giveaway)
nn-Contains a comic bound with new cover. Several combinations possible; contents determine price (40 - 60 percent of contents).

WEEKLY COMIC MAGAZINE
Fox Publications: May 12, 1940 (16 pgs.) (Others exist w/o super-heroes)
(1st Version)-8 pg. Blue Beetle story, 7 pg. Patty O'Day story; two copies known to exist. (a VF copy sold in 5/07 for $1553)
(2nd Version)-7 two-pg. adventures of Blue Beetle, Patty O'Day, Yarko, Dr. Fung, Green Mask, Spark Stevens, & Rex Dexter (two known copies, a FN sold in 2007 for $1912, other is GD)
(3rd version)-Captain Valor (only one known copy, in VG+; it sold in 2005 for $480) -
Discovered with business papers, letters and exploitation material promoting **Weekly Comic Magazine** for use by newspapers in the same manner of **The Spirit** weeklies. Interesting note: these are dated three weeks before the first Spirit comic. Letters indicate that samples may have been sent to a few newspapers. These sections were actually 15-1/2x22" pages which will fold down to an approximate 8x10" comic booklet. Other various comic sections were found with the above, but were more like the Sunday comic sections in format.

WE HIT THE JACKPOT
General Comics, Inc./American Affairs: 1947 (Promotional comic)
nn 6 12 18 31 38 45

WHAT DO YOU KNOW ABOUT THIS COMICS SEAL OF APPROVAL?
No publisher listed (DC Comics Giveaway): nd (1955) (4 pgs., slick paper-c)
nn-(Rare) 77 154 231 489 845 1200

WHAT'S BEHIND THESE HEADLINES
William C. Popper Co.: 1948 (16 pgs.)
nn-Comic insert "The Plot to Steal the World" 6 12 18 31 38 45

WHAT'S IN IT FOR YOU?
Harvey Publications Inc.: (16 pgs., paper cover)
nn-National Guard recruitment 4 7 10 14 17 20

WHEATIES (Premiums)
Walt Disney Productions: 1950 & 1951 (32 titles, pocket-size, 32 pgs.)
Mailing Envelope (no art on front)(Designates sets A,B,C or D on front) 7 14 21 37 46 55

(Set A-1 to A-8, 1950)
A-1-Mickey Mouse & the Disappearing Island, A-5-Mickey Mouse, Roving Reporter each... 6 12 18 28 34 40
A-2-Grandma Duck, Homespun Detective, A-6-Li'l Bad Wolf, Forest Ranger, A-7-Goofy, Tightrope Acrobat, A-8-Pluto & the Bogus Money each... 5 10 15 24 30 35
A-3-Donald Duck & the Haunted Jewels, A-4-Donald Duck & the Giant Ape each... 8 16 24 42 54 65

(Set B-1 to B-8, 1950)
B-1-Mickey Mouse & the Pharoah's Curse, B-4-Mickey Mouse & the Mystery Sea Monster each... 6 12 18 31 38 45
B-2-Pluto, Canine Cowpoke, B-5-Li'l Bad Wolf in the Hollow Tree Hideout, B-7-Goofy & the Gangsters each... 5 10 15 24 30 35
B-3-Donald Duck & the Buccaneers, B-6-Donald Duck,Trail Blazer, B-8 Donald Duck, Klondike Kid each... 8 16 24 42 54 65

(Set C-1 to C-8, 1951)
C-1-Donald Duck & the Inca Idol, C-5-Donald Duck in the Lost Lakes, C-8-Donald Duck Deep-Sea Diver each... 8 16 24 42 54 65
C-2-Mickey Mouse & the Magic Mountain, C-6-Mickey Mouse & the Stagecoach Bandits

The Wheel of Progress © AAR

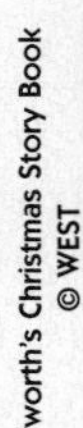

Woolworth's Christmas Story Book © WEST

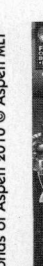

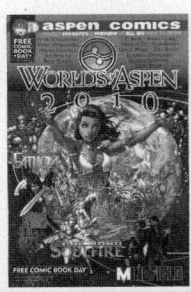

Worlds of Aspen 2010 © Aspen MLT

each... 6 12 18 31 38 45
C-3-Li'l Bad Wolf, Fire Fighter, C-4-Gus & Jaq Save the Ship, C-7-Goofy, Big Game Hunter
each... 5 10 15 24 30 35
(Set D-1 to D-8, 1951)
D-1-Donald Duck in Indian Country, D-5-Donald Duck, Mighty Mystic
each... 8 16 24 42 54 65
D-2-Mickey Mouse and the Abandoned Mine, D-6-Mickey Mouse & the Medicine Man
each... 6 12 18 31 38 45
D-3-Pluto & the Mysterious Package, D-4-Bre'r Rabbit's Sunken Treasure, D-7-Li'l Bad Wolf and the Secret of the Woods, D-8-Minnie Mouse, Girl Explorer
each... 5 10 15 24 30 35
NOTE: *Some copies lack the Wheaties ad.*

WHEEL OF PROGRESS, THE
Assoc. of American Railroads: Oct, 1957 (16 pgs.)
nn-Bill Bunce 6 12 18 28 34 40

WHIZ COMICS (Formerly Flash Comics & Thrill Comics #1)
Fawcett Publications
Wheaties Giveaway(1946, Miniature, 6-1/2x8-1/4", 32 pgs.); all copies were taped at each corner to a box of Wheaties and are never found in very fine or mint condition; "Capt. Marvel & the Water Thieves", plus Golden Arrow, Ibis, Crime Smasher stories
90 180 405 - - -

WILD KINGDOM (TV) (Mutual of Omaha's...)
Western Printing Co.: 1965, 1966 (Giveaway, regular size, slick-c, 16 pgs.)
nn-Front & back-c are different on 1966 edition 2 4 6 9 12 15

WISCO/KLARER COMIC BOOK (Miniature)
Marvel Comics/Vital Publ./Fawcett Publ.: 1948 - 1964 (3-1/2x6-3/4", 24 pgs.)
Given away by Wisco "99" Service Stations, Carnation Malted Milk, Klarer Health Wieners, Fleers Dubble Bubble Gum, Rodeo All-Meat Wieners, Perfect Potato Chips, & others; see ad in Tom Mix #21
Blackstone & the Gold Medal Mystery (1948) 8 16 24 42 54 65
Blackstone "Solves the Sealed Vault Mystery" (1950) 8 16 24 42 54 65
Blaze Carson in "The Sheriff Shoots It Out" (1950) 8 16 24 42 54 65
Captain Marvel & Billy's Big Game (r/Capt. Marvel Adv. #76)
24 48 72 145 238 330
(Prices vary widely on this book)
China Boy in "A Trip to the Zoo" #10 (1948) 5 10 15 24 30 35
Indoors-Outdoors Game Book 4 7 10 14 17 20
Jim Solar Space Sheriff in "Battle for Mars", "Between Two Worlds", "Conquers Outer Space", "The Creatures on the Comet", "Defeats the Moon Missile Men", "Encounter Creatures on Comet", "Meet the Jupiter Jumpers", "Meets the Man From Mars", "On Traffic Duty", "Outlaws of the Spaceways", "Pirates of the Planet X", "Protects Space Lanes", "Raiders From the Sun", "Ring Around Saturn", "Robots of Rhea", "The Sky Ruby", "Spacetts of the Sky", "Spidermen of Venus", "Trouble on Mercury"
7 14 21 35 43 50
Johnny Starboard & the Underseas Pirates (1948) 5 10 15 22 26 30
Kid Colt in "He Lived by His Guns" (1950) 8 16 24 44 57 70
Little Aspirin as the "Crook Catcher" #2 (1950) 4 7 10 14 17 20
Little Aspirin in "Naughty But Nice" #6 (1950) 4 7 10 14 17 20
Return of the Black Phantom (not M.E. character)(Roy Dare)(1948)
6 12 18 28 34 40
Secrets of Magic 4 8 11 16 19 22
Slim Morgan "Brings Justice to Mesa City" #3 4 8 11 16 19 22
Super Rabbit(1950)-Cuts Red Tape, Stops Crime Wave!
9 18 27 50 65 80
Tex Farnum, Frontiersman (1948) 5 10 15 22 26 30
Tex Taylor in "Draw or Die, Cowpoke!" (1950) 7 14 21 35 43 50
Tex Taylor in "An Exciting Adventure at the Gold Mine" (1950)
6 12 18 31 38 45
Wacky Quacky in "All-Aboard" 3 6 8 12 14 16
When School Is Out 3 6 8 12 14 16
Willie in a "Comic-Comic Book Fall" #1 4 8 11 16 19 22
Wonder Duck "An Adventure at the Rodeo of the Fearless Quacker!" (1950)
9 18 27 47 61 75
Rare uncut version of three; includes Capt. Marvel, Tex Farnum, Black Phantom
Estimated value... 700.00
Rare uncut version of three; includes China Boy, Blackstone, Johnny Starboard & the Underseas Pirates Estimated value... 250.00
Rare uncut version of three; includes Willie in a "Comic-Comic Book Fall", Little Aspirin #2, Slim Morgan Brings Justice to Mesa City (a VF/FN copy sold for $54 in Nov. 2007)

WOLVERINE
Marvel Comics
145-(1999 Nabisco mail-in offer) Sienkiewicz-c 8 16 24 54 90 125
: Origin of an X-Man Free Comic Book Day 2009 (5/09) Gurihiru-a/McGuinness-c 2.50
...Son of Canada (4/01, ed. of 65,000) Spider-Man & The Hulk app.; Lim-a 3.00

WOMAN OF THE PROMISE, THE
Catechetical Guild: 1950 (General Distr.) (Paper cover, 32 pgs.)
nn 6 12 18 28 34 40

WONDERFUL WORLD OF DUCKS (See Golden Picture Story Book)
Colgate Palmolive Co.: 1975
1-Mostly-r 1 3 4 6 8 10

WONDER WOMAN
DC Comics: 1977
Pizza Hut Giveaways (12/77)-Reprints #60,62 2 4 6 9 13 16
... - The Minotaur (1981, General Foods giveaway, 8 pages, 3-1/2 x 6-3/4", oblong) 2 4 6 13 18 22

WONDER WORKER OF PERU
Catechetical Guild: No date (5x7", 16 pgs., B&W, giveaway)
nn 5 10 15 27 33 38

WOODY WOODPECKER
Dell Publishing Co.
Clover Stamp-Newspaper Boy Contest('56)-9 pg. story-(Giveaway)
7 14 21 37 46 55
In Chevrolet Wonderland(1954-Giveaway)(Western Publ.)-20 pgs., full story line; Chilly Willy app. 18 36 54 103 162 220
...Meets Scotty MacTape(1953-Scotch Tape giveaway)-16 pgs., full size
18 36 54 103 162 220

WOOLWORTH'S CHRISTMAS STORY BOOK
Promotional Publ. Co.(Western Printing Co.): 1952 - 1954 (16 pgs., paper-c) (See Jolly Christmas Book)
nn: 1952 issue-Marv Levy c/a 6 12 18 33 41 48

WOOLWORTH'S HAPPY TIME CHRISTMAS BOOK
F. W. Woolworth Co. (Western Printing Co.): 1952 (Christmas giveaway)
nn-36 pgs. 6 12 18 31 38 45

WORLD'S FINEST COMICS
National Periodical Publ./DC Comics
Giveaway (c. 1944-45, 8 pgs., in color, paper-c)-Johnny Everyman-r/World's Finest
20 40 60 118 194 270
Giveaway (c. 1949, 8 pgs., in color, paper-c)- "Make Way For Youth" r/World's Finest; based on film of same name 18 36 54 107 169 230
#176, #179- Best Western reprint edition (1997) 3.00

WORLD'S GREATEST SUPER HEROES
DC Comics (Nutra Comics) (Child Vitamins, Inc.): 1977 (Giveaway, 3-3/4x3-3/4", 24 pgs.)
nn-Batman & Robin app.; health tips 2 4 6 9 13 16

WORLDS OF ASPEN
Aspen MLT, Inc.: 2006 - 2010 (Free Comic Book Day giveaways)
...: FCBD 2006, 2007, #3, #4 Editions; Fathom, Soulfire, Shrugged short stories; Turner-c 2.50
... 2010 (5/10) Previews Fathom, Mindfield, Soulfire, Executive Assistant: Iris and Dellec 2.50

XMAS FUNNIES
Kinney Shoes: No date (Giveaway, paper cover, 36 pgs.?)
Contains 1933 color strip-r; Mutt & Jeff, etc. 29 58 87 172 281 390

X-MEN
Marvel Comics: 2006; May, 2008 (Free Comic Book Day giveaways)
FCBD 2008 Edition #1-(5/08) Features Pixie; Carey-s/Land-a/c 2.50
.../Runaways: FCBD 2006 Edition; new x-over story; Mighty Avengers preview; Chen-c 2.50

X-MEN THE MOVIE
Marvel Comics/Toys R' Us: 2000
Special Movie Prequel Edition 5.00

X2 PRESENTS THE ULTIMATE X-MEN #2
Marvel Comics/New York Post: July, 2003
Reprint distributed inside issue of the New York Post 2.50

YALTA TO KOREA (Also see Korea My Home)
M. Phillip Corp. (Republican National Committee): 1952 (Giveaway, paper-c)
nn-(8 pgs.)-Anti-communist propaganda book 18 36 54 103 162 220

YOGI BEAR (TV)
Dell Publishing Co.
Giveaway ('84, '86)-City of Los Angeles, "Creative First Aid" & "Earthquake Preparedness for Children" 1 2 3 4 5 7

YOUR TRIP TO NEWSPAPERLAND
Philadelphia Evening Bulletin (Printed by Harvey Press): June, 1955 (14x11-1/2", 12 pgs.)
nn-Joe Palooka takes kids on newspaper tour 5 10 15 24 30 35

YOUR VOTE IS VITAL!
Harvey Publications Inc.: 1952 (5" x 7", 16 pgs., paper cover)
nn-The importance of voting 4 8 12 18 22 25

THE PIONEER AGE

The American Comic Book: 1500s-1828

For the last few years, we have featured a tremendous article by noted historian and collector Eric C. Caren on the foundations of what we now call "The Pioneer Age" of comics. We look forward to a new article on this significant topic in *The Overstreet Comic Book Price Guide* #41. In the meantime, should you need it, Caren's article may be found in our previous edition.

That said, even with the space constraints in this special 40th anniversary edition of the *Guide*, we could not possibly exclude reference to these incredible, formative works.

German broadsheet, dated 1569.

Why are these illustrations and sequences of illustrations important to the comic books of today?

Quite frankly, because we can see in them the very building blocks of the comic art form.

The Murder of King Henry III (1589).

The shooting of the Italian Concini (1617).

Over the course of just a few hundred years, we the evolution of narration, word balloons, panel-to-panel progression of story, and so much more. If these stories aren't developed first, how would be every have reached the point that that *The Adventures of Mr. Obadiah Oldbuck* could have come along in 1842?

As the investigation of comic book history has blown away the notion that comic books were a 20 century invention, it hasn't been easy to convince some, even with the clear, linear progression of the artful melding of illustration and words.

"Want to avoid an argument in social discourse? Steer clear of politics and religion. In the latter category, the most controversial subject is human evolution. Collectors can become just as squeamish when you start messing with the evolution of a particular collectible," Eric Caren wrote in his article. "In most cases, the origin of a particular comic character will be universally agreed upon, but try tackling the origin of printed comics and you are asking for trouble."

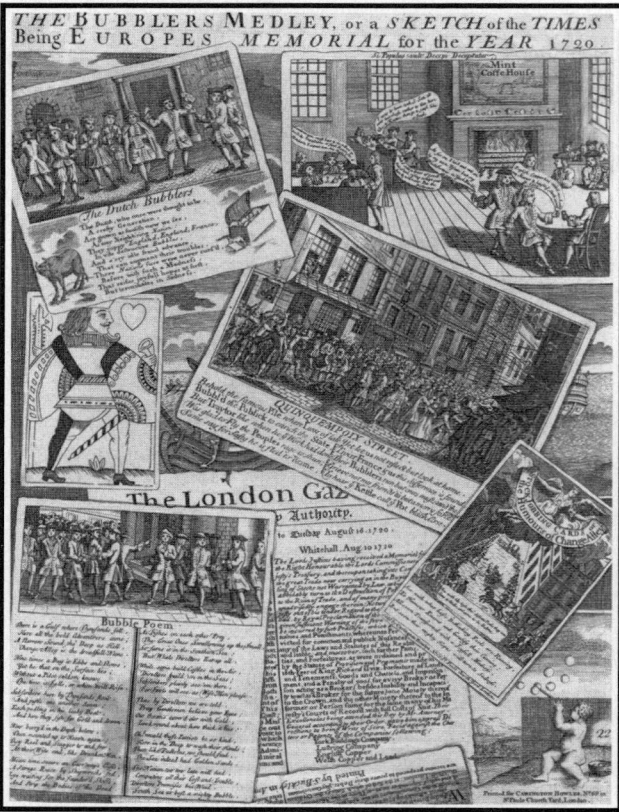

THE BUBBLERS MEDLEY, or a SKETCH of the TIMES Being EUROPES MEMORIAL for the YEAR 1720.

The London Gaz

"The Bubblers Medley" (1720).

"Join, or Die" from the Pennsylvania Gazette, *May 9, 1754.*

"Amusement for John Bull..." from The European Magazine *(1783).*

But the evidence is there for any who choose to look. Before the original comics of the Golden Age, there were comic strip reprints collected in comic book form. The practice dated back decades earlier, of course, but coalesced into the current form when the realities of the Great Depression spawned the modern incarnation of the comic book and its immediate cousin, the Big Little Book.

Everything that came later, though, did so because the acceptance of the visual language had already been worked out. Before Spider-Man and the Hulk, before Superman and Batman, before the Yellow Kid, Little Nemo, and the Brownies, cartoonists and editorial illustrators were working out how to tell a story or simply convey their ideas in this new artform.

Without this sort of work, without these pioneers, we simply wouldn't be where we are today.

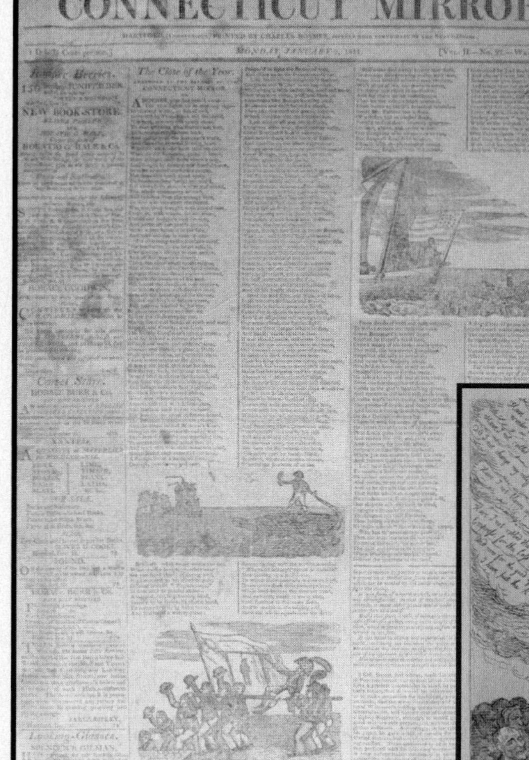
CONNECTICUT MIRROR.

Cartoons satirizing Napoleon on the front page of the Connecticut Mirror, *dated January 7, 1811.*

Another Napoleon cartoon, this time dubbing him "The Corsican Munchausen," from the London Strand, December 4, 1813.

"A Consultation at the Medical Board" from The Pasquin or General Satirist *(1821)*.

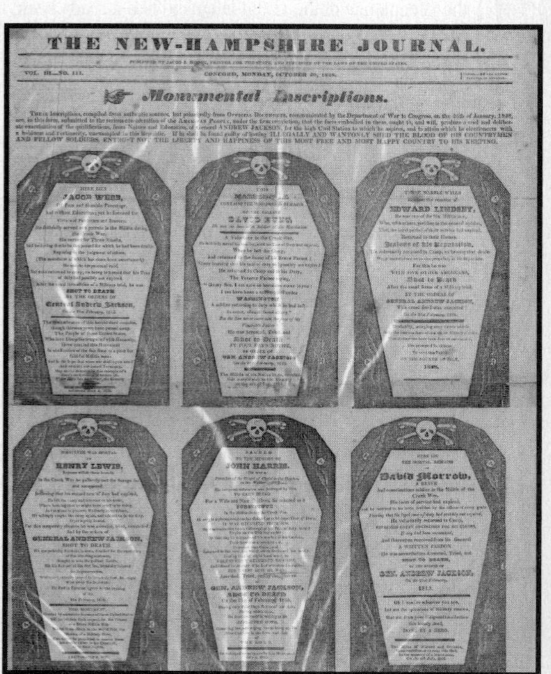

THE NEW-HAMPSHIRE JOURNAL.

VOL. III.—NO. 111. CONCORD, MONDAY, OCTOBER 20, 1828.

Monumental Inscriptions.

HERE LIES JACOB WEBB,

THESE MARBLE WALLS ... EDWARD LINDSEY,

HENRY LEWIS,

JOHN HARRIS.

David Morrow,

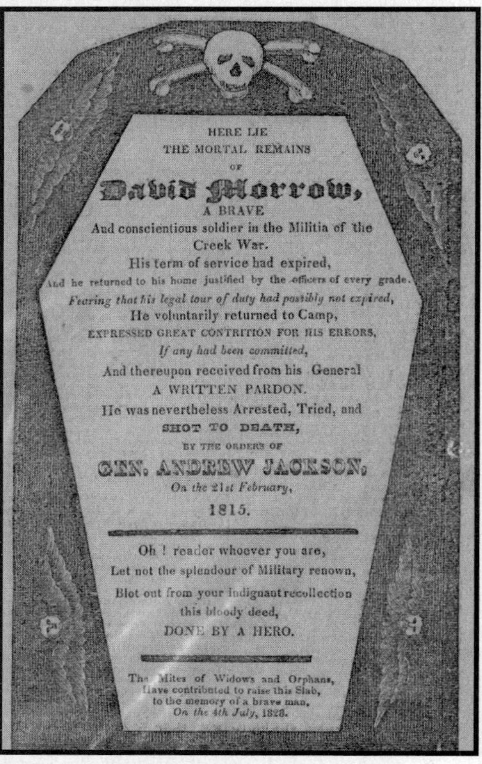

HERE LIE
THE MORTAL REMAINS
OF
David Morrow,
A BRAVE
And conscientious soldier in the Militia of the
Creek War.
His term of service had expired,
And he returned to his home justified by the officers of every grade.
Fearing that his legal tour of duty had possibly not expired,
He voluntarily returned to Camp,
EXPRESSED GREAT CONTRITION FOR HIS ERRORS,
If any had been committed,
And thereupon received from his General
A WRITTEN PARDON.
He was nevertheless Arrested, Tried, and
SHOT TO DEATH,
BY THE ORDERS OF
GEN. ANDREW JACKSON,
On the 21st February,
1815.

Oh! reader whoever you are,
Let not the splendour of Military renown,
Blot out from your indignant recollection
this bloody deed,
DONE BY A HERO.

The Mites of Widows and Orphans,
Have contributed to raise this Slab,
to the memory of a brave man,
On the 4th July, 1828.

Above left, the front page of The New Hampshire Journal, *dated October 20, 1828, with multiple tombstone "panels." To the right is a detail of the bottom right tombstone.*

THE VICTORIAN AGE

Comic Strips and Books: 1646-1900

For each of the past few years, Robert Beerbohm, Richard Samuel West, Richard Olson, Ph.D., and other contributors have provided detailed insight into what has been dubbed "The Victorian Age," a key, formative era through which the path to the modern comic book would travel. It is in this era, in 1842, that *The Adventures of Mr. Obadiah Olbuck*, a 40-page story told in a panel-to-panel progression that would be familiar to any comic book fan, first appeared in the pages of the literary publication *Brother Jonathan*.

Look for a newly revised article on the subject to appear in *The Overstreet Comic Book Price Guide* #41. Until then, we hope you'll enjoy images of some of the landmark comic work of The Victorian Age.

"God's Revenge For Murder" By John Reynolds, unknown artist, 1656.
Earliest-known sequential comic "panel" strip created in the English language.

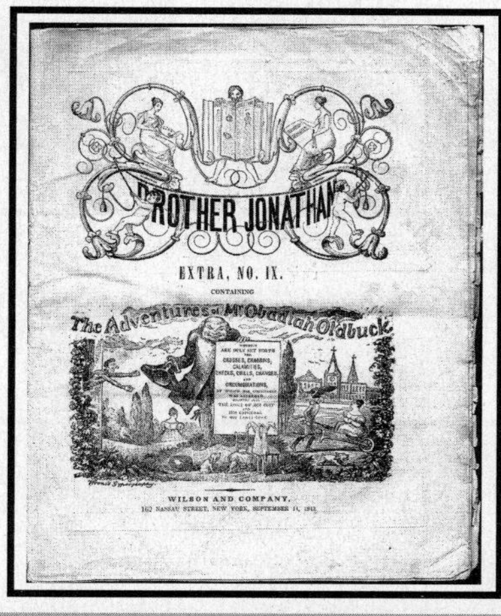

Cover to the subscriber version of the earliest-known sequential comic book published in America, The Adventures of Mr. Obadiah Oldbuck, Sept. 1842, Wilson & Co. New York, originally conceived in 1828 in Geneva Switzerland by creator Rodolphe Töpffer.

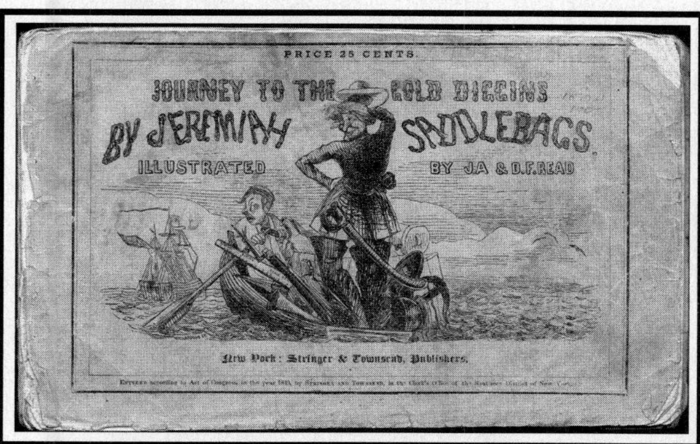

Journey to the Gold Diggins By Jeremiah Saddlebags, June 1849, so far the earliest known sequential comic book by American creators, J.A. and D.F. Read.

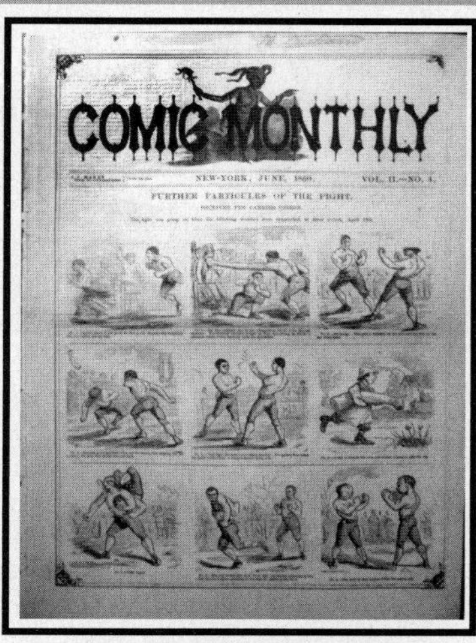

Comic Monthly v2#4 June 1860.

Sample panels from Frank Bellew Sr's The Flying Machine; And Professor High's Adventure therein in a Trip across the Ocean, Merryman's Monthly V3#5, May 1865.

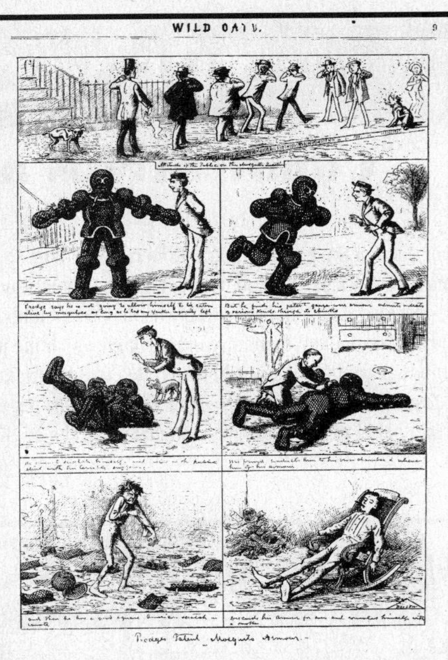

Wild Oats #190, August 16, 1876 by Frank Bellew Sr., Father of American Comic Strips. This one titled "Rodger's Patent Mosquito Armour."

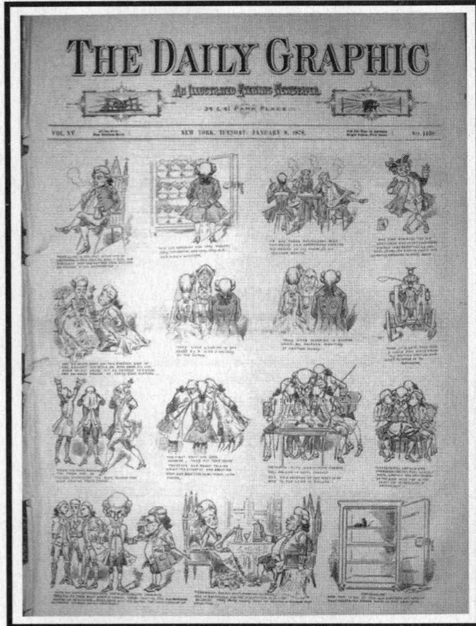

The Daily Graphic #1498, Jan 8, 1878, New York. Artist: Gray Parkxxx. This innovative paper carried all kinds of comic strips beginning more than 20 years before both Pulitzer and then Hearst got into the comic strip business. Largely overlooked by later historians, it is only recently being sought after once again.

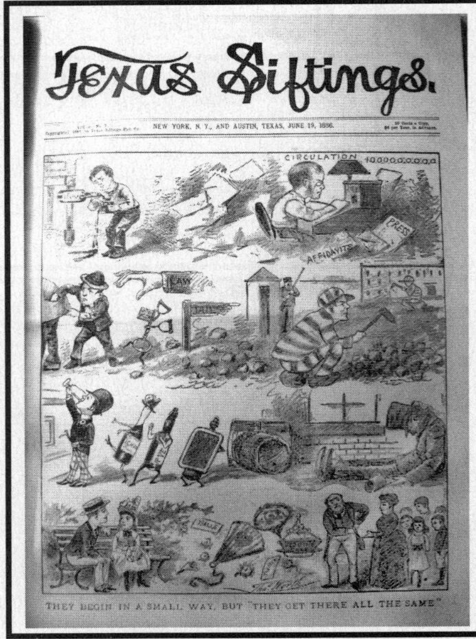

Texas Siftings v6#7, June 19, 1886 ran a whole slew of sequential comic strips for many years and is yet another sleeper for collectors to hunt.

The American Comic Almanac #5
1835 © Charles Ellms, NYC

The Strange and Wonderful Adventures
of Bachelor Butterfly by Rodolphe Töpffer
1870s © Dick & Fitzgerald, NYC

Barker's "Komic" Picture Souvenir, 3rd Edition
1894 © Barker, Moore & Klein Medicine Co.

FR1.0 GD2.0 FN6.0

COLLECTOR'S NOTE: Most of the books listed in this section were published well over a century before organized comics fandom began archiving and helping to preserve these fragile popular culture artifacts. With some of these comics now over 160 years old, they almost never surface in Fine+ or better shape. Be happy when you simply find a copy.

This year has seen price growth in quite a few comic books in this era. Since this section began growing almost a decade now, comic books from Wilson, Brother Jonathan, Huestis & Cozans, Garrett, Dick & Fitzgerald, Frank Leslie, Street & Smith and others continue to be recognized by the more savvy in this fine hobby as legitimate comic book collectors' items. We had been more concerned with simply establishing what is known to exist. For the most part, that work is now a *fait accompli* in this section compiled, revised, and expanded by Robert Beerbohm with special thanks this year to Terrance Keegan plus acknowledgment to Bill Blackbeard, Chris Brown, Alfredo Castelli, Darrell Coons, Leonardo De Sá, Scott Deschaine, Joe Evans, Ron Friggle, Tom Gordon III, Michel Kempeneers, Andy Konkykru, Don Kurtz, Richard Olson, Robert Quesinberry, Joseph Rainone, Steve Rowe, Randy Scott, John Snyder, Art Spiegelman, Steve Thompson, Richard Samuel West, Doug Wheeler and Richard Wright. Special kudos to long-time collector and scholar Gabriel Laderman.

The prices given for Fair, Good and Fine categories are for strictly graded editions. If you need help grading your item, we refer you to the grading section in this book or contact the authors of this essay. Items marked Scarce, Rare or Very Rare we are still trying to figure out how many copies might still be in existence. We welcome additions and corrections from any interested collectors and scholars at robert@BLBcomics.com

For ease ascertaining the contents of each item of this listing and the Platinum index list, we offer the following list of categories found immediately following most of the titles:

E - EUROPEAN ORIGINAL COMICS MATERIAL; Printed in Europe or reprinted in USA
G - GRAPHIC NOVEL (LONGER FORMAT COMIC TELLING A SINGLE STORY)
H - "HOW TO DRAW CARTOONS" BOOKS
I - ILLUSTRATED BOOKS NOTABLE FOR THE ARTIST, BUT NOT A COMIC.
M - MAGAZINE / PERIODICAL COMICS MATERIAL REPRINTS
N - NEWSPAPER COMICS MATERIAL REPRINTS
O - ORIGINAL COMIC MATERIAL NOT REPRINTED FROM ANOTHER SOURCE
P - PROMOTIONAL COMIC, EITHER GIVEN AWAY FOR FREE, OR A PREMIUM GIVEN IN CONJUNCTION WITH THE PURCHASE OF A PRODUCT.
S - SINGLE PANEL / NON-SEQUENTIAL CARTOONS

Measurements are in inches. The first dimension given is Height and the second is Width. Some original British editions are included in the section, so as to better explain and differentiate their American counterparts.

ACROBATIC ANIMALS
R.H. Russell: 1899 (9x11-7/8", 72 pgs, B&W, hard-c)

nn (Scarce) 150.00 300.00 600.00
NOTE: *Animal strips by Gustave Verbeck, presented 1 panel per page.*

ALMY'S SANTA CLAUS (P,E)
Edward C. Almy & Co., Providence, R.I.: nd (1880's) (5-3/4x4-5/8", 20 pgs, B&W, paper-c

nn - (Rare) 12.50 40.00 80.00
NOTE: *Department store Christmas giveaway containing an abbreviated 28-panel reprinting of George Cruikshank's* ***The Tooth-ache****. Santa Claus cover.*

AMERICAN COMIC ALMANAC, THE (OLD AMERICAN COMIC ALMANAC 1839-1846)
Charles Ellms: 1831-1846 (5x8, 52 pgs, B&W)

1 first American comic almanac ever prrinted 500.00 1000.00 2000.00
2-16 100.00 200.00 400.00
NOTE:#1 from 1831 is the First American Comic Almanac

AMERICAN PUNCH
American Punch Publishing Co: Jan 1879-March 1881, J.A. Cummings Engraving Co (last 3 issues) (Quarto Monthly)

Most issues 25.00 50.00 150.00

THE AMERICAN WIT
Richardson & Collins, NY: 1867-68 (18-1/2x13. 8 pgs, B&W)
2/3 Frank Bellew single panels 50.00 100.00 200.00

AMERICAN WIT AND HUMOR
Harper & Bros, NY: 1859 (

nn - numerous McLenan sequential comic strips 100.00 200.00 400.00

ATTWOOD'S PICTURES - AN ARTIST'S HISTORY OF THE LAST TEN YEARS OF THE NINETEENTH CENTURY (M,S)
Life Publishing Company, New York: 1900 (11-1/4x9-1/8", 156 pgs, B&W, gilted blue hard-c)

nn - By Attwood 40.00 80.00 160.00
NOTE: *Reprints monthly calendar cartoons which appeared in* ***LIFE****, for 1887 through 1899.*

BACHELOR BUTTERFLY, THE VERITABLE HISTORY OF MR. (E,G)
D. Bogue, London: 1845 (5-1/2x10-1/4", 74 pgs, B&W, gilted hardcover)

nn - By Rodolphe Töpffer (Scarce) 500.00 1250.00 2500.00
nn - Hand colored edition (Very Rare) (no known sales)
NOTE: *This is the British Edition, translated from the re-engraved by Cham serialization found in* ***L'Illustration*** *- a periodical from Paris publisher Dubochet. Predates the first French collected edition. Third Töpffer comic book published in English. The first story page is numbered Page 3. Page 17 shows Bachelor Butterfly being swallowed by a whale.*

BACHELOR BUTTERFLY, THE STRANGE ADVENTURES OF (E,G)
Wilson & Co., New York: 1846 (5-3/8x10-1/8", 68 pgs, B&W, soft-c)

FR1.0 GD2.0 FN6.0

nn - By Rodolphe Töpffer (Very Rare) 600.00 1500.00 3000.00
nn - At least one hand colored copy exists (Very Rare) (no known sales)
NOTE: *2nd Töpffer comic book printed in the U.S., 3rd earliest known sequential comic book in the USA. Reprinted from the British D. Bogue 1845 edition, itself from the earlier French language* ***Histoire de Mr. Cryptogame****. Released the same year as the French Dubochet edition. Two variations known, the earlier printing with Page number 17 placed on the inside (left) bottom corner in error, with slightly later printings corrected to place page number 17 on the outside (right) bottom corner of that page. Another first printing indicator is pages 17 and 20 are printed on the wrong side of the page. For both printings: the first story page is numbered 2. Page 17 shows Bachelor Butterfly already in the whale. In most panels with 3 lines of text, the third line is indented further than the second, which is in turn indented further than the first.*

BACHELOR BUTTERFLY, THE STRANGE ADVENTURES
Brother Jonathan Press, NY: 1854 (5-1/2x10-5/8", 68 pgs, paper-c, B&W) (Very Rare)

nn - By Rodolphe Töpffer 250.00 500.00 1000.00

BACHELOR BUTTERFLY,THE STRANGE & WONDERFUL ADVENTURES OF
Dick & Fitzgerald, New York: 1870s-1888 (various printings 30 Cent cover price, 68 pgs, B&W, paper cover) (all versions Rare) (E,G)

nn - Black print on blue cover (5-1/2x10-1/2"); string bound 112.00 225.00 450.00
nn - Black print on green cover (5-1/2x10-1/2"); string bound 100.00 200.00 400.00
NOTE: *Reprints the earlier Wilson & Co. edition. Page 2 is the first story page. Page 17 shows Bachelor Butterfly already in the whale. In most panels with 3 lines of text, the second and third lines are equally indented in from the first. Unknown which cover (blue or green) is earlier.*

BACHELOR'S OWN BOOK. BEING THE PROGRESS OF MR. LAMBKIN, (GENT.) IN THE PURSUIT OF PLEASURE AND AMUSEMENT (E,O,G)
(See also PROGRESS OF MR. LAMBKIN)
D. Bogue, London: August 1, 1844 (5x8-1/4", 28 pgs printed one side only, cardboard cover & interior) (all versions Rare)

nn - First printing hand colored 200.00 400.00 800.00
nn - First printing black & white 200.00 400.00 800.00
NOTE: *First printing has misspellings in the title. "PURSUIT" is spelled "PERSUIT", and "AMUSEMENT" is spelled "AMUSEMEMT".*
nn - Second printing hand colored 200.00 400.00 800.00
nn - Second printing black & white 200.00 400.00 800.00
NOTE: Second printing. The misspelling of "PURSUIT" has been corrected, but "AMUSEMEMT" error is still present.
nn - Third printing hand colored No misspellings 200.00 400.00 800.00
nn - Third printing black & white 200.00 400.00 800.00
NOTE: *By George Cruikshank. This is the British Edition. Issued both in black & white, and professionally hand-colored editions. Hand-colored editions have survived in higher quantities than uncolored. Originally made with thin paper sheets covering the plates.*

BACHELOR'S OWN BOOK; OR, THE PROGRESS OF MR. LAMBKIN, (GENT.), IN THE PURSUIT OF PLEASURE AND AMUSEMENT, AND ALSO IN SEARCH OF HEALTH AND HAPPINESS, THE (E,O,G)
David Bryce & Son: Glasgow: 1884 (one shilling; 7-5/8 x5-7/8", 62 pgs printed one side only, illustrated hardcover, page edges guilt

nn - Reprints the 1844 edition with altered title 17.50 35.00 70.00
nn - soft cover edition exists 15.00 30.00 60.00

BACHELOR'S OWN BOOK. BEIN-G TWENTY-FOUR PASSAGES IN THE LIFE OF MR. LAMBKIN, GENT. (E,G)
Burgess, Stringer & Co., New York on cover; Carey & Hart, Philadelphia on title page: 1845 (31-1/4 cents, 7-1/2x4-5/8", 52 pgs, B&W, paper cover)

nn - By George Cruikshank (Very Rare) (no known sales)
NOTE: *This is the second known sequential comic book story published in America. Reprints the earlier British edition. Pages printed on one side only. New cover art by an unknown artist.*

BAD BOY'S FIRST READER (O,S)
G.W. Carleton & Co.: 1881 (5-3/4 x 4-1/8", 44 pgs, B&W, paper cover)

nn - By Frank Bellew (Senior) 50.00 100.00 200.00
NOTE: *Parody of a children's ABC primer, one cartoon illustration plus text per page. Includes one panel of Boss Tweed. Frank Bellew is considered the "Father of the American Sequential Comics."*

BALL OF YARN OR, QUEER, QUIANT & QUIZZICAL STORIES, UNRAVELED WITH NEARLY 200 COMIC ENGRAVINGS OF FREAKS, FOLLIES & FOIBLES OF QUEER FOLKS BY THAT PRINCE OF COMICS, ELTON, THE (M)
Philip. J. Cozans, 116 Nassau St, NY: early 1850s (7-1/4x3-1/2", 76 pgs, yellow-wraps)

nn - sequential comic strips plus singles (no known sales)
NOTE: Mose Keyser-r, Jones, Smith & Robinson Goes To A Ball-r; The Adventures of Mr Goliah Starvemouse-r are all sequential comic strips printed in a number of sources

BARKER'S ILLUSTRATED ALMANAC (O,P,S)
Barker, Moore & Mein Medicine Co: 1878-1932+ (36 pgs, B&W, color paper-cr)

1878-1879 (Rare) 40.00 80.00 160.00
NOTE: *Not known yet what the cover art is.*
1880 Farmer Plowing Field-c 30.00 60.00 120.00
1881-1883 (Scarce,7-3/4x6-1/8") *4-mast ships & lighthouse-c* 30.00 60.00 120.00
1884-1889 (8x6-1/4") *Horse & Rider jumping picket fence-c* 20.00 40.00 80.00
1890-1897 (8-1/8x6-1/4") 20.00 40.00 80.00
1898-1899 (7-3/8x5-7/8") 20.00 40.00 80.00
1900+: see the Platinum Age Comics section (7x5-7/8")
NOTE: *Barker's Almanacs were actually issued in November of the year preceding the year which appears on the almanac. For example, the 1878 dated almanac was issued November 1877. They were given away to retailers of Barker's farm animal medicinal products, to in turn be given away to customers. Each Barker's Almanac contains 10 full page cartoons. These frequently included racist stereotypes of blacks. Each cartoon*

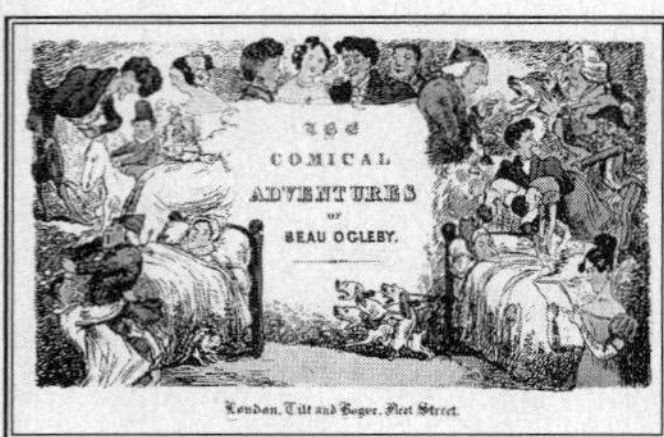

The Comical Adventures of Beau Ogleby
1843 © Tlit & Bogue, London

The Bottle by George Cruickshank
1871 © Geo. Gebbie, Philadelphia

Buzz A Buzz Or The Bees By Wilhelm Busch
1873 © Henry Holt And Company, New York

FR1.0 GD2.0 FN6.0

contained advertisements for Barker's products. It is unknown whether the cartoons appeared only in the almanacs, or if they also ran as newspaper ads or flyers. Originally issued with a metal hook attached in the upper left hand corner, which could be used to hang the almanac.

BARKER'S "KOMIC" PICTURE SOUVENIR (P,S)
Barker, Moore & Mein Medicine Co: nd (1892-94) (color cardboard cover, B&W interior) (all unnumbered editions Very Rare)

nn - (1892) (1st edition, 6-7/8x10-1/2, 150 pgs) wraparound cover showing people headed towards Chicago for the 1893 World's Fair 150.00 300.00 650.00
nn - (1893) (2nd edition, ??? pgs) same cover as 1st edition 150.00 300.00 650.00
nn - (1894) (3rd edition, 180 pgs, 6-3/4x10-3/8") 150.00 300.00 650.00
NOTE: *New cover art showing crowd of people laughing with a copy of Barker's Almanac.The crowd picture is flanked on both sides by picture of a tall thin person.*
nn - (1894) (4th edition, 124 pgs, 6-3/8x9-3/8") same-c as 3rd edition 150.00 300.00 650.00
NOTE: *Essentially same-c as 3rd edition, except flanking picture on left edge is now gone. The 2nd through 4th editions state their printing on the first interior page, in the paragraph beneath the picture of the Barker's Building. These have been confirmed as premium comic books, predating the Buster Brown premiums. They reprint advertising cartoons from Barker's Illustrated Almanac. For the 50 page booklets by this same name, numbered as "Part"s, see the PLATINUM AGE SECTION. All "Editions in Parts", without exception, were published after 1900.*

BEAU OGLEBY, THE COMICAL ADVENTURES OF (E,G)
Tilt & Bogue: nd (c1843) (5-7/8x9-1/8", 72 pgs, printed one side only, green gilted hard-c, B&W)

nn - By Rodolphe Töpffer (Rare) 300.00 600.00 1500.00
nn - Hand coloured edition (Very Rare) (no known sales)
NOTE: *British Edition; no known American Edition. 2nd Töpffer comic book published in English. Translated from Paris publisher Aubert's unauthorized redrawn 1839 bootleg edition of Töpffer's* ***Histoire de Mr. Jabot****. The back most interior page is an advertisement for* ***Obadiah Oldbuck****, showing its comic book cover*

BEE, THE
Bee Publishing Co: May 16 1898-Aug 2 1898 (Chromolithographic Weekly)

most issues 50.00 100.00 200.00
8 June Yellow Kid Hearst cover issue 150.00 300.00 650.00

BEFORE AND AFTER. A LOCOFOCO CHRISTMAS PRESENT. (O, C)
D.C. Johnston, Boston: 1837 (4-3/4x3", 1 page, hand colored cardboard)

nn - (Very Rare) by David Claypoole Johnston (sold at auction for $400 in GD)
NOTE: *Pull-tab cartoon envelope, parodying the 1836 New York City mayoral election, picturing the candidate of the Locofoco Party smiling "Before the N.York election", then, when the tab is pulled, picturing him with an angry sneer "After the N.York election".*

BILLY GOAT AND OTHER COMICALITIES, THE (M)
Charles Scribner's Sons: 1898 (6-3/4x8-1/2", 116 pgs., B&W, Hardcover)

nn - By E. W. Kemble 125.00 250.00 600.00

BLACKBERRIES, THE (N.S) (see Coontown's 400)
R. H. Russell: 1897 (9"x12", 76 pgs, hard-c, every other page in color, every other page in one color sepia tone)

nn - By E. W. Kemble 162.00 325.00 1300.00
NOTE: *Tastefully done comics about Black Americana during the USA's Jim Crow days.*

BOOK OF BUBBLES, YE (S)
Endicott & Co., New York: March 1864 (6-1/4 x 9-7/8",160 pgs, guilt-illus. hard-c, B&W

nn - By unknown 150.00 300.00 600.00
NOTE: *Subtitle: A contribution to the New York Fair in aid of the Sanitary Commission; 68 single-sided pages of B&W cartoons, each with an accompanying limerick. A few are sequential.*

BOOK OF DRAWINGS BY FRED RICHARDSON (N,S)
Lakeside Press, Chicago: 1899 (13-5/8x10-1/2", 116 pgs, B&W, hard-c)

nn - 80.00 160.00 320.00
NOTE: *Reprinted from the* ***Chicago Daily News****. Mostly single panel. Includes one* ***Yellow Kid*** *parody, some Spanish-American War cartoons.*

BOTTLE, THE (E,O) (see also THE DRUNKARD'S CHILDREN, and TEA GARDEN TO TEA POT, and TEMPERANCE TALES; OR, SIX NIGHTS WITH THE WASHINGTONIANS)
D. Bogue, London, with others in later editions: nd (1846) (16-1/2x11-1/2", 16 pgs, printed one side only, paper cover)

D. Bogue, London (nd; 1846): first edition:
nn - Black & white (Scarce) 200.00 400.00 900.00
nn - Hand colored (Rare) (no known sales)

D. Bogue, London, and Wiley and Putnam, New York (nd; 1847) : second edition, misspells American publisher "Putnam" as "Putman":
nn - Black & white (Scarce) 150.00 300.00 600.00
nn - Hand colored (Rare) (no known sales)

D. Bogue, London, and Wiley and Putnam, New York (nd; 1847) : third edition has "Putnam" spelled correctly.
nn - Black & white (Scarce) 150.00 300.00 600.00
nn - Hand colored (Rare) (no known sales)

D. Bogue, London, Wiley and Putnam, New York, and J. Sands, Sydney, New South Wales: (nd; 1847) : fourth edition with no misspellings
nn - Black & white (Scarce) 150.00 300.00 600.00
nn - Hand colored (Rare) (no known sales)
NOTE: *By George Cruikshank. Temperance/anti-alcohol story. All editions are in precisely identical format. The only difference is to be found on the cover, where it lists who published it. Cover is text only - no cover art.*

BOTTLE, THE HISTORY OF THE
J.C. Becket, 22 Grea St James St, Montreal, Canada: 1851 (9-1/8x6", B&W)

nn - From Engravings by Cruikshank 150.00 300.00 650.00
NOTE: *As published in The Canada Temperance Advocate.*

BOTTLE, THE (E)
W. Tweedie, London: nd (1862) (11-1/2x17-1/3", 16 pgs, printed one side only, paper cover)

nn - Black & white; By George Cruikshank (Scarce) 100.00 200.00 400.00
nn - Hand colored (Scarce) (no known sales)

BOTTLE, THE (E)
Geo. Gebbie, Philadelphia: nd (c.1871) (11-3/8x17-1/8", 42 pgs, tinted interior, hard-c)

nn - By George Cruikshank 100.00 200.00 400.00
NOTE: *New cover art (cover not by Cruikshank).*

BOTTLE, THE (E)
National Temperance, London: nd (1881) (11-1/2x16-1/2", 16 pgs, printed one side only, paper-c, color)

nn - By George Cruikshank 100.00 200.00 400.00
NOTE: *See Platinum Age section for 1900s printings.*

BOTTLE, THE (E)
Marques, Pittsburgh, PA: 1884/85 (6x8", 8 plates, full color, illustrated envelope)
nn - art not by Cruickshank; New Art 50.00 100.00 200.00
NOTE: Says Presented by J.M. Gusky, Dealer in Boots and Shoes

BROAD GRINS OF THE LAUGHING PHILOSOPHER
Dick & Fitzgerald,NY: 1870s
nn - (4) panel sequential strip 25.00 50.00 150.00

BROTHER JONATHAN
Wilson & Co/Benj H Day, 48 Beekman, NYC: 1839-???

July 4 1846 - ads for Obadiah & Butterfly 50.00 100.00 200.00
July 4 1856 catalog list - front cover comic strip 100.00 200.00 400.00
Xmas/New Years 1856 75.00 150.00 300.00
average large size issues 25.00 50.00 100.00
NOTE: has full page advert for Fredinand Flipper comic book**116**

BULL CALF, THE (P,M)
Various: nd (c1890's) (3-7/8x4-1/8", 16 pgs, B&W, paper-c)

nn - By A.B. Frost Creme Oatmeal Toilet Soap 25.00 50.00 150.00
nn - By A.B. Frost Thompson & Taylor Spice Co, Chicago 25.00 50.00 150.00
NOTE: *Reprints the popular strip story by Frost, with the art modified to place a sign for Creme Oatmeal Soap within each panel. The back cover advertises the specific merchant who gave this booklet away - multiple variations exist.*

BULL CALF AND OTHER TALES, THE (M)
Charles Scribner's Sons: 1892 (120 pgs., 6-3/4x8-7/8", B&W, illus. hard cover)

nn - By Arthur Burdett Frost 50.00 150.00 500.00
NOTE: *Blue, grey, tan hard covers known to exist.*

BULL CALF, THE STORY OF THE MAN OF HUMANITY AND THE (P,M)
C.H. Fargo & Co.: 1890 (5-1/4x6-1/4", 24 pgs, B&W, color paper-c)

nn - By A.B. Frost 42.50 85.00 185.00
NOTE: *Fargo shoe company giveaway; pages alternate between shoe advertisements and the strip story.*

BUSHEL OF MERRY THOUGHTS, A (see Mischief Book, The) (E)
Sampson Low Son & Marsten: 1868 (68 pgs, handcolored hardcover, B&W)

nn - (6-1/4 x 9-7/8", 138 pgs) red binding, publisher's name on title page only 200.00 400.00 800.00
nn - (6-1/2 x 10", 134 pgs) green binding, publisher's name on cover & title page 200.00 400.00 800.00
NOTE: *Cover plus story title pages designed by Leighton Brothers, based on Busch art. Translated by Harry Rogers (who is credited instead of Busch). This is a British publication, notable as the earliest known English language anthology collection of Wilhelm Busch comic strips. Page 13 of second story missing from all editions (panel dropped). Unknown which of the two editions was published first. A modern reprint, by Dover in 1971.*

BUTTON BURSTER, THE (M) (says on cover "ten cents hard cash")
M.J. Ivers & Co., 86 Nassau St., New York: 1873 (11x8-1/8", soft paper, B&W)

By various cartoonists (Very Rare) 125.00 250.00 500.00
NOTE: *Reprints from various 1873 issues of Wild Oats; has (5) different sequential comic strips: (3) by Livingston Hopkins, (1) by Thomas Worth, other one creator presently unknown; Bellew, Sr. single panel cartoons.*

BUZZ A BUZZ OR THE BEES (E)
Griffith & Farran, London: September 1872 (8-1/2x5-1/2", 168 pgs, printed one side only, orange, black & white hardcover, B&W interior)

nn - By Wilhelm Busch (Scarce) 112.00 225.00 450.00
NOTE: *Reprint published by Phillipson & Golder, Chester; text written by English to accompany Busch art.*

BUZZ A BUZZ OR THE BEES (E)
Henry Holt & Company, New York: 1873 (9x6", 96 pgs, gilted hardcover, hand colored)

nn - By Wilhelm Busch (Scarce) 100.00 200.00 450.00
NOTE: *Completely different translation than the Griffith & Farran version. Also, contains 28 additional illustrations by Park Benjamin. The lower page count is because the Henry Holt edition prints on both sides of each page, and the Griffith & Farran edition is printed one side only.*

CALENDAR FOR THE MONTH; YE PICTORIAL LYSTE OF YE MATTERS OF

The Carpet Bag #14
1851 © Snow & Wilder

Keppler Cover to Centennial Fun
July 1876 © Frank Leslie

Comic Monthly v2 #7
Sept. 1860 © J.C. Haney, NY

FR1.0 GD2.0 FN6.0

INTEREST FOR SUMMER READING (P,M)
S.E. Bridgman & Company, Northampton, Mass: nd (c. late 1880's-1890's) (5-5/8x7-1/4", 64 pgs, paper-c, B&W)
nn - (Very Rare) T.S. Sullivant-c/a 100.00 200.00 400.00
NOTE: Book seller's catalog, with every other page reprinting cartoons and strips (from Life??). Art by: Chips Bellew, Gibson, Howarth, Kemble, Sullivant, Townsend, Woolf.

CARICATURE AND OTHER COMIC ART
Harper & Brothers, NY: 1877 (9-5/16x7-1/8", 360 pgs, B&W, green hard-c)
nn - By James Parton (over 200 illustrations) 30.00 60.00 200.00
NOTE: This is the earliest known serious history of comics & related genre from around the world produced by an American. Parton was a cousin of Thomas Nast's wife Sarah. A large portion of this book was first serialized in ***Harper's Monthly*** *in 1875.*

CARPET BAG, THE
Snow & Wilder, later Wilder & Pickard, Boston: March 21 1851-March 26 1853
Each average issue 25.00 50.00 100.00
Samuel "Mark Twain" Clemmons issues (first app in print) 500.00 1000.00 2000.00
NOTE: Many issues contain cartoons by DC Johnston, Frank Bellew, others; literature includes Artemus Ward's Miss Partington who had a mischevious little Katzenjammer Kids-like brat. Carpet Bag was not considered derogatory pre-Civil War.

CARROT-POMADE (O.G)
James G. Gregory, Publisher, New York: 1864 (9x6-7/8", 36 pgs, B&W)
nn - By Augustus Hoppin 70.00 140.00 280.00
NOTE: The story of a quack remedy for baldness, sequentially told in the format parodying ABC primers. Has protective tissue pages (not part of page count).

CARTOONS BY HOMER C. DAVENPORT (M,N,S)
De Witt Publishing House: 1898 (16-1/8x12", 102 pgs, hard-c, B&W)
nn 100.00 200.00 400.00
NOTE: Reprinted from Harper's Weekly and the New York Journal. Includes cartoons about the Spanish-American War. Title page reads "Davenport's Cartoons".

CARTOONS BY WILL E. CHAPIN (P,N,S)
The Times-Mirror Printing and Binding House, Los Angeles: 1899 (15-1/4x12", 98 pgs, hard-c, B&W)
nn - scarce 100.00 200.00 400.00
NOTE: Premium item for subscribing to the Los-Angeles Times-Mirror newspaper, from which these cartoons were reprinted. Includes cartoons about the Spanish-American War.

CARTOONS OF OUR WAR WITH SPAIN (N,S)
Frederick A. Stokes Company: 1898 (11-1/2x10", 72 pgs, hardcover, B&W)
nn - By Charles Nelan (r-New York Herald) 40.00 100.00 200.00
nn - 2nd printing noted on copy right page 30.00 60.00 120.00

CARTOONS OF THE WAR OF 1898 (E,M,N,S)
Belford, Middlebrook & Co., Chicago: 1898 (7x10-3/8",190 pgs, B&W, hard-c)
nn 50.00 100.00 200.00
NOTE: Reprints single panel editorial cartoons on the Spanish-American War, from American, Spanish, Latino, and European newspapers and magazines, at rate of 2 to 6 cartoons per page. Art by Bart, Berryman, Bowman, Bradley, Chapin, Gillam, Nelan, Tenniel, others.

CENTENNIAL FUN (O,S) (Rare)
Frank Leslie, Philadelphia: (July) 1876 (25¢, 11x8", 32 pgs, paper cover, B&W)
nn - By Joseph Keppler-c/a;Thomas Worth-a 150.00 300.00 600.00
NOTE: Issued for the 1876 Centennial Exposition in Philadelphia. Exists with both black & white, and orange, black & white covers. One copy of the latter had an embossed newstand label from Partland, Maine, implying that the orange cover version, at least, was distributed and sold outside of Philadelphia.

CHAMPAIGNE
Frank Leslie: June-Dec 1871
1-7 scarce 150.00 225.00 350.00

CHIC
Chic Publishing Co: 1880-81 (Chromolithographic Weekly)
1-38 Livingston Hopkins, Charles Kendrick, CW Weldon 75.00 150.00 300.00

CHILDREN'S CHRISTMAS BOOK, THE
The New York Sunday World: 1897 (10-1/4x8-3/4", 16 pgs, full color)
Dec 12, 1897 - By George Luks, G.H. Grant, Will Crawford, others) (Rare) 50.00 100.00 280.00

CHIP'S DOGS (M)
R.H. Russell and Son Publishers: 1895 hardcover, B&W)
nn - By Frank P. W. "Chip" Bellew 25.00 50.00 100.00
Early printing 80 pgs, 8-7/8x11-7/8"; dark green border of hardcover surrounds all four sides of pasted on cover image; pages arranged in error -- see NOTE below. (more scarce)
nn - By Frank P. W. "Chip" Bellew 12.50 25.00 50.00
Later printing 72 pgs, 8-7/8x11-3/4";green border only on the binding side (one side) of the cover image.
NOTE: Both are strip reprints from ***LIFE****. The difference in page count is due to more blank pages in the first printing -- all printings have the same comics contents, but with the pages in the first printing arranged differently. This is noticeable particularly in the 2-page strip "Getting a Pointer", which appears on the 2nd & 3rd to last pages of the later printings, but in the early printing the first half of this strip is near the middle of the book, while the last half appears on the 2nd to last story page.*

CHIP'S OLD WOOD CUTS (M,S)
R.H. Russell & Son: 1895 (8-7/8x11-3/4", 72 pgs, hardcover, B&W)
nn - By Frank P. W. ("Chip") Bellew 25.00 50.00 100.00
nn - 1897 reprint 15.00 30.00 60.00

CHIP'S UN-NATURAL HISTORY (O,S)
Frederick A. Stokes & Brother: 1888 (7x5-1/4", 64 pgs, hardcover, B&W)
nn - By Frank P. W. ("Chip") Bellew 12.50 25.00 50.00
NOTE: Title page lists publisher as "Successors to White, Stokes & Allen."

CLOWN, OR THE BANQUET OF WIT, THE (E,M,O)
Fisher & Brother, Philadelphia, Baltimore, New York, Boston: nd (c.1851) (7-3/8x4-1/2", 88 pgs, paper cover, B&W)
nn - (Very Rare; 3 known copies) 400.00 800.00 1500.00
NOTE: Earliest known multi-artist anthology of sequential comics; contains multiple sequential comics, plus numerous single panel cartoons. A mixture of reprinted and original material, involving both European and American artists. "Jones, Smith, and Robinson Goes to a Ball" by Richard Doyle (1st app. of Doyle's "Foreign Tour" in America, reprinted from PUNCH, August 24, 1850); "Moses Keyser The Bowery Bully's Trip to the Californian Gold Mines", by John H. Manning; "The Adventures of Mr. Gulp" (by the Read brothers?); more comics by artists unknown; cartoons by George Cruikshank, Grandville, Elton.

COLD CUTS AND PICKLED EELS' FEET; DONE BROWN BY JOHN BROWN
P.J. Cozans, New York: nd (c1855-60) (B&W)
nn (Very Rare) 100.00 200.00 300.00
NOTE: Mostly a children's book. But, pages 87 to 110, and 111 to 122, contain narrative sequential stories.

COLLEGE SCENES (O,G)
N. Hayward, Boston: 1850 (5x6-3/4", 72 pgs, printed one side only, B&W lithography)
nn - (Rare) by Nathan Hayward 200.00 400.00 600.00
NOTE: This is the 2nd such production for an American University; the first issued at Yale circa 1845, decent funny art of story about life of a Harvard student from his entrance thru graduation entirely in caricature. Has art on back cover as well.

COLLEGE CUTS Chosen From The Columbia Spectator 1880-81-82 (S)
White & Stokes, NY: 1882 (8x9-5/8", 92 pgs, B&W)
By F. Benedict Herzog, H. McVickar, W. Bard McVickar, others 20.00 40.00 80.00
nn - 2nd edition reprint (1888) (8-1/4x10-3/8) 10.00 20.00 40.00

COMICAL COONS (M)
R.H. Russell: 1898 (8-7/8 x 11-7/8", 68 pgs, hardcover, B&W)
nn - By E. W. Kemble 300.00 600.00 1200.00
NOTE: Black Americana collection of 2-panel stories.

COMICAL ALMANAC
Anton Bicker, Cinncinati, OH: 1885 (9x6, 260 pgs, B&W, illustrated-c)
nn - two (12) page sequential Busch comic strips 50.00 100.00 200.00

COMIC ALMANAC, THE
John Berger. Baltimore: 1854-? (7-1/2x6-1/4, 36 pgs, B&W)
nn - 60.00 120.00 240.00

COMIC ANNUAL, AMERICAN (O,I)
Richardson, Lord, & Holbrook, Boston: 1831 (6-7/8x4-3/8", 268 pgs, B&W, hard-c)
nn - (Scarce) 150.00 300.00 600.00
NOTE: Mostly text; front & back cover illustrations, 13 full page, and scattered smaller illustrations by David Claypoole Johnston; edited by Henry J. Finn.

COMIC HISTORY OF THE UNITED STATES, (I)
Carleton & Co., NY: 1876 (6-7/8x5-1/8", 336 pgs, hardcover, B&W)
nn - By Livingston Hopkins. 12.50 25.00 50.00
2nd printing: Cassell, Petter, Galpin & Co.: 1880 (6-7/8x5-1/8", 336 pgs, hardcover, B&W)
nn - By Livingston Hopkins. 12.50 25.00 50.00
NOTE: Text with many B&W illustrations; some are multi-panel comics. Not to beconfused with ***Bill Nye's Comic History Of The U.S.*** *which contains Frederick Opper illustrations.*

COMIC MONTHLY, THE
J.C. Haney, N.Y.: March 1859-1880 (16 x 11-1/2", 30 pgs average, B&W)
Certain average issues with sequential comics 50.00 100.00 200.00
11 (Jan 1860) Bellew-c 25.00 50.00 100.00
v2#2 (Apr 1860) Bellew-c 25.00 50.00 100.00
v2#3 (May 1860) Bellew-c 25.00 50.00 100.00
v2#4 (June 1860) Comic Strip Cover 50.00 100.00 200.00
v2#5 (July 1860) Bellew-c; (12) panel Explaining American Politics To An Intelligent Foreigner; (10) panel The Art of Stump Speaking; (15) panel Mr. Dibbs Goes to Pike's Peak and Comes Back Again 100.00 200.00 400.00
v2#7 (Sept 1860) Comic Strip Cover; (24) panel double page spread The Prince of Wales In America 50.00 100.00 200.00
v2#8 (18) panel The Three Young Friends Sillouette Strip 25.00 50.00 100.00
v2#9 (Nov 1860) (9) panel sequential 25.00 50.00 100.00
v2#10 11 not indexed 25.00 50.00 100.00
v2#12 (Jan 1861) (12) panel double page spread 25.00 50.00 100.00

COMIC TOKEN FOR 1836, A COMPANION TO THE COMIC ALMANAC, THE
Charles Ellms, Boston: 1836 (8x5', 48 pgs, B&W)
nn - 50.00 100.00 200.00

COMIC WEEKLY, THE
???, NYC: 1881-???
issues with comic strips (Chips, etc) 60.00 125.00 250.00

The Comus Offering
1830-31 © B. Franklin Edmands

The Daily Graphic #158 Frank Bellew-c
Sept 4, 1873 © The Graphic Company, NY

Elton's Californian Comic All-My-Nack #17
1850 © Elton's, NY

COMIC WORLD
???: 1876-1879 (Quarto Monthly)

issues with comic strips 37.50 75.00 150.00

COMICS FROM SCRIBNER'S MAGAZINE (M)
Scribner's: nd (1891) (10 cents, 9-1/2x6-5/8", 24 pgs, paper cover, side stapled, B&W)

nn - (Rare) F.M.Howarth C&A 100.00 200.00 400.00
NOTE: *Advertised in SCRIBNER'S MAGAZINE in the June 1891 issue, page 793, as available by mail order for 10 cents. Collects together comics material which ran in the back pages of Scribner's Magazine. Art by Attwood, "Chip" Bellew, Döes, Frost, Gibson, Zim.*

COMUS OFFERING CONTAINING HUMOROUS SCRAPS OF DIVERTING COMICALITIES, THE (O, S)
B. Franklin Edmands, 25 Court St, Boston: c1830-31 (8-7/8x10-3/4", 16 pgs, thin brown paper-c, blank on backs,

nn - (William F Straton, Engraver, 15 Water St, Boston) (no known sales)
NOTE: All hand-colored single panel cartoons format definitely inspired by D.C. Johnston's Scraps with every panel character using well-defined word balloons. Might become a seminal step in the evolution of the American comic book. More research is needed.

CONTRASTS AND CONCEITS FOR CONTEMPLATION BY LUKE LIMNER (O)
Ackerman & Co, 96 Strand, London: c1848 (9-3/4x6-1/4, 48 pgs, B&W)
nn - By John Leighton 50.00 100.00 200.00

COONTOWN'S 400 (M) (see **Blackberries**) (M)
The Life (Magazine) Co.: 1899 (10-15/16x8-7/8, 68 pgs, cloth light-brown hard-c, B&W
nn - By E.W. Kemble (scarce) 250.00 500.00 1500.00
NOTE: *Tastefully drawn depictions of Black Americana over one hundred years ago during Jim Crow days.*

CROSSING THE ATLANTIC (O,G)
James R. Osgood & Co., Boston: 1872 (10-7/8x16", 68 pgs, hardcover, B&W);
Houghton, Osgood & Co., Boston: 1880

1st printing - by Augustus Hoppin 50.00 100.00 200.00
2nd printing (1880; 66 pgs; 8-1/8x11-1/8") 32.50 65.00 150.00

C.R. PITT'S COMIC ALMANAC
C.R. Pitt: 1880 (7-1/2x4-5/8", 28 pgs)

nn - contains (8) panel sequential 50.00 100.00 200.00

CRUIKSHANK'S OMNIBUS: A VEHICLE FOR FUN AND FROLIC (E,S)
E. Ferrett & Co., Philadelphia: 1845 (25 cents, 7-1/2" x 4-5/8", 96 pgs, B&W, paper-c)

nn - By George Cruikshank c/a (Very Rare) 150.00 300.00 600.00
NOTE: *Mostly prose, with 10 plates of cartoons printed on one-side (about half the plates with multiple cartoons), plus illustrated cover, all by George Cruikshank. First (perhaps only) American printing of Cruikshank's Omnibus, which was published first in Britain. It is only a partial reprinting.*

CYCLISTS' DICTIONARY (S)
Morgan & Wright, Chicago: 1894 (5 x3-3/4, 80 pgs, soft-c, B&W

nn - By Unknown 37.50 75.00 150.00

THE DAILY GRAPHIC
The Graphic Company, 39 Park Place, NY: 1873-Sept 23, 1889 (14x20-1/2, 8 pgs, B&W)

Average issues with comic strips 7.50 15.00 30.00
Average issues without comic strips 5.00 10.00 20.00
NOTE:

DAVY CROCKETT'S COMIC ALMANACK
???, Nashville, TN, then elsewhere: 1835-end (32 pages plus wraps)

1 500.00 1000.00 2000.00
2-13 15 end 250.00 500.00 1000.00
14 contains (17) panel Crocket comic strip bio 1848 1000.00 1500.00 3000.00

DAY'S DOINGS (was The Last Sensation) (Becomes New York Illustrated Times)
James Watts, NYC: #1 June 6 1868-early 1876 (11x16, 16 pgs, B&W)

average issue with comic strips 10.00 15.00 25.00
Paul Pry & Alley Sloper character issues 25.00 50.00 100.00
Aug 19 1871 - First Alley Sloper in America?? 50.00 100.00 200.00
NOTE: *James Watts was a shadow company for Frank Leslie; outright sold to Frank Leslie in 1873. There are a lot of issues with comic strips from 1868 up.*

DAY'S SPORT - OR, HUNTING ADVENTURES OF S. WINKS WATTLES, A SHOPKEEPER, THOMAS TITT, A "LEGAL GENT," AND MAJOR NICHOLAS NOGGIN, A JOLLY GOOD FELLOW GENERALLY, A (O)
Brother Jonathan, NY: c1850s (5-7/8x8-1/4, 44 pgs)

nn - By Henry L. Stephens, Philadelphia (Very Rare) (no known sales)

DEVIL'S COMICAL OLDMANICK WITH COMIC ENGRAVINGS OF THE PRINCIPAL EVENTS OF TEXAS, THE
Turner & Fisher, NY & Philadelphia: 1837 (7-7/8x5", 24 pgs)

nn - many single panel cartoons 100.00 200.00 400.00

DIE VEHME, ILLUSTRIRTES WOCHENBLATT FUR SCHERZ UND ERNEST (M,O)
Heinrich Binder, St. Louis: No.1 Aug 28, 1869 - No.?? Aug 20, 1870 (10 cents, 8 pgs, B&W, paper-c) (see also PUCK)

1-?? (Very Rare) by Joseph Keppler 100.00 200.00 400.00
NOTE: *Joseph Keppler's first attempt at a weekly American humor periodical. Entirely in German. The title translates into: **"The Star Chamber: An Illustrated Weekly Paper in Fun and Ernest"**.*

DOMESTIC MANNERS OF THE AMERICANS
The Imprint Society, Barre, Mass: 1969 (9-3/4 x 7-1/4", 390 pgs, hard-c in slipcase, B&W)

nn - 10.00 20.00 40.00
NOTE: *Reprints the 1832 edition of this book by Mrs. Trollope with an added insert. The 28-page insert is what is of primary interest to us -- it reproduces SCRAPS No. 4 (1833) by D.C. Johnston.*

DRUNKARD'S CHILDREN, THE (see also THE BOTTLE) (E,O)
David Bogue, London; John Wiley and G.P. Putnam, New York; J. Sands, Sydney, New South Wales: July 1, 1848 (16x11", 16 pgs, printed on one side only, paper-c)

nn - Black & white edition (Scarce) 300.00 600.00 950.00
nn - Hand colored edition (Rare) (no known sales)
NOTE: *Sequel story to THE BOTTLE, by George Cruikshank. Temperance/anti-alcohol story. British-American-Australian co-publication. Cover is text only - no cover art.*

DRUNKARD'S PROGRESS, OR THE DIRECT ROAD TO POVERTY, WRETCHEDNESS & RUIN, THE
J. W. Barber, New Haven, Conn.: Sept 1826 (single sheet)

nn - By John Warner Barber (Very Rare) (no known sales)
NOTE: *Broadside designed and printed by barber contains four large wood engravings showing "The Morning Dram" which is "The Beginning of Sorrow"; "The Grog Shop" with its "Bad Company"; "The Confirmed Drunkard" in a state of "Beastly Intoxication"; and the "Concluding Scene" with the family being drive off to the alms house. It is an interesting set of cuts, faintly reminiscent of Hogarth. Many modern reprints exist.*

DUEL FOR LOVE, A (O,P)
E.C. DeWitt & Co., Chicago: nd (c1880's) (3-3/8" x 2-5/8", 12 pgs, B&W, paper-c)

nn - Art by F.M. Howarth (Rare) 25.00 50.00 100.00
NOTE: *Advertising giveaway for DeWitt's Little Early Risers, featuring an 8-panel strip story, spread out 1 panel per page.*

DURHAM WHIFFS (O, P)
Blackwells Durham Tobacco Co: Jan 8 1878 (9x6.5", 8 pgs, color-c, B&W)

v1 #1 w/Trade Card Insert 37.50 75.00 150.00
NOTE: Sold in 2008 CGC 9.4 $1250

DYNALENE LAFLETS (P)
The Dynalene Company: nd (3 x 3-1/2", 16 pgs, B&W, paper cover)

nn - Dynalene Dyes promo (9) panel comic strip 25.00 50.00 75.00

ELEPHANT, THE
William H Graham, Tribune Building, NYC: Jan 22 1848-Feb 19 1848 (11x8.5", B&W)

1-5 Rare - single panel cartoons 150.00 300.00 600.00

ELTON'S COMIC ALL-MY-NACK (E,O.S)
Elton, Publisher, 18 Division & 98 Nassau St, NY: 1833-1852 (7-1/2x4-1/2", 36pgs, B&W

1-5 99% single panel cartoons 100.00 200.00 400.00
6 (1839) 100.00 200.00 400.00
NOTE: Two different covers & different interiors exist for this title and number
7-15 - 99% single panel cartoons 100.00 200.00 400.00
16 - contains 6 panel "A Tales of A Tayl-or" 1848-49 200.00 400.00 600.00
17 - contains "Moses Keyser, The Bowery Bully's Trip To the California Gold Mines" 1850
By John H. Manning, early comics creator, told in 15 panels 200.00 400.00 600.00
18-19 presently unknown contents 100.00 200.00 400.00
NOTE: *Contains both original American, and pirated European, cartoons. All single panel material, except where noted. Almanacs are published near the end of the year prior to that for which they are printed -- like calendars today. Thus, the 1833 No. 1 issue was really published in the last months of 1832. #17 has Elton's Californian Comic-All-My-Nack on the cover.*

ELTON'S COMIC ALMANAC (Publsiher change)
GW Cottrell & Co, Publishers & C Cornhill, Boston, Mass: 1853 (7-7/8x4-5/8,36pgs,B&W
20 - (2) sequential comic strips (9) panel "Jones, Smith and Robinson Goes To A Ball; (21) panel "The Adventures of Mr. Gulp" Rare 300.00 600.00 1200.00
NOTE: *Both strips appear in* The Clown, Or The Banquet of Wit

ELTON'S FUNNY ALMANACK (title change to Almanac)
Elton Publisher and Engraver, New York: 1846 (8x6-1/2", 36 pgs)

1 1846 50.00 100.00 200.00

ELTON'S FUNNY ALMANAC (#1 titled Almanack)
Elton & Co, New York: 1847-1853 (8x6-1/4, 36 pgs, B&W)
2 (1847) #3 (1848) 50.00 100.00 200.00
nn 1853 (8-1/8x4-7/8"; (5) panel comic strip "The Adventures of Mr. Goliah Starvemouse"

ELTON'S RIPSNORTER COMIC ALMANAC
Elton, 90 Nassau St, NY: 1850 (8x5, 24 pgs, B&W, paper-c)
nn - scarce 50.00 100.00 200.00

ENGLISH SOCIETY (S)
Harper & Brothers, Publishers, New York: 1897 (9-5/8x12-1/4", 206 pgs, B&W)

nn - by George Du Maurier 25.00 50.00 75.00

ENGLISH SOCIETY AT HOME (S)
James R. Osgood and Company: 1881 (10-7/8x8-5/8, 182 pgss, protective sheets on some pages - not included in pages count, hard-c, B&W 25.00 50.00 75.00

nn - by George Du Maurier

ENTER: THE COMICS (E,G)
University of Nebraska Press: 1965 (6-7/8x9-1/4", 120 pgs, hard-c)

The Evolution Of A Democrat
1888 © Paquet & Co, NY

Flying Leaves
1880s © E.R. Herrick & Company, New York

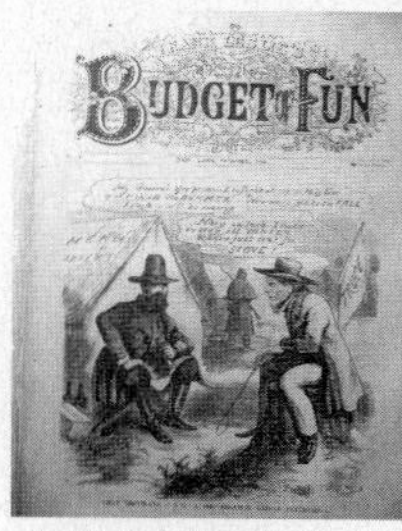

Frank Leslie's Budget of Fun #79
Oct 1864 © Frank Leslie, NY

	FR1.0	GD2.0	FN6.0
nn - By Ellen Weisse	25.00	50.00	100.00

NOTE: *Contains overview of Töpffer's life and career plus only published English translation of Töpffer's Monsieur Crepin (1837); appears to have been re-drawn by Weisse in the days before xerox machines.*

ESQUIRE BROWN AND HIS MULE, STORY OF
A.C. Meyer, Baltimore, Maryland: 1880s (5x3/7/8", 28 pgs, B&W)

Booklet (9 panel story plus cough remedies catalog)	25.00	50.00	100.00
Fold-Out of Booklet (9 panel version)	25.00	50.00	100.00

"EVENTS OF THE WEEK" REPRINTED FROM THE CHICAGO TRIBUNE
Henry O. Shepard Co, Chicago: 1894 (5-3/8x15-7/8", 110 pg, B&W, hard-c)

First Series, Second Series - By HR Heaton	37.50	75.00	150.00

EVERYBODY'S COMICK ALMANACK
Turner & Fisher, NY & Philadelphia: 1837 (7-7/8x5", 36 pgs, B&W)

nn	50.00	100.00	200.00

EVOLUTION OF A DEMOCRAT - A DARWINIAN TALE, THE (O,G)
Paquet & Co., New York: 1888 (25 cents, 7-7/8x5-1/2", 100 pgs, printed one side only, orange paper cover, B&W) (Very Rare)

nn - Written by Henry Liddell, art by G. Roberty	300.00	600.00	1200.00

NOTE: *Political parody about the rise of an Irishman through Tammany Hall. Grover Cleveland appears as linked with Tammany. Ireland becomes the next state in the USA.*

FABLES FOR THE TIMES (S, I)
R.H. Russell & Son, New York: 1896 (9-1/8x12-1/8", 52 pgs, yellow hard-c)

nn - By H.W. Phillips and T.S. Sullivant Scarce	75.00	150.00	300.00

FERDINAND FLIPPER, ESQ., THE FORTUNES OF (O,G)
Brother Jonathan, Publisher, NY: nd (1851) (5-3/4 x 9-3/8", 84 pgs, B&W, printed both sides)

nn - By Various (Very Rare)	500.00	1000.00	2500.00

NOTE: *Extended title: "...Commencing With A Period of Four Months And Anterior To His Birth Going Thru The Various Stages of His Infancy, Childhood, Verdant Years, Manhood, Middle Life, and Green and Ripe Old Age, And Ending A Short Time Subsequent to His Sudden Decease With His Final Exit, Funeral And Burial." Extremely unique comic book, put together by gathering 145 independent single illustrations and cartoons, by various artists, and stringing them together into a sequential story. The majority of panels are by Grandville. Also included are at least 19 signed Charles Martin, reprinted from 1847 issues of Yankee Doodle, 5 panels from D.C. Johnston, plus other panels by F.O.C. Darley, T.H. Matheson, and others. The story also contains several panels of Gold Rush content . Printed by E.A. Alverds. The 1851 date is derived from an advertisement found in the Oct-Dec 1851 issue of the Brother Jonathan newspaper. It ispossible, however, that it actually came out even earlier.*

FERDINAND FLIPPER, ESQ., THE FORTUNES OF (G)
Dick & Fitzgerald, New York: nd (1870's to 1888) (30 Cents, 84 pgs, B&W, paper cover)

nn - (Very Rare reprint - several editions possible)	375.00	750.00	1500.00

FINN'S COMIC ALMANAC
Marsh, Capen, & Lyon; Boston: 1835-??? (4.5x7.5, 36 pgs, B&W)

nn	100.00	200.00	400.00

FINN'S COMIC SKETCHBOOK (S)
Peabody & Co., 223 Broadway, NY: 1831 (10-1/2x16", 12 pgs, B&W)

nn - By Henry J. Finn (Very Rare) (no known sales)

NOTE: *Designs on copper plates; etched by J. Harris, NY; should have tissue paper in front of each plate.*

50 GREAT CARTOONS (M,P,S)
Ram's Horn Press: 1899 (14x10-3/4, 112 pgs, hard-c)

nn - By Frank Beard	30.00	60.00	120.00

NOTE: *Premium in return for a subscription to* ***The Ram's Horn*** *magazine.*

FISHER'S COMIC ALMANAC
Ames Fisher and Brother, No 12 North Sixth St, Philadelphia , Charles Small in NYC, Also in Boston: 1841-1868 (4-1/2 x 7-1/4, 36 pgs, B&W)

1-7 (1841-1847)	100.00	200.00	400.00
12 reprints mermaid-c with word balloon (1868)	100.00	200.00	400.00

F**** A*** K*****, OUTLINES ILLUSTRATIVE OF THE JOURNAL OF** (O,S)
D.C. Johnston, Boston: 1835 (9-5/16 x 6", 12 pgs, printed one side only, blue paper cover, B&W interior) (see also **SCRAPS**)

nn - by David Claypoole Johnston (Scarce)	600.00	1000.00	1600.00

NOTE: *This is a series of 8 plates parodying passages from the Journal of Fanny (Frances) A. Kemble, a British woman who wrote a highly negative book about American Culture after returning from the U.S. Though remembered now for her campaign against slavery, she was prejudiced against most everything American culture, thus inspiring Johnston's satire. Contains 4 protective sheets (not part of page count.)*

FLYING DUTCHMAN; OR, THE WRATH OF HERR VONSTOPPELNOZE, THE (E)
Carleton Publishing, New York: 1862 (7-5/8x5-1/4", 84 pgs, printed on one side only, gilted hardcover, B&W)

nn - By Wilhelm Busch (Scarce)	35.00	70.00	160.00
nn - 1975 Scarce 100 copy-r 74 pgs Visual Studies Workshop	5.00	10.00	20.00

NOTE: *This is the earliest known English language book publication of a Wilhelm Busch work. The story is plagiarized by American poet John G. Saxe, who is credited with the text, while the uncredited Busch cartoons are described merely as accompanying illustrations.*

FLYING LEAVES (E)
E.R. Herrick & Company, New York: nd (c1889/1890's) (8-1/4" x 11-1/2", 76 pgs, B&W interior, orange, b&w hard-c)

nn- (Scarce)	85.00	175.00	260.00

NOTE: *Reprints strips and single panel cartoons from 1888 Fliegende Blatter issues, translated into English. Various artists, including Bechstein, Adolf Hengeler, Lothar Meggendorfer, Emil Reinicke.*

FOOLS PARADISE WITH THE MANY ADVENTURES THERE AS SEEN IN THE STRANGE SURPRISING PEEP SHOW OF PROFESSOR WOLLEY COBBLE, THE (E)
(see also THE COMICAL PEEP SHOW)
John Camden Hotten, London: Nov 1871 (1 crown, 9-7/8x7-3/8", 172 pgs, printed one side only, gilted green hardcover, hand colored interior)

	FR1.0	GD2.0	FN6.0
nn - By Wilhelm Busch (Rare)	400.00	800.00	1750.00

NOTE: *Title on cover is:* ***WALK IN! WALK IN!! JUST ABOUT TO BEGIN!!! the FOOLS PARADISE****; below the above title page. Anthology of Wilhelm Busch comics, translated into English.*

FOOLS PARADISE WITH THE MANY WONDERFUL SIGHTS AS SEEN IN THE STRANGE SURPRISING PEEP SHOW OF PROFESSOR WOLLEY COBBLE, FURTHER ADVENTURES IN (E)
Chatto & Windus, London: 1873 (10x7-3/8", 128 pgs, printed one side only, brown hardcover, hand colored interior)

nn - By Wilhelm Busch (Rare)	300.00	600.00	1320.00

NOTE: *Sequel to the 1871* ***FOOLS PARADISE****, containing a completely different set of Busch stories, translated into English.*

FOOLS PARADISE MIRTH AND FUN FOR THE OLD & YOUNG (E)
Griffith & Farran, London: May 1883 (9-3/4x7-5/8", 78 pgs, color cover, color interior)

nn - By Wilhelm Busch (Rare)	100.00	200.00	420.00

NOTE: *Collection of selected stories reprinted from both the 1871 & 1873* ***FOOLS PARADISE.***

FOOLS PARADISE - MIRTH AND FUN FOR THE OLD & YOUNG (E)
E.P. Dutton and Co., NY: May 1883 (9-3/4x7-5/8", 78 pgs, color cover, color interior)

nn - By Wilhelm Busch (Rare)	100.00	200.00	420.00

NOTE: *Collection of selected stories reprinted from both the 1871 & 1873* ***FOOLS PARADISE.***

FOREIGN TOUR OFMESSRS. BROWN, JONES, AND ROBINSON, THE (see Messrs....)

FRANK LESLIE'S BOYS AND GIRLS
Frank Leslie, NYC: Oct 13 1866-#905 Feb 9 1884

average issue with comic strip	10.00	20.00	40.00

FRANK LESLIE'S BUDGET OF FUN
Frank Leslie, Ross & Tousey, 121 Nassau St, NYC: Jan 1859-1878 (newspaper size)

1-5 no comic strips	50.00	100.00	200.00
6 June 1859 (9) panel "The Wonderful Hunting Tour of Mr Borridge After the Deer"	75.00	150.00	300.00
7-9 no comic strips	25.00	50.00	100.00
10 Sept 1859 sequential comic strip	50.00	100.00	200.00
11 (8) panel sequential "Apropos of the Great Eastern"	50.00	100.00	200.00
12-14	25.00	50.00	100.00
15 Feb 1860 (12) panel "The Ballet Girl" strip	50.00	100.00	200.00
16-18	25.00	50.00	100.00
19 June 1860 comic strip front cover	100.00	200.00	300.00

NOTE: Cover is (11) panel "The Very Latest Fashionable Amusement..."; Back cover comic strip "Mr Jogg's Reasons For Preferring to Board to Keeping House" (7) panels using word balloons. Plus centerfold double page (18) panel spread "The New York May, Moving in General, and Mrs. Grundy's In Particular."

20 24 25 no comic strips	25.00	50.00	100.00
21 (7/15/60) (8) panel Mr Septimus Verdilater Visits the Baltimore Convention"	50.00	100.00	200.00
22 (8/1/60) (3) panel	25.00	50.00	100.00
23 (8/15/60) (12) panel "Superb Scheme For Perfecting of Dramatic Entertainment"	50.00	100.00	200.00
25 (9/15/60 (9) panel sequential	25.00	50.00	100.00
27 AbrahamLincoln Word Balloon cover	50.00	100.00	200.00
28 Wilhelm Busch sequential strip-r begin	50.00	100.00	200.00
29, 31-51 to be indexed next year	25.00	50.00	100.00
30 (12/15/60) (3) panel sequential strip	25.00	50.00	100.00
31 (Jan 1861) (12) panel The Boarding School Miss	25.00	50.00	100.00
32 (Feb 1861) (10) panel Telegraphic Horrors; Or, Mr Buchanan Undergoing A Series of Electric Shocks	50.00	100.00	200.00
35 (4/1/61) Abraham Lincoln Word Balloon cover	50.00	100.00	200.00
43 44 no sequential comic strips	25.00	50.00	100.00
45 (Nov 1861) (6) panel sequential; (11) panel The Budget Army and Infantry Tactics; First Bellew here? - Many Bellew full pagers begin	50.00	100.00	200.00
48 (Feb 1862) Bellew-c; (2) panel Bellew strip plus singles	50.00	100.00	200.00
49 (Mar 1862) Bellew-c; (16) panel Wilhelm Busch "The Fly Or The Disturbed Ducthman A Story without Words"	50.00	100.00	200.00
50 (April 1862) Bellew-c "Succession Bath" plus singles	25.00	50.00	100.00
51 (May 1862) Bellew-c; (25) panel Busch The Toothache (6) panel Definitions of the Day	50.00	100.00	200.00
52 (June 1862) Bellew-c; (9) panel A Cock & A Bull Expedition; (6) panel Bellew The First Campaign of the Home Guard	50.00	100.00	200.00

NOTE: Johnny Bull & Louis Napolean with Brother Jonathan

53-67 To Be Indexed in the Future	25.00	50.00	100.00
68 (11/18//63) (6) panel Bellew strip "Cuts On Cowards"	25.00	50.00	100.00

NOTE: contains (1) panel William Newman 1817-1870, mentor to Thomas Nast

71 (Feb 1864) Wiord Balloon Jefferson Davis-c	25.00	50.00	100.00
72 (Mar 1864) Word Balloon-c	25.00	50.00	100.00

Frank Tousey's Illustrated New York Monthly #9
June 1882 © Frank Tousey

The Funnyest Of Awl And The Funniest Sort Of Phun v4#4
1865 © A.T. Bellew Word Balloon Cover

Funny Fellow's Own Book
1852 © Philip Cozans

	FR1.0	GD2.0	FN6.0
73 (April 1864) Word Balloon-c in (6) panels	25.00	50.00	100.00
74 (May 1864) Newman Word Balloon-c	25.00	50.00	100.00
75 77 78 no sequentials	25.00	50.00	100.00
76 (July 1864) Newman Word Balloon-c	25.00	50.00	100.00
79 (Oct 1864) Word Balloon-c	25.00	50.00	100.00
80 (Nov 1864) Robt E Lee & JeffDavis-c; no sequentials	25.00	50.00	100.00
81 (Dec 1864) Word Balloon "Abyss of War"-c	25.00	50.00	100.00
83 (2/18/65) Back-c (6) panel "Petroleum"	25.00	50.00	100.00
84 (Mar 1865) (6) panel sequential	25.00	50.00	100.00
85 (Apr 1865) Word Balloon-c	25.00	50.00	100.00
86 89 90 92 no sequentials	25.00	50.00	100.00
88 (7/6/65) (6) panel "Marriage"	25.00	50.00	100.00
91 (Oct 1865) (6) panel "Brief Confab At The Corner	25.00	50.00	100.00
93-98 yet to be indexed	25.00	50.00	100.00
99 (June 1866) (18) panel Mr Paul Peters Adventures While Trout-Fishing In The Adirondacks	50.00	100.00	200.00
100 (July 1866) (4) panel sequential comic strip	25.00	50.00	100.00
102 (Sept 1866) (6) panel sequential comic strip	25.00	50.00	100.00
103 (Oct 1866) (9) panel strip; (12) pane;l back cover Adventures of McTiffin At Long Branch	50.00	100.00	200.00
104 (Nov 1866) (4) panel; (23) panel "The Budget Rebuses; (2) panel Glut On Treason Market;back-c; (6) sequential strip	25.00	50.00	100.00
105 (12/18/66) Word Balloon-c; (20) panel sequential back-c	37.50	65.00	130.00

NOTE: Artists include William Newman (1863-1868), William Henry Shelton, Joseph Keppler (1873-1876), James A. Wales (1876-1878), Frederick Burr Opper (1878)

FRANK LESLIE'S LADY'S MAGAZINE
Frank Leslie, NYC: Feb 1863-Dec 1882 (8.5x12", typically 152 pgs)

issues with comic strips	10.00	20.00	40.00

FRANK LESLIE'S PICTORIAL WEEKLY
Frank Leslie, Ross & Tousey, 121 Nassau St, NYC:

average issue (Very Rare)	50.00	100.00	200.00

FRANK TOUSEY'S NEW YORK COMIC MONTHLY
Frank Tousey, NYC: (no known sales)

FREAKS
???, Philadelphia: Jan 8, 1881-April? 1881 (Chromolithographic Weekly)

(Very Rare)	50.00	100.00	300.00

FREELANCE, THE
A.M. Soteldo Jr, Edito, 292 Broadway, NYC: 1874-75 (Folio Weekly)

(Rare)	25.00	50.00	100.00

FREE MASONRY EXPOSED
Winchell & Small, 113 Fulton, NY: 1871 (7-5/8x10-1/2", 36pgs, blue paper-c, B&W)

nn- Thomas Worth Scarce	100.00	200.00	400.00

NOTE: Scathing satircal look at Free Masons thru many cartoons, their power waning by the 1870s

FREETHINKERS' PICTORIAL TEXT-BOOK, THE (S,O)
The Truth Seeker Company, New York: 1890, 1896, 1898 (9x12, hard-c, B&W)

1 (1890 edition) - Scarce 382 pgs By Watson Heston	200.00	400.00	800.00
1 (1896 edition) - Scarce 378 pgs By Watson Heston (1890-r)	100.00	200.00	450.00
2 (1898 edition) - Scarce 408 pgs By Watson Heston	125.00	250.00	450.00

NOTE: *Sought after by collectors of Freethought/Atheism material. There is also 200 copy Modern Reprint.*

FRITZ SPINDLE-SHANKS, THE RAVEN BLACK
Cosack & C o, Buffalo, NY: 1870/80s (4-3/8x2-3/4", color)

(10) card comic strip set by Wilhelm Busch	25.00	50.00	100.00

FUN BY RALL
Unknown: circa 1865 (11x7-7/8", 68 pgs, soft-c, B&W)

nn - By presently unknown (Very Rare)	100.00	200.00	350.00

NOTE: *Wraparound soft cover like modern comic book; yellow paper cover with red & black ink.*

FUN FOR THE FAMILY IN PICTURES
D. Lothrop and Company: 1886 (4 x 7", 48 pgs, Silver & Red stiff-c; interior pages have various single color inks)

nn - By unknown hand	50.00	100.00	200.00

NOTE: *Single panel cartoons and sequential stories.*

FUN FROM LIFE
Frederick A Stokes & Brother, New York: 1889 (9 1/8 by 7 1/8, 72 pages, hard-c)

nn - Mostly by Frank "Chips" Bellew Jr	62.50	125.00	250.00

NOTE: *Contains both single panel and many sequential comics reprints from Life.*

FUNNYEST OF AWL AND THE FUNNIEST SORT OF PHUN, THE
AT Bellew Or W. Jennings Demorest, 121 Nassau St, NY : 1865-67 (30 issues, 16x11 tabloid 16 pgs B&W Monthly, 1-8 © American News; 9-on © A.T. Bellews)

1 (April 1864) Bellew-c	50.00	100.00	200.00
4 (1865) Bellew-c	50.00	100.00	200.00
5 (1865) Busch (20) panel comic srtip The Toothache	75.00	150.00	300.00
7 (1865) Bellew-c	50.00	100.00	200.00
8 (1865) Special Petroleum oil issue - much cartoon art	100.00	200.00	400.00
9 (July 1865) Bellew Bullfrog-c; centerfold double page spread hanging many Confederates; (6) panel strip hanging Jeff Davis	100.00	200.00	400.00
10 (Aug 1865) Bellew-c (13) panel Busch strip with two ducks, a frog and a butcher who gets the ducks in the end	100.00	200.00	400.00
11 (Sept 1865) Bellew Bull Frog Anti-French-c	50.00	100.00	200.00
13 14 15 (12/65-1/66) Bellew-c no sequential comic strips	50.00	100.00	200.00
16 (March 1866) address change to 39 Park Ave	50.00	100.00	200.00
22 (Sept 1866) 133 Nassau St	50.00	100.00	200.00
34 (Oct 1867) 133 Nassau St (7) panel Baseball comic strip; Last Known Issue - were there more?	100.00	200.00	400.00

NOTE: *Radical Republican politics distributed by Great American News Company; owned by Frank Bellew's wife as a front for her husband. When the Civil War ended, the brutal anti-Confederate comic strips and jokes switched to frogs and began attacking France. Funny thing, history says without France's help in the 1700s, there just might not have been a United States.*

FUNNY ALMANAC
Elton & Co., NY: 1853 (8-1/8x4-7/8, 36 pgs)

nn - sequential comic strip	50.00	100.00	200.00

NOTE: (5) panel strip "The Adventures of Mr. Goliah Starvemouse"

FUNNY FELLOWS OWN BOOK, A COMPANION FOR THE LOVERS OF FROLIC AND GLEE, THE (M,N)
Philip. J. Cozans, 116 Nassau ST, NY: 1852 (4-1/2x7-1/2", 196 pgs, burnt orange paper-c)

nn - contains many sequential comic strips (Very Rare) (no known sales)

NOTE: Collected from many different Comic Alamac(k)s including Mose Keyser (Calif Gold Rush); Jones, Smith and Robinson Goes To A Ball; Adventures of Mr. Gulp, Or the Effects of A Dinner Party; The Bowery Bully's Trip To The California Gold Mines plus lots more. This one is a sleeper so far.

FUNNY FOLK (M)
E. P. Dutton: 1899 (12x16-1/2", 90 pgs,14 strips in color-rest in b&w, hard-c)

nn - By Franklin Morris Howarth	162.50	325.00	1500.00
nn - London: J.M. Dent, 1899 embossed-c; same interior	200.00	450.00	900.00

NOTE: *Reprints many sequential strips & single panel cartoons from* ***Puck****. This is considered by many to be yet another "missing link" between Victorian & Platinum Age comic books. Most comic books 1900-1917 re-printing Sunday newspaper comic strips follow this size format, except using cardboard-c rather than hard-c.*

FUNNY SKETCHES...Also Embracing Comic Illustrations
Frank Harrison, New York: 1881 (6-5/8x5", 68 pgs, B&W, Color-c)

nn - contains (3) sequential comic strips; one strip is (6) pages long; plus one (3) pages; one more (2) pager	75.00	150.00	300.00

GIBSON BOOK, THE (M,S)
Charles Scribner's Sons & R.H. Russell, New York: 1906 (11-3/8x17-5/8", gilted red hard-c, B&W)

Book I	50.00	100.00	200.00

NOTE: *Reprints in whole the books: Drawings, Pictures of People, London,Sketches and Cartoons, Education of Mr. Pipp, Americans. 414 pgs. 1907 2nd editions exist same value.*

Book II	50.00	100.00	200.00

NOTE: *Reprints in whole the books: A Widow and Her Friends, The Weaker Sex, Everyday People, Our Neighbors. 314 pgs 1907 second edition for both also exists. Same value.*

GIBSON'S PUBLISHED DRAWINGS, MR. (M,S) (see Plat index for later issues post 1900)
R.H. Russell, New York: No.1 1894 - No. 9 1904 (11x17-3/4", hard-c, B&W)

nn (No.1; 1894) Drawings 96 pgs	30.00	60.00	120.00
nn (No.2; 1896) Pictures of People 92 pgs	30.00	60.00	120.00
nn (No.3; 1898) Sketches and Cartoons 94 pgs	30.00	60.00	120.00
nn (No.4; 1899) The Education of Mr. Pipp 88 pgs	30.00	60.00	120.00
nn (No.5; 1900) Americans	30.00	60.00	120.00

NOTE: *By Charles Dana Gibson cartoons, reprinted from magazines, primarily* ***LIFE****. The Education of Mr. Pipp tells a story. Series continues how long after 1904? Each of these books originally came in a boxx and are worth more with the box.*

GIRL WHO WOULDN'T MIND GETTING MARRIED, THE (O)
Frederick Warne & Co., London & New York: nd (c1870's) (9-1/2x11-1/2", 28 pgs, printed 1 side, paper-c, B&W)

nn - By Harry Parkes	62.50	125.00	250.00

NOTE: *Published simultaneously with its companion volume,* ***The Man Who Would Like to Marry****.*

GOBLIN SNOB, THE (O)
DeWitt & Davenport, New York: nd (c1853-56) (24 x 17 cm, 96 pgs, B&W, color hard-c)

nn - (Rare) by H.L. Stephens	250.00	500.00	1000.00

GOLDEN ARGOSY
Frank A. Munsey, 81 Warren St, NYC: 1880s (10-1/2x12, 16 pgs, B&W)

issues with full page comic strips by Chips and Bisbee	12.50	25.00	50.00

GOLDEN DAYS, THE
James Elverson, Publisher, NYC: March 6 1880-May 11 1907 weekly, 16 pgs

issues with comic strips	4.00	7.50	15.00
Horatio Alger issues	10.00	20.00	40.00
v10 #49-v11#1 1889 first Stratemeyer story	25.00	50.00	100.00

GOLDEN WEEKLY, THE
Frank Tousey, NYC: #1 Sept 25 1889-#145 Aug 18 1892 (10-3/4x14-1/2, 16 pgs, B&W)

average issue with comic striips	15.00	25.00	50.00

GREAT LOCOFOCO JUGGERNAUT, THE (S)
publisher unknown: Fall/Winter 1837 (7-5/8x3-1/4, handbill single page)

The Story of Han's The Swapper Cover & First Two Panels
1865 © L. Pranc & Co, Boston

The Home Circle #20
August 1855 © Garrett & Co., NY

Imagerie d'Epinal
1888 © Mumoristic Publishing Co.

FR1.0 GD2.0 FN6.0

nn - By David Claypoole Johnston (a VG copy sold for $2000 in 2005)
nn - **Imprint Society:** 1971 (reprint) 6.00 12.00 25.00

HALF A CENTURY OF ENGLISH HISTORY (S. M)
G.P. Putnam's Sons - The Knickerbocker Press, New York and London: 1884 (7-3/4 x 5-3/4", 316 pgs., illustrated hard-c)
nn - By Various 25.00 50.00 175.00
NOTE: Subtitle: Pictorially Presented in a Series of Cartoons from the Collection of Mr. Punch. Comprising 150 plates by Doyle, Leech, Tenniel, and others, in which are portrayed the political careers of Peel, Palmerston, Russell, Cobden, Bright, Beaconsfield, Derby, Salisbury, Gladstone and other English statesmen.

HAIL COLUMBIA! HISTORICAL, COMICAL, AND CENTENNIAL (O,S)
The Graphic Co., New York & Walter F. Brown, Providence, RI: 1876 (10x11-3/8", 60 pgs, red gilted hard-c, B&W)
nn - by Walter F. Brown (Scarce) 100.00 200.00 450.00

HANS HUCKEBEIN'S BATCH OF ODD STORIES ODDLY ILLUSTRATEDED
McLoughlin Bros., New York: 1880s (9-3/4x7-3/8, 36?? pg?
nn - By Wilhelm Busch (Rare) 75.00 150.00 300.00

HANS THE SWAPPER, THE STORY OF (O)
L. Pranc & Co., 159 Washington St, Boston: 1865 (33 inch long fold out in colors)
nn - unique fold out comic book on one long piece of paper 75.00 150.00 300.00

HARPER'S NEW MONTHLY MAGAZINE
Harper & Brothers, Franklin Square, NY: 1850-1870s (6-3/4x10, 140 pgs, paper-c, B&W)
1850s issues with comic strips in back advert section 10.00 20.00 40.00

HEALTH GUYED (I)
Frederick A. Stokes Company: 1890 (5-3/8 x 8-3/8, 56 pgs, hardcover, B&W)
nn - By Frank P.W. ("Chip") Bellew (Junior) 25.00 50.00 175.00
NOTE: Text & cartoon illustration parody of a health guide.

HEATHEN CHINEE, THE (O)
Western News Co.: 1870 (5-1/32x7-1/4, B&W, paper)
nn - 10 sheets printed on one side came in envelope 75.00 150.00 300.00

HITS AT POLITICS (M,S)
R.H. Russell, New York: 1899 (15" x 12", 156 pgs, B&W, hard-c)
nn - W.A. Rogers c/a 100.00 200.00 300.00
NOTE: Collection of W.A. Rogers cartoons, all reprinted from Harper's Weekly. Includes Spanish-American War cartoons.

THE HOME CIRCLE
Garrett & Co, NY: 1854-56 (26x19", 4 pgs, B&W)

	FR1.0	GD2.0	FN6.0
1 (1/54) beautiful ad of Garrett Building	100.00	200.00	400.00
2/4 (4/66) Cover ad for Yale College Scraps	100.00	200.00	400.00
2/5 (5/55) First ad for Oscas Snanghai	75.00	150.00	300.00
2/6 (6/55) another ad forOscas Snanghai	75.00	150.00	300.00
2/8 (#20) (8/55) Oscar Shanghai comic book cover repro	200.00	400.00	800.00
3/1 (#25) (1/56)	200.00	400.00	800.00

NOTE: Garrett's 2nd comic book Courtship of Chavalier Slyfox-Wikoff

3/8 (#32) (8/56)	50.00	100.00	200.00

NOTE: First print ad for Foreign Tour of Messrs. Brown, Jones, and Robinson

35 (11/56) first official Garrett, Dick & Fitzgerald issue	50.00	100.00	200.00
37 (1/57)	100.00	200.00	400.00

NOTE: Front page comic strip repro ad for Messrs. Brown, Jones, and Robinson's Foreign Tour; Back cover full of short sequentials, singles panel

HOME MADE HAPPY. A ROMANCE FOR MARRIED MEN IN SEVEN CHAPTERS (O,P)
Genuine Durham Smoking Tobacco & The Graphic Co.: nd (c1870's) (5-1/4 tall x 3-3/8" wide folded, 27" wide unfolded, color cardboard)
nn - With all 8 panels attached (Scarce) 30.00 60.00 200.00
nn - Individual panels/cards 5.00 10.00 25.00
NOTE: Consists of 8 attached cards, printed on one side, which unfold into a strip story of title card & 7 panels. Scrapbook hobbyists in the 19th Century tended to pull the panels apart to paste into their scrapbooks, making copies with all panels still attached scarce.

HOME PICTURE BOOK FOR LITTLE CHILDREN (E,P)
Home Insurance Company, New York: July 1887 (8 x 6-1/8", 36 pgs, b&w, color paper-c)
nn (Scarce) 40.00 80.00 160.00
NOTE: Contains an abbreviated 32-panel reprinting of "The Toothache" by George Cruikshank. Remainder of booklet does not contain comics. Some copies known to exist do not contain The Toothache - buyer beware!

HOOD'S COMICALITIES. COMICAL PICTURES FROM HIS WORKS (E,S)
Porter & Coates: 1880 (8-1/2x10-3/8", 104 pgs, printed one side, hard-c, B&W)
nn 20.00 40.00 80.00
NOTE: Reprints 4 cartoon illustrations per page from the British Hood's Comic Annuals, which were poetry books by Thomas Hood.

HOOKEYBEAK THE RAVEN, AND OTHER TALES (see also JACK HUCKABACK, THE SCAPEGRACE RAVEN) (E)
George Routledge and Sons, London & New York: nd (1878) (7-1/4x5-5/8", 104 pgs, hardcover, B&W)
nn - By Wilhelm Busch (Rare) 100.00 200.00 400.00

HOW ADOLPHUS SLIM-JIM USED JACKSON'S BEST, AND WAS HAPPY. A LENGTHY TALE IN 7 ACTS. (O,P)
Jackson's Best Chewing Tobacco & Donaldson Brothers: nd(c1870's) (5-1/8 tall x 3-3/8" wide folded, 27" wide unfolded, color cardboard)
nn - With all 8 panels attached (Scarce) 30.00 60.00 200.00
nn - Individual panels/cards 5.00 10.00 25.00
NOTE: Consists of 8 attached cards, printed on one side, which unfold into a strip story of title card & 7 panels. Scrapbook hobbyists in the 19th Century tended to pull the panels apart topaste into their scrapbooks, making copies with all panels still attached scarce.

HOW DAYS' DURHAM STANDARD OF THE WORLD SMOKING TOBACCO MADE TWO PAIRS OF TWINS HAPPY (O,P)
J.R. Day & Bro. Standard Durham Smoking Tobacco, Durham, NC: nd (c late 1870's/early 1880's) (3-5/8" x 5-1/2", folded, 21-3/4" tall unfolded, color cardboard)
nn- With all 6 panels attached (Scarce) 120.00 240.00 480.00
nn- Individual panels/cards 20.00 40.00 60.00
NOTE: Highly sought by both Black Americana and Tobacciana collectors. Recurring mid-19th Century story about two African-American twin brothers who romance and marry a pair of African-American twin sisters. Although the text is racist at points, the art is not. Consists of 6 attached cards, printed on one side, which unfold downwards into a strip story of title card & 5 panels. Scrapbook hobbyists in the 19th Century tended to pull the panels apart and paste into their scrapbooks, making copies with all panels attached scarce. Note, there are numerous cartoon tellings of this same story, including several card series versions (with different art, and story variations, each time). But, the above is the only version which unfolds as a strip of attached cards. The cards from all the unattached versions are smaller sized, and thus distinguishable.

HUGGINIANA; OR, HUGGINS' FANTASY, BEING A COLLECTION OF THE MOST ESTEEMED MODERN LITERARY PRODUCTIONS (I,S,P)
H.C. Southwick, New York: 1808 (296 pgs, printed one side, B&W, hard-c)
nn - (Very Rare)) (no known sales)
NOTE: The earliest known surviving collected promotional cartoons in America. This is a booklet collecting 7 folded plus 1 full page flyer advertisements for barber John Richard Desborus Huggins, who hired American artists Elkanah Tisdale and William S. Leney to modify previously published illustrations into cartoons referring to his barber shop.

HUMOROUS MASTERPIECES - PICTURES BY JOHN LEECH (E,M)
Frederick A. Stokes: nd (late 1900's - early 1910's) No.1-2 (5-5/8x3-7/8", 68 pgs, cardboard covers, B&W)
1- John Leech (single panel cartoon-r from **Punch**) 17.50 35.00 70.00
2- John Leech (single panel cartoon-r from **Punch**) 17.50 35.00 70.00

HUMOURIST, THE (E,I,S)
C.V. Nickerson and Lucas and Deaver, Baltimore: No.1 Jan 1829 - No.12 Dec 1829 (5-3/4x3-1/2", B&W text w/hand colored cartoon pg.)
Bound volume No.1-12 (Very Rare; copies in libraries 270 pgs) (no known sales)
NOTE: Earliest known American published periodical to contain a cartoon every issue. Surviving individual issues currently unknown -- all information comes from 1 surviving bound volume. Each issue is mostly text, with one full page hand-colored cartoon. Bound volume contains an additional hand-colored cartoons at front of each six month set (total of 14 cartoons in volume). Cartoons appear to be of British origin, possibly by George Cruikshank.

HUMPTY DUMPTY, ADVENTURES OF...(I,P)
1877 (Promotional 4x3-1/2", 12 page chapbook from Gantz, Jones & Co, 10¢-c.)
nn-Promotes Gantz Sea Foam Baking Powder; early app. of a costumed character, dressed as Humpty Dumpty 50.00 100.00 350.00

HUSBAND AND WIFE, OR THE STORY OF A HAIR. (O,P)
Garland Stoves and Ranges, Michigan Stove Co.: 1883 (4-3/16 tall x 2-11/16" wide folded, 16" wide unfolded, color cardboard)
nn - With all 6 panels attached (Scarce) 25.00 50.00 125.00
nn - Individual panels/cards 5.00 10.00 25.00
NOTE: Consists of 6 attached cards, printed on one side, which unfold into a strip story of title card & 5 panels. Scrapbook hobbyists in the 19th Century tended to pull the panels apart topaste into their scrapbooks, making copies with all panels still attached scarce.

ICHABOD ACADEMICUS, THE COLLEGE EXPERIENCES OF (O,G)
William T. Peters, New Haven, CT: 1850 (5-1/2x9-3/4",108 pgs, B&W)
nn - By William T. Peters (Rare) 1000.00 2000.00 4000.00
NOTE: Pages are not uniform in size. Also, a copy showed up on eBay with misspelled Academicus. Has "n" instead of "m" - not known yet which printing is earliest version.

ICHABOD ACADEMICUS, THE COLLEGE EXPERIENCES OF (O,G)
Dick & Fitzgerald, New York: nd (1870s-1888) (paper-c, B&W)
nn - By William T. Peters (Very Rare) 250.00 500.00 1000.00
NOTE: Pages are uniform in size.

ILLUSTRATED SCRAP-BOOK OF HUMOR AND INTELLIGENCE (M)
John J. Dyer & Co.: nd (c1859-1860)
nn - Very Rare 200.00 400.00 800.00
NOTE: A "printed scrapbook" of images culled from some unidentified periodical. About half of it is illustrations that would have accompanied prose pieces. There are pages of single panel cartoons (multiple per page). And there are roughly 8 to 12 pages of sequential comics (all different stories, but appears to all be by the same presently unidentified artist).

THE ILLUSTRATED WEEKLY
Chars C Lucas & Co, 11 Dey St, NY: 1876 (15x18", 8pgs, 8¢ per issue)

	FR1.0	GD2.0	FN6.0
2/8 (2/19/76) back-c all sequential comic strips	100.00	200.00	400.00
2/12 (3/18/76) full page of British-r sequentials	100.00	200.00	400.00
2/14 (4/1/76) April Fool Issue - (6) panel center; plus more	100.00	200.00	400.00
2/15 (4/8/76) (6) panel sequential	100.00	200.00	400.00
issues without comic strips	12.50	25.00	50.00

Jingo No. 3, Sept 24
1884 © Art Newspaper Co, Boston & NYC

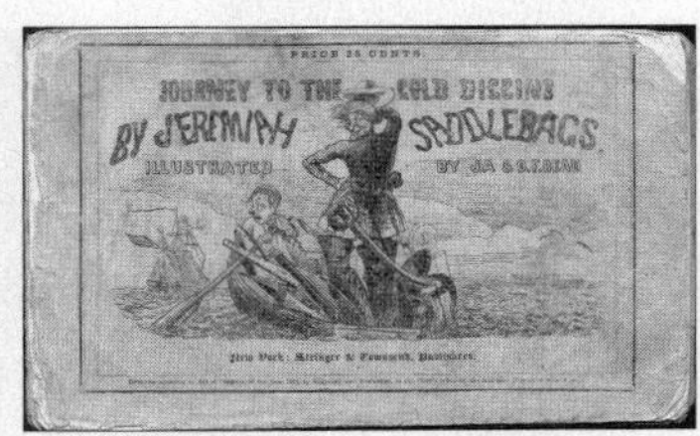

Journey To The Gold Diggings By Jeremiah Saddlebags
1849 © Various - First Original USA Comic Book

The Judge #1 Oct 29, 1881
1881 © Judge Publishing Co.

ILLUSTRATIONS OF THE POETS: FROM PASSAGES IN THE LIFE OF LITTLE BILLY VIDKINS (See A Day's Sport...)
S. Robinson, Philadelphia: May 1849 (14.7 cm x 11.3 cm, 32 pgs, B&W)

nn - by Henry Stephens (very rare) (no known sales)
NOTE: Predates Journey to the Gold Diggins By Jeremiah Saddlebags by a few months and is an original American proto-comic strip book. More research needs to be done. A later edition brought $800 in G/VG 2007

IMAGERIE d'EPINAL (untrimmed individual sheets) (E)
Pellerin for Humoristic Publishing Co, Kansas City, Mo.: nd (1888) No.1-60 (15-7/8x11-3/4",single sheets, hand colored) (All are Rare)

1-14, 21, 22, 25-46, 49-60 - in the Album d'Images 17.50 35.00 70.00
15-20, 23,24, 47, 48 - not in the Album d'Images 30.00 60.00 120.00
NOTE: Printed and hand colored in France expressly for the Humoristic Publishing Company . Printed on one side only. These are single sheets, sold separately. Reprints and translates the sheets from their original French.

IMAGERIE d'EPINAL ALBUM d'IMAGES (E)
Pellerin for Humoristic Publishing Co., Kansas City. Mo: nd (1888) (15-1/2x11-1/2",108 pgs plus full color hard-c, hand colored interior)

nn - Various French artists (Rare) 300.00 600.00 1800.00
NOTE: Printed and hand colored in France expressly for the Humoristic Publishing Company . Printed on one side only. This is supposedly a collection of sixty broadsheets, originally sold separately. All copies known only have fifty of the sixty known of these broadsheets (slightly bigger, before binding, trimming the margins in the process, down to 15-1/4x11-3/8".). Three slightly different covers known to exist, with or without the indication in French "Textes en Anglais" ("Texts in Englishl), with or without the general title "Contes de FEes" ("Fairy Tales"). All known copies were collected with sheets 15-20, 23,24, 47, and 48 missing.

IN LAUGHLAND (M)
R.H. Russell, New York: 1899 (14-9/16x12", 72 pgs, hard-c)

nn - By Henry "Hy" Mayer (scarce) 150.00 300.00 600.00
NOTE: Mostly strips plus single panel cartoon-r from various magazines. The majority are reprinted from Life, with the rest from: Truth, Dramatic Mirror, Black and White, Figaro Illustre, Le Rire, and Fliegende Blatter.

IN THE "400" AND OUT (M,S) (see also **THE TAILOR-MADE GIRL**)
Keppler & Schwarzmann, New York: 1888 (8-1/4x12", 64 pgs, hardc, B&W)

nn - By C.J. Taylor 42.50 85.00 170.00
*NOTE: Cartoons reprinted from **Puck**. The "400" is a reference to New York City's aristocratic elite.*

IN VANITY FAIR (M,S)
R.H.Russell & Son, New York: 1896 (11-7/8x17-7/8", 80 pgs, hard-c, B&W)

nn - By A.B.Wenzell, r-LIFE and HARPER'S 45.00 90.00 180.00

JACK HUCKABACK, THE SCAPEGRACE RAVEN (see also HOOKEYBEAK THE RAVEN) (E)
Stroefer & Kirchner, New York: nd (c1877) (9-3/8x6-3/8", 56 pgs, printed one side only, hand colored hardcover, B&W interior)

nn - By Wilhelm Busch (Rare) 75.00 150.00 350.00
NOTE: The 1877 date is derived from a gift signature on one known copy. The publication date might in truth be earlier. There are also professionally hand colored copies known to exist which would be worth more.

JEFF PETTICOATS
American News Company, NY: July 1865 (23 inches folded out; 6-1/4x8 folded,, B&W)
nn - Very Rare Frank Bellew (6) panel sequential foldout (10¢) (no known sales)
*NOTE: printed also in **FUNNYEST OF AWL AND THE FUNNIEST SORT OF PHUN** #9 (July 1865) (6) panel strip hanging Jeff Davis; This sold hundreds of thousand of copies in its day*

JINGO (M,O)
Art Newspaper Co., Boston & New York: No.1 Sept 10, 1884 - No.11 Nov 19, 1884 (10 cents, 13-7/8" x 10-1/4",16 pgs, color front/back-c and center, remainder B&W, paper-c)

1-11(Rare) 50.00 100.00 200.00
*NOTE: Satirical Republican propaganda magazine, modeled after **Puck** and **Judge**, which was published during the last couple months of the 1884 Presidential Election campaign. The Republicans lost, **Jingo** ceased publication, and Republican backers soon after purchased **Judge** magazine.*

JOHN-DONKEY, THE (O, S)
George Dexter, Burgess, Stringer & Co., NYC: 1848 (10x7.5",16 pgs,B&W, 6¢

1 Jan 1 1848 75.00 150.00 300.00
2-end (last issue Aug 12 1848) 50.00 100.00 200.00

JOLLY JOKER
Frank Leslie, NY: 1862-1878 (B&W, 10¢)

20/6 (July 1877) (Bellew Opper cover & single panels 150.00 300.00 600.00

JOLLY JOKER, OR LAUGH ALL-ROUND
Dick & Fitzgerald, NY: 1870s? (8-1/4x4-7/8", 148, B&W, illustrated green cover)

nn - cartoons on every page 100.00 200.00 400.00

JONATHAN'S WHITTLINGS OF THE WAR (O, S)
T.W. Strong, 98 Nassau St, NYC: April 1854-July 8 1854 (11.5x8.5", 16 pgs, B&W)

1 April 1854 100.00 200.00 400.00
NOTE: Begins Frank Bellew's sequential comic strip "Mr. Hookemcumsnivey, A Russian Gentleman, Hears That His Country Is In A State of War"
2-12 (July 8 1854) Many Bellew & Hopkins 100.00 200.00 400.00

JOURNAL CARRIER'S GREETING
???, Minn, Minn: 1897-98? (giveaway promo, 10-1/8x8-1/4, 36, B&W, paper-c)
nn - rare 50.00 100.00 200.00

JOURNEY TO THE GOLD DIGGINS BY JEREMIAH SADDLEBAGS (O,G)
Various publishers: 1849 (25 cents, 5-5/8 x 8-3/4", 68 pgs, green & black paper cover, B&W interior)

nn -- New York edition, Stringer & Townsend, Publishers
(Very Rare) By J.A. and D.F. Read. 4500.00 7500.00 12000.00
nn -- Cincinnati, Ohio edition, published by U.P. James
(Very Rare) By J.A. and D.F. Read. 4500.00 7500.00 12000.00
nn -- 1950 reprint, with introduction, published by William P. Wreden, Burlingame, California: 1950 (5-7/8 x 9", 92 pgs, hardcover, color interior)
(390 copies printed) By J.A. and D.F. Read. 67.50 125.00 250.00
*NOTE: Earliest known original sequential comic book by an American creator; directly inspired by Töpffer's **Obadiah Oldbuck** and **Bachelor Butterfly** The New York and Cincinnati editions were both published in 1849, one soon after the other. Antiquarian Book sources have traditionally cited that the Cincinnati edition preceded the New York, but without referencing their evidence. Conflicting with this, the Cincinnati edition lists the New York publishers' 1849 copyright, while the New York edition makes no reference to the Cincinnati publishers. Such would indicate that the New York edition was first. Both are very rare, and until resolved both will be regarded as published simultaneously. A New York copy with missing back cover, detached front cover, and G/VG interior sold for $2000 in 2000. Two copies sold at auction in 2006 for $11,500 and 12,000. (Prices vary widely.)*

JUDGE (M,O)
Judge Publishing, New York: No.1 Oct 29, 1881 - No. 950, Dec ??, 1899 (10 cents, color front/back c and centerspread, remainder B&W, paper-c)

1 (Scarce) (no known sales)
2-26 (Volume 1; Scarce) 20.00 40.00 80.00
27-790,792-950 12.50 25.00 50.00
791 (12/12/1896; Vol.31) - classic satirical-c depicting Tammany Hall politicians as the Yellow Kid & Cox's Brownies 50.00 150.00 350.00
Bound Volumes (six month, 26 issue run each):
Vol. 1 (Scarce) (no known sales)
Vol. 2-30,32-37 140.00 280.00 600.00
Vol. 31 - includes issue 791 **YK/Brownies** parody 165.00 230.00 725.00
NOTE: Rival publication to Puck. Purchased by Republican Party backers, following their loss in the 1884 Presidential Election, to become a Republican propaganda satire magazine.

JUDGE, GOOD THINGS FROM
Judge Publishing Co., NY: 1887 (13-3/4x10.5", 68 pgs, color paper-c)

1 first printing 50.00 100.00 200.00
NOTE: Zimmerman, Hamilton, Victor, Woolf, Beard, Ehrhart, De Meza, Howarth, Smith, Alfred Mitchell

JUDGE'S LIBRARY (M)
Judge Publishing, New York: No.1, April 1890 - No. 141, Dec 1899 (10 cents, 11x8-1/8", 36 pgs, color paper-c, B&W)

1 10.00 20.00 40.00
2-141 10.00 20.00 40.00
151-??? (post-1900 issues; see Platinum Age section)
*NOTE: **Judge's Library** was a monthly magazine reprinting cartoons & prose from **Judge**, with each issue's material organized around the same subject. The cover art was often original. All issues were kept in print for the duration of the series, so later issues are more scarce than earlier ones.*

JUDGE'S QUARTERLY (M)
Judge Publishing Company/Arkell Publishing Company, New York: No.1 April 1892 - 31 Oct 1899 (25¢, 13-3/4x10-1/4", 64 pgs, color paper-c, B&W)

1-11 13-31 contents presently unknown to us 15.00 30.00 60.00
12 ZIM Sketches From Judge Jan 1895 100.00 200.00 400.00
*NOTE: Similar to **Judge's Library**, except larger in size, and issued quarterly. All reprint material, except for the cover art.*

JUDGE'S SERIALS (M,S)
Judge Publishing, New York: March 1888 (10x7.5", 36 pgs)

#3 - Eugene Zimmerman 100.00 200.00 400.00
NOTE: A bit of sequential comic strips; mostly single panel cartoons. This series runs to at least #8.

JUDY
Burgess, Stringer & Co., 17 Ann St, NYC: Nov 28 1846-Feb 20 47 (11x8.5",12 pgs,B&W)

1 Nov 28 1846 67.50 125.00 250.00
2-13 50.00 100.00 200.00

JUVENILE GEM, THE (see also THE ADVENTURES OF MR. TOM PLUMP, and OLD MOTHER MITTEN) (O,I)
Huestis & Cozans: nd (1850-1852) (6x3-7/8", 64 pgs, hand colored paper-c, B&W) (all versions Very Rare)

nn - First printing(s) publisher's address is 104 Nassau Street (1850-1851) (1 copy sold for $800.00 in Fair)
nn - 2nd printing(s) publisher's address is 116 Nassau Street (1851-1852) (no known sales)
nn - 3rd printing(s) publisher's address is 107 Nassau Street (1852+) (no known sales)
*NOTE: The JUVENILE GEM is a gathering of multiple booklets under a single, hand colored cover (none of the interior booklets have the covers which they were given when sold separately). The publisher appears to have gathered whichever printings of each booklet were available when copies of THE JUVENILE GEM was assembled, so that the booklets within, and the conglomerate cover, may be from a mixture of printings. Contains two sequential comic booklets: THE ADVENTURES OF MR. TOM PLUMP, and OLD MOTHER MITTEN AND HER FUNNY KITTEN, plus five heavily illustrated children's booklets - **The Pretty Primer**, **The Funny Book**, **The Picture Book**, **The Two Sisters**, and **Story Of The Little Drummer**. Six of these -- including the two comic books -- were reprinted in the 1960's by Americana Review as a set of individual booklets, and included in a folder collectively titled "Six Children's Books of the 1850's".*

LANTERN, THE
Stringer & Townsend:1852-1853 (11x8-3/8", 12 pgs, soft paper, 6 ¢)

Leslie's Young America #1
1881 © Leslie & Company, NYC

Life Jan 3
1884 © J.A. Mitchell

Max and Maurice by Wilhelm Busch
1871 © Roberts Bros, Boston

	FR1.0	GD2.0	FN6.0
1 Jan 10, 1852	37.50	75.00	150.00
2	25.00	50.00	100.00
3 First Frank Bellew cartoons onwards each issue	37.50	75.00	150.00
4 Bellew 's Mr Blobb begins 1/31/52	50.00	100.00	200.00

NOTE: *Bellew serial sequential comic strip "Mr Blobb In Search Of A Physician" becomes 2nd earliest known recurring character in American comic strips plus full page single panel Bellew cartoon "The Modern Frankenstein" take-off on Shelly's story.*

	FR1.0	GD2.0	FN6.0
5 Hunsdale 2-panel "The Horrors of Slavery"; Mr Blobb	50.00	100.00	200.00
6 DF Read 15 panel "A Volley of Valentines"; Mr Blobb	50.00	100.00	200.00
7-8 10 Bellew's Mr Blobb continues	25.00	50.00	100.00
9 (4) panel "The Perils of Leap Year" MrBlobb	50.00	100.00	200.00
11 no Mr Blobb	20.00	40.00	80.00
12 Bellew's Mr Blobb continues 3/27/52	50.00	100.00	200.00
13 Bellew (10) panel sequential "Stump Speaking Studied"	50.00	100.00	200.00
14 no comic strips	20.00	40.00	80.00
15 Bellew's Mr Blobb ends (5) panel 4/17/52	50.00	100.00	200.00
16 Bellew begins new comic strip serial, "Mr. Bulbear, A Stockbroker, After having Supped at Delmonicos, Has A Dream", Part One, (6) panels	50.00	100.00	200.00
17 Bellew's Mr Bulbear continues	25.00	50.00	100.00
18 Bellew (8) panel "Trials of a Witness"	50.00	100.00	200.00
19 Bellew's Mr Bulbear's Dream continues	25.00	50.00	100.00
20-23 no comic strips	20.00	40.00	80.00
24 Bellew "Trials of a Publisher" (6) panel	50.00	100.00	200.00
25 comic strip "Travels of Jonathan Verdant" recurring character	25.00	50.00	100.00
26-49 contents to be indexed soon			
50 (12/18/52) (2) panel Impertinent Smile	25.00	50.00	100.00
58 (2/12/53) (6) panel Trip to California	25.00	50.00	100.00
66 (4/9/53) (3) panel sequential strip	25.00	50.00	100.00

LAST SENSATION, THE (Becomes Day's Doings)
James Watts, NYC: Dec 27 1867-May 30 1868 (11x16 folio-size, 16 pgs, B&W)

	FR1.0	GD2.0	FN6.0
issues with comic strips	50.00	100.00	200.00

LAUGH AND GROW FAT COMIC ALMANAC
Fisher & Brother, Philadelphia, New York & Boston: 1860-? (36 pgs)

	FR1.0	GD2.0	FN6.0
nn	60.00	120.00	240.00

LEGEND OF SAM'L OF POSEN (O)
M.B. Curtis Company: 1884-85 (8x3-3/8", 44 pgs, Color-c, B&W interior)

	FR1.0	GD2.0	FN6.0
nn - By M.B. Curtis	50.00	100.00	200.00

NOTE: Cover blurb says: From Early Days in Fatherland to affluence And Success in the Land of His Adoption, America

LESLIE'S YOUNG AMERICA (O. S)
Leslie & Co, 98 Chamber St, NY: 1881-82 (11-1/2x8", 5¢, B&W)

	FR1.0	GD2.0	FN6.0
1 (7/9/81) back cover (6) panel strip	125.00	250.00	500.00
2 (7/16/81) back cover (9) panel strip	50.00	100.00	200.00
3 (7/23/81) back cover (16) panel Busch strip	67.50	125.00	250.00
9 (9/3/81) sequentials; Hopkins singles	50.00	100.00	200.00
15 (10/15/81) Zim or Frost? (6) panel strip	50.00	100.00	200.00
19 (11/12/81) (9) panel back-c strip	50.00	100.00	200.00
24 (4) panel strip 25 (2) panel back-c strip	50.00	100.00	200.00
26 27 (6) panel back-c strip	50.00	100.00	200.00
29 31 (12) panel strip	50.00	100.00	200.00
32 (2/11/82) (8) panel strip	50.00	100.00	200.00
issues without comic strips or Jules Verne	25.00	50.00	100.00

NOTE: Jules Verne stories begin with #1 and run thru at least #42

LIFE (M,O) (continues with Vol.35 No. 894+ in the Platinum Age section)
J.A.Mitchell: Vol.1 No.1 Jan. 4, 1883 - Vol.1 No.26 June 29, 1883 (10-1/4x8", 16 pgs, B&W, paper cover); J.A. Mitchell: Vol. 2 No. 27, July 5, 1883 - Vol. 6 No.148, Oct 29, 1885 (10-1/4x8-1/4", 16 pgs., B&W, paper cover); Mitchell & Miller: Vol.6 No.149, Nov. 5, 1885 - Vol. 31, No. 796, March 17, 1898 (10-3/8x8-3/8", 16 pgs., B&W, paper cover); Life Publishing Company: Vol. 31 No. 797, March 24, 1898 - Vol. 34 No. 893, Dec 28, 1899 (10-3/8 x 8-1/2", 20 pgs., B&W, paper cover)

	FR1.0	GD2.0	FN6.0
1-26 (Scarce)		(no known sales)	
27-799	5.00	10.00	20.00
800 (4/7/1898) parody Yellow Kid / Spanish-American War cover (not by Outcault)	67.50	125.00	250.00
801-893	5.00	10.00	20.00

NOTE: *All covers for issues 1 - 26 are identical, apart from issue number & date.*

Hard bound collected volumes:

	FR1.0	GD2.0	FN6.0
V. 1 (No.1-26) (Scarce)	67.50	125.00	250.00
V. 2-34	45.00	90.00	180.00
V. 31 YK #800 parody-c not by RFO	70.00	140.00	280.00

NOTE: *Because the covers of all issues in Volume 1 are identical, it was common practice to remove the covers before binding the issues together. This is not true of later volumes, though, in all volumes it was common to drop the advertising pages which appeared at the rear of each issue. Information on many more individual issues will expand next Guide.*

LIFE AND ADVENTURES OF JEFF DAVIS (I)
J.C. Haney & Co., NY: 1865 (10 cents, 7-1/2" x 4", 36 pgs, B&W, paper-c)

	FR1.0	GD2.0	FN6.0
nn - By McArone (Scarce)	150.00	300.00	650.00
nn - 1974 Reprint (350) copies 6-3/4x4-3/8	50.00	10.00	20.00
nn - 1997 Reprint (7th Fla. Sutler, Clearwater, 6-3/4x4-1/4")	–	–	2.00

NOTE: *Humorous telling of the capture of Confederate President Jeff Davis in women's clothing, from the publisher of Merryman's Monthly. It contains an ad page for that publication; the material is perhaps reprinted from it. J.C. Haney licensed it to local printers, and so various publishers are found -- all printings currently regarded as simultaneous. (The Geo. H. Hees printing, Oswego, NY, contains an ad for the upcoming October 1865 issue of Merryman's Monthly, thus placing that printing in September 1865). Modern facsimile editions have been produced.*

LIFE IN PHILADELPHIA
W. Simpson, 66 Chestnut, Philadelphia; Siltart, No. 65 South Third St, Philadelphia: 1830 (7-3/4x6-7/8", 15 loose plates, hand colored copies exist, maybe B&W also)

nn - By Edward Williams Clay (1799-1857) (Very Rare) (no known sales)

NOTE: *First 13 plates etched, with many word balloons; scenes of exaggerated Black Americana in Philadelphia viewed one by one as broadsides. Had several publishers over the years. Was also eventually collected into a book of same name but only with the first 13 plates used; the last two not used in book. Collected book not yet viewed to share info.*

LIFE'S BOOK OF ANIMALS (M.S)
Doubleday & McClure Co.: 1898 (7-1/4x10-1/8", 88 pgs, color hardcover, B&W)

	FR1.0	GD2.0	FN6.0
nn	25.00	50.00	100.00

NOTE: *Reprints funny animal single panel and strip cartoons reprinted from LIFE. Art by Blaisdell, Chip Bellew, Kemble, Hy Mayer, Sullivant, Woolf.*

LIFE'S COMEDY (M,S)
Charles Scribner's Sons: Series 1 1897 - Series 3 1898 (12x9-3/8", hardcover, B&W)

	FR1.0	GD2.0	FN6.0
1 (142 pgs). 2, 3 (138 pgs)	60.00	120.00	240.00

NOTE: *Gibson a-1-3; c-3. Hy Mayer a-1-3. Rose O'Neill a-2-3. Stanlaws a-2-3. Sullivant a-1-2. Verbeek a-2. Wenzell a-1-3; c(painted)-2.*

LIFE, THE GOOD THINGS OF (M,S)
White, Stokes, & Allen, NY: 1884 - No.3 1886 ; Frederick A. Stokes, NY: No.4 1887; Frederick Stokes & Brother, NY: No.5 1888 - No.6 1889; Frederick A. Stokes Company, NY: No. 7 1890 - No.10 1893 (8-3/8x10-1/2", 74 pgs, gilted hardcover, B&W)

	FR1.0	GD2.0	FN6.0
nn - 1884 (most common issue)	32.50	65.00	130.00
2 - 1885	32.50	65.00	130.00
3 - 1886 (76 pgs)	32.50	65.00	130.00
4 - 1887 (76 pgs)	32.50	65.00	130.00
5 - 1888	32.50	65.00	130.00
6 - 1889	32.50	65.00	130.00
7 - 1890	32.50	65.00	130.00
8 - 1891 (scarce)	50.00	100.00	200.00
9 - 1892	32.50	65.00	130.00
10 - 1893	32.50	65.00	130.00

NOTE: *Contains mostly single panel, and some sequential, comics reprinted from LIFE. Attwood a-1-4,10. Roswell Bacon a-5. Chip Bellew a-4-6. Frank Bellew a-4,6. Palmer Cox a-1. H. E. Dey a-5. C. D. Gibson a-4-10. F.M. Howarth a-5-6. Kemble a-1-3. Klapp a-5. Walt McDougall a-1-2. H. McVickar a-5; J. A. Mitchell a-5. Peter Newell a-2-3. Gray Parker a-4-5,7. J. Smith a-5. Albert E. Steiner a-5; T. S. Sullivant a-7-9. Wenzell a-8-10. Wilder a-3. Woolf a-3-6.*)

LIFE, THE SPICE OF (E,M,)
White and Allen: NY & London: 1888 (8-3/8x10-1/2",76 pgs, hard-c, B&W)

	FR1.0	GD2.0	FN6.0
nn	50.00	100.00	200.00

NOTE: *Resembles **THE GOOD THINGS OF LIFE** in layout and format, and appears to be an attempt to compete with their former partner Frederick A. Stokes. However, the material is not from **LIFE**, but rather is reprinted and translated German sequential and single panel comics.*

LIFE'S PICTURE GALLERY (becomes LIFE'S PRINTS) (M,S,P)
Life Publishing Company, New York: nd (1898-1899) (paper cover, B&W) (all are scarce)

	FR1.0	GD2.0	FN6.0
nn - (nd; 1898, 100 pgs, 5-1/4x8-1/2") Gibson-c of a woman with closed umbrella; 1st interior page announcing that after January 1, 1899 Gibson will draw exclusively for LIFE; the word "SPECIMEN" is printed in red, diagonally, across every print; a-Gibson, Rose O'Neill, Sullivant	37.50	75.00	150.00
nn - (nd; 1899, 128 pgs, 4-7/8x7-3/8") Gibson-c of a woman golfer; 1st interior page announcing that Gibson & Hanna, Jr. draw exclusively for LIFE; the word "SPECIMEN" is printed in red, horizontally, across every print. Includes prints from Gibson's **THE EDUCATION OF MR. PIPP**; a-Gibson, Sullivant	37.50	75.00	150.00

NOTE: *Catalog of prints reprinted from **LIFE** covers & centerspreads. The first catalog was given away free to anyone requesting it, but after many people got the catalog without ordering anything, subsequent catalogs were sold at 10 cents.*

LITTLE SICK BEAR, THE
Edwin W. Joy Co, San Francisco, CA: 1897 (6-1/4x5", 20 pgs, B&W, Scarce)

	FR1.0	GD2.0	FN6.0
nn - By James Swinnerton one long sequential comic strip	200.00	400.00	800.00

LIGHT AND SHADE
William Drey Doppel Soap: 1892 (3-3/4x5-3/8", 20 pgs, B&W, color cover)

	FR1.0	GD2.0	FN6.0
nn - By J.C.	50.00	100.00	200.00

NOTE: Contains (8) panel comic strip of black boy whose skin turns white using this soap.

LONDON OUT OF TOWN, OR THE ADVENTURES OF THE BROWNS AT THE SEA SIDE BY LUKE LIMNER, ESQ. (O)
David Bogue, 86 Fleet St, London: c1847 (5-1/2x4-1/4, 32 pgs, yellow paper hard-c, B&W

	FR1.0	GD2.0	FN6.0
nn - By John Leighton	150.00	300.00	600.00

NOTE: one long sequential comic strip multiple-panel per page story; each page crammed with panels inspired by the Töpffer comic books Bogue began several years earlier.

LORGNETTE, THE (S)

The Merry Thought, Or Laughter From Year To Year
early 1850s © Fisher & Brother, Phila, Baltimore

Merryman's Monthly v3#5 with Bellew strip
May 1865 © J. C. Haney & Co., New York

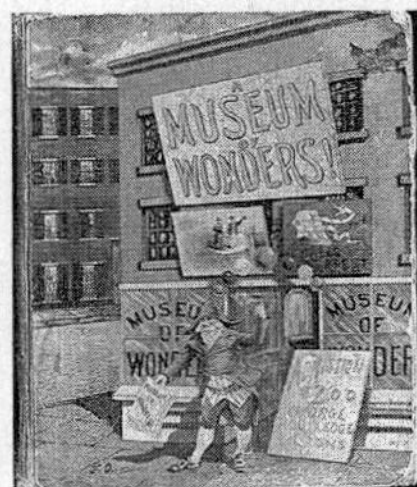
Museum of Wonders by F. Opper
1894 © Routledge & Sons

George J Coombes, New York: 1886 (6-1/2x8-3/4, 38 pgs, hard-c, B&W)
nn - By J.K. Bangs 50.00 100.00 200.00

LOVING BALLAD OF LORD BATEMAN, THE (E,I)
G.W. Carleton & Co., Publishers, Madison Square, NY: 1871 (9x5-7/8",16 pgs, soft-c, 6¢)
nn - By George Cruikshank 50.00 100.00 200.00

MADISON'S EXPOSITION OF THE AWFUL & TERRIFYING CEREMONIES OF THE ODD FELLOWS
T.E. Peterson & Brothers, 306 Chestnut St, Phila: 1870s? (5-3/4x9-1/4, 68 pgs, B&W)
nn - single panel cartoons 50.00 100.00 200.00

MANNERS AND CUSTOMS OF YE HARVARD STUDENTE (M,S)
Houghton Mifflin & Co., Boston & Moses King, Cambridge: 1877 (7-7/8x11", 72 pgs, printed one side, hardc, B&W)
nn - by F.G. Attwood 75.00 150.00 300.00
NOTE: *Collection of cartoons originally serialized in the* ***Harvard Lampoon****. Attwood later became a major cartoonist for* ***Life****.*

MAN WHO WOULD LIKE TO MARRY, THE (O)
Frederick Warne & Co., London & New York: nd (c 1880's) (9-1/2x11-1/2", 28 pgs, printed 1 side, paper-c, B&W)
nn - By Harry Parkes 62.50 125.00 250.00
NOTE: *Published simultaneously with its companion volume,* ***The Girl Who Wouldn't Mind Getting Married****.*

MAX AND MAURICE: A JUVENILE HISTORY IN SEVEN TRICKS (E)
(see also Teasing Tom and Naughty Ned)
Roberts Brothers, Boston: 1871 first edition (8-1/8 x 5-1/2", 76 pgs, hard & soft-c B&W)
nn - By Wilhelm Busch (green or brown cloth hardbound) 275.00 550.00 1000.00
nn - exactly the same, but soft paper cover 162.00 325.00 650.00
NOTE: *Page count includes 56 pgs of art, two blank endpapers at the front (one colored), 8 pgs of ads at the back, two blank endpapers at the end (one colored), and the covers. Green or brown illustrated hardcover. The name of the author is given on the title page as "William Busch." We assume this to be the 1st edition. Back side of title page states: Entered according to Act of Congress, in the year 1870, by Roberts Brothers, In the office of the Librarian of Congress at Washington.*
nn - By Wilhelm Busch (1872 edition) 225.00 470.00 900.00
nn - 1875 reprint 100.00 200.00 450.00
nn - 1882 reprint (76 pgs, hand colored- c/a, 75¢) 100.00 200.00 400.00
nn- 1889 reprint with new art on cover printed in full color 100.00 200.00 400.00
NOTE: *Each of the above contains 56 pages of art and text in a transitional format between a regular children's book and a comic book (the page count difference is ad pages in back). Seminal inspiration for William Randolph Hearst to acquire as a "new comic" (following the wild success of Outcault's Yellow Kid) to license M&M from Busch and hire Rudolph Dirks in late 1897 to create a New York American newspaper incarnation. In Hearst's English language newspapers it was called The Katzenjammer Kids and in his German language NYC newspaper it was titled Max & Moritz, Busch's original title. At least 50 other reprints versions are reputed to exist printed thru 1900. Translated from the 1865 German original. We are still sorting out the edition confusion.*

MAX AND MAURICE: A JUVENILE HISTORY IN SEVEN TRICKS (E)
(see also Teasing Tom and Naughty Ned)
Little, Brown, and Company, Boston: 1898-1902 (8-1/8 x 5-3/4", 72 pgs, hardcover, black ink on orange paper) (various early reprints)
nn - 1898 , 1899 By Wilhelm Busch 50.00 100.00 200.00
nn - 1902 (64 pages, B&W) 10.00 30.00 90.00

MERRY MAPLE LEAVES Or A Summer In The Country (S)
E.P. Dutton And Company, New York: 1872 (9-3/8x7-3/8", 90 and 86 pgs pgs, hard-c)
nn - By Abner Perk 25.00 50.00 150.00
NOTE: *Each drawing contained in a maple leaf motif by Livingston Hopkins and others.*

MERRYMAN'S MONTHLY A COMIC MAGAZINE FOR THE FAMILY (M,O,E)
J.C. Haney & Co, NY: 1863-1875 (10-7/8x7-13/16", 30 pgs average, B&W)
Certain issues with sequential comics 100.00 200.00 400.00
NOTE: *Sequential strips by Frank Bellew Sr, Wilhelm Busch found so far; others?*

MERRYTHOUGHT, OR LAUGHTER FROM YEAR TO YEAR, THE
Fisher & Brother, Phila, Baltimore: early 1850s (4-1/2x7", B&W)
nn - many singles, some sequential (Very Rare) (no known sales)
NOTE: See Vict article for back cover pic which is earliest known use of the term Comic Book

MESSRS. BROWN, JONES, AND ROBINSON, THE FOREIGN TOUR OF
(see also **THE CLOWN, OR THE BANQUET OF WIT**) (E,M,O,G)
Bradbury & Evans, London: 1854 (11-5/8x9-1/2", 196 pgs, gilted hard-c, B&W)
nn - By Richard Doyle 35.00 70.00 200.00
nn - Bradbury & Evans 1900 reprint 20.00 40.00 80.00
NOTE: *Protective sheets between each page (not part of page count). Expanded and redrawn sequential comics story from the serialized episodes originally published in PUNCH. Also comes in a 174 pg 8-3/4x11" version.*

MESSRS. BROWN, JONES, AND ROBINSON, THE LAUGHABLE ADVENTURES OF (E,M,G)
Garrett, Dick & Fitzgerald, NY: nd (1856 or 1857) (5-3/4x9-1/4", 100 pgs, printed one side only, paper-c, B&W)
nn - (Very Rare) by Richard Doyle c/a 300.00 500.00 1000.00
NOTE: *1st American reprinting of the "Foreign Tour"; reformatted into a small oblong format. Links the earlier Garrett & Co. to the later Dick & Fitzgerald. Back cover reprints full size the Garrett & Co. version cover for Oscar Shanghai. Interior front cover reprints full size the Garrett & Co. version cover for Slyfox-Wikof. Issued without a title page.*

FR1.0 GD2.0 FN6.0

MESSRS. BROWN, JONES, AND ROBINSON, THE FOREIGN TOUR OF (E,M,G)
D. Appleton & Co., New York: 1860 & 1877 (11-5/8x9-1/2", 196 pgs, gilted hard-c, B&W)
nn - (1860 printing) by Richard Doyle 30.00 60.00 200.00
nn - (1871 printing) by Richard Doyle 30.00 60.00 150.00
nn - (1877 printing) by Richard Doyle 30.00 60.00 150.00
NOTE: *Protective sheets between each page (not part of page count). Reprints the Bradbury & Evans edition.*

MESSRS BROWN JONES AND ROBINSON, THE AMERICAN TOUR OF (O,G)
D. Appleton & Co., New York: 1872 (11-5/8x9-1/2", 158 pgs, printed one side only, B&W, green gilted hard-c)
nn - By Toby 70.00 140.00 400.00
NOTE: *Original American graphic novel sequel to Richard Doyle's Foreign Tour of Brown, Jones, and Robinson, with the same characters visiting New York, Canada, and Cuba. Protective sheets between each page (not part of page count).*

MESSRS. BROWN, JONES, AND ROBINSON, THE LAUGHABLE ADVEN. OF (E,M,G)
Dick & Fitzgerald, NY: nd (late 1870's - 1888) (5-3/4x9-1/4", 100 pgs, printed one side only, green paper-c, B&W)
nn - (Scarce) by Richard Doyle 100.00 200.00 450.00
NOTE: *Reprints the Garrett, Dick & Fitzgerald printing, with the following changes: Takes what had been page 12 in the Garrett, D&F printing (art by M.H. Henry), and makes it a title page, which is numbered page 1. The first story page, "Go to the Races", is numbered 2 (whereas it is numbered 1 in the Garrett, Dick & Fitzgerald version). Numbering stays ahead of the G,D&F edition by 1 page up through page 12, after which the page numbering becomes identical.*

MINNEAPOLIS JOURNAL CARTOONS (N,S)
Minneapolis Journal: nn 1894 - No.2 1895 (7-3/4" x 10-7/8", 76 pgs, B&W, paper-c)
nn (1894) (Rare) 50.00 100.00 200.00
Second Series (1895) (Rare) 50.00 100.00 200.00
nn- "War Cartoons" Jan 1899 (9x8", 160 pgs, paperback, punched & string bound) (Scarce) 24.00 96.00 170.00
NOTE: *Reprints single panel cartoons from the prior year, by Charles "Bart" L. Bartholomew.*

MISCHIEF BOOK, THE (E)
R. Worthington, New York: 1880 (7-1/8 x 10-3/4", 176 pgs, hard-c, B&W)
nn - Green cloth binding; green on brown cover; cover art by R. Lewis based on Busch art by Wilhelm Busch 175.00 350.00 735.00
nn - Blue cloth binding; hand colored cover; completely different cover art based on Busch by Wilhelm Busch 175.00 350.00 735.00
NOTE: *Translated by Abby Langdon Alger. American published anthology collection of Wilhelm Busch comic strips. Includes two of the strips found in the British "Bushel of Merry-Thoughts" collection, translated better, and with the dropped panel restored. Unknown which cover version was first.*

MISSES BROWN, JONES AND ROBINSON, THE FOREIGN TOUR OF THE (E,O,G)
Bickers & Sons, London: nd (c1850's) (12-1/4" x 9-7/8", 108 pgs, printed on one side, B&W, hard-c)
nn- "by Miss Brown" (Rare) 100.00 200.00 400.00
NOTE: *A female take on Doyle's Foreign Tour, by an unknown woman artist, using the pseudonym "Miss Brown."*

MISS MILLY MILLEFLEUR'S CAREER (S)
Sheldon & Co., NY: 1869 (10-3/4x9-7/8", 74 pgs, purple hard-c)
nn - Artist unknown (Rare) 75.00 150.00 300.00

MR PODGER AT COUP'S GREATEST SHOW ON EARTH HIS HAPS AND MISHAPS, THE ADVENTURES OF (O,S)
W.C. Coup, New York: 1884 (5-5/8x4-1/4", 20 pgs, color-c, B&W)
nn - Circus Themes; Similar to Barker's Comic Almanacs 20.00 40.00 80.00

MR. TOODLES' GREAT ELEPHANT HUNT (See Peter Piper in Bengal)
Brother Jonathan, NYC: 1850s (4-1/4x7-7/8", page count presently unknown)
nn - catalog contains comic strip (Very Rare) (no known sales)

MR. TOODLES' TERRIFIC ELEPHANT HUNT
Dick & Fitzgerald, NYC: 1860s (5-3/4x9-1/4", 32 pgs, paper-c, B&W) (Very Rare)
nn - catalog reprint contains 28 panel comic strip 150.00 300.00 600.00

MRS GRUNDY
Mrs Grundy Publishing Co, NYC: July 8 1865-Sept 30 1865 (weekly)
1-13 Thomas Nast, Hoppin, Stephens, 50.00 100.00 200.00

MUSEUM OF WONDERS, A (O,I)
Routledge & Sons: 1894 (13x10", 64 pgs, color-c, color thru out)
nn - By Frederick Opper 100.00 200.00 450.00

MY FRIEND WRIGGLES, A (Laughter) Moving Panorama, of His Fortunes And Misfortunes, Illustrated With Over 200 Engravings, of Most Comic Catastrophes And Side-Splitting Merriment) (O,G)
Stearn & Co, 202 Williams St, NY: 1850s (5-7/8x9-3/4", 100 pgs, B&W)
nn - By S. P. Avery (also the engraver) (Very Rare) 200.00 400.00 800.00

MY SKETCHBOOK (E,S)
Dana Estes & Charles E. Lauriat, Boston; J. Sabins & Sons, New York: circa 1880s (9-3/8x12", brown hard-c)
nn - By George Cruikshank 25.00 50.00 150.00
NOTE: *Reprints British editions 1834-36; extensive usage of word balloons.*

Nasby's Life Of Andy Jonson
1866 © Jesse Haney Company

Nonsense Or, A Treasure Box of Unconsidered Trifles
early 1850s © Fisher & Brother, Phila.

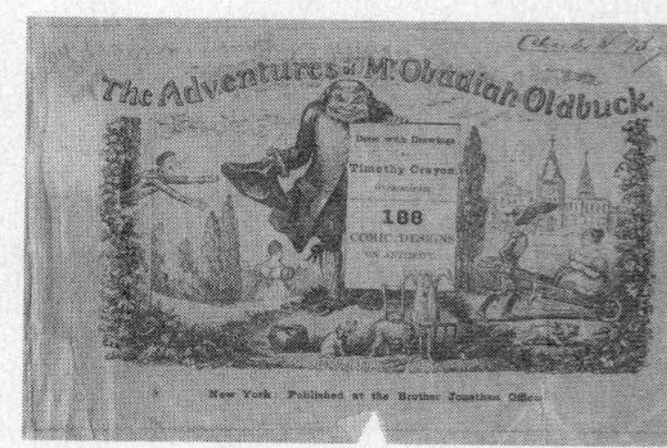

The Adventures of Obadiah Oldbuck 4th printing
mid-1850s © Brother Jonathan Offices, NY

FR1.0 GD2.0 FN6.0

NASBY'S LIFE OF ANDY JONSON (O, M)
Jesse Haney Co., Publishers No. 119 Nassau St, NY: 1866 (4-1/2x7-1/2, 48 pgs, B&W)
nn - President Andrew Johnson satire 100.00 200.00 450.00
NOTE: Blurb further reads: With a True Pictorial History of His STumping Tour Out West By Petroleum V. Nasby, A Dimmicrat of Thirty Years Standing, And Who Allus Tuk His Licker Straight. Front of book has long sequential comic strip satire on President Andrew Johnson, misspelling his name on the cover on purpose.

NAST'S ILLUSTRATED ALMANAC
Harper & Brothers, Franklin Square, NYC: 1872-1874 (8x5.5", 80 pgs, B&W, 35¢)
nn 60.00 120.00 240.00

NAST'S WEEKLY (O,S)
???: 1892-93 (Quarto Weekly)
all issues scarce 50.00 100.00 200.00

NATIONAL COMIC ALMANAC
An Association of Gentlemen, Boston: 1838-?? (8.25x4.75", 34 pgs, B&W)
nn 60.00 120.00 240.00

NEW AMERICAN COMIC ALL-IMAKE (ELTON'S BASKET OF COMICAL SCRAPS), THE
Elton, Publisher, New York: 1839 (7-1/2x4-5/8, 24 pgs)
1 100.00 200.00 400.00

NEW BOOK OF NONSENSE, THE: A Contribution To The Great Central Fair In Aid of the Sanitary Commission (O,S)
Ashmead & Evans, No. 724 Chestnut St, Philadelphia: June 1864 (red hard-c)
nn - Artists unknown (Scarce) 50.00 150.00 300.00

NEW YORK ILLUSTRATED NEWS
Frank Leslie, NYC: 10/14/76-June 1884
average issues with comic strips 10.00 20.00 40.00

NEW YORK PICAYUNE (see PHUN FOTOCRAFT)
Woodward & Hutchings: 1850-1855 newspaper-size weekly; 1856-1857 Folio Monthly 16x10.5; 1857-1858 Quarto Weekly; 1858-1860 Quarto Weekly
Average Issue With Comic Strips 50.00 100.00 200.00
Issues with Full Front Page Comic Strip 100.00 200.00 400.00
NOTE: *Many issues contain Frank Bellew sequential comic strips & single panel cartoons. Later issues published by Woodward, Levison & Robert Gun (1853-1857) ; Levison & Thompson (1857-1860)*

NICK-NAX
Levison & Haney, NY: 1857-1858? (11x7-3/4", 32 pgs, B&W, paper-c)
v2 #10 Feb 1858 has many single panel cartoons 50.00 100.00 200.00

99 "WOOLFS" FROM TRUTH (see Sketches of Lowly Life in a Great City, Truth)
Truth Company, NY: 1896 (9x5-1/2", 72 pgs, varnished paper-like cloth hard-c, 25 cents)
nn - By Michael Angelo Woolf (Rare) 150.00 300.00 600.00
NOTE: *Woolf's cartoons are regarded as a primary influence on R.F. Outcault in the later development of The Yellow Kid newspaper strip. Copy sold in 2002 on eBay for $800.00.*

NONSENSE OR, THE TREASURE BOX OF UNCONSIDERED TRIFLES
Fisher & Brother, 12 North Sixth St, Phila, PA, 64 Baltimore St, Baltimore, MD: early 1850s (4-1/2x7", 128 pgs, B&W)
nn - much Davy Crocket sequential story-telling comic strips 250.00 500.00 1000.00

OBADIAH OLDBUCK, THE ADVENTURES OF MR. (E,G)
Tilt & Bogue, London: nd (1840-41) (5-15/16x9-3/16", 176 pgs,B&W, gilted hard-c)
nn - By Rodolphe Töpffer 700.00 1200.00 2800.00
nn - Hand coloured edition (Very Rare) (no known sales)
NOTE: *This is the British edition, translating the unauthorized redrawn 1839 edition from Parisian publisher Aubert, adapted from Töpffer's "Les Amours de Mr. Vieux Bois" (aka "Histoire de Mr. Vieux Bois"), originally published in French in Switzerland, in 1837 (2nd ed. 1839). Early 19th century books are often found rebound, with original cover and/or title page gone. To distinguish editions having no cover or title page: the British oblong editions (published by Tilt & Bogue) use Roman Numerals to number pages. American oblong shaped editions use Arabic Numerals. British are printed on one side only. This is the earliest known English language sequential comic book. Has a new title page with art by Robert Cruikshank.*

OBADIAH OLDBUCK, THE ADVENTURES OF MR. (E,G)
Wilson and Company, New York: September 14, 1842 (11-3/4x9", 44 pgs, B&W, yellow paper-c on bookstand editions, hemp paper interior)
Brother Jonathan Extra No. IX - Rare bookstand edition 2500.00 5000.00 10000.00
Brother Jonathan Extra No. IX Very Rare subscriber/mailorder 2500.00 5000.00 10000.00
NOTE: *By Rodolphe Töpffer. Earliest known sequential American comic book, reprinting the 1841 British edition. Pages are numbered via Roman numerals. States "BROTHER JONATHAN EXTRA - ADVENTURES OF MR. OBADIAH OLDBUCK." at the top of each page. Prints 2 to 3 tiers of panels on both sides of each page. Copies could be had for ten cents according to adverts in* **Brother Jonathan**. *By Rodolphe Töpffer with cover masthead design by David Claypool Johnston, and cover art beneath the masthead reprinting Robert Cruikshank's title page art from the Tilt & Bogue edition. A special, additional cover was added for copies sold on stands (it was not issued with mail order or subscriber copies). Only 1 known copy possesses (partially) this very thin outer yellow cover. A decent (subscriber) copy sold on eBay in later October 2002 for over $3500.00. In 2005, a FR copy sold for $10,000; a G/VG for $20,000; and a VG for $20,000. A copy GVG sold in auction in 2007 for $9500. (Prices vary widely.)*

OBADIAH OLDBUCK, THE ADVENTURES OF MR. (E,G)
Wilson & Co, New York: nd (1849) (5-11/16x8-3/8", 84 pgs, B&W,paper-c)
nn - by Rodolphe Töpffer; title page by Robert Cruikshank (Very Rare) 500.00 1200.00 4000.00
NOTE: *2nd Wilson & Co printing, reformatted into a small oblong format, with nine panels edited out, and text modified to smooth out this removal. Results in four less printed tiers/strips. Pages are numbered via Arabic numerals. Every panel on Pages 11, 14, 19, 21, 24, 34, 35 has one line of text. Reformatted to conform with British first edition.*

OBADIAH OLDBUCK, THE ADVENTURES OF MR. (E,G)
Wilson & Co, 162 Nassau, NY: nd (early-1850s) (5-11/16x8-3/8", 84 pgs, B&W, yellow-c
nn - 3rd USA Printing by Rodolphe Töpffer; title page by Robert Cruikshank (Very Rare) Says By Timothy Crayon, an obvious pseudonym 800.00 1600.00 4500.00
NOTE: Front cover banner the giant is holding says "Done With Drawings By Timothy Crayon, Gypsographer, 188 Comic Etchings On Antimony" Title page changes address to No. 15 Spruce-Street. (Late 162 Nassau Street.)

OBADIAH OLDBUCK, THE ADVENTURES OF MR..
Brother Jonathan Offices: ND (mid-1850s) (5-11/16x8-3/8", 84 pages, B&W, oblong)
nn - 4th printing; Originally by Rodolphe Töpffer (Very Rare) 500.00 1200.00 4000.00
NOTE: *Cover States: "New York: Published at the Brother Jonathan Office". Front cover banner the giant is holding says "Done With Drawings By Timothy Crayon, Gypsographer, 188 Comic Designs On Antimony."*

OBADIAH OLDBUCK, THE ADVENTURES OF MR. (E,G)
Dick & Fitzgerald, New York: nd (various printings; est. 1870s to 1888) (Thirty Cents, 84 pgs, B&W, paper-c) (all versions scarce)
nn - Black print on green cover(5-11/16x8-15/16"); string bound 200.00 400.00 800.00
nn - Black print on blue cover; same format as green-c 200.00 400.00 800.00
nn - Black print on white cover(5-13/16x9-3/16"); staple bound beneath cover); this is a later printing than the blue or green-c 200.00 400.00 800.00
NOTE: *Reprints the abbreviated 1849 Wilson & Co. 2nd printing. Pages are numbered via Arabic numerals. Many of the panels on Pages 11, 14, 19, 21, 24, 34, 35 take two lines to print the same words found in the Wilson & Co version, which used only one text line for the same panels. Unknown whether the blue or green cover is earlier. White cover version has "thirty cents" line blackened out on the two copies known to exist. Robert Cruikshank's title page has been made the cover in the D&F editions.*

OLD FOGY'S COMIC ALMANAC
Philip J. Cozans, NY: 1858 (4-7/8x7-1/4, 48 pgs)
nn - sequential comic strip told one panel per page 50.00 100.00 200.00
NOTE: Contains (12) panel "Fourth of July in New York" sequential

OLD MOTHER MITTEN AND HER FUNNY KITTEN (see also **The Juvenile Gem**) (O)
Huestis & Cozans: nd(1850-1852) (6x3-7/8"12pgs, hand colored paper-c, B&W)
nn - first printing(s) publisher's address is 104 Nassau Street (1850-1851) (Very Rare) (no known sales)
NOTE: *A hand colored outer cover is highly rare, with only 1 recorded copy possessing it. Front cover image and text is repeated precisely on page 3 (albeit b&w), and only interior pages are numbered, together leading owners of coverless copies to believe they have the cover. The true back cover has ads for the publisher. Cover was issued only with copies which were sold separately - books which were bound together as part of THE JUVENILE GEM never had such covers.*

OLD MOTHER MITTEN AND HER FUNNY KITTEN (see JUVENILE GEM) (O)
Philip J. Cozans: nd (1850-1852) (6x3-7/8",12 pgs, hand colored paper-c, B&W)
nn - Second printing(s) publisher's address is 116 Nassau Street (1851-1852) (Very Rare) (no known sales)
nn - Third printing(s) publisher's address is 107 Nassau Street (1852+) (Very Rare) (no known sales)

OLD MOTHER MITTEN AND HER FUNNY KITTEN
Americana Review, Scotia, NY: nd (1960's) (6-1/4x4-1/8", 8 pgs, side-stapled, cardboard, B&W)
nn - Modern reprint 2.50 5.00 10.00
NOTE: *Issued within a folder titled SIX CHILDREN'S BOOKS OF THE 1850'S. States "Reprinted by American Review" at bottom of front cover. Reprints the 104 Nassau Street address.*

ON THE NILE (O,G)
James R. Osgood & Co., Boston: 1874 ; **Houghton, Osgood & Co., Boston:** 1880 (112 pgs, gilted green hardcover, B&W)
1st printing (1874; 10-3/4x16") - by Augustus Hoppin 45.00 90.00 180.00
2nd printing (1880; smaller sized) 32.50 65.00 130.00

OSCAR SHANGHAI, THE EXTRAORDINARY AND MIRTH-PROVKING ADVENTURES BY SEA & LAND OF (O, G)
Garrett & Co., Publishers, No. 18 Ann Street, New York: May 1855 (5-3/4x9-1/4", 100 pgs, printed one side only, paper-c, 25¢, B&W)
nn - Samuel Avery-c; interior by ALC Very Rare) 1000.00 2000.00 4000.00
NOTE: *Not much is known of this first edition as the data comes from a recently rediscovered* **Brother Jonathan** *catalog issued circa 1853-55. No original known yet to exist.*

OSCAR SHANGHAI, THE WONDERFUL AND AMUSING DOINGS BY SEA AND LAND OF (G)
Dick & Fitzgerald, 10 Ann St, NY: nd (1870s-1888) (25 ¢, 5-3/4x9-1/4", 100 pgs, printed one side only, green paper c, B&W)
nn - Cover by Samuel Avery; interior by ALC (Rare) 300.00 500.00 1000.00
NOTE: Exact reprint of Garrett & Co original.

OUR ARTIST IN CUBA (O)
Carleton, New York: 1865 (6-5/8x4-3/8", 120 pgs, printed one side only, gilted hard-c, B&W)
nn - By Geo. W. Carleton 37.50 75.00 150.00

OUR ARTIST IN CUBA, PERU, SPAIN, AND ALGIERS (O)
Carleton: 1877 (6-1/2x5-1/8", 156 pgs, hard-c, B&W)
nn - By Geo. W. Carleton 50.00 100.00 200.00
nn - By Geo. W. Carleton (wraps paper cover) (Rare) 45.00 90.00 180.00

The Wonderful and Amusing Doings by Sea & Land of Oscar Shanghai
1870s © Dick & Fitzgerald, New York

Phun Fotocraft, Kewreus Konsweets Komically Illustrated By A Kweer Feller
1850s © The New York Picayune

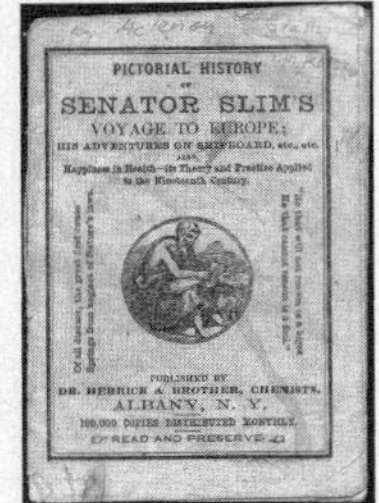
Pictorial History of Senator Slim's Voyage To Europe
1860 © Dr. Herrick & Brother, Albany, NY

NOTE: *Reprints OUR ARTIST IN CUBA and OUR ARTIST IN PERU, then adds new section on Spain and Algiers.*

OUR ARTIST IN PERU (O)
Carleton, New York: 1866 (7-3/4x5-7/8", 68 pgs, gilted hardcover, B&W)
nn- By Geo. W. Carleton 37.50 75.00 150.00
NOTE: *Contains advertisement for the upcoming books* ***OUR ARTIST IN ITALY*** *and* ***OUR ARTIST IN FRANCE****, but no such publications have been found to date.*

PARSON SOURBALL'S EUROPEAN TOUR (O)
Duff and Ashmead: 1867 (6x7-1/2", 76 pgs, blue embossed title hard-c)
nn - By Horace Cope 100.00 200.00 400.00
NOTE: see **REV. MR. SOURBALL'S EUROPEAN TOUR, THE** for the soft paper cover version

PEN AND INK SKETCHES OF YALE NOTABLES (O,S)
Soule, Thomas and Winsor, St. Louis: 1872 (12-1/4x9-3/4", B&W)
By Squills 25.00 50.00 100.00
NOTE: *Printed by Steamlith Press, The R.P. Studley Company, St Louis.*

PETER PIPER IN BENGAL
Bengamin H Day.Publisher, Brother Jonathan Cheap Book Establishment, 48 Beekman, NY: 1953-55 (6-5/8x4-1/4, 36 pgs, yellow paper-c, B&W, 3 cents - two dollars per hundred) (Very Rare)
nn - By John Tenniel - 32 panel comic strip Punch-r 500.00 1000.00 2000.00
NOTE: *Actually also a catalog of inexpensive books, prints, maps and half a dozen comic books for sale on separate pages from publishers Day and Garrett - see full story of this brand new find in the Victorian Era essay. A complete copy with split spine sold in November 2002 for $750.00. Published date most likely 1855.*

THE PHILADELPHIA COMIC ALMANAC (S)
G. Strong, 44 Strawberry St, NYC: 1835 (8-1/2x5", 36 pgs)
nn - 100.00 200.00 600.00
NOTE: *77 engravings full of recurring cartoon characters but not sequential; early use of recurring characters.*

PHIL MAY'S SKETCH BOOK (E,S,M)
R.H. Russell, New York: 1899 (14-5/8x10", 64 pgs, brown hard-c, B&W)
nn - By Phil May 32.50 65.00 130.00
NOTE: *American reprint of the British edition.*

PHUNNY PHELLOW, THE
Oakie, Dayton & Jones: Oct 1859-1876; **Street & Smith** 1876: (Folio Monthly)
average issue with Thomas Nast 50.00 100.00 200.00

PHUN FOTOCRAFT, KEWREUS KONSEETS KOMICALLY ILLUSTRATED BY A KWEER FELLER (N) (see **NEW YORK PICAYUNE)**
The New York Picayune, NY: 1850s (104 pgs)
nn - Mostly Frank Bellew, some John Leach 250.00 500.00 1000.00
NOTE: Many sequential comic strips as well as single cartoons all collected from The New York Picayune. Ross & Tousey, Agents, 121 Nassau St, NY. The Picayune ran many sequential comic strips in its decade.

PICTORIAL HISTORY OF SENATOR SLIM'S VOYAGE TO EUROPE
Dr. Herrick & Brother, Chemists, Albany, NY: 1860 (3-1/4x4-3/4", 32 pgs, B&W)
nn - By John McLenan Very Rare 150.00 300.00 600.00

PICTURES OF ENGLISH SOCIETY (Parchment-Paper Series, No.4) (M,S,E)
D. Appleton & Co., New York: 1884 (5-5/8x4-3/8", 108 pgs, paper-c, B&W)
4 - By George du Maurier; Punch-r 15.00 30.00 60.00
NOTE: *Every other page is a full page cartoon, with the opposite page containing the cartoon's caption.*

PICTURES OF LIFE AND CHARACTER (M,S,E)
Bradbury and Evans, London: No.1 1855 - No.5 c1864 (12-1/2x18", 100 pgs, illustrated hard-c, B&W)
nn (No.1) (1855) 32.50 65.00 130.00
2 (1858), 3 (1860) 32.50 65.00 130.00
4 (nd; c1862) 5 (nd; c1864) 32.50 65.00 130.00
nn (nd (late 1860's) 32.50 65.00 130.00
NOTE: 2-1/2x18-1/4", 494 pgs, green gilted-c) reprints 1-5 in one book
1-3 John Leech's... (nd; 12-3/8x10", ? pgs, red gilted-c). 25.00 50.00 100.00
NOTE: *Reprints John Leech cartoons from* ***Punch****. note that the Volume Number is mentioned only on the last page of these versions.*

PICTURES OF LIFE AND CHARACTER (E,M,S)
G.P. Putnam's Sons: 1880's (8-5/8x6-1/4", 218 pgs, hardcover, color-cr, B&W)
nn - John Leech (single panel **Punch** cartoon-r) 20.00 40.00 160.00
NOTE: *Leech reprints which extend back to the 1850s.*

PICTURES OF LIFE AND CHARACTER (Parchment-Paper Series) (E,M,S)
(see also Humerous Masterpieces)
D. Appleton & Co., NY: 1884 (30¢, 5-3/4 x 4-1/2", 104 pgs, paper-c, B&W)
nn - John Leech (single panel **Punch** cartoon-r) 20.00 40.00 160.00
NOTE: *An advertisment in the back refers to a cloth-bound edition for 50 cents.*

PIPPIN AMONG THE WIDE-AWAKES (O,S)
Werill & Chapin, 113 Nassau St, NYC, NY): 1860 (6x4-1/2", 36 pgs, 6 cents)
nn - Artist unknown (Very Rare) 100.00 200.00 400.00

PLISH AND PLUM (E.G)
Roberts Brothers, Boston: 1883 (8-1/8x5-3/4", 80 pgs, hardcover, B&W)
nn - By Wilhelm Busch 40.00 80.00 200.00
nn - Reprint (Roberts Brothers, 1895) 40.00 80.00 200.00
nn - Reprint (Little, Brown & Co., 1899) 40.00 80.00 200.00
NOTE: *The adventures of two dogs.*

POUNDS OF FUN
Frank Tousey, 34 North Moore St, NY: 1881 (6-1/2x9-1/2", 68pgs, B&W)
nn - Bellew, Worth, Woolf, Chips 40.00 80.00 200.00

PRESIDENTS MESSAGE, THE
G.P. Putnam's Sons, NY: 1887 (5-3/4x7-5/8, 44 pgs)
nn - (19) Thomas Nast single panel full page cartoons 40.00 80.00 200.00

PROTECT THE U.S. FROM JOHN BULL - PROTECTION PICTURES FROM JUDGE
Judge Publishing, New York: 1888 ((10 cents, 6-7/8x10-3/8", 36 pgs, paper-c, B&W)
nn - (Scarce) 25.00 50.00 100.00
NOTE: *Reprints both cartoons and commentary from* ***Puck****, concerning the issue of tariffs which were then being debated in Congress. Art by Gillam, Hamilton, Victor.*

PUCK (German language edition, St. Louis) (M,O) (see also Die Vehme)
Publisher unknown, St. Louis: No.1, March 18, 1871 - No. ??, Aug. 24, 1872 (B&W, paper-c)
1-?? (Very Rare) by Joseph Keppler (no known sales)
NOTE: *Joseph Keppler's second attempt at a weekly humor periodical, following* ***Die Vehme*** *one year earlier. This was his first attempt to launch using the title* ***Puck****. This German language version ran for a full year before being joined by an English language version.*

PUCK (English language edition, St. Louis) (M,O)
Publisher unknown, St. Louis: No.1, March ?? 1872 - No. ??, Aug. 24, 1872 (B&W, paper c)
1-?? (Very Rare) by Joseph Keppler (no known sales)
NOTE: *Same material as in the German language edition, but in English.*

PUCK, ILLUSTRIRTES HUMORISTISCHES WOCHENBLATT (German language edition, NYC) (M,O)
Keppler & Schwarzmann, New York: No.1 Sept (27) 1876 - 1164 Dec ?? 1899 (10 cents, color front/back-c and centerspread, remainder B&W, paper-c)
1-26 (Volume 1; Rare) by Joseph Keppler - these issues precede the English language version, and contain cartoons not found in them. Includes cartoons on the controversial Tilden-Hayes 1876 Presidential Election debacle. (no known sales)
27-52 (Volume 2; Rare) by Joseph Keppler - contains some cartoon material not found in the English language editions. Particularly in the earlier issues. (no known sales)
53-1164 7.50 15.00 30.00
Bound Volumes (six month, 26 issue run each):
Vol. 1 (Rare) (no known sales)
Vol. 2-4 (Rare) (no known sales)
Vol. 5-47 62.50 125.00 250.00
NOTE: *Joseph Keppler's second, and successful, attempt to launch* ***Puck****. In German. The first six months precede the launch of the English language edition. Soon after (but not immediately after) the launch of the English edition, both editions began sharing the same cartoons, but, their prose material always remained different. The German language edition ceased publication at the end of 1899, while the English language edition continued into the early 20th Century. First American periodical to feature printed color every issue.*

PUCK (English language edition, NYC) (M,O)
Keppler & Schwarzmann, New York: No.1 March (14) 1877 - 1190 Dec ?? 1899 (10 cents, color front/back-c and centerspread, remainder B&W, paper-c)
1 (Rare) by Joseph Keppler (no known sales)
2-26 (Rare) by Joseph Keppler (no known sales)
27-1190 12.50 25.00 50.00
(see Platinum Age section for year 1900+ issues)
Bound volumes (six month, 26 issue run each):
Vol. 1 (Rare) (one set sold on eBay for $2300.00)
Vol. 2 (Scarce) (one set sold on eBay for $1500.00)
Vol. 3-6 (pre-1880 issues) 175.00 375.00 750.00
Vol. 7-46 140.00 300.00 600.00
NOTE: *The English language editions began six months after the German editions, and so the English edition numbering is always one volume number, and 26 issue numbers, behind its parallel German language edition. Pre-1880 & post-1900 issues are more scarce than 1880's & 1890's.*

PUCK (miniature) (M,P,I)
Keppler & Schwarzmann, New York: nd (c1895) (7x5-1/8", 12 pgs, color front & back paper-c, B&W interior)
nn - Scarce 25.00 50.00 110.00
NOTE: *C.J.Taylor-c; F.M.Howarth-a; F.Opper-a; giveaway item promoting* ***Puck's*** *various publications. Mostly text, with art reprinted from* ***Puck****.*

PUCK, CARTOONS FROM (M,S)
Keppler & Schwarzmann, New York: 1893 (14-1/4x11-1/2", 244 pgs, hard-c, mostly B&W)
nn - by Joseph Keppler (Signed and Numbered) 100.00 200.00 400.00
NOTE: *Reprints Keppler cartoons from 1877 to 1893, mostly in B&W, though a few in color, with a text opposite each cartoon explaining the situation then being satirized. Issued only in an edition of 300 numbered issues, signed by Keppler. Only 1/4 of the pages are cartoons.*

PUCK'S LIBRARY (M)
Keppler & Schwarzmann, New York: No.1, July, 1887 - No. 174, Dec, 1899 (10 cents, 11-1/2x8-1/4", 36 pgs, color paper-c, B&W)
1- "The National Game" (Baseball) 50.00 100.00 200.00
2-149 10.00 20.00 40.00
NOTE: ***Puck's Library*** *was a monthly magazine reprinting cartoons & prose from* ***Puck****, with each issue's*

Rays of Light
1886 © Morse Bros., Canton, Mass.

Sam Slick's Comic Almanac
1857 © Philip J Cozans, Publisher, NYC

Shakespeare Would Ride The Bicycle If Alive Today
1896 © Cleveland Bicycles, Toledo, OH.

material organized around the same subject. The cover art was often original. All issues were kept in print for the duration of the series, so later issues are more scarce than earlier ones.

PUCK, PICKINGS FROM (M)
Keppler & Schwarzmann, New York: No.1, Sept, 1891 - No. 34, Dec, 1899 (25 cents, 13-1/4x10-1/4", 68 pgs, color paper-c, B&W)

1-34 Scarce 15.00 30.00 60.00

NOTE: *Similar to **Puck's Library**, except larger in size, and issued quarterly. All reprint material, except for the cover art. There also exist variations with "RAILROAD EDITION 30 CENTS" printed on the cover in place of the standard 25 cent price.*

PUCK'S OPPER BOOK (M)
Keppler & Schwarzmann, New York: 1888 (11-3/4x13-7/8", color paper-c, 68 pgs,interior B&W, 30¢)

nn - (Very Rare) by F. Opper 225.00 450.00 750.00

NOTE: *Puck's first book collecting work by a single artist.; mostly sequential comic strips.*

PUCK'S PRINTING BOOK FOR CHILDREN (S,O.I)
Keppler & Schwarzman, Pubs, NY: 1891 (10-3/8x7-7/8", 52 pgs, color-c, B&W and color)

nn - Frederick B Opper (Very Rare) (no known sales)

NOTE: *Left side printed in color; Right side B&W to be colored in.*

PUCK PROOFS (M,P,S)
Keppler & Schwarzmann, New York: nd (1906-1909) (74 pgs, paper cover; B&W) (all are Scarce)

nn - (c.1906, no price, 4-1/8x5-1/4") B&W painted -c of couple kissing over a chess board; 1905 & 1906-r 25.00 50.00 100.00

nn- (c.1909, 10 cents, 4-3/8x5-3/8") plain green paper-c; 76 pgs 1905-1909-r 25.00 50.00 100.00

NOTE: *Catalog of prints available from **Puck**, reprinting mostly cover & centerspread art from **Puck**. There likely exist more as yet unreported **Puck Proofs** catalogs. Art by Rose O'Neill.*

PUCK, THE TARIFF ?, CARTOONS AND COMMENTS FROM (M,S)
Keppler & Schwarzmann, New York: 1888 (10 cents, 6-7/8x10-3/8", 36 pgs, paper-c, B&W)

nn - (Scarce) 37.50 75.00 200.00

NOTE: *Reprints both cartoons and commentary from **Puck**, concerning the issue of tariffs which were then being debated in Congress. Art by Gillam, Keppler, Opper, Taylor.*

PUCK, WORLD'S FAIR
Keppler & Schwarzmann, PUCK BUILDING, World's Fair Grounds, Chicago: No.1 May 1, 1893 - No.26 Oct 30, 1893 (10 cents, 11-1/4x8-3/4, 14 pgs, paper-c, color front/back/center pages, rest B&W)(All issues Scarce to Rare)

1-26 30.00 60.00 130.00
1-26 bound volume: 500.00 1100.00 2200.00

NOTE: *Art by Joseph Keppler, F. Opper, F.M. Howarth, C.J. Taylor, W.A. Rogers. This was a separate, parallel run of **Puck**, published during the 1893 Chicago World's Fair from within the fairgrounds, and containing all new and different material than the regular weekly **Puck**. Smaller sized and priced the same, this originally sold poorly, and had not as wide distribution as **Puck**, and so consequently issues are much more rare than regular **Puck** issues from the same period. Not to be confused with the larger sized regular **Puck** issues from 1893 which sometimes also contained World's Fair related material, and sometimes had the words "World's Fair" appear on the cover. Can also be distinguished by the fact that **Puck's** issue numbering was in the 800's in 1893, while these issue number 1 through 26.*

PUNCHINELLO
Punchinello Publishing Co, NYC: April 2-Dec 24 1870 (weekly)

1-39 Henry L. Stephens, Frank Bellew, Bowlend 12.50 25.00 50.00

NOTE: *Funded by the Tweed Ring, mild politics attacking Grant Admin & other NYC newspapers. Bound copies exist.*

QUIDDITIES OF AN ALASKAN TRIP (O,G)
G.A. Steel & Co., Portland, OR: 1873 (6-3/4x10-1/2", 80 pgs, gilted hard-c, Red-c and Blue-c exist, B&W)

nn - By William H. Bell (Scarce) 350.00 750.00 1500.00

NOTE: *Highly sought Western Americana collectors. Parody of a trip from Washington DC to Alaska, by a member of the team which went to survey Alaska, purchase commonly known then as "Seward's Folly".*

"RAG TAGS" AND THEIR ADVENTURES, THE (N,S)
A. M. Robertson, San Francisco: 1899 (10-1/4x13-7/8, 84 pgs, color hard-c, B&W inside)

nn - By Arthur M. Lewis (SF Chronicle newspaper-r) (Scarce) 60.00 120.00 240.00

RAYS OF LIGHT (O,P)
Morse Bros., Canton, Mass.: No.1 1886 (7-1/8x5-1/8", 8 pgs, color paper-c, B&W)

1- (Rare) 50.00 100.00 200.00

NOTE: *Giveaway pamphlet in guise of an educational publication, consisting entirely of a sequential story in which a teacher instructs her classroom of young girls in the use of Rising Sun Stove Polish. Color front & back covers.*

RELIC OF THE ITALIAN REVOLUTION OF 1849, A
Gabici's Music Stores, New Orleans: 1849 (10-1/8x12-3/4", 144 pgs, hardcover)

nn - By G. Daelli (Scarce) 100.00 200.00 400.00

NOTE: *From the title page: "Album of fifty line engravings, executed on copper, by the most eminent artists at Rome in 1849; secreted from the papal police after the 'Restoration of Order,' And just imported into America."*

REMARKS ON THE JACOBINIAD (I,S)
E.W. Weld & W. Greenough, Boston: 1795-98 (8-1/4x5-1/8", 72 pgs, a number of B&W plates with text)

nn - Written by Rev. James Sylvester Gardner,artist unknown (Rare) (no known sales)

NOTE: *Early comics-type characters. Not sequential comics, but uses word balloons. Satire directed against "The Jacobin Club," supporters of the French Revolution and Radical Republicans. Gardner came to America from England in 1783, was minister of Trinity Church, Boston. There appears to be some reprints of this done as late as 1798.*

REV. MR. SOURBALL'S EUROPEAN TOUR, THE RECREATION OF A CITY, THE
Duffield Ashmead, Philadelphia: 1867 (7-5/8x6-1/4", 72 pgs, turquoise blue soft wrappers)

By Horace Cope (Rare) 50.00 100.00 200.00

NOTE: see **PARSON SOURBALL'S EUROPEAN TOUR** for the hard cover version.

RHYMES OF NONSENSE TRUTH & FICTION (S)
G.W. Carleton & Co, Publishers, NY: 1874 (10x7-3/4", 44 pgs, hard-c, B&W) (Very Rare)

nn - By Chaucer Jones and Michael Angelo Raphael Smith 100.00 200.00 400.00

NOTE: *Creator names obviously pseudonyms; looks like weak A.B. Frost.*

ROMANCE OF A HAMMOCK, THE - AS RECITED BY MR. GUS WILLIAMS IN "ONE OF THE FINEST" (O,P)
Unknown: 1880s (5-1/2x3-5/8" folded, 7 attached cardboard cards which fold out into a strip, color)

nn - By presently unknown Scarce 75.00 150.00 300.00

NOTE: *12-panel story, which one begins reading on one side of the folded-out strip, then flip to the other side to continue -- unlike the vast majority of folded strips, which are printed on only one side. This was a promotional handout, for a play titled "One of the Finest". The story pictured comes from a poem read in the play by then famous New York stage actor Gus Williams, who is pictured on the "cover"/title card."*

SAD TALE OF THE COURTSHIP OF CHEVALIER SLYFOX-WIKOF, SHOWING HIS HEART-RENDING ASTOUNDING & MOST WONDERFUL LOVE ADVENTURES WITH FANNY ELSSLER AND MISS GAMBOL, THE (O,G)
Garrett & Co., NY: Jan 1856 (25 ¢, 5-3/4x9-1/4", 100 pages, paper-c, B&W)

nn - By T.C. Bond ?? (Very Rare) 500.00 1000.00 2000.00

NOTE: *No surviving copies yet reported -- known via ads in Home Circle published by Garrett. Cover art by John McLenan and Samuel Avery. Graphic novel parodying the real-life romance between European actress/dancer Fanny Elssler and American aristocrat Henry Wikoff. The entire graphic novel is reprinted in the 1976 book "Fanny Elssler in America."*

SAD TALE OF THE COURTSHIP OF CHEVALIER SLYFOX-WIKOF, SHOWING HIS HEART-RENDING ASTOUNDING & MOST WONDERFUL LOVE ADVENTURES WITH FANNY ELSSLER AND MISS GUMBEL, THE (G) (25 cents printed on cover)
Dick And Fitzgerald, NY: 1870s-1888 (5-3/4x9-1/4", ??? pages, soft paper-c, B&W)

nn - By T.C. Bond ?? (Very Rare) 250.00 500.00 1000.00

NOTE: *Reprint of Garrett original printing before G,D&F partnership begins.*

SALT RIVER GUIDE FOR DISAPPOINTED POLITICIANS
Winchell, Small & Co., 113 Fulton St, NY: 1870s (16 pgs, 10¢)

nn - single panel cartoons from Wild Oats (Rare) 75.00 150.00 300.00

SAM SLICK'S COMIC ALMANAC
Philip J. Cozans, NYC: 1857 (7.5x4.5, 48 pgs, B&W) 100.00 200.00 400.00

NOTE: *Contains reprint of "Moses Keyser the Bowery Bully's Trip to the California Gold Mines" from Elton's Comic Almanac #17 1850.*

SCRAPS (O,S) (see also **F****** A*** K*****)
D.C. Johnston, Boston: 1828 - No.8 1840; New Series No.1 1849 (12 pgs, printed one side only, paper-c, B&W)

1 - 1828 (9-1/4 x 11-3/4") (Very Rare) (no known sales)
2 - 1830 (9-3/4 x 12-3/4") (Very Rare) (no known sales)
3 - 1832 (10-7/8 x 13-1/8") (Very Rare) (no known sales)
4 - 1833 (11 x 13-5/8") (Very Rare) (no known sales)
5- 1834 (10-3/8 x 13-3/8") (Very Rare) (no known sales)
6 - 1835 (10-3/8 x 13-1/4") red lettering in title SCRAPS (Very Rare) 250.00 500.00 1000.00
6 - 1835 (10-3/8 x 13-1/4") no red lettering in title (Rare) 200.00 400.00 880.00
7 - 1837 (10-3/4 x 13-7/8") 1st Edition (Very Rare) 200.00 400.00 880.00
7 - 1837 (10-3/4 x 13-3/4") 2nd Edition (so stated) 100.00 175.00 375.00

NOTE: *20 pgs. of text (double-sided), 4 pgs. of art (single-sided), plus the covers. There are no protective sheets between the art pages.*

8 - 1840 (10-1/2 x 13-7/8") (Rare) 200.00 400.00 880.00
New Series 1- 1849 (10-7/8 x 13-3/4") 125.00 250.00 475.00

NOTE: *By David Claypoole Johnston. All issues consist of four one-sided sheets with 9 to 12 single panel cartoons per sheet. The other pages are blank or text. With #1-5 the size of the pages can vary up to an inch. Contains 4 protective sheets (not part of page count) Only 1 3 4 and the 1849 New Series Number 1 has cover art along with 4 art pgs. (single sided) with 4 protective sheets and no text pages.New Series Number 1, as well as #6 with bo red lettering and the second printing of issue 7, have survived in higher numbers due to a 1940s warehouse discovery.*

THE SETTLEMENT OF RHODE ISLAND (O)
The Graphic Co. Photo-Lith 39 & 41, Park Place, New York: 1874 (11-3/8x10, 40 pgs, gilted blue hard-c

nn - Charles T. Miller & Walter F. Brown 50.00 100.00 250.00

NOTE: *This is also the Same Walter F. Brown that did "Hail Columbia".*

SHAKESPEARE WOULD RIDE THE BICYCLE IF ALIVE TODAY. "THE REASON WHY" (O,P,S)
Cleveland Bicycles H.A. Lozier & Co., Toledo, OH: 1896 (5-1/2x4",16 pgs, paper-c, color)

nn - By F. Opper (Rare) 70.00 140 .00 300.00

NOTE: *Original cartoons of Shakespearian characters riding bicycles; also popular amongst collectors of bicycle ephemera.*

Stuff and Nonsense by A.B. Frost
1884 © Charles Scribner's Sons

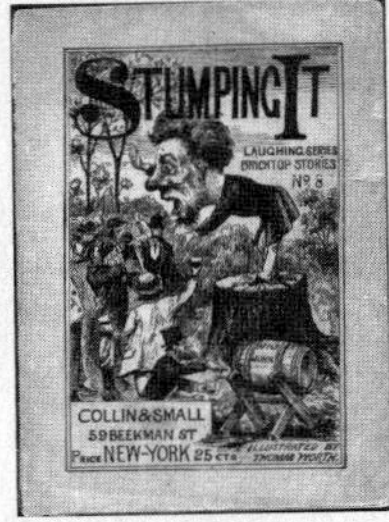

Stumping It
1876 © Collin & Lee, NY

The Adventures Of Mr. Tom Plump
1851 © Huestis & Cozans, NY

FR1.0 GD2.0 FN6.0

SHAKINGS - ETCHINGS FROM THE NAVAL ACADEMY BY A MEMBER OF THE CLASS OF '67 (O,S)
Lee & Shepard, Boston: 1867 (7-7/8x10", 132 pages, blue hard-c)
By: Park Benjamin 38.00 75.00 150.00
NOTE: *Park Benjamin later became editor of Harper's Bazaar magazine.*

SHOO FLY PICTORIAL (S)
John Stetson, Chestnut sT Theatre, Phila, PA: June 1870 (15-1/2x11-1/2", 8 pgs, B&W)
1 67.50 125.00 250.00

SHYS AT SHAKSPEARE
J.P. and T.C.P., Philadelphia: 1869 (9-1/4x6", 52 pgs)
nn - Artist unknown 75.00 150.00 300.00

SKETCHES OF LOWLY LIFE IN A GREAT CITY (M,S) (See 99 "Woolfs" From Truth)
G. P. Puntam's Sons: 1899 (8-5/8x11-1/4", 200 pgs, hard-c, B&W)
(reprints from Life and Judge of Woolf's cartoons of NYC slum children)
nn - By Michael Angelo Woolf 75.00 150.00 350.00
NOTE: *Woolf's cartoons are regarded as a primary influence on R.F. Outcault in the later development of The Yellow Kid newspaper strip.*

SNAP (O,S)
Valentine & Townsend, Tribune Bldg, NYC: March 13,1885 (17x11, 8 pgs, B&W)
1-Contains a sequential comic strip 50.00 100.00 150.00

SOCIETY PICTURES (M,S,E)
Charles H. Sergel Company, Chicago: 1895 (5-1/4x7-3/4", 168 pgs, printed 1 side, paper-c, B&W)
nn - By George du Maurier; reprints from **Punch.** 12.50 25.00 50.00

SOLDIERS AND SAILORS HALF DIME TALES OF THE LATE REBELLION
Soldiers & Sailors Publishing Co: 1868 (5-1/4x7-7/8", 32 pgs)
v1#1-#16 v2#1-#10 10.00 20.00 40.00
v2 #11 contains (5) page comic strip 20.00 40.00 80.00
NOTE: *Changes to Soldiers & Sailors Half Dime Magazine with v2 #1.*

SOUVENIR CONTAINING CARTOONS ISSUED BY THE PRESS BUREAU OF THE OHIO STATE REPUBLICAN EXECUTIVE COMMITTEE, A (S)
Ohio State Republican Executive Committee, Columbus, OH: 1899 (10-3/8x13-1/2, 248 pgs, Hard-c, B&W
nn - By William L. Bloomer (Scarce) 100.00 200.00 400.00

SOUVENIR OF SOHMER CARTOONS FROM PUCK, JUDGE, AND FRANK LESLIE'S (M,S,P)
Sohmer Piano Co.: nd(c.1893) (6x4-3/4", 16 pgs, paper-c, B&W)
nn 20.00 40.00 80.00
NOTE: *Reprints painted "cartoon" Sohmer Piano advertisements which appeared in the above publications. Artists include Keppler, Gillam, others.*

SPORTING NEW YORKER, THE
Ornum & Co, Beekman ST, NYC: 1870s
issues with sequential comic strips (Rare) 50.00 100.00 200.00

STORY OF THE MAN OF HUMANITY AND THE BULL CALF, THE
(see Bull Calf, The Story of The Man Of Humanity And The)
NOTE: *Reprints of two of A. B. Frost's mostfamous sequential comic strips.*

STREET & SMITH'S LITERARY ALBUM
Street & Smith, NY: #1 Dec 23 1865-#225 Apr 9 1870 (11-3/4x16-3/4", 16 pgs, B&W)
1 (23 Dec 1865) 10.00 30.00 50.00
2-129 131-225 (issues with short sequential strips) 7.50 15.00 30.00
130 (Steam Man satire parody) 100.00 200.00 300.00

STUFF AND NONSENSE (Harper's Monthly strip-r) (M)
Charles Scribner's Sons: 1884 (10-1/4x7-3/4", 100 pgs, hardcover, B&W)
nn - By Arthur Burdett Frost 100.00 185.00 375.00
nn - By A.B. Frost (1888 reprint, 104 pgs) 40.00 80.00 180.00
NOTE: *Earliest known anthology devoted to collecting the comic strips of a single American artist. 1888 2nd printing has a different cover and is layed out somewhat differently inside with a new title page, 3 added pages of cartoons, and a couple more illustrations. For more Frost, the 2nd is worth checki ng out also.*

STUMPING IT (LAUGHING SERIES BRICKTOP STORIES #8) (O,S)
Collin & Small, NY: 1876 (6-5/8x9-1/4, 68 pgs, perfect bound, B&W)
nn - Thomas Worth art abounds (some sequentials) 75.00 150.00 300.00
NOTE: Mainly single panel cartoons w/text; however, some sequential comic strips inside worth picking up

SUMMER SCHOOL OF PHILOSOPHY AT MT. DESERT, THE
Henry Holt & Co.: 1881 (10-3/8x8-5/8", 60 pgs, illus. gilt hard-c, B&W)
nn - By J. A. Mitchell 60.00 120.00 240.00
NOTE: *J.A.Mitchell went on to found **LIFE** two years later in 1883. Also, the long-running mascot for **LIFE** was Cupid - which you see multitudes of Cupids flying around in this story.*

SURE WATER CURE, THE
Carey Grey & Hart, Phila, PA: c1841-43 (8-/2x5, 32 pgs, B&W
nn - proto-comic-strip Very Rare 150.00 300.00 600.00

TAILOR-MADE GIRL, HER FRIENDS, HER FASHIONS, AND HER FOLLIES, THE
(see also IN THE "400" AND OUT) (M)
Charles Scribner's Sons, New York: 1888 (8-3/8x10-1/2", 68 pgs, hard-c, B&W)
nn - Art by C.J. Taylor 17.50 35.00 70.00
NOTE: *Format is a full page cartoon on every other page, with a script style vignette, written by Philip H. Welch, on every page opposite the art.*

TALL STUDENT, THE
Roberts Brothers, Boston: 1873 (7x5", 48 pgs, printed one side only, gilted hard-c, B&W)
nn - By Wilhelm Busch (Scarce) 37.50 75.00 150.00

TARIFF ?, CARTOONS AND COMMENTS FROM PUCK, THE (see Puck, The Tariff...)

TEASING TOM AND NAUGHTY NED WITH A SPOOL OF CLARK'S COTTON, THE ADVENTURES OF (O,P)
Clark's O.N.T. Spool Cotton: 1879 (4-1/4x3", 12 pgs, B&W, paper-c)
nn 17.50 35.00 70.00
NOTE: *Knock-off of the "First Trick" in Wilhelm Busch's **Max and Maurice**, modified to involve Clark's Spool Cotton in the story, with similar but new art by an artist identified as "HB". The back cover advertises the specific merchant who gave this booklet away -- multiple variations of back cover suspected.*

TEMPERANCE TALES; OR, SIX NIGHTS WITH THE WASHINGTONIANS, VOL I & II
W.A. Leary & Co., Philadelphia: 1848 (50¢, 6-1/8x4", 328 pgs, B&W, hard-c)
nn 100.00 200.00 400.00
NOTE: *Mostly text. This edition gathers Volume I & II together. The first 8 pages reprints George Cruikshank's **THE BOTTLE**, re-drawn & re-engraved by Phil A. Pilliner. Later editions of this book do not include **THE BOTTLE** reprint and are therefore of little interest to comics collectors.*

TEXAS SIFTINGS
Texas Siftings Publishing Co, Austin, Texas (1881-1887), **NYC** (1887-1897): 1881-1885 newspaper-size weekly; 1886-1897 folio weekly (15x10-3/4", 16 pgs, B&W 10¢
1881-1885 issues 25.00 50.00 100.00
v6#1 (5/8/86) (8) panel strip Afterwhich He Emigrated;
(16) panel The Tenor's Triumph Veni Vidi Vici 12.50 25.00 50.00
v6#2 (5/16/86 (5) panel sewuential 12.50 25.00 50.00
v6#3 no sequentials 12.50 25.00 50.00
v6#4 (5/29/86) Worth-c (4) panel Worth strip; (2) panel 12.50 25.00 50.00
v6#5 no sequentials 12.50 25.00 50.00
v6#6 (6/12/86) Comic Strip Cover (11) panels The Rise of a Great Artist
(5) panel sequential 50.00 100.00 200.00
v6#7 (6/19/86) Worth-c (2) panel Wiorth;
(10) panel Ha! Ha! The Honest Youth & the Lordly Villain 25.00 50.00 100.00
v6#8 (6/26/86) Worth-c; (15) panel The Kangaroo Hunter 25.00 50.00 100.00
v6#9 (7/3/86) Worth-c; Bellew (2) panel How Wives Get What They Want
12.50 25.00 50.00
v6#10 ((7/10/86) Baseball-c; (3) panel;
(5) panel A Story Without Words from Fliegende Blätter 12.50 25.00 50.00
v6 #11 12 13 Worth-c no sequentials 12.50 25.00 50.00
v6#14 (8/7/86) Wiorth-c; (7) panel Mrs Cleveland Presents
The President With A New Rocking Chair 12.50 25.00 50.00
v6#15 (8/14/86) Worth-c; (6) panel Worth strip 12.50 25.00 50.00
v6#16 (8/21/86) Worth-c Asleep At Post USA/Mexico Border
(6) panel sequential 12.50 25.00 50.00
v6#17 no sequrntials 12.50 25.00 50.00
v6#18 (9/4/86) Worth-c; (3) panel from Fliegende 12.50 25.00 50.00
v6#19 (9/11/86) Worth Anarchist & Uncle Sam-c;
(5) panel Duel of the Dudes 12.50 25.00 50.00
v6#20 (9/18/86) Worth-c (6) panel sequential 12.50 25.00 50.00
v6#21 (9/25/86) Worth-c; Verbeck single panel; (9) panel 12.50 25.00 50.00
v6#22 (10/2/86) Verbeck-c plus interiors 12.50 25.00 50.00
v6#23 (10/9/86) Worth-c Geronimo & Devil cover;
Verbeck and Chips singles 25.00 50.00 100.00
v6#24 (10/16/86) Worth-c Verbeck strip "Evolution" 12.50 25.00 50.00
v6#25 no sequential strips 12.50 25.00 50.00
v6#26 (10/30/86) Worth-c; (6) panel Verbeck "A Warning To Smokers"
12.50 25.00 50.00
NOTE: *Many Thomas Worth sequential comic strips. Frank Bellew and Dan McCarthy appear. Wilhelm Busch-r from German Fligende Blaetter. Later issues in 1890s comics become sporadic*

THAT COMIC PRIMER (S)
G.W. Carleton & Co., Publishers: 1877 (6-5/8x5", 52 pgs, paper soft-c, B&W)
nn - By Frank Bellew 75.00 150.00 300.00
NOTE: *Premium for the United States Life Insurance Company, New York.*

TIGER, THE LEFTENANT AND THE BOSUN, THE
Prudential Insurance Home Office, 878 & 880 Broad St, Newark, NJ: 1889 (4.5x3.25", 12 pgs) (Scarce)
nn - 8 panel sequential story in color 50.00 100.00 200.00

TOM PLUMP, THE ADVENTURES OF MR. (see also The Juvenile Gem) (O)
Huestis & Cozans, New York: nd (c1850-1851) (6x3-7/8", 12 pgs, hand colored paper-c, B&W)
nn- First printing(s) publisher's address is 104 Nassau Street (1850-1851)
(Very Rare) 625.00 1250.00 2500.00
NOTE: *California Gold Rush story. The hand colored outer cover is highly rare, with only 1 recorded copy possessing it. The front cover image and text is repeated precisely on page 3 (albeit b&w), and only interior pages are numbered, together leading owners of coverless copies to believe they have the cover. The true back*

The Tramp Exposed #1 By Bellew Family
1878 © Dick & Fitzgerald

Uncle Josh's Trunk Full Of Fun
1870s © Dick & Fitzgerald

Wild Oats #115 March 10
1875 © Winchell & Small, NYC

FR1.0 GD2.0 FN6.0

cover contains ads for the publisher. The cover was issued only with copies which were sold separately - booklets which were bound together as part of ***THE JUVENILE GEM*** *never had such covers.*

TOM PLUMP, THE ADVENTURES OF MR. (see also The Juvenile Gem) (O)
Philip J. Cozans: nd (1851-1852) (6x3-7/8", 12 pgs,hand colored paper-c, B&W)

	FR1.0	GD2.0	FN6.0
nn- Second printing(s) publisher's address is 116 Nassau Street (1851-1852) (Very Rare)	400.00	800.00	1600.00
nn- Third printing(s) publisher's address is 107 Nassau Street (1852+) (Very Rare)	400.00	800.00	1600.00

TOM PLUMP, THE ADVENTURES OF MR.
Americana Review, Scotia, NY: nd(1960's) (6-1/4x4-1/8", 8 pgs, side-stapled, cardboard-c, B&W)

	FR1.0	GD2.0	FN6.0
nn - Modern reprint	-	12.00	24.00

NOTE: *Issued within a folder titled SIX CHILDREN'S BOOKS OF THE 1850'S. States "Reprinted by American Review" at bottom of front cover. Reprints the 104 Nassau Street address.)*

	FR1.0	GD2.0	FN6.0
nn - Modern reprint (Scarce 1980s) (5-1/2x4-1/4", 8 pgs,side-stapled)	-	5.00	10.00

NOTE: *Photocopy reprint by a comix zine publisher, from an Americana Review cop; vailable by mail order*

TOOTH-ACHE, THE (E,O)
D. Bogue, London: 1849 (5-1/4x3-3/4)

	FR1.0	GD2.0	FN6.0
nn - By Cruikshank, B&W (Very Rare)	250.00	500.00	1000.00
nn - By Cruikshank, hand colored (Rare)	(no known sales)		

NOTE: *Scripted by Horace Mayhew, art by George Cruikshank. This is the British edition. Price 1/6 b&w, 3 hand colored. In British editions, the panels are not numbered. Publisher's name appears on cover. Booklet's "pages" unfold into a single, long, strip.*

J.L. Smith, Philadelphia, PA: nd (1849) (5-1/8"x 3-3/4" folded, 86-7/8" wide unfolded, 26 pgs, cardboard-c, color, 15¢)

	FR1.0	GD2.0	FN6.0
nn - By Cruikshank, hand colored (Very Rare)	400.00	800.00	1600.00

NOTE: *Reprints the D. Bogue edition. In American editions, the panels are numbered (43 panels, not counting front & back cover). Publisher's name stamped on inside front cover, plus printed along left-hand side of first interior page. Page 1 is pasted to inside back cover, and unfolds from there. Front cover not attached to back cover by design. Booklet's "pages" unfold into a single, long, strip (made from four individual strips pasted together on the blank back side). There is a fairly common1974 British Arts Council reprint.*

TRAMP, THE: His Tricks, Tallies, and Tell-Tales, with His Signs, Countersigns, Grips, Passwords and Villainies Exposed (0,S)
Dick & Fitzgerald, New York: 1878 (11-3/8x8, 36 pgs, paper-c, B&W, 25¢) (Rare)

	FR1.0	GD2.0	FN6.0
1 Frank Bellew	150.00	300.00	600.00

NOTE: *Edited by Frank Bellew, A Bee And A Chip (Bellew's daughter and son Frank).*

TRUTH (See Platinum Age section for 1900-1906 issues)
Truth Company, NY: 1886-1906? (13-11/16x10-5/16", 16 pgs, process color-c & centerfolds, rest B&W)

	FR1.0	GD2.0	FN6.0
1886-1887 issues	20.00	40.00	100.00
1888-1895 issues non Outcault issues	15.00	30.00	80.00
Mar 10 1894 - precursor Yellow Kid RFO	60.00	180.00	400.00
#372 June 2 1894 - first app Yellow Kid RFO	215.00	650.00	1300.00
June 23 1894 - precursor Yellow Kid R. F. Outcault	60.00	180.00	400.00
July 14 1894 -2nd app Yellow Kid RFO	110.00	330.00	700.00
Sept 15 1894 - (2) 3rd app YK RFO plus YK precursor	110.00	330.00	700.00
Feb 9 1895 - 4th app Yellow Kid RFO	110.00	330.00	700.00
1896-1899 issues	10.00	20.00	55.00

NOTE: *This magazine contains the earliest known appearances of* ***The Yellow Kid*** *by Richard Felton Outcault. Feb 9 1895 issue's YK cartoon was reprinted one week later in the* ***New York World*** *Feb 17 1895 edition. We are still sorting out further Outcault appearances. Truth also contained full color sequential strips by Hy Mayer on the back plus Woolf, Verbeek, etc.*

TRUTH, SELECTIONS FROM
Truth Company, NY: 1894-Spr 1897 (13-11/16x10-1/4, color-c, quarterly)

	FR1.0	GD2.0	FN6.0
1-4	25.00	50.00	100.00
5-Outcault's early Yellow Kid	100.00	200.00	400.00
6-13	20.00	40.00	80.00

NOTE: *#5 reprints all early Outcault Yellow Kid appearances*

TURNER'S COMIC ALMANAC
Charles Strong, 298 Pearl St, NYC: ???-1843 (7.25x4.5", 36 pgs, B&W)

	FR1.0	GD2.0	FN6.0
nn	60.00	120.00	240.00

TURNER'S COMICK ALMA-NACK
Turner & Fisher, NYC: 1844-?? (7.25x4.5", 36 pgs, B&W)

	FR1.0	GD2.0	FN6.0
nn	60.00	120.00	240.00

TWO HUNDRED SKETCHES, HUMOROUS AND GROTESQUE, BY GUSTAVE DORE (E)
Frederick Warne & Co, London: 1867 (13-3/4x11-3/8, 94 pgs, hard-c, B&W)

	FR1.0	GD2.0	FN6.0
nn - (1867) by Gustave Dore	100.00	200.00	500.00
nn - (Second Edition; 1871)- by Gustave Dore	50.00	100.00	240.00
nn - (Third Edition; 1870's)- by Gustave Dore	50.00	100.00	240.00
nn - (Fourth Edition; 1870's- by Gustave Dore	50.00	100.00	240.00

NOTE: *Contains sequential comics stories, single panel cartoons, and sketches. Reprints and translates material which originally appeared in the French publications "Le Journal pour Rire", circa 1848-49. Although dated 1867, it was likely published & available for the 1866 Christmas Season, as has been confirmed for the American edition. Printed by Dalziel. The American & first British editions were printed simultaneously, the American edition is not a reprint of the British.*

TWO HUNDRED SKETCHES, HUMOROUS AND GROTESQUE, BY GUSTAVE DORE (E)
Roberts Brothers, Boston: 1867 (13-3/4x11-3/8", 96 pgs, hard-c, B&W)

FR1.0 GD2.0 FN6.0

	FR1.0	GD2.0	FN6.0
nn - By Gustave Dore	100.00	200.00	500.00

NOTE: *Although dated 1867, it was published & available for the 1866 Christmas Season. Printed by Dalziel, in England, and imported to the USA expressly for a USA publisher.*

UNCLE JOSH'S TRUNK-FUL OF FUN
Dick & Fitzgerald, 18 Ann St, NY: 1870s (5-3/4x9", 68 pgs, B&W & Red-c, B&W inside)

	FR1.0	GD2.0	FN6.0
nn - Rare	75.00	125.00	200.00

NOTE: *Many single panel cartoons; (2) pages of early boxing sequential strip*

UNCLE SAM'S COMIC ALMANAC
M.J. Meyers, NY: 1879 (11x8", 32 pgs)

	FR1.0	GD2.0	FN6.0
nn -	50.00	100.00	200.0

UNDER THE GASLIGHT
Gaslight Publishing Co (Frank Tousey): Oct 13 1878-Apr 12 1879 (Folio, 16pgs)

	FR1.0	GD2.0	FN6.0
1-27	75.00	125.00	200.00

UNITED STATES COMIC ALMANAC
King & Baird, Philadelphia: 1851-?? (7.5x4.5", 36 pgs, B&W)

	FR1.0	GD2.0	FN6.0
nn	60.00	120.00	240.00

UPS AND DOWNS ON LAND AND WATER (O.G)
James R. Osgood & Co., Boston: 1871 ; **Houghton, Osgood & Co., Boston:** 1880 (108 pgs, gilted hard-c, B&W)

	FR1.0	GD2.0	FN6.0
1st printing (1871; 10-3/4x16") - By Augustus Hoppin	45.00	90.00	180.00
2nd printing (1880; smaller sized)	32.50	65.00	130.00

NOTE: *Exists as blue or orange hard covers.*

VANITY FAIR
William A. Stephens (for Thompson & Camac): Dec 29 1859-July 4 1863 Quarto Weekly

	FR1.0	GD2.0	FN6.0
average issues with comic strips	12.50	25.00	50.00

VERDICT, THE
Verdict Publishing Co: Dec 19 1898-Nov 12 1900 (Chromolithographic Weekly)

	FR1.0	GD2.0	FN6.0
Average Issues	50.00	100.00	200.00

NOTE: *Artists included George B. Luks, Horace Taylor, MIRS. Striking anti-Republican weekly full o fsome of the most savage political cartoons of the era. The last brilliant burst of energy for the political cartoon weekly*

VERY VERY FUNNY (M,S)
Dick & Fitzgerald, New York: nd(c1880's) (10¢, 7-1/2x5", 68 pgs, paper-c, B&W)

	FR1.0	GD2.0	FN6.0
nn - (Rare)	75.00	150.00	300.00

NOTE: *Unauthorized reprints of prose and cartoons extracted from Puck, Texas Siftings, and other publications. Includes art by Chips Bellew, Bisbee, Graetz, Opper, Wales, Zim.*

VIM
H. Wimmel, NYC: June 22-Aug 24 1898 (Chromolithographic Weekly)

	FR1.0	GD2.0	FN6.0
average issue	50.00	100.00	200.00
Yellow Kid by Leon Barritt issues	75.00	150.00	300.00

WAR IN THE MIDST OF AMERICA. FROM A NEW POINT OF VIEW. (E,O,G)
Ackermann & Co., London: 1864 (4-3/8" x 5-7/8", folded, 36 feet wide unfolded, 80 pgs, hard-c, B&W)

	FR1.0	GD2.0	FN6.0
nn- by Charles Dryden (rare)	375.00	750.00	1500.00

NOTE: *British graphic novel about the American Civil War, with a pro-Confederate bent. Adventures of a British artist who decides to visually summarize the American Civil War for his countrymen, from newspaper accounts. Reaching current events, he finds he can not finish the story until the War ends, and so he travels to America, to end it. Book unfolds into a single long strip (binding was issued split, to enable the unfolding).*

WASP, THE ILLUSTRATED SAN FRANCISCO
F. Korbel & Bros and Numerous Others: August 5 1876-April 25 1941 (Chromolithographic Weekly)

	FR1.0	GD2.0	FN6.0
average 1800s issues with comic strips	50.00	100.00	200.00

WHAT I KNOW OF FARMING: Founded On The Experience of Horace Greeley (S)
The American News Company, New York: 1871 (7-1/4x4-1/2", paper-c, B&W)

	FR1.0	GD2.0	FN6.0
nn - By Joseph Hull (Scarce)	35.00	70.00	140.00

NOTE: *Pay & Cox, Printers & Engravers, NY; political tract regarding Presidential elections.*

WILD FIRE
Wild Fire Co, NYC: Nov 30 1877-at least#16 Mar 1878 (Folio, 16 pgs)

	FR1.0	GD2.0	FN6.0
1-16	12.50	25.00	50.00

WILD OATS, An Illustrated Weekly Journal of Fun, Satire, Burlesque, and Nits at Persons and Events of the Day (O)
Winchell & Small, 113 Fulton St /48 Ann St, NYC: Feb 1870-1881 (16-1/4x11", generally 16 pages, B&W, began as monthly, then bi-weekly, then weekly) All loose issues Very Rare (See *The Overstreet Price Guide* #35 2005 for a detailed index of single issue contents)

	FR1.0	GD2.0	FN6.0
1-25 Very Rare - contents to be indexed next year	50.00	100.00	200.00
26-28 30 32 35 36 39 40 41 43-46 1872 (sequential strips)	50.00	100.00	200.00
29 33 37 42 no sequential strips	40.00	80.00	160.00
31 34 38 47 Hopkins sequential comic strips	50.00	100.00	200.00
48 (1/16/73) Worth 13 panel sequential; first Woolf-c	50.00	100.00	200.00
49 51 53 54 60 62 61 64 65 66 67 69 1873 sequential strips	50.00	100.00	200.00
50 52 56 59 63 71 no sequential strips	40.00	80.00	160.00
51 (Worth 18 panel double page spread, Woolf 9 panel	50.00	100.00	200.00
55 Hopkins 22 panel double page spread; Bellew-c	50.00	150.00	300.00

57 intense unknown 6 panel "Two Relics of Barbarism, or A Few Contrasted Pictures,

Wild Oats #139 August 25 1875 © Winchell & Small, NY

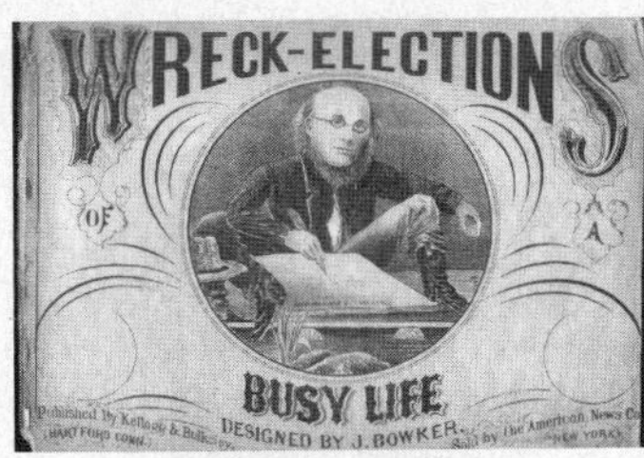

Wreck-Elections Of Busy Life Kellogg & Buckeley © 1864?

Yankee Notions #7 (v2#1) July 1852 © T.W. Strong, NY

FR1.0 GD2.0 FN6.0

Showing the origin of the North American Indian 50.00 100.00 200.00
58 (6/5/73) unknown 19 panel double pager "The Terrible Adventures of Messrs Buster & Stumps, About Exterminating the Indians" reads across both pages like Popeye #2095 (1933); Woolf-c 100.00 200.00 400.00
68 (10/16/73) unknown 9 panel "Adv of New jersey Mosquito" looks like Winsor McCay type style: early inspiration for McCay's animated cartoon? 50.00 100.00 200.00
70 unknown 6 panel; Hopkins 6 panel "Hopkins novel: A Tale of True Love, with all the variations"; Bellew-c 50.00 100.00 200.00
72 (12/11/73) Worth 11 panel; Wales President Grant war-c 50.00 100.00 200.00
73 74 75 Hopkins sequential comic strip 75.00 150.00 300.00
76 77 sequential strips 50.00 100.00 200.00
78 Bellew 5 panel double pager 50.00 100.00 200.00
79-105 (March 1874-Dec 1874) contents presently unknown 50.00 100.00 200.00
106 107 111 no sequentials;Bellew-c #106 110;Wales-c #107 50.00 100.00 200.00
108 (1/20/75) Wales 12 panel double pg spread; Bellew-c 50.00 100.00 200.00
109 (1/27/75) unknown 6 panel; Wales-c 50.00 100.00 200.00
111 Busch 13 panel "The Conundrum of the Day - Is Lager Beer Intoxicating?"; Bellew-c 50.00 100.00 200.00
112 116 sequential comic strips 50.00 100.00 200.00
113 114 115 no sequentials Worth-c #114 40.00 80.00 160.00
117 intense Wales 6 panel "One of the Oppresions of the Civil Rights Laws" Bellew-c 75.00 150.00 300.00
118-137 (3/31/75-8/4/75) no sequential comic strips 40.00 80.00 160.00
138 (8/18/75) Bellew Sr & Bellew "Chips" Jr singles appear 50.00 100.00 200.00
139-143 145-147 154-157 159 no sequentials 40.00 80.00 160.00
144 (9/29/75) Hopkins 8 panel sequential; Wales-c 50.00 100.00 200.00
148 (10/27/75) Opper's first cover; many Opper singles 75.00 150.00 300.00
149 150 151 152 153 all Opper-c and much interior work 50.00 100.00 200.00
158 (1/5/76) Palmer Cox 1rst comic strip 24 panel double page spread "The Adv of Mr & Mrs Sprowl And Their Christmas Turkey - A Crashing Chasing Tearful Tragedy But Happily Ending Well"; Opper-c 100.00 200.00 400.00
159 160 162 165 167 169-173 no sequentials 40.00 80.00 160.00
161 163 164 166 168 179 182 Palmer Cox sequential strips 100.00 200.00 400.00
174 (4/26/76) Cox 24 panel double pager "The Tramp's Progress; A Story of the West And the Union Pacific Railroad" 100.00 200.00 400.00
175-178 183-189 no sequentials 40.00 80.00 160.00
180 (6/7/76) Beard & Opper jam; Woolf, Bellew singles 50.00 100.00 200.00
181 more Mann two panel jobs; Opper-c 50.00 100.00 200.00
190 Bellew 9 panel "Rodger's Patent Mosquito Armour" 75.00 150.00 300.00
191-end contents to be indexed in the near future 40.00 80.00 160.00
NOTE: *There are very few lknown oose issues. All loose issues are Very Rare. Prices vary widely on this magazine. Issues with sequential comic strips would be in higher demand than issues with no comic strips. We present this index from the Library of Congress and New York Historical Society bound sets. We would love to hear from any one who turns up loose copies. This scarce humor bi-weekly contains easily a couple hundred original first-time published sequential comic strips found in most issues plus innumerable single panel cartoons in every issue*

WYMAN'S COMIC ALMANAC FOR THE TIMES
T.W.Strong, NY: 1854 (8x5", 24 pgs)
nn - 50.00 100.00 200.00

WOMAN IN SEARCH OF HER RIGHTS, THE ADVENTURES OF (G)
Lee & Shepard, Boston And New York: early 1870s (8-3/8x13", 40 pgs, hard-c)
By Florence Claxton (Very Rare) 400.00 800.00 1600.00
NOTE: *Earliest known original comic book sequential story by a woman; contains "nearly 100 original drawings by the author, which have been reproduced in fac-simile by the graphotype process of engraving." Tinted two color lithography; orange tint printed first, then printed 2nd time with black ink; early women's sufferage.*

WORLD OVER, THE (I)
G. W. Dillingham Company, New York: 1897 (192 pgs, hard-c)
nn - By Joe Kerr; 80 illustrations by R.F. Outcault (Rare) 250.00 500.00 1000.00
NOTE: *soft cover editions also exist*

WRECK-ELECTIONS OF BUSY LIFE (S)
Kellogg & Bulkeley: 1867 (9-1/4x11-3/4", ??? pages, soft-c)
nn - By J. Bowker (Rare) 100.00 200.00 400.00
NOTE: *Says "Sold by American News Company, New York" on cover.*

YANKEE DOODLE
W.H. Graham, Tribune Building, NYC: Oct 10 1846-Oct 2 1847 (Quarto weekly)
average issue 50.00 100.00 200.00

YANKEE NOTIONS, OR WHITTLINGS OF JONATHAN'S JACK-KNIFE
T.W. Strong, 98 Nassau St, NYC: Jan. 1852-1875 (11x8, 32 pgs, paper-c, 12.5¢, monthly)
1 Brother Jonathan character single panel cartoons 50.00 100.00 200.00
NOTE: *Begins continuing character sequential comic strip, "The Adventures of Jeremiah Oldpot" in "A Bird in the Hand Is Worth Two in The Bush"*
2-4 25.00 50.00 100.00
5 British X-Over 25.00 50.00 100.00
NOTE: *Single panel of John Bull & Brother Jonathan exchanging civilities (issues of Punch & Yankee Notions)*
6 end of Jeremiah Oldpot continued strip 25.00 50.00 100.00
v2#1 begin "Hoosier Bragg" sequential strip - six issue serial 25.00 50.00 100.00
v2#2 Feb 1853 two pg 12 panel sequential "Mr Vanity's Exploits, Arising Out Of A Valentine" 37.50 75.00 150.00
v2#3-v2#5 continues Hoosier Bragg 25.00 50.00 100.00
v2#6 Juen 1853 Lion Eats Hoosier Bragg, end of story 25.00 50.00 100.00
v3#1 begins referring to its cartoons as "Comic Art" 37.50 75.00 150.00

FR1.0 GD2.0 FN6.0

v4#1-V4#6 v5#1-v5#2 no sequential comic strips 20.00 40.00 80.00
v5#3 two sequential comic strips 37.50 75.00 150.00
NOTE: *Mr Take-A-Drop And The Maine Law (5) panels and The First Segar (7) panels (about smoking tobacco)*
v5#4 April 1856 begin Billy Vidkins 37.50 75.00 150.00
NOTE: *Begins reprinting "From Passages in the Life of Little Billy Vidkins, first issued as a stand alone proto-comic book in 1849 Illustrations of the Poets*
v5#5 The McBargem Guards (9) panel sequential; Vidkins 25.00 50.00 100.00
v5#6 v5 #9 no comics 20.00 40.00 80.00
v5#7 Billy Vidkins continues 25.00 50.00 100.00
v5#8 end of Vidkins By HL Stephens, Esq. 25.00 50.00 100.00
v5#10 (6) panel "How We Learn To Ride"; Timber is hero 25.00 50.00 100.00
v5#11 (7) panel "How Mr. Green Sparrowgrass Voted-A Warning For the Benefit of Quiet Citizens About To Excercize the Elective Franchise" plus Pt Two "How We Learn to Ride" 37.50 75.00 150.00
v5#12 (6) panel "How Mr Pipp Got Struck"; "The Eclipse" featuring Mr Phips; Pt 3 "How We Learn to Ride" 25.00 50.00 100.00
v6#1 (Jan 1857) (12) panel "A Tale of An Umbrella; (4) panel begins a serial "The Man Who Bought The Elephant; (8) panel How Our Young New Yorkers Celebrate New Years Day 25.00 50.00 100.00
v6#2 (Feb 1857) Pt 2 (4) panels The Man Who Bought the Elephant; (7) panel A Game of All Fours 25.00 50.00 100.00
v6#3 (Mar 1857) Pt 3 (4) panels The Man Who Bought the Elephant ending; (4) panel Ye Great Crinoline Monopoly 25.00 50.00 100.00
v6#4 no comic strips 25.00 50.00 100.00
v6#5 (May 1850) (3) panel A Short Trip to Mr Bumps, And How It Ended; (2) panel How mr Trembles Was Garrotted 25.00 50.00 100.00
v6#6 no comic strips 25.00 50.00 100.00
v6#7 (July 1857) (5) panel Alma Mater; (3) panel Three Tableaux In the Life of A Broadway Swell 25.00 50.00 100.00
v6 #8 9 no comic strips 25.00 50.00 100.00
v6#10 (Oct 1857) (3) panel Adv of Mr Near-Sight 25.00 50.00 100.00
v6#11 (Nov 1857) (11) panel Mrs Champignon's Dinner Party And the Way She Arranged Her Guests; (4) panel A Stroll in August 25.00 50.00 100.00
v6#12 (Dec 1857) (8) panel strip; (12) panel Young Fitz At A Blow Out in the Fifth Ave 25.00 50.00 100.00
v10#1 (Jan 1860) comic strip Bibbs at Central Park Skating Pond using word balloons 25.00 50.00 100.00

YE TRUE ACCOUNTE OF YE VISIT TO SPRINGFIELDE BY YE CONSTABEL HIS SPECIAL REPORTER
Frank Leslie: 1861 (5-1/8 x 5-1/4 or 93 inches when folded out, paper-c, B&W)
nn - Very Rare fold-out of 18 comic strip panels plus covers - - -
NOTE: *8 panels contain word balloons (Very Rare - only one copy known to exist.) First printed in Frank Leslie's Budget of Fun Jan 1 1861 issue. Abraham Lincoln Biography.*

YE VERACIOUS CHRONICLE OF GRUFF & POMPEY IN 7 TABLEAUX. (O,P)
Jackson's Best Chewing Tobacco & Donaldson Brothers: nd (c1870's) (5-1/8 tall x 3-3/8" wide folded, 27" wide unfolded, color cardboard)
nn - With all 8 panels attached (Scarce) 40.00 80.00 160.00
nn - Individual panels/cards 6.00 12.00 24.00
NOTE: *Black Americana interest. Consists of 8 attached cards, printed on one side, which unfold into a strip story of title card & 7 panels. Scrapbook hobbyists in the 19th Century tended to pull the panels apart and paste into their scrapbooks, making copies with all panels attached scarce.*

YOUNG AMERICA (continues as Yankee Doodle)
T.W. Strong, NYC: 1856
1-30 John McLennon 50.00 100.00 200.00

YOUNG AMERICA'S COMIC ALMANAC
T.W. Strong, NY: 1857 (7-1/2x5", 24 pgs)
nn 50.00 100.00 200.00

THE YOUNG MEN OF AMERICA (becomes Golden Weekly) (S)
Frank Tousey, NYC: 1887-88 (14x10-1/4", 16 pgs, B&W)
527 (10/13/87) Bellew strip "Story of A Black Eye" 25.00 50.00 100.00
530 (11/3/87) Thomas Worth (6) panel strip 125
531 (11/10/87) Thomas Worth(3) panel strip
537 (12/22/87) H.E. Patterson (3) panel strip
544 (2/9/88) Caran s'Ache (6) panel strip-r 37.50 75.00 100.00
555 (4/26/88) Thomas Worth (3) panel strip
556 (5/3/88) Thomas Worth (6) panel strip; Kit Carson-c 75.00 150.00 300.00
569 (8/21/88) Frank Bellew (2) panel strip
570 (8/9/88) Kemble (2) panel strip
571 (8/16/88) Kemble (2) panel strip; first Davy Crockett 75.00 150.00 300.00
Issues with just single panel cartoons 10.00 20.00 40.00

ZIM'S QUARTERLY (M)
(13-13/16x10-1/4", 60 pgs, color-c; most;y B&W, some interior color)
1 - Eugene Zimmerman 112.50 225.00 450.00
NOTE: *Approx. half sequential comic strips, other half single panel cartoons.*

For a free, lively e-mail discussion group of Victorian & Platinum Age comics collectors, fans, dealers, enthusiasts, and scholars you can join to look, listen, learn, and share at **PlatinumAgeComics@Yahoogroups.com/subscribe**.
Any addititions or corrections to this section are always welcome, very much encouraged and can be sent to **robert@BLBcomics.com** to be processed for next year's Guide.

THE PLATINUM AGE

The American Comic Book: 1883-1938

The Brownies. The Yellow Kid. Foxy Grandpa. Pore Lil Mose. The Katzenjammer Kids. Happy Hooligan. Little Sammy Sneeze. Mutt and Jeff. Barney Google. Bringing Up Father. Popeye. The Platinum Age, as it is called, saw the newspaper companies harness the power of comic characters – many of whom are still highly recognizable today – to drive sales, and it worked. During this period, comic strip reprint books became common, some selling millions of copies each.

Palmer Cox's Brownies created the road map that so many successful characters have followed into licensing. With the exception of new technologies that didn't exist back then, anything we've seen Mickey Mouse or Superman do in terms of licensed products was probably done first by the Brownies.

Since *The Overstreet Comic Book Price Guide* #29, we've featured a constantly evolving examination of this key period in comic book history. A newly revised article will be featured in our next edition. Until then, we hope you'll enjoy a few visual icons from this bygone era that continues to so richly influence us today.

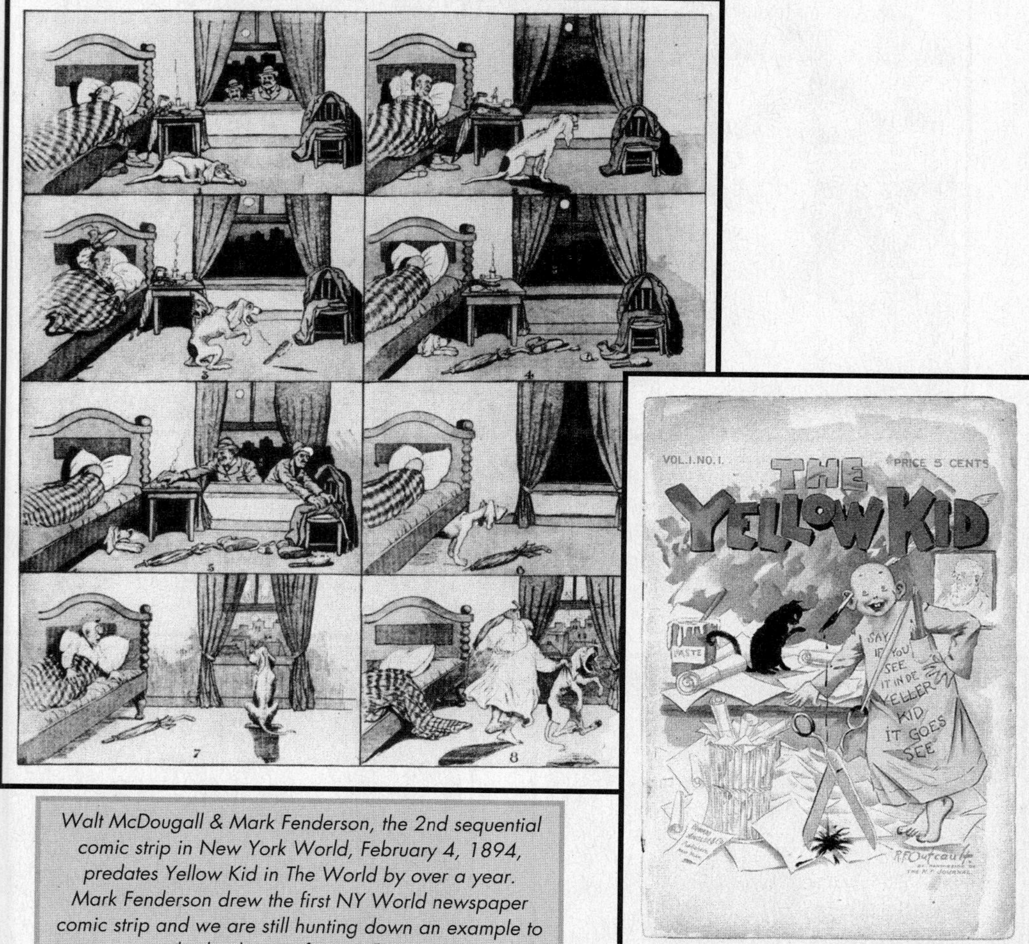

Walt McDougall & Mark Fenderson, the 2nd sequential comic strip in New York World, February 4, 1894, predates Yellow Kid in The World by over a year. Mark Fenderson drew the first NY World newspaper comic strip and we are still hunting down an example to display here in future editions.

The Yellow Kid #1, March 20, 1897, Street & Smith as Howard Ainslee, NY.

Pore Li'l Mose by Richard Outcault, 1901.
Bridges in between Yellow Kid and Buster Brown.
Becoming scarce because many copies have been cut up.

Katzenjammer Kids #1, 1902,
by Rudolph Dirks was inspired by Wilhelm Busch.

The Chicago Tribune introduced a straight super hero with obvious super strength called "Hugo Hercules" by the unknown artist J. Koerner. This Sunday strip ran September 7, 1902 through January 11, 1903 and ran only in this one paper. It is entirely possible a very young Chicago-resident named Philip Wylie read "Hugo" since that was the same name he gave his super-heroic main character in his much-later book The Gladiator (1930). Other appearances have Hugo running with almost super speed.

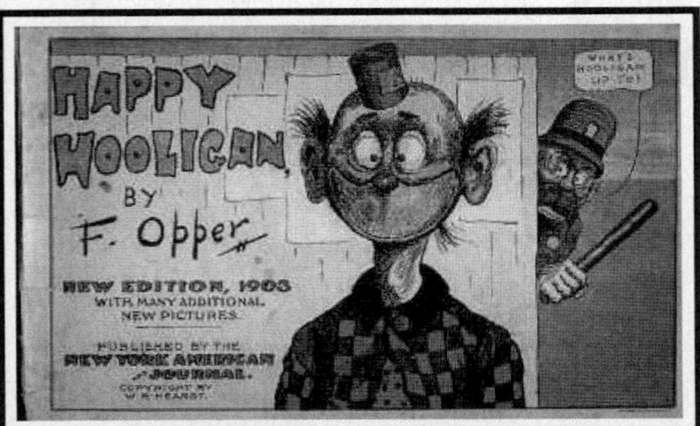

The second Happy Hooligan comic book,
1903, by Frederick Opper set a high standard.

Little Sammy Sneeze, 1905, by Winsor McCay.

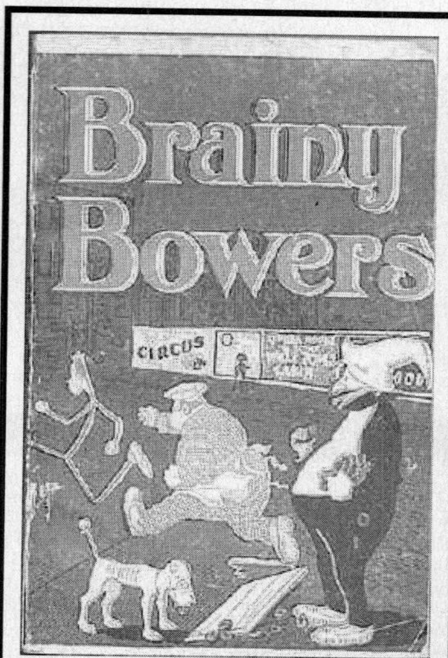

Brainy Bowers and Drowsy Duggan by R.W. Taylor 1905 © Star Publishing Co - appears to be the first daily newspaper reprint comic book compilation ever. As such, this is a sleeper investment comic book.

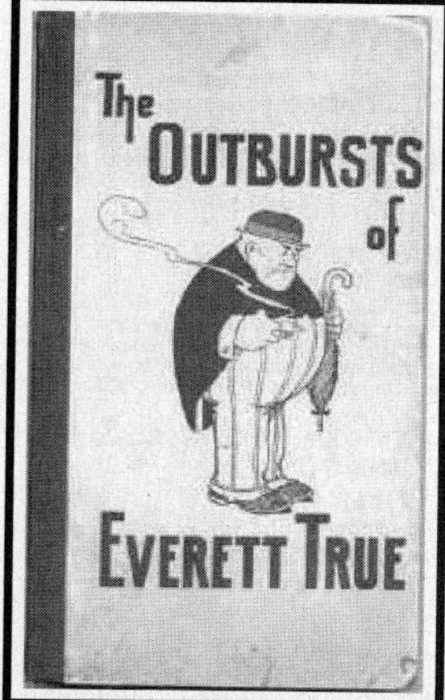

The Outbursts of Everett True. 2nd daily strip collection, published 1907

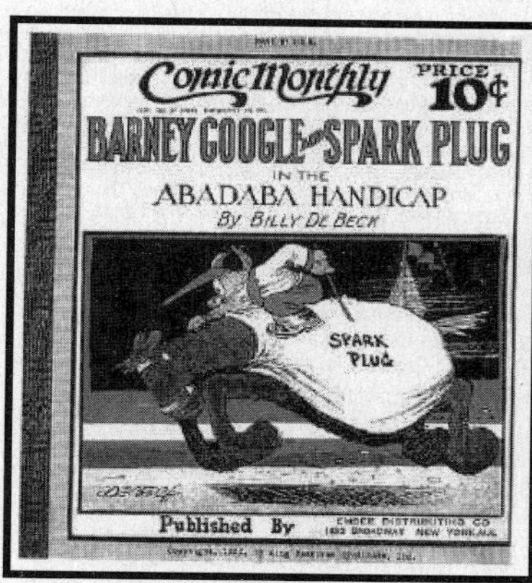

Comic Monthly #11 1922 the first 10¢ monthly newsstand comic book title.

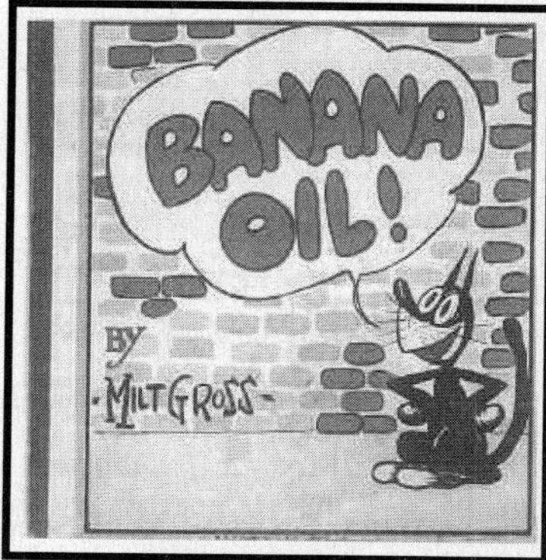

Banana Oil, a 1924 example of Cupples & Leon's then-revolutionary format from M.S. Publishers

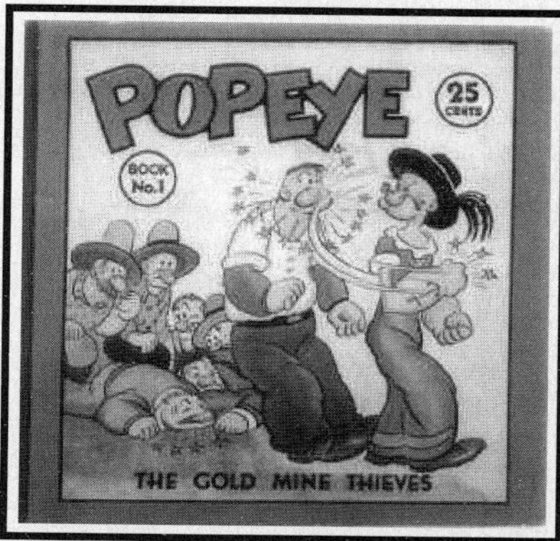

David McKay published the last of the 10x10 comic books in 1935 as Famous Funnies grew in popularity.

The Adventures of Willie Green
© Frank M. Acton

Alphonse and Gaston by Opper
1902 © Hearst's NY American & Journal

Banana Oil by Milt Gross
1924 © M.S. Publishing Company

GD2.0 FN6.0 VF8.0

COLLECTOR'S NOTE: The books listed in this section were published many decades before organized comics fandom began archiving and helping to preserve these fragile popular culture artifacts. Consequently, copies of most all of these comics do not often surface in Fine+ or better shape. eBay has proven after more than a decade that many items once considered rare actually are not, though they almost always are in higher grades. For items marked scarce, we are trying to ascertain how many copies might still be in existence. Your input is always welcome.

Most Platinum Age comic books are in the Fair to VG range. If you want to collect these only in high grade, your collection will be extremely small. The prices given for Good, Fine and Very Fine categories are for strictly graded editions. If you need help grading your item, we refer you to the grading section in the front of this price guide or contact the authors of the Platinum essay. Most measurements are in inches. A few measurements are in centimeters. The first dimension given is Height and the second is Width.

For ease of ascertaining the contents of each item of this listing, there is a code letter or two following most titles we have been adding in over the years to aid you. A helpful list of categories pertaining to these codes can be found at the beginning of the Victorian Age pricing sections.This section created, revised, and expanded by Robert Beerbohm and Richard Olson with able assistance from Ray Agricola, Jon Berk, Bill Blackbeard, Roy Bonario, Ray Bottorff Jr., Chris Brown, Alfredo Castelli, Darrell Coons, Sol Davidson, Leonardo De Sá, Scott Deschaine, Mitchell Duval, Joe Evans, Tom Gordon III, Bruce Hamilton, Andy Konkykru, Don Kurtz, Gabriel Laderman, Bruce Mason, Donald Puff, Robert Quesinberry, Steve Rowe, Randy Scott, John Snyder, Art Spiegelman, Steve Thompson, Joan Crosby Tibbets, Richard Samuel West, Doug Wheeler, Richard Wright and Craig Yoe.

ADVENTURES OF EVA, PORA AND TED (M)
Evaporated Milk Association: 1932 (5x15", 16 pgs, B&W)
nn - By Steve 10.00 30.00 70.00
NOTE: *Appears to have had green, blue or white paper cover versions.*

ADVENTURES OF HAWKSHAW (N) (See Hawkshaw The Detective)
The Saalfield Publishing Co.: 1917 (9-3/4x13-1/2", 48 pgs., color & two-tone)
nn - By Gus Mager (only 24 pgs. of strips, reverse of each pg. is blank) 50.00 175.00 300.00
nn - 1927 Reprints 1917 issue 30.00 150.00 260.00
NOTE: *Started Feb 23, 1913-Sept 4, 1922, then begins again Dec 13, 1931-Feb 11, 1952.*

ADVENTURES OF SLIM AND SPUD, THE (M)
Prairie Farmer Publ. Co.: 1924 (3-3/4x 9-3/4", 104 pgs., B&W strip reprints)
nn 21.00 84.00 150.00
NOTE: *Illustrated mailing envelope exists postmarked out of Chicago, add 50%.*

ADVENTURES OF WILLIE WINTERS, THE (O,P)
Kelloggs Toasted Corn Flake Co.: 1912 (6-7/8x9-1/2", 20 pgs, full color)
nn - By Byron Williams & Dearborn Melvill 54.00 189.00 350.00

ADVENTURES OF WILLIE GREEN, THE (N) (see The Willie Green Comics)
Frank M. Acton Co.: 1915 (50¢, 52 pgs, 8-1/2X16", B&W, soft-c)
Book 1 - By Harris Brown; strip-r 54.00 189.00 350.00

A. E. F. IN CARTOONS BY WALLY, THE (N)
Don Sowers & Co.: 1933 (12x10-1/8", 88 pgs, hardcover B&W)
nn - By Wally Wallgren (WW One Stars & Stripes-r) 25.00 90.00 150.00

AFTER THE TOWN GOES DRY (I)
The Howell Publishing Co, Chicago: 1919 (48 pgs, 6-1/2x4", hardbound two color-c)
nn - By Henry C. Taylor; illus by Frank King 25.00 75.00 150.00

AIN'T IT A GRAND & GLORIOUS FEELING? (N) (Also see Mr. & Mrs.)
Whitman Publishing Co.: 1922 (9x9-3/4", 52 pgs., stiff cardboard-c)
nn - 1921 daily strip-r; B&W, color-c; Briggs-a 36.00 143.00 250.00
nn -(9x9-1/2", 28pgs., stiff cardboard-c)-Sunday strip-r in color (inside front-c says "More of the Married Life of Mr. & Mrs".) 36.00 143.00 250.00
NOTE: *Strip started in 1917; This is the 2nd Whitman comic book, after Brigg's MR. & MRS.*

ALL THE FUNNY FOLKS (I)
World Press Today, Inc.: 1926 (11-1/2x8-1/2", 112 pgs., color, hard-c)
nn-Barney Google, Spark Plug, Jiggs & Maggie, Tillie The Toiler, Happy Hooligan, Hans & Fritz, Toots & Casper, etc. 100.00 400.00 700.00
With Dust Jacket By Louis Biedermann 200.00 800.00 1600.00
NOTE: *Booklength race horse story masterfully enveloping all major King Features characters.*

ALPHONSE AND GASTON AND THEIR FRIEND LEON (N)
Hearst's New York American & Journal: 1902,1903 (10x15-1/4", Sunday strip reprints in color)
nn - (1902) - By Frederick Opper (scarce) 500.00 1800.00 -
nn - (1903) - By Frederick Opper (scarce) (72 pages) 500.00 1800.00 -
NOTE: *Strip ran Sept 22, 1901to at least July 17, 1904.*

ALWAYS BELITTLIN' (see Skippy; That Rookie From the 13th Squad; Between Shots)
Henry Holt & Co.: 1927 (6x8", hard-c with DJ,
nn -By Percy Crosby (text with cartoons) 43.00 172.00 300.00

ALWAYS BELITTLIN' (I) (see Skippy; That Rookie From the 13th Squad, Between Shots)
Percy Crosby, Publisher: 1933 (14 1/4 x 11", 72 pgs, hard-c, B&W)
nn - By Percy Crosby 43.00 172.00 300.00
NOTE: *Self-published; primarily political cartoons with text pages denouncing prohibition's gang warfare effects and cuts in the national defense budget as Crosby saw war looming in Europe and with Japan.*

GD2.0 FN6.0 VF8.0

AMERICAN-JOURNAL-EXAMINER JOKE BOOK SPECIAL SUPPLEMENT (O)
New York American: 1911-12 (12 x 9 3/4", 16 pgs) (known issues) (Very Rare)
1 Tom Powers Joke Book(12/10/11) 80.00 280.00 -
2 Mutt & Jeff Joke Book (Bud Fisher 12/17/11) 100.00 350.00 -
3 TAD's Joke Book (Thomas Dorgan 12/24/11) 80.00 300.00 -
4 F. Opper's Joke Book (Frederick Burr Opper 12/31/11) (contains Happy Hooligan) 100.00 350.00 -
5 not known to exist
6 Swinnerton's Joke Book (Jimmy Swinnerton 01/14/12) (contains Mr. Jack) 100.00 350.00 -
7 The Monkey's Joke Book (Gus Mager 01/21/12) (contains Sherlocko the Monk) 100.00 350.00 -
8 Joys And Glooms Joke Book (T. E. Powers 01/28/12) 80.00 280.00 -
9 The Dingbat Family's Joke Book (George Herriman 02/04/12) (contains early Krazy Kat & Ignatz) 200.00 700.00 -
10 Valentine Joke Book, A (Opper, Howarth, Mager, T. E. Powers 02/11/12) 80.00 280.00 -
11 Little Hatchet Joke Book (T. E. Powers 02/18/12) 80.00 280.00 -
12 Jungle Joke Book (Dirks, McCay 02/25/12) 100.00 400.00 -
13 The Hayseeds Joke Book (03/03/12) 80.00 280.00 -
14 Married Life Joke Book (T.E. Powers 03/10/12) 80.00 280.00 -
NOTE: *These were insert newspaper supplements similar to Eisner's later Spirit sections. A Valentine Joke Book recently surfaced from Hearst's Boston Sunday American proving that other cities besides New York City had these special supplements. Each issue also contains work by other cartoonists besides the cover featured creator and those already listed above such as Sidney Smith, Winsor McCay, Hy Mayer, Grace Weiderseim (later Drayton), others.*

AMERICA'S BLACK & WHITE BOOK 100 Pictured Reasons Why We Are At War (N,S)
Cupples & Leon: 1917 (10 3/4 x 8", 216 pgs)
nn - W. A. Rogers (New York Herald-r) 32.00 114.00 195.00

AMONG THE FOLKS IN HISTORY
Rand McNally Print Guild: 1935 (192 pgs, 8-1/2x9-1/2", hard-c, B&W)
nn - By Gaar Williams 21.00 84.00 150.00

AMONG THE FOLKS IN HISTORY
The Book and Print Guild: 1935 (200 pgs, 8-1/2x9-1/2:,
nn - By Gaar Williams 21.00 84.00 150.00
NOTE: *Both the above are evidently different editions and contain largely full-page, single panel cartoons similar to Briggs' work of that sort. 8 or 10 pages are broken into panels, usually with a this is how it was in the old days, this is how it is today theme.*

ANGELIC ANGELINA (N)
Cupples & Leon Company: 1909 (11-1/2x17", 56 pgs., 2 colors)
nn - By Munson Paddock 67.00 233.00 400.00
NOTE: *Strip ran March 22, 1908-Feb 7, 1909.*

ANDY GUMP, HIS LIFE STORY (I)
The Reilly & Lee Co, Chicago: 1924 (192 pgs, hardbound)
nn - By Sidney Smith (over 100 illustrations) 20.00 80.00 150.00

ANIMAL CIRCUS, THE (from Puggery Wee)
Rand McNally + Company: 1908 (48 pgs, 11x8-1/2", color-c, 3-color insides)
nn - By unknown 20.00 80.00 150.00
NOTE: *Illustrated verse, many pages with multiple illustrations.*

ANIMAL SERIALS
T. Y. Crowell: 1906 (9x6-7/8", 214 pgs, hard-c, B&W)
nn - By E Warde Blaisdell 20.00 80.00 150.00
NOTE: *Multi-page comic strip stories. Reprints of Sunday strip "Bunny Bright He's All-Right".*

A NOBODY'S SCRAP BOOK
Frederik A. Stokes Co., New York: 1900 (11" x 8-5/8", hard-c, color)
nn- (Scarce) 67.00 233.00 400.00
NOTE: *Designed in England, printed in Holland, on English paper -- which likely explains the mispelling of Frederick Stokes' name. Highly fragile paper. Strips and cartoons, all by the same unidentified artist, "A Nobody", almost certainly reprinted from somewhere, as they are very professional.*

AT THE BOTTOM OF THE LADDER (M)
J.P. Lippincott Company: 1926 (11x8-1/4", 296 pgs, hardcover, B&W)
nn - By Camillus Kessler 45.00 157.50 300.00
NOTE: *Hilarious single panel cartoons showing first jobs of then important "captains of industry."*

AUTO FUN, PICTURES AND COMMENTS FROM "LIFE"
Thomas Y. Crowell & Co.: 1905 (152 pgs, 9x7", hard-c, B&W)
nn -By various 45.00 157.00 300.00
NOTE: *The cover just has "Auto Fun" but the title page also has the subheading listed here. This is similar to other reprint books of Life cartoons printed in the guide. Largely single panel cartoons but also several sequential. One or more cartoons by Kemble, Levering, Dirks, Flagg, Sullivant. Sequential cartoons by Kemble, Levering, Sullivant, and the highpoint, a 2 pg 6 panel piece by Winsor McCay.*

BANANA OIL (N) (see also HE DONE HER WRONG)

Barney Google and Spark Plug #1
© C&L

Bill the Boy Artist's Book by Ed Payne
1910 © C.M. Clark Publishing Co

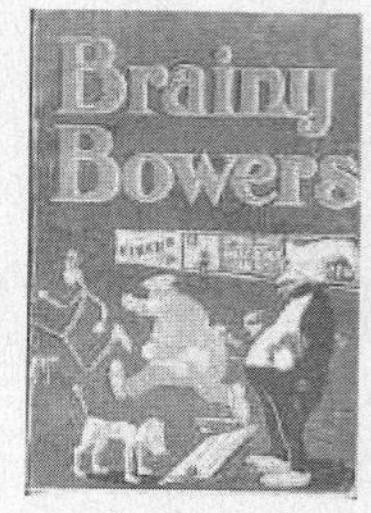

Brainy Bowers and Drowsy Duggan by R.W. Taylor
1905 © Star Publishing Co. - the first daily reprints

GD2.0 FN6.0 VF8.0

MS Publ. Co.: 1924 (9-7/8x10", 52 pgs., B&W)

nn - Milt Gross comic strips; not reprints 150.00 450.00 750.00

BARKER'S ILLUSTRATED ALMANAC (O,P,S) (See Barkers in Victorian Era section)
Barker, Moore & Mein Medicine Co: 1900-1932+ (36 pgs, B&W, color paper-c)

1900-1932+ (7x5-7/8") 20.00 70.00 125.00

BARKER'S "KOMIC" PICTURE SOUVENIR (P,S) (see Barker's in Victorian)
Barker, Moore & Mein Medicine Co: nd (Parts 1-3, 1901-1903; Parts 1-4, 1906+) (color cardboard-c, B&W interior, 50 pages)

Parts 1-3 (Rare, earliest printing, nd (1901)) 60.00 300.00 600.00
NOTE: *Same cover as 4th edition in Victorian Age Section, except has "Part 1", "Part 2", or "Part 3" printed in the blank space beneath the crate on which central figure is sitting. States "Edition in 3 Parts" on the first interior page, beneath the picture of the Barker's Building.*
Parts 1-3 (nd, c1901-1903) 40.00 200.00 400.00
NOTE: *New cover art on all Parts. States "Edition in 3 Parts" on the first interior page.*
Parts 1-4 (nd, c1906+) 25.00 100.00 300.00
NOTE: *States "Edition in 4 Parts" on the first interior page. Various printings known.These have been confirmed as premium comic books, predating the Buster Brown premiums. They reprint advertising cartoons from Barker's Illustrated Almanac. For the 50 page booklets by this same name, numbered as "Part"s, without exception, were published after 1900. Some editions are found to have 54 pages.*

BARNEY GOOGLE AND SPARK PLUG (N) (See **Comic Monthly**)
Cupples & Leon Co.: 1923 - No.6, 1928 (9-7/8x9-3/4"; 52 pgs., B&W, daily-r)

1 (nn)-By Billy DeBeck 60.00 240.00 450.00
2-4 (#5 & #6 do not exist) 46.00 186.00 350.00
NOTE: *Started June 17, 1919 as newspaper strip; Spark Plug introduced July 17, 1922; strip still running making it one of the oldest still in existence.*

BART'S CARTOONS FOR 1902 FROM THE MINNEAPOLIS JOURNAL (N,S)
Minneapolis Journal: 1903 (11x9", 102 pgs, paperback, B&W)

nn - By Charles L. Bartholomew 28.00 99.00 170.00

BELIEVE IT OR NOT! by Ripley (N,S)
Simon & Schuster: 1929 (8x 5-1/4", 68 pgs, red, B&W cover, B&W interior)

nn - By Robert Ripley (strip-r text & art) 40.00 120.00 240.00
NOTE: *1929 was the first printing of many reprintings . Strip began Dec 19, 1918 and is still running.*

BEN WEBSTER (N)
Standard Printing Company: 1928-1931 (13-3/4x4-7/16", 768 pgs, soft-c)

1 - "Bound to Win" 40.00 120.00 280.00
2 - "...in old Mexico 40.00 120.00 280.00
3 - "...At Wilderness Lake 40.00 120.00 280.00
4 - "...in the Oil Fields 40.00 120.00 280.00
NOTE: *Self Published by Edwin Alger, also contains fan's letter pages.*

BIG SMOKER
W.T. Blackwell & Co.: 1908 (16 pgs, 5-1/2x3-1/2", color-c & interior)

nn - By unknown 12.00 48.00 80.00
NOTE: *Stated reprint of 1878 version. no known copies yet of original printing.*

BILLY BOUNCE (I)
Donohue & Co.: 1906 (288 pgs, hardbound)

nn - By W.W. Denslow & Dudley Bragdon 150.00 525.00 900.00
NOTE: *Billy Bounce was created in 1901 as a comic strip by W. W. Denslow (strip ran from 1901 NOV 11 to 1905 DEC 3), but the series is best remembered in the C. W. Kahles version (from 1902 SEP 28). Denslow resumed his character in the above illustrated book.*

BILLY HON'S FAMOUS CARTOON BOOK (H)
Wasley Publishing Co.: 1927 (7-1/2x10", 68 pgs, softbound wraparound)

nn - By Billy Hon 12.00 48.00 80.00

BILLY THE BOY ARTIST'S BOOK OF FUNNY PICTURES (N)
C.M.Clark Publishing Co.: 1910 (9x12", hardcover-c, Boston Globe strip-r)

nn - By Ed Payne 125.00 400.00 750.00
NOTE: *This long lived strip ran in **The Boston Globe** from Nov 5 1899-Jan 7 1955; one of the longer run strips.*

BILLY THE BOY ARTIST'S PAINTING BOOK OF FUNNY PICTURES
(known to exist; more data required) – – –

BIRD CENTER CARTOONS: A Chronicle of Social Happenings (N,S)
A. C. McClurg & Co.: 1904 (12-3/8x9-1/2", 216 pgs, hardcover, B&W, single panels)

nn - By John McCutcheon 40.00 140.00 260.00
NOTE: *Strip began in **The Chicago Tribune** in 1903. Satirical cartoons and text concerning a mythical town.*

BLASTS FROM THE RAM'S HORN
The Rams Horn Company: 1902 (330 pgs, 7x9", B&W)

nn - By various 20.00 70.00 120.00
NOTE: *Cartoons reprinted from what was, apparently, a religious newspaper. Many cartoons by Frank Beard. Mostly single panel but occasionally sequential. Allegorical cartoons similar to the Christian Cartoons book. This book mixes cartoons and text sort of like the Caricature books. One or more cartoons on every page.*

BOBBY THATCHER & TREASURE CAVE (N)
Altemus Co.: 1932 (9x7", 86 pgs., B&W, hard-c)

nn - Reprints; Storm-a 54.00 189.00 400.00

BOBBY THATCHER'S ROMANCE (N)
The Bell Syndicate/Henry Altemus Co.: 1931 (8-3/4x7", color cover, B&W)

nn - By Storm 54.00 189.00 400.00

BOOK OF CARTOONS, A (M,S)
Edward T. Miller: 1903 (12-1/4x9-1/4", 120 pgs, hardcover, B&W)

nn - By Harry J. Westerman (Ohio State Journal-r) 20.00 70.00 120.00

BOOK OF DRAWINGS BY A.B. FROST, A (M,S)
P.F. Collier & Son: 1904 (15-3/8 x 11", 96 pgs, B&W)

nn - A.B. Frost 50.00 100.00 300.00
NOTE: *Pages alternate verses by Wallace Irwin and full-page plated by A.B.Frost. 39 plates.*

BOTTLE, THE (E) (see Victorian Age section for earlier printings)
Gowans & Gray, London & Glasgow: June 1905 (3-3/4x6", 72 pgs, printed one side only, paper cover, B&W)

nn - 1st printing (June 1905) 17.50 35.00 70.00
nn - 2nd printing (March 1906) 17.50 35.00 70.00
nn - 3rd printing (January 1911) 17.50 35.00 70.00
NOTE: *By George Cruikshank. Reprints both THE BOTTLE and THE DRUNKARD'S CHILDREN. Cover is text only - no cover art.*

BOTTLE, THE (E)
Frederick A. Stokes: nd (c1906) (3-3/4x6", 72 pgs, printed one side only, paper-c, B&W)

nn- by George Cruikshank 17.50 35.00 70.00
NOTE: *Reprint of the Gowans & Gray edition. Reprints both THE BOTTLE and THE DRUNKARD'S CHILDREN. Cover is text only - no cover art.*

BOYS AND FOLKS (N).
George H. Dornan Company: 1917 (10-1/4 x 8-1/4", 232 pgs. (single-sided), B&W strip-r.

nn - By Webster 21.00 64.00 150.00
NOTE: *Four sections: Life's Darkest Moments, Mostly About Folks, The Thrill That Comes Once in a Lifetime, and Our Boyhood Ambitions. Most are single-panel cartoons, but there are some sequential comic strips.*

BOY'S & GIRLS' BIG PAINTING BOOK OF INTERESTING COMIC PICTURES (N)
M. A. Donohue & Co.: 1914-16 (9x15, 70 pgs)

nn - By Carl "Bunny" Schultze (Foxy Grandpa-r) 81.00 284.00 –
#2 (1914) 81.00 284.00 –
#337 (1914) (sez "Big Painting & Drawing Book") 81.00 284.00 –
nn - (1916) (sez "Big Painting Book")(9-1/4x15") 81.00 284.00 –
NOTE: *These are all **Foxy Grandpa** items.*

BRAIN LEAKS: Dialogues of Mutt & Flea (N)
O. K. Printing Co. (Rochester Evening Times): 1911 (76 pgs, 6-5/8x4-5/8, hard-c, B&W)

nn - By Leo Edward O'Melia; newspaper strip-r 29.00 100.00 171.00

BRAINY BOWERS AND DROWSY DUGGAN (N)
Star Publishing: 1905 (7-1/4 x 4-9/16", 98 pgs., blue, brown & white color cover, B&W interior, 25¢) (daily strip-r 1902-04 Chicago Daily News)

#74 - By R. W. Taylor (Scarce) 500.00 1700.00 –
NOTE: *Part of a series of Atlantic Library Heart Series. Strip begins in 1901 and runs thru 1915. Taylor also created Yen the Janitor for the **New York World.***

BRAIN BOWERS AND DROWSY DUGAN (N)
Max Stein Pub. House, Chicago: 1905 (6-3/16x4-3/8", 64 pgs, B&W)

nn - By R.W. Taylor (Scarce) 500.00 1700.00 –
NOTE: *A coverless copy of this surfaced on eBay in 2002 selling for $700.00.;*

BRAINY BOWERS AND DROWSY DUGGAN GETTING ON IN THE WORLD WITH NO VISIBLE MEANS OF SUPPORT (STORIES TOLD IN PICTURES TO MAKE THEIR TELLING SHORT) (N)
Max Stein/Star Publishing: 1905 (7-3/8x5 1/8", 164 pgs, slick black, red & tan color cover, interior newsprint) (daily strip-r 1902-04 Chicago Daily News)

nn - By R. W. Taylor (Scarce) 500.00 1700.00 –
nn - Possible hard cover edition also? – – –
NOTE: *These Brainy Bowers editions are the earliest known daily newspaper strip reprint books.*

BRINGING UP FATHER (N)
Star Co. (King Features): 1917 (5-1/2x16-1/2", 100 pgs., B&W, cardboard-c)

nn - (Scarcer)-Daily strip- by George McManus 158.00 553.00 950.00

BRINGING UP FATHER (N)
Cupples & Leon Co.: 1919 - No. 26, 1934 (10x10", 52 pgs., B&W, stiff cardboard-c)
(No. 22 is 9-1/4x9-1/2")

1-Daily strip-r by George McManus in all 25.00 100.00 260.00
2-10 25.00 100.00 250.00
11-20 40.00 200.00 375.00
21-26 (Scarcer) 60.00 300.00 550.00
The Big Book 1 (1926)-Thick book (hardcover, 142 pgs.) 127.00 508.00 1000.00
w/dust jacket (rare) 183.00 732.00 1325.00
The Big Book 2 (1929) 96.00 384.00 700.00
w/dust jacket (rare) 183.00 732.00 1325.00
NOTE: *The Big Books contain 3 regular issues rebound.* Strip began Jan 2 1913-May 28 2000

BRINGING UP FATHER, THE TROUBLE OF (N)
Embee Publ. Co.: 1921 (9-3/4x15-3/4", 46 pgs, Sunday-r in color)

nn - (Rare) 100.00 350.00 600.00
NOTE: *Ties with Mutt & Jeff (EmBee) and Jimmie Dugan And The Reg'lar Fellers (C&L) as the last of the*

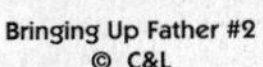

Bringing Up Father #2
© C&L

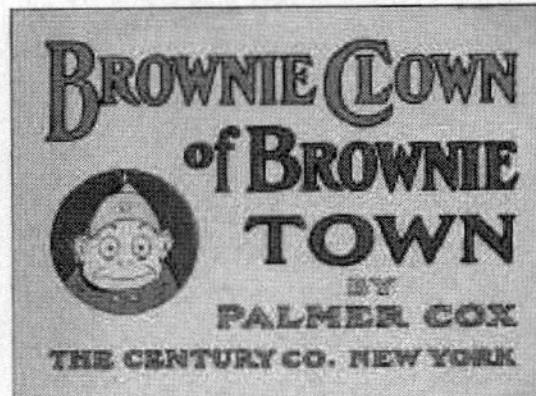

Brownie Clown of Brownie Town
© The Century Co.

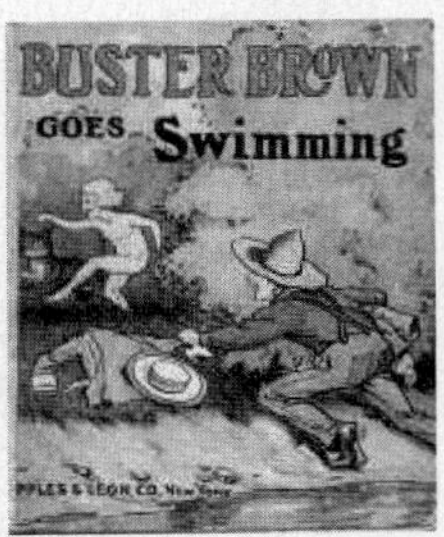

Buster Brown Nuggets - Goes Swimming
1907 © Cupples & Leon

GD2.0 FN6.0 VF8.0

oblong size era. This was self published by George McManus.

BRINGING UP FATHER (N) (see SAGARA'S ENGLISH CARTOONS
Publisher unknown (actually, unreadable), Tokyo: October 1924 (9-7/8" x 7-1/2", 90 pgs, color hard-c, B&W)

nn- (Scarce) by George McManus C&A (no known sales)
NOTE: *Published in Tokyo, Japan, with all strips in both English and Japanese, to facilitate learning English. Introduction by George McManus. Scarce in USA.*

BRONX BALLADS (I)
Simon & Schuster, NY: 1927 (9-1/2x7-1/4", hard-c, B&W)

nn - By Robert Simon and Harry Hershfield 36.00 143.00 250.00

BROWNIES, THE (not sequential comic strips)
The Century Co.: 1887 - 1914 (all came with dust jackets; add $100-150 to value if original dust jacket is included and intact)

Book 1 - The Brownies: Their Book (1887) 200.00 850.00 1320.00
Book 2 - Another Brownies Book (1890) 150.00 635.00 1000.00
Book 3 - The Brownies at Home (1893) 125.00 530.00 825.00
Book 4 - The Brownies Around the World (1894) 100.00 425.00 660.00
Book 5 - The Brownies Through the Union (1895) 100.00 425.00 660.00
Book 6 - The Brownies Abroad (1899) 100.00 425.00 660.00
Book 7 - The Brownies in the Philippines (1904) 100.00 425.00 660.00
Book 8 - The Brownies' Latest Adventures (1910) 100.00 425.00 660.00
Book 9 - The Brownies Many More Nights (1914) 100.00 425.00 660.00
...Raid on Kleinmaier Bros. (c. 1910, 16 pages) Kleinmaier Bros. Clothing, Marion, Ohio (no known sales)

BROWNIE CLOWN OF BROWNIE TOWN (N)
The Century Co.: 1908 (6-7/8 x 9-3/8", 112 pgs, color hardcover & interior)

nn - By Palmer Cox (rare; 1907 newspaper comic strip-r) 250.00 800.00 1400.00
NOTE: *The Brownies created 1883 in* **St Nicholas Magazine.**

BUDDY TUCKER & HIS FRIENDS (N) (Also see **Buster Brown Nuggets**)
Cupples & Leon Co.: 1906 (11-5/8 x17", 58 pgs, color) (Scarce)

nn - 1905 Sunday strip-r by R. F. Outcault 500.00 1500.00 2500.00
NOTE: *Strip began Apr 30, 1905 thru at least Oct 1905.*

BUFFALO BILL'S PICTURE STORIES
Street & Smith Publications: 1909 (Soft cardboard cover)

nn - Very rare 67.00 233.00 400.00

BUGHOUSE FABLES (N) (see also **Comic Monthly**)
Embee Distributing Co. (King Features): 1921 (10¢, 4x4-1/2", 48 pgs.)

1-By Barney Google (Billy DeBeck) 46.00 186.00 350.00

BUG MOVIES (O) (Also see Clancy The Cop & Deadwood Gulch)
Dell Publishing Co.: 1931 (9-13/16x9-7/8", 52 pgs., B&W)

nn - Original material; Stookie Allen-a 150.00 300.00 500.00

BULL
Bull Publishing Company, New York: No.1, March, 1916 - No.12, Feb, 1917 (10 cents, 10-3/4x8-3/4", 24 pgs, color paper-c, B&W)

1-12 (Very Rare) – – –
NOTE: *Pro-German, Anti-British cartoon/humor monthly, whose goal was to keep the U.S. neutral and out of World War I. We know of no copies which have sold in the past few years.*

BUNNY'S BLUE BOOK (see also Foxy Grandpa) (N)
Frederick A. Stokes Co.: 1911 (10x15, 60¢)

nn - By Carl "Bunny" Schultze strip-r 100.00 350.00 –

BUNNY'S RED BOOK (see also Foxy Grandpa) (N)
Frederick A. Stokes Co.: 1912 (10-1/4x15-3/4", 64 pgs.)

nn - By Carl "Bunny" Schultze strip-r 100.00 350.00 –

BUNNY'S GREEN BOOK (see also Foxy Grandpa) (N)
Frederick A. Stokes Co.: 1913 (10x15")

nn - By Carl "Bunny" Schultze 100.00 350.00 –

BUSTER BROWN (C) (Also see Brown's Blue Ribbon Book of Jokes and Jingles & Buddy Tucker & His Friends)
Frederick A. Stokes Co.: 1903 - 1916 (Daily strip-r in color)

1903...& His Resolutions (11-1/4x16", 66 pgs.) by R. F. Outcault (Rare)-1st nationally distributed comic. Distr. through Sears & Roebuck 1600.00 5500.00 –
1904...His Dog Tige & Their Troubles (11-1/4x16-1/4", 66 pgs.)(Rare) 600.00 1875.00 –
1905...Pranks (11-1/4x16-3/8", 66 pgs.) 400.00 1450.00 –
1906...Antics (11x16-3/8", 66 pgs.) 400.00 1450.00 –
1906...And Company (11x16-1/2", 66 pgs.) 300.00 1050.00 –
1906...Mary Jane & Tige (11-1/4x16, 66 pgs.) 300.00 1050.00 –
NOTE: ***Yellow Kid*** *pictured on two pages.*
1908 Collection of Buster Brown Comics 250.00 835.00 –
1909 Outcault's Real Buster and The Only Mary Jane (11x16, 66 pgs, Stokes) 250.00 835.00 –
1910...Up to Date (10-1/8x15-3/4", 66 pgs.) 208.00 729.00 1315.00
1911...Fun And Nonsense (10-1/8x15-3/4", 66 pgs.) 183.00 642.00 1150.00
1912...The Fun Maker (10-1/8x15-3/4", 66 pgs.) -Yellow Kid (4 pgs.) 183.00 642.00 1150.00
1913...At Home (10-1/8x15-3/4", 56 pgs.) 167.00 583.00 1050.00
1914...And Tige Here Again (10x16, 62 pgs, Stokes) 153.00 535.00 1000.00
1915...And His Chum Tige (10x16, Stokes) 153.00 535.00 1000.00
1916...The Little Rogue (10-1/8x15-3/4", 62 pgs.) 162.00 567.00 1025.00
1917...And the Cat (5-1/2x 6-1/2, 26 pgs, Stokes) 115.00 402.00 750.00
1917...Disturbs the Family (5-1/2x 6 1/2, 26 pgs, Stokes
NOTE: *Story featuring statue of "the Chinese Yellow Kid"* 115.00 402.00 750.00
1917...The Real Buster Brown (5-1/2x 6 -/2, 26 pgs, Stokes 115.00 402.00 750.00

Frederick A. Stokes Co. Hard Cover Series (I)

...Abroad (1904, 10-1/4x8", 86 pgs., B&W, hard-c)-R. F. Outcault-a (Rare) 200.00 700.00 1260.00
...Abroad (1904, B&W, 67 pgs.)-R. F. Outcault-a 200.00 700.00 1260.00
NOTE: *Buster Brown Abroad is not an actual comic book, but prose with illustrations.*
..."Tige" His Story 1905 (10x8", 63 pgs., B&W) (63 illos.)
nn-By RF Outcault 143.00 500.00 –
...My Resolutions 1906 (10x8", B&W, 68 pgs.)-R.F. Outcault-a (Rare) 233.00 817.00 1475.00
...Autobiography 1907 (10x8", B&W, 71 pgs.) (16 color plates & 36 B&W illos) 67.00 233.00 440.00
...And Mary Jane's Painting Book 1907 (10x13-1/4", 60 pgs, both card & hardcover versions exist
nn-RFO (first printing blank on top of cover) 67.00 233.00 440.00
First Series- this is a reprint if it says First Series 67.00 233.00 440.00
Volume Two - By RFO 67.00 233.00 440.00
... My Resolutions by Buster Brown (1907, 68 pgs, small size, cardboard covers) scarce 43.00 150.00 285.00
NOTE: *Not actual comic book per se, but a compilation of the Resolutions panels found at the end of Outcault's Buster Brown newspaper strips.*

BUSTER BROWN (N)
Cupples & Leon Co./N. Y. Herald Co.: 1906 - 1917 (11x17", color, strip-r)
NOTE: *Early issues by R. F. Outcault; most C&L editions are not by Outcault.*

1906...His Dog Tige And Their Jolly Times (11-3/8x16-5/8", 68 pgs.) 300.00 1100.00 1900.00
1906...His Dog Tige & Their Jolly Times (11x16, 46 pgs.) 163.00 600.00 1025.00
1907...Latest Frolics (11-3/8x16-5/8", 66 pgs., r/'05-06 strips) 163.00 600.00 1025.00
1908...Amusing Capers (58 pgs.) 129.00 475.00 815.00
1909...The Busy Body (11-3/8x16-5/8", 62 pgs.) 129.00 475.00 815.00
1910...On His Travels (11x16", 58 pgs.) 115.00 402.00 750.00
1911...Happy Days (11-3/8x16-5/8", 58 pgs.) 115.00 402.00 750.00
1912...In Foreign Lands (10x16", 58 pgs) 115.00 402.00 750.00
1913...And His Pets (11x16", 58 pgs.) STOKES???? 115.00 402.00 750.00
1913...And His Pets (26 pg partial reprint) – – –
1914...Funny Tricks (11-3/8x16-5/8", 58 pgs.) 115.00 402.00 750.00
1916...At Play (10x16, 58 pgs) 115.00 402.00 750.00

BUSTER BROWN NUGGETS (N)
Cupples & Leon Co./N.Y.Herald Co.: 1907 (1905, 7-1/2x6-1/2", 36 pgs., color, strip-r, hard-c)(By R. F. Outcault) (NOTE: books are all unnumbered)

Buster Brown Goes Fishing, Goes Swimming, Plays Indian, Goes Shooting, Plays Cowboy, On Uncle Jack's Farm, Tige And the Bull, And Uncle Buster 39.00 137.00 275.00
Buddy Tucker Meets Alice in Wonderland 56.00 200.00 400.00
Buddy Tucker Visits The House That Jack Built 39.00 137.00 275.00

BUSTER BROWN MUSLIN SERIES (N)
Saalfield: 1907 (also contain copyright Cupples & Leon)

...Goes Fishing, Plays Indian, And the Donkey (1907, 6-7/8x6-1/8", 24 pgs., color)-r/1905 Sunday comics page by Outcault (Rare) 50.00 175.00 315.00
...Plays Cowboy (1907, 6-3/4x6", 10 pgs., color)-r/1905 Sunday comics page by Outcault (Rare) 50.00 175.00 315.00
NOTE: *These are muslin versions of the C&L BB Nugget series. Muslin books are all cloth books, made to be washable so as not easily stained/destroyed by very young children. The Muslin books contain one strip each (the title strip), to the more common NUGGET's three strips.*

BUSTER BROWN PREMIUMS (Advertising premium booklets)
Various Publishers: 1904 - 1912 (3x5" to 5x7"; sizes vary)

American Fruit Product Company, Rochester, NY

Buster Brown Duffy's 1842 Cider (1904, 7x5". 12 pgs, C.E. Sherin Co, NYC)
nn - By R. F. Outcault (scarce) 100.00 350.00 600.00

The Brown Shoe Company, St. Louis, USA
Set of five books (5x7", 16 pgs., color)

Brown's Blue Ribbon Book of Jokes and Jingles Book 1 (nn, 1904)-By R. F. Outcault; Buster Brown & Tige, Little Tommy Tucker, Jack & Jill, Little Boy Blue, Dainty Jane; The Yellow Kid app. on back-c (1st BB comic book premium) 300.00 1050.00 1900.00

Buster Brown Nuggets -Buster Brown Plays Cowboy © C&L

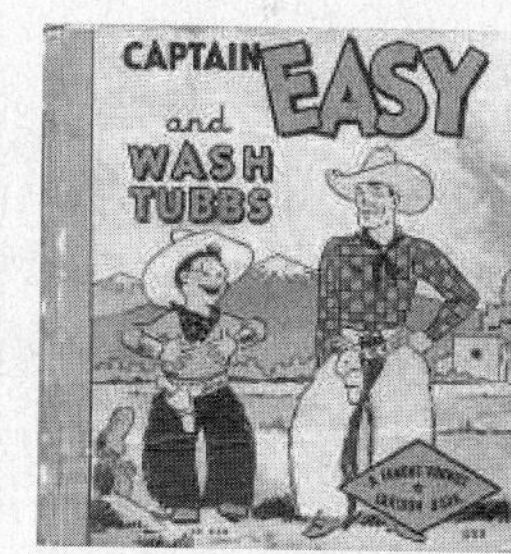

Captain Easy and Wash Tubbs by Roy Crane 1934 © Whitman Famous Comics Cartoon Book

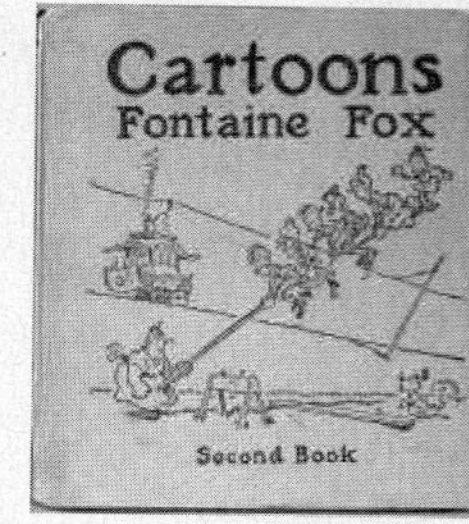

Cartoons Fontaine Fox Second Book early 1920s © Harper & Bros, NY

GD2.0 FN6.0 VF8.0

Buster Brown's Blue Ribbon Book of Jokes and Jingles Book 2 (1905)-Original color art by Outcault 200.00 600.00 1260.00
Buster's Book of Jokes & Jingles Book 3 (1909) not by R.F. Outcault 150.00 400.00 840.00
NOTE: *Reprinted from the Blue Ribbon post cards with advert jingles added.*
Buster's Book of Instructive Jokes and Jingles Book 4 (1910)-Original color art not by R.F. Outcault 150.00 585.00 1050.00
...Book of Travels nn (1912, 3x5")-Original color art not signed by Outcault 117.00 408.00 735.00
NOTE: *Estimated 5 or 6 known copies exist of books #1-4.*

The Buster Brown Bread Company

"Buster Brown" Bread Book of Rhymes, The (1904, 4x6", 12 pgs., half color, half B&W)- Original color art not signed by RFO 158.00 553.00 1000.00

Buster Brown's Hosiery Mills

"How Buster Brown Got The Pie" nn (nd, 7x5-1/4". 16 pgs, color paper cover and color interior By R.F. Outcault 83.00 292.00 525.00
"The Autobiography of Buster Brown" nn (nd,9x6-1/8", 36 pgs, text story & art by R.F. Outcault 83.00 292.00 525.00
NOTE: *Similar to, but a distinctly different item than "Buster Brown's Autobiography."*

The Buster Brown Stocking Company

Buster Brown Drawing Book, The nn (nd, 5x6", 20 pgs.)-B&W reproductions of 1903 R.F. Outcault art to trace 50.00 150.00 315.00
NOTE: *Reprints a comic strip from Burr McIntosh Magazine, which includes Buster, Yellow Kid, and Pore Li'l Mose (only known story involving all three.)*
Buster Brown Stocking Magazine nn (Jan. 1906, 7-3/4x5-3/8", 36 pgs.) R.F. Outcault 50.00 100.00 200.00
NOTE: *This was actually a store bought item selling for 5 cents per copy.*

Collins Baking Company

Buster Brown Drawing Book nn (1904, 5x3", 12 pgs.)-Original B&W art to trace, not signed by R.F. Outcault 50.00 150.00 315.00

C. H. Morton, St. Albans, VT

Merry Antics of Buster Brown, Buddy Tucker & Tige nn (nd, 3-1/2x5-1/2", 16 pgs.) -Original B&W art by R.F. Outcault 83.00 292.00 525.00

Ivan Frank & Company

Buster Brown nn (1904, 3x5", 12 pgs.)-B&W repros of R. F. Outcault Sunday pages (First premium to actually reproduce Sunday comic pages – may be first premium comic strip-r book?) 125.00 438.00 785.00
Buster Brown's Pranks (1904, 3-1/2x5-1/8", 12 pgs.)-reprints intro of Buddy Tucker into the BB newspaper strip before he was spun off into his own short lived newspaper strip 125.00 438.00 785.00

Kaufmann & Strauss

Buster Brown Drawing Book (1906, 28 pages, 5x3-1/2") Color Cover, B+W original story signed by Outcault, tracing paper inserted as alternate pages. Back cover imprinted for Nox' Em All Shoes 50.00 150.00 315.00

Pond's Extract

Buster Brown's Experiences With Pond's Extract nn (1904, 6-3/4x4-1/2", 28 pgs.) Original color art by R.F. Outcault (may be the first BB premium comic book with original art) 100.00 250.00 525.00

C. A. Cross & Co.

Red Cross Drawing Book nn (1906, 4-7/8x3-1/2", color paper -c, B&W interior, 12 pgs.) 50.00 150.00 315.00
NOTE: *This is for Red Cross coffee; not the health organization.*

Ringen Stove Company

Quick Meal Steel Ranges nn (nd, 5x3", 16 pgs.)-Original B&W art not signed by R.F. Outcault 50.00 150.00 315.00

Steinwender Stoffregen Coffee Co.

"Buster Brown Coffee" (1905, 4-7/8x3", color paper cover, B&W interior, 12 printed pages, plus 1 tracing paper page above each interior image (total of 8 sheets) (Very Rare) 83.00 292.00 525.00
NOTE: *Part of a BB drawing contest. If instructions had been followed, most copies would have ended up destroyed.*

U. S. Playing Card Company

Buster Brown - My Own Playing Cards (1906, 2-1/2x1-3/4", full color)
nn - By R. F. Outcault 42.00 147.00 250.00
NOTE: *Series of full color panels tell stories, average about 5 cards per story.*

Publisher Unknown

The Drawing Book nn (1906, 3-9/16x5", 8 pgs.)-Original B&W art to trace not by R.F. Outcault 50.00 150.00 300.00

BUTLER BOOK A Series of Clever Cartoons of Yale Undergraduate Life
Yale Record: June 16, 1913 (10-3/4 x 17", 34 pgs, paper cover B&W)
nn - By Alban Bernard Butler 21.00 73.00 130.00
NOTE: *Cartoons and strips reprinted from The Yale Record student newspaper.*

BUTTONS & FATTY IN THE FUNNIES
Whitman Publishing Co.: nd 1927 (10-1/4x15-1/2", 28pg., color)
W936 - Signed "M.E.B.", probably M.E. Brady; strips in color copyright The Brooklyn Daily Eagle; (very rare) 61.00 244.00 425.00

BY BRIGGS (M,N,P) (see also OLD GOLD THE SMOOTHER AND BETTER CIGARETTE)
Old Gold Cigarettes: nd (c1920's) (11" x 9-11/16", 44 pgs, cardboard-c, B&W)
nn- (Scarce) 20.00 70.00 130.00
NOTE: *Collection reprinting strip cartoons by Clare Briggs, advertising Old Gold Cigarettes. These strips originally appeared in various magazines, play program booklets, newspapers, etc. Some of the strips involve regular Briggs strip series. Contains all of the strips in the smaller, color "OLD GOLD" giveaways, plus more.*

CAMION CARTOONS
Marshall Jones Company: 1919 (7-1/2x5", 136 pgs, B&W)
nn - By Kirkland H. Day (W.W.One occupation) 20.00 70.00 120.00

CANYON COUNTRY KIDDIES (M)
Doubleday, Page & Co: 1923 (8x10-1/4", 88 pgs, hard-c, B&W)
nn - By James Swinnerton 39.00 137.00 260.00

CARLO (H)
Doubleday, Page & Co.: 1913 (8 x 9-5/8, 120 pgs, hardcover, B&W)
nn - By A.B. Frost 40.00 140.00 300.00
NOTE: *Original sequential strips about a dog. Became short lived newspaper comic strip in 1914. Originally published with a dust jacket which increases value 50%.*

CARTOON BOOK, THE
Bureau of Publicity, War Loan Organization, Treasury Department, Washington, D.C.: 1918 (6-1/2x4-7/8", 48 pgs, paper cover, B&W)
nn - By various artists 31.00 108.00 185.00
NOTE: *U.S. government issued booklet of WW I propaganda cartoons by 46 artists promoting the third sale of Liberty Loan bonds. The artists include: Berryman, Clare Briggs, Cesare, J. N. "Ding" Darling, Rube Goldberg, Kemble, McCutcheon, George McManus, F. Opper, T. E. Powers, Ripley, Satterfield, H. T. Webster, Gaar Williams.*

CARTOON CATALOGUE (S)
The Lockwood Art School, Kalamazoo, Mich.: 1919 (11-5/8x9, 52 pgs, B&W)
nn - Edited by Mr. Lockwood 20.00 60.00 140.00
NOTE: *Jammed with 100s of single panel cartoons and some sequential comics; Mr Lockwood began the very first cartoonist school back in 1892. Clare Briggs was one of his students.*

CARTOON COMICS
Lasco Publications, Detroit, Mich: #1, April 1930 - #2, May 1930 (8-3/6x5-1/5")
1, 2 - By Lu Harris 20.00 60.00 100.00
NOTE: *Contains recurring characters Hollywood Horace, Campus Charlie, Pair-A-Dice Alley and Jocko Monkey. Not much is presently known about the creator(s) or publisher.*

CARTOON HISTORY OF ROOSEVELT'S CAREER, A
The Review of Reviews Company: 1910 (276 pgs, 8-1/4x11",
nn - By various 43.00 129.00 325.00
NOTE: *Reprints editorial cartoons about Teddy Roosevelt from U.S. and international newspapers and cartoons from the humor magaines (Puck, Judge, etc.). A few cartoonists whose work is included are Dalrymple, Opper, McDougall, McCutcheon, Remington, Rogers, Kemble. Mostly single panel but 10 or so are sequential strips.*

CARTOON HUMOR
Collegian Press: 1938 (102 pgs, squarebound, B&W)
nn 20.00 70.00 120.00
NOTE: *Contains cartoons & strips by Otto Soglow, Syd Hoff, Peter Arno, Abner Dean, others.*

CARTOONIST'S PHILOSOPHY, A
Percy Crosby: 1931, HC, 252 pgs, 5-1/2x7-1/2", hard-c, celluloid dust wrapper
nn - By Percy Crosby (10 plates, 6 are of Skippy) 20.00 60.00 130.00
NOTE: *Crosby's partial autobiography regarding his return to France in 1929, and portrayals of Normandy, the "cliff dwellers" on Normandy cliffs (destroyed in WWII), his visit to London, comments on art, philosophy, several poems, and political dialogue. His description of his Cockney driver, " Harold" is amusing. Also describes his experience visiting Chicago to speak out against Capone, his concerns over the evils of Prohibition, and the economy prior to the 1929 crash. This book reveals he was aware of the dangers of his outspoken views, and is prophetic, re: his later years as political prisoner. Also reveals his religious beliefs.*

CARTOONS BY BRADLEY: CARTOONIST OF THE CHICAGO DAILY NEWS
Rand McNally & Company: 1917 (11-1/4x8-3/4", 112 pgs, hardcover, B&W)
nn - By Luther D. Bradley (editorial) 20.00 70.00 120.00

CARTOONS BY FONTAINE FOX (Toonerville Trolley) (S)
Harper & Brothers Publishers: nd early '20s (9x7-7/8",102 pgs., hard-c, B&W)
Second Book- By Fontaine Fox (Toonerville-r) 150.00 300.00 500.00

CARTOONS BY HALLADAY (N,S)
Providence Journal Co., Rhode Island: Dec 1914 (116 pgs, 10-1/2x 7-3/4", hard-c, B&W)
nn- (Scarce) 50.00 125.00 250.00
NOTE: *Cartoons on Rhode Island politics, plus some Teddy Roosevelt & WW I cartoons.*

CARTOONS BY McCUTCHEON (S)
A. C. McClurg & Co.: 1903 (12-3/8x9-3/4", 212 pgs., hardcover, B&W)
nn - By John McCutcheon 20.00 70.00 120.00

CARTOONS BY W. A. IRELAND (S)
The Columbus-Evening Dispatch: 1907 (13-3/4 x 10-1/2", 66 pgs, hardcover)
nn - By W. A. Ireland (strip-r) 20.00 70.00 120.00

CARTOONS MAGAZINE (I,N,S)
H. H. Windsor, Publisher: Jan 1912-June 1921; July 1921-1923; 1923-1924; 1924-1927 (1912-July 1913 issues 12x9-1/4", 68-76 pgs; 1913-1921 issues 10x7", average 112 to 188 pgs, color covers)
1912-Jan-Dec 30.00 75.00 125.00

Cartoons Magazine Sept, 1917
by various creators © H. H. Windsor, Chicago

Charlie Chaplin in the Army by Segar
1917 © Essaney

Comic Monthly #2
© Embee Dist. Co.

GD2.0 FN6.0 VF8.0

1913-1917 30.00 75.00 125.00
1917-(Apr) "How Comickers Regard Their Characters" 30.00 105.00 150.00
1917-(June) "A Genius of the Comic Page" - long article on George Herriman, Krazy Kat, etc with lots of Herriman art; "Cartoonists and Their Cars" 125.00 250.00 500.00
1918-1919 30.00 75.00 125.00
1920-June 1921 30.00 75.00 125.00
July 1921-1923 titled Wayside Tales & Cartoons Magazine 30.00 75.00 125.00
1923-1924 becomes Cartoons Magazine again 30.00 75.00 125.00
1924-1927 becomes Cartoons & Movie Magazine 30.00 75.00 125.00
NOTE: *Many issues contain a wealth of historical background on then current cartoonists of the day with an international slant; each issue profusely illustrated with many cartoons. We are unsure if this magazine continued after 1927.*

CARTOONS BY J. N. DARLING (S,N - some sequential strips)
The Register & Tribune Co., Des Moines, Iowa: 1909?-1920 (12x8-7/8",B&W)
Book 1 15.00 51.00 90.00
Book 2 Education of Alonzo Applegate (1910) 15.00 51.00 90.00
2nd printing 10.00 30.00 90.00
Book 3 Cartoons From The Files (1911) 15.00 51.00 90.00
Book 4 15.00 51.00 90.00
Book 5 In Peace And War (1916) 15.00 51.00 90.00
Book 6 Aces & Kings War Cartoons (Dec 1, 1918) 15.00 51.00 90.00
Book 7 The Jazz Era (Dec 1920) 15.00 51.00 90.00
Book 8 Our Own Outlines of History (1922) 15.00 51.00 90.00
NOTE: *Some of the most inspired hard hitting cartoons ever printed. Are there more?*

CARTOONS THAT MADE PRINCE HENRY FAMOUS, THE (N,S)
The Chicago Record-Herald: Feb/March 1902 (12-1/8" x 9", 32 pgs, paper-c, B&W)
nn- (Scarce) by McCutcheon 15.00 51.00 90.00
NOTE: *Cartoons about the visit of the British Prince Henry to the U.S.*

CAVALRY CARTOONS (O)
R. Montalboddi: nd (c1918) (14-1/4" x 11", 30 pgs, printed on one side, olive & black construction paper-c, B&W interior)
nn - By R.Montalboddi 15.00 51.00 90.00
NOTE: *Comics about life in the U.S.Cavalry during World War I, by a soldier who was in the 1st Cavalry.*

CHARLIE CHAPLIN (N)
Essanay/M. A. Donohue & Co.: 1917 (9x16", B&W, large size soft-c)
Series 1, #315-Comic Capers (9-3/4x15-3/4")-20 pgs. by Segar;
Series 1, #316-In the Movies 165.00 525.00 1200.00
#317-Up in the Air (20 pgs), #318-In the Army 165.00 525.00 1400.00
Funny Stunts-(12-1/2x16-3/8",16 color pgs) 165.00 525.00 1400.00
NOTE: *All contain pre-Thimble Theatre Segar art. The thin paper used makes high grade copies very scarce.*

CHASING THE BLUES
Doubleday Page: 1912 (7-1/2x10", 108 pgs., B&W, hard-c)
nn - By Rube Goldberg 150.00 525.00 900.00
NOTE: *Contains a dozen Foolish Questions, baseball, a few Goldberg poems and lots of sequential strips.*

CHRISTIAN CARTOONS (N,S)
The Sunday School Times Company: 1922 (7-1/4 x 6-1/8,104 pgs, brown hard-c, B&W)
nn - E.J. Pace 15.00 51.00 90.00
NOTE: *Religious cartoons reprinted from The Sunday School Times.*

CLANCY THE COP (O))
Dell Publishing Co.: 1930 - No. 2, 1931 (10x10", 52 pgs., B&W, cardboard-c)
(Also see Bug Movies & Deadwood Gulch)
1, 2-By VEP Victor Pazimino (original material; not reprints) 10000 250.00 500.00

CLIFFORD MCBRIDE'S IMMORTAL NAPOLEON & UNCLE ELBY (N)
The Castle Press: 1932 (12x17"; soft-c cartoon book)
nn - Intro. by Don Herod 36.00 144.00 250.00

COLLECTED DRAWINGS OF BRUCE BAIRNSFATHER, THE
W. Colston Leigh: 1931 (11-1/4x8-1/4 ", 168 pages, hardcover, B&W)
nn - By Bruce Bairnsfather 24.00 96.00 165.00

COMICAL PEEP SHOW
McLoughlin Bros: 1902 (36 pgs, B&W)
nn 24.00 96.00 165.00
NOTE: *Comic stories of Wilhelm Busch redrawn; two versions with green or gold front cover logos; back covers different.*

COMIC ANIMALS (I)
Charles E. Graham & Co.: 1903 (9-3/4x7-1/4", 90 pgs, color cover)
nn - By Walt McDougall (not comic strips) 43.00 150.00 260.00

COMIC CUTS (O)
H. L. Baker Co., Inc.: 5/19/34-7/28/34 (Tabloid size 10-1/2x15-1/2", 24 pgs., 5¢)
(full color, not reprints; published weekly; created for news stand sales)
V1#1 - V1#7(6/30/34), V1#8(7/14/34), V1#9(7/28/34)-Idle Jack strips 200.00 400.00 800.00
NOTE: *According to a 1958 Lloyd Jacquet interview, this short-lived comics mag was the direct inspiration for Major Malcolm Wheeler-Nicholson's* ***New Fun Comics****, not* ***Famous Funnies****.*

GD2.0 FN6.0 VF8.0

COMIC MONTHLY (N)
Embee Dist. Co.: Jan, 1922 - No. 12, Dec, 1922 (10¢, 8-1/2"x9", 28 pgs., 2-color covers) (1st monthly newsstand comic publication) (Reprints 1921 B&W dailies)
1-Polly & Her Pals by Cliff Sterrett 375.00 1125.00 2225.00
2-Mike & Ike by Rube Goldberg 140.00 490.00 1000.00
3-S'Matter, Pop? 140.00 490.00 1000.00
4-Barney Google by Billy DeBeck 140.00 490.00 1000.00
5-Tillie the Toiler by Russ Westover 140.00 490.00 1000.00
6-Indoor Sports by Tad Dorgan 140.00 490.00 1000.00
NOTE: *#6 contains more Judge Rummy than Indoor Sports.*
7-Little Jimmy by James Swinnerton 140.00 490.00 1000.00
8-Toots and Casper b y Jimmy Murphy 140.00 490.00 1000.00
9-New Bughouse Fables by Barney Google 140.00 490.00 1000.00
10-Foolish Questions by Rube Goldberg 140.00 490.00 1000.00
11-Barney Google & Spark Plug by Billy DeBeck 140.00 490.00 1000.00
12-Polly & Her Pals by Cliff Sterrett 214.00 752.00 1500.00
NOTE: *This series was published by George McManus (Bringing Up Father) as Em & Rudolph Block, Jr., son of Hearst's cartoon editor for many years, as "Bee." One would have thought this series would have done very well considering the tremendous amount of talent assembled. All issues are extremely hard to find these days and rarely show up in any type of higher grade.*

COMIC PAINTING AND CRAYONING BOOK (H)
Saalfield Publ. Co.: 1917 (13-1/2x10", 32 pgs.) (No price on-c)
nn - Tidy Teddy by F. M. Follett, Clarence the Cop, Mr. & Mrs. Butt-In; regular comic stories to read or color 50.00 175.00 300.00

COMPLETE TRIBUNE PRIMER, THE (I)
Mutual Book Company: 1901 (7 1/4 x 5", 152 pgs, red hard-c)
nn - By Frederick Opper; has 75 Opper cartoons 25.00 88.00 150.00

COURTSHIP OF TAGS, THE (N)
McCormick Press: pre-1910 (9x4", 88 pgs, red & B&W-c, B&W interior)
nn - By O. E. Wertz (strip-r Wichita Daily Beacon) 25.00 88.00 150.00

DAFFYDILS (N)
Cupples & Leon Co.: 1911 (5-3/4x7-7/8", 52 pgs., B&W, hard-c)
nn - By "Tad" Dorgan 58.00 204.00 350.00
NOTE: *Also exists in self-published TAD edition: The T.A. Dorgan Company; unknown which is first printing.*

DAN DUNN SECRET OPERATIVE 48 (Also See Detective Dan) (N)
Whitman Publishing: 1937 ((5 1/2 x 7 1/4", 68pgs., color cardboard-c, B&W)
1010 And The Gangsters' Frame-Up 50.00 150.00 300.00
NOTE: *There are two versions of the book the later printing has a 5 cent cover price. Dick Tracy look-alike character by Norman Marsh.*

DANGERS OF DOLLY DIMPLE, THE (N)
Penn Tobacco Co.: nd (1930's) (9-3/8x7-7/8", 28 pgs, red cardboard-c, B&W)
nn - (Rare) by Walter Enright 25.00 88.00 150.00
NOTE: *Reprints newspaper comic strip advertisements, in which in every episode, Dolly Dimple's life is saved by Penn's Smoking Tobacco. - how very un-P.C. by today's standards.*

DEADWOOD GULCH (O) (See The Funnies 1929)(also see Bug Movies & Clancy The Cop)
Dell Publishing Co.: 1931 (10x10", 52 pgs., B&W, color covers, B&W interior)
nn - By Charles "Boody" Rogers (original material) 150.00 300.00 600.00

DESTINY A Novel In Pictures (O)
Farrar & Rinehart: 1930 (8x7", 424 pgs, B&W, hard-c, dust jacket?)
nn - By Otto Nuckel (original graphic novel) 25.00 100.00 175.00

DICK TRACY & DICK TRACY JR. CAUGHT THE RACKETEERS, HOW
Cupples & Leon Co.: 1933 (8-1/2x7", 88 pgs., hard-c) (See Treasure Box of Famous Comics) (N)
2-(Numbered on pg. 84)-Continuation of Stooge Viller book (daily strip reprints from 8/3/33 thru 11/8/33)(Rarer than #1) 94.00 376.00 750.00
With dust jacket... 175.00 500.00 1000.00

DICK TRACY & DICK TRACY JR. AND HOW THEY CAPTURED "STOOGE" VILLER (N)
Cupples & Leon Co.: 1933 (8-1/2x7", 100 pgs., hard-c, one-shot)
Reprints 1932 & 1933 Dick Tracy daily strips
nn(No.1)-1st app. of "Stooge" Viller 94.00 376.00 750.00
With dust jacket... 175.00 500.00 1000.00

DIMPLES By Grace Drayton (N) (See Dolly Dimples)
Hearst's International Library Co.: 1915 (6 1/4 x 5 1/4, 12 pgs) (5 known)
nn-Puppy and Pussy; nn-She Goes For a Walk; nn-She Had A Sneeze; nn-She Has a Naughty Play Husband; nn-Wait Till Fido Comes Home 21.00 74.00 150.00

DOINGS OF THE DOO DADS, THE (N)
Detroit News (Universal Feat. & Specialty Co.): 1922 (50¢, 7-3/4x7-3/4", 34 pgs, B&W, red & white-c, square binding)
nn-Reprints 1921 newspaper strip "Text & Pictures" given away as prize in the Detroit News Doo Dads contest; by Arch Dale 43.00 173.00 360.00

DOING THE GRAND CANYON
Fred Harvey: 1922 (7 x 4-3/4", 24 pgs, B&W, paper cover)

'Erbie And 'Is Playmates By F. Opper
1932 © Democratic National Committee

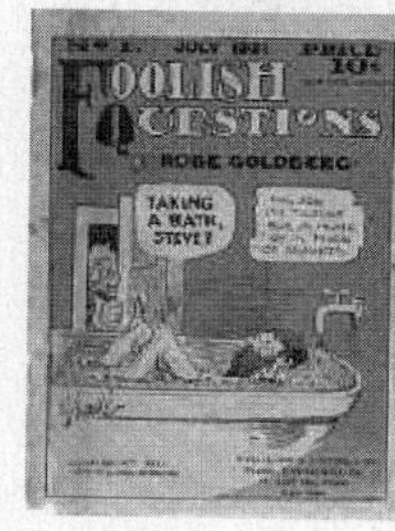

Foolish Questions by Rube Goldberg
1921 © EmBee Distributing Co., NY.

The Latest Adventures of Foxy Grandpa 1905
© Bunny Publ.

	GD2.0	FN6.0	VF8.0
nn - John McCutcheon	20.00	40.00	100.00

NOTE: *Text & 8 cartoons about visiting the Grand Canyon.*

DOINGS OF THE VAN-LOONS (N) (from same company as Mutt & Jeff #1-#5)
Ball Publications: 1912 (5-3/4X15-1/2", 68pg., B&W, hard-c)

nn - By Fred I. Leipziger (scarce) 72.00 252.00 600.00

DOLLY DIMPLES & BOBBY BOUNCE (See Dimples)
Cupples & Leon Co.: 1933 (8-3/4x7", color hardcover, B&W)

nn - Grace Drayton-a 24.00 96.00 165.00

DOO DADS, THE (Sleepy Sam and Tiny the Elephant)
Universal Feature * Specialty Co: 1922 (5-1/4x14", 36 pgs.,B&W, R&W-c,square binding)

nn - By Arch Dale 35.00 125.00 250.00

DRAWINGS BY HOWARD CHANDLER CHRISTIE (S, M)
Moffat, Yard & Company, NY: 1905 (11-7/8x16-1/2", 68 pgs, hard-c, B&W)

nn - Howard C. Christie 30.00 60.00 120.00
NOTE: *Reprints1898-1905 from Hapfer & Bros, Ch. Scribners Sons, Leslie's, MacMillians, McLurg, Russell.*

DREAMS OF THE RAREBIT FIEND (N)
Frederick A. Stokes Co.:1905 (10-1/4x7-1/2", 68 pgs, thin paper cover all B&W) newspaper reprints from the New York Evening Telegram printed on yellow paper

nn-By Winsor "Silas" McCay (Very Rare) (Five copies known to exist)
Estimated value.... 750.00 2500.00 –
NOTE: *A G/VG copy sold for $2,045 in May 2004. This item usually turns up with fragile paper.*

DRISCOLL'S BOOK OF PIRATES (O)
David McKay Publ.: 1934 (9x7", 124 pgs, B&W, hardcover)

nn - By Montford Amory ("Pieces of Eight strip-r) 21.00 64.00 150.00

DUCKY DADDLES
Frederick A. Stokes Co: July 1911 (15x10")

nn - By Grace Weiderseim (later Drayton) strip-r 50.00 175.00 300.00

DUMBUNNIES AND THEIR FRIENDS IN RABBITBORO, THE (O)
Albertine Randall Wheelan: 1931 (8-3/4x7-1/8", 82 pgs, color hardcover, B&W)

nn - By Albertine Randall Wheelan (self-pub) 34.00 103.00 240.00

EDISON - INSPIRATION TO YOUTH (N)(Also see Life of Thomas---)
Thomas A. Edison, Incorporated: 1939 (9-1/2 x 6-1/2, paper cover, B&W)

nn - Photo-c 46.00 138.00 275.00
NOTE: *Reprints strip material found in the 1928 Life of Thomas A. Edison in Word and Picture.*

'ERBIE AND 'IS PLAYMATES
Democratic National Committee: 1932 (8x9-1/2, 16 pgs, B&W)

nn - By Frederick Opper (Rare) 100.00 200.00 400.00
NOTE: *Anti-Hoover/Pro-Roosevelt political comics.*

EXPANSION BEING BART'S BEST CARTOONS FOR 1899
Minneapolis Journal: 1900 (10-1/4x8-1/4", 124 pgs, paperback, B&W)

v2#1 - By Charles L. Bartholomew 24.00 84.00 145.00

FAMOUS COMICS (N)
King Features Synd. (Whitman Pub. Co.): 1934 (100 pgs., daily newspaper-r) (3-1/2x8-1/2"; paper cover)(came in an illustrated box)

684 (#1) - Little Jimmy, Katz Kids & Barney Google 34.00 103.00 240.00
684 (#2) - Polly, Little Jimmy, Katzenjammer Kids 34.00 103.00 240.00
684 (#3) - Little Annie Rooney, Polly and Her Pals, Katzenjammer Kids
34.00 103.00 240.00
Box price... 75.00 150.00 375.00

FAMOUS COMICS CARTOON BOOKS (N)
Whitman Publishing Co.: 1934 (8x7-1/4", 72 pgs, B&W hard-c, daily strip-r)

1200-The Captain & the Kids; Dirks reprints credited to Bernard Dibble 29.00 86.00 200.00
1202-Captain Easy & Wash Tubbs by Roy Crane; 2 slightly different versions of cover exist 34.00 103.00 240.00
1203-Ella Cinders By Conselman & Plumb 28.00 84.00 195.00
1204-Freckles & His Friends 25.00 75.00 175.00
NOTE: *Called Famous Funnies Cartoon Books inside back area sales advertisement.*

FANTASIES IN HA-HA (M)
Meyer Bros & Co.: 1900 (14 x 11-7/8", 64 pgs, color cover hardcover, B&W)

nn - By Hy Mayer 50.00 150.00 300.00

FELIX (N)
Henry Altemus Company: 1931 (6-1/2"x8-1/4", 52 pgs., color, hard-c w/dust jacket)

1-3-Sunday strip reprints of Felix the Cat by Otto Messmer. Book No. 2 r/1931 Sunday panels mostly two to a page in a continuity format oddly arranged so each tier of panels reads across two pages, then drops to the next tier. (Books 1 & 3 have not been documented.)(Rare)
Each 104.00 416.00 900.00
With dust jacket 250.00 750.00 1200.00

FELIX THE CAT BOOK (N)
McLoughlin Bros.: 1927 (8"x15-3/4", 52 pgs, half in color-half in B&W)

nn - Reprints 23 Sunday strips by Otto Messmer from 1926 & 1927, every other one in color, two pages per strip. (Rare) 200.00 800.00 1550.00
260-Reissued (1931), reformatted to 9-1/2"x10-1/4" (same color plates, but one strip per every three pages), retitled ("Book" dropped from title) and abridged (only eight strips repeated from first issue, 28 pgs.).(Rare) 79.00 316.00 600.00

F. FOX'S FUNNY FOLK (see Toonerville Trolley; Cartoons by Fontaine Fox) (C)
George H. Doran Company: 1917 (10-1/4x8-1/4", 228 pgs, red, B&W cover, B&W interior, hardcover; dust jacket?)

nn - By Fontaine Fox (Toonerville Trolley strip-r) 150.00 450.00 750.00

52 CAREY CARTOONS (O,S)
Carey Cartoon Service, NY: 1915 (25 cents, 6-3/4" x 10-1/2", 118 pgs, printed on one side, color cardboard-c, B&W)

nn - (1915) War – – –
NOTE: *The Carey Cartoon Service supplied a weekly, hand-colored single panel cartoon broadsheet, on current news events, starting in 1906 or 1907, for window display in Carey Fountain Pen chain stores. These broadsheets were 22-1/2" x 33" in size. Starting circa 1915, Carey Fountain Pens began offering subscriptions for the broadsheets to other merchants, for window display in their stores as well. This collects, in B&W, the cartoons for 1915. An "Edition Deluxe" was also advertised, with all cartoons hand colored. It is currently unknown whether a reprint collection was only issued in 1915, or if other editions exist.*

52 LETTERS TO SALESMEN
Steven-Davis Company: 1927 (???)

nn - (Rare) 23.00 92.00 140.00
NOTE: *52 motivational letters to salesmen, with page of comics for each week, bound into embossed leather binder.*

FOLKS IN FUNNYVILLE (S)
R.H. Russell: 1900 (12"x9-1/4", 48 pgs.)(cardboard-c)

nn - By Frederick Opper 271.00 950.00 –
NOTE: *Reprinted from Hearst's NY Journal American Humorist supplements.*

FOOLISH QUESTIONS (S)
Small, Maynard & Co.: 1909 (6-7/8 x 5-1/2", 174 pgs, hardcover, B&W)

nn - By Rube Goldberg (first Goldberg item) 100.00 300.00 500.00
NOTE: *Comic strip began Oct 23, 1908 running thru 1941. Also drawn by George Frink in 1909.*

FOOLISH QUESTIONS THAT ARE ASKED BY ALL
Levi Strauss & Co./Small, Maynard & Co.: 1909 (5-1/2x5-3/4", 24 pgs, paper-c, B&W)

nn- (Rare) by Rube Goldberg 65.00 175.00 350.00

FOOLISH QUESTIONS (Boxed card set) (S)
Wallie Dorr Co., N.Y.: 1919 (5-1/4x3-3/4")(box & card backs are red)

nn - Boxed set w/52 B&W comics on cards; each a single panel gag complete set w/box 75.00 263.00 450.00
NOTE: *There are two diff sets put out simultaneously with the first set, by the same company. One set continues/picks up the numbering of the cards from the other set.*

FOOLISH QUESTIONS (S)
EmBee Distributing Co.: 1921 (10¢, 4x5 1/2; 52 pgs, 3 color covers; B&W)

1-By Rube Goldberg 46.00 160.00 300.00

FOXY GRANDPA
Foxy Grandpa Company, 33 Wall St, NY : 1900 (9x15", 84 pgs, full color, cardboard-c)

nn - By Carl Schultze (By Permission of New York Herald) 271.00 1200.00 –
NOTE: *This seminal comic strip began Jan 7, 1900 and was collected later that same year.*

FOXY GRANDPA (Also see The Funnies, 1st series) (N)
N. Y. Herald/Frederick A. Stokes Co./M. A. Donahue & Co./Bunny Publ. (L. R. Hammersly Co.): 1901 - 1916 (Strip-r in color, hard-c)

1901- 9x15" in color-N. Y. Herald 313.00 1100.00 –
1902- "Latest Larks of...", 32 pgs., 9-1/2x15-1/2" 164.00 575.00 –
1902- "The Many Advs. of...", 9x12", 148 pgs., Hammersly Co. 179.00 625.00 –
1903- "Latest Advs.", 9x15", 24 pgs., Hammersly Co. 164.00 575.00 –
1903- "...'s New Advs.", 11x15", 66 pgs., Stokes 164.00 575.00 –
1904- "Up to Date", 10x15", 66 pgs., Stokes 146.00 510.00 950.00
1904- "The Many Adventures of...", 9x15, 144pgs, Donohue 146.00 510.00 950.00
1905- "& Flip-Flaps", 9-1/2x15-1/2", 52 pgs. 146.00 510.00 950.00
1905- "The Latest Advs. of...", 9x15", 28, 52, & 68 pgs, M.A. Donohue Co.; re-issue of 1902 issue 104.00 365.00 700.00
1905- "Latest Larks of...", 9-1/2x15-1/2", 52 pgs., Donahue; re-issue of 1902 issue with more pages added 104.00 365.00 700.00
1905- "Latest Larks of...", 9-1/2x15-1/2", 24 pgs. edition, Donahue; re-issue of 1902 issue 104.00 365.00 700.00
1905- "Merry Pranks of...", 9-1/2x15-1/2", 28, 52 & 62 pgs., Donahue 104.00 365.00 700.00
1905-"...Surprises",10x15", color, 64 pg,Stokes, 60¢ 104.00 365.00 700.00
1906- "Frolics", 10x15", 30 pgs., Stokes 104.00 365.00 700.00
1907?-"...& His Boys",10x15", 64 color pgs, Stokes 104.00 365.00 700.00
1907- "Triumphs", 10x15", 62 pgs, Stokes 104.00 365.00 700.00
1908-"...Mother Goose", Stokes 104.00 365.00 700.00

Giggles
© Pratt Food Co.

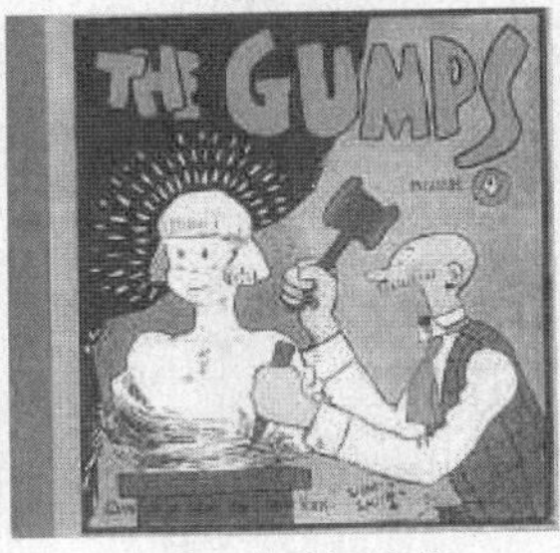

The Gumps by Sidney Smith
1927? © Cupples & Leon

Happy Hooligan Book 1 1902
© Frederick A. Stokes

GD2.0 FN6.0 VF8.0

1909- "...& Little Brother", 10x15, 58 pgs, Stokes 104.00 365.00 700.00
1911- "Latest Tricks", r-1910,1911 Sundays-Stokes Co. 104.00 365.00 700.00
1914-(9-1/2x15-1/2", 24 pgs.)-6 color cartoons/page, Bunny Publ. Co. 88.00 306.00 575.00
1915 - ...Always Jolly (10x16, Stokes) 88.00 306.00 575.00
1916- "Merry Book", (10x15", 64 pgs, Stokes) 88.00 306.00 575.00
1917-"...Adventures (5 1/2 x 6 1/2, 26 pgs, Stokes) 57.00 200.00 400.00
1917-"...Frolics (5 1/2 x 6 1/2, 26 pgs, Stokes) 57.00 200.00 400.00
1917-"...Triumphs (5 1/2 x 6 1/2, 26 pgs, Stokes) 57.00 200.00 400.00

FOXY GRANDPA, FUNNY TRICKS OF (The Stump Books)
M.A. Donahue Co, Chicago: approx 1903 (1-7/8x6-3/8", 44 pgs, blue hardcover)
nn - By Carl Schultze 54.00 189.00 325.00
NOTE: *One of a series of ten "stump" books; the only comics one.*

FOXY GRANDPA'S MOTHER GOOSE (I)
Stokes: October 1903 (10-11/16x8-1/2", 86 pgs, hard-c)
nn - By Carl Schultze (not comics - illustrated book) 54.00 189.00 325.00

FOXY GRANDPA SPARKLETS SERIES (N)
M. A. Donahue & Co.: 1908 (7-3/4x6-1/2"; 24 pgs., color)
"... Rides the Goat", "...& His Boys", "...Playing Ball", "...Fun on the Farm", "...Fancy Shooting", "...Show His Boys Up-To-Date Sports", "...Plays Santa Claus"
each.... 88.00 306.00 525.00
900- "Playing Ball"; Bunny illos; 8 pgs., linen like pgs., no date 73.00 254.00 435.00

FOXY GRANDPA VISITS RICHMOND (O,P)
Dietz Printing Co., Richmond, VA / Hotel Rueger: nd (c1920's) (5-7/8" x 4-1/2", 16 pgs, paper-c, B&W)
nn - (Scarce) By Bunny 25.00 88.00 175.00
NOTE: *Promotional comic given away to its guests by the Hotel Rueger, about Foxy Grandpa visiting and enjoying the Hotel. Originally came in an envelope, with the words "Foxy Grandpa Visits Richmond -- and Rueger's" printed on it.*

FOXY GRANDPA VISITS WASHINGTON, D.C. (P)
Dietz Printing Co., Richmond, VA / Hamilton Hotel: nd (c1920's) (5-7/8" x 4-1/2", 16 pgs, paper-c, B&W)
nn - (Scarce) By Bunny 25.00 88.00 150.00
NOTE: *Mostly reprints "... Visits Richmond", changing all references to Hotel Rueger, to Hamilton Hotel instead. Also, changes depictions of a waiter and a cook from black to white, plus incompletely erases the cover art on a book Foxy Grandpa falls asleep with (the latter is how we know that the Richmond version was first).*

FRAGMENTS FROM FRANCE (S)
G. P. Putnam & Sons: 1917 (9x6-1/4", 168 pgs, hardcover, $1.75)
nn - By Bruce Bairnsfather 25.00 88.00 150.00
NOTE: *WW1 trench warfare cartoons; color dust jacket.*

FUNNIES, THE (H) (See Clancy the Cop, Deadwood Gulch, Bug Movies)
Dell Publishing Co.: 1929 - No. 36, 10/18/30 (10¢; 5¢ No. 22 on) (16 pgs.)
Full tabloid size in color; not reprints; published every Saturday
1-My Big Brudder, Jonathan, Jazzbo & Jim, Foxy Grandpa, Sniffy, Jimmy Jams & other strips begin; first four-color comic newsstand publication; also contains magic, puzzles & stories 200.00 700.00 1500.00
2-21 (1930, 10¢) 150.00 300.00 600.00
22(nn-7/12/30-5¢) 150.00 300.00 600.00
23(nn-7/19/30-5¢), 24(nn-7/26/30-5¢), 25(nn-8/2/30), 26(nn-8/9/30), 27(nn-8/16/30), 28(nn-8/23/30), 29(nn-8/30/30), 30(nn-9/6/30), 31(nn-9/13/30), 32(nn-9/20/30), 33(nn-9/27/30), 34(nn-10/4/30), 35(nn-10/11/30), 36(nn, no date-10/18/30)
each.... 150.00 300.00 600.00

GASOLINE ALLEY (Also see Popular Comics & Super Comics) (N)
Reilly & Lee Publishers: 1929 (8-3/4x7", B&W daily strip-r, hard-c)
nn - By King (96 pgs.) 125.00 300.00 600.00
with scarce Dust Wrapper 250.00 500.00 900.00
NOTE: *Of all the Frank King reprint books, this is the only one to reprint actual complete newspaper strips - all others are illustrated prose text stories.*

GIBSON'S PUBLISHED DRAWINGS, MR. (M,S) (see Victorian index for earlier issues)
R.H. Russell, New York: No.1 1894 - No. 9 1904 (11x17-3/4", hard-c, B&W)
nn (No.6; 1901) A Widow and her Friends (90 pgs.) 30.00 60.00 120.00
nn (No.7; 1902) The Social Ladder (88 pgs.) 30.00 60.00 120.00
8 - 1903 The Weaker Sex (88 pgs.) 30.00 60.00 120.00
9 - 1904 Everyday People (88 pgs.) 30.00 60.00 120.00
NOTE: *By Charles Dana Gibson cartoons, reprinted from magazines, primarily LIFE. The Education of Mr. Pipp tells a story. Series continues how long after 1904?*

GIGGLES
Pratt Food Co., Philadelphia, PA: 1908-09? (12x9", 8 pgs, color, 5 cents-c)
1-8: By Walt McDougall (#8 dated March 1909) 40.00 175.00 –
NOTE: *Appears to be monthly; almost tabloid size; yearly subscriptions was 25 cents.*

GOD'S MAN (H)
Jonathan Cape and Harrison Smith Inc.: 1929 (8-1/4x6", 298 pgs, B&W hardcover w/dust jacket) (original graphic novel in wood cuts)
nn - By Lynd Ward 43.00 171.00 300.00

GOLD DUST TWINS
N. K. Fairbank Co.: 1904 (4-5/8x6-3/4", 18 pgs, color and B&W)
nn - By E. W. Kemble (Rare) 30.00 60.00 130.00
NOTE: *Promo comic for Gold DustWashing Powder; includes page of watercolor paints.*

GOLF
Volland Co.: 1916 (9x12-3/4", 132 pgs, hard-c, B&W)
nn - By Clair Briggs 100.00 200.00 400.00

GUMPS, THE (N)
Landfield-Kupfer: No. 1, 1918 - No. 6, 1921; (B&W Daily strip-r)
Book No. 1(1918)(scarce)-cardboard-c, 5-1/4x13-1/3", 64 pgs., daily strip-r by Sidney Smith 75.00 250.00 500.00
Book No.2(1918)-(scarce); 5-1/4x13-1/3"; paper cover; 36 pgs. daily strip reprints by Sidney Smith 75.00 250.00 500.00
Book No. 3 100.00 350.00 700.00
Book No. 4 (1918) 5-3/8x13-7/8", 20 pgs. Color card-c 100.00 350.00 700.00
Book No. 5 10-1/4x13-1/2", 20 pgs. Color paper-c 100.00 350.00 700.00
Book No. 6 (Rare, 20 pgs, 8x13-3/8, strip-r 1920-21) 121.00 423.00 725.00

GUMPS, ANDY AND MIN, THE (N)
Landfield-Kupfer Printing Co., Chicago/Morrison Hotel: nd (1920s) (Giveaway, 5-1/2"x14", 20 pgs., B&W, soft-c)
nn - Strip-r by Sidney Smith; art & logo embossed on cover w/hotel restaurant menu on back-c or a hotel promo ad; 4 different contents of issues known 50.00 175.00 300.00

GUMPS, THE (N)
Cupples & Leon: 1924-1930 (10x10, 52 pgs, B&W)
1 - By Sidney Smith 61.00 244.00 450.00
2-7 39.00 154.00 300.00

THE GUMPS (P)
Cupples & Leon Company: 1924 (9 x 7-1/2", 28 pgs, paper cover)
nn (1924) 50.00 175.00 300.00
NOTE: *Promotional comic for Sunshine Andy Gump Biscuits. Daily strip-r from 1922-24.*

GUMP'S CARTOON BOOK, THE (N)
The National Arts Company: 1931 (13-7/8x10", 36 pgs, color covers, B&W)
nn - By Sidney Smith 57.00 228.00 450.00

GUMPS PAINTING BOOK, THE (N)
The National Arts Company: 1931 (11 x 15 1/4", 20 pgs, half in full color)
nn - By Sidney Smith 57.00 228.00 450.00

HALT FRIENDS! (see also **HELLO BUDDY**)
???: 1918? (4-3/8x5-3/4", 36 pgs, color-c, B&W, no cover price listed)
nn - Unknown 10.00 30.00 70.00
NOTE: *Says on front cover: "Comics of War Facts of Service Sold on its merits by Unemployed or Disabled Ex-Service Men. Credentials Shown On Request. Price - Pay What You Please." These are very common; contents vary widely.*

HAMBONE'S MEDITATIONS
Jahl & Co.: no date 1920 (6-1/8 x 7-1/2, 108 pgs, paper cover, B&W)
nn - By J. P. Alley 33.00 132.00 250.00
NOTE: *Reprint of racist single panel newspaper series, 2 cartoons per page.*

HAN OLA OG PER (N)
Anundsen Publishing Co, Decorah, Iowa: 1927 (10-3/8 x 15-3/4", 54 pgs, paper-c, B&W)
nn - American origin Norwegian language strips-r 33.00 131.00 230.00
NOTE: *1940s and modern reprints exist.*

HANS UND FRITZ (N)
The Saalfield Publishing Co.: 1917, 1927-29 (10x13-1/2", 28 pgs., B&W)
nn - By R. Dirks (1917, r-1916 strips) 96.00 335.00 600.00
nn - By R. Dirks (1923 edition- reprint of 1917 edition) 58.00 204.00 350.00
nn - By R. Dirks (1926 edition- reprint of 1917 edition) 58.00 204.00 350.00
The Funny Larks Of... By R. Dirks (©1917 outside cover; ©1916 inside indicia) 96.00 335.00 600.00
The Funny Larks Of... (1927) reprints 1917 edition of 1916 strips Halloween-c 58.00 204.00 350.00
The Funny Larks Of... 2 (1929) 58.00 204.00 350.00
193 - By R. Dirks; contains 1916 Sunday strip reprints of Katzenjammer Kids & Hawkshaw the Detective - reprint of 1917 nn edition (1929) this edition is not rare 58.00 204.00 350.00

HAPPY DAYS (S)
Coward-McCann Inc.: 1929 (12-1/2x9-5/8", 110 pgs, hardcover B&W)
nn - By Alban Butler (WW 1 cartoons) 20.00 60.00 120.00

HAPPY HOOLIGAN (See Alphonse...) (N)
Hearst's New York American & Journal: 1902,1903
Book 1-(1902)-"And His Brother Gloomy Gus", By Fred Opper; has 1901-02-r;

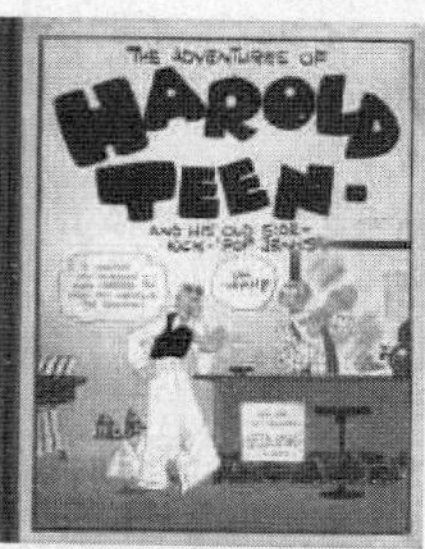

Harold Teen #2 by Carl Ed
1931 © Cupples & Leon

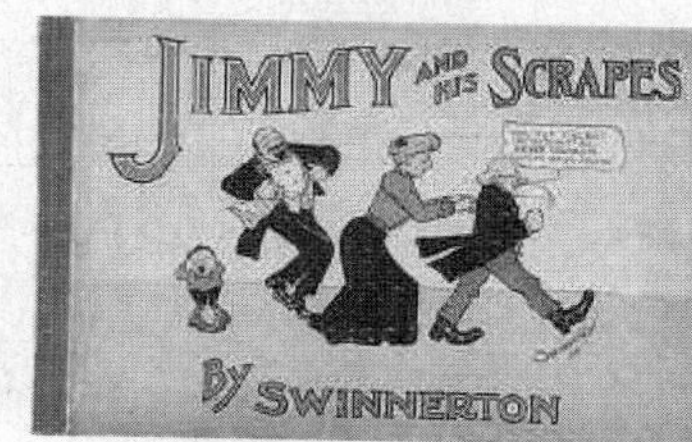

Jimmy and His Scrapes
© Frederick A. Stokes

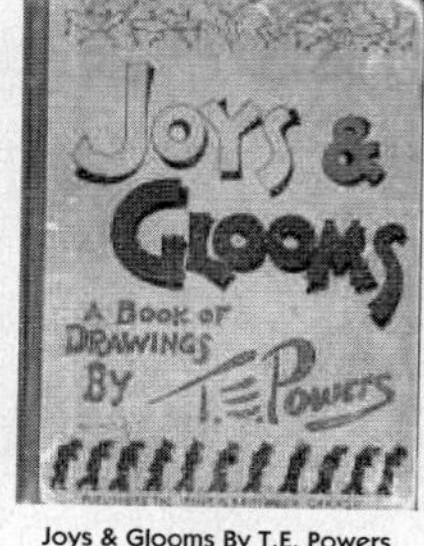

Joys & Glooms By T.E. Powers
1912 © Reilly & Britton Co.

	GD2.0	FN6.0	VF8.0
(yellow & black)(86 pgs.)(10x15-1/4")	600.00	1800.00	3000.00
New Edition, 1903 -10x15" 82 pgs. in color	350.00	1400.00	–

NOTE: *Strip ran March 26, 1900-Aug 14, 1932 and is widely recognized as setting the format standard for all newspaper comic strips which came after it. Opper (1857-1937) was going blind towards the end.*

HAPPY HOOLIGAN (N) (By Fredrick Opper)
Frederick A. Stokes Co.: 1906-08 (10-1/4x15-3/4", cardboard color-c)

	GD2.0	FN6.0	VF8.0
1906 - :Travels of...), 68 pgs,10-1/4x15-3/4", 1905-r	300.00	900.00	–
1907 - "--Home Again", 68 pgs., 10x15-3/4", 60¢; full color-c	300.00	900.00	–
1908 - "Handy--", 68 pgs, color	300.00	900.00	–

HAPPY HOOLIGAN, THE STORY OF (G)
McLoughlin Bros.: No. 281, 1932 (12x9-1/2", 20 pgs., soft-c)

	GD2.0	FN6.0	VF8.0
281-Three-color text, pictures on heavy paper	57.00	228.00	400.00

NOTE: *An homage to Opper's creation on its 30th Anniversary in 1932.*

HAROLD HARDHIKE'S REJUVENATION
O'Sullivan Rubber: 1917 (6-1/4x3-1/2, 16 pgs, B&W)

	GD2.0	FN6.0	VF8.0
nn	25.00	100.00	175.00

NOTE: *Comic book to promote rubber shoe heels.*

HAROLD TEEN (N)
Cupples & Leon Co.: 1929 (9-7/8x9-7/8", 52 pgs, cardboard covers)

	GD2.0	FN6.0	VF8.0
1 - By Carl Ed	50.00	200.00	500.00
nn - (1931, 8-11/16x6-7/8", 96 pgs, hardcover w/dj)	41.00	164.00	290.00

NOTE: *Title 2nd book:* ***HAROLD TEEN AND HIS OLD SIDE-KICK– POP JENKINS,*** *(Adv. of...). Precursor for Archie Andrews & crew; strip began May 4, 1919 running into 1959.*

HAROLD TEEN PAINT AND COLOR BOOK (N)
McLoughlin Bros Inc.: 1932 (13x9-3/4, 28 pgs, B&W and color)

	GD2.0	FN6.0	VF8.0
#2054	25.00	100.00	175.00

HAWKSHAW THE DETECTIVE (See Advs. of..., Hans Und Fritz & Okay) (N)
The Saalfield Publishing Co.: 1917 (10-1/2x13-1/2", 24 pgs., B&W)

	GD2.0	FN6.0	VF8.0
nn - By Gus Mager (Sunday strip-r)	54.00	190.00	350.00
nn - By Gus Mayer (1923 reprint of 1917 edition)	25.00	100.00	175.00
nn - By Gus Mager (1926 reprint of 1917 edition)	25.00	100.00	175.00

NOTE: *Runs Feb 23, 1913-Sept 4, 1922, starts again from Dec 13, 1931-Feb 11, 1952; Sherlock Holmes spoof.*

HEALTH IN PICTURES
American Public Health Association, NYC: 1930 (6-1/2" x 5-3/16", 76 pgs, green & black paper-c, B&W interior)

	GD2.0	FN6.0	VF8.0
nn - By various	15.00	51.00	90.00

NOTE: *Collection of strips and cartoons put out by the Public Health Association, on topics ranging from boating and food safety, to small pox and typhoid prevention.*

HE DONE HER WRONG (O) (see also BANANA OIL)
Doubleday, Doran & Company: 1930 (8-1/4x 7-1/4", 276pgs, hard-c with dust jacket, B&W interiors)

	GD2.0	FN6.0	VF8.0
nn - By Milt Gross	75.00	225.00	400.00

NOTE: *A seminal original-material wordless graphic novel, not reprints. Several modern reprints.*

HELLO BUDDY (see also **HALT FRIENDS**)
???: 1919? (4-3/8x5-3/4", 36 pgs, color-c, B&W, 15¢)

	GD2.0	FN6.0	VF8.0
nn - Unknown	10.00	30.00	70.00

NOTE: *Says on front cover: "Comics of War Facts of Service Sold on its merits by Unemployed or Disabled Ex-Service Men." These are very common; contents vary widely.*

HENRY (N)
David McKay Co.: 1935 (25¢, soft-c)

	GD2.0	FN6.0	VF8.0
Book 1 - By Carl Anderson	57.00	200.00	400.00

NOTE: *Strip began March 19 1932; this book ties with Popeye (David McKay) and Little Annie Rooney (David McKay) as the last of the 10x10" Platinum Age comic books.*

HENRY (M)
Greenberg Publishers Inc.: 1935 (11-1/4x 8-5/8", 72 pgs, red & blue color hard-c, dust jacket, B&W interiors) (strip-r from Saturday Evening Post)

	GD2.0	FN6.0	VF8.0
nn - By Carl Anderson	57.00	200.00	400.00

HIGH KICKING KELLYS, THE (M)
Vaudeville News Corporation, NY: 1926 (5x11", B&W, two color soft-c)

	GD2.0	FN6.0	VF8.0
nn - By Jack A. Ward (scarce)	40.00	160.00	280.00

HIGHLIGHTS OF HISTORY (N)
World Syndicate Publishing Co.: 1933-34 (4-1/2x4", 288 pgs)

	GD2.0	FN6.0	VF8.0
nn - 5 different unnumbered issues; daily strip-r	10.00	40.00	70.00

NOTE: *Titles include Buffalo Bill, Daniel Boone, Kit Carson, Pioneers of the Old West, Winning of the Old Northwest. There are line drawing color covers and embossed hardcover versions. It is unknown which came out first.*

HOMER HOLCOMB AND MAY (N)
no publisher listed: 1920s (4 x 9-1/2", 40 pgs, paper cover, B&W)

	GD2.0	FN6.0	VF8.0
nn - By Doc Bird Finch (strip-r)	10.00	40.00	70.00

HOME, SWEET HOME (N)
M.S. Publishing Co.: 1925 (10-1/4x10")

	GD2.0	FN6.0	VF8.0
nn - By Tuthill	33.00	134.00	235.00

HOW THEY DRAW PROHIBITION (S)
Association Against Prohibition: 1930 (10x9", 100 pgs.)

	GD2.0	FN6.0	VF8.0
nn - Single panel and multi-panel comics (rare)	71.00	285.00	500.00

NOTE: *Contains art by J.N. "Ding" Darling, James Flagg, Rollin Kirby, Winsor McCay, T.E. Powers, H.T. Webster, others. Also comes with a loose sheet listing all the newspapers where the cartoons originally appeared.*

HOW TO BE A CARTOONIST (H)
Saalfield Pub. Co: 1936 (10-3/8x12-1/2", 16 pgs, color-c, B&W)

	GD2.0	FN6.0	VF8.0
nn - By Chas. H. Kuhn	10.00	40.00	70.00

HOW TO DRAW: A PRACTICAL BOOK OF INSTRUCTION (H)
Harper & Brothers: 1904 (9-1/4x12-3/8", 128 pgs, hardcover, B&W)

	GD2.0	FN6.0	VF8.0
nn - Edited By Leon Barritt	57.00	228.00	400.00

NOTE: *Strips reprinted include: "Buster Brown" by Outcault, "Foxy Grandpa" by Bunny, "Happy Hooligan" by Opper, "Katzenjammer Kids" by Dirks, "Lady Bountiful" by Gene Carr, "Mr. Jack" by Swinnerton, "Panhandle Pete" by George McManus, "Mr E.Z. Mark" by F.M. Howarth others; non-character strips by Hy Mayer, Winsor McCay, T.E. Powers, others; single panel cartoons by Davenport, Frost, McDougall, Nast, W.A. Rogers, Sullivant, others.*

HOW TO DRAW CARTOONS (H)
Garden City Publishing Co.: 1926, 1937 (10 1/4 x 7 1/2, 150 pgs)

	GD2.0	FN6.0	VF8.0
1926 first edition By Clare Briggs	25.00	75.00	150.00
1937 2nd edition By Clare Briggs	20.00	60.00	120.00

NOTE: *Seminal "how to" break into the comics syndicates with art by Briggs, Fisher, Goldberg, King, Webster, Opper, Tad, Hershfield, McCay, Ding, others. Came with Dust Jacket -add 50%.*

HOW TO DRAW FUNNY PICTURES: A Complete Course in Cartooning (H)
Frederick J. Drake & Co., Chicago: 1936 (10-3/8x6-7/8", 168 pgs, hardcover, B&W)

	GD2.0	FN6.0	VF8.0
nn - By E.C. Matthews (200 illus by Eugene Zimmerman)	20.00	60.00	120.00

HY MAYER (M)
Puck Publishing: 1915 (13-1/2 x 20-3/4", 52 pgs, hardcover cover, color & B&W interiors)

	GD2.0	FN6.0	VF8.0
nn - By Hy Mayer(strip reprints from Puck)	40.00	140.00	300.00

HYSTERICAL HISTORY OF THE CIVILIAN CONSERVATION CORPS
Peerless Engraving: 1934 (10-3/4x7-1/2", 104 pgs, soft-c, B&W)

	GD2.0	FN6.0	VF8.0
nn - By various	20.00	60.00	120.00

NOTE: *Comics about CCC life, includes two color insert postcards in back.*

INDOOR SPORTS (N,S)
National Specials Co., New York: nd circa 1912 (25 cents, 6 x 9", 68 pgs, B&W)

	GD2.0	FN6.0	VF8.0
nn - Tad	35.00	125.00	225.00

NOTE: *Cartoons reprinted from Hearst papers.*

IT HAPPENS IN THE BEST FAMILIES (N)
Powers Photo Engraving Co.: 1920 (52 pgs.)(9-1/2x10-3/4")

	GD2.0	FN6.0	VF8.0
nn - By Briggs; B&W Sunday strips-r	29.00	114.00	200.00
Special Railroad Edition (30¢)-r/strips from 1914-1920	26.00	103.00	180.00

JIMMIE DUGAN AND THE REG'LAR FELLERS (N)
Cupples & Leon: 1921, 46 pgs. (11"x16")

	GD2.0	FN6.0	VF8.0
nn - By Gene Byrne	71.00	284.00	500.00

NOTE: *Ties with EmBee's Mutt & Jeff and Trouble of Bringing Up Father as the last of this size.*

JIMMY (N) (see Little Jimmy Picture & Story Book)
N. Y. American & Journal: 1905 (10x15", 84 pgs., color)

	GD2.0	FN6.0	VF8.0
nn - By Jimmy Swinnerton (scarce)	300.00	800.00	1500.00

NOTE: *James Swinnerton was one of the original first pioneers of the American newspaper comic strip.*

JIMMY AND HIS SCRAPES (N)
Frederick A. Stokes: 1906, (10-1/4x15-1/4", 66 pgs, cardboard-c, color)

	GD2.0	FN6.0	VF8.0
nn - By Jimmy Swinnerton (scarce)	300.00	800.00	1500.00

JOE PALOOKA (N)
Cupples & Leon Co.: 1933 (9-13/16x10", 52 pgs., B&W daily strip-r)

	GD2.0	FN6.0	VF8.0
nn - By Ham Fisher (scarce)	114.00	456.00	800.00

JOHN, JONATHAN AND MR. OPPER BY F. OPPER (S,I,N)
Grant, Richards, 48 Leicester Square, W.C.: 1903 (9-5/8x8-3/8", 108 pgs, hard-c B&W)

	GD2.0	FN6.0	VF8.0
nn - Opper (Scarce)	50.00	200.00	380.00

NOTE: *British precursor-type companion to* Willie And His Poppa *reprints from Hearst's* NY American & Journal *Opper cartoons interfacing* Uncle Sam *precursor* Brother Jonathan, John Bull. *Uses name* Happy Hooligan *in one cartoon, has* John Bull *smoking opium in another.*

JOLLY POLLY'S BOOK OF ENGLISH AND ETIQUETTE (S)
Jos. J. Frisch: 1931 (60 cents, 8 x 5-1/8, 88 pgs, paper-c, B&W)

	GD2.0	FN6.0	VF8.0
nn - By Jos. J. Frisch	20.00	60.00	120.00

NOTE: *Reprint of single panel newspaper series, 4 per page, of English and etiquette lessons taught by a flapper.*

JOYS AND GLOOMS (N)
Reilly & Britton Co.: 1912 (11x8", 72 pgs, hard-c, B&W interior)

	GD2.0	FN6.0	VF8.0
nn - By T. E. Powers (newspaper strip-r)	39.00	156.00	325.00

JUDGE - yet to be indexed

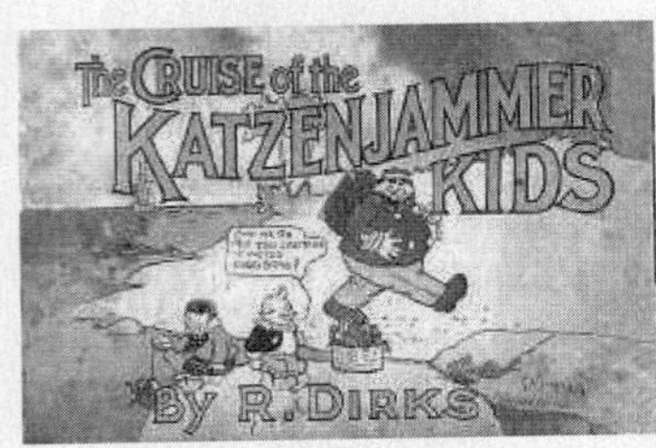

The Cruise of the Katzenjammer Kids
© NY American & Journal

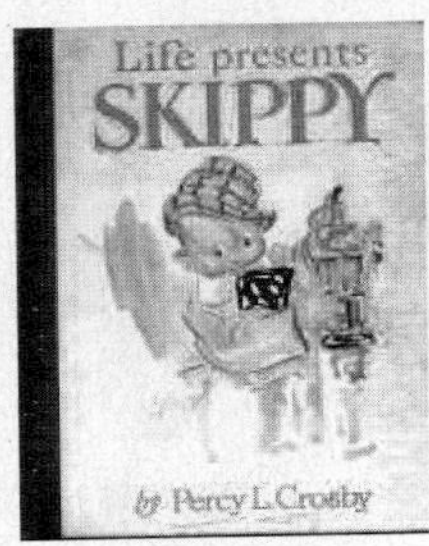

Life Presents Skippy by Percy L. Crosby
1924 © Life Publishing Company

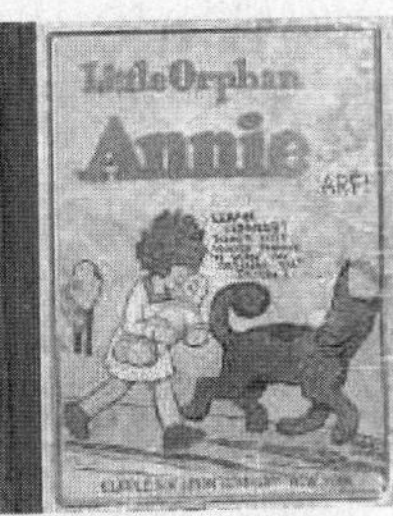

Little Orphan Annie 1926
© C&L

GD2.0 FN6.0 VF8.0

JUDGE'S LIBRARY - yet to be indexed

JUST KIDS COMICS FOR CRAYON COLORING
King Features. NYC: 1928 (11x8-1/2, 16 pgs, soft-c)

nn - By Ad Carter 33.00 100.00 200.00
NOTE: *Porous better grade paper; top pics printed in color; lower in b&w to color.*

JUST KIDS, THE STORY OF (I)
McLoughlin Bros.: 1932 (12x9-1/2", 20 pgs., paper-c)

283-Three-color text, pictures on heavy paper 39.00 156.00 275.00

KAPTIN KIDDO AND PUPPO (N)
Frederick A. Stokes Co.: 1910-1913 (11x16-1/2", 62 pgs)

1910-By Grace Wiederseim (later Drayton) 40.00 140.00 240.00
1910-Turr-ble Tales of... By Grace Wiederseim (Edward Stern & Co., 11x16-1/2", 64 pgs.) 40.00 140.00 240.00
1913- ...'Speriences By Grace Drayton 40.00 140.00 240.00
NOTE: *Strip ran approx. 1909-1912.*

KATZENJAMMER KIDS, THE (Also see Hans Und Fritz) (N)
New York American & Journal: 1902,1903 (10x15-1/4", 86 pgs., color)
(By Rudolph Dirks; strip first appeared in 1897) © W.R. Hearst
NOTE: *All KK books 1902-1905 all have the same exact title page with a 1902 copyright by W.R. Hearst; almost always look instead on the front cover.*

1902 (Rare) (red & black); has 1901-02 strips 1000.00 2400.00 -
1903- **A New Edition** (Rare), 86 pgs 750.00 2000.00 -
1904- 10x15", 84 pgs 250.00 900.00 -
1905?-The Cruise of the, 10x15", 60¢, in color 250.00 900.00 -
1905-A Series of Comic Pictures, 10x15", 84 pgs. in color, possible reprint of 1904 edition 250.00 800.00 -
1905-Tricks of... (10x15", 66 pgs, Stokes) 250.00 800.00 -
1906-Stokes (10x16", 32 pgs. in color) 186.00 800.00 -
1907- The Cruise of the, 10x15", 62 pgs 1905-r? 186.00 800.00 -
1910-The Komical...(10x15) 150.00 450.00 800.00
1921-Embee Dist. Co., 10x16", 20 pgs. in color 150.00 450.00 800.00

KATZENJAMMER KIDS MAGIC DRAWING AND COLORING BOOK (N)
Sam L Gabriel Sons And Company: 1931 (8 1/2 x 12", 36 pages, stiff-c

838-By Knerr 50.00 200.00 350.00

KEEPING UP WITH THE JONESES (N)
Cupples & Leon Co.: 1920 - No. 2, 1921 (9-1/4x9-1/4",52 pgs.,B&W daily strip-r)

1,2-By Pop Momand 39.00 154.00 270.00

KID KARTOONS (N,S)
The Century Co.: 1922 (232 pgs, printed 1 side, 9-3/4 x 7-3/4", hard-c, B&W)

nn - By Gene Carr (Metropolitan Movies strip-r) 60.00 240.00 -

KING OF THE ROYAL MOUNTED (Also See Dan Dunn) (N)
Whitman Publishing: 1937 (5 1/2 x 7 1/4", 68 pgs., color cardboard-c, B&W)

1010 36.00 144.00 250.00

LADY BOUNTIFUL (N)
Saalfield Publ. Co./Press Publ. Co.: 1917 (13-3/8x10", 36 pgs, color cardboard-c, B&W interiors)

nn - By Gene Carr; 2 panels per page 50.00 175.00 300.00
193S - 2nd printing (13-1/8x10",28 pgs color-c, B&W) 33.00 117.00 200.00

LAUGHS YOU MIGHT HAVE HAD From The Comic Pages of Six Week Day Issues of the Post-Dispatch (N)
St. Louis Post-Dispatch: 1921 (9 x 10 1/2", 28 pgs, B&W, red ink cover)

nn - Various comic strips 39.00 154.00 270.00

LIFE, DOGS FROM (M)
Doubleday, Page & Company: nn 1920 - No.2 1926 (130 pgs, 11-1/4 x 9", color painted-c, hard-c, B&W)

nn (No.1) 120.00 360.00 -
Second Litter 80.00 320.00 -
NOTE: *Reprints strips & cartoons featuring dogs, from Life Magazine. Edited by Thomas L. Masson. Highly sought by collectors of dog ephemera. Art in both books is mostly by Robert L. Dickey. Other art: Carl Anderson-1,2; Barbes-1; Chip Bellew-1; Lang Campbell-1,2; Percy Crosby-1,2; Edwina-2; Frueh-2; R.B. Fuller-1; Gibson-1,2; Don Herold-2; Gus Mager-2; Orr-1; J.R. Shaver-1,2; T.S. Sullivant-2; Russ Westover-1,2; Crawford Young-1.*

LIFE OF DAVY CROCKETT IN PICTURE AND STORY, THE
Cupples & Leon: 1935 (8-3/4x7", 64 pgs, B&W hard-c, dust jacket?)

nn - By C. Richard Schaare 29.00 116.00 200.00

LIFE OF THOMAS A. EDISON IN WORD AND PICTURE, THE (N)(Also see Edison...)
Thomas A. Edison Industries: 1928 (10x8", 56 pgs, paper cover, B&W)

nn - Photo-c 100.00 250.00 400.00
NOTE: *Reprints newspaper strip which ran August to November 1927.*

LIFE'S LITTLE JOKES (S)
M.S. Publ. Co.: No date (1924)(10-1/16x10", 52 pgs., B&W)

GD2.0 FN6.0 VF8.0

nn - By Rube Goldberg 64.00 257.00 525.00

LIFE, MINIATURE (see also LIFE (miniature reprint of of issue No. 1)) (M,P,S)
Life Publishing Co.: No. 1 - No. 4 1913, 1916, 1919 (5-3/4x4-5/8", 20 pgs, color paper-c

1- 3 (1913) 4 (1916) 5 (1919) (no known sales)
NOTE: *Giveaway item from Life, to promote subscriptions. All reprint material. No.2: James Montgomery Flagg-c; a-Chip Bellew, Gus Dirks, Gibson, F.M.Howarth, Art Young.*

LIFE'S PRINTS (was **LIFE'S PICTURE GALLERY** - See Victorian Age section) (M,S,P)
Life Publishing Company, New York: nd (c1907) (7x4-1/2", 132 pgs, paper cover, B&W)

nn - (nd; c1907) unillustrated black construction paper cover; reprints art from 1895-1907; art by J.M.Flagg, A.B.Frost, Gibson (Scarce) - - -
nn - (nd; c1908) b&w cardboard painted cover by Gibson, showing angel raising a champagne glass; reprints art from 1901-1908; art by J.M.Flagg, A.B.Frost, Gibson, Walt Kuhn, Art Young (Scarce) - - -
NOTE: *Catalog of prints reprinted from LIFE covers & centerspreads. There are likely more as yet unreported catalogs.*

LIFE, THE COMEDY OF LIFE
Life Publishing Company: 1907 (130 pgs, 11-3/4x9-1/4",embossed printed cloth covered board-c, B+W

nn - By various 20.00 80.00 120.00
NOTE: *Single cartoons and some sequential cartoons). Artists include Charles Dana Gibson, Harrison Cady, E.W. Kemble, James Montgomery Flagg.*

LILY OF THE ALLEY IN THE FUNNIES
Whitman Publishing Co.: No date (1927) (10-1/4x15-1/2"; 28 pgs., color)

W936 - By T. Burke (Rare) 57.00 228.00 400.00

LITTLE ANNIE ROONEY (N)
David McKay Co.: 1935 (25¢, soft-c)

Book 1 43.00 172.00 340.00
NOTE: *Ties with Henry & Popeye (David McKay) as the last of the 10x10" size Plat comic books.*

LITTLE ANNIE ROONEY WISHING BOOK (G) (See Happy Hooligan, Story of #281)
McLoughlin Bros.: 1932 (12x9-1/2", 16 pgs., soft-c, 3-color text, heavier paper)

282 - By Darrell McClure 41.00 144.00 250.00

LITTLE BIRD TOLD ME, A (E)
Life Publishing Co.: 1905? (96 pgs, hardbound)

nn - By Walt Kuhn (Life-r) 41.00 144.00 250.00

LITTLE FOLKS PAINTING BOOK (N)
The National Arts Company: 1931 (10-7/8 x 15-1/4", 20 pgs, half in full color)

nn - By "Tack" Knight (strip-r) 41.00 144.00 250.00

LITTLE JIMMY PICTURE AND STORY BOOK (I) (see Jimmy)
McLaughlin Bros., Inc.: 1932 (13-1/4 x 9-3/4", 20 pgs, cardstock color cover)

284 Text by Marion Kincaird; illus by Swinnerton 57.00 228.00 400.00

LITTLE JOHNNY & THE TEDDY BEARS (Judge-r) (M) (see Teddy Bear Books)
Reilly & Britton Co.: 1907 (10x14".; 68 pgs, green, red, black interior color)

nn - By J. R. Bray-a/Robert D. Towne-s 67.00 233.00 400.00

LITTLE JOURNEY TO THE HOME OF BRIGGS THE SKY-ROCKET, THE
Lockhart Art School: 1917 (10-3/4x7-7/8", 20 pgs, B&W) (I)

nn - About Clare Briggs (bio & lots of early art) 41.00 144.00 250.00

LITTLE KING, THE (see New Yorker Cartoon Albums for 1st appearance) (M)
Farrar & Reinhart, Inc: 1933 (10-1/4 x 8-3/4, 80 pgs, hardcover w/dust jacket

nn - By Otto Soglow (strip-r The New Yorker) 125.00 250.00 450.00
NOTE: *Copies with dust jacket are worth 50% more. Also exists in a 12x8-3/4 edition.*

LITTLE LULU BY MARGE (M)
Rand McNally & Company, Chicago: 1936 (6-9/16x6", 68 pgs, yellow hard-c, B&W)

nn - By Marjorie Henderson Buell 25.00 100.00 250.00
NOTE: *Begins reprinting single panel Little Lulu cartoons which began with Saturday Evening Post Feb. 23, 1935. This book was reprinted several times as late as 1940.*

LITTLE NAPOLEON
No publisher listed: 1924 , 50 pages, 10" by 10"; Color cardstock-c, B&W

nn - By Bud Counihan (Cupples &Leon format) 25.00 100.00 240.00

LITTLE NEMO (...in Slumberland) (N) (see also Little Sammy Sneeze, Dreams...Rarebit F)
Doffield & Co.(1906)/Cupples & Leon Co.(1909): 1906, 1909 (Sunday strip-r in color, cardboard covers)

1906-11x16-1/2" by Winsor McCay; 30 pgs. (scarce) 1500.00 5000.00 -
1909-10x14" by Winsor McCay (scarce) 1300.00 4000.00 -

LITTLE ORPHAN ANNIE (See Treasure Box of Famous Comics) (N)
Cupples & Leon Co.: 1926 - 1934 (8-3/4x7", 100 pgs., B&W daily strip-r, hard-c)

1 (1926)-Little Orphan Annie (softback see Treasure Box) 50.00 200.00 375.00
2 (1927)-In the Circus (softback see Wonder Box...) 36.00 144.00 275.00
3 (1928)-The Haunted House (softback see Wonder Box...) 36.00 144.00 275.00
4 (1929)-Bucking the World 36.00 144.00 275.00

The Trials of Lulu and Leander by Howarth
1906 © NY American & Journal

Maud the Mirthful Mule by Opper
1908 © Frederick A. Stokes

Mickey Mouse Book
1930 © Bibo & Lang

	GD2.0	FN6.0	VF8.0
5 (1930)-Never Say Die	30.00	120.00	225.00
6 (1931)-Shipwrecked	30.00	120.00	225.00
7 (1932)-A Willing Helper	25.00	100.00	200.00
8 (1933)-In Cosmic City	25.00	100.00	200.00
9 (1934)-Uncle Dan (not rare)	25.00	100.00	200.00

NOTE: *Each book reprints dailies from the previous year. Each hardcover came with a dust jacket. Books with out dust jackets are worth 50% less. Many of copies of #9 Uncle Dan have been turning up on eBay recently.*

LITTLE ORPHAN ANNIE RUMMY CARDS (N)
Whitman Publishing Co., Racine: 1935 (box: 5 x 6 1/2" Cards: 3 1/2 x 2 1/4")

nn-Harold Gray 20.00 60.00 120.00
NOTE: *36 cards, including 1 instruction card, 5 character cards and 30 cards forming 5 sequential stories (6 cards each).*

LITTLE SAMMY SNEEZE (N) (see also Little Nemo, Dreams of A Rarebit Fiend)
New York Herald Co.: Dec 1905 (11x16-1/2", 72 pgs., color)

nn - By Winsor McCay (Very Rare) 2500.00 6000.00 –
NOTE: *Rarely found in fine to mint condition.*

LIVE AND LET LIVE
Travelers Insurance Co.: 1936 (5-3/4x7/3/4", 16 pgs. color and B&W)

nn - Bill Holman, Carl Anderson, etc 20.00 60.00 120.00

LULU AND LEANDER (N) (see also Funny Folk, 1899, in Victorian section)
New York American & Journal: 1904 (76 pgs); **William A Stokes & Co:** 1906

nn - By F.M. Howarth 300.00 750.00 1500.00
nn - The Trials of...(1906, 10x16", 68 pgs. in color) 300.00 750.00 1500.00
NOTE: *F. M. Howarth helped pioneer the American comic strip in the pages of PUCK magazine in the early 1890s before the Yellow Kid.*

MADMAN'S DRUM (O)
Jonathan Cape and Harrison Smith Inc.: 1930 (8-1/4x6", 274 pgs, B&W hardcover w/dust jacket) (original graphic novel in wood cuts)

nn - By Lynd Ward 50.00 175.00 300.00

MAMA'S ANGEL CHILD IN TOYLAND (I)
Rand McNally, Chicago: 1915 (128 pgs, hardbound)

nn - By M.T. "Penny" Ross & Marie C, Sadler 40.00 140.00 240.00
NOTE: *Mamma's Angel Child published as a comic strip by the "Chicago Tribune" 1908 Mar 1 to 1920 Oct 17.This novel dedicated to Esther Starring Richartz, "the original Mamma's Angel Kid."*

MAUD (N) (see also **Happy Hooligan**)
Frederick A. Stokes Co.: 1906 - 1908? (10x15-1/2", cardboard-c)

1906-By Fred Opper (Scarce), 66 pgs. color 400.00 1200.00 –
1907-The Matchless, 10x15" 70 pgs in color 300.00 900.00 –
1908-The Mirthful Mule, 10x15", 64 pgs in color 300.00 900.00 –
NOTE: *First run of strip began July 24, 1904 to at least Oct 6, 1907, spun out of* ***Happy Hooligan.***

MEMORIAL EDITION The Drawings of Clare Briggs (S)
Wm H. Wise & Company: 1930 (7-1/2x8-3/4", 284 pgs, pebbled false black leather, B&W) (posthumous boxed set of 7 books by Clare Briggs)

nn - The Days of Real Sport; nn-Golf; nn-Real Folks at Home; nn-Ain't it a Grand and Glorious Feeling?; nn-That Guiltiest Feeling; nn-Somebody's Always Taking the Joy Out of Life; nn-When a Feller Needs a Friend
Each book... 30.00 120.00 210.00
NOTE: *Also exists in a whitish cream colored paper back edition; first edition unknown presently.*

MENACE CARTOONS (M, S)
Menace Publishing Company, Aurora, Missouri: 1914 (10-3/8x8", 80 pgs, cardboard-c, B&W)

nn - (Rare) 50.00 150.00 450.00
NOTE: *Reprints anti-Catholic cartoons from K.K.K. related publication* ***The Menace.***

MEN OF DARING (N)
Cupples & Leon Co.: 1933 (8-3/4x7", 100 pgs)

nn - By Stookie Allen, intro by Lowell Thomas 30.00 90.00 200.00

MICKEY MOUSE BOOK
Bibo & Lang: 1930-1931 (12x9", stapled-c, 20 pgs., 4 printings)

nn - First Disney licensed publication (a magazine, not a book–see first book, Adventures of Mickey Mouse). Contains story of how Mickey met Walt and got his name; games, cartoons & song "Mickey Mouse (You Cute Little Feller)," written by Irving Bibo; Minnie, Clarabelle Cow, Horace Horsecollar & caricature of Walt shaking hands with Mickey. The changes made with the 2nd printing have been verified by billing affidavits in the Walt Disney Archives and include:Two Win Smith Mickey strips from 4/15/30 and 4/17/30 added to page 8 & back-c; "Printed in U.S.A." added to front cover; Bobette Bibo's age of 11 years added to title page; faulty type on the word "tail" corrected top of page 3; the word "start" added to bottom of page 7, removing the words "start 1 2 3 4" from the top of page 7; music and lyrics were rewritten on pages 12-14. A green ink border was added beginning with 2nd printing and some covers have inking variations. Art by Albert Barbelle, drawn in an Ub Iwerks style. Total circulation : 97,938 copies varying from 21,000 to 26,000 per printing.

1st printing. Contains the song lyrics **censored** in later printings, "When little Minnie's pursued by a big bad villain we feel so bad then we're glad when you up and kill him." Attached to the Nov. 15, 1930 issue of the Official Bulletin of the Mickey Mouse Club notes: "Attached to this Bulletin is a new Mickey Mouse Book that has just been published." This is thought to be the reason why a slightly disproportionate larger number of copies of the first printing still exist 1200.00 6000.00 12,000.00
2nd printing with a theater/advertising. Christmas greeting added to inside front cover (1 copy known with Dec. 27, 1930 date) – 12,000.00 –
2nd-4th printings 1050.00 5000.00 10,000.00
NOTE: *Theater/advertising copies do not qualify as separate printings. Most copies are missing pages 9 & 10 which had a puzzle to be cut out. Puzzle (pages 9 and 10) cut out or missing, subtract 60% to 75%.*

MICKEY MOUSE COLORING BOOK (S)
Saalfield Publishing Company:1931 (15-1/4x10-3/4", 32 pgs, color soft cover, half printed in full color interior, rest B&W

871 - By Ub Iwerks & Floyd Gottfredson (rare) 400.00 1200.00 2520.00
NOTE: *Contains reprints of first MM daily strip ever, including the "missing" speck the chicken is after found only on the original daily strip art by Iwerks plus other very early MM art. There were several other Saalfield Mickey Mouse coloring books manufactured around the same time.*

MICKEY MOUSE, THE ADVENTURES OF (I)
David McKay Co., Inc.: Book I, 1931 - Book II, 1932 (5-1/2"x8-1/2", 32 pgs.)

Book I-First Disney book, by strict definition (1st printing-50,000 copies)(see Mickey Mouse Book by Bibo & Lang). Illustrated text refers to Clarabelle Cow as "Carolyn" and Horace Horsecollar as "Henry". The name "Donald Duck" appears with a non-costumed generic duck on back cover & inside, not in the context of the character that later debuted in the Wise Little Hen.
Hardback w/characters on back-c 75.00 300.00 650.00
Softcover w/characters on back-c 38.00 151.00 350.00
Version without characters on back-c 45.00 180.00 400.00
Book II-Less common than Book I. Character development brought into conformity with the Mickey Mouse cartoon shorts and syndicated strips. Captain Church Mouse, Tanglefoot, Peg-Leg Pete and Pluto appear with Mickey & Minnie 46.00 186.00 400.00

MICKEY MOUSE COMIC (N)
David McKay Co.: 1931 - No. 4, 1934 (10"x9-3/4", 52 pgs., card board-c)
(Later reprints exist)

1 (1931)-Reprints Floyd Gottfredson daily strips in black & white from 1930 & 1931, including the famous two week sequence in which Mickey tries to commit suicide 229.00 914.00 1680.00
2 (1932)-1st app. of Pluto reprinted from 7/8/31 daily. All pgs. from 1931 164.00 656.00 1200.00
3 (1933)-Reprints 1932 & 1933 Sunday pages in color, one strip per page, including the "Lair of Wolf Barker" continuity pencilled by Gottfredson and inked by Al Taliaferro & Ted Thwaites. First app. Mickey's nephews, Morty & Ferdie, one identified by name of Mortimer Fieldmouse, not to be confused with Uncle Mortimer Mouse who is introduced in the Wolf Barker story 214.00 856.00 1600.00
4 (1934)-1931 dailies, include the only known reprint of the infamous strip of 2/4/31 where the villainous Kat Nipp snips off the end of Mickey's tail with a pair of scissors 140.00 560.00 1050.00

MICKEY MOUSE (N)
Whitman Publishing Co.: 1933-34 (10x8-3/4", 34 pgs, cardboard-c)

948-1932 & 1933 Sunday strips in color, printed from the same plates as Mickey Mouse Book #3 by David McKay, but only pages 5-17 & 32-48 (including all of the "Wolf Barker" continuity) 157.00 629.00 1100.00
NOTE: *Some copies bound with back cover upside down. Variance doesn't affect value. Same art appears on front and back covers of all copies. Height of Whitman reissue trimmed 1/2 inch.*

MILITARY WILLIE
J. I. Austen Co.: 1907 (7x9-1/2", 12 pgs., every other page in color, stapled)

nn - By F. R. Morgan 70.00 245.00 400.00

MINNEAPOLIS TRIBUNE CARTOON BOOK (S)
Minneapolis Tribune: 1899-1903 (11-3/8x9-3/8", B&W, paper cover)

nn (#1) (1899) 28.00 99.00 170.00
nn (#2) (1900) 28.00 99.00 170.00
nn (#3) (1901) (published Jan 01, 1901) 28.00 99.00 170.00
nn (#4) (1902) (114 pgs) 28.00 99.00 170.00
nn (#5) (1903) (9x10-3/4",110 pgs, B&W; color-c) 28.00 99.00 170.00
NOTE: *All by Roland C. Bowman (editorial-r).*

MINUTE BIOGRAPHIES: INTIMATE GLIMPSES INTO THE LIVES OF 150 FAMOUS MEN AND WOMEN
Grossett & Dunlap: 1931, 1933 (10-1/4x7-3/4", 168 pgs, hardcover, B&W)

nn - By Nisenson (art) & Parker(text) 21.00 63.00 125.00
More.... (1933) 21.00 63.00 125.00

MISCHIEVOUS MONKS OF CROCODILE ISLE, THE (N)
J. I. Austen Co., Chicago: 1908 (8-1/2x11-1/2", 12 pgs., 4 pgs. in color)

nn - By F. R. Morgan; reads longwise 125.00 375.00 600.00

MR. & MRS. (Also see Ain't It A Grand and Glorious Feeling?) (N)
Whitman Publishing Co.: 1922 (9x9-1/2", 52 & 28 pgs., cardboard-c)

nn - By Briggs (B&W, 52 pgs.) 37.00 149.00 260.00
nn - 28 pgs.-(9x9-1/2")-Sunday strips-r in color 41.00 163.00 285.00

Moon Mullins #5 by Frank Willard
1931 @ Cupples & Leon

The Nebbs
© C&L

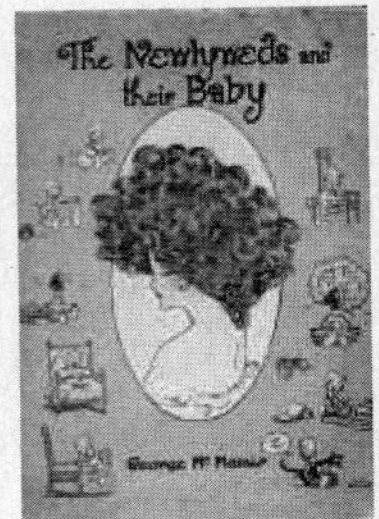

The Newlyweds by George McManus
1907 © Saalfield Publishing Co.

GD2.0 FN6.0 VF8.0

NOTE: The earliest presently-known Whitman comic books

MR. BLOCK (N)
Industrial Workers of the World (IWW): 1913, 1919
nn - By Ernest Riebe (C) 50.00 150.00 –
...And The Profiteers (original material) (H) 50.00 150.00 –
NOTE: Mr Block was a daily strip published from 1912 NOV 7 to 1913 SEP ? by the socialist newspaper "Industrial Worker"; Mr Block was a "square" guy (his head was in fact a block) who enthusiastically supported the same system that exploited him. The noted Joe Hill wrote a song about him (Mr Block,1913, on the air of "It loooks me like a big time tonight") for the "Industrial Worker Songbook".

MR. TWEE-DEEDLE (N)
Cupples & Leon: 1913, 1917 (11-3/8 x 16-3/4" color strips-r from NY Herald)
nn - By John B. Gruelle (later of Raggedy Ann fame) 350.00 900.00 1800.00
nn - "Further Adventures of..." By Gruelle 350.00 900.00 1800.00
NOTE: Strip ran Feb 5, 1911-March 10, 1918.

MONKEY SHINES OF MARSELEEN AND SOME OF HIS ADVENTURES (C)
McLaughlin Bros. New York: 1906 (10 x 12-3/8", 36 pgs, full color hardcover)
nn - By Norman E. Jennett strip-r NY Evening Telegram 100.00 250.00 450.00
NOTE: Strip began in 1906 until at least March 13, 1910.

MONKEY SHINES OF MARSELEEN (N)
Cupples & Leon Co.: 1909 (11-1/2 x 17", 58 pgs. in two colors)
nn - By Norman E. Jennett (strip-r New York Herald) 100.00 250.00 450.00

MOON MULLINS (N)
Cupples & Leon Co.: 1927 - 1933 (52 pgs., B&W daily strip-r)
Series 1 ('27)-By Willard 63.00 250.00 500.00
Series 2 ('28), Series 3 ('29), Series 4 ('30) 39.00 156.00 300.00
Series 5 ('31), 6 ('32), 7 ('33) 39.00 156.00 300.00
Big Book 1 ('30)-B&W (scarce) 100.00 400.00 750.00
w/dust jacket (rare) 183.00 732.00 1300.00

MOVING PICTURE FUNNIES
Saml Gabriel Sons & Company: 1918 (5-1/4 x 10-1/4", 52 pgs, B&W, illustrated hard-c)
nn 20.00 40.00 80.00
NOTE: 823 Comical illustrations that show a different scene when folded.

MUTT & JEFF (...Cartoon, The) (N)
Ball Publications: 1911 - No. 5, 1916 (5-3/4 x 15-1/2", 72 pgs, B&W, hard-c)
1 (1910)(50¢) very common 71.00 286.00 500.00
2,3: 2 (1911)-Opium den panels; Jeff smokes opium (pipe dreams).
3 (1912) both very common 71.00 286.00 500.00
2-(1913) Reprint of 1911 edition with black ink cover 50.00 175.00 300.00
4 (1915) (50¢) (Scarce) 150.00 350.00 650.00
5 (1916) (Rare) -Photos of Fisher, 1st pg. (68 pages) 200.00 480.00 900.00
5-Scarce 84 page reprint edition 150.00 450.00 800.00
NOTE: Mutt & Jeff first appeared in newspapers in 1907. Cover variations exist showing Mutt & Jeff reading various newspapers; i.e., The Oregon Journal, The American, and The Detroit News. Reprinting of each issue began soon after publication. No. 4 and 5 may not have been reprinted. Values listed include the reprints. Mutt & Jeff was the first successful American daily newspaper comic strip and as such remains one of the seminal strips of all time.

MUTT & JEFF (N)
Cupples & Leon Co.: No. 6, 1919 - No. 22, 1934? (9-1/2x9-1/2", 52 pgs., B&W dailies, stiff-c)
6, 7 - By Bud Fisher (very common) 32.00 128.00 225.00
8-10 46.00 186.00 325.00
11-18 (Somewhat Scarcer) (#19-#22 do not exist) 60.00 â240.00 420.00
nn (1920) (Advs. of...) 11x16"; 44 pgs.; full color reprints of 1919 Sunday strips 93.00 372.00 650.00
Big Book nn (1926, 144 pgs., hardcovers) 114.00 456.00 800.00
w/dust jacket 193.00 772.00 1350.00
Big Book 1 (1928) - Thick book (hardcovers) 114.00 456.00 800.00
w/dust jacket (rare) 182.00 729.00 1275.00
Big Book 2 (1929) - Thick book (hardcovers) 114.00 456.00 800.00
w/dust jacket (rare) 182.00 729.00 1275.00
NOTE: The Big Books contain three previous issues rebound.

MUTT & JEFF (N)
Embee Publ. Co.: 1921 (9x15", color cardboard-c & interior)
nn - Sunday strips in color (Rare)- BY Bud Fisher 143.00 572.00 1000.00
NOTE: Ties with The Trouble of Bringing Up Father (EmBee) and Jimmie Dugan & The Reg'lar Fellers (C&L) as the last of this size.

MYSTERIOUS STRANGER AND OTHER CARTOONS, THE
McClure, Phillips & Co.: 1905 (12-3/8x9-3/4", 338 pgs, hardcover, B&W)
nn - By John McCutcheon 32.00 128.00 225.00

MY WAR - Szeged (Szuts)
Wm. Morrow Co.: 1932 (7x10-1/2", 210 pgs, hard-c, B&W)
nn - (All story panels, no words - powerful) 32.00 128.00 225.00

NAUGHTY ADVENTURES OF VIVACIOUS MR. JACK, THE
New York American & Journal: 1904 (15x10", color strips)
nn - By James Swinnerton; (Very Rare - 3 known copies) 800.00 1500.00 2000.00

GD2.0 FN6.0 VF8.0

NEBBS, THE (N)
Cupples & Leon Co.: 1928 (52 pgs., B&W daily strip-r)
nn - By Sol Hess; Carlson-a 40.00 160.00 280.00

NERVY NAT'S ADVENTURES (E)
Leslie-Judge Co.: 1911 (90 pgs, 85¢, 1903 strip reprints from **Judge**)
nn - By James Montgomery Flagg 75.00 263.00 450.00

THE NEWLYWEDS AND THEIR BABY (N)
Saalfield Publ. Co.: 1907 (13x10", 52 pgs., hardcover)
...& Their Baby' by McManus; daily strips 50% color 300.00 900.00 –
NOTE: Strip ran Apr 10, 1904 thru Jan 14, 1906 and then May 19, 1907-Dec 5, 1916; was a huge success with Baby Snookums long before McManus invented Bringing Up Father; Snookums brought back as a topper strip over BUF Nov 19, 1944-Dec 30, 1956.

THE NEWLYWEDS AND THEIR BABY'S COMIC PICTURES FOR PAINTING AND CRAYONING (N)
Saalfield Publishign Company: 1916 (10-1/4x14-3/4", 52 pgs. Cardboard-c)
nn - 44 B&W pages, covers, and one color wrap glued to B&W title page.
Color wrap: color title pg. & 3 pgs of color strips 83.00 290.00 500.00
nn - (1917, 10x14", 20 pgs, oblong, cardboard-c) partial reprint of 1916 edition 31.00 124.00 275.00

THE NEWLYWEDS AND THEIR BABY (N)
Saalfield Publishing Company: 1917 (10-1/8x13-9/16 ", 52 pgs, full color cardstock-c, some pages full color, others two color (orange, blue))
nn 83.00 290.00 500.00

NEW YORKER CARTOON ALBUM, THE (M)
Doubleday, Doran & Company Inc.: (1928-1931); **Harper & Brothers.:** (1931-1933); **Random House** (1935-1937), 12x9", various pg counts, hardcovers w/dust jackets)
1928: nn-114 pgs Arno, Held, Soglow, Williams, etc 20.00 60.00 120.00
1928: SECOND-114 pgs Arno, Bairnsfather, Gross, Held, Soglow, Williams 10.00 30.00 60.00
1930: THIRD-172 pgs Arno, Bairnsfather, Held, Soglow, Art Young 10.00 30.00 60.00
1931: FOURTH-154 pgs Arno, Held, Soglow, Steig, Thurber, Williams, Art Young, "Little King" by Soglow begins 10.00 30.00 60.00
1932: FIFTH-156 pgs Arno, Bairnsfather, Held, Hoff, Soglow, Steig, Thurber, Williams 10.00 30.00 60.00
1933: SIXTH-156 pgs same as above 10.00 30.00 60.00
1935: SEVENTH-164 pgs 10.00 30.00 60.00
1937: 168 pgs; Charles Addams plus same as above but no Little King, two page "Gone With The Wind" parody strip 10.00 30.00 60.00
NOTE: Some sequential strips but mostly single panel cartoons.

NIPPY'S POP (N)
The Saalfield Publishing Co.: 1917 (10-1/2x13-1/2", 36 pgs., B&W, Sunday strip-r)
nn - Charles M Payne (better known as S'Matter Pop) 43.00 152.00 260.00

OH, MAN (A Bully Collection of Those Inimitable Humor Cartoons) (S)
P.F. Volland & Co.: 1919 (8-1/2x13"; 136 pgs.)
nn - By Briggs 43.00 152.00 260.00
NOTE: Originally came in illustrated box with Briggs art (box is Rare - worth 50% more with box).

OH SKIN-NAY! (S)
P.F. Volland & Co.: 1913 (8-1/2x13", 136 pgs.)
nn - The Days Of Real Sport by Briggs 43.00 152.00 260.00
NOTE: Originally came in illustrated box with Briggs art (box is Rare - worth 50% more with box).

OLD GOLD THE SMOOTHER AND BETTER CIGARETTE...NOT A COUGH IN A CARLOAD (M,N,P) (see also BY BRIGGS)
Old Gold Cigarettes: nd (c1920's) (16 pgs, paper-c, color) (both Scarce)
nn- (4-1/4" x 3-7/8") cover strip is "Oh, Man!"; also contains: "Real Folks at Home", "Ain't It a Grand and Glorious Feelin?", "It Happens in the Best Regulated Families", and "Mr. and Mrs." (no known sales)
1440- (5-9/16" x 5-1/4") cover strip is "Frank and Ernest"; also contains: "That Guiltiest Feeling", "Real Folks at Home", "Oh, Man!", "When a Feller Needs a Friend". (no known sales)
NOTE: Collection reprinting strip cartoons by Clare Briggs, advertising Old Gold Cigarettes. These strips originally appeared in various magazines, play program booklets, newspapers, etc. Some of the strips involve regular Briggs strip series. The two booklets contain a completely different set of comics.

ON AND OFF MOUNT ARARAT (also see **Tigers**) (N)
Hearst's New York American & Journal: 1902, 86pgs. 10x15-1/4"
nn - Rare Noah's Ark satire by Jimmy Swinnerton (rare) 450.00 1500.00 –

ON THE LINKS (N)
Associated Feature Service: Dec, 1926 (9x10", 48 pgs.)
nn - Daily strip-r 25.00 100.00 175.00

ONE HUNDRED WAR CARTOONS (S)
Idaho Daily Statesman: 1918 (7-3/4x10", 102 pgs, paperback, B&W)
nn - By Villeneuve (WW I cartoons) 20.00 60.00 120.00

OUR ANTEDILUVIAN ANCESTORS (N,S)

Oh Skin-nay! by Claire Briggs
1913 © P.F. Volland

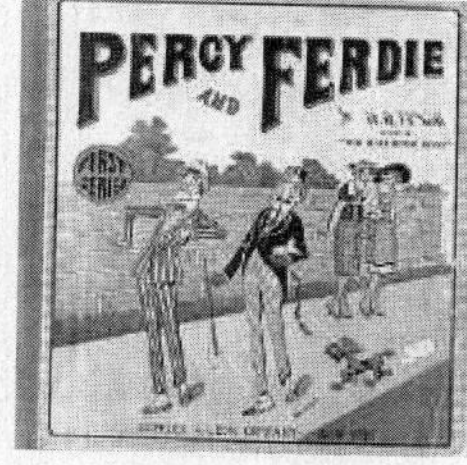

Percy and Ferdie
1921 © Cupples & Leon

Roger Bean, R.G. #4
© C&L

GD2.0 FN6.0 VF8.0

New York Evening Journal, NY: 1903 (11-3/8x8-7/8", hardcover)
nn - By F Opper 75.00 200.00 400.00
NOTE: *There is a simultaneously published British edition, identical size and contents, from C. Arthur Pearson Ltd, London. A collection of single panel cartoons about cavemen. Similar to an earlier British cartoon book "Prehistoric Peeps from Punch", by E.T. Reed.*

OUTBURSTS OF EVERETT TRUE, THE (N)
Saalfield Publ. Co.(Werner Co.): 1907 (92 pgs, 9-7/16x5-1/4")
1907 (2-4 panel strips-r)-By Condo & Raper 125.00 350.00 675.00
1921-Full color-c; reprints 56 of 88 cartoons from 1907 ed. (10x10", 32 pgs B&W) 125.00 225.00 350.00

OVER THERE COMEDY FROM FRANCE
Observer House Printing: nd (WW 1 era) (6x14", 60 pgs, paper cover)
nn - Artist(s) unknown 15.00 53.00 90.00

OWN YOUR OWN HOME (I)
Bobbs-Merrill Company, Indianapolis: 1919 (7-7/16x5-1/4")
nn - By Fontaine Fox – – –

PECKS BAD BOY (N)
Charles C. Thompson Co, Chicago (by Walt McDougal): 1906-1908 (strip-r)
The Adventures of... (1906) 11-1/2x16-1/4", 68 pgs 100.00 400.00 800.00
...& His Country Cousin Cynthia (1907) 12x16-1/2," 34 pgs In color 100.00 400.00 800.00
Advs. of...And His Country Cousins (1907) 5-1/2x10 1/2", 18 pgs In color 50.00 175.00 300.00
Advs. of...And His Country Cousins (1907) 11-1/2x16-1/4", 36 pgs 50.00 175.00 300.00
...& Their Advs With The Teddy Bear (1907) 5-1/2x10-1/2", 18 pgs in color 50.00 175.00 300.00
...& Their Balloon Trip To the Country (1907) 5-1/2x 10-1/2, 18 pgs in color 50.00 175.00 300.00
...With the Teddy Bear Show (1907) 5-1/2x 10-1/2 50.00 175.00 300.00
...With The Billy Whiskers Goats (1907) 5-1/2 x 10-1/2, 18 pgs in color 50.00 175.00 300.00
...& His Chums (1908) - 11x16-3/8", 36 pgs. Stanton & Van Vliet Co 100.00 400.00 750.00
...& His Chums (1908)-Hardcover; full color;16 pgs. 100.00 350.00 600.00
Advs. of...in Pictures (1908) (11x17, 36 pgs)-In color; Stanton & Van V. Liet Co. 100.00 400.00 700.00

PERCY & FERDIE (N)
Cupples & Leon Co.: 1921 (10x10", 52 pgs., B&W dailies, cardboard-c)
nn - By H. A. MacGill (Rare) 61.00 244.00 450.00

PETER RABBIT (N)
John H. Eggers Co. The House of Little Books Publishers: 1922 - 1923
B1-B4-(Rare)-(Set of 4 books which came in a cardboard box)-Each book reprints half of a Sunday page per page and contains 8 B&W and 2 color pages; by Harrison Cady (9-1/4x6-1/4", paper-c) each.... 43.00 172.00 300.00
Box only 57.00 228.00 400.00

PHILATELIC CARTOONS (M)
Essex Publishing Company, Lynn, Mass.: 1916 (8-11/16" x 5-7/8", 40 pgs, light blue construction paper-c, B&W interior)
nn - By Leroy S. Bartlett 25.00 75.00 175.00
NOTE: *Comics reprinted from The New England Philatelist.*

PICTORIAL HISTORY OF THE DEPARTMENT OF COMMERCE UNDER HERBERT HOOVER (see Picture Life of a Great American) (O)
Hoover-Curtis Campaign Committee of New York State: no date, 1928 (3-1/4 x 5-1/4, 32 pgs, paper cover, B&W)
nn - By Satterfield (scarce) 50.00 140.00 260.00
NOTE: *1928 Presidential Campaign giveaway. Original material, contents completely different from Picture Life of a Great American.*

PICTURE LIFE OF A GREAT AMERICAN (see Pictorial History of the Department of Commerce under Herbert Hoover) (O)
Hoover-Curtis Campaign Committee of New York State: no date, 1928 (paper cover, B&W)
nn - (8-3/4 x 7, 20 pgs) Text cover, 2 page text introduction, 18 pgs of comics (scarcer first print) 43.00 129.00 260.00
nn - (9 x 6-3/4,24 pgs) Illustrated cover,5 page text introduction, 18 pgs of comics (scarce) 43.00 129.00 260.00
NOTE: *1928 Presidential Campaign giveaway. Unknown which above version was published first. Both contain the same original comics material by Satterfield.*

PINK LAFFIN (I)
Whitman Publishing Co.: 1922 (9x12")(Strip-r; some of these actually text joke books)
...the Lighter Side of Life, ...He Tells 'Em, ...and His Family, ...Knockouts; Ray Gleason-a (All rare) each... 26.00 104.00 185.00

POLLY (AND HER PALS) - (N)

GD2.0 FN6.0 VF8.0

Newspaper Feature Service: 1916 (3x2-1/2", color)
Altogether: Three Rahs and a Tiger! by Cliff Sterrett 21.00 63.00 130.00
There Is A Limit To Pa's Patience by Cliff Sterrett 21.00 63.00 130.00
Pa's Lil Book Has Some Uncut Pages by Sterrett 21.00 63.00 130.00
NOTE: *Single newsprint sheet printed in full color on both sides, unfolds to show 12 panel story.*

POPEYE PAINT BOOK (N)
McLaughlin Bros, Inc., Springfield, Mass.: 1932 (9-7/8x13", 28 pgs, color-c)
2052 - By E. C. Segar 90.00 300.00 600.00
NOTE: *Contains a full color panel above and the exact same art in below panel n B&W which one was to color in; strip-r panels.*

POPEYE CARTOON BOOK (N)
The Saalfield Co.: 1934 (8-1/2x13", 40 pgs, cardboard-c)
2095-(scarce)-1933 strip reprints in color by Segar. Each page contains a vertical half of a Sunday strip, so the continuity reads row by row completely across each double page spread. If each page is read by itself, the continuity makes no sense. Each double page spread reprints one complete Sunday page from 1933 300.00 900.00 2700.00
12 Page Version 100.00 300.00 900.00

POPEYE (See **Thimble Theatre** for earlier Popeye-r from Sonnett) (N)
David McKay Publications: 1935 (25¢; 52 pgs, B&W) (By Segar)
1-Daily strip reprints- "The Gold Mine Thieves" 200.00 400.00 800.00
2-Daily strip-r (scarce) 200.00 400.00 900.00
NOTE: *Ties with Henry & Little Annie Rooney (David McKay) as the last of the 10x10" size books.*

PORE LI'L MOSE (N)
New York Herald Publ. by Grand Union Tea
Cupples & Leon Co.: 1902 (10-1/2x15", 78 pgs., color)
nn - By R. F. Outcault; Earliest known C&L comic book (scarce in high grade - very high demand) 1750.00 5775.00 –
NOTE: *Black Americana one page newspaper strips; falls in between Yellow Kid & Buster Brown. Complete copies have become scarce. Some have cut this book apart thinking that reselling individual pages will bring them more money.*

PRETTY PICTURES (M)
Farrar & Rinehart: 1931 (12 x 8-7/8", 104 pgs, color hardcover w/dust jacket, B&W; reprints from New Yorker, Judge, Life, Collier's Weekly)
nn - By Otto Soglow (contains "The Little King") 33.00 134.00 235.00

QUAINT OLD NEW ENGLAND (S)
Triton Syndicate: 1936 (5-1/4x6-1/4", 100 pgs, soft-c squarebound, B&W)
nn - By Jack Withycomb 36.00 144.00 250.00
NOTE: *Comics about weird doings in Old New England.*

RED CARTOONS (S)
Daily Worker Publishing Company: 1926 (12 x 9", 68 pgs,cardboard cover, B&W)
nn - By Various (scarce) 40.00 160.00 280.00
NOTE: *Reprint of American Communist Party editorial cartoons, from The Daily Worker, The Workers Monthly, and the Liberator. Art by Fred Ellis, William Gropper, Clive Weed, Art Young.*

REG'LAR FELLERS (See All-American Comics, Jimmie Dugan & The..., Popular Comics & Treasure Box of Famous Comics) (N)
Cupples & Leon Co./MS Publishing Co.: 1921-1929
1 (1921)-52 pgs. B&W dailies (Cupples & Leon, 10x10") 43.00 171.00 300.00
1925, 48 pgs. B&W dailies (MS Publ.) 39.00 157.00 275.00
Hardcover (1929, 8-3/4x7-1/2"; 96 pgs.)-B&W-r 54.00 214.00 375.00

REG'LAR FELLERS STORY PAINT BOOK
Whitman, Racine, Wisc.: 1932 (8-3/4x12-1/8", 132 pgs, red soft-c)
By Gene Byrnes 25.00 75.00 150.00

ROGER BEAN, R. G. (Regular Guy) (N)
The Indiana News Co, Distributers.: 1915 - No. 2, 1915 (5-3/8x17", 68 pgs., B&W, hardcovers); #3-#5 published by **Chas. B. Jackson:** 1916-1919
(No. 1 2 4 & 5 bound on side, No. 3 bound at top)
1-By Chas B. Jackson (68pgs.)(Scarce) 60.00 210.00 360.00
2- 5-5/8x17-1/8", 66 pgs (says 1913 inside - an obvious printing error) (red or green binding) 60.00 210.00 360.00
3-Along the Firing Line... (1916; 68 pgs, 6x17") 60.00 210.00 360.00
3-Along the Firing Line side-bound version 60.00 210.00 360.00
4-Into the Trenches and Out Again with... (1917, 68 pgs) 60.00 210.00 360.00
5 ...And The Reconstruction Period (1919, 5-3/8x15-1/2", 84 pgs) (Scarce) (has $1 printed on cover) 60.00 210.00 360.00
Baby Grand Editions 1-5 (10x10", cardboard-c) 60.00 210.00 360.00
NOTE: *No. 1 & 2 of the Twin Baby Grands (nd) 8-1/4x10-7/8", 52 pgs. #3 & #4 9x10-7/8" Cardboard cover. B&W strip reprints. Cover also says "Politics Pickles People Police."*
nn - 9x11, 68 pgs 60.00 210.00 360.00
NOTE: *Has picture of Chic Jackson and a posthumous dedication from his three children. strip-r 1931-32*

ROGER BEAN PHILOSOPHER
Schnull & Co: 1917 (5-1/2x17", 36 pgs., B&W, brown & black paper-c, square binding)
nn - By Chic Jackson (no known sales)

ROOKIE FROM THE 13TH SQUAD, THAT (N) (also Between Shots; Always Belittlin';Skippy)

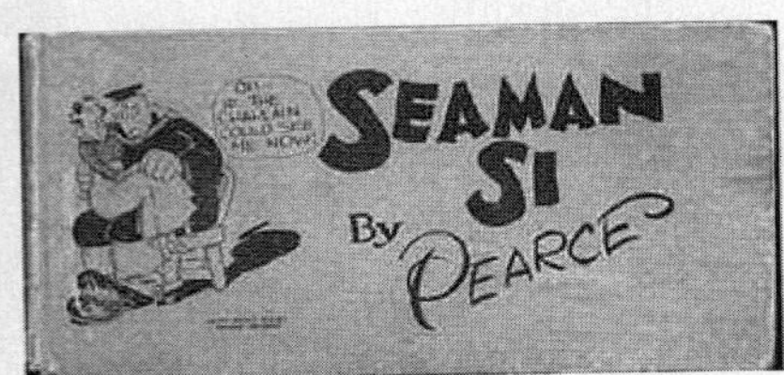

Seaman Si
© Pierce Publ. Co.

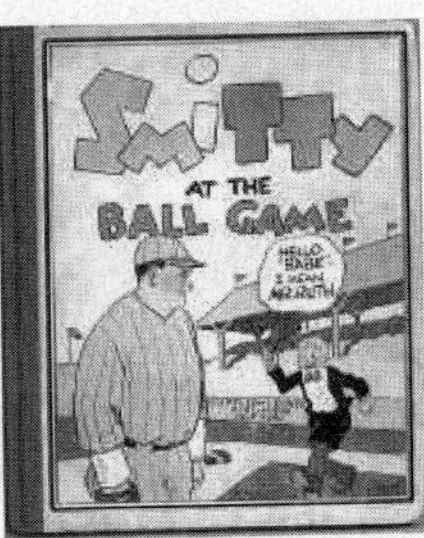

Smitty #2 By Walter Berndt
1929 © Cupples & Leon

Tailspin Tommy Story & Picture Book
By Hal Forest and Glenn Chappin
1932 © Cupples & Leon

GD2.0 FN6.0 VF8.0

Harper & Brothers Publishers: Feb. 1918 (8x9-1/4", 72 pgs, hardcover, B&W)
nn - By Lieut. P(ercy) L. Crosby 75.00 225.00 400.00
NOTE: *Strip began in 1917 at an Army base during basic training.*

ROUND THE WORLD WITH THE DOO-DADS (see Doings of the Doo-Dads, Doo Dads)
Universal Feature And Specialty Co, Chicago: 1922 (12x10-1/2", 52 pgs, B&W, red & light blue-c, square binding)
nn - By Arch Dale newspaper strip-r 43.00 173.00 300.00
NOTE: *Intermixed single panel and sequential comic strips with scenes from Scotland, Ireland, England, Holland, Italy, Spain, Egypt, Africa, and Lions & Elephants along the Nile River, China, Australia & back home.*

RUBAIYKT OF THE EGG
The John C Winston Co, Philadelphia: 1905 (7x5/12", 64 pgs, purple-c, B&W)
nn - By Clare Victor Dwiggins 20.00 60.00 125.00
NOTE: *Book is printed & cut into the shape of an egg.*

RULING CLAWSS, THE (N,S)
The Daily Worker: 1935 (192 pgs, 10-1/4 x 7-3/8", hard-c, B&W)
nn - By Redfield 60.00 240.00 –
NOTE: *Reprints cartoons from the American Communist Party newspaper The Daily Worker.*

SAGARA'S ENGLISH CARTOONS AND CARTOON STORIES (N)
Bunkosha, Tokyo: nd (c1925) (6-5/8" x 4-1/4", 272 pgs, hard-c, B&W)
nn- (Scarce) – – –
NOTE: *Published in Tokyo, Japan, with all strips in both English and Japanese, to facilitate learning English. Majority of book is Bringing Up Father by George McManus. Also contains Japanese strip Father Takes it Easy, by T. Sagara, reprinted from the Kokusai News Agency.*

SAM AND HIS LAUGH (N)
Frederick A. Stokes: 1906 (10x15", cardboard-c, Sunday strip-r in color)
nn - By Jimmy Swinnerton (Extremely Rare) 600.00 1200.00 2400.00
NOTE: *Strip ran July 24, 1904-Dec 26 1906; its ethnic humor might be considered racist by today's standards.*

SCHOOL DAYS (N)
Harper & Bros.: 1919 (9x8", 104 pgs.)
nn - By Clare Victor Dwiggins 75.00 150.00 300.00

SEAMAN SI - A Book of Cartoons About the Funniest "Gob" in the Navy (N)
Pierce Publishing Co.: 1916 (4x8-1/2, 200 pgs, hardcover, B&W); 1918 (4-1/8x8-1/4, 104 pgs, hardcover, B&W)
nn - By Perce Pearce (1916) 50.00 150.00 300.00
nn - 1918 - (Reilly & Britton Co.) 30.00 125.00 200.00
NOTE: *There exists two different covers for the 1918 reprints. The earlier edition was self published by the artist. The newspaper strip is sometimes also known as "The American Sailor."*

SECRET AGENT X-9 (N)
David McKay Pbll.: 1934 (Book 1: 84 pgs; Book 2: 124 pgs.) (8x7-1/2")
Book 1-Contains reprints of the first 13 weeks of the strip by Dashiell Hammett & Alex Raymond, complete except for 2 dailies 100.00 300.00 750.00
Book 2-Contains reprints immediately following contents of Book 1, for 20 weeks by Dashiell Hammett & Alex Raymond; complete except for two dailies. Last 5 strips misdated from 6/34, continuity correct 100.00 300.00 750.00

SILK HAT HARRY'S DIVORCE SUIT (N)
M. A. Donoghue & Co.: 1912 (5-3/4x15-1/2", oblong, B&W)
nn - Newspaper-r by Tad (Thomas A. Dorgan) 33.00 117.00 400.00

SINBAD A DOG'S LIFE (M)
Coward - McCann, Inc.: 1930 (11x 8-3/4", 104 pgs., single-sided, illustrated hard-c, B&W
nn - By Edwina 11.00 33.00 100.00
Sinbad...Again (1932, 10-15/16x 8-9/16", 104 pgs.) 11.00 33.00 100.00
NOTE: *Wordless comic strips from LIFE.*

SIS HOPKINS OWN BOOK AND MAGAZINE OF FUN
Leslie-Judge Co.: 1899-July 1911 (36 pgs, color-c, B&W) (merged into Judge's Library, later titled Film Fun)
any issue - By various 11.00 33.00 100.00
NOTE: *Zim, Flagg, Young, Newell, Adams, etc.*

SKEEZIX (Also see Gasoline Alley & Little Skeezix Books listed below) (I)
Reilly & Lee Co.: 1925 - 1928 (Strip-r, soft covers) (pictures & text)
...and Uncle Walt (1924)-Origin 26.00 104.00 180.00
...and Pal (1925), ...at the Circus (1926) 21.00 84.00 160.00
...& Uncle Walt (1927) (does this actually exist? reprint? never seen one yet)
...Out West (1928) 30.00 100.00 200.00
Hardback Editions... 34.00 136.00 235.00

SKEEZIX BOOKS, LITTLE (Also see Skeezix, Gasoline Alley) (G)
Reilly & Lee Co.: No date (1928, 1929) (Boxed set of three Skeezix books)
nn - Box with 3 issues of Skeezix. Skeezix & Pal, Skeezix at the Circus, Skeezix & Uncle Walt known. 1928 Set... 60.00 180.00 360.00
nn - Box with 4 issues of (3) above Skeezix plus "Out West" 80.00 330.00 550.00

SKEEZIX COLOR BOOK (N)
McLaughlin Bros. Inc, Springfield, Mass: 1929 (9-1/2x10-1/4", 28 pgs, one third in full color, rest in B&W)

GD2.0 FN6.0 VF8.0

2023 - By Frank King; strip-r to color 20.00 75.00 135.00

SKIPPY (see also Life Presents Skippy, Always Belittlin', That Rookie From 13th Squad)
No publisher listed: Circa 1920s (10x8", 16 pgs., color/B&W cartoons)
nn - By Percy Crosby 20.00 84.00 150.00

SKIPPY, LIFE PRESENTS (M)
Life Publishing Company & Henry Holt, NY: nd 1924 (134 pgs, 10-13/16x8-3/4", color hard-c, B&W
nn - By Percy L Crosby 100.00 300.00 500.00
NOTE: *Many sequential & single panel reprints from Skippy's earliest appearances in Life Magazine.*

SKIPPY
Greenberg, Publisher, Inc, NY: 1925. (11-14x8-5/8, 72 pgs, hard-c, B&W and color
nn - By Percy L. Crosby 50.00 150.00 300.00
NOTE: *Some but not all of these comics were also in Life Presents Skippy; issued with dust wrapper.*

SKIPPY AND OTHER HUMOR
Greenberg: Publisher, NY: 1929 (11-1/4x8-1/2",72 pgs,tan hard-c, B&W and color)
nn - By Percy L. Crosby 25.00 75.00 150.00
NOTE: *Came with a dust jacket.*

SKIPPY (I)
Grossett & Dunlap: 1929 (7-3/8x6, 370 pgs, hardcover text with some art)
nn - By Percy Crosby (issued with a dust jacket) 23.00 92.00 160.00
NOTE: *This is worth very little without the dust wrapper; very common without athe dust jacket.*

SKIPPY
Greenberg Press: 1930 (soft cover, ca. 16 pp.,
nn - By Percy Crosby (scarce) 50.00 175.00 300.00
NOTE: *Reprints from LIFE cartoons, color, b/w. Crosby told Greenberg to withdraw from the market as it cheapened the hard cover prior editions. Greenberg then stopped publishing per agreement, and sent Crosby all the copper & zinc bookplates, which were in Crosby estate until 1996.*

SKIPPY CRAYON AND COLORING BOOK (N)
McLoughlin Bros., Inc., Springfield, MA: 1931 (13x9-3/4", 28 pgs, color-c, color & B&W)
2050 - By Percy Crosby 28.00 84.00 195.00
NOTE: *This item says on the front cover: "Licensed by Percy Crosby" because he owned his creation. About half the pages have one panel pre-printed in full color with same one b&w below for person to copy the colors.*

SKIPPY RAMBLES (I)
G.P. Putnam's Sons: 1932 (7 1/8 x 5 1/8, 202 pgs)
nn - By Percy Crosby 21.00 84.00 150.00
NOTE: *Issued with a dustjacket. Has Skippy plates by Crosby every 4 or 5 pages.*

SKUDDABUD STARRY STORY SERIES - FOLK FROM THE FUTURE (O,G)
no publisher listed: 1936 (9" x 11-7/8", 48 pgs, cardboard-c, B&W)
Book One (Rare) "Parachuting" 21.00 84.00 150.00
NOTE: *By Columba Krebs. Top half of each page is a continuing strip story, while bottom half are different stories, in prose, about the same characters -- a race of aliens who have migrated to Earth, from their dying world.*

S'MATTER POP? (N)
Saalfield Publ. Co.: 1917 (10x14", 44 pgs., B&W, cardboard-c,)
nn - By Charlie Payne; in full color; pages printed on one side 48.00 169.00 290.00

S'MATTER POP? (N) (25 ¢ cover price)
E.I. Company, New York: 1927 (8-15/16x7-1/8", 52 pgs, yellow soft-c perfect bound
nn - By C.M. Payne (scarce) 24.00 84.00 145.00
NOTE: *First comic book published by Hugo Gernsback, noted for inventing Amazing Stories among other memorable science fiction pulps. The World Science Fiction Convention Award, The Hugo, is named for him.*

SMITTY (See Treasure Box of Famous Comics) (N)
Cupples & Leon Co.: 1928 - 1933 (9x7", 96 pgs., B&W strip-r, hardcover)
1928-(96 pgs. 7x8-3/4") By Walter Berndt 43.00 172.00 300.00
1929-At the Ball Game (Babe Ruth on cover) 57.00 229.00 450.00
1930-The Flying Office Boy, 1931-The Jockey, 1932-In the North Woods each... 31.00 126.00 250.00
1933-At Military School 31.00 126.00 250.00
NOTE: *Each hardbound was published with a dust jacket; worth 50% more with dust jacket. The 1929 edition is very popular with baseball collectors. Strip debuted Nov 27, 1922.*

SMOKEY STOVER (See Dan Dunn & King of the Royal Mounted) (N)
Whitman Publishing: 1937 (5 1/2 x 7 1/4", 68pgs., color cardboard-c, B&W)
1010 36.00 144.00 250.00

SOCIAL COMEDY (M)
Life Publishing Company: 1902 (11-3/4 x 9-1/2", 128 pgs, B&W, illustrated hardcover)
nn - Artists include C.D. Gibson & Kemble. 20.00 70.00 120.00
NOTE: *Reprints cartoons and a few sequential comics from LIFE. Came in unmarked slipcase.*

SOCIAL HELL, THE (O)
Rich Hill: 1902
nn - By Ryan Walker 21.00 74.00 130.00
NOTE: *"The conditions of workers and the corruption of a political system beholden to corporate interests have been a major focus of human rights concerns since the 19th century. This early graphic novel depicts the social evils of unreformed capitalism. Ryan Walker was a syndicate cartoonist for many mainstream newspapers as well as for the communist Daily Worker." This description comes from http://www.lib.uconn.edu/DoddCenter/ascexh3.html, where*

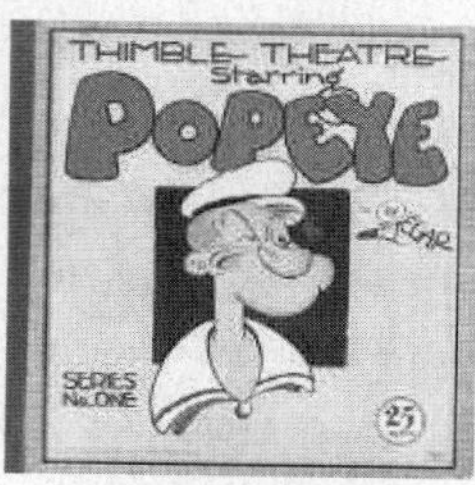

Thimble Theater #1 by E.C. Segar
1931 © Sonnet Publishing Co.

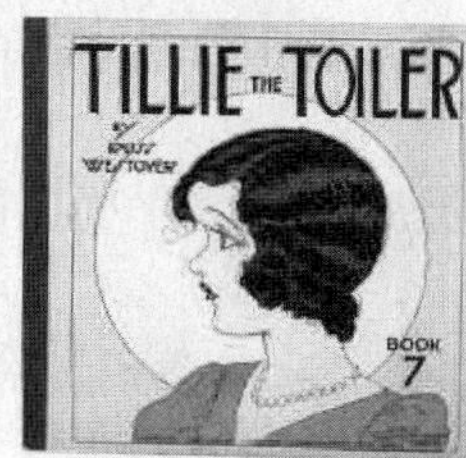

Tillie the Toiler #7 by Russ Westover
1932 © Cupples & Leon

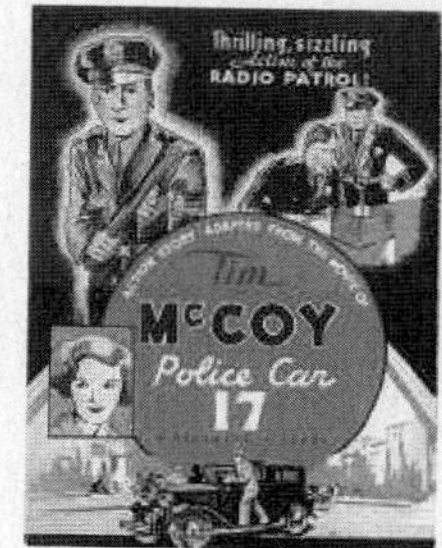

Tim McCoy, Police Car 17
© Whitman Publ. Co.

GD2.0 FN6.0 VF8.0

you can find also a reproduction of the cover. I add that Ryan Walker was the editor of "The Saint Louis Republic" comic section since its inception in 1897; the supplement published "Alma and Oliver", George McManus's first series.

SPORT AND THE KID (see The Umbrella Man) (N)
Lowman & Hanford Co.: 1913 (6-1/4x6-5/8",114 pgs, hardcover, B&W&orange)
nn - By J.R. "Dok" Hager 20.00 70.00 120.00

STORY OF CONNECTICUT (N)
The Hartford Times: Vol.1 1935 - Vol.3 1936 (10-1/2" x 7-3/8",304 pgs,color hard-c, B&W)
Vol.1 - 3 20.00 70.00 120.00
NOTE: *Collects a newspaper strip on Connecticut State history, which ran in the Hartford Times. Strip is in a similar format to "Texas History Movies". Also published in a plain, blue hardcover.*

STORY OF JAPAN IN CHINA, THE (N,S)
Trans-Pacific News Service, NYC: Vol. 3, No.1 March 10, 1938 (9" x 6", 36 pgs, construction paper-c, B&W)
Vol.3 No.1 21.00 64.00 150.00
NOTE: *Part of the "China Reference Series" of booklets, detailing the Japanese occupation and brutalization of China. Consists entirely of cartoons. The other booklets in the series have no cartoons. Art by: Ding, Fitzpatrick, Herblock, Herman, Rollin Kirby, Knox, Low, Manning, Orr, Shoemaker, Talburt.*

STRANGE AS IT SEEMS (S)
Blue-Star Publishing Co.: 1932 (64 pgs., B&W, square binding)
1-Newspaper-r (*Published with & without No. 1 and price on cover.*) 32.00 128.00 225.00
Ex-Lax giveaway (1936, B&W, 24 pgs., 5x7") - McNaught Synd. 13.00 52.00 90.00

SULLIVANT'S ABC ZOO (I)
The Old Wine Press: 1946 (11-3/4x9-3/8", hardcover)
nn - By T.S. Sullivant (Rare) – – –
NOTE: *Reprints Mitchell & Miller material 1895-1898 and Life Publishing 1898-1926.*

TAILSPIN TOMMY STORY & PICTURE BOOK (N)
McLoughlin Bros.: No. 266, 1931? (nd) (10x10-1/2", color strip-r)
266 - By Forrest 43.00 172.00 300.00

TAILSPIN TOMMY (Also see Famous Feature Stories & The Funnies)(N)
Cupples & Leon Co.: 1932 (100 pgs., hard-c) (B&W 1930 strip reprints)
nn - (Scarce)- by Hal Forrest & Glenn Chaffin 50.00 150.00 375.00

TALES OF DEMON DICK AND BUNKER BILL (O)
Whitman Publishing Co.: 1934 (5-1/4x10-1/2", 80 pgs, color hardcover, B&W)
793 - By Spencer 33.00 100.00 300.00

TARZAN BOOK (The Illustrated...) (N)
Grosset & Dunlap: 1929 (9x7", 80 pgs.)
1(Rare)-Contains 1st B&W Tarzan newspaper comics from 1929. By Hal Foster Cloth reinforced spine & dust jacket (50¢); Foster-c
With dust jacket... 86.00 344.00 630.00
Without dust jacket... 43.00 172.00 315.00
2nd Printing(1934, 25¢, 76 pgs.)-4 Foster pgs. dropped; paper spine, circle in lower right cover with 25¢ price. The 25¢ is barely visible on some copies 34.00 136.00 250.00
1967-House of Greystoke reprint-7x10", using the complete 300 illustrations/text from the 1929 edition minus the original indicia, foreword, etc. Initial version bound in gold paper & sold for $5.00. Officially titled **Burroughs Bibliophile #2**. A very few additional copies were bound in heavier blue paper. Gold binding... 2.25 6.75 20.00
Blue binding... 2.50 7.50 27.00

TARZAN OF THE APES TO COLOR (N)
Saalfield Publishing Co.: No. 988, 1933 (15-1/4x10-3/4", 24 pgs)
(Coloring book)
988-(Very Rare)-Contains 1929 daily reprints with some new art by Hal Foster. Two panels blown up large on each page with one at the top of opposing pages on every other double-page spread. Believed to be the only time these panels appeared in color. Most color panels are reproduced a second time in B&W to be colored 271.00 1084.00 2000.00

TARZAN OF THE APES The Big Little Cartoon Book (N)
Whitman Publishing Company: 1933 (4-1/2x3 5/8", 320 pgs, color-c, B&W)
744 - By Hal Foster (comic strips on every page) 60.00 175.00 325.00

TECK HASKINS AT OHIO STATE (S)
Lea-Mar Press: 1908 (7-1/4x5-3/8", 84 pgs, B&W hardcover)
nn - By W.A. Ireland; football cartoons-r from Columbus Ohio Evening Dispatch 28.00 99.00 170.00
NOTE: *Small blue & white patch of cover art pasted atop a color cloth quilt patter; pasted patch can easily peel off some copies.*

TECK 1909 (S)
Lea-Mar Press: 1909 (8-5/8 x 8-1/8", 124 pgs., B&W hardcover, 25¢)
nn - By W.A. Ireland; Ohio State University baseball cartoons-r from Columbus Evening Dispatch 28.00 99.00 170.00

TEDDY BEAR BOOKS, THE (M) (see also LITTLE JOHNNY AND THE TEDDY BEARS)
Reilly & Britton Co., Chicago: 1907 (7-1/16" x 5-3/8", 24 pgs, hard-c, color

GD2.0 FN6.0 VF8.0

The Teddy Bears Come to Life, The Teddy Bears at the Circus, The Teddy Bears in a Smashup, The Teddy Bears on a Lark, The Teddy Bears on a Toboggan, The Teddy Bears at School, The Teddy Bears Go Fishing, The Teddy Bears in Hot Water 21.00 63.00 130.00
NOTE: *Books are all unnumbered. C & A by J.R. Bray; s-Robert D. Towne. Reprints "Little Johnny & the Teddy Bears" strips, from Judge Magazine. Similar in format to the Buster Brown Nuggets series. All eight books debuted simultaneously.*

TEDDY BEARS IN FUN AND FROLIC (M) (see LITTLE JOHNNY & THE TEDDY BEARS)
Reilly & Britton Co., Chicago: 1908 (8-3/4" x 8-3/4", 50 pgs, cardboard-c, color)
nn - (Rare) by J.R. Bray-a; Robert D. Towne-s 100.00 400.00 700.00
NOTE: *Reprints "Little Johnny & the Teddy Bears" strips, from Judge Magazine. Unknown if there were any other "Teddy Bear" titles published in this format.*

THE TEENIE WEENIES
Reilly & Britton, Chicago: 1916 (16-3/8x10-1/2", 52 pgs, cardboard-c, full color)
nn - By Wm. Donahey (Chicago Tribune-r) 200.00 550.00 900.00

TERROR OF THE TINY TADS (see also UPSIDE DOWNS OF LITTLE LADY LOVEKINS AND OLD MAN MUFFAROO)
Cupples & Leon: 1909 (11x17, 26 Sunday strips in Black & Red, Stiff cardboard-c)
nn - By Gustave Verbeek (Very Rare) (no known sales)

TEXAS HISTORY MOVIES (N)
Various editions, 1928 to 1986 (B&W)
Book I -1928 Southwest Press (7-1/4 x 5-3/8, 56 pgs, cardboard cover) for the Magnolia Petroleum Company 50.00 125.00 250.00
nn - 1928 Southwest Press (12-3/8 x 9-1/4, 232 pgs, HC) 75.00 200.00 400.00
nn - 1935 Magnolia Petroleum Company (6 x 9, 132 pgs, paper cover) 21.00 63.00 130.00
NOTE: *Exists with either Wagon Train or Texas Flag & Lafitte/pirate covers.*
nn - 1943 Magnolia Petroleum Company (132 pgs, paper cover) 16.00 48.00 100.00
nn - 1963 Graphic Ideas Inc (11 x 8-1/2, softcover) 12.00 37.00 75.00
NOTE: *Reprints daily newspaper strips from the Dallas News, on Texas history. 1935 editions onward distributed within the Texas Public School System. Prior to that they appear to be giveaway comic books for the Magnolia Petroleum Company. There are many more editions than the ones pointed out above.*

THAT SON-IN-LAW OF PA'S! (N)
Newspaper Feature Service: 1914 (2-1/2 by 3", color)
nn - *Imprinted on back for THE LESTER SHOE STORE.* 15.00 25.00 50.00
NOTE: *Single sheet printed in full color on both sides, unfolds to show 12 panel story.*

THIMBLE THEATRE STARRING POPEYE (See also Popeye) (N)
Sonnet Publishing Co.: 1931 - No. 2, 1932 (25¢, B&W, 52 pgs.)(Rare)
1-Daily strip serial-r in both by Segar 157.00 650.00 1300.00
2 136.00 544.00 1100.00
NOTE: *The very first Popeye reprint book. The first Thimble Theatre Sunday page appeared Dec 19, 1919. Popeye first entered Thimble Theatre on Jan 17, 1929.*

THREE FUN MAKERS, THE (N)
Stokes and Company: 1908 (10x15", 64 pgs., color) (1904-06 Sunday strip-r)
nn - Maud, Katzenjammer Kids, Happy Hooligan 800.00 2000.00 –
NOTE: *This is the first comic book to compile more than one newspaper strip together.*

TIGERS (Also see On and Off Mount Ararat) (N)
Hearst's New York American & Journal: 1902, 86 pgs. 10x15-1/4"
nn - Funny animal strip-r by Jimmy Swinnerton 600.00 1600.00 –
NOTE: *The strip began as The Journal Tigers in The New York Journal Dec 12, 1897-Sept 28 1903*

TILLIE THE TOILER (N)
Cupples & Leon Co.: 1925 - No. 8, 1933 (52 pgs., B&W, daily strip-r)
nn (#1) By Russ Westover 54.00 216.00 450.00
2-8 50.00 175.00 360.00
NOTE: *First newspaper strip appearance was in January, 1921.*

TILLIE THE TOILER MAGIC DRAWING AND COLORING BOOK
Sam L Gabriel Sons And Company: 1931 (8-1/2 x 12", 36 pages, stiff-c)
838-By Russ Westover 39.00 156.00 275.00

TIMID SOUL, THE (N)
Simon & Schuster: 1931 (12-1/4x9", 136 pgs, B&W hardcover, dust jacket?)
nn - By H. T. Webster (newspaper strip-r) 40.00 120.00 260.00

TIM McCOY, POLICE CAR 17 (O)
Whitman Publishing Co.: 1934 (14-3/4x11", 32 pgs, stiff color covers)
674-1933 original material 75.00 300.00 600.00
NOTE: *Historically important as first movie adaptation in comic books.*

TOAST BOOK
John C. Winston Co: 1905 (7-1/4 x 6,104 pgs, skull-shaped book, feltcover, B&W)
nn - By Clare Dwiggins 50.00 175.00 300.00
NOTE: *Cartoon illustrations accompanying toasts/poems, most involving alcohol.*

TOM SAWYER & HUCK FINN (N)
Stoll & Edwards Co.:1925 (10x10-3/4", 52 pgs, stiff covers)
nn - By "Dwig" Dwiggins; 1923, 1924-r color Sunday strips 5000 200.00 350.00

When a Feller Needs a Friend
© P.F. Volland & Co.

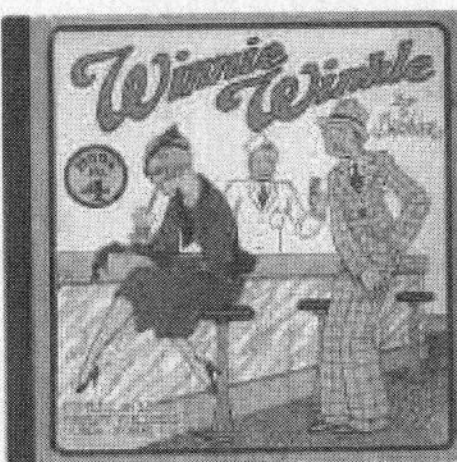

Winnie Winkle #4 by Branner
1933 © Cupples & Leon

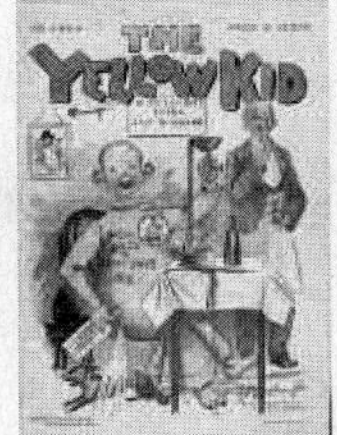

The Yellow Kid #4 cover by Outcault
1897 © Howard Ainslee & Co.

	GD2.0	FN6.0	VF8.0

NOTE: *By Permission of the Estate of Samuel L. Clemons and the Mark Twain Company.*

TOONERVILLE TROLLEY AND OTHER CARTOONS (N) (See Cartoons by Fontaine Fox)
Cupples & Leon Co.: 1921 (10 x10", 52 pgs., B&W, daily strip-r)

	GD2.0	FN6.0	VF8.0
1 - By Fontaine Fox	100.00	350.00	600.00

TRAINING FOR THE TRENCHES (M)
Palmer Publishing Company: 1917 (5-3/8 x 7", 20 pgs., paper-c, 10¢)

	GD2.0	FN6.0	VF8.0
nn - By Lieut. Alban B. Butler, Jr.	21.00	84.00	150.00

NOTE: *Subtitle: "A book of humorous cartoons on a serious subject." Single-panels about military training.*

TREASURE BOX OF FAMOUS COMICS (N) (see Wonder Chest of Famous Comics)
Cupples & Leon Co.: 1934 8-1/2x(6-7/8", 36 pgs, soft covers) (Boxed set of 5 books)

	GD2.0	FN6.0	VF8.0
Little Orphan Annie (1926)	21.00	84.00	165.00
Reg'lar Fellers (1928)	19.00	76.00	145.00
Smitty (1928)	19.00	76.00	145.00
Harold Teen (1931)	19.00	76.00	145.00
How Dick Tracy & Dick Tracy Jr. Caught The Racketeers (1933)	26.00	104.00	205.00
Softcover set of five books in box	160.00	640.00	1250.00
Box only	57.00	228.00	450.00

NOTE: *Dates shown are copyright dates; all books actually came out in 1934 or later. The softcovers are abbreviated versions of the hardcover editions listed under each character.*

T.R. IN CARTOONS (N)
A.C. McClurg & Co., Chicago: June 13, 1910 (10-5/8" x 8", 104? pgs, paper-c, B&W)

	GD2.0	FN6.0	VF8.0
nn - By McCutcheon about Teddy Roosevelt	-	-	–

TRUTH (See Victorian section for earlier issues including the first Yellow Kid appearances)
Truth Company, NY: 1886-1906? (13-11/16x10-5/16", 16 pgs, process color-c & center-folds, rest B&W)

	GD2.0	FN6.0	VF8.0
1900-1906 issues	10.00	20.00	50.00

TRUTH SAVE IT FROM ABUSE & OVERWORK BEING THE EPISODE OF THE HIRED HAND & MRS. STIX PLASTER, CONCERTIST (N)
Radio Truth Society of WBAP: no date, 1924 (6-3/8 x 4-7/8, 40 pgs, paper cover, B&W)

	GD2.0	FN6.0	VF8.0
nn - By V.T. Hamlin (Very Rare)	100.00	400.00	700.00

NOTE: *Radio station WBAP giveaway reprints strips from the Ft. Worth Texas Star-Telegram set at local radio station. 1st collected work by V.T. Hamlin, pre-Alley Oop.*

TWENTY FIVE YEARS AGO (see At The Bottom Of The Ladder) (M,S)
Coward-McCann: 1931 (5-3/4x8-1/4, 328 pgs, hardcover, B&W)

	GD2.0	FN6.0	VF8.0
nn - By Camillus Kessler	32.00	128.00	225.00

NOTE: *Multi-image panel cartoons showing historical events for dates during the year.*

UMBRELLA MAN, THE (N) (See Sport And The Kid)
Lowman & Hanford Co.: 1911 (8-7/8x5-7/8",112 pgs, hard-c, B&W & orange)

	GD2.0	FN6.0	VF8.0
nn - By J.R. "Dok" Hager (Seattle Times-r)	20.00	70.00	120.00

UNCLE REMUS AND BRER RABBIT (N)
Frederick A. Stokes Co.: 1907 (64 pgs, hardbound, color)

	GD2.0	FN6.0	VF8.0
nn - By Joel C Harris & J.M. Conde	50.00	175.00	300.00

UPSIDE DOWNS OF LITTLE LADY LOVEKINS AND OLD MAN MUFFAROO
(see also TERROR OF THE TINY TADS)
New York Herald: 1905 (?) (N)

	GD2.0	FN6.0	VF8.0
nn - By Gustav Verbeck	150.00	450.00	750.00

VAUDEVILLES AND OTHER THINGS (N)
Isaac H. Blandiard Co.: 1900 (13x10-1/2", 22 pgs., color) plus two reprints

	GD2.0	FN6.0	VF8.0
nn - By Bunny (Scarce)	400.00	1200.00	–
nn - 2nd print "By the Creator of Foxy Grandpa" on-c but only has copyright info of 1900 (10-1/2x15 1/2, 28 pgs, color)	450.00	900.00	–
nn - 3rd print. "By the creator of Foxy Grandpa" on-c; has both 1900 and 1901 copyright info (11x13")	350.00	700.00	–

WALLY - HIS CARTOONS OF THE A.E.F. (N)
Stars & Stripes: 1917 (96 and 108 pgs, B&W)

	GD2.0	FN6.0	VF8.0
nn - By Abian A "Wally" Wallgren (7x18; 96 pgs)	25.00	75.00	150.00
nn - another edition (108 pgs, 7x17-1/2)	25.00	75.00	150.00

NOTE: *World War One cartoons reprints from Stars & Stripes; sold to U.S. servicemen with profits to go to French War Orphans Fund. various editions from 1917-1920; there might be more than what we list here.*

WAR CARTOONS (S)
Dallas News: 1918 (11x9", 112 pgs, hardcover, B&W)

	GD2.0	FN6.0	VF8.0
nn - By John Knott (WWOne cartoons)	20.00	70.00	125.00

WAR CARTOONS FROM THE CHICAGO DAILY NEWS (N,S)
Chicago Daily News: 1914 (10 cents, 7-3/4x10-3/4", 68 pgs, paper-c, B&W)

	GD2.0	FN6.0	VF8.0
nn - By L.D. Bradley	20.00	70.00	125.00

WEBER & FIELD'S FUNNYISMS (S,M,O)
Arkell Comoany, NY: 1904 (10-7/8x8", 112 pgs, color-c, B&W)

	GD2.0	FN6.0	VF8.0
1 - By various (only issue?)	20.00	70.00	150.00

NOTE: *Contains some sequential & many single panel strips by Outcault, George Luks, CA David, Houston, L Smith, Hy Mayer, Verbeck, Woolf, Sydney Adams, Frank "Chip" Bellew, Eugene "ZIM" Zimmerman, Phil May, FT Richards, Billy Marriner, Grosvenor and many others.*

WE'RE NOT HEROES (O,S)
E.C. Wells and J.W. Moss: 1933 (8-11/16" x 5-7/8", 52 pgs, B&W interior)

	GD2.0	FN6.0	VF8.0
nn - By Eddie Wells; red & black paper-c	10.00	30.00	60.00

NOTE: *Amateurish cartoons about World War I vets in the Walter Reed Veteran's Hospital.*

WHEN A FELLER NEEDS A FRIEND (S)
P. F. Volland & Co.: 1914 (11-11/16x8-7/8)

	GD2.0	FN6.0	VF8.0
nn - By Clare Briggs	37.00	131.00	225.00

NOTE: *Originally came in box with Briggs art (box is Rare); also numerous more modern reprints)*

WILD PILGRIMAGE (O)
Harrison Smith & Robert Haas: 1932 (9-7/8x7", 210 pgs, B&W hardcover w/dust jacket) (original wordless graphic novel in woodcuts)

	GD2.0	FN6.0	VF8.0
nn - By Lynd Ward	50.00	175.00	300.00

WILLIE AND HIS PAPA AND THE REST OF THE FAMILY (I)
Grossett & Dunlap: 1901 (9-1/2x8", 200 pgs, hardcover from N.Y. Evening Journal by Permission of W. R. Hearst) (pictures & text)

	GD2.0	FN6.0	VF8.0
nn - By Frederick Opper	100.00	260.00	450.00

NOTE: *Political satire series of single panel cartoons, involving whiny child Willie (President William McKinley), his rambunctious and uncontrollable cousin Teddy (Vice President Roosevelt), and Willie's Papa (trusts/monopolies) and their Maid (Senator) Hanna.*

WILLIE GREEN COMICS, THE (N) (see Adventures of Willie Green)
Frank M. Acton Co./Harris Brown: 1915 (8x15, 36 pgs); 1921 (6x10-1/8", 52 pgs, color paper cover, B&W interior, 25¢)

	GD2.0	FN6.0	VF8.0
Book No. 1 By Harris Brown	45.00	158.00	270.00
Book 2 (#2 sold via mail order directly from the artist)(very rare)	45.00	172.00	300.00

NOTE: *Book No. 1 possible reprint of Adv. of Willie Green; definitely two different editions.*

WILLIE WESTINGHOUSE EDISON SMITH THE BOY INVENTOR (N)
William A. Stokes Co.: 1906 (10x16", 36 pgs. in color)

	GD2.0	FN6.0	VF8.0
nn - By Frank Crane (Scarce)	350.00	850.00	1500.00

NOTE: *Comic strip began May 27, 1900 and ran thru 1914. Parody of inventors Westinghouse and Edison.*

WINNIE WINKLE (N)*Strip began as a daily Sept 20, 1920.*
Cupples & Leon Co.: 1930 - No. 4, 1933 (52 pgs., B&W daily strip-r)

	GD2.0	FN6.0	VF8.0
1	43.00	172.00	400.00
2-4	29.00	116.00	300.00

WISDOM OF CHING CHOW, THE (see also The Gumps)
R. J. Jefferson Printing Co.: 1928 (4x3", 100 pgs, red & B&W cardboard cover) (newspaper strip-r The Chicago Tribune)

	GD2.0	FN6.0	VF8.0
nn - By Sidney Smith (scarce)	30.00	90.00	150.00

WONDER CHEST OF FAMOUS COMICS (N) see Treasure Chest of Famous Comics)
Cupples & Leon Co.: 1935? 8-1/2x(6-7/8", 36 pgs, soft covers) (Boxed set of 5 books)

	GD2.0	FN6.0	VF8.0
Little Orphan Annie #2 (1927) (Haunted House)	21.00	84.00	130.00
Little Orphan Annie #3 (1928) (in the Circus)	19.00	76.00	130.00
Smitty #2 (1929) (Babe Ruth app.)	19.00	76.00	130.00
Dolly Dimples and Bobby Bounce (1933) by Grace Drayton	19.00	76.00	130.00
How Dick Tracy & Dick Tracy Jr. Caught The Racketeers (1933)	26.00	104.00	185.00
Softcover set of five books in box	160.00	640.00	1125.00
Box only	57.00	228.00	400.00

NOTE: *Dates shown are original copyright dates of the first printings; all actually came out in 1934 or later. Extremely abbreviated versions of the hardcover editions listed under each character. It is suspected this came out the Christmas season following Teasure Chest of Famous Comics. which contains earlier editions.*

WORLD OF TROUBLE, A (S)
Minneapolis Journal: 1901 (10x8-3/4", 100 pgs, 40 pgs full color)

	GD2.0	FN6.0	VF8.0
v3#1 - By Charles L. Bartholomew (editorial-r)	28.00	99.00	170.00

WRIGLEY'S "MOTHER GOOSE"
Wm. Wrigley Jr. Company, Chicago: 1915 (6" x 4", 28 pgs, full color)

	GD2.0	FN6.0	VF8.0
nn - *Promotional comics for Wrigley's gum. Intro Wrigley's "Spearmen*	20.00	70.00	120.00
Book No. 2	20.00	70.00	120.00

YELLOW KID, THE (Magazine)(I) (becomes **The Yellow Book** #10 on)
Howard Ainslee & Co., N.Y.: Mar. 20, 1897 - #9, July 17, 1897
(5¢, B&W w/color covers, 52p., stapled) (not a comic book)

	GD2.0	FN6.0	VF8.0
1-R.F. Outcault Yellow kid on-c only #1-6. The same Yellow Kid color ad app. on back-c #1-6 (advertising the New York Sunday Journal)	857.00	3500.00	–
2-6 (#2 4/3/97, #5 5/22/97, #6, 6/5/97)	743.00	2800.00	–
7-9 (Yellow Kid not on-c)	121.00	425.00	–

NOTE: *Richard Outcault's Yellow Kid from the Hearst New York American represents the very first successful newspaper comic strip in America. Listed here due to historical importance.*

YELLOW KID IN MCFADDEN'S FLATS, THE (N)
G. W. Dillingham Co., New York: 1897 (50¢, 7-1/2x5-1/2", 196 pgs., B&W, squarebound)

	GD2.0	FN6.0	VF8.0
nn - The first "comic" book featuring The Yellow Kid; E. W. Townsend narrative w/R. F. Outcault Sunday comic page art-r & some original drawings	7000.00	14000.00	–

NOTE: *A Fair condition copy sold for $2,901 in August 2004.; restored app VF sold for $10,500 in 2005. A copy in Fine+ (spine intact) and loose bacl cover sold for $17,000 in 2006.*

YESTERDAYS (S)
The Reilly & Lee Co.: 1930 (8-3/4 x 7-1/2", 128 pgs, illustrated hard-c with dust jacket

	GD2.0	FN6.0	VF8.0
nn - Text and cartoons about Victorian times by Frank Wing	20.00	40.00	80.00

Any addititions or corrections to this section are always welcome, very much encouraged and can be sent to **feedback@gemstonepub.com** to be processed for next year's Guide.

The American Comic Book: 1929-Present

A Concise History Of The Field As Of 2010

THE MODERN COMICS MAGAZINE SUPPLANTS THE EARLIER FORMATS

by Robert Lee Beerbohm & Richard D. Olson, PhD ©2010

(This article was originally created by Robert Beerbohm and Richard Olson for CBPG #27 1997.)

Although somewhat similar in appearance to comic books of the Golden Age of the superhero, the varied formats that comic publishing pioneers Stokes, Cupples & Leon and others popularized beginning in 1899 are quite different in appearance from today's comics. Even so, those many formats were consistently successful until the early 1930s, when they then had to compete against The Great Depression; the Depression eventually won. One major reason for a format change was that at a cost of 25¢ per book for the 10" x 10" cardboard style and 60¢ for the 7" x 8 1/2" dustjacketed hardcovers, the price became increasingly prohibitive for most consumers already stifled by the crushed economy. As a result, all Cupples & Leon style books published between 1929-1935 are much rarer than their earlier counterparts because most Americans had little money to spend after paying for necessities like food and shelter.

By the early 1930s, the era of the Prestige Format black & white reprint comic book was over. In 1932-33 a lot of format variations arose, collecting such newspaper strips as *Bobby Thatcher, Bringing Up Father, Buck Rogers, Dick Tracy, Happy Hooligan, Joe Palooka, The Little King, Little Orphan Annie, Mickey Mouse, Moon Mullins, Mutt & Jeff, Smitty, Tailspin Tommy, Tarzan, Thimble Theater starring Popeye, Tillie the Toiler, Winnie Winkle, and the Highlights of History.*

There had been Embee's *Comic Monthly's* dozen issues a decade earlier in 1922, and several dozen of Dell & Eastern's *The Funnies* tabloid in 1929-30. It contained only original material, went from a dime to a nickel and still it failed to catch a decent circulation.

A couple years ago it was discovered that Eastern Color and Dell were also co-partners in *The Funnies*. It is possible that Eastern came up with the idea and Delecorte agreed to publish it for general stand-alone distribution. Similar format Sunday sections of the same material have been discovered by comics historian Ken Barker to be published at the same time in the *Montreal Standard*, a Canadian newspaper; it appears to have been an effort to get a new comics syndicate off the ground. The effort was not too successful as *The Standard* dropped the sections after just a few months. Allan Holtz went through the *E&P* yearbooks and found that this section (presumably a preprint) was advertised from 1930-34 by Eastern Color Printing out of New York City.

This is a re-discovery of important magnitude as it pushes back the time known for Eastern Color Printing Company and Dell Publishing Company to be partners by four years into late 1928. They had almost discovered the winning formula which has ruled the format of comic books in America for the last 70 years. Unfortunately, it would be another four years before they successfully figured it out.

With another format change including four colors, page counts beginning at 32 (soon hitting a whopping 68), and a hefty price reduction (starting for free as promotional premiums due to the nationwide numbing effects of worldwide deflation), the birthing pangs of the modern American comic book occurred in late 1932. Created out of desperation, to keep the printing presses rolling, the modern American comic book was born when a 45-year-old sales manager for Eastern Color Printing Company of New York reinvented the format from the failed tabloid *The Funnies.*

The Funnies #1, early 1929, Dell Publishing Company and Eastern Color. This was the very first original material newsstand comic book!

Harry I. Wildenberg's job was to come up with ideas that would sell color printing for Eastern, a company which also printed the comic sections for a score of newspapers along the eastern seaboard, including the *Boston Globe, the Brooklyn Times, the Providence Journal, and the Newark Ledger.* Down-time meant less take-home pay, so Wildenberg was always racking his brains to keep the color presses running. He was fascinated by the miles of funny sheets which rolled off Eastern's presses each week, and he constantly sought new ways to exploit their commercial possibilities. If the funny papers were this popular, he reasoned, they should prove a good advertising medium. He decided to pitch a comics tabloid to various oil company clients.

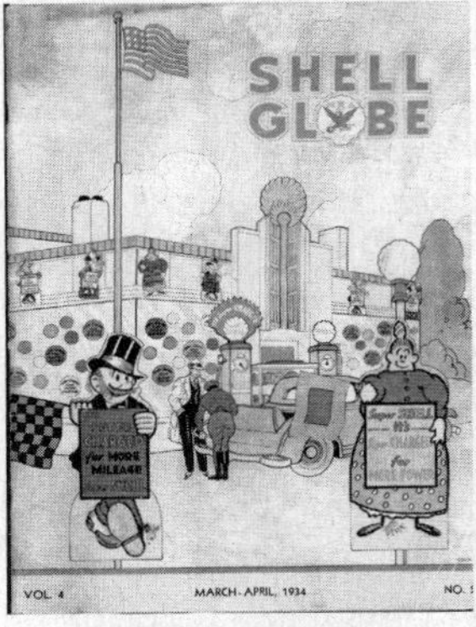

Top: Newly discovered Standard Oil Comics from Dec 1932. One copy presently known to exist. This rare give-away ended in late in 1934. Standard Oil was the first to issue a regular give-away using comics to bring in customers; Middle: Gulf Comic Weekly #1, April, 1933, copied what Standard Oil began. Gulf's weekly changed its name to Gulf Funny Weekly with #5; Bottom: Not to be outdone, by March 1934, Shell Oil began a huge comics promotion to compete with Standard and Gulf.

Brand new research conducted late in December 2005 has discovered the existence of a no number introduction issue of *Standard Oil Comics* dated to December 1932. Evidently it was Rockefeller's Standard Oil which decided before Gulf Oil to entice customers with a comics giveaway.

There are at least 14 issues each of at least a 1933 A and a 1934 B series of a four page tabloid-size full color comics giveaway titled *Standard Oil Comics*. The A issues all contain Fred Opper's *Si & Mirandi*, an older couple who interact with perennial favorites, *Happy Hooligan & Maud the Mule*, drawn by the grand old master himself, Frederick Opper, who had been a professional cartoonist for over 60 years by this time. This new "no number" 1932 precursor instructed readers to listen to the Si & Miandi radio show, come in regularly to Standard Oil stations and pick up *Standard Oil Comics*.

The 1934 B series front Goofus "He's From The Big City" McVittle by Walter O'Ehrle, set in humorous farming scenarios. Interior strips include *Pesty And His Pop & Smiling Slim* by Sid Hicks. Considering the concept of *Gulf Funny Weekly* has been well known for decades while *Standard Oil Comics* remains virtually unknown, what we now know is Gulf copied Standard in almost all respects.

Gulf Oil Company also liked the idea and hired a few artists to create an original comic called *Gulf Comic Weekly*. Their first issue was dated April 1933 and was 10 1/2" x 15". Gulf copied Standard Oil by advertising their giveaway nationally on the radio beginning April 30th. Its first artists were Stan Schendel doing *The Uncovered Wagon*, Victor doing *Curly and the Kids*, and Svess on a strip named *Smileage*. All were full page, full color comic strips. Wildenberg promptly had Eastern print this four page comic, making it probably the first tabloid newsprint comic published for American distribution outside of a newspaper in the 20th Century. Wildenberg and Gulf were astonished when the tabloids were grabbed up as fast as Gulf service stations could offer them. Distribution shot up to 3,000,000 copies a week after Gulf changed the name to *Gulf Funny Weekly* with its 5th issue. It remained a tabloid until early 1939 & ran for 422 issues until May 23, 1941.

Recent research has also turned up "new" rediscovered comics material from other oil companies from this same time span of 1933-34. Perhaps spurred by the runaway success of first *Standard Oil Comics, then Gulf Funny Weekly*, these other oil companies found they had to compete with licensed comic strip material of their own in order to remain profitable.

Beginning with the March-April 1934 issue of *Shell Globe* (V4 #2), characters from Bud Fisher (*Mutt & Jeff*) and Fontaine Fox (*Toonerville Folks*) were licensed to sell gas & oil for this company. 52,000 eight foot standees were made for Fisher's *Mutt and Jeff* and Fox's *Powerful Katrinka* and *The Skipper* for placement around 13,000 Shell gas stations. Augmenting them was an army of 250,000 miniature figures of the same characters. In addition, more than 1,000,000 play masks were given away to children along with more than 285,000 window stickers. If that wasn't enough, hundreds of thousands of 3x5 foot posters featuring these characters were released in conjunction with twenty-four sheet outdoor billboards. Radio announcements of this promotion began running April 7th, 1934. It is presently unknown if Shell had a comics tabloid created to give away to customers.

In addition, new research has uncovered the Gilmore Oil Company issuing an eight page giveaway titled *The Gilmore Cub*. It appears to have carried "Strange As It Seems" among other cartoon features by John Hix. At least one issue, v4 #2, May, 1938, is known to exist.

The authors of this essay are actively soliciting help in uncovering more information regarding these and potentially other oil comics giveaways.

With the 1933 newsstand appearance of Humor's *Detective Dan, Adventures of Detective Ace King, Bob Scully, Two Fisted Hick Detective*, and possibly the still unrediscovered, but definitely advertised, *Happy Mulligan*, these little understood original-material comic books from Humor were the direct inspiration for Jerry Siegel and Joe Shuster to transform their fanzine's evil character The Superman from *Science Fiction* #3 (January 1933) into a comic strip that would stand as a watershed heroic mark in American pop culture. The stage was set for a new frontier. The idea for creating an actual comic book as we know it

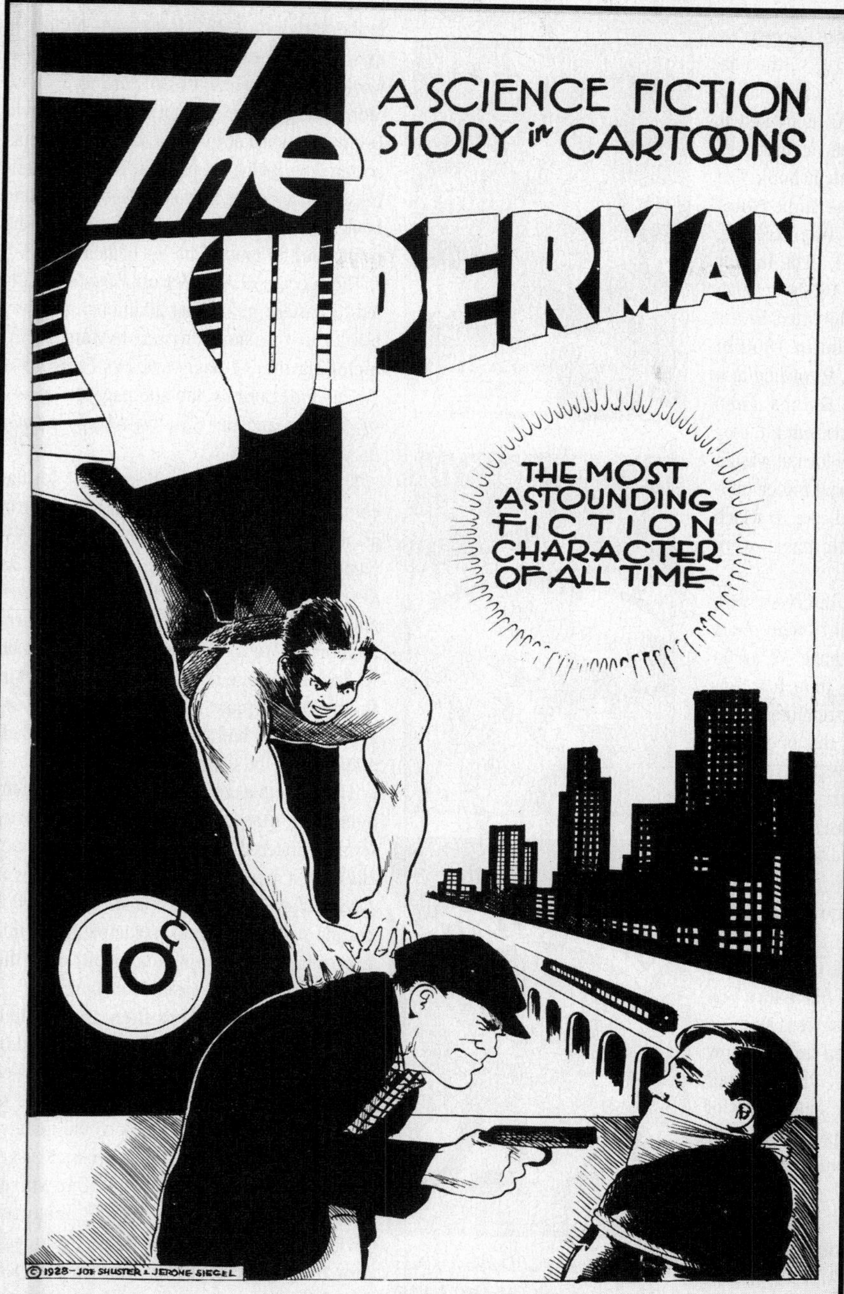

THE SUPERMAN *#1, art by Joseph Shuster, 1933.*

This long lost front cover to the proposed Superman comic book to be published by Humor Publishing was originally discovered in four pieces in late 1969 by Bill Gaines. They were crumpled up behind a drawer of Max Gaines' desk. He had been killed in a boating accident on August 20, 1947. The desk had sat untouched since his death.

In early 1970, Bill Gaines gave the four pieces to Russ Cochran, who in turn, traded them to me for $100 worth of vintage comic books.

Wishing to preserve it for posterity, I went down to my local printer and had the fellow make a negative on film of the art, and a few hundred printed up twice the size of the original art. More on this significant rediscovered treasure in our next edition.

today, however, did not occur to Wildenberg until later in 1933, when he said he was idly folding a newspaper in halves, then in quarters. As he looked at the twice-folded paper, it occurred to him that it was a convenient book size (actually it was late stage Dime Novel size, which companies like Street & Smith were pumping out). The format had its heyday from the 1880s through the 1910s, having been invented by the firm of Beadle and Adam in 1860 in more of a digest format. According to a 1942 article by Max Gaines (née Ginzberg), another contributing factor in the development of the format was an inspection of a promotional folder published by the Ledger Syndicate, in which four-color Sunday comic pages were printed in 7"x9".

According to a 1949 interview with Wildenberg, he thought "why not a comic book? It would have 32 or 64 pages and make a fine item for concerns which distribute premiums." All they did at Eastern Color that one fateful day is fold a tabloid newspaper format down to "dime novel" size running full color throughout on most of the comic strips, then staple it, and they hit upon their winning formula.

But they did not yet know this...as we will find out.

Working for Eastern Color at this same time were quite a few future legends of the comics business, such as Max Gaines, Lev Gleason and a fellow named Harold Moore (all sales staff directly underneath the supervision of Wilden-berg), Sol Harrison as a color separator, and George Dougherty Sr. as a printer.

Janosik, Wildenberg, Gaines, Gleason and crew obtained publishing rights to certain Associated, Bell, Fisher, McNaught and Public Ledger Syndicate comics, had an artist make up a few dummies by hand. The sales staff then walked them around to their biggest prospects. Wildenberg received a telegram from Proctor & Gamble for an order of a million copies for a 32-page color comic magazine called **Funnies on Parade**. The entire print run was given away in just a few weeks

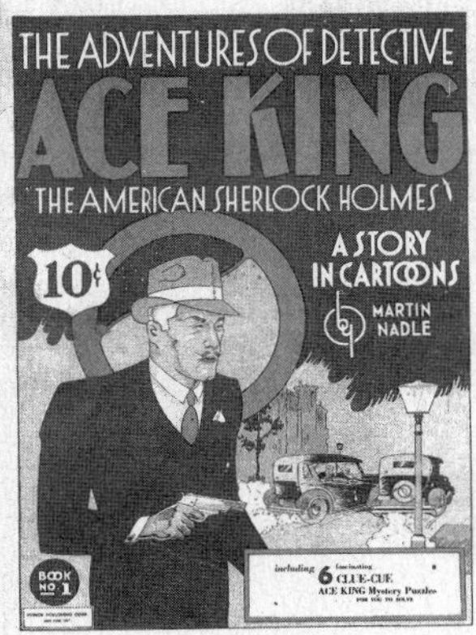

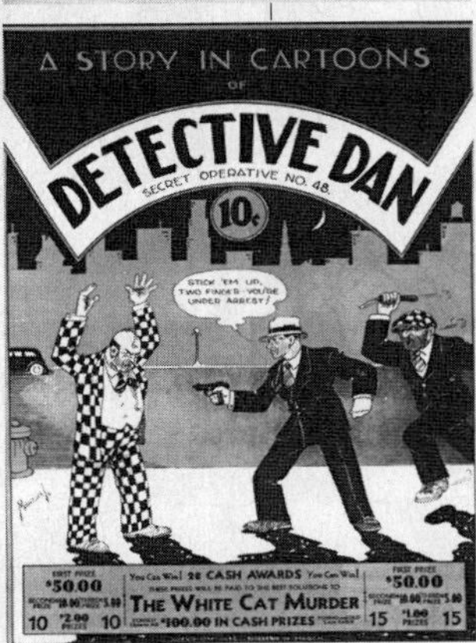

The Adventures of Detective Ace King, Bob Scully The Two Fisted Hick Detective & Detective Dan Secret Op. #48, early 1933, Humor Publishing Co. All issues Very Rare from the 2nd original newsstand comic book publisher; the direct inspiration for Jerry Siegel & Joe Shuster's 1933 conversion of The Superman into a comic book due to a promise of publication. This earliest Superman was never published.

in the Spring of 1933. Most copies no longer exist and it is now hard to find. All of them worked on the *Funnies on Parade* project. Morris Margolis was brought in from Charlton in Derby, Connecticut to solve binding problems centered on getting the pages in proper numerical sequence on that last fold to "modern" comic book size. Most of them were infected with the comics bug for most of the rest of their lives.

The success of *Funnies on Parade* quickly led to Eastern publishing additional giveaway books in the same format by late 1933, including the 32-page *Famous Funnies A Carnival of Comics*, the 100-page *A Century of Comics* and the 52-page *Skippy's Own Book of Comics*.

The latter became the first "new" format comic book about a single character. Out of all the comic strips on the market in 1933, Eastern Color's growing comics market as devised by Harry Wildenberg, M.C. Gaines and Lev Gleason chose the Percy Crosby creation in *Skippy's Own Book of Comics* to be its first standalone title. This first solo effort in their new 52-page newsprint *Funnies On Parade* format had an initial print run of half a million, as did their 100-pager.

The idea that anyone would pay for them seemed fantastic to Wildenberg, so Max Gaines stickered ten cents on several dozen of the latest premium, *Famous Funnies A Carnival of Comics*, as a test, and talked a couple newsstands into participating in this experiment. The copies sold out over the weekend and newsies asked for more.

Eastern sales staffers then approached Woolworth's. The late Oscar Fitz-Alan Douglas, sales brains of Woolworth, showed some interest, but after several months of deliberation decided the book would not give enough value for ten cents. Kress, Kresge, McCrory, and several other dime stores turned them down even more abruptly. Wildenberg next went to George Hecht, editor of *Parents Magazine*, and tried to persuade him to run a comic supplement or publish a "higher level" comic magazine. Hecht also frowned on the idea.

In Wildenberg's 1949 interview, he noted that "even the comic syndicates couldn't see it. 'Who's going to read old comics?' they asked." With the failures of EmBee's *Comic Monthly* (1922) and Dell's *The Funnies* (1929) still fresh in some minds, no one could see why children would pay ten cents for a comic magazine when they could get all they wanted for free in a Sunday newspaper. But Wildenberg had become convinced that children as well as grown-ups were not getting all the comics they wanted in the Sunday papers; otherwise, *Standard Oil Comics, Gulf Comic Weekly* and the premium comics would not have met with such success. Wildenberg said, "I decided that if boys and girls were willing to work for premium coupons to obtain comic books, they might be willing to pay ten cents on the newsstands." This conviction was also strengthened by Max Gaines' ten cent sticker experiment.

George Janosik, the president of Eastern Color, then called on George Delacorte to form another 50-50 joint venture to publish and market a comic book "magazine" for retail sales as they did with *The Funnies* just a few years previously, but this time American News turned them down cold. The magazine monopoly remembered the abortive *The Funnies* from just a few years before. After much discussion on how to proceed, Delacorte finally agreed to publish it and a partnership was formed. Feeling cautious, they printed 40,000 copies for distribution to a few chain stores who agreed to try it out. Known today as *Famous Funnies Series One*, it clocks in at 68 pages, with half its pages coming from reprints of the reprints in *Funnies on Parade* and half from *Famous Funnies A Carnival of Comics*. It is the scarcest issue.

With 68 full-color pages at only ten cents a piece, it sold out in thirty days with not a single returned copy. Delacorte refused to print a second edition. "Advertisers won't use it," he complained. "They say it's not dignified enough." The profit, however, was approximately $2,000. This particular edition is the rarest of all these early Eastern comic book experiments.

In early 1934, while riding the train, another Eastern Color employee named Harold A. Moore read an account from a prominent New York newspaper that indicated they owed much of their circulation success to their comics section. Mr. Moore went back to Harry Gold, President of American News, with the article in hand. He succeeded in acquiring a print order for 250,000 copies for a proposed monthly comics magazine. In May 1934, *Famous Funnies* #1 (with a July cover date) hit the newsstands with Steven O. Douglass as its only editor (even though Harold Moore was listed as such in #1) until it ceased publication some twenty years later. It was a 64-page version of the 32-page giveaways, and more importantly, it still sold for a dime! The first issue lost $4,150.60. Ninety percent of the copies sold out and a second issue dated September debuted in July. From then on, the comic book was published monthly. *Famous Funnies* also began carrying original material, apparently as early as the second issue. With #3, Buck Rogers took center stage and stayed there for the next twenty years, with covers by Frank Frazetta towards the end of the run–some of his best comics work ever.

Funnies on Parade, 1933 - what we recognize today as the first "modern" comic book with its slick cover.

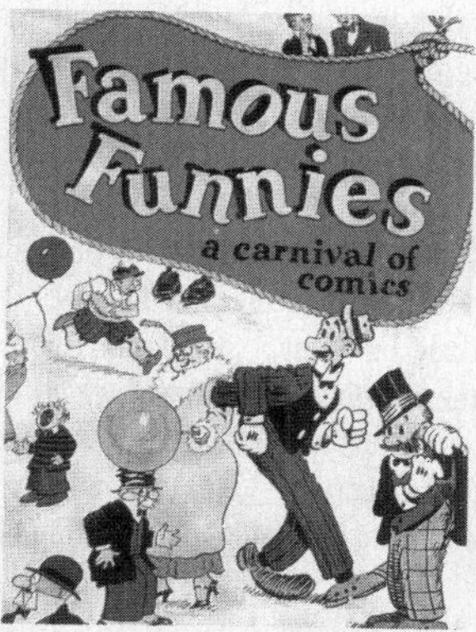

The fateful version Charlie Gaines stickered 10¢ a copy one weekend in late '33 which sold out over a weekend.

Famous Funnies Series One is the rare one, only 40,000 copies were printed.

Delacorte got cold feet and sold back his interest to Eastern, even though the seventh issue cleared a profit of $2,664.25. Wildenberg emphasized that Eastern could make a manufacturer's profit by printing its own books as well as the publishing profits once it was distributed. Every issue showed greater sales than the preceding one, until within a year, close to a million 64-page books were being sold monthly at ten cents apiece; Eastern received the lion's share of the receipts, and soon found it was netting $30,000 per issue. The comic syndicates received $640 ($10 a page) for publishing rights. Original material could be obtained from budding professionals for just $5 a page. According to Will Eisner in R. C. Harvey's *The Art of the Comic Book*, the prices then paid for original material had a long range effect of keeping creator wages low for years.

Initially, Eastern's experiment was eyed with skepticism by the publishing world, but within a year or so after *Famous Funnies* was nonchalantly placed on sale alongside slicker magazines like *Atlantic Monthly* or *Harper's*, at least five other competitors tried this brand new format.

However, one other abortive periodical comics experiment was launched cover dated a full two months before the highly successful newsstand *Famous Funnies* format would have an important influence on a chain of events which led ultimately to *Superman* being published.

Comic Cuts #1, May 19, 1934, debuted published by H.L. Baker Co., Inc., 195 Main St, Buffalo, New York with editorial

Famous Funnies #1, July 1934, was the first successful newsstand comic book, lasting until 1955.

and executive offices at 381 Fourth St, NYC, same address as ULTEM (Centaur) would use just a couple years later - this address housed a number of publishers fighting to exist during the Great Depression. The indica says H. L. Baker was President & Treasurer and J. D. Geller was Vice President and Secretary. It lasted nine issues with the final one cover-dated July 28. It appears Jake Geller, Windsor, Ontario, Canada, acquired American rights to a number of comic strips from the publisher Amalgamated Press, publisher of *Comic Cuts* in England. He partnered in the publishing with H. L. Baker and they acquired the backing of S-M News Co., Inc. as their distributor. Most distributors back then functioned on many important levels. It was common practice for the distributor back then to front the funds to pay the paper company and the printer, collecting the revenue from the 900 I.D. distributors located around the country after months of on-sale time, then paying the publisher.

In late 1934, army officer/diplomat turned pulp writer turned publisher Major Wheeler-Nicholson (1890-1968) formed the under-funded National Allied Publishing which introduced *New Fun #1* (Feb 1935) at almost tabloid-size. *New Fun* was also distributed by S-M News. It is entirely possible Wheeler-Nicholson somehow convinced them he could produce a superior "home-grown" package as the imported strips were not selling well. *New Fun* was basically the same as *Comic Cuts* while also containing all original USA material such as carried in *The Funnies* (1929-30) from Dell/Eastern. With *New Fun*, what S-M News offered was more familiar American home grown. Coulton Waugh speculated in his 1947 history book *The Comics* on page 342: "...The Major had gone back to the 1929 idea of *The Funnies*, for the contents of *New Fun* were original material. (It should be recorded here that original art work had appeared in a one-color book called *Detective Dan*."

Comic Cuts #8, July 14, 1934, issued weekly by H.L. Baker Co. Inc., Buffalo, New York; editorial offices at 381 Fourth Ave, NYC; co-owner Jake D. Geller was Canadian. Title provided inspiration for New Fun.

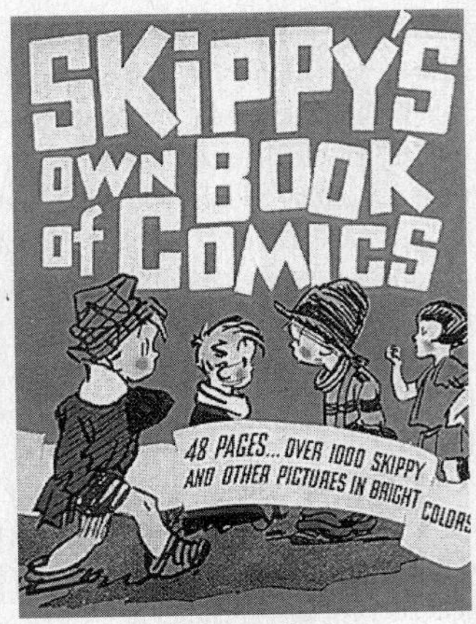

Skippy's Own Book of Comics, 1934, had half a million issues printed. It was the very first single character comic book in this "new" format.

However, Lloyd Jacquet, a person definitely in a position to know better, wrote as Chapter One of a proposed "History of the Comic Book" in 1957, "When Major Malcolm Wheeler-Nicholson set up his card table and chair in an eleventh floor office of the Hathaway Building in New York that Fall of 1934, these most modest beginnings sparked off what can rightly be called the 'comic book era.' When he came back to the U.S. after his last stay abroad, he looked over the American newsstand, and thought that the European juvenile weekly papers, with their picture-story continuities, their colorful illustrations, and their low price would appeal to the American boys and girls in the same way. He knew that those European publications were made up of new material, specially drawn and produced for each little magazine. He also knew that the American presentation of such material would have to be different, and merely importing, or translating European produced features for republication here was not the answer. This was about the time I joined with him in his project. It was still embryonic, but beginning to take form under Nicholson's direction. We were in the depression then, & it was not too difficult to secure writers and artists - but it was a task to instruct them as to exactly what was wanted. We finally rounded up a small but gifted group of creative people, and we produced our first issue of a monthly magazine composed of original features and material, and which was called,

New Fun #1, Feb 1935. According to first-employee Lloyd Jacquet, the format Major Malcolm Wheeler-Nicholson used was directly inspired by Comic Cuts. Many of the non-comics features were the same.

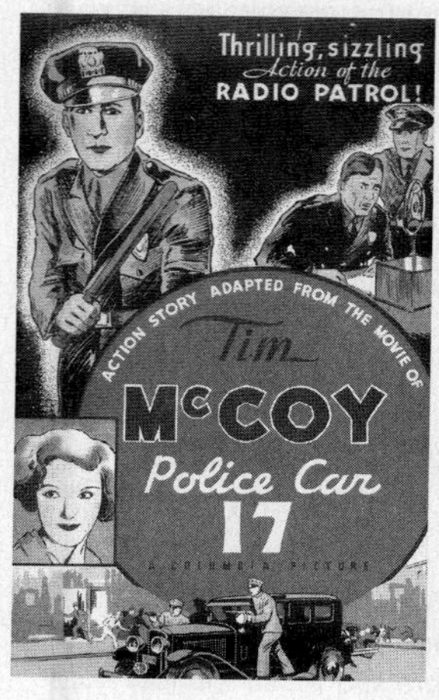

Tim McCoy Police Car #17, Whitman's first 1930s comic book (1934); the first movie adaptation

simply, *'FUN'*."

Around this same time in late 1934, M.C. Gaines left Eastern Color moving over to the McClure Newspaper Syndicate to become their manager of their Color Printing Department He immediately went to work convincing clients to issue promotional comics. Also, long-time comics publisher Whitman brought out the first original material movie adaptation, Tim McCoy Police Car 17, in the tabloid New Fun format with stiff card covers. A few years before, they had introduced the new comics formats known as the Big Little Book and the Big Big Book. The BLB and BBB formats would go toe-to-toe with Eastern's creation throughout the 1930s, but Eastern would win out with their new comics magazine format.

The very last 10" x 10" comic books pioneered by Cupples & Leon were published by the David McKay Publishing Company around mid-1935. Around this same time the Major published his 2nd comic book in which the editorial mentions amongst other exciting stories they were going to be showcasing the adventures of "hero supermen of the days to come."

By late 1935, Max Gaines (with his youthful assistant Sheldon Mayer) reached a business agreement with George Delacorte (who was re-entering the comic book business a third time) and McClure Syndicate (a growing newspaper comic strip enterprise) to be come editor of reprint newspaper comic strips in *Popular Comics.*

New Comics #1, Dec. 1935, was the Major's second entry into comic books, re-emphasizing the concept of "New!"

Also by late '35, Lev Gleason, another pioneer who participated in mercantiling *Funnies on Parade* and the early *Famous Funnies*, had become the first editor of United Feature's own *Tip Top Comics* with its first issue cover dated April 1936. In 1939 he would begin publishing his own titles starting with *Silver Streak*, created by the comics genius, Jack Cole, best known for Plastic Man. Gleason later created the crime comic book as a separate popular genre by 1942 with *Crime Does Not Pay* with a long run until 1955.

Wheeler-Nicholson introduced the concept of "the annual" into this new format with *Big Book of Fun Comics* #1 cover dated March 1936. It featured reprints from his earlier efforts in *New Fun* #1-5 as he struggled to make a go of it.

Industry giant King Features introduced *King Comics* #1 cover dated April 1936 through publisher David McKay, with Ruth Plumly Thompson as editor. McKay had already been issuing various format comic books with King Feature characters for a few years, including Mickey Mouse, Henry, Popeye and Secret Agent X-9, wherein Dashiell Hammett received cover billing and Alex Raymond was listed inside simply as "illustrator." McKay readily adapted to trying several formats. Soon many young comic book illustrators were copying Raymond.

The next month, William Cook & John Mahon, former disgruntled employees of Major Wheeler-Nicholson, issued their first issue of *Comics Magazine* #1 in May 1936.

Left, Charlie Gaines & Sheldon Mayer packaged Popular Comics #1, Feb. 1936, for George Delecorte in late 1935 after the former left Eastern Color. Middle, King Comics #1, April 1936, marked King Features Syndicate's entry into the new 64-page color comic market with their new heavyweights, Flash Gordon and Popeye. By this point, Hearst had been involved in publishing comic books for close to 40 years. Right, Lev Gleason left Eastern & Wildenberg about the same time as Gaines to edit Tip Top Comics #1, April 1936, for United Features.

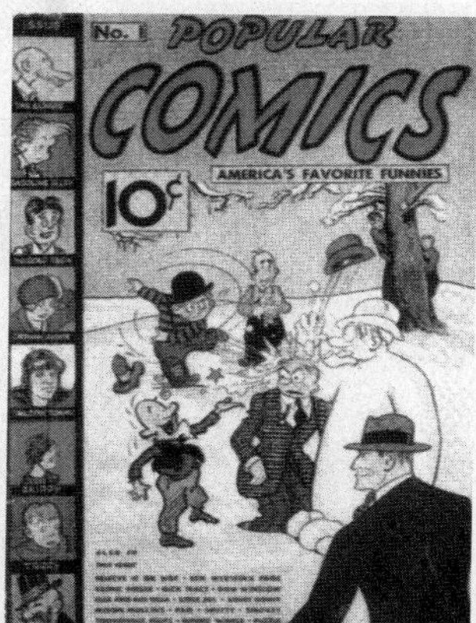

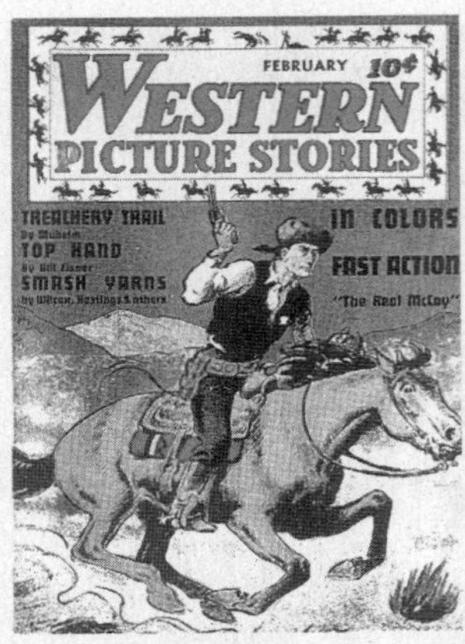

Left, The Comics Magazine #2, June 1936, was the first title of what later became Centaur. Soon it had a name change and quickly made history. Middle, Wow What A Magazine is a rare title which ran four issues beginning in June 1936 with the first published work by youthful, eager Bernard Baily, Dick Briefer, Will Eisner & Bob Kane. Painted cover by Will Eisner. Western Picture Stories #1, Feb. 1937 has more art by Eisner, ties with Star Ranger Funnies #1 as first western comic book. Centaur also introduced the earliest crime comic book, Detective Picture Stories #1 dated December 1936.

This was followed by Henle Publishing issuing *Wow What A Magazine*, which contained the earliest comic work of Will Eisner, Bob Kane, Dick Briefer & others. By the end of 1936, Cook and Mahon pioneered the first single theme comic books: *Funny Picture Stories* #1 in Nov. 1936 (adventure), *Detective Picture Stories* #1 in Feb. 1937 (crime), as well as *Western Picture Stories* #1 in Feb. 1937 (the Western). The company would eventually be known historically as Centaur Comics, and serve as the subject of endless debate among fan historians regarding their earliest origins as to who the owners were, where they came from and where they went.

Dell issued the second western genre comic book titled *Western Action Thrillers* #1 in April 1937. It was ten cents for one hundred pages as well as *100 Pages of Comics 101*, containing Big Little Book art reworked back into sequential comics.

Harry 'A' Chesler jumped ship from the Major, issuing his first comic books with **Star Comics** and **Star Ranger Funnies**, dated Feb 1937. Later that year, he sold these two titles to Ultem while remaining editor, and his newly set up art shop supplied contents. He then began **Feature Funnies** #1 in Oct. 1937, headlining Joe Palooka, at one time the #1 newspaper comic strip in America. Issue #2 sported a Rube Goldberg cover while #3 contains "Hawk of the Sea," Will Eisner's first work for what would soon become the Quality Comics Group when Everett "Busy" Arnold bought the company. **Feature Funnies** #3 also contains the first appearance of The Clock by George Brenner - the first costumed comic book hero.

Almost forty years after the first newspaper strip comic book compilations were issued at the dawn of international

Left, Feature Funnies #3, Dec. 1937, contains George Brenner's The Clock, the first comic book costumed hero plus Eisner's first work for Quality Comics, when still owned by Chesler. Circus the Comic Riot #1, June 1938, contains Basil Wolverton's earliest professional comic book work plus more Will Eisner and Bob Kane. Right, Action Comics #1, June 1938, began revolutionizing the industry when Superman by Jerome Siegel & Joseph Shuster debuted. The publishers did not understand what they had at first as Superman does not appear on a cover again until #7. Nobody knew at first, it seemed, except book-keeper Victor Fox counting copies sold, who quit and formed his own comic book company.

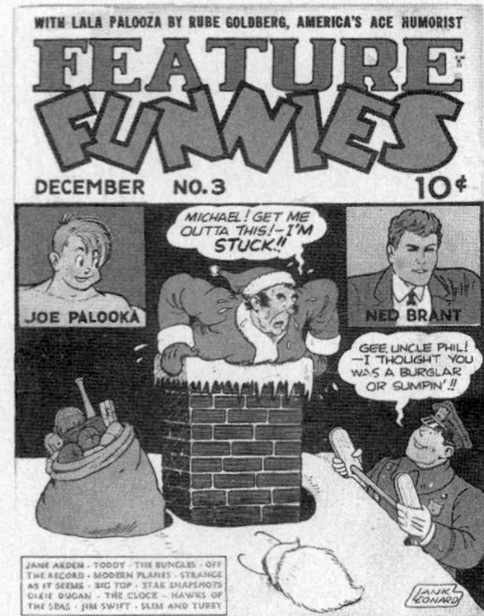

Left, Jumbo Comics #1, Sept. 1938, debuts pulp publisher Fiction House's entry into the growing comic book industry. Middle, Detective Comics #27 introduced Batman created by Bob Kane and Bill Finger - need we say more? Right, Wonder Comics #1, May 1939, became Victor Fox's first entry into the comics biz when he fast-talked a youthful Will Eisner into creating a near-exact clone of the creation of Siegel & Shuster's brainchild, Superman. There was a quick lawsuit and #2 featured Yarko The Great instead. Bob Kane was busy that May as he is also in Wonder #1.

popularity for American comic strips, the race was on to get titles out of the starting block. In late 1937 the Major began stumbling when he couldn't pay his printing bill to Harry Donenfeld. In recent interviews, Harry's son, Irwin, who as a 12-year old read the original art to the first issue of *Action Comics* #1 and *Detective Comics* #27 said "in 1932 my father and Paul Sampliner started Independent News with Liebowitz as the accountant. The company was begun with Paul Sampliner's mother's money. If it hadn't been for her investments into building the distribution as well as purchasing color printing presses, there might never have been a DC Comics. My father took over Wheeler-Nicholson's company with the Major's books literally on the printing presses. Harry had to absorb debt that could not otherwise be paid." Irwin told this writer "my dad did not originally willingly enter the comics business"

Soon after the Major lost control of his company, *Action Comics* #1 was published with a cover date of June 1938, and the first Golden Age of superhero comics had begun. Early in 1938 at McClure Syndicate, Max Gaines and Shelly Mayer showed editor Vin Sullivan a many times rejected sample strip. Sullivan then talked Donenfeld, Paul Sampliner and Jack Liebowitz into publishing Jerry Siegel & Joe Shuster's creation of "The Last Son of Krypton." This was followed in 1939 by a lucrative partnership for Gaines beginning with Harry Donenfeld as the All-American Comics Group.

While there's a great deal of controversy surrounding such labeling, the "Golden Age" is viewed by many these days as beginning with *Action Comics* #1 and continuing through the end of World War II. There was a time not that long ago that the newspaper reprint comic book was collected with more fervor than the heroic comics of the '40s. *Prince Valiant FB*

Left, Marvel Comics #1, Oct. 1939, was the first Martin Goodman comic book, introducing Human Torch by Carl Burgos and Sub-Mariner by Bill Everett. Middle, Silver Streak #1, Dec. 1939, Lev Gleason's first published comic book, introduced Jack Cole's classic, The Claw, running until #24, when the title changed to Crime Does Not Pay. Right, Whiz Comics #2 (#1), Feb. 1940, ushered Fawcett onto the comic book scene with yet another Superman clone - Captain Marvel, who was successful from the get-go. At one time his main title was issued every three weeks.

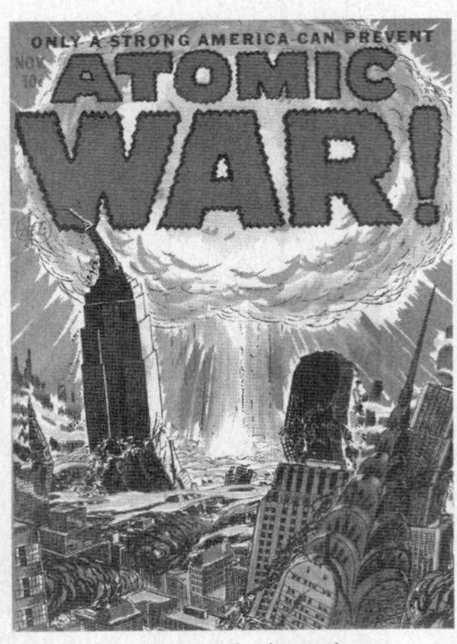

Left, Crime Does Not Pay #43, Nov. 1945. Lev Gleason instigated a popular new genre which brought the industry unfairly under heavy fire from church and state. Middle, My Date #1, July 1947. Joe Simon and Jack Kirby created the romance genre when they developed the older female audience which lasted into the '70s. Right, Atomic War #1, Nov. 1952. Nuclear obliteration was heavy on the minds of most Americans. Due to the Korean War, there was a plethora of war titles and the genre survived well into the 1970s before being eventually marginalized by the super hero revival.

#26, *Flash Gordon 4C* #10 and *Tarzan SS* #20 were some of the highest Holy Grails of collecting, but no more even though they contain fantastic art & story.

Today's marketplace dictates super heroes command the highest prices and are seemingly the most desirable. Maybe one day that pendulum will swing once again as there have been many years since they were introduced when super heroes almost disappeared completely from the racks.

The Atomic/Romance Age debuted with a bang by early 1946, revamping the industry once again as circulations soon hit their all-time highs with well over 1.3 billion periodical issues sold a year by the consignment honor system. By the early 1950s one in three periodicals sold in the USA was a comic book. 90% of all children admitted they read and enjoyed comics. There were dozens of genres being published. There were comic books for every taste and style. Hundreds of titles were being issued every month.

For many readers, the pinnacle was reached with the "New Trend" Entertaining Comics (E.C.) began delivering to the newsstands in 1950. The company still has a large following even today - a testament to its emphasis on quality art & story.

Comic book publishers glutted the market place by 1952-53. The attacks on comics begun the late 1940s came back anew in 1954 brought on by over-zealous church people and district attorneys with an agenda.

This continued until the advent of the self-censoring, industry-stifling Comics Code, created in response to a public outcry spearheaded by Dr. Frederic Wertham's tirade against

Left, Crime Detective #9, July 1948. Some say the tied-up figure represents Dr. Fredric Wertham following his earliest attacks on the crime comic book. Hillman joined the first Code. Middle, Justice Traps the Guilty #56, Nov. 1953. The S&K studio placed themselves in the spotlight, with a pretty mother pointing out Joe Simon as the tall, dastardly ringleader. Jack Kirby is on the right end. Right, Thing #15, Apr. 1954. Ditko wreaks havoc on a world rising against comics as a giant worm eats Brooklyn in one of the most gruesome titles created. His early work is intense.

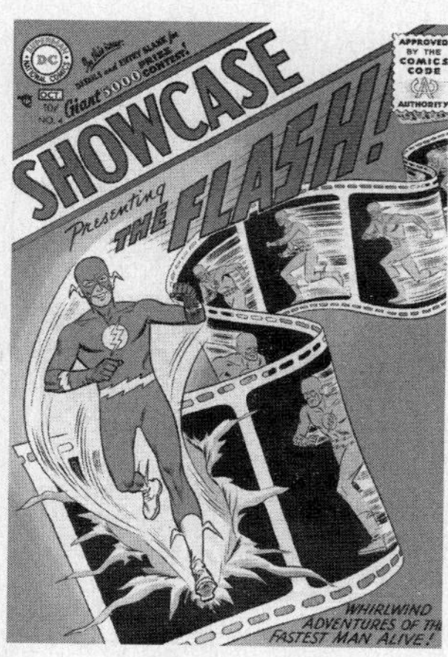

Left, By the early 1950s, Carl Barks increased the circulation of Walt Disney's C&S to over 4 million per issue & in 1952 his creation, Uncle Scrooge, got his own book, selling over a million an issue through the '50s while superheroes slumbered. Middle, Harvey Kurtzman created Mad Comics #1, 1952, as the comics industry went in an entirely "New" Direction and has directly inspired countless comics creators for years. Right, Showcase #4, Sept. 1956, the superhero revival starts a year after the Code, though it was three years before the Flash earned his own title once again.

the American comics industry, published as a book titled *Seduction of the Innocent*, which removed crime and horror comic books from the marketplace. Some of them were quite gruesome; however in his last book, *The World of Fanzines*, Wertham exhonerated comics fans for misinterpreting his data more than 20 years previous.

It took a year or two to recover from that moralistic assault, with many historians speculating the Silver Age of Superheroes began with the publication of *Showcase* #4 in 1956. Others point to the 1952 successful releases of Kurtzman's *MAD* #1 and Bark's *Uncle Scrooge Four Color* #386 as true Silver, since those titles soon broke the "million sold per issue" mark when the rest of the comic book industry was reeling from the effects of the public uproar fueled by Wertham. Within the Silver Era the term Bronze Age has been stated by some to begin when the Code approved newsstand comic book industry raised its standard cover price from 12 to 15 cents and Jack Kirby left Marvel for DC. As circulations plummeted after the Batman TV craze wore off by 1968 and the ensuing superhero glut withered on the stands, out in the Bay Area cartoonist Robert Crumb's creator-owned *Zap Comics* #1 appeared in Feb 1968, printed by Charles Plymell & Don Donahue on a small printing press. Soon after in Chicago, Jay Lynch and Skip Williamson brought out *Bijou Funnies*, Gilbert Shelton self-published *Feds 'N' Heads* while still in Austin, Texas, with Print Mint reprinting it almost immediately & Crumb let S. Clay Wilson, Victor Moscoso & Rick Griffin into Zap #2.

As originally published by the Print Mint beginning with #2 in 1968, *Zap Comics* almost single-handedly spawned an industry with tremendous growth in alternative comix run-

Left, Brave & Bold #28, Feb/Mar. 1960, gathered together the revived DC heroes, further expanding the resurging superhero market DC Comics ushered in. Middle, Fantastic Four #1, Nov. 1961, began the revitalization of Martin Goodman's moribund Marvel Comics Group, directly inspired by the success of the JLA's own regular series begun 2 years earlier in late 1960. Right, Amazing Fantasy #15, Aug. 1962, introduced the Amazing Spider-Man, created almost completely by Steve Ditko with some assists from Stan Lee and Jack Kirby, which revolutionized the way comic book stories could be told.

Left, Zap Comics #1, Plymell first printing, Feb. 1968, was the "direct" inspiration for the earliest successful origins of the Direct Market and has sold over a million copies. Most issues have been continuously in print for over 30 years. High grade first printings have sold for over $4500. Middle, soon afterwards Gilbert Shelton brought Feds 'N' Heads to Print Mint and later joined Zap. It has sold for $1000. Right, famed poster artist Rick Griffin edited his own comic book, Tales From the Tube in 1973, with most of the Zap crew joining him. It currently brings over $200 in NM high grade.

ning through the 1970s. During this decade the San Francisco Bay Area was an intense hotbed of comix being issued without a comics code "seal of approval" from companies such as Rip Off Press, Last Gasp, San Francisco Comic Book Company, Company & Sons, Weirdom Publications, Star*Reach, and Comics & Comix. Kitchen Sink prospered for many years in Wisconsin and many small press comix publishers scattered across the USA and Canada - all of whom created the Direct Sales Market. There were hundreds of people involved with an independent mind producing & distributing alternative underground comix, creating the direct market. Phil Seuling introduced DC, Marvel and Warren to this already developed for five years, San Francisco Bay Area-based, comix business system as a "new" way of selling comics in late 1973, acknowedged by Phil himself in his last interview in *Will Eisner's Quarterly* #3, Summer 1984.

After DC and Marvel joined the DM in a serious way in 1979, the last 20 years have generally been called the "Modern Age", although there are hints of a new age emerging since the mid-'90s. The jury is still out on naming it.

The comic book store as an industry came into its own in the 1980s. Thousands of fans & entrepreneurs opened stores, fulfilling a life's dream for many of them - fueled by a vibrant speculator's market which lasted until the early 1990s, its last hurrah being when DC "killed" Superman in 1992. The comic book marketplace has been rebuilding ever since. Much of that growth has been outside the super hero genre.

In each of the preceding eras, however, the secret for collectors has remained the same: buy what you enjoy. We did, and we are still collectors today! *Portions excerpted from* **Comics Archeology 101** © *2006 Robert L. Beerbohm, a detailed, heavily researched book in progress covering the more than 160 year history of the American comic book business. You may contact him thru his web site at* www.BLBComics.com

Left, Conan #1, Oct. 1970, by Roy Thomas and Barry Windsor-Smith intro'd the sword & sorcery genre. Middle, StarReach #1, April 1974, published by Mike Friedrich, was the first comic book directed specifically at comic book stores. Right, Giant-Size X-Men #1, Summer, 1975, introduced the new X-team, which later on revolutionized the comic book store system with its phenomenal sales once Chris Claremont and John Byrne teamed up on the title.

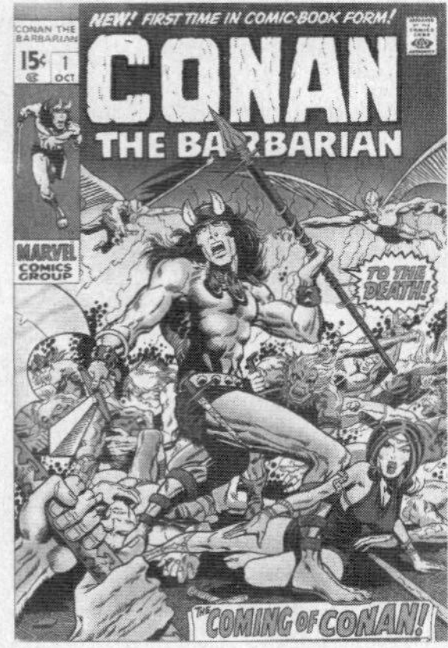

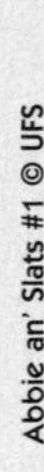
Abbie an' Slats #1 © UFS

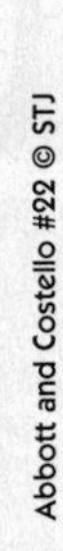
Abbott and Costello #22 © STJ

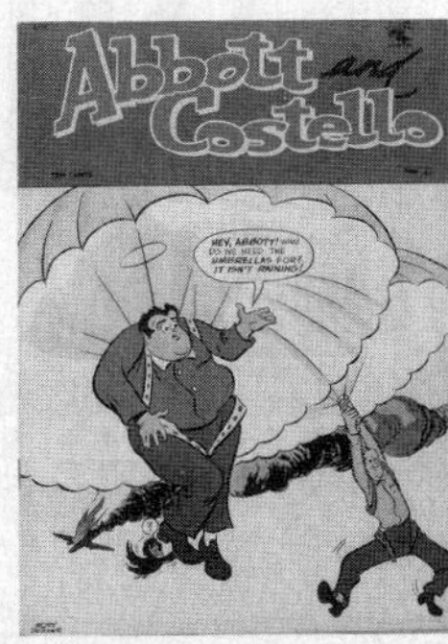

Ace Comics #26 © DMP

	GD 2.0	VG 4.0	FN 6.0	VF 8.0	VF/NM 9.0	NM- 9.2

The correct title listing for each comic book can be determined by consulting the indicia (publication data) on the beginning interior pages of the comic. The official title is determined by those words of the title in capital letters only, and not by what is on the cover. Titles are listed in this book as if they were one word, ignoring spaces, hyphens, and apostrophes, to make finding titles easier. Exceptions are made in rare cases. Comic books listed should be assumed to be in color unless noted "B&W".

Comic publishers are invited to send us sample copies for possible inclusion in future guides.

PRICING IN THIS GUIDE: Prices for **GD 2.0** (Good), **VG 4.0** (Very Good), **FN 6.0** (Fine), **VF 8.0** (Very Fine), **VF/NM 9.0** (Very Fine/Near Mint),and **NM– 9.2** (Near Mint–) are listed in whole U.S. dollars except for prices below $7 which show dollars and cents. **The minimum price listed is $2.25**, the cover price for current new comics. Many books listed at this price can be found in $1.00 boxes at conventions and dealers stores.

A-1 (See A-One)

ABADAZAD
CrossGen (Code 6): Mar, 2004 - No. 3, May, 2004 ($2.95)

	GD	VG	FN	VF	VF/NM	NM-
1-3-Ploog-a/c; DeMatteis-s						3.00
1-2nd printing with new cover						3.00

ABBIE AN' SLATS (...With Becky No. 1-4) (See Comics On Parade, Fight for Love, Giant Comics Edition 2, Giant Comics Editions #1, Sparkler Comics, Tip Topper, Treasury of Comics, & United Comics)
United Features Syndicate: 1940; March, 1948 - No. 4, Aug, 1948 (Reprints)

	GD	VG	FN	VF	VF/NM	NM-
Single Series 25 ('40)	39	78	117	236	388	540
Single Series 28	33	66	99	194	317	440
1 (1948)	17	34	51	98	154	210
2-4: 3-r/Sparkler #68-72	10	20	30	58	79	100

ABBOTT AND COSTELLO (...Comics)(See Giant Comics Editions #1 & Treasury of Comics)
St. John Publishing Co.: Feb, 1948 - No. 40, Sept, 1956 (Mort Drucker-a in most issues)

	GD	VG	FN	VF	VF/NM	NM-
1	61	122	183	387	664	940
2	35	70	105	208	339	470
3-9 (#8, 8/49; #9, 2/50)	22	44	66	132	216	300
10-Son of Sinbad story by Kubert (new)	27	54	81	158	259	360
11,13-20 (#11, 10/50; #13, 8/51; #15, 12/52)	17	34	51	98	154	210
12-Movie issue	18	36	54	105	165	225
21-30: 28-r/#8. 29,30-Painted-c	14	28	42	76	108	140
31-40: 33,38-Reprints	10	20	30	56	76	95
3-D #1 (11/53, 25¢)-Infinity-c	32	64	96	188	307	425

ABBOTT AND COSTELLO (TV)
Charlton Comics: Feb, 1968 - No. 22, Aug, 1971 (Hanna-Barbera)

	GD	VG	FN	VF	VF/NM	NM-
1	8	16	24	54	90	125
2	4	8	12	28	44	60
3-10	4	8	12	22	34	45
11-22	3	6	9	18	27	35

ABC (See America's Best TV Comics)

ABC: A-Z (one-shots)
America's Best Comics: Nov, 2005 - July, 2006 ($3.99, one-shots)

	GD	VG	FN	VF	VF/NM	NM-
... Greyshirt and Cobweb (1/06) character bios; Veitch-s/a; Gebbie-a; Dodson-c						4.00
... Terra Obscura and Splash Brannigan (3/06) character bios; Barta-a; Dodson-c						4.00
... Tom Strong and Jack B. Quick (11/05) character bios; Sprouse-a; Nowlan-a; Dodson-c						4.00
... Top Ten and Teams (7/06) character bios; Ha & Cannon-a; Veitch-a; Dodson-c						4.00

ABE SAPIEN... (Hellboy character)
Dark Horse Comics

	GD	VG	FN	VF	VF/NM	NM-
...: Drums of the Dead (3/98, $2.95) 1-Thompson-a. Hellboy back-up; Mignola-s/a/c						3.00
...: The Drowning (2/08 - No. 5, 6/08, $2.99) 1-5-Mignola-s/c; Alexander-a						3.00
...: The Haunted Boy (10/09, $3.50) 1-Mignola & Arcudi-s/Reynolds-a/Johnson-c						3.50

A. BIZARRO
DC Comics: Jul, 1999 - No. 4, Oct, 1999 (2.50, limited series)

	GD	VG	FN	VF	VF/NM	NM-
1-4-Gerber-s/Bright-a						2.50

ABOMINATIONS (See Hulk)
Marvel Comics: Dec, 1996 - No. 3, Feb, 1997 (1.50, limited series)

	GD	VG	FN	VF	VF/NM	NM-
1-3-Future Hulk storyline						2.50

ABRAHAM LINCOLN LIFE STORY (See Dell Giants)

ABRAHAM STONE
Marvel Comics (Epic): July, 1995 - No. 2, Aug, 1995 ($6.95, limited series)

	GD	VG	FN	VF	VF/NM	NM-
1,2-Joe Kubert-s/a						7.00

ABSENT-MINDED PROFESSOR, THE
Dell Publishing Co.: Apr, 1961 (Disney)

	GD	VG	FN	VF	VF/NM	NM-
Four Color #1199-Movie, photo-c; variant edition has a "Fabulous Formula" strip on back-c	8	16	24	56	93	130

ABSOLUTE VERTIGO
DC Comics (Vertigo): Winter, 1995 (99¢, mature)

	GD	VG	FN	VF	VF/NM	NM-
nn-1st app. Preacher. Previews upcoming titles including Jonah Hex: Riders of the Worm, The Invisibles (King Mob), The Eaters, Ghostdancing & Preacher	1	2	3	5	7	9

ABYSS, THE (Movie)
Dark Horse Comics: June, 1989 - No. 2, July, 1989 ($2.25, limited series)

	GD	VG	FN	VF	VF/NM	NM-
1,2-Adaptation of film; Kaluta & Moebius-a						3.00

ACCELERATE
DC Comics (Vertigo): Aug, 2000 - No. 4, Nov, 2000 ($2.95, limited series)

	GD	VG	FN	VF	VF/NM	NM-
1-4-Pander Bros.-a/Kadrey-s						3.00

ACCLAIM ADVENTURE ZONE
Acclaim Books: 1997 ($4.50, digest size)

	GD	VG	FN	VF	VF/NM	NM-
1-Short stories of Turok, Troublemakers, Ninjak and others						4.50

ACE COMICS
David McKay Publications: Apr, 1937 - No. 151, Oct-Nov, 1949 (All contain some newspaper strip reprints)

	GD	VG	FN	VF	VF/NM	NM-
1-Jungle Jim by Alex Raymond, Blondie, Ripley's Believe It Or Not, Krazy Kat begin (1st app. of each)	324	648	972	2203	3852	5500
2	95	190	285	599	1012	1425
3-5	63	126	189	397	674	950
6-10	47	94	141	291	486	680
11-The Phantom begins (1st app., 2/38) (in brown costume)	82	164	246	517	871	1225
12-20	39	78	117	231	378	525
21-25,27-30	34	68	102	199	325	450
26-Origin & 1st app. Prince Valiant (5/39); begins series?	102	204	306	648	1112	1575
31-40: 37-Krazy Kat ends	24	48	72	142	234	325
41-60	19	38	57	109	172	235
61-64,66-76-(7/43; last 68 pgs.)	15	30	45	94	147	200
65-(8/42)-Flag-c	19	38	57	109	172	235
77-84 (3/44; all 60 pgs.)	14	28	42	80	115	150
85-99 (52 pgs.)	12	24	36	69	97	125
100 (7/45; last 52 pgs.)	14	28	42	80	115	150
101-134: 128-(11/47)-Brick Bradford begins. 134-Last Prince Valiant (all 36 pgs.)	10	20	30	56	76	95
135-151: 135-(6/48)-Lone Ranger begins	9	18	27	52	69	85

ACE KELLY (See Tops Comics & Tops In Humor)

ACE KING (See Adventures of Detective...)

ACES
Acme Press (Eclipse): Apr, 1988 - No. 5, Dec, 1988 ($2.95, B&W, magazine)

	GD	VG	FN	VF	VF/NM	NM-
1-5						3.00

ACES HIGH
E.C. Comics: Mar-Apr, 1955 - No. 5, Nov-Dec, 1955

	GD	VG	FN	VF	VF/NM	NM-
1-Not approved by code	23	46	69	184	292	400
2	13	26	39	104	167	230
3-5	12	24	36	96	153	210

NOTE: *All have stories by* ***Davis, Evans, Krigstein,*** *and* ***Wood. Evans*** *c-1-5.*

ACES HIGH
Gemstone Publishing: Apr, 1999 - No. 5, Aug, 1999 ($2.50)

	GD	VG	FN	VF	VF/NM	NM-
1-5-Reprints E.C. issues						2.50
Annual 1 ($13.50) r/#1-5						13.50

ACME NOVELTY LIBRARY, THE
Fantagraphics Books: Winter 1993-94 - Present (quarterly, various sizes)

	GD	VG	FN	VF	VF/NM	NM-
1-Introduces Jimmy Corrigan; Chris Ware-s/a in all	1	3	4	6	8	10
1-2nd and later printings						4.00
2,3: 2-Quimby						6.00
4-Sparky's Best Comics & Stories	1	2	3	4	5	7
5-12: Jimmy Corrigan in all						5.00
13,15-($10.95-c)						11.00
14-($12.95-c) Concludes Jimmy Corrigan saga						13.00

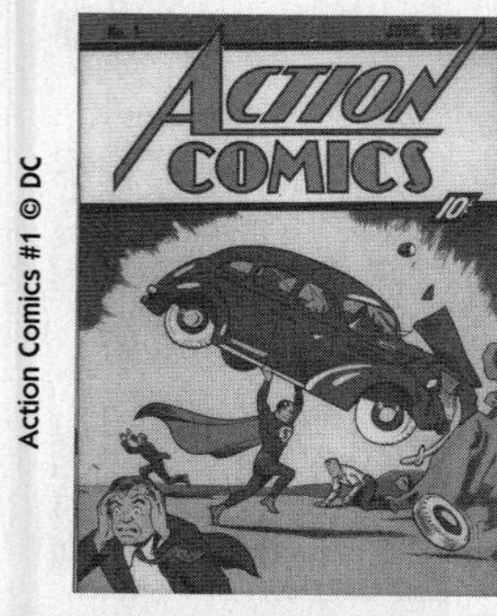

Action Comics #1 © DC

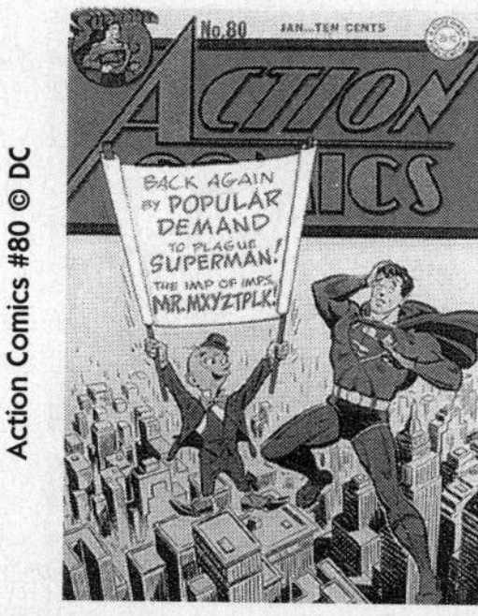

Action Comics #80 © DC

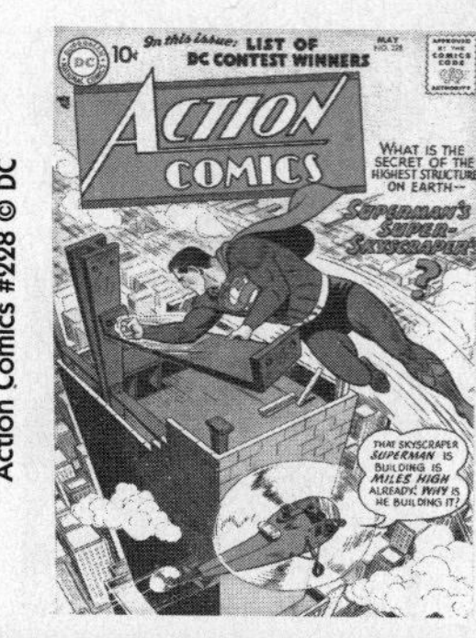

Action Comics #228 © DC

GD 2.0 VG 4.0 FN 6.0 VF 8.0 VF/NM 9.0 NM- 9.2

16,19-($15.95, hardcover) Rusty Brown 16.00
17-($16.95, hardcover) Rusty Brown 17.00
18-($17.95, hardcover) 18.00
Jimmy Corrigan, The Smartest Kid on Earth (2000, Pantheon Books, Hardcover, $27.50, 380 pgs.) Collects Jimmy Corrigan stories; folded dust jacket 27.50
Jimmy Corrigan, The Smartest Kid on Earth (2003, Softcover, $17.95) 18.00
NOTE: *Multiple printings exist for most issues.*

ACROSS THE UNIVERSE: THE DC UNIVERSE STORIES OF ALAN MOORE (Also see DC Universe: The Stories of Alan Moore)
DC Comics: 2003 ($19.95, TPB)
nn-Reprints selected Moore stories from '85-'87; Superman, Batman, Swamp Thing app. 20.00

ACTION ADVENTURE (War) (Formerly Real Adventure)
Gillmor Magazines: V1#2, June, 1955 - No. 4, Oct, 1955
V1#2-4 6 12 18 31 38 45

ACTION COMICS (...Weekly #601-642) (Also see The Comics Magazine #1, More Fun #14-17 & Special Edition) (Also see Promotional Comics section)
National Periodical Publ./Detective Comics/DC Comics: 6/38 - No. 583, 9/86; No. 584, 1/87 - Present

1-Origin & 1st app. Superman by Siegel & Shuster, Marco Polo, Tex Thompson, Pep Morgan, Chuck Dawson & Scoop Scanlon; 1st app. Zatara & Lois Lane; Superman story missing 4 pgs. which were included when reprinted in Superman #1; Clark Kent works for Daily Star; story continued in #2 80,000 160,000 240,000 600,000 900,000 1,200,000
1-Reprint, Oversize 13-1/2x10". **WARNING:** This comic is an exact reprint of the original except for its size. DC published it in 1974 with a second cover titling it as a Famous First Edition. There have been many reported cases of the outer cover being removed and the interior sold as the original edition. The reprint with the new outer cover removed is practically worthless. See Famous First Edition for value.
2-O'Mealia non-Superman covers thru #6 5100 10,200 15,300 37,740 60,870 84,000
3 (Scarce)-Superman apps. in costume in only one panel 3273 6546 9819 24,220 39,110 54,000
4-6: 6-1st Jimmy Olsen (called office boy) 1879 3758 5637 13,905 22,453 31,000
7-2nd Superman cover 6060 12,120 18,180 44,844 72,422 100,000
8,9 1212 2424 3636 8969 14,485 20,000
10-3rd Superman cover by Siegel & Shuster; splash panel used as cover art for Superman #1 3333 6666 10,000 24,664 39,832 55,000
11,14: 1st X-Ray Vision? 14-Clip Carson begins, ends #41; Zatara-c 697 1394 2091 5158 8329 11,500
12-Has 1 panel Batman ad for Det. #27 (5/39); Zatara sci-fi cover 758 1516 2274 5609 9055 12,500
13-Shuster Superman-c; last Scoop Scanlon 1515 3030 4545 11,211 18,106 25,000
15-Guardineer Superman-c; has ad for Detective Comics #27 1030 2060 3090 7622 12,311 17,000
16 485 970 1455 3589 5795 8000
17-Superman cover; last Marco Polo 849 1698 2547 6283 10,142 14,000
18-Origin 3 Aces; has a 1 panel ad for New York World's Fair 1939 at the end of the Superman story (ad also in #19) 485 970 1455 3589 5795 8000
19-Superman covers begin 788 1576 2364 5831 9416 13,000
20-The 'S' left off Superman's chest; Clark Kent works at 'Daily Star' 758 1516 2274 5609 9055 12,500
21-Has 2 ads for More Fun #52 (1st Spectre) 389 758 1167 2723 4762 6800
22,24,25: 24-Kent at Daily Planet. 25-Last app. Gargantua T. Potts, Tex Thompson's sidekick 383 746 1149 2681 4691 6700
23-1st app. Luthor (w/red hair) & Black Pirate; Black Pirate by Moldoff; 1st mention of The Daily Planet (4/40)-Has 1 panel ad for Spectre in More Fun 865 1730 2595 6315 11,158 16,000
26-28,30 331 662 993 2317 4059 5800
29-1st Lois Lane-c (10/40) 366 732 1098 2562 4481 6400
31,32: 32-Intro/1st app. Krypto Ray Gun in Superman story by Burnley 232 464 696 1485 2543 3600
33-Origin Mr. America; Superman by Burnley; has half page ad for All Star Comics #3 239 478 717 1530 2615 3700
34,35,38,39 226 452 678 1446 2473 3500
36, 40: 36-Classic robot-c. 40-(9/41)-Intro/1st app. Star Spangled Kid & Stripesy; Jerry Siegel photo 234 468 702 1486 2556 3625
37-Origin Congo Bill 229 458 687 1454 2502 3550
41 200 400 600 1280 2190 3100
42-1st app./origin Vigilante; Bob Daley becomes Fat Man; origin Mr. America's magic flying carpet; The Queen Bee & Luthor app; Black Pirate ends; not in #41 226 452 678 1446 2473 3500
43-46,48-50: 44-Fat Man's i.d. revealed to Mr. America. 45-1st app. Stuff (Vigilante's oriental sidekick) 187 374 561 1197 2049 2900
47-1st Luthor cover in comics (4/42) 271 542 813 1734 2967 4200
51-1st app. The Prankster 194 388 582 1242 2121 3000
52-Fat Man & Mr. America become the Ameri-commandos; origin Vigilante retold; classic Superman and back-ups-c 219 438 657 1402 2401 3400
53-56,59,60: 56-Last Fat Man. 59-Kubert Vigilante begins?, ends #70. 60-First app. Lois Lane as Super-woman 148 296 444 947 1624 2300
57-2nd Lois Lane-c in Action (3rd anywhere, 2/43) 168 336 504 1075 1838 2600
58-"Slap a Jap-c" 168 336 504 1075 1838 2600
61-Historic Atomic Radiation-c (6/43) 155 310 465 992 1696 2400
62,63-Japan war-c: 63-Last 3 Aces 148 296 444 947 1624 2300
64-Intro Toyman 155 310 465 992 1696 2400
65-70 123 246 369 787 1344 1900
71-79: 74-Last Mr. America 97 194 291 621 1061 1500
80-2nd app. & 1st Mr. Mxyztplk-c (1/45) 126 252 378 806 1378 1950
81-88,90: 83-Intro Hocus & Pocus 90 180 270 576 988 1400
89-Classic rainbow cover 94 188 282 597 1024 1450
91-99: 93-X-Mas-c. 99-1st small logo (8/46) 77 154 231 493 847 1200
100 115 230 345 730 1253 1775
101-Nuclear explosion-c (10/46) 148 296 444 947 1624 2300
102-107,109-120: 102-Mxyztplk-c. 105,117-X-Mas-c 71 142 213 454 777 1100
108-Classic molten metal-c 79 158 237 502 864 1225
121,122,124-126,128-140: 135,136,138-Zatara by Kubert 66 132 198 419 722 1025
123-(8/48) 1st time Superman flies, not leaps 67 134 201 425 730 1035
127-Vigilante by Kubert; Tommy Tomorrow begins (12/48, see Real Fact #6) 68 136 204 435 743 1050
141-157,159-161: 151-Luthor/Mr. Mxyztplk/Prankster team-up. 156-Lois as Super Woman. 161- Last 52 pgs. 63 126 189 403 689 975
158-Origin Superman retold 129 258 387 826 1413 2000
162-180: 168,176-Used in **POP**, pg. 90. 173-Robot-c 61 122 183 390 670 950
181-201: 191-Intro. Janu in Congo Bill. 198-Last Vigilante. 201-Last pre-code issue 58 116 174 371 636 900
202-220,232: 212-(1/56)-Includes 1956 Superman calendar that is part of story. 232-1st Curt Swan-c in Action 53 106 159 334 567 800
221-231,233-240: 221-1st S.A. issue. 224-1st Golden Gorilla story. 228-(5/57)-Kongorilla in Congo Bill story (Congorilla try-out) 45 90 135 284 480 675
241,243-251: 241-Batman x-over. 248-Origin/1st app. Congorilla; Congo Bill renamed Congorilla. 251-Last Tommy Tomorrow 39 78 117 240 395 550
242-Origin & 1st app. Brainiac (7/58); 1st mention of Shrunken City of Kandor 185 370 555 1619 3210 4800
252-Origin & 1st app. Supergirl (5/59); 1st app. Metallo 200 400 600 1750 3475 5200
253-2nd app. Supergirl 58 116 174 371 636 900
254-1st meeting of Bizarro & Superman-c/story; 3rd app. Supergirl 42 84 126 265 445 625
255-1st Bizarro Lois Lane-c/story & both Bizarros leave Earth to make Bizarro World; 4th app. Supergirl 39 78 117 231 378 525
256-260: 259-Red Kryptonite used 27 54 81 158 259 360
261-1st X-Kryptonite which gave Streaky his powers; last Congorilla in Action; origin & 1st app. Streaky The Super Cat 30 60 90 177 289 400
262,264-266,268-270 23 46 69 136 223 310
263-Origin Bizarro World (continues in #264) 30 60 90 177 289 400
267(8/60)-3rd Legion app; 1st app. Chameleon Boy, Colossal Boy, & Invisible Kid, 1st app. of Supergirl as Superwoman. 53 106 159 334 567 800
271-275,277-282: 274-Lois Lane as Superwoman; 282-Last 10¢ issue 20 40 60 118 192 265
276(5/61)-6th Legion app; 1st app. Brainiac 5, Phantom Girl, Triplicate Girl, Bouncing Boy, Sun Boy, & Shrinking Violet; Supergirl joins Legion 36 72 108 216 351 485
283(12/61)-Legion of Super-Villains app. 1st 12¢ 14 28 42 98 184 270
284(1/62)-Mon-El app. 14 28 42 98 184 270
285(2/62)-12th Legion app; Brainiac 5 cameo; Supergirl's existence revealed to world; JFK & Jackie cameos 21 42 63 148 287 425
286-287,289-292,294-299: 286(3/62)-Legion of Super Villains app. 287(4/62)-15th Legion app. (cameo). 289(6/62)-16th Legion app. (Adult); Lightning Man & Saturn Woman's marriage 1st revealed. 290(7/62)-Legion app. (cameo); Phantom Girl app. 1st Supergirl emergency squad. 291-1st meeting Supergirl & Mr. Mxyzptlk. 292-2nd app. Superhorse (see Adv.#293). 297-Mon-El app. 298-Legion cameo 12 24 36 85 155 225
288-Mon-El app.; r-origin Supergirl 12 24 36 88 162 235
293-Origin Comet (Superhorse) 14 28 42 100 188 275
300-(5/63) 13 26 39 94 175 255
301-303,305,307,308,310-312,315-320: 307-Saturn Girl app. 317-Death of Nor-Kan of Kandor. 319-Shrinking Violet app. 9 18 27 63 107 150
304,306,313: 304-Origin/1st app. Black Flame (9/63). 306-Brainiac 5, Mon-El app. 313-Batman app. 9 18 27 64 110 155
309-(2/64)-Legion app.; Batman & Robin-c & cameo; JFK app. (he died 11/22/63; on stands last week of Dec, 1963) 10 20 30 67 116 165

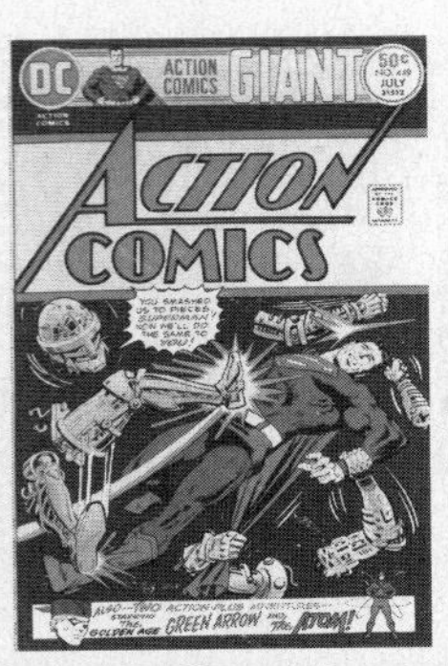

Action Comics #449 © DC

Action Comics #750 © DC

Action Comics Annual #10 © DC

	GD 2.0	VG 4.0	FN 6.0	VF 8.0	VF/NM 9.0	NM- 9.2
314-Retells origin Supergirl; J.L.A. x-over	9	18	27	64	110	155
321-333,335-339: 336-Origin Akvar (Flamebird)	7	14	21	50	83	115
334-Giant G-20; origin Supergirl, Streaky, Superhorse & Legion (all-r)	11	22	33	80	145	210
340-Origin, 1st app. of the Parasite; 2 pg. pin-up	8	16	24	54	90	125
341,344,350,358: 341-Batman app. in Supergirl back-up story. 344-Batman x-over. 350-Batman, Green Arrow & Green Lantern app. in Supergirl back-up story. 358-Superboy meets Supergirl	7	14	21	45	73	100
342,343,345,346,348,349,351-357,359: 342-UFO story. 345-Allen Funt/Candid Camera story.	6	12	18	43	69	95
347,360-Giant Supergirl G-33,G-45; 347-Origin Comet-r plus Bizarro story. 360-Legion app.-r; r/origin Supergirl	9	18	27	60	100	140
361-364,367-372,374-378: 361-2nd app. Parasite. 362-366-Leper/Death story. 370-New facts about Superman's origin. 376-Last Supergirl in Action; last 12¢-c. 377-Legion begins (thru #392)	5	10	15	34	55	75
365,366: 365-JLA & Legion app. 366-JLA app.	6	12	18	37	59	80
373-Giant Supergirl G-57; Legion-r	8	16	24	56	93	130
379-399,401: 388-Sgt. Rock app. 392-Batman-c/app.; last Legion in Action; Saturn Girl gets new costume. 393-401-All Superman issues	3	6	9	20	30	40
400	4	8	12	23	36	48
402-Last 15¢ issue; Superman vs. Supergirl duel	3	6	9	20	30	40
403-413: All 52 pg. issues. 411-Origin Eclipso-(r). 413-Metamorpho begins, ends #418	3	6	9	20	30	40
414-424: 419-Intro. Human Target. 421-Intro Capt. Strong; Green Arrow begins. 422,423-Origin Human Target	2	4	6	9	13	16
425-Neal Adams-a(p); The Atom begins	3	6	9	14	19	24
426-431,433-436,438,439	2	4	6	8	10	12
432-1st Bronze Age Toyman app. (2/74)	2	4	6	13	18	22
437,443-(100 pg. Giants)	4	8	12	26	41	55
440-1st Grell-a on Green Arrow	2	4	6	9	13	16
441,442,444-448: 441-Grell-a on Green Arrow continues	1	3	4	6	8	10
449-(68 pgs.)	2	4	6	9	13	16
450-465,467-483,486,489-499: 454-Last Atom. 456-Grell Jaws-c. 458-Last Green Arrow.	1	2	3	4	5	7
466,485,487,488: 466-Batman, Flash app. 485-Adams-c. 487,488-(44 pgs.). 487-Origin & 1st app. Microwave Man; origin Atom retold	1	2	3	5	7	9
481-483,485-492,495-499,501-505,507,508-Whitman variants (low print run; none show issue # on cover)	1	3	4	6	8	10
484-Earth II Superman & Lois Lane wed; 40th anniversary issue(6/78)	2	4	6	8	10	12
484-Variant includes 3-D Superman punchout doll in cello. pack; 4 different inserts; Canadian promo?)	3	6	9	16	22	28
500-($1.00, 68 pgs.)-Infinity-c; Superman life story retold; shows Legion statues in museum	1	3	4	6	8	10
501-543,545,547-551: 511-514-Airwave II solo stories. 513-The Atom begins. 517-Aquaman begins; ends #541. 521-1st app. The Vixen. 532,536-New Teen Titans cameo. 535,536-Omega Men app. 551-Starfire becomes Red-Star						5.00
504,505,507,508-Whitman variants (no cover price)	1	3	4	6	8	10
544-(6/83, Mando paper, 68 pgs.)-45th Anniversary issue; origins new Luthor & Brainiac; Omega Men cameo; Shuster-a (pin-up); article by Siegel	1	2	3	4	5	7
546-J.L.A., New Teen Titans app.	1	2	3	5	6	8
552,553-Animal Man-c & app. (2/84 & 3/84)						5.00
554-582						3.00
583-Alan Moore scripts; last Earth 1 Superman story (cont'd from Superman #423)	2	4	6	8	10	12
584-Byrne-a begins; New Teen Titans app.						6.00
585-599: 586-Legends x-over. 596-Millennium x-over; Spectre app. 598-1st Checkmate						3.00
600-($2.50, 84 pgs., 5/88)						6.00
601-610,619-642: (#601-642 are weekly issues) ($1.50, 52 pgs.) 601-Re-intro The Secret Six; death of Katma Tui						3.00
611-618: 611-614-Catwoman stories (new costume in #611). 613-618-Nightwing stories						3.00
643-Superman & monthly issues begin again; Perez-c/a/scripts begin; swipes cover to Superman #1						4.00
644-649,651-661,663-673,675-683: 645-1st app. Maxima. 654-Part 3 of Batman storyline. 655-Free extra 8 pgs. 660-Death of Lex Luthor. 661-Begin $1.00-c. 667-($1.75, 52 pgs.). 675-Deathstroke cameo. 679-Last $1.00 issue. 683-Doomsday cameo						2.50
650-($1.50, 52 pgs.)-Lobo cameo (last panel)						3.00
662-Clark Kent reveals i.d. to Lois Lane; story cont'd in Superman #53						4.00
674-Supergirl logo & c/story (reintro)						6.00
683-685-2nd & 3rd printings						2.50
684-Doomsday battle issue						3.00
685,686-Funeral for a Friend issues; Supergirl app.						3.00
687-($1.95)-Collector's Ed.w/die-cut-c						3.00
687-($1.50)-Newsstand Edition with mini-poster						2.50
688-699,701-703-($1.50): 688-Guy Gardner-c/story. 697-Bizarro-c/story. 703-(9/94)-Zero Hour						2.50
695-($2.50)-Collector's Edition w/embossed foil-c						3.00
700-($2.95, 68 pgs.)-Fall of Metropolis Pt 1, Guice-a; Pete Ross marries Lana Lang and Smallville flashbacks with Curt Swan art & Murphy Anderson inks						3.00
700-Platinum						15.00
700-Gold						18.00
0(10/94), 704(11/94)-719,721-731: 710-Begin $1.95-c. 714-Joker app. 719-Batman-c/app. 721-Mr. Mxyzptlk app. 723-Dave Johnson-c. 727-Final Night x-over.						2.50
720-Lois breaks off engagement w/Clark						3.00
720-2nd print.						2.50
732-749,751-767: 732-New powers. 733-New costume, Ray app. 738-Immonen-s/a(p) begins. 741-Legion app. 744-Millennium Giants x-over. 745-747-70's-style Superman vs. Prankster. 753-JLA-c/app. 757-Hawkman-c. 760-1st Encantadora. 761-Wonder Woman app. 765-Joker & Harley-c/app. 766-Batman-c/app.						2.50
750-($2.95)						3.00
768,769,771-774: 768-Begin $2.25-c; Marvel Family-c/app. 771-Nightwing-c/app. 772,773-Ra's al Ghul app. 774-Martian Manhunter-c/app.						2.50
770-($3.50) Conclusion of Emperor Joker x-over						3.50
775-($3.75) Bradstreet-c; intro. The Elite						3.75
776-799: 776-Farewell to Krypton; Rivoche-c. 780-782-Our Worlds at War x-over. 781-Hippolyta and Major Lane killed. 782-War ends. 784-Joker: Last Laugh; Batman & Green Lantern app. 793-Return to Krypton. 795-The Elite app. 798-Van Fleet-c						2.50
800-(4/03, $3.95) Struzan painted-c; guest artists include Ross, Jim Lee, Jurgens, Sale						4.00
801-811: 801-Raney-a. 809-The Creeper app. 811-Mr. Majestic app.						2.50
812-Godfall part 1; Turner-c; Caldwell-a(p)						4.00
812-2nd printing; B&W sketch-c by Turner						3.00
813-Godfall pt. 4; Turner-c; Caldwell-a(p)						3.00
814-824, 826-828,830-836: 814-Reis-a/Art Adams-c; Darkseid app.; begin $2.50-c. 815,816-Teen Titans-c/app. 820-Doomsday app. 826-Capt. Marvel app. 827-Byrne-c/a begin. 831-Villains United tie-in. 835-Livewire app. 836-Infinite Crisis; revised origin						2.50
825-($2.99, 40 pgs.) Doomsday app.						3.00
829-Omac Project x-over Sacrifice pt. 2						5.00
829-(2nd printing) red tone cover						2.50
837-843-One Year Later; powers return after Infinite Crisis; Johns & Busiek-s						3.00
844-Donner & Johns-s/Adam Kubert-a/c begin; brown-toned cover						4.00
844-Andy Kubert variant-c						5.00
844-2nd printing with red-toned Adam Kubert cover						3.00
845-849,851-857: 845-Bizarro-c/app.; re-intro. General Zod, Ursa & Non. 846-Jax-Ur app. 847-849-No Kubert-a. 851-Kubert-a/c. 855-857-Bizarro app.; Powell-a/c						3.00
850-($3.99) Supergirl and LSH app., origin re-told; Guedes-a/c						4.00
858-($3.50) Legion of Super-Heroes app.; 1st meeting re-told; Johns-s/Frank-a/c						4.00
858-Variant-c (Superman & giant Brainiac robot) by Frank						5.00
858-Second printing with regular cover with red background instead of yellow						3.00
859-878: 859-863-Legion of Super-Heroes app.; var-c on each (859-Andy Kubert. 860-Lightle. 861-Grell. 862-Giffen. 863-Frank) 864-Batman and Lightning Lad app. 866-Brainiac returns 869-"Soda Pop" cover edition, 870-Pa Kent dies. 871-New Krypton; Ross-c						3.00
869-Initial printing recalled because of beer bottles on cover						10.00
879-885: 879-($3.99) Back-up Capt. Atom feature begins						4.00
#1,000,000 (11/98) Gene Ha-c; 853rd Century x-over						2.50
Annual 1-6 ('87-'94, $2.95)-1-Art Adams-c/a(p); Batman app. 2-Perez-c/a(i). 3-Armageddon 2001. 4-Eclipso vs. Shazam. 5-Bloodlines; 1st app. Loose Cannon. 6-Elseworlds story						3.00
Annual 7,9 ('95, '97, $3.95) 7-Year One story. 9-Pulp Heroes sty						4.00
Annual 8 (1996, $2.95) Legends of the Dead Earth story						3.00
Annual 10 ('07, $3.99) Short stories by Johns & Donner and various incl. A. Adams, J. Kubert, Wight, Morales; origin of Phantom Zone, Mon-El; Metallo app.; Adam & Joe Kubert-c						4.00
Annual 11 (7/08, $4.99) Conclusion to General Zod story continued from #851; Kubert-a						5.00
Annual 12 (8/09, $4.99) Origin of Nightwing and Flamebird						5.00

NOTE: *Supergirl's origin in 262, 280, 285, 291, 305, 309.* **N. Adams** *c-356, 358, 359, 361-364, 366, 367, 370-374, 377-379i, 398-400, 402, 404,405, 419p, 466, 468, 469, 473i, 485.* **Aparo** *a-642.* **Austin** *c/a-682i.* **Baily** *a-24, 25.* **Boring** *a-164, 194, 211, 223, 233, 241, 250, 261, 266-268, 346, 348, 352, 356, 357.* **Burnley** *a-28-33; c-48?, 53-55, 58, 59?, 60-63, 65, 66p, 67p, 70p, 71p, 79p, 82p, 84-86p, 90-92p, 93p?, 94p, 107p, 108p.* **Byrne** *a-584-598p, 599i, 600p; c-584-591, 596-600.* **Ditko** *a-642.* **Giffen** *a-560, 563, 565, 577, 579; c-539, 560, 563, 565, 577, 579.* **Grell** *a-440-442, 444-446, 450-452, 456-458; c-456.* **Guardineer** *a-24, 25; c-8, 11, 12, 14-16, 18. 25.* **Guice** *a(p)-676-681, 683-698, 700; c-683, 685, 686, 687(direct), 688-693i, 694-696, 697i, 698-700.* **Infantino** *a-642.* **Kaluta** *c-613.* **Bob Kane's** *Clip Carson-14-41.* **Gil Kane** *a-443r, 493r, 539-541, 544-546, 551-554, 601-605, 642; c-535p, 540, 541, 544p, 545-549, 551-554, 580, 627.* **Kirby** *c-638.* **Meskin** *a-42-121(most).* **Mignola** *a-600, Annual 2; c-c-614.* **Moldoff** *a-23-25, 443r.* **Mooney** *a-667p.* **Mortimer** *c-153, 154, 159-172, 174, 178-181, 184, 186-189, 191-193, 196, 200, 206.* **Orlando** *a-617p; c-621.* **Perez** *a-600i, 643-652p, Annual 2p; c-529p, 643-651, Annual 2p.* **Quesada** *c-Annual 4p.* **Fred Ray** *c-34, 36-46, 50-52.* **Siegel & Shuster** *a-1-27.* **Paul Smith** *c-608.* **Starlin** *a-509; c-631.* **Leonard Starr** *a-597i(part),* **Staton** *a-525p, 526p, 531p, 535p, 536p.* **Swan/Moldoff** *c-281, 286, 287, 293, 298, 334.* **Thibert** *c-676, 677p, 678-681, 684.* **Toth** *a-406, 407, 413, 431; c-616.* **Tuska** *a-486p, 550.* **Williamson** *a-568i.* **Zeck** *c-Annual 5*

ACTION COMICS

Adam Strange Special #1 © DC

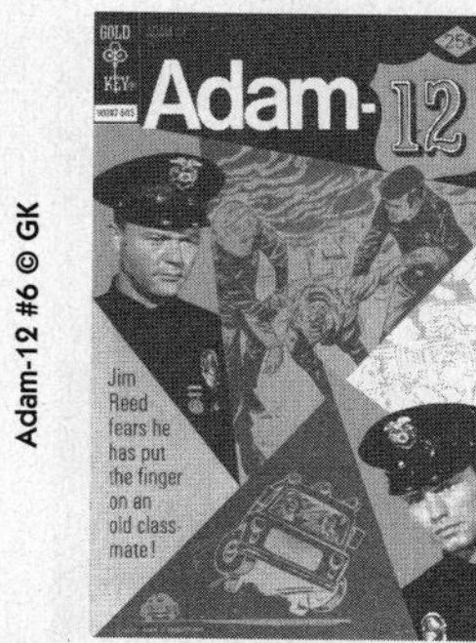

Adam-12 #6 © GK

Adventure Comics #46 © DC

GD VG FN VF VF/NM NM-
2.0 4.0 6.0 8.0 9.0 9.2

DC Comics: (no date)

1-Ashcan comic, not distributed to newsstands, only for in-house use. Cover art is the rejected art to Detective Comics #2 and interior from Detective Comics #1. A CGC certified 9.0 copy sold for $17,825 in 2002 and for $29,000 in 2008.

ACTION FORCE (Also see G.I. Joe European Missions)
Marvel Comics Ltd. (British): Mar, 1987 - No. 50, 1988 ($1.00, weekly, magazine)

1,3: British G.I. Joe series. 3-w/poster insert 2 3 4 6 8 10
2,4 1 2 3 4 5 7
5-10 5.00
11-50 3.00
...Special 1 (7/87) Summer holiday special; Snake Eyes-c/app. 1 2 3 5 6 8
...Special 2 (10/87) Winter special; 5.00

ACTION FUNNIES
DC Comics: 1938

nn - Ashcan comic, not distributed to newsstands, only for in house use. Cover art is Action Comics #3 and interior from Detective Comics #10. The Mallette/Brown copy in VG+ condition sold for $15,000 in 2005.

ACTION GIRL
Slave Labor Graphics: Oct, 1994 - No. 19 ($2.50/$2.75/$2.95, B&W)

1-19: 4-Begin $2.75-c. 19-Begin $2.95-c 3.00
1-6 ($2.75, 2nd printings): All read 2nd Print in indicia. 1-(2/96). 2-(10/95). 3-(2/96). 4-(7/96). 5-(2/97). 6-(9/97) 2.75
1-4 ($2.75, 3rd printings): All read 3rd Print in indicia. 2.75

ACTION PLANET COMICS
Action Planet: 1996 - No. 3, Sept, 1997 ($3.95, B&W, 44 pgs.)

1-3: 1-Intro Monster Man by Mike Manley & other stories 4.00
Giant Size Action Planet Halloween Special (1998, $5.95, oversized) 6.00

ACTUAL CONFESSIONS (Formerly Love Adventures)
Atlas Comics (MPI): No. 13, Oct, 1952 - No. 14, Dec, 1952

13,14 9 18 27 50 65 80

ACTUAL ROMANCES (Becomes True Secrets #3 on?)
Marvel Comics (IPS): Oct, 1949 - No. 2, Jan, 1950 (52 pgs.)

1 14 28 42 82 121 160
2-Photo-c 10 20 30 56 76 95

ADAM AND EVE
Spire Christian Comics (Fleming H. Revell Co.): 1975,1978 (35¢/39¢/49¢)

nn-By Al Hartley 2 4 6 9 13 16

ADAM: LEGEND OF THE BLUE MARVEL
Marvel Comics: Jan, 2009 - No. 5, May, 2009 ($3.99, limited series)

1-5-Grevioux-s/Broome-a; Avengers app. 4.00

ADAM STRANGE (Also see Green Lantern #132, Mystery In Space #53 & Showcase #17)
DC Comics: 1990 - No. 3, 1990 ($3.95, 52 pgs, limited series, squarebound)

Book One - Three: Andy & Adam Kubert-c/a 4.00
...: The Man of Two Worlds (2003, $19.95, TPB) r/#1-3; sketch pages by Andy Kubert 20.00

ADAM STRANGE (Leads into the Rann/Thanagar War mini-series)
DC Comics: Nov, 2004 - No. 8, June, 2005 ($2.95, limited series)

1-8-Andy Diggle-s/Pascal Ferry-a/c. 1-Superman app. 3.00
...: Planet Heist TPB (2005, $19.99) r/series; sketch pages 20.00
... Special (11/08, $3.50) Takes place durng Rann/Thanagar Holy War series; Starlin-s 3.50

ADAM-12 (TV)
Gold Key: Dec, 1973 - No. 10, Feb, 1976 (Photo-c)

1 6 12 18 43 69 95
2-10 4 8 12 22 34 45

ADDAMS FAMILY (TV cartoon)
Gold Key: Oct, 1974 - No. 3, Apr, 1975 (Hanna-Barbera)

1 8 16 24 54 90 125
2,3 6 12 18 37 59 80

ADLAI STEVENSON
Dell Publishing Co.: Dec, 1966

12-007-612-Life story; photo-c 4 8 12 22 34 45

ADOLESCENT RADIOACTIVE BLACK BELT HAMSTERS (See Clint)
Comic Castle/Eclipse Comics: 1986 - No. 9, Jan, 1988 ($1.50, B&W)

1-9: 1st & 2nd printings exist 2.50
1-Limited Edition 6.00
1-In 3-D (7/86), 2-4 ($2.50) 2.50
Massacre The Japanese Invasion #1 (8/89, $2.00) 2.50

ADOLESCENT RADIOACTIVE BLACK BELT HAMSTERS
Dynamite Entertainment: 2008 - No. 4, 2008 ($3.50, limited series)

1-4-Tom Nguyen-a/Keith Champagne-s; 2 covers by Nguyen and Oeming 3.50

ADRENALYNN (See The Tenth)
Image Comics: Aug, 1999 - No. 4, Feb, 2000 ($2.50)

1-4-Tony Daniel-s/Marty Egeland-a; origin of Adrenalynn 2.50

ADULT TALES OF TERROR ILLUSTRATED (See Terror Illustrated)

ADVANCED DUNGEONS & DRAGONS (Also see TSR Worlds)
DC Comics: Dec, 1988 - No. 36, Dec, 1991 (Newsstand #1 is Holiday, 1988-89) ($1.25-$1.75)

1-Based on TSR role playing game 4.00
2-36: 25-$1.75-c begins 2.50
Annual 1 (1990, $3.95, 68 pgs.) 4.00

ADVENTURE BOUND
Dell Publishing Co.: Aug, 1949

Four Color 239 6 12 18 39 62 85

ADVENTURE COMICS (Formerly New Adventure)(...Presents Dial H For Hero #479-490)
National Periodical Publications/DC Comics: No. 32, 11/38 - No. 490, 2/82; No. 491, 9/82 - No. 503, 9/83

32-Anchors Aweigh (ends #52), Barry O'Neil (ends #60, not in #33), Captain Desmo (ends #47), Dale Daring (ends #47), Federal Men (ends #70), The Golden Dragon (ends #36), Rusty & His Pals (ends #52) by Bob Kane, Todd Hunter (ends #38) and Tom Brent (ends #39) begin 430 860 1290 2408 3454 4500
33-38: 37-Cover used on Double Action #2 210 420 630 1176 1688 2200
39(6/39)- Jack Wood begins, ends #42; early mention of Marijuana in comics 210 420 630 1176 1688 2200
40-(Rare, 7/39, on stands 6/10/39)-The Sandman begins by Bert Christman (who died in WWII); believed to be 1st conceived story (see N.Y. World's Fair for 1st published app.); Socko Strong begins, ends #54 6000 12,000 18,000 45,000 80,000 115,000
41-O'Mealia shark-c 595 1190 1785 4344 7672 11,000
42,44-Sandman-c by Flessel. 44-Opium story 730 1460 2190 5329 9415 13,500
43,45: 45-Full page ad for Flash Comics #1 331 662 993 2317 4059 5800
46,47-Sandman covers by Flessel. 47-Steve Conrad Adventurer begins, ends #76 514 1018 1542 3750 6625 9500
48-Intro & 1st app. The Hourman by Bernard Baily; Baily-c (Hourman c-48,50,52-59) 2600 5200 7800 19,500 35,750 52,000
49,50: 50-Cotton Carver by Jack Lehti begins, ends #64 281 562 843 1784 3070 4355
51,60-Sandman-c: 51-Sandman-c by Flessel. 354 708 1062 2478 4339 6200
52-59: 53-1st app. Jimmy "Minuteman" Martin & the Minutemen of America in Hourman; ends #78. 58-Paul Kirk Manhunter begins (1st app.), ends #72 245 490 735 1568 2684 3800
61-1st app. Starman by Jack Burnley (4/41); Starman c-61-72; Starman by Burnley in #61-80 1200 2400 3600 9000 16,500 24,000
62-65,67,68,70: 67-Origin & 1st app. The Mist; classic Burnley-c. 70-Last Federal Men 206 412 618 1318 2259 3200
66-Origin/1st app. Shining Knight (9/41) 252 504 756 1613 2757 3900
69-1st app. Sandy the Golden Boy (Sandman's sidekick) by Paul Norris (in a Bob Kane style); Sandman dons new costume 216 432 648 1372 2361 3350
71-Jimmy Martin becomes costumed aide to the Hourman; 1st app. Hourman's Miracle Ray machine 200 400 600 1280 2190 3100
72-1st Simon & Kirby Sandman (3/42, 1st DC work) 919 1838 2757 6709 11,855 17,000
73-Origin Manhunter by Simon & Kirby; begin new series; Manhunter-c (scarce) 1275 2550 3825 9550 17,275 25,000
74-78,80: 74-Thorndyke replaces Jimmy, Hourman's assistant; new Sandman-c begin by S&K. 75-Thor app. by Kirby; 1st Kirby Thor (see Tales of the Unexpected #16). 77-Origin Genius Jones; Mist story. 80-Last S&K Manhunter & Burnley Starman 194 388 582 1242 2121 3000
79-Classic Manhunter-c 265 530 795 1694 2897 4100
81-90: 83-Last Hourman. 84-Mike Gibbs begins, ends #102 119 238 357 762 1306 1850
91-Last Simon & Kirby Sandman 110 220 330 704 1202 1700
92-99,101,102: 92-Last Manhunter. 101-Shining Knight origin retold. 102-Last Starman, Sandman, & Genius Jones; most-S&K-c (Genius Jones cont'd in More Fun #108) 97 194 291 621 1061 1500
100-S&K-c 132 264 396 838 1444 2050
103-Aquaman, Green Arrow, Johnny Quick & Superboy all move over from More Fun Comics #107; 8th app. Superboy; Superboy-c begin; 1st small logo (4/46) 300 600 900 1950 3375 4800

Adventure Comics #247 © DC

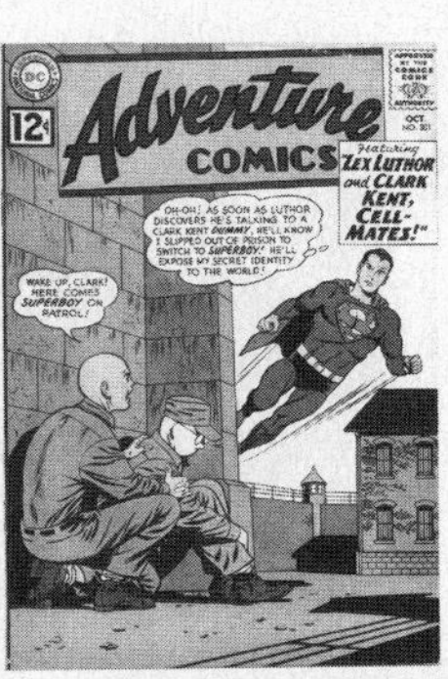

Adventure Comics #301 © DC

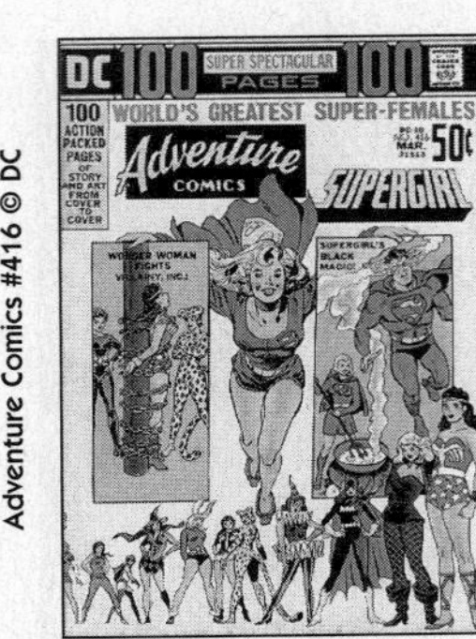

Adventure Comics #416 © DC

	GD 2.0	VG 4.0	FN 6.0	VF 8.0	VF/NM 9.0	NM- 9.2
104	108	216	324	686	1181	1675
105-110	77	154	231	493	847	1200
111-120: 113-X-Mas-c	69	138	207	438	752	1065
121,122-126,128-130: 128-1st meeting Superboy & Lois Lane	61	122	183	390	670	950
127-Brief origin Shining Knight retold	62	124	186	394	680	965
131-141,143-149: 132-Shining Knight 1st return to King Arthur time; origin aide Sir Butch	53	106	159	334	567	800
142-Origin Shining Knight & Johnny Quick retold	55	110	165	352	601	850
150,151,153,155,157,159,161,163-All have 6 pg. Shining Knight stories by Frank Frazetta. 159-Origin Johnny Quick. 161-1st Lana Lang app. in this title	66	132	198	419	722	1025
152,154,156,158,160,162,164-169: 166-Last Shining Knight. 168-Last 52 pg. issue	47	94	141	296	498	700
170-180	44	88	132	277	469	660
181-199: 189-B&W and color illo in **POP**	42	84	126	265	450	635
200 (5/54)	55	110	165	352	601	850
201-208: 207-Last Johnny Quick (not in 205)	40	80	120	246	411	575
209-Last pre-code issue; origin Speedy	41	82	123	256	428	600
210-1st app. Krypto (Superdog)-c/story (3/55)	320	640	960	2500	4750	7000
211-213,215-219	39	78	117	231	378	525
214-2nd app. Krypto	65	130	195	416	708	1000
220-Krypto-c/sty	42	84	126	265	445	625
221-246: 229-1st S.A. issue. 237-1st Intergalactic Vigilante Squadron (6/57). 239-Krypto-c	33	66	99	194	317	440
247(4/58)-1st Legion of Super Heroes app.; 1st app. Cosmic Boy, Saturn Girl & Lightning Boy (later Lightning Lad in #267) (origin)	500	1000	1500	4500	9000	13,500
248-252,254,255-Green Arrow in all: 255-Intro. Red Kryptonite in Superboy (used in #252 but with no effect)	28	56	84	165	270	375
253-1st meeting of Superboy & Robin; Green Arrow by Kirby in #250-255 (also see World's Finest #96-99)	32	64	96	192	314	435
256-Origin Green Arrow by Kirby	66	132	198	419	722	1025
257-259: 258-Green Arrow x-over in Superboy	24	48	72	142	234	325
260-1st Silver-Age origin Aquaman (5/59)	76	152	228	486	831	1175
261-265,268,270: 262-Origin Speedy in Green Arrow. 270-Congorilla begins, ends #281,283	20	40	60	118	192	265
266-(11/59)-Origin & 1st app. Aquagirl (tryout, not same as later character)	21	42	63	122	199	275
267(12/59)-2nd Legion of Super Heroes; Lightning Boy now called Lightning Lad; new costumes for Legion	97	194	291	611	1206	1800
269-Intro. Aqualad (2/60); last Green Arrow (not in #206)	32	64	96	192	314	435
271-Origin Luthor retold	37	74	111	222	361	500
272-274,277-280: 279-Intro White Kryptonite in Superboy. 280-1st meeting Superboy & Lori Lemaris	19	38	57	111	176	240
275-Origin Superman-Batman team retold (see World's Finest #94)	25	50	75	147	241	335
276-(9/60) Robinson Crusoe-like story	20	40	60	114	182	250
281,284,287-289: 281-Last Congorilla. 284-Last Aquaman in Adv.; Mooney-a. 287,288-Intro Dev-Em, the Knave from Krypton. 287-1st Bizarro Perry White & Jimmy Olsen. 288-Bizarro-c. 289-Legion cameo (statues)	18	36	54	103	162	220
282(3/61)-5th Legion app; intro/origin Star Boy	36	72	108	211	343	475
283-Intro. The Phantom Zone	28	56	84	165	270	375
285-1st Tales of the Bizarro World-c/story (ends #299) in Adv. (see Action #255)	23	46	69	136	223	310
286-1st Bizarro Mxyzptlk; Bizarro-c	22	44	66	132	216	300
290(11/61)-9th Legion app; origin Sunboy in Legion (last 10¢ issue)	32	64	96	188	307	425
291,292,295-298: 291-1st 12¢ ish, (12/61). 292-1st Bizarro Lana Lang & Lucy Lane. 295-Bizarro-c; 1st Bizarro Titano	11	22	33	76	136	195
293(2/62)-13th Legion app; Mon-El & Legion of Super Pets (1st app./origin) app. (1st Superhorse). 1st Bizarro Luthor & Kandor	16	32	48	115	220	325
294-1st Bizarro Marilyn Monroe, Pres. Kennedy.	12	24	36	88	162	235
299-1st Gold Kryptonite (8/62)	11	22	33	78	139	200
300-Tales of the Legion of Super-Heroes series begins (9/62); Mon-El leaves Phantom Zone (temporarily), joins Legion	43	86	129	344	672	1000
301-Origin Bouncing Boy	15	30	45	107	204	300
302-305: 303-1st app. Matter-Eater Lad. 304-Death of Lightning Lad in Legion	12	24	36	85	155	225
306-310: 306-Intro. Legion of Substitute Heroes. 307-1st app. Element Lad in Legion. 308-1st app. Lightning Lass in Legion	11	22	33	80	145	210
311-320: 312-Lightning Lad back in Legion. 315-Last new Superboy story; Colossal Boy app. 316-Origins & powers of Legion given. 317-Intro. Dream Girl in Legion; Lightning Lass becomes Light Lass; Hall of Fame series begins. 320-Dev-Em 2nd app.	10	20	30	67	116	165

	GD 2.0	VG 4.0	FN 6.0	VF 8.0	VF/NM 9.0	NM- 9.2
321-Intro. Time Trapper	9	18	27	60	100	140
322-330: 327-Intro/1st app. Lone Wolf in Legion. 329-Intro The Bizarro Legionnaires; intro. Legion flight rings	8	16	24	56	93	130
331-340: 337-Chlorophyll Kid & Night Girl app. 340-Intro Computo in Legion	8	16	24	52	86	120
341-Triplicate Girl becomes Duo Damsel	7	14	21	48	78	105
342-345,347-351: 345-Last Hall of Fame; returns in 356,371. 348-Origin Sunboy; intro Dr. Regulus in Legion. 349-Intro Universo & Rond Vidar. 351-1st app. White Witch	7	14	21	47	76	100
346-1st app. Karate Kid, Princess Projectra, Ferro Lad, & Nemesis Kid.	9	18	27	63	107	150
352,354-360: 354,355-Superman meets the Adult Legion. 355-Insect Queen joins Legion (4/67)	6	12	18	41	66	90
353-Death of Ferro Lad in Legion	7	14	21	49	80	110
361-364,366,368-370: 369-Intro Mordru in Legion	6	12	18	37	59	80
365,367: 365-Intro Shadow Lass (memorial to Shadow Woman app. in #354's Adult Legion-s); lists origins & powers of L.S.H. 367-New Legion headquarters	6	12	18	39	62	85
371,372: 371-Intro. Chemical King (mentioned in #354's Adult Legion-s). 372-Timber Wolf & Chemical King join	6	12	18	39	62	85
373,374,376-380: 373-Intro. Tornado Twins (Barry Allen Flash descendants). 374-Article on comics fandom. 380-Last Legion in Adventure; last 12¢-c	5	10	15	34	55	75
375-Intro Quantum Queen & The Wanderers	6	12	18	39	62	85
381-Supergirl begins; 1st full length Supergirl story & her 1st solo book (6/69)	11	22	33	80	145	210
382-389	5	10	15	30	48	65
390-Giant Supergirl G-69	7	14	21	45	73	100
391-396,398	4	8	12	24	37	50
397-1st app. new Supergirl	5	10	15	32	51	70
399-Unpubbed G.A. Black Canary story	4	8	12	26	41	55
400-New costume for Supergirl (12/70)	5	10	15	32	51	70
401,402,404-408-(15¢-c)	3	6	9	18	27	35
403-68 pg. Giant G-81; Legion-r/#304,305,308,312	7	14	21	45	73	100
409-411,413-415,417-420-(52 pgs.): 413-Hawkman by Kubert r/B&B #44; G.A. Robotman-r/Det. #178; Zatanna by Morrow. 414-r-2nd Animal Man/Str. Advs. #184. 415-Animal Man-r/Str. Adv.#190 (origin recap). 417-Morrow Vigilante; Frazetta Shining Knight-r/Adv. #161; origin The Enchantress; no Zatanna. 418-Prev. unpub. Dr. Mid-Nite story from 1948; no Zatanna. 420-Animal Man-r/Str. Adv. #195	3	6	9	19	29	38
412-(52 pgs.) Reprints origin & 1st app. of Animal Man from Strange Adventures #180	3	6	9	19	29	38
416-Also listed as DC 100 Pg. Super Spectacular #10; Golden Age-r; r/1st app. Black Canary from Flash #86; no Zatanna (see DC 100 Pg. Super Spectacular #10 for price)						
421-424: 424-Last Supergirl in Adventure	3	6	9	14	20	25
425-New look, content change to adventure; Kaluta-c; Toth-a, origin Capt. Fear	3	6	9	16	23	30
426,427: 426-1st Adventurers Club. 427-Last Vigilante	2	4	6	9	12	15
428-Origin/1st app. Black Orchid (c/story, 6-7/73)	6	12	18	37	59	80
429,430-Black Orchid-c/stories	3	6	9	21	32	42
431-Spectre by Aparo begins, ends #440.	6	12	18	41	66	90
432-439-Spectre app. 433-437-Cover title is Weird Adventure Comics. 436-Last 20¢ issue	4	8	12	22	34	45
440-New Spectre origin.	4	8	12	28	44	60
441-458: 441-452-Aquaman app. 443-Fisherman app. 445-447-The Creeper app. 446-Flag-c. 449-451-Martian Manhunter app. 450-Weather Wizard app. in Aquaman story. 453-458-Superboy app. 453-Intro. Mighty Girl. 457,458-Eclipso app.	1	3	4	6	8	10
459,460 (68 pgs.): 459-New Gods/Darkseid storyline concludes from New Gods #19 (#459 is dated 9-10/78) without missing a month. 459-Flash (ends #466), Deadman (ends #466), Wonder Woman (ends #464), Green Lantern (ends #460). 460-Aquaman (ends #478)	3	6	9	14	20	26
461,462 ($1.00, 68 pgs.): 461-Justice Society begins; ends 466. 461,462-Death Earth II Batman	4	8	12	26	41	55
463-466 ($1.00 size, 68 pgs.)	2	4	6	10	14	18
467-Starman by Ditko & Plastic Man begins; 1st app. Prince Gavyn (Starman).	2	4	6	8	11	14
468-490: 470-Origin Starman. 479-Dial 'H' For Hero begins, ends #490. 478-Last Starman & Plastic Man. 480-490: Dial 'H' For Hero						5.00
491-503: 491-100pg. Digest size begins; r/Legion of Super Heroes/Adv. #247, 267; Spectre, Aquaman, Superboy, S&K Sandman, Black Canary-r & new Shazam by Newton begin. 492,495,496,499-S&K Sandman-r/Adventure in all. 493-Challengers of the Unknown begins by Tuska w/brief origin. 493-495,497-499-G.A. Captain Marvel-r. 494-499-Spectre-r/Spectre						

Adventure Comics (2009 series) #5 © DC

Adventure Into Mystery #4 © MAR

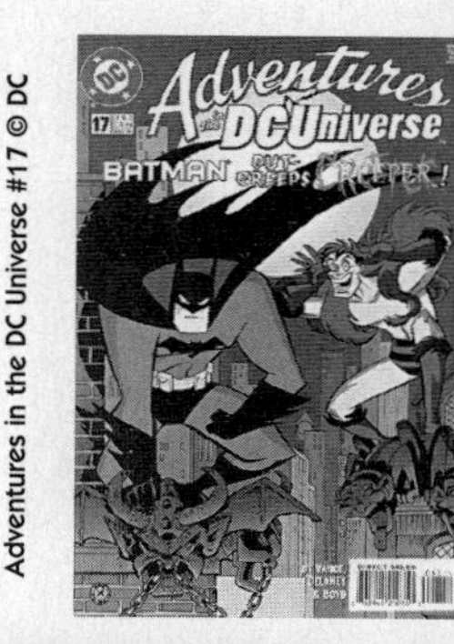

Adventures in the DC Universe #17 © DC

	GD	VG	FN	VF	VF/NM	NM-
	2.0	4.0	6.0	8.0	9.0	9.2

1-3, 5-7. 496-Capt. Marvel Jr. new-s, Cockrum-a. 498-Mary Marvel new-s; Plastic Man-r begin; origin Bouncing Boy-r/ #301. 500-Legion-r (Digest size, 148 pgs.).
501-503: G.A.-r 2 4 6 9 13 16
... 80 Page Giant (10/98, $4.95) Wonder Woman, Shazam, Superboy, Supergirl, Green Arrow, Legion, Bizarro World stories 5.00

NOTE: *Bizarro covers-285, 286, 288, 294, 295, 329. Vigilante app.-420, 426, 427.* **N. Adams** *a(r)-495i-498i; c-365-369, 371-373, 375-379, 381-383.* **Aparo** *a-431-433, 434i, 435, 436, 437i, 438i, 439-452, 503r; c-431-452.* **Austin** *a-449i 451i.* **Bernard Baily** *c-48, 50, 52-59.* **Bolland** *c-475.* **Burnley** *c-61-72, 116-120p.* **Chaykin** *a-438.* **Ditko** *a-467-478p; c-467p.* **Creig Flessel** *c-32, 33, 40, 42, 44, 46, 47, 51, 60.* **Giffen** *c-491p-494p, 500p.* **Grell** *a-435-437, 440.* **Guardineer** *c-34, 35, 45.* **Infantino** *a-416r.* **Kaluta** *c-425.* **Bob Kane** *a-38.* **G. Kane** *a-414r, 425; c-496-499, 537.* **Kirby** *a-250-256.* **Kubert** *a-413.* **Meskin** *a-81,127.* **Moldoff** *a-494i; c-49.* **Morrow** *a-413-415, 417, 422, 502r, 503r.* **Netzer/Nasser** *a-449-451.* **Newton** *a-459-461, 464-466, 491p, 492p.* **Paul Norris** *a-69.* **Orlando** *a-457p, 458p.* **Perez** *c-484-486, 490p.* **Simon/Kirby** *a-503r; c-73-97, 100-102.* **Starlin** *c-471.* **Staton** *a-445-447i, 456-458p, 459, 460, 461p-465p, 466,467p-478p, 502p(r); c-458, 461(back).* **Toth** *a-418, 419, 425, 431, 495p-497p.* **Tuska** *a-494p.*

ADVENTURE COMICS (Also see All Star Comics 1999 crossover titles)
DC Comics: May, 1999 ($1.99, one-shot)
1-Golden Age Starman and the Atom; Snejbjerg-a 2.50

ADVENTURE COMICS (See Final Crisis: Legion of Three Worlds)
DC Comics: No. 0, Apr, 2009 - Present ($1.00/$3.99)
0-($1.00) R/Adventure Comics #247; new Luthor & Brainiac back-up-s; Lopresti-c 2.50
1-6-($3.99) Superboy stories; Johns-s/Manapul-a; Legion back-up-s. 5-Blackest Night 4.00
1-4-Variant 7-panel cover by Manapul numbered with original #504-#507 5.00

ADVENTURE COMICS SPECIAL (See New Krypton issues in 2009 Superman titles)
DC Comics: Jan, 2009 ($2.99, one-shot)
... Featuring the Guardian - James Robinson-s/Pere Pérez-a; origin re-told; intro. Gwen 3.00

ADVENTURE INTO MYSTERY
Atlas Comics (BFP No. 1/OPI No. 2-8): May, 1956 - No. 8, July, 1957
1-Powell s/f-a; Forte-a; Everett-c 39 78 117 240 395 550
2-Flying Saucer story 22 44 66 132 216 300
3,6-Everett-c 20 40 60 117 189 260
4,5,7: 4-Williamson-a, 4 pgs; Powell-a. 5-Everett-c/a, Orlando-a. 7-Torres-a; Everett-c 21 42 63 124 202 280
8-Moreira, Sale, Torres, Woodbridge-a, Severin-c 20 40 60 117 189 260

ADVENTURE IS MY CAREER
U.S. Coast Guard Academy/Street & Smith: 1945 (44 pgs.)
nn-Simon, Milt Gross-a 21 42 63 122 199 275

ADVENTURERS, THE
Aircel Comics/Adventure Publ.: Aug, 1986 - No. 10, 1987? ($1.50, B&W)
V2#1, 1987 - V2#9, 1988; V3#1, Oct, 1989 - V3#6, 1990
1-Peter Hsu-a 1 2 3 5 6 8
1-Cover variant, limited ed. 2 4 6 9 12 15
1-2nd print (1986); 1st app. Elf Warrior 3.00
2,3, 0 (#4, 12/86)-Origin, 5-10, Book II, reg. & Limited Ed. #1 3.50
Book II, #2,3,0,4-9 2.50
Book III, #1 (10/89, $2.25)-Reg. & limited-c, Book III, #2-6 2.50

ADVENTURES (No. 2 Spectacular... on cover)
St. John Publishing Co.: Nov, 1949 - No. 2, Feb, 1950 (No. 1 ...in Romance on cover) (Slightly larger size)
1(Scarce); Bolle, Starr-a(2) 27 54 81 158 259 360
2(Scarce)-Slave Girl; China Bombshell app.; Bolle, L. Starr-a 39 78 117 240 395 550

ADVENTURES FOR BOYS
Bailey Enterprises: Dec, 1954
nn-Comics, text, & photos 8 16 24 40 50 60

ADVENTURES IN PARADISE (TV)
Dell Publishing Co.: Feb-Apr, 1962
Four Color#1301 6 12 18 39 62 85

ADVENTURES IN ROMANCE (See Adventures)

ADVENTURES IN SCIENCE (See Classics Illustrated Special Issue)

ADVENTURES IN THE DC UNIVERSE
DC Comics: Apr, 1997 - No. 19, Oct, 1998 ($1.75/$1.95/$1.99)
1-Animated style in all: JLA-c/app 5.00
2-11,13-17,19: 2-Flash app. 3-Wonder Woman. 4-Green Lantern. 6-Aquaman. 7-Shazam Family. 8-Blue Beetle & Booster Gold. 9-Flash. 10-Legion. 11-Green Lantern & Wonder Woman. 13-Impulse & Martian Manhunter. 14-Superboy/Flash race 3.50
12,18-JLA-c/app 3.50
Annual 1(1997, $3.95)-Dr. Fate, Impulse, Rose & Thorn, Superboy, Mister Miracle app. 4.50

ADVENTURES IN THE RIFLE BRIGADE
DC Comics (Vertigo): Oct, 2000 - No. 3, Dec, 2000 ($2.50, limited series)
1-3-Ennis-s/Ezquerra-a/Bolland-c 2.50
TPB (2004, $14.95) r/series and Operation Bollock series 15.00

ADVENTURES IN THE RIFLE BRIGADE: OPERATION BOLLOCK
DC Comics (Vertigo): Oct, 2001 - No. 3, Jan, 2002 ($2.50, limited series)
1-3-Ennis-s/Ezquerra-a/Fabry-c 2.50

ADVENTURES IN 3-D (With glasses)
Harvey Publications: Nov, 1953 - No. 2, Jan, 1954 (25¢)
1-Nostrand, Powell-a, 2-Powell-a 15 30 45 86 133 180

ADVENTURES INTO DARKNESS (See Seduction of the Innocent 3-D)
Better-Standard Publications/Visual Editions: No. 5, Aug, 1952- No. 14, 1954
5-Katz-c/a; Toth-a(p) 42 84 126 265 445 625
6-Tuska, Katz-a 30 60 90 177 289 400
7-9: 7-Katz-c/a. 8,9-Toth-a(p) 30 60 90 177 289 400
10-12: 10,11-Jack Katz-a. 12-Toth-a; lingerie panel 27 54 81 158 259 360
13-Toth-a(p); Cannibalism story cited by T. E. Murphy articles 34 68 102 199 325 450
14 20 40 60 117 189 260

NOTE: **Fawcette** *a-13.* **Moreira** *a-5.* **Sekowsky** *a-10, 11, 13(2).*

ADVENTURES INTO TERROR (Formerly Joker Comics)
Marvel/Atlas Comics (CDS): No. 43, Nov, 1950 - No. 31, May, 1954
43(#1) 69 138 207 442 759 1075
44(#2, 2/51)-Sol Brodsky-c 42 84 126 265 445 625
3(4/51), 4 31 62 93 186 303 420
5-Wolverton-c panel/Mystic #6; Rico-c panel also; Atom Bomb story 35 70 105 210 338 465
6,8: 8-Wolverton text illo r-/Marvel Tales #104; prototype of Spider-Man villain The Lizard 29 58 87 174 285 395
7-Wolverton-a "Where Monsters Dwell", 6 pgs.; Tuska-c; Maneely-c panels 60 120 180 381 653 925
9,10,12-Krigstein-a. 9-Decapitation panels 25 50 75 150 245 340
11,13-20 22 44 66 130 213 295
21-24,26-31 20 40 60 120 195 270
25-Matt Fox-a 25 50 75 150 245 340

NOTE: **Ayers** *a-21.* **Colan** *a-3, 5, 14, 21, 24, 25, 28, 29; c-27.* **Colletta** *a-30.* **Everett** *c-13, 21, 25.* **Fass** *a-28, 29.* **Forte** *a-28.* **Heath** *a-43, 44, 4-6, 22, 24, 26; c-43, 9, 11.* **Lazarus** *a-7.* **Maneely** *a-7(3 pg.), 10, 11, 21., 22 c-15, 29.* **Don Rico** *a-4, 5(3 pg.).* **Sekowsky** *a-43, 3, 4.* **Sinnott** *a-8, 9, 11, 28.* **Tuska** *a-14; c-7.*

ADVENTURES INTO THE UNKNOWN
American Comics Group: Fall, 1948 - No. 174, Aug, 1967 (No. 1-33: 52 pgs.)
(1st continuous series Supernatural comic; see Eerie #1)
1-Guardineer-a; adapt. of 'Castle of Otranto' by Horace Walpole 226 452 678 1446 2473 3500
2,3: 3-Feldstein-a (9 pgs) 79 158 237 502 864 1225
4,5: 5- 'Spirit Of Frankenstein' series begins, ends #12 (except #11) 41 82 123 256 428 600
6-10 34 68 102 204 332 460
11-16,18-20: 13-Starr-a 29 58 87 170 278 385
17-Story similar to movie 'The Thing' 34 68 102 199 325 450
21-26,28-30 25 50 75 147 241 335
27-Williamson/Krenkel-a (8 pgs.) 31 62 93 182 296 410
31-50: 38-Atom bomb panels 20 40 60 114 182 250
51-(1/54)-(3-D effect-c/story)-Only white cover 39 78 117 240 395 550
52-58: (3-D effect-c/stories with black covers). 52-E.C. swipe/Haunt Of Fear #14 37 74 111 222 361 500
59-3-D effect story only; new logo 29 58 87 172 281 390
60-Wood*esque*-a by Landau 15 30 45 86 133 180
61-Last pre-code issue (1-2/55) 15 30 45 86 133 180
62-70 8 16 24 54 90 125
71-90 6 12 18 43 69 95
91,96(#95 on inside),107,116-All have Williamson-a 7 14 21 47 76 105
92-95,97-99,101-106,108-115,117-128: 109-113,118-Whitney painted-c. 128-Williamson/Krenkel/Torres-a(r)/Forbidden Worlds #63; last 10¢ issue 5 10 15 34 55 75
100 6 12 18 39 62 85
129-153,157: 153,157-Magic Agent app. 4 8 12 24 37 50
154-Nemesis series begins (origin), ends #170 5 10 15 30 48 65
155,156,158-167,170-174 4 8 12 23 36 48
168-Ditko-a(p) 4 8 12 28 44 60
169-Nemesis battles Hitler 4 8 12 28 44 60
Nemesis Archives: Vol. One (Dark Horse Books, 9/08, $59.95) r/#154-170; creator bios 60.00

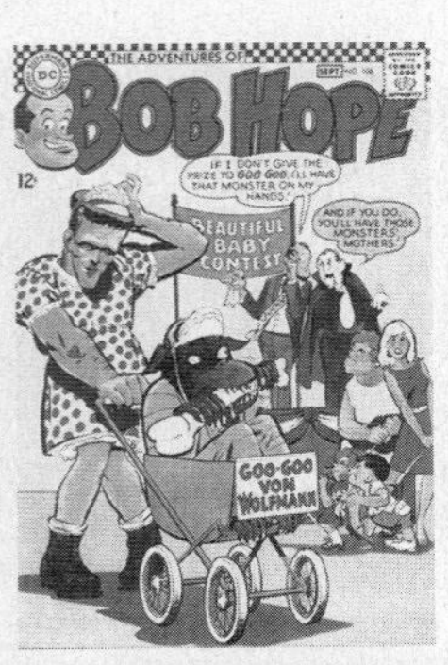

Adventures of Bob Hope #106 © DC

Adventures of Cyclops and Phoenix #3 © MAR

Adventures of Jerry Lewis #105 © DC

NOTE: *"Spirit of Frankenstein" series in 5, 6, 8-10, 12, 16.* ***Buscema*** *a-100, 106, 108-110, 158r, 165r.* ***Cameron*** *a-34.* ***Craig*** *a-152, 160.* ***Goode*** *a-45, 47, 60.* ***Landau*** *a-51, 59-63.* ***Lazarus*** *a-34, 48, 51, 52, 56, 58, 79, 87; c-31-56, 58.* ***Reinman*** *a-102, 111, 112, 115-118, 124, 130, 137, 141, 145, 164.* ***Whitney*** *c-12-30, 57, 59-on (most.)* ***Torres/Williamson*** *a-116.*

ADVENTURES INTO WEIRD WORLDS
Marvel/Atlas Comics (ACI): Jan, 1952 - No. 30, June, 1954

	GD 2.0	VG 4.0	FN 6.0	VF 8.0	VF/NM 9.0	NM- 9.2
1-Atom bomb panels	74	148	222	470	810	1150
2-Sci/fic stories (2); one by Maneely	39	78	117	240	395	550
3-10: 7-Tongue ripped out. 10-Krigstein, Everett-a	29	58	87	170	278	385
11-20	22	44	66	132	216	300
21-Hitler in Hell story	28	56	84	165	270	375
22-26: 24-Man holds hypo & splits in two	20	40	60	120	195	270
27-Matt Fox end of world story-a; severed head-c	39	78	117	240	395	550
28-Atom bomb story; decapitation panels	22	44	66	132	216	300
29,30	18	36	54	107	169	230

NOTE: ***Ayers*** *a-8, 26.* ***Everett*** *a-4, 5; c-6, 8, 10-13, 18, 19, 22, 24, 25; a-4, 25.* ***Fass*** *a-7.* ***Forte*** *a-21, 24.* ***Al Hartley*** *a-2.* ***Heath*** *a-1, 4, 17, 22; c-7, 9, 20.* ***Maneely*** *a-2, 3, 11, 20, 22, 23, 25; c-1, 3, 22, 25-27, 29.* ***Reinman*** *a-24, 28.* ***Rico*** *a-13.* ***Robinson*** *a-13.* ***Sinnott*** *a-25, 30.* ***Tuska*** *a-1, 2, 12, 15.* ***Whitney*** *a-7.* ***Wildey*** *a-28. Bondage c-22.*

ADVENTURES IN WONDERLAND
Lev Gleason Publications: April, 1955 - No. 5, Feb, 1956 (Jr. Readers Guild)

	GD 2.0	VG 4.0	FN 6.0	VF 8.0	VF/NM 9.0	NM- 9.2
1-Maurer-a	11	22	33	62	86	110
2-4	7	14	21	37	46	55
5-Christmas issue	8	16	24	40	50	60

ADVENTURES OF ALAN LADD, THE
National Periodical Publ.: Oct-Nov, 1949 - No. 9, Feb-Mar, 1951 (All 52 pgs.)

	GD 2.0	VG 4.0	FN 6.0	VF 8.0	VF/NM 9.0	NM- 9.2
1-Photo-c	78	156	234	491	833	1175
2-Photo-c	41	82	123	253	419	585
3-6: Last photo-c	32	64	96	190	305	420
7-9	26	52	78	154	247	340

NOTE: ***Dan Barry*** *a-1.* ***Moreira*** *a-3-7.*

ADVENTURES OF ALICE (Also see Alice in Wonderland & ...at Monkey Island)
Civil Service Publ./Pentagon Publishing Co.: 1945

	GD 2.0	VG 4.0	FN 6.0	VF 8.0	VF/NM 9.0	NM- 9.2
1	15	30	45	83	124	165
2-Through the Magic Looking Glass	11	22	33	62	86	110

ADVENTURES OF BARON MUNCHAUSEN, THE
Now Comics: July, 1989 - No. 4, Oct, 1989 ($1.75, limited series)

	GD 2.0	VG 4.0	FN 6.0	VF 8.0	VF/NM 9.0	NM- 9.2
1-4: Movie adaptation						2.50

ADVENTURES OF BARRY WEEN, BOY GENIUS, THE (Also see Free Comic Book Day Edition in the Promotional Comics section)
Image Comics: Mar, 1999 - No. 3, May, 1999 ($2.95, B&W, limited series)

	GD 2.0	VG 4.0	FN 6.0	VF 8.0	VF/NM 9.0	NM- 9.2
1-3-Judd Winick-s/a						3.00
TPB (Oni Press, 11/99, $8.95)						9.00

ADVENTURES OF BARRY WEEN, BOY GENIUS 2.0, THE
Oni Press: Feb, 2000 - No. 3, Apr, 2000 ($2.95, B&W, limited series)

	GD 2.0	VG 4.0	FN 6.0	VF 8.0	VF/NM 9.0	NM- 9.2
1-3-Judd Winick-s/a						3.00
TPB (2000, $8.95)						9.00

ADVENTURES OF BARRY WEEN, BOY GENIUS 3, THE : MONKEY TALES
Oni Press: Feb, 2001 - No. 6, Feb, 2002 ($2.95, B&W, limited series)

	GD 2.0	VG 4.0	FN 6.0	VF 8.0	VF/NM 9.0	NM- 9.2
1-6-Judd Winick-s/a						3.00
TPB (2001, $8.95) r/#1-3; intro. by Peter David						9.00
...4 TPB (5/02, $8.95) r/#4-6						9.00

ADVENTURES OF BAYOU BILLY, THE (Based on video game)
Archie Comics: Sept, 1989 - No. 5, June, 1990 ($1.00)

	GD 2.0	VG 4.0	FN 6.0	VF 8.0	VF/NM 9.0	NM- 9.2
1-5: Esposito-c/a(i). 5-Kelley Jones-c						3.00

ADVENTURES OF BOB HOPE, THE (Also see True Comics #59)
National Per. Publ.: Feb-Mar, 1950 - No. 109, Feb-Mar, 1968 (#1-10: 52pgs.)

	GD 2.0	VG 4.0	FN 6.0	VF 8.0	VF/NM 9.0	NM- 9.2
1-Photo-c	194	388	582	1242	2121	3000
2-Photo-c	84	168	252	538	919	1300
3,4-Photo-c	52	104	156	328	557	785
5-10	40	80	120	241	401	560
11-20	28	56	84	165	270	375
21-31 (2-3/55; last precode)	20	40	60	114	182	250
32-40	10	20	30	70	123	175
41-50	9	18	27	61	103	145
51-70	7	14	21	50	83	115
71-93	6	12	18	37	59	80
94-Aquaman cameo	6	12	18	37	59	80
95-1st app. Super-Hip & 1st monster issue (11/65)	7	14	21	50	83	115
96-105: Super-Hip and monster stories in all. 103-Batman, Robin, Ringo Starr cameos	6	12	18	37	59	80
106-109-All monster-c/stories by N. Adams-c/a	8	16	24	52	86	120

NOTE: *Buzzy in #34. Kitty Karr of Hollywood in #15, 17-20, 23, 28. Liz in #26, 109. Miss Beverly Hills of Hollywood in #7, 8, 10, 13, 14. Miss Melody Lane of Broadway in #15. Rusty in #23, 25. Tommy in #24. No 2nd feature in #2-4, 6, 8, 11, 12, 28-108.*

ADVENTURES OF CAPTAIN AMERICA
Marvel Comics: Sept, 1991 - No. 4, Jan, 1992 ($4.95, 52 pgs., squarebound, limited series)

	GD 2.0	VG 4.0	FN 6.0	VF 8.0	VF/NM 9.0	NM- 9.2
1-4: 1-Origin in WW2; embossed-c; Nicieza scripts; Maguire-c/a(p) begins, ends #3. 2-4-Austin-c/a(i). 3,4-Red Skull app.						5.00

ADVENTURES OF CYCLOPS AND PHOENIX (Also See Askani'son & The Further Adventures of Cyclops And Phoenix)
Marvel Comics: May, 1994 - No. 4, Aug, 1994 ($2.95, limited series)

	GD 2.0	VG 4.0	FN 6.0	VF 8.0	VF/NM 9.0	NM- 9.2
1-4-Characters from X-Men; origin of Cable						4.00
Trade paperback ($14.95)-reprints #1-4						15.00

ADVENTURES OF DEAN MARTIN AND JERRY LEWIS, THE
(The Adventures of Jerry Lewis #41 on) (See Movie Love #12)
National Periodical Publications: July-Aug, 1952 - No. 40, Oct, 1957

	GD 2.0	VG 4.0	FN 6.0	VF 8.0	VF/NM 9.0	NM- 9.2
1	110	220	330	704	1202	1700
2-3 pg origin on how they became a team	52	104	156	328	552	775
3-10: 3- I Love Lucy text featurette	31	62	93	186	303	420
11-19: Last precode (2/55)	20	40	60	117	189	260
20-30	15	30	45	88	137	185
31-40	14	28	42	78	112	145

ADVENTURES OF DETECTIVE ACE KING, THE (Also see Bob Scully-- & Detective Dan)
Humor Publ. Corp.: No date (1933) (36 pgs., 9-1/2x12") (10¢, B&W, one-shot) (paper-c)

	GD 2.0	VG 4.0	FN 6.0	VF 8.0	VF/NM 9.0	NM- 9.2
Book 1-Along with Bob Scully & Detective Dan, the first comic w/original art & the first of a single theme.; Not reprints; Ace King by Martin Nadle (The American Sherlock Holmes). A Dick Tracy look-alike	375	750	1125	3000	-	-

ADVENTURES OF EVIL AND MALICE, THE
Image Comics: June, 1999 - No. 3, Nov, 1999 ($3.50/$3.95, limited series)

	GD 2.0	VG 4.0	FN 6.0	VF 8.0	VF/NM 9.0	NM- 9.2
1,2-Jimmie Robinson-s/a						3.50
3-(3.95)						4.00

ADVENTURES OF FELIX THE CAT, THE
Harvey Comics: May, 1992 ($1.25)

	GD 2.0	VG 4.0	FN 6.0	VF 8.0	VF/NM 9.0	NM- 9.2
1-Messmer-r						4.00

ADVENTURES OF FORD FAIRLANE, THE
DC Comics: May, 1990 - No. 4, Aug, 1990 ($1.50, limited series, mature)

	GD 2.0	VG 4.0	FN 6.0	VF 8.0	VF/NM 9.0	NM- 9.2
1-4: Andrew Dice Clay movie tie-in; Don Heck inks						3.00

ADVENTURES OF HOMER COBB, THE
Say/Bart Prod. : Sept, 1947 (Oversized) (Published in the U.S., but printed in Canada)

	GD 2.0	VG 4.0	FN 6.0	VF 8.0	VF/NM 9.0	NM- 9.2
1-(Scarce)-Feldstein-c/a	32	64	96	188	307	425

ADVENTURES OF HOMER GHOST (See Homer The Happy Ghost)
Atlas Comics: June, 1957 - No. 2, Aug, 1957

	GD 2.0	VG 4.0	FN 6.0	VF 8.0	VF/NM 9.0	NM- 9.2
V1#1,2: 2-Robot-c	11	22	33	64	90	115

ADVENTURES OF JERRY LEWIS, THE (Adventures of Dean Martin & Jerry Lewis No. 1-40) (See Super DC Giant)
National Periodical Publ.: No. 41, Nov, 1957 - No. 124, May-June, 1971

	GD 2.0	VG 4.0	FN 6.0	VF 8.0	VF/NM 9.0	NM- 9.2
41	9	18	27	64	110	155
42-60	7	14	21	50	83	115
61-67,69-73,75-80	6	12	18	43	69	95
68,74-Photo-c (movie)	9	18	27	63	107	150
81,82,85-87,90,91,94,96,98,99	6	12	18	37	59	80
83,84,88: 83-1st Monsters-c/s. 84-Jerry as a Super-hero-c/s. 88-1st Witch, Miss Kraft	6	12	18	43	69	95
89-Bob Hope app.; Wizard of Oz & Alfred E. Neuman in MAD parody	7	14	21	47	76	105
92-Superman cameo	7	14	21	47	76	105
93-Beatles parody as babies	6	12	18	43	69	95
95-1st Uncle Hal Wack-A-Boy Camp-c/s	6	12	18	43	69	95
97-Batman/Robin/Joker-c/story; Riddler & Penguin app; Dick Sprang-c.	9	18	27	64	110	155
100	7	14	21	45	73	100
101,103,104-Neal Adams-c/a	8	16	24	52	86	120
102-Beatles app.; Neal Adams c/a	9	18	27	65	113	160
105-Superman x-over	7	14	21	47	76	105
106-111,113-116	4	8	12	28	44	60
112,117: 112-Flash x-over. 117-W. Woman x-over	7	14	21	45	73	100
118-124	4	8	12	26	41	55

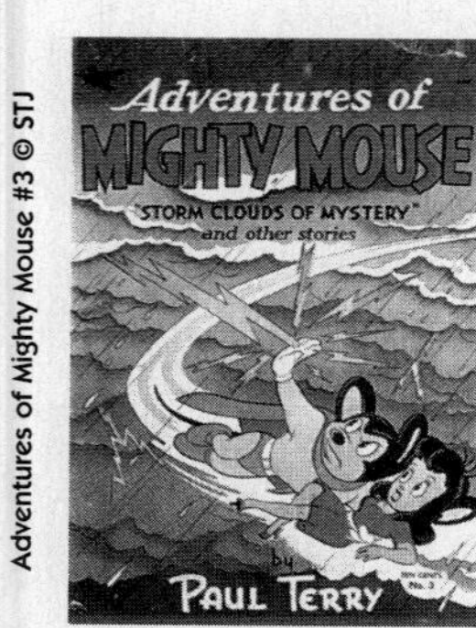

Adventures of Mighty Mouse #3 © STJ

Adventures of Rex the Wonder Dog #5 © DC

Adventures of Superman #628 © DC

	GD 2.0	VG 4.0	FN 6.0	VF 8.0	VF/NM 9.0	NM- 9.2

NOTE: *Monster-c/s-90,93,96,98,101. Wack-A-Buy Camp-c/s-96,99,102,107,108.*

ADVENTURES OF JO-JOY, THE (See Jo-Joy)

ADVENTURES OF LASSIE, THE (See Lassie)

ADVENTURES OF LUTHER ARKWRIGHT, THE
Valkyrie Press/Dark Horse Comics: Oct, 1987 - No. 9, Jan, 1989 ($2.00, B&W) V2, #1, Mar, 1990 - V2#9, 1990 ($1.95, B&W)

	GD	VG	FN	VF	VF/NM	NM-
1-9: 1-Alan Moore intro., V2#1-9 (Dark Horse): r-1st series; new-c						4.00
TPB (1997, $14.95) r/#1-9 w/Michael Moorcock intro.						15.00

ADVENTURES OF MIGHTY MOUSE (Mighty Mouse Adventures No. 1)
St. John Publishing Co.: No. 2, Jan, 1952 - No. 18, May, 1955

	GD	VG	FN	VF	VF/NM	NM-
2	24	48	72	144	237	330
3-5	15	30	45	83	124	165
6-18	11	22	33	62	86	110

ADVENTURES OF MIGHTY MOUSE (2nd Series) (Becomes Mighty Mouse #161 on)
(Two No. 144's; formerly Paul Terry's Comics; No. 129-137 have nn's)
St. John/Pines/Dell/Gold Key: No. 126, Aug, 1955 - No. 160, Oct, 1963

	GD	VG	FN	VF	VF/NM	NM-
126(8/55), 127(10/55), 128(11/55)-St. John	10	20	30	54	72	90
nn(129, 4/56)-144(8/59)-Pines	5	10	15	30	48	65
144(10-12/59)-155(7-9/62) Dell	4	8	12	28	44	60
156(10/62)-160(10/63) Gold Key	4	8	12	28	44	60

NOTE: *Early issues titled "Paul Terry's Adventures of ...."*

ADVENTURES OF MIGHTY MOUSE (Formerly Mighty Mouse)
Gold Key: No. 166, Mar, 1979 - No. 172, Jan, 1980

	GD	VG	FN	VF	VF/NM	NM-
166-172	1	2	3	5	6	8

ADVS. OF MR. FROG & MISS MOUSE (See Dell Junior Treasury No. 4)

ADVENTURES OF OZZIE & HARRIET, THE (See Ozzie & Harriet)

ADVENTURES OF PATORUZU
Green Publishing Co.: Aug, 1946 - Winter, 1946

	GD	VG	FN	VF	VF/NM	NM-
nn's-Contains Animal Crackers reprints	6	12	18	28	34	40

ADVENTURES OF PINKY LEE, THE (TV)
Atlas Comics: July, 1955 - No. 5, Dec, 1955

	GD	VG	FN	VF	VF/NM	NM-
1	24	48	72	140	230	320
2-5	15	30	45	86	133	180

ADVENTURES OF PIPSQUEAK, THE (Formerly Pat the Brat)
Archie Publications (Radio Comics): No. 34, Sept, 1959 - No. 39, July, 1960

	GD	VG	FN	VF	VF/NM	NM-
34	3	6	9	21	32	42
35-39	3	6	9	17	25	32

ADVENTURES OF QUAKE & QUISP, THE (See Quaker Oats "Plenty of Glutton")

ADVENTURES OF REX THE WONDER DOG, THE (Rex...No. 1)
National Periodical Publ.: Jan-Feb, 1952 - No. 45, May-June, 1959; No. 46, Nov-Dec, 1959

	GD	VG	FN	VF	VF/NM	NM-
1-(Scarce)-Toth-c/a	132	264	396	838	1444	2050
2-(Scarce)-Toth-c/a	60	120	180	381	653	925
3-(Scarce)-Toth-a	47	94	141	296	498	700
4,5	39	78	117	240	395	550
6-10	31	62	93	186	303	420
11-Atom bomb-c/story; dinosaur-c/sty	37	74	111	222	361	500
12-19: 19-Last precode (1-2/55)	20	40	60	117	189	260
20-46	15	30	45	85	130	175

NOTE: ***Infantino, Gil Kane** art in 5-19 (most)*

ADVENTURES OF ROBIN HOOD, THE (Formerly Robin Hood)
Magazine Enterprises (Sussex Publ. Co.): No. 7, 9/57 - No. 8, 11/57
(Based on Richard Greene TV Show)

	GD	VG	FN	VF	VF/NM	NM-
7,8-Richard Greene photo-c. 7-Powell-a	15	30	45	83	124	165

ADVENTURES OF ROBIN HOOD, THE
Gold Key: Mar, 1974 - No. 7, Jan, 1975 (Disney cartoon) (36 pgs.)

	GD	VG	FN	VF	VF/NM	NM-
1(90291-403)-Part-r of $1.50 editions	2	4	6	13	18	22
2-7: 1-7 are part-r	2	4	6	8	11	14

ADVENTURES OF SNAKE PLISSKEN
Marvel Comics: Jan, 1997 ($2.50, one-shot)

	GD	VG	FN	VF	VF/NM	NM-
1-Based on Escape From L.A. movie; Brereton-c						4.00

ADVENTURES OF SPAWN, THE
Image Comics (Todd McFarlane Prods.): Jan, 2007; Nov, 2008 ($5.99)

	GD	VG	FN	VF	VF/NM	NM-
1,2-Printed adaptation of the Spawn.com web comic; Khary Randolph-a						6.00

ADVENTURES OF SPIDER-MAN, THE (Based on animated TV series)
Marvel Comics: Apr, 1996 - No. 12, Mar, 1997 (99¢)

	GD	VG	FN	VF	VF/NM	NM-
1-12: 1-Punisher app. 2-Venom cameo. 3-X-Men. 6-Fantastic Four						3.00

ADVENTURES OF SUPERBOY, THE (See Superboy, 2nd Series)

ADVENTURES OF SUPERMAN (Formerly Superman)
DC Comics: No. 424, Jan, 1987 - No. 499, Feb, 1993; No. 500, Early June, 1993 - No. 649, Apr, 2006 (This title's numbering continues with Superman #650, May, 2006)

	GD	VG	FN	VF	VF/NM	NM-
424-Ordway-c/a/Wolfman-s begin following Byrne's Superman revamp						3.00
425-435,437-462: 426-Legends x-over. 432-1st app. Jose Delgado who becomes Gangbuster in #434. 437-Millennium x-over. 438-New Brainiac app. 440-Batman app. 449-Invasion						3.00
436-Byrne scripts begin; Millennium x-over						3.50
463-Superman/Flash race; cover swipe/Superman #199						5.00
464-Lobo-c & app. (pre-dates Lobo #1)						4.00
465-495: 467-Part 2 of Batman story. 473-Hal Jordan, Guy Gardner x-over. 477-Legion app. 491-Last $1.00-c. 480-($1.75, 52 pgs.). 495-Forever People-c/story; Darkseid app.						2.50
496,497: 496-Doomsday cameo. 497-Doomsday battle issue						3.00
496,497-2nd printings						2.50
498,499-Funeral for a Friend; Supergirl app.						2.50
498-2nd & 3rd printings						2.50
500-($2.95, 68 pgs.)-Collector's edition w/card						3.50
500-($2.50, 68 pgs.)-Regular edition w/different-c						2.50
500-Platinum edition						30.00
501-($1.95)-Collector's edition with die-cut-c						2.50
501-($1.50)-Regular edition w/mini-poster & diff.-c						2.50
502-516: 502-Supergirl-c/story. 508-Challengers of the Unknown app. 510-Bizarro-c/story. 516-(9/94)-Zero Hour						2.50
505-($2.50)-Holo-grafx foil-c edition						2.50
0,517-523: 0-(10/94). 517-(11/94)						2.50
524-549,551-580: 524-Begin $1.95-c. 527-Return of Alpha Centurion (Zero Hour). 533-Impulse-c/app. 535-Luthor-c/app. 536-Brainiac app. 537-Parasite app. 540-Final Night x-over. 541-Superboy-c/app.; Lois & Clark honeymoon. 545-New powers. 546-New costume. 555-Red & Blue Supermen battle. 557-Millennium Giants x-over. 558-560: Superman Silver Age-style story; Krypto app. 561-Begin $1.99-c. 565-JLA app.						2.50
550-($3.50)-Double sized						3.50
581-588: 581-Begin $2.25-c. 583-Emperor Joker. 588-Casey-s						2.50
589-595: 589-Return to Krypton; Rivoche-c. 591-Wolfman-s. 593-595-Our Worlds at War x-over. 593-New Suicide Squad formed. 594-Doomsday-c/app.						2.50
596-Aftermath of "War" x-over has panel showing damaged World Trade Center buildings; issue went on sale the day after the Sept. 11 attack						5.00
597-599,601-624: 597-Joker: Last Laugh. 604,605-Ultraman, Owlman, Superwoman app. 606-Return to Krypton. 612-616,619-623-Nowlan-c. 624-Mr. Majestic app.						2.50
600-($3.95) Wieringo-a; painted-c by Adel; pin-ups by various						4.00
625,626-Godfall parts 2,5; Turner-c; Caldwell-a(p)						3.00
627-641,643-648: 627-Begin $2.50-c, Rucka-s/Clark-a/Ha-c begin. 628-Wagner-c. 631-Bagged with Sky Captain CD; Lois shot. 634-Mxyzptlk visits DC offices. 639-Capt. Marvel & Eclipso app. 641-OMAC app. 643-Sacrifice aftermath; Batman & Wonder Woman app.						2.50
642-OMAC Project x-over Sacrifice pt. 3; JLA app.						5.00
642-(2nd printing) red tone cover						2.50
649-Last issue; Infinite Crisis x-over, Superman vs. Earth-2 Superman						3.00
#1,000,000 (11/98) Gene Ha-c; 853rd Century x-over						3.00
Annual 1 (1987, $1.25, 52 pgs.)-Starlin-c & scripts						4.00
Annual 2,3 (1990, 1991, $2.00, 68 pgs.): 2-Byrne-c/a(i); Legion '90 (Lobo) app. 3-Armageddon 2001 x-over						3.00
Annual 4-6 ('92-'94, $2.50, 68 pgs.): 4-Guy Gardner/Lobo-c/story; Eclipso storyline; Quesada-c(p). 5-Bloodlines storyline. 6-Elseworlds sty.						3.00
Annual 7,9('95, '97, $3.95)-7-Year One story. 9-Pulp Heroes sty						4.00
Annual 8 (1996, $2.95)-Legends of the Dead Earth story						3.00

NOTE: ***Erik Larsen** a-431.*

ADVENTURES OF THE DOVER BOYS
Archie Comics (Close-up): September, 1950 - No. 2, 1950 (No month given)

	GD	VG	FN	VF	VF/NM	NM-
1,2	9	18	27	52	69	85

ADVENTURES OF THE FLY (The Fly #1-6; Fly Man No. 32-39; See The Double Life of Private Strong, The Fly, Laugh Comics & Mighty Crusaders)
Archie Publications/Radio Comics: Aug, 1959 - No. 30, Oct, 1964; No. 31, May, 1965

	GD	VG	FN	VF	VF/NM	NM-
1-Shield app.; origin The Fly; S&K-c/a	50	100	150	413	807	1200
2-Williamson, S&K-a	27	54	81	197	386	575
3-Origin retold; Davis, Powell-a	23	46	69	163	314	465
4-Neal Adams-a(p)(1 panel); S&K-c; Powell-a; 2 pg. Shield story	15	30	45	107	204	300
5,6,9,10: 9-Shield app. 9-1st app. Cat Girl. 10-Black Hood app.	11	22	33	78	139	200
7,8: 7-1st S.A. app. Black Hood (7/60). 8-1st S.A. app. Shield (9/60)	12	24	36	86	158	230

Adventures on the Planet of the Apes #10 © MAR

African Lion Four Color #665 © DIS

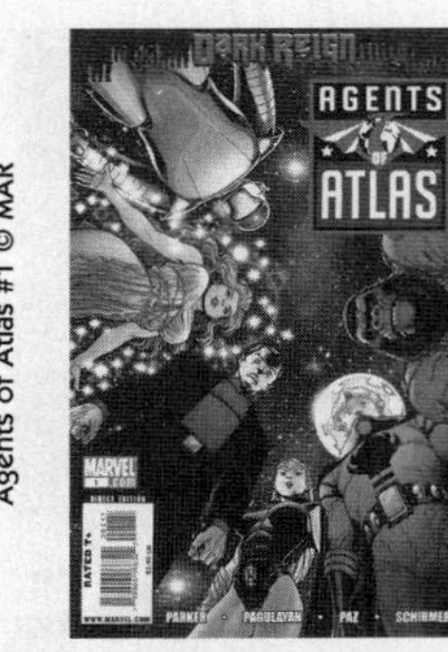

Agents of Atlas #1 © MAR

GD 2.0 | VG 4.0 | FN 6.0 | VF 8.0 | VF/NM 9.0 | NM- 9.2

11-13,15-20: 13-1st app. Fly Girl w/o costume. 16-Last 10¢ issue. 20-Origin Fly Girl retold 8 16 24 54 90 125
14-Origin & 1st app. Fly Girl in costume 9 18 27 61 103 145
21-30: 23-Jaguar cameo. 27-29-Black Hood 1 pg. strips. 30-Comet x-over (1st S.A. app.) in Fly Girl 6 12 18 43 69 95
31-Black Hood, Shield, Comet app. 7 14 21 45 73 100
Vol. 1 TPB ('04, $12.95) r/#1-4 & Double Life of Private Strong #1,2; foreward by Joe Simon 13.00
NOTE: *Simon c-2-4. Tuska a-1. Cover title to #31 is Flyman; Advs. of the Fly inside.*

ADVENTURES OF THE JAGUAR, THE (See Blue Ribbon Comics, Laugh Comics & Mighty Crusaders)
Archie Publications (Radio Comics): Sept, 1961 - No. 15, Nov, 1963
1-Origin Jaguar (1st app?) by J. Rosenberger 21 42 63 153 297 440
2,3: 3-Last 10¢ issue 11 22 33 80 145 210
4-6-Catgirl app. (#4's-c is same as splash pg.) 9 18 27 63 107 150
7-10 8 16 24 52 86 120
11-15: 13,14-Catgirl, Black Hood app. in both 7 14 21 45 73 100

ADVENTURES OF THE MASK (TV cartoon)
Dark Horse Comics: Jan, 1996 - No. 12, Dec, 1996 ($2.50)
1-12: Based on animated series 2.50

ADVENTURES OF THE NEW MEN (Formerly Newmen #1-21)
Maximum Press: No. 22, Nov, 1996; No. 23, March, 1997 ($2.50)
22,23-Sprouse-c/a 2.50

ADVENTURES OF THE OUTSIDERS, THE (Formerly Batman & The Outsiders; also see The Outsiders)
DC Comics: No. 33, May, 1986 - No. 46, June, 1987
33-46: 39-45-r/Outsiders #1-7 by Aparo 2.50

ADVENTURES OF THE SUPER MARIO BROTHERS (See Super Mario Bros.)
Valiant: 1990 - No. 9, Oct, 1991 ($1.50)
V2#1-9 5.00

ADVENTURES OF THE THING, THE (Also see The Thing)
Marvel Comics: Apr, 1992 - No. 4, July, 1992, ($1.25, limited series)
1-4: 1-r/Marvel Two-In-One #50 by Byrne; Kieth-c. 2-4-r/Marvel Two-In-One #80,51 & 77; 2-Ghost Rider-c/story; Quesada-c. 3-Miller-r/Quesada-c; new Perez-a (4 pgs.) 2.50

ADVENTURES OF THE X-MEN, THE (Based on animated TV series)
Marvel Comics: Apr, 1996 - No. 12, Mar, 1997 (99¢)
1-12: 1-Wolverine/Hulk battle. 3-Spider-Man-c. 5,6-Magneto-c/app. 3.00

ADVENTURES OF TINKER BELL (See Tinker Bell, 4-Color No. 896 & 982)

ADVENTURES OF TOM SAWYER (See Dell Junior Treasury No. 10)

ADVENTURES OF YOUNG DR. MASTERS, THE
Archie Comics (Radio Comics): Aug, 1964 - No. 2, Nov, 1964
1 3 6 9 20 30 40
2 3 6 9 14 20 26

ADVENTURES ON OTHER WORLDS (See Showcase #17 & 18)

ADVENTURES ON THE PLANET OF THE APES (Also see Planet of the Apes)
Marvel Comics Group: Oct, 1975 - No. 11, Dec, 1976
1-Planet of the Apes magazine-r in color; Starlin-c; adapts movie thru #6 3 6 9 18 27 35
2-5: 5-(25¢-c edition) 2 4 6 10 14 18
5-7-(30¢-c variants, limited distribution) 4 8 12 24 37 50
6-10: 6,7-(25¢-c edition). 7-Adapts 2nd movie (thru #11) 2 4 6 11 16 20
11-Last issue; concludes 2nd movie adaptation 3 6 9 14 20 26
NOTE: *Alcala a-6-11r.* ***Buckler*** *c-2p.* ***Nasser*** *c-7.* ***Ploog*** *a-1-9.* ***Starlin*** *c-6.* ***Tuska*** *a-1-5r.*

AEON FLUX (Based on the 2005 movie which was based on the MTV animated series)
Dark Horse Comics: Oct, 2005 - No. 4, Jan, 2006 ($2.99, limited series)
1-4-Timothy Green II-a/Mike Kennedy-s 3.00
TPB (5/06, $12.95) r/series; cover gallery 13.00

AFRICA
Magazine Enterprises: 1955
1(A-1 #137)-Cave Girl, Thun'da; Powell-c/a(4) 27 54 81 158 259 360

AFRICAN LION (Disney movie)
Dell Publishing Co.: Nov, 1955
Four Color #665 6 12 18 37 59 80

AFTER DARK
Sterling Comics: No. 6, May, 1955 - No. 8, Sept, 1955
6-8-Sekowsky-a in all 9 18 27 52 69 85

AFTER THE CAPE
Image Comics (Shadowline): Mar, 2007 - No. 3, May, 2007 ($2.99, B&W, limited series)
1-3-Jim Valentino-s/Marco Rudy-a 3.00
... Volume One TPB (9/07, $12.99) r/series; scripts, sketch pages, character profiles 13.00
...II (11/07 - No. 3, 1/08, $2.99) 1-3-Jim Valentino-s/Sergio Carrera-a 3.00

AGAINST BLACKSHARD 3-D (Also see SoulQuest)
Sirius Comics: August, 1986 ($2.25)
1 3.50

AGENCY, THE
Image Comics (Top Cow): August, 2001 - No. 6, Mar, 2002 ($2.50/$2.95/$4.95)
1,2: 1-Jenkins-s/Hotz-a; three covers by Hotz, Turner, Silvestri 2.50
3-5 ($2.95) 3.00
6-($4.95) Flip-c preview of Jeremiah TV series 5.00
Preview (2001, 16 pgs.) B&W pages, cover previews, sketch pages 2.25

AGENT LIBERTY SPECIAL (See Superman, 2nd Series)
DC Comics: 1992 ($2.00, 52 pgs, one-shot)
1-1st solo adventure; Guice-c/a(i) 2.50

AGENTS, THE
Image Comics: Apr, 2003 - No. 6, Sept, 2003 ($2.95, B&W)
1-5-Ben Dunn-c/a in all 3.00
6-Five pg. preview of Walking Dead #1 2 4 6 9 12 15

AGENTS OF ATLAS
Marvel Comics: Oct, 2006 - No. 6, Mar, 2007 ($2.99, limited series)
1-6: 1-Golden Age heroes Marvel Boy & Venus app.; Kirk-a 3.00
HC (2007, $24.99, dustjacket) r/#1-6, What If? #9, agents' debuts in '40s-'50s Atlas comics, creator interviews, character design art 25.00

AGENTS OF ATLAS (Dark Reign)
Marvel Comics: Apr, 2009 - Present ($3.99)
1-11: 1-Pagulayan-a; 2 covers by Art Adams and McGuinness; back-up with Wolverine app. 5-New Avengers app. 8-Hulk app. 4.00

AGENTS OF LAW (Also see Comic's Greatest World)
Dark Horse Comics: Mar, 1995 - No. 6, Sept, 1995 ($2.50)
1-6: 5-Predator app. 6-Predator app.; death of Law 2.50

AGENT X (Continued from Deadpool)
Marvel Comics: Sept. 2002 - No. 15, Dec, 2003 ($2.99/$2.25)
1-($2.99) Simone-s/Udon Studios-a; Taskmaster app. 3.00
2-9-($2.25) 2-Punisher app. 2.50
10-15-($2.99) 10,11-Evan Dorkin-s. 12-Hotz-a 3.00

AGE OF APOCALYPSE: THE CHOSEN
Marvel Comics: Apr, 1995 ($2.50, one-shot)
1-Wraparound-c 3.00

AGE OF BRONZE
Image Comics: Nov, 1998 - Present ($2.95/$3.50, B&W, limited series)
1-6-Eric Shanower-c/s/a 3.00
7-29-($3.50) 3.50
...Behind the Scenes (5/02, $3.50) background info and creative process 3.50
...Special (6/99, $2.95) Story of Agamemnon and Menelaus 3.00
A Thousand Ships (7/01, $19.95, TPB) r/#1-9 20.00
Sacrifice (9/04, $19.95, TPB) r/#10-19 20.00

AGE OF HEROES, THE
Halloween Comics/Image Comics #3 on: 1996 - No. 5, 1999 ($2.95, B&W)
1-5: James Hudnall scripts; John Ridgway-c/a 3.00
...Special ($4.95) r/#1,2 5.00
...Special 2 ($6.95) r/#3,4 7.00
...Wex 1 ('98, $2.95) Hudnall-s/Angel Fernandez-a 3.00

AGE OF INNOCENCE: THE REBIRTH OF IRON MAN
Marvel Comics: Feb, 1996 ($2.50, one-shot)
1-New origin of Tony Stark 3.00

AGE OF REPTILES
Dark Horse Comics: Nov, 1993 - No. 4, Feb, 1994 ($2.50, limited series)
1-4: Delgado-c/a/scripts in all 3.00
... The Hunt 1-5 (5/96 - No. 5, 9/96, $2.95) Delgado-c/a/scripts in all; wraparound-c 3.00
... The Journey 1,2 (11/09 - No. 4, $3.50) Delgado-c/a/scripts in all; wraparound-c 3.50

AGE OF THE SENTRY, THE

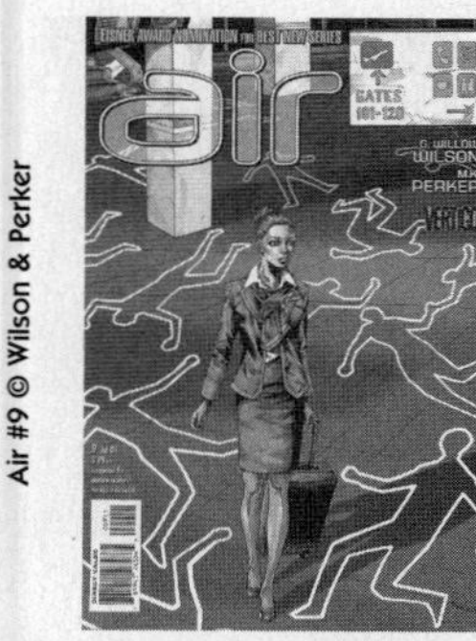

Air #9 © Wilson & Perker

Airboy Comics V3 #10 © HILL

Air War Stories #1 © DELL

GD VG FN VF VF/NM NM-
2.0 4.0 6.0 8.0 9.0 9.2

Marvel Comics: Nov, 2008 - No. 6, Mar, 2010 ($2.99, limited series)
1-6-Silver Age style stories. 1-Origin retold; Bullock-c. 3-Coover-a 3.00

AGGIE MACK
Four Star Comics Corp./Superior Comics Ltd.: Jan, 1948 - No. 8, Aug, 1949
1-Feldstein-a, "Johnny Prep" 40 80 120 243 402 560
2,3-Kamen-c 21 42 63 124 202 280
4-Feldstein "Johnny Prep"; Kamen-c 28 56 84 165 270 375
5-8-Kamen-c/a 22 44 66 132 216 300

AGGIE MACK
Dell Publishing Co.: Apr - Jun, 1962
Four Color #1335 5 10 15 30 48 65

AIR
DC Comics (Vertigo): Oct, 2008 - Present ($2.99)
1-6,8-17-G. Willow Wilson-s/M.K. Perker-a 3.00
7-($1.00) Includes story re-cap 2.00
... Flying Machine TPB (2009, $12.99) r/#6-10; Wilson intro. 13.00
... Letters From Lost Countries TPB (2009, $9.99) r/#1-5; character sketch pages 10.00

AIR ACE (Formerly Bill Barnes No. 1-12)
Street & Smith Publications: V2#1, Jan, 1944 - V3#8(No. 20), Feb-Mar, 1947
V2#1-Nazi concentration camp-c 43 86 129 271 461 650
V2#2-Classic-c 58 116 174 371 636 900
V2#3-12: 7-Powell-a 16 32 48 94 147 200
V3#1-6: 2-Atomic explosion on-c 14 28 42 80 115 150
V3#7-Powell bondage-c/a; all atomic issue 23 46 69 136 223 310
V3#8 (V5#8 on-c)-Powell-c/a 15 30 45 84 127 170

AIRBOY (Also see Airmaidens, Skywolf, Target: Airboy & Valkyrie)
Eclipse Comics: July, 1986 - No. 50, Oct, 1989 (#1-8, 50¢, 20 pgs., bi-weekly; #9-on, 36 pgs.; #34-on monthly)
1-4: 2-1st Marisa; Skywolf gets new costume. 3-The Heap begins 4.00
5-Valkyrie returns; Dave Stevens-c 6.00
6-49: 9-Begin $1.25-c; Skywolf begins. 11-Origin of G.A. Airboy & his plane Birdie. 28-Mr. Monster vs. The Heap. 33-Begin $1.75-c. 38-40-The Heap by Infantino. 41-r/1st app. Valkyrie from Air Fighters. 42-Begin $1.95-c. 46,47-part-r/Air Fighters. 48-Black Angel-r/A.F 3.00
50 ($4.95, 52 pgs.)-Kubert-c 5.00
NOTE: *Evans* c-21. *Gulacy* c-7, 20. *Spiegle* a-34, 35, 37. *Ken Steacy* painted c-17, 33.

AIRBOY COMICS (Air Fighters Comics No. 1-22)
Hillman Periodicals: V2#11, Dec, 1945 - V10#4, May, 1953 (No V3#3)
V2#11 74 148 222 470 810 1150
12-Valkyrie-c/app. 52 104 156 323 549 775
V3#1,2(no #3) 40 80 120 246 411 575
4-The Heap app. in Skywolf 37 74 111 222 361 500
5,7,8,10,11 33 66 99 194 317 440
6-Valkyrie-c/app. 36 72 108 216 351 485
9-Origin The Heap 37 74 111 222 361 500
12-Skywolf & Airboy x-over; Valkyrie-c/app. 39 78 117 240 395 550
V4#1-Iron Lady app. 33 66 99 194 317 440
2,3,12: 2-Rackman begins 25 50 75 147 241 335
4-Simon & Kirby-c 30 60 90 177 289 400
5-9,11-All S&K-a 28 56 84 165 270 375
10-Valkyrie-c/app. 31 62 93 182 296 410
V5#1-4,6-11: 4-Infantino Heap. 10-Origin The Heap 19 38 57 112 179 245
5-Skull-c. 21 42 63 126 206 285
12-Krigstein-a(p) 20 40 60 115 185 255
V6#1-3,5-12: 6,8-Origin The Heap 18 36 54 107 169 230
4-Origin retold 21 42 63 126 206 285
V7#1-12: 7,8,10-Origin The Heap 18 36 54 105 165 225
V8#1-3,5-12 16 32 48 96 151 205
4-Krigstein-a 17 34 51 100 158 215
V9#1,3,4,6-12: 7-One pg. Frazetta ad 15 30 45 84 127 170
2-Valkyrie app. 15 30 45 88 137 185
5(#100) 15 30 45 88 137 185
V10#1-4 14 28 42 81 118 155
NOTE: *Barry* a-V2#3, 7. *Bolle* a-V4#12. *McWilliams* a-V3#7, 9. *Powell* a-V7#2, 3, V8#1, 6. *Starr* a-V5#1, 12. *Dick Wood* a-V4#12. Bondage-c V5#8.

AIRBOY MEETS THE PROWLER
Eclipse Comics: Aug, 1987 ($1.95, one-shot)
1-John Snyder, III-c/a 3.00

AIRBOY-MR. MONSTER SPECIAL
Eclipse Comics: Aug, 1987 ($1.75, one-shot)
1 3.00

AIRBOY VERSUS THE AIR MAIDENS
Eclipse Comics: July, 1988 ($1.95)
1 3.00

AIR FIGHTERS CLASSICS
Eclipse Comics: Nov, 1987 - No. 6, May, 1989 ($3.95, 68 pgs., B&W)
1-6: Reprints G.A. Air Fighters #2-7. 1-Origin Airboy 4.00

AIR FIGHTERS COMICS (Airboy Comics #23 (V2#11) on)
Hillman Periodicals: Nov, 1941; No. 2, Nov, 1942 - V2#10, Fall, 1945
V1#1-(Produced by Funnies, Inc.); No Airboy; Black Commander only app. 226 452 678 1446 2473 3500
2(11/42)-(Produced by Quality artists & Biro for Hillman); Origin & 1st app. Airboy & Iron Ace; Black Angel (1st app.), Flying Dutchman & Skywolf (1st app.) begin; Fuje-a; Biro-c/a 423 846 1269 3067 5384 7700
3-Origin/1st app. The Heap; origin Skywolf; 2nd Airboy app./c 187 374 561 1197 2049 2900
4-Japan war-c 145 290 435 921 1586 2250
5-Japanese octopus War-c 123 246 369 787 1344 1900
6-Japanese soldiers as rats-c 161 322 483 1030 1765 2500
7-Classic Nazi swastika-c 158 316 474 1003 1727 2450
8-12: 8,10,11-War covers 84 168 252 538 919 1300
V2#1-Classic Nazi War-c 89 178 267 565 970 1375
2-Skywolf by Giunta; Flying Dutchman by Fuje; 1st meeting Valkyrie & Airboy (she worked for the Nazis in beginning); 1st app. Valkyrie (11/43); Valkyrie-c 119 238 357 762 1306 1850
3,4,6,8,9 60 120 180 381 658 935
5,7: 5-Flag-c; Fuje-a. 7-Valkyrie app. 64 128 192 406 696 985
10-Origin The Heap & Skywolf 69 138 207 442 759 1075
NOTE: *Fuje* a-V1#2, 5, 7, V2#2, 3, 5, 7-9. *Giunta* a-V2#2, 3, 7, 9.

AIRFIGHTERS MEET SGT. STRIKE SPECIAL, THE
Eclipse Comics: Jan, 1988 ($1.95, one-shot, stiff-c)
1-Airboy, Valkyrie, Skywolf app. 3.00

AIR FORCES (See American Air Forces)

AIRMAIDENS SPECIAL
Eclipse Comics: August, 1987 ($1.75, one-shot, Baxter paper)
1-Marisa becomes La Lupina (origin) 3.00

AIR RAIDERS
Marvel Comics (Star Comics)/Marvel #3 on: Nov, 1987- No. 5, Mar, 1988 ($1.00)
1,5: Kelley Jones-a in all 4.00
2-4: 2-Thunderhammer app. 3.00

AIRTIGHT GARAGE, THE (Also see Elsewhere Prince)
Marvel Comics (Epic Comics): July, 1993 - No. 4, Oct, 1993 ($2.50, lim. series, Baxter paper)
1-4: Moebius-c/a/scripts 5.00

AIR WAR STORIES
Dell Publishing Co.: Sept-Nov, 1964 - No. 8, Aug, 1966
1-Painted-c; Glanzman-c/a begins 4 8 12 28 44 60
2-8: 2,3-Painted-c 3 6 9 18 27 35

A.K.A. GOLDFISH
Caliber Comics: 1994 - 1995 (B&W, $3.50/$3.95)
...:Ace; ...:Jack; ...:Queen; ...:Joker; ...:King -Brian Michael Bendis-s/a 4.00
TPB (1996, $17.95) 20.00
Goldfish: The Definitive Collection (Image, 2001, $19.95) r/series plus promo art and new prose story; intro. by Matt Wagner 20.00
10th Anniversary HC (Image, 2002, $49.95) 50.00

AKIKO
Sirius: Mar, 1996 - Present ($2.50/$2.95, B&W)
1-Crilley-c/a/scripts in all 5.00
2 4.00
3-39: 25-($2.95, 32 pgs.)-w/Asala back-up pages 3.00
40-49,51,52: 40-Begin $2.95-c 3.00
50-($3.50) 3.50
Flights of Fancy TPB (5/02, $12.95) r/various features, pin-ups and gags 13.00
TPB Volume 1,4 ('97, 2/00, $14.95) 1-r/#1-7. 4-r/#19-25 15.00
TPB Volume 2,3 ('98, '99, $11.95) 2-r/#8-13. 3- r/#14-18 12.00
TPB Volume 5 (12/01, $12.95) r/#26-31 13.00
TPB Volume 6,7 (6/03, 4/04, $14.95) 6-r/#32-38. 7-r/#40-47 15.00

Akira #31 © K. Otomo

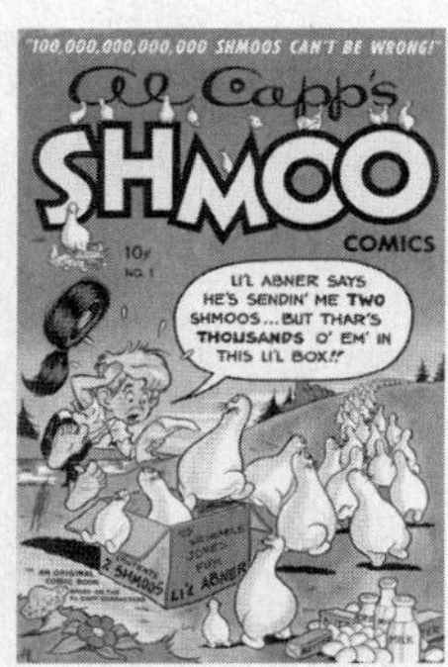

Al Capp's Shmoo #1 © HARV

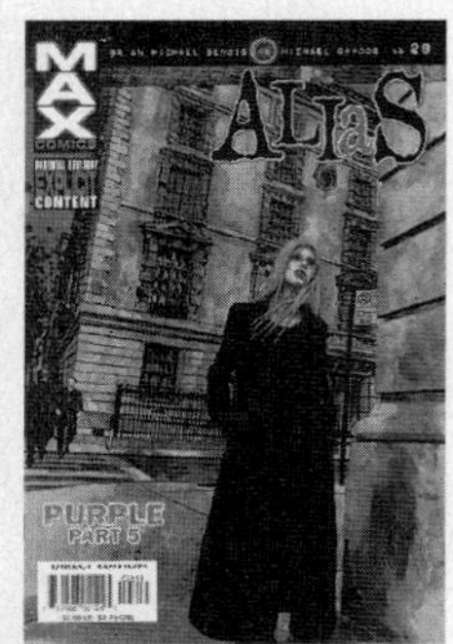

Alias #28 © MAR

	GD 2.0	VG 4.0	FN 6.0	VF 8.0	VF/NM 9.0	NM- 9.2

AKIKO ON THE PLANET SMOO
Sirius: Dec, 1995 ($3.95, B&W)

V1#1-($3.95)-Crilley-c/a/scripts; gatefold-c						5.00
Ashcan ('95, mail offer)						3.00
Hardcover V1#1 (12/95, $19.95, B&W, 40 pgs.)						20.00
The Color Edition(2/00,$4.95)						5.00

AKIRA
Marvel Comics (Epic): Sept, 1988 - No. 38, Dec, 1995 ($3.50/$3.95/$6.95, deluxe, 68 pgs.)

1-Manga by Katsuhiro Otomo	3	6	9	16	23	30
1,2-2nd printings (1989, $3.95)						5.00
2	2	4	6	9	12	15
3-5	2	4	6	8	10	12
6-16	1	2	3	5	7	9
17-33: 17-$3.95-c begins						6.00
34-37: 34-(1994)-$6.95-c begins. 35-37: 35-(1995). 37-Texeira back-up, Gibbons, Williams pin-ups	2	4	6	8	10	12
38-Moebius, Allred, Pratt, Toth, Romita, Van Fleet, O'Neill, Madureira pin-ups	2	4	6	8	11	14

ALADDIN & HIS WONDERFUL LAMP (See Dell Jr Treasury #2)

ALAN LADD (See The Adventures of...)

ALAN MOORE'S AWESOME UNIVERSE HANDBOOK (Also see Across the Universe:...)
Awesome Entertainment: Apr, 1999 ($2.95, B&W)

1-Alan Moore-text/ Alex Ross-sketch pages and 2 covers						5.00

ALAN MOORE...
DC Comics (WildStorm): TPB

...'s Complete WildC.A.T.S. (2007, $29.99) r/#21-34,50; ...Homecoming & ...Gang War						30.00
...: Wild Worlds (2007, $24.99) r/various WildStorm one-shots and limited series						25.00

ALARMING ADVENTURES
Harvey Publications: Oct, 1962 - No. 3, Feb, 1963

1-Crandall/Williamson-a	8	16	24	54	90	125
2-Williamson/Crandall-a	5	10	15	35	55	75
3-Torres-a	5	10	15	30	48	65

NOTE: **Bailey** a-1, 3. **Crandall** a-1p, 2i. **Powell** a-2(2). **Severin** c-1-3. **Torres** a-2? **Tuska** a-1. **Williamson** a-1i, 2p.

ALARMING TALES
Harvey Publications (Western Tales): Sept, 1957 - No. 6, Nov, 1958

1-Kirby-c/a(4); Kamandi prototype story by Kirby	30	60	90	177	289	400
2-Kirby-a(4)	20	40	60	118	192	265
3,4-Kirby-a. 4-Powell, Wildey-a	16	32	48	94	147	200
5-Kirby/Williamson-a; Wildey-a; Severin-c	17	34	51	100	158	215
6-Williamson-a?; Severin-c	14	28	42	80	115	150

ALBEDO
Thoughts And Images: Apr, 1985 - No. 14, Spring, 1989 (B&W)
Antarctic Press: (Vol. 2) Jun, 1991 - No. 10 ($2.50)

0-Yellow cover; 50 copies	14	28	42	102	194	285
0-White cover, 450 copies	8	16	24	52	86	120
0-Blue, 1st printing, 500 copies	7	14	21	49	80	110
0-Blue, 2nd printing, 1000 copies	4	8	12	26	41	55
0-3rd & 4th printing	3	6	9	14	19	24
1-Dark red - low print run	8	16	24	58	97	135
1-Bright red - low print run	6	12	18	37	59	80
2 -1st app. Usagi Yojimbo by Stan Sakai; 2000 copies - no 2nd printing	32	64	96	245	473	700
3	3	6	9	20	30	40
4-Usagi Yojimbo-c	4	8	12	22	34	45
5-14	1	2	3	5	7	9
(Vol. 2) 1-10, Color Special						4.00

ALBEDO ANTHROPOMORPHICS
Antarctic Press: (Vol. 3) Spring, 1994 - No. 4, Jan, 1996 ($2.95, color); (Vol. 4) Dec, 1999 - No. 2, Jan, 1999 ($2.95/$2.99, B&W)

V3#1-4-Steve Gallacci-c/a. V4#1,2						3.00

ALBERTO (See The Crusaders)

ALBERT THE ALLIGATOR & POGO POSSUM (See Pogo Possum)

ALBION (Inspired by 1960s IPC British comics characters)
DC Comics (WildStorm): Aug, 2005 - No. 6, Nov, 2006 ($2.99, limited series)

1-6-Alan Moore, Leah Moore & John Reppion-s/Shane Oakley-a; Dave Gibbons-c						3.00
TPB (2007, $19.99) r/series; intro by Neil Gaiman; reprints from 1960s British comics						20.00

ALBUM OF CRIME (See Fox Giants)

ALBUM OF LOVE (See Fox Giants)

AL CAPP'S DOGPATCH (Also see Mammy Yokum)
Toby Press: No. 71, June, 1949 - No. 4, Dec, 1949

71(#1)-Reprints from Tip Top #112-114	15	30	45	86	133	180
2-4: 4-Reprints from Li'l Abner #73	12	24	36	67	94	120

AL CAPP'S SHMOO (Also see Oxydol-Dreft & Washable Jones & Shmoo)
Toby Press: July, 1949 - No. 5, Apr, 1950 (None by Al Capp)

1-1st app. Super-Shmoo	28	56	84	165	270	375
2-5: 3-Sci-fi trip to moon. 4-X-Mas-c	20	40	60	114	182	250

AL CAPP'S WOLF GAL
Toby Press: 1951 - No. 2, 1952

1,2-Edited-r from Li'l Abner #63,64	20	40	60	120	195	270

ALEISTER ARCANE
IDW Publishing: Apr, 2004 - No. 3, June, 2004 ($3.99, limited series)

1-3-Steve Niles-s/Breehn Burns-a						4.00
TPB (10/04, $17.99) r/series; sketch pages						18.00

ALEXANDER THE GREAT (Movie)
Dell Publishing Co.: No. 688, May, 1956

Four Color 688-Buscema-a; photo-c	7	14	21	49	80	110

ALF (TV) (See Star Comics Digest)
Marvel Comics: Mar, 1988 - No. 50, Feb, 1992 ($1.00)

1-Photo-c						4.00
1-2nd printing						2.50
2-19: 6-Photo-c						2.50
20-22: 20-Conan parody. 21-Marx Brothers. 22-X-Men parody						3.00
23-30: 24-Rhonda-c/app. 29-3-D cover						2.50
31-43,46,47,49:						3.00
44,45: 44-X-Men parody. 45-Wolverine, Punisher, Capt. America-c						4.00
48-(12/91) Risqué Alf with seal cover	2	4	6	8	10	12
50-($1.75, 52 pgs.)-Final issue; photo-c						4.00
Annual 1-3: 1-Rocky & Bullwinkle app. 2-Sienkiewicz-c. 3-TMNT parody						3.00
...Comics Digest 1,2: 1-(1988)-Reprints Alf #1,2	1	3	4	6	8	10
Holiday Special 1,2 ('88, Wint. '89, 68 pgs.): 2-X-Men parody-c						3.00
Spring Special 1 (Spr/89, $1.75, 68 pgs.) Invisible Man parody						3.00
TPB (68 pgs.) r/#1-3; photo-c						5.00

ALFRED HARVEY'S BLACK CAT
Lorne-Harvey Productions: 1995 ($3.50, B&W/color)

1-Origin by Mark Evanier & Murphy Anderson; contains history of Alfred Harvey & Harvey Publications; 5 pg. B&W Sad Sack story; Hildebrandts-c						6.00

ALGIE (LITTLE...)
Timor Publ. Co.: Dec, 1953 - No. 3, 1954

1-Teenage	8	16	24	40	50	60
1-Algie #1 cover w/Secret Mysteries #19 inside	9	18	27	50	65	80
2,3	5	10	15	24	30	35
Accepted Reprint #2(nd)	3	6	8	12	14	16
Super Reprint #15	2	4	6	8	11	14

ALIAS:
Now Comics: July, 1990 - No. 5, Nov, 1990 ($1.75)

1-5: 1-Sienkiewicz-c						2.50

ALIAS (Also see The Pulse)
Marvel Comics (MAX Comics): Nov, 2001 - No. 28, Jan, 2004 ($2.99)

1-Bendis-s/Gaydos-a/Mack-c; intro Jessica Jones; Luke Cage app.	1	2	3	5	6	8
2-4						5.00
5-28: 7,8-Sienkiewicz-a (2 pgs.) 16-21-Spider-Woman app. 22,23-Jessica's origin. 24-28-Purple; Avengers app.; flashback-a by Bagley						3.00
HC (2002, $29.99) r/#1-9; intro. by Jeph Loeb						30.00
Omnibus (2006, $69.99, hardcover with dustjacket) r/#1-28 and What If Jessica Jones Had Joined the Avengers?; original pitch, script and sketch pages						70.00
Vol. 1: TPB (2003, $19.99) r/#1-9						20.00
Vol. 2: Come Home TPB (2003, $13.99) r/#11-15						14.00
Vol. 3: The Underneath TPB (2003, $16.99) r/#10,16-21						17.00

ALICE (New Adventures in Wonderland)
Ziff-Davis Publ. Co.: No. 10, 7-8/51 - No. 11(#2), 11-12/51

10-Painted-c; Berg-a	26	52	78	154	252	350
11-(#2 on inside) Dave Berg-a	16	32	48	94	147	200

ALICE AT MONKEY ISLAND (See The Adventures of Alice)

Alice #11 © Z-D

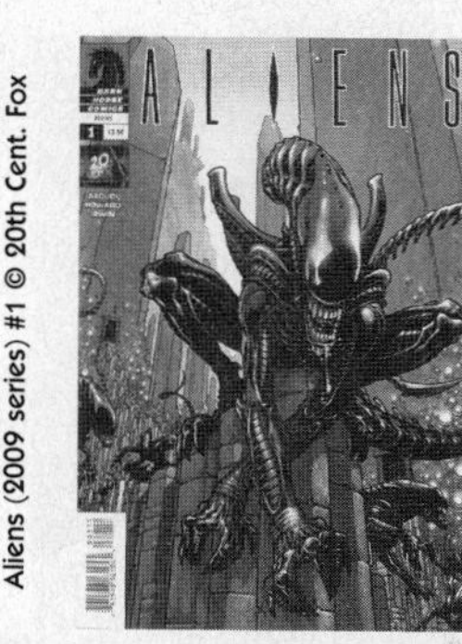

Aliens (2009 series) #1 © 20th Cent. Fox

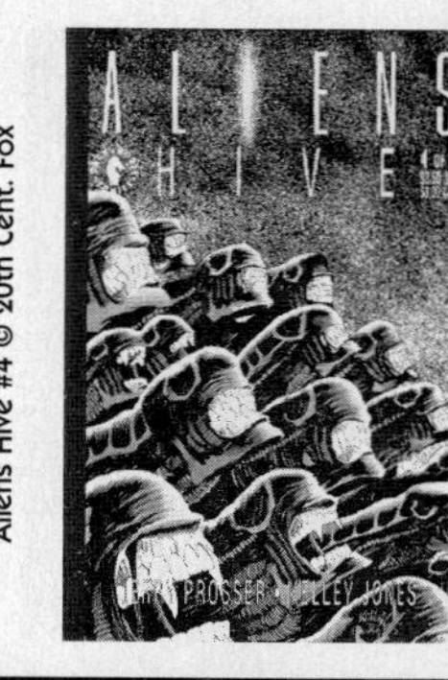

Aliens Hive #4 © 20th Cent. Fox

GD 2.0 | VG 4.0 | FN 6.0 | VF 8.0 | VF/NM 9.0 | NM- 9.2

Pentagon Publ. Co. (Civil Service): No. 3, 1946
3 10 20 30 54 72 90

ALICE IN WONDERLAND (Disney; see Advs. of Alice, Dell Jr. Treasury #1, The Dreamery, Movie Comics,Walt Disney Showcase #22, and World's Greatest Stories)
Dell Publishing Co.: No. 24, 1940; No. 331, 1951; No. 341, July, 1951
Single Series 24 (#1)(1940) 48 96 144 302 514 725
Four Color 331, 341-"Unbirthday Party w/..." 15 30 45 104 197 290
1-(Whitman, 3/84, pre-pack only)-r/4-Color #331 2 4 6 11 16 20

ALIEN ENCOUNTERS (Replaces Alien Worlds)
Eclipse Comics: June, 1985 - No. 14, Aug, 1987 ($1.75, Baxter paper, mature)
1-10: Nudity, strong language in all. 9-Snyder-a 4.00
11-14-Low print run 5.00

ALIEN LEGION (See Epic & Marvel Graphic Novel #25)
Marvel Comics (Epic Comics): Apr, 1984 - No. 20, Sept, 1987
nn-With bound-in trading card; Austin-i 4.00
2-20: 2-$1.50-c. 7,8-Portacio-i 3.00

ALIEN LEGION (2nd Series)
Marvel Comics (Epic): Aug, 1987(indicia)(10/87 on-c) - No. 18, Aug, 1990
V2#1-18-Stroman-a in all. 7-18-Farmer-i 2.50
...: Force Nomad TPB (Checker Book Pub. Group, 2001, $24.95) r/#1-11 25.00
...: Piecemaker TPB (Checker Book Pub. Group, 2002, $19.95) r/#12-18 20.00

ALIEN LEGION: (Series of titles; all Marvel/Epic Comics)
--BINARY DEEP, 1993 ($3.50, one-shot, 52 pgs.), nn-With bound-in trading card 3.50
--JUGGER GRIMROD, 8/92 ($5.95, one-shot, 52 pgs.) Book 1 6.00
--ONE PLANET AT A TIME, 5/93 - Book 3, 7/93 ($4.95, squarebound, 52 pgs.)
Book 1-3: Hoang Nguyen-a 5.00
--ON THE EDGE (The... #2 & 3), 11/90 - No. 3, 1/91 ($4.50, 52 pgs.)
1-3-Stroman & Farmer-a 4.50
--TENANTS OF HELL, '91 - No. 2, '91 ($4.50, squarebound, 52 pgs.)
Book 1,2-Stroman-c/a(p) 4.50

ALIEN NATION (Movie)
DC Comics: Dec, 1988 ($2.50; 68 pgs.)
1-Adaptation of film; painted-c 4.00

ALIEN PIG FARM 3000
Image Comics (RAW Studios): Apr, 2007 - No. 4, July, 2007 ($2.99, limited series)
1-4-Steve Niles, Thomas Jane & Todd Farmer-s/Don Marquez-a 3.00

ALIEN RESURRECTION (Movie)
Dark Horse Comics: Oct, 1997 - No. 2, Nov, 1997 ($2.50; limited series)
1,2-Adaptation of film; Dave McKean-c 3.00

ALIENS, THE (Captain Johner and...)(Also see Magnus Robot Fighter...)
Gold Key: Sept-Dec, 1967; No. 2, May, 1982
1-Reprints from Magnus #1,3,4,6-10; Russ Manning-a in all
3 6 9 20 30 40
2-(Whitman) Same contents as #1 1 2 3 5 6 8

ALIENS (Movie) (See Alien: The Illustrated..., Dark Horse Comics & Dark Horse Presents #24)
Dark Horse Comics: May, 1988 - No. 6, July, 1989 ($1.95, B&W, limited series)
1-Based on movie sequel;1st app. Aliens in comics 3 6 9 14 20 26
1-2nd - 6th printings; 4th w/new inside front-c 3.00
2 2 4 6 8 10 12
2-2nd & 3rd printing, 3-6-2nd printings 3.00
3 1 2 3 5 7 9
4-6 5.00
Mini Comic #1 (2/89, 4x6")-Was included with Aliens Portfolio 4.00
Collection 1 ($10.95,)-r/#1-6 plus Dark Horse Presents #24 plus new-a 12.00
Collection 1-2nd printing (1991, $11.95)-On higher quality paper than 1st print; Dorman painted-c 12.00
Hardcover ('90, $24.95, B&W)-r/1-6, DHP #24 30.00
... Omnibus Vol. 1 (7/07, $24.95, 9x6") r/1st & 2nd series and Aliens: Earth War 25.00
... Omnibus Vol. 2 (12/07, $24.95, 9x6") r/Genocide, Harvest and Colonial Marines series 25.00
... Omnibus Vol. 3 (3/08, $24.95, 9x6") r/Rogue, Salvation and Sacrifice, Labyrinth series 25.00
... Omnibus Vol. 4 (8/08, $24.95, 9x6") r/Music of the Spears, Stronghold, Berserker, Mondo Pest and Mondo Heat series and one-shots 25.00
... Omnibus Vol. 5 (11/08, $24.95, 9x6") r/Alchemy, Survival, Havoc series and various 25.00
... Omnibus Vol. 6 (2/09, $24.95, 9x6") r/Apocalypse GN, Xenogenesis & one-shots 25.00
... Outbreak (3rd printing, 8/96, $17.95)-Bolton-c 18.00
Platinum Edition - (See Dark Horse Presents: Aliens Platinum Edition) -

ALIENS
Dark Horse Comics: V2#1, Aug, 1989 - No. 4, 1990 ($2.25, limited series)
V2#1-Painted art by Denis Beauvais 5.00
1-2nd printing (1990), 2-4 3.00
...: Nightmare Asylum TPB (12/96, $16.95) r/series; Bolton-c 17.00

ALIENS
Dark Horse Comics: May, 2009 - No. 4, Nov, 2009 ($3.50, limited series)
1-4-John Arcudi-s/Zach Howard-a. 1,2-Howard-c. 3,4-Swanland-c 3.50

ALIENS: (Series of titles, all Dark Horse)
--ALCHEMY, 10/97 - No. 3, 11/97 ($2.95),1-3-Corben-c/a, Arcudi-s 3.00
--APOCALYPSE - THE DESTROYING ANGELS, 1/99 - No. 4, 4/99 ($2.95)
1-4-Doug Wheatly-a/Schultz-s 3.00
--BERSERKERS, 1/95 - No. 4, 4/95 ($2.50) 1-4 3.00
--COLONIAL MARINES, 1/93 - No. 10, 7/94 ($2.50) 1-10 3.00
--EARTH ANGEL. 8/94 ($2.95) 1-Byrne-a/story; wraparound-c 3.00
--EARTH WAR, 6/90 - No. 4, 10/90 ($2.50) 1-All have Sam Kieth-a & Bolton painted-c 5.00
1-2nd printing, 3,4 3.00
2 4.00
--GENOCIDE, 11/91 - No. 4, 2/92 ($2.50) 1-4-Suydam painted-c. 4-Wraparound-c, poster 3.00
--GLASS CORRIDOR, 6/98 ($2.95) 1-David Lloyd-s/a 3.00
--HARVEST (See Aliens: Hive)
--HAVOC, 6/97 - No. 2, 7/97 ($2.95) 1,2: Schultz-s, Kent Williams-c, 40 artists including Art Adams, Kelley Jones, Duncan Fegredo, Kevin Nowlan 3.00
--HIVE, 2/92 - No. 4,5/92 ($2.50) 1-4: Kelley Jones-c/a in all 3.00
...Harvest TPB ('98, $16.95) r/series; Bolton-c 17.00
--KIDNAPPED, 12/97 - No. 3, 2/98 ($2.50) 1-3 3.00
--LABYRINTH, 9/93 - No. 4, 1/94 ($2.50)1-4: 1-Painted-c 3.00
--LOVESICK, 12/96 ($2.95) 1 3.00
--MONDO HEAT, 2/96 ($2.50) nn-Sequel to Mondo Pest 3.00
--MONDO PEST, 4/95 ($2.95, 44 pgs.)nn-r/Dark Horse Comics #22-24 3.00
--MUSIC OF THE SPEARS, 1/94 - No. 4, 4/94 ($2.50) 1-4 3.00
--NEWT'S TALE, 6/92 - No. 2, 7/92 ($4.95) 1,2-Bolton-c 5.00
--PIG, 3/97 ($2.95)1 3.00
--PREDATOR: THE DEADLIEST OF THE SPECIES, 7/93 - No. 12,8/95 ($2.50)
1-Bolton painted-c; Guice-a(p) 5.00
1-Embossed foil platinum edition 10.00
2-12: Bolton painted-c. 2,3-Guice-a(p) 3.00
--PURGE, 8/97 ($2.95) nn-Hester-a 3.00
--ROGUE, 4/993 - No. 4, 7/93 ($2.50)1-4: Painted-c 3.00
--SACRIFICE, 5/93 ($4.95, 52 pgs.) nn-P. Milligan scripts; painted-c/a 5.00
--SALVATION, 11/93 ($4.95, 52 pgs.) nn-Mignola-c/a(p); Gibbons script 5.00
--SPECIAL, 6/97 ($2.50) 1 3.00
--STALKER, 6/98 ($2.50)1-David Wenzel-s/a 3.00
--STRONGHOLD, 5/94 - No. 4, 9/94 ($2.50) 1-4 3.00
--SURVIVAL, 2/98 - No. 3, 4/98 ($2.95) 1-3-Tony Harris-c 3.00
--TRIBES, 1992 ($24.95, hardcover graphic novel) Bissette text-s with Dorman painted-a 25.00
...softcover ($9.95) 10.00

ALIENS VS. PREDATOR (See Dark Horse Presents #36)
Dark Horse Comics: June, 1990 - No. 4, Dec, 1990 ($2.50, limited series)
1-Painted-c 1 2 3 5 6 8
1-2nd printing 3.00
0-(7/90, $1.95, B&W)-r/Dark Horse Pres. #34-36 1 2 3 5 7 9
2,3 5.00
4-Dave Dorman painted-c 4.00
Annual (7/99, $4.95) Jae Lee-c 5.00
... : Booty (1/96, $2.50) painted-c 3.00
... Omnibus Vol. 1 (5/07, $24.95, 9x6") r/#1-4 & Annual; ...: War; ...: Eternal 25.00
... Omnibus Vol. 2 (10/07, $24.95, 9x6") r/...: Xenogenesis #1-4; ...: Deadliest of the Species; ...: Booty and stories from ... Annual 25.00
... : Thrill of the Hunt (9/04, $6.95, digest-size TPB) Based on 2004 movie 7.00
... Wraith 1 (7/98, $2.95) Jay Stephens-s 3.00
--VS. PREDATOR: DUEL, 3/95 - No. 2, 4/95 ($2.50) 1,2 3.00

Aliens/Predator: The Deadliest of the Species #11 © 20th Cent. Fox

All-American Comics #95 © DC

All-American Men of War #8 © DC

GD VG FN VF VF/NM NM-
2.0 4.0 6.0 8.0 9.0 9.2

GD VG FN VF VF/NM NM-
2.0 4.0 6.0 8.0 9.0 9.2

--VS. PREDATOR: ETERNAL, 6/98 - No. 4, 9/98 ($2.50)1-4: Edginton-s/Maleev-a; Fabry-c 3.00

--VS. PREDATOR: THREE WORLD WAR, 1/10 - Present ($3.50) 1-Leonardi-a 3.50

--VS. PREDATOR VS. THE TERMINATOR, 4/00 - No. 4, 7/00 ($2.95) 1-4: Ripley app. 3.00

--VS. PREDATOR: WAR, No. 0, 5/95 - No. 4, 8/95 ($2.50) 0-4: Corben painted-c 3.00

--VS. PREDATOR: XENOGENESIS, 12/99 - No. 4, 3/00 ($2.95) 1-4: Watson-s/Mel Rubi-a 3.00

--XENOGENESIS, 8/99 - No. 4, 11/99 ($2.95) 1-4: T&M Bierbaum-s 3.00

ALIEN TERROR (See 3-D Alien Terror)

ALIEN: THE ILLUSTRATED STORY (Also see Aliens)
Heavy Metal Books: 1980 ($3.95, soft-c, 8x11")

nn-Movie adaptation; Simonson-a 3 6 9 14 19 24

ALIEN[3] (Movie)
Dark Horse Comics: June, 1992 - No. 3, July, 1992 ($2.50, limited series)

1-3: Adapts 3rd movie; Suydam painted-c 3.00

ALIEN WORLDS (Also see Eclipse Graphic Album #22)
Pacific Comics/Eclipse: Dec, 1982 - No. 9, Jan, 1985

1,2,4: 2,4-Dave Stevens-c/a 6.00
3,5-7 4.00
8,9 1 2 3 4 5 7
3-D No. 1-Art Adams 1st published art 1 2 3 4 5 7

ALISON DARE, LITTLE MISS ADVENTURES (Also see Return of ...)
Oni Press: Sept, 2000 ($4.50, B&W, one-shot)

1-J. Torres-s/J.Bone-c/a 4.50

ALISON DARE & THE HEART OF THE MAIDEN
Oni Press: Jan, 2002 - No. 2, Feb, 2002 ($2.95, B&W, limited series)

1,2-J. Torres-s/J.Bone-c/a 3.00

ALISTER THE SLAYER
Midnight Press: Oct, 1995 ($2.50)

1-Boris-c 2.50

ALL-AMERICAN COMICS (...Western #103-126, ...Men of War #127 on; also see The Big All-American Comic Book)
All-American/National Periodical Publ.: April, 1939 - No. 102, Oct, 1948

1-Hop Harrigan (1st app.), Scribbly by Mayer (1st DC app.), Toonerville Folks, Ben Webster, Spot Savage, Mutt & Jeff, Red White & Blue (1st app.), Adventures in the Unknown, Tippie, Reg'lar Fellers, Skippy, Bobby Thatcher, Mystery Men of Mars, Daiseybelle, Wiley of West Point begin 607 1214 1821 3794 6147 8500
2-Ripley's Believe It or Not begins, ends #24 179 358 537 1119 1810 2500
3-5: 5-The American Way begins, ends #10 143 286 429 894 1447 2000
6,7: 6-Last Spot Savage; Popsicle Pete begins, ends #26, 28. 7-Last Bobby Thatcher
110 220 330 704 1202 1700
8-The Ultra Man begins & 1st-c app. 297 594 891 1901 3251 4600
9,10: 10-X-Mas-c 95 190 285 599 1037 1475
11,15: 11-Ultra Man-c. 15-Last Tippie & Reg'lar Fellars; Ultra Man-c
116 232 348 742 1271 1800
12-14: 12-Last Toonerville Folks 90 180 270 576 988 1400
16-(Rare)-Origin/1st app. Green Lantern by Sheldon Moldoff (c/a)(7/40) & begin series; appears in costume on-c & only one panel inside; created by Martin Nodell. Inspired in 1940 by a switchman's green lantern that would give trains the go ahead to proceed
15,000 30,000 45,000 120,000 235,000 350,000
17-2nd Green Lantern 1000 2000 3000 7400 13,200 19,000
18-N.Y. World's Fair-c/story (scarce) 1100 2200 3300 8250 15,125 22,000
19-Origin/1st app. The Atom (10/40); last Ultra Man
1850 3700 5550 14,000 25,500 37,000
20-Atom dons costume; Ma Hunkle becomes Red Tornado (1st app.)(1st DC costumed heroine, before Wonder Woman, 11/40); Rescue on Mars begins, ends #25; 1 pg. origin Green Lantern 514 1028 1542 3750 6625 9500
21-Last Wiley of West Point & Skippy; classic Moldoff-c
423 846 1269 3000 5250 7500
22,23: 23-Last Daiseybelle; 3 Idiots begin, end #82
326 652 978 2282 3991 5700
24-Sisty & Dinky become the Cyclone Kids; Ben Webster ends; origin Dr. Mid-Nite & Sargon, The Sorcerer in text with app. 343 686 1029 2400 4200 6000
25-Origin & 1st story app. Dr. Mid-Nite by Stan Asch; Hop Harrigan becomes Guardian Angel; last Adventure in the Unknown (scarce) 1075 2150 3225 8000 14,500 21,000
26-Origin/1st story app. Sargon, the Sorcerer 377 754 1131 2639 4620 6600
27: #27-32 are misnumbered in indicia with correct No. appearing on-c. Intro. Doiby Dickles, Green Lantern's sidekick 389 778 1167 2723 4762 6800
28-Hop Harrigan gives up costumed i.d. 200 400 600 1280 2190 3100
29,30 200 400 600 1280 2190 3100
31-40: 35-Doiby learns Green Lantern's i.d. 148 296 444 947 1624 2300
41-50: 50-Sargon ends 119 238 357 762 1306 1850
51-60: 59-Scribbly & the Red Tornado ends 103 206 309 659 1130 1600
61-Origin/1st app. Solomon Grundy (11/44) 757 1514 2271 5526 9763 14,000
62-70: 70-Kubert Sargon; intro Sargon's helper, Maximillian O'Leary
90 180 270 576 988 1400
71-88: 71-Last Red White & Blue. 72-Black Pirate begins (not in #74-82); last Atom. 73-Winky, Blinky & Noddy begins, ends #82. 79,83-Mutt & Jeff-c.
71 142 213 454 777 1100
89-Origin & 1st app. Harlequin 123 246 369 787 1344 1900
90-99: 90-Origin/1st app. Icicle. 99-Last Hop Harrigan
119 238 357 762 1306 1850
100-1st app. Johnny Thunder by Alex Toth (8/48); western theme begins (Scarce) 200 400 600 1280 2190 3100
101-Last Mutt & Jeff (Scarce) 135 270 405 864 1482 2100
102-Last Green Lantern, Black Pirate & Dr. Mid-Nite (Scarce)
258 516 774 1651 2826 4000

NOTE: *No Atom in 47, 62-69.* ***Kinstler*** *Black Pirate-89.* ***Stan Aschmeier*** *a (Dr. Mid-Nite) 25-84; c-7.* ***Mayer*** *c-1, 2(part), 6, 10.* ***Moldoff*** *c-16-23.* ***Nodell*** *c-31.* ***Paul Reinman*** *a (Green Lantern)-53-55p, 56-84, 87; (Black Pirate)-83-88, 90; c-52, 55-76, 78, 80, 81, 87.* ***Toth*** *a-88, 92, 96, 98-102; c(p)-92, 96-102. Scribbly by* ***Mayer*** *in #1-59. Ultra Man by* ***Mayer*** *in #8-19.*

ALL AMERICAN COMICS
DC Comics: April 1939

nn - Ashcan comic, not distributed to newsstands, only for in house use. Cover art is Advenure Comics #33 and interior from Detective Comics #23 (no known sales)

ALL-AMERICAN COMICS (Also see All Star Comics 1999 crossover titles)
DC Comics: May, 1999 ($1.99, one-shot)

1-Golden Age Green Lantern and Johnny Thunder; Barreto-a 2.50

ALL-AMERICAN MEN OF WAR (Previously All-American Western)
National Periodical Publ.: No. 127, Aug-Sept, 1952 - No. 117, Sept-Oct, 1966

127 (#1, 1952) 108 216 324 918 1809 2700
128 (1952) 52 104 156 442 871 1300
2(12-1/'52-53)-5 48 96 144 384 742 1100
6-Devil Dog story; Ghost Squadron story 38 76 114 288 557 825
7-10: 8-Sgt. Storm Cloud-s 38 76 114 288 557 825
11-16,18: 18-Last precode; 1st Kubert-c (2/55) 33 66 99 254 490 725
17-1st Frogman-s in this title 34 68 102 262 506 750
19,20,22-27 26 52 78 190 370 550
21-Easy Co. prototype 31 62 93 236 456 675
28 (12/55)-1st Sgt. Rock prototype; Kubert-a 43 86 129 344 672 1000
29,30,32-Wood-a 26 52 78 190 370 550
31,33,34,36-38,40: 34-Gunner prototype-s. 36-Little Sure Shot prototype-s. 38-1st S.A. issue 23 46 69 166 321 475
35-Greytone-c 25 50 75 183 354 525
39 (11/56)-2nd Sgt. Rock prototype; 1st Easy Co.? 33 66 99 254 490 725
41,43-47,49,50: 46-Tankbusters-c/s 19 38 57 139 270 400
42-Pre-Sgt. Rock Easy Co.-c/s 24 48 72 175 338 500
48-Easy Co.-c/s; Nick app.; Kubert-a 24 48 72 175 338 500
51-56,58-62,65,66: 61-Gunner-c/s 15 30 45 107 204 300
57(5/58),63,64 -Pre-Sgt. Rock Easy Co.-c/s 20 40 60 146 283 420
67-1st Gunner & Sarge by Andru & Esposito 40 80 120 314 607 900
68,69: 68-2nd app. Gunner & Sarge. 69-1st Tank Killer-c/s
18 36 54 129 252 375
70 13 26 39 95 178 260
71-80: 71,72,76-Tank Killer-c/s. 74-Minute Commandos-c/s
11 22 33 80 145 210
81,84-88: 88-Last 10¢ issue 10 20 30 70 123 175
82-Johnny Cloud begins(1st app.), ends #117 18 36 54 129 252 375
83-2nd Johnny Cloud 12 24 36 88 162 235
89-100: 89-Battle Aces of 3 Wars begins, ends #98 8 16 24 54 90 125
101-111,113-116: 111,114,115-Johnny Cloud 6 12 18 39 62 85
112-Balloon Buster series begins, ends #114,116 6 12 18 41 66 90
117-Johnny Cloud-c & 3-part story 6 12 18 41 66 90

NOTE: *Frogman stories in 17, 38, 44, 45, 50, 51, 53, 55-58, 63, 65, 66, 72, 76, 77.* ***Colan*** *a-112.* ***Drucker*** *a-47, 58, 61, 63, 65, 69, 71, 74, 77.* ***Grandenetti*** *c(p)-127, 128, 2-17(most).* ***Heath*** *a-14, 27, 32, 38, 41, 45, 47, 50, 51, 55-58, 62, 64, 71, 75, 76, 78, 95, 111-117; c-85, 91, 94-96, 100, 101, 110-112, others?* ***Infantino*** *a-8.* ***Kirby*** *a-29.* ***Krigstein*** *a-128('52), 2, 3, 5.* ***Kubert*** *a-22, 24, 28, 29, 33, 34, 36, 38, 39, 41-43, 47-50, 52, 53, 55, 56, 59, 60, 63-65, 69, 71-73, 76, 102, 103, 105, 106, 108, 114; c-41, 44, 52, 54, 55, 58, 64, 69, 76, 77, 79, 102-106, 108, 113-117, others? Tank Killer in 69, 71, 76 by* ***Kubert***. ***P. Reinman*** *c-55, 57, 61, 62, 71, 72, 74-76, 80.* ***J. Severin*** *a-58.*

ALL AMERICAN MEN OF WAR
DC Comics: Aug/Sept. 1952

nn - Ashcan comic, not distributed to newsstands, only for in-house use. Cover art is All Star Western #58 and interior from Mr. District Attorney #21 (no known sales)

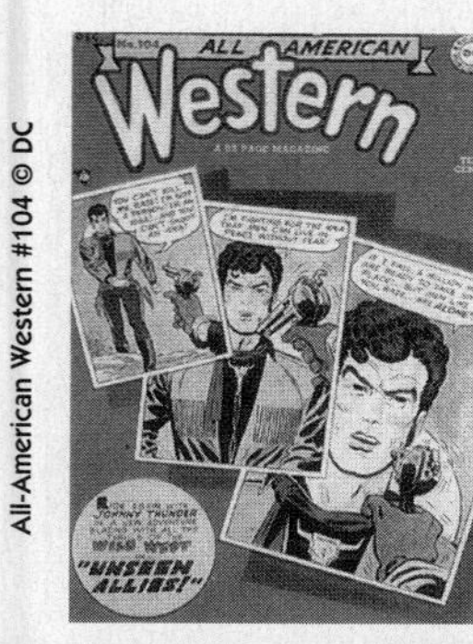

All-American Western #104 © DC

Alley Oop #13 © NEA

All-Flash #10 © DC

ALL-AMERICAN SPORTS
Charlton Comics: Oct, 1967

	GD 2.0	VG 4.0	FN 6.0	VF 8.0	VF/NM 9.0	NM- 9.2
1	3	6	9	20	30	40

ALL-AMERICAN WESTERN (Formerly All-American Comics; Becomes All-American Men of War)
National Periodical Publ.: No. 103, Nov, 1948 - No. 126, June-July, 1952 (103-121: 52 pgs.)

	GD 2.0	VG 4.0	FN 6.0	VF 8.0	VF/NM 9.0	NM- 9.2
103-Johnny Thunder & his horse Black Lightning continues by Toth, ends #126; Foley of The Fighting 5th, Minstrel Maverick, & Overland Coach begin; Captain Tootsie by Beck; mentioned in Love and Death	50	100	150	315	533	750
104-Kubert-a	36	72	108	216	351	485
105,107-Kubert-a	31	62	93	182	296	410
106,108-110,112: 112-Kurtzman's "Pot-Shot Pete" (1 pg.)	25	50	75	150	245	340
111,114-116-Kubert-a	26	52	78	156	256	355
113-Intro. Swift Deer, J. Thunder's new sidekick (4-5/50); classic Toth-c; Kubert-a	28	56	84	165	270	375
117-126: 121-Kubert-a; bondage-c	19	38	57	111	176	240

NOTE: *G. Kane c(p)-112, 119, 120, 123. Kubert a-103-105, 107, 111, 112(1 pg.), 113-116, 121. Toth a 103-125; c(p)-103-111,113-116, 121, 122, 124-126. Some copies of #125 have #12 on-c.*

ALL COMICS
Chicago Nite Life News: 1945

	GD 2.0	VG 4.0	FN 6.0	VF 8.0	VF/NM 9.0	NM- 9.2
1	15	30	45	83	124	165

ALLEGRA
Image Comics (WildStorm): Aug, 1996 - No. 4, Dec, 1996 ($2.50)

	GD 2.0	VG 4.0	FN 6.0	VF 8.0	VF/NM 9.0	NM- 9.2
1-4						2.50

ALLEY CAT (Alley Baggett)
Image Comics: July, 1999 - No. 6, Mar, 2000 ($2.50/$2.95)

	GD 2.0	VG 4.0	FN 6.0	VF 8.0	VF/NM 9.0	NM- 9.2
Preview Edition						6.00
Prelude						5.00
Prelude w/variant-c						6.00
1-Photo-c						2.50
1-Painted-c by Dorian						3.50
1-Another Universe Edition, 1-Wizard World Edition						7.00
2-4: 4-Twin towers on-c						2.50
5,6-($2.95)						3.00
Lingerie Edition (10/99, $4.95) Photos, pin-ups, cover gallery						5.00
...Vs. Lady Pendragon ('99, $3.00) Stinsman-c						3.00

ALLEY OOP (See The Comics, The Funnies, Red Ryder and Super Book #9)
Dell Publishing Co.: No. 3, 1942

	GD 2.0	VG 4.0	FN 6.0	VF 8.0	VF/NM 9.0	NM- 9.2
Four Color 3 (#1)	42	84	126	336	656	975

ALLEY OOP
Argo Publ.: Nov, 1955 - No. 3, Mar, 1956 (Newspaper reprints)

	GD 2.0	VG 4.0	FN 6.0	VF 8.0	VF/NM 9.0	NM- 9.2
1	16	32	48	92	144	195
2,3	12	24	36	67	94	120

ALLEY OOP
Dell Publishing Co.: 12-2/62-63 - No. 2, 9-11/63

	GD 2.0	VG 4.0	FN 6.0	VF 8.0	VF/NM 9.0	NM- 9.2
1	6	12	18	41	66	90
2	5	10	15	34	55	75

ALLEY OOP
Standard Comics: No. 10, Sept, 1947 - No. 18, Oct, 1949

	GD 2.0	VG 4.0	FN 6.0	VF 8.0	VF/NM 9.0	NM- 9.2
10	25	50	75	145	233	320
11-18: 17,18-Schomburg-c	20	40	60	115	183	250

ALLEY OOP ADVENTURES
Antarctic Press: Aug, 1998 - No. 3, Dec, 1998 ($2.95)

	GD 2.0	VG 4.0	FN 6.0	VF 8.0	VF/NM 9.0	NM- 9.2
1-3-Jack Bender-s/a						3.00

ALLEY OOP ADVENTURES (Alley Oop Quarterly in indicia)
Antarctic Press: Sept, 1999 - No. 3, Mar, 2000 ($2.50/$2.99, B&W)

	GD 2.0	VG 4.0	FN 6.0	VF 8.0	VF/NM 9.0	NM- 9.2
1-3-Jack Bender-s/a						3.00

ALL-FAMOUS CRIME (2nd series - Formerly Law Against Crime #1-3; becomes All-Famous Police Cases #6 on)
Star Publications: No. 8, 5/51 - No. 10, 11/51; No. 4, 2/52 - No. 5, 5/52;

	GD 2.0	VG 4.0	FN 6.0	VF 8.0	VF/NM 9.0	NM- 9.2
8 (#1-1st series)	22	44	66	128	209	290
9 (#2)-Used in **SOTI**, illo- "The wish to hurt or kill couples in lovers' lanes is a not uncommon perversion;" L.B. Cole-c/a(r)/Law-Crime #3	37	74	111	222	361	500
10 (#3)	20	40	60	114	182	250
4 (#4-2nd series)-Formerly Law-Crime	19	38	57	109	172	235
5 (#5) Becomes All-Famous Police Cases #6	19	38	57	109	172	235

NOTE: *All have **L.B. Cole** covers.*

ALL FAMOUS CRIME STORIES (See Fox Giants)

ALL-FAMOUS POLICE CASES (Formerly All Famous Crime #5)
Star Publications: No. 6, Feb, 1952 - No. 16, Sept, 1954

	GD 2.0	VG 4.0	FN 6.0	VF 8.0	VF/NM 9.0	NM- 9.2
6	19	38	57	112	176	240
7,8: 7-Baker story. 8-Marijuana story	18	36	54	105	165	225
9-16	16	32	48	94	147	200

NOTE: ***L. B. Cole** c-all; a-15, 1pg. **Hollingsworth** a-15.*

ALL-FLASH (...Quarterly No. 1-5)
National Per. Publ./All-American: Summer, 1941 - No. 32, Dec-Jan, 1947-48

	GD 2.0	VG 4.0	FN 6.0	VF 8.0	VF/NM 9.0	NM- 9.2
1-Origin The Flash retold by E. E. Hibbard; Hibbard c-1-10,12-14,16,31p.	1451	2902	4353	11,028	19,264	27,500
2-Origin recap	314	628	942	2198	3849	5500
3,4	177	354	531	1124	1937	2750
5-Winky, Blinky & Noddy begins (1st app.), ends #32	129	258	387	826	1413	2000
6-10	106	212	318	673	1162	1650
11-13: 12-Origin/1st The Thinker. 13-The King app.	90	180	270	576	988	1400
14-Green Lantern cameo	106	212	318	673	1162	1650
15-20: 18-Mutt & Jeff begins, ends #22	77	154	231	493	847	1200
21-31	65	130	195	416	708	1000
32-Origin/1st app. The Fiddler; 1st Star Sapphire	123	246	369	787	1344	1900

NOTE: *Book length stories in 2-13, 16. Bondage c-31, 32. **Martin Nodell** c-15, 17-28.*

ALL FLASH (Leads into Flash [2nd series] #231)
DC Comics: Sept, 2007 ($2.99, one-shot)

	GD 2.0	VG 4.0	FN 6.0	VF 8.0	VF/NM 9.0	NM- 9.2
1-Wally West hunts down Bart's killers; Waid-s; two covers by Middleton & Sienkiewicz						3.00

ALL FOR LOVE (Young Love V3#5-on)
Prize Publications: Apr-May, 1957 - V3#4, Dec-Jan, 1959-60

	GD 2.0	VG 4.0	FN 6.0	VF 8.0	VF/NM 9.0	NM- 9.2
V1#1	8	16	24	54	90	125
2-6: 5-Orlando-c	5	10	15	30	48	65
V2#1-5(1/59), 5(3/59)	4	8	12	26	41	55
V3#1(5/59), 1(7/59)-4: 2-Powell-a	4	8	12	22	34	45

ALL FUNNY COMICS
Tilsam Publ./National Periodical Publications (Detective): Winter, 1943-44 - No. 23, May-June, 1948

	GD 2.0	VG 4.0	FN 6.0	VF 8.0	VF/NM 9.0	NM- 9.2
1-Genius Jones (1st app.), Buzzy (1st app., ends #4), Dover & Clover (see More Fun #93) begin; Bailey-a	47	94	141	296	498	700
2	22	44	66	132	216	300
3-10	15	30	45	83	124	165
11-13,15,18,19-Genius Jones app.	14	28	42	80	115	150
14,17,20-23	10	20	30	56	76	95
16-DC Super Heroes app.	31	62	93	182	296	410

ALL GOOD
St. John Publishing Co.: Oct, 1949 (50¢, 260 pgs.)

	GD 2.0	VG 4.0	FN 6.0	VF 8.0	VF/NM 9.0	NM- 9.2
nn-(8 St. John comics bound together)	69	138	207	442	759	1075

NOTE: *Also see Li'l Audrey Yearbook & Treasury of Comics.*

ALL GOOD COMICS (See Fox Giants)
Fox Features Syndicate: No.1, Spring, 1946 (36 pgs.)

	GD 2.0	VG 4.0	FN 6.0	VF 8.0	VF/NM 9.0	NM- 9.2
1-Joy Family, Dick Transom, Rick Evans, One Round Hogan	27	54	81	158	259	360

ALL GREAT
William H. Wise & Co.: nd (1945?) (132 pgs.)

	GD 2.0	VG 4.0	FN 6.0	VF 8.0	VF/NM 9.0	NM- 9.2
nn-Capt. Jack Terry, Joan Mason, Girl Reporter, Baron Doomsday; Torture scenes	41	82	123	256	428	600

ALL GREAT COMICS (See Fox Giants)
Fox Feature Syndicate: 1946 (36 pgs.)

	GD 2.0	VG 4.0	FN 6.0	VF 8.0	VF/NM 9.0	NM- 9.2
1-Crazy House, Bertie Benson Boy Detective, Gussie the Gob	27	54	81	158	259	360

ALL GREAT COMICS (Formerly Phantom Lady #13? Dagar, Desert Hawk No. 14 on)
Fox Feature Syndicate: No. 14, Oct, 1947 - No. 13, Dec, 1947 (Newspaper strip reprints)

	GD 2.0	VG 4.0	FN 6.0	VF 8.0	VF/NM 9.0	NM- 9.2
14(#12)-Brenda Starr & Texas Slim-r (Scarce)	57	114	171	362	621	880
13-Origin Dagar, Desert Hawk; Brenda Starr (all-r); Kamen-c; Dagar covers begin	65	130	195	416	708	1000

ALL-GREAT CONFESSIONS (See Fox Giants)

ALL GREAT CRIME STORIES (See Fox Giants)

ALL GREAT JUNGLE ADVENTURES (See Fox Giants)

ALL HALLOW'S EVE
Innovation Publishing: 1991 ($4.95, 52 pgs.)

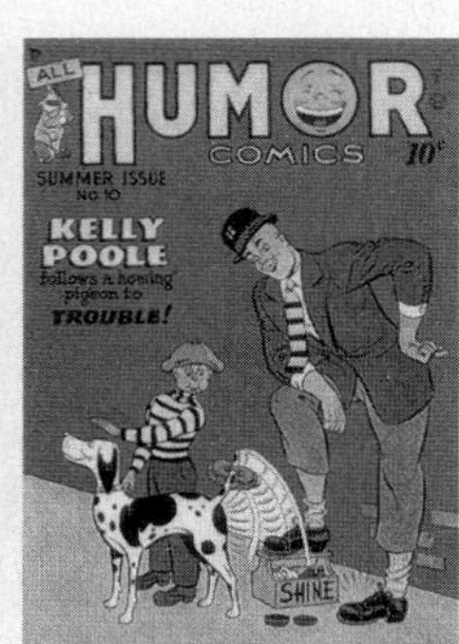

All Humor Comics #10 © QUA

All-Select Comics #2 © MAR

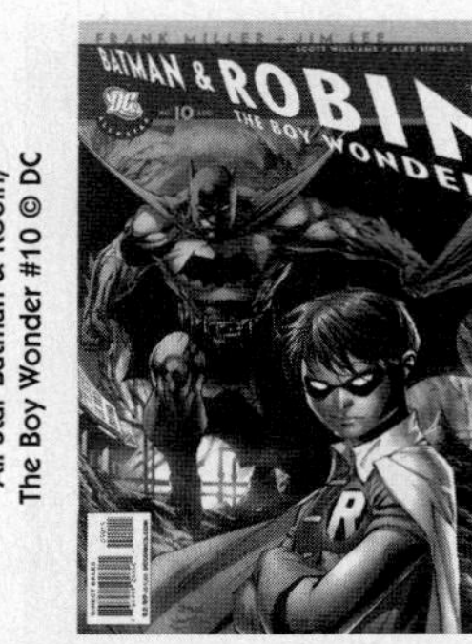

All Star Batman & Robin, The Boy Wonder #10 © DC

GD 2.0 | VG 4.0 | FN 6.0 | VF 8.0 | VF/NM 9.0 | NM- 9.2

1-Painted-c/a 1 2 3 4 5 7

ALL HERO COMICS
Fawcett Publications: Mar, 1943 (100 pgs., cardboard-c)

1-Capt. Marvel Jr., Capt. Midnight, Golden Arrow, Ibis the Invincible, Spy Smasher, Lance O'Casey; 1st Banshee O'Brien; Raboy-c 174 348 522 1114 1907 2700

ALL HUMOR COMICS
Quality Comics Group: Spring, 1946 - No. 17, December, 1949

1 21 42 63 122 199 275
2-Atomic Tot story; Gustavson-a 13 26 39 74 105 135
3-9: 3-Intro Kelly Poole who is cover feature #3 on. 5-1st app. Hickory? 8-Gustavson-a 9 18 27 47 61 75
10-17 8 16 24 42 54 65

ALLIANCE, THE
Image Comics (Shadowline Ink): Aug, 1995 - No. 3, Nov, 1995 ($2.50)

1-3: 2-(9/95) 2.50

ALL LOVE (...Romances No. 26)(Formerly Ernie Comics)
Ace Periodicals (Current Books): No. 26, May, 1949 - No. 32, May, 1950

26 (No. 1)-Ernie, Lily Belle app. 10 20 30 58 79 100
27-L. B. Cole-a 14 28 42 76 108 140
28-32 8 16 24 40 50 60

ALL-NEGRO COMICS
All-Negro Comics: June, 1947 (15¢)

1 (Rare) 1400 2800 4200 7500 10,000 12,500

NOTE: *Seldom found in fine or mint condition; many copies have brown pages.*

ALL-NEW ATOM, THE (See The Atom and DCU Brave New World)
DC Comics: Sept, 2006 - No. 25, Sept, 2008 ($2.99)

1-25: 1-18-Simone-s. 1-Intro Ryan Choi; Byrne-a thru #3. 4-11-Barrows-a. 12,13-Chronos app. 14,15-Countdown x-over. 17,18-Wonder Woman app. 3.00
...: Future/Past TPB (2007, $14.99) r/#7-11 15.00
...: My Life in Miniature TPB (2007, $14.99) r/#1-6 and app. in DCU Brave New World #1 15.00
...: Small Wonder TPB (2008, $17.99) r/#17,18,21-25 18.00
...: The Hunt For Ray Palmer TPB (2008, $14.99) r/#12-16 15.00

ALL-NEW COLLECTORS' EDITION (Formerly Limited Collectors' Edition: see for C-57, C-59)
DC Comics, Inc.: Jan, 1978 - Vol. 8, No. C-62, 1979 (No. 54-58: 76 pgs.)

C-53-Rudolph the Red-Nosed Reindeer 5 10 15 30 48 65
C-54-Superman Vs. Wonder Woman 4 8 12 26 41 55
C-55-Superboy & the Legion of Super-Heroes; Wedding of Lightning Lad & Saturn Girl; Grell-c/a 4 8 12 26 41 55
C-56-Superman Vs. Muhammad Ali: story & wraparound N. Adams-c/a 7 14 21 45 73 100
C-56-Superman Vs. Muhammad Ali (Whitman variant)-low print 8 16 24 54 90 125
C-57,C-59-(See Limited Collectors' Edition)
C-58-Superman Vs. Shazam; Buckler-c/a 4 8 12 26 41 55
C-60-Rudolph's Summer Fun(8/78) 4 8 12 26 41 55
C-61-(See Famous First Edition-Superman #1)
C-62-Superman the Movie (68 pgs.; 1979)-Photo-c from movie plus photos inside (also see DC Special Series #25) 3 6 9 16 22 28

ALL-NEW COMICS (...Short Story Comics No. 1-3)
Family Comics (Harvey Publications): Jan, 1943 - No. 14, Nov, 1946; No. 15, Mar-Apr, 1947 (10 x 13-1/2")

1-Steve Case, Crime Rover, Johnny Rebel, Kayo Kane, The Echo, Night Hawk, Ray O'Light, Detective Shane begin (all 1st app.?); Red Blazer on cover only; Sultan-a 300 600 900 1920 3310 4700
2-Origin Scarlet Phantom by Kubert 110 220 330 704 1202 1700
3-Nazi war-c 87 174 261 552 951 1350
4 71 142 213 454 777 1100
5-11: 5-Schomburg-c thru #11. 6-The Boy Heroes & Red Blazer (text story) begin, end #12; Black Cat app.; intro. Sparky in Red Blazer. 7-Kubert, Powell-a; Black Cat & Zebra app. 8,9: 8-Shock Gibson app.; Kubert, Powell-a; Schomburg-c. 9-Black Cat app.; Kubert-a. 10-The Zebra app. (from Green Hornet Comics); Kubert-a(3). 11-Girl Commandos, Man In Black app. 87 174 261 552 951 1350
12,13: 12-Kubert-a. 13-Stuntman by Simon & Kirby; Green Hornet, Joe Palooka, Flying Fool app.; Green Hornet-c 58 116 174 371 636 900
14-The Green Hornet & The Man in Black Called Fate by Powell, Joe Flying Fool app.; Flying Fool app.; J. Palooka-c by Ham Fisher 45 90 135 284 480 675
15-(Rare)-Small size (5-1/2x8-1/2"; B&W; 32 pgs.). Distributed to mail subscribers only. Black Cat and Joe Palooka app. 135 270 405 864 1482 2100

NOTE: *Also see Boy Explorers No. 2, Flash Gordon No. 5, and Stuntman No. 3.* ***Powell*** *a-11.* ***Schomburg*** *c-5-11. Captain Red Blazer & Spark on c-5-11 (w/Boy Heroes #12).*

GD 2.0 | VG 4.0 | FN 6.0 | VF 8.0 | VF/NM 9.0 | NM- 9.2

ALL-NEW OFFICIAL HANDBOOK OF THE MARVEL UNIVERSE A TO Z
Marvel Comics: 2006 - No. 12, 2006 ($3.99, limited series)

1-12-Profile pages of Marvel characters not covered in 2004-2005 Official Handbooks 4.00
...: Update 1-4 (2007, $3.99) Profile pages 4.00

ALL-OUT WAR
DC Comics: Sept-Oct, 1979 - No. 6, Aug, 1980 ($1.00, 68 pgs.)

1-The Viking Commando(origin), Force Three(origin), & Black Eagle Squadron begin 2 4 6 10 14 18
2-6 2 3 4 6 8 10

NOTE: ***Ayers*** *a(p)-1-6.* ***Elias*** *r-2.* ***Evans*** *a-1-6.* ***Kubert*** *c-16.*

ALL PICTURE ADVENTURE MAGAZINE
St. John Publishing Co.: Oct, 1952 - No. 2, Nov, 1952 (100 pg. Giants, 25¢, squarebound)

1-War comics 33 66 99 194 317 440
2-Horror-crime comics 47 94 141 296 498 700

NOTE: *Above books contain three St. John comics rebound; variations possible.* ***Baker*** *art known in both.*

ALL PICTURE ALL TRUE LOVE STORY
St. John Publishing Co.: Oct., 1952 - No. 2, Nov., 1952 (100 pgs., 25¢)

1-Canteen Kate by Matt Baker 52 104 156 322 549 775
2-Baker-c/a 37 74 111 222 361 500

ALL-PICTURE COMEDY CARNIVAL
St. John Publishing Co.: October, 1952 (100 pgs., 25¢)(Contains 4 rebound comics)

1-Contents can vary; Baker-a 43 86 129 271 461 650

ALL REAL CONFESSION MAGAZINE (See Fox Giants)

ALL ROMANCES (Mr. Risk No. 7 on)
A. A. Wyn (Ace Periodicals): Aug, 1949 - No. 6, June, 1950

1 13 26 39 74 105 135
2 8 16 24 44 57 70
3-6 8 16 24 40 50 60

ALL-SELECT COMICS (Blonde Phantom No. 12 on)
Timely Comics (Daring Comics): Fall, 1943 - No. 11, Fall, 1946

1-Capt. America (by Rico #1), Human Torch, Sub-Mariner begin; Black Widow story (4 pgs.); Classic Schomburg-c 1433 2866 4300 10,750 19,375 28,000
2-Red Skull app. 459 918 1377 3350 5925 8500
3-The Whizzer begins 300 600 900 2070 3635 5200
4,5-Last Sub-Mariner 245 490 735 1568 2684 3800
6-9: 6-The Destroyer app. 8-No Whizzer 194 388 582 1242 2121 3000
10-The Destroyer & Sub-Mariner app.; last Capt. America & Human Torch issue 194 388 582 1242 2121 3000
11-1st app. Blonde Phantom; Miss America app.; all Blonde Phantom-c by Shores 274 548 822 1740 2995 4250

NOTE: ***Schomburg*** *c-1-10.* ***Sekowsky*** *a-7. #7 & 8 show 1944 in indicia, but should be 1945.*

ALL SELECT COMICS 70th ANNIVERARY SPECIAL
Marvel Comics: Sept, 2009 ($3.99, one-shot)

1-New stories of Blonde Phantom and Marvex the Super Robot; r/Marvex G.A. app. 4.00

ALL SPORTS COMICS (Formerly Real Sports Comics; becomes All Time Sports Comics No. 4 on)
Hillman Periodicals: No. 2, Dec-Jan, 1948-49; No. 3, Feb-Mar, 1949

2-Krigstein-a(p), Powell, Starr-a 34 68 102 199 325 450
3-Mort Lawrence-a 22 44 66 132 216 300

ALL STAR BATMAN & ROBIN, THE BOY WONDER
DC Comics: Sept, 2005 - No. 10, Aug, 2008 ($2.99)

1-Two covers; retelling of Robin's origin; Frank Miller-s/Jim Lee-a/c 3.00
1-Diamond Retailer Summit Edition (9/05) sketch-c 100.00
2-10: 2-7-Two covers by Lee and Miller. 3-Black Canary app. 4-Six pg. Batcave gatefold. 10-Edition without profanity 3.00
8-10: 8,9-Variant cover by Neal Adams. 10-Variant-c by Quitely 5.00
10-Recalled edition with insufficiently covered profanity inside; Jim Lee-c 20.00
10-Recalled edition with variant Quitely-c 40.00
... Special Edition (2/06, $3.99) r/#1 with Lee pencil pages and Miller script; new Miller-c 4.00
Vol. 1 HC (2008, $24.99, dustjacket) r/#1-9; cover gallery, sketch pages; Schreck intro. 25.00
Vol. 1 SC (2009, $19.99) r/#1-9; cover gallery, sketch pages; Schreck intro. 20.00

ALL STAR COMICS
DC Comics: Spring 1940

1-Ashcan comic, not distributed to newsstands, only for in-house use. Cover art is Flash Comics #1 and interior from Detective Comics #37. A CGC certified 7.0 copy sold for $15,600 in 2002.

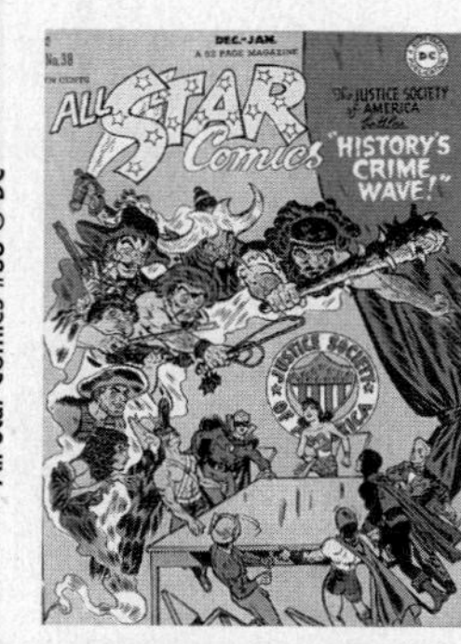

All Star Comics #38 © DC

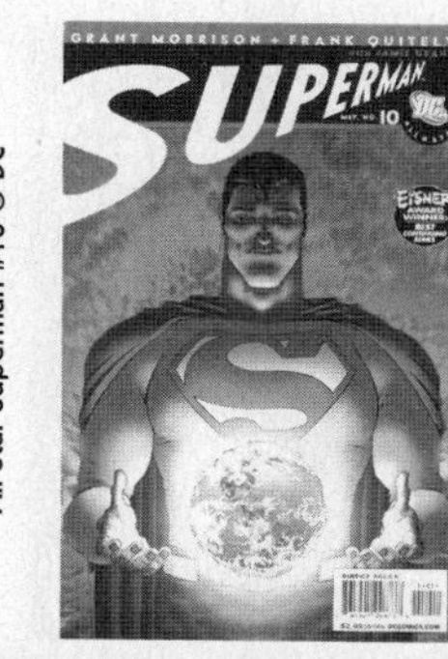

All Star Superman #10 © DC

All Star Western #87 © DC

GD VG FN VF VF/NM NM-
2.0 4.0 6.0 8.0 9.0 9.2

ALL STAR COMICS (All Star Western No. 58 on)
National Periodical Publ./All-American/DC Comics: Sum, 1940 - No. 57, Feb-Mar, 1951; No. 58, Jan-Feb, 1976 - No. 74, Sept-Oct, 1978

1-The Flash (#1 by E.E. Hibbard), Hawkman (by Shelly), Hourman (by Bernard Baily), The Sandman (by Creig Flessel), The Spectre (by Baily), Biff Bronson, Red White & Blue (ends #2) begin; Ultra Man's only app. (#1-3 are quarterly; #4 begins bi-monthly issues) 1170 2340 3510 8800 15,900 23,000
2-Green Lantern (by Martin Nodell), Johnny Thunder begin; Green Lantern figure swipe from the cover of All-American Comics #16; Flash figure swipe from cover of Flash Comics #8; Moldoff/Bailey-c (cut & paste-c.) 503 1006 1509 3672 6486 9300
3-Origin & 1st app. The Justice Society of America (Win/40); Dr. Fate & The Atom begin, Red Tornado cameo 4250 8500 12,750 32,000 58,500 85,000
3-Reprint, Oversize 13-1/2x10". **WARNING:** This comic is an exact reprint of the original except for its size. DC published it in 1974 with a second cover titling it as a Famous First Edition. There have been many reported cases of the outer cover being removed and the interior sold as the original edition. The reprint with the new outer cover removed is practically worthless. See Famous First Edition for value.
4-1st adventure for J.S.A. 530 1060 1590 3869 6835 9800
5-1st app. Shiera Sanders as Hawkgirl (1st costumed super-heroine, 6-7/41) 459 918 1377 3350 5925 8500
6-Johnny Thunder joins JSA 300 600 900 1935 3343 4750
7-Batman, Superman, Flash cameo; last Hourman; Doiby Dickles app. 331 662 993 2317 4059 5800
8-Origin & 1st app. Wonder Woman (12-1/41-42)(added as 9 pgs. making book 76 pgs.; origin cont'd in Sensation #1; see W.W. #1 for more detailed origin); Dr. Fate dons new helmet; Hop Harrigan text stories & Starman begin; Shiera app.; Hop Harrigan JSA guest; Starman & Dr. Mid-Nite become members 3500 7000 10,500 26,000 48,000 70,000
9-11: 9-JSA's girlfriends cameo; Shiera app.; J. Edgar Hoover of FBI made associate member of JSA. 10-Flash, Green Lantern cameo; Sandman new costume. 11-Wonder Woman begins; Spectre cameo; Shiera app.; Moldoff Hawkman-c 300 600 900 1920 3310 4700
12-Wonder Woman becomes JSA Secretary 274 548 822 1740 2995 4250
13,15: Sandman w/Sandy in #14 & 15. 15-Origin & 1st app. Brain Wave; Shiera app. 252 504 756 1613 2757 3900
14-(12/42) Junior JSA Club begins; w/membership offer & premiums 258 516 774 1651 2826 4000
16-20: 19-Sandman w/Sandy. 20-Dr. Fate & Sandman cameo 213 426 639 1363 2332 3300
21-23: 21-Spectre & Atom cameo; Dr. Fate by Kubert; Dr. Fate, Sandman end. 22-Last Hop Harrigan; Flag-c. 23-Origin/1st app. Psycho Pirate; last Spectre & Starman 165 330 495 1048 1799 2550
24-Flash & Green Lantern cameo; Mr. Terrific only app.; Wildcat, JSA guest; Kubert Hawkman begins; Hitler-c 165 330 495 1048 1799 2550
25-27: 25-Flash & Green Lantern start again. 26-Robot-c. 27-Wildcat, JSA guest (#24-26: only All-American imprint) 139 278 417 883 1517 2150
28-32 123 246 369 787 1344 1900
33-Solomon Grundy & Doiby Dickles app; classic Solomon Grundy cover & last G.A. app. 349 698 1047 2443 4272 6100
34,35-Johnny Thunder cameo in both 118 236 354 749 1292 1835
36-Batman & Superman JSA guests 284 568 852 1818 3109 4400
37-Johnny Thunder cameo; origin & 1st app. Injustice Society; last Kubert Hawkman 158 316 474 1003 1727 2450
38-Black Canary begins; JSA Death issue 219 438 657 1402 2401 3400
39,40: 39-Last Johnny Thunder 116 232 348 742 1271 1800
41-Black Canary joins JSA; Injustice Society app. (2nd app.?) 116 232 348 742 1271 1800
42-Atom & the Hawkman don new costumes 116 232 348 742 1271 1800
43-49,51-56: 43-New logo; Robot-c. 55-Sci/Fi story. 56-Robot-c 116 232 348 742 1271 1800
50-Frazetta art, 3 pgs. 124 248 372 787 1356 1925
57-Kubert-a, 6 pgs. (Scarce); last app. G.A. Green Lantern, Flash & Dr. Mid-Nite 168 336 504 1075 1838 2600
V12 #58-(1976) JSA (Flash, Hawkman, Dr. Mid-Nite, Wildcat, Dr. Fate, Green Lantern, Robin & Star Spangled Kid) app.; intro. Power Girl 6 12 18 39 62 85
V12 #59,60: 59-Estrada & Wood-a 3 6 9 17 25 32
V12 #61-68: 62-65-Superman app. 64,65-Wood-c/a; Vandal Savage app. 66-Injustice Society app. 68-Psycho Pirate app. 3 6 9 17 25 32
V12 #69-1st Earth-2 Huntress (Helena Wayne) 4 8 12 28 44 60
V12 #70-73: 70-Full intro. of Huntress 3 6 9 17 25 32
V12 #74-(44 pgs.) Last issue, story continues in Adventure Comics #461 & 462 (death of Earth-2 Batman; Staton-c/a 4 8 12 26 41 55
(See Justice Society Vol. 1 TPB for reprints of V12 revival)
NOTE: *No Atom-27, 36; no Dr. Fate-13; no Flash-8, 9, 11-23; no Green Lantern-8, 9,11-23; Hawkman in 1-57 (only one to app. in all 57 issues); no Johnny Thunder-5, 36; no Wonder Woman-9, 10, 23. Book length stories in 4-9, 11-14, 18-22, 25, 26, 29, 30, 32-36, 40, 42, 43. Johnny Peril in #42-46, 48, 49, 51, 52,54-57.* **Baily** *a-1-10, 12, 13, 14i, 15-20.* **Burnley** *Starman-8-13; c-12, 13.* **Grell** *c-58.* **E.E. Hibbard** *c-3, 4, 6-10.* **Infantino** *c-40.* **Kubert** *Hawkman-24-30, 33-37.* **Lampert/Baily/Flessel** *c-1, 2.* **Moldoff** *Hawkman-3-23; c-11.* **Mart Nodell** *c-25i, 26i, 27-32.* **Purcell** *c-5.* **Simon & Kirby** *Sandman 14-17, 19.* **Staton** *a-66-74p. c-74p.* **Toth** *a-37(2), 38(2), 40, 41; c-38, 41.* **Wood** *a-58i-63i, 64, 65; c-63i, 64, 65. Issues 1-7, 9-16 are 68 pgs.; #8 is 76 pgs.; #17-19 are 60 pgs.; #20-57 are 52 pgs.*

ALL STAR COMICS (Also see crossover 1999 editions of Adventure, All-American, National, Sensation, Smash, Star Spangled and Thrilling Comics)
DC Comics: May, 1999 - No. 2, May, 1999 ($2.95, bookends for JSA x-over)

1,2-Justice Society in World War 2; Robinson-s/Johnson-c 3.00
1-RRP Edition (price will be based on future sales)
...80-Page Giant (9/99, $4.95) Phantom Lady app. 5.00

ALL STAR INDEX, THE
Independent Comics Group (Eclipse): Feb, 1987 ($2.00, Baxter paper)

1 1 2 3 5 6 8

ALL-STAR SQUADRON (See Justice League of America #193)
DC Comics: Sept, 1981 - No. 67, Mar, 1987

1-Original Atom, Hawkman, Dr. Mid-Nite, Robotman (origin), Plastic Man, Johnny Quick, Liberty Belle, Shining Knight begin 1 2 3 5 6 8
2-10: 3-Solomon Grundy app. 4,7-Spectre app. 8-Re-intro Steel, the Indestructable Man 5.00
11-46,48,49: 12-Origin G.A. Hawkman retold. 23-Origin/1st app. The Amazing Man. 24-Batman app. 25-1st app. Infinity, Inc. (9/83), 26-Origin Infinity, Inc.(2nd app.); Robin app. 27-Dr. Fate vs. The Spectre. 30-35-Spectre app. 33-Origin Freedom Fighters of Earth-X. 36,37-Superman vs. Capt. Marvel; Ordway-c. 41-Origin Starman 4.00
47-Origin Dr. Fate; McFarlane-a (1st full story)/part-c (7/85) 2 4 6 8 10 12
50-Double size; Crisis x-over 1 2 3 4 5 7
51-66: 51-56-Crisis x-over. 61-Origin Liberty Belle. 62-Origin The Shining Knight. 63-Origin Robotman. 65-Origin Johnny Quick. 66-Origin Tarantula 5.00
67-Last issue; retells first case of the Justice Society 1 2 3 4 5 7
Annual 1-3: 1(11/82)-Retells origin of G.A. Atom, Guardian & Wildcat; Jerry Ordway's 1st pencils for DC. (1st work was inking Carmine Infantino in Mystery in Space #117). 2(11/83)-Infinity, Inc. app. 3(9/84) 5.00
NOTE: **Buckler** *a-1-5; c-1, 3-5, 51.* **Kubert** *c-2, 7-18. JLA app. in 14, 15. JSA app. in 4, 14, 15, 19, 27, 28.*

ALL-STAR STORY OF THE DODGERS, THE
Stadium Communications: Apr, 1979 ($1.00)

1 2 4 6 9 13 16

ALL-STAR SUPERMAN (Also see FCBD edition in the Promotional Comics section)
DC Comics: Jan, 2006 - No. 12, Oct, 2008 ($2.99)

1-Grant Morrison-s/Frank Quitely-a/c 5.00
1-Variant-c by Neal Adams 20.00
1-Special Edition (2009, $1.00) r/#1 with "After Watchmen" cover logo frame 1.00
2-12: 3-Lois gets super powers. 7,8-Bizarro app. 3.00
Vol. 1 HC (2007, $19.99, dustjacket) r/#1-6; Bob Schreck intro. 20.00
Vol. 1 SC (2008, $12.99) r/#1-6; Schreck intro. 13.00
Vol. 2 HC (2009, $19.99, dustjacket) r/#7-12; Mark Waid intro. 20.00
Vol. 2 SC (2009, $12.99) r/#7-12; Mark Waid intro. 13.00

ALL STAR WESTERN (Formerly All Star Comics No. 1-57)
National Periodical Publ.: No. 58, Apr-May, 1951 - No. 119, June-July, 1961

58-Trigger Twins (ends #116), Strong Bow, The Roving Ranger & Don Caballero begin 45 90 135 284 480 675
59,60: Last 52 pgs. 27 54 81 158 259 360
61-66: 61-64-Toth-a 22 44 66 128 209 290
67-Johnny Thunder begins; Gil Kane-a 28 56 84 165 270 375
68-81: Last precode (2-3/55) 15 30 45 84 127 170
82-98: 97-1st S.A. issue 14 28 42 76 108 140
99-Frazetta-r/Jimmy Wakely #4 14 28 42 78 112 145
100 14 28 42 78 112 145
101-107,109-116,118,119 12 24 36 67 94 120
108-Origin J. Thunder; J. Thunder logo begins 22 44 66 128 209 290
117-Origin Super Chief 14 28 42 82 121 160
NOTE: **Gil Kane** *c(p)-58, 59, 61, 63, 64, 68, 69, 70-95(most), 97-199(most).* **Infantino** *art in most issues. Madame .44 app.- #117-119.*

ALL-STAR WESTERN (Weird Western Tales No. 12 on)
National Periodical Publications: Aug-Sept, 1970 - No. 11, Apr-May, 1972

1-Pow-Wow Smith-r; Infantino-a 5 10 15 34 55 75
2-Outlaw begins; El Diablo by Morrow begins; has cameos by Williamson, Torres, Kane, Giordano & Phil Seuling 5 10 15 32 51 70
3-Origin El Diablo 5 10 15 30 48 65
4-6: 5-Last Outlaw issue. 6-Billy the Kid begins, ends #8 3 6 9 21 32 42
7-9-(52 pgs.) 9-Frazetta-a, 3pgs.(r) 4 8 12 24 37 50
10-(52 pgs.) Jonah Hex begins (1st app., 2-3/72) 36 72 108 280 540 800
11-(52 pgs.) 2nd app. Jonah Hex; 1st cover 15 30 45 107 204 300

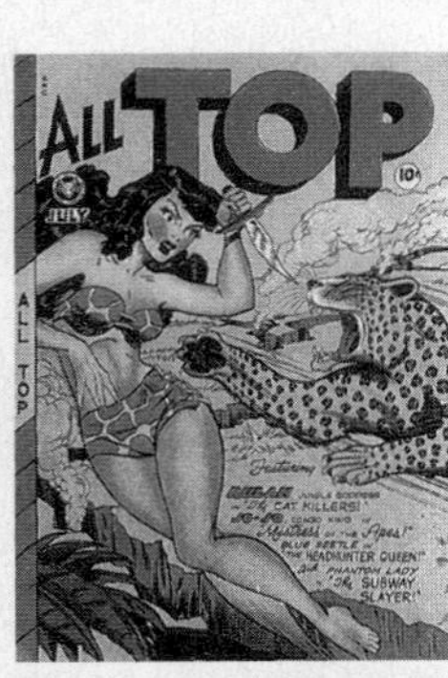

All Top Comics #12 © FOX

All Winners Comics 70th Anniversary Special #1 © MAR

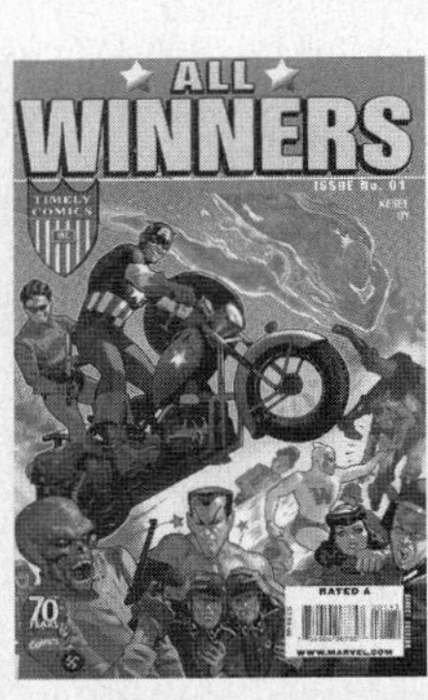

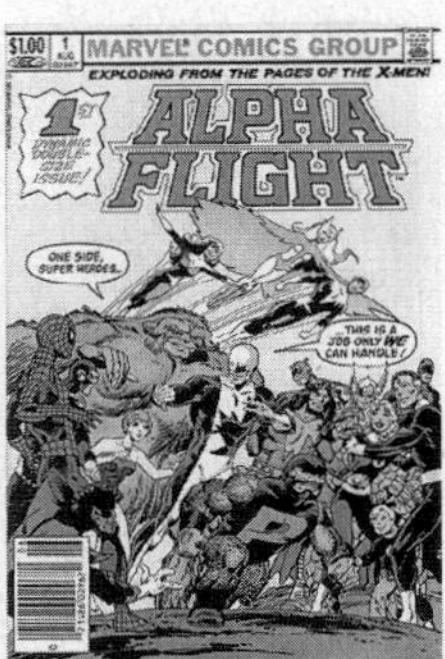

Alpha Flight #1 © MAR

GD VG FN VF VF/NM NM-
2.0 4.0 6.0 8.0 9.0 9.2

NOTE: ***Neal Adams** c-2-5; **Aparo** a-5. **G. Kane** a-3, 4, 6, 8. **Kubert** a-4r, 7-9r. **Morrow** a-2-4, 10, 11. No. 7-11 have 52 pgs..*

ALL SURPRISE (Becomes Jeanie #13 on) (Funny animal)
Timely/Marvel (CPC): Fall, 1943 - No. 12, Winter, 1946-47

1-Super Rabbit, Gandy & Sourpuss begin 39 78 117 231 378 525
2 19 38 57 111 176 240
3-10,12 15 30 45 86 133 180
11-Kurtzman "Pigtales" art 15 30 45 90 140 190

ALL TEEN (Formerly All Winners; All Winners & Teen Comics No. 21 on)
Marvel Comics (WFP): No. 20, January, 1947

20-Georgie, Mitzi, Patsy Walker, Willie app.; Syd Shores-c
16 32 48 94 147 200

ALL-TIME SPORTS COMICS (Formerly All Sports Comics)
Hillman Per.: V2, No. 4, Apr-May, 1949 - V2, No. 7, Oct-Nov, 1949 (All 52 pgs.)

V2#4 23 46 69 136 223 310
5-7: 5-(V1#5 inside)-Powell-a; Ty Cobb sty. 7-Krigstein-p; Walter Johnson & Knute Rockne sty 18 36 54 105 165 225

ALL TOP
William H. Wise Co.: 1944 (132 pgs.)

nn-Capt. V, Merciless the Sorceress, Red Robbins, One Round Hogan, Mike the M.P., Snooky, Pussy Katnip app. 33 66 99 194 317 440

ALL TOP COMICS (My Experience No. 19 on)
Fox Features Synd./Green Publ./Norlen Mag.: 1945; No. 2, Sum, 1946 - No. 18, Mar, 1949; 1957 - 1959

1-Cosmo Cat & Flash Rabbit begin (1st app.) 24 48 72 142 234 325
2 (#1-7 are funny animal) 14 28 42 76 108 140
3-7: 7-Two diff. issues (7/47 & 9/47) 10 20 30 56 76 95
8-Blue Beetle, Phantom Lady, & Rulah, Jungle Goddess begin (11/47); Kamen-c 284 568 852 1818 3109 4400
9-Kamen-c 145 290 435 921 1586 2250
10-Kamen bondage-c 152 304 456 965 1658 2350
11-13,15-17: 11,12-Rulah-c. 15-No Blue Beetle 119 238 357 762 1306 1850
14-No Blue Beetle; used in **SOTI**, illo- "Corpses of colored people strung up by their wrists" 168 336 504 1075 1838 2600
18-Dagar, Jo-Jo app; no Phantom Lady or Blue Beetle 76 152 228 486 831 1175
6(1957-Green Publ.)-Patoruzu the Indian; Cosmo Cat on cover only. 6(1958-Literary Ent.)-Muggy Doo; Cosmo Cat on cover only. 6(1959-Norlen)-Atomic Mouse; Cosmo Cat on-c only. 6(1959)-Little Eva. 6(Cornell)-Supermouse on-c 5 10 15 24 30 35

NOTE: *Jo-Jo by **Kamen**-12,18.*

ALL TRUE ALL PICTURE POLICE CASES
St. John Publishing Co.: Oct, 1952 - No. 2, Nov, 1952 (100 pgs.)

1-Three rebound St. John crime comics 44 88 132 277 469 660
2-Three comics rebound 33 66 99 194 317 440

NOTE: *Contents may vary.*

ALL-TRUE CRIME (...Cases No. 26-35; formerly Official True Crime Cases)
Marvel/Atlas Comics: No. 26, Feb, 1948 - No. 52, Sept, 1952
(OFI #26,27/CFI #28,29/LCC #30-46/LMC #47-52)

26(#1)-Syd Shores-c 34 68 102 199 325 450
27(4/48)-Electric chair-c 28 56 84 165 270 375
28-41,43-48,50-52: 35-37-Photo-c 14 28 42 78 112 145
42,49-Krigstein-a. 49-Used in **POP**, Pg 79 14 28 42 81 118 155

NOTE: ***Colan** a-46. **Keller** a-46. **Robinson** a-47, 50. **Sale** a-46. **Shores** c-26. **Tuska** a-48(3).*

ALL-TRUE DETECTIVE CASES (Kit Carson No. 5 on)
Avon Periodicals: #2, Apr-May, 1954 - No. 4, Aug-Sept, 1954

2(#1)-Wood-a 23 46 69 136 223 310
3-Kinstler-c 14 28 42 81 118 155
4-r/Gangsters And Gun Molls #2; Kamen-a 18 36 54 105 165 225
nn(100 pgs.)-7 pg. Kubert-a, Kinstler back-c 40 80 120 241 398 555

ALL TRUE ROMANCE (...Illustrated No. 3)
Artful Publ. #1-3/Harwell(Comic Media) #4-20?/Ajax-Farrell(Excellent Publ.) No. 22 on/Four Star Comic Corp.: 3/51 - No. 20, 12/54; No. 22, 3/55 - No. 30?, 7/57; No. 3(#31), 9/57;No. 4(#32), 11/57; No. 33, 2/58 - No. 34, 6/58

1 (3/51) 18 36 54 107 169 230
2 (10/51; 11/51 on-c) 11 22 33 64 90 115
3(12/51) - #5(5/52) 10 20 30 54 72 90
6-Wood-a, 9 pgs. (exceptional) 18 36 54 107 169 230
7-10 [two #7s: #7(11/52, 9/52 inside), #7(11/52, 11/52 inside)]. 10-Hollingsworth-c 9 18 27 50 65 80

GD VG FN VF VF/NM NM-
2.0 4.0 6.0 8.0 9.0 9.2

11-13,16-19(9/54),20(12/54) (no #21): 11,13-Heck-a 8 16 24 40 50 60
14-Marijuana story 8 16 24 42 54 65
22: Last precode issue (1st Ajax, 3/55) 8 16 24 40 50 60
23-27,29,30(7/57): 29-Disbrow-a 7 14 21 35 43 50
28 (9/56)-L. B. Cole, Disbrow-a 11 22 33 64 90 115
3(#31, 9/57),4(#32, 11/57),33,34 (Farrell, '57- '58) 6 12 18 31 38 45

ALL WESTERN WINNERS (Formerly All Winners; becomes Western Winners with No. 5; see Two-Gun Kid No. 5)
Marvel Comics(CDS): No. 2, Winter, 1948-49 - No. 4, April, 1949

2-Black Rider (origin/1st app.) & his horse Satan, Kid Colt & his horse Steel, & Two-Gun Kid & his horse Cyclone begin; Shores c-2-4 74 148 222 470 810 1150
3-Anti-Wertham editorial 37 74 111 222 361 500
4-Black Rider i.d. revealed; Heath, Shores-a 37 74 111 222 361 500

ALL WINNERS COMICS (All Teen #20) (Also see Timely Presents: ...)
USA No. 1-7/WFP No. 10-19/YAI No. 21: Summer, 1941 - No. 19, Fall, 1946; No. 21, Winter, 1946-47; (No #20) (No. 21 continued from Young Allies No. 20)

1-The Angel & Black Marvel only app.; Capt. America by Simon & Kirby, Human Torch & Sub-Mariner begin (#1 was advertised as All Aces); 1st app. All-Winners Squad in text story by Stan Lee 1950 3900 5850 14,625 25,812 38,000
2-The Destroyer & The Whizzer begin; Simon & Kirby Captain America 508 1016 1524 3708 6554 9400
3 383 766 1149 2681 4690 6700
4-Classic War-c by Al Avison 411 822 1233 2877 5039 7200
5 284 568 852 1818 3109 4400
6-The Black Avenger only app.; no Whizzer story; Hitler, Hirohito & Mussolini-c 309 618 927 2163 3782 5400
7-10 252 504 756 1613 2757 3900
11,13-18: 11-1st Atlas globe on-c (Winter, 1943-44; also see Human Torch #14). 14-16-No Human Torch 174 348 522 1114 1907 2700
12-Red Skull story; last Destroyer; no Whizzer story 232 464 696 1485 2543 3600
19-(Scarce)-1st story app. & origin All Winners Squad (Capt. America & Bucky, Human Torch & Toro, Sub-Mariner, Whizzer, & Miss America; r-in Fantasy Masterpieces #10 676 1352 2028 4935 8718 12,500
21-(Scarce)-All Winners Squad; bondage-c 541 1082 1623 3950 6975 10,000

NOTE: ***Everett** Sub-Mariner-1, 3, 4; **Burgos** Torch-1, 3, 4. **Schomburg** c-1, 7-18. **Shores** c-19p, 21.*

(2nd Series - August, 1948, Marvel Comics (CDS))
(Becomes All Western Winners with No. 2)

1-The Blonde Phantom, Capt. America, Human Torch, & Sub-Mariner app. 300 600 900 1920 3310 4700

ALL WINNERS COMICS 70th ANNIVERARY SPECIAL
Marvel Comics: Oct, 2009 ($3.99, one-shot)

1-New story of All Winners Squad; r/G.A. Capt Anerica app. from All Winners #12 4.00

ALL YOUR COMICS (See Fox Giants)
Fox Feature Syndicate (R. W. Voight): Spring, 1946 (36 pgs.)

1-Red Robbins, Merciless the Sorceress app. 22 44 66 128 209 290

ALMANAC OF CRIME (See Fox Giants)

AL OF FBI (See Little Al of the FBI)

ALONE IN THE DARK (Based on video game)
Image Comics: Feb, 2003 ($4.95)

1-Matt Haley-c/a; Jean-Marc & Randy Lofficier-s 5.00

ALPHA AND OMEGA
Spire Christian Comics (Fleming H. Revell): 1978 (49¢)

nn 2 4 6 8 11 14

ALPHA CENTURION (See Superman, 2nd Series & Zero Hour)
DC Comics: 1996 ($2.95, one-shot)

1 3.00

ALPHA FLIGHT (See X-Men #120,121 & X-Men/Alpha Flight)
Marvel Comics: Aug, 1983 - No. 130, Mar, 1994 (#52-on are direct sales only)

1-(52 pgs.) Byrne-a begins (thru #28) -Wolverine & Nightcrawler cameo 4.00
2-28: 2-Vindicator becomes Guardian; origin Marrina & Alpha Flight. 3-Concludes origin Alpha Flight. 6-Origin Shaman. 7-Origin Snowbird. 10,11-Origin Sasquatch. 12-(52 pgs.)-Death of Guardian. 13-Wolverine app. 16,17-Wolverine cameo. 17-X-Men x-over (mostly r-/X-Men #109); 20-New headquarters. 25-Return of Guardian. 28-Last Byrne issue 3.00
29-32,35-50: 39-47,49-Portacio-a(i). 50-Double size; Portacio-a(i) 2.50
33,34-1st & 2nd app. Lady Deathstrike; Wolverine app. 34-Origin Wolverine 3.00
51-Jim Lee's 1st work at Marvel (10/87); Wolverine cameo; 1st Lee Wolverine; Portacio-a(i) 5.00
52,53-Wolverine app.; Lee-a on Wolverine; Portacio-a(i); 53-Lee/Portacio-a 3.00

Alpha Flight V2 #11 © MAR

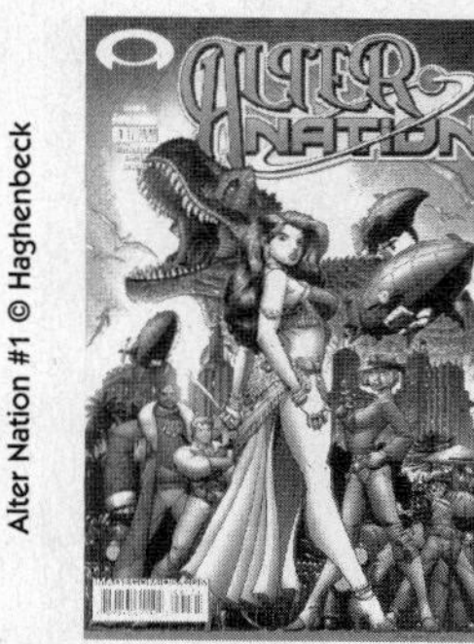

Alter Nation #1 © Haghenbeck

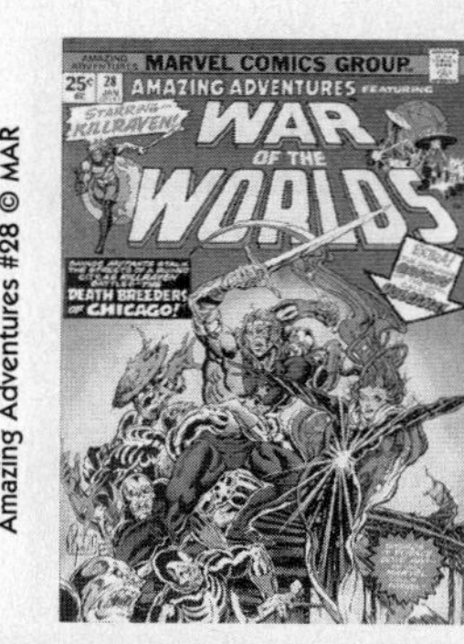

Amazing Adventures #28 © MAR

GD 2.0 | VG 4.0 | FN 6.0 | VF 8.0 | VF/NM 9.0 | NM- 9.2

54-73,76-86,91-99,101-105: 54,63,64-No Jim Lee-a. 54-Portacio-a(i). 55-62-Jim Lee-a(p). 71-Intro The Sorcerer (villain). 91-Dr. Doom app. 94-F.F. x-over. 99-Galactus, Avengers app. 102-Intro Weapon Omega 2.50
74,75,87-90,100: 74-Wolverine, Spider-Man & The Avengers app. 75-Double size ($1.95, 52 pgs.). 87-90-Wolverine. 4 part story w/Jim Lee-c. 89-Original Guardian returns. 100-($2.00, 52 pgs.)-Avengers & Galactus app. 3.00
106-Northstar revelation issue 2.50
106-2nd printing (direct sale only) 2.25
107-109,112-119,121-129: 107-X-Factor x-over. 112-Infinity War x-overs 2.50
110,111: Infinity War x-overs, Wolverine app. (brief). 111-Thanos cameo 3.00
120-($2.25)-Polybagged w/Paranormal Registration Act poster 2.50
130-($2.25, 52 pgs.) 3.00
Annual 1,2 (9/86, 12/87) 3.00
...Classics Vol. 1 TPB (2007, $24.99) r/#1-8; character profile pages; Byrne interview 25.00
Special V2#1(6/92, $2.50, 52 pgs.)-Wolverine-c/story 2.50
NOTE: ***Austin*** *c-1i, 2i, 53i.* ***Byrne*** *c-81, 82.* ***Guice*** *c-85, 91-99.* ***Jim Lee*** *a(p)-51, 53, 55-62, 64; c-53, 87-90.* ***Mignola*** *a-29-31p.* ***Whilce Portacio*** *a(i)-39-47, 49-54.*

ALPHA FLIGHT (2nd Series)
Marvel Comics: Aug, 1997 - No. 20, Mar, 1999 ($2.99/$1.99)

1-($2.99)-Wraparound cover 6.00
2,3: 2-Variant-c 4.00
4-11: 8,9-Wolverine-c/app. 3.00
12-($2.99) Death of Sasquatch; wraparound-c 4.00
13-20 3.00
.../Inhumans '98 Annual ($3.50) Raney-a 3.50

ALPHA FLIGHT (3rd Series)
Marvel Comics: May, 2004 - No. 12, April, 2005 ($2.99)

1-12: 1-6-Lobdell-s/Henry-c/a 3.00
... Vol. 1: You Gotta Be Kiddin' Me (2004, $14.99) r/#1-6 15.00

ALPHA FLIGHT: IN THE BEGINNING
Marvel Comics: July, 1997 ($1.95, one-shot)

(-1)-Flashback w/Wolverine 2.50

ALPHA FLIGHT SPECIAL
Marvel Comics: July, 1991 - No. 4, Oct, 1991 ($1.50, limited series)

1-4: 1-3-r-A. Flight #97-99 w/covers. 4-r-A.Flight #100 2.50

ALPHA KORPS
Diversity Comics: Sept, 1996 ($2.50)

1-Origin/1st app. Alpha Korps 2.50

ALTERED IMAGE
Image Comics: Apr, 1998 - No. 3, Sept, 1998 ($2.50, limited series)

1-3-Spawn, Witchblade, Savage Dragon; Valentino-s/a 3.00

ALTER EGO
First Comics: May, 1986 - No. 4, Nov, 1986 (Mini-series)

1-4 2.50

ALTER NATION
Image Comics: Feb, 2004 - No. 4, Jun, 2004 ($2.95, limited series)

1-4: 1-Two covers by Art Adams and Barberi; Barberi-a 3.00

ALVIN (TV) (See Four Color Comics No. 1042 or Three Chipmunks #1)
Dell Publishing Co.: Oct-Dec, 1962 - No. 28, Oct, 1973

	GD	VG	FN	VF	VF/NM	NM-
12-021-212 (#1)	9	18	27	60	100	140
2	5	10	15	35	55	75
3-10	5	10	15	30	48	65
11-"Chipmunks sing the Beatles' Hits"	5	10	15	34	55	75
12-28	4	8	12	24	37	50
Alvin For President (10/64)	5	10	15	30	48	65
...& His Pals in Merry Christmas with Clyde Crashcup & Leonardo 1 (02-120-402)-(12-2/64)	7	14	21	50	83	115
Reprinted in 1966 (12-023-604)	4	8	12	24	37	50

ALVIN & THE CHIPMUNKS
Harvey Comics: July, 1992 - No. 5, May, 1994

1-5: 1-Richie Rich app. 5.00

AMALGAM AGE OF COMICS, THE: THE DC COMICS COLLECTION
DC Comics: 1996 ($12.95, trade paperback)

nn-r/Amalgam, Assassins, Doctor Strangefate, JLX, Legends of the Dark Claw, & Super Soldier 13.00

AMANDA AND GUNN
Image Comics: Apr, 1997 - No. 4, Oct, 1997 ($2.95, B&W, limited series)

GD 2.0 | VG 4.0 | FN 6.0 | VF 8.0 | VF/NM 9.0 | NM- 9.2

1-4 3.00

AMAZING ADULT FANTASY (Formerly Amazing Adventures #1-6; becomes Amazing Fantasy #15) (See Amazing Fantasy for Omnibus HC reprint of #1-15)
Marvel Comics Group (AMI): No. 7, Dec, 1961 - No. 14, July, 1962

	GD	VG	FN	VF	VF/NM	NM-
7-Ditko-c/a begins, ends #14	47	94	141	376	701	1025
8-Last 10¢ issue	38	76	114	293	547	800
9-13: 12-1st app. Mailbag. 13-Anti-communist sty	36	72	108	282	529	775
13-2nd printing (1994)	2	4	6	8	10	12
14-Prototype issue (Professor X)	39	78	117	300	563	825

AMAZING ADVENTURE FUNNIES (Fantoman No. 2 on)
Centaur Publications: June, 1940 - No. 2, Sept. 1940

	GD	VG	FN	VF	VF/NM	NM-
1-The Fantom of the Fair by Gustavson (r/Amaz. Mystery Funnies V2#7,V2#8), The Arrow, Skyrocket Steele From the Year X by Everett (r/AMF #2); Burgos-a	174	348	522	1114	1907	2700
2-Reprints; Published after Fantoman #2	114	228	342	724	1242	1760

NOTE: ***Burgos*** *a-1(2).* ***Everett*** *a-1(3).* ***Gustavson*** *a-1(5), 2(3).* ***Pinajian*** *a-2.*

AMAZING ADVENTURES (Also see Boy Cowboy & Science Comics)
Ziff-Davis Publ. Co.: 1950; No. 1, Nov, 1950 - No. 6, Fall, 1952 (Painted covers)

	GD	VG	FN	VF	VF/NM	NM-
1950 (no month given) (8-1/2x11) (8 pgs.) Has the front & back cover plus Schomburg story used in Amazing Advs. #1 (Sent to subscribers of Z-D s/f magazines & ordered through mail for 10¢. Used to test market)	58	116	174	371	636	900
1-Wood, Schomburg, Anderson, Whitney-a	81	162	243	518	884	1250
2-5: 2-Schomburg-a. 2,4,5-Anderson-a. 3,5-Starr-a	40	80	120	246	411	575
6-Krigstein-a	40	80	120	249	417	585

AMAZING ADVENTURES (Becomes Amazing Adult Fantasy #7 on) (See Amazing Fantasy for Omnibus HC reprint of #1-15)
Atlas Comics (AMI)/Marvel Comics No. 3 on: June, 1961 - No. 6, Nov, 1961

	GD	VG	FN	VF	VF/NM	NM-
1-Origin Dr. Droom (1st Marvel-Age Superhero) by Kirby; Kirby/Ditko-a (5 pgs.) Ditko & Kirby-a in all; Kirby monster c-1-6	113	226	339	961	1831	2700
2	47	94	141	376	701	1025
3-6: 6-Last Dr. Droom	40	80	120	318	597	875

AMAZING ADVENTURES
Marvel Comics Group: Aug, 1970 - No. 39, Nov, 1976

	GD	VG	FN	VF	VF/NM	NM-
1-Inhumans by Kirby(p) & Black Widow (1st app. in Tales of Suspense #52) double feature begins	7	14	21	45	73	100
2-4: 2-F.F. brief app. 4-Last Inhumans by Kirby	4	8	12	22	34	45
5-8: Adams-a(p); 8-Last Black Widow; last 15¢-c	5	10	15	32	51	70
9,10: Magneto app. 10-Last Inhumans (origin-r by Kirby)	3	6	9	20	30	40
11-New Beast begins(1st app. in mutated form; origin in flashback); X-Men cameo in flashback (#11-17 are X-Men tie-ins)	17	34	51	122	236	350
12-17: 12-Beast battles Iron Man. 13-Brotherhood of Evil Mutants x-over from X-Men. 15-X-Men app. 16-Rutland Vermont - Bald Mountain Halloween x-over; Juggernaut app. 17-Last Beast (origin); X-Men app.	8	16	24	52	86	120
18-War of the Worlds begins (5/73); 1st app. Killraven; Neal Adams-a(p)	3	6	9	19	29	38
19-35,38,39: 19-Chaykin-a. 25-Buckler-a. 35-Giffen's first published story (art), along with Deadly Hands of Kung-Fu #22 (3/76)	1	3	4	6	8	10
36,37-(Regular 25¢ edition)(7-8/76)	1	3	4	6	8	10
36,37-(30¢-c variants, limited distribution)	6	12	18	37	59	80

NOTE: ***N. Adams*** *c-6-8.* ***Buscema*** *a-1p, 2p.* ***Colan*** *a-3-5p, 26p.* ***Ditko*** *a-24r.* ***Everett*** *a(i)3-5, 7-9.* ***Giffen*** *a-35i, 38p.* ***G. Kane*** *c-11, 25p, 29p.* ***Ploog*** *a-12i.* ***Russell*** *a-27-32, 34-37, 39; c-28, 30-32, 33i, 34, 35, 37, 39i.* ***Starliing*** *a-17.* ***Starlin*** *c-15p, 16, 17, 27.* ***Sutton*** *a-11-15p.*

AMAZING ADVENTURES
Marvel Comics Group: Dec, 1979 - No. 14, Jan, 1981

	GD	VG	FN	VF	VF/NM	NM-
V2#1-Reprints story/X-Men #1 & 38 (origins)	1	2	3	5	6	8
2-14: 2-6-Early X-Men-r. 7,8-Origin Iceman						6.00

NOTE: ***Byrne*** *c-6p, 9p.* ***Kirby*** *a-1-14r; c-7, 9.* ***Steranko*** *a-12r.* ***Tuska*** *a-7-9.*

AMAZING ADVENTURES
Marvel Comics: July, 1988 ($4.95, squarebound, one-shot, 80 pgs.)

1-Anthology; Austin, Golden-a 5.00

AMAZING ADVENTURES OF CAPTAIN CARVEL AND HIS CARVEL CRUSADERS, THE
(See Carvel Comics in the Promotional Comics section)

AMAZING CHAN & THE CHAN CLAN, THE (TV)
Gold Key: May, 1973 - No. 4, Feb, 1974 (Hanna-Barbera)

	GD	VG	FN	VF	VF/NM	NM-
1-Warren Tufts-a in all	4	8	12	22	34	45
2-4	3	6	9	16	23	30

AMAZING COMICS (Complete Comics No. 2)
Timely Comics (EPC): Fall, 1944

Amazing Fantasy #15 © MAR

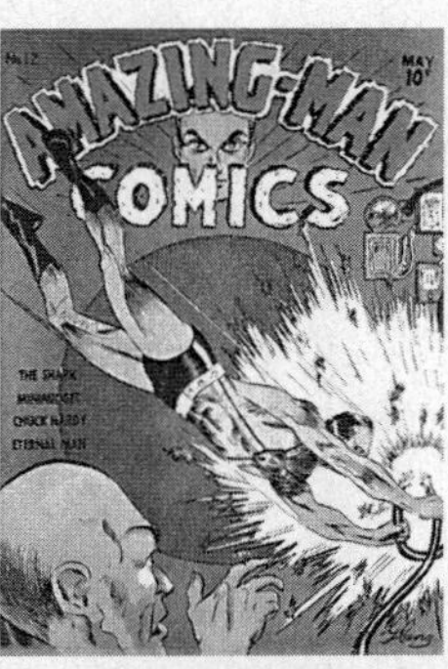

Amazing-Man Comics #12 © CEN

Amazing Spider-Girl #25 © MAR

GD VG FN VF VF/NM NM-
2.0 4.0 6.0 8.0 9.0 9.2

GD VG FN VF VF/NM NM-
2.0 4.0 6.0 8.0 9.0 9.2

1-The Destroyer, The Whizzer, The Young Allies (by Sekowsky), Sergeant Dix; Schomburg-c 258 516 774 1651 2826 4000

AMAZING DETECTIVE CASES (Formerly Suspense No. 2?)
Marvel/Atlas Comics (CCC): No. 3, Nov, 1950 - No. 14, Sept, 1952

3 30 60 90 177 289 400
4-6 18 36 54 103 162 220
7-10 16 32 48 92 144 195
11,12: 11-(3/52)-Horror format begins. 12-Krigstein-a 39 78 117 231 378 525
13-(Scarce)-Everett-a; electrocution-c/story 40 80 120 246 411 575
14 34 68 102 205 335 465

NOTE: ***Colan** a-9. **Maneely** c-13. **Sekowsky** a-12. **Sinnott** a-13. **Tuska** a-10.*

AMAZING FANTASY (Formerly Amazing Adult Fantasy #7-14)
Atlas Magazines/Marvel: #15, Aug, 1962 (Sept, 1962 shown in indicia); #16, Dec, 1995 - #18, Feb, 1996

15-Origin/1st app. of Spider-Man by Steve Ditko (11 pgs.); 1st app. Aunt May & Uncle Ben; Kirby/Ditko-c 3000 6000 12,000 36,000 68,000 100,000
16-18 ('95-'96, $3.95): Kurt Busiek scripts; painted-c/a by Paul Lee 4.00
Amazing Fantasy Omnibus HC ("Amazing Adult Fantasy" on-c) (2007, $75.00, dustjacket) r/Amazing Adventures #1-6, Amazing Adult Fantasy #7-14 and Amazing Fantasy #15 with letter pages; foreword by Bissette; cover gallery from '70s reprint titles 75.00

AMAZING FANTASY (Continues from #6 in Araña: The Heart of the Spider)
Marvel Comics: Aug, 2004 - No. 20, June, 2006 ($2.99)

1-Intro. Anya Corazon; Fiona Avery-s/Mark Brooks-c/a 4.00
2-14,16-20: 3,4-Roger Cruz-a. 7-Intro. new Scorpion; Kirk-a. 10-Intro. Vampire By Night 13,14-Back-up Captain Universe stories. 16-20-Death's Head 3.00
15-($3.99) Spider-Man app.; intro 6 new characters incl. Mastermind Excello seen in World War Hulk series; s/a by various 4.00
Death's Head 3.0: Unnatural Selection TPB (2006, $13.99) r/#16-20 14.00
Scorpion: Poison Tomorrow (2005, $7.99, digest) r/#7-13 8.00

AMAZING GHOST STORIES (Formerly Nightmare)
St. John Publishing Co.: No. 14, Oct, 1954 - No. 16, Feb, 1955

14-Pit & the Pendulum story by Kinstler; Baker-c 34 68 102 206 336 465
15-r/Weird Thrillers #5; Baker-c, Powell-a 25 50 75 147 241 335
16-Kubert reprints of Weird Thrillers #4; Baker-c; Roussos, Tuska-a; Kinstler-a (1 pg.) 25 50 75 150 245 340

AMAZING HIGH ADVENTURE
Marvel Comics: 8/84; No. 2, 10/85; No. 3, 10/86 - No. 5, 1986 ($2.00)

1-5: Painted-c on all. 3,4-Baxter paper. 4-Bolton-c/a. 5-Bolton-a 4.00

NOTE: ***Bissette** a-4. **Severin** a-1, 3. **Sienkiewicz** a-1,2. **Paul Smith** a-2. **Williamson** a-2i.*

AMAZING JOY BUZZARDS
Image Comics: 2005 - No. 4, 2005 ($2.95, B&W with pink spot color in #1)

1-4-Mark Andrew Smith-s/Dan Hipp-a. 1-Mahfood back-c. 2-Morse back-c 3.00
Vol. 1 TPB (2005, $11.95) r/#1-4; bonus art and character design sketches 12.00
TPB (2008, $19.99) r/#1-4 and Vol. 2 #1-5 20.00

AMAZING JOY BUZZARDS (Volume 2)
Image Comics: Oct, 2005 - No. 5, Aug, 2006 ($2.99, B&W)

1-5: 1-Mark Andrew Smith-s/Dan Hipp-a. 4-Mahfood-a; Crosland-a. 5-Holgate-a 3.00
Vol. 2 TPB (2006, $12.99) r/#1-4; bonus art, pin-ups and character sketches 13.00

AMAZING-MAN COMICS (Formerly Motion Picture Funnies Weekly?)
(Also see Stars And Stripes Comics)
Centaur Publications: No. 5, Sept, 1939 - No. 26, Jan, 1942

5(#1)(Rare)-Origin/1st app. A-Man the Amazing Man by Bill Everett; The Cat-Man by Tarpe Mills (also #8), Mighty Man by Filchock, Minimidget & sidekick Ritty, & The Iron Skull by Burgos begins 1500 3000 4500 11,250 20,125 29,000
6-Origin The Amazing Man retold; The Shark begins; Ivy Menace by Tarpe Mills app. 337 674 1011 2359 4130 5900
7-Magician From Mars begins; ends #11 245 490 735 1568 2684 3800
8-Cat-Man dresses as woman 184 368 552 1168 2009 2850
9-Magician From Mars battles the 'Elemental Monster,' swiped into The Spectre in More Fun #54 & 55. Ties w/Marvel Mystery #4 for 1st Nazi War-c on a comic (2/40) 194 388 582 1242 2121 3000
10,11: 11-Zardi, the Eternal Man begins; ends #16; Amazing Man dons costume; last Everett issue 139 278 417 883 1517 2150
12,13 129 258 387 826 1413 2000
14-Reef Kinkaid, Rocke Wayburn (ends #20), & Dr. Hypno (ends #21) begin; no Zardi or Chuck Hardy 103 206 309 659 1130 1600
15,17-20: 15-Zardi returns; no Rocke Wayburn. 17-Dr. Hypno returns; no Zardi 92 184 276 584 1005 1425
16-Mighty Man's powers of super strength & ability to shrink & grow explained; Rocke Wayburn returns; no Dr. Hypno; Al Avison (a character) begins, ends #18 (a tribute to the famed artist) 97 194 291 621 1061 1500
21-Origin Dash Dartwell (drug-use story); origin & only app. T.N.T. 107 214 321 680 1165 1650
22-Dash Dartwell, the Human Meteor & The Voice app; last Iron Skull & The Shark; Silver Streak app. (classic-c) 194 388 582 1242 2121 3000
23-Two Amazing Man stories; intro/origin Tommy the Amazing Kid; The Marksman only app. 81 162 243 518 884 1250
24-King of Darkness, Nightshade, & Blue Lady begin; end #26; 1st app. Super-Ann 81 162 243 518 884 1250
25,26 (Scarce): Meteor Martin by Wolverton in both; 26-Electric Ray app. 129 258 387 826 1413 2000

NOTE: ***Everett** a-5-11; c-5-11. **Gilman** a-14-20. **Giunta/Mirando** a-7-10. **Sam Glanzman** a-14-16, 18-21, 23. **Louis Glanzman** a-6, 9-11, 14-21; c-13-19, 21. **Robert Golden** a-9. **Gustavson** a-6; c-22, 23. **Lubbers** a-14-21. **Simon** a-10. **Frank Thomas** a-6, 9-11, 14, 15, 17-21.*

AMAZING MYSTERIES (Formerly Sub-Mariner Comics No. 31)
Marvel Comics (CCC): No. 32, May, 1949 - No. 35, Jan, 1950 (1st Marvel Horror Comic)

32-The Witness app. 86 172 258 546 936 1325
33-Horror format 40 80 120 246 411 575
34,35: Changes to Crime. 34,35-Photo-c 21 42 63 124 202 280

AMAZING MYSTERY FUNNIES
Centaur Publications: Aug, 1938 - No. 24, Sept, 1940 (All 52 pgs.)

V1#1-Everett-c(1st); Dick Kent Adv. story; Skyrocket Steele in the Year X on cover only 371 742 1113 2600 4550 6500
2-Everett 1st-a (Skyrocket Steele) 194 388 582 1242 2121 3000
3 107 214 321 680 1165 1650
3(#4, 12/38)-nn on cover, #3 on inside; bondage-c 97 194 291 621 1061 1500
V2#1-4,6: 2-Drug use story. 3-Air-Sub DX begins by Burgos. 4-Dan Hastings, Sand Hog begins (ends #5). 6-Last Skyrocket Steele 81 162 243 518 884 1250
5-Classic Everett-c 174 348 522 1114 1907 2700
7 (Scarce)-Intro. The Fantom of the Fair & begins; Everett, Gustavson, Burgos-a 354 708 1062 2478 4339 6200
8-Origin & 1st app. Speed Centaur 147 294 441 934 1605 2275
9-11: 11-Self portrait and biog. of Everett; Jon Linton begins; early Robot cover (11/39) 81 162 243 518 884 1250
12 (Scarce)-1st Space Patrol; Wolverton-a (12/39); new costume Phantom of the Fair 194 388 582 1242 2121 3000
V3#1(#17, 1/40)-Intro. Bullet; Tippy Taylor serial begins, ends #24 (continued in The Arrow #2) 81 162 243 518 884 1250
18,20: 18-Fantom of the Fair by Gustavson 77 154 231 493 847 1200
19,21-24: Space Patrol by Wolverton in all 94 188 282 597 1024 1450

NOTE: ***Burgos** a-V2#3-9. **Eisner** a-V1#2, 3(2). **Everett** a-V1#2-4, V2#1, 3-6; c-V1#1-4,V2#3, 5, 18. **Filchock** a-V2#9. **Flessel** a-V2#6. **Guardineer** a-V1#4, V2#4-6; **Gustavson** a-V2#4, 5, 9-12, V3#1, 18, 19; c-V2#7, 9, 12, V3#1, 21, 22; **McWilliams** a-V2#9, 10. **TarpeMills** a-V2#2, 4-6, 9-12, V3#1. **Leo Morey**(Pulp artist) c-V2#10; text illo-V2#11. **FrankThomas** a-6-V2#11. **Webster** a-V2#4.*

AMAZING SAINTS
Logos International: 1974 (39¢)

nn-True story of Phil Saint 2 4 6 9 13 16

AMAZING SCARLET SPIDER
Marvel Comics: Nov, 1995 - No. 2, Dec, 1995 ($1.95, limited series)

1,2: Replaces "Amazing Spider-Man" for two issues. 1-Venom/Carnage cameos. 2-Green Goblin & Joystick-c/app. 2.50

AMAZING SCREW-ON HEAD, THE
Dark Horse Comics (Maverick): May, 2002 ($2.99, one-shot)

1-Mike Mignola-s/a/c 3.00

AMAZING SPIDER-GIRL (Also see Spider-Girl and What If...? (2nd series) #105)
Marvel Comics: No. 0, 2006; No. 1, Dec, 2006 - No. 30, May, 2009 ($2.99)

0-($1.99) Recap of the Spider-Girl series and character profiles; A.F. #15 cover swipe 2.50
1-14,16-24,26--($2.99) Frenz & Buscema-a. 9-Carnage returns. 19-Has #17 on cover3.00
15,25,30-($3.99) 15-10th Anniversary issue. 25-Three covers 4.00
... Vol. 1: What Ever Happened to the Daughter of Spider-Man? TPB (2007, $14.99) r/#0-6 15.00
... Vol. 2: Comes the Carnage! TPB (2007, $13.99) r/#7-12 14.00
... Vol. 3: Mind Games TPB (2008, $13.99) r/#13-18 14.00

AMAZING SPIDER-MAN, THE (See All Detergent Comics, Amazing Fantasy, America's Best TV Comics, Aurora, Deadly Foes of..., Fireside Book Series, Friendly Neighborhood...., Giant-Size..., Giant Size Super-Heroes Featuring..., Marvel Age..., Marvel Collectors Item Classics, Marvel Fanfare, Marvel Graphic Novel, Marvel Knoghts..., Marvel Spec. Ed., Marvel Tales, Marvel Team-Up, Marvel Treasury Ed., New Avengers, Nothing Can Stop the Juggernaut, Official Marvel Index To..., Peter Parker..., Power Record Comics, Spectacular...., Spider-Man, Spider-Man Digest, Spider-Man Saga, Spider-Man 2099, Spider-Man Vs. Wolverine, Spidey Super Stories, Strange Tales Annual #2, Superman Vs. ..., Try-Out Winner Book, Ultimate Marvel Team-Up, Ultimate Spider-Man, Web of Spider- Man & Within Our Reach)

Amazing Spider-Man #3 © MAR

Amazing Spider-Man #45 © MAR

Amazing Spider-Man #194 © MAR

	GD 2.0	VG 4.0	FN 6.0	VF 8.0	VF/NM 9.0	NM- 9.2
AMAZING SPIDER-MAN, THE						
Marvel Comics Group: March, 1963 - No. 441, Nov, 1998						
1-Retells origin by Steve Ditko; 1st Fantastic Four x-over (ties with F.F. #12 as first Marvel x-over); intro. John Jameson & The Chameleon; Spider-Man's 2nd app.; Kirby/Ditko-c; Ditko-c/a #1-38	1500	3000	4500	13,500	31,750	50,000
1-Reprint from the Golden Record Comic set	17	34	51	122	236	350
With record (1966)	24	48	72	175	338	500
2-1st app. the Vulture & the Terrible Tinkerer	370	740	1110	3330	6665	10,000
3-1st app. Doc Octopus; 1st full-length story; Human Torch cameo; Spider-Man pin-up by Ditko	315	630	945	2835	5668	8500
4-Origin & 1st app. The Sandman (see Strange Tales #115 for 2nd app.); 1st monthly issue; intro. Betty Brant & Liz Allen	262	524	786	2293	4547	6800
5-Dr. Doom app.	212	424	636	1855	3678	5500
6-1st app. Lizard	171	342	513	1496	2973	4450
7-Vs. The Vulture	115	230	345	978	1927	2875
8-Fantastic Four app. in back-up story by Kirby & Ditko	90	180	270	765	1508	2250
9-Origin & 1st app. Electro (2/64)	118	236	354	1003	1977	2950
10-1st app. Big Man & The Enforcers	100	200	300	850	1675	2500
11-1st app. Bennett Brant	96	192	288	816	1608	2400
12-Doc Octopus unmasks Spider-Man-c/story	80	160	240	680	1340	2000
13-1st app. Mysterio	110	220	330	935	1843	2750
14-(7/64)-1st app. The Green Goblin (c/story)(Norman Osborn); Hulk x-over	169	338	507	1479	2940	4400
15-1st app. Kraven the Hunter; 1st mention of Mary Jane Watson (not shown)	84	168	252	714	1407	2100
16-Spider-Man battles Daredevil (1st x-over 9/64); still in old yellow costume	72	144	216	612	1206	1800
17-2nd app. Green Goblin (c/story); Human Torch x-over (also in #18 & #21)	80	160	240	680	1340	2000
18-1st app. Ned Leeds who later becomes Hobgoblin; Fantastic Four cameo; 3rd app. Sandman	51	102	153	408	792	1175
19-Sandman app.	40	80	120	308	592	875
20-Origin & 1st app. The Scorpion	64	128	192	544	1072	1600
21-2nd app. The Beetle (see Strange Tales #123)	40	80	120	314	607	900
22-1st app. Princess Python	40	80	120	308	592	875
23-3rd app. The Green Goblin-c/story; Norman Osborn app.	49	98	147	392	759	1125
24	36	72	108	280	540	800
25-(6/65)-1st brief app. Mary Jane Watson (face not shown); 1st app. Spencer Smythe; Norman Osborn app.	40	80	120	314	607	900
26-4th app. The Green Goblin-c/story; 1st app. Crime Master; dies in #27	40	80	120	321	623	925
27-5th app. The Green Goblin-c/story; Norman Osborn app.	40	80	120	314	607	900
28-Origin & 1st app. Molten Man (9/65, scarcer in high grade)	80	160	240	680	1340	2000
29,30	29	58	87	212	406	600
31-1st app. Harry Osborn who later becomes 2nd Green Goblin, Gwen Stacy & Prof. Warren.	32	64	96	245	473	700
32-38: 34-4th app. Kraven the Hunter. 36-1st app. Looter. 37-Intro. Norman Osborn. 38-(7/66)-2nd brief app. Mary Jane Watson (face not shown); last Ditko issue	23	46	69	169	327	485
39-The Green Goblin-c/story; Green Goblin's i.d. revealed as Norman Osborn; Romita-a begins (8/66; see Daredevil #16 for 1st Romita-a on Spider-Man)	34	68	102	262	506	750
40-1st told origin The Green Goblin-c/story	40	80	120	307	591	875
41-1st app. Rhino	33	66	99	254	490	725
42-(11/66)-3rd app. Mary Jane Watson (cameo in last 2 panels); 1st time face is shown	21	42	63	148	287	425
43-49: 44,45-2nd & 3rd app. The Lizard. 46-Intro. Shocker. 47-M. J. Watson & Peter Parker 1st date. 47-Green Goblin cameo; Harry & Norman Osborn app. 47,49-5th & 6th app. Kraven the Hunter	16	32	48	115	220	325
50-1st app. Kingpin (7/67)	58	116	174	493	972	1450
51-2nd app. Kingpin; Joe Robertson 1-panel cameo	22	44	66	157	304	450
52-58,60: 52-1st app. Joe Robertson & 3rd app. Kingpin. 56-1st app. Capt. George Stacy. 57,58-Ka-Zar app.	12	24	36	86	158	230
59-1st app. Brainwasher (alias Kingpin); 1st-c app. M. J. Watson	13	26	39	90	165	240
61-74: 61-1st Gwen Stacy cover app. 67-1st app. Randy Robertson. 69-Kingpin-c. 69,70-Kingpin app. 73-1st app. Silvermane. 74-Last 12¢ issue	10	20	30	70	123	175
75-83,87-89,91,92,95,99: 78,79-1st app. The Prowler. 83-1st app. Schemer & Vanessa (Kingpin's wife)	9	18	27	61	103	145
84-86,93: 84,85-Kingpin-c/story. 86-Re-intro & origin Black Widow in new costume. 93-1st app. Arthur Stacy	9	18	27	63	107	150
90-Death of Capt. Stacy	10	20	30	73	129	185
94-Origin retold	11	22	33	74	132	190
96-98-Green Goblin app. (97,98-Green Goblin-c); drug books not approved by CCA	11	22	33	76	136	195
100-Anniversary issue (9/71); Green Goblin cameo (2 pgs.)	15	30	45	107	204	300
101-1st app. Morbius the Living Vampire; Wizard cameo; last 15¢ issue (10/71)	17	34	51	122	236	350
101-Silver ink 2nd printing (9/92, $1.75)						2.50
102-Origin & 2nd app. Morbius (25¢, 52 pgs.)	12	24	36	85	155	225
103-118: 104,111-Kraven the Hunter-c/stories. 108-1st app. Sha-Shan. 109-Dr. Strange-c/story (6/72). 110-1st app. Gibbon. 113-1st app. Hammerhead. 116-118-reprints story from Spectacular Spider-Man Mag. in color with some changes	7	14	21	45	73	100
119,120-Spider-Man vs. Hulk (4 & 5/73)	9	18	27	63	107	150
121-Death of Gwen Stacy (6/73) (killed by Green Goblin) (reprinted in Marvel Tales #98 & 192)	19	38	57	139	270	400
122-Death of The Green Goblin-c/story (7/73) (reprinted in Marvel Tales #99 & 192)	20	40	60	142	276	410
123,126-128: 123-Cage app. 126-1st mention of Harry Osborn becoming Green Goblin	6	12	18	41	66	90
124-1st app. Man-Wolf (9/73)	7	14	21	47	76	105
125-Man-Wolf origin	6	12	18	43	69	95
129-1st app. The Punisher (2/74); 1st app. Jackal	40	80	120	314	607	900
130-133: 131-Last 20¢ issue	5	10	15	34	55	75
134-(7/74); 1st app. Tarantula; Harry Osborn discovers Spider-Man's ID; Punisher cameo	6	12	18	39	62	85
135-2nd full Punisher app. (8/74)	9	18	27	60	100	140
136-1st app. Harry Osborn Green Goblin in costume	8	16	24	54	90	125
137-Green Goblin-c/story (2nd Harry Osborn Goblin)	6	12	18	41	66	90
138-141: 139-1st Grizzly. 140-1st app. Glory Grant	4	8	12	23	36	48
142,143-Gwen Stacy clone cameos: 143-1st app. Cyclone	4	8	12	24	37	50
144-147: 144-Full app. of Gwen Stacy clone. 145,146-Gwen Stacy clone storyline continues. 147-Spider-Man learns Gwen Stacy is clone	4	8	12	24	37	50
148-Jackal revealed	4	8	12	26	41	55
149-Spider-Man clone story begins, clone dies (?); origin of Jackal	7	14	21	45	73	100
150-Spider-Man decides he is not the clone	4	8	12	26	41	55
151-Spider-Man disposes of clone body	4	8	12	26	41	55
152-160-(Regular 25¢ editions). 159-Last 25¢ issue(8/76)	3	6	9	19	29	38
155-159-(30¢-c variants, limited distribution)	7	14	21	49	80	110
161-Nightcrawler app. from X-Men; Punisher cameo; Wolverine & Colossus app.	4	8	12	23	36	48
162-Punisher, Nightcrawler app.; 1st Jigsaw	4	8	12	23	36	48
163-168: 167-1st app. Will O' The Wisp	3	6	9	16	22	28
169-173-(Regular 30¢ edition). 169-Clone story recapped. 171-Nova app.	3	6	9	16	22	28
169-173-(35¢-c variants, limited dist.)(6-10/77)	14	28	42	101	191	280
174,175-Punisher app.	3	6	9	17	25	32
176-180-Green Goblin app.	3	6	9	18	27	35
181-188: 181-Origin retold; gives life history of Spidey; Punisher cameo in flashback (1 panel). 182-(7/78)-Peter's first proposal to Mary Jane, but she declines (in #183)	3	6	9	14	20	25
189,190-Byrne-a	3	6	9	16	23	30
191-193,196-199: 193-Peter & Mary Jane break up. 196-Faked death of Aunt May	2	4	6	11	16	20
NOTE: *Whitman 3-packs containing #192-194,196 exist.*						
194-1st app. Black Cat	5	10	15	30	48	65
195-2nd app. Black Cat	3	6	9	16	22	28
200-Giant origin issue (1/80)	4	8	12	22	34	45
201,202-Punisher app.	3	6	9	14	19	24
203-205,207,208,210-219: 203-3rd app. Dazzler (4/80). 210-1st app. Madame Web. 212-1st app. Hydro Man; origin Sandman	2	4	6	8	10	12
206-Byrne-a	2	4	6	9	12	15
209-Origin & 1st app. Calypso (10/80)	2	4	6	11	16	20
220-237: 225-(2/82)-Foolkiller-c/story. 226,227-Black Cat returns. 234-Free 16 pg. insert "Marvel Guide to Collecting Comics". 235-Origin Will-'O-The-Wisp. 236-Tarantula dies	1	3	4	6	8	10
238-(3/83)-1st app. Hobgoblin (Ned Leeds); came with skin "Tattooz" decal.						
NOTE: The same decal appears in the more common Fantastic Four #252 which is being removed & placed in this issue as incentive to increase value						

Amazing Spider-Man #252 © MAR

Amazing Spider-Man #386 © MAR

Amazing Spider-Man #425 © MAR

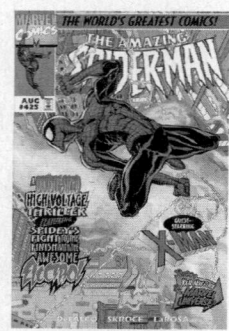

	GD 2.0	VG 4.0	FN 6.0	VF 8.0	VF/NM 9.0	NM- 9.2
(Value listed is with or without tattooz)	8	16	24	52	86	120
239-2nd app. Hobgoblin & 1st battle w/Spidey	4	8	12	28	44	60
240-243,246-248: 241-Origin The Vulture. 242-Mary Jane Watson cameo (last panel). 243-Reintro Mary Jane after 4 year absence	1	2	3	5	7	9
244-3rd app. Hobgoblin (cameo)	2	4	6	9	12	15
245-(10/83)-4th app. Hobgoblin (cameo); Lefty Donovan gains powers of Hobgoblin & battles Spider-Man	2	4	6	9	12	15
249-251: 3 part Hobgoblin/Spider-Man battle. 249-Retells origin & death of 1st Green Goblin. 251-Last old costume	2	4	6	9	13	16
252-Spider-Man dons new black costume (5/84); ties with Marvel Team-Up #141 & Spectacular Spider-Man #90 for 1st new costume in regular title (See Marvel Super-Heroes Secret Wars #8 (12/84) for acquisition of costume)	4	8	12	28	44	60
253-1st app. The Rose	2	4	6	8	11	14
254-258: 256-1st app. Puma. 257-Hobgoblin cameo; 2nd app. Puma; M.J. Watson reveals she knows Spidey's i.d. 258-Hobgoblin app.	1	2	3	5	7	9
259-Full Hobgoblin app.; Spidey back to old costume; origin Mary Jane Watson	2	4	6	8	11	14
260-Hobgoblin app.	1	3	4	6	8	11
261-Hobgoblin-c/story; painted-c by Vess	2	4	6	8	10	12
262-Spider-Man unmasked; photo-c	1	2	3	5	7	9
263,264,266-274,277-280,282,283: 274-Zarathos (The Spirit of Vengeance) app. 277-Vess back-up art. 279-Jack O'Lantern-c/story. 282-X-Factor x-over	1	2	3	4	5	7
265-1st app. Silver Sable (6/85)	2	4	6	9	13	16
265-Silver ink 2nd printing ($1.25)						2.50
275-($1.25, 52 pgs.)-Hobgoblin-c/story; origin-r by Ditko	2	4	6	13	18	22
276-Hobgoblin app.	1	3	4	6	8	10
281-Hobgoblin battles Jack O'Lantern	1	3	4	6	8	10
284,285: 284-Punisher cameo; Gang War story begins; Hobgoblin-c/story. 285-Punisher app.; minor Hobgoblin app.	1	3	4	6	8	10
286-288: 286-Hobgoblin-c & app. (minor). 287-Hobgoblin app. (minor). 288-Full Hobgoblin app.; last Gang War	1	3	4	6	8	10
289-(6/87, $1.25, 52 pgs.)-Hobgoblin's i.d. revealed as Ned Leeds; death of Ned Leeds; Macendale (Jack O'Lantern) becomes new Hobgoblin (1st app.)	3	6	9	14	19	24
290-292,295-297: 290-Peter proposes to Mary Jane. 292-She accepts; leads into wedding in Amazing Spider-Man Annual #21	1	2	3	4	5	7
293,294-Part 2 & 5 of Kraven story from Web of Spider-Man. 294-Death of Kraven	2	4	6	8	11	14
298-Todd McFarlane-c/a begins (3/88); 1st brief app. Eddie Brock who becomes Venom; (last pg.)	5	10	15	32	51	70
299-1st brief app. Venom with costume	3	6	9	20	30	40
300 ($1.50, 52 pgs.; 25th Anniversary)-1st full Venom app.; last black costume (5/88)	9	18	27	60	100	140
301-305: 301 ($1.00 issues begin). 304-1st bi-weekly issue	2	4	6	9	13	16
306-311,313,314: 306-Swipes-c from Action #1	2	4	6	8	11	14
312-Hobgoblin battles Green Goblin	2	4	6	11	16	20
315-317-Venom app.	3	6	9	14	19	24
318-323,325: 319-Bi-weekly begins again	1	2	3	5	7	9
324-Sabretooth app.; McFarlane cover only	1	2	3	5	7	9
326,327,329: 327-Cosmic Spidey continues from Spectacular Spider-Man (no McFarlane-c/a)						5.00
328-Hulk x-over; last McFarlane issue	1	3	4	6	8	10
330,331-Punisher app. 331-Minor Venom app.						5.00
332,333-Venom-c/story	1	3	4	6	8	10
334-336,338-343: 341-Tarantula app.						4.00
337-Hobgoblin app.						5.00
344-(2/91) 1st app. Cletus Kasady (Carnage)	2	4	6	9	12	15
345-1st full app. Cletus Kasady; Venom cameo on last pg.	2	4	6	9	12	15
346,347-Venom app.	1	3	4	6	8	10
348,349,351-359: 348-Avengers x-over. 351,352-Nova of New Warriors app. 353-Darkhawk app.; brief Punisher app. 354-Punisher cameo & Nova, Night Thrasher (New Warriors), Darkhawk & Moon Knight app. 357,358-Punisher, Darkhawk, Moon Knight, Night Thrasher, Nova x-over. 358-3 part gatefold-c; last $1.00-c. 360-Carnage cameo						3.00
350-($1.50, 52pgs.)-Origin retold; Spidey vs. Dr. Doom; pin-ups; Uncle Ben app.						5.00
360-Carnage cameo						4.00
361-(4/92) Intro Carnage (the Spawn of Venom); begin 3 part story; recap of how Spidey's alien costume became Venom	2	4	6	9	12	15
361-($1.25)-2nd printing; silver-c						2.50
362,363-Carnage & Venom-c/story	1	2	3	5	7	9
362-2nd printing						2.50

	GD 2.0	VG 4.0	FN 6.0	VF 8.0	VF/NM 9.0	NM- 9.2
364,366-374,376-387: 364-The Shocker app. (old villain). 366-Peter's parents-c/story. 369-Harry Osborn back-up (Gr. Goblin II). 373-Venom back-up. 374-Venom-c/story. 376-Cardiac app. 378-Maximum Carnage part 3. 381,382-Hulk app. 383-The Jury app. 384-Venom/carnage app. 387-New costume Vulture						2.50
365-($3.95, 84 pgs.)-30th anniversary issue w/silver hologram on-c; Spidey/Venom/Carnage pull-out poster; contains 5 pg. preview of Spider-Man 2099 (1st app.); Spidey's origin retold; Lizard app.; reintro Peter's parents in Stan Lee 3 pg. text w/illo (story continues thru #370)						5.00
375-($3.95, 68 pgs.)-Holo-grafx foil-c; vs. Venom story; ties into Venom: Lethal Protector #1; Pat Olliffe-a.						5.00
388-($2.25, 68 pgs.)-Newsstand edition; Venom back-up & Cardiac & chance back-up						2.50
388-($2.95, 68 pgs.)-Collector's edition w/foil-c						3.00
389-396,398,399,401-420: 389-$1.50-c begins; bound-in trading card sheet; Green Goblin app. 394-Power & Responsibility Pt. 2. 396-Daredevil-c & app. 403-Carnage app. 406-1st New Doc Octopus. 407-Human Torch, Silver Sable, Sandman app. 409-Kaine, Rhino app. 410-Carnage app. 414-The Rose app. 415-Onslaught story; Spidey vs. Sentinels. 416-Epilogue to Onslaught; Garney-a(p); Williamson-a(i)						2.50
390-($2.95)-Collector's edition polybagged w/16 pg. insert of new animated Spidey TV show plus animation cel						3.00
394-($2.95, 48 pgs.)-Deluxe edition; flip book w/Birth of a Spider-Man Pt. 2; silver foil both-c; Power & Responsibility Pt. 2						3.00
397-($2.25)-Flip book w/Ultimate Spider-Man						2.50
400-($2.95)-Death of Aunt May						3.00
400-($3.95)-Death of Aunt May; embossed double-c						5.00
400-Collector's Edition; white-c	1	2	3	5	7	9
408-($2.95) Polybagged version with TV theme song cassette						8.00
421-424,426,428-433: 426-Begin $1.99-c. 432-Spiderhunt pt. 2						2.50
425-($2.99)-48 pgs., wraparound-c						3.00
427-($2.25) Return of Dr. Octopus; double gatefold-c						2.50
434-440: 434-Double-c with "Amazing Ricochet #1". 438-Daredevil app. 439-Avengers-c/app. 440-Byrne-s						2.50
441-Final issue; Byrne-s						4.00
#500-up (See Amazing Spider-Man Vol. 2; series resumed original numbering after Vol. 2 #58)						
#(-1) Flashback issue (7/97, $1.95-c)						2.50
Annual 1 (1964, 72 pgs.)-Origin Spider-Man; 1st app. Sinister Six (Dr. Octopus, Electro, Kraven the Hunter, Mysterio, Sandman, Vulture) (new 41 pg. story); plus gallery of Spidey foes; early X-Men app.	86	172	258	731	1441	2150
Annual 2 (1965, 25¢, 72 pgs.)-Reprints from #1,2,5 plus new Doctor Strange story	35	70	105	271	523	775
Special 3 (11/66, 25¢, 72 pgs.)-New Avengers story & Hulk x-over; Doctor Octopus-r from #11,12; Romita-a	17	34	51	119	230	340
Special 4 (11/67, 25¢, 68 pgs.)-Spidey battles Human Torch (new 41 pg. story)	14	28	42	100	188	275
Special 5 (11/68, 25¢, 68 pgs.)-New 40 pg. Red Skull story; 1st app. Peter Parker's parents; last annual with new-a	12	24	36	85	155	225
Special 5-2nd printing (1994)	2	4	6	8	10	12
Special 6 (11/69, 25¢, 68 pgs.)-Reprints 41 pg. Sinister Six story from annual #1 plus 2 Kirby/Ditko stories (r)	5	10	15	34	55	75
Special 7 (12/70, 25¢, 68 pgs.)-All-r(#1,2) new Vulture-c	5	10	15	34	55	75
Special 8 (12/71)-All-r	5	10	15	34	55	75
King Size 9 ('73)-Reprints Spectacular Spider-Man (mag.) #2; 40 pg. Green Goblin-c/story (re-edited from 58 pgs.)	5	10	15	34	55	75
Annual 10 (1976)-Origin Human Fly (vs. Spidey); new-a begins	3	6	9	16	22	28
Annual 11-13 ('77-'79):12-Spidey vs. Hulk-r/#119,120. 13-New Byrne/Austin-a; Dr. Octopus x-over w/Spectacular S-M Ann. #1	2	4	6	10	14	18
Annual 14 (1980)-Miller-c/a(p); Dr. Strange app.	3	6	9	14	19	24
Annual 15 (1981)-Miller-c/a(p); Punisher app.	3	6	9	17	25	32
Annual 16-20:16 ('82)-Origin/1st app. new Capt. Marvel (female heroine). 17 ('83)-Kingpin app. 18 ('84)-Scorpion app.; JJJ weds. 19 ('85). 20 ('86)-Origin Iron Man of 2020	1	2	3	4	5	7
Annual 21 (1987)-Special wedding issue; newsstand & direct sale versions exist & are worth same	2	4	6	8	10	12
Annual 22 (1988, $1.75, 68 pgs.)-1st app. Speedball; Evolutionary War x-over; Daredevil app.						6.00
Annual 23 (1989, $2.00, 68 pgs.)-Atlantis Attacks; origin Spider-Man retold; She-Hulk app.; Byrne-c; Liefeld-a(p), 23 pgs.						4.00
Annual 24 (1990, $2.00, 68 pgs.)-Ant-Man app.						3.00
Annual 25 (1991, $2.00, 68 pgs.)-3 pg. origin recap; Iron Man app.; 1st Venom solo story; Ditko-a (6 pgs.)						5.00
Annual 26 (1992, $2.25, 68 pgs.)-New Warriors-c/story; Venom solo story cont'd in Spectacular Spider-Man Annual #12						4.00
Annual 27,28 ('93, '94, $2.95, 68 pgs.)-27-Bagged w/card; 1st app. Annex. 28-Carnage-c/story;						

Amazing Spider-Man V2 #9 © MAR

Amazing Spider-Man #512 © MAR

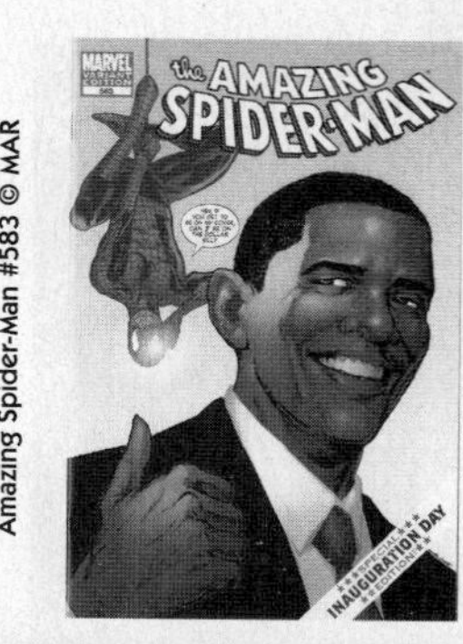

Amazing Spider-Man #583 © MAR

GD VG FN VF VF/NM NM-
2.0 4.0 6.0 8.0 9.0 9.2

Rhino & Cloak and Dagger back-ups 3.00
'96 Special-($2.95, 64 pgs.)-"Blast From The Past" 3.00
'97 Special-($2.99)-Wraparound-c,Sundown app. 3.00
Marvel Graphic Novel - Parallel Lives (3/89, $8.95) 2 4 6 8 10 12
Marvel Graphic Novel - Spirits of the Earth (1990, $18.95, HC) 3 6 9 16 22 28
Super Special 1 (4/95, $3.95)-Flip Book 4.00
...: Skating on Thin Ice 1(1990, $1.25, Canadian)-McFarlane-c; anti-drug issue; Electro app. 1 2 3 5 7 9
...: Skating on Thin Ice 1 (2/93, $1.50, American) 4.00
...: Double Trouble 2 (1990, $1.25, Canadian) 6.00
...: Double Trouble 2 (2/93, $1.50, American) 3.00
...: Hit and Run 3 (1990, $1.25, Canadian)-Ghost Rider-c/story 1 2 3 5 7 9
...: Hit and Run 3 (2/93. $1.50, American) 3.00
...: Carnage (6/93, $6.95)-r/ASM #344,345,359-363 1 2 3 4 5 7
...: Chaos in Calgary 4 (Canadian; part of 5 part series)-Turbine,Night Rider, Frightful app. 2 4 6 8 11 14
...: Chaos in Calgary 4 (2/93, $1.50, American) 3.00
...: Deadball 5 (1993, $1.60, Canadian)-Green Goblin-c/story; features Montreal Expos 2 4 6 10 14 18
Note: Prices listed above are for English Canadian editions. French editions are worth double.
...: Soul of the Hunter nn (8/92, $5.95, 52 pgs.)-Zeck-c/a(p) 6.00
Wizard #1 Ace Edition ($13.99) r/#1 w/ new Ramos acetate-c 14.00
Wizard #129 Ace Edition ($13.99) r/#129 w/ new Ramos acetate-c 14.00

NOTE: ***Austin*** *a(i)-248, 335, 337, Annual 13; c(i)-188, 241, 242, 248, 331, 334, 343, Annual 25.* ***J. Buscema*** *a(p)-72, 73, 76-81, 84, 85.* ***Byrne*** *a-189p, 190p, 206p, Annual 3r, 6r, 7r, 13p; c-189p, 268, 296, Annual 12.* ***Ditko*** *a-1-38, Annual 1, Special 3(r), 2, 24(2); c-1i, 2-38.* ***Guice*** *c/a-Annual 18i.* ***Gil Kane*** *a(p)-89-105, 120-124, 150, Annual 10, 12i, 24p; c-90p, 96, 98, 99, 101-105p, 129p, 131p, 132p, 137-140p, 143p, 148p, 149p, 151p, 153p, 160p, 161p, Annual 10p, 24.* ***Kirby*** *a-8.* ***Erik Larsen*** *a-324, 327, 329-350; c-327, 329-350, 354i, Annual 25.* ***McFarlane*** *a-298p, 299p, 300-303, 304-323p, 325p, 328; c-298-325, 328.* ***Miller*** *c-218, 219.* ***Mooney*** *a-65i, 67-82i, 84-88i, 173i, 178i, 189i, 190i, 192i, 193i, 196-202i, 207i, 211-219i, 221i, 222i, 226i, 227i, 229-233i, Annual 11i, 17i.* ***Nasser*** *c-228p.* ***Nebres*** *a-Annual 24i.* ***Russell*** *c-357i.* ***Simonson*** *c-222, 337i.* ***Starlin*** *a-113i, 114i, 187p.* ***Williamson*** *a-365i.*

AMAZING SPIDER-MAN (Volume 2) (Some issues reprinted in "Spider-Man, Best Of" hardcovers)
Marvel Comics: Jan, 1999 - Present ($2.99/$1.99/$2.25)

1-($2.99)-Byrne-a 6.00
1-Sunburst variant-c 1 2 3 5 6 8
1-($6.95) Dynamic Forces variant-c by the Romitas 1 3 4 6 8 10
1-Marvel Matrix sketch variant-c 1 3 4 6 8 10
2-($1.99) Two covers -by John Byrne and Andy Kubert 4.00
3-11: 4-Fantastic Four app. 5-Spider-Woman-c 2.50
12-($2.99) Sinister Six return (cont. in Peter Parker #12) 3.00
13-17: 13-Mary Jane's plane explodes 2.50
18,19,21-24,26-28: 18-Begin $2.25-c. 19-Venom-c. 24-Maximum Security 2.50
20-($2.99, 100 pgs.) Spider-Slayer issue; new story and reprints 3.00
25-($2.99) Regular cover; Peter Parker becomes the Green Goblin 3.00
25-($3.99) Holo-foil enhanced cover 4.00
29-Peter is reunited with Mary Jane 2.50
30-Straczynski-s/Campbell-c begin; intro. Ezekiel 6.00
31-35: Battles Morlun 4.00
36-Black cover; aftermath of the Sept. 11 tragedy in New York 10.00
37-49: 39-'Nuff Said issue 42-Dr. Strange app. 43-45-Doctor Octopus app. 46-48-Cho-c 2.50
50-Peter and MJ reunite; Captain America & Dr. Doom app.; Campbell-c 3.00
51-58: 51,52-Campbell-c. 55,56-Avery scripts. 57,58-Avengers, FF, Cyclops app. 2.50
(After #58 [Nov, 2003] numbering reverts back to original Vol. 1 with #500, Dec, 2003)
500-($3.50) J. Scott Campbell-c; Romita Jr. & Sr.-a; Uncle Ben app. 3.50
501-524: 501-Harris-c. 503-504-Loki app. 506-508-Ezekiel app. 509-514-Sins Past; intro. Gabriel and Sarah Osborn; Deodato-a. 519-Moves into Avengers HQ. 521-Begin $2.50-c 524-Harris-c 2.50
525,526-Evolve or Die x-over. 525-David-s. 526-Hudlin-s; Spider-Man loses eye 4.00
525-528-2nd printings with variant-c. 525-Ben Reilly costume. 526-Six-Armed Spidey. 527-Spider-Man 2099. 528-Spider-Ham 5.00
527,528: Evolve or Die pt.9, 12 2.50
529-Debut of red and gold costume; Garney-a 10.00
529-2nd printing 5.00
529-3rd printing with Wieringo-c 3.00
530,531-Titanium Man app.; Kirkham-a. 531-Begin $2.99-c 6.00
532-538-Civil War tie-in. 538-Aunt May shot 5.00
539-543-Back in Black. 539-Peter wears the black costume 3.00
544-($3.99) "One More Day" pt. 1; Quesada-a/Straczynski-s 4.00
545-(12/08, $3.99) "One More Day" pt. 4; Quesada-a/Straczynski-s, Peter & MJ's marriage un-done; r/wedding from ASM Annual #21; 2 covers by Quesada and Djurdjevic 4.00
546-($3.99) Brand New Day begins; McNiven-a; Deodato, Winslade, Land, Romita Jr.-a; 1st app. Mr. Negative 5.00
546-Variant-c by Bryan Hitch 8.00

GD VG FN VF VF/NM NM-
2.0 4.0 6.0 8.0 9.0 9.2

546-Second printing with new McNiven-c of Peter Parker 4.00
547-567: 547,548-McNiven-a. 549-551-Larroca-a. 550-Intro. Menace. 555-557-Bachalo-a. 559-Intro. Screwball. 560,561-MJ app. 565-New Kraven intro. 566,567-Spidey in Daredevil costume 3.00
568-($3.99) Romita Jr.-a begins; two covers by Romita Jr. and Alex Ross 6.00
568-Variant-c by John Romita Sr. 20.00
568-2nd printing with Romita Jr. Anti-Venom costume cover 4.00
569-Debut of Anti-Venom; Norman Osborn and Thunderbolts app.;Romita Jr.-c 3.00
569-Variant Venom-c by Granov 5.00
570-572-Two covers on each 3.00
573-($3.99) New Ways to Die conclusion; Spidey meets Stephen Colbert back-up; Ollife-a; two covers by Romita Jr. and Maguire 5.00
573-Variant cover with Stephen Colbert; cover swipe of AF #15 by Quesada 10.00
574-582: 577-Punisher app. 3.00
583-($3.99) Spidey meets Obama back-up story; regular Romita Sr. "Cougars" cover 8.00
583-($3.99) Obama variant-c with Spidey on left; Spidey meets Obama back-up story 40.00
583-($3.99) Second printing Obama variant-c with Spidey on right and yellow bkgrd 8.00
583-($3.99) 3rd-5th printings Obama variant-c: 3rd-Blue bkgrd w/flag. 4th-White bkgrd w/flag. 5th-Lincoln Memorial bkgrd 5.00
584-587, 589-599: 585-Menace ID revealed. 590,591-Fantastic Four app. 594-Aunt May engaged. 595-599-American Son; Osborn Avengers app. app. 3.00
588-($3.99) Conclusion to "Character Assassination"; Romita Jr.-a 4.00
600-(9/09, $4.99) Aunt May's wedding; Romita Jr.-a; Doc Octopus, FF app.; Mary Jane cameo; back-up story by Stan Lee; back-up with Doran-a; 2 covers by Romita Jr. & Ross 5.00
600-Variant covers by Romita Sr. and Quesada 10.00
601-604,606-611,613-616,618-621,623,624: 601-Back-up w/Quesada-a. 606,607-Black Cat app.; Campbell-c. 611-Deadpool-c/app. 612-The Gauntlet begins; Waid-s. 615,616-Sandman app. 621-Black Cat app. 624-Peter Parker fired 3.00
605,612,617,622-($3.99): 605-Mayhew-c. 613-Rhino back-up story. 617-New Rhino. 622-Bianchi-c; Morbius app. 4.00
1999, 2000 Annual (6/99, '00, $3.50) 1999-Buscema-a 3.50
2001 Annual ($2.99) Follows Peter Parker: S-M #29; last Mackie-s 3.00
Annual 1 (2008, $3.99) McKone-a; secret of Jackpot revealed; death of Jackpot 4.00
Annual 36 (9/09, $3.99) Debut of Raptor; Olliffe-a 4.00
Collected Edition #30-32 ($3.95) reprints #30-32 w/cover #30 4.00
... 500 Covers HC (2004, $49.99) reprints covers for #1-500 & Annuals; yearly re-caps 50.00
... Omnibus HC (2007, $99.99, dustjacket) r/Amazing Fantasy #15, Amazing Spider-Man #1-38, Annual #1,2, Strange Tales Annual #2 & Fantastic Four Annual #1; letter pages, bonus art, intro. by Stan Lee; bios, essays, Marvel Tales cover gallery 100.00
Spider-Man: Brand New Day - Extra!! #1 (9/08, $3.99) short stories; Bachalo,Olliffe-a 4.00
Spider-Man: Brand New Day Yearbook #1 (2008, $4.99) plot synopses; profile pages 5.00
...: Swing Shift Director's Cut (2008, $3.99) story from 2007 FCBD; Brand New Day info 4.00
...: The Short Halloween (7/09, $3.99) Bill Hader & Seth Meyers-s/Maguire-a 4.00
...Vol. 1: Coming Home (2001, $15.95) r/#30-35; J. Scott Campbell-c 16.00
...Vol. 2: Revelations (2002, $8.99) r/#36-39; Kaare Andrews-c 9.00
...Vol. 3: Until the Stars Turn Cold (2002, $12.99) r/#40-45; Romita Jr.-c 13.00
...Vol. 4: The Life and Death of Spiders (2003, $11.99) r/#46-50; Campbell-c 12.00
...Vol. 5: Unintended Consequences (2003, $12.99) r/#51-56; Dodson-c 13.00
...Vol. 6: Happy Birthday (2003, $12.99) r/#57,58,500-502 13.00
...Vol. 7: The Book of Ezekiel (2004, $12.99) r/#503-508; Romita Jr.-c 13.00
...Vol. 8: Sins Past (2005, $12.99) r/#509-514; cover sketch gallery 13.00
...Vol. 9: Skin Deep (2005, $9.99) r/#515-518 10.00
...Vol. 10: New Avengers (2005, $14.99) r/#519-524 15.00
Brand New Day #1-3 (11/08-1/09, $3.99) reprints #546-551 4.00
Civil War: Amazing Spider-Man TPB (2007, $17.99) r/#532-538; variant covers 18.00

AMAZING SPIDER-MAN EXTRA! (Continued from Spider-Man: Brand New Day - Extra!! #1)
Marvel Comics: No. 2, Mar, 2009 - No. 3, May, 2009 ($3.99)

2,3: 2-Anti-Venom app.; Bachalo-a. 3-Ana Kraven app.; Jimenez-a 4.00

AMAZING SPIDER-MAN FAMILY (Also see Spider-Man Family)
Marvel Comics: Oct, 2008 - No. 8, Sept, 2009 ($4.99, anthology)

1-8-New tales and reprints. 1-Includes r/ASM #300; Granov-c. 2-Deodato-c. 5-Spider-Girl new story. 6-Origin of Jackpot 5.00

AMAZING SPIDER-MAN FAMILY PRESENTS: ANTI-VENOM - NEW WAYS TO LIVE
Marvel Comics: Nov, 2009 - No. 3, Feb, 2010 ($3.99, limited series)

1-3-Wells-s/Siqueira-a; Punisher app. 4.00

AMAZING WILLIE MAYS, THE
Famous Funnies Publ.: No date (Sept, 1954)

nn 81 162 243 518 884 1250

AMAZING WORLD OF DC COMICS
DC Comics: Jul, 1974 - No. 17, 1978 ($1.50, B&W, mail-order DC Pro-zine)

1-Kubert interview; unpublished Kirby-a; Infantino-c 7 14 21 47 76 105

Amazons Attack #6 © DC

American Flagg Definitive Collection Vol. 1 © Howard Chaykin

American Splendor #1 © Harvey Pekar & DC

GD VG FN VF VF/NM NM-
2.0 4.0 6.0 8.0 9.0 9.2

2-4: 3-Julie Schwartz profile. 4-Batman; Robinson-c 5 10 15 32 51 70
5-Sheldon Mayer 4 8 12 28 44 60
6,8,13: 6-Joe Orlando; EC-r; Wrightson pin-up. 8-Infantino; Batman-r from Pop Tart giveaway. 13-Humor; Aragonés-c; Wood/Ditko-a; photos from serials of Superman, Batman, Captain Marvel 4 8 12 22 34 45
7,10-12: 7-Superman; r/1955 Pep comic giveaway. 10-Behind the scenes at DC; Showcase article. 11-Super-Villains; unpubl. Secret Society of S.V. story. 12-Legion; Grell-c/interview; 4 8 12 23 36 48
9-Legion of Super-Heroes; lengthy bios and history; Cockrum-c 7 14 21 49 80 110
14-Justice League 4 8 12 24 37 50
15-Wonder Woman; Nasser-c 5 10 15 30 48 65
16-Golden Age heroes 4 8 12 28 44 60
17-Shazam; G.A., 70s, TV and Fawcett heroes 4 8 12 24 37 50
Special 1 (Digest size) 3 6 9 20 30 40

AMAZING WORLD OF SUPERMAN (See Superman)

AMAZING X-MEN
Marvel Comics: Mar, 1995 - No. 4, July, 1995 ($1.95, limited series)
1-Age of Apocalypse; Andy Kubert-c/a 3.50
2-4 2.50

AMAZON
Comico: Mar, 1989 - No. 3, May, 1989 ($1.95, limited series)
1-3: Ecological theme; Steven Seagle-s/Tim Sale-a 2.50
1-3-(Dark Horse, 3/09 - No. 3, 5/09, $3.50) recolored reprint with creator interviews 3.50

AMAZON (Also see Marvel Versus DC #3 & DC Versus Marvel #4)
DC Comics (Amalgam): Apr, 1996 ($1.95, one-shot)
1-John Byrne-c/a/scripts 2.50

AMAZON ATTACK 3-D
The 3-D Zone: Sept, 1990 ($3.95, 28 pgs.)
1-Chaykin-a 6.00

AMAZONS ATTACK (See Wonder Woman #8 - 2006 series)
DC Comics: Jun, 2007 - No. 6, Late Oct, 2007 ($2.99, limited series)
1-6-Queen Hippolyta and Amazons attacks Wash., DC; Pfeifer-s/Woods-a 3.00

AMAZON WOMAN (1st Series)
FantaCo: Summer, 1994 - No. 2, Fall, 1994 ($2.95, B&W, limited series, mature)
1,2: Tom Simonton-c/a/scripts 3.00

AMAZON WOMAN (2nd Series)
FantaCo: Feb, 1996 - No. 4, May, 1996 ($2.95, B&W, limited series, mature)
1-4: Tom Simonton-a/scripts 3.00
...: Invaders of Terror ('96, $5.95) Simonton-a/s 6.00

AMBUSH (See Zane Grey, Four Color 314)

AMBUSH BUG (Also see Son of...)
DC Comics: June, 1985 - No. 4, Sept, 1985 (75¢, limited series)
1-4: Giffen-c/a in all 3.00
Nothing Special 1 (9/92, $2.50, 68pg.)-Giffen-c/a 3.00
Stocking Stuffer (2/86, $1.25)-Giffen-c/a 3.00

AMBUSH BUG: YEAR NONE
DC Comics: Sept, 2008 - No. 5, Jan, 2009; No. 7, Dec, 2009 ($2.99, limited series, no #6)
1-5,7-Giffen-s/a; Jonni DC app. 4-Conner-c. 7-Baltazar & Franco-a; Giffen-a 3.00

AMERICA AT WAR - THE BEST OF DC WAR COMICS (See Fireside Book Series)

AMERICA IN ACTION
Dell (Imp. Publ. Co.)/ Mayflower House Publ.: 1942; Winter, 1945 (36 pgs.)
1942-Dell-(68 pgs.) 17 34 51 98 154 210
1-(1945)-Has 3 adaptations from American history; Kiefer, Schrotter & Webb-a 14 28 42 76 108 140

AMERICAN, THE
Dark Horse Comics: July, 1987 - No. 8, 1989 ($1.50/$1.75, B&W)
1-8: ($1.50) 2.50
Collection ($5.95, B&W)-Reprints 6.00
Special 1 (1990, $2.25, B&W) 2.50

AMERICAN AIR FORCES, THE (See A-1 Comics)
William H. Wise(Flying Cadet Publ. Co./Hasan(No.1)/Life's Romances/ Magazine Ent. No. 5 on): Sept-Oct, 1944-No. 4, 1945; No. 5, 1951-No. 12, 1954
1-Article by Zack Mosley, creator of Smilin' Jack; German war-c 22 44 66 132 216 300

GD VG FN VF VF/NM NM-
2.0 4.0 6.0 8.0 9.0 9.2

2-Classic-Japan war-c 43 86 129 271 461 650
3,4-Japan war-c 15 30 45 88 137 185
NOTE: *All part comic, part magazine. Art by* ***Whitney, Chas. Quinlan, H. C. Kiefer,*** *and* ***Tony Dipreta.***
5(A-1 45)(Formerly Jet Powers), 6(A-1 54), 7(A-1 58), 8(A-1 65), 9(A-1 67), 10(A-1 74), 11(A-1 79), 12(A-1 91) 9 18 27 50 65 80
NOTE: ***Powell*** *c/a-5-12.*

AMERICAN CENTURY
DC Comics (Vertigo): May, 2001 - No. 27, Oct, 2003 ($2.50/$2.75)
1-Chaykin-s/painted-c; Tischman-a 4.00
2-27: 5-New story arc begins. 10-16,22-27-Orbik-c. 17-21-Silke-c. 18-$2.75-c begins 2.75
Hollywood Babylon (2002, $12.95, TPB) r/#5-9; w/sketch-to-art pages 13.00
Scars & Stripes (2001, $8.95, TPB) r/#1-4; Tischman intro. 9.00

AMERICAN DREAM (From the M2 Avengers)
Marvel Comics: Jul, 2008 - No. 5, Sept, 2008 ($2.99, limited series)
1-5-DeFalco-s/Nauck-a 3.00

AMERICAN FLAGG! (See First Comics Graphic Novel 3,9,12,21 & Howard Chaykin's..)
First Comics: Oct, 1983 - No. 50, Mar, 1988
1,21-27: 1-Chaykin-c/a begins. 21-27-Alan Moore scripts 4.00
2-20,28-49: 31-Origin Bob Violence 3.00
50-Last issue 4.00
Special 1 (11/86)-Introduces Chaykin's Time² 4.00
...: Hard Times TPB (6/85, $11.95) r/#1-7; intro. by Michael Moorcock; bonus materials 12.00
...: Definitive Collection Volume 1 HC (2008, $49.99) r/#1-14 and material from the...: Hard Times TPB; intro by Michael Chabon; afterword by Jim Lee 50.00

AMERICAN FREAK: A TALE OF THE UN-MEN
DC Comics (Vertigo): Feb, 1994 - No. 5, Jun, 1994 ($1.95, mini-series, mature)
1-5 2.50

AMERICAN GRAPHICS
Henry Stewart: No. 1, 1954; No. 2, 1957 (25¢)
1-The Maid of the Mist, The Last of the Eries (Indian Legends of Niagara) (sold at Niagara Falls) 11 22 33 60 83 105
2-Victory at Niagara & Laura Secord (Heroine of the War of 1812) 8 16 24 40 50 60

AMERICAN INDIAN, THE (See Picture Progress)

AMERICAN LIBRARY
David McKay Publ.: 1943 - No. 6, 1944 (15¢, 68 pgs., B&W, text & pictures)
nn (#1)-Thirty Seconds Over Tokyo (movie) 39 78 117 231 378 525
nn (#2)-Guadalcanal Diary; painted-c (only 10¢) 28 56 84 165 270 375
3-6: 3-Look to the Mountain. 4-Case of the Crooked Candle (Perry Mason). 5-Duel in the Sun. 6-Wingate's Raiders 15 30 45 88 137 185

AMERICAN: LOST IN AMERICA, THE
Dark Horse Comics: July, 1992 - No. 4, Oct, 1992 ($2.50, limited series)
1-4: 1-Dorman painted-c. 2-Phillips painted-c. 3-Mignola-c. 4-Jim Lee-c 2.50

AMERICAN SPLENDOR: (Series of titles)
Dark Horse Comics: Aug, 1996 - Present (B&W, all one-shots)
--**COMIC-CON COMICS** (8/96) 1-H. Pekar script. --**MUSIC COMICS** (11/97) nn-H. Pekar-s/ Sacco-a; r/Village Voice jazz strips. --**ODDS AND ENDS** (12/97) 1-Pekar-s. --**ON THE JOB** (5/97) 1-Pekar-s. --**A STEP OUT OF THE NEST** (8/94) 1-Pekar-s. --**TERMINAL** (9/99) 1-Pekar-s. --**TRANSATLANTIC** (7/98) 1-"American Splendour" on cover; Pekar-s 3.00
--**A PORTRAIT OF THE AUTHOR IN HIS DECLINING YEARS** (4/01, $3.99) 1-Photo-c. --**BEDTIME STORIES** (6/00, $3.95) 4.00

AMERICAN SPLENDOR
DC Comics: Nov, 2006 - No. 4, Feb, 2007 ($2.99, B&W)
1-4-Pekar-s/art by Haspiel and various. 1-Fabry-c 3.00
...: Another Day TPB (2007, $14.99) r/#1-4 15.00

AMERICAN SPLENDOR (Volume 2)
DC Comics (Vertigo): Jun, 2008 - No. 4, Sept, 2008 ($2.99, B&W)
1-4-Pekar-s/art by Haspiel and various. 1-Bond-c. 3-Cooke-c 3.00
...: Another Dollar TPB (2009, $14.99) r/#1-4 15.00

AMERICAN SPLENDOR: UNSUNG HERO
Dark Horse Comics: Aug, 2002 - No. 3, Oct, 2002 ($3.99, B&W, limited series)
1-3-Pekar script/Collier-a; biography of Robert McNeill 4.00
TPB (8/03, $11.95) r/#1-3 12.00

AMERICAN SPLENDOR: WINDFALL
Dark Horse Comics: Sept, 1995 - No. 2, Oct,1995 ($3.95, B&W, limited series)
1,2-Pekar script 4.00

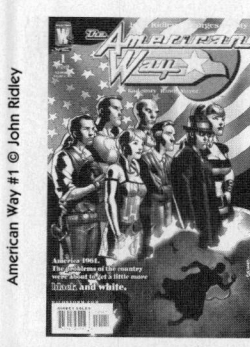

American Way #1 © John Ridley

America's Best Comics #24 © STD

Amory Wars #1 © Evil Ink

	GD 2.0	VG 4.0	FN 6.0	VF 8.0	VF/NM 9.0	NM- 9.2

AMERICAN TAIL: FIEVEL GOES WEST, AN
Marvel Comics: Early Jan, 1992 - No. 3, Early Feb, 1992 ($1.00, limited series)

1-3-Adapts Universal animated movie; Wildman-a 3.00
1-($2.95-c, 69 pgs.) Deluxe squarebound edition 5.00

AMERICAN VIRGIN
DC Comics (Vertigo): May, 2006 - No. 23, Mar, 2008 ($2.99)

1-23-Steven Seagle-s/Becky Cloonan-a in most. 1-3-Quitely-c. 4-14-Middleton-c 3.00
...: Head (2006, $9.99, TPB) r/#1-4; interviews with the creators and page development 10.00
...: Going Down (2007, $14.99, TPB) r/#5-9 15.00
...: Wet (2007, $12.99, TPB) r/#10-14 13.00
...: Around the World (Vol. 4) (2008, $17.99, TPB) r/#15-23 18.00

AMERICAN WAY, THE
DC Comics (WildStorm): Apr, 2006 - No. 8, Nov, 2006 ($2.99, limited series)

1-8-John Ridley-s/Georges Jeanty-a/c 3.00
TPB (2007, $19.99) r/series; covers; Jeanty sketch pages 20.00

AMERICA'S BEST COMICS
Nedor/Better/Standard Publications: Feb, 1942; No. 2, Sept, 1942 - No. 31, July, 1949 (New logo with #9)

1-The Woman in Red, Black Terror, Captain Future, Doc Strange, The Liberator, & Don Davis, Secret Ace begin 300 600 900 2010 3505 5000
2-Origin The American Eagle; The Woman in Red ends 110 220 330 704 1202 1700
3-Pyroman begins (11/42, 1st app.; also see Startling Comics #18, 12/42) 84 168 252 538 919 1300
4-6: 5-Last Capt. Future (not in #4); Lone Eagle app. 6-American Crusader app. 64 128 192 406 696 985
7-Hitler, Mussolini & Hirohito-c 135 270 405 864 1482 2100
8-Last Liberator 61 122 183 390 670 950
9-The Fighting Yank begins; The Ghost app. 68 136 204 435 743 1050
10-Flag-c 57 114 171 362 619 875
11-Hirohito & Tojo-c. (10/44) 79 158 237 502 864 1225
12-17,19-21: 14-American Eagle ends; Doc Strange vs. Hitler story. 21-Infinity-c 54 108 162 347 594 840
18-Classic-c 73 146 219 467 796 1125
22-Capt. Future app. 47 94 141 296 498 700
23-Miss Masque begins; last Doc Strange 54 108 162 347 594 840
24-Miss Masque bondage-c 54 108 162 336 573 810
25-Last Fighting Yank; Sea Eagle app. 41 82 123 249 417 585
26-31: 26-The Phantom Detective & The Silver Knight app.; Frazetta text illo & some panels in Miss Masque. 27,28-Commando Cubs. 27-Doc Strange. 28-Tuska Black Terror. 29-Last Pyroman 40 80 120 245 408 570

NOTE: *American Eagle not in 3, 8, 9, 13. Fighting Yank not in 10, 12. Liberator not in 2, 6, 7. Pyroman not in 9, 11, 14-16, 23, 25-27.* ***Schomburg (Xela)*** *c-5, 7-31. Bondage c-18, 24.*

AMERICA'S BEST COMICS
America's Best Comics: 1999 - 2008

... Preview (1999, Wizard magazine supplement) - Previews Tom Strong, Top Ten, Promethea, Tomorrow Stories 2.25
... Primer (2008, $4.99, TPB) r/Tom Strong #1, Tom Strong's Terrific Tales, Top Ten #1, Promethea #1, Tomorrow Stories #1,6 5.00
... Sketchbook (2002, $5.95, square-bound)-Design sketches by Sprouse, Ross, Adams, Nowlan, Ha and others 6.00
Special 1 (2/01, $6.95)-Short stories of Alan Moore's characters; art by various; Ross-c 7.00
TPB (2004, $17.95) Reprints short stories and sketch pages from ABC titles 18.00

AMERICA'S BEST TV COMICS (TV)
American Broadcasting Co. (Prod. by Marvel Comics): 1967 (25¢, 68 pgs.)

1-Spider-Man, Fantastic Four (by Kirby/Ayers), Casper, King Kong, George of the Jungle, Journey to the Center of the Earth stories (promotes new TV cartoon show) 12 24 36 85 155 225

AMERICA'S BIGGEST COMICS BOOK
William H. Wise: 1944 (196 pgs., one-shot)

1-The Grim Reaper, The Silver Knight, Zudo, the Jungle Boy, Commando Cubs, Thunderhoof app. 39 78 117 240 395 550

AMERICA'S FUNNIEST COMICS
William H. Wise: 1944 - No. 2, 1944 (15¢, 80 pgs.)

nn(#1), 2 30 60 90 177 289 400

AMERICA'S GREATEST COMICS
Fawcett Publications: May?, 1941 - No. 8, Summer, 1943 (15¢, 100 pgs., soft cardboard-c)

1-Bulletman, Spy Smasher, Capt. Marvel, Minute Man & Mr. Scarlet begin; Classic Mac Raboy-c. 1st time that Fawcett's major super-heroes appear together as a group on a cover. Fawcett's 1st squarebound comic 337 674 1011 2359 4130 5900
2 145 290 435 921 1586 2250
3 103 206 309 659 1130 1600
4,5: 4-Commando Yank begins; Golden Arrow, Ibis the Invincible & Spy Smasher cameo in Captain Marvel 76 152 228 486 831 1175
6,7: 7-Balbo the Boy Magician app.; Captain Marvel, Bulletman cameo in Mr. Scarlet 67 134 201 430 733 1035
8-Capt. Marvel Jr. & Golden Arrow app.; Spy Smasher x-over in Capt. Midnight; no Minute Man or Commando Yank 67 134 201 430 733 1035

AMERICA'S SWEETHEART SUNNY (See Sunny, ...)

AMERICA VS. THE JUSTICE SOCIETY
DC Comics: Jan, 1985 - No. 4, Apr, 1985 ($1.00, limited series)

1-Double size; Alcala-a(i) in all 2 3 4 6 8 10
2-4: 3,4-Spectre cameo 1 2 3 5 6 8

AMERICOMICS
Americomics: April, 1983 - No. 6, Mar, 1984 ($2.00, Baxter paper/slick paper)

1-Intro/origin The Shade; Intro. The Slayer, Captain Freedom and The Liberty Corps; Perez-c 5.00
1,2-2nd printings ($2.00) 2.25
2-6: 2-Messenger app. & 1st app. Tara on Jungle Island. 3-New & old Blue Beetle battle. 4-Origin Dragonfly & Shade. 5-Origin Commando D. 6-Origin the Scarlet Scorpion 3.00
Special 1 (8/83, $2.00)-Sentinels of Justice (Blue Beetle, Captain Atom, Nightshade & The Question) 4.50

AMETHYST
DC Comics: Jan, 1985 - No. 16, Aug, 1986 (75¢)

1-16: 8-Fire Jade's i.d. revealed 2.50
Special 1 (10/86, $1.25), 1-4 (11/87 - 2/88)(Limited series) 2.50

AMETHYST, PRINCESS OF GEMWORLD (See Legion of Super-Heroes #298)
DC Comics: May, 1983 - No. 12, Apr, 1984 (Maxi-series)

1-(60¢) 2.50
1,2-(75¢): tested in Austin & Kansas City 3 6 9 20 30 40
2-12, Annual 1(9/84): 5-11-Pérez-c(p) 2.50

AMORY WARS (Based on the Coheed and Cambria album The Second Stage Turbine Blade)
Image Comics: Jun, 2007 - No. 5, Jan, 2008 ($2.99, limited series)

1-5: 1-Claudio Sanchez-s/Gus Vasquez-a 3.00

AMORY WARS II
Image Comics: Jun, 2008 - No. 5, Oct, 2008 ($2.99, limited series)

1-5-Claudio Sanchez-s/Gabriel Guzman-a 3.00

AMY RACECAR COLOR SPECIAL (See Stray Bullets)
El Capitán Books: July, 1997; Oct, 1999 ($2.95/$3.50)

1,2-David Lapham-a/scripts. 2-($3.50) 3.50

ANARCHO DICTATOR OF DEATH (See Comics Novel)

ANARKY (See Batman titles)
DC Comics: May, 1997 - No. 4, Aug, 1997 ($2.50, limited series)

1 3.50
2-4 2.50

ANARKY (See Batman titles)
DC Comics: May, 1999 - No. 8, Dec, 1999 ($2.50)

1-8: 1-JLA app.; Grant-s/Breyfogle-a. 3-Green Lantern app. 7-Day of Judgment; Haunted Tank app. 8-Joker-c/app. 2.50

ANCHORS ANDREWS (The Saltwater Daffy)
St. John Publishing Co.: Jan, 1953 - No. 4, July, 1953 (Anchors the Saltwater... No. 4)

1-Canteen Kate by Matt Baker (9 pgs.) 21 42 63 122 199 275
2-4 9 18 27 52 69 85

ANDY & WOODY (See March of Comics No. 40, 55, 76)

ANDY BURNETT (TV, Disney)
Dell Publishing Co.: Dec, 1957

Four Color 865-Photo-c 8 16 24 58 97 135

ANDY COMICS (Formerly Scream Comics; becomes Ernie Comics)
Current Publications (Ace Magazines): No. 20, June, 1948-No. 21, Aug, 1948

20,21: Archie-type comic 8 16 24 42 54 65

ANDY DEVINE WESTERN
Fawcett Publications: Dec, 1950 - No. 2, 1951

1 48 96 144 298 499 700
2 38 76 114 226 363 500

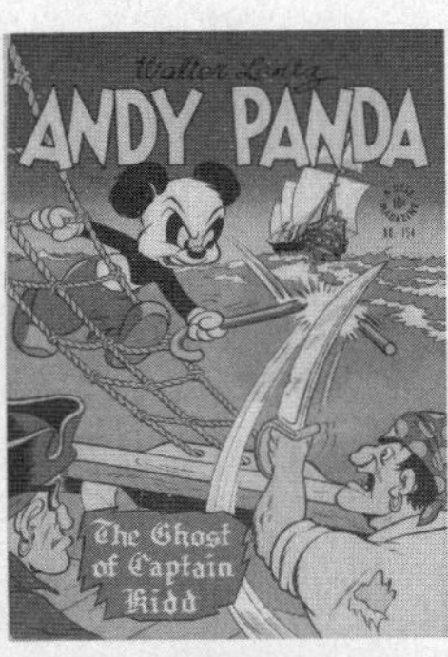

Andy Panda Four Color #154 © W. Lantz

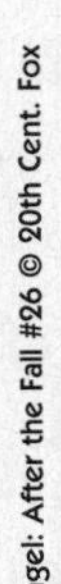
Angel: After the Fall #26 © 20th Cent. Fox

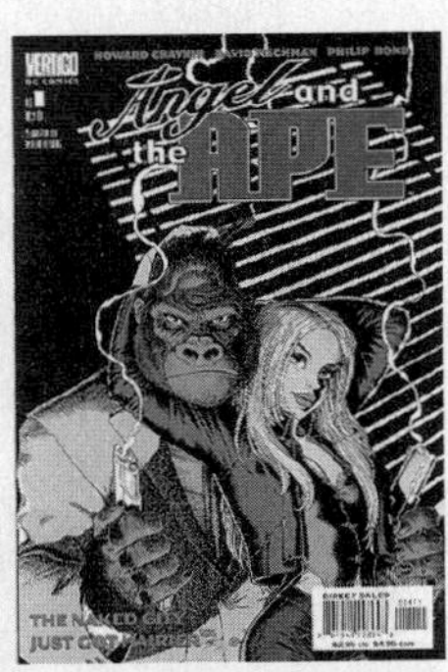

Angel and the Ape (2001 series) #1 © DC

	GD 2.0	VG 4.0	FN 6.0	VF 8.0	VF/NM 9.0	NM- 9.2
ANDY GRIFFITH SHOW, THE (TV)(1st show aired 10/3/60)						
Dell Publishing Co.: #1252, Jan-Mar, 1962; #1341, Apr-Jun, 1962						
Four Color 1252(#1)	35	70	105	266	513	760
Four Color 1341-Photo-c	32	64	96	247	479	710
ANDY HARDY COMICS (See Movie Comics #3 by Fiction House)						
Dell Publishing Co.: April, 1952 - No. 6, Sept-Nov, 1954						
Four Color 389(#1)	5	10	15	34	55	75
Four Color 447,480,515, #5,#6	4	8	12	26	41	55
ANDY PANDA (Also see Crackajack Funnies #39, The Funnies, New Funnies & Walter Lantz...)						
Dell Publishing Co.: 1943 - No. 56, Nov-Jan, 1961-62 (Walter Lantz)						
Four Color 25(#1, 1943)	50	100	150	413	807	1200
Four Color 54(1944)	29	58	87	212	406	600
Four Color 85(1945)	16	32	48	115	220	325
Four Color 130(1946),154,198	11	22	33	80	145	210
Four Color 216,240,258,280,297	8	16	24	58	97	135
Four Color 326,345,358	6	12	18	43	69	95
Four Color 383,409	5	10	15	34	55	75
16(11-1/52-53) - 30	4	8	12	28	44	60
31-56	4	8	12	22	34	45
(See March of Comics #5, 22, 79, & Super Book #4, 15, 27.)						
A-NEXT (See Avengers)						
Marvel Comics: Oct, 1998 - No. 12, Sept, 1999 ($1.99)						
1-Next generation of Avengers; Frenz-a						3.00
2-12: 2-Two covers. 3-Defenders app.						2.50
Spider-Girl Presents Avengers Next Vol. 1: Second Coming (2006, $7.99, digest) r/#1-6						8.00
ANGEL						
Dell Publishing Co.: Aug, 1954 - No. 16, Nov-Jan, 1958-59						
Four Color 576(#1, 8/54)	4	8	12	26	41	55
2(5-7/55) - 16	3	6	9	18	27	35
ANGEL (TV) (Also see Buffy the Vampire Slayer)						
Dark Horse Comics: Nov, 1999 - No. 17, Apr, 2001 ($2.95/$2.99)						
1-17: 1-3,5-7,10-14-Zanier-a. 1-4,7,10-Matsuda & photo-c. 16-Buffy-c/app.						3.00
...: Earthly Possessions TPB (4/01, $9.95) r/#5-7, photo-c						10.00
...: Surrogates TPB (12/00, $9.95) r/#1-3; photo-c						10.00
ANGEL (Buffy the Vampire Slayer)						
Dark Horse Comics: Sept, 2001 - No. 4, May, 2002 ($2.99, limited series)						
1-4-Joss Whedon & Matthews-s/Rubi-a; photo-c and Rubi-c on each						3.00
ANGEL (one-shots) (Buffy the Vampire Slayer)						
IDW Publishing: ($3.99/$7.49)						
...: Connor (8/06, $3.99) Jay Faerber-s/Bob Gill-a; 4 covers + 1 retailer cover						4.00
...: Doyle (7/06, $3.99) Jeff Mariotte-s/David Messina-a; 4 covers + 1 retailer cover						4.00
...: Gunn (5/06, $3.99) Dan Jolley-s/Mark Pennington-a; 4 covers + 2 retailer covers						4.00
...: Illyria (4/06, $3.99) Peter David-s/Nicola Scott-a; 4 covers + 2 retailer covers						4.00
...: Masks (10/06, $7.49) short stories of Angel, Illyria, Cordilia & Lindsay; puppet Angel app.						8.00
...: Vs. Frankenstein (10/09, $3.99) John Byrne-s/a/c						4.00
...: Wesley (6/06, $3.99) Scott Tipton-s/Mike Norton-a; 4 covers + 1 retailer cover						4.00
Spotlight TPB (12/06, $19.99) r/Connor, Doyle, Gunn, Illyria & Wesley one-shots						20.00
ANGELA						
Image Comics (Todd McFarlane Prod.): Dec, 1994 - No. 3, Feb, 1995 ($2.95, lim. series)						
1-Gaiman scripts & Capullo-c/a in all; Spawn app.	1	2	3	5	6	8
2						6.00
3						5.00
Special Edition (1995)-Pirate Spawn-c	3	6	9	14	20	25
Special Edition (1995)-Angela-c	3	6	9	14	20	25
TPB ($9.95, 1995) reprints #1-3 & Special Ed. w/additional pin-ups						10.00
ANGEL: AFTER THE FALL (Buffy the Vampire Slayer) (Follows the last TV episode)						
IDW Publishing: Nov, 2007 - Present ($3.99)						
1-Whedon & Lynch-s; multiple covers						5.00
2-29: Multiple covers on all. 25-Juliet Landau-s						4.00
ANGELA/GLORY: RAGE OF ANGELS (See Glory/Angela: Rage of Angels)						
Image Comics (Todd McFarlane Productions): Mar, 1996 ($2.50, one-shot)						
1-Liefeld-c/Cruz-a(p); Darkchylde preview flip book						4.00
1-Variant-c						4.00
ANGEL: A HOLE IN THE WORLD (Adaptation of the 2-part TV episode)						
IDW Publishing: Dec, 2009 - No. 5 ($3.99, limited series)						
1-3-Fred becomes Illyria; Casagrande-a/c						4.00

	GD 2.0	VG 4.0	FN 6.0	VF 8.0	VF/NM 9.0	NM- 9.2
ANGEL AND THE APE (Meet Angel No. 7) (See Limited Collector's Edition C-34 & Showcase No. 77)						
National Periodical Publications: Nov-Dec, 1968 - No. 6, Sept-Oct, 1969						
1-(11-12/68)-Not Wood-a	5	10	15	30	48	65
2-5-Wood inks in all. 4-Last 12¢ issue	3	6	9	20	30	40
6-Wood inks	4	8	12	22	34	45
ANGEL AND THE APE (2nd Series)						
DC Comics: Mar, 1991 - No. 4, June, 1991 ($1.00, limited series)						
1-4						3.00
ANGEL AND THE APE (3rd Series)						
DC Comics (Vertigo): Oct, 2001 - No. 4, Jan 2002 ($2.95, limited series)						
1-4-Chaykin & Tischman-s/Bond-a/Art Adams-c						3.00
ANGEL: AULD LANG SYNE (Buffy the Vampire Slayer)						
IDW Publishing: Nov, 2006 - No. 5, Mar, 2007 ($3.99, limited series)						
1-5: 1-Three covers plus photo-c; Tipton-s/Messina-a						4.00
ANGEL: BLOOD & TRENCHES (Buffy the Vampire Slayer)						
IDW Publishing: Mar, 2009 - No. 4, June, 2009 ($3.99, B&W&Red, limited series)						
1-4-Angel in World War II Europe; John Byrne-s/a/c						4.00
ANGEL LOVE						
DC Comics: Aug, 1986 - No. 8, Mar, 1987 (75¢, limited series)						
1-8, Special 1 (1987, $1.25, 52 pgs.)						2.50
ANGEL: NOT FADE AWAY (Buffy the Vampire Slayer)						
IDW Publishing: May, 2009 - No. 3, July, 2009 ($3.99, limited series)						
1-3-Adaptation of TV show's final episodes; Mooney-a						4.00
ANGEL OF LIGHT, THE (See The Crusaders)						
ANGEL: OLD FRIENDS (Buffy the Vampire Slayer)						
IDW Publishing: Nov, 2005 - No. 5, Mar, 2006 ($3.99, limited series)						
1-5: Four covers plus photo-c on each; Mariotte-s/Messina-a; Gunn, Spike and Illyria app.						4.00
... Cover Gallery (6/06, $3.99) gallery of variant covers for the series						4.00
... Cover Gallery (12/06, $3.99) gallery of variant covers; preview of Angel: Auld Lang Syne						4.00
TPB (2006, $19.99) r/series; gallery of Messina covers						20.00
ANGEL: ONLY HUMAN (Buffy the Vampire Slayer)						
IDW Publishing: Aug, 2009 - No. 5, Dec, 2009 ($3.99, limited series)						
1-5-Lobdell-s/Messina-a; covers by Messina and Dave Dorman						4.00
ANGEL: REVELATIONS (X-Men character)						
Marvel Comics: July, 2008 - No. 5, Nov, 2008 ($3.99, limited series)						
1-5-Origin from childhood re-told; Adam Pollina-a/Aquirre-Sacasa-s						4.00
ANGEL: SMILE TIME (Buffy the Vampire Slayer)						
IDW Publishing: Dec, 2008 - No. 3, Apr, 2009 ($3.99, limited series)						
1-3-Adaptation of TV episode; Messina-a; Messina and photo covers for each						4.00
ANGEL: THE CURSE (Buffy the Vampire Slayer)						
IDW Publishing: June, 2005 - No. 5, Oct, 2005 ($3.99, limited series)						
1-5-Four covers on each; Mariotte-s/Messina-a						4.00
TPB (1/06, $19.99) r/#1-5; cover gallery of Messina covers						20.00
ANGELTOWN						
DC Comics (Vertigo): Jan, 2005 - No. 5, May, 2005 ($2.95, limited series)						
1-5-Gary Phillips-s/Shawn Martinbrough-a						3.00
ANGELUS						
Image Comics (Top Cow): Dec, 2007; Dec, 2009 - Present ($2.99)						
... Pilot Season 1-(12/07) Sejic-a/c; Edington-s; origin re-told						3.00
1,2-Marz-s/Sejic-a; multiple covers on each						3.00
ANGRY CHRIST COMIX (See Cry For Dawn)						
ANIMA						
DC Comics: Mar, 1994 - No. 15, July, 1995 ($1.75/$1.95/$2.25)						
1-7,0,8-15: 7-(9/94)-Begin $1.95-c; Zero Hour x-over						2.50
ANIMAL ADVENTURES						
Timor Publications/Accepted Publ. (reprints): Dec, 1953 - No. 3, May?, 1954						
1-Funny animal	8	16	24	40	50	60
2,3: 2-Featuring Soopermutt (2/54)	6	12	18	28	34	40
1-3 (reprints, nd)	3	6	8	11	13	15
ANIMAL ANTICS						
DC Comics: Feb, 1946						
nn - Ashcan comic, not distributed to newsstands, only for in-house use. Cover art is Star						

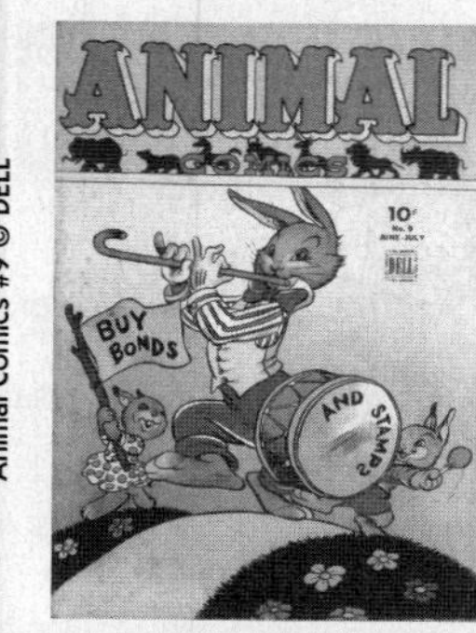

Animal Comics #9 © DELL

Animaniacs #38 © WB

Anita Blake - Vampire Hunter: Guilty Pleasures #7 © Laurell K. Hamilton

GD VG FN VF VF/NM NM-
2.0 4.0 6.0 8.0 9.0 9.2

Spangled Comics #49 and interior is Boy Commandos #12 ; a cover sold for $600 in 2006.

ANIMAL ANTICS (Movietown... No. 24 on)
National Periodical Publ: Mar-Apr, 1946 - No. 23, Nov-Dec, 1949 (All 52 pgs.?)
1-Raccoon Kids begins by Otto Feuer; many-c by Grossman; Seaman Sy Wheeler by Kelly in some issues; Grossman-a in most issues 45 90 135 279 465 650
2 25 50 75 145 233 320
3-10: 10-Post-c/a 16 32 48 92 144 195
11-23: 14,15,18,19-Post-a 12 24 36 67 94 120

ANIMAL COMICS
Dell Publishing Co.: Dec-Jan, 1941-42 - No. 30, Dec-Jan, 1947-48
1-1st Pogo app. by Walt Kelly (Dan Noonan art in most issues) 100 200 300 635 1093 1550
2-Uncle Wiggily begins 52 104 156 322 549 775
3,5 28 56 84 202 394 585
4,6,7-No Pogo 16 32 48 115 220 325
8-10 19 38 57 133 259 385
11-15 13 26 39 90 165 240
16-20 9 18 27 63 107 150
21-30: 24-30- "Jigger" by John Stanley 8 16 24 52 86 120
NOTE: *Dan Noonan a-18-30. Gollub art in most later issues; c-29, 30. Kelly c-7-26, part #27-30.*

ANIMAL CRACKERS (Also see Adventures of Patoruzu)
Green Publ. Co./Norlen/Fox Feat.(Hero Books): 1946; No. 31, July, 1950; No. 9, 1959
1-Super Cat begins (1st app.) 19 38 57 111 176 240
2 10 20 30 58 79 100
31(Fox)-Formerly My Love Secret 8 16 24 42 54 65
9(1959-Norlen)-Infinity-c 5 10 14 20 24 28
nn, nd ('50s), no publ.; infinity-c 5 10 14 20 24 28

ANIMAL FABLES
E. C. Comics (Fables Publ. Co.): July-Aug, 1946 - No. 7, Nov-Dec, 1947
1-Freddy Firefly (clone of Human Torch), Korky Kangaroo, Petey Pig, Danny Demon begin 52 104 156 322 549 775
2-Aesop Fables begin 32 64 96 192 314 435
3-6 27 54 81 160 263 365
7-Origin Moon Girl 68 136 204 435 743 1050

ANIMAL FAIR (Fawcett's...)
Fawcett Publications: Mar, 1946 - No. 11, Feb, 1947
1 28 56 84 165 270 375
2 14 28 42 82 121 160
3-6 12 24 36 67 94 120
7-11 10 20 30 54 72 90

ANIMAL FUN
Premier Magazines: 1953 (25¢, came w/glasses)
1-(3-D)-Ziggy Pig, Silly Seal, Billy & Buggy Bear 35 70 105 208 334 470

ANIMAL MAN (See Action Comics #552, 553, DC Comics Presents #77, 78, Last Days of Animal Man, Secret Origins #39, Strange Adventures #180 & Wonder Woman #267, 268)
DC Comics (Vertigo imprint #57 on): Sept, 1988 - No. 89, Nov, 1995 ($1.25/$1.50/$1.75/$1.95/$2.25, mature)
1-Grant Morrison scripts begin, ends #26 2 4 6 8 10 12
2-10: 2-Superman cameo. 6-Invasion tie-in. 9-Manhunter-c/story. 10-Psycho Pirate app. 1 2 3 4 5 7
11-49,51-55,57-89: 23,24-Psycho Pirate app. 24-Arkham Asylum story; Bizarro Superman app. 25-Inferior Five app. 26-Morrison apps. in story; part photo-c (of Morrison?) 3.00
50-($2.95, 52 pgs.)-Last issue w/Veitch scripts 5.00
56-($3.50, 68 pgs.) 5.00
Annual 1 (1993, $3.95, 68 pgs.)-Bolland-c; Children's Crusade Pt. 3 6.00
...: Deus Ex Machina TPB (2003, $19.95) r/#18-26; Morrison-s; new Bolland-c 20.00
...: Origin of the Species TPB (2002, $19.95) r/#10-17 & Secret Origins #39 20.00
NOTE: *Bolland c-1-63. 71-Sutton-a(i)*

ANIMAL MYSTIC (See Dark One...)
Cry For Dawn/Sirius: 1993 - No. 4, 1995 ($2.95?/$3.50, B&W)
1 3 6 9 14 19 24
1-Alternate 4 8 12 22 34 45
1-2nd printing 5.00
2 2 4 6 10 14 18
2,3-2nd prints (Sirius) 3.50
3 ,4: 4-Color poster insert, Linsner-s 1 2 3 5 7 9
TPB ($14.95) r/series 18.00

ANIMAL MYSTIC WATER WARS
Sirius: 1996 - No. 6 ($2.95, limited series)
1-6-Dark One-c/a/scripts 5.00

ANIMAL WORLD, THE (Movie)
Dell Publishing Co.: No. 713, Aug, 1956
Four Color 713 4 8 12 26 41 55

ANIMANIACS (TV)
DC Comics: May, 1995 - No. 59, Apr, 2000 ($1.50/$1.75/$1.95/$1.99)
1 1 2 3 4 5 7
2-20: 13-Manga issue. 19-X-Files parody; Miran Kim-c; Adlard-a (4 pgs.) 4.00
21-59: 26-E.C. parody-c. 34-Xena parody. 43-Pinky & the Brain take over 3.00
A Christmas Special (12/94, $1.50, "1" on-c) 3.00

ANIMATED COMICS
E. C. Comics: No date given (Summer, 1947?)
1 (Rare) 81 162 243 518 884 1250

ANIMATED FUNNY COMIC TUNES (See Funny Tunes)

ANIMATED MOVIE-TUNES (Movie Tunes No. 3)
Margood Publishing Corp. (Timely): Fall, 1945 - No. 2, Sum, 1946
1,2-Super Rabbit, Ziggy Pig & Silly Seal 34 68 102 199 325 450

ANIMAX
Marvel Comics (Star Comics): Dec, 1986 - No. 4, June, 1987
1-4: Based on toys; Simonson-a 3.00

ANITA BLAKE: VAMPIRE HUNTER GUILTY PLEASURES
Marvel Comics (Dabel Brothers): Dec, 2006 - No. 12, Aug, 2008 ($2.99)
1-Laurell K. Hamilton-s/Brett Booth-a; blue cover 6.00
1-Variant-c by Greg Horn 20.00
1-Sketch cover 25.00
1-2nd printing with red cover 3.00
2-Two covers 5.00
3-12 3.00
...: Handbook (2007, $3.99) profile pages of characters; glossary 4.00
... Volume One HC (6/07, $19.99, dust jacket) r/#1-6; cover gallery 20.00

ANITA BLAKE: VAMPIRE HUNTER THE FIRST DEATH, (LAURELL K. HAMILTON'S...)
Marvel Comics (Dabel Brothers): July, 2007 - No. 2, Dec, 2007 ($3.99)
1,2-Laurell K. Hamilton & Jonathon Green-s/Wellington Alves-a. 2-Marvel Zombie var-c 4.00
... HC (2008, $19.99, dust jacket) r/#1,2 & Guilty Pleasures Handbook 20.00

ANITA BLAKE, VAMPIRE HUNTER: THE LAUGHING CORPSE
Marvel Comics: Dec, 2008 - No. 5, Apr, 2009 ($3.99)
... - Book One (12/08 - No. 5, 4/09) 1-5-Laurell K. Hamilton-s/Ron Lim-a/c 4.00
... - Necromancer 1-5 (6/09 - No. 5, 11/09, $3.99) Lim-a/c 4.00
Anita Blake (Executioner on-c) #11-15 (12/09 - No. 15, 5/10) numbering continued; Lim-a 4.00

ANNE RICE'S INTERVIEW WITH THE VAMPIRE
Innovation Books: 1991 - No. 12, Jan, 1994 ($2.50, limited series)
1-12: Adapts novel; Moeller-a 3.00

ANNE RICE'S THE MASTER OF RAMPLING GATE
Innovation Books: 1991 ($6.95, one-shot)
1-Bolton painted-c; Colleen Doran painted-a 7.00

ANNE RICE'S THE MUMMY OR RAMSES THE DAMNED
Millennium Publications: Oct, 1990 - No. 12, Feb, 1992 ($2.50, limited series)
1-12: Adapts novel; Mooney-p in all 3.00

ANNE RICE'S THE WITCHING HOUR
Millennium Publ./Comico: 1992 - No. 13, Jan, 1993 ($2.50, limited series)
1-13 3.00

ANNETTE (Disney, TV)
Dell Publishing Co.: No. 905, May, 1958; No. 1100, May, 1960 (Mickey Mouse Club)
Four Color 905-Annette Funicello photo-c 24 48 72 175 338 500
Four Color 1100-...'s Life Story (Movie); A. Funicello photo-c 19 38 57 139 270 400

ANNEX (See Amazing Spider-Man Annual #27 for 1st app.)
Marvel Comics: Aug, 1994 - No. 4, Nov, 1994 ($1.75)
1-4: 1,4-Spider-Man app. 2.50

ANNIE
Marvel Comics Group: Oct, 1982 - No. 2, Nov, 1982 (60¢)

Annie Oakley #8 © DELL

Annihilation: Heralds of Galactus #2 © MAR

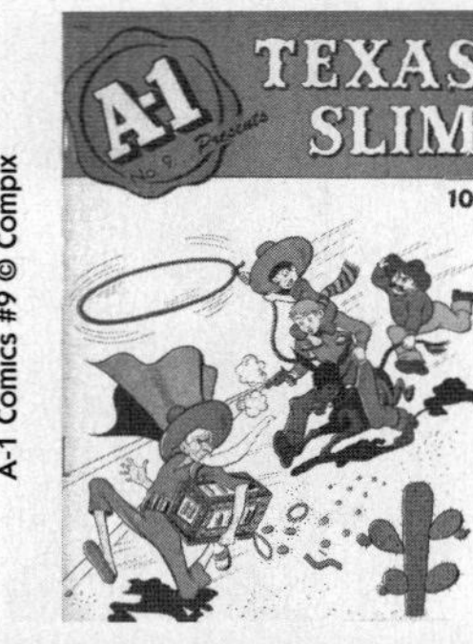

A-1 Comics #9 © Compix

	GD 2.0	VG 4.0	FN 6.0	VF 8.0	VF/NM 9.0	NM- 9.2
1,2-Movie adaptation						4.00
Treasury Edition ($2.00, tabloid size)	3	6	9	18	27	35

ANNIE OAKLEY (See Tessie The Typist #19, Two-Gun Kid & Wild Western)
Marvel/Atlas Comics(MPI No. 1-4/CDS No. 5 on): Spring, 1948 - No. 4, 11/48; No. 5, 6/55 - No. 11, 6/56

	GD	VG	FN	VF	VF/NM	NM-
1 (1st Series, 1948)-Hedy Devine app.	45	90	135	284	480	675
2 (7/48, 52 pgs.)-Kurtzman-a, "Hey Look", 1 pg; Intro. Lana; Hedy Devine app; Captain Tootsie by Beck	26	52	78	154	252	350
3,4	22	44	66	128	209	290
5 (2nd Series, 1955)-Reinman-a ; Maneely-c	17	34	51	98	154	210
6-9: 6,8-Woodbridge-a. 9-Williamson-a (4 pgs.)	14	28	42	80	115	150
10,11: 11-Severin-c	13	26	39	74	105	135

ANNIE OAKLEY AND TAGG (TV)
Dell Publishing Co./Gold Key: 1953 - No. 18, Jan-Mar, 1959; July, 1965 (Gail Davis photo-c #3 on)

	GD	VG	FN	VF	VF/NM	NM-
Four Color 438 (#1)	14	28	42	103	184	265
Four Color 481,575 (#2,3)	9	18	27	64	110	155
4(7-9/55)-10	8	16	24	54	90	125
11-18(1-3/59)	7	14	21	45	73	100
1(7/65-Gold Key)-Photo-c (c-r/#6)	4	8	12	28	44	60

NOTE: *Manning a-13. Photo back c-4, 9, 11.*

ANNIHILATION
Marvel Comics: May, 2006 - No. 6, Mar, 2007 ($3.99/$2.99, limited x-over series)

	NM-
Prologue (5/06, $3.99, one-shot) Nova, Thanos and Silver Surfer app.	4.00
1-6: 1-(10/06) Giffen-s/DiVito-a; Annihilus app.	3.00
...: Heralds of Galactus 1,2 (4/07-5/07, $3.99) 2-Silver Surfer app.	4.00
...: Nova 1-4 (6/06-9/06, $2.99) Abnett & Lanning-s/Walker-a/Dell'Otto-c. 2,3-Quasar app.	3.00
...: Ronan 1-4 (6/06-9/06, $2.99) Furman-s/Lucas-a/Dell'Otto-c	3.00
... Saga (2007, $1.99) re-cap of the series; DiVito-c	2.50
...: Silver Surfer 1-4 (6/06-9/06, $2.99) Giffen-s/Arlem-a/Dell'Otto-c	3.00
...: Super-Skrull 1-4 (6/06-9/06, $2.99) Grillo-Marxuach-s/Titus-a/Dell'Otto-c	3.00
...: The Nova Corps Files (2006, $3.99) profile pages of characters and alien races	4.00
Annihilation Book 1 HC (2007, $29.99, dustjacket) r/Drax the Destroyer #1-4, Annihilation Prologue and Annihilation: Nova #1-4; sketch and layout pages	30.00
Annihilation Book 1 SC (2007, $24.99) same content as HC	25.00
Annihilation Book 2 HC (2007, $29.99, dustjacket) r/Annihilation: Silver Surfer #1-4, ...: Super Skrull #1-4 and ...: Ronan #1-4; sketch and layout pages	30.00
Annihilation Book 2 SC (2007, $24.99) same content as HC	25.00
Annihilation Book 3 HC (2007, $29.99, dustjacket) r/Annihilation #1-6, Annihilation: Heralds of Galactus #1,2 and Annihilation: Nova Corps Files; sketch pages	30.00
Annihilation Book 3 SC (2007, $24.99) same content as HC	25.00

ANNIHILATION: CONQUEST (Also see Nova 2007 series)
Marvel Comics: Jan, 2008 - No. 6, Jun, 2008 ($3.99/$2.99, limited x-over series)

	NM-
Prologue (8/07, $3.99, one-shot) the new Quasar, Moondragon app.; Perkins-a	4.00
1-5-Raney-a; Ultron app. 3-Moondragon dies	3.00
6-($3.99)	4.00
... - Quasar 1-4 (9/07-No. 4, 12/07, $2.99) Gage-s/Lilly-a. 1-Super-Adaptoid app.	3.00
... - Starlord 1-4 (9/07-No. 4, 12/07, $2.99) Giffen-s/Green-a	3.00
... - Wraith 1-4 (9/07-No. 4, 12/07, $2.99) Hotz-a/Grillo-Marxuach-s	3.00
Annihilation: Conquest Book 1 HC (2008, $29.99, dustjacket) r/Prologue; ...Quasar #1-4, ...Star-Lord #1-4; Annihilation Saga; design pages	30.00

ANOTHER WORLD (See Strange Stories From...)

ANT
Image Comics: Aug, 2005 - Present ($2.99)

	NM-
1-11: 1-Mario Gulley-s/a. 2-Savage Dragon & Spawn app. 3-Spawn-c/app.	3.00
Vol. 1: Reality Bites TPB (2006, $12.99) r/#1-4; sketch and concept art	13.00

ANTHRO (See Showcase #74)
National Periodical Publications: July-Aug, 1968 - No. 6, July-Aug, 1969

	GD	VG	FN	VF	VF/NM	NM-
1-(7-8/68)-Howie Post-a in all	6	12	18	37	59	80
2-5: 5-Last 12¢ issue	4	8	12	22	34	45
6-Wood-c/a (inks)	4	8	12	24	37	50

ANTI-HITLER COMICS
New England Comics Press: Summer, 1992 ($2.75, B&W, one-shot)

	NM-
1-Reprints Hitler as Devil stories from wartime comics	5.00

ANT-MAN (See Irredeemable Ant-Man, The)

ANT-MAN'S BIG CHRISTMAS
Marvel Comics: Feb, 2000 ($5.95, square-bound, one-shot)

	NM-
1-Bob Gale-s/Phil Winslade-a; Avengers app.	6.00

ANTONY AND CLEOPATRA (See Ideal, a Classical Comic)

ANYTHING GOES
Fantagraphics Books: Oct, 1986 - No. 6, 1987 ($2.00, #1-5 color & B&W/#6 B&W, lim. series)

	NM-
1-6: 1-Flaming Carrot app. (1st in color?); G. Kane-c. 2-6: 2-Miller-c(p); Alan Moore scripts; Kirby-a; early Sam Kieth-a (2 pgs.). 3-Capt. Jack, Cerebus app.; Cerebus-c by N. Adams. 4-Perez-c. 5-3rd color Teenage Mutant Ninja Turtles app.	3.50

A-1
Marvel Comics (Epic Comics): 1992 - No. 4, 1993 ($5.95, limited series, mature)

	GD	VG	FN	VF	VF/NM	NM-
1-4: 1-Fabry-c/a, Russell-a, S. Hampton-a. 3-Bisley-c; Kent Williams-a. 4-McKean-a; Dorman-s/a	1	2	3	4	5	7

A-1 COMICS (A-1 appears on covers No. 1-17 only)(See individual title listings for #11-139) (1st two issues not numbered.)
Life's Romances Publ.-No. 1/Compix/Magazine Ent.: 1944 - No. 139, Sept-Oct, 1955 (No #2)

	GD	VG	FN	VF	VF/NM	NM-
nn-(1944) (See Kerry Drake Detective Cases)						
1-Dotty Dripple (1 pg.), Mr. Ex, Bush Berry, Rocky, Lew Loyal (20 pgs.)	15	30	45	85	130	175
3-8,10: Texas Slim & Dirty Dalton, The Corsair, Teddy Rich, Dotty Dripple, Inca Dinca, Tommy Tinker, Little Mexico & Tugboat Tim, The Masquerader & others. 7-Corsair-c/s. 8-Intro Rodeo Ryan	10	20	30	54	72	90
9-All Texas Slim	10	20	30	56	76	95

(See Individual Alphabetical listings for prices)

11-Teena; Ogden Whitney-c	12,15-Teena
13-Guns of Fact & Fiction (1948). Used in **SOTI**, pg. 19; Ingels & Johnny Craig-a	14-Tim Holt Western Adventures #1
17-Tim Holt #2; photo-c; last issue to carry A-1 on cover (9-10/48)	16-Vacation Comics; The Pixies, Tom Tom, Flying Fredd, & Koko & Kola
19-Tim Holt #3; photo-c	18,20-Jimmy Durante; photo covers on both
22-Dick Powell (1949)-Photo-c	21-Joan of Arc (1949)-Movie adapta tion; Ingrid Bergman photo-covers & interior photos; Whitney-a
23-Cowboys and Indians #6; Doc Holiday-c/story	24-Trail Colt #1-Frazetta-r in-Manhunt #13; Ingels-c; L. B. Cole-a
25-Fibber McGee & Molly (1949) (Radio)	
26-Trail Colt #2-Ingels-c	27-Ghost Rider #1(1950)-Origin
28-Christmas-(Koko & Kola #6) ("50)	29-Ghost Rider #2-Frazetta-c (1950)
30-Jet Powers #1-Powell-a	31-Ghost Rider #3-Frazetta-c & origin ('51)
32-Jet Powers #2	
33-Muggsy Mouse #1('51)	34-Ghost Rider #4-Frazetta-c (1951)
35-Jet Powers #3-Williamson/Evans-a	36-Muggsy Mouse #2; Racist-c
37-Ghost Rider #5-Frazetta-c (1951)	38-Jet Powers #4-Williamson/Wood-a
39-Muggsy Mouse #3	40-Dogface Dooley #1('51)
41-Cowboys 'N' Indians #7 (1951)	42-Best of the West #1-Powell-a
43-Dogface Dooley #2	44-Ghost Rider #6
45-American Air Forces #5-Powell-c/a	46-Best of the West #2
47-Thun'da, King of the Congo #1-Frazetta-c/a('52)	48-Cowboys 'N' Indians #8
	49-Dogface Dooley #3
50-Danger Is Their Business #11 ('52)-Powell-a	51-Ghost Rider #7 ('52)
	52-Best of the West #3
53-Dogface Dooley #4	54-American Air Forces #6(8/52)-Powell-a
55-U.S. Marines #5-Powell-a	
56-Thun'da #2-Powell-c/a	57-Ghost Rider #8
58-American Air Forces #7-Powell-a	59-Best of the West #4
60-The U.S. Marines #6-Powell-a	61-Space Ace #5('53)-Guardineer-a
62-Starr Flagg, Undercover Girl #5 (#1) reprinted from A-1 #24	63-Manhunt #13-Frazetta
	64-Dogface Dooley #5
65-American Air Forces #8-Powell-a	66-Best of the West #5
67-American Air Forces #9-Powell-a	68-U.S. Marines #7-Powell-a
69-Ghost Rider #9(10/52)	70-Best of the West #6
71-Ghost Rider #10(12/52)-Vs. Frankenstein	72-U.S. Marines #8-Powell-a(3)
	73-Thun'da #3-Powell-c/a
74-American Air Forces #10-Powell-a	75-Ghost Rider #11(3/52)
76-Best of the West #7	77-Manhunt #14
78-Thun'da #4-Powell-c/a	79-American Air Forces #11-Powell-a
80-Ghost Rider #12(6/52)-One-eyed Devil-c	81-Best of the West #8
	82-Cave Girl #11(1953)-Powell-c/a; origin (#1)
83-Thun'da #5-Powell-c/a	
84-Ghost Rider #13(7-8/53)	85-Best of the West #9
86-Thun'da #6-Powell-c/a	87-Best of the West #10(9-10/53)
88-Bobby Benson's B-Bar-B Riders #20	89-Home Run #3-Powell-a; Stan Musial photo-c
90-Red Hawk #11(1953)-Powell-c/a	
91-American Air Forces #12-Powell-a	92-Dream Book of Romance #5-Photo-c; Guardineer-a
93-Great Western #8('54)-Origin The Ghost Rider; Powell-a	94-White Indian #11-Frazetta-a(r);

A-1 Comics #77 © ME

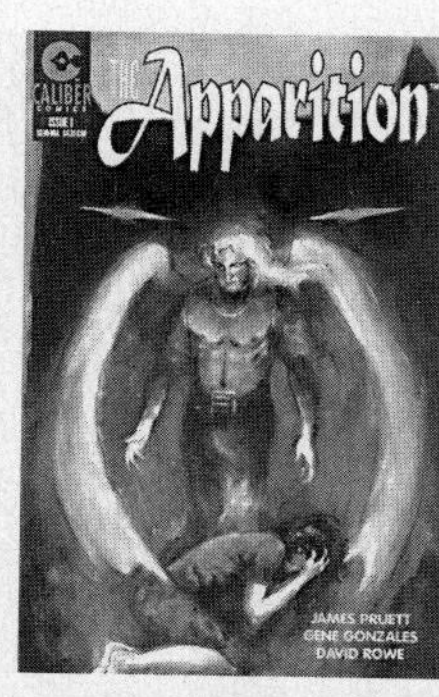

Apparition #1 © CAL

Aquaman #27 © DC

	GD	VG	FN	VF	VF/NM	NM-
	2.0	4.0	6.0	8.0	9.0	9.2

95-Muggsy Mouse #4
96-Cave Girl #12, with Thun'da; Powell-c/a
99-Muggsy Mouse #5
101-White Indian #12-Frazetta-a(r)
101-Dream Book of Romance #6 (4-6/54); Marlon Brando photo-c; Powell, Bolle, Guardineer-a
105-Great Western #9-Ghost Rider app.; Powell-a, 6 pgs.; Bolle-c
107-Hot Dog #1
108-Red Fox #15 (1954)-L.B. Cole-c/a; Powell-a
110-Dream Book of Romance #8 (10/54)-Movie photo-c
112-Ghost Rider #14 ('54)
114-Dream Book of Love #2- Guardineer, Bolle-a; Piper Laurie, Victor Mature photo-c
118-Undercover Girl #7-Powell-c
120-Badmen of the West #2
121-Mysteries of Scotland Yard #1; reprinted from Manhunt (5 stories)
124-Dream Book of Romance #8 (10-11/54)
126-I'm a Cop #2-Powell-a
128-I'm a Cop #3-Powell-a
130-Strongman #1-Powell-a (2-3/55)
132-Strongman #2
134-Strongman #3
136-Hot Dog #4
138-The Avenger #4-Powell-c/a
Powell-c
97-Best of the West #11
98-Undercover Girl #6-Powell-c
100-Badmen of the West #1-Meskin-a(?)
103-Best of the West #12-Powell-a
104-White Indian #13-Frazetta-a(r) ('54)
106-Dream Book of Love #1 (6-7/54) -Powell, Bolle-a; Montgomery Clift, Donna Reed photo-c
109-Dream Book of Romance #7 (7-8/54). Powell-a; movie photo-c
111-I'm a Cop #1 ('54); drug mention story; Powell-a
113-Great Western #10; Powell-a
115-Hot Dog #3
116-Cave Girl #13-Powell-c/a
117-White Indian #14
119-Straight Arrow's Fury #1 (origin); Fred Meagher-c/a
122-Black Phantom #1 (11/54)
123-Dream Book of Love #3 (10-11/54)-Movie photo-c
125-Cave Girl #14-Powell-c/a
127-Great Western #11('54)-Powell-a
129-The Avenger #1('55)-Powell-c
131-The Avenger #2('55)-Powell-c/a
133-The Avenger #3-Powell-c/a
135-White Indian #15
137-Africa #1-Powell-c/a(4)
139-Strongman #4-Powell-a

NOTE: ***Bolle** a-110. Photo-c-17-22, 89, 92, 101, 106, 109, 110, 114, 123, 124.*

APACHE
Fiction House Magazines: 1951

	GD	VG	FN	VF	VF/NM	NM-
1	22	44	66	132	216	300
I.W. Reprint No. 1-r/#1 above	3	6	9	18	27	35

APACHE KID (Formerly Reno Browne; Western Gunfighters #20 on)
(Also see Two-Gun Western & Wild Western)
Marvel/Atlas Comics(MPC No. 53-10/CPS No. 11 on): No. 53, 12/50 - No. 10, 1/52; No. 11, 12/54 - No. 19, 4/56

	GD	VG	FN	VF	VF/NM	NM-
53(#1)-Apache Kid & his horse Nightwind (origin), Red Hawkins by Syd Shores begins	35	70	105	203	327	450
2(2/51)	17	34	51	98	154	210
3-5	13	26	39	72	101	130
6-10 (1951-52): 7-Russ Heath-a	11	22	33	60	83	105
11-19 (1954-56)	9	18	27	50	65	80

NOTE: ***Heath** a-7. c-11, 13. **Maneely** a-53; c-53(#1), 12, 14-16. **Powell** a-14. **Severin** c-17.*

APACHE MASSACRE (See Chief Victorio's...)

APACHE SKIES
Marvel Comics: Sept, 2002 - No. 4, Dec, 2002 ($2.99, limited series)

	NM-
1-4-Apache Kid app.; Ostrander-s/Manco-c/a	3.00
TPB (2003, $12.99) r/#1-4	13.00

APACHE TRAIL
Steinway/America's Best: Sept, 1957 - No. 4, June, 1958

	GD	VG	FN	VF	VF/NM	NM-
1	11	22	33	62	86	110
2-4: 2-Tuska-a	8	16	24	40	50	60

APE (Magazine)
Dell Publishing Co.: 1961 (52 pgs., B&W)

	GD	VG	FN	VF	VF/NM	NM-
1-Comics and humor	4	8	12	24	37	50

APHRODITE IX
Image Comics (Top Cow): Sept, 2000 - No. 4, Mar, 2002 ($2.50)

	NM-
1-3: 1-Four covers by Finch, Turner, Silvestri, Benitez	4.00
1-Tower Record Ed.; Finch-c	3.00
1-DF Chrome ($14.99)	15.00
4-($4.95) Double-sized issue; Finch-c	5.00
Convention Preview	10.00
...: Time Out of Mind TPB (6/04, $14.99) r/#1-4, & #0; cover gallery	15.00
Wizard #0 (4/00, bagged w/Tomb Raider magazine) Preview & sketchbook	5.00
#0-(6/01, $2.95) r/Wizard #0 with cover gallery	3.00

	GD	VG	FN	VF	VF/NM	NM-
	2.0	4.0	6.0	8.0	9.0	9.2

APOCALYPSE NERD
Dark Horse Comics: January, 2005 - No. 6, Oct, 2007 ($2.99, B&W)

	NM-
1-6-Peter Bagge-s/a	3.00

APPARITION
Caliber Comics: 1995 ($3.95, 52 pgs., B&W)

	NM-
1 ($3.95)	4.00
V2#1-6 ($2.95)	3.00
Visitations	4.00

APPLESEED
Eclipse Comics: Sept, 1988 - Book 4, Vol. 4, Aug, 1991 ($2.50/$2.75/$3.50, 52/68 pgs, B&W)

	NM-
Book One, Vol. 1-5: 5-(1/89), Book Two, Vol. 1(2/89) -5(7/89): Art Adams-c, Book Three, Vol. 1(8/89) -4 ($2.75), Book Three, Vol. 5 ($3.50), Book Four, Vol. 1 (1/91) - 4 (8/91) ($3.50, 68 pgs.)	6.00

APPLESEED DATABOOK
Dark Horse Comics: Apr, 1994 - No. 2, May, 1994 ($3.50, B&W, limited series)

	NM-
1,2: 1-Flip book format	3.50

APPROVED COMICS (Also see Blue Ribbon Comics)
St. John Publishing Co. (Most have no c-price): March, 1954 - No. 12, Aug, 1954 (Painted-c on #1-5,7,8,10)

	GD	VG	FN	VF	VF/NM	NM-
1-The Hawk #5-r	10	20	30	56	76	95
2-Invisible Boy (3/54)-Origin; Saunders-c	16	32	48	92	144	195
3-Wild Boy of the Congo #11-r (4/54)	10	20	30	56	76	95
4,5: 4-Kid Cowboy-r. 5-Fly Boy-r	10	20	30	56	76	95
6-Daring Adv.-r (5/54); Krigstein-a(2); Baker-c	14	28	42	76	108	140
7-The Hawk #6-r	10	20	30	56	76	95
8-Crime on the Run (6/54); Powell-a; Saunders-c	10	20	30	56	76	95
9-Western Bandit Trails #3-r, with new-c; Baker-c/a	14	28	42	76	108	140
10-Dinky Duck (Terrytoons)	6	12	18	31	38	45
11-Fightin' Marines #3-r (8/54); Canteen Kate app; Baker-c/a	14	28	42	76	108	140
12-Northwest Mounties #4-r(8/54); new Baker-c	14	28	42	76	108	140

AQUAMAN (See Adventure Comics #260, Brave & the Bold, DC Comics Presents #5, DC Special #28, DC Special Series #1, DC Super Stars #7, Detective Comics, JLA, Justice League of America, More Fun #73, Showcase #30-33, Super DC Giant, Super Friends, and World's Finest Comics)

AQUAMAN (1st Series)
National Periodical Publications/DC Comics: Jan-Feb, 1962 - #56, Mar-Apr, 1971; #57, Aug-Sept,1977 - #63, Aug-Sept, 1978

	GD	VG	FN	VF	VF/NM	NM-
1-(1-2/62)-Intro. Quisp	88	176	264	748	1474	2200
2	32	64	96	245	473	700
3-5	19	38	57	139	270	400
6-10	13	26	39	93	172	250
11,18: 11-1st app. Mera. 18-Aquaman weds Mera; JLA cameo	11	22	33	76	136	195
12-17,19,20	10	20	30	73	129	185
21-32: 23-Birth of Aquababy. 26-Huntress app.(3-4/66). 29-1st app. Ocean Master, Aquaman's step-brother. 30-Batman & Superman-c & cameo	7	14	21	49	80	110
33-1st app. Aqua-Girl (see Adventure #266)	8	16	24	52	86	120
34-40: 35-1st app. Black Manta. 40-Jim Aparo's 1st DC work (8/68)	6	12	18	39	62	85
41-46,47,49: 45-Last 12¢-c	5	10	15	34	55	75
48-Origin reprinted	6	12	18	37	59	80
50-52-Deadman by Neal Adams	8	16	24	56	93	130
53-56('71): 56-1st app. Crusader; last 15¢-c	3	6	9	17	25	32
57('77)-63: 58-Origin retold	2	3	4	6	8	10

NOTE: ***Aparo** a-40-45, 46p, 47-59; c-58-63. **Nick Cardy** c-1-40. **Newton** a-60-63.*

AQUAMAN (1st limited series)
DC Comics: Feb, 1986 - No. 4, May, 1986 (75¢, limited series)

	GD	VG	FN	VF	VF/NM	NM-
1-New costume; 1st app. Nuada of Thierna Na Oge	1	2	3	4	5	7
2-4: 3-Retelling of Aquaman & Ocean Master's origins.						5.00
Special 1 (1988, $1.50, 52 pgs.)						4.00

NOTE: ***Craig Hamilton** c/a-1-4p. **Russell** c-2-4i.*

AQUAMAN (2nd limited series)
DC Comics: June, 1989 - No. 5, Oct, 1989 ($1.00, limited series)

	NM-
1-5: Giffen plots/breakdowns; Swan-a(p).	3.00
Special 1 (Legend of..., $2.00, 1989, 52 pgs.)-Giffen plots/breakdowns; Swan-a(p)	3.00

AQUAMAN (2nd Series)
DC Comics: Dec, 1991 - No. 13, Dec, 1992 ($1.00/$1.25)

	NM-
1-5	2.50
6-13: 6-Begin $1.25-c. 9-Sea Devils app.	2.50

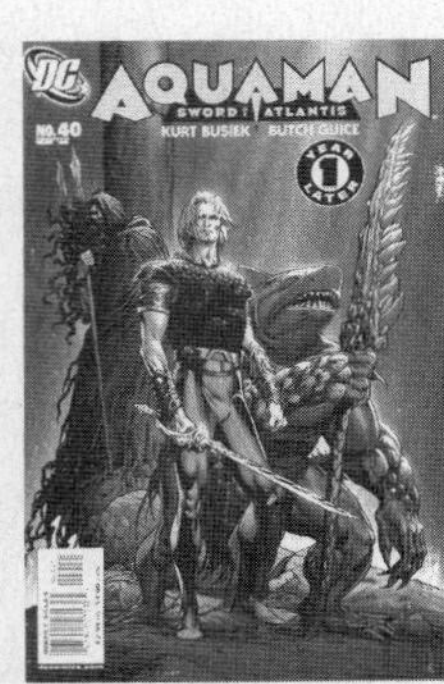

Aquaman: Sword of Atlantis #40 © DC

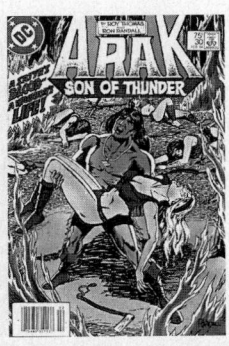

Arak/Son of Thunder #30 © DC

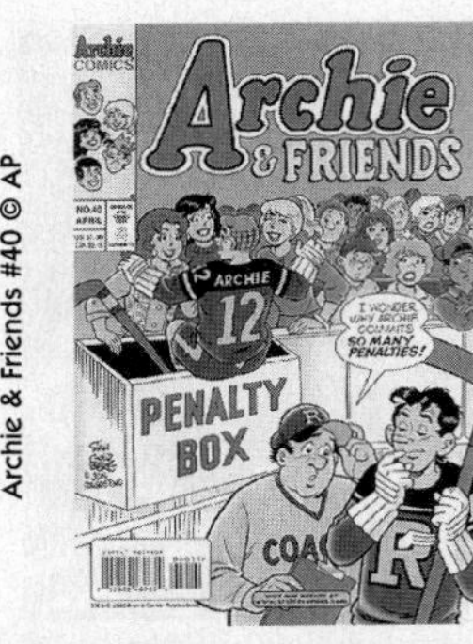

Archie & Friends #40 © AP

GD 2.0 | VG 4.0 | FN 6.0 | VF 8.0 | VF/NM 9.0 | NM- 9.2

GD 2.0 | VG 4.0 | FN 6.0 | VF 8.0 | VF/NM 9.0 | NM- 9.2

AQUAMAN (3rd Series)(Also see Atlantis Chronicles)
DC Comics: Aug, 1994 - No. 75, Jan, 2001 ($1.50/$1.75/$1.95/$1.99/$2.50)

1-(8/94)-Peter David scripts begin; reintro Dolphin 6.00
2-(9/94)-Aquaman loses hand 6.50
0-(10/94)-Aquaman replaces lost hand with hook. 6.50
3-8: 3-(11/94)-Superboy-c/app. 4-Lobo app. 6-Deep Six app. 3.50
9-69: 9-Begin $1.75-c. 10-Green Lantern app. 11-Reintro Mera. 15-Re-intro Kordax. 16-vs. JLA. 18-Reintro Ocean Master & Atlan (Aquaman's father). 19-Reintro Garth (Aqualad). 23-1st app. Deep Blue (Neptune Perkins & Tsunami's daughter). 23,24-Neptune Perkins, Nuada, Tsunami, Arion, Power Girl, & The Sea Devils app. 26-Final Night. 28-Martian Manhunter-c/app. 29-Black Manta-c/app. 32-Swamp Thing-c/app. 37-Genesis x-over. 41-Maxima-c/app. 43-Millennium Giants x-over; Superman-c/app. 44-G.A. Flash & Sentinel app. 50-Larsen-s begins. 53-Superman app. 60-Tempest marries Dolphin; Teen Titans app. 63-Kaluta covers begin. 66-JLA app. 2.50
70-75: 70-Begin $2.50-c. 71-73-Warlord-c/app. 75-Final issue 2.50
#1,000,000 (11/98) 853rd Century x-over 3.00
Annual 1 (1995, $3.50)-Year One story 3.50
Annual 2 (1996, $2.95)-Legends of the Dead Earth story 3.00
Annual 3 (1997, $3.95)-Pulp Heroes story 4.00
Annual 4,5 ('98, '99, $2.95)-4-Ghosts; Wrightson-c. 5-JLApe 3.00
...Secret Files 1 (12/98, $4.95) Origin-s and pin-ups 5.00
NOTE: ***Art Adams**-c, Annual 5. **Mignola** c-6. **Simonson** c-15.*

AQUAMAN (4th Series)(Titled Aquaman: Sword of Atlantis #40-on) (Also see JLA #69-75)
DC Comics: Feb, 2003 - No. 57, Dec, 2007 ($2.50/$2.99)

1-Veitch-s/Guichet-a/Maleev-c 3.00
2-14: 2-Martian Manhunter app. 8-11-Black Manta app. 2.50
15-39: 15-San Diego flooded; Pfeifer-s/Davis-c begin. 23,24-Sea Devils app. 33-Mera returns. 39-Black Manta app. 2.50
40-Sword of Atlantis; One Year Later begins ($2.99-c) Guice-a ; two covers 4.00
41-49,51-57: 41-Two covers. 42-Sea Devils app. 44-Ocean Master app. 3.00
50-($3.99) Tempest app.; McManus-a 4.00
...Secret Files 2003 (5/03, $4.95) background on Aquaman's new powers; pin-ups 5.00
...: Once and Future TPB (2006, $12.99) r/#40-45 13.00
...: The Waterbearer TPB (2003, $12.95) r/#1-4, stories from Aquaman Secret Files and JLA/JSA Secret Files #1; JG Jones-c 13.00

AQUAMAN: TIME & TIDE (3rd limited series) (Also see Atlantis Chronicles)
DC Comics: Dec, 1993 - No. 4, Mar, 1994 ($1.50, limited series)

1-4: Peter David scripts; origin retold. 3.00
Trade paperback ($9.95) 10.00

AQUANAUTS (TV)
Dell Publishing Co.: May - July, 1961

Four Color 1197-Photo-c 7 14 21 47 76 105

ARABIAN NIGHTS (See Cinema Comics Herald)

ARACHNOPHOBIA (Movie)
Hollywood Comics (Disney Comics): 1990 ($5.95, 68 pg. graphic novel)

nn-Adaptation of film; Spiegle-a 6.00
Comic edition ($2.95, 68 pgs.) 3.00

ARAK/SON OF THUNDER (See Warlord #48)
DC Comics: Sept, 1981 - No. 50, Nov, 1985

1,24,50: 1-1st app. Angelica, Princess of White Cathay. 24,50-(52 pgs.) 3.00
2-23,25-49: 3-Intro Valda. 12-Origin Valda. 20-Origin Angelica 2.50
Annual 1(10/84) 3.00

ARAÑA THE HEART OF THE SPIDER (See Amazing Fantasy (2004) #1-6)
Marvel Comics: March, 2005 - No. 12, Feb, 2006 ($2.99)

1-12: 1-Avery-s/Cruz-a. 4-Spider-Man-c/app. 3.00
Vol. 1: Heart of the Spider (2005, $7.99, digest) r/Amazing Fantasy (2004) #1-6 8.00
Vol. 2: In the Beginning (2005, $7.99, digest) r/#1-6 8.00
Vol. 3: Night of the Hunter (2006, $7.99, digest) r/#7-12 8.00

ARCANA (Also see Books of Magic limited & ongoing series and Mister E)
DC Comics (Vertigo): 1994 ($3.95, 68 pgs., annual)

1-Bolton painted-c; Children's Crusade/Tim Hunter story 4.00

ARCANUM
Image Comics (Top Cow Productions): Apr, 1997 - No. 8, Feb, 1998 ($2.50)

1/2 Gold Edition 12.00
1-Brandon Peterson-s/a(p), 1-Variant-c, 4-American Ent. Ed. 3.00
2-8 2.50
3-Variant-c 4.00
...: Millennium's End TPB (2005, $16.99) r/#1-8 & #1/2; cover gallery and sketch pages 17.00

ARCHANGEL (See Uncanny X-Men, X-Factor & X-Men)
Marvel Comics: Feb, 1996 ($2.50, B&W, one-shot)

1-Milligan story 2.50

ARCHARD'S AGENTS (See Ruse)
CrossGeneration Comics: Jan, 2003; Nov, 2003; Apr, 2004 ($2.95)

1-Dixon-s/Perkins-a 3.00
...: The Case of the Puzzled Pugilist (11/03) Dixon-s/Perkins-a 3.00
Vol. 3 - Deadly Dare (4/04) Dixon-s/McNiven-a; preview of Lady Death: The Wild Hunt 3.00

ARCHENEMIES
Dark Horse Comics: Apr, 2006 - No. 4, July, 2006 ($2.99, limited series)

1-4-Melbourne-s/Guichet-a 3.00

ARCHER & ARMSTRONG
Valiant: July (June inside), 1992 - No. 26, Oct, 1994 ($2.50)

0-(7/92)-B. Smith-c/a; Reese-i assists 4.00
0-(with Gold Valiant Logo) 2 4 6 8 10 12
1-7,9-26: 1-(8/92)-Origin & 1st app. Archer; Miller-c; B. Smith/Layton-a. 2-2nd app. Turok (c/story); Smith/Layton-a; Simonson-c. 3,4-Smith-c&a(p) & scripts. 10-2nd app. Ivar. 10,11-B. Smith-c. 21,22-Shadowman app. 22-w/bound-in trading card. 25-Eternal Warrior app. 26-Flip book w/Eternal Warrior #26 2.50
8-($4.50, 52 pgs.)-Combined with Eternal Warrior #8; B. Smith-c/a & scripts; 1st app. Ivar the Time Walker 4.50
...: First Impressions HC (2008, $24.95) recolored reprints #0-6; new "Formation of the Sect" story by Jim Shooter and Sal Velutto; Shooter commentary; new cover by Golden 25.00

ARCHIE (See Archie Comics) (Also see Christmas & Archie, Everything's..., Explorers of the Unknown, Jackpot, Little..., Oxydol-Dreft, Pep, Riverdale High, Teenage Mutant Ninja Turtles Adventures & To Riverdale and Back Again)

ARCHIE ALL CANADIAN DIGEST
Archie Publications: Aug, 1996 ($1.75, 96 pgs.)

1 1 2 3 5 6 8

ARCHIE AMERICANA SERIES, BEST OF THE FORTIES
Archie Publications: 1991,2002 ($10.95, trade paperback)

Vol. 1,2-r/early strips from 1940s 1-Intro. by Steven King. 2-Intro. by Paul Castiglia 11.00

ARCHIE AMERICANA SERIES, BEST OF THE FIFTIES
Archie Publications: 1991 ($8.95, trade paperback)

Vol. 2-r/strips from 1950's; 10.00
2nd printing (1998, $9.95) 12.00
Book 2 (2003, $10.95) 13.00

ARCHIE AMERICANA SERIES, BEST OF THE SIXTIES
Archie Publications: 1995 ($9.95, trade paperback)

Vol. 3-r/strips from 1960s; intro. by Frankie Avalon. 12.00

ARCHIE AMERICANA SERIES, BEST OF THE SEVENTIES
Archie Publications: 1997, 2008 ($9.95/$10.95, trade paperback)

Vol. 4 (1997, $9.95)-r/strips from 1970s 12.00
Vol. 8 Book 2 (2008, $10.95)-r/other strips from 1970s 13.00

ARCHIE AMERICANA SERIES, BEST OF THE EIGHTIES
Archie Publications: 2001 ($10.95, trade paperback)

Vol. 5-r/strips from 1980s; foreward by Steve Geppi 13.00

ARCHIE AMERICANA SERIES, BEST OF THE '90S
Archie Publications: 2008 ($11.95, trade paperback)

Vol. 9-r/strips from 1990s; new Lindsey cover 14.00

ARCHIE AND BIG ETHEL
Spire Christian Comics (Fleming H. Revell Co.): 1982 (69¢)

nn-(Low print run) 2 4 6 11 16 20

ARCHIE & FRIENDS
Archie Comics: Dec, 1992 - Present ($1.25/$1.50/$1.75/$1.79/$1.99/$2.19/$2.25, bi-monthly)

1 5.00
2,4,10-14,17,18,20-Sabrina app. 20-Archie's Band-c 4.00
3,5-9,16 2.50
15-Babewatch-s with Sabrina app. 6.00
19-Josie and the Pussycats app.; E.T. parody-c/s 5.00
21-46 2.50
47-All Josie and the Pussycats issue; movie and actress profiles/photos 3.00
48-142: 48-56,58,60,96-Josie and the Pussycats-c/s. 79-Cheryl Blossom returns. 100-The Veronicas-c/app. 101-Katy Keene begins. 129-Begin $2.50. 130,131-Josie and the Pussycats. 137-Cosmo, Super Duck, Pat the Brat and other old characters app. 2.50

ARCHIE AND ME (See Archie Giant Series Mag. #578, 591, 603, 616, 626)

Archie Comics #42 © AP

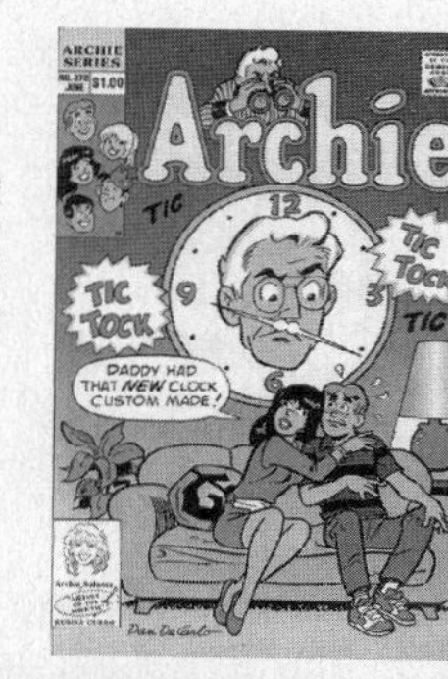

Archie Comics #378 © AP

Archie Comics #601 © AP

	GD 2.0	VG 4.0	FN 6.0	VF 8.0	VF/NM 9.0	NM- 9.2
Archie Publications: Oct, 1964 - No. 161, Feb, 1987						
1	15	30	45	104	197	290
2	9	18	27	61	103	145
3-5	6	12	18	41	66	90
6-10	4	8	12	26	41	55
11-20	3	6	9	18	27	35
21(6/68)-26,28-30: 21-UFO story. 26-X-Mas-c	3	6	9	16	22	28
27-Groovyman & Knowman superhero-s; UFO-sty	3	6	9	18	27	35
31-42: 37-Japan Expo '70-c/s	2	4	6	11	16	20
43-48,50-63-(All Giants): 43-(8/71) Mummy-s. 44-Mermaid-s. 62-Elvis cameo-c. 63-(2/74)	3	6	9	15	21	26
49-(Giant) Josie & the Pussycats-c/app.	3	6	9	18	27	35
64-66,68-99-(Regular size): 85-Bicentennial-s. 98-Collectors Comics	1	3	4	6	8	10
67-Sabrina app.(8/74)	2	4	6	9	13	16
100-(4/78)	2	4	6	8	10	12
101-120: 107-UFO-s						6.00
121(8/80)-159: 134-Riverdale 2001						5.00
160,161: 160-Origin Mr. Weatherbee. 161-Last issue						6.00

ARCHIE AND MR. WEATHERBEE
Spire Christian Comics (Fleming H. Revell Co.): 1980 (59¢)

	GD	VG	FN	VF	VF/NM	NM-
nn - (Low print run)	2	4	6	10	14	18

ARCHIE...ARCHIE ANDREWS, WHERE ARE YOU? (...Comics Digest #9, 10; ...Comics Digest Mag. No. 11 on)
Archie Publications: Feb, 1977 - No. 114, May, 1998 (Digest size, 160-128 pgs., quarterly)

	GD	VG	FN	VF	VF/NM	NM-
1	3	6	9	18	27	35
2,3,5,7-9-N. Adams-a; 8-r-/origin The Fly by S&K. 9-Steel Sterling-r	2	4	6	10	14	18
4,6,10 ($1.00/$1.50)	2	4	6	8	11	14
11-20: 17-Katy Keene story	2	3	4	6	8	10
21-50,100	1	2	3	5	6	8
51-70						4.00
71-99,101-114: 113-Begin $1.95-c						3.00

ARCHIE AS PUREHEART THE POWERFUL (Also see Archie Giant Series #142; Jughead as Captain Hero, Life With Archie & Little Archie)
Archie Publications (Radio Comics): Sept, 1966 - No. 6, Nov, 1967

	GD	VG	FN	VF	VF/NM	NM-
1-Super hero parody	11	22	33	74	132	190
2	6	12	18	43	69	95
3-6	6	12	18	37	59	80

NOTE: *Evilheart cameos in all. Title: Archie As Pureheart the Powerful #1-3; ...As Capt. Pureheart-#4-6.*

ARCHIE AT RIVERDALE HIGH (See Archie Giant Series Magazine #573, 586, 604 & Riverdale High)
Archie Publications: Aug, 1972 - No. 113, Feb, 1987

	GD	VG	FN	VF	VF/NM	NM-
1	6	12	18	41	66	90
2	4	8	12	22	34	45
3-5	3	6	9	16	23	30
6-10	2	4	6	11	16	20
11-30	2	4	6	8	10	12
31(12/75)-46,48-50(12/77)	1	2	3	5	7	9
47-Archie in drag-s; Betty mud wrestling-s	2	4	6	9	13	16
51-80,100 (12/84)						6.00
81(8/81)-88, 91,93-95,98						5.00
89,90-Early Cheryl Blossom app. 90-Archies Band app.	3	6	9	14	19	24
92,96,97,99-Cheryl Blossom app. 96-Anti-smoking issue	2	4	6	10	14	18
101,102,104-109,111,112: 102-Ghost-c						6.00
103-Archie dates Cheryl Blossom-s	2	4	6	10	14	18
110,113: 110-Godzilla-s. 113-Last issue	1	2	3	5	6	8

ARCHIE COMICS (Archie #114 on; 1st Teen-age comic; Radio show aired 6/2/45 by NBC)
MLJ Magazines No. 1-19/Archie Publ. No. 20 on: Winter, 1942-43 - No. 19, 3-4/46; No. 20, 5-6/46 - Present

	GD	VG	FN	VF	VF/NM	NM-
1 (Scarce)-Jughead, Veronica app.; 1st app. Mrs. Andrews	3200	6400	9600	24,000	37,000	50,000
2 (Scarce)	514	1028	1542	3750	6625	9500
3 (60 pgs.)(scarce)	371	742	1113	2600	4550	6500
4,5: 4-Article about Archie radio series. 5-Halloween-c	239	478	717	1530	2615	3700
6,8-10: 6-X-Mas-c. 9-1st Miss Grundy cover	168	336	504	1075	1838	2600
7-1st definitive love triangle story	181	362	543	1158	1979	2800
11-20: 15,17,18-Dotty & Ditto by Woggon. 16,19-Woggon-a. 18-Halloween pumpkin-c.	107	214	321	680	1165	1650
21-30: 23-Betty & Veronica by Woggon. 25-Woggon-a. 30-Coach Piffle app., a Coach Kleets prototype. 34-Pre-Dilton try-out (named Dilbert)	65	130	195	416	708	1000
31-40	41	82	123	256	428	600
41-50	32	64	96	188	307	425
51-60	13	26	39	95	178	260
61-70 (1954): 65-70, Katy Keene app.	11	22	33	74	132	190
71-80: 72-74-Katy Keene app.	9	18	27	60	100	140
81-93,95-99	7	14	21	50	83	115
94-1st Coach Kleets	8	16	24	56	93	130
100	9	18	27	61	103	145
101-122,126,128-130 (1962)	5	10	15	34	55	75
123-125,127-Horror/SF covers. 123-UFO-c/s	7	14	21	45	73	100
131,132,134-157,159,160: 137-1st Caveman Archie gang story	3	6	9	20	30	40
133 (12/62)-1st app. Cricket O'Dell	4	8	12	24	37	50
158-Archie in drag story	3	6	9	21	32	42
161(2/66)-184,186-188,190-195,197-199: 168-Superhero gag-c. 176,178-Twiggy-c 183-Caveman Archie gang story	3	6	9	16	22	28
185-1st "The Archies" Band story	4	8	12	23	36	48
189 (3/69)-Archie's band meets Don Kirshner who developed the Monkees	3	6	9	18	27	35
196 (12/69)-Early Cricket O'Dell app.	3	6	9	18	27	35
200 (6/70)	3	6	9	16	23	30
201-230(11/73): 213-Sabrina/Josie-c cameos. 229-Lost Child issue	2	4	6	9	13	16
231-260(3/77): 253-Tarzan parody	1	3	4	6	8	10
261-282, 284-299	1	2	3	5	6	8
283(8/79)-Cover/story plugs "International Children's Appeal" which was a fraudulent charity, according to TV's 20/20 news program broadcast July 20, 1979	1	2	3	5	7	9
300(1/81)-Anniversary issue	1	3	4	6	8	10
301-321,323-325,327-335,337-350: 323-Cheryl Blossom pin-up. 325-Cheryl Blossom app.						5.00
322-E.T. story						6.00
326-Early Cheryl Blossom story	2	4	6	9	13	16
336-Michael Jackson/Boy George parody	1	2	3	5	6	8
351-399: 356-Calgary Olympics Special. 393-Infinity-c; 1st comic book printed on recycled paper						4.00
400 (6/92)-Shows 1st meeting of Little Archie and Veronica						6.00
401-428						3.00
429-Love Showdown part 1						5.00
430-599: 467- "A Storm Over Uniforms" x-over parts 3,4. 538-Comic-Con issue						2.50
600-602: 600-(10/09) Archie proposes to Veronica. 601-Marries Veronica. 602-Twins born						2.50
603-607: 603-(1/10) Archie proposes to Betty. 604-Marries Betty. 605-Twins born						2.50
Annual 1 ('50)-116 pgs. (Scarce)	226	452	678	1446	2473	3500
Annual 2 ('51)	103	206	309	659	1130	1600
Annual 3 ('52)	60	120	180	381	653	925
Annual 4,5 (1953-54)	42	84	126	266	451	635
Annual 6-10 (1955-59): 8,9-(100 pgs.) 10-(84 pgs.) Elvis record on-c	16	32	48	115	220	325
Annual 11-15 (1960-65): 12,13-(84 pgs.) 14,15-(68 pgs.)	10	20	30	67	116	165
Annual 16-20 (1966-70)(all 68 pgs.): 20-Archie's band-c	6	12	18	41	66	90
Annual 21,22,24-26 (1971-75): 21,22-(68 pgs.). 22-Archie's band-s. 24-26-(52 pgs.). 25-Cavemen-s	4	8	12	22	34	45
Annual 23-Archie's band-c/s; Josie/Sabrina-c	5	10	15	30	48	65
Annual Digest 27 ('75)	4	8	12	24	37	50
...28-30	3	6	9	14	20	25
...31-34	2	4	6	9	13	16
...35-40 (...Magazine #35 on)	1	3	4	6	8	10
...41-65 ('94)						5.00
...66-69						3.00
...All-Star Specials (Winter '75, $1.25)-6 remaindered Archie comics rebound in each; titles: "The World of Giant Comics", "Giant Grab Bag of Comics", "Triple Giant Comics" & "Giant Spec. Comics	5	10	15	30	48	65

NOTE: *Archies Band-s-185, 188-192, 197, 198, 201, 204, 205, 208, 209, 215, 329, 330; Band-c-191, 330. Cavemen Archie Gang-s-183, 192, 197, 208, 210, 220, 223, 282, 333, 335, 338, 340.* ***Al Fagly*** *c-17-35.* ***Bob Montana*** *c-38, 41-50, 58, Annual 1-4.* ***Bill Woggon*** *c-53, 54.*

ARCHIE COMICS DIGEST (...Magazine No. 37-95)
Archie Publications: Aug, 1973 - Present (Small size, 160-128 pgs.)

	GD	VG	FN	VF	VF/NM	NM-
1-1st Archie digest	9	18	27	63	107	150
2	5	10	15	32	51	70
3-5	4	8	12	24	37	50

Archie Giant Series #9 © AP

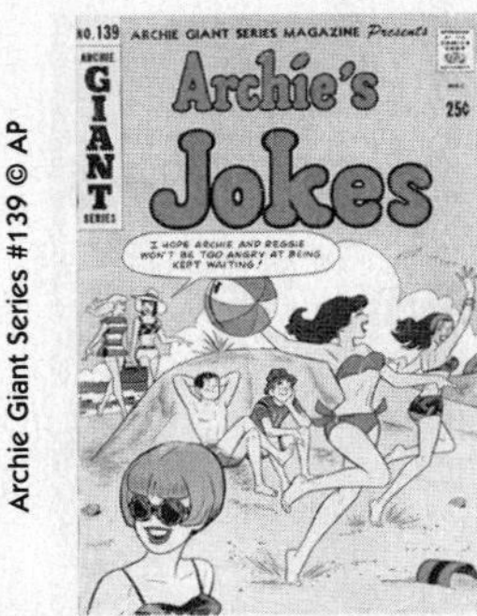

Archie Giant Series #139 © AP

Archie Giant Series #457 © AP

	GD 2.0	VG 4.0	FN 6.0	VF 8.0	VF/NM 9.0	NM- 9.2

6-10 3 6 9 16 23 30
11-33: 32,33-The Fly-r by S&K 2 4 6 10 14 18
34-60 1 3 4 6 8 10
61-80,100 1 2 3 5 6 8
81-99 5.00
101-140: 36-Katy Keene story 4.00
141-165 3.00
166-263: 194-Begin $2.39-c. 225-Begin $2.49-c. 236-65th Anniversary issue, r/1st app. in Pep #22 and entire Archie Comics #1 (1942) 2.50
NOTE: ***Neal Adams** a-1, 2, 4, 5, 19-21, 24, 25, 27, 29, 31, 33. X-mas c-88, 94, 100, 106.*

ARCHIE COMICS PRESENTS: THE LOVE SHOWDOWN COLLECTION
Archie Publications: 1994 ($4.95, squarebound)
nn-r/Archie #429, Betty #19, Betty & Veronica #82, & Veronica #39 1 2 3 5 6 8

ARCHIE GETS A JOB
Spire Christian Comics (Fleming H. Revell Co.): 1977
nn 2 4 6 11 16 20

ARCHIE GIANT SERIES MAGAZINE
Archie Publications: 1954 - No. 632, July, 1992 (No #36-135, no #252-451)
(#1 not code approved) (#1-233 are Giants; #12-184 are 68 pgs.,#185-194,197-233 are 52 pgs.; #195,196 are 84 pgs.; #234-up are 36 pgs.)
1-Archie's Christmas Stocking 142 284 426 909 1555 2200
2-Archie's Christmas Stocking('55) 76 152 228 486 831 1175
3-6-Archie's Christmas Stocking('56- '59) 52 104 156 322 549 775
7-10: 7-Katy Keene Holiday Fun(9/60); Bill Woggon-c. 8-Betty & Veronica Summer Fun (10/60); baseball story w/Babe Ruth & Lou Gehrig. 9-The World of Jughead (12/60); Neal Adams-a. 10-Archie's Christmas Stocking(1/61) 39 78 117 240 395 550
11,13,16,18: 11-Betty & Veronica Spectacular (6/61). 13-Betty & Veronica Summer Fun (10/61). 16-Betty & Veronica Spectacular (6/62). 18-Betty & Veronica Summer Fun (10/62) 25 50 75 150 245 340
12,14,15,17,19,20: 12-Katy Keene Holiday Fun (9/61). 14-The World of Jughead (12/61); Vampire-s. 15-Archie's Christmas Stocking (1/62). 17-Archie's Jokes (9/62); Katy Keene app. 19-The World of Jughead (12/62). 20-Archie's Christmas Stocking (1/63) 19 38 57 112 179 245
21,23,28: 21-Betty & Veronica Spectacular (6/63). 23-Betty & Veronica Summer Fun (10/63). 28-Betty & Veronica Summer Fun (9/64) 10 20 30 70 123 175
22,24,25,27,29,30: 22-Archie's Jokes (9/63). 24-The World of Jughead (12/63). 25-Archie's Christmas Stocking (1/64). 27-Archie's Jokes (8/64). 29-Around the World with Archie (10/64); Doris Day-s. 30-The World of Jughead (12/64) 9 18 27 63 107 150
26-Betty & Veronica Spectacular (6/64); all pin-ups; DeCarlo-c/a 10 20 30 71 126 180
31,33-35: 31-Archie's Christmas Stocking (1/65). 33-Archie's Jokes (8/65). 34-Betty & Veronica Summer Fun (9/65). 35-Around the World with Archie (10/65). 7 14 21 45 73 100
32-Betty & Veronica Spectacular (6/65); all pin-ups; DeCarlo-c/a 8 16 24 54 90 125
36-135-**Do not exist**
136-141: 136-The World of Jughead (12/65). 137-Archie's Christmas Stocking (1/66). 138-Betty & Veronica Spect. (6/66). 139-Archie's Jokes (6/66). 140-Betty & Veronica Summer Fun (8/66). 141-Around the World with Archie (9/66) 7 14 21 45 73 100
142-Archie's Super-Hero Special (10/66)-Origin Capt. Pureheart, Capt. Hero, and Evilheart 8 16 24 58 97 135
143-The World of Jughead (12/66); Capt. Hero-c/s; Man From R.I.V.E.R.D.A.L.E., Pureheart, Superteen app. 7 14 21 45 73 100
144-160: 144-Archie's Christmas Stocking (1/67). 145-Betty & Veronica Spectacular (6/67). 146-Archie's Jokes (6/67). 147-Betty & Veronica Summer Fun (8/67) 148-World of Archie (9/67). 149-World of Jughead (10/67). 150-Archie's Christmas Stocking (1/68). 151-World of Archie (2/68). 152-World of Jughead (2/68). 153-Betty & Veronica Spectacular (6/68). 154-Archie Jokes (6/68). 155-Betty & Veronica Summer Fun (8/68). 156-World of Archie (10/68). 157-World of Jughead (12/68). 158-Archie's Christmas Stocking (1/69). 159-Betty & Veronica Christmas Spectacular (1/69). 160-World of Archie (2/69); Frankenstein-s each... 4 8 12 24 37 50
161-World of Jughead (2/69); Super-Jughead-s; 11 pg.early Cricket O'Dell-s 4 8 12 26 41 55
162-183: 162-Betty & Veronica Spectacular (6/69). 163-Archie's Jokes(8/69). 164-Betty & Veronica Summer Fun (9/69). 165-World of Archie (9/69). 166-World of Jughead (9/69). 167-Archie's Christmas Stocking (1/70). 168-Betty & Veronica Christmas Spect. (1/70). 169-Archie's Christmas Love-In (1/70). 170-Jughead's Eat-Out Comic Book Mag. (12/69). 171-World of Archie (2/70). 172-World of Jughead (2/70). 173-Betty & Veronica Spectacular (6/70). 174-Archie's Jokes (8/70). 175-Betty & Veronica Summer Fun (9/70). 176-Li'l Jinx Giant Laugh-Out (8/70). 177-World of Archie (9/70). 178-World of Jughead (9/70). 179-Archie's Christmas Stocking(1/71). 180-Betty & Veronica Christmas Spect. (1/71). 181-Archie's Christmas Love-In (1/71). 182-World of Archie (2/71). 183-World of Jughead (2/71)-Last squarebound each... 3 6 9 18 27 35
184-189,193,194,197-199 (52 pgs.): 184-Betty & Veronica Spectacular (6/71). 185-Li'l Jinx Giant Laugh-Out (6/71). 186-Archie's Jokes (8/71). 187-Betty & Veronica Summer Fun (9/71). 188-World of Archie (9/71). 189-World of Jughead (9/71). 193-World of Archie (3/72).194-World of Jughead (4/72). 197-Betty & Veronica Spectacular (6/72). 198-Archie's Jokes (8/72). 199-Betty & Veronica Summer Fun (9/72) each... 3 6 9 16 22 28
190-Archie's Christmas Stocking (12/71); Sabrina-c 4 8 12 28 44 60
191-Betty & Veronica Christmas Spect.(2/72); Sabrina app. 4 8 12 24 37 50
192-Archie's Christmas Love-In (1/72); Archie Band-c/s 3 6 9 21 32 42
195-(84 pgs.)-Li'l Jinx Christmas Bag (1/72). 4 8 12 22 34 45
196-(84 pgs.)-Sabrina's Christmas Magic (1/72) 6 12 18 37 59 80
200-(52 pgs.)-World of Archie (10/72) 3 6 9 21 32 42
201-206,208-219,221-230,232,233 (All 52 pgs.): 201-Betty & Veronica Spectacular (10/72). 202-World of Jughead (11/72). 203-Archie's Christmas Stocking (12/72). 204-Betty & Veronica Christmas Spectacular (2/73). 205-Archie's Christmas Love-In (1/73). 206-Li'l Jinx Christmas Bag (12/72). 208-World of Archie (3/73). 209-World of Jughead (4/73). 210-Betty & Veronica Spectacular (6/73). 211-Archie's Jokes (8/73). 212-Betty & Veronica Summer Fun (9/73). 213-World of Archie (10/73). 214-Betty & Veronica Spectacular (10/73). 215-World of Jughead (11/73). 216-Archie's Christmas Stocking (12/73). 217-Betty & Veronica Christmas Spectacular (2/74). 218-Archie's Christmas Love-In (1/74). 219-Li'l Jinx Christmas Bag (12/73). 221-Betty & Veronica Spectacular (Advertised as World of Archie) (6/74). 222-Archie's Jokes (advertised as World of Jughead) (8/74). 223-Li'l Jinx (8/74). 224-Betty & Veronica Summer Fun (9/74). 225-World of Archie (9/74). 226-Betty & Veronica Spectacular (10/74). 227-World of Jughead (10/74). 228-Archie's Christmas Stocking (12/74). 229-Betty & Veronica Christmas Spectacular (12/74). 230-Archie's Christmas Love-In (1/75). 232-World of Archie (3/75). 233-World of Jughead (4/75) each... 2 4 6 11 16 20
207,220,231,243: Sabrina's Christmas Magic. 207-(12/72). 220-(12/73). 231-(1/75). 243-(1/76) each... 3 6 9 17 25 32
234-242,244-251 (36 pgs.): 234-Betty & Veronica Spectacular (6/75). 235-Archie's Jokes (8/75). 236-Betty & Veronica Summer Fun (9/75). 237-World of Archie (9/75) 238-Betty & Veronica Spectacular (10/75). 239-World of Jughead (10/75). 240-Archie's Christmas Stocking (12/75). 241-Betty & Veronica Christmas Spectacular (12/75). 242-Archie's Christmas Love-In (1/76). 244-World of Archie (3/76). 245-World of Jughead (4/76). 246-Betty & Veronica Spectacular (6/76). 247-Archie's Jokes (8/76). 248-Betty & Veronica Summer Fun (9/76). 249-World of Archie (9/76). 250-Betty & Veronica Spectacular (10/76). 251-World of Jughead each.... 2 4 6 9 12 15
252-451-**Do not exist**
452-454,456-466,468-478, 480-490,492-499: 452-Archie's Christmas Stocking (12/76). 453-Betty & Veronica Christmas Spectacular (12/76). 454-Archie's Christmas Love-In (1/77). 456-World of Archie (3/77). 457-World of Jughead (4/77). 458-Betty & Veronica Spectacular (6/77). 459-Archie's Jokes (8/77)-Shows 8/76 in error. 460-Betty & Veronica Summer Fun (9/77). 461-World of Archie (9/77). 462-Betty & Veronica Spectacular (10/77). 463-World of Jughead (10/77). 464-Archie's Christmas Stocking (12/77). 465-Betty & Veronica Christmas Spectacular (12/77). 466-Archie's Christmas Love-In (1/78). 468-World of Archie (2/78). 469-World of Jughead (2/78). 470-Betty & Veronica Spectacular(6/78). 471-Archie's Jokes (8/78). 472-Betty & Veronica Summer Fun (9/78). 473-World of Archie (9/78). 474-Betty & Veronica Spectacular (10/78). 475-World of Jughead (10/78). 476-Archie's Christmas Stocking (12/78). 477-Betty & Veronica Christmas Spectacular (12/78). 478-Archie's Christmas Love-In (1/79). 480-The World of Archie (3/79). 481-World of Jughead (4/79). 482-Betty & Veronica Spectacular (6/79). 483-Archie's Jokes (8/79). 484-Betty & Veronica Summer Fun(9/79). 485-The World of Archie (9/79). 486-Betty & Veronica Spectacular (10/79). 487-The World of Jughead (10/79). 488-Archie's Christmas Stocking (12/79). 489-Betty & Veronica Christmas Spectacular (1/80). 490-Archie's Christmas Love-in (1/80). 492-The World of Archie (2/80). 493-The World of Jughead (4/80). 494-Betty & Veronica Spectacular (6/80). 495-Archie's Jokes (8/80). 496-Betty & Veronica Summer Fun (9/80). 497-The World of Archie (9/80). 498-Betty & Veronica Spectacular (10/80). 499-The World of Jughead (10/80) each... 2 4 6 8 10 12
455,467,479,491,503-Sabrina's Christmas Magic: 455-(1/77). 467-(1/78). 479-(1/79) Dracula/Werewolf-s. 491-(1/80), 503(1/81) 2 4 6 11 16 20
500-Archie's Christmas Stocking (12/80) 2 4 6 8 11 14
501-514,516-527,529-532,534-539,541-543,545-550: 501-Betty & Veronica Christmas Spectacular (12/80). 502-Archie's Christmas Love-in (1/81). 504-The World of Archie (3/81). 505-The World of Jughead (4/81). 506-Betty & Veronica Spectacular (6/81). 507-Archie's Jokes (8/81). 508-Betty & Veronica Summer Fun (9/81). 509-The World of Archie (9/81). 510-Betty & Vernonica Spectacular (9/81). 511-The World of Jughead (10/81). 512-Archie's Christmas Stocking (12/81). 513-Betty & Veronica Christmas Spectacular (12/81). 514-Archie's Christmas Love-in (1/82). 516-The World of Archie(3/82). 517-The World of Jughead (4/82). 518-Betty & Veronica Spectacular (6/82). 519-Archie's Jokes (8/82). 520-Betty & Veronica Summer Fun (9/82). 521-The World of Archie (9/82). 522-Betty &

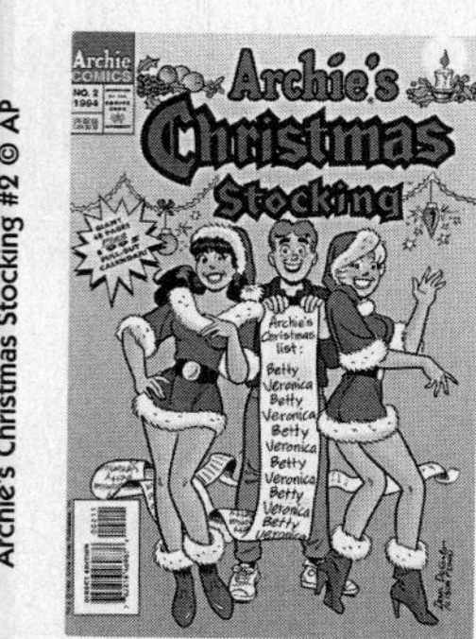

Archie's Christmas Stocking #2 © AP

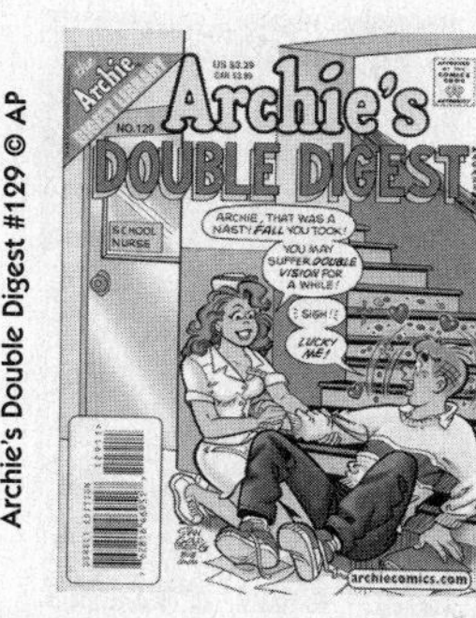

Archie's Double Digest #129 © AP

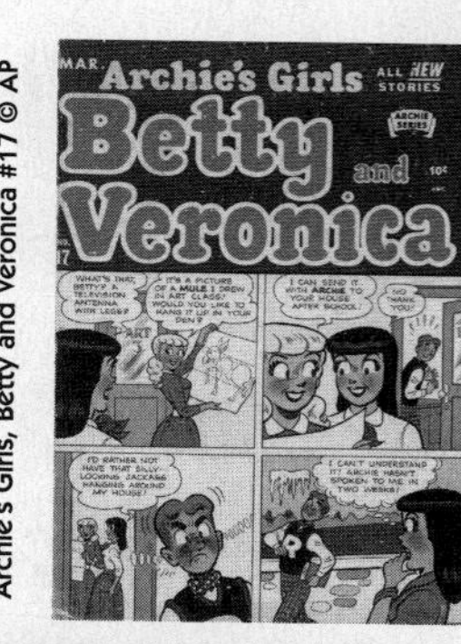

Archie's Girls, Betty and Veronica #17 © AP

GD VG FN VF VF/NM NM-
2.0 4.0 6.0 8.0 9.0 9.2

Veronica Spectacular (10/82). 523-The World of Jughead (10/82).524-Archie's Christmas Stocking (1/83). 525-Betty and Veronica Christmas Spectacular (1/83). 526-Betty and Veronica Spectacular (5/83). 527-Little Archie (8/83). 529-Betty and Veronica Summer Fun (8/83). 530-Betty and Veronica Spectacular (9/83). 531-The World of Jughead (9/83). 532-The World of Archie (10/83). 534-Little Archie (1/84). 535-Archie's Christmas Stocking (1/84). 536-Betty and Veronica Christmas Spectacular (1/84). 537-Betty and Veronica Spectacular (6/84). 538-Little Archie (8/84). 539-Betty and Veronica Summer Fun (8/84). 541-Betty and Veronica Spectacular (9/84). 542-The World of Jughead (9/84). 543-The World of Archie (10/84). 545-Little Archie (12/84). 546-Archie's Christmas Stocking (12/84). 547-Betty and Veronica Christmas Spectacular (12/84). 548-?. 549-Little Archie. 550-Betty and Veronica Summer Fun each... 1 2 3 5 7 9

515,528,533,540,544: 515-Sabrina's Christmas Magic (1/82). 528-Josie and the Pussycats (8/83). 533-Sabrina; Space Pirates by Frank Bolling (10/83). 540-Josie and the Pussycats (8/84). 544-Sabrina the Teen-Age Witch (10/84).
each... 2 4 6 10 14 18

551,562,571,584,597-Josie and the Pussycats 2 4 6 8 10 12

552-561,563-570,572-583,585-596,598-600: 552-Betty & Veronica Spectacular. 553-The World of Jughead. 554-The World of Archie. 555-Betty's Diary. 556-Little Archie (1/86). 557-Archie's Christmas Stocking (1/86). 558-Betty & Veronica Christmas Spectacular (1/86). 559-Betty & Veronica Spectacular. 560-Little Archie. 561-Betty & Veronica Summer Fun. 563-Betty & Veronica Spectacular. 564-World of Jughead. 565-World of Archie. 566-Little Archie. 567-Archie's Christmas Stocking. 568-Betty & Veronica Christmas Spectacular. 569-Betty & Veronica Spring Spectacular. 570-Little Archie. 571-Dracula-c/s. 572-Betty & Veronica Summer Fun. 573-Archie At Riverdale High. 574-World of Archie. 575-Betty & Veronica Spectacular. 576-Pep. 577-World of Jughead. 578-Archie And Me. 579-Archie's Christmas Stocking. 580-Betty and Veronica Christmas Spectacular. 581-Little Archie Christmas Special. 582-Betty & Veronica Spring Spectacular. 583-Little Archie. 585-Betty & Veronica Summer Fun. 586-Archie At Riverdale High. 587-The World of Archie (10/88); 1st app. Explorers of the Unknown. 588-Betty & Veronica Spectacular. 589-Pep (10/88). 590-The World of Jughead. 591-Archie & Me. 592-Archie's Christmas Stocking. 593-Betty & Veronica Christmas Spectacular. 594-Little Archie. 595-Betty & Veronica Spring Spectacular. 596-Little Archie. 598-Betty & Veronica Summer Fun. 599-The World of Archie (10/89); 2nd app. Explorers of the Unknown. 600-Betty and Veronica Spectacular
each.... 6.00

601,602,604-609,611-629: 601-Pep. 602-The World of Jughead. 604-Archie at Riverdale High. 605-Archie's Christmas Stocking. 606-Betty and Veronica Christmas Spectacular. 607-Little Archie. 608-Betty and Veronica Spectacular. 609-Little Archie. 611-Betty and Veronica Summer Fun. 612-The World of Archie. 613-Betty and Veronica Spectacular. 614-Pep (10/90). 615-Veronica's Summer Special. 616-Archie and Me. 617-Archie's Christmas Stocking. 618-Betty & Veronica Christmas Spectacular. 619-Little Archie. 620-Betty and Veronica Spectacular. 621-Betty and Veronica Summer Fun. 622-Josie & the Pussycats; not published. 623-Betty and Veronica Spectacular. 624-Pep Comics. 625-Veronica's Summer Special. 626-Archie and Me. 627-World of Archie. 628-Archie's Pals 'n' Gals Holiday Special. 629-Betty & Veronica Christmas Spectacular.
each.... 4.00

603-Archie and Me; Titanic app. 5.00

610-Josie and the Pussycats 1 2 3 4 5 7

630-631: 630-Archie's Christmas Stocking. 631-Archie's Pals 'n' Gals 4.00

632-Last issue; Betty & Veronica Spectacular 1 2 3 4 5 7

NOTE: *Archies Band-c-173,180,192; s-189,192. Archie Cavemen-165,225,232,244,249. Little Sabrina-527,534, 538,545,556,566. UFO-s-178,487,594.*

ARCHIE MEETS THE PUNISHER (Same contents as The Punisher Meets Archie)
Marvel Comics & Archie Comics Publ.: Aug, 1994 ($2.95, 52 pgs., one-shot)

1-Batton Lash story, J. Buscema-a on Punisher, S. Goldberg-a on Archie 6.00

ARCHIE'S ACTIVITY COMICS DIGEST MAGAZINE
Archie Enterprises: 1985 - No. 4 (Annual, 128 pgs., digest size)

1 (Most copies are marked) 2 4 6 9 13 16
2-4 1 2 3 5 7 9

ARCHIE'S CAR
Spire Christian Comics (Fleming H. Revell co.): 1979 (49¢)

nn 2 4 6 9 13 16

ARCHIE'S CHRISTMAS LOVE-IN (See Archie Giant Series Mag. No. 169, 181,192, 205, 218, 230, 242, 454, 466, 478, 490, 502, 514)

ARCHIE'S CHRISTMAS STOCKING (See Archie Giant Series Mag. No. 1-6,10, 15, 20, 25, 31, 137, 144, 150, 158, 167, 179, 190, 203, 216, 228, 240, 452, 464, 476, 488, 500, 512, 524, 535, 546, 557, 567, 579, 592, 605, 617, 630)

ARCHIE'S CHRISTMAS STOCKING
Archie Comics: 1993 - No. 7, 1999 ($2.00-$2.29, 52 pgs.)(Bound-in calendar poster in all)

1-Dan DeCarlo-c/a 5.00
2-5 4.00
6,7: 6-(1998, $2.25). 7-(1999, $2.29) 3.00

GD VG FN VF VF/NM NM-
2.0 4.0 6.0 8.0 9.0 9.2

ARCHIE'S CIRCUS
Barbour Christian Comics: 1990 (69¢)

nn 2 4 6 9 13 16

ARCHIE'S CLASSIC CHRISTMAS STORIES
Archie Comics: 2002 ($10.95, TPB)

Volume 1 - Reprints stories from 1955-1964 Archie's Christmas Stocking issues 11.00

ARCHIE'S CLEAN SLATE
Spire Christian Comics (Fleming H. Revell Co.): 1973 (35/49¢)

1-(35¢-c edition)(Some issues have nn) 2 4 6 11 16 20
1-(49¢-c edition) 2 4 6 9 13 16

ARCHIE'S DATE BOOK
Spire Christian comics (Fleming H. Revell Co.): 1981

nn-(Low print) 2 4 6 11 16 20

ARCHIE'S DOUBLE DIGEST QUARTERLY MAGAZINE
Archie Comics: 1981 - Present ($1.95-$3.99, 256 pgs.) (Archie's Double Digest Magazine No. 10 on)

1 3 6 9 16 23 30
2-10; 6-Katy Keene story. 2 4 6 10 14 18
11-30: 29-Pureheart story 2 4 6 8 10 12
31-50 1 2 3 4 5 7
51-70,100 5.00
71-99 4.00
101-209: 115-Begin $3.19-c. 123-Begin $3.29-c. 170-Begin $3.69. 197-Begin $3.99-c. 4.00

ARCHIE'S FAMILY ALBUM
Spire Christian Comics (Fleming H. Revell Co.): 1978 (39¢/49¢, 36 pgs.)

nn 2 4 6 9 13 16
nn (49¢-c edition) 2 4 6 8 10 12

ARCHIE'S FESTIVAL
Spire Christian Comics (Fleming H. Revell Co.): 1980 (49¢)

nn 2 4 6 9 13 16

ARCHIE'S GIRLS, BETTY AND VERONICA (Becomes Betty & Veronica)(Also see Veronica)
Archie Publications (Close-Up): 1950 - No. 347, Apr, 1987

1 265 530 795 1694 2897 4100
2 106 212 318 673 1162 1650
3-5: 3-Betty's 1st ponytail. 4-Dan DeCarlo's 1st Archie work
61 122 183 390 670 950
6-10: 10-Katy Keene app. (2 pgs.) 48 96 144 302 514 725
11-20: 11,13,14,17-19-Katy Keene app. 17-Last pre-code issue (3/55). 20-Debbie's Diary (2 pgs.) 39 78 117 231 378 525
21-30: 27,30-Katy Keene app. 29-Tarzan 27 54 81 158 259 360
31-43,45-50: 41-Marilyn Monroe and Brigitte Bardot mentioned. 45-Fabian 1 pg. photo & bio. 46-Bobby Darin 1 pg. photo & bio 19 38 57 112 179 245
44-Elvis Presley 1 pg. photo & bio 21 42 63 122 199 275
51-55,57-74: 67-Jackie Kennedy homage. 73-Sci-fi-c 9 18 27 61 103 145
56-Elvis and Bobby Darin records parody 10 20 30 70 123 175
75-Betty & Veronica sell souls to Devil 16 32 48 115 220 325
76-99: 82-Bobby Rydell 1 pg. illustrated bio; Elvis mentioned on-c. 84-Connie Francis 1 pg. illustrated bio 6 12 18 41 66 90
100 7 14 21 47 76 105
101-104, 106-117,120 (12/65): 113-Monsters-s 5 10 15 30 48 65
105-Beatles wig parody (5 pg. story)(9/64) 5 10 15 32 51 70
118-(10/65) 1st app./origin Superteen (also see Betty & Me #3)
7 14 21 47 76 105
119-2nd app./last Superteen story 5 10 15 34 55 75
121,122,124-126,128-140 (8/67): 135,140-Mod-c. 136-Slave Girl-s
3 6 9 20 30 40
123-"Jingo"-Ringo parody-c 4 8 12 23 36 48
127-Beatles Fan Club-s 5 10 15 32 51 70
141-156,158-163,165-180 (12/70) 3 6 9 16 22 28
157,164-Archies Band 3 6 9 19 29 38
181-193,195-199 2 4 6 11 16 20
194-Sabrina-c/s 3 6 9 19 29 38
200-(8/72) 3 6 9 14 19 24
201-205,207,209,211-215,217-240 2 4 6 8 10 12
206,208,210, 216: 206,208,216-Sabrina c/app. 206-Josie-c. 210-Sabrina app.
3 6 9 16 22 28
241 (1/76)-270 (6/78) 1 3 4 6 8 10
271-299: 281-UFO-s 1 2 3 5 7 9
300 (12/80)-Anniversary issue 2 4 6 8 10 12

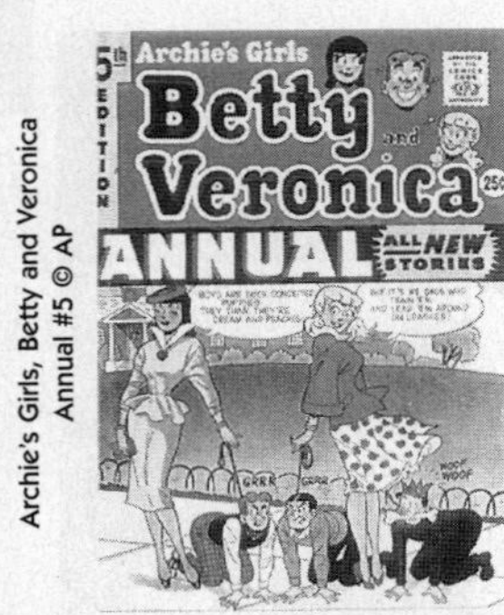

Archie's Girls, Betty and Veronica Annual #5 © AP

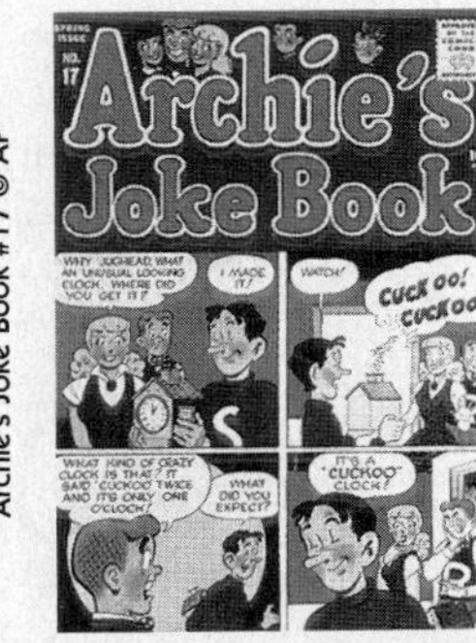

Archie's Joke Book #17 © AP

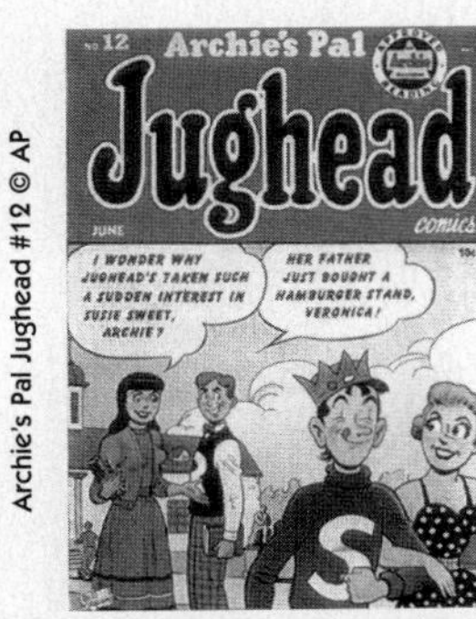

Archie's Pal Jughead #12 © AP

	GD 2.0	VG 4.0	FN 6.0	VF 8.0	VF/NM 9.0	NM- 9.2
301-309	1	2	3	4	5	7
310-John Travolta parody story	1	3	4	6	8	10
311-319						6.00
320 (10/82)-Intro. of Cheryl Blossom on cover and inside story (she also appears, but not on the cover, in Jughead #325 with same 10/82 publication date)	8	16	24	54	90	125
321,322-Cheryl Blossom app. 322-Cheryl meets Archie for the 1st time	3	6	9	19	29	38
323,326,329,330,331,333-338: 333-Monsters-s	2	3	4	6	8	10
324,325-Crickett O'Dell app.	2	4	6	8	11	14
327,328-Cheryl Blossom app.	3	6	9	17	25	32
332,339: 332-Superhero costume party. 339-(12/85) Betty dressed as Madonna.	2	4	6	8	11	14
340-346 Low print	1	2	3	5	7	9
347 (4/87) Last issue; low print	2	3	4	6	8	10
Annual 1 (1953)	116	232	348	742	1271	1800
Annual 2 (1954)	47	94	141	296	498	700
Annual 3-5 (1955-1957)	39	78	117	231	378	525
Annual 6-8 (1958-1960)	26	52	78	154	252	350

ARCHIE'S HOLIDAY FUN DIGEST
Archie Comics: 1997 - Present ($1.75/$1.95/$1.99/$2.19/$2.39/$2.49, annual)

	GD 2.0	VG 4.0	FN 6.0	VF 8.0	VF/NM 9.0	NM- 9.2
1-12-Christmas stories						2.50

ARCHIE'S JOKEBOOK COMICS DIGEST ANNUAL (See Jokebook...)

ARCHIE'S JOKE BOOK MAGAZINE (See Joke Book ...)
Archie Publ: 1953 - No. 3, Sum, 1954; No. 15, Fall, 1954 - No. 288, 11/82 (subtitled...Laugh-In #127-140; ...Laugh-Out #141-194)

	GD 2.0	VG 4.0	FN 6.0	VF 8.0	VF/NM 9.0	NM- 9.2
1953-One Shot (#1)	106	212	318	673	1162	1650
2	48	96	144	302	514	725
3 (no #4-14)	39	78	117	240	395	550
15-20: 15-Formerly Archie's Rival Reggie #14; last pre-code issue (Fall/54).						
15-17-Katy Keene app.	24	48	72	142	234	325
21-30	15	30	45	90	140	190
31-43: 42-Bio of Ed "Kookie" Byrnes. 43-story about guitarist Duane Eddy	13	26	39	74	105	135
44-1st professional comic work by Neal Adams, 4 pgs.	30	60	90	177	289	400
45-47-N. Adams-a in all, 2-6 pgs.	18	36	54	103	162	220
48-Four pgs. N. Adams-a	18	36	54	103	162	220
49,50	6	12	18	39	62	85
51-56,60 (1962)	4	8	12	28	44	60
57-Elvis mentioned; Marilyn Monroe cameo	6	12	18	37	59	80
58,59-Horror/Sci-Fi-c	6	12	18	37	59	80
61-80 (8/64): 66-(12¢ cover)	3	6	9	18	27	35
66-(15¢ cover variant)	4	8	12	22	34	45
81-89,91,92,94-99	3	6	9	14	20	25
90,93: 90-Beatles gag. 93-Beatles cameo	3	6	9	17	25	32
100 (5/66)	3	6	9	16	23	30
101,103-117,119-123,127,129,131-140 (9/69): 105-Superhero gag-c. 108-110-Archies Archers Band-s. 116-Beatles/Monkees/Bob Dylan cameos (posters)	2	4	6	11	16	20
102 (7/66) Archie Band prototype-c; Elvis parody panel, Rolling Stones mention	3	6	9	18	27	35
118,124,125,126,128,130: 118-Archie Band-c; Veronica & Groovers band-s. 124-Archies Band-c/app. 125-Beatles cameo (poster). 126,130-Monkees cameo. 128-Veronica/Archies Band app.	3	6	9	16	23	30
141-173,175-181,183-199	2	4	6	8	11	14
174-Sabrina-c. 182-Sabrina cameo	2	4	6	9	13	16
200 (9/74)	2	4	6	9	13	16
201-230 (3/77)	1	2	3	5	6	8
231-239,241-287						6.00
240-Elvis record-c	2	3	4	6	8	10
288-Last issue	1	2	3	4	5	7

NOTE: *Archies Band-c-118,124,147,172; 1 pg.-s-127,128,138,140,143,147,167; 2 pg.-s-124,131, 155. Sabrina app.-247,248,252-259,261,262,264,266-270,274,277,284-286.*

ARCHIE'S JOKES (See Archie Giant Series Mag. No. 17, 22, 27, 33, 139, 146, 154, 163, 174, 186, 198, 211, 222, 235, 247, 459, 471, 483, 495, 519)

ARCHIE'S LOVE SCENE
Spire Christian Comics (Fleming H. Revell Co.): 1973 (35¢/39¢/49¢/no price)

	GD 2.0	VG 4.0	FN 6.0	VF 8.0	VF/NM 9.0	NM- 9.2
1-(35¢ Edition)	2	4	6	11	16	20
1-(39¢/49¢ Edition/no price) (Some copies have nn)	2	4	6	8	11	14

ARCHIE'S LOVE SHOWDOWN SPECIAL
Archie Publications: 1994 ($2.00, one-shot)

	GD 2.0	VG 4.0	FN 6.0	VF 8.0	VF/NM 9.0	NM- 9.2
1-Concludes x-over from Archie #429, Betty #19, B&V #82, Veronica #39						4.00

ARCHIE'S MADHOUSE (Madhouse Ma-ad No. 67 on)
Archie Publications: Sept, 1959 - No. 66, Feb, 1969

	GD 2.0	VG 4.0	FN 6.0	VF 8.0	VF/NM 9.0	NM- 9.2
1-Archie begins	21	42	63	153	297	440
2	12	24	36	83	152	220
3-5	9	18	27	60	100	140
6-10	6	12	18	43	69	95
11-17 (Last w/regular characters)	5	10	15	34	55	75
18-21,23,29: 18-New format begins. 23-No Sabrina	4	8	12	28	44	60
22-1st app. Sabrina, the Teen-age Witch (10/62)	24	48	72	175	338	500
24-2nd app.Sabrina a	11	22	33	74	132	190
25,26,28-Sabrina app. 25-1st app. Captain Sprocket (4/63); 3rd app. Sabrina; sci-fi/horror-c	8	16	24	58	97	135
27-Sabrina-c; no story	7	14	21	45	73	100
30,34,38-40: No Sabrina. 34-Bordered-c begin.	3	6	9	19	29	38
31,33,37-Sabrina app.	6	12	18	43	69	95
32-Sabrina app.?	3	6	9	19	29	38
35-Beatles cameo. No Sabrina	4	8	12	22	34	45
36-1st Salem the Cat w/Sabrina story	9	18	27	60	100	140
41-48,51-57,60-62,64-66; No Sabrina 43-Mighty Crusaders cameo. 44-Swipes Mad #4 (Super-Duperman) in "Bird Monsters From Outer Space"	3	6	9	16	23	30
49,50,58,59,63-Sabrina stories	5	10	15	32	51	70
Annual 1 (1962-63) no Sabrina	7	14	21	49	80	110
Annual 2 (1964) no Sabrina	5	10	15	32	51	70
Annual 3 (1965)-Origin Sabrina the Teen-Age Witch	10	20	30	70	123	175
Annual 4,5('66-68)(Becomes Madhouse Ma-ad Annual #7 on); no Sabrina	3	6	9	20	30	40
Annual 6 (1969)-Sabrina the Teen-Age Witch-sty	6	12	18	41	66	90

NOTE: *Cover title to #61-65 is "Madhouse" and to #66 is "Madhouse Ma-ad Jokes". Sci-Fi/Horror covers 6, 8, 11, 13, 15-26, 29, 35, 36, 38, 42, 43, 48, 51, 58, 60.*

ARCHIE'S MECHANICS
Archie Publications: Sept, 1954 - No. 3, 1955

	GD 2.0	VG 4.0	FN 6.0	VF 8.0	VF/NM 9.0	NM- 9.2
1-(15¢; 52 pgs.)	85	170	255	540	933	1325
2-(10¢)-Last pre-code issue	48	96	144	302	514	725
3-(10¢)	40	80	120	250	418	585

ARCHIE'S MYSTERIES (Continued from Archie's Weird Mysteries)
Archie Comics: No. 25, Feb, 2003 - No. 34, June, 2004 ($2.19)

	GD 2.0	VG 4.0	FN 6.0	VF 8.0	VF/NM 9.0	NM- 9.2
25-34- Archie and gang as "Teen Scene Investigators"						2.50

ARCHIE'S ONE WAY
Spire Christian Comics (Fleming H. Revell Co.): 1972 (35¢/39¢/49¢, 36 pgs.)

	GD 2.0	VG 4.0	FN 6.0	VF 8.0	VF/NM 9.0	NM- 9.2
nn-(35¢ Edition)	2	4	6	11	16	20
nn-(39¢, 49¢, no price editions)	2	4	6	8	11	14

ARCHIE'S PAL, JUGHEAD (Jughead No. 127 on)
Archie Publications: 1949 - No. 126, Nov, 1965

	GD 2.0	VG 4.0	FN 6.0	VF 8.0	VF/NM 9.0	NM- 9.2
1 (1949)-1st app. Moose (see Pep #33)	226	452	678	1446	2473	3500
2 (1950)	84	168	252	538	919	1300
3-5	50	100	150	315	533	750
6-10: 7-Suzie app.	36	72	108	211	343	475
11-20: 20-Jughead as Sherlock Holmes parody	23	46	69	136	223	310
21-30: 23-25,28-30-Katy Keene app. 23-Early Dilton-s. 28-Debbie's Diary app.	16	32	48	94	147	200
31-50: 49-Archies Rock 'N' Rollers band-c	7	14	21	49	80	110
51-57,59-70: 59- Bio of Will Hutchins of TV's Sugarfoot. 67-Betty seducing Jughead-c. 68-Early Archie Gang Cavemen-s	5	10	15	34	55	75
58-Neal Adams-a	6	12	18	43	69	95
71-76,83,84,89-99: 72-Jughead dates Betty & Veronica. 83 (4/62) 1st mention of Secret Society of Jughead Hating Girls. 84-1st app. Big Ethyl (5/62). 95-2nd app. Cricket O'Dell	4	8	12	24	37	50
77,78,80-82,85,86,88-Horror/Sci-Fi-c. 86(7/62) 1st app. The Brain	6	12	18	39	62	85
79-Creature From the Black Lagoon-c	7	14	21	47	76	105
87-2nd app. of Big Ethyl; UGAJ (United Girls Against Jughead)-s	5	10	15	30	48	65
100	4	8	12	28	44	60
101-Return of Big Ethyl	4	8	12	26	41	55
102-126	3	6	9	18	27	35
Annual 1 (1953, 25¢)	74	148	222	470	810	1150
Annual 2 (1954, 25¢)-Last pre-code issue	40	80	120	246	411	575
Annual 3-5 (1955-57, 25¢)	29	58	87	172	281	390
Annual 6-8 (1958-60, 25¢)	19	38	57	112	179	245

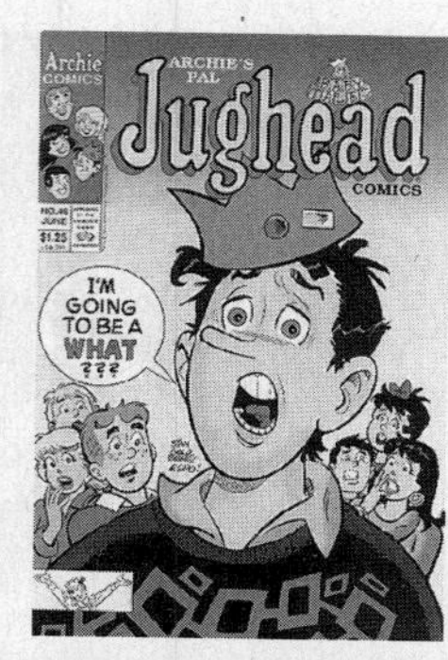

Archie's Pal Jughead #46 © AP

Archie's Rival Reggie #1 © AP

Archie's TV Laugh-Out #8 © AP

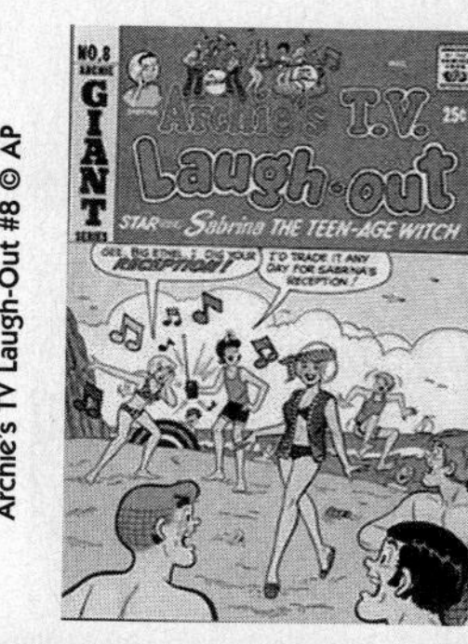

GIANT SERIES
Archie's T.V. Laugh-out
25¢
STARRING Sabrina THE TEEN-AGE WITCH

ARCHIE'S PAL JUGHEAD COMICS (Formerly Jughead #1-45)
Archie Comic Publ.: No. 46, June, 1993 - Present ($1.25-$2.50)

	GD 2.0	VG 4.0	FN 6.0	VF 8.0	VF/NM 9.0	NM- 9.2
46-60						3.00
61-200: 100-"A Storm Over Uniforms" x-over part 1,2. 166-Three Geeks cameo						2.50

ARCHIE'S PALS 'N' GALS (Also see Archie Giant Series Magazine #628)
Archie Publ: 1952-53 - No. 6, 1957-58; No. 7, 1958 - No. 224, Sept, 1991
(...All News Stories on-c #49-59)

	GD 2.0	VG 4.0	FN 6.0	VF 8.0	VF/NM 9.0	NM- 9.2
1-(116 pgs., 25¢)	90	180	270	576	988	1400
2(Annual)('54, 25¢)	43	86	129	271	461	650
3-5(Annual, '55-57, 25¢): 3-Last pre-code issue	32	64	96	192	314	435
6-10('58-'60)	20	40	60	117	189	260
11,13,14,16,17,20-(84 pgs.): 17-B&V paper dolls	13	26	39	72	101	130
12,15-(84 pgs.) Neal Adams-a. 12-Harry Belafonte 2 pg. photos & bio.	14	28	42	82	121	160
18-(84 pgs.) Horror/Sci-Fi-c	14	28	42	80	115	150
19-Marilyn Monroe app.	18	36	54	103	162	220
21,22,24-28,30 (68 pgs.)	6	12	18	43	69	95
23-(Wint./62) 6 pg. Josie-s with Pepper and Melody (1st app.) by DeCarlo; Betty in towel pin-up	16	32	48	115	220	325
29-Beatles satire (68 pgs.)	9	18	27	64	110	155
31(Wint. 64/65)-39 -(68 pgs.)	6	12	18	37	59	80
40-Early Superteen-s; with Pureheart	7	14	21	49	80	110
41(8/67)-43,45-50(2/69) (68 pgs.)	4	8	12	26	41	55
44-Archies Band-s; WEB cameo	5	10	15	30	48	65
51(4/69),52,55-64(6/71): 62-Last squarebound	3	6	9	19	29	38
53-Archies Band-c/s	4	8	12	22	34	45
54-Satan meets Veronica-s	5	10	15	32	51	70
65(8/70),67-70,73,74,76-81,83(6/74) (52 pgs.)	3	6	9	14	20	25
66,82-Sabrina-c	3	6	9	21	32	42
71,72-Two part drug story (8/72,9/72)	3	6	9	21	32	42
75-Archies Band-s	3	6	9	17	25	32
84-99	2	4	6	8	10	12
100 (12/75)	2	4	6	9	13	16
101-130(3/79): 125,126-Riverdale 2001-s	1	2	3	5	6	8
131-160,162-170 (7/84)						6.00
161 (11/82) 3rd app./1st solo Cheryl Blossom-s and pin-up; 2nd Jason Blossom	4	8	12	22	34	45
171-173,175,177-197,199: 197-G. Colan-a						4.00
174,176,198: 174-New Archies Band-s. 176-Cyndi Lauper-c. 198-Archie gang on strike at Archie Ent. offices						6.00
200(9/88)-Illiteracy-s						6.00
201,203-223: Later issues $1.00 cover						3.00
202-Explains end of Archie's jalopy; Dezerland-c/s; James Dean cameo						6.00
224-Last issue						5.00

NOTE: *Archies Band-c-45,47,49,53,56; s-44,53,75,174. UFO-s-50,63,209,220.*

ARCHIE'S PALS 'N' GALS DOUBLE DIGEST MAGAZINE
Archie Comic Publications: Nov, 1992 - Present ($2.50-$3.99)

	GD 2.0	VG 4.0	FN 6.0	VF 8.0	VF/NM 9.0	NM- 9.2
1-Capt. Hero story; Pureheart app.	2	4	6	8	10	12
2-10: 2-Superduck story; Little Jinx in all. 4-Begin $2.75-c	1	2	3	4	5	7
11-29						4.00
30-138: 40-Begin $2.99-c. 48-Begin $3.19-c. 56-Begin $3.29-c. 72-Begin $3.59-c. 100-Story uses screen captures from classic animated series. 102-Begin $3.69-c 125-128-"New Look" art; Moose and Midge break up. 130-Begin $3.99-c. 133-Reggie spotlight, also reprints early apps.						4.00

ARCHIE'S PARABLES
Spire Christian Comics (Fleming H. Revell Co.): 1973,1975 (39/49¢, 36 pgs.)

	GD 2.0	VG 4.0	FN 6.0	VF 8.0	VF/NM 9.0	NM- 9.2
nn-By Al Hartley; 39¢ Edition	2	4	6	11	16	20
49¢, no price editions	2	4	6	8	11	14

ARCHIE'S R/C RACERS (Radio controlled cars)
Archie Comics: Sept, 1989 - No. 10, Mar, 1991 (95¢/$1)

	GD 2.0	VG 4.0	FN 6.0	VF 8.0	VF/NM 9.0	NM- 9.2
1						6.00
2,5-7,10: 5-Elvis parody. 7-Supervillain-c/s. 10-UFO-c/s						4.00
3,4,8,9						3.00

ARCHIE'S RIVAL REGGIE (Reggie & Archie's Joke Book #15 on)
Archie Publications: 1949 - No. 14, Aug, 1954

	GD 2.0	VG 4.0	FN 6.0	VF 8.0	VF/NM 9.0	NM- 9.2
1-Reggie 1st app. in Jackpot Comics #5	87	174	261	553	952	1350
2	41	82	123	256	428	600
3-5	32	64	96	188	307	425
6-10	22	44	66	128	209	290
11-14: Katy Keene in No. 10-14, 1-2 pgs.	17	34	51	98	154	210

ARCHIE'S RIVERDALE HIGH (See Riverdale High)

ARCHIE'S ROLLER COASTER
Spire Christian Comics (Fleming H. Revell Co.): 1981 (69¢)

	GD 2.0	VG 4.0	FN 6.0	VF 8.0	VF/NM 9.0	NM- 9.2
nn-(Low print)	2	4	6	11	16	20

ARCHIE'S SOMETHING ELSE
Spire Christian Comics (Fleming H. Revell Co.): 1975 (39/49¢, 36 pgs.)

	GD 2.0	VG 4.0	FN 6.0	VF 8.0	VF/NM 9.0	NM- 9.2
nn-(39¢-c) Hell's Angels Biker on motorcycle-c	2	4	6	11	16	20
nn-(49¢-c)	2	4	6	8	11	14
Barbour Christian Comics Edition ('86, no price listed)	2	3	4	6	8	10

ARCHIE'S SONSHINE
Spire Christian Comics (Fleming H. Revell Co.): 1973, 1974 (39/49¢, 36 pgs.)

	GD 2.0	VG 4.0	FN 6.0	VF 8.0	VF/NM 9.0	NM- 9.2
39¢ Edition	2	4	6	11	16	20
49¢, no price editions	2	4	6	8	11	14

ARCHIE'S SPORTS SCENE
Spire Christian Comics (Fleming H. Revell Co.): 1983 (no cover price)

	GD 2.0	VG 4.0	FN 6.0	VF 8.0	VF/NM 9.0	NM- 9.2
nn-(Low print)	2	4	6	11	16	20

ARCHIE'S SPRING BREAK
Archie Comics: 1996 - Present ($2.00, 48 pgs., annual)

	GD 2.0	VG 4.0	FN 6.0	VF 8.0	VF/NM 9.0	NM- 9.2
1-Dan DeCarlo-c						4.00
2-4: 2-Dan DeCarlo-c						3.00

ARCHIE'S STORY & GAME COMICS DIGEST MAGAZINE
Archie Enterprises: Nov, 1986 - No. 39, Jan, 1998 ($1.25-$1.95, 128 pgs., digest-size)

	GD 2.0	VG 4.0	FN 6.0	VF 8.0	VF/NM 9.0	NM- 9.2
1: Marked-up copies are common	2	4	6	11	16	20
2-10	2	4	6	8	10	12
11-20	1	2	3	4	5	7
21-38						4.00
39-($1.95)						3.00

ARCHIE'S SUPER HERO SPECIAL (See Archie Giant Series Mag. No. 142)

ARCHIE'S SUPER HERO SPECIAL (...Comics Digest Mag. 2)
Archie Publications (Red Circle): Jan, 1979 - No. 2, Aug, 1979 (95¢, 148 pgs.)

	GD 2.0	VG 4.0	FN 6.0	VF 8.0	VF/NM 9.0	NM- 9.2
1-Simon & Kirby r-/Double Life of Pvt. Strong #1,2; Black Hood, The Fly, Jaguar, The Web app.	2	4	6	11	16	20
2-Contains contents to the never published Black Hood #1; origin Black Hood; N. Adams, Wood, McWilliams, Morrow, S&K-a(r); N. Adams-c. The Shield, The Fly, Jaguar, Hangman, Steel Sterling, The Web, The Fox-r	2	4	6	11	16	20

ARCHIE'S SUPER TEENS
Archie Comic Publications, Inc.: 1994 - No. 4, 1996 ($2.00, 52 pgs.)

	GD 2.0	VG 4.0	FN 6.0	VF 8.0	VF/NM 9.0	NM- 9.2
1-Staton/Esposito-c/a; pull-out poster						4.00
2-4: 2-Fred Hembeck script; Bret Blevins/Terry Austin-a						3.00

ARCHIE'S TV LAUGH-OUT ("...Starring Sabrina" on-c #1-50)
Archie Publications: Dec, 1969 - No. 105, Feb, 1986 (#1-7: 68 pgs.)

	GD 2.0	VG 4.0	FN 6.0	VF 8.0	VF/NM 9.0	NM- 9.2
1-Sabrina begins, thru #106	10	20	30	71	126	180
2 (68 pgs.)	6	12	18	41	66	90
3-6 (68 pgs.)	5	10	15	32	51	70
7-Josie begins, thru #105; Archie's & Josie's Bands cover logos begin	7	14	21	50	83	115
8-23 (52 pgs.): 10-1st Josie on-c. 12-1st Josie and Pussycats on-c. 14-Beatles cameo on poster	4	8	12	26	41	55
24-40: 37,39,40-Bicenntennial-c	3	6	9	14	20	25
41,47,56: 41-Alexandra rejoins J&P band. 47-Fonz cameo; voodoo-s. 56-Fonz parody; B&V with Farrah hair-c	3	6	9	16	22	28
42-46,48-55,57-60	2	4	6	9	12	15
61-68,70-80: 63-UFO-s. 79-Mummy-s	1	3	4	6	8	10
69-Sherlock Holmes parody	1	3	4	6	8	10
81-90,94,95,97-99: 84 Voodoo-s	1	2	3	5	6	8
91-Early Cheryl Blossom-s; Sabrina/Archies Band-c	3	6	9	14	20	26
92-A-Team parody	1	3	4	6	8	10
93-(2/84) Archie in drag-s; Hill Street Blues-s; Groucho Marx parody; cameo parody app. of Batman, Spider-Man, Wonder Woman and others	2	4	6	9	12	15
96-MASH parody-s; Jughead in drag; Archies Band-c	1	3	4	6	8	10
100-(4/85) Michael Jackson parody-c/s; J&P band and Archie band on-c	2	4	6	10	14	18
101-104-Lower print run. 104-Miami Vice parody-c	1	2	3	5	7	9
105-Wrestling/Hulk Hogan parody-c; J&P band-s	2	4	6	9	12	15

NOTE: ***Dan DeCarlo-a*** *78-up(most),* ***c****-89-up(most).* ***Archies Band-s*** *2,7,9-11,15,20,25,37,64,65,67,68,70,73, 76,78,79,83,84,86,90,96,100,101;* ***Archies Band-c*** *2,17,20,91,94,96,99-103.* ***Josie-s*** *12,21,26,35,52,78,80,90.* ***Josie-c*** *10,91,94.* ***Josie and the Pussycats (as a band in costume)-s*** *7,9,10,37,38,41,42,66,84,99-101,105.* ***Josie w/Pussycats member Valerie &/or Melody-s*** *17,20,22,25,27-29,31,33,36,39,40,43-51,53-65,67-77,79,81-*

Archie 3000 #1 © AP

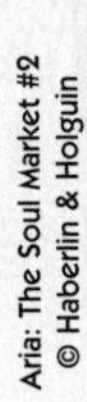

Aria: The Soul Market #2 © Haberlin & Holguin

Armegeddon #1 © Chaos!

	GD 2.0	VG 4.0	FN 6.0	VF 8.0	VF/NM 9.0	NM- 9.2

83,85-89,92-94,102-104. ***Josie w/Pussycats band-c*** *12,14,17,18,22,24.* ***Sabrina-s*** *1-9,11-86,88-106.* ***Sabrina-c*** *1-18,21,23,27,49,91,94.*

ARCHIE'S VACATION SPECIAL
Archie Publications: Winter, 1994 - Present ($2.00/$2.25/$2.29/$2.49, annual)

1 — 4.00
2-8: 8-(2000, $2.49) — 3.00

ARCHIE'S WEIRD MYSTERIES (Continues as Archie's Mysteries)
Archie Comics: Feb, 2000 - No. 24, Dec, 2002 ($1.79/$1.99)

1 — 3.50
2-10: 3-Mighty Crusaders app. — 3.00
11-24: 14-Super Teens-c/app.; Mighty Crusaders app. — 2.50

ARCHIE'S WORLD
Spire Christian Comics (Fleming H. Revell Co.): 1973, 1976 (39/49¢)

	GD	VG	FN	VF	VF/NM	NM-
39¢ Edition	2	4	6	11	16	20
49¢ Edition, no price editions	2	4	6	8	11	14

ARCHIE 3000
Archie Comics: May, 1989 - No. 16, July, 1991 (75¢/95¢/$1.00)

1,16: 16-Aliens-c/s — 4.00
2-15: 6-Begin $1.00-c; X-Mas-c — 3.00

ARCOMICS PREMIERE
Arcomics: July, 1993 ($2.95)

1-1st lenticular-c on a comic (flicker-c) — 3.00

AREA 52
Image Comics: Jan, 2001 - No. 4, June, 2001 ($2.95)

1-4-Haberlin-s/Henry-a — 3.00

ARES
Marvel Comics: Mar, 2006 - No. 5, July, 2006 ($2.99, limited series)

1-5-Oeming-s/Foreman-a — 3.00
...: God of War TPB (2006, $13.99) r/series — 14.00

ARGUS (See Flash, 2nd Series) (Also see Showcase '95 #1,2)
DC Comics: Apr, 1995 - No. 6, Oct, 1995 ($1.50, limited series)

1-6: 4-Begin $1.75-c — 2.50

ARIA
Image Comics (Avalon Studios): Jan, 1999 - Present ($2.50)

	GD	VG	FN	VF	VF/NM	NM-
Preview (11/98, $2.95)						5.00
1-Anacleto-c/a	1	2	3	5	6	8
1-Variant-c by Michael Turner	1	2	3	5	6	8
1-($10.00) Alternate-c by Turner	1	3	4	6	8	10
1,2-(Blanc & Noir) Black and white printing of pencil art						3.00
1-(Blanc & Noir) DF Edition						5.00
2-4: 2,4-Anacleto-c/a. 3-Martinez-a						3.00
4-($6.95) Glow in the Dark-c	1	3	4	6	8	10

Aria Angela 1 (2/00, $2.95) Anacleto-a; 4 covers by Anacleto, JG Jones, Portacio and Quesada — 3.00
Aria Angela Blanc & Noir 1 (4/00, $2.95) Anacleto-c — 3.00
Aria Angela European Ashcan — 10.00
Aria Angela 2 (10/00, $2.95) Anacleto-a/c — 3.00
...: A Midwinter's Dream 1 (1/02, $4.95, 7"x7") text-s w/Anacleto panels — 5.00
...: The Enchanted Collection (5/04, $16.95) r/Summer's Spell & The Uses of Enchantment — 17.00

ARIA: SUMMER'S SPELL
Image Comics (Avalon Studios): Mar, 2002 - No. 2, Jun, 2002 ($2.95)

1,2-Anacleto-c/Holguin-s/Pajarillo & Medina-a — 3.00

ARIA: THE SOUL MARKET
Image Comics (Avalon Studios): Mar, 2001 - No. 6, Dec, 2001 ($2.95)

1-6-Anacleto-c/Holguin-s — 3.00
HC (2002, $26.95, 8.25" x 12.25") oversized r/#1-6 — 27.00
SC (2004, $16.95, 8.25" x 12.25") oversized r/#1-6 — 17.00

ARIA: THE USES OF ENCHANTMENT
Image Comics (Avalon Studios): Feb, 2003 - No. 4, Sept, 2003 ($2.95)

1-4-Anacleto-c/Holguin-s/Medina-a — 3.00

ARIANE AND BLUEBEARD (See Night Music #8)

ARIEL & SEBASTIAN (See Cartoon Tales & The Little Mermaid)

ARION, LORD OF ATLANTIS (Also see Warlord #55)
DC Comics: Nov, 1982 - No. 35, Sept, 1985

1-Story cont'd from Warlord #62 — 3.00
2-35, Special #1 (11/85) — 2.50

ARION THE IMMORTAL (Also see Showcase '95 #7)
DC Comics: July, 1992 - No. 6, Dec, 1992 ($1.50, limited series)

1 — 3.00
2-6: 4-Gustovich-a(i) — 2.50

ARISTOCATS (See Movie Comics & Walt Disney Showcase No. 16)

ARISTOKITTENS, THE (...Meet Jiminy Cricket No. 1)(Disney)
Gold Key: Oct, 1971 - No. 9, Oct, 1975

	GD	VG	FN	VF	VF/NM	NM-
1	3	6	9	20	30	40
2-5,7-9	3	6	9	14	19	24
6-(52 pgs.)	3	6	9	16	22	28

ARIZONA KID, THE (Also see The Comics & Wild Western)
Marvel/Atlas Comics(CSI): Mar, 1951 - No. 6, Jan, 1952

	GD	VG	FN	VF	VF/NM	NM-
1	22	44	66	128	209	290
2-4: 2-Heath-a(3)	12	24	36	69	97	125
5,6	10	20	30	56	76	95

NOTE: ***Heath*** *a-1-3; c-1-3.* ***Maneely*** *c-4-6.* ***Morisi*** *a-4-6.* ***Sinnott*** *a-6.*

ARK, THE (See The Crusaders)

ARKAGA
Image Comics: Sept, 1997 ($2.95, one-shot)

1-Jorgensen-s/a — 3.00

ARKANIUM
Dreamwave Productions: Sept, 2002 - No. 5 ($2.95)

1-5: 1-Gatefold wraparound-c — 3.00

ARKHAM ASYLUM: LIVING HELL
DC Comics: July, 2003 - No. 6, Dec, 2003 ($2.50, limited series)

1-6-Ryan Sook-a; Batman app. 3-Batgirl-c/app. — 2.50

ARKHAM REBORN
DC Comics: Dec, 2009 - No. 3, Feb, 2010 ($2.99, limited series)

1-3-David Hine-s/Jeremy Haun-a — 3.00

ARMAGEDDON
Chaos! Comics: Oct, 1999 - No. 4, Jan, 2000 ($2.95, limited series)

Preview — 5.00
1-4-Lady Death, Evil Ernie, Purgatori app. — 3.00

ARMAGEDDON: ALIEN AGENDA
DC Comics: Nov, 1991 - No. 4, Feb, 1992 ($1.00, limited series)

1-4 — 2.50

ARMAGEDDON FACTOR, THE
AC Comics: 1987 - No. 2, 1987; No. 3, 1990 ($1.95)

1,2: Sentinels of Justice, Dragonfly, Femforce — 2.50
3-($3.95, color)-Almost all AC characters app. — 4.00

ARMAGEDDON: INFERNO
DC Comics: Apr, 1992 - No. 4, July, 1992 ($1.00, limited series)

1-4: Many DC heroes app. 3-A. Adams/Austin-a — 2.50

ARMAGEDDON 2001
DC Comics: May, 1991 - No. 2, Oct, 1991 ($2.00, squarebound, 68 pgs.)

1-Features many DC heroes; intro Waverider — 4.00
1-2nd & 3rd printings; 3rd has silver ink-c — 2.50
2 — 3.00

ARMED & DANGEROUS
Acclaim Comics (Armada): Apr, 1996 - No.4, July, 1996 ($2.95, B&W)

1-4-Bob Hall-c/a & scripts — 3.00
Special 1 (8/96, $2.95, B&W)-Hall-c/a & scripts. — 3.00

ARMED & DANGEROUS HELL'S SLAUGHTERHOUSE
Acclaim Comics (Armada): Oct, 1996 - No. 4, Jan, 1997 ($2.95, B&W)

1-4: Hall-c/a/scripts. — 3.00

ARMOR (AND THE SILVER STREAK) (Revengers Featuring... in indicia for #1-3)
Continuity Comics: Sept, 1985 - No.13, Apr, 1992 ($2.00)

1-13: 1-Intro/origin Armor & the Silver Streak; Neal Adams-c/a. 7-Origin Armor; Nebres-i — 3.50

ARMOR (DEATHWATCH 2000)
Continuity Comics: Apr, 1993 - No. 6, Nov, 1993 ($2.50)

1-6: 1-3-Deathwatch 2000 x-over — 3.00

ARMORINES (See X-O Manowar #25 for 16 pg. bound-in Armorines #0)

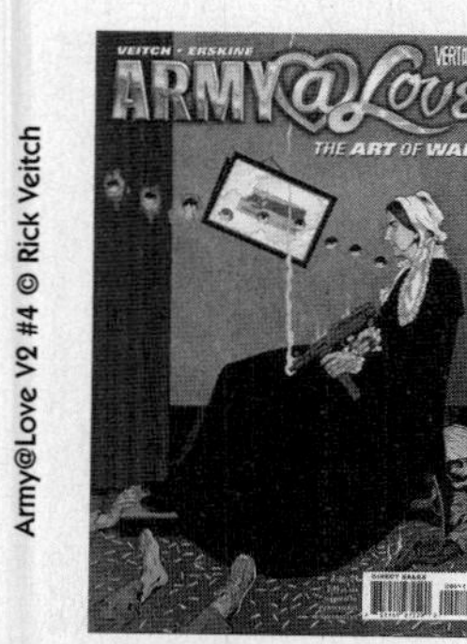

Army@Love V2 #4 © Rick Veitch

Army of Darkness: Ash Saves Obama #1 © Orion

Arrowsmith #1 © Busiek & Pacheco

GD 2.0 | VG 4.0 | FN 6.0 | VF 8.0 | VF/NM 9.0 | NM- 9.2

Valiant: June, 1994 - No. 12, June, 1995 ($2.25)
0-Stand-alone edition with cardstock-c 25.00
0-Gold 15.00
1-12: 7-Wraparound-c. 12-Byrne-c/swipe (X-Men, 1st Series #138) 2.50

ARMORINES (Volume 2)
Acclaim Comics: Oct, 1999 - No. 4 ($3.95/$2.50, limited series)
1-($3.95) Calafiore & P. Palmiotti-a 4.00
2,3-($2.50) 2.50

ARMOR X
Image Comics: March, 2005 - No. 4, June, 2005 ($2.95, limited series)
1-Keith Champagne-s/Andy Smith-a; flip covers on #2-4 3.00

ARMY AND NAVY COMICS (Supersnipe No. 6 on)
Street & Smith Publications: May, 1941 - No. 5, July, 1942
1-Cap Fury & Nick Carter 53 106 159 329 550 770
2-Cap Fury & Nick Carter 31 62 93 181 291 400
3,4: 4-Jack Farr-c/a 23 46 69 133 214 295
5-Supersnipe app.; see Shadow V2#3 for 1st app.; Story of Douglas MacArthur; George Marcoux-c/a 53 106 159 332 556 780

ARMY @ LOVE
DC Comics (Vertigo): May, 2007 - No. 12, Apr, 2008; V2 #1, Oct, 2008 - No. 6, Mar, 2009 ($2.99)
1-12-Rick Veitch-s/a(p); Gary Erskine-a(i) 3.00
(Vol. 2) 1-6-Veitch-s/a(p); Erskine-a(i) 3.00
...: Generation Pwned TPB (2008, $12.99) r/#6-12 10.00
...: The Hot Zone Club TPB (2007, $9.99) r/#1-5; intro. by Peter Kuper 10.00

ARMY ATTACK
Charlton Comics: July, 1964 - No. 4, Feb, 1965; V2#38, July, 1965 - No. 47, Feb, 1967
V1#1 5 10 15 30 48 65
2-4(2/65) 3 6 9 19 29 38
V2#38(7/65)-47 (formerly U.S. Air Force #1-37) 3 6 9 16 22 28
NOTE: *Glanzman a-1-3. Montes/Bache a-44.*

ARMY AT WAR (Also see Our Army at War & Cancelled Comic Cavalcade)
DC Comics: Oct-Nov, 1978
1-Kubert-c; all new story and art 2 4 6 10 14 18

ARMY OF DARKNESS (Movie)
Dark Horse Comics: Nov, 1992 - No. 2, Dec, 1992; No. 3, Oct, 1993 ($2.50, limited series)
1-3-Bolton painted-c/a 2 4 6 9 12 15
... Movie Adaptation TPB (2006, $14.99) r/#1-3; intro. by Busiek; Bruce Campbell interview 15.00

ARMY OF DARKNESS (Also see Marvel Zombies vs. Army of Darkness)
Dynamite Entertainment: 2005 - No. 13, 2007 ($2.99)
1-4 (Vs. Re-Animator):1,2-Four covers; Greene-a/Kuhoric-s. 3,4-Three covers 3.00
5-13: 5-7-Kuhoric-s/Sharpe-a; four covers. 8-11-Ash Vs. Dracula. 12,13-Death of Ash 3.00

ARMY OF DARKNESS: ...
Dynamite Entertainment: 2007 - Present ($3.50)
... From the Ashes 1-4-Kuhoric-s/Blanco-a; covers by Blanco & Suydam 3.50
5-8-(The Long Road Home); two covers on each 3.50
9-25: 9-12-(Home Sweet Hell), 13-King For a Day. 14-17-Hellbillies and Deadnecks 3.50
...: Ash's Christmas Horror Special (2008, $4.99) Kuhoric-s/Simons-a; 2 covers 5.00

ARMY OF DARKNESS: ASHES 2 ASHES (Movie)
Devil's Due Publ.: July, 2004 - No. 4, 2004 ($2.99, limited series)
1-4-Four covers for each; Nick Bradshaw-a 3.00
1-Director's Cut (12/04, $4.99) r/#1, cover gallery, script and sketch pages 5.00
TPB (2005, $14.99) r/series; cover gallery; Bradshaw interview and sketch pages 15.00

ARMY OF DARKNESS: ASH SAVES OBAMA
Dynamite Entertainment: 2009 - No. 4, 2009 ($3.50, limited series)
1-4-Serrano-s/Padilla-a; covers by Parrillo and Nauck. 4-Obama app. 3.50

ARMY OF DARKNESS: SHOP TILL YOU DROP DEAD (Movie)
Devil's Due Publ.: Jan, 2005 - No. 4, July, 2005 ($2.99, limited series)
1-4:1-Five covers; Bradshaw-a/Kuhoric-s. 2-4: Two covers. 3-Greene-a 3.00

ARMY OF DARKNESS / XENA
Dynamite Entertainment: 2008 - No. 4, 2008 ($3.50, limited series)
1-4-Layman-s/Montenegro-a; two covers on each 3.50

ARMY SURPLUS KOMIKZ FEATURING CUTEY BUNNY
Army Surplus Komikz/Eclipse Comics: 1982 - No. 5, 1985 ($1.50, B&W)
1-Cutey Bunny begins 2 4 6 8 10 12
2-5: 5-(Eclipse)-JLA/X-Men/Batman parody 4.50

ARMY WAR HEROES (Also see Iron Corporal)
Charlton Comics: Dec, 1963 - No. 38, June, 1970
1 5 10 15 34 55 75
2-10 3 6 9 19 29 38
11-21,23-30: 24-Intro. Archer & Corp. Jack series 3 6 9 16 22 28
22-Origin/1st app. Iron Corporal series by Glanzman 4 8 12 24 37 50
31-38 2 4 6 10 14 18
Modern Comics Reprint 36 ('78) 4.00
NOTE: *Montes/Bache a-1, 16, 17, 21, 23-25, 27-30.*

AROUND THE BLOCK WITH DUNC & LOO (See Dunc and Loo)

AROUND THE WORLD IN 80 DAYS (Movie) (See A Golden Picture Classic)
Dell Publishing Co.: Feb, 1957
Four Color 784-Photo-c 7 14 21 50 83 115

AROUND THE WORLD UNDER THE SEA (See Movie Classics)

AROUND THE WORLD WITH ARCHIE (See Archie Giant Series Mag. #29, 35, 141)

AROUND THE WORLD WITH HUCKLEBERRY & HIS FRIENDS (See Dell Giant No. 44)

ARRGH! (Satire)
Marvel Comics Group: Dec, 1974 - No. 5, Sept, 1975 (25¢)
1-Dracula story; Sekowsky-a(p) 3 6 9 18 27 35
2-5: 2-Frankenstein. 3-Mummy. 4-Nightstalker(TV); Dracula-c/app., Hunchback. 5-Invisible Man, Dracula 2 4 6 13 18 22
NOTE *Alcala a-2; c-3. Everett a-1r, 2r. Grandenetti a-4. Maneely a-4r. Sutton a-1-3.*

ARROW (See Protectors)
Malibu Comics: Oct, 1992 ($1.95, one-shot)
1-Moder-a(p) 2.50

ARROW, THE (See Funny Pages)
Centaur Publications: Oct, 1940 - No. 2, Nov, 1940; No. 3, Oct, 1941
1-The Arrow begins(r/Funny Pages) 309 618 927 2163 3782 5400
2,3: 2-Tippy Taylor serial continues from Amazing Mystery Funnies #24. 3-Origin Dash Dartwell, the Human Meteor; origin The Rainbow-r; bondage-c 139 278 417 883 1517 2150
NOTE: *Gustavson a-1, 2; c-3.*

ARROWHEAD (See Black Rider and Wild Western)
Atlas Comics (CPS): April, 1954 - No. 4, Nov, 1954
1-Arrowhead & his horse Eagle begin 15 30 45 88 137 185
2-4: 4-Forte-a 10 20 30 54 72 90
NOTE: *Heath c-3. Jack Katz a-3. Maneely c-2. Pakula a-2. Sinnott a-1-4; c-1.*

ARROWSMITH (Also see Astro City/Arrowsmith flip book)
DC Comics (Cliffhanger): Sept, 2003 - No. 6, May, 2004 ($2.95)
1-6-Pacheco-a/Busiek-s 3.00
...: So Smart in Their Fine Uniforms TPB (2004, $14.95) r/#1-6 15.00

ARSENAL (Teen Titans' Speedy)
DC Comics: Oct, 1998 - No. 4, Jan, 1999 ($2.50, limited series)
1-4: Grayson-s. 1-Black Canary app. 2-Green Arrow app. 2.50

ARSENAL SPECIAL (See New Titans, Showcase '94 #7 & Showcase '95 #8)
DC Comics: 1996 ($2.95, one-shot)
1 3.00

ARTBABE
Fantagraphics Books: May, 1996 - Apr, 1999 ($2.50/$2.95/$3.50, B&W)
V1 #5, V2 #1-3 3.00
#4-($3.50) 3.50

ARTEMIS: REQUIEM (Also see Wonder Woman, 2nd Series #90)
DC Comics: June, 1996 - No. 6, Nov, 1996 ($1.75, limited series)
1-6: Messner-Loebs scripts & Benes-c/a in all. 1,2-Wonder Woman app. 3.00

ART OF HOMAGE STUDIOS, THE
Image Comics: Dec, 1993 ($4.95, one-shot)
1-Short stories and pin-ups by Jim Lee, Silvestri, Williams, Portacio & Chiodo 5.00

ART OF ZEN INTERGALACTIC NINJA, THE
Entity Comics: 1994 - No. 2, 1994 ($2.95)
1,2 3.00

ARZACH (See Moebius...)
Dark Horse Comics: 1996 ($6.95, one-shot)
nn-Moebius-c/a/scripts 1 2 3 4 5 7

Ash #4 © Q&P

Astonishing #4 © MAR

Astonishing Tales (2009 series) #3 © MAR

GD VG FN VF VF/NM NM-
2.0 4.0 6.0 8.0 9.0 9.2

ASCENSION
Image Comics (Top Cow Productions): Oct, 1997 - No. 22, Mar, 2000 ($2.50)
Preview 5.00
Preview Gold Edition 8.00
Preview San Diego Edition 2 4 6 8 10 12
0 4.00
1/2 6.00
1-David Finch-s/a(p)/Batt-s/a(i) 4.00
1-Variant-c w/Image logo at lower right 6.00
2-6 3.00
7-22 2.50
Fan Club Edition 5.00
...COLLECTED EDITION
1998 - No. 2 ($4.95, squarebound) 1,2: 1-r/#1,2. 2-r/#3,4 5.00

ASH
Event Comics: Nov, 1994 - No. 6, Dec, 1995; No. 0, May, 1996 ($2.50/$3.00)
0-Present & Future (Both 5/96, $3.00, foil logo-c)-w/pin-ups 3.00
0-Blue Foil logo-c (Present and Future) (1000 each) 4.00
0-Silver Prism logo-c (Present and Future) (500 each) 10.00
0-Red Prism logo-c (Present and Future) (250 each) 20.00
0-Gold Hologram logo-c (Present and Future) (1000 each) 8.00
1-Quesada-p/story; Palmiotti-i/story: Barry Windsor-Smith pin-up
2 4 6 8 10 12
2-Mignola Hellboy pin-up 1 2 3 4 5 7
3,4: 3-Big Guy pin-up by Geoff Darrow. 4-Jim Lee pin-up 4.00
4-Fahrenheit Gold 7.00
4-6-Fahrenheit Red (5,6-1000) 8.00
4-6-Fahrenheit White 12.00
5, 6-Double-c w/Hildebrandt Bros.-a, Quesada & Palmiotti. 6-Texeira-c 3.00
5,6-Fahrenheit Gold (2000) 4.00
6-Fahrenheit White (500)-Texeira-c 12.00
Volume 1 (1996, $14.95, TPB)-r/#1-5, intro by James Robinson 15.00
Wizard Mini-Comic (1996, magazine supplement) 2.25
Wizard #1/2 (1997, mail order) 4.00

ASH: CINDER & SMOKE
Event Comics: May, 1997 - No. 6, Oct, 1997 ($2.95, limited series)
1-6: Ramos-a/Waid, Augustyn-s in all. 2-6-variant covers by Ramos and Quesada 3.00

ASH: FILES
Event Comics: Mar, 1997 ($2.95, one-shot)
1-Comics w/text 3.00

ASH: FIRE AND CROSSFIRE
Event Comics: Jan, 1999 - No. 5 ($2.95, limited series)
1,2-Robinson-s/Quesada & Palmiotti-c/a 3.00

ASH: FIRE WITHIN, THE
Event Comics: Sept, 1996 - No. 2, Jan, 1997 ($2.95, unfinished limited series)
1,2: Quesada & Palmiotti-c/s/a 3.00

ASH/ 22 BRIDES
Event Comics: Dec, 1996 - No. 2, Apr, 1997 ($2.95, limited series)
1,2: Nicieza-s/Ramos-c/a 3.00

ASKANI'SON (See Adventures of Cyclops & Phoenix limited series)
Marvel Comics: Jan, 1996 - No. 4, May, 1996 ($2.95, limited series)
1-4: Story cont'd from Advs. of Cyclops & Phoenix; Lobdell/Loeb story; Gene Ha-c/a(p) 3.00
TPB (1997, $12.99) r/#1-4; Gene Ha painted-c 13.00

ASPEN (MICHAEL TURNER PRESENTS:...) (Also see Fathom)
Aspen MLT, Inc.: July, 2003 - No. 3, Aug, 2003 ($2.99)
1-Fathom story; Turner-a/Johns-s; interviews w/Turner & Johns; two covers by Turner 3.00
2,3:2-Fathom story; Turner-a/Johns-s; two covers by Turner; pin-ups and interviews 3.00
... Seasons: Fall 2005 (12/05, $2.99) short stories by various; Turner-c 3.00
... Seasons: Spring 2005 (4/05, $2.99) short stories by various; Turner-c 3.00
... Seasons: Summer 2006 (10/06, $2.99) short stories by various; Turner-c 3.00
... Seasons: Winter 2009 (3/09, $2.99) short stories by various; Benitez-c 3.00
... Showcase: Aspen Matthews 1 (7/08, $2.99) Caldwell-a 3.00
... Showcase: Kiani 1 (10/09, $2.99) Scott Clark-a; covers by Clark and Caldwell 3.00
... Sketchbook 1 (2003, $2.99) sketch pages by Michael Turner and Talent Caldwell 3.00
... Splash: 2006 Swimsuit Spectacular 1 (3/06, $2.99) pin-up pages by various; Turner-c 3.00
... Splash: 2007 Swimsuit Spectacular 1 (8/07, $2.99) pin-up pages by various; Turner-c 3.00
... Splash: 2008 Swimsuit Spectacular 1 (7/08, $2.99) pin-up pages by various; Turner-c 3.00

ASPEN SHOWCASE
Aspen MLT: Oct, 2008 ($2.99)
...: Benoist 1 (10/08) - Krul-s/Gunnell-a; two covers by Gunnell & Manapul 3.00
...: Ember 1 (2/09) - Randy Green-a; two covers by Gunnell & Green 3.00

ASSASSINS
DC Comics (Amalgam): Apr, 1996 ($1.95)
1 2.50

ASSAULT ON NEW OLYMPUS PROLOGUE
Marvel Comics: Jan, 2010 ($3.99, one-shot)
1-Spider-Man, Hercules, Amadeus Cho app.; Granov-c; leads into Inc. Hercules #138 4.00

ASTONISHING (Formerly Marvel Boy No. 1, 2)
Marvel/Atlas Comics(20CC): No. 3, Apr, 1951 - No. 63, Aug, 1957
3-Marvel Boy continues; 3-5-Marvel Boy-c 94 188 282 597 1024 1450
4-6-Last Marvel Boy; 4-Stan Lee app. 66 132 198 419 722 1025
7-10: 7-Maneely s/f story. 10-Sinnott s/f story 36 72 108 211 343 475
11,12,15,17,20 31 62 93 182 296 410
13,14,16,18,19-Krigstein-a. 18-Jack The Ripper sty
31 62 93 186 303 420
21,22,24 26 52 78 154 252 350
23-E.C. swipe "The Hole In The Wall" from Vault Of Horror #16
27 54 81 158 259 360
25,29: 25-Crandall-a. 29-Decapitation-c 24 48 72 142 234 325
26-28 22 44 66 132 216 300
30-Tentacled eyeball-c/story; classic-c 45 90 135 284 480 675
31-37-Last pre-code issue 20 40 60 117 189 260
38-43,46,48-52,56,58,59,61 16 32 48 94 147 200
44,45,47,53-55,57,60: 44-Crandall swipe/Weird Fantasy #22. 45,47-Krigstein-a. 53-Ditko-a. 54-Torres-a, 55-Crandall, Torres-a. 57-Williamson/Krenkel-a (4 pgs.).
60-Williamson/Mayo-a (4 pgs.) 17 34 51 100 158 215
62,63: 62-Torres, Powell-a. 63-Woodbridge-a 17 34 51 98 154 210
NOTE: ***Ayers** a-16, 49. **Berg** a-36, 53, 56. **Cameron** a-50. **Gene Colan** a-12, 20, 29, 56. **Ditko** a-53. **Drucker** a-41, 62. **Everett** a-3-6(3), 6, 10, 12, 37, 47, 48, 58; c-3-5, 13,15, 16, 18, 29, 47, 49, 51, 53-55, 57, 59-63. **Fass** a-11, 34. **Forte** a-26, 48, 53, 58, 60. **Fuje** a-11. **Heath** a-8, 29; c-8, 9, 19, 22, 25, 26. **Kirby** a-56. **Lawrence** a-28, 37, 38, 42. **Maneely** a-7(2), 19; c-7, 31, 33, 34, 56. **Moldoff** a-33. **Morisi** a-10, 60. **Morrow** a-52, 61. **Orlando** a-47, 58, 61. **Pakula** a-10. **Powell** a-43, 44, 48. **Ravielli** a-26, 28. **Reinman** a-32, 34, 38. **Robinson** a-20. **J. Romita** a-7, 18, 24, 43, 57,61. **Roussos** a-55. **Sale** a-28, 38, 59; c-32. **Sekowsky** a-13. **Severin** c-46. **Shores** a-16, 60. **Sinnott** a-11, 30, 31. **Whitney** a-13. **Ed Win** a-20. Canadian reprints exist.*

ASTONISHING TALES (See Ka-Zar)
Marvel Comics Group: Aug, 1970 - No. 36, July, 1976 (#1-7: 15¢; #8: 25¢)
1-Ka-Zar (by Kirby(p) #1,2; by B. Smith #3-6) & Dr. Doom (by Wood #1-4; by Tuska #5,6; by Colan #7,8; 1st Marvel villain solo series) double feature begins; Kraven the Hunter-c/story; Nixon cameo 7 14 21 45 73 100
2-Kraven the Hunter-c/story; Kirby, Wood-a 4 8 12 22 34 45
3-6: B. Smith-p; Wood-a-#3,4. 5,6-Red Skull 2-part story
4 8 12 24 37 50
7-Last 15¢ issue; Black Panther app. 3 6 9 16 23 30
8-(25¢, 52 pgs.)-Last Dr. Doom of series 4 8 12 22 34 45
9-All Ka-Zar issues begin; Lorna-r/Lorna #14 2 4 6 11 16 20
10-B. Smith/Sal Buscema-a. 3 6 9 14 20 25
11-Origin Ka-Zar & Zabu; death of Ka-Zar's father 2 4 6 13 18 22
12-2nd app.Man-Thing; by Neal Adams (see Savage Tales #1 for 1st app.)
4 8 12 26 41 55
13-3rd app.Man-Thing 3 6 9 19 29 38
14-20: 14-Jann of the Jungle-r (1950s); reprints censored Ka-Zar-s from Savage Tales #1. 17-S.H.I.E.L.D. begins. 19-Starlin-a(p). 20-Last Ka-Zar (continues into 1974 Ka-Zar series)
1 3 4 6 8 10
21-(12/73)-It! the Living Colossus begins, ends #24 (see Supernatural Thrillers #1)
4 8 12 22 34 45
22-24: 23,24-IT vs. Fin Fang Foom 3 6 9 18 27 35
25-1st app. Deathlok the Demolisher; full length stories begin, end #36; Perez's 1st work, 2 pgs. (8/74) 5 10 15 34 55 75
26-28,30 2 4 6 11 16 20
29-r/origin/1st app. Guardians of the Galaxy from Marvel Super-Heroes #18 plus-c w/4 pgs. omitted; no Deathlok story 1 3 4 6 8 10
31-34: 31-Watcher-r/Silver Surfer #3 2 4 6 9 12 15
35,36-(Regular 25¢ edition)(5,7/76) 2 4 6 9 12 15
35,36-(30¢-c, low distribution) 5 10 15 32 51 70
NOTE: ***Buckler** a-13i, 16p, 25, 26p, 27p, 28, 29p-36p; c-13, 25p, 26-30, 32-35p, 36. **John Buscema** a-9, 12p-14p, 16p; c-4-6p, 12p. **Colan** a-7p, 8p. **Ditko** a-21r. **Everett** a-6i. **G. Kane** a-11p, 15p; c-9, 10p, 11p, 14, 15p, 21p. **McWilliams** a-30i. **Starlin** a-19p; c-16p. **Sutton & Trimpe** a-8. **Tuska** a-5p, 6p, 8p. **Wood** a-1-4. **Wrightson** c-31i.*

ASTONISHING TALES (Anthology)
Marvel Comics: Apr, 2009 - No. 6, Sept, 2009 ($3.99, limited series)
1-6-Wolverine, Punisher, Iron Man and Iron Man 2020 app. 1-Wraparound-c 4.00

Astonishing X-Men #4 © MAR

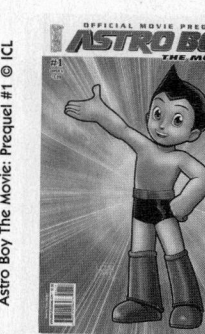

Astro Boy The Movie: Prequel #1 © ICL

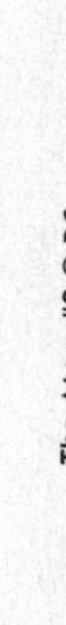
The Atom #8 © DC

GD 2.0 | VG 4.0 | FN 6.0 | VF 8.0 | VF/NM 9.0 | NM- 9.2

ASTONISHING X-MEN
Marvel Comics: Mar, 1995 - No. 4, July, 1995 ($1.95, limited series)
1-Age of Apocalypse; Magneto-c 4.00
2-4 3.00

ASTONISHING X-MEN
Marvel Comics: Sept, 1999 - No.3, Nov, 1999 ($2.50, limited series)
1-3-New team, Cable & X-Man app.; Peterson-a 2.50
TPB (11/00, $15.95) r/#1-3, X-Men #92 & #95, Uncanny X-Men #375 16.00

ASTONISHING X-MEN (See Giant-Size Astonishing X-Men for story folllowing #24)
Marvel Comics: July, 2004 - Present ($2.99)
1-Whedon-s/Cassaday-c/a; team of Cyclops, Beast, Wolverine, Emma Frost & Kitty Pryde 3.00
1-Director's Cut (2004, $3.99) different Cassaday partial sketch-c; cover gallery, sketch pages and script excerpt 4.00
1-Variant-c by Cassaday 10.00
1-Variant-c by Dell'Otto 5.00
2,3,5,6-X-Men battle Ord 3.00
4-Colossus returns 4.00
4-Variant Colossus cover by Cassaday 5.00
7-24: 7-Fantastic Four app. 9,10-X-Men vs. the Danger Room 3.00
7,9,10-12,19-24-Second printing variant covers 3.00
25-33: 25-Ellis-s/Bianchi-a begins; Bianchi wraparound-c. 31-Jimenez-a begins 3.00
.../Amazing Spider-Man: The Gauntlet Sketchbook ('09, giveaway) flip book preview 1.00
...: Ghost Boxes 1,2 (12/08-1/09, $3.99) Ellis-s/Davis & Granov-a; full Ellis script 4.00
... Saga (2006, $3.99) reprints highlights from #1-12; sketch pages and cover gallery 4.00
... Sketchbook Special ('08, $2.99) Costume sketches & blueprints by Bianchi & Larroca 3.00
...Vol. 1 HC (2006, $29.99, dust jacket) r/#1-12; interviews, sketch pages and covers 30.00
...Vol. 1: Gifted (2004, $14.99) r/#1-6; variant cover gallery 15.00
...Vol. 2: Dangerous (2005, $14.99) r/#7-12; variant cover gallery 15.00
...Vol. 3: Torn (2007, $14.99) r/#13-18; variant & sketch cover gallery 15.00

ASTOUNDING SPACE THRILLS: THE COMIC BOOK
Image Comics: Apr, 2000 - No. 4, Dec, 2000 ($2.95, limited series)
1-4-Steve Conley-s/a. 2,3-Flip book w/Crater Kid 3.00
Galaxy-Sized Astounding Space Thrills 1 (10/01, $4.95) 5.00

ASTOUNDING WOLF-MAN
Image Comics: Jun, 2007 - Present ($2.99)
1-Free Comic Boy Day issue; Kirkman-s/Howard-a; origin story 3.00
2-21: 11-Invincible x-over from Invincble #57 3.00
Vol. 1 TPB (2008, $14.99) r/#1-7; sketch pages; Kirkman intro. 15.00

ASTRA
CPM Manga: 2001 - No. 8 ($2.95, B&W, limited series)
1-8: Created by Jerry Robinson; Tanaka-a. 1-Balent variant-c 3.00
TPB (2002, $15.95) r/#1-8; JH Williams III-c from #3 16.00

ASTRO BOY (TV) (See March of Comics #285 & The Original...)
Gold Key: August, 1965 (12¢)
1(10151-508)-Scarce;1st app. Astro Boy in comics 26 52 78 190 370 550

ASTRO BOY THE MOVIE (Based on the 2009 CGI movie)
IDW Publishing: 2009 ($3.99, limited series)
...Official Movie Adaptation 1-4 (8/09 - No. 4, 9/09, $3.99) EJ Su-a 4.00
...Official Movie Prequel 1-4 (5/09 - No. 4, 8/09) Jourdan-a/c; Ashley Wood var-c on each 4.00

ASTRO CITY / ARROWSMITH (Flip book)
DC Comics (WildStorm Productions): Jun, 2004 ($2.95, one-shot flip book)
1-Intro. Black Badge; Ross-c; Arrowsmith a/c by Pacheco 3.00

ASTRO CITY (Also see Kurt Busiek's Astro City)
DC Comics (WildStorm Productions): Dec, 2004 - Dec, 2009 (one-shots)
...: Astra Special 1,2 (11/09, 12/09, $3.99) Busiek-s/Anderson-a/Ross-c 4.00
... A Visitor's Guide (12/04, $5.95) short story, city guide and pin-ups by various; Ross-c 6.00
...: Beautie (4/08, $3.99) Busiek-s/Anderson-a/Ross-c; origin 4.00
...: Samaritan (9/06, $3.99) Busiek-s/Anderson-a/Ross-c; origin of Infidel 4.00

ASTRO CITY: DARK AGE
DC Comics (WildStorm Productions): Aug, 2005 - No. 4, Dec, 2005 ($2.95, limited series)
Book One 1-4-Busiek-s/Anderson-a/Ross-c; Silver Agent and The Blue Knight app. 3.00
Book Two #1-4 (1/07-11/07, $2.99) Busiek-s/Anderson-a/Ross-c 3.00
Book Three #1-4 (7/09-10/09, $3.99) Busiek-s/Anderson-a/Ross-c 4.00
Book Four #1 (3/10, $3.99) Busiek-s/Anderson-a/Ross-c 4.00
... 1: Brothers and Other Strangers HC (2008, $29.99, d.j.) r/Book One #1-4, Book Two #1-4, and story from Astro City/Arrowsmith #1; Marc Guggenheim intro.; new Ross-c 30.00
... 1: Brothers and Other Strangers SC (2009, $19.99) same contents as HC 20.00

GD 2.0 | VG 4.0 | FN 6.0 | VF 8.0 | VF/NM 9.0 | NM- 9.2

ASTRO CITY: LOCAL HEROES
DC Comics (WildStorm Productions): Apr, 2003 - No. 5, Feb, 2004 ($2.95, limited series)
1-5-Busiek-s/Anderson-a/Ross-c 3.00
HC (2005, $24.95) r/series; Kurt Busiek's Astro City V2 #21,22; stories from Astro City/Arrowsmith #1; and 9-11, The World's Finest... Vol. 2; Alex Ross sketch pages 25.00
SC (2005, $17.99) same contents as HC 18.00

ASYLUM
Millennium Publications: 1993 ($2.50)
1-3: 1-Bolton-c/a; Russell 2-pg. illos 2.50

ASYLUM
Maximum Press: Dec, 1995 - No. 11, Jan, 1997 ($2.95/$2.99, anthology) (#1-6 are flip books)
1-11: 1-Warchild by Art Adams, Beanworld, Avengelyne, Battlestar Galactica. 2-Intro Mike Deodato's Deathkiss. 4-1st app.Christian; painted Battlestar Galactica story begins. 6-Intro Bionix (Six Million Dollar Man & the Bionic Woman). 7-Begin $2.99-c. 8-B&W-a. 9- Foot Soldiers & Kid Supreme. 10-Lady Supreme by Terry Moore-c/app. 4.00

ATARI FORCE (Also see Promotional comics section)
DC Comics: Jan, 1984 - No. 20, Aug, 1985 (Mando paper)
1-(1/84)-Intro Tempest, Packrat, Babe, Morphea, & Dart 4.00
2-20 3.00
Special 1 (4/86) 3.00
NOTE: *Byrne c-Special 1i. Giffen a-12p, 13i. Rogers a-18p, Special 1p.*

A-TEAM, THE (TV) (Also see Marvel Graphic Novel)
Marvel Comics Group: Mar, 1984 - No. 3, May, 1984 (limited series)
1-3 5.00
1,2-(Whitman bagged set) w/75¢-c 2 4 6 8 10 12
3-(Whitman, no bag) w/75¢-c 1 2 3 5 6 8

ATHENA INC. THE MANHUNTER PROJECT
Image Comics: Dec, 2001; Apr, 2002 - No. 6 ($2.95/$4.95/$5.95)
...The Beginning (12/01, $5.95) Anacleto-c/a; Haberlin-s 6.00
1-5: 1-(4/02, $2.95) two covers by Anacleto 3.00
6-($4.95) 5.00
...: Agents Roster #1 (11/02, $5.95, 8 1/2 x 11") bios and sketch pages by Anacleto 6.00
Vol. 1 TPB (4/03, $19.95) r/#1-6 & Agents Roster; cover gallery 20.00

ATHENA
Dynamite Entertainment: 2009 - No. 4, 2010 ($3.50)
1-4-Murray-s/Neves-a; multiple covers on each. 1-Obama flip cover 3.50

ATLANTIS CHRONICLES, THE (Also see Aquaman, 3rd Series & Aquaman: Time & Tide)
DC Comics: Mar, 1990 - No. 7, Sept, 1990 ($2.95, limited series, 52 pgs.)
1-7: 1-Peter David scripts. 7-True origin of Aquaman; nudity panels 3.25

ATLANTIS, THE LOST CONTINENT
Dell Publishing Co.: May, 1961
Four Color #1188-Movie, photo-c 10 20 30 68 119 170

ATLAS (See 1st Issue Special)

ATLAS
Dark Horse Comics: Feb, 1994 - No. 4, 1994 ($2.50, limited series)
1-4 2.50

ATMOSPHERICS
Avatar Press: June, 2002 ($5.95, B&W, one-shot graphic novel)
1-Warren Ellis-s/Ken Meyer Jr.-painted-a/c 6.00

ATOM, THE (See Action #425, All-American #19, Brave & the Bold, D.C. Special Series #1, Detective Comics, Flash Comics #80, Hawkman, Identity Crisis, JLA, Power Of The Atom, Showcase #34 -36, Super Friends, Sword of The Atom, Teen Titans & World's Finest)

ATOM, THE (...& the Hawkman No. 39 on)
National Periodical Publ.: June-July, 1962 - No. 38, Aug-Sept, 1968
1-(6-7/62)-Intro Plant-Master; 1st app. Maya 88 176 264 748 1474 2200
2 32 64 96 245 473 700
3-1st Time Pool story; 1st app. Chronos (origin) 22 44 66 157 304 450
4,5: 4-Snapper Carr x-over 16 32 48 117 226 335
6,9,10 13 26 39 91 168 245
7-Hawkman x-over (6-7/63; 1st Atom & Hawkman team-up); 1st app. Hawkman since Brave & the Bold tryouts 29 58 87 212 406 600
8-Justice League, Dr. Light app. 13 26 39 94 175 255
11-15: 13-Chronos-c/story 10 20 30 71 126 180
16-20: 19-Zatanna x-over 8 16 24 54 90 125
21-28,30: 26-Two-page pin-up. 28-Chronos-c/story 7 14 21 49 80 110

Atom-Age Comics #5 © STJ

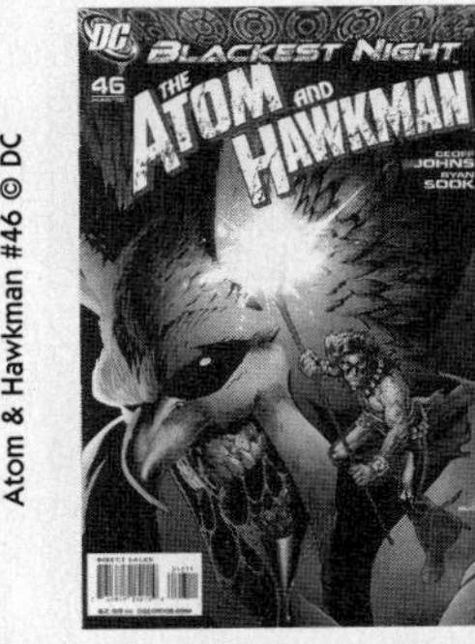

Atom & Hawkman #46 © DC

Atomic Rabbit #6 © CC

GD 2.0 | VG 4.0 | FN 6.0 | VF 8.0 | VF/NM 9.0 | NM- 9.2

29-1st solo Golden Age Atom x-over in S.A. 14 28 42 97 181 265
31-35,37,38: 31-Hawkman x-over. 37-Intro. Major Mynah; Hawkman cameo
6 12 18 41 66 90
36-G.A. Atom x-over 7 14 21 49 80 110
NOTE: ***Anderson** a-1-11i, 13i; c-inks-1-25, 31-35, 37. **Sid Greene** a-8i-37i. **Gil Kane** a-1p-37p; c-1p-28p, 29, 33p, 34; c-26i. **George Roussos** a-38i. **Mike Sekowsky** a-38p. Time Pool stories also in 6, 9,12, 17, 21, 27, 35.*

ATOM, THE (See All New Atom and Tangent Comics/ The Atom)

ATOM AGE (See Classics Illustrated Special Issue)

ATOM-AGE COMBAT
St. John Publishing Co.: June, 1952 - No. 5, Apr, 1953; Feb, 1958
1-Buck Vinson in all 48 96 144 302 514 725
2-Flying saucer story 30 60 90 177 289 400
3,5: 3-Mayo-a (6 pgs.). 5-Flying saucer-c/story 26 52 78 154 252 350
4 (Scarce) 30 60 90 177 289 400
1(2/58-St. John) 22 44 66 128 209 290

ATOM-AGE COMBAT
Fago Magazines: No. 2, Jan, 1959 - No. 3, Mar, 1959
2-A-Bomb explosion-c; 27 54 81 160 263 365
3 21 42 63 124 202 280

ATOMAN
Spark Publications: Feb, 1946 - No. 2, April, 1946
1-Origin & 1st app. Atoman; Robinson/Meskin-a; Kidcrusaders, Wild Bill Hickok, Marvin the Great app. 66 132 198 419 722 1025
2-Robinson/Meskin-a; Robinson c-1,2 41 82 123 256 428 600

ATOM & HAWKMAN, THE (Formerly The Atom)
National Periodical Publ: No. 39, Oct-Nov, 1968 - No. 45, Oct-Nov, 1969; No. 46, Mar, 2010
39-43: 40-41-Kubert/Anderson-a. 43-(7/69)-Last 12¢ issue; 1st S.A. app. Gentleman Ghost
6 12 18 39 62 85
44,45: 44-(9/69)-1st 15¢-c; origin Gentleman Ghost 6 12 18 39 62 85
46-(3/10, $2.99) Blackest Night crossover one-shot; Geoff Johns-s/Ryan Sook-a/c 3.00
NOTE: ***M. Anderson** a-39, 40i, 41i, 43, 44. **Sid Greene** a-40i-45i. **Kubert** a-40p, 41p; c-39-45.*

ATOM ANT (TV) (See Golden Comics Digest #2) (Hanna-Barbera)
Gold Key: January, 1966 (12¢)
1(10170-601)-1st app. Atom Ant, Precious Pup, and Hillbilly Bears
17 34 51 122 236 350

ATOM ANT & SECRET SQUIRREL (See Hanna-Barbera Presents)

ATOMIC AGE
Marvel Comics (Epic Comics): Nov, 1990 - No. 4, Feb, 1991 ($4.50, limited series, squarebound, 52 pgs.)
1-4: Williamson-a(i); sci-fi story set in 1957 4.50

ATOMIC ATTACK (True War Stories; formerly Attack, first series)
Youthful Magazines: No. 5, Jan, 1953 - No. 8, Oct, 1953 (1st story is sci/fi in all issues)
5-Atomic bomb-c; science fiction stories in all 39 78 117 240 395 550
6-8 25 50 75 150 245 340

ATOMIC BOMB
Jay Burtis Publications: 1945 (36 pgs.)
1-Airmale & Stampy (scarce) 69 138 207 442 759 1075

ATOMIC BUNNY (Formerly Atomic Rabbit)
Charlton Comics: No. 12, Aug, 1958 - No. 19, Dec, 1959
12 12 24 36 69 97 125
13-19 8 16 24 42 54 65

ATOMIC COMICS
Daniels Publications (Canadian): Jan, 1946 (Reprints, one-shot)
1-Rocketman, Yankee Boy, Master Key app. 39 78 117 240 395 550

ATOMIC COMICS
Green Publishing Co.: Jan, 1946 - No. 4, July-Aug, 1946 (#1-4 were printed w/o cover gloss)
1-Radio Squad by Siegel & Shuster; Barry O'Neal app.; Fang Gow cover-r/ Detective Comics (Classic-c) 93 186 279 586 993 1400
2-Inspector Dayton; Kid Kane by Matt Baker; Lucky Wings, Congo King, Prop Powers (only app.) begin 59 118 177 369 610 850
3,4: 3-Zero Ghost Detective app.; Baker-a(2) each; 4-Baker-c
41 82 123 248 404 560

ATOMIC KNIGHTS (See Strange Adventures #117)

ATOMIC MOUSE (TV, Movies) (See Blue Bird, Funny Animals, Giant Comics Edition & Wotalife Comics)
Capitol Stories/Charlton Comics: 3/53 - No. 54, 6/63; No. 1, 12/84; V2#10, 19/85 - No. 12, 1/86

GD 2.0 | VG 4.0 | FN 6.0 | VF 8.0 | VF/NM 9.0 | NM- 9.2

1-Origin & 1st app.; Al Fago-c/a in most 33 66 99 194 317 440
2 15 30 45 84 127 170
3-10: 5-Timmy The Timid Ghost app.; see Zoo Funnies
10 20 30 58 79 100
11-13,16-25 8 16 24 40 50 60
14,15-Hoppy The Marvel Bunny app. 9 18 27 50 65 80
26-(68 pgs.) 12 24 36 67 94 120
27-40: 36,37-Atom The Cat app. 6 12 18 29 36 42
41-54 5 10 15 22 26 30
1 (1984)-Low print run; rep/#7-c w/diff. stories 2 4 6 8 10 12
V2#10 (9/85) -12(1/86)-Low print run 1 3 4 6 8 10

ATOMIC RABBIT (Atomic Bunny #12 on; see Giant Comics #3 & Wotalife)
Charlton Comics: Aug, 1955 - No. 11, Mar, 1958
1-Origin & 1st app.; Al Fago-c/a in all? 30 60 90 177 289 400
2 14 28 42 80 115 150
3-10 10 20 30 56 76 95
11-(68 pgs.) 14 28 42 80 115 150

ATOMICS, THE
AAA Pop Comics: Jan, 2000 - No. 15, Nov, 2001 ($2.95)
1-11-Mike Allred-s/a; 1-Madman-c/app. 3.00
12-15-($3.50): 13-15-Savage Dragon-c/app. 15-Afterword by Alex Ross; colored reprint of 1st Frank Einstein story 3.50
...King-Size Giant Spectacular: Jigsaw (2000, $10.00) r/#1-4 10.00
...King-Size Giant Spectacular: Lessons in Light, Lava, & Lasers (2000, $8.95) r/#5-8 9.00
...King-Size Giant Spectacular: Running With the Dragon ('02, $8.95) r/#13-15 and r/1st Frank Einstein app. in color 9.00
...King-Size Giant Spectacular: Worlds Within Worlds ('01, $8.95) r/#9-12 9.00
Madman and the Atomics, Vol. 1 TPB (2007, $24.99) r/#1-15, cover gallery, pin-ups, afterword by Alex Ross 25.00
...: Spaced Out & Grounded in Snap City TPB (10/03, $12.95) r/one-shots - It Girl, Mr. Gum, Spaceman and Crash Metro & the Star Squad; sketch pages 13.00

ATOMIC SPY CASES
Avon Periodicals: Mar-Apr, 1950 (Painted-c)
1-No Wood-a; A-bomb blast panels; Fass-a 35 70 105 208 339 470

ATOMIC THUNDERBOLT, THE
Regor Company: Feb, 1946 (one-shot) (scarce)
1-Intro. Atomic Thunderbolt & Mr. Murdo 63 126 189 403 689 975

ATOMIC TOYBOX
Image Comics: Dec, 1999 ($2.95)
1- Aaron Lopresti-c/s/a 3.00

ATOMIC WAR!
Ace Periodicals (Junior Books): Nov, 1952 - No. 4, Apr, 1953
1-Atomic bomb-c 113 226 339 718 1234 1750
2,3: 3-Atomic bomb-c 61 122 183 390 670 950
4-Used in **POP**, pg. 96 & illo. 61 122 183 390 670 950

ATOMIKA
Speakeasy Comics/Mercury Comics: Mar, 2005 - No. 6 ($2.99)
1-6: 1-Alex Ross-c/Sal Abbinanti-a/Dabb-s. 3-Fabry-c. 4-Four covers; Romita back-c 3.00
... God is Red TPB (5/06, $19.99) r/#1-6; cover gallery; Dabb foreword 20.00

ATOMIK ANGELS
Crusade Comics: May, 1996 - No. 4, Nov. 1996 ($2.50)
1-4: 1-Freefall from Gen 13 app. 3.00
1-Variant-c 4.00
Intrep-Edition (2/96, B&W, giveaway at launch party)-Previews Atomik Angels #1; includes Billy Tucci interview. 4.00

ATOM SPECIAL (See Atom & Justice League of America)
DC Comics: 1993/1995 ($2.50/$2.95)(68pgs.)
1,2: 1-Dillon-c/a. 2-McDonnell-a/Bolland-c/Peyer-s 3.00

ATOM THE CAT (Formerly Tom Cat; see Giant Comics #3)
Charlton Comics: No. 9, Oct, 1957 - No. 17, Aug, 1959
9 10 20 30 54 72 90
10,13-17 7 14 21 35 43 50
11,12: 11(64 pgs)-Atomic Mouse app. 12(100 pgs.) 11 22 33 62 86 110

ATTACK
Youthful Mag./Trojan No. 5 on: May, 1952 - No. 4, Nov, 1952; No. 5, Jan, 1953 - No. 5, Sept, 1953
1-(1st series)-Extreme violence 34 68 102 199 325 450

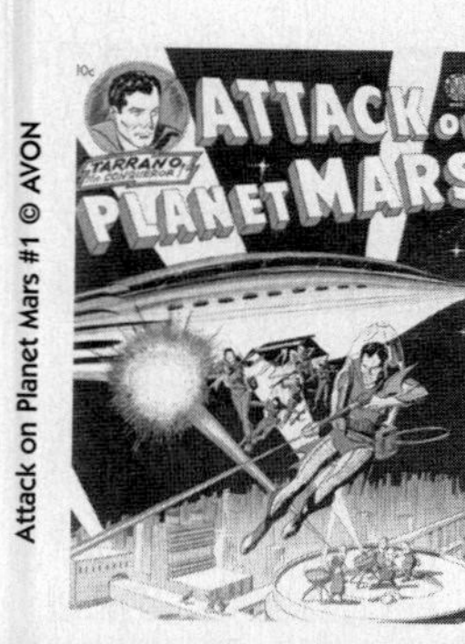

Attack on Planet Mars #1 © AVON

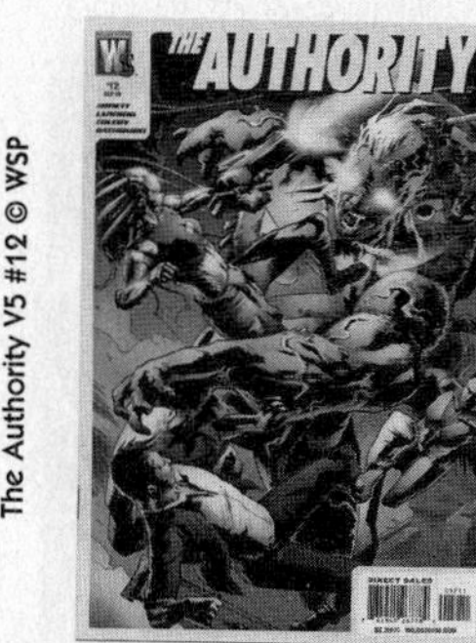

The Authority V5 #12 © WSP

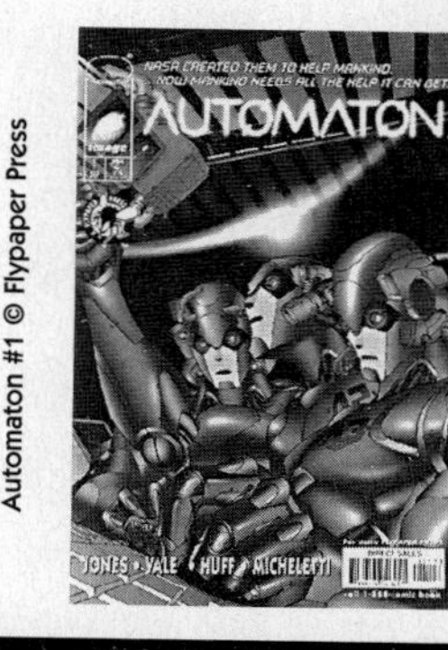

Automaton #1 © Flypaper Press

	GD 2.0	VG 4.0	FN 6.0	VF 8.0	VF/NM 9.0	NM- 9.2
2,3-Both Harrison-c/a; bondage, whipping	19	38	57	109	172	235
4-Krenkel-a (7 pgs.); Harrison-a (becomes Atomic Attack #5 on)	19	38	57	109	172	235
5-(#1, Trojan, 2nd series)	15	30	45	83	124	165
6-8 (#2-4), 5	11	22	33	64	90	115

ATTACK
Charlton Comics: No. 54, 1958 - No. 60, Nov, 1959

	GD	VG	FN	VF	VF/NM	NM-
54 (25¢, 100 pgs.)	12	24	36	69	97	125
55-60	7	14	21	35	43	50

ATTACK!
Charlton Comics: 1962 - No. 15, 3/75; No. 16, 8/79 - No. 48, 10/84

	GD	VG	FN	VF	VF/NM	NM-
nn(#1)-('62) Special Edition	5	10	15	34	55	75
2('63), 3(Fall, '64)	3	6	9	21	32	42
V4#3(10/66), 4(10/67)-(Formerly Special War Series #2; becomes Attack At Sea V4#5)	3	6	9	17	25	32
1(9/71)	3	6	9	16	23	30
2-5: 4-American Eagle app.	2	4	6	9	12	15
6-15(3/75):	1	3	4	6	8	10
16(8/79) - 40						5.00
41-47 Low print run						7.00
48(10/84)-Wood-r; S&K-c (low print)	1	3	4	6	8	10
Modern Comics 13('78)-r						4.00

NOTE: *Sutton a-9,10,13.*

ATTACK!
Spire Christian Comics (Fleming H. Revell Co.): 1975 (39¢/49¢, 36 pgs.)

	GD	VG	FN	VF	VF/NM	NM-
nn	2	4	6	9	13	16

ATTACK AT SEA (Formerly Attack!, 1967)
Charlton Comics: V4#5, Oct, 1968 (one-shot)

	GD	VG	FN	VF	VF/NM	NM-
V4#5	3	6	9	17	25	32

ATTACK ON PLANET MARS (See Strange Worlds #18)
Avon Periodicals: 1951

	GD	VG	FN	VF	VF/NM	NM-
nn-Infantino, Fawcette, Kubert & Wood-a; adaptation of Tarrano the Conqueror by Ray Cummings	81	162	243	518	884	1250

ATTITUDE LAD
Slave Labor Graphics: Apr, 1994 - No. 3, Nov, 1994 ($2.95, B&W)

	GD	VG	FN	VF	VF/NM	NM-
1-3						3.00

AUDREY & MELVIN (Formerly Little...)(See Little Audrey & Melvin)
Harvey Publications: No. 62, Sept, 1974

	GD	VG	FN	VF	VF/NM	NM-
62	2	4	6	9	13	16

AUGIE DOGGIE (TV) (See Hanna-Barbera Band Wagon, Quick-Draw McGraw, Spotlight #2, Top Cat & Whitman Comic Books)
Gold Key: October, 1963 (12¢)

	GD	VG	FN	VF	VF/NM	NM-
1-Hanna-Barbera character	17	34	51	119	230	340

AUTHENTIC POLICE CASES
St. John Publishing Co.: 2/48 - No. 6, 11/48; No. 7, 5/50 - No. 38, 3/55

	GD	VG	FN	VF	VF/NM	NM-
1-Hale the Magician by Tuska begins	45	90	135	284	480	675
2-Lady Satan, Johnny Rebel app.	28	56	84	165	270	375
3-Veiled Avenger app.; blood drainage story plus 2 Lucky Coyne stories; used in **SOTI**, illo. from Red Seal #16	48	96	144	302	514	725
4,5: 4-Masked Black Jack app. 5-Late 1930s Jack Cole-a(r); transvestism story	28	56	84	165	270	375
6-Matt Baker-c; used in **SOTI**, illo- "An invitation to learning", r-in Fugitives From Justice #3; Jack Cole-a; also used by the N.Y. Legis. Comm.	52	104	156	328	552	775
7,8,10-14: 7-Jack Cole-a; Matt Baker-a begins #8, ends #?; Vic Flint in #10-14. 10-12-Baker-a(2 each)	27	54	81	158	259	360
9-No Vic Flint	22	44	66	128	209	290
15-Drug-c/story; Vic Flint app.; Baker-c	28	56	84	165	270	375
16,18,20,21,23: Baker-a(i)	18	36	54	105	165	225
17,19,22-Baker-c	21	42	63	122	199	275
24-28 (All 100 pgs.): 26-Transvestism	37	74	111	222	361	500
29,31,32-Baker-c	15	30	45	88	137	185
30	14	28	42	81	118	155
33-38: 33-Baker-c. 34-Baker-c; r/#9. 35-Baker-c/a(2); r/#10. 36-r/#11; Vic Flint strip-r; Baker-c/a(2) unsigned. 37-Baker-c; r/#17. 38- Baker-c/a; r/#18	17	34	51	100	158	215

NOTE: ***Matt Baker** c-6-16, 17, 19, 22, 27, 29, 31-38; a-13, 16. Bondage c-1, 3.*

AUTHORITY, THE (See Stormwatch and Jenny Sparks: The Secret History of...)
DC Comics (WildStorm): May, 1999 - No. 29, Jul, 2002 ($2.50)

	GD 2.0	VG 4.0	FN 6.0	VF 8.0	VF/NM 9.0	NM- 9.2
1-Wraparound-c; Warren Ellis-s/Bryan Hitch and Paul Neary-a	2	4	6	8	11	14
2-4	1	3	4	6	8	10
5-12: 12-Death of Jenny Sparks; last Ellis-s	1	2	3	5	6	8
13-Mark Millar-s/Frank Quitely-c/a begins	2	4	6	8	10	12
14-16-Authority vs. Marvel-esque villains	1	2	3	4	5	7
17-22: 17,18-Weston-a. 19,20,22-Quitely-a. 21-McCrea-a						5.00
23-29: 23-26-Peyer-s/Nguyen-a; new Authority. 24-Preview of "The Establishment." 25,26-Jenny Sparks app. 27,28-Millar-s/Adams-a/c						4.00
Annual 2000 ($3.50) Devil's Night x-over; Hamner-a/Bermejo-c	1	2	3	4	5	7
Absolute Authority Slipcased Hardcover (2002, $49.95) oversized r/#1-12 plus script pages by Ellis and sketch pages by Hitch						50.00
...: Earth Inferno and Other Stories TPB (2002, $14.95) r/#17-20, Annual 2000, and Wildstorm Summer Special; new Quitely-c						15.00
...: Human on the Inside HC (2004, $24.95, dust jacket) Ridley-s/Oliver-a/c						25.00
...: Human on the Inside SC (2004, $17.99) Ridley-s/Oliver-a/c						18.00
...: Kev (10/02, $4.95) Ennis-s/Fabry-c/a						5.00
...: Relentless TPB (2000, $17.95) r/#1-8						18.00
...: Scorched Earth (2/03, $4.95) Robbie Morrison-s/Frazer Irving-a/Ashley Wood-c						5.00
...: Transfer of Power TPB (2002, $17.95) r/#22-29						18.00
...: Under New Management TPB (2000, $17.95) r/#9-16; new Quitely-c						18.00

AUTHORITY, THE (See previews in Sleeper, Stormwatch: Team Achilles and Wildcats Version 3.0)
DC Comics (WildStorm): Jul, 2003 - No. 14, Oct, 2004 ($2.95)

	GD	VG	FN	VF	VF/NM	NM-
1-14: 1-Robbie Morrison-s/Dwayne Turner-a. 5-Huat-a. 14-Portacio-a						3.00
#0 (10/03, $2.95) r/preview back-up-s listed above; Turner sketch pages						3.00
...: Fractured Worlds TPB (2005, $17.95) r/#6-14; cover gallery						18.00
...: Harsh Realities TPB (2004, $14.95) r/#0-5; cover gallery						15.00
.../Lobo: Jingle Hell (2/04, $4.95) Bisley-c/a; Giffen & Grant-s						5.00
.../Lobo: Spring Break Massacre (8/05, $4.99) Bisley-c/a; Giffen & Grant-s						5.00

AUTHORITY, THE (Volume 4) (The Lost Year)
DC Comics (WildStorm): Dec, 2006 - No. 2, May 2007; No. 3, Jan, 2010 - No. 6 ($2.99)

	GD	VG	FN	VF	VF/NM	NM-
1,2-Grant Morrison-s/Gene Ha-a/c						3.00
1-Variant cover by Art Adams						5.00
3-5: 3-(1/10) Morrison & Giffen-s/Robertson-a						3.00
...Reader: The Lost Year (1/10, $2.99) r/#1,2						3.00

AUTHORITY, THE (Volume 5) (World's End)
DC Comics (WildStorm): Oct, 2008 - Present ($2.99)

	GD	VG	FN	VF	VF/NM	NM-
1-19: 1-5-Simon Coleby-a/c; Lynch back-up story w/Hairsine-a/Gage-s						3.00
...: World's End TPB (2009, $17.99) r/#1-7						18.00

AUTHORITY, THE: MORE KEV
DC Comics (WildStorm): Jul, 2004 - No. 4, Dec, 2004 ($2.95, limited series)

	GD	VG	FN	VF	VF/NM	NM-
1-4-Garth Ennis-s/Glenn Fabry-c/a						3.00
...: Kev TPB (2005, $14.99) r/Authority: Kev one-shot and Authority: More Kev series						15.00

AUTHORITY, THE: PRIME
DC Comics (WildStorm): Dec, 2007 - No. 6, May, 2008 ($2.99, limited series)

	GD	VG	FN	VF	VF/NM	NM-
1-6-Gage-s/Robertson-c/a; Bendix app.						3.00
TPB (2008, $17.99) r/#1-6						18.00

AUTHORITY, THE: REVOLUTION
DC Comics (WildStorm): Dec, 2004 - No. 12, Dec, 2005 ($2.95/$2.99)

	GD	VG	FN	VF	VF/NM	NM-
1-12-Brubaker-s/Nguyen-a. 5-Henry Bendix returns. 7-Jenny Sparks app.						3.00
...: Book One TPB (2005, $14.99) r/#1-6; cover gallery and Nguyen sketch pages						15.00
...: Book Two TPB (2006, $14.99) r/#7-12; cover gallery and Nguyen sketch pages						15.00

AUTHORITY, THE: THE MAGNIFICENT KEV
DC Comics (WildStorm): Nov, 2005 - No. 5, Feb, 2006 ($2.99, limited series)

	GD	VG	FN	VF	VF/NM	NM-
1-5-Garth Ennis-s/Carlos Ezquerra-a/Glenn Fabry-c						3.00
TPB (2006, $14.99) r/#1-5						15.00

AUTOMATIC KAFKA
DC Comics (WildStorm): Sept, 2002 - No. 9, Jul, 2003 ($2.95)

	GD	VG	FN	VF	VF/NM	NM-
1-9-Ashley Wood-c/a; Joe Casey-s						3.00

AUTOMATON
Image Comics (Flypaper Press): Sept, 1998 - No. 3, 1998 ($2.95, lim. series)

	GD	VG	FN	VF	VF/NM	NM-
1-3-R.A. Jones-s/Peter Vale-a						3.00

AUTUMN
Caliber Comics: 1995 - No. 3, 1995 ($2.95, B&W)

	GD	VG	FN	VF	VF/NM	NM-
1-3						3.00

AUTUMN ADVENTURES (Walt Disney's...)

Avengelyne: Deadly Sins #1 © R. Liefeld

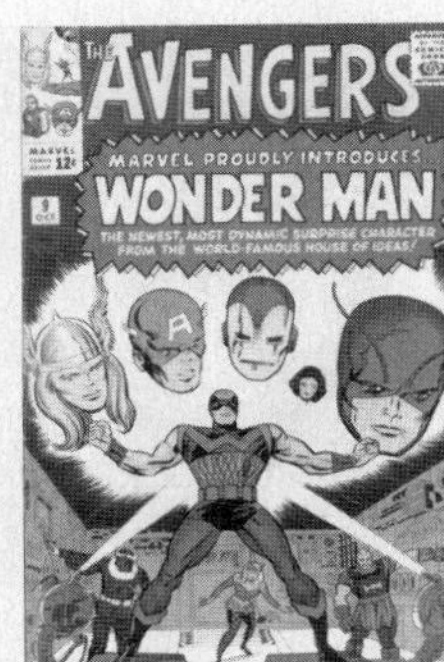

Avengers #9 © MAR

Avengers #160 © MAR

	GD 2.0	VG 4.0	FN 6.0	VF 8.0	VF/NM 9.0	NM- 9.2
Disney Comics: Autumn, 1990; No. 2, Autumn, 1991 ($2.95, 68 pgs.)						
1-Donald Duck-r(2) by Barks, Pluto-r, & new-a						4.00
2-D. Duck-r by Barks; new Super Goof story						4.00

AVATAARS: COVENANT OF THE SHIELD
Marvel Comics: Sept, 2000 - No. 3, Nov, 2000 ($2.99, limited series)

	GD	VG	FN	VF	VF/NM	NM-
1-3-Kaminski-s/Oscar Jimenez-a						3.00

AVATAR
DC Comics: Feb, 1991 - No. 3, Apr, 1991 ($5.95, limited series, 100 pgs.)

	GD	VG	FN	VF	VF/NM	NM-
1-3: Based on TSR's Forgotten Realms						6.00

AVENGELYNE
Maximum Press: May, 1995 - No. 3, July, 1995 ($2.50/$3.50, limited series)

	GD	VG	FN	VF	VF/NM	NM-
1/2	2	4	6	8	10	12
1/2 Platinum						15.00
1-Newstand ($2.50)-Photo-c; poster insert						6.00
1-Direct Market ($3.50)-Chromium-c; poster	1	2	3	4	5	7
1-Glossy edition	2	4	6	12	16	20
1-Gold						12.00
2-3: 2-Polybagged w/card						3.00
3-Variant-c; Deodato pin-up						5.00
...Bible (10/96, $3.50)						4.00
.../Glory (9/95, $3.95) 2 covers						4.00
.../Glory Swimsuit Special (6/96, $2.95) photo and illos. covers						3.00
.../Glory: The Godyssey (9/96, $2.99) 2 covers (1 photo)						3.00
...Revelation One (Avatar, 1/01, $3.50) 3 covers by Haley, Rio, Shaw; Shaw-a						3.50
.../Shi (Avatar, 11/01, $3.50) Eight covers; Waller-a						3.50
...Swimsuit (8/95, $2.95)-Pin-ups/photos. 3-Variant-c exist (2 photo, 1 Liefeld-a)						4.00
...Swimsuit (1/96, $3.50, 2nd printing)-photo-c						4.00
Trade paperback (12/95, $9.95)						10.00
.../Warrior Nun Areala 1 (11/96, $2.99) also see Warrior Nun/Avengelyne						3.00

AVENGELYNE
Maximum Press: V2#1, Apr, 1996 - No. 14, Apr, 1997 ($2.95/$2.50)

	GD	VG	FN	VF	VF/NM	NM-
V2#1-Four covers exist (2 photo-c).						4.00
V2#2-Three covers exist (1 photo-c); flip book w/Darkchylde						5.00
V2#0, 3-14: 0-(10/96).3-Flip book w/Priest preview. 5-Flip book w/Blindside						3.00

AVENGELYNE (Volume 3)
Awesome Comics: Mar, 1999 ($2.50)

	GD	VG	FN	VF	VF/NM	NM-
1-Fraga & Liefeld-a						3.00

AVENGELYNE: ARMAGEDDON
Maximum Press: Dec, 1996 - No. 3, Feb, 1997 ($2.99, limited series)

	GD	VG	FN	VF	VF/NM	NM-
1-3-Scott Clark-a(p)						3.00

AVENGELYNE: DEADLY SINS
Maximum Press: Feb, 1996 - No. 2, Mar, 1996 ($2.95, limited series)

	GD	VG	FN	VF	VF/NM	NM-
1,2: 1-Two-c exist (1 photo, 1 Liefeld-a). 2-Liefeld-c; Pop Mhan-a(p)						3.00

AVENGELYNE/POWER
Maximum Press: Nov, 1995 - No.3, Jan, 1996 ($2.95, limited series)

	GD	VG	FN	VF	VF/NM	NM-
1-3: 1,2-Liefeld-c. 3-Three variant-c. exist (1 photo-c)						3.00

AVENGELYNE • PROPHET
Maximum Press: May, 1996; No. 2, Feb. 1997 ($2.95, unfinished lim. series)

	GD	VG	FN	VF	VF/NM	NM-
1,2-Liefeld-c/a(p)						3.00

AVENGER, THE (See A-1 Comics)
Magazine Enterprises: Feb-Mar, 1955 - No. 4, Aug-Sept, 1955

	GD	VG	FN	VF	VF/NM	NM-
1(A-1 #129)-Origin	39	78	117	240	395	550
2(A-1 #131), 3(A-1 #133) Robot-c, 4(A-1 #138)	27	54	81	158	259	360
IW Reprint #9('64)-Reprints #1 (new cover)	4	8	12	20	29	38

NOTE: *Powell a-2-4; c-1-4.*

AVENGERS, THE (TV)(Also see Steed and Mrs. Peel)
Gold Key: Nov, 1968 ("John Steed & Emma Peel" cover title) (15¢)

	GD	VG	FN	VF	VF/NM	NM-
1-Photo-c	15	30	45	107	204	300
1-(Variant with photo back-c)	19	38	57	139	270	400

AVENGERS, THE (See Essential..., Giant-Size..., JLA/..., Kree/Skrull War Starring..., Marvel Graphic Novel #27, Marvel Super Action, Marvel Super Heroes('66), Marvel Treasury Ed., Marvel Triple Action, New Avengers, Solo Avengers, Tales Of Suspense #49, West Coast Avengers & X-Men Vs....)

AVENGERS, THE (The Mighty Avengers on cover only #63-69)
Marvel Comics Group: Sept, 1963 - No. 402, Sept, 1996

	GD	VG	FN	VF	VF/NM	NM-
1-Origin & 1st app. The Avengers (Thor, Iron Man, Hulk, Ant-Man, Wasp); Loki app.	463	926	1389	4167	8334	12,500
2-Hulk leaves Avengers	96	192	288	816	1608	2400
3-2nd Sub-Mariner x-over outside the F.F. (see Strange Tales #107 for 1st); Sub-Mariner & Hulk team-up & battle Avengers; Spider-Man cameo (1/64)	64	128	192	544	1072	1600
4-Revival of Captain America who joins the Avengers; 1st Silver Age app. of Captain America & Bucky (3/64)	162	324	486	1418	2809	4200
4-Reprint from the Golden Record Comic set	13	26	39	90	165	240
With Record (1966)	17	34	51	124	242	360
5-Hulk app.	43	86	129	344	672	1000
6,8: 6-Intro/1st app. original Zemo & his Masters of Evil. 8-Intro Kang	33	66	99	254	490	725
7-Rick Jones app. in Bucky costume	36	72	108	280	540	800
9-Intro Wonder Man who dies in same story	46	92	138	368	709	1050
10-Intro/1st app. Immortus; early Hercules app. (11/64)	26	52	78	190	370	550
11-Spider-Man-c & x-over (12/64)	34	68	102	262	506	750
12-15: 15-Death of original Zemo	18	36	54	129	252	375
16-New Avengers line-up (Hawkeye, Quicksilver, Scarlet Witch join; Thor, Iron Man, Giant-Man, Wasp leave)	26	52	78	190	370	550
17,18	13	26	39	95	178	260
19-1st app. Swordsman; origin Hawkeye (8/65)	14	28	42	102	194	285
20-22: Wood inks	10	20	30	70	123	175
23-30: 23-Romita Sr. inks (1st Silver Age Marvel work). 25-Dr. Doom-c/story. 28-Giant-Man becomes Goliath (5/66)	9	18	27	63	107	150
31-40	8	16	24	54	90	125
41-46,49-52,54-56: 43-1st app. Red Guardian (dies in #44) . 46-Ant-Man returns (re-intro, 11/67). 52-Black Panther joins; 1st app. The Grim Reaper. 54-1st app. new Masters of Evil. 56-Zemo app; story explains how Capt. America became imprisoned in ice during WWII, only to be rescued in Avengers #4	7	14	21	45	73	100
47-Magneto-c/story	7	14	21	47	76	105
48-Origin/1st app. new Black Knight (1/68)	7	14	21	47	76	105
53-X-Men app.	9	18	27	64	110	155
57-1st app. S.A. Vision (10/68)	17	34	51	122	236	350
58-Origin The Vision	10	20	30	67	116	165
59-65: 59-Intro. Yellowjacket. 60-Wasp & Yellowjacket wed. 63-Goliath becomes Yellowjacket; Hawkeye becomes the new Goliath. 65-Last 12¢ issue	6	12	18	37	59	80
66,67-B. Smith-a	6	12	18	39	62	85
68-70: 69-Nighthawk cameo. 70-1st full app. Nighthawk	5	10	15	34	55	75
71-1st app. The Invaders (12/69); Black Knight joins	8	16	24	54	90	125
72-79,81,82,84-86,89-91: 82-Daredevil app	5	10	15	32	51	70
80-Intro. Red Wolf (9/70)	5	10	15	34	55	75
83-Intro. The Liberators (Wasp, Valkyrie, Scarlet Witch, Medusa & the Black Widow)	6	12	18	37	59	80
87-Origin The Black Panther	6	12	18	37	59	80
88-Written by Harlan Ellison	5	10	15	34	55	75
88-2nd printing (1994)	2	4	6	8	10	12
92-Last 15¢ issue; Neal Adams-c	6	12	18	41	66	90
93-(52 pgs.)-Neal Adams-c/a	13	26	39	93	172	250
94-96-Neal Adams-c/a	8	16	24	52	86	120
97-G.A. Capt. America, Sub-Mariner, Human Torch, Patriot, Vision, Blazing Skull, Fin, Angel, & new Capt. Marvel x-over	6	12	18	39	62	85
98,99: 98-Goliath becomes Hawkeye; Smith c/a(i). 99-Smith-c, Smith/Sutton-a	5	10	15	32	51	70
100-(6/72)-Smith-c/a; featuring everyone who was an Avenger	9	18	27	64	110	155
101-Harlan Ellison scripts	4	8	12	23	36	48
102-106,108,109	3	6	9	21	32	42
107-Starlin-a(p)	4	8	12	23	36	48
110,111-X-Men app.	6	12	18	37	59	80
112-1st app. Mantis	4	8	12	28	44	60
113-115,119-124,126-130: 123-Origin Mantis	3	6	9	18	27	35
116-118-Defenders/Silver Surfer app.	5	10	15	32	51	70
125-Thanos-c & brief app.	4	8	12	22	34	45
131-133,136-140: 136-Ploog-r/Amazing Advs. #12	3	6	9	14	20	25
134,135-Origin of the Vision revised (also see Avengers Forever mini-series)	3	6	9	21	32	42
141-143,145,152-163	2	4	6	8	11	14
144-Origin & 1st app. Hellcat	3	6	9	14	19	24
146-149-(Reg.25¢ editions)(4-7/76)	2	4	6	8	11	14
146-149-(30¢-c variants, limited distribution)	4	8	12	22	34	45
150-Kirby-a(r); new line-up: Capt. America, Scarlet Witch, Iron Man, Wasp, Yellowjacket, Vision & The Beast	2	4	6	10	14	18

Avengers #236 © MAR

Avengers V3 #23 © MAR

Avengers V3 #83 © MAR

GD VG FN VF VF/NM NM-
2.0 4.0 6.0 8.0 9.0 9.2

150-(30¢-c variant, limited distribution) 4 8 12 26 41 55
151-Wonder Man returns w/new costume 2 4 6 9 13 16
160-164-(35¢-c variants, limited dist.)(6-10/77) 7 14 21 47 76 105
164-166: Byrne-a 2 4 6 9 13 16
167-180: 168-Guardians of the Galaxy app. 174-Thanos cameo. 176-Starhawk app. 1 2 3 5 6 8
181-191-Byrne-a: 181-New line-up: Capt. America, Scarlet Witch, Iron Man, Wasp, Vision, Beast & The Falcon. 183-Ms. Marvel joins. 185-Origin Quicksilver & Scarlet Witch 2 4 6 8 10 12
192-194,197-199 6.00
195,196: 195-1st Taskmaster cameo. 196-1st Taskmaster full app. 1 3 4 6 8 10
200-(10/80, 52 pgs.)-Ms. Marvel leaves. 1 3 4 6 8 10
201-213,217-238: 211-New line-up: Capt. America, Iron Man, Tigra, Thor, Wasp & Yellowjacket. 213-Yellowjacket leaves. 217-Yellowjacket & Wasp return. 221-Hawkeye & She-Hulk join. 227-Capt. Marvel (female) joins; origins of Ant-Man, Wasp, Giant-Man, Goliath, Yellowjacket, & Avengers. 230-Yellowjacket quits. 231-Iron Man leaves. 232-Starfox (Eros) joins. 234-Origin Quicksilver, Scarlet Witch. 238-Origin Blackout 4.50
214-Ghost Rider-c/story 6.00
215,216,239,240,250: 215,216-Silver Surfer app. 216-Tigra leaves. 239-(1/84) Avengers app. on David Letterman show. 240-Spider-Woman revived. 250-($1.00, 52 pgs.) 4.00
241-249, 251-262 3.50
263-(1/86) Return of Jean Grey, leading into X-Factor #1(story continues in FF #286) 6.00
264-299: 272-Alpha Flight app. 291-$1.00 issues begin. 297-Black Knight, She-Hulk & Thor resign. 298-Inferno tie-in 3.00
300 (2/89, $1.75, 68 pgs.)-Thor joins; Simonson-a 4.00
301-304,306-313,319-325,327,329-343: 302-Re-intro Quasar. 320-324-Alpha Flight app. (320-cameo). 327-2nd app. Rage. 341,342-New Warriors app. 343-Last $1.00-c 3.00
305,314-318: 305-Byrne scripts begin. 314-318-Spider-Man x-over 3.50
326-1st app. Rage (11/90) 4.00
328,344-349,351-359,361,362,364,365,367: 328-Origin Rage. 365-Contains coupon for Hunt for Magneto contest 3.00
350-($2.50, 68 pgs.)-Double gatefold-c showing-c to #1; r/#53 w/cover in flip book format; vs. The Starjammers 3.50
360-($2.95, 52 pgs.)-Embossed all-foil-c; 30th ann. 4.00
363-($2.95, 52 pgs.)-All silver foil-c 4.00
366-($3.95, 68 pgs.)-Embossed all gold foil-c 4.00
368,370-374,376-399: 368-Bloodties part 1; Avengers/X-Men x-over. 374-bound-in trading card sheet. 380-Deodato-a. 390,391-"The Crossing." 395-Death of "old" Tony Stark; wraparound-c. 3.00
369-($2.95)-Foil embossed-c; Bloodties part 5 4.00
375-($2.00, 52 pgs.)-Regular ed.; Thunderstrike returns; leads into Malibu Comics' Black September. 3.00
375-($2.50, 52 pgs.)-Collector's ed. w/bound-in poster; leads into Malibu Comics' Black September. 3.50
400-402: Waid-s; 402-Deodato breakdowns; cont'd in X-Men #56 & Onslaught: Marvel Universe. 4.00
#500-503 (See Avengers Vol. 3; series resumed original numbering after Vol. 3 #84)
Special 1 (9/67, 25¢, 68 pgs.)-New-a; original & new Avengers team-up 11 22 33 78 139 200
Special 2 (9/68, 25¢, 68 pgs.)-New-a; original vs. new Avengers 7 14 21 47 76 105
Special 3 (9/69, 25¢, 68 pgs.)-r/Avengers #4 plus 3 Capt. America stories by Kirby (art); origin Red Skull 4 8 12 28 44 60
Special 4 (1/71, 25¢, 68 pgs.)-Kirby-r/Avengers #5,6 3 6 9 18 27 35
Special 5 (1/72, 52 pgs.)-Spider-Man x-over 3 6 9 18 27 35
Annual 6 (11/76) Peréz-a; Kirby-c 2 4 6 11 16 20
Annual 7 (11/77)-Starlin-c/a; Warlock dies; Thanos app. 5 10 15 32 51 70
Annual 8 (1978)-Dr. Strange, Ms. Marvel app. 2 4 6 8 11 14
Annual 9 (1979)-Newton-a(p) 2 3 4 6 8 10
Annual 10 (1981)-Golden-p; X-Men cameo; 1st app. Rogue & Madelyne Pryor 5 10 15 32 51 70
Annual 11-13: 11(1982)-Vs. The Defenders. 12('83), 13('84) 4.00
Annual 14-18: 14('85),15('86),16('87),17('88)-Evolutionary War x-over, 18('89)-Atlantis Attacks 4.00
Annual 19-23 (90-'94, 68 pgs.). 22-Bagged/card 3.00
...: Galactic Storm Vol. 1 ('06, $29.99, TPB) r/Kree-Shi'ar war from Avengers #345-346, Capt. America #398-399, Avengers West Coast #80-81, Quasar #32-33, Wonder Man #7-8, Iron Man #278 and Thor #445; new Epting-c 30.00
...: Galactic Storm Vol. 2 ('06, $29.99, TPB) r/Kree-Shi'ar war from Avengers #347, Capt. America #400-401, Avengers West Coast #82, Quasar #34-36, Wonder Man #9, Iron Man #279, Thor #446 and What If #55-56 30.00
...: Kang - Time and Time Again ('05, $19.99, TPB) r/Avengers #69-71 & 267-269, Thor #140 and Incredible Hulk #135 20.00
...Kree-Skrull War ('00, $24.95, TPB) new Neal Adams-c 25.00
...: Legends Vol. 3: George Perez ('03, $16.99)-r/#161,162,194-196,201, Ann. #6 & 8 17.00
Marvel Double Feature...Avengers/Giant-Man #379 ($2.50, 52 pgs.)-Same as Avengers #379 w/Giant-Man flip book 2.50
Marvel Graphic Novel - Deathtrap: The Vault (1991, $9.95) Venom-c/app. 2 4 6 8 10 12
The Korvac Saga TPB (2003, $19.95)-r/#167,168,170-177; Perez-c 20.00
The Serpent Crown TPB (2005, $15.99)-r/#141-144,147-149; Hellcat app. 16.00
The Yesterday Quest ($6.95)-r/#181,182,185-187 1 2 3 4 5 7
Under Siege ('98, $16.95, TPB) r/#270,271,273-277 17.00
...: Vision and the Scarlet Witch TPB (2005, $15.99) r/wedding from Giant-Size Avengers #4 and "Vision and the Scarlet Witch" mini-series #1-4 16.00
...: Visionaries ('99, $16.95)-r/early George Perez art 17.00

NOTE: ***Austin*** *c(i)-157, 167, 168, 170-177, 181, 183-188, 198-201, Annual 8.* ***John Buscema*** *a-41-44p, 46p, 47p, 49, 50, 51-62p, 74-77, 79-85, 87-91, 97, 105p, 121p, 124p,125p, 152, 153p, 255-279p, 281-302p; c-41-66, 68-71, 73-91, 97-99, 178, 256-259p, 261-279p, 281-302p.* ***Byrne*** *a-164-166p, 181-191p, 233p, Annual 13i, 14p; c-186-190p, 233p, 260, 305p; scripts-305-312.* ***Colan*** *a(p)-63-65, 111, 206-208, 210, 211; c(p)-65, 206-208, 210, 211.* ***Ditko*** *a-Annual 13.* ***Guice*** *a-Annual 12p.* ***Don Heck*** *a-9-15, 17-40, 157.* ***Kane*** *c-37p, 159p.* ***Kane/Everett*** *c-97.* ***Kirby*** *a-1-8p, Special 3r, 4r(p); c-1-30, 148, 151-158; layouts-14-16.* ***Ron Lim*** *c(p)-335-341.* ***Miller*** *c-193p.* ***Mooney*** *a-86i, 179p, 180p.* ***Nebres*** *a-178i; c-179i.* ***Newton*** *a-204p, Annual 9p.* ***Perez*** *a(p)-141, 143, 144, 148, 150, 154, 155, 160, 161, 162, 167,168, 170, 171, 194-196, 198-202, Annual 6, 8; c(p)-160-162, 164-166, 170-174, 181,183-185, 191, 192, 194-201, 379-382, Annual 8.* ***Starlin*** *c-121, 135.* ***Staton*** *a-127-134i.* ***Tuska*** *a-47i,48i, 51i, 53i, 54i, 106p, 107p, 135p, 137-140p, 163p. Guardians of the Galaxy app. in #167, 168, 170, 173, 175, 181.*

AVENGERS, THE (Volume Two)
Marvel Comics: V2#1, Nov, 1996 - No. 13, Nov, 1997 ($2.95/$1.95/$1.99) (Produced by Extreme Studios)

1-($2.95)-Heroes Reborn begins; intro new team (Captain America, Swordsman, Scarlet Witch, Vision, Thor, Hellcat & Hawkeye); 1st app. Avengers Island; Loki & Enchantress app.; Rob Liefeld-p & plot; Chap Yaep-p; Jim Valentino scripts; variant-c exists 5.00
1-($1.95)-Variant-c 6.00
2-13: 2,3-Jeph Loeb scripts begin, Kang app. 4-Hulk-c/app. 5-Thor/Hulk battle; 2 covers. 10,11,13-"World War 3"-pt. 2, x-over w/Image characters. 12-($2.99) "Heroes Reunited"-pt. 2 4.00
Heroes Reborn: Avengers (2006, $29.99, TPB) r/#1-12; pin-up and cover gallery 30.00

AVENGERS, THE (Volume Three)(See New Avengers for next series)
Marvel Comics: Feb, 1998 - No. 84, Aug, 2004; No. 500, Sept, 2004 - No. 503, Dec, 2004 ($2.99/$1.99/$2.25)

1-($2.99, 48 pgs.) Busiek-s/Perez-a/wraparound-c; Avengers reassemble after Heroes Return 5.00
1-Variant Heroes Return cover 1 2 3 4 5 7
1-Rough Cut-Features original script and pencil pages 3.00
2-($1.99)Perez-c, 2-Lago painted-c 4.00
3,4: 3-Wonder Man-c/app. 4-Final roster chosen; Perez poster 3.00
5-11: 5,6-Squadron Supreme-c/app. 8-Triathlon-c/app. 2.50
12-($2.99) Thunderbolts app. 3.00
12-Alternate-c of Avengers w/white background; no logo 15.00
13-24,26,28: 13-New Warriors app. 16-18-Ordway-s/a. 19-Ultron returns. 26-Immonen-a 2.50
16-Variant-c with purple background 5.00
25,27-($2.99) 25-vs. the Exemplars; Spider-Man app. 27-100 pgs. 3.00
29-33,35-47: 29-Begin $2.25-c. 35-Maximum Security x-over; Romita Jr.-a. 36-Epting-a; poster by Alan Davis. 38-Davis-a begins ($1.99-c) 2.50
34-($2.99) Last Pérez-a; Thunderbirds app. 3.00
48-($3.50, 100 pgs.) new story w/Dwyer-a & r/#98-100 3.50
49,51-59: 49-'Nuff Said story. 51-Anderson-a. 52-Reis-a. 57-Johns-s begin 2.50
50,60-($3.50): 50 Dwyer-a; Quasar app. 3.50
61-84: 61,62-Frank-a; new line-up. 63-Davis-a. 64-Reis-a. 65-70-Coipel-a. 75-Hulk app. 76-Jack of Hearts dies; Jae Lee-c. 77-(50¢-c) Coipel-a/Cassaday-c. 78,80,81Coipel-a. 83,84-New Invaders app. 2.50
(After #84 [Aug, 2004], numbering reverted back to original Vol. 1 with #500, Sept, 2004)
500-($3.50) "Avengers Disassembled" begins; Bendis-s/Finch-a; Ant-Man (Scott Lang) killed, Vision destroyed 3.50
500-Director's Cut ($4.99) Cassaday foil variant-c plus interviews and galleries 5.00
501, 502-($2.25): 502-Hawkeye killed 2.50
503-($3.50) "Avengers Disassembled" ends; reprint pages from Avengers V1#16 3.50
#11 1/2 (12/99, $2.50) Timm-c/a/Stern-s; 1963-style issue 2.50
.../ Squadron Supreme '98 Annual ($2.99) 3.00
1999, 2000 Annual (7/99, '00, $3.50) 1999-Manco-a. 2000-Breyfogle-a 3.50
2001 Annual ($2.99) Reis-a; back-up-s art by Churchill 3.00
...: Above and Beyond TPB ('05, $24.99) r/#36-40,56, Annual 2001, & Avengers: The Ultron Imperative; Alan Davis-c 25.00
... Assemble HC ('04, $29.95, oversized) r/#1-11 & '98 Annual; Busiek intro.; Pérez pencil art and Busiek script from Avengers #1 30.00
... Assemble Vol. 2 HC ('05, $29.95, oversized) r/#12-22, #0 & Ann. 1999; Ordway intro. 30.00
... Assemble Vol. 3 HC ('06, $34.99, oversized) r/#23-34, #1 1/2 & Thunderbolts #42-44 35.00

Avengers Forever #2 © MAR

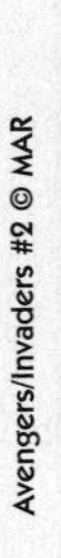
Avengers/Invaders #2 © MAR

Avengers: The Initiative #10 © MAR

GD 2.0 | VG 4.0 | FN 6.0 | VF 8.0 | VF/NM 9.0 | NM- 9.2

... Assemble Vol. 4 HC ('07, $34.99, oversized) r/#35-40, Avengers 2000, Avengers 2001, Avengers: The Ultron Imperative, Maximum Security #1-3 & ...Dangerous Planet 35.00
... Assemble Vol. 5 HC ('07, $39.99, oversized) r/#41-56 and Avengers 2001 40.00
...: Clear and Present Dangers TPB ('01, $19.95) r/#8-15 20.00
...: Defenders War HC ('07, $19.99) r/#115-118 & Defenders #8-11; Englehart intro. 20.00
...: Disassembled HC ('06, $24.99) r/#500-503 & Avengers Finale; Director's Cut extras 25.00
...: Disassembled TPB ('05, $15.99) r/#500-503 & Avengers Finale; Director's Cut extras 16.00
...Finale 1 (1/05, $3.50) Epilogue to Avengers Disassembled; Neal Adams-c; art by various incl. Peréz, Maleev, Oeming, Powell, Mayhew, Mack, McNiven, Cheung, Frank 3.50
...: Living Legends TPB ('04, $19.99) r/#23-30; last Busiek/Pérez arc 20.00
...Supreme Justice TPB (4/01, $17.95) r/Squadron Supreme appearances in Avengers #5-7, '98 Annual, Iron Man #7, Capt. America #8, Quicksilver #10; Pérez-c 18.00
The Kang Dynasty TPB ('02, $29.99) r/#41-55 & 2001 Annual 30.00
The Morgan Conquest TPB ('00, $14.95) r/#1-4 15.00
.../Thunderbolts Vol. 1: The Nefaria Protocols (2004, $19.99) r/#31-34, 42-44 20.00
Ultron Unleashed TPB (8/99, $3.50) reprints early app. 3.50
Ultron Unlimited TPB (4/01, $14.95) r/#19-22 & #0 prelude 15.00
Wizard #0-Ultron Unlimited prelude 2.50
Vol. 1: World Trust TPB ('03, $14.99) r/#57-62 & Marvel Double-Shot #2 15.00
Vol. 2: Red Zone TPB ('04, $14.99) r/#64-70 15.00
Vol. 3: The Search For She-Hulk TPB ('04, $12.99) r/#71-76 13.00
Vol. 4: The Lionheart of Avalon TPB ('04, $11.99) r/#77-81 12.00
Vol. 5: Once an Invader TPB ('04, $14.99) r/#82-84, V1 #71; Invaders #0 & Ann #1 ('77) 15.00

AVENGERS AND POWER PACK ASSEMBLE!
Marvel Comics: June, 2006 - No. 4, Sept, 2006 ($2.99, limited series)
1-4-GuriHiru-a/Sumerak-s. 1-Capt. America app. 2-Iron Man. 3-Spider-Man, Kang app. 3.00
TPB (2006, $6.99, digest-size) r/#1-4 7.00

AVENGERS: CELESTIAL QUEST
Marvel Comics: Nov, 2001 - No. 8, June, 2002 ($2.50/$3.50, limited series)
1-7-Englehart-s/Santamaría-a; Thanos app. 2.50
8-($3.50) 3.50

AVENGERS: CLASSIC
Marvel Comics: Aug, 2007 - No. 12, Juy, 2008 ($3.99/$2.99)
1,12-($3.99) 1-Reprints Avengers #1 ('63) with new stories about that era; Art Adams-c 4.00
2-11-($2.99) R/#2-11 with back-up w/art by Oeming and others 3.00

AVENGERS COLLECTOR'S EDITION, THE
Marvel Comics: 1993 (Ordered through mail w/candy wrapper, 20 pgs.)
1-Contains 4 bound-in trading cards 5.00

AVENGERS: EARTH'S MIGHTIEST HEROES
Marvel Comics: Jan, 2005 - No. 8, Apr, 2005 ($3.50, limited series)
1-8-Retells origin; Casey-s/Kolins-a 3.50
HC (2005, $24.99, 7 1/2" x 11" with dustjacket) r/#1-8 25.00

AVENGERS: EARTH'S MIGHTIEST HEROES II
Marvel Comics: Jan, 2007 - No. 8, May, 2007 ($3.99, limited series)
1-8-Retells time when the Vision joined; Casey-s/Rosado-a. 6-Hank & Janet's wedding 4.00
HC (2007, $24.99, 7 1/2" x 11" with dustjacket) r/#1-8; cover sketches 25.00

AVENGERS FAIRY TALES
Marvel Comics: May, 2008 - No. 4, Dec, 2008 ($2.99, limited series)
1-4: 1-Peter Pan-style tale; Cebulski-a/Lemos-a. 2-The Vision. 3-Miyazawa-a 3.00

AVENGERS FOREVER
Marvel Comics: Dec, 1998 - No. 12, Feb, 2000 ($2.99)
1-Busiek-s/Pacheco-a in all 4.00
2-12: 4-Four covers. 6-Two covers. 8-Vision origin revised. 12-Rick Jones becomes Capt. Marvel 3.00
TPB (1/01, $24.95) r/#1-12; Busiek intro.; new Pacheco-c 25.00

AVENGERS INFINITY
Marvel Comics: Sept, 2000 - No. 4, Dec, 2000 ($2.99, limited series)
1-4-Stern-s/Chen-a 3.00

AVENGERS/ INVADERS
Marvel Comics: Jul, 2008 - No. 12, Aug, 2009 ($2.99, limited series)
1-Invaders journey to the present; Alex Ross-c/Sadowski-a; Thunderbolts app. 3.00
2-12: 2-New Avengers app.; Perkins variant-c. 3-12-Variant-c on each 3.00
... Sketchbook (2008, giveaway) Ross and Sadowski sketch art; Krueger commentary 2.50

AVENGERS/ JLA (See JLA/Avengers for #1 & #3)
DC Comics: No, 2, 2003; No. 4, 2003 ($5.95, limited series)
2-Busiek-s/Pérez-a; wraparound-c; Krona, Galactus app. 6.00
4-Busiek-s/Pérez-a; wraparound-c 6.00

AVENGERS LOG, THE
Marvel Comics: Feb, 1994 ($1.95)
1-Gives history of all members; Perez-c 2.50

AVENGERS NEXT (See A-Next and Spider-Girl)
Marvel Comics: Jan, 2007 - No. 5 ($2.99, limited series)
1-5-Lim-a/Wieringo-c; Spider-Girl app. 1-Avengers vs. zombies. 2-Thena app. 3.00
...: Rebirth TPB (2007, $13.99) r/#1-5 14.00

AVENGERS SPOTLIGHT (Formerly Solo Avengers #1-20)
Marvel Comics: No. 21, Aug, 1989 - No. 40, Jan, 1991 (75¢/$1.00)
21-Byrne-c/a 3.00
22-40: 26-Acts of Vengeance story. 31-34-U.S. Agent series. 36-Heck-i. 37-Mortimer-i. 40-The Black Knight app. 2.50

AVENGERS STRIKEFILE
Marvel Comics: Jan, 1994 ($1.75, one-shot)
1 2.50

AVENGERS: THE CROSSING
Marvel Comics: July, 1995 ($4.95, one-shot)
1-Deodato-c/a; 1st app. Thor's new costume 5.00

AVENGERS: THE INITIATIVE (See Civil War and related titles)
Marvel Comics: Jun, 2007 - Present ($2.99)
1-Caselli-a/Slott-s/Cheung-c; War Machine app. 4.00
2-33: 4,5-World War Hulk. 6-Uy-a. 14-19-Secret Invasion; 3-D Man app. 16-Skrull Kill Krew returns. 20-Tigra pregnancy revealed, 21-25-Ramos-a. 32,33-Siege 3.00
Annual 1 (1/08, $3.99) Secret Invasion tie-in; Cheung-c 4.00
... Featuring Reptil (5/09, $3.99) Gage-s/Uy-a 4.00
... Special 1 (1/09, $3.99) Slott & Gage-s/Uy-a 4.00
...: Vol. 1 - Basic Training HC (2007, $19.99, d.j.) r/#1-6 20.00
...: Vol. 1 - Basic Training SC (2008, $14.99) r/#1-6 15.00

AVENGERS: THE TERMINATRIX OBJECTIVE
Marvel Comics: Sept, 1993 - No. 4, Dec, 1993 ($1.25, limited series)
1 ($2.50)-Holo-grafx foil-c 3.00
2-4-Old vs. current Avengers 2.50

AVENGERS: THE ULTRON IMPERATIVE
Marvel Comics: Nov, 2001 ($5.99, one-shot)
1-Follow-up to the Ultron Unlimited ending in Avengers #42; BWS-c 6.00

AVENGERS/THUNDERBOLTS
Marvel Comics: May, 2004 - No. 6, Sept, 2004 ($2.99, limited series)
1-6: Busiek & Nicieza-s/Kitson-c. 1,2-Kitson-a. 3-6-Grummett-a 3.00
Vol. 2: Best Intentions (2004, $14.99) r/#1-6 15.00

AVENGERS: TIMESLIDE
Marvel Comics: Feb, 1996 ($4.95, one-shot)
1-Foil-c 5.00

AVENGERS TWO: WONDER MAN & BEAST
Marvel Comics: May, 2000 - No. 3, July, 2000 ($2.99, limited series)
1-3: Stern-s/Bagley-c/a 3.00

AVENGERS/ULTRAFORCE (See Ultraforce/Avengers)
Marvel Comics: Oct, 1995 ($3.95, one-shot)
1-Wraparound foil-c by Perez 4.00

AVENGERS UNITED THEY STAND
Marvel Comics: Nov, 1999 - No. 7, June, 2000 ($2.99/$1.99)
1-Based on the animated series 3.00
2-6-($1.99) 2-Avengers battle Hydra 2.50
7-($2.99) Devil Dinosaur-c/app.; reprints Avengers Action Figure Comic 3.00

AVENGERS UNIVERSE
Marvel Comics: Jun, 2000 - No. 3, Oct, 2000 ($3.99)
1-3-Reprints recent stories 4.00

AVENGERS UNPLUGGED
Marvel Comics: Oct, 1995 - No. 6, Aug, 1996 (99¢, bi-monthly)
1-6 2.50

AVENGERS VS. ATLAS
Marvel Comics: Mar, 2010 - No. 4 ($3.99, limited series)
1-3-Hardman-a; Ramos-c. 1-Back-up w/Miyazawa-a. 2-Original Avengers app. 4.00

AVENGERS WEST COAST (Formerly West Coast Avengers)
Marvel Comics: No. 48, Sept, 1989 - No. 102, Jan, 1994 ($1.00/$1.25)

Avengers West Coast #68 © MAR

Azrael: Death's Dark Knight #3 © DC

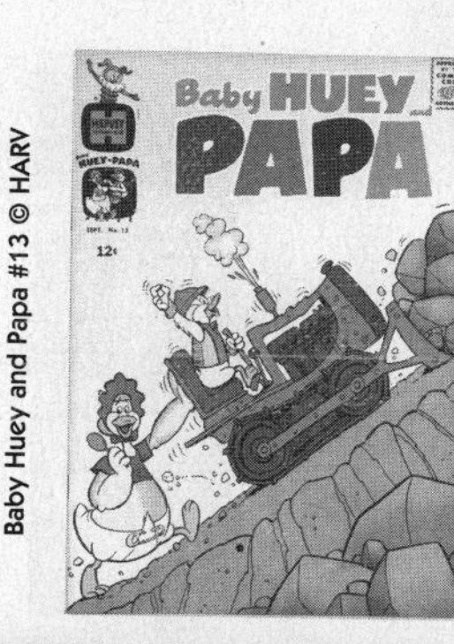

Baby Huey and Papa #13 © HARV

	GD 2.0	VG 4.0	FN 6.0	VF 8.0	VF/NM 9.0	NM- 9.2

48,49: 48-Byrne-c/a & scripts continue thru #57 — 3.00
50-Re-intro original Human Torch — 4.00
51-69,71-74,76-83,85,86,89-99: 54-Cover swipe/F.F. #1. 78-Last $1.00-c. 79-Dr. Strange x-over. 93-95-Darkhawk app. — 2.50
70,75,84,87,88: 70-Spider-Woman app. 75 (52 pgs.)-Fantastic Four x-over. 84-Origin Spider-Woman retold; Spider-Man app. (also in #85,86). 87,88-Wolverine-c/story — 3.00
100-($3.95, 68 pgs.)-Embossed all red foil-c — 4.00
101,102: 101-X-Men x-over — 5.00
Annual 5-8 ('90- '93, 68 pgs.)-5,6-West Coast Avengers in indicia. 7-Darkhawk app. 8-Polybagged w/card — 3.00
...: Darker Than Scarlet TPB (2008, $24.99) r/#51-57,60-62; Byrne-s/a — 25.00
...: Vision Quest TPB (2005, $24.99) r/#42-50; Byrne-s/a — 25.00

AVIATION ADVENTURES AND MODEL BUILDING (True Aviation Advs. ...No. 15)
Parents' Magazine Institute: No. 16, Dec, 1946 - No. 17, Feb, 1947
16,17-Half comics and half pictures — 8 16 24 42 54 65

AVIATION CADETS
Street & Smith Publications: 1943
nn — 19 37 57 109 172 235

A-V IN 3-D
Aardvark-Vanaheim: Dec, 1984 ($2.00, 28 pgs. w/glasses)
1-Cerebus, Flaming Carrot, Normalman & Ms. Tree — 4.00

AWAKENING, THE
Image Comics: Oct, 1997 - No. 4, Apr, 1998 ($2.95, B&W, limited series)
1-4-Stephen Blue-s/c/a — 3.00

AWESOME ADVENTURES
Awesome Entertainment: Aug, 1999 ($2.50)
1-Alan Moore-s/ Steve Skroce-a; Youngblood story — 3.00

AWESOME HOLIDAY SPECIAL
Awesome Entertainment: Dec, 1997 ($2.50, one-shot)
1-Flip book w/covers of Fighting American & Coven. Holiday stories also featuring Kaboom and Shaft by regular creators. — 3.00
1-Gold Edition — 5.00

AWFUL OSCAR (Formerly & becomes Oscar Comics with No. 13)
Marvel Comics: No. 11, June, 1949 - No. 12, Aug, 1949
11,12 — 14 28 42 80 115 150

AWKWARD UNIVERSE
Slave Labor Graphics: 12/95 ($9.95, graphic novel)
nn — 10.00

AXA
Eclipse Comics: Apr, 1987 - No. 2, Aug, 1987 ($1.75)
1,2 — 2.50

AXEL PRESSBUTTON (Pressbutton No. 5; see Laser Eraser &...)
Eclipse Comics: Nov, 1984 - No. 6, July, 1985 ($1.50/$1.75, Baxter paper)
1-6: Reprints Warrior (British mag.). 1-Bolland-c; origin Laser Eraser & Pressbutton — 3.00

AXIS ALPHA
Axis Comics: Feb, 1994 ($2.50, one-shot)
V1-Previews Axis titles including, Tribe, Dethgrip, B.E.A.S.T.I.E.S. & more; Pitt app. in Tribe story. — 3.00

AZRAEL (...Agent of the Bat #47 on)(Also see Batman: Sword of Azrael)
DC Comics: Feb, 1995 - No. 100, May, 2003 ($1.95/$2.25/$2.50/$2.95)
1-Dennis O'Neil scripts begin — 5.00
2,3 — 3.00
4-46,48-62: 5,6-Ras Al Ghul app. 13-Nightwing-c/app. 15-Contagion Pt. 5 (Pt. 4 on-c). 16-Contagion Pt. 10. 22-Batman-c/app. 23,27-Batman app. 27,28-Joker app. 35-Hitman app. 36-39-Batman, Bane app. 50-New costume. 53-Joker-c/app. 56,57,60-New Batgirl app. — 2.50
47-($3.95) Flip book with Batman: Shadow of the Bat #80 — 4.00
63-74,76-92: 63-Huntress-c/app.; Azrael returns to old costume. 67-Begin $2.50-c. 70-79-Harris-c. 83-Joker x-over. 91-Bruce Wayne: Fugitive pt. 15 — 2.50
75-($3.95) New costume; Harris-c — 4.00
93-100: 93-Begin $2.95-c. 95,96-Two-Face app. 100-Last issue; Zeck-c — 3.00
#1,000,000 (11/98) Giarrano-a — 2.50
Annual 1 (1995, $3.95)-Year One story — 4.00
Annual 2 (1996, $2.95)-Legends of the Dead Earth story — 3.00
Annual 3 (1997, $3.95)-Pulp Heroes story; Orbik-c — 4.00
.../Ash (1997, $4.95) O'Neil-s/Quesada, Palmiotti-a — 5.00

	GD 2.0	VG 4.0	FN 6.0	VF 8.0	VF/NM 9.0	NM- 9.2

Plus (12/96, $2.95)-Question-c/app. — 3.00

AZRAEL
DC Comics: Dec, 2009 - Present ($2.99)
1-4-Nicieza-s/Bachs-a. 1-3-Jock-c — 3.00

AZRAEL: DEATH'S DARK KNIGHT
DC Comics: May, 2009 - No. 3, Jul, 2009 ($2.99, limited series)
1-Battle For the Cowl tie-in; Nicieza-s/Irving-a/March-c — 3.00

AZTEC ACE
Eclipse Comics: Mar, 1984 - No. 15, Sept, 1985 ($2.25/$1.50/$1.75, Baxter paper)
1-$2.25-c (52 pgs.) — 3.00
2-15: 2-Begin 36 pgs. — 2.50
NOTE: *N. Redondo a-1i-8i, 10i. c-6-8i.*

AZTEK: THE ULTIMATE MAN
DC Comics: Aug, 1996 - No. 10, May 1997 ($1.75)
1-1st app. Aztek & Synth; Grant Morrison & Mark Millar scripts in all — 6.00
2-9: 2-Green Lantern app. 3-1st app. Death-Doll. 4-Intro The Lizard King. 5-Origin. 6-Joker app.; Batman cameo. 7-Batman app. 8-Luthor app. 9-vs. Parasite-c/app. — 4.00
10-JLA-c/app. — 1 2 4 6 8 10
JLA Presents: Aztek the Ultimate Man TPB (2008, $19.99) r/#1-10 — 20.00
NOTE: *Breyfogle c-5p. N. Steven Harris a-1-5p. Porter c-1p. Wieringo c-2p.*

BABE (...Darling of the Hills, later issues)(See Big Shot and Sparky Watts)
Prize/Headline/Feature: June-July, 1948 - No. 11, Apr-May, 1950
1-Boody Rogers-a — 27 54 81 158 259 360
2-Boody Rogers-a — 15 30 45 90 140 190
3-11-All by Boody Rogers — 15 30 45 83 124 165

BABE
Dark Horse Comics (Legend): July, 1994 - No. 4, Jan, 1994 ($2.50, lim. series)
1-4: John Byrne-c/a/scripts; ProtoTykes back-up story — 2.50

BABE RUTH SPORTS COMICS (Becomes Rags Rabbit #11 on?)
Harvey Publications: April, 1949 - No. 11, Feb, 1951
1-Powell-a — 41 82 123 250 413 575
2-Powell-a — 28 56 84 162 261 360
3-11: Powell-a in most — 23 46 69 133 214 295
NOTE: *Baseball c-2-4, 9. Basketball c-1, 6. Football c-5. Yogi Berra c/story-8. Joe DiMaggio c/story-3. Bob Feller c/story-4. Stan Musial c-9.*

BABES IN TOYLAND (Disney, Movie) (See Golden Pix Story Book ST-3)
Dell Publishing Co.: No. 1282, Feb-Apr, 1962
Four Color 1282-Annette Funicello photo-c — 13 26 39 95 178 260

BABES OF BROADWAY
Broadway Comics: May, 1996 ($2.95, one-shot)
1-Pin-ups of Broadway Comics' female characters; Alan Davis, Michael Kaluta, J. G. Jones, Alan Weiss, Guy Davis & others-a; Giordano-c. — 3.00

BABE 2
Dark Horse Comics (Legend): Mar, 1995 - No. 2, May, 1995 ($2.50, lim. series)
1,2: John Byrne-c/a/scripts — 2.50

BABY HUEY
Harvey Comics: No. 1, Oct, 1991 - No. 9, June, 1994 ($1.00/$1.25/$1.50, quarterly)
1 ($1.00): 1-Cover says "Big Baby Huey" — 5.00
2-9 ($1.25-$1.50) — 3.00

BABY HUEY AND PAPA (See Paramount Animated...)
Harvey Publications: May, 1962 - No. 33, Jan, 1968 (Also see Casper The Friendly Ghost)
1 — 15 30 45 104 197 290
2 — 8 16 24 58 97 135
3-5 — 6 12 18 37 59 80
6-10 — 3 6 9 21 32 42
11-20 — 3 6 9 16 22 28
21-33 — 2 4 6 13 18 22

BABY HUEY DIGEST
Harvey Publications: June, 1992 (Digest-size, one-shot)
1-Reprints — 1 3 4 6 8 10

BABY HUEY DUCKLAND
Harvey Publications: Nov, 1962 - No. 15, Nov, 1966 (25¢ Giants, 68 pgs.)
1 — 11 22 33 80 145 210
2-5 — 6 12 18 39 62 85
6-15 — 4 8 12 22 34 45

Backlash #3 © WSP

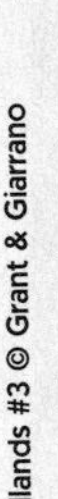
The Badger #14 © FC

Badlands #3 © Grant & Giarrano

BABY HUEY, THE BABY GIANT (Also see Big Baby Huey, Casper, Harvey Hits #22, Harvey Comics Hits #60, & Paramount Animated Comics)
Harvey Publ: 9/56 - #97, 10/71; #98, 10/72; #99, 10/80; #100, 10/90; #101, 11/90

	GD 2.0	VG 4.0	FN 6.0	VF 8.0	VF/NM 9.0	NM- 9.2
1-Infinity-c	48	96	144	384	742	1100
2	23	46	69	163	314	465
3-Baby Huey takes anti-pep pills	15	30	45	104	197	290
4,5	10	20	30	73	129	185
6-10	7	14	21	47	76	105
11-20	5	10	15	35	55	75
21-40	4	8	12	24	37	50
41-60	3	6	9	16	23	30
61-79 (12/67)	2	4	6	13	18	22
80(12/68) - 95-All 68 pg. Giants	3	6	9	17	25	32
96,97-Both 52 pg. Giants	3	6	9	14	19	24
98-Regular size	2	4	6	9	12	15
99-Regular size	1	2	3	5	6	8
100,101 ($1.00)						4.00

BABYLON 5 (TV)
DC Comics: Jan, 1995 - No. 11, Dec, 1995 ($1.95/$2.50)

	GD 2.0	VG 4.0	FN 6.0	VF 8.0	VF/NM 9.0	NM- 9.2
1	2	4	6	8	11	14
2-5	1	2	3	5	7	9
6-11: 7-Begin $2.50-c	1	2	3	4	5	7
... The Price of Peace (1998, $9.95, TPB) r/#1-4,11						10.00

BABYLON 5: IN VALEN'S NAME
DC Comics: Mar, 1998 - No. 3, May, 1998 ($2.50, limited series)

	GD 2.0	VG 4.0	FN 6.0	VF 8.0	VF/NM 9.0	NM- 9.2
1-3						4.00

BABY SNOOTS (Also see March of Comics #359,371,396,401,419,431,443,450,462,474,485)
Gold Key: Aug, 1970 - No. 22, Nov, 1975

	GD 2.0	VG 4.0	FN 6.0	VF 8.0	VF/NM 9.0	NM- 9.2
1	3	6	9	20	30	40
2-11	2	4	6	11	16	20
12-22: 22-Titled Snoots, the Forgetful Elefink	2	4	6	8	10	12

BACCHUS (Also see Eddie Campbell's ...)
Harrier Comics (New Wave): 1988 - No. 2, Aug, 1988 ($1.95, B&W)

	GD 2.0	VG 4.0	FN 6.0	VF 8.0	VF/NM 9.0	NM- 9.2
1,2: Eddie Campbell-c/a/scripts.						3.00

BACHELOR FATHER (TV)
Dell Publishing Co.: No. 1332, 4-6/62 - No. 2, Sept.-Nov., 1962

	GD 2.0	VG 4.0	FN 6.0	VF 8.0	VF/NM 9.0	NM- 9.2
Four Color 1332 (#1), 2-Written by Stanley	7	14	21	50	83	115

BACHELOR'S DIARY
Avon Periodicals: 1949 (15¢)

	GD 2.0	VG 4.0	FN 6.0	VF 8.0	VF/NM 9.0	NM- 9.2
1(Scarce)-King Features panel cartoons & text-r; pin-up, girl wrestling photos; similar to Sideshow	68	136	204	435	743	1050

BACK DOWN THE LINE
Eclipse Books: 1991 (Mature adults, 8-1/2 x 11", 52 pgs.)

	GD 2.0	VG 4.0	FN 6.0	VF 8.0	VF/NM 9.0	NM- 9.2
nn (Soft-c, $8.95)-Bolton-c/a						9.00
nn (Limited Hard-c, $29.95)						30.00

BACKLASH (Also see The Kindred)
Image Comics (WildStorm Prod.): Nov,1994 - No. 32, May, 1997 ($1.95/$2.50)

	GD 2.0	VG 4.0	FN 6.0	VF 8.0	VF/NM 9.0	NM- 9.2
1-Double-c; variant-double-c						3.00
2-7,9-32: 5-Intro Mindscape; 2 pinups. 19-Fire From Heaven Pt 2. 20-Fire From Heaven Pt 10. 31-WildC.A.T.S app.						2.50
8-($1.95, newsstand)-Wildstorm Rising Pt. 8						2.50
8-($2.50, direct market)-Wildstorm Rising Pt. 8						2.50
25-($3.95)-Double-size						4.00
...& Taboo's African Holiday (9/99, $5.95) Booth-s/a(p)						6.00

BACKLASH/SPIDER-MAN
Image Comics (WildStorm Productions): Aug, 1996 - No. 2, Sept, 1996 ($2.50, lim. series)

	GD 2.0	VG 4.0	FN 6.0	VF 8.0	VF/NM 9.0	NM- 9.2
1,2: Pike (villain from WildC.A.T.S) & Venom app.						3.00

BACKPACK MARVELS (B&W backpack-sized reprint collections)
Marvel Comics: Nov, 2000 ($6.95, B&W, digest-size)

	GD 2.0	VG 4.0	FN 6.0	VF 8.0	VF/NM 9.0	NM- 9.2
Avengers 1 -r/Avengers #181-189; profile pages						7.00
Spider-Man 1-r/ASM #234-240						7.00
X-Men 1-r/Uncanny X-Men #167-173						7.00
X-Men 2-r/Uncanny X-Men #174-179; new painted-c by Greg Horn						7.00

BACK TO THE FUTURE (Movie, TV cartoon)
Harvey Comics: Nov, 1991 - No. 4, June, 1992 ($1.25)

	GD 2.0	VG 4.0	FN 6.0	VF 8.0	VF/NM 9.0	NM- 9.2
1-4: 1,2-Gil Kane-c; based on animated cartoon						3.00

BACK TO THE FUTURE: FORWARD TO THE FUTURE
Harvey Comics: Oct, 1992 - No. 3, Feb, 1993 ($1.50, limited series)

	GD 2.0	VG 4.0	FN 6.0	VF 8.0	VF/NM 9.0	NM- 9.2
1-3						3.00

BAD BOY
Oni Press: Dec, 1997 ($4.95, one-shot)

	GD 2.0	VG 4.0	FN 6.0	VF 8.0	VF/NM 9.0	NM- 9.2
1-Frank Miller-s/Simon Bisley-a/painted-c						5.00

BAD COMPANY
Quality Comics/Fleetway Quality #15 on: Aug, 1988 - No. 19?, 1990 ($1.50/$1.75, high quality paper)

	GD 2.0	VG 4.0	FN 6.0	VF 8.0	VF/NM 9.0	NM- 9.2
1-19: 5,6-Guice-c						2.50

BADGE OF JUSTICE (Formerly Crime And Justice #21)
Charlton Comics: No. 22, 1/55 - No. 2, 4/55 - No. 4, 10/55

	GD 2.0	VG 4.0	FN 6.0	VF 8.0	VF/NM 9.0	NM- 9.2
22(#1)(1/55)	10	20	30	58	79	100
2-4	7	14	21	35	43	50

BADGER, THE
Capital Comics(#1-4)/First Comics: Dec, 1983 - No. 70, Apr, 1991; V2#1, Spring, 1991

	GD 2.0	VG 4.0	FN 6.0	VF 8.0	VF/NM 9.0	NM- 9.2
1						5.00
2-70: 52-54-Tim Vigil-c/a						3.00
50-($3.95, 52 pgs.)						4.00
V2#1 (Spring, 1991, $4.95)						5.00

BADGER, THE
Image Comics: V3#78, May, 1997 - V3#88 ($2.95, B&W)

	GD 2.0	VG 4.0	FN 6.0	VF 8.0	VF/NM 9.0	NM- 9.2
78-Cover lists #1, Baron-s						3.00
79/#2, 80/#3, 81(indicia lists #80)/#4,82-88/#5-11						3.00

BADGER GOES BERSERK
First Comics: Sept, 1989 - No. 4, Dec, 1989 ($1.95, lim. series, Baxter paper)

	GD 2.0	VG 4.0	FN 6.0	VF 8.0	VF/NM 9.0	NM- 9.2
1-4: 2-Paul Chadwick-c/a(2pgs.)						3.00

BADGER: SHATTERED MIRROR
Dark Horse Comics: July, 1994 - No. Oct, 1994 ($2.50, limited series)

	GD 2.0	VG 4.0	FN 6.0	VF 8.0	VF/NM 9.0	NM- 9.2
1-4						3.00

BADGER: ZEN POP FUNNY-ANIMAL VERSION
Dark Horse Comics: July, 1994 - No. 2, Aug, 1994 ($2.50, limited series)

	GD 2.0	VG 4.0	FN 6.0	VF 8.0	VF/NM 9.0	NM- 9.2
1,2						3.00

BAD GIRLS
DC Comics: Oct, 2003 - No. 5, Feb, 2004 ($2.50, limited series)

	GD 2.0	VG 4.0	FN 6.0	VF 8.0	VF/NM 9.0	NM- 9.2
1-5-Steve Vance-s/Jennifer Graves-a/Darwyn Cooke-c						2.50
TPB (2009, $14.99) r/#1-5; Graves sketch pages						15.00

BAD IDEAS
Image Comics: Apr, 2004 - No. 2, July, 2004 ($5.95, B&W, limited series)

	GD 2.0	VG 4.0	FN 6.0	VF 8.0	VF/NM 9.0	NM- 9.2
1,2-Chinsang-s/Mahfood & Crosland-a						6.00
..., Vol. 1: Collected! (2005, $12.99) r/#1,2						13.00

BADLANDS
Vortex Comics: May, 1990 ($3.00, glossy stock, mature)

	GD 2.0	VG 4.0	FN 6.0	VF 8.0	VF/NM 9.0	NM- 9.2
1-Chaykin-c						3.00

BADLANDS
Dark Horse Comics: July, 1991 - No. 6, Dec, 1991 ($2.25, B&W, limited series)

	GD 2.0	VG 4.0	FN 6.0	VF 8.0	VF/NM 9.0	NM- 9.2
1-6: 1-John F. Kennedy-c; reprints Vortex Comics issue						2.50

BADMEN OF THE WEST
Avon Periodicals: 1951 (Giant) (132 pgs., painted-c)

	GD 2.0	VG 4.0	FN 6.0	VF 8.0	VF/NM 9.0	NM- 9.2
1-Contains rebound copies of Jesse James, King of the Bad Men of Deadwood, Badmen of Tombstone; other combinations possible. Issues with Kubert-a...	39	78	117	240	395	550

BADMEN OF THE WEST! (See A-1 Comics)
Magazine Enterprises: 1953 - No. 3, 1954

	GD 2.0	VG 4.0	FN 6.0	VF 8.0	VF/NM 9.0	NM- 9.2
1 (A-1 100)-Meskin-a?	22	44	66	132	216	300
2 (A-1 120), 3: 2-Larsen-a	15	30	45	85	130	175

BADMEN OF TOMBSTONE
Avon Periodicals: 1950

	GD 2.0	VG 4.0	FN 6.0	VF 8.0	VF/NM 9.0	NM- 9.2
nn	15	30	45	94	147	200

BAD PLANET
Image Comics (Raw Studios): Dec, 2005 - Present ($2.99)

	GD 2.0	VG 4.0	FN 6.0	VF 8.0	VF/NM 9.0	NM- 9.2
1-6: 1-Thomas Jane & Steve Niles-s/Larosa & Bradstreet-a/c. 2-Wrightson-c. 3-3-D pages						3.00

BADROCK (Also see Youngblood)

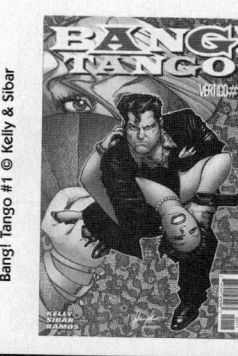

Baffling Mysteries #9 © ACE

Bang! Tango #1 © Kelly & Sibar

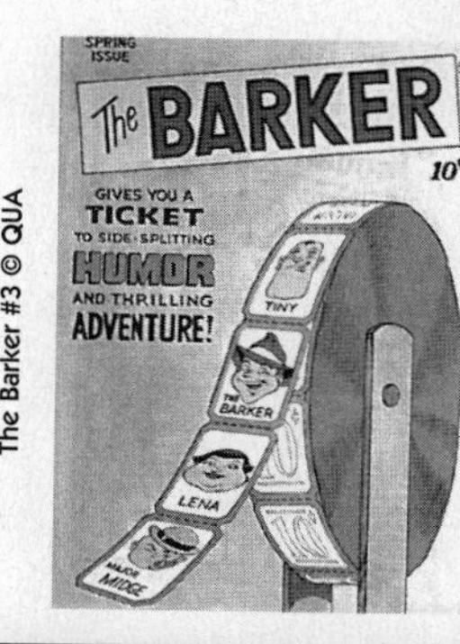

The Barker #3 © QUA

GD 2.0 | VG 4.0 | FN 6.0 | VF 8.0 | VF/NM 9.0 | NM- 9.2

Image Comics (Extreme Studios): Mar, 1995 - No. 2, Jan, 1996 ($1.75/$2.50)
1-Variant-c (3) 3.00
2-Liefeld-c/a & story; Savage Dragon app, flipbook w/Grifter/Badrock #2; variant-c exist 2.50
Annual 1(1995,$2.95)-Arthur Adams-c 3.00
Annual 1 Commemorative ($9.95)-3,000 printed 10.00
.../Wolverine (6/96, $4.95, squarebound)-Sauron app; pin-ups; variant-c exists 5.00
.../Wolverine (6/96)-Special Comicon Edition 5.00

BADROCK AND COMPANY (Also see Youngblood)
Image Comics (Extreme Studios): Sept, 1994 - No.6, Feb, 1995 ($2.50)
1-6 : 6-Indicia reads "October 1994"; story cont'd in Shadowhawk #17 2.50

BAFFLING MYSTERIES (Formerly Indian Braves No. 1-4; Heroes of the Wild Frontier No. 26-on)
Periodical House (Ace Magazines): No. 5, Nov, 1951 - No. 26, Oct, 1955
5 40 80 120 246 411 575
6-19,21-24: 8-Woodish-a by Cameron. 10-E.C. Crypt Keeper swipe on-c.
24-Last pre-code issue 25 50 75 150 245 340
20-Classic-c 34 68 102 199 325 450
25-Reprints; surrealistic-c 19 38 57 111 176 240
26-Reprints 17 34 51 100 158 215
NOTE: ***Cameron** a-8, 10, 16-18, 20-22. **Colan** a-5, 11, 25r/5. **Sekowsky** a-5, 6, 22. Bondage c-20, 23. Reprints in 18(1), 19(1), 24(3).*

BALBO (See Master Comics #33 & Mighty Midget Comics)

BALDER THE BRAVE
Marvel Comics Group: Nov, 1985 - No. 4, 1986 (Limited series)
1-4: Simonson-c/a; character from Thor 3.00

BALLAD OF HALO JONES, THE
Quality Comics: Sept, 1987 - No. 12, Aug, 1988 ($1.25/$1.50)
1-12: Alan Moore scripts in all 2.50

BALL AND CHAIN
DC Comics (Homage): Nov, 1999 - No. 4, Feb, 2000 ($2.50, limited series)
1-4-Lobdell-s/Garza-a 2.50

BALLISTIC (Also See Cyberforce)
Image Comics (Top Cow Productions): Sept, 1995 - No. 3, Dec, 1995 ($2.50, limited series)
1-3: Wetworks app, Turner-c/a 3.00
... Action (5/96, $2.95) Pin-ups of Top Cow characters participating in outdoor sports 3.00
... Imagery (1/96, $2.50, anthology) Cyberforce app. 2.50
.../ Wolverine (2/97, $2.95) Devil's Reign pt. 4; Witchblade cameo (1 page) 4.00

BALOO & LITTLE BRITCHES (Disney)
Gold Key: Apr, 1968
1-From the Jungle Book 4 8 12 24 37 50

BAMBI (Disney) (See Movie Classics, Movie Comics, and Walt Disney Showcase No. 31)
Dell Publishing Co.: No. 12, 1942; No. 30, 1943; No. 186, Apr, 1948; 1984
Four Color 12-Walt Disney's... 50 100 150 400 775 1150
Four Color 30-Bambi's Children (1943) 45 90 135 360 693 1025
Four Color 186-Walt Disney's...; reprinted as Movie Classic Bambi #3 (1956)
16 32 48 115 220 325
1-(Whitman, 1984; 60¢)-r/Four Color #186 (3-pack) 2 4 6 10 14 18

BAMBI (Disney)
Grosset & Dunlap: 1942 (50¢, 7"x8-1/2", 32pg, hard-c w/dust jacket)
nn-Given away w/a copy of Thumper for a $2.00, 2-yr. subscription to WDC&S
in 1942 (Xmas offer). Book only 22 44 66 132 216 300
w/dust jacket 39 78 117 240 395 550

BAMM BAMM & PEBBLES FLINTSTONE (TV)
Gold Key: Oct, 1964 (Hanna-Barbera)
1 9 18 27 60 100 140

BANANA SPLITS, THE (TV) (See Golden Comics Digest & March of Comics No. 364)
Gold Key: June, 1969 - No. 8, Oct, 1971 (Hanna-Barbera)
1-Photo-c on all 9 18 27 65 113 160
2-8 6 12 18 39 62 85

BANANA SUNDAY
Oni Press: July, 2005 - No. 4, Oct, 2005 ($2.99, B&W, limited series)
1-4-Root Nibot-s/Colleen Coover-a 3.00
TPB (3/06, $11.95) r/#1-4; sketch gallery 12.00

BAND WAGON (See Hanna-Barbera Band Wagon)

BANG! TANGO
DC Comics (Vertigo): Apr, 2009 - No. 6, Sept, 2009 ($2.99, limited series)
1-6-Kelly-s/Sibar-a/Chaykin-c 3.00

BANG-UP COMICS
Progressive Publishers: Dec, 1941 - No. 3, June, 1942
1-Cosmo Mann & Lady Fairplay begin; Buzz Balmer by Rick Yager in all (origin #1)
94 188 282 597 1024 1450
2,3 45 90 135 284 480 675

BANISHED KNIGHTS (See Warlands)
Image Comics: Dec, 2001 - No. 4, June, 2002 ($2.95)
1-4-Two covers (Alvin Lee, Pat Lee) 3.00

BANNER COMICS (Becomes Captain Courageous No. 6)
Ace Magazines: No. 3, Sept, 1941 - No. 5, Jan, 1942
3-Captain Courageous (1st app.) & Lone Warrior & Sidekick Dicky begin;
Jim Mooney-c 106 212 318 673 1162 1650
4,5: 4-Flag-c 66 132 198 425 725 1025

BARACK OBAMA (See Presidential Material: Barack Obama, Amazing Spider-Man #583, Savage Dragon #137)

BARACK THE BARBARIAN
Devil's Due Publishing: Jun, 2009 - No. 4, Oct, 2009 ($3.50/$3.99, limited series)
...Quest For The Treasure of Stimuli 1-3-($3.50) Conan spoof with Barack Obama; Hama-s 3.50
...Quest For The Treasure of Stimuli 4-($3.99) 4.00
...: The Red of Red Sarah 1 ($5.99, B&W) Sarah Palin satire; Hama-s 6.00

BARBARIANS, THE
Atlas Comics/Seaboard Periodicals: June, 1975
1-Origin, only app. Andrax; Iron Jaw app.; Marcos-a 2 4 6 9 12 15

BARBIE
Marvel Comics: Jan, 1991 - No. 63, Mar, 1996 ($1.00/$1.25/$1.50)
1-Polybagged w/doorknob hanger; Romita-c 2 4 6 9 12 15
2-49,51-62 1 2 3 5 7 9
50,63: 50-(Giant). 63-Last issue 2 4 6 8 10 12
... And Baby Sister Kelly (1995, 99¢-c, part of a Marvel 4-pack) scarce
3 6 9 14 20 25

BARBIE & KEN
Dell Publishing Co.: May-July, 1962 - No. 5, Nov-Jan, 1963-64
01-053-207(#1)-Based on Mattel toy dolls 36 72 108 275 530 785
2-4 29 58 87 212 406 600
5 (Rare) 30 60 90 218 422 625

BARBIE FASHION
Marvel Comics: Jan, 1991 - No. 53, May, 1995 ($1.00/$1.25/$1.50)
1-Polybagged w/Barbie Pink Card 2 4 6 9 12 15
2-49,51,52: 4-Contains preview to Sweet XVI 1 2 3 5 7 9
50,53: 50-(Giant). 53-Last issue 2 4 6 8 10 12

BARB WIRE (See Comics' Greatest World)
Dark Horse Comics: Apr, 1994 - No. 9, Feb, 1995 ($2.00/$2.50)
1-9: 1-Foil logo 3.00
Trade paperback (1996, $8.95)-r/#2,3,5,6 w/Pamela Anderson bio 9.00

BARB WIRE: ACE OF SPADES
Dark Horse Comics: May, 1996 - No. 4, Sept, 1996 ($2.95, limited series)
1-4: Chris Warner-c/a(p)/scripts; Tim Bradstreet-c/a(i) in all 3.00

BARB WIRE COMICS MAGAZINE SPECIAL
Dark Horse Comics: May, 1996 ($3.50, B&W, magazine, one-shot)
nn-Adaptation of film; photo-c; poster insert. 3.50

BARB WIRE MOVIE SPECIAL
Dark Horse Comics: May, 1996 ($3.95, one-shot)
nn-Adaptation of film; photo-c; 1st app. new look 4.00

BARKER, THE (Also see National Comics #42)
Quality Comics Group/Comic Magazine: Autumn, 1946 - No. 15, Dec, 1949
1 23 46 69 136 223 310
2 14 28 42 80 115 150
3-10 11 22 33 62 86 110
11-14 9 18 27 50 65 80
15-Jack Cole-a(p) 9 18 27 52 69 85
NOTE: ***Jack Cole** art in some issues.*

BARNABY
Civil Service Publications Inc.: 1945 (25¢,102 pgs., digest size)
V1#1-r/Crocket Johnson strips from 1942 5 10 14 20 24 28

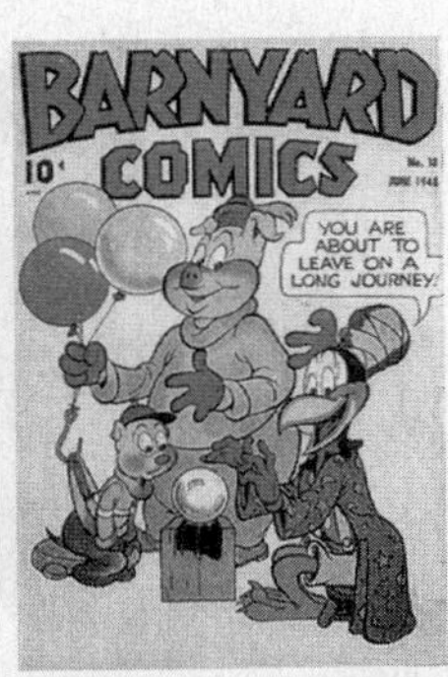

Barnyard Comics #18 © Nedor

Baseball Thrills #2 © Z-D

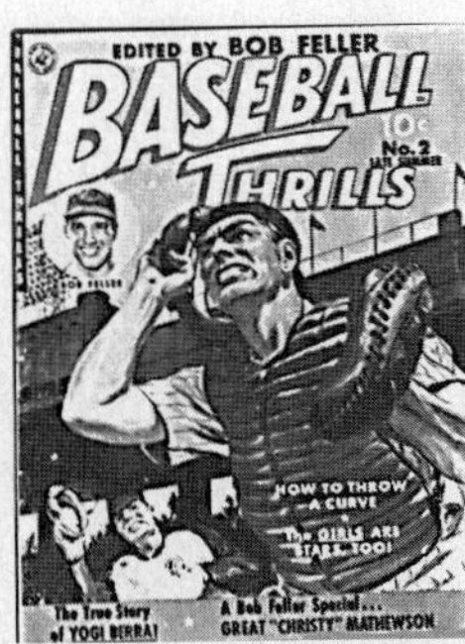

Batgirl #25 © DC

GD VG FN VF VF/NM NM-
2.0 4.0 6.0 8.0 9.0 9.2

BARNEY AND BETTY RUBBLE (TV) (Flintstones' Neighbors)
Charlton Comics: Jan, 1973 - No. 23, Dec, 1976 (Hanna-Barbera)

	GD 2.0	VG 4.0	FN 6.0	VF 8.0	VF/NM 9.0	NM- 9.2
1	4	8	12	24	37	50
2-11: 11(2/75)-1st Mike Zeck-a (illos)	3	6	9	14	20	25
12-23	2	4	6	10	14	18
Digest Annual (1972, B&W, 100 pgs.) (scarce)	4	8	12	24	37	50

BARNEY BAXTER (Also see Magic Comics)
David McKay/Dell Publishing Co./Argo: 1938 - No. 2, 1956

	GD 2.0	VG 4.0	FN 6.0	VF 8.0	VF/NM 9.0	NM- 9.2
Feature Books 15(McKay-1938)	40	80	120	246	411	575
Four Color 20(1942)	25	50	75	183	354	525
1,2 (1956-Argo)	9	18	27	50	65	80

BARNEY BEAR ...
Spire Christian Comics (Fleming H. Revell Co.): 1977-1981

	GD 2.0	VG 4.0	FN 6.0	VF 8.0	VF/NM 9.0	NM- 9.2
...Home Plate nn-(1979, 49¢), ...Lost and Found nn-(1979, 49¢), Out of The Woods nn-(1980, 49¢), Sunday School Picnic nn-(1981, 69¢, The Swamp Gang!-(1977, 39¢)	2	4	6	8	11	14

BARNEY GOOGLE & SNUFFY SMITH
Dell Publishing Co./Gold Key: 1942 - 1943; April, 1964

	GD 2.0	VG 4.0	FN 6.0	VF 8.0	VF/NM 9.0	NM- 9.2
Four Color 19(1942)	47	94	141	296	498	700
Four Color 40(1944)	21	42	63	148	287	425
Large Feature Comic 11(1943)	38	76	114	225	368	510
1(10113-404)-Gold Key (4/64)	4	8	12	26	41	55

BARNEY GOOGLE & SNUFFY SMITH
Toby Press: June, 1951 - No. 4, Feb, 1952 (Reprints)

	GD 2.0	VG 4.0	FN 6.0	VF 8.0	VF/NM 9.0	NM- 9.2
1	14	28	42	76	108	140
2,3	8	16	24	44	57	70
4-Kurtzman-a "Pot Shot Pete", 5 pgs.; reprints John Wayne #5	12	24	36	69	97	125

BARNEY GOOGLE AND SNUFFY SMITH
Charlton Comics: Mar, 1970 - No. 6, Jan, 1971

	GD 2.0	VG 4.0	FN 6.0	VF 8.0	VF/NM 9.0	NM- 9.2
1	3	6	9	17	25	32
2-6	2	4	6	11	16	20

BARNUM!
DC Comics (Vertigo): 2003; 2005 ($29.95, $19.95)

	GD 2.0	VG 4.0	FN 6.0	VF 8.0	VF/NM 9.0	NM- 9.2
Hardcover (2003, $29.95, with dust jacket)-Chaykin & Tischman-s/Henrichon-a						30.00
Softcover (2005, $19.95)-Chaykin & Tischman-s/Henrichon-a						20.00

BARNYARD COMICS (Dizzy Duck No. 32 on)
Nedor/Polo Mag./Standard(Animated Cartoons): June, 1944 - No. 31, Sept, 1950; No. 10, 1957

	GD 2.0	VG 4.0	FN 6.0	VF 8.0	VF/NM 9.0	NM- 9.2
1 (nn, 52 pgs.)-Funny animal	20	40	60	114	182	250
2 (52 pgs.)	12	24	36	69	97	125
3-5	9	18	27	52	69	85
6-12,16	8	16	24	44	57	70
13-15,17,21,23,26,27,29-All contain Frazetta text illos	10	20	30	54	72	90
18-20,22,24,25-All contain Frazetta-a & text illos	12	24	36	69	97	125
28,30,31	7	14	21	37	46	50
10 (1957)(Exist?)	4	7	10	14	17	20

BARRY M. GOLDWATER
Dell Publishing Co.: Mar, 1965 (Complete life story)

	GD 2.0	VG 4.0	FN 6.0	VF 8.0	VF/NM 9.0	NM- 9.2
12-055-503-Photo-c	4	8	12	24	37	50

BARRY WINDSOR-SMITH: STORYTELLER
Dark Horse Comics: Oct, 1996 - No. 9, July, 1997 ($4.95, oversize)

	GD 2.0	VG 4.0	FN 6.0	VF 8.0	VF/NM 9.0	NM- 9.2
1-9: 1-Intro Young Gods, Paradox Man & the Freebooters; Barry Smith-c/a/scripts						5.00
Preview						4.00

BAR SINISTER (Also see Shaman's Tears)
Acclaim Comics (Windjammer): Jun, 1995 - No. 4, Sept, 1995 ($2.50, lim. series)

	GD 2.0	VG 4.0	FN 6.0	VF 8.0	VF/NM 9.0	NM- 9.2
1-4: Mike Grell-c/a/scripts						2.50

BARTMAN (Also see Simpson's Comics & Radioactive Man)
Bongo Comics: 1993 - No. 6, 1994 ($1.95/$2.25)

	GD 2.0	VG 4.0	FN 6.0	VF 8.0	VF/NM 9.0	NM- 9.2
1-($2.95)-Foil-c; bound-in jumbo Bartman poster						6.00
2-6: 3-w/trading card						4.00

BART SIMPSON (See Simpsons Comics Presents Bart Simpson)

BASEBALL COMICS
Will Eisner Productions: Spring, 1949 (Reprinted later as a Spirit section)

	GD 2.0	VG 4.0	FN 6.0	VF 8.0	VF/NM 9.0	NM- 9.2
1-Will Eisner-c/a	68	136	204	435	743	1050

GD VG FN VF VF/NM NM-
2.0 4.0 6.0 8.0 9.0 9.2

BASEBALL COMICS
Kitchen Sink Press: 1991 ($3.95, coated stock)

	GD 2.0	VG 4.0	FN 6.0	VF 8.0	VF/NM 9.0	NM- 9.2
1-r/1949 ish. by Eisner; contains trading cards						6.00

BASEBALL HEROES
Fawcett Publications: 1952 (one-shot)

	GD 2.0	VG 4.0	FN 6.0	VF 8.0	VF/NM 9.0	NM- 9.2
nn (Scarce)-Babe Ruth photo-c; baseball's Hall of Fame biographies	81	162	243	518	884	1250

BASEBALL'S GREATEST HEROES
Magnum Comics: Dec, 1991 - No. 2, May, 1992 ($1.75)

	GD 2.0	VG 4.0	FN 6.0	VF 8.0	VF/NM 9.0	NM- 9.2
1-Mickey Mantle #1; photo-c; Sinnott-a(p)						5.00
2-Brooks Robinson #1; photo-c; Sinnott-a(i)						4.00

BASEBALL THRILLS
Ziff-Davis Publ. Co.: No. 10, Sum, 1951 - No. 3, Sum, 1952 (Saunders painted-c No.1,2)

	GD 2.0	VG 4.0	FN 6.0	VF 8.0	VF/NM 9.0	NM- 9.2
10(#1)-Bob Feller, Musial, Newcombe & Boudreau stories	43	86	129	271	461	650
2-Powell-a(2)(Late Sum, '51); Feller, Berra & Mathewson stories	31	62	93	186	303	420
3-Kinstler-c/a; Joe DiMaggio story	31	62	93	186	303	420

BASEBALL THRILLS 3-D
The 3-D Zone: May, 1990 ($2.95, w/glasses)

	GD 2.0	VG 4.0	FN 6.0	VF 8.0	VF/NM 9.0	NM- 9.2
1-New L.B. Cole-c; life stories of Ty Cobb & Ted Williams						6.00

BASICALLY STRANGE (Magazine)
John C. Comics (Archie Comics Group): Dec, 1982 ($1.95, B&W)

	GD 2.0	VG 4.0	FN 6.0	VF 8.0	VF/NM 9.0	NM- 9.2
1-(21,000 printed; all but 1,000 destroyed; pgs. out of sequence)	3	6	9	16	23	30
1-Wood, Toth-a; Corben-c; reprints & new art	2	4	6	13	18	22

BASIC HISTORY OF AMERICA ILLUSTRATED
Pendulum Press: 1976 (B&W) (Soft-c $1.50; Hard-c $4.50)

07-1999-America Becomes a World Power 1890-1920. 07-2251-The Industrial Era 1865-1915. 07-226x-Before the Civil War 1830-1860. 07-2278-Americans Move Westward 1800-1850. 07-2286-The Civil War 1850-1876; Redondo-a. 07-2294-The Fight for Freedom 1750-1783. 07-2308-The New World 1500-1750. 07-2316-Problems of the New Nation 1800-1830. 07-2324-Roaring Twenties and the Great Depression 1920-1940. 07-2332-The United States Emerges 1783-1800. 07-2340-America Today 1945-1976. 07-2359-World War II 1940-1945

	GD 2.0	VG 4.0	FN 6.0	VF 8.0	VF/NM 9.0	NM- 9.2
Softcover editions each	1	2	3	4	5	7
Hardcover editions each						14.00

BASIL (...the Royal Cat)
St. John Publishing Co.: Jan, 1953 - No. 4, Sept, 1953

	GD 2.0	VG 4.0	FN 6.0	VF 8.0	VF/NM 9.0	NM- 9.2
1-Funny animal	7	14	21	37	46	55
2-4	5	10	15	22	26	30
I.W. Reprint 1	2	4	6	9	12	15

BASIL WOLVERTON'S FANTASTIC FABLES
Dark Horse Comics: Oct, 1993 - No. 2, Dec, 1993 ($2.50, B&W, limited series)

	GD 2.0	VG 4.0	FN 6.0	VF 8.0	VF/NM 9.0	NM- 9.2
1,2-Wolverton-c/a(r)						6.00

BASIL WOLVERTON'S GATEWAY TO HORROR
Dark Horse Comics: June, 1988 ($1.75, B&W, one-shot)

	GD 2.0	VG 4.0	FN 6.0	VF 8.0	VF/NM 9.0	NM- 9.2
1-Wolverton-r						6.00

BASIL WOLVERTON'S PLANET OF TERROR
Dark Horse Comics: Oct, 1987 ($1.75, B&W, one-shot)

	GD 2.0	VG 4.0	FN 6.0	VF 8.0	VF/NM 9.0	NM- 9.2
1-Wolverton-r; Alan Moore-c						6.00

BASTARD SAMURAI
Image Comics: Apr, 2002 - No. 3, Aug, 2002 ($2.95)

	GD 2.0	VG 4.0	FN 6.0	VF 8.0	VF/NM 9.0	NM- 9.2
1-3-Oeming & Gunter-s; Shannon-a/Oeming-i						3.00
TPB (2003, $12.95) r/#1-3; plus sketch pages and pin-ups						13.00

BATGIRL (See Batman: No Man's Land stories)
DC Comics: Apr, 2000 - No. 73, Apr, 2006 ($2.50)

	GD 2.0	VG 4.0	FN 6.0	VF 8.0	VF/NM 9.0	NM- 9.2
1-Scott & Campanella-a						6.00
1-(2nd printing)						2.50
2-10: 8-Lady Shiva app.						4.50
11-24: 12-"Officer Down" x-over. 15-Joker-c/app. 24-Bruce Wayne: Murderer pt. 2.						4.00
25-($3.25) Batgirl vs Lady Shiva						3.50
26-29: 27- Bruce Wayne: Fugitive pt. 5; Noto-a. 29-B.W.:F. pt. 13						3.50
30-49,51-73: 30-32-Connor Hawke app. 39-Intro. Black Wind. 41-Superboy-c/app. 53-Robin (Spoiler) app. 54-Bagged with Sky Captain CD. 55-57-War Games. 63,64-Deathstroke app. 67-Birds of Prey app. 73-Lady Shiva origin; Sale-c						2.50
50-($3.25) Batgirl vs Batman						3.25
Annual 1 ('00, $3.50) Planet DC; intro. Aruna						5.00

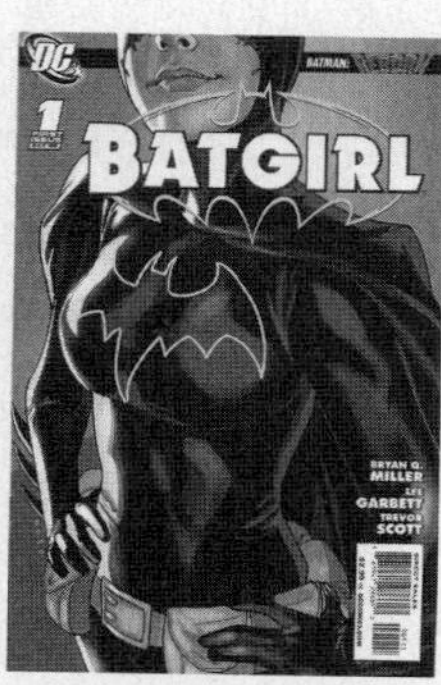

Batgirl (2009 series) #1 © DC

Batman #4 © DC

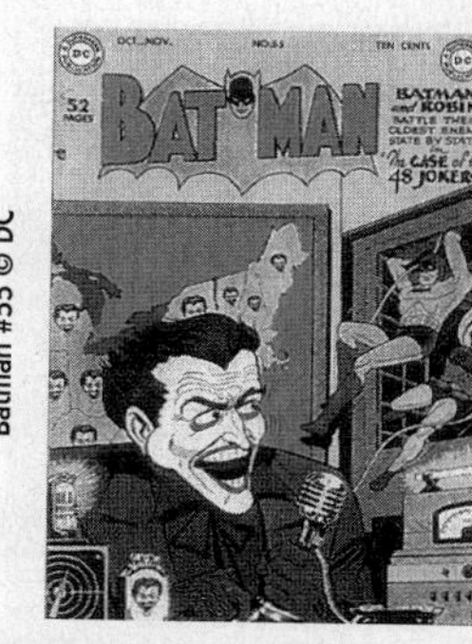

Batman #55 © DC

GD VG FN VF VF/NM NM-
2.0 4.0 6.0 8.0 9.0 9.2

...: A Knight Alone (2001, $12.95, TPB) r/#7-11,13,14 13.00
...: Death Wish (2003, $14.95, TPB) r/#17-20,22,23,25 & Secret Files and Origins #1 15.00
...: Destruction's Daughter (2006, $19.99, TPB) r/#65-73 20.00
...: Fists of Fury (2004, $14.95, TPB) r/#15,16,21,26-28 15.00
...: Kicking Assassins (2005, $14.99, TPB) r/#60-64 15.00
... Secret Files and Origins (8/02, $4.95) origin-s Noto-a; profile pages and pin-ups 5.00
...: Silent Running (2001, $12.95, TPB) r/#1-6 13.00

BATGIRL (Cassandra Cain)
DC Comics: Sept, 2008 - No. 6, Feb, 2009 ($2.99)
1-6-Beechen-s/Calafiore-a 3.00

BATGIRL (Spoiler/Stephanie Brown)(Batman: Reborn)
DC Comics: Oct, 2009 - Present ($2.99)
1-6-Garbett-a/Noto-c. 3-New costume 3.00
1-Variant-c by Hamner 5.00

BATGIRL ADVENTURES (See Batman Adventures, The)
DC Comics: Feb, 1998 ($2.95, one-shot) (Based on animated series)
1-Harley Quinn and Poison Ivy app.; Timm-c 5.00

BATGIRL SPECIAL
DC Comics: 1988 ($1.50, one-shot, 52 pgs)
1-Kitson-a/Mignola-c 1 2 3 5 7 9

BATGIRL: YEAR ONE
DC Comics: Feb, 2003 - No. 9, Oct, 2003 ($2.95, limited series)
1-9-Barbara Gordon becomes Batgirl; Killer Moth app.; Beatty & Dixon-s 3.00
TPB (2003, $17.95) r/#1-9 18.00

BAT LASH (See DC Special Series #16, Showcase #76, Weird Western Tales)
National Periodical Publications: Oct-Nov, 1968 - No. 7, Oct-Nov, 1969
(All 12¢ issues)
1-(10-11/68)-2nd app. Bat Lash; classic Nick Cardy-c/a in all
6 12 18 41 66 90
2-7 4 8 12 26 41 55

BAT LASH
DC Comics: Feb, 2008 - No. 6, Jul, 2008 ($2.99, limited series)
1-6-Aragonés & Brandvold-s/John Severin-a. 1-Two covers by Severin and Simonson 3.00
...: Guns and Roses TPB (2008, $17.99) r/#1-6 18.00

BATMAN (See All Star Batman & Robin, Anarky, Aurora [in Promo. Comics section], Azrael, The Best of DC #2, Blind Justice, The Brave & the Bold, Cosmic Odyssey, DC 100-Page Super Spec. #14,20, DC Special, DC Special Series, Detective, Dynamic Classics, 80-Page Giants, Gotham By Gaslight, Gotham Nights, Greatest Batman Stories Ever Told, Greatest Joker Stories Ever Told, Heroes Against Hunger, JLA,The Joker, Justice League of America, Justice League Int., Legends of the Dark Knight, Limited Coll. Ed., Man-Bat, Nightwing, Power Record Comics, Real Fact #5, Robin, Saga of Ra's Al Ghul, Shadow of the..., Star Spangled, Super Friends, 3-D Batman, Untold Legend of..., Wanted... & World's Finest Comics)

BATMAN
National Per. Publ./Detective Comics/DC Comics: Spring, 1940 - Present
(#1-5 were quarterly)
1-Origin The Batman reprinted (2 pgs.) from Det. #33 w/splash from #34 by Bob Kane; see Detective #33 for 1st origin; 1st app. Joker (2 stories intended for 2 separate issues of Det. Comics which would have been 1st & 2nd app.); splash pg. to 2nd Joker story is similar to cover of Det. #40 (story intended for #40); 1st app. The Cat (Catwoman) (1st villainess in comics); has Batman story (w/Hugo Strange) without Robin originally planned for Det. #38; mentions location (Manhattan) where Batman lives (see Det. #31). This book was created entirely from the inventory of Det. Comics; 1st Batman/Robin pin-up on back-c; has text piece & photo of Bob Kane
12,000 24,000 36,000 85,000 167,500 250,000
1-Reprint, oversize 13-1/2x10". **WARNING**: This comic is an exact duplicate reprint of the original except for its size. DC published it in 1974 with a second cover titling it as a Famous First Edition. There have been many reported cases of the outer cover being removed and the interior sold as the original edition. The reprint with the new outer cover removed is practically worthless. See Famous First Edition for value.
2-2nd app. The Joker; 2nd app. Catwoman (out of costume) in Joker story; 1st time called Catwoman (NOTE: A 15¢-c for Canadian distr. exists.)
1560 3120 4680 11,700 21,850 32,000
3-3rd app Catwoman (1st in costume & 1st costumed villainess); 1st Puppet Master app.; classic Kane & Robinson-c 975 1950 2919 7100 12,550 18,000
4-4th app. The Joker (see Det. #45 for 3rd); 1st mention of Gotham City in a Batman comic (on newspaper)(Win/40) 741 1482 2223 5409 9,555 13,700
5-1st app. the Batmobile with its bat-head front 541 1082 1623 3950 6975 10,000
6,7: 7-Bullseye-c; Joker app. 465 930 1395 3395 5998 8600
8-Infinity-c by Fred Ray; Joker app. 389 778 1167 2723 4762 6800
9-10:9-1st Batman x-mas story; Burnley-c. 10-Catwoman story (gets new costume)
377 754 1131 2639 4620 6600
11-Classic Joker-c by Ray/Robinson (3rd Joker-c, 6-7/42); Joker & Penguin app.

GD VG FN VF VF/NM NM-
2.0 4.0 6.0 8.0 9.0 9.2

757 1514 2271 5526 9763 14,000
12,15: 12-Joker app. 15-New costume Catwoman 300 600 900 2040 3570 5100
13-Jerry Siegel (Superman's co-creator) appears in a Batman story.
300 600 900 2070 3635 5200
14-2nd Penguin-c; Penguin app. (12-1/42-43) 303 606 909 2121 3711 5300
16-Intro/origin Alfred (4-5/43); cover is a reverse of #9 cover by Burnley; 1st small logo
541 1082 1623 3950 6975 10,000
17,20: 17-Classic war-c; Penguin app. 20-1st Batmobile-c (12-1/43-44); Joker app.
265 530 795 1694 2897 4100
18-Hitler, Hirohito, Mussolini-c. 309 618 927 2163 3782 5400
19-Joker app. 207 414 621 1318 2259 3200
21,22,24,26,28-30: 21-1st skinny Alfred in Batman (2-3/44). 21,30-Penguin app. 22-1st Alfred solo-c/story (Alfred solo stories in 22-32,36); Catwoman & The Cavalier app. 28-Joker story
156 312 468 991 1708 2425
23-Joker-c/story; classic black-c 271 542 813 1734 2967 4200
25-Only Joker/Penguin team-up; 1st team-up between two major villains
245 490 735 1568 2684 3800
27-Classic Burnley Christmas-c; Penguin app. 210 420 630 1334 2292 3250
31,32,34-36,39: 32-Origin Robin retold; Joker app. 35-Catwoman story (in new costume w/o cat head mask). 36-Penguin app. 119 238 357 762 1306 1850
33-Christmas-c 140 280 420 889 1532 2175
37,40,44-Joker-c/stories 171 342 513 1086 1868 2650
38-Penguin-c/story 140 280 420 889 1532 2175
41,45,46: 41-1st Sci-fi cover/story in Batman; Penguin app.(6-7/47). 45-Christmas-c/story; Catwoman story. 46-Joker app. 87 174 261 553 952 1350
42-2nd Catwoman-c (1st in Batman)(8-9/47); Catwoman story also.
161 322 483 1030 1765 2500
43-Penguin-c/story 123 246 369 787 1344 1900
47-1st detailed origin The Batman (6-7/48); 1st Bat-signal-c this title (see Detective #108); Batman tracks down his parent's killer and reveals i.d. to him
360 720 1080 2520 4410 6300
48-1000 Secrets of the Batcave; r-in #203; Penguin story
119 238 357 762 1306 1850
49-Joker-c/story; 1st app. Mad Hatter; 1st app. Vicki Vale
194 388 582 1242 2121 3000
50-Two-Face impostor app. 102 204 306 648 1112 1575
51,54,56,57,59,60: 57-Centerfold is a 1950 calendar; Joker app. 59-1st app. Deadshot; Batman in the future-c/story 87 174 261 553 952 1350
52,55-Joker-c/stories 126 252 378 806 1378 1950
53-Joker story 90 180 270 576 988 1400
58,61: 58-Penguin-c. 61-Origin Batman Plane II 97 194 291 621 1061 1500
62-Origin Catwoman; Catwoman-c 148 296 444 947 1624 2300
63,80-Joker stories. 63-1st app. Killer Moth; flying saucer story(2-3/51)
82 164 246 528 902 1275
64,70-72,74-77,79: 70-Robot-c. 72-Last 52 pg. issue. 74-Used in **POP**, Pg. 90. 76-Penguin story. 79-Vicki Vale in "The Bride of Batman"
69 138 207 442 759 1075
65,69-Catwoman-c/stories 106 212 318 673 1162 1650
66,73-Joker-c/stories. 66-Pre-2nd Batman & Robin team try-out. 73-Vicki Vale story
110 220 330 704 1202 1700
67-Joker story 82 164 246 528 902 1275
68,81-Two-Face-c/stories 87 174 261 553 952 1350
78-(8-9/53)-Roh Kar, The Man Hunter from Mars story-the 1st lawman of Mars to come to Earth (green skinned) 84 168 252 538 919 1300
82,83,87-89: 89-Last pre-code issue 66 132 198 419 722 1025
84-Catwoman-c/story; Two-Face app. 100 200 300 635 1093 1550
85,86-Joker story. 86-Intro Batmarine (Batman's submarine)
68 136 204 435 743 1050
90,91,93-96,98,99: 99-(4/56)-Last G.A. Penguin app.
58 116 174 371 636 900
92-1st app. Bat-Hound-c/story 97 194 291 621 1061 1500
97-2nd app. Bat-Hound-c/story; Joker story 63 126 189 403 689 975
100-(6/56) 281 562 843 1784 3067 4350
101-(8/56)-Clark Kent x-over who protects Batman's i.d. (3rd story)
59 118 177 375 645 915
102-104,106-109: 103-1st S.A. issue; 3rd Bat-Hound-c/story
54 108 162 340 583 825
105-1st Batwoman in Batman (2nd anywhere) 84 168 252 538 919 1300
110-Joker story 55 110 165 352 601 850
111-120: 112-1st app. Signalman (super villain). 113-1st app. Fatman; Batman meets his counterpart on Planet X w/a chest plate similar to S.A. Batman's design (yellow oval w/black design inside). 47 94 141 296 498 700
121- Origin/1st app. of Mr. Zero (Mr. Freeze). 68 136 204 435 743 1050
122,124-126,128,130: 122,126-Batwoman-c/story. 124-2nd app. Signal Man.

Batman #137 © DC

Batman #311 © DC

Batman #477 © DC

	GD 2.0	VG 4.0	FN 6.0	VF 8.0	VF/NM 9.0	NM- 9.2
128-Batwoman cameo. 130-Lex Luthor app.	39	78	117	240	395	550
123,127: 123-Joker story; Bat-Hound app. 127-(10/59)-Batman vs. Thor the Thunder God c/story; Joker story; Superman cameo	40	80	120	246	411	575
129-Origin Robin retold; bondage-c; Batwoman-c/story (reprinted in Batman Family #8)	47	94	141	296	498	700
131-135,137-139,141-143: 131-Intro 2nd Batman & Robin series (see #66; also in #135,145, 154,159,163). 133-1st Bat-Mite in Batman (3rd app. anywhere). 134-Origin The Dummy (not Vigilante's villain). 139-Intro 1st original Bat-Girl; only app. Signalman as the Blue Bowman. 141-2nd app. original Bat-Girl. 143-(10/61)-Last 10¢ issue	34	68	102	199	325	450
136-Joker-c/story	39	78	117	231	378	525
140-Joker story, Batwoman-c/s; Superman cameo	34	68	102	206	336	465
144-(12/61)-1st 12¢ issue; Joker story	22	44	66	161	311	460
145,148-Joker-c/stories	24	48	72	175	338	500
146,147,149,150	18	36	54	129	252	375
151-154,156-158,160-162,164-168,170: 152-Joker story. 156-Ant-Man/Robin team-up(6/63). 164-New Batmobile(6/64) new look & Mystery Analysts series begins	15	30	45	107	204	300
155-1st S.A. app. The Penguin (5/63)	32	64	96	245	473	700
159,163-Joker-c/stories. 159-Bat-Girl app. 163-Last Bat-Girl app. until Teen Titans #50	17	34	51	124	242	360
169-2nd SA Penguin app.	17	34	51	122	236	350
171-1st Riddler app.(5/65) since Dec. 1948	40	80	120	320	623	925
172-175,177,178,180,184	11	22	33	78	139	200
176-(80-Pg. Giant G-17); Joker-c/story; Penguin app. in strip-r; Catwoman reprint	13	26	39	93	172	250
179-2nd app. Silver Age Riddler	17	34	51	122	236	350
181-Batman & Robin poster insert; intro. Poison Ivy	23	46	69	166	321	475
182,187-(80 Pg. Giants G-24, G-30); Joker-c/stories	12	24	36	82	149	215
183-2nd app. Poison Ivy	14	28	42	100	188	275
185-(80 Pg. Giant G-27)	11	22	33	80	145	210
186-Joker-c/story	12	24	36	82	149	215
188,191,192,194-196,199	9	18	27	60	100	140
189-1st S.A. app. Scarecrow; retells origin of G.A. Scarecrow from World's Finest #3(1st app.)	15	30	45	107	204	300
190-Penguin-c/app.	11	22	33	78	139	200
193-(80-Pg. Giant G-37)	11	22	33	74	132	190
197-4th S.A. Catwoman app. cont'd from Det. #369; 1st new Batgirl app. in Batman (5th anywhere)	13	26	39	93	172	250
198-(80-Pg. Giant G-43); Joker-c/story-r/World's Finest #61; Catwoman-r/Det. #211; Penguin-r; origin-r/#47	11	22	33	78	139	200
200-(3/68)-Joker cameo; retells origin of Batman & Robin; 1st Neal Adams work this title (cover only)	13	26	39	93	172	250
201-Joker story	7	14	21	49	80	110
202,204-207,209-212: 210-Catwoman-c/app. 212-Last 12¢ issue	7	14	21	45	73	100
203-(80 Pg. Giant G-49); r/#48, 61, & Det. 185; Batcave Blueprints	9	18	27	60	100	140
208-(80 Pg. Giant G-55); New origin Batman by Gil Kane plus 3 G.A. Batman reprints w/Catwoman, Vicki Vale & Batwoman	9	18	27	60	100	140
213-(80-Pg. Giant G-61); 30th anniversary issue (7-8/69); origin Alfred (r/Batman #16), Joker(r/Det. #168), Clayface; new origin Robin with new facts	10	20	30	67	116	165
214-217: 214-Alfred given a new last name- "Pennyworth" (see Detective #96)	6	12	18	37	59	80
218-(80-Pg. Giant G-67)	7	14	21	49	80	110
219-Neal Adams-a	7	14	21	50	83	115
220,221,224-226,229-231	5	10	15	32	51	70
222-Beatles take-off; art lesson by Joe Kubert	7	14	21	45	73	100
223,228,233: 223,228-(80-Pg. Giants G-73,G-79). 233-G-85-(68 pgs., "64 pgs." on-c)	7	14	21	47	76	105
227-Neal Adams cover swipe of Detective #31	12	24	36	85	155	225
232-(6/71) Adams-a. Intro/1st app. Ra's al Ghul; origin Batman & Robin retold; last 15¢ issue (see Detective #411 (5/71) for Talia's debut)	16	32	48	115	220	325
234-(9/71)-1st modern app. of Harvey Dent/Two-Face; (see World's Finest #173 for Batman as Two-Face; only S.A. mention of character); N. Adams-a; 52 pg. issues begin, end #242	17	34	51	122	236	350
235,236,239-242: 239-XMas-c. 241-Reprint/#5	6	12	18	37	59	80
237-N. Adams-a. 1st Rutland Vermont - Bald Mountain Halloween x-over. G.A. Batman-r/ Det. #37; 1st app. The Reaper; Wrightson/Ellison plots	12	24	36	88	162	235
238-Also listed as DC 100 Page Super Spectacular #8; Batman, Legion, Aquaman-r; G.A. Atom, Sargon (r/Sensation #57), Plastic Man (r/Police #14) stories; Doom Patrol origin-r; N. Adams wraparound-c (see DC 100 Pg. Super Spectacular #8 for price)						
243-245-Neal Adams-a	8	16	24	54	90	125
246-250,252,253: 246-Scarecrow app. 253-Shadow-c & app.	5	10	15	32	51	70
251-(9/73)-N. Adams-c/a; Joker-c/story	9	18	27	65	113	160
254,256-259,261-All 100 pg. editions; part-r: 254-(2/74)-Man-Bat-c & app. 256-Catwoman app. 257-Joker & Penguin app. 258-The Cavalier-r. 259-Shadow-c/app.	7	14	21	45	73	100
255-(100 pgs.)-N. Adams-c/a; tells of Bruce Wayne's father who wore bat costume & fought crime (r/Det. #235); r/story Batman #22	8	16	24	52	86	120
260-Joker-c/story (100 pgs.)	8	16	24	52	86	120
262 (68pgs.)	5	10	15	32	51	70
263,264,266-285,287-290,292,293,295-299: 266-Catwoman back to old costume	2	4	6	13	18	22
265-Wrightson-a(i)	3	6	9	14	19	24
286,291,294: 294-Joker-c/stories	3	6	9	17	25	32
300-Double-size	3	6	9	18	27	35
301-(7/78)-310,312-315,317-320,325-331,333-352: 304-(44 pgs.). 306-3rd app. Black Spider. 308-Mr. Freeze app. 310-1st modern app. The Gentleman Ghost in Batman; Kubert-c. 312,314,346-Two-Face-c/stories. 313-2nd app. Calendar Man. 318-Intro Firebug. 319-2nd modern age app. The Gentleman Ghost; Kubert-c. 344-Poison Ivy app. 345-1st app. new Dr. Death. 345,346,351-Catwoman back-ups	2	4	6	8	10	12
306-308,311-320,323,324,326-(Whitman variants; low print run; none show issue # on cover)	2	4	6	10	14	18
311,316,322-324: 311-Batgirl-c/story; Batgirl reteams w/Batman. 316-Robin returns. 322-324-Catwoman (Selina Kyle) app. 322,323-Cat-Man cameos (1st in Batman, 1 panel each). 323-1st meeting Catwoman & Cat-Man. 324-1st full app. Cat-Man this title	2	4	6	9	12	15
321,353,359-Joker-c/stories	2	4	6	13	18	22
332-Catwoman's 1st solo	2	4	6	10	14	18
354-356,358,360-365,369,370: 361-1st app Harvey Bullock	1	2	3	5	7	9
357-1st app. Jason Todd (3/83); see Det. #524; 1st brief app. Croc	2	4	6	9	13	16
366-Jason Todd 1st in Robin costume; Joker-c/story	2	4	6	11	16	20
367-Jason in red & green costume (not as Robin)	2	4	6	8	10	12
368-1st new Robin in costume (Jason Todd)	2	4	6	9	13	16
371-399,401-403: 371-Cat-Man-c/story; brief origin Cat-Man (cont'd in Det. #538). 386,387-Intro Black Mask (villain). 380-391-Catwoman app. 398-Catwoman & Two-Face app. 401-2nd app. Magpie (see Man of Steel #3 for 1st). 403-Joker cameo						6.00
NOTE: *Issues 397-399, 401-403, 408-416, 421-425, 430-432 all have 2nd printings in 1989; some with up to 8 printings. Some are not identified as reprints but have newer ads copyrighted after cover dates. All reprints have different back-c ads. All reprints are scarcer than 1st prints and have same value to variant collectors.*						
400 ($1.50, 68pgs.)-Dark Knight special; intro by Stephen King; Art Adams/Austin-a	3	6	9	16	23	30
404-Miller scripts begin (end 407); Year 1; 1st modern app. Catwoman (2/87)	3	6	9	16	22	28
405-407: 407-Year 1 ends (See Detective Comics #575-578 for Year 2)	2	4	6	13	18	22
408-410: New Origin Jason Todd (Robin)	2	4	6	13	18	22
411-416,421-425: 411-Two-face app. 412-Origin/1st app. Mime. 414-Starlin scripts begin, end #429. 416-Nightwing-c/story. 423-McFarlane-c						5.00
417-420: "Ten Nights of the Beast" storyline	2	4	6	8	10	12
426-($1.50, 52 pgs.)- "A Death In The Family" storyline begins, ends #429	2	4	6	11	16	20
427- "A Death In The Family" part 2.	2	4	6	9	12	15
428-Death of Robin (Jason Todd)	2	4	6	11	16	20
429-Joker-c/story; Superman app.	2	4	6	8	10	12
430-432						3.00
433-435-Many Deaths of the Batman story by John Byrne-c/scripts						3.00
436-Year 3 begins (ends #439); origin original Robin retold by Nightwing (Dick Grayson); 1st app. Timothy Drake (8/89)						4.00
436-441: 436-2nd printing. 437-Origin Robin cont. 440,441: "A Lonely Place of Dying" Parts 1 & 3						3.00
442-1st app. Timothy Drake in Robin costume						4.00
443-456,458,459,462-464: 445-447-Batman goes to Russia. 448,449-The Penguin Affair Pts 1 & 3. 450-Origin Joker. 450,451-Joker-c/stories. 452-454-Dark Knight Dark City storyline; Riddler app. 455-Alan Grant scripts begin, ends #466, 470. 464-Last solo Batman story; free 16 pg. preview of Impact Comics line						3.00
457-Timothy Drake officially becomes Robin & dons new costume						5.00
457-Direct sale edition (has #000 in indicia)						5.00
460,461,465-487: 460,461-Two part Catwoman story. 465-Robin returns to action with Batman. 470-War of the Gods x-over. 475-1st app. Renee Montoya. 475,476-Return of Scarface. 476-Last $1.00-c. 477,478-Photo-c						3.00

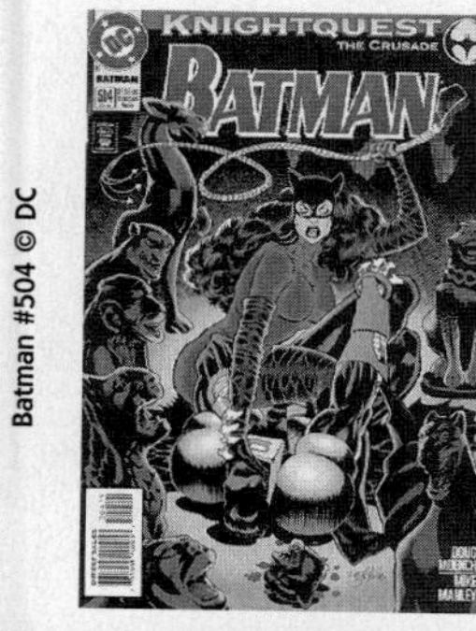

Batman #504 © DC

Batman #624 © DC

Batman #686 © DC

	GD 2.0	VG 4.0	FN 6.0	VF 8.0	VF/NM 9.0	NM- 9.2
488-Cont'd from Batman: Sword of Azrael #4; Azrael-c & app.	1	2	3	5	6	8

489-Bane-c/story; 1st app. Azrael in Bat-costume 5.00
490-Riddler-c/story; Azrael & Bane app. 6.00
491,492: 491-Knightfall lead-in; Joker-c/story; Azrael & Bane app.; Kelley Jones-c begin. 492-Knightfall part 1; Bane app. 4.00
492-Platinum edition (promo copy) 10.00
493-496: 493-Knightfall Pt. 3. 494-Knightfall Pt. 5; Joker-c & app. 495-Knightfall Pt. 7; brief Bane & Joker apps. 496-Knightfall Pt. 9, Joker-c/story; Bane cameo 3.00
497-(Late 7/93)-Knightfall Pt. 11; Bane breaks Batman's back; B&W outer-c; Aparo-a(p); Giordano-a(i) 5.00
497-499: 497-2nd printing. 497-Newsstand edition w/o outer cover. 498-Knightfall part 15; Bane & Catwoman-c & app. (see Showcase 93 #7 & 8) 499-Knightfall Pt. 17; Bane app. 3.00
500-($2.50, 68 pgs.)-Knightfall Pt. 19; Azrael in new Bat-costume; Bane-c/story 3.00
500-($3.95, 68 pgs.)-Collector's Edition w/die-cut double-c w/foil by Joe Quesada & 2 bound-in post cards 5.00
501-508,510,511: 501-Begin $1.50-c. 501-508-Knightquest. 503,504-Catwoman app. 507-Ballistic app.; Jim Balent-a(p). 510-KnightsEnd Pt. 7. 511-(9/94)-Zero Hour; Batgirl-c/story 2.50
509-($2.50, 52 pgs.)-KnightsEnd Pt. 1 3.00
512-514,516-518: 512-(11/94)-Dick Grayson assumes Batman role 2.50
515-Special Ed.($2.50)-Kelley Jones-a begins; all black embossed-c; Troika Pt. 1 3.00
515-Regular Edition 2.50
519-534,536-549: 519-Begin $1.95-c. 521-Return of Alfred, 522-Swamp Thing app. 525-Mr. Freeze app. 527,528-Two Face app. 529-Contagion Pt. 6. 530-532-Deadman app. 533-Legacy prelude. 534-Legacy Pt. 5. 536-Final Night x-over; Man-Bat-c/app. 540,541-Spectre-c-app. 544-546-Joker & The Demon. 548,549-Penguin-c/app. 2.50
530-532 ($2.50)-Enhanced edition; glow-in-the-dark-c. 3.00
535-(10/96, $2.95)-1st app. The Ogre 3.00
535-(10/96, $3.95)-1st app. The Ogre; variant, cardboard, foldout-c 4.00
550-($3.50)-Collector's Ed., includes 4 collector cards; intro. Chase, return of Clayface; Kelley Jones-c 3.50
550-($2.95)-Standard Ed.; Williams & Gray-c 3.00
551,552,554-562: 551,552-Ragman c/app. 554-Cataclysm pt. 12. 2.50
553-Cataclysm pt.3 4.00
563-No Man's Land; Joker-c by Campbell; Bob Gale-s 5.00
564-574: 569-New Batgirl-c/app. 572-Joker and Harley app. 2.50
575-579: 575-New look Batman begins; McDaniel-a 2.50
580-598: 580-Begin $2.25-c. 587-Gordon shot. 591,592-Deadshot-c/app. 2.50
599-Bruce Wayne: Murderer pt. 7 2.50
600-($3.95) Bruce Wayne: Fugitive pt. 1; back-up homage stories in '50s, 60's, & 70s styles; by Aragonés, Gaudiano, Shanower and others 5.00
600-(2nd printing) 4.00
601-604, 606,607: 601,603-Bruce Wayne: Fugitive pt.3,13. 606,607-Deadshot-c/app. 2.50
605-($2.95) Conclusion to Bruce Wayne: Fugitive x-over; Noto-c 3.00
608-(12/02) Jim Lee-a/c & Jeph Loeb-s begin; Poison Ivy & Catwoman app. 8.00
608-2nd printing; has different cover with Batman standing on gargoyle 12.00
608-Special Edition; has different cover; 200 printed; used for promotional purposes (a CGC certified 9.2 copy sold for $700, and a CGC certified 9.8 copy sold for $2,100)
608-Special Edition (9/09, $1.00) printing has new "After Watchmen" logo cover frame 2.00
609-Huntress app. 9.00
610,611: 610-Killer Croc-c/app.; Batman & Catwoman kiss 8.00
612-Batman vs. Superman; 1st printing with full color cover 9.00
612-2nd printing with B&W sketch cover 15.00
613,614: 614-Joker-c/app. 7.00
615-617: 615-Reveals ID to Catwoman. 616-Ra's al Ghul app. 617-Scarecrow app. 5.00
618- Batman vs. "Jason Todd" 4.00
619-Newsstand cover; Hush story concludes; Riddler app. 5.00
619-Two variant tri-fold covers; one Heroes group, one Villains group 5.00
619-2nd printing with Riddler chess cover 5.00
620-Broken City pt. 1; Azzarello-s/Risso-a/c begin; Killer Croc app. 3.00
621-633: 621-625-Azzarello-s/Risso-a/c. 626-630-Winick-s/Nguyen-a/Wagner-c; Penguin & Scarecrow app. 631-633-War Games. 633-Conclusion to War Games x-over 3.00
634-638-Winick-s/Nguyen-a/Wagner-c; Red Hood app. 637-Amazo app. 638-Red Hood unmasked as Jason Todd 2.50
639-650: 640-Superman app. 641-Begin $2.50-c. 643,644-War Crimes; Joker app. 650-Infinite Crisis; Joker and Jason Todd app. 2.50
651-654-One Year Later; Bianchi-c 3.00
655-Begin Grant Morrison-s/Andy Kubert-a; Kubert-c w/red background 5.00
655-Variant cover by Adam Kubert, brown-toned image 15.00
656-665: 656-Intro. Damien, son of Talia and Batman (see Batman: Son of the Demon). 657-Damien in Robin costume. 659-662-Mandrake-a. 663-Van Fleet-a. 664-Bane app. 3.00
666-675: 666-Future story of adult Damien; Andy Kubert-a. 667-669-Williams III-a. 670,671-Resurrection of Ra's al Ghul; Daniel-a. 671-2nd printing 3.00

	GD 2.0	VG 4.0	FN 6.0	VF 8.0	VF/NM 9.0	NM- 9.2

676-Batman R.I.P. begins; Morrison-s/Daniel-a/Alex Ross-c 4.00
676-Variant-c by Tony Daniel 12.00
676-Second (red-tinted Daniel-c) & third (B&W Daniel-c) printings 3.00
677-680,682-685: Batman R.I.P.; Alex Ross-c. 678-Bat-Mite app. 682-685-Last Rites 3.00
677-Variant-c by Tony Daniel 10.00
677-Second printing with B&W&red-tinted Daniel-c 3.00
681-($3.99) Batman R.I.P. conclusion 4.00
686-($3.99) Gaiman-s/Andy Kubert-a; continues in Detective #853; Kubert sketch pgs.; covers by Kubert and Ross; 2nd & 3rd printings exist 4.00
687-($3.99) Batman: Reborn begins; Dick Grayson becomes Batman; Winick-s/Benes-a 4.00
688-695: 688-691-Bagley-a. 692-695-Tony Daniel-s/a. 692-Catwoman app. 3.00
#0 (10/94)-Zero Hour issue released between #511 & #512; Origin retold 2.50
#1,000,000 (11/98) 853rd Century x-over 2.50

	GD	VG	FN	VF	VF/NM	NM-
Annual 1 (8-10/61)-Swan-c	56	112	168	476	938	1400
Annual 2	27	54	81	195	380	565
Annual 3 (Summer, '62)-Joker-c/story	27	54	81	197	386	575
Annual 4,5	14	28	42	101	191	280
Annual 6,7 (7/64, 25¢, 80 pgs.)	12	24	36	83	152	220
Annual V5#8 (1982)-Painted-c	1	2	3	5	6	8

Annual 9,10,12: 9(7/85). 10(1986). 12(1988, $1.50) 6.00

	GD	VG	FN	VF	VF/NM	NM-
Annual 11 (1987, $1.25)-Penguin-c/story; Moore-s	1	2	3	5	6	8

Annual 13 (1989, $1.75, 68 pgs.)-Gives history of Bruce Wayne, Dick Grayson, Jason Todd, Alfred, Comm. Gordon, Barbara Gordon (Batgirl) & Vicki Vale; Morrow-i 5.00
Annual 14-17 ('90-'93, 68 pgs.)-14-Origin Two-Face. 15-Armageddon 2001 x-over; Joker app. 15 (2nd printing). 16-Joker-c/s; Kieth-c. 17 (1993, $2.50, 68 pgs.)-Azrael in Bat-costume; intro Ballistic 4.00
Annual 18 (1994, $2.95) 3.00
Annual 19 (1995, $3.95)-Year One story; retells Scarecrow's origin 4.00
Annual 20 (1996, $2.95)-Legends of the Dead Earth story; Giarrano-a 3.00
Annual 21 (1997, $3.95)-Pulp Heroes story 4.00
Annual 22,23 ('98, '99, $2.95)-22-Ghosts; Wrightson-c. 23-JLApe; Art Adams-c 3.00
Annual 24 ('00, $3.50) Planet DC; intro. The Boggart; Aparo-a 3.50
Annual 25 ('06, $4.99) Infinite Crisis-revised story of Jason Todd; unused Aparo page 6.00
Annual 26 ('07, $3.99) Origin of Ra's al Ghul; Damien app. 4.00
Annual 27 ('09, $4.99) Azrael app.; Calafiore-a; back-up story w/Kelley Jones-a 5.00

NOTE: **Art Adams** *a-400p.* **Neal Adams** *c-200, 203, 210, 217, 219-222, 224-227, 229, 230, 232, 234, 236-241, 243-246, 251, 255, Annual 14.* **Aparo** *a-414-420, 426-435, 440-448, 450, 451, 480-483, 486-491, 494-500; c-414-416, 481, 482, 463i, 486, 487i.* **Bolland** *a-400; c-445-447.* **Burnley** *a-10, 12-18, 20, 22, 25, 27; c-9, 15, 16, 27, 28p, 40p, 42p.* **Byrne** *c-401, 433-435, 533-535, Annual 11.* **Travis Charest** *c-488-490p.* **Colan** *a-340p, 343-345p, 348-351p, 373p, 383p; c-343p, 345p, 350p.* **J. Cole** *a-238r.* **Cowan** *a-Annual 10p.* **Golden** *a-295p, 303p, 484, 485.* **Alan Grant** *scripts-455-466, 470, 474-476, 479, 480, Annual 16(part).* **Grell** *a-287, 288p, 289p, 290; c-287-290.* **Infantino/Anderson** *c-167, 173, 175, 181, 186, 191, 192, 194, 195, 198, 199.* **Infantino/Giella** *c-190.* **Kelley Jones** *a-513-519, 521-525, 527; c-491-499, 500(newsstand), 501-510, 513.* **Kaluta** *c-242, 248, 253, Annual 12.* **G. Kane/Anderson** *c-178-180.* **Bob Kane** *a-1, 2, 5; c-1-5, 7, 17.* **G. Kane** *a-(r)-254, 255, 259, 261, 353i.* **Kubert** *a-238r, 400; c-310, 319p, 327, 328, 344.* **McFarlane** *c-423.* **Mignola** *c-426-429, 452-454, Annual 18.* **Moldoff** *c-101-140.* **Moldoff/Giella** *a-164-175, 177-181, 183, 184, 186.* **Moldoff/Greene** *a-169, 172-174, 177-179, 181, 184.* **Mooney** *a-255r.* **Morrow** *a-Annual 13i.* **Newton** *a-305, 306, 328p, 331p, 332p, 337p, 338p, 346p, 352-357p, 360-372p, 374-378p; c-374p, 378p.* **Nino** *a-Annual 9.* **Irv Novick** *c-201, 202.* **Perez** *a-400; c-436-442.* **Fred Ray** *c-8, 10; w/***Robinson***-11.* **Robinson/Roussos** *a-12-17, 20, 22, 24, 25, 27, 28, 31, 33, 37.* **Robinson** *a-12, 14, 18, 22-32,34, 36, 37, 255r, 260r, 261r; c-6, 10, 12-14, 18, 21, 24, 26, 30, 37, 39.* **Simonson** *a-300p, 312p, 321p; c-300p, 312p, 366, 413i.* **P. Smith** *a-Annual 9.* **Dick Sprang** *c-19, 20, 22, 23, 25, 29, 31-36, 38, 51, 55, 66, 73, 76.* **Starlin** *c/a-402.* **Staton** *a-334.* **Sutton** *a-400.* **Wrightson** *a-265i, 400; c-320r. Bat-Hound app. in 92, 97, 103, 123, 125, 133, 156, 158. Bat-Mite app. in 133, 136, 144, 146, 158, 161. Batwoman app. in 105, 116, 122, 125, 128, 129, 131, 133, 139, 140, 141, 144, 145, 150, 151, 153, 154, 157, 159, 162, 163.* **Zeck** *c-417-420. Catwoman back-ups in 332, 345, 346, 348-351. Joker app. in 1, 2, 4, 5, 7-9, 11-13, 19, 20, 23, 25, 28, 32 & many more. Robin solo back-up stories in 337-339, 341-343.*

BATMAN (Hardcover books and trade paperbacks)
...: ABSOLUTION (2002, $24.95)-Hard-c.; DeMatteis-s/Ashmore painted-a 25.00
...: ABSOLUTION (2003, $17.95)-Soft-c.; DeMatteis-s/Ashmore painted-a 18.00
...: A LONELY PLACE OF DYING (1990, $3.95, 132 pgs.)-r/Batman #440-442 & New Titans #60,61; Perez-c 4.00
...: ANARKY TPB (1999, $12.95) r/early appearances 13.00
...AND DRACULA: RED RAIN nn (1991, $24.95)-Hard-c.; Elseworlds storyline 32.00
...AND DRACULA: RED RAIN nn (1992, $9.95)-SC 12.00
...AND SON HC (2007, $24.99, dustjacket) r/Batman #655-658,663-666 25.00
...AND SON SC (2008, $14.99) r/Batman #655-658,663-666 15.00
...ANNUALS (See DC Comics Classics Library for reprints of early Annuals)
ARKHAM ASYLUM Hard-c; Morrison-s/McKean-a (1989, $24.95) 30.00
ARKHAM ASYLUM Soft-c ($14.95) 15.00
ARKHAM ASYLUM 15TH ANNIVERSARY EDITION Hard-c (2004, $29.95) reprint with Morrison's script and annotations, original page layouts; Karen Berger afterword 30.00
ARKHAM ASYLUM 15TH ANNIVERSARY EDITION Soft-c (2005, $17.99) 18.00
...: AS THE CROW FLIES-(2004, $12.95) r/#626-630; Nguyen sketch pages 13.00
BIRTH OF THE DEMON Hard-c (1992, $24.95)-Origin of Ra's al Ghul 25.00
BIRTH OF THE DEMON Soft-c (1993, $12.95) 13.00
BLIND JUSTICE nn (1992, $7.50)-r/Det. #598-600 7.50
BLOODSTORM (1994, $24.95,HC) Kelley Jones-c/a 28.00

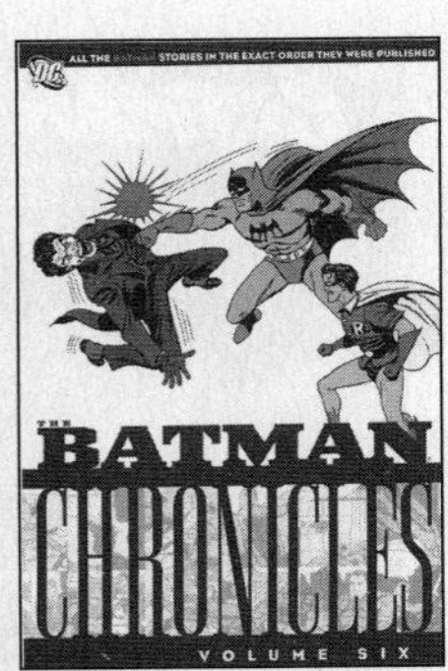

Batman Chronicles Vol. 6 © DC

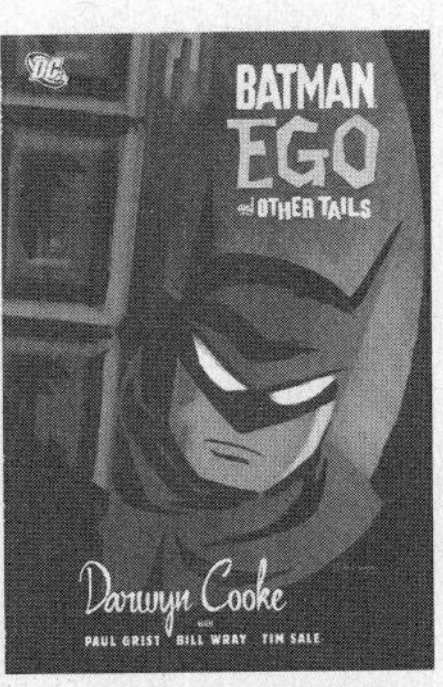

Batman: Ego and Other Tales HC © DC

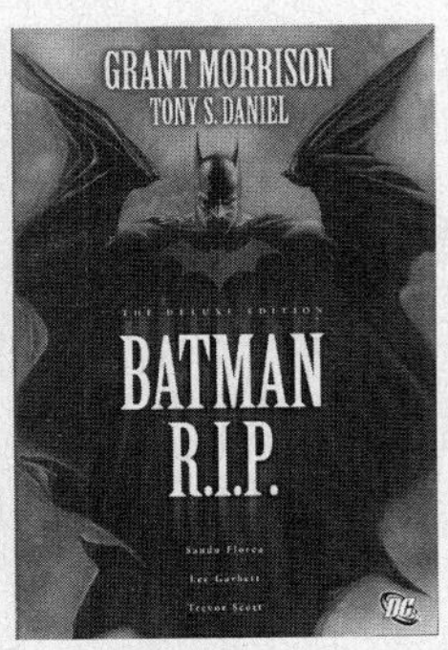

Batman: R.I.P. HC © DC

GD 2.0 | VG 4.0 | FN 6.0 | VF 8.0 | VF/NM 9.0 | NM- 9.2

BRIDE OF THE DEMON Hard-c (1990, $19.95) 20.00
BRIDE OF THE DEMON Soft-c ($12.95) 13.00
...: BROKEN CITY HC-(2004, $24.95) r/#620-625; new Johnson-c; intro by Schreck 25.00
...: BROKEN CITY SC-(2004, $14.99) r/#620-625; new Johnson-c; intro by Schreck 15.00
...: BRUCE WAYNE: FUGITIVE Vol. 1 ('02, $12.95)-r/ story arc 13.00
...: BRUCE WAYNE: FUGITIVE Vol. 2 ('03, $12.95)-r/ story arc 13.00
...: BRUCE WAYNE: FUGITIVE Vol. 3 ('03, $12.95)-r/ story arc 13.00
...: BRUCE WAYNE-MURDERER? ('02, $19.95)-r/ story arc 20.00
...: CASTLE OF THE BAT ($5.95)-Elseworlds story 6.00
...: CATACLYSM ('99, $17.95)-r/ story arc 18.00
...: CHILD OF DREAMS (2003, $24.95, B&W, HC) Reprint of Japanese manga with Kia Asamiya-s/a/c; English adaptation by Max Allan Collins; Asamiya interview 25.00
...: CHILD OF DREAMS (2003, $19.95, B&W, SC) 20.00
...CHRONICLES VOL. 1 (2005, $14.99)-r/apps. in Detective Comics #27-38; Batman #1 15.00
...CHRONICLES VOL. 2 (2006, $14.99)-r/apps. in Detective Comics #39-45 and NY World's Fair 1940; Batman #2,3 15.00
...CHRONICLES VOL. 3 (2007, $14.99)-r/apps. in Detective Comics #46-50 and World's Best Comics #1; Batman #4,5 15.00
...CHRONICLES VOL. 4 (2007, $14.99)-r/apps. in Detective Comics #51-56 and World's Finest Comics #2,3; Batman #6,7 15.00
...CHRONICLES VOL. 5 (2008, $14.99)-r/apps. in Detective Comics #57-61 and World's Finest Comics #4; Batman #8,9 15.00
...CHRONICLES VOL. 6 (2008, $14.99)-r/apps. in Detective Comics #62-65 and World's Finest Comics #5,6; Batman #10,11 15.00
...CHRONICLES VOL. 7 (2009, $14.99)-r/apps. in Detective Comics #66-70 and World's Finest Comics #7; Batman #12,13 15.00
...CHRONICLES VOL. 8 (2009, $14.99)-r/apps. in Detective Comics #71-74 and World's Finest Comics #8,9; Batman #14,15 15.00
...: CITY OF CRIME (2006, $19.99) r/Detective Comics #800-808,811-814; Lapham-s 20.00
...: COLLECTED LEGENDS OF THE DARK KNIGHT nn (1994, $12.95)-r/Legends of the Dark Knight #32-34,38,42,43 13.00
...: CRIMSON MIST (1999, $24.95,HC)-Vampire Batman Elseworlds story Doug Moench-s/Kelley Jones-c/a 25.00
...: CRIMSON MIST (2001, $14.95,SC) 25.00
...: DARK JOKER-THE WILD (1993, $24.95,HC)-Elseworlds story; Moench-s/Jones-c/a 25.00
...: DARK JOKER-THE WILD (1993, $9.95,SC) 10.00
...DARK KNIGHT DYNASTY nn (1997, $24.95)-Hard-c.; 3 Elseworlds stories; Barr-s/ S. Hampton painted-a, Gary Frank, McDaniel-a(p) 25.00
...DARK KNIGHT DYNASTY Softcover (2000, $14.95) Hampton-c 15.00
...DEADMAN: DEATH AND GLORY nn (1996, $24.95)-Hard-c.; Robinson-s/ Estes-c/a 25.00
...DEADMAN: DEATH AND GLORY ($12.95)-SC 13.00
DEATH AND THE CITY (2007, $14.99, TPB)-r/Detective #827-834 15.00
DEATH IN THE FAMILY (1988, $3.95, trade paperback)-r/Batman #426-429 by Aparo 5.00
DEATH IN THE FAMILY: (2nd - 5th printings) 4.00
...: DETECTIVE (2007, $14.99, SC)-r/Detective Comics #821-826 15.00
...: DETECTIVE #27 HC (2003, $19.95)-Elseworlds; Uslan-s/Snejbjerg-a 20.00
...: DETECTIVE #27 SC (2004, $12.95)-Elseworlds; Uslan-s/Snejbjerg-a 13.00
DIGITAL JUSTICE nn (1990, $24.95, Hard-c.)-Computer generated art 25.00
... : EGO AND OTHER TALES HC (2007, $24.99)-r/Batman: Ego, Catwoman: Selina's Big Score, and stories from Batman Black and White and Solo; Darwyn Cooke-s/a 25.00
... : EGO AND OTHER TALES SC (2008, $17.99) same contents as HC 18.00
... :EVOLUTION (2001, $12.95, SC)-r/Detective Comics #743-750 13.00
... FACES (1995, $9.95, TPB) r/Legends of the Dark Knight #28-30 10.00
... FACES (2008, $12.99, TPB) Second printing 13.00
...: FACE THE FACE (2006, $14.99, TPB)-r/Batman #651-654, Detective #817-820 15.00
...: FALSE FACES HC (2008, $19.99)-r/Batman #588-590, Wonder Woman #160,161; Batman: Gotham City Secret Files #1 and Detective #787; Brian K. Vaughn intro. 20.00
...: FALSE FACES SC (2008, $14.99)-r/Batman #588-590, Wonder Woman #160,161; Batman: Gotham City Secret Files #1 and Detective #787; Brian K. Vaughn intro. 15.00
...: FORTUNATE SON HC (1999, $24.95) Gene Ha-a 25.00
...: FORTUNATE SON SC (2000, $14.95) Gene Ha-a 15.00
FOUR OF A KIND TPB (1998, $14.95)-r/1995 Year One Annuals featuring Poison Ivy, Riddler, Scarecrow, & Man-Bat 15.00
... GOING SANE (2008, $14.95, TPB) r/Legends of the Dark Knight #65-68,200 15.00
...: GOTHAM BY GASLIGHT (2006, $12.99, TPB) r/Gotham By Gaslight & Master of the Future one-shots; Elseworlds Batman vs. Jack the Ripper 13.00
...GOTHIC (1992, $12.95, TPB)-r/Legends of the Dark Knight #6-10 13.00
...GOTHIC (2007, $14.99, TPB)-r/Legends of the Dark Knight #6-10 15.00
...: HARVEST BREED-(2000, $24.95) George Pratt-s/painted-a 25.00
...: HARVEST BREED-(2003, $17.95) George Pratt-s/painted-a 18.00
...: HAUNTED KNIGHT-(1997, $12.95) r/ Halloween specials 13.00
...: HEART OF HUSH HC-(2009, $19.99) r/#Detective #846-850; pin-ups 20.00
...: HONG KONG HC (2003, $24.95, with dustjacket) Doug Moench-s/Tony Wong-a 25.00
...: HONG KONG SC (2004, $17.95) Doug Moench-s/Tony Wong-a 18.00
...: HUSH SC-(2009, $24.99) r/#608-619; Wizard 0; variant cover gallery; Loeb intro 25.00
...: HUSH DOUBLE FEATURE-(2003, $3.95) r/#608,609(1st 2 Jim Lee-a issues) 4.00
...: HUSH VOLUME 1 HC-(2003, $19.95) r/#608-612; & new 2 pg. origin w/Lee-a 20.00
...: HUSH VOLUME 1 SC-(2004, $12.95) r/#608-612; includes CD of DC GN art 13.00
...: HUSH VOLUME 2 HC-(2003, $19.95) r/#613-619; Lee intro & sketchpages 20.00
...: HUSH VOLUME 2 SC-(2004, $12.95) r/#613-619; Lee intro & sketchpages 13.00
...: ILLUSTRATED BY NEAL ADAMS VOLUME 1 HC-(2003, $49.95) r/Batman, Brave and the Bold, and Detective Comics stories and covers 50.00
...: ILLUSTRATED BY NEAL ADAMS VOLUME 2 HC-(2004, $49.95) r/Adams' Batman art from 1969-71; intro. by Dick Giordano 50.00
...: ILLUSTRATED BY NEAL ADAMS VOLUME 3 HC-(2006, $49.99) r/Adams' Batman art from 1971-74; covers, pin-ups and design art; intro. by Denny O'Neil 50.00
... IN THE FORTIES TPB ($19.95) Intro. by Bill Schelly 20.00
... IN THE FIFTIES TPB ($19.95) Intro. by Michael Uslan 20.00
... IN THE SIXTIES TPB ($19.95) Intro. by Adam West 20.00
... IN THE SEVENTIES TPB ($19.95) Intro. by Dennis O'Neil 20.00
... IN THE EIGHTIES TPB ($19.95) Intro. by John Wells 20.00
.../ JUDGE DREDD FILES (2004, $14.95) reprints cross-overs 15.00
... LEGACY-(1996, $17.95) reprints Legacy 18.00
...: LOVERS & MADMEN-(See Batman Confidential)
...: MAD LOVE AND OTHER STORIES HC (2009, $19.99) r/Batman Adventures: Mad Love, Batman Advs. Holiday Special and other Dini/Timm collaborations; commentary 20.00
...: THE MANY DEATHS OF THE BATMAN (1992, $3.95, 84 pgs.)-r/Batman #433-435 w/new Byrne-c 4.00
...: MONSTERS (2009, $19.99, TPB)-r/Legends of the Dark Knight #71-73,83,84,89,90 20.00
...: THE MOVIES (1997, $19.95)-r/movie adaptations of Batman, Batman Returns, Batman Forever, Batman and Robin 20.00
...: NINE LIVES HC (2002, $24.95, sideways format) Motter-s/Lark-a 25.00
...: NINE LIVES SC (2003, $17.95, sideways format) Motter-s/Lark-a 18.00
...: OFFICER DOWN (2001, $12.95)-r/Commissioner shot x-over; Talon-c 13.00
...: PREY (1992, $12.95)-Gulacy/Austin-a 13.00
...: PRIVATE CASEBOOK HC (2008, $19.99)-r/Detective Comics #840-845 and story from DC Infinite Halloween Special #1 20.00
...: PRODIGAL (1997, $14.95)-Gulacy/Austin-a 15.00
...: R.I.P.: THE DELUXE EDITION HC (2009, $24.99)-r/Batman #676-683 and story from DC Universe #0 25.00
... SCARECROW TALES (2005, $19.99, TPB) r/Scarecrow stories & pin-ups from World's Finest #3 to present 20.00
...: SECRETS OF THE BATCAVE (2007, $17.99, TPB) r/Batcave stories 18.00
SHAMAN (1993, $12.95)-r/Legends/D.K. #1-5 13.00
...: SNOW (2007, $14.99, TPB)-r/Legends of the Dark Knight #192-196; Fisher-a 15.00
...: SON OF THE DEMON Hard-c (9/87, $14.95) (see Batman #655-658) 30.00
...: SON OF THE DEMON limited signed & numbered Hard-c (1,700) 45.00
...: SON OF THE DEMON Soft-c w/new-c ($8.95) 10.00
...: SON OF THE DEMON Soft-c (1989, $9.95, 2nd printing - 5th printing) 10.00
... : STRANGE APPARITIONS ($12.95) r/'77-'78 Englehart/Rogers stories from Detective #469-479; also Simonson-a 13.00
...: TALES OF THE DEMON (1991, $17.95, 212 pgs.)-Intro by Sam Hamm; reprints by Neal Adams(3) & Golden; contains Saga of Ra's al Ghul #1 18.00
TALES OF THE MULTIVERSE: BATMAN - VAMPIRE (2007, $19.99) r/Batman & Dracula: Red Rain, Batman: Bloodstorm and Batman: Crimson Mist; Van Lustbader foreword 20.00
...: TEN NIGHTS OF THE BEAST (1994, $5.95)-r/Batman #417-420 6.00
...: TERROR (2003, $12.95, TPB)-r/Legends of the Dark Knight #137-141; Gulacy-c 13.00
...: THE BLACK GLOVE (2009, $17.99, TPB) r/Batman #667-669,672-675 18.00
...: THE CHALICE (HC, '99, $24.95) Van Fleet painted-a 25.00
...: THE CHALICE (SC, '00, $14.95) Van Fleet painted-a 15.00
...: THE GREATEST STORIES EVER TOLD (2005, $19.99, TPB) Les Daniels intro. 20.00
...: THE GREATEST STORIES EVER TOLD VOLUME TWO (2007, $19.99, TPB) 20.00
...: THE JOKER'S LAST LAUGH ('08, $17.99) r/Joker's Last Laugh series #1-6 18.00
...: THE LAST ANGEL (1994, $12.95, TPB) Lustbader-s 13.00
...: THE RESURRECTION OF RA'S AL GHUL (2008, $29.99, HC w/DJ) r/x-over 30.00
...: THE RESURRECTION OF RA'S AL GHUL (2009, $19.99, SC) r/x-over 20.00
...: THE RING, THE ARROW AND THE BAT (2003, $19.95, TPB) r/Legends of the DCU #7-9 & Batman: Legends of the Dark Knight #127-131; Green Lantern & Green Arrow app. 20.00
...: THE STRANGE DEATHS OF BATMAN ('09, $19.99) r/Batman #291-294, Det. #347, World's Finest #184,269, Brave & the Bold #115, Nightwing #52; Aparo-c 20.00
...: THE WRATH ('09, $17.99) r/Batman Special #1 and Batman Confidential #13-16 18.00
...: THRILLKILLER (1998, $12.95, TPB)-r/series & Thrillkiller '62 13.00
...: TWO-FACE AND SCARECROW YEAR ONE (2009, $19.99, TPB)-r/Year One: Batman Scarecrow #1,2 and Two Face: Year One #1,2 20.00
...: UNDER THE COWL (2010, $17.99, TPB)-r/app. Dick Grayson, Tim Drake, Damien Wayne, Jean Paul Valley and Terry McGinnis as Batman 18.00
...: UNDER THE HOOD (2005, $9.99, TPB)-r/Batman #635-641 10.00
...: UNDER THE HOOD Vol. 2 (2006, $9.99, TPB)-r/Batman #645-650 & Annual #25 10.00

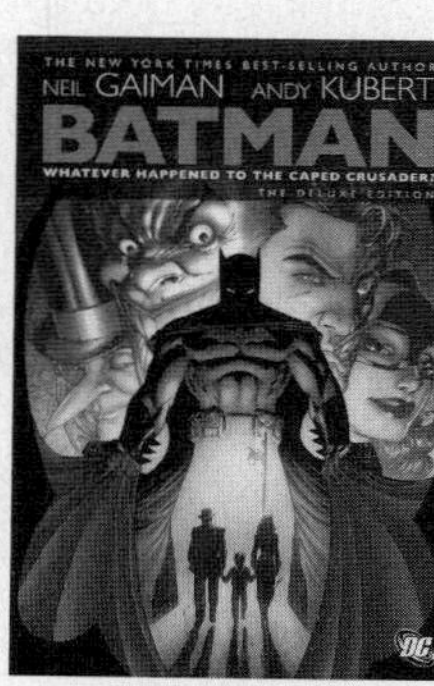

Batman: Whatever Happened to the Caped Crusader? HC © DC

Batman: Batgirl #1 © DC

Batman: The Man Who Laughs © DC

	GD 2.0	VG 4.0	FN 6.0	VF 8.0	VF/NM 9.0	NM- 9.2
...: VENOM (1993, $9.95, TPB)-r/Legends of the Dark Knight #16-20; embossed-c						10.00
... VS. TWO-FACE (2008, $19.99, TPB) r/initial (Det. #80) & classic battles; Bianchi-c						20.00
...: WAR CRIMES (2006, $12.99, TPB) r/x-over; James Jean-c						13.00
... WAR DRUMS (2004, $17.95) r/Detective #790-796 & Robin #126-128						18.00
...: WAR GAMES ACT 1,2,3 (2005, $14.95/$14.99, TPB) r/x-over; James Jean-c; each..						15.00
...: WHATEVER HAPPENED TO THE CAPED CRUSADER? HC-(2009, $24.99, d.j.) r/Batman #686, Detective #853 and other Gaiman Batman stories; Gaiman intro.; Andy Kubert sketch pages; new Kubert cover						25.00
YEAR ONE Hard-c (1988, $12.95) r/Batman #404-407						18.00
YEAR ONE (1988, $9.95, TPB)-r/Batman #404-407 by Miller; intro by Miller						10.00
YEAR ONE (TPB, 2nd & 3rd printings)						10.00
YEAR ONE Deluxe HC (2005, $19.99, die-cut d.j.) new intro. by Miller and developmental material from Mazzucchelli; script pages and sketches						20.00
YEAR ONE (Deluxe) SC (2007, $14.99) r/story plus bonus material from 2005 HC						15.00
YEAR TWO (1990, $9.95, TPB)-r/Det. 575-578 by McFarlane; wraparound-c						10.00
BATMAN (one-shots)						
... ABDUCTION, THE (1998, $5.95)						6.00
... ALLIES SECRET FILES AND ORIGINS 2005 (8/05, $4.99) stories/pin-ups by various						5.00
... & ROBIN (1997, $5.95)-Movie adaptation						6.00
...: ARKHAM ASYLUM - TALES OF MADNESS (5/98, $2.95) Cataclysm x-over pt. 16						3.00
... : BANE (1997, $4.95)-Dixon-s/Burchett-a; Stelfreeze-c; cover art interlocks w/Batman:(Batgirl, Mr. Freeze, Poison Ivy)						5.00
... : BATGIRL (1997, $4.95)-Puckett-s/Haley,Kesel-a; Stelfreeze-c; cover art interlocks w/Batman:(Bane, Mr. Freeze, Poison Ivy)						5.00
... : BATGIRL (6/98, $1.95)-Girlfrenzy; Balent-a						2.50
... : BLACKGATE (1/97, $3.95) Dixon-s						4.00
... : BLACKGATE - ISLE OF MEN (4/98, $2.95) Cataclysm x-over pt. 8; Moench-s/Aparo-a						3.00
... BOOK OF SHADOWS, THE (1999, $5.95)						6.00
BROTHERHOOD OF THE BAT (1995, $5.95)-Elseworlds-s						6.00
... BULLOCK'S LAW (8/99, $4.95) Dixon-s						5.00
.../CAPTAIN AMERICA (1996, $5.95, DC/Marvel) Elseworlds story; Byrne-c/s/a						6.00
... : CATWOMAN DEFIANT nn (1992, $4.95, prestige format)-Milligan scripts; cover art interlocks w/Batman: Penguin Triumphant; special foil logo						5.00
... /DANGER GIRL (2/05, $4.95)-Leinil Yu-a/c; Joker, Harley Quinn & Catwoman app.						5.00
... /DAREDEVIL (2000, $5.95)-Barreto-a						6.00
...: DARK ALLEGIANCES (1996, $5.95)-Elseworlds story, Chaykin-c/a						6.00
... : DARK KNIGHT GALLERY (1/96, $3.50)-Pin-ups by Pratt, Balent, & others						3.50
...:DAY OF JUDGMENT (11/99, $3.95)						4.00
...:DEATH OF INNOCENTS (12/96, $3.95)-O'Neil-s/ Staton-a(p)						4.00
.../DEMON (1996, $4.95)-Alan Grant scripts						5.00
.../DEMON: A TRAGEDY (2000, $5.95)-Grant-s/Murray painted-a						6.00
...:D.O.A. (1999, $6.95)-Bob Hall-s/a						7.00
...:/DOC SAVAGE SPECIAL (2010, $4.99)-Azzarello-s/Noto-a/covers by JG Jones & Morales; preview of First Wave line (Batman, Doc Savage, The Spirit, Blackhawks)						5.00
...:DREAMLAND (2000, $5.95)-Grant-s/Breyfogle-a						6.00
... : EGO (2000, $6.95)-Darwyn Cooke-s/a						7.00
... 80-PAGE GIANT (8/98, $4.95) Stelfreeze-c						6.00
... 80-PAGE GIANT 1 (2/10, $5.99) Andy Kubert-c; Catwoman, Poison Ivy app.						6.00
... 80-PAGE GIANT 2 (10/99, $4.95) Luck of the Draw						6.00
... 80-PAGE GIANT 3 (7/00, $5.95) Calendar Man						6.00
... FOREVER (1995, $5.95, direct market)						6.00
... FOREVER (1995, $3.95, newsstand)						4.00
FULL CIRCLE nn (1991, $5.95, 68 pgs.)-Sequel to Batman: Year Two						6.00
...GALLERY, The 1 (1992, $2.95)-Pin-ups by Miller, N. Adams & others						3.00
...GOLDEN STREETS OF GOTHAM (2003, $6.95) Elseworlds in early 1900s						7.00
...GOTHAM BY GASLIGHT (1989, $3.95) Elseworlds; Mignola-a/Augustyn-s						4.00
...GOTHAM CITY SECRET FILES 1 (4/00, $4.95) Batgirl app.						5.00
...: GOTHAM NOIR (2001, $6.95)-Elseworlds; Brubaker-s/Phillips-c/a						7.00
.../GREEN ARROW: THE POISON TOMORROW nn (1992, $5.95, square-bound, 68 pgs.) Netzer-c/a						6.00
HOLY TERROR nn (1991, $4.95, 52 pgs.)-Elseworlds story						5.00
.../HOUDINI: THE DEVIL'S WORKSHOP (1993, $5.95)						6.00
... :HUNTRESS/SPOILER - BLUNT TRAUMA (5/98, $2.95) Cataclysm pt. 13; Dixon-s/Barreto & Sienkiewicz-a						3.00
...: I, JOKER nn (1998, $4.95)-Elseworlds story; Bob Hall-s/a						5.00
...: IN BARCELONA: DRAGON'S KNIGHT 1 (7/09, $3.99) Waid-s/Olmos-a/Jim Lee-c						4.00
...: IN DARKEST KNIGHT nn (1994, $4.95, 52 pgs.)-Elseworlds story; Batman w/Green Lantern's ring.						5.00
...:JOKER'S APPRENTICE (5/99, $3.95) Von Eeden-a						4.00
.../ JOKER: SWITCH (2003, $6.95)-Bolton-a/Grayson-s						7.00
...:JUDGE DREDD: JUDGEMENT ON GOTHAM nn (1991, $5.95, 68 pgs.) Simon Bisley-c/a; Grant/Wagner scripts						6.00
...:JUDGE DREDD: JUDGEMENT ON GOTHAM nn (2nd printing)						6.00
...:JUDGE DREDD: THE ULTIMATE RIDDLE (1995, $4.95)						5.00
...:JUDGE DREDD: VENDETTA IN GOTHAM (1993, $5.95)						6.00
...: KNIGHTGALLERY (1995, $3.50)-Elseworlds sketchbook.						3.50
.../ LOBO (2000, $5.95)-Elseworlds; Joker app.; Bisley-a						6.00
...: MASK OF THE PHANTASM (1994, $2.95)-Movie adapt.						3.00
...: MASK OF THE PHANTASM (1994, $4.95)-Movie adapt.						5.00
...: MASQUE (1997, $6.95)-Elseworlds; Grell-c/s/a						7.00
...: MASTER OF THE FUTURE nn (1991, $5.95, 68 pgs.)-Elseworlds; sequel to Gotham By Gaslight; Barreto-a; embossed-c						6.00
...: MITEFALL (1995, $4.95)-Alan Grant script, Kevin O'Neill-a						5.00
... : MR. FREEZE (1997, $4.95)-Dini-s/Buckingham-a; Stelfreeze-c; cover art interlocks w/Batman:(Bane, Batgirl, Poison Ivy)						5.00
... /NIGHTWING: BLOODBORNE (2002, $5.95) Cypress-a; McKeever-c						6.00
...: NOSFERATU (1999, $5.95) McKeever-a						6.00
...: OF ARKHAM (2000, $5.95)-Elseworlds; Grant-s/Alcatena-a						6.00
...: OUR WORLDS AT WAR (8/01, $2.95)-Jae Lee-c						3.00
...: PENGUIN TRIUMPHANT nn (1992, $4.95)-Staton-a(p); foil logo						5.00
...•PHANTOM STRANGER nn (1997, $4.95) nn-Grant-s/Ransom-a						5.00
... : PLUS (2/97, $2.95) Arsenal-c/app.						3.00
... : POISON IVY (1997, $4.95)-J.F. Moore-s/Apthorp-a; Stelfreeze-c; cover art interlocks w/Batman:(Bane, Batgirl, Mr. Freeze)						5.00
.../POISON IVY: CAST SHADOWS (2004, $6.95) Van Fleet-c/a; Nocenti-s						7.00
.../PUNISHER: LAKE OF FIRE (1994, $4.95, DC/Marvel)						5.00
... :REIGN OF TERROR ('99, $4.95) Elseworlds						5.00
...RETURNS MOVIE SPECIAL (1992, $3.95)						4.00
...RETURNS MOVIE PRESTIGE (1992, $5.95, squarebound)-Dorman painted-c						6.00
...:RIDDLER-THE RIDDLE FACTORY (1995, $4.95)-Wagner script						5.00
...: ROOM FULL OF STRANGERS (2004, $5.95) Scott Morse-s/c/a						6.00
...: SCARECROW 3-D (12/98, $3.95) w/glasses						4.00
.../ SCARFACE: A PSYCHODRAMA (2001, $5.95)-Adlard-a/Sienkiewicz-c						6.00
...: SCAR OF THE BAT nn (1996, $4.95)-Elseworlds; Max Allan Collins script; Barreto-a						5.00
... :SCOTTISH CONNECTION (1998, $5.95) Quitely-a						6.00
... :SEDUCTION OF THE GUN nn (1992, $2.50, 68 pgs.)						3.00
.../SPAWN: WAR DEVIL nn (1994, $4.95, 52 pgs.)						5.00
... SPECIAL 1 (4/84)-Mike W. Barr story; Golden-c/a	1	2	3	5	6	8
.../SPIDER-MAN (1997, $4.95) Dematteis-s/Nolan & Kesel-a						5.00
... : THE ABDUCTION ('98, $5.95)						6.00
...: THE BLUE, THE GREY, & THE BAT (1992, $5.95)-Weiss/Lopez-a						6.00
... :THE HILL (5/00, $2.95)-Priest-s/Martinbrough-a						3.00
... :THE KILLING JOKE (1988, deluxe 52 pgs., mature readers)-Bolland-c/a; Alan Moore scripts; Joker cripples Barbara Gordon	2	4	6	11	16	20
...: THE KILLING JOKE (2nd thru 11th printings)	2	4	6	8	10	12
...: THE KILLING JOKE : THE DELUXE EDITION (2008, $17.99, HC) re-colored version along with Bolland-s/a from Batman Black and White #4; sketch pages; Tim Sale intro.						18.00
...: THE MAN WHO LAUGHS (2005, $6.95)-Retells 1st meeting with the Joker; Mahnke-a						7.00
...: THE OFFICIAL COMIC ADAPTATION OF THE WARNER BROS. MOTION PICTURE (1989, $2.50, regular format, 68 pgs.)-Ordway-c						3.00
...: THE OFFICIAL COMIC ADAPTATION OF THE WARNER BROS. MOTION PICTURE (1989, $4.95, prestige format, 68 pgs.)-same interiors but different-c						5.00
...: THE ORDER OF BEASTS (2004, $5.95)-Elseworlds; Eddie Campbell-a						6.00
...: THE SPIRIT (1/07, $4.99)-Loeb-s/Cooke-a; P'Gell & Commissioner Dolan app.						5.00
...: THE 10-CENT ADVENTURE (3/02, 10¢) intro. to the "Bruce Wayne: Murderer" x-over; Rucka-s/Burchett & Janson-a/Dave Johnson-c						2.00
NOTE: (Also see Promotional Comics section for alternate copies with special outer half-covers promoting local comic shops)						
...: THE 12-CENT ADVENTURE (10/04, 12¢) intro. to the "War Games" x-over; Grayson-s/Bachs-a; Catwoman & Spoiler app.						2.00
...: TWO-FACE-CRIME AND PUNISHMENT-(1995, $4.95)-McDaniel-a						5.00
... : TWO FACES (11/98, $4.95) Elseworlds						5.00
...: VENGEANCE OF BANE SPECIAL 1 (1992, $2.50, 68 pgs.)-Origin & 1st app. Bane (see Batman #491)	2	4	6	8	10	12
...: VENGEANCE OF BANE SPECIAL 1 (2nd printing)						3.00
....:VENGEANCE OF BANE II nn (1995, $3.95)-sequel						4.00
...Vs. THE INCREDIBLE HULK (1995, $3.95)-r/DC Special Series #27						4.00
...: VILLAINS SECRET FILES (10/98, $4.95) Origin-s						5.00
... VILLAINS SECRET FILES AND ORIGINS 2005 (7/05, $4.99) Clayface origin w/ Mignola-a; Black Mask story, pin-up of villains by various; Barrionuevo-c						5.00
BATMAN ADVENTURES, THE (Based on animated series)						
DC Comics: Oct, 1992 - No. 36, Oct, 1995 ($1.25/$1.50)						
1-Penguin-c/story						5.00
1 ($1.95, Silver Edition)-2nd printing						3.00
2-6,8-19: 2,12-Catwoman-c/story. 3-Joker-c/story. 5-Scarecrow-c/story. 10-Riddler-c/story. 11-Man-Bat-c/story. 12-Batgirl & Catwoman-c/story. 16-Joker-c/story; begin $1.50-c. 18-Batgirl-c/story. 19-Scarecrow-c/story.						3.50
7-Special edition polybagged with Man-Bat trading card						6.00

Batman and Robin #1 © DC

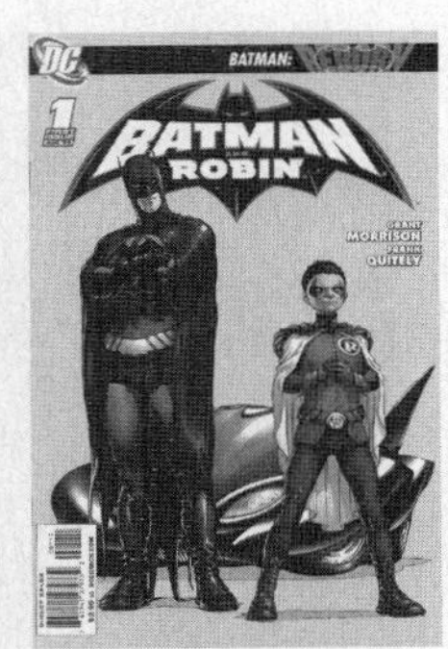

Batman and Robin Adventures #16 © DC

Batman Cacophony #1 © DC

GD 2.0 | VG 4.0 | FN 6.0 | VF 8.0 | VF/NM 9.0 | NM- 9.2

20-24,26-32: 26-Batgirl app. 3.00
25-($2.50, 52 pgs.)-Superman app. 3.50
33-36: 33-Begin $1.75-c 3.00
Annual 1,2 ('94, '95): 2-Demon-c/story; Ra's al Ghul app. 4.00
...: Dangerous Dames & Demons (2003, $14.95, TPB) r/Annual 1,2, Mad Love & Adventures in the DC Universe #3; Bruce Timm painted-c 30.00
Holiday Special 1 (1995, $2.95) 5.00
The Collected Adventures Vol. 1,2 ('93, '95, $5.95) 6.00
TPB ('98, $7.95) r/#1-6; painted wraparound-c 8.00

BATMAN ADVENTURES (Based on animated series)
DC Comics: Jun, 2003 - No. 17, Oct, 2004 ($2.25)

1-Timm-c (2003 Free Comic Book Day edition is listed in Promotional Comics section) 2.25
2-17: 3,16-Joker-c/app. 4-Ra's al Ghul app. 6-8-Phantasm app. 14-Grey Ghost app. 2.50
Vol. 1: Rogues Gallery (2004, $6.95, digest size) r/#1-4 & Batman: Gotham Advs. #50 7.00
Vol. 2: Shadows & Masks (2004, $6.95, digest size) r/#5-9 7.00

BATMAN ADVENTURES, THE: MAD LOVE
DC Comics: Feb, 1994 ($3.95/$4.95)

1-Origin of Harley Quinn; Dini-s/Timm-c/a 3 6 9 14 19 24
1-($4.95, Prestige format) new Timm painted-c 2 3 4 6 8 10

BATMAN ADVENTURES, THE: THE LOST YEARS (TV)
DC Comics: Jan, 1998 - No. 5, May, 1998 ($1.95) (Based on animated series)

1-5-Leads into Fall '97's new animated episodes. 4-Tim Drake becomes Robin. 5-Dick becomes Nightwing 2.50
TPB-(1999, $9.95) r/series 10.00

BATMAN/ALIENS
DC Comics/Dark Horse: Mar, 1997 - No. 2, Apr, 1997 ($4.95, limited series)

1,2: Wrightson-c/a. 5.00
TPB-(1997, $14.95) w/prequel from DHP #101,102 15.00

BATMAN/ALIENS II
DC Comics/Dark Horse: 2003 - No. 3, 2003 ($5.95, limited series)

1-3-Edginton-s/Staz Johnson-a 6.00
TPB-(2003, $14.95) r/#1-3 15.00

BATMAN AND ROBIN (See Batman R.I.P. and Batman: Battle For The Cowl series)
DC Comics: Aug, 2009 - Present ($2.99)

1-Grant Morrison-s/Frank Quitely-a/c 5.00
1-Variant cover by J.G. Jones 20.00
1-Second thru Fourth printings - recolored Quitely covers 3.00
2-7-Quitely-c. 2-Three printings. 4-6-Tan-a. 7-Stewart-a; Squire-a 3.00
2-Variant-c by Adam Kubert 10.00

BATMAN AND ROBIN ADVENTURES (TV)
DC Comics: Nov, 1995 - No. 25, Dec, 1997 ($1.75) (Based on animated series)

1-Dini-s. 3.00
2-24: 2-4-Dini script. 4-Penguin-c/story. 5-Joker-c/story; Poison Ivy, Harley Quinn-c/app. 9-Batgirl & Talia-c/story. 10-Ra's al Ghul-c/story. 11-Man-Bat app. 12-Bane-c/app. 13-Scarecrow-c/app. 15 Deadman-c/app. 16-Catwoman-c/app. 18-Joker-c/app. 24-Poison Ivy app. 2.50
25-($2.95, 48 pgs.) 3.00
Annual 1,2 (11/96, 11/97): 1-Phantasm-c/app. 2-Zatara & Zatanna-c/app. 4.00
...: Sub-Zero(1998, $3.95) Adaptation of animated video 4.00

BATMAN AND SUPERMAN ADVENTURES: WORLD'S FINEST
DC Comics: 1997 ($6.95, square-bound, one-shot) (Based on animated series)

1-Adaptation of animated crossover episode; Dini-s/Timm-c. 7.00

BATMAN AND SUPERMAN: WORLD'S FINEST
DC Comics: Apr, 1999 - No. 10, Jan, 2000 ($4.95/$1.99, limited series)

1,10-($4.95, squarebound) Taylor-a 5.00
2-9-($1.99) 5-Batgirl app. 8-Catwoman-c/app. 2.50
TPB (2003, $19.95) r/#1-10 20.00

BATMAN AND THE OUTSIDERS (The Adventures of the Outsiders #33 on)
(Also see Brave & The Bold #200 & The Outsiders) (Replaces The Brave and the Bold)
DC Comics: Aug, 1983 - No. 32, Apr, 1986 (Mando paper #5 on)

1-Batman, Halo, Geo-Force, Katana, Metamorpho & Black Lightning begin 4.50
2-32: 5-New Teen Titans x-over. 9-Halo begins. 11,12-Origin Katana. 18-More info on Metamorpho's origin. 28-31-Lookers origin. 32-Team disbands 3.00
Annual 1,2 (9/84, 9/85): 2-Metamorpho & Sapphire Stagg wed 3.50
NOTE: ***Aparo** a-1-9, 11-13p, 16-20; c-1-4, 5i, 6-21, Annual 1, 2. **B. Kane** a-3r. **Layton** a-19i, 20i. **Lopez** a-3p. **Miller** c-Annual 1. **Perez** c-5p. **B. Willingham** a-14p.*

BATMAN AND THE OUTSIDERS (Resumes as The Outsiders with #15)
DC Comics: Dec, 2007 - No. 14, Feb, 2009 ($2.99)

1-14: 1-Batman, Catwoman, Martian Manhunter, Katana, Metamorpho, Thunder & Grace begin. 4-Batgirl joins. 11-13-Batman R.I.P. 3.00
... Special (3/09, $3.99) Alfred assembles a new team; Andy Kubert-a; two covers 4.00
...: The Chrysalis TPB (2008, $14.99) r/#1-5 15.00
...: The Snare TPB (2008, $14.99) r/#6-10 15.00

BATMAN: BANE OF THE DEMON
DC Comics: Mar, 1998 - No. 4, June, 1998 ($1.95, limited series)

1-4-Dixon-s/Nolan-a; prelude to Legacy x-over 2.50

BATMAN: BATTLE FOR THE COWL (Follows Batman R.I.P. storyline)
DC Comics: May, 2009 - No. 3, Jul, 2009 ($3.99, limited series)

1-3-Tony Daniel-s/a/c; 2 covers on each 4.00
...: Arkham Asylum (6/09, $2.99) Hine-s/Haun-a/Ladronn-c 3.00
...: Commissioner Gordon (5/09, $2.99) Mandrake-a/Ladronn-c; Mr. Freeze app. 3.00
...: Man-Bat (6/09, $2.99) Harris-s/Calafiore-a/Ladronn-c; Dr. Phosphorus app. 3.00
...: The Network (7/09, $2.99) Nicieza-s/Calafiore & Kramer-a/Ladronn-c 3.00
...: The Underground (6/09, $2.99) Yost-s/Raimondi-a/Ladronn-c 3.00
Companion SC (2009, $14.99) r/ five one-shots 15.00
HC (2009, $19.99) r/#1-3 & Gotham Gazette: Batman Dead & Gotham Gazette: Batman Alive; gallery of variant covers and sketch art 20.00

BATMAN BEYOND (Based on animated series)
DC Comics: Mar, 1999 - No. 6, Aug, 1999 ($1.99, limited series)

1-6: 1,2-Adaptation of pilot episode, Timm-c 2.50
TPB (1999, $9.95) r/#1-6 10.00

BATMAN BEYOND (Based on animated series)(Continuing series)
DC Comics: Nov, 1999 - No. 24, Oct, 2001 ($1.99)

1-24: 1-Rousseau-a; Batman vs. Batman. 14-Demon-c/app. 21,22-Justice League Unlimited-c/app. 3.00
...: Return of the Joker (2/01, $2.95) adaptation of video release 4.00

BATMAN: BLACK & WHITE
DC Comics: June, 1996 - No. 4, Sept, 1996 ($2.95, B&W, limited series)

1-Stories by McKeever, Timm, Kubert, Chaykin, Goodwin; Jim Lee-c; Allred inside front-c; Moebius inside back-c 4.00
2-4: 2-Stories by Simonson, Corben, Bisley & Gaiman; Miller-c. 3-Stories by M. Wagner, Janson, Sienkiewicz, O'Neil & Kristiansen; B. Smith-c; Russell inside front-c; Silvestri inside back-c. 4-Stories by Bolland, Goodwin & Gianni, Strnad & Nowlan, O'Neil & Stelfreeze; Toth-c; pin-ups by Neal Adams & Alex Ross 3.00
Hardcover ('97, $39.95) r/series w/new art & cover plate 40.00
Softcover ('00, $19.95) r/series 20.00
Volume 2 HC ('02, $39.95, 7 3/4"x12") r/B&W back-up-s from Batman: Gotham Knights #1-16; stories and art by various incl. Ross, Buscema, Byrne, Ellison, Sale; Mignola-c 40.00
Volume 2 SC ('03, $19.95, 7 3/4"x12") same contents as HC 20.00
Volume 2 SC ('08, $19.99, reg. size) same contents as HC 20.00
Volume 3 HC ('07, $24.99, reg. size) r/B&W back-up-s from Batman: Gotham Knights #17-49; stories and art by various incl. Davis, DeCarlo, Morse, Schwartz, Thompson; Miller-c 25.00

BATMAN: BOOK OF THE DEAD
DC Comics: Jun, 1999 - No. 2, July, 1999 ($4.95, limited series, prestige format)

1,2-Elseworlds; Kitson-a 5.00

BATMAN CACOPHONY
DC Comics: Jan, 2009 - No. 3, Mar, 2009 ($3.99, limited series)

1-3-Kevin Smith-s/Walt Flanagan-a; Joker and Onomatoapoeia app.; Adam Kubert-c 4.00
1-3-Variant-c by Sienkiewicz 10.00
HC (2009, $19.99, d.j.) r/#1-3; Kevin Smith intro.; script for #3, cover gallery 20.00

BATMAN: CATWOMAN DEFIANT (See Batman one-shots)

BATMAN/ CATWOMAN: TRAIL OF THE GUN
DC Comics: 2004 - No. 2, 2004 ($5.95, limited series, prestige format)

1,2-Elseworlds; Van Sciver-a/Nocenti-s 6.00

BATMAN CHRONICLES, THE (See the Batman TPB listings for the Golden Age reprint series that shares this title)
DC Comics: Summer, 1995 - No. 23, Winter, 2001 ($2.95, quarterly)

1-3,5-19: 1-Dixon/Grant/Moench script. 3-Bolland-c. 5-Oracle Year One story, Richard Dragon app.,Chaykin-c. 6-Kaluta-c; Ra's al Ghul story. 7-Superman-c/app.11-Paul Pope-s/a. 12-Cataclysm pt. 10. 18-No Man's Land 3.50
4-Hitman story by Ennis, Contagion tie-in; Balent-c 2 4 6 8 10 12
20-23: 20-Catwoman and Relative Heroes-c/app. 21-Pander Bros.-a 3.00
...Gallery (3/97, $3.50) Pin-ups 3.50
...Gauntlet, The (1997, $4.95, one-shot) 5.00

BATMAN: CITY OF LIGHT
DC Comics: Dec, 2003 - No. 8, July, 2004 ($2.95, limited series)

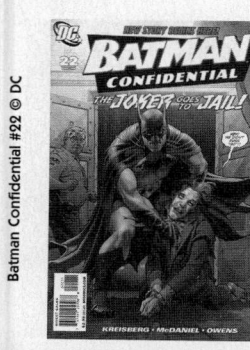

Batman Confidential #22 © DC

Batman: Gotham Knights #1 © DC

Batman: Harley Quinn © DC

GD 2.0 | VG 4.0 | FN 6.0 | VF 8.0 | VF/NM 9.0 | NM- 9.2

1-8-Pander Brothers-a/s; Paniccia-s 3.00

BATMAN CONFIDENTIAL
DC Comics: Feb, 2007 - Present ($2.99)

1-41: 1-6-Diggle-s/Portacio-a/c. 7-12-Cowan-a; Joker's origin. 13-16-Morales-a. 17-21-Batgirl vs. Catwoman; Maguire-a. 22-25-McDaniel-a; Joker app. 26-28-King Tut app.; Garcia-Lopez-a. 40,41-Kieth-s/a 3.00
...: Lovers and Madmen HC (2008, $24.99, dustjacket) r/#7-12; Brad Meltzer intro. 25.00
...: Lovers and Madmen SC (2009, $14.99) r/#7-12; Brad Meltzer intro. 15.00
...: Rules of Engagement HC (2007, $24.99, dustjacket) r/#1-6 25.00
...: The Cat and the Bat SC (2009, $12.99) r/#17-21 13.00

BATMAN: DARK DETECTIVE
DC Comics: Early July, 2005 - No. 6, Late September, 2005 ($2.99, limited series)

1-6-Englehart-s/Rogers & Austin-a; Silver St. Cloud and The Joker app. 3.00

BATMAN: DARK KNIGHT OF THE ROUND TABLE
DC Comics: 1999 - No. 2, 1999 ($4.95, limited series, prestige format)

1,2-Elseworlds; Giordano-a 5.00

BATMAN: DARK VICTORY
DC Comics: 1999 - No. 13, 2000 ($4.95/$2.95, limited series)

Wizard #0 Preview 2.25
1-($4.95) Loeb-s/Sale-c/a 5.00
2-12-($2.95) 3.00
13-($4.95) 5.00
Hardcover (2001, $29.95) with dust jacket; r/#0,1-13 30.00
Softcover (2002, $19.95) r/#0,1-13 20.00

BATMAN: DEATH AND THE MAIDENS
DC Comics: Oct, 2003 - No. 9, Aug, 2004 ($2.95, limited series)

1-Ra's al Ghul app.; Rucka-s/Janson-a 4.00
2-9: 9-Ra's al Ghul dies 3.00
TPB (2004, $19.95) r/#1-9 & Detective #783 20.00

BATMAN/ DEATHBLOW: AFTER THE FIRE
DC Comics/WildStorm: 2002 - No. 3, 2002 ($5.95, limited series)

1-3-Azzarello-s/Bermejo & Bradstreet-a 6.00
TPB (2003, $12.95) r/#1-3; plus concept art 13.00

BATMAN: DEATH MASK
DC Comics/CMX: Jun, 2008 - No. 4, Sept, 2008 ($2.99, B&W, limited series, right-to-left manga style)

1-4-Yoshinori Natsume-s/a 3.00
TPB (2008, $9.99, digest size) r/#1-4; interview with Yoshinori Natsume 10.00

BATMAN FAMILY, THE
National Periodical Pub./DC Comics: Sept-Oct, 1975 - No. 20, Oct-Nov, 1978 (#1-4, 17-on: 68 pgs.) (Combined with Detective Comics with No. 481)

1-Origin/2nd app. Batgirl-Robin team-up (The Dynamite Duo); reprints plus one new story begins; N. Adams-a(r); r/1st app. Man-Bat from Det. #400
4 8 12 24 37 50
2-5: 2-r/Det. #369. 3-Batgirl & Robin learn each's i.d.; r/Batwoman app. from Batman #105. 4-r/1st Fatman app. from Batman #113. 5-r/1st Bat-Hound app. from Batman #92
3 6 9 16 22 28
6,9-Joker's daughter on cover (1st app?) 3 6 9 16 23 30
7,8,14-16: 8-r/Batwoman app.14-Batwoman app. 15-3rd app. Killer Moth. 16-Bat-Girl cameo (last app. in costume until New Teen Titans #47) 2 4 6 11 16 20
10-1st revival Batwoman; Cavalier app.; Killer Moth app.
3 6 9 18 27 35
11-13,17-20: 11-13-Rogers-a(p): 11-New stories begin; Man-Bat begins. 13-Batwoman cameo. 17-($1.00 size)-Batman, Huntress begin; Batwoman & Catwoman 1st meet. 18-20: Huntress by Staton in all. 20-Origin Ragman retold
3 6 9 17 25 32

NOTE: *Aparo a-17; c-11-16.* ***Austin*** *a-12i.* ***Chaykin*** *a-14p.* ***Michael Golden*** *a-15-17,18-20p.* ***Grell*** *a-1; c-1.* ***Gil Kane*** *a-2r.* ***Kaluta*** *c-17, 19.* ***Newton*** *a-13.* ***Robinson*** *a-1r, 3i(r), 9r.* ***Russell*** *a-18i, 19i.* ***Starlin*** *a-17; c-18, 20.*

BATMAN: FAMILY
DC Comics: Dec, 2002 - No. 8, Feb, 2003 ($2.95/$2.25, weekly limited series)

1,8-($2.95). John Francis Moore-s/Hoberg & Gaudiano-a 3.00
2-7-($2.25). 3-Orpheus & Black Canary app. 2.50

BATMAN: GCPD
DC Comics: Aug, 1996 - No. 4, Nov, 1996 ($2.25, limited series)

1-4: Features Jim Gordon; Aparo/Sienkiewicz-a 2.50

BATMAN: GORDON OF GOTHAM
DC Comics: June, 1998 - No. 4, Sept, 1998 ($1.95, limited series)

1-4: Gordon's early days in Chicago 2.50

BATMAN: GORDON'S LAW
DC Comics: Dec, 1996 - No. 4, Mar, 1997 ($1.95, limited series)

1-4: Dixon-s/Janson-c/a 2.50

BATMAN: GOTHAM ADVENTURES (TV)
DC Comics: June, 1998 - No. 60, May, 2003 ($2.95/$1.95/$1.99/$2.25)

1-($2.95) Based on Kids WB Batman animated series 3.00
2-3-($1.95): 2-Two-Face-c/app. 2.50
4-22: 4-Begin $1.99-c. 5-Deadman-c. 13-MAD #1 cover swipe 2.50
23-60: 31,60-Joker-c/app. 50-Catwoman-c/app. 53-Begin $2.25-c. 58-Creeper-c/app. 2.50
TPB (2000, $9.95) r/#1-6 10.00

BATMAN: GOTHAM AFTER MIDNIGHT
DC Comics: July, 2008 - No. 12, Jun, 2009 ($2.99, limited series)

1-12-Steve Niles-s/Kelley Jones-a/c. 1-Scarecrow app. 2-Man-Bat app. 5,6-Joker app. 3.00
TPB (2009, $19.99) r/#1-12; John Carpenter intro.; Jones sketch pages 20.00

BATMAN: GOTHAM COUNTY LINE
DC Comics: 2005 - No. 3, 2005 ($5.99, square-bound, limited series)

1-3-Steve Niles-s/Scott Hampton-a. 2,3-Deadman app. 6.00
TPB (2006, $17.99) r/#1-3 18.00

BATMAN: GOTHAM KNIGHTS
DC Comics: Mar, 2000 - No. 74, Apr, 2006 ($2.50/$2.75)

1-Grayson-s; B&W back-up by Warren Ellis & Jim Lee 4.00
2-10-Grayson-s; B&W back-ups by various 2.75
11-($3.25) Bolland-c; Kyle Baker back-up story 3.25
12-24: 13-Officer Down x-over; Ellison back-up-s. 15-Colan back-up. 20-Superman-c/app. 2.75
25,26-Bruce Wayne: Murderer pt. 4,10 3.00
27-31: 28,30,31-Bruce Wayne: Fugitive pt. 7,14,17 2.75
32-49: 32-Begin $2.75-c; Kaluta-a back-up. 33,34-Bane-c/app. 35-Mahfood-a back-up. 38-Bolton-a back-up. 43-Jason Todd & Batgirl app. 44-Jason Todd flashback 2.75
50-54-Hush returns-Barrionuevo-a/Bermejo-c. 53,54-Green Arrow app. 3.00
55-($3.75) Batman vs. Hush; Joker & Riddler app. 4.00
56-74: 56-58-War Games; Jae Lee-c. 60-65-Hush app. 66-Villains United tie-in; Talia app. 2.50
Batman: Hush Returns TPB (2006, $12.99) r/#50-55,66; cover gallery 13.00

BATMAN: GOTHAM NIGHTS II (First series listed under Gotham Nights)
DC Comics: Mar, 1995 - No. 4, June, 1995 ($1.95, limited series)

1-4 2.50

BATMAN/GRENDEL (1st limited series)
DC Comics: 1993 - No. 2, 1993 ($4.95, limited series, squarebound; 52 pgs.)

1,2: Batman vs. Hunter Rose. 1-Devil's Riddle; Matt Wagner-c/a/scripts. 2-Devil's Masque; Matt Wagner-c/a/scripts 6.00

BATMAN/GRENDEL (2nd limited series)
DC Comics: June, 1996 - No. 2, July, 1996 ($4.95, limited series, squarebound)

1,2: Batman vs. Grendel Prime. 1-Devil's Bones. 2-Devil's Dance; Wagner-c/a/s 5.00

BATMAN: HARLEY & IVY
DC Comics: Jun, 2004 - No. 3, Aug, 2004 ($2.50, limited series)

1-3-Paul Dini-s/Bruce Timm-c/a 2.50
TPB (2007, $14.99) r/series; newly colored story from Batman: Gotham Knights #14 and Harley and Ivy: Love on the Lam series 15.00

BATMAN: HARLEY QUINN
DC Comics: 1999 ($5.95, prestige format)

1-Intro. of Harley Quinn into regular DC continuity; Dini-s/Alex Ross-c 9.00
1-(2nd printing) 6.00

BATMAN: HAUNTED GOTHAM
DC Comics: 2000 - No. 4, 2000 ($4.95, limited series, squarebound)

1-4-Doug Moench-s/Kelley Jones-c/a 5.00
TPB (2009, $19.99) r/#1-4 13.00

BATMAN/ HELLBOY/STARMAN
DC Comics/Dark Horse: Jan, 1999 - No. 2, Feb, 1999 ($2.50, limited series)

1,2: Robinson-s/Mignola-a. 2-Harris-c 2.50

BATMAN: HOLLYWOOD KNIGHT
DC Comics: Apr, 2001 - No. 3, Jun, 2001 ($2.50, limited series)

1-3-Elseworlds Batman as a 1940's movie star; Giordano-a/Layton-s 2.50

BATMAN/ HUNTRESS: CRY FOR BLOOD
DC Comics: Jun, 2000 - No. 6, Nov, 2000 ($2.50, limited series)

1-6: Rucka-s/Burchett-a; The Question app. 2.50

Batman: Legends of the Dark Knight #47 © DC

Batman: Manbat #2 © DC

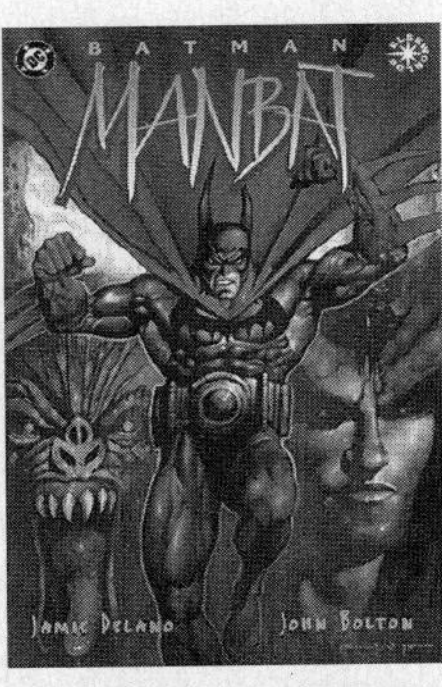

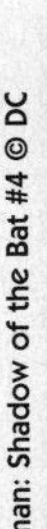

Batman: Shadow of the Bat #4 © DC

GD VG FN VF VF/NM NM-
2.0 4.0 6.0 8.0 9.0 9.2

TPB (2002, $12.95) r/#1-6 13.00

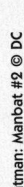

BATMAN: JEKYLL & HYDE
DC Comics: June, 2005 - No. 6, Nov, 2005 ($2.99, limited series)
1-6-Paul Jenkins-s; Two-Face app. 1-3-Jae Lee-a. 4-6-Sean Phillips-a 3.00
TPB (2008, $14.99) r/#1-6 15.00

BATMAN: JOKER TIME (...: It's Joker Time! on cover)
DC Comics: 2000 - No. 3 ($4.95, limited series, squarebound)
1-3-Bob Hall-s/a 5.00

BATMAN: JOURNEY INTO KNGHT
DC Comics: Oct, 2005 - No. 12, Nov, 2006 ($2.50/$2.99, limited series)
1-9-Andrew Helfer-s/Tan Eng Huat-a/Pat Lee-c 2.50
10-12-($2.99) Joker app. 3.00

BATMAN/ JUDGE DREDD "DIE LAUGHING"
DC Comics: 1998 - No. 2, 1999 ($4.95, limited series, squarebound)
1,2: 1-Fabry-c/a. 2-Jim Murray-c/a 5.00

BATMAN: KNIGHTGALLERY (See Batman one-shots)

BATMAN: LEAGUE OF BATMEN
DC Comics: 2001 - No. 2, 2001 ($5.95, limited series, squarebound)
1,2-Elseworlds; Moench-s/Bright & Tanghal-a/Van Fleet-c 6.00

BATMAN: LEGENDS OF THE DARK KNIGHT (Legends of the Dark...#1-36)
DC Comics: Nov, 1989 - No. 214, Mar, 2007 ($1.50/$1.75/$1.95/$1.99/$2.25/$2.50/$2.99)
1- "Shaman" begins, ends #5; outer cover has four different color variations, all worth same 4.00
2-10: 6-10- "Gothic" by Grant Morrison (scripts) 3.00
11-15: 11-15-Gulacy/Austin-a. 13-Catwoman app. 3.00
16-Intro drug Bane uses; begin Venom story 5.00
17-20 4.00
21-49,51-63: 38-Bat-Mite-c/story. 46-49-Catwoman app. w/Heath-c/a. 51-Ragman app.; Joe Kubert-c. 59,60,61-Knightquest x-over. 62,63-KnightsEnd Pt. 4 & 10 3.00
50-($3.95, 68 pgs.)-Bolland embossed gold foil-c; Joker-c/story; pin-ups by Chaykin, Simonson, Williamson, Kaluta, Russell, others 5.00
64-99: 64-(9/94)-Begin $1.95-c. 71-73-James Robinson-s,Watkiss-c/a. 74,75-McKeever-c/a/s. 76-78-Scott Hampton-c/a/s. 81-Card insert. 83,84-Ellis-s. 85-Robinson-s. 91-93-Ennis-s. 94-Michael T. Gilbert-s/a. 3.00
100-($3.95) Alex Ross painted-c; gallery by various 5.00
101-115: 101-Ezquerra-a. 102-104-Robinson-s 2.50
116-No Man's Land stories begin; Huntress-c 4.00
117-119,121-126: 122-Harris-c 2.50
120-ID of new Batgirl revealed 4.00
127-131: Return to Legends stories; Green Arrow app. 2.50
132-199, 201-204: 132-136 ($2.25-c) Archie Goodwin-s/Rogers-a. 137-141-Gulacy-a. 142-145-Joker and Ra's al Ghul app. 146-148-Kitson-a. 158-Begin $2.50-c 169-171-Tony Harris-c/a. 182-184-War Games. 182-Bagged with Sky Captain CD 2.50
200-($4.99) Joker-c/app. 5.00
205-214: 205-Begin $2.99-c. 207,208-Olivetti-a. 214-Deadshot app. 3.00
#0-(10/94)-Zero Hour; Quesada/Palmiotti-c; released between #64&65 3.00
Annual 1-7 ('91-'97, $3.50-$3.95, 68 pgs.): 1-Joker app. 2-Netzer-c/a. 3-New Batman (Azrael) app. 4-Elseworlds story. 5-Year One; Man-Bat app. 6-Legend of the Dead Earth story. 7-Pulp Heroes story 4.00
Halloween Special 1 (12/93, $6.95, 84 pgs.)-Embossed & foil stamped-c
1 2 3 4 5 7
Batman Madness-...Halloween Special (1994, $4.95) 5.00
Batman Ghosts-...Halloween Special (1995, $4.95) 5.00
NOTE: *Aparo a-Annual 1.* ***Chaykin*** *scripts-24-26.* ***Giffen*** *a-Annual 1.* ***Golden*** *a-Annual 1.* ***Alan Grant*** *scripts-38, 52, 53.* ***Gil Kane*** *c/a-24-26.* ***Mignola*** *a-54; c-54, 62.* ***Morrow*** *a-Annual 3i.* ***Quesada*** *a-Annual 1.* ***James Robinson*** *scripts- 71-73.* ***Russell*** *c/a-42, 43.* ***Sears*** *a-21, 23; c-21, 23.* ***Zeck*** *a-69, 70; c-69, 70.*

BATMAN-LEGENDS OF THE DARK KNIGHT: JAZZ
DC Comics: Apr, 1995 - No. 3, June, 1995 ($2.50, limited series)
1-3 2.50

BATMAN/LOBO
DC Comics: Oct, 2007 - No. 2, Nov, 2007 ($5.99, squarebound, limited series)
1,2-Sam Kieth-s/a 6.00

BATMAN: MANBAT
DC Comics: Oct, 1995 - No. 3, Dec, 1995 ($4.95, limited series)
1-3-Elseworlds-Delano-script; Bolton-a. 5.00
TPB-(1997, $14.95) r/#1-3 15.00

BATMAN: MITEFALL (See Batman one-shots)

BATMAN MINIATURE (See Batman Kellogg's)

GD VG FN VF VF/NM NM-
2.0 4.0 6.0 8.0 9.0 9.2

BATMAN: NEVERMORE
DC Comics: June, 2003 - No. 5, Oct, 2003 ($2.50, limited series)
1-5-Elseworlds Batman & Edgar Allan Poe; Wrightson-c/Guy Davis-a/Len Wein-s 2.50

BATMAN: NO MAN'S LAND (Also see 1999 Batman titles)
DC Comics: (one shots)
nn (3/99, $2.95) Alex Ross-c; Bob Gale-s; begins year-long story arc 3.00
Collector's Ed. (3/99, $3.95) Ross lenticular-c 5.00
#0 (: Ground Zero on cover) (12/99, $4.95) Orbik-c 5.00
...: Gallery (7/99, $3.95) Jim Lee-c 4.00
...: Secret Files (12/99, $4.95) Maleev-c 5.00
TPB ('99, $12.95) r/early No Man's Land stories; new Batgirl early app. 13.00
No Law and a New Order TPB(1999, $5.95) Ross-c 6.00
Volume 2 ('00, $12.95) r/later No Man's Land stories; Batgirl(Huntress) app.; Deodato-c 13.00
Volume 3-5 ('00,'01 $12.95) 3-Intro. new Batgirl. 4-('00). 5-('01) Land-c 13.00

BATMAN: ORPHEUS RISING
DC Comics: Oct, 2001 - No. 5, Feb, 2002 ($2.50, limited series)
1-5-Intro. Orpheus; Simmons-s/Turner & Miki-a 2.50

BATMAN: OUTLAWS
DC Comics: 2000 - No. 3, 2000 ($4.95, limited series)
1-3-Moench-s/Gulacy-a 5.00

BATMAN: PENGUIN TRIUMPHANT (See Batman one-shots)

BATMAN/PREDATOR III: BLOOD TIES
DC Comics/Dark Horse Comics: Nov, 1997 - No. 4, Feb, 1998 ($1.95, lim. series)
1-4: Dixon-s/Damaggio-c/a 2.50
TPB-(1998, $7.95) r/#1-4 8.00

BATMAN/RA'S AL GHUL (See Year One:...)

BATMAN RETURNS MOVIE SPECIAL (See Batman one-shots)

BATMAN: RIDDLER-THE RIDDLE FACTORY (See Batman one-shots)

BATMAN: RUN, RIDDLER, RUN
DC Comics: 1992 - Book 3, 1992 ($4.95, limited series)
Book 1-3: Mark Badger-a & plot 5.00

BATMAN SCARECROW (See Year One:...)

BATMAN: SECRET FILES
DC Comics: Oct, 1997 ($4.95)
1-New origin-s and profiles 5.00

BATMAN: SECRETS
DC Comics: May, 2006 - No. 5, Sept, 2006 ($2.99, limited series)
1-5-Sam Kieth-s/a/c; Joker app. 3.00
TPB (2007, $12.99) r/series 13.00

BATMAN: SHADOW OF THE BAT
DC Comics: June, 1992 - No. 94, Feb, 2000 ($1.50/$1.75/$1.95/$1.99)
1-The Last Arkham-c/story begins; Alan Grant scripts in all 4.00
1-($2.50)-Deluxe edition polybagged w/poster, pop-up & book mark 5.00
2-7: 4-The Last Arkham ends. 7-Last $1.50-c 3.00
8-28: 14,15-Staton-a(p). 16-18-Knightfall tie-ins. 19-28-Knightquest tie-ins w/Azrael as Batman. 25-Silver ink-c; anniversary issue 2.50
29-($2.95, 52 pgs.)-KnightsEnd Pt. 2 3.00
30-72: 30-KnightsEnd Pt. 8. 31-(9.94)-Begin $1.95-c; Zero Hour. 32-(11/94). 33-Robin-c. 35-Troika-Pt.2. 43,44-Cat-Man & Catwoman-c. 48-Contagion Pt. 1; card insert. 49-Contagion Pt.7. 56,57,58-Poison Ivy-c/app. 62-Two-Face app. 69,70-Fate app. 2.50
35-($2.95)-Variant embossed-c 3.00
73,74,76-78: Cataclysm x-over pts. 1,9. 76-78-Orbik-c 2.50
75-($2.95) Mr. Freeze & Clayface app.; Orbik-c 3.00
79,81,82: 79-Begin $1.99-c; Orbik-c 2.50
80-($3.95) Flip book with Azrael #47 4.00
83-No Man's Land; intro. new Batgirl (Huntress) 12.00
84,85-No Man's Land 4.00
86-94: 87-Deodato-a. 90-Harris-c. 92-Superman app. 93-Joker and Harley app. 94-No Man's Land ends 3.00
#0 (10/94) Zero Hour; released between #31&32 3.00
#1,000,000 (11/98) 853rd Century x-over; Orbik-c 2.50
Annual 1-5 ('93-'97 $2.95-$3.95, 68 pgs.): 3-Year One story; Poison Ivy app. 4-Legends of the Dead Earth story; Starman cameo. 5-Pulp Heroes story; Poison Ivy app. 4.00

BATMAN: SON OF THE DEMON (Also see Batman #655-658 and Batman Hardcovers)
DC Comics: 2006 ($5.99, reprints the 1987 HC in comic book format)
nn-Talia has Batman's son; Mike W. Barr-s/Jerry Bingham-a; new Andy Kubert-c 6.00

The Batman Strikes! #45 © DC

Batman: The Brave and the Bold #1 © DC

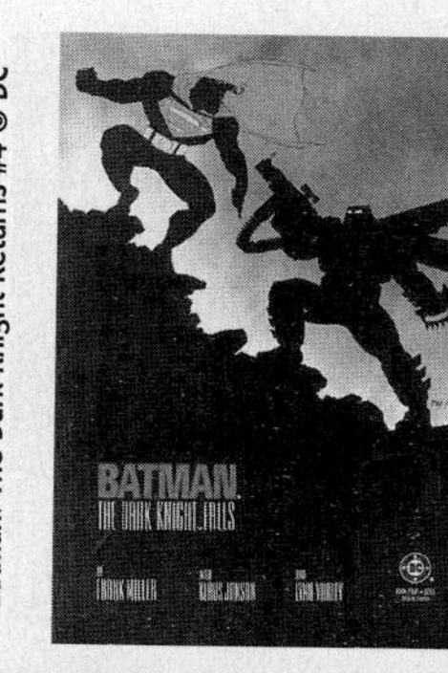

Batman: The Dark Knight Returns #4 © DC

GD 2.0 | VG 4.0 | FN 6.0 | VF 8.0 | VF/NM 9.0 | NM- 9.2

BATMAN-SPAWN: WAR DEVIL (See Batman one-shots)

BATMAN SPECTACULAR (See DC Special Series No. 15)

BATMAN: STREETS OF GOTHAM (Follows Batman: Battle For The Cowl series)
DC Comics: Aug, 2009 - Present ($3.99)
1-8: 1-Dini-s/Nguyen-a; back-up Manhunter feature; Jeanty-a 4.00

BATMAN STRIKES!, THE (Based on the 2004 animated series) (2005 Free Comic Book Day edition is listed in Promotional Comics section)
DC Comics: Nov, 2004 - No. 50, Dec, 2008 ($2.25)
1,2,4-50: 1,11-Penguin app. 2-Man-Bat app. 4-Bane app. 9-Joker app. 18-Batgirl debut. 29-Robin debuts. 32,33-Cal Ripken 8-pg. insert. 44-Superman app. 2.50
3-($2.95) Joker-c/app.; Catwoman & Wonder Woman-r from Advs. in the DCU 3.00
Jam Packed Action (2005, $7.99, digest) adaptations of two TV episodes 8.00
... Vol. 1: Crime Time (2005, $6.99, digest) r/#1-5 7.00
... Vol. 2: In Darkest Knight (2005, $6.99, digest) r/#6-10 7.00

BATMAN/ SUPERMAN/WONDER WOMAN: TRINITY
DC Comics: 2003 - No. 3, 2003 ($6.95, limited series, squarebound)
1-3-Matt Wagner-s/a/c. 1-Ra's al Ghul & Bizarro app. 7.00
HC (2004, $24.95, with dust-jacket) r/series; intro. by Brad Meltzer 30.00
SC (2004, $17.99) r/series; intro. by Brad Meltzer 18.00

BATMAN: SWORD OF AZRAEL (Also see Azrael & Batman #488,489)
DC Comics: Oct, 1992 - No. 4, Jan, 1993 ($1.75, limited series)
1-Wraparound gatefold-c; Quesada-c/a(p) in all; 1st app. Azrael 2 4 6 8 10 12
2-4: 4-Cont'd in Batman #488 1 2 3 5 6 8
Silver Edition 1-4 (1993, $1.95)-Reprints #1-4 2.50
Trade Paperback (1993, $9.95)-Reprints #1-4 10.00
Trade Paperback Gold Edition 15.00

BATMAN/ TARZAN: CLAWS OF THE CAT-WOMAN
Dark Horse Comics/DC Comics: Sept, 1999 - No. 4, Dec, 1999 ($2.95, limited series)
1-4: Marz-s/Kordey-a 3.00

BATMAN: TENSES
DC Comics: 2003 - No. 2, 2003 ($6.95, limited series)
1,2-Joe Casey-s/Cully Hamner-a; Bruce Wayne's first year back in Gotham 7.00

BATMAN: THE ANKH
DC Comics: 2002 - No. 2, 2002 ($5.95, limited series)
1,2-Dixon-s/Van Fleet-a 6.00

BATMAN: THE BRAVE AND THE BOLD (Based on the 2008 animated series)
DC Comics: Mar, 2009 - Present ($2.50)
1-13: 1-Power Girl app. 4-Sugar & Spike cameo. 7-Doom Patrol app. 9-Catman app. 2.50
TPB (2009, $12.99) r/#1-6 13.00

BATMAN: THE CULT
DC Comics: 1988 - No. 4, Nov, 1988 ($3.50, deluxe limited series)
1-Wrightson-a/painted-c in all 6.00
2-4 5.00
Trade Paperback (1991, $14.95)-New Wrightson-c; Starlin intro. 15.00
Trade Paperback (2009, $19.99) 20.00

BATMAN: THE DARK KNIGHT RETURNS (Also see Dark Knight Strikes Again)
DC Comics: Mar, 1986 - No. 4, 1986 ($2.95, squarebound, limited series)
1-Miller story & c/a(p); set in the future 5 10 15 30 48 65
1,2-2nd & 3rd printings, 3-2nd printing 6.00
2-Carrie Kelly becomes 1st female Robin 3 6 9 16 23 30
3-Death of Joker; Superman app. 3 6 9 14 20 25
4-Death of Alfred; Superman app. 2 4 6 11 16 20
Hardcover, signed & numbered edition ($40.00)(4000 copies) 250.00
Hardcover, trade edition 50.00
Softcover, trade edition (1st printing only) 2 4 6 9 12 15
Softcover, trade edition (2nd thru 8th printings) 1 2 3 4 5 7
10th Anniv. Slipcase set ('96, $100.00): Signed & numbered hard-c edition (10,000 copies), sketchbook, copy of script for #1, 2 color prints 100.00
10th Anniv. Hardcover ('96, $45.00) 45.00
10th Anniv. Softcover ('97, $14.95) 15.00
Hardcover 2nd printing ('02, $24.95) with 3 1/4" tall partial dustjacket 25.00
NOTE: *The #2 second printings can be identified by matching the grey background colors on the inside front cover and facing page. The inside front cover of the second printing has a dark grey background which does not match the lighter grey of the facing page. On the true 1st printings, the backgrounds are both light grey. All other issues are clearly marked.*

BATMAN: THE DOOM THAT CAME TO GOTHAM
DC Comics: 2000 - No. 3, 2001 ($4.95, limited series)
1-3-Elseworlds; Mignola-c/s; Nixey-a; Etrigan app. 5.00

BATMAN: THE KILLING JOKE (See Batman one-shots)

BATMAN: THE LONG HALLOWEEN
DC Comics: Oct, 1996 - No. 13, Oct, 1997 ($2.95/$4.95, limited series)
1-($4.95)-Loeb-s/Sale-c/a in all 1 2 3 5 6 8
2-5($2.95): 2-Solomon Grundy-c/app. 3-Joker-c/app., Catwoman, Poison Ivy app. 6.00
6-10: 6-Poison Ivy-c. 7-Riddler-c/app. 5.00
11,12 4.00
13-($4.95, 48 pgs.)-Killer revelations 5.00
Absolute Batman: The Long Halloween (2007, $75.00, oversized HC) r/series; interviews with the creators; Sale sketch pages; action figure line; unpubbed 4-page sequence 75.00
HC-($29.95) r/series 30.00
SC-($19.95) 20.00

BATMAN: THE MAD MONK ("Batman & the Mad Monk" on cover)
DC Comics: Oct, 2006 - No. 6, ($3.50, limited series)
1-5-Matt Wagner-s/a/c. 1-Catwoman app. 3.50
TPB (2007, $14.99) r/#1-6 15.00

BATMAN: THE MONSTER MEN ("Batman & the Monster Men" on cover)
DC Comics: Jan, 2006 - No. 6, June, 2006 ($2.99, limited series)
1-6-Matt Wagner-s/a/c 3.00
TPB (2006, $14.99) r/#1-6 15.00

BATMAN: THE OFFICIAL COMIC ADAPTATION OF THE WARNER BROS. MOTION PICTURE (See Batman one-shots)

BATMAN: THE ULTIMATE EVIL
DC Comics: 1995 ($5.95, limited series, prestige format)
1,2-Barrett, Jr. adaptation of Vachss novel. 6.00

BATMAN: THE WIDENING GYRE
DC Comics: Oct, 2009 - No. 6 ($3.99, limited series)
1-4-Kevin Smith-s/Walt Flanagan-a; Demon app.; Sienkiewicz-c. 2-Silver St. Cloud app. 4.00

BATMAN 3-D (Also see 3-D Batman)
DC Comics: 1990 ($9.95, w/glasses, 8-1/8x10-3/4")
nn-Byrne-a/scripts; Riddler, Joker, Penguin & Two-Face app. plus r/1953 3-D Batman; pin-ups by many artists 2 4 6 8 10 12

BATMAN: TOYMAN
DC Comics: Nov, 1998 - No. 4, Feb, 1999 ($2.25, limited series)
1-4-Hama-s 2.50

BATMAN: TURNING POINTS
DC Comics: Jan, 2001 - No. 5, Jan, 2001 ($2.50, weekly limited series)
1-5: 2-Giella-a. 3-Kubert-c/Giordano-a. 4-Chaykin-c/Brent Anderson-a. 5-Pope-c/a 2.50
TPB (2007, $14.99) r/#1-5 15.00

BATMAN: TWO-FACE-CRIME AND PUNISHMENT (See Batman one-shots)

BATMAN: TWO-FACE STRIKES TWICE
DC Comics: 1993 - No. 2, 1993 ($4.95, 52 pgs.)
1,2-Flip book format w/Staton-a (G.A. side) 5.00

BATMAN UNSEEN
DC Comics: Early Dec, 2009 - No. 5, Feb, 2010 ($2.99, limited series)
1-5-Doug Moench-s/Kelley Jones-a/c. Black Mask app. 3.00

BATMAN VERSUS PREDATOR
DC Comics/Dark Horse Comics: 1991 - No. 3, 1992 ($4.95/$1.95, limited series) (1st DC/Dark Horse x-over)
1 (Prestige format, $4.95)-1 & 3 contain 8 Batman/Predator trading cards; Andy & Adam Kubert-a; Suydam painted-c 6.00
1-3 (Regular format, $1.95)-No trading cards 3.00
2,3-(Prestige)-2-Extra pin-ups inside; Suydam-c 5.00
TPB (1993, $5.95, 132 pgs.)-r/#1-3 w/new introductions & forward plus new wraparound-c by Dave Gibbons 6.00

BATMAN VERSUS PREDATOR II: BLOODMATCH
DC Comics: Late 1994 - No. 4, 1995 ($2.50, limited series)
1-4-Huntress app.; Moench scripts; Gulacy-a 3.00
TPB (1995, $6.95)-r/#1-4 7.00

BATMAN VS. THE INCREDIBLE HULK (See DC Special Series No. 27)

BATMAN: WAR ON CRIME
DC Comics: Nov, 1999 ($9.95, treasury size, one-shot)

Batman/Wildcat #3 © DC

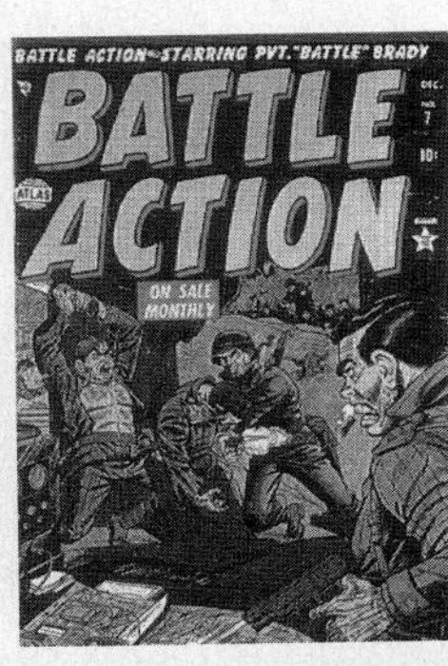

Battle Action #7 © ATLAS

Battlefield #4 © ATLAS

	GD 2.0	VG 4.0	FN 6.0	VF 8.0	VF/NM 9.0	NM- 9.2
nn-Painted art by Alex Ross; story by Alex Ross and Paul Dini						10.00

BATMAN/ WILDCAT
DC Comics: Apr, 1997 - No. 3, June, 1997 ($2.25, mini-series)

	GD 2.0	VG 4.0	FN 6.0	VF 8.0	VF/NM 9.0	NM- 9.2
1-3: Dixon/Smith-s: 1-Killer Croc app.						2.50

BATMAN: YEAR 100
DC Comics: 2006 - No. 4, 2006 ($5.99, squarebound, limited series)

	GD 2.0	VG 4.0	FN 6.0	VF 8.0	VF/NM 9.0	NM- 9.2
1-4-Paul Pope-s/a/c						6.00
TPB (2007, $19.99) r/series						20.00

BAT MASTERSON (TV) (Also see Tim Holt #28)
Dell Publishing Co.: Aug-Oct, 1959; Feb-Apr, 1960 - No. 9, Nov-Jan, 1961-62

	GD 2.0	VG 4.0	FN 6.0	VF 8.0	VF/NM 9.0	NM- 9.2
Four Color 1013 (#1) (8-10/59)	11	22	33	79	140	200
2-9: Gene Barry photo-c on all. 2,3,6-Two different back-c exist; variants have a comic strip on the back-c	7	14	21	45	73	100

BATS (See Tales Calculated to Drive You Bats)

BATS, CATS & CADILLACS
Now Comics: Oct, 1990 - No. 2, Nov, 1990 ($1.75)

	GD 2.0	VG 4.0	FN 6.0	VF 8.0	VF/NM 9.0	NM- 9.2
1,2: 1-Gustovich-a(i); Snyder-c						2.50

BAT-THING
DC Comics (Amalgam): June, 1997 ($1.95, one-shot)

	GD 2.0	VG 4.0	FN 6.0	VF 8.0	VF/NM 9.0	NM- 9.2
1-Hama-s/Damaggio & Sienkiewicz-a						2.50

BATTLE
Marvel/Atlas Comics(FPI #1-62/ Male #63 on): Mar, 1951 - No. 70, Jun, 1960

	GD 2.0	VG 4.0	FN 6.0	VF 8.0	VF/NM 9.0	NM- 9.2
1	34	68	102	199	325	450
2	18	36	54	105	165	225
3-10: 4-1st Buck Pvt. O'Toole. 10-Pakula-a	14	28	42	82	121	160
11-20: 11-Check-a	12	24	36	67	94	120
21,23-Krigstein-a	13	26	39	72	101	130
22,24-36: 32-Tuska-a. 36-Everett-a	10	20	30	58	79	100
37-Kubert-a (Last precode, 2/55)	11	22	33	62	86	110
38-40,42-48	10	20	30	56	76	95
41,49: 41-Kubert/Moskowitz-a. 49-Davis-a	11	22	33	60	83	105
50-54,56-58: 56-Colan-a; Ayers-a	10	20	30	54	72	90
55-Williamson-a (5 pgs.)	11	22	33	60	83	105
59-Torres-a	10	20	30	56	76	95
60-62: 60,62-Combat Kelly app. 61-Combat Casey app.	10	20	30	54	72	90
63-Ditko-a	15	30	45	83	124	165
64-66-Kirby-a. 66-Davis-a; has story of Fidel Castro in pre-Communism days (an admiring profile)	16	32	48	92	144	195
67,68: 67-Williamson/Crandall-a (4 pgs.); Kirby, Davis-a. 68-Kirby/Williamson-a (4 pgs.); Kirby/Ditko-a	16	32	48	94	147	200
69,70: 69-Kirby-a. 70-Kirby/Ditko-a	16	32	48	92	144	195

NOTE: ***Andru** a-37. **Berg** a-38, 14, 60-62. **Colan** a-19, 33, 55. **Everett** a-36, 50, 70; c-56, 57. **Heath** a-6, 9, 13, 31, 69; c-6, 9, 12, 26, 35, 37. **Kirby** c-64-69. **Maneely** a-4, 6, 31, 61; c-4, 22, 33, 48, 59, 61. **Orlando** a-47. **Powell** a-53, 55. **Reinman** a-4, 8-10, 14, 26, 32, 48. **Robinson** a-9, 39. **Romita** a-14, 26. **Severin** a-28, 32-34, 66-69; c-36, 50, 55. **Sinnott** a-33, 37, 63, 66. **Whitney** s-10.**Woodbridge** a-52, 55.*

BATTLE ACTION
Atlas Comics (NPI): Feb, 1952 - No. 12, 5/53; No. 13, 10/54 - No. 30, 8/57

	GD 2.0	VG 4.0	FN 6.0	VF 8.0	VF/NM 9.0	NM- 9.2
1-Pakula-a	26	52	78	154	252	350
2	15	30	45	85	130	175
3,4,6,7,9,10: 6-Robinson-c/a. 7-Partial nudity	11	22	33	60	83	105
5-Used in **POP**, pg. 93,94	11	22	33	62	86	110
8-Krigstein-a	11	22	33	64	90	115
11-15 (Last precode, 2/55)	10	20	30	58	79	100
16-30: 20-Romita-a. 22-Pakula-a. 27,30-Torres-a	10	20	30	54	72	90

NOTE: *Battle Brady app. 5-7, 10-12. **Berg** a-3. **Check** a-11. **Everett** a-7; c-13, 25. **Heath** a-3, 8, 18; c-3,15, 18, 21. **Maneely** a-1; c-5. **Reinman** a-1, 2, 20. **Robinson** a-6, 7; c-6. **Shores** a-7(2), 12, 20; c-11. **Sinnott** a-3, 27. **Woodbridge** a-28, 30.*

BATTLE ATTACK
Stanmor Publications: Oct, 1952 - No. 8, Dec, 1955

	GD 2.0	VG 4.0	FN 6.0	VF 8.0	VF/NM 9.0	NM- 9.2
1	14	28	42	76	108	140
2	8	16	24	44	57	70
3-8: 3-Hollingsworth-a	8	16	24	40	50	60

BATTLEAXES
DC Comics (Vertigo): May, 2000 - No. 4, Aug, 2000 ($2.50, limited series)

	GD 2.0	VG 4.0	FN 6.0	VF 8.0	VF/NM 9.0	NM- 9.2
1-4: Terry LaBan-s/Alex Horley-a						2.50

BATTLE BEASTS
Blackthorne Publishing: Feb, 1988 - No. 4, 1988 ($1.50/$1.75, B&W/color)

	GD 2.0	VG 4.0	FN 6.0	VF 8.0	VF/NM 9.0	NM- 9.2
1-4: 1-3- (B&W)-Based on Hasbro toys. 4-Color						2.50

BATTLE BRADY (Formerly Men in Action No. 1-9; see 3-D Action)
Atlas Comics (IPC): No. 10, Jan, 1953 - No. 14, June, 1953

	GD 2.0	VG 4.0	FN 6.0	VF 8.0	VF/NM 9.0	NM- 9.2
10: 10-12-Syd Shores-c	17	34	51	98	154	210
11-Used in **POP**, pg. 95 plus B&W & color illos	11	22	33	62	86	110
12-14	10	20	30	56	76	95

BATTLE CHASERS
Image Comics (Cliffhanger): Apr, 1998 - No. 4, Dec, 1998;
DC Comics (Cliffhanger): No. 5, May, 1999 - No. 8, May, 2001 ($2.50)
Image Comics: No. 9, Sept, 2001 ($3.50)

	GD 2.0	VG 4.0	FN 6.0	VF 8.0	VF/NM 9.0	NM- 9.2
Prelude (2/98)	1	3	4	6	8	10
Prelude Gold Ed.	1	3	4	6	8	10
1-Madureira & Sharrieff-s/Madureira-a(p)/Charest-c	1	2	3	5	7	9
1-American Ent. Ed. w/"racy" cover	1	3	4	6	8	10
1-Gold Edition						9.00
1-Chromium cover						40.00
1-2nd printing						3.00
2						5.00
2-Dynamic Forces BattleChrome cover	2	4	6	8	10	12
3-Red Monika cover by Madureira						4.00
4-8: 4-Four covers. 6-Back-up by Adam Warren-s/a. 7-Three covers (Madureira, Ramos, Campbell)						3.00
9-($3.50, Image) Flip cover/story by Adam Warren						3.50
...: A Gathering of Heroes HC ('99, $24.95) r/#1-5, Prelude, Frank Frazetta Fantasy Ill.; cover gallery						25.00
...: A Gathering of Heroes SC ('99, $14.95)						15.00
...Collected Edition 1,2 (11/98, 5/99, $5.95) 1-r/#1,2. 2-r/#3,4						6.00

BATTLE CLASSICS (See Cancelled Comic Cavalcade)
DC Comics: Sept-Oct, 1978 (44 pgs.)

	GD 2.0	VG 4.0	FN 6.0	VF 8.0	VF/NM 9.0	NM- 9.2
1-Kubert-r; new Kubert-c	2	4	6	8	10	12

BATTLE CRY
Stanmor Publications: 1952 (May) - No. 20, Sept, 1955

	GD 2.0	VG 4.0	FN 6.0	VF 8.0	VF/NM 9.0	NM- 9.2
1	15	30	45	90	140	190
2	10	20	30	56	76	95
3,5-10: 8-Pvt. Ike begins, ends #13,17	8	16	24	44	57	70
4-Classic E.C. swipe	9	18	27	52	69	85
11-20	8	16	24	40	50	60

NOTE: ***Hollingsworth** a-9; c-20.*

BATTLEFIELD (War Adventures on the...)
Atlas Comics (ACI): April, 1952 - No. 11, May, 1953

	GD 2.0	VG 4.0	FN 6.0	VF 8.0	VF/NM 9.0	NM- 9.2
1-Pakula, Reinman-a	22	44	66	128	209	290
2-5: 2-Heath, Maneely, Pakula, Reinman-a	14	28	42	76	108	140
6-11	10	20	30	58	79	100

NOTE: ***Colan** a-11. **Everett** a-8. **Heath** a-1, 2, 5p,7; c-2, 8, 9, 11. **Ravielli** a-11.*

BATTLEFIELD ACTION (Formerly Foreign Intrigues)
Charlton Comics: No. 16, Nov, 1957 - No. 62, 2-3/66; No. 63, 7/80 - No. 89, 11/84

	GD 2.0	VG 4.0	FN 6.0	VF 8.0	VF/NM 9.0	NM- 9.2
V2#16	8	16	24	44	57	70
17,20-30	6	12	18	27	33	38
18,19-Check-a (2 stories in #18)	3	6	9	21	32	42
31-62(1966)	3	6	9	16	22	28
63-80(1983-84)						5.00
81-83,85-89 (Low print run)	1	2	3	4	5	7
84-Kirby reprints; 3 stories	1	3	4	6	8	10

NOTE: ***Montes/Bache** a-43, 55, 62. **Glanzman** a-87r.*

BATTLEFIELDS
Dynamite Entertainment: (Limited series)

	GD 2.0	VG 4.0	FN 6.0	VF 8.0	VF/NM 9.0	NM- 9.2
...: Dear Billy 1-3 ('09 - No. 3, '09, $3.50) Ennis-s/Snejbjerg-a/Cassaday-c.1-Leach var-c						3.50
...: Happy Valley 1-3 ('09 - No. 3, '09, $3.50) Ennis-s/Holden-a/Leach-c						3.50
...: The Night Witches 1-3 ('08 - No. 3, '09, $3.50) Ennis-s/Braun-a/Cassaday-c; Russian female pilots in WW2. 1-Leach var-c						3.50
...: The Tankies 1-3 ('09 - No. 3, '09, $3.50) Ennis-s/Ezquerra-a/Cassaday-c.1-Leach var-c						3.50

BATTLE FIRE
Aragon Magazine/Stanmor Publications: Apr, 1955 - No. 7, 1955

	GD 2.0	VG 4.0	FN 6.0	VF 8.0	VF/NM 9.0	NM- 9.2
1	13	26	39	72	101	130
2	8	16	24	44	57	70
3-7	8	16	24	40	50	60

BATTLE FOR A THREE DIMENSIONAL WORLD
3D Cosmic Publications: May, 1983 (20 pgs., slick paper w/stiff-c, $3.00)

	GD 2.0	VG 4.0	FN 6.0	VF 8.0	VF/NM 9.0	NM- 9.2
nn-Kirby c/a in 3-D; shows history of 3-D	2	4	6	8	11	14

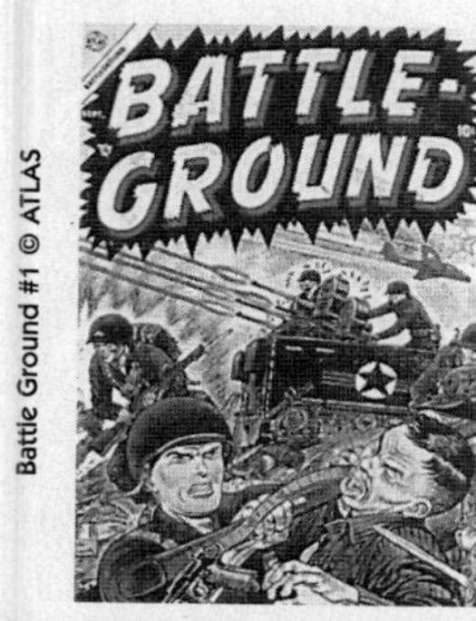

Battle Ground #1 © ATLAS

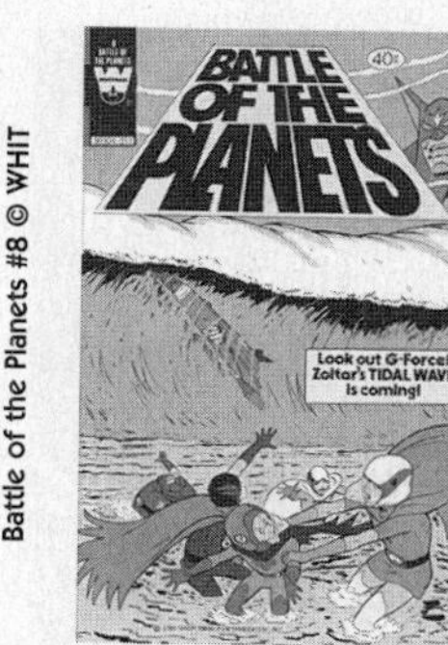

Battle of the Planets #8 © WHIT

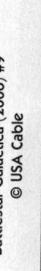

Battlestar Galactica (2006) #9 © USA Cable

GD VG FN VF VF/NM NM-
2.0 4.0 6.0 8.0 9.0 9.2

BATTLEFORCE
Blackthorne Publishing: Nov, 1987 - No. 2, 1988 ($1.75, color/B&W)
1,2: Based on game. 1-In color. 2-B&W 2.50

BATTLE FOR INDEPENDENTS, THE (Also See Cyblade/Shi & Shi/Cyblade: The Battle For Independents)
Image Comics (Top Cow Productions)/Crusade Comics: 1995 ($29.95)
nn-boxed set of all editions of Shi/Cyblade & Cyblade/Shi plus new variant. 3 6 9 20 30 40

BATTLE FOR THE PLANET OF THE APES (See Power Record Comics)

BATTLEFRONT
Atlas Comics (PPI): June, 1952 - No. 48, Aug, 1957
1-Heath-c 30 60 90 177 289 400
2-Robinson-a(4) 15 30 45 90 140 190
3-5-Robinson-a 14 28 42 80 115 150
6-10: Combat Kelly in No. 6-10. 6-Romita-a 12 24 36 67 94 120
11-22,24-28: 14,16-Battle Brady app. 22-Teddy Roosevelt & His Rough Riders story. 28-Last pre-code (2/55) 10 20 30 58 79 100
23,43-Check-a 11 22 33 60 83 105
29-39,41,44-47 10 20 30 54 72 90
40,42-Williamson-a 11 22 33 62 86 110
48-Crandall-a 10 20 30 58 79 100
NOTE: *Ayers a-19, 32, 35. Berg a-44. Colan a-21, 22, 32, 33, 35, 38, 40, 42. Drucker a-28, 29. Everett a-44. Heath c-23, 26, 27, 29, 32. Maneely a-22, 23, 26; c-2, 7, 13, 22, 34, 35, 41. Morisi a-42. Morrow a-41. Orlando a-47. Powell a-19, 21, 25, 29, 32, 40, 47. Robinson a-1-3, 4&5(4); c-4, 5. Robert Sale a-19. Severin a-32; c-40, 42, 45. Sinnott a-26; 48. Woodbridge a-45, 46.*

BATTLEFRONT
Standard Comics: No. 5, June, 1952
5-Toth-a 15 30 45 83 124 165

BATTLE GODS: WARRIORS OF THE CHAAK
Dark Horse Comics: Apr, 2000 - No. 4, July, 2000 ($2.95)
1-4-Francisco Ruiz Velasco-s/a 3.00

BATTLE GROUND
Atlas Comics (OMC): Sept, 1954 - No. 20, Aug, 1957
1 22 44 66 128 209 290
2-Jack Katz-a 14 28 42 78 112 145
3,4: 3-Jack Katz-a. 4-Last precode (3/55) 11 22 33 62 86 110
5-8,10 10 20 30 58 79 100
9,11,13,18: 9-Krigstein-a. 11,13,18-Williamson-a in each 12 24 36 67 94 120
12,15-17,19,20 10 20 30 54 72 90
14-Kirby-a 14 28 42 76 108 140
NOTE: *Ayers a-4, 13, 16. Colan a-3, 11, 13. Drucker a-7, 12, 13, 20. Heath c-2, 3, 5, 7, 13. Maneely a-3, 14, 19; c-1, 18, 19. Orlando a-17. Pakula a-11. Reinman a-2. Severin a-4, 5, 12, 19. c-20. Sinnott a-7, 16. Tuska a-11.*

BATTLE HEROES
Stanley Publications: Sept, 1966 - No. 2, Nov, 1966 (25¢, squarebound giants)
1 4 8 12 22 34 45
2 3 6 9 16 23 30

BATTLE HYMN
Image Comics: Jan, 2005 - No. 5, Oct, 2005 ($2.95/$2.99, limited series)
1-5-WW2 super team; B. Clay Moore-s/Jeremy Haun-a; flip cover on #1-4 3.00

BATTLE OF THE BULGE (See Movie Classics)

BATTLE OF THE PLANETS (Based on syndicated cartoon by Sandy Frank)
Gold Key/Whitman No. 6 on: 6/79 - No. 10, 12/80
1: Mortimer a-1-4,7-10 4 8 12 26 41 55
2-6,10 3 6 9 18 27 35
7-Low print run 5 10 15 32 51 70
8,9-Low print run: 8(11/80). 9-(3-pack only?) 4 8 12 28 44 60

BATTLE OF THE PLANETS (Also see Thundercats/...)
Image Comics (Top Cow): Aug, 2002 - No. 12, Sept, 2003 ($2.95/$2.99)
1-($2.95) Alex Ross-c & art director; Tortosa-a(p); re-intro. G-Force 3.00
1-($5.95) Holofoil-c by Ross 6.00
2-11-($2.99) Ross-c on all 3.00
12-($4.99) 5.00
#1/2 (7/03, $2.99) Benitez-c; Alex Ross sketch pages 3.00
... Battle Book 1 (5/03, $4.99) background info on characters, equipment, stories 5.00
... : Jason 1 (7/03, $4.99) Ross-c; Erwin David-a; preview of Tomb Raider: Epiphany 5.00
... : Mark 1 (5/03, $4.99) Ross-c; Erwin David-a; preview of BotP: Jason 5.00
.../Thundercats 1 (Image/WildStorm, 5/03, $4.99) 2 covers by Ross & Campbell 5.00

GD VG FN VF VF/NM NM-
2.0 4.0 6.0 8.0 9.0 9.2

.../Witchblade 1 (2/03, $5.95) Ross-c; Christina and Jo Chen-a 6.00
Vol. 1: Trial By Fire (2003, $7.99) r/#1-3 8.00
Vol. 2: Blood Red Sky (9/03, $16.95) r/#4-9 17.00
Vol. 3: Destroy All Monsters (11/03, $19.95) r/#10-12, ...: Jason, ...: Mark, .../Witchblade 20.00
Vol. 1: Digest (1/04, $9.99, 7-3/8x5", B&W) r/#1-9 & ...: Mark 10.00
Vol. 2: Digest (8/04, $9.99, B&W) r/#10-12, ...: Jason, ...: Manga #1-3, .../Witchblade 10.00

BATTLE OF THE PLANETS: MANGA
Image Comics (Top Cow): Nov, 2003 - No. 3, Jan, 2004 ($2.99, B&W)
1-3-Edwin David-a/David Wohl-s; previews for Wanted & Tomb Raider #35 3.00

BATTLE OF THE PLANETS: PRINCESS
Image Comics (Top Cow): Nov, 2004 - No. 6, May, 2005 ($2.99, B&W, limited series)
1-6-Tortosa-a/Wohl-s. 1-Ross-c. 2-Tortosa-c 3.00

BATTLE POPE
Image Comics: June, 2005 - No. 14, Apr, 2007 ($2.99/$3.50, reprints 2000 B&W series in color)
1-5-Kirkman-s/Moore-a 3.00
6-10,12-14-($3.50) 14-Wedding 3.50
11-($4.99) Christmas issue 5.00
... Vol. 1: Genesis TPB (2006, $12.95) r/#1-4; sketch pages 13.00
... Vol. 2: Mayhem TPB (2006, $12.99) r/#5-8; sketch pages 13.00
... Vol. 3: Pillow Talk TPB (2007, $12.99) r/#9-11; sketch pages 13.00

BATTLER BRITTON (British comics character who debuted in 1956)
DC Comics (WildStorm): Sept, 2006 - No. 5, Jan, 2007 ($2.99, limited series)
1-5-WWII fighter pilots; Garth Ennis-s/Colin Wilson-a 3.00
TPB (2007, $19.99) r/#1-5; background of the character's British origins in the 1950s 20.00

BATTLE REPORT
Ajax/Farrell Publications: Aug, 1952 - No. 6, June, 1953
1 12 24 36 67 94 120
2-6 8 16 24 40 50 60

BATTLE SQUADRON
Stanmor Publications: April, 1955 - No. 5, Dec, 1955
1 11 22 33 62 86 110
2-5: 3-Iwo Jima & flag-c 7 14 21 37 46 55

BATTLESTAR GALACTICA (TV) (Also see Marvel Comics Super Special #8)
Marvel Comics Group: Mar, 1979 - No. 23, Jan, 1981
1: 1-5 adapt TV episodes 2 4 6 8 11 14
2-23: 1-3-Partial-r 1 2 3 5 7 9
NOTE: *Austin c-9i, 10i. Golden c-18. Simonson a(p)-4, 5, 11-13, 15-20, 22, 23; c(p)-4, 5,11-17, 19, 20, 22, 23.*

BATTLESTAR GALACTICA (TV) (Also see Asylum)
Maximum Press: July, 1995 - No. 4, Nov, 1995 ($2.50, limited series)
1-4: Continuation of 1978 TV series 4.00
Trade paperback (12/95, $12.95)-reprints series 13.00

BATTLESTAR GALACTICA (1978 TV series)
Realm Press: Dec, 1997 - No. 5, July, 1998 ($2.99)
1-5-Chris Scalf-s/painted-a/c 3.00
...Search For Sanctuary (9/98, $2.99) Scalf & Kuhoric-s 3.00
...Search For Sanctuary Special (4/00, $3.99) Kuhoric-s/Scalf & Scott-a 4.00

BATTLESTAR GALACTICA (2003-2009 TV series)
Dynamite Entertainment: No. 0, 2006 - No. 12, 2007 (25¢/$2.99)
0-(25¢-c) Two covers; Pak-s/Raynor-a 2.25
1-($2.99) Covers by Turner, Tan, Raynor & photo-c; Pak-s/Raynor-a 3.00
2-12-Four covers on each 3.00
... Pegasus (2007, $4.99) story of Battlestar Pegasus & Admiral Cain; 2 covers 5.00
... Volume 1 HC (2007, $19.99) r/#0-4; cover gallery; Raynor sketch pages; commentary 20.00
... Volume 1 TPB (2007, $14.99) r/#0-4; cover gallery; Raynor sketch pages; commentary 15.00
... Volume 2 HC (2007, $19.99) r/#5-8; cover gallery; Raynor sketch pages 20.00
... Volume 2 TPB (2007, $14.99) r/#5-8; cover gallery; Raynor sketch pages 15.00

BATTLESTAR GALACTICA, (Classic...) (1978 TV series characters)
Dynamite Entertainment: 2006 - Present ($2.99)
1-5: 1-Two covers by Dorman & Caldwell; Rafael-a. 2-Two covers 3.00

BATTLESTAR GALACTICA: APOLLO'S JOURNEY (1978 TV series)
Maximum Press: Apr, 1996 - No. 3, June, 1996 ($2.95, limited series)
1-3: Richard Hatch scripts 4.00

BATTLESTAR GALACTICA: CYLON APOCALYPSE (1978 TV series characters)
Dynamite Entertainment: 2007 - No. 4, 2007 ($2.99, limited series)
1-4-Carlos Rafael-a; 4 covers on each 3.00
TPB (2007, $14.99) r/series with cover gallery 15.00

Battlestar Galactica: Origins #1 © USA Cable

Battle Stories #6 © FAW

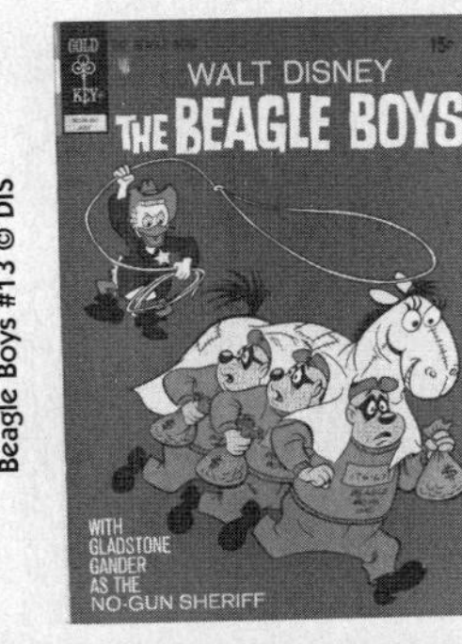

Beagle Boys #13 © DIS

	GD	VG	FN	VF	VF/NM	NM-
	2.0	4.0	6.0	8.0	9.0	9.2

BATTLESTAR GALACTICA: CYLON WAR (2003-2009 TV series)
Dynamite Entertainment: 2009 - No. 4, 2010 ($3.99, limited series)
1-3-First cylon war 40 years before the Caprica attack; Raynor-a; 2 covers 4.00

BATTLESTAR GALACTICA: GHOSTS (2003-2009 TV series)
Dynamite Entertainment: 2008 - No. 4, 2009 ($4.99, 40 pgs., limited series)
1-4-Intro. of the Ghost Squadron; Jerwa-s/Lau-a/Calero-c 5.00

BATTLESTAR GALACTICA: JOURNEY'S END (1978 TV series)
Maximum Press: Aug, 1996 - No. 4, Nov, 1996 ($2.99, limited series)
1-4-Continuation of the T.V. series 4.00

BATTLESTAR GALACTICA: ORIGINS (2003-2009 TV series)
Dynamite Entertainment: 2007 - No. 11, 2008 ($3.50)
1-11: 1-4-Baltar's origin; multiple covers. 5-8-Adama's origin. 9-11-Starbuck & Helo 3.50

BATTLESTAR GALACTICA: SEASON III
Realm Press: June/July, 1999 - No. 3, Sept, 1999 ($2.99)
1-3: 1-Kuhoric-s/Scalf & Scott-a; two covers by Scalf & Jae Lee. 2,3-Two covers 3.00
Gallery (4/00, $3.99) short story and pin-ups 4.00
1999 Tour Book (5/99, $2.99) 3.00
1999 Tour Book Convention Edition (6.99) 7.00
...Special: Centurion Prime (12/99, $3.99) Kuhoric-s 4.00

BATTLESTAR GALACTICA: SEASON ZERO (2003-2009 TV series)
Dynamite Entertainment: 2007 - No. 12, 2008 ($2.99)
1-12-Set 2 years before the Cylon attack; multiple covers 3.00

BATTLESTAR GALACTICA: SPECIAL EDITION (TV)
Maximum Press: Jan, 1997 ($2.99, one-shot)
1-Fully painted; Scalf-c/s/a; r/Asylum 3.00

BATTLESTAR GALACTICA: STARBUCK (TV)
Maximum Press: Dec, 1995 - No. 3, Mar, 1996 ($2.50, limited series)
1-3 4.00

BATTLESTAR GALACTICA: THE COMPENDIUM (TV)
Maximum Press: Feb, 1997 ($2.99, one-shot)
1 3.00

BATTLESTAR GALACTICA: THE ENEMY WITHIN (TV)
Maximum Press: Nov, 1995 - No. 3, Feb, 1996 ($2.50, limited series)
1-3: 3-Indicia reads Feb, 1995 in error. 4.00

BATTLESTAR GALACTICA: THE FINAL FIVE (2003 series)
Dynamite Entertainment: 2009 - No. 4, 2009 ($3.99, limited series)
1-4-Raynor-a; 2 covers on each 4.00

BATTLESTAR GALACTICA ZAREK (2003 series)
Dynamite Entertainment: 2007 - No. 4, 2007 ($3.50, limited series)
1-4-Origin story of political activist Tom Zarek; 2 covers on each 3.50

BATTLE STORIES (See XMas Comics)
Fawcett Publications: Jan, 1952 - No. 11, Sept, 1953

	GD	VG	FN	VF	VF/NM	NM-
1-Evans-a	16	32	48	92	144	195
2	10	20	30	56	76	95
3-11	9	18	27	47	61	75

BATTLE STORIES
Super Comics: 1963 - 1964

	GD	VG	FN	VF	VF/NM	NM-
Reprints #10-13,15-18: 10-r/U.S Tank Commandos #? 11-r/? 11, 12,17-r/Monty Hall #?; 13-Kintsler-a (1pg).15-r/American Air Forces #7 by Powell; Bolle-r. 18-U.S. Fighting Air Force #?	2	4	6	9	13	16

BATTLETECH (See Blackthorne 3-D Series #41 for 3-D issue)
Blackthorne Publishing: Oct, 1987 - No. 6, 1988 ($1.75/$2.00)
1-6: Based on game. 1-Color. 2-Begin B&W 3.00
Annual 1 ($4.50, B&W) 5.00

BATTLETECH
Malibu Comics: Feb, 1995 ($2.95)
0 3.00

BATTLETECH FALLOUT
Malibu Comics: Dec, 1994 - No. 4, Mar, 1995 ($2.95)
1-4-Two edi. exist #1; normal logo 3.00
1-Gold version w/foil logo stamped "Gold Limited Edition 8.00
1-Full-c holographic limited edition 6.00

BATTLETIDE (Death's Head II & Killpower...)
Marvel Comics UK, Ltd.: Dec, 1992 - No. 4, Mar, 1993 ($1.75, mini-series)
1-4: Wolverine, Psylocke, Dark Angel app. 2.50

BATTLETIDE II (Death's Head II & Killpower...)
Marvel Comics UK, Ltd.: Aug, 1993 - No. 4, Nov, 1993 ($1.75, mini-series)
1-($2.95)-Foil embossed logo 3.00
2-4: 2-Hulk-c/story 2.50

BAY CITY JIVE
DC Comics (WildStorm): Jul, 2001 - No. 3, Sept, 2001 ($2.95, limited series)
1-3: Intro Sugah Rollins in 1970s San Francisco; Layman-s/Johnson-a 3.00

BAYWATCH COMIC STORIES (TV) (Magazine)
Acclaim Comics (Armada): May, 1996 - No. 4, 1997 ($4.95) (Photo-c on all)
1-4: Photo comics based on TV show 5.00

BEACH BLANKET BINGO (See Movie Classics)

	GD	VG	FN	VF	VF/NM	NM-
	2.0	4.0	6.0	8.0	9.0	9.2

BEAGLE BOYS, THE (Walt Disney)(See The Phantom Blot)
Gold Key: 11/64; No. 2, 11/65; No. 3, 8/66 - No. 47, 2/79 (See WDC&S #134)

	GD	VG	FN	VF	VF/NM	NM-
1	5	10	15	32	51	70
2-5	3	6	9	18	27	35
6-10	3	6	9	16	22	28
11-20: 11,14,19-r	2	4	6	11	16	20
21-30: 27-r	2	4	6	8	11	14
31-47	1	3	4	6	8	10

BEAGLE BOYS VERSUS UNCLE SCROOGE
Gold Key: Mar, 1979 - No. 12, Feb, 1980

	GD	VG	FN	VF	VF/NM	NM-
1	2	4	6	9	13	16
2-12: 9-r	1	2	3	5	6	8

BEANBAGS
Ziff-Davis Publ. Co. (Approved Comics): Winter, 1951 - No. 2, Spring, 1952

	GD	VG	FN	VF	VF/NM	NM-
1,2	12	24	36	69	97	125

BEANIE THE MEANIE
Fago Publications: No. 3, May, 1959

	GD	VG	FN	VF	VF/NM	NM-
3	5	10	15	24	30	35

BEANY AND CECIL (TV) (Bob Clampett's...)
Dell Publishing Co.: Jan, 1952 - 1955; July-Sept, 1962 - No. 5, July-Sept, 1963

	GD	VG	FN	VF	VF/NM	NM-
Four Color 368	23	46	69	166	321	475
Four Color 414,448,477,530,570,635(1/55)	14	28	42	100	188	275
01-057-209 (#1)	13	26	39	94	175	255
2-5	10	20	30	68	119	170

BEAR COUNTRY (Disney)
Dell Publishing Co.: No. 758, Dec, 1956

	GD	VG	FN	VF	VF/NM	NM-
Four Color 758-Movie	5	10	15	34	55	75

BEAST (See X-Men)
Marvel Comics: May, 1997 - No. 3, 1997 ($2.50, mini-series)
1-3-Giffen-s/Nocon-a 3.00

BEAST BOY (See Titans)
DC Comics: Jan, 2000 - No. 4, Apr, 2000 ($2.95, mini-series)
1-4-Justiano-c/a; Raab & Johns-s 3.00

B.E.A.S.T.I.E.S. (Also see Axis Alpha)
Axis Comics: Apr, 1994 ($1.95)
1-Javier Saltares-c/a/scripts 2.50

BEASTS OF BURDEN
Dark Horse Comics: Sept, 2009 - No. 4, Dec, 2009 ($2.99, limited series)
1-4-Evan Dorkin-s/Jill Thompson-a/c 3.00

BEATLES, THE (See Girls' Romances #109, Go-Go, Heart Throbs #101, Herbie #5, Howard the Duck Mag. #4, Laugh #166, Marvel Comics Super Special #4, My Little Margie #54, Not Brand Echh, Strange Tales #130, Summer Love, Superman's Pal Jimmy Olsen #79, Teen Confessions #37, Tippy's Friends & Tippy Teen)

BEATLES, THE (Life Story)
Dell Publishing Co.: Sept-Nov, 1964 (35¢)

	GD	VG	FN	VF	VF/NM	NM-
1-(Scarce)-Stories with color photo pin-ups; Paul S. Newman-s	40	80	120	314	607	900

BEATLES EXPERIENCE, THE
Revolutionary Comics: Mar, 1991 - No. 8, 1991 ($2.50, B&W, limited series)
1-8: 1-Gold logo 5.00

BEATLES YELLOW SUBMARINE (See Movie Comics under Yellow...)

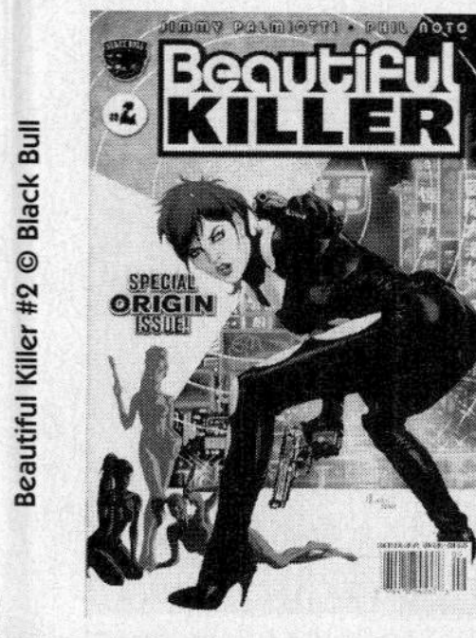

Beautiful Killer #2 © Black Bull

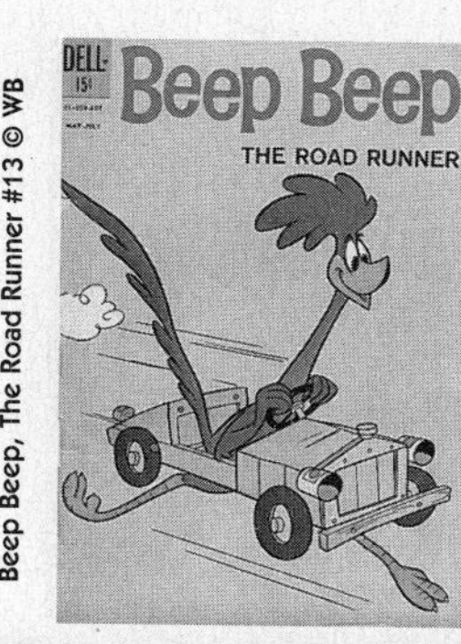

Beep Beep, The Road Runner #13 © WB

Beetle Bailey #70 © CC

	GD 2.0	VG 4.0	FN 6.0	VF 8.0	VF/NM 9.0	NM- 9.2

BEAUTIFUL KILLER
Black Bull Comics: Sept., 2002 - No. 3, Jan, 2003 ($2.99, limited series)

...Limited Preview Edition (5/02, $5.00) preview pgs. & creator interviews 5.00
1-Noto-a/Palmiotti-s; Hughes-c; intro Brigit Cole 3.00
2,3: 2-Jusko-c. 3-Noto-c 3.00
TPB (5/03, $9.99) r/#1-3; cover gallery and Adam Hughes sketch pages 10.00

BEAUTIFUL PEOPLE
Slave Labor Graphics: Apr, 1994 ($4.95, 8-1/2x11", one-shot)

nn 5.00

BEAUTIFUL STORIES FOR UGLY CHILDREN
DC Comics (Piranha Press): 1989 - No. 30, 1991 ($2.00/$2.50, B&W, mature)

Vol. 1-20: 12-$2.50-c begins 4.00
21-25 5.00
26-30-(Lower print run) 1 2 3 4 5 7
A Cotton Candy Autopsy ($12.95, B&W)-Reprints 1st two volumes 13.00

BEAUTY AND THE BEAST, THE
Marvel Comics Group: Jan, 1985 - No. 4, Apr, 1985 (limited series)

1-4: Dazzler & the Beast from X-Men; Sienkiewicz-c on all 3.00

BEAUTY AND THE BEAST (Graphic novel)(Also see Cartoon Tales & Disney's New Adventures of...)
Disney Comics: 1992

nn-($4.95, prestige edition)-Adapts animated film 7.00
nn-($2.50, newsstand edition) 3.00

BEAUTY AND THE BEAST
Disney Comics: Sept., 1992 - No. 2, 1992 ($1.50, limited series)

1,2 3.00

BEAUTY AND THE BEAST: PORTRAIT OF LOVE (TV)
First Comics: May, 1989 - No. 2, Mar, 1990 ($5.95, 60 pgs., squarebound)

1,2: 1-Based on TV show, Wendy Pini-a/scripts. 2-...: Night of Beauty; by Wendy Pini 6.00

BEAVER VALLEY (Movie)(Disney)
Dell Publishing Co.: No. 625, Apr, 1955

Four Color 625 6 12 18 41 66 90

BEAVIS AND BUTTHEAD (MTV's...)(TV cartoon)
Marvel Comics: Mar, 1994 - No. 28, June, 1996 ($1.95)

1-Silver ink-c. 1, 2-Punisher & Devil Dinosaur app. 4.00
1-2nd printing 2.50
2,3: 2-Wolverine app. 3-Man-Thing, Spider-Man, Venom, Carnage, Mary Jane & Stan Lee cameos; John Romita, Sr. art (2 pgs.) 2.50
4-28: 5-War Machine, Thor, Loki, Hulk, Captain America & Rhino cameos. 6-Psylocke, Polaris, Daredevil & Bullseye app. 7-Ghost Rider & Sub-Mariner app. 8-Quasar & Eon app. 9-Prowler & Nightwatch app. 11-Black Widow app. 12-Thunderstrike & Bloodaxe app. 13-Night Thrasher app. 14-Spider-Man 2099 app. 15-Warlock app. 16-X-Factor app. 25-Juggernaut app. 2.50

BECK & CAUL INVESTIGATIONS
Gauntlet Comics (Caliber): Jan, 1994 - No. 5, 1995? ($2.95, B&W)

1-5 3.00
Special 1 ($4.95) 5.00

BEDKNOBS AND BROOMSTICKS (See Walt Disney Showcase No. 6 & 50)

BEDLAM!
Eclipse Comics: Sept, 1985 - No. 2, Sept, 1985 (B&W-r in color)

1,2: Bissette-a 3.00

BEDTIME STORY (See Cinema Comics Herald)

BEELZELVIS
Slave Labor Graphics: Feb, 1994 ($2.95, B&W, one-shot)

1 3.00

BEEP BEEP, THE ROAD RUNNER (TV) (See Dell Giant Comics Bugs Bunny Vacation Funnies #8 for 1st app.) (Also see Daffy & Kite Fun Book)
Dell Publishing Co./Gold Key No. 1-88/Whitman No. 89 on: July, 1958 - No. 14, Aug-Oct, 1962; Oct, 1966 - No. 105, 1984

Four Color 918 (#1, 7/58) 11 22 33 78 139 200
Four Color 1008,1046 (11-1/59-60) 7 14 21 45 73 100
4(2-4/60)-14(Dell) 6 12 18 41 66 90
1(10/66, Gold Key) 6 12 18 41 66 90
2-5 4 8 12 26 41 55
6-14 3 6 9 19 29 38
15-18,20-40 3 6 9 16 22 28
19-With pull-out poster 4 8 12 24 37 50
41-50 2 4 6 13 18 22
51-70 2 4 6 9 12 15
71-88 2 3 4 6 8 10
89,90,94-101: 100(3/82), 101(4/82) 2 4 6 8 10 12
91(8/80), 92(9/80), 93 (3-pack?) (low printing) 4 8 12 22 34 45
102-105 (All #90189 on-c; nd or date code; pre-pack) 102(6/83), 103(7/83), 104(5/84), 105(6/84) 3 6 9 16 22 28
#63-2970 (Now Age Books/Pendulum Pub. Comic Digest, 1971, 75¢, 100 pages, B&W) collection of one-page gags 4 8 12 26 41 55

NOTE: *See March of Comics #351, 353, 375, 387, 397, 416, 430, 442, 455. #5, 8-10, 35, 53, 59-62, 68-r; 96-102, 104 are 1/3-r.*

BEETLE BAILEY (See Giant Comic Album, Sarge Snorkel; also Comics Reading Libraries in the Promotional Comics section)
Dell Publishing Co./Gold Key #39-53/King #54-66/Charlton #67-119/Gold Key #120-131/ Whitman #132: #459, 5/53 - #38, 5-7/62; #39, 11/62 - #53, 5/66; #54, 8/66 - #65, 12/67;#67, 2/69 - #119, 11/76; #120, 4/78 - #132, 4/80

Four Color 469 (#1)-By Mort Walker 11 22 33 78 139 200
Four Color 521,552,622 7 14 21 45 73 100
5(2-4/56)-10(5-7/57) 6 12 18 39 62 85
11-20(4-5/59) 4 8 12 28 44 60
21-38(5-7/62) 3 6 9 20 30 40
39-53(5/66) 3 6 9 17 25 32
54-65 (No. 66 publ. overseas only?) 3 6 9 16 22 28
67-69: 69-Last 12¢ issue 3 6 9 14 19 24
70-99 2 4 6 9 13 16
100 2 4 6 11 16 20
101-111,114-119 1 3 4 6 8 10
112,113-Byrne illos. (4 each) 2 4 6 9 12 18
120-132 1 2 3 4 5 7

BEETLE BAILEY
Harvey Comics: V2#1, Sept, 1992 - V2#9, Aug, 1994 ($1.25/$1.50)

V2#1 5.00
2-9-($1.50) 3.50
Big Book 1(11/92),2(5/93)(Both $1.95, 52 pgs.) 4.00
Giant Size V2#1(10/92),2(3/93)(Both $2.25,68 pgs.) 4.00

BEETLEJUICE (TV)
Harvey Comics: Oct, 1991 ($1.25)

1 3.50

BEETLEJUICE CRIMEBUSTERS ON THE HAUNT
Harvey Comics: Sept, 1992 - No. 3, Jan, 1993 ($1.50, limited series)

1-3 3.50

BEE 29, THE BOMBARDIER
Neal Publications: Feb, 1945

1-(Funny animal) 34 68 102 199 325 450

BEFORE THE FANTASTIC FOUR: BEN GRIMM AND LOGAN
Marvel Comics: July, 2000 - No. 3, Sept, 2000 ($2.99, limited series)

1-3-The Thing and Wolverine app.; Hama-s 3.00

BEFORE THE FANTASTIC FOUR: REED RICHARDS
Marvel Comics: Sept, 2000 - No. 3, Dec, 2000 ($2.99, limited series)

1-3-Peter David-s/Duncan Fegredo-c/a 3.00

BEFORE THE FANTASTIC FOUR: THE STORMS
Marvel Comics: Dec, 2000 - No. 3, Feb, 2001 ($2.99, limited series)

1-3-Adlard-a 3.00

BEHIND PRISON BARS
Realistic Comics (Avon): 1952

1-Kinstler-c 32 64 96 188 307 425

BEHOLD THE HANDMAID
George Pflaum: 1954 (Religious) (25¢ with a 20¢ sticker price)

nn 6 12 18 31 38 45

BELIEVE IT OR NOT (See Ripley's...)

BELLE STARR: QUEEN OF BANDITS
Moonstone: 2005 - Present ($2.95, B&W)

1,2-Ricketts-s/Buccallato-a/Beck-c 3.00

BEN AND ME (Disney)
Dell Publishing Co.: No. 539, Mar, 1954

Ben Casey #2 © DELL

Berserker #3 © TCOW

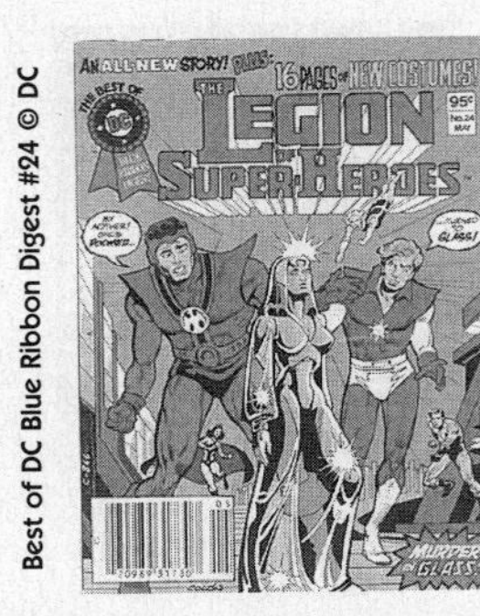

Best of DC Blue Ribbon Digest #24 © DC

	GD 2.0	VG 4.0	FN 6.0	VF 8.0	VF/NM 9.0	NM- 9.2
Four Color 539	4	8	12	26	41	55

BEN BOWIE AND HIS MOUNTAIN MEN
Dell Publishing Co.: 1952 - No. 17, Nov-Jan, 1958-59

Four Color 443 (#1) 9 18 27 60 100 140
Four Color 513,557,599,626,657 5 10 15 32 51 70
7(5-7/56)-11: 11-Intro/origin Yellow Hair 4 8 12 26 41 55
12-17 4 8 12 24 37 50

BEN CASEY (TV)
Dell Publishing Co.: June-July, 1962 - No. 10, June-Aug, 1965 (Photo-c)

12-063-207 (#1) 6 12 18 41 66 90
2(10/62),3,5-10 4 8 12 24 37 50
4-Marijuana & heroin use story 4 8 12 28 44 60

BEN CASEY FILM STORIES (TV)
Gold Key: Nov, 1962 (25¢) (Photo-c)

30009-211-All photos 7 14 21 45 73 100

BENEATH THE PLANET OF THE APES (See Movie Comics & Power Record Comics)

BEN FRANKLIN (See Kite Fun Book)

BEN HUR
Dell Publishing Co.: No. 1052, Nov, 1959

Four Color 1052-Movie, Manning-a 10 20 30 67 116 165

BEN ISRAEL
Logos International: 1974 (39¢)

nn-Christian religious 2 4 6 10 14 18

BEOWULF (Also see First Comics Graphic Novel #1)
National Periodical Publications: Apr-May, 1975 - No. 6, Feb-Mar, 1976

1 2 4 6 8 11 14
2,3,5,6: 5-Flying saucer-c/story 1 2 3 5 6 8
4-Dracula-c/s 1 2 3 5 7 9

BERNI WRIGHTSON, MASTER OF THE MACABRE
Pacific Comics/Eclipse Comics No. 5: July, 1983 - No. 5, Nov, 1984 ($1.50, Baxter paper)

1-5: Wrightson-c/a(r). 4-Jeff Jones-r (11 pgs.) 6.00

BERRYS, THE (Also see Funny World)
Argo Publ.: May, 1956

1-Reprints daily & Sunday strips & daily Animal Antics by Ed Nofziger
6 12 18 29 36 42

BERZERKER (Milo Ventimiglia Presents...)
Image Comics (Top Cow): No. 0, Feb, 2009 - Present ($2.99)

0-4-Jeremy Haun-a/Rick Loverd-s/Dale Keown-c. 0-Creator interviews 3.00

BERZERKERS (See Youngblood V1#2)
Image Comics (Extreme Studios): Aug, 1995 - No. 3, Oct, 1995 ($2.50, limited series)

1-3: Beau Smith scripts, Fraga-a 2.50

BEST COMICS
Better Publications: Nov, 1939 - No. 4, Feb, 1940(10-11/16" wide x 8" tall, reads sideways)

1-(Scarce)-Red Mask begins(1st app.) & c/s-all 87 174 261 553 952 1350
2-4: 4-Cannibalism story 48 96 144 302 514 725

BEST FROM BOY'S LIFE, THE
Gilberton Company: Oct, 1957 - No. 5, Oct, 1958 (35¢)

1-Space Conquerors & Kam of the Ancient Ones begin, end #5; Bob Cousy photo/story
13 26 39 72 101 130
2,3,5 8 16 24 42 54 65
4-L.B. Cole-a 8 16 24 44 57 70

BEST LOVE (Formerly Sub-Mariner Comics No. 32)
Marvel Comics (MPI): No. 33, Aug, 1949 - No. 36, April, 1950 (Photo-c 33-36)

33-Kubert-a 14 28 42 81 118 155
34 10 20 30 54 72 90
35,36-Everett-a 11 22 33 60 83 105

BEST OF ARCHIE, THE
Perigee Books: 1980 ($7.95, softcover TPB)

nn-Intro by Michael Uslan & Jeffrey Mendel 6 12 18 37 59 80

BEST OF BUGS BUNNY, THE
Gold Key: Oct, 1966 - No. 2, Oct, 1968

1,2-Giants 4 8 12 28 44 60

BEST OF DC, THE (Blue Ribbon Digest) (See Limited Coll. Ed. C-52)
DC Comics: Sept-Oct, 1979 - No. 71, Apr, 1986 (100-148 pgs; mostly reprints)

1-Superman, w/"Death of Superman"-r 2 4 6 11 16 20
2,5-9: 2-Batman 40th Ann. Special. 5-Best of 1979. 6,8-Superman. 7-Superboy. 9-Batman, Creeper app.
2 4 6 8 10 12
3-Superfriends 2 4 6 9 12 15
4-Rudolph the Red Nosed Reindeer 2 4 6 9 13 16
10-Secret Origins of Super Villains; 1st ever Penguin origin-s
3 6 9 16 22 28
11-16,18-20: 11-The Year's Best Stories. 12-Superman Time and Space Stories.13-Best of DC Comics Presents. 14-New origin stories of Batman villains. 15-Superboy. 16-Superman Anniv. 18-Teen Titans new-s., Adams, Kane-a; Perez-c. 19-Superman. 20-World's Finest
1 2 3 5 7 9
17-Supergirl 2 4 6 8 10 12
21,22: 21-Justice Society. 22-Christmas; unpublished Sandman story w/Kirby-a
2 4 6 10 14 18
23-27: 23-(148 pgs.)-Best of 1981. 24 Legion, new story and 16 pgs. new costumes. 25-Superman. 26-Brave & Bold. 27-Superman vs. Luthor
2 4 6 9 12 15
28,29: 28-Binky, Sugar & Spike app. 29-Sugar & Spike, 3 new stories; new Stanley & his Monster story
2 4 6 9 13 16
30,32-36,38,40: 30-Detective Comics. 32-Superman. 33-Secret origins of Legion Heroes and Villains. 34-Metal Men; has #497 on-c from Adv. Comics. 35-The Year's Best Comics Stories (148 pgs.). 36-Superman vs. Kryptonite. 38-Superman. 40-World of Krypton
2 4 6 9 12 15
31-JLA 2 4 6 10 14 18
37,39: 37-"Funny Stuff", Mayer-a. 39-Binky 2 4 6 10 14 18
41,43,45,47,49,53,55,58,60,63,65,68,70: 41-Sugar & Spike new stories with Mayer-a. 43,49,55-Funny Stuff. 45,53,70-Binky. 47,65,68-Sugar & Spike. 58-Super Jrs. Holiday Special; Sugar & Spike. 60-Plop!; Wood-c(r) & Aragonés-r (5/85). 63-Plop!; Wrightson-a(r)
3 6 9 14 19 24
42,44,46,48,50-52,54,56,57,59,61,62,64,66,67,69,71: 42,56-Superman vs. Aliens. 44,57,67-Superboy & LSH. 46-Jimmy Olsen. 48-Superman Team-ups. 50-Year's best Superman. 51-Batman Family. 52 Best of 1984. 54,56,59-Superman. 61-(148 pgs.)Year's best. 62-Best of Batman 1985. 69-Year's best Team stories. 71-Year's best
2 4 6 10 14 18

NOTE: ***N. Adams*** *a-2r, 14r, 18r, 26, 51.* ***Aparo*** *a-9, 14, 26, 30; c-9, 14, 26.* ***Austin*** *a-51i.* ***Buckler*** *a-40p; c-16, 22.* ***Giffen*** *a-50, 52; c-33p.* ***Grell*** *a-33p.* ***Grossman*** *a-37.* ***Heath*** *a-26.* ***Infantino*** *a-10r, 18.* ***Kaluta*** *a-40.* ***G. Kane*** *a-10r, 18r; c-40, 44.* ***Kubert*** *a-10r, 21, 26.* ***Layton*** *a-21.* ***S. Mayer*** *c-29, 37, 41, 43, 47; a-28, 29, 37, 41, 43, 47, 58, 65, 68.* ***Moldoff*** *c-64p.* ***Morrow*** *a-40; c-40.* ***W. Mortimer*** *a-39p.* ***Newton*** *a-5, 51.* ***Perez*** *a-24, 50p; c-18, 21, 23.* ***Rogers*** *a-14, 51p.* ***Simonson*** *a-11r.* ***Spiegle*** *a-52.* ***Starlin*** *a-51.* ***Staton*** *a-5, 21.* ***Tuska*** *a-24.* ***Wolverton*** *a-60.* ***Wood*** *a-60, 63; c-60, 63.* ***Wrightson*** *a-60. New art in #14, 18, 24.*

BEST OF DENNIS THE MENACE, THE
Hallden/Fawcett Publications: Summer, 1959 - No. 5, Spring, 1961 (100 pgs.)

1-All reprints; Wiseman-a 7 14 21 45 73 100
2-5 4 8 12 28 44 60

BEST OF DONALD DUCK, THE
Gold Key: Nov, 1965 (12¢, 36 pgs.)(Lists 2nd printing in indicia)

1-Reprints Four Color #223 by Barks 8 16 24 54 90 125

BEST OF DONALD DUCK & UNCLE SCROOGE, THE
Gold Key: Nov, 1964 - No. 2, Sept, 1967 (25¢ Giants)

1(30022-411)('64)-Reprints 4-Color #189 & 408 by Carl Barks; cover of F.C. #189 redrawn by Barks
9 18 27 63 107 150
2(30022-709)('67)-Reprints 4-Color #256 & "Seven Cities of Cibola" & U.S. #8 by Barks
8 16 24 52 86 120

BEST OF HORROR AND SCIENCE FICTION COMICS
Bruce Webster: 1987 ($2.00)

1-Wolverton, Frazetta, Powell, Ditko-r 5.00

BEST OF JOSIE AND THE PUSSYCATS
Archie Comics: 2001 ($10.95, TPB)

1-Reprints 1st app. and noteworthy stories 12.00

BEST OF MARMADUKE, THE
Charlton Comics: 1960

1-Brad Anderson's strip reprints 3 6 9 20 30 40

BEST OF MS. TREE, THE
Pyramid Comics: 1987 - No. 4, 1988 ($2.00, B&W, limited series)

1-4 2.50

BEST OF RAY BRADBURY, THE
ibooks: 2003 ($18.95, TPB)

The Graphic Novel - Reprints from Ray Bradbury Comics; adaptations by various 19.00

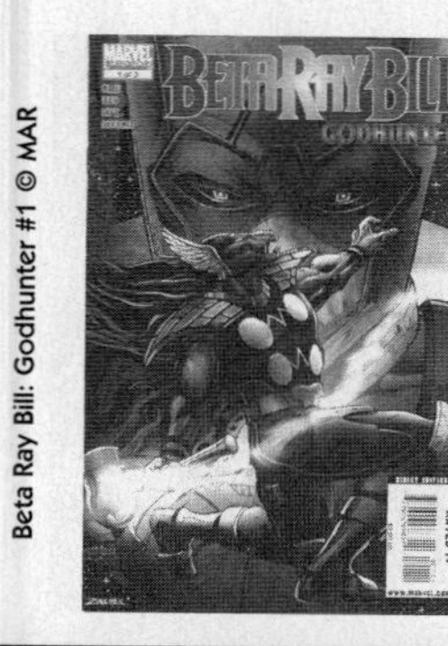
Beta Ray Bill: Godhunter #1 © MAR

Bettie Page: Queen of the Nile #3 © J. Silke

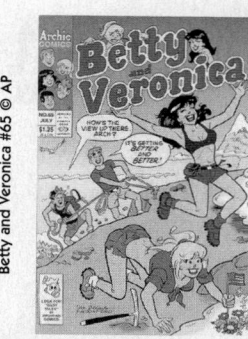

Betty and Veronica #65 © AP

	GD 2.0	VG 4.0	FN 6.0	VF 8.0	VF/NM 9.0	NM- 9.2

BEST OF THE BRAVE AND THE BOLD, THE (See Super DC Giant)
DC Comics: Oct, 1988 - No. 6, Jan, 1989 ($2.50, limited series)
1-6: Neal Adams-r, Kubert-r & Heath-r in all 4.00

BEST OF THE SPIRIT, THE
DC Comics: 2005 ($14.99, TPB)
nn-Reprints 1st app. and noteworthy stories; intro by Neil Gaiman; Eisner bio. 15.00

BEST OF THE WEST (See A-1 Comics)
Magazine Enterprises: 1951 - No. 12, April-June, 1954
1(A-1 42)-Ghost Rider, Durango Kid, Straight Arrow, Bobby Benson begin
41 82 123 256 428 600
2(A-1 46) 22 44 66 128 209 290
3(A-1 52), 4(A-1 59), 5(A-1 66) 18 36 54 105 165 225
6(A-1 70), 7(A-1 76), 8(A-1 81), 9(A-1 85), 10(A-1 87), 11(A-1 97),
12(A-1 103) 15 30 45 84 127 170
NOTE: *Bolle a-9. Borth a-12. Guardineer a-5, 12. Powell a-1, 12.*

BEST OF UNCLE SCROOGE & DONALD DUCK, THE
Gold Key: Nov, 1966 (25¢)
1(30030-611)-Reprints part 4-Color #159 & 456 & Uncle Scrooge #6,7 by Carl Barks
8 16 24 52 86 120

BEST OF WALT DISNEY COMICS, THE
Western Publishing Co.: 1974 ($1.50, 52 pgs.) (Walt Disney)
(8-1/2x11" cardboard covers; 32,000 printed of each)
96170-Reprints 1st two stories less 1 pg. each from 4-Color #62
6 12 18 41 66 90
96171-Reprints Mickey Mouse and the Bat Bandit of Inferno Gulch from 1934
(strips) by Gottfredson 6 12 18 41 66 90
96172-r/Uncle Scrooge #386 & two other stories 6 12 18 41 66 90
96173-Reprints "Ghost of the Grotto" (from 4-Color #159) & "Christmas on
Bear Mountain" (from 4-Color #178) 6 12 18 41 66 90

BEST ROMANCE
Standard Comics (Visual Editions): No. 5, Feb-Mar, 1952 - No. 7, Aug, 1952
5-Toth-a; photo-c 14 28 42 80 115 150
6,7-Photo-c 9 18 27 47 61 75

BEST SELLER COMICS (See Tailspin Tommy)

BEST WESTERN (Formerly Terry Toons? or Miss America Magazine
Marvel Comics (IPC): V7#24(#57)?; Western Outlaws & Sheriffs No. 60 on)
No. 58, June, 1949 - No. 59, Aug, 1949
58,59-Black Rider, Kid Colt, Two-Gun Kid app.; both have Syd Shores-c
20 40 60 115 185 255

BETA RAY BILL: GODHUNTER
Marvel Comics: Aug, 2009 - No. 3, Oct, 2009 ($3.99, limited series)
1-3-Kano-a; Thor and Galactus app.; reprints form Thor #337-339. 2,3-Silver Surfer app. 4.00

BETTIE PAGE COMICS
Dark Horse Comics: Mar, 1996 ($3.95)
1-Dave Stevens-c; Blevins & Heath-a; Jaime Hernandez pin-up
1 2 3 5 6 8

BETTIE PAGE COMICS: QUEEN OF THE NILE
Dark Horse Comics: Dec, 1999 - No. 3, Apr, 2000 ($2.95, limited series)
1-3-Silke-s/a; Stevens-c 4.00

BETTIE PAGE COMICS: SPICY ADVENTURE
Dark Horse Comics: Jan, 1997 ($2.95, one-shot, mature)
nn-Silke-c/s/a 5.00

BETTY (See Pep Comics #22 for 1st app.)
Archie Comics: Sept, 1992 - Present ($1.25-$2.50)
1 5.00
2-18,20-24: 20-1st Super Sleuther-s 3.00
19-Love Showdown part 2 5.00
25-Pin-up page of Betty as Marilyn Monroe, Madonna, Lady Di 5.00
26-50 3.00
51-185: 57- "A Storm Over Uniforms" x-over part 5,6. 179-Begin $2.50-c 2.50

BETTY AND HER STEADY (Going Steady with Betty No. 1)
Avon Periodicals: No. 2, Mar-Apr, 1950
2 10 20 30 56 76 95

BETTY AND ME
Archie Publications: Aug, 1965 - No. 200, Aug, 1992
1 10 20 30 68 119 170
2,3: 3-Origin Superteen 6 12 18 39 62 85
4-8: Superteen in new costume #4-7; dons new helmet in #5,
ends #8. 4 8 12 28 44 60
9,10: Girl from R.I.V.E.R.D.A.L.E. 9-UFO-s 4 8 12 22 34 45
11-15,17-20(4/69) 3 6 9 18 27 35
16-Classic cover; w/risqué cover dialogue 4 8 12 28 44 60
21,24-35: 33-Paper doll page 3 6 9 16 22 28
22-Archies Band-s 3 6 9 16 23 30
23-I Dream of Jeannie parody 3 6 9 18 27 35
36(8/71),37,41-55 (52 pgs.): 42-Betty as vamp-s 3 6 9 16 22 28
38-Sabrina app. 4 8 12 22 34 45
39-Josie and Sabrina cover cameos 3 6 9 18 27 35
40-Archie & Betty share a cabin 3 6 9 16 23 30
56(4/71)-80(12/76): 79 Betty Cooper mysteries thru #86. 79-81-Drago the Vampire-s
2 4 6 9 12 15
81-99: 83-Harem-c. 84-Jekyll & Hyde-c/s 2 4 6 8 10 12
100(3/79) 2 4 6 9 12 15
101,118: 101-Elvis mentioned. 118-Tarzan mentioned 1 2 3 5 7 9
102-117,119-130(9/82): 103,104-Space-s. 124-DeCarlo-c begins 7.00
131-138,140,142-147,149-154,156-158: 135,136-Jason Blossom app. 136-Cheryl Blossom
cameo. 137-Space-s. 138-Tarzan parody 5.00
139,141,148: 139-Katy Keene collecting-s; Archie in drag-s. 141-Tarzan parody-s.
148-Cyndi Lauper parody-s 6.00
155,159,160(8/87): 155-Archie in drag-s. 159-Superhero gag-c. 160-Wheel of Fortune parody
6.00
161-169,171-199 4.00
170,200: 170-New Archie Superhero-s 6.00

BETTY AND VERONICA (Also see Archie's Girls...)
Archie Enterprises: June, 1987 - Present (75¢-$2.50)
1 2 3 4 6 8 10
2-10 6.00
11-30 4.00
31-50 3.00
51-81 2.50
82-Love Showdown part 3 5.00
83-246: 242-Begin $2.50-c 2.50
NOTE: *2005 Free Comic Book Day edition is listed in Promotional Comics section.*

BETTY & VERONICA ANNUAL DIGEST (...Digest Magazine #1-4, 44 on; ...Comics Digest
Mag. #5-43)
Archie Publications: Nov, 1980 - Present ($1.00/-$2.69, digest size)
1 3 6 9 16 22 28
2-10: 2(11/81-Katy Keene story), 3(8/82) 2 4 6 9 13 16
11-30 1 3 4 6 8 10
31-50 1 2 3 4 5 7
51-70 4.00
71-191: 110-Begin $2.19-c. 135-Begin $2.39-c. 165-Begin $2.49. 185-Includes reprint of
Archie's Girls B&V #1 (1950) and new story where 1950 & 2008 B&V meet 2.50
192-204: 192-Begin $2.69-c 2.69

BETTY & VERONICA ANNUAL DIGEST MAGAZINE
Archie Comics: Sept, 1989 - No. 16, Aug, 1997 ($1.50/$1.75/$1.79, 128 pgs.)
1 1 2 3 5 7 9
2-10: 9-Neon ink logo 5.00
11-16: 16-Begin $1.79-c 3.00

BETTY & VERONICA CHRISTMAS SPECTACULAR (See Archie Giant Series Magazine #159, 168, 180, 191, 204, 217, 229, 241, 453, 465, 477, 489, 501, 513, 525, 536, 547, 558, 568, 580, 593, 606, 618)

BETTY & VERONICA DOUBLE DIGEST MAGAZINE
Archie Enterprises: 1987 - Present ($2.25-$3.99, digest size, 256 pgs.)(...Digest #12 on)
1 2 4 6 8 10 12
2-10 1 2 3 4 5 7
11-25: 5,17-Xmas-c. 16-Capt. Hero story 5.00
26-50 4.00
51-150: 87-Begin $3.19-c. 95-Begin $3.29-c. 114-Begin $3.59-c. 142-Begin $3.69-c 3.75
151-181: 151-(7/07)-Realistic style Betty & Veronica debuts (thru #154). 160-Cheryl Blossom
spotlight. 170-173-Realistic style 4.00
Betty & Veronica: in Bad Boy Trouble Vol.1 TPB (2007, $7.49) r/new style from #151-154 8.00

BETTY & VERONICA SPECTACULAR (See Archie Giant Series Mag. #11, 16, 21, 26, 32, 138, 145, 153, 162, 173, 184, 197, 201, 210, 214, 221, 226, 234, 238, 246, 250, 458, 462, 470, 482, 486, 494, 498, 506, 510, 518, 522, 526, 530, 537, 552, 559, 563, 569, 575, 582, 588, 600, 608, 613, 620, 623, and Betty & Veronica)

BETTY AND VERONICA SPECTACULAR
Archie Comics: Oct, 1992 - No. 90, Sept, 2009 ($1.25/$1.50/$1.75/$1.99/$2.19/$2.25/$2.50)

Beverly Hillbillies #18 © CBS

Beware #13(#1) © Trojan

Beware the Creeper (2003 series) #5 © DC

	GD	VG	FN	VF	VF/NM	NM-
	2.0	4.0	6.0	8.0	9.0	9.2

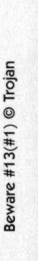

1-Dan DeCarlo-c/a 5.00
2-20 3.00
21-90: 48-Cheryl Blossom leaves Riverdale. 64-Cheryl Blossom returns 2.50

BETTY & VERONICA SPRING SPECTACULAR (See Archie Giant Series Magazine #569, 582, 595)

BETTY & VERONICA SUMMER FUN (See Archie Giant Series Mag. #8, 13, 18, 23, 28, 34, 140, 147, 155, 164, 175, 187, 199, 212, 224, 236, 248, 460, 484, 496, 508, 520, 529, 539, 550, 561, 572, 585, 598, 611, 621)
Archie Comics: 1994 - Present ($2.00/$2.25/$2.29)

1-6: 1-($2.00, 52 pgs. plus poster). 5-($2.25-c). 6-($2.29-c) 3.00
Vol. 1 (2003, $10.95) reprints stories from Archie Giant Series editions 12.00

BETTY BOOP'S BIG BREAK
First Publishing: 1990 ($5.95, 52 pgs.)

nn-By Joshua Quagmire; 60th anniversary ish. 6.00

BETTY PAGE 3-D COMICS
The 3-D Zone: 1991 ($3.95, "7-1/2x10-1/4," 28 pgs., no glasses)

1-Photo inside covers; back-c nudity 2 3 4 6 8 10

BETTY'S DIARY (See Archie Giant Series Magazine No. 555)
Archie Enterprises: April, 1986 - No. 40, Apr, 1991 (#1:65¢; 75¢/95¢)

1 1 2 3 4 5 7
2-10 4.00
11-40 2.50

BETTY'S DIGEST
Archie Enterprises: Nov, 1996 - No. 2 ($1.75/$1.79)

1,2 3.00

BEVERLY HILLBILLIES (TV)
Dell Publishing Co.: 4-6/63 - No. 18, 8/67; No. 19, 10/69; No. 20, 10/70; No. 21, Oct, 1971

1-Photo-c 14 28 42 101 191 280
2-Photo-c 9 18 27 60 100 140
3-9: All have photo covers 7 14 21 47 76 105
10: No photo cover 5 10 15 32 51 70
11-21: All have photo covers. 18-Last 12¢ issue. 19-21-Reprint #1-3 (covers and insides) 6 12 18 37 59 80

NOTE: *#1-9, 11-21 are photo covers.*

BEWARE (Formerly Fantastic; Chilling Tales No. 13 on)
Youthful Magazines: No. 10, June, 1952 - No. 12, Oct, 1952

10-E.A. Poe's Pit & the Pendulum adaptation by Wildey; Harrison/Bache-a; atom bomb and shrunken head-c 58 116 174 371 636 900
11-Harrison-a; Ambrose Bierce adapt. 39 78 117 231 378 525
12-Used in **SOTI**, pg. 388; Harrison-a 39 78 117 231 378 525

BEWARE
Trojan Magazines/Merit Publ. No. ?: No. 13, 1/53 - No. 16, 7/53; No. 5, 9/53 - No. 15, 5/55

13(#1)-Harrison-a 56 112 168 356 616 875
14(#2, 3/53)-Krenkel/Harrison-c; dismemberment, severed head panels 39 78 117 231 378 525
15,16(#3, 5/53; #4, 7/53)-Harrison-a 34 68 102 204 332 460
5,9,12,13 34 68 102 199 325 450
6-Ill. in **SOTI**- "Children are first shocked and then desensitized by all this brutality." Corpse on cover swipe/V.O.H. #26; girl on cover swipe/Advs. Into Darkness #10 62 124 186 394 677 960
7,8-Check-a 34 68 102 204 332 460
10-Frazetta/Check-c; Disbrow, Check-a 71 142 213 454 777 1100
11-Disbrow-a; heart torn out, blood drainage 39 78 117 231 378 525
14,15: 14-Myron Fass-c. 15-Harrison-a 28 56 84 165 270 375

NOTE: ***Fass** a-5, 6, 8; c-6, 11, 14. **Forte** a-8. **Hollingsworth** a-15(#3), 16(#4), 9; c-16(#4), 8, 9. **Kiefer** a-16(#4), 5, 6, 10.*

BEWARE (Becomes Tomb of Darkness No. 9 on)
Marvel Comics Group: Mar, 1973 - No. 8, May, 1974 (All reprints)

1-Everett-c; Kirby & Sinnott-r ('54) 3 6 9 17 25 32
2-8: 2-Forte, Colan-r. 6-Tuska-a. 7-Torres-r/Mystical Tales #7 2 4 6 11 16 20

NOTE: ***Infantino** a-4r. **Gil Kane** c-4. **Wildey** a-7r.*

BEWARE TERROR TALES
Fawcett Publications: May, 1952 - No. 8, July, 1953

1-E.C. art swipe/Haunt of Fear #5 & Vault of Horror #26 47 94 141 298 504 710
2 32 64 96 188 307 425
3-5,7 26 52 78 154 252 350
6-Classic skeleton-c 28 56 84 165 270 375
8-Tothish-a; people being cooked-c 32 64 96 188 307 425

NOTE: ***Andru** a-2. **Bernard Bailey** a-1; c-1-5. **Powell** a-1, 2, 8. **Sekowsky** a-2.*

BEWARE THE CREEPER (See Adventure, Best of the Brave & the Bold, Brave & the Bold, 1st Issue Special, Flash #318-323, Showcase #73, World's Finest Comics #249)
National Periodical Publications: May-June, 1968 - No. 6, Mar-Apr, 1969 (All 12¢ issues)

1-(5-6/68)-Classic Ditko-c; Ditko-a in all 9 18 27 63 107 150
2-6: 2-5-Ditko-c. 2-Intro. Proteus. 6-Gil Kane-c 5 10 15 34 55 75

BEWARE THE CREEPER
DC Comics (Vertigo): June, 2003 - No. 5, Oct, 2003 ($2.95, limited series)

1-5-Female vigilante in 1920s Paris; Jason Hall-s/Cliff Chiang-a 3.00

BEWITCHED (TV)
Dell Publishing Co.: 4-6/65 - No. 11, 10/67; No. 12, 10/68 - No. 13, 1/69; No. 14, 10/69

1-Photo-c 14 28 42 100 188 275
2-No photo-c 8 16 24 54 90 125
3-13-All have photo-c. 12-Rep. #1. 13-Last 12¢-c 7 14 21 47 76 105
14-No photo-c; reprints #2 5 10 15 34 55 75

BEYOND!
Marvel Comics: Sept, 2006 - No. 6, Feb, 2007 ($2.99, limited series)

1-6-McDuffie-s/Kolins-a; Spider-Man, Venom, Gravity, Wasp app. 6-Gravity dies 3.00
HC (2007, $19.99, dustjacket) r/series; cover sketches and sketch design pages 20.00
SC (2008, $14.99) r/series; cover sketches and sketch design pages 15.00

BEYOND, THE
Ace Magazines: Nov, 1950 - No. 30, Jan, 1955

1-Bakerish-a(p) 43 86 129 271 461 650
2-Bakerish-a(p) 28 56 84 165 270 375
3-10: 10-Woodish-a by Cameron 20 40 60 118 192 265
11-20: 18-Used in **POP**, pgs. 81,82 17 34 51 98 154 210
21-26,28-30 16 32 48 94 147 200
27-Used in **SOTI**, pg. 111 17 34 51 98 154 210

NOTE: ***Cameron** a-10, 11p, 12p, 15, 16, 21-27, 30; c-20. **Colan** a-6, 13, 17. **Sekowsky** a-2, 3, 5, 7, 11, 14, 27r. No. 1 was to appear as Challenge of the Unknown No. 7.*

BEYOND THE GRAVE
Charlton Comics: July, 1975 - No. 6, June, 1976; No. 7, Jan, 1983 - No. 17, Oct, 1984

1-Ditko-a (6 pgs.); Sutton painted-c 3 6 9 19 29 38
2-6: 2-5-Ditko-a; Ditko c-2,3,6 2 4 6 11 16 20
7-17: ('83-'84) Reprints. 13-Aparo-c(r). 15-Sutton-c (low print run) 1 2 3 4 5 7
Modern Comics Reprint 2('78) 4.00

NOTE: ***Howard** a-4. **Kim** a-1. **Larson** a-4, 6.*

BIBLE, THE: EDEN
IDW Publishing: 2003 ($21.99, hardcover graphic novel)

HC-Scott Hampton painted-a; adaptation of Genesis by Dave Elliot and Keith Giffen 22.00

BIBLE TALES FOR YOUNG FOLK (...Young People No. 3-5)
Atlas Comics (OMC): Aug, 1953 - No. 5, Mar, 1954

1 27 54 81 158 259 360
2-Everett, Krigstein-a; Robinson-c 18 36 54 105 165 225
3-5: 4,5-Robinson-c 15 30 45 88 137 185

BIG (Movie)
Hit Comics (Dark Horse Comics): Mar, 1989 ($2.00)

1-Adaptation of film; Paul Chadwick-c 2.50

BIG ALL-AMERICAN COMIC BOOK, THE (See All-American Comics)
All-American/National Per. Publ.: 1944 (132 pgs., one-shot) (Early DC Annual)

1-Wonder Woman, Green Lantern, Flash, The Atom, Wildcat, Scribbly, The Whip, Ghost Patrol, Hawkman by Kubert (1st on Hawkman), Hop Harrigan, Johnny Thunder, Little Boy Blue, Mr. Terrific, Mutt & Jeff app.; Sargon on cover only; cover by Kubert/Hibbard/Mayer and others 649 1298 1947 4738 8369 12,000

BIG BABY HUEY (See Baby Huey)

BIG BANG COMICS (Becomes Big Bang #4)
Caliber Press: Spring, 1994 - No. 4, Feb, 1995; No. 0, May, 1995 ($1.95, lim. series)

1-4-($1.95-c) 2.50
0-(5/95, $2.95) Alex Ross-c; color and B&W pages 3.00
Your Big Book of Big Bang Comics TPB ('98, $11.00) r/#0-2 11.00

BIG BANG COMICS (Volume 2)
Image Comics (Highbrow Ent.): V2#1, May, 1996 - No. 35, Jan, 2001 ($1.95-$3.95)

1-23,26: 1-Mighty Man app. 2-4-S.A. Shadowhawk app. 5-Begin $2.95-c. 6-Curt Swan/Murphy Anderson-c. 7-Begin B&W. 12-Savage Dragon-c/app. 16,17,21-Shadow Lady 3.00
24,25,27-35-($3.95): 35-Big Bang vs. Alan Moore's "1963" characters 4.00

Big Black Kiss #3 © Howard Chaykin

Big Hero 6 #2 © MAR

Big Shot Comics #64 © CCG

	GD 2.0	VG 4.0	FN 6.0	VF 8.0	VF/NM 9.0	NM- 9.2
...Presents the Ultiman Family (2/05, $3.50)						3.50
...Round Table of America (2/04, $3.95) Don Thomas-a						4.00
...Summer Special (8/03, $4.95) World's Nastiest Nazis app.						5.00

BIG BANG PRESENTS (Volume 3)
Big Bang Comics: July, 2006 - No. 5 ($2.95/$3.95, B&W)

	GD	VG	FN	VF	VF/NM	NM-
1,2: 1-Protoplasman (Plastic Man homage)						3.00
3-5-($3.95) 3-Origin of Protoplasman. 4-Flip book						4.00

BIG BLACK KISS
Vortex Comics: Sep, 1989 - No, 3, Nov, 1989 ($3.75, B&W, lim. series, mature)

	GD	VG	FN	VF	VF/NM	NM-
1-3-Chaykin-s/a						4.00

BIG BLOWN BABY (Also see Dark Horse Presents)
Dark Horse Comics: Aug, 1996 - No. 4, Nov, 1996 ($2.95, lim. series, mature)

	GD	VG	FN	VF	VF/NM	NM-
1-4: Bill Wray-c/a/scripts						3.00

BIG BOOK OF ..., THE
DC Comics (Paradox Press): 1994 - 1999 (B&W)($12.95 - $14.95)

	GD	VG	FN	VF	VF/NM	NM-
nn-...**BAD**,1998 ($14.95),...**CONSPIRACIES**, 1995 ($12.95), ...**DEATH**,1994 ($12.95), ...**FREAKS**, 1996 ($14.95), ...**GRIMM**, 1999 ($14.95), ...**HOAXES**, 1996 ($14.95), ...**LITTLE CRIMINALS**, 1996 ($14.95), ...**LOSERS**,1997 ($14.95), **MARTYRS**, 1997 ($14.95), ...**SCANDAL**,1997 ($14.95), ...**THE WEIRD WILD WEST**,1998 ($14.95), ...**THUGS**, 1997 ($14.95), ...**UNEXPLAINED**, 1997 ($14.95), ...**URBAN LEGENDS**, 1994 ($12.95), ...**VICE**, 1999 ($14.95), ...**WEIRDOS**, 1995 ($12.95)						cover price

BIG BOOK OF FUN COMICS (See New Book of Comics)
National Periodical Publications: Spring, 1936 (Large size, 52 pgs.)
(1st comic book annual & DC annual)

	GD	VG	FN	VF	VF/NM	NM-
1 (Very rare)-r/New Fun #1-5	2300	4600	6900	15,000	-	-

BIG BOOK ROMANCES
Fawcett Publications: Feb, 1950 (no date given) (148 pgs.)

	GD	VG	FN	VF	VF/NM	NM-
1-Contains remaindered Fawcett romance comics - several combinations possible	41	82	123	256	428	600

BIG CHIEF WAHOO
Eastern Color Printing/George Dougherty (distr. by Fawcett): July, 1942 - No. 7, Wint., 1943/44?(no year given)(Quarterly)

	GD	VG	FN	VF	VF/NM	NM-
1-Newspaper-r (on sale 6/15/42)	42	84	126	265	445	625
2-Steve Roper app.	23	46	69	136	223	310
3-5: 4-Chief is holding a Katy Keene comic	18	36	54	105	165	225
6-7	14	28	42	82	121	160

NOTE: *Kerry Drake in some issues.*

BIG CIRCUS, THE (Movie)
Dell Publishing Co.: No. 1036, Sept-Nov, 1959

	GD	VG	FN	VF	VF/NM	NM-
Four Color 1036-Photo-c	6	12	18	43	69	95

BIG COUNTRY, THE (Movie)
Dell Publishing Co.: No. 946, Oct, 1958

	GD	VG	FN	VF	VF/NM	NM-
Four Color 946-Photo-c	7	14	21	47	76	105

BIG DADDY DANGER
DC Comics: Oct, 2002 - No. 9, June, 2003 ($2.95, limited series)

	GD	VG	FN	VF	VF/NM	NM-
1-9-Adam Pollina-s/a/c						3.00

BIG DADDY ROTH (Magazine)
Millar Publications: Oct-Nov, 1964 - No. 4, Apr-May, 1965 (35¢)

	GD	VG	FN	VF	VF/NM	NM-
1-Toth-a	17	34	51	119	230	340
2-4-Toth-a	11	22	33	80	145	210

BIGFOOT
IDW Publishing: Feb, 2005 - No. 4, May, 2005 ($3.99, limited series)

	GD	VG	FN	VF	VF/NM	NM-
1-4-Steve Niles & Rob Zombie-s/Richard Corben-a/c						4.00

BIGG TIME
DC Comics (Vertigo): 2002 ($14.95, B&W, graphic novel)

	GD	VG	FN	VF	VF/NM	NM-
nn-Ty Templeton-s/c/a						15.00

BIG GUY AND RUSTY THE BOY ROBOT, THE (Also See Madman Comics #6,7 & Martha Washington Stranded In Space)
Dark Horse (Legend): July, 1995 - No. 2, Aug, 1995 ($4.95, oversize, limited series)

	GD	VG	FN	VF	VF/NM	NM-
1,2-Frank Miller scripts & Geoff Darrow-c/a	1	2	3	4	5	7
Trade paperback (10/96, $14.95)-r/1,2 w/cover gallery						15.00

BIG HAIR PRODUCTIONS
Image Comics: Feb, 2000 - No. 2, Mar, 2000 ($3.50, B&W)

	GD	VG	FN	VF	VF/NM	NM-
1,2						3.50

GD VG FN VF VF/NM NM-
2.0 4.0 6.0 8.0 9.0 9.2

BIG HERO ADVENTURES (See Jigsaw)

BIG HERO 6 (Also see Sunfire & Big Hero Six)
Marvel Comics: Nov, 2008 - No. 5, Mar, 2009 ($3.99, limited series)

	GD	VG	FN	VF	VF/NM	NM-
1-5-Claremont-s/Nakayama-a; 1-Character design pages & Handbook entries						4.00

BIG JON & SPARKIE (Radio)(Formerly Sparkie, Radio Pixie)
Ziff-Davis Publ. Co.: No. 4, Sept-Oct, 1952 (Painted-c)

	GD	VG	FN	VF	VF/NM	NM-
4-Based on children's radio program	18	36	54	107	169	230

BIG LAND, THE (Movie)
Dell Publishing Co.: No. 812, July, 1957

	GD	VG	FN	VF	VF/NM	NM-
Four Color 812-Alan Ladd photo-c	9	18	27	60	100	140

BIG RED (See Movie Comics)

BIG SHOT COMICS
Columbia Comics Group: May, 1940 - No. 104, Aug, 1949

	GD	VG	FN	VF	VF/NM	NM-
1-Intro. Skyman; The Face (1st app.; Tony Trent), The Cloak (Spy Master), Marvelo, Monarch of Magicians, Joe Palooka, Charlie Chan, Tom Kerry, Dixie Dugan, Rocky Ryan begin; Charlie Chan moves over from Feature Comics #31 (4/40)	258	516	774	1651	2826	4000
2	89	178	267	565	970	1375
3-The Cloak called Spy Chief; Skyman-c	79	158	237	502	864	1225
4,5	57	114	171	362	624	885
6-10: 8-Christmas-c	46	92	138	290	488	685
11-13	42	84	126	265	445	625
14-Origin & 1st app. Sparky Watts (6/41)	45	90	135	284	480	675
15-Origin The Cloak	46	92	138	290	488	685
16-20	35	70	105	208	339	470
21-23,26,27,29,30: 29-Intro. Capt. Yank; Bo (a dog) newspaper strip-r by Frank Beck begin, ends #104. 30-X-Mas-c	30	60	90	177	289	400
24-Classic Tojo-c.	54	108	162	343	584	825
25-Hitler-c	43	86	129	271	461	650
28-Hitler, Tojo & Mussolini-c	58	116	174	371	636	900
31,33-40	22	44	66	128	209	290
32-Vic Jordan newspaper strip reprints begin, ends #52; Hitler, Tojo & Mussolini-c	48	96	144	302	514	725
41,42,44,45,47-50: 42-No Skyman. 50-Origin The Face retold	19	38	57	112	179	245
43-Hitler-c	39	78	117	240	395	550
46-Hitler, Tojo-c (6/44)	39	78	117	231	378	525
51-56,58-60: 51-Tojo Japanese war-c	15	30	45	94	147	200
57-Hitler, Tojo Halloween mask-c	30	60	90	177	289	400
61-70: 63 on-Tony Trent, the Face	14	28	42	80	115	150
71-80: 73-The Face cameo. 74-(2/47)-Mickey Finn begins. 74,80-The Face app. in Tony Trent. 78-Last Charlie Chan strip-r	14	28	42	76	108	140
81-90: 85-Tony Trent marries Babs Walsh. 86-Valentines-c	11	22	33	62	86	110
91-99,101-104: 69-94-Skyman in Outer Space. 96-Xmas-c	10	20	30	56	76	95
100	11	22	33	64	90	115

NOTE: ***Mart Bailey** art on "The Face" No. 1-104. **Guardineer** a-5. Sparky Watts by **Boody Rogers**-No. 14-42, 77-104, (by others No. 43-76). Others than Tony Trent wear "The Face" mask in No. 46-63, 93. Skyman by **Ogden Whitney**-No. 1, 2, 4, 12-37, 49, 70-101. Skyman covers-No. 1, 3, 7-12, 14, 16, 20, 27, 89, 95, 100.*

BIG SMASH BARGAIN COMICS
No publisher listed: Early 1950s (25¢, 160pgs., Canadian reprints)

	GD	VG	FN	VF	VF/NM	NM-
1-4: Contains 4 comics from various companies bundled with new cover (scarce)	29	58	87	170	278	385

BIG TEX
Toby Press: June, 1953

	GD	VG	FN	VF	VF/NM	NM-
1-Contains (3) John Wayne stories-r with name changed to Big Tex	10	20	30	58	79	100

BIG-3
Fox Features Syndicate: Fall, 1940 - No. 7, Jan, 1942

	GD	VG	FN	VF	VF/NM	NM-
1-Blue Beetle, The Flame, & Samson begin	226	452	678	1446	2473	3500
2	84	168	252	538	919	1300
3-5	60	120	180	381	653	925
6,7: 6-Last Samson. 7-V-Man app.	45	90	135	284	480	675

BIG TOP COMICS, THE (TV's Great Circus Show)
Toby Press: 1951 - No. 2, 1951 (No month)

	GD	VG	FN	VF	VF/NM	NM-
1	10	20	30	58	79	100
2	9	18	27	47	61	75

BIG TOWN (Radio/TV) (Also see Movie Comics, 1946)

Bill Boyd Western #1 © FAW

Billy Batson and the Magic of Shazam! #2 © DC

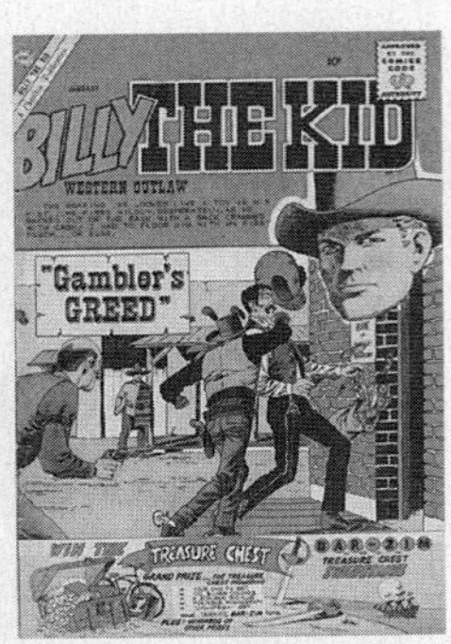

Billy the Kid #26 © CC

	GD 2.0	VG 4.0	FN 6.0	VF 8.0	VF/NM 9.0	NM- 9.2

National Periodical Publ: Jan, 1951 - No. 50, Mar-Apr, 1958 (No. 1-9: 52pgs.)

	GD 2.0	VG 4.0	FN 6.0	VF 8.0	VF/NM 9.0	NM- 9.2
1-Dan Barry-a begins	66	132	198	419	722	1025
2	35	70	105	208	339	470
3-10	21	42	63	122	199	275
11-20	15	30	45	90	140	190
21-31: Last pre-code (1-2/55)	13	26	39	72	101	130
32-50: 46-Grey tone cover	10	20	30	56	76	95

BIG VALLEY, THE (TV)
Dell Publishing Co.: June, 1966 - No. 5, Oct, 1967; No. 6, Oct, 1969

	GD 2.0	VG 4.0	FN 6.0	VF 8.0	VF/NM 9.0	NM- 9.2
1: Photo-c #1-5	5	10	15	34	55	75
2-6: 6-Reprints #1	4	8	12	22	34	45

BIKER MICE FROM MARS (TV)
Marvel Comics: Nov, 1993 - No. 3, Jan, 1994 ($1.50, limited series)

	GD 2.0	VG 4.0	FN 6.0	VF 8.0	VF/NM 9.0	NM- 9.2
1-3: 1-Intro Vinnie, Modo & Throttle. 2-Origin						4.00

BILL & TED'S BOGUS JOURNEY
Marvel Comics: Sept, 1991 ($2.95, squarebound, 84 pgs.)

	GD 2.0	VG 4.0	FN 6.0	VF 8.0	VF/NM 9.0	NM- 9.2
1-Adapts movie sequel						3.00

BILL & TED'S EXCELLENT COMIC BOOK (Movie)
Marvel Comics: Dec, 1991 - No. 12, 1992 ($1.00/$1.25)

	GD 2.0	VG 4.0	FN 6.0	VF 8.0	VF/NM 9.0	NM- 9.2
1-12: 3-Begin $1.25-c						2.50

BILL BARNES COMICS (...America's Air Ace Comics No. 2 on) (Becomes Air Ace V2#1 on; also see Shadow Comics)
Street & Smith Publications: Oct, 1940(No. month given) - No. 12, Oct, 1943

	GD 2.0	VG 4.0	FN 6.0	VF 8.0	VF/NM 9.0	NM- 9.2
1-23 pgs.-comics; Rocket Rooney begins	87	174	261	553	952	1350
2-Barnes as The Phantom Flyer app.; Tuska-a	43	86	129	271	461	650
3-5	39	78	117	240	395	550
6-12	34	68	102	199	325	450

BILL BATTLE, THE ONE MAN ARMY (Also see Master Comics No. 133)
Fawcett Publications: Oct, 1952 - No. 4, Apr, 1953 (All photo-c)

	GD 2.0	VG 4.0	FN 6.0	VF 8.0	VF/NM 9.0	NM- 9.2
1	14	28	42	76	108	140
2	8	16	24	44	57	70
3,4	8	16	24	40	50	60

BILL BLACK'S FUN COMICS
Paragon #1-3/Americomics #4: Dec, 1982 - No. 4, Mar, 1983 ($1.75/$2.00, Baxter paper) (1st AC comic)

	GD 2.0	VG 4.0	FN 6.0	VF 8.0	VF/NM 9.0	NM- 9.2
1-(B&W fanzine; 7x8-1/2"; low print) Intro. Capt. Paragon, Phantom Lady & Commando D	2	4	6	13	18	22
2-4: 2,3-(B&W fanzines; 8-1/2x11"). 3-Kirby-c. 4-($2.00, color)-Origin Nightfall (formerly Phantom Lady); Nightveil app.; Kirby-a	1	3	4	6	8	10

BILL BOYD WESTERN (Movie star; see Hopalong Cassidy & Western Hero)
Fawcett Publ: Feb, 1950 - No. 23, June, 1952 (1-3,7,11,14-on: 36 pgs.)

	GD 2.0	VG 4.0	FN 6.0	VF 8.0	VF/NM 9.0	NM- 9.2
1-Bill Boyd & his horse Midnite begin; photo front/back-c	40	80	120	240	390	540
2-Painted-c	20	40	60	120	193	265
3-Photo-c begin, end #23; last photo back-c	15	30	45	94	147	200
4-6(52 pgs.)	15	30	45	84	127	170
7,11(36 pgs.)	13	26	39	72	101	130
8-10,12,13(52 pgs.)	13	26	39	74	105	135
14-22	12	24	36	67	94	120
23-Last issue	13	26	39	72	101	130

BILL BUMLIN (See Treasury of Comics No. 3)

BILL ELLIOTT (See Wild Bill Elliott)

BILLI 99
Dark Horse Comics: Sept, 1991 - No. 4, 1991 ($3.50, B&W, lim. series, 52 pgs.)

	GD 2.0	VG 4.0	FN 6.0	VF 8.0	VF/NM 9.0	NM- 9.2
1-4: Tim Sale-c/a						3.50

BILL STERN'S SPORTS BOOK
Ziff-Davis Publ. Co.(Approved Comics): Spring-Sum, 1951 - V2#2, Win, 1952

	GD 2.0	VG 4.0	FN 6.0	VF 8.0	VF/NM 9.0	NM- 9.2
V1#10-(1951) Whitney painted-c	21	42	63	122	199	275
2-(Sum/52; reg. size)	16	32	48	94	147	200
V2#2-(1952, 96 pgs.)-Krigstein, Kinstler-a	21	42	63	126	206	285

BILL THE BULL: ONE SHOT, ONE BOURBON, ONE BEER
Boneyard Press: Dec, 1994 ($2.95, B&W, mature)

	GD 2.0	VG 4.0	FN 6.0	VF 8.0	VF/NM 9.0	NM- 9.2
1						3.00

BILLY AND BUGGY BEAR (See Animal Fun)
I.W. Enterprises/Super: 1958; 1964

	GD 2.0	VG 4.0	FN 6.0	VF 8.0	VF/NM 9.0	NM- 9.2
I.W. Reprint #1, #7('58)-All Surprise Comics #?(Same issue-r for both)	2	4	6	10	14	18
Super Reprint #10(1964)	2	4	6	8	11	14

BILLY BATSON AND THE MAGIC OF SHAZAM! (Follows Shazam: The Monster Society of Evil mini-series)
DC Comics: Sept, 2008 - Present ($2.25/$2.50, all ages title)

	GD 2.0	VG 4.0	FN 6.0	VF 8.0	VF/NM 9.0	NM- 9.2
1-12: 1-4-Mike Kunkel-s/a/c; Theo (Black) Adam app. 5-DeStefano-a						2.50
1-Variant B&W sketch cover						3.00

BILLY BUCKSKIN WESTERN (2-Gun Western No. 4)
Atlas Comics (IMC No. 1/MgPC No. 2,3): Nov, 1955 - No. 3, Mar, 1956

	GD 2.0	VG 4.0	FN 6.0	VF 8.0	VF/NM 9.0	NM- 9.2
1-Mort Drucker-a; Maneely-c/a	16	32	48	88	137	185
2-Mort Drucker-a	10	20	30	56	76	95
3-Williamson, Drucker-a	12	24	36	67	94	120

BILLY BUNNY (Black Cobra No. 6 on)
Excellent Publications: Feb-Mar, 1954 - No. 5, Oct-Nov, 1954

	GD 2.0	VG 4.0	FN 6.0	VF 8.0	VF/NM 9.0	NM- 9.2
1	9	18	27	50	65	80
2	6	12	18	28	34	40
3-5	5	10	15	24	30	35

BILLY BUNNY'S CHRISTMAS FROLICS
Farrell Publications: 1952 (25¢ Giant, 100 pgs.)

	GD 2.0	VG 4.0	FN 6.0	VF 8.0	VF/NM 9.0	NM- 9.2
1	20	40	60	117	189	260

BILLY COLE
Cult Press: May, 1994 - No. 4, Aug, 1994 ($2.75, B&W, limited series)

	GD 2.0	VG 4.0	FN 6.0	VF 8.0	VF/NM 9.0	NM- 9.2
1-4						2.75

BILLY MAKE BELIEVE
United Features Syndicate: No. 14, 1939

	GD 2.0	VG 4.0	FN 6.0	VF 8.0	VF/NM 9.0	NM- 9.2
Single Series 14	30	60	90	177	289	400

BILLY NGUYEN, PRIVATE EYE
Caliber Press: V2#1, 1990 ($2.50)

	GD 2.0	VG 4.0	FN 6.0	VF 8.0	VF/NM 9.0	NM- 9.2
V2#1						2.50

BILLY THE KID (Formerly The Masked Raider; also see Doc Savage Comics & Return of the Outlaw)
Charlton Publ. Co.: No. 9, Nov, 1957 - No. 121, Dec, 1976; No. 122, Sept, 1977 - No. 123, Oct, 1977; No. 124, Feb, 1978 - No. 153, Mar, 1983

	GD 2.0	VG 4.0	FN 6.0	VF 8.0	VF/NM 9.0	NM- 9.2
9	10	20	30	58	79	100
10,12,14,17-19: 12-2 pg Check-sty	8	16	24	40	50	60
11-(68 pgs.)-Origin & 1st app. The Ghost Train	9	18	27	50	65	80
13-Williamson/Torres-a	8	16	24	44	57	70
15-Origin; 2 pgs. Williamson-a	8	16	24	44	57	70
16-Williamson-a, 2 pgs.	8	16	24	42	54	65
20-26-Severin-a(3-4 each)	8	16	24	44	57	70
27-30: 30-Masked Rider app.	3	6	9	19	29	38
31-40	3	6	9	16	22	28
41-60	2	4	6	13	18	22
61-65	2	4	6	10	14	18
66-Bounty Hunter series begins.	3	6	9	14	20	25
67-80: Bounty Hunter series; not in #79,82,84-86	2	4	6	10	14	18
81-84,86-90: 87-Last Bounty Hunter	2	4	6	8	10	12
85-Early Kaluta-a (4 pgs.)	2	4	6	9	13	16
91-123: 110-Dr. Young of Boothill app. 111-Origin The Ghost Train. 117-Gunsmith & Co., The Cheyenne Kid app.	1	2	3	5	6	8
124(2/78)-153						6.00
Modern Comics 109 (1977 reprint)						4.00

NOTE: ***Boyette*** *a-91-110.* ***Kim*** *a-73.* ***Morsi*** *a-12,14.* ***Sattler*** *a-118-123.* ***Severin*** *a(r)-121-129, 134; c-23, 25.* ***Sutton*** *a-111.*

BILLY THE KID ADVENTURE MAGAZINE
Toby Press: Oct, 1950 - No. 29, 1955

	GD 2.0	VG 4.0	FN 6.0	VF 8.0	VF/NM 9.0	NM- 9.2
1-Williamson/Frazetta-a (2 pgs) r/from John Wayne Adventure Comics #2; photo-c	31	62	93	182	296	410
2-Photo-c	12	24	36	69	97	125
3-Williamson/Frazetta "The Claws of Death", 4 pgs. plus Williamson art	34	68	102	199	325	450
4,5,7,8,10: 4,7-Photo-c	9	18	27	52	69	85
6-Frazetta assist on "Nightmare"; photo-c	15	30	45	83	124	165
9-Kurtzman Pot-Shot Pete; photo-c	11	22	33	64	90	115
11,12,15-20: 11-Photo-c	8	16	24	42	54	65
13-Kurtzman-r/John Wayne #12 (Genius)	9	18	27	47	61	75
14-Williamson/Frazetta; r-of #1 (2 pgs.)	10	20	30	56	76	95
21,23-29	7	14	21	37	46	55

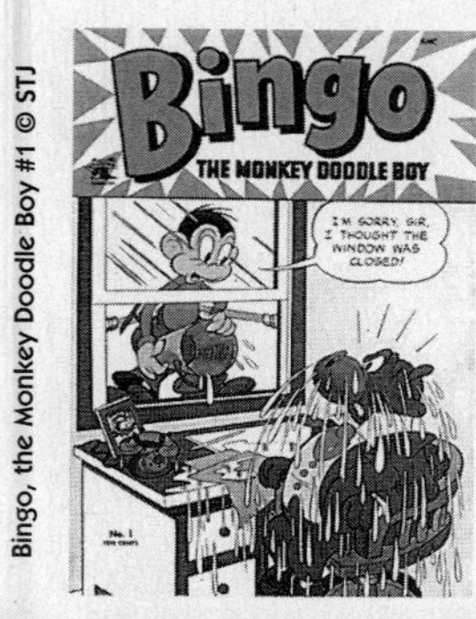

Bingo, the Monkey Doodle Boy #1 © STJ

Birds of Prey #115 © DC

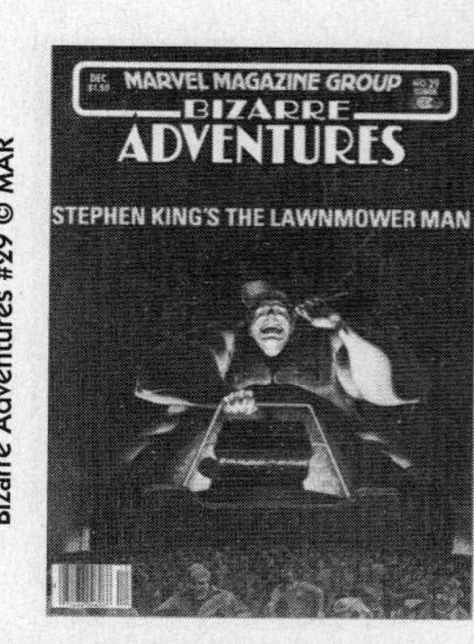

Bizarre Adventures #29 © MAR

	GD 2.0	VG 4.0	FN 6.0	VF 8.0	VF/NM 9.0	NM- 9.2

22-Williamson/Frazetta-r(1pg.)/#1; photo-c 8 16 24 42 54 65

BILLY THE KID AND OSCAR (Also see Fawcett's Funny Animals)
Fawcett Publications: Winter, 1945 - No. 3, Fall, 1946 (Funny animal)
1 15 30 45 84 127 170
2,3 10 20 30 56 76 95

BILLY THE KID'S OLD TIMEY ODDITIES
Dark Horse Comics: Apr, 2005 - No. 4, July, 2005 ($2.99, limited series)
1-4-Eric Powell-s/c; Kyle Hotz-a 3.00
TPB (2005, $13.95) r/series 14.00

BILLY WEST (Bill West No. 9,10)
Standard Comics (Visual Editions): 1949-No. 9, Feb, 1951; No. 10, Feb, 1952
1 14 28 42 82 121 160
2 9 18 27 50 65 80
3-6,9,10 8 16 24 42 54 65
7,8-Schomburg-c 9 18 27 47 61 75
NOTE: *Celardo a-1-6, 9; c-1-3.* ***Moreira*** *a-3.* ***Roussos*** *a-2.*

BING CROSBY (See Feature Films)

BINGO (...Comics) (H. C. Blackerby)
Howard Publ.: 1945 (Reprints National material)
1-L. B. Cole opium-c; blank back-c 36 72 108 211 343 475

BINGO, THE MONKEY DOODLE BOY
St. John Publishing Co.: Aug, 1951; Oct, 1953
1(8/51)-By Eric Peters 8 16 24 40 50 60
1(10/53) 6 12 18 28 34 40

BINKY (Formerly Leave It to...)
National Periodical Publ./DC Comics: No. 72, 4-5/70 - No. 81, 10-11/71; No. 82, Summer/77
72-76 4 8 12 22 34 45
77-79: (68 pgs.). 77-Bobby Sherman 1pg. story w/photo. 78-1 pg. sty on Barry Williams of Brady Bunch. 79-Osmonds 1pg. story 6 12 18 37 59 80
80,81 (52 pgs.)-Sweat Pain story 5 10 15 30 48 65
82 (1977, one-shot) 4 8 12 24 37 50

BINKY'S BUDDIES
National Periodical Publications: Jan-Feb, 1969 - No. 12, Nov-Dec, 1970
1 7 14 21 45 73 100
2-12: 3-Last 12¢ issue 4 8 12 24 37 50

BIONIC WOMAN, THE (TV)
Charlton Publications: Oct, 1977 - No. 5, June, 1978
1 3 6 9 20 30 40
2-5 3 6 9 14 20 25

BIRDS OF PREY (Also see Black Canary/Oracle: Birds of Prey)
DC Comics: Jan, 1999 - No. 127, Apr, 2009 ($1.99/$2.50/$2.99)
1-Dixon-s/Land-c/a 1 3 4 6 8 10
2-4 6.00
5-7,9-15: 15-Guice-a begins. 4.00
8-Nightwing-c/app.; Barbara & Dick's circus date 2 4 6 9 12 15
16-38: 23-Grodd-c/app. 26-Bane app. 32-Noto-c begin 2.50
39,40-Bruce Wayne: Murderer pt. 5,12 3.00
41-Bruce Wayne: Fugitive pt. 2 4.00
42-46: 42-Fabry-a. 45-Deathstroke-c/app. 2.50
47-74,76-91: 47-49-Terry Moore-s/Conner & Palmiotti-a; Noto-c. 50-Gilbert Hernandez-s begin. 52,54-Metamorpho app. 56-Simone-s/Benes-a begin. 65,67,68,70-Land-c. 76-Debut of Black Alice (from Day of Vengeance). 86-Timm-a (7 pgs.) 2.50
75-($2.95) Pearson-c; back-up story of Lady Blackhawk 3.00
92-99,101-127: 92-One Year Later. 94-Begin $2.99-c; Prometheus app. 96,97-Black Alice app. 98,99-New Batgirl app. 99-Black Canary leaves the team. 104-107-Secret Six app. 3.00
100-($3.99) new team recruited; Black Canary origin re-told 4.00
TPB (1999, $17.95) r/ previous series and one-shots 18.00
...: Batgirl 1 (2/98, $2.95) Dixon-s/Frank-c 5.00
...: Batgirl/Catwoman 1 ('03, $5.95) Robertson-a; cont'd in BOP: Catwoman/Oracle 1 6.00
...: Between Dark & Dawn TPB (2006, $14.99) r/#69-75 15.00
...: Blood and Circuits TPB (2007, $17.99) r/#96-103 18.00
...: Catwoman/Oracle 1 ('03, $5.95) Cont'd from BOP: Batgirl/Catwoman 1; David Ross-a 6.00
...: Club Kids TPB (2008, $17.99) r/#109-112,118 18.00
...: Dead of Winter TPB (2008, $17.99) r/#104-108 18.00
...: Metropolis or Dust TPB (2008, $17.99) r/#113-117 18.00
...: Of Like Minds TPB (2004, $14.95) r/#55-61 15.00
...: Old Friends, New Enemies TPB (2003, $17.95) r/#1-6, ...: Batgirl, ...: Wolves 18.00
...: Perfect Pitch TPB (2007, $17.99) r/#86-90,92-95 18.00
...: Platinum Flats TPB (2009, $17.99) r/#119-124 18.00
...: Revolution 1 (1997, $2.95) Frank-c/Dixon-s 5.00
... Secret Files 2003 (8/03, $4.95) Short stories, pin-ups and profile pages; Noto-c 5.00
...: Sensei and Student TPB (2005, $17.95) r/#62-68 18.00
...: The Battle Within TPB (2006, $17.99) r/#76-85 18.00
...: The Ravens 1 (6/98, $1.95)-Dixon-s; Girlfrenzy issue 4.00
...: Wolves 1 (10/97, $2.95) Dixon-s/Giordano & Faucher-a 5.00

BIRDS OF PREY: MANHUNT
DC Comics: Sept, 1996 - No. 4, Dec, 1996 ($1.95, limited series)
1-Features Black Canary, Oracle, Huntress, & Catwoman; Chuck Dixon scripts; Gary Frank-c on all. 1-Catwoman cameo only 1 2 3 5 6 8
2-4 6.00
NOTE: ***Gary Frank*** *c-1-4.* ***Matt Haley*** *a-1-4p.* ***Wade Von Grawbadger*** *a-1i.*

BIRTH CAUL, THE
Eddie Campbell Comics: 1999 ($5.95, B&W, one-shot)
1-Alan Moore-s/Eddie Campbell-a 6.00

BIRTH OF THE DEFIANT UNIVERSE, THE
Defiant Comics: May, 1993
nn-Contains promotional artwork & text; limited print run of 1000 copies. 2 4 6 8 10 12

BISHOP (See Uncanny X-Men & X-Men)
Marvel Comics: Dec, 1994 - No.4, Mar, 1995 ($2.95, limited series)
1-4: Foil-c; Shard & Mountjoy in all. 1-Storm app. 3.00

BISHOP THE LAST X-MAN
Marvel Comics: Oct, 1999 - No. 16, Jan, 2001 ($2.99/$1.99/$2.25)
1-($2.99)-Jeanty-a 3.50
2-8-($1.99): 2-Two covers 2.50
9-11,13-16: 9-Begin $2.25-c. 15-Maximum Security x-over; Xavier app. 2.50
12-($2.99) 3.00

BISHOP: XAVIER SECURITY ENFORCER
Marvel Comics: Jan, 1998 - No.3, Mar, 1998 ($2.50, limited series)
1-3: Ostrander-s 3.00

BITE CLUB
DC Comics (Vertigo): Jun, 2004 - No. 6, Nov, 2004 ($2.95, limited series)
1-6-Chaykin-s/Tischman-a/Quitely-c 3.00
TPB Digest (2005, $9.99) r/#1-6; cover gallery 10.00
The Complete Bite Club TPB (2007, $19.99) r/#1-6 and ...: Vampire Crime Unit #1-5 20.00

BITE CLUB: VAMPIRE CRIME UNIT
DC Comics (Vertigo): Jun, 2006 - No. 5 ($2.99, limited series)
1-5:1-Chaykin & Tischman-s/Hahn-a/Quitely-c. 4-Chaykin-c 3.00

BIZARRE ADVENTURES (Formerly Marvel Preview)
Marvel Comics Group: No. 25, 3/81 - No. 34, 2/83 (#25-33: Magazine-$1.50)
25,26: 25-Lethal Ladies. 26-King Kull; Bolton-c/a 2 4 6 8 10 12
27,28: 27-Phoenix, Iceman & Nightcrawler app. 28-The Unlikely Heroes; Elektra by Miller; Neal Adams-a 2 4 6 10 14 18
29,30,32,33: 29-Stephen King's Lawnmower Man. 30-Tomorrow; 1st app. Silhouette. 32-Gods; Thor-c/s. 33-Horror; Dracula app.; photo-c 2 3 4 6 8 10
31-After The Violence Stops; new Hangman story; Miller-a 2 4 6 8 10 12
34 ($2.00, Baxter paper, comic size)-Son of Santa; Christmas special; Howard the Duck by Paul Smith 1 2 3 5 7 9
NOTE: ***Alcala*** *a-27i.* ***Austin*** *a-25i, 28i.* ***Bolton*** *a-26, 32.* ***J. Buscema*** *a-27p, 29, 30p; c-26.* ***Byrne*** *a-31 (2 pg.).* ***Golden*** *a-25p, 28p.* ***Perez*** *a-27p.* ***Rogers*** *a-25p.* ***Simonson*** *a-29; c-29.* ***Paul Smith*** *a-34.*

BIZARRO COMICS!
DC Comics: 2001 ($29.95, hardcover, one-shot)
HC-Short stories of DC heroes by various alternative cartoonists including Dorkin, Pope, Haspiel, Kidd, Kochalka, Millionaire, Stephens, Wray; includes "Superman's Babysitter" by Kyle Baker from Elseworlds 80-Page Giant recalled by DC; Groening-c 30.00
Softcover (2003, $19.95) 20.00

BIZARRO WORLD
DC Comics: 2005 ($29.95, hardcover, one-shot)
HC-Short stories by various alternative cartoonists including Bagge, Baker, Dorkin, Dunn, Kupperman, Morse, Oswalt, Pekar, Simpson, Stewart; Jaime Hernandez-c 30.00
Softcover (2006, $19.99) 20.00

BLACK ADAM (See 52 and Countdown)
DC Comics: Oct, 2007 - No. 6, Mar, 2008 ($2.99, limited series)

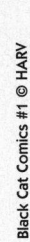

Black Canary (2007 series) #3 © DC

Black Cat Comics #1 © HARV

Black Condor #12 © DC

	GD 2.0	VG 4.0	FN 6.0	VF 8.0	VF/NM 9.0	NM- 9.2
1-6: 1-Mahnke-a/c; Isis returns; Felix Faust app.						3.00
...: The Dark Age TPB (2008, $17.99) r/#1-6; Alex Ross-c						18.00

BLACK AND WHITE (See Large Feature Comic, Series I)

BLACK & WHITE (Also see Codename: Black & White)
Image Comics (Extreme): Oct, 1994 - No. 3, Jan, 1995 ($1.95, limited series)

	GD	VG	FN	VF	VF/NM	NM-
1-3: Thibert-c/story						2.50

BLACK & WHITE MAGIC
Innovation Publishing: 1991 ($2.95, 98 pgs., B&W w/30 pgs. color, squarebound)

	GD	VG	FN	VF	VF/NM	NM-
1-Contains rebound comics w/covers removed; contents may vary						3.00

BLACK AXE
Marvel Comics (UK): Apr, 1993 - No. 7, Oct, 1993 ($1.75)

	GD	VG	FN	VF	VF/NM	NM-
1-4: 1-Romita Jr.-c. 2-Sunfire-c/s						3.00
5-7: 5-Janson-c; Black Panther app. 6,7-Black Panther-c/s						3.00

BLACKBALL COMICS
Blackball Comics: Mar, 1994 ($3.00)

	GD	VG	FN	VF	VF/NM	NM-
1-Trencher-c/story by Giffen; John Pain by O'Neill						3.00

BLACKBEARD'S GHOST (See Movie Comics)

BLACK BEAUTY (See Son of Black Beauty)
Dell Publishing Co.: No. 440, Dec, 1952

	GD	VG	FN	VF	VF/NM	NM-
Four Color 440	5	10	15	30	48	65

BLACKBURNE COVENANT, THE
Dark Horse Comics: Apr, 2003 - No. 4, July, 2003 ($2.99, limited series)

	GD	VG	FN	VF	VF/NM	NM-
1-4-Nicieza-s/Raffaele-a						3.00
TPB (2003, $12.95) r/#1-4						13.00

BLACK CANARY (See All Star Comics #38, Flash Comics #86, Justice League of America #75 & World's Finest #244)
DC Comics: Nov, 1991 - No. 4, Feb, 1992 ($1.75, limited series)

	GD	VG	FN	VF	VF/NM	NM-
1-4						2.50

BLACK CANARY
DC Comics: Jan, 1993 - No. 12, Dec, 1993 ($1.75)

	GD	VG	FN	VF	VF/NM	NM-
1-7						2.50
8-12: 8-The Ray-c/story. 9,10-Huntress-c/story						3.00

BLACK CANARY (Follows Oliver Queen's marriage proposal in Green Arrow #75)
DC Comics: Early Sept, 2007 - No. 4, Late Oct, 2007 ($2.99, bi-weekly limited series)

	GD	VG	FN	VF	VF/NM	NM-
1-4-Bedard-s/Siqueira-a						3.00
... Wedding Planner 1 (11/07, $2.99) Roux-c/Ferguson & Norrie-a						3.00

BLACK CANARY/ORACLE: BIRDS OF PREY (Also see Showcase '96 #3)
DC Comics: 1996 ($3.95, one-shot)

	GD	VG	FN	VF	VF/NM	NM-
1-Chuck Dixon scripts & Gary Frank-c/a.	1	2	3	5	7	9

BLACK CAT COMICS (...Western #16-19; ...Mystery #30 on)
(See All-New #7,9, The Original Black Cat, Pocket & Speed Comics)
Harvey Publications (Home Comics): June-July, 1946 - No. 29, June, 1951

	GD	VG	FN	VF	VF/NM	NM-
1-Kubert-a; Joe Simon c-1,2	74	148	222	470	810	1150
2-Kubert-a	39	78	117	240	395	550
3,4: 4-The Red Demons begin (The Demon #4 & 5)	33	66	99	194	317	440
5,6,7: 5,6-The Scarlet Arrow app. in ea. by Powell; S&K-a in both. 6-Origin Red Demon. 7-Vagabond Prince by S&K plus 1 more story	39	78	117	240	395	550
8-S&K-a; Kerry Drake begins, ends #13	35	70	105	208	339	470
9-Origin Stuntman (r/Stuntman #1)	38	76	114	226	368	510
10-20: 14,15,17-Mary Worth app. plus Invisible Scarlet O'Neil-#15,20,24	26	52	78	154	252	350
21-26	21	42	63	124	202	280
27,28: 27-Used in **SOTI**, pg. 193; X-Mas-c; 2 pg. John Wayne story. 28-Intro. Kit, Black Cat's new sidekick	23	46	69	134	220	305
29-Black Cat bondage-c; Black Cat stories	22	44	66	128	209	290

BLACK CAT MYSTERY (Formerly Black Cat; ...Western Mystery #54; ...Western #55,56; ...Mystery #57; ...Mystic #58-62; Black Cat #63-65)
Harvey Publications: No. 30, Aug, 1951 - No. 65, Apr, 1963

	GD	VG	FN	VF	VF/NM	NM-
30-Black Cat on cover and splash page only	31	62	93	186	303	420
31,32,34,37,38,40	26	52	78	152	249	345
33-Used in **POP**, pg. 89; electrocution-c	28	56	84	165	270	375
35-Atomic disaster cover/story	31	62	93	182	296	410
36,39-Used in **SOTI**: #36-Pgs. 270,271; #39-Pgs. 386-388	30	60	90	177	289	400
41-43	25	50	75	147	241	335
44-Eyes, ears, tongue cut out; Nostrand-a	27	54	81	158	259	360
45-Classic "Colorama" by Powell; Nostrand-a	42	84	126	265	445	625
46-49,51-Nostrand-a in all. 51-Story has blank panel covering censored art (post-Code)	26	52	78	152	249	345
50-Check-a; classic Warren Kremer-c showing a man's face & hands burning away	103	206	309	659	1130	1600
52,53 (r/#34 & 35)	16	32	48	94	147	200
54-Two Black Cat stories (2/55, last pre-code)	18	36	54	107	169	230
55,56-Black Cat app.	16	32	48	94	147	200
57(7/56)-Kirby-c	18	36	54	103	162	220
58-60-Kirby-a(4). 58,59-Kirby-c. 60,61-Simon-c	21	42	63	124	202	280
61-Nostrand-a; "Colorama" r/#45	19	38	57	109	172	235
62 (3/58)-E.C. story swipe	16	32	48	94	147	200
63-65: Giants(10/62,1/63, 4/63); Reprints; Black Cat app. 63-origin Black Kitten. 65-1 pg. Powell-a	19	38	57	112	179	245

NOTE: ***Kremer*** *a-37, 39, 43; c-36, 37, 47.* ***Meskin*** *a-51.* ***Palais*** *a-30, 31(2), 32(2), 33-35, 37-40.* ***Powell*** *a-32-35, 36(2), 40, 41, 43-53, 57.* ***Simon*** *c-63-65.* ***Sparling*** *a-44. Bondage c-32, 34, 43.*

BLACK COBRA (Bride's Diary No. 4 on) (See Captain Flight #8)
Ajax/Farrell Publications(Excellent Publ.): No. 1, 10-11/54; No. 6(No. 2), 12-1/54-55; No. 3, 2-3/55

	GD	VG	FN	VF	VF/NM	NM-
1-Re-intro Black Cobra & The Cobra Kid (costumed heroes)	36	72	108	211	343	475
6(#2)-Formerly Billy Bunny	19	38	57	111	176	240
3-(Pre-code)-Torpedoman app.	18	36	54	105	165	225

BLACK CONDOR (Also see Crack Comics, Freedom Fighters & Showcase '94 #10,11)
DC Comics: June, 1992 - No. 12, May, 1993 ($1.25)

	GD	VG	FN	VF	VF/NM	NM-
1-8-Heath-c						2.50
9-12: 9,10,12-Heath-c. 9,10-The Ray app. 12-Batman-c/app.						3.00

BLACK CROSS SPECIAL (See Dark Horse Presents)
Dark Horse Comics: Jan, 1988 ($1.75, B&W, one-shot)(Reprints & new-a)

	GD	VG	FN	VF	VF/NM	NM-
1-1st printing						3.00
1-(2nd printing) has 2 pgs. new-a						2.50

BLACK CROSS: DIRTY WORK (See Dark Horse Presents)
Dark Horse Comics: Apr, 1997 ($2.95, one-shot)

	GD	VG	FN	VF	VF/NM	NM-
1-Chris Warner-c/s/a						3.00

BLACK DIAMOND
Americomics: May, 1983 - No. 5, 1984 (no month)($2.00-$1.75, Baxter paper)

	GD	VG	FN	VF	VF/NM	NM-
1-3-Movie adapt.; 1-Colt back-up begins						4.00
4,5						3.00

NOTE: ***Bill Black*** *a-1i; c-1.* ***Gulacy*** *c-2-5. Sybil Danning photo back-c-1.*

BLACK DIAMOND WESTERN (Formerly Desperado No. 1-8)
Lev Gleason Publ: No. 9, Mar, 1949 - No. 60, Feb, 1956 (No. 9-28: 52 pgs.)

	GD	VG	FN	VF	VF/NM	NM-
9-Black Diamond & his horse Reliapon begin; origin & 1st app. Black Diamond	21	42	63	122	199	275
10	12	24	36	69	97	125
11-15	10	20	30	54	72	90
16-28(11/49-11/51)-Wolverton's Bingbang Buster	14	28	42	76	108	140
29-40: 31-One pg. Frazetta anti-drug ad	9	18	27	47	61	75
41-50,53-59	8	16	24	40	50	60
51-3-D effect-c/story	15	30	45	85	130	175
52-3-D effect story	14	28	42	81	118	155
60-Last issue	8	16	24	44	57	70

NOTE: ***Biro*** *c-9-35?.* ***Fass*** *a-58, c-54-56, 58.* ***Guardineer*** *a-9, 15, 18.* ***Kida*** *a-9.* ***Maurer*** *a-10.* ***Ed Moore*** *a-16.* ***Morisi*** *a-55.* ***Tuska*** *a-10, 48.*

BLACK DRAGON, THE
Marvel Comics (Epic Comics): 5/85 - No. 6, 10/85 (Baxter paper, mature)

	GD	VG	FN	VF	VF/NM	NM-
1-6: 1-Chris Claremont story & John Bolton painted-c/a in all						3.00
TPB (Dark Horse, 4/96, $17.95, B&W, trade paperback) r/#1-6; intro by Anne McCaffrey						18.00

BLACKEST NIGHT (2009 Green Lantern & DC crossover) (Leads into Brightest Day series)
DC Comics: No. 0, Jun, 2009 - No. 8, May, 2010 ($3.99, limited series)

	GD	VG	FN	VF	VF/NM	NM-
0-Free Comic Book Day edition; Johns-s/Reis-a; profile pages of different corps						2.50
1-8: 1-($3.99) Black Lantern Corps arises; Johns-s/Reis-c/a; Hawkman & Hawkgirl killed. 4-Nekron rises. 8-Dead heroes return						4.00
1-Variant cover by Van Sciver						15.00
1-3,5: 2nd-4th printings						4.00
2-8: 2-Cascioli variant-c. 3-Van Sciver variant-c. 4-7-Migliari variant-c. 8-Mahnke var-c						8.00

BLACKEST NIGHT: BATMAN (2009 Green Lantern & DC crossover)
DC Comics: Oct, 2009 - No. 3, Dec, 2009 ($2.99, limited series)

Blackest Night #1 © DC

Black Goliath #1 © MAR

Blackhawk #122 © DC

	GD 2.0	VG 4.0	FN 6.0	VF 8.0	VF/NM 9.0	NM- 9.2
1-3: 1-Bat-parents rise as Black Lanterns; Deadman app.; Syaf-a/Andy Kubert-c; 2 printings. 3-Flying Graysons return						3.00
1-3-Variant-c by Sienkiewicz						5.00

BLACKEST NIGHT: JSA (2009 Green Lantern & DC crossover)
DC Comics: Feb, 2010 - No. 3, Apr, 2010 ($2.99, limited series)

	GD 2.0	VG 4.0	FN 6.0	VF 8.0	VF/NM 9.0	NM- 9.2
1-Original Sandman, Dr. Midnite and Mr. Terrific rise; Barrows-a/c						3.00
1-Variant-c by Gene Ha						5.00

BLACKEST NIGHT: SUPERMAN (2009 Green Lantern & DC crossover)
DC Comics: Oct, 2009 - No. 3, Dec, 2009 ($2.99, limited series)

	GD 2.0	VG 4.0	FN 6.0	VF 8.0	VF/NM 9.0	NM- 9.2
1-3-Earth-2 Superman and Lois become Black Lanterns; Barrows-a/c; 2 printings						3.00
1-3-Variant-c by Shane Davis						5.00

BLACKEST NIGHT: TALES OF THE CORPS (2009 Green Lantern & DC crossover)
DC Comics: Sept, 2009 - No. 3, Sept, 2009 ($3.99, weekly limited series)

	GD 2.0	VG 4.0	FN 6.0	VF 8.0	VF/NM 9.0	NM- 9.2
1-3-Short stories by various; interlocking cover images. 3-Commentary on B.N. #0						4.00

BLACKEST NIGHT: THE FLASH (2009 Green Lantern & DC crossover)
DC Comics: Feb, 2010 - No. 3, Apr, 2010 ($2.99, limited series)

	GD 2.0	VG 4.0	FN 6.0	VF 8.0	VF/NM 9.0	NM- 9.2
1,2-Rogues vs. Dead Rogues; Johns-s/Kolins-a						3.00
1-Variant-c by Manapul						5.00

BLACKEST NIGHT: TITANS (2009 Green Lantern & DC crossover)
DC Comics: Oct, 2009 - No. 3, Dec, 2009 ($2.99, limited series)

	GD 2.0	VG 4.0	FN 6.0	VF 8.0	VF/NM 9.0	NM- 9.2
1-3-Terra and the original Hawk return; Benes-a/c						3.00
1-3-Variant-c by Brian Haberlin						5.00

BLACKEST NIGHT: WONDER WOMAN (2009 Green Lantern & DC crossover)
DC Comics: Feb, 2010 - No. 3, Apr, 2010 ($2.99, limited series)

	GD 2.0	VG 4.0	FN 6.0	VF 8.0	VF/NM 9.0	NM- 9.2
1-3-Maxwell Lord returns; Rucka-s/Scott-a/Horn-c. 2,3-Mera app.; Star Sapphire						3.00
1-3-Variant-c by Ryan Sook						5.00

BLACK FLAG (See Asylum #5)
Maximum Press: Jan, 1995 - No.4, 1995; No. 0, July, 1995 ($2.50, B&W) (No. 0 in color)

	GD 2.0	VG 4.0	FN 6.0	VF 8.0	VF/NM 9.0	NM- 9.2
Preview Edition (6/94, $1.95, B&W)-Fraga/McFarlane-c.						3.00
0-4: 0-(7/95)-Liefeld/Fraga-c. 1-(1/95).						3.00
1-Variant cover						5.00
2,4-Variant covers						3.00

NOTE: ***Fraga** a-0-4, Preview Edition; c-1-4. **Liefeld/Fraga** c-0. **McFarlane/Fraga** c-Preview Edition.*

BLACK FURY (Becomes Wild West No. 58) (See Blue Bird)
Charlton Comics Group: May, 1955 - No. 57, Mar-Apr, 1966 (Horse stories)

	GD 2.0	VG 4.0	FN 6.0	VF 8.0	VF/NM 9.0	NM- 9.2
1	12	24	36	67	94	120
2	7	14	21	37	46	55
3-10	6	12	18	28	34	40
11-15,19,20	4	8	10	18	22	25
16-18-Ditko-a	12	24	36	67	94	120
21-30	4	7	10	14	17	20
31-57	3	6	8	12	14	16

BLACK GOLIATH (See Avengers #32-35,41,54 and Civil War #4)
Marvel Comics Group: Feb, 1976 - No. 5, Nov, 1976

	GD 2.0	VG 4.0	FN 6.0	VF 8.0	VF/NM 9.0	NM- 9.2
1-Tuska-a(p) thru #3	2	4	6	11	16	20
2-5: 2-4-(Regular 25¢ editions). 4-Kirby-c/Buckler-a	2	4	6	8	11	14
2-4-(30¢-c variants, limited distribution)(4,6,8/76)	4	8	12	24	37	50

BLACKHAWK (Formerly Uncle Sam #1-8; see Military Comics & Modern Comics)
Comic Magazines(Quality)No. 9-107(12/56); National Periodical Publications No. 108 (1/57) -250; DC Comics No. 251 on: No. 9, Winter, 1944 - No. 243, 10-11/68; No. 244, 1-2/76 - No. 250, 1-2/77; No. 251, 10/82 - No. 273, 11/84

	GD 2.0	VG 4.0	FN 6.0	VF 8.0	VF/NM 9.0	NM- 9.2
9 (1944)	300	600	900	2070	3635	5200
10 (1946)	103	206	309	659	1130	1600
11-15: 14-Ward-a; 13,14-Fear app.	71	142	213	454	777	1100
16-19	61	122	183	390	670	950
20-Classic Crandall bondage-c; Ward Blackhawk	77	154	231	493	847	1200
21-30 (1950)	45	90	135	284	480	675
31-40: 31-Chop Chop by Jack Cole	38	76	114	225	368	510
41-49,51-60: 42-Robot-c	31	62	93	184	300	415
50-1st Killer Shark; origin in text	34	68	102	204	332	460
61,62: 61-Used in **POP**, pg. 91. 62-Used in **POP**, pg. 92 & color illo	27	54	81	162	266	370
63-70,72-80: 65-H-Bomb explosion panel. 66-B&W & color illos **POP**. 67-Hitler-s. 70-Return of Killer Shark; atomic explosion panel. 75-Intro. Blackie the Hawk	26	52	78	154	252	350
71-Origin retold; flying saucer-c; A-Bomb panels	30	60	90	177	289	400
81-86: Last precode (3/55)	23	46	69	136	223	310
87-92,94-99,101-107: 91-Robot-c. 105-1st S.A.	19	38	57	112	179	245
93-Origin in text	20	40	60	114	182	250
100	23	46	69	136	223	310
108-1st DC issue (1/57); re-intro. Blackie, the Hawk, their mascot; not in #115	39	78	117	297	574	850
109-117: 117-(10/57)-Mr. Freeze app.	14	28	42	102	194	285
118-(11/57)-Frazetta-r/Jimmy Wakely #4 (3 pgs.)	15	30	45	107	204	300
119-130 (11/58): 120-Robot-c	11	22	33	80	145	210
131-140 (9/59): 133-Intro. Lady Blackhawk	10	20	30	68	119	170
141-150,152-163,165,166: 141-Cat-Man returns-c/s. 143-Kurtzman-r/Jimmy Wakely #4. 150-(7/60)-King Condor returns. 166-Last 10¢ issue	8	16	24	54	90	125
151-Lady Blackhawk receives & loses super powers	8	16	24	58	97	135
164-Origin retold	8	16	24	58	97	135
167-180	6	12	18	39	62	85
181-190	5	10	15	32	51	70
191-196,199: 196-Combat Diary series begins	4	8	12	26	41	55
197,198,200: 197-New look for Blackhawks. 198-Origin retold	4	8	12	28	44	60
201,202,204-210	4	8	12	22	34	45
203-Origin Chop Chop (12/64)	4	8	12	26	41	55
211-227,229-243(1968): 230-Blackhawks become superheroes; JLA cameo 242-Return to old costumes	3	6	9	18	27	35
228-Batman, Green Lantern, Superman, The Flash cameos.	3	6	9	20	30	40
244 ('76) -250: 250-Chuck dies	1	2	3	4	5	7
251-273: 251-Origin retold; Black Knights return. 252-Intro Domino. 253-Part origin Hendrickson. 258-Blackhawk's Island destroyed. 259-Part origin Chop-Chop. 265-273 (75¢ cover price)						3.00

NOTE: ***Chaykin** a-260; c-257-260, 262. **Crandall** a-10, 11, 13, 16?, 18-20, 22-26, 30-33, 35p, 36(2), 37, 38?, 39-44, 46-50, 52-58, 60, 63, 64, 66, 67; c-14-20, 22-63(most except #28-33, 36, 37, 39). **Evans** a-244, 245,246i, 248-250i. **G. Kane** c-263, 264. **Kubert** c-244, 245. **Newton** a-266p. **Severin** a-257.**Spiegle** a-261-267, 269-273; c-265-272. **Toth** a-260p. **Ward** a-16-27(Chop Chop, 8pgs. ea.); pencilled stories-No. 17-63(approx.). **Wildey** a-268. Chop Chop solo stories in #10-95?*

BLACKHAWK
DC Comics: Mar, 1988 - No. 3, May, 1988 ($2.95, limited series, mature)

	GD 2.0	VG 4.0	FN 6.0	VF 8.0	VF/NM 9.0	NM- 9.2
1-3: Chaykin painted-c/a/scripts						4.00

BLACKHAWK (Also see Action Comics #601)
DC Comics: Mar, 1989 - No. 16, Aug, 1990 ($1.50, mature)

	GD 2.0	VG 4.0	FN 6.0	VF 8.0	VF/NM 9.0	NM- 9.2
1						3.50
2-6,8-16: 16-Crandall-c swipe						2.50
7-($2.50, 52 pgs.)-Story-r/Military #1						3.00
Annual 1 (1989, $2.95, 68 pgs.)-Recaps origin of Blackhawk, Lady Blackhawk, and others						3.50
Special 1 (1992, $3.50, 68 pgs.)-Mature readers						3.50

BLACKHAWK INDIAN TOMAHAWK WAR, THE
Avon Periodicals: 1951 (Also see Fighting Indians of the Wild West)

	GD 2.0	VG 4.0	FN 6.0	VF 8.0	VF/NM 9.0	NM- 9.2
nn-Kinstler-c; Kit West story	20	40	60	114	182	250

BLACK HEART ASSASSIN
Iguana Comics: Jan, 1994 ($2.95)

	GD 2.0	VG 4.0	FN 6.0	VF 8.0	VF/NM 9.0	NM- 9.2
1						3.00

BLACK HOLE (See Walt Disney Showcase #54) (Disney, movie)
Whitman Publishing Co.: Mar, 1980 - No. 4, Sept, 1980

	GD 2.0	VG 4.0	FN 6.0	VF 8.0	VF/NM 9.0	NM- 9.2
11295(#1) (1979, Golden, $1.50-c, 52 pgs., graphic novel; 8 1/2x11") Photo-c; Spiegle-a.	3	6	9	14	19	24
1-3: 1,2-Movie adaptation. 2,3-Spiegle-a. 3-McWilliams-a; photo-c. 3-New stories	2	4	6	8	11	14
4-Sold only in pre-packs; new story; Spiegle-a	7	14	21	50	83	115

BLACK HOOD, THE (See Blue Ribbon, Flyman & Mighty Comics)
Red Circle Comics (Archie): June, 1983 - No. 3, Oct, 1983 (Mandell paper)

	GD 2.0	VG 4.0	FN 6.0	VF 8.0	VF/NM 9.0	NM- 9.2
1-Morrow, McWilliams, Wildey-a; Toth-c						6.00
2,3: The Fox by Toth-c/a; Boyette-a. 3-Morrow-a; Toth wraparound-c						4.00

(Also see Archie's Super-Hero Special Digest #2)

BLACK HOOD
DC Comics (Impact Comics): Dec, 1991 - No. 12, Dec, 1992 ($1.00)

	GD 2.0	VG 4.0	FN 6.0	VF 8.0	VF/NM 9.0	NM- 9.2
1						3.50
2-12: 11-Intro The Fox. 12-Origin Black Hood						2.50
Annual 1 (1992, $2.50, 68 pgs.)-w/Trading card						3.00

BLACK HOOD COMICS (Formerly Hangman #2-8; Laugh Comics #20 on; also see Black Swan, Jackpot, Roly Poly & Top-Notch #9)
MLJ Magazines: No. 9, Wint., 1943-44 - No. 19, Sum., 1946 (on radio in 1943)

	GD 2.0	VG 4.0	FN 6.0	VF 8.0	VF/NM 9.0	NM- 9.2
9-The Hangman & The Boy Buddies cont'd	110	220	330	704	1202	1700

Black Lightning: Year One #5 © DC

Black Orchid Annual #1 © DC

Black Panther V2 #2 © MAR

	GD 2.0	VG 4.0	FN 6.0	VF 8.0	VF/NM 9.0	NM- 9.2
10-Hangman & Dusty, the Boy Detective app.	62	124	186	394	680	965
11-Dusty app.; no Hangman	48	96	144	302	514	725
12-18: 14-Kinstler blood-c. 17-Hal Foster swipe from Prince Valiant; 1st issue with "An Archie Magazine" on-c	43	86	129	271	456	640
19-I.D. exposed; last issue	52	104	156	322	549	775

NOTE: *Hangman by* ***Fuje*** *in 9, 10.* ***Kinstler*** *a-15, c-14-16.*

BLACK JACK (Rocky Lane's...; formerly Jim Bowie)
Charlton Comics: No. 20, Nov, 1957 - No. 30, Nov, 1959

	GD 2.0	VG 4.0	FN 6.0	VF 8.0	VF/NM 9.0	NM- 9.2
20	9	18	27	52	69	85
21,27,29,30	6	12	18	31	38	45
22,23: 22-(68 pgs.). 23-Williamson/Torres-a	8	16	24	42	54	65
24-26,28-Ditko-a	10	20	30	56	76	95

BLACK KNIGHT, THE
Toby Press: May, 1953; 1963

	GD 2.0	VG 4.0	FN 6.0	VF 8.0	VF/NM 9.0	NM- 9.2
1-Bondage-c	27	54	81	160	263	365
Super Reprint No. 11 (1963)-Reprints 1953 issue	3	6	9	19	25	32

BLACK KNIGHT, THE
Atlas Comics (MgPC): May, 1955 - No. 5, April, 1956

	GD 2.0	VG 4.0	FN 6.0	VF 8.0	VF/NM 9.0	NM- 9.2
1-Origin Crusader; Maneely-c/a	89	178	267	565	970	1375
2-Maneely-c/a(4)	60	120	180	381	658	935
3-5: 4-Maneely-c/a. 5-Maneely-c, Shores-a	47	94	141	296	498	700

BLACK KNIGHT (See The Avengers #48, Marvel Super Heroes & Tales To Astonish #52)
Marvel Comics: June, 1990 - No. 4, Sept, 1990 ($1.50, limited series)

	GD 2.0	VG 4.0	FN 6.0	VF 8.0	VF/NM 9.0	NM- 9.2
1-4: 1-Original Black Knight returns. 3,4-Dr. Strange app.						2.50
... (MDCU) 1 (01/10, $3.99) Origin re-told; Frenz-a; originally from Marvel Digital Comics						4.00

NOTE: ***Buckler*** *c-1-4p*

BLACK KNIGHT: EXODUS
Marvel Comics: Dec, 1996 ($2.50, one-shot)

	GD 2.0	VG 4.0	FN 6.0	VF 8.0	VF/NM 9.0	NM- 9.2
1-Raab-s; Apocalypse-c/app.						2.50

BLACK LAMB, THE
DC Comics (Helix): Nov, 1996 - No, 6, Apr, 1997 ($2.50, limited series)

	GD 2.0	VG 4.0	FN 6.0	VF 8.0	VF/NM 9.0	NM- 9.2
1-6: Tim Truman-c/a/scripts						2.50

BLACKLIGHT (From ShadowHawk)
Image Comics: June, 2005 - Present ($2.99)

	GD 2.0	VG 4.0	FN 6.0	VF 8.0	VF/NM 9.0	NM- 9.2
1,2-Toledo & Deering-a/Wherle-s						3.00

BLACK LIGHTNING (See The Brave & The Bold, Cancelled Comic Cavalcade, DC Comics Presents #16, Detective #490 and World's Finest #257)
National Periodical Publ./DC Comics: Apr, 1977 - No. 11, Sept-Oct, 1978

	GD 2.0	VG 4.0	FN 6.0	VF 8.0	VF/NM 9.0	NM- 9.2
1-Origin Black Lightning	2	4	6	8	11	14
2,3,6-10	1	2	3	4	5	7
4,5-Superman-c/s. 4-Intro Cyclotronic Man	1	2	3	5	6	8
11-The Ray new solo story	2	3	4	6	8	10

NOTE: ***Buckler*** *c-1-3p, 6-11p. #11 is 44 pgs.*

BLACK LIGHTNING (2nd Series)
DC Comics: Feb, 1995 - No. 13, Feb, 1996 ($1.95/$2.25)

	GD 2.0	VG 4.0	FN 6.0	VF 8.0	VF/NM 9.0	NM- 9.2
1-5-Tony Isabella scripts begin, ends #8						3.00
6-13: 6-Begin $2.25-c. 13-Batman-c/app.						3.00

BLACK LIGHTNING: YEAR ONE
DC Comics: Mar, 2009 - No. 6, May, 2009 ($2.99, bi-weekly limited series)

	GD 2.0	VG 4.0	FN 6.0	VF 8.0	VF/NM 9.0	NM- 9.2
1-6-Van Meter-s/Hamner-a. 1-Two printings (white and yellow cover title logos)						3.00
TPB (2009, $17.99) r/#1-6						18.00

BLACK MAGIC (...Magazine) (Becomes Cool Cat V8#6 on)
Crestwood Publ. V1#1-4,V6#1-V7#5/Headline V1#5-V5#3,V7#6-V8#5: 10-11/50 - V4#1, 6-7/53: V4#2, 9-10/53 - V5#3, 11-12/54; V6#1, 9-10/57 - V7#2, 11-12/58: V7#3, 7-8/60 - V8#5, 11-12/61 (V1#1-5, 52pgs.; V1#6-V3#3, 44pgs.)

	GD 2.0	VG 4.0	FN 6.0	VF 8.0	VF/NM 9.0	NM- 9.2
V1#1-S&K-a, 10 pgs.; Meskin-a(2)	142	284	426	909	1555	2200
2-S&K-a, 17 pgs.; Meskin-a	62	124	186	394	677	960
3-6(8-9/51)-S&K, Roussos, Meskin-a	54	108	162	340	575	810
V2#1(10-11/51),4,5,7(#13),9(#15),12(#18)-S&K-a	38	76	114	226	368	510
2,3,6,8,10,11(#17)	29	58	87	172	281	390
V3#1(#19, 12/52) - 6(#24, 5/53)-S&K-a	30	60	90	177	289	400
V4#1(#25, 6-7/53), 2(#26, 9-10/53)-S&K-a(3-4)	31	62	93	182	296	410
3(#27, 11-12/53)-S&K-a; Ditko-a (2nd published-a); also see Captain 3-D, Daring Love #1, Strange Fantasy #9, & Fantastic Fears #5 (Fant. Fears was 1st drawn, but not 1st publ.)	50	100	150	315	533	750
4(#28)-Eyes ripped out/story-S&K, Ditko-a	41	82	123	248	417	585
5(#29, 3-4/54)-S&K, Ditko-a	32	64	96	192	314	435
6(#30, 5-6/54)-S&K, Powell?-a	26	52	78	154	252	350
V5#1(#31, 7-8/54 - 3(#33, 11-12/54)-S&K-a	19	38	57	112	179	245
V6#1(#34, 9-10/57), 2(#35, 11-12/57)	12	24	36	67	94	120
3(1-2/58) - 6(7-8/58)	12	24	36	67	94	120
V7#1(9-10/58) - 3(7-8/60), 4(9-10/60)	10	20	30	56	76	95
5(11-12/60)-Hitler-c; Torres-a	15	30	45	85	130	175
6(1-2/61)-Powell-a(2)	10	20	30	56	76	95
V8#1(3-4/61)-Powell-c/a	10	20	30	56	76	95
2(5-6/61)-E.C. story swipe/W.F. #22; Ditko, Powell-a	11	22	33	60	83	105
3(7-8/61)-E.C. story swipe/W.F. #22; Powell-a(2)	11	22	33	60	83	105
4(9-10/61)-Powell-a(5)	10	20	30	56	76	95
5-E.C. story swipe/W.S.F. #28; Powell-a(3)	11	22	33	60	83	105

NOTE: ***Bernard Baily*** *a-V4#6?, V5#3(2).* ***Grandenetti*** *a-V2#3, 11.* ***Kirby*** *c-V1#1-6, V2#1-12, V3#1-6, V4#1, 2, 4-6, V5#1-3.* ***McWilliams*** *a-V3#2i.* ***Meskin*** *a-V1#1(2), 2, 3, 4(2), 5(2), 6, V2/1, 2, 3(2), 4(3), 5, 6(2), 7-9, 11, 12i, V3#1(2), 5, 6, V5#1(2), 2.* ***Orlando*** *a-V6#1, 4, V7#2; c-V6/1-6.* ***Powell*** *a-V5#1?.* ***Roussos*** *a-V1#3-5, 6(2), V2#3(2), 4, 5(2), 6, 8, 9, 10(2), 11, 12p, V3#1(2), 2i, 5, V5#2.* ***Simon*** *a-V2#12, V3#2, V7#5? c-V4#3?, V7#3?, 4, 5?, 6?, V8#1-5.* ***Simon & Kirby*** *a-V1#1, 2(2), 3-6, V2#1, 4, 5, 7, 9, 12, V3#1-6, V4#1(3), 2(4), 3(2), 4(2), 5, 6, V5#1-3; c-V2#1.* ***Leonard Starr*** *a-V1#1.* ***Tuska*** *a-V6#3, 4.* ***Woodbridge*** *a-V7#4.*

BLACK MAGIC
National Periodical Publications: Oct-Nov, 1973 - No. 9, Apr-May, 1975

	GD 2.0	VG 4.0	FN 6.0	VF 8.0	VF/NM 9.0	NM- 9.2
1-S&K reprints	3	6	9	17	25	32
2-8-S&K reprints	2	4	6	10	14	18
9-S&K reprints	2	4	6	11	16	20

BLACKMAIL TERROR (See Harvey Comics Library)

BLACK MASK
DC Comics: 1993 - No. 3, 1994 ($4.95, limited series, 52 pgs.)

	GD 2.0	VG 4.0	FN 6.0	VF 8.0	VF/NM 9.0	NM- 9.2
1-3						5.00

BLACK OPS
Image Comics (WildStorm): Jan, 1996 - No. 5, May, 1996 ($2.50, lim. series)

	GD 2.0	VG 4.0	FN 6.0	VF 8.0	VF/NM 9.0	NM- 9.2
1-5						2.50

BLACK ORCHID (See Adventure Comics #428 & Phantom Stranger)
DC Comics: Holiday, 1988-89 - No. 3, 1989 ($3.50, lim. series, prestige format)

	GD 2.0	VG 4.0	FN 6.0	VF 8.0	VF/NM 9.0	NM- 9.2
Book 1,3: Gaiman scripts & McKean painted-a in all						6.00
Book 2-Arkham Asylum story; Batman app.	1	2	3	5	6	8
TPB (1991, $19.95) r/#1-3; new McKean-c						20.00

BLACK ORCHID
DC Comics: Sept, 1993 - No. 22, June, 1995 ($1.95/$2.25)

	GD 2.0	VG 4.0	FN 6.0	VF 8.0	VF/NM 9.0	NM- 9.2
1-22: Dave McKean-c all issues						2.50
1-Platinum Edition						12.00
Annual 1 (1993, $3.95, 68 pgs.)-Children's Crusade						4.00

BLACKOUTS (See Broadway Hollywood...)

BLACK PANTHER, THE (Also see Avengers #52, Fantastic Four #52, Jungle Action & Marvel Premiere #51-53)
Marvel Comics Group: Jan, 1977 - No. 15, May, 1979

	GD 2.0	VG 4.0	FN 6.0	VF 8.0	VF/NM 9.0	NM- 9.2
1-Jack Kirby-s/a thru #12	3	6	9	20	30	40
2-13: 4,5-(Regular 30¢ editions). 8-Origin	2	4	6	9	12	15
4,5-(35¢-c variants, limited dist.)(7,9/77)	6	12	18	39	62	85
14,15-Avengers x-over. 14-Origin	3	6	9	14	19	24
...By Jack Kirby Vol. 1 TPB (2005, $19.99) r/#1-7; unused covers and sketch pages						20.00
...By Jack Kirby Vol. 2 TPB (2006, $19.99) r/#8-12 by Kirby and #13 non-Kirby						20.00

NOTE: ***J. Buscema*** *c-15p.* ***Layton*** *c-13i.*

BLACK PANTHER
Marvel Comics Group: July, 1988 - No. 4, Oct, 1988 ($1.25)

	GD 2.0	VG 4.0	FN 6.0	VF 8.0	VF/NM 9.0	NM- 9.2
1-4-Gillis-s/Cowan & Delarosa-a						2.50

BLACK PANTHER (Marvel Knights)
Marvel Comics: Nov, 1998 - No. 62, Sept, 2003 ($2.50)

	GD 2.0	VG 4.0	FN 6.0	VF 8.0	VF/NM 9.0	NM- 9.2
1-Texeira-a/c; Priest-s						6.00
1-($6.95) DF edition w/Quesada & Palmiotti-c	1	2	3	5	6	8
2-4: 2-Two covers by Texeira and Timm. 3-Fantastic Four app.						3.50
5-35,37-40: 5-Evans-a. 6-8-Jusko-a. 8-Avengers-c/app. 15-Hulk app. 22-Moon Knight app. 23-Avengers app. 25-Maximum Security x-over. 26-Storm-c/app. 28-Magneto & Sub-Mariner-c/app. 29-WWII flashback meeting w/Captain America. 35-Defenders-c/app. 37-Luke Cage and Falcon-c/app.						2.50
36-($3.50, 100 pgs.) 35th Anniversary issue incl. r/1st app. in FF #52						3.50
41-56: 41-44-Wolverine app. 47-Thor app. 48,49-Magneto app.						2.50
57-62: 57-Begin $2.99-c. 59-Falcon app.						3.00
...: The Client (6/01, $14.95, TPB) r/#1-5						15.00
... 2099 #1 (11/04, $2.99) Kirkman-s/Hotz-a/Pat Lee-c						3.00

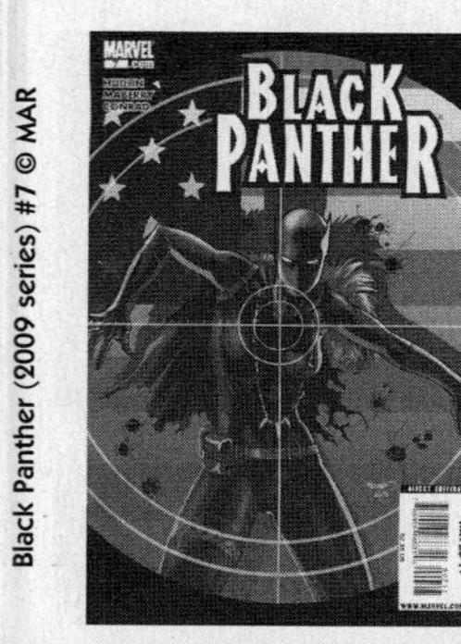

Black Panther (2009 series) #7 © MAR

Black Rider Rides Again #1 © MAR

Black Terror #1 © Super Power Heroes

GD VG FN VF VF/NM NM-
2.0 4.0 6.0 8.0 9.0 9.2

BLACK PANTHER (Marvel Knights)
Marvel Comics: Apr, 2005 - No. 41, Nov, 2008 ($2.99)

1-Reginald Hudlin-s/John Romita Jr. & Klaus Janson-a; covers by Romita & Ribic 5.00
1-2nd printing; variant-c by Ribic 3.00
2-7,9-15,17-20: 7-House of M; Hairsine-a. 10-14-Luke Cage app. 12,13-Blade app. 17-Linsner-c. 19-Doctor Doom app. 3.00
8-Cho-c; X-Men app. 4.00
8-2nd printing variant-c 3.00
16-($3.99) Wedding of T'Challa and Storm; wraparound Cho-c; Hudlin-s/Eaton-a 4.00
21-Civil War x-over; Namor app. 8.00
21-2nd printing with new cover and Civil War logo 3.00
22-25-Civil War: 23-25-Turner-c 4.00
26-41: 26-30-T'Challa and Storm join the Fantastic Four. 27-30-Marvel Zombies app. 28-30-Suydam-c. 39-41-Secret Invasion 3.00
Annual 1 (4/08, $3.99) Hudlin-s/Stroman & Lashley-a; alternate future; Uatu app. 4.00
...: Bad Mutha TPB (2006, $10.99) r/#10-13 11.00
...: Civil War TPB (2007, $17.99) r/#19-25 18.00
...: Four the Hard Way TPB (2007, $13.99) r/#26-30; page layouts and character designs 14.00
...: Little Green Men TPB (2008, $10.99) r/#31-34 11.00
...: The Bride TPB (2006, $14.99) r/#14-18; interview with the dress designer 15.00
...: Who Is The Black Panther HC (2005, $21.99) r/#1-6; Hudlin afterword; cover gallery 22.00
...: Who Is The Black Panther SC (2006, $14.99) r/#1-6; Hudlin afterword; cover gallery 15.00

BLACK PANTHER
Marvel Comics: Apr, 2009 - Present ($3.99/$2.99)

1-($3.99) Hudlin-s/Lashley-a; covers by Campbell & Lashley; Dr. Doom app. 4.00
2-12-($2.99) 2-6-Campbell-c. 6-Shuri becomes female Black Panther 3.00

BLACK PANTHER: PANTHER'S PREY
Marvel Comics: May, 1991 - No. 4, Oct, 1991 ($4.95, squarebound, lim. series, 52 pgs.)

1-4: McGregor-s/Turner-a 5.00

BLACK PEARL, THE
Dark Horse Comics: Sept, 1996 - No. 5, Jan, 1997 ($2.95, limited series)

1-5: Mark Hamill scripts 3.00

BLACK PHANTOM (See Tim Holt #25, 38)
Magazine Enterprises: Nov, 1954 (one-shot) (Female outlaw)

1 (A-1 #122)-The Ghost Rider story plus 3 Black Phantom stories; Headlight-c/a
36 72 108 216 351 485

BLACK PHANTOM
AC Comics: 1989 - No. 3, 1990 ($2.50, B&W; #2 color)(Reprints & new-a)

1-3: 1-Ayers-r, Bolle-r/B.P. #1-3-Redmask-r 2.75

BLACK PHANTOM, RETURN OF THE (See Wisco)

BLACK RIDER (Western Winners #1-7; Western Tales of Black Rider #28-31; Gunsmoke Western #32 on)(See All Western Winners, Best Western, Kid Colt, Outlaw Kid, Rex Hart, Two-Gun Kid, Two-Gun Western, Western Gunfighters, Western Winners, & Wild Western)
Marvel/Atlas Comics(CDS No. 8-17/CPS No. 19 on): No. 8, 3/50 - No. 18, 1/52; No. 19, 11/53 - No. 27, 3/55

8 (#1)-Black Rider & his horse Satan begin; 36 pgs; Stan Lee photo-c as Black Rider) 42 84 126 265 445 625
9-52 pgs. begin, end #14 22 44 66 132 216 300
10-Origin Black Rider 27 54 81 158 259 360
11-14: 14-Last 52pgs. 17 34 51 98 154 210
15-19: 19-Two-Gun Kid app. 15 30 45 85 130 175
20-Classic-c; Two-Gun Kid app. 16 32 48 92 144 195
21-27: 21-23-Two-Gun Kid app. 24,25-Arrowhead app. 26-Kid Colt app. 27-Last issue; last precode. Kid Colt app. The Spider (a villain) burns to death
14 28 42 81 118 155

NOTE: *Ayers c-22. Jack Keller a-15, 26, 27. Maneely a-14; c-16, 17, 25, 27. Syd Shores a-19, 21, 22, 23(3), 24(3), 25-27; c-19, 21, 23. Sinnott a-24, 25. Tuska a-12, 19-21.*

BLACK RIDER RIDES AGAIN!, THE
Atlas Comics (CPS): Sept, 1957

1-Kirby-a(3); Powell-a; Severin-c 25 50 75 147 241 335

BLACK SEPTEMBER (Also see Avengers/Ultraforce, Ultraforce (1st series) #10 & Ultraforce/Avengers)
Malibu Comics (Ultraverse): 1995 ($1.50, one-shot)

Infinity-Intro to the new Ultraverse; variant-c exists. 2.50

BLACKSTONE (See Super Magician Comics & Wisco Giveaways)

BLACKSTONE, MASTER MAGICIAN COMICS
Vital Publ./Street & Smith Publ.: Mar-Apr, 1946 - No. 3, July-Aug, 1946

1 32 64 96 188 307 425
2,3 19 38 57 111 176 240

BLACKSTONE, THE MAGICIAN (...Detective on cover only #3 & 4)
Marvel Comics (CnPC): No. 2, May, 1948 - No. 4, Sept, 1948 (No #1) (Cont'd from E.C. #1?)

2-The Blonde Phantom begins, ends #4 69 138 207 442 759 1075
3,4: 3-Blonde Phantom by Sekowsky 41 82 123 256 428 600

BLACKSTONE, THE MAGICIAN DETECTIVE FIGHTS CRIME
E. C. Comics: Fall, 1947

1-1st app. Happy Houlihans 50 100 150 315 533 750

BLACK SUN (X-Men Black Sun on cover)
Marvel Comics: Nov, 2000 - No. 5, Nov, 2000 ($2.99, weekly limited series)

1-(...: X-Men), 2-(...: Storm), 3-(...: Banshee and Sunfire), 4-(...: Colossus and Nightcrawler), 5-(...: Wolverine and Thunderbird); Claremont-s in all; Evans interlocking painted covers; Magik returns 3.00

BLACK SUN
DC Comics (WildStorm): Nov, 2002 - No. 6, Jun, 2003 ($2.95, limited series)

1-6-Andreyko-s/Scott-a 3.00

BLACK SWAN COMICS
MLJ Magazines (Pershing Square Publ. Co.): 1945

1-The Black Hood reprints from Black Hood No. 14; Bill Woggon-a; Suzie app. Caribbean Pirates-c 21 42 63 122 199 275

BLACK TARANTULA (See Feature Presentations No. 5)

BLACK TERROR (See America's Best Comics & Exciting Comics)
Better Publications/Standard: Winter, 1942-43 - No. 27, June, 1949

1-Black Terror, Crime Crusader begin 300 600 900 2070 3635 5200
2 119 238 357 762 1306 1850
3 82 164 246 528 902 1275
4,5 68 136 204 432 746 1060
6-10: 7-The Ghost app. 58 116 174 371 636 900
11-20: 20-The Scarab app. 50 100 150 315 533 750
21-Miss Masque app. 53 106 159 334 567 800
22-Part Frazetta-a on one Black Terror story 50 100 150 315 533 750
23,25-27 45 90 135 284 480 675
24-Frazetta-a (1/4 pg.) 46 92 138 290 488 685

NOTE: *Schomburg (Xela) c-2-27; bondage c-2, 17, 24. Meskin a-27. Moreira a-27. Robinson/Meskin a-23, 24(3), 25, 26. Roussos/Mayo a-24. Tuska a-26, 27.*

BLACK TERROR, THE (Also see Total Eclipse)
Eclipse Comics: Oct, 1989 - No. 3, June, 1990 ($4.95, 52 pgs., squarebound, limited series)

1-3: Beau Smith & Chuck Dixon scripts; Dan Brereton painted-c/a 5.00

BLACK TERROR (Also see Project Superpowers)
Dynamite Entertainment: 2008 - Present ($3.50)

1-8-Golden Age hero; Alex Ross-c/Mike Lilly-a; various variant-c exist 3.50

BLACKTHORNE 3-D SERIES
Blackthorne Publishing Co.: May, 1985 - No. 80, 1989 ($2.25/$2.50)

1-Sheena in 3-D #1. D. Stevens-c/retouched-a 1 2 3 5 6 8
2-10: 2-MerlinRealm in 3-D #1. 3-3-D Heroes #1. Goldyn in 3-D #1. 5-Bizarre 3-D Zone #1. 6-Salimba in 3-D #1. 7-Twisted Tales in 3-D #1. 8-Dick Tracy in 3-D #1. 9-Salimba in 3-D #2. 10-Gumby in 3-D #1 6.00
11-19: 11-Betty Boop in 3-D #1. 12-Hamster Vice in 3-D #1. 13-Little Nemo in 3-D #1. 14-Gumby in 3-D #2. 15-Hamster Vice #6 in 3-D. 16-Laffin' Gas #6 in 3-D. 17-Gumby in 3-D #3. 18-Bullwinkle and Rocky in 3-D #1. 19-The Flintstones in 3-D #1 6.00
20(#1),26(#2),35(#3),39(#4),52(#5),62,71(#6)-G.I. Joe in 3-D. 62-G.I. Joe Annual
2 4 6 8 11 14
21-24,27-28: 21-Gumby in 3-D #4. 22-The Flintstones in 3-D #2. 23-Laurel & Hardy in 3-D #1. 24-Bozo the Clown in 3-D #1. 27-Bravestarr in 3-D #1. 28- Gumby in 3-D #5 6.00
25,29,37-The Transformers in 3-D 2 4 6 10 14 18
30-Star Wars in 3-D #1 3 6 9 14 19 24
31-34,36,38,40: 31-The California Raisins in 3-D #1. 32-Richie Rich & Casper in 3-D #1. 33-Gumby in 3-D #6. 34-Laurel & Hardy in 3-D #2. 36-The Flintstones in 3-D #3. 38-Gumby in 3-D #7. 40-Bravestarr in 3-D #2 6.00
41-46,49,50: 41-Battletech in 3-D #1. 42-The Flintstones in 3-D #4. 43-Underdog in 3-D #1 44-The California Raisins in 3-D #2. 45-Red Heat in 3-D #1 (movie adapt.). 46-The California Raisins in 3-D #3. 49-Rambo in 3-D #1. 49-Sad Sack in 3-D #1. 50-Bullwinkle For President in 3-D #1 6.00
47,48-Star Wars in 3-D #2,3 2 4 6 9 13 16
51,53-60: 51-Kull in 3-D #1. 53-Red Sonja in 3-D #1. 54-Bozo in 3-D #2. 55-Waxwork in 3-D #1 (movie adapt.). 57-Casper in 3-D #1. 58-Baby Huey in 3-D #1. 59-Little Dot in 3-D #1. 60-Solomon Kane in 3-D #1 6.00
61,63-70,72-80: 61-Werewolf in 3-D #1. 63-The California Raisins in 3-D #4. 64-To Die For in

Black Widow: Deadly Origin #1 © MAR

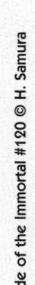

Blade of the Immortal #120 © H. Samura

Blaze #4 © MAR

	GD 2.0	VG 4.0	FN 6.0	VF 8.0	VF/NM 9.0	NM- 9.2

3-D #1. 65-Capt. Holo in 3-D #1. 66-Playful Little Audrey in 3-D #1. 67-Kull in 3-D #2. 69-The California Raisins in 3-D #5. 70-Wendy in 3-D #1. 72-Sports Hall of Shame #1. 74-The Noid in 3-D #1. 75-Moonwalker in 3-D #1 (Michael Jackson movie adapt.). 76-79. 80-The Noid in 3-D #2 1 2 3 4 5 7

BLACK WIDOW (Marvel Knights) (Also see Marvel Graphic Novel)
Marvel Comics: May, 1999 - No. 3, Aug, 1999 ($2.99, limited series)
1-(June on-c) Devin Grayson-s/J.G. Jones-c/a; Daredevil app. 5.00
1-Variant-c by J.G. Jones 6.00
2,3 4.00
...Web of Intrigue (6/99, $3.50) r/origin & early appearances 3.50
TPB (7/01, $15.95) r/Vol. 1 & 2; Jones-c 16.00

BLACK WIDOW (Marvel Knights) (Volume 2)
Marvel Comics: Jan, 2001 - No. 3, May, 2001 ($2.99, limited series)
1-3-Grayson & Rucka-s/Scott Hampton-c/a; Daredevil app. 3.00

BLACK WIDOW (Marvel Knights)
Marvel Comics: Nov, 2004 - No. 6, Apr, 2005 ($2.99, limited series)
1-6-Sienkiewicz-a/Land-c 3.00

BLACK WIDOW & THE MARVEL GIRLS
Marvel Comics: Feb, 2010 - No. 4, Apr, 2010 ($2.99, limited series)
1-4-Tobin-s. 1-Enchantress app. 2-Avengers app. 4-Storm app.; Miyazawa-a 3.00

BLACK WIDOW: DEADLY ORIGIN
Marvel Comics: Jan, 2010 - No. 4, Apr, 2010 ($3.99, limited series)
1-4-Granov-c; origin retold. 1-Wolverine and Bucky app. 3-Daredevil app. 4.00

BLACK WIDOW: PALE LITTLE SPIDER (Marvel Knights) (Volume 3)
Marvel Comics: Jun, 2002 - No. 3, Aug, 2002 ($2.99, limited series)
1-3-Rucka-s/Kordey-a/Horn-c 3.00

BLACK WIDOW 2 (THE THINGS THEY SAY ABOUT HER) (Marvel Knights)
Marvel Comics: Nov, 2005 - No. 6, Apr, 2006 ($2.99, limited series)
1-6-Phillips & Sienkiewicz-a/Morgan-s; Daredevil app. 3.00
TPB (2006, $15.99) r/#1-6 16.00

BLACKWULF
Marvel Comics: June, 1994 - No. 10, Mar, 1995 ($1.50)
1-($2.50)-Embossed-c; Angel Medina-a 3.00
2-10 2.50

BLADE (The Vampire Hunter)
Marvel Comics
1-(3/98, $3.50) Colan-a(p)/Christopher Golden-s 3.50
... Black & White TPB (2004, $15.99, B&W) reprints from magazines Vampire Tales #8,9; Marvel Preview #3,6; Crescent City Blues #1 and Marvel Shadow and Light #1 16.00
San Diego Con Promo (6/97) Wesley Snipes photo-c 3.00
...Sins of the Father (10/98, $5.99) Sears-a; movie adaption 6.00
Blade 2: Movie Adaptation (5/02, $5.95) Ponticelli-a/Bradstreet-c 6.00

BLADE (The Vampire Hunter)
Marvel Comics: Nov, 1998 - No. 3, Jan, 1999 ($3.50/$2.99)
1-($3.50) Contains Movie insider pages; McKean-a 3.50
2,3-($2.99): 2-Two covers 3.00

BLADE (Volume 2)
Marvel Comics (MAX): May, 2002 -No. 6, Oct, 2002 ($2.99)
1-6-Bradstreet-c/Hinz-s. 1-5-Pugh-a. 6-Homs-a 3.00

BLADE
Marvel Comics: Nov, 2006 - No. 12, Oct, 2007 ($2.99)
1-12: 1-Chaykin-a/Guggenheim-s; origin retold; Spider-Man app. 2-Dr. Doom-c/app. 5-Civil War tie-in; Wolverine app. 6-Blade loses a hand. 10-Spider-Man app. 3.00
...: Sins of the Father TPB (2007, $14.99) r/#7-12; afterword by Guggenheim 15.00
...: Undead Again TPB (2007, $14.99) r/#1-6; letters pages from #1&2 15.00

BLADE OF THE IMMORTAL (Manga)
Dark Horse Comics: June, 1996 - No. 131, Nov, 2007 ($2.95/$2.99/$3.95, B&W)
1-Hiroaki Samura-s/a in all 1 3 4 6 8 10
2-5: 2-#1 on cover in error 6.00
6-10 5.00
11,19,20,34-($3.95, 48 pgs.): 34-Food one-shot 4.00
12-18,21-33,35-41,43-105,107-131: 12-20-Dreamsong. 21-28-On Silent Wings. 29-33-Dark Shadow. 35-42-Heart of Darkness. 43-57-The Gathering 3.00
42-($3.50) Ends Heart of Darkness 3.50
106-($3.99) 4.00

BLADE RUNNER (Movie)
Marvel Comics Group: Oct, 1982 - No. 2, Nov, 1982
1,2-r/Marvel Super Special #22; 1-Williamson-c/a. 2-Williamson-a 3.50

BLADE: THE VAMPIRE-HUNTER
Marvel Comics: July, 1994 - No. 10, Apr, 1995 ($1.95)
1-($2.95)-Foil-c; Dracula returns; Wheatley-c/a 3.50
2-10: 2,3,10-Dracula-c/app. 8-Morbius app. 2.50

BLADE: VAMPIRE-HUNTER
Marvel Comics: Dec, 1999 - No. 6, May, 2000 ($3.50/$2.50)
1-($3.50)-Bart Sears-s; Sears and Smith-a 3.50
2-6-($2.50): 2-Regular & Wesley Snipes photo-c 2.50

BLAIR WITCH CHRONICLES, THE
Oni Press: Mar, 2000 - No. 4, July, 2000 ($2.95, B&W, limited series)
1-4-Van Meter-s.1-Guy Davis-a. 2-Mireault-a 3.00
1-DF Alternate-c by John Estes 7.00
TPB (9/00, $15.95) r/#1-4 & Blair Witch Project one-shot 16.00

BLAIR WITCH: DARK TESTAMENTS
Image Comics: Oct, 2000 ($2.95, one-shot)
1-Edington-s/Adlard-a; story of murderer Rustin Parr 3.00

BLAIR WITCH PROJECT, THE (Movie companion, not adaptation)
Oni Press: July, 1999 ($2.95, B&W, one-shot)
1-(1st printing) History of the Blair Witch, art by Edwards, Mireault, and Davis; Van Meter-s; only the stick figure is red on the cover 12.00
1-(2nd printing) Stick figure and title lettering are red on cover 4.00
1-(3rd printing) Stick figure, title, and creator credits are red on cover 3.00
DF Glow in the Dark variant-c ($10.00) 10.00

BLAST (Satire Magazine)
G & D Publications: Feb, 1971 - No. 2, May, 1971
1-Wrightson & Kaluta-a/Everette-c 8 16 24 52 86 120
2-Kaluta-c/a 6 12 18 39 62 85

BLAST CORPS
Dark Horse Comics: Oct, 1998 ($2.50, one-shot, based on Nintendo game)
1-Reprints from Nintendo Power magazine; Mahn-a 2.50

BLASTERS SPECIAL
DC Comics: 1989 ($2.00, one-shot)
1-Peter David scripts; Invasion spin-off 2.50

BLAST-OFF (Three Rocketeers)
Harvey Publications (Fun Day Funnies): Oct, 1965 (12¢)
1-Kirby/Williamson-a(2); Williamson/Crandall-a; Williamson/Torres/Krenkel-a; Kirby/Simon-c 7 14 21 45 73 100

BLAZE
Marvel Comics: Aug, 1994 - No. 12, July, 1995 ($1.95)
1-($2.95)-Foil embossed-c 3.50
2-12: 2-Man-Thing-c/story. 11,12-Punisher app. 2.50

BLAZE CARSON (Rex Hart #6 on)(See Kid Colt, Tex Taylor, Wild Western, Wisco)
Marvel Comics (USA): Sept, 1948 - No. 5, June, 1949
1: 1,2-Shores-c 27 54 81 158 259 360
2,4,5: 4-Two-Gun Kid app. 5-Tex Taylor app. 18 36 54 105 165 225
3-Used by N.Y. State Legis. Comm. (injury to eye splash); Tex Morgan app. 19 38 57 111 176 240

BLAZE: LEGACY OF BLOOD (See Ghost Rider & Ghost Rider/Blaze)
Marvel Comics (Midnight Sons imprint): Dec, 1993 - No. 4, Mar, 1994 ($1.75, limited series)
1-4 2.50

BLAZE OF GLORY
Marvel Comics: Feb, 2000 - No. 4, Mar, 2000 ($2.99, limited series)
1-4-Ostrander-s/Manco-a; Two-Gun Kid, Rawhide Kid, Red Wolf and Ghost Rider app. 3.00
TPB (7/02, $9.99) r/#1-4 10.00

BLAZE THE WONDER COLLIE (Formerly Molly Manton's Romances #1?)
Marvel Comics(SePI): No. 2, Oct, 1949 - No. 3, Feb, 1950 (Both have photo-c)
2(#1), 3-(Scarce) 23 46 69 136 223 310

BLAZING BATTLE TALES
Seaboard Periodicals (Atlas): July, 1975
1-Intro. Sgt. Hawk & the Sky Demon; Severin, McWilliams, Sparling-a; Nazi-c by Thorne 2 4 6 9 13 16

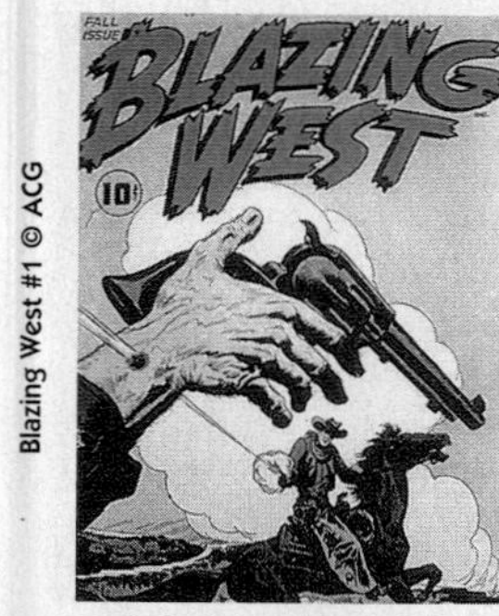

Blazing West #1 © ACG

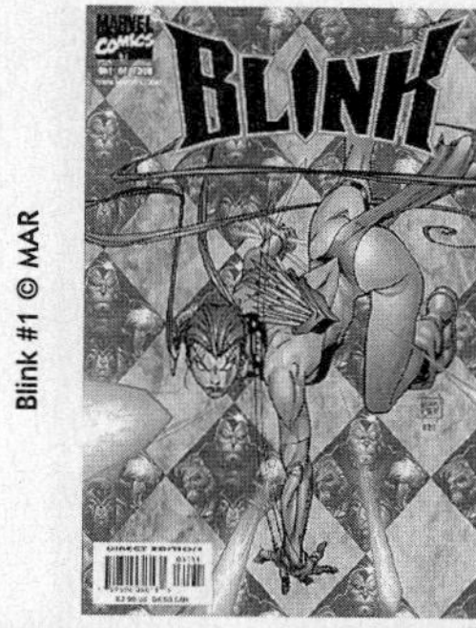

Blink #1 © MAR

Blondie Comics #187 © HARV

GD VG FN VF VF/NM NM-
2.0 4.0 6.0 8.0 9.0 9.2

BLAZING COMBAT (Magazine)
Warren Publishing Co.: Oct, 1965 - No. 4, July, 1966 (35¢, B&W)
1-Frazetta painted-c on all 26 52 78 190 370 550
2 8 16 24 54 90 125
3,4: 4-Frazetta half pg. ad 7 14 21 49 80 110
nn-Anthology (reprints from No. 1-4) (low print) 8 16 24 56 93 130
NOTE: ***Adkins** a-4. **Colan** a-3,4,nn. **Crandall** a-all. **Evans** a-1,4. **Heath** a-4,nn. **Morrow** a-1-3,nn. **Orlando** a-1-3,nn. **J. Severin** a-all. **Torres** a-1-4. **Toth** a-all. **Williamson** a-2. and **Wood** a-3,4,nn.*

BLAZING COMBAT: WORLD WAR I AND WORLD WAR II
Apple Press: Mar, 1994 ($3.75, B&W)
1,2: 1-r/Colan, Toth, Goodwin, Severin, Wood-a. 2-r/Crandall, Evans, Severin, Torres, Williamson-a 4.00

BLAZING COMICS (Also see Blue Circle Comics and Red Circle Comics)
Enwil Associates/Rural Home: 6/44 - #3, 9/44; #4, 2/45; #5, 3/45; #5(V2#2), 3/55 - #6(V2#3), 1955?
1-The Green Turtle, Red Hawk, Black Buccaneer begin; origin Jun-Gal
51 102 153 321 541 760
2-5: 3-Briefer-a. 5-(V2#2 inside) 34 68 102 204 332 460
5(3/55, V2#2-inside)-Black Buccaneer-c, 6(V2#3-inside, 1955)-Indian/Japanese-c; cover is from Apr. 1945 19 38 57 111 176 240
NOTE: *No. 5 & 6 contain remaindered comics rebound and the contents can vary. Cloak & Daggar, Will Rogers, Superman 64, Star Spangled 130, Kaanga known. Value would be half of contents.*

BLAZING SIXGUNS
Avon Periodicals: Dec, 1952
1-Kinstler-c/a; Larsen/Alascia-a(2), Tuska?-a; Jesse James, Kit Carson, Wild Bill Hickok app. 18 36 54 103 162 220

BLAZING SIXGUNS
I.W./Super Comics: 1964
I.W. Reprint #1,8,9: 1-r/Wild Bill Hickok #26, Western True Crime #? & Blazing Sixguns #1 by Avon; Kinstler-c. 8-r/Blazing Western #?; Kinstler-c. 9-r/Blazing Western #1; Ditko-r; Kintsler-c reprinted from Dalton Boys #1 2 4 6 10 14 18
Super Reprint #10,11,15-17: 10,11-r/The Rider #2,1. 15-r/Silver Kid Western #?. 16-r/Buffalo Bill #?; Wildey-r; Severin-c. 17(1964)-r/Western True Crime #?
2 4 6 10 14 18
12-Reprints Bullseye #3; S&K-a 4 8 12 19 29 38
18-r/Straight Arrow #? by Powell; Severin-c 2 4 6 10 14 18

BLAZING SIX-GUNS (Also see Sundance Kid)
Skywald Comics: Feb, 1971 - No. 2, Apr, 1971 (52 pgs.)
1-The Red Mask (3-D effect, not true 3-D), Sundance Kid begin (new-s), Avon's Geronimo reprint by Kinstler; Wyatt Earp app. 3 6 9 14 20 25
2-Wild Bill Hickok, Jesse James, Kit Carson-r plus M.E. Red Mask-r (3-D effect)
2 4 6 10 14 18

BLAZING WEST (The Hooded Horseman #21 on)
American Comics Group (B&I Publ./Michel Publ.): Fall, 1948 - No. 20, Nov-Dec, 1951
1-Origin & 1st app. Injun Jones, Tenderfoot & Buffalo Belle; Texas Tim & Ranger begins, ends #13 20 40 60 114 182 250
2,3 (1-2/49) 11 22 33 62 86 110
4-Origin & 1st app. Little Lobo; Starr-a (3-4/49) 10 20 30 56 76 95
5-10: 5-Starr-a 9 18 27 50 65 80
11-13 8 16 24 42 54 65
14(11-12/50)-Origin/1st app. The Hooded Horseman 13 26 39 74 105 135
15-20: 15,16,18,19-Starr-a 9 18 27 50 65 80

BLAZING WESTERN
Timor Publications: Jan, 1954 - No. 5, Sept, 1954
1-Ditko-a (1st Western-a?); text story by Bruce Hamilton
17 34 51 98 154 210
2-4 9 18 27 50 65 80
5-Disbrow-a 9 18 27 52 69 85

BLINDSIDE
Image Comics (Extreme Studios): Aug, 1996 ($2.50)
1-Variant-c exists 2.50

BLINK (See X-Men Age of Apocalypse storyline)
Marvel Comics: March, 2001 - No. 4, June, 2001 ($2.99, limited series)
1-4-Adam Kubert-c/Lobdell-s/Winick-script; leads into Exiles #1 3.00

BLIP
Marvel Comics Group: 2/1983 - 1983 (Video game mag. in comic format)
1-1st app. Donkey Kong & Mario Bros. in comics, 6pgs. comics; photo-c
2 3 4 6 8 10
2-Spider-Man photo-c; 6pgs. Spider-Man comics w/Green Goblin
2 4 6 8 10 12
3,4,6 6.00
5-E.T., Indiana Jones; Rocky-c 1 2 3 4 5 7
7-6pgs. Hulk comics; Pac-Man & Donkey Kong Jr. Hints 1 2 3 5 6 8

BLISS ALLEY
Image Comics: July, 1997 - No. 2, Sept, 1997 ($2.95, B&W)
1,2-Messner-Loebs-s/a 3.00

BLITZKRIEG
National Periodical Publications: Jan-Feb, 1976 - No. 5, Sept-Oct, 1976
1-Kubert-c on all 4 8 12 24 37 50
2-5 3 6 9 16 23 30

BLONDE PHANTOM (Formerly All-Select #1-11; Lovers #23 on)(Also see Blackstone, Marvel Mystery, Millie The Model #2, Sub-Mariner Comics #25 & Sun Girl)
Marvel Comics (MPC): No. 12, Winter, 1946-47 - No. 22, Mar, 1949
12-Miss America begins, ends #14 171 342 513 1086 1868 2650
13-Sub-Mariner begins (not in #16) 100 200 300 635 1093 1550
14,15: 15-Kurtzman's "Hey Look" 94 188 282 597 1024 1450
16-Captain America with Bucky story by Rico(p), 6 pgs.; Kurtzman's "Hey Look" (1 pg.)
126 252 378 806 1378 1950
17-22: 22-Anti Wertham editorial 79 158 237 502 864 1225
NOTE: ***Shores** c-12-18.*

BLONDIE (See Ace Comics, Comics Reading Libraries (Promotional Comics section), Dagwood, Daisy & Her Pups, Eat Right to Work…, King & Magic Comics)
David McKay Publications: 1942 - 1946
Feature Books 12 (Rare) 82 164 246 528 902 1275
Feature Books 27-29,31,34(1940) 21 42 63 122 199 275
Feature Books 36,38,40,42,43,45,47 20 40 60 114 182 250
…1944 (Hard-c, 1938, B&W, 128 pgs.)-1944 daily strip-r
16 32 48 94 147 200

BLONDIE & DAGWOOD FAMILY
Harvey Publ. (King Features Synd.): Oct, 1963 - No. 4, Dec, 1965 (68 pgs.)
1 5 10 15 32 51 70
2-4 3 6 9 20 30 40

BLONDIE COMICS (…Monthly No. 16-141)
David McKay #1-15/Harvey #16-163/King #164-175/Charlton #177 on:
Spring, 1947 - No. 163, Nov, 1965; No. 164, Aug, 1966 - No. 175, Dec, 1967; No. 177, Feb, 1969 - No. 222, Nov, 1976
1 33 66 99 194 317 440
2 17 34 51 98 154 210
3-5 14 28 42 82 121 160
6-10 13 26 39 72 101 130
11-15 9 18 27 52 69 85
16-(3/50; 1st Harvey issue) 11 22 33 60 83 105
17-20: 20-(3/51)-Becomes Daisy & Her Pups #21 & Chamber of Chills #21
6 12 18 37 59 80
21-30 5 10 15 32 51 70
31-50 4 8 12 24 37 50
51-80 4 8 12 22 34 45
81-99 3 6 9 20 30 40
100 4 8 12 24 37 50
101-124,126-130 3 6 9 16 23 30
125 (80 pgs.) 4 8 12 26 41 55
131-136,138,139 3 6 9 16 22 28
137,140-(80 pgs.) 4 8 12 25 39 52
141-147,149-154,156,160,164-167 3 6 9 16 22 28
148,155,157-159,161-163 are 68 pgs. 3 6 9 21 32 42
168-175 2 4 6 11 16 20
177-199 (no #176) 2 4 6 9 13 16
200 2 4 6 10 14 18
201-210,213-222 2 4 6 8 10 12
211,212-1st & 2nd app. Super Dagwood 2 4 6 9 13 16
Blondie, Dagwood & Daisy by Chic Young #1(Harvey, 1953, 100 pg. squarebound giant) new stories; Popeye (1 pg.) and Felix (1pg.) app. 29 58 87 172 281 390

BLOOD
Marvel Comics (Epic Comics): Feb, 1988 - No. 4, Apr, 1988 ($3.25, mature)
1-4: DeMatteis scripts & Kent Williams-c/a 3.50

BLOOD AND GLORY (Punisher & Captain America)
Marvel Comics: Oct, 1992 - No. 3, Dec, 1992 ($5.95, limited series)

Blood and Water #1 © Winick & Coker

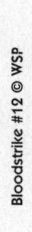

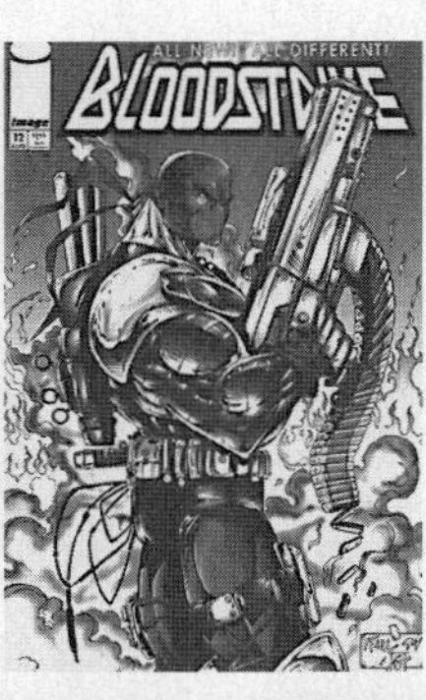
Bloodstrike #12 © WSP

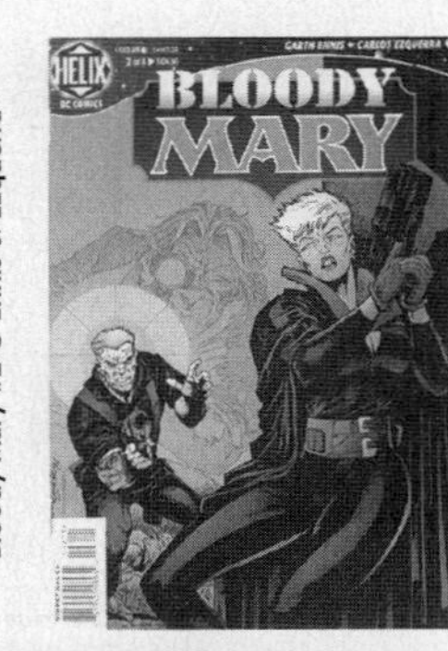

Bloody Mary #2 © Ennis & Ezquerra

	GD 2.0	VG 4.0	FN 6.0	VF 8.0	VF/NM 9.0	NM- 9.2

1-3: 1-Embossed wraparound-c by Janson; Chichester & Clarke-s 6.00

BLOOD & ROSES: FUTURE PAST TENSE (Bob Hickey's...)
Sky Comics: Dec, 1993 ($2.25)

1-Silver ink logo 2.50

BLOOD & ROSES: SEARCH FOR THE TIME-STONE (Bob Hickey's...)
Sky Comics: Apr, 1994 ($2.50)

1 2.50

BLOOD AND SHADOWS
DC Comics (Vertigo): 1996 - Book 4, 1996 ($5.95, squarebound, mature)

Books 1-4: Joe R. Lansdale scripts; Mark A. Nelson-c/a. 6.00

BLOOD AND WATER
DC Comics (Vertigo): May, 2003 - No. 5, Sept, 2003 ($2.95, limited series)

1-5-Judd Winick-s/Tomm Coker-a/Brian Bolland-c 3.00
TPB (2009, $14.99) r/#1-5 15.00

BLOOD: A TALE
DC Comics (Vertigo): Nov, 1996 - No. 4, Feb, 1997 ($2.95, limited series)

1-4: Reprints Epic series w/new-c; DeMatteis scripts; Kent Williams-c/a 3.00
TPB (2004, $19.95) r/#1-4 20.00

BLOODBATH
DC Comics: Early Dec, 1993 - No. 2, Late Dec, 1993 ($3.50, 68 pgs.)

1-Neon ink-c; Superman app.; new Batman-c /app. 3.50
2-Hitman 2nd app. 1 2 3 4 5 7

BLOODHOUND
DC Comics: Sept, 2004 - No. 10, June, 2005 ($2.95)

1-10: 1-Jolley-s/Kirk-a/Johnson-c. 5-Firestorm app. (cont. from Firestorm #7) 3.00

BLOOD LEGACY
Image Comics (Top Cow): May, 2000 - No. 4, Nov, 2000; Apr, 2003 ($2.50/$4.99)

...: The Story of Ryan 1-4-Kerri Hawkins-s. 1-Andy Park-a(p); 3 covers 2.50
...: The Young Ones 1 (4/03, $4.99, one-shot) Basaldua-c/a 5.00
Preview Special ('00, $4.95) B&W flip-book w/The Magdalena Preview 5.00

BLOODLINES: A TALE FROM THE HEART OF AFRICA (See Tales From the Heart of Africa)
Marvel Comics (Epic Comics): 1992 ($5.95, 52 pgs.)

1-Story cont'd from Tales From... 6.00

BLOOD OF DRACULA
Apple Comics: Nov, 1987 - No. 20?, 1990 ($1.75/$1.95, B&W)($2.25 #14,16 on)

1-3,5-14,20: 1-10-Chadwick-c 4.00
4,16-19-Lost Frankenstein pgs. by Wrightson 1 2 3 4 5 7
15-Contains stereo flexidisc ($3.75) 5.00

BLOOD OF THE DEMON (Etrigan the Demon)
DC Comics: May, 2005 - No. 17, Sept, 2006 ($2.50/$2.99)

1-14-Byrne-a(p) & plot/Pfeifer-script. 3,4-Batman app. 13-One Year Later 2.50
15-17-($2.99) 3.00

BLOOD OF THE INNOCENT (See Warp Graphics Annual)
WaRP Graphics: 1/7/86 - No. 4, 1/28/86 (Weekly mini-series, mature)

1-4 2.50

BLOODPACK
DC Comics: Mar, 1995 - No. 4, June,1995 ($1.50, limited series)

1-4 2.50

BLOODPOOL
Image Comics (Extreme): Aug, 1995 - No. 4, Nov, 1995 ($2.50, limited series)

1-4: Jo Duffy scripts in all 2.50
Special (3/96, $2.50)-Jo Duffy scripts 2.50
Trade Paperback (1996, $12.95)-r/#1-4 13.00

BLOODSCENT
Comico: Oct, 1988 ($2.00, one-shot, Baxter paper)

1-Colan-p 2.50

BLOODSEED
Marvel Comics (Frontier Comics): Oct, 1993 - No. 2, Nov, 1993 ($1.95)

1,2: Sharp/Cam Smith-a 3.00

BLOODSHOT (See Eternal Warrior #4 & Rai #0)
Valiant/Acclaim Comics (Valiant): Feb, 1993 - No. 51, Aug, 1996 ($2.25/$2.50)

0-(3/94, $3.50)-Wraparound chromium-c by Quesada(p); origin 4.00
0-Gold variant; no cover price 10.00

Note: There is a "Platinum variant" ; press run error of Gold ed. (25 copies exist)
(A CGC certified 9.8 copy sold for $2,067 in 2004)

1-($3.50)-Chromium embossed-c by B. Smith w/poster 4.00
2-5,8-14: 3-$2.25-c begins; cont'd in Hard Corps #5. 4-Eternal Warrior-c/story. 5-Rai & Eternal Warrior app. 14-(3/94)-Reese-c(i) 2.50
6,7: 6-1st app. Ninjak (out of costume). 7-In costume 2.50
15(4/94)-51: 16-w/bound-in trading card. 51-Bloodshot dies? 2.50
Yearbook 1 (1994, $3.95) 4.00
Special 1 (3/94, $5.95)-Zeck-c/a(p); Last Stand 6.00

BLOODSHOT (Volume Two)
Acclaim Comics (Valiant): July, 1997 - No. 16, Oct, 1998 ($2.50)

1-16: 1-Two covers. 5-Copycat-c. X-O Manowar-c/app 2.50

BLOODSTONE
Marvel Comics: Dec, 2001 - No. 4, Mar, 2002 ($2.99)

1-4-Intro. Elsa Bloodstone; Abnett & Lanning-s/Lopez-a 3.00

BLOODSTREAM
Image Comics: Jan, 2004 - No. 4, Dec, 2004 ($2.95)

1-4-Adam Shaw painted-a 3.00

BLOODSTRIKE (See Supreme V2#3)
Image Comics (Extreme Studios): 1993 - No. 22, May, 1995; No. 25, May, 1994 ($1.95/$2.50)

1-22, 25: Liefeld layouts in early issues. 1-Blood Brothers prelude. 2-1st app. Lethal. 5-1st app. Noble. 9-Black and White part 6 by Art Thibert; Liefeld pin-up. 9,10-Have coupon #3 & 7 for Extreme Prejudice #0. 10-(4/94). 11-(7/94). 16:Platt-c; Prophet app. 17-19-polybagged w/card . 25-(5/94)-Liefeld/Fraga-c 3.00

NOTE: ***Giffen*** *story/layouts-4-6.* ***Jae Lee*** *c-7, 8.* ***Rob Liefeld*** *layouts-1-3.* ***Art Thibert*** *c-6i.*

BLOODSTRIKE ASSASSIN
Image Comics (Extreme Studios): June, 1995 - No. 3, Aug, 1995; No. 0, Oct, 1995 ($2.50, limited series)

0-3: 3-(8/95)-Quesada-c. 0-(10/95)-Battlestone app. 3.00

BLOOD SWORD, THE
Jademan Comics: Aug, 1988 - No. 53, Dec, 1992 ($1.50/$1.95, 68 pgs.)

1-53-Kung Fu stories in all 3.00

BLOOD SWORD DYNASTY
Jademan Comics: 1989 -No. 41, Jan, 1993 ($1.25, 36 pgs.)

1-Ties into Blood Sword 2.50
2-41: Ties into Blood Sword 2.50

BLOOD SYNDICATE
DC Comics (Milestone): Apr, 1993 - No. 35, Feb, 1996 ($1.50/-$3.50)

1-($2.95)-Collector's Edition; polybagged with poster, trading card, & acid-free backing board (direct sale only) 3.50
1-9,11-24,26,27,29,33-34: 8-Intro Kwai. 15-Byrne-c. 16-Worlds Collide Pt. 6; Superman-c/app. 17-Worlds Collide Pt. 13. 29-(99¢); Long Hot Summer x-over 2.50
10,28,30-32: 10-Simonson-c. 30-Long Hot Summer x-over 2.50
25-($2.95, 52 pgs.) 3.00
35-Kwai disappears; last issue 3.50

BLOODWULF
Image Comics (Extreme): Feb, 1995 - No. 4, May, 1995 ($2.50, limited series)

1-4: 1-Liefeld-c w/4 diferent captions & alternate-c. 2.50
Summer Special (8/95, $2.50)-Jeff Johnson-c/a; Supreme app; story takes place between Legend of Supreme #3 & Supreme #23. 2.50

BLOODY MARY
DC Comics (Helix): Oct, 1996 - No. 4, Jan, 1997 ($2.25, limited series)

1-4: Garth Ennis scripts; Ezquerra-c/a in all 3.50
TPB (2005, $19.99) r/#1-4 and Bloody Mary: Lady Liberty #1-4 20.00

BLOODY MARY: LADY LIBERTY
DC Comics (Helix): Sept, 1997 - No. 4, Dec, 1997 ($2.50, limited series)

1-4: Garth Ennis scripts; Ezquerra-c/a in all 3.00

BLUE
Image Comics (Action Toys): Aug, 1999 - No. 2, Apr, 2000 ($2.50)

1,2-Aronowitz-s/Struzan-c 2.50

BLUEBEARD
Slave Labor Graphics: Nov, 1993 - No. 3, Mar, 1994 ($2.95, B&W, lim. series)

1-3: James Robinson scripts. 2-(12/93) 3.00
Trade paperback (6/94, $9.95) 13.00
Trade paperback (2nd printing, 7/96, $12.95)-New-c 13.00

Blue Beetle #24 © FOX

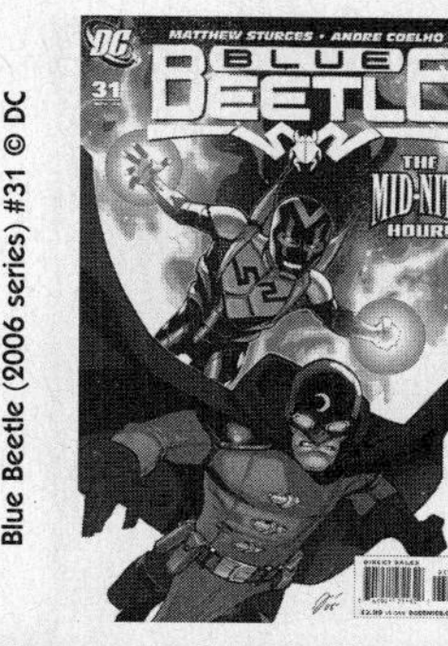

Blue Beetle (2006 series) #31 © DC

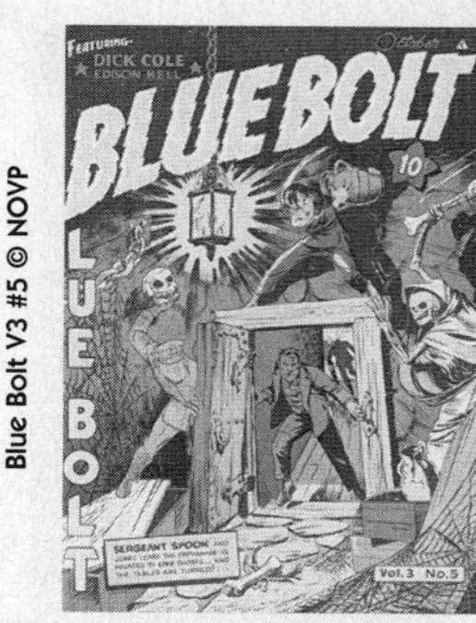

Blue Bolt V3 #5 © NOVP

BLUE BEETLE, THE (Also see All Top, Big-3, Mystery Men & Weekly Comic Magazine)
Fox Publ. No. 1-11, 31-60; Holyoke No. 12-30: Winter, 1939-40 - No. 57, 7/48; No. 58, 4/50 - No. 60, 8/50

	GD 2.0	VG 4.0	FN 6.0	VF 8.0	VF/NM 9.0	NM- 9.2
1-Reprints from Mystery Men #1-5; Blue Beetle origin; Yarko the Great-r/from Wonder Comics /Wonderworld #2-5 all by Eisner; Master Magician app.; (Blue Beetle in 4 different costumes)	459	918	1377	3350	5925	8500
2-K-51-r by Powell/Wonderworld #8,9	161	322	483	1030	1765	2500
3-Simon-c	118	236	354	749	1287	1825
4-Marijuana drug mention story	79	138	237	502	864	1225
5-Zanzibar The Magician by Tuska	68	136	204	432	746	1060
6-Dynamite Thor begins (1st); origin Blue Beetle	65	130	195	416	708	1000
7,8-Dynamo app. in both. 8-Last Thor	58	116	174	371	636	900
9-12: 9,10-The Blackbird & The Gorilla app. in both. 10-Bondage/hypo-c. 11(2/42)-The Gladiator app. 12(6/42)-The Black Fury app.	52	104	156	328	557	785
13-V-Man begins (1st app.), ends #19; Kubert-a; centerfold spread	60	120	180	381	658	935
14,15-Kubert-a in both. 14-Intro. side-kick (c/text only), Sparky (called Spunky #17-19)	53	106	159	334	567	800
16-18: 17-Brodsky-c	43	86	129	271	461	650
19-Kubert-a	45	90	135	284	480	675
20-Origin/1st app. Tiger Squadron; Arabian Nights begin	47	94	141	296	503	710
21-26: 24-Intro. & only app. The Halo. 26-General Patton story & photo	37	74	111	222	361	500
27-Tamaa, Jungle Prince app.	34	68	102	204	332	460
28-30(2/44)	30	60	90	177	289	400
31(6/44), 33,34,36-40: 34-38-"The Threat from Saturn" serial.	28	56	84	165	270	375
32-Hitler-c	53	106	159	334	567	800
35-Extreme violence	34	68	102	204	332	460
41-45 (#43 exist?)	26	52	78	154	252	350
46-The Puppeteer app.	29	58	87	172	281	390
47-Kamen & Baker-a begin	135	270	405	864	1482	2100
48-50	102	204	306	648	1112	1575
51,53	87	174	261	553	952	1350
52-Kamen bondage-c; true crime stories begin	129	258	387	826	1413	2000
54-Used in **SOTI**. Illo, "Children call these 'headlights' comics"	184	368	552	1168	2009	2850
55-57: 56-Used in **SOTI**, pg. 145. 57(7/48)-Last Kamen issue; becomes Western Killers?	84	168	252	538	919	1300
58(4/50)-60-No Kamen-a	18	36	54	105	165	225

NOTE: ***Kamen** a-47-51, 53, 55-57; c-47, 49-52. **Powell** a-4(2). Bondage-c 9-12, 46, 52.*

BLUE BEETLE (Formerly The Thing; becomes Mr. Muscles No. 22 on) (See Charlton Bullseye & Space Adventures)
Charlton Comics: No. 18, Feb, 1955 - No. 21, Aug, 1955

	GD 2.0	VG 4.0	FN 6.0	VF 8.0	VF/NM 9.0	NM- 9.2
18,19-(Pre-1944-r). 18-Last pre-code issue. 19-Bouncer, Rocket Kelly-r	20	40	60	117	189	260
20-Joan Mason by Kamen	25	50	75	147	241	335
21-New material	20	40	60	114	182	250

BLUE BEETLE (Unusual Tales #1-49; Ghostly Tales #55 on)(See Captain Atom #83 & Charlton Bullseye)
Charlton Comics: V2#1, June, 1964 - V2#5, Mar-Apr, 1965; V3#50, July, 1965 - V3#54, Feb-Mar, 1966; #1, June, 1967 - #5, Nov, 1968

	GD 2.0	VG 4.0	FN 6.0	VF 8.0	VF/NM 9.0	NM- 9.2
V2#1-Origin/1st S.A. app. Dan Garrett-Blue Beetle	9	18	27	61	103	145
2-5: 5-Weiss illo; 1st published-a?	6	12	18	37	59	80
V3#50-54-Formerly Unusual Tales	5	10	15	34	55	75
1(1967)-Question series begins by Ditko	10	20	30	71	126	180
2-Origin Ted Kord-Blue Beetle (see Capt. Atom #83 for 1st Ted Kord Blue Beetle); Dan Garrett x-over	6	12	18	41	66	90
3-5 (All Ditko-c/a in #1-5)	6	12	18	37	59	80
1,3(Modern Comics-1977)-Reprints	1	2	3	5	6	8

NOTE: *#6 only appeared in the fanzine 'The Charlton Portfolio.'*

BLUE BEETLE (Also see Americomics, Crisis On Infinite Earths, Justice League & Showcase '94 #2-4)
DC Comics: June, 1986 - No. 24, May, 1988

	GD 2.0	VG 4.0	FN 6.0	VF 8.0	VF/NM 9.0	NM- 9.2
1-Origin retold; intro. Firefist						4.00
2-10,15-19,21-24: 2-Origin Firefist. 5-7-The Question app. 21-Millennium tie-in						2.50
11-14-New Teen Titans x-over						3.00
20-Justice League app.; Millennium tie-in						3.00

BLUE BEETLE (See Infinite Crisis, Teen Titans, and Booster Gold #21)
DC Comics: May, 2006 - No. 36, Apr, 2009 ($2.99)

	GD 2.0	VG 4.0	FN 6.0	VF 8.0	VF/NM 9.0	NM- 9.2
1-Hamner-a/Giffen & Rogers-s; Guy Gardner app.						4.00
1-2nd & 3rd printings						3.00
2-36: 2-2nd printing exists. 2-4-Oracle app. 5-Phantom Stranger app. 16-Eclipso app. 18,33-Teen Titans app. 20-Sinestro Corps. 21-Spectre app. 26-Spanish issue						3.00
...: Boundaries TPB (2009, $14.99) r/#29-34						15.00
...: End Game TPB (2008, $14.99) r/#20-26; English script for #26						15.00
...: Reach For the Stars TPB (2008, $14.99) r/#13-19						15.00
...: Road Trip TPB (2007, $12.99) r/#7-12						13.00
...: Shellshocked TPB (2006, $12.99) r/#1-6						13.00

BLUEBERRY (See Lt. Blueberry & Marshal Blueberry)
Marvel Comics (Epic Comics): 1989 - No. 5, 1990 ($12.95/$14.95, graphic novel)

	GD 2.0	VG 4.0	FN 6.0	VF 8.0	VF/NM 9.0	NM- 9.2
1,3,4,5-($12.95)-Moebius-a in all	3	6	9	14	19	24
2-($14.95)	3	6	9	14	20	26

BLUE BOLT
Funnies, Inc. No. 1/Novelty Press/Premium Group of Comics: June, 1940 - No. 101 (V10#2), Sept-Oct, 1949

	GD 2.0	VG 4.0	FN 6.0	VF 8.0	VF/NM 9.0	NM- 9.2
V1#1-Origin Blue Bolt by Joe Simon, Sub-Zero Man, White Rider & Super Horse, Dick Cole, Wonder Boy & Sgt. Spook (1st app. of each)	320	640	960	2240	3920	5600
2-Simon & Kirby's 1st art & 1st super-hero (Blue Bolt)	181	362	543	1158	1979	2800
3-1 pg. Space Hawk by Wolverton; 2nd S&K-a on Blue Bolt (same cover date as Red Raven #1); 1st time S&K names app. in a comic; Simon-c	158	316	474	1003	1727	2450
4-S&K-a; classic Everett shark-c	155	310	465	992	1696	2400
5-S&K-a; Everett-a begins on Sub-Zero	134	268	402	851	1463	2075
6,8-10-S&K-a	123	246	369	787	1344	1900
7-S&K-c/a	142	284	426	909	1555	2200
11,12: 11-Robot-c	116	232	348	742	1271	1800
V2#1-Origin Dick Cole & The Twister; Twister x-over in Dick Cole, Sub-Zero, & Blue Bolt; origin Simba Karno who battles Dick Cole thru V2#5 & becomes main supporting character V2#6 on; battle-c	41	82	123	249	417	585
2-Origin The Twister retold in text	34	68	102	204	332	460
3-5: 5-Intro. Freezum	30	60	90	177	289	400
6-Origin Sgt. Spook retold	26	52	78	154	252	350
7-12: 7-Lois Blake becomes Blue Bolt's costume aide; last Twister. 12-Text-sty by Mickey Spillaine	22	44	66	128	209	290
V3#1-3	18	36	54	107	169	230
4-12: 4-Blue Bolt abandons costume	15	30	45	86	133	180
V4#1-Hitler, Tojo, Mussolini-c	41	82	123	256	428	600
V4#2-12: 3-Shows V4#3 on-c, V4#4 inside (9-10/43). 5-Infinity-c. 8-Last Sub-Zero	13	26	39	72	101	130
V5#1-8, V6#1-3,5-10, V7#1-12	11	22	33	64	90	115
V6#4-Racist cover	20	40	60	114	182	250
V8#1-6,8-12, V9#1-4,7,8, V10#1(#100),V10#2(#101)-Last Dick Cole, Blue Bolt	10	20	30	56	76	95
V8#7,V9#6,9-L. B. Cole-c	22	44	66	128	209	290
V9#5-Classic fish in the face-c	22	44	66	128	209	290

NOTE: ***Everett** c-V1#4, 11, V2#1, 2. **Gustavson** a-V1#1-12, V2#1-7. **Kiefer** c-V3#1. **Rico** a-V6#10, V7#4. Blue Bolt not in V9#8.*

BLUE BOLT (Becomes Ghostly Weird Stories #120 on; continuation of Novelty Blue Bolt) (...Weird Tales of Terror #111,112,...Weird Tales #113-119)
Star Publications: No. 102, Nov-Dec, 1949 - No. 119, May-June, 1953

	GD 2.0	VG 4.0	FN 6.0	VF 8.0	VF/NM 9.0	NM- 9.2
102-The Chameleon, & Target app.	39	78	117	235	385	535
103,104-The Chameleon app. 104-Last Target	38	76	114	228	369	510
105-Origin Blue Bolt (from #1) retold by Simon; Chameleon & Target app.; opium den story	56	112	168	356	611	865
106-Blue Bolt by S&K begins; Spacehawk reprints from Target by Wolverton begin, ends #110; Sub-Zero begins; ends #109	54	108	162	340	575	810
107-110: 108-Last S&K Blue Bolt reprint. 109-Wolverton-c(r)/inside Spacehawk splash. 110-Target app.	52	104	156	328	557	785
111,112: 111-Red Rocket & The Mask-r; last Blue Bolt; 1pg. L. B. Cole-a. 112-Last Torpedo Man app.	48	96	144	302	514	725
113-Wolverton's Spacehawk-r/Target V3#7	50	100	150	315	533	750
114,116: 116-Jungle Jo-r	48	96	144	302	514	725
115-Sgt. Spook app.	50	100	150	315	533	750
117-Jo-Jo & Blue Bolt-r	49	98	147	309	525	740
118-"White Spirit" by Wood	50	100	150	315	533	750
119-Disbrow/Cole-c; Jungle Jo-r	49	98	147	309	525	740
Accepted Reprint #103(1957?, nd)	14	28	42	80	115	150

NOTE: ***L. B. Cole** c-102-108, 110 on. **Disbrow** a-112(2), 113(3), 114(2), 115(2), 116-118. **Hollingsworth** a-117. **Palais** a-112r. Sci/Fi c-105-110. Horror c-111.*

BLUE BULLETEER, THE (Also see Femforce Special)
AC Comics: 1989 ($2.25, B&W, one-shot)

Blue Circle Comics #1 © Enwil

Blue Monday: Thieves Like Us #1 © Chynna Clugston

Bobby Benson's B-Bar-B Riders #5 © ME

GD VG FN VF VF/NM NM-
2.0 4.0 6.0 8.0 9.0 9.2

GD VG FN VF VF/NM NM-
2.0 4.0 6.0 8.0 9.0 9.2

1-Origin by Bill Black; Bill Ward-a 4.00

BLUE BULLETEER (Also see Femforce Special)
AC Comics: 1996 ($5.95, B&W, one-shot)
1-Photo-c 6.00

BLUE CIRCLE COMICS (Also see Red Circle Comics, Blazing Comics & Roly Poly Comic Book)
Enwil Associates/Rural Home: June, 1944 - No. 6, Apr, 1945
1-The Blue Circle begins (1st app.); origin & 1st app. Steel Fist
32 64 96 188 307 425
2 20 40 60 114 182 250
3-Hitler parody-c 36 72 108 211 343 475
4-6: 5-Last Steel Fist. 18 36 54 105 165 225
6-(Dated 4/45, Vol. 2#3 inside)-Leftover covers to #6 were later restapled over early 1950's coverless comics; variations of the coverless comics exist.
Colossal Features known. 18 36 54 105 165 225

BLUE DEVIL (See Fury of Firestorm #24, Underworld Unleashed, Starman (2nd) #38, Infinite Crisis and Shadowpact)
DC Comics: June, 1984 - No. 31, Dec, 1986 (75¢/$1.25)
1 4.00
2-16,19-31: 4-Origin Nebiros. 7-Gil Kane-a. 8-Giffen-a 2.50
17,18-Crisis x-over 3.00
Annual 1 (11/85)-Team-ups w/Black Orchid, Creeper, Demon, Madame Xanadu, Man-Bat & Phantom Stranger 3.00

BLUE MONDAY: ... (one-shots)
Oni Press: Feb, 2002 - Present (B&W, Chynna Clugston-Major-s/a/c in all)
Dead Man's Party (10/02, $2.95) Dan Brereton painted back-c 3.00
Inbetween Days (9/03, $9.95, 8" x 5-1/2") r/Dead Man's Party, Lovecats, & Nobody's Fool 10.00
Lovecats (2/02, $2.95) Valentine's Day themed 3.00
Nobody's Fool (2/03, $2.95) April Fool's Day themed 3.00

BLUE MONDAY: ABSOLUTE BEGINNERS
Oni Press: Feb, 2001 - No. 4, Sept, 2001 ($2.95, B&W, limited series)
1-4-Chynna Clugston-Major-s/a/c 3.00
TPB (12/01, $11.95, 8" x 6") r/series 12.00

BLUE MONDAY: PAINTED MOON
Oni Press: Feb, 2004 - No. 4, Mar, 2005 ($2.99, B&W, limited series)
1-4-Chynna Clugston-Major-s/a/c 3.00
TPB (4/05, $11.95, digest-sized) r/series; sketch pages 12.00

BLUE MONDAY: THE KIDS ARE ALRIGHT
Oni Press: Feb, 2000 - No. 3, May, 2000 ($2.95, B&W, limited series)
1-3-Chynna Clugston-Major-s/a/c. 1-Variant-c by Warren. 2-Dorkin-c 3.00
3-Variant cover by J. Scott Campbell 4.00
TPB (12/00, $10.95, digest-sized) r/#1-3 & earlier short stories 11.00

BLUE MONDAY: THIEVES LIKE US
Oni Press: Dec, 2008 - No. 5 ($3.50, B&W, limited series)
1-Chynna Clugston-s/a/c 3.50

BLUE PHANTOM, THE
Dell Publishing Co.: June-Aug, 1962
1(01-066-208)-by Fred Fredericks 3 6 9 21 32 42

BLUE RIBBON COMICS (...Mystery Comics No. 9-18)
MLJ Magazines: Nov, 1939 - No. 22, Mar, 1942 (1st MLJ series)
1-Dan Hastings, Richy the Amazing Boy, Rang-A-Tang the Wonder Dog begin (1st app. of each); Little Nemo app. (not by W. McCay); Jack Cole-a(3) (1st MLJ comic) 284 568 852 1818 3109 4400
2-Bob Phantom, Silver Fox (both in #3), Rang-A-Tang Club & Cpl. Collins begin (1st app. of each); Jack Cole-a 118 236 354 749 1287 1825
3-J. Cole-a 77 154 231 493 847 1200
4-Doc Strong, The Green Falcon, & Hercules begin (1st app. each); origin & 1st app. The Fox & Ty-Gor, Son of the Tiger 85 170 255 540 933 1325
5-8: 8-Last Hercules; 6,7-Biro, Meskin-a. 7-Fox app. on-c
63 126 189 403 689 975
9-(Scarce)-Origin & 1st app. Mr. Justice (2/41) 297 594 891 1990 3445 4900
10-13: 12-Last Doc Strong. 13-Inferno, the Flame Breather begins, ends #19; Devil-c
103 206 309 659 1130 1600
14,15,17,18: 15-Last Green Falcon 87 174 261 553 952 1350
16-Origin & 1st app. Captain Flag (9/41) 161 322 483 1030 1765 2500
19-22: 20-Last Ty-Gor. 22-Origin Mr. Justice retold 87 174 261 553 952 1350
NOTE: *Biro c-3-5; a-2 (Cpl. Collins & Scoop Cody).* ***S. Cooper*** *c-9-17. 20-22 contain "Tales From the Witch's Cauldron" (same strip as "Stories of the Black Witch" in Zip Comics). Mr. Justice c-9-18. Captain Flag c-16-18 (w/Mr. Justice), 19-22.*

BLUE RIBBON COMICS (Becomes Teen-Age Diary Secrets #4)
(Also see Approved Comics, Blue Ribbon Comics and Heckle &Jeckle)
Blue Ribbon (St. John): Feb, 1949 - No. 6, Aug, 1949
1-Heckle & Jeckle (Terrytoons) 14 28 42 80 115 150
2(4/49)-Diary Secrets; Baker-c 32 64 96 188 307 425
3-Heckle & Jeckle (Terrytoons) 11 22 33 60 83 105
4(6/49)-Teen-Age Diary Secrets; Baker c/a(2) 32 64 96 188 307 425
5(8/49)-Teen-Age Diary Secrets; Oversize; photo-c; Baker-a(2)- Continues as Teen-Age Diary Secrets 37 74 111 222 361 500
6-Dinky Duck(8/49)(Terrytoons) 8 16 24 42 54 65

BLUE RIBBON COMICS
Red Circle Prod./Archie Ent. No. 5 on: Nov, 1983 - No. 14, Dec, 1984
1-S&K-r/Advs. of the Fly #1,2; Williamson/Torres-r/Fly #2; Ditko-c
1 2 3 5 6 8
2-7,9,10: 3-Origin Steel Sterling. 5-S&K Shield-r; new Kirby-c. 6,7-The Fox app. 6.00
8-Toth centerspread; Black Hood app.; Neal Adams-a(r)
1 2 3 4 5 7
11,13,14: 11-Black Hood. 13-Thunder Bunny. 14-Web & Jaguar 6.00
12-Thunder Agents; Noman new Ditko-a 1 2 3 5 6 8
NOTE: ***N. Adams*** *a(r)-8.* ***Buckler*** *a-4i.* ***Nino*** *a-2i.* ***McWilliams*** *a-8.* ***Morrow*** *a-8.*

BLUE STREAK (See Holyoke One-Shot No. 8)

BLUNTMAN AND CHRONIC TPB(Also see Jay and Silent Bob, Clerks, and Oni Double Feature)
Image Comics: Dec, 2001 ($14.95, TPB)
nn-Tie-in for "Jay & Silent Bob Strike Back" movie; new Kevin Smith-s/Michael Oeming-a; r/app. from Oni Double Feature #12 in color; Ben Affleck & Jason Lee afterwords 15.00

BLYTHE (Marge's)
Dell Publishing Co.: No. 1072, Jan-Mar, 1960
Four Color 1072 6 12 18 37 59 80

B-MAN (See Double-Dare Adventures)

BO (Tom Cat #4 on) (Also see Big Shot #29 & Dixie Dugan)
Charlton Comics Group: June, 1955 - No. 3, Oct, 1955 (A dog)
1-3: Newspaper reprints by Frank Beck 8 16 24 40 50 60

BOATNIKS, THE (See Walt Disney Showcase No. 1)

BOB BURDEN'S ORIGINAL MYSTERYMEN PRESENTS
Dark Horse Comics: 1999 - No. 4 ($2.95/$3.50)
1-3-Bob Burden-s/Sadowski-a(p) 3.50
4-($3.50) All Villain issue 3.50

BOBBY BENSON'S B-BAR-B RIDERS (Radio) (See Best of The West, The Lemonade Kid & Model Fun)
Magazine Enterprises/AC Comics: May-June, 1950 - No. 20, May-June, 1953
1-The Lemonade Kid begins; Powell-a (Scarce) 41 82 123 256 428 600
2 17 34 51 98 154 210
3-5: 4,5-Lemonade Kid-c (#4-Spider-c) 14 28 42 76 108 140
6-8,10 13 26 39 72 101 130
9,11,13-Frazetta-c; Ghost Rider in #13-15 by Ayers-a. 13-Ghost Rider-c
37 74 111 222 361 500
12,17-20: 20-(A-1 #88) 11 22 33 64 90 115
14-Decapitation/Bondage-c & story; classic horror-c 29 58 87 170 278 385
15-Ghost Rider-c 22 44 66 132 216 300
16-Photo-c 14 28 42 80 115 150
1 (1990, $2.75, B&W)-Reprints; photo-c & inside covers 3.00
NOTE: ***Ayers*** *a-13-15, 20.* ***Powell*** *a-1-12(4 ea.), 13(3), 14-16(Red Hawk only); c-1-8,1 0, 12. Lemonade Kid in most 1-13.*

BOBBY COMICS
Universal Phoenix Features: May, 1946
1-By S. M. Iger 9 18 27 47 61 75

BOBBY SHERMAN (TV)
Charlton Comics: Feb, 1972 - No. 7, Oct, 1972
1-Based on TV show "Getting Together" 6 12 18 37 59 80
2-7: 2,4-Photo-c 4 8 12 24 37 50

BOB COLT (Movie star)(See XMas Comics)
Fawcett Publications: Nov, 1950 - No. 10, May, 1952
1-Bob Colt, his horse Buckskin & sidekick Pablo begin; photo front/back-c begin 33 66 99 192 309 425
2 17 34 51 98 154 210
3-5 15 30 45 83 124 165

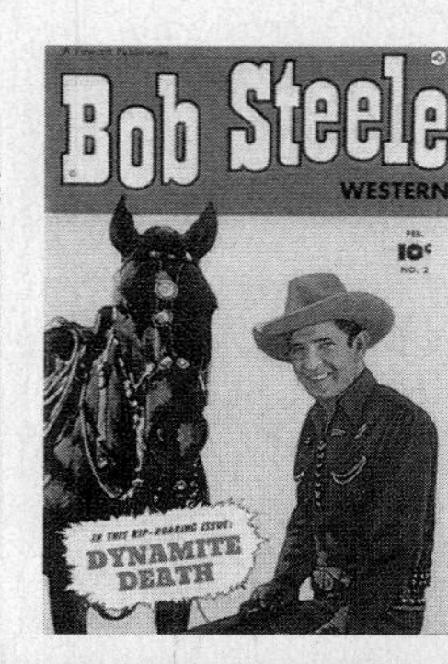

Bob Steele Western #2 © FAW

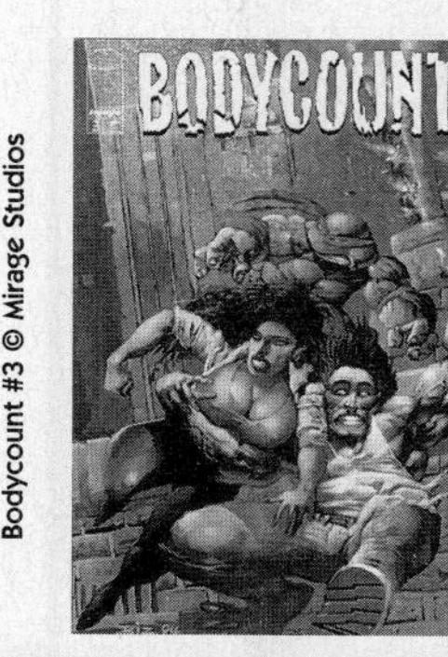

Bodycount #3 © Mirage Studios

Bonanza #16 © CBS

	GD 2.0	VG 4.0	FN 6.0	VF 8.0	VF/NM 9.0	NM- 9.2

6-Flying Saucer story 14 28 42 76 108 140
7-10: 9-Last photo back-c 12 24 36 69 97 125

BOB HOPE (See Adventures of... & Calling All Boys #12)

BOB MARLEY, TALE OF THE TUFF GONG (Music star)
Marvel Comics: Aug, 1994 - No, 3, Nov, 1994 ($5.95, limited series)
1-3 6.00

BOB POWELL'S TIMELESS TALES
Eclipse Comics: March, 1989 ($2.00, B&W)
1-Powell-r/Black Cat #5 (Scarlet Arrow), 9 & Race for the Moon #1 3.00

BOB SCULLY, THE TWO-FISTED HICK DETECTIVE (Also see Advs. of Detective Ace King and Detective Dan)
Humor Publ. Co.: No date (1933) (36 pgs., 9-1/2x11", B&W, paper-c; 10¢-c)
nn-By Howard Dell; not reprints; along with Advs. of Det. Ace King and Detective Dan, the first comic w/original art & the first of a single theme; has a blue 2-tone cover 375 750 1125 3000 - -

BOB SON OF BATTLE
Dell Publishing Co.: No. 729, Nov, 1956
Four Color 729 4 8 12 24 37 50

BOB STEELE WESTERN (Movie star)
Fawcett Publications/AC Comics: Dec, 1950 - No. 10, June, 1952; 1990
1-Bob Steele & his horse Bullet begin; photo front/back-c begin 40 80 120 244 397 550
2 20 40 60 115 183 250
3-5: 4-Last photo back-c 15 30 45 85 130 175
6-10: 10-Last photo-c 14 28 42 76 108 140
1 (1990, $2.75, B&W)-Bob Steele & Rocky Lane reprints; photo-c & inside covers 3.00

BOB SWIFT (Boy Sportsman)
Fawcett Publications: May, 1951 - No. 5, Jan, 1952
1 10 20 30 58 79 100
2-5: Saunders painted-c #1-5 7 14 21 35 43 50

BOB, THE GALACTIC BUM
DC Comics: Feb, 1995 - No. 4, June, 1995 ($1.95, limited series)
1-4: 1-Lobo app. 2.50

BODY BAGS
Dark Horse Comics (Blanc Noir): Sept, 1996 - No. 4, Jan, 1997 ($2.95, mini-series, mature) (1st Blanc Noir series)
1-Jason Pearson-c/a/scripts in all. 1-Intro Clownface & Panda. 1 2 3 5 6 8
2 1 3 4 6 8 10
3,4 6.00
Body Bags 1 (Image Comics, 7/05, $5.99) r/#1&2 6.00
Body Bags 2 (Image Comics, 8/05, $5.99) r/#3&4 6.00
...: 3 The Hard Way (Image, 2/06, $5.99) new story & r/Dark Horse Presents Annual 1997 and Dark Horse Maverick 2000; Pearson-c 6.00
...: One Shot (Image, 11/08, $5.99) wraparound-c; Pearson-c/a/s 6.00

BODYCOUNT (Also see Casey Jones & Raphael)
Image Comics (Highbrow Entertainment): Mar, 1996 - No. 4, July, 1996 ($2.50, lim. series)
1-4: Kevin Eastman-a(p)/scripts; Simon Bisley-c/a(i); Turtles app. 2.50

BODY DOUBLES (See Resurrection Man)
DC Comics: Oct, 1999 - No. 4, Jan, 2000 ($2.50, limited series)
1-4-Lanning & Abnett-s. 2-Black Canary app. 4-Wonder Woman app. 2.50
...(Villains) (2/98, $1.95, one-shot) 1-Pearson-c; Deadshot app. 2.50

BOFFO LAFFS
Paragraphics: 1986 - No. 5 ($2.50/$1.95)
1-($2.50) First comic cover with hologram 3.00
2-5 2.50

BOLD ADVENTURES
Pacific Comics: Oct, 1983 - No. 3, June, 1984 ($1.50)
1-Time Force, Anaconda, & The Weirdling begin 3.00
2,3: 2-Soldiers of Fortune begins. 3-Spitfire 3.00
NOTE: ***Kaluta*** *c-3.* ***Nebres*** *a-1-3.* ***Nino*** *a-2, 3.* ***Severin*** *a-3.*

BOLD STORIES (Also see Candid Tales & It Rhymes With Lust)
Kirby Publishing Co.: Mar, 1950 - July, 1950 (Digest size, 144 pgs.)
March issue (Very Rare) - Contains "The Ogre of Paris" by Wood 155 310 465 992 1696 2400
May issue (Very Rare) - Contains "The Cobra's Kiss" by Graham Ingels (21 pgs.) 135 270 405 864 1482 2100
July issue (Very Rare) - Contains "The Ogre of Paris" by Wood 123 246 369 787 1344 1900

BOLT AND STAR FORCE SIX
Americomics: 1984 ($1.75)
1-Origin Bolt & Star Force Six 3.00
Special 1 (1984, $2.00, 52pgs., B&W) 3.00

BOMBARDIER (See Bee 29, the Bombardier & Cinema Comics Herald)

BOMBAST
Topps Comics: 1993 ($2.95, one-shot) (Created by Jack Kirby)
1-Polybagged w/Kirbychrome trading card; Savage Dragon app.; Kirby-c; has coupon for Amberchrome Secret City Saga #0 3.00

BOMBA THE JUNGLE BOY (TV)
National Periodical Publ.: Sept-Oct, 1967 - No. 7, Sept-Oct, 1968 (12¢)
1-Intro. Bomba; Infantino/Anderson-c 4 8 12 24 37 50
2-7 3 6 9 16 23 30

BOMBER COMICS
Elliot Publ. Co./Melverne Herald/Farrell/Sunrise Times: Mar, 1944 - No. 4, Winter, 1944-45
1-Wonder Boy, & Kismet, Man of Fate begin 81 162 243 518 884 1250
2-Hitler-c and 8 pg. story 90 180 270 576 988 1400
3: 2-4-Have Classics Comics ad to HRN 20 45 90 135 284 480 675
4-Hitler, Tojo & Mussolini-c; Sensation Comics #13-c/swipe; has Classics Comics ad to HRN 20. 84 168 252 538 919 1300

BOMB QUEEN
Image Comics (Shadowline): Feb, 2006 - No. 4, May, 2006 ($3.50, mature)
1-4-Jimmie Robinson-s/a 3.50
... Vs. Blacklight One Shot #1 (8/06, $3.50) Robinson-a; Shadowhawk app. 3.50
..., Vol. 1: WMD: Woman of Mass Destruction TPB (7/06, $12.99) r/#1-4; bonus art 13.00

BOMB QUEEN II
Image Comics (Shadowline): Oct, 2006 - No. 3, Dec, 2006 ($3.50, mature)
1-3-Jimmie Robinson-s/a; intro. The Four Queens 3.50
..., Vol. 2: Dirty Bomb - Queen of Hearts TPB (7/07, $14.99) r/#1-3 & Blacklight One Shot; bonus art; Robinson interview 15.00

BOMB QUEEN III THE GOOD, THE BAD & THE LOVELY
Image Comics (Shadowline): Mar, 2007 - No. 4, Jun, 2007 ($3.50, mature)
1-4-Jimmie Robinson-a/Jim Valentino-s; Blacklight & Rebound app. 1-Linsner-c 3.50

BOMB QUEEN IV SUICIDE BOMBER
Image Comics (Shadowline): Aug, 2007 - No. 4, Dec, 2007 ($3.50, mature)
1-4-Jim Robinson-s/a. 3-She-Spawn app. 3.50

BOMB QUEEN (Volume 5)
Image Comics (Shadowline): May, 2008 - No. 6, Mar, 2009 ($3.50, mature)
Vol. 5 #1-6-Jim Robinson-s/a 3.50
Vol. 6 #1 (9/09, $3.50) Obama-c 3.50
... Presents: All Girl Comics (5/09, $3.50) Dee Rail, Blacklight, Rebound, Tempest app. 3.50

BONANZA (TV)
Dell/Gold Key: June-Aug, 1960 - No. 37, Aug, 1970 (All Photo-c)
Four Color 1110 (6-8/60) 31 62 93 236 456 675
Four Color 1221,1283, & #01070-207, 01070-210 17 34 51 119 230 340
1(12/62-Gold Key) 18 36 54 126 246 365
2 10 20 30 68 119 170
3-10 8 16 24 52 86 120
11-20 6 12 18 39 62 85
21-37: 29-Reprints 5 10 15 32 51 70

BONE
Cartoon Books #1-20, 28 on/Image Comics #21-27: Jul, 1991 - No. 55, Jun, 2004 ($2.95, B&W)
1-Jeff Smith-c/a in all 15 30 45 107 204 300
1-2nd printing 2 4 6 9 12 15
1-3rd thru 5th printings 4.00
2-1st printing 7 14 21 45 73 100
2-2nd & 3rd printings 4.00
3-1st printing 5 10 15 34 55 75
3-2nd thru 4th printings 4.00
4,5 4 8 12 24 37 50
6-10 2 4 6 11 16 20
11-20 6.00

Bone #52 © Jeff Smith

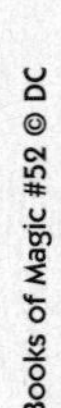
Books of Magic #52 © DC

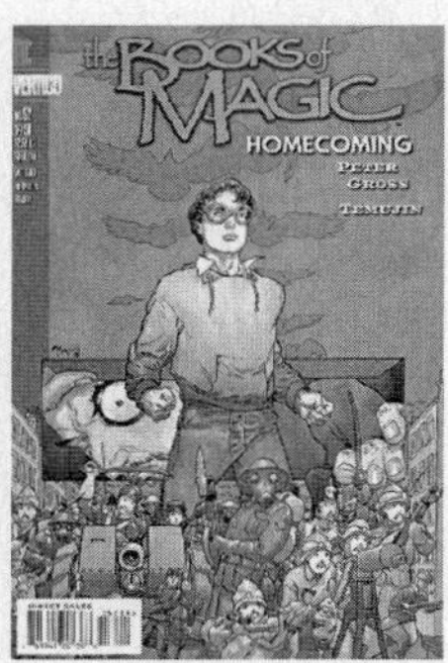

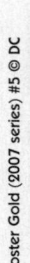

Booster Gold (2007 series) #5 © DC

	GD 2.0	VG 4.0	FN 6.0	VF 8.0	VF/NM 9.0	NM- 9.2
13 1/2 (1/95, Wizard)	2	4	6	8	10	12
13 1/2 (Gold)	2	4	6	9	12	15
21-37: 21-1st Image issue						5.00
38-($4.95) Three covers by Miller, Ross, Smith	1	2	3	4	5	7
39-55-($2.95)						4.00
1-27-($2.95): 1-Image reprints begin w/new-c. 2-Allred pin-up.						3.00
... Holiday Special (1993, giveaway)	2	3	4	6	8	10
... Reader -($9.95) Behind the scenes info						10.00
... Sourcebook-San Diego Edition						3.00
...10th Anniversary Edition (8/01, $5.95) r/#1 in color; came with figure						6.00
Complete Bone Adventures Vol 1,2 ('93, '94, $12.95, r/#1-6 & #7-12)						13.00
...: One Volume Edition (2004, $39.95, 1300 pgs.) r/#1-54; extra material						40.00
Volume 1-($19.95, hard-c)-"Out From Boneville"						20.00
Volume 1-($12.95, soft-c)						13.00
Volume 2,5-($22.95, hard-c)-"The Great Cow Race" & "Rock Jaw"						23.00
Volume 2,5-($14.95, soft-c)						15.00
Volume 3,4-($24.95, hard-c)-"Eyes of the Storm" & "The Dragonslayer"						25.00
Volume 3,4,7-($16.95, soft-c)						17.00
Volume 6-($15.95, soft-c)-"Old Man's Cave"						16.00
Volume 7-($24.95, hard-c)-"Ghost Circles"						25.00
Volume 8-($23.95, hard-c)-"Treasure Hunters"						24.00

NOTE: *Printings not listed sell for cover price.*

BONGO (See Story Hour Series)

BONGO & LUMPJAW (Disney, see Walt Disney Showcase #3)
Dell Publishing Co.: No. 706, June, 1956; No. 886, Mar, 1958

	GD	VG	FN	VF	VF/NM	NM-
Four Color 706 (#1)	6	12	18	37	59	80
Four Color 886	5	10	15	30	48	65

BONGO COMICS PRESENTS RADIOACTIVE MAN (See Radioactive Man)

BON VOYAGE (See Movie Classics)

BOOF
Image Comics (Todd McFarlane Prod.): July, 1994 - No. 6, Dec, 1994 ($1.95)

1-6 — 2.50

BOOF AND THE BRUISE CREW
Image Comics (Todd McFarlane Prod.): July, 1994 - No. 6, Dec, 1994 ($1.95)

1-6 — 2.50

BOOK AND RECORD SET (See Power Record Comics)

BOOK OF ALL COMICS
William H. Wise: 1945 (196 pgs.)(Inside f/c has Green Publ. blacked out)

	GD	VG	FN	VF	VF/NM	NM-
nn-Green Mask, Puppeteer & The Bouncer	43	86	129	271	461	650

BOOK OF ANTS, THE
Artisan Entertainment: 1998 ($2.95, B&W)

1-Based on the movie Pi; Aronofsky-s — 3.00

BOOK OF BALLADS AND SAGAS, THE
Green Man Press: Oct, 1995 - No. 4 ($2.95/$3.50/$3.25, B&W)

1-4: 1-Vess-c/a; Gaiman story. — 3.50

BOOK OF COMICS, THE
William H. Wise: No date (1944) (25¢, 132 pgs.)

	GD	VG	FN	VF	VF/NM	NM-
nn-Captain V app.	41	82	123	248	417	585

BOOK OF FATE, THE (See Fate)
DC Comics: Feb, 1997 - No. 12, Jan, 1998 ($2.25/$2.50)

1-12: 4-Two-Face-c/app. 6-Convergence. 11-Sentinel app. — 3.00

BOOK OF LOST SOULS, THE
Marvel Comics (Icon): Dec, 2005 - No. 6, June, 2006 ($2.99)

1-6-Colleen Doran-a/c; J. Michael Straczynski-s — 3.00
... Vol. 1: Introductions All Around TPB (2006, $16.99) r/series — 17.00

BOOK OF LOVE (See Fox Giants)

BOOK OF NIGHT, THE
Dark Horse Comics: July, 1987 - No. 3, 1987 ($1.75, B&W)

1-3: Reprints from Epic Illustrated; Vess-a — 2.50
TPB-r/#1-3 — 15.00
Hardcover-Black-c with red crest — 100.00
Hardcover w/slipcase (1991) signed and numbered — 50.00

BOOK OF THE DEAD
Marvel Comics: Dec, 1993 - No. 4, Mar, 1994 ($1.75, limited series, 52 pgs.)

	GD	VG	FN	VF	VF/NM	NM-
1-4: 1-Ploog Frankenstein & Morrow Man-Thing-r begin; Wrightson-r/Chamber of Darkness #7. 2-Morrow new painted-c; Chaykin/Morrow Man-Thing; Krigstein-r/Uncanny Tales #54; r/Fear #10. 3-r/Astonishing Tales #10 & Starlin Man-Thing. 3,4-Painted-c	1	2	3	5	6	8

BOOKS OF DOOM (Dr. Doom from Fantastic Four)
Marvel Comics: Jan, 2006 - No. 6, June, 2006 ($2.99, limited series)

1-6-Life story/origin of Dr. Doom; Brubaker-s/Raimondi-a/Rivera-c — 3.00
Fantastic Four: Books of Doom HC (2006, $19.99) r/#1-6 — 20.00
Fantastic Four: Books of Doom SC (2007, $14.99) r/#1-6 — 15.00

BOOKS OF FAERIE, THE
DC Comics (Vertigo): Mar, 1997 - No. 3, May, 1997 ($2.50, limited series)

1-3-Gross-a — 3.00
TPB (1998, $14.95) r/#1-3 & Arcana Annual #1 — 15.00

BOOKS OF FAERIE, THE : AUBERON'S TALE
DC Comics (Vertigo): Aug, 1998 - No. 3, Oct, 1998 ($2.50, limited series)

1-3-Gross-a — 3.00

BOOKS OF FAERIE, THE : MOLLY'S STORY
DC Comics (Vertigo): Sept, 1999 - No. 4, Dec, 1999 ($2.50, limited series)

1-4-Ney Rieber-s/Mejia-a — 3.00

BOOKS OF MAGIC
DC Comics: 1990 - No. 4, 1991 ($3.95, 52 pgs., limited series, mature)

	GD	VG	FN	VF	VF/NM	NM-
1-Bolton painted-c/a; Phantom Stranger app.; Gaiman scripts in all	1	3	4	6	8	10
2,3: 2-John Constantine, Dr. Fate, Spectre, Deadman app. 3-Dr. Occult app.; minor Sandman app.	1	2	3	4	5	7
4-Early Death-c/app. (early 1991)	1	2	3	5	6	8
Trade paperback-($19.95)-Reprints limited series						20.00

BOOKS OF MAGIC (Also see Hunter: The Age of Magic and Names of Magic)
DC Comics (Vertigo): May, 1994 - No. 75, Aug, 2000 ($1.95/$2.50, mature)

	GD	VG	FN	VF	VF/NM	NM-
1-Charles Vess-c	2	4	6	8	10	12
1-Platinum	2	4	6	13	18	22
2-4: 4-Death app.	1	2	3	4	5	7
5-14; Charles Vess-c						4.00
15-50: 15-$2.50-c begins. 22-Kaluta-c. 25-Death-c/app; Bachalo-c						3.00
51-75: 51-Peter Gross-s/a begins. 55-Medley-a						2.50
Annual 1-3 (2/97, 2/98, '99, $3.95)						4.00
Bindings (1995, $12.95, TPB)-r/#1-4						13.00
Death After Death (2001, $19.95, TPB)-r/#42-50						20.00
Girl in the Box (1999, $14.95, TPB)-r/#26-32						15.00
Reckonings (1997, $12.95, TPB)-r/#14-20						13.00
Summonings (1996, $17.50, TPB)-r/#5-13, Vertigo Rave #1						17.50
The Burning Girl (2000, $17.95, TPB)-r/#33-41						18.00
Transformations (1998, $12.95, TPB)-r/#21-25						13.00

BOOKS OF MAGICK, THE : LIFE DURING WARTIME (See Books of Magic)
DC Comics (Vertigo): Sept, 2004 - No. 15, Dec, 2005 ($2.50/$2.75)

1-15: 1-Spencer-s/Ormston-a/Quitely-c; Constantine app. 2-Bagged with Sky Captain CD 6-Fegredo-a. 7-Constantine & Zatanna-c — 2.75
... Book One TPB (2005, $9.95) r/#1-5 — 10.00

BOOSTER GOLD (See Justice League #4)
DC Comics: Feb, 1986 - No. 25, Feb, 1988 (75¢)

1-Dan Jurgens-s/a(p) — 3.00
2-25: 4-Rose & Thorn app. 6-Origin. 6,7,23-Superman app. 8,9-LSH app. 22-JLI app. 24,25-Millennium tie-ins — 2.50

NOTE: *Austin c-22i. **Byrne** c-23i.*

BOOSTER GOLD (See DC's weekly series 52)
DC Comics: Oct, 2007 - Present ($3.50/$2.99/$3.99)

1-Geoff Johns-s/Dan Jurgens-a(p); covers by Jurgens and Art Adams; Rip Hunter app. — 5.00
2-20: 3-Jonah Hex app. 4-Barry Allen app. 5-Joker and Batgirl app. 8-Superman app. — 3.00
21-28-($3.99) 21-Blue Beetle back-ups begin. 22-New Teen Titans app. 23-Photo-c. 26,27-Blackest Night; Ted Kord rises — 4.00
#0-(4/08) Blue Beetle (Ted Cord) returns; takes place between #6&7 — 3.00
#1,000,000-(9/08) Michelle Carter returns; takes place between #10&11 — 3.00
...: Blue and Gold (2008, $24.99, HC w/d.j.) r/#0,7-10,#1,000,000; cover sketches — 25.00
...: 52 Pick-Up (2008, $24.99, HC w/d.j.) r/#1-6, original design sketches from Jurgens — 25.00
...: Reality Lost (2009, $14.99, SC) r/#11,12,15-19 — 15.00

BOOTS AND HER BUDDIES
Standard Comics/Visual Editions/Argo (NEA Service):
No. 5, 9/48 - No. 9, 9/49; 12/55 - No. 3, 1956

	GD	VG	FN	VF	VF/NM	NM-
5-Strip-r	16	32	48	94	147	200

Born #1 © MAR

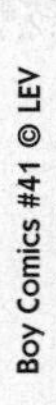
Boy Comics #41 © LEV

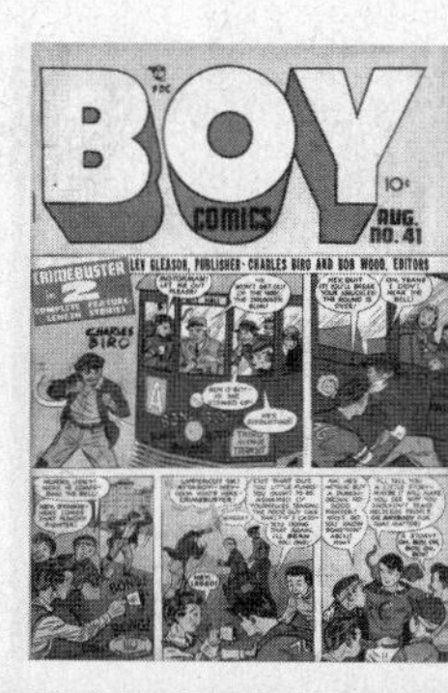

Boy Commandos #3 © DC

	GD 2.0	VG 4.0	FN 6.0	VF 8.0	VF/NM 9.0	NM- 9.2
6,8	11	22	33	64	90	115
7-(Scarce)	14	28	42	80	115	150
9-(Scarce)-Frazetta-a (2 pgs.)	26	52	78	154	252	350
1-3(Argo-1955-56)-Reprints	6	12	18	31	38	45

BOOTS & SADDLES (TV)
Dell Publ. Co.: No. 919, July, 1958; No. 1029, Sept, 1959; No. 1116, Aug, 1960

	GD 2.0	VG 4.0	FN 6.0	VF 8.0	VF/NM 9.0	NM- 9.2
Four Color 919 (#1)-Photo-c	7	14	21	50	83	115
Four Color 1029, 1116-Photo-c	5	10	15	34	55	75

BORDERLINE
Friction Press: June, 1992 ($2.25, B&W)

	GD 2.0	VG 4.0	FN 6.0	VF 8.0	VF/NM 9.0	NM- 9.2
0-Ashcan edition; 1st app. of Cliff Broadway						2.25
1-Painted-c						3.00
1-Special Edition (bagged w/ photo, S&N)						4.00

BORDER PATROL
P. L. Publishing Co.: May-June, 1951 - No. 3, Sept-Oct, 1951

	GD 2.0	VG 4.0	FN 6.0	VF 8.0	VF/NM 9.0	NM- 9.2
1	14	28	42	80	115	150
2,3	10	20	30	54	72	90

BORDER WORLDS (Also see Megaton Man)
Kitchen Sink Press: 7/86 - No. 7, 1987; V2#1, 1990 - No. 4, 1990 ($1.95-$2.00, B&W, mature)

	GD 2.0	VG 4.0	FN 6.0	VF 8.0	VF/NM 9.0	NM- 9.2
1-7, V2#1-4: Donald Simpson-c/a/scripts						3.00

BORIS KARLOFF TALES OF MYSTERY (TV) (...Thriller No. 1,2)
Gold Key: No. 3, April, 1963 - No. 97, Feb, 1980

	GD 2.0	VG 4.0	FN 6.0	VF 8.0	VF/NM 9.0	NM- 9.2
3-5-(Two #5's, 10/63,11/63): 5-(10/63)-11 pgs. Toth-a.	5	10	15	32	51	70
6-8,10: 10-Orlando-a	4	8	12	24	37	50
9-Wood-a	4	8	12	26	41	55
11-Williamson-a, 8 pgs.; Orlando-a, 5 pgs.	4	8	12	26	41	55
12-Torres, McWilliams-a; Orlando-a(2)	3	6	9	21	32	42
13,14,16-20	3	6	9	18	27	35
15-Crandall	3	6	9	19	29	38
21-Jeff Jones-a(3 pgs.) "The Screaming Skull"	3	6	9	19	29	38
22-Last 12¢ issue	3	6	9	16	22	28
23-30: 23-Reprint; photo-c	3	6	9	14	20	26
31-50: 36-Weiss-a	2	4	6	13	18	22
51-74: 74-Origin & 1st app. Taurus	2	4	6	9	13	16
75-79,87-97: 90-r/Torres, McWilliams-a/#12; Morrow-c	2	4	6	8	11	14
80-86-(52 pgs.)	2	4	6	9	13	16
Story Digest 1(7/70-Gold Key)-All text/illos.; 148 pp.	5	10	15	34	55	75

(See Mystery Comics Digest No. 2, 5, 8, 11, 14, 17, 20, 23, 26)
NOTE: ***Bolle** a-51-54, 56, 58, 59. **McWilliams** a-12, 14, 18, 19, 72, 80, 81, 93. **Orlando** a-11-15, 21. Reprints: 78, 81-86, 88, 90, 92, 95, 97.*

BORIS KARLOFF THRILLER (TV) (Becomes Boris Karloff Tales...)
Gold Key: Oct, 1962 - No. 2, Jan, 1963 (84 pgs.)

	GD 2.0	VG 4.0	FN 6.0	VF 8.0	VF/NM 9.0	NM- 9.2
1-Photo-c	10	20	30	70	123	175
2	7	14	21	45	73	100

BORIS THE BEAR
Dark Horse Comics/Nicotat Comics #13 on: Aug, 1986 - No. 34, 1990 ($1.50/$1.75/$1.95, B&W)

	GD 2.0	VG 4.0	FN 6.0	VF 8.0	VF/NM 9.0	NM- 9.2
1, Annual 1 (1988, $2.50)						3.00
1 (2nd printing),2,3,4A,4B,5-12, 14-34: 8-(44 pgs.)						2.50
13-1st Nicotat Comics issue						3.00

BORIS THE BEAR INSTANT COLOR CLASSICS
Dark Horse Comics: July, 1987 - No. 3, 1987 ($1.75/$1.95)

	GD 2.0	VG 4.0	FN 6.0	VF 8.0	VF/NM 9.0	NM- 9.2
1-3						2.50

BORN
Marvel Comics: 2003 - No. 4, 2003 ($3.50, limited series)

	GD 2.0	VG 4.0	FN 6.0	VF 8.0	VF/NM 9.0	NM- 9.2
1-4-Frank Castle (the Punisher) in 1971 Vietnam; Ennis-s/Robertson-a						3.50
HC (2004, $17.99) oversized reprint of series; proposal, layout pages						18.00
Punisher: Born SC (2004, $13.99) r/series; proposal, layout pages						14.00

BORN AGAIN
Spire Christian Comics (Fleming H. Revell Co.): 1978 (39¢)

	GD 2.0	VG 4.0	FN 6.0	VF 8.0	VF/NM 9.0	NM- 9.2
nn-Watergate, Nixon, etc.	2	4	6	10	14	18

BOUNCER, THE (Formerly Green Mask #9)
Fox Features Syndicate: 1944 - No. 14, Jan, 1945

	GD 2.0	VG 4.0	FN 6.0	VF 8.0	VF/NM 9.0	NM- 9.2
nn(1944, #10?)	31	62	93	182	296	410
11 (9/44)-Origin; Rocket Kelly, One Round Hogan app.	23	46	69	136	223	310
12-14: 14-Reprints no # issue	19	38	57	111	176	240

BOUNTY GUNS (See Luke Short's..., Four Color 739)

BOX OFFICE POISON
Antarctic Press: 1996 - No. 21, Sept, 2000 ($2.95, B&W)

	GD 2.0	VG 4.0	FN 6.0	VF 8.0	VF/NM 9.0	NM- 9.2
1-Alex Robinson-s/a in all	1	2	3	4	5	7
2-5						4.00
6-21, ...Kolor Karnival 1 (5/99, $2.99)						3.00
...Super Special 0 (5/97, $4.95)						5.00
Sherman's March: Collected BOP Vol. 1 (9/98, $14.95) r/#0-4						15.00
TPB (2002, $29.95, 608 pgs.) r/entire series						30.00

BOY AND HIS 'BOT, A
Now Comics: Jan, 1987 ($1.95)

	GD 2.0	VG 4.0	FN 6.0	VF 8.0	VF/NM 9.0	NM- 9.2
1-A Holiday Special						3.00

BOY AND THE PIRATES, THE (Movie)
Dell Publishing Co.: No. 1117, Aug, 1960

	GD 2.0	VG 4.0	FN 6.0	VF 8.0	VF/NM 9.0	NM- 9.2
Four Color 1117-Photo-c	6	12	18	43	69	95

BOY COMICS (Captain Battle No. 1 & 2; Boy Illustories No. 43-108) (Stories by Charles Biro) (Also see Squeeks)
Lev Gleason Publ. (Comic House): No. 3, Apr, 1942 - No. 119, Mar, 1956

	GD 2.0	VG 4.0	FN 6.0	VF 8.0	VF/NM 9.0	NM- 9.2
3(No.1)-1st app. & origin Crimebuster, Bombshell & Young Robin Hood; Yankee Longago, Case 1001-1008, Swoop Storm, & Boy Movies begin; 1st app. Iron Jaw; Crimebuster's pet monkey Squeeks begins	309	618	927	2163	3782	5400
4-Hitler, Tojo, Mussolini-c	135	270	405	864	1482	2100
5	90	180	270	576	988	1400
6-Origin Iron Jaw; origin & death of Iron Jaw's son; Little Dynamite begins, ends #39; 1st Iron Jaw-c	303	606	909	2121	3711	5300
7-Flag & Hitler, Tojo, Mussolini-c	103	206	309	659	1130	1600
8-Death of Iron Jaw; Iron Jaw-c	100	200	300	635	1093	1550
9-Iron Jaw-c	90	180	270	576	988	1400
10-Return of Iron Jaw; classic Biro-c; Iron Jaw-c	135	270	405	864	1482	2100
11-Classic Iron Jaw-c	94	188	282	597	1024	1450
12,13: 12-Torture-c	56	112	168	356	616	875
14-Iron Jaw-c	66	132	198	419	722	1025
15-Death of Iron Jaw	76	152	228	486	831	1175
16,18-20	41	82	123	249	417	585
17-Flag-c	41	82	123	256	428	600
21-29,31,32-(All 68 pgs.). 28-Yankee Longago ends. 32-Swoop Storm & Young Robin Hood end	29	58	87	170	278	385
30-(68 pgs.)-Origin Crimebuster retold	37	74	111	222	361	500
33-40: 34-Crimebuster story(2); suicide-c/story	22	44	66	128	209	290
41-50	18	36	54	107	169	230
51-59: 57-Dilly Duncan begins, ends #71	15	30	45	90	140	190
60-Iron Jaw returns	17	34	51	98	154	210
61-Origin Crimebuster & Iron Jaw retold	19	38	57	109	172	235
62-Death of Iron Jaw explained	18	36	54	105	165	225
63-73: 63-McWilliams-a. 73-Frazetta 1-pg. ad	13	26	39	74	105	135
74-88: 80-1st app. Rocky X of the Rocketeers; becomes "Rocky X" #101; Iron Jaw, Sniffer & the Deadly Dozen in 80-118	11	22	33	60	83	105
89-92-The Claw serial app. in all	11	22	33	62	86	110
93-Claw cameo; Rocky X by Sid Check	11	22	33	60	83	105
94-97,99	10	20	30	58	79	100
98,100: 98-Rocky X by Sid Check	11	22	33	60	83	105
101-107,109,111,119: 101-Rocky X becomes spy strip. 106-Robin Hood app. 119-Last Crimebuster. 111-Crimebuster becomes Chuck Chandler.	9	18	27	52	69	85
108,110,112-118-Kubert-a; 108-Ditko-a	10	20	30	56	76	95

(See Giant Boy Book of Comics)
NOTE: *Boy Movies in 3-5,40,41. Iron Jaw app.-3, 4, 6, 8, 10, 11, 13-15; returns-60-62, 68, 69, 72-79, 81-118. **Biro** c-all. **Briefer** a-5, 13, 14, 16-20 among others. **Fuje** a-55, 18 pgs. **Palais** a-14, 16, 17, 19, 20 among others.*

BOY COMMANDOS (See Detective #64 & World's Finest Comics #8)
National Periodical Publications: Winter, 1942-43 - No. 36, Nov-Dec, 1949

	GD 2.0	VG 4.0	FN 6.0	VF 8.0	VF/NM 9.0	NM- 9.2
1-Origin Liberty Belle; The Sandman & The Newsboy Legion x-over in Boy Commandos; S&K-a, 48 pgs.; S&K cameo? (classic WWII-c)	503	1006	1509	3672	6486	9300
2-Last Liberty Belle; Hitler-c; S&K-a, 46 pgs.; WWII-c	239	478	717	1530	2615	3700
3-S&K-a, 45 pgs.; WWII-c	135	270	405	864	1482	2100
4-6: All WWII-c. 6-S&K-a	84	168	252	538	919	1300
7-10: All WWII-c	53	106	159	334	567	800
11-13: All WWII-c. 11-Infinity-c	39	78	117	240	395	550
14,16,18-19-All have S&K-a. 18-2nd Crazy Quilt-c	32	64	96	188	307	425

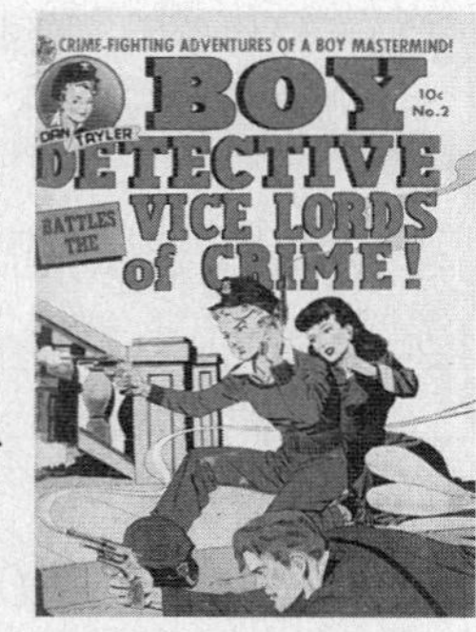

Boy Detective #2 © AVON

The Boys #31 © Spitfire

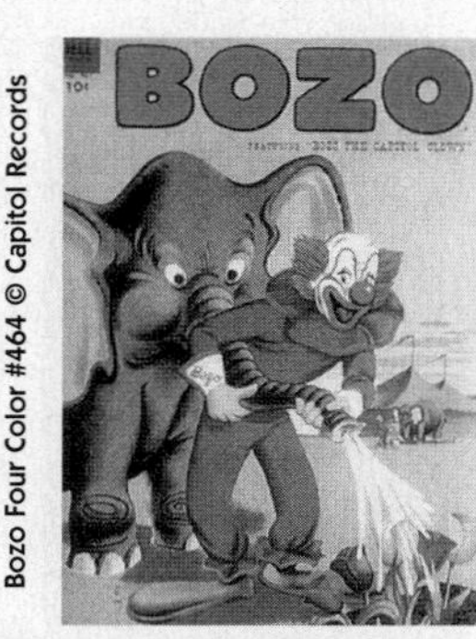

Bozo Four Color #464 © Capitol Records

GD VG FN VF VF/NM NM-
2.0 4.0 6.0 8.0 9.0 9.2

15-1st app. Crazy Quilt, their arch nemesis 40 80 120 246 411 575
17,20-Sci/fi-c/stories 39 78 117 231 378 525
21,22,25: 22-3rd Crazy Quilt-c; Judy Canova x-over 25 50 75 150 245 340
23-S&K-c/a(all) 34 68 102 204 332 460
24-1st costumed superhero satire-c (11-12/47). 30 60 90 177 289 400
26-Flying Saucer story (3-4/48)-4th of this theme; see The Spirit 9/28/47(1st), Shadow Comics V7#10 (2nd, 1/48) & Captain Midnight #60 (3rd, 2/48)
31 62 93 182 296 410
27,28,30: 30-Cleveland Indians story 24 48 72 144 237 330
29-S&K story (1) 26 52 78 154 252 350
31-35: 32-Dale Evans app. on-c & in story. 33-Last Crazy Quilt-c. 34-Intro. Wolf, their mascot 22 44 66 128 209 290
36-Intro The Atomobile c/sci-fi story (Scarce) 40 80 120 246 411 575

NOTE: *Most issues signed by **Simon & Kirby** are not by them.* ***S&K** c-1-9, 13, 14, 17, 21, 23, 24, 30-32. **Feller** c-30.*

BOY COMMANDOS
National Per. Publ.: Sept-Oct, 1973 - No. 2, Nov-Dec, 1973 (G.A. S&K reprints)

1,2: 1-Reprints story from Boy Commandos #1 plus-c & Detective #66 by S&K. 2-Infantino/Orlando-c 2 4 6 10 14 18

BOY COMMANDOS COMICS
DC Comics: Sept/Oct. 1942

1-Ashcan comic, not distributed to newsstands, only for in-house use. Cover art is the splash page from the Boy Commandos story in Detective Comics #68 interior is from an unidentified issue of Detective Comics (no known sales)
nn - (9-10/42) Ashcan comic, not distributed to newsstands, only for in-house use. Cover art is the splash page from the Boy Commandos story in Detective Comics #68 interior is from Detective Comics #68 (no known sales)

BOY COWBOY (Also see Amazing Adventures & Science Comics)
Ziff-Davis Publ. Co.: 1950 (8 pgs. in color)

nn-Sent to subscribers of Ziff-Davis mags. & ordered through mail for 10¢; used to test market for Kid Cowboy 28 56 84 165 270 375

BOY DETECTIVE
Avon Periodicals: May-June, 1951 - No. 4, May, 1952

1 20 40 60 115 183 250
2-4: 3,4-Kinstler-c 14 28 42 80 115 150

BOY EXPLORERS COMICS (Terry and The Pirates No. 3 on)
Family Comics (Harvey Publ.): May-June, 1946 - No. 2, Sept-Oct, 1946

1-Intro The Explorers, Duke of Broadway, Calamity Jane & Danny Dixon...Cadet; S&K-c/a, 24 pgs. 65 130 195 416 708 1000
2-(Rare)-Small size (5-1/2x8-1/2"; B&W; 32 pgs.) Distributed to mail subscribers only; S&K-a 155 310 465 992 1696 2400

(Also see All New No. 15, Flash Gordon No. 5, and Stuntman No. 3)

BOY ILLUSTORIES (See Boy Comics)

BOY LOVES GIRL (Boy Meets Girl No. 1-24)
Lev Gleason Publications: No. 25, July, 1952 - No. 57, June, 1956

25(#1) 10 20 30 58 79 100
26,27,29-33: 30-33-Serial, 'Loves of My Life 8 16 24 42 54 65
34-42: 39-Lingerie panels 8 16 24 40 50 60
28-Drug propaganda story 8 16 24 42 54 65
43-Toth-a 8 16 24 44 57 70
44-50: 47-Toth-a? 50-Last pre-code (2/55) 7 14 21 37 46 55
51-57: 57-Ann Brewster-a 6 12 18 31 38 45

BOY MEETS GIRL (Boy Loves Girl No. 25 on)
Lev Gleason Publications: Feb, 1950 - No. 24, June, 1952 (No. 1-17: 52 pgs.)

1-Guardineer-a 15 30 45 86 133 180
2 10 20 30 54 72 90
3-10 9 18 27 50 65 80
11-24 9 18 27 47 61 75

NOTE: ***Briefer** a-24. **Fuje** c-3,7. Painted-c 1-17. Photo-c 19-21, 23.*

BOYS, THE
DC Comics (WildStorm)/Dynamite Ent. #7 on: Oct, 2006 - Present ($2.99, mature)

1-Garth Ennis-s/Darick Robertson-a 6.00
2-6 4.00
7-40-(Dynamite Ent.,). 19-Origin of the Homelander. 23-Variant-c by Cassaday 3.00
#1: Dynamite Edition (2009, $1.00) r/#1; flip book with Battlefields Night Witches 1.00
...: Herogasm 1-6 (2009 - No. 6, 2009, $2.99) Ennis-s/McCrea-a 3.00
... Volume 1: The Name of the Game TPB (2007, $14.99) r/#1-6; intro. by Simon Pegg 15.00
... Volume 2: Get Some TPB (2008, $19.99) r/#7-14 20.00
... Volume 3: Good For The Soul TPB (2008, $19.99) r/#15-22 20.00
... Volume 4: We Gotta Go Now TPB (2009, $19.99) r/#23-30; cover gallery 20.00

BOYS' AND GIRLS' MARCH OF COMICS (See March of Comics)

BOYS' RANCH (Also see Western Tales & Witches' Western Tales)
Harvey Publ.: Oct, 1950 - No. 6, Aug, 1951 (No.1-3, 52 pgs.; No. 4-6, 36 pgs.)

1-S&K-c/a(3) 60 120 180 378 639 900
2-S&K-c/a(3) 41 82 123 250 413 575
3-S&K-c/a(2); Meskin-a 40 80 120 235 380 525
4-S&K-c/a, 5 pgs. 35 70 105 203 327 450
5,6-S&K-c, splashes & centerspread only; Meskin-a 20 40 60 115 183 250

BOZO (Larry Harmon's Bozo, the World's Most Famous Clown)
Innovation Publishing: 1992 ($6.95, 68 pgs.)

1-Reprints Four Color #285(#1) 1 2 3 4 5 7

BOZO THE CLOWN (TV) (Bozo No. 7 on)
Dell Publishing Co.: July, 1950 - No. 4, Oct-Dec, 1963

Four Color 285(#1) 18 36 54 126 246 365
2(7-9/51)-7(10-12/52) 11 22 33 74 132 190
Four Color 464,508,551,594(10/54) 9 18 27 65 113 160
1(nn, 5-7/62) 7 14 21 50 83 115
2 - 4(1963) 6 12 18 39 62 85

BOZZ CHRONICLES, THE
Marvel Comics (Epic Comics): Dec, 1985 - No. 6, 1986 (Lim. series, mature)

1-6-Logan/Wolverine look alike in 19th century. 1,3,5-Blevins-a 3.00

B.P.R.D. (Bureau of Paranormal Research and Defense) (Also see Hellboy titles)
Dark Horse Comics: (one-shots)

... Dark Waters (7/03, $2.99) Guy Davis-c/a; Augustyn-s 3.00
... Night Train (9/03, $2.99) Johns & Kolins-s; Kolins & Stewart-a 3.00
... The Ectoplasmic Man (6/08, $2.99) Stenbeck-a/Mignola-c; origin of Johann Kraus 3.00
... There's Something Under My Bed (11/03, $2.99) Pollina-a/c 3.00
... The Soul of Venice (5/03, $2.99) Oeming-a/c; Gunter & Oeming-s 3.00
... The Soul of Venice and Other Stories TPB (8/04, $17.95) r/one-shots & new story by Mignola and Cam Stewart; sketch pages by various 18.00
... War on Frogs (6/08,12/08, 6/09, 12/09, $2.99) 1-Trimpe-a/Mignola-c; Abe Sapien app. 2-Severin-a. 3-Moline-a. 4-Snejbjerg 3.00

B.P.R.D.: GARDEN OF SOULS
Dark Horse Comics: Mar, 2007 - No. 5, July, 2007 ($2.99, limited series)

1-5-Mignola & Arcudi-s/Guy Davis-a/Mignola-c 3.00

B.P.R.D.: HOLLOW EARTH (Mike Mignola's...)
Dark Horse Comics: Jan, 2002 - No. 3, June, 2002 ($2.99, limited series)

1-3-Mignola, Golden & Sniegoski-s/Sook-a/Mignola-c; Hellboy and Abe Sapien app. 3.00
... and Other Stories TPB (1/03; 7/04, $17.95) r/#1-3, Hellboy: Box Full of Evil, Abe Sapien: Drums of the Dead, and Dark Horse Extra; plus sketch pages 18.00

B.P.R.D.: KILLING GROUND
Dark Horse Comics: Aug, 2007 - No. 5, Dec, 2007 ($2.99, limited series)

1-5-Mignola & Arcudi-s/Guy Davis-a/c 3.00

B.P.R.D.: KING OF FEAR
Dark Horse Comics: Jan, 2010 - Present ($2.99, limited series)

1,2-Mignola & Arcudi-s/Guy Davis-a/c 3.00

B.P.R.D.: 1946
Dark Horse Comics: Jan, 2008 - No. 5, May, 2008 ($2.99, limited series)

1-5-Mignola & Dysart-s/Azaceta-a; Mignola/c 3.00

B.P.R.D.: 1947
Dark Horse Comics: Jul, 2009 - No. 5, Nov, 2009 ($2.99, limited series)

1-5-Mignola & Dysart-s/Bá & Moon-a; Mignola/c 3.00

B.P.R.D.: PLAGUE OF FROGS
Dark Horse Comics: Mar, 2004 - No. 5, July, 2004 ($2.99, limited series)

1-5-Mignola-s/Guy Davis-c/a 3.00
TPB (1/05, $17.95) r/series; sketchbook pages & afterword by Davis & Mignola 18.00

B.P.R.D.: THE BLACK FLAME
Dark Horse Comics: Sept, 2005 - No. 6, Jan, 2006 ($2.99, limited series)

1-6-Mignola & Arcudi-s/Guy Davis-a/ Mignola-c 3.00
TPB (7/06, $17.95) r/series; sketchbook pages & afterword by Davis & Mignola 18.00

B.P.R.D.: THE BLACK GODDESS
Dark Horse Comics: Jan, 2009 - No. 5, May, 2009 ($2.99, limited series)

1-5-Mignola & Arcudi-s/Guy Davis-a/Nowlan-c 3.00

B.P.R.D.: THE DEAD

B.P.R.D.: The War on Frogs #3 © Mike Mignola

Brave and the Bold #46 © DC

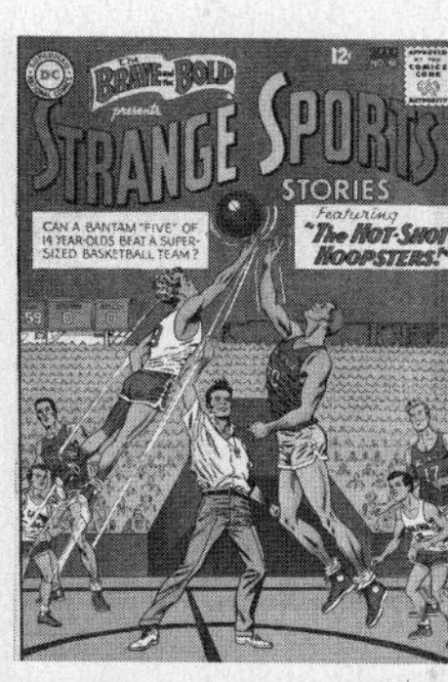

Brave and the Bold #62 © DC

	GD	VG	FN	VF	VF/NM	NM-
	2.0	4.0	6.0	8.0	9.0	9.2

Dark Horse Comics: Nov, 2004 - No. 5, Mar, 2005 ($2.99, limited series)

1-5-Mignola-s/Guy Davis-c/a 3.00

B.P.R.D.: THE UNIVERSAL MACHINE
Dark Horse Comics: Apr, 2006 - No. 5, Aug, 2006 ($2.99, limited series)

1-5-Mignola & Arcudi-s/Guy Davis-a/Mignola-c. 5-Mignola-a (5 pgs.) 3.00
TPB (1/07, $17.95) r/series; sketchbook pages by Davis; Mignola afterword 18.00

B.P.R.D.: THE WARNING
Dark Horse Comics: July, 2008 - No. 5, Nov, 2008 ($2.99, limited series)

1-5-Mignola & Arcudi-s/Guy Davis-c/a 3.00

BRADLEYS, THE (Also see Hate)
Fantagraphics Books: Apr, 1999 - No. 6, Jan, 2000 ($2.95, B&W, limited series)

1-6-Reprints Peter Bagge's-s/a 3.00

BRADY BUNCH, THE (TV)(See Kite Fun Book and Binky #78)
Dell Publishing Co.: Feb, 1970 - No. 2, May, 1970

1 11 22 33 78 139 200
2 8 16 24 58 97 135

BRAIN, THE
Sussex Publ. Co./Magazine Enterprises: Sept, 1956 - No. 7, 1958

1-Dan DeCarlo-a in all including reprints 12 24 36 67 94 120
2,3 8 16 24 40 50 60
4-7 4 8 12 24 37 50
I.W. Reprints #1-4,8-10('63),14: 2-Reprints Sussex #2 with new cover added 2 4 6 9 13 16
Super Reprint #17,18(nd) 2 4 6 9 13 16

BRAINBANX
DC Comics (Helix): Mar, 1997 - No. 6, Aug, 1997 ($2.50, limited series)

1-6: Elaine Lee-s/Temujin-a 2.50

BRAIN BOY
Dell Publishing Co.: Apr-June, 1962 - No. 6, Sept-Nov, 1963 (Painted c-#1-6)

Four Color 1330(#1)-Gil Kane-a; origin 11 22 33 78 139 200
2(7-9/62),3-6: 4-Origin retold 7 14 21 49 80 110

BRAM STOKER'S BURIAL OF THE RATS (Movie)
Roger Corman's Cosmic Comics: Apr, 1995 - No.3, June, 1995 ($2.50)

1-3: Adaptation of film; Jerry Prosser scripts 2.50

BRAM STOKER'S DRACULA (Movie)(Also see Dracula: Vlad the Impaler)
Topps Comics: Oct, 1992 - No. 4, Jan, 1993 ($2.95, limited series, polybagged)

1-(1st & 2nd printing)-Adaptation of film begins; Mignola-c/a in all; 4 trading cards & poster; photo scenes of movie 3.00
1-Crimson foil edition (limited to 500) 8.00
2-4: 2-Bound-in poster & cards. 4 trading cards in both. 3-Contains coupon to win 1 of 500 crimson foil-c edition of #1. 4-Contains coupon to win 1 of 500 uncut sheets of all 16 trading cards 3.00

BRAND ECHH (See Not Brand Echh)

BRAND OF EMPIRE (See Luke Short's...Four Color 771)

BRASS
Image Comics (WildStorm Productions): Aug, 1996 - No. 3, May, 1997 ($2.50, lim. series)

1-($4.50) Folio Ed.; oversized 4.50
1-3: Wiesenfeld-s/Bennett-a. 3-Grunge & Roxy(Gen 13) cameo 2.50

BRASS
DC Comics (WildStorm): Aug, 2000 - No. 6, Jan, 2001 ($2.50, limited series)

1-6-Arcudi-s 2.50

BRATH
CrossGeneration Comics: Feb, 2003 - No. 14, June, 2004 ($2.95)

Prequel-Dixon-s/Di Vito-a 3.00
1-14: 1-(3/03)-Dixon-s/Di Vito-a 3.00
Vol. 1: Hammer of Vengeance (2003, $9.95) Digest-sized reprint of Prequel & #1-6 10.00

BRATPACK/MAXIMORTAL SUPER SPECIAL
King Hell Press: 1996 ($2.95, B&W, limited series)

1,2: Veitch-s/a 3.00

BRATS BIZARRE
Marvel Comics (Epic/Heavy Hitters): 1994 - No. 4, 1994 ($2.50, limited series)

1-4: All w/bound-in trading cards 2.50

BRAVADOS, THE (See Wild Western Action)
Skywald Publ. Corp.: Aug, 1971 (52 pgs., one-shot)

1-Red Mask, The Durango Kid, Billy Nevada-r; Bolle-a; 3-D effect story 3 6 9 14 19 24

BRAVE AND THE BOLD, THE (See Best Of... & Super DC Giant) (Replaced by Batman & The Outsiders)
National Periodical Publ./DC Comics: Aug-Sept, 1955 - No. 200, July, 1983

1-Viking Prince by Kubert, Silent Knight, Golden Gladiator begin; part Kubert-c 288 576 864 2520 5010 7500
2 116 232 348 986 1943 2900
3,4 62 124 186 527 1039 1550
5-Robin Hood begins (4-5/56, 1st DC app.), ends #15; see Robin Hood Tales #7 64 128 192 544 1072 1600
6-10: 6-Robin Hood by Kubert; last Golden Gladiator app.; Silent Knight; no Viking Prince. 8-1st S.A. issue 46 92 138 368 709 1050
11-22,24: 12,14-Robin Hood-c. 18,21-23-Grey tone-c. 22-Last Silent Knight. 24-Last Viking Prince by Kubert (2nd solo book) 36 72 108 280 540 800
23-Viking Prince origin by Kubert; 1st B&B single theme issue & 1st Viking Prince solo book 46 92 138 368 709 1050
25-1st app. Suicide Squad (8-9/59) 43 86 129 344 672 1000
26,27-Suicide Squad 30 60 90 218 422 625
28-(2-3/60)-Justice League intro./1st app.; origin/1st app. Snapper Carr 533 1066 1600 5200 10,600 16,000
29-Justice League (4-5/60)-2nd app. battle the Weapons Master; robot-c 200 400 600 1750 3475 5200
30-Justice League (6-7/60)-3rd app.; vs. Amazo 162 324 486 1418 2809 4200
31-1st app. Cave Carson (8-9/60); scarce in high grade; 1st try-out series 39 78 117 300 583 865
32,33-Cave Carson 23 46 69 166 321 475
34-Origin/1st app. Silver-Age Hawkman, Hawkgirl & Byth (2-3/61); Gardner Fox story, Kubert-c/a ; 1st S.A. Hawkman tryout series; 2nd in #42-44; both series predate Hawkman #1 (4-5/64) 177 354 531 1549 3075 4600
35-Hawkman by Kubert (4-5/61)-2nd app. 43 86 129 344 672 1000
36-Hawkman by Kubert; origin & 1st app. Shadow Thief (6-7/61)-3rd app. 39 78 117 300 583 865
37-Suicide Squad (2nd tryout series) 21 42 63 148 287 425
38,39-Suicide Squad. 38-Last 10¢ issue 18 36 54 126 246 365
40,41-Cave Carson Inside Earth (2nd try-out series). 40-Kubert-a. 41-Meskin-a 14 28 42 100 188 275
42-Hawkman by Kubert (2nd tryout series); Hawkman earns helmet wings; Byth app. 26 52 78 190 370 550
43-Hawkman by Kubert; more detailed origin 31 62 93 236 456 675
44-Hawkman by Kubert; grey-tone-c 25 50 75 183 354 525
45-49-Strange Sports Stories by Infantino 9 18 27 65 113 160
50-The Green Arrow & Manhunter From Mars (10-11/63); 1st Manhunter x-over outside of Detective Comics (pre-dates House of Mystery #143); team-ups begin 19 38 57 133 259 385
51-Aquaman & Hawkman (12-1/63-64); pre-dates Hawkman #1 21 42 63 148 287 425
52-(2-3/64)-3 Battle Stars; Sgt. Rock, Haunted Tank, Johnny Cloud, & Mlle. Marie team-up for 1st time by Kubert (c/a) 22 44 66 157 304 450
53-Atom & The Flash by Toth 10 20 30 68 119 170
54-Kid Flash, Robin & Aqualad; 1st app./origin Teen Titans (6-7/64) 30 60 90 228 439 650
55-Metal Men & The Atom 9 18 27 61 103 145
56-The Flash & Manhunter From Mars 9 18 27 61 103 145
57-Origin & 1st app. Metamorpho (12-1/64-65) 17 34 51 122 236 350
58-2nd app. Metamorpho by Fradon 10 20 30 70 123 175
59-Batman & Green Lantern; 1st Batman team-up in Brave and the Bold 12 24 36 86 158 230
60-Teen Titans (2nd app.)-1st app. new Wonder Girl (Donna Troy), who joins Titans (6-7/65) 15 30 45 107 204 300
61-Origin Starman & Black Canary by Anderson 13 26 39 90 165 240
62-Origin Starman & Black Canary cont'd. 62-1st S.A. app. Wildcat (10-11/65); 1st S.A. app. of G.A. Huntress (W.W. villain) 11 22 33 80 145 210
63-Supergirl & Wonder Woman 9 18 27 60 100 140
64-Batman Versus Eclipso (see H.O.S. #61) 8 16 24 58 97 135
65-Flash & Doom Patrol (4-5/66) 6 12 18 43 69 95
66-Metamorpho & Metal Men (6-7/66) 6 12 18 43 69 95
67-Batman & The Flash by Infantino; Batman team-ups begin, end #200 (8-9/66) 7 14 21 50 83 115
68-Batman/Metamorpho/Joker/Riddler/Penguin-c/story; Batman as Bat-Hulk (Hulk parody) 9 18 27 60 100 140
69-Batman & Green Lantern 7 14 21 45 73 100
70-Batman & Hawkman; Craig-a(p) 7 14 21 45 73 100
71-Batman & Green Arrow 7 14 21 45 73 100

Brave and the Bold #75 © DC

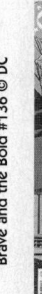

Brave and the Bold #136 © DC

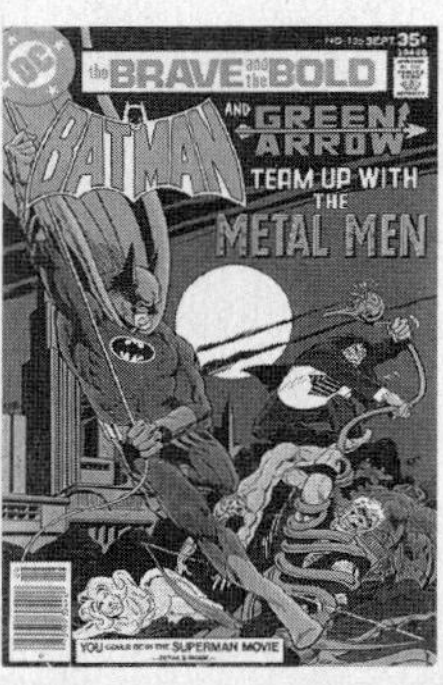

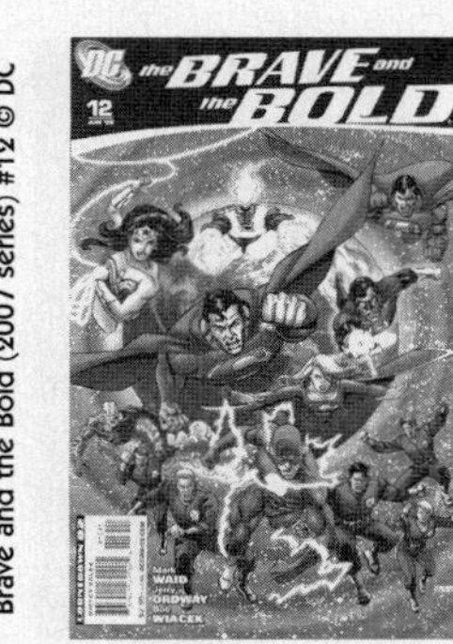

Brave and the Bold (2007 series) #12 © DC

GD VG FN VF VF/NM NM-
2.0 4.0 6.0 8.0 9.0 9.2

72-Spectre & Flash (6-7/67); 4th app. The Spectre; predates Spectre #1 7 14 21 47 76 105
73-Aquaman & The Atom 6 12 18 43 69 95
74-Batman & Metal Men 6 12 18 43 69 95
75-Batman & The Spectre (12-1/67-68); 6th app. Spectre; came out between Spectre #1 & #2 7 14 21 45 73 100
76-Batman & Plastic Man (2-3/68); came out between Plastic Man #8 & #9 6 12 18 43 69 95
77-Batman & The Atom 6 12 18 43 69 95
78-Batman, Wonder Woman & Batgirl 6 12 18 43 69 95
79-Batman & Deadman by Neal Adams (8-9/68); early Deadman app. 9 18 27 63 107 150
80-Batman & Creeper (10-11/68); N. Adams-a; early app. The Creeper; came out between Creeper #3 & #4 8 16 24 54 90 125
81-Batman & Flash; N. Adams-a 8 16 24 54 90 125
82-Batman & Aquaman; N. Adams-a; origin Ocean Master retold (2-3/69) 8 16 24 54 90 125
83-Batman & Teen Titans; N. Adams-a (4-5/69) 8 16 24 54 90 125
84-Batman (G.A., 1st S.A. app.) & Sgt. Rock; N. Adams-a; last 12¢ issue (6-7/69) 8 16 24 54 90 125
85-Batman & Green Arrow; 1st new costume for Green Arrow by Neal Adams (8-9/69) 9 18 27 63 107 150
86-Batman & Deadman (10-11/69); N. Adams-a; story concludes from Strange Adventures #216 (1-2/69) 8 16 24 54 90 125
87-Batman & Wonder Woman 4 8 12 28 44 60
88-Batman & Wildcat 4 8 12 28 44 60
89-Batman & Phantom Stranger (4-5/70); early Phantom Stranger app. (came out between Phantom Stranger #6 & 7 4 8 12 26 41 55
90-Batman & Adam Strange 4 8 12 26 41 55
91-Batman & Black Canary (8-9/70) 4 8 12 26 41 55
92-Batman; intro the Bat Squad 4 8 12 26 41 55
93-Batman-House of Mystery; N. Adams-a 7 14 21 45 73 100
94-Batman-Teen Titans 4 8 12 23 36 48
95-Batman & Plastic Man 3 6 9 21 32 42
96-Batman & Sgt. Rock; last 15¢ issue 4 8 12 22 34 45
97-Batman & Wildcat; 52 pg. issues begin, end #102; reprints origin & 1st app. Deadman from Strange Advs. #205 4 8 12 22 34 45
98-Batman & Phantom Stranger; 1st Jim Aparo Batman-a? 4 8 12 22 34 45
99-Batman & Flash 4 8 12 22 34 45
100-(2-3/72, 25¢, 52 pgs.)-Batman-Green Lantern-Green Arrow-Black Canary-Robin; Deadman-r by Adams/Str. Advs. #210 6 12 18 41 66 90
101-Batman & Metamorpho; Kubert Viking Prince 3 6 9 21 32 42
102-Batman-Teen Titans; N. Adams-a(p) 5 10 15 32 51 70
103-107,109,110: Batman team-ups: 103-Metal Men. 104-Deadman. 105-Wonder Woman. 106-Green Arrow. 107-Black Canary. 109-Demon. 110-Wildcat 3 6 9 14 20 26
108-Sgt. Rock 3 6 9 16 22 28
111-Batman/Joker-c/story 3 6 9 19 29 38
112-117: All 100 pgs.; Batman team-ups: 112-Mr. Miracle. 113-Metal Men; reprints origin/1st Hawkman from Brave and the Bold #34; r/origin Multi-Man/Challengers #14. 114-Aquaman. 115-Atom; r/origin Viking Prince from #23; r/Dr. Fate/Hourman/Solomon Grundy/Green Lantern from Showcase #55. 116-Spectre. 117-Sgt. Rock; last 100 pg. issue 5 10 15 32 51 70
118-Batman/Wildcat/Joker-c/story 3 6 9 17 25 32
119,121-123,125-128,132-140: Batman team-ups: 119-Man-Bat. 121-Metal Men. 122-Swamp Thing. 123-Plastic Man/Metamorpho. 125-Flash. 126-Aquaman. 127-Wildcat. 128-Mr. Miracle. 132-Kung-Fu Fighter. 133-Deadman. 134-Green Lantern. 135-Metal Men. 136-Metal Men/Green Arrow. 137-Demon. 138-Mr. Miracle. 139-Hawkman. 140-Wonder Woman 2 4 6 8 10 12
120-Kamandi (68 pgs.) 3 6 9 14 19 24
124-Sgt. Rock 2 4 6 9 12 15
129,130-Batman/Green Arrow/Atom parts 1 & 2; Joker & Two Face-c/stories 2 4 6 13 18 22
131-Batman & Wonder Woman vs. Catwoman-c/sty 2 4 6 10 14 18
141-Batman/Black Canary vs. Joker-c/story 2 4 6 13 18 22
142-160: Batman team-ups: 142-Aquaman. 143-Creeper; origin Human Target (44 pgs.). 144-Green Arrow; origin Human Target part 2 (44 pgs.). 145-Phantom Stranger. 146-G.A. Batman/Unknown Soldier. 147-Supergirl. 148-Plastic Man; X-Mas-c. 149-Teen Titans. 150-Anniversary issue; Superman. 151-Flash. 152-Atom. 153-Red Tornado. 154-Metamorpho. 155-Green Lantern. 156-Dr. Fate. 157-Batman vs. Kamandi (ties into Kamandi #59). 158-Wonder Woman. 159-Ra's Al Ghul. 160-Supergirl. 1 3 4 6 8 10
145(11/79)-147,150-159,165(8/80)-(Whitman variants; low print run; none show issue # on cover) 2 4 6 9 13 16

GD VG FN VF VF/NM NM-
2.0 4.0 6.0 8.0 9.0 9.2

161-181,183-190,192-195,198,199: Batman team-ups: 161-Adam Strange. 162-G.A. Batman/Sgt. Rock. 163-Black Lightning. 164-Hawkman. 165-Man-Bat. 166-Black Canary; Nemesis (intro) back-up story begins, ends #192; Penguin-c/story. 167-G.A. Batman/Blackhawk; origin Nemesis. 168-Green Arrow. 169-Zatanna. 170-Nemesis. 171-Scalphunter. 172-Firestorm. 173-Guardians of the Universe. 174-Green Lantern. 175-Lois Lane. 176-Swamp Thing. 177-Elongated Man. 178-Creeper. 179-Legion. 180-Spectre. 181-Hawk & Dove. 183-Riddler. 184-Huntress & Earth II Batman. 185-Green Arrow. 186-Hawkman. 187-Metal Men. 188,189-Rose & the Thorn. 190-Adam Strange. 192-Superboy vs. Mr. I.Q. 194-Flash. 195-I...Vampire. 198-Karate Kid. 199-Batman vs. The Spectre 6.00
182-G.A. Robin; G.A. Starman app.; 1st modern app. G.A. Batwoman 2 4 6 8 10 12
191-Batman/Joker-c/story; Nemesis app. 2 4 6 8 11 14
196-Ragman; origin Ragman retold. 1 2 3 5 6 8
197-Catwoman; Earth II Batman & Catwoman marry; 2nd modern app. of G.A. Batwoman; Scarecrow story in Golden Age style 2 4 6 9 12 15
200-Double-sized (64 pgs.); printed on Mando paper; Earth One & Earth Two Batman app. in separate stories; intro/1st app. Batman & The Outsiders 2 4 6 8 10 12

NOTE: ***Neal Adams** a-79-86, 93, 100r, 102; c-75, 76, 79-86, 88-90, 93, 95, 99, 100r. **M. Anderson** a-115r; c-72i, 96i. **Andru/Esposito** c-25-27. **Aparo** a-98, 100-102, 104-125, 126i, 127-136, 138-145, 147, 148i, 149-152, 154, 155, 157-162, 168-170, 173-178, 180-182, 184, 186i-189i, 191i-193i, 195, 196, 200; c-105-109, 111-136, 137i, 138-175, 177, 180-184, 186-200. **Austin** a-166i. **Bernard Baily** c-32, 33, 58. **Buckler** a-185, 186p; c-137, 178p, 185p, 186p. **Giordano** a-143, 144. **Infantino** a-67p, 72p, 97r, 98r, 115r, 172p, 183p, 190p, 194p; c-45-49, 67p, 69p, 70p, 72p, 96p, 98r. **Kaluta** c-176. **Kane** a-115r; c-59, 64. **Kubert** &/or **Heath** a-1-24; reprints-101, 113, 115, 117. **Kubert** a-99r; c-22-24, 34-36, 40, 42-44, 52. **Mooney** a-114r. **Mortimer** a-64, 69. **Newton** a-153p, 156p, 165p. **Irv Novick** c-1(part), 2-21. **Fred Ray** a-78r. **Roussos** a-50, 76i, 114r. **Staton** 148p. 52 pgs.-97, 100; 68 pgs.-120; 100 pgs.-112-117.*

BRAVE AND THE BOLD, THE
DC Comics: Dec, 1991 - No. 6, June, 1992 ($1.75, limited series)

1-6: Green Arrow, The Butcher, The Question in all; Grell scripts in all 2.50
NOTE: ***Grell** c-3, 4-6.*

BRAVE AND THE BOLD, THE
DC Comics: Apr, 2007 - Present ($2.99)

1-Batman & Green Lantern team-up; Roulette app.; Waid-s/Peréz-c/a; 2 covers 4.00
2-31: 2-GL & Supergirl. 3-Batman & Blue Beetle vs. Fatal Five; Lobo app. 4-6-LSH app. 12-Megistus conclusion; Ordway-a. 14-Kolins-a. 16-Superman & Catwoman. 28-Blackhawks app. 29-Batman/Brother Power the Geek. 31-Atom/Joker 3.00
...: Demons and Dragons HC (2009, $24.99, dustjacket) r/#13-16; Brave & the Bold V1 #181, Flash V3 #107 and Impulse #17; Mark Waid commentary 25.00
...: Milestone SC (2010, $17.99) r/#24-26 and Static #12, Hardware #16, Xombi #6 18.00
...: The Book of Destiny HC (2008, $24.99, dustjacket) r/#7-12; Ordway sketch pages 25.00
...: The Book of Destiny SC (2009, $17.99) r/#7-12; Ordway sketch pages 18.00
...: The Lords of Luck HC (2007, $24.99, dustjacket) r/#1-6 with Waid intro & annotations 25.00
...: The Lords of Luck SC (2008, $17.99) r/#1-6 with Waid intro & annotations 18.00
...: Without Sin SC (2009, $17.99) r/#17-22 18.00

BRAVE AND THE BOLD ANNUAL NO. 1 1969 ISSUE, THE
DC Comics: 2001 ($5.95, one-shot)

1-Reprints silver age team-ups in 1960s-style 80 pg. Giant format 6.00

BRAVE AND THE BOLD SPECIAL, THE (See DC Special Series No. 8)

BRAVE EAGLE (TV)
Dell Publishing Co.: No. 705, June, 1956 - No. 929, July, 1958

Four Color 705 (#1)-Photo-c 6 12 18 43 69 95
Four Color 770, 816, 879 (2/58), 929-All photo-c 4 8 12 26 41 55

BRAVE NEW WORLD (See DCU Brave New World)

BRAVE OLD WORLD (V2K)
DC Comics (Vertigo): Feb, 2000 - No. 4, May, 2000 ($2.50, mini-series)

1-4-Messner-Loeb-s/Guy Davis & Phil Hester-a 2.50

BRAVE ONE, THE (Movie)
Dell Publishing Co.: No. 773, Mar, 1957

Four Color 773-Photo-c 5 10 15 34 55 75

BRAVURA
Malibu Comics (Bravura): 1995 (mail-in offer)

0-wraparound holographic-c; short stories and promo pin-ups of Chaykin's Power & Glory, Gil Kane's & Steven Grant's Edge, Starlin's Breed, & Simonson's Star Slammers 5.00
1 1/2 7.00

BREACH
DC Comics: Mar, 2005 - No. 11, Jan, 2006 ($2.95/$2.50)

1-11: 1-Marcos Martin-a/Bob Harras-s; origin. 4-JLA-c/app. 3.00

BREAKDOWN

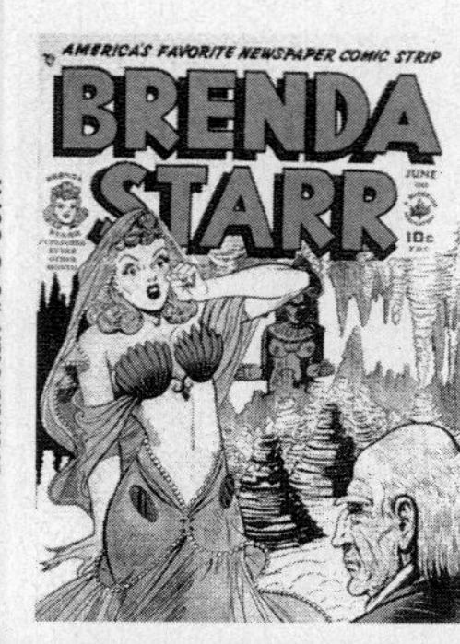

Brenda Starr #3 © SUPR

Brer Rabbit Four Color #129 © DIS

Brigade #7 © Rob Liefeld

Devil's Due Publ.: Oct, 2004 - No. 6, Apr, 2005 ($2.95)

	GD 2.0	VG 4.0	FN 6.0	VF 8.0	VF/NM 9.0	NM- 9.2
1-6: 1-Two covers by Dave Ross and Leinil Yu; Dixon-s/Ross-a						3.00

BREAKFAST AFTER NOON
Oni Press: May, 2000 - No. 6, Jan, 2001($2.95, B&W, limited series)

	GD	VG	FN	VF	VF/NM	NM-
1-6-Andi Watson-s/a						3.00
TPB (2001, $19.95) r/series						20.00

BREAKNECK BLVD.
MotioN Comics/Slave Labor Graphics Vol. 2: No. 0, Feb, 1994 - No. 2, Nov, 1994; Vol. 2#1, Jul, 1995 - #6, Dec., 1996 ($2.50/$2.95, B&W)

	GD	VG	FN	VF	VF/NM	NM-
0-2, V2#1-6: 0-Perez/Giordano-c						3.00

BREAK-THRU (Also see Exiles V1#4)
Malibu Comics (Ultraverse): Dec, 1993 - No. 2, Jan, 1994 ($2.50, 44 pgs.)

	GD	VG	FN	VF	VF/NM	NM-
1,2-Perez-c/a(p); has x-overs in Ultraverse titles						2.50

BREATHTAKER
DC Comics: 1990 - No. 4, 1990 ($4.95, 52 pgs., prestige format, mature)

	GD	VG	FN	VF	VF/NM	NM-
Book 1-4: Mark Wheatley-painted-c/a & scripts; Marc Hempel-a						5.00
TPB (1994, $14.95) r/#1-4; intro by Neil Gaiman						15.00

'BREED
Malibu Comics (Bravura): Jan, 1994 - No. 6, 1994 ($2.50, limited series)

	GD	VG	FN	VF	VF/NM	NM-
1-6: 1-(48 pgs.)-Origin/1st app. of 'Breed by Starlin; contains Bravura stamps; spot varnish-c. 2-5-contains Bravura stamps. 6-Death of Rachel						3.00
...:Book of Genesis (1994, $12.95)-reprints #1-6						13.00

'BREED II
Malibu Comics (Bravura): Nov, 1994 - No. 6, Apr, 1995 ($2.95, limited series)

	GD	VG	FN	VF	VF/NM	NM-
1-6: Starlin-c/a/scripts in all. 1-Gold edition						3.00

BREEZE LAWSON, SKY SHERIFF (See Sky Sheriff)

BRENDA LEE'S LIFE STORY
Dell Publishing Co.: July-Sept., 1962

	GD	VG	FN	VF	VF/NM	NM-
01-078-209	8	16	24	52	86	120

BRENDA STARR (Also see All Great)
Four Star Comics Corp./Superior Comics Ltd.: No. 13, 9/47; No. 14, 3/48; V2#3, 6/48 - V2#12, 12/49

	GD	VG	FN	VF	VF/NM	NM-
V1#13-By Dale Messick	84	168	252	538	919	1300
14-Classic Kamen bondage-c	155	310	465	992	1696	2400
V2#3-Baker-a?	68	136	204	435	743	1050
4-Used in **SOTI**, pg. 21; Kamen-c	82	164	246	528	902	1275
5-10	66	132	198	425	725	1025
11,12 (Scarce)	69	138	207	438	752	1065

NOTE: *Newspaper reprints plus original material through #6. All original #7 on.*

BRENDA STARR (...Reporter)(Young Lovers No. 16 on?)
Charlton Comics: No. 13, June, 1955 - No. 15, Oct, 1955

	GD	VG	FN	VF	VF/NM	NM-
13-15-Newspaper-r	32	64	96	188	307	425

BRENDA STARR REPORTER
Dell Publishing Co.: Oct, 1963

	GD	VG	FN	VF	VF/NM	NM-
1	12	24	36	86	153	220

BRER RABBIT (See Kite Fun Book, Walt Disney Showcase #28 and Wheaties)
Dell Publishing Co.: No. 129, 1946; No. 208, Jan, 1949; No. 693, 1956 (Disney)

	GD	VG	FN	VF	VF/NM	NM-
Four Color 129 (#1)-Adapted from Disney movie "Song of the South"	25	50	75	183	354	525
Four Color 208 (1/49)	11	22	33	78	139	200
Four Color 693-Part-r #129	8	16	24	56	93	130

BRIAN BOLLAND'S BLACK BOOK
Eclipse Comics: July, 1985 (one-shot)

	GD	VG	FN	VF	VF/NM	NM-
1-British B&W-r in color						3.00

BRIAN PULIDO'S LADY DEATH... (See Lady Death)

BRICK BRADFORD (Also see Ace Comics & King Comics)
King Features Syndicate/Standard: No. 5, July, 1948 - No. 8, July, 1949 (Ritt & Grey reprints)

	GD	VG	FN	VF	VF/NM	NM-
5	19	38	57	112	176	240
6-Robot-c (by Schomburg?).	36	72	108	211	343	475
7-Schomburg-c. 8-Says #7 inside, #8 on-c	15	30	45	94	147	200

BRIDE'S DIARY (Formerly Black Cobra No. 3)
Ajax/Farrell Publ.: No. 4, May, 1955 - No. 10, Aug, 1956

	GD	VG	FN	VF	VF/NM	NM-
4 (#1)	9	18	27	52	69	85
5-8	7	14	21	35	43	50
9,10-Disbrow-a	8	16	24	44	57	70

BRIDES IN LOVE (Hollywood Romances & Summer Love No. 46 on)
Charlton Comics: Aug, 1956 - No. 45, Feb, 1965

	GD	VG	FN	VF	VF/NM	NM-
1	12	24	36	67	94	120
2	8	16	24	40	50	60
3-6,8-10	4	8	12	22	34	45
7-(68 pgs.)	4	8	12	28	44	60
11-20	3	6	9	16	23	30
21-45	2	4	6	11	16	20

BRIDES ROMANCES
Quality Comics Group: Nov, 1953 - No. 23, Dec, 1956

	GD	VG	FN	VF	VF/NM	NM-
1	15	30	45	86	133	180
2	9	18	27	50	65	80
3-10: Last precode (3/55)	9	18	27	47	61	75
11-17,19-22: 15-Baker-a(p)?; Colan-a	8	16	24	42	54	65
18-Baker-a	9	18	27	50	65	80
23-Baker-c/a	13	26	39	74	105	135

BRIDE'S SECRETS
Ajax/Farrell(Excellent Publ.)/Four-Star: Apr-May, 1954 - No. 19, May, 1958

	GD	VG	FN	VF	VF/NM	NM-
1	13	26	39	72	101	130
2	8	16	24	42	54	65
3-6: Last precode (3/55)	7	14	21	35	43	50
7-11,13-19: 18-Hollingsworth-a	6	12	18	31	38	45
12-Disbrow-a	7	14	21	37	46	55

BRIDE-TO-BE ROMANCES (See True...)

BRIGADE
Image Comics (Extreme Studios): Aug, 1992 - No. 4, 1993 ($1.95, lim. series)

	GD	VG	FN	VF	VF/NM	NM-
1-Liefeld part plots/scripts in all, Liefeld-c(p); contains 2 Brigade trading cards						3.00
1-Gold foil stamped logo edition						8.00
2-Contains coupon for Image Comics #0 & 2 trading cards						3.00
2-With coupon missing						2.25
3,4: 3-Contains 2 trading cards; 1st Birds of Prey. 4-Flip book featuring Youngblood #5						2.50

BRIGADE
Image Comics (Extreme): V2#1, May, 1993 - V2#22, July, 1995, V2#25, May, 1996 ($1.95/$2.50)

	GD	VG	FN	VF	VF/NM	NM-
V2#1-22,25: 1-Gatefold-c; Liefeld co-plots; Blood Brothers part 1; Bloodstrike app. 2-(6/93, V2#1 on inside)-Foil merricote-c (newsstand ed. w/out foil-c exists). 3-Perez-c(i); Liefeld scripts. 8,9-Coupons #2 & 6 for Extreme Prejudice #0 bound-in. 11-(8/94, $2.50) WildC.A.T.S app. 16-Polybagged w/ trading card. 22-"Supreme Apocalypse" Pt. 4; w/ trading card						2.50
0-(9/93)-Liefeld scripts; 1st app. Warcry; Youngblood & Wildcats app.;						2.50
20-Variant-c. by Quesada & Palmiotti						2.50
Sourcebook 1 (8/94, $2.95)						3.00

BRIGADE
Awesome Entertainment: July, 2000 ($2.99)

	GD	VG	FN	VF	VF/NM	NM-
1-Flip book w/Century preview						3.00

BRIGAND, THE (See Fawcett Movie Comics No. 18)

BRINGING UP FATHER
Dell Publishing Co.: No. 9, 1942 - No. 37, 1944

	GD	VG	FN	VF	VF/NM	NM-
Large Feature Comic 9	30	60	90	177	289	400
Four Color 37	19	38	57	133	259	385

BRING BACK THE BAD GUYS (Also see Fireside Book Series)
Marvel Comics: 1998 ($24.95, TPB)

	GD	VG	FN	VF	VF/NM	NM-
1-Reprints stories of Marvel villains' secrets						25.00

BRING ON THE BAD GUYS (See Fireside Book Series)

BROADWAY HOLLYWOOD BLACKOUTS
Stanhall: Mar-Apr, 1954 - No. 3, July-Aug, 1954

	GD	VG	FN	VF	VF/NM	NM-
1	14	28	42	78	112	145
2,3	9	18	27	52	69	85

BROADWAY ROMANCES
Quality Comics Group: January, 1950 - No. 5, Sept, 1950

	GD	VG	FN	VF	VF/NM	NM-
1-Ward-c/a (9 pgs.); Gustavson-a	38	76	114	225	368	510
2-Ward-a (9 pgs.); photo-c	26	52	78	154	252	350
3-5: All-Photo-c	15	30	45	83	124	165

BROKEN ARROW (TV)
Dell Publishing Co.: No. 855, Oct, 1957 - No. 947, Nov, 1958

	GD	VG	FN	VF	VF/NM	NM-
Four Color 855 (#1)-Photo-c	6	12	18	37	59	80

Brotherhood #5 © MAR

Brownies Four Color #293 © DELL

Bruce Lee #4 © Bruce Lee Estate

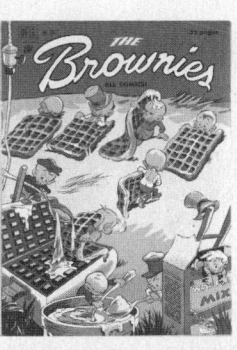

	GD 2.0	VG 4.0	FN 6.0	VF 8.0	VF/NM 9.0	NM- 9.2
Four Color 947-Photo-c	5	10	15	32	51	70
BROKEN CROSS, THE (See The Crusaders)						
BROKEN TRILOGY						
Image Comics (Top Cow): July, 2008 - No. 3, Nov, 2008 ($2.99, limited series)						
1-3-Witchblade, Darkness & Angelus app.; Marz-s/Sejic & Hester-a; two covers						3.00
...: Aftermath 1 (4/09, $2.99) Marz & Hill-s/Lucas & Kirkham-a						3.00
...: Angelus 1 (12/08, $2.99) Marz-s/Stelfreeze-a; two covers						3.00
...: Pandora's Box 1 (2/10, $3.99) Tommy Lee Edwards-c						4.00
...: The Darkness 1 (8/08, $2.99) Hester-s/Lucas-a; two covers						3.00
...: Witchblade 1 (12/08, $2.99) Marz-s/Blake-a; two covers						3.00
BRONCHO BILL (See Comics On Parade, Sparkler & Tip Top Comics)						
United Features Syndicate/Standard(Visual Editions) No. 5-on: 1939 - 1940; No. 5, 1?/48 - No. 16, 8?/50						
Single Series 2 ('39)	52	104	156	328	552	775
Single Series 19 ('40)(#2 on cvr)	42	84	126	265	445	625
5	15	30	45	84	127	170
6(4/48)-10(4/49)	10	20	30	54	72	90
11(6/49)-16	9	18	27	47	61	75
NOTE: *Schomburg c-6, 7, 9-13, 15, 16.*						
BROOKS ROBINSON (See Baseball's Greatest Heroes #2)						
BROTHER BILLY THE PAIN FROM PLAINS						
Marvel Comics Group: 1979 (68pgs.)						
1-B&W comics, satire, Jimmy Carter-c & x-over w/Brother Billy peanut jokes. Joey Adams-a (scarce)	4	8	12	22	34	45
BROTHERHOOD, THE (Also see X-Men titles)						
Marvel Comics: July, 2001 - No. 9, Mar, 2002 ($2.25)						
1-Intro. Orwell & the Brotherhood; Ribic-a/X-s/Sienkiewicz-c						2.50
2-9: 2-Two covers (JG Jones & Sienkiewicz). 4-6-Fabry-c. 7-9-Phillips-c/a						2.50
BROTHER POWER, THE GEEK (See Saga of Swamp Thing Annual & Vertigo Visions)						
National Periodical Publications: Sept-Oct, 1968 - No. 2, Nov-Dec, 1968						
1-Origin; Simon-c(i?)	5	10	15	34	55	75
2	3	6	9	20	30	40
BROTHERS, HANG IN THERE, THE						
Spire Christian Comics (Fleming H. Revell Co.): 1979 (49¢)						
nn	2	4	6	9	13	16
BROTHERS IN ARMS (Based on the World War II military video game)						
Dynamite Entertainment: 2008 - No. 4, 2008 ($3.99/$3.50)						
1-($3.99) Fabbri-a; two covers by Fabbri & Sejic						4.00
2-4-($3.50) Two covers by Fabbri & Sejic on each						3.50
BROTHERS OF THE SPEAR (Also see Tarzan)						
Gold Key/Whitman No. 18: June, 1972 - No. 17, Feb, 1976; No. 18, May, 1982						
1	5	10	15	32	51	70
2-Painted-c begin, end #17	3	6	9	18	27	35
3-10	3	6	9	14	20	26
11-18: 12-Line drawn-c. 13-17-Spiegle-a. 18(5/82)-r/#2; Leopard Girl-r	2	4	6	10	14	18
BROTHERS, THE CULT ESCAPE, THE						
Spire Christian Comics (Fleming H. Revell Co.): 1980 (49¢)						
nn	2	4	6	10	14	18
BROWNIES (See New Funnies)						
Dell Publishing Co.: No. 192, July, 1948 - No. 605, Dec, 1954						
Four Color 192(#1)-Kelly-a	13	26	39	93	172	250
Four Color 244(9/49), 293 (9/50)-Last Kelly c/a	10	20	30	68	119	170
Four Color 337(7-8/51), 365(12-1/51-52), 398(5/52)	6	12	18	37	59	80
Four Color 436(11/52), 482(7/53), 522(12/53), 605	5	10	15	34	55	75
BRUCE GENTRY						
Better/Standard/Four Star Publ./Superior No. 3: Jan, 1948 - No. 8, Jul, 1949						
1-Ray Bailey strip reprints begin, end #3; E. C. emblem appears as a monogram on stationery in story; negligee panels	58	116	174	371	636	900
2,3	37	74	111	222	361	500
4-8	25	50	75	147	241	335
NOTE: *Kamenish a-2-7; c-1-8.*						
BRUCE LEE (Also see Deadly Hands of Kung Fu)						
Malibu Comics: July, 1994 - No. 6, Dec, 1994 ($2.95, 36 pgs.)						
1-6: 1-(44 pgs.)-Mortal Kombat prev., 1st app. in comics. 2,6-(36 pgs.)						5.00
BRUCE JONES' OUTER EDGE						
Innovation: 1993 ($2.50, B&W, one-shot)						
1-Bruce Jones-c/a/script						2.50
BRUCE WAYNE: AGENT OF S.H.I.E.L.D. (Also see Marvel Vs. DC #3 & DC Vs. Marvel #4)						
Marvel Comics (Amalgam): Apr, 1996 ($1.95, one-shot)						
1-Chuck Dixon scripts & Cary Nord-c/a.						2.50
BRUISER						
Anthem Publications: Feb, 1994 ($2.45)						
1						2.50
BRUTE, THE						
Seaboard Publ. (Atlas): Feb, 1975 - No. 3, July, 1975						
1-Origin & 1st app; Sekowsky-a(p)	2	4	6	9	12	15
2-Sekowsky-a(p); Fleisher-s	2	3	4	6	8	10
3-Brunner/Starlin/Weiss-a(p)	2	4	6	8	10	12
BRUTE & BABE						
Ominous Press: July, 1994 - No. 2, Aug, 1994						
1-($3.95, 8 tablets plus-c)-"...It Begins..."; tablet format						4.00
2-($2.50, 36 pgs.)-"Mael's Rage", 2-(40 pgs.)-Stiff additional variant-c						2.50
BRUTE FORCE						
Marvel Comics: Aug, 1990 - No. 4, Nov, 1990 ($1.00, limited series)						
1-4: Animal super-heroes; Delbo & DeCarlo-a						2.50
B-SIDES (The Craptacular...)						
Marvel Comics: Nov, 2002 - No. 3, Jan, 2003 ($2.99, limited series)						
1-3-Kieth-c/Weldele-a. 2-Dorkin-a (1 pg.) 2-FF cameo. 3-FF app.						3.00
BUBBLEGUM CRISIS: GRAND MAL						
Dark Horse Comics: Mar, 1994 - No. 4, June, 1994 ($2.50, limited series)						
1-4-Japanese manga						2.50
BUCCANEER						
I. W. Enterprises: No date (1963)						
I.W. Reprint #1(r-/Quality #20), #8(r-/#23): Crandall-a in each	3	6	9	16	23	30
BUCCANEERS (Formerly Kid Eternity)						
Quality Comics: No. 19, Jan, 1950 - No. 27, May, 1951 (No. 24-27: 52 pgs.)						
19-Captain Daring, Black Roger, Eric Falcon & Spanish Main begin; Crandall-a	48	96	144	302	514	725
20,23-Crandall-a	36	72	108	215	350	485
21-Crandall-c/a	39	78	117	236	388	540
22-Bondage-c	28	56	84	165	270	375
24-26: 24-Adam Peril, U.S.N. begins. 25-Origin & 1st app. Corsair Queen. 26-last Spanish Main	24	48	72	142	234	325
27-Crandall-c/a	34	68	102	205	335	465
Super Reprint #12 (1964)-Crandall-r/#21	3	6	9	16	23	30
BUCCANEERS, THE (TV)						
Dell Publishing Co.: No. 800, 1957						
Four Color 800-Photo-c	7	14	21	47	76	105
BUCKAROO BANZAI (Movie)						
Marvel Comics Group: Dec, 1984 - No. 2, Feb, 1985						
1,2-Movie adaptation; r/Marvel Super Special #33; Texiera-c/a						3.00
BUCKAROO BANZAI: RETURN OF THE SCREW						
Moonstone: 2006 - No. 3, 2006 ($3.50, limited series)						
1-3: 1-Three covers by Haley, Stribling, Beck; Thompson-a						3.50
Preview (2006, 50¢) B&W preview; history of movie and spin-off projects						2.25
BUCK DUCK						
Atlas Comics (ANC): June, 1953 - No. 4, Dec, 1953						
1-Funny animal stories in all	15	30	45	86	133	180
2-4: 2-Ed Win-a(5)	10	20	30	54	72	90
BUCK JONES (Also see Crackajack Funnies, Famous Feature Stories, Master Comics #7 & Wow Comics #1, 1936)						
Dell Publishing Co.: No. 299, Oct, 1950 - No. 850, Oct, 1957 (All Painted-c)						
Four Color 299(#1)-Buck Jones & his horse Silver-B begin; painted back-c begins, ends #5	13	26	39	90	165	240
2(4-6/51)	8	16	24	52	86	120
3-8(10-12/52)	6	12	18	43	69	95
Four Color 460,500,546,589	6	12	18	41	66	90
Four Color 652,733,850	5	10	15	32	51	70

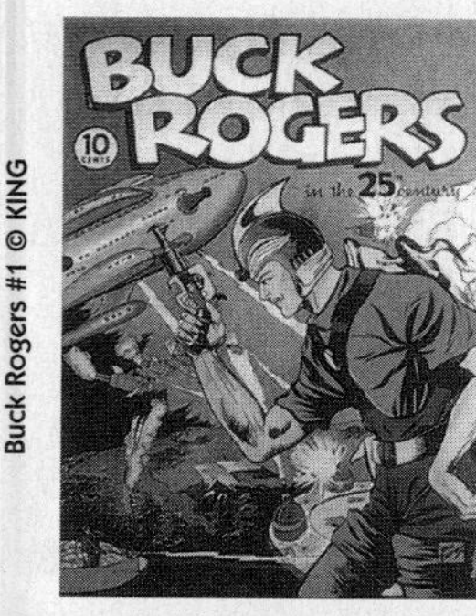

Buck Rogers #1 © KING

Buffalo Bill #3 © YM

Buffy the Vampire Slayer (2007 series) #32 © 20th Cent. Fox

	GD 2.0	VG 4.0	FN 6.0	VF 8.0	VF/NM 9.0	NM- 9.2

BUCK ROGERS (Also see Famous Funnies, Pure Oil Comics, Salerno Carnival of Comics, 24 Pages of Comics, & Vicks Comics)
Famous Funnies: Winter, 1940-41 - No. 6, Sept, 1943
NOTE: Buck Rogers first appeared in the pulp magazine Amazing Stories Vol. 3 #5 in Aug, 1928.

1-Sunday strip reprints by Rick Yager; begins with strip #190; Calkins-c
309 618 927 2163 3782 5400
2 (7/41)-Calkins-c 131 262 393 832 1429 2025
3 (12/41), 4 (7/42) 113 226 339 718 1234 1750
5,6: 5-Story continues with Famous Funnies No. 80; Buck Rogers, Sky Roads. 6-Reprints of 1939 dailies; contains B.R. story "Crater of Doom" (2 pgs.) by Calkins not-r from Famous Funnies 95 190 285 603 1039 1475

BUCK ROGERS
Toby Press: No. 100, Jan, 1951 - No. 9, May-June, 1951

100(#7)-All strip-r begin 30 60 90 177 289 400
101(#8), 9-All Anderson-a(1947-49-r/dailies) 23 46 69 136 223 310

BUCK ROGERS (...in the 25th Century No. 5 on) (TV)
Gold Key/Whitman No. 7 on: Oct, 1964; No. 2, July, 1979 - No. 16, May, 1982 (No #10; story was written but never released. #17 exists only as a press proof without covers and was never published)

1(10128-410, 12¢)-1st S.A. app. Buck Rogers & 1st new B. R. in comics since 1933 giveaway; painted-c; back-c pin-up 10 20 30 70 123 175
2(7/79)-6: 3,4,6-Movie adaptation; painted-c 2 4 6 9 12 15
7,11 (Whitman) 2 4 6 11 16 20
8,9 (prepack)(scarce) 3 6 9 18 27 35
12-16: 14(2/82), 15(3/82), 16(5/82) 2 4 6 8 10 12
Giant Movie Edition 11296(64pp, Whitman, $1.50), reprints GK #2-4 minus cover; tabloid size; photo-c (See Marvel Treasury) 3 6 9 18 27 35
Giant Movie Edition 02489(Western/Marvel, $1.50), reprints GK #2-4 minus cover
3 6 9 17 25 32
NOTE: *Bolle a-2p,3p, Movie Ed.(p).* ***McWilliams*** *a-2i,3i, 5-11, Movie Ed.(i). Painted c-1-9,11-13.*

BUCK ROGERS (Comics Module)
TSR, Inc.: 1990 - No. 10, 1991 ($2.95, 44 pgs.)

1-10 (1990): 1-Begin origin in 3 parts. 2-Indicia says #1. 2,3-Black Barney back-up story. 4-All Black Barney issue; B. B.-c. 5-Indicia says #6; Black Barney-c & lead story; Buck Rogers back-up story. 10-Flip book (72pgs.) 3.00

BUCK ROGERS
Dynamite Entertainment: No. 0, 2009 - Present (25¢/$3.50)

0-(25¢) Beatty-s/Rafael-a/Cassaday-c 2.00
1-9: 1-($3.50) Three covers by Cassaday, Ross and Wagner; origin re-told 3.50

BUCKSKIN (TV)
Dell Publishing Co.: No. 1011, July, 1959 - No. 1107, June-Aug, 1960

Four Color 1011 (#1)-Photo-c 7 14 21 47 76 105
Four Color 1107-Photo-c 6 12 18 43 69 95

BUCKY O'HARE (Funny Animal)
Continuity Comics: 1988 ($5.95, graphic novel)

1-Golden-c/a(r); r/serial-Echo of Futurepast #1-6 1 2 3 4 5 7
Deluxe Hardcover ($40.00, 52 pg., 8 x 11") 40.00

BUCKY O'HARE
Continuity Comics: Jan, 1991 - No. 5, 1991 ($2.00)

1-6: 1-Michael Golden-c/a 2.50

BUDDIES IN THE U.S. ARMY
Avon Periodicals: Nov, 1952 - No. 2, 1953

1-Lawrence-c 14 28 42 80 115 150
2-Mort Lawrence-c/a 10 20 30 54 72 90

BUFFALO BEE (TV)
Dell Publishing Co.: No. 957, Nov, 1958 - No. 1061, Dec-Feb, 1959-60

Four Color 957 (#1) 8 16 24 58 97 135
Four Color 1002 (8-10/59), 1061 7 14 21 45 73 100

BUFFALO BILL (See Frontier Fighters, Super Western Comics & Western Action Thrillers)
Youthful Magazines: No. 2, Oct, 1950 - No. 9, Dec, 1951

2-Annie Oakley story 14 28 42 78 112 145
3-9: 2-4-Walter Johnson-c/a. 9-Wildey-a 10 20 30 54 72 90

BUFFALO BILL CODY (See Cody of the Pony Express)

BUFFALO BILL, JR. (TV) (See Western Roundup)
Dell/Gold Key: Jan, 1956 - No. 13, Aug-Oct, 1959; 1965 (All photo-c)

Four Color 673 (#1) 9 18 27 60 100 140
Four Color 742,766,798,828,856(11/57) 6 12 18 39 62 85
7(2-4/58)-13 5 10 15 34 55 75
1(6/65, Gold Key)-Photo-c(r/F.C. #798); photo-b/c 4 8 12 24 37 50

BUFFALO BILL PICTURE STORIES
Street & Smith Publications: June-July, 1949 - No. 2, Aug-Sept, 1949

1,2-Wildey, Powell-a in each 14 28 42 78 112 145

BUFFY THE VAMPIRE SLAYER (Based on the TV series)(Also see Tales of the Vampires)
Dark Horse Comics: 1998 - No. 63, Nov, 2003 ($2.95/$2.99)

1-Bennett-a/Watson-s; Art Adams-c 1 2 3 5 7 9
1-Variant photo-c 1 2 3 5 7 9
1-Gold foil logo Art Adams-c 15.00
1-Gold foil logo photo-c 20.00
2-15-Regular and photo-c. 4-7-Gomez-a. 5,8-Green-c 5.00
16-48: 29,30-Angel x-over. 43-45-Death of Buffy. 47-Lobdell-s begin. 48-Pike returns 3.00
50-($3.50) Scooby gang battles Adam; back-up story by Watson 3.50
51-63: 51-54-Viva Las Buffy; pre-Sunnydale Buffy & Pike in Vegas 3.00
Annual '99 ($4.95)-Two stories and pin-ups 1 2 3 4 5 7
...: A Stake to the Heart TPB (3/04, $12.95) r/#60-63 13.00
...: Chaos Bleeds (6/03, $2.99) Based on the video game; photo & Campbell-c 3.00
...: Creatures of Habit (3/02, $17.95) text with Horton & Paul Lee-a 18.00
...: Jonathan 1 (1/01, $2.99) two covers; Richards-a 3.00
...: Lost and Found 1 (3/02, $2.99) aftermath of Buffy's death; Richards-a 3.00
... Lovers Walk (2/01, $2.99) short stories by various; Richards & photo-c 3.00
...: Note From the Underground (3/03, $12.95) r/#47-50 13.00
...: Omnibus Vol. 1 (7/07, $24.95, 9x6") r/Spike & Dru #3, Origin #1-3 and Buffy #51-59 25.00
...: Omnibus Vol. 2 (9/07, $24.95, 9x6") r/Buffy #60-63 and various one-shots & specials 25.00
...: Omnibus Vol. 3 (1/08, $24.95, 9x6") r/Buffy #1-8,12,16, Annual '99 25.00
...: Omnibus Vol. 4 (5/08, $24.95, 9x6") r/Buffy #9-11,13-15,17-20,50 and various 25.00
...: Omnibus Vol. 5 (9/08, $24.95, 9x6") r/Buffy #21-28 and various one-shots & specials 25.00
...: Omnibus Vol. 6 (2/09, $24.95, 9x6") r/Buffy #29-38 and various one-shots & specials 25.00
...: Reunion (6/02, $3.50) Buffy & Angel's; Espenson-s; art by various 3.50
...: Slayer Interrupted TPB (2003, $14.95) r/#56-59 15.00
...: Tales of the Slayers (10/02, $3.50) art by Matsuda and Colan; art & photo-c 3.50
...: The Death of Buffy TPB (8/02, $15.95) r/#43-46 16.00
...: Viva Las Buffy TPB (7/03, $12.95) r/#51-54 13.00
Wizard #1/2 1 2 3 6 8 9

BUFFY THE VAMPIRE SLAYER ("Season Eight" of the TV series)
Dark Horse Comics: Mar, 2007 - Present ($2.99)

1-Joss Whedon-s/Georges Jeanty-a/Jo Chen-c 7.00
1-Variant cover by Jeanty 10.00
1-RRP with B&W Jeanty cover (edition of 1000) 70.00
1-4: 1-2nd thru 5th printings. 2-2nd-4th printings. 3,4-2nd & 3rd printings 3.00
2-5-Chen-c/Jeanty-a 4.00
2-5-Variant-c by Jeanty 6.00
6-19: 6-9-Faith app.; Vaughan-s. 10,11-Whedon-s. 12-15-Goddard-s; Dracula app. 16-19-Fray app.; Whedon-s/Moline-a 3.00
6-19-Variant-c by Jeanty 4.00
20-32: 20-28-Two covers by Chen and Jeanty. 20-Animation style flashback. 21,26-30-Espenson-s. 30-Hughes-c. 31-Whedon-s. 32-Meltzer-s 3.00
... Tales of the Vampires (6/09, $2.99) Cloonan-s/Lolos-a; covers by Chen & Bá/Moon 3.00
...: Willow (12/09, $3.50) Whedon-s/Moline-a; Willow meets the Snake Guide 3.50
...: Volume One: The Long Way Home TPB (11/07, $15.95) r/#1-5 and variant covers 16.00
...: Volume Two: No Future for You TPB (6/08, $15.95) r/#6-10 and variant covers 16.00
...: Volume Three: Wolves at the Gate TPB (11/08, $15.95) r/#11-15 and variant covers 16.00
...: Volume Four: Time of Your Life TPB (5/09, $15.95) r/#16-20 and variant covers 16.00
...: Volume Five: Predators and Prey TPB (9/09, $15.95) r/#21-25 and variant covers 16.00
...: Volume Six: Retreat TPB (3/10, $15.99) r/#26-30 and stories from MySpace DHP 16.00
NOTE: *Later printings have Jo Chen cover art with different credit graphics.*

BUFFY THE VAMPIRE SLAYER: ANGEL
Dark Horse Comics: May, 1999 - No. 3, July, 1999 ($2.95, limited series)

1-3-Gomez-a; Matsuda-c & photo-c for each 3.00

BUFFY THE VAMPIRE SLAYER: GILES
Dark Horse Comics: Oct, 2000 ($2.95, one-shot)

1-Eric Powell-a; Powell & photo-c 3.00

BUFFY THE VAMPIRE SLAYER: HAUNTED
Dark Horse Comics: Dec, 2001 - No. 4, Mar, 2002 ($2.99, limited series)

1-4-Faith and the Mayor app.; Espenson-s/Richards-a 3.00
TPB (9/02, $12.95) r/series; photo-c 13.00

BUFFY THE VAMPIRE SLAYER: OZ
Dark Horse Comics: July, 2001 - No. 3, Sept, 2001 ($2.99, limited series)

Buffy the Vampire Slayer: Willow & Tara - Wilderness #2 © 20th Cent. Fox

Bugs Bunny #88 © WB

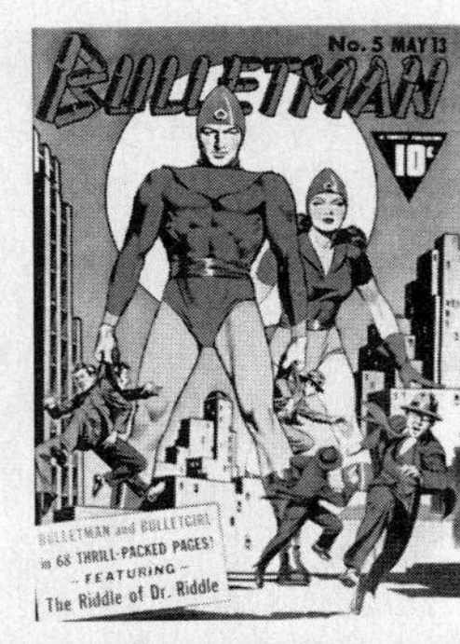

Bulletman #5 © FAW

	GD 2.0	VG 4.0	FN 6.0	VF 8.0	VF/NM 9.0	NM- 9.2
1-3-Totleben & photo-c; Golden-s						3.00

BUFFY THE VAMPIRE SLAYER: SPIKE AND DRU
Dark Horse Comics: Apr, 1999; No. 2, Oct, 1999; No. 3, Dec, 2000 ($2.95)

	GD	VG	FN	VF	VF/NM	NM-
1-3: 1,2-Photo-c. 3-Two covers (photo & Sook)						3.00

BUFFY THE VAMPIRE SLAYER: THE ORIGIN (Adapts movie screenplay)
Dark Horse Comics: Jan, 1999 - No. 3, Mar, 1999 ($2.95, limited series)

	GD	VG	FN	VF	VF/NM	NM-
1-3-Brereton-s/Bennett-a; reg & photo-c for each						3.00

BUFFY THE VAMPIRE SLAYER: WILLOW & TARA
Dark Horse Comics: Apr, 2001 ($2.99, one-shot)

	GD	VG	FN	VF	VF/NM	NM-
1-Terry Moore-a/Chris Golden & Amber Benson-s; Moore-c & photo-c						3.00
TPB (4/03, $9.95) r/#1 & W&T - Wilderness; photo-c						10.00

BUFFY THE VAMPIRE SLAYER: WILLOW & TARA - WILDERNESS
Dark Horse Comics: Jul, 2002 - No. 2, Sept, 2002 ($2.99, limited series)

	GD	VG	FN	VF	VF/NM	NM-
1,2-Chris Golden & Amber Benson-s; Jothikaumar-c & photo-c						3.00

BUG
Marvel Comics: Mar, 1997 ($2.99, one-shot)

	GD	VG	FN	VF	VF/NM	NM-
1-Micronauts character						3.00

BUGALOOS (Sid & Marty Krofft TV show)
Charlton Comics: Sept, 1971 - No. 4, Feb, 1972

	GD	VG	FN	VF	VF/NM	NM-
1	5	10	15	32	51	70
2-4	3	6	9	20	30	40

NOTE: *No. 3(1/72) went on sale late in 1972 (after No. 4) with the 1/73 issues.*

BUGHOUSE (Satire)
Ajax/Farrell (Excellent Publ.): Mar-Apr, 1954 - No. 4, Sept-Oct, 1954

	GD	VG	FN	VF	VF/NM	NM-
V1#1	21	42	63	124	202	280
2-4	14	28	42	80	115	150

BUGS BUNNY (See The Best of..., Camp Comics, Comic Album #2, 6, 10, 14, Dell Giant #28, 32, 46, Dynabrite, Golden Comics Digest #1, 3, 5, 6, 8, 10, 14, 15, 17, 21, 26, 30, 34, 39, 42, 47, Kite Fun Book, Large Feature Comic #8, Looney Tunes and Merry Melodies, March of Comics #44, 59, 75, 83, 97, 115, 132, 149, 160, 179, 188, 201, 220, 231, 245, 259, 273, 287, 301, 315, 329, 343, 363, 367, 380, 392, 403, 415, 428, 440, 452, 464, 476, 487, Porky Pig, Puffed Wheat, Story Hour Series #802, Super Book #14, 26 and Whitman Comic Books)

BUGS BUNNY (See Dell Giants for annuals)
Dell Publishing Co./Gold Key No. 86-218/Whitman No. 219 on: 1942 - No. 245, April, 1984

	GD	VG	FN	VF	VF/NM	NM-
Large Feature Comic 8(1942)-(Rarely found in fine-mint condition)	194	388	582	1242	2121	3000
Four Color 33 ('43)	96	192	288	816	1608	2400
Four Color 51	32	64	96	248	479	710
Four Color 88	23	46	69	163	314	465
Four Color 123('46),142,164	15	30	45	110	210	310
Four Color 187,200,217,233	12	24	36	83	152	220
Four Color 250-Used in **SOTI**, pg. 309	12	24	36	86	158	230
Four Color 266,274,281,289,298('50)	10	20	30	67	116	165
Four Color 307,317(#1),327(#2),338,347,355,366,376,393	9	18	27	60	100	140
Four Color 407,420,432(10/52)	7	14	21	50	83	115
Four Color 498(9/53),585(9/54), 647(9/55)	6	12	18	41	66	90
Four Color 724(9/56),838(9/57),1064(12/59)	5	10	15	34	55	75
28(12-1/52-53)-30	6	12	18	39	62	85
31-50	5	10	15	30	48	65
51-85(7-9/62)	4	8	12	24	37	50
86(10/62)-88-Bugs Bunny's Showtime-(25¢, 80pgs.)	6	12	18	41	66	90
89-99	3	6	9	17	25	32
100	3	6	9	18	27	35
101-118: 108-1st Honey Bunny. 118-Last 12¢ issue	3	6	9	14	19	24
119-140	2	4	6	11	16	20
141-170	2	4	6	9	12	15
171-218: 218-Publ. by Whitman only?	2	4	6	8	10	12
219,220,225-237(5/82): 229-Swipe of Barks story/WDC&S #223. 233(2/82)	2	4	6	8	10	12
221(9/80),222(11/80)-Pre-pack? (Scarce)	3	6	9	21	32	42
223 (1/81, 50¢-c), 224 (3/81)-Low distr.	2	4	6	11	16	20
223 (1/81, 40¢-c) Cover price error variant	3	6	9	16	22	28
238-245 (#90070 on-c, nd, nd code; pre-pack): 238(5/83), 239(6/83), 240(7/83), 241(7/83), 242(8/83), 243(8/83), 244(3/84), 245(4/84)	3	6	9	14	19	24

NOTE: *Reprints-100,102-104,110,115,123,143,144,147,167,173,175-177,179-185,187,190.*

	GD	VG	FN	VF	VF/NM	NM-
nn (Xerox Pub. Comic Digest, 1971, 100 pages, B&W) collection of one-page gags	4	8	12	22	34	45
...Comic-Go-Round 11196-(224 pgs.)($1.95)(Golden Press, 1979)	4	8	12	25	39	52
...Winter Fun 1(12/67-Gold Key)-Giant	5	10	15	32	51	70

BUGS BUNNY
DC Comics: June, 1990 - No. 3, Aug, 1990 ($1.00, limited series)

	GD	VG	FN	VF	VF/NM	NM-
1-3: Daffy Duck, Elmer Fudd, others app.						4.00

BUGS BUNNY (...Monthly on-c)
DC Comics: 1993 - No. 3, 1994? ($1.95)

	GD	VG	FN	VF	VF/NM	NM-
1-3-Bugs, Porky Pig, Daffy, Road Runner						3.50

BUGS BUNNY (Digest-size reprints from Looney Tunes)
DC Comics: 2005 - Present ($6.99, digest)

	GD	VG	FN	VF	VF/NM	NM-
Vol. 1: What's Up Doc? - Reprints from Looney Tunes #37,41,43-45,48,52,55,57-59,63						7.00

BUGS BUNNY & PORKY PIG
Gold Key: Sept, 1965 (Paper-c, giant, 100 pgs.)

	GD	VG	FN	VF	VF/NM	NM-
1(30025-509)	7	14	21	45	73	100

BUGS BUNNY'S ALBUM (See Bugs Bunny, Four Color No. 498,585,647,724)

BUGS BUNNY LIFE STORY ALBUM (See Bugs Bunny, Four Color No. 838)

BUGS BUNNY MERRY CHRISTMAS (See Bugs Bunny, Four Color No. 1064)

BUILDING, THE
Kitchen Sink Press: 1987; 2000 (8 1/2" x 11" sepia toned graphic novel)

	GD	VG	FN	VF	VF/NM	NM-
nn-Will Eisner-s/c/a						10.00
nn-(DC Comics, 9/00, $9.95) reprints 1987 edition						10.00

BULLET CROW, FOWL OF FORTUNE
Eclipse Comics: Mar, 1987 - No. 2, Apr, 1987 ($2.00, B&W, limited series)

	GD	VG	FN	VF	VF/NM	NM-
1,2-The Comic Reader-r & new-a						2.50

BULLETMAN (See Fawcett Miniatures, Master Comics, Mighty Midget Comics, Nickel Comics & XMas Comics)
Fawcett Publications: Sum, 1941 - #12, 2/12/43; #14, Spr, 1946 - #16, Fall, 1946 (No #13)

	GD	VG	FN	VF	VF/NM	NM-
1-Silver metallic-c	377	754	1131	2639	4620	6600
2-Raboy-c	165	330	495	1048	1799	2550
3,5-Raboy-c each	129	258	387	826	1413	2000
4	97	194	291	621	1061	1500
6,8-10: 10-Intro. Bulletdog	81	162	243	518	884	1250
7-Ghost Stories told by night watchman of cemetery begins; Eisnerish-a; hidden message "Chic Stone is a jerk".	84	168	252	538	919	1300
11,12,14-16 (nn 13): 12-Robot-c	60	120	180	381	653	925

NOTE: ***Mac Raboy** c-1-3, 5, 6, 10. "Bulletman the Flying Detective" on cover #8 on.*

BULLET POINTS
Marvel Comics: Jan, 2007 - No. 5 ($2.99, limited series)

	GD	VG	FN	VF	VF/NM	NM-
1-5: 1-Steve Rogers becomes Iron Man; Straczynski-s/Edwards-a. 4,5-Galactus app.						3.00
TPB (2007, $13.99) r/#1-5; layout pages by Edwards						14.00

BULLETPROOF MONK (Inspired the 2003 film)
Image Comics (Flypaper Press): 1998 - No. 3, 1999 ($2.95, limited series)

	GD	VG	FN	VF	VF/NM	NM-
1-3-Oeming-a						3.00
...: Tales of the BPM (3/03, $2.95) Flip book; 2 covers by Sale; art by Sale, Oeming, Dave Johnson; Seann William Scott afterword						3.00
TPB (2002, $9.95) r/#1-3; foreword by John Woo						10.00

BULLETS AND BRACELETS (Also see Marvel Versus DC #3 & DC Versus Marvel #4)
Marvel Comics (Amalgam): Apr, 1996 ($1.95)

	GD	VG	FN	VF	VF/NM	NM-
1-John Ostrander script & Gary Frank-c/a						2.50

BULLSEYE: GREATEST HITS (Daredevil villain)
Marvel Comics: Nov, 2004 - No. 5, Mar, 2005 ($2.99, limted series)

	GD	VG	FN	VF	VF/NM	NM-
1-5-Origin of Bullseye; Steve Dillon-a/Deodato-c. 3-Punisher app.						3.00
TPB (2005, $13.99) r/#1-5						14.00

BULLS-EYE (Cody of The Pony Express No. 8 on)
Mainline No. 1-5/Charlton No. 6,7: 7-8/54-No. 5, 3-4/55; No. 6, 6/55; No. 7, 8/55

	GD	VG	FN	VF	VF/NM	NM-
1-S&K-c, 2 pgs.-a	56	112	168	356	616	875
2-S&K-c/a	47	94	141	296	498	700
3-5-S&K-c/a(2 each). 4-Last pre-code issue (1-2/55). 5-Censored issue with tomahawks removed in battle scene	40	80	120	245	408	570
6-S&K-c/a	36	72	108	214	347	480
7-S&K-c/a(3)	40	80	120	245	408	570

BULLS-EYE COMICS (Formerly Komik Pages #10; becomes Kayo #12)
Harry 'A' Chesler: No. 11, 1944

	GD	VG	FN	VF	VF/NM	NM-
11-Origin K-9, Green Knight's sidekick, Lance; The Green Knight, Lady Satan, Yankee Doodle Jones app.	43	86	129	271	461	650

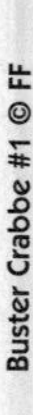

Buster Crabbe #1 © FF

The Buzz #3 © MAR

Cable #14 © MAR

	GD 2.0	VG 4.0	FN 6.0	VF 8.0	VF/NM 9.0	NM- 9.2

BULLWHIP GRIFFIN (See Movie Comics)

BULLWINKLE (...and Rocky No. 22 on; See March of Comics #233 and Rocky & Bullwinkle) (TV) (Jay Ward)
Dell/Gold Key: 3-5/62 - #11, 4/74; #12, 6/76 - #19, 3/78; #20, 4/79 - #25, 2/80

	GD	VG	FN	VF	VF/NM	NM-
Four Color 1270 (3-5/62)	18	36	54	129	252	375
01-090-209 (Dell, 7-9/62)	15	30	45	104	197	290
1(11/62, Gold Key)	14	28	42	97	181	265
2(2/63)	9	18	27	63	107	150
3(4/72)-11(4/74-Gold Key)	5	10	15	34	55	75
12-14: 12(6/76)-Reprints. 13(9/76), 14-New stories	3	6	9	18	27	35
15-25	2	4	6	11	16	20
Mother Moose Nursery Pomes 01-530-207 (5-7/62, Dell)	17	34	51	119	230	340

NOTE: *Reprints: 6, 7, 20-24.*

BULLWINKLE (...& Rocky No. 2 on)(TV)
Charlton Comics: July, 1970 - No. 7, July, 1971

	GD	VG	FN	VF	VF/NM	NM-
1	7	14	21	47	76	105
2-7	5	10	15	32	51	70

BULLWINKLE AND ROCKY
Star Comics/Marvel Comics No. 3 on: Nov, 1987 - No. 9, Mar, 1989

	GD	VG	FN	VF	VF/NM	NM-
1-9: Boris & Natasha in all. 3,5,8-Dudley Do-Right app. 4-Reagan-c						4.50
Marvel Moosterworks (1/92, $4.95)	2	4	6	8	10	12

BUMMER
Fantagraphics Books: June, 1995 ($3.50, B&W, mature)

	GD	VG	FN	VF	VF/NM	NM-
1						3.50

BUNNY (Also see Harvey Pop Comics)
Harvey Publications: Dec, 1966 - No. 20, Dec, 1971; No. 21, Nov, 1976

	GD	VG	FN	VF	VF/NM	NM-
1-68 pg. Giants begin	8	16	24	52	86	120
2-10	4	8	12	28	44	60
11-18: 18-Last 68 pg. Giant	4	8	12	26	41	55
19-21-52 pg. Giants: 21-Fruitman app.	4	8	12	24	37	50

BURKE'S LAW (TV)
Dell Publ.: 1-3/64; No. 2, 5-7/64; No. 3, 3-5/65 (All have Gene Barry photo-c)

	GD	VG	FN	VF	VF/NM	NM-
1-Photo-c	5	10	15	34	55	75
2,3-Photo-c	4	8	12	24	37	50

BURNING ROMANCES (See Fox Giants)

BUSTER BEAR
Quality Comics Group (Arnold Publ.): Dec, 1953 - No. 10, June, 1955

	GD	VG	FN	VF	VF/NM	NM-
1-Funny animal	11	22	33	60	83	105
2	7	14	21	35	43	50
3-10	6	12	18	28	34	40
I.W. Reprint #9,10 (Super on inside)	2	4	6	9	13	16

BUSTER BROWN COMICS (See Promotional Comics section)

BUSTER BUNNY
Standard Comics(Animated Cartoons)/Pines: Nov, 1949 - No. 16, Oct, 1953

	GD	VG	FN	VF	VF/NM	NM-
1-Frazetta 1 pg. text illo.	11	22	33	60	83	105
2	7	14	21	35	43	50
3-14,16	6	12	18	28	34	40
15-Racist-c	9	18	27	47	61	75

BUSTER CRABBE (TV)
Famous Funnies Publ.: Nov, 1951 - No. 12, 1953

	GD	VG	FN	VF	VF/NM	NM-
1-1st app.(?) Frazetta anti-drug ad; text story about Buster Crabbe & Billy the Kid	40	80	120	235	380	525
2-Williamson/Evans-c; text story about Wild Bill Hickok & Pecos Bill	38	76	114	222	356	490
3-Williamson/Evans-c/a	40	80	120	235	380	525
4-Frazetta-c/a, 1pg.; bondage-c	48	96	144	298	499	700
5-Frazetta-c; Williamson/Krenkel/Orlando-a, 11pgs. (per Mr. Williamson)	127	254	381	800	1350	1900
6,8	19	38	57	109	172	235
7-Frazetta one pg. ad	19	38	57	111	176	240
9-One pg. Frazetta Boy Scouts ad (1st?)	15	30	45	94	147	200
10-12	12	24	36	69	97	125

NOTE: Eastern Color sold 3 dozen each NM file copies of #s 9-12 a few years ago.

BUSTER CRABBE (The Amazing Adventures of...)(Movie star)
Lev Gleason Publications: Dec, 1953 - No. 4, June, 1954

	GD	VG	FN	VF	VF/NM	NM-
1,4: 1-Photo-c. 4-Flash Gordon-c	21	42	63	122	199	275
2,3-Toth-a	19	38	57	111	176	240

BUTCH CASSIDY
Skywald Comics: June, 1971 - No. 3, Oct, 1971 (52 pgs.)

	GD	VG	FN	VF	VF/NM	NM-
1-Pre-code reprints and new material; Red Mask reprint, retitled Maverick; Bolle-a; Sutton-a	3	6	9	16	22	28
2,3: 2-Whip Wilson-r. 3-Dead Canyon Days reprint/Crack Western No. 63; Sundance Kid app.; Crandall-a	2	4	6	10	14	18

BUTCH CASSIDY (...& the Wild Bunch)
Avon Periodicals: 1951

	GD	VG	FN	VF	VF/NM	NM-
1-Kinstler-c/a	19	38	57	111	176	240

NOTE: *Reinman story; Issue number on inside spine.*

BUTCH CASSIDY (See Fun-In No. 11 & Western Adventure Comics)

BUTCHER, THE (Also see Brave and the Bold, 2nd Series)
DC Comics: May, 1990 - No. 5, Sept, 1990 ($1.50, mature)

	GD	VG	FN	VF	VF/NM	NM-
1-5: 1-No indicia inside						2.50

BUTCHER KNIGHT
Image Comics (Top Cow): Jan, 2001 - No. 4, June, 2001 ($2.95, limited series)

	GD	VG	FN	VF	VF/NM	NM-
Preview (B&W, 16 pgs.) Dwayne Turner-c/a						2.25
1-4-Dwayne Turner-c/a						3.00

BUZ SAWYER (Sweeney No. 4 on)
Standard Comics: June, 1948 - No. 3, 1949

	GD	VG	FN	VF	VF/NM	NM-
1-Roy Crane-a	26	52	78	154	252	350
2-Intro his pal Sweeney	15	30	45	86	133	180
3	12	24	36	69	97	125

BUZ SAWYER'S PAL, ROSCOE SWEENEY (See Sweeney)

BUZZ, THE (Also see Spider-Girl)
Marvel Comics: July, 2000 - No. 3, Sept, 2000 ($2.99, limited series)

	GD	VG	FN	VF	VF/NM	NM-
1-3-Buscema-a/DeFalco & Frenz-s						3.00

BUZZ BUZZ COMICS MAGAZINE
Horse Press: May, 1996 ($4.95, B&W, over-sized magazine)

	GD	VG	FN	VF	VF/NM	NM-
1-Paul Pope-c/a/scripts; Moebius-a						5.00

BUZZY (See All Funny Comics)
National Periodical Publications/Detective Comics: Winter, 1944-45 - No. 75, 1-2/57; No. 76, 10/57; No. 77, 10/58

	GD	VG	FN	VF	VF/NM	NM-
1 (52 pgs. begin); "America's favorite teenster"	31	62	93	186	303	420
2 (Spr, 1945)	16	32	48	94	147	200
3-5	13	26	39	72	101	130
6-10	10	20	30	58	79	100
11-20	9	18	27	52	69	85
21-30	8	16	24	44	57	70
31,35-38	8	16	24	42	54	65
32-34,39-Last 52 pgs. Scribbly story by Mayer in each (these four stories were done for Scribbly #14 which was delayed for a year)	9	18	27	47	61	75
40-77: 62-Last precode (2/55)	8	16	24	40	50	60

BUZZY THE CROW (See Harvey Comics Hits #60 & 62, Harvey Hits #18 & Paramount Animated Comics #1)

BY BIZARRE HANDS
Dark Horse Comics: Apr, 1994 - No. 3, June, 1994 ($2.50, B&W, mature)

	GD	VG	FN	VF	VF/NM	NM-
1-3: Lansdale stories						2.50

CABBOT: BLOODHUNTER (Also see Bloodstrike & Bloodstrike: Assassin)
Maximum Press: Jan, 1997 ($2.50, one-shot)

	GD	VG	FN	VF	VF/NM	NM-
1-Rick Veitch-a/script; Platt-c; Thor, Chapel & Prophet cameos						2.50

CABLE (See Ghost Rider &..., & New Mutants #87) (Title becomes Soldier X)
Marvel Comics: May, 1993 - No. 107, Sept, 2002 ($3.50/$1.95/$1.50-$2.25)

	GD	VG	FN	VF	VF/NM	NM-
1-($3.50, 52 pgs.)-Gold foil & embossed-c; Thibert a-1-4p; c-1-3						5.00
2-15: 3-Extra 16 pg. X-Men/Avengers ann. preview. 4-Liefeld-a assist; last Thibert-a(p). 6-8-Reveals that Baby Nathan is Cable; gives background on Stryfe. 9-Omega Red-c/story. 11-Bound-in trading card sheet						3.50
16-Newsstand edition						2.50
16-Enhanced edition						5.00
17-20-($1.95)-Deluxe edition, 20-w/bound in '95 Fleer Ultra cards						3.00
17-20-($1.50)-Standard edition						2.50

21-24, 26-44, -1(7/97): 21-Begin $1.95-c; return from Age of Apocalyse. 24-Grizzly dies. 28-vs. Sugarman; Mr. Sinister app. 30-X-Man-c/app.; Exodus app. 31-vs. X-Man. 32-Post app. 33-Post-c/app; Mandarin app (flashback); includes "Onslaught Update". 34-Onslaught x-over; Hulk-c/app; Apocalypse app. (cont'd in Hulk #444). 35-Onslaught x-over; Apocalypse vs. Cable. 36-w/card insert. 38-Weapon X-c/app; Psycho Man & Micronauts

Cable/Deadpool #39 © MAR

Cadillacs and Dinosaurs #1 © Topps

Calling All Girls #9 © PMI

GD 2.0 | VG 4.0 | FN 6.0 | VF 8.0 | VF/NM 9.0 | NM- 9.2

app. 40-Scott Clark-a(p). 41-Bishop-c/app. 3.00
25 ($3.95)-Foil gatefold-c 4.00
45-49,51-74: 45-Operation Zero Tolerance. 51-1st Casey-s. 54-Black Panther. 55-Domino-c/app. 62-Nick Fury-c/app.63-Stryfe-c/app. 67,68-Avengers-c/app. 71,73-Liefeld-a 2.50
50-($2.99) Double sized w/wraparound-c 3.00
75 -($2.99) Liefeld-c/a; Apocalypse: The Twelve x-over 3.00
76-79: 76-Apocalypse: The Twelve x-over 2.50
80-96: 80-Begin $2.25-c. 87-Mystique-c/app. 2.50
97-99,101-107: 97-Tischman-s/Kordey-a/c begin 2.50
100-($3.99) Dialogue-free 'Nuff Said back-up story 4.00
... Classic Vol. 1 TPB (2008, $29.99) r/#1-4, New Mutants #87, Cable: Blood & Metal #1,2 30.00
.../Machine Man '98 Annual ($2.99) Wraparound-c 3.00
.../X-Force '96 Annual ($2.95) Wraparound-c 3.00
...'99 Annual ($3.50) vs. Sinister; computer photo-c 3.50
...Second Genesis 1 (9/99, $3.99) r/New Mutants #99, 100 and X-Force #1; Liefeld-c 4.00
...: The End (2002, $14.99, TPB) r/#101-107 15.00

CABLE
Marvel Comics: May, 2008 - Present ($2.99)

1-23: 1-10-Olivetti-c/a. 1-Liefeld var-c. 2-Finch var-c. 3-Romita Jr. var-c. 4-Bishop app.; Djurdjevic var-c. 5-Silvestri var-c. 6-Liefeld var-c. 13-15-Messiah War x-over; Deadpool app. 16,17-Gulacy-a 3.00

CABLE - BLOOD AND METAL (Also see New Mutants #87 & X-Force #8)
Marvel Comics: Oct, 1992 - No. 2, Nov, 1992 ($2.50, limited series, 52 pgs.)

1-Fabian Nicieza scripts; John Romita, Jr.-c/a in both; Cable vs. Stryfe; 2nd app. of The Wild Pack (becomes The Six Pack); wraparound-c 4.00
2-Prelude to X-Cutioner's Song 3.00

CABLE/DEADPOOL ("Cable & Deadpool" on cover)
Marvel Comics: May, 2004 - No. 50, Apr, 2008 ($2.99)

1-49: 1-Nicieza-s/Liefeld-c. 7-9-X-Men app. 17-House of M. 21-Heroes For Hire app. 30,31-Civil War. 30-Great Lakes Avengers app. 33-Liefeld-c. 43,44-Wolverine app. 3.00
50-($3.99) Final issue; Spider-Man and the Avengers app. 4.00
... Vol. 1: If Looks Could Kill TPB (2004, $14.99) r/#1-6 15.00
... Vol. 2: The Burnt Offering TPB (2005, $14.99) r/#7-12 15.00
... Vol. 3: The Human Race TPB (2005, $14.99) r/#13-18 15.00
... Vol. 4: Bosom Buddies TPB (2006, $14.99) r/#19-24 15.00
... Vol. 5: Living Legends TPB (2006, $13.99) r/#25-29 14.00
... Vol. 6: Paved With Good Intentions TPB (2007, $14.99) r/#30-35 15.00
... Vol. 7: Separation Anxiety TPB (2007, $17.99) r/#36-42; sketch pages 18.00
Deadpool Vs. The Marvel Universe TPB (2008, $24.99) r/#43-50 25.00

CADET GRAY OF WEST POINT (See Dell Giants)

CADILLACS & DINOSAURS (TV)
Marvel Comics (Epic Comics): Nov, 1990 - No. 6, Apr, 1991 ($2.50, limited series)

1-6: r/Xenozoic Tales in color w/new-c 3.00
...In 3-D #1 (7/92, $3.95, Kitchen Sink)-With glasses 6.00

CADILLACS AND DINOSAURS (TV)
Topps Comics: V2#1, Feb, 1994 - V2#9, 1995 ($2.50, limited series)

V2#1-($2.95)-Collector's edition w/Stout-c & bound-in poster; Buckler-a; foil stamped logo; Giordano-a in all 6.00
V2#1-9: 1-Newsstand edition w/Giordano-c. 2,3-Collector's editions w/Stout-c & posters. 2,3-Newsstand ed. w/Giordano-c; w/o posters. 4-6-Collectors & Newsstand editions; Kieth-c. 7-9-Linsner-c 3.00

CAGE (Also see Hero for Hire, Power Man & Punisher)
Marvel Comics: Apr, 1992 - No. 20, Nov, 1993 ($1.25)

1,3,10,12: 3-Punisher-c & minor app. 10-Rhino & Hulk-c/app. 12-(52 pgs.)-Iron Fist app. 3.00
2,4-9,11,13-20: 9-Rhino-c/story; Hulk cameo 2.50

CAGE (Volume 3)
Marvel Comics (MAX): Mar, 2002 - No. 5, Sept, 2002 ($2.99, mature)

1-5-Corben-c/a; Azzarello-s 3.00
HC (2002, $19.99, with dustjacket) r/#1-5; intro. by Darius James; sketch pages 20.00
SC (2003, $13.99) r/#1-5; intro. by Darius James 14.00

CAGED HEAT 3000 (Movie)
Roger Corman's Cosmic Comics: Nov, 1995 - No. 3, Jan, 1996 ($2.50)

1-3: Adaptation of film 2.50

CAGES
Tundra Publ.: 1991 - No. 10, May, 1996 ($3.50/$3.95/$4.95, limited series)

1-Dave McKean-c/a in all 2 4 6 8 10 12
2-Misprint exists 1 2 3 5 6 8
3-9: 5-$3.95-c begins 4.00
10-($4.95) 5.00

CAIN'S HUNDRED (TV)
Dell Publishing Co.: May-July, 1962 - No. 2, Sept-Nov, 1962

nn(01-094-207) 3 6 9 20 30 40
2 3 6 9 16 22 28

CAIN/VAMPIRELLA FLIP BOOK
Harris Comics: Oct, 1994 ($6.95, one-shot, squarebound)

nn-contains Cain #3 & #4; flip book is r/Vampirella story from 1993 Creepy Fearbook 1 2 3 5 7 9

CALIBER PRESENTS
Caliber Press: Jan, 1989 - No. 24, 1991 ($1.95/$2.50, B&W, 52 pgs.)

1-Anthology; 1st app. The Crow; Tim Vigil-c/a 6 12 18 39 62 85
2-Deadworld story; Tim Vigil-a 2 4 6 9 13 16
3-24: 15-24 ($3.50, 68 pgs.) 3.50

CALIBER PRESENTS: CINDERELLA ON FIRE
Caliber Press: 1994 ($2.95, B&W, mature)

1 3.00

CALIBER SPOTLIGHT
Caliber Press: May, 1995 ($2.95, B&W)

1-Kabuki app 3.50

CALIFORNIA GIRLS
Eclipse Comics: June, 1987 - No. 8, May, 1988 ($2.00, 40 pgs, B&W)

1-8: All contain color paper dolls 3.00

CALL, THE
Marvel Comics: June, 2003 - No. 4, Sept, 2003 ($2.25)

1-4-Austen-s/Olliffe-a 2.50

CALLING ALL BOYS (Tex Granger No. 18 on)
Parents' Magazine Institute: Jan, 1946 - No. 17, May, 1948 (Photo c-1-5,7,8)

1 14 28 42 81 118 155
2-Contains Roy Rogers article 9 18 27 47 61 75
3-7,9,11,14-17: 6-Painted-c. 11-Rin Tin Tin photo on-c; Tex Granger begins. 14-J. Edgar Hoover photo on-c. 15-Tex Granger-c begin 7 14 21 35 43 50
8-Milton Caniff story 9 18 27 50 65 80
10-Gary Cooper photo on-c 9 18 27 50 65 80
12-Bob Hope photo on-c 14 28 42 76 108 140
13-Bing Crosby photo on-c 12 24 36 67 94 120

CALLING ALL GIRLS
Parents' Magazine Institute: Sept, 1941 - No. 89, Sept, 1949 (Part magazine, part comic)

1 18 36 54 105 165 225
2-Photo-c 10 20 30 58 79 100
3-Shirley Temple photo-c 14 28 42 81 118 155
4-10: 4,5,7,9-Photo-c. 9-Flag-c 9 18 27 50 65 80
11-Tina Thayer photo-c; Mickey Rooney photo-b/c; B&W photo inside of Gary Cooper as Lou Gehrig in "Pride of Yankees" 11 22 33 60 83 105
12-20 8 16 24 42 54 65
21-39,41-43(10-11/45)-Last issue with comics 8 16 24 40 50 60
40-Liz Taylor photo-c 21 42 63 122 199 275
44-51(7/46)-Last comic book size issue 7 14 21 35 43 50
52-89 6 12 18 28 34 40

NOTE: ***Jack Sparling*** art in many issues; becomes a girls' magazine *"Senior Prom"* with #90.

CALLING ALL KIDS (Also see True Comics)
Parents' Magazine Institute: Dec-Jan, 1945-46 - No. 26, Aug, 1949

1-Funny animal 14 28 42 80 115 150
2 8 16 24 44 57 70
3-10 7 14 21 35 43 50
11-26 6 12 18 31 38 45

CALL OF DUTY, THE : THE BROTHERHOOD
Marvel Comics: Aug, 2002 - No. 6, Jan, 2003 ($2.25)

1-Exploits of NYC Fire Dept.; Finch-c/a; Austen & Bruce Jones-s 4.00
2-6-Austen-s 2.50
...Vol 1: The Brotherhood & The Wagon TPB (2002, $14.99) r/#1-6 & ...The Wagon #1-4 15.00

CALL OF DUTY, THE : THE PRECINCT
Marvel Comics: Sept, 2002 - No. 5, Jan, 2003 ($2.25, limited series)

1-Exploits of NYC Police Dept.; Finch-c; Bruce Jones-s/Mandrake-a 3.00
2-4 2.50
...Vol 2: The Precinct TPB (2003, $9.99) r/#1-4 10.00

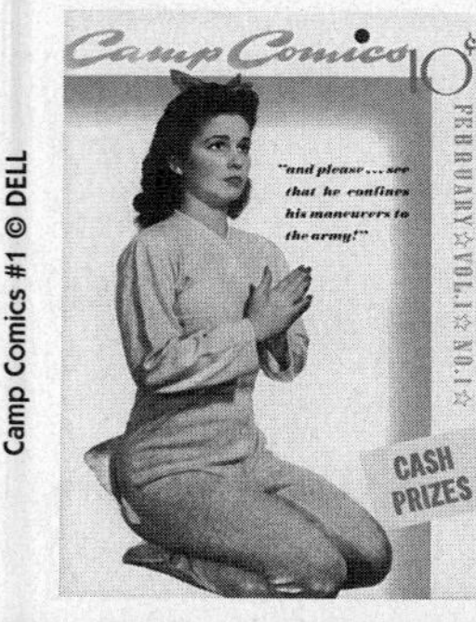

Camp Comics #1 © DELL

Cannonball Comics #2 © RH

Captain Action #1 © DC

	GD 2.0	VG 4.0	FN 6.0	VF 8.0	VF/NM 9.0	NM- 9.2

CALL OF DUTY, THE : THE WAGON
Marvel Comics: Oct, 2002 - No. 4, Jan, 2003 ($2.25, limited series)

	GD	VG	FN	VF	VF/NM	NM-
1-4-Exploits of NYC EMS Dept.; Finch-c; Austen-s/Zelzej-a						2.50

CALVIN (See Li'l Kids)

CALVIN & THE COLONEL (TV)
Dell Publishing Co.: No. 1354, Apr-June, 1962 - No. 2, July-Sept, 1962

	GD	VG	FN	VF	VF/NM	NM-
Four Color 1354(#1)	8	16	24	56	93	130
2	6	12	18	39	62	85

CAMELOT 3000
DC Comics: Dec, 1982 - No. 11, July, 1984; No. 12, Apr, 1985 (Direct sales, maxi series, Mando paper)

	GD	VG	FN	VF	VF/NM	NM-
1-12: 1-Mike Barr scripts & Brian Bolland-c/a begin. 5-Intro Knights of New Camelot						4.00
TPB (1988, $12.95) r/#1-12						15.00
...: The Deluxe Edition (2008, $34.99, HC) r/#1-12; oversized & recolored; Barr intro.; design and promotional art; original proposal page						35.00

NOTE: ***Austin** a-7i-12i. **Bolland** a-1-12p; c-1-12.*

CAMERA COMICS
U.S. Camera Publishing Corp./ME: July, 1944 - No. 9, Summer, 1946

	GD	VG	FN	VF	VF/NM	NM-
nn (7/44)	25	50	75	147	241	335
nn (9/44)	19	38	57	109	172	235
1(10/44)-The Grey Comet (slightly smaller page size than subsequent issues)	19	38	57	109	172	235
2-16 pgs. of photos with 32 pgs. of comics	14	28	42	82	121	160
3-Nazi WW II-c; photos	15	30	45	85	130	175
4-9: All 1/3 photos	13	26	39	74	105	135

CAMP CANDY (TV)
Marvel Comics: May, 1990 - No. 6, Oct, 1990 ($1.00, limited series)

	GD	VG	FN	VF	VF/NM	NM-
1-6: Post-c/a(p); featuring John Candy						4.00

CAMP COMICS
Dell Publishing Co.: Feb, 1942 - No. 3, April, 1942 (All have photo-c)

	GD	VG	FN	VF	VF/NM	NM-
1- "Seaman Sy Wheeler" by Kelly, 7 pgs.; Bugs Bunny app.; Mark Twain adaptation (scarce)	81	162	243	518	884	1250
2-Kelly-a, 12 pgs.; Bugs Bunny app.; classic-c	81	162	243	518	884	1250
3-(Scarce)-Dave Berg & Walt Kelly-a	61	122	183	390	670	950

CAMP RUNAMUCK (TV)
Dell Publishing Co.: Apr, 1966

	GD	VG	FN	VF	VF/NM	NM-
1-Photo-c	4	8	12	22	34	45

CAMPUS LOVES
Quality Comics Group (Comic Magazines): Dec, 1949 - No. 5, Aug, 1950

	GD	VG	FN	VF	VF/NM	NM-
1-Ward-c/a (9 pgs.)	35	70	105	208	339	470
2-Ward-c/a	26	52	78	154	252	350
3-5	15	30	45	83	124	165

NOTE: ***Gustavson** a-1-5. Photo c-3-5.*

CAMPUS ROMANCE (...Romances on cover)
Avon Periodicals/Realistic: Sept-Oct, 1949 - No. 3, Feb-Mar, 1950

	GD	VG	FN	VF	VF/NM	NM-
1-Walter Johnson-a; c-/Avon paperback #348	27	54	81	158	259	360
2-Grandenetti-a; c-/Avon paperback #151	20	40	60	114	182	250
3-c-/Avon paperback #201	20	40	60	114	182	250
Realistic reprint	10	20	30	58	79	100

CANADA DRY PREMIUMS (See Swamp Fox, The & Terry & The Pirates in the Promotional Comics section)

CANCELLED COMIC CAVALCADE (See the Promotional Comics section)

CANDID TALES (Also see Bold Stories & It Rhymes With Lust)
Kirby Publ. Co.: April, 1950; June, 1950 (Digest size) (144 pgs.) (Full color)

	GD	VG	FN	VF	VF/NM	NM-
nn-(Scarce) Contains Wood female pirate story, 15 pgs., and 14 pgs. in June issue; Powell-a	116	232	348	742	1271	1800

NOTE: *Another version exists with Dr. Kilmore by Wood; no female pirate story.*

CANDY
William H. Wise & Co.: Fall, 1944 - No. 3, Spring, 1945

	GD	VG	FN	VF	VF/NM	NM-
1-Two Scoop Scuttle stories by Wolverton	39	78	117	240	395	550
2,3-Scoop Scuttle by Wolverton, 2-4 pgs.	26	52	78	154	252	350

CANDY (Teen-age)(Also see Police Comics #37)
Quality Comics Group (Comic Magazines): Autumn, 1947 - No. 64, Jul, 1956

	GD	VG	FN	VF	VF/NM	NM-
1-Gustavson-a	23	46	69	136	223	310
2-Gustavson-a	14	28	42	80	115	150
3-10	10	20	30	54	72	90
11-30	8	16	24	40	50	60
31-64: 64-Ward-c(p)?	7	14	21	35	43	50
Super Reprint No. 2,10,12,16,17,18('63- '64):17-Candy #12	2	4	6	10	14	18

NOTE: ***Jack Cole** 1-2 pg. art in many issues.*

CANNON (See Heroes, Inc. Presents Cannon)

CANNON: DAWN OF WAR (Michael Turner's...)
Aspen MLT, Inc.: Nov, 2004 ($2.99)

	GD	VG	FN	VF	VF/NM	NM-
1-Turnbull-a; two covers by Turnbull and Turner						3.00

CANNONBALL COMICS
Rural Home Publishing Co.: Feb, 1945 - No. 2, Mar, 1945

	GD	VG	FN	VF	VF/NM	NM-
1-The Crash Kid, Thunderbrand, The Captive Prince & Crime Crusader begin; skull-c	97	194	291	621	1061	1500
2-Devil-c	71	142	213	454	777	1100

CANTEEN KATE (See All Picture All True Love Story & Fightin' Marines)
St. John Publishing Co.: June, 1952 - No. 3, Nov, 1952

	GD	VG	FN	VF	VF/NM	NM-
1-Matt Baker-c/a	71	142	213	454	777	1100
2-Matt Baker-c/a	45	90	135	284	480	675
3-(Rare)-Used in **POP**, pg. 75; Baker-c/a	53	106	159	334	567	800

CAPER
DC Comics: Dec, 2003 - No. 12, Nov, 2004 ($2.95, limited series)

	GD	VG	FN	VF	VF/NM	NM-
1-12: 1-4-Judd Winick-s/Farel Dalrymple-a. 5-8-John Severin-a. 9-12-Fowler-a						3.00

CAPES
Image Comics: Sept, 2003 - No. 3, Nov, 2003 ($3.50)

	GD	VG	FN	VF	VF/NM	NM-
1-3-Robert Kirkman-s/Mark Englert-a/c						3.50

CAP'N QUICK & A FOOZLE (Also see Eclipse Mag. & Monthly)
Eclipse Comics: July, 1984 - No. 3, Nov, 1985 ($1.50, color, Baxter paper)

	GD	VG	FN	VF	VF/NM	NM-
1-3-Rogers-c/a						3.00

CAPTAIN ACTION (Toy)
National Periodical Publications: Oct-Nov, 1968 - No. 5, June-July, 1969 (Based on Ideal toy)

	GD	VG	FN	VF	VF/NM	NM-
1-Origin; Wood-a; Superman-c app.	7	14	21	45	73	100
2,3,5-Kane/Wood-a	5	10	15	34	55	75
4	4	8	12	28	44	60

CAPTAIN ACTION COMICS (Toy)
Moonstone: No. 0, 2008 - Present (Based on the Ideal toy)

	GD	VG	FN	VF	VF/NM	NM-
0-($1.99) Origin re-told; Sparacio-a; three covers; character history by Michael Eury						2.50
1-5: 1-($3.99) Sparacio-a; intro. by Jim Shooter						4.00
...: First Mission, Last Day (2008, $3.99) origin story re-told; Nicieza-s/Procopio-a						4.00

CAPTAIN AERO COMICS (Samson No. 1-6; also see Veri Best Sure Fire & Veri Best Sure Shot Comics)
Holyoke Publishing Co.: V1#7(#1), Dec, 1941 - V2#4(#10), Jan, 1943; V3#9(#11), Sept, 1943 -V4#3(#17), Oct, 1944; #21, Dec, 1944 - #26, Aug, 1946 (No #18-20)

	GD	VG	FN	VF	VF/NM	NM-
V1#7(#1)-Flag-Man & Solar, Master of Magic, Captain Aero, Cap Stone, Adventurer begin; Nazi WWII-c	181	362	543	1158	1979	2800
8,10: 8(#2)-Pals of Freedom app. 10(#4)-Origin The Gargoyle; Kubert-a	90	180	270	576	988	1400
9(#3)-Hitler-sty; Catman back-c; Alias X begins; Pals of Freedom app.	103	206	309	659	1130	1600
11,12(#5,6)-Kubert-a; Miss Victory in #6	73	146	219	467	796	1125
V2#1,2(#7,8): 8-Origin The Red Cross; Miss Victory app.; Brodsky-c(i)	43	86	129	271	461	650
3(#9)-Miss Victory app.	41	82	123	252	421	590
4(#10)-Miss Victory app.; Japanese WWII-c	37	74	111	222	361	500
V3#9 - V3#12(#11-14): 9-Quinlan Japanese WWII-c; Miss Victory app.	29	58	87	170	278	385
V3#13(#15),V4#2(#16): Schomburg Japanese WWII-c. 13-Miss Victory app.	37	74	111	222	361	500
V4#3(#17), 21-24-L. B. Cole Japanese WWII covers. 22-Intro/origin Mighty Mite.	50	100	150	315	533	750
25-L. B. Cole SciFi-c	52	104	156	322	549	775
26-L. B. Cole SciFi-c; Palais-a(2) (scarce)	116	232	348	742	1271	1800

NOTE: ***L.B. Cole** c-17. **Hollingsworth** a-23. **Infantino** a-23, 26. **Schomburg** c-15, 16.*

CAPTAIN AMERICA (See Adventures of..., All-Select, All Winners, Aurora, Avengers #4, Blood and Glory, Captain Britain 16-20, Giant-Size..., The Invaders, Marvel Double Feature, Marvel Fanfare, Marvel Mystery, Marvel Super-Action, Marvel Super Heroes V2#3, Marvel Team-Up, Marvel Treasury Special, Power Record Comics, Ultimates, USA Comics, Young Allies & Young Men)

CAPTAIN AMERICA (Formerly Tales of Suspense #1-99) (Captain America and the Falcon #134-223 & Steve Rogers: Captain America #444-454 appears on cover only)
Marvel Comics Group: No. 100, Apr, 1968 - No. 454, Aug, 1996

Captain America #202 © MAR

Captain America #372 © MAR

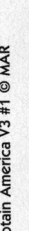

Captain America V3 #1 © MAR

GD VG FN VF VF/NM NM-
2.0 4.0 6.0 8.0 9.0 9.2

100-Flashback on Cap's revival with Avengers & Sub-Mariner; story continued
from Tales of Suspense #99; Kirby-c/a begins 29 58 87 212 406 600
101-The Sleeper-c/story; Red Skull app. 9 18 27 60 100 140
102-104: 102-Sleeper-c/s. 103,104-Red Skull-c/sty 7 14 21 45 73 100
105-108 6 12 18 39 62 85
109-Origin Capt. America retold in detail 8 16 24 54 90 125
109-2nd printing (1994) 2 4 6 8 10 12
110-Rick Jones dons Bucky's costume & becomes Cap's partner; Hulk x-over; Steranko-a
Classic Steranko-c 10 20 30 68 119 170
111,113-Classic Steranko-c/a: 111-Death of Steve Rogers. 113-Cap's funeral; Avengers app.
9 18 27 61 105 145
112-S.A. recovery retold; last Kirby-c/a 5 10 15 34 55 75
114-116,119,120: 115-Last 12¢ issue 4 8 12 24 37 50
117-1st app. The Falcon (9/69) 11 22 33 78 139 200
118-2nd app. The Falcon 5 10 15 34 55 75
121-136,139,140: 121-Retells origin. 133-The Falcon becomes Cap's partner; origin Modok.
140-Origin Grey Gargoyle retold 3 6 9 18 27 35
137,138-Spider-Man x-over 4 8 12 22 34 45
141,142: 142-Last 15¢ issue 3 6 9 16 22 28
143-(52 pgs). 3 6 9 18 27 35
144-153: 144-New costume Falcon. 153-1st brief app. Jack Monroe
2 4 6 13 18 22
154-1st full app. Jack Monroe (Nomad)(10/72) 3 6 9 14 19 24
155-Origin re-told; origin Jack Monroe 3 6 9 14 19 24
156-171,176-179: 155-158-Cap's strength increased. 160-1st app. Solarr. 164-1st app.
Nightshade. 176-End of Capt. America. 2 4 6 8 11 14
172-175: X-Men x-over 2 4 6 13 18 22
180-Intro/origin of Nomad (Steve Rogers) 3 6 9 14 19 24
181-Intro/origin new Cap. 2 4 6 11 16 20
182,184-192: 186-True origin The Falcon 2 3 4 6 8 10
183-Death of new Cap; Nomad becomes Cap 2 4 6 9 12 15
193-Kirby-c/a begins 2 4 6 13 18 22
194-199-(Regular 25¢ edition)(4-7/76) 2 4 6 10 14 18
196-199-(30¢-c variants, limited distribution) 5 10 15 32 51 70
200-(Regular 25¢ edition)(8/76) 2 4 6 11 16 20
200-(30¢-c variant, limited distribution) 6 12 18 37 59 80
201-214-Kirby-c/a 2 4 6 8 11 14
210-214-(35¢-c variants, limited dist.)(6-10/77) 7 14 21 45 73 100
215,216,218-229,231-234,236-240,242-246: 215-Retells Cap's origin. 216-r/story from Strange
Tales #114. 229-Marvel Man app. 233-Death of Sharon Carter. 234-Daredevil x-over.
244,245-Miller-c 6.00
217,230,235: 217-1st app. Marvel Man (later Quasar). 230-Battles Hulk-c/story cont'd in
Hulk #232. 235-(7/79) Daredevil x-over; Miller-a(p) 1 2 3 4 5 7
241-Punisher app.; Miller-c. 3 6 9 17 25 32
241-2nd print 3.00
247-255-Byrne-a. 255-Origin; Miller-c. 1 2 3 5 7 9
256-281,284,285,289-322,324-326,328-331: 264-Old X-Men cameo in flashback.
265,266-Nick Fury & Spider-Man app. 267-1st app. Everyman. 269-1st Team America.
279-(3/83)-Contains Tattooz skin decals. 281-1950s Bucky returns. 284-Patriot (Jack Mace)
app. 285-Death of Patriot. 298-Origin Red Skull. 328-Origin & 1st app. D-Man 3.00
282-Bucky becomes new Nomad (Jack Monroe) 5.00
282-Silver ink 2nd print ($1.75) w/original date (6/83) 2.50
283,327,333-340: 283-2nd app. Nomad. 327-Capt. Amer. battles Super Patriot. 333-Intro &
origin new Captain (Super Patriot). 339-Fall of the Mutants tie-in 4.00
286-288-Deathlok app. 4.00
323-1st app. new Super Patriot (see Nick Fury) 4.00
332-Old Cap resigns 1 2 3 5 6 8
341-343,345-349 3.00
344-($1.50, 52 pgs.)-Ronald Reagan cameo 4.00
350-($1.75, 68 pgs.)-Return of Steve Rogers (original Cap) to original costume 4.00
351-382,384-396: 351-Nick Fury app. 354-1st app. U.S. Agent (6/89, see Avengers West
Coast). 360-1st app. Crossbones. 375-Daredevil app. 386-U.S. Agent app. 387-389-Red
Skull back-up stories. 396-Last $1.00-c. 396,397-1st app. all new Jack O'Lantern 2.50
383-($2.00, 68 pgs.)-50th anniversary issue; Red Skull story; Jim Lee-c(i) 4.00
397-399,401-424,425: 402-Begin 6 part Man-Wolf story w/Wolverine in #403-407.
405-410-New Jack O'Lantern app. in back-up story. 406-Cable & Shatterstar cameo.
407-Capwolf vs. Cable-c/story. 408-Infinity War x-over; Falcon solo back-up.
423-Vs. Namor-c/story 2.50
400-($2.25, 84 pgs.)-Flip book format w/double gatefold-c; r/Avengers #4 plus-c; contains
cover pin-ups. 3.00
425-($2.95, 52 pgs.)-Embossed Foil-c ed.n; Fighting Chance Pt. 1 3.00
426-443,446,447,449-453: 427-Begin $1.50-c; bound-in trading card sheet. 449-Thor app.
450-"Man Without A Country" storyline begins, ends #453; Bill Clinton app; variant-c exists.
451-1st app.Cap's new costume. 453-Cap gets old costume back; Bill Clinton app. 2.50
444-Mark Waid scripts & Ron Garney-c/a(p) begins, ends #454; Avengers app. 5.00
445,454: 445-Sharon Carter & Red Skull return. 3.00
448-($2.95, double-sized issue)-Waid script & Garney-c/a; Red Skull "dies" 4.00
#600-up (See Captain America 2005 series, resumed original numbering after #50)
Special 1(1/71)-Origin retold 5 10 15 34 55 75
Special 2(1/72, 52 pgs.)-Colan-r/Not Brand Echh; all-r 3 6 9 21 32 42
Annual 3('76, 52 pgs.)-Kirby-c/a(new) 3 6 9 16 22 28
Annual 4('77, 34 pgs.)-Magneto-c/story 3 6 9 16 22 28
Annual 5-7: (52 pgs.)('81-'83) 5.00
Annual 8(9/86)-Wolverine-c/story 3 6 9 19 29 38
Annual 9-13('90-'94, 68 pgs.)-9-Nomad back-up. 10-Origin retold (2 pgs.). 11-Falcon solo story.
12-Bagged w/card. 13-Red Skull-c/story 3.00
...Ashcan Edition ('95, 75¢) 3.00
... and the Falcon: Madbomb TPB (2004, $16.99) r/#193-200; Kirby-s/a 17.00
... and the Falcon: Nomad TPB (2006, $24.99) r/#177-186; Cap becomes Nomad 25.00
... and the Falcon: Secret Empire TPB (2005, $19.99) r/#169-176 20.00
... and the Falcon: The Swine TPB (2006, $29.99) r/#206-214 & Annual #3,4 30.00
... By Jack Kirby: Bicentennial Battles TPB (2005, $19.99) r/#201-205 & Marvel Treasury
Special Featuring Captain America's Bicentennial Battles; Kirby-s/a 20.00
...: Deathlok Lives! nn(10/93, $4.95)-r/#286-288 5.00
...Drug War 1-(1994, $2.00, 52 pgs.)-New Warriors app. 3.00
...Man Without a Country(1998, $12.99, TPB)-r/#450-453 13.00
...Medusa Effect 1 (1994, $2.95, 68 pgs.)-Origin Baron Zemo 3.00
...Operation Rebirth (1996, $9.95)-r/#445-448 10.00
... 65th Anniversary Special (5/06, $3.99) WWII flashback with Bucky; Brubaker-s 4.00
...Streets of Poison ($15.95)-r/#372-378 16.00
...: The Movie Special nn (5/92, $3.50, 52 pgs.)-Adapts movie; printed on coated stock;
The Red Skull app. 3.50

NOTE: ***Austin*** *c-225i, 239i, 246i.* ***Buscema*** *a-115p, 217p; c-136p, 217, 297.* ***Byrne*** *c-223(part), 238, 239, 247p-254p, 290, 291, 313p; a-247-254p, 255, 313p, 350.* ***Colan*** *a(p)-116-137, 256, Annual 5; c(p)-116-123, 126, 129.* ***Everett*** *a-136i, 137i; c-126i.* ***Garney*** *a(p)-444-454.* ***Gil Kane*** *a-145p; c-147p, 149p, 150p, 170p, 172-174, 180, 181p, 183-190p, 215, 216, 220, 221.* ***Kirby*** *a(p)-100-109, 112, 193-214, 216, Special 1, 2(layouts), Annual 3, 4; c-100-109, 112, 126p, 193-214.* ***Ron Lim*** *a(p)-366, 368-378, 380-386; c-366p, 368-378p, 379, 380-393p.* ***Miller*** *c-241p, 244p, 245p, 255p, Annual 5.* ***Mooney*** *a-149i.* ***Morrow*** *a-144.* ***Perez*** *c-243p, 246p.* ***Robbins*** *c(p)-183-187, 189-192, 225.* ***Roussos*** *a-140i, 168i.* ***Shores*** *a-102i, 107i, 109i.* ***Starlin/Sinnott*** *c-162.* ***Sutton*** *a-244i.* ***Tuska*** *a-112i, 215p, Special 2.* ***Waid*** *scripts-444-454.* ***Williamson*** *a-313i.* ***Wood*** *a-127i.* ***Zeck*** *a-263-289; c-300.*

CAPTAIN AMERICA (Volume Two)
Marvel Comics: V2#1, Nov, 1996 - No. 13, Nov, 1997($2.95/$1.95/$1.99)
(Produced by Extreme Studios)

1-($2.95)-Heroes Reborn begins; Liefeld-c/a; Loeb scripts; reintro Nick Fury 6.00
1-($2.95)-(Variant-c)-Liefeld-c/a 6.00
1-(7/96, $2.95)-(Exclusive Comicon Ed.)-Liefeld-c/a. 1 2 3 5 6 8
2-11,13: 5-Two-c. 6-Cable-c/app. 13-"World War 3"-pt. 4, x-over w/Image 3.00
12-($2.99) "Heroes Reunited"-pt. 4 4.00
Heroes Reborn: Captain America (2006, $29.99, TPB) r/#1-12 & Heroes Reborn #1/2 30.00

CAPTAIN AMERICA (Vol. Three) (Also see Capt. America: Sentinel of Liberty)
Marvel Comics: Jan, 1998 - No. 50, Feb, 2002 ($2.99/$1.99/$2.25)

1-($2.99) Mark Waid-s/Ron Garney-a 4.00
1-Variant cover 6.00
2-($1.99): 2-Two covers 3.00
3-11: 3-Returns to old shield. 4-Hawkeye app. 5-Thor-c/app. 7-Andy Kubert-c/a begin.
9-New shield 2.50
12-($2.99) Battles Nightmare; Red Skull back-up story 3.50
13-17,19-Red Skull returns 2.50
18-($2.99) Cap vs. Korvac in the Future 3.00
20-24,26-29: 20,21-Sgt. Fury back-up story painted by Evans 2.50
25-($2.99) Cap & Falcon vs. Hatemonger 3.00
30-49: 30-Begin $2.25-c. 32-Ordway-a. 33-Jurgens-s/a begins; U.S. Agent app. 36-Maximum
Security x-over. 41,46-Red Skull app. 2.50
50-($5.95) Stories by various incl. Jurgens, Quitely, Immonen; Ha-c 6.00
.../Citizen V '98 Annual ($3.50) Busiek & Kesel-s 3.50
1999 Annual ($3.50) Flag Smasher app. 3.50
2000 Annual ($3.50) Continued from #35 vs. Protocide; Jurgens-s 3.50
2001 Annual ($2.99) Golden Age flashback; Invaders app. 3.00
...: To Serve and Protect TPB (2/02, $17.95) r/Vol. 3 #1-7 18.00

CAPTAIN AMERICA (Volume 4)
Marvel Comics: Jun, 2002 - No. 32, Dec, 2004 ($3.99/$2.99)

1-Ney Rieber-s/Cassaday-c/a 4.00
2-9-($2.99) 3-Cap reveals Steve Rogers ID. 7-9-Hairsine-a 3.00
10-32: 10-16-Jae Lee-a. 17-20-Gibbons-s/Weeks-a. 21-26-Bachalo-a. 26-Bucky flashback.
27,28-Eddie Campbell-a. 29-32-Red Skull app. 3.00
...Vol. 1: The New Deal HC (2003, $22.99) r/#1-6; foreward by Max Allan Collins 23.00
...Vol. 2: The Extremists TPB (2003, $13.99) r/#7-11; Cassaday-c 14.00
...Vol. 3: Ice TPB (2003, $12.99) r/#12-16; Jae Lee-a; Cassaday-c 13.00

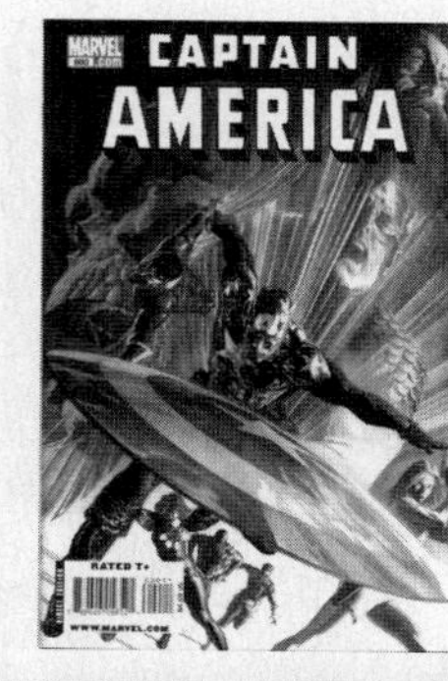

Captain America #600 © MAR

Captain America Comics #73 © MAR

Captain America: Reborn #1 © MAR

GD 2.0 | VG 4.0 | FN 6.0 | VF 8.0 | VF/NM 9.0 | NM- 9.2

...Vol. 4: Cap Lives TPB (2004, $12.99) r/#17-22 & Tales of Suspense #66 13.00
Avengers Disassembled: Captain America TPB (2004, $17.99) r/#29-32 and Captain America and the Falcon #5-7 18.00

CAPTAIN AMERICA
Marvel Comics: Jan, 2005 - Present ($2.99)

1-Brubaker-s/Epting-c/a; Red Skull app. 4.00
2-24: 10-House of M. 11-Origin of the Winter Soldier. 13-Iron Man app. 24-Civil War 3.00
6,8-Retailer variant covers 6.00
25-($3.99) Captain America shot dead; handcuffed red glove cover by Epting 10.00
25-($3.99) Variant edition with running Cap cover by McGuinness 12.00
25-($3.99) 2nd printing with "The Death of The Dream" cover by Epting 4.00
25 Director's Cut-($4.99) w/script with Brubaker commentary; pencil pages, variant and un-used covers gallery; article on media hype 5.00
26-33-Falcon & Winter Soldier app. 3.00
34-(3/08) Bucky becomes the new Captain America; Alex Ross-c 3.00
34-Variant-c by Steve Epting 3.00
34-($3.99) Director's Cut; includes script; pencil art, costume designs, cover gallery 4.00
34-DF Edition with Alex Ross portrait cover; signed by Ross 25.00
35-49-Bucky as Captain America. 43-45-Batroc app. 46,47-Sub-Mariner app. 3.00
50-(7/09, $3.99) Bucky's birthday flashbacks; Captain America's lifr synopsis; Martin-a 4.00
(After #50, numbering reverts to original with #600, Aug, 2009)
600-(8/09, $4.99) Covers by Ross and Epting; leads into Captain America: Reborn series; art by Guice, Chaykin, Ross, Eaglesham; commentary by Joe Simon; cover gallery 5.00
601-604-($3.99) 601-Gene Colan-a; 3 covers. 602-Nomad back-up feature begins 4.00
... By Ed Brubaker Omnibus Vol. 1 HC (2007, $74.99, dustjacket) r/#1-25; Capt. America 65th Anniv. Spec. and Winter Soldier: Winter Kills; Brubaker intro.; bonus material 75.00
Civil War: Captain America TPB (2007, $11.99) r/#22-24 & Winter Soldier: Winter Kills 12.00
...: Red Menace Vol. 1 SC (2006, $11.99) r/#15-17 and 65th Anniversary Special 12.00
...: Red Menace Vol. 2 SC (2006, $10.99) r/#18-21; Brubaker interview 11.00
... Theater of War: America First! (2/09, $3.99) 1950s era tale; Chaykin-s/a; reprints 4.00
... Theater of War: America the Beautiful (3/09, $4.99) WW2 tale; Jenkins-s/Erskine-a 5.00
... Theater of War: Operation Zero-Point (12/08, $3.99) WW2 tale; Breitweiser-a 4.00
...: The Death of Captan America Vol. 1 HC (2007, $19.99) r/#25-30; variant covers 20.00
...: The Death of Captan America Vol. 2 HC (2008, $19.99) r/#31-36; variant covers 20.00
...Vol. 1: Winter Soldier HC (2005, $21.99) r/#1-7; concept sketches 22.00
...Vol. 1: Winter Soldier SC (2006, $16.99) r/#1-7; concept sketches 17.00
...: Winter Soldier Vol. 2 HC (2006, $19.99) r/#8,9,11-14 20.00
...: Winter Soldier Vol. 2 SC (2006, $14.99) r/#8,9,11-14 15.00

CAPTAIN AMERICA AND THE FALCON
Marvel Comics: May, 2004 - No. 14, June, 2005 ($2.99, limited series)

1-4-Priest-s/Sears-a 3.00
5-14: 5-8-Avengers Disassembled x-over. 6,7-Scarlet Witch app. 8-12-Modok app. 3.00
... Vol. 1: Two Americas (2005, $9.99) r/#1-4 10.00
... Vol. 2: Brothers and Keepers (2005, $17.99) r/#8-14 18.00

CAPTAIN AMERICA COMICS
Timely/Marvel Comics (TCI 1-20/CmPS 21-68/MjMC 69-75/Atlas Comics (PrPI 76-78): Mar, 1941 - No. 75, Feb, 1950; No. 76, 5/54 - No. 78, 9/54
(No. 74 & 75 titled Capt. America's Weird Tales)

Issue	GD 2.0	VG 4.0	FN 6.0	VF 8.0	VF/NM 9.0	NM- 9.2
1-Origin & 1st app. Captain America & Bucky by S&K; Hurricane, Tuk the Caveboy begin by S&K; 1st app. Red Skull; Hitler-c (by Simon?); intro of the "Capt. America Sentinels of Liberty Club" (advertised on inside front-c.); indicia reads Vol. 2, Number 1	9100	18,200	27,300	63,700	132,500	215,000
2-S&K Hurricane; Tuk by Avison (Kirby splash); classic Hitler-c	1700	3400	5100	12,600	23,800	35,000
3-Classic Red Skull-c & app; Stan Lee's 1st text (1st work for Marvel)	1317	2634	3951	9800	18,400	27,000
4-Early use of full pg. panel in comic	865	1730	2595	6315	11,158	16,000
5	811	1622	2433	5920	10,460	15,000
6-Origin Father Time; Tuk the Caveboy ends	703	1406	2109	5132	9066	13,000
7-Red Skull app.; classic-c	773	1546	2319	5643	9972	14,300
8-10-Last S&K issue, (S&K centerfold #6-10)	541	1082	1623	3950	6975	10,000
11-Last Hurricane, Headline Hunter; Al Avison Captain America begins, ends #20; Avison-c(p)	438	876	1314	3197	5649	8100
12-The Imp begins, ends #16; last Father Time	423	846	1269	3067	5384	7700
13-Origin The Secret Stamp; classic-c	486	972	1458	3550	6275	9000
14,15	423	846	1269	3067	5384	7700
16-Red Skull unmasks Cap; Red Skull-c	541	1082	1623	3950	6975	10,000
17-The Fighting Fool only app.	383	766	1149	2681	4691	6700
18-Classic-c	400	800	1200	2800	4900	7000
19-Human Torch begins #19	337	674	1011	2359	4130	5900
20-Sub-Mariner app.; no H. Torch	331	662	993	2317	4059	5800
21-25: 25-Cap drinks liquid opium	314	628	942	2198	3849	5500
26-30: 27-Last Secret Stamp; last 68 pg. issue. 28-60 pg. issues begin.	303	606	909	2121	3711	5300
31-35,38-40: 34-Centerfold poster of Cap	297	594	891	1901	3251	4600
36-Classic Hitler-c	371	742	1113	2600	4550	6500
37-Red Skull app.	320	640	960	2240	3920	5600
41-45,47: 41-Last Japan War-c. 47-Last German War-c	236	472	708	1499	2575	3650
46-German Holocaust-c; classic	371	742	1113	2600	4550	6500
48-58,60	168	336	504	1075	1838	2600
59-Origin retold	314	628	942	2198	3849	5500
61-Red Skull-c/story	314	628	942	2198	3849	5500
62,64,65: 65-Kurtzman's "Hey Look"	213	426	639	1363	2332	3300
63-Intro/origin Asbestos Lady	219	438	657	1402	2401	3400
66-Bucky is shot; Golden Girl teams up with Captain America & learns his i.d; origin Golden Girl	277	554	831	1759	3030	4300
67-69: 67-Captain America/Golden Girl team-up; Mxyztplk swipe; last Toro in Human Torch. 68-Sub-Mariner/Namora, and Captain America/Golden Girl team-up. 69-Human Torch/Sun Girl team-up.	274	548	822	1740	2995	4250
70-73: 70-Sub-Mariner/Namora, and Captain America/Golden Girl team-up. 70-SciFi-c/story. 71-Anti Wertham editorial; The Witness, Bucky app.	290	580	870	1856	3178	4500
74-(Scarce)(10/49)-Titled "Captain America's Weird Tales"; Red Skull-c & app.; classic-c	811	1622	2433	5920	10,460	15,000
75(2/50)-Titled "C.A.'s Weird Tales"; no C.A. app.; horror cover/stories	290	580	870	1856	3178	4500
76-78(1954): Human Torch/Toro stories; all have communist-c/stories	152	304	456	965	1658	2350
132-Pg. Issue (B&W-1942)(Canadian)-Very rare. Has blank inside-c and back-c; contains Marvel Mystery #33 & Captain America #18 w/cover from Captain America #22; same contents as one version of the Marvel Mystery annuals	5500	11,000	16,500	33,000	-	-

NOTE: ***Crandall*** *a-2i, 3i, 9i, 10i.* ***Kirby*** *c-1, 2, 5-8p.* ***Rico*** *c-69-71.* ***Romita*** *c-77, 78.* ***Schomburg*** *c-3, 4, 26-29, 31, 33, 37-39, 41, 42, 45-54, 58.* ***Sekowsky*** *c-55, 56.* ***Shores*** *c-1i, 2i, 5-7i, 11i, 20-25, 30, 32, 34, 35, 40, 57, 59-67.* ***S&K*** *c-9, 10. Bondage c-3, 7, 15, 16, 34, 38.*

CAPTAIN AMERICA COMICS 70TH ANNIVERSARY SPECIAL
Marvel Comics: June, 2009 ($3.99, one-shot)

1-WWII flashback; Marcos Martin-a; Marcos-2 covers; r/Capt. America Comics #7 4.00

CAPTAIN AMERICA: DEAD MEN RUNNING
Marvel Comics: Mar, 2002 - No. 3, May, 2002 ($2.99, limited series)

1-3-Macan-s/Zezelj-a 3.00

CAPTAIN AMERICA/NICK FURY: BLOOD TRUCE
Marvel Comics: Feb, 1995 ($5.95, one-shot, squarebound)

nn-Chaykin story 6.00

CAPTAIN AMERICA/NICK FURY: THE OTHERWORLD WAR
Marvel Comics: Oct, 2001 ($6.95, one-shot, squarebound)

nn-Manco-a; Bucky and Red Skull app. 7.00

CAPTAIN AMERICA: REBORN (Titled Reborn in #1-3)
Marvel Comics: Sept, 2009 - No. 6, Mar, 2010 ($3.99, limited series)

1-6-Steve Rogers returns from the dead; Brubaker-s/Hitch & Guice-a. 1-Covers by Hitch, Ross & Quesada. 2-Origin re-told. 4-Joe Kubert var-c. 5-Cassaday var-c 4.00
1-4-Variant-c by Cassaday. 2-Variant-c by Sale. 5-Finch var-c 10.00
...: Who Will Wield the Shield? (2/10, $3.99) Aftermath of series; Guice & Luke Ross-a 4.00

CAPTAIN AMERICA: RED, WHITE & BLUE
Marvel Comics: Sept, 2002 ($29.99, one-shot, hardcover with dustjacket)

nn-Reprints from Lee & Kirby, Steranko, Miller and others; and new short stories and pin-ups by various incl. Ross, Dini, Timm, Waid, Dorkin, Sienkiewicz, Miller, Bruce Jones, Collins, Piers-Rayner, Pope, Deodato, Quitely, Nino; Stelfreeze-c 30.00
TPB (2007, $19.99) 20.00

CAPTAIN AMERICA, SENTINEL OF LIBERTY (See Fireside Book Series)

CAPTAIN AMERICA: SENTINEL OF LIBERTY
Marvel Comics: Sept, 1998 - No. 12, Aug, 1999 ($1.99)

1-Waid-s/Garney-a 3.00
1-Rough Cut ($2.99) Features original script and pencil pages 3.00
2-5: 2-Two-c; Invaders WW2 story 2.50
6-($2.99) Iron Man-c/app. 3.00
7-11: 8-Falcon-c/app. 9-Falcon poses as Cap 2.50
12-($2.99) Final issue; Bucky-c/app. 3.00

CAPTAIN AMERICA SPECIAL EDITION
Marvel Comics Group: Feb, 1984 - No. 2, Mar, 1984 ($2.00, Baxter paper)

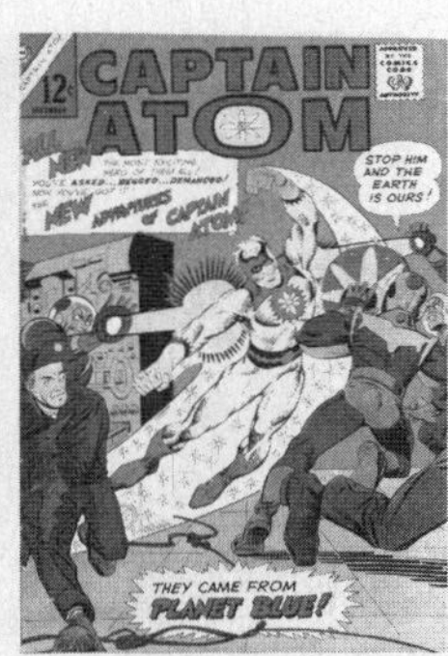

Captain Atom #78 © CC

Captain Britain #1 © MAR

Captain Carrot and His Amazing Zoo Crew #1 © DC

GD VG FN VF VF/NM NM-
2.0 4.0 6.0 8.0 9.0 9.2

GD VG FN VF VF/NM NM-
2.0 4.0 6.0 8.0 9.0 9.2

1-Steranko-c/a(r) in both; r/ Captain America #110,111 6.00
2-Reprints the scarce Our Love Story #5, and C.A. #113
1 2 3 5 6 8

CAPTAIN AMERICA THEATER OF WAR
Marvel Comics: 2009 - 2010 ($3.99, series of one-shots)
...: A Brother in Arms (6/09) Jenkins-s/McCrea-a; WWII story 4.00
...: Ghosts of My Country (12/09) Jenkins-s/Bonetti-a/Guice-c 4.00
...: Prisoners of Duty (2/10) Higgins & Siegel-s/Padilla-a; WWII story 4.00
...: To Soldier On (10/09) Jenkins-s/Blanco-a/Noto-c; Captain America in Iraq 4.00

CAPTAIN AMERICA: THE CHOSEN
Marvel Comics: Nov, 2007 - No. 6 ($3.99, limited series)
1-6-Breitweiser-a/Morrell-s 4.00

CAPTAIN AMERICA: THE CLASSIC YEARS
Marvel Comics: Jun, 1998 -No. 2 (trade paperbacks)
1-($19.95) Reprints Captain America Comics #1-5 25.00
2-($24.95) Reprints Captain America Comics #6-10 25.00

CAPTAIN AMERICA: THE LEGEND
Marvel Comics: Sept, 1996 ($3.95, one-shot)
1-Tribute issue; wraparound-c 4.00

CAPTAIN AMERICA: WHAT PRICE GLORY
Marvel Comics: May, 2003 - No. 4, May, 2003 ($2.99, weekly limited series)
1-4-Bruce Jones-s/Steve Rude & Mike Royer-a 3.00

CAPTAIN AMERICA: WHITE
Marvel Comics: No. 0, Sept, 2008 ($2.99, unfinished limited series)
0-Bucky's origin retold; Loeb-s/Sale-a; interviews with creators; Sale sketch art 3.00

CAPTAIN AND THE KIDS, THE (See Famous Comics Cartoon Books)

CAPTAIN AND THE KIDS, THE (See Comics on Parade, Katzenjammer Kids, Okay Comics & Sparkler Comics)
United Features Syndicate/Dell Publ. Co.: 1938 -12/39; Sum, 1947 - No. 32, 1955; Four Color No. 881, Feb, 1958
Single Series 1(1938) 97 194 291 621 1061 1500
Single Series 1(Reprint)(12/39- "Reprint" on-c) 48 96 144 302 514 725
1(Summer, 1947-UFS)-Katzenjammer Kids 17 34 51 98 154 210
2 11 22 33 60 83 105
3-10 9 18 27 52 69 85
11-20 8 16 24 42 54 65
21-32 (1955) 8 16 24 40 50 60
50th Anniversary issue-(1948)-Contains a 2 pg. history of the strip, including an account of the famous Supreme Court decision allowing both Pulitzer & Hearst to run the same strip under different names 15 30 45 94 147 200
Special Summer issue, Fall issue (1948) 11 22 33 60 83 105
Four Color 881 (Dell) 4 8 12 28 44 60

CAPTAIN ATOM
Nationwide Publishers: 1950 - No. 7, 1951 (5¢, 5x7-1/4", 52 pgs.)
1-Science fiction 41 82 123 256 428 600
2-7 22 44 66 132 216 300

CAPTAIN ATOM (Formerly Strange Suspense Stories #77)(Also see Space Adventures)
Charlton Comics: V2#78, Dec, 1965 - V2#89, Dec, 1967
V2#78-Origin retold; Bache-a (3 pgs.) 8 16 24 56 93 130
79-82: 79-1st app. Dr. Spectro; 3 pg. Ditko cut & paste /Space Adventures #24. 82-Intro. Nightshade (9/66) 6 12 18 37 59 80
83-86: Ted Kord Blue Beetle in all. 83-(11/66)-1st app. Ted Kord. 84-1st app. new Captain Atom 5 10 15 32 51 70
87-89: Nightshade by Aparo in all 5 10 15 32 51 70
83-85(Modern Comics-1977)-reprints 1 2 3 4 5 7
NOTE: *Aparo a-87-89. Ditko c/a(p) 78-89. #90 only published in fanzine 'The Charlton Bullseye' #1, 2.*

CAPTAIN ATOM (Also see Americomics & Crisis On Infinite Earths)
DC Comics: Mar, 1987 - No. 57, Sept, 1991 (Direct sales only #35 on)
1-(44 pgs.)-Origin/1st app. with new costume 4.00
2-49: 5-Firestorm x-over. 6-Intro. new Dr. Spectro. 11-Millennium tie-in. 14-Nightshade app. 16-Justice League app. 17-$1.00-c begins; Swamp Thing app. 20-Blue Beetle x-over. 24,25-Invasion tie-in 2.50
51-57: 50-($2.00, 52 pgs.). 57-War of the Gods x-over 2.50
Annual 1,2 ('88, '89)-1-Intro Major Force 3.00

CAPTAIN ATOM: ARMAGEDDON (Restarts the WildStorm Universe)
DC Comics (WildStorm): Dec, 2005 - No. 9, Aug, 2006 ($2.99, limited series)
1-9-Captain Atom appears in WildStorm Universe; Pfeifer-s/Camuncoli-a. 1-Lee-c 3.00
TPB (2007, $19.99) r/series 20.00

CAPTAIN BATTLE (Boy Comics #3 on) (See Silver Streak Comics)
New Friday Publ./Comic House: Summer, 1941 - No. 2, Fall, 1941
1-Origin Blackout by Rico; Captain Battle begins (1st appeared in Silver Streak #10, 5/41) 145 290 435 921 1586 2250
2 81 162 243 518 884 1250

CAPTAIN BATTLE (2nd Series)
Magazine Press/Picture Scoop No. 5: No. 3, Wint, 1942-43; No. 5, Sum, 1943 (No #4)
3-Origin Silver Streak-r/SS#3; origin Lance Hale-r/Silver Streak; Simon-a(r) (52 pgs., nd) 71 142 213 454 777 1100
5-Origin Blackout retold (68 pgs.) 50 100 150 315 533 750

CAPTAIN BATTLE, JR.
Comic House (Lev Gleason): Fall, 1943 - No. 2, Winter, 1943-44
1-The Claw vs. The Ghost 135 270 405 864 1482 2100
2-Wolverton's Scoop Scuttle; Don Rico-c/a; The Green Claw story is reprinted from Silver Streak #6; bondage/torture-c 81 162 243 518 884 1250

CAPTAIN BEN DIX (See Promotional Comics section)

CAPTAIN BRITAIN (Also see Marvel Team-Up No. 65, 66)
Marvel Comics International: Oct. 13, 1976 - No. 39, July 6, 1977 (Weekly)
1-Origin; with Capt. Britain's face mask inside 2 4 6 11 16 20
2-Origin, part II; Capt. Britain's Boomerang inside 2 4 6 8 11 14
3-11: 3,8-Vs. Bank Robbers. 4-7-Vs. Hurricane. 9-11: Vs. Dr. Synne 1 2 3 4 5 7
12-23,25-27: (scarce)-12,13-Vs. Dr. Synne. 14,15-Vs. Mastermind. 16-23,25,26-With Captain America. 17-Misprinted & color section reprinted in #18. 27-Origin retold 2 4 6 9 13 16
24-With C.B.'s Jet Plane inside 2 4 6 11 16 20
28-32,36-39: 28-32-Vs. Lord Hawk. 37-39-Vs. Highwayman & Munipulator 4.00
33-35-More on origin 4.50
Annual (1978, Hardback, 64 pgs.)-Reprints #1-7 with pin-ups of Marvel characters 2 4 6 10 14 18
Summer Special (1980, 52 pgs.)-Reprints 6.00
NOTE: *No. 1, 2, & 24 are rarer in mint due to inserts. Distributed in Great Britain only. Nick Fury-r by* ***Steranko*** *in 1-20, 24-31, 35-37. Fantastic Four-r by* ***J. Buscema*** *in all. New* ***Buscema****-a in 24-30. Story from No. 39 continues in Super Spider-Man (British weekly) No. 231-247. Following cancellation of his series, new Captain Britain stories appeared in "Super Spider-Man" (British weekly) No. 231-247. Captain Britain stories which appear in Super-Spider-Man No 248-253 are reprints of Marvel Team-Up No. 65&66. Capt. Britain strips also appeared in Hulk Comic (weekly) 1, 3-30, 42-55, 57-60, in Marvel Superheroes (monthly) 377-388, in Daredevils (monthly) 1-11, Mighty World of Marvel (monthly) 7-16 & Captain Britain (monthly) 1-14. Issues 1-23 have B&W & color, paper-c, & are 32 pgs. Issues 24 on are all B&W w/glossy-c & are 36 pgs.*

CAPTAIN BRITAIN AND MI: 13 (Also see Secret Invasion x-over titles)
Marvel Comics: Jul, 2008 - No. 15, Sept, 2009 ($2.99)
1-Skrull invasion; Black Knight app.; Kirk-a 4.00
1-2nd printing with Kirk variant-c; 3rd printing with B&W cover 3.00
2-15: 5-Blade app. 9,10-Dracula app. 3.00
... Annual 1 (8/09, $3.99) Land-c; Meggan in Hell; Dr. Doom cameo; Collins-a 4.00

CAPTAIN CANUCK
Comely Comix (Canada)(All distr. in U. S.): 7/75 - No. 4, 7/77; No. 4, 7-8/79 - No. 14, 3-4/81
1-1st app. Bluefox 5.00
2,3(5-7/76)-2-1st app. Dr. Walker, Redcoat & Kebec. 3-1st app. Heather 4.00
4(1st printing-2/77)-10x14-1/2"; (5.00); B&W; 300 copies serially numbered and signed with one certificate of authenticity 7 14 21 49 80 110
4(2nd printing-7/77)-11x17", B&W; only 15 copies printed; signed by creator Richard Comely, serially #'d and two certificates of authenticity inserted; orange cardboard covers (Very Rare) 10 20 30 72 126 180
4-14: 4(7-8/79)-1st app. Tom Evans & Mr. Gold; origin The Catman. 5-Origin Capt. Canuck's powers; 1st app. Earth Patrol & Chaos Corps. 8-Jonn 'The Final Chapter'. 9-1st World Beyond. 11-1st 'Chariots of Fire' story 4.00
15-(8/04, $15.00) Limited edition of unpublished issue from 1981; serially #'d edition of 150; signed by creator Richard Comely 4 8 12 24 37 50
... Legacy 1 (9-10/06) Comely-s/a 3.00
... Legacy Special Edition ($7.95, 52 pgs., limited ed. of 1000) Comely-s/a 1 2 3 5 6 8
Special Collectors Pack (polybagged) 1 3 4 6 8 10
Summer Special 1(7-9/80, 95¢, 64 pgs.) 4.00
NOTE: *30,000 copies of No. 2 were destroyed in Winnipeg.*

CAPTAIN CANUCK: UNHOLY WAR
Comely Comix: Oct, 2004 - No. 3 ($2.50, limited series)
1-Riel Langlois-s/Drue Langlois-a 2.50

CAPTAIN CARROT AND HIS AMAZING ZOO CREW (Also see New Teen Titans &

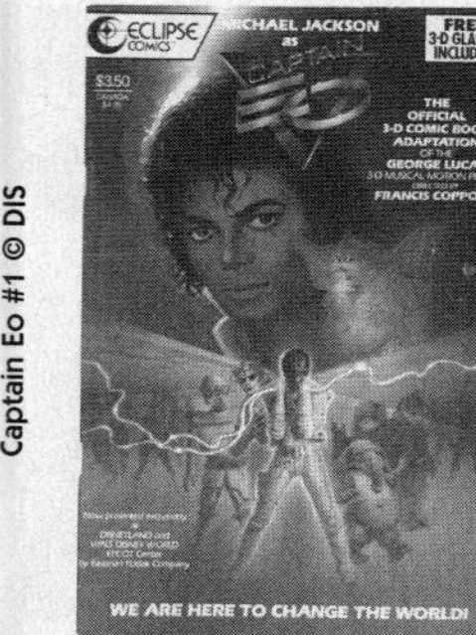

Captain Eo #1 © DIS

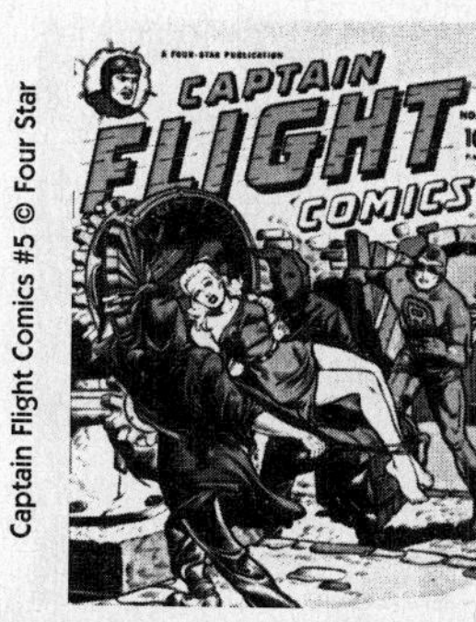

Captain Flight Comics #5 © Four Star

Captain Marvel #8 © MAR

GD 2.0 | VG 4.0 | FN 6.0 | VF 8.0 | VF/NM 9.0 | NM- 9.2

Oz-Wonderland War)
DC Comics: Mar, 1982 - No. 20, Nov, 1983

1-20: 1-Superman app. 3-Re-intro Dodo & The Frog. 9-Re-intro Three Mouseketeers, the Terrific Whatzit. 10,11-Pig Iron reverts back to Peter Porkchops. 20-Changeling app. 3.00

CAPTAIN CARROT AND THE FINAL ARK (DC Countdown tie-in)
DC Comics: Dec, 2007 - No. 3, Feb, 2008 ($2.99, limited series)

1-3-Bill Morrison-s/Scott Shaw!-a. 3-Batman, Red Arrow, Hawkgirl & Zatanna app. 3.00
TPB (2008, $19.99) r/#1-3; Captain Carrot and His Amazing Zoo Crew #1,14,15; New Teen Titans #16 and stories from Teen Titans (2003 series) #30,31; cover gallery 20.00

CAPTAIN CARVEL AND HIS CARVEL CRUSADERS (See Carvel Comics)

CAPTAIN CONFEDERACY
Marvel Comics (Epic Comics): Nov, 1991 - No. 4, Feb, 1992 ($1.95)

1-4: All new stories 2.50

CAPTAIN COURAGEOUS COMICS (Banner #3-5; see Four Favorites #5)
Periodical House (Ace Magazines): No. 6, March, 1942

6-Origin & 1st app. The Sword; Lone Warrior, Capt. Courageous app.; Capt. moves to Four Favorites #5 in May 77 154 231 493 847 1200

CAPT'N CRUNCH COMICS (See Cap'n...)

CAPTAIN DAVY JONES
Dell Publishing Co.: No. 598, Nov, 1954

Four Color 598 5 10 15 30 48 65

CAPTAIN EASY (See The Funnies & Red Ryder #3-32)
Hawley/Dell Publ./Standard(Visual Editions)/Argo: 1939 - No. 17, Sept, 1949; April, 1956

nn-Hawley(1939)-Contains reprints from The Funnies & 1938 Sunday strips by Roy Crane 89 178 267 565 970 1375
Four Color 24 (1943) 50 100 150 315 533 750
Four Color 111(6/46) 13 26 39 93 172 250
10(Standard-10/47) 13 26 39 72 101 130
11,12,14,15,17: 11-17 all contain 1930s & '40s strip-r 10 20 30 54 72 90
13,16: Schomburg-c 11 22 33 62 86 110
Argo 1(4/56)-Reprints 7 14 21 37 46 55

CAPTAIN EASY & WASH TUBBS (See Famous Comics Cartoon Books)

CAPTAIN ELECTRON
Brick Computer Science Institute: Aug, 1986 ($2.25)

1-Disbrow-a 2.50

CAPTAIN EO 3-D (Michael Jackson Disney theme parks movie)
Eclipse Comics: July, 1987 (Eclipse 3-D Special #18, $3.50, Baxter)

1-Adapts 3-D movie; Michael Jackson-c/app. 6.00
1-2-D limited edition 2 4 6 9 12 15
1-Large size (11x17", 8/87)-Sold only at Disney Theme parks ($6.95) 3 6 9 14 20 25

CAPTAIN FEARLESS COMICS (Also see Holyoke One-Shot #6, Old Glory Comics & Silver Streak #1)
Helnit Publishing Co. (Holyoke Publ. Co.): Aug, 1941 - No. 2, Sept, 1941

1-Origin Mr. Miracle, Alias X, Captain Fearless, Citizen Smith Son of the Unknown Soldier; Miss Victory (1st app.) begins (1st patriotic heroine? before Wonder Woman) 84 168 252 538 919 1300
2-Grit Grady, Captain Stone app. 50 100 150 315 533 750

CAPTAIN FLAG (See Blue Ribbon Comics #16)

CAPTAIN FLASH
Sterling Comics: Nov, 1954 - No. 4, July, 1955

1-Origin; Sekowsky-a; Tomboy (female super hero) begins; only pre-code issue; atomic rocket-c 39 78 117 240 395 550
2-4: 4-Flying saucer invasion-c 22 44 66 128 209 290

CAPTAIN FLEET (Action Packed Tales of the Sea)
Ziff-Davis Publishing Co.: Fall, 1952

1-Painted-c 15 30 45 88 137 185

CAPTAIN FLIGHT COMICS
Four Star Publications: Mar, 1944 - No. 10, Dec, 1945; No. 11, Feb-Mar, 1947

nn 44 88 132 277 469 660
2-4: 4-Rock Raymond begins, ends #7 25 50 75 150 245 340
5-Bondage, classic torture-c; Red Rocket begins; the Grenade app. (scarce) 115 230 345 730 1253 1775
6 24 48 72 140 230 320
7-10: 7-L. B. Cole covers begin, end #11. 8-Yankee Girl begins; intro. Black Cobra & Cobra Kid & begins. 9-Torpedoman app.; last Yankee Girl; Kinstler-a. 10-Deep Sea Dawson, Zoom of the Jungle, Rock Raymond, Red Rocket, & Black Cobra app; bondage-c 52 104 156 322 549 775
11-Torpedoman, Blue Flame (Human Torch clone) app.; last Black Cobra, Red Rocket; classic L. B. Cole robot-c (scarce) 161 322 483 1030 1765 2500

CAPTAIN GALLANT (...of the Foreign Legion) (TV) (Texas Rangers in Action No. 5 on?)
Charlton Comics: 1955; No. 2, Jan, 1956 - No. 4, Sept, 1956

Non-Heinz version (#1)-Buster Crabbe photo on-c; full page Buster Crabbe photo inside front-c 8 16 24 44 57 70
(Heinz version is listed in the Promotional Comics section)
2-4: Buster Crabbe in all 6 12 18 31 38 45

CAPTAIN GLORY
Topps Comics: Apr, 1993 ($2.95) (Created by Jack Kirby)

1-Polybagged w/Kirbychrome trading card; Ditko-a & Kirby-c; has coupon for Amberchrome Secret City Saga #0 3.00

CAPTAIN HERO (See Jughead as...)

CAPTAIN HERO COMICS DIGEST MAGAZINE
Archie Publications: Sept, 1981

1-Reprints of Jughead as Super-Guy 2 4 6 10 14 18

CAPTAIN HOBBY COMICS
Export Publication Ent. Ltd. (Dist. in U.S. by Kable News Co.): Feb, 1948 (Canadian)

1 8 16 24 40 50 60

CAPT. HOLO IN 3-D (See Blackthorne 3-D Series #65)

CAPTAIN HOOK & PETER PAN (Movie)(Disney)
Dell Publishing Co.: No. 446, Jan, 1953

Four Color 446 9 18 27 60 100 140

CAPTAIN JET (Fantastic Fears No. 7 on)
Four Star Publ./Farrell/Comic Media: May, 1952 - No. 5, Jan, 1953

1-Bakerish-a 22 44 66 132 216 300
2 14 28 42 80 115 150
3-5,6(?) 12 24 36 67 94 120

CAPTAIN JOHNER & THE ALIENS
Valiant: May, 1995 - No. 2, May, 1995 ($2.95, shipped in same month)

1,2: Reprints Magnus Robot Fighter 4000 A.D. back-up stories; new Paul Smith-c 3.00

CAPTAIN JUSTICE (TV)
Marvel Comics: Mar, 1988 - No. 2, Apr, 1988 (limited series)

1,2-Based on the 1987 "Once a Hero" television series 2.50

CAPTAIN KANGAROO (TV)
Dell Publishing Co.: No. 721, Aug, 1956 - No. 872, Jan, 1958

Four Color 721 (#1)-Photo-c 15 30 45 104 197 290
Four Color 780, 872-Photo-c 12 24 36 88 162 235

CAPTAIN KIDD (Formerly Dagar; My Secret Story #26 on)(Also see Comic Comics & Fantastic Comics)
Fox Feature Syndicate: No. 24, June, 1949 - No. 25, Aug, 1949

24,25: 24-Features Blackbeard the Pirate 15 30 45 83 124 165

CAPTAIN MARVEL (See All Hero, All-New Collectors' Ed., America's Greatest, Fawcett Miniature, Gift, JSA, Kingdom Come, Legends, Limited Collectors' Ed., Marvel Family, Master No. 21, Mighty Midget Comics, Power of Shazam!, Shazam, Special Edition Comics, Whiz, Wisco (in Promotional Comics section), World's Finest #253 and XMas Comics)

CAPTAIN MARVEL (Becomes ...Presents the Terrible 5 No. 5)
M. F. Enterprises: April, 1966 - No. 4, Nov, 1966 (25¢ Giants)

nn-(#1 on pg. 5)-Origin; created by Carl Burgos 5 10 15 30 48 65
2-4: 3-(#3 on pg. 4)-Fights the Bat 3 6 9 20 30 40

CAPTAIN MARVEL (Marvel's Space-Born Super-Hero! Captain Marvel #1-6; see Giant-Size..., Life Of..., Marvel Graphic Novel #1, Marvel Spotlight V2#1 & Marvel Super-Heroes #12)
Marvel Comics Group: May, 1968 - No. 19, Dec, 1969; No. 20, June, 1970 - No. 21, Aug, 1970; No. 22, Sept, 1972 - No. 62, May, 1979

1 13 26 39 93 172 250
2-Super Skrull-c/story 6 12 18 43 69 95
3-5: 4-Captain Marvel battles Sub-Mariner 5 10 15 34 55 75
6-11: 11-Capt. Marvel given great power by Zo the Ruler; Smith/Trimpe-c; Death of Una 4 8 12 22 34 45
12,13,15-20: 16,17-New costume 3 6 9 16 22 28
14,21: 14-Capt. Marvel vs. Iron Man; last 12¢ issue. 21-Capt. Marvel battles Hulk; last 15¢ issue 4 8 12 22 34 45
22-24 3 6 9 14 19 24
25,26: 25-Starlin-c/a begins; Starlin's 1st Thanos saga begins (3/73), ends #34; Thanos

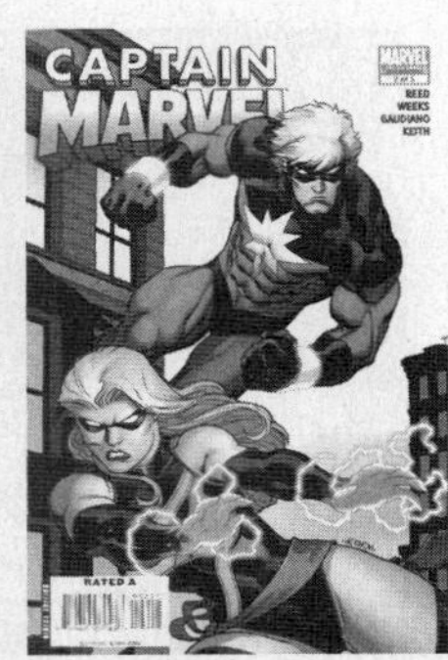

Captain Marvel V5 #2 © MAR

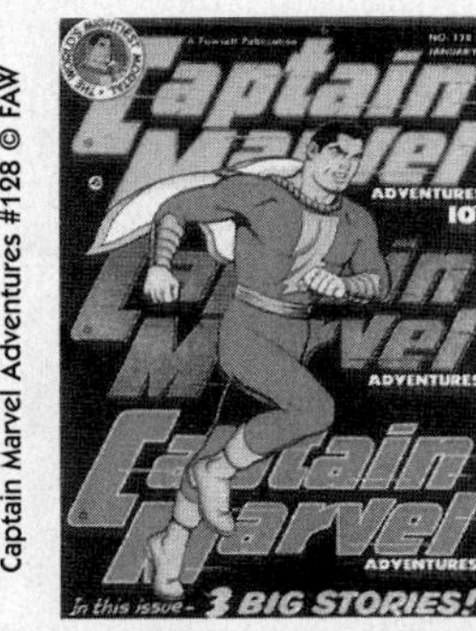

Captain Marvel Adventures #128 © FAW

Captain Marvel, Jr. #10 © FAW

GD VG FN VF VF/NM NM-
2.0 4.0 6.0 8.0 9.0 9.2

GD VG FN VF VF/NM NM-
2.0 4.0 6.0 8.0 9.0 9.2

cameo (5 panels). 26-Minor Thanos app. (see Iron Man #55); 1st Thanos-c
5 10 15 30 48 65
27,28-2nd & 3rd app. Thanos. 28-Thanos-c/s 4 8 12 24 37 50
29,30-Thanos cameos. 29-C.M. gains more powers 3 6 9 17 25 32
31,32: Thanos app. 31-Last 20¢ issue. 32-Thanos-c 3 6 9 18 27 35
33-Thanos-c & app.; Capt. Marvel battles Thanos; Thanos origin re-told
4 8 12 24 37 50
34-1st app. Nitro; C.M. contracts cancer which eventually kills him; last Starlin-c/a
3 6 9 17 25 32
35,37-40,42,46-48,50,53-56,58-62: 39-Origin Watcher. 58-Thanos cameo
2 4 6 8 10 12
36,41,43,49: 36-R-origin/1st app. Capt. Marvel from Marvel Super-Heroes #12. 41,43-Wrightson part inks; #43-c(i). 49-Starlin & Weiss-p assists
2 4 6 8 11 14
44,45-(Regular 25¢ editions)(5,7/76) 2 4 6 8 10 12
44,45-(30¢-c variants, limited distribution) 4 8 12 28 44 60
51,52-(Regular 30¢ editions)(7,9/77) 2 4 6 8 10 12
51,52-(35¢-c variants, limited distribution) 5 10 15 32 51 70
57-Thanos appears in flashback 2 4 6 9 12 15

NOTE: *Alcala a-35. Austin a-46i, 49-53i; c-52i. Buscema a-18p-21p. Colan a(p)-1-4; c(p)-1-4, 8, 9. Heck a-5-10p, 16p. Gil Kane a-17-21p; c-17-24p, 37p, 53. Starlin a-36. McWilliams a-40i. #25-34 were reprinted in The Life of Captain Marvel.*

CAPTAIN MARVEL
Marvel Comics: Nov, 1989 ($1.50, one-shot, 52 pgs.)

1-Super-hero from Avengers; new powers 3.00

CAPTAIN MARVEL
Marvel Comics: Feb, 1994 ($1.75, 52 pgs.)

1-(Indicia reads Vol 2 #2)-Minor Captain America app. 2.50

CAPTAIN MARVEL
Marvel Comics: Dec, 1995 - No. 6, May, 1996 ($2.95/$1.95)

1 ($2.95)-Advs. of Mar-Vell's son begins; Fabian Nicieza scripts; foil-c 3.50
2-6: 2-Begin $1.95-c 2.50

CAPTAIN MARVEL (Vol. 3) (See Avengers Forever)
Marvel Comics: Jan, 2000 - No. 35, Oct, 2002 ($2.50)

1-Peter David-s in all; two covers 4.00
2-10: 2-Two covers; Hulk app. 9-Silver Surfer app. 3.00
11-35: 12-Maximum Security x-over. 17,18-Starlin-a. 27-30-Spider-Man 2099 app. 2.50
Wizard #0-Preview and history of Rick Jones 4.00
...: First Contact (8/01, $16.95, TPB) r/#0,1-6 17.00

CAPTAIN MARVEL (Vol. 4) (See Avengers Forever)
Marvel Comics: Nov, 2002 - No. 25, Sept, 2004 ($2.25/$2.99)

1-Peter David-s/Chriscross-a ; 3 covers by Ross, Jusko & Chriscross 3.00
2-7: 2,3-Punisher app. 3-Alex Ross-c; new costume debuts. 4-Noto-c. 7-Thor app. 2.50
3-Sketchbook Edition-($3.50) includes Ross' concept design pages for new costume 3.50
8-25: 8-Begin $2.99-c; Thor app.; Manco-c. 10-Spider-Man-c/app. 15-Neal Adams-c 3.00
Vol. 1: Nothing To Lose (2003, $14.99, TPB) r/#1-6 15.00
Vol. 2: Coven (2003, $14.99, TPB) r/#7-12 15.00
Vol. 3: Crazy Like a Fox (2004, $14.99, TPB) r/#13-18 15.00
Vol. 4: Odyssey (2004, $16.99, TPB) r/#19-25 17.00

CAPTAIN MARVEL (Vol. 5) (See Secret Invasion x-over titles)
Marvel Comics: Jan, 2008 - No. 5, Jun, 2008 ($2.99)

1-5-Mar-Vell "from the past in the present"; McGuinness-c/Weeks-a 3.00
3,4-Skrull variant-c 4.00

CAPTAIN MARVEL ADVENTURES (See Special Edition Comics for pre #1)
Fawcett Publications: 1941 (March) - No. 150, Nov, 1953 (#1 on stands 1/16/41)

nn(#1)-Captain Marvel & Sivana by Jack Kirby. The cover was printed on unstable paper stock and is rarely found in Fine or Mint condition; blank back inside-c
2900 5800 8700 22,000 38,500 55,000
2-(Advertised as #3, which was counting Special Edition Comics as the real #1); Tuska-a 423 846 1269 3000 5250 7500
3-Metallic silver-c 300 600 900 1950 3375 4800
4-Three Lt. Marvels app. 206 412 618 1318 2259 3200
5 161 322 483 1030 1765 2500
6-10: 9-1st Otto Binder scripts on Capt. Marvel 123 246 369 787 1344 1900
11-15: 12-Capt. Marvel joins the Army. 13-Two pg. Capt. Marvel pin-up. 15-Comic cards on back-c begin, end #26 94 188 282 597 1024 1450
16,17: 17-Painted-c 89 178 267 565 970 1375
18-Origin & 1st app. Mary Marvel & Marvel Family (12/11/42); painted-c; Mary Marvel by Marcus Swayze 248 496 744 1575 2713 3850
19-Mary Marvel x-over; Christmas-c 76 152 228 486 831 1175
20,21,23-Attached to the cover, each has a miniature comic just like the Mighty Midget Comics #11, except that each has a full color promo ad on the back cover. Most copies were circulated without the miniature comic. These issues with miniatures attached are very rare, and should not be mistaken for copies with the similar Mighty Midget glued in its place. The Mighty Midgets had blank back covers except for a small victory stamp seal. Only the Capt. Marvel, Captain Marvel Jr. and Golden Arrow No. 11 miniatures have been positively documented as having been affixed to these covers. Each miniature was only partially glued by its back cover to the Captain Marvel comic making it easy to see if it's the genuine miniature rather than a Mighty Midget.
with comic attached.... 366 732 1098 2562 4481 6400
20,23-Without miniature 68 136 204 432 746 1060
21-Without miniature; Hitler-c 116 232 348 742 1271 1800
22-Mr. Mind serial begins; Mr. Mind first heard 95 190 285 603 1039 1475
24,25 67 134 201 425 730 1035
26-28,30: 26-Flag-c; subtle Mr. Mind 2-panel cameo. 27-1st full Mr. Mind app. (his voice was only heard over the radio before now) (9/43) 55 110 165 352 601 850
29-1st Mr. Mind-c (11/43) 58 116 174 371 636 900
31-35: 35-Origin Radar (5/44, see Master #50) 49 98 147 309 522 735
36-40: 37-Mary Marvel x-over 46 92 138 290 488 685
41-46: 42-Christmas-c. 43-Capt. Marvel 1st meets Uncle Marvel; Mary Batson cameo. 46-Mr. Mind serial ends 39 78 117 240 395 550
47-50 37 74 111 222 361 500
51-53,55-60: 51-63-Bi-weekly issues. 52-Origin & 1st app. Sivana Jr.; Capt. Marvel Jr. x-over
32 64 96 190 310 430
54-Special oversize 68 pg. issue 33 66 99 194 317 440
61-The Cult of the Curse serial begins 34 68 102 205 335 465
62-65-Serial cont.; Mary Marvel x-over in #65 32 64 96 190 310 430
66-Serial ends; Atomic War-c 37 74 111 218 354 490
67-77,79: 69-Billy Batson's Christmas; Uncle Marvel, Mary Marvel, Capt. Marvel Jr. x-over. 71-Three Lt. Marvels app. 79-Origin Mr. Tawny 29 58 87 172 281 390
78-Origin Mr. Atom 33 66 99 194 317 440
80-Origin Capt. Marvel retold 66 132 198 419 722 1025
81-84,86-90: 81,90-Mr. Atom app. 82-Infinity-c. 82,86,88,90-Mr. Tawny app.
27 54 81 160 263 365
85-Freedom Train issue 32 64 96 188 307 425
91-99: 92-Mr. Tawny app. 96-Gets 1st name "Tawky" 26 52 78 156 256 355
100-Origin retold; silver metallic-c 47 94 141 296 498 700
101-115,117-120 26 52 78 154 252 350
116-Flying Saucer issue (1/51) 30 60 90 177 289 400
121-Origin retold 34 68 102 204 332 460
122-137,139,140 26 52 78 154 252 350
138-Flying Saucer issue (11/52) 30 60 90 177 289 400
141-Pre-code horror story "The Hideous Head-Hunter"
28 56 84 165 270 375
142-149: 142-used in **POP**, pgs. 92,96 27 54 81 160 263 365
150-(Low distribution) 48 96 144 302 514 725

NOTE: *Swayze a-12, 14, 15, 18, 19, 40; c-12, 15, 19.*

CAPTAIN MARVEL AND THE GOOD HUMOR MAN (Movie)
Fawcett Publications: 1950

nn-Partial photo-c w/Jack Carson & the Captain Marvel Club Boys
47 94 141 296 498 700

CAPTAIN MARVEL COMIC STORY PAINT BOOK (See Comic Story...)

CAPTAIN MARVEL, JR. (See Fawcett Miniatures, Marvel Family, Master Comics, Mighty Midget Comics, Shazam & Whiz Comics)

CAPTAIN MARVEL, JR.
Fawcett Publications: Nov, 1942 - No. 119, June, 1953 (No #34)

1-Origin Capt. Marvel Jr. retold (Whiz #25); Capt. Nazi app. Classic Raboy-c
551 1102 1653 4022 7111 10,200
2-Vs. Capt. Nazi; origin Capt. Nippon 200 400 600 1280 2190 3100
3 113 226 339 718 1234 1750
4-Classic Raboy-c 119 238 357 762 1306 1850
5-Vs. Capt. Nazi 95 190 285 603 1039 1475
6-8: 8-Vs. Capt. Nazi 79 158 237 502 864 1225
9-Classic flag-c 86 172 258 546 936 1325
10-Hitler-c 123 246 369 787 1344 1900
11,12,15-Capt. Nazi app. 67 134 201 426 731 1035
13-Classic Hitler, Tojo and Mussolini football-c 123 246 369 787 1344 1900
14,16-20: 14-X-Mas-c. 16-Capt. Marvel & Sivana x-over. 19-Capt. Nazi & Capt. Nippon app.
55 110 165 349 605 860
21-30: 25-Flag-c 45 90 135 284 480 675
31-33,36-40: 37-Infinity-c 32 64 96 188 307 425
35-#34 on inside; cover shows origin of Sivana Jr. which is not on inside. Evidently the cover to #35 was printed out of sequence and bound with contents to #34
32 64 96 188 307 425
41-70: 42-Robot-c. 53-Atomic Bomb-c/story 26 52 78 154 252 350
71-99,101-104: 87-Robot-c. 104-Used in **POP**, pg. 89

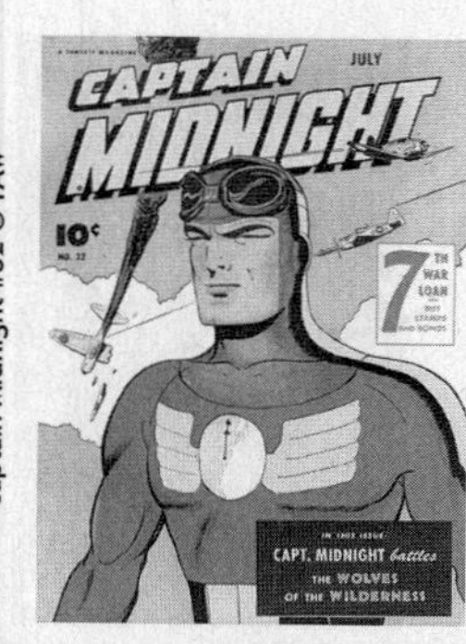

Captain Midnight #32 © FAW

Captain Science #6 © YM

Capt. Storm #15 © DC

GD VG FN VF VF/NM NM-
2.0 4.0 6.0 8.0 9.0 9.2

21 42 63 122 199 275
100 24 48 72 142 234 325
105-114,116-118: 116-Vampira, Queen of Terror app.
20 40 60 120 195 270
115-Injury to eye-c; Eyeball story w/injury-to-eye panels
50 100 150 315 533 750
119-Electric chair-c (scarce) 55 110 165 347 586 825
NOTE: *Mac Raboy c-1-28, 30-32, 57, 59 among others.*

CAPTAIN MARVEL PRESENTS THE TERRIBLE FIVE
M. F. Enterprises: Aug, 1966; V2#5, Sept, 1967 (No #2-4) (25¢)
1 4 8 12 28 44 60
V2#5-(Formerly Captain Marvel) 3 6 9 18 27 35

CAPTAIN MARVEL'S FUN BOOK
Samuel Lowe Co.: 1944 (1/2" thick) (cardboard covers)(25¢)
nn-Puzzles, games, magic, etc.; infinity-c 37 74 111 218 354 490

CAPTAIN MARVEL SPECIAL EDITION (See Special Edition)

CAPTAIN MARVEL STORY BOOK
Fawcett Publications: Summer, 1946 - No. 4, Summer?, 1948
1-Half text 52 104 156 322 549 775
2-4 37 74 111 222 361 500

CAPTAIN MARVEL THRILL BOOK (Large-Size)
Fawcett Publications: 1941 (B&W w/color-c)
1-Reprints from Whiz #8,10, & Special Edition #1 (Rare)
300 600 900 3000 - -
NOTE: *Rarely found in Fine or Mint condition.*

CAPTAIN MIDNIGHT (TV, radio, films) (See The Funnies, Popular Comics & Super Book of Comics)(Becomes Sweethearts No. 68 on)
Fawcett Publications: Sept, 1942 - No. 67, Fall, 1948 (#1-14: 68 pgs.)
1-Origin Captain Midnight, star of radio and movies; Captain Marvel cameo on cover
300 600 900 2070 3635 5200
2-Smashes the Jap Juggarnaut 135 270 405 864 1482 2100
3-Classic Nazi war-c 126 252 378 806 1378 1950
4,5: 4-Grapples the Gremlins 107 214 321 680 1165 1650
6-8 65 130 195 416 708 1000
9-Raboy-c 67 134 201 426 731 1035
10-Raboy Flag-c 68 136 204 432 746 1060
11-20: 11,17,18-Raboy-c. 16 (1/44) 48 96 144 302 514 725
21-Classic WWII-c 50 100 150 315 533 750
22,25-30: 22-War savings stamp-c 40 80 120 246 411 575
23-WWII Concentration Camp-c 47 94 141 296 498 700
24-Japan flag sunburst-c 53 106 159 334 567 800
31-40 31 62 93 182 296 410
41-59,61-67: 50-Sci/fi theme begins? 23 46 69 136 223 310
60-Flying Saucer issue (2/48)-3rd of this theme; see The Spirit 9/28/47(1st), Shadow Comics V7#10 (2nd, 1/48) & Boy Commandos #26 (4th, 3-4/48)
34 68 102 199 325 450

CAPTAIN NICE (TV)
Gold Key: Nov, 1967 (one-shot)
1(10211-711)-Photo-c 6 12 18 43 69 95

CAPTAIN N: THE GAME MASTER (TV)
Valiant Comics: 1990 - No. 6? ($1.95, thick stock, coated-c)
1-6: 4-6-Layton-c 3.00

CAPTAIN PARAGON (See Bill Black's Fun Comics)
Americomics: Dec, 1983 - No. 4, 1985
1-Intro/1st app. Ms. Victory 4.00
2-4 3.00

CAPTAIN PARAGON AND THE SENTINELS OF JUSTICE
AC Comics: April, 1985 - No. 6, 1986 ($1.75)
1-6: 1-Capt. Paragon, Commando D., Nightveil, Scarlet Scorpion, Stardust & Atoman 3.00

CAPTAIN PLANET AND THE PLANETEERS (TV cartoon)
Marvel Comics: Oct, 1991 - No. 12, Oct, 1992 ($1.00/$1.25)
1-N. Adams painted-c 4.00
2-12: 3-Romita-c 3.00

CAPTAIN POWER AND THE SOLDIERS OF THE FUTURE (TV)
Continuity Comics: Aug, 1988 - No. 2, 1988 ($2.00)
1,2: 1-Neal Adams-c/layouts/inks; variant-c exists. 3.00

CAPTAIN PUREHEART (See Archie as...)

GD VG FN VF VF/NM NM-
2.0 4.0 6.0 8.0 9.0 9.2

CAPTAIN ROCKET
P. L. Publ. (Canada): Nov, 1951
1 43 86 129 271 461 650

CAPT. SAVAGE AND HIS LEATHERNECK RAIDERS (...And His Battlefield Raiders #9 on)
Marvel Comics Group (Animated Timely Features): Jan, 1968 - No. 19, Mar, 1970 (See Sgt. Fury No. 10)
1-Sgt. Fury & Howlers cameo 5 10 15 32 51 70
2,7,11: 2,4-Origin Hydra. 7-Pre-"Thing" Ben Grimm story. 11-Sgt. Fury app.
3 6 9 18 27 35
3-6,8-10,12-14: 14-Last 12¢ issue 3 6 9 16 23 30
15-19 3 6 9 14 19 24
NOTE: *Ayres/Shores a-1-8,11. Ayres/Severin a-9,10,17-19. Heck/Shores a-12-15.*

CAPTAIN SCIENCE (Fantastic No. 8 on)
Youthful Magazines: Nov, 1950; No. 2, Feb, 1951 - No. 7, Dec, 1951
1-Wood-a; origin; 2 pg. text w/ photos of George Pal's "Destination Moon."
89 178 267 565 970 1375
2-Flying saucer-c swipes Weird Science #13(#2)-c 48 96 144 302 514 725
3,6,7; 3,6-Bondage c-swipes/Wings #94,91 41 82 123 256 428 600
4,5-Wood/Orlando-c/a(2) each 81 162 243 518 884 1250
NOTE: *Fass a-4. Bondage c-3, 6, 7.*

CAPTAIN SILVER'S LOG OF SEA HOUND (See Sea Hound)

CAPTAIN SINBAD (Movie Adaptation) (See Fantastic Voyages of... & Movie Comics)

CAPTAIN STERNN: RUNNING OUT OF TIME
Kitchen Sink Press: Sept, 1993 - No. 5, 1994 ($4.95, limited series, coated stock, 52 pgs.)
1-5: Berni Wrightson-c/a/scripts 6.00
1-Gold ink variant 10.00

CAPTAIN STEVE SAVAGE (...& His Jet Fighters, No. 2-13)
Avon Periodicals: 1950 - No. 8, 1/53; No. 5, 9-10/54 - No. 13, 5-6/56
nn(1st series)-Harrison/Wood art, 22 pgs. (titled "...Over Korea")
39 78 117 240 395 550
1(4/51)-Reprints nn issue (Canadian) 18 36 54 105 165 225
2-Kamen-a 14 28 42 80 115 150
3-11 (#6, 11-12/54, last precode) 10 20 30 58 79 100
12-Wood-a (6 pgs.) 14 28 42 81 118 155
13-Check, Lawrence-a 11 22 33 60 83 105
NOTE: *Kinstler c-2-5, 7-9, 11. Lawrence a-8. Ravielli a-5, 9.*
5(9-10/54-2nd series)(Formerly Sensational Police Cases)
10 20 30 54 72 90
6-Reprints nn issue; Harrison/Wood-a 10 20 30 58 79 100
7-13: 9,10-Kinstler-c. 10-r/cover #2 (1st series). 13-r/cover #8 (1st series)
8 16 24 44 57 70

CAPTAIN STONE (See Holyoke One-Shot No. 10)

CAPT. STORM (Also see G. I. Combat #138)
National Periodical Publications: May-June, 1964 - No. 18, Mar-Apr, 1967
1-Origin 9 18 27 65 113 160
2-7,9-18: 3,6,13-Kubert-a. 4-Colan-a. 12-Kubert-c 6 12 18 41 66 90
8-Grey-tone-c 7 14 21 49 80 110

CAPTAIN 3-D (Super hero)
Harvey Publications: December, 1953 (25¢, came with 2 pairs of glasses)
1-Kirby/Ditko-a (Ditko's 3rd published work tied with Strange Fantasy #9, see also Daring Love #1 & Black Magic V4 #3); shows cover in 3-D on inside; Kirby/Meskin-c
12 24 36 69 97 125
NOTE: *Half price without glasses*

CAPTAIN THUNDER AND BLUE BOLT
Hero Comics: Sept, 1987 - No. 10, 1988 ($1.95)
1-10: 1-Origin Blue Bolt. 3-Origin Capt. Thunder. 6-1st app. Wicket. 8-Champions x-over 2.50

CAPTAIN TOOTSIE & THE SECRET LEGION (Advs. of...)(Also see Monte Hale #30,39 & Real Western Hero)
Toby Press: Oct, 1950 - No. 2, Dec, 1950
1-Not Beck-a; both have sci/fi covers 32 64 96 188 307 425
2-The Rocketeer Patrol app.; not Beck-a 20 40 60 114 182 250

CAPTAIN TRIUMPH (See Crack Comics #27)

CAPTAIN UNIVERSE... (5-part x-over)
Marvel Comics: 2005; Jan, 2006
.../ Daredevil 1 (1/06, $2.99) Part 2; Faerber-s/Santacruz-a 3.00
.../ Hulk 1 (1/06, $2.99) Part 1; Faerber-s/Magno-a 3.00
.../ Invisible Woman 1 (1/06, $2.99) Part 4; Faerber-s/Raiz-a; Gladiator app. 3.00

Captain Video #4 © FAW

Cars #0 © DIS/Pixar

Cartoon Network Action Pack #35 © CN

	GD 2.0	VG 4.0	FN 6.0	VF 8.0	VF/NM 9.0	NM- 9.2

.../ Silver Surfer 1 (1/06, $2.99) Part 5; Faerber-s/Magno-a 3.00
.../ X-23 1 (1/06, $2.99) Part 3; Faerber-s/Portella-a; Scorpion app. 3.00
...: Power Unimaginable TPB (2005, $19.99)-Reprints from Marvel Spotlight #9-11, Incredible Hulk Ann. #10, Marvel Fanfare #25, Web of Spider-Man Ann. #5&6, Marvel Comics Presents #148, Cosmic Power Unlimited #5 20.00
...: Universal Heroes TPB (2005, $13.99) reprints .../Hulk, .../Daredevil, ...X-23 and back-up stories from Amazing Fantasy (2005) #13,14 14.00

CAPTAIN VENTURE & THE LAND BENEATH THE SEA (See Space Family Robinson)
Gold Key: Oct, 1968 - No. 2, Oct, 1969

1-r/Space Family Robinson serial; Spiegle-a 4 8 12 28 44 60
2-Spiegle-a 4 8 12 24 37 50

CAPTAIN VICTORY AND THE GALACTIC RANGERS
Pacific Comics: Nov, 1981 - No. 13, Jan, 1984 ($1.00, direct sales, 36-48 pgs.)
(Created by Jack Kirby)

1-1st app. Mr. Mind 4.00
2-13: 3-N. Adams-a 3.00
Special 1-(10/83)-Kirby c/a(p) 4.00
*NOTE: **Conrad** a-10, 11. **Ditko** a-6. **Kirby** a-1-3p; c-1-13.*

CAPTAIN VICTORY AND THE GALACTIC RANGERS
Jack Kirby Comics: July, 2000 - No. 2, Sept, 2000 ($2.95, B&W)

1,2-New Jeremy Kirby-s with reprinted Jack Kirby-a; Liefeld pin-up art 3.00

CAPTAIN VIDEO (TV) (See XMas Comics)
Fawcett Publications: Feb, 1951 - No. 6, Dec, 1951 (No. 1,5,6-36pgs.; 2-4, 52 pgs.)

1-George Evans-a(2); 1st TV hero comic 103 206 309 649 1100 1550
2-Used in **SOTI**, pg. 382 67 134 201 422 711 1000
3-6-All Evans-a except #5 mostly Evans 55 110 165 347 586 825
*NOTE: Minor **Williamson** assists on most issues. Photo c-1, 5, 6; painted c-2-4.*

CAPTAIN WILLIE SCHULTZ (Also see Fightin' Army)
Charlton Comics: No. 76, Oct, 1985 - No. 77, Jan, 1986

76,77-Low print run 1 2 3 5 6 8

CAPTAIN WIZARD COMICS (See Meteor, Red Band & Three Ring Comics)
Rural Home: 1946

1-Capt. Wizard dons new costume; Impossible Man, Race Wilkins app.
34 68 102 204 332 460

CARE BEARS (TV, Movie)(See Star Comics Magazine)
Star Comics/Marvel Comics No. 15 on: Nov, 1985 - No. 20, Jan, 1989

1-20: Post-a begins. 11-$1.00-c begins. 13-Madballs app. 4.00

CAREER GIRL ROMANCES (Formerly Three Nurses)
Charlton Comics: June, 1964 - No. 78, Dec, 1973

V4#24-31 3 6 9 14 20 25
32-Elvis Presley, Herman's Hermits, Johnny Rivers line drawn-c
10 20 30 70 123 175
33-38,40-50 2 4 6 13 18 22
39-(4/67) 1st app. Tiffany Sinn, C.I.A. Sweetheart, Undercover Agent (also see Secret Agent #10; Dominguel-a 3 6 9 17 25 32
51-78: 70-David Cassidy poster 2 4 6 10 14 18

CAR 54, WHERE ARE YOU? (TV)
Dell Publishing Co.: Mar-May, 1962 - No. 7, Sept-Nov, 1963; 1964 - 1965 (All photo-c)

Four Color 1257(#1, 3-5/62) 8 16 24 56 93 130
2(6-8/62)-7 5 10 15 32 51 70
2,3(10-12/64), 4(1-3/65)-Reprints #2,3,&4 of 1st series
3 6 9 20 30 40

CARL BARKS LIBRARY OF WALT DISNEY'S GYRO GEARLOOSE COMICS AND FILLERS IN COLOR, THE
Gladstone: 1993 ($7.95, 8-1/2x11", limited series, 52 pgs.)

1-6: Carl Barks reprints 1 3 4 6 8 10

CARL BARKS LIBRARY OF WALT DISNEY'S COMICS AND STORIES IN COLOR, THE
Gladstone: Jan, 1992 - No. 51, Mar, 1996 ($8.95, 8-1/2x11", 60 pgs.)

1,2,6,8-51: 1-Barks Donald Duck-r/WDC&S #31-35; 2-r/#36,38-41; 6-r/#57-61; 8-r/#67-71; 9-r/#72-76; 10-r/#77-81; 11-r/#82-86; 12-r/#87-91; 13-r/#92-96; 14-r/#97-101; 15-r/#102-106; 16-r/#107-111; 17-r/#112,114,117,124,125; 18-r/#126-130; 19-r/#131,132(2),133,134; 20-r/#135-139; 21-r/#140-144; 22-r/#145-149; 23-r/#150-154; 24-r/#155-159; 25-r/#160-164; 26-r/#165-169; 27-r/#170-174;28-r/#175-179; 29-r/#180-184; 30-r/#185-189; 31-r/#190-194; 32-r/#195-199;33-r/#200-204; 34-r/#205-209; 35-r/#210-214; 36-r/#215-219; 37-r/#220-224; 38-r/#225-229; 39-r/#230-234; 40-r/#235-239; 41-r/#240-244; 42r/#245-249; 43-r/#250-254; 44-50; All contain one Heroes & Villains trading card each
2 4 6 9 12 15

3,4,7: 3-r/#42-46. 4-r/#47-51. 7-r/#62-66. 2 4 6 11 16 20
5-r/#52-56 3 6 9 16 23 30

CARL BARKS LIBRARY OF WALT DISNEY'S DONALD DUCK ADVENTURES IN COLOR, THE
Gladstone: Jan, 1994 - No. 25, Jan, 1996 ($7.95-$9.95, 44-68 pgs., 8-1/2"x11")
(all contain one Donald Duck trading card each)

1-5,7-25-Carl Barks-r: 1-r/FC #9; 2-r/FC #29; 3-r/FC #62; 4-r/FC #108; 5-r/FC #147 & #79(Mickey Mouse); 7-r/FC #159. 8-r/FC #178 & 189. 9-r/FC #199 & 203; 10-r/FC 223 & 238; 11-r/Christmas Parade #1 & 2; 12-r/FC #296; 13-r/FC #263; 14-r/MOC #20 & 41; 15-r/FC 275 & 282; 16-r/FC #291&300; 17-r/FC #308 & 318; 18-r/Vac. Parade #1 & Summer Fun #2; 19-r/FC #328 & 367 2 4 6 9 12 15
6-r/MOC #4, Cheerios "Atom Bomb," D.D. Tells About Kites
3 6 9 14 20 25

CARL BARKS LIBRARY OF WALT DISNEY'S DONALD DUCK CHRISTMAS STORIES IN COLOR, THE
Gladstone: 1992 ($7.95, 44pgs., one-shot)

nn-Reprints Firestone giveaways 1945-1949 2 4 6 10 14 18

CARL BARKS LIBRARY OF WALT DISNEY'S UNCLE SCROOGE COMICS ONE PAGERS IN COLOR, THE
Gladstone: 1992 - No. 2, 1993 ($8.95, limited series, 60 pgs., 8-1/2x11")

1-Carl Barks one pg. reprints 3 6 9 16 23 30
2-Carl Barks one pg. reprints 2 4 6 10 14 18

CARNAGE: IT'S A WONDERFUL LIFE
Marvel Comics: Oct, 1996 ($1.95, one-shot)

1-David Quinn scripts 3.00

CARNAGE: MIND BOMB
Marvel Comics: Feb, 1996 ($2.95, one-shot)

1-Warren Ellis script; Kyle Hotz-a 3.00

CARNATION MALTED MILK GIVEAWAYS (See Wisco)

CARNEYS, THE
Archie Comics: Summer, 1994 ($2.00, 52 pgs)

1-Bound-in pull-out poster 2.50

CARNIVAL COMICS (Formerly Kayo #12; becomes Red Seal Comics #14)
Harry 'A' Chesler/Pershing Square Publ. Co.: 1945

nn (#13)-Guardineer-a 18 36 54 105 165 225

CAROLINE KENNEDY
Charlton Comics: 1961 (one-shot)

nn-Interior photo covers of Kennedy family 9 18 27 61 103 145

CAROUSEL COMICS
F. E. Howard, Toronto: V1#8, April, 1948

V1#8 8 16 24 42 54 65

CARS (Based on the 2006 Pixar movie)
Boom Entertainment: No. 0, Nov, 2009 - Present ($2.99)

0,1-Three covers on each 3.00
...: Radiator Springs 1-4 (7/09 - No. 4, 10/09, $2.99) Two covers on each 3.00
...: The Rookie 1-4 (3/09 - No. 4, 6/09, $2.99) Origin of Lightning McQueen 3.00

CARTOON CARTOONS (Anthology)
DC Comics: Mar, 2001 - No. 33, Oct, 2004 ($1.99/$2.25)

1-33-Short stories of Cartoon Network characters. 3,6,10,13,15-Space Ghost. 13-Begin $2.25-c. 17-Dexter's Laboratory begins 2.50

CARTOON KIDS
Atlas Comics (CPS): 1957 (no month)

1-Maneely-c/a; Dexter The Demon, Willie The Wise-Guy, Little Zelda app.
11 22 33 62 86 110

CARTOON NETWORK ACTION PACK (Anthology)
DC Comics: July, 2006 - Present ($2.25/$2.50)

1-31-Short stories of Cartoon Network characters. 1,4,6-Rowdyruff Boys app. 2.25
32-46: 32-Begin $2.50-c 2.50

CARTOON NETWORK BLOCK PARTY (Anthology)
DC Comics: Nov, 2004 - No. 59, Sept, 2009 ($2.25/$2.50)

1,2,4-51-Short stories of Cartoon Network characters 2.25
3-($2.95) Bonus pages 3.00
52-59: 52-Begin $2.50-c. 59-Last issue; Powerpuff Girls app. 2.50
... Vol. 1: Get Down! (2005, $6.99, digest) reprints from Dexter's Lab and Cartoon Cartoons 7.00
... Vol. 2: Read All About It! (2005, $6.99, digest) reprints 7.00
... Vol. 3: Can You Dig It?; ... Vol. 4: Blast Off! (2006, $6.99, digest) reprints 7.00

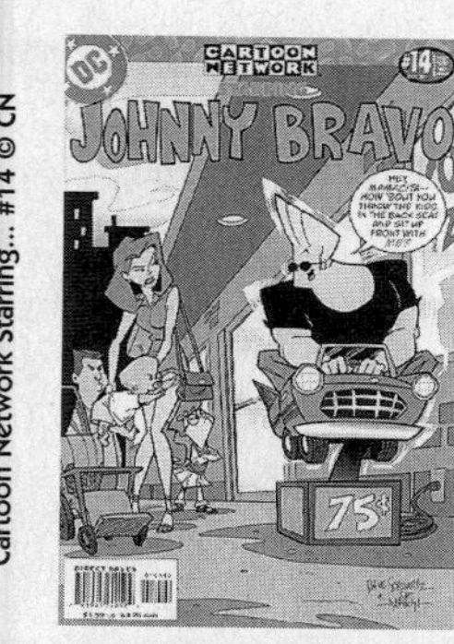
Cartoon Network Starring... #14 © CN

Casey Crime Photographer #2 © MAR

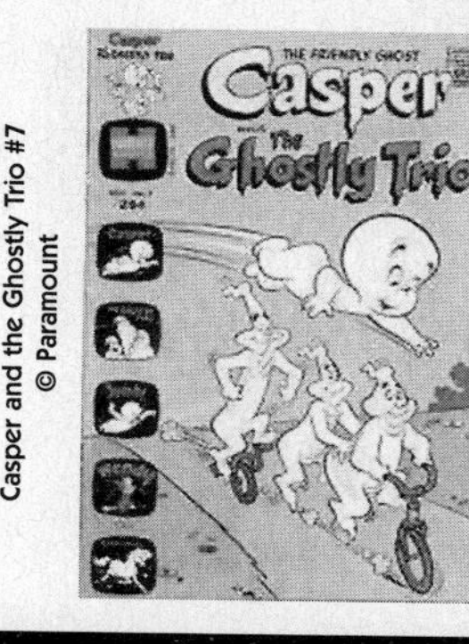
Casper and the Ghostly Trio #7 © Paramount

	GD 2.0	VG 4.0	FN 6.0	VF 8.0	VF/NM 9.0	NM- 9.2

CARTOON NETWORK PRESENTS
DC Comics: Aug, 1997 - No. 24, Aug, 1999 ($1.75-$1.99, anthology)

1-Dexter's Lab						5.00
1-Platinum Edition	1	2	3	5	7	9
2-10: 2-Space Ghost						3.50
11-24: 12-Bizarro World						2.50

CARTOON NETWORK PRESENTS SPACE GHOST
Archie Comics: Mar, 1997 ($1.50)

1-Scott Rosema-p 6.00

CARTOON NETWORK STARRING... (Anthology)
DC Comics: Sept, 1999 - No. 18, Feb, 2001 ($1.99)

1-Powerpuff Girls 5.00
2-18: 2,8,11,14,17-Johnny Bravo. 12,15,18-Space Ghost 3.00

CARTOON TALES (Disney's...)
W.D. Publications (Disney): nd, nn (1992) ($2.95, 6-5/8x9-1/2", 52 pgs.)

nn-Ariel & Sebastian-Serpent Teen; Beauty and the Beast; A Tale of Enchantment; Darkwing Duck - Just Us Justice Ducks; 101 Dalmatians - Canine Classics; Tale Spin - Surprise in the Skies; Uncle Scrooge - Blast to the Past 4.00

CARVERS
Image Comics (Flypaper Press): 1998 - No. 3, 1999 ($2.95)

1-3-Pander Bros.-a/Fleming-s 3.00

CAR WARRIORS
Marvel Comics (Epic): June, 1991 - No. 4, Sept, 1991 ($2.25, lim. series)

1-4: 1-Says April in indicia 2.50

CASANOVA
Image Comics: June, 2006 - No. 14, May, 2008 ($1.99, B&W& olive green or blue)

1-14: 1-7-Matt Fraction-s/Gabriel Bá-a/c. 8-14-Fabio Moon-a 2.50
...: Luxuria TPB (2008, $12.99) r/#1-7; sketch pages and cover gallery 13.00

CASE FILES: SAM & TWITCH (Also see the Spawn titles)
Image Comics: May, 2003 - No. 25, July, 2006 ($2.50/$2.95, color #1-6/B&W #7-on)

1-25: 1-5-Scott Morse-a/Marc Andreyko-s. 7-13-Paul Lee-a. 13-Niles-s 3.00

CASE OF THE SHOPLIFTER'S SHOE (See Perry Mason, Feature Book No.50)

CASE OF THE WINKING BUDDHA, THE
St. John Publ. Co.: 1950 (132 pgs.; 25¢; B&W; 5-1/2x7-5-1/2x8")

nn-Charles Raab-a; reprinted in Authentic Police Cases No. 25	30	60	90	177	289	400

CASEY BLUE
DC Comics (WildStorm): Jul, 2008 - No. 6, Dec, 2008 ($2.99, limited series)

1-6-B. Clay Moore-s/Carlos Barberi-a 3.00
...: Beyond Tomorrow TPB (2009, $19.99) r/#1-6; Barberi sketch pages 20.00

CASEY-CRIME PHOTOGRAPHER (Two-Gun Western No. 5 on)(Radio)
Marvel Comics (BFP): Aug, 1949 - No. 4, Feb, 1950

1-Photo-c; 52 pgs.	25	50	75	150	245	340
2-4: Photo-c	18	36	54	105	165	225

CASEY JONES (TV)
Dell Publishing Co.: No. 915, July, 1958

Four Color 915-Alan Hale photo-c	5	10	15	34	55	75

CASEY JONES & RAPHAEL (See Bodycount)
Mirage Studios: Oct, 1994 ($2.75, unfinished limited series)

1-Bisley-c; Eastman story & pencils 2.75

CASEY JONES: NORTH BY DOWNEAST
Mirage Studios: May, 1994 - No. 2, July, 1994 ($2.75, limited series)

1,2-Rick Veitch script & pencils; Kevin Eastman story & inks 2.75

CASPER ADVENTURE DIGEST
Harvey Comics: V2#1, Oct, 1992 - V2#8, Apr, 1994 ($1.75/$1.95, digest-size)

V2#1: Casper, Richie Rich, Spooky, Wendy 5.00
2-8 3.50

CASPER AND...
Harvey Comics: Nov, 1987 - No. 12, June, 1990 (.75/$1.00, all reprints)

1-Ghostly Trio 5.00
2-12: 2-Spooky; begin $1.00-c. 3-Wendy. 4-Nightmare. 5-Ghostly Trio. 6-Spooky. 7-Wendy. 8-Hot Stuff. 9-Baby Huey. 10-Wendy.11-Ghostly Trio. 12-Spooky 3.00

CASPER AND FRIENDS
Harvey Comics: Oct, 1991 - No. 5, July, 1992 ($1.00/$1.25)

1-Nightmare, Ghostly Trio, Wendy, Spooky 4.00
2-5 3.00

CASPER AND FRIENDS MAGAZINE: Mar, 1997 - No. 3, July, 1997 ($3.99)

1-3 4.00

CASPER AND NIGHTMARE (See Harvey Hits# 37, 45, 52, 56, 59, 62, 65, 68,71, 75)

CASPER AND NIGHTMARE (Nightmare & Casper No. 1-5)
Harvey Publications: No. 6, 11/64 - No. 44, 10/73; No. 45, 6/74 - No. 46, 8/74 (25¢)

6: 68 pg. Giants begin, ends #32	5	10	15	34	55	75
7-10	4	8	12	22	34	45
11-20	3	6	9	18	27	35
21-37: 33-37-(52 pg. Giants)	3	6	9	14	20	26
38-46	2	4	6	10	14	18

NOTE: *Many issues contain reprints.*

CASPER AND SPOOKY (See Harvey Hits No. 20)
Harvey Publications: Oct, 1972 - No. 7, Oct, 1973

1	3	6	9	18	27	35
2-7	2	4	6	10	14	18

CASPER AND THE GHOSTLY TRIO
Harvey Pub.: Nov, 1972 - No. 7, Nov, 1973; No. 8, Aug, 1990 - No. 10, Dec, 1990

1	3	6	9	18	27	35
2-7	2	4	6	10	14	18
8-10						6.00

CASPER AND WENDY
Harvey Publications: Sept, 1972 - No. 8, Nov, 1973

1: 52 pg. Giant	3	6	9	18	27	35
2-8	2	4	6	10	14	18

CASPER BIG BOOK
Harvey Comics: V2#1, Aug, 1992 - No. 3, May, 1993 ($1.95, 52 pgs.)

V2#1-Spooky app. 4.00
2,3 3.00

CASPER CAT (See Dopey Duck)
I. W. Enterprises/Super: 1958; 1963

1,7:1-Wacky Duck #?.7-Reprint, Super No. 14('63)	2	4	6	9	13	16

CASPER DIGEST (...Magazine #?; ...Halloween Digest #8, 10)
Harvey Publications: Oct, 1986 - No. 18, Jan, 1991 ($1.25/$1.75, digest-size)

1	1	3	4	6	8	10
2-18: 11-Valentine-c. 18-Halloween-c						6.00

CASPER DIGEST (...Magazine #? on)
Harvey Comics: V2#1, Sept, 1991 - V2#14, Nov, 1994 ($1.75/$1.95, digest-size)

V2#1 5.00
2-14 3.50

CASPER DIGEST STORIES
Harvey Publications: Feb, 1980 - No. 4, Nov, 1980 (95¢, 132 pgs., digest size)

1	2	4	6	9	13	16
2-4	1	2	3	5	7	9

CASPER DIGEST WINNERS
Harvey Publications: Apr, 1980 - No. 3, Sept, 1980 (95¢, 132 pgs., digest size)

1	2	4	6	9	13	16
2,3	1	2	3	5	7	9

CASPER ENCHANTED TALES DIGEST
Harvey Comics: May, 1992 - No. 10, Oct, 1994 ($1.75, digest-size, 98 pgs.)

1-Casper, Spooky, Wendy stories 5.00
2-10 3.50

CASPER GHOSTLAND
Harvey Comics: May, 1992 ($1.25)

1 3.00

CASPER GIANT SIZE
Harvey Comics: Oct, 1992 - No. 4, Nov, 1993 ($2.25, 68 pgs.)

V2#1-Casper, Wendy, Spooky stories 5.00
2-4 4.00

CASPER HALLOWEEN TRICK OR TREAT
Harvey Publications: Jan, 1976 (52 pgs.)

1	3	6	9	18	27	35

Casper's Ghostland #73 © Paramount

Casper The Friendly Ghost #6 © Paramount

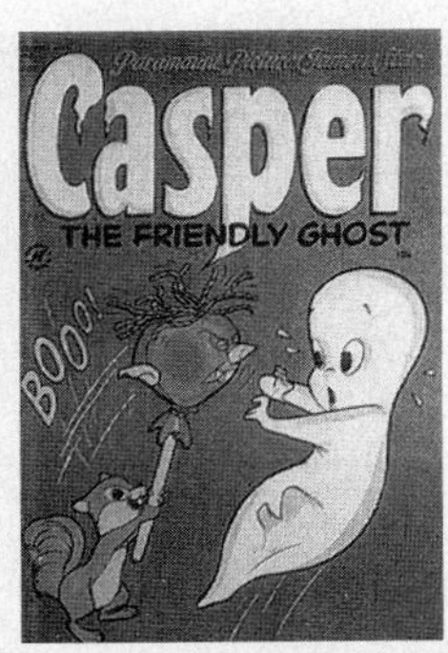

Catman Comics #3 © HOKE

	GD 2.0	VG 4.0	FN 6.0	VF 8.0	VF/NM 9.0	NM- 9.2

CASPER IN SPACE (Formerly Casper Spaceship)
Harvey Publications: No. 6, June, 1973 - No. 8, Oct, 1973

	GD	VG	FN	VF	VF/NM	NM-
6-8	2	4	6	10	14	18

CASPER'S GHOSTLAND
Harvey Publications: Winter, 1958-59 - No. 97, 12/77; No. 98, 12/79 (25¢)

	GD	VG	FN	VF	VF/NM	NM-
1-84 pgs. begin, ends #10	18	36	54	129	252	375
2	10	20	30	70	123	175
3-10	8	16	24	52	86	120
11-20: 11-68 pgs. begin, ends #61. 13-X-Mas-c	6	12	18	41	66	90
21-40	5	10	15	30	48	65
41-61	3	6	9	17	25	32
62-77: 62-52 pgs. begin	2	4	6	9	13	16
78-98: 94-X-Mas-c	2	4	6	8	10	12

NOTE: *Most issues contain reprints w/new stories.*

CASPER SPACESHIP (Casper in Space No. 6 on)
Harvey Publications: Aug, 1972 - No. 5, April, 1973

	GD	VG	FN	VF	VF/NM	NM-
1: 52 pg. Giant	3	6	9	19	27	38
2-5	2	4	6	11	16	20

CASPER STRANGE GHOST STORIES
Harvey Publications: October, 1974 - No. 14, Jan, 1977 (All 52 pgs.)

	GD	VG	FN	VF	VF/NM	NM-
1	3	6	9	19	29	38
2-14	2	4	6	11	16	20

CASPER, THE FRIENDLY GHOST (See America's Best TV Comics, Famous TV Funday Funnies, The Friendly Ghost..., Nightmare &..., Richie Rich and..., Tastee-Freez, Treasury of Comics, Wendy the Good Little Witch & Wendy Witch World)

CASPER, THE FRIENDLY GHOST (Becomes Harvey Comics Hits No. 61 (No. 6), and then continued with Harvey issue No. 7)(1st Series)
St. John Publishing Co.: Sept, 1949 - No. 5, Aug, 1951

	GD	VG	FN	VF	VF/NM	NM-
1(1949)-Origin & 1st app. Baby Huey & Herman the Mouse (1st comic app. of Casper and the 1st time the name Casper app. in any media, even films)	290	580	870	1856	3178	4500
2,3 (2/50 & 8/50)	97	194	291	621	1061	1500
4,5 (3/51 & 8/51)	71	142	213	454	777	1100

CASPER, THE FRIENDLY GHOST (Paramount Picture Star...)(2nd Series)
Harvey Publications (Family Comics): No. 7, Dec, 1952 - No. 70, July, 1958
Note: No. 6 is Harvey Comics Hits No. 61 (10/52)

	GD	VG	FN	VF	VF/NM	NM-
7-Baby Huey begins, ends #9	33	66	99	254	490	725
8,9	20	40	60	146	283	420
10-Spooky begins (1st app., 6/53), ends #70?	26	52	78	190	370	550
11,12: 2nd & 3rd app. Spooky	14	28	42	101	191	280
13-18: Alfred Harvey app. in story	13	26	39	93	172	250
19-1st app. Nightmare (4/54)	21	42	63	153	297	440
20-Wendy the Witch begins (1st app., 5/54)	25	50	75	185	360	535
21-30: 24-Infinity-c	10	20	30	68	119	170
31-40: 38-Early Wendy app. 39-1st app. Samson Honeybun. 40-1st app. Dr. Brainstorm	8	16	24	54	90	125
41-1st Wendy app. on-c	9	18	27	60	100	140
42-50: 43-2nd Wendy-c. 46-1st app. Spooky's girl Pearl.	6	12	18	43	69	95
51-70 (Continues as Friendly Ghost... 8/58) 58-Early app. Bat Balfrey. 63-2nd app. Something the Baby Ghost. 66-1st app. Wildcat Witch	5	10	15	34	55	75
Harvey Comics Classics Vol. 1 TPB (Dark Horse Books, 6/07, $19.95) Reprints Casper's earliest appearances in this title, Little Audrey, and The Friendly Ghost Casper, mostly B&W with some color stories; history, early concept drawings and animation art						20.00

NOTE: *Baby Huey app. 7-9, 11, 121, 14, 16, 20. Buzzy app. 14, 16, 20. Nightmare app. 19, 27, 36, 37, 42, 46, 51, 53, 56, 70. Spooky app. 10-70. Wendy app. 20, 29-31, 35, 37, 38, 41-49, 51, 52, 54-58, 61, 64, 68.*

CASPER THE FRIENDLY GHOST (Formerly The Friendly Ghost...)(3rd Series)
Harvey Comics: No. 254, July, 1990 - No. 260, Jan, 1991 ($1.00)

	GD	VG	FN	VF	VF/NM	NM-
254-260						3.00

CASPER THE FRIENDLY GHOST (4th Series)
Harvey Comics: Mar, 1991 - No. 28, Nov, 1994 ($1.00/$1.25/$1.50)

	GD	VG	FN	VF	VF/NM	NM-
1-Casper becomes Mighty Ghost; Spooky & Wendy app.						5.00
2-10: 7,8-Post-a						3.00
11-28-($1.50)						2.50

CASPER T.V. SHOWTIME
Harvey Comics: Jan, 1980 - No. 5, Oct, 1980

	GD	VG	FN	VF	VF/NM	NM-
1	2	4	6	9	13	16
2-5	1	2	3	5	7	9

CASSETTE BOOKS (Classics Illustrated)
Cassette Book Co./I.P.S. Publ.: 1984 (48 pgs, b&w comic with cassette tape)
NOTE: *This series was illegal. The artwork was illegally obtained, and the Classics Illustrated copyright owner, Twin Circle Publ. sued to get an injunction to prevent the continued sale of this series. Many C.I. collectors obtained copies before the 1987 injunction, but now they are already scarce. Here again the market is just developing, but sealed mint copies of com ic and tape should be worth at least $25.*

1001 (CI#1-A2)New-PC 1002(CI#3-A2)CI-PC 1003(CI#13-A2)CI-PC
1004(CI#25)CI-LDC 1005(CI#10-A2)New-PC 1006(CI#64)CI-LDC

CASTILIAN (See Movie Classics)

CASTLEVANIA: THE BELMONT LEGACY
IDW Publishing: March 2005 - No. 5, July, 2005 ($3.99, limited series)

	GD	VG	FN	VF	VF/NM	NM-
1-5-Marc Andreyko-s/E.J. Su-a						4.00

CASTLE WAITING
Olio: 1997 - No. 7, 1999 ($2.95, B&W)
Cartoon Books: Vol. 2, Aug, 2000 - No. 16 ($2.95/$3.95, B&W)
Fantagraphics Books: Vol. 3, 2006 - Present ($5.95/$3.95, B&W)

	GD	VG	FN	VF	VF/NM	NM-
1-Linda Medley-s/a in all	1	2	3	5	6	8
2						4.00
3-7						3.00
The Lucky Road TPB r/#1-7						17.00
Hiatus Issue (1999) Crilley-c; short stories and previews						3.00
Vol. 2 #1-6,14-16 (#5&6 also have #12&13 on cover, for series numbering)						3.00
Vol. 3 #1 ($5.95) r/#15,16 and new story						6.00
Vol. 3 #2-15 ($3.95)						4.00

CASUAL HEROES
Image Comics (Motown Machineworks): Apr, 1996 ($2.25, unfinished lim. series)

	GD	VG	FN	VF	VF/NM	NM-
1-Steve Rude-c						2.50

CAT, T.H.E. (TV) (See T.H.E. Cat)

CAT, THE (See Movie Classics)

CAT, THE (Female hero)
Marvel Comics Group: Nov, 1972 - No. 4, June, 1973

	GD	VG	FN	VF	VF/NM	NM-
1-Origin & 1st app. The Cat (who later becomes Tigra); Mooney-a(i); Wood-c(i)/a(i)	4	8	12	24	37	50
2,3: 2-Marie Severin/Mooney-a. 3-Everett inks	3	6	9	14	20	25
4-Starlin/Weiss-a(p)	3	6	9	16	22	28

CATALYST: AGENTS OF CHANGE (Also see Comics' Greatest World)
Dark Horse Comics: Feb, 1994 - No.7, Nov, 1994 ($2.00, limited series)

	GD	VG	FN	VF	VF/NM	NM-
1-7: 1-Foil stamped logo						2.50

CAT & MOUSE
EF Graphics (Silverline): Dec, 1988 ($1.75, color w/part B&W)

	GD	VG	FN	VF	VF/NM	NM-
1-1st printing (12/88, 32 pgs.), 1-2nd printing (5/89, 36 pgs.)						2.50

CAT FROM OUTER SPACE (See Walt Disney Showcase #46)

CATHOLIC COMICS (See Heroes All Catholic...)
Catholic Publications: June, 1946 - V3#10, July, 1949

	GD	VG	FN	VF	VF/NM	NM-
1	30	60	90	177	289	400
2	16	32	48	94	147	200
3-13(7/47): 11-Hollingsworth-a	14	28	42	82	121	160
V2#1-10	11	22	33	62	86	110
V3#1-10: Reprints 10-part Treasure Island serial from Target V2#2-11 (see Key Comics #5)	11	22	33	64	90	115

NOTE: ***Orlando** c-V2#10, V3#5, 6, 8.*

CATHOLIC PICTORIAL
Catholic Guild: 1947

	GD	VG	FN	VF	VF/NM	NM-
1-Toth-a(2) (Rare)	39	78	117	240	395	550

CATMAN COMICS (Formerly Crash Comics No. 1-5)
Holyoke Publishing Co./Continental Magazines V2#12, 7/44 on:
5/41 - No. 17, 1/43; No. 18, 7/43 - No. 22, 12/43; No. 23, 3/44 - No. 26, 11/44; No. 27, 4/45 - No. 30, 12/45; No. 31, 6/46 - No. 32, 8/46

	GD	VG	FN	VF	VF/NM	NM-
1(V1#6)-Origin The Deacon & Sidekick Mickey, Dr. Diamond & Rag-Man; The Black Widow app.; The Catman by Chas. Quinlan & Blaze Baylor begin	400	800	1200	2800	4900	7000
2(V1#7)	174	348	522	1114	1907	2700
3(V1#8)-The Pied Piper begins; classic Hitler, Stalin & Mussolini-c	161	322	483	1030	1765	2500
4(V1#9)	113	226	339	718	1234	1750
5(V2#10)-1st app. Kitten; The Hood begins (c-redated), 6,7(V2#11,12)	95	190	285	603	1039	1475
8(V2#13,3/42)-Origin Little Leaders; Volton by Kubert begins (his 1st comic book work)	116	232	348	742	1271	1800

Catwoman #19 © DC

Catwoman (2002 series) #74 © DC

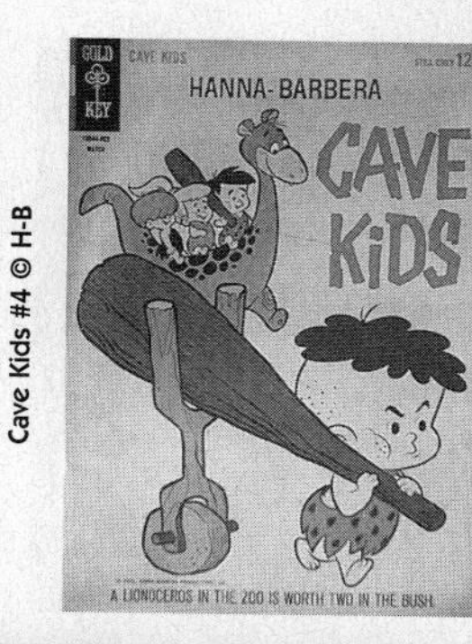

Cave Kids #4 © H-B

GD 2.0 | VG 4.0 | FN 6.0 | VF 8.0 | VF/NM 9.0 | NM- 9.2

9,10(V2#14,15): 10-Origin Blackout; Phantom Falcon begins 81 162 243 518 884 1250
11 (V3#1)-Kubert-a 81 162 243 518 884 1250
12 (V3#2), 14, 15, 17. 12-Volton by Brodsky, not Kubert. 14-Brodsky-a 68 136 204 435 743 1050
13-(scarce) 116 232 348 742 1271 1800
16 (V3#5)-Hitler, Tojo, Mussolini, Goehring-c 116 232 348 742 1271 1800
18(V3#8, 7/43)-(scarce) 82 164 246 528 902 1275
19,20: 19 (V2#6)-Hitler, Tojo, Mussolini-c. 20 (V2#7): Classic Hitler-c 119 238 357 762 1306 1850
21-23 (V2#10, 3/44) 66 132 198 419 722 1025
nn(V3#13, 5/44)-Rico-a; Schomburg bondage-c 65 130 195 416 708 1000
nn(V2#12, 7/44, nn(V3#1, 9/44)-Origin The Golden Archer; Leatherface app. 60 120 180 381 653 925
nn(V3#2, 11/44)-L. B. Cole-c 102 204 306 648 1112 1575
27-Origins Catman & Kitten retold; L. B. Cole Flag-c; Infantino-a 116 232 348 742 1271 1800
28-Dr. Macabre app.; L. B. Cole-c/a 129 258 387 826 1413 2000
29-32-L. B. Cole-c; bondage-#30 113 226 339 718 1234 1750
NOTE: *Fuje a-11, 27, 28(2), 29(3), 30.* ***Palais*** *a-11, 16, 27, 28, 29(2), 30(2), 32; c-25(7/44).* ***Rico*** *a-11(2), 23, 27, 28.*

CAT TALES (3-D)
Eternity Comics: Apr, 1989 ($2.95)
1-Felix the Cat-r in 3-D 5.00

CATWOMAN (Also see Action Comics Weekly #611, Batman #404-407, Detective Comics, & Superman's Girlfriend Lois Lane #70, 71)
DC Comics: Feb, 1989 - No. 4, May, 1989 ($1.50, limited series, mature)
1 1 3 4 6 8 10
2-4: 3-Batman cameo. 4-Batman app. 1 2 3 5 7 9
Her Sister's Keeper (1991, $9.95, trade paperback)-r/#1-4 10.00

CATWOMAN (Also see Showcase '93, Showcase '95 #4, & Batman #404-407)
DC Comics: Aug, 1993 - No. 94, Jul, 2001 ($1.50-$2.25)
0-(10/94)-Zero Hour; origin retold. Released between #14&15 3.00
1-($1.95)-Embossed-c; Bane app.; Balent c-1-10; a-1-10p 4.00
2-20: 3-Bane flashback cameo. 4-Brief Bane app. 6,7-Knightquest tie-ins; Batman (Azrael) app. 8-1st app. Zephyr. 12-KnightsEnd pt. 6. 13-new Knights End Aftermath. 14-(9/94)-Zero Hour 3.00
21-24, 26-30, 33-49: 21-$1.95-c begins. 28,29-Penguin cameo app. 36-Legacy pt. 2. 38-40-Year Two; Batman, Joker, Penguin & Two-Face app. 46-Two-Face app. 2.50
25,31,32: 25-($2.95)-Robin app. 31,32-Contagion pt. 4 (Reads pt. 5 on-c) & pt. 9. 3.00
50-($2.95, 48 pgs.)-New armored costume 3.00
50-($2.95, 48 pgs.)-Collector's Ed.w/metallic ink-c 3.00
51-77: 51-Huntress-c/app. 54-Grayson-s begins. 56-Cataclysm pt.6. 57-Poison Ivy-c/app. 63-65-Joker-c/app. 72-No Man's Land; Ostrander-s begins 2.50
78-82: 80-Catwoman goes to jail 2.50
83-94: 83-Begin $2.25-c. 83,84,89-Harley Quinn-c/app. 2.50
#1,000,000 (11/98) 853rd Century x-over 2.50
Annual 1 (1994, $2.95, 68 pgs.)-Elseworlds story; Batman app.; no Balent-a 3.00
Annual 2,4 ('95, '97, $3.95) 2-Year One story. 4-Pulp Heroes 4.00
Annual 3 (1996, $2.95)-Legends of the Dead Earth story 3.00
...Plus 1 (11/97, $2.95) Screamqueen (Scare Tactics) app. 3.00
TPB ($9.95) r/#15-19, Balent-c 10.00

CATWOMAN (Also see Detective Comics #759-762)
DC Comics: Jan, 2002 - No. 82, Oct, 2008; No. 83, Mar, 2010 ($2.50/$2.99)
1-Darwyn Cooke & Mike Allred-a; Ed Brubaker-s 6.00
2-4 3.00
5-54: 5-9-Rader-a/Paul Pope-c. 10-Morse-c. 16-JG Jones-c. 22-Batman-c/app. 34-36-War Games. 43-Killer Croc app. 44-Hughes-c begin. 50-Zatanna app. 52-Catwoman kills Black Mask. 53-One Year Later; Helena born 2.50
55-82: 55-Begin $2.99-c. 56-58-Wildcat app. 74-Zatanna app. 75-78-Salvation Run 3.00
83-(3/10, $2.99) Blackest Night one-shot; Black Mask app.; Hughes-c 3.00
...: Catwoman Dies TPB (2008, $14.99) r/#66-72; Hughes cover gallery 15.00
...: Crime Pays TPB (2008, $14.99) r/#73-77 15.00
...: Crooked Little Town TPB (2003, $14.95) r/#5-10 & Secret Files; Oeming-c 15.00
...: It's Only a Movie TPB (2007, $19.99) r/#59-65 20.00
...: Relentless TPB (2005, $19.95) r/#12-19 & Secret Files 20.00
... Secret Files and Origins (10/02, $4.95) origin-s Oeming-a; profiles and pin-ups 5.00
...Selina's Big Score HC (2002, $24.95) Cooke-s/a; pin-ups by various 25.00
...Selina's Big Score SC (2003, $17.95) Cooke-s/a; pin-ups by various 18.00
...: The Dark End of the Street TPB (2002, $12.95) r/#1-4 & Slam Bradley back-up stories from Detective Comics #759-762 13.00
...: The Long Road Home TPB (2009, $17.99) r/#78-82 18.00

GD 2.0 | VG 4.0 | FN 6.0 | VF 8.0 | VF/NM 9.0 | NM- 9.2

...: The Replacements TPB (2007, $14.99) r/#53-58 15.00
...: Wild Ride TPB (2005, $14.99) r/#20-24 & Secret Files #1 15.00

CATWOMAN/ GUARDIAN OF GOTHAM
DC Comics: 1999 - No. 2, 1999 ($5.95, limited series)
1,2-Elseworlds; Moench-s/Balent-a 6.00

CATWOMAN: NINE LIVES OF A FELINE FATALE
DC Comics: 2004 ($14.95, TPB)
nn-Reprints notable stories from Batman #1 to the present; pin-ups by various; Bolland-c 15.00

CATWOMAN: THE MOVIE (2004 Halle Berry movie)
DC Comics: 2004 ($4.95/$9.95)
1-($4.95) Movie adaptation; Jim Lee-c and sketch pages; Derenick-a 5.00
... & Other Cat Tales TPB (2004, $9.95)-r/Movie adaptation; Jim Lee sketch pages, r/Catwoman #0, Catwoman (2nd series) #11 & 25; photo-c 10.00

CATWOMAN/VAMPIRELLA: THE FURIES
DC Comics/Harris Publ.: Feb, 1997 ($4.95, squarebound, 46 pgs.) (1st DC/Harris x-over)
nn-Reintro Pantha; Chuck Dixon scripts; Jim Balent-c/a 5.00

CATWOMAN: WHEN IN ROME
DC Comics: Nov, 2004 - No. 6, Aug, 2005 ($3.50, limited series)
1-6-Jeph Loeb-s/Tim Sale-a/c; Riddler app. 3.50
HC (2005, $19.99, dustjacket) r/series; intro by Mark Chiarello; sketch pages 20.00
SC (2007, $12.99) r/series; intro by Mark Chiarello; sketch pages 13.00

CATWOMAN/WILDCAT
DC Comics: Aug, 1998 - No. 4, Nov, 1998 ($2.50, limited series)
1-4-Chuck Dixon & Beau Smith-s; Stelfreeze-c 3.00

CAUGHT
Atlas Comics (VPI): Aug, 1956 - No. 5, Apr, 1957
1 22 44 66 128 209 290
2-4: 3-Maneely, Pakula, Torres-a. 4-Maneely-a 13 26 39 74 105 135
5-Crandall, Krigstein-a 14 28 42 78 112 145
NOTE: ***Drucker*** *a-2.* ***Heck*** *a-4.* ***Severin*** *c-1, 2, 4, 5.* ***Shores*** *a-4.*

CAVALIER COMICS
A. W. Nugent Publ. Co.: 1945; 1952 (Early DC reprints)
2(1945)-Speed Saunders, Fang Gow 20 40 60 115 185 255
2(1952) 11 22 33 64 90 115

CAVE GIRL (Also see Africa)
Magazine Enterprises: No. 11, 1953 - No. 14, 1954
11(A-1 82)-Origin; all Cave Girl stories 47 94 141 296 498 700
12(A-1 96), 13(A-1 116), 14(A-1 125)-Thunda by Powell in each 37 74 111 222 361 500
NOTE: ***Powell*** *c/a in all.*

CAVE GIRL
AC Comics: 1988 ($2.95, 44 pgs.) (16 pgs. of color, rest B&W)
1-Powell-r/Cave Girl #11; Nyoka photo back-c from movie; Powell/Bill Black-c; Special Limited Edition on-c 4.00

CAVE KIDS (TV) (See Comic Album #16)
Gold Key: Feb, 1963 - No. 16, Mar, 1967 (Hanna-Barbera)
1 7 14 21 45 73 100
2-5 4 8 12 24 37 50
6-16: 7,12-Pebbles & Bamm Bamm app. 16-1st Space Kidettes 3 6 9 20 30 40

CAVEWOMAN
Basement Comics: Jan, 1994 - No. 6, 1995 ($2.95)
1 3 6 9 16 23 30
2 2 4 6 9 12 15
3-6 1 2 3 5 6 8
...: Meets Explorers ('97, $2.95) 3.00
...: One-Shot Special (7/00, $2.95) Massey-s/a 3.00

CELESTINE (See Violator Vs. Badrock #1)
Image Comics (Extreme): May, 1996 - No. 2, June, 1996 ($2.50, limited series)
1,2: Warren Ellis scripts 2.50

CENTURION OF ANCIENT ROME, THE
Zondervan Publishing House: 1958 (no month listed) (B&W, 36 pgs.)
(Rare) All by Jay Disbrow 65 130 195 416 708 1000

CENTURIONS (TV)
DC Comics: June, 1987 - No. 4, Sept, 1987 (75¢, limited series)

Cerebus #200 © Dave Sim & Gerhard

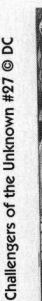

Challengers of the Unknown #27 © DC

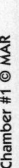

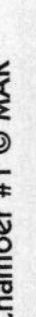
Chamber #1 © MAR

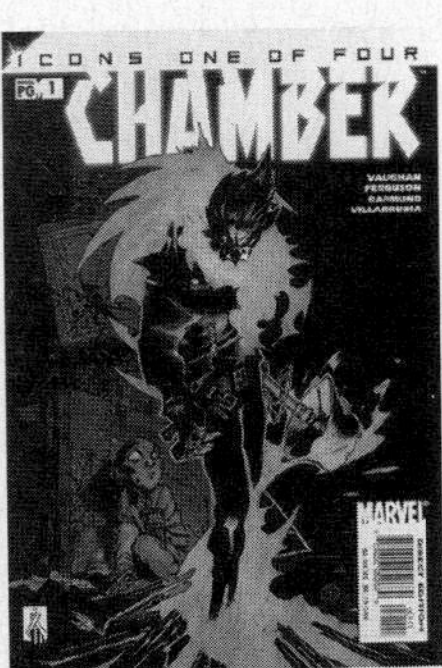

GD 2.0 | VG 4.0 | FN 6.0 | VF 8.0 | VF/NM 9.0 | NM- 9.2

1-4 2.50

CENTURY: DISTANT SONS
Marvel Comics: Feb, 1996 ($2.95, one-shot)
1-Wraparound-c 3.00

CENTURY OF COMICS (See Promotional Comics section)

CEREBUS BI-WEEKLY
Aardvark-Vanaheim: Dec. 2, 1988 - No. 26, Nov. 11, 1989 ($1.25, B&W)
Reprints Cerebus The Aardvark #1-26
1-16, 18, 19, 21-26: 3.00
17-Hepcats app. 2 4 6 8 10 12
20-Milk & Cheese app. 2 4 6 10 12 15

CEREBUS: CHURCH & STATE
Aardvark-Vanaheim: Feb, 1991 - No. 30, Apr, 1992 ($2.00, B&W, bi-weekly)
1-30: r/Cerebus #51-80 3.00

CEREBUS: HIGH SOCIETY
Aardvark-Vanaheim: Feb, 1990 - No. 25, 1991 ($1.70, B&W)
1-25: r/Cerebus #26-50 3.00

CEREBUS JAM
Aardvark-Vanaheim: Apr, 1985
1-Eisner, Austin, Dave Sim-a (Cerebus vs. Spirit) 6.00

CEREBUS THE AARDVARK (See A-V in 3-D, Nucleus, Power Comics)
Aardvark-Vanaheim: Dec, 1977 - No. 300, March, 2004 ($1.70/$2.00/$2.25, B&W)
0 3.00
0-Gold 20.00
1-1st app. Cerebus; 2000 print run; most copies poorly printed
48 96 144 384 742 1100

Note: *There is a counterfeit version known to exist. It can be distinguished from the original in the following ways: inside cover is glossy instead of flat, black background on the front cover is blotted or spotty. Reports show that a counterfeit #2 also exists.*

2-Dave Sim art in all 13 26 39 93 172 250
3-Origin Red Sophia 11 22 33 78 139 200
4-Origin Elrod the Albino 9 18 27 63 107 150
5,6 8 16 24 52 86 120
7-10 6 12 18 41 66 90
11,12: 11-Origin The Cockroach 5 10 15 32 51 70
13-15: 14-Origin Lord Julius 4 8 12 28 44 60
16-20 3 6 9 20 30 40
21-B. Smith letter in letter column 6 12 18 41 66 90
22-Low distribution; no cover price 4 8 12 24 37 50
23-30: 23-Preview of Wandering Star by Teri S. Wood. 26-High Society begins, ends #50
3 6 9 16 22 28
31-Origin Moonroach 3 6 9 16 23 30
32-40, 53-Intro. Wolveroach (brief app.) 2 4 6 8 10 12
41-50,52: 52-Church & State begins, ends #111; Cutey Bunny app.
1 2 3 5 7 9
51,54: 51-Cutey Bunny app. 54-1st full Wolveroach story
2 4 6 8 11 14
55,56-Wolveroach app.; Normalman back-ups by Valentino
1 3 4 6 8 10
57-100: 61,62: Flaming Carrot app. 65-Gerhard begins 4.00
101-160: 104-Flaming Carrot app. 112/113-Double issue. 114-Jaka's Story begins, ends #136.
139-Melmoth begins, ends #150. 151-Mothers & Daughters begins, ends #200 3.00
161-Bone app. 1 3 4 6 8 10
162-231: 175-($2.25, 44 pgs). 186-Strangers in Paradise cameo. 201-Guys storyline begins;
Eddie Campbell's Bacchus app. 220-231-Rick's Story 2.50
232-265-Going Home 2.50
266-288,291-299-Latter Days: 267-Five-Bar Gate. 276-Spore (Spawn spoof) 2.50
289&290 ($4.50) Two issues combined 5.00
300-Final issue 2.50
Free Cerebus (Giveaway, 1991-92?, 36 pgs.)-All-r 4.00

CHAIN GANG WAR
DC Comics: July, 1993 - No. 12, June, 1994 ($1.75)
1-($2.50)-Embossed silver foil-c, Dave Johnson-c/a 3.00
2-4,6-12: 3-Deathstroke app. 4-Brief Deathstroke app. 6-New Batman (Azrael) cameo.
11-New Batman-c/story. 12-New Batman app. 2.50
5-($2.50)-Foil-c; Deathstroke app; new Batman cameo (1 panel) 3.00

CHAINS OF CHAOS
Harris Comics: Nov, 1994 - No. 3, Jan, 1995 ($2.95, limited series)
1-3-Re-Intro of The Rook w/ Vampirella 3.00

GD 2.0 | VG 4.0 | FN 6.0 | VF 8.0 | VF/NM 9.0 | NM- 9.2

CHALLENGE OF THE UNKNOWN (Formerly Love Experiences)
Ace Magazines: No. 6, Sept, 1950 (See Web Of Mystery No. 19)
6- "Villa of the Vampire" used in N.Y. Joint Legislative Comm. Publ; Sekowsky-a
36 72 108 216 351 485

CHALLENGER, THE
Interfaith Publications/T.C. Comics: 1945 - No. 4, Oct-Dec, 1946
nn; nd; 32 pgs.; Origin the Challenger Club; Anti-Fascist with funny animal filler
52 104 156 328 552 775
2-4: Kubert-a; 4-Fuje-a 40 80 120 246 411 575

CHALLENGERS OF THE FANTASTIC
Marvel Comics (Amalgam): June 1997 ($1.95, one-shot)
1-Karl Kesel-s/Tom Grummett-a 2.50

CHALLENGERS OF THE UNKNOWN (See Showcase #6, 7, 11, 12, Super DC Giant, and Super Team Family) (See Showcase Presents for B&W reprints)
National Per. Publ./DC Comics: 4-5/58 - No. 77, 12-1/70-71; No. 78, 2/73 - No. 80, 6-7/73; No. 81, 6-7/77 - No. 87, 6-7/78
1-(4-5/58)-Kirby/Stein-a(2); Kirby-c 208 416 624 1820 3610 5400
2-Kirby/Stein-a(2) 66 132 198 561 1106 1650
3-Kirby/Stein-a(2); Rocky returns from space with powers similar to the Fantastic Four (9/58)
56 112 168 476 938 1400
4-8-Kirby/Wood-a plus cover to #8 43 86 129 344 672 1000
9,10 26 52 78 186 361 535
11-Grey tone-c 24 48 72 175 338 500
12-15: 14-Origin/1st app. Multi-Man (villain) 18 36 54 129 252 375
16-22: 18-Intro. Cosmo, the Challengers Spacepet. 22-Last 10¢ issue
13 26 39 93 172 250
23-30 9 18 27 60 100 140
31-Retells origin of the Challengers 9 18 27 61 103 145
32-40 6 12 18 43 69 95
41-47,49,50,52-60: 43-New look begins. 49-Intro. Challenger Corps. 55-Death of Red Ryan.
60-Red Ryan returns 5 10 15 30 48 65
48,51: 48-Doom Patrol app. 51-Sea Devils app. 5 10 15 32 51 70
61-68: 64,65-Kirby origin-r, parts 1 & 2. 66-New logo. 68-Last 12¢ issue.
4 8 12 22 34 45
69-73,75-80: 69-1st app. Corinna. 77-Last 15¢ issue 3 6 9 14 20 25
74-Deadman by Tuska/Adams; 1 pg. Wrightson-a 6 12 18 39 62 85
81,83-87: 81-(6-7/77). 83-87-Swamp Thing app. 84-87-Deadman app.
1 3 4 6 8 10
82-Swamp Thing begins (thru #87, c/s 2 4 6 8 11 14

NOTE: ***N. Adams*** *c-67, 68, 70, 72, 74i, 81i.* ***Buckler*** *c-83-86p.* ***Giffen*** *a-83-87p.* ***Kirby*** *a-75-80r; c-75, 77, 78.* ***Kubert*** *c-64, 66, 69, 76, 79.* ***Nasser*** *c/a-81p, 82p.* ***Tuska*** *a-73.* ***Wood*** *r-76.*

CHALLENGERS OF THE UNKNOWN
DC Comics: Mar, 1991 - No. 8, Oct, 1991 ($1.75, limited series)
1-Jeph Loeb scripts & Tim Sale-a in all (1st work together); Bolland-c 3.00
2-8: 2-Superman app. 3-Dr. Fate app. 6-G. Kane-c(p). 7-Steranko-c/swipe by Art Adams 2.50
... Must Die! (2004, $19.95, TPB) r/series; intro by Bendis; Sale sketch pages 20.00

NOTE: ***Art Adams*** *c-7.* ***Hempel*** *c-5.* ***Gil Kane*** *c-6p.* ***Sale*** *a-1-8; c-3, 8.* ***Wagner*** *c-4.*

CHALLENGERS OF THE UNKNOWN
DC Comics: Feb, 1997 - No. 18, July, 1998 ($2.25)
1-18: 1-Intro new team; Leon-c/a(p) begins. 4-Origin of new team. 11,12-Batman app.
15-Millennium Giants x-over; Superman-c/app. 2.50

CHALLENGERS OF THE UNKNOWN
DC Comics: Aug, 2004 - No. 6, Jan, 2005 ($2.95, limited series)
1-6-Intro. new team; Howard Chaykin-s/a 3.00

CHALLENGE TO THE WORLD
Catechetical Guild: 1951 (10¢, 36 pgs.)
nn 6 12 18 28 34 40

CHAMBER (See Generation X and Uncanny X-Men)
Marvel Comics: Oct, 2002 - No. 4, Jan, 2003 ($2.99, limited series)
1-4-Bachalo-c/Vaughan-s/Ferguson-a. 1-Cyclops app. 3.00

CHAMBER OF CHILLS (Formerly Blondie Comics #20; ...of Clues No. 27 on)
Harvey Publications/Witches Tales: No. 21, June, 1951 - No. 26, Dec, 1954
21 (#1) 48 96 144 302 514 725
22,24 (#2,4) 36 72 108 211 343 475
23 (#3)-Excessive violence; eyes torn out 37 74 111 222 361 500
5(2/52)-Decapitation, acid in face scene 37 74 111 222 361 500
6-Woman melted alive 36 72 108 216 351 485
7-Used in **SOTI**, pg. 389; decapitation/severed head panels

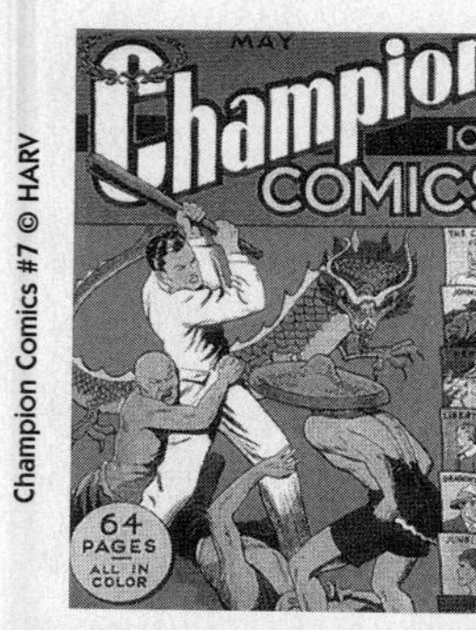

Champion Comics #7 © HARV

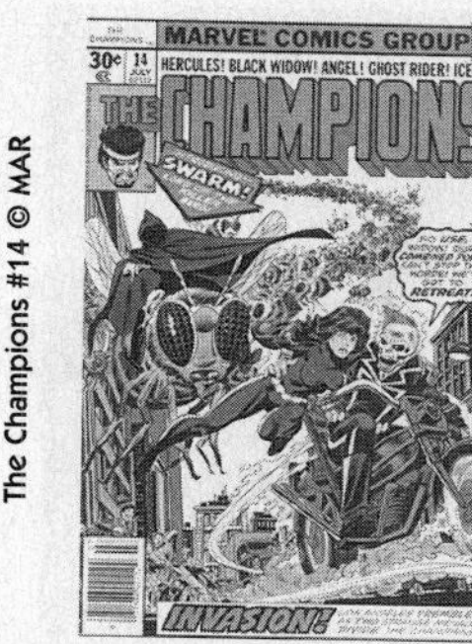

The Champions #14 © MAR

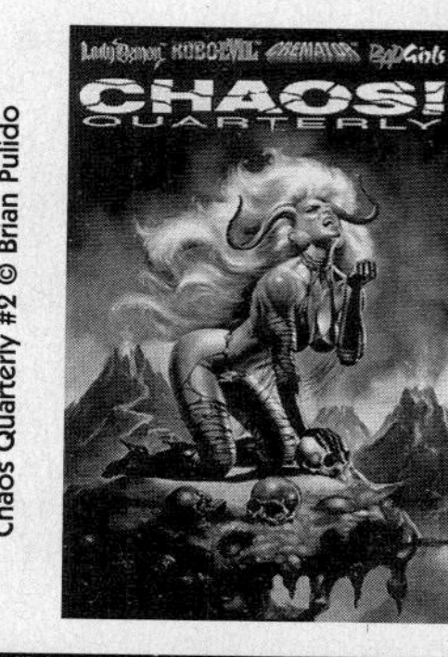

Chaos Quarterly #2 © Brian Pulido

	GD 2.0	VG 4.0	FN 6.0	VF 8.0	VF/NM 9.0	NM- 9.2
	34	68	102	204	332	460
8-10: 8-Decapitation panels	28	56	84	168	274	380
11,12,14	23	46	69	136	223	310
13,15-24-Nostrand-a in all. 13,21-Decapitation panels. 18-Atom bomb panels. 20-Nostrand-c	28	56	84	165	270	375
25,26	19	38	57	111	176	240

NOTE: *About half the issues contain bondage, torture, sadism, perversion, gore, cannabalism, eyes ripped out, acid in face, etc.* ***Elias*** *c-4-11, 14-19, 21-26.* ***Kremer*** *a-12, 17.* ***Palais*** *a-21(1), 23.* ***Nostrand/Powell*** *a-13, 15, 16.* ***Powell*** *a-21, 23, 24('51), 5-8, 11, 13, 18-21, 23-25. Bondage-c-21, 24('51), 7. 25-r/#5; 26-r/#9.*

CHAMBER OF CHILLS
Marvel Comics Group: Nov, 1972 - No. 25, Nov, 1976

	GD	VG	FN	VF	VF/NM	NM-
1-Harlan Ellison adaptation	4	8	12	22	34	45
2-5: 2-1st app. John Jakes' Brak the Barbarian	2	4	6	11	16	20
6-25: 22,23-(Regular 25¢ editions)	2	4	6	9	13	16
22,23-(30¢-c variants, limited distribution)(5,7/76)	4	8	12	24	37	50

NOTE: ***Adkins*** *a-1i, 2i.* ***Brunner*** *a-2-4; c-4.* ***Chaykin*** *a-4.* ***Ditko*** *r-14, 16, 19, 23, 24.* ***Everett*** *a-3i, 11r,21r.* ***Heath*** *a-1r.* ***Gil Kane*** *c-2p.* ***Kirby*** *r-11, 18, 19, 22.* ***Powell*** *a-13r.* ***Russell*** *a-1p, 2p.* ***Shores*** *a-5 .* ***Williamson/Mayo*** *a-13r.* ***Robert E. Howard*** *horror story adaptation-2, 3.*

CHAMBER OF CLUES (Formerly Chamber of Chills)
Harvey Publications: No. 27, Feb, 1955 - No. 28, April, 1955

	GD	VG	FN	VF	VF/NM	NM-
27-Kerry Drake-r/#19; Powell-a; last pre-code	7	14	21	35	43	50
28-Kerry Drake	6	12	18	28	34	40

CHAMBER OF DARKNESS (Monsters on the Prowl #9 on)
Marvel Comics Group: Oct, 1969 - No. 8, Dec, 1970

	GD	VG	FN	VF	VF/NM	NM-
1-Buscema-a(p)	8	16	24	52	86	120
2,3: 2-Neal Adams scripts. 3-Smith, Buscema-a	4	8	12	28	44	60
4-A Conan-esque tryout by Smith (4/70); reprinted in Conan #16; Marie Severin/Everett-c	9	18	27	63	107	150
5,8: 5-H.P. Lovecraft adaptation. 8-Wrightson-c	4	8	12	24	37	50
6	3	6	9	20	30	40
7-Wrightson-c/a, 7pgs. (his 1st work at Marvel); Wrightson draws himself in 1st & last panels; Kirby/Ditko-r; last 15¢-c	6	12	18	37	59	80
1-(1/72; 25¢ Special, 52 pgs.)	4	8	12	24	37	50

NOTE: ***Adkins/Everett*** *a-8.* ***Buscema*** *a-Special 1r.* ***Craig*** *a-5.* ***Ditko*** *a-6-8r.* ***Heck*** *a-1, 2, 8, Special 1r.* ***Kirby*** *a(p)-4, 5, 7r.* ***Kirby/Everett*** *c-5.* ***Severin/Everett*** *c-6.* ***Shores*** *a-2, 3i, Special 1r.* ***Sutton*** *a-1, 2i, 4, 7, Special 1r.* ***Wrightson*** *c-7, 8.*

CHAMP COMICS (Formerly Champion No. 1-10)
Worth Publ. Co./Champ Publ./Family Comics(Harvey Publ.): No. 11, Oct, 1940 - No. 24, Dec, 1942; No. 25, April, 1943

	GD	VG	FN	VF	VF/NM	NM-
11-Human Meteor cont'd. from Champion	94	188	282	597	1024	1450
12-17,20: 14,15-Crandall-c. 20-The Green Ghost app.	73	146	219	467	796	1125
18,19-Simon-c. 19-The Wasp app.	92	184	276	584	1005	1425
21-23,25: 22-The White Mask app. 23-Flag-c	53	106	159	334	567	800
24-Hitler, Tojo & Mussolini-c	71	142	213	454	777	1100

CHAMPION (See Gene Autry's...)

CHAMPION COMICS
Worth Publ. Co.: Oct, 1939 (ashcan)

nn-Ashcan comic, not distributed to newsstands, only for in house use (no known sales)

CHAMPION COMICS (Formerly Speed Comics #1?; Champ Comics No. 11 on)
Worth Publ. Co.(Harvey Publications): No. 2, Dec, 1939 - No. 10, Aug, 1940 (no No.1)

	GD	VG	FN	VF	VF/NM	NM-
2-The Champ, The Blazing Scarab, Neptina, Liberty Lads, Jungleman, Bill Handy, Swingtime Sweetie begin	174	348	522	1114	1907	2700
3-7: 7-The Human Meteor begins?	79	158	237	502	864	1225
8-10: 8-Simon-c. 9-1st S&K-c (1st collaboration together). 10-Bondage-c by Kirby	168	336	504	1075	1838	2600

CHAMPIONS, THE
Marvel Comics Group: Oct, 1975 - No. 17, Jan, 1978

	GD	VG	FN	VF	VF/NM	NM-
1-Origin & 1st app. The Champions (The Angel, Black Widow, Ghost Rider, Hercules, Iceman); Venus x-over	4	8	12	24	37	50
2-4,8-10,16: 2,3-Venus x-over	2	4	6	11	16	20
5-7-(Regular 25¢ edition)(4-8/76) 6-Kirby-c	2	4	6	11	16	20
5-7-(30¢-c variants, limited distribution)	5	10	15	30	48	65
11-14,17-Byrne-a. 14-(Regular 30¢ edition)	2	4	6	13	18	22
14,15-(35¢-c variant, limited distribution)	6	12	18	37	59	80
15-(Regular 30¢ edition)(9/77)-Byrne-a	2	4	6	13	18	22
... Classic Vol. 1 TPB (2006, $19.99) r/#1-11; unused cover to #7						20.00
... Classic Vol. 2 TPB (2007, $19.99) r/#12-17, Iron Man Ann. #4, Avengers #163, Super-Villain Team-Up #14 and Peter Parker, The Spectacular Spider-Man #17-18						20.00

NOTE: ***Buckler/Adkins*** *c-3.* ***Byrne*** *a-11-15, 17.* ***Kane/Adkins*** *c-1.* ***Kane/Layton*** *c-11.* ***Tuska*** *a-3p, 4p, 6p, 7p. Ghost Rider c-1-4, 7, 8, 10, 14, 16, 17 (4, 10, 14 are more prominent).*

CHAMPIONS (Game)
Eclipse Comics: June, 1986 - No. 6, Feb, 1987 (limited series)

1-6: 1-Intro Flare; based on game. 5-Origin Flare 2.50

CHAMPIONS (Also see The League of Champions)
Hero Comics: Sept, 1987 - No. 12, 1989 ($1.95)

1-12: 1-Intro The Marksman & The Rose. 14-Origin Malice 2.50
Annual 1(1988, $2.75, 52pgs.)-Origin of Giant 2.75

CHAMPION SPORTS
National Periodical Publications: Oct-Nov, 1973 - No. 3, Feb-Mar, 1974

	GD	VG	FN	VF	VF/NM	NM-
1	3	6	9	16	23	30
2,3	2	4	6	9	12	15

CHANNEL ZERO
Image Comics: Feb, 1998 - No. 5 ($2.95, B&W, limited series)

1-5, ...Dupe (1/99) -Brian Wood-s/a 3.00

CHAOS (See The Crusaders)

CHAOS! BIBLE
Chaos! Comics: Nov, 1995 ($3.30, one-shot)

1-Profiles of characters & creators 3.50

CHAOS! CHRONICLES
Chaos! Comics: Feb, 2000 ($3.50, one-shot)

1-Profiles of characters, checklist of Chaos! comics and products 3.50

CHAOS EFFECT, THE
Valiant: 1994

Alpha (Giveaway w/trading card checklist) 2.25
Alpha-Gold variant, Alpha-Red variant, Omega-Gold variant 5.00
Omega (11/94, $2.25); Epilogue Pt. 1, 2 (12/94, 1/95; $2.95) 3.00

CHAOS! GALLERY
Chaos! Comics: Aug, 1997 ($2.95, one-shot)

1-Pin-ups of characters 3.00

CHAOS! QUARTERLY
Chaos! Comics: Oct, 1995 -No. 3, May, 1996 ($4.95, quarterly)

1-3: 1-anthology; Lady Death-c by Julie Bell. 2-Boris "Lady Demon"-c 5.00
1-Premium Edition (7,500) 25.00

CHAPEL (Also see Youngblood & Youngblood Strikefile #1-3)
Image Comics (Extreme Studios): No. 1 Feb, 1995 - No. 2, Mar, 1995 ($2.50, limited series)

1,2 2.50

CHAPEL (Also see Youngblood & Youngblood Strikefile #1-3)
Image Comics (Extreme Studios): V2 #1, Aug, 1995 - No. 7, Apr, 1996 ($2.50)

V2#1-7: 4-Babewatch x-over. 5-vs. Spawn. 7-Shadowhawk-c/app; Shadowhunt x-over 2.50
#1-Quesada & Palmiotti variant-c 2.50

CHAPEL (Also see Youngblood & Youngblood Strikefile #1-3)
Awesome Entertainment: Sept, 1997 ($2.99, one-shot)

1 (Reg. & alternate covers) 3.00

CHARLEMAGNE (Also see War Dancer)
Defiant Comics: Mar, 1994 - No. 5, July, 1994 ($2.50)

1/2 (Hero Illustrated giveaway)-Adam Pollina-c/a.
1-(3/94, $3.50, 52 pgs.)-Adam Pollina-c/a. 3.50
2,3,5: Adam Pollina-c/a. 2-War Dancer app. 5-Pre-Schism issue. 2.50
4-($3.25, 52 pgs.) 3.25

CHARLIE CHAN (See Big Shot Comics, Columbia Comics, Feature Comics & The New Advs. of...)

CHARLIE CHAN (The Adventures of...) (Zaza The Mystic No. 10 on) (TV)
Crestwood(Prize) No. 1-5; Charlton No. 6(6/55) on: 6-7/48 - No. 5, 2-3/49; No.6, 6/55 - No. 9, 3/56

	GD	VG	FN	VF	VF/NM	NM-
1-S&K-c, 2 pgs.; Infantino-a	87	174	261	553	952	1350
2-5-S&K-c: 3-S&K-c/a	50	100	150	315	533	750
6 (6/55-Charlton)-S&K-c	37	74	111	222	361	500
7-9	20	40	60	118	192	265

CHARLIE CHAN
Dell Publishing Co.: Oct-Dec, 1965 - No. 2, Mar, 1966

	GD	VG	FN	VF	VF/NM	NM-
1-Springer-a/c	5	10	15	35	55	75
2	4	8	12	22	34	45

CHARLIE McCARTHY (See Edgar Bergen Presents...)
Dell Publishing Co.: No. 171, Nov, 1947 - No. 571, July, 1954 (See True Comics #14)

Charlton Bullseye #4 © CC

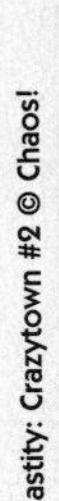
Chastity: Crazytown #2 © Chaos!

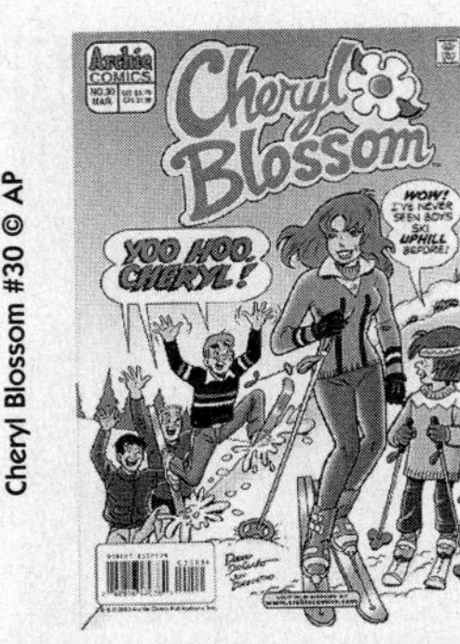

Cheryl Blossom #30 © AP

	GD 2.0	VG 4.0	FN 6.0	VF 8.0	VF/NM 9.0	NM- 9.2
Four Color 171	24	48	72	175	338	500
Four Color 196-Part photo-c; photo back-c	15	30	45	107	204	300
1(3-5/49)-Part photo-c; photo back-c	14	28	42	98	184	270
2-9(7/52; #5,6-52 pgs.)	8	16	24	56	93	130
Four Color 445,478,527,571	6	12	18	39	62	85

CHARLTON BULLSEYE
CPL/Gang Publications: 1975 - No. 5, 1976 ($1.50, B&W, bi-monthly, magazine format)

	GD	VG	FN	VF	VF/NM	NM-
1: 1 & 2 are last Capt. Atom by Ditko/Byrne intended for the never published Capt. Atom #90; Nightshade app.; Jeff Jones-a	5	10	15	30	48	65
2-Part 2 Capt. Atom story by Ditko/Byrne	3	6	9	21	32	42
3-Wrong Country by Sanho Kim	2	4	6	13	18	22
4-Doomsday + 1 by John Byrne	3	6	9	17	25	32
5-Doomsday + 1 by Byrne, The Question by Toth; Neal Adams back-c; Toth-c	4	8	12	24	37	50

CHARLTON BULLSEYE
Charlton Publications: June, 1981 - No. 10, Dec, 1982; Nov, 1986

	GD	VG	FN	VF	VF/NM	NM-
1-Blue Beetle, The Question app.; 1st app. Rocket Rabbit	1	2	3	5	7	9
2-5: 2-1st app. Neil The Horse; Rocket Rabbit app. 4-Vanguards						6.00
6-10: Low print run. 6-Origin & 1st app. Thunderbunny	1	2	3	5	7	9

NOTE: *Material intended for issue #11-up was published in **Scary Tales** #37-up.*

CHARLTON CLASSICS
Charlton Comics: Apr, 1980 - No. 9, Aug, 1981

1-Hercules-r by Glanzman in all — 6.00
2-9 — 5.00

CHARLTON CLASSICS LIBRARY (1776)
Charlton Comics: V10 No.1, Mar, 1973 (one-shot)

	GD	VG	FN	VF	VF/NM	NM-
1776 (title) - Adaptation of the film musical "1776"; given away at movie theatres; also a newsstand version	3	6	9	14	19	24

CHARLTON PREMIERE (Formerly Marine War Heroes)
Charlton Comics: V1#19, July, 1967; V2#1, Sept, 1967 - No. 4, May, 1968

	GD	VG	FN	VF	VF/NM	NM-
V1#19, V2#1,2,4: V1#19-Marine War Heroes. V2#1-Trio; intro. Shape, Tyro Team & Spookman. 2-Children of Doom; Boyette classic-a. 4-Unlikely Tales; Aparo, Ditko-a	3	6	9	16	22	28
V2#3-Sinistro Boy Fiend; Blue Beetle & Peacemaker x-over	3	6	9	18	27	35

CHARLTON SPORT LIBRARY - PROFESSIONAL FOOTBALL
Charlton Comics: Winter, 1969-70 (Jan. on cover) (68 pgs.)

	GD	VG	FN	VF	VF/NM	NM-
1	3	6	9	20	30	40

CHASE (See Batman #550 for 1st app.)
DC Comics: Feb, 1998 - No. 9, Oct, 1998; #1,000,000 Nov, 1998 ($2.50)

1-9: Williams III & Gray-a. 1-Includes 4 Chase cards. 4-Teen Titans app. 7,8-Batman app. 9-GL Hal Jordan-c/app. — 2.50
#1,000,000 (11/98) Final issue; 853rd Century x-over — 2.50

CHASING DOGMA (See Jay and Silent Bob)

CHASSIS
Millenium Publications: 1996 - No. 3 ($2.95)

1-3: 1-Adam Hughes-c. 2-Conner var-c. — 3.00

CHASSIS
Hurricane Entertainment: 1998 - No. 3 ($2.95)

0,1-3: 1-Adam Hughes-c. 0-Green var-c. — 3.00

CHASSIS (Vol. 3)
Image Comics: Nov, 1999 - No. 4 ($2.95, limited series)

1-4: 1-Two covers by O'Neil and Green. 2-Busch var-c. — 3.00
1-($6.95) DF Edition alternate-c by Wieringo — 7.00

CHASTITY
Chaos! Comics: (one-shots)

#1/2 (1/01, $2.95) Batista-a — 3.00
Heartbreaker (3/02, $2.99) Adrian-a/Molenaar-c — 3.00
Love Bites (3/01, $2.99) Vale-a/Romano-c — 3.00
Reign of Terror 1 (10/00, $2.95) Grant-s/Ross-a/Rio-c — 3.00
Re-Imagined 1 (7/02, $2.99) Conner-c; Toledo-a — 3.00

CHASTITY: CRAZYTOWN
Chaos! Comics: Apr, 2002 - No. 3, June, 2002 ($2.99, limited series)

1-3-Nicieza-s/Batista-c/a — 3.00

CHASTITY: LUST FOR LIFE
Chaos! Comics: May, 1999 - No. 3, July, 1999 ($2.95, limited series)

1-3-Nutman-s/Benes-c/a — 3.00

CHASTITY: ROCKED
Chaos! Comics: Nov, 1998 - No. 4, Feb, 1999 ($2.95, limited series)

1-4-Nutman-s/Justiniano-c/a — 3.00

CHASTITY: SHATTERED
Chaos! Comics: Jun, 2001 - No. 3, Sept, 2001 ($2.99, limited series)

1-3-Kaminski & Pulido-s/Batista-c/a — 3.00

CHASTITY: THEATER OF PAIN
Chaos! Comics: Feb, 1997 - No. 3, June, 1997 ($2.95, limited series)

1-3-Pulido-s/Justiniano-c/a — 3.00
TPB (1997, $9.95) r/#1-3 — 10.00

CHECKMATE (TV)
Gold Key: Oct, 1962 - No. 2, Dec, 1962

	GD	VG	FN	VF	VF/NM	NM-
1-Photo-c on both	6	12	18	37	59	80
2	5	10	15	32	51	70

CHECKMATE! (See Action Comics #598 and The OMAC Project)
DC Comics: Apr, 1988 - No. 33, Jan, 1991 ($1.25)

1-33: 13: New format begins — 2.50

NOTE: ***Gil Kane** c-2, 4, 7, 8, 10, 11, 15-19.*

CHECKMATE (See Infinite Crisis and The OMAC Project)
DC Comics: Jun, 2006 - No. 31, Dec, 2008 ($2.99)

1-Rucka-s/Saiz-a/Bermejo-c; Alan Scott, Mr. Terrific, Sasha Bordeaux app. — 4.00
1-2nd printing with B&W cover — 3.00
2-31: 2,3-Kobra, King Faraday, Amanda Waller, Fire app. 13-15-Outsiders app. 26-Chimera origin — 3.00
...: A King's GameTPB (2007, $14.99) r/#1-7 — 15.00
...: Chimera TPB (2009, $17.99) r/#26-31 — 18.00
...: Fall of the Wall TPB (2008, $14.99) r/#16-22 — 15.00
...: Pawn Breaks TPB (2007, $14.99) r/#8-12 — 15.00

CHERYL BLOSSOM (See Archie's Girls, Betty and Veronica #320 for 1st app.)
Archie Publications: Sept, 1995 - No. 3, Nov, 1995 ($1.50, limited series)

	GD	VG	FN	VF	VF/NM	NM-
1-3	1	2	3	4	5	7
Special 1-4 ('95, '96, $2.00)	1	2	3	4	5	7

CHERYL BLOSSOM (Cheryl's Summer Job)
Archie Publications: July, 1996 - No. 3, Sept, 1996 ($1.50, limited series)

1-3 — 5.00

CHERYL BLOSSOM (...Goes Hollywood)
Archie Publications: Dec, 1996 - No. 3, Feb, 1997 ($1.50, limited series)

1-3 — 5.00

CHERYL BLOSSOM
Archie Publications: Apr, 1997 - No. 37, Mar, 2001 ($1.50/$1.75/$1.79/$1.99)

	GD	VG	FN	VF	VF/NM	NM-
1-Dan DeCarlo-c/a	1	2	3	5	7	9
2-10: 2-7-Dan DeCarlo-c/a						5.00
11-37: 32-Begin $1.99-c. 34-Sabrina app.						3.00

CHESTY SANCHEZ
Antarctic Press: Nov, 1995 - No. 2, Mar, 1996 ($2.95, B&W)

1,2 — 3.00
...Super Special (2/99, $5.99) — 6.00

CHEVAL NOIR
Dark Horse Comics: 1989 - No. 48, Nov, 1993 ($3.50, B&W, 68 pgs.)

1-8,10 ($3.50): 6-Moebius poster insert — 3.50
9,11,13,15,17,20,22 ($4.50, 84 pgs.) — 4.50
12,18,19,21,23 ($3.95): 12-Geary-a; Mignola-c — 4.00
14 ($4.95, 76 pgs.)(7 pgs. color) — 5.00
16,24 ($3.75): 16-19-Contain trading cards — 3.75
25,26 ($3.95): 26-Moebius-a begins — 4.00
27-48 ($2.95): 33-Snyder III-c — 3.00

NOTE: ***Bolland** a-2, 6, 7, 13, 14. **Bolton** a-2, 4, 45; c-4, 20. **Chadwick** c-13. **Dorman** painted c-16. **Geary** a-13, 14. **Kelley Jones** c-27. **Kaluta** a-6; c-6, 18. **Moebius** c-5, 9, 26. **Dave Stevens** c-1, 7. **Sutton** painted c-36.*

CHEW
Image Comics: Jun, 2009 - Present ($2.99)

1-Layman-s/Guillory-a — 20.00
1-2nd-4th printings — 3.00
2-1st printing — 5.00

Chew #8 © John Layman

Children of the Voyager #4 © MAR

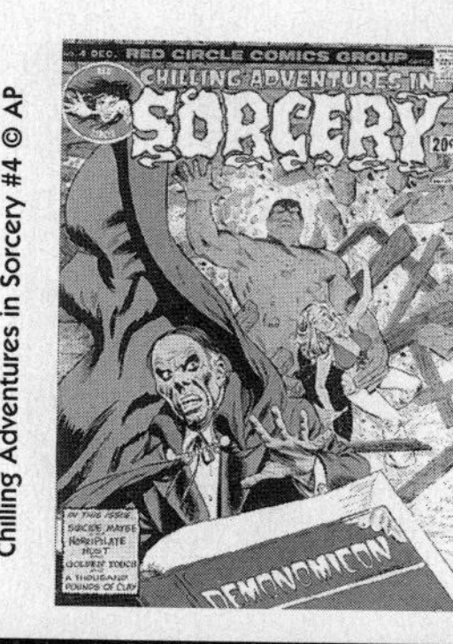

Chilling Adventures in Sorcery #4 © AP

	GD 2.0	VG 4.0	FN 6.0	VF 8.0	VF/NM 9.0	NM- 9.2
2-(2nd printing) - 8: Multiple printings exist						3.00
CHEYENNE (TV)						
Dell Publishing Co.: No. 734, Oct, 1956 - No. 25, Dec-Jan, 1961-62						
Four Color 734(#1)-Clint Walker photo-c	14	28	42	102	194	285
Four Color 772,803: Clint Walker photo-c	9	18	27	60	100	140
4(8-10/57) - 20: 4-9,13-20-Clint Walker photo-c. 10-12-Ty Hardin photo-c	6	12	18	43	69	95
21-25-Clint Walker photo-c on all	7	14	21	45	73	100
CHEYENNE AUTUMN (See Movie Classics)						
CHEYENNE KID (Formerly Wild Frontier No. 1-7)						
Charlton Comics: No. 8, July, 1957 - No. 99, Nov, 1973						
8 (#1)	8	16	24	40	50	65
9,15-19	6	12	18	29	36	42
10-Williamson/Torres-a(3); Ditko-c	11	22	33	60	83	105
11-(68 pgs.)-Cheyenne Kid meets Geronimo	10	20	30	58	79	100
12-Williamson/Torres-a(2)	10	20	30	58	79	100
13-Williamson/Torres-a (5 pgs.)	8	16	24	44	57	70
14-Williamson-a (5 pgs.?)	8	16	24	42	54	65
20-22,24,25-Severin c/a(3) each	4	8	12	22	34	45
23,27-29	3	6	9	16	22	28
26,30-Severin-a	3	6	9	18	27	35
31-59	2	4	6	10	14	18
60-65,67-80	2	4	6	8	11	14
66-Wander by Aparo begins, ends #87	2	4	6	10	14	18
81-99: Apache Red begins #88, origin in #89	2	4	6	8	11	14
Modern Comics Reprint 87,89(1978)						4.00
CHIAROSCURO (THE PRIVATE LIVES OF LEONARDO DA VINCI)						
DC Comics (Vertigo): July, 1995 - No. 10, Apr, 1996 ($2.50/$2.95, limited series, mature)						
1-9: McGreal and Rawson-s/Truog & Kayanan-a						2.50
10-($2.95)						3.00
TPB (2005, $24.99) r/series; intro. by Alisa Kwitney, afterword by Pat McGreal						25.00
CHICAGO MAIL ORDER (See C-M-O Comics)						
CHIEF, THE (Indian Chief No. 3 on)						
Dell Publishing Co.: No. 290, Aug, 1950 - No. 2, Apr-June, 1951						
Four Color 290(#1)	7	14	21	49	80	110
2	6	12	18	39	62	85
CHIEF CRAZY HORSE (See Wild Bill Hickok #21)						
Avon Periodicals: 1950 (Also see Fighting Indians of the Wild West!)						
nn-Fawcette-c	21	42	63	124	202	280
CHIEF VICTORIO'S APACHE MASSACRE (See Fight Indians of/Wild West!)						
Avon Periodicals: 1951						
nn-Williamson/Frazetta-a (7 pgs.); Larsen-a; Kinstler-c	45	90	135	284	480	675
CHILDREN OF FIRE						
Fantagor Press: Nov, 1987 - No. 3, 1988 ($2.00, limited series)						
1-3: by Richard Corben						4.00
CHILDREN OF THE VOYAGER (See Marvel Frontier Comics Unlimited)						
Marvel Frontier Comics: Sept, 1993 - No. 4, Dec, 1993 ($1.95, limited series)						
1-($2.95)-Embossed glow-in-the-dark-c; Paul Johnson-c/a						3.00
2-4						2.50
CHILDREN'S BIG BOOK						
Dorene Publ. Co.: 1945 (25¢, stiff-c, 68 pgs.)						
nn-Comics & fairy tales; David Icove-a	14	28	42	78	112	145
CHILDREN'S CRUSADE, THE						
DC Comics (Vertigo): Dec, 1993 - No. 2, Jan, 1994 ($3.95, limited series)						
1,2-Gaiman scripts & Bachalo-a; framing issues for Children's Crusade x-over						4.00
CHILD'S PLAY: THE SERIES (Movie)						
Innovation Publishing: May, 1991 - #3, 1991 ($2.50, 28pgs.)						
1-3						2.50
CHILD'S PLAY 2 THE OFFICIAL MOVIE ADAPTATION (Movie)						
Innovation Publishing: 1990 - No. 3, 1990 ($2.50, bi-weekly limited series)						
1-3: Adapts movie sequel						2.50
CHILI (Millie's Rival)						
Marvel Comics Group: 5/69 - No. 17, 9/70; No. 18, 8/72 - No. 26, 12/73						
1	9	18	27	63	107	150

	GD 2.0	VG 4.0	FN 6.0	VF 8.0	VF/NM 9.0	NM- 9.2
2,4,5	5	10	15	34	55	75
3-Millie & Chili visit Marvel and meet Stan Lee & Stan Goldberg (6 pgs.)	6	12	18	37	59	80
6-17	4	8	12	28	44	60
18-26	4	8	12	24	37	50
Special 1(12/71, 52 pgs.)	6	12	18	37	59	80
CHILLER						
Marvel Comics (Epic): Nov, 1993 - No. 2, Dec, 1993 ($7.95, lim. series)						
1,2-(68 pgs.)	1	2	3	5	6	8
CHILLING ADVENTURES IN SORCERY (...as Told by Sabrina #1, 2) (Red Circle Sorcery No. 6 on)						
Archie Publications (Red Circle Prods.): 9/72 - No. 2, 10/72; No. 3, 10/73 - No. 5, 2/74						
1-Sabrina cameo as narrator	5	10	15	32	51	70
2-Sabrina cameo as narrator	3	6	9	18	27	35
3-5: Morrow-c/a, all. 4,5-Alcazar-a	2	4	6	11	16	20
CHILLING TALES (Formerly Beware)						
Youthful Magazines: No. 13, Dec, 1952 - No. 17, Oct, 1953						
13(No.1)-Harrison-a; Matt Fox-c/a	68	136	204	435	743	1050
14-Harrison-a	45	90	135	284	480	675
15-Has #14 on-c; Matt Fox-c; Harrison-a	53	106	159	334	567	800
16-Poe adapt.-'Metzengerstein'; Rudyard Kipling adapt.- 'Mark of the Beast,' by Kiefer; bondage-c	40	80	120	246	411	575
17-Matt Fox-c; Sir Walter Scott & Poe adapt.	45	90	135	284	480	675
CHILLING TALES OF HORROR (Magazine)						
Stanley Publications: V1#1, 6/69 - V1#7, 12/70; V2#2, 2/71 - V2#6, 10/71(50¢, B&W, 52 pgs.)						
V1#1	7	14	21	49	80	110
2-4,(no #5),6,7: 7-Cameron-a	5	10	15	32	51	70
V2#2-6: 2-Two different #2 issues exist (2/71 & 4/71). 2-(2/71) Spirit of Frankenstein -r/Adventures into the Unknown #16. 4-(8/71) different from other V2#4(6/71)	5	10	15	30	48	65
V2#4-(6/71) r/9 pg. Feldstein-a from Adventures into the Unknown #3	5	10	15	32	51	70

NOTE: *Two issues of V2#2 exist, Feb, 1971 and April, 1971. Two issues of V2#4 exist, Jun, 1971 and Aug, 1971.*

	GD	VG	FN	VF	VF/NM	NM-
CHILLY WILLY (Also see New Funnies #211)						
Dell Publ. Co.: No. 740, Oct, 1956 - No. 1281, Apr-June, 1962 (Walter Lantz)						
Four Color 740 (#1)	7	14	21	45	73	100
Four Color 852 (2/58),967 (2/59),1017 (9/59),1074 (2-4/60),1122 (8/60), 1177 (4-6/61), 1212 (7-9/61), 1281	5	10	15	30	48	65
CHIMERA						
CrossGeneration Comics: Mar, 2003 - No. 4, July, 2003 ($2.95, limited series)						
1-4-Marz-s/Peterson-c/a						3.00
Vol. 1 TPB (2003, $15.95) r/#1-4 plus sketch pages, 3-D models, how-to guides						16.00
CHIMICHANGA						
Albatross Exploding Funny Books: 2010 ($3.00, B&W)						
1-Eric Powell-s/a/c						3.00
CHINA BOY (See Wisco in the Promotional Comics section)						
CHIP 'N' DALE (Walt Disney)(See Walt Disney's C&S #204)						
Dell Publishing Co./Gold Key/Whitman No. 65 on: Nov, 1953 - No. 30, June-Aug, 1962; Sept, 1967 - No. 83, July, 1984						
Four Color 517(#1)	10	20	30	73	129	185
Four Color 581	6	12	18	43	69	95
Four Color 636	6	12	18	43	69	95
4(12/55-2/56)-10	6	12	18	37	59	80
11-30	5	10	15	30	48	65
1(Gold Key, 1967)-Reprints	3	6	9	19	29	38
2-10	2	4	6	11	16	20
11-20	2	4	6	8	11	14
21-40	1	3	4	6	8	10
41-64,70-77: 75(2/82), 76(2-3/82), 77(3/82)	1	2	3	5	6	8
65,66 (Whitman)	2	4	6	8	10	12
67-69 (3-pack? 1980): 67(8/80), 68(10/80) (scarce)	4	8	12	22	34	45
78-83 (All #90214; 3-pack, nd, nd code): 78(4/83), 79(5/83), 80(7/83), 81(8/83), 82(5/84), 83(7/84)	3	6	9	14	20	26

NOTE: *All Gold Key/Whitman issues have reprints except No. 32-35, 38-41, 45-47. No. 23-28, 30-42, 45-47, 49 have new covers.*

	GD	VG	FN	VF	VF/NM	NM-
CHIP 'N DALE RESCUE RANGERS						
Disney Comics: June, 1990 - No. 19, Dec, 1991 ($1.50)						
1-New stories; origin begins						3.00

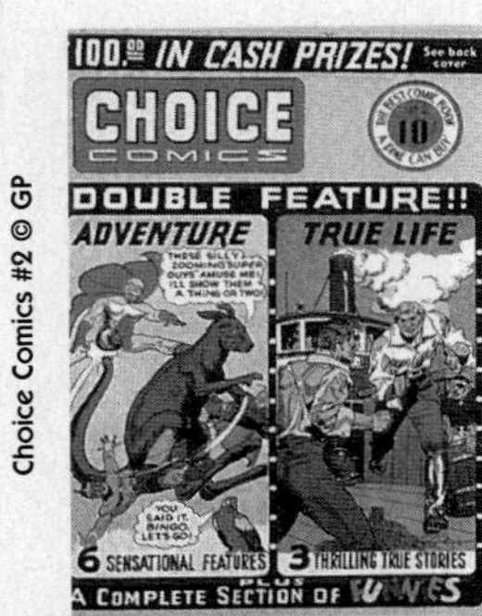

Choice Comics #2 © GP

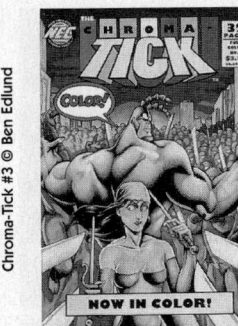

Chroma-Tick #3 © Ben Edlund

Chucky #1 © Universal Studios

	GD 2.0	VG 4.0	FN 6.0	VF 8.0	VF/NM 9.0	NM- 9.2
2-19: 2-Origin continued						2.50

CHITTY CHITTY BANG BANG (See Movie Comics)

C.H.I.X.
Image Comics (Studiosaurus): Jan, 1998 ($2.50)

	GD	VG	FN	VF	VF/NM	NM-
1-Dodson, Haley, Lopresti, Randall, and Warren-s/c/a						3.00
1-($5.00) "X-Ray Variant" cover						5.00
C.H.I.X. That Time Forgot 1 (8/98, $2.95)						3.00

CHOICE COMICS
Great Publications: Dec, 1941 - No. 3, Feb, 1942

	GD	VG	FN	VF	VF/NM	NM-
1-Origin Secret Circle; Atlas the Mighty app.; Zomba, Jungle Fight, Kangaroo Man, & Fire Eater begin	152	304	456	965	1658	2350
2	76	152	228	486	831	1175
3-Double feature; Features movie "The Lost City" (classic cover); continued from Great Comics #3	142	284	426	909	1555	2200

CHOLLY AND FLYTRAP (Arthur Suydam's...)
Image Comics: Nov, 2004 - No. 4, June, 2005 ($4.95/$5.95, limited series)

	GD	VG	FN	VF	VF/NM	NM-
1-($4.95) Arthur Suydam-s/a/c						5.00
2-4-($5.95)						6.00

CHOO CHOO CHARLIE
Gold Key: Dec, 1969

	GD	VG	FN	VF	VF/NM	NM-
1-John Stanley-a	9	18	27	63	107	150

CHOSEN
Dark Horse Comics: Jan, 2004 - No. 3, Aug, 2004 ($2.99, limited series)

	GD	VG	FN	VF	VF/NM	NM-
1-Story of the second coming; Mark Millar-s/Peter Gross-a						4.00
2,3						3.00

CHRISTIAN (See Asylum)
Maximum Press: Jan, 1996 ($2.99, one-shot)

	GD	VG	FN	VF	VF/NM	NM-
1-Pop Mhan-a						3.00

CHRISTIAN HEROES OF TODAY
David C. Cook: 1964 (36 pgs.)

	GD	VG	FN	VF	VF/NM	NM-
nn	3	6	9	17	25	32

CHRISTMAS (Also see A-1 Comics)
Magazine Enterprises: No. 28, 1950

	GD	VG	FN	VF	VF/NM	NM-
A-1 28	8	16	24	40	50	60

CHRISTMAS ADVENTURE, A (See Classics Comics Giveaways, 12/69)

CHRISTMAS ALBUM (See March of Comics No. 312)

CHRISTMAS ANNUAL
Golden Special: 1975 ($1.95, 100 pgs., stiff-c)

	GD	VG	FN	VF	VF/NM	NM-
nn-Reprints Mother Goose stories with Walt Kelly-a	4	8	12	22	34	45

CHRISTMAS & ARCHIE
Archie Comics: Jan, 1975 ($1.00, 68 pgs., 10-1/4x13-1/4" treasury-sized)

	GD	VG	FN	VF	VF/NM	NM-
1-(scarce)	6	12	18	39	62	85

CHRISTMAS BELLS (See March of Comics No. 297)

CHRISTMAS CARNIVAL
Ziff-Davis Publ. Co./St. John Publ. Co. No. 2: 1952 (25¢, one-shot, 100 pgs.)

	GD	VG	FN	VF	VF/NM	NM-
nn	35	70	105	208	339	470
2-Reprints Ziff-Davis issue plus-c	17	34	51	98	154	210

CHRISTMAS CAROL, A (See March of Comics No. 33)

CHRISTMAS EVE, A (See March of Comics No. 212)

CHRISTMAS IN DISNEYLAND (See Dell Giants)

CHRISTMAS PARADE (See Dell Giant No. 26, Dell Giants, March of Comics No. 284, Walt Disney Christmas Parade & Walt Disney's...)

CHRISTMAS PARADE (Walt Disney's)
Gold Key: 1962 (no month listed) - No. 9, Jan, 1972 (#1,5: 80 pgs.; #2-4,7-9: 36 pgs.)

	GD	VG	FN	VF	VF/NM	NM-
1 (30018-301)-Giant	9	18	27	60	100	140
2-6: 2-r/F.C. #367 by Barks. 3-r/F.C. #178 by Barks. 4-r/F.C. #203 by Barks. 5-r/Christmas Parade #1 (Dell) by Barks; giant. 6-r/Christmas Parade #2 (Dell) by Barks (64 pgs.); giant	6	12	18	41	66	90
7-Pull-out poster (half price w/o poster)	5	10	15	32	51	70
8-r/F.C. #367 by Barks; pull-out poster	6	12	18	41	66	90
9	4	8	12	26	41	55

CHRISTMAS PARTY (See March of Comics No. 256)

CHRISTMAS STORIES (See Little People No. 959, 1062)

CHRISTMAS STORY (See March of Comics No. 326 in the Promotional Comics section)

CHRISTMAS STORY BOOK (See Woolworth's Christmas Story Book)

CHRISTMAS TREASURY, A (See Dell Giants & March of Comics No. 227)

CHRISTMAS WITH ARCHIE
Spire Christian Comics (Fleming H. Revell Co.): 1973, 1974 (49¢, 52 pgs.)

	GD	VG	FN	VF	VF/NM	NM-
nn-Low print run	2	4	6	11	16	20

CHRISTMAS WITH MOTHER GOOSE
Dell Publishing Co.: No. 90, Nov, 1945 - No. 253, Nov, 1949

	GD	VG	FN	VF	VF/NM	NM-
Four Color 90 (#1)-Kelly-a	16	32	48	116	223	330
Four Color 126 ('46), 172 (11/47)-By Walt Kelly	13	26	39	90	165	240
Four Color 201 (10/48), 253-By Walt Kelly	11	22	33	78	139	200

CHRISTMAS WITH SANTA (See March of Comics No. 92)

CHRISTMAS WITH THE SUPER-HEROES (See Limited Collectors' Edition)
DC Comics: 1988; No. 2, 1989 ($2.95)

	GD	VG	FN	VF	VF/NM	NM-
1,2: 1-(100 pgs.)-All reprints; N. Adams-r, Byrne-c; Batman, Superman, JLA, LSH Christmas stories; r-Miller's 1st Batman/DC Special Series #21. 2-(68 pgs.)-Superman by Chadwick; Batman, Wonder Woman, Deadman, Green Lantern, Flash app.; Morrow-a; Enemy Ace by Byrne; all new-a						5.00

CHROMA-TICK, THE (...Special Edition, #1,2) (Also see The Tick)
New England Comics Press: Feb, 1992 - No. 8, Nov, 1993 ($3.95/$3.50, 44 pgs.)

	GD	VG	FN	VF	VF/NM	NM-
1,2-Includes serially numbered trading card set						5.00
3-8 ($3.50, 36 pgs.): 6-Bound-in card						4.00

CHROME
Hot Comics: 1986 - No. 3, 1986 ($1.50, limited series)

	GD	VG	FN	VF	VF/NM	NM-
1-3						2.50

CHROMIUM MAN, THE
Triumphant Comics: Aug, 1993 - No.10, May, 1994 ($2.50)

	GD	VG	FN	VF	VF/NM	NM-
1-1st app. Mr. Death; all serially numbered						2.50
2-10: 2-1st app. Prince Vandal. 3-1st app. Candi, Breaker & Coil. 4,5-Triumphant Unleashed x-over. 8,9-(3/94). 10-(5/94)						2.50
0-(4/94)-Four color-c, 0-All pink-c & all blue-c; no cover price						2.50

CHROMIUM MAN: VIOLENT PAST, THE
Triumphant Comics: Jan, 1994 - No. 2, Jan, 1994 ($2.50, limited series)

	GD	VG	FN	VF	VF/NM	NM-
1,2-Serially numbered to 22,000 each						2.50

CHRONICLES OF CONAN, THE (See Conan the Barbarian)

CHRONICLES OF CORUM, THE (Also see Corum...)
First Comics: Jan, 1987 - No. 12, Nov, 1988 ($1.75/$1.95, deluxe series)

	GD	VG	FN	VF	VF/NM	NM-
1-12: Adapts Michael Moorcock's novel						2.50

CHRONOS
DC Comics: Mar, 1998 - No. 11, Feb. 1999 ($2.50)

	GD	VG	FN	VF	VF/NM	NM-
1-11-J.F. Moore-s/Guinan-a						2.50
#1,000,000 (11/98) 853rd Century x-over						2.50

CHUCK (Based on the NBC TV series)
DC Comics (WildStorm): Aug, 2008 - No. 6, Jan, 2009 ($2.99, limited series)

	GD	VG	FN	VF	VF/NM	NM-
1-6-Jeremy Haun-a/Kristian Donaldson-c; Noto back-up-a						3.00
TPB (2009, $19.99) r/#1-6; photo-c						20.00

CHUCKLE, THE GIGGLY BOOK OF COMIC ANIMALS
R. B. Leffingwell Co.: 1945 (132 pgs., one-shot)

	GD	VG	FN	VF	VF/NM	NM-
1-Funny animal	22	44	66	128	209	290

CHUCK NORRIS (TV)
Marvel Comics (Star Comics): Jan, 1987 - No. 4, July, 1987

	GD	VG	FN	VF	VF/NM	NM-
1-3: Ditko-a						3.50
4-No Ditko-a (low print run)						5.00

CHUCK WAGON (See Sheriff Bob Dixon's...)

CHUCKY (Based on the 1988 killer doll movie Child's Play)
Devil's Due Publishing: Apr, 2007 - No. 4, Nov, 2007 ($3.50/$5.50)

	GD	VG	FN	VF	VF/NM	NM-
1-3-Pulido-s/Medors-a; art & photo covers						3.50
4-($5.50)						5.50
TPB (2007, $18.99) r/series; gallery of variant covers; 4 pages of script and sketch art						19.00

CHYNA (WWF Wrestling)
Chaos! Comics: Sept, 2000; July, 2001 ($2.95/$2.99, one-shots)

	GD	VG	FN	VF	VF/NM	NM-
1-Grant-s/Barrows-a; photo-c						3.00
1-($9.95) Premium Edition; Cleavenger-c						10.00

Cinderella: From Fabletown With Love #1 © Bill Willingham & DC

City of Heroes #18 © Cryptic Studios

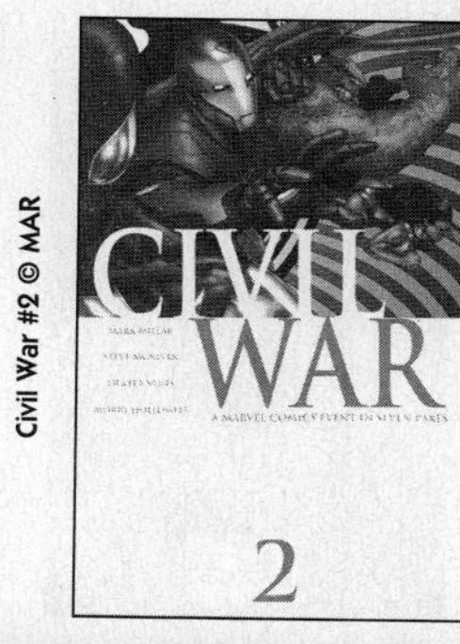
Civil War #2 © MAR

	GD 2.0	VG 4.0	FN 6.0	VF 8.0	VF/NM 9.0	NM- 9.2
II -(7/01, $2.99) Deodato-a; photo-c						3.00

CICERO'S CAT
Dell Publishing Co.: July-Aug, 1959 - No. 2, Sept-Oct, 1959

	GD	VG	FN	VF	VF/NM	NM-
1-Cat from Mutt & Jeff	5	10	15	30	48	65
2	4	8	12	26	41	55

CIMARRON STRIP (TV)
Dell Publishing Co.: Jan, 1968

	GD	VG	FN	VF	VF/NM	NM-
1-Stuart Whitman photo-c	4	8	12	24	37	50

CINDER AND ASHE
DC Comics: May, 1988 - No. 4, Aug, 1988 ($1.75, limited series)

	GD	VG	FN	VF	VF/NM	NM-
1-4: Mature readers						2.50

CINDERELLA (Disney) (See Movie Comics)
Dell Publishing Co.: No. 272, Apr, 1950 - No. 786, Apr, 1957

	GD	VG	FN	VF	VF/NM	NM-
Four Color 272	12	24	36	85	155	225
Four Color 786-Partial-r #272	7	14	21	45	73	100

CINDERELLA
Whitman Publishing Co.: Apr, 1982

	GD	VG	FN	VF	VF/NM	NM-
nn-Reprints 4-Color #272	1	2	3	4	5	7

CINDERELLA: FROM FABLETOWN WITH LOVE (See Fables)
DC Comics (Vertigo): Jan, 2010 - Present ($2.99)

	GD	VG	FN	VF	VF/NM	NM-
1-4: Roberson-s/McManus-a/Zullo-c						3.00

CINDERELLA LOVE
Ziff-Davis/St. John Publ. Co. No. 12 on: No. 10, 1950; No. 11, 4-5/51; No. 12, 9/51; No. 4, 10-11/51 - No. 11, Fall, 1952; No. 12, 10/53 - No. 15, 8/54; No. 25, 12/54 - No. 29, 10/55 (No #16-24)

	GD	VG	FN	VF	VF/NM	NM-
10(#1)(1st Series, 1950)-Painted-c	17	34	51	98	154	210
11(#2, 4-5/51)-Crandall-a; Saunders painted-c	12	24	36	67	94	120
12(#3, 9/51)-Photo-c	10	20	30	58	79	100
4-8: 4,6,7-Photo-c	10	20	30	54	72	90
9-Kinstler-a; photo-c	11	22	33	60	83	105
10,11(Fall/'52): 10,11-Photo-c	10	20	30	54	72	90
12(St. John-10/53)-#13:13-Painted-c.	9	18	27	52	69	85
14-Baker-a	11	22	33	62	86	110
15(8/54)-Matt Baker-c	14	28	42	76	108	140
25(2nd Series)(Formerly Romantic Marriage) Baker-c	14	28	42	76	108	140
26-Baker-c; last precode (2/55)	14	28	42	76	108	140
27,29: Both Matt Baker-c	14	28	42	76	108	140
28	9	18	27	47	61	75

CINDY COMICS (...Smith No. 39, 40; Crime Can't Win No. 41 on)(Formerly Krazy Komics) (See Junior Miss & Teen Comics)
Timely Comics: No. 27, Fall, 1947 - No. 40, July, 1950

	GD	VG	FN	VF	VF/NM	NM-
27-Kurtzman-a, 3 pgs: Margie, Oscar begin	22	44	66	132	216	300
28-31-Kurtzman-a	15	30	45	83	124	165
32-40: 33-Georgie story; anti-Wertham editorial	11	22	33	64	90	115

NOTE: *Kurtzman's "Hey Look"-#27(3), 29(2), 30(2), 31; "Giggles 'n' Grins"-28.*

CINNAMON: EL CICLO
DC Comics: Oct, 2003 - No. 5, Feb, 2004 ($2.50, limited series)

	GD	VG	FN	VF	VF/NM	NM-
1-5-Van Meter-s/Chaykin-c/Paronzini-a						2.50

CIRCUS (...the Comic Riot)
Globe Syndicate: June, 1938 - No. 3, Aug, 1938

	GD	VG	FN	VF	VF/NM	NM-
1-(Scarce)-Spacehawks (2 pgs.), & Disk Eyes by Wolverton (2 pgs.), Pewee Throttle by Cole (2nd comic book work; see Star Comics V1#11), Beau Gus, Ken Craig & The Lords of Crillon, Jack Hinton by Eisner, Van Bragger by Kane	500	1000	1500	3600	6300	9000
2,3-(Scarce)-Eisner, Cole, Wolverton, Bob Kane-a in each	280	5560	840	1764	2982	4200

CIRCUS BOY (TV) (See Movie Classics)
Dell Publishing Co.: No. 759, Dec, 1956 - No. 813, July, 1957

	GD	VG	FN	VF	VF/NM	NM-
Four Color 759 (#1)-The Monkees' Mickey Dolenz photo-c	12	24	36	85	155	225
Four Color 785 (4/57),813-Mickey Dolenz photo-c	10	20	30	70	123	175

CIRCUS COMICS
Farm Women's Pub. Co./D. S. Publ.: 1945 - No. 2, Jun, 1945; Wint., 1948-49

	GD	VG	FN	VF	VF/NM	NM-
1-Funny animal	14	28	42	80	115	150
2	9	18	27	50	65	80
1(1948)-D.S. Publ.; 2 pgs. Frazetta	24	48	72	140	230	320

CIRCUS OF FUN COMICS
A. W. Nugent Publ. Co.: 1945 - No. 3, Dec, 1947 (A book of games & puzzles)

	GD	VG	FN	VF	VF/NM	NM-
1	15	30	45	83	124	165
2,3	10	20	30	54	72	90

CISCO KID, THE (TV)
Dell Publishing Co.: July, 1950 - No. 41, Oct-Dec, 1958

	GD	VG	FN	VF	VF/NM	NM-
Four Color 292(#1)-Cisco Kid, his horse Diablo, & sidekick Pancho & his horse Loco begin; painted-c begin	22	44	66	157	304	450
2(1/51)	11	22	33	78	139	200
3-5	10	20	30	70	123	175
6-10	9	18	27	60	100	140
11-20	8	16	24	52	86	120
21-36-Last painted-c	6	12	18	43	69	95
37-41: All photo-c	8	16	24	54	90	125

NOTE: ***Buscema** a-40. **Ernest Nordli** painted c-5-16, 20, 35.*

CISCO KID COMICS
Bernard Bailey/Swappers Quarterly: Winter, 1944 (one-shot)

	GD	VG	FN	VF	VF/NM	NM-
1-Illustrated Stories of the Operas: Faust; Funnyman by Giunta; Cisco Kid (1st app.) & Superbaby begin; Giunta-c	43	86	129	271	461	650

CITIZEN SMITH (See Holyoke One-Shot No. 9)

CITIZEN V AND THE V-BATTALION (See Thunderbolts)
Marvel Comics: June, 2001 - No. 3, Aug, 2001 ($2.99, limited series)

	GD	VG	FN	VF	VF/NM	NM-
1-3-Nicieza-a; Michael Ryan-c/a						3.00
...: The Everlasting 1-4 (3/02 - No. 4, 7/02) Nicieza-s/LaRosa-a(p)						3.00

CITY OF HEROES (Online game)
Dark Horse Comics/Blue King Studios: Sept, 2002; May, 2004 - No. 7 ($2.95)

	GD	VG	FN	VF	VF/NM	NM-
1-(no cover price) Dakan-s/Zombo-a						2.50
1-7-($2.95)						3.00

CITY OF HEROES (Online game)
Image Comics: June, 2005 - No. 20, Aug, 2007 ($2.99)

	GD	VG	FN	VF	VF/NM	NM-
1-20: 1-Waid-s; Pérez-c. 6-Flp-c with City of Villains. 7-9-Jurgens-s						3.00

CITY OF OTHERS
Dark Horse Comics: Apr, 2007 - No. 4, Aug, 2007 ($2.99, limited series)

	GD	VG	FN	VF	VF/NM	NM-
1-4-Bernie Wrightson-a/c; Steve Niles & Wrightson-s						3.00
TPB (2/08, $14.95) r/#1-4; Wrightson sketch pages						15.00

CITY OF SILENCE
Image Comics: May, 2000 - No. 3, July, 2000 ($2.50)

	GD	VG	FN	VF	VF/NM	NM-
1-3-Ellis-s/Erskine-a						2.50
TPB (6/04, $9.95) r/#1-3; pin-up gallery						10.00

CITY OF THE LIVING DEAD (See Fantastic Tales No. 1)
Avon Periodicals: 1952

	GD	VG	FN	VF	VF/NM	NM-
nn-Hollingsworth-c/a	48	96	144	302	514	725

CITY OF TOMORROW
DC Comics (WildStorm): June, 2005 - No. 6, Nov, 2005 ($2.99, limited series)

	GD	VG	FN	VF	VF/NM	NM-
1-6-Howard Chaykin-s/a						3.00
TPB (2006, $19.99) r/#1-6						20.00

CITY PEOPLE NOTEBOOK
Kitchen Sink Press: 1989 ($9.95, B&W, magazine sized)

	GD	VG	FN	VF	VF/NM	NM-
nn-Will Eisner-s/a						10.00
nn-(DC Comics, 2000) Reprint						10.00

CITY SURGEON (Blake Harper...)
Gold Key: August, 1963

	GD	VG	FN	VF	VF/NM	NM-
1(10075-308)-Painted-c	4	8	12	24	37	50

CIVIL WAR (Also see Amazing Spider-Man for TPB)
Marvel Comics: July, 2006 - No. 7, Jan, 2007 ($3.99/$2.99, limited series)

	GD	VG	FN	VF	VF/NM	NM-
1-($3.99) Millar-s/McNiven-a & wraparound-c	1	2	3	5	6	8
1-Variant cover by Michael Turner	2	4	6	9	12	15
1-Aspen Comics Variant cover by Turner	2	4	6	9	12	15
1-Director's Cut (2006, $4.99) r/#1 plus promo art, variant covers, sketches and script						5.00
2-($2.99) Spider-Man unmasks	1	2	3	4	5	7
2-Turner variant cover						5.00
2-B&W sketch variant cover						20.00
2-2nd printing						4.00
3-7: 3-Thor returns. 4-Goliath killed						4.00
3-7-Turner variant covers						5.00
3-7-B&W sketch variant covers						15.00
TPB (2007, $24.99) r/#1-7; gallery of variant covers						25.00

Civil War War Crimes #1 © MAR

Claire Voyant #2 © STD

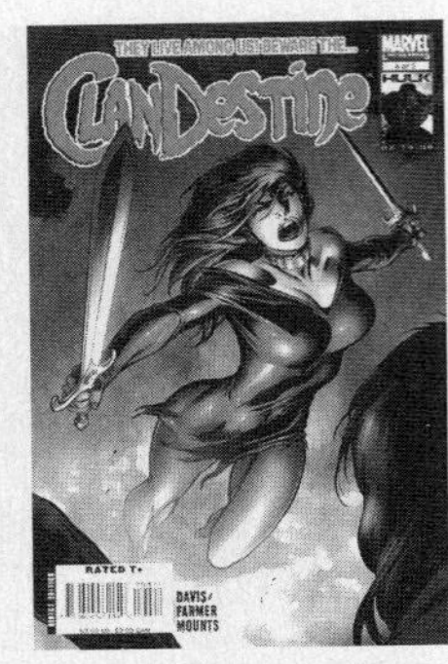

Clandestine (2008 series) #4 © MAR

	GD 2.0	VG 4.0	FN 6.0	VF 8.0	VF/NM 9.0	NM- 9.2

...: Battle Damage Report (2007, $3.99) Post-Civil War character profiles; McGuinness-c 4.00
...: Choosing Sides (2/07, $3.99) Colan-c; Howard the Duck app.; 2 covers by Yu & Colan 4.00
... Companion TPB (2007, $13.99) r/Civil War Files, ...:Battle Damage Report, Marvel Spotlight: Millar/McNiven, Marvel Spotlight: Civil War Aftermath and Daily Bugle CW 14.00
Daily Bugle Civil War Newspaper Special #1 (9/06, 50¢, newsprint) Daily Bugle "newspaper" overview of the crossover; Mayhew-a 2.50
...Files (2006, $3.99) profile pages of major Civil War characters; McNiven-c 4.00
...: Marvel Universe TPB (2007, $11.99) r/Civil War: Choosing Sides, CW: The Return, She-Hulk #8, CW: The Initiative; She-Hulk sketch page; variant cover gallery 12.00
...: The Confession (5/07, $2.99) Maleev-c/a; Bendis-s 3.00
...: The Initiative (4/07, $4.99) Silvestri-c/a; previews of post-Civil War series 5.00
...: The Return (3/07, $2.99) Captain Marvel returns; The Sentry app.; Raney-a 3.00
...: The Road to Civil War TPB (2007, $14.99) r/New Avengers: Illuminati, Fantastic Four #536 & 537, Amazing Spider-Man #529-531; Spider-Man costume sketches by Bachalo 15.00
... War Crimes (2/07, $3.99) Kingpin in prison; Tieri-s/Staz Johnson-a 4.00
... War Crimes TPB (2007, $17.99) r/Civil War: War Crimes one-shot and Underworld #1-5 18.00
... X-Men Universe TPB (2007, $13.99) r/Cable & Deadpool #30-32; X-Factor #8,9 14.00

CIVIL WAR CHRONICLES (Reprints of Civil War and related Marvel issues)
Marvel Comics: Oct, 2007 - No. 12, Sept, 2008 ($4.99, limited series)

1-12: Reprints Civil War, Civil War: Frontline and x-over issues 5.00

CIVIL WAR: FRONTLINE (Tie-in to Civil War and related Marvel issues)
Marvel Comics: Aug, 2006 - No. 11, Apr, 2007 ($2.99, limited series)

1-Jenkins-s/Bachs-a/Watson-c; back-up stories by various 4.00
2-11: 3-Green Goblin app. 11-Aftermath of Civil War #7 3.00
... Book 1 TPB (2007, $14.99) r/#1-6 15.00
... Book 2 TPB (2007, $14.99) r/#7-11 15.00

CIVIL WAR: HOUSE OF M
Marvel Comics: Nov, 2008 - No. 5, Mar, 2009 ($2.99, limited series)

1-5-Gage-s/DiVito-a 3.00

CIVIL WAR MUSKET, THE (Kadets of America Handbook)
Custom Comics, Inc.: 1960 (25¢, half-size, 36 pgs.)

nn 3 6 9 16 22 28

CIVIL WAR: X-MEN (Tie-in to Civil War)
Marvel Comics: Sept, 2006 - No. 4, Dec, 2006 ($2.99, limited series)

1-4-Paquette-a/Hine-s; Bishop app. 3.00
1-Variant cover by Michael Turner 10.00
TPB (2007, $11.99) r/#1-4, profile pages of minor characters 12.00

CIVIL WAR: YOUNG AVENGERS & RUNAWAYS (Tie-in to Civil War)
Marvel Comics: Sept, 2006 - No. 4, Dec, 2006 ($2.99, limited series)

1-4-Caselli-a/Wells-s/Cheung-c 3.00
TPB (2007, $11.99) r/#1-4, profile pages of characters 12.00

CLAIRE VOYANT (Also see Keen Teens)
Leader Publ./Standard/Pentagon Publ.: 1946 - No. 4, 1947 (Sparling strip reprints)

nn 66 132 198 419 722 1025
2,4: 2-Kamen-c. 4-Kamen bondage-c 49 98 147 309 522 735
3-Kamen bridal-c; contents mentioned in Love and Death, a book by Gershom Legman(1949) referenced by Dr. Wertham in **SOTI** 58 116 174 371 636 900

CLANDESTINE (Also see Marvel Comics Presents & X-Men: ClanDestine)
Marvel Comics: Oct, 1994 - No.12, Sept, 1995 ($2.95/$2.50)

1-($2.95)-Alan Davis-c/a(p)/scripts & Mark Farmer-c/a(i) begin, ends #8; Modok app.; Silver Surfer cameo; gold foil-c 3.00
2-12: 2-Wraparound-c. 2,3-Silver Surfer app. 5-Origin of ClanDestine. 6-Capt. America, Hulk, Spider-Man, Thing & Thor-c; Spider-Man cameo. 7-Spider-Man-c/app; Punisher cameo. 8-Invaders & Dr. Strange app. 10-Captain Britain-c/app. 11-Sub-Mariner app. 2.50
Preview (10/94, $1.50) 2.50
... Classic HC (2008, $29.99, DJ) r/#1-8, Marvel Comics Presents #158, X-Men and Clandestine #1&2, sketch pages and cover gallery; Alan Davis afterword 30.00

CLANDESTINE
Marvel Comics: Apr, 2008 - No. 5, Aug, 2008 ($2.99, limited series)

1-5: 1-Alan Davis-c/a(p)/scripts & Mark Farmer-c/a(i). 2-5-Excalibur app. 3.00

CLASH
DC Comics: 1991 - No. 3, 1991 ($4.95, limited series, 52 pgs.)

Book One - Three: Adam Kubert-c/a 5.00

CLASSIC BATTLESTAR GALACTICA (See Battlestar Galactica, Classic...)

CLASSIC COMICS/ILLUSTRATED - INTRODUCTION
by Dan Malan

Since the first publication of this special introduction to the **Classics** section, a number of revisions have been made to further clarify the listings. **Classics** reprint editions prior to 1963 had either incorrect dates or no dates listed. Those reprint editions should be identified only by the highest number on the reorder list (HRN). Past *Guides* listed what were calculated to be approximately correct dates, but many people found it confusing for the *Guide* to list a date not listed in the comic itself.

We have also attempted to clear up confusion about edition variations, such as color, printer, etc. Such variations are identified by letters. Editions are determined by three categories. Original edition variations are designated as Edition 1A, 1B, etc. All reprint editions prior to 1963 are identified by HRN only. All reprint editions from 9/63 on are identified by the correct date listed in the comic.

Information is also included on four reprintings of **Classics**. From 1968-1976, Twin Circle, the Catholic newspaper, serialized over 100 **Classics** titles. That list can be found under non-series items at the end of this section. In 1972, twelve **Classics** were reissued as **Now Age Books Illustrated**. They are listed under **Pendulum Illustrated Classics**. In 1982, 20 **Classics** were reissued, adapted for teaching English as a second language. They are listed under **Regents Illustrated Classics**. Then in 1984, six **Classics** were reissued with cassette tapes. See the listing under **Cassette Books**.

UNDERSTANDING CLASSICS ILLUSTRATED
by Dan Malan

Since **Classics Illustrated** is the most complicated comic book series, with all its reprint editions and variations, changes in covers and artwork, a variety of means of identifying editions, and the most extensive worldwide distribution of any comic-book series, this introductory section is provided to assist you in gaining expertise about this series.

THE HISTORY OF CLASSICS
The **Classics** series was the brain child of Albert L. Kanter, who saw in the new comic-book medium a means of introducing children to the great classics of literature. In October of 1941 his Gilberton Co. began the **Classic Comics** series with **The Three Musketeers**, with 64 pages of storyline. In those early years, the struggling series saw irregular schedules and numerous printers, not to mention variable art quality and liberal story adaptations. With No.13 the page total was reduced to 56 (except for No. 33, originally scheduled to be No. 9), and with No. 15 the coming-next ad on the outside back cover moved inside. In 1945 the Jerry Iger Shop began producing all new CC titles, beginning with No. 23. In 1947 the search for a classier logo resulted in **Classics Illustrated**, beginning with No. 35, **Last Days of Pompeii**. With No. 45 the page total dropped again to 48, which was to become the standard.

Two new developments in 1951 had a profound effect upon the success of the series. One was the introduction of painted covers, instead of the old line drawn covers, beginning with No. 81, **The Odyssey**. The second was the switch to the major national distributor Curtis. They raised the cover price from 10 to 15 cents, making it the highest priced comic-book, but it did not slow the growth of the series, because they were marketed as books, not comics. Because of this higher quality image, **Classics** flourished during the fifties while other comic series were reeling from outside attacks. They diversified with their new **Juniors**, **Specials**, and **World Around Us** series.

Classics artwork can be divided into three distinct periods. The pre-Iger era (1941-44) was mentioned above for its variable art quality. The Iger era (1945-53) was a major improvement in art quality and adaptations. It came to be dominated by artists Henry Kiefer and Alex Blum, together accounting for some 50 titles. Their styles gave the first real personality to the series. The EC era (1954-62) resulted from the demise of the EC horror series, when many of their artists made the major switch to classical art.

But several factors brought the production of new CI titles to a complete halt in 1962. Gilberton lost its 2nd class mailing permit. External factors like television, cheap paperback books, and Cliff Notes were all eating away at their market. Production halted with No.167, **Faust**, even though many more titles were already in the works. Many of those found their way into foreign series, and are very desirable to collectors. In 1967, **Classics Illustrated** was sold to Patrick Frawley and his Catholic publication, Twin Circle. They issued two new titles in 1969 as part of an attempted revival, but succumbed to major distribution problems in 1971. In 1988, First Publishing acquired the rights to use the old CI series art, logo, and name from the Frawley Group, and released a short-lived series featuring contributions of modern creators. Acclaim Books and Twin Circles issued a series of **Classics** reprints from 1997-1998.

One of the unique aspects of the **Classics Illustrated** (CI) series was the proliferation of reprint variations. Some titles had as many as 25 editions. Reprinting began in 1943. Some **Classic Comics** (CC) reprints (r) had the logo format revised to a banner logo, and added a motto under the banner. In 1947 CC titles changed to the CI logo, but kept their line drawn covers (LDC). In 1948, Nos. 13, 18, 29 and 41 received second covers (LDC2), replacing covers considered too violent, and reprints of Nos. 13-44 had pages reduced to 48, except for No. 26, which had 48 pages to begin with.

Starting in the mid-1950s, 70 of the 80 LDC titles were reissued with new painted covers (PC). Thirty of them also received new interior artwork (A2). The new artwork was generally higher quality with larger art panels and more faithful but abbreviated storylines. Later on, there were 29 second painted covers (PC2), mostly by Twin Circle. Altogether there were 199 interi-

Classic Comics #1 © GIL

Classic Comics #2 © GIL

Classic Comics #3 © GIL

GD 2.0 | VG 4.0 | FN 6.0 | VF 8.0 | VF/NM 9.0 | NM- 9.2

or art variations (169 (O)s and 30 A2 editions) and 272 different covers (169 (O)s, four LDC2s, 70 new PCs of LDC (O)s, and 29 PC2s). It is mildly astounding to realize that there are nearly 1400 different editions in the U.S. CI series.

FOREIGN CLASSICS ILLUSTRATED

If U.S. Classics variations are mildly astounding, the veritable plethora of foreign CI variations will boggle your imagination. While we still anticipate additional discoveries, we presently know about series in 25 languages and 27 countries. There were 250 new CI titles in foreign series, and nearly 400 new foreign covers of U.S. titles. The 1400 U.S. CI editions pale in comparison to the 4000 plus foreign editions. The very nature of CI lent itself to flourishing as an international series. Worldwide, they published over one billion copies! The first foreign CI series consisted of six Canadian Classic Comic reprints in 1946.

The following chart shows when CI series first began in each country:
1946: Canada. 1947: Australia. 1948: Brazil/The Netherlands. 1950: Italy. 1951: Greece/Japan/Hong Kong(?)/England/Argentina/Mexico. 1952: West Germany. 1954: Norway. 1955: New Zealand/South Africa. 1956: Denmark/Sweden/Iceland. 1957: Finland/France. 1962: Singapore(?). 1964: India (8 languages). 1971: Ireland (Gaelic). 1973: Belgium(?) /Philippines(?) & Malaysia(?).

Significant among the early series were Brazil and Greece. In 1950, Brazil was the first country to begin doing its own new titles. They issued nearly 80 new CI titles by Brazilian authors. In Greece in 1951 they actually had debates in parliament about the effects of Classics Illustrated on Greek culture, leading to the inclusion of 88 new Greek History & Mythology titles in the CI series.

But by far the most important foreign CI development was the joint European series which began in 1956 in 10 countries simultaneously. By 1960, CI had the largest European distribution of any American publication, not just comics! So when all the problems came up with U.S. distribution, they literally moved the CI operation to Europe in 1962, and continued producing new titles in all four CI series. Many of them were adapted and drawn in the U.S., the most famous of which was the British CI #158A. Dr. No, drawn by Norman Nodel. Unfortunately, the British CI series ended in late 1963, which limited the European CI titles available in English to 15. Altogether there were 82 new CI art titles in the joint European series, which ran until 1976.

IDENTIFYING CLASSICS EDITIONS

HRN: This is the highest number on the reorder list. It should be listed in ( ) after the title number. It is crucial to understanding various CI editions.

ORIGINALS (O): This is the all-important First Edition. To determine (O)s,there is one primary rule and two secondary rules (with exceptions):

Rule No. 1: All (O)s and only (O)s have coming-next ads for the next number. **Exceptions**: No. 14(15) (reprint) has an ad on the last inside text page only. No. 14(0) also has a full-page outside back cover ad (also rule 2). Nos.55(75) and 57(75) have coming-next ads. (Rules 2 and 3 apply here). Nos. 168(0) and 169(0) do not have coming-next ads. No.168 was never reprinted; No. 169(0) has HRN (166). No. 169(169) is the only reprint.

Rule No. 2: On nos.1-80, all (O)s and only (O)s list 10c on the front cover. **Exceptions**: Reprint variations of Nos. 37(62), 39(71), and 46(62) list 10c on the front cover. (Rules 1 and 3 apply here.)

Rule No. 3: All (O)s have HRN close to that title No. **Exceptions**: Some reprints also have HRNs close to that title number: a few CC(r)s, 58(62), 60(62), 149(149), 152(149) 153(149), and title nos. in the 160's. (Rules 1 and 2 apply here.)

DATES: Many reprint editions list either an incorrect date or no date. Since Gilberton apparently kept track of CI editions by HRN, they often left the (O) date on reprints. Often, someone with a CI collection for sale will swear that all their copies are originals. That is why we are so detailed in pointing out how to identify original editions. Except for original editions, which should have a coming-next ad, etc., all CI dates prior to 1963 are incorrect! So you want to go by HRN only if it is (165) or below, and go by listed date if it is 1963 or later. There are a few (167) editions with incorrect dates. They could be listed either as (167) or (62/3), which is meant to indicate that they were issued sometime between late 1962 and early 1963.

COVERS: A change from CC to LDC indicates a logo change, not a cover change; while a change from LDC to LDC2, LDC to PC, or from PC to PC2 does indicate a new cover. New PCs can be identified by HRN, and PC2s can be identified by HRN and date. Several covers had color changes, particularly from purple to blue.

Notes: If you see 15 cents in Canada on a front cover, it does not necessarily indicate a Canadian edition. Editions with an HRN between 44 and 75, with 15 cents on the cover are Canadian. Check the publisher's address. An HRN listing two numbers with a / between them indicates that there are two different reorder lists in the front and back covers. Official Twin Circle editions have a full-page back cover ad for their TC magazine, with no CI reorder list. Any CI with just a Twin Circle sticker on the front is not an official TC edition.

TIPS ON LISTING CLASSICS FOR SALE

It may be easy to just list Edition 17, but Classics collectors keep track of CI editions in terms of HRN and/or date, (O) or (r), CC or LDC, PC or PC2, A1 or A2, soft or stiff cover, etc. Try to help them out. For originals, just list (0), unless there are variations such as color (Nos. 10 and 61), printer (Nos. 18-22), HRN (Nos. 95, 108, 160), etc. For reprints, just list HRN if it's (165) or below. Above that, list HRN and date. Also, please list type of logo/cover/art for the convenience of buyers. They will appreciate it.

CLASSIC COMICS (Also see Best from Boys Life, Cassette Books, Famous Stories, Fast Fiction, Golden Picture Classics, King Classics, Marvel Classics Comics, Pendulum Illustrated Classics, Picture Parade, Picture Progress, Regents Ill. Classics, Spitfire, Stories by Famous Authors, Superior Stories, and World Around Us.)

CLASSIC COMICS (Classics Illustrated No. 35 on)
Elliot Publishing #1-3 (1941-1942)/Gilberton Publications #4-167 (1942-1967) /Twin Circle Pub. (Frawley) #168-169 (1968-1971):
10/41 - No. 34, 2/47; No. 35, 3/47 - No. 169, Spring 1969
(Reprint Editions of almost all titles 5/43 - Spring 1971)
(Painted Covers (0)s No. 81 on, and (r)s of most Nos. 1-80)

Abbreviations:
A–Art; C or c–Cover; CC–Classic Comics; CI–Classics Ill.; Ed–Edition; LDC–Line Drawn Cover; PC–Painted Cover; r–Reprint

1. The Three Musketeers

Ed	HRN	Date	Details	A	C	GD 2.0	VG 4.0	FN 6.0	VF 8.0	VF/NM 9.0	NM- 9.2
1	–	10/41	Date listed-1941; Elliot Pub; 68 pgs.	1	1	449	898	1347	3278	5789	8300
2	10	–	10¢ price removed on all (r)s; Elliot Pub; CC-r	1	1	34	68	102	199	325	450
3	15	–	Long Isl. Ind. Ed.; CC-r	1	1	24	48	72	140	230	320
4	18/20	–	Sunrise Times Ed.; CC-r	1	1	18	36	54	105	165	225
5	21	–	Richmond Courier Ed.; CC-r	1	1	16	32	48	94	147	200
6	28	1946	CC-r	1	1	14	28	42	80	115	150
7	36	–	LDC-r	1	1	8	16	24	42	54	65
8	60	–	LDC-r	1	1	6	12	18	27	33	38
9	64	–	LDC-r	1	1	5	10	15	22	26	30
10	78	–	C-price 15¢;LDC-r	1	1	4	9	13	18	22	26
11	93	–	LDC-r	1	1	4	9	13	18	22	26
12	114	–	Last LDC-r	1	1	4	8	11	16	19	22
13	134	–	New-c; old-a; 64 pg. PC-r	1	2	3	6	9	19	29	38
14	143	–	Old-a; PC-r; 64 pg.	1	2	2	4	6	11	16	20
15	150	–	New-a; PC-r; Evans/Crandall-a	2	2	3	6	9	17	25	32
16	149	–	PC-r	2	2	2	4	6	8	10	12
17	167	–	PC-r	2	2	2	4	6	8	10	12
18	167	4/64	PC-r	2	2	2	4	6	8	10	12
19	167	1/65	PC-r	2	2	2	4	6	8	10	12
20	167	3/66	PC-r	2	2	2	4	6	8	10	12
21	166	11/67	PC-r	2	2	2	4	6	8	10	12
22	166	Spr/69	C-price 25¢ ; stiff-c; PC-r	2	2	2	4	6	8	10	12
23	169	Spr/71	PC-r; stiff-c	2	2	2	4	6	8	10	12

2. Ivanhoe

Ed	HRN	Date	Details	A	C	GD 2.0	VG 4.0	FN 6.0	VF 8.0	VF/NM 9.0	NM- 9.2
1	(O)	12/41?	Date listed-1941; Elliot Pub; 68 pgs.	1	1	232	464	696	1485	2543	3600
2	10	–	Price & 'Presents' removed; Elliot Pub; CC-r	1	1	31	62	93	182	296	410
3	15	–	Long Isl. Ind. ed.; CC-r	1	1	20	40	60	117	189	260
4	18/20	–	Sunrise Times ed.; CC-r	1	1	18	36	54	105	165	225
5	21	–	Richmond Courier ed.; CC-r	1	1	16	32	48	94	147	200
6	28	1946	Last 'Comics'-r	1	1	14	28	42	80	115	150
7	36	–	1st LDC-r	1	1	9	18	27	47	61	75
8	60	–	LDC-r	1	1	6	12	18	27	33	38
9	64	–	LDC-r	1	1	5	10	15	22	26	30
10	78	–	C-price 15¢; LDC-r	1	1	4	9	13	18	22	26
11	89	–	LDC-r	1	1	4	8	12	17	21	24
12	106	–	LDC-r	1	1	4	7	10	14	17	20
13	121	–	Last LDC-r	1	1	4	7	10	14	17	20
14	136	–	New-c&a; PC-r	2	2	5	10	15	25	31	36
15	142	–	PC-r	2	2	2	4	6	8	11	14
16	153	–	PC-r	2	2	2	4	6	8	11	14
17	149	–	PC-r	2	2	2	4	6	8	11	14

Classic Comics #4 © GIL

Classic Comics #5 © GIL

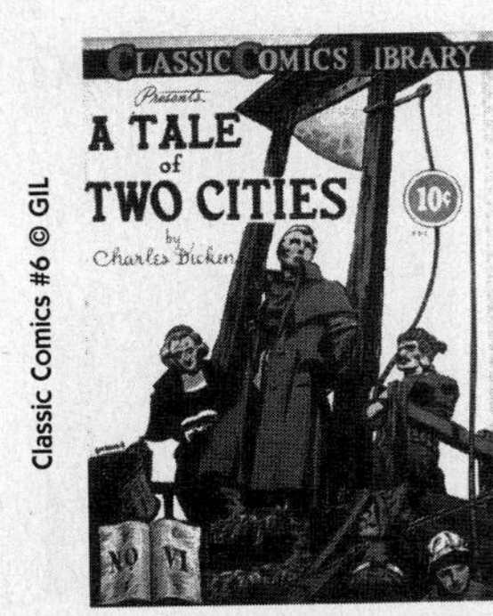

Classic Comics #6 © GIL

Ed	HRN	Date	Details	A	C	GD 2.0	VG 4.0	FN 6.0	VF 8.0	VF/NM 9.0	NM- 9.2
18	167	–	PC-r	2	2	2	4	6	8	10	12
19	167	5/64	PC-r	2	2	2	4	6	8	10	12
20	167	1/65	PC-r	2	2	2	4	6	8	10	12
21	167	3/66	PC-r	2	2	2	4	6	8	10	12
22A	166	9/67	PC-r	2	2	2	4	6	8	10	12
22B	166	–	Center ad for Children's Digest & Young Miss; rare; PC-r	2	2	7	14	21	47	76	105
23	166	R/68	C-Price 25¢; PC-r	2	2	2	4	6	8	10	12
24	169	Win/69	Stiff-c	2	2	2	4	6	8	10	12
25	169	Win/71	PC-r; stiff-c	2	2	2	4	6	8	10	12

3. The Count of Monte Cristo

Ed	HRN	Date	Details	A	C	GD 2.0	VG 4.0	FN 6.0	VF 8.0	VF/NM 9.0	NM- 9.2
1	(O)	3/42	Elliot Pub; 68 pgs.	1	1	148	296	444	947	1624	2300
2	10	–	Conray Prods; CC-r	1	1	26	52	78	154	252	350
3	15	–	Long Isl. Ind. ed.; CC-r	1	1	20	40	60	117	189	260
4	18/20	–	Sunrise Times ed.; CC-r	1	1	18	36	54	107	169	230
5	20	–	Sunrise Times ed.; CC-r	1	1	17	34	51	98	154	210
6	21	–	Richmond Courier ed.; CC-r	1	1	16	32	48	94	147	200
7	28	1946	CC-r; new Banner logo	1	1	14	28	42	80	115	150
8	36	–	1st LDC-r	1	1	9	18	27	47	61	75
9	60	–	LDC-r	1	1	6	12	18	27	33	38
10	62	–	LDC-r	1	1	6	12	18	29	36	42
11	71	–	LDC-r	1	1	5	10	14	20	24	28
12	87	–	C-price 15¢; LDC-r	1	1	4	9	13	18	22	26
13	113	–	LDC-r	1	1	4	7	10	14	17	20
14	135	–	New-c&a; PC-r; Cameron-a	2	2	3	6	9	18	27	35
15	143	–	PC-r	2	2	2	4	6	8	11	14
16	153	–	PC-r	2	2	2	4	6	8	11	14
17	161	–	PC-r	2	2	2	4	6	8	11	14
18	167	–	PC-r	2	2	2	4	6	8	10	12
19	167	7/64	PC-r	2	2	2	4	6	8	10	12
20	167	7/65	PC-r	2	2	2	4	6	8	10	12
21	167	7/66	PC-r	2	2	2	4	6	8	10	12
22	166	R/68	C-price 25¢; PC-r	2	2	2	4	6	8	10	12
23	169	–	Win/69 Stiff-c; PC-r	2	2	2	4	6	8	10	12

4. The Last of the Mohicans

Ed	HRN	Date	Details	A	C	GD 2.0	VG 4.0	FN 6.0	VF 8.0	VF/NM 9.0	NM- 9.2
1	(O)	8/42	Date listed-1942; Gilberton #4(0) on; 68 pgs.	1	1	126	252	378	806	1378	1950
2	12	–	Elliot Pub; CC-r	1	1	26	52	78	154	252	350
3	15	–	Long Isl. Ind. ed.; CC-r	1	1	20	40	60	117	189	260
4	20	–	Long Isl. Ind. ed.; CC-r; banner logo	1	1	18	36	54	105	165	225
5	21	–	Queens Home News ed.; CC-r	1	1	16	32	48	94	147	200
6	28	1946	Last CC-r; new	1	1	14	28	42	80	115	150
7	36	–	1st LDC-r	1	1	9	18	27	47	61	75
8	60	–	LDC-r	1	1	6	12	18	27	33	38
9	64	–	LDC-r	1	1	5	10	14	20	24	28
10	78	–	C-price 15¢; LDC-r	1	1	4	9	13	18	22	26
11	89	–	LDC-r	1	1	4	8	12	17	21	24
12	117	–	Last LDC-r	1	1	4	7	10	14	17	20
13	135	–	New-c; PC-r	1	2	5	10	15	24	30	35
14	141	–	PC-r	1	2	3	6	8	12	14	16
15	150	–	New-a; PC-r; Severin, L.B. Cole-a	2	2	6	12	18	27	33	38
16	161	–	PC-r	2	2	2	4	6	8	10	12
17	167	–	PC-r	2	2	2	4	6	8	10	12
18	167	6/64	PC-r	2	2	2	4	6	8	10	12
19	167	8/65	PC-r	2	2	2	4	6	8	10	12
20	167	8/66	PC-r	2	2	2	4	6	8	10	12
21	166	R/67	C-price 25¢; PC-r	2	2	2	4	6	8	10	12
22	169	Spr/69	Stiff-c; PC-r	2	2	2	4	6	8	10	12

5. Moby Dick

Ed	HRN	Date	Details	A	C	GD 2.0	VG 4.0	FN 6.0	VF 8.0	VF/NM 9.0	NM- 9.2
1A	(O)	9/42	Date listed-1942; Gilberton; 68 pgs.	1	1	152	304	456	965	1658	2350
1B			inside-c, rare free promo			232	464	696	1485	2543	3600
2	10	–	Conray Prods; Pg. 64 changed from 105 title list to letter from Editor; CC-r	1	1	27	54	81	158	259	360
3	15	–	Long Isl. Ind. ed.; Pg. 64 changed from Letter to the Editor to Ill. poem-Concord Hymn; CC-r	1	1	22	44	66	132	216	300
4	18/20	–	Sunrise Times ed.; CC-r	1	1	18	36	54	107	169	230
5	20	–	Sunrise Times ed.; CC-r	1	1	18	36	54	103	162	220
6	21	–	Sunrise Times ed.; CC-r	1	1	16	32	48	94	147	200
7	28	1946	CC-r; new banner logo	1	1	14	28	42	81	118	155
8	36	–	1st LDC-r	1	1	9	18	27	47	61	75
9	60	–	LDC-r	1	1	6	12	18	27	33	38
10	62	–	LDC-r	1	1	6	12	18	29	36	42
11	71	–	LDC-r	1	1	5	10	15	22	26	30
12	87	–	C-price 15¢; LDC-r	1	1	5	10	14	20	24	28
13	118	–	LDC-r	1	1	4	8	12	17	21	24
14	131	–	New c&a; PC-r	2	2	5	10	15	25	31	36
15	138	–	PC-r	2	2	2	4	6	8	11	14
16	148	–	PC-r	2	2	2	4	6	8	11	14
17	158	–	PC-r	2	2	2	4	6	8	11	14
18	167	–	PC-r	2	2	2	4	6	8	10	12
19	167	6/64	PC-r	2	2	2	4	6	8	10	12
20	167	7/65	PC-r	2	2	2	4	6	8	10	12
21	167	3/66	PC-r	2	2	2	4	6	8	10	12
22	166	9/67	PC-r	2	2	2	4	6	8	10	12
23	166	Win/69	New-c & c-price 25¢; Stiff-c; PC-r	2	3	3	6	9	16	22	28
24	169	Win/71	PC-r	2	3	2	4	6	13	18	22

6. A Tale of Two Cities

Ed	HRN	Date	Details	A	C	GD 2.0	VG 4.0	FN 6.0	VF 8.0	VF/NM 9.0	NM- 9.2
1	(O)	10/42	Date listed-1942; 68 pgs. Zeckerberg c/a	1	1	126	252	378	806	1378	1950
2	14	–	Elliot Pub; CC-r	1	1	24	48	72	142	234	325
3	18	–	Long Isl. Ind. ed.; CC-r	1	1	20	40	60	114	182	250
4	20	–	Sunrise Times ed.; CC-r	1	1	18	36	54	105	165	225
5	28	1946	Last CC-r; new banner logo	1	1	14	28	42	80	115	150
6	51	–	1st LDC-r	1	1	8	16	24	42	54	65
7	64	–	LDC-r	1	1	5	10	15	23	28	32
8	78	–	C-price 15¢; LDC-r	1	1	5	10	14	20	24	28
9	89	–	LDC-r	1	1	4	7	10	14	17	20
10	117	–	LDC-r	1	1	4	7	10	14	17	20
11	132	–	New-c&a; PC-r; Joe Orlando-a	2	2	5	10	15	25	31	36
12	140	–	PC-r	2	2	2	4	6	8	10	12
13	147	–	PC-r	2	2	2	4	6	8	10	12
14	152	–	PC-r; very rare	2	2	17	34	51	98	154	210
15	153	–	PC-r	2	2	2	4	6	8	11	14
16	149	–	PC-r	2	2	2	4	6	8	11	14
17	167	–	PC-r	2	2	2	4	6	8	10	12
18	167	6/64	PC-r	2	2	2	4	6	8	10	12
19	167	8/65	PC-r	2	2	2	4	6	8	10	12
20	166	5/67	PC-r	2	2	2	4	6	8	10	12
21	166	Fall/68	New-c & 25¢; PC-r	2	3	3	6	9	16	23	30
22	169	Sum/70	Stiff-c; PC-r	2	3	2	4	6	11	16	20

7. Robin Hood

Ed	HRN	Date	Details	A	C	GD 2.0	VG 4.0	FN 6.0	VF 8.0	VF/NM 9.0	NM- 9.2
1	(O)	12/42	Date listed-1942;	1	1	94	188	282	597	1024	1450

Classic Comics #7 © GIL

Classic Comics #10 © GIL

Classic Comics #12 © GIL

Ed	HRN	Date	Details	A	C	GD 2.0	VG 4.0	FN 6.0	VF 8.0	VF/NM 9.0	NM- 9.2
			first Gift Box ad-bc; 68 pgs.								
2	12	–	Elliot Pub; CC-r	1	1	23	46	69	136	223	310
3	18	–	Long Isl. Ind. ed.; CC-r	1	1	19	38	57	111	176	240
4	20	–	Nassau Bulletin ed.; CC-r	1	1	18	36	54	103	162	220
5	22	–	Queens Cty. Times ed.; CC-r	1	1	16	32	48	94	147	200
6	28	–	CC-r	1	1	14	28	42	81	118	155
7	51	–	LDC-r	1	1	8	16	24	42	54	65
8	64	–	LDC-r	1	1	5	10	15	24	30	35
9	78	–	LDC-r	1	1	4	9	13	18	22	26
10	97	–	LDC-r	1	1	4	8	12	17	21	24
11	106	–	LDC-r	1	1	4	7	10	14	17	20
12	121	–	LDC-r	1	1	4	7	10	14	17	20
13	129	–	New-c; PC-r	1	2	5	10	15	25	31	36
14	136	–	New-a; PC-r	2	2	5	10	15	24	29	34
15	143	–	PC-r	2	2	2	4	6	8	11	14
16	153	–	PC-r	2	2	2	4	6	8	11	14
17	164	–	PC-r	2	2	2	4	6	8	10	12
18	167	–	PC-r	2	2	2	4	6	8	10	12
19	167	6/64	PC-r	2	2	2	4	6	8	10	12
20	167	5/65	PC-r	2	2	2	4	6	8	10	12
21	167	7/66	PC-r	2	2	2	4	6	8	10	12
22	166	12/67	PC-r	2	2	2	4	6	8	10	12
23	169	Sum/69	Stiff-c; c-price 25¢; PC-r	2	2	2	4	6	8	10	12

8. Arabian Nights

Ed	HRN	Date	Details	A	C	GD 2.0	VG 4.0	FN 6.0	VF 8.0	VF/NM 9.0	NM- 9.2
1	(O)	2/43	Original; 68 pgs. Lilian Chestney-c/a	1	1	150	300	450	953	1639	2325
2	17	–	Long Isl. ed.; pg. 64 changed from Gift Box ad to Letter from British Medical Worker; CC-r	1	1	52	104	156	328	552	775
3	20	–	Nassau Bulletin; Pg. 64 changed from letter to article-Three Men Named Smith; CC-r	1	1	42	84	126	265	445	625
4A	28	1946	CC-r; new banner logo, slick-c	1	1	31	62	93	182	296	410
4B	28	1946	Same, but w/stiff-c	1	1	31	62	93	182	296	410
5	51	–	LDC-r	1	1	22	44	66	128	209	290
6	64	–	LDC-r	1	1	19	38	57	111	176	240
7	78	–	LDC-r	1	1	18	36	54	105	165	225
8	164	–	New-c&a; PC-r	2	2	15	30	45	90	140	190

9. Les Miserables

Ed	HRN	Date	Details	A	C	GD 2.0	VG 4.0	FN 6.0	VF 8.0	VF/NM 9.0	NM- 9.2
1A	(O)	3/43	Original; slick paper cover; 68 pgs.	1	1	94	188	282	597	1024	1450
1B	(O)	3/43	Original; rough, pulp type-c; 68 pgs.	1	1	110	220	330	704	1202	1700
2	14	–	Elliot Pub; CC-r	1	1	26	52	78	154	252	350
3	18	3/44	Nassau Bul. Pg. 64 changed from Gift Box ad to Bill of Rights article; CC-r	1	1	22	44	66	128	209	290
4	20	–	Richmond Courier ed.; CC-r	1	1	19	38	57	111	176	240
5	28	1946	Gilberton; pgs. 60-64 rearranged/ illos added; CC-r	1	1	14	28	42	81	118	155
6	51	–	LDC-r	1	1	9	18	27	47	61	75
7	71	–	LDC-r	1	1	6	12	18	29	36	42
8	87	–	C-price 15¢; LDC-r	1	1	6	12	18	27	33	38
9	161	–	New-c&a; PC-r	2	2	7	14	21	37	46	55
10	167	9/63	PC-r	2	2	2	4	6	11	16	20
11	167	12/65	PC-r	2	2	2	4	6	11	16	20
12	166	R/1968	New-c & price 25¢; PC-r	2	3	3	6	9	18	27	35

10. Robinson Crusoe (Used in **SOTI**, pg. 142)

Ed	HRN	Date	Details	A	C	GD 2.0	VG 4.0	FN 6.0	VF 8.0	VF/NM 9.0	NM- 9.2
1A	(O)	4/43	Original; Violet-c; 68 pgs; Zuckerberg c/a	1	1	84	168	252	538	919	1300
1B	(O)	4/43	Original; blue-grey-c, 68 pgs.	1	1	92	184	276	584	1005	1425
2A	14	–	Elliot Pub; violet-c; 68 pgs; CC-r	1	1	29	58	87	170	278	385
2B	14	–	Elliot Pub; blue-grey-c; CC-r	1	1	25	50	75	147	241	335
3	18	–	Nassau Bul. Pg. 64 changed from Gift Box ad to Bill of Rights article; CC-r	1	1	19	38	57	111	176	240
4	20	–	Queens Home News ed.; CC-r	1	1	16	32	48	94	147	200
5	28	1946	Gilberton; pg. 64 changes from Bill of Rights to WWII article-One Leg Shot Away; last CC-r	1	1	14	28	42	80	115	150
6	51	–	LDC-r	1	1	8	16	24	42	54	65
7	64	–	LDC-r	1	1	6	12	18	27	33	38
8	78	–	C-price 15¢; LDC-r	1	1	5	10	14	20	24	28
9	97	–	LDC-r	1	1	4	9	13	18	22	26
10	114	–	LDC-r	1	1	4	7	10	14	17	20
11	130	–	New-c; PC-r	1	2	5	10	15	25	31	36
12	140	–	New-a; PC-r	2	2	5	10	15	24	29	34
13	153	–	PC-r	2	2	2	4	6	8	10	12
14	164	–	PC-r	2	2	2	4	6	8	10	12
15	167	–	PC-r	2	2	2	4	6	8	10	12
16	167	7/64	PC-r	2	2	2	4	6	10	13	16
17	167	5/65	PC-r	2	2	2	4	6	10	13	16
18	167	6/66	PC-r	2	2	2	4	6	8	10	12
19	166	Fall/68	C-price 25¢; PC-r	2	2	2	4	6	8	10	12
20	166	R/68	(No Twin Circle ad)	2	2	2	4	6	8	11	14
21	169	Sm/70	Stiff-c; PC-r	2	2	2	4	6	8	11	14

11. Don Quixote

Ed	HRN	Date	Details	A	C	GD 2.0	VG 4.0	FN 6.0	VF 8.0	VF/NM 9.0	NM- 9.2
1	10	5/43	First (O) with HRN list; 68 pgs.	1	1	87	174	261	553	952	1350
2	18	–	Nassau Bulletin ed.; CC-r	1	1	23	46	69	136	223	310
3	21	–	Queens Home News ed.; CC-r	1	1	19	38	57	111	176	240
4	28	–	CC-r	1	1	14	28	42	81	118	155
5	110	–	New-PC; PC-r	1	2	7	14	21	35	43	50
6	156	–	Pgs. reduced 68 to 52; PC-r	1	2	4	7	10	14	17	20
7	165	–	PC-r	1	2	2	4	6	9	11	14
8	167	1/64	PC-r	1	2	2	4	6	9	11	14
9	167	11/65	PC-r	1	2	2	4	6	9	11	14
10	166	R/1968	New-c & price 25¢; PC-r	1	3	3	6	9	18	27	36

12. Rip Van Winkle and the Headless Horseman

Ed	HRN	Date	Details	A	C	GD 2.0	VG 4.0	FN 6.0	VF 8.0	VF/NM 9.0	NM- 9.2
1	11	6/43	Original; 68 pgs.	1	1	87	174	261	553	952	1350
2	15	–	Long Isl. Ind. ed.; CC-r	1	1	23	46	69	136	223	310
3	20	–	Long Isl. Ind. ed.;	1	1	19	38	57	111	176	240
4	22	–	Queens Cty. Times ed.; CC-r	1	1	16	32	48	94	147	200
5	28	–	CC-r	1	1	14	28	42	80	115	150
6	60	–	1st LDC-r	1	1	8	16	24	40	50	60
7	62	–	LDC-r	1	1	5	10	15	23	28	32
8	71	–	LDC-r	1	1	4	9	13	18	22	26
9	89	–	C-price 15¢; LDC-r	1	1	4	8	12	17	21	24
10	118	–	LDC-r	1	1	4	7	10	14	17	20
11	132	–	New-c; PC-r	1	2	5	10	15	25	31	36
12	150	–	New-a; PC-r	2	2	5	10	15	24	29	34
13	158	–	PC-r	2	2	2	4	6	8	11	14
14	167	–	PC-r	2	2	2	4	6	8	11	14
15	167	12/63	PC-r	2	2	2	4	6	8	10	12
16	167	4/65	PC-r	2	2	2	4	6	8	10	12

Classic Comics #13 © GIL

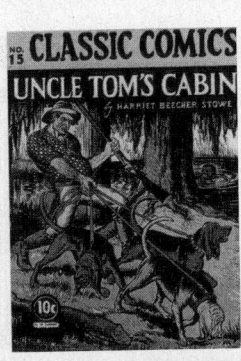

Classic Comics #15 © GIL

Classic Comics #17 © GIL

Ed	HRN	Date	Details	A	C	GD 2.0	VG 4.0	FN 6.0	VF 8.0	VF/NM 9.0	NM- 9.2
17	167	4/66	PC-r	2	2	2	4	6	8	10	12
18	166	R/1968	New-c&price 25¢; PC-r; stiff-c	2	3	3	6	9	14	19	24
19	169	Sm/70	PC-r; stiff-c	2	3	2	4	6	9	13	16

13. Dr. Jekyll and Mr. Hyde (Used in **SOTI**, pg. 143)(1st horror comic?)

Ed	HRN	Date	Details	A	C	GD 2.0	VG 4.0	FN 6.0	VF 8.0	VF/NM 9.0	NM- 9.2
1	12	8/43	Original 60 pgs.	1	1	129	258	387	826	1413	2000
2	15	–	Long Isl. Ind. ed.; CC-r	1	1	34	68	102	199	325	450
3	20	–	Long Isl. Ind. ed.; CC-r	1	1	23	46	69	136	223	310
4	28	–	No c-price; CC-r	1	1	18	36	54	105	165	225
5	60	–	New-c; Pgs. reduced from 60 to 52; H.C. Kiefer-c; LDC-r	1	2	9	18	27	47	61	75
6	62	–	LDC-r	1	2	6	12	18	28	34	40
7	71	–	LDC-r	1	2	5	10	15	23	28	32
8	87	–	Date returns (erroneous); LDC-r	1	2	5	10	15	22	26	30
9	112	–	New-c&a; PC-r; Cameron-a	2	3	7	14	21	35	43	50
10	153	–	PC-r	2	3	2	4	6	9	12	15
11	161	–	PC-r	2	3	2	4	6	9	12	15
12	167	–	PC-r	2	3	2	4	6	8	10	12
13	167	8/64	PC-r	2	3	2	4	6	8	10	12
14	167	11/65	PC-r	2	3	2	4	6	8	10	12
15	166	R/68	C-price 25¢; PC-r	2	3	2	4	6	8	10	12
16	169	Wn/69	PC-r; stiff-c	2	3	2	4	6	8	10	12

14. Westward Ho!

Ed	HRN	Date	Details	A	C	GD 2.0	VG 4.0	FN 6.0	VF 8.0	VF/NM 9.0	NM- 9.2
1	13	9/43	Original; last outside bc coming-next ad; 60 pgs.	1	1	194	388	582	1242	2121	3000
2	15	–	Long Isl. Ind. ed.; CC-r	1	1	57	114	171	362	624	885
3	21	–	Queens Home News; Pg. 56 changed from coming-next ad to Three Men Named Smith; CC-r	1	1	45	90	135	284	480	675
4	28	1946	Gilberton; Pg. 56 changed again to WWII article-Speaking for America; last CC-r	1	1	39	78	117	240	395	550
5	53	–	Pgs. reduced from 60 to 52; LDC-r	1	1	36	72	108	211	343	475

15. Uncle Tom's Cabin (Used in **SOTI**, pgs. 102, 103)

Ed	HRN	Date	Details	A	C	GD 2.0	VG 4.0	FN 6.0	VF 8.0	VF/NM 9.0	NM- 9.2
1	14	11/43	Original; Outside-bc ad: 2 Gift Boxes; 60 pgs.; color var. on-c; green trunk,root on left & brown trunk, root on left	1	1	74	148	222	470	810	1150
2	15	–	Long Isl. Ind. listed- bottom inside-fc; also Gilberton listed bottom-pg. 1; CC-r; green root vs. brown root var. occurs again	1	1	25	50	75	147	241	335
3	21	–	Nassau Bulletin ed.; CC-r	1	1	20	40	60	114	182	250
4	28	–	No c-price; CC-r	1	1	14	28	42	81	118	155
5	53	–	Pgs. reduced 60 to 52; LDC-r	1	1	8	16	24	42	54	65
6	71	–	LDC-r	1	1	6	12	18	27	33	38
7	89	–	C-price 15¢; LDC-r	1	1	5	10	15	24	30	35
8	117	–	New-c/lettering changes; PC-r	1	2	5	10	15	25	31	36
9	128	–	'Picture Progress' promo; PC-r	1	2	2	4	6	9	13	16
10	137	–	PC-r	1	2	2	4	6	8	11	14
11	146	–	PC-r	1	2	2	4	6	8	11	14
12	154	–	PC-r	1	2	2	4	6	8	11	14
13	161	–	PC-r	1	2	2	4	6	8	10	12
14	167	–	PC-r	1	2	2	4	6	8	10	12
15	167	6/64	PC-r	1	2	2	4	6	8	10	12
16	167	5/65	PC-r	1	2	2	4	6	8	10	12
17	166	5/67	PC-r	1	2	2	4	6	8	10	12
18	166	Wn/69	New-stiff-c; PC-r	1	3	3	6	9	16	22	28
19	169	Sm/70	PC-r; stiff-c	1	3	2	4	6	10	13	16

16. Gullivers Travels

Ed	HRN	Date	Details	A	C	GD 2.0	VG 4.0	FN 6.0	VF 8.0	VF/NM 9.0	NM- 9.2
1	15	12/43	Original-Lilian Chestney c/a; 60 pgs.	1	1	76	152	228	486	831	1175
2	18/20	–	Price deleted; Queens Home News ed; CC-r	1	1	22	44	66	128	209	290
3	22	–	Queens Cty. Times ed.; CC-r	1	1	18	36	54	105	165	225
4	28	–	CC-r	1	1	14	28	42	80	115	150
5	60	–	Pgs. reduced to 48; LDC-r	1	1	6	12	18	31	38	45
6	62	–	LDC-r	1	1	5	10	15	23	28	32
7	78	–	C-price 15¢; LDC-r	1	1	5	10	14	20	24	28
8	89	–	LDC-r	1	1	4	8	12	17	21	24
9	155	–	New-c; PC-r	1	2	5	10	15	25	31	36
10	165	–	PC-r	1	2	2	4	6	8	10	12
11	167	5/64	PC-r	1	2	2	4	6	8	10	12
12	167	11/65	PC-r	1	2	2	4	6	8	10	12
13	166	R/1968	C-price 25¢; PC-r	1	2	2	4	6	8	10	12
14	169	Wn/69	PC-r; stiff-c	1	2	2	4	6	8	10	12

17. The Deerslayer

Ed	HRN	Date	Details	A	C	GD 2.0	VG 4.0	FN 6.0	VF 8.0	VF/NM 9.0	NM- 9.2
1	16	1/44	Original; Outside-bc ad: 3 Gift Boxes; 60 pgs.	1	1	64	128	192	406	696	985
2A	18	–	Queens Cty Times (inside-fc); CC-r	1	1	23	46	69	136	223	310
2B	18	–	Gilberton (bottom-pg. 1); CC-r; Scarce	1	1	33	66	99	194	317	440
3	22	–	Queens Cty. Times ed.; CC-r	1	1	19	38	57	109	172	235
4	28	–	CC-r	1	1	14	28	42	81	118	155
5	60	–	Pgs.reduced to 52; LDC-r	1	1	7	14	21	37	46	55
6	64	–	LDC-r	1	1	5	10	15	22	26	30
7	85	–	C-price 15¢; LDC-r	1	1	4	8	12	17	21	24
8	118	–	LDC-r	1	1	4	7	10	14	17	20
9	132	–	LDC-r	1	1	4	7	10	14	17	20
10	167	11/66	Last LDC-r	1	1	2	4	6	11	16	20
11	166	R/1968	New-c & price 25¢; PC-r	1	2	3	6	9	18	27	35
12	169	Spr/71	Stiff-c; letters from parents & educators; PC-r	1	2	2	4	6	10	14	18

18. The Hunchback of Notre Dame

Ed	HRN	Date	Details	A	C	GD 2.0	VG 4.0	FN 6.0	VF 8.0	VF/NM 9.0	NM- 9.2
1A	17	3/44	Orig.; Gilberton ed; 60 pgs.	1	1	87	174	261	553	952	1350
1B	17	3/44	Orig.; Island Pub. Ed.; 60 pgs.	1	1	77	154	231	493	847	1200
2	18/20	–	Queens Home News ed.; CC-r	1	1	24	48	72	142	234	325
3	22	–	Queens Cty. Times ed.; CC-r	1	1	19	38	57	111	176	240
4	28	–	CC-r	1	1	16	32	48	94	147	200
5	60	–	New-c; 8pgs. deleted; Kiefer-c; LDC-r	1	2	9	18	27	47	61	75
6	62	–	LDC-r	1	2	5	10	15	22	26	30
7	78	–	C-price 15¢; LDC-r	1	2	5	10	14	20	24	28
8A	89	–	H.C.Kiefer on bottom right-fc; LDC-r	1	2	4	9	13	18	22	26
8B	89	–	Name omitted; LDC-r	1	2	5	10	15	24	30	35

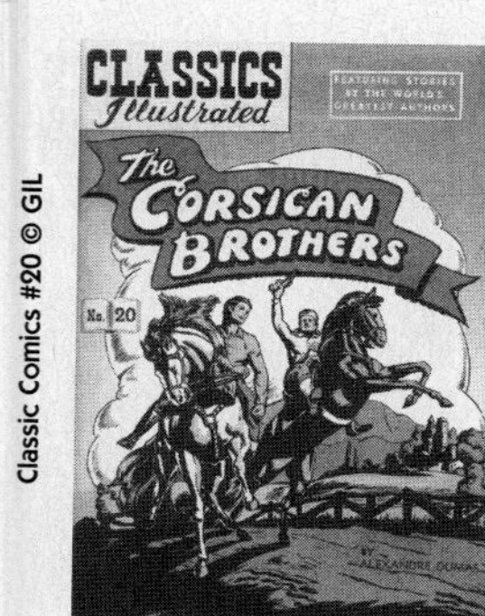

Classic Comics #20 © GIL

Classic Comics #21 © GIL

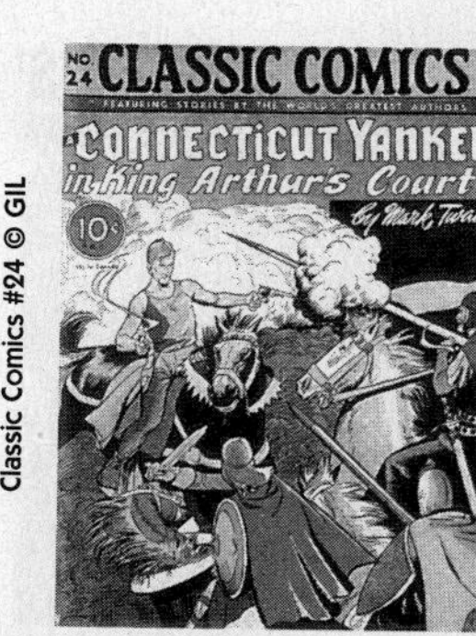

Classic Comics #24 © GIL

Ed	HRN	Date	Details	A	C	GD 2.0	VG 4.0	FN 6.0	VF 8.0	VF/NM 9.0	NM- 9.2
9	118	–	LDC-r	1	2	4	8	12	17	21	24
10	140	–	New-c; PC-r	1	3	7	14	21	35	43	50
11	146	–	PC-r	1	3	4	9	13	18	22	26
12	158	–	New-c&a; PC-r; Evans/Crandall-a	2	4	5	10	15	25	31	36
13	165	–	PC-r	2	4	2	4	6	8	11	14
14	167	9/63	PC-r	2	4	2	4	6	8	11	14
15	167	10/64	PC-r	2	4	2	4	6	8	11	14
16	167	4/66	PC-r	2	4	2	4	6	8	11	14
17	166	R/1968	New price 25¢; PC-r	2	4	2	4	6	8	10	12
18	169	Sp/70	Stiff-c; PC-r	2	4	2	4	6	8	10	12

19. Huckleberry Finn

Ed	HRN	Date	Details	A	C	GD	VG	FN	VF	VF/NM	NM-
1A	18	4/44	Orig.; Gilberton ed.; 60 pgs.	1	1	53	106	159	334	567	800
1B	18	4/44	Orig.; Island Pub.; 60 pgs.	1	1	55	110	165	352	601	850
2	18	–	Nassau Bulletin ed.; fc-price 15¢-Canada; no coming-next ad; CC-r	1	1	23	46	69	136	223	310
3	22	–	Queens City Times ed.; CC-r	1	1	19	38	57	111	176	240
4	28	–	CC-r	1	1	14	28	42	80	115	150
5	60	–	Pgs. reduced to 48; LDC-r	1	1	6	12	18	31	38	45
6	62	–	LDC-r	1	1	5	10	15	23	28	32
7	78	–	LDC-r	1	1	4	9	13	18	22	26
8	89	–	LDC-r	1	1	4	8	12	17	21	24
9	117	–	LDC-r	1	1	4	7	10	14	17	20
10	131	–	New-c&a; PC-r	2	2	5	10	15	24	30	35
11	140	–	PC-r	2	2	2	4	6	8	11	14
12	150	–	PC-r	2	2	2	4	6	8	11	14
13	158	–	PC-r	2	2	2	4	6	8	11	14
14	165	–	PC-r (scarce)	2	2	3	6	9	14	19	24
15	167	–	PC-r	2	2	2	4	6	8	10	12
16	167	6/64	PC-r	2	2	2	4	6	8	10	12
17	167	6/65	PC-r	2	2	2	4	6	8	10	12
18	167	10/65	PC-r	2	2	2	4	6	8	10	12
19	166	9/67	PC-r	2	2	2	4	6	8	10	12
20	166	Win/69	C-price 25¢; PC-r; stiff-c	2	2	2	4	6	8	10	12
21	169	Sm/70	PC-r; stiff-c	2	2	2	4	6	9	11	12

20. The Corsican Brothers

Ed	HRN	Date	Details	A	C	GD	VG	FN	VF	VF/NM	NM-
1A	20	6/44	Orig.; Gilberton ed.; bc-ad: 4 Gift Boxes; 60 pgs.	1	1	47	94	141	296	498	700
1B	20	6/44	Orig.; Courier ed.; 60 pgs.	1	1	40	80	120	246	411	575
1C	20	6/44	Orig.; Long Island Ind. ed.; 60 pgs.	1	1	40	80	120	246	411	575
2	22	–	Queens Cty. Times ed.; white logo banner; CC-r	1	1	20	40	60	114	182	250
3	28	–	CC-r	1	1	19	38	57	109	172	235
4	60	–	CI logo; no price; 48 pgs.; LDC-r	1	1	15	30	45	90	140	190
5A	62	–	LDC-r; Classics Ill. logo at top of pgs.	1	1	15	30	45	83	124	165
5B	62	–	w/o logo at top of pg. (scarcer)	1	1	15	30	45	86	133	180
6	78	–	C-price 15¢; LDC-r	1	1	14	28	42	81	118	155
7	97	–	LDC-r	1	1	14	28	42	78	112	145

21. 3 Famous Mysteries ("The Sign of the 4", "The Murders in the Rue Morgue", "The Flayed Hand")

Ed	HRN	Date	Details	A	C	GD	VG	FN	VF	VF/NM	NM-
1A	21	7/44	Orig.; Gilberton ed.; 60 pgs.	1	1	94	188	282	597	1024	1450
1B	21	7/44	Orig. Island Pub. Co.; 60 pgs.	1	1	97	194	291	621	1061	1500
1C	21	7/44	Original; Courier Ed.; 60 pgs.	1	1	84	168	252	538	919	1300
2	22	–	Nassau Bulletin ed.; CC-r	1	1	39	78	117	231	378	525
3	30	–	CC-r	1	1	28	56	84	165	270	375
4	62	–	LDC-r; 8 pgs. deleted; LDC-r	1	1	22	44	66	128	209	290
5	70	–	LDC-r	1	1	20	40	60	117	189	260
6	85	–	C-price 15¢; LDC-r	1	1	18	36	54	107	169	230
7	114	–	New-c; PC-r	1	2	18	36	54	107	169	230

22. The Pathfinder

Ed	HRN	Date	Details	A	C	GD	VG	FN	VF	VF/NM	NM-
1A	22	10/44	Orig.; No printer listed; ownership statement inside fc lists Gilberton & date; 60 pgs.	1	1	45	90	135	284	480	675
1B	22	10/44	Orig.; Island Pub. ed.; 60 pgs.	1	1	40	80	120	246	411	575
1C	22	10/44	Orig.; Queens Cty Times ed. 60 pgs.	1	1	40	80	120	246	411	575
2	30	–	C-price removed; CC-r	1	1	15	30	45	85	130	175
3	60	–	Pgs. reduced to 52; LDC-r	1	1	6	12	18	27	33	38
4	70	–	LDC-r	1	1	5	10	15	22	26	30
5	85	–	C-price 15¢; LDC-r	1	1	4	9	13	18	22	26
6	118	–	LDC-r	1	1	4	8	12	17	21	24
7	132	–	LDC-r	1	1	4	7	10	14	17	20
8	146	–	LDC-r	1	1	4	7	10	14	17	20
9	167	11/63	New-c; PC-r	1	2	4	8	12	24	37	50
10	167	12/65	PC-r	1	2	2	4	6	11	16	20
11	166	8/67	PC-r	1	2	2	4	6	11	16	20

23. Oliver Twist (1st Classic produced by the Iger Shop)

Ed	HRN	Date	Details	A	C	GD	VG	FN	VF	VF/NM	NM-
1	23	7/45	Original; 60 pgs.	1	1	45	90	135	284	480	675
2A	30	–	Printers Union logo on bottom left-fc same as 23(Orig.) (very rare); CC-r	1	1	30	60	90	177	289	400
2B	30	–	Union logo omitted; CC-r	1	1	15	30	45	84	127	170
3	60	–	Pgs. reduced to 48; LDC-r	1	1	6	12	18	29	36	42
4	62	–	LDC-r	1	1	5	10	15	23	28	32
5	71	–	LDC-r	1	1	5	10	14	20	24	28
6	85	–	C-price 15¢; LDC-r	1	1	4	9	13	18	22	26
7	94	–	LDC-r	1	1	4	7	10	14	17	20
8	118	–	LDC-r	1	1	4	7	10	14	17	20
9	136	–	New-PC, old-a; PC-r	1	2	5	10	15	24	30	35
10	150	–	Old-a; PC-r	1	2	4	7	10	14	17	20
11	164	–	Old-a; PC-r	1	2	4	8	11	16	19	22
12	164	–	New-a; PC-r; Evans/Crandall-a	2	2	4	8	12	24	37	50
13	167	–	PC-r	2	2	2	4	6	11	16	20
14	167	8/64	PC-r	2	2	2	4	6	8	10	12
15	167	12/65	PC-r	2	2	2	4	6	8	10	12
16	166	R/1968	New 25¢; PC-r	2	2	2	4	6	8	10	12
17	169	Win/69	Stiff-c; PC-r	2	2	2	4	6	8	10	12

24. A Connecticut Yankee in King Arthur's Court

Ed	HRN	Date	Details	A	C	GD	VG	FN	VF	VF/NM	NM-
1	–	9/45	Original	1	1	40	80	120	246	411	575
2	30	–	No price circle; CC-r	1	1	15	30	45	84	127	170
3	60	–	8 pgs. deleted; LDC-r	1	1	6	12	18	27	33	38
4	62	–	LDC-r	1	1	5	10	15	23	28	32
5	71	–	LDC-r	1	1	5	10	15	22	26	30
6	87	–	C-price 15¢; LDC-r	1	1	4	9	13	18	22	26
7	121	–	LDC-r	1	1	4	8	12	17	21	24
8	140	–	New-c&a; PC-r	2	2	5	10	15	25	31	36
9	153	–	PC-r	2	2	2	4	6	8	11	14
10	164	–	PC-r	2	2	2	4	6	8	10	12

Classic Comics #26 © GIL

Classic Comics #30 © GIL

Classic Comics #32 © GIL

Ed	HRN	Date	Details	A	C	GD 2.0	VG 4.0	FN 6.0	VF 8.0	VF/NM 9.0	NM- 9.2
11	167	–	PC-r	2	2	2	4	6	8	10	12
12	167	7/64	PC-r	2	2	2	4	6	8	10	12
13	167	6/66	PC-r	2	2	2	4	6	8	10	12
14	166	R/1968	C-price 25¢; PC-r	2	2	2	4	6	8	10	12
15	169	Spr/71	PC-r; stiff-c	2	2	2	4	6	8	10	12

25. Two Years Before the Mast

Ed	HRN	Date	Details	A	C	GD 2.0	VG 4.0	FN 6.0	VF 8.0	VF/NM 9.0	NM- 9.2
1	–	10/45	Original; Webb/Heames-a&c	1	1	40	80	120	246	411	575
2	30	–	Price circle blank; CC-r	1	1	15	30	45	84	127	170
3	60	–	8 pgs. deleted; LDC-r	1	1	6	12	18	27	33	38
4	62	–	LDC-r	1	1	5	10	15	23	28	32
5	71	–	LDC-r	1	1	4	9	13	18	22	26
6	85	–	C-price 15¢; LDC-r	1	1	4	8	12	17	21	24
7	114	–	LDC-r	1	1	4	7	10	14	17	20
8	156	–	3 pgs. replaced by fillers; new-c; PC-r	1	2	5	10	15	25	31	36
9	167	12/63	PC-r	1	2	2	4	6	8	10	12
10	167	12/65	PC-r	1	2	2	4	6	8	10	12
11	166	9/67	PC-r	1	2	2	4	6	8	10	12
12	169	Win/69	C-price 25¢; stiff-c PC-r	1	2	2	4	6	8	10	12

26. Frankenstein (2nd horror comic?)

Ed	HRN	Date	Details	A	C	GD 2.0	VG 4.0	FN 6.0	VF 8.0	VF/NM 9.0	NM- 9.2
1	26	12/45	Orig.; Webb/Brewster a&c; 52 pgs.	1	1	105	210	315	667	1146	1625
2A	30	–	Price circle blank; no indicia; CC-r	1	1	30	60	90	177	289	400
2B	30	–	With indicia; scarce; CC-r	1	1	34	68	102	204	332	460
3	60	–	LDC-r	1	1	16	32	48	94	147	200
4	62	–	LDC-r	1	1	15	30	45	85	130	175
5	71	–	LDC-r	1	1	8	16	24	40	50	60
6A	82	–	C-price 15¢; soft-c LDC-r	1	1	7	14	21	35	43	50
6B	82	–	Stiff-c; LDC-r	1	1	8	16	24	40	50	60
7	117	–	LDC-r	1	1	4	8	12	18	22	25
8	146	–	New Saunders-c; PC-r	1	2	6	12	18	29	36	42
9	152	–	Scarce; PC-r	1	2	8	16	24	40	50	60
10	153	–	PC-r	1	2	2	4	6	8	11	14
11	160	–	PC-r	1	2	2	4	6	8	11	14
12	165	–	PC-r	1	2	2	4	6	8	10	12
13	167	–	PC-r	1	2	2	4	6	8	10	12
14	167	6/64	PC-r	1	2	2	4	6	8	10	12
15	167	6/65	PC-r	1	2	2	4	6	8	10	12
16	167	10/65	PC-r	1	2	2	4	6	8	10	12
17	166	9/67	PC-r	1	2	2	4	6	8	10	12
18	169	Fall/69	C-price 25¢; stiff-c PC-r	1	2	2	4	6	8	10	12
19	169	Spr/71	PC-r; stiff-c	1	2	2	4	6	8	10	12

27. The Adventures of Marco Polo

Ed	HRN	Date	Details	A	C	GD 2.0	VG 4.0	FN 6.0	VF 8.0	VF/NM 9.0	NM- 9.2
1	–	4/46	Original	1	1	40	80	120	246	411	575
2	30	–	Last 'Comics' reprint; CC-r	1	1	15	30	45	84	127	170
3	70	–	8 pgs. deleted; no c-price; LDC-r	1	1	5	10	15	24	30	35
4	87	–	C-price 15¢; LDC-r	1	1	4	9	13	18	22	26
5	117	–	LDC-r	1	1	4	7	10	14	17	20
6	154	–	New-c; PC-r	1	2	5	10	15	24	30	35
7	165	–	PC-r	1	2	2	4	6	8	10	12
8	167	4/64	PC-r	1	2	2	4	6	8	10	12
9	167	6/66	PC-r	1	2	2	4	6	8	10	12
10	169	Spr/69	New price 25¢; stiff-c; PC-r	1	2	2	4	6	8	10	12

28. Michael Strogoff

Ed	HRN	Date	Details	A	C	GD 2.0	VG 4.0	FN 6.0	VF 8.0	VF/NM 9.0	NM- 9.2
1	–	6/46	Original	1	1	40	80	120	246	411	575
2	51	–	8 pgs. cut; LDC-r	1	1	15	30	45	84	127	170
3	115	–	New-c; PC-r	1	2	6	12	18	31	38	45
4	155	–	PC-r	1	2	4	7	10	14	17	20
5	167	11/63	PC-r	1	2	2	4	6	9	13	16
6	167	7/66	PC-r	1	2	2	4	6	9	13	16
7	169	Sm/69	C-price 25¢; stiff-c PC-r	1	3	3	6	9	15	21	26

29. The Prince and the Pauper

Ed	HRN	Date	Details	A	C	GD 2.0	VG 4.0	FN 6.0	VF 8.0	VF/NM 9.0	NM- 9.2
1	–	7/46	Orig.; "Horror"-c	1	1	57	114	171	362	619	875
2	60	–	8 pgs. cut; new-c by Kiefer; LDC-r	1	2	9	18	27	50	65	80
3	62	–	LDC-r	1	2	5	10	15	24	30	35
4	71	–	LDC-r	1	2	4	9	13	18	22	26
5	93	–	LDC-r	1	2	4	8	12	17	21	24
6	114	–	LDC-r	1	2	4	7	10	14	17	20
7	128	–	New-c; PC-r	1	3	5	10	15	24	30	35
8	138	–	PC-r	1	3	2	4	6	8	11	14
9	150	–	PC-r	1	3	2	4	6	8	11	14
10	164	–	PC-r	1	3	2	4	6	8	10	12
11	167	–	PC-r	1	3	2	4	6	8	10	12
12	167	7/64	PC-r	1	3	2	4	6	8	10	12
13	167	11/65	PC-r	1	3	2	4	6	8	10	12
14	166	R/68	C-price 25¢; PC-r	1	3	2	4	6	8	10	12
15	169	Sm/70	PC-r; stiff-c	1	3	2	4	6	8	10	12

30. The Moonstone

Ed	HRN	Date	Details	A	C	GD 2.0	VG 4.0	FN 6.0	VF 8.0	VF/NM 9.0	NM- 9.2
1	–	9/46	Original; Rico-c/a	1	1	40	80	120	246	411	575
2	60	–	LDC-r; 8pgs. cut	1	1	9	18	27	47	61	75
3	70	–	LDC-r	1	1	8	16	24	42	54	65
4	155	–	New L.B. Cole-c; PC-r	1	2	4	8	12	28	44	60
5	165	–	PC-r; L.B. Cole-c	1	2	3	6	9	16	23	30
6	167	1/64	PC-r; L.B. Cole-c	1	2	2	4	6	10	14	18
7	167	9/65	PC-r; L.B. Cole-c	1	2	2	4	6	9	13	16
8	166	R/1968	C-price 25¢; PC-r	1	2	2	4	6	8	11	14

31. The Black Arrow

Ed	HRN	Date	Details	A	C	GD 2.0	VG 4.0	FN 6.0	VF 8.0	VF/NM 9.0	NM- 9.2
1	30	10/46	Original	1	1	39	78	117	231	378	525
2	51	–	CI logo; LDC-r 8pgs. deleted	1	1	6	12	18	33	41	48
3	64	–	LDC-r	1	1	4	9	13	18	22	26
4	87	–	C-price 15¢; LDC-r	1	1	4	8	12	17	21	24
5	108	–	LDC-r	1	1	4	7	10	14	17	20
6	125	–	LDC-r	1	1	4	7	10	14	17	20
7	131	–	New-c; PC-r	1	2	5	10	15	24	30	35
8	140	–	PC-r	1	2	2	4	6	8	11	14
9	148	–	PC-r	1	2	2	4	6	8	11	14
10	161	–	PC-r	1	2	2	4	6	8	10	12
11	167	–	PC-r	1	2	2	4	6	8	10	12
12	167	7/64	PC-r	1	2	2	4	6	8	10	12
13	167	11/65	PC-r	1	2	2	4	6	8	10	12
14	166	R/1968	C-price 25¢; PC-r	1	2	2	4	6	8	10	12

32. Lorna Doone

Ed	HRN	Date	Details	A	C	GD 2.0	VG 4.0	FN 6.0	VF 8.0	VF/NM 9.0	NM- 9.2
1	–	12/46	Original; Matt Baker c&a	1	1	40	80	120	246	411	575
2	53/64	–	8 pgs. deleted; LDC-r	1	1	9	18	27	47	61	75
3	85	1951	C-price 15¢; LDC-r; Baker c&a	1	1	7	14	21	37	46	55
4	118	–	LDC-r	1	1	4	9	13	18	22	26
5	138	–	New-c; old-c becomes new title pg.; PC-r	1	2	6	12	18	28	34	40
6	150	–	PC-r	1	2	2	4	6	8	10	12
7	165	–	PC-r	1	2	2	4	6	8	10	12
8	167	1/64	PC-r	1	2	2	4	6	8	11	14
9	167	11/65	PC-r	1	2	2	4	6	8	11	14
10	166	R/1968	New-c; PC-r	1	3	3	6	9	17	25	32

33. The Adventures of Sherlock Holmes

Ed	HRN	Date	Details	A	C	GD 2.0	VG 4.0	FN 6.0	VF 8.0	VF/NM 9.0	NM- 9.2
1	33	1/47	Original; Kiefer-c; contains Study in Scarlet & Hound of	1	1	123	246	369	787	1344	1900

Classics Illustrated #36 © GIL

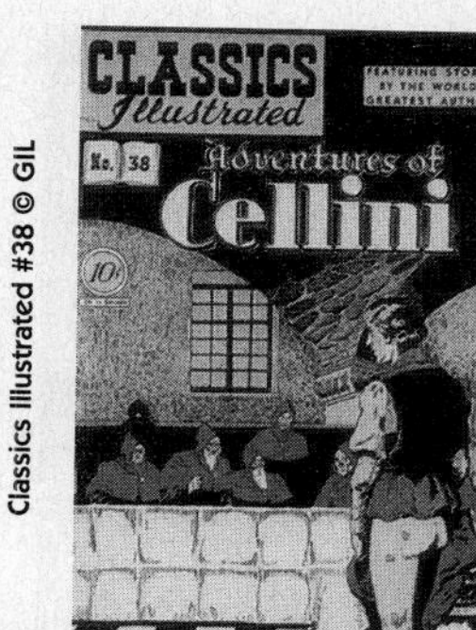

Classics Illustrated #38 © GIL

Classics Illustrated #44 © GIL

Ed	HRN	Date	Details	A	C	GD 2.0	VG 4.0	FN 6.0	VF 8.0	VF/NM 9.0	NM- 9.2
			the Baskervilles; 68 pgs.								
2	53	–	"A Study in Scarlet" (17 pgs.) deleted; LDC-r	1	1	45	90	135	284	480	675
3	71	–	LDC-r	1	1	37	74	111	222	361	500
4A	89	–	C-price 15¢; LDC-r	1	1	29	58	87	170	278	385
4B	89	–	Kiefer's name omitted from-c	1	1	30	60	90	177	289	400

34. Mysterious Island (Last "Classic Comic")

Ed	HRN	Date	Details	A	C	GD 2.0	VG 4.0	FN 6.0	VF 8.0	VF/NM 9.0	NM- 9.2
1	35	2/47	Original; Webb/ Heames-c/a	1	1	40	80	120	246	411	575
2	60	–	8 pgs. deleted; LDC-r	1	1	7	14	21	37	46	55
3	62	–	LDC-r	1	1	5	10	15	23	28	32
4	71	–	LDC-r	1	1	6	12	18	31	38	45
5	78	–	C-price 15¢ in circle; LDC-r	1	1	5	10	14	20	24	28
6	92	–	LDC-r	1	1	4	9	13	18	22	26
7	117	–	LDC-r	1	1	4	7	10	14	17	20
8	140	–	New-c; PC-r	1	2	5	10	15	24	30	35
9	156	–	PC-r	1	2	2	4	6	8	11	14
10	167	10/63	PC-r	1	2	2	4	6	8	10	12
11	167	5/64	PC-r	1	2	2	4	6	8	10	12
12	167	6/66	PC-r	1	2	2	4	6	8	10	12
13	166	R/1968	C-price 25¢; PC-r	1	2	2	4	6	8	10	12

35. Last Days of Pompeii (First "Classics Illustrated")

Ed	HRN	Date	Details	A	C	GD 2.0	VG 4.0	FN 6.0	VF 8.0	VF/NM 9.0	NM- 9.2
1	35	3/47	Original; LDC; Kiefer-c/a	1	1	40	80	120	246	411	575
2	161	–	New c&a; 15¢; PC-r; Kirby/Ayers-a	2	2	5	10	15	30	48	65
3	167	1/64	PC-r	2	2	3	6	9	15	21	26
4	167	7/66	PC-r	2	2	3	6	9	15	21	26
5	169	Spr/70	New price 25¢; stiff-c; PC-r	2	2	3	6	9	15	21	26

36. Typee

Ed	HRN	Date	Details	A	C	GD 2.0	VG 4.0	FN 6.0	VF 8.0	VF/NM 9.0	NM- 9.2
1	36	4/47	Original	1	1	26	52	78	154	252	350
2	64	–	No c-price; 8 pg. ed.; LDC-r	1	1	7	14	21	37	46	55
3	155	–	New-c; PC-r	1	2	5	10	15	24	30	35
4	167	9/63	PC-r	1	2	2	4	6	9	12	15
5	167	7/65	PC-r	1	2	2	4	6	9	12	15
6	169	Sm/69	C-price 25¢; stiff-c PC-r	1	2	2	4	6	9	12	15

37. The Pioneers

Ed	HRN	Date	Details	A	C	GD 2.0	VG 4.0	FN 6.0	VF 8.0	VF/NM 9.0	NM- 9.2
1	37	5/47	Original; Palais-c/a	1	1	24	48	72	142	234	325
2A	62	–	8 pgs. cut; LDC-r; price circle blank	1	1	6	12	18	28	34	40
2B	62	–	10¢; LDC-r;	1	1	26	52	78	154	252	350
3	70	–	LDC-r	1	1	4	8	12	17	21	24
4	92	–	15¢; LDC-r	1	1	4	8	11	16	19	22
5	118	–	LDC-r	1	1	4	7	10	14	17	20
6	131	–	LDC-r	1	1	4	7	10	14	17	20
7	132	–	LDC-r	1	1	4	7	10	14	17	20
8	153	–	LDC-r	1	1	4	7	10	14	17	20
9	167	5/64	LDC-r	1	1	2	4	6	8	11	14
10	167	6/66	LDC-r	1	1	2	4	6	8	11	14
11	166	R/1968	New-c; 25¢; PC-r	1	2	3	6	9	18	27	36

38. Adventures of Cellini

Ed	HRN	Date	Details	A	C	GD 2.0	VG 4.0	FN 6.0	VF 8.0	VF/NM 9.0	NM- 9.2
1	–	6/47	Original; Froehlich c/a	1	1	32	64	96	188	307	425
2	164	–	New-c&a; PC-r	2	2	3	6	9	18	27	36
3	167	12/63	PC-r	2	2	2	4	6	10	14	18
4	167	7/66	PC-r	2	2	2	4	6	10	14	18
5	169	Spr/70	Stiff-c; new price 25¢; PC-r	2	2	2	4	6	11	16	20

39. Jane Eyre

Ed	HRN	Date	Details	A	C	GD 2.0	VG 4.0	FN 6.0	VF 8.0	VF/NM 9.0	NM- 9.2
1	–	7/47	Original	1	1	31	62	93	182	296	410
2	60	–	No c-price; 8 pgs. cut; LDC-r	1	1	6	12	18	31	38	45
3	62	–	LDC-r	1	1	5	10	15	24	30	35
4	71	–	LDC-r; c-price 10¢	1	1	5	10	15	22	26	30
5	92	–	C-price 15¢; LDC-r	1	1	4	9	13	18	22	26
6	118	–	LDC-r	1	1	4	8	12	17	21	24
7	142	–	New-c; old-a; PC-r	1	2	6	12	18	28	34	40
8	154	–	Old-a; PC-r	1	2	4	8	12	17	21	24
9	165	–	New-a; PC-r	2	2	3	6	9	18	27	35
10	167	12/63	PC-r	2	2	3	6	9	14	19	24
11	167	4/65	PC-r	2	2	2	4	6	13	18	22
12	167	8/66	PC-r	2	2	2	4	6	13	18	22
13	166	R/1968	New-c; PC-r	2	3	5	10	15	34	55	75

40. Mysteries ("The Pit and the Pendulum", "The Advs. of Hans Pfall" & "The Fall of the House of Usher")

Ed	HRN	Date	Details	A	C	GD 2.0	VG 4.0	FN 6.0	VF 8.0	VF/NM 9.0	NM- 9.2
1	40	8/47	Original; Kiefer-c/a, Froehlich, Griffiths-a	1	1	58	116	174	371	636	900
2	62	–	LDC-r; 8pgs. cut	1	1	22	44	66	132	216	300
3	75	–	LDC-r	1	1	19	38	57	109	172	235
4	92	–	C-price 15¢; LDC-r	1	1	15	30	45	94	147	200

41. Twenty Years After

Ed	HRN	Date	Details	A	C	GD 2.0	VG 4.0	FN 6.0	VF 8.0	VF/NM 9.0	NM- 9.2
1	–	9/47	Original; 'horror'-c	1	1	39	78	117	231	378	525
2	62	–	New-c; no c-price 8 pgs. cut; LDC-r; Kiefer-c	1	2	7	14	21	37	46	55
3	78	–	C-price 15¢; LDC-r	1	2	5	10	15	23	28	32
4	156	–	New-c; PC-r	1	3	5	10	15	24	30	35
5	167	12/63	PC-r	1	3	2	4	6	8	10	12
6	167	11/66	PC-r	1	3	2	4	6	8	10	12
7	169	Spr/70	New price 25¢; stiff-c; PC-r	1	3	2	4	6	8	10	12

42. Swiss Family Robinson

Ed	HRN	Date	Details	A	C	GD 2.0	VG 4.0	FN 6.0	VF 8.0	VF/NM 9.0	NM- 9.2
1	42	10/47	Orig.; Kiefer-c&a;	1	1	23	46	69	136	223	310
2A	62	–	8 pgs. cut; outside bc: Gift Box ad; LDC-r	1	1	6	12	18	31	38	45
2B	62	–	8 pgs. cut; outside-bc: Reorder list; scarce; LDC-r	1	1	10	20	30	58	79	100
3	75	–	LDC-r	1	1	5	10	14	20	24	28
4	93	–	LDC-r	1	1	5	10	14	20	24	28
5	117	–	LDC-r	1	1	3	6	9	14	19	24
6	131	–	New-c; old-a; PC-r	1	2	3	6	9	15	21	26
7	137	–	Old-a; PC-r	1	2	2	4	6	10	14	18
8	141	–	Old-a; PC-r	1	2	2	4	6	10	14	18
9	152	–	New-a; PC-r	2	2	3	6	9	16	23	30
10	158	–	PC-r	2	2	2	4	6	8	10	12
11	165	–	PC-r	2	2	3	6	9	17	25	32
12	167	12/63	PC-r	2	2	2	4	6	8	11	14
13	167	4/65	PC-r	2	2	2	4	6	8	10	12
14	167	5/66	PC-r	2	2	2	4	6	8	10	12
15	166	11/67	PC-r	2	2	2	4	6	8	10	12
16	169	Spr/69	PC-r; stiff-c	2	2	2	4	6	8	10	12

43. Great Expectations (Used in **SOTI**, pg. 311)

Ed	HRN	Date	Details	A	C	GD 2.0	VG 4.0	FN 6.0	VF 8.0	VF/NM 9.0	NM- 9.2
1	43	11/47	Original; Kiefer-a/c	1	1	89	178	267	565	970	1375
2	62	–	No c-price; 8 pgs. cut; LDC-r	1	1	57	114	171	362	624	885

44. Mysteries of Paris (Used in **SOTI**, pg. 323)

Ed	HRN	Date	Details	A	C	GD 2.0	VG 4.0	FN 6.0	VF 8.0	VF/NM 9.0	NM- 9.2
1A	44	12/47	Original; 56 pgs.; Kiefer-c/a	1	1	64	128	192	406	696	985
1B	44	12/47	Orig.; printed on white/heavier paper; (rare)	1	1	75	150	225	476	818	1160
2A	62	–	8 pgs. cut; outside-bc: Gift Box ad;	1	1	30	60	90	177	289	400

Classics Illustrated #47 © GIL

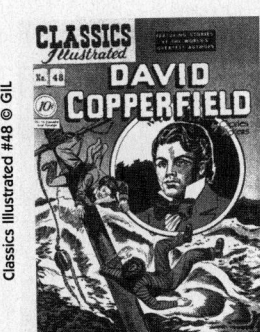

Classics Illustrated #48 © GIL

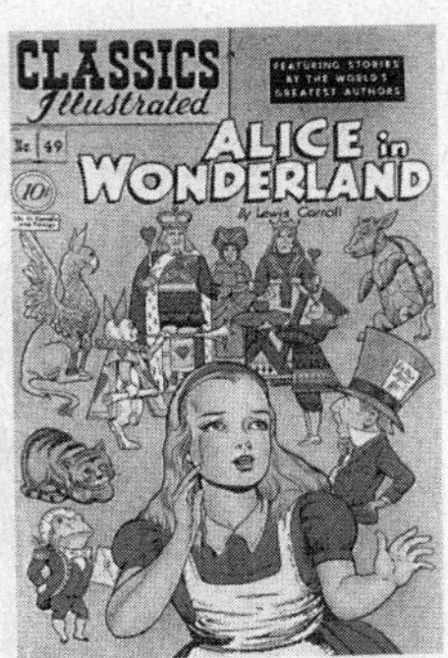

Classics Illustrated #49 © GIL

Ed	HRN	Date	Details	A	C	GD 2.0	VG 4.0	FN 6.0	VF 8.0	VF/NM 9.0	NM- 9.2
			LDC-r								
2B	62	–	8 pgs. cut; outside-bc: reorder list; LDC-r	1	1	30	60	90	177	289	400
3	78	–	C-price 15¢; LDC-r	1	1	25	50	75	147	241	335

45. Tom Brown's School Days

Ed	HRN	Date	Details	A	C	GD	VG	FN	VF	VF/NM	NM-
1	44	1/48	Original; 1st 48pg. issue	1	1	18	36	54	105	165	225
2	64	–	No c-price; LDC-r	1	1	7	14	21	35	43	50
3	161	–	New-c&a; PC-r	2	2	3	6	9	17	25	32
4	167	2/64	PC-r	2	2	2	4	6	8	11	14
5	167	8/66	PC-r	2	2	2	4	6	8	11	14
6	166	R/1968	C-price 25¢; PC-r	2	2	2	4	6	8	11	14

46. Kidnapped

Ed	HRN	Date	Details	A	C	GD	VG	FN	VF	VF/NM	NM-
1	47	4/48	Original; Webb-c/a	1	1	18	36	54	105	165	225
2A	62	–	Price circle blank; LDC-r	1	1	7	14	21	35	43	50
2B	62	–	C-price 10¢; rare; LDC-r	1	1	30	60	90	177	289	400
3	78	–	C-price 15¢; LDC-r	1	1	5	10	14	20	24	28
4	87	–	LDC-r	1	1	4	9	13	18	22	26
5	118	–	LDC-r	1	1	4	7	10	14	17	20
6	131	–	New-c; PC-r	1	2	5	10	15	23	28	32
7	140	–	PC-r	1	2	2	4	6	8	11	14
8	150	–	PC-r	1	2	2	4	6	8	11	14
9	164	–	Reduced pg.width; PC-r	1	2	2	4	6	8	10	12
10	167	–	PC-r	1	2	2	4	6	8	10	12
11	167	3/64	PC-r	1	2	2	4	6	8	10	12
12	167	6/65	PC-r	1	2	2	4	6	8	10	12
13	167	12/65	PC-r	1	2	2	4	6	8	10	12
14	166	9/67	PC-r	1	2	2	4	6	8	10	12
15	166	Win/69	New price 25¢; PC-r; stiff-c	1	2	2	4	6	8	10	12
16	169	Sm/70	PC-r; stiff-c	1	2	2	4	6	8	10	12

47. Twenty Thousand Leagues Under the Sea

Ed	HRN	Date	Details	A	C	GD	VG	FN	VF	VF/NM	NM-
1	47	5/48	Orig.; Kiefer-a&c	1	1	19	38	57	111	176	240
2	64	–	No c-price; LDC-r	1	1	6	12	18	27	33	38
3	78	–	C-price 15¢; LDC-r	1	1	4	9	13	18	22	26
4	94	–	LDC-r	1	1	4	8	12	17	21	24
5	118	–	LDC-r	1	1	4	7	10	14	17	20
6	128	–	New-c; PC-r	1	2	5	10	15	24	30	35
7	133	–	PC-r	1	2	2	4	6	9	13	16
8	140	–	PC-r	1	2	2	4	6	8	11	14
9	148	–	PC-r	1	2	2	4	6	8	11	14
10	156	–	PC-r	1	2	2	4	6	8	11	14
11	165	–	PC-r	1	2	2	4	6	8	11	14
12	167	–	PC-r	1	2	2	4	6	8	11	14
13	167	3/64	PC-r	1	2	2	4	6	8	11	14
14	167	8/65	PC-r	1	2	2	4	6	8	11	14
15	167	10/66	PC-r	1	2	2	4	6	8	11	14
16	166	R/1968	C-price 25¢; new-c PC-r	1	3	3	6	9	14	20	25
17	169	Spr/70	Stiff-c; PC-r	1	3	2	4	6	11	16	20

48. David Copperfield

Ed	HRN	Date	Details	A	C	GD	VG	FN	VF	VF/NM	NM-
1	47	6/48	Original; Kiefer-c/a	1	1	18	36	54	105	165	225
2	64	–	Price circle replaced by motif of boy reading; LDC-r	1	1	6	12	18	27	33	38
3	87	–	C-price 15¢; LDC-r	1	1	4	8	12	17	21	24
4	121	–	New-c; PC-r	1	2	5	10	15	22	26	30
5	130	–	PC-r	1	2	2	4	6	8	11	14
6	140	–	PC-r	1	2	2	4	6	8	11	14
7	148	–	PC-r	1	2	2	4	6	8	11	14
8	156	–	PC-r	1	2	2	4	6	8	11	14
9	167	–	PC-r	1	2	2	4	6	8	10	12
10	167	4/64	PC-r	1	2	2	4	6	8	10	12
11	167	6/65	PC-r	1	2	2	4	6	8	10	12
12	166	5/67	PC-r	1	2	2	4	6	8	10	12
13	166	R/67	PC-r; C-price 25¢	1	2	2	4	6	9	13	16
14	166	Spr/69	C-price 25¢; stiff-c PC-r	1	2	2	4	6	8	10	12
15	169	Win/69	Stiff-c; PC-r	1	2	2	4	6	8	10	12

49. Alice in Wonderland

Ed	HRN	Date	Details	A	C	GD	VG	FN	VF	VF/NM	NM-
1	47	7/48	Original; 1st Blum a & c	1	1	21	42	63	124	202	280
2	64	–	No c-price; LDC-r	1	1	8	16	24	42	54	65
3A	85	–	C-price 15¢; soft-c LDC-r	1	1	7	14	21	37	46	55
3B	85	–	Stiff-c; LDC-r	1	1	8	16	24	40	50	60
4	155	–	New PC, similar to orig.; PC-r	1	2	4	8	12	26	41	55
5	165	–	PC-r	1	2	3	6	9	18	27	35
6	167	3/64	PC-r	1	2	3	6	9	16	23	30
7	167	6/66	PC-r	1	2	3	6	9	16	23	60
8A	166	Fall/68	New-c; soft-c; 25¢ c-price; PC-r	1	3	4	8	12	26	41	55
8B	166	Fall/68	New-c; stiff-c; 25¢ c-price; PC-r	1	3	7	14	21	45	73	100

50. Adventures of Tom Sawyer (Used in **SOTI**, pg. 37)

Ed	HRN	Date	Details	A	C	GD	VG	FN	VF	VF/NM	NM-
1A	51	8/48	Orig.; Aldo Rubano a&c	1	1	18	36	54	105	165	225
1B	51	9/48	Orig.; Rubano c&a	1	1	18	36	54	105	165	225
1C	51	9/48	Orig.; outside-bc: blue & yellow only; rare	1	1	23	46	69	136	223	310
2	64	–	No c-price; LDC-r	1	1	5	10	15	23	28	32
3	78	–	C-price 15¢; LDC-r	1	1	4	8	12	17	21	24
4	94	–	LDC-r	1	1	4	7	10	14	17	20
5	117	–	LDC-r	1	1	2	4	6	10	14	18
6	132	–	LDC-r	1	1	2	4	6	10	14	18
7	140	–	New-c; PC-r	1	2	3	6	9	18	27	35
8	150	–	PC-r	1	2	2	4	6	8	11	14
9	164	–	New-a; PC-r	2	2	3	6	9	18	27	35
10	167	–	PC-r	2	2	2	4	6	8	11	14
11	167	1/65	PC-r	2	2	2	4	6	8	10	12
12	167	5/66	PC-r	2	2	2	4	6	8	10	12
13	166	12/67	PC-r	2	2	2	4	6	8	10	12
14	169	Fall/69	C-price 25¢; stiff-c; PC-r	2	2	2	4	6	8	10	12
15	169	Win/71	PC-r	2	2	2	4	6	8	10	12

51. The Spy

Ed	HRN	Date	Details	A	C	GD	VG	FN	VF	VF/NM	NM-
1A	51	9/48	Original; inside-bc illo: Christmas Carol	1	1	17	34	51	100	158	215
1B	51	9/48	Original; inside-bc illo: Man in Iron Mask	1	1	17	34	51	100	158	215
1C	51	8/48	Original; outside-bc: full color	1	1	17	34	51	100	158	215
1D	51	8/48	Original; outside-bc: blue & yellow only; scarce	1	1	19	38	57	109	172	235
2	89	–	C-price 15¢; LDC-r	1	1	5	10	14	20	24	28
3	121	–	LDC-r	1	1	4	8	12	17	21	24
4	139	–	New-c; PC-r	1	2	3	6	9	18	27	35
5	156	–	PC-r	1	2	2	4	6	8	11	14
6	167	11/63	PC-r	1	2	2	4	6	8	10	12
7	167	7/66	PC-r	1	2	2	4	6	8	10	12
8A	166	Win/69	C-price 25¢; soft-c; scarce; PC-r	1	2	3	6	9	15	21	26
8B	166	Win/69	C-price 25¢; stiff-c; PC-r	1	2	2	4	6	8	10	12

52. The House of the Seven Gables

Ed	HRN	Date	Details	A	C	GD	VG	FN	VF	VF/NM	NM-
1	53	10/48	Orig.; Griffiths a&c	1	1	17	34	51	100	158	215
2	89	–	C-price 15¢; LDC-r	1	1	5	10	14	20	24	28
3	121	–	LDC-r	1	1	4	8	12	17	21	24
4	142	–	New-c&a; PC-r; Woodbridge-a	2	2	5	10	15	25	31	36

Classics Illustrated #55 © GIL

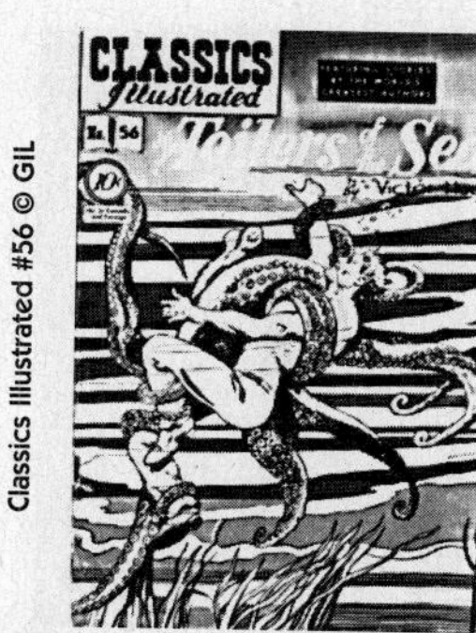

Classics Illustrated #56 © GIL

Classics Illustrated #61 © GIL

Ed	HRN	Date	Details	A	C	GD 2.0	VG 4.0	FN 6.0	VF 8.0	VF/NM 9.0	NM- 9.2
5	156	–	PC-r	2	2	2	4	6	8	11	14
6	165	–	PC-r	2	2	2	4	6	8	10	12
7	167	5/64	PC-r	2	2	2	4	6	8	11	14
8	167	3/66	PC-r	2	2	2	4	6	8	10	12
9	166	R/1968	C-price 25¢; PC-r	2	2	2	4	6	8	10	12
10	169	Spr/70	Stiff-c; PC-r	2	2	2	4	6	8	10	12

53. A Christmas Carol

Ed	HRN	Date	Details	A	C	GD 2.0	VG 4.0	FN 6.0	VF 8.0	VF/NM 9.0	NM- 9.2
1	53	11/48	Original & only ed; Kiefer-c/a	1	1	24	48	72	140	230	320

54. Man in the Iron Mask

Ed	HRN	Date	Details	A	C	GD 2.0	VG 4.0	FN 6.0	VF 8.0	VF/NM 9.0	NM- 9.2
1	55	12/48	Original; Froehlich-a, Kiefer-c	1	1	17	34	51	100	158	215
2	93	–	C-price 15¢; LDC-r	1	1	5	10	15	23	28	32
3A	111	–	(O) logo lettering; scarce; LDC-r	1	1	6	12	18	31	38	45
3B	111	–	New logo as PC; LDC-r	1	1	5	10	15	23	28	32
4	142	–	New-c&a; PC-r	2	2	5	10	15	24	30	35
5	154	–	PC-r	2	2	2	4	6	8	11	14
6	165	–	PC-r	2	2	2	4	6	8	10	12
7	167	5/64	PC-r	2	2	2	4	6	8	10	12
8	167	4/66	PC-r	2	2	2	4	6	8	10	12
9A	166	Win/69	C-price 25¢; soft-c PC-r	2	2	3	6	9	15	21	26
9B	166	Win/69	Stiff-c	2	2	2	4	6	8	10	12

55. Silas Marner (Used in **SOTI**, pgs. 311, 312)

Ed	HRN	Date	Details	A	C	GD 2.0	VG 4.0	FN 6.0	VF 8.0	VF/NM 9.0	NM- 9.2
1	55	1/49	Original-Kiefer-c	1	1	17	34	51	100	158	215
2	75	–	Price circle blank; 'Coming Next' ad; LDC-r	1	1	5	10	15	24	30	35
3	97	–	LDC-r	1	1	3	6	9	14	19	24
4	121	–	New-c; PC-r	1	2	3	6	9	18	27	35
5	130	–	PC-r	1	2	2	4	6	8	11	14
6	140	–	PC-r	1	2	2	4	6	8	11	14
7	154	–	PC-r	1	2	2	4	6	8	11	14
8	165	–	PC-r	1	2	2	4	6	8	10	12
9	167	2/64	PC-r	1	2	2	4	6	8	10	12
10	167	6/65	PC-r	1	2	2	4	6	8	10	12
11	166	5/67	PC-r	1	2	2	4	6	8	10	12
12A	166	Win/69	C-price 25¢; soft-c PC-r	1	2	3	6	9	15	21	26
12B	166	Win/69	C-price 25¢; stiff-c PC-r	1	2	2	4	6	8	10	12

56. The Toilers of the Sea

Ed	HRN	Date	Details	A	C	GD 2.0	VG 4.0	FN 6.0	VF 8.0	VF/NM 9.0	NM- 9.2
1	55	2/49	Original; A.M. Froehlich-c/a	1	1	24	48	72	140	230	320
2	165	–	New-c&a; PC-r; Angelo Torres-a	2	2	8	16	24	40	50	60
3	167	3/64	PC-r	2	2	3	6	9	16	23	30
4	167	10/66	PC-r	2	2	3	6	9	16	23	30

57. The Song of Hiawatha

Ed	HRN	Date	Details	A	C	GD 2.0	VG 4.0	FN 6.0	VF 8.0	VF/NM 9.0	NM- 9.2
1	55	3/49	Original; Alex Blum-c/a	1	1	16	32	48	94	147	200
2	75	–	No c-price w/15¢ sticker; 'Coming Next' ad; LDC-r	1	1	5	10	15	24	30	35
3	94	–	C-price 15¢; LDC-r	1	1	5	10	14	20	24	28
4	118	–	LDC-r	1	1	3	6	9	14	19	24
5	134	–	New-c; PC-r	1	2	3	6	9	18	27	35
6	139	–	PC-r	1	2	2	4	6	8	11	14
7	154	–	PC-r	1	2	2	4	6	8	11	14
8	167	–	Has orig.date; PC-r	1	2	2	4	6	8	10	12
9	167	9/64	PC-r	1	2	2	4	6	8	10	12
10	167	10/65	PC-r	1	2	2	4	6	8	10	12
11	166	F/1968	C-price 25¢; PC-r	1	2	2	4	6	8	10	12

58. The Prairie

Ed	HRN	Date	Details	A	C	GD 2.0	VG 4.0	FN 6.0	VF 8.0	VF/NM 9.0	NM- 9.2
1	60	4/49	Original; Palais c/a	1	1	16	32	48	94	147	200
2A	62	–	No c-price; no coming-next ad; LDC-r	1	1	9	18	27	47	61	75
2B	62		10¢ (rare)	1	1	18	36	54	105	165	225
3	78	–	C-price 15¢ in dbl. circle; LDC-r	1	1	5	10	15	22	26	30
4	114	–	LDC-r	1	1	4	8	12	17	21	24
5	131	–	LDC-r	1	1	4	7	10	14	17	20
6	132	–	LDC-r	1	1	4	7	10	14	17	20
7	146	–	New-c; PC-r	1	2	5	10	15	23	28	32
8	155	–	PC-r	1	2	2	4	6	8	11	14
9	167	5/64	PC-r	1	2	2	4	6	8	10	12
10	167	4/66	PC-r	1	2	2	4	6	8	10	12
11	169	Sm/69	New price 25¢; stiff-c; PC-r	1	2	2	4	6	8	10	12

59. Wuthering Heights

Ed	HRN	Date	Details	A	C	GD 2.0	VG 4.0	FN 6.0	VF 8.0	VF/NM 9.0	NM- 9.2
1	60	5/49	Original; Kiefer-c/a	1	1	17	34	51	100	158	215
2	85	–	C-price 15¢; LDC-r	1	1	6	12	18	28	34	40
3	156	–	New-c; PC-r	1	2	5	10	15	25	31	36
4	167	1/64	PC-r	1	2	2	4	6	8	11	14
5	167	10/66	PC-r	1	2	2	4	6	8	11	14
6	169	Sm/69	C-price 25¢; stiff-c; PC-r	1	2	2	4	6	8	11	14

60. Black Beauty

Ed	HRN	Date	Details	A	C	GD 2.0	VG 4.0	FN 6.0	VF 8.0	VF/NM 9.0	NM- 9.2
1	62	6/49	Original; Froehlich-c/a	1	1	16	32	48	94	147	200
2	62	–	No c-price; no coming-next ad; LDC-r (rare)	1	1	18	36	54	107	169	230
3	85	–	C-price 15¢; LDC-r	1	1	5	10	15	23	28	32
4	158	–	New L.B. Cole-c/a; PC-r	2	2	7	14	21	35	43	50
5	167	2/64	PC-r	2	2	2	4	6	11	16	20
6	167	3/66	PC-r	2	2	2	4	6	11	16	20
7	166	R/1968	New-c&price, 25¢; PC-r	2	3	5	10	15	32	51	70

61. The Woman in White

Ed	HRN	Date	Details	A	C	GD 2.0	VG 4.0	FN 6.0	VF 8.0	VF/NM 9.0	NM- 9.2
1A	62	7/49	Original; Blum-c/a fc-purple; bc: top illos light blue	1	1	17	34	51	100	158	215
1B	62	7/49	Original; Blum-c/a fc-pink; bc: top illos light violet	1	1	17	34	51	100	158	215
2	156	–	New-c; PC-r	1	2	6	12	18	28	34	40
3	167	1/64	PC-r	1	2	2	4	6	11	16	20
4	166	R/1968	C-price 25¢; PC-r	1	2	2	4	6	11	16	20

62. Western Stories ("The Luck of Roaring Camp" and "The Outcasts of Poker Flat")

Ed	HRN	Date	Details	A	C	GD 2.0	VG 4.0	FN 6.0	VF 8.0	VF/NM 9.0	NM- 9.2
1	62	8/49	Original; Kiefer-c/a	1	1	15	30	45	90	140	190
2	89	–	C-price 15¢; LDC-r	1	1	5	10	15	23	28	32
3	121	–	LDC-r	1	1	3	6	9	15	21	26
4	137	–	New-c; PC-r	1	2	3	6	9	18	27	35
5	152	–	PC-r	1	2	2	4	6	8	10	12
6	167	10/63	PC-r	1	2	2	4	6	8	10	12
7	167	6/64	PC-r	1	2	2	4	6	8	10	12
8	167	11/66	PC-r	1	2	2	4	6	8	10	12
9	166	R/1968	New-c&price 25¢; PC-r	1	3	3	6	9	17	25	32

63. The Man Without a Country

Ed	HRN	Date	Details	A	C	GD 2.0	VG 4.0	FN 6.0	VF 8.0	VF/NM 9.0	NM- 9.2
1	62	9/49	Original; Kiefer-c/a	1	1	16	32	48	94	147	200
2	78	–	C-price 15¢ in double circle; LDC-r	1	1	5	10	15	23	28	32
3	156	–	New-c, old-a; PC-r	1	2	6	12	18	28	34	40
4	165	–	New-a & text pgs.; PC-r; A. Torres-a	2	2	5	10	15	23	28	32
5	167	3/64	PC-r	2	2	2	4	6	8	10	12
6	167	8/66	PC-r	2	2	2	4	6	8	10	12

Classics Illustrated #66 © GIL

Classics Illustrated #73 © GIL

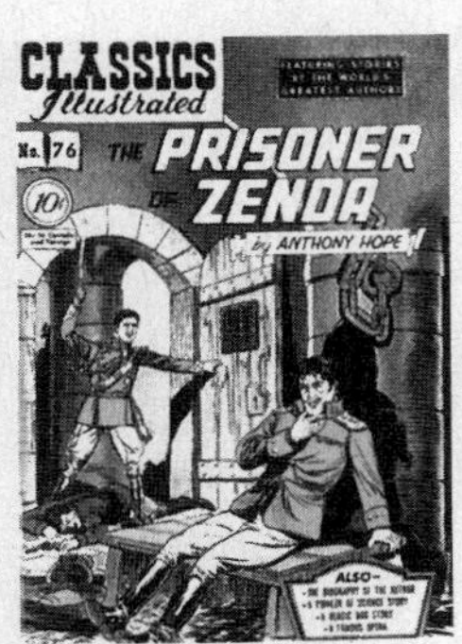

Classics Illustrated #76 © GIL

Ed	HRN	Date	Details	A	C	GD 2.0	VG 4.0	FN 6.0	VF 8.0	VF/NM 9.0	NM- 9.2
7	169	Sm/69	New price 25¢; stiff-c; PC-r	2	2	2	4	6	8	10	12

64. Treasure Island

Ed	HRN	Date	Details	A	C	GD 2.0	VG 4.0	FN 6.0	VF 8.0	VF/NM 9.0	NM- 9.2
1	62	10/49	Original; Blum-c/a	1	1	17	34	51	100	158	215
2A	82	–	C-price 15¢; soft-c LDC-r	1	1	5	10	15	22	26	30
2B	82	–	Stiff-c; LDC-r	1	1	5	10	15	23	28	32
3	117	–	LDC-r	1	1	3	6	9	15	21	26
4	131	–	New-c; PC-r	1	2	3	6	9	18	27	35
5	138	–	PC-r	1	2	2	4	6	8	11	14
6	146	–	PC-r	1	2	2	4	6	8	11	14
7	158	–	PC-r	1	2	2	4	6	8	11	14
8	165	–	PC-r	1	2	2	4	6	8	10	12
9	167	–	PC-r	1	2	2	4	6	8	10	12
10	167	6/64	PC-r	1	2	2	4	6	8	10	12
11	167	12/65	PC-r	1	2	2	4	6	8	10	12
12A	166	10/67	PC-r	1	2	2	4	6	8	10	12
12B	166	10/67	w/Grit ad stapled in book	1	2	9	18	27	65	113	160
13	169	Spr/69	New price 25¢; stiff-c; PC-r	1	2	2	4	6	8	11	14
14	–	1989	Long John Silver's Seafood Shoppes; $1.95, First/Berkley Publ.; Blum-r	1	2						5.00

65. Benjamin Franklin

Ed	HRN	Date	Details	A	C	GD 2.0	VG 4.0	FN 6.0	VF 8.0	VF/NM 9.0	NM- 9.2
1	64	11/49	Original; Kiefer-c; Iger Shop-a	1	1	16	32	48	94	147	200
2	131	–	New-c; PC-r	1	2	5	10	15	24	30	35
3	154	–	PC-r	1	2	2	4	6	9	12	15
4	167	2/64	PC-r	1	2	2	4	6	8	11	14
5	167	4/66	PC-r	1	2	2	4	6	8	11	14
6	169	Fall/69	New price 25¢; stiff-c; PC-r	1	2	2	4	6	8	11	14

66. The Cloister and the Hearth

Ed	HRN	Date	Details	A	C	GD 2.0	VG 4.0	FN 6.0	VF 8.0	VF/NM 9.0	NM- 9.2
1	67	12/49	Original & only ed; Kiefer-a & c	1	1	30	60	90	177	289	400

67. The Scottish Chiefs

Ed	HRN	Date	Details	A	C	GD 2.0	VG 4.0	FN 6.0	VF 8.0	VF/NM 9.0	NM- 9.2
1	67	1/50	Original; Blum-a&c	1	1	15	30	45	85	130	175
2	85	–	C-price 15¢; LDC-r	1	1	5	10	15	23	28	32
3	118	–	LDC-r	1	1	3	6	9	15	21	26
4	136	–	New-c; PC-r	1	2	3	6	9	18	27	36
5	154	–	PC-r	1	2	2	4	6	8	11	14
6	167	11/63	PC-r	1	2	2	4	6	9	13	16
7	167	8/65	PC-r	1	2	2	4	6	8	11	14

68. Julius Caesar (Used in **SOTI**, pgs. 36, 37)

Ed	HRN	Date	Details	A	C	GD 2.0	VG 4.0	FN 6.0	VF 8.0	VF/NM 9.0	NM- 9.2
1	70	2/50	Original; Kiefer-c/a	1	1	15	30	45	85	130	175
2	85	–	C-price 15¢; LDC-r	1	1	5	10	15	22	26	30
3	108	–	LDC-r	1	1	4	9	13	18	22	26
4	156	–	New L.B. Cole-c; PC-r	1	2	6	12	18	28	34	40
5	165	–	New-a by Evans, Crandall; PC-r	2	2	5	10	15	24	30	35
6	167	2/64	PC-r	2	2	2	4	6	8	10	12
7	167	10/65	Tarzan books inside cover; PC-r	2	2	2	4	6	8	10	12
8	166	R/1967	PC-r	2	2	2	4	6	8	10	12
9	169	Win/69	PC-r; stiff-c	2	2	2	4	6	8	10	12

69. Around the World in 80 Days

Ed	HRN	Date	Details	A	C	GD 2.0	VG 4.0	FN 6.0	VF 8.0	VF/NM 9.0	NM- 9.2
1	70	3/50	Original; Kiefer-c/a	1	1	15	30	45	85	130	175
2	87	–	C-price 15¢; LDC-r	1	1	5	10	15	22	26	30
3	125	–	LDC-r	1	1	4	9	13	18	22	26
4	136	–	New-c; PC-r	1	2	5	10	15	25	31	36
5	146	–	PC-r	1	2	2	4	6	8	11	14
6	152	–	PC-r	1	2	2	4	6	8	11	14
7	164	–	PC-r	1	2	2	4	6	8	10	12
8	167	–	PC-r	1	2	2	4	6	8	10	12
9	167	7/64	PC-r	1	2	2	4	6	8	10	12
10	167	11/65	PC-r	1	2	2	4	6	8	10	12
11	166	7/67	PC-r	1	2	2	4	6	8	10	12
12	169	Spr/69	C-price 25¢; stiff-c; PC-r	1	2	2	4	6	8	10	12

70. The Pilot

Ed	HRN	Date	Details	A	C	GD 2.0	VG 4.0	FN 6.0	VF 8.0	VF/NM 9.0	NM- 9.2
1	71	4/50	Original; Blum-c/a	1	1	14	28	42	76	108	140
2	92	–	C-price 15¢; LDC-r	1	1	5	10	15	23	28	32
3	125	–	LDC-r	1	1	4	9	13	18	22	26
4	156	–	New-c; PC-r	1	2	6	12	18	28	34	40
5	167	2/64	PC-r	1	2	2	4	6	11	16	20
6	167	5/66	PC-r	1	2	2	4	6	9	13	16

71. The Man Who Laughs

Ed	HRN	Date	Details	A	C	GD 2.0	VG 4.0	FN 6.0	VF 8.0	VF/NM 9.0	NM- 9.2
1	71	5/50	Original; Blum-c/a	1	1	19	38	57	111	176	240
2	165	–	New-c&a; PC-r	2	2	14	28	42	80	115	155
3	167	4/64	PC-r	2	2	11	22	33	62	86	115

72. The Oregon Trail

Ed	HRN	Date	Details	A	C	GD 2.0	VG 4.0	FN 6.0	VF 8.0	VF/NM 9.0	NM- 9.2
1	73	6/50	Original; Kiefer-c/a	1	1	14	28	42	81	118	140
2	89	–	C-price 15¢; LDC-r	1	1	5	10	15	23	28	32
3	121	–	LDC-r	1	1	4	9	13	18	22	26
4	131	–	New-c; PC-r	1	2	5	10	15	25	31	36
5	140	–	PC-r	1	2	2	4	6	8	11	14
6	150	–	PC-r	1	2	2	4	6	8	11	14
7	164	–	PC-r	1	2	2	4	6	8	10	12
8	167	–	PC-r	1	2	2	4	6	8	10	12
9	167	8/64	PC-r	1	2	2	4	6	8	10	12
10	167	10/65	PC-r	1	2	2	4	6	8	10	12
11	166	R/1968	C-price 25¢; PC-r	1	2	2	4	6	8	10	12

73. The Black Tulip

Ed	HRN	Date	Details	A	C	GD 2.0	VG 4.0	FN 6.0	VF 8.0	VF/NM 9.0	NM- 9.2
1	75	7/50	1st & only ed.; Alex Blum-c/a	1	1	35	70	105	208	339	470

74. Mr. Midshipman Easy

Ed	HRN	Date	Details	A	C	GD 2.0	VG 4.0	FN 6.0	VF 8.0	VF/NM 9.0	NM- 9.2
1	75	8/50	1st & only edition	1	1	35	70	105	208	339	470

75. The Lady of the Lake

Ed	HRN	Date	Details	A	C	GD 2.0	VG 4.0	FN 6.0	VF 8.0	VF/NM 9.0	NM- 9.2
1	75	9/50	Original; Kiefer-c/a	1	1	14	28	42	76	108	140
2	85	–	C-price 15¢; LDC-r	1	1	5	10	15	24	30	35
3	118	–	LDC-r	1	1	5	10	14	20	24	28
4	139	–	New-c; PC-r	1	2	5	10	15	25	31	36
5	154	–	PC-r	1	2	2	4	6	8	11	14
6	165	–	PC-r	1	2	2	4	6	8	10	12
7	167	4/64	PC-r	1	2	2	4	6	8	10	12
8	167	5/66	PC-r	1	2	2	4	6	8	10	12
9	169	Spr/69	New price 25¢; stiff-c; PC-r	1	2	2	4	6	8	10	12

76. The Prisoner of Zenda

Ed	HRN	Date	Details	A	C	GD 2.0	VG 4.0	FN 6.0	VF 8.0	VF/NM 9.0	NM- 9.2
1	75	10/50	Original; Kiefer-c/a	1	1	14	28	42	76	108	140
2	85	–	C-price 15¢; LDC-r	1	1	5	10	15	23	28	32
3	111	–	LDC-r	1	1	3	6	9	16	21	26
4	128	–	New-c; PC-r	1	2	3	6	9	18	27	35
5	152	–	PC-r	1	2	2	4	6	8	11	14
6	165	–	PC-r	1	2	2	4	6	8	10	12
7	167	4/64	PC-r	1	2	2	4	6	8	10	12
8	167	9/66	PC-r	1	2	2	4	6	8	10	12
9	169	Fall/69	New price 25¢; stiff-c; PC-r	1	2	2	4	6	8	10	12

77. The Iliad

Ed	HRN	Date	Details	A	C	GD 2.0	VG 4.0	FN 6.0	VF 8.0	VF/NM 9.0	NM- 9.2
1	78	11/50	Original; Blum-c/a	1	1	14	28	42	76	108	140
2	87	–	C-price 15¢; LDC-r	1	1	5	10	15	24	30	35
3	121	–	LDC-r	1	1	3	6	9	15	21	26
4	139	–	New-c; PC-r	1	2	3	6	9	17	25	32
5	150	–	PC-r	1	2	2	4	6	8	11	14
6	165	–	PC-r	1	2	2	4	6	8	10	12
7	167	10/63	PC-r	1	2	2	4	6	8	10	12

Classics Illustrated #79 © GIL

Classics Illustrated #84 © GIL

Classics Illustrated #89 © GIL

Ed	HRN	Date	Details	A	C	GD 2.0	VG 4.0	FN 6.0	VF 8.0	VF/NM 9.0	NM- 9.2
8	167	7/64	PC-r	1	2	2	4	6	8	10	12
9	167	5/66	PC-r	1	2	2	4	6	8	10	12
10	166	R/1968	C-price 25¢; PC-r	1	2	2	4	6	8	10	12

78. Joan of Arc

Ed	HRN	Date	Details	A	C	GD 2.0	VG 4.0	FN 6.0	VF 8.0	VF/NM 9.0	NM- 9.2
1	78	12/50	Original; Kiefer-c/a	1	1	14	28	42	76	108	140
2	87	–	C-price 15¢; LDC-r	1	1	5	10	15	23	28	32
3	113	–	LDC-r	1	1	3	6	9	15	21	26
4	128	–	New-c; PC-r	1	2	3	6	9	18	27	35
5	140	–	PC-r	1	2	2	4	6	8	11	14
6	150	–	PC-r	1	2	2	4	6	8	11	14
7	159	–	PC-r	1	2	2	4	6	8	11	14
8	167	–	PC-r	1	2	2	4	6	8	11	14
9	167	12/63	PC-r	1	2	2	4	6	8	10	12
10	167	6/65	PC-r	1	2	2	4	6	8	10	12
11	166	6/67	PC-r	1	2	2	4	6	8	10	12
12	166	Win/69	New-c&price, 25¢; PC-r; stiff-c	1	3	3	6	9	16	23	30

• **79. Cyrano de Bergerac**

Ed	HRN	Date	Details	A	C	GD 2.0	VG 4.0	FN 6.0	VF 8.0	VF/NM 9.0	NM- 9.2
1	78	1/51	Orig.; movie promo inside front-c; Blum-c/a	1	1	14	28	42	76	108	140
2	85	–	C-price 15¢; LDC-r	1	1	5	10	15	23	28	32
3	118	–	LDC-r	1	1	3	6	9	17	23	28
4	133	–	New-c; PC-r	1	2	3	6	9	17	25	32
5	156	–	PC-r	1	2	2	4	6	11	16	20
6	167	8/64	PC-r	1	2	2	4	6	11	16	20

80. White Fang (Last line drawn cover)

Ed	HRN	Date	Details	A	C	GD 2.0	VG 4.0	FN 6.0	VF 8.0	VF/NM 9.0	NM- 9.2
1	79	2/51	Orig.; Blum-c/a	1	1	14	28	42	76	108	140
2	87	–	C-price 15¢; LDC-r	1	1	5	10	15	24	30	35
3	125	–	LDC-r	1	1	3	6	9	15	21	26
4	132	–	New-c; PC-r	1	2	3	6	9	17	25	32
5	140	–	PC-r	1	2	2	4	6	8	11	14
6	153	–	PC-r	1	2	2	4	6	8	11	14
7	167	–	PC-r	1	2	2	4	6	8	10	12
8	167	9/64	PC-r	1	2	2	4	6	8	10	12
9	167	7/65	PC-r	1	2	2	4	6	8	10	12
10	166	6/67	PC-r	1	2	2	4	6	8	10	12
11	169	Fall/69	New price 25¢; PC-r; stiff-c	1	2	2	4	6	8	10	12

81. The Odyssey (1st painted cover)

Ed	HRN	Date	Details	A	C	GD 2.0	VG 4.0	FN 6.0	VF 8.0	VF/NM 9.0	NM- 9.2
1	82	3/51	First 15¢ Original; Blum-c	1	1	14	28	42	76	108	140
2	167	8/64	PC-r	1	1	2	4	6	11	16	20
3	167	10/66	PC-r	1	1	2	4	6	11	16	20
4	169	Spr/69	New, stiff-c; PC-r	1	2	3	6	9	18	27	36

82. The Master of Ballantrae

Ed	HRN	Date	Details	A	C	GD 2.0	VG 4.0	FN 6.0	VF 8.0	VF/NM 9.0	NM- 9.2
1	82	4/51	Original; Blum-c	1	1	11	22	33	64	90	115
2	167	8/64	PC-r	1	1	3	6	9	14	19	24
3	166	Fall/68	New, stiff-c; PC-r	1	2	3	6	9	18	27	36

83. The Jungle Book

Ed	HRN	Date	Details	A	C	GD 2.0	VG 4.0	FN 6.0	VF 8.0	VF/NM 9.0	NM- 9.2
1	85	5/51	Original; Blum-c Bossert/Blum-a	1	1	11	22	33	64	90	115
2	110	–	PC-r	1	1	2	4	6	9	13	16
3	125	–	PC-r	1	1	2	4	6	8	11	14
4	134	–	PC-r	1	1	2	4	6	8	11	14
5	142	–	PC-r	1	1	2	4	6	8	11	14
6	150	–	PC-r	1	1	2	4	6	8	11	14
7	159	–	PC-r	1	1	2	4	6	8	11	14
8	167	–	PC-r	1	1	2	4	6	8	10	12
9	167	3/65	PC-r	1	1	2	4	6	8	10	12
10	167	11/65	PC-r	1	1	2	4	6	8	10	12
11	167	5/66	PC-r	1	1	2	4	6	8	10	12
12	166	R/1968	New c&a; stiff-c; PC-r	2	2	3	6	9	18	27	36

84. The Gold Bug and Other Stories ("The Gold Bug", "The Tell-Tale Heart", "The Cask of Amontillado")

Ed	HRN	Date	Details	A	C	GD 2.0	VG 4.0	FN 6.0	VF 8.0	VF/NM 9.0	NM- 9.2
1	85	6/51	Original; Blum-c/a; Palais, Laverly-a	1	1	15	30	45	83	124	165
2	167	7/64	PC-r	1	1	11	22	33	62	86	110

85. The Sea Wolf

Ed	HRN	Date	Details	A	C	GD 2.0	VG 4.0	FN 6.0	VF 8.0	VF/NM 9.0	NM- 9.2
1	85	7/51	Original; Blum-c/a	1	1	11	22	33	60	83	105
2	121	–	PC-r	1	1	2	4	6	8	11	14
3	132	–	PC-r	1	1	2	4	6	8	11	14
4	141	–	PC-r	1	1	2	4	6	8	11	14
5	161	–	PC-r	1	1	2	4	6	8	10	12
6	167	2/64	PC-r	1	1	2	4	6	8	10	12
7	167	11/65	PC-r	1	1	2	4	6	8	10	12
8	169	Fall/69	New price 25¢; stiff-c; PC-r	1	1	2	4	6	8	10	12

86. Under Two Flags

Ed	HRN	Date	Details	A	C	GD 2.0	VG 4.0	FN 6.0	VF 8.0	VF/NM 9.0	NM- 9.2
1	87	8/51	Original; first delBourgo-a	1	1	11	22	33	60	83	105
2	117	–	PC-r	1	1	2	4	6	9	13	16
3	139	–	PC-r	1	1	2	4	6	8	11	14
4	158	–	PC-r	1	1	2	4	6	8	11	14
5	167	2/64	PC-r	1	1	2	4	6	8	10	12
6	167	8/66	PC-r	1	1	2	4	6	8	10	12
7	169	Sm/69	New price 25¢; stiff-c; PC-r	1	1	2	4	6	8	10	12

87. A Midsummer Nights Dream

Ed	HRN	Date	Details	A	C	GD 2.0	VG 4.0	FN 6.0	VF 8.0	VF/NM 9.0	NM- 9.2
1	87	9/51	Original; Blum c/a	1	1	11	22	33	60	83	105
2	161	–	PC-r	1	1	2	4	6	8	11	14
3	167	4/64	PC-r	1	1	2	4	6	8	10	12
4	167	5/66	PC-r	1	1	2	4	6	8	10	12
5	169	Sm/69	New price 25¢; stiff-c; PC-r	1	1	2	4	6	8	10	12

88. Men of Iron

Ed	HRN	Date	Details	A	C	GD 2.0	VG 4.0	FN 6.0	VF 8.0	VF/NM 9.0	NM- 9.2
1	89	10/51	Original	1	1	11	22	33	60	83	105
2	154	–	PC-r	1	1	2	4	6	8	11	14
3	167	1/64	PC-r	1	1	2	4	6	8	10	12
4	166	R/1968	C-price 25¢; PC-r	1	1	2	4	6	8	10	12

89. Crime and Punishment (Cover illo. in **POP**)

Ed	HRN	Date	Details	A	C	GD 2.0	VG 4.0	FN 6.0	VF 8.0	VF/NM 9.0	NM- 9.2
1	89	11/51	Original; Palais-a	1	1	11	22	33	60	83	105
2	152	–	PC-r	1	1	2	4	6	8	11	14
3	167	4/64	PC-r	1	1	2	4	6	8	10	12
4	167	5/66	PC-r	1	1	2	4	6	8	10	12
5	169	Fall/69	New price 25¢ stiff-c; PC-r	1	1	2	4	6	8	10	12

90. Green Mansions

Ed	HRN	Date	Details	A	C	GD 2.0	VG 4.0	FN 6.0	VF 8.0	VF/NM 9.0	NM- 9.2
1	89	12/51	Original; Blum-c/a	1	1	11	22	33	60	83	105
2	148	–	New L.B. Cole-c; PC-r	1	2	5	10	15	22	26	30
3	165	–	PC-r	1	2	2	4	6	8	10	12
4	167	4/64	PC-r	1	2	2	4	6	8	10	12
5	167	9/66	PC-r	1	2	2	4	6	8	10	12
6	169	Sm/69	New price 25¢; stiff-c; PC-r	1	2	2	4	6	8	10	12

91. The Call of the Wild

Ed	HRN	Date	Details	A	C	GD 2.0	VG 4.0	FN 6.0	VF 8.0	VF/NM 9.0	NM- 9.2
1	92	1/52	Orig.; delBourgo-a	1	1	11	22	33	60	83	105
2	112	–	PC-r	1	1	2	4	6	8	11	14
3	125	–	'Picture Progress' on back-c; PC-r	1	1	2	4	6	8	11	14
4	134	–	PC-r	1	1	2	4	6	8	11	14
5	143	–	PC-r	1	1	2	4	6	8	11	14
6	165	–	PC-r	1	1	2	4	6	8	11	14
7	167	–	PC-r	1	1	2	4	6	8	10	12
8	167	4/65	PC-r	1	1	2	4	6	8	10	12
9	167	3/66	PC-r	1	1	2	4	6	8	10	12
10	166	11/67	PC-r	1	1	2	4	6	8	10	12
11	169	Spr/70	New price 25¢;	1	1	2	4	6	8	10	12

Classics Illustrated #94 © GIL

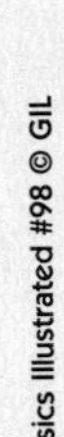

Classics Illustrated #98 © GIL

Classics Illustrated #102 © GIL

						GD 2.0	VG 4.0	FN 6.0	VF 8.0	VF/NM 9.0	NM- 9.2
			stiff-c; PC-r								

92. The Courtship of Miles Standish

Ed	HRN	Date	Details	A	C	GD 2.0	VG 4.0	FN 6.0	VF 8.0	VF/NM 9.0	NM- 9.2
1	92	2/52	Original; Blum-c/a	1	1	11	22	33	60	83	105
2	165	–	PC-r	1	1	2	4	6	8	11	14
3	167	3/64	PC-r	1	1	2	4	6	8	11	14
4	166	5/67	PC-r	1	1	2	4	6	8	11	14
5	169	Win/69	New price 25¢ stiff-c; PC-r	1	1	2	4	6	8	11	14

93. Pudd'nhead Wilson

Ed	HRN	Date	Details	A	C	GD 2.0	VG 4.0	FN 6.0	VF 8.0	VF/NM 9.0	NM- 9.2
1	94	3/52	Orig.; Kiefer-c/a;	1	1	11	22	33	60	83	105
2	165	–	New-c; PC-r	1	2	2	4	6	11	16	25
3	167	3/64	PC-r	1	2	2	4	6	8	11	14
4	166	R/1968	New price 25¢; soft-c; PC-r	1	2	2	4	6	9	12	15

94. David Balfour

Ed	HRN	Date	Details	A	C	GD 2.0	VG 4.0	FN 6.0	VF 8.0	VF/NM 9.0	NM- 9.2
1	94	4/52	Original; Palais-a	1	1	11	22	33	60	83	105
2	167	5/64	PC-r	1	1	2	4	6	11	16	20
3	166	R/1968	C-price 25¢; PC-r	1	1	2	4	6	13	18	22

95. All Quiet on the Western Front

Ed	HRN	Date	Details	A	C	GD 2.0	VG 4.0	FN 6.0	VF 8.0	VF/NM 9.0	NM- 9.2
1A	96	5/52	Orig.; del Bourgo-a	1	1	14	28	42	80	115	150
1B	99	5/52	Orig.; del Bourgo-a	1	1	12	24	36	69	97	125
2	167	10/64	PC-r	1	1	3	6	9	16	22	28
3	167	11/66	PC-r	1	1	3	6	9	16	22	28

96. Daniel Boone

Ed	HRN	Date	Details	A	C	GD 2.0	VG 4.0	FN 6.0	VF 8.0	VF/NM 9.0	NM- 9.2
1	97	6/52	Original; Blum-a	1	1	10	20	30	58	79	100
2	117	–	PC-r	1	1	2	4	6	8	11	14
3	128	–	PC-r	1	1	2	4	6	8	11	14
4	132	–	PC-r	1	1	2	4	6	8	11	14
5	134	–	"Story of Jesus" on back-c; PC-r	1	1	2	4	6	8	11	14
6	158	–	PC-r	1	1	2	4	6	8	11	14
7	167	1/64	PC-r	1	1	2	4	6	8	10	12
8	167	5/65	PC-r	1	1	2	4	6	8	10	12
9	167	11/66	PC-r	1	1	2	4	6	8	10	12
10	166	Win/69	New-c; price 25¢; PC-r; stiff-c	1	2	3	6	9	16	22	28

97. King Solomon's Mines

Ed	HRN	Date	Details	A	C	GD 2.0	VG 4.0	FN 6.0	VF 8.0	VF/NM 9.0	NM- 9.2
1	96	7/52	Orig.; Kiefer-a	1	1	10	20	30	58	79	100
2	118	–	PC-r	1	1	2	4	6	8	11	14
3	131	–	PC-r	1	1	2	4	6	8	11	14
4	141	–	PC-r	1	1	2	4	6	8	11	14
5	158	–	PC-r	1	1	2	4	6	8	11	14
6	167	2/64	PC-r	1	1	2	4	6	8	10	12
7	167	9/65	PC-r	1	1	2	4	6	8	10	12
8	169	Sm/69	New price 25¢; stiff-c; PC-r	1	1	2	4	6	8	10	12

98. The Red Badge of Courage

Ed	HRN	Date	Details	A	C	GD 2.0	VG 4.0	FN 6.0	VF 8.0	VF/NM 9.0	NM- 9.2
1	98	8/52	Original	1	1	10	20	30	58	79	100
2	118	–	PC-r	1	1	2	4	6	8	11	14
3	132	–	PC-r	1	1	2	4	6	8	11	14
4	142	–	PC-r	1	1	2	4	6	8	11	14
5	152	–	PC-r	1	1	2	4	6	8	11	14
6	161	–	PC-r	1	1	2	4	6	8	11	14
7	167	–	Has orig.date; PC-r	1	1	2	4	6	8	11	14
8	167	9/64	PC-r	1	1	2	4	6	8	11	14
9	167	10/65	PC-r	1	1	2	4	6	8	11	14
10	166	R/1968	New-c&price 25¢; PC-r; stiff-c	1	2	3	6	9	16	23	30

99. Hamlet (Used in **POP**, pg. 102)

Ed	HRN	Date	Details	A	C	GD 2.0	VG 4.0	FN 6.0	VF 8.0	VF/NM 9.0	NM- 9.2
1	98	9/52	Original; Blum-a	1	1	11	22	33	60	83	105
2	121	–	PC-r	1	1	2	4	6	8	11	14
3	141	–	PC-r	1	1	2	4	6	8	11	14
4	158	–	PC-r	1	1	2	4	6	8	11	14
5	167	–	Has orig.date; PC-r	1	1	2	4	6	8	10	12
6	167	7/65	PC-r	1	1	2	4	6	8	10	12
7	166	4/67	PC-r	1	1	2	4	6	8	10	12
8	169	Spr/69	New-c&price 25¢; PC-r; stiff-c	1	2	3	6	9	16	23	30

100. Mutiny on the Bounty

Ed	HRN	Date	Details	A	C	GD 2.0	VG 4.0	FN 6.0	VF 8.0	VF/NM 9.0	NM- 9.2
1	100	10/52	Original	1	1	10	20	30	58	79	100
2	117	–	PC-r	1	1	2	4	6	8	11	14
3	132	–	PC-r	1	1	2	4	6	8	11	14
4	142	–	PC-r	1	1	2	4	6	8	11	14
5	155	–	PC-r	1	1	2	4	6	8	11	14
6	167	–	Has orig. date;PC-r	1	1	2	4	6	8	10	12
7	167	5/64	PC-r	1	1	2	4	6	8	10	12
8	167	3/66	PC-r	1	1	2	4	6	8	10	12
9	169	Spr/70	PC-r; stiff-c	1	1	2	4	6	8	10	12

101. William Tell

Ed	HRN	Date	Details	A	C	GD 2.0	VG 4.0	FN 6.0	VF 8.0	VF/NM 9.0	NM- 9.2
1	101	11/52	Original; Kiefer-c delBourgo-a	1	1	10	20	30	58	79	100
2	118	–	PC-r	1	1	2	4	6	8	11	14
3	141	–	PC-r	1	1	2	4	6	8	11	14
4	158	–	PC-r	1	1	2	4	6	8	11	14
5	167	–	Has orig.date; PC-r	1	1	2	4	6	8	10	12
6	167	11/64	PC-r	1	1	2	4	6	8	10	12
7	166	4/67	PC-r	1	1	2	4	6	8	10	12
8	169	Win/69	New price 25¢; stiff-c; PC-r	1	1	2	4	6	8	10	12

102. The White Company

Ed	HRN	Date	Details	A	C	GD 2.0	VG 4.0	FN 6.0	VF 8.0	VF/NM 9.0	NM- 9.2
1	101	12/52	Original; Blum-a	1	1	13	26	39	74	105	135
2	165	–	PC-r	1	1	3	6	9	16	23	30
3	167	4/64	PC-r	1	1	3	6	9	16	23	30

103. Men Against the Sea

Ed	HRN	Date	Details	A	C	GD 2.0	VG 4.0	FN 6.0	VF 8.0	VF/NM 9.0	NM- 9.2
1	104	1/53	Original; Kiefer-c; Palais-a	1	1	11	22	33	60	83	105
2	114	–	PC-r	1	1	4	8	11	16	19	22
3	131	–	New-c; PC-r	1	2	5	10	15	24	30	35
4	158	–	PC-r	1	2	4	7	10	14	17	20
5	149	–	White reorder list; came after HRN-158; PC-r	1	2	5	10	15	22	26	30
6	167	3/64	PC-r	1	2	2	4	6	8	11	14

104. Bring 'Em Back Alive

Ed	HRN	Date	Details	A	C	GD 2.0	VG 4.0	FN 6.0	VF 8.0	VF/NM 9.0	NM- 9.2
1	105	2/53	Original; Kiefer-c/a	1	1	10	20	30	58	79	100
2	118	–	PC-r	1	1	2	4	6	8	11	14
3	133	–	PC-r	1	1	2	4	6	8	11	14
4	150	–	PC-r	1	1	2	4	6	8	11	14
5	158	–	PC-r	1	1	2	4	6	8	11	14
6	167	10/63	PC-r	1	1	2	4	6	8	10	12
7	167	9/65	PC-r	1	1	2	4	6	8	10	12
8	169	Win/69	New price 25¢; stiff-c; PC-r	1	1	2	4	6	8	10	12

105. From the Earth to the Moon

Ed	HRN	Date	Details	A	C	GD 2.0	VG 4.0	FN 6.0	VF 8.0	VF/NM 9.0	NM- 9.2
1	106	3/53	Original; Blum-a	1	1	10	20	30	58	79	100
2	118	–	PC-r	1	1	2	4	6	8	11	14
3	132	–	PC-r	1	1	2	4	6	8	11	14
4	141	–	PC-r	1	1	2	4	6	8	11	14
5	146	–	PC-r	1	1	2	4	6	8	11	14
6	156	–	PC-r	1	1	2	4	6	8	11	14
7	167	–	Has orig. date; PC-r	1	1	2	4	6	8	10	12
8	167	5/64	PC-r	1	1	2	4	6	8	10	12
9	167	5/65	PC-r	1	1	2	4	6	8	10	12
10A	166	10/67	PC-r	1	1	2	4	6	8	10	12
10B	166	10/67	w/Grit ad stapled in book	1	1	8	16	24	54	90	125
11	169	Sm/69	New price 25¢; stiff-c; PC-r	1	1	2	4	6	8	10	12
12	169	Spr/71	PC-r	1	1	2	4	6	8	10	12

Classics Illustrated #111 © GIL

Classics Illustrated #115 © GIL

Classics Illustrated #124 © GIL

106. Buffalo Bill

Ed	HRN	Date	Details	A	C	GD 2.0	VG 4.0	FN 6.0	VF 8.0	VF/NM 9.0	NM- 9.2
1	107	4/53	Orig.; delBourgo-a	1	1	10	20	30	56	76	95
2	118	–	PC-r	1	1	2	4	6	8	11	14
3	132	–	PC-r	1	1	2	4	6	8	11	14
4	142	–	PC-r	1	1	2	4	6	8	11	14
5	161	–	PC-r	1	1	2	4	6	8	10	12
6	167	3/64	PC-r	1	1	2	4	6	8	10	12
7	166	7/67	PC-r	1	1	2	4	6	8	10	12
8	169	Fall/69	PC-r; stiff-c	1	1	2	4	6	8	10	12

107. King of the Khyber Rifles

Ed	HRN	Date	Details	A	C	GD 2.0	VG 4.0	FN 6.0	VF 8.0	VF/NM 9.0	NM- 9.2
1	108	5/53	Original	1	1	10	20	30	56	76	95
2	118	–	PC-r	1	1	2	4	6	8	11	14
3	146	–	PC-r	1	1	2	4	6	8	11	14
4	158	–	PC-r	1	1	2	4	6	8	11	14
5	167	–	Has orig.date; PC-r	1	1	2	4	6	8	10	12
6	167	–	PC-r	1	1	2	4	6	8	10	12
7	167	10/66	PC-r	1	1	2	4	6	8	10	12

108. Knights of the Round Table

Ed	HRN	Date	Details	A	C	GD 2.0	VG 4.0	FN 6.0	VF 8.0	VF/NM 9.0	NM- 9.2
1A	108	6/53	Original; Blum-a	1	1	11	22	33	60	83	105
1B	109	6/53	Original; scarce	1	1	11	22	33	62	86	110
2	117	–	PC-r	1	1	2	4	6	8	11	14
3	165	–	PC-r	1	1	2	4	6	8	10	12
4	167	4/64	PC-r	1	1	2	4	6	8	10	12
5	166	4/67	PC-r	1	1	2	4	6	8	10	12
6	169	Sm/69	New price 25¢; stiff-c; PC-r	1	1	2	4	6	8	10	12

109. Pitcairn's Island

Ed	HRN	Date	Details	A	C	GD 2.0	VG 4.0	FN 6.0	VF 8.0	VF/NM 9.0	NM- 9.2
1	110	7/53	Original; Palais-a	1	1	11	22	33	60	83	105
2	165	–	PC-r	1	1	2	4	6	8	11	14
3	167	3/64	PC-r	1	1	2	4	6	8	11	14
4	166	6/67	PC-r	1	1	2	4	6	8	11	14

110. A Study in Scarlet

Ed	HRN	Date	Details	A	C	GD 2.0	VG 4.0	FN 6.0	VF 8.0	VF/NM 9.0	NM- 9.2
1	111	8/53	Original	1	1	15	30	45	83	124	165
2	165	–	PC-r	1	1	11	22	33	62	86	110

111. The Talisman

Ed	HRN	Date	Details	A	C	GD 2.0	VG 4.0	FN 6.0	VF 8.0	VF/NM 9.0	NM- 9.2
1	112	9/53	Original; last H.C. Kiefer-a	1	1	11	22	33	60	83	105
2	165	–	PC-r	1	1	2	4	6	8	11	14
3	167	5/64	PC-r	1	1	2	4	6	8	11	14
4	166	Fall/68	C-price 25¢; PC-r	1	1	2	4	6	8	11	14

112. Adventures of Kit Carson

Ed	HRN	Date	Details	A	C	GD 2.0	VG 4.0	FN 6.0	VF 8.0	VF/NM 9.0	NM- 9.2
1	113	10/53	Original; Palais-a	1	1	10	20	30	58	79	100
2	129	–	PC-r	1	1	2	4	6	8	11	14
3	141	–	PC-r	1	1	2	4	6	8	11	14
4	152	–	PC-r	1	1	2	4	6	8	11	14
5	161	–	PC-r	1	1	2	4	6	8	10	12
6	167	–	PC-r	1	1	2	4	6	8	10	12
7	167	2/65	PC-r	1	1	2	4	6	8	10	12
8	167	5/66	PC-r	1	1	2	4	6	8	10	12
9	166	Win/69	New-c&price 25¢; PC-r; stiff-c	1	2	3	6	9	14	20	25

113. The Forty-Five Guardsmen

Ed	HRN	Date	Details	A	C	GD 2.0	VG 4.0	FN 6.0	VF 8.0	VF/NM 9.0	NM- 9.2
1	114	11/53	Orig.; delBourgo-a	1	1	12	24	36	69	97	125
2	166	7/67	PC-r	1	1	3	6	9	20	30	40

114. The Red Rover

Ed	HRN	Date	Details	A	C	GD 2.0	VG 4.0	FN 6.0	VF 8.0	VF/NM 9.0	NM- 9.2
1	115	12/53	Original	1	1	12	24	36	69	97	125
2	166	7/67	PC-r	1	1	3	6	9	20	30	40

115. How I Found Livingstone

Ed	HRN	Date	Details	A	C	GD 2.0	VG 4.0	FN 6.0	VF 8.0	VF/NM 9.0	NM- 9.2
1	116	1/54	Original	1	1	13	26	39	74	105	135
2	167	1/67	PC-r	1	1	4	8	12	26	41	55

116. The Bottle Imp

Ed	HRN	Date	Details	A	C	GD 2.0	VG 4.0	FN 6.0	VF 8.0	VF/NM 9.0	NM- 9.2
1	117	2/54	Orig.; Cameron-a	1	1	13	26	39	74	105	135
2	167	1/67	PC-r	1	1	4	8	12	26	41	55

117. Captains Courageous

Ed	HRN	Date	Details	A	C	GD 2.0	VG 4.0	FN 6.0	VF 8.0	VF/NM 9.0	NM- 9.2
1	118	3/54	Orig.; Costanza-a	1	1	12	24	36	69	97	125
2	167	2/67	PC-r	1	1	3	6	9	14	20	26
3	169	Fall/69	New price 25¢; stiff-c; PC-r	1	1	3	6	9	14	20	26

118. Rob Roy

Ed	HRN	Date	Details	A	C	GD 2.0	VG 4.0	FN 6.0	VF 8.0	VF/NM 9.0	NM- 9.2
1	119	4/54	Original; Rudy & Walter Palais-a	1	1	13	26	39	74	105	135
2	167	2/67	PC-r	1	1	4	8	12	26	41	55

119. Soldiers of Fortune

Ed	HRN	Date	Details	A	C	GD 2.0	VG 4.0	FN 6.0	VF 8.0	VF/NM 9.0	NM- 9.2
1	120	5/54	Schaffenberger-a	1	1	11	22	33	64	90	115
2	166	3/67	PC-r	1	1	3	6	9	14	20	26
3	169	Spr/70	New price 25¢; stiff-c; PC-r	1	1	3	6	9	14	20	26

120. The Hurricane

Ed	HRN	Date	Details	A	C	GD 2.0	VG 4.0	FN 6.0	VF 8.0	VF/NM 9.0	NM- 9.2
1	121	6/54	Orig.; Cameron-a	1	1	11	22	33	64	90	115
2	166	3/67	PC-r	1	1	3	6	9	21	32	42

121. Wild Bill Hickok

Ed	HRN	Date	Details	A	C	GD 2.0	VG 4.0	FN 6.0	VF 8.0	VF/NM 9.0	NM- 9.2
1	122	7/54	Original	1	1	10	20	30	56	76	95
2	132	–	PC-r	1	1	2	4	6	8	11	14
3	141	–	PC-r	1	1	2	4	6	8	11	14
4	154	–	PC-r	1	1	2	4	6	8	11	14
5	167	–	PC-r	1	1	2	4	6	8	10	12
6	167	8/64	PC-r	1	1	2	4	6	8	10	12
7	166	4/67	PC-r	1	1	2	4	6	8	10	12
8	169	Win/69	PC-r; stiff-c	1	1	2	4	6	8	10	12

122. The Mutineers

Ed	HRN	Date	Details	A	C	GD 2.0	VG 4.0	FN 6.0	VF 8.0	VF/NM 9.0	NM- 9.2
1	123	9/54	Original	1	1	11	22	33	60	83	105
2	136	–	PC-r	1	1	2	4	6	8	11	14
3	146	–	PC-r	1	1	2	4	6	8	11	14
4	158	–	PC-r	1	1	2	4	6	8	11	14
5	167	11/63	PC-r	1	1	2	4	6	8	10	12
6	167	3/65	PC-r	1	1	2	4	6	8	10	12
7	166	8/67	PC-r	1	1	2	4	6	8	10	12

123. Fang and Claw

Ed	HRN	Date	Details	A	C	GD 2.0	VG 4.0	FN 6.0	VF 8.0	VF/NM 9.0	NM- 9.2
1	124	11/54	Original	1	1	11	22	33	60	83	105
2	133	–	PC-r	1	1	2	4	6	8	11	14
3	143	–	PC-r	1	1	2	4	6	8	11	14
4	154	–	PC-r	1	1	2	4	6	8	11	14
5	167	–	Has orig.date; PC-r	1	1	2	4	6	8	10	12
6	167	9/65	PC-r	1	1	2	4	6	8	10	12

124. The War of the Worlds

Ed	HRN	Date	Details	A	C	GD 2.0	VG 4.0	FN 6.0	VF 8.0	VF/NM 9.0	NM- 9.2
1	125	1/55	Original; Cameron-c/a	1	1	13	26	39	74	105	135
2	131	–	PC-r	1	1	2	4	6	9	13	16
3	141	–	PC-r	1	1	2	4	6	9	13	16
4	148	–	PC-r	1	1	2	4	6	9	13	16
5	156	–	PC-r	1	1	2	4	6	9	13	16
6	165	–	PC-r	1	1	2	4	6	11	16	20
7	167	–	PC-r	1	1	2	4	6	8	11	14
8	167	11/64	PC-r	1	1	2	4	6	9	13	16
9	167	11/65	PC-r	1	1	2	4	6	8	11	14
10	166	R/1968	C-price 25¢; PC-r	1	1	2	4	6	8	11	14
11	169	Sm/70	PC-r; stiff-c	1	1	2	4	6	8	11	14

125. The Ox Bow Incident

Ed	HRN	Date	Details	A	C	GD 2.0	VG 4.0	FN 6.0	VF 8.0	VF/NM 9.0	NM- 9.2
1	–	3/55	Original; Picture Progress replaces reorder list	1	1	10	20	30	56	76	95

Classics Illustrated #127 © GIL

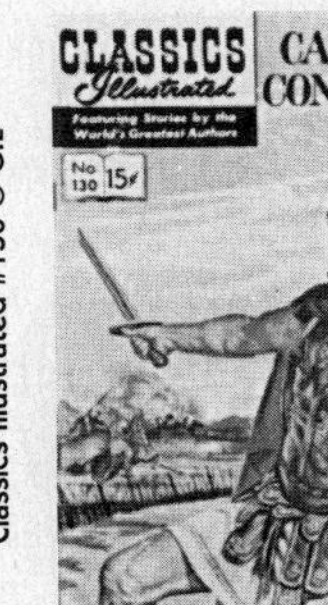

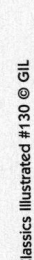

Classics Illustrated #130 © GIL

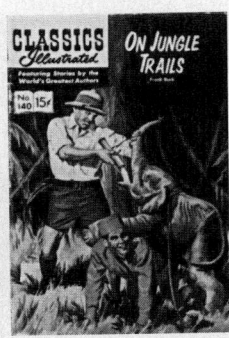

Classics Illustrated #140 © GIL

Ed	HRN	Date	Details	A	C	GD 2.0	VG 4.0	FN 6.0	VF 8.0	VF/NM 9.0	NM- 9.2
2	143	–	PC-r	1	1	2	4	6	8	11	14
3	152	–	PC-r	1	1	2	4	6	8	11	14
4	149	–	PC-r	1	1	2	4	6	8	11	14
5	167	–	PC-r	1	1	2	4	6	8	10	12
6	167	11/64	PC-r	1	1	2	4	6	8	10	12
7	166	4/67	PC-r	1	1	2	4	6	8	10	12
8	169	Win/69	New price 25¢; stiff-c; PC-r	1	1	2	4	6	8	10	12

126. The Downfall

Ed	HRN	Date	Details	A	C	GD 2.0	VG 4.0	FN 6.0	VF 8.0	VF/NM 9.0	NM- 9.2
1	5/55	–	Orig.; 'Picture Progress' replaces reorder list; Cameron-c/a	1	1	11	22	33	60	83	105
2	167	8/64	PC-r	1	1	2	4	6	13	18	22
3	166	R/1968	C-price 25¢; PC-r	1	1	2	4	6	13	18	22

127. The King of the Mountains

Ed	HRN	Date	Details	A	C	GD 2.0	VG 4.0	FN 6.0	VF 8.0	VF/NM 9.0	NM- 9.2
1	128	7/55	Original	1	1	11	22	33	60	83	105
2	167	6/64	PC-r	1	1	2	4	6	10	14	18
3	166	F/1968	C-price 25¢; PC-r	1	1	2	4	6	10	14	18

128. Macbeth (Used in **POP**, pg. 102)

Ed	HRN	Date	Details	A	C	GD 2.0	VG 4.0	FN 6.0	VF 8.0	VF/NM 9.0	NM- 9.2
1	128	9/55	Orig.; last Blum-a	1	1	11	22	33	60	83	105
2	143	–	PC-r	1	1	2	4	6	8	11	14
3	158	–	PC-r	1	1	2	4	6	8	11	14
4	167	–	PC-r	1	1	2	4	6	8	10	12
5	167	6/64	PC-r	1	1	2	4	6	8	10	12
6	166	4/67	PC-r	1	1	2	4	6	8	10	12
7	166	R/1968	C-Price 25¢; PC-r	1	1	2	4	6	8	10	12
8	169	Spr/70	Stiff-c; PC-r	1	1	2	4	6	8	10	12

129. Davy Crockett

Ed	HRN	Date	Details	A	C	GD 2.0	VG 4.0	FN 6.0	VF 8.0	VF/NM 9.0	NM- 9.2
1	129	11/55	Orig.; Cameron-a	1	1	14	28	42	81	118	155
2	167	9/66	PC-r	1	1	11	22	33	62	86	110

130. Caesar's Conquests

Ed	HRN	Date	Details	A	C	GD 2.0	VG 4.0	FN 6.0	VF 8.0	VF/NM 9.0	NM- 9.2
1	130	1/56	Original; Orlando-a	1	1	11	22	33	60	83	105
2	142	–	PC-r	1	1	2	4	6	8	11	14
3	152	–	PC-r	1	1	2	4	6	8	11	14
4	149	–	PC-r	1	1	2	4	6	8	11	14
5	167	–	PC-r	1	1	2	4	6	8	10	12
6	167	10/64	PC-r	1	1	2	4	6	8	10	12
7	167	4/66	PC-r	1	1	2	4	6	8	10	12

131. The Covered Wagon

Ed	HRN	Date	Details	A	C	GD 2.0	VG 4.0	FN 6.0	VF 8.0	VF/NM 9.0	NM- 9.2
1	131	3/56	Original	1	1	6	12	18	43	69	95
2	143	–	PC-r	1	1	2	4	6	8	11	14
3	152	–	PC-r	1	1	2	4	6	8	11	14
4	158	–	PC-r	1	1	2	4	6	8	11	14
5	167	–	PC-r	1	1	2	4	6	8	10	12
6	167	11/64	PC-r	1	1	2	4	6	8	10	12
7	167	4/66	PC-r	1	1	2	4	6	8	10	12
8	169	Win/69	New price 25¢; stiff-c; PC-r	1	1	2	4	6	8	10	12

132. The Dark Frigate

Ed	HRN	Date	Details	A	C	GD 2.0	VG 4.0	FN 6.0	VF 8.0	VF/NM 9.0	NM- 9.2
1	132	5/56	Original	1	1	11	22	33	60	83	105
2	150	–	PC-r	1	1	2	4	6	9	12	15
3	167	1/64	PC-r	1	1	2	4	6	8	11	14
4	166	5/67	PC-r	1	1	2	4	6	8	11	14

133. The Time Machine

Ed	HRN	Date	Details	A	C	GD 2.0	VG 4.0	FN 6.0	VF 8.0	VF/NM 9.0	NM- 9.2
1	132	7/56	Orig.; Cameron-a	1	1	7	14	21	50	83	115
2	142	–	PC-r	1	1	2	4	6	9	13	16
3	152	–	PC-r	1	1	2	4	6	9	13	16
4	158	–	PC-r	1	1	2	4	6	9	13	16
5	167	–	PC-r	1	1	2	4	6	8	11	14
6	167	6/64	PC-r	1	1	2	4	6	9	13	16
7	167	3/66	PC-r	1	1	2	4	6	8	11	14
8	166	12/67	PC-r	1	1	2	4	6	8	11	14
9	169	Win/71	New price 25¢; stiff-c; PC-r	1	1	2	4	6	8	11	14

134. Romeo and Juliet

Ed	HRN	Date	Details	A	C	GD 2.0	VG 4.0	FN 6.0	VF 8.0	VF/NM 9.0	NM- 9.2
1	134	9/56	Original; Evans-a	1	1	7	14	21	47	76	105
2	161	–	PC-r	1	1	2	4	6	8	11	14
3	167	9/63	PC-r	1	1	2	4	6	8	10	12
4	167	5/65	PC-r	1	1	2	4	6	8	10	12
5	166	6/67	PC-r	1	1	2	4	6	8	10	12
6	166	Win/69	New c&price 25¢; stiff-c; PC-r	1	2	3	6	9	17	25	32

135. Waterloo

Ed	HRN	Date	Details	A	C	GD 2.0	VG 4.0	FN 6.0	VF 8.0	VF/NM 9.0	NM- 9.2
1	135	11/56	Orig.; G. Ingels-a	1	1	7	14	21	47	76	105
2	153	–	PC-r	1	1	2	4	6	8	11	14
3	167	–	PC-r	1	1	2	4	6	8	10	12
4	167	9/64	PC-r	1	1	2	4	6	8	10	12
5	166	R/1968	C-price 25¢; PC-r	1	1	2	4	6	8	10	12

136. Lord Jim

Ed	HRN	Date	Details	A	C	GD 2.0	VG 4.0	FN 6.0	VF 8.0	VF/NM 9.0	NM- 9.2
1	136	1/57	Original; Evans-a	1	1	7	14	21	47	76	105
2	165	–	PC-r	1	1	2	4	6	8	10	12
3	167	3/64	PC-r	1	1	2	4	6	8	10	12
4	167	9/66	PC-r	1	1	2	4	6	8	10	12
5	169	Sm/69	New price 25 ¢; stiff-c; PC-r	1	1	2	4	6	8	10	12

137. The Little Savage

Ed	HRN	Date	Details	A	C	GD 2.0	VG 4.0	FN 6.0	VF 8.0	VF/NM 9.0	NM- 9.2
1	136	3/57	Original; Evans-a	1	1	7	14	21	47	76	105
2	148	–	PC-r	1	1	2	4	6	8	11	14
3	156	–	PC-r	1	1	2	4	6	8	11	14
4	167	–	PC-r	1	1	2	4	6	8	10	12
5	167	10/64	PC-r	1	1	2	4	6	8	10	12
6	166	8/67	PC-r	1	1	2	4	6	8	10	12
7	169	Spr/70	New price 25¢; stiff-c; PC-r	1	1	2	4	6	8	10	12

138. A Journey to the Center of the Earth

Ed	HRN	Date	Details	A	C	GD 2.0	VG 4.0	FN 6.0	VF 8.0	VF/NM 9.0	NM- 9.2
1	136	5/57	Original	1	1	8	16	24	56	93	130
2	146	–	PC-r	1	1	2	4	6	10	14	18
3	156	–	PC-r	1	1	2	4	6	10	14	18
4	158	–	PC-r	1	1	2	4	6	10	14	18
5	167	–	PC-r	1	1	2	4	6	8	11	14
6	167	6/64	PC-r	1	1	2	4	6	11	16	20
7	167	4/66	PC-r	1	1	2	4	6	11	16	20
8	166	R/68	C-price 25¢; PC-r	1	1	2	4	6	9	13	16

139. In the Reign of Terror

Ed	HRN	Date	Details	A	C	GD 2.0	VG 4.0	FN 6.0	VF 8.0	VF/NM 9.0	NM- 9.2
1	139	7/57	Original; Evans-a	1	1	6	12	18	43	69	95
2	154	–	PC-r	1	1	2	4	6	8	11	14
3	167	–	Has orig.date; PC-r	1	1	2	4	6	8	10	12
4	167	7/64	PC-r	1	1	2	4	6	8	10	12
5	166	R/1968	C-price 25¢; PC-r	1	1	2	4	6	8	10	12

140. On Jungle Trails

Ed	HRN	Date	Details	A	C	GD 2.0	VG 4.0	FN 6.0	VF 8.0	VF/NM 9.0	NM- 9.2
1	140	9/57	Original	1	1	6	12	18	43	69	95
2	150	–	PC-r	1	1	2	4	6	8	11	14
3	160	–	PC-r	1	1	2	4	6	8	11	14
4	167	9/63	PC-r	1	1	2	4	6	8	10	12
5	167	9/65	PC-r	1	1	2	4	6	8	10	12

141. Castle Dangerous

Ed	HRN	Date	Details	A	C	GD 2.0	VG 4.0	FN 6.0	VF 8.0	VF/NM 9.0	NM- 9.2
1	141	11/57	Original	1	1	7	14	21	49	80	110
2	152	–	PC-r	1	1	2	4	6	8	11	14
3	167	–	PC-r	1	1	2	4	6	8	11	14
4	166	7/67	PC-r	1	1	2	4	6	8	11	14

142. Abraham Lincoln

Ed	HRN	Date	Details	A	C	GD 2.0	VG 4.0	FN 6.0	VF 8.0	VF/NM 9.0	NM- 9.2
1	142	1/58	Original	1	1	7	14	21	47	76	105
2	154	–	PC-r	1	1	2	4	6	8	11	14
3	158	–	PC-r	1	1	2	4	6	8	11	14
4	167	10/63	PC-r	1	1	2	4	6	8	10	12

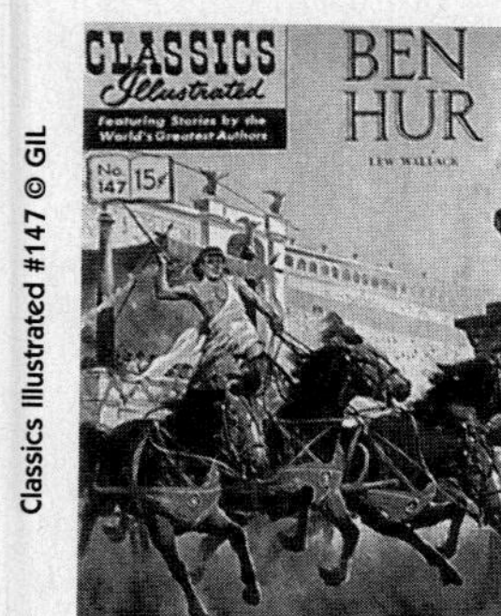

Classics Illustrated #147 © GIL

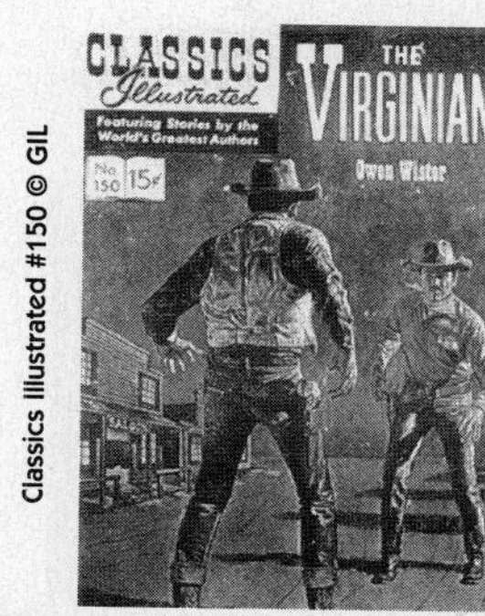

Classics Illustrated #150 © GIL

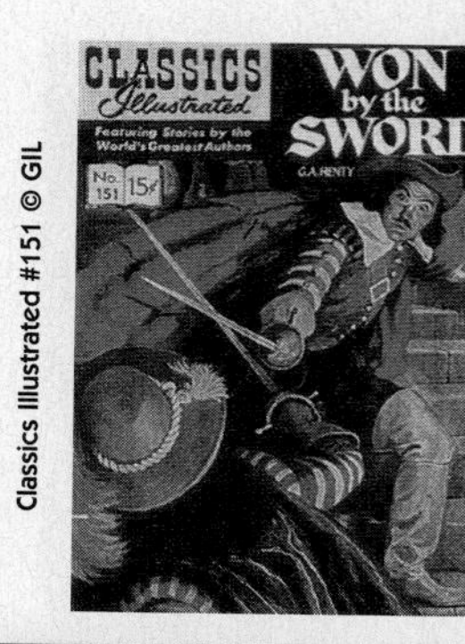

Classics Illustrated #151 © GIL

Ed	HRN	Date	Details	A	C	GD 2.0	VG 4.0	FN 6.0	VF 8.0	VF/NM 9.0	NM- 9.2
5	167	7/65	PC-r	1	1	2	4	6	8	10	12
6	166	11/67	PC-r	1	1	2	4	6	8	10	12
7	169	Fall/69	New price 25¢; stiff-c; PC-r	1	1	2	4	6	8	10	12

143. Kim

Ed	HRN	Date	Details	A	C	GD 2.0	VG 4.0	FN 6.0	VF 8.0	VF/NM 9.0	NM- 9.2
1	143	3/58	Original; Orlando-a	1	1	6	12	18	43	69	95
2	165	–	PC-r	1	1	2	4	6	8	10	12
3	167	11/63	PC-r	1	1	2	4	6	8	10	12
4	167	8/65	PC-r	1	1	2	4	6	8	10	12
5	169	Win/69	New price 25¢; stiff-c; PC-r	1	1	2	4	6	8	10	12

144. The First Men in the Moon

Ed	HRN	Date	Details	A	C	GD 2.0	VG 4.0	FN 6.0	VF 8.0	VF/NM 9.0	NM- 9.2
1	143	5/58	Original; Woodbridge/Williamson/Torres-a	1	1	7	14	21	50	83	115
2	152	–	(Rare)-PC-r	1	1	8	16	24	56	93	130
3	153	–	PC-r	1	1	2	4	6	8	11	14
4	161	–	PC-r	1	1	2	4	6	8	10	12
5	167	–	PC-r	1	1	2	4	6	8	10	12
6	167	12/65	PC-r	1	1	2	4	6	8	10	12
7	166	Fall/68	New-c&price 25¢; PC-r; stiff-c	1	2	3	6	9	16	22	28
8	169	Win/69	Stiff-c; PC-r	1	2	2	4	6	10	14	18

145. The Crisis

Ed	HRN	Date	Details	A	C	GD 2.0	VG 4.0	FN 6.0	VF 8.0	VF/NM 9.0	NM- 9.2
1	143	7/58	Original; Evans-a	1	1	7	14	21	47	76	105
2	156	–	PC-r	1	1	2	4	6	8	11	14
3	167	10/63	PC-r	1	1	2	4	6	8	10	12
4	167	3/65	PC-r	1	1	2	4	6	8	10	12
5	166	R/68	C-price 25¢; PC-r	1	1	2	4	6	8	10	12

146. With Fire and Sword

Ed	HRN	Date	Details	A	C	GD 2.0	VG 4.0	FN 6.0	VF 8.0	VF/NM 9.0	NM- 9.2
1	143	9/58	Original; Woodbridge-a	1	1	7	14	21	47	76	105
2	156	–	PC-r	1	1	2	4	6	9	13	16
3	167	11/63	PC-r	1	1	2	4	6	8	11	14
4	167	3/65	PC-r	1	1	2	4	6	8	11	14

147. Ben-Hur

Ed	HRN	Date	Details	A	C	GD 2.0	VG 4.0	FN 6.0	VF 8.0	VF/NM 9.0	NM- 9.2
1	147	11/58	Original; Orlando-a	1	1	7	14	21	45	73	100
2	152	–	Scarce; PC-r	1	1	7	14	21	47	76	105
3	153	–	PC-r	1	1	2	4	6	8	11	14
4	158	–	PC-r	1	1	2	4	6	8	11	14
5	167	–	Orig.date; but PC-r	1	1	2	4	6	8	10	12
6	167	2/65	PC-r	1	1	2	4	6	8	10	12
7	167	9/66	PC-r	1	1	2	4	6	8	10	12
8A	166	Fall/68	New-c&price 25¢; PC-r; soft-c	1	2	3	6	9	17	25	32
8B	166	Fall/68	New-c&price 25¢; PC-r; stiff-c; scarce	1	2	4	8	12	22	34	45

148. The Buccaneer

Ed	HRN	Date	Details	A	C	GD 2.0	VG 4.0	FN 6.0	VF 8.0	VF/NM 9.0	NM- 9.2
1	148	1/59	Orig.; Evans/Jenny-a; Saunders-c	1	1	6	12	18	43	69	95
2	568	–	Juniors list only PC-r	1	1	2	4	6	8	11	14
3	167	–	PC-r	1	1	2	4	6	8	10	12
4	167	9/65	PC-r	1	1	2	4	6	8	10	12
5	169	Sm/69	New price 25¢; PC-r; stiff-c	1	1	2	4	6	8	10	12

149. Off on a Comet

Ed	HRN	Date	Details	A	C	GD 2.0	VG 4.0	FN 6.0	VF 8.0	VF/NM 9.0	NM- 9.2
1	149	3/59	Orig.;G.McCann-a; blue reorder list	1	1	7	14	21	47	76	105
2	155	–	PC-r	1	1	2	4	6	8	11	14
3	149	–	PC-r; white reorder list; no coming-next ad	1	1	2	4	6	8	11	14
4	167	12/63	PC-r	1	1	2	4	6	8	10	12
5	167	2/65	PC-r	1	1	2	4	6	8	10	12
6	167	10/66	PC-r	1	1	2	4	6	8	10	12
7	166	Fall/68	New-c & price 25¢; PC-r	1	2	3	6	9	16	23	30

150. The Virginian

Ed	HRN	Date	Details	A	C	GD 2.0	VG 4.0	FN 6.0	VF 8.0	VF/NM 9.0	NM- 9.2
1	150	5/59	Original	1	1	7	14	21	49	80	110
2	164	–	PC-r	1	1	2	4	6	11	16	20
3	167	10/63	PC-r	1	1	3	6	9	15	21	26
4	167	12/65	PC-r	1	1	2	4	6	11	16	20

151. Won By the Sword

Ed	HRN	Date	Details	A	C	GD 2.0	VG 4.0	FN 6.0	VF 8.0	VF/NM 9.0	NM- 9.2
1	150	7/59	Original	1	1	7	14	21	47	76	105
2	164	–	PC-r	1	1	2	4	6	9	13	16
3	167	10/63	PC-r	1	1	2	4	6	9	13	16
4	166	7/67	PC-r	1	1	2	4	6	9	13	16

152. Wild Animals I Have Known

Ed	HRN	Date	Details	A	C	GD 2.0	VG 4.0	FN 6.0	VF 8.0	VF/NM 9.0	NM- 9.2
1	152	9/59	Orig.; L.B. Cole c/a	1	1	7	14	21	50	83	115
2A	149	–	PC-r; white reorder list; no coming-next ad; IBC: Jr. list #572	1	1	2	4	6	8	11	14
2B	149	–	PC-r; inside-bc: Jr. list to #555	1	1	2	4	6	9	12	15
2C	149	–	PC-r; inside-bc: has World Around Us ad; scarce	1	1	3	6	9	15	21	26
3	167	9/63	PC-r	1	1	2	4	6	8	10	12
4	167	8/65	PC-r	1	1	2	4	6	8	10	12
5	169	Fall/69	New price 25¢; stiff-c; PC-r	1	1	2	4	6	8	10	12

153. The Invisible Man

Ed	HRN	Date	Details	A	C	GD 2.0	VG 4.0	FN 6.0	VF 8.0	VF/NM 9.0	NM- 9.2
1	153	11/59	Original	1	1	8	16	24	54	90	125
2A	149	–	PC-r; white reorder list; no coming-next ad; inside-bc: Jr. list to #572	1	1	2	4	6	10	14	18
2B	149	–	PC-r; inside-bc: Jr. list to #555	1	1	2	4	6	11	16	20
3	167	–	PC-r	1	1	2	4	6	9	12	15
4	167	2/65	PC-r	1	1	2	4	6	9	12	15
5	167	9/66	PC-r	1	1	2	4	6	9	12	15
6	166	Win/69	New price 25¢; PC-r; stiff-c	1	1	2	4	6	9	12	15
7	169	Spr/71	Stiff-c; letters spelling 'Invisible Man' are 'solid' not 'invisible;' PC-r	1	1	2	4	6	9	12	15

154. The Conspiracy of Pontiac

Ed	HRN	Date	Details	A	C	GD 2.0	VG 4.0	FN 6.0	VF 8.0	VF/NM 9.0	NM- 9.2
1	154	1/60	Original	1	1	7	14	21	49	80	110
2	167	11/63	PC-r	1	1	2	4	6	13	18	22
3	167	7/64	PC-r	1	1	2	4	6	13	18	22
4	166	12/67	PC-r	1	1	2	4	6	13	18	22

155. The Lion of the North

Ed	HRN	Date	Details	A	C	GD 2.0	VG 4.0	FN 6.0	VF 8.0	VF/NM 9.0	NM- 9.2
1	154	3/60	Original	1	1	7	14	21	47	76	105
2	167	1/64	PC-r	1	1	2	4	6	11	16	20
3	166	R/1967	C-price 25¢; PC-r	1	1	2	4	6	10	14	18

156. The Conquest of Mexico

Ed	HRN	Date	Details	A	C	GD 2.0	VG 4.0	FN 6.0	VF 8.0	VF/NM 9.0	NM- 9.2
1	156	5/60	Orig.; Bruno Premiani-c/a	1	1	7	14	21	47	76	105
2	167	1/64	PC-r	1	1	2	4	6	10	14	18
3	166	8/67	PC-r	1	1	2	4	6	10	14	18
4	169	Spr/70	New price 25¢; stiff-c; PC-r	1	1	2	4	6	9	12	15

157. Lives of the Hunted

Ed	HRN	Date	Details	A	C	GD 2.0	VG 4.0	FN 6.0	VF 8.0	VF/NM 9.0	NM- 9.2
1	156	7/60	Orig.; L.B. Cole-c	1	1	7	14	21	49	80	110
2	167	2/64	PC-r	1	1	2	4	6	13	18	22
3	166	10/67	PC-r	1	1	2	4	6	13	18	22

Classics Illustrated #160 © GIL

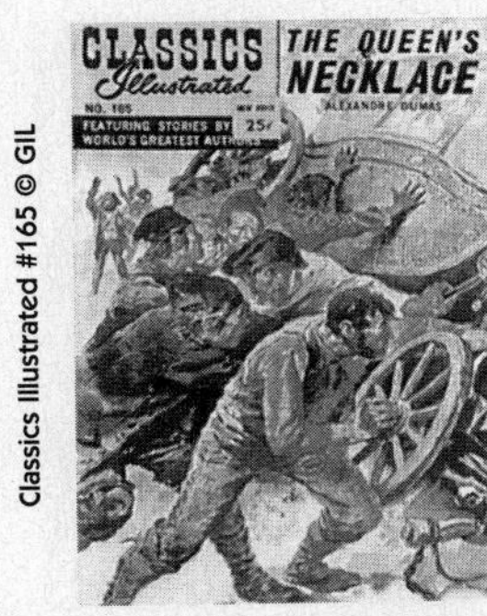

Classics Illustrated #165 © GIL

Classics Illustrated Junior #503 © GIL

	GD 2.0	VG 4.0	FN 6.0	VF 8.0	VF/NM 9.0	NM- 9.2

158. The Conspirators

Ed	HRN	Date	Details	A	C	GD	VG	FN	VF	VF/NM	NM-
1	156	9/60	Original	1	1	7	14	21	49	80	110
2	167	7/64	PC-r	1	1	2	4	6	13	18	22
3	166	10/67	PC-r	1	1	2	4	6	13	18	22

159. The Octopus

Ed	HRN	Date	Details	A	C	GD	VG	FN	VF	VF/NM	NM-
1	159	11/60	Orig.; Gray Morrow-a; L.B. Cole-c	1	1	7	14	21	49	80	110
2	167	2/64	PC-r	1	1	2	4	6	13	18	22
3	166	R/1967	C-price 25¢; PC-r	1	1	2	4	6	13	18	22

160. The Food of the Gods

Ed	HRN	Date	Details	A	C	GD	VG	FN	VF	VF/NM	NM-
1A	159	1/61	Original	1	1	7	14	21	50	83	115
1B	160	1/61	Original; same, except for HRN	1	1	7	14	21	49	80	110
2	167	1/64	PC-r	1	1	2	4	6	13	18	22
3	166	6/67	PC-r	1	1	2	4	6	13	18	22

161. Cleopatra

Ed	HRN	Date	Details	A	C	GD	VG	FN	VF	VF/NM	NM-
1	161	3/61	Original	1	1	7	14	21	49	80	110
2	167	1/64	PC-r	1	1	3	6	9	14	19	24
3	166	8/67	PC-r	1	1	3	6	9	14	19	24

162. Robur the Conqueror

Ed	HRN	Date	Details	A	C	GD	VG	FN	VF	VF/NM	NM-
1	162	5/61	Original	1	1	7	14	21	49	80	110
2	167	7/64	PC-r	1	1	3	6	9	14	19	24
3	166	8/67	PC-r	1	1	3	6	9	14	19	24

163. Master of the World

Ed	HRN	Date	Details	A	C	GD	VG	FN	VF	VF/NM	NM-
1	163	7/61	Original; Gray Morrow-a	1	1	7	14	21	49	80	110
2	167	1/65	PC-r	1	1	2	4	6	13	18	22
3	166	R/1968	C-price 25¢; PC-r	1	1	2	4	6	13	18	22

164. The Cossack Chief

Ed	HRN	Date	Details	A	C	GD	VG	FN	VF	VF/NM	NM-
1	164	(1961)	Orig.; nd(10/61?)	1	1	7	14	21	45	73	100
2	167	4/65	PC-r	1	1	2	4	6	13	18	22
3	166	Fall/68	C-price 25¢; PC-r	1	1	2	4	6	13	18	22

165. The Queen's Necklace

Ed	HRN	Date	Details	A	C	GD	VG	FN	VF	VF/NM	NM-
1	164	1/62	Original; Morrow-a	1	1	7	14	21	49	80	110
2	167	4/65	PC-r	1	1	2	4	6	13	18	22
3	166	Fall/68	C-price 25¢; PC-r	1	1	2	4	6	13	18	22

166. Tigers and Traitors

Ed	HRN	Date	Details	A	C	GD	VG	FN	VF	VF/NM	NM-
1	165	5/62	Original	1	1	9	18	27	63	107	150
2	167	2/64	PC-r	1	1	4	8	12	22	34	45
3	167	11/66	PC-r	1	1	4	8	12	22	34	45

167. Faust

Ed	HRN	Date	Details	A	C	GD	VG	FN	VF	VF/NM	NM-
1	165	8/62	Original	1	1	13	26	39	90	165	240
2	167	2/64	PC-r	1	1	6	12	18	39	62	85
3	166	6/67	PC-r	1	1	6	12	18	39	62	85

168. In Freedom's Cause

Ed	HRN	Date	Details	A	C	GD	VG	FN	VF	VF/NM	NM-
1	169	Win/69	Original; Evans/ Crandall-a; stiff-c; 25¢; no coming-next ad;	1	1	14	28	42	100	188	275

169. Negro Americans The Early Years

Ed	HRN	Date	Details	A	C	GD	VG	FN	VF	VF/NM	NM-
1	166	Spr/69	Orig. & last issue; 25¢; Stiff-c; no coming-next ad; other sources indicate publication date of 5/69	1	1	13	26	39	93	172	250
2	169	Spr/69	Stiff-c	1	1	7	14	21	50	83	115

NOTE: *Many other titles were prepared or planned but were only issued in British/European series.*

CLASSIC PUNISHER (Also see Punisher)
Marvel Comics: Dec, 1989 ($4.95, B&W, deluxe format, 68 pgs.)

1-Reprints Marvel Super Action #1 & Marvel Preview #2 plus new story 5.00

CLASSICS ILLUSTRATED
First Publishing/Berkley Publishing: Feb, 1990 - No. 27, July, 1991 ($3.75/$3.95, 52 pgs.)

1-27: 1-Gahan Wilson-c/a. 4-Sienkiewicz painted-c/a. 6-Russell scripts/layouts. 7-Spiegle-a. 9-Ploog-c/a. 16-Staton-a. 18-Gahan Wilson-c/a; 20-Geary-a. 26-Aesop's Fables (6/91). 26,27-Direct sale only 5.00

CLASSICS ILLUSTRATED
Acclaim Books/Twin Circle PublishingCo.: Feb, 1997 - Present ($4.99, digest-size) (Each book contains study notes)

A Christmas Carol-(12/97), A Connecticut Yankee in King Arthur's Court-(5/97), All Quiet on the Western Front-(1/98), A Midsummer's Night Dream-(4/97) Around the World in 80 Days-(1/98), A Tale of Two Cities-(2/97)Joe Orlando-r, Captains Courageous-(11/97), Crime and Punishment-(3/97), Dr. Jekyll and Mr. Hyde-(10/97), Don Quixote-(12/97), Frankenstein-(10/97), Great Expectations-(4/97), Hamlet-(3/97), Huckleberry Finn-(3/97), Jane Eyre-(2/97), Kidnapped-(1/98), Les Miserables-(5/97), Lord Jim-(9/97),Macbeth-(5/97), Moby Dick-(4/97), Oliver Twist-(5/97), Robinson Crusoe-(9/97), Romeo & Juliet-(2/97), Silas Marner-(11/97), The Call of the Wild-(9/97), The Count of Monte Cristo-(1/98), The House of the Seven Gables-(9/97), The Iliad-(12/97), The Invisible Man-(10/97), The Last of the Mohicans-(12/97), The Master of Ballantrae-(11/97), The Odyssey-(3/97), The Prince and the Pauper-(4/97), The Red Badge Of Courage-(9/97), Tom Sawyer-(2/97) Wuthering Heights-(11/97) 5.00

NOTE: *Stories reprinted from the original Gilberton Classic Comics and Classics Illustrated.*

CLASSICS ILLUSTRATED GIANTS
Gilberton Publications: Oct, 1949 (One-Shots - "OS")
These Giant Editions, all with new front and back covers, were advertised from 10/49 to 2/52. They were 50¢ on the newsstand and 60¢ by mail. They are actually four Classics in one volume. All the stories are reprints of the Classics Illustrated Series.
NOTE: There were also British hardback Adventure & Indian Giants in 1952, with the same covers but different contents: Adventure - 2, 7, 10; Indian - 17, 22, 37, 58. They are also rare.

	GD	VG	FN	VF	VF/NM	NM-
"An Illustrated Library of Great Adventure Stories" - reprints of No. 6,7,8,10 (Rare); Kiefer-c	148	296	444	947	1624	2300
"An Illustrated Library of Exciting Mystery Stories" - reprints of No. 30,21,40, 13 (Rare); Blum-c	160	320	480	1016	1746	2475
"An Illustrated Library of Great Indian Stories" - reprints of No. 4,17,22,37 (Rare); Blum-c	148	296	444	947	1624	2300

INTRODUCTION TO CLASSICS ILLUSTRATED JUNIOR

Collectors of Juniors can be put into one of two categories: those who want any copy of each title, and those who want all the originals. Those seeking every original and reprint edition are a limited group, primarily because Juniors have no changes in art or covers to spark interest, and because reprints are so low in value it is difficult to get dealers to look for specific reprint editions.

In recent years it has become apparent that most serious Classics collectors seek Junior originals. Those seeking reprints seek them for low cost. This has made the previous note about the comparative market value of reprints inadequate. Three particular reprint editions are worth even more. For the 535-Twin Circle edition, see Giveaways. There are also reprint editions of 501 and 503 which have a full-page bc ad for the very rare Junior record. Those may sell as high as $10-$15 in mint. Original editions of 557 and 558 also have that ad.

There are no reprint editions of 577. The only edition, from 1969, is a 25 cent stiff-cover edition with no ad for the next issue. All other original editions have coming-next ad. But 577, like C.I. #168, was prepared in 1962 but not issued. Copies of 577 can be found in 1963 British/European series, which then continued with dozens of additional new Junior titles.

PRICES LISTED BELOW ARE FOR ORIGINAL EDITIONS, WHICH HAVE AN AD FOR THE NEXT ISSUE.

NOTE: *Non HRN 576 copies- many are written on or colored . Reprints with 576 HRN are worth about 1/3 original prices. All other HRN #'s are 1/2 original price*

CLASSICS ILLUSTRATED JUNIOR
Famous Authors Ltd. (Gilberton Publications): Oct, 1953 - Spring, 1971

	GD	VG	FN	VF	VF/NM	NM-
501-Snow White & the Seven Dwarfs; Alex Blum-a	12	24	36	69	97	125
502-The Ugly Duckling	9	18	27	47	61	75
503-Cinderella	8	16	24	40	50	60
504-512: 504-The Pied Piper. 505-The Sleeping Beauty. 506-The Three Little Pigs. 507-Jack & the Beanstalk. 508-Goldilocks & the Three Bears. 509-Beauty and the Beast. 510-Little Red Riding Hood. 511-Puss-N Boots. 512-Rumpelstiltskin	6	12	18	27	33	38
513-Pinocchio	7	14	21	37	46	55
514-The Steadfast Tin Soldier	8	16	24	44	57	70
515-Johnny Appleseed	6	12	18	27	33	38
516-Aladdin and His Lamp	6	12	18	29	36	42
517-519: 517-The Emperor's New Clothes. 518-The Golden Goose. 519-Paul Bunyan	6	12	18	27	33	38

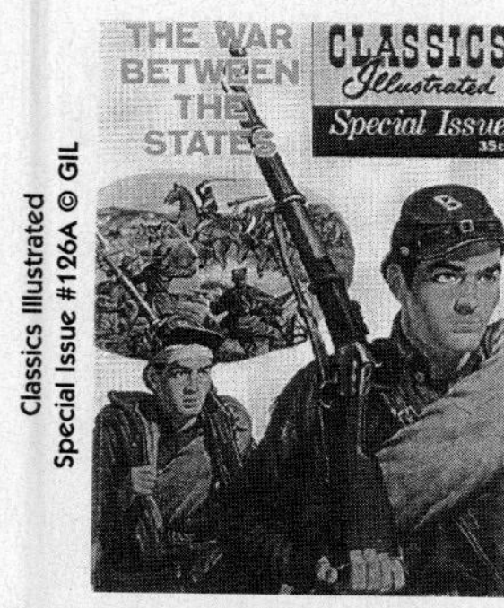

Classics Illustrated Special Issue #126A © GIL

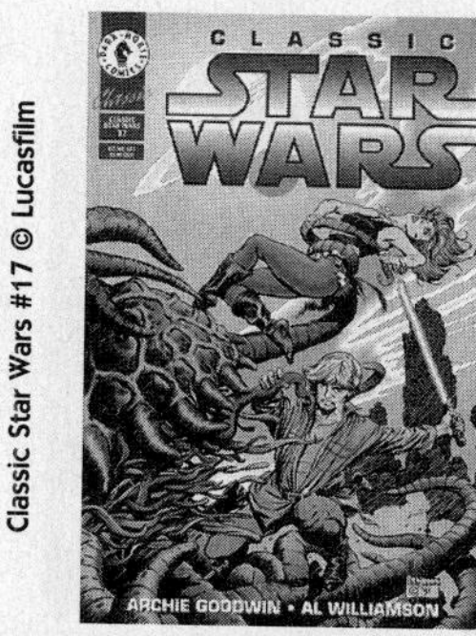

Classic Star Wars #17 © Lucasfilm

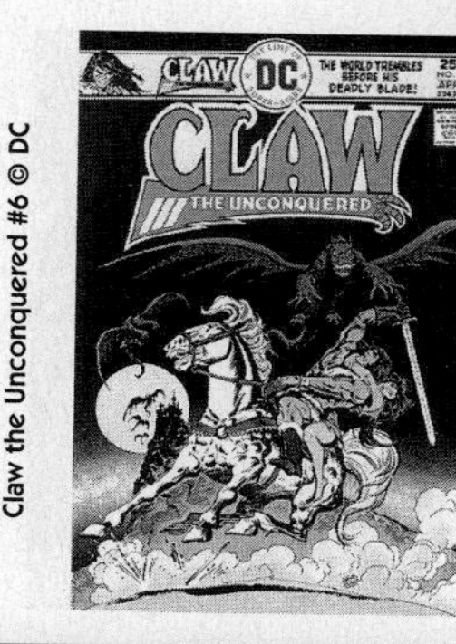

Claw the Unconquered #6 © DC

	GD 2.0	VG 4.0	FN 6.0	VF 8.0	VF/NM 9.0	NM- 9.2
520-Thumbelina	6	12	18	29	36	42
521-King of the Golden River	6	12	18	27	33	38
522,523,530: 522-The Nightingale. 523-The Gallant Tailor. 530-The Golden Bird	5	10	15	24	30	35
524-The Wild Swans	6	12	18	29	36	42
525,526: 525-The Little Mermaid. 526-The Frog Prince	6	12	18	29	36	42
527-The Golden-Haired Giant	6	12	18	27	33	38
528-The Penny Prince	6	12	18	27	33	38
529-The Magic Servants	6	12	18	27	33	38
531-Rapunzel	6	12	18	27	33	38
532-534: 532-The Dancing Princesses. 533-The Magic Fountain. 534-The Golden Touch	5	10	15	23	28	32
535-The Wizard of Oz	8	16	24	44	57	70
536-The Chimney Sweep	6	12	18	27	33	38
537-The Three Fairies	6	12	18	28	34	40
538-Silly Hans	5	10	15	23	28	32
539-The Enchanted Fish	6	12	18	31	38	45
540-The Tinder-Box	6	12	18	31	38	45
541-Snow White & Rose Red	5	10	15	24	30	35
542-The Donkey's Tale	5	10	15	24	30	35
543-The House in the Woods	6	12	18	27	33	38
544-The Golden Fleece	6	12	18	31	38	45
545-The Glass Mountain	5	10	15	24	30	35
546-The Elves & the Shoemaker	5	10	15	24	30	35
547-The Wishing Table	6	12	18	27	33	38
548-551: 548-The Magic Pitcher. 549-Simple Kate. 550-The Singing Donkey. 551-The Queen Bee	5	10	15	23	28	32
552-The Three Little Dwarfs	6	12	18	27	33	38
553,556: 553-King Thrushbeard. 556-The Elf Mound	5	10	15	23	28	32
554-The Enchanted Deer	6	12	18	29	36	42
555-The Three Golden Apples	5	10	15	24	30	35
557-Silly Willy	6	12	18	28	34	40
558-The Magic Dish; L.B. Cole-c; soft and stiff-c exist on original	7	14	21	35	43	50
559-The Japanese Lantern; 1 pg. Ingels-a; L.B. Cole-c	7	14	21	35	43	50
560-The Doll Princess; L.B. Cole-c	7	14	21	35	43	50
561-Hans Humdrum; L.B. Cole-c	6	12	18	29	36	42
562-The Enchanted Pony; L.B. Cole-c	7	14	21	35	43	50
563,565-568,570: 563-The Wishing Well; L.B. Cole-c. 565-The Silly Princess; L.B. Cole-c. 566-Clumsy Hans; L.B. Cole-c. 567-The Bearskin Soldier; L.B. Cole-c. 570-The Pearl Princess	6	12	18	27	33	38
564-The Salt Mountain; L.B.Cole-c. 568-The Happy Hedgehog; L.B. Cole-c.	6	12	18	28	34	40
569,573: 569-The Three Giants.573-The Crystal Ball	5	10	15	23	28	32
571,572: 571-How Fire Came to the Indians. 572-The Drummer Boy	6	12	18	29	36	42
574-Brightboots	5	10	15	24	30	35
575-The Fearless Prince	6	12	18	28	34	40
576-The Princess Who Saw Everything	7	14	21	35	43	50
577-The Runaway Dumpling	8	16	24	44	57	70

NOTE: *Prices are for original editions. Last reprint - Spring, 1971.* ***Costanza*** *&* ***Schaffenberger*** *art in many issues.*

CLASSICS ILLUSTRATED SPECIAL ISSUE
Gilberton Co.: (Came out semi-annually) Dec, 1955 - Jul, 1962 (35¢, 100 pgs.)

	GD 2.0	VG 4.0	FN 6.0	VF 8.0	VF/NM 9.0	NM- 9.2
129-The Story of Jesus (titled ...Special Edition) "Jesus on Mountain" cover	14	28	42	82	121	160
"Three Camels" cover (12/58)	15	30	45	85	130	175
"Mountain" cover (no date)-Has checklist on inside b/c to HRN #161 & different testimonial on back-c	12	24	36	67	94	120
"Mountain" cover (1968 re-issue; has white 50¢ circle)	9	18	27	50	65	80
132A-The Story of America (6/56); Cameron-a	11	22	33	62	86	110
135A-The Ten Commandments(12/56)	10	20	30	58	79	100
138A-Adventures in Science(6/57); HRN to 137	10	20	30	56	76	95
138A-(6/57)-2nd version w/HRN to 149	7	14	21	35	43	50
138A-(12/61)-3rd version w/HRN to 149	7	14	21	35	43	50
141A-The Rough Rider (Teddy Roosevelt)(12/57); Evans-a	10	20	30	58	79	100
144A-Blazing the Trails West(6/58)- 73 pgs. of Crandall/Evans plus Severin-a	11	22	33	60	83	105
147A-Crossing the Rockies(12/58)-Crandall/Evans-a	10	20	30	58	79	100
150A-Royal Canadian Police(6/59)-Ingels, Sid Check-a	10	20	30	58	79	100
153A-Men, Guns & Cattle(12/59)-Evans-a (26 pgs.); Kinstler-a	10	20	30	58	79	100
156A-The Atomic Age(6/60)-Crandall/Evans, Torres-a	10	20	30	58	79	100
159A-Rockets, Jets and Missiles(12/60)-Evans, Morrow-a	10	20	30	58	79	100
162A-War Between the States(6/61)-Kirby & Crandall/Evans-a; Ingels-a	15	30	45	90	140	190
165A-To the Stars(12/61)-Torres, Crandall/Evans, Kirby-a	12	24	36	67	94	120
166A-World War II('62)-Torres, Crandall/Evans, Kirby-a	14	28	42	76	108	140
167A-Prehistoric World(7/62)-Torres & Crandall/Evans-a; two versions exist (HRN to 165 & HRN to 167)	13	26	39	72	101	130
nn Special Issue-The United Nations (1964; 50¢; scarce); this is actually part of the European Special Series, which cont'd on after the U.S. series stopped issuing new titles in 1962. This English edition was prepared specifically for sale at the U.N. It was printed in Norway	40	80	120	246	411	575

NOTE: *There was another U.S. Special Issue prepared in 1962 with artwork by* ***Torres*** *entitled World War I. Unfortunately, it was never issued in any English-language edition. It was issued in 1964 in West Germany, The Netherlands, and some Scandanavian countries, with another edition in 1974 with a new cover.*

CLASSICS LIBRARY (See King Classics)

CLASSIC STAR WARS (Also see Star Wars)
Dark Horse Comics: Aug, 1992 - No. 20, June, 1994 ($2.50)

1-Begin Star Wars strip-r by Williamson; Williamson redrew portions of the panels to fit comic book format 6.00
2-10: 8-Polybagged w/Star Wars Galaxy trading card. 8-M. Schultz-c 4.00
11-19: 13-Yeates-c. 17-M. Schultz-c. 19-Evans-c 3.00
20-($3.50, 52 pgs.)-Polybagged w/trading card 3.50
Escape To Hoth TPB ($16.95) r/#15-20 17.00
The Rebel Storm TPB - r/#8-14 17.00
Trade paperback ($29.95, slip-cased)-Reprints all movie adaptations 30.00
NOTE: *Williamson c-1-5,7,9,10,14,15,20.*

CLASSIC STAR WARS: (Title series). **Dark Horse Comics**

--A NEW HOPE, 6/94 - No. 2, 7/94 ($3.95)
1,2: 1-r/Star Wars #1-3, 7-9 publ; 2-r/Star Wars #4-6, 10-12 publ. by Marvel Comics 4.00

--DEVILWORLDS, 8/96 - No.2, 9/96 ($2.50s)1,2: r/Alan Moore-s 2.50

--HAN SOLO AT STARS' END, 3/97 - No. 3, 5/97 ($2.95)
1-3: r/strips by Alfredo Alcala 3.00

--RETURN OF THE JEDI, 10/94 - No.2, 11/94 ($3.50)
1,2: 1-r/1983-84 Marvel series; polybagged with w/trading card 3.50

--THE EARLY ADVENTURES, 8/94 - No. 9, 4/95 ($2.50)1-9 2.50

--THE EMPIRE STRIKES BACK, 8/94 - No. 2, 9/94 ($3.95)
1-r/Star Wars #39-44 published by Marvel Comics 4.00

CLASSIC X-MEN (Becomes X-Men Classic #46 on)
Marvel Comics Group: Sept, 1986 - No. 45, Mar, 1990

1-Begins-r of New X-Men 5.00
2-10: 10-Sabretooth app. 4.00
11-45: 11-1st origin of Magneto in back-up story. 17-Wolverine-c. 27-r/X-Men #121. 26-r/X-Men #120; Wolverine-c/app. 35-r/X-Men #129. 39-New Jim Lee back-up story (2nd-a on X-Men). 43-Byrne-c/a(r); $1.75, double-size 3.00
NOTE: ***Art Adams*** *c(p)-1-10, 12-16, 18-23.* ***Austin*** *c-10,15-21,24-28i.* ***Bolton*** *back up stories in 1-28,30-35.* ***Williamson*** *c-12-14i.*

CLAW (See Capt. Battle, Jr., Daredevil Comics & Silver Streak Comics)

CLAWS
Marvel Comics: Oct, 2006 - No. 3, Dec, 2006 ($3.99, limited series)

1-3-Wolverine and Black Cat team-up; Linsner-a/c 4.00
Wolverine & Black Cat: Claws HC (2007, $17.99, dustjacket) r/#1-3 & bonus Linsner art 18.00

CLAW THE UNCONQUERED (See Cancelled Comic Cavalcade)
National Periodical Publications/DC Comics: 5-6/75 - No. 9, 9-10/76; No. 10, 4-5/78 - No. 12, 8-9/78

	GD 2.0	VG 4.0	FN 6.0	VF 8.0	VF/NM 9.0	NM- 9.2
1-1st app. Claw	2	4	6	8	10	12
2-12: 3-Nudity panel. 9-Origin	1	2	3	4	5	7

NOTE: ***Giffen*** *a-8-12p.* ***Kubert*** *c-10-12.* ***Layton*** *a-9i, 12i.*

CLAW THE UNCONQUERED (See Red Sonja/Claw: The Devil's Hands)
DC Comics: Aug, 2006 - No. 6, Jan, 2007 ($2.99)

1-6: 1,2-Chuck Dixon-s/Andy Smith; two covers by Smith & Van Sciver 3.00
TPB (2007, $17.99) r/#1-6; cover gallery 18.00

CLAY CODY, GUNSLINGER
Pines Comics: Fall, 1957

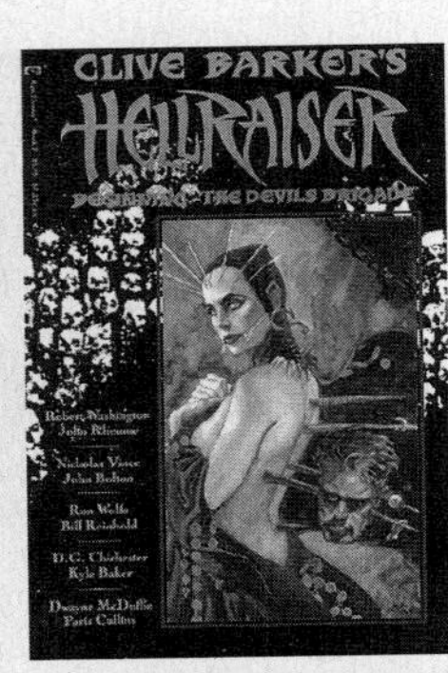

Clive Barker's Hellraiser #7 © MAR

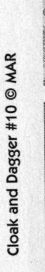

Cloak and Dagger #10 © MAR

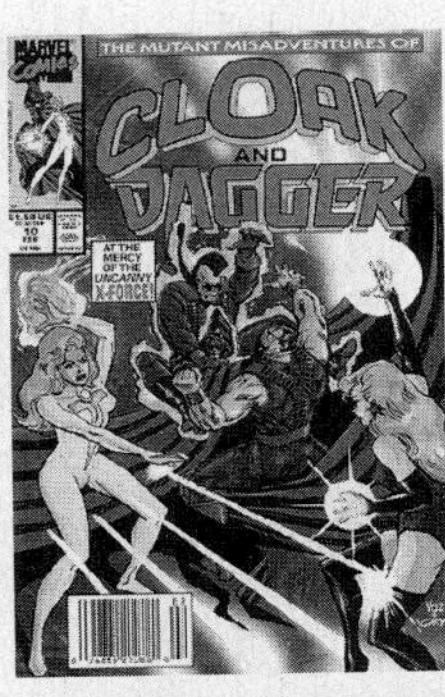

Club "16" #3 © FF

GD 2.0 | VG 4.0 | FN 6.0 | VF 8.0 | VF/NM 9.0 | NM- 9.2

1-Painted-c 6 12 18 31 38 45

CLEAN FUN, STARRING "SHOOGAFOOTS JONES"
Specialty Book Co.: 1944 (10¢, B&W, oversized covers, 24 pgs.)
nn-Humorous situations involving Negroes in the Deep South
White cover issue... 16 32 48 94 147 200
Dark grey cover issue... 17 34 51 98 154 210

CLEMENTINA THE FLYING PIG (See Dell Jr. Treasury)

CLEOPATRA (See Ideal, a Classical Comic No. 1)

CLERKS: THE COMIC BOOK (Also see Tales From the Clerks and Oni Double Feature #1)
Oni Press: Feb, 1998 ($2.95, B&W, one-shot)
1-Kevin Smith-s 2 4 6 8 10 12
1-Second printing 4.00
...Holiday Special (12/98, $2.95) Smith-s 5.00
...The Lost Scene (12/99, $2.95) Smith-s/Hester-a 5.00

CLIFFHANGER (See Battle Chasers, Crimson, and Danger Girl)
WildStorm Prod./Wizard Press: 1997 (Wizard supplement)
0-Sketchbook preview of Cliffhanger titles 6.00

CLIMAX! (Mystery)
Gillmor Magazines: July, 1955 - No. 2, Sept, 1955
1 16 32 48 94 147 200
2 14 28 42 76 108 140

CLINT (Also see Adolescent Radioactive Black Belt Hamsters)
Eclipse Comics: Sept, 1986 - No. 2, Jan, 1987 ($1.50, B&W)
1,2 2.50

CLINT & MAC (TV, Disney)
Dell Publishing Co.: No. 889, Mar, 1958
Four Color 889-Alex Toth-a, photo-c 11 22 33 78 139 200

CLIVE BARKER'S BOOK OF THE DAMNED: A HELLRAISER COMPANION
Marvel Comics (Epic): Oct, 1991 - No. 3, Nov, 1992 ($4.95, semi-annual)
Volume 1-3-(52 pgs.): 1-Simon Bisley-c. 2-(4/92). 3-(11/92)-McKean-a (1 pg.) 5.00

CLIVE BARKER'S HELLRAISER (Also see Epic, Hellraiser Nightbreed –Jihad, Revelations, Son of Celluloid, Tapping the Vein & Weaveworld)
Marvel Comics (Epic Comics): 1989 - No. 20, 1993 ($4.50-6.95, mature, quarterly, 68 pgs.)
Book 1-4,10-16,18,19: Based on Hellraiser & Hellbound movies; Bolton-c/a;
Spiegle & Wrightson-a (graphic album). 10-Foil-c. 12-Sam Kieth-a 6.00
Book 5-9 ($5.95): 7-Bolton-a. 8-Morrow-a 6.00
Book 17-Alex Ross-a, 34 pgs. 2 4 6 8 10 12
Book 20-By Gaiman/McKean 1 2 3 5 6 8
...Collected Best (Checker Books, '02, $21.95)-r/by various incl. Ross, Gaiman, Mignola 22.00
...Collected Best II ('03, $19.95)-r/by various incl. Bolton, L. Wachowski, Dorman 20.00
...Collected Best III ('04, $26.95)-r/by various incl. Bolton, L. Wachowski, Wrightson 27.00
...Dark Holiday Special ('92, $4.95)-Conrad-a 6.00
...Spring Slaughter 1 ('94, $6.95, 52 pgs.)-Painted-c 7.00
...Summer Special 1 ('92, $5.95, 68 pgs.) 6.00

CLIVE BARKER'S NIGHTBREED (Also see Epic)
Marvel Comics (Epic Comics): Apr, 1990 - No. 25, Mar, 1993 ($1.95/$2.25/$2.50, mature readers)
1-25: 1-4-Adapt horror movie. 5-New stories; Guice-a(p) 2.50

CLIVE BARKER'S THE HARROWERS
Marvel Comics (Epic Comics): Dec, 1993 - No. 6, May, 1994 ($2.50)
1-($2.95)-Glow-in-the-dark-c; Colan-c/a in all 3.00
2-6 2.50
NOTE: *Colan a(p)-1-6; c-1-3, 4p, 5p.* ***Williamson*** *a(i)-2, 4, 5(part).*

CLOAK AND DAGGER
Ziff-Davis Publishing Co.: Fall, 1952
1-Saunders painted-c 28 56 84 165 270 375

CLOAK AND DAGGER (Also see Marvel Fanfare)
Marvel Comics Group: Oct, 1983 - No. 4, Jan, 1984 (Mini-series)
(See Spectacular Spider-Man #64)
1-4-Austin-c/a(i) in all. 4-Origin 3.00

CLOAK AND DAGGER (2nd Series)(Also see Marvel Graphic Novel #34 & Strange Tales)
Marvel Comics Group: July, 1985 - No. 11, Jan, 1987
1-11: 9-Art Adams-p 2.50
...And Power Pack (1990, $7.95, 68 pgs.) 8.00
NOTE: ***Mignola*** *c-7, 8.*

CLOAK AND DAGGER (3rd Series listed as Mutant Misadventures Of...)

CLOBBERIN' TIME
Marvel Comics: Sept, 1995 ($1.95) (Based on card game)
nn-Overpower game guide; Ben Grimm story 2.50

CLOCK MAKER, THE
Image Comics: Jan, 2003 - No. 4, May, 2003 ($2.50, comic unfolds to 10"x13" pages)
1-4-Krueger-s 2.50
... Act Two (4/04, $4.95, standard format) Krueger-s/Matt Smith-c 5.00

CLONEZONE SPECIAL
Dark Horse Comics/First Comics: 1989 ($2.00, B&W)
1-Back-up series from Badger & Nexus 2.50

CLOSE ENCOUNTERS (See Marvel Comics Super Special & Marvel Special Edition)

CLOSE SHAVES OF PAULINE PERIL, THE (TV cartoon)
Gold Key: June, 1970 - No. 4, March, 1971
1 3 6 9 21 32 42
2-4 3 6 9 16 22 28

CLOWN COMICS (No. 1 titled Clown Comic Book)
Clown Comics/Home Comics/Harvey Publ.: 1945 - No. 3, Win, 1946
nn (#1) 13 26 39 74 105 135
2,3 9 18 27 47 61 75

CLOUDBURST
Image Comics: June, 2004 ($7.95, squarebound)
1-Gray & Palmiotti-s/Shy & Gouveia-a 8.00

CLOUDFALL
Image Comics: Nov, 2003 ($4.95, B&W, squarebound)
1-Kirkman-s/Su-a/c 5.00

CLOWNS, THE (I Pagliacci)
Dark Horse Comics: 1998 ($2.95, B&W, one-shot)
1-Adaption of the opera; P. Craig Russell-script 3.00

CLUBHOUSE RASCALS (#1 titled ...Presents?) (Also see Three Rascals)
Sussex Publ. Co. (Magazine Enterprises): June, 1956 - No. 2, Oct, 1956
1-The Brain app. in both; DeCarlo-a 8 16 24 44 57 70
2 7 14 21 35 43 50

CLUB "16"
Famous Funnies: June, 1948 - No. 4, Dec, 1948
1-Teen-age humor 14 28 42 76 108 140
2-4 8 16 24 44 57 70

CLUE COMICS (Real Clue Crime V2#4 on)
Hillman Periodicals: Jan, 1943 - No. 15(V2#3), May, 1947
1-Origin The Boy King, Nightmare, Micro-Face, Twilight, & Zippo
161 322 483 1030 1765 2500
2 (scarce) 82 164 246 521 893 1265
3-5 (9/43) 44 88 132 277 469 660
6,8,9: 8-Palais-c/a(2) 34 68 102 199 325 450
7-Classic concentration camp torture-c (3/44) 68 136 204 435 743 1050
10-Origin/1st app. The Gun Master & begin series; content changes to crime
(10/46) 36 72 108 211 343 475
11 (12/46) 24 48 72 144 237 330
12-Origin Rackman; McWilliams-a, Guardineer-a(2) 30 60 90 177 289 400
V2#1-Nightmare new origin; Iron Lady app.; Simon & Kirby-a (3/47)
53 106 159 334 567 800
V2#2-S&K-a(2)-Bondage/torture-c; man attacks & kills people with electric iron.
Infantino-a 68 136 204 432 746 1060
V2#3-S&K-a(3) 55 110 165 347 586 825

CLUELESS SPRING SPECIAL (TV)
Marvel Comics: May, 1997 ($3.99, magazine sized, one-shot)
1-Photo-c from TV show 4.00

CLUTCHING HAND, THE
American Comics Group: July-Aug, 1954
1 39 78 117 240 395 550

CLYDE BEATTY COMICS (Also see Crackajack Funnies)
Commodore Productions & Artists, Inc.: October, 1953 (84 pgs.)
1-Photo front/back-c; movie scenes and comics 23 46 69 135 218 300

CLYDE CRASHCUP (TV)

Codename: Stryke Force #10 © TCOW

The Coffin #3 © Hester & Huddleston

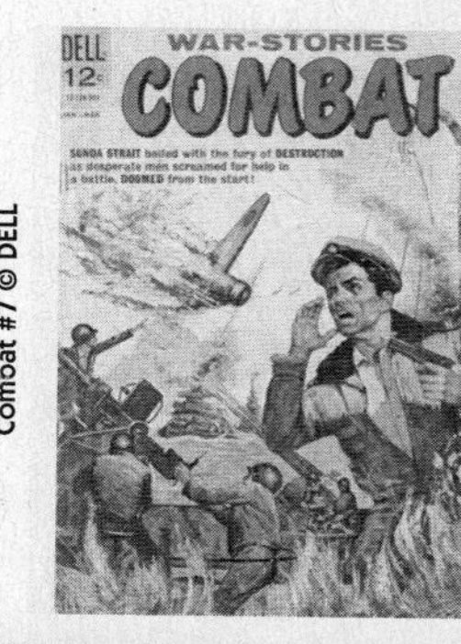

Combat #7 © DELL

	GD 2.0	VG 4.0	FN 6.0	VF 8.0	VF/NM 9.0	NM- 9.2

Dell Publishing Co.: Aug-Oct, 1963 - No. 5, Sept-Nov, 1964

1-All written by John Stanley	9	18	27	63	107	150
2-5	8	16	24	52	86	120

COBALT BLUE (Also see Power Comics)
Innovation Publishing: Sept, 1989 - No. 2, Oct, 1989 ($1.95, 28 pgs.)

1,2-Gustovich-c/a/scripts						2.50
The Graphic Novel ($6.95, color, 52 pgs.)-r/1,2						7.00

COBB
IDW Publishing: May, 2006 - No. 3, July, 2007 ($3.99, B&W)

1-3-Beau Smith-s/Eduardo Barreto-a/c; regular and retailer incentive covers						4.00

CODE NAME: ASSASSIN (See 1st Issue Special)

CODENAME: DANGER
Lodestone Publishing: Aug, 1985 - No. 4, May, 1986 ($1.50)

1-4						2.50

CODENAME: FIREARM (Also see Firearm)
Malibu Comics (Ultraverse): June, 1995 - No. 5, Sept, 1995 ($2.95, bimonthly limited series)

0-5: 0-2-Alec Swan back-up story by James Robinson						3.00

NOTE: *Perez c-0.*

CODENAME: GENETIX
Marvel Comics UK: Jan, 1993 - No. 4, May, 1993 ($1.75, limited series)

1-4: Wolverine in all						3.00

CODENAME: KNOCKOUT
DC Comics (Vertigo): No. 0, Jun, 2001 - No. 23, June, 2003 ($2.50/$2.75)

0-15: Rodi-s in all. 0-6-Small Jr. -a. 1-Two covers by Chiodo & Cho. 7,8,10,11,12-Paquette-a. 9,13,14-Conner-a						2.50
16-23: 16-Begin $2.75-c. 23-Last issue; JG Jones-c						2.75

CODENAME SPITFIRE (Formerly Spitfire And The Troubleshooters)
Marvel Comics Group: No. 10, July, 1987 - No. 13, Oct, 1987

10-13: 10-Rogers-c/a (low printing)						3.50

CODENAME: STRYKE FORCE (Also See Cyberforce V1#4 & Cyberforce/Stryke Force: Opposing Forces
Image Comics (Top Cow Productions): Jan, 1994 - No. 14, Sept, 1995 ($1.95-$2.25)

0,1-14: 1-12-Silvestri stories, Peterson-a. 4-Stormwatch app. 14-Story continues in Cyberforce/Stryke Force: Opposing Forces; Turner-a						2.50
1-Gold, 1-Blue						4.00

CODE NAME: TOMAHAWK
Fantasy General Comics: Sept, 1986 ($1.75, high quality paper)

1-Sci/fi						2.50

CODE OF HONOR
Marvel Comics: Feb, 1997 - No. 4, May, 1997 ($5.95, limited series)

1-4-Fully painted by various; Dixon-s						6.00

CODY OF THE PONY EXPRESS (See Colossal Features Magazine)
Fox Features Syndicate: Sept, 1950 (See Women Outlaws)(One shot)

1-Painted-c	14	28	42	81	118	155

CODY OF THE PONY EXPRESS (Buffalo Bill...) (Outlaws of the West #11 on; Formerly Bullseye)
Charlton Comics: No. 8, Oct, 1955; No. 9, Jan, 1956; No. 10, June, 1956

8-Bullseye on splash pg; not S&K-a	8	16	24	44	57	70
9,10: Buffalo Bill app. in all	6	12	18	29	36	42

CODY STARBUCK (1st app. in Star Reach #1)
Star Reach Productions: July, 1978

nn-Howard Chaykin-c/a	3	6	9	14	20	25
2nd printing	2	4	6	8	10	12

NOTE: *Both printings say First Printing. True first printing is on lower-grade paper, somewhat off-register, and snow in snow sequence has green tint.*

CO-ED ROMANCES
P. L. Publishing Co.: November, 1951

1	9	18	27	47	61	75

COFFEE WORLD
World Comics: Oct, 1995 ($1.50, B&W, anthology)

1-Shannon Wheeler's Too Much Coffee Man story						3.00

COFFIN, THE
Oni Press: Sept, 2000 - No. 4, May, 2001 ($2.95, B&W, limited series)

1-4-Hester-s/Huddleston-a						3.00
TPB (8/01, $11.95, TPB) r/#1-4						12.00

COLLECTORS DRACULA, THE
Millennium Publications: 1994 - No. 2, 1994 ($3.95, color/B&W, 52 pgs., limited series)

1,2-Bolton-a (7 pgs.)						4.00

COLLECTORS ITEM CLASSICS (See Marvel Collectors Item Classics)

COLORS IN BLACK
Dark Horse Comics: Mar, 1995 - No. 4, June, 1995 ($2.95, limited series)

1-4						3.00

COLOSSAL FEATURES MAGAZINE (Formerly I Loved) (See Cody of the Pony Express)
Fox Features Syndicate: No. 33, 5/50 - No. 34, 7/50; No. 3, 9/50 (Based on Columbia serial)

33,34: Cody of the Pony Express begins. 33-Painted-c. 34-Photo-c	14	28	42	80	115	150
3-Authentic criminal cases	14	28	42	80	115	150

COLOSSAL SHOW, THE (TV cartoon)
Gold Key: Oct, 1969

1	5	10	15	32	51	70

COLOSSUS (See X-Men)
Marvel Comics: Oct, 1997 ($2.99, 48 pgs., one-shot)

1-Raab-s/Hitch & Neary-a, wraparound-c						3.00

COLOSSUS COMICS (See Green Giant & Motion Picture Funnies Weekly)
Sun Publications (Funnies, Inc.?): March, 1940

1-(Scarce)-Tulpa of Tsang(hero); Colossus app.	676	1352	2028	4935	8718	12,500

NOTE: *Cover by artist that drew Colossus in Green Giant Comics.*

COLOUR OF MAGIC, THE (Terry Pratchett's...)
Innovation Publishing: 1991 - No. 4, 1991 ($2.50, limited series)

1-4: Adapts 1st novel of the Discworld series						3.00

COLT .45 (TV)
Dell Publishing Co.: No. 924, 8/58 - No. 1058, 11-1/59-60; No. 4, 2-4/60 - No. 9, 5-7/61

Four Color 924(#1)-Wayde Preston photo-c on all	10	20	30	70	123	175
Four Color 1004,1058, #4,5,7-9: 1004-Photo-b/c	8	16	24	56	93	130
6-Toth-a	9	18	27	60	100	140

COLUMBIA COMICS
William H. Wise Co.: 1943

1-Joe Palooka, Charlie Chan, Capt. Yank, Sparky Watts, Dixie Dugan app.	27	54	81	158	259	360

COMANCHE
Dell Publishing Co.: No. 1350, Apr-Jun, 1962

Four Color 1350-Disney movie; reprints FC #966 with title change from "Tonka" to "Comanche"; Sal Mineo photo-c	5	10	15	35	55	75

COMANCHEROS, THE
Dell Publishing Co.: No. 1300, Mar-May, 1962

Four Color 1300-Movie, John Wayne photo-c	14	28	42	101	191	280

COMBAT
Atlas Comics (ANC): June, 1952 - No. 11, April, 1953

1	26	52	78	154	252	350
2-Heath-c/a	15	30	45	85	130	175
3,5-9,11: 3-Romita-a. 6-Robinson-c; Romita-a	12	24	36	67	94	120
4-Krigstein-a	12	24	36	69	97	125
10-B&W and color illos. in **POP**; Sale-a, Forte-a	12	24	36	69	97	125

NOTE: *Combat Casey in 7-11.* ***Heath*** *a-2, 3; c-1, 2, 5, 9.* ***Maneely*** *a-1; c-3, 10.* ***Pakula*** *a-1.* ***Reinman*** *a-1.*

COMBAT
Dell Publishing Co.: Oct-Nov, 1961 - No. 40, Oct, 1973 (No #9)

1	7	14	21	45	73	100
2,3,5	4	8	12	26	41	55
4-John F. Kennedy c/story (P.T. 109)	5	10	15	34	55	75
6,7,8(4-6/63), 8(7-9/63)	4	8	12	24	37	50
10-26: 26-Last 12¢ issue	3	6	9	20	30	40
27-40(reprints #1-14). 30-r/#4	3	6	9	14	19	24

COMBAT CASEY (Formerly War Combat)
Atlas Comics (SAI): No. 6, Jan, 1953 - No. 34, July, 1957

6 (Indicia shows 1/52 in error)	18	36	54	103	162	220
7-R.Q. Sale-a	11	22	33	62	86	110
8-Used in **POP**, pg. 94	10	20	30	56	76	95
9,10,13-19-Violent art by R.Q. Sale; Battle Brady x-over #10						

Combat Kelly and the Deadly Dozen #2 © MAR

Comedy Comics #17 © MAR

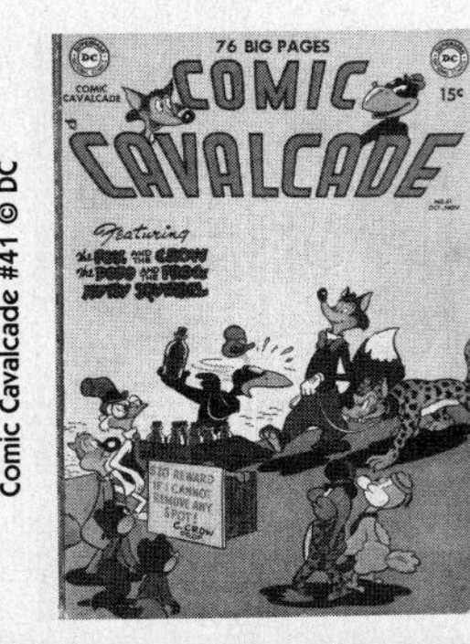

Comic Cavalcade #41 © DC

GD VG FN VF VF/NM NM-
2.0 4.0 6.0 8.0 9.0 9.2

13 26 39 74 105 135
11,12,20-Last Precode (2/55) 9 18 27 52 69 85
21-34: 22,25-R.Q. Sale-a 9 18 27 50 65 80
NOTE: *Everett a-6. Heath c-10, 17, 19, 23, 30. Maneely c-6, 8, 15. Powell a-29(5), 30(5), 34. Severin c-26, 33.*

COMBAT KELLY
Atlas Comics (SPI): Nov, 1951 - No. 44, Aug, 1957

1-1st app. Combat Kelly; Heath-a 31 62 93 182 296 410
2 15 30 45 90 140 190
3-10 14 28 42 76 108 140
11-Used in **POP**, pgs. 94,95 plus color illo. 12 24 36 67 94 120
12-Color illo. in **POP** 12 24 36 67 94 120
13-16 10 20 30 58 79 100
17-Violent art by R. Q. Sale; Combat Casey app. 14 28 42 78 112 145
18-20,22-44: 18-Battle Brady app. 28-Last precode (1/55). 38-Green Berets story (8/56)
10 20 30 54 72 90
21-Transvestism-c 10 20 30 56 76 95
NOTE: *Berg a-8, 12-14, 15-17, 19-23, 25, 26, 28, 31-37, 39, 41-44; c-2. Colan a-42. Heath a-4, 18; c-31. Lawrence a-23. Maneely a-4(2), 6, 7(3), 8; c-4, 5, 7, 8, 10, 25, 29, 39. R.Q. Sale a-17, 25. Severin c-41, 42. Whitney a-5.*

COMBAT KELLY (...and the Deadly Dozen)
Marvel Comics Group: June, 1972 - No. 9, Oct, 1973

1-Intro & origin new Combat Kelly; Ayers/Mooney-a; Severin-c (20¢)
3 6 9 20 30 40
2,5-8 2 4 6 11 16 20
3,4: 3-Origin. 4-Sgt. Fury-c/s 3 6 9 14 19 24
9-Death of the Deadly Dozen 3 6 9 16 23 30

COMBAT ZONE: TRUE TALES OF GIS IN IRAQ
Marvel Comics: 2005 ($19.99, squarebound)

Vol. 1-Karl Zinsmeister scripts adapted from his non-fiction books; Dan Jurgens-a 20.00

COMBINED OPERATIONS (See The Story of the Commandos)

COMEBACK (See Zane Grey 4-Color 357)

COMEDY CARNIVAL
St. John Publishing Co.: no date (1950's) (100 pgs.)

nn-Contains rebound St. John comics 35 70 105 208 339 470

COMEDY COMICS (1st Series) (Daring Mystery #1-8) (Becomes Margie Comics #35 on)
Timely Comics (TCI 9,10): No. 9, April, 1942 - No. 34, Fall, 1946

9-(Scarce)-The Fin by Everett, Capt. Dash, Citizen V, & The Silver Scorpion app.; Wolverton-a; 1st app. Comedy Kid; satire on Hitler & Stalin; The Fin, Citizen V & Silver Scorpion cont. from Daring Mystery 296 592 888 1895 3248 4600
10-(Scarce)-Origin The Fourth Musketeer, Victory Boys; Monstro, the Mighty app.
213 426 639 1363 2332 3300
11-Vagabond, Stuporman app. 53 106 159 334 567 800
12,13 18 36 54 105 165 225
14-Origin/1st app. Super Rabbit (3/43) plus-c 55 110 165 352 601 850
15-19 17 34 51 98 154 210
20-Hitler parody-c 22 44 66 132 216 300
21-Tojo-c 16 32 48 94 147 200
22-Hitler parody-c 20 40 60 114 182 250
23-32 14 28 42 80 115 150
33-Kurtzman-a (5 pgs.) 15 30 45 85 130 175
34-Intro Margie; Wolverton-a (5 pgs.) 23 46 69 136 223 310

COMEDY COMICS (2nd Series)
Marvel Comics (ACI): May, 1948 - No. 10, Jan, 1950

1-Hedy, Tessie, Millie begin; Kurtzman's "Hey Look" (he draws himself)
37 74 111 222 361 500
2 17 34 51 98 154 210
3,4-Kurtzman's "Hey Look" (?&3) 18 36 54 103 162 220
5-10 12 24 36 67 94 120

COMET, THE (See The Mighty Crusaders & Pep Comics #1)
Red Circle Comics (Archie): Oct, 1983 - No. 2, Dec, 1983

1-Re-intro & origin The Comet; The American Shield begins. Nino & Infantino art in both. Hangman in both 6.00
2-Origin continues. 4.50

COMET, THE
DC Comics (Impact Comics): July, 1991 - No. 18, Dec, 1992 ($1.00/$1.25)

1 3.00
2-18: 4-Black Hood app. 6-Re-intro Hangman. 8-Web x-over. 10-Contains Crusaders trading card. 4-Origin. Netzer(Nasser) c(p)-11,14-17 2.50
Annual 1 (1992, $2.50, 68 pgs.)-Contains Impact trading card; Shield back-up story 2.50

GD VG FN VF VF/NM NM-
2.0 4.0 6.0 8.0 9.0 9.2

COMET MAN, THE (Movie)
Marvel Comics Group: Feb, 1987 - No. 6, July, 1987 (limited series)

1-6: 3-Hulk app. 4-She-Hulk shower scene-c/s. Fantastic 4 app. 5-Fantastic 4 app. 2.50
NOTE: *Kelley Jones a-1-6p.*

COMIC ALBUM (Also see Disney Comic Album)
Dell Publishing Co.: Mar-May, 1958 - No. 18, June-Aug, 1962

1-Donald Duck 9 18 27 60 100 140
2-Bugs Bunny 5 10 15 32 51 70
3-Donald Duck 7 14 21 47 76 105
4-6,8-10: 4-Tom & Jerry. 5-Woody Woodpecker. 6,10-Bugs Bunny. 8-Tom & Jerry. 9-Woody Woodpecker 4 8 12 28 44 60
7,11,15: Popeye. 11-(9-11/60) 6 12 18 33 49 65
12-14: 12-Tom & Jerry. 13-Woody Woodpecker. 14-Bugs Bunny
5 10 15 30 48 60
16-Flintstones (12-2/61-62)-3rd app. Early Cave Kids app.
8 16 24 54 90 125
17-Space Mouse (3rd app.) 5 10 15 32 51 70
18-Three Stooges; photo-c 8 16 24 54 90 125

COMIC BOOK
Marvel Comics-#1/Dark Horse Comics-#2: 1995 ($5.95, oversize)

1-Spumco characters by John K. 1 2 3 4 5 7
2-(Dark Horse) 6.00

COMIC CAPERS
Red Circle Mag./Marvel Comics: Fall, 1944 - No. 6, Summer, 1946

1-Super Rabbit, The Creeper, Silly Seal, Ziggy Pig, Sharpy Fox begin
30 60 90 177 289 400
2 16 32 48 94 147 200
3-6 14 28 42 82 121 160

COMIC CAVALCADE
All-American/National Periodical Publications: Winter, 1942-43 - No. 63, June-July, 1954
(Contents change with No. 30, Dec-Jan, 1948-49 on)

1-The Flash, Green Lantern, Wonder Woman, Wildcat, The Black Pirate by Moldoff (also #2), Ghost Patrol, and Red White & Blue begin; Scribbly app.; Minute Movie
865 1730 2595 6315 11,158 16,000
2-Mutt & Jeff begin; last Ghost Patrol & Black Pirate; Minute Movies
245 490 735 1568 2684 3800
3-Hop Harrigan & Sargon, the Sorcerer begin; The King app.
161 322 483 1030 1765 2500
4,5: 4-The Gay Ghost, The King, Scribbly, & Red Tornado app. 5-Christmas-c. 5-Prints ad for Jr. JSA membership kit that includes "The Minute Man Answers The Call"
145 290 435 921 1586 2250
6-10: 7-Red Tornado & Black Pirate app.; last Scribbly. 9-Fat & Slat app.; X-Mas-c
116 232 348 742 1271 1800
11,12,14: 12-Last Red White & Blue 97 194 291 621 1061 1500
13-Solomon Grundy app.; X-Mas-c 168 336 504 1075 1838 2600
15-Just a Story begins 98 196 294 622 1074 1525
16-20: 19-Christmas-c 90 180 270 576 988 1400
21-23: 22-Johnny Peril begins. 23-Harry Lampert-c (Toth swipes)
86 172 258 546 936 1325
24-Solomon Grundy x-over in Green Lantern 115 230 345 730 1253 1775
25-28: 25-Black Canary app.; X-Mas-c. 26-28-Johnny Peril app. 28-Last Mutt & Jeff
76 152 228 486 831 1175
29-(10-11/48)-Last Flash, Wonder Woman, Green Lantern & Johnny Peril; Wonder Woman invents "Thinking Machine"; 2nd computer in comics (after Flash Comics #52); Leave It to Binky story (early app.) 87 174 261 552 951 1350
30-(12-1/48-49)-The Fox & the Crow, Dodo & the Frog & Nutsy Squirrel begin
41 82 123 256 428 600
31-35 23 46 69 136 223 310
36-49: 41-Last squarebound issue 17 34 51 100 158 215
50-62(Scarce) 21 42 63 122 199 275
63(Rare) 34 68 102 204 332 460
NOTE: *Grossman a-30-63. E.E. Hibbard c-(Flash only)-1-4, 7-14, 16-19, 21. Sheldon Mayer a(2-3)-40-63. Moulson c(G.L.)-7, 15. Nodell c(G.L.)-9. H.G. Peter c(W. Woman only)-1, 3-21, 24. Post a-31, 36. Purcell c(G.L.)-2-5, 10. Reinman a(Green Lantern)-4-6, 8, 9, 13, 15-21; c(Gr. Lantern)-6, 8, 19. Toth a(Green Lantern)-26-28; c-27. Atom app.-22, 23.*

COMIC COMICS
Fawcett Publications: Apr, 1946 - No. 10, Feb, 1947

1-Captain Kid; Nutty Comics #1 in indicia 15 30 45 83 124 165
2-10-Wolverton-a, 4 pgs. each. 5-Captain Kidd app. Mystic Moot by Wolverton in #2-10? 15 30 45 84 127 170

The Comics #8 © DELL

Comics Greatest World V4 #3 King Tiger © DH

Comics on Parade #57 © UFS

GD VG FN VF VF/NM NM-
2.0 4.0 6.0 8.0 9.0 9.2

COMIC LAND
Fact and Fiction Publ.: March, 1946
1-Sandusky & the Senator, Sam Stupor, Sleuth, Marvin the Great, Sir Passer, Phineas Gruff app.; Irv Tirman & Perry Williams art 15 30 45 84 127 170

COMICO CHRISTMAS SPECIAL
Comico: Dec, 1988 ($2.50, 44pgs.)
1-Rude/Williamson-a; Dave Stevens-c 4.00

COMICO COLLECTION (Also see Grendel)
Comico: 1987 ($9.95, slipcased collection)
nn-Contains exclusive Grendel: Devil's Vagary, 9 random Comico comics, a poster and newsletter in black slipcase w/silver ink 25.00

COMICO PRIMER (See Primer)

COMIC PAGES (Formerly Funny Picture Stories)
Centaur Publications: V3#4, July, 1939 - V3#6, Dec, 1939
V3#4-Bob Wood-a 53 106 159 334 567 800
5,6: 6-Schwab-c 43 86 129 271 461 650

COMICS (See All Good)

COMICS, THE
Dell Publ. Co.: Mar, 1937 - No. 11, Nov, 1938 (Newspaper strip-r; bi-monthly)
1-1st app. Tom Mix in comics; Wash Tubbs, Tom Beatty, Myra North, Arizona Kid, Erik Noble & International Spy w/Doctor Doom begin 187 374 561 1197 2049 2900
2 82 164 246 528 902 1275
3-11: 3-Alley Oop begins 66 132 198 419 722 1025

COMICS AND STORIES (See Walt Disney's Comics and Stories)

COMICS & STORIES (Also see Wolf & Red)
Dark Horse Comics: Apr, 1996 - No. 4, July, 1996 ($2.95, lim. series) (Created by Tex Avery)
1-4: Wolf & Red app; reads Comics and Stories on-c. 1-Terry Moore-a. 2-Reed Waller-a 3.00

COMICS CALENDAR, THE (The 1946...)
True Comics Press (ordered through the mail): 1946 (25¢, 116 pgs.) (Stapled at top)
nn-(Rare) Has a "strip" story for every day of the year in color
39 78 117 240 395 550

COMICS DIGEST (Pocket size)
Parents' Magazine Institute: Winter, 1942-43 (B&W, 100 pgs)
1-Reprints from True Comics (non-fiction World War II stories)
10 20 30 54 72 90

COMICS EXPRESS
Eclipse Comics: Nov, 1989 - No. 2, Jan, 1990 ($2.95, B&W, 68pgs.)
1,2: Collection of strip-r; 2(12/89-c, 1/90 inside) 3.00

COMICS FOR KIDS
London Publ. Co./Timely: 1945 (no month); No. 2, Sum, 1945 (Funny animal)
1,2-Puffy Pig, Sharpy Fox 18 36 54 103 162 220

COMICS' GREATEST WORLD
Dark Horse Comics: Jun, 1993 - V4#4, Sept, 1993 ($1.00, weekly, lim. series)
Arcadia (Wk 1): V1#1,2,4: 1-X: Frank Miller-c. 2-Pit Bulls. 4-Monster. 2.50
1-B&W Press Proof Edition (1500 copies) 1 3 4 6 8 10
1-Silver-c; distr. retailer bonus w/print & cards 1 2 3 5 6 8
3-Ghost, Dorman-c; Hughes-a 4.00
Retailer's Prem. Emb. Silver Foil Logo-r/V1#1-4 1 3 4 6 8 10
Golden City (Wk 2: V2#1-4: 1-Rebel; Ordway-c. 2-Mecha; Dave Johnson-c.
3-Titan; Walt Simonson-c. 4-Catalyst; Perez-c. 2.50
1-Gold-c; distr. retailer bonus w/print & cards. 6.00
Retailer's Prem. Embos. Gold Foil Logo-r/V2#1-4 1 2 3 5 6 8
Steel Harbor (Week 3): V3#1-Barb Wire; Dorman-c; Gulacy-a(p) 4.00
2-4: 2-The Machine. 3-Wolfgang. 4-Motorhead 2.50
1-Silver-c; distr. retailer bonus w/print & cards 1 2 3 5 6 8
Retailer's Prem. Emb. Red Foil Logo-r/V3#1-4. 1 3 4 6 8 10
Vortex (Week 4): V4#1-4: 1-Division 13; Dorman-c. 2-Hero Zero; Art Adams-c.
3-King Tiger; Chadwick-a(p); Darrow-c. 4-Vortex; Miller-c. 2.50
1-Gold-c; distr. retailer bonus w/print & cards. 6.00
Retailer's Prem. Emb. Blue Foil Logo-r/V4#1-4. 1 2 3 5 6 8

COMICS' GREATEST WORLD: OUT OF THE VORTEX (See Out of The Vortex)

COMICS HITS (See Harvey Comics Hits)

COMICS MAGAZINE, THE (...Funny Pages #3)(Funny Pages #6 on)
Comics Magazine Co. (1st Comics Mag./Centaur Publ.): May, 1936 - No. 5, Sept, 1936 (Paper covers)
1-1st app. Dr. Mystic (a.k.a. Dr. Occult) by Siegel & Shuster (the 1st app. of a Superman prototype in comics). Dr. Mystic is not in costume but later appears in costume as a more pronounced prototype in More Fun #14-17. (1st episode of "The Koth and the Seven"; continues in More Fun #14; originally scheduled for publication at DC). 1 pg. Kelly-a; Sheldon Mayer-a 3167 6334 9500 19,000 - -
2-Federal Agent (a.k.a. Federal Men) by Siegel & Shuster; 1 pg. Kelly-a
360 720 1080 2160 2880 3600
3-5 310 620 930 1860 2480 3100

COMICS NOVEL (Anarcho, Dictator of Death)
Fawcett Publications: 1947
1-All Radar; 51 pg anti-fascism story 32 64 96 188 307 425

COMICS ON PARADE (No. 30 on are a continuation of Single Series)
United Features Syndicate: Apr, 1938 - No. 104, Feb, 1955
1-Tarzan by Foster; Captain & the Kids, Little Mary Mixup, Abbie & Slats, Ella Cinders, Broncho Bill, Li'l Abner begin 360 720 1080 2520 4410 6300
2 (Tarzan & others app. on-c of #1-3,17) 127 254 381 806 1391 1975
3 97 194 291 621 1061 1500
4,5 76 152 228 486 831 1175
6-10 53 106 159 334 567 800
11-16,18-20 42 84 126 265 445 625
17-Tarzan-c 49 98 147 309 522 735
21-29: 22-Son of Tarzan begins. 22,24,28-Tailspin Tommy-c. 29-Last Tarzan issue
36 72 108 216 351 485
30-Li'l Abner 20 40 60 114 182 250
31-The Captain & the Kids 15 30 45 85 130 175
32-Nancy & Fritzi Ritz 14 28 42 78 112 145
33,36,39,42-Li'l Abner 16 32 48 94 147 200
34,37,40-The Captain & the Kids (10/41,6/42,3/43) 15 30 45 83 124 165
35,38-Nancy & Fritzi Ritz. 38-Infinity-c 14 28 42 76 108 140
41-Nancy & Fritzi Ritz 11 22 33 60 83 105
43-The Captain & the Kids 15 30 45 83 124 165
44 (3/44),47,50: Nancy & Fritzi Ritz 11 22 33 60 83 105
45-Li'l Abner 15 30 45 84 127 170
46,49-The Captain & the Kids 13 26 39 74 105 135
48-Li'l Abner (3/45) 15 30 45 84 127 170
51,54-Li'l Abner 14 28 42 76 108 140
52-The Captain & the Kids (3/46) 10 20 30 56 76 95
53,55,57-Nancy & Fritzi Ritz 10 20 30 56 76 95
56-The Captain & the Kids (r/Sparkler) 10 20 30 56 76 95
58-Li'l Abner; continues as Li'l Abner #61? 14 28 42 76 108 140
59-The Captain & the Kids 9 18 27 47 61 75
60-70-Nancy & Fritzi Ritz 8 16 24 44 57 70
71-99,101-104-Nancy & Sluggo: 71-76-Nancy only 8 16 24 42 54 65
100-Nancy & Sluggo 14 28 42 76 108 140
Special Issue, 7/46; Summer, 1948 - The Captain & the Kids app.
12 24 36 69 97 125
NOTE: Bound Volume (Very Rare) includes No. 1-12; bound by publisher in pictorial comic boards & distributed at the 1939 World's Fair and through mail order from ads in comic books (also see Tip Top)
284 568 852 1818 3109 4400
NOTE: *Li'l Abner reprinted from Tip Top.*

COMICS READING LIBRARIES (See the Promotional Comics section)

COMICS REVUE
St. John Publ. Co. (United Features Synd.): June, 1947 - No. 5, Jan, 1948
1-Ella Cinders & Blackie 11 22 33 64 90 115
2,4: 2-Hap Hopper (7/47). 4-Ella Cinders (9/47) 9 18 27 47 61 75
3,5: 3-Iron Vic (8/47). 5-Gordo No. 1 (1/48) 8 16 24 44 57 70

COMIC STORY PAINT BOOK
Samuel Lowe Co.: 1943 (Large size, 68 pgs.)
1055-Captain Marvel & a Captain Marvel Jr. story to read & color; 3 panels in color per pg. (reprints) 76 152 228 486 831 1175

COMIX BOOK
Marvel Comics Group/Krupp Comics Works No. 4,5: 1974 - No. 5, 1976 ($1.00, B&W, magazine) (#1-3 newsstand; #4,5 were direct distribution only)
1-Underground comic artists; 2 pgs. Wolverton-a 3 6 9 16 22 28
2,3: 2-Wolverton-a (1 pg.) 3 6 9 14 19 24
4(2/76), 4(5/76), 5 (Low distribution) 3 6 9 16 23 30
NOTE: *Print run No. 1-3: 200-250M; No. 4&5: 10M each.*

COMIX INTERNATIONAL
Warren Magazines: Jul, 1974 - No. 5, Spring, 1977 (Full color, stiff-c, mail only)
1-Low distribution; all Corben story remainders from Warren; Corben-c on all
9 18 27 63 107 150

Complete Dracula #1 © Savage Tales

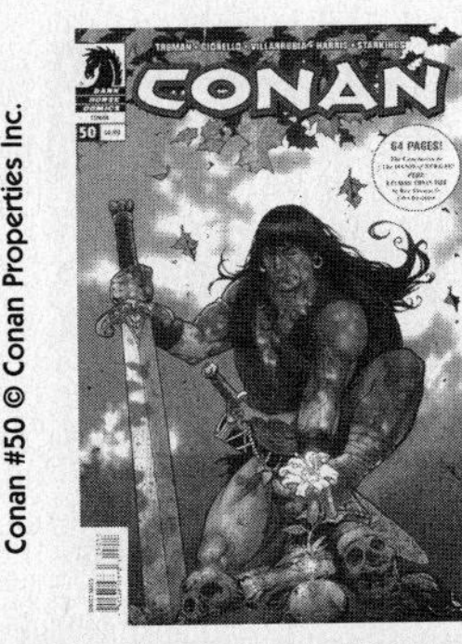

Conan #50 © Conan Properties Inc.

Conan and the Demons of Khitai #3 © Conan Properties Inc.

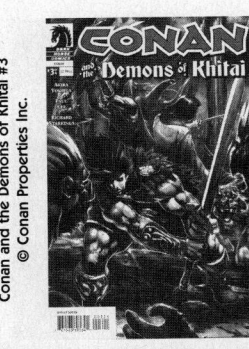

GD 2.0 | VG 4.0 | FN 6.0 | VF 8.0 | VF/NM 9.0 | NM- 9.2

2,4: 2-Two Dracula stories; Wood, Wrightson-r; Crandall-a; Maroto-a.
4-Printing w/ 3 Corben sty 5 10 15 34 55 75

3-5: 3-Dax story. 4-(printing without Corben story). 4-Crandall-a. 4,5-Vampirella stories.
5-Spirit story; Eisner-a 4 8 12 28 44 60

NOTE: *No. 4 had two printings with extra* **Corben** *story in one. No. 3 may also have a variation. No. 3 has two Jeff Jones reprints from Vampirella.*

COMMANDER BATTLE AND THE ATOMIC SUB
Amer. Comics Group (Titan Publ. Co.): Jul-Aug, 1954 - No. 7, Aug-Sep, 1955

1 (3-D effect)-Moldoff flying saucer-c 47 94 141 296 498 700

2,4-7: 2-Moldoff-c. 4-(1-2/55)-Last pre-code; Landau-a. 5-3-D effect story (2 pgs.). 6,7-Landau-a. 7-Flying saucer-c 31 62 93 182 296 410

3-H-Bomb-c; Atomic Sub becomes Atomic Spaceship 32 64 96 188 307 425

COMMANDO ADVENTURES
Atlas Comics (MMC): June, 1957 - No. 2, Aug, 1957

1-Severin-c 14 28 42 76 108 140

2-Severin-c; Drucker-a? 10 20 30 54 72 90

COMMANDOS
DC Comics: Oct. 1942

1-Ashcan comic, not distributed to newsstands, only for in-house use. Cover art is Boy Commandos #1 with interior being a Boy Commandos story from an unidentified issue of Detective Comics (no known sales)

COMMANDO YANK (See The Mighty Midget Comics & Wow Comics)

COMMON GROUNDS
Image Comics (Top Cow): Feb, 2004 - No. 6, July, 2004 ($2.99)

1-6: 1-Two covers; art by Jurgens and Oeming. 3-Bachalo, Jurgens-a. 4-Peréz-a 3.00

...: Baker's Dozen TPB (12/04, $14.99) r/#1-6; cover gallery; Holey Crullers pages 15.00

COMPLETE ALICE IN WONDERLAND (Adaptation of Carroll's original story)
Dynamite Entertainment: 2009 - Present ($4.99, limited series)

1-Leah Moore & John Reppion-s/Erica Awano-a/John Cassaday-c 5.00

COMPLETE BOOK OF COMICS AND FUNNIES
William H. Wise & Co.: 1944 (25¢, one-shot, 196 pgs.)

1-Origin Brad Spencer, Wonderman; The Magnet, The Silver Knight by Kinstler, & Zudo the Jungle Boy app. 43 86 129 271 461 650

COMPLETE BOOK OF TRUE CRIME COMICS
William H. Wise & Co.: No date (Mid 1940's) (25¢, 132 pgs.)

nn-Contains Crime Does Not Pay rebound (includes #22) 129 258 387 826 1413 2000

COMPLETE COMICS (Formerly Amazing Comics No. 1)
Timely Comics (EPC): No. 2, Winter, 1944-45

2-The Destroyer, The Whizzer, The Young Allies & Sergeant Dix; Schomburg-c 165 330 495 1048 1799 2550

COMPLETE DRACULA (Adaptation of Stoker's original story)
Dynamite Entertainment: 2009 - No. 5, 2009 ($4.99, limited series)

1-5-Leah Moore & John Reppion-s/Colton Worley-a/John Cassaday-c 5.00

COMPLETE FRANK MILLER BATMAN, THE
Longmeadow Press: 1989 ($29.95, hardcover, silver gilded pages)

HC-Reprints Batman: Year One, Wanted: Santa Claus--Dead or Alive, and The Dark Knight Returns 30.00

COMPLETE GUIDE TO THE DEADLY ARTS OF KUNG FU AND KARATE
Marvel Comics: 1974 (68 pgs., B&W magazine)

V1#1-Bruce Lee-c and 5 pg. story (scarce) 6 12 18 41 66 90

COMPLETE LOVE MAGAZINE (Formerly a pulp with same title)
Ace Periodicals (Periodical House): V26#2, May-June, 1951 - V32#4(#191), Sept, 1956

	GD	VG	FN	VF	VF/NM	NM-
V26#2-Painted-c (52 pgs.)	11	22	33	60	83	105
V26#3-6(2/52), V27#1(4/52)-6(1/53)	9	18	27	47	61	75
V28#1(3/53), V28#2(5/53), V29#3(7/53)-6(12/53)	8	16	24	44	57	70
V30#1(2/54), V30#1(#176, 4/54),2,4-6(#181, 1/55)	8	16	24	44	57	70
V30#3(#178)-Rock Hudson photo-c	9	18	27	47	61	75
V31#1(#182, 3/55)-Last precode	8	16	24	42	54	65
V31#2(5/55)-6(#187, 1/56)	8	16	24	40	50	60
V32#1(#188, 3/56)-4(#191, 9/56)	8	16	24	40	50	60

NOTE: *(34 total issues). Photo-c V27#5-on. Painted-c V26#3.*

COMPLETE MYSTERY (True Complete Mystery No. 5 on)
Marvel Comics (PrPI): Aug, 1948 - No. 4, Feb, 1949 (Full length stories)

1-Seven Dead Men 45 90 135 284 480 675

2-4: 2-Jigsaw of Doom!; Shores-a. 3-Fear in the Night; Burgos-c/a (28 pgs.).
4-A Squealer Dies Fast 39 78 117 231 378 525

COMPLETE ROMANCE
Avon Periodicals: 1949

1-(Scarce)-Reprinted as Women to Love 40 80 120 246 411 575

CONAN (See Chamber of Darkness #4, Giant-Size..., Handbook of..., King Conan, Marvel Graphic Novel #19, 28, Marvel Treasury Ed., Power Record Comics, Robert E. Howard's.., Savage Sword of Conan, and Savage Tales)

CONAN
Dark Horse Comics: Feb, 2004 - No. 50, May, 2008 ($2.99)

0-(11/03, 25¢-c) Busiek-s/Nord-a 2.25
1-($2.99) Linsner-c/Busiek-s/Nord-a 5.00
1-(2nd printing) J. Scott Campell-c 3.00
1-(3rd printing) Nord-c 3.00
2-49: 18-Severin & Timm-a. 22-Kaluta-a (6 pgs.) 24-Harris-c. 29-31-Mignola-s 3.00
24-Variant-c with nude woman (also see Conan and the Demons of Khitai #3 for ad) 20.00
50-($4.99) Harris-c; new story and reprint from Conan the Barbarian #30 5.00
... and the Daughters of Midora (10/04, $4.99) Texiera-a/c 5.00
...: Born on the Battlefield TPB (6/08, $17.95) r/#0,8,15,23,32,45,46; Ruth sketch pages 18.00
...: The Blood-Stained Crown and Other Stories TPB (1/08, $14.95) r/#18,26-28,39 15.00
...: The Frazetta Cover Series (12/07 - No. 8, $3.50) 1,2-Reprints with Frazetta covers 3.50
...: The Weight of the Crown (1/10, $3.50) Darick Robertson-s/a; 2 covers by Robertson 3.50
HC Vol. 1: The Frost Giant's Daughter and Other Stories (2005, $24.95) r/#1-6, partial #7; signed by Busiek; Nord sketch pages 25.00
Vol. 1: The Frost Giant's Daughter and Other Stories (2005, $15.95) r/#1-6, partial #7 16.00
Vol. 2: The God in the Bowl and Other Stories HC (2005, $24.95) r/#9-14 25.00
Vol. 2: The God in the Bowl and Other Stories SC (2006, $15.95) r/#9-14 16.00
Vol. 3: The Tower of the Elephant and Other Stories HC (5/06, $24.95) r/#0,16,17,19-22 25.00
Vol. 3: The Tower of the Elephant and Other Stories SC (6/06, $15.95) r/#0,16,17,19-22 16.00
Vol. 4: The Hall of the Dead and Other Stories HC (5/07, $24.95) r/#0,24,25,29-31,33,34 25.00
Vol. 4: The Hall of the Dead and Other Stories SC (6/07, $17.95) r/#0,24,25,29-31,33,34 18.00
Vol. 5: Rogues in the House and Other Stories SC (3/08, $17.95) r/#0,37,38,41-44 18.00
Vol. 6: The Hand of Nergal HC (10/08, $24.95) r/#0,47-50; sketch pages 25.00

CONAN AND THE DEMONS OF KHITAI
Dark Horse Comics: Oct, 2005 - No. 4, Jan, 2006 ($2.99, limited series)

1,2,4-Paul Lee-a/Akira Yoshida-s/Pat Lee-c 3.00
3-1st printing with red cover logo; letters page has image of Conan #24 nude variant-c 5.00
3-2nd printing with black cover logo; letters page has image of Conan #24 regular-c 3.00
TPB (7/06, $12.95) r/series 13.00

CONAN AND THE JEWELS OF GWAHLUR
Dark Horse Comics: Apr, 2005 - No. 3, June, 2005 ($2.99, limited series)

1-3-P. Craig Russell-s/a/c 3.00
HC (12/05, $13.95) r/series; P. Craig Russell interview and sketch pages 14.00

CONAN AND THE MIDNIGHT GOD
Dark Horse Comics: Dec, 2006 - No. 5, May, 2007 ($2.99, limited series)

1-5-Dysart-s/Conrad-a/Alexander-c 3.00
TPB (10/07, $14.95) r/#1-5 and Age of Conan: Hyborian Adventures one-shot 15.00

CONAN AND THE SONGS OF THE DEAD
Dark Horse Comics: July, 2006 - No. 5, Nov, 2006 ($2.99, limited series)

1-5-Timothy Truman-a/c; Joe Lansdale-s 3.00
TPB (4/07, $14.95) r/series; Truman sketch pages 15.00

CONAN: (Title Series): Marvel Comics

CONAN, 8/95 - No. 11, 6/96 ($2.95), 1-11: 4-Malibu Comic's Rune app. 3.00

...CLASSIC, 6/94 - No. 11, 4/95 ($1.50), 1-11: 1-r/Conan #1 by B. Smith, r/covers w/changes. 2-11-r/Conan #2-11 by Smith. 2-Bound w/cover to Conan The Adventurer #2 by mistake 2.50

...DEATH COVERED IN GOLD, 9/99 - No. 3, 11/99 ($2.99), 1-3-Roy Thomas-s/ John Buscema-a 3.00

...FLAME AND THE FIEND, 8/00 - No. 3, 10/00 ($2.99), 1-3-Thomas-s 3.00

...RETURN OF STYRM, 9/98 - No. 3, 11/98 ($2.99), 1-3-Parente & Soresina-a; painted-c 3.00

...RIVER OF BLOOD, 6/98 - No. 3, 8/98 ($2.50), 1-3 2.50

...SCARLET SWORD, 12/98 - No. 3, 2/99 ($2.99), 1-3-Thomas-s/Raffaele-a 3.00

CONAN SAGA, THE
Marvel Comics: June, 1987 - No. 97, Apr, 1995 ($2.00/$2.25, B&W, magazine)

1-Barry Smith-r; new Smith-c 1 2 3 5 6 8
2-27: 2-9,11-new Barry Smith-c. 13,15-Boris-c. 17-Adams-r.18,25-Chaykin-r. 22-r/Giant-Size Conan 1,2 4.00

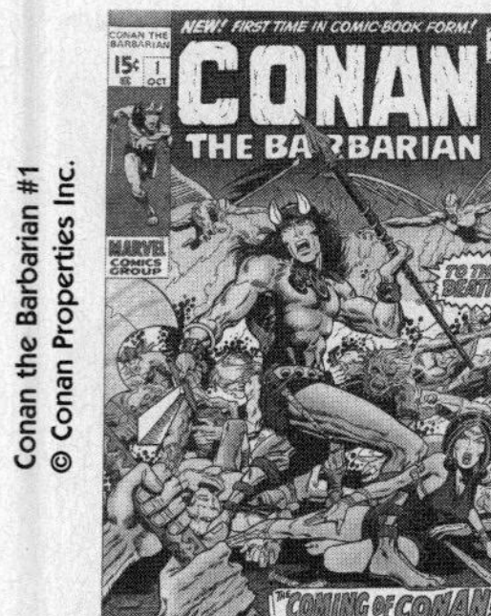

Conan the Barbarian #1
© Conan Properties Inc.

Conan the Barbarian #241
© Conan Properties Inc.

Conan the Cimmerian #16
© Conan Properties Inc.

	GD 2.0	VG 4.0	FN 6.0	VF 8.0	VF/NM 9.0	NM- 9.2
28-90: 28-Begin $2.25-c. 31-Red Sonja-r by N. Adams/SSOC #1; 1 pg. Jeff Jones-r. 32-Newspaper strip-r begin by Buscema. 33-Smith/Conrad-a. 39-r/Kull #1('71) by Andru & Wood. 44-Swipes-c/Savage Tales #1. 57-Brunner-r/SSOC #30. 66-r/Conan Annual #2 by Buscema. 79-r/Conan #43-45 w/Red Sonja. 85-Based on Conan #57-63						3.00
91-96						4.50
97-Last issue	1	2	3	4	5	7

NOTE: ***J. Buscema*** *r-32-on; c-86.* ***Chaykin*** *r-34.* ***Chiodo*** *painted c-63, 65, 66, 82.* ***G. Colan*** *a-47p.* ***Jusko*** *painted c-64, 83.* ***Kaluta*** *c-84.* ***Nino*** *a-37.* ***Ploog*** *a-50.* ***N. Redondo*** *painted c-48, 50, 51, 53, 57, 62.* ***Simonson*** *r-50-54, 56.* ***B. Smith*** *r-51.* ***Starlin*** *c-34.* ***Williamson*** *r-50i.*

CONAN THE ADVENTURER
Marvel Comics: June, 1994 - No. 14, July, 1995 ($1.50)

	GD	VG	FN	VF	VF/NM	NM-
1-($2.50)-Embossed foil-c; Kayaran-a						3.00
2-14						2.50
2-Contents are Conan Classics #2 by mistake						2.50

CONAN THE BARBARIAN
Marvel Comics: Oct, 1970 - No. 275, Dec, 1993

	GD	VG	FN	VF	VF/NM	NM-
1-Origin/1st app. Conan (in comics) by Barry Smith; 1st brief app. Kull; #1-9 are 15¢ issues	21	42	63	148	287	425
2	9	18	27	63	107	150
3-(Low distribution in some areas)	14	28	42	97	181	265
4,5	8	16	24	54	90	125
6-9: 8-Hidden panel message, pg. 14. 9-Last 15¢-c	6	12	18	41	66	90
10,11 (25¢ 52 pg. giants): 10-Black Knight-r; Kull story by Severin	7	14	21	49	80	110
12,13: 12-Wrightson-c(i)	6	12	18	37	59	80
14,15-Elric app.	6	12	18	43	69	95
16,19,20: 16-Conan-r/Savage Tales #1	5	10	15	34	55	75
17,18-No Barry Smith-a	4	8	12	26	41	55
21,22: 22-Has reprint from #1	4	8	12	28	44	60
23-1st app. Red Sonja (2/73)	6	12	18	41	66	90
24-1st full Red Sonja story; last Smith-a	6	12	18	39	62	85
25-John Buscema-c/a begins	3	6	9	16	23	30
26-30	2	4	6	13	18	22
31-36,38-40	2	4	6	9	12	15
37-Neal Adams-c/a; last 20¢ issue; contains pull-out subscription form	3	6	9	17	25	32
41-43,46-50: 48-Origin retold	2	4	6	8	10	12
44,45-N. Adams-i(Crusty Bunkers). 45-Adams-c	2	4	6	9	12	15
51-57,59,60: 59-Origin Belit	1	2	3	5	6	8
58-2nd Belit app. (see Giant-Size Conan #1)	2	4	6	8	11	14
61-65-(Regular 25¢ editions)(4-8/76)	1	2	3	4	5	7
61-65-(30¢-c variants, limited distribution)	5	10	15	32	51	70
66-99: 68-Red Sonja story cont'd from Marvel Feature #7. 75-79-(Reg. 30¢-c). 84-Intro. Zula. 85-Origin Zula. 87-r/Savage Sword of Conan #3 in color						6.00
75-79-(35¢-c variants, limited distribution)	4	8	12	28	44	60
100-(52 pg. Giant)-Death of Belit	1	2	3	5	7	9
101-114						3.50
115-Double size						4.50
116-199,201-231,233-249: 116-r/Power Record Comic PR31. 244-Zula returns						3.50
200,232: 200-(52 pgs.). 232-Young Conan storyline begins; Conan is born						5.00
250-(60 pgs.)						5.00
251-270: 262-Adapted from R.E. Howard story						4.00
271-274						6.00
275-($2.50, 68 pgs.)-Final issue; painted-c (low print)	2	4	6	11	16	20
King Size 1(1973, 35¢)-Smith-r/#2,4; Smith-c	3	6	9	18	27	35
Annual 2(1976, 50¢)-New full length story	2	4	6	9	13	16
Annual 3,4: 3('78)-Chaykin/N. Adams-r/SSOC #2. 4('78)-New full length story	2	4	6	8	10	12
Annual 5,6: 5(1979)-New full length Buscema story & part-c, 6(1981)-Kane-c/a						6.00
Annual 7-12: 7('82)-Based on novel "Conan of the Isles" (new-a). 8(1984). 9(1984). 10(1986). 11(1986). 12(1987)						4.00
Special Edition 1 (Red Nails)						4.00
The Chronicles of Conan Vol. 1: Tower of the Elephant and Other Stories (Dark Horse, 2003, $15.95) r/#1-8; afterword by Roy Thomas						16.00
The Chronicles of Conan Vol. 2: Rogues in the House and Other Stories (Dark Horse, 2003, $15.95) r/#9-13,16; afterword by Roy Thomas						16.00
The Chronicles of Conan Vol. 3: The Monster of the Monoliths and Other Stories (Dark Horse, 2003, $15.95) r/#14,15,17-21; afterword by Roy Thomas						16.00
The Chronicles of Conan Vol. 4: The Song of Red Sonja and Other Stories (Dark Horse, 2004, $15.95) r/#23-26 & "Red Nails" from Savage Tales; afterword by Roy Thomas						16.00
The Chronicles of Conan Vol. 5: The Shadow in the Tomb and Other Stories (Dark Horse, 2004, $15.95) r/#27-34; afterword by Roy Thomas						16.00
The Chronicles of Conan Vol. 6: The Curse of the Skull and Other Stories (Dark Horse, 2004, $15.95) r/#35-42; afterword by Roy Thomas						16.00
The Chronicles of Conan Vol. 7: The Dweller in the Pool and Other Stories (Dark Horse, 2005, $15.95) r/#43-51; afterword by Roy Thomas						16.00
The Chronicles of Conan Vol. 8: Brothers of the Blade and Other Stories (Dark Horse, 2005, $16.95) r/#52-59; afterword by Roy Thomas						17.00
The Chronicles of Conan Vol. 9: Riders of the River-Dragons and Other Stories (Dark Horse, 11/05, $16.95) r/#60-63,65,69-71; afterword by Roy Thomas						17.00
The Chronicles of Conan Vol. 10: When Giants Walk the Earth and Other Stories (Dark Horse, 3/06, $16.95) r/#72-77,79-82; afterword by Roy Thomas						17.00
The Chronicles of Conan Vol. 11: The Dance of the Skull and Other Stories (Dark Horse, 2/07, $16.95) r/#82-86,88-90; afterword by Roy Thomas						17.00
The Chronicles of Conan Vol. 12: The King Beast of Abombi and Other Stories (Dark Horse, 7/07, $16.95) r/#91,93-100; afterword by Roy Thomas						17.00
The Chronicles of Conan Vol. 13: Whispering Shadows and Other Stories (Dark Horse, 12/07, $16.95) r/#92,100-107; afterword by Roy Thomas						17.00
The Chronicles of Conan Vol. 14: Shadow of the Beast and Other Stories (Dark Horse, 3/08, $16.95) r/#92,108-115; afterword by Roy Thomas						17.00
The Chronicles of Conan Vol. 15: The Corridor of Mullah-Kajar and Other Stories (Dark Horse, 7/08, $16.95) r/#116-121 & Annual #2; afterword by Roy Thomas						17.00

NOTE: ***Arthur Adams*** *c-248, 249.* ***Neal Adams*** *a-116r(i); c-49i.* ***Austin*** *a-125, 126; c-125i, 126i.* ***Brunner*** *c-17i. c-40.* ***Buscema*** *a-25-36p, 38, 39, 41-56p, 58-63p, 65-67p, 68, 70-78p, 84-86p, 88-91p, 93-126p, 136p, 140, 141-144p, 146-158p, 159, 161, 162, 163p, 165-185p, 187-190p, Annual 2(3pgs.). 3-5p, 7p; c(p)-26, 36, 44, 46, 52, 56, 58, 59, 64, 65, 72, 78-80, 83-91, 93-103, 105-126, 136-151, 155-159, 161, 162, 168, 169, 171, 172, 174, 175, 178-185, 188, 189, Annual 4, 5, 7.* ***Chaykin*** *a-79-83.* ***Golden*** *c-152.* ***Kaluta*** *c-167.* ***Gil Kane*** *a-12p, 17p, 18p, 127-130, 131-134p; c-12p, 17p, 18p, 23, 25, 27-32, 34, 35, 38, 39, 41-43, 45-51, 53-55, 57, 60-63, 65-71, 73p, 76p, 127-134.* ***Jim Lee*** *c-242.* ***McFarlane*** *c-241p.* ***Ploog*** *a-57.* ***Russell*** *a-21; c-251i.* ***Simonson*** *c-135.* ***B. Smith*** *a-1-11p, 12, 13-15p, 16, 19-21, 23, 24; c-1-11, 13-16, 19-24p.* ***Starlin*** *a-64.* ***Wood*** *a-47r. Issue Nos. 3-5, 7-9, 11, 16-18, 21, 23, 25, 27-30, 35, 37, 38, 42, 45, 52, 57, 58, 65, 69-71, 73, 79-83, 99, 100, 104, 114, Annual 2 have original Robert E. Howard stories adapted. Issues #32-34 adapted from Norvell Page's novel* ***Flame Winds****.*

CONAN THE BARBARIAN (Volume 2)
Marvel Comics: July, 1997 - No. 3, Oct, 1997 ($2.50, limited series)

1-3-Castellini-a — 3.00

CONAN THE BARBARIAN MOVIE SPECIAL (Movie)
Marvel Comics Group: Oct, 1982 - No. 2, Nov, 1982

1,2-Movie adaptation; Buscema-a — 3.50

CONAN THE BARBARIAN: THE USURPER
Marvel Comics: Dec, 1997 - No. 3, Feb, 1998 ($2.50, limited series)

1-3-Dixon-s — 3.00

CONAN: THE BOOK OF THOTH
Dark Horse Comics: Mar, 2006 - No. 4, June, 2006 ($4.99, limited series)

	NM-
1-4-Origin of Thoth-amon; Len Wein & Kurt Busiek-s/Kelley Jones-a/c	5.00
TPB (12/06, $17.95) r/#1-4	18.00

CONAN THE CIMMERIAN
Dark Horse Comics: No. 0, Jun, 2008 - Present (99¢/$2.99)

	NM-
0-Follows Conan #50; Truman-s/Giorello-a/c	3.00
1-(7/08, $2.99) Two covers by Joe Kubert and Cho; Giorello & Corben-a	3.00
2-18: 2-7-Cho-c; Giorello & Corben-a. 8-18-Linsner-c. 14-Joe Kubert-a (7 pgs.)	3.00

CONAN THE DESTROYER (Movie)
Marvel Comics Group: Jan, 1985 - No. 2, Mar, 1985

1,2-r/Marvel Super Special — 3.00

CONAN THE KING (Formerly King Conan)
Marvel Comics Group: No. 20, Jan, 1984 - No. 55, Nov, 1989

	GD	VG	FN	VF	VF/NM	NM-
20-49						4.00
50-54						5.00
55-Last issue	1	2	3	5	6	8

NOTE: ***Kaluta*** *c-20-23, 24i, 26, 27, 30, 50, 52.* ***Williamson*** *a-37i; c-37i, 38i.*

CONAN: THE LEGEND (See Conan 2004 series)

CONAN: THE LORD OF THE SPIDERS
Marvel Comics: Mar, 1998 - No. 3, May, 1998 ($2.50, limited series)

1-3-Roy Thomas-s/Raffaele-a — 3.00

CONAN THE SAVAGE
Marvel Comics: Aug, 1995 - No. 10, May, 1996 ($2.95, B&W, Magazine)

1-10: 1-Bisley-c. 4-vs. Malibu Comics' Rune. 5,10-Brereton-c — 4.00

CONAN VS. RUNE (Also See Conan #4)
Marvel Comics: Nov, 1995 ($2.95, one-shot)

1-Barry Smith-c/a/scripts — 4.00

CONCRETE (Also see Dark Horse Presents & Within Our Reach)
Dark Horse Comics: March, 1987 - No. 10, Nov, 1988 ($1.50, B&W)

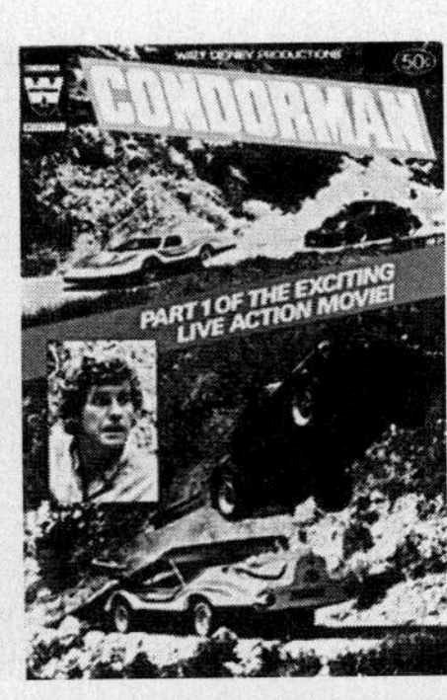

Condorman #1 © DIS

Confessions of Love #12 © STAR

Contact Comics #12 © Aviation

	GD 2.0	VG 4.0	FN 6.0	VF 8.0	VF/NM 9.0	NM- 9.2
1-Paul Chadwick-c/a in all	1	3	4	6	8	10
1-2nd print						3.00
2						6.00
3-Origin						5.00
4-10						4.00
A New Life 1 (1989, $2.95, B&W)-r/#3,4 plus new-a (11 pgs.)						3.00
Celebrates Earth Day 1990 ($3.50, 52 pgs.)						6.00
Color Special 1 (2/89, $2.95, 44 pgs.)-r/1st two Concrete apps. from Dark Horse Presents #1,2 plus new-a						6.00
Depths TPB (7/05, $12.95)-r/#1-5, stories from DHP #1,8,10,150; other short stories						13.00
Land And Sea 1 (2/89, $2.95, B&W)-r/#1,2						6.00
Odd Jobs 1 (7/90, $3.50)-r/5,6 plus new-a						3.50
...Vol. 1: Depths ('05, $12.95, 9"x6") r/#1-5 & short stories						13.00
...Vol. 2: Heights ('05, $12.95, 9"x6") r/#6-10 & short stories						13.00
...Vol. 3: Fragile Creatures (1/06, $12.95, 9"x6") r/mini-series & short stories from DHP						13.00
...Vol. 4: Killer Smile (3/06, $12.95, 9"x6") r/mini-series & short stories from various						13.00
...Vol. 5: Think Like a Mountain (5/06, $12.95, 9"x6") r/mini-series & short stories						13.00
...Vol. 6: Strange Armor (7/06, $12.95, 9"x6") r/mini-series & short stories						13.00
...Vol. 7: The Human Dilemma (4/06, $12.95, 9"x6") r/mini-series						13.00

CONCRETE: (Title series), **Dark Horse Comics**

	GD 2.0	VG 4.0	FN 6.0	VF 8.0	VF/NM 9.0	NM- 9.2
--ECLECTICA, 4/93 - No. 2, 5/93 ($2.95) 1,2						3.00
--FRAGILE CREATURE, 6/91 - No. 4, 2/92 ($2.50) 1-4						3.00
--KILLER SMILE, (Legend), 7/94 - No. 4, 10/94 ($2.9) 1-4						3.00
--STRANGE ARMOR, 12/97 - No. 5, 5/98 ($2.95, color) 1-5-Chadwick-s/c/a; retells origin						3.00
--THE HUMAN DILEMMA, 12/04 - No. 6, 5/05 ($3.50) 1-6: Chadwick-a/c & scripts; Concrete has a child						3.50
--THINK LIKE A MOUNTAIN, (Legend), 3/96 - No. 6, 8/96 ($2.95) 1-6: Chadwick-a/scripts & Darrow-c in all						3.00

CONDORMAN (Walt Disney)
Whitman Publishing: Oct, 1981 - No. 3, Jan, 1982

	GD 2.0	VG 4.0	FN 6.0	VF 8.0	VF/NM 9.0	NM- 9.2
1-3: 1,2-Movie adaptation; photo-c	1	3	4	6	8	10

CONEHEADS
Marvel Comics: June, 1994 - No. 4, 1994 ($1.75, limited series)

	GD 2.0	VG 4.0	FN 6.0	VF 8.0	VF/NM 9.0	NM- 9.2
1-4						2.50

CONFESSIONS ILLUSTRATED (Magazine)
E. C. Comics: Jan-Feb, 1956 - No. 2, Spring, 1956

	GD 2.0	VG 4.0	FN 6.0	VF 8.0	VF/NM 9.0	NM- 9.2
1-Craig, Kamen, Wood, Orlando-a	29	58	87	172	281	390
2-Craig, Crandall, Kamen, Orlando-a	21	42	63	126	206	285

CONFESSIONS OF LOVE
Artful Publ.: Apr, 1950 - No. 2, July, 1950 (25¢, 7-1/4x5-1/4", 132 pgs.)

	GD 2.0	VG 4.0	FN 6.0	VF 8.0	VF/NM 9.0	NM- 9.2
1-Bakerish-a	30	60	90	177	289	400
2-Art & text; Bakerish-a	19	38	57	111	176	240

CONFESSIONS OF LOVE (Formerly Startling Terror Tales #10; becomes Confessions of Romance No. 7 on)
Star Publications: No. 11, 7/52 - No. 14, 1/53; No. 4, 3/53- No. 6, 8/53

	GD 2.0	VG 4.0	FN 6.0	VF 8.0	VF/NM 9.0	NM- 9.2
11-13: 12,13-Disbrow-a	15	30	45	90	140	190
14,5,6	14	28	42	78	112	145
4-Disbrow-a	14	28	42	81	118	155

NOTE: *All have* ***L. B. Cole*** *covers.*

CONFESSIONS OF ROMANCE (Formerly Confessions of Love)
Star Publications: No. 7, Nov, 1953 - No. 11, Nov, 1954

	GD 2.0	VG 4.0	FN 6.0	VF 8.0	VF/NM 9.0	NM- 9.2
7	15	30	45	90	140	190
8	14	28	42	78	112	145
9-Wood-a	15	30	45	84	127	170
10,11-Disbrow-a	14	28	42	81	118	155

NOTE: *All have* ***L. B. Cole*** *covers.*

CONFESSIONS OF THE LOVELORN (Formerly Lovelorn)
American Comics Group (Regis Publ./Best Synd. Features): No. 52, Aug, 1954 - No. 114, June-July, 1960

	GD 2.0	VG 4.0	FN 6.0	VF 8.0	VF/NM 9.0	NM- 9.2
52 (3-D effect)	29	58	87	172	281	390
53,55	11	22	33	62	86	110
54 (3-D effect)	29	58	87	172	281	390
56-Anti-communist propaganda story, 10 pgs; last pre-code (2/55)	14	28	42	82	121	160
57-90,100	9	18	27	47	61	75
91-Williamson-a	10	20	30	56	76	95
92-99,101-114	8	16	24	40	50	60

NOTE: ***Whitney*** *a-most issues; c-52, 53. Painted c-106, 107.*

CONFIDENTIAL DIARY (Formerly High School Confidential Diary; Three Nurses #18 on)
Charlton Comics: No. 12, May, 1962 - No. 17, Mar, 1963

	GD 2.0	VG 4.0	FN 6.0	VF 8.0	VF/NM 9.0	NM- 9.2
12-17	3	6	9	15	21	26

CONGO BILL (See Action Comics & More Fun Comics #56)
National Periodical Publication: Aug-Sept, 1954 - No. 7, Aug-Sept, 1955

	GD 2.0	VG 4.0	FN 6.0	VF 8.0	VF/NM 9.0	NM- 9.2
1 (Scarce)	200	400	600	1600	-	-
2,7 (Scarce)	125	250	375	1000	-	-
3-6 (Scarce). 4-Last pre-code issue	100	200	300	800	-	-

NOTE: *(Rarely found in fine to mint condition.)* ***Nick Cardy*** *c-1-7.*

CONGO BILL
DC Comics (Vertigo): Oct, 1999 - No. 4, Jan, 2000 ($2.95, limited series)

	GD 2.0	VG 4.0	FN 6.0	VF 8.0	VF/NM 9.0	NM- 9.2
1-4-Corben-c						3.00

CONGORILLA (Also see Actions Comics #224)
DC Comics: Nov, 1992 - No. 4, Feb, 1993 ($1.75, limited series)

	GD 2.0	VG 4.0	FN 6.0	VF 8.0	VF/NM 9.0	NM- 9.2
1-4: 1,2-Brian Bolland-c						3.00

CONJURORS
DC Comics: Apr, 1999 - No. 3, Jun, 1999 ($2.95, limited series)

	GD 2.0	VG 4.0	FN 6.0	VF 8.0	VF/NM 9.0	NM- 9.2
1-3-Elseworlds; Phantom Stranger app.; Barreto-c/a						3.00

CONNECTICUT YANKEE, A (See King Classics)

CONNOR HAWKE: DRAGON'S BLOOD (Also see Green Arrow titles)
DC Comics: Jan, 2007 - No. 6, Jun, 2007 ($2.99, limited series)

	GD 2.0	VG 4.0	FN 6.0	VF 8.0	VF/NM 9.0	NM- 9.2
1-6-Chuck Dixon-s/Derec Donovan-a/c						3.00
SC (2008, $19.99) r/#1-6						20.00

CONQUEROR, THE
Dell Publishing Co.: No., 690, Mar, 1956

	GD 2.0	VG 4.0	FN 6.0	VF 8.0	VF/NM 9.0	NM- 9.2
Four Color 690-Movie, John Wayne photo-c	15	30	45	107	204	300

CONQUEROR COMICS
Albrecht Publishing Co.: Winter, 1945

	GD 2.0	VG 4.0	FN 6.0	VF 8.0	VF/NM 9.0	NM- 9.2
nn	21	42	63	124	202	280

CONQUEROR OF THE BARREN EARTH (See The Warlord #63)
DC Comics: Feb, 1985 - No. 4, May, 1985 (Limited series)

	GD 2.0	VG 4.0	FN 6.0	VF 8.0	VF/NM 9.0	NM- 9.2
1-4: Back-up series from Warlord						2.50

CONQUEST
Store Comics: 1953 (6¢)

	GD 2.0	VG 4.0	FN 6.0	VF 8.0	VF/NM 9.0	NM- 9.2
1-Richard the Lion Hearted, Beowulf, Swamp Fox	7	14	21	35	43	50

CONQUEST
Famous Funnies: Spring, 1955

	GD 2.0	VG 4.0	FN 6.0	VF 8.0	VF/NM 9.0	NM- 9.2
1-Crandall-a, 1 pg.; contains contents of 1953 ish.	5	10	15	22	26	30

CONSPIRACY
Marvel Comics: Feb, 1998 - No. 2, Mar, 1998 ($2.99, limited series)

	GD 2.0	VG 4.0	FN 6.0	VF 8.0	VF/NM 9.0	NM- 9.2
1,2-Painted art by Korday/Abnett-s						3.00

CONSTANTINE (Also see Hellblazer)
DC Comics (Vertigo): 2005 (Based on the 2005 Keanu Reeves movie)

	GD 2.0	VG 4.0	FN 6.0	VF 8.0	VF/NM 9.0	NM- 9.2
...: The Hellblazer Collection (2005, $14.95) Movie adaptation and r/#1, 27, 41; photo-c						15.00
...: The Official Movie Adaptation (2005, $6.95) Seagle-s/Randall-a/photo-c						7.00

CONSTRUCT
Caliber (New Worlds): 1996 - No. 6, 1997 ($2.95, B&W, limited series)

	GD 2.0	VG 4.0	FN 6.0	VF 8.0	VF/NM 9.0	NM- 9.2
1-6: Paul Jenkins scripts						3.00

CONSUMED
Platinum Studios: July, 2007 - No. 4, Oct, 2007 ($2.99, limited series)

	GD 2.0	VG 4.0	FN 6.0	VF 8.0	VF/NM 9.0	NM- 9.2
1-4-Linsner-c/Budd-a/Shumskas-Tait-s						3.00

CONTACT COMICS
Aviation Press: July, 1944 - No. 12, May, 1946

	GD 2.0	VG 4.0	FN 6.0	VF 8.0	VF/NM 9.0	NM- 9.2
nn-Black Venus, Flamingo, Golden Eagle, Tommy Tomahawk begin	54	108	162	343	584	825
2-5: 3-Last Flamingo. 3,4-Black Venus by L. B. Cole. 5-The Phantom Flyer app.	40	80	120	243	402	560
6,11-Kurtzman's Black Venus; 11-Last Golden Eagle, last Tommy Tomahawk; Feldstein-a	47	94	141	296	498	700
7-10	39	78	117	240	395	550
12-Sky Rangers, Air Kids, Ace Diamond app.; L.B. Cole sci-fi cover	113	226	339	718	1234	1750

NOTE: ***L. B. Cole*** *a-3, 9; c-1-12.* ***Giunta*** *a-3.* ***Hollingsworth*** *a-5, 7, 10.* ***Palais*** *a-11, 12.*

Cookie #6 © ACG

Cosmic Boy #4 © DC

Cosmo Cat #3 © FOX

	GD 2.0	VG 4.0	FN 6.0	VF 8.0	VF/NM 9.0	NM- 9.2

CONTEMPORARY MOTIVATORS
Pendelum Press: 1977 - 1978 ($1.45, 5-3/8x8", 31 pgs., B&W)

	GD	VG	FN	VF	VF/NM	NM-
14-3002 The Caine Mutiny; 14-3010 Banner in the Sky; 14-3029 God Is My Co-Pilot; 14-3037 Guadalcanal Diary; 14-3045 Hiroshima; 14-3053 Hot Rod; 14-3061 Just Dial a Number; 14-3088 The Diary of Anne Frank; 14-3096 Lost Horizon	2	4	6	8	10	12

NOTE: *Also see Pendulum Illustrated Classics. Above may have been distributed the same.*

CONTEST OF CHAMPIONS (See Marvel Super-Hero...)

CONTEST OF CHAMPIONS II
Marvel Comics: Sept, 1999 - No. 5 ($2.50, limited series)

1-5-Claremont-s/Jimenez-a 2.50

CONTRACTORS
Eclipse Comics: June, 1987 ($2.00, B&W, one-shot)

1-Funny animal 2.50

CONTRACT WITH GOD, A
Baronet Publishing Co./Kitchen Sink Press: 1978 ($4.95/$7.95, B&W, graphic novel)

	GD	VG	FN	VF	VF/NM	NM-
nn-Will Eisner-s/a	3	6	9	14	20	25
Reprint (DC Comics, 2000, $12.95)						13.00

CONVOCATIONS: A MAGIC THE GATHERING GALLERY
Acclaim Comics (Armada): Jan, 1996 ($2.50, one-shot)

1-pin-ups by various artists including Kaluta, Vess, and Dringenberg 2.50

COO COO COMICS (...the Bird Brain No. 57 on)
Nedor Publ. Co./Standard (Animated Cartoons): Oct, 1942 - No. 62, Apr, 1952

	GD	VG	FN	VF	VF/NM	NM-
1-Origin/1st app. Super Mouse & begin series (cloned from Superman); the first funny animal super hero series (see Looney Tunes #5 for 1st funny animal super hero)	31	62	93	182	296	410
2	15	30	45	86	133	180
3-10: 10-(3/44)	11	22	33	60	83	105
11-33: 33-1 pg. Ingels-a	9	18	27	50	65	80
34-40,43-46,48-Text illos by Frazetta in all. 36-Super Mouse covers begin	11	22	33	64	90	115
41-Frazetta-a (6-pg. story & 3 text illos)	21	42	63	126	206	285
42,47-Frazetta-a & text illos.	15	30	45	86	133	180
49-(1/50)-3-D effect story; Frazetta text illo	14	28	42	76	108	140
50,51-3-D effect-c only. 50-Frazetta text illo	13	26	39	72	101	130
52-62: 56-58,61-Super Mouse app.	8	16	24	42	54	65

"COOKIE" (Also see Topsy-Turvy)
Michel Publ./American Comics Group(Regis Publ.): Apr, 1946 - No. 55, Aug-Sept, 1955

	GD	VG	FN	VF	VF/NM	NM-
1-Teen-age humor	23	46	69	136	223	310
2	14	28	42	81	118	155
3-10	11	22	33	64	90	115
11-20	10	20	30	56	76	95
21-23,26,28-30	9	18	27	47	61	75
24,25,27-Starlett O'Hara stories	9	18	27	50	65	80
31-34,37-48,50,52-55	8	16	24	40	50	60
35,36-Starlett O'Hara stories	8	16	24	44	57	70
49,51: 49-(6-7/54)-3-D effect-c/s. 51-(10-11/54) 8pg. TrueVision 3-D effect story	12	24	36	69	97	125

COOL CAT (Formerly Black Magic)
Prize Publications: V8#6, Mar-Apr, 1962 - V9#2, July-Aug, 1962

	GD	VG	FN	VF	VF/NM	NM-
V8#6, nn(V9#1, 5-6/62), V9#2	3	6	9	18	27	35

COOL WORLD (Movie by Ralph Bakshi)
DC Comics: Apr, 1992 - No. 4, Sept, 1992 ($1.75, limited series)

1-4: Prequel to animated/live action movie. 1-Bakshi-c. Bill Wray inks in all 2.50
Movie Adaptation nn ('92, $3.50, 68pg.)-Bakshi-c 3.50

COPPER CANYON (See Fawcett Movie Comics)

COPS (TV)
DC Comics: Aug, 1988 - No. 15, Aug, 1989 ($1.00)

1 ($1.50, 52 pgs.)-Based on Hasbro Toys 3.00
2-15: 14-Orlando-c(p) 2.50

COPS: THE JOB
Marvel Comics: June, 1992 - No. 4, Sept, 1992 ($1.25, limited series)

1-4: All have Jusko scripts & Golden-c 2.50

CORBEN SPECIAL, A
Pacific Comics: May, 1984 (one-shot)

1-Corben-c/a; E.A. Poe adaptation 5.00

CORE, THE
Image Comics: July, 2008 ($3.99)

Pilot Season - Hickman-s/Rocafort-a 4.00

CORKY & WHITE SHADOW (Disney, TV)
Dell Publishing Co.: No. 707, May, 1956 (Mickey Mouse Club)

	GD	VG	FN	VF	VF/NM	NM-
Four Color 707-Photo-c	7	14	21	47	76	105

CORLISS ARCHER (See Meet Corliss Archer)

CORMAC MAC ART (Robert E. Howard's...)
Dark Horse Comics: 1990 - No. 4, 1990 ($1.95, B&W, mini-series)

1-4: All have Bolton painted-c; Howard adapts. 3.00

CORNY'S FETISH
Dark Horse Comics: Apr, 1998 ($4.95, B&W, one-shot)

1-Renée French-s/a; Bolland-c 5.00

CORPORAL RUSTY DUGAN (See Holyoke One-Shot #2)

CORPSES OF DR. SACOTTI, THE (See Ideal a Classical Comic)

CORSAIR, THE (See A-1 Comics No. 5, 7, 10 under Texas Slim)

CORTEZ AND THE FALL OF THE AZTECS
Tome Press: 1993 ($2.95, B&W, limited series)

1,2 3.00

CORUM: THE BULL AND THE SPEAR (See Chronicles Of Corum)
First Comics: Jan, 1989 - No. 4, July, 1989 ($1.95)

1-4: Adapts Michael Moorcock's novel 2.50

COSMIC BOOK, THE
Ace Comics: Dec, 1986 - No. 1, 1987 ($1.95)

1,2: 1-(44pgs.)-Wood, Toth-a. 2-(B&W) 2.50

COSMIC BOY (Also see The Legion of Super-Heroes)
DC Comics: Dec, 1986 - No. 4, Mar, 1987 (limited series)

1-4: Legends tie-ins all issues 2.50

COSMIC GUARD
Devil's Due Publ.: Aug, 2004 - No. 6, Dec, 2005 ($2.99)

1-6-Jim Starlin-s/a 3.00

COSMIC HEROES
Eternity/Malibu Graphics: Oct, 1988 - No. 11, Dec, 1989 ($1.95, B&W)

1-11: Reprints 1934-1936's Buck Rogers newspaper strips #1-728 2.50

COSMIC ODYSSEY
DC Comics: 1988 - No. 4, 1988 ($3.50, limited series, squarebound)

1-4: Reintro. New Gods into DC continuity; Superman, Batman, Green Lantern (John Stewart) app; Starlin scripts, Mignola-c/a in all. 2-Darkseid merges Demon & Jason Blood (separated in Demon limited series #4) 5.00
TPB (1992,2009, $19.99) r/#1-4; Robert Greenberger intro. 20.00

COSMIC POWERS
Marvel Comics: Mar, 1994 - No. 6, Aug, 1994 ($2.50, limited series)

1-6: 1-Ron Lim-c/a(p). 1,2-Thanos app. 2-Terrax. 3-Ganymede & Jack of Hearts app. 2.50

COSMIC POWERS UNLIMITED
Marvel Comics: May, 1995 - No. 5, May, 1996 ($3.95, quarterly)

1-5 4.00

COSMIC RAY
Image Comics: June, 1999 - No. 2 ($2.95, B&W)

1,2-Steven Blue-s/a 3.00

COSMIC SLAM
Ultimate Sports Entertainment: 1999 ($3.95, one-shot)

1-McGwire, Sosa, Bagwell, Justice battle aliens; Sienkiewicz-c 4.00

COSMO CAT (Becomes Sunny #11 on; also see All Top & Wotalife Comics)
Fox Publications/Green Publ. Co./Norlen Mag.: July-Aug, 1946 - No. 10, Oct, 1947; 1957; 1959

	GD	VG	FN	VF	VF/NM	NM-
1	26	52	78	152	249	345
2	15	30	45	84	127	170
3-Origin (11-12/46)	18	36	54	107	169	230
4-Robot-c	14	28	42	76	108	140
5-10	11	22	33	60	83	105
2-4(1957-Green Publ. Co.)	6	12	18	27	33	38
2-4(1959-Norlen Mag.)	5	10	15	23	28	32
I.W. Reprint #1	2	4	6	11	16	20

Countdown #9 © DC

Count Duckula #15 © Cosgrove-Hall

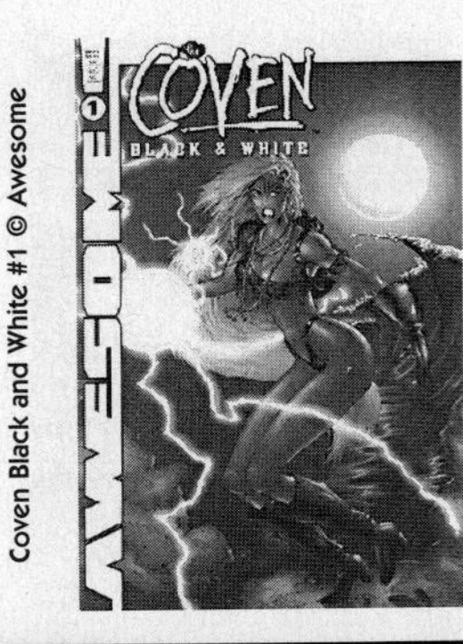

Coven Black and White #1 © Awesome

	GD 2.0	VG 4.0	FN 6.0	VF 8.0	VF/NM 9.0	NM- 9.2

COSMO THE MERRY MARTIAN
Archie Publications (Radio Comics): Sept, 1958 - No. 6, Oct, 1959

1-Bob White-a in all	15	30	45	84	127	170
2-6	11	22	33	60	83	105

COTTON WOODS
Dell Publishing Co.: No. 837, Sept, 1957

Four Color 837	4	8	12	24	37	50

COUGAR, THE (Cougar No. 2)
Seaboard Periodicals (Atlas): April, 1975 - No. 2, July, 1975

1,2: 1-Vampire; Adkins-a(p). 2-Cougar origin; werewolf-s; Buckler-c(p)	2	4	6	8	10	12

COUNTDOWN (See Movie Classics)

COUNTDOWN
DC Comics (WildStorm): June, 2000 - No. 8, Jan, 2001 ($2.95)

1-8-Mariotte-s/Lopresti-a 3.00

COUNTDOWN (Continued from 52 weekly series)
DC Comics: No. 51, July, 2007 - No. 1, June, 2008 ($2.99, weekly, limited series) (issue #s go in reverse)

51-Gatefold wraparound-c by Andy Kubert; Duela Dent killed; the Monitors app. 3.00
50-1: 50-Joker-c. 48-Lightray dies. 47-Mary Marvel gains Black Adam's powers. 46-Intro. Forerunner. 43-Funeral for Bart Allen. 39-Karate Kid-c 3.00
Countdown to Final Crisis Vol. 1 TPB (2008, $19.99) r/#51-39 20.00
Countdown to Final Crisis Vol. 2 TPB (2008, $19.99) r/#38-26 20.00
Countdown to Final Crisis Vol. 3 TPB (2008, $19.99) r/#25-13 20.00
Countdown to Final Crisis Vol. 4 TPB (2008, $19.99) r/#12-1 20.00

COUNTDOWN: ARENA (Takes place during Countdown #21-18)
DC Comics: Feb, 2008 - No. 4, Feb, 2008 ($3.99, weekly, limited series)

1-4-Battles between alternate Earth heroes; McDaniel-a; Andy Kubert variant-c on each 4.00
TPB (2008, $17.99) r/#1-4; variant covers 18.00

COUNTDOWN PRESENTS: LORD HAVOK & THE EXTREMISTS
DC Comics: Dec, 2007 - No. 8 ($2.99, limited series)

1-6: 1-Tieri-s/Sharp-a/c; Challengers From Beyond app. 3.00
TPB (2008, $17.99) r/#1-6 18.00

COUNTDOWN PRESENTS THE SEARCH FOR RAY PALMER (Leads into Countdown #18)
DC Comics: Nov, 2007 - Feb, 2008 ($2.99, series of one-shots)

...: Wildstorm (11/07) Part 1; The Authority app.; Art Adams-c/Unzueta-a 3.00
...: Crime Society (12/07) Earth-3 Owlman & Jokester app.; Igle-a 3.00
...: Red Rain (1/08) Vampire Batman app.; Kelley Jones-c; Jones, Battle & Unzueta-a 3.00
...: Gotham By Gaslight (1/08) Victorian Batman app.; Tocchini-a/Nguyen-c 3.00
...: Red Son (2/08) Soviet Superman app.; Foreman-a 3.00
...: Superwoman/Batwoman (2/08) Conclusion; gender-reversed heroes; Sook-c 3.00
TPB (2008, $17.99) r/one-shots 18.00

COUNTDOWN SPECIAL
DC Comics: Dec, 2007 - Jun, 2008 ($4.99, collection of reprints related to Countdown)

...: Eclipso (5/08) r/Eclipso #10 & Spectre #17,18 (1994); Sook-c 5.00
...: Jimmy Olsen (1/08) r/Superman's Pal, Jimmy Olsen #136,147,148; Kirby-s/a; Sook-c 5.00
...: Kamandi (6/08) r/Kamandi: The Last Boy on Earth #1,10,29; Kirby-s/a; Sook-c 5.00
...: New Gods (3/08) r/Forever People #1, Mr. Miracle #1, New Gods #7; Kirby-s/a; Sook-c 5.00
...: Omac (4/08) r/Omac (1974) #1, Warlord #37-39, DC Comics Presents #61; Sook-c 5.00
...: The Atom 1,2 (2/08) r/stories from Super-Team Family #11-14; Sook-c on both 5.00
...: The Flash (12/07) r/Rogues Gallery in Flash (1st series) #106,113,155,174; Sook-c 5.00

COUNTDOWN TO ADVENTURE
DC Comics: Oct, 2007 - No. 8, May, 2008 ($3.99, limited series)

1-8: 1-Adam Strange, Animal Man and Starfire app.; origin of Forerunner 4.00
TPB (2008, $17.99) r/#1-8 18.00

COUNTDOWN TO INFINITE CRISIS (See DC Countdown)

COUNTDOWN TO MYSTERY (See Eclipso: The Music of the Spheres TPB for reprint)
DC Comics: Nov, 2007 - No. 8, Jun, 2008 ($3.99, limited series)

1-8: 1-Doctor Fate, Eclipso, The Spectre and Plastic Man app. 4.00
TPB (2008, $17.99) r/#1-8 18.00

COUNT DUCKULA (TV)
Marvel Comics: Nov, 1988 - No. 15, Jan, 1991 ($1.00)

1,8: 1-Dangermouse back-up. 8-Geraldo Rivera photo-c/& app.; Sienkiewicz-a(i) 5.00
2-7,9-15: Dangermouse back-ups in all 4.00

COUNT OF MONTE CRISTO, THE
Dell Publishing Co.: No. 794, May, 1957

	GD 2.0	VG 4.0	FN 6.0	VF 8.0	VF/NM 9.0	NM- 9.2

Four Color 794-Movie, Buscema-a	8	16	24	56	93	130

COUP D'ETAT (Oneshots)
DC Comics (WildStorm): April, 2004 ($2.95, weekly limited series)

...: Sleeper 1 (part 1 of 4) Jim Lee-a; 2 covers by Lee and Bermejo 3.00
...: Stormwatch 1 (part 2 of 4) D'Anda-a; 2 covers by D'Anda and Bermejo 3.00
...: Wildcats Version 3.0 1 (part 3 of 4) Garza-a; 2 covers by Garza and Bermejo 3.00
...: The Authority 1 (part 4 of 4) Portacio-a; 2 covers by Portacio and Bermejo 3.00
...: Afterword 1 (5/04) Profile pages and prelude stories for Sleeper & Wetworks 3.00
TPB (2004, $12.95) r/series and profile pages from Afterword 13.00

COURAGE COMICS
J. Edward Slavin: 1945

1,2,77	14	28	42	80	115	150

COURTNEY CRUMRIN...
Oni Press: July, 2005; July 2007; Dec, 2008 ($5.95, B&W, series of one-shots)

... And The Fire Thief's Tale (7/07) Naifeh-s/a 6.00
... And The Prince of Nowhere (12/08) Naifeh-s/a 6.00
... Tales Portrait of the Warlock as a Young Man (7/05) origin Uncle Aloysius; Naifeh-s/a 6.00

COURTNEY CRUMRIN & THE COVEN OF MYSTICS
Oni Press: Dec, 2002 - No. 4, March, 2003 ($2.95, B&W, limited series)

1-4-Ted Naifeh-s/a 3.00
TPB (9/03, $11.95, 8" x 5-1/2") r/#1-4 12.00

COURTNEY CRUMRIN & THE NIGHT THINGS (Also see Promotional Section for FCBD Ed.)
Oni Press: Mar, 2002 - No. 4, June, 2002 ($2.95, B&W, limited series)

1-4-Ted Naifeh-s/a 3.00
TPB (12/02, $11.95) r/#1-4 12.00

COURTNEY CRUMRIN IN THE TWILIGHT KINGDOM
Oni Press: Dec, 2003 - No. 4, May, 2004 ($2.99, B&W, limited series)

1-4-Ted Naifeh-s/a 3.00
TPB (9/04, $11.95, digest-size) r/#1-4 12.00

COURTSHIP OF EDDIE'S FATHER (TV)
Dell Publishing Co.: Jan, 1970 - No. 2, May, 1970

1-Bill Bixby photo-c on both	6	12	18	37	59	80
2	4	8	12	24	37	50

COVEN
Awesome Entertainment: Aug, 1997 - No. 5, Mar, 1998 ($2.50)

Preview	1	2	3	5	6	8
1-Loeb-s/Churchill-a; three covers by Churchill, Liefeld, Pollina	1	2	3	5	6	8
1-Fan Appreciation Ed.(3/98); new Churchill-c						3.00
1+ :Includes B&W art from Kaboom	1	3	4	6	8	10
2-Regular-c w/leaping Fantom						6.00
2-Variant-c w/circle of candles	1	2	3	5	6	8
3-6-Contains flip book preview of ReGex						3.00
3-White variant-c	1	2	3	4	5	7
3,4: 3-Halloween wraparound-c. 4-Purple variant-c						3.00
...Black & White (9/98) Short stories						3.00
...Fantom Special (2/98) w/sketch pages						5.00

COVEN
Awesome Entertainment: Jan, 1999 - No. 3, June, 1999 ($2.50)

1-3: 1-Loeb-s/Churchill-a; 6 covers by various. 2-Supreme-c/app. 3-Flip book w/Kaboom preview 2.50
... Dark Origins (7/99, 2.50) w/Lionheart gallery 2.50

COVENANT, THE
Image Comics (Top Cow): 2005 ($9.99, squarebound, one-shot)

nn-Tone Rodriguez-a/Aron Coleite-s 10.00

COVERED WAGONS, HO (Disney, TV)
Dell Publishing Co.: No. 814, June, 1957 (Donald Duck)

Four Color 814-Mickey Mouse app.	5	10	15	34	55	75

COWBOY ACTION (Formerly Western Thrillers No. 1-4; Becomes Quick-Trigger Western No. 12 on)
Atlas Comics (ACI): No. 5, March, 1955 - No. 11, March, 1956

5	14	28	42	76	108	140
6-10: 6-8-Heath-c	10	20	30	54	72	90
11-Williamson-a (4 pgs.); Baker-a	11	22	33	62	86	110

NOTE: ***Ayers** a-8. **Drucker** a-6. **Maneely** c/a-5, 6. **Severin** c-10. **Shores** a-7.*

COWBOY COMICS (Star Ranger #12, Stories #14)(Star Ranger Funnies #15)

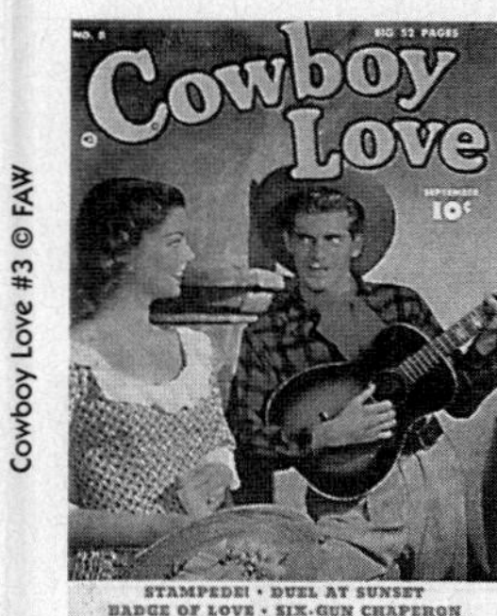

Cowboy Love #3 © FAW

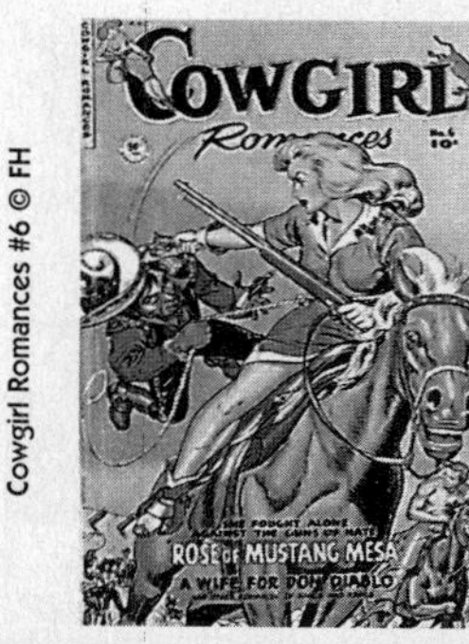

Cowgirl Romances #6 © FH

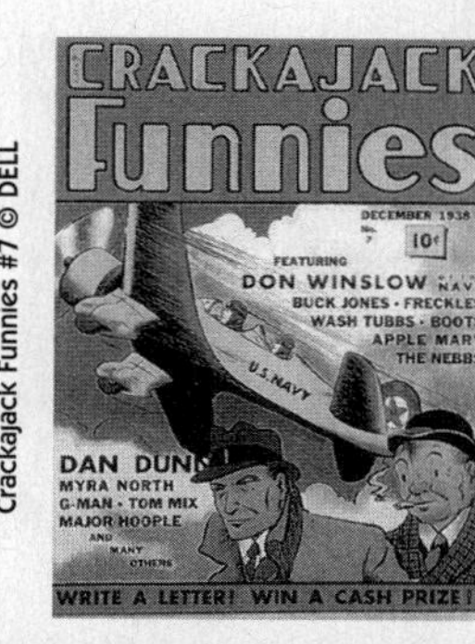

Crackajack Funnies #7 © DELL

	GD	VG	FN	VF	VF/NM	NM-
	2.0	4.0	6.0	8.0	9.0	9.2

Centaur Publishing Co.: No. 13, July, 1938 - No. 14, Aug, 1938

13-(Rare)-Ace and Deuce, Lyin Lou, Air Patrol, Aces High, Lee Trent, Trouble Hunters begin
129 258 387 826 1413 2000
14-Filchock-c 87 174 261 553 952 1350
NOTE: *Guardineer a-13, 14. Gustavson a-13, 14.*

COWBOY IN AFRICA (TV)
Gold Key: Mar, 1968
1(10219-803)-Chuck Connors photo-c 4 8 12 26 41 55

COWBOY LOVE (Becomes Range Busters?)
Fawcett Publications/Charlton Comics No. 28 on: 7/49 - V2#10, 6/50; No. 11, 1951; No. 28, 2/55 - No. 31, 8/55
V1#1-Rocky Lane photo back-c 15 30 45 88 137 185
2 8 16 24 44 57 70
V1#3,4,6 (12/49) 8 16 24 40 50 60
5-Bill Boyd photo back-c (11/49) 9 18 27 47 61 75
V2#7-Williamson/Evans-a 10 20 30 54 72 90
V2#8-11 7 14 21 35 43 50
V1#28 (Charlton)-Last precode (2/55) (Formerly Romantic Story?)
6 12 18 31 38 45
V1#29-31 (Charlton; becomes Sweetheart Diary #32 on)
6 12 18 28 34 40
NOTE: *Powell a-10. Marcus Swayze a-2, 3. Photo c-1-11. No. 1-3, 5-7, 9, 10 are 52 pgs.*

COWBOY ROMANCES (Young Men No. 4 on)
Marvel Comics (IPC): Oct, 1949 - No. 3, Mar, 1950 (All photo-c & 52 pgs.)
1-Photo-c 22 44 66 132 216 300
2-William Holden, Mona Freeman "Streets of Laredo" photo-c
16 32 48 94 147 200
3-Photo-c 15 30 45 84 127 170

COWBOYS 'N' INJUNS (...and Indians No. 6 on)
Compix No. 1-5/Magazine Enterprises No. 6 on: 1946 - No. 5, 1947; No. 6, 1949 - No. 8, 1952
1-Funny animal western 14 28 42 82 121 160
2-5-All funny animal western 10 20 30 54 72 90
6(A-1 23)-Half violent, half funny; Ayers-a 14 28 42 76 108 140
7(A-1 41, 1950), 8(A-1 48)-All funny 9 18 27 47 61 75
I.W. Reprint No. 1,7 (Reprinted in Canada by Superior, No. 7)
2 4 6 11 16 20
Super Reprint #10 (1963) 2 4 6 11 16 20

COWBOY WESTERN COMICS (TV)(Formerly Jack In The Box; Becomes Space Western No. 40-45 & Wild Bill Hickok & Jingles No. 68 on; title:Cowboy Western Heroes No. 47 & 48; Cowboy Western No. 49 on)
Charlton (Capitol Stories): No. 17, 7/48 - No. 39, 8/52; No. 46, 10/53; No. 47, 12/53; No. 48, Spr, '54; No. 49, 5-6/54 - No. 67, 3/58 (nn 40-45)
17-Jesse James, Annie Oakley, Wild Bill Hickok begin; Texas Rangers app.
16 32 48 94 147 200
18,19-Orlando-c/a. 18-Paul Bunyan begins. 19-Wyatt Earp story
10 20 30 58 79 100
20-25: 21-Buffalo Bill story. 22-Texas Rangers-c/story. 24-Joel McCrea photo-c & adaptation from movie "Three Faces West". 25-James Craig photo-c & adaptation from movie "Northwest Stampede" 9 18 27 52 69 85
26-George Montgomery photo-c and adaptation from movie "Indian Scout"; 1 pg. bio on Will Rogers 10 20 30 58 79 100
27-Sunset Carson photo-c & adapts movie "Sunset Carson Rides Again" plus 1 other Sunset Carson story 40 80 120 244 397 550
28-Sunset Carson line drawn-c; adapts movies "Battling Marshal" & "Fighting Mustangs" starring Sunset Carson 20 40 60 115 183 250
29-Sunset Carson line drawn-c; adapts movies "Rio Grande" with Sunset Carson & "Winchester '73" w/James Stewart plus 5 pg. life history of Sunset Carson featuring Tom Mix 20 40 60 115 183 250
30-Sunset Carson photo-c; adapts movie "Deadline" starring Sunset Carson plus 1 other Sunset Carson story 40 80 120 244 397 550
31-34,38,39,47-50 (no #40-45): 50-Golden Arrow, Rocky Lane & Blackjack (r?) stories
9 18 27 47 61 75
35,36-Sunset Carson-c/stories (2 in each). 35-Inside front-c photo of Sunset Carson plus photo on-c 21 42 63 123 197 270
37-Sunset Carson stories (2) 15 30 45 94 147 200
46-(Formerly Space Western)-Space western story 15 30 45 94 147 200
51-57,59-66: 51-Golden Arrow(r?) & Monte Hale-r renamed Rusty Hall. 53,54-Tom Mix-r. 55-Monte Hale story(r?). 66-Young Eagle story. 67-Wild Bill Hickok and Jingles-c/story
7 14 21 35 43 50
58-(1/56, 15¢, 68 pgs.)-Wild Bill Hickok, Annie Oakley & Jesse James stories; Forgione-a
8 16 24 44 57 70
67-(15¢, 68 pgs.)-Williamson/Torres-a, 5 pgs. 9 18 27 50 65 80
NOTE: *Many issues trimmed 1" shorter. Maneely a-67(5). Inside front/back photo c-29.*

COWGIRL ROMANCES
Marvel Comics (CCC): No. 28, Jan, 1950 (52 pgs.)
28(#1)-Photo-c 21 42 63 124 202 280

COWGIRL ROMANCES
Fiction House Magazines: 1950 - No. 12, Winter, 1952-53 (No. 1-3: 52 pgs.)
1-Kamen-a 40 80 120 246 411 575
2 21 42 63 122 199 275
3-5: 5-12-Whitman-c (most) 19 38 57 109 172 235
6-9,11,12 18 36 54 105 165 225
10-Frazetta?/Williamson?-a; Kamen?/Baker-a; r/Mitzi story from Movie Comics #4 w/all new dialogue 31 62 93 182 296 410

COW PUNCHER (...Comics)
Avon Periodicals: Jan, 1947; No. 2, Sept, 1947 - No. 7, 1949
1-Clint Cortland, Texas Ranger, Kit West, Pioneer Queen begin; Kubert-a; Alabam stories begin 44 88 132 277 469 660
2-Kubert, Kamen/Feldstein-a; Kamen-c 38 76 114 226 368 510
3-5,7: 3-Kiefer story 27 54 81 158 259 360
6-Opium drug mention story; bondage, headlight-c; Reinman-a
36 72 108 211 343 475

COWPUNCHER
Realistic Publications: 1953 (nn) (Reprints Avon's No. 2)
nn-Kubert-a 12 24 36 67 94 120

COWSILLS, THE (See Harvey Pop Comics)

COW SPECIAL, THE
Image Comics (Top Cow): Spring-Summer 2000; 2001 ($2.95)
1-Previews upcoming Top Cow projects; Yancy Butler photo-c 3.00
Vol. 2 #1-Witchblade-c; previews and interviews 3.00

COYOTE
Marvel Comics (Epic Comics): June, 1983 - No. 16, Mar, 1986
1-10,15: 7-10-Ditko-a 2.50
11-1st McFarlane-a. 6.00
12-14,16: 12-14-McFarlane-a. 14-Badger x-over. 16-Reagan c/app. 4.00
Coyote Collection Vol. 1 (2005, $14.99) reprints from Coyote #1-7 & Scorpio Rose #1,2 plus Rogers layout pages for unpublished #3; Englehart intro. 15.00
Coyote Collection Vol. 2 (2005, $12.99) reprints from Coyote #1-4 13.00
Coyote Collection Vol. 3 (2006, $12.99) reprints from Coyote #5-8 13.00
Coyote Collection Vol. 4 (2007, $14.99) reprints from Coyote #9-12 15.00
Coyote Collection Vol. 5 (2007, $12.99) reprints from Coyote #13-16 13.00

CRACKAJACK FUNNIES (Also see The Owl)
Dell Publishing Co.: June, 1938 - No. 43, Jan, 1942
1-Dan Dunn, Freckles, Myra North, Wash Tubbs, Apple Mary, The Nebbs, Don Winslow, Tom Mix, Buck Jones, Major Hoople, Clyde Beatty, Boots begin
206 412 618 1318 2259 3200
2 77 154 231 493 847 1200
3 57 114 171 362 619 875
4 45 90 135 284 480 675
5-Nude woman on cover 47 94 141 296 498 700
6-8,10: 8-Speed Bolton begins (1st app.) 40 80 120 246 411 575
9-(3/39)-Red Ryder strip-r begin by Harman; 1st app. in comics & 1st cover app.
161 322 483 1030 1765 2500
11-14 37 74 111 222 361 500
15-Tarzan text feature begins by Burroughs (9/39); not in #26,35
39 78 117 240 395 550
16-24: 18-Stratosphere Jim begins (1st app., 12/39). 23-Ellery Queen begins plus-c (1st comic book app., 5/40) 30 60 90 177 289 400
25-The Owl begins (1st app., 7/40); in new costume #26 by Frank Thomas (also see Popular Comics #72) 71 142 213 454 777 1100
26-30: 28-Part Owl-c 48 96 144 302 509 715
31-Owl covers begin, end #42 48 96 144 302 514 725
32-Origin Owl Girl 55 110 165 347 586 825
33-38: 36-Last Tarzan issue. 37-Cyclone & Midge begin (1st app.)
47 94 141 296 503 710
39-Andy Panda begins (intro/1st app., 9/41) 57 114 171 362 619 875
40-42: 42-Last Owl-c. 37 74 111 222 361 500
43-Terry & the Pirates-r 26 52 78 154 252 350
NOTE: *McWilliams art in most issues.*

Crack Comics #34 © QUA

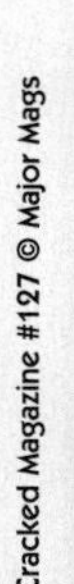
Cracked Magazine #127 © Major Mags

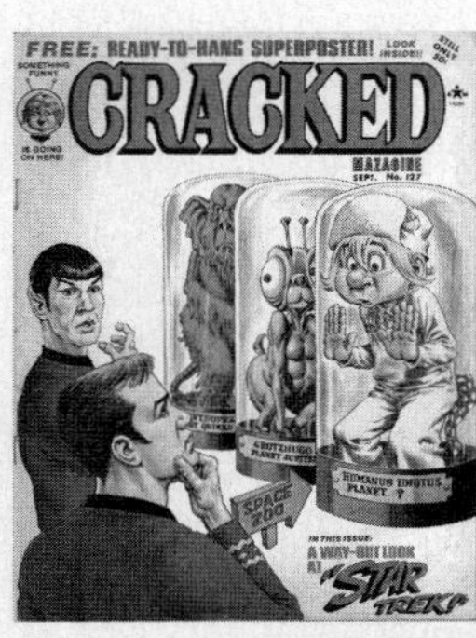

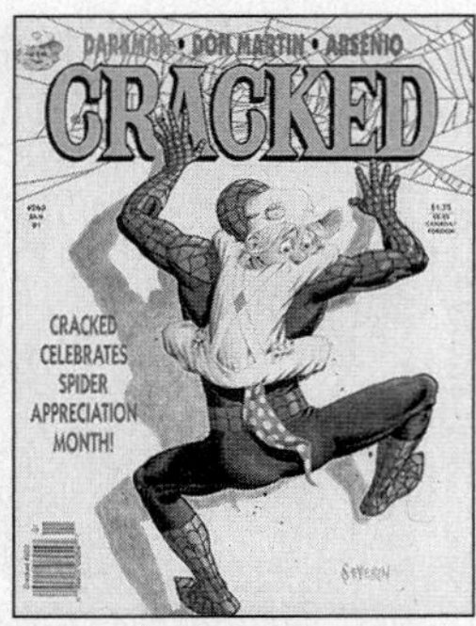

Cracked Magazine #260 © Globe Comm.

	GD 2.0	VG 4.0	FN 6.0	VF 8.0	VF/NM 9.0	NM- 9.2

CRACK COMICS (Crack Western No. 63 on)
Quality Comics Group: May, 1940 - No. 62, Sept, 1949

1-Origin & 1st app. The Black Condor by Lou Fine, Madame Fatal, Red Torpedo, Rock Bradden & The Space Legion; The Clock, Alias the Spider (by Gustavson), Wizard Wells, & Ned Brant begin; Powell-a; Note: Madame Fatal is a man dressed as a woman 465 930 1395 3395 5998 8600
2 219 438 657 1402 2401 3400
3 152 304 456 965 1658 2350
4 123 246 369 787 1344 1900
5-10: 5-Molly The Model begins. 10-Tor, the Magic Master begins 92 184 276 584 1005 1425
11-20: 13-1 pg. J. Cole-a. 15-1st app. Spitfire 81 162 243 514 887 1260
21-24: 23-Pen Miller begins; continued from National Comics #22. 24-Last Fine Black Condor 64 128 192 406 696 985
25,26: 26-Flag-c 48 96 144 302 514 725
27-(1/43)-Intro & origin Captain Triumph by Alfred Andriola (Kerry Drake artist) & begin series 90 180 270 576 988 1400
28-30 41 82 123 256 428 600
31-39: 31-Last Black Condor 24 48 72 142 234 325
40-46 17 34 51 100 158 215
47-57,59,60-Capt. Triumph by Crandall 18 36 54 107 169 230
58,61,62-Last Captain Triumph 15 30 45 85 130 175

NOTE: *Black Condor by* ***Fine****: No. 1, 2, 5, 6, 8, 10-24; by* ***Sultan****: No. 3, 7; by* ***Fugitani****: No. 9.* ***Cole*** *a-34.* ***Crandall*** *a-61(unsigned); c-48, 49, 51-61.* ***Guardineer*** *a-17.* ***Gustavson*** *a-1, 2, 4, 7, 13, 17, 23.* ***McWilliams*** *a-15-27. Black Condor c-2, 4, 6, 8, 10, 12, 14, 16, 18, 20-26. Capt. Triumph c-27-62. The Clock c-1, 3, 5, 7, 9, 11, 13, 15, 17, 19.*

CRACK COMICS
Quality Comics: May 1940

1-Ashcan comic, not distributed to newsstands, only for in-house use. Cover art is the same as published version of Crack Comics #1with exception of text panel on bottom left of cover. A CGC certified 4.0 copy sold for $1,495 in 2005.

CRACKED (Magazine) (Satire) (Also see The 3-D Zone #19)
Major Magazines(#1-212)/Globe Communications(#213-346/American Media #347 on):
Feb-Mar, 1958 - No. 365, Nov, 2004

1-One pg. Williamson-a; Everett-c; Gunsmoke-s 17 34 51 122 236 350
2-1st Shut-Ups & Bonus Cut-Outs; Superman parody-c by Severin (his 1st cover on the title) Frankenstein-s 10 20 30 67 116 165
3-5 7 14 21 50 83 115
6-10: 7-Reprints 1st 6 covers on-c. 8-Frankenstein-c. 10-Wolverton-a 6 12 18 41 66 90
11-12, 13(nn,3/60), 5 10 15 34 55 75
14-Kirby-a 6 12 18 41 66 90
15-17, 18(nn,2/61), 19,20 5 10 15 32 51 70
21-27(11/62), 27(No.28, 2/63; mis-#d), 29(5/63) 4 8 12 28 44 60
30-40(11/64): 37-Beatles and Superman cameos 4 8 12 24 37 50
41-45,47-56,59,60: 47,49,52-Munsters. 51-Beatles inside-c. 59-Laurel and Hardy photos 3 6 9 20 30 40
46,57,58: 46,58-Man From U.N.C.L.E. 46-Beatles. 57-Rolling Stones 4 8 12 22 34 45
61-80: 62-Beatles cameo. 69-Batman, Superman app. 70-(8/68) Elvis cameo. 71-Garrison's Gorillas; W.C. Fields photos 3 6 9 16 22 28
81-99: 99-Alfred E. Neuman on-c 3 6 9 14 19 24
100 3 6 9 18 27 35
101-119: 104-Godfather-c/s. 108-Archie Bunker-s. 112,119-Kung Fu (TV). 113-Tarzan-s. 115-MASH. 117-Cannon. 118-The Sting-c/s 2 4 6 10 14 18
120(12/74) Six Million Dollar Man-c/s; Ward-a 2 4 6 13 18 22
121,122,124-126,128-133,136-140: 121-American Graffiti. 122-Korak-c/s. 124,131-Godfather-c/s. 128-Capone-c. 129,131-Jaws. 132-Baretta-c/s. 133-Space 1999. 136-Laverne and Shirley/Fonz-c. 137-Travolta/Kotter-c/s. 138-Travolta/Laverne and Shirley/ Fonz-c. 139-Barney Miller-c/s. 140-King Kong-c/s; Fonz-s 2 4 6 10 14 18
123-Planet of the Apes-c/s; Six Million Dollar Man 2 4 6 13 18 22
127,134,135: 127-Star Trek-c/s; Ward-a. 134-Fonz-c/s; Starsky and Hutch. 135-Bionic Woman-c/s; Ward-a 2 4 6 11 16 20
141,151-Charlie's Angels-c/s. 151-Frankenstein 2 4 6 11 16 20
142,143,150,152-155,157: 142-MASH-c/s. 143-Rocky-c/s; King Kong-s. 150-(5/78) Close Encounters-c/s. 152-Close Enc./Star Wars-c/s. 153-Close Enc./Fonz-c/s. 154-Jaws II-c/s; Star Wars-s. 155-Star Wars/Fonz-c 2 4 6 9 13 16
144,149,156,158-160: 144-Fonz/Happy Days-c. 149-Star Wars/Six Mil.$ Man-c/s. 156-Grease/Travolta-c. 158-Mork & Mindy. 159-Battlestar Galactica-c/s; MASH-s. 160-Superman-c/s 2 4 6 11 16 20
145,147-Both have insert postcards: 145-Fonz/Rocky/L&S-c/s. 147-Star Wars-s; Farrah photo page (missing postcards-1/2 price) 3 6 9 14 20 26
146,148: 46-Star Wars-c/s with stickers insert (missing stickers-1/2 price). 148-Star Wars-c/s with inside-c color poster 3 6 9 16 23 30
161,170-Ward-a: 161-Mork & Mindy-c/s. 170-Dukes of Hazzard-c/s 2 4 6 8 11 14
162,165-168,171,172,175-178,180-Ward-a: 162-Sherlock Holmes-s. 165-Dracula-c/s. 167-Mork-c/s. 168,175-MASH-c/s. 168-Mork-s. 172-Dukes of Hazzard/CHiPs-c/s. 176-Barney Miller-c/s 2 4 6 8 10 12
163,179:163-Postcard insert; Mork & Mindy-c/s. 179-Insult cards insert; Popeye, Dukes of Hazzard-c/s 3 6 9 14 19 24
164,169,173,174: 164-Alien movie-c/s; Mork & Mindy-s. 169-Star Trek. 173,174-Star Wars-Empire Strikes Back. 173-SW poster 2 4 6 9 13 16
181,182,185-191,193,194,196-198-most Ward-a: 182-MASH-c/s. 185-Dukes of Hazzard-c/s; Jefferson-s. 187-Love Boat. 188-Fall Guy-s. 189-Fonz/Happy Days-c. 190,194-MASH-c/s. 191-Magnum P.I./Rocky-c; Magnum-s. 193-Knight Rider-s. 196-Dukes of Hazzard/Knight Rider-c/s. 198-Jaws III-c/s; Fall Guy-s 1 2 3 5 7 9
183,184,192,195,199,200-Ward-a in all: 183-Superman-c/s. 184-Star Trek-c/s. 192-E.T.-c/s; Rocky-s. 195-E.T.-c/s. 199-Jabba-c; Star Wars-s. 200-(12/83) 1 3 4 6 8 10
201,203,210-A-Team-c/s 6.00
202,204-206,211-224,226,227,230-233: 202-Knight Rider-s. 204-Magnum P.I.; A-Team-s. 206-Michael Jackson/Mr. T-c/s. 212-Prince-s; Cosby-s. 213-Monsters issue-c/s. 215-Hulk Hogan/Mr. T-c/s. 216-Miami Vice-s; James Bond-s. 217-Rambo-s; Cosby-s; A-Team-s. 218-Rocky-c/s. 219-Arnold/Commando-c/s; Rocky-s; Godzilla. 220-Rocky-c/s. 221-Stephen King app. 223-Miami Vice-s. 224-Cosby-s. 226-29th Anniv.; Tarzan-s; Aliens-s; Family Ties-s. 227-Cosby, Family Ties, Miami Vice-s. 230-Monkees-c/s; Elvis on-c; 232-Alf, Cheers, StarTrek-s. 233-Superman/James Bond-c/s; Robocop, Predator-s 5.00
207-209,225,234: 207-Michael Jackson-c/s. 208-Indiana Jones-c/s. 209-MichaelJackson/ Gremlins-c/s; Star Trek III-s. 225-Schwarzenegger/Stallone/G.I. Joe-c/s. 234-Don Martin-a begins; Batman/Robocop/Clint Eastwood-c/s 6.00
228,229: 228-Star Trek-c/s; Alf, Pee Wee Herman-s. 229-Monsters issue-c/s; centerfold with many superheroes 6.00
235,239,243,249: 235-1st Martin-c; Star Trek:TNG-s; Alf-s. 239-Beetlejuice-c/s; Mike Tyson-s. 243-X-Men and other heroes app. 249-Batman/Indiana Jones/Ghostbusters-c/s 6.00
236,244,245,248: 236-Madonna/Stallone-c/s; Twilight Zone-s. 244-Elvis-c/s; Martin-c. 245-Roger Rabbit-c/s. 248-Batman issue 6.00
237,238,240-242,246,247,250: 237-Robocop-s. 238-Rambo-c/s; Star Trek-s. 242-Dirty Harry-s, Ward-a. 246-Alf-s; Star Trek-s., Ward-a. 247-Star Trek-s. 250-Batman/Ghostbusters-s 4.00
251-253,255,256,259,261-265,275-278,281,284,286-297,299: 252-Star Trek-s. 253-Back to the Future-c/s. 255-TMNT-c/s. 256-TMNT-c/s; Batman, Bart Simpson on-c. 259-Die Hard II, Robocop-s. 261-TMNT, Twin Peaks-s. 262-Rocky-c/s; Rocky Horror-s. 265-TMNT-s. 276-Aliens III, Batman-s. 277-Clinton-c. 284-Bart Simpson-c; 90210-s. 297-Van Damme-s/photo-c. 299-Dumb & Dumber-c/s 4.00
254,257,266,267,272,280,282,285,298,300: 254-Back to the Future, Punisher-s; Wolverton-a, Batman-s, Ward-a. 257-Batman, Simpsons-s; Spider-Man and other heroes app. 266-Terminator-c/s. 267-Toons-c/s. 272-Star Trek VI-s. 280-Swimsuit issue. 282-Cheers-c/s. 285-Jurassic Park-c/s. 298-Swimsuit issue; Martin-c. 300-(8/95) Brady Bunch-c/s 5.00
258,260,274,279,283: 258-Simpsons-c/s; Back to the Future-s. 260-Spider-Man-c/s; Simpsons-s. 274-Batman-c/s. 279-Madonna-c/s. 283-Jurassic Park-c/s; Wolverine app. inside back-c 5.00
301-305,307-365: 365-Freas-c 2.50
306-Toy Story-c/s 4.00
Biggest... (Winter, 1977) 2 4 6 13 18 22
Biggest, Greatest... nn('65) 5 10 15 30 48 65
Biggest, Greatest... 2('66/67) - #5('69/70) 3 6 9 20 30 40
Biggest, Greatest... 6('70) - #12(Wint. '77) 3 6 9 14 19 24
Biggest, Greatest...13(Fall '78) - #21(Fall/Wint. '86) 2 4 6 8 11 14
...Blockbuster 1(Sum '87), 2('88), 3(Sum. '89) 1 3 4 6 8 10
...Blockbuster 4 - 6(Sum. '92) 6.00
...Collectors' Edition 4 ('73; formerly ...Special) 2 4 6 13 18 22
5-9,10(10/75) 2 4 6 11 16 20
11-19,20(11/17) 2 4 6 8 11 14
21,22,23(5/78): 23-Ward-a 2 4 6 8 11 14
(#24-62,64 not numbered)
1978 (nn; July, Sept, Nov, Dec) (#24-27) 2 4 6 8 11 14
1979 (nn; May, July, Sept, Nov, Dec) (#28-33) 2 4 6 8 11 14
1980 (nn; Feb, May, July, Sept, Nov, Dec) (#34-39) 1 3 4 6 8 10
1981 (nn; Feb, May, July, Sept, Nov, Dec) (#40-45) 1 3 4 6 8 10
1982 (nn; Feb, May, July, Sept, Nov, Dec) (#46-51) 1 3 4 6 8 10
1983 (nn; Feb, May, Sept, Nov, Dec) (#52-56) 1 3 4 6 8 10
1984 (nn; Feb, May, July, Nov) (#57-60) 1 2 3 4 5 7
1985 (nn; Feb) (#61) 1 2 3 4 5 7
62(9/85), nn(#63,11/85), 64(12/85), 65-69, 70(4/87) 1 2 3 4 5 7
71,72,73(100 pgs., 1/88), 74-79, 80(9/89) 5.00
81-96, 97(two diff. issues), 98-115: 83-Elvis, Batman parodies 5.00
116('98)-Last issue? 6.00

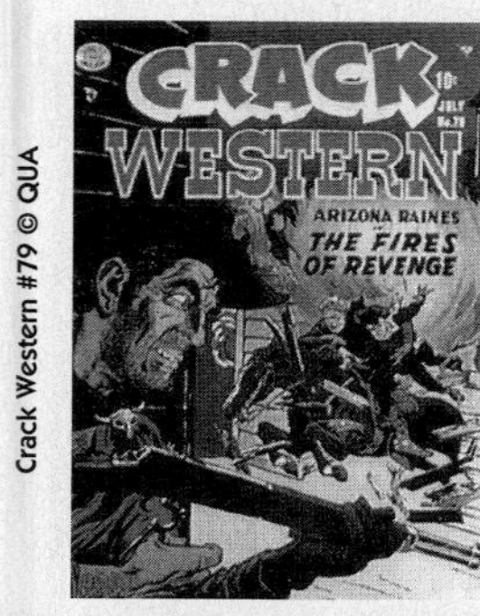

Crack Western #79 © QUA

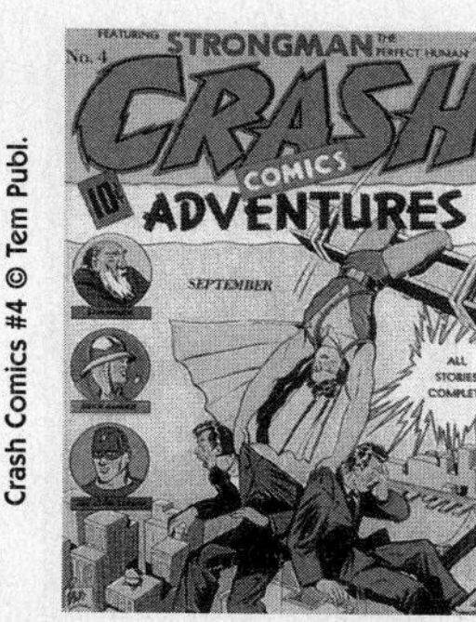

Crash Comics #4 © Tem Publ.

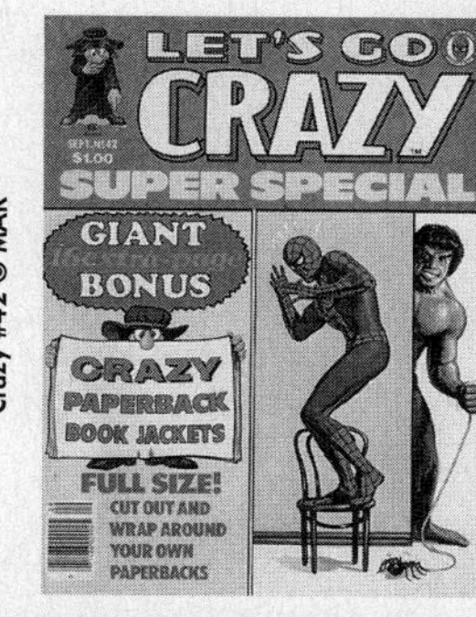

Crazy #42 © MAR

	GD 2.0	VG 4.0	FN 6.0	VF 8.0	VF/NM 9.0	NM- 9.2
...Digest 1(Fall, '86, 148 pgs.), 2(1/87)	1	2	3	6	8	10
...Digest 3-5	1	2	3	4	5	7
...Party Pack 1,2('88) - 4('90)						4.00
...Shut-Ups 1(2/72)	3	6	9	18	27	35
...Shut-Ups 2('72) becomes Cracked Spec. #3	3	6	9	14	19	24
...Special 3('73; formerly Cracked Shut-Ups; ...Collectors' Edition#4 on)	2	4	6	13	18	22
... Summer Special 1(Sum. '91), 2(Sum. '92)-Don Martin-a						4.00
... Summer Special 3(Sum. '93) - 8(Sum. '98)						3.00
... Super (Vol. 2, formerly Super Cracked) 5(Wint. '91/92) - 14(Wint.'97/98)						3.00
Extra Special... 1(Spr. '76)	2	4	6	11	16	20
Extra Special... 2(Spr./Sum. '77)	2	4	6	10	14	18
Extra Special... 3(Wint. '79) - 9(Wint. '86)	1	2	3	4	5	7
Giant... nn('65)	6	12	18	37	59	80
Giant... 2('66) - 5('69)	4	8	12	22	34	45
Giant...6('70) - 12('76)	3	6	9	17	25	32
Giant...nn(9/77, #13), nn(1/78, #14), nn(3/78, #15), nn(5/78, #16), nn(7/78, #17), nn(11/78, #18), nn(3/79, #19), nn(7/79, #20), nn(10/79, #21), nn(12/79, #22), nn(3/80, #23), nn(7/80, #24)	2	4	6	11	16	20
Giant...nn(10/80, #25), nn(12/80, #26), nn(3/81, #27), nn(7/81, #28), nn(10/81, #29), nn(12/81, #30), nn(7/82, #31), nn(10/82, #32), nn(12/82, #33), nn(7/83, #34),	2	4	6	8	11	14
Giant...nn(10/83, #35), nn(12/83, #36), nn(3/84, #37), nn(7/84, #38), nn(10/84, #39), nn(3/85, #40), nn(7/85, #41), nn(10/85, #42)	1	2	3	5	7	9
Giant...43(3/86) - 46(1/87), 47(Wint. '88), 48(Wint. '89)	1	2	3	4	5	7
King Sized... 1('67)	4	8	12	26	41	55
King Sized... 2('68) - 5('71)	3	6	9	18	27	35
King Sized... 6('72) - 11('77)	3	6	9	14	20	26
King Sized... 12(Fall '78) - 17(Sum. '83)	2	4	6	8	11	14
King Sized... 18-20 (Sum/'86) (#21,22 exist?)	1	3	4	6	8	10
Spaced Out... 1-4 ('93 - '94)						5.00
Super... 1('68)	4	8	12	26	41	55
Super... 2('69) - 6('73)	3	6	9	20	30	40
Super... 7('74), 8(Spr. '75) - 10(Spr. '77)	3	6	9	16	22	28
Super... 11(Sum. '78) - 16(Fall '81)	2	4	6	11	16	20
Super... 17(Spr. '82) - 22(Fall '83)	2	4	6	8	11	14
Super... 23(Sum. '84, mis-numbered as #24)	2	4	6	8	11	14
Super... 24(Fall '84, correctly numbered)	2	4	6	8	11	14
Super... 25(Wint. '85) - 32(Fall '86)	2	4	6	8	10	12
Super... (Vol. 2) 1('87, 100 pgs.)-Severin & Elder-a	1	3	4	6	8	10
Super... (Vol. 2) 2(Sum. '88), 3(Wint. '89), 4(exist?)(Becomes Cracked Super)						6.00

NOTE: ***Burgos** a-1-10. **Colan** a-257. **Davis** a-5, 11-17, 24, 40, 80; c-12-14, 16. **Elder** a-5, 6, 10-13; c-10. **Everett** a-1-10, 23-25, 61; c-1. **Heath** a-1-3, 6, 13, 14, 17, 110; c-6. **Jaffee** a-5, 6. **Don Martin** c-235, 244, 247, 259, 261, 264. **Morrow** a-8-10. **Reinman** a-1-4. **Severin** c/a-in most all issues. **Shores** a-3-7. **Torres** a-7-10. **Ward** a-22-24, 27, 35, 40, 120-193, 195, 197-205, 242, 244, 246, 247, 250, 252-257. **Williamson** a-1 (1 pg.). **Wolverton** a-10 (2 pgs.), Giant nn('65). **Wood** a-27, 35, 40. Alfred E. Neuman c-177, 200, 202. Batman c-234, 248, 249, 256, 274. Captain America c-256. Christmas c-234, 243. Spider-Man c-260. Star Trek c-127, 169, 207, 228. Star Wars c-145, 146, 148, 149, 152, 155, 173, 174, 199. Superman c-183, 233. #144, 146 have free full-color pre-glued stickers. #145, 147, 155, 163 have free full-color postcards. #123, 137, 154, 157 have free iron-ons.*

CRACKED MONSTER PARTY
Globe Communications: July, 1988 - No. 27, Wint. 1999/2000

	GD 2.0	VG 4.0	FN 6.0	VF 8.0	VF/NM 9.0	NM- 9.2
1	2	4	6	10	14	18
2-10	2	4	6	8	10	12
11-26	1	2	3	4	5	7
27-Interview with a Vampire-c/s	2	4	6	8	10	12

CRACKED'S FOR MONSTERS ONLY
Major Magazines: Sept, 1969 - No. 9, Sept, 1969; June, 1972

	GD 2.0	VG 4.0	FN 6.0	VF 8.0	VF/NM 9.0	NM- 9.2
1	5	10	15	30	48	65
2-9, nn(6/72)	3	6	9	20	30	40

CRACK WESTERN (Formerly Crack Comics; Jonesy No. 85 on)
Quality Comics Group: No. 63, Nov, 1949 - No. 84, May, 1953 (36 pgs., 63-68,74-on)

	GD 2.0	VG 4.0	FN 6.0	VF 8.0	VF/NM 9.0	NM- 9.2
63(#1)-Ward-c; Two-Gun Lil (origin & 1st app.)(ends #84), Arizona Ames, his horse Thunder (with sidekick Spurs & his horse Calico), Frontier Marshal (ends #70), & Dead Canyon Days (ends #69) begin; Crandall-a	18	36	54	107	169	230
64,65: 64-Ward-c. Crandall-a in both.	15	30	45	83	124	165
66,68-Photo-c. 66-Arizona Ames becomes A. Raines (ends #84)	13	26	39	72	101	130
67-Randolph Scott photo-c; Crandall-a	14	28	42	80	115	150
69(52pgs.)-Crandall-a	13	26	39	72	101	130
70(52pgs.)-The Whip (origin & 1st app.) & his horse Diablo begin (ends #84); Crandall-a	13	26	39	72	101	130
71(52pgs.)-Frontier Marshal becomes Bob Allen F. Marshal (ends #84); Crandall-c/a	14	28	42	80	115	150
72(52pgs.)-Tim Holt photo-c	12	24	36	67	94	120
73(52pgs.)-Photo-c	10	20	30	58	79	100
74-76,78,79,81,83-Crandall-c. 83-Crandall-a(p)	11	22	33	62	86	110
77,80,82	8	16	24	44	57	70
84-Crandall-c/a	12	24	36	67	94	120

NOTE: ***Crandall** c-71p, 74-81, 83p(w/**Cuidera**-i).*

CRASH COMICS (Catman Comics No. 6 on)
Tem Publishing Co.: May, 1940 - No. 5, Nov, 1940

	GD 2.0	VG 4.0	FN 6.0	VF 8.0	VF/NM 9.0	NM- 9.2
1-The Blue Streak, Strongman (origin), The Perfect Human, Shangra begin (1st app. of each); Kirby-a	320	640	960	2240	3920	5600
2-Simon & Kirby-a	161	322	483	1030	1765	2500
3,5-Simon & Kirby-a	135	270	405	864	1482	2100
4-Origin & 1st app. The Catman; S&K-a	331	662	993	2317	4059	5800

NOTE: *Solar Legion by **Kirby** No. 1-5 (5 pgs. each). Strongman c-1-4. Catman c-5.*

CRASH DIVE (See Cinema Comics Herald)

CRASH METRO AND THE STAR SQUAD
Oni Press: May, 1999 ($2.95, B&W, one-shot)

	GD 2.0	VG 4.0	FN 6.0	VF 8.0	VF/NM 9.0	NM- 9.2
1-Allred-s/Ontiveros-a						3.00

CRASH RYAN (Also see Dark Horse Presents #44)
Marvel Comics (Epic): Oct, 1984 - No. 4, Jan, 1985 (Baxter paper, lim. series)

	GD 2.0	VG 4.0	FN 6.0	VF 8.0	VF/NM 9.0	NM- 9.2
1-4						2.50

CRAZY (Also see This Magazine is Crazy)
Atlas Comics (CSI): Dec, 1953 - No. 7, July, 1954

	GD 2.0	VG 4.0	FN 6.0	VF 8.0	VF/NM 9.0	NM- 9.2
1-Everett-c/a	30	60	90	177	289	400
2	20	40	60	118	192	265
3-7: 4-I Love Lucy satire. 5-Satire on censorship	17	34	51	100	158	215

NOTE: ***Ayers** a-5. **Berg** a-1, 2. **Burgos** c-5, 6. **Drucker** a-6. **Everett** a-1-4. **Al Hartley** a-4. **Heath** a-3, 7; c-7. **Maneely** a-1-7, c-3, 4. **Post** a-3-6. Funny monster c-1-4.*

CRAZY (Satire)
Marvel Comics Group: Feb, 1973 - No. 3, June, 1973

	GD 2.0	VG 4.0	FN 6.0	VF 8.0	VF/NM 9.0	NM- 9.2
1-Not Brand Echh-r; Beatles cameo (r)	3	6	9	16	23	30
2,3-Not Brand Echh-r; Kirby-a	2	4	6	10	16	20

CRAZY MAGAZINE (Satire)
Oct, 1973 - No. 94, Apr, 1983 (40-90¢, B&W magazine)
Marvel Comics: (#1, 44 pgs; #2-90, reg. issues, 52 pgs; #92-95, 68 pgs)'

	GD 2.0	VG 4.0	FN 6.0	VF 8.0	VF/NM 9.0	NM- 9.2
1-Wolverton(1 pg.), Bode-a; 3 pg. photo story of Neal Adams & Dick Giordano; Harlan Ellison story; TV Kung Fu sty.	5	10	15	30	48	65
2-"Live & Let Die" c/s; 8pgs; Adams/Buscema-a; McCloud w5 pgs. Adams-a; Kurtzman's "Hey Look" 2 pg.-r	3	6	9	20	30	40
3-5: 3-"High Plains Drifter" w/Clint Eastwood c/s; Waltons app; Drucker, Reese-a. 4-Shaft-c/s; Ploog-a; Nixon 3 pg. app; Freas-a. 5-Michael Crichton's "Westworld" c/s; Nixon app.	3	6	9	17	25	32
6,7,18: 6-Exorcist c/s; Nixon app. 7-TV's Kung Fu c/s; Nixon app.; Ploog & Freas-a. 18-Six Million Dollar Man/Bionic Woman c/s; Welcome Back Kotter story	3	6	9	16	22	28
8-10: 8-Serpico c/s; Casper parody; TV's Police Story. 9-Joker cameo; Chinatown story; Eisner s/a begins; Has 1st 8 covers on-c. 10-Playboy Bunny-c; M. Severin-a; Lee Marrs-a begins; "Deathwish" story	3	6	9	14	20	26
11-17,19: 11-Towering Inferno. 12-Rhoda. 13-"Tommy" the Who Rock Opera. 14-Mandingo. 15-Jaws story. 16-Santa/Xmas-c; "Good Times" TV story; Jaws. 17-Bicentennial issue; Baretta; Woody Allen. 19-King Kong c/s; Reagan, J. Carter, Howard the Duck cameos, "Laverne & Shirley"	2	4	6	11	16	20
20,24,27: 20-Bicentennial-c; Space 1999 sty; Superheroes song sheet, 4pgs. 24-Charlie's Angels. 27-Charlie's Angels/Travolta/Fonz-c; Bionic Woman sty	3	6	9	14	19	24
21-23,25,26,28-30: 21-Starsky & Hutch. 22-Mount Rushmore/J. Carter-c; TV's Barney Miller; Superheroes spoof. 23-Santa/Xmas-c; "Happy Days" sty; "Omen" sty. 25-J. Carter-c/s; Grandenetti-a begins; TV's Alice; Logan's Run. 26-TV Stars-c; Mary Hartman, King Kong. 28-Donny & Marie Osmond-c/s; Marathon Man. 29-Travolta/Kotter-c; "One Day at a Time", Gong Show. 30-1977, 84 pgs. w/bonus; Jaws, Baretta, King Kong, Happy Days	2	4	6	9	12	15
31,33-35,38,40: 31-"Rocky"-c/s; TV game shows. 33-Peter Benchley's "Deep". 34-J. Carter-c; TV's "Fish". 35-Xmas-c with Fonz/Six Million Dollar Man/Wonder Woman/Darth Vader/ Travolta, TV's "Mash" & "Family Matters". 38-Close Encounters of the Third Kind-c/s. 40-"Three's Company-c/s	1	3	4	6	8	11
32-Star Wars/Darth Vader-c/s; "Black Sunday"	3	6	9	14	19	24
36,42,47,49: 36-Farrah Fawcett/Six Million Dollar Man-c; TV's Nancy Drew & Hardy Boys; 1st app. Howard The Duck in Crazy, 2 pgs. 42-84 pgs. w/bonus; TV Hulk/Spider-Man-c; Mash, Gong Show, One Day at a Time, Disco, Alice. 47-Battlestar Galactica xmas-c; movie "Foul Play". 49-1979, 84 pgs. w/bonus; Mork & Mindy-c; Jaws, Saturday Night Fever, Three's Company	2	4	6	9	12	15

37-1978, 84 pgs. w/bonus. Darth Vader-c; Barney Miller, Laverne & Shirley, Good Times,

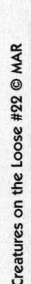

Crazy #57 © MAR

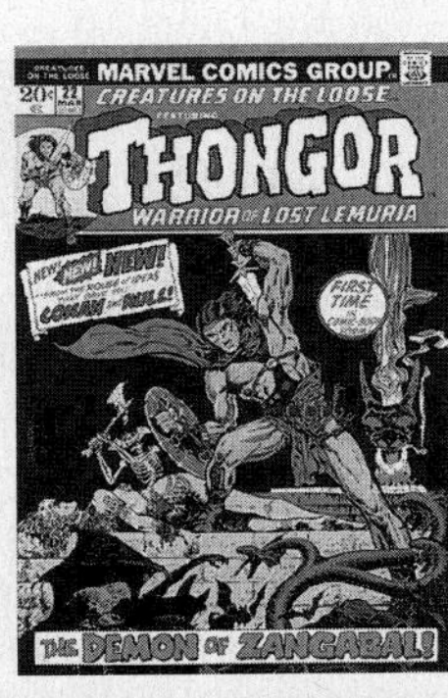

Creatures on the Loose #22 © MAR

The Creeper #9 © DC

GD VG FN VF VF/NM NM-
2.0 4.0 6.0 8.0 9.0 9.2

Rocky, Donny & Marie Osmond, Bionic Woman 2 4 6 13 18 22

39,44: 39-Saturday Night Fever-c/s. 44-"Grease"-c w/Travolta/O. Newton-John
2 4 6 11 16 20

41-Kiss-c & 1pg. photos; Disaster movies, TV's "Family", Annie Hall
4 8 12 28 44 60

43,45,46,48,51: 43-Jaws-c; Saturday Night Fever. 43-E.C. swipe from Mad #131. 45-Travolta/O. Newton-John/J. Carter-c; Eight is Enough. 46-TV Hulk-c/s; Punk Rock. 48-"Wiz"-c, Battlestar Galactica-s. 51-Grease/Mork & Mindy/D&M Osmond-c, Mork & Mindy-sty. "Boys from Brazil" 1 3 4 6 8 11

50,58: 50-Superman movie-c/sty, Playboy Mag., TV Hulk, Fonz; Howard the Duck, 1 pg. 58-1980, 84 pgs. w/32 pg. color comic bonus insert-Full reprint of Crazy Comic #1, Battlestar Galactica, Charlie's Angels, Starsky & Hutch
2 4 6 11 16 20

52,59,60,64: 52-1979, 84 pgs. w/bonus. Marlon Brando-c; TV Hulk, Grease. Kiss, 1 pg. photos. 59-Santa Ptd-c by Larkin; "Alien", "Moonraker", Rocky-2, Howard the Duck, 1 pg. 60-Star Trek w/Muppets-c; Star Trek sty; 1st app/origin Teen Hulk; Severin-a. 64-84 pgs. w/bonus Monopoly game satire. "Empire Strikes Back", 8 pgs., One Day at a Time
2 4 6 11 16 20

53,54,65,67-70: 53-"Animal House"-c/sty; TV's "Vegas", Howard the Duck, 1 pg. 54-Love at First Bite-c/sty, Fantasy Island sty, Howard the Duck 1 pg. 65-(Has #66 on-c, Aug/'80). "Black Hole" w/Janson-a; Kirby,Wood/Severin-a(r), 5 pgs. Howard the Duck, 3 pgs.; Broderick-a; Buck Rogers, Mr. Rogers. 67-84 pgs. w/bonus; TV's Kung Fu, Exorcist; Ploog-a(r). 68-American Gigolo, Dukes of Hazzard, Teen Hulk; Howard the Duck, 3 pgs. Broderick-a; Monster sty/5 pg. Ditko-a(r). 69-Obnoxio the Clown-c/sty; Stephen King's "Shining", Teen Hulk, Richie Rich, Howard the Duck, 3pgs; Broderick-a. 70-84 pgs. Towering Inferno, Daytime TV; Trina Robbins-a 1 3 4 6 8 10

55-57,61,63: 55-84 pgs. w/bonus; Love Boat, Mork & Mindy, Fonz, TV Hulk. 56-Mork/Rocky/J. Carter-c; China Syndrome. 57-TV Hulk with Miss Piggy-c, Dracula, Taxi, Muppets. 61-1980, 84 pgs. Adams-a(r), McCloud, Pro wrestling, Casper, TV's Police Story. 63-Apocalypse Now-Coppola's cult movie; 3rd app. Teen Hulk, Howard the Duck, 3 pgs.
2 4 6 8 11 14

62-Kiss-c & 2 pg. app; Quincy, 2nd app. Teen Hulk 4 8 12 24 37 50

66-Sept/'80, Empire Strikes Back-c/sty; Teen Hulk by Severin, Howard the Duck, 3pgs. by Broderick 2 4 6 10 14 18

71,72,75-77,79: 71-Blues Brothers parody, Teen Hulk, Superheroes parody, WKRP in Cincinnati, Howard the Duck, 3pgs. by Broderick. 72-Jackie Gleason/Smokey & the Bandit II-c/sty, Shogun, Teen Hulk. Howard the Duck, 3pgs. by Broderick. 75-Flash Gordon movie c/sty; Teen Hulk, Cat in the Hat, Howard the Duck 3pgs. by Broderick. 76-84 pgs. w/bonus; Monster-sty w/ Crandall-a(r), Monster-stys(2) w/Kirby-a(r), 5pgs. ea; Mash, TV Hulk, Chinatown. 77-Popeye movie/R. Williams-c/sty; Teen Hulk, Love Boat, Howard the Duck 3 pgs. 79-84 pgs. w/bonus color stickers; has new material; "9 to 5" w/Dolly Parton, Teen Hulk, Magnum P.I., Monster-sty w/5pgs, Ditko-a(r), "Rat" w/Sutton-a(r), Everett-a, 4 pgs.(r)
1 3 4 6 8 10

73,74,78,80: 73-84 pgs. w/bonus Hulk/Spiderman Finger Puppets-c & bonus; "Live & Let Die, Jaws, Fantasy Island. 74-Dallas/"Who Shot J.R."-c/sty; Elephant Man, Howard the Duck 3pgs. by Broderick. 78-Clint Eastwood-c/sty; Teen Hulk, Superheroes parody, Lou Grant. 80-Star Wars, 2 pg. app; "Howling", TV's "Greatest American Hero"
2 4 6 8 11 14

81,84,86,87,89: 81-.Superman Movie II-c/sty; Wolverine cameo, Mash, Teen Hulk. 84-American Werewolf in London, Johnny Carson app; Teen Hulk. 86-Time Bandits-c/sty; Private Benjamin. 87-Rubix Cube-c; Hill Street Blues, "Ragtime", Origin Obnoxio the Clown; Teen Hulk. 89-Burt Reynolds "Sharkey's Machine", Teen Hulk
1 3 4 6 8 10

82-X-Men-c w/new Byrne-a, 84 pgs. w/new material; Fantasy Island, Teen Hulk, "For Your Eyes Only", Spiderman/Human Torch-r by Kirby/Ditko; Sutton-a(r); Rogers-a; Hunchback of Notre Dame, 5 pgs. 2 4 6 11 16 20

83-Raiders of the Lost Ark-c/sty; Hart to Hart; Reese-a; Teen Hulk
2 4 6 9 13 20

85,88: 85-84 pgs; Escape from New York, Teen Hulk; Kirby-a(r), 5 pgs, Poseidon Adventure, Flintstones, Sesame Street. 88-84 pgs. w/bonus Dr. Strange Game; some new material; Jeffersons, X-Men/Wolverine, 10 pgs.; Byrne-a; Apocalypse Now, Teen Hulk
1 3 4 6 8 11

90-94: 90-Conan-c/sty; M. Severin-a; Teen Hulk. 91-84 pgs, some new material; Bladerunner-c/sty, "Deathwish-II, Teen Hulk, Black Knight, 10 pgs.-'50s-r w/Maneely-a. 92-Wrath of Khan Star Trek-c/sty; Joanie & Chachi, Teen Hulk. 93-"E.T."-c/sty, Teen Hulk, Archie Bunkers Place, Dr. Doom Game. 94-Poltergeist, Smurfs, Teen Hulk, Casper, Avengers parody-8pgs. Adams-a 2 4 6 10 14 18

Crazy Summer Special #1 (Sum, '75, 100 pgs.)-Nixon, TV Kung Fu, Babe Ruth, Joe Namath, Waltons, McCloud, Chariots of the Gods 3 6 9 14 19 24

NOTE: ***N. Adams** a-2, 61r, 94p. **Austin** a-82i. **Buscema** a-2, 82. **Byrne** c-82p. **Nick Cardy** c-7, 8, 10, 12-16, Super Special 1. **Crandall** a-76r. **Ditko** a-68r, 79r, 82r. **Drucker** a-3. **Eisner** a-9-16. **Kelly Freas** c-1-6, 9, 11; a-7. **Kirby/Wood** a-66r. **Ploog** a-1, 4, 7, 67r, 73r. **Rogers** a-82. **Sparling** a-92. **Wood** a-65r. Howard the Duck in 36, 50, 51, 53, 54, 59, 63, 65, 66, 68, 69, 71, 72, 74, 75, 77. Hulk in 46, c-42, 46, 57, 73. Star Wars in 32, 66; c-37.*

CRAZYMAN
Continuity Comics: Apr, 1992 - No. 3, 1992 ($2.50, high quality paper)

1-($3.95, 52 pgs.)-Embossed-c; N. Adams part-i 4.00
2,3 ($2.50): 2-N. Adams/Bolland-c 2.50

CRAZYMAN
Continuity Comics: V2#1, 5/93 - No. 4, 1/94 ($2.50, high quality paper)

V2#1-4: 1-Entire book is die-cut. 2-(12/93)-Adams-c(p) & part scripts. 3-(12/93). 4-Indicia says #3, Jan. 1993 2.50

CRAZY, MAN, CRAZY (Magazine) (Becomes This Magazine is...?)
(Formerly From Here to Insanity)
Humor Magazines (Charlton): V2#1, Dec, 1955 - V2#2, June, 1956

V2#1,V2#2-Satire; Wolverton-a, 3 pgs. 15 30 45 85 130 175

CREATURE, THE (See Movie Classics)

CREATURE COMMANDOS (See Weird War Tales #93 for 1st app.)
DC Comics: May, 2000 - No. 8, Dec, 2000 ($2.50, limited series)

1-8: Truman-s/Eaton-a 2.50

CREATURES OF THE ID
Caliber Press: 1990 ($2.95, B&W)

1-Frank Einstein (Madman) app.; Allred-a 3 6 9 16 23 30

CREATURES OF THE NIGHT
Dark Horse Books: Nov, 2004 ($12.95, hardcover graphic novel)

HC-Neil Gaiman-s/Michael Zulli-a/c 13.00

CREATURES ON THE LOOSE (Formerly Tower of Shadows No. 1-9)(See Kull)
Marvel Comics: No. 10, March, 1971 - No. 37, Sept, 1975 (New-a & reprints)

10-(15¢)-1st full app. King Kull; see Kull the Conqueror; Wrightson-a
7 14 21 49 80 110

	GD	VG	FN	VF	VF/NM	NM-
11-15: 13-Last 15¢ issue	3	6	9	17	25	32
16-Origin Warrior of Mars (begins, ends #21)	2	4	6	13	18	22
17-20	2	4	6	8	11	14
21-Steranko-c	3	6	9	14	20	26
22-Steranko-c; Thongor stories begin	3	6	9	16	22	28
23-29-Thongor-c/stories	1	2	3	5	7	9
30-Manwolf begins	3	6	9	17	25	32
31-33	2	4	6	9	12	15
34-37	2	4	6	8	10	12

NOTE: ***Crandall** a-13. **Ditko** r-15, 17, 18, 20, 22, 24, 27, 28. **Everett** a-16i(new). **Matt Fox** r-21i. **Howard** a-26i. **Gil Kane** a-16p, 17p, 19i; c-16, 17, 19, 20, 25, 29, 33p, 35p, 36p. **Kirby** a-10-15r, 16(2)r, 17r, 19r. **Morrow** a-20, 21. **Perez** a-33-37; c-34p. **Shores** a-11. **innott** r-21. **Sutton** c-10. **Tuska** a-30-32p.*

CREECH, THE
Image Comics: Oct, 1997 - No. 3, Dec, 1997 ($1.95/$2.50, limited series)

1-3: 1-Capullo-s/c/a(p) 2.50
TPB (1999, $9.95) r/#1-3, McFarlane intro. 10.00
Out for Blood 1-3 (7/01 - No. 3, 11/01; $4.95) Capullo-s/c/a 5.00

CREED
Hall of Heroes Comics: Dec, 1994 - No. 2, Jan, 1995 ($2.50, B&W)

1 2 4 6 9 12 15
2 2 4 6 8 10 12

CREED
Lightning Comics: June, 1995 - No. 3 ($2.75/$3.00, B&W/color)

1-($2.75) 4.00
1-($3.00, color) 5.00
1-($9.95)-Commemorative Edition 10.00
1-TwinVariant Edition (1250? print run) 10.00
1-Special Edition; polybagged w/certificate 4.00
1 Gold Collectors Edition; polybagged w/certificate 3.00
2,3-($3.00, color)-Butt Naked Edition & regular-c 3.00
3-($9.95)-Commemorative Edition; polybagged w/certificate & card 10.00

CREED: CRANIAL DISORDER
Lightning Comics: Oct, 1996 ($3.00, limited series)

1-3-Two covers 3.00
1-($5.95)-Platinum Edition 6.00
2,3-($9.95)Ltd.l Edition 10.00

CREED/TEENAGE MUTANT NINJA TURTLES
Lightning Comics: May, 1996 ($3.00, one-shot)

1-Kaniuga-a(p)/scripts; Laird-c; variant-c exists 3.00
1-($9.95)-Platinum Edition 10.00
1-Special Edition; polybagged w/certificate 5.00

CREEPER, THE (See Beware... , Showcase #73 & 1st Issue Special #7)
DC Comics: Dec, 1997 - No. 11; #1,000,000 Nov, 1998 ($2.50)

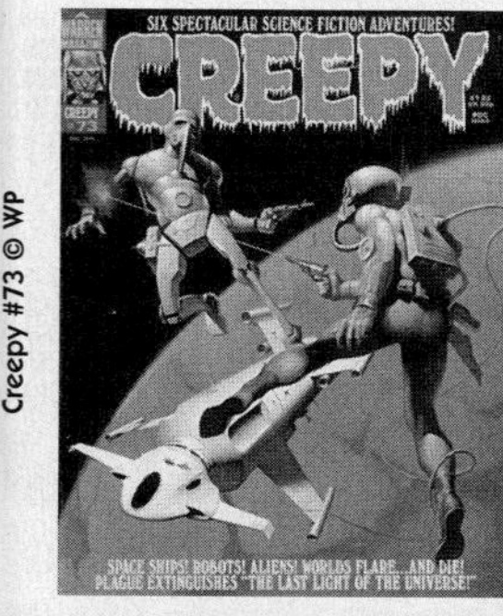

Creepy #73 © WP

Creepy (2009) #1 © New Comic Co.

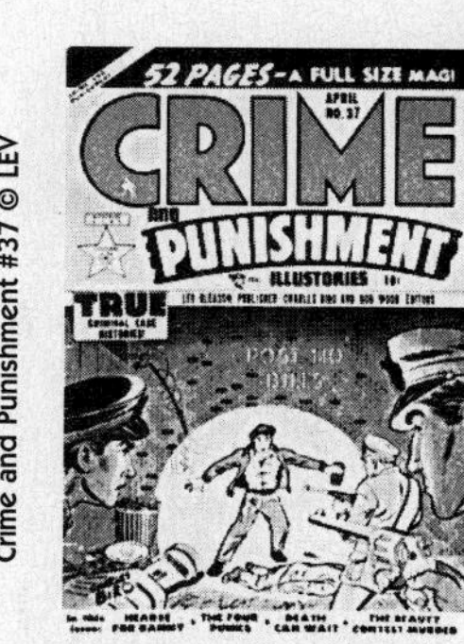

Crime and Punishment #37 © LEV

1-11-Kaminski-s/Martinbrough-a(p). 7,8-Joker-c/app. 3.00
#1,000,000 (11/98) 853rd Century x-over 3.00

CREEPER, THE (See DCU Brave New World)
DC Comics: Oct, 2006 - No. 6, Mar, 2007 ($2.99, limited series)

1-6-Niles-s/Justiniano-a/c; Jack Ryder becomes the Creeper. 2-6-Batman app. 3.00
... - Welcome to Creepsville TPB ('07, $19.99) r/#1-6 & story from DCU Brave New World 20.00

CREEPS
Image Comics: Oct, 2001 - No. 4, May, 2002 ($2.95)

1-4-Mandrake-a/Mishkin-s 3.00

CREEPSHOW
Plume/New American Library Pub.: July, 1982 (softcover graphic novel)

1st edition-nn-(68 pgs.) Kamen-c/Wrightson-a; screenplay by Stephen King for the George Romero movie 4 8 12 24 37 50
2nd-7th printings 3 6 9 18 27 35

CREEPSVILLE
Laughing Reindeer Press: V2#1, Winter, 1995 ($4.95)

V2#1-Comics w/text 5.00

CREEPY (See Warren Presents)
Warren Publishing Co./Harris Publ. #146: 1964 - No. 145, Feb, 1983; No. 146, 1985 (B&W, magazine)

1-Frazetta-a (his last story in comics?); Jack Davis-c; 1st Warren all comics magazine; 1st app. Uncle Creepy 12 24 36 83 152 220
2-Frazetta-c & 1 pg. strip 7 14 21 50 83 115
3-8,11-13,15-17: 3-7,9-11,15-17-Frazetta-c. 7-Frazetta 1 pg. strip. 15,16-Adams-a. 16-Jeff Jones-a 5 10 15 32 51 70
9-Creepy fan club sketch by Wrightson (1st published-a); has 1/2 pg. anti-smoking strip by Frazetta; Frazetta-c; 1st Wood and Ditko art on this title; Toth-a (low print) 7 14 21 49 80 110
10-Brunner fan club sketch (1st published work) 5 10 15 34 55 75
14-Neal Adams 1st Warren work 5 10 15 34 55 75
18-28,30,31: 27-Frazetta-c 4 8 12 24 37 50
29,34: 29-Jones-a 4 8 12 26 41 55
32-(scarce) Frazetta-c; Harlan Ellison sty 6 12 18 41 66 90
33,35,37,39,40,42-47,49: 35-Hitler/Nazi-s. 39-1st Uncle Creepy solo-s, Cousin Eerie app.; early Brunner-a. 42-1st San Julian-c. 44-1st Ploog-a. 46-Corben-a 3 6 9 21 32 42
36-(11/70)1st Corben art at Warren 4 8 12 26 41 55
38,41-(scarce): 38-1st Kelly-c. 41-Corben-a 5 10 15 30 48 65
48,55,65-(1972, 1973, 1974 Annuals) #55 & 65 contain an 8 pg. slick comic insert. 48-(84 pgs.). 55-Color poster bonus (1/2 price if missing). 65-(100 pgs.) Summer Giant 4 8 12 26 41 55
50-Vampirella/Eerie/Creepy-c 5 10 15 30 48 65
51,54,56-61,64: All contain an 8 pg. slick comic insert in middle. 59-Xmas horror. 54,64-Chaykin-a 4 8 12 23 36 48
52,53,66,71,72,75,76,78-80: 71-All Bermejo-a; Space & Time issue. 72-Gual-a. 78-Fantasy issue. 79,80-Monsters issue 3 6 9 17 25 32
62,63-1st & 2nd full Wrightson story art; Corben-a; 8 pg. color comic insert 4 8 12 23 36 48
67,68,73 3 6 9 19 29 38
69,70-Edgar Allan Poe issues; Corben-a 3 6 9 18 27 35
74,77: 74-All Crandell-a. 77-Xmas Horror issue; Corben-a,Wrightson-a 3 6 9 21 32 42
81,84,85,88-90,92-94,96-99,102,104-112,114-118,120,122-130: 84,93-Sports issue. 85,97,102-Monster issue. 89-All war issue; Nino-a. 94-Weird Children issue. 96,109-Aliens issue. 99-Disasters. 103-Corben-a. 104-Robots issue. 106-Sword & Sorcery.107-Sci-fi. 116-End of Man. 125-Xmas Horror 2 4 6 9 12 15
82,100,101: 82-All Maroto issue. 100-(8/78) Anniversary. 101-Corben-a 2 4 6 13 18 22
83,95-Wrightson-a. 83-Corben-a. 95-Gorilla/Apes. 2 4 6 10 14 18
86,87,91,103-Wrightson-a. 86-Xmas Horror 2 4 6 10 14 18
113-All Wrightson-r issue 3 6 9 17 25 32
119,121: 119-All Nino issue.121-All Severin-r issue 2 4 6 10 14 18
131,133-136,138,140: 135-Xmas issue 2 4 6 10 14 18
132,137,139: 132-Corben. 137-All Williamson-r issue. 139-All Toth-r issue 2 4 6 13 18 22
141,143,144 (low dist.): 144-Giant, $2.25; Frazetta-c 3 6 9 15 21 26
142,145 (low dist.): 142-(10/82, 100 pgs.) All Torres issue. 145-(2/83) last Warren issue 3 6 9 16 23 30
146 ($2.95)-1st from Harris; resurrection issue 6 12 18 43 69 95
Year Book '68-'70: '70-Neal Adams, Ditko-a(r) 5 10 15 32 51 70
Annual 1971,1972 5 10 15 30 48 65
1993 Fearbook ($3.95)-Harris Publ.; Brereton-c; Vampirella by Busiek-s/Art Adams-a; David-s; Paquette-a 4 8 12 24 37 50
... Archives - Volume One HC (Dark Horse, 8/08, $49.95) r/#1-5; Jon B. Cooke intro. 50.00
... Archives - Volume Two HC (Dark Horse, 12/08, $49.95) r/#6-10; Roy Thomas intro. 50.00
... Archives - Volume Three HC (Dark Horse, 6/09, $49.95) r/#11-15 50.00
...:The Classic Years TPB (Harris/Dark Horse, '91, $12.95) Kaluta-c; art by Frazetta,Torres, Crandall, Ditko, Morrow, Williamson, Wrightson 25.00

NOTE: *All issues contain many good artists works:* ***Neal Adams, Brunner, Corben, Craig (Taycee), Crandall, Ditko, Evans, Frazetta, Heath, Jeff Jones, Krenkel, McWilliams, Morrow, Nino, Orlando, Ploog, Severin, Torres, Toth, Williamson, Wood, & Wrightson****; covers by* ***Crandall, Davis, Frazetta, Morrow, San Julian, Todd/Bode****; Otto Binder's "Adam Link" stories in No. 2, 4, 6, 8, 9, 12, 13, 15 with* ***Orlando*** *art.* ***Frazetta*** *c-2-7, 9-11, 15-17, 27, 32, 83r, 89r, 91r.* ***E.A. Poe*** *adaptations in 66, 69, 70.*

CREEPY (Mini-series)
Harris Comics/Dark Horse: 1992 - Book 4, 1992 (48 pgs, B&W, squarebound)

Book 1-4: Brereton painted-c on all. Stories and art by various incl. David (all), Busiek(2), Infantino(2), Guice(3), Colan(1) 2 4 6 8 10 12

CREEPY
Dark Horse Comics: July, 2009 - Present ($4.99, 48 pgs, B&W, quarterly)

1,2: 1-Powell-c; art by Wrightson, Toth, Alexander 5.00

CREEPY THINGS
Charlton Comics: July, 1975 - No. 6, June, 1976

1-Sutton-c/a 2 4 6 13 18 22
2-6: Ditko-a in 3,5. Sutton c-3,4. 6-Zeck-c 2 4 6 8 10 12
Modern Comics Reprint 2-6(1977) 4.00

NOTE: ***Larson*** *a-2,6.* ***Sutton*** *a-1,2,4,6.* ***Zeck*** *a-2.*

CREW, THE
Marvel Comics: July, 2003 - No. 7, Jan, 2004 ($2.50)

1-7-Priest-s/Bennett-a; James Rhodes (War Machine) app. 2.50

CRIME AND JUSTICE (Badge Of Justice #22 on; Rookie Cop? No. 27 on)
Capitol Stories/Charlton Comics: March, 1951 - No. 21; No. 23 - No. 26, Sept, 1955 (No #22)

1 34 68 102 199 325 450
2 15 30 45 85 130 175
3-8,10-13: 6-Negligee panels 14 28 42 78 112 145
9-Classic story "Comics Vs. Crime" 25 50 75 147 241 335
14-Color illos in **POP**; gory story of man who beheads women 21 42 63 124 202 280
15-17,19-21,23,24: 15-Negligee panels. 23-Rookie Cop (1st app.) 10 20 30 58 79 100
18-Ditko-a 25 50 75 150 245 340
25,26: (scarce) 15 30 45 85 130 175

NOTE: ***Alascia*** *c-20.* ***Ayers*** *a-17.* ***Shuster*** *a-19-21; c-19. Bondage c-11, 12.*

CRIME AND PUNISHMENT (Title inspired by 1935 film)
Lev Gleason Publications: April, 1948 - No. 74, Aug, 1955

1-Mr. Crime app. on-c 37 74 111 222 361 500
2 19 38 57 111 176 240
3-Used in **SOTI**, pg. 112; injury-to-eye panel; Fuje-a 21 42 63 122 199 275
4,5 15 30 45 86 133 180
6-10 14 28 42 76 108 140
11-20 12 24 36 67 94 120
21-30 10 20 30 58 79 100
31-38,40-44,46: 46-One pg. Frazetta-a 9 18 27 52 69 85
39-Drug mention story "The 5 Dopes" 14 28 42 80 115 150
45- "Hophead Killer" drug story 14 28 42 80 115 150
47-57,60-65,70-74: 9 18 27 50 65 80
58-Used in **POP**, pg. 79 10 20 30 54 72 90
59-Used in **SOTI**, illo "What comic-book America stands for" 32 64 96 188 307 425
66-Toth-c/a(4); 3-D effect issue (3/54); 1st "Deep Dimension" process 39 78 117 240 395 550
67- "Monkey on His Back" heroin story; 3-D effect issue 37 74 111 222 361 500
68-3-D effect issue; Toth-c (7/54) 31 62 93 182 296 410
69- "The Hot Rod Gang" dope crazy kids 14 28 42 80 115 150

NOTE: ***Biro*** *c-most.* ***Everett*** *a-31.* ***Fuje*** *a-2-4, 12, 13, 17, 18, 20, 26, 27.* ***Guardineer*** *a-2-4, 10, 14, 17, 18, 20, 26-28, 32, 38-44,54.* ***Kinstler*** *c-69.* ***McWilliams*** *a-41, 48, 49.* ***Tuska*** *a-28, 30, 51, 64, 70.*

CRIME AND PUNISHMENT: MARSHALL LAW TAKES MANHATTAN
Marvel Comics (Epic Comics): 1989 ($4.95, 52 pgs., direct sales only, mature)

nn-Graphic album featuring Marshall Law 5.00

CRIME BIBLE: THE FIVE LESSONS (Aftermath of DC's 52 series)
DC Comics: Dec, 2007 - No. 5, Apr, 2008 ($2.99, limited series)

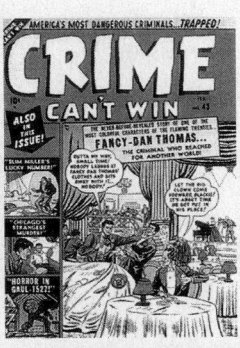

Crime Can't Win #43 © MAR

Crime Detector #5 © Timor

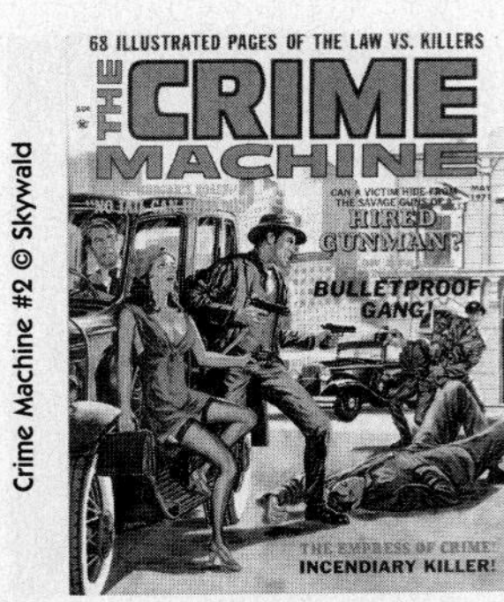

Crime Machine #2 © Skywald

	GD 2.0	VG 4.0	FN 6.0	VF 8.0	VF/NM 9.0	NM- 9.2
1-5-Rucka-s; The Question (Renee Montoya) app. 3-Batwoman app.						3.00
The Question: The Five Books of Blood HC (2008, $19.99) r/#1-5						20.00
The Question: The Five Books of Blood SC (2009, $14.99) r/#1-5						15.00

CRIME CAN'T WIN (Formerly Cindy Smith)
Marvel/Atlas Comics (TCI 41/CCC 42,43,4-12): No. 41, 9/50 - No. 43, 2/51; No. 4, 4/51 - No. 12, 9/53

	GD 2.0	VG 4.0	FN 6.0	VF 8.0	VF/NM 9.0	NM- 9.2
41(#1)	26	52	78	154	252	350
42(#2)	15	30	45	86	133	180
43(#3)-Horror story	18	36	54	107	169	230
4(4/51),5-12: 10-Possible use in **SOTI**, pg. 161	14	28	42	78	112	145

NOTE: ***Robinson** a-9-11. **Tuska** a-43.*

CRIME CASES COMICS (Formerly Willie Comics)
Marvel/Atlas Comics(CnPC No.24-8/MJMC No.9-12): No. 24, 8/50 - No. 27, 3/51; No. 5, 5/51 - No. 12, 7/52

	GD 2.0	VG 4.0	FN 6.0	VF 8.0	VF/NM 9.0	NM- 9.2
24 (#1, 52 pgs.)-True police cases	18	36	54	105	165	225
25-27(#2-4): 27-Morisi-a	14	28	42	78	112	145
5-12: 11-Robinson-a. 12-Tuska-a	12	24	36	69	97	125

CRIME CLINIC
Ziff-Davis Publishing Co.: No. 10, July-Aug, 1951 - No. 5, Summer, 1952

	GD 2.0	VG 4.0	FN 6.0	VF 8.0	VF/NM 9.0	NM- 9.2
10(#1)-Painted-c; origin Dr. Tom Rogers	28	56	84	165	270	375
11(#2),4,5: 4,5-Painted-c	19	38	57	111	176	240
3-Used in **SOTI**, pg. 18	20	40	60	114	182	250

NOTE: *All have painted covers by **Saunders**. **Starr** a-10.*

CRIME CLINIC
Slave Labor Graphics: May, 1995 - No. 2, Oct, 1995 ($2.95, B&W, limited series)

	GD 2.0	VG 4.0	FN 6.0	VF 8.0	VF/NM 9.0	NM- 9.2
1,2						3.00

CRIME DETECTIVE COMICS
Hillman Periodicals: Mar-Apr, 1948 - V3#8, May-June, 1953

	GD 2.0	VG 4.0	FN 6.0	VF 8.0	VF/NM 9.0	NM- 9.2
V1#1-The Invisible 6, costumed villains app; Fuje-c/a, 15 pgs.	30	60	90	177	289	400
2,5: 5-Krigstein-a	15	30	45	85	130	175
3,4,6,7,10-12: 6-McWilliams-a	14	28	42	76	108	140
8-Kirbyish-a by McCann	13	26	39	76	108	140
9-Used in **SOTI**, pg. 16 & "Caricature of the author in a position comic book publishers wish he were in permanently" illo.	37	74	111	222	361	500
V2#1,4,7-Krigstein-a: 1-Tuska-a	13	26	39	72	101	130
2,3,5,6,8-12 (1-2/52)	11	22	33	60	83	105
V3#1-Drug use-c	11	22	33	62	86	110
2-8	9	18	27	50	65	80

NOTE: ***Briefer** a-11, V3#1. **Kinstlerish**-a by **McCann**-V2#7, V3#2. **Powell** a-10, 11. **Starr** a-10.*

CRIME DETECTOR
Timor Publications: Jan, 1954 - No. 5, Sept, 1954

	GD 2.0	VG 4.0	FN 6.0	VF 8.0	VF/NM 9.0	NM- 9.2
1	21	42	63	124	202	280
2	13	26	39	74	105	135
3,4	11	22	33	62	86	110
5-Disbrow-a (classic)	22	44	66	130	213	295

CRIME DOES NOT PAY (Formerly Silver Streak Comics No. 1-21)
Comic House/Lev Gleason/Golfing: No. 22, June, 1942 - No. 147, July, 1955
(1st crime comic)(Title inspired by film)

	GD 2.0	VG 4.0	FN 6.0	VF 8.0	VF/NM 9.0	NM- 9.2
22 (23 on cover, 22 on indicia)-Origin The War Eagle & only app.; Chip Gardner begins; #22 was rebound in Complete Book of True Crime (Scarce)	423	846	1269	3000	5250	7500
23-(7/42) (Scarce)	194	388	582	1242	2121	3000
24-(11/42) Intro. & 1st app. Mr. Crime; classic Biro-c showing woman's head on fire being pushed onto hot stovetop burner	290	580	870	1856	3178	4500
25-(1/43) 2nd app. Mr. Crime; classic '40s crime-c	90	180	270	576	988	1400
26-(3/43) 3rd app. Mr. Crime	77	154	231	493	847	1200
27-Classic Biro-c pushing man into hot oven	84	168	252	538	919	1300
28-30: 30-Wood and Biro app.	68	136	204	435	743	1050
31,32,34-40	40	80	120	246	411	575
33-(5/44) Classic Biro hanging & hatchet-c	77	154	231	493	847	1200
41-(9/45) Origin & 1st app. Officer Common Sense	34	68	102	199	325	450
42-(11/45) Classic electrocution-c	43	86	129	271	461	650
43-46,48-50: 44,45,46,50 are 68 pg. issues; 44-"legs" diamond story	22	44	66	132	216	300
47-(9/46) Electric chair-c; photo of Gleason & Biro	39	78	117	231	378	525
51-70: 63,64-Possible use in **SOTI**, pg. 306. 63-Contains Biro & Gleason's self censorship code of 12 listed restrictions (5/48)	18	36	54	105	165	225
71-99: 87-Chip Gardner begins, ends #100	15	30	45	86	133	180
100	16	32	48	94	147	200
101-104,107-110: 102-Chip Gardner app	13	26	39	74	105	135
105-Used in **POP**, pg. 84	14	28	42	80	115	150
106,114-Frazetta-a, 1 pg.	13	26	39	74	105	135
111-Used in **POP**, pgs. 80 & 81; injury-to-eye sty illo	14	28	42	80	115	150
112,113,115-130	10	20	30	58	79	100
131-140	9	18	27	52	69	85
141,142-Last pre-code issue; Kubert-a(1)	11	22	33	60	83	105
143-Kubert-a in one story	11	22	33	60	83	105
144-146	9	18	27	52	69	85
147-Last issue (scarce); Kubert-a	15	30	45	85	130	175
1(Golfing-1945)	9	18	27	47	61	75
The Best of...(1944, 128 pgs.)-Series contains 4 rebound issues	84	168	252	538	919	1300
...1945 issue	61	122	183	390	670	950
...1946-48 issues	46	92	138	290	488	685
...1949-50 issues	41	82	123	256	428	600
...1951-53 issues	37	74	111	218	354	490

NOTE: *Many issues contain violent covers and stories. Who Dunnit by **Guardineer**-39-42, 44-105, 108-110; Chip Gardner by **Bob Fujitani (Fuje)**-88-103. **Alderman** a-29, 41-44, 49. **Dan Barry** a-67, 75. **Biro** c-1-76, 122, 142. **Briefer** a-29(2), 30, 31, 33, 37, 39. **G. Colan** a-105. **Fuje** c-88, 89, 91-94, 96, 98, 99, 102, 103. **Guardineer** a-47, 51, 57, 67, 68, 71, 74. **Kubert** c-143. **Landau** a-118. **Maurer** a-29, 39, 41, 42. **McWilliams** a-91, 93, 95, 100-103. **Palais** a-30, 33, 37, 39, 41-43, 44(2), 46, 49. **Powell** a-146, 147. **Tuska** a-48, 50(2), 51, 52, 56, 57(2), 60-64, 66, 67, 68, 71, 74. Painted c-87-102. Bondage c-43, 62, 98.*

CRIME EXPOSED
Marvel Comics (PPI)/Marvel Atlas Comics (PrPI): June, 1948; Dec, 1950 - No. 14, June, 1952

	GD 2.0	VG 4.0	FN 6.0	VF 8.0	VF/NM 9.0	NM- 9.2
1(6/48)	34	68	102	199	325	450
1(12/50)	20	40	60	117	189	260
2	14	28	42	81	118	155
3-9,11,14	12	24	36	69	97	125
10-Used in **POP**, pg. 81	13	26	39	74	105	135
12-Krigstein & Robinson-a	13	26	39	74	105	135
13-Used in **POP**, pg. 81; Krigstein-a	14	28	42	76	108	140

NOTE: ***Keller** a-8, 10. **Maneely** c-8. **Robinson** a-11, 12. **Sale** a-4. **Tuska** a-3, 4.*

CRIMEFIGHTERS
Marvel Comics (CmPS 1-3/CCC 4-10): Apr, 1948 - No. 10, Nov, 1949

	GD 2.0	VG 4.0	FN 6.0	VF 8.0	VF/NM 9.0	NM- 9.2
1-Some copies are undated & could be reprints	25	50	75	147	241	335
2,3: 3-Morphine addict story	15	30	45	83	124	165
4-10: 4-Early John Buscema-a. 6-Anti-Wertham editorial. 9,10-Photo-c	14	28	42	76	108	140

CRIME FIGHTERS (...Always Win)
Atlas Comics (CnPC): No. 11, Sept, 1954 - No. 13, Jan, 1955

	GD 2.0	VG 4.0	FN 6.0	VF 8.0	VF/NM 9.0	NM- 9.2
11-13: 11-Maneely-a,13-Pakula, Reinman, Severin-a	12	24	36	69	97	125

CRIME-FIGHTING DETECTIVE (Shock Detective Cases No. 20 on; formerly Criminals on the Run)
Star Publications: No. 11, Apr-May, 1950 - No. 19, June, 1952 (Based on true crime cases)

	GD 2.0	VG 4.0	FN 6.0	VF 8.0	VF/NM 9.0	NM- 9.2
11-L. B. Cole-c/a (2 pgs.); L. B. Cole-c on all	18	36	54	107	169	230
12,13,15-19: 17-Young King Cole & Dr. Doom app.	15	30	45	83	124	165
14-L. B. Cole-c/a, r/Law-Crime #2	15	30	45	90	140	190

CRIME FILES
Standard Comics: No. 5, Sept, 1952 - No. 6, Nov, 1952

	GD 2.0	VG 4.0	FN 6.0	VF 8.0	VF/NM 9.0	NM- 9.2
5-1pg. Alex Toth-a; used in **SOTI**, pg. 4 (text)	23	46	69	136	223	310
6-Sekowsky-a	14	28	42	80	115	150

CRIME ILLUSTRATED (Magazine)
E. C. Comics: Nov-Dec, 1955 - No. 2, Spring, 1956 (25¢, Adult Suspense Stories on-c)

	GD 2.0	VG 4.0	FN 6.0	VF 8.0	VF/NM 9.0	NM- 9.2
1-Ingels & Crandall-a	18	36	54	105	165	225
2-Ingels & Crandall-a	14	28	42	82	121	160

NOTE: ***Craig** a-2. **Crandall** a-1, 2; c-2. **Evans** a-1. **Davis** a-2. **Ingels** a-1, 2. **Krigstein/Crandall** a-1. **Orlando** a-1, 2; c-1.*

CRIME INCORPORATED (Formerly Crimes Incorporated)
Fox Features Syndicate: No. 2, Aug, 1950; No. 3, Aug, 1951

	GD 2.0	VG 4.0	FN 6.0	VF 8.0	VF/NM 9.0	NM- 9.2
2	26	52	78	154	252	350
3(1951)-Hollingsworth-a	18	36	54	105	165	225

CRIME MACHINE (Magazine reprints pre-code crime and gangster comics)
Skywald Publications: Feb, 1971 - No. 2, May, 1971 (B&W, 68 pgs., roundbound)

	GD 2.0	VG 4.0	FN 6.0	VF 8.0	VF/NM 9.0	NM- 9.2
1-Kubert-a(2)(r)(Avon); bikini girl in cake-c	6	12	18	41	66	90
2-Torres, Wildey-a; violent-c/a	4	8	12	28	44	60

CRIME MUST LOSE! (Formerly Sports Action?)
Sports Action (Atlas Comics): No. 4, Oct, 1950 - No. 12, April, 1952

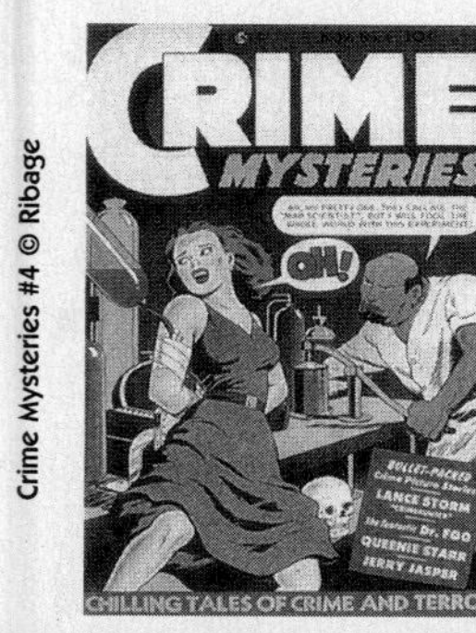

Crime Mysteries #4 © Ribage

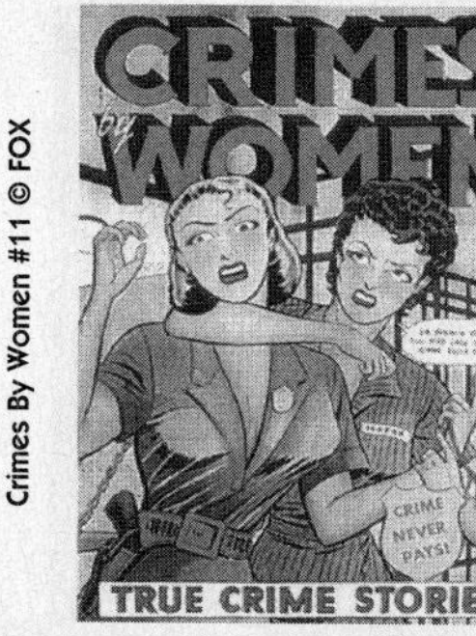

Crimes By Women #11 © FOX

Criminal #8 © Brubaker & Phillips

GD VG FN VF VF/NM NM-
2.0 4.0 6.0 8.0 9.0 9.2

GD VG FN VF VF/NM NM-
2.0 4.0 6.0 8.0 9.0 9.2

4-Ann Brewster-a in all; c-used in N.Y. Legis. Comm. documents
19 38 57 109 172 235
5-12: 9-Robinson-a. 11-Used in **POP**, pg. 89 14 28 42 80 115 150

CRIME MUST PAY THE PENALTY (Formerly Four Favorites; Penalty #47, 48)
Ace Magazines (Current Books): No. 33, Feb, 1948; No. 2, Jun, 1948 - No. 48, Jan, 1956

33(#1, 2/48)-Becomes Four Teeners #34? 37 74 111 222 361 500
2(6/48)-Extreme violence; Palais-a? 22 44 66 132 216 300
3,4,8: 3- "Frisco Mary" story used in Senate Investigation report, pg. 7. 4,8-Transvestism stories 18 36 54 105 165 225
5-7,9,10 14 28 42 80 115 150
11-19 13 26 39 74 105 135
20-Drug story "Dealers in White Death" 17 34 51 98 154 210
21-32,34-40,42-48: 44-Last pre-code 10 20 30 58 79 100
33(7/53)- "Dell Fabry-Junk King" drug story; mentioned in Love and Death
15 30 45 83 124 165
41-reprints "Dealers in White Death" 11 22 33 60 83 105
NOTE: ***Cameron** a-29-31, 34, 35, 39-41. **Colan** a-20, 31. **Kremer** a-3, 37r. **Larsen** a-32. **Palais** a-5?,37.*

CRIME MUST STOP
Hillman Periodicals: October, 1952 (52 pgs.)

V1#1(Scarce)-Similar to Monster Crime; Mort Lawrence, Krigstein-a
90 180 270 576 988 1400

CRIME MYSTERIES (Secret Mysteries #16 on; combined with Crime Smashers #7 on)
Ribage Publ. Corp. (Trojan Magazines): May, 1952 - No. 15, Sept, 1954

1-Transvestism story; crime & terror stories begin 58 116 174 371 636 900
2-Marijuana story (7/52) 40 80 120 246 411 575
3-One pg. Frazetta-a 37 74 111 222 361 500
4-Cover shows girl in bondage having her blood drained; 1 pg. Frazetta-a
60 120 180 381 653 925
5-10 32 64 96 188 307 425
11,12,14 29 58 87 172 281 390
13-(5/54)-Angelo Torres 1st comic work (inks over Check's pencils); Check-a
35 70 105 208 339 470
15-Acid in face-c 43 86 129 271 461 650
NOTE: ***Fass** a-13; c-4, 6, 10. **Hollingsworth** a-10-13, 15; c-2, 12, 13, 15. **Kiefer** a-4. **Woodbridge** a-13? Bondage-c-1, 8, 12.*

CRIME ON THE RUN (See Approved Comics #8)

CRIME ON THE WATERFRONT (Formerly Famous Gangsters)
Realistic Publications: No. 4, May, 1952 (Painted cover)

4 28 56 84 165 270 375

CRIME PATROL (Formerly International #1-5; International Crime Patrol #6; becomes Crypt of Terror #17 on)
E. C. Comics: No. 7, Summer, 1948 - No. 16, Feb-Mar, 1950

7-Intro. Captain Crime 73 146 219 467 796 1125
8-14: 12-Ingels-a 63 126 189 403 689 975
15-Intro. of Crypt Keeper (inspired by Witches Tales radio show) & Crypt of Terror (see Tales From the Crypt #33 for origin); used by N.Y. Legis. Comm.; last pg. Feldstein-a
269 538 807 2152 3426 4700
16-2nd Crypt Keeper app.; Roussos-a 171 342 513 1368 2184 3000
NOTE: ***Craig** c/a in most issues. **Feldstein** a-9-16. **Kiefer** a-8, 10, 11. **Moldoff** a-7.*

CRIME PATROL
Gemstone Publishing: Apr, 2000 - No. 10, Jan, 2001 ($2.50)

1-10: E.C. reprints 2.50
Volume 1,2 (2000, $13.50) 1-r/#1-5. 2-r/#6-10 14.00

CRIME PHOTOGRAPHER (See Casey...)

CRIME REPORTER
St. John Publ. Co.: Aug, 1948 - No. 3, Dec, 1948 (Indicia shows Oct.)

1-Drug club story 55 110 165 347 586 825
2-Used in **SOTI**: illo- "Children told me what the man was going to do with the red-hot poker;" r/Dynamic #17 with editing; Baker-c; Tuska-a 77 154 231 493 847 1200
3-Baker-c; Tuska-a 42 84 126 265 445 625

CRIMES BY WOMEN
Fox Features Syndicate: June, 1948 - No. 15, Aug, 1951; 1954 (True crime cases)

1-True story of Bonnie Parker 123 246 369 787 1344 1900
2,3: 3-Used in **SOTI**, pg. 234 64 128 192 406 696 985
4,5,7-9,11-15: 8-Used in **POP**. 14-Bondage-c 59 118 177 375 643 910
6-Classic girl fight-c; acid-in-face panel 66 132 198 419 722 1025
10-Used in **SOTI**, pg. 72; girl fight-c 59 118 177 378 649 920
54(M.S. Publ.-'54)-Reprint; (formerly My Love Secret)
24 48 72 140 230 320

CRIMES INCORPORATED (Formerly My Past)
Fox Features Syndicate: No. 12, June, 1950 (Crime Incorporated No. 2 on)

12 21 42 63 124 202 280

CRIMES INCORPORATED (See Fox Giants)

CRIME SMASHER (See Whiz #76)
Fawcett Publications: Summer, 1948 (one-shot)

1-Formerly Spy Smasher 41 82 123 256 428 600

CRIME SMASHERS (Becomes Secret Mysteries No. 16 on)
Ribage Publishing Corp.(Trojan Magazines): Oct, 1950 - No. 15, Mar, 1953

1-Used in **SOTI**, pg. 19,20, & illo "A girl raped and murdered;" Sally the Sleuth begins
89 178 267 565 970 1375
2-Kubert-c 47 94 141 296 498 700
3,4 39 78 117 231 378 525
5-Wood-a 45 90 135 284 480 675
6,8-11: 8-Lingerie panel 30 60 90 177 289 400
7-Female heroin junkie story 34 68 102 199 325 450
12-Injury to eye panel; 1 pg. Frazetta-a 32 64 96 192 314 435
13-Used in **POP**, pgs. 79,80; 1 pg. Frazetta-a 32 64 96 192 314 435
14,15 24 48 72 142 234 325
NOTE: ***Hollingsworth** a-14. **Kiefer** a-15. Bondage c-7, 9.*

CRIME SUSPENSTORIES (Formerly Vault of Horror No. 12-14)
E. C. Comics: No. 15, Oct-Nov, 1950 - No. 27, Feb-Mar, 1955

15-Identical to #1 in content; #1 printed on outside front cover. #15 (formerly "The Vault of Horror") printed and blackened out on inside front cover with Vol. 1, No. 1 printed over it. Evidently, several of No. 15 were printed before a decision was made not to drop the Vault of Horror and Haunt of Fear series. The print run was stopped on No. 15 and continued on No. 1. All of the No. 15 issues were changed as described above.
154 308 462 1232 1966 2700
1 120 240 360 960 1530 2100
2 63 126 189 504 802 1100
3-5: 3-Poe adaptation. 3-Old Witch stories begin 43 86 129 344 547 750
6-10: 9-Craig bio. 37 74 111 296 473 650
11,12,14,15: 15-The Old Witch guest stars 29 58 87 232 366 500
13,16-Williamson-a 31 62 93 248 394 540
17-Williamson/Frazetta-a (6 pgs.) Williamson bio. 37 74 111 296 473 650
18,19: 19-Used in **SOTI**, pg. 235 25 50 75 200 320 440
20-Cover used in **SOTI**, illo "Cover of a children's comic book"
33 66 99 264 420 575
21,24-26: 24- "Food For Thought" similar to "Cave In" in Amazing Detective Cases #13 (1952)
18 36 54 144 232 320
22-Used in Senate investigation on juvenile delinquency; Ax decapitation-c
57 114 171 456 728 1000
23-Used in Senate investigation on juvenile delinquency
25 50 75 200 320 440
27-Last issue (Low distribution) 23 46 69 184 292 400
NOTE: ***Craig** a-1-21; c-1-18, 20-22. **Crandall** a-18-26. **Davis** a-4, 5, 7, 9-12, 20. **Elder** a-17,18. **Evans** a-15, 19, 21, 23, 25, 27; c-23, 24. **Feldstein** c-19. **Ingels** a-1-12, 14, 15, 27. **Kamen** a-2, 4-18, 20-27; c-25-27. **Krigstein** a-22, 24, 25, 27. **Kurtzman** a-1, 3. **Orlando** a-16, 22, 24, 26. **Wood** a-1, 3. Issues No. 1-3 were printed in Canada as "Weird Suspenstories." Issues No. 11-15 have E. C. "quickie" stories. No. 25 contains the famous "Are You a Red Dupe?" editorial. Ray Bradbury adaptations-15, 17.*

CRIME SUSPENSTORIES
Russ Cochran/Gemstone Publ.: Nov, 1992 - No. 27, May, 1999 ($1.50/$2.00/$2.50)

1-27: Reprints Crime SuspenStories series 3.00

CRIMINAL (Also see Criminal: The Sinners)
Marvel Comics (Icon): Oct, 2006 - No. 10, Oct, 2007 ($2.99)
Volume 2: Feb, 2008 - No. 7, Nov, 2008 ($3.50)

1-10-Ed Brubaker-s/Sean Phillips-a/c 3.00
Volume 2: 1-7-Brubaker-s/Phillips-a 3.50
... Vol. 1: Coward TPB (2007, $14.99) r/#1-5; intro. by Tom Fontana 15.00
... Vol. 2: Lawless TPB (2007, $14.99) r/#6-10; intro. by Frank Miller 15.00
... Vol. 3: The Dead and the Dying TPB (2008, $11.99) r/V2#1-4; intro. by John Singleton 12.00

CRIMINAL MACABRE: A CAL MCDONALD MYSTERY (Also see Last Train to Deadsville)
Dark Horse Comics: May, 2003 - No. 5, Sept, 2003 ($2.99)

1-5-Niles-s/Templesmith-a 3.00

CRIMINAL MACABRE: (limited series and one-shots)
Dark Horse Comics: ($2.99)

...: Cellblock 666 (9/08 - No. 4, 5/09)(#25-28 in series) 1-4-Niles-s/Stakal-a/Bradstreet-c 3.00
... :Feat of Clay (6/06, $2.99) Niles-s/Hotz-a/c 3.00
...: My Demon Baby (9/07 - No. 4, 4/08)(#21-24 in the series) 1-4-Niles-s/Stakal-a 3.00
...: Two Red Eyes (12/06 - No. 4, 3/07) 1-4-Niles-s/Hotz-a/Bradstreet-c 3.00

CRIMINALS ON THE RUN (Formerly Young King Cole) (Crime Fighting Detective No. 11 on)

Crimson #15 © H. Ramos

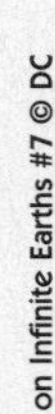
Crisis on Infinite Earths #7 © DC

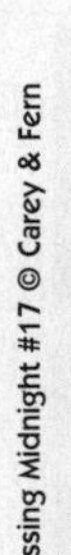
Crossing Midnight #17 © Carey & Fern

GD 2.0 | VG 4.0 | FN 6.0 | VF 8.0 | VF/NM 9.0 | NM- 9.2

GD 2.0 | VG 4.0 | FN 6.0 | VF 8.0 | VF/NM 9.0 | NM- 9.2

Premium Group (Novelty Press): V4#1, Aug-Sep, 1948-#10, Dec-Jan, 1949-50

V4#1-Young King Cole continues 27 54 81 158 254 350
2-6: 6-Dr. Doom app. 23 46 69 135 218 300
7-Classic "Fish in the Face" c by L. B. Cole 53 106 159 330 553 775
V5#1,2 (#8,9),10: 9,10-L. B. Cole-c 20 40 60 120 193 265

NOTE: *Most issues have* **L. B. Cole** *covers.* **McWilliams** *a-V4#6, 7, V5#2; c-V4#5.*

CRIMINAL: THE SINNERS
Marvel Comics (Icon): Sept, 2009 - No. 5 ($3.50)

1-4-Ed Brubaker-s/Sean Phillips-a/c 3.50

CRIMSON (Also see Cliffhanger #0)
Image Comics (Cliffhanger Productions): May, 1998 - No. 7, Dec, 1998;
DC Comics (Cliffhanger Prod.): No. 8, Mar, 1999 - No. 24, Apr, 2001 ($2.50)

1-Humberto Ramos-a/Augustyn-s 5.00
1-Variant-c by Warren 8.00
1-Chromium-c 20.00
2-Ramos-c with street crowd, 2-Variant-c by Art Adams 3.00
2-Dynamic Forces CrimsonChrome cover 15.00
3-7: 3-Ramos Moon background-c. 7-Three covers by Ramos, Madureira, & Campbell 3.50
8-23: 8-First DC issue 2.50
24-($3.50) Final issue; wraparound-c 3.50
DF Premiere Ed. 1998 ($6.95) covers by Ramos and Jae Lee 7.00
Crimson: Scarlet X Blood on the Moon (10/99, $3.95) 4.00
Crimson Sourcebook (11/99, $2.95) Pin-ups and info 3.00
Earth Angel TPB (2001, $14.95) r/#13-18 15.00
Heaven and Earth TPB (1/00, $14.95) r/#7-12 15.00
Loyalty and Loss TPB ('99, $12.95) r/#1-6 13.00
Redemption TPB ('01, $14.95) r/#19-24 15.00

CRIMSON AVENGER, THE (See Detective Comics #20 for 1st app.)(Also see Leading Comics #1 & World's Best/Finest Comics)
DC Comics: June, 1988 - No. 4, Sept, 1988 ($1.00, limited series)

1-4 2.50

CRIMSON DYNAMO
Marvel Comics (Epic): Oct, 2003 - No. 6, Apr, 2004 ($2.50/$2.99)

1-4,6: 1-John Jackson Miller-s/Steve Ellis-a/c 2.50
5-($2.99) Iron Man-c/app. 3.00

CRIMSON PLAGUE
Event Comics: June, 1997 ($2.95, unfinished mini-series)

1-George Perez-a 3.00

CRIMSON PLAGUE (George Pérez's...)
Image Comics (Gorilla): June, 2000 - No. 2, Aug, 2000 ($2.95, mini-series)

1-George Perez-a; reprints 6/97 issue with 16 new pages 3.00
2-($2.50) 2.50

CRISIS AFTERMATH: THE BATTLE FOR BLUDHAVEN (Also see Infinite Crisis)
DC Comics: Jun, 2006 - No. 6, Sept, 2006 ($2.99, limited series)

1-Atomic Knights return; Teen Titans app.; Jurgens-a/Acuna-c 4.00
1-2nd printing with pencil cover 3.00
2-6: 2-Intro S.H.A.D.E. (new Freedom Fighters) 3.00
TPB (2007, $12.99) r/#1-6 13.00

CRISIS AFTERMATH: THE SPECTRE (Also see Infinite Crisis, Gotham Central and Tales of the Unexpected)
DC Comics: Jul, 2006 - No. 3, Sept, 2006 ($2.99, limited series)

1-3-Crispus Allen becomes the Spectre; Pfeifer-s/Chiang-a/c 3.00
TPB (2007, $12.99) r/#1-3 and Tales of the Unexpected #1-3 13.00

CRISIS ON INFINITE EARTHS (Also see Official... Index and Legends of the DC Universe)
DC Comics: Apr, 1985 - No. 12, Mar, 1986 (maxi-series)

1-1st DC app. Blue Beetle & Detective Karp from Charlton; Pérez-c on all 2 4 6 9 13 16
2-6: 6-Intro Charlton's Capt. Atom, Nightshade, Question, Judomaster, Peacemaker & Thunderbolt into DC Universe 1 3 4 6 8 10
7-Double size; death of Supergirl 2 4 6 13 16 22
8-Death of the Flash (Barry Allen) 2 4 6 11 16 20
9-11: 9-Intro. Charlton's Ghost into DC Universe. 10-Intro. Charlton's Banshee, Dr. Spectro, Image, Punch & Jewellee into DC Universe; Starman (Prince Gavyn) dies 1 3 4 6 8 10
12-(52 pgs.)-Deaths of Dove, Kole, Lori Lemaris, Sunburst, G.A. Robin & Huntress; Kid Flash becomes new Flash; 3rd & final DC app. of the 3 Lt. Marvels; Green Fury gets new look (becomes Green Flame in Infinity, Inc. #32) 2 4 6 8 11 14
Slipcased Hardcover (1998, $99.95) Wraparound dust-jacket cover by Pérez and Alex Ross; sketch pages by Pérez; intro by Wolfman 125.00
TPB (2000, $29.95) Wraparound-c by Pérez and Ross 30.00

NOTE: *Crossover issues: All Star Squadron 50-56,60; Amethyst 13; Blue Devil 17,18; DC Comics Presents 78,86-88,95; Detective Comics 558; Fury of Firestorm 41,42; G.I. Combat 274; Green Lantern 194-196,198; Infinity, Inc. 18-25 & Annual 1, Justice League of America 244,245 & Annual 3; Legion of Super-Heroes 16,18; Losers Special 1; New Teen Titans 13,14; Omega Men 31,33; Superman 413-415; Swamp Thing 44,46; Wonder Woman 327-329.*

CRISIS ON MULTIPLE EARTHS
DC Comics: 2002, 2003, 2004 ($14.95, trade paperbacks)

TPB-(2003) Reprints 1st 4 Silver Age JLA/JSA crossovers from J.L.ofA. #21,22; 29,30; 37,38; 46,47; new painted-c by Alex Ross; intro. by Mark Waid 15.00
Volume 2 (2003, $14.95) r/J.L.ofA. #55,56; 64,65; 73,74; 82,83; new Ordway-c 15.00
Volume 3 (2004, $14.95) r/J.L.ofA. #91,92; 100-102; 107,108; 113; Wein intro., Ross-c 15.00
Volume 4 (2006, $14.99) r/J.L.ofA. #123-124 (Earth-Prime),135-137 (Fawcett's Shazam characters), 147-148 (Legion of Super-Heroes); Ross-c 15.00
... The Team-Ups Volume 1 (2005, $14.99) r/Flash #123,129,137,151; Showcase #55,56; Green Lantern #40, Brave and the Bold #61 and Spectre #7; new Ordway-c 15.00

CRITICAL MASS (See A Shadowline Saga: Critical Mass)

CRITTERS (Also see Usagi Yojimbo Summer Special)
Fantagraphics Books: 1986 - No. 50, 1990 ($1.70/$2.00, B&W)

1-Cutey Bunny, Usagi Yojimbo app. 1 3 4 6 8 10
2,4,5,8,9 6.00
3,6,7,10-Usagi Yojimbo app. 1 2 3 4 5 7
11-22,24-37,39,40: 11,14-Usagi Yojimbo app. 11-Christmas Special (68 pgs.); Usagi Yojimbo. 22-Watchmen parody; two diff. covers exist 2.50
23-With Alan Moore Flexi-disc ($3.95) 5.00
38-($2.75-c) Usagi Yojimbo app. 3.00
41-49 4.00
50 ($4.95, 84 pgs.)-Neil the Horse, Capt. Jack, Sam & Max & Usagi Yojimbo app.; Quagmire, Shaw-a 1 2 3 4 5 7
Special 1 (1/88, $2.00) 3.00

CROSS
Dark Horse Comics: No. 0, Oct, 1995 - No. 6, Apr, 1995 ($2.95, limited series, mature)

0-6: Darrow-c & Vachss scripts in all 3.00

CROSS AND THE SWITCHBLADE, THE
Spire Christian Comics (Fleming H. Revell Co.): 1972 (35-49¢)

1-Some issues have nn 2 4 6 10 14 18

CROSS BRONX, THE
Image Comics: Sept, 2006 - No. 4, Dec, 2006 ($2.99, limited series)

1-4: 1-Oeming-a/c; Oeming & Brandon-s; Ribic var-c. 2-Johnson var-c. 4-Mack var-c 3.00

CROSSFIRE
Spire Christian Comics (Fleming H. Revell Co.): 1973 (39/49¢)

nn 2 4 6 9 13 16

CROSSFIRE (Also see DNAgents)
Eclipse Comics: 5/84 - No. 17, 3/86; No. 18, 1/87 - No. 26, 2/88 ($1.50, Baxter paper) (#18-26 are B&W)

1-11,14-26: 1-DNAgents x-over; Spiegle-c/a begins 2.50
12,13-Death of Marilyn Monroe. 12-Dave Stevens-c 4.00

CROSSFIRE AND RAINBOW (Also see DNAgents)
Eclipse Comics: June, 1986 - No. 4, Sept, 1986 ($1.25, deluxe format)

1-3: Spiegle-a. 4-Dave Stevens-c 2.50

CROSSGEN...
CrossGeneration Comics

CrossGenesis (1/00) Previews CrossGen universe; cover gallery 3.00
...Primer (1/00) Wizard supplement; intro. to the CrossGen universe 2.50
...Sampler (2/00) Retailer preview book 3.00

CROSSGEN CHRONICLES
CrossGeneration Comics: June, 2000 - No. 8 ($3.95)

1-Intro. to CrossGen characters & company 4.00
1-(no cover price) same contents, customer preview 4.00
2-8: 2-(3/01) George Pérez-c/a. 3-5-Pérez-a/Waid-s. 6,7-Nebres-c/a 4.00

CROSSING MIDNIGHT
DC Comics (Vertigo): Jan, 2007 - No. 19, Jul, 2008 ($2.99)

1-19: 1-Carey-s/Fern-a/Williams III-c. 10-12-Nguyen-a 3.00
...: Cut Here TPB (2007, $9.99) r/#1-5 10.00
...: A Map of Midnight TPB (2008, $14.99) r/#6-12; afterword by Carey 15.00
...: The Sword in the Soul TPB (2008, $14.99) r/#13-19 15.00

CROSSING THE ROCKIES (See Classics Illustrated Special Issue)

Crown Comics #6 © Golfing

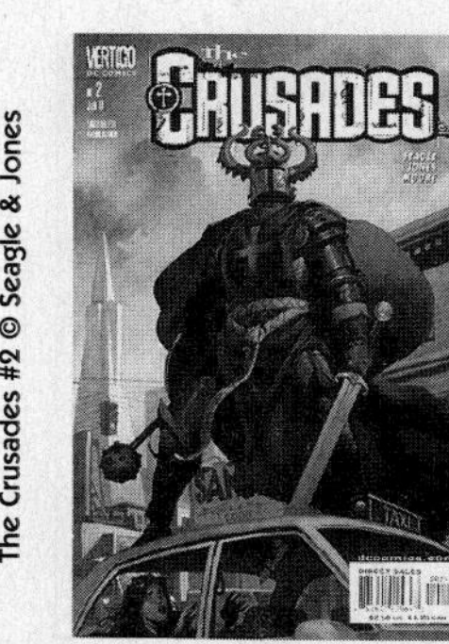

The Crusades #2 © Seagle & Jones

Crux #7 © CRO

CROSSOVERS, THE
CrossGeneration Comics: Feb, 2003 - No. 12 ($2.95)

	GD 2.0	VG 4.0	FN 6.0	VF 8.0	VF/NM 9.0	NM- 9.2
1-12-Robert Rodi-s. 1-6-Mauricet & Ernie Colon-a. 7-Staton-a begins						3.00
Vol. 1: Cross Currents (2003, $9.95) digest-sized reprints #1-6						10.00

CROW, THE (Also see Caliber Presents)
Caliber Press: Feb, 1989 - No. 4, 1989 ($1.95, B&W, limited series)

	GD 2.0	VG 4.0	FN 6.0	VF 8.0	VF/NM 9.0	NM- 9.2
1-James O'Barr-c/a/scripts	6	12	18	37	59	80
1-3-2nd printing						6.00
2-4	4	8	12	22	34	45
2-3rd printing						4.00

CROW, THE
Tundra Publishing, Ltd.: Jan, 1992 - No. 3, 1992 ($4.95, B&W, 68 pgs.)

	GD 2.0	VG 4.0	FN 6.0	VF 8.0	VF/NM 9.0	NM- 9.2
1-3: 1-r/#1,2 of Caliber series. 2-r/#3 of Caliber series w/new material. 3-All new material	1	2	3	5	6	8

CROW, THE
Kitchen Sink Press: 1/96 - No. 3, 3/96 ($2.95, B&W)

	GD 2.0	VG 4.0	FN 6.0	VF 8.0	VF/NM 9.0	NM- 9.2
1-3: James O'Barr-c/scripts						5.00
#0-A Cycle of Shattered Lives (12/98, $3.50) new story by O'Barr						4.00

CROW, THE
Image Comics (Todd McFarlane Prod.): Feb, 1999 - No. 10, Nov, 1999 ($2.50)

	GD 2.0	VG 4.0	FN 6.0	VF 8.0	VF/NM 9.0	NM- 9.2
1-10: 1-Two covers by McFarlane and Kent Williams; Muth-s in all. 2-6,10-Paul Lee-a						3.00
Book 1 - Vengeance (2000, $10.95, TPB) r/#1-3,5,6						11.00
Book 2 - Evil Beyond Reach (2000, $10.95, TPB) r/#4,7-10						11.00
Todd McFarlane Presents The Crow Magazine 1 (3/00, $4.95)						5.00

CROW, THE: CITY OF ANGELS (Movie)
Kitchen Sink Press: July, 1996 - No. 3, Sept, 1996 ($2.95, limited series)

	GD 2.0	VG 4.0	FN 6.0	VF 8.0	VF/NM 9.0	NM- 9.2
1-3: Adaptation of film; two-c (photo & illos.). 1-Vincent Perez interview						3.00

CROW, THE: FLESH AND BLOOD
Kitchen Sink Press: May, 1996 - No. 3, July, 1996 ($2.95, limited series)

	GD 2.0	VG 4.0	FN 6.0	VF 8.0	VF/NM 9.0	NM- 9.2
1-3: O'Barr-c						3.00

CROW, THE: RAZOR - KILL THE PAIN
London Night Studios: Apr, 1998 - No. 3, July, 1998 ($2.95, B&W, lim. series)

	GD 2.0	VG 4.0	FN 6.0	VF 8.0	VF/NM 9.0	NM- 9.2
1-3-Hartsoe-s/O'Barr-painted-c						3.00
0(10/98) Dorien painted-c, Finale (2/99)						3.00
The Lost Chapter (2/99, $4.95), Tour Book-(12/97) pin-ups; 4 diff.-c						5.00

CROW, THE: WAKING NIGHTMARES
Kitchen Sink Press: Jan, 1997 - No. 4, 1998 ($2.95, B&W, limited series)

	GD 2.0	VG 4.0	FN 6.0	VF 8.0	VF/NM 9.0	NM- 9.2
1-4-Miran Kim-c						5.00

CROW, THE: WILD JUSTICE
Kitchen Sink Press: Oct, 1996 - No. 3, Dec, 1996 ($2.95, B&W, limited series)

	GD 2.0	VG 4.0	FN 6.0	VF 8.0	VF/NM 9.0	NM- 9.2
1-3-Prosser-s/Adlard-a						3.00

CROWN COMICS (Also see Vooda)
Golfing/McCombs Publ.: Wint, 1944-45; No. 2, Sum, 1945 - No. 19, July, 1949

	GD 2.0	VG 4.0	FN 6.0	VF 8.0	VF/NM 9.0	NM- 9.2
1- "The Oblong Box" E.A. Poe adaptation	42	84	126	265	445	625
2,3-Baker-a; 3-Voodah by Baker	30	60	90	177	289	400
4-6-Baker-c/a; Voodah app. #4,5	32	64	96	188	307	425
7-Feldstein, Baker, Kamen-a; Baker-c	31	62	93	184	300	415
8-Baker-a; Voodah app.	25	50	75	150	245	340
9-11,13-19: Voodah in #10-19. 13-New logo	18	36	54	103	162	220
12-Master Marvin by Feldstein, Starr-a; Voodah-c	18	36	54	107	169	230

NOTE: ***Bolle** a-11, 13-16, 18, 19; c-11p, 15. **Powell** a-19. **Starr** a-11-13; c-11i.*

CRUCIBLE
DC Comics (Impact): Feb, 1993 - No. 6, July, 1993 ($1.25, limited series)

	GD 2.0	VG 4.0	FN 6.0	VF 8.0	VF/NM 9.0	NM- 9.2
1-6: 1-(99¢)-Neon ink-c. 1,2-Quesada-c(p). 1-4-Quesada layouts						2.50

CRUEL AND UNUSUAL
DC Comics (Vertigo): June, 1999 - No. 4, Sept, 1999 ($2.95, limited series)

	GD 2.0	VG 4.0	FN 6.0	VF 8.0	VF/NM 9.0	NM- 9.2
1-4-Delano & Peyer-s/McCrea-c/a						3.00

CRUSADER FROM MARS (See Tops in Adventure)
Ziff-Davis Publ. Co.: Jan-Mar, 1952 - No. 2, Fall, 1952 (Painted-c)

	GD 2.0	VG 4.0	FN 6.0	VF 8.0	VF/NM 9.0	NM- 9.2
1-Cover is dated Spring	75	150	225	476	818	1160
2-Bondage-c	53	106	159	334	567	800

CRUSADER RABBIT (TV)
Dell Publishing Co.: No. 735, Oct, 1956 - No. 805, May, 1957

	GD 2.0	VG 4.0	FN 6.0	VF 8.0	VF/NM 9.0	NM- 9.2
Four Color 735 (#1)	24	48	72	175	338	500
Four Color 805	18	36	54	131	256	380

CRUSADERS, THE (Religious)
Chick Publications: 1974 - Vol. 17, 1988 (39/69¢, 36 pgs.)

	GD 2.0	VG 4.0	FN 6.0	VF 8.0	VF/NM 9.0	NM- 9.2
Vol.1-Operation Bucharest ('74). Vol.2-The Broken Cross ('74). Vol.3-Scarface ('74). Vol.4-Exorcists ('75). Vol.5-Chaos ('75)	2	4	6	11	16	20
Vol.6-Primal Man? ('76)-(Disputes evolution theory). Vol.7-The Ark-(claims proof of existence, destroyed by Bolsheviks). Vol.8-The Gift-(Life story of Christ). Vol.9-Angel of Light-(Story of the Devil). Vol.10-Spellbound?-(Tells how rock music is Satanic & produced by witches). 11-Sabotage?. 12-Alberto. 13-Double Cross. 14-The Godfathers. (No. 6-14 low in distribution; loaded with religious propaganda.). 15-The Force. 16-The Four Horsemen	2	4	6	11	16	20
Vol. 17-The Prophet (low print run)	2	4	6	13	18	22

CRUSADERS (Southern Knights No. 2 on)
Guild Publications: 1982 (B&W, magazine size)

	GD 2.0	VG 4.0	FN 6.0	VF 8.0	VF/NM 9.0	NM- 9.2
1-1st app. Southern Knights	2	4	6	9	12	16

CRUSADERS, THE (Also see Black Hood, The Jaguar, The Comet, The Fly, Legend of the Shield, The Mighty... & The Web)
DC Comics (Impact): May, 1992 - No. 8, Dec, 1992 ($1.00/$1.25)

	GD 2.0	VG 4.0	FN 6.0	VF 8.0	VF/NM 9.0	NM- 9.2
1-8-Contains 3 Impact trading cards						2.50

CRUSADES, THE
DC Comics (Vertigo): 2001 - No. 20, Dec, 2002 ($3.95/$2.50)

	GD 2.0	VG 4.0	FN 6.0	VF 8.0	VF/NM 9.0	NM- 9.2
...: Urban Decree ('01, $3.95) Intro. the Knight; Seagle-s/Kelley Jones-c/a						4.00
1-(5/01, $2.50) Sienkiewicz-c						3.00
2-20: 2-Moeller-c. 18-Begin $2.95-c						3.00

CRUSH
Dark Horse Comics: Oct, 2003 - No. 4, Jan, 2004 ($2.99, limited series)

	GD 2.0	VG 4.0	FN 6.0	VF 8.0	VF/NM 9.0	NM- 9.2
1-4-Jason Hall-s/Sean Murphy-a						3.00

CRUSH, THE
Image Comics (Motown Machineworks): Jan, 1996 - No. 5, July, 1996 ($2.25, limited series)

	GD 2.0	VG 4.0	FN 6.0	VF 8.0	VF/NM 9.0	NM- 9.2
1-5: Baron scripts						3.00

CRUX
CrossGeneration Comics: May, 2001 - No. 33, Feb, 2004 ($2.95)

	GD 2.0	VG 4.0	FN 6.0	VF 8.0	VF/NM 9.0	NM- 9.2
1-33: 1-Waid-s/Epting & Magyar-a/c. 6-Pelletier-a. 13-Dixon-s begin. 25-Cover has fake creases and other aging						3.00
Atlantis Rising Vol. 1 TPB (2002, $15.95) r/#1-6						16.00
Test of Time Vol. 2 TPB (12/02, $15.95) r/#7-12						16.00
Vol. 3: Strangers in Atlantis (2003, $15.95) r/#13-18						16.00
Vol. 4: Chaos Reborn (2003, $15.95) r/#19-24						16.00

CRY FOR DAWN
Cry For Dawn Pub.: 1989 - No. 9 ($2.25, B&W, mature)

	GD 2.0	VG 4.0	FN 6.0	VF 8.0	VF/NM 9.0	NM- 9.2
1	8	16	24	52	86	120
1-2nd printing	3	6	9	18	27	35
1-3rd printing	3	6	9	14	20	25
2	5	10	15	32	51	70
2-2nd printing	2	4	6	11	16	20
3	4	8	12	24	37	50
3a-HorrorCon Edition (1990, less than 400 printed, signed inside-c)						200.00
4-6	3	6	9	14	19	24
5-2nd printing	1	2	3	5	6	8
7-9	2	4	6	10	14	18
4-9-Signed & numbered editions	3	6	9	14	20	25
Angry Christ Comix HC (4/03, $29.99) reprints various stories; and 30 pgs. new material						30.00
...Calendar (1993)						35.00

CRYIN' LION COMICS
William H. Wise Co.: Fall, 1944 - No. 3, Spring, 1945

	GD 2.0	VG 4.0	FN 6.0	VF 8.0	VF/NM 9.0	NM- 9.2
1-Funny animal	15	30	45	83	124	165
2-Hitler and Tojo app.	13	26	39	74	105	135
3	10	20	30	56	76	95

CRYPT
Image Comics (Extreme): Aug, 1995 - No.2, Oct. 1995 ($2.50, limited series)

	GD 2.0	VG 4.0	FN 6.0	VF 8.0	VF/NM 9.0	NM- 9.2
1,2-Prophet app.						2.50

CRYPTIC WRITINGS OF MEGADETH
Chaos! Comics: Sept, 1997 - No. 4, Jun, 1998 ($2.95, quarterly)

	GD 2.0	VG 4.0	FN 6.0	VF 8.0	VF/NM 9.0	NM- 9.2
1-4-Stories based on song lyrics by Dave Mustaine						3.00

CRYPT OF DAWN (see Dawn)
Sirius: 1996 ($2.95, B&W, limited series)

	GD 2.0	VG 4.0	FN 6.0	VF 8.0	VF/NM 9.0	NM- 9.2
1-Linsner-c/s; anthology.						5.00
2, 3 (2/98)						4.00

CSI: Dying in the Gutters #1 © CBS

C•23 #2 © Wizards of the Coast

Cursed #1 © TCOW

	GD	VG	FN	VF	VF/NM	NM-
	2.0	4.0	6.0	8.0	9.0	9.2

4,5: 4- (6/98), 5-(11/98) 3.00
Ltd. Edition 20.00

CRYPT OF SHADOWS
Marvel Comics Group: Jan, 1973 - No. 21, Nov, 1975 (#1-9 are 20¢)

	GD	VG	FN	VF	VF/NM	NM-
1-Wolverton-r/Advs. Into Terror #7	3	6	9	18	27	35
2-10: 2-Starlin/Everett-c	2	4	6	11	16	20
11-21: 18,20-Kirby-a	2	4	6	10	14	18

NOTE: ***Briefer** a-2r. **Ditko** a-13r, 18-20r. **Everett** a-6, 14r; c-2i. **Heath** a-1r. **Gil Kane** c-1, 6. **Mort Lawrence** a-1r, 8r. **Maneely** a-2r. **Moldoff** a-8. **Powell** a-12r, 14r. **Tuska** a-2r.*

CRYPT OF TERROR (Formerly Crime Patrol; Tales From the Crypt No. 20 on)
(Also see EC Archives • Tales From the Crypt)
E. C. Comics: No. 17, Apr-May, 1950 - No. 19, Aug-Sept, 1950

	GD	VG	FN	VF	VF/NM	NM-
17-1st New Trend to hit stands	291	582	873	2328	3714	5100
18,19	166	332	498	1328	2114	2900

NOTE: ***Craig** c/a-17-19. **Feldstein** a-17-19. **Ingels** a-19. **Kurtzman** a-18. **Wood** a-18. Canadian reprints known; see Table of Contents.*

CSI: CRIME SCENE INVESTIGATION (Based on TV series)
IDW Publishing: Jan, 2003 - No. 5, May, 2003 ($3.99, limited series)

1-Two covers (photo & Ashley Wood); Max Allan Collins-s 4.00
2-5 4.00
...: Case Files Vol. 1 TPB (8/06, $19.99) B&W rep/Serial TPB, CSI - Bad Rap and CSI - Demon House limited series 20.00
...: Serial TPB (2003, $19.99) r/#1-5; bonus short story by Collins/Wood 20.00
...: Thicker Than Blood (7/03, $6.99) Mariotte-s/Rodriguez-a 7.00

CSI: CRIME SCENE INVESTIGATION - BAD RAP
IDW Publishing: Aug, 2003 - No. 5, Dec, 2003 ($3.99, limited series)

1-5-Two photo covers; Max Allan Collins-s/Rodriguez-a 4.00
TPB (3/04, $19.99) r/#1-5 20.00

CSI: CRIME SCENE INVESTIGATION - DEMON HOUSE
IDW Publishing: Feb, 2004 - No. 5, Jun, 2004 ($3.99, limited series)

1-5-Photo covers on all; Max Allan Collins-s/Rodriguez-a 4.00
TPB (10/04, $19.99) r/#1-5 20.00

CSI: CRIME SCENE INVESTIGATION - DOMINOS
IDW Publishing: Aug, 2004 - No. 5, Dec, 2004 ($3.99, limited series)

1-5-Photo covers on all; Oprisko-s/Rodriguez-a 4.00

CSI: CRIME SCENE INVESTIGATION - DYING IN THE GUTTERS
IDW Publishing: Aug, 2006 - No. 5, Dec, 2006 ($3.99, limited series)

1-5-"Rich Johnston" murdered; comic creators (Quesada, Rucka, David, Brubaker, Silvestri and others) appear as suspects; Stephen Mooney-a; photo-c 4.00

CSI: CRIME SCENE INVESTIGATION - SECRET IDENTITY
IDW Publishing: Feb, 2005 - No. 5, Jun, 2005 ($3.99, limited series)

1-5-Photo covers on all; Steven Grant-s/Gabriel Rodriguez-a 4.00

CSI: MIAMI
IDW Publishing: Oct, 2003; Apr, 2004 ($6.99, one-shots)

... - Blood Money (9/04)-Oprisko-s/Guedes & Perkins-a 7.00
... - Smoking Gun (10/03)-Mariotte-s/Avilés & Wood-a 7.00
... - Thou Shalt Not... (4/04)-Oprisko-s/Guedes & Wood-a 7.00
TPB (2/05, $19.99) reprints one-shots 20.00

CSI: NY - BLOODY MURDER
IDW Publishing: July, 2005 - No. 5, Nov, 2005 ($3.99, limited series)

1-5-Photo covers on all; Collins-s/Woodward-a 4.00

C•23 (Jim Lee's...) (Based on Wizards of the Coast card game)
Image Comics: Apr, 1998 - No. 8, Nov, 1998 ($2.50)

1-8: 1,2-Choi & Mariotte-s/ Charest-c. 2-Variant-c by Jim Lee. 4-Ryan Benjamin-c. 5,8-Corben var-c. 6-Flip book with Planetary preview; Corben-c 3.00

CUD
Fantagraphics Books: 8/92 - No. 8, 12/94 ($2.25-$2.75, B&W, mature)

1-8: Terry LaBan scripts & art in all. 6-1st Eno & Plum 3.00

CUD COMICS
Dark Horse Comics: Jan, 1995 - No. 8, Sept, 1997 ($2.95, B&W)

1-8: Terry LaBan-c/a/scripts. 5-Nudity; marijuana story 3.00
Eno and Plum TPB (1997, $12.95) r/#1-4, DHP #93-95 13.00

CUPID
Marvel Comics (U.S.A.): Dec, 1949 - No. 2, Mar, 1950

	GD	VG	FN	VF	VF/NM	NM-
1-Photo-c	17	34	51	98	154	210
2-Bettie Page ('50s pin-up queen) photo-c; Powell-a (see My Love #4)	43	86	129	271	461	650

CURIO
Harry 'A' Chesler: 1930's(?) (Tabloid size, 16-20 pgs.)

	GD	VG	FN	VF	VF/NM	NM-
nn	18	36	54	107	169	230

CURLY KAYOE COMICS (Boxing)
United Features Syndicate/Dell Publ. Co.: 1946 - No. 8, 1950; Jan, 1958

	GD	VG	FN	VF	VF/NM	NM-
1 (1946)-Strip-r (Fritzi Ritz); biography of Sam Leff, Kayoe's artist	18	36	54	103	162	220
2	11	22	33	62	86	110
3-8	10	20	30	54	72	90
United Presents...(Fall, 1948)	10	20	30	54	72	90
Four Color 871 (Dell, 1/58)	4	8	12	24	37	50

CURSED
Image Comics (Top Cow): Oct, 2003 - No. 4, Feb, 2004 ($2.99)

1-4-Avery & Blevins-s/Molenaar-a 3.00

CURSE OF DRACULA, THE
Dark Horse Comics: July, 1998 - No. 3, Sept, 1998 ($2.95, limited series)

1-3-Marv Wolfman-s/Gene Colan-a 3.00
TPB (2005, $9.95) r/series; intro. by Marv Wolfman 10.00

CURSE OF DREADWOLF
Lightning Comics: Sept, 1994 ($2.75, B&W)

1 2.75

CURSE OF RUNE (Becomes Rune, 2nd Series)
Malibu Comics (Ultraverse): May, 1995 - No. 4, Aug, 1995 ($2.50, lim. series)

1-4: 1-Two covers form one image 2.50

CURSE OF THE SPAWN
Image Comics (Todd McFarlane Prod.): Sept, 1996 - No. 29, Mar, 1999 ($1.95)

	GD	VG	FN	VF	VF/NM	NM-
1-Dwayne Turner-a(p)						6.00
1-B&W Edition	2	4	6	9	13	16
2-3						4.00
4-29: 12-Movie photo-c of Melinda Clarke (Priest)						2.50
Blood and Sutures ('99, $9.95, TPB) r/#5-8						10.00
Lost Values ('00, $10.95, TPB) r/#12-14,22; Ashley Wood-c						11.00
Sacrifice of the Soul ('99, $9.95, TPB) r/#1-4						10.00
Shades of Gray ('00, $9.95, TPB) r/#9-11,29						10.00
The Best of the Curse of the Spawn (6/06, $16.99, TPB) B&W r/#1-8,12-16,20-29						17.00

CURSE OF THE WEIRD
Marvel Comics: Dec, 1993 - No. 4, Mar, 1994 ($1.25, limited series)
(Pre-code horror-r)

	GD	VG	FN	VF	VF/NM	NM-
1-4: 1,3,4-Wolverton-r(1-Eye of Doom; 3-Where Monsters Dwell; 4-The End of the World). 2-Orlando-r. 4-Zombie-r by Everett; painted-c	1	2	3	5	6	8

NOTE: ***Briefer** r-2. **Davis** a-4r. **Ditko** a-1r, 2r, 4r; c-1r. **Everett** r-1. **Heath** r-1-3. **Kubert** r-3. **Wolverton** a-1r, 3r, 4r.*

CUSTER'S LAST FIGHT
Avon Periodicals: 1950

	GD	VG	FN	VF	VF/NM	NM-
nn-Partial reprint of Cowpuncher #1	15	30	45	88	137	185

CUTEY BUNNY (See Army Surplus Komikz Featuring...)

CUTIE PIE
Junior Reader's Guild (Lev Gleason): May, 1955 - No. 3, Dec, 1955; No. 4, Feb, 1956; No. 5, Aug, 1956

	GD	VG	FN	VF	VF/NM	NM-
1	8	16	24	42	54	65
2-5: 4-Misdated 2/55	6	12	18	28	34	40

CUTTING EDGE
Marvel Comics: Dec, 1995 ($2.95)

1-Hulk-c/story; Messner-Loebs scripts 3.00

CVO: COVERT VAMPIRIC OPERATIONS
IDW Publishing: June, 2003 ($5.99, one-shot)

1-Alex Garner-s/Mindy Lee-a(p) 6.00
... - Human Touch 1 (8/04, $3.99, one-shot) Hernandez & Garner-a 4.00
TPB (9/04, $19.99) r/#1 and ... - Artifact #1-3; intro. by Garner 20.00

CVO: COVERT VAMPIRIC OPERATIONS - AFRICAN BLOOD
IDW Publishing: Sept, 2006 - No. 4, May, 2007 ($3.99, limited series)

1-4-El Torres-s/Luis Czerniawski-a 4.00

CVO: COVERT VAMPIRIC OPERATIONS - ARTIFACT
IDW Publishing: Oct, 2003 - No. 3, Dec, 2003 ($3.99, limited series)

1-3-Jeff Mariotte-s/Gabriel Hernandez-a/Alex Garner-c 4.00

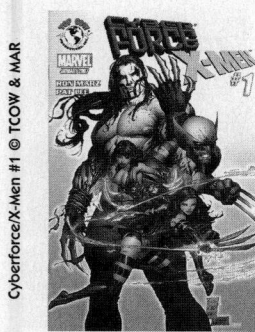

Cyberforce/X-Men #1 © TCOW & MAR

Cybernary #2 © WSP

Daffodil #2 © MC Prods.

GD 2.0 | VG 4.0 | FN 6.0 | VF 8.0 | VF/NM 9.0 | NM- 9.2

CVO: COVERT VAMPIRIC OPERATIONS - ROGUE STATE
IDW Publishing: Nov, 2004 - No. 5, Mar, 2005 ($3.99, limited series)

1-5-Jeff Mariotte-s/Vazquez-a 4.00
TPB (7/05, $19.99) r/#1-5; cover gallery 20.00

CYBERELLA
DC Comics (Helix): Sept, 1996 - No. 12, Aug, 1997 ($2.25/$2.50)(1st Helix series)

1-12: 1-5-Chaykin & Cameron-a. 1,2-Chaykin-c. 3-5-Cameron-c 2.50

CYBERFORCE
Image Comics (Top Cow Productions): Oct, 1992 - No. 4, 1993; No. 0, Sept, 1993 ($1.95, limited series)

1-Silvestri-c/a in all; coupon for Image Comics #0; 1st Top Cow Productions title 6.00
1-With coupon missing 2.50
2-4,0: 2-(3/93). 3-Pitt-c/story. 4-Codename: Stryke Force back-up (1st app.); foil-c. 0-(9/93)-Walt Simonson-c/a/scripts 3.00

CYBERFORCE
Image Comics (Top Cow Productions)/Top Cow Comics No. 28 on: V2#1, Nov, 1993 - No. 35, Sept. 1997 ($1.95)

V2#1-24: 1-7-Marc Silvestri/Keith Williams-c/a. 8-McFarlane-c/a. 10-Painted variant-c exists. 18-Variant-c exists. 23-Velocity-c. 2.50
1-3: 1-Gold Logo-c. 2-Silver embossed-c. 3-Gold embossed-c 10.00
1-(99¢, 3/96, 2nd printing) 2.50
25-($3.95)-Wraparound, foil-c 4.00
26-35: 28-(11/96)-1st Top Cow Comics iss. Quesada & Palmiotti's Gabriel app. 27-Quesada & Palmiotti's Ash app. 2.50
Annual 1,2 (3/95, 8/96, $2.50, $2.95) 3.00
NOTE: *Annuals read Volume One in the indica.*

CYBERFORCE (Volume 2)
Image Comics (Top Cow): Apr, 2006 - No. 6, Nov, 2006 ($2.99)

1-6: 1-Pat Lee-a/Ron Marz-s; three covers by Pat Lee, Marc Silvestri and Dave Finch 3.00
#0-(6/06, $2.99) reprints origin story from Image Comics Hardcover Vol. 1 3.00
.../X-Men 1 (1/07, $3.99) Pat Lee-a/Ron Marz-s; 2 covers by Lee and Silvestri 4.00
Vol. 1 TPB (12/06, $14.99) r/#1-6, #0 & story from The Cow Quarterly; cover gallery 15.00

CYBERFORCE/HUNTER-KILLER
Image Comics (Top Cow Productions): July, 2009 - Present ($2.99)

1-4-Waid-s/Rocafort-a; multiple covers on each 3.00

CYBERFORCE ORIGINS
Image Comics (Top Cow Productions): Jan, 1995 - No. 3, Nov, 1995 ($2.50)

1-Cyblade (1/95) 5.00
1-Cyblade (3/96, 99¢, 2nd printing) 2.25
1A-Exclusive Ed.; Tucci-c 4.00
2,3: 2-Stryker (2/95)-1st Mike Turner-a. 3-Impact 2.50
(#4) Misery (12/95, $2.95) 3.00

CYBERFORCE/STRYKEFORCE: OPPOSING FORCES (See Codename: Stryke Force #15)
Image Comics (Top Cow Productions): Sept, 1995 - No. 2, Oct, 1995 ($2.50, limited series)

1,2: 2-Stryker disbands Strykeforce. 2.50

CYBERFORCE UNIVERSE SOURCEBOOK
Image Comics (Top Cow Productions): Aug, 1994/Feb, 1995 ($2.50)

1,2-Silvestri-c 2.50

CYBERFROG
Hall of Heroes: June, 1994 - No. 2, Dec, 1994 ($2.50, B&W, limited series)

1,2 3.00

CYBERFROG
Harris Comics: Feb, 1996 - No. 3, Apr, 1996 ($2.95)

0-3: Van Sciver-c/a/scripts. 2-Variant-c exists 5.00

CYBERFROG: (Title series), **Harris Comics**

--RESERVOIR FROG, 9/96 - No. 2, 10/96 ($2.95) 1,2: Van Sciver-c/a/scripts; wraparound-c 3.00
--3RD ANNIVERSARY SPECIAL, 1/97 - #2, ($2.50, B&W) 1,2 3.00
--VS. CREED, 7/97 ($2.95, B&W)1 3.00

CYBERNARY (See Deathblow #1)
Image Comics (WildStorm Productions): Nov, 1995 - No.5, Mar, 1996 ($2.50)

1-5 2.50

CYBERNARY 2.0
DC Comics (WildStorm): Sept, 2001 - No. 6, Apr, 2002 ($2.95, limited series)

1-6: Joe Harris-s/Eric Canete-a. 6-The Authority app. 3.00

CYBERPUNK
Innovation Publishing: Sept, 1989 - No. 2, Oct, 1989 ($1.95, 28 pgs.) Book 2, #1, May, 1990 - No. 2, 1990 ($2.25, 28 pgs.)

1,2, Book 2 #1,2:1,2-Ken Steacy painted-covers (Adults) 2.50

CYBERPUNK: THE SERAPHIM FILES
Innovation Publishing: Nov, 1990 - No. 2, Dec, 1990 ($2.50, 28 pgs., mature)

1,2: 1-Painted-c; story cont'd from Seraphim 2.50

CYBERPUNX
Image Comics (Extreme Studios): Mar, 1996 ($2.50)

1 3.00

CYBERRAD
Continuity Comics: 1991 - No. 7, 1992 ($2.00)(Direct sale & newsstand-c variations) V2#1, 1993 ($2.50)

1-7: 5-Glow-in-the-dark-c by N. Adams (direct sale only). 6-Contains 4 pg. fold-out poster; N. Adams layouts 2.50
V2#1-($2.95, direct sale ed.)-Die-cut-c w/B&W hologram on-c; Neal Adams sketches 3.00
V2#1-($2.50, newsstand ed.)-Without sketches 2.50

CYBERRAD DEATHWATCH 2000 (Becomes CyberRad w/#2, 7/93)
Continuity Comics: Apr, 1993 - No. 2, 1993 ($2.50)

1,2: 1-Bagged w/2 cards; Adams-c & layouts & plots. 2-Bagged w/card; Adams scripts 2.50

CYBER 7
Eclipse Comics: Mar, 1989 - #7, Sept, 1989; V2#1, Oct, 1989 - #10, 1990 ($2.00, B&W)

1-7, Book 2 #1-10: Stories translated from Japanese 2.50

CYBLADE
Image Comics (Top Cow Productions): Oct, 2008 - No. 4, Mar, 2009 ($2.99)

1-4: 1,2-Mays-a/Fialkov-s. 1-Two covers. 3,4-Ferguson-a 3.00
.../ Ghost Rider 1 (Marvel/Top Cow, 1/97, $2.95) Devil's Reign pt. 2 4.00
...: Pilot Season 1 (9/07, $2.99) Rick Mays-a 3.00

CYBLADE/SHI (Also see Battle For The Independents & Shi/Cyblade: The Battle For The Independents)
Image Comics (Top Cow Productions): 1995 ($2.95, one-shot)

	GD 2.0	VG 4.0	FN 6.0	VF 8.0	VF/NM 9.0	NM- 9.2
San Diego Preview	3	6	9	16	20	25
1-($2.95)-1st app. Witchblade	2	4	6	12	16	20
1-($2.95)-variant-c; Tucci-a	2	4	6	10	12	15

CYBRID
Maximum Press: July, 1995; No. 0, Jan, 1997 ($2.95/$3.50)

1-(7/95) 3.50
0-(1/97)-Liefeld-a/script; story cont'd in Avengelyne #4 3.50

CYCLONE COMICS (Also see Whirlwind Comics)
Bilbara Publishing Co.: June, 1940 - No. 5, Nov, 1940

	GD 2.0	VG 4.0	FN 6.0	VF 8.0	VF/NM 9.0	NM- 9.2
1-Origin Tornado Tom; Volton (the human generator), Tornado Tom, Kingdom of the Moon, Mister Q begin (1st app. of each)	120	240	360	756	1278	1800
2	60	120	180	378	639	900
3-Classic-c (scarce)	105	210	315	662	1119	1575
4	63	126	189	397	669	940
5-(Scarce)	79	158	237	498	842	1185

Ashcan - Not distributed to newsstands, only for in house use. Cover produced on green stock paper. A CGC certified FN (6.0) copy sold for $2,000 in 2006.

CYCLOPS (X-Men)
Marvel Comics: Oct, 2001 - No. 4, Jan, 2002 ($2.50, limited series)

1-4-Texeira-c/a. 1,2-Black Tom and Juggernaut app. 2.50

CYCLOPS: RETRIBUTION
Marvel Comics: 1994 ($5.95, trade paperback)

nn-r/Marvel Comics Presents #17-24 6.00

CY-GOR (See Spawn #38 for 1st app.)
Image Comics (Todd McFarlane Prod.): July, 1999 - No. 6, Dec, 1999 ($2.50)

1-6-Veitch-s 2.50

CYNTHIA DOYLE, NURSE IN LOVE (Formerly Sweetheart Diary)
Charlton Publications: No. 66, Oct, 1962 - No. 74, Feb, 1964

	GD 2.0	VG 4.0	FN 6.0	VF 8.0	VF/NM 9.0	NM- 9.2
66-74	3	6	9	14	19	24

DAFFODIL
Marvel Comics (Soleil): 2010 - No. 3, 2010 ($5.99, limited series)

1-3-English version of French comic; Brrémaud-s/Rigano-a 6.00

DAFFY (Daffy Duck No. 18 on)(See Looney Tunes)

Daffy Duck #22 © WB

Dagwood Comics #69 © HARV

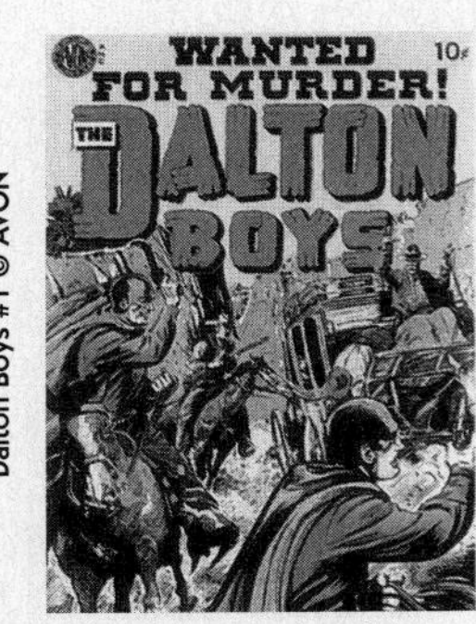

Dalton Boys #1 © AVON

Dell Publishing Co./Gold Key No. 31-127/Whitman No. 128 on: #457, 3/53 - #30, 7-9/62; #31, 10-12/62 - #145, 6/84 (No #132,133)

	GD 2.0	VG 4.0	FN 6.0	VF 8.0	VF/NM 9.0	NM- 9.2
Four Color 457(#1)-Elmer Fudd x-overs begin	10	20	30	71	126	180
Four Color 536,615('55)	6	12	18	41	66	90
4(1-3/56)-11('57)	5	10	15	32	51	70
12-19(1958-59)	4	8	12	24	37	50
20-40(1960-64)	3	6	9	17	25	32
41-60(1964-68)	3	6	9	14	20	25
61-90(1969-74)-Road Runner in most. 76-82-"Daffy Duck and the Road Runner" on-c	2	4	6	10	14	18
91-110	2	4	6	8	10	12
111-127	1	2	3	5	6	8
128,134-141: 139(2/82), 140(2-3/82), 141(4/82)	1	3	4	6	8	10
129(8/80),130,131 (pre-pack?) (scarce). 129-Sherlock Holmes parody-s	3	6	9	21	32	42
142-145(#90029 on-c; nd, nd code, pre-pack): 142(6/83), 143(8/83), 144(3/84), 145(6/84)	3	6	9	16	22	28
Mini-Comic 1 (1976; 3-1/4x6-1/2")	1	2	3	5	6	8

NOTE: *Reprint issues-No.41-46, 48, 50, 53-55, 58, 59, 65, 67, 69, 73, 81, 96, 103-108; 136-142, 144, 145(1/3-2/3-r). (See March of Comics No. 277, 288, 303, 313, 331, 347, 357,375, 387, 397, 402, 413, 425, 437, 460).*

DAFFY DUCK (Digest-size reprints from Looney Tunes)
DC Comics: 2005 - Present ($6.99, digest)

	GD 2.0	VG 4.0	FN 6.0	VF 8.0	VF/NM 9.0	NM- 9.2
Vol. 1: You're Despicable! - Reprints from Looney Tunes #38,43,45,47,51,53,54,58,61,62,66,70						7.00

DAFFY TUNES COMICS
Four-Star Publications: June, 1947; No. 12, Aug, 1947

	GD 2.0	VG 4.0	FN 6.0	VF 8.0	VF/NM 9.0	NM- 9.2
nn	9	18	27	52	69	85
12-Al Fago-c/a; funny animal	9	18	27	47	61	75

DAGAR, DESERT HAWK (Captain Kidd No. 24 on; formerly All Great)
Fox Features Syndicate: No. 14, Feb, 1948 - No. 23, Apr, 1949 (No #17,18)

	GD 2.0	VG 4.0	FN 6.0	VF 8.0	VF/NM 9.0	NM- 9.2
14-Tangi & Safari Cary begin; Good bondage-c/a	82	164	246	528	902	1275
15,16-E. Good-a; 15-Bondage-c	50	100	150	315	533	750
19,20,22: 19-Used in **SOTI**, pg. 180 (Tangi)	45	90	135	284	480	675
21,23: 21-Bondage-c; "Bombs & Bums Away" panel in "Flood of Death" story used in **SOTI.** 23-Bondage-c	48	96	144	302	514	725

NOTE: *Tangi by **Kamen**-14-16, 19, 20; c-20, 21.*

DAGAR THE INVINCIBLE (Tales of Sword & Sorcery...) (Also see Dan Curtis Giveaways & Gold Key Spotlight)
Gold Key: Oct, 1972 - No. 18, Dec, 1976; No. 19, Apr, 1982

	GD 2.0	VG 4.0	FN 6.0	VF 8.0	VF/NM 9.0	NM- 9.2
1-Origin; intro. Villains Olstellon & Scor	4	8	12	24	37	50
2-5: 3-Intro. Graylin, Dagar's woman; Jarn x-over	3	6	9	14	19	24
6-1st Dark Gods story	2	4	6	9	13	16
7-10: 9-Intro. Torgus. 10-1st Three Witches story	2	4	6	9	13	16
11-18: 13-Durak & Torgus x-over; story continues in Dr. Spektor #15. 14-Dagar's origin retold. 18-Origin retold	2	4	6	8	10	12
19(4/82)-Origin-r/#18						6.00

NOTE: *Durak app. in 7, 12, 13. Tragg app. in 5, 11.*

DAGWOOD (Chic Young's) (Also see Blondie Comics)
Harvey Publications: Sept, 1950 - No. 140, Nov, 1965

	GD 2.0	VG 4.0	FN 6.0	VF 8.0	VF/NM 9.0	NM- 9.2
1	15	30	45	107	204	300
2	9	18	27	63	107	150
3-10	8	16	24	52	86	120
11-20	6	12	18	41	66	90
21-30	5	10	15	34	55	75
31-50	5	10	15	30	48	65
51-70	4	8	12	22	34	45
71-100	3	6	9	18	27	35
101-121,123-128,130,135	3	6	9	16	23	30
122,129,131-134,136-140-All are 68-pg. issues	4	8	12	22	34	45

NOTE: *Popeye and other one page strips appeared in early issues.*

DAI KAMIKAZE!
Now Comics: June, 1987 - No. 12, Aug, 1988 ($1.75)

	GD 2.0	VG 4.0	FN 6.0	VF 8.0	VF/NM 9.0	NM- 9.2
1-1st app. Speed Racer; 2nd print exists						4.00
2-12						2.50

DAILY BUGLE (See Spider-Man)
Marvel Comics: Dec, 1996 - No. 3, Feb, 1997 ($2.50, B&W, limited series)

	GD 2.0	VG 4.0	FN 6.0	VF 8.0	VF/NM 9.0	NM- 9.2
1-3-Paul Grist-s						2.50

DAISY AND DONALD (See Walt Disney Showcase No. 8)
Gold Key/Whitman No. 42 on: May, 1973 - No. 59, July, 1984 (no No. 48)

	GD 2.0	VG 4.0	FN 6.0	VF 8.0	VF/NM 9.0	NM- 9.2
1-Barks-r/WDC&S #280,308	3	6	9	20	30	40
2-5: 4-Barks-r/WDC&S #224	2	4	6	11	16	20
6-10	2	4	6	9	12	15
11-20	1	3	4	6	8	10
21-41: 32-r/WDC&S #308	1	2	3	5	6	8
42-44 (Whitman)	2	4	6	8	11	14
45 (8/80),46-(pre-pack?)(scarce)	4	8	12	22	34	45
47-(12/80)-Only distr. in Whitman 3-pack (scarce)	5	10	15	35	55	75
48(3/81)-50(8/81): 50-r/#3	2	4	6	10	14	18
51-54: 51-Barks-r/4-Color #1150. 52-r/#2. 53(2/82), 54(4/82)	2	4	6	9	13	16
55-59-(all #90284 on-c, nd, nd code, pre-pack): 55(5/83), 56(7/83), 57(8/83), 58(8/83), 59(7/84)	3	6	9	14	19	24

DAISY & HER PUPS (Dagwood & Blondie's Dogs)(Formerly Blondie Comics #20)
Harvey Publications: No. 21, 7/51 - No. 27, 7/52; No. 8, 9/52 - No. 18, 5/54

	GD 2.0	VG 4.0	FN 6.0	VF 8.0	VF/NM 9.0	NM- 9.2
21 (#1)-Blondie's dog Daisy and her 5 pups led by Elmer begin. Rags Rabbit app.	6	12	18	41	66	90
22-27 (#2-7): 26 has No. 6 on cover but No. 26 on inside. 23,25-The Little King app. 24-Bringing Up Father by McManus app. 25-27-Rags Rabbit app.	4	8	12	28	44	60
8-18: 8,9-Rags Rabbit app. 8,17-The Little King app. 11-The Flop Family Swan begins. 22-Cookie app. 11-Felix The Cat app. by 17,18-Popeye app.	4	8	12	26	41	55

DAISY DUCK & UNCLE SCROOGE PICNIC TIME (See Dell Giant #33)

DAISY DUCK & UNCLE SCROOGE SHOW BOAT (See Dell Giant #55)

DAISY DUCK'S DIARY (See Dynabrite Comics, & Walt Disney's C&S #298)
Dell Publishing Co.: No. 600, Nov, 1954 - No. 1247, Dec-Fef, 1961-62 (Disney)

	GD 2.0	VG 4.0	FN 6.0	VF 8.0	VF/NM 9.0	NM- 9.2
Four Color 600 (#1)	7	14	21	47	76	105
Four Color 659, 743 (11/56)	6	12	18	37	59	80
Four Color 858 (11/57), 948 (11/58), 1247 (12-2/61-62)	5	10	15	32	51	70
Four Color 1055 (11-1/59-60), 1150 (12-1/60-61)-By Carl Barks	9	18	27	60	100	140

DAISY HANDBOOK
Daisy Manufacturing Co.: 1946; No. 2, 1948 (10¢, pocket-size, 132 pgs.)

	GD 2.0	VG 4.0	FN 6.0	VF 8.0	VF/NM 9.0	NM- 9.2
1-Buck Rogers, Red Ryder; Wolverton-a (2 pgs.)	25	50	75	147	236	325
2-Captain Marvel & Ibis the Invincible, Red Ryder, Boy Commandos & Robotman; Wolverton-a (2 pgs.); contains 8 pg. color catalog	25	50	75	147	236	325

DAISY MAE (See Oxydol-Dreft)

DAISY'S RED RYDER GUN BOOK
Daisy Manufacturing Co.: 1955 (25¢, pocket-size, 132 pgs.)

	GD 2.0	VG 4.0	FN 6.0	VF 8.0	VF/NM 9.0	NM- 9.2
nn-Boy Commandos, Red Ryder; 1pg. Wolverton-a	18	36	54	105	165	225

DAKKON BLACKBLADE ON THE WORLD OF MAGIC: THE GATHERING
Acclaim Comics (Armada): June, 1996 ($5.95, one-shot)

	GD 2.0	VG 4.0	FN 6.0	VF 8.0	VF/NM 9.0	NM- 9.2
1-Jerry Prosser scripts; Rags Morales-c/a.						6.00

DAKOTA LIL (See Fawcett Movie Comics)

DAKTARI (Ivan Tors) (TV)
Dell Publishing Co.: July, 1967 - No. 3, Oct, 1968; No. 4, Oct, 1969

	GD 2.0	VG 4.0	FN 6.0	VF 8.0	VF/NM 9.0	NM- 9.2
1-Marshall Thompson photo-c on all	4	8	12	24	37	50
2-4	3	6	9	18	27	35

DALE EVANS COMICS (Also see Queen of the West...)(See Boy Commandos #32)
National Periodical Publications: Sept-Oct, 1948 - No. 24, Jul-Aug, 1952 (No. 1-19: 52 pgs.)

	GD 2.0	VG 4.0	FN 6.0	VF 8.0	VF/NM 9.0	NM- 9.2
1-Dale Evans & her horse Buttermilk begin; Sierra Smith begins by Alex Toth	67	134	201	422	711	1000
2-Alex Toth-a	35	70	105	203	327	450
3-11-Alex Toth-a	21	42	63	125	200	275
12-20: 12-Target-c	15	30	45	83	124	165
21-24	15	30	45	85	130	175

NOTE: *Photo-c-1, 2, 4-14.*

DALGODA
Fantagraphics Books: Aug, 1984 - No. 8, Feb, 1986 (High quality paper)

	GD 2.0	VG 4.0	FN 6.0	VF 8.0	VF/NM 9.0	NM- 9.2
1,8: 1- Fujitake-c/a in all. 8-Alan Moore story						4.00
2-7: 2,3-Debut Grimwood's Daughter.						2.50

DALTON BOYS, THE
Avon Periodicals: 1951

	GD 2.0	VG 4.0	FN 6.0	VF 8.0	VF/NM 9.0	NM- 9.2
1-(Number on spine)-Kinstler-c	17	34	51	100	158	215

DAMAGE
DC Comics: Apr, 1994 - No. 20, Jan, 1996 ($1.75/$1.95/$2.25)

Dan Dare #3 © Dan Dare Corp.

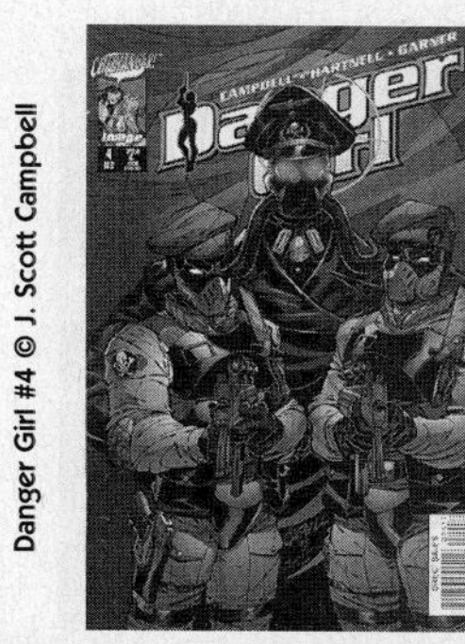
Danger Girl #4 © J. Scott Campbell

Danger Trail #2 © DC

GD VG FN VF VF/NM NM-
2.0 4.0 6.0 8.0 9.0 9.2

1-20: 6-(9/94)-Zero Hour. 0-(10/94). 7-(11/94). 14-Ray app. 3.00

DAMAGE CONTROL (See Marvel Comics Presents #19)
Marvel Comics: 5/89 - No. 4, 8/89; V2#1, 12/89 - No. 4, 2/90 ($1.00)
V3#1, 6/91 - No. 4, 9/91 ($1.25, all are limited series)

V1#1-4,V2#1-4,V3#1-4: V1#4-Wolverine app. V2#2,4-Punisher app. 1-Spider-Man app. 2-New Warriors app. 3,4-Silver Surfer app. 4-Infinity Gauntlet parody 2.50

DAMNED
Image Comics (Homage Comics): June, 1997 - No. 4, Sept, 1997 ($2.50, limited series)

1-4-Steven Grant-s/Mike Zeck-c/a in all 2.50

DAMN NATION
Dark Horse Comics: Feb, 2005 - No. 3, Apr, 2005 ($2.99, limited series)

1-3-J. Alexander-a/Andrew Cosby-s 3.00

DANCES WITH DEMONS (See Marvel Frontier Comics Unlimited)
Marvel Frontier Comics: Sept, 1993 - No. 4, Dec, 1993 ($1.95, limited series)

1-($2.95)-Foil embossed-c; Charlie Adlard & Rod Ramos-a 3.00
2-4 2.50

DAN DARE
Virgin Comics: Nov, 2007 - No. 7, July, 2008 ($2.99/$5.99)

1-6-Ennis-s/Erskine-a. 1-Two covers by Talbot and Horn. 2-6-Two covers on each 3.00
7-($5.99) Double sized finale with wraparound Erskine-c; Gibbons variant-c 6.00

DANDEE: Four Star Publications: 1947 (Advertised, not published)

DAN DUNN (See Crackajack Funnies, Detective Dan, Famous Feature Stories & Red Ryder)

DANDY COMICS (Also see Happy Jack Howard)
E. C. Comics: Spring, 1947 - No. 7, Spring, 1948

1-Funny animal; Vince Fago-a in all; Dandy in all 39 78 117 240 395 550
2 27 54 81 158 259 360
3-7: 3-Intro Handy Andy who is c-feature #3 on 21 42 63 126 206 285

DANGER
Comic Media/Allen Hardy Assoc.: Jan, 1953 - No. 11, Aug, 1954

1-Heck-c/a 28 56 84 165 270 375
2,3,5,7,9-11: 15 30 45 88 137 185
4-Marijuana cover/story 19 38 57 109 172 235
6- "Narcotics" story; begin spy theme 17 34 51 98 154 210
8-Bondage/torture/headlights panels 20 40 60 114 182 250
NOTE: *Morisi a-2, 5, 6(3), 10; c-2. Contains some reprints from Danger & Dynamite.*

DANGER (Formerly Comic Media title)
Charlton Comics Group: No. 12, June, 1955 - No. 14, Oct, 1955

12(#1) 12 24 36 69 97 125
13,14: 14-r/#12 10 20 30 56 76 95

DANGER
Super Comics: 1964

Super Reprint #10-12 (Black Dwarf; #10-r/Great Comics #1 by Novack. #11-r/Johnny Danger #1. #12-r/Red Seal #14), #15-r/Spy Cases #26. #16-Unpublished Chesler material (Yankee Girl), #17-r/Scoop #8 (Capt. Courage & Enchanted Dagger), #18(nd)-r/Guns Against Gangsters #5 (Gun-Master, Annie Oakley, The Chameleon; L.B. Cole-r)
2 4 6 11 16 20

DANGER AND ADVENTURE (Formerly This Magazine Is Haunted; Robin Hood and His Merry Men No. 28 on)
Charlton Comics: No. 22, Feb, 1955 - No. 27, Feb, 1956

22-Ibis the Invincible-c/story; Nyoka app.; last pre-code issue
11 22 33 62 86 110
23-Lance O'Casey-c/sty; Nyoka app.; Ditko-a thru #27
13 26 39 72 101 130
24-27: 24-Mike Danger & Johnny Adventure begin 9 18 27 50 65 80

DANGER GIRL (Also see Cliffhanger #0)
Image Comics (Cliffhanger Productions): Mar, 1998 - No. 4, Dec, 1998;
DC Comics (Cliffhanger Prod.): No. 5, July, 1999 - No. 7, Feb, 2001

Preview-Bagged in DV8 #14 Voyager Pack 4.00
Preview Gold Edition 8.00
1-($2.95) Hartnell & Campbell-s/Campbell/Garner-a 1 2 3 5 6 8
1-($4.95) Chromium cover 45.00
1-American Entertainment Ed. 8.00
1-American Entertainment Gold Ed., 1-Tourbook edition 10.00
1-"Danger-sized" ed.; over-sized format 3 6 9 16 23 30
2-($2.50) 4.00
2-Smoking Gun variant cover, 2-Platinum Ed., 2-Dynamic Forces Omnichrome variant-c 2 4 6 9 13 16
2-Gold foil cover 9.00
2-Ruby red foil cover 90.00
3,4: 3-c by Campbell, Charest and Adam Hughes. 4-Big knife variant-c 3.00
3,5: 3-Gold foil cover. 5-DF Bikini variant-c 5.00
4-6 3.00
7-($5.95) Wraparound gatefold-c; Last issue 6.00
...: Hawaiian Punch (5/03, $4.95) Campbell-c; Phil Noto-a 5.00
...: Odd Jobs TPB (2004, $14.95) r/one-shots Hawaiian Punch, Viva Las Danger & Special; Campbell-c 15.00
San Diego Preview (8/98, B&W) flip book w/Wildcats preview 5.00
Sketchbook (2001, $6.95) Campbell-a; sketches for comics, toys, games 7.00
...Special (2/00, $3.50) art by Campbell, Chiodo, and Art Adams 3.50
... 3-D #1 (4/03, $4.95, bagged with 3-D glasses) r/ Preview & #1 in 3-D 5.00
...: Viva Las Danger (1/04, $4.95) Noto-a/Campbell-c 5.00
... :The Dangerous Collection nn(8/98; r-#1) 6.00
... :The Dangerous Collection 2,3: 2-(11/98, $5.95) r/#2,3. 3-('99) r/#4,5 6.00
... :The Dangerous Collection nn, 2-($10.00) Gold foil logo 10.00
... :The Ultimate Collection HC ($29.95) r/#1-7; intro by Bruce Campbell 30.00
... :The Ultimate Collection SC ($19.95) r/#1-7; intro by Bruce Campbell 20.00

DANGER GIRL: BACK IN BLACK
DC Comics (Cliffhanger): Jan, 2006 - No. 4, Apr, 2006 ($2.99, limited series)

1-4-Hartnell-s/Bradshaw-a. 1-Campbell-c 3.00
TPB (2007, $12.99) r/series & covers 13.00

DANGER GIRL: BODY SHOTS
DC Comics (WildStorm): Jun, 2007 - No. 4, Sept, 2007 ($2.99, limited series)

1-4-Hartnell-s/Bradshaw-a 3.00
TPB (2007, $12.99) r/series & covers 13.00

DANGER GIRL KAMIKAZE
DC Comics (Cliffhanger): Nov, 2001 - No. 2, Dec., 2001 ($2.95, lim. series)

1,2-Tommy Yune-s/a 3.00

DANGER IS OUR BUSINESS!
Toby Press: 1953(Dec.) - No. 10, June, 1955

1-Captain Comet by Williamson/Frazetta-a, 6 pgs. (science fiction)
44 88 132 277 471 665
2 14 28 42 80 115 150
3-10 12 24 36 67 94 120
I.W. Reprint #9('64)-Williamson/Frazetta-r/#1; Kinstler-c
8 16 24 52 86 120

DANGER IS THEIR BUSINESS (Also see A-1 Comic)
Magazine Enterprises: No. 50, 1952

A-1 50-Powell-a 14 28 42 80 115 150

DANGER MAN (TV)
Dell Publishing Co.: No. 1231, Sept-Nov, 1961

Four Color 1231-Patrick McGoohan photo-c 10 20 30 71 126 180

DANGER TRAIL (Also see Showcase #50, 51)
National Periodical Publ.: July-Aug, 1950 - No. 5, Mar-Apr, 1951 (52 pgs.)

1-King Faraday begins, ends #4; Toth-a in all 126 252 378 806 1378 1950
2 87 174 261 552 951 1350
3-(Rare) one of the rarest early '50s DCs 126 252 378 806 1378 1950
4,5: 5-Johnny Peril-c/story (moves to Sensation Comics #107); new logo (also see Comic Cavalcade #15-29) 67 134 201 425 730 1035

DANGER TRAIL
DC Comics: Apr, 1993 - No. 4, July, 1993 ($1.50, limited series)

1-4: Gulacy-c on all 2.50

DANGER UNLIMITED (See San Diego Comic Con Comics #2 & Torch of Liberty Special)
Dark Horse (Legend): Feb, 1994 - No. 4, May, 1994 ($2.00, limited series)

1-4: Byrne-c/a/scripts in all; origin stories of both original team (Doc Danger, Thermal, Miss Mirage, & Hunk) & future team (Thermal, Belebet, & Caucus). 1-Intro Torch of Liberty & Golgotha (cameo) in back-up story. 4-Hellboy & Torch of Liberty cameo in lead story 2.50
TPB (1995, $14.95)-r/#1-4; includes last pg. originally cut from #4 15.00

DAN HASTINGS (See Syndicate Features)

DANIEL BOONE (See The Exploits of..., Fighting... Frontier Scout...,The Legends of... & March of Comics No. 306)
Dell Publishing Co.: No. 1163, Mar-May, 1961

Four Color 1163-Marsh-a 5 10 15 35 55 75

Daredevil #2 © LEV

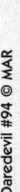

Daredevil #63 © LEV

Daredevil #94 © MAR

DANIEL BOONE (TV) (See March of Comics No. 306)
Gold Key: Jan, 1965 - No. 15, Apr, 1969 (All have Fess Parker photo-c)

	GD 2.0	VG 4.0	FN 6.0	VF 8.0	VF/NM 9.0	NM- 9.2
1-Back-c and last eight pages fold in half to form "Official Handbook Fess Parker as Daniel Boone Trail Blazers Club"	8	16	24	56	93	130
2-Back-c pin-up	5	10	15	32	51	70
3-5-Back-c pin-ups	4	8	12	26	41	55
6-15: 7,8-Back-c pin-up	3	6	9	20	30	40

DAN'L BOONE
Sussex Publ. Co.: Sept, 1955 - No. 8, Sept, 1957

	GD 2.0	VG 4.0	FN 6.0	VF 8.0	VF/NM 9.0	NM- 9.2
1	14	28	42	80	115	150
2	10	20	30	54	72	90
3-8	8	16	24	40	50	60

DANNY BLAZE (...Firefighter) (Nature Boy No. 3 on)
Charlton Comics: Aug, 1955 - No. 2, Oct, 1955

	GD 2.0	VG 4.0	FN 6.0	VF 8.0	VF/NM 9.0	NM- 9.2
1-Authentic stories of fire fighting	13	26	39	74	105	135
2	9	18	27	50	65	80

DANNY DINGLE (See Sparkler Comics)
United Features Syndicate: No. 17, 1940

	GD 2.0	VG 4.0	FN 6.0	VF 8.0	VF/NM 9.0	NM- 9.2
Single Series 17	26	52	78	154	252	350

DANNY THOMAS SHOW, THE (TV)
Dell Publishing Co.: No. 1180, Apr-June, 1961 - No. 1249, Dec-Feb, 1961-62

	GD 2.0	VG 4.0	FN 6.0	VF 8.0	VF/NM 9.0	NM- 9.2
Four Color 1180-Toth-a, photo-c	14	28	42	100	188	275
Four Color 1249-Manning-a, photo-c	13	26	39	93	172	250

DANTE'S INFERNO (Based on the video game)
DC Comics (WildStorm): Feb, 2010 - No. 6 ($3.99, limited series)

	GD 2.0	VG 4.0	FN 6.0	VF 8.0	VF/NM 9.0	NM- 9.2
1,2-Christos Gage-s/Diego Latorre-a						4.00

DARBY O'GILL & THE LITTLE PEOPLE (Movie)(See Movie Comics)
Dell Publishing Co.: 1959 (Disney)

	GD 2.0	VG 4.0	FN 6.0	VF 8.0	VF/NM 9.0	NM- 9.2
Four Color 1024-Toth-a; photo-c.	9	18	27	65	113	160

DAREDEVIL ("Daredevil Comics" on cover of #2) (See Silver Streak Comics)
Lev Gleason Publications (Funnies, Inc. No. 1): July, 1941 - No. 134, Sept, 1956
(Charles Biro stories)

	GD 2.0	VG 4.0	FN 6.0	VF 8.0	VF/NM 9.0	NM- 9.2
1-No. 1 titled "Daredevil Battles Hitler"; The Silver Streak, Lance Hale, Cloud Curtis, Dickey Dean, Pirate Prince team up w/Daredevil and battle Hitler; Daredevil battles the Claw; Origin of Hitler feature story. Hitler photo app. on-c	1250	2500	3750	9375	16,188	23,000
2-London, Pat Patriot (by Reed Crandall), Nightro, Real American No. 1 (by Briefer #2-11), Dickie Dean, Pirate Prince, & Times Square begin; intro. & only app. The Pioneer, Champion of America	318	636	954	2162	3781	5400
3-Origin of 13	242	484	726	1537	2644	3750
4	184	368	552	1168	2009	2850
5-Intro. Sniffer & Jinx; Ghost vs. Claw begins by Bob Wood, ends #20	135	270	405	864	1482	2100
6	115	230	345	730	1253	1775
7,9: 7-(2/42; shows #6 on cover).	92	184	276	584	1005	1425
8,10: 8-Nazi WWII-c; Nightro ends. 10-"Remember Pearl Harbor Japanese War-c	98	196	294	622	1074	1525
11-London, Pat Patriot end; classic Quasimodo (Hunchback) bondage/torture-c	206	412	618	1318	2259	3200
12-Origin of The Claw; Scoop Scuttle by Wolverton begins (2-4 pgs.), ends #22, not in #21	132	264	396	838	1444	2050
13-Intro. of Little Wise Guys (10/42)	107	214	321	680	1165	1650
14	65	130	195	416	708	1000
15-Death of Meatball	92	184	276	584	1005	1425
16,17: World War II covers	59	118	177	375	648	920
18-New origin of Daredevil (not same as Silver Streak #6). Hitler, Mussolini Tojo and Mickey Mouse app. on-c	118	236	354	749	1287	1825
19,20	56	112	168	356	616	875
21-Reprints cover of Silver Streak #6 (on inside) plus intro. of The Claw from Silver Streak #1	84	168	252	538	919	1300
22,23	42	84	126	265	445	625
24-Bloody puppet show-c	47	94	141	296	498	700
25-Wise Guys only-c	34	68	102	199	325	450
26,28-30	41	82	123	256	428	600
27-Bondage/torture-c	53	106	159	334	567	800
31-Death of The Claw	77	154	231	493	847	1200
32-37,39-41: 35-Two Daredevil stories begin, end #68 (35-41 are 64 pgs.)	31	62	93	186	303	420
38-Origin Daredevil retold from #18	45	90	135	284	480	675
42-50: 42-Intro. Kilroy in Daredevil	26	52	78	154	252	350
51-69-Last Daredevil issue (12/50)	19	38	57	111	176	240
70-Little Wise Guys take over book; McWilliams-a; Hot Rock Flanagan begins, ends #80	13	26	39	72	101	130
71-78,81	10	20	30	54	72	90
79,80: 79-Daredevil returns. 80-Daredevil x-over	10	20	30	58	79	100
82,90,100: 82,90-One pg. Frazetta ad in both	10	20	30	54	72	90
83-89,91-99,101-134	9	18	27	50	65	80

NOTE: *Biro c/a-all? Bolle a-125. Maurer a-75. McWilliams a-73, 75, 79, 80.*

DAREDEVIL (...& the Black Widow #92-107 on-c only; see Giant-Size...,Marvel Advs., Marvel Graphic Novel #24, Marvel Super Heroes, '66 & Spider-Man &...)
Marvel Comics Group: Apr, 1964 - No. 380, Oct, 1998

	GD 2.0	VG 4.0	FN 6.0	VF 8.0	VF/NM 9.0	NM- 9.2
1-Origin/1st app. Daredevil; intro Foggy Nelson & Karen Page; death of Battling Murdock; Bill Everett-c/a; reprinted in Marvel Super Heroes #1 (1966)	288	576	864	2520	5010	7500
2-Fantastic Four cameo; 2nd app. Electro (Spidey villain); Thing guest star	64	128	192	544	1072	1600
3-Origin & 1st app. The Owl (villain)	41	82	123	328	639	950
4-Origin & 1st app. The Purple Man	35	70	105	271	523	775
5-Minor costume change; Wood-a begins	26	52	78	190	370	550
6-Mr. Fear app.	18	36	54	129	252	375
7-Daredevil battles Sub-Mariner & dons red costume for 1st time (4/65)	67	134	201	536	1043	1550
8-10: 8-Origin/1st app. Stilt-Man	15	30	45	107	204	300
11-15: 12-1st app. Plunderer; Ka-Zar app. 13-Facts about Ka-Zar's origin; Kirby-a	11	22	33	78	139	200
16,17-Spider-Man x-over. 16-1st Romita-a on Spider-Man (5/66)	17	34	51	124	242	360
18-Origin & 1st app. Gladiator	10	20	30	73	129	185
19,20	9	18	27	60	100	140
21-26,28-30: 24-Ka-Zar app.	7	14	21	45	73	100
27-Spider-Man x-over	7	14	21	50	83	115
31-40: 38-Fantastic Four x-over; cont'd in F.F. #73. 39-1st Exterminator (later becomes Death-Stalker)	6	12	18	39	62	85
41,42,44-49: 41-Death Mike Murdock. 42-1st app. Jester. 45-Statue of Liberty photo-c	5	10	15	34	55	75
43-Daredevil battles Captain America; origin partially retold	7	14	21	45	73	100
50-53: 50-52-B. Smith-a. 53-Origin retold; last 12¢ issue	6	12	18	37	59	80
54-56,58-60: 54-Spider-Man cameo. 56-1st app. Death's Head (9/69); story cont'd in #57 (not same as new Death's Head)	4	8	12	24	37	50
57-Reveals i.d. to Karen Page; Death's Head app.	4	8	12	28	44	60
61-76,78-80: 79-Stan Lee cameo. 80-Last 15¢ issue	3	6	9	20	30	40
77-Spider-Man x-over	4	8	12	26	41	55
81-(52 pgs.) Black Widow begins (11/71).	5	10	15	30	48	65
82,84-99: 87-Electro-c/story	3	6	9	16	23	30
83-B. Smith layouts/Weiss-p	3	6	9	18	27	35
100-Origin retold	4	8	12	24	37	50
101-104,106-120: 107-Starlin-c; Thanos cameo. 113-1st brief app. Deathstalker. 114-1st full app. Deathstalker	3	6	9	14	20	26
105-Origin Moondragon by Starlin (12/73); Thanos cameo in flashback (early app.)	3	6	9	16	23	30
121-130,137: 124-1st app. Copperhead; Black Widow leaves. 126-1st new Torpedo	2	4	6	13	18	22
131-Origin/1st app. new Bullseye (see Nick Fury #15)	8	16	24	58	97	135
132-2nd app. new Bullseye (Regular 25¢ edition)	5	10	15	34	55	75
132-(30¢-c variant, limited distribution)(4/76)	9	18	27	63	107	150
133-136-(Regular 25¢ editions). 133-Uri Geller app.	2	4	6	13	18	22
133-136-(30¢-c variants, limited distribution)(5-8/76)	4	8	12	22	34	45
138-Ghost Rider-c/story; Death's Head is reincarnated; Byrne-a	3	6	9	18	27	35
139,140,142-145,147-157: 142-Nova cameo. 147,148-(Reg. 30¢-c). 150-1st app. Paladin. 151-Reveals i.d. to Heather Glenn. 155-Black Widow returns. 156-The '60s Daredevil app.	2	4	6	11	16	20
141,146-Bullseye app.	3	6	9	20	30	40
146-(35¢-c variant, limited distribution)	7	14	21	45	73	100
147,148-(35¢-c variants, limited distribution)	5	10	15	32	51	70
158-Frank Miller art begins (5/79); origin/death of Deathstalker (see Captain America #235 & Spectacular Spider-Man #27	8	16	24	58	97	135
159	5	10	15	30	48	65
160,161-Bullseye app.	4	8	12	24	37	50
162-Ditko-a; no Miller-a	2	4	6	11	16	20
163,164: 163-Hulk cameo. 164-Origin retold	3	6	9	18	27	35

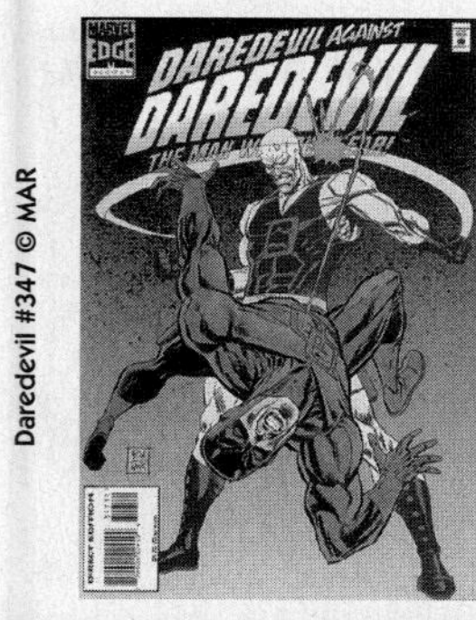

Daredevil #347 © MAR

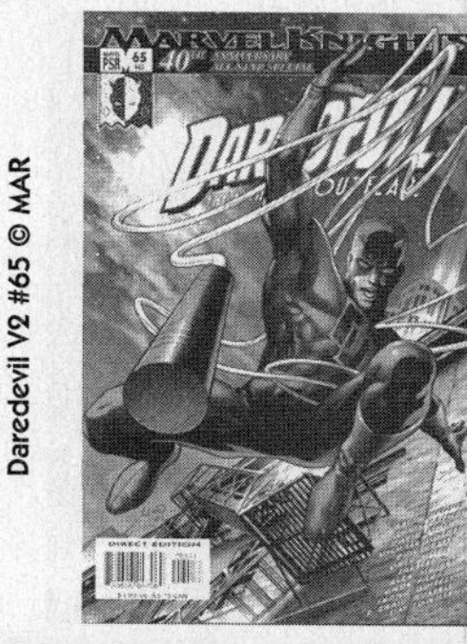

Daredevil V2 #65 © MAR

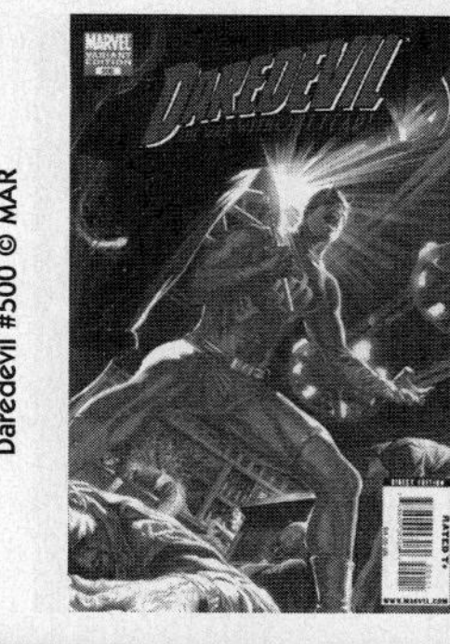

Daredevil #500 © MAR

	GD 2.0	VG 4.0	FN 6.0	VF 8.0	VF/NM 9.0	NM- 9.2

165-167,170 3 6 9 16 23 30
168-Origin/1st app. Elektra; 1st Miller scripts 10 20 30 73 129 185
169-2nd Elektra app. 5 10 15 32 51 70
171-173 3 6 9 16 22 28
174,175-Elektra app. 3 6 9 17 25 32
176-180-Elektra app. 178-Cage app. 179-Anti-smoking issue mentioned in the Congressional Record 3 6 9 16 23 30
181-(52 pgs.)-Death of Elektra; Punisher cameo out of costume 4 8 12 24 37 50
182-184-Punisher app. by Miller (drug issues) 3 6 9 14 19 24
185-191: 187-New Black Widow. 189-Death of Stick. 190-($1.00, 52 pgs.)-Elektra returns, part origin. 191-Last Miller Daredevil 2 4 6 8 10 12
192-195,198,199,201-207,209-218,220-226,234-237: 226-Frank Miller plots begin 3.50
196-Wolverine-c/app. 2 4 6 9 13 16
197-Bullseye-c/app.; 1st app. Yuriko Oyama (who becomes Lady Deathstrike) 5.00
200,238: 200-Bullseye app. 238-Mutant Massacre; Sabretooth app. 6.00
208,219,228-233: 208-Harlan Ellison scripts borrowed from Avengers TV episode "House that Jack Built". 219-Miller-c/script. 228-233-Last Miller scripts 4.00
227-Miller scripts begin 6.00
239,240,242-247 3.00
241-Todd McFarlane-a(p) 5.00
248,249-Wolverine app. 6.00
250,251,253,258: 250-1st app. Bullet. 258-Intro The Bengal (a villain) 3.00
252,260 (52 pgs.): 252-Fall of the Mutants. 260-Typhoid Mary app. 5.00
254-Origin & 1st app. Typhoid Mary (5/88) 1 2 3 4 5 8
255,256,258: 255,256-2nd/3rd app. Typhoid Mary. 259-Typhoid Mary app. 5.00
257-Punisher app. (x-over w/Punisher #10) 1 3 4 6 8 10
261-281,283-294,296-299,301-304,307-318: 270-1st app. Black Heart. 272-Intro Shotgun (villain). 281-Silver Surfer cameo. 283-Capt. America app. 297-Typhoid Mary app.; Kingpin storyline begins. 292-D.G. Chichester scripts begin. 293-Punisher app. 303-Re-intro the Owl. 304-Garney-c/a. 309-Punisher-c.; Terror app. 310-Calypso-c 2.50
282,295,300,305,306: 282-Silver Surfer app. 295-Ghost Rider app. 300-($2.00, 52 pgs.) Kingpin story ends. 305,306-Spider-Man-c 3.00
319-Prologue to Fall From Grace; Elektra returns 6.00
319-2nd printing w/black-c 2.50
320-Fall From Grace Pt 1 5.00
321-Fall From Grace regular ed.; Pt 2; new costume; Venom app. 3.00
321-($2.00)-Wraparound Glow-in-the-dark-c ed. 5.00
322-Fall From Grace Pt 3; Eddie Brock app. 4.00
323,324-Fall From Grace Pt. 4 & 5: 323-Vs. Venom-c/story. 324-Morbius-c/story 4.00
325-($2.50, 52 pgs.)-Fall From Grace ends; contains bound-in poster 4.00
326-349,351-353: 326-New logo. 328-Bound-in trading card sheet. 330-Gambit app. 348-1st Cary Nord art in DD (1/96);"Dec" on-c. 353-Karl Kesel scripts; Nord-c/a begins; Mr. Hyde-c/app. 2.50
350-($2.95)-Double-sized 3.00
350-($3.50)-Double-sized; gold ink-c 3.50
354-374,376-379: Kesel scripts, Nord-c/a in all. 354-$1.50-c begins. 355-Larry Hama layouts; Pyro app. 358-Mysterio-c/app. 359-Absorbing Man cameo. 360-Absorbing Man-c/app. 361-Black Widow-c/app. 363,366-370-Gene Colan-a(p). 368-Omega Red-c/app. 372-Ghost Rider-c/app. 376-379-"Flying Blind", DD goes undercover for S.H.I.E.L.D. 2.50
375-($2.99) Wraparound-c; Mr. Fear-c/app. 3.00
380-($2.99) Final issue; flashback story 4.00
Special 1(9/67, 25¢, 68 pgs.)-New art/story 7 14 21 45 73 100
Special 2,3: 2(2/71, 25¢, 52 pgs.)-Entire book has Powell/Wood-r; Wood-c. 3(1/72, 52 pgs.)-Reprints 3 6 9 18 27 35
Annual 4(10/76) 2 4 6 8 11 14
Annual 4(#5)-10: ('89-94 68 pgs.)-5-Atlantis Attacks. 6-Sutton-a. 7-Guice-a (7 pgs.). 8-Deathlok-c/story. 9-Polybagged w/card 3.00
... :Born Again TPB ($17.95)-r/#227-233; Miller-s/Mazzucchelli-a & new-c 20.00
... By Frank Miller and Klaus Janson Onmibus HC (2007, $99.99, dustjacket) r/#158-161, 163-191 and What If...? #28; intros by Miller and Janson; interviews, bonus art 100.00
... By Frank Miller and Klaus Janson Onmibus Companion HC (2007, $59.99, die-cut d.j.) r/#219,226-233, Daredevil: The Man Without Fear #1-5, Daredevil: Love and War, and Peter Parker, the Spect. Spider-Man #27-28; bonus materials 60.00
.../Deadpool- (Annual '97, $2.99)-Wraparound-c 3.00
...:Fall From Grace TPB ($19.95)-r/#319-325 20.00
... :Gang War TPB ($15.95)-r/#169-172,180; Miller-s/a(p) 16.00
...Legends: (Vol. 4) Typhoid Mary TPB (2003, $19.95) r/#254-257,259-263 20.00
... :Love's Labors Lost TPB ($19.99)-r/#215-217,219-222,225,226; Mazzucchelli-c 20.00
.../Punisher TPB (1988, $4.95)-r/D.D. #182-184 (all printings) 5.00
...Visionaries: Frank Miller Vol. 1 TPB ($17.95) r/#158-161,163-167 18.00
...Visionaries: Frank Miller Vol. 2 TPB ($24.95) r/#168-182; new Miller-c 25.00
...Visionaries: Frank Miller Vol. 3 TPB ($24.95) r/#183-191, What If? #28,35 & Bizarre Adventures #28; new Miller-c 25.00

... Vs. Bullseye Vol. 1 TPB (2004, $15.99) r/#131-132,146,169,181,191 16.00
Wizard Ace Edition: Daredevil (Vol. 1) #1 (4/03, $13.99) Acetate Campbell-c 14.00
NOTE: ***Art Adams*** *c-238p, 239.* ***Austin*** *a-191i; c-151i, 200i.* ***John Buscema*** *a-136, 137p, 234p, 235p; c-86p, 136i, 137p, 142, 219.* ***Byrne*** *c-200p, 201, 203, 223.* ***Capullo*** *a-286p.* ***Colan*** *a(p)-20-49, 53-82, 84-98, 100, 110, 112, 124, 153, 154, 156, 157, 363, 366-370, Spec. 1p; c(p)-20-42, 44-49, 53-60, 71, 92, 98, 138, 153, 154, 156, 157, Annual 1.* ***Craig*** *a-50i, 52i.* ***Ditko*** *a-162, 234p, 235p, 264p; c-162.* ***Everett*** *c/a-1; inks-21, 83.* ***Garney*** *c/a-304.* ***Gil Kane*** *a-141p, 146-148p, 151p; c(p)-85, 90, 91, 93, 94, 115, 116, 119, 120, 125-128, 133, 139, 147, 152.* ***Kirby*** *c-2-4, 5p, 12p, 13p, 43, 136p.* ***Layton*** *c-202.* ***Miller*** *scripts-168-182, 183(part), 184-191, 219, 227-233; a-158-161p, 163-184p, 191p; c-158-161p, 163-184p, 185-189, 190p, 191.* ***Orlando*** *a-2-4p.* ***Powell*** *a-9p, 11p, Special 1r, 2r.* ***Simonson*** *c-199, 236p.* ***B. Smith*** *a-236p; c-51p, 52p, 217.* ***Starlin*** *a-105p.* ***Steranko*** *c-44i.* ***Tuska*** *a-39i, 145p.* ***Williamson*** *a(i)-237, 239, 240, 243, 248-257, 259-282, 283(part), 284, 285, 287, 288(part), 289(part), 293-300; c(i)-237, 243, 244, 248-257, 259-263, 265-278, 280-289, Annual 8.* ***Wood*** *a-5-8, 9i, 10, 11i, Spec. 2i; c-5i, 6-11, 164i.*

DAREDEVIL (Volume 2) (Marvel Knights)
Marvel Comics: Nov, 1998 - Present ($2.50/$2.99)

1-Kevin Smith-s/Quesada & Palmiotti-a 12.00
1-($6.95) DF Edition w/Quesada & Palmiotti var.-c 15.00
1-($6.00) DF Sketch Ed. w/B&W-c 10.00
2-Two covers by Campbell and Quesada/Palmiotti 9.00
3-8: 4,5-Bullseye app. 5-Variant-c exists. 8-Spider-Man-c/app.; last Smith-s 6.00
9-15: 9-11-David Mack-s; intro Echo. 12-Begin $2.99-c; Haynes-a. 13,14-Quesada-a 3.00
16-19-Direct editions; Bendis-s/Mack-c/painted-a 3.00
18,19,21,22-Newsstand editions with variant cover logo "Marvel Unlimited Featuring... 3.00
20-($3.50) Gale-s/Winslade-a; back-up by Stan Lee-s/Colan-a; Mack-c 3.50
21-40: 21-25-Gale-s. 26-38-Bendis-s/Maleev-a. 32-Daredevil's ID revealed. 35-Spider-Man-c/app. 38-Iron Fist & Luke Cage app. 40-Dodson-a 3.50
41-(25¢-c) Begins "Lowlife" arc; Maleev-a; intro Milla Donovan 2.50
41-(Newsstand edition with 2.99¢-c) 4.00
42-45-"Lowlife" arc; Maleev-a 2.50
46-50-($2.99). 46-Typhoid Mary returns. 49-Bullseye app. 50-Art panels by various incl. Romita, Colan, Mack, Janson, Oeming, Quesada 3.00
51-64,66-74,76-81: 51-55-Mack-s/a; Echo app. 54-Wolverine-c/app. 61-64-Black Widow app. 71-Decalogue begins. 76-81-The Murdock Papers. 81-Last Bendis-s/Maleev-a 3.00
65-($3.99) 40th Anniversary issue; Land-c; art by Maleev, Horn, Bachalo and others 4.00
75-($3.99) Decalogue ends; Jester app. 4.00
82-99,101-119: 82-Brubaker-s/Lark-a begin; Foggy "killed". 84-86-Punisher app. 87-Other Daredevil ID revealed. 94-Romita-c. 111-Lady Bullseye debut 3.00
82-Variant-c by McNiven 4.00
100-($3.99) Three covers (Djurdjevic, Bermejo and Turner); art by Romita Sr., Colan, Lark, Sienkiewicz, Maleev, Bermejo & Djurdjevic; sketch art gallery; r/Daredevil #90 (1972) 4.00

(After Vol. 2 #119, Aug, 2009, numbering reverts to original Vol. 1 with #500)

500-(10/09, $4.99) Kingpin, Lady Bullseye app.; back-up stories, pin-up & cover galleries; r/#191; five covers by Djurdjevic, Darrow, Dell'Otto, Ross and Zircher 5.00
501-505: 501-Daredevil takes over The Hand; Diggle-s begins; Ribic-c 3.00
Annual #1 (12/07, $3.99) Brubaker-s/Fernandez-a/Djurdjevic-c; Black Tarantula app. 4.00
... & Captain America: Dead on Arrival (2008, $4.99) English version of Italian story 5.00
... Blood of the Tarantula (6/08, $3.99) Parks & Brubaker-s/Samnee-a/Djurdjevic-c 4.00
... By Brian Michael Bendis Omnibus Vol. 1 HC (2008, $99.99) oversized r/#16-19,26-50, and 56-60 100.00
... By Ed Brubaker Saga (2008, giveaway) synopsis of issues #82-110, preview of #111 1.00
...2099 #1 (11/04, $2.99) Kirkman-s/Moline-a 3.00
TPB ($9.95) r/#1-3 10.00
...Vol. 1 HC (2001, $29.99, with dustjacket) r/#1-11,13-15 30.00
...Vol. 1 HC (2003, $29.99, with dustjacket) r/#1-11,13-15; larger page size 30.00
...Vol. 2 HC (2002, $29.99, with dustjacket) r/#26-37; afterword by Bendis 30.00
...Vol. 3 HC (2004, $29.99, with dustjacket) r/#38-50; Maleev sketch pages 30.00
...Vol. 4 HC (2005, $29.99, with dustjacket) r/#56-65; Vol. 1 #81 (1971) Black Widow 30.00
...Vol. 5 HC (2006, $29.99, with dustjacket) r/#66-75 30.00
...Vol. 6 HC (2006, $34.99, with dustjacket) r/#76-81 & What If Karen Page Had Lived? 35.00
(Vol. 1) Visionaries TPB ($19.95) r/#1-8; Ben Affleck intro. 20.00
(Vol. 2) Parts of a Hole TPB (1/02, $17.95) r/#9-15; David Mack intro. 18.00
(Vol. 3) Wake Up TPB (7/02, $9.99) r/#16-19 10.00
...Vol. 4: Underboss TPB (8/02, $14.99) r/#26-31 15.00
...Vol. 5: Out TPB (2003, $19.99) r/#32-40 20.00
...Vol. 6: Lowlife TPB (2003, $13.99) r/#41-45 14.00
...Vol. 7: Hardcore TPB (2003, $13.99) r/#46-50 14.00
...Vol. 8: Echo - Vision Quest TPB (2004, $13.99) r/#51-55; David Mack-s/a 14.00
...Vol. 9: King of Hell's Kitchen TPB (2004, $13.99) r/#56-60 14.00
...Vol. 10: The Widow TPB (2004, $16.99) r/#61-65 & Vol. 1 #81 17.00
...Vol. 11: Golden Age TPB (2005, $13.99) r/#66-70 14.00
...Vol. 12: Decalogue TPB (2005, $14.99) r/#71-75 15.00
...Vol. 13: The Murdock Papers TPB (2006, $14.99) r/#76-81 15.00
...: The Devil Inside and Out Vol. 1 (2006, $14.99) r/#82-87; Brubaker & Lark interview 15.00
...: The Devil Inside and Out Vol. 2 (2007, $14.99) r/#88-93; Bermejo cover sketches 15.00
...: Hell To Pay Vol. 1 TPB (2007, $14.99) r/#94-99; Djurdjevic cover sketches 15.00
...: Hell To Pay Vol. 2 TPB (2008, $15.99) r/#100-105 16.00

Daredevil Noir #1 © MAR

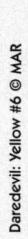

Daredevil: Yellow #6 © MAR

Daring Mystery Comics #5 © MAR

	GD 2.0	VG 4.0	FN 6.0	VF 8.0	VF/NM 9.0	NM- 9.2

DAREDEVIL/ BATMAN (Also see Batman/Daredevil)
Marvel Comics/ DC Comics: 1997 ($5.99, one-shot)
nn-McDaniel-c/a 6.00

DAREDEVIL BATTLES HITLER (See Daredevil #1[1941 series])

DAREDEVIL: BATTLIN' JACK MURDOCK
Marvel Comics: Aug, 2007 - No. 4, Nov, 2007 ($3.99, limited series)
1-4-Wells-s/DiGiandomenico-a; flashback to the fixed fight 4.00
TPB (2007, $12.99) r/#1-4; page layouts and cover inks 13.00

DAREDEVIL COMICS (Golden Age title) (See Daredevil)

DAREDEVIL/ ELEKTRA: LOVE AND WAR
Marvel Comics: 2003 ($29.99, hardcover with dust jacket)
HC-Larger-size reprints of Daredevil: Love and War (Marvel Graphic Novel #24) & Elektra: Assassin; Frank Miller-s; Bill Sienkiewicz-a 30.00

DAREDEVIL: FATHER
Marvel Comics: June, 2004 - No. 6, Feb, 2007 ($3.50/$2.99, limited series)
1-Quesada-s/a; Isanove-painted color 3.50
1-Director's Cut ($2.99) cover and page development art; partial sketch-c 3.00
2-6: 2-($2.99,10/05). 3-Santerians app. 3.00
HC (2006, $24.99) r/series; Lindelof intro.; sketch pages, cover pencils and bonus art 25.00

DAREDEVIL: NINJA
Marvel Comics: Dec, 2000 - No. 3, Feb, 2001 ($2.99, limited series)
1-3: Bendis-s/Haynes-a 3.00
1-Dynamic Forces foil-c 10.00
TPB (7/01, $12.95) r/#1-3 with cover and sketch gallery 13.00

DAREDEVIL NOIR
Marvel Comics: June, 2009 - No. 4, Sept, 2009 ($3.99, limited series)
1-4-Irvine-s/Coker-a; covers by Coker and Calero 4.00

DAREDEVIL: REDEMPTION
Marvel Comics: Apr, 2005 - No. 6, Aug, 2005 ($2.99, limited series)
1-6-Hine-s/Gaydos-a/Sienkiewicz-c 3.00
TPB (2005, $14.99) r/#1-6 15.00

DAREDEVIL/ SHI (See Shi/ Daredevil)
Marvel Comics/ Crusade Comics: Feb,1997 ($2.95, one-shot)
1 3.00

DAREDEVIL/ SPIDER-MAN
Marvel Comics: Jan, 2001 - No. 4, Apr, 2001 ($2.99, limited series)
1-4-Jenkins-s/Winslade-a/Alex Ross-c; Stilt Man app. 3.00
TPB (8/01, $12.95) r/#1-4; Ross-c 13.00

DAREDEVIL THE MAN WITHOUT FEAR
Marvel Comics: Oct, 1993 - No. 5, Feb, 1994 ($2.95, limited series) (foil embossed covers)
1-Miller scripts; Romita, Jr./Williamson-c/a 6.00
2-5 5.00
Hardcover 100.00
Trade paperback 20.00

DAREDEVIL: THE MOVIE (2003 movie adaptation)
Marvel Comics: March, 2003 ($3.50/$12.95, one-shot)
1-Photo-c of Ben Affleck; Bruce Jones-s/Manuel Garcia-a 3.50
TPB ($12.95) r/movie adaptation; Daredevil #32; Ultimate Daredevil & Elektra #1 and Spider-Man's Tangled Web #4; photo-c of Ben Affleck 13.00

DAREDEVIL: THE TARGET (Daredevil Bullseye on cover)
Marvel Comics: Jan, 2003 ($3.50, unfinished limited series)
1-Kevin Smith-s/Glenn Fabry-c/a 3.50

DAREDEVIL VS. PUNISHER
Marvel Comics: Sept, 2005 - No. 6, Jan, 2006 ($2.99, limited series)
1-5-David Lapham-s/a 3.00
TPB (2005, $15.99) r/#1-6 16.00

DAREDEVIL: YELLOW
Marvel Comics: Aug, 2001 - No. 6, Jan, 2002 ($3.50, limited series)
1-6-Jeph Loeb-s/Tim Sale-a/c; origin & yellow costume days retold 3.50
HC (5/02, $29.95) r/#1-6 with dustjacket; intro by Stan Lee; sketch pages 30.00
Daredevil Legends Vol. 1: Daredevil Yellow (2002, $14.99, TPB) r/#1-6 15.00

DARING ADVENTURES (Also see Approved Comics)
St. John Publishing Co.: Nov, 1953 (25¢, 3-D, came w/glasses)
1 (3-D)-Reprints lead story from Son of Sinbad #1 by Kubert 26 52 78 154 252 350

DARING ADVENTURES
I.W. Enterprises/Super Comics: 1963 - 1964
I. W. Reprint #8-r/Fight Comics #53; Matt Baker-a 5 10 15 30 48 65
I.W. Reprint #9-r/Blue Bolt #115; Disbrow-a(3) 5 10 15 32 51 70
Super Reprint #10,11('63)-r/Dynamic #24,16; 11-Marijuana story; Yankee Boy app.; Mac Raboy-a 4 8 12 22 34 45
Super Reprint #12('64)-Phantom Lady from Fox (r/#14 only? w/splash pg. omitted); Matt Baker-a 10 20 30 67 116 165
Super Reprint #15('64)-r/Hooded Menace #1 6 12 18 43 69 95
Super Reprint #16('64)-r/Dynamic #12 3 6 9 20 30 40
Super Reprint #17('64)-r/Green Lama #3 by Raboy 4 8 12 26 41 55
Super Reprint #18-Origin Atlas from unpublished Atlas Comics #1 4 8 12 24 37 50

DARING COMICS (Formerly Daring Mystery) (Jeanie Comics No. 13 on)
Timely Comics (HPC): No. 9, Fall, 1944 - No. 12, Fall, 1945
9-Human Torch, Toro & Sub-Mariner begin 135 270 405 864 1482 2100
10-12: 10-The Angel only app. 11,12-The Destroyer app. 110 220 330 704 1202 1700
NOTE: ***Schomburg*** *c-9-11.* ***Sekowsky*** *c-12? Human Torch, Toro & Sub-Mariner c-9-12.*

DARING CONFESSIONS (Formerly Youthful Hearts)
Youthful Magazines: No. 4, 11/52 - No. 7, 5/53; No. 8, 10/53
4-Doug Wildey-a; Tony Curtis story 16 32 48 92 144 195
5-8: 5-Ray Anthony photo on-c. 6,8-Wildey-a 13 26 39 72 101 130

DARING ESCAPES
Image Comics: Sept, 1998 - No. 4, Mar, 1999 ($2.95/$2.50, mini-series)
1-Houdini; following app. in Spawn #19,20 3.00
2-4-($2.50) 2.50

DARING LOVE (Radiant Love No. 2 on)
Gilmor Magazines: Sept-Oct, 1953
1–Steve Ditko's 1st published work (1st drawn was Fantastic Fears #5)(Also see Black Magic #27)(scarce) 84 168 252 538 919 1300

DARING LOVE (Formerly Youthful Romances)
Ribage/Pix: No. 15, 12/52; No. 16, 2/53-c, 4/53-Indicia; No. 17-4/53-c & indicia
15 12 24 36 69 97 125
16,17: 17-Photo-c 11 22 33 60 83 105
NOTE: ***Colletta*** *a-15.* ***Wildey*** *a-17.*

DARING LOVE STORIES (See Fox Giants)

DARING MYSTERY COMICS (Comedy Comics No. 9 on; title changed to Daring Comics with No. 9)
Timely Comics (TPI 1-6/TCI 7,8): 1/40 - No. 5, 6/40; No. 6, 9/40; No. 7, 4/41 - No. 8, 1/42
1-Origin The Fiery Mask (1st app.) by Joe Simon; Monako, Prince of Magic (1st app.), John Steele, Soldier of Fortune (1st app.), Doc Denton (1st app.) begin; Flash Foster & Barney Mullen, Sea Rover only app; bondage-c 1950 3900 5850 14,625 26,312 38,000
2-(Rare)-Origin The Phantom Bullet (1st & only app.); The Laughing Mask & Mr. E only app.; Trojak the Tiger Man begins, ends #6; Zephyr Jones & K-4 & His Sky Devils app., also #4 1000 2000 3000 7600 13,800 20,000
3-The Phantom Reporter, Dale of FBI, Captain Strong only app.; Breeze Barton, Marvex the Super-Robot, The Purple Mask begin 514 1028 1542 3750 6625 9500
4,5: 4-Last Purple Mask; Whirlwind Carter begins; Dan Gorman, G-Man app. 5-The Falcon begins (1st app.); The Fiery Mask, Little Hercules app. by Sagendorf in the Segar style; bondage-c 354 708 1062 2478 4339 6200
6-Origin & only app. Marvel Boy by S&K; Flying Flame, Dynaman, & Stuporman only app.; The Fiery Mask by S&K; S&K-c 432 864 1296 3154 5577 8000
7-Origin and 1st app. The Blue Diamond, Captain Daring by S&K, The Fin by Everett, The Challenger, The Silver Scorpion & The Thunderer by Burgos; Mr. Millions app 360 720 1080 2520 4410 6300
8-Origin Citizen V; Last Fin, Silver Scorpion, Capt. Daring by Borth, Blue Diamond & The Thunderer; Kirby & part solo Simon-c; Rudy the Robot only app.; Citizen V, Fin & Silver Scorpion continue in Comedy #9 300 600 900 2040 3570 5100
NOTE: ***Schomburg*** *c-1-4, 7.* ***Simon*** *a-2, 3, 5. Cover features: 1-Fiery Mask; 2-Phantom Bullet; 3-Purple Mask; 4-G-Man; 5-The Falcon; 6-Marvel Boy; 7, 8-Multiple characters.*

DARING MYSTERY COMICS 70th ANNIVERARY SPECIAL
Marvel Comics: Nov, 2009 ($3.99, one-shot)
1-New story of The Phantom Reporter; r/app. in Daring Mystery #3 (1940); 2 covers 4.00

DARING NEW ADVENTURES OF SUPERGIRL, THE
DC Comics: Nov, 1982 - No. 13, Nov, 1983 (Supergirl No. 14 on)
1-Origin retold; Lois Lane back-ups in #2-12 1 2 3 5 6 8

Dark Avengers #11 © MAR

Darkchylde #2 © Randy Queen

Darkhawk #6 © MAR

GD 2.0 | VG 4.0 | FN 6.0 | VF 8.0 | VF/NM 9.0 | NM- 9.2

2-13: 8,9-Doom Patrol app. 13-New costume; flag-c 4.00
NOTE: ***Buckler*** *c-1p, 2p.* ***Giffen*** *c-3p, 4p.* ***Gil Kane*** *c-6,8, 9, 11-13.*

DARK, THE
Continum Comics: Nov, 1990 - No. 4, Feb, 1993; V2#1, May, 1993 - V2#7, Apr?, 1994 ($1.95)
1-4: 1-Bright-p; Panosian, Hanna-i; Stroman-c. 2-(1/92)-Stroman-c/a(p). 4-Perez-c & part-i 3.00
V2#1,V2#2-6: V2#1-Red foil Bart Sears-c. V2#1-Red non-foil variant-c. V2#1-2nd printing w/blue foil Bart Sears-c. V2#2-Stroman/Bryant-a. 3-Perez-c(i). 3-6-Foil-c. 4-Perez-c & part-i; bound-in trading cards. 5,6-(2,3/94)-Perez-c(i). 7-(B&W)-Perez-c(i) 2.50
Convention Book 1 ,2(Fall/94, 10/94)-Perez-c 2.50

DARK ANGEL (Formerly Hell's Angel)
Marvel Comics UK, Ltd.: No. 6, Dec, 1992 - No. 16, Dec, 1993 ($1.75)
6-8,13-16: 6-Excalibur-c/story. 8-Psylocke app. 2.50
9-12-Wolverine/X-Men app. 3.00

DARK ANGEL: PHOENIX RESURRECTION (Kia Asamiya's...)
Image Comics: May, 2000 - No. 4, Oct, 2001 ($2.95)
1-4-Kia Asamiya-s/a. 3-Van Fleet variant-c 3.00

DARK AVENGERS (See Secret Invasion and Dark Reign titles)
Marvel Comics: Mar, 2009 - Present ($3.99)
1-Norman Osborn assembles his Avengers; Bendis-s/Deodato-a/c 4.00
1-Variant Iron Patriot armor cover by Djurdjevic 8.00
2-15: 2-6-Bendis-s/Deodato-a/c. 2-4 Dr. Doom app. 7,8-Utopia x-over; X-Men app. 9-Nick Fury app. 11,12-Deodato & Horn-a. 13-15-Siege. 13-Sentry origin 4.00
Annual 1 (2/10, $4.99) Bendis-s/Bachalo-a; Marvel Boy new costume; Siege preview 5.00
,,,/ Uncanny X-Men: Exodus (11/09, $3.99) Conclusion of x-over; Deodato & Dodson-a 4.00
,,,/ Uncanny X-Men: Utopia (8/09, $3.99) Part 1 of x-over w/Uncanny X-Men #513,514 4.00

DARK AVENGERS: ARES
Marvel Comics: Dec, 2009 - No. 3, Feb, 2010 ($3.99, limited series)
1-3-Garcia-a/Gillen-s. 1-Nord-c. 2-Tan-c. 3-McGuinness-c 4.00

DARKCHYLDE (Also see Dreams of the Darkchylde)
Maximum Press #1-3/ Image Comics #4 on: June, 1996 - No. 5, Sept, 1997 ($2.95/ $2.50)
1-Randy Queen-c/a/scripts; "Roses" cover 6.00
1-American Entertainment Edition-wraparound-c 6.00
1-"Fashion magazine-style" variant-c 1 2 3 4 5 7
1-Special Comicon Edition (contents of #1) Winged devil variant-c 5.00
1-($2.50)-Remastered Ed.-wraparound-c 4.00
2(Reg-c),2-Spiderweb and Moon variant-c 6.00
3(Reg-c),3-"Kalvin Clein" variant-c by Drew 3.00
4,5(Reg-c), 4-Variant-c 4.00
5-B&W Edition, 5-Dynamic Forces Gold Ed. 8.00
0-(3/98, $2.50) 2.50
0-Remastered (1/01, $2.95) includes Darkchylde: Redemption preview 3.00
1/2-WIzard offer 4.00
1/2 Variant-c 6.00
... The Descent TPB ('98, $19.95) r/#1-5; bagged with Darkchylde The Legacy Preview Special 1998; listed price is for TPB only 20.00

DARKCHYLDE LAST ISSUE SPECIAL
Darkchylde Entertainment: June, 2002 ($3.95)
1-Wraparound-c; cover gallery 4.00

DARKCHYLDE REDEMPTION
Darkchylde Entertainment: Feb, 2001 - No. 2, Dec, 2001 ($2.95)
1,2: 1-Wraparound-c 3.00
1-Dynamic Forces alternate-c 6.00
1-Dynamic Forces chrome-c 16.00

DARKCHYLDE SKETCH BOOK
Image Comics (Dynamic Forces): 1998
1-Regular-c 8.00
1-DarkChrome cover 16.00

DARKCHYLDE SUMMER SWIMSUIT SPECTACULAR
DC Comics (WildStorm): Aug, 1999 ($3.95, one-shot)
1-Pin-up art by various 4.00

DARKCHYLDE SWIMSUIT ILLUSTRATED
Image Comics: 1998 ($2.50, one-shot)
1-Pin-up art by various 2.50
1-(6.95) Variant cover 7.00
1-Chromium cover 15.00

DARKCHYLDE THE DIARY
Image Comics: June, 1997 ($2.50, one-shot)
1-Queen-c/s/ art by various 2.50
1-Variant-c 5.00
1-Holochrome variant-c 8.00

DARKCHYLDE THE LEGACY
Image Comics/DC (WildStorm) #3 on: Aug, 1998 - No. 3, June, 1999 ($2.50)
1-3: 1-Queen-c. 2-Two covers by Queen and Art Adams 2.50

DARK CLAW ADVENTURES
DC Comics (Amalgam): June, 1997 ($1.95, one-shot)
1-Templeton-c/s/a & Burchett-a 2.50

DARK CROSSINGS: DARK CLOUDS RISING
Image Comics (Top Cow): June, 2000; Oct, 2000 ($5.95, limited series)
1-Witchblade, Darkness, Tomb Raider crossover; Dwayne Turner-a 6.00
1-(Dark Clouds Overhead) 6.00

DARK CRYSTAL, THE (Movie)
Marvel Comics Group: April, 1983 - No. 2, May, 1983
1,2-Adaptation of film 3.00

DARK DAYS (See 30 Days of Night)
IDW Publishing: June, 2003 - No. 6, Dec, 2003 ($3.99, limited series)
1-6-Sequel to 30 Days of Night; Niles-s/Templesmith-a 4.00
1-Retailer variant (Diamond/Alliance Fort Wayne 5/03 summit) 15.00
TPB (2004, $19.99) r/#1-6; cover gallery; intro. by Eric Red 20.00

DARKDEVIL (See Spider-Girl)
Marvel Comics: Nov, 2000 - No. 3, Jan, 2001 ($2.99, limited series)
1-3: 1-Origin of Darkdevil; Kingpin-c/app. 3.00

DARK DOMINION
Defiant: Oct, 1993 - No. 10, July, 1994 ($2.50)
1-10-Len Wein scripts begin. 4-Free extra 16 pgs. 7-9-J.G. Jones-c/a. 10-Pre-Schism issue; Shooter/Wein script; John Ridgway-a 2.50

DARKER IMAGE (Also see Deathblow, The Maxx, & Bloodwulf)
Image Comics: Mar, 1993 ($1.95, one-shot)
1-The Maxx by Sam Kieth begins; Bloodwulf by Rob Liefeld & Deathblow by Jim Lee begin (both 1st app.); polybagged w/1 of 3 cards by Kieth, Lee or Liefeld 2.50
1-B&W interior pgs. w/silver foil logo 6.00

DARKEWOOD
Aircel Publishing: 1987 - No. 5, 1988 ($2.00, 28pgs, limited series)
1-5 2.50

DARK FANTASIES
Dark Fantasy: 1994 - No. 8, 1995 ($2.95)
1-Test print Run (3,000)-Linsner-c 1 2 3 5 6 8
1-Linsner-c 5.00
2-8: 2-4 (Deluxe), 2-4 (Regular), 5-8 (Deluxe; $3.95) 4.00
5-8 (Regular; $3.50) 3.50

DARK GUARD
Marvel Comics UK: Oct, 1993 - No. 4, Jan, 1994 ($1.75)
1-($2.95)-Foil stamped-c 3.00
2-4 2.50

DARKHAWK (Also see War of Kings)
Marvel Comics: Mar, 1991 - No. 50, Apr, 1995 ($1.00/$1.25/$1.50)
1-Origin/1st app. Darkhawk; Hobgoblin cameo 4.00
2,3,13,14: 2-Spider-Man & Hobgoblin app. 3-Spider-Man & Hobgoblin app. 13,14-Venom-c/story 3.00
4-12,15-24,26-49: 6-Capt. America & Daredevil x-over. 9-Punisher app. 11,12-Tombstone app. 19-Spider-Man & Brotherhood of Evil Mutants-c/story. 20-Spider-Man app. 22-Ghost Rider-c/story. 23-Origin begins, ends #25. 27-New Warriors-c/story. 35-Begin 3 part Venom story. 39-Bound-in trading card sheet 2.50
25,50: (52 pgs.)-Red holo-grafx foil-c w/double gatefold poster; origin of Darkhawk armor 3.00
Annual 1-3 ('92-'94,68 pgs.)-1-Vs. Iron Man. 2 -Polybagged w/card 3.00

DARKHOLD: PAGES FROM THE BOOK OF SINS (See Midnight Sons Unlimited)
Marvel Comics (Midnight Sons imprint #15 on): Oct, 1992 - No. 16, Jan, 1994
1-($2.75, 52 pgs.)-Polybagged w/poster by Andy & Adam Kubert; part 4 of Rise of the Midnight Sons storyline 3.00
2-10,12-16: 3-Reintro Modred the Mystic (see Marvel Chillers #1). 4-Sabertooth-c/sty. 5-Punisher & Ghost Rider app. 15-Spot varnish-c. 15,16-Siege of Darkness pt. 4&12 2.50
11-($2.25)-Outer-c is a Darkhold envelope made of black parchment w/gold ink 2.50

Dark Horse Comics #22 © DH

Dark Horse Presents #71 © DH

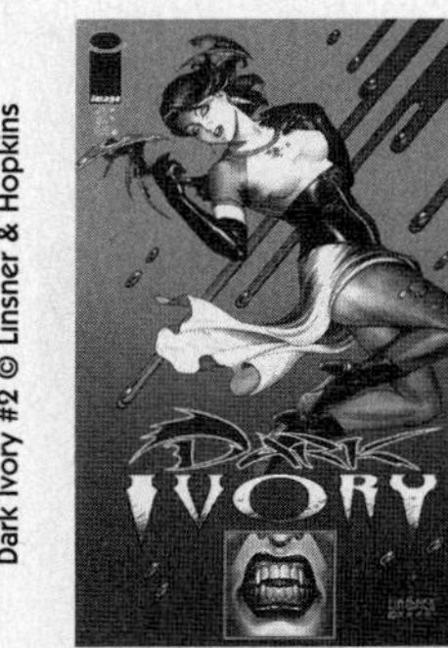

Dark Ivory #2 © Linsner & Hopkins

GD VG FN VF VF/NM NM-
2.0 4.0 6.0 8.0 9.0 9.2

DARK HORSE BOOK OF..., THE
Dark Horse Comics: Aug, 2003 - Nov, 2006 ($14.95/$15.95, HC, 9 1/4" x 6 1/4")
... Hauntings (8/03, $14.95)-Short stories by various incl. Mignola (Hellboy), Thompson, Dorkin, Russell; Gianni-c 15.00
... Monsters (11/06, $15.95)-Short-s by Mignola, Thompson, Dorkin, Giffen, Busiek; Gianni-c 16.00
... The Dead (6/05, $14.95)-Short-s by Mignola, Thompson, Dorkin, Powell; Gianni-c 15.00
... Witchcraft (6/04, $14.95)-Short-s by Mignola, Thompson, Dorkin, Millionaire; Gianni-c 15.00

DARK HORSE CLASSICS (Title series), **Dark Horse Comics**
1992 ($3.95, B&W, 52 pgs. nn's): The Last of the Mohicans. 20,000 Leagues Under the Sea 4.00

DARK HORSE CLASSICS, 5/96 ($2.95) 1-r/Predator: Jungle Tales 3.00

--ALIENS VERSUS PREDATOR, 2/97 - No. 6, 7/97 ($2.95,) 1-6: r/Aliens Versus Predator 3.00

--GODZILLA: KING OF THE MONSTERS, 4/98 ($2.95) 1-6: 1-r/Godzilla: Color Special; Art Adams-a 3.00

--STAR WARS: DARK EMPIRE, 3/97 - No. 6, 8/97 ($2.95) 1-6: r/Star Wars: Dark Empire 3.00

--TERROR OF GODZILLA, 8/98 - No. 6, 1/99 ($2.95) 1-6-r/manga Godzilla in color; Art Adams-c 3.00

DARK HORSE COMICS
Dark Horse Comics: Aug, 1992 - No. 25, Sept, 1994 ($2.50)
1-Dorman double gategold painted-c; Predator, Robocop, Timecop (3-part) & Renegade stories begin 3.00
2-6,11-25: 2-Mignola-c. 3-Begin 3-part Aliens story; Aliens-c. 4-Predator-c. 6-Begin 4 part Robocop story. 12-Begin 2-part Aliens & 3-part Predator stories. 13-Thing From Another World begins w/Nino-a(i). 15-Begin 2-part Aliens: Cargo story. 16-Begin 3-part Predator story. 17-Begin 3-part StarWars: Droids story & 3-part Aliens: Alien story; Droids-c. 19-Begin 2-part X story; X cover 2.50
7-Begin Star Wars: Tales of the Jedi 3-part story 1 2 3 4 5 7
8-1st app. X and begins; begin 4-part James Bond 6.00
9,10: 9-Star Wars ends. 10-X ends; Begin 3-part Predator & Godzilla stories 4.00
NOTE: *Art Adams c-11.*

DARK HORSE DOWN UNDER
Dark Horse Comics: June, 1994 - No. 3, Oct, 1994 ($2.50, B&W, limited series)
1-3 2.50

DARK HORSE MAVERICK
Dark Horse Comics: July, 2000; July, 2001; Sept, 2002 (B&W, annual)
2000-($3.95) Short stories by Miller, Chadwick, Sakai, Pearson 4.00
2001-($4.99) Short stories by Sakai, Wagner and others; Miller-c 5.00
...: Happy Endings (9/02, $9.95) Short stories by Bendis, Oeming, Mahfood, Mignola, Miller, Kieth and others; Miller-c 10.00

DARK HORSE MONSTERS
Dark Horse Comics: Feb, 1997 ($2.95, one-shot)
1-reprints 3.00

DARK HORSE PRESENTS
Dark Horse Comics: July, 1986 - No. 157, Sept, 2000 ($1.50-$2.95, B&W)
1-1st app. Concrete by Paul Chadwick 2 4 6 8 11 14
1-2nd printing (1988, $1.50) 2.50
1-Silver ink 3rd printing (1992, $2.25)-Says 2nd printing inside 2.50
2-9: 2-6,9-Concrete app. 6.00
10-1st app. The Mask; Concrete app. 2 4 6 9 12 15
11-19,21-23: 11-19,21-Mask stories. 12,14,16,18,22-Concrete app. 15(2/88). 17-All Roachmill issue 6.00
20-(68 pgs.)-Concrete, Flaming Carrot, Mask 1 3 4 6 8 10
24-Origin Aliens-c/story (11/88); Mr. Monster app. 2 4 6 10 14 18
25-31,33,37-41,44,45,47-49: 28-(52 pgs.)-Concrete app.; Mr. Monster story (homage to Graham Ingels). 33-(44 pgs.). 38-Concrete. 40-(52 pgs.)-1st Argosy story. 44-Crash Ryan. 48,49-Contain 2 trading cards 3.00
32,34,35: 32-(68 pgs.)-Annual; Concrete, American. 34-Aliens-c/story. 35-Predator-c/app. 4.00
36-1st Aliens Vs. Predator story; painted-c, 36-Variant line drawn-c 5.00
42,43,46: 42,43-Aliens-c/stories. 46-Prequel to new Predator II mini-series 3.00
50-S/F story by Perez; contains 2 trading cards 4.00
51-53-Sin City by Frank Miller, parts 2-4; 51,53-Miller-c (see D.H.P. Fifth Anniversary Special for pt. 1) 1 2 3 4 6 8
54-61: 54-(9/91) The Next Men begins (1st app.) by Byrne; Miller-a/Morrow-c. Homocide by Morrow (also in #55). 55-2nd app. The Next Men; parts 5 & 6 of Sin City by Miller; Miller-c. 56-(68 pg. annual)-part 7 of Sin City by Miller; part prologue to Aliens: Genocide; Next Men by Byrne. 57-(52 pgs.)-Part 8 of Sin City by Miller; Next Men by Byrne; Byrne & Miller-c; Alien Fire story; swipes cover to Daredevil #1. 58,59-Alien Fire stories. 58-61- Part 9-12 Sin City by Miller 5.00
62-Last Sin City (entire book by Miller, c/a; 52 pgs.) 1 3 4 6 8 10
63-66,68-79,81-84-($2.25): 64-Dr. Giggles begins (1st app.), ends #66; Boris the Bear story. 66-New Concrete-c/story by Chadwick. 71-Begin 3 part Dominque story by Jim Balent; Balent-c. 72-(3/93)-Begin 3-part Eudaemon (1st app.) story by Nelson 3.00
67-($3.95, 68 pgs.)-Begin 3-part prelude to Predator: Race War mini-series; Oscar Wilde adapt. by Russell 4.00
80-Art Adams-c/a (Monkeyman & O'Brien) 4.00
85-87,92-99: 85-Begin $2.50-c. 92, 93, 95-Too Much Coffee Man 3.00
88-91-Hellboy by Mignola. 6.00
NOTE: *There are 5 different Dark Horse Presents #100 issues*
100-1-Intro Lance Blastoff by Miller; Milk & Cheese by Evan Dorkin 4.00
100-2-Hellboy-c by Wrightson; Hellboy story by Mignola; includes Roberta Gregory & Paul Pope stories 6.00
100-3-100-5: 100-3-Darrow-c, Concrete by Chadwick; Pekar story. 100-4-Gibbons-c: Miller story, Geary story/a. 100-5-Allred-c, Adams, Dorkin, Pope 3.00
101-125: 101-Aliens c/a by Wrightson, story by Pope. 103-Kirby gatefold-c. 106-Big Blown Baby by Bill Wray. 107-Mignola-c/a. 109-Begin $2.95-c; Paul Pope-c. 110-Ed Brubaker-a/s. 114-Flip books begin; Lance Blastoff by Miller; Star Slammers by Simonson. 115-Miller-c. 117-Aliens-c/app. 118-Evan Dorkin-c/a. 119-Monkeyman & O'Brien. 124-Predator. 125-Nocturnals 3.00
126-($3.95, 48 pgs.)-Flip book: Nocturnals, Starship Troopers 4.00
127-134,136-140: 127-Nocturnals. 129-The Hammer. 132-134-Warren-a 3.00
135-($3.50) The Mark 3.50
141-All Buffy the Vampire Slayer issue 4.00
142-149: 142-Mignola-c. 143-Tarzan. 146,147-Aliens vs. Predator. 148-Xena 3.00
150-($4.50) Buffy-c by Green; Buffy, Concrete, Fish Police app. 4.50
151-157: 151-Hellboy-c/app. 153-155-Angel flip-c. 156,157-Witch's Son 3.00
Annual 1997 ($4.95, 64 pgs.)-Flip book; Body Bags, Aliens. Pearson-c; stories by Allred & Stephens, Pope, Smith & Morrow 1 2 3 5 6 8
Annual 1998 ($4.95, 64 pgs.) 1st Buffy the Vampire Slayer comic app.; Hellboy story and cover by Mignola 1 2 3 4 5 7
Annual 1999 (7/99, $4.95) Stories of Xena, Hellboy, Ghost, Luke Skywalker, Groo, Concrete, the Mask and Usagi Yojimbo in their youth. 5.00
Annual 2000 ($4.95) Girl sidekicks; Chiodo-c and flip photo Buffy-c 5.00
...Aliens Platinum Edition (1992)-r/DHP #24,43,43,56 & Special 11.00
...Fifth Anniversary Special nn (4/91, $9.95)-Part 1 of Sin City by Frank Miller (c/a); Aliens, Aliens vs. Predator, Concrete, Roachmill, Give Me Liberty & The American stories 25.00
The One Trick Rip-off (1997, $12.95, TPB)-r/stories from #101-112 13.00
NOTE: ***Geary** a-59, 60. **Miller** a-Special, 51-53, 55-62; c-59-62, 100-1; c-51, 53, 55, 59-62, 100-1. **Moebius** a-63; c-63, 70. **Vess** a-78; c-75, 78.*

DARK HORSE TWENTY YEARS
Dark Horse Comics: 2006 (25¢, one-shot)
nn-Pin-ups by Dark Horse artists of other artists' Dark Horse characters; Mignola-c 2.50

DARK IVORY
Image Comics: Mar, 2008 - No. 4, Jan, 2009 ($2.99, limited series)
1-4-Eva Hopkins & Joseph Michael Linsner-s/Linsner-a/c 3.00

DARK KNIGHT (See Batman: The Dark Knight Returns & Legends of the...)

DARK KNIGHT STRIKES AGAIN, THE (Also see Batman: The Dark Knight Returns)
DC Comics: 2001 - No. 3, 2002 ($7.95, prestige format, limited series)
1-Frank Miller-s/a/c; sequel 3 years after Dark Knight Returns; 2 covers 8.00
2,3 8.00
HC (2002, $29.95) intro. by Miller; sketch pages and exclusive artwork; cover has 3 1/4" tall partial dustjacket 30.00
SC (2002, $19.95) intro. by Miller; sketch pages 20.00

DARKLON THE MYSTIC (Also see Eerie Magazine #79,80)
Pacific Comics: Oct, 1983 (one-shot)
1-Starlin-c/a(r) 4.00

DARKMAN (Movie)
Marvel Comics: Sept, 1990; Oct, 1990 - No. 3, Dec, 1990 ($1.50)
1 (9/90, $2.25, B&W mag., 68 pgs.)-Adaptation of film 3.00
1-3: Reprints B&W magazine 2.50

DARKMAN
Marvel Comics: V2#1, Apr, 1993 -No. 6, Sept, 1993 ($2.95, limited series)
V2#1 ($3.95, 52 pgs.) 4.00
2-6 3.00

DARKMAN VS. THE ARMY OF DARKNESS (Movie crossover)
Dynamite Entertanment: 2006 - No. 4, 2007 ($3.50)
1-4: 1-Busiek & Stern-s/Fry-a; photo-c and Perez and Bradshaw covers 3.50

DARK MANSION OF FORBIDDEN LOVE, THE (Becomes Forbidden Tales of Dark Mansion No. 5 on)

Dark Mysteries #24 © Merit Publ.

Darkness #81 © TCOW

Dark Reign: Elektra #5 © MAR

	GD 2.0	VG 4.0	FN 6.0	VF 8.0	VF/NM 9.0	NM- 9.2

National Periodical Publ.: Sept-Oct, 1971 - No. 4, Mar-Apr, 1972 (52 pgs.)
1 18 36 54 129 252 375
2-4: 2-Adams-c. 3-Jeff Jones-c 9 18 27 65 113 160

DARKMINDS
Image Comics (Dreamwave Prod.): July, 1998 - No. 8, Apr, 1999 ($2.50)
1-Manga; Pat Lee-s/a; 2 covers 1 3 4 6 8 10
1-2nd printing 2.50
2, 0-(1/99, $5.00) Story and sketch pages 5.00
3-8, 1/2-(5/99, $2.50) Story and sketch pages 2.50
... Collected 1,2 (1/99,3/99; $7.95) 1-r/#1-3. 2-r/#4-6 8.00
... Collected 3 (5/99; $5.95) r/#7,8 6.00

DARKMINDS (Volume 2)
Image Comics (Dreamwave Prod.): Feb, 2000 - No. 10, Apr, 2001 ($2.50)
1-10-Pat Lee-c 2.50
0-(7/00) Origin of Mai Murasaki; sketchbook 2.50

DARKMINDS: MACROPOLIS
Image Comics (Dreamwave Prod.): Jan, 2002 - No. 4, Dec, 2002 ($2.95)
Preview (8/01) Flip book w/Banished Knights preview 2.50
1-4-Jo Chen-a 3.00

DARKMINDS: MACROPOLIS (Volume 2)
Dreamwave Prod.: Sept, 2003 - No. 4, Jul, 2004 ($2.95)
1-4-Chris Sarracini-s/Kwang Mook Lim-a 3.00

DARKMINDS / WITCHBLADE (Also see Witchblade/Dark Minds)
Image Comics (Top Cow/Dreamwave Prod.): Aug, 2000 ($5.95, one-shot)
1-Wohl-s/Pat Lee-a; two covers by Silvestri and Lee 6.00

DARK MYSTERIES (Thrilling Tales of Horror & Suspense)
"Master" - "Merit" Publications: June-July, 1951 - No. 24, July, 1955
1-Wood-c/a (8 pgs.) 126 252 378 806 1378 1950
2-Wood/Harrison-c/a (8 pgs.) 84 168 252 538 919 1300
3-9: 7-Dismemberment, hypo blood drainage stys 47 94 141 296 498 700
10-Cannibalism story; witch burning-c 50 100 150 315 533 750
11-13,15-18: 11-Severed head panels. 13-Dismemberment-c/story. 17-The Old Gravedigger host 41 82 123 256 428 600
14-Several E.C. Craig swipes 41 82 123 259 435 610
19-Injury-to-eye panel; E.C. swipe; torture-c 50 100 150 315 533 750
20-Female bondage, blood drainage story 45 90 135 284 480 675
21,22: 21-Devil-c. 22-Last pre-code issue, misdated 3/54 instead of 3/55 32 64 96 188 307 425
23,24 22 44 66 132 216 300
NOTE: ***Cameron** a-1, 2. **Myron Fass** c/a-21. **Harrison** a-3, 7; c-3. **Hollingsworth** a-7-17, 20, 21, 23. **Wildey** a-5. Woodish art by **Fleishman**-9; c-10, 14-17. Bondage c-10, 18, 19.*

DARK NEMESIS (VILLAINS) (See Teen Titans)
DC Comics: Feb, 1998 ($1.95, one-shot)
1-Jurgens-s/Pearson-c 2.50

DARKNESS, THE (See Witchblade #10)
Image Comics (Top Cow Productions): Dec, 1996 - No. 40, Aug, 2001 ($2.50)
Special Preview Edition-(7/96, B&W)-Ennis script; Silvestri-a(p) 2 4 6 9 13 16
0 2 4 6 8 10 12
0-Gold Edition 16.00
1/2 1 3 4 6 8 10
1/2-Christmas-c 3 6 9 14 19 24
1/2-(3/01, $2.95) r/#1/2 w/new 6 pg. story & Silvestri-c 3.00
1-Ennis-s/Silvestri-a, 1-Black variant-c 2 4 6 9 12 15
1-Platinum variant-c 20.00
1-DF Green variant-c 12.00
1,2: 1-Fan Club Ed. 1 3 4 6 8 10
3-5 6.00
6-10: 9,10-Witchblade "Family Ties" x-over pt. 2,3 4.00
7-Variant-c w/concubine 1 2 3 5 7 9
8-American Entertainment 6.00
8-10-American Entertainment Gold Ed. 7.00
11-Regular Ed.; Ennis-s/Silverstri & D-Tron-c 3.00
11-Nine (non-chromium) variant-c (Benitez, Cabrera, the Hildebrandts, Finch, Keown, Peterson, Portacio, Tan, Turner 4.50
11-Chromium-c by Silvestri & Batt 20.00
12-19: 13-Begin Benitez-a(p) 3.00
20-24,26-40: 34-Ripclaw app. 2.50
25-($3.99) Two covers (Benitez, Silvestri) 4.00
25-Chromium-c variant by Silvestri 8.00
.../ Batman (8/99, $5.95) Silvestri, Finch, Lansing-a(p) 6.00
...Collected Editions #1-4 ($4.95,TPB) 1-r/#1,2. 2-r/#3,4. 3- r/#5,6. 4- r/#7,8 6.00
...Collected Editions #5,6 ($5.95, TPB)5- r/#11,12. 6-r/#13,14 6.00
Deluxe Collected Editions #1 (12/98, $14.95, TPB) r/#1-6 & Preview 15.00
...: Heart of Darkness (2001, $14.95, TPB) r/ #7,8, 11-14 15.00
Holiday Pin-up-American Entertainment 5.00
Holiday Pin-up Gold Ed.-American Entertainment 7.00
Infinity #1 (8/99, $3.50) Lobdell-s 3.50
Prelude-American Entertainment 4.00
Prelude Gold Ed.-American Entertainment 9.00
Volume 1 Compendium (2006, $59.99) r/#1-40, V2 #1, Tales of the Darkness #1-4; #1/2, Darkness/Witchblade #1/2, Darkness: Wanted Dead; cover and sketch gallery 60.00
...: Wanted Dead 1 (8/03, $2.99) Texiera-a/Tieri-s 3.00
Wizard ACE Ed.- Reprints #1 2 4 6 8 10 12

DARKNESS (Volume 2)
Image Comics (Top Cow Productions): Dec, 2002 - No. 24, Oct, 2004 ($2.99)
1-24: 1-6-Jenkins-s/Keown-a. 17-20-Lapham-s. 23,24-Magdalena app. 3.00
... Black Sails (3/05, $2.99) Marz-s/Cha-a; Hunter-Killer preview 3.00
... and Tomb Raider (4/05, $2.99) r/Darkness Prelude & Tomb Raider/Darkness Special 3.00
...: Resurrection TPB (2/04, $16.99) r/#1-6 & Vol. 1 #40 17.00
.../ The Incredible Hulk (7/04, $2.99) Keown-a/Jenkins-s 3.00
.../ Vampirella (7/05, $2.99) Terry Moore-s; two covers by Basaldua and Moore 3.00
... Vol. 5 TPB (2006, $19.99) r/#7-16 & The Darkness: Wanted Dead #1; cover gallery 20.00
... vs. Mr Hyde Monster War 2005 (9/05, $2.99) x-over w/Witchblade, Tomb Raider and Magdalena; two covers 3.00
.../ Wolverine (2006, $2.99) Kirkham-a/Tieri-s 3.00

DARKNESS (Volume 3) (Numbering jumps from #10 to #75)
Image Comics (Top Cow Productions): Dec, 2007 - Present ($2.99)
1-10: 1-Hester-s/Broussard-a. 1-Three covers. 7-9-Lucas-a. 8-Aphrodite IV app. 3.00
75 (2/09, $4.99) Four covers; Hester-s/art by various 5.00
76-82-($2.99) Multiple covers on each 3.00
...: Butcher (4/08, $3.99) Story of Butcher Joyce; Levin-s/Broussard-a/c 4.00
... First Look (11/07, 99¢) Previews series; sketch pages 2.25
...: Lodbrok's Hand (12/08, $2.99) Hester-s/Oeming-a/c; variant-c by Carnevale 3.00
...: Shadows and Flame 1 (1/10, $2.99) Lucas-c/a 3.00

DARKNESS: LEVEL...
Image Comics (Top Cow): No. 0, Dec, 2006 - No. 5, Aug, 2007 ($2.99, limited series)
0-5: 0-Origin of The Darkness in WW1; Jenkins-s. 1-Jackie's origin retold; Sejic-a 3.00

DARKNESS/ PITT
Image Comics (Top Cow): Dec, 2006; Aug, 2009 - No. 3, Nov, 2009 ($2.99)
...: First Look (12/06) Jenkins script pages with Keown B&W and color art 3.00
1-3: 1-(8/09) Jenkins-s/Keown-a; covers by Keown and Sejic. 2,3-Two covers 3.00

DARKNESS/ SUPERMAN
Image Comics (Top Cow Productions): Jan, 2005 - No. 2, Feb, 2005 ($2.99, limited series)
1,2-Marz-s/Kirkham & Banning-a/Silvestri-c 3.00

DARKNESS VS. EVA: DAUGHTER OF DRACULA
Dynamite Entertainment: 2008 - No. 4, 2008 ($3.50, limited series)
1-4-Leah Moore & John Reppion-s/Salazar-a; three covers on each 3.50

DARK REIGN (Follows Secret Invasion crossover)
Marvel Comics: 2009 ($3.99/$4.99, one-shots)
...: Files 1 (2009, $4.99) profile pages of villains tied in to Dark Reign x-over 4.00
...: Made Men 1 (11/09, $3.99) short stories by various incl. Pham, Leon, Oliver 4.00
...: New Nation 1 (2/09, $3.99) previews of various series tied in to Dark Reign x-over 4.00
...: The Cabal 1 (6/09, $3.99) Cabal members stories by various incl. Granov, Acuña 4.00
...: The Goblin Legacy 1 (2009, $3.99) r/ASM #39,40; Osborn history; Mayhew-a 4.00

DARK REIGN: ELEKTRA
Marvel Comics: May, 2009 - No. 5, Oct, 2009 ($3.99, limited series)
1-5-Mann-a/Bermejo-c; Elektra after the Skrull replacement. 2,3-Bullseye app. 4.00

DARK REIGN: FANTASTIC FOUR
Marvel Comics: May, 2009 - No. 5, Sept, 2009 ($2.99, limited series)
1-5-Chen-a 3.00

DARK REIGN: HAWKEYE
Marvel Comics: June, 2009 - No. 5, Mar, 2010 ($3.99, limited series)
1-5-Bullseye in the Dark Avengers; Raney-a/Langley-c. 5-Guinaldo-a 4.00

DARK REIGN: LETHAL LEGION
Marvel Comics: Aug, 2009 - No. 3, Nov, 2009 ($3.99, limited series)

Dark Reign: Young Avengers #5 © MAR

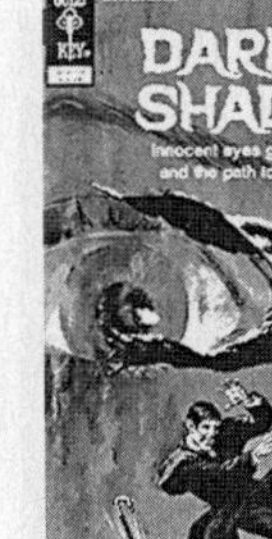
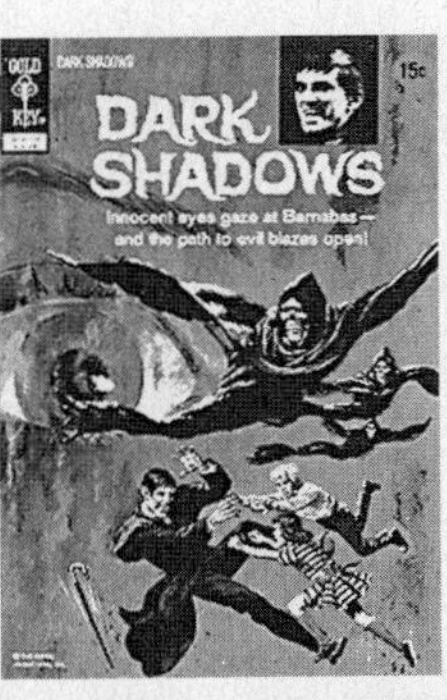

Dark Shadows #15 © GK

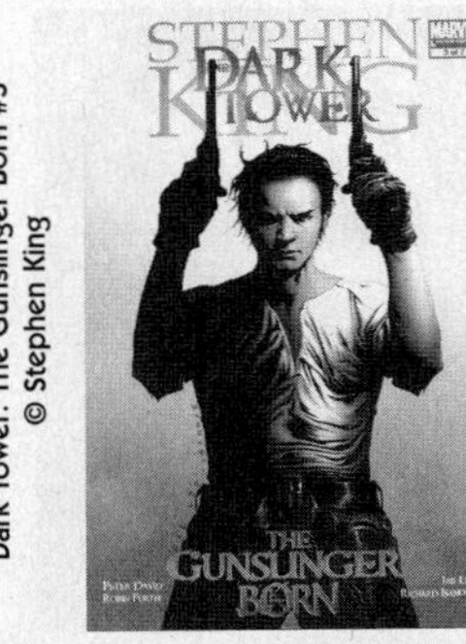

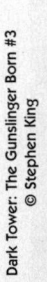

Dark Tower: The Gunslinger Born #3 © Stephen King

	GD 2.0	VG 4.0	FN 6.0	VF 8.0	VF/NM 9.0	NM- 9.2

GD VG FN VF VF/NM NM- 2.0 4.0 6.0 8.0 9.0 9.2

1-3-Santolouco-a/Edwards-c; Grim Reaper and Wonder Man app. 4.00

DARK REIGN: MR. NEGATIVE (Also see Amazing Spider-Man #546)
Marvel Comics: Aug, 2009 - No. 3, Oct, 2009 ($3.99, limited series)

1-3-Jae Lee-c/Gugliotta-a; Spider-Man app. 4.00

DARK REIGN: SINISTER SPIDER-MAN
Marvel Comics: Aug, 2009 - No. 4, Nov, 2009 ($3.99, limited series)

1-4-Bachalo-c/a; Venom/Scorpion as Dark Avenger Spider-Man 4.00

DARK REIGN: THE HOOD
Marvel Comics: Jul, 2009 - No. 5, Nov, 2009 ($3.99, limited series)

1-5-Hotz-a/Djurdjevic-c 4.00

DARK REIGN: THE LIST
Marvel Comics: 2009 - 2010 ($3.99, one-shots)

... - Amazing Spider-Man (1/10, $3.99) Adam Kubert-c/a; back-up r/Pulse #5 4.00
... - Avengers (11/09, $3.99) Bendis-s/Djurdjevic-c/a; Ronin (Hawkeye) app. 4.00
... - Daredevil (11/09, $3.99) Diggle-s/Tan-c/a; Bullseye app.; leads into Daredevil #501 4.00
... - Hulk (12/09, $3.99) Pak-s/Oliver-a; Skaar app.; back-up r/Amaz. Spider-Man #14 4.00
... - Punisher (12/09, $3.99) Romita Jr.-a/c; Castle killed by Daken; preview of Franken-Castle in Punisher #11 6.00
... - Secret Warriors (12/09, $3.99) McGuinness-a/c; Nick Fury; back-up r/Steranko-a 4.00
... - Wolverine (12/09, $3.99) Ribic-a/c; Marvel Boy and Fantomex app. 4.00
... - X-Men (11/09, $3.99) Alan Davis-a/c; Namor app.; back-up r/Kieth-a 4.00

DARK REIGN: YOUNG AVENGERS
Marvel Comics: Jul, 2009 - No. 5, Dec, 2009 ($3.99, limited series)

1-5-Brooks-a; Osborn's Young Avengers vs. original Young Avengers 4.00

DARK REIGN: ZODIAC
Marvel Comics: Aug, 2009 - No. 3, Nov, 2009 ($3.99, limited series)

1-3-Casey-s/Fox-a. 1-Human Torch app. 4.00

DARKSEID (VILLAINS) (See Jack Kirby's New Gods and New Gods)
DC Comics: Feb, 1998 ($1.95, one-shot)

1-Byrne-s/Pearson-c 2.50

DARKSEID VS. GALACTUS: THE HUNGER
DC Comics: 1995 ($4.95, one-shot) (1st DC/Marvel x-over by John Byrne)

nn-John Byrne-c/a/script 5.00

DARK SHADOWS
Steinway Comic Publ. (Ajax)(America's Best): Oct, 1957 - No. 3, May, 1958

	GD	VG	FN	VF	VF/NM	NM-
1	27	54	81	158	259	360
2,3	19	38	57	111	176	240

DARK SHADOWS (TV) (See Dan Curtis Giveaways)
Gold Key: Mar, 1969 - No. 35, Feb, 1976 (Photo-c: 1-7)

	GD	VG	FN	VF	VF/NM	NM-
1(30039-903)-With pull-out poster (25¢)	22	44	66	157	304	450
1-With poster missing	8	16	24	56	93	130
2	8	16	24	52	86	120
3-With pull-out poster	10	20	30	71	126	180
3-With poster missing	6	12	18	41	66	90
4-7: 7-Last photo-c	7	14	21	45	73	100
8-10	5	10	15	32	51	70
11-20	4	8	12	28	44	60
21-35: 30-Last painted-c	4	8	12	24	37	50
Story Digest 1 (6/70, 148pp.)-Photo-c (low print)	8	16	24	54	90	125

DARK SHADOWS (TV) (See Nightmare on Elm Street)
Innovation Publishing: June, 1992 - No. 4, Spring, 1993 ($2.50, limited series, coated stock)

1-Based on 1991 NBC TV mini-series; painted-c 5.00
2-4 4.00

DARK SHADOWS: BOOK TWO
Innovation Publishing: 1993 - No. 4, July, 1993 ($2.50, limited series)

1-4-Painted-c. 4-Maggie Thompson scripts 4.00

DARK SHADOWS: BOOK THREE
Innovation Publishing: Nov, 1993 ($2.50)

1-(Whole #9) 4.00

DARKSTARS, THE
DC Comics: Oct, 1992 - No. 38, Jan, 1996 ($1.75/$1.95)

1-1st app. The Darkstars 3.00
2-24,0,25-38: 5-Hawkman & Hawkwoman app. 18-20-Flash app. 24-(9/94)-Zero Hour. 0-(10/94). 25-(11/94). 30-Green Lantern app. 31-...vs. Darkseid. 32-Green Lantern app. 2.50
NOTE: *Travis Charest a(p)-4-7; c(p)-2-5; c-6-11. **Stroman** a-1-3; c-1.*

DARK TOWER: THE BATTLE OF JERICHO HILL (Based on Stephen King's Dark Tower)
Marvel Comics: Feb, 2010 - No. 5, May, 2010 ($3.99, limited series)

1-5-Peter David & Robin Furth-s/Jae Lee & Richard Isanove-a/c; variant-c for each 4.00

DARK TOWER: THE FALL OF GILEAD (Based on Stephen King's Dark Tower)
Marvel Comics: July, 2009 - No. 6, Jan, 2010 ($3.99, limited series)

1-6-Peter David & Robin Furth-s/Richard Isanove-a/Jae Lee-c; variant-c for each 4.00
Dark Tower: Guide to Gilead (2009, $3.99) profile pages of people and places 4.00

DARK TOWER: THE GUNSLINGER BORN (Based on Stephen King's Dark Tower series)
Marvel Comics: Apr, 2007 - No. 7, Oct, 2007 ($3.99, limited series)

1-Peter David & Robin Furth-s/Jae Lee & Richard Isanove-a; boyhood of Roland Deschain; afterword by Ralph Macchio; map of New Canaan 6.00
1-Variant cover by Quesada 8.00
1-Second printing with variant-c by Quesada 5.00
1-Sketch cover variant by Jae Lee 40.00
2-6-Jae Lee-c 4.00
2-Second printing with variant-c by Immonen 4.00
2-7-Variant covers. 2-Finch-c. 3-Yu-c. 4-McNiven-c. 5-Land-c. 6-Campbell. 7-Coipel 6.00
2-7-B&W sketch-c by Jae Lee 20.00
... Sketchbook (2006, no cover price) pencil art and designs by Lee; coloring process 5.00
Dark Tower: Gunslinger's Guidebook (2007, $3.99) profile pages with Jae Lee-a 4.00
HC (2007, $24.99) r/#1-7; variant covers and sketch pages; Macchio intro. 25.00

DARK TOWER: THE LONG ROAD HOME (Based on Stephen King's Dark Tower series)
Marvel Comics: May, 2008 - No. 5, Sept, 2008 ($3.99, limited series)

1-Peter David & Robin Furth-s/Jae Lee & Richard Isanove-a 4.00
1-Variant cover by Deodato 6.00
1-Sketch cover variant by Jae Lee 40.00
2-5-Jae Lee-c 4.00
2-5: 2-Variant-c by Quesada. 3-Djurdjevic var-c. 4-Garney var-c. 5-Bermejo var-c 6.00
2-5-B&W sketch-c by Jae Lee 20.00
2-Second printing with variant-c by Lee 4.00
Dark Tower: End-World Almanac (2008, $3.99) guide to locations and inhabitants 4.00

DARK TOWER: THE SORCEROR (Based on Stephen King's Dark Tower)
Marvel Comics: June, 2009 ($3.99, one-shot)

1-Robin Furth-s/Richard Isanove-a/c; the story of Marten Broadcloak 4.00

DARK TOWER: TREACHERY (Based on Stephen King's Dark Tower series)
Marvel Comics: Nov, 2008 - No. 6, Apr, 2009 ($3.99, limited series)

1-6-Peter David & Robin Furth-s/Jae Lee & Richard Isanove-a 4.00
1-Variant cover by Dell'otto 10.00

DARKWING DUCK (TV cartoon) (Also see Cartoon Tales)
Disney Comics: Nov, 1991 - No. 4, Feb, 1992 ($1.50, limited series)

1-4: Adapts hour-long premiere TV episode 3.00

DARK WOLVERINE (See Wolverine 2003 series)

DARK X-MEN (See Dark Avengers and the Dark Reign mini-series)
Marvel Comics: Jan, 2010 - No. 5, May, 2010 ($3.99, limited series)

1-5-Cornell-s/Kirk-a. 1-3-Bianchi-c. 1-Nate Grey returns 4.00
...: The Confession (11/09, $3.99) Cansino-a; Paquette-c 4.00

DARK X-MEN: THE BEGINNING (See Dark Avengers and the Dark Reign mini-series)
Marvel Comics: Sept, 2009 - No. 3, Oct, 2009 ($3.99, limited series)

1-3: 1-Cornell-s/Kirk-a; Jae Lee-c on all. 2-Daken app. 3-Mystique app.; Jock-a 4.00

DARLING LOVE
Close Up/Archie Publ. (A Darling Magazine): Oct-Nov, 1949 - No. 11, 1952 (no month) (52 pgs.)(Most photo-c)

	GD	VG	FN	VF	VF/NM	NM-
1-Photo-c	19	38	57	111	176	240
2-Photo-c	12	24	36	69	97	125
3-8,10,11: 3-6-photo-c	10	20	30	58	79	100
9-Krigstein-a	11	22	33	62	86	110

DARLING ROMANCE
Close Up (MLJ Publications): Sept-Oct, 1949 - No. 7, 1951 (All photo-c)

	GD	VG	FN	VF	VF/NM	NM-
1-(52 pgs.)-Photo-c	22	44	66	132	216	300
2	13	26	39	72	101	130
3-7	10	20	30	56	76	95

DARQUE PASSAGES (See Master Darque)
Acclaim (Valiant): April, 1998 ($2.50)

1-Christina Z.-s/Manco-c/a 2.50

DART (Also see Freak Force & Savage Dragon)
Image Comics (Highbrow Entertainment): Feb, 1996 - No. 3, May, 1996 ($2.50, lim. series)

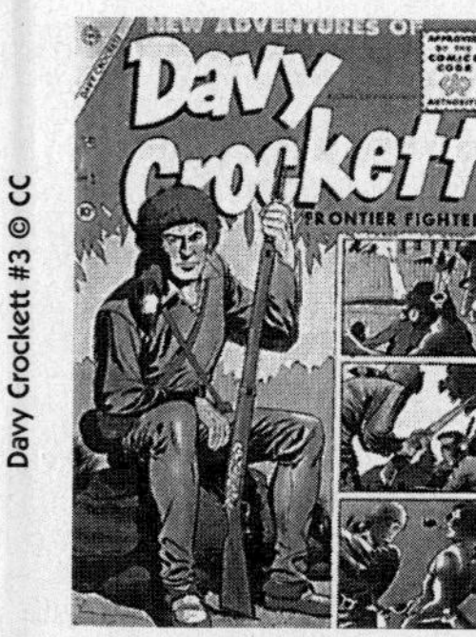

Davy Crockett #3 © CC

Dawn #4 © JM Linsner

Dazzler #26 © MAR

	GD 2.0	VG 4.0	FN 6.0	VF 8.0	VF/NM 9.0	NM- 9.2
1-3						3.00

DASTARDLY & MUTTLEY (See Fun-In No. 1-4, 6 and Kite Fun Book)

DATE WITH DANGER
Standard Comics: No. 5, Dec, 1952 - No. 6, Feb, 1953

	GD 2.0	VG 4.0	FN 6.0	VF 8.0	VF/NM 9.0	NM- 9.2
5,6-Secret agent stories: 6-Atom bomb story	9	18	27	52	69	85

DATE WITH DEBBI (Also see Debbi's Dates)
National Periodical Publ.: Jan-Feb, 1969 - No. 17, Sept-Oct, 1971; No. 18, Oct-Nov, 1972

	GD 2.0	VG 4.0	FN 6.0	VF 8.0	VF/NM 9.0	NM- 9.2
1-Teenage	6	12	18	41	66	90
2-5,17-(52 pgs) James Taylor sty.	4	8	12	22	34	45
6-12,18-Last issue	3	6	9	20	30	40
13-16-(68 pgs.): 14-1 pg. story on Jack Wild. 15-Marlo Thomas/"That Girl" story	4	8	12	24	37	50

DATE WITH JUDY, A (Radio/TV, and 1948 movie)
National Periodical Publications: Oct-Nov, 1947 - No. 79, Oct-Nov, 1960 (No. 1-25: 52 pgs.)

	GD 2.0	VG 4.0	FN 6.0	VF 8.0	VF/NM 9.0	NM- 9.2
1-Teenage	29	58	87	172	281	390
2	15	30	45	84	127	170
3-10	13	26	39	72	101	130
11-20	10	20	30	54	72	90
21-40	9	18	27	50	65	80
41-45: 45-Last pre-code (2-3/55)	8	16	24	44	57	70
46-79: 79-Drucker-c/a	8	16	24	42	54	65

DATE WITH MILLIE, A (Life With Millie No. 8 on)(Teenage)
Atlas/Marvel Comics (MPC): Oct, 1956 - No. 7, Aug, 1957; Oct, 1959 - No. 7, Oct, 1960

	GD 2.0	VG 4.0	FN 6.0	VF 8.0	VF/NM 9.0	NM- 9.2
1(10/56)-(1st Series)-Dan DeCarlo-a in #1-7	27	54	81	160	263	365
2	15	30	45	86	133	180
3-7	13	26	39	72	101	130
1(10/59)-(2nd Series)	15	30	45	86	133	180
2-7	11	22	33	60	83	105

DATE WITH PATSY, A (Also see Patsy Walker)
Atlas Comics: Sept, 1957 (One-shot)

	GD 2.0	VG 4.0	FN 6.0	VF 8.0	VF/NM 9.0	NM- 9.2
1-Starring Patsy Walker	13	26	39	72	101	130

DAUGHTERS OF THE DRAGON (See Heroes For Hire)
Marvel Comics: 2005; Mar, 2006 - No. 6, Aug, 2006 ($2.99, limited series)

	GD 2.0	VG 4.0	FN 6.0	VF 8.0	VF/NM 9.0	NM- 9.2
1-6-Palmiotti & Gray-s/Evans-a. 1-Rhino app. 5,6-Iron Fist app.						3.00
... Deadly Hands Special (2005, $3.99) reprints app. from Deadly Hands of Kung Fu #32,33 & Bizarre Adventures #25; Claremont-s/Rogers-a; new Rogers-c & interview						4.00
...: Samurai Bullets TPB (2006, $15.99) r/#1-6						16.00

DAVID AND GOLIATH (Movie)
Dell Publishing Co.: No. 1205, July, 1961

	GD 2.0	VG 4.0	FN 6.0	VF 8.0	VF/NM 9.0	NM- 9.2
Four Color 1205-Photo-c	6	12	18	43	69	95

DAVID BORING (See Eightball)
Pantheon Books: 2000 ($24.95, hardcover w/dust jacket)

	GD 2.0	VG 4.0	FN 6.0	VF 8.0	VF/NM 9.0	NM- 9.2
Hardcover - reprints David Boring stories from Eightball; Clowes-s/a						25.00

DAVID CASSIDY (TV)(See Partridge Family, Swing With Scooter #33 & Time For Love #30)
Charlton Comics: Feb, 1972 - No. 14, Sept, 1973

	GD 2.0	VG 4.0	FN 6.0	VF 8.0	VF/NM 9.0	NM- 9.2
1-Most have photo covers	6	12	18	41	66	90
2-5	4	8	12	24	37	50
6-14	4	8	12	22	34	45

DAVID LADD'S LIFE STORY (See Movie Classics)

DAVY CROCKETT (See Dell Giants, Fightin..., Frontier Fighters, It's Game Time, Power Record Comics, Western Tales & Wild Frontier)

DAVY CROCKETT (Frontier Fighter...)
Avon Periodicals: 1951

	GD 2.0	VG 4.0	FN 6.0	VF 8.0	VF/NM 9.0	NM- 9.2
nn-Tuska?, Reinman-a; Fawcette-c	18	36	54	105	165	225

DAVY CROCKETT (...King of the Wild Frontier No. 1,2)(TV)
Dell Publishing Co./Gold Key: 5/55 - No. 671, 12/55; No. 1, 12/63; No. 2, 11/69 (Walt Disney)

	GD 2.0	VG 4.0	FN 6.0	VF 8.0	VF/NM 9.0	NM- 9.2
Four Color 631(#1)-Fess Parker photo-c	16	32	48	115	220	325
Four Color 639-Photo-c	13	26	39	95	178	260
Four Color 664,671(Marsh-a)-Photo-c	13	26	39	91	168	245
1(12/63-Gold Key)-Fess Parker photo-c; reprints	8	16	24	54	90	125
2(11/69)-Fess Parker photo-c; reprints	4	8	12	28	44	60

DAVY CROCKETT (...Frontier Fighter #1,2; Kid Montana #9 on)
Charlton Comics: Aug, 1955 - No. 8, Jan, 1957

	GD 2.0	VG 4.0	FN 6.0	VF 8.0	VF/NM 9.0	NM- 9.2
1	10	20	30	56	76	95
2	7	14	21	35	43	50
3-8	5	10	15	24	30	35

DAWN
Sirius Entertainment/Image Comics: June, 1995 - No. 6, 1996 ($2.95)

	GD 2.0	VG 4.0	FN 6.0	VF 8.0	VF/NM 9.0	NM- 9.2
1/2-w/certificate	1	2	3	5	6	8
1/2-Variant-c	2	4	6	10	14	18
1-Linsner-c/a	1	2	3	5	6	8
1-Black Light Edition	2	4	6	9	13	16
1-White Trash Edition	3	6	9	16	23	30
1-Look Sharp Edition	3	6	9	19	29	38
2-4: Linsner-c/a						4.50
2-Variant-c, 3-Limited Edition	2	4	6	13	18	22
4-6-Vibrato-c						3.50
4, 5-Limited Edition	2	4	6	8	10	12
6-Limited Edition	2	4	6	8	10	12
...Convention Sketchbook (Image Comics, 2002, $2.95) pin-ups						3.00
...2003 Convention Sketchbook (Image Comics, 3/03, $2.95) pin-ups						3.00
...2004 Convention Sketchbook (Image Comics, 4/04, $2.95) pin-ups						3.00
...2005 Convention Sketchbook (Image Comics, 5/05, $2.95) pin-ups						3.00
Genesis Edition ('99, Wizard supplement) previews Return of the Goddess						2.50
Lucifer's Halo TPB (11/97, $19.95) r/Drama, Dawn #1-6 plus 12 pages of new artwork						20.00
...: Tenth Anniversary Special (9/99, $2.95) Interviews						3.00
The Portable Dawn ($9.95, 5"x4", 64 pgs.) Pocket-sized cover gallery						10.00

DAWN OF THE DEAD (George A. Romaro's...)
IDW Publishing: Apr, 2004 - No. 3, Jun, 2004 ($3.99, limited series)

	GD 2.0	VG 4.0	FN 6.0	VF 8.0	VF/NM 9.0	NM- 9.2
1-3-Adaptation of the 2004 movie; Niles-s						4.00
TPB (9/04, $17.99) r/#1-3; intro. by George A. Romero						18.00

DAWN: THE RETURN OF THE GODDESS
Sirius Entertainment: Apr, 1999 - No. 4, July, 2000 ($2.95, limited series)

	GD 2.0	VG 4.0	FN 6.0	VF 8.0	VF/NM 9.0	NM- 9.2
1-4-Linsner-s/a						3.00
TPB (4/02, $12.95) r/#1-4; intro. by Linsner						13.00

DAWN: THREE TIERS
Image Comics: Jun, 2003 - No. 6, Aug, 2005 ($2.95, limited series)

	GD 2.0	VG 4.0	FN 6.0	VF 8.0	VF/NM 9.0	NM- 9.2
1-6-Linsner-s/a. 2-Preview of Vampire's Christmas						3.00

DAYDREAMERS (See Generation X)
Marvel Comics: Aug, 1997 - No. 3, Oct, 1997 ($2.50, limited series)

	GD 2.0	VG 4.0	FN 6.0	VF 8.0	VF/NM 9.0	NM- 9.2
1-3-Franklin Richards, Howard the Duck, Man-Thing app.						2.50

DAY OF JUDGMENT
DC Comics: Nov, 1999 - No. 5, Nov, 1999 ($2.95/$2.50, limited series)

	GD 2.0	VG 4.0	FN 6.0	VF 8.0	VF/NM 9.0	NM- 9.2
1-($2.95) Spectre possessed; Matt Smith-a						3.00
2-5: Parallax returns. 5-Hal Jordan becomes the Spectre						3.00
...Secret Files 1 (11/99, $4.95) Harris-c						5.00

DAY OF VENGEANCE (Prelude to Infinite Crisis)(Also see Birds of Prey #76 for 1st app. of Black Alice)
DC Comics: June, 2005 - No. 6, Nov, 2005 ($2.50, limited series)

	GD 2.0	VG 4.0	FN 6.0	VF 8.0	VF/NM 9.0	NM- 9.2
1-6: 1-Jean Loring becomes Eclipso; Spectre, Ragman, Enchantress, Detective Chimp, Shazam app.; Justiniano-a. 2,3-Capt. Marvel app. 4-6-Black Alice app.						2.50
...: Infinite Crisis Special 1 (3/06, $4.99) Justiniano-a/Simonson-c						5.00
TPB (2005, $12.99) r/series & Action #826, Advs. of Superman #639, Superman #216						13.00

DAYS OF THE DEFENDERS (See Defenders, The)
Marvel Comics: Mar, 2001 ($3.50, one-shot)

	GD 2.0	VG 4.0	FN 6.0	VF 8.0	VF/NM 9.0	NM- 9.2
1-Reprints early team-ups of members, incl. Marvel Feature #1; Larsen-c						3.50

DAYS OF THE MOB (See In the Days of the Mob)

DAYTRIPPER
DC Comics (Vertigo): Feb, 2010 - No. 10 ($2.99, limited series)

	GD 2.0	VG 4.0	FN 6.0	VF 8.0	VF/NM 9.0	NM- 9.2
1,2-Gabriel Bá & Fábio Moon-s/a						3.50

DAZEY'S DIARY
Dell Publishing Co.: June-Aug, 1962

	GD 2.0	VG 4.0	FN 6.0	VF 8.0	VF/NM 9.0	NM- 9.2
01-174-208: Bill Woggon-c/a	4	8	12	28	44	60

DAZZLER, THE (Also see Marvel Graphic Novel & X-Men #130)
Marvel Comics Group: Mar, 1981 - No. 42, Mar, 1986

	GD 2.0	VG 4.0	FN 6.0	VF 8.0	VF/NM 9.0	NM- 9.2
1,22,24,27,28,38,42: 1-X-Men app. 22 (12/82)-vs. Rogue Battle-c/sty. 24-Full app. Rogue w/Powerman (Iron Fist). 27-Rogue app. 28-Full app. Rogue; Mystique app. 38-Wolverine-c/app.; X-Men app. 42-Beast-c/app.						4.00
2-21,23,25,26,29-32,34-37,39-41: 2-X-Men app. 10,11-Galactus app. 21-Double size; photo-c. 23-Rogue/Mystique 1 pg. app. 26-Jusko-c. 40-Secret Wars II						3.00
33-Michael Jackson "Thriller" swipe-c/sty						3.00

DC Comics Classics Library: Batman Annuals © DC

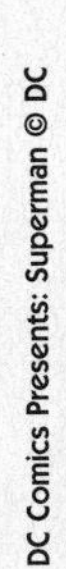
DC Comics Presents: Superman © DC

DC 100 Page Super Spectacular #22 © DC

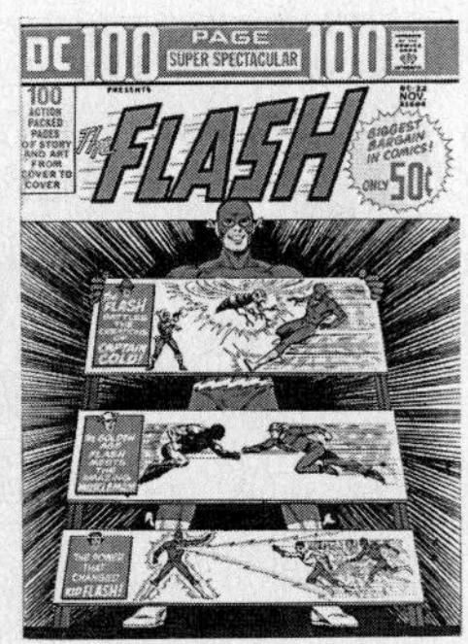

	GD	VG	FN	VF	VF/NM	NM-
	2.0	4.0	6.0	8.0	9.0	9.2

	GD	VG	FN	VF	VF/NM	NM-
	2.0	4.0	6.0	8.0	9.0	9.2

NOTE: *No. 1 distributed only through comic shops.* ***Alcala*** *a-1i, 2i.* ***Chadwick*** *a-38-42p; c(p)-39, 41, 42.* ***Guice*** *a-38i, 42i; c-38, 40.*

DC CHALLENGE (Most DC superheroes appear)
DC Comics: Nov, 1985 - No. 12, Oct, 1986 ($1.25/$2.00, maxi-series)

1-11: 1-Colan-a. 2,8-Batman-c/app. 4-Gil Kane-c/a 2.50
12-($2.00-c) Giant; low print 3.00

NOTE: *Batman app. in 1-4, 6-12. Joker app. in 7.* ***Infantino*** *a-3.* ***Ordway*** *c-12.* ***Swan/Austin*** *c-10.*

DC COMICS CLASSICS LIBRARY (Hardcover collections of classic DC stories)
DC Comics: 2009 - Present ($39.99, hardcover with dustjacket)

Batman: A Death in the Family ('09)- r/Batman #426-429, 440-442, New Titans #60,61 40.00
Batman Annuals ('09)- r/Batman Annual #1-3; afterword by Richard Bruning 40.00
Flash of Two Worlds ('09)- r/Flash #123,129,137,151,170&173 team-ups with G.A. Flash 40.00
Justice League of America by George Pérez ('09) r/J.L.of A. #184-186, 192-194 40.00
Legion of Super-Heroes: The Life and Death of Ferro Lad ('09) - r/Adventure Comics # 346, 347,352-355,357; intro. by Paul Levitz; afterword by Jim Shooter 40.00
Roots of the Swamp Thing ('09)- r/House of Secrets #92 & Swamp Thing #1-13; Wein intro. 40.00
Superman: Kryptonite Nevermore ('09)- r/Superman #233-238,240-242; afterword by Denny O'Neil 40.00

DC COMICS PRESENTS
DC Comics: July-Aug, 1978 - No. 97, Sept, 1986 (Superman team-ups in all)

1-4th Superman/Flash race 4 8 12 22 34 45
1-(Whitman variant) 4 8 12 24 37 50
2-Part 2 of Superman/Flash race 2 4 6 13 18 22
2-4,9-12,14-16,19,21,22-(Whitman variants, low print run, none have issue # on cover) 2 4 6 13 18 22
3-10: 4-Metal Men. 6-Green Lantern. 8-Swamp Thing. 9-Wonder Woman 2 4 6 8 10 12
11-25,27-40: 13-Legion of Super-Heroes. 19-Batgirl. 31-Robin. 35-Man-Bat 6.00
26-(10/80)-Green Lantern; intro Cyborg, Starfire, Raven (1st app. New Teen Titans in 16 pg. preview); Starlin-c/a; Sargon the Sorcerer back-up 5 10 15 30 48 65
41,72,77,78,97: 41-Superman/Joker-c/story. 72-Joker/Phantom Stranger-c/story. 77,78-Animal Man app. (77-c also). 97-Phantom Zone 6.00
42-46,48-50,52-71,73-76,79-83: 42-Sandman. 43,80-Legion of Super-Heroes. 52-Doom Patrol. 58-Robin. 82-Adam Strange. 83-Batman & Outsiders 4.00
47-He-Man-c/s (1st app. in comics) 2 4 6 10 14 18
51-Preview insert (16 pgs.) of He-Man (2nd app.) 1 2 3 5 6 8
84-Challengers of the Unknown; Kirby-c/s. 6.00
85-Swamp Thing; Alan Moore scripts 6.00
86,88-96: 86-88-Crisis x-over. 88-Creeper 4.00
87-Origin/1st app. Superboy of Earth Prime 1 3 4 6 8 10
Annual 1,4: 1(9/82)-G.A. Superman; 1st app. Alexander Luthor. 4(10/85)-Superwoman 4.00
Annual 2,3: 2(7/83)-Intro/origin Superwoman. 3(9/84)-Shazam 4.00

NOTE: ***Adkins*** *a-2, 54; c-2.* ***Buckler*** *a-33, 34; c-30, 33, 34.* ***Giffen*** *a-39; c-59.* ***Gil Kane*** *a-28, 35, Annual 3; c-48p, 56, 58, 60, 62, 64, 68, Annual 2, 3.* ***Kirby*** *c/a-84.* ***Kubert*** *c/a-66.* ***Morrow*** *c/a-65.* ***Newton*** *c/a-54p.* ***Orlando*** *c-53i.* ***Perez*** *a-26p, 61p; c-38, 61, 94.* ***Starlin*** *a-26-29p, 36p, 37p; c-26-29, 36, 37, 93.* ***Toth*** *a-84.* ***Williamson*** *i-79, 85, 87.*

DC COMICS PRESENTS: ...(Julie Schwartz tribute series of one-shots based on classic covers)
DC Comics: Sept, 2004 - Oct, 2004 ($2.50)

The Atom -(Based on cover of Atom #10) Gibbons-s/Oliffe-a; Waid-s/Jurgens-a; Bolland-c 2.50
Batman -(Batman #183) Johns-s/Infantino-a; Wein-s/Kuhn-a; Hughes-c 2.50
The Flash -(Flash #163) Loeb-s/McGuinness-a; O'Neil-s/Mahnke-a; Ross-c 2.50
Green Lantern -(Green Lantern #31) Azzarello-s/Breyfogle-a; Pasko-s/McDaniel-a; Bolland-c 2.50
Hawkman -(Hawkman #6) Bates-s/Byrne-a; Busiek-s/Simonson-a; Garcia-Lopez-c 2.50
Justice League of America -(J.L. of A. #53) Ellison & David-s/Giella-a; Wolfman-s/Nguyen-a; Garcia-Lopez-c 2.50
Mystery in Space -(M.I.S. #82) Maggin-s/Williams-a; Morrison-s/Ordway-a; Ross-c 2.50
Superman -(Superman #264) Stan Lee-s/Cooke-a; Levitz-s/Giffen-a; Hughes-c 2.50

DC COUNTDOWN (To Infinite Crisis)
DC Comics: May, 2005 ($1.00, 80 pages, one-shot)

1-Death of Blue Beetle; prelude to OMAC Project, Day of Vengeance, Rann/Thanagar War and Villains United mini-series; s/a by various; Jim Lee/Alex Ross-c 3.00

DC FIRST: ...(series of one-shots)
DC Comics: July, 2002 ($3.50)

Batgirl/Joker 1-Sienkiewicz & Terry Moore-a; Nowlan-c 3.50
Green Lantern/Green Lantern 1-Alan Scott & Hal Jordan vs. Krona 3.50
Flash/Superman 1-Superman races Jay Garrick; Abra Kadabra app. 3.50
Superman/Lobo 1-Giffen-s; Nowlan-c 3.50

DC GOES APE
DC Comics: 2008 ($19.99, trade paperback)

Vol. 1 - Reprints app. of Grodd, Beppo, Titano and other monkey tales; Art Adams-c 20.00

DC GRAPHIC NOVEL (Also see DC Science Fiction...)
DC Comics: Nov, 1983 - No. 7, 1986 ($5.95, 68 pgs.)

1-3,5,7: 1-Star Raiders. 2-Warlords; not from regular Warlord series. 3-The Medusa Chain; Ernie Colon story/a. 5-Me and Joe Priest; Chaykin-c. 7-Space Clusters; Nino-c/a 2 4 6 9 12 15
4-The Hunger Dogs by Kirby; Darkseid kills Himon from Mister Miracle & destroys New Genesis 5 10 15 34 55 75
6-Metalzoic; Sienkiewicz-c ($6.95) 2 4 6 9 12 15

DC HOLIDAY SPECIAL '09
DC Comics: Feb, 2010 ($5.99, one-shot)

1-Christmas short stories by various incl. Dragotta, Tucci, Chaykin; Dustin Nguyen-c 6.00

DC INFINITE HALLOWEEN SPECIAL
DC Comics: Dec, 2007 ($5.99, one-shot)

1-Halloween short stories by various incl. Dini, Waid, Hairsine, Kelley Jones; Gene Ha-c 6.00

DC KIDS MEGA SAMPLER
DC Comics: June, 2009 (Free Comic Book Day giveaway, one-shot)

1-Tiny Titans, Batman: The Brave and the Bold, Billy Batson/Shazam short stories 2.50

DC/MARVEL: ALL ACCESS (Also see DC Versus Marvel & Marvel Versus DC)
DC Comics: 1996 - No. 4, 1997 ($2.95, limited series)

1-4: 1-Superman & Spider-Man app. 2-Robin & Jubilee app. 3-Dr. Strange & Batman-c/app., X-Men, JLA app. 4-X-Men vs. JLA-c/app. rebirth of Amalgam 3.00

DC/MARVEL: CROSSOVER CLASSICS
DC Comics: 1998; 2003 ($14.95, TPB)

Vol. II-Reprints Batman/Punisher: Lake of Fire, Punisher/Batman: Deadly Knights, Silver Surfer/Superman, Batman & Capt. America 15.00
Vol. 4 (2003, $14.95) Reprints Green Lantern/Silver Surfer: Unholy Alliances, Darkseid/ Galactus: The Hunger, Batman & Spider-Man, and Superman/Fantastic Four 15.00

DC 100 PAGE SUPER SPECTACULAR
(Title is 100 Page... No. 14 on)(Square bound) (Reprints, 50¢)
National Periodical Publications: No. 4, Summer, 1971 - No. 13, 6/72; No. 14, 2/73 - No. 22, 11/73 (No #1-3)

4-Weird Mystery Tales; Johnny Peril & Phantom Stranger; cover & splashes by Wrightson; origin Jungle Boy of Jupiter 18 36 54 129 252 375
5-Love Stories; Wood inks (7 pgs.)(scarcer) 46 92 138 368 709 1050
6- "World's Greatest Super-Heroes"; JLA, JSA, Spectre, Johnny Quick, Vigilante & Hawkman; contains unpublished Wildcat story; N. Adams wrap-around-c; r/JLA #21,22 18 36 54 129 252 375
6-Replica Edition (2004, $6.95) complete reprint w/wraparound-c 7.00
7-(Also listed as Superman #245) Air Wave, Kid Eternity, Hawkman-r; Atom-r/Atom #3 9 18 27 65 113 160
8-(Also listed as Batman #238) Batman, Legion, Aquaman-r; G.A. Atom, Sargon (r/Sensation #57), Plastic Man (r/Police #14) stories; Doom Patrol origin-r; Neal Adams wraparound-c 12 24 36 83 152 220
9-(Also listed as Our Army at War #242) Kubert-c 9 18 27 65 113 160
10-(Also listed as Adventure Comics #416) Golden Age-reprints; r/1st app. Black Canary from Flash #86; no Zatanna 11 22 33 78 139 200
11-(Also listed as Flash #214) origin Metal Men-r/Showcase #37; never before published G.A. Flash story. 9 18 27 60 100 140
12,14: 12-(Also listed as Superboy #185) Legion-c/story; Teen Titans, Kid Eternity (r/Hit #46), Star Spangled Kid-r(S.S. #55). 14-Batman-r/Detective #31,32,156; Atom-r/Showcase #34 8 16 24 52 86 120
13-(Also listed as Superman #252) Ray(r/Smash #17), Black Condor, (r/Crack #18), Hawkman(r/Flash #24); Starman-r/Adv. #67; Dr. Fate & Spectre-r/More Fun #57; Neal Adams-c 11 22 33 74 132 190
15,16,18,19,21,22: 15-r/2nd Boy Commandos/Det. #64. 21-Superboy; r/Brave & the Bold #54. 22-r/All-Flash #13. 6 12 18 41 66 90
17,20: 17-JSA-r/All Star #37 (10-11/47, 38 pgs.), Sandman-r/Adv. #65 (8/41), JLA #23 (11/63) & JLA #43 (3/66). 20-Batman-r/Det. #66,68, Spectre; origin Two-Face 6 12 18 43 69 95
... : Love Stories Replica Edition (2000, $6.95) reprints #5 7.00

NOTE: ***Anderson*** *r-11, 14, 18i, 22.* ***B. Baily*** *r-18, 20.* ***Burnley*** *r-18, 20.* ***Crandall*** *r-14p, 20.* ***Drucker*** *r-4.* ***Grandenetti*** *a-22(2)r.* ***Heath*** *a-22r.* ***Infantino*** *r-17, 20, 22.* ***G. Kane*** *r-18.* ***Kirby*** *r-15.* ***Kubert*** *r-6, 7, 16, 17; c-16, 19.* ***Manning*** *a-19r.* ***Meskin*** *r-4, 22.* ***Mooney*** *r-15, 21.* ***Toth*** *r-17, 20.*

DC ONE MILLION (Also see crossover #1,000,000 issues and JLA One Million TPB)
DC Comics: Nov, 1998 - No. 4, Nov, 1998 ($2.95/$1.99, weekly lim. series)

1-($2.95) JLA travels to the 853rd century; Morrison-s 3.00
2-4-($1.99) 2.50
... Eighty-Page Giant (8/99, $4.95) 5.00
TPB ('99, $14.95) r/#1-4 and several x-over stories 15.00

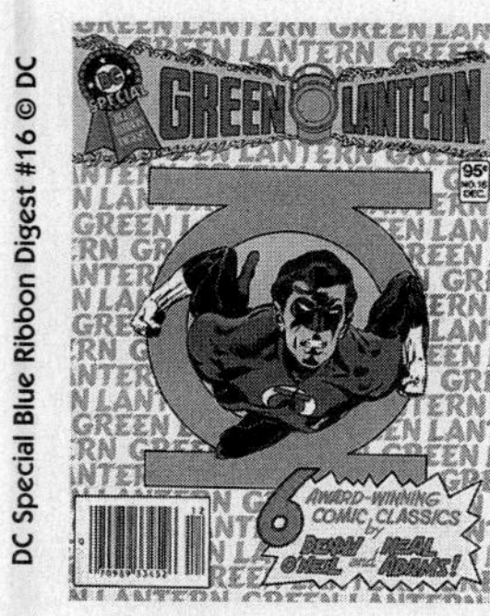

DC Special Blue Ribbon Digest #16 © DC

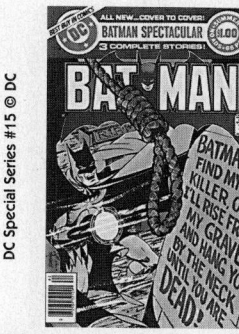

DC Special Series #15 © DC

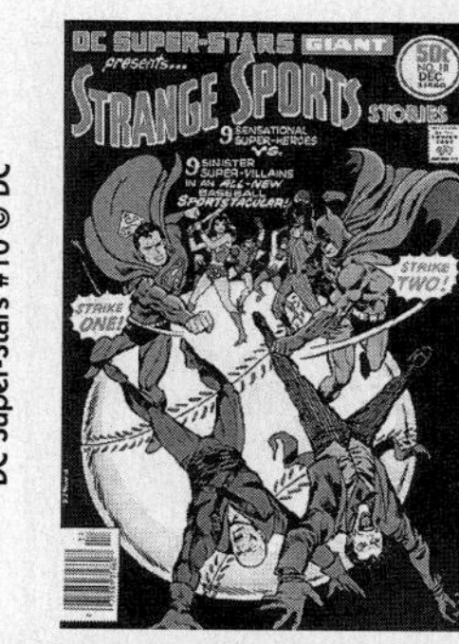

DC Super-Stars #10 © DC

GD 2.0 | VG 4.0 | FN 6.0 | VF 8.0 | VF/NM 9.0 | NM- 9.2

DC SCIENCE FICTION GRAPHIC NOVEL
DC Comics: 1985 - No. 7, 1987 ($5.95)

SF1-SF7: SF1-Hell on Earth by Robert Bloch; Giffen-p. SF2-Nightwings by Robert Silverberg; G. Colan-p. SF3-Frost & Fire by Bradbury. SF4-Merchants of Venus. SF5-Demon With A Glass Hand by Ellison; M. Rogers-a. SF6-The Magic Goes Away by Niven. SF7-Sandkings by George R.R. Martin 2 4 6 8 11 14

DC SILVER AGE CLASSICS
DC Comics: 1992 ($1.00, all reprints)

...Action Comics #252-r/1st Supergirl. Adventure Comics #247-r/1st Legion of Super-Heroes. The Brave and the Bold #28-r/1st JLA. Detective Comics #225-r/1st Martian Manhunter. Detective Comics #327-r/1st new look Batman. Green Lantern #76-r/1st Green Lantern/ Green Arrow. House of Secrets #92-r/1st Swamp Thing. Showcase #4-r/1st S.A. Flash. Showcase #22-r/1st S.A. Green Lantern 2.50
...Sugar and Spike #99; includes 2 unpublished stories 4.00

DC SPECIAL (Also see Super DC Giant)
National Per. Publ.: 10-12/68 - No. 15, 11-12/71; No. 16, Spr/75 - No. 29, 8-9/77

1-All Infantino issue; Flash, Batman, Adam Strange-r; begin 68 pg. issues, end #21 9 18 27 60 100 140
2-Teen humor; Binky, Buzzy, Harvey app. 10 20 30 70 123 175
3-All-Girl issue; unpubl. GA Wonder Woman story 9 18 27 63 107 150
4,11: 4-Horror (1st Abel, brief). 11-Monsters 5 10 15 34 55 75
5-10,12-15: 5-All Kubert issue; Viking Prince, Sgt. Rock-r. 6-Western. 7,9,13-Strangest Sports. 12-Viking Prince; Kubert-c/a (r/B&B almost entirely). 15-G.A. Plastic Man origin-r/Police #1; origin Woozy by Cole; 14,15-(52 pgs.) 4 8 12 28 44 60
16-27: 16-Super Heroes Battle Super Gorillas; r/Capt. Storm #1, 1st Johnny Cloud/All-Amer. Men of War #82. 17-Early S.A. Green Lantern-r. 22-Origin Robin Hood. 26-Enemy Ace. 27-Captain Comet story 3 6 9 16 23 30
28-Earth Shattering Disaster Stories; Legion of Super-Heroes story 3 6 9 17 25 32
29-New "The Untold Origin of the Justice Society"; Staton-a/Neal Adams-c; Hitler app. in story and on cover 4 8 12 24 37 50

NOTE: *N. Adams c-3, 4, 6, 11, 29.* ***Grell*** *a-20; c-17, 20.* ***Heath*** *a-12r.* ***G. Kane*** *a-6p, 13r, 17r, 19-21r.* ***Kirby*** *a-4,11.* ***Kubert*** *a-6r, 12r, 22.* ***Meskin*** *a-10.* ***Moreira*** *a-10.* ***Staton*** *a-29p.* ***Toth*** *a-13, 20r. #1-15: 25¢; 16-27: 50¢; 28, 29: 60¢. #1-13, 16-21: 68 pgs.; 14, 15: 52 pgs.; 25-27: oversized.*

DC SPECIAL BLUE RIBBON DIGEST
DC Comics: Mar-Apr, 1980 - No. 24, Aug, 1982

1,2,4,5: 1-Legion reprints. 2-Flash. 4-Green Lantern. 5-Secret Origins; new Zatara and Zatanna 2 4 6 8 11 14
3-Justice Society 2 4 6 10 14 18
6,8-10: 6-Ghosts. 8-Legion. 9-Secret Origins. 10-Warlord-"The Deimos Saga"-Grell-s/c/a 2 4 6 8 11 14
7-Sgt. Rock's Prize Battle Tales 2 4 6 13 18 22
11,16: 11-Justice League. 16-Green Lantern/Green Arrow-r; all Adams-a 2 4 6 11 16 20
12-Haunted Tank; reprints 1st app. 2 4 6 13 18 22
13-15,17-19: 13-Strange Sports Stories. 14-UFO Invaders; Adam Strange app. 15-Secret Origins of Super Villains; JLA app. 17-Ghosts. 18-Sgt. Rock; Kubert front & back-c. 19-Doom Patrol; new Perez-c 2 4 6 9 13 16
20-Dark Mansion of Forbidden Love (scarce) 5 10 15 30 48 65
21-Our Army at War 3 6 9 16 22 28
22-24: 22-Secret Origins. 23-Green Arrow, w/new 7 pg. story. 24-House of Mystery; new Kubert wraparound-c 2 4 6 13 18 22

NOTE: ***N. Adams*** *a-16(6)r, 17r, 23r; c-16.* ***Aparo*** *a-6r, 24r; c-23.* ***Grell*** *a-8, 10; c-10.* ***Heath*** *a-14.* ***Infantino*** *a-15r.* ***Kaluta*** *a-17r.* ***Gil Kane*** *a-15r, 22r.* ***Kirby*** *a-5, 9, 23r.* ***Kubert*** *a-3, 18r, 21r; c-7, 12, 14, 17, 18, 21, 24.* ***Morrow*** *a-24r.* ***Orlando*** *a-17r, 22r; c-1, 20.* ***Toth*** *a-21r, 24r.* ***Wood*** *a-3, 17r, 24r.* ***Wrightson*** *a-16r, 17r, 24r.*

DC SPECIAL: CYBORG (From Teen Titans) (See Teen Titans 2003 series for TPB collection)
DC Comics: Jul, 2008 - No. 6, Dec, 2008 ($2.99, limited series)

1-6: 1-Sable-s/Lashley-a; origin re-told. 3-6-Magno-a 3.00

DC SPECIAL: RAVEN (From Teen Titans) (See Teen Titans 2003 series for TPB collection)
DC Comics: May, 2008 - No. 5, Sept, 2008 ($2.99, limited series)

1-5-Marv Wolfman-s/Damion Scott-a 3.00

DC SPECIAL SERIES
National Periodical Publications/DC Comics: 9/77 - No. 16, Fall, 1978; No. 17, 8/79 - No. 27, Fall, 1981 (No. 18, 19, 23, 24 - digest size, 100 pgs.; No. 25-27 - Treasury sized)

1-"5-Star Super-Hero Spectacular 1977"; Batman, Atom, Flash, Green Lantern, Aquaman, in solo stories, Kobra app.; N. Adams-c 4 8 12 24 37 50
2(#1)-"The Original Swamp Thing Saga 1977"-r/Swamp Thing #1&2 by Wrightson; new Wrightson wraparound-c. 2 4 6 10 14 18
3,4,6-8: 3-Sgt Rock. 4-Unexpected. 6-Secret Society of Super Villains, Jones-a. 7-Ghosts Special. 8-Brave and Bold w/ new Batman, Deadman & Sgt Rock team-up 2 4 6 11 16 20
5-"Superman Spectacular 1977"-(84 pg, $1.00)-Superman vs. Brainiac & Lex Luthor, new 63 pg. story 3 6 9 14 20 26
9-Wonder Woman; Ditko-a (11 pgs.) 3 6 9 14 20 26
10-"Secret Origins of Superheroes Special 1978"-(52 pgs.)-Dr. Fate, Lightray & Black Canary on-c/new origin stories; Staton, Newton-a 3 6 9 14 19 24
11-"Flash Spectacular 1978"-(84 pgs.) Flash, Kid Flash, GA Flash & Johnny Quick vs. Grodd; Wood-i on Kid Flash chapter 2 4 6 11 16 20
12-"Secrets of Haunted House Special Spring 1978" 2 4 6 11 16 20
13-"Sgt. Rock Special Spring 1978", 50 pg new story 2 4 6 13 18 22
14,17,20-"Original Swamp Thing Saga", Wrightson-a: 14-Sum '78, r/#3,4. 17-Sum '79 r/#5-7. 20-Jan/Feb '80, r/#8-10 2 4 6 8 11 14
15-"Batman Spectacular Summer 1978", Ra's Al Ghul-app.; Golden-a. Rogers-a/front & back-c 3 6 9 19 29 38
16-"Jonah Hex Spectacular Fall 1978"; death of Jonah Hex, Heath-a; Bat Lash and Scalphunter stories 6 12 18 41 66 90
18,19-Digest size: 18-"Sgt. Rock's Prize Battle Tales Fall 1979". 19-"Secret Origins of Super-Heroes Fall 1979"; origins Wonder Woman (new-a),r/Robin, Batman-Superman team, Aquaman, Hawkman and others 2 4 6 11 16 20
21-"Super-Star Holiday Special Spring 1980", Frank Miller-a in "Batman--Wanted Dead or Alive" (1st Batman story); Jonah Hex, Sgt. Rock, Superboy & LSH and House of Mystery/ Witching Hour-c/stories 4 8 12 24 37 50
22-"G.I. Combat Sept. 1980", Kubert-c. Haunted Tank-s 2 4 6 13 18 22
23,24-Digest size: 23-World's Finest-r. 24-Flash 2 4 6 10 14 18
V5#25-($2.95)-"Superman II, the Adventure Continues Summer 1981"; photos from movie & photo-c (see All-New Coll. Ed. C-62) 3 6 9 14 19 24
26-($2.50)-"Superman and His Incredible Fortress of Solitude Summer 1981" 3 6 9 14 19 24
27-($2.50)-"Batman vs. The Incredible Hulk Fall 1981" 4 8 12 24 37 50

NOTE: ***Aparo*** *c-8.* ***Heath*** *a-12i, 16.* ***Infantino*** *a-19r.* ***Kirby*** *a-23, 19r.* ***Kubert*** *c-13, 19r.* ***Nasser/Netzer*** *a-1, 10i, 15.* ***Newton*** *a-10.* ***Nino*** *a-4, 7.* ***Starlin*** *c-12.* ***Staton*** *a-1.* ***Tuska*** *a-19r. #25 & 26. were advertised as All-New Collectors' Edition C-63, C-64. #26 was originally planned as All-New Collectors' Ed. C-30?; has C-630 & A.N.C.E. on cover.*

DC SPECIAL: THE RETURN OF DONNA TROY
DC Comics: Aug, 2005 - No. 4, Late Oct, 2005 ($2.99, limited series)

1-4-Jimenez-s/Garcia-Lopez-a(p)/Pérez-i 3.00

DC SUPER-STARS
National Periodical Publications/DC Comics: March, 1976 - No. 18, Winter, 1978 (No. 3-18: 52 pgs.)

1-(68 pgs.)-Re-intro Teen Titans (predates T. T. #44 (11/76); tryout iss.) plus r/Teen Titans; W.W. as girl was original Wonder Girl 3 6 9 18 27 35
2-7,9,11,12,16: 2,4,6,8-Adam Strange; 2-(68 pgs.)-r/1st Adam Strange/Hawkman team-up from Mystery in Space #90 plus Atomic Knights origin-r. 3-Legion issue. 4-r/Tales/Unexpected #45 2 4 6 8 10 12
8-r/1st Space Ranger from Showcase #15, Adam Strange-r/Mystery in Space #89 & Star Rovers-r/M.I.S. #80 2 4 6 8 11 14
10-Strange Sports Stories; Batman/Joker-c/story 2 4 6 9 13 16
13-Sergio Aragonés Special 3 6 9 14 20 26
14,15,18: 15-Sgt. Rock 2 4 6 8 11 14
17-Secret Origins of Super-Heroes (origin of The Huntress); origin Green Arrow by Grell; Legion app.; Earth II Batman & Catwoman marry (1st revealed; also see B&B #197 & Superman Family #211) 5 10 15 32 51 70

NOTE: ***M. Anderson*** *r-2, 4, 6.* ***Aparo*** *c-7, 14, 18.* ***Austin*** *a-11i.* ***Buckler*** *a-14p; c-10.* ***Grell*** *a-17.* ***G. Kane*** *a-1r, 10r.* ***Kubert*** *c-15.* ***Layton*** *c/a-16i, 17i.* ***Mooney*** *a-4r, 6r.* ***Morrow*** *c/a-11r.* ***Nasser*** *a-11.* ***Newton*** *c/a-16p.* ***Staton*** *a-17; c-17. No. 10, 12-18 contain all new material; the rest are reprints. #1 contains new and reprint material.*

DC: THE NEW FRONTIER (Also see Justice League: The New Frontier Special)
DC Comics: Mar, 2004 - No. 6, Nov, 2004 ($6.95, limited series)

1-6-DCU in the 1940s-60s; Darwyn Cooke-c/s/a in all. 1-Hal Jordan and The Losers app. 2-Origin Martian Manhunter; Barry Allen app. 3-Challengers of the Unknown 7.00
...Volume One (2004, $19.95, TPB) r/#1-3; cover gallery & intro. by Paul Levitz 20.00
...Volume Two (2005, $19.99, TPB) r/#4-6; cover gallery & afterword by Cooke 20.00

DC TOP COW CROSSOVERS
DC Comics/Top Cow Productions: 2007 ($14.99, TPB)

SC-r/The Darkness/Batman; JLA/Witchblade; The Darkness/Superman; JLA/Cyberforce 15.00

DC 2000
DC Comics: 2000 - No. 2, 2000 ($6.95, limited series)

1,2-JLA visit 1941 JSA; Semeiks-a 7.00

DCU BRAVE NEW WORLD (See Infinite Crisis and tie-ins)
DC Comics: Aug, 2006 ($1.00, 80 pgs., one-shot)

1-Previews 2006 series Martian Manhunter, OMAC, The Creeper, The All-New Atom, The Trials of Shazam, and Uncle Sam and the Freedom Fighters; the Monitor app. 3.00

DCU (Halloween and Christmas one-shot anthologies)

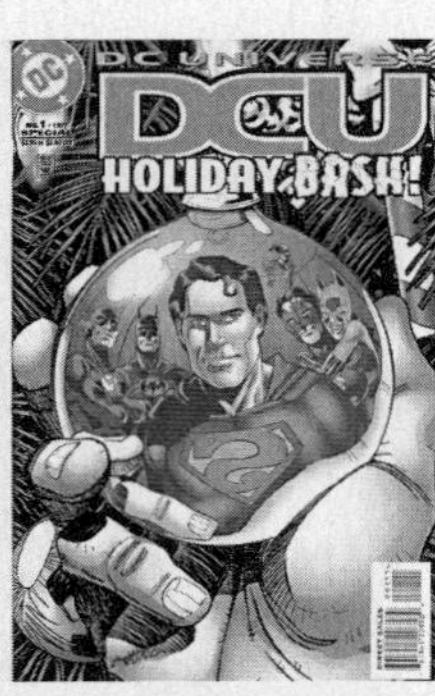

DC Universe Holiday Bash #1 © DC

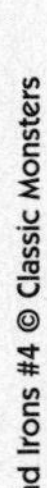
Dead Irons #4 © Classic Monsters

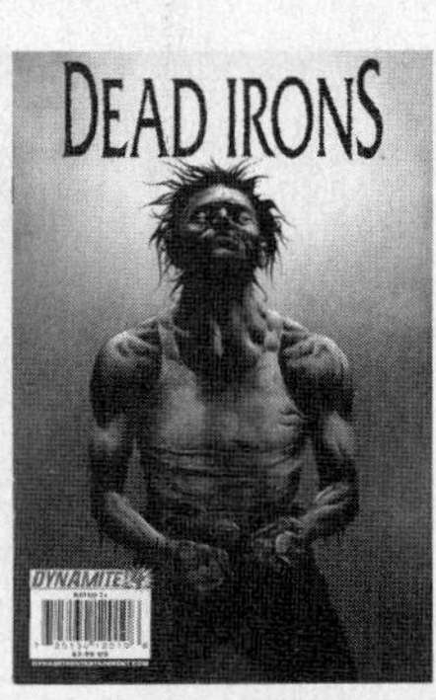

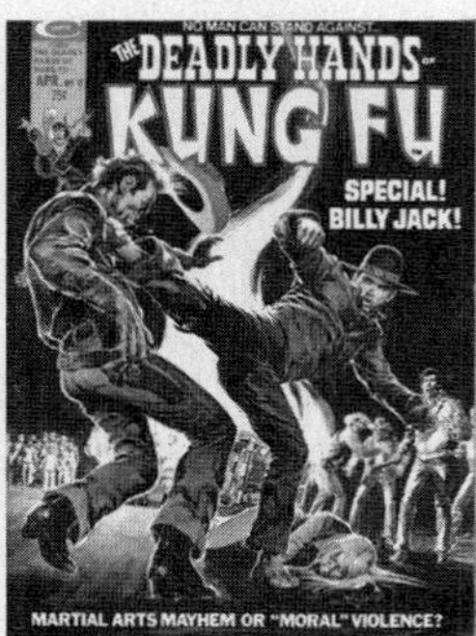

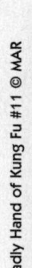

Deadly Hand of Kung Fu #11 © MAR

GD VG FN VF VF/NM NM-
2.0 4.0 6.0 8.0 9.0 9.2

DC Comics

... Halloween Special '09 (12/09, $5.99) Ha-c; art from Bagley, Tucci, K. Jones, Nguyen 6.00
... Holiday Special (2/09, $5.99) Christmas by various incl. Dini, Maguire, Reis; Quitely-c 6.00
... Infinite Halloween Special (12/08, $5.99) Ralph & Sue Dibny app.; Gene Ha-c 6.00
... Infinite Holiday Special (2/07, $4.99) by various; Batwoman app.; Porter-c 5.00

DCU HEROES SECRET FILES
DC Comics: Feb, 1999 ($4.95, one-shot)

1-Origin-s and pin-ups; new Star Spangled Kid app. 5.00

DC UNIVERSE CHRISTMAS, A
DC Comics: 2000 ($19.95)

TPB-Reprints DC Christmas stories by various 20.00

DC UNIVERSE: DECISIONS
DC Comics: Early Nov, 2008 - No. 4, Late Dec, 2008 ($2.99, limited series)

1-4-Assassination plot in the Presidential election; Winick & Willingham-s/Porter-a 3.00

DC UNIVERSE HOLIDAY BASH
DC Comics: 1997- 1999 ($3.95)

I,II-(X-mas '96,'97) Christmas stories by various 5.00
III (1999, for Christmas '98, $4.95) 5.00

DC UNIVERSE ILLUSTRATED BY NEAL ADAMS (Also see Batman Illustrated by Neal Adams HC Vol. 1-3)
DC Comics: 2008 ($39.99, hardcover with dustjacket)

Vol. 1 - Reprints Adams' non-Batman/non-Green Lantern work from 1967-1972; incl. Teen Titans, DC war, Enemy Ace, Superman and PSAs; promo art; Levitz foreword 40.00

DC UNIVERSE: LAST WILL AND TESTAMENT
DC Comics: Oct, 2008 ($3.99, one-shot)

1-Geo-Force vs. Deathstroke; DC heroes prepare for Final Crisis; Brad Meltzer-s; Adam Kubert & Joe Kubert-a; two covers 4.00

DC UNIVERSE: ORIGINS
DC Comics: 2009 ($14.99, TPB)

nn-Reprints 2-page origins of DC characters from back-ups in 52, Countdown and Justice League: Cry For Justice #1-3; s/a by various; Alex Ross-c 15.00

DC UNIVERSE SPECIAL
DC Comics: July, 2008 - Aug, 2008 ($4.99, collection of reprints related to Final Crisis)

...: Justice League of America (7/08) r/J.L. of A. #111,166-168 & Detective #274; Sook-c 5.00
...: Reign in Hell (8/08) r/Blaze/Satanus War x-over; Sook-c 5.00
...: Superman (7/08) r/Mongul app. in Superman #32, Showcase '95 #7,8, Flash #102 5.00

DC UNIVERSE: THE STORIES OF ALAN MOORE (Also see Across the Universe:...)
DC Comics: 2006 ($19.99)

TPB-Reprints Batman: The Killing Joke, "Whatever Happened to the Man of Tomorrow", "For The Man Who Has Everything, and other classic Moore DC stories; Bolland-c 20.00

DC UNIVERSE: TRINITY
DC Comics: Aug, 1993 - No. 2, Sept, 1993 ($2.95, 52 pgs, limited series)

1,2-Foil-c; Green Lantern, Darkstars, Legion app. 3.50

DCU VILLAINS SECRET FILES
DC Comics: Apr, 1999 ($4.95, one-shot)

1-Origin-s and profile pages 5.00

DC VERSUS MARVEL (See Marvel Versus DC) (Also see Amazon, Assassins, Bruce Wayne: Agent of S.H.I. E. L.D., Bullets & Bracelets, Doctor Strangefate, JLX, Legend of the Dark Claw, Magneto & The Magnetic Men, Speed Demon, Spider-Boy, Super Soldier, X-Patrol)
DC Comics: No. 1, 1996, No. 4, 1996 ($3.95, limited series)

1,4: 1-Marz script, Jurgens-a(p); 1st app. of Access. 4.00
.../Marvel Versus DC ($12.95, trade paperback) r/1-4 13.00

DC/WILDSTORM DREAMWAR
DC Comics: Jun, 2008 - No. 6, Nov, 2008 ($2.99, limited series)

1-6-Giffen-s; Silver Age JLA, Teen Titans, JSA, Legion app. on WildStorm Earth 3.00
1-Variant-c of Superman & Midnighter by Garbett 6.00
TPB (2009, $19.99) r/series 20.00

DC: WORLD WAR III (See 52/WWIII)

D-DAY (Also see Special War Series)
Charlton Comics (no No. 3): Sum/63; No. 2, Fall/64; No. 4, 9/66; No. 5, 10/67; No. 6, 11/68

	GD	VG	FN	VF	VF/NM	NM-
1,2: 1(1963)-Montes/Bache-c. 2(Fall '64)-Wood-a(4)	4	8	12	22	34	45
4-6('66-'68)-Montes/Bache-a #5	3	6	9	14	20	25

DEAD AIR
Slave Labor Graphics: July, 1989 ($5.95, graphic novel)

nn-Mike Allred's 1st published work 6.00

DEAD CORPSE
DC Comics (Helix): Sept, 1998 - No. 4, Dec, 1998 ($2.50, limited series)

1-4-Pugh-a/Hinz-s 2.50

DEAD END CRIME STORIES
Kirby Publishing Co.: April, 1949 (52 pgs.)

	GD	VG	FN	VF	VF/NM	NM-
nn-(Scarce)-Powell, Roussos-a; painted-c	51	102	153	318	539	760

DEAD ENDERS
DC Comics (Vertigo): Mar, 2000 - No. 16, June, 2001 ($2.50)

1-16-Brubaker-s/Pleece & Case-a 2.50
Stealing the Sun (2000, $9.95, TPB) r/#1-4, Vertigo Winter's Edge #3 10.00

DEAD-EYE WESTERN COMICS
Hillman Periodicals: Nov-Dec, 1948 - V3#1, Apr-May, 1953

	GD	VG	FN	VF	VF/NM	NM-
V1#1-(52 pgs.)-Krigstein, Roussos-a	20	40	60	114	182	250
V1#2,3-(52 pgs.)	12	24	36	69	97	125
V1#4-12-(52 pgs.)	9	18	27	47	61	75
V2#1,2,5-8,10-12: 1-7-(52 pgs.)	8	16	24	40	50	60
3,4-Krigstein-a	8	16	24	44	57	70
9-One pg. Frazetta ad	8	16	24	40	50	60
V3#1	8	16	24	40	50	60

NOTE: *Briefer a-V1#8. Kinstleresque stories by* **McCann**-*12, V2#1, 2, V3#1.* **McWilliams** *a-V1#5.* **Ed Moore** *a-V1#4.*

DEADFACE: DOING THE ISLANDS WITH BACCHUS
Dark Horse Comics: July, 1991 - No. 3, Sept, 1991 ($2.95, B&W, lim. series)

1-3: By Eddie Campbell 3.00

DEADFACE: EARTH, WATER, AIR, AND FIRE
Dark Horse Comics: July, 1992 - No. 4, Oct, 1992 ($2.50, B&W, limited series; British-r)

1-4: By Eddie Campbell 3.00

DEAD IN THE WEST
Dark Horse Comics: Oct, 1993 - No. 2, Mar, 1994 ($3.95, B&W, 52 pgs.)

1,2-Timothy Truman-c 4.00

DEAD IRONS
Dynamite Entertainment: 2009 - No. 4, 2009 ($3.99)

1-4-Kuhoric-s/Alexander-a/Jae Lee-c 4.00

DEADLANDER (Becomes Dead Rider for #2)
Dark Horse Comics: Oct, 2007 - No. 4, ($2.99, limited series)

1-2-Kevin Ferrara-s/a 3.00

DEADLIEST HEROES OF KUNG FU (Magazine)
Marvel Comics Group: Summer, 1975 (B&W)(76 pgs.)

	GD	VG	FN	VF	VF/NM	NM-
1-Bruce Lee vs. Carradine painted-c; TV Kung Fu, 4pgs. photos/article; Enter the Dragon, 24 pgs. photos/article w/ Bruce Lee; Bruce Lee photo pinup	4	8	12	28	44	60

DEADLINE
Marvel Comics: June, 2002 - No. 4, Sept, 2002 ($2.99, limited series)

1-4: 1-Intro. Kat Farrell; Bill Rosemann-s/Guy Davis-a; Horn painted-c 3.00
TPB (2002. $9.99) r/#1-4 10.00

DEADLY DUO, THE
Image Comics (Highbrow Entertainment): Nov, 1994 - No. 3, Jan, 1995 ($2.50, lim. series)

1-3: 1-1st app. of Kill Cat 2.50

DEADLY DUO, THE
Image Comics (Highbrow Entertainment): June, 1995 - No. 4, Oct, 1995 ($2.50, lim. series)

1-4: 1-Spawn app. 2-Savage Dragon app. 3-Gen 13 app. 2.50

DEADLY FOES OF SPIDER-MAN (See Lethal Foes of...)
Marvel Comics: May, 1991 - No. 4, Aug, 1991 ($1.00, limited series)

1-4: 1-Punisher, Kingpin, Rhino app. 2.50

DEADLY HANDS OF KUNG FU, THE (See Master of Kung Fu)
Marvel Comics Group: April, 1974 - No. 33, Feb, 1977 (75¢) (B&W, magazine)

	GD	VG	FN	VF	VF/NM	NM-
1(V1#4 listed in error)-Origin Sons of the Tiger; Shang-Chi, Master of Kung Fu begins (ties w/Master of Kung Fu #17 as 3rd app. Shang-Chi); Bruce Lee painted-c by Neal Adams; 2pg. memorial photo pinup w/8 pgs. photos/articles; TV Kung Fu, 9 pgs. photos/articles; 15 pgs. Starlin-a	6	12	18	37	59	80
2-Adams painted-c; 1st time origin of Shang-Chi, 34 pgs. by Starlin. TV Kung Fu, 6 pgs. photos & article w/2 pg. pinup. Bruce Lee, 11 pgs. ph/a	4	8	12	28	44	60

3,4,7,10: 3-Adams painted-c; Gulacy-a. Enter the Dragon, photos/articles, 8 pgs. 4-TV Kung

Deadman (2002 series) #1 © DC

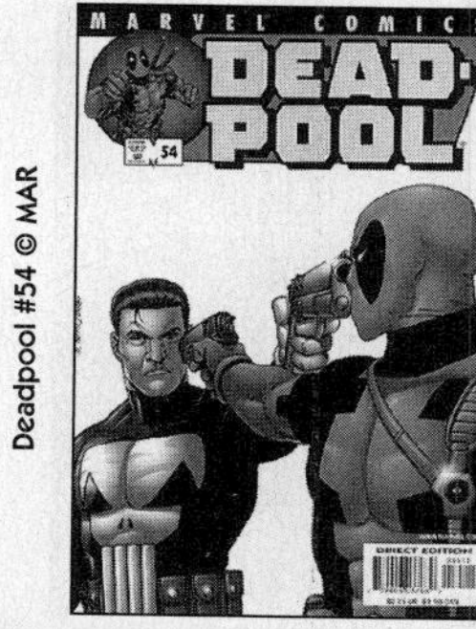

Deadpool #54 © MAR

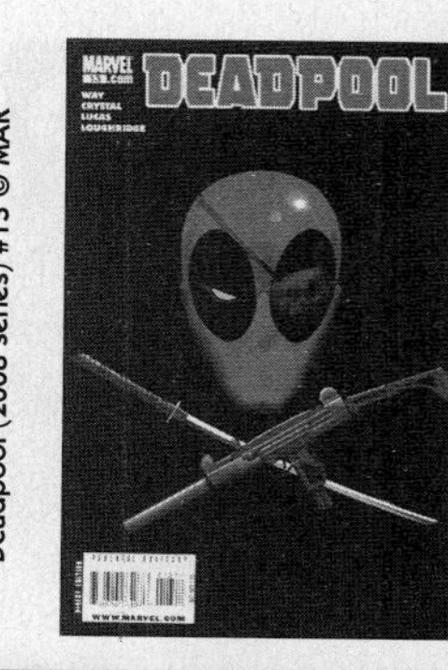

Deadpool (2008 series) #13 © MAR

GD VG FN VF VF/NM NM-
2.0 4.0 6.0 8.0 9.0 9.2

Fu painted-c by Neal Adams; TV Kung Fu 7 pg. article/art; Fu Manchu; Enter the Dragon, 10 pg. photos/article w/Bruce Lee. 7-Bruce Lee painted-c & 9 pgs. photos/articles-Return of Dragon plus 1 pg. photo pinup. 10-(3/75)-Iron Fist painted-c & 34 pg. sty-Early app.
3 6 9 20 30 40

5,6: 5-1st app. Manchurian, 6 pgs. Gulacy-a. TV Kung Fu, 4 pg. article; reprints books w/Barry Smith-a. Capt. America-sty, 10 pgs. Kirby-a(r). 6-Bruce Lee photos/article, 6 pgs.; 15 pgs. early Perez-a 3 6 9 19 29 38

8,9,11: 9-Iron Fist, 2 pg. Preview pinup; Nebres-a. 11-Billy Jack painted-c by Adams; 17 pgs. photos/article 3 6 9 18 27 35

12,13: 12-James Bond painted-c by Adams; 14 pg. photos/article. 13-16 pgs. early Perez-a; Piers Anthony, 7 pgs. photos/article 3 6 9 17 25 32

14-Classic Bruce Lee painted-c by Adams. Lee pinup by Chaykin. Lee 16 pg. photos/article w/2 pgs. Green Hornet TV 6 12 18 43 69 95

15,19: 15-Sum, '75 Giant Annual #1. 20pgs. Starlin-a. Bruce Lee photo pinup & 3 pg. photos/article re book; Man-Thing app. Iron Fist-c/sty; Gulacy-a 18pgs. 19-Iron Fist painted-c & series begins; 1st White Tiger 3 6 9 18 27 35

16,18,20: 16-1st app. Corpse Rider, a Samurai w/Sanho Kim-a. 20-Chuck Norris painted-c & 16 pgs. interview w/photos/article; Bruce Lee vs. C. Norris pinup by Ken Barr. Origin The White Tiger, Perez-a 3 6 9 16 23 30

17-Bruce Lee painted-c by Adams; interview w/R. Clouse, director Enter Dragon 7 pgs. w/B. Lee app. 1st Giffen-a (1pg. 11/75) 4 8 12 28 44 60

21-Bruce Lee 1pg. photos/article 3 6 9 16 23 30

22,30-32: 22-1st brief app. Jack of Hearts. 1st Giffen sty-a (along w/Amazing Adv. #35, 3/76). 30-Swordquest-c/sty & conclusion; Jack of Hearts app. 31-Jack of Hearts app; Staton-a. 32-1st Daughters of the Dragon-c/sty, 21 pgs. M. Rogers-a/Claremont-sty; Iron Fist pinup 3 6 9 16 22 28

23-26,29: 23-1st full app. Jack of Hearts. 24-Iron Fist-c & centerfold pinup. early Zeck-a; Shang Chi pinup; 6 pgs. Piers Anthony text sty w/Perez/Austin-a; Jack of Hearts app. early Giffen-a. 25-1st app. Shimuru, "Samurai", 20 pgs. Mantlo-sty/Broderick-a; "Swordquest"-c & begins 17 pg. sty by Sanho Kim; 11 pg. photos/article; partly Bruce Lee. 26-Bruce Lee painted-c & pinup; 16 pgs. interviews w/Kwon & Clouse; talk about Bruce Lee re-filming of Lee legend. 29-Ironfist vs. Shang Chi battle-c/sty; Jack of Hearts app.
3 6 9 18 27 35

27 3 6 9 14 20 26

28-All Bruce Lee Special Issue; (1st time in comics). Bruce Lee painted-c by Ken Barr & pinup. 36 pgs. comics chronicaling Bruce Lee's life; 15 pgs. B. Lee photos/article (Rare in high grade) 8 16 24 52 86 120

33-Shang Chi-c/sty; Classic Daughters of the Dragon, 21 pgs. M. Rogers-a/Claremont-story with nudity; Bob Wall interview, photos/article, 14 pgs.
3 6 9 20 30 40

...Special Album Edition 1(Summer, '74)-Iron Fist-c/story (early app., 3rd?); 10 pgs. Adams-i; Shang Chi/Fu Manchu, 10 pgs.; Sons of Tiger, 11 pgs.; TV Kung Fu, 6 pgs. photos/article
4 8 12 22 34 45

NOTE: ***Bruce Lee:*** *1-7, 14, 15, 17, 25, 26, 28.* ***Kung Fu (TV):*** *1, 2, 4.* ***Jack of Hearts****: 22, 23, 29-33.* ***Shang Chi Master of Kung Fu****: 1-9, 11-18, 29, 31, 33.* ***Sons of Tiger:*** *1, 3, 4, 6-14, 16-19.* ***Swordquest:*** *25-27, 29-33.* ***White Tiger:*** *19-24, 26, 27, 29-33.* ***N. Adams*** *a-1i(part), 27i; c-1, 2-4, 11, 12, 14, 17.* ***Giffen*** *a-22p, 24p.* ***G. Kane*** *a-23p.* ***Kirby*** *a-5r.* ***Nasser*** *a-27p, 28.* ***Perez*** *a(p)-6-14, 16, 17, 19, 21.* ***Rogers*** *a-26, 32, 33.* ***Starlin*** *a-1, 2r, 15r.* ***Staton*** *a-28p, 31, 32.*

DEADMAN (See The Brave and the Bold & Phantom Stranger #39)
DC Comics: May, 1985 - No. 7, Nov, 1985 ($1.75, Baxter paper)

1-7: 1-Deadman-r by Infantino, N. Adams in all. 5-Batman-c/story-r/Strange Adventures. 7-Batman-r 3.00

DEADMAN
DC Comics: Mar, 1986 - No. 4, June, 1986 (75¢, limited series)

1-4: Lopez-c/a. 4-Byrne-c(p) 3.00

DEADMAN
DC Comics: Feb, 2002 - No. 9, Oct, 2002 ($2.50)

1-9: 1-4-Vance-s/Beroy-a. 3,4-Mignola-c. 5,6-Garcia-Lopez-a 2.50

DEADMAN
DC Comics (Vertigo): Oct, 2006 - No. 13, Oct, 2007 ($2.99)

1-13: 1-Bruce Jones-s/John Watkiss-a/c; intro Brandon Cayce 3.00
...: Deadman Walking TPB (2007, $9.99) r/#1-5 10.00

DEADMAN: DEAD AGAIN (Leads into 2002 series)
DC Comics: Oct, 2001 - No. 5, Oct, 2001 ($2.50, weekly limited series)

1-5: Deadman at the deaths of the Flash, Robin, Superman, Hal Jordan 2.50

DEADMAN: EXORCISM
DC Comics: 1992 - No. 2, 1992 ($4.95, limited series, 52 pgs.)

1,2: Kelley Jones-c/a in both 5.00

DEADMAN: LOVE AFTER DEATH
DC Comics: 1989 - No. 2, 1990 ($3.95, 52 pgs., limited series, mature)

GD VG FN VF VF/NM NM-
2.0 4.0 6.0 8.0 9.0 9.2

Book One, Two: Kelley Jones-c/a in both. 1-contains nudity 4.00

DEAD OF NIGHT
Marvel Comics Group: Dec, 1973 - No. 11, Aug, 1975

1-Horror reprints 3 6 9 17 25 32
2-10: 10-Kirby-a. 6-Jack the Ripper-c/s 2 4 6 11 16 20
11-Intro Scarecrow; Kane/Wrightson-c 3 6 9 21 32 42
NOTE: ***Ditko*** *r-7, 10.* ***Everett*** *c-2.* ***Sinnott*** *r-1.*

DEAD OF NIGHT FEATURING DEVIL-SLAYER
Marvel Comics (MAX): Nov, 2008 - No. 4, Feb, 2009 ($3.99, limited series)

1-4-Keene-s/Samnee-a/Andrews-c 4.00

DEAD OF NIGHT FEATURING MAN-THING
Marvel Comics (MAX): Apr, 2008 - No. 4, July, 2008 ($3.99, limited series)

1-4: 1-Man-Thing origin re-told; Kano-a. 2-4-Jennifer Kale app. 4.00

DEAD OF NIGHT FEATURING WEREWOLF BY NIGHT
Marvel Comics (MAX): Mar, 2009 - No. 4, Jun, 2009 ($3.99, limited series)

1-4: 1-Werewolf By Night origin re-told; Swierczynski-s/Suayan-a 4.00

DEAD OR ALIVE - A CYBERPUNK WESTERN
Image Comics (Shok Studio): Apr, 1998 - No. 4, July, 1998 ($2.50, limited series)

1-4 3.00

DEADPOOL (See New Mutants #98 for 1st app.)
Marvel Comics: Aug, 1994 - No. 4, Nov, 1994 ($2.50, limited series)

1-4: Mark Waid's 1st Marvel work; Ian Churchill-c/a 4.00

DEADPOOL (... : Agent of Weapon X on cover #57-60) (title becomes Agent X)
Marvel Comics: Jan, 1997 - No. 69, Sept, 2002 ($2.95/$1.95/$1.99)

1-($2.95)-Wraparound-c 1 2 3 4 5 7
2-Begin-$1.95-c. 5.00
3-10,12-22,24: 4-Hulk-c/app. 12-Variant-c. 14-Begin McDaniel-a. 22-Cable app. 5.00
11-($3.99)-Deadpool replaces Spider-Man from Amazing Spider-Man #47; Kraven, Gwen Stacy app. 6.00
23,25-($2.99); 23-Dead Reckoning pt. 1; wraparound-c 4.00
26-40: 27-Wolverine-c/app. 37-Thor app. 3.00
41-53,56-60: 41-Begin $2.25-c. 44-Black Panther-c/app. 46-49-Chadwick-a 51-Cover swipe of Detective #38. 57-60-BWS-c 3.00
54,55-Punisher-c/app. 54-Dillon-c. 55-Bradstreet-c 3.00
61-69: 61-64-Funeral For a Freak on cover. 65-69-Udon Studios-a. 67-Dazzler-c/app. 2.50
#(-1) Flashback (7/97) Lopresti-a; Wade Wilson's early days 3.00
.../Death '98 Annual ($2.99) Kelly-s, ... Team-Up (12/98, $2.99) Widdle Wade-c/app., Baby's First Deadpool Book (12/98, $2.99), Encyclopædia Deadpoolica (12/98, $2.99) Synopses 3.00
.../GLI - Summer Fun Spectacular #1 (9/07, $3.99) short stories; Pelletier-c 4.00
... Classic Vol. 1 TPB (2008, $29.99) r/#1, New Mutants #98, Deadpool: The Circle Chase #1-4 and Deadpool (1994 series) #1-4 30.00
Mission Improbable TPB (9/98, $14.95) r/#1-5 15.00
Wizard #0 ('98, bagged with Wizard #87) 2.50

DEADPOOL
Marvel Comics: Nov, 2008 - Present ($3.99/$2.99)

1-($3.99) Medina-a; Secret Invasion x-over; 2 covers by Crain & Liefeld 4.00
2-20-($2.99) Variant covers for most. 4-20-Pearson-c. 8,9-Thunderbolts x-over. 10-Dark Reign. 16-18-X-Men app. 19-Spider-Man & Hit-Monkey app. 3.00
900-(12/09, $4.99) Stories by various incl. Liefeld, Baker; wraparound-c by Johnson 5.00
...: Games of Death 1 (5/09, $3.99) Benson-s/Crystal-a/Land-c 4.00

DEADPOOL: MERC WITH A MOUTH
Marvel Comics: Sept, 2009 - Present ($3.99/$2.99)

1-($3.99) Suydam-c/Dazo-a; Zombie-head Deadpool & Ka-Zar app.; r/Deadpool #4 ('97) 4.00
2-6,8,9-($2.99) Suydam zombie-c on all. 8-Deadpool goes to Zombie dimension 3.00
7-($3.99) Covers by Suydam & Liefeld; art by Liefeld, Baker, Pastoras, Dazo 4.00

DEADPOOL: SUICIDE KINGS
Marvel Comics: Jun, 2009 - No. 5, Oct, 2009 ($3.99, limited series)

1-5-Barberi-a; Punisher, Daredevil, & Spider-Man app. 4.00

DEADPOOL TEAM-UP
Marvel Comics: No. 899, Jan, 2010 - Present ($2.99, numbering runs in reverse)

899-895: 899-Hercules app.; Ramos-c. 897-Ghost Rider app. 3.00

DEADPOOL: THE CIRCLE CHASE (See New Mutants #98)
Marvel Comics: Aug, 1993 - No. 4, Nov, 1993 ($2.00, limited series)

1-($2.50)-Embossed-c 4.00
2-4 3.00

The Dead Who Walk © AVON

Deathblow #11 © WSP

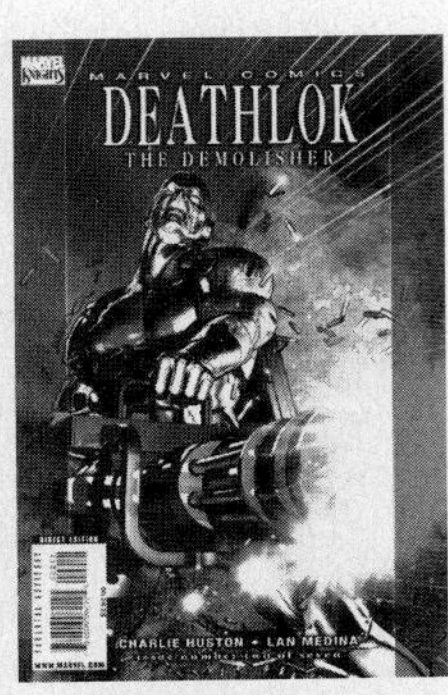

Deathlok (2009 series) #2 © MAR

	GD 2.0	VG 4.0	FN 6.0	VF 8.0	VF/NM 9.0	NM- 9.2

GD VG FN VF VF/NM NM-
2.0 4.0 6.0 8.0 9.0 9.2

DEAD RIDER (See Deadlander)

DEAD ROMEO
DC Comics: June, 2009 - No. 6, Nov, 2009 ($2.99, limited series)
1-6-Ryan Benjamin-a/Jesse Snider-s 3.00
TPB (2010, $19.99) r/#1-6; cover gallery 20.00

DEAD, SHE SAID
IDW Publishing: May, 2008 - No. 3, Sept, 2008 ($3.99, limited series)
1-3-Bernie Wrightson-a/Steve Niles-s 4.00

DEADSHOT (See Batman #59, Detective Comics #474, & Showcase '93 #8)
DC Comics: Nov, 1988 - No. 4, Feb, 1989 ($1.00, limited series)
1-4 2.50

DEADSHOT
DC Comics: Feb, 2005 - No. 5, June 2005 ($2.95, limited series)
1-5-Zeck-c/Gage-s/Cummings-a. 3-Green Arrow app. 3.00

DEAD SPACE (Based on the Electronics Arts videogame)
Image Comics: Mar, 2008 - No. 6, Sept, 2008 ($2.99, limited series)
1-6-Templesmith-a/Johnston-s 3.00
... Extraction (9/09, $3.50) Templesmith-a/Johnston-s 3.50

DEAD WHO WALK, THE (See Strange Mysteries, Super Reprint #15, 16)
Realistic Comics: 1952 (one-shot)
nn 54 108 162 338 574 810

DEADWORLD (Also see The Realm)
Arrow Comics/Caliber Comics: Dec, 1986 - No. 26 ($1.50/$1.95/#15-28: $2.50, B&W)
1-4 4.00
5-26-Graphic cover version 4.00
5-26-Tame cover version 3.00
...Archives 1-3 (1992, $2.50) 3.00

DEAN MARTIN & JERRY LEWIS (See Adventures of...)

DEAR BEATRICE FAIRFAX
Best/Standard Comics (King Features): No. 5, Nov, 1950 - No. 9, Sept, 1951
(Vern Greene art)
5-All have Schomburg air brush-c 13 26 39 74 105 135
6-9 9 18 27 52 69 85

DEAR HEART (Formerly Lonely Heart)
Ajax: No. 15, July, 1956 - No. 16, Sept, 1956
15,16 7 14 21 37 46 55

DEAR LONELY HEART (...Illustrated No. 1-6)
Artful Publications: Mar, 1951; No. 2, Oct, 1951 - No. 8, Oct, 1952
1 17 34 51 98 154 210
2 10 20 30 54 72 90
3-Matt Baker Jungle Girl story 20 40 60 114 182 250
4-8 9 18 27 50 65 80

DEAR LONELY HEARTS (Lonely Heart #9 on)
Harwell Publ./Mystery Publ. Co. (Comic Media): Aug, 1953 -No. 8, Oct, 1954
1 13 26 39 74 105 135
2-8 9 18 27 52 69 85

DEARLY BELOVED
Ziff-Davis Publishing Co.: Fall, 1952
1-Photo-c 17 34 51 100 158 215

DEAR NANCY PARKER
Gold Key: June, 1963 - No. 2, Sept, 1963
1-Painted-c on both 4 8 12 23 36 48
2 3 6 9 17 25 32

DEATH, THE ABSOLUTE... (From Neil Gaiman's Sandman titles)
DC Comics (Vertigo): 2009 ($99.99, oversized hardcover in slipcase)
nn-Reprints 1st app. in Sandman #8, Sandman #20, Death: The High Cost of Living #1-3, Death: the Time of Your Life #1-3, Death Talks About Life; short stories and pin-ups; merchandise pics; script and sketch art for Sandman #8; Gaiman afterword 100.00

DEATH: AT DEATH'S DOOR (See Sandman: The Season of Mists)
DC Comics (Vertigo): 2003 ($9.95, graphic novel one-shot, B&W, 7-1/2" x 5")
1-Jill Thompson-s/a/c; manga-style; Morpheus and the Endless app. 10.00

DEATHBLOW (Also see Batman/Deathblow and Darker Image)
Image Comics (WildStorm Productions): May (Apr. inside), 1993 - No. 29, Aug, 1996
($1.75/$1.95/$2.50)
0-(8/96, $2.95, 32 pgs.)-r/Darker Image w/new story & art; Jim Lee & Trevor Scott-a; new Jim Lee-c 3.00
1-($2.50)-Red foil stamped logo on black varnish-c; Jim Lee-c/a; flip-book side has Cybernary -c/story (#2 also) 3.00
1-($1.95)-Newsstand version w/o foil-c & varnish 2.50
2-29: 2-(8/93)-Lee-a; with bound-in poster. 2-($1.75)-Newsstand version w/o poster. 4-Jim Lee-c/Tim Sale-a begin. 13-W/pinup poster by Tim Sale & Jim Lee. 16-($1.95 Newsstand & $2.50 Direct Market editions)-Wildstorm Rising Pt. 6. 17-Variant "Chicago Comicon" edition exists. 20,21-Gen 13 app. 23-Backlash-c/app. 24,25-Grifter-c/app; Gen 13 & Dane from Wetworks app. 28-Deathblow dies. 29-Memorial issue 2.50
5-Alternate Portacio-c (Forms larger picture when combined with alternate-c for Gen 13 #5, Kindred #3, Stormwatch #10, Team 7 #1, Union #0, Wetworks #2 & WildC.A.T.S #11) 6.00
...:Sinners and Saints TPB ('99, $19.95) r/#1-12; Sale-c 20.00

DEATHBLOW (Volume 2)
DC Comics (WildStorm): Dec, 2006 - No. 9, Apr, 2008 ($2.99)
1-9: 1-Azzarello-s/D'Anda-a; two covers by D'Anda & Platt 3.00
...: And Then You Live! TPB (2008, $19.99) r/#1-9 20.00

DEATHBLOW BY BLOWS
DC Comics (WildStorm): Nov, 1999 - No. 3, Jan, 2000 ($2.95, limited series)
1-3-Alan Moore-s/Jim Baikie-a 3.00

DEATHBLOW/WOLVERINE
Image Comics (WildStorm Productions)/ Marvel Comics: Sept, 1996 - No. 2, Feb, 1997 ($2.50, limited series)
1,2: Wiesenfeld-s/Bennett-a 2.50
TPB (1997, $8.95) r/#1,2 9.00

DEATHDEALER (Also see Frank Frazetta's...)
Verotik: July, 1995 - No. 4, July, 1997 ($5.95)
1-Frazetta-c; Bisley-a 1 2 3 5 6 8
1-2nd print, 2-4-($6.95)-Frazetta-c; embossed logo 1 2 3 4 5 7

DEATH-DEFYING 'DEVIL, THE (Also see Project Superpowers)
Dynamite Entertainment: 2008 - No. 4, 2009 ($3.50, limited series)
1-4-Casey & Ross-s/Salazar-a; multiple covers; the Dragon app. 3.50

DEATH, JR.
Image Comics: Apr, 2005 - No. 3, Aug, 2005 ($4.99, squarebound, limited series)
1-3-Gary Whitta-s/Ted Naifeh-a 5.00
Vol. 1 TPB (2005, $14.99) r/series; concept and promotional art 15.00

DEATH, JR. (Volume 2)
Image Comics: Jul, 2006 - No. 3, May, 2007 ($4.99, squarebound, limited series)
1-3-Gary Whitta-s/Ted Naifeh-a. 1-Dan Brereton-c 5.00
Vol. 2 TPB (2007, $14.99) r/series; Halloween story w/Guy Davis-a; promotional art 15.00

DEATHLOK (Also see Astonishing Tales #25)
Marvel Comics: July, 1990 - No. 4, Oct, 1990 ($3.95, limited series, 52 pgs.)
1-4: 1,2-Guice-a(p). 3,4-Denys Cowan-a, c-4 4.00

DEATHLOK
Marvel Comics: July, 1991 - No. 34, Apr, 1994 ($1.75)
1-Silver ink cover; Denys Cowan-c/a(p) begins 3.00
2-18,20-24,26-34: 2-Forge (X-Men) app. 3-Vs. Dr. Doom. 5-X-Men & F.F. x-over. 6,7-Punisher x-over. 9,10-Ghost Rider-c/story. 16-Infinity War x-over. 17-Jae Lee-c. 22-Black Panther app. 27-Siege app. 2.50
19-($2.25)-Foil-c 3.00
25-($2.95, 52 pgs.)-Holo-grafx foil-c 3.00
Annual 1 (1992, $2.25, 68 pgs.)-Guice-p; Quesada-c(p) 3.00
Annual 2 (1993, $2.95, 68 pgs.)-Bagged w/card; intro Tracer 3.00
NOTE: ***Denys Cowan** a(p)-9-13, 15, Annual 1; c-9-12, 13p, 14. **Guice/Cowan** c-8.*

DEATHLOK
Marvel Comics: Sept, 1999 - No. 11, June, 2000 ($1.99)
1-11: 1-Casey-s/Manco-a. 2-Two covers. 4-Canete-a 2.50

DEATHLOK (... The Demolisher on cover)
Marvel Comics: Jan, 2010 - No. 7 ($3.99, limited series)
1-5-Huston-s/Medina-a/Peterson-c 4.00

DEATHLOK SPECIAL
Marvel Comics: May, 1991 - No. 4, June, 1991 ($2.00, bi-weekly lim. series)
1-4: r/1-4(1990) w/new Guice-c #1,2; Cowan c-3,4 2.50
1-2nd printing w/white-c 2.50

DEATHMASK

Death of the New Gods #1 © DC

Deathstroke the Terminator #21 © DC

Deathwish #3 © Milestone

	GD	VG	FN	VF	VF/NM	NM-
	2.0	4.0	6.0	8.0	9.0	9.2

Future Comics: Mar, 2003 - No. 3, June, 2003 ($2.99)
1-3-Giordano-a(p)/Michelinie & Layton-s 3.00

DEATHMATE
Valiant (Prologue/Yellow/Blue)/Image Comics (Black/Red/Epilogue): Sept, 1993 - Epilogue (#6), Feb, 1994 ($2.95/$4.95, limited series)
Preview-(7/93, 8 pgs.) 2.25
Prologue (#1)–Silver foil; Jim Lee/Layton-c; B. Smith/Lee-a; Liefeld-a(p) 3.00
Prologue–Special gold foil ed. of silver ed. 4.00
Black (#2)-(9/93, $4.95, 52 pgs.)-Silvestri/Jim Lee-c; pencils by Peterson/Silvestri/Capullo/Jim Lee/Portacio; 1st story app. Gen 13 telling their rebellion against the Troika (see WildC.A.T.S. Trilogy) 6.00
Black-Special gold foil edition 7.00
Yellow (#3)-(10/93, $4.95, 52 pgs)-Yellow foil-c; Indicia says Prologue Sept 1993 by mistake; 3rd app. Ninjak; Thibert-c(i) 5.00
Yellow-Special gold foil edition 6.00
Blue (#4)-(10/93, $4.95, 52 pgs.)-Thibert blue foil-c(i); Reese-a(i) 5.00
Blue-Special gold foil edition 6.00
Red (#5), Epilogue (#6)-(2/94, $2.95)-Silver foil Quesada/Silvestri-c; Silvestri-a(p) 3.00

DEATH METAL
Marvel Comics UK: Jan, 1994 - No. 4, Apr, 1994 ($1.95, limited series)
1-4: 1-Silver ink-c. Alpha Flight app. 2.50

DEATH METAL VS. GENETIX
Marvel Comics UK: Dec, 1993 - No. 2, Jan, 1994 (Limited series)
1-($2.95)-Polybagged w/2 trading cards 3.00
2-($2.50)-Polybagged w/2 trading cards 2.50

DEATH OF CAPTAIN MARVEL (See Marvel Graphic Novel #1)

DEATH OF MR. MONSTER, THE (See Mr. Monster #8)

DEATH OF SUPERMAN (See Superman, 2nd Series)

DEATH OF THE NEW GODS (Tie-in to the Countdown series)
DC Comics: Early Dec, 2007 - No. 8, Jun, 2008 ($3.50, limited series)
1-8-Jim Starlin-s/a/c. 1-Barda killed. 6-Orion dies. 7-Scott Free and Metron die 3.50
TPB (2009, $19.99) r/#1-8; Starlin intro.; cover gallery 20.00

DEATH RACE 2020
Roger Corman's Cosmic Comics: Apr, 1995 - No. 8, Nov, 1995 ($2.50)
1-8: Sequel to the Movie 2.50

DEATH RATTLE (Formerly an Underground)
Kitchen Sink Press: V2#1, 10/85 - No. 18, 1988, 1994 ($1.95, Baxter paper, mature); V3#1, 11/95 - No. 5, 6/96 ($2.95, B&W)
V2#1-7,9-18: 1-Corben-c. 2-Unpubbed Spirit story by Eisner. 5-Robot Woman-r by Wolverton. 6-B&W issues begin. 10-Savage World-r by by Williamson/Torres/ Krenkel/Frazetta from Witzend #1. 16-Wolverton Spacehawk-r 5.00

	GD	VG	FN	VF	VF/NM	NM-
8-(12/86)-1st app. Mark Schultz's Xenozoic Tales/Cadillacs & Dinosaurs	2	4	6	8	10	12

8-(1994)-r plus interview w/Mark Schultz 3.50
V3#1-5 ($2.95-c) 3.50

DEATH'S HEAD (See Daredevil #56, Dragon's Claws #5 & Incomplete…)(See Amazing Fantasy (2004) for Death's Head 3.0)
Marvel Comics: Dec, 1988 - No. 10, Sept, 1989 ($1.75)
1-Dragon's Claws spin-off 3.00
2-Fantastic Four app.; Dragon's Claws x-over 3.00
3-10: 8-Dr. Who app. 9-F. F. x-over; Simonson-c(p) 2.50

DEATH'S HEAD II (Also see Battletide)
Marvel Comics UK, Ltd.: Mar, 1992 - No. 4, June (May inside), 1992 ($1.75, color, lim. series)
1-4: 2-Fantastic Four app. 4-Punisher, Spider-Man, Daredevil, Dr. Strange, Capt. America & Wolverine in the year 2020 2.50
1,2-Silver ink 2nd printiings 2.50

DEATH'S HEAD II (Also see Battletide)
Marvel Comics UK, Ltd.: Dec, 1992 - No. 16, Mar, 1994 ($1.75/$1.95)
V2#1-13,15,16: 1-Gatefold-c. 1-4-X-Men app.15-Capt. America & Wolverine app. 2.50
14-($2.95)-Foil flip-c w/Death's Head II Gold #0 3.00
...Gold 1 (1/94, $3.95, 68 pgs.)-Gold foil-c 4.00

DEATH'S HEAD II & THE ORIGIN OF DIE CUT
Marvel Comics UK, Ltd.: Aug, 1993 - No. 2, Sept, 1993 (limited series)
1-($2.95)-Embossed-c 3.00
2 ($1.75) 2.50

DEATHSTROKE: THE TERMINATOR (Deathstroke: The Hunted #0-47; Deathstroke #48-60)
(Also see Marvel & DC Present, New Teen Titans #2, New Titans, Showcase '93 #7,9 & Tales of the Teen Titans #42-44)
DC Comics: Aug, 1991 - No. 60, June, 1996 ($1.75-$2.25)
1-New Titans spin-off; Mike Zeck c-1-28 4.00
1-Gold ink 2nd printing ($1.75) 2.50
2 3.00
3-40,0(10/94),41(11/94)-49,51-60: 6,8-Batman cameo. 7,9-Batman-c/story. 9-1st brief app. new Vigilante (female). 10-1st full app. new Vigilante; Perez-i. 13-Vs. Justice League; Team Titans cameo on last pg. 14-Total Chaos, part 1; TeamTitans-c/story cont'd in New Titans #90. 40-(9/94). 0-(10/94)-Begin Deathstroke, The Hunted, ends #47. 2.50
50 ($3.50) 3.50
Annual 1-4 ('92-'95, 68 pgs.): 1-Nightwing & Vigilante app.; minor Eclipso app. 2-Bloodlines Deathstorm; 1st app. Gunfire. 3-Elseworlds story. 4-Year One story 4.00
NOTE: *Golden a-12. Perez a-11i. Zeck c-Annual 1, 2.*

DEATH: THE HIGH COST OF LIVING (See Sandman #8) (Also see the Books of Magic limited & ongoing series)
DC Comics (Vertigo): Mar, 1993 - No. 3, May, 1993 ($1.95, limited series)
1-Bachalo/Buckingham-a; Dave McKean-c; Neil Gaiman scripts in all 6.00
1-Platinum edition 40.00
2 3.50
3-Pgs. 19 & 20 had wrong placement 3.00
3-Corrected version w/pgs. 19 & 20 facing each other; has no-c & ads for Sebastion O & The Geek added 4.00
Death Talks About Life-giveaway about AIDS prevention 5.00
Hardcover (1994, $19.95)-r/#1-3 & Death Talks About Life; intro. by Tori Amos 20.00
Trade paperback (6/94, $12.95, Titan Books)-r/#1-3 & Death Talks About Life; prism-c 13.00

DEATH: THE TIME OF YOUR LIFE (See Sandman #8)
DC Comics (Vertigo): Apr, 1996 - No. 3, July, 1996 ($2.95, limited series)
1-3: Neil Gaiman story & Bachalo/Buckingham-a; Dave McKean-c. 2-(5/96) 3.00
Hardcover (1997, $19.95)-r/#1-3 w/3 new pages & gallery art by various 20.00
TPB (1997, $12.95)-r/#1-3 & Visions of Death gallery; Intro. by Claire Danes 13.00

DEATH 3
Marvel Comics UK: Sept, 1993 - No. 4, Dec, 1993 ($1.75, limited series)
1-($2.95)-Embossed-c 3.00
2-4 2.50

DEATH VALLEY (Cowboys and Indians)
Comic Media: Oct, 1953 - No. 6, Aug, 1954

	GD	VG	FN	VF	VF/NM	NM-
1-Billy the Kid; Morisi-a; Andru/Esposito-c/a	18	36	54	107	169	230
2-Don Heck-c	12	24	36	67	94	120
3-6: 3,5-Morisi-a. 5-Discount-a	11	22	33	62	86	110

DEATH VALLEY (Becomes Frontier Scout, Daniel Boone No.10-13)
Charlton Comics: No. 7, 6/55 - No. 9, 10/55 (Cont'd from Comic Media series)

	GD	VG	FN	VF	VF/NM	NM-
7-9: 8-Wolverton-a (half pg.)	9	18	27	50	65	80

DEATHWISH
DC Comics (Milestone Media): Dec, 1994 - No. 4, Mar, 1995 (2.50, lim. series)
1-4 2.50

DEATH WRECK
Marvel Comics UK: Jan, 1994 - No. 4, Apr, 1994 ($1.95, limited series)
1-4: 1-Metallic ink logo; Death's Head II app. 2.50

DEBBIE DEAN, CAREER GIRL
Civil Service Publ.: April, 1945 - No. 2, July, 1945

	GD	VG	FN	VF	VF/NM	NM-
1,2-Newspaper reprints by Bert Whitman	14	28	42	76	108	140

DEBBI'S DATES (Also see Date With Debbi)
National Periodical Publications: Apr-May, 1969 - No. 11, Dec-Jan, 1970-71

	GD	VG	FN	VF	VF/NM	NM-
1	6	12	18	41	66	90
2,3,5,7-11: 2-Last 12¢ issue	4	8	12	22	34	45
4-Neal Adams text illo	4	8	12	26	41	55
6-Superman cameo	6	12	18	39	62	85

DECADE OF DARK HORSE, A
Dark Horse Comics: Jul, 1996 - No. 4, Oct, 1996 ($2.95, B&W/color, lim. series)
1-4: 1-Sin City-c/story by Miller; Grendel by Wagner; Predator. 2-Star Wars wraparound-c. 3-Aliens-c/story; Nexus, Mask stories 3.00

DECAPITATOR (Randy Bowen's...)
Dark Horse Comics: Jun, 1998 - No. 4, ($2.95)
1-4-Bowen-s/art by various. 1-Mahnke-c. 3-Jones-c 4.00

DECEPTION, THE

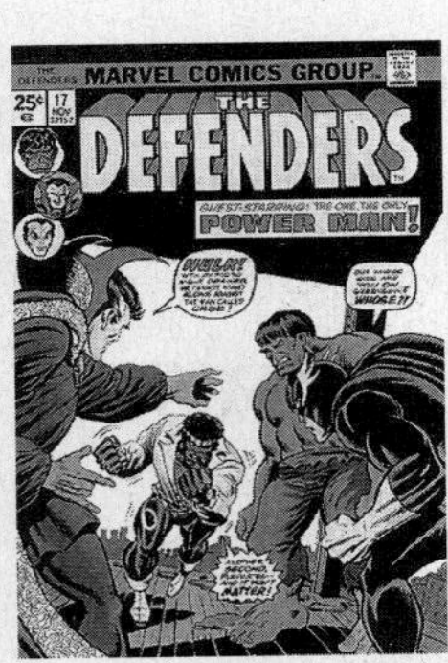

The Defenders #17 © MAR

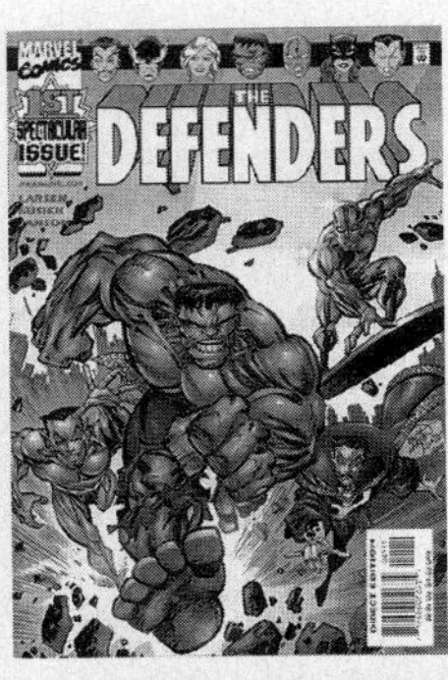

The Defenders V2 #1 © MAR

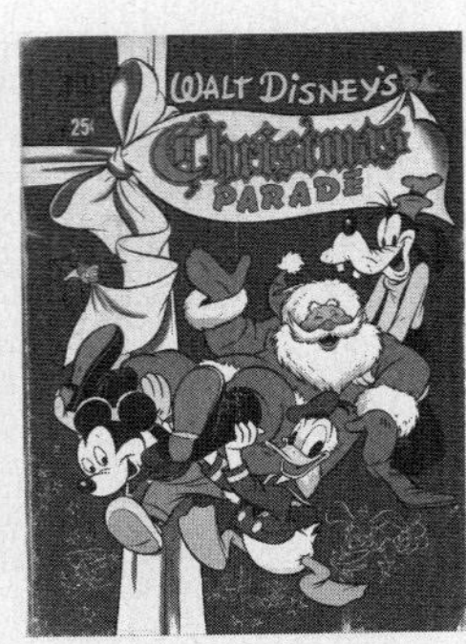

Dell Giant - Christmas Parade #2 © DIS

	GD 2.0	VG 4.0	FN 6.0	VF 8.0	VF/NM 9.0	NM- 9.2

Image Comics (Flypaper Press): 1999 - No. 3, 1999 ($2.95, B&W, mini-series)

	GD	VG	FN	VF	VF/NM	NM-
1-3-Horley painted-c						3.00

DECIMATION: THE HOUSE OF M
Marvel Comics: Jan, 2006 ($3.99)

	GD	VG	FN	VF	VF/NM	NM-
... - The Day After (one-shot) Claremont-s/Green-a						4.00

DEEP, THE (Movie)
Marvel Comics Group: Nov, 1977 (Giant)

	GD	VG	FN	VF	VF/NM	NM-
1-Infantino-c/a	1	3	4	6	8	10

DEEP SLEEPER
Oni Press/Image Comics: Feb, 2004 - No. 4, Sept, 2004 ($3.50/$2.95, B&W, limited series)

	GD	VG	FN	VF	VF/NM	NM-
1,2-(Oni Press, $3.50)-Hester-s/Huddleston-a						3.50
3,4-(Image Comics, $2.95)						3.00
... Omnibus (Image, 8/04, $5.95) r/#1,2						6.00
... Vol. 1 TPB (2005, $12.95) r/#1-4; cover gallery						13.00

DEFCON 4
Image Comics (WildStorm Productions): Feb, 1996 - No. 4, Sept, 1996 ($2.50, lim. series)

	GD	VG	FN	VF	VF/NM	NM-
1/2	1	2	3	5	7	9
1/2 Gold-(1000 printed)						14.00
1-Main Cover by Mat Broome & Edwin Rosell						3.00
1-Hordes of Cymulants variant-c by Michael Golden						5.00
1-Backs to the Wall variant-c by Humberto Ramos & Alex Garner						5.00
1-Defcon 4-Way variant-c by Jim Lee	1	2	3	4	5	7
2-4						2.50

DEFENDERS, THE (TV)
Dell Publishing Co.: Sept-Nov, 1962 - No. 2, Feb-Apr, 1963

	GD	VG	FN	VF	VF/NM	NM-
12-176-211(#1)	4	8	12	26	41	55
12-176-304(#2)	3	6	9	21	32	42

DEFENDERS, THE (Also see Giant-Size..., Marvel Feature, Marvel Treasury Edition, Secret Defenders & Sub-Mariner #34, 35; The New...#140-on)
Marvel Comics Group: Aug, 1972 - No. 152, Feb, 1986

	GD	VG	FN	VF	VF/NM	NM-
1-The Hulk, Doctor Strange, Sub-Mariner begin	12	24	36	83	152	220
2-Silver Surfer x-over	7	14	21	45	73	100
3-5: 3-Silver Surfer x-over. 4-Valkyrie joins	5	10	15	30	48	65
6,7: 6-Silver Surfer x-over	3	6	9	20	30	40
8,9,11: 8-11-Defenders vs. the Avengers (Crossover with Avengers #115-118) 8,11-Silver Surfer x-over	4	8	12	26	41	55
10-Hulk vs. Thor battle	8	16	24	54	90	125
12-14: 12-Last 20¢ issue	2	4	6	13	18	22
15,16-Magneto & Brotherhood of Evil Mutants app. from X-Men	3	6	9	14	20	25
17-20: 17-Power Man x-over (11/74)	2	4	6	8	10	12
21-25: 24,25-Son of Satan app.	1	2	3	5	6	8
26-29-Guardians of the Galaxy app. (#26 is 8/75; pre-dates Marvel Presents #3): 28-1st full app. Starhawk (1st brief app. #27). 29-Starhawk joins Guardians	1	3	4	6	8	10
30-33,39-50: 31,32-Origin Nighthawk. 44-Hellcat joins. 45-Dr. Strange leaves. 47-49-Early Moon Knight app. (5/77). 48-50-(Reg. 30¢-c)						5.00
34-38-(Regular 25¢ editions): 35-Intro New Red Guardian						5.00
34-38-(30¢-c variants, limited distribution)(4-8/76)	3	6	9	20	30	40
48-52-(35¢-c variants, limited distribution)(6-10/77)	4	8	12	28	44	60
51-60: 51,52-(Reg. 30¢-c). 53-1st brief app. Lunatik (Lobo lookalike). 55-Origin Red Guardian; Lunatik cameo. 56-1st full Lunatik story						4.00
61-75: 61-Lunatik & Spider-Man app. 70-73-Lunatik (origin #71). 73-75-Foolkiller II app. (Greg Salinger). 74-Nighthawk resigns						3.00
76-93,95,97-99,102-119,123,124,126-149,151: 77-Origin Omega. 78-Original Defenders return thru #101. 104-The Beast joins. 105-Son of Satan joins. 106-Death of Nighthawk. 129-New Mutants cameo (3/84, early x-over)						2.50
94,101,120-122: 94-1st Gargoyle. 101-Silver Surfer-c & app. 120,121-Son of Satan-c/stories. 122-Final app. Son of Satan (2 pgs.)						4.00
96-Ghost Rider app.						4.00
100-(52 pgs.)-Hellcat (Patsy Walker) revealed as Satan's daughter						5.00
125,150: 125-(52 pgs.)-Intro new Defenders. 150-(52 pgs.)-Origin Cloud						4.00
152-(52 pgs.)-Ties in with X-Factor & Secret Wars II						4.00
Annual 1 (1976, 52 pgs.)-New book-length story	3	6	9	18	27	35

NOTE: ***Art Adams** c-142p. **Austin** a-53i; c-65i, 119i, 145i. **Frank Bolle** a-7i, 10i, 11i. **Buckler** c(p)-34, 38, 76, 77, 79-86, 90, 91. **J. Buscema** c-66. **Giffen** a-42-49p, 50, 51-54p. **Golden** a-53p, 54p; c-94, 96. **Guice** c-129. **G. Kane** c(p)-13, 16, 18, 19, 21-26, 31-33, 35-37, 40, 41, 52, 55. **Kirby** c-42-45. **Mooney** a-3i, 31-34i, 62i, 63i, 85i. **Nasser** c-88p. **Perez** c(p)-51, 53, 54. **Rogers** c-98. **Starlin** c-110. **Tuska** a-57p. Silver Surfer in No. 2, 3, 6, 8-11, 92, 98-101, 107, 112-115, 122-125.*

DEFENDERS, THE (Volume 2) (Continues in The Order)
Marvel Comics: Mar, 2001 - No. 12, Feb, 2002 ($2.99/$2.25)

	GD	VG	FN	VF	VF/NM	NM-
1-Busiek & Larsen-s/Larsen & Janson-a/c						3.00
2-11: 2-Two covers by Larsen & Art Adams; Valkyrie app. 4-Frenz-a						2.50
12-($3.50) 'Nuff Said issue; back-up-s Reis-a						3.50

DEFENDERS, THE
Marvel Comics: Sept, 2005 - No. 5, Jan, 2006 ($2.99, limited series)

	GD	VG	FN	VF	VF/NM	NM-
1-5-Giffen & DeMatteis-s/Maguire-a. 2-Dormammu app.						3.00
...: Indefensible HC (2006, $19.99, dust jacket) r/#1-5; Giffen & Maguire sketch page						20.00
...: Indefensible SC (2007, $13.99) r/#1-5; Giffen & Maguire sketch page						14.00

DEFENDERS OF DYNATRON CITY
Marvel Comics: Feb, 1992 - No. 6, July, 1992 ($1.25, limited series)

	GD	VG	FN	VF	VF/NM	NM-
1-6-Lucasarts characters. 2-Origin						3.00

DEFENDERS OF THE EARTH (TV)
Marvel Comics (Star Comics): Jan, 1987 - No. 4, July, 1987

	GD	VG	FN	VF	VF/NM	NM-
1-4: The Phantom, Mandrake The Magician, Flash Gordon begin. 3-Origin Phantom. 4-Origin Mandrake						4.00

DEFEX
Devil's Due Publ.: Oct, 2004 - No. 6, Apr, 2005 ($2.95)

	GD	VG	FN	VF	VF/NM	NM-
1-6: 1-Wolfman-s/Caselli-a. 6-Pérez-c						3.00

DEFIANCE
Image Comics: Feb, 2002 - No. 8, Jun, 2003 ($2.95)

	GD	VG	FN	VF	VF/NM	NM-
Preview Edition (12/01)						2.50
1-8-Barré-s/Kang & Suh-a						3.00

DEFINITIVE DIRECTORY OF THE DC UNIVERSE, THE (See Who's Who...)

DELECTA OF THE PLANETS (See Don Fortune & Fawcett Miniatures)

DELICATE CREATURES
Image Comics (Top Cow): 2001 ($16.95, hardcover with dust jacket)

	GD	VG	FN	VF	VF/NM	NM-
nn-Fairy tale storybook; J. Michael Straczynski-s; Michael Zulli-a						17.00

DELLA VISION (...The Television Queen) (Patty Powers #4 on)
Atlas Comics: April, 1955 - No. 3, Aug, 1955

	GD	VG	FN	VF	VF/NM	NM-
1-Al Hartley-c	15	30	45	92	144	195
2,3	11	22	33	62	86	110

DELL GIANT COMICS

Dell Publishing began to release square bound comics in 1949 with a 132-page issue called Christmas Parade #1. The covers were of a heavier stock to accommodate the increased number of pages. The books proved profitable at 25 cents, but the average number of pages was quickly reduced to 100. Ten years later they were converted to a numbering system similar to the Four Color Comics, for greater ease in distribution and the page counts cut back to mostly 84 pages. The label "Dell Giant" began to appear on the covers in 1954. Because of the size of the books and the heavier, less pliant cover stock, they are rarely found in high grade condition, and with the exception of a small quantity of copies released from Western Publishing's warehouse–are almost never found in near mint.

	GD	VG	FN	VF	VF/NM	NM-
Abraham Lincoln Life Story 1(3/58)	8	16	24	64	107	150
Bugs Bunny Christmas Funnies 1(11/50, 116pp)	19	38	57	152	261	370
...Christmas Funnies 2(11/51, 116pp)	11	22	33	88	157	225
...Christmas Funnies 3-5(11/52-11/54,)-Becomes Christmas Party #6	10	20	30	80	138	195
...Christmas Funnies 7-9(12/56-12/58)	9	18	27	72	124	175
...Christmas Party 6(11/55)-Formerly Bugs Bunny Christmas Funnies	9	18	27	72	124	175
...County Fair 1(9/57)	11	22	33	88	149	210
...Halloween Parade 1(10/53)	11	22	33	88	157	225
...Halloween Parade 2(10/54)-Trick 'N' Treat Halloween Fun #3 on	9	18	27	72	129	185
...Trick 'N' Treat Halloween Fun 3,4(10/55-10/56)-Formerly Halloween Parade #2	9	18	27	72	129	185
...Vacation Funnies 1(7/51, 112pp)	18	36	54	144	252	360
...Vacation Funnies 2('52)	13	26	39	104	180	255
...Vacation Funnies 3-5('53-'55)	10	20	30	80	138	195
...Vacation Funnies 6,7,9('56-'59)	9	18	27	72	124	175
...Vacation Funnies 8('58) 1st app. Beep Beep the Road Runner, Wile E. Coyote (1st meeting), Mathilda (Mrs. Beep Beep) and their 3 children who hatch from eggs; one month before Four Color #918	11	22	33	88	149	210
Cadet Gray of West Point 1(4/58)-Williamson-a, 10pgs.; Buscema-a; photo-c	8	16	24	64	107	150
Christmas In Disneyland 1(12/57)-Barks-a, 18 pgs.	25	50	75	200	350	500

Christmas Parade 1(11/49)(132 pgs.)(1st Dell Giant)-Donald Duck (25 pgs. by Barks, r-in G.K. Christmas Parade #5); Mickey Mouse & other film oriented stories; Cinderella (prior to

Dell Giant - Marge's Lulu and Tubby Halloween Fun #6 © M. Buell

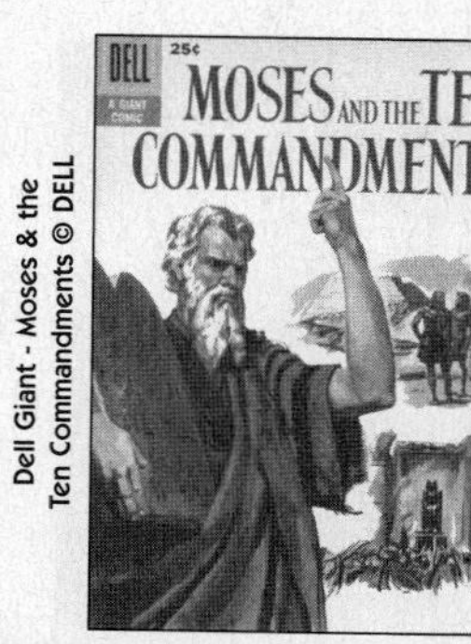

Dell Giant - Moses & the Ten Commandments © DELL

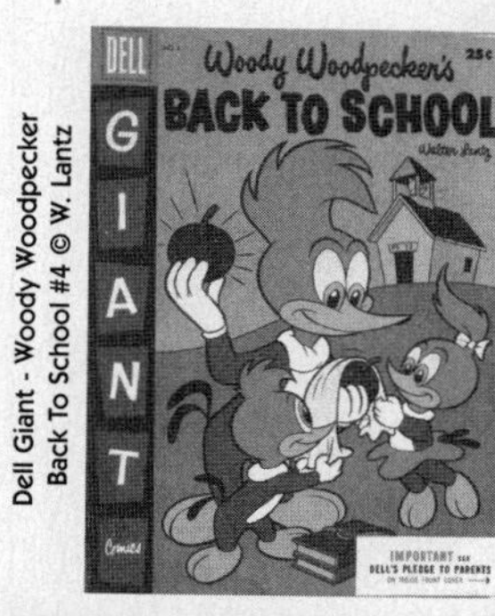

Dell Giant - Woody Woodpecker Back To School #4 © W. Lantz

	GD 2.0	VG 4.0	FN 6.0	VF 8.0	VF/NM 9.0	NM- 9.2
movie), 7 Dwarfs, Bambi & Thumper, So Dear To My Heart, Flying Mouse, Dumbo, Cookieland & others	63	126	189	504	877	1250
Christmas Parade 2('50)-Donald Duck (132 pgs.)(25 pgs. by Barks, r-in Gold Key's Christmas Parade #6). Mickey, Pluto, Chip & Dale, etc. Contents shift to a holiday expansion of W.D. C&S type format	42	84	126	336	588	840
Christmas Parade 3-7('51-'55, #3-116pgs; #4-7, 100 pgs.)	14	28	42	112	196	280
Christmas Parade 8(12/56)-Barks-a, 8 pgs.	22	44	66	176	306	435
Christmas Parade 9(12/58)-Barks-a, 20 pgs.	25	50	75	200	350	500
Christmas Treasury, A 1(11/54)	9	18	27	72	126	180
Davy Crockett, King Of The Wild Frontier 1(9/55)-Fess Parker photo-c; Marsh-a	19	38	57	152	269	385
Disneyland Birthday Party 1(10/58)-Barks-a, 16 pgs. r-by Gladstone	25	50	75	200	350	500
Donald and Mickey In Disneyland 1(5/58)	11	22	33	88	157	225
Donald Duck Beach Party 1(7/54)-Has an Uncle Scrooge story (not by Barks) that prefigures the later rivalry with Flintheart Glomgold and tells of Scrooge's wild rivalry with another millionaire	16	32	48	128	224	320
...Beach Party 2(1955)-Lady & Tramp	11	22	33	88	157	225
...Beach Party 3-5(1956-58)	11	22	33	88	152	215
...Beach Party 6(8/59, 84pp)-Stapled	8	16	24	64	115	165
Donald Duck Fun Book 1,2 (1953 & 10/54)-Games, puzzles, comics & cut-outs (very rare in unused condition)(most copies commonly have defaced interior pgs.)	63	126	189	504	877	1250
Donald Duck In Disneyland 1(9/55)-1st Disneyland Dell Giant	15	30	45	120	210	300
Golden West Rodeo Treasury 1(10/57)	10	20	30	80	135	190
Huey, Dewey and Louie Back To School 1(9/58)	9	18	27	72	126	180
Lady and The Tramp 1(6/55)	17	34	51	136	233	330
Life Stories of American Presidents 1(11/57)-Buscema-a	8	16	24	64	107	150
Lone Ranger Golden West 3(8/55)-Formerly Lone Ranger Western Treasury	18	36	54	144	255	365
Lone Ranger Movie Story nn(3/56)-Origin Lone Ranger in text; Clayton Moore photo-c	36	72	108	288	507	725
...Western Treasury 1(9/53)-Origin Lone Ranger, Silver, & Tonto; painted cover	23	46	69	184	325	465
...Western Treasury 2(8/54)-Becomes Lone Ranger Golden West #3	18	36	54	144	255	365
Marge's Little Lulu & Alvin Story Telling Time 1(3/59)-r/#2,5,3,11,30,10,21,17,8, 14,16; Stanley-a	14	28	42	112	196	280
...& Her Friends 4(3/56)-Tripp-a	14	28	42	112	191	270
...& Her Special Friends 3(3/55)-Tripp-a	15	30	45	120	210	300
...& Tubby At Summer Camp 5,2: 5(10/57)-Tripp-a. 2(10/58)-Tripp-a	13	26	39	104	182	260
...& Tubby Halloween Fun 6,2: 6(10/57)-Tripp-a. 2(10/58)-Tripp-a	13	26	39	104	182	260
...& Tubby In Alaska 1(7/59)-Tripp-a	13	26	39	104	177	250
...On Vacation 1(7/54)-r/4C-110,14,4C-146,5,4C-97,4,4C-158,3,1;Stanley-a	25	50	75	200	350	500
...& Tubby Annual 1(3/53)-r/4C-165,4C-74,4C-146,4C-97,4C-158, 4C-139, 4C-131; Stanley-a (1st Lulu Dell Giant)	30	60	90	240	420	600
...& Tubby Annual 2('54)-r/4C-139,6,4C-115,4C-74,5,4C-97,3,4C-146,18; Stanley-a	25	50	75	200	350	500
Marge's Tubby & His Clubhouse Pals 1(10/56)-1st app. Gran'pa Feeb;1st app. Janie; written by Stanley; Tripp-a	15	30	45	120	210	300
Mickey Mouse Almanac 1(12/57)-Barks-a, 8pgs.	27	54	81	216	378	540
...Birthday Party 1(9/53)-r/entire 48pgs. of Gottfredson's "Mickey Mouse in Love Trouble" from WDC&S 36-39. Quality equal to original. Also reprints one story each from Four Color 27, 79, & 181 plus 6 panels of highlights in the career of Mickey Mouse	31	62	93	248	434	620
...Club Parade 1(12/55)-r/4-Color 16 with some death trap scenes redrawn by Paul Murry & recolored with night turned into day; quality less than original	22	44	66	176	308	440
...In Fantasy Land 1(5/57)	13	26	39	104	180	255
...In Frontier Land 1(5/56)-Mickey Mouse Club iss.	13	26	39	104	180	255
...Summer Fun 1(8/58)-Mobile cut-outs on back-c; becomes Summer Fun with #2; Canadian version exists with 30¢-c price	13	26	39	104	180	255
Moses & The Ten Commandments 1(8/57)-Not based on movie; Dell's adaptation; Sekowsky-a; variant version has "Gods of Egypt" comic back-c	7	14	21	56	98	140
Nancy & Sluggo Travel Time 1(9/58)	8	16	24	64	115	165
Peter Pan Treasure Chest 1(1/53, 212pp)-Disney; contains 54-page movie adaptation & other Peter Pan stories; plus Donald & Mickey stories w/P. Pan; a 32-page retelling of "D. Duck Finds Pirate Gold" with yellow beak, called "Capt. Hook & the Buried Treasure"						

	GD 2.0	VG 4.0	FN 6.0	VF 8.0	VF/NM 9.0	NM- 9.2
	125	250	375	1000	1750	2500
Picnic Party 6,7(7/55-6/56)(Formerly Vacation Parade)-Uncle Scrooge, Mickey & Donald	12	24	36	96	166	235
Picnic Party 8(7/57)-Barks-a, 6pgs	21	42	63	168	289	410
Pogo Parade 1(9/53)-Kelly-a(r-/Pogo from Animal Comics in this order: #11,13,21,14,27,16,23,9,18,15,17)	25	50	75	200	350	500
Raggedy Ann & Andy 1(2/55)	16	32	48	128	224	320
Santa Claus Funnies 1(11/52)-Dan Noonan -A Christmas Carol adaptation	9	18	27	72	126	180
Silly Symphonies 1(9/52)-Redrawing of Gotfredson's Mickey Mouse strip of "The Brave Little Tailor;" 2 Good Housekeeping pages (from 1943); Lady and the Two Siamese Cats, three years before "Lady & the Tramp;" a retelling of Donald Duck's first app. in "The Wise Little Hen" & other stories based on 1930's Silly Symphony cartoons	29	58	87	232	409	585
Silly Symphonies 2(9/53)-M. Mouse in "The Sorcerer's Apprentice", 2 Good Housekeeping pages (from 1944); The Pelican & the Snipe, Elmer Elephant, Peculiar Penguins, Little Hiawatha, & others	24	48	72	192	336	480
Silly Symphonies 3(2/54)-r/Mickey & The Beanstalk (4-Color #157, 39pgs.), Little Minnehaha, Pablo, The Flying Gauchito, Pluto, & Bongo, & 2 Good Housekeeping pages (1944)	20	40	60	160	275	390
Silly Symphonies 4(8/54)-r/Dumbo (4-Color 234), Morris The Midget Moose, The Country Cousin, Bongo, & Clara Cluck	20	40	60	160	275	390
Silly Symphonies 5-8: 5(2/55)-r/Cinderella (4-Color 272), Bucky Bug, Pluto, Little Hiawatha, The 7 Dwarfs & Dumbo, Pinocchio. 6(8/55)-r/Pinocchio (WDC&S 63), The 7 Dwarfs & Thumper (WDC&S 45), M. Mouse "Adventures With Robin Hood" (40 pgs.), Johnny Appleseed, Pluto & Peter Pan, & Bucky Bug; Cut-out on back-c. 7(2/57)-r/Reluctant Dragon, Ugly Duckling, M. Mouse & Peter Pan, Jiminy Cricket, Peter & The Wolf, Brer Rabbit, Bucky Bug; Cut-out on back-c. 8(2/58)-r/Thumper Meets The 7 Dwarfs (4-Color #19), Jiminy Cricket, Niok, Brer Rabbit; Cut-out on back-c	16	32	48	128	224	320
Silly Symphonies 9(2/59)-r/Paul Bunyan, Humphrey Bear, Jiminy Cricket, The Social Lion, Goliath II; cut-out on back-c	15	30	45	120	210	300
Sleeping Beauty 1(4/59)	25	50	75	200	350	500
Summer Fun 2(8/59, 84pp, stapled binding)(Formerly Mickey Mouse...)-Barks-a(2), 24 pgs.	24	48	72	192	336	480
Tarzan's Jungle Annual 1(8/52)-Lex Barker photo on-c of #1,2	15	30	45	120	210	300
...Annual 2(8/53)	11	22	33	88	152	215
...Annual 3-7('54-9/58)(two No. 5s)-Manning-a-No. 3,5-7; Marsh-a in No. 1-7 plus painted-c 1-7	9	18	27	72	124	175
Tom And Jerry Back To School 1(9/56) 2 different back-c, variant has "Apple for the Teacher" cut-out	12	24	36	96	168	240
...Picnic Time 1(7/58)	10	20	30	80	135	190
...Summer Fun 1(7/54)-Droopy written by Barks	15	30	45	120	205	290
...Summer Fun 2-4(7/55-7/57)	8	16	24	64	107	150
...Toy Fair 1(6/58)	9	18	27	72	126	180
...Winter Carnival 1(12/52)-Droopy written by Barks	20	40	60	160	280	400
...Winter Carnival 2(12/53)-Droopy written by Barks	16	32	48	128	224	320
...Winter Fun 3(12/54)	8	16	24	64	115	165
...Winter Fun 4-7(12/55-11/58)	7	14	21	56	101	145
Treasury of Dogs, A 1(10/56)	7	14	21	56	101	145
Treasury of Horses, A (9/55)	7	14	21	56	101	145
Uncle Scrooge Goes To Disneyland 1(8/57p)-Barks-a, 20 pgs. r-by Gladstone; 2 different back-c; variant shows 6 snapshots of Scrooge	26	52	78	208	359	510
Vacation In Disneyland 1(8/58)	11	22	33	88	157	225
Vacation Parade 1(7/50, 132pp)-Donald Duck & Mickey Mouse; Barks-a, 55 pgs.	93	186	276	744	1297	1850
Vacation Parade 2(7/51,116pp)	25	50	75	200	350	500
Vacation Parade 3-5(7/52-7/54)-Becomes Picnic Party No. 6 on. #4-Robin Hood Advs.	14	28	42	112	194	275
Western Roundup 1(6/52)-Photo-c; Gene Autry, Roy Rogers, Johnny Mack Brown, Rex Allen, & Bill Elliott begin; photo back-c begin, end No. 14,16,18	25	50	75	200	350	500
Western Roundup 2(2/53)-Photo-c	14	28	42	112	196	280
Western Roundup 3-5(7-9/53 - 1-3/54)-Photo-c	11	22	33	88	157	225
Western Roundup 6-10(4-6/54 - 4-6/55)-Photo-c	11	22	33	88	149	210
Western Roundup 11-17,25: 11-17-Photo-c; 11-13,16,17-Manning-a. 11-Flying A's Range Rider, Dale Evans begin	9	18	27	72	129	185
Western Roundup 18-Toth-a; last photo-c; Gene Autry ends	11	22	33	88	149	210
Western Roundup 19-24-Manning-a. 19-Buffalo Bill Jr. begins (7-9/57; early app.). 19,20,22-Toth-a. 21-Rex Allen, Johnny Mack Brown end. 22-Jace Pearson's Texas Rangers, Rin Tin Tin, Tales of Wells Fargo (2nd app., 4-6/58) & Wagon Train (2nd app.) begin	9	18	27	72	129	185

Dell Giant #35 © DIS

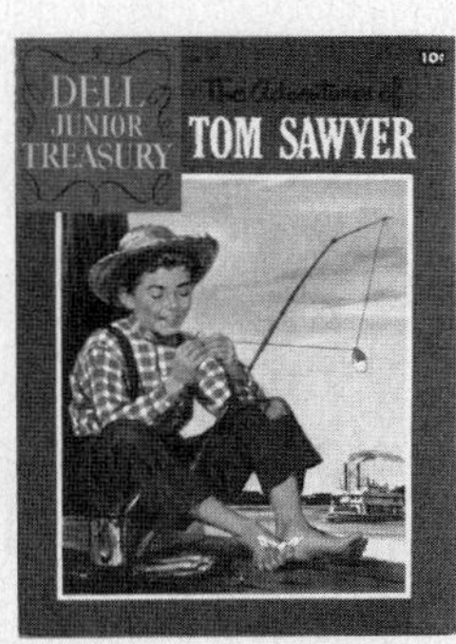

Dell Junior Treasury #10 © DELL

The Demon #5 © DC

	GD 2.0	VG 4.0	FN 6.0	VF 8.0	VF/NM 9.0	NM- 9.2

Woody Woodpecker Back To School 1(10/52) 10 20 30 80 140 200
...Back To School 2-4,6('53-10/57)-County Fair No. 5 8 16 24 64 112 160
...County Fair 5(9/56)-Formerly Back To School 8 16 24 64 112 160
...County Fair 2(11/58) 7 14 21 56 101 145

DELL GIANTS (Consecutive numbering)
Dell Publishing Co.: No. 21, Sept, 1959 - No. 55, Sept, 1961 (Most 84 pgs., 25¢)

21-(#1)-M.G.M.'s Tom & Jerry Picnic Time (84pp, stapled binding)-Painted-c
11 22 33 88 157 225
22-Huey, Dewey & Louie Back to School (Disney; 10/59, 84pp, square binding begins)
9 18 27 72 129 185
23-Marge's Little Lulu & Tubby Halloween Fun (10/59)-Tripp-a
12 24 36 96 168 240
24-Woody Woodpecker's Family Fun (11/59)(Walter Lantz)
8 16 24 64 112 160
25-Tarzan's Jungle World(11/59)-Marsh-a; painted-c 11 22 33 88 152 215
26-Christmas Parade(Disney; 12/59)-Barks-a, 16pgs.; Barks draws himself on wanted poster on pg. 13 21 42 63 168 289 410
27-Walt Disney's Man in Space (10/59) r-/4-Color 716,866, & 954 (100 pgs., 35¢)(TV)
9 18 27 72 129 185
28-Bugs Bunny's Winter Fun (2/60) 9 18 27 72 126 180
29-Marge's Little Lulu & Tubby in Hawaii (4/60)-Tripp-a
12 24 36 96 166 235
30-Disneyland USA(Disney; 6/60) 9 18 27 72 124 175
31-Huckleberry Hound Summer Fun (7/60)(TV)(HannaBarbera)-Yogi Bear & Pixie & Dixie app. 12 24 36 96 173 250
32-Bugs Bunny Beach Party 7 14 21 56 101 145
33-Daisy Duck & Uncle Scrooge Picnic Time (Disney; 9/60)
9 18 27 72 124 175
34-Nancy & Sluggo Summer Camp (8/60) 7 14 21 56 101 145
35-Huey, Dewey & Louie Back to School (Disney; 10/60)-1st app. Daisy Duck's Nieces, April, May & June 12 24 36 96 163 230
36-Marge's Little Lulu & Witch Hazel Halloween Fun (10/60)-Tripp-a
11 22 33 88 157 225
37-Tarzan, King of the Jungle (11/60)-Marsh-a; painted-c
9 18 27 72 129 185
38-Uncle Donald & His Nephews Family Fun (Disney; 11/60)-Cover painting based on a pencil sketch by Barks 12 24 36 96 173 250
39-Walt Disney's Merry Christmas (Disney; 12/60)-Cover painting based on a pencil sketch by Barks 12 24 36 96 173 250
40-Woody Woodpecker Christmas Parade (12/60)(Walter Lantz)
6 12 18 48 87 125
41-Yogi Bear's Winter Sports (12/60)(TV)(Hanna-Barbera)-Huckleberry Hound, Pixie & Dixie, Augie Doggie app. 12 24 36 96 173 250
42-Marge's Little Lulu & Tubby in Australia (4/61) 11 22 33 88 157 225
43-Mighty Mouse in Outer Space (5/61) 18 36 54 144 252 360
44-Around the World with Huckleberry and His Friends (7/61)(TV)(Hanna-Barbera)-Yogi Bear, Pixie & Dixie, Quick Draw McGraw, Augie Doggie app.; 1st app. Yakky Doodle
13 26 39 104 182 260
45-Nancy & Sluggo Summer Camp (8/61) 7 14 21 56 96 135
46-Bugs Bunny Beach Party (8/61) 7 14 21 56 96 135
47-Mickey & Donald in Vacationland (Disney; 8/61) 8 16 24 64 115 165
48-The Flintstones (No. 1)(Bedrock Bedlam)(7/61)(TV)(Hanna-Barbera) 1st app. in comics 19 38 57 152 269 385
49-Huey, Dewey & Louie Back to School (Disney; 9/61)
9 18 27 72 124 175
50-Marge's Little Lulu & Witch Hazel Trick 'N' Treat (10/61)
11 22 33 88 157 225
51-Tarzan, King of the Jungle by Jesse Marsh (11/61)-Painted-c
8 16 24 64 110 155
52-Uncle Donald & His Nephews Dude Ranch (Disney; 11/61)
8 16 24 64 115 165
53-Donald Duck Merry Christmas (Disney; 12/61) 8 16 24 64 112 160
54-Woody Woodpecker's Christmas Party (12/61)-Issued after No. 55
7 14 21 56 98 140
55-Daisy Duck & Uncle Scrooge Showboat (Disney; 9/61)
8 16 24 64 117 170

NOTE: All issues printed with & without ad on back cover.

DELL JUNIOR TREASURY
Dell Publishing Co.: June, 1955 - No. 10, Oct, 1957 (15¢) (All painted-c)

1-Alice in Wonderland; r/4-Color #331 (52 pgs.) 9 18 27 63 107 150
2-Aladdin & the Wonderful Lamp 7 14 21 49 80 110
3-Gulliver's Travels (1/56) 6 12 18 43 69 95
4-Adventures of Mr. Frog & Miss Mouse 7 14 21 45 73 100
5-The Wizard of Oz (7/56) 7 14 21 49 80 110
6-10: 6-Heidi (10/56). 7-Santa and the Angel. 8-Raggedy Ann and the Camel with the Wrinkled Knees. 9-Clementina the Flying Pig. 10-Adventures of Tom Sawyer
6 12 18 43 69 95

DEMOLITION MAN
DC Comics: Nov, 1993 - No. 4, Feb, 1994 ($1.75, color, limited series)

1-4-Movie adaptation 2.50

DEMON, THE (See Detective Comics No. 482-485)
National Periodical Publications: Aug-Sept, 1972 - V3#16, Jan, 1974

1-Origin; Kirby-c/a in all 7 14 21 45 73 100
2-5 4 8 12 24 37 50
6-16 3 6 9 18 27 35

DEMON, THE (1st limited series)(Also see Cosmic Odyssey #2)
DC Comics: Nov, 1986 - No. 4, Feb, 1987 (75¢, limited series)(#2 has #4 of 4 on-c)

1-4: Matt Wagner-a(p) & scripts in all. 4-Demon & Jason Blood become separate entities. 3.00

DEMON, THE (2nd Series)
DC Comics: July, 1990 - No. 58, May, 1995 ($1.50/$1.75/$1.95)

1-Grant scripts begin, ends #39: 1-4-Painted-c 4.00
2-18,20-27,29-39,41,42: 3,8-Batman app. (cameo #4). 12-Bisley painted-c. 12-15,21-Lobo app. (1 pg. cameo #11). 23-Robin app. 29-Superman app. 31,33-39-Lobo app. 2.50
19,28,40: 19-($2.50, 44 pgs.)-Lobo poster stapled inside. 28-Superman-c/story; begin $1.75-c. 40-Garth Ennis scripts begin 4.00
43-45-Hitman app. 1 2 3 5 7 9
46-48 Return of The Haunted Tank-c/s. 48-Begin $1.95-c. 5.00
49,51,0-(10/94),55-58: 51-(9/94) 2.50
50 ($2.95, 52 pgs.) 3.00
52-54-Hitman-s 5.00
Annual 1 (1992, $3.00, 68 pgs.)-Eclipso-c/story 3.00
Annual 2 (1993, $3.50, 68 pgs.)-1st app. of Hitman 2 4 6 9 13 16

NOTE: ***Alan Grant** scripts in #1-16, 20, 21, 23-25, 30-39, Annual 1. **Wagner** a/scripts-22.*

DEMON DREAMS
Pacific Comics: Feb, 1984 - No. 2, May, 1984

1,2-Mostly r-/Heavy Metal 2.50

DEMON: DRIVEN OUT
DC Comics: Nov, 2003 - No. 6, Apr, 2004 ($2.50, limited series)

1-6-Dysart-s/Mhan-a 2.50

DEMON-HUNTER
Seaboard Periodicals (Atlas): Sept, 1975

1-Origin/1st app. Demon-Hunter; Buckler-c/a 2 4 6 8 10 12

DEMON KNIGHT: A GRIMJACK GRAPHIC NOVEL
First Publishing: 1990 ($8.95, 52 pgs.)

nn-Flint Henry-a 9.00

DEMONWARS (R.A. Salvatore's...) ("The Demon Awakens" on cover)
Devil's Due Publishing: Jan, 2007 - No. 3, May, 2007 ($4.99/$5.50, limited series)

1-Daab-s/Seeley-a 5.00
2,3-($5.50) 5.50
Volume 2 (The Demon Spirit) (3/08 - Present, $5.50, B&W) 1-Balan-a 5.50

DEMONWARS: EYE FOR AN EYE (R.A. Salvatore's...)
CrossGeneration Comics (Code 6 Comics): Jun, 2003 - No. 5, Nov, 2003 ($2.95, lim. series)

1-5-Ciencin-s/Tocchini-a 3.00

DEMONWARS: TRIAL BY FIRE (R.A. Salvatore's...)
CrossGeneration Comics (Code 6 Comics): Jan, 2003 - No. 5, May, 2003 ($2.95, lim. series)

1-5-Ciencin-s/Wagner-a 3.00
TPB (2003, $9.95) r/#1-5; new short story by Salvatore 10.00

DENNIS THE MENACE (TV with 1959 issues) (Becomes ...Fun Fest Series; See The Best of... & The Very Best of...)(...Fun Fest on-c only to #156-166)
Standard Comics/Pines No.15-31/Hallden (Fawcett) No.32 on: 8/53 - #14, 1/56; #15, 3/56 - #31, 11/58; #32, 1/59 - #166, 11/79

1-1st app. Dennis, Mr. & Mrs. Wilson, Ruff & Dennis' mom & dad; Wiseman-a, written by Fred Toole-most issues 84 168 252 538 919 1300
2 35 70 105 208 339 470
3-10: 8-Last pre-code issue 20 40 60 114 182 250
11-20 14 28 42 80 115 150
21,23-30 10 20 30 58 79 100
22-1st app. Margaret w/blonde hair 13 26 39 74 105 135

Dennis the Menace #98 © FAW

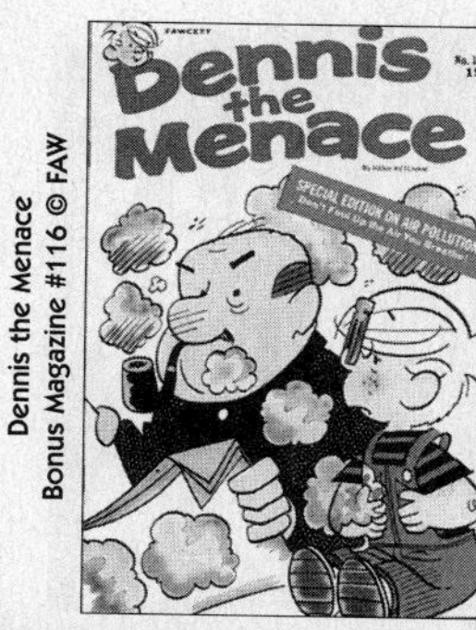

Dennis the Menace Bonus Magazine #116 © FAW

Deputy Dawg #1 © Terrytoons

	GD 2.0	VG 4.0	FN 6.0	VF 8.0	VF/NM 9.0	NM- 9.2
31-1st app. Joey	13	26	39	74	105	135
32-38,40(1/60): 37-A-Bomb blast panel	8	16	24	40	50	60
39-1st app. Gina (11/59)	9	18	27	47	61	75
41-60(7/62)	4	8	12	21	30	40
61-80(9/65),100(1/69)	3	6	9	14	19	24
81-99	2	4	6	11	16	20
101-117: 102-Last 12¢ issue	2	4	6	9	12	15
118(1/72)-131 (All 52 pages)	2	4	6	10	14	18
132(1/74)-142,144-160	1	2	3	5	7	9
143(3/76) Olympic-c/s; low print	2	4	6	10	14	18
161-166	1	3	4	6	8	10

NOTE: *Wiseman c/a-1-46, 53, 68, 69.*

DENNIS THE MENACE (Giants) (No. 1 titled Giant Vacation Special; becomes Dennis the Menace Bonus Magazine No. 76 on)
(#1-8,18,23,25,30,38: 100 pgs.; rest to #41: 84 pgs.; #42-75: 68 pgs.)
Standard/Pines/Hallden(Fawcett): Summer, 1955 - No. 75, Dec, 1969

	GD	VG	FN	VF	VF/NM	NM-
nn-Giant Vacation Special(Summ/55-Standard)	18	36	54	103	162	220
nn-Christmas issue (Winter '55)	15	30	45	88	137	185
2-Giant Vacation Special (Summer '56-Pines)	14	28	42	78	112	145
3-Giant Christmas issue (Winter '56-Pines)	13	26	39	72	101	130
4-Giant Vacation Special (Summer '57-Pines)	12	24	36	67	94	120
5-Giant Christmas issue (Winter '57-Pines)	12	24	36	67	94	120
6-In Hawaii (Giant Vacation Special)(Summer '58-Pines)	11	22	33	62	86	110
6-In Hawaii (Summer '59-Hallden)-2nd printing; says 3rd large printing on-c 6-In Hawaii (Summer '60)-3rd printing; says 4th large printing on-c 6-In Hawaii (Summer '62)-4th printing; says 5th large printing on-c each....	8	16	24	42	54	65
6-Giant Christmas issue (Winter '58)	11	22	33	62	86	110
7-In Hollywood (Winter '59-Hallden)	5	10	15	32	51	70
7-In Hollywood (Summer '61)-2nd printing	3	6	9	21	32	42
8-In Mexico (Winter '60, 100 pgs.-Hallden/Fawcett)	5	10	15	32	51	70
8-In Mexico (Summer '62, 2nd printing)	3	6	9	21	32	42
9-Goes to Camp (Summer '61, 84 pgs.)-1st CCA approved issue	5	10	15	32	51	70
9-Goes to Camp (Summer '62)-2nd printing	3	6	9	21	32	42
10-12: 10-X-Mas issue (Winter '61), 11-Giant Christmas issue (Winter '62), 12-Triple Feature (Winter '62)	6	12	18	37	59	80
13-17: 13-Best of Dennis the Menace (Spring '63)-Reprints, 14-And His Dog Ruff (Summer '63), 15-In Washington, D.C. (Summer '63), 16-Goes to Camp (Summer '63)-Reprints No. 9, 17-& His Pal Joey (Winter '63)	4	8	12	24	37	50
18-In Hawaii (Reprints No. 6)	3	6	9	20	30	40
19-Giant Christmas issue (Winter '63)	4	8	12	24	37	50
20-Spring Special (Spring '64)	4	8	12	24	37	50
21-40 (Summer '66): 30-r/#6. #35-Xmas spec.Wint,'65	3	6	9	18	27	35
41-60 (Fall '68)	3	6	9	14	19	24
61-75 (12/69): 68-Partial-r/#6	2	4	6	11	16	20

NOTE: *Wiseman c/a-1-8, 12, 14, 15, 17, 20, 22, 27, 28, 31, 35, 36, 41, 49.*

DENNIS THE MENACE
Marvel Comics Group: Nov, 1981 - No. 13, Nov, 1982

	GD	VG	FN	VF	VF/NM	NM-
1-New-a	2	4	6	8	10	12
2-13: 2-New art. 3-Part-r. 4,5-r. 5-X-Mas-c & issue, 7-Spider Kid-c/sty	1	2	3	4	5	7

NOTE: ***Hank Ketcham** c-most; a-3, 12. **Wiseman** a-4, 5.*

DENNIS THE MENACE AND HIS DOG RUFF
Hallden/Fawcett: Summer, 1961

	GD	VG	FN	VF	VF/NM	NM-
1-Wiseman-c/a	5	10	15	32	51	70

DENNIS THE MENACE AND HIS FRIENDS
Fawcett Publ.: 1969; No. 5, Jan, 1970 - No. 46, April, 1980 (All reprints)

	GD	VG	FN	VF	VF/NM	NM-
Dennis the Menace & Joey No. 2 (7/69)	2	4	6	13	18	22
Dennis the Menace & Ruff No. 2 (9/69)	2	4	6	13	18	22
Dennis the Menace & Mr. Wilson No. 1 (10/69)	3	6	9	16	22	28
Dennis & Margaret No. 1 (Winter '69)	3	6	9	16	22	28
5-12: 5-Dennis the Menace & Margaret. 6-...& Joey. 7-...& Ruff. 8-...& Mr. Wilson	2	4	6	8	11	14
13-21-(52 pg Giants): 13-(1/72). 21-(1/74)	2	4	6	10	14	18
22-37	1	3	4	6	8	10
38-46 (Digest size, 148 pgs., 4/78, 95¢)	2	4	6	8	11	14

NOTE: *Titles rotate every four issues, beginning with No. 5. Joey issues: #2(7/69),6,10,14,18,22,26,30,34. Ruff issues: #2(9/69), 7,11,15,19,23,27,31,35. Mr. Wilson issues: #1(10/69),8,12,16,20,24,28,32,36. Margaret issues: #1(Wint./69),5,9,13,17,21,25,29,33,37.*

DENNIS THE MENACE AND HIS PAL JOEY
Fawcett Publ.: Summer, 1961 (10¢) (See Dennis the Menace Giants No. 45)

	GD	VG	FN	VF	VF/NM	NM-
1-Wiseman-c/a	5	10	15	34	55	75

DENNIS THE MENACE AND THE BIBLE KIDS
Word Books: 1977 (36 pgs.)

	GD	VG	FN	VF	VF/NM	NM-
1-6: 1-Jesus. 2-Joseph. 3-David. 4-The Bible Girls. 5-Moses. 6-More About Jesus	2	4	6	9	12	15
7-9-Low print run: 7-The Lord's Prayer. 8-Stories Jesus told. 9-Paul, God's Traveller	3	6	9	20	30	40
10-Low print run; In the Beginning	6	12	18	37	59	80

NOTE: ***Ketcham** c/a in all.*

DENNIS THE MENACE BIG BONUS SERIES
Fawcett Publications: No. 10, Feb, 1980 - No. 11, Apr, 1980

	GD	VG	FN	VF	VF/NM	NM-
10,11	1	2	3	5	6	8

DENNIS THE MENACE BONUS MAGAZINE (Formerly Dennis the Menace Giants Nos. 1-75) (...Big Bonus Series on-c for #174-194)
Fawcett Publications: No. 76, 1/70 - No. 95, 7/71; No. 95, 7/71; No. 97, '71; No. 194, 10/79; (No. 76-124: 68 pgs.; No. 125-163: 52 pgs.; No. 164 on: 36 pgs.)

	GD	VG	FN	VF	VF/NM	NM-
76-90(3/71)	2	4	6	10	14	18
91-95, 97-110(10/72): Two #95's with same date(7/71) A-Summer Games, and B-That's Our Boy. No #96	2	4	6	9	13	16
111-124	2	4	6	8	10	12
125-163-(52 pgs.)	2	4	6	8	10	12
164-194: 166-Indicia printed backwards	1	2	3	4	5	7

DENNIS THE MENACE COMICS DIGEST
Marvel Comics Group: April, 1982 - No. 3, Aug, 1982 ($1.25, digest-size)

	GD	VG	FN	VF	VF/NM	NM-
1-3-Reprints	1	3	4	6	8	10
1-Mistakenly printed with DC emblem on cover	2	4	6	10	12	15

NOTE: ***Ketcham** c-all. **Wiseman** a-all. A few thousand #1's were published with a DC emblem on cover.*

DENNIS THE MENACE FUN BOOK
Fawcett Publications/Standard Comics: 1960 (100 pgs.)

	GD	VG	FN	VF	VF/NM	NM-
1-Part Wiseman-a	6	12	18	41	66	90

DENNIS THE MENACE FUN FEST SERIES (Formerly Dennis the Menace #166)
Hallden (Fawcett): No. 16, Jan, 1980 - No. 17, Mar, 1980 (40¢)

	GD	VG	FN	VF	VF/NM	NM-
16,17-By Hank Ketcham	1	2	3	4	5	7

DENNIS THE MENACE POCKET FULL OF FUN!
Fawcett Publications (Hallden): Spring, 1969 - No. 50, March, 1980 (196 pgs.) (Digest size)

	GD	VG	FN	VF	VF/NM	NM-
1-Reprints in all issues	6	12	18	37	59	80
2-10	4	8	12	24	37	50
11-20	3	6	9	16	22	28
21-28	2	4	6	11	16	20
29-50: 35,40,46-Sunday strip-r	2	4	6	8	11	14

NOTE: *No. 1-28 are 196 pgs.; No. 29-36: 164 pgs.; No. 37: 148 pgs.; No. 38 on: 132 pgs. No. 8, 11, 15, 21, 25, 29 all contain strip reprints.*

DENNIS THE MENACE TELEVISION SPECIAL
Fawcett Publ. (Hallden Div.): Summer, 1961 - No. 2, Spring, 1962 (Giant)

	GD	VG	FN	VF	VF/NM	NM-
1	6	12	18	39	62	85
2	4	8	12	22	34	45

DENNIS THE MENACE TRIPLE FEATURE
Fawcett Publications: Winter, 1961 (Giant)

	GD	VG	FN	VF	VF/NM	NM-
1-Wiseman-c/a	6	12	18	39	62	85

DEPUTY, THE (TV)
Dell Publishing Co.: No. 1077, Feb-Apr, 1960 - No. 1225, Oct-Dec, 1961 (all-Henry Fonda photo-c)

	GD	VG	FN	VF	VF/NM	NM-
Four Color 1077 (#1)-Buscema-a	11	22	33	79	140	200
Four Color 1130 (9-11/60)-Buscema-a,1225	9	18	27	63	107	150

DEPUTY DAWG (TV) (Also see New Terrytoons)
Dell Publishing Co./Gold Key: Oct-Dec, 1961 - No. 1299, 1962; No. 1, Aug, 1965

	GD	VG	FN	VF	VF/NM	NM-
Four Color 1238,1299	10	20	30	73	129	185
1(10164-508)(8/65)-Gold Key	10	20	30	73	129	185

DEPUTY DAWG PRESENTS DINKY DUCK AND HASHIMOTO-SAN (TV)
Gold Key: August, 1965

	GD	VG	FN	VF	VF/NM	NM-
1(10159-508)	9	18	27	64	110	155

DESERT GOLD (See Zane Grey 4-Color 467)

DESIGN FOR SURVIVAL (Gen. Thomas S. Power's...)
American Security Council Press: 1968 (36 pgs. in color) (25¢)

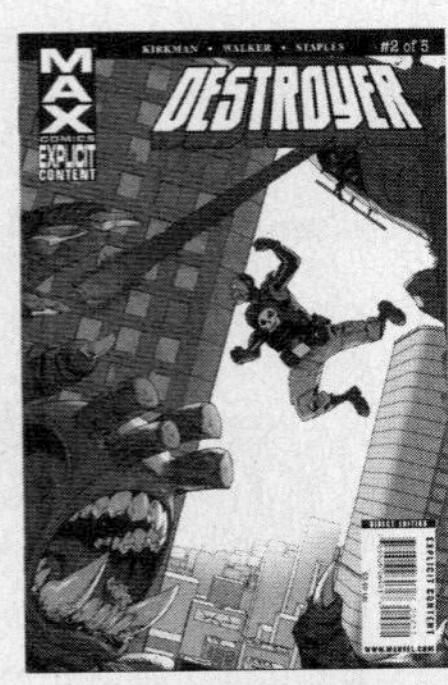

Destroyer #2 © MAR

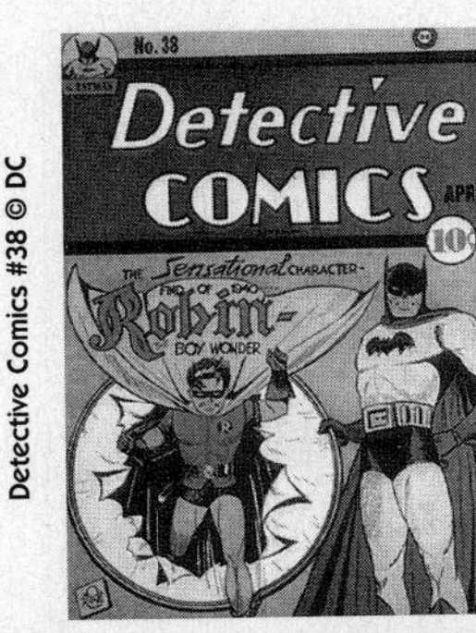

Detective Comics #38 © DC

Detective Comics #47 © DC

	GD 2.0	VG 4.0	FN 6.0	VF 8.0	VF/NM 9.0	NM- 9.2

GD VG FN VF VF/NM NM-
2.0 4.0 6.0 8.0 9.0 9.2

nn-Propaganda against the Threat of Communism-Aircraft cover; H-Bomb panel
3 6 9 17 25 32
Twin Circle Edition-Cover shows panels from inside 2 4 6 11 16 20

DESOLATION JONES
DC Comics (WildStorm): July, 2005 - Present ($2.95/$2.99)
1-8: 1-6-Warren Ellis-s/J.H. Williams-a. 7,8-Zezelj-a 3.00
...: Made in England TPB (2006, $14.99) r/series; cover gallery 15.00

DESPERADO (Becomes Black Diamond Western No. 9 on)
Lev Gleason Publications: June, 1948 - No. 8, Feb, 1949 (All 52 pgs.)
1-Biro-c on all; contains inside photo-c of Charles Biro, Lev Gleason & Bob Wood
15 30 45 86 133 180
2 10 20 30 54 72 90
3-Story with over 20 killings 10 20 30 56 76 95
4-8 8 16 24 42 54 65
NOTE: *Barry a-2. Fuje a-4, 8. Guardineer a-5-7. Kida a-3-7. Ed Moore a-4, 6.*

DESPERADO PRIMER
Image Comics (Desperado): Apr, 2005 ($1.99, one-shot)
1-Previews of Roundeye, World Traveler, A Mirror To The Soul; Bolland-c 2.50

DESPERADOES
Image Comics (Homage): Sept, 1997 - No. 5, June, 1998 ($2.50/$2.95)
1-5-Mariotte-s/Cassaday-c/a: 1-($2.50-c). 2-5-($2.95) 3.00
...: A Moment's Sunlight TPB ('98, $16.95) r/#1-5 17.00
...: Epidemic! (11/99, $5.95) Mariotte-s 6.00

DESPERADOES: BANNERS OF GOLD
IDW Publishing: Dec, 2004 - No. 5, Apr, 2005 ($3.99, limited series)
1-5: Mariotte-s/Haun-a. 1-Cassaday-c 4.00

DESPERADOES: BUFFALO DREAMS
IDW Publishing: Jan, 2007 - No. 4, Apr, 2007 ($3.99, limited series)
1-4: Mariotte-s/Dose-a/c 4.00

DESPERADOES: QUIET OF THE GRAVE
DC Comics (Homage): Jul, 2001 - No. 5, Nov, 2001 ($2.95)
1-5-Jeff Mariotte-s/John Severin-c/a 3.00
TPB (2002, $14.95) r/#1-5; intro. by Brian Keene 15.00

DESPERATE TIMES (See Savage Dragon)
Image Comics: Jun, 1998 - No. 4, Dec, 1998; Nov, 2000 - No. 4, July, 2001 ($2.95, B&W)
1-4-Chris Eliopoulos-s/a 3.00
(Vol. 2) 1-4 3.00
(Vol. 3) 0-(1/04, $3.50) Pages read sideways 3.50
(Vol. 3) 1-Pages read sideways 3.00

DESTINATION MOON (See Fawcett Movie Comics, Space Adventures #20, 23, & Strange Adventures #1)

DESTINY: A CHRONICLE OF DEATHS FORETOLD (See Sandman)
DC Comics (Vertigo): 1997 - No.3, 1998 ($5.95, limited series)
1-3-Alisa Kwitney-s in all: 1-Kent Williams & Michael Zulli-a, Williams painted-c. 2-Williams & Scott Hampton-painted-c/a. 3-Williams & Guay-a 6.00
TPB (2000, $14.95) r/series 15.00

DESTROY!!
Eclipse Comics: 1986 ($4.95, B&W, magazine-size, one-shot)
1 5.00
3-D Special 1-r-/#1 ($2.50) 5.00

DESTROYER
Marvel Comics: June, 2009 - No. 5, Oct, 2009 ($3.99, limited series)
1-5-Kirkman-s/Walker-a/Pesrson-c 4.00

DESTROYER, THE
Marvel Comics (MAX): Nov, 1989 - No. 9, Jun, 1990 ($2.25, B&W, magazine, 52 pgs.)
1-Based on Remo Williams movie, paperbacks 6.00
2-9: 2-Williamson part inks. 4-Ditko-a 4.00

DESTROYER, THE
Marvel Comics: V2#1, March, 1991 ($1.95, 52 pgs.)
V3#1, Dec, 1991 - No. 4, Mar, 1992 ($1.95, mini-series)
V2#1,V3#1-4: Based on Remo Williams paperbacks. V3#1-4-Simonson-c. 3-Morrow-a 2.50

DESTROYER, THE (Also see Solar, Man of the Atom)
Valiant: Apr, 1995 ($2.95, color, one-shot)
0-Indicia indicates #1 3.00

DESTROYER DUCK
Eclipse Comics: Feb, 1982 - No. 7, May, 1984 (#2-7: Baxter paper) ($1.50)
1-Origin Destroyer Duck; 1st app. Groo; Kirby-c/a(p) 1 3 4 6 8 10
2-5: 2-Starling back-up begins; Kirby-c/a(p) thru #5 5.00
6,7 4.00
NOTE: *Neal Adams c-1i. Kirby c/a-1-5p. Miller c-7.*

DESTRUCTOR, THE
Atlas/Seaboard: February, 1975 - No. 4, Aug, 1975
1-Origin/1st app.; Ditko/Wood-a; Wood-c(i) 2 4 6 8 10 12
2-4: 2-Ditko/Wood-a. 3,4-Ditko-a(p) 2 3 4 6 8 10

DETECTIVE COMICS (Also see other Batman titles)
National Periodical Publications/DC Comics: Mar, 1937 - Present
1-(Scarce)-Slam Bradley & Spy by Siegel & Shuster, Speed Saunders by Stoner and Flessel, Cosmo, the Phantom of Disguise, Buck Marshall, Bruce Nelson begin; Chin Lung in 'Claws of the Red Dragon' serial begins; Vincent Sullivan-c
11,000 22,000 33,000 77,000 - -
2 (Rare)-Creig Flessel-c begin; new logo 3143 6286 9429 22,000 - -
3 (Rare) 2357 4714 7071 16,500 - -
4,5: 5-Larry Steele begins 1200 2400 3600 6600 9300 12,000
6,7,9,10 850 1700 2550 4675 6588 8500
8-Mister Chang-c; classic-c 1280 2560 3840 7040 9920 12,800
11-17,19: 15,16-Have interior ad for Action Comics #1. 17-1st app. Fu Manchu in Detective
650 1300 1950 3575 5038 6500
18-Fu Manchu-c; last Flessel-c 1050 2100 3150 5775 8138 10,500
20-The Crimson Avenger begins (1st app.) 1000 2000 3000 5500 7750 10,000
21,23-25 530 1060 1590 2915 4108 5300
22-1st Crimson Avenger-c by Chambers (12/38) 720 1440 2160 3960 5580 7200
26 500 1000 1500 2750 3875 5000
27-The Bat-Man & Commissioner Gordon begin (1st app.), created by Bill Finger & Bob Kane (5/39); Batman-c (1st)(by Kane). Bat-Man's secret identity revealed as Bruce Wayne in six pg. story. Signed Rob't Kane (also see Det. PIcture Stories #5 & Funny Pages V3#1)
70,000 140,000 210,000 525,000 787,500 1,050,000
27-Reprint, Oversize 13-1/2x10". WARNING: This comic is an exact duplicate reprint of the original except for its size. DC published it in 1974 with a second cover titling it as Famous First Edition. There have been many reported cases of the outer cover being removed and the interior sold as the original edition. The reprint with the new outer cover removed is practically worthless; see Famous First Edition for value.
28-2nd app. The Batman (6 pg. story); non-Bat-Man-c; signed Rob't Kane
2700 5400 8100 20,250 35,125 50,000
29-1st app. Doctor Death-c/story, Batman's 1st name villain. 1st 2 part story (10 pgs.). 2nd Batman-c by Kane 4325 8650 12,975 32,500 56,250 80,000
30-Dr. Death app. Story concludes from issue #29. Classic Batman splash panel by Kane.
946 1892 2838 6906 12,203 17,500
31-Classic Batman over castle cover; 1st app. The Monk & 1st Julie Madison (Bruce Wayne's 1st love interest); 1st Batplane (Bat-Gyro) and Batarang; 2nd 2-part Batman adventure. Gardner Fox takes over script from Bill Finger. 1st mention of locale (New York City) where Batman lives 4865 9730 14,595 36,500 63,250 90,000
32-Batman story concludes from issue #31. 1st app. Dala (Monk's assistant). Batman uses gun for 1st time to slay The Monk and Dala. This was the 1st time a costumed hero used a gun in comic books. 1st Batman head logo on cover
838 1676 2514 6117 10,809 15,500
33-Origin The Batman (2 pgs.)(1st told origin); Batman gun holster-c; Batman w/smoking gun panel at end of story. Batman story now 12 pgs. Classic Batman-c
4975 9950 14,925 37,400 64,700 92,000
34-2nd Crimson Avenger-c by Creig Flessel and last non Batman-c. Story from issue #32 x-over as Bruce Wayne sees Julie Madison off to America from Paris. Classic Batman splash panel used later in Batman #1 for origin story. Steve Malone begins
622 1244 1866 4541 8021 11,500
35-Classic Batman hypodermic needle-c that reflects story in issue #34. Classic Batman with smoking .45 automatic splash panel. Batman-c begin
2166 4332 6500 16,250 28,125 40,000
36-Batman-c that reflects adventure in issue #35. Origin/1st app. of Dr. Hugo Strange (1st major villain, 2/40). 1st finned-gloves worn by Batman
1000 2000 3000 7600 13,800 20,000
37-Last solo Golden-Age Batman adventure in Detective Comics. Panel at end of story reflects solo Batman adventure in Batman #1 that was originally planned for Detective #38. Cliff Crosby begins 946 1892 2838 6906 12,203 17,500
38-Origin/1st app. Robin the Boy Wonder (4/40); Batman and Robin-c begin; cover by Kane
4600 9200 13,800 34,500 59,750 85,000
39-Opium story; Clayface app. in 1 panel ad at the end of the Batman story
703 1406 2109 5132 9066 13,000
40-Origin & 1st app. Clayface (Basil Karlo); 1st Joker cover app. (6/40); Joker story intended for this issue was used in Batman #1 instead; cover is similar to splash page in 2nd Joker story in Batman #1 838 1676 2514 6117 10,809 15,500
41-Robin's 1st solo 389 778 1167 2723 4762 6800

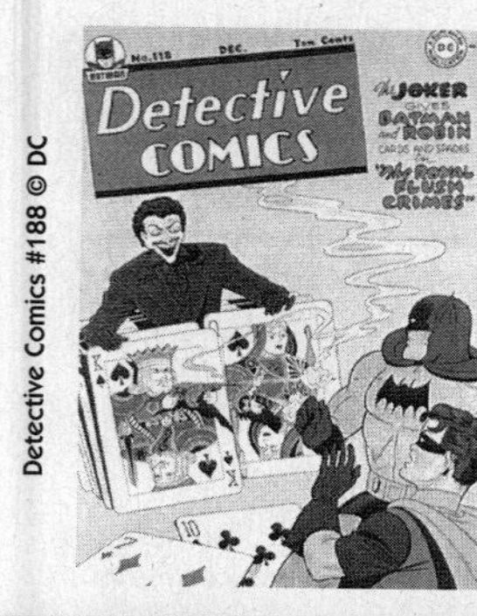

Detective Comics #188 © DC

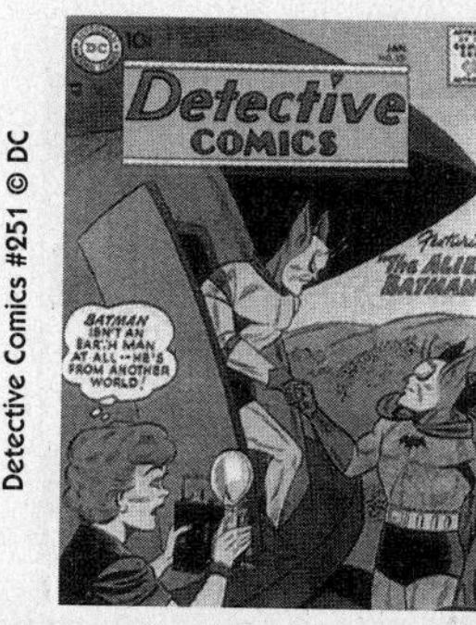

Detective Comics #251 © DC

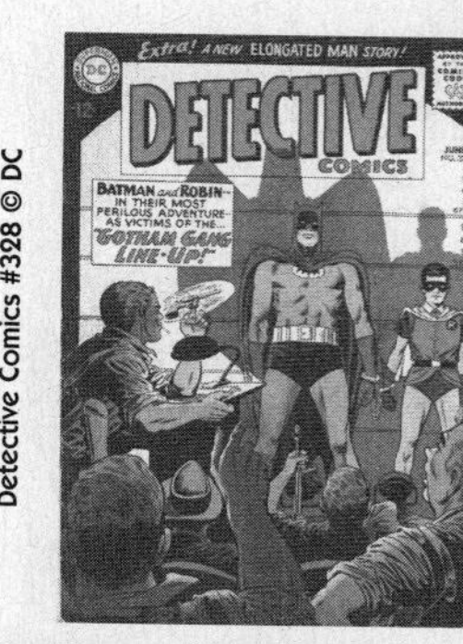

Detective Comics #328 © DC

	GD 2.0	VG 4.0	FN 6.0	VF 8.0	VF/NM 9.0	NM- 9.2
42-44: 44-Crimson Avenger-new costume	300	600	900	2010	3505	5000
45-1st Joker story in Det. (3rd book app. & 4th story app. over all, 11/40)	411	822	1233	2877	5039	7200
46-50: 46-Death of Hugo Strange. 48-1st time car called Batmobile (2/41); Gotham City 1st mention in Detective (1st mentioned in Wow #1; also see Batman #4). 49-Last Clay Face	300	600	900	1920	3310	4700
51-57	200	400	600	1280	2190	3100
58-1st Penguin app. (12/41); last Speed Saunders; Fred Ray-c	486	972	1458	3550	6275	9000
59,60: 59-Last Steve Malone; 2nd Penguin; Wing becomes Crimson Avenger's aide. 60-Intro. Air Wave; Joker app. (2nd in Det.)	206	412	618	1318	2259	3200
61,63: 63-Last Cliff Crosby; 1st app. Mr. Baffle	184	368	552	1168	2009	2850
62-Joker-c/story (2nd Joker-c, 4/42)	300	600	900	2070	3635	5200
64-Origin & 1st app. Boy Commandos by Simon & Kirby (6/42); Joker app.	400	800	1200	2800	4900	7000
65-1st Boy Commandos-c (S&K-a on Boy Commandos & Ray/Robinson-a on Batman & Robin on-c; 4 artists on one-c)	300	600	900	1965	3408	4850
66-Origin & 1st app. Two-Face	454	908	1362	3314	5857	8400
67-1st Penguin-c (9/42)	300	600	900	1980	3440	4900
68-Two-Face-c/story; 1st Two-Face-c	232	464	696	1485	2543	3600
69-Joker-c/story	258	516	774	1651	2826	4000
70	158	316	474	1003	1727	2450
71-Joker-c/story	252	504	756	1613	2757	3900
72,74,75: 74-1st Tweedledum & Tweedledee plus-c; S&K-a	135	270	405	864	1482	2100
73-Scarecrow-c/story (1st Scarecrow-c)	181	362	543	1158	1979	2800
76-Newsboy Legion & The Sandman x-over in Boy Commandos; S&K-a; Joker-c/story	213	426	639	1363	2332	3300
77-79: All S&K-a	132	264	396	838	1444	2050
80-Two-Face app.; S&K-a	152	304	456	965	1658	2350
81,82,84,86-90: 81-1st Cavalier-c & app. 89-Last Crimson Avenger; 2nd Cavalier-c & app.	100	200	300	635	1093	1550
83-1st "skinny" Alfred (1/44)(see Batman #21; last S&K Boy Commandos (also #92,128); most issues #84 on signed S&K are not by them	108	216	324	686	1181	1675
85-Joker-c/story; last Spy; Kirby/Klech Boy Commandos	155	310	465	992	1696	2400
91,102-Joker-c/story	148	296	444	947	1624	2300
92-98: 96-Alfred's last name 'Beagle' revealed, later changed to 'Pennyworth' in #214	84	168	252	538	919	1300
99-Penguin-c/story	139	278	417	883	1517	2150
100 (6/45)	123	246	369	787	1344	1900
101,103-108,110-113,115-117,119: 108-1st Bat-signal-c (2/46). 114-1st small logo (8/46)	76	152	228	486	831	1175
109,114,118-Joker-c/stories	132	264	396	838	1444	2050
120-Penguin-c/story	148	296	444	947	1624	2300
121,123,125,127,129,130	73	146	219	467	796	1125
122-1st Catwoman-c (4/47)	187	374	561	1197	2049	2900
124,128-Joker-c/stories	119	238	357	762	1306	1850
126-Penguin-c	116	232	348	742	1271	1800
131-134,136,139: 134-Penguin-c/story	68	136	204	435	743	1050
135-Frankenstein-c/story	86	172	258	546	936	1325
137-Joker-c/story; last Air Wave	100	200	300	635	1093	1550
138-Origin Robotman (see Star Spangled #7 for 1st app.); series ends #202	110	220	330	704	1202	1700
140-The Riddler-c/story (1st app., 10/48)	503	1006	1509	3672	6486	9300
141,143-148,150: 150-Last Boy Commandos	68	136	204	435	743	1050
142-2nd Riddler-c/story	142	284	426	909	1555	2200
149-Joker-c/story	100	200	300	635	1093	1550
151-Origin & 1st app. Pow Wow Smith, Indian lawman (9/49) & begins series	77	154	231	493	847	1200
152,154,155,157-160: 152-Last Slam Bradley	68	136	204	435	743	1050
153-1st app. Roy Raymond TV Detective (11/49); origin The Human Fly	71	142	213	454	777	1100
156(2/50)-The new classic Batmobile	95	190	285	603	1039	1475
161-167,169,170,172-176: Last 52 pg. issue	65	130	195	416	708	1000
168-Origin the Joker	400	800	1200	2800	4900	7000
171-Penguin-c	94	188	282	547	1024	1450
177-179,181-186,188,189,191,192,194-199,201,202,204,206-210,212,214-216: 184-1st app. Fire Fly. 185-Secret of Batman's utility belt. 187-Two-Face app. 202-Last Robotman & Pow Wow Smith. 215-1st app. of Batmen of all Nations. 216-Last precode (2/55)	61	122	183	390	670	950
180,193-Joker-c/story	77	154	231	493	847	1200
187-Two-Face-c/story	71	142	213	454	777	1100
190-Origin Batman retold	84	168	252	538	919	1300
200(10/53), 205: 205-Origin Batcave	77	154	231	493	847	1200
203,211-Catwoman-c/stories	77	154	231	493	847	1200
213-Origin & 1st app. Mirror Man	73	146	219	467	796	1125
217-224: 218-Batman Jr. & Robin Sr. app.	53	106	159	334	567	800
225-(11/55)-1st app. Martian Manhunter (J'onn J'onzz); origin begins; also see Batman #78	389	778	1167	3500	7000	10,500
226-Origin Martian Manhunter cont'd (2nd app.)	145	290	435	921	1586	2250
227-229: Martian Manhunter stories in all	58	116	174	371	636	900
230-1st app. Mad Hatter; brief recap origin of Martian Manhunter	65	130	195	416	708	1000
231-Brief origin recap Martian Manhunter	47	94	141	298	504	710
232,234,237-240: 239-Early DC grey tone-c	44	88	132	277	469	660
233-Origin & 1st app. Batwoman (7/56)	181	362	543	1158	1979	2800
235-Origin Batman & his costume; tells how Bruce Wayne's father (Thomas Wayne) wore Bat costume & fought crime (reprinted in Batman #255)	73	146	219	467	796	1125
236-1st S.A. issue; J'onn J'onzz talks to parents and Mars-1st since being stranded on Earth; 1st app. Bat-Tank?	46	92	138	290	488	685
241-260: 246-Intro. Diane Meade, John Jones' girl. 249-Batwoman-c/app. 253-1st app. The Terrible Trio. 254-Bat-Hound-c/story. 257-Intro. & 1st app. Whirly Bats. 259-1st app. The Calendar Man	39	78	117	234	385	535
261-264,266,268-271: 261-J. Jones tie-in to sci/fi movie "Incredible Shrinking Man"; 1st app. Dr. Double X. 262-Origin Jackal. 268,271-Manhunter origin recap	31	62	93	186	303	420
265-Batman's origin retold with new facts	42	84	126	265	445	625
267-Origin & 1st app. Bat-Mite (5/59)	47	94	141	296	498	700
272,274,275,277-280	26	52	78	154	252	350
273-J'onn J'onzz i.d. revealed for 1st time	27	54	81	158	259	360
276-2nd app. Bat-Mite	32	64	96	188	307	425
281-292, 294-297: 286,292-Batwoman-c/app. 287-Origin J'onn J'onzz retold. 289-Bat-Mite-c/story. 292-Last Roy Raymond. 297-Last 10¢ issue (11/61)	21	42	63	122	197	275
293-(7/61)-Aquaman begins (pre #1); ends #300	21	42	63	126	206	285
298-(12/61)-1st modern Clayface (Matt Hagen)	25	50	75	183	354	525
299, 300-(2/62)-Aquaman ends	13	26	39	93	172	250
301-(3/62)-J'onn J'onzz returns to Mars (1st time since stranded on Earth six years before)	11	22	33	79	142	200
302-317,319-321,323,324,326,329,330: 302,307-Batwoman-c/app. 311-Intro. Zook in John Jones; 1st app. Cat-Man. 321-2nd Terrible Trio. 326-Last J'onn J'onzz, story cont'd in House of Mystery #143; intro. Idol-Head of Diabolu	10	20	30	67	116	165
318,322,325: 318,325-Cat-Man-c/story (2nd & 3rd app.); also 1st & 2nd app. Batwoman as the Cat-Woman. 322-Bat-Girl's 1st/only app. in Det. (6th in all); Batman cameo in J'onn J'onzz (only hero to app. in series)	10	20	30	68	119	170
327-(5/64)-Elongated Man begins, ends #383; 1st new look Batman with new costume; Infantino/Giella new look-a begins; Batman with gun	13	26	39	91	168	245
328-Death of Alfred; Bob Kane biog, 2 pgs.	12	24	36	85	155	225
331,333-340: 334-1st app. The Outsider	8	16	24	56	93	130
332,341,365-Joker-c/stories	10	20	30	67	116	165
342-358,360,361,366-368: 345-Intro Block Buster. 347-"What If" theme story (1/66). 350-Elongated Man new costume. 355-Zatanna x-over in Elongated Man. 356-Alfred brought back in Batman, early SA app.	7	14	21	49	80	110
359-Intro/origin Batgirl (Barbara Gordon)-c/story (1/67); 1st Silver Age app. Killer Moth	21	42	63	148	287	425
362-364: 362,364-S.A. Riddler app. (early). 363-2nd app. new Batgirl	9	18	27	60	100	140
369(11/67)-N. Adams-a (Elongated Man); 3rd app. S.A. Catwoman (cameo; leads into Batman #197); 4th app. new Batgirl	10	20	30	71	126	180
370-1st Neal Adams-a on Batman (cover only, 12/67)	8	16	24	58	97	135
371-(1/68) 1st new Batmobile from TV show; classic Batgirl-c	9	18	27	64	110	155
372-376,378-386,389,390: 375-New Batmobile-c	6	12	18	41	66	90
377-S.A. Riddler-c/sty	7	14	21	49	80	110
387-r/1st Batman story from #27 (30th anniversary, 5/69); Joker-c; last 12¢ issue	9	18	27	60	100	140
388-Joker-c/story	8	16	24	56	93	130
391-394,396,398,399,401,403,405,406,409: 392-1st app. Jason Bard. 401-2nd Batgirl/Robin team-up. 405-Debut League of Assassins	5	10	15	34	55	75
395,397,402,404,407,408,410-Neal Adams-a. 404-Tribute to Enemy Ace	9	18	27	63	107	150
400-(6/70)-Origin & 1st app. Man-Bat; 1st Batgirl/Robin team-up (cont'd in #401); Neal Adams-a	18	36	54	129	252	375

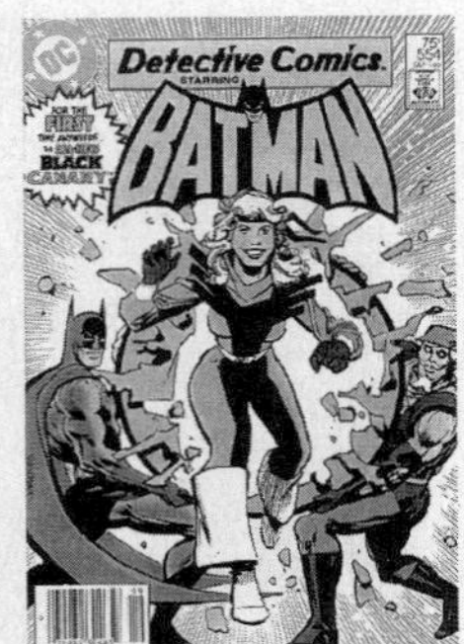

Detective Comics #554 © DC

Detective Comics #766 © DC

Detective Comics #854 © DC

GD 2.0 | VG 4.0 | FN 6.0 | VF 8.0 | VF/NM 9.0 | NM- 9.2

411-(5/71) Intro. Talia, daughter of Ra's al Ghul (Ra's mentioned, but doesn't appear until Batman #232 (6/71); Bob Brown-a 6 12 18 39 62 85
412-413: 413-Last 15¢ issue 4 8 12 28 44 60
414-424: All-25¢, 52 pgs. 418-Creeper x-over. 424-Last Batgirl. 5 10 15 30 48 65
425-436: 426,430,436-Elongated Man app. 428,434-Hawkman begins, ends #467 3 6 9 20 40 60
437-New Manhunter begins (10-11/73, 1st app.) by Simonson, ends #443 5 10 15 34 55 75
438-445 (All 100 Page Super Spectaculars): 438-Kubert Hawkman-r. 439-Origin Manhunter. 440-G.A. Manhunter(Adv. #79) by S&K, Hawkman, Dollman, Green Lantern; Toth-a. 441-G.A. Plastic Man, Batman, Ibis-r. 442-G.A. Newsboy Legion, Black Canary, Elongated Man, Dr. Fate-r. 443-Origin The Creeper-r; death of Manhunter; G.A. Green Lantern, Spectre-r; Batman-r/Batman #18. 444-G.A. Kid Eternity-r. 445-G.A. Dr. Midnite-r 6 12 18 43 69 95
446-460: 457-Origin retold & updated 3 6 9 16 22 28
461-465,470,480: 480-(44 pgs.). 463-1st app. Black Spider. 464-2nd app. Black Spider 470-Intro. Silver St. Cloud. 3 6 9 14 19 24
466-468,471-474,478,479-Rogers-a in all: 466-1st app. Signalman since Batman #139. 470,471-1st modern app. Hugo Strange. 474-1st app. new Deadshot. 478-1st app. 3rd Clayface (Preston Payne). 479-(44 pgs.) 4 8 12 24 37 50
469-Intro/origin Dr. Phosphorous; Simonson-a 4 8 12 22 34 45
475,476-Joker-c/stories; Rogers-a 7 14 21 49 80 110
477-Neal Adams-a(r); Rogers-a (3 pgs.) 4 8 12 22 34 45
481-(Combined with Batman Family, 12-1/78-79, begin $1.00, 68 pg. issues, ends #495); 481-495-Batgirl, Robin solo stories 3 6 9 16 22 28
482-Starlin/Russell, Golden-a; The Demon begins (origin-r), ends #485 (by Ditko #483-485) 2 4 6 11 16 20
483-40th Anniversary issue; origin retold; Newton Batman begins 3 6 9 14 19 24
484-495 (68 pgs): 484-Origin Robin. 485-Death of Batwoman. 486-Killer Moth app. 487-The Odd Man by Ditko. 489-Robin/Batgirl team-up. 490-Black Lightning begins. 491-(#492 on inside). 493-Intro. The Swashbuckler 2 4 6 8 11 14
496-499: 496-Clayface app. 2 3 4 6 8 10
500-($1.50, 52 pgs.)-Batman/Deadman team-up with Infantino-a; new Hawkman story by Joe Kubert; incorrectly says 500th Anniv. of Det. 2 4 6 11 16 20
501-503,505-523: 509-Catman-c. 510-Mad Hatter-c. 512-2nd app. new Dr. Death. 519-Last Batgirl. 521-Green Arrow series begins. 523-Solomon Grundy app. 6.00
504-Joker-c/story 2 4 6 8 11 14
524-2nd app. Jason Todd (cameo)(3/83) 1 2 3 5 7 9
525-3rd app. Jason Todd (See Batman #357) 1 2 3 5 7 9
526-Batman's 500th app. in Detective Comics ($1.50, 68 pgs.); Death of Jason Todd's parents, Joker-c/story (55 pgs.); Bob Kane pin-up 2 4 6 13 18 22
527-531,533,534,536-568,571,573: 538-Cat-Man-c/story cont'd from Batman #371. 542-Jason Todd quits as Robin (becomes Robin again #547). 549,550-Alan Moore scripts (Green Arrow). 554-1st new Black Canary (9/85). 566-Batman villains profiled. 567-Harlan Ellison scripts. 6.00
532,569,570-Joker-c/stories 2 4 6 8 11 14
535-Intro new Robin (JasonTodd)-1st appeared in Batman 1 2 3 5 7 9
572-(3/87, $1.25, 60 pgs.)-50th Anniv. of Det. Comics 1 2 3 4 5 7
574-Origin Batman & Jason Todd retold 1 2 3 5 7 9
575-Year 2 begins, ends #578 3 6 9 14 20 25
576-578: McFarlane-c/a; The Reaper app. 3 6 9 14 20 25
579-597,599,601-610: 579-New bat wing logo. 583-1st app. villains Scarface & Ventriloquist. 589-595-(52 pgs.)-Each contain free 16 pg. Batman stories. 604-607-Mudpack storyline; 604,607-Contain Batman mini-posters. 610-Faked death of Penguin; artists names app. on tombstone on-c 3.00
598-($2.95, 84 pgs.)- "Blind Justice" storyline begins by Batman movie writer Sam Hamm, ends #600 4.00
600-(5/89, $2.95, 84 pgs.)-50th Anniv. of Batman in Det.; 1 pg. Neal Adams pin-up, among other artists 4.00
611-626,628-658: 612-1st new look Cat-Man; Catwoman app. 615- "The Penguin Affair" part 2 (See Batman #448,449). 617-Joker-c/story. 624-1st new Catwoman (w/death) & 1st new Batwoman. 626-Batman's 600th app. in Detective. 642-Return of Scarface, part 2. 644-Last $1.00-c. 652,653-Huntress-c/story w/new costume plus Charest-c on both 3.00
627-($2.95, 84 pgs.)-Batman's 601st app. in Det.; reprints 1st story/#27 plus 3 versions (2 new) of same story 4.00
659-664: 659-Knightfall part 2; Kelley Jones-c. 660-Knightfall part 4; Bane-c by Sam Kieth. 661-Knightfall part 6; brief Joker & Riddler app. 662-Knightfall part 8; Riddler app.; Sam Kieth-c. 663-Knightfall part 10; Kelley Jones-c. 664-Knightfall part 12; Bane-c/story; Joker app.; continued in Showcase 93 #7 & 8; Jones-c 3.00
665-675: 665,666-Knightfall parts 16 & 18; 666-Bane-c/story. 667-Knightquest: The Crusade & new Batman begins (1st app. in Batman #500). 669-Begin $1.50-c; Knightquest, cont'd in Robin #1. 671,673-Joker app. 2.75

GD 2.0 | VG 4.0 | FN 6.0 | VF 8.0 | VF/NM 9.0 | NM- 9.2

675-($2.95)-Collectors edition w/foil-c 3.50
676-($2.50, 52 pgs.)-KnightsEnd pt. 3 3.00
677,678: 677-KnightsEnd pt. 9. 678-(9/94)-Zero Hour tie-in. 2.75
679-685: 679-(11/94). 682-Troika pt. 3 2.75
682-($2.50) Embossed-c Troika pt. 3 3.00
686-699,701-719: 686-Begin $1.95-c. 693,694-Poison Ivy-c/app. 695-Contagion pt. 2; Catwoman, Penguin app. 696-Contagion pt. 8. 698-Two-Face-c/app. 701-Legacy pt. 6; Batman vs. Bane-c/app. 702-Legacy Epilogue. 703-Final Night x-over. 705-707-Riddler-app. 714,715-Martian Manhunter-app. 2.75
700-($4.95, Collectors Edition)-Legacy pt. 1; Ra's Al Ghul-c/app; Talia & Bane app; book displayed at shops in envelope 5.00
700-($2.95, Regular Edition)-Different-c 3.00
720-740: 720,721-Cataclysm pts. 5,14. 723-Green Arrow app. 730-740-No Man's Land stories 2.75
741-($2.50) Endgame; Joker-c/app. 3.00
742-749,751-765: 742-New look Batman begins; 1st app. Crispus Allen (who later becomes the Spectre). 751,752-Poison Ivy app. 756-Superman-c/app. 759-762-Catwoman back-up 2.75
750-($4.95, 64 pgs.) Ra's al Ghul-c 5.00
766-772: 766,767-Bruce Wayne: Murderer pt. 1,8. 769-772-Bruce Wayne: Fugitive pts. 4,8,12,16 3.00
773,774,776-799: 773-Begin $2.75-c; Sienkiewicz-c. 777-784-Sale-c. 784-786-Alan Scott app. 787-Mad Hatter app. 793-Begin $2.95-c. 797-799-War Games 3.00
775-($3.50) Sienkiewicz-c 3.50
800-($3.50) Jock-c; aftermath of War Games; back-up by Lapham 3.50
801-816: 801-814-Lapham-s. 804-Mr. Freeze app. 809-War Crimes 3.00
817-849,851,852: 817-820: One Year Later 8-part x-over with Batman #651-654; Robinson-s/ Bianchi-c. 819-Begin $2.99-c. 820-Dini-s/Williams III-a. 825-Doctor Phosphorus app. 827-Debut of new Scarface. 831-Harley app.; Dini-s. 833,834-Zatanna & Joker app. 838,839-Resurrection of Ra's al Ghul x-over. 846-847-Batman R.I.P. x-over 3.00
817,818,838,839-2nd printings. 817-Combo-c of #817̳ cover images. 818-Combo-c of #818 and Batman #653 cover images. 838-Andy Kubert variant-c. 839-Red bkgd-c 3.00
850-($3.99) Batman vs. Hush; Dini-s/Nguyen-a 4.00
853-($3.99) Gaiman-s/Andy Kubert-a; continued from Batman #686; Kubert sketch pgs. 4.00
853-Variant-c with red background by Andy Kubert 12.00
854-861-($3.99) 854-Batwoman features begin; Rucka-a/J.H. Williams-a/c; The Question back-ups begin. 858-860-Batwoman origin 4.00
854,858,859,860-Variant-c: 854-JG Jones. 858-Hughes. 859-Jock. 860-Alex Ross 6.00
#0-(10/94) Zero Hour tie-in 2.75
#1,000,000 (11/98) 853rd Century x-over 2.75
Annual 1 (1988, $1.50) 5.00
Annual 2-7,9 ('89-'94, '96, 68 pgs.)-4-Painted-c. 5-Joker-c/story (54 pgs.) continued in Robin Annual #1; Sam Kieth-c; Eclipso app. 6-Azrael as Batman in new costume; intro Geist the Twilight Man; Bloodlines storyline. 7-Elseworlds story. 9-Legends of the Dead Earth story 3.00
Annual 8 (1995, $3.95, 68 pgs.)-Year One story 4.00
Annual 10 (1997, $3.95)-Pulp Heroes story 4.00
Annual 11 (12/09, $4.99)-Azrael & The Question app.; continued from Batman Ann. #27 5.00

NOTE: ***Neal Adams*** *c-370, 372, 385, 389, 391, 392, 394-422, 439.* ***Aparo*** *a-437, 438, 444-446, 500, 625-632p, 638-643p; c-430, 437, 440-446, 448, 468-470, 480, 484(back), 492-502,508, 509, 515, 518-522, 641, 716, 719, 722, 724.* ***Austin*** *a(i)-450, 451, 463-468, 471-476; c(i)-474-476, 478.* ***Baily*** *a-443r.* ***Buckler*** *a-434, 446p, 479p; c(p)-467, 482, 505-507, 511, 513-516, 518.* ***Burnley*** *a(Batman)-65, 75, 78, 83, 100, 103, 125; c-62i, 63i, 64, 73i, 78, 83p, 96p, 103p, 105p, 106, 108, 121p, 123p, 125p.* ***Chaykin*** *a-441.* ***Colan*** *a(p)-510, 512, 517, 523, 528-538, 540-546, 555-567; c(p)-510, 512, 528, 530-535, 537, 538, 540, 541, 543-545, 556-558, 560-564.* ***J. Craig*** *a-488.* ***Ditko*** *a-443r, 483-485, 487.* ***Golden*** *a-482p; c-625, 626, 628-631, 633, 644-646.* ***Alan Grant*** *scripts-584-597, 601-621, 641, 642, Annual 5.* ***Grell*** *a-445, 455, 463p, 464p; c-455.* ***Guardineer*** *c-23, 24, 26, 28, 30, 32.* ***Gustavson*** *a-441r.* ***Infantino*** *a-354, 442(2)r, 500, 572.* ***Infantino/Anderson*** *c-333, 337-340, 343, 344, 347, 351, 352, 359, 361-368, 371.* ***Kelley Jones*** *c-651, 657i, 658i, 659, 661, 663-675.* ***Kaluta*** *c-423, 424, 426-428, 431, 434, 438, 484, 486, 572.* ***Bob Kane*** *a-Most early issues #27 on, 297r, 356r, 438-440r, 442r, 443r.* ***Kane/Robinson*** *c-33.* ***Gil Kane*** *a(p)-368, 370-374, 384, 385, 388-407, 438r, 439r, 520.* ***Kane/Anderson*** *c-369.* ***Sam Kieth*** *c-654-656 (657, 658 w/****Kelley Jones****), 660, 662, Annual #5.* ***Kubert*** *a-438r, 439r, 500; c-348, 350.* ***McFarlane*** *c/a(p)-576-578.* ***Meskin*** *a-420r.* ***Mignola*** *c-583.* ***Moldoff*** *c-233-354, 259, 266, 267, 275, 287, 289, 290, 297, 300.* ***Moldoff/Giella*** *a-328, 330, 332, 334, 336, 338, 340, 342, 344, 346, 348, 350, 352, 354, 356.* ***Mooney*** *a-444r.* ***Moreira*** *a-153-300, 419r, 444r, 445r.* ***Nasser/Netzer*** *a-654, 655, 657, 658.* ***Newton*** *a(p)-480, 481, 483-499, 501-509, 511, 513-516, 518-520, 524, 526, 539; c-526p.* ***Irv Novick*** *c-375-377, 383.* ***Robbins*** *a-426p, 429p.* ***Robinson*** *a-part: 66, 68, 71-73; all: 74-76, 79, 80; c-62, 64, 66, 68-74, 76, 79, 82, 86, 88, 442r, 443r.* ***Rogers*** *a-466-468, 471-479p, 481p; c-471p, 472p, 473, 474-479p.* ***Roussos*** *Airwave-76-105(most); c(i)-71, 72, 74-76, 79, 107.* ***Russell*** *a-481i, 482i.* ***Simon/Kirby*** *a-440r, 442r.* ***Simonson*** *a-437-443, 450, 469, 470, 500.* ***Dick Sprang*** *c-77, 82, 84, 85, 87, 89-93, 95-100, 102, 103i, 104i, 106, 108, 114, 117, 118, 122, 123, 128, 129, 131, 133, 135, 141, 148, 149, 168, 622-624.* ***Starlin*** *a-481p, 482p; c-503, 504, 567p.* ***Starr*** *a-444r.* ***Toth*** *a-442; r-414, 416, 418, 424, 440-441, 443, 444.* ***Tuska*** *a-486p, 490p.* ***Matt Wagner*** *c-647-649.* ***Wrightson*** *c-425.*

DETECTIVE DAN, SECRET OP. 48 (Also see Adventures of Detective Ace King and Bob Scully, The Two-Fisted Hick Detective)
Humor Publ. Co. (Norman Marsh): 1933 (10¢, 10x13", 36 pgs., B&W, one-shot) (3 color, cardboard-c)

nn-By Norman Marsh, 1st comic w/ original-a; 1st newsstand-c; Dick Tracy look-alike; forerunner of Dan Dunn. (Title and Wu Fang character inspired Detective Comics #1 four

Detective Eye #1 © CEN

Dethklok vs. The Goon #1 © CN & Eric Powell

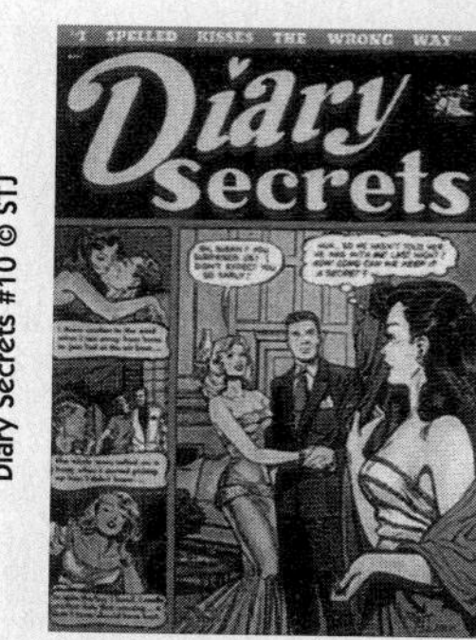

Diary Secrets #10 © STJ

	GD 2.0	VG 4.0	FN 6.0	VF 8.0	VF/NM 9.0	NM- 9.2

years later.) (1st comic of a single theme) 1600 3200 4800 9600 - -

DETECTIVE EYE (See Keen Detective Funnies)
Centaur Publications: Nov, 1940 - No. 2, Dec, 1940

1-Air Man (see Keen Detective) & The Eye Sees begins; The Masked Marvel & Dean Denton app. 232 464 696 1485 2543 3600
2-Origin Don Rance and the Mysticape; Binder-a; Frank Thomas-c 123 246 369 787 1344 1900

DETECTIVE PICTURE STORIES (Keen Detective Funnies No. 8 on?)
Comics Magazine Company: Dec, 1936 - No. 5, Apr, 1937 (1st comic of a single theme)

1 (all issues are very scarce) 580 1160 1740 3074 4437 5800
2-The Clock app. (1/37, early app.) 250 500 750 1325 1913 2500
3,4: 4-Eisner-a 170 340 510 901 1301 1700
5-The Clock-c/story (4/37); 1st detective/adventure art by Bob Kane; Bruce Wayne prototype app.(see Funny Pages V3/1) 195 390 585 1034 1492 1950

DETECTIVES, THE (TV)
Dell Publishing Co.: No. 1168, Mar-May, 1961 - No. 1240, Oct-Dec, 1961

Four Color 1168 (#1)-Robert Taylor photo-c 9 18 27 65 113 160
Four Color 1219-Robert Taylor, Adam West photo-c 8 16 24 56 93 130
Four Color 1240-Tufts-a; Robert Taylor photo-c; 2 different back-c 8 16 24 56 93 130

DETECTIVES, INC. (See Eclipse Graphic Album Series)
Eclipse Comics: Apr, 1985 - No. 2, Apr, 1985 ($1.75, both w/April dates)

1,2: 2-Nudity 2.50

DETECTIVES, INC.: A TERROR OF DYING DREAMS
Eclipse Comics: Jun, 1987 - No. 3, Dec, 1987 ($1.75, B&W& sepia)

1-3: Colan-a 2.50
TPB ('99, $19.95) r/series 20.00

DETENTION COMICS
DC Comics: Oct, 1996 ($3.50, 56 pgs., one-shot)

1-Robin story by Dennis O'Neil & Norm Breyfogle; Superboy story by Ron Marz & Ron Lim; Warrior story by Ruben Diaz & Joe Phillips; Phillips-c 5.00

DETHKLOK VERSUS THE GOON (Based on the animated series Metalocalypse)
Dark Horse Comics: July, 2009 ($3.50, one-shot)

1-Eric Powell-s/a/c; Dethklok visits the Goon universe; Rockzo app. 3.50
1-Variant cover by Jon Schnepp 5.00

DETONATOR (Mike Baron's...)
Image Comics: Nov, 2004 - No. 4 ($2.50/$2.95)

1-4-Mike Baron-s/Mel Rubi-a 3.00

DEVASTATOR
Image Comics/Halloween: 1998 - No. 3 ($2.95, B&W, limited series)

1,2-Hudnall-s/Horn-c/a 3.00

DEVI (Shekhar Kapur's...)
Virgin Comics: July, 2006 - Present ($2.99)

1-20: 1-Mukesh Singh-a/Siddharth Kotian-s. 2-Greg Horn-c 3.00
.../Witchblade (4/08, $2.99) Singh-a/Land-c; continued from Witchblade/Devi 3.00
... Vol. 1 TPB (5/07, $14.99) r/#1-5 and Story from Virgin Comics Preview #0 15.00
... Vol. 2 TPB (9/07, $14.99) r/#6-10; character and cover sketches 15.00

DEVIL CHEF
Dark Horse Comics: July, 1994 ($2.50, B&W, one-shot)

nn 2.50

DEVIL DINOSAUR
Marvel Comics Group: Apr, 1978 - No. 9, Dec, 1978

1-Kirby/Royer-a in all; all have Kirby-c 3 6 9 14 20 25
2-9: 4-7-UFO/sci. fic. 8-Dinoriders-c/sty 2 4 6 8 11 14
... By Jack Kirby Omnibus HC (2007, $29.99, dustjacket) r/#1-9; intro. by Brevoort 30.00

DEVIL DINOSAUR SPRING FLING
Marvel Comics: June, 1997 ($2.99. one-shot)

1-(48pgs.) Moon-Boy-c/app. 3.00

DEVIL-DOG DUGAN (Tales of the Marines No. 4 on)
Atlas Comics (OPI): July, 1956 - No. 3, Nov, 1956

1-Severin-c 14 28 42 76 108 140
2-Iron Mike McGraw x-over; Severin-c 9 18 27 47 61 75
3 8 16 24 42 54 65

DEVIL DOGS
Street & Smith Publishers: 1942

1-Boy Rangers, U.S. Marines 28 56 84 165 270 375

DEVILINA (Magazine)
Atlas/Seaboard: Feb, 1975 - No. 2, May, 1975 (B&W)

1-Art by Reese, Marcos; "The Tempest" adapt. 3 6 9 20 30 40
2 (Low printing) 4 8 12 22 34 45

DEVIL KIDS STARRING HOT STUFF
Harvey Publications (Illustrated Humor): July, 1962 - No. 107, Oct, 1981 (Giant-Size #41-55)

1 (12¢ cover price #1-#41-9/69) 22 44 66 157 304 450
2 11 22 33 80 145 210
3-10 (1/64) 8 16 24 58 97 135
11-20 6 12 18 37 59 80
21-30 4 8 12 26 41 55
31-40: 40-(6/69) 3 6 9 20 30 40
41-50: All 68 pg. Giants 4 8 12 22 34 45
51-55: All 52 pg. Giants 3 6 9 20 30 40
56-70 2 4 6 11 16 20
71-90. 2 4 6 8 11 14
91-107 1 2 3 5 6 8

DEVIL'S FOOTPRINTS, THE
Dark Horse Comics: March, 2003 - No. 4, June, 2003 ($2.99, limited series)

1-4-Paul Lee-c/a; Scott Allie-s 3.00

DEXTER COMICS
Dearfield Publ.: Summer, 1948 - No. 5, July, 1949

1-Teen-age humor 11 22 33 60 83 105
2-Junie Prom app. 8 16 24 42 54 65
3-5 7 14 21 35 43 50

DEXTER'S LABORATORY (Cartoon Network)
DC Comics: Sept, 1999 - No. 34, Apr, 2003 ($1.99/$2.25)

1 4.00
2-10: 2-McCracken-s 3.00
11-24, 26-34: 31-Begin $2.25-c. 32-34-Wray-c 2.50
25-(50¢-c) Tartakovsky-s/a; Action Hank-c/app. 2.50

DEXTER THE DEMON (Formerly Melvin The Monster)(See Cartoon Kids & Peter the Little Pest)
Atlas Comics (HPC): No. 7, Sept, 1957

7 8 16 24 42 54 65

DHAMPIRE: STILLBORN
DC Comics (Vertigo): 1996 ($5.95, one-shot, mature)

1-Nancy Collins script; Paul Lee-c/a 6.00

DIARY CONFESSIONS (Formerly Ideal Romance)
Stanmor/Key Publ.(Medal Comics): No. 9, May, 1955 - No. 14, Apr, 1955

9 9 18 27 50 65 80
10-14 7 14 21 37 46 55

DIARY LOVES (Formerly Love Diary #1; G. I. Sweethearts #32 on)
Quality Comics Group: No. 2, Nov, 1949 - No. 31, April, 1953

2-Ward-c/a, 9 pgs. 18 36 54 105 165 225
3 (1/50)-Photo-c begin, end #27? 10 20 30 56 76 95
4-Crandall-a 11 22 33 62 86 110
5-7,10 9 18 27 50 65 80
8,9-Ward-a 6,8 pgs. 8-Gustavson-a; Esther Williams photo-c 14 28 42 78 112 145
11,13,14,17-20 9 18 27 47 61 75
12,15,16-Ward-a 9,7,8 pgs. 13 26 39 72 101 130
21-Ward-a, 7 pgs. 11 22 33 64 90 115
22-31: 31-Whitney-a 8 16 24 44 57 70

NOTE: *Photo c-3-10, 12-27.*

DIARY OF HORROR
Avon Periodicals: December, 1952

1-Hollingsworth-c/a; bondage-c 44 88 132 277 469 660

DIARY SECRETS (Formerly Teen-Age Diary Secrets)(See Giant Comics Ed.)
St. John Publishing Co.: No. 10, Feb, 1952 - No. 30, Sept, 1955

10-Baker-c/a most issues 26 52 78 154 252 350
11-16,18,19 20 40 60 114 182 250
17,20: Kubert-r/Hollywood Confessions #1. 17-r/Teen Age Romances #9 20 40 60 114 182 250
21-30: 22,27-Signed stories by Estrada. 28-Last precode (3/55)

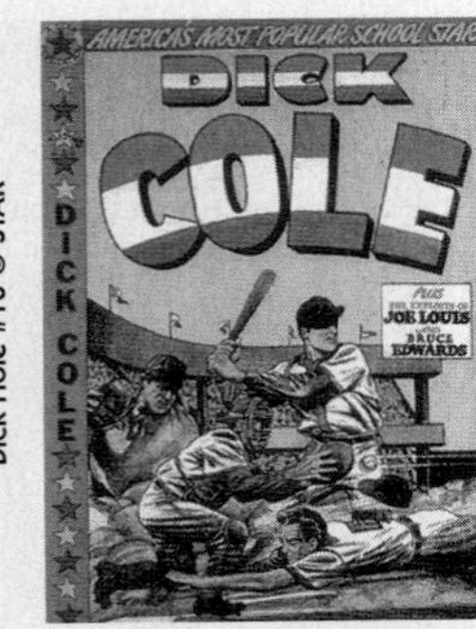

Dick Hole #10 © STAR

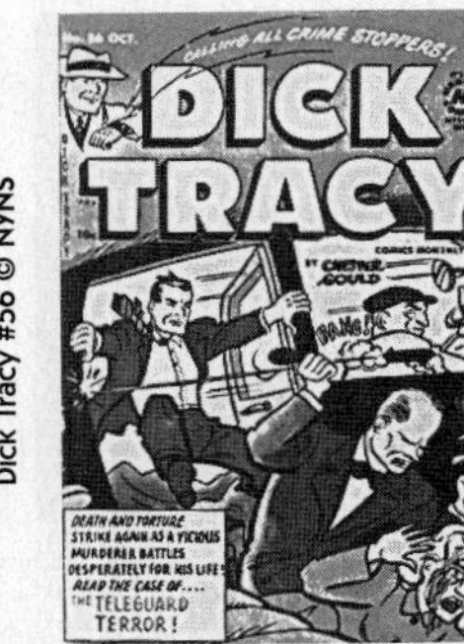

Dick Tracy #56 © NYNS

Die Hard: Year One #1
© 20th Century Fox

	GD 2.0	VG 4.0	FN 6.0	VF 8.0	VF/NM 9.0	NM- 9.2
	15	30	45	85	130	175
nn-(25¢ giant, nd (1950?)-Baker-c & rebound St. John comics	68	136	204	435	743	1050

DICK COLE (Sport Thrills No. 11 on)(See Blue Bolt & Four Most #1)
Curtis Publ./Star Publications: Dec-Jan, 1948-49 - No. 10, June-July, 1950

	GD 2.0	VG 4.0	FN 6.0	VF 8.0	VF/NM 9.0	NM- 9.2
1-Sgt. Spook; L. B. Cole-c; McWilliams-a; Curt Swan's 1st work	34	68	102	199	325	450
2,5	15	30	45	92	144	195
3,4,6-10: All-L.B. Cole-c. 10-Joe Louis story	22	44	66	130	213	295
Accepted Reprint #7(V1#6 on-c)(1950's)-Reprints #7; L.B. Cole-c	9	18	27	47	61	75
Accepted Reprint #9(nd)-(Reprints #9 & #8-c)	9	18	27	47	61	75

NOTE: *L. B. Cole c-1, 3, 4, 6-10. Al McWilliams a-6. Dick Cole in 1-9. Baseball c-10. Basketball c-9. Football c-8.*

DICKIE DARE
Eastern Color Printing Co.: 1941 - No. 4, 1942 (#3 on sale 6/15/42)

	GD 2.0	VG 4.0	FN 6.0	VF 8.0	VF/NM 9.0	NM- 9.2
1-Caniff-a, bondage-c by Everett	60	120	180	383	659	935
2	28	56	84	165	270	375
3,4-Half Scorchy Smith by Noel Sickles who was very influential in Milton Caniff's development	30	60	90	177	289	400

DICK POWELL (Also see A-1 Comics)
Magazine Enterprises: No. 22, 1949 (one shot)

	GD 2.0	VG 4.0	FN 6.0	VF 8.0	VF/NM 9.0	NM- 9.2
A-1 22-Photo-c	22	44	66	132	216	300

DICK QUICK, ACE REPORTER (See Picture News #10)

DICKS
Caliber Comics: 1997 - No. 4, 1998 ($2.95, B&W)

	GD 2.0	VG 4.0	FN 6.0	VF 8.0	VF/NM 9.0	NM- 9.2
1-4-Ennis-s/McCrea-c/a; r/Fleetway						3.00
TPB ('98, $12.95) r/series						13.00

DICK'S ADVENTURES
Dell Publishing Co.: No. 245, Sept, 1949

	GD 2.0	VG 4.0	FN 6.0	VF 8.0	VF/NM 9.0	NM- 9.2
Four Color 245	6	12	18	41	66	90

DICK TRACY (See Famous Feature Stories, Harvey Comics Library, Limited Collectors' Ed., Mammoth Comics, Merry Christmas, The Original..., Popular Comics, Super Book No. 1, 7, 13, 25, Super Comics & Tastee-Freez)

DICK TRACY
David McKay Publications: May, 1937 - Jan, 1938

	GD 2.0	VG 4.0	FN 6.0	VF 8.0	VF/NM 9.0	NM- 9.2
Feature Books nn - 100 pgs., partially reprinted as 4-Color No. 1 (appeared before Large Feature Comics, 1st Dick Tracy comic book) (Very Rare-five known copies; two incomplete)	1000	2000	3000	7400	13,200	19,000
Feature Books 4 - Reprints nn issue w/new-c	131	262	393	832	1429	2025
Feature Books 6,9	95	190	285	603	1039	1475

DICK TRACY (...Monthly #1-24)
Dell Publishing Co.: 1939 - No. 24, Dec, 1949

	GD 2.0	VG 4.0	FN 6.0	VF 8.0	VF/NM 9.0	NM- 9.2
Large Feature Comic 1 (1939) -Dick Tracy Meets The Blank	181	362	543	1158	1979	2800
Large Feature Comic 4,8	94	188	282	597	1024	1450
Large Feature Comic 11,13,15	82	164	246	528	902	1275
Four Color 1(1939)('35-r)	975	1950	2919	7100	12,550	18,000
Four Color 6(1940)('37-r)-(Scarce)	213	426	639	1363	2332	3300
Four Color 8(1940)('38-'39-r)	107	214	321	680	1165	1650
Large Feature Comic 3(1941, Series II)	82	164	246	528	902	1275
Four Color 21('41)('38-r)	79	158	237	502	864	1225
Four Color 34('43)('39-'40-r)	40	80	120	309	597	885
Four Color 56('44)('40-r)	36	72	108	275	530	785
Four Color 96('46)('40-r)	24	48	72	175	338	500
Four Color 133('47)('40-'41-r)	19	38	57	133	259	385
Four Color 163('47)('41-r)	17	34	51	119	230	340
Four Color 215('48)-Titled "Sparkle Plenty", Dick Tracy-r	11	22	33	80	145	210
1(1/48)('34-r)	37	74	111	284	530	775
2,3	20	40	60	148	274	400
4-10	17	34	51	126	233	340
11-18: 13-Bondage-c	14	28	42	99	175	250
19-1st app. Sparkle Plenty, B.O. Plenty & Gravel Gertie in a 3-pg. strip not by Gould	14	28	42	103	184	265
20-1st app. Sam Catchem; c/a not by Gould	13	26	39	95	168	240
21-24-Only 2 pg. Gould-a in each	13	26	39	90	160	230

NOTE: *No. 19-24 have a 2 pg. biography of a famous villain illustrated by* ***Gould****: 19-Little Face; 20-Flattop; 21-Breathless Mahoney; 22-Measles; 23-Itchy; 24-The Brow.*

DICK TRACY (Continued from Dell series)(...Comics Monthly #25-140)
Harvey Publications: No. 25, Mar, 1950 - No. 145, April, 1961

	GD 2.0	VG 4.0	FN 6.0	VF 8.0	VF/NM 9.0	NM- 9.2
25-Flat Top-c/story (also #26,27)	14	28	42	99	175	250
26-28,30: 28-Bondage-c. 28,29-The Brow-c/stories	10	20	30	73	129	185
29-1st app. Gravel Gertie in a Gould-r	12	24	36	87	156	225
31,32,34,35,37-40: 40-Intro/origin 2-way wrist radio (6/51)	9	18	27	61	103	145
33- "Measles the Teen-Age Dope Pusher"	10	20	30	73	129	185
36-1st app. B.O. Plenty in a Gould-r	10	20	30	73	129	185
41-50	8	16	24	54	90	125
51-56,58-80: 51-2pgs Powell-a	7	14	21	47	76	105
57-1st app. Sam Catchem in a Gould-r	8	16	24	54	90	125
81-99,101-140: 99-109-Painted-c	6	12	18	43	69	95
100, 141-145 (25¢)(titled "Dick Tracy")	7	14	21	47	76	105

NOTE: ***Powell*** *a(1-2pgs.)-43, 44, 104, 108, 109, 145. No. 110-120, 141-145 are all reprints from earlier issues.*

DICK TRACY ("Reuben Award" series)
Blackthorne Publishing: 12/84 - No. 24, 6/89 (1-12: $5.95; 13-24: $6.95, B&W, 76 pgs.)

	GD 2.0	VG 4.0	FN 6.0	VF 8.0	VF/NM 9.0	NM- 9.2
1-8-1st printings; hard-c ed. ($14.95)						20.00
1-3-2nd printings, 1986; hard-c ed.						20.00
1-12-1st & 2nd printings; squarebound. thick-c						12.00
13-24 ($6.95): 21,22-Regular-c & stapled						14.00

NOTE: *Gould daily & Sunday strip-r in all. 1-12 r-12/31/45-4/5/49; 13-24 r-7/13/41-2/20/44.*

DICK TRACY (Disney)
WD Publications: 1990 - No. 3, 1990 (color) (Book 3 adapts 1990 movie)

	GD 2.0	VG 4.0	FN 6.0	VF 8.0	VF/NM 9.0	NM- 9.2
Book One ($3.95, 52pgs.)-Kyle Baker-c/a						6.00
Book Two, Three ($5.95, 68pgs.)-Direct sale						6.00
Book Two, Three ($2.95, 68pgs.)-Newsstand						3.00

DICK TRACY ADVENTURES
Gladstone Publishing: May, 1991 ($4.95, 76 pgs.)

	GD 2.0	VG 4.0	FN 6.0	VF 8.0	VF/NM 9.0	NM- 9.2
1-Reprints strips 2/1/42-4/18/42						5.00

DICK TRACY, EXPLOITS OF
Rosdon Books, Inc.: 1946 ($1.00, hard-c strip reprints)

	GD 2.0	VG 4.0	FN 6.0	VF 8.0	VF/NM 9.0	NM- 9.2
1-Reprints the near complete case of "The Brow" from 6/12/44 to 9/24/44 (story starts a few weeks late)	25	50	75	147	241	335
with dust jacket...	39	78	117	240	395	550

DICK TRACY MONTHLY/WEEKLY
Blackthorne Publishing: May, 1986 - No. 99, 1989 ($2.00, B&W)
(Becomes Weekly #26 on)

	GD 2.0	VG 4.0	FN 6.0	VF 8.0	VF/NM 9.0	NM- 9.2
1-60: Gould-r. 30,31-Mr. Crime app.						3.00
61-90						4.00
91-95						6.00
96-99-Low print	1	2	3	5	7	9

NOTE: *#1-10 reprint strips 3/10/40-7/13/41; #10(pg.8)-51 reprint strips 4/6/49-12/31/55; #52-99 reprint strips 12/26/56-4/26/64.*

DICK TRACY SPECIAL
Blackthorne Publ.: Jan, 1988 - No. 3, Aug. (no month), 1989 ($2.95, B&W)

	GD 2.0	VG 4.0	FN 6.0	VF 8.0	VF/NM 9.0	NM- 9.2
1-3: 1-Origin D. Tracy; 4/strips 10/12/31-3/30/32						3.00

DICK TRACY: THE EARLY YEARS
Blackthorne Publishing: Aug, 1987 - No. 4, Aug (no month) 1989 ($6.95, B&W, 76 pgs.)

	GD 2.0	VG 4.0	FN 6.0	VF 8.0	VF/NM 9.0	NM- 9.2
1-3: 1-4-r/strips 10/12/31(1st daily)-8/31/32 & Sunday strips 6/12/32-8/28/32; Big Boy apps. in #1-3	1	2	3	4	5	7
4 ($2.95, 52pgs.)						3.00

DICK TRACY UNPRINTED STORIES
Blackthorne Publishing: Sept, 1987 - No. 4, June, 1988 ($2.95, B&W)

	GD 2.0	VG 4.0	FN 6.0	VF 8.0	VF/NM 9.0	NM- 9.2
1-4: Reprints strips 1/1/56-12/25/56						3.00

DICK TURPIN (See Legend of Young...)

DIE-CUT
Marvel Comics UK, Ltd: Nov, 1993 - No. 4, Feb, 1994 ($1.75, limited series)

	GD 2.0	VG 4.0	FN 6.0	VF 8.0	VF/NM 9.0	NM- 9.2
1-4: 1-Die-cut-c; The Beast app.						2.50

DIE-CUT VS. G-FORCE
Marvel Comics UK, Ltd: Nov, 1993 - No. 2, Dec, 1993 ($2.75, limited series)

	GD 2.0	VG 4.0	FN 6.0	VF 8.0	VF/NM 9.0	NM- 9.2
1,2-($2.75)-Gold foil-c on both						2.75

DIE HARD: YEAR ONE (Based on the John McClane character)
BOOM! Studios: Aug, 2009 - Present ($3.99, limited series)

	GD 2.0	VG 4.0	FN 6.0	VF 8.0	VF/NM 9.0	NM- 9.2
1-7-Chaykin-s; Officier McClane in 1976 NYC; 3 covers on each						4.00

DIE, MONSTER, DIE (See Movie Classics)

DIGIMON DIGITAL MONSTERS (TV)
Dark Horse Comics: May, 2000 - No. 12, Nov, 2000 ($2.95/$2.99)

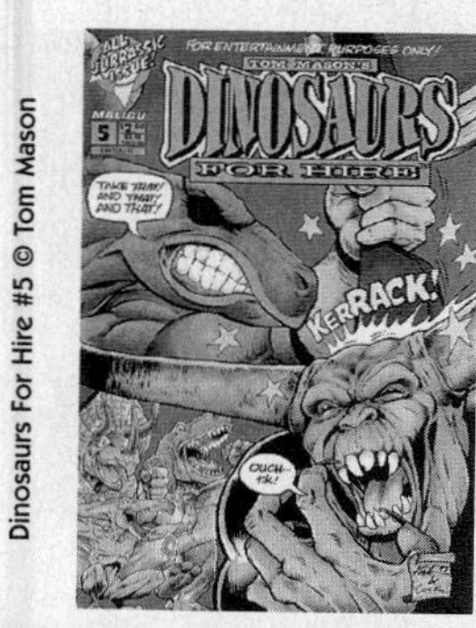

Dinosaurs For Hire #5 © Tom Mason

Dippy Duck #1 © MAR

Disney's Action Club #1 © DIS

GD 2.0 | VG 4.0 | FN 6.0 | VF 8.0 | VF/NM 9.0 | NM- 9.2

1-12 3.00

DIGITEK
Marvel UK, Ltd: Dec, 1992 - No. 4, Mar, 1993 ($1.95/$2.25, mini-series)
1-4: 3-Deathlock-c/story 2.50

DILLY (Dilly Duncan from Daredevil Comics; see Boy Comics #57)
Lev Gleason Publications: May, 1953 - No. 3, Sept, 1953
1-Teenage; Biro-c 7 14 21 37 46 55
2,3-Biro-c 5 10 15 24 30 35

DILTON'S STRANGE SCIENCE (See Pep Comics #78)
Archie Comics: May, 1989 - No. 5, May, 1990 (75¢/$1.00)
1-5 3.00

DIME COMICS
Newsbook Publ. Corp.: 1945; 1951
1-Silver Streak-c/sty; L.B. Cole-c; Japanese war-c 97 194 291 621 1061 1500
1(1951) 12 24 36 67 94 120

DINGBATS (See 1st Issue Special)

DING DONG
Compix/Magazine Enterprises: Summer?, 1946 - No. 5, 1947 (52 pgs.)
1-Funny animal 27 54 81 158 259 360
2 (9/46) 14 28 42 82 121 160
3 (Wint '46-'47) - 5 12 24 36 67 94 120

DINKY DUCK (Paul Terry's...) (See Approved Comics, Blue Ribbon, Giant Comics Edition #5A & New Terrytoons)
St. John Publishing Co./Pines No. 16 on: Nov, 1951 - No. 16, Sept, 1955; No. 16, Fall, 1956; No. 17, May, 1957 - No. 19, Summer, 1958
1-Funny animal 13 26 39 72 101 130
2 8 16 24 42 54 65
3-10 6 12 18 29 36 42
11-16(9/55) 6 12 18 27 33 38
16(Fall, '56) - 19 5 10 15 22 26 30

DINKY DUCK & HASHIMOTO-SAN (See Deputy Dawg Presents...)

DINO (TV)(The Flintstones)
Charlton Publications: Aug, 1973 - No. 20, Jan, 1977 (Hanna-Barbera)
1 3 6 9 18 27 35
2-10 2 4 6 10 14 18
11-20 2 4 6 8 10 12
Digest nn (w/Xerox Pub., 1974) (low print run) 2 4 6 11 16 20

DINO ISLAND
Mirage Studios: Feb, 1994 - No. 2, Mar, 1994 ($2.75, limited series)
1,2-By Jim Lawson 2.75

DINO RIDERS
Marvel Comics: Feb, 1989 - No. 3, 1989 ($1.00)
1-3: Based on toys 3.00

DINOSAUR REX
Upshot Graphics (Fantagraphics): 1986 - No. 3, 1986 ($2.00, limited series)
1-3 2.50

DINOSAURS, A CELEBRATION
Marvel Comics (Epic): Oct, 1992 - No. 4, Oct, 1992 ($4.95, lim. series, 52 pgs.)
1-4: 2-Bolton painted-c 5.00

DINOSAURS ATTACK! THE GRAPHIC NOVEL
Eclipse Comics: 1991 ($3.95, coated stock, stiff-c)
Book One- Based on Topps trading cards 4.00

DINOSAURS FOR HIRE
Malibu Comics: Feb, 1993 - No. 12, Feb, 1994 ($1.95/$2.50)
1-12: 1,10-Flip bk. 8-Bagged w/Skycap; Staton-c. 10-Flip book 2.50

DINOSAURS GRAPHIC NOVEL (TV)
Disney Comics: 1992 - No. 2, 1993 ($2.95, 52 pgs.)
1,2-Staton-a; based on Dinosaurs TV show 3.00

DINOSAURUS
Dell Publishing Co.: No. 1120, Aug, 1960
Four Color 1120-Movie, painted-c 8 16 24 56 93 130

DIPPY DUCK
Atlas Comics (OPI): October, 1957

GD 2.0 | VG 4.0 | FN 6.0 | VF 8.0 | VF/NM 9.0 | NM- 9.2

1-Maneely-a; code approved 10 20 30 56 76 95

DIRECTORY TO A NONEXISTENT UNIVERSE
Eclipse Comics: Dec, 1987 ($2.00, B&W)
1 2.50

DIRTY DOZEN (See Movie Classics)

DIRTY PAIR (Manga)
Eclipse Comics: Dec, 1988 - No. 4, Apr, 1989 ($2.00, B&W, limited series)
1-4: Japanese manga with original stories 3.00
...: Start the Violence (Dark Horse, 9/99, $2.95) r/B&W stories in color from Dark Horse Presents #132-134; covers by Warren & Pearson 3.00

DIRTY PAIR: FATAL BUT NOT SERIOUS (Manga)
Dark Horse Comics: July, 1995 - No. 5, Nov, 1995 ($2.95, limited series)
1-5 3.00

DIRTY PAIR: RUN FROM THE FUTURE (Manga)
Dark Horse Comics: Jan, 2000 - No. 4, Mar, 2000 ($2.95, limited series)
1-4-Warren-s/c/a. Var.-c by Hughes(1), Stelfreeze(2), Timm(3), Ramos(4) 3.00

DIRTY PAIR: SIM HELL (Manga)
Dark Horse Comics: May, 1993 - No. 4, Aug, 1993 ($2.50, B&W, limited series)
1-4 3.00
...Remastered #1-4 (5/01 - 8/01) reprints in color, with pin-up gallery 3.00

DIRTY PAIR II (Manga)
Eclipse Comics: June, 1989 - No. 5, Mar, 1990 ($2.00, B&W, limited series)
1-5: 3-Cover is misnumbered as #1 3.00

DIRTY PAIR III, THE (A Plague of Angels) (Manga)
Eclipse Comics: Aug, 1990 - No. 5, Aug, 1991 ($2.00/$2.25, B&W, lim. series)
1-5 3.00

DISHMAN
Eclipse Comics: Sept, 1988 ($2.50, B&W, 52 pgs.)
1 2.50

DISNEY AFTERNOON, THE (TV)
Marvel Comics: Nov, 1994 - No. 10?, Aug, 1995 ($1.50)
1-10: 3-w/bound-in Power Ranger Barcode Card 3.00

DISNEY COMIC ALBUM
Disney Comics: 1990(no month, year) - No. 8, 1991 ($6.95/$7.95)
1,2 ($6.95): 1-Donald Duck and Gyro Gearloose by Barks(r). 2-Uncle Scrooge by Barks(r); Jr. Woodchucks app. 9.00
3-8: 3-Donald Duck-r/F.C. 308 by Barks; begin $7.95-c. 4-Mickey Mouse Meets the Phantom Blot; r/M.M Club Parade (censored 1956 version of story). 5-Chip 'n' Dale Rescue Rangers; new-a. 6-Uncle Scrooge. 7-Donald Duck in Too Many Pets; Barks-r(4) including F.C. #29. 8-Super Goof; r/S.G. #1, D.D. #102 9.00

DISNEY COMIC HITS
Marvel Comics: Oct, 1995 - No. 16, Jan, 1997 ($1.50/$2.50)
1-16: 4-Toy Story. 6-Aladdin. 7-Pocahontas. 10-The Hunchback of Notre Dame (Same story in Disney's The Hunchback of Notre Dame). 13-Aladdin and the Forty Thieves 4.00

DISNEY COMICS
Disney Comics: June, 1990
Boxed set of #1 issues includes Donald Duck Advs., Ducktales, Chip 'n Dale Rescue Rangers, Roger Rabbit, Mickey Mouse Advs. & Goofy Advs.; limited to 10,000 sets 2 4 6 9 12 15

DISNEYLAND BIRTHDAY PARTY (Also see Dell Giants)
Gladstone Publishing Co.: Aug, 1985 ($2.50)
1-Reprints Dell Giant with new-photo-c 2 4 6 8 10 12
...Comics Digest #1-(Digest) 2 4 6 8 11 14

DISNEYLAND MAGAZINE
Fawcett Publications: Feb. 15, 1972 - ? (10-1/4"x12-5/8", 20 pgs, weekly)
1-One or two page painted art features on Dumbo, Snow White, Lady & the Tramp, the Aristocats, Brer Rabbit, Peter Pan, Cinderella, Jungle Book, Alice & Pinocchio. Most standard characters app. 3 6 9 16 23 30

DISNEYLAND, USA (See Dell Giant No. 30)

DISNEY MOVIE BOOK
Walt Disney Productions (Gladstone): 1990 ($7.95, 8-1/2"x11", 52 pgs.) (w/pull-out poster)
1-Roger Rabbit in Tummy Trouble; from the cartoon film strips adapted to the comic format. Ron Dias-c 2 4 6 8 10 12

DISNEY'S ACTION CLUB

Disney's Hero Squad #1 © DIS

A Distant Soil #13 © Colleen Doran

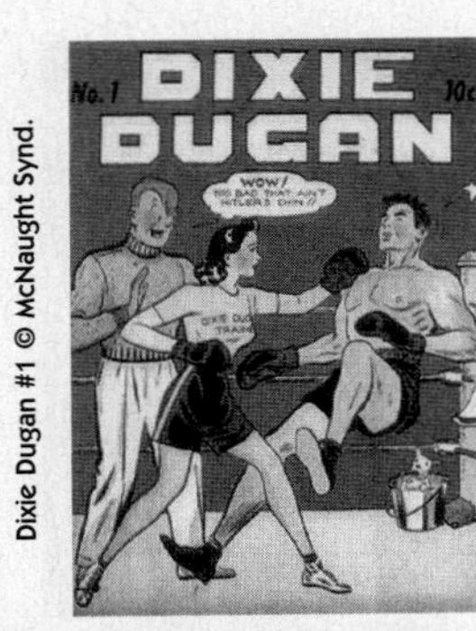

Dixie Dugan #1 © McNaught Synd.

	GD 2.0	VG 4.0	FN 6.0	VF 8.0	VF/NM 9.0	NM- 9.2

Acclaim Books: 1997 - No. 4 ($4.50, digest size)

1-4: 1-Hercules. 4-Mighty Ducks — 4.50

DISNEY'S ALADDIN (Movie)
Marvel Comics: Oct, 1994 - No. 11, 1995 ($1.50)

1-11 — 3.00

DISNEY'S BEAUTY AND THE BEAST (Movie)
Marvel Comics: Sept, 1994 - No. 13, 1995 ($1.50)

1-13 — 3.00

DISNEY'S BEAUTY AND THE BEAST HOLIDAY SPECIAL
Acclaim Books: 1997 ($4.50, digest size, one-shot)

1-Based on The Enchanted Christmas video — 4.50

DISNEY'S COLOSSAL COMICS COLLECTION
Disney Comics: 1991 - No. 10, 1993 ($1.95, digest-size, 96/132 pgs.)

1-10: Ducktales, Talespin, Chip 'n Dale's Rescue Rangers. 4-r/Darkwing Duck #1-4. 6-Goofy begins. 8-Little Mermaid — 5.00

DISNEY'S COMICS IN 3-D
Disney Comics: 1992 ($2.95, w/glasses, polybagged)

1-Infinity-c; Barks, Rosa, Gottfredson-r — 5.00

DISNEY'S ENCHANTING STORIES
Acclaim Books: 1997 - No. 5 ($4.50, digest size)

1-5: 1-Hercules. 2-Pocahontas — 4.50

DISNEY'S HERO SQUAD
BOOM! Studios: Jan, 2010 - Present ($2.99)

1,2-Phantom Blot app. 1-Back-up reprint of Super Goof #1 — 3.00

DISNEY'S NEW ADVENTURES OF BEAUTY AND THE BEAST (Also see Beauty and the Beast & Disney's Beauty and the Beast)
Disney Comics: 1992 - No. 2, 1992 ($1.50, limited series)

1,2-New stories based on movie — 3.00

DISNEY'S POCAHONTAS (Movie)
Marvel Comics: 1995 ($4.95, one-shot)

1-Movie adaptation — 1 2 3 4 5 7

DISNEY'S TALESPIN LIMITED SERIES: "TAKE OFF" (TV) (See Talespin)
W. D. Publications (Disney Comics): Jan, 1991 - No. 4, Apr, 1991 ($1.50, lim. series, 52 pgs.)

1-4: Based on animated series; 4 part origin — 2.50

DISNEY'S TARZAN (Movie)
Dark Horse Comics: June, 1999 - No. 2, July, 1999 ($2.95, limited series)

1,2: Movie adaptation — 3.00

DISNEY'S THE LION KING (Movie)
Marvel Comics: July, 1994 - No. 2, July, 1994 ($1.50, limited series)

1,2: 2-part movie adaptation — 3.00
1-($2.50, 52 pgs.)-Complete story — 5.00

DISNEY'S THE LITTLE MERMAID (Movie)
Marvel Comics: Sept, 1994 - No. 12, 1995 ($1.50)

1-12 — 4.00

DISNEY'S THE LITTLE MERMAID LIMITED SERIES (Movie)
Disney Comics: Feb, 1992 - No. 4, May, 1992 ($1.50, limited series)

1-4: Peter David scripts — 3.00

DISNEY'S THE LITTLE MERMAID: UNDERWATER ENGAGEMENTS
Acclaim Books: 1997 ($4.50, digest size)

1-Flip book — 4.50

DISNEY'S THE HUNCHBACK OF NOTRE DAME (Movie)(See Disney's Comic Hits #10)
Marvel Comics: July, 1996 ($4.95, squarebound, one-shot)

1-Movie adaptation. — 1 2 3 4 5 7

NOTE: A different edition of this series was sold at Wal-Mart stores with new covers depicting scenes from the 1989 feature film. Inside contents and price were identical.

DISNEY'S THE THREE MUSKETEERS (Movie)
Marvel Comics: Jan, 1994 - No. 2, Feb, 1994 ($1.50, limited series)

1,2-Morrow-c; Spiegle-a; Movie adaptation — 2.50

DISNEY'S TOY STORY (Movie)
Marvel Comics: Dec, 1995 ($4.95, one-shot)

nn-Adaptation of film — 1 2 3 4 5 7

DISTANT SOIL, A (1st Series)
WaRP Graphics: Dec, 1983 - No. 9, Mar 1986 ($1.50, B&W)

1-Magazine size — 4.00
2-9: 2-4 are magazine size — 3.00

NOTE: Second printings exist of #1, 2, 3 & 6.

DISTANT SOIL, A
Donning (Star Blaze): Mar, 1989 ($12.95, trade paperback)

nn-new material — 13.00

DISTANT SOIL, A (2nd Series)
Aria Press/Image Comics (Highbrow Entertainment) #15 on: June, 1991 - Present ($1.75/$2.50/$2.95/$3.95, B&W)

1-27: 13-$2.95-c begins. 14-Sketchbook. 15-(8/96)-1st Image issue — 3.00
29-33,35,37-($3.95) — 4.00
34-($4.95, 64 pages) includes sketchbook pages — 5.00
36,38-($4.50) 36-Back-up story by Darnall & Doran. 38-Includes sketch pages — 4.50
The Aria ('01, $16.95,TPB) r/#26-31 — 17.00
The Ascendant ('98, $18.95,TPB) r/#13-25 — 19.00
The Gathering ('97, $18.95,TPB) r/#1-13; intro. Neil Gaiman — 19.00
Vol. 4: Coda (2005, $17.99, TPB) r/#32-38 — 18.00

NOTE: Four separate printings exist for #1 and are clearly marked. Second printings exist of #2-4 and are also clearly marked.

DISTANT SOIL, A: IMMIGRANT SONG
Donning (Star Blaze): Aug, 1987 ($6.95, trade paperback)

nn-new material — 7.00

DISTRICT X (Also see X-Men titles) (Also see Mutopia X)
Marvel Comics: July, 2004 - No. 14, Aug, 2005 ($2.99)

1-14: 1-3-Bishop app.; Yardin-a/Hine-s — 3.00
...Vol. 1: Mr. M (2005, $14.99) r/#1-6; sketch page by Yardin — 15.00
...Vol. 2: Underground (2005, $19.99) r/#7-14; prologue from X-Men Unlimited #2 — 20.00

DIVER DAN (TV)
Dell Publishing Co.: Feb-Apr, 1962 - No. 2, June-Aug, 1962

Four Color 1254(#1), 2 — 5 10 15 34 55 75

DIVINE RIGHT
Image Comics (WildStorm Prod.): Sept, 1997 - No. 12, Nov, 1999 ($2.50)

Preview — 5.00
1,2: 1-Jim Lee-s/a(p)/c, 1-Variant-c by Charest — 4.00
1-($3.50)-Voyager Pack w/Stormwatch preview — 3.50
1-American Entertainment Ed. — 6.00
2-Variant-c of Exotica & Blaze — 5.00
3-Chromium-c by Jim Lee — 5.00
3-12: 3-5-Fairchild & Lynch app. 4-American Entertainment Ed. 8-Two covers. 9-1st DC issue. 11,12-Divine Intervention pt. 1,4 — 3.00
5-Pacific Comicon Ed. — 6.00
6-Glow in the dark variant-c, European Tour Edition — 20.00
...Book One TPB (2002, $17.95) r/#1-7 — 18.00
...Book Two TPB (2002, $17.95) r/#8-12 & Divine Intervention Gen13, ...Wildcats — 18.00
...Collected Edition #1-3 ($5.95, TPB) 1-r/#1,2. 2-r/#3,4. 3-r/#5,6 — 6.00
Divine Intervention/Gen 13 (11/99, $2.50) Part 3; D'Anda-a — 2.50
Divine Intervention/Wildcats (11/99, $2.50) Part 2; D'Anda-a — 2.50

DIVISION 13 (See Comic's Greatest World)
Dark Horse Comics: Sept, 1994 - Jan, 1995 ($2.50, color)

1-4: Giffen story in all. 1-Art Adams-c — 2.50

DIXIE DUGAN (See Big Shot, Columbia Comics & Feature Funnies)
McNaught Syndicate/Columbia/Publication Ent.: July, 1942 - No. 13, 1949
(Strip reprints in all)

1-Joe Palooka x-over by Ham Fisher — 27 54 81 160 263 365
2 — 15 30 45 86 133 180
3 — 12 24 36 69 97 125
4,5(1945-46)-Bo strip-r — 10 20 30 54 72 90
6-13(1/47-49): 6-Paperdoll cut-outs — 9 18 27 47 61 75

DIXIE DUGAN
Prize Publications (Headline): V3#1, Nov, 1951 - V4#4, Feb, 1954

V3#1 — 10 20 30 54 72 90
2-4 — 7 14 21 35 43 50
V4#1-4(#5-8) — 6 12 18 28 34 40

DIZZY DAMES
American Comics Group (B&M Distr. Co.): Sept-Oct, 1952 - No. 6, Jul-Aug, 1953

1-Whitney-c — 17 34 51 98 154 210
2 — 11 22 33 60 83 105

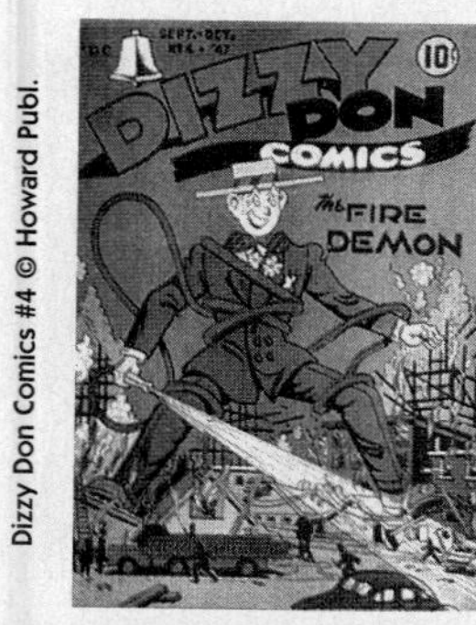

Dizzy Don Comics #4 © Howard Publ.

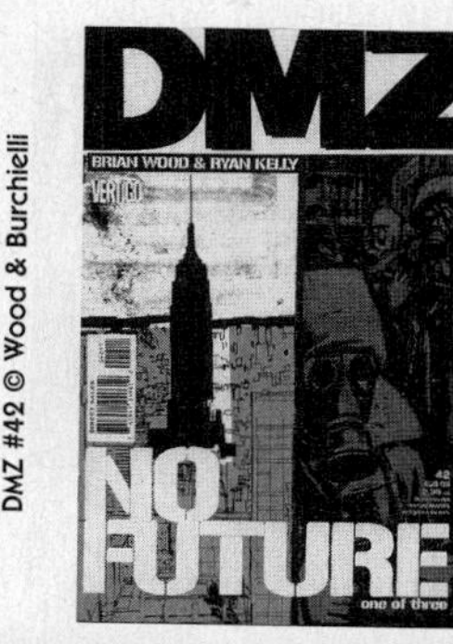

DMZ #42 © Wood & Burchielli

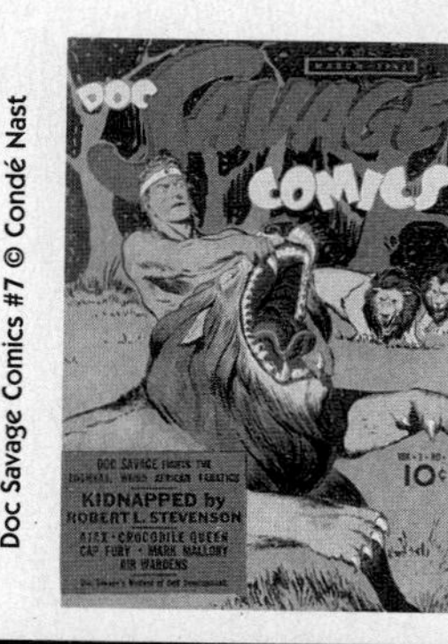

Doc Savage Comics #7 © Condé Nast

GD 2.0 | VG 4.0 | FN 6.0 | VF 8.0 | VF/NM 9.0 | NM- 9.2

3-6 9 18 27 50 65 80

DIZZY DON COMICS
F. E. Howard Publications/Dizzy Don Ent. Ltd (Canada): 1942 - No. 22, Oct, 1946; No. 3, Apr, 1947 - No. 4, Sept./Oct., 1947 (Most B&W)

1 (B&W) 22 44 66 128 209 290
2 (B&W) 14 28 42 80 115 150
4-21 (B&W) 12 24 36 67 94 120
22-Full color, 52 pgs. 22 44 66 128 209 290
3 (4/47), 4 (9-10/47)-Full color, 52 pgs. 22 44 66 128 209 290

DIZZY DUCK (Formerly Barnyard Comics)
Standard Comics: No. 32, Nov, 1950 - No. 39, Mar, 1952

32-Funny animal 10 20 30 54 72 90
33-39 6 12 18 31 38 45

DMZ
DC Comics (Vertigo): Jan, 2006 - Present ($2.99)

1-Brian Wood-s/Riccardo Burchielli-a 4.00
1-(2008, no cover price) Convention Exclusive promotional edition 3.00
2-49: 2-10-Brian Wood-s/Riccardo Burchielli-a. 11-Donaldson-a. 12-Wood-s/a 3.00
...: Blood in the Game TPB (2009, $12.99) r/#29-34; intro. by Greg Palast 13.00
...: Body of a Journalist TPB (2007, $12.99) r/#6-12; intro. by D. Randall Blythe 13.00
...: Friendly Fire TPB (2008, $12.99) r/#18-22; intro. by Sgt. John G. Ford 13.00
...: On the Ground TPB (2006, $9.99) r/#1-5; intro. by Brian Azzarello 10.00
...: Public Works TPB (2007, $12.99) r/#13-17; intro. by Cory Doctorow 13.00
...: The Hidden War TPB (2008, $12.99) r/#23-28 13.00
...: War Powers TPB (2009, $14.99) r/#35-41 15.00

DNAGENTS (The New DNAgents V2/1 on)(Also see Surge)
Eclipse Comics: March, 1983 - No. 24, July, 1985 ($1.50, Baxter paper)

1,24: 1-Origin. 4-Amber app. 24-Dave Stevens-c 3.00
2-23: 8-Infinity-c 2.50
... Industrial Strength Edition TPB (Image, 2008, $24.99) B&W r/#1-14; Evanier intro. 25.00

DOBERMAN (See Sgt. Bilko's Private...)

DOBIE GILLIS (See The Many Loves of...)

DOC CHAOS: THE STRANGE ATTRACTOR
Vortex Comics: Apr, 1990 - No. 3, 1990 ($3.00, 32 pgs.)

1-3: The Lust For Order 3.00

DOC FRANKENSTEIN
Burlyman Entertainment: Nov, 2004 - Present ($3.50)

1-6-Wachowski brothers-s/Skroce-a 3.50

DOCK WALLOPER (Ed Burns' ...)
Virgin Comics: Nov, 2007 - No. 5, Jun, 2008 ($2.99)

1-5-Burns & Palmiotti-s/Siju Thomas-a; Prohibition time 3.00

DOC SAMSON (Also see Incredible Hulk)
Marvel Comics: Jan, 1996 - No. 4, Apr, 1996 ($1.95, limited series)

1-4: 1-Hulk c/app. 2-She-Hulk-c/app. 3-Punisher-c/app. 4-Polaris-c/app. 2.50

DOC SAMSON (Incredible Hulk)
Marvel Comics: Mar, 2006 - No. 5, July, 2006 ($2.99, limited series)

1-5: 1-DiFilippo-s/Fiorentino-a. 3-Conner-c 3.00

DOC SAVAGE
Gold Key: Nov, 1966

1-Adaptation of the Thousand-Headed Man; James Bama c-r/1964 Doc Savage paperback 11 22 33 74 132 190

DOC SAVAGE (Also see Giant-Size...)
Marvel Comics Group: Oct, 1972 - No. 8, Jan, 1974

1 3 6 9 19 29 38
2,3-Steranko-c 3 6 9 14 20 25
4-8 2 4 6 9 12 15

NOTE: ***Gil Kane** c-5, 6. **Mooney** a-1i. No. 1, 2 adapts pulp story "The Man of Bronze"; No. 3, 4 adapts "Death in Silver"; No. 5, 6 adapts "The Monsters"; No. 7, 8 adapts "The Brand of The Werewolf".*

DOC SAVAGE (Magazine)
Marvel Comics Group: Aug, 1975 - No. 8, Spring, 1977 ($1.00, B&W)

1-Cover from movie poster; Ron Ely photo-c 3 6 9 16 22 28
2-5: 3-Buscema-a. 5-Adams-a(1 pg.), Rogers-a(1 pg) 2 4 6 9 13 16
6-8 2 4 6 10 14 18

DOC SAVAGE
DC Comics: Nov, 1987 - No. 4, Feb, 1988 ($1.75, limited series)

GD 2.0 | VG 4.0 | FN 6.0 | VF 8.0 | VF/NM 9.0 | NM- 9.2

1-4: Dennis O'Neil-s/Adam & Andy Kubert-a/c in all 3.00
...: The Silver Pyramid TPB (2009, $19.99) r/#1-4 20.00

DOC SAVAGE
DC Comics: Nov, 1988 - No. 24, Oct, 1990 ($1.75/$2.00: #13-24)

1-16,19-24 3.00
17,18-Shadow x-over 4.00
Annual 1 (1989, $3.50, 68 pgs.) 4.00

DOC SAVAGE COMICS (Also see Shadow Comics)
Street & Smith Publ.: May, 1940 - No. 20, Oct, 1943 (1st app. in Doc Savage pulp, 3/33)

1-Doc Savage, Cap Fury, Danny Garrett, Mark Mallory, The Whisperer, Captain Death, Billy the Kid, Sheriff Pete & Treasure Island begin; Norgil, the Magician app. 497 994 1491 3628 6414 9200
2-Origin & 1st app. Ajax, the Sun Man; Danny Garrett, The Whisperer end; classic sci-fi cover 203 406 609 1289 2220 3150
3 129 258 387 826 1413 2000
4-Treasure Island ends; Tuska-a 103 206 309 659 1130 1600
5-Origin & 1st app. Astron, the Crocodile Queen, not in #9 & 11; Norgi the Magician app.; classic-c 94 188 282 597 1024 1450
6-10: 6-Cap Fury ends; origin & only app. Red Falcon in Astron story. 8-Mark Mallory ends; Charlie McCarthy app. on-c plus true life story. 9-Supersnipe app. 10-Origin & only app. The Thunderbolt 61 122 183 384 662 940
11,12 52 104 156 322 549 775
V2#1-6,8(#13-18,20): 15-Origin of Ajax the Sun Man; Jack Benny on-c; Hitler app. 16-The Pulp Hero, The Avenger app.; Fanny Brice story. 17-Sun Man ends; Nick Carter begins; Duffy's Tavern part photo-c & story. 18-Huckleberry Finn part-c/story. 19-Henny Youngman part photo-c & life story. 20-Only all funny-c w/Huckleberry Finn 47 94 141 296 498 700
V2#7-Classic Devil-c 52 104 156 322 549 775

DOC SAVAGE: CURSE OF THE FIRE GOD
Dark Horse Comics: Sept, 1995 - No. 4, Dec, 1995 ($2.95, limited series)

1-4 3.00

DOC SAVAGE: THE MAN OF BRONZE
Skylark Pub: Mar, 1979, 68pgs. (B&W comic digest, 5-1/4x7-5/8")(low print)

15406-0: Whitman-a, 60 pgs., new comics 4 8 12 24 37 50

DOC SAVAGE: THE MAN OF BRONZE
Millennium Publications: 1991 - No. 4, 1991 ($2.50, limited series)

1-4: 1-Bronze logo 3.00
...: The Manual of Bronze 1 ($2.50, B&W, color, one-shot)-Unpublished proposed Doc Savage strip in color, B&W strip-r 3.00

DOC SAVAGE: THE MAN OF BRONZE, DOOM DYNASTY
Millennium Publ.: 1992 (Says 1991) - No. 2, 1992 ($2.50, limited series)

1,2 3.00

DOC SAVAGE: THE MAN OF BRONZE - REPEL
Innovation Publishing: 1992 ($2.50)

1-Dave Dorman painted-c 3.00

DOC SAVAGE: THE MAN OF BRONZE THE DEVIL'S THOUGHTS
Millennium Publ.: 1992 (Says 1991) - No. 3, 1992 ($2.50, limited series)

1-3 3.00

DOC STEARN...MR. MONSTER (See Mr. Monster)

DR. ANTHONY KING, HOLLYWOOD LOVE DOCTOR
Minoan Publishing Corp./Harvey Publications No. 4: 1952(Jan) - No. 3, May, 1953; No. 4, May, 1954

1 14 28 42 82 121 160
2-4: 4-Powell-a 9 18 27 52 69 85

DR. ANTHONY'S LOVE CLINIC (See Mr. Anthony's...)

DR. BOBBS
Dell Publishing Co.: No. 212, Jan, 1949

Four Color 212 6 12 18 37 59 80

DOCTOR CYBORG
Attention! Publishing: 1996 - No. 5 ($2.95, B&W)

1-5 3.00
The Clone Conspiracy TPB (1998, $14.95) r/#1-5 15.00

DOCTOR DOOM AND THE MASTERS OF EVIL (All ages title)
Marvel Comics: Mar, 2009 - No. 4, Jun, 2009 ($2.99)

1-4: 1-Sinister Six app. 4-Magneto app. 3.00

Dr. Horrible #1 © Timescape

Doctor Solar, Man of the Atom #5 © GK

Doctor Strange #56 © MAR

	GD	VG	FN	VF	VF/NM	NM-
	2.0	4.0	6.0	8.0	9.0	9.2

DR. DOOM'S REVENGE
Marvel Comics: 1989 (Came w/computer game from Paragon Software)
V1#1-Spider-Man & Captain America fight Dr. Doom 3.00

DR. FATE (See 1st Issue Special, The Immortal..., Justice League, More Fun #55, & Showcase)

DOCTOR FATE
DC Comics: July, 1987 - No. 4, Oct, 1987 ($1.50, limited series, Baxter paper)
1-4: Giffen-c/a in all 3.00

DOCTOR FATE
DC Comics: Winter, 1988-'89 - No. 41, June, 1992 ($1.25/$1.50 #5 on)
1,15: 15-Justice League app. 3.50
2-14 3.00
16-41: 25-1st new Dr. Fate. 36-Original Dr. Fate returns 2.50
Annual 1(1989, $2.95, 68 pgs.)-Sutton-a 3.50

DOCTOR FATE
DC Comics: Oct, 2003 - No. 5, Feb, 2004 ($2.50, limited series)
1-5-Golden-s/Kramer-a 2.50

DR. FU MANCHU (See The Mask of...)
I.W. Enterprises: 1964
1-r/Avon's "Mask of Dr. Fu Manchu"; Wood-a 7 14 21 49 80 110

DR. GIGGLES (See Dark Horse Presents #64-66)
Dark Horse Comics: Oct, 1992 - No. 2, Oct, 1992 ($2.50, limited series)
1,2-Based on movie 2.50

DOCTOR GRAVES (Formerly The Many Ghosts of...)
Charlton Comics: No. 73, Sept, 1985 - No. 75, Jan, 1986
73-75-Low print run 1 2 3 5 6 8

DR. HORRIBLE (Based on Joss Whedon's internet feature)
Dark Horse Comics: Nov, 2009 ($3.50, one-shot)
1-Zack Whedon-s/Joëlle Jones-a; Captain Hammer pin-up by Gene Ha; 3 covers 3.50

DR. JEKYLL AND MR. HYDE (See A Star Presentation & Supernatural Thrillers #4)

DR. KILDARE (TV)
Dell Publishing Co.: No. 1337, 4-6/62 - No. 9, 4-6/65 (All Richard Chamberlain photo-c)
Four Color 1337(#1, 1962) 8 16 24 58 97 135
2-9 6 12 18 43 69 95

DR. MASTERS (See The Adventures of Young...)

DOCTOR MID-NITE (Also see All-American #25)
DC Comics: 1999 - No. 3, 1999 ($5.95, square-bound, limited series)
1-3-Matt Wagner-s/John K. Snyder III-painted art 6.00
TPB (2000, $19.95) r/series 20.00

DOCTOR OCTOPUS: NEGATIVE EXPOSURE
Marvel Comics: Dec, 2003 - No. 5, Apr, 2004 ($2.99, limited series)
1-5-Vaughan-s/Staz Johnson-a; Spider-Man app. 3.00
Spider-Man/Doctor Octopus: Negative Exposure TPB (2004, $13.99) r/series 14.00

DR. ROBOT SPECIAL
Dark Horse Comics: Apr, 2000 ($2.95, one-shot)
1-Bernie Mireault-s/a; some reprints from Madman Comics #12-15 3.00

DOCTOR SOLAR, MAN OF THE ATOM (See The Occult Files of Dr. Spektor #14 & Solar)
Gold Key/Whitman No. 28 on: 10/62 - No. 27, 4/69; No. 28, 4/81 - No. 31, 3/82 (1-27 have painted-c)
1-(#10000-210)-Origin/1st app. Dr. Solar (1st original Gold Key character)
18 36 54 129 252 375
2-Prof. Harbinger begins 9 18 27 63 107 150
3,4 6 12 18 41 66 90
5-Intro. Man of the Atom in costume 6 12 18 43 69 95
6-10 5 10 15 32 51 70
11-14,16-20 4 8 12 24 37 50
15-Origin retold 4 8 12 26 41 55
21-23: 23-Last 12¢ issue 3 6 9 20 30 40
24-27 3 6 9 19 29 38
28-31: 29-Magnus Robot Fighter begins. 31-(3/82)The Sentinel app.
2 4 6 11 16 20
Hardcover Volume One (Dark Horse Books, 2004, $49.95) r/#1-7; creator bios 50.00
Hardcover Volume Two (Dark Horse Books, 6/05, $49.95) r/#8-14; Jim Shooter foreword 50.00
Hardcover Volume Three (Dark Horse Books, 9/05, $49.95) r/#15-22; Mike Baron foreword 50.00
Hardcover Volume Four (Dark Horse Books, 11/07, $49.95) r/#23-31 and The Occult Files of Dr. Spektor #14; Batton Lash foreword 50.00

	GD	VG	FN	VF	VF/NM	NM-
	2.0	4.0	6.0	8.0	9.0	9.2

NOTE: ***Frank Bolle** a-6-19, 29-31; c-29i, 30i. **Bob Fugitani** a-1-5. **Spiegle** a-29-31. **Al McWilliams** a-20-23.*

DOCTOR SOLAR, MAN OF THE ATOM
Valiant Comics: 1990 - No. 2, 1991 ($7.95, card stock-c, high quality, 96 pgs.)
1,2: Reprints Gold Key series 1 2 3 4 5 7

DOCTOR SPECTRUM (See Supreme Power)
Marvel Comics: Oct, 2004 - No. 6, Mar, 2005 ($2.99, limited series)
1-6-Origin; Sara Barnes-s/Travel Foreman-a 3.00
TPB (2005, $16.99) r/#1-6 17.00

DOCTOR SPEKTOR (See The Occult Files of..., & Spine-Tingling Tales)

DOCTOR STRANGE (Formerly Strange Tales #1-168) (Also see The Defenders, Giant-Size..., Marvel Fanfare, Marvel Graphic Novel, Marvel Premiere, Marvel Treasury Edition, Strange & Strange Tales, 2nd Series)
Marvel Comics Group: No. 169, 6/68 - No. 183, 11/69; 6/74 - No. 81, 2/87
169(#1)-Origin retold; panel swipe/M.D. #1-c 13 26 39 93 172 250
170-177: 177-New costume 5 10 15 30 48 65
178-183: 178-Black Knight app. 179-Spider-Man story-r. 180-Photo montage-c. 181-Brunner-c(part-i), last 12¢ issue 4 8 12 28 44 60
1(6/74, 2nd series)-Brunner-c/a 7 14 21 49 80 110
2 4 8 12 26 41 55
3-5 3 6 9 16 23 30
6-10 2 4 6 9 13 16
11-13,15-20: 13,15-17-(Regular 25¢ editions) 1 2 3 5 7 9
13,15-17-(30¢-c variants, limited distribution) 4 8 12 22 34 45
14-(5/76) Dracula app.; (regular 25¢ edition) 2 4 6 9 13 16
14-(30¢-c variant, limited distribution) 5 10 15 32 51 70
21-40: 21-Origin-r/Doctor Strange #169. 23-25-(Regular 30¢ editions). 31-Sub-Mariner-c/story 6.00
23-25-(35¢-c variants, limited distribution)(6,8,10/77) 2 4 6 8 10 12
41-57,63-77,79-81: 56-Origin retold 4.00
58-62: 58-Re-intro Hannibal King (cameo). 59-Hannibal King full app. 59-62-Dracula app. (Darkhold storyline). 61,62-Doctor Strange, Blade, Hannibal King & Frank Drake team-up to battle. Dracula. 62-Death of Dracula & Lilith 6.00
78-New costume 5.00
Annual 1(1976, 52 pgs.)-New Russell-a (35 pgs.) 2 4 6 11 16 20
.../Silver Dagger Special Edition 1 (3/83, $2.50)-r/#1,2,4,5; Wrightson-c 3.00
... Vs. Dracula TPB (2006, $19.99) r/#14,58-62 and Tomb of Dracula #44 20.00
...What Is It That Disturbs You, Stephen? #1 (10/97, $5.99, 48 pgs.) Russell-a/Andreyko & Russell-s, retelling of Annual #1 story 6.00
NOTE: ***Adkins** a-169, 170, 171i; c-169-171, 172i, 173. **Adams** a-4i. **Austin** a(i)-48-60, 66, 68, 70, 73; c(i)-38, 47-53, 55, 58-60, 70. **Brunner** a-1-5p; c-1-6, 22, 28-30, 33. **Colan** a(p)-172-178, 180-183, 6-18, 36-45, 47; c(p)-172, 174-183, 11-21, 23, 27, 35, 36, 47. **Ditko** a-179r, 3r. **Everett** c-183i. **Golden** a-46p, 55p; c-42-44, 46, 55p. **G. Kane** c(p)-8-10. **Miller** c-46p. **Nebres** a-20, 22, 23, 24i, 26i, 32i; c-32i, 34. **Rogers** a-48-53p; c-47p-53p. **Russell** a-34i, 46i, Annual 1. **B. Smith** c-179. **Paul Smith** a-54p, 56p, 65, 66p, 68p, 69, 71-73; c-56, 65, 66, 68, 71. **Starlin** a-23p, 26; c-25, 26. **Sutton** a-27-29p, 31i, 33, 34p. Painted c-62, 63.*

DOCTOR STRANGE (Volume 2)
Marvel Comics: Feb, 1999 - No. 4, May, 1999 ($2.99, limited series)
1-4: 1,2-Tony Harris-a/painted cover. 3,4-Chadwick-a 3.00

DOCTOR STRANGE CLASSICS
Marvel Comics Group: Mar, 1984 - No. 4, June, 1984 ($1.50, Baxter paper)
1-4: Ditko-r; Byrne-c. 4-New Golden pin-up 3.00
NOTE: ***Byrne** c-1i, 2-4.*

DOCTOR STRANGEFATE (See Marvel Versus DC #3 & DC Versus Marvel #4)
DC Comics (Amalgam): Apr, 1996 ($1.95)
1-Ron Marz script w/Jose Garcia-Lopez-(p) & Kevin Nowlan-(i). Access & Charles Xavier app. 2.50

DOCTOR STRANGE MASTER OF THE MYSTIC ARTS (See Fireside Book Series)

DOCTOR STRANGE, SORCERER SUPREME
Marvel Comics (Midnight Sons imprint #60 on): Nov, 1988 - No. 90, June, 1996 ($1.25/$1.50/$1.75/$1.95, direct sales only, Mando paper)
1 ($1.25) 4.00
2-9,12-14,16-25,27,29-40,42-49,51-64: 3-New Defenders app. 5-Guice-c/a begins. 14-18-Morbius story line. 31-36-Infinity Gauntlet x-overs. 31-Silver Surfer app. 33-Thanos-c & cameo. 36-Warlock app. 37-Silver Surfer app. 40-Daredevil x-over. 41-Wolverine-c/story. 42-47-Infinity War x-overs. 47-Gamora app. 52,53-Morbius-c/stories. 60,61-Siege of Darkness pt. 7 & 15. 60-Spot varnish-c. 61-New Doctor Strange begins (cameo, 1st app.). 62-Dr. Doom & Morbius app. 2.50
10,11,26,28,41: 10-Re-intro Morbius w/new costume (11/89). 11-Hobgoblin app. 26-Werewolf by Night app. 28-Ghost Rider-s cont'd from G.R. #12; published at same time as Doctor Strange/Ghost Rider Special #1(4/91) 3.00
15-Unauthorized Amy Grant photo-c 4.00

Doctor Voodoo: Avenger of the Supernatural #5 © MAR

Do-Do #1 © Nation-Wide

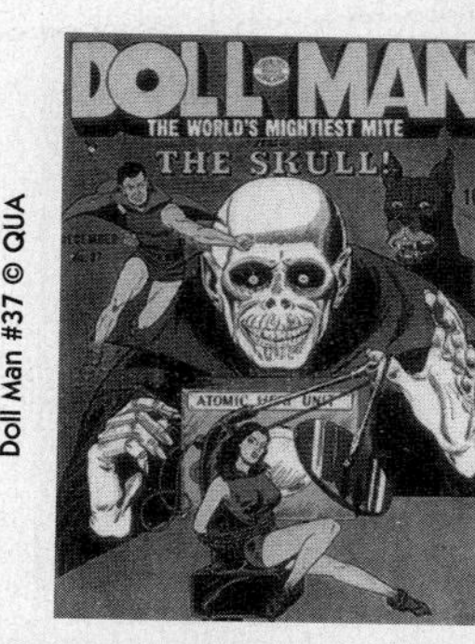

Doll Man #37 © QUA

	GD 2.0	VG 4.0	FN 6.0	VF 8.0	VF/NM 9.0	NM- 9.2
50-($2.95, 52 pgs.)-Holo-grafx foil-c; Hulk, Ghost Rider & Silver Surfer app.; leads into new Secret Defenders series						3.00
65-74, 76-90: 65-Begin $1.95-c; bound-in card sheet. 72-Silver ink-c. 80-82- Ellis-s. 84-DeMatteis story begins. 87-Death of Baron Mordo						2.50
75 ($2.50)						3.00
75 ($3.50)-Foil-c						4.00
Annual 2-4 ('92-'94, 68 pgs.)-2-Defenders app. 3-Polybagged w/card						3.00
Ashcan (1995, 75¢)						2.25
.../Ghost Rider Special 1 (4/91, $1.50)-Same book as D.S.S.S. #28						2.50
...Vs. Dracula 1 (3/94, $1.75, 52 pgs.)-r/Tomb of Dracula #44 & Dr. Strange #14						2.50

NOTE: *Colan c/a-19.* ***Golden*** *c-28.* ***Guice*** *a-5-16, 18, 20-24; c-5-12, 20-24. See 1st series for Annual #1.*

DOCTOR STRANGE: THE OATH
Marvel Comics: Dec, 2006 - No. 5, Apr, 2007 ($2.99, limited series)

1-5-Vaughan-s/Martin-a; Night Nurse app. 3.00
TPB (2007, $13.99) r/#1-5; sketch pages and promotional art 14.00

DR. TOM BRENT, YOUNG INTERN
Charlton Publications: Feb, 1963 - No. 5, Oct, 1963

	GD	VG	FN	VF	VF/NM	NM-
1	3	6	9	16	23	30
2-5	2	4	6	11	16	20

DR. TOMORROW
Acclaim Comics (Valiant): Sept, 1997 - No. 12 ($2.50)

1-12: 1-Mignola-c 2.50

DR. VOLTZ (See Mighty Midget Comics)

DOCTOR VOODOO: AVENGER OF THE SUPERNATURAL
Marvel Comics: Dec, 2009 - No. 5, Apr, 2010 ($2.99, limited series)

1-5-Dr. Doom, Son of Satan & Ghost Rider app.; Palo-a 3.00
Doctor Voodoo: The Origin of Jericho Drumm (1/10, $4.99) r/Strange Tales #169,170 5.00

DR. WEIRD
Big Bang Comics: Oct, 1994 - No. 2, May, 1995 ($2.95, B&W)

1,2: 1-Frank Brunner-c 4.00

DR. WEIRD SPECIAL
Big Bang Comics: Feb, 1994 ($3.95, B&W, 68 pgs.)

1-Origin-r by Starlin; Starlin-c. 4.00

DOCTOR WHO (Also see Marvel Premiere #57-60)
Marvel Comics Group: Oct, 1984 - No. 23, Aug, 1986 ($1.50, direct sales, Baxter paper)

1-15-British-r 4.00
16-23 5.00
Graphic Novel Voyager (1985, $8.95) color reprints of B&W comic pages from Doctor Who Magazine #88-99; Colin Baker afterword 12.00

DOCTOR WHO (Based on the 2005 TV series with David Tennant)
IDW Publishing: Jan, 2008 - No. 6, Jun, 2008 ($3.99)

1-6: 1-Nick Roche-a/Gary Russell-s; two covers 4.00

DOCTOR WHO (Based on the 2005 TV series with David Tennant)
IDW Publishing: Jul, 2009 - Present ($3.99)

1-8-Grist variant-c on all. 3-5-Art by Matt Smith (not the actor) 4.00
...: Autopia (6/09, $3.99) Ostrander-s; Yates-a/c; variant photo-c 4.00
...: Black Death White Life (9/09, $3.99) Mandrake-a; Guy Davis- c; variant photo-c 4.00
...: Cold-Blooded War (8/09, $3.99) Salmon-a/c; variant photo-c 4.00
...: Room With a Déjà View (6/09, $3.99) Eric J-a; Mandrake-c; variant photo-c 4.00
...: The Whispering Gallery (2/09, $3.99) Moore & Reppion-s; Templesmith-a/2 covers 4.00
...: Time Machination (5/09, $3.99) Paul Grist-a/c; variant photo-c 4.00

DR. WHO & THE DALEKS (See Movie Classics)

DOCTOR WHO CLASSICS
IDW Publishing: Nov, 2005 - Present ($3.99)

1-10: Reprints from Doctor Who Weekly (1979); art by Gibbons, Neary and others 4.00
Series 2 (12/08 - No. 12, 11/09, $3.99) 1-12 4.00

DOCTOR WHO: THE FORGOTTEN (Based on the 2005 TV series with David Tennant)
IDW Publishing: Aug, 2008 - No. 6, Jan, 2009 ($3.99)

1-6: 1,2-Pia Guerra-a/Tony Lee-s; two covers 4.00

DR. WONDER
Old Town Publishing: June, 1996 - No. 5 ($2.95, B&W)

1-5: 1-Intro & origin of Dr. Wonder; Dick Ayers-c/a; Irwin Hasen-a 3.00

DOCTOR ZERO
Marvel Comics (Epic Comics): Apr, 1988 - No. 8, Aug, 1989 ($1.25/$1.50)

1-8: 1-Sienkiewicz-c. 6,7-Spiegle-a 2.50

NOTE: ***Sienkiewicz*** *a-3i, 4i; c-1.* ***Spiegle*** *a-6, 7.*

DO-DO (Funny Animal Circus Stories)
Nation-Wide Publishers: 1950 - No. 7, 1951 (5¢, 5x7-1/4" Miniature)

	GD	VG	FN	VF	VF/NM	NM-
1 (52 pgs.)	26	52	78	154	252	350
2-7	15	30	45	85	130	175

DODO & THE FROG, THE (Formerly Funny Stuff; also see It's Game Time #2)
National Periodical Publications: No. 80, 9-10/54 - No. 88, 1-2/56; No. 89, 8-9/56; No. 90, 10-11/56; No. 91, 9/57; No. 92, 11/57 (See Comic Cavalcade and Captain Carrot)

	GD	VG	FN	VF	VF/NM	NM-
80-1st app. Doodles Duck by Sheldon Mayer	20	40	60	114	182	250
81-91: Doodles Duck by Mayer in #81,83-90	14	28	42	76	108	140
92-(Scarce)-Doodles Duck by S. Mayer	18	36	54	105	165	225

DOGFACE DOOLEY
Magazine Enterprises: 1951 - No. 5, 1953

	GD	VG	FN	VF	VF/NM	NM-
1(A-1 40)	8	16	24	40	50	60
2(A-1 43), 3(A-1 49), 4(A-1 53), 5(A-1 64)	6	12	18	28	34	40
I.W. Reprint #1('64), Super Reprint #17	2	4	6	9	13	16

DOG MOON
DC Comics (Vertigo): 1996 ($6.95, one-shot)

1-Robert Hunter-scripts; Tim Truman-c/a. 7.00

DOG OF FLANDERS, A
Dell Publishing Co.: No. 1088, Mar, 1960

	GD	VG	FN	VF	VF/NM	NM-
Four Color 1088-Movie, photo-c	5	10	15	30	48	65

DOGPATCH (See Al Capp's... & Mammy Yokum)

DOGS OF WAR (Also see Warriors of Plasm)
Defiant: Apr, 1994 - No. 5, Aug, 1994 ($2.50)

1-5 2.50

DOGS-O-WAR
Crusade Comics: June, 1996 - No. 3, Jan, 1997 ($2.95, B&W, limited series)

1-3: 1,2-Photo-c 3.00

DOLLFACE & HER GANG (Betty Betz'...)
Dell Publishing Co.: No. 309, Jan, 1951

	GD	VG	FN	VF	VF/NM	NM-
Four Color 309	5	10	15	35	55	75

DOLLMAN (Movie)
Eternity Comics: Sept, 1991 - No. 4, Dec, 1991 ($2.50, limited series)

1-4: Adaptation of film 2.50

DOLL MAN QUARTERLY, THE (Doll Man #17 on; also see Feature Comics #27 & Freedom Fighters)
Quality Comics: Fall, 1941 - No. 7, Fall, '43; No. 8, Spr, '46 - No. 47, Oct, 1953

	GD	VG	FN	VF	VF/NM	NM-
1-Dollman (by Cassone), Justin Wright begin	331	662	993	2317	4059	5800
2-The Dragon begins; Crandall-a(5)	145	290	435	921	1586	2250
3,4	89	178	267	565	970	1375
5-Crandall-a	86	172	258	546	936	1325
6,7(1943)	54	108	162	343	584	825
8(1946)-1st app. Torchy by Bill Ward	165	330	495	1048	1799	2550
9	53	106	159	334	567	800
10-20	41	82	123	256	428	600
21-30: 28-Vs. The Flame	36	72	108	216	351	485
31-36,38,40: 31-(12/50)-Intro Elmo, the wonder dog (Dollman's faithful dog). 32-34-Jeb Rivers app.; 34 by Crandall(p)	33	66	99	194	317	440
37-Origin & 1st app. Dollgirl; Dollgirl bondage-c	47	94	141	296	498	700
39- "Narcotics...the Death Drug" c-/story	37	74	111	222	361	500
41-47	24	48	72	140	230	320
Super Reprint #11('64, r/#20),15(r/#23),17(r/#28): 15,17-Torchy app.; Andru/Esposito-c	3	6	9	20	30	40

NOTE: ***Ward*** *Torchy in 8, 9, 11, 12, 14-24, 27; by Fox-#26, 30, 35-47.* ***Crandall*** *a-2, 5, 10, 13 & Super #11, 17, 18.* ***Crandall/Cuidera*** *c-40-42.* ***Guardineer*** *a-3. Bondage c-27, 37, 38, 39.*

DOLLS
Sirius: June, 1996 ($2.95, B&W, one-shot)

1 3.00

DOLLY
Ziff-Davis Publ. Co.: No. 10, July-Aug, 1951 (Funny animal)

	GD	VG	FN	VF	VF/NM	NM-
10-Painted-c	8	16	24	44	57	70

DOLLY DILL
Marvel Comics/Newsstand Publ.: 1945

	GD	VG	FN	VF	VF/NM	NM-
1	18	36	54	105	165	225

Dominic Fortune #1 © MAR

Donald Duck Large Feature Comic #20 © DIS

Donald Duck #106 © DIS

GD VG FN VF VF/NM NM-
2.0 4.0 6.0 8.0 9.0 9.2

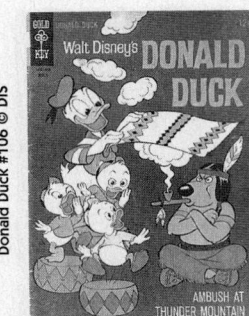

DOLLZ, THE
Image Comics: Apr, 2001 - No. 2, June, 2001 ($2.95)
1,2: 1-Four covers; Sniegoski & Green-s/Green-a 3.00

DOMINATION FACTOR
Marvel Comics: Nov, 1999 - 4.8, Feb, 2000 ($2.50, interconnected mini- series)
1.1, 2.3, 3.5, 4.7-Fantastic Four; Jurgens-s/a 2.50
1.2, 2.4, 3.6, 4.8-Avengers; Ordway-s/a 2.50

DOMINIC FORTUNE
Marvel Comics (MAX): Oct, 2009 - No. 4, Jan, 2010 ($3.99, limited series)
1-4-Howard Chaykin-s/a/c 4.00

DOMINION
Image Comics: Jan, 2003 - No. 2 ($2.95)
1,2-Keith Giffen-s/a 3.00

DOMINION (Manga)
Eclipse Comics: Dec, 1990 - No. 6., July, 1990 ($2.00, B&W, limited series)
1-6 3.00

DOMINION: CONFLICT 1 (Manga)
Dark Horse Comics: Mar, 1996 - No. 6, Aug, 1996 ($2.95, B&W, limited series)
1-6: Shirow-c/a/scripts 3.00

DOMINIQUE: KILLZONE
Caliber Comics: May, 1995 ($2.95, B&W)
1 3.00

DOMINO (See X-Force)
Marvel Comics: Jan, 1997 - No. 3, Mar, 1997 ($1.95, limited series)
1-3: 2-Deathstrike-c/app. 2.50

DOMINO (See X-Force)
Marvel Comics: June, 2003 - No. 4, Aug, 2003 ($2.50, limited series)
1-4-Stelfreeze-c/a; Pruett-s. 2.50

DOMINO CHANCE
Chance Enterprises: May-June, 1982 - No. 9, May, 1985 (B&W)
1-9: 7-1st app. Gizmo, 2 pgs. 8-1st full Gizmo story. 1-Reprint, May, 1985 2.50

DONALD AND MICKEY IN DISNEYLAND (See Dell Giants)

DONALD AND SCROOGE
Disney Comics: 1992 ($8.95, squarebound, 100 pgs.)
nn-Don Rosa reprint special; r/U.S., D.D. Advs. 1 3 4 6 8 10
1-3 (1992, $1.50)-r/D.D. Advs. (Disney) #1,22,24 & U.S. #261-263,269 3.00

DONALD AND THE WHEEL (Disney)
Dell Publishing Co.: No. 1190, Nov, 1961
Four Color 1190-Movie, Barks-c 8 16 24 54 90 125

DONALD DUCK (See Adventures of Mickey Mouse, Cheerios, Donald & Mickey, Ducktales, Dynabrite Comics, Gladstone Comic Album, Mickey & Donald, Mickey Mouse Mag., Story Hour Series, Uncle Scrooge, Walt Disney's Comics & Stories, W. D.'s Donald Duck, Wheaties & Whitman Comic Books, Wise Little Hen, The)

DONALD DUCK
Whitman Publishing Co./Grosset & Dunlap/K.K.: 1935, 1936 (All pages on heavy linen-like finish cover stock in color;1st book ever devoted to Donald Duck; see Advs. of Mickey Mouse for 1st app.) (9-1/2x13")
978(1935)-16 pgs.; Illustrated text story book 206 412 618 1318 2259 3200
nn(1936)-36 pgs.plus hard cover & dust jacket. Story completely rewritten with B&W illos added. Mickey appears and his nephews are named Morty & Monty
Book only 194 388 582 1242 2121 3000
Dust jacket only.... 39 78 117 240 395 550

DONALD DUCK (Walt Disney's) (10¢)
Whitman/K.K. Publications: 1938 (8-1/2x11-1/2", B&W, cardboard-c)
(Has D. Duck with bubble pipe on-c)
nn-The first Donald Duck & Walt Disney comic book; 1936 & 1937 Sunday strip-r(in B&W); same format as the Feature Books; 1st strips with Huey, Dewey & Louie from 10/17/37 258 516 774 1651 2826 4000

DONALD DUCK (Walt Disney's...#262 on; see 4-Color listings for titles & Four Color No. 1109 for origin story)
Dell Publ. Co./Gold Key #85-216/Whitman #217-245/Gladstone #246 on: 1940 - No. 84, Sept-Nov, 1962; No. 85, Dec, 1962 - No. 245, July, 1984; No. 246, Oct, 1986 - No. 279, May, 1990; No. 280, Sept, 1993 - No. 307, Mar,1998
Four Color 4(1940)-Daily 1939 strip-r by Al Taliaferro 1500 3000 4500 11,250 17,625 24,000

GD VG FN VF VF/NM NM-
2.0 4.0 6.0 8.0 9.0 9.2

Large Feature Comic 16(1/41?)-1940 Sunday strips-r in B&W 568 1136 1704 4146 7323 10,500
Large Feature Comic 20('41)-Comic Paint Book, r-single panels from Large Feature #16 at top of each pg. to color; daily strip-r across bottom of each pg. (Rare) 595 1190 1785 4350 7675 11,000
Four Color 9('42)- "Finds Pirate Gold"; 64 pgs. by Carl Barks & Jack Hannah (pgs. 1,2,5,12-40 are by Barks, his 1st Donald Duck comic book art work; © 8/17/42) 1000 2000 3000 7400 13,200 19,000
Four Color 29(9/43)- "Mummy's Ring" by Barks; reprinted in Uncle Scrooge & Donald Duck #1('65), W. D. Comics Digest #44('73) & Donald Duck Advs. #14 730 1460 2190 5329 9415 13,500
Four Color 62(1/45)- "Frozen Gold"; 52 pgs. by Barks, reprinted in The Best of W.D. Comics & Donald Duck Advs. #4 212 424 636 1855 3678 5500
Four Color 108(1946)- "Terror of the River"; 52 pgs. by Carl Barks; reprinted in Gladstone Comic Album #2 156 312 468 1326 2613 3900
Four Color 147(5/47)-in "Volcano Valley" by Barks 106 212 318 901 1776 2650
Four Color 159(8/47)-in "The Ghost of the Grotto";52 pgs. by Carl Barks; reprinted in Best of Uncle Scrooge & Donald Duck #1 ('66) & The Best of W.D. Comics & D.D. Advs. #9; two Barks stories 90 180 270 765 1508 2250
Four Color 178(12/47)-1st app. Uncle Scrooge by Carl Barks; reprinted in Gold Key Christmas Parade #3 & The Best of Walt Disney Comics 122 244 366 1037 2044 3050
Four Color 189(6/48)-by Carl Barks; reprinted in Best of Donald Duck & Uncle Scrooge #1('64) & D.D. Advs. #19 74 148 222 629 1240 1850
Four Color 199(10/48)-by Carl Barks; mentioned in Love and Death; r/in Gladstone Comic Album #5 80 160 240 680 1340 2000
Four Color 203(12/48)-by Barks; reprinted as Gold Key Christmas Parade #4 56 112 168 476 938 1400
Four Color 223(4/49)-by Barks; reprinted as Best of Donald Duck #1 & Donald Duck Advs. #3 74 148 222 629 1240 1850
Four Color 238(8/49)-in "Voodoo Hoodoo" by Barks 56 112 168 476 938 1400
Four Color 256(12/49)-by Barks; reprinted in Best of Donald Duck & Uncle Scrooge #2('67), Gladstone Comic Album #16 & W.D. Comics Digest 44('73) 49 98 147 392 754 1125
Four Color 263(2/50)-Two Barks stories; r-in D.D. #278 48 96 144 384 742 1100
Four Color 275(5/50), 282(7/50), 291(9/50), 300(11/50)-All by Carl Barks; 275, 282 reprinted in W.D. Comics Digest #44('73). #275 r/in Gladstone Comic Album #10. #291 r/in D. Duck Advs. #16 47 94 141 376 726 1075
Four Color 308(1/51), 318(3/51)-by Barks; #318-reprinted in W.D. Comics Digest #34 & D.D. Advs. #2,19 43 86 129 344 672 1000
Four Color 328(5/51)-by Carl Barks 43 86 129 342 664 985
Four Color 339(7-8/51), 379-2nd Uncle Scrooge-c; art not by Barks. 13 26 39 90 165 240
Four Color 348(9-10/51), 356,394-Barks-c only 21 42 63 148 287 425
Four Color 367(1-2/52)-by Barks; reprinted as Gold Key Christmas Parade #2 & #8 34 68 102 262 506 750
Four Color 408(7-8/52), 422(9-10/52)-All by Carl Barks. #408-r-in Best of Donald Duck & Uncle Scrooge #1('64) & Gladstone Comic Album #13 34 68 102 262 506 750
26(11-12/52)-In "Trick or Treat" (Barks-a, 36pgs.) 1st story r-in Walt Disney Digest #16 & Gladstone C.A. #23 34 68 102 262 506 750
27-30-Barks-c only 13 26 39 90 165 240
31-44,47-50 7 14 21 50 83 115
45-Barks-a (6 pgs.) 14 28 42 101 191 280
46- "Secret of Hondorica" by Barks, 24 pgs.; reprinted in Donald Duck #98 & 154 19 38 57 139 270 400
51-Barks-a,1/2 pg. 7 14 21 50 83 115
52- "Lost Peg-Leg Mine" by Barks, 10 pgs. 14 28 42 102 194 285
53,55-59 6 12 18 43 69 95
54- "Forbidden Valley" by Barks, 26 pgs. (10¢ & 15¢ versions exist) 16 32 48 115 220 325
60- "Donald Duck & the Titanic Ants" by Barks, 20 pgs. plus 6 more pgs. 16 32 48 115 220 325
61-67,69,70 6 12 18 37 59 80
68-Barks-a, 5 pgs. 10 20 30 73 129 185
71-Barks-r, 1/2 pg. 6 12 18 37 59 80
72-78,80,82-97,99,100: 96-Donald Duck Album 5 10 15 34 55 75
79,81-Barks-a, 1pg. 6 12 18 37 59 80
98-Reprints #46 (Barks) 6 12 18 37 59 80
101,103-111,113-135: 120-Last 12¢ issue. 134-Barks-r/#52 & WDC&S 194. 135-Barks-r/WDC&S 198, 19 pgs. 4 8 12 22 34 45
102-Super Goof. 112-1st Moby Duck 4 8 12 23 36 48
136-153,155,156,158: 149-20¢-c begin 3 6 9 14 20 26
154-Barks-r(#46) 3 6 9 17 25 32

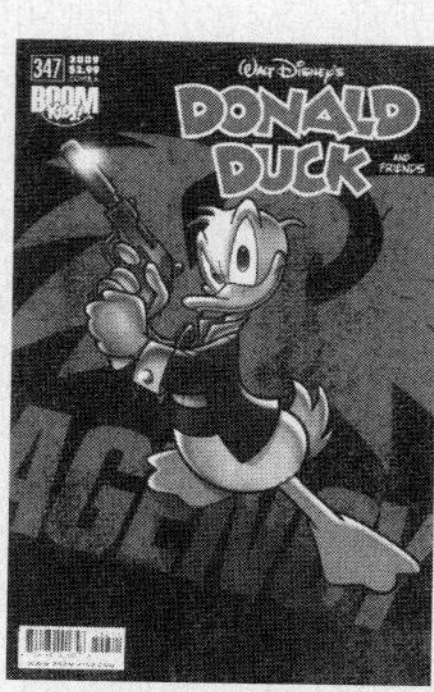

Donald Duck and Friends #347 © DIS

Don Fortune Magazine #3 © DFP

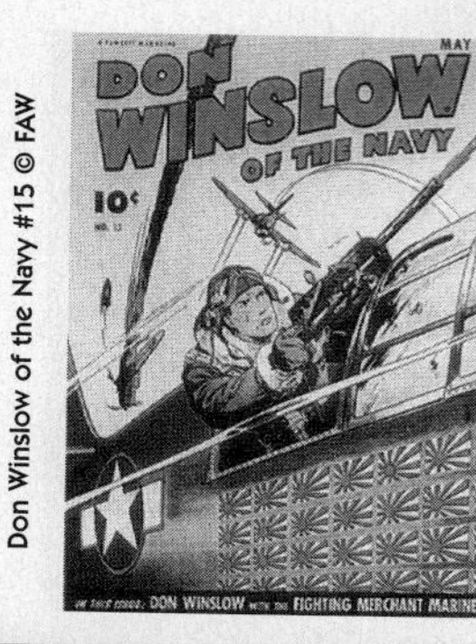

Don Winslow of the Navy #15 © FAW

GD VG FN VF VF/NM NM-
2.0 4.0 6.0 8.0 9.0 9.2

157,159,160,164: 157-Barks-r(#45); 25¢-c begin. 159-Reprints/WDC&S #192 (10 pgs.). 160-Barks-r(#26). 164-Barks-r(#79) 3 6 9 14 20 26
161-163,165-173,175-187,189-191: 175-30¢-c begin. 187-Barks r/#68. 2 4 6 13 18 22
174,188: 174-r/4-Color #394. 3 6 9 14 19 24
192-Barks-r(40 pgs.) from Donald Duck #60 & WDC&S #226,234 (52 pgs.) 3 6 9 16 22 28
193-200,202-207,209-211,213-216 2 4 6 9 13 16
201,208,212: 201-Barks-r/Christmas Parade #26, 16pgs. 208-Barks-r/#60 (6 pgs.). 212-Barks-r/WDC&S #130 2 4 6 9 13 16
217-219: 217 has 216 on-c. 219-Barks-r/WDC&S #106,107, 10 pgs. ea. 2 4 6 10 14 18
220,225-228: 228-Barks-r/F.C. #275 2 4 6 13 18 22
221,223,224: Scarce; only sold in pre-packs. 221(8/80), 223(11/80), 224(12/80) 6 12 18 37 59 80
222-(9-10/80)-(Very low distribution) 16 32 48 115 220 325
229-240: 229-Barks-r/F.C. #282. 230-Barks-r/ #52 & WDC&S #194. 236(2/82), 237(2-3/82), 238(3/82), 239(4/82), 240(5/82) 2 4 6 9 13 16
241-245: 241(4/83), 242(5/83), 243(3/84), 244(4/84), 245(7/84)(low print) 3 6 9 14 19 24
246-(1st Gladstone issue)-Barks-r/FC #422 3 6 9 15 21 26
247-249,251: 248,249-Barks-r/DD #54 & 26. 251-Barks-r/1945 Firestone 2 4 6 9 13 16
250-($1.50, 68 pgs.)-Barks-r/4-Color #9 2 4 6 10 14 18
252-277,280: 254-Barks-r/FC #328. 256-Barks-r/FC #147. 257-($1.50, 52 pgs.)-Barks-r/ Vacation Parade #1. 261-Barks-r/FC #300. 275-Kelly-r/FC #92. 280 (#1, 2nd Series) 1 2 3 5 6 8
278,279,286: 278,279 ($1.95, 68 pgs.): 278-Rosa-a; Barks-r/FC #263. 279-Rosa-c; Barks-r/MOC #4. 286-Rosa-a 1 2 3 5 7 9
281,282,284 1 2 3 4 5 7
283-Don Rosa-a, part-c & scripts 1 2 3 5 6 8
285,287-307 5.00
286 ($2.95, 68 pgs.)-Happy Birthday, Donald 6.00
Mini-Comic #1(1976)-(3-1/4x6-1/2"); r/D.D. #150 2 4 6 8 11 14

NOTE: ***Carl Barks*** *wrote all issues he illustrated, but #117, 126, 138 contain his script only. Issues 4-Color #189, 199, 203, 223, 238, 256, 263, 275, 282, 308, 348, 356, 367, 394, 408, 422, 26-30, 35, 44, 46, 52, 55, 57, 60, 65, 70-73, 77-80, 83, 101, 103, 105, 106, 111, 126, 246r, 266r, 268r, 271r, 275r, 278r(F.C. 263) all have* ***Barks*** *covers.* ***Barks*** *r-263-267, 269-278-282, 284, 285. #96 titled "Comic Album", #99-"Christmas Album". New art issues (not reprints)-106-46, 148-63, 167, 169, 170, 172, 173, 175, 178, 179, 196, 209, 223, 225, 236.* ***Taliaferro*** *daily newspaper strips #258-260, 264, 284, 285; Sunday strips #247, 280-283.*

DONALD DUCK ADVENTURES (See Walt Disney's Donald Duck Adventures)

DONALD DUCK ALBUM (See Comic Album No. 1,3 & Duck Album)
Dell Publishing Co./Gold Key: 5-7/59 - F.C. No. 1239, 10-12/61; 1962; 8/63 - No. 2, Oct, 1963

Four Color 995 (#1) 6 12 18 43 69 95
Four Color 1099,1140,1239-Barks-c 7 14 21 45 73 100
Four Color 1182, 01204-207 (1962-Dell) 5 10 15 32 51 70
1(8/63-Gold Key)-Barks-c 6 12 18 39 62 85
2(10/63) 5 10 15 30 48 65

DONALD DUCK AND FRIENDS (Numbering continues from Walt Disney's ...)
BOOM! Studios: No. 347, Oct, 2009 - Present ($2.99)

347-351 3.00

DONALD DUCK AND THE BOYS (Also see Story Hour Series)
Whitman Publishing Co.: 1948 (5-1/4x5-1/2", 100pgs., hard-c; art & text)

845-(49) new illos by Barks based on his Donald Duck 10-pager in WDC&S #74, Expanded text not written by Barks; Cover not by Barks 50 100 150 350 600 850
(Prices vary widely on this book)

DONALD DUCK AND THE CHRISTMAS CAROL
Whitman Publishing Co.: 1960 (A Little Golden Book, 6-3/8"x7-5/8", 28 pgs.)

nn-Story book pencilled by Carl Barks with the intended title "Uncle Scrooge's Christmas Carol." Finished art adapted by Norman McGary. (Rare)-Reprinted in Uncle Scrooge in Color. 30 60 90 150 210 270

DONALD DUCK BEACH PARTY (Also see Dell Giants)
Gold Key: Sept, 1965 (12¢)

1(#10158-509)-Barks-r/WDC&S #45; painted-c 6 12 18 43 69 95

DONALD DUCK BOOK (See Story Hour Series)

DONALD DUCK COMICS DIGEST
Gladstone Publishing: Nov, 1986 - No. 5, July, 1987 ($1.25/$1.50, 96 pgs.)

1,3: 1-Barks-c/a-r 1 3 4 6 8 10
2,4,5: 4,5-$1.50-c 6.00

GD VG FN VF VF/NM NM-
2.0 4.0 6.0 8.0 9.0 9.2

DONALD DUCK FUN BOOK (See Dell Giants)

DONALD DUCK IN DISNEYLAND (See Dell Giants)

DONALD DUCK MARCH OF COMICS (See March of Comics #4,20,41,56,69,263)

DONALD DUCK MERRY CHRISTMAS (See Dell Giant No. 53)

DONALD DUCK PICNIC PARTY (See Picnic Party listed under Dell Giants)

DONALD DUCK TELLS ABOUT KITES (See Kite Fun Book)

DONALD DUCK, THIS IS YOUR LIFE (Disney, TV)
Dell Publishing Co.: No. 1109, Aug-Oct, 1960

Four Color 1109-Gyro flashback to WDC&S #141; origin Donald Duck (1st told) 13 26 39 95 178 260

DONALD DUCK XMAS ALBUM (See regular Donald Duck No. 99)

DONALD IN MATHMAGIC LAND (Disney)
Dell Publishing Co.: No. 1051, Oct-Dec, 1959 - No. 1198, May-July, 1961

Four Color 1051 (#1)-Movie 9 18 27 63 107 150
Four Color 1198-Reprint of above 6 12 18 43 69 95

DONATELLO, TEENAGE MUTANT NINJA TURTLE
Mirage Studios: Aug, 1986 ($1.50, B&W, one-shot, 44 pgs.)

1 1 2 3 5 7 9

DONDI
Dell Publishing Co.: No. 1176, Mar-May, 1961 - No. 1276, Dec, 1961

Four Color 1176 (#1)-Movie; origin, photo-c 5 10 15 35 55 75
Four Color 1276 4 8 12 22 34 45

DON FORTUNE MAGAZINE
Don Fortune Publishing Co.: Aug, 1946 - No. 6, Feb, 1947

1-Delecta of the Planets by C.C. Beck in all 26 52 78 154 252 350
2 15 30 45 84 127 170
3-6: 3-Bondage-c 14 28 42 76 108 140

DONKEY KONG (See Blip #1)

DONNA MATRIX
Reactor, Inc.: Aug, 1993 ($2.95, 52 pgs.)

1-Computer generated-c/a by Mike Saenz; 3-D effects 3.00

DON NEWCOMBE
Fawcett Publications: 1950 (Baseball)

nn-Photo-c 43 86 129 271 461 650

DON ROSA'S COMICS AND STORIES
Fantagraphics Books (CX Comics): 1983 ($2.95)

1,2: 1-(68 pgs.) Reprints Rosa's The Pertwillaby Papers episodes #128-133. 2-(60 pgs.) Reprints episodes #134-138 2 4 6 11 16 20

DON SIMPSON'S BIZARRE HEROES (Also see Megaton Man)
Fiasco Comics: May, 1990 - No. 17, Sept, 1996 ($2.50/$2.95, B&W)

1-10,0,11-17: 0-Begin $2.95-c; r/Bizarre Heroes #1. 17-(9/96)-Indicia also reads Megaton Man #0; intro Megaton Man and the Fiascoverse to new readers 3.00

DON'T GIVE UP THE SHIP
Dell Publishing Co.: No. 1049, Aug, 1959

Four Color 1049-Movie, Jerry Lewis photo-c 9 18 27 61 103 145

DON WINSLOW OF THE NAVY
Merwil Publishing Co.: Apr, 1937 - No. 2, May, 1937 (96 pgs.)(A pulp/comic book cross; stapled spine)

V1#1-Has 16 pgs. comics in color. Captain Colorful & Jupiter Jones by Sheldon Mayer; complete Don Winslow novel 653 1306 1959 4900 - -
2-Sheldon Mayer-a 177 354 531 1325 - -

DON WINSLOW OF THE NAVY (See Crackajack Funnies, Famous Feature Stories, Popular Comics & Super Book #5,6)
Dell Publishing Co.: No. 2, Nov, 1939 - No. 22, 1941

Four Color 2 (#1)-Rare 187 374 561 1197 2049 2900
Four Color 22 45 90 135 284 480 675

DON WINSLOW OF THE NAVY (See TV Teens; Movie, Radio, TV) (Fightin' Navy No. 74 on)
Fawcett Publications/Charlton No. 70 on: 2/43 - #64, 12/48; #65, 1/51 - #69, 9/51; #70, 3/55 - #73, 9/55

1-(68 pgs.)-Captain Marvel on cover 112 224 336 706 1191 1675
2 43 86 129 267 446 625
3 35 70 105 203 327 450
4-6: 6-Flag-c 27 54 81 158 254 350

Doom Patrol (2009 series) #1 © DC

Doomdasy + 1 #4 © CC

Dorothy Lamour #2 © FOX

	GD 2.0	VG 4.0	FN 6.0	VF 8.0	VF/NM 9.0	NM- 9.2
7-10: 8-Last 68 pg. issue?	20	40	60	115	183	250
11-20	15	30	45	90	140	190
21-40	14	28	42	76	108	140
41-43,45-64: 51,60-Singapore Sal (villain) app. 64-(12/48)	12	24	36	67	94	120
44-Classic spider-c	26	52	78	154	252	350
65(1/51)-Flying Saucer attack; photo-c	19	38	57	109	172	235
66 - 69(9/51): All photo-c. 66-sci-fi story	14	28	42	80	115	150
70(3/55)-73: 70-73 r-/#26,58 & 59	9	18	27	50	65	80

DOOM
Marvel Comics: Oct, 2000 - No. 3, Dec, 2000 ($2.99, limited series)

1-3-Dr. Doom; Dixon-s/Manco-a						3.00

DOOM FORCE SPECIAL
DC Comics: July, 1992 ($2.95, 68 pgs., one-shot, mature) (X-Force parody)

1-Morrison scripts; Simonson, Steacy, & others-a; Giffen/Mignola-c						3.00

DOOM PATROL, THE (Formerly My Greatest Adventure No. 1-85; see Brave and the Bold, DC Special Blue Ribbon Digest 19, Official... Index & Showcase No. 94-96)
National Periodical Publ.: No. 86, 3/64 - No. 121, 9-10/68; No. 122, 2/73 - No. 124, 6-7/73

86-1 pg. origin (#86-121 are 12¢ issues)	11	22	33	76	136	195
87-98: 88-Origin The Chief. 91-Intro. Mento	8	16	24	56	93	130
99-Intro. Beast Boy (later becomes the Changeling in New Teen Titans)	10	20	30	67	116	165
100-Origin Beast Boy; Robot-Maniac series begins (12/65)	10	20	30	67	116	165
101-110: 102-Challengers of the Unknown app. 105-Robot-Maniac series ends. 106-Negative Man begins (origin)	6	12	18	41	66	90
111-120	5	10	15	32	51	70
121-Death of Doom Patrol; Orlando-c.	10	20	30	70	123	175
122-124: All reprints	2	4	6	8	10	12

DOOM PATROL
DC Comics (Vertigo imprint #64 on): Oct, 1987 - No, 87, Feb, 1995 (75¢-$1.95, new format)

1-Wraparound-c; Lightle-a						5.00
2-18: 3-1st app. Lodestone. 4-1st app. Karma. 8,15,16-Art Adams-c(i). 18-Invasion tie-in						3.00
19-(2/89)-Grant Morrison scripts begin, ends #63; 1st app Crazy Jane; $1.50-c & new format begins.	1	2	3	5	6	8
20-30: 29-Superman app. 30-Night Breed fold-out						5.00
31-34,37-41,45-49,51-56,58-60: 39-World Without End preview						2.50
35-1st brief app. of Flex Mentallo						5.00
36-1st full app. of Flex Mentallo						6.00
42-44-Origin of Flex Mentallo						4.00
50,57 ($2.50, 52 pgs.)						2.50
61-87: 61,70-Photo-c. 73-Death cameo (2 panels)						3.00
...And Suicide Squad 1 (3/88, $1.50, 52 pgs.)-Wraparound-c						2.50
Annual 1 (1988, $1.50, 52 pgs.)						2.50
Annual 2 (1994, $3.95, 68 pgs.)-Children's Crusade tie-in.						4.00
...: Crawling From the Wreckage TPB (2004, $19.95) r/#19-25; Morrison-s						20.00
...: Down Paradise Way TPB (2005, $19.99) r/#35-41; Morrison-s						20.00
...: Magic Bus TPB (2007, $19.99) r/#51-57; Morrison-s; new Bolland-c						20.00
...: Musclebound TPB (2006, $19.99) r/#42-50; Morrison-s; new Bolland-c						20.00
...: Planet Love TPB (2008, $19.99) r/#58-63 & Doom Force Special #1; Morrison-s						20.00
...: The Painting That Ate Paris TPB (2004, $19.95) r/#26-34; Morrison-s						20.00

NOTE: *Bisley painted c-26-48, 55-58.* ***Bolland** c-64, 75.* ***Dringenberg** a-42(p).* ***Steacy** a-53.*

DOOM PATROL
DC Comics: Dec, 2001 - No. 22, Sept, 2003 ($2.50)

1-Intro. new team with Robotman; Tan Eng Huat-c/a; John Arcudi-s						3.00
2-22: 4,5-Metamorpho & Elongated Man app. 13,14-Fisher-a. 20-Geary-a						2.50

DOOM PATROL (see JLA #94-99)
DC Comics: Aug, 2004 - No. 18, Jan, 2006 ($2.50)

1-18-John Byrne-s/a. 1-Green Lantern, Batman app.						2.50

DOOM PATROL
DC Comics: Oct, 2009 - Present ($3.99)

1-7: 1-Giffen-s/Clark-a; back-up Metal Men feature w/Maguire-a. 1-Two covers. 4-5-Blackest Night. 6-Negative Man origin re-told						4.00

DOOM PATROL (See Tangent Comics/ Doom Patrol)

DOOMSDAY
DC Comics: 1995 ($3.95, one-shot)

1-Year One story by Jurgens, L. Simonson, Ordway, and Gil Kane; Superman app.						4.00

DOOMSDAY + 1 (Also see Charlton Bullseye)
Charlton Comics: July, 1975 - No. 6, June, 1976; No. 7, June, 1978 - No. 12, May, 1979

	GD 2.0	VG 4.0	FN 6.0	VF 8.0	VF/NM 9.0	NM- 9.2
1: #1-5 are 25¢ issues	3	6	9	15	20	25
2-6: 4-Intro Lor. 5-Ditko-a(1 pg.) 6-Begin 30¢-c	2	4	6	10	13	16
V3#7-12 (reprints #1-6)						6.00
5 (Modern Comics reprint, 1977)						4.00

NOTE: ***Byrne** c/a-1-12; Painted covers-2-7.*

DOOMSDAY SQUAD, THE
Fantagraphics Books: Aug, 1986 - No. 7, 1987 ($2.00)

1-7: Byrne-a in all. 1-3-New Byrne-c. 3-Usagi Yojimbo app. (1st in color). 4-Neal Adams-c. 5-7-Gil Kane-c						3.00

DOOM'S IV
Image Comics (Extreme): July, 1994 - No.4, Oct, 1994 ($2.50, limited series)

1-4-Liefeld story						2.50
1,2-Two alternate Liefeld-c each, 4 covers form 1 picture						5.00

DOOM: THE EMPEROR RETURNS
Marvel Comics: Jan, 2002 - No. 3, Mar, 2002 ($2.50, limited series)

1-3-Dixon-s/Manco-a; Franklin Richards app.						2.50

DOOM 2099 (See Marvel Comics Presents #118 & 2099: World of Tomorrow)
Marvel Comics: Jan, 1993 - No. 44, Aug, 1996 ($1.25/$1.50/$1.95)

1-24,26-44: 1-Metallic foil stamped-c. 4-Ron Lim-c(p). 17-bound-in trading card sheet. 40-Namor & Doctor Strange app. 41-Daredevil app., Namor-c/app. 44-Intro The Emissary; story contin'd in 2099: World of Tomorrow						2.50
1-2nd printing						2.50
18-Variant polybagged with Sega Sub-Terrania poster						4.00
25 ($2.25, 52 pgs.)						2.50
25 ($2.95, 52pgs.) Foil embossed cover						3.00
29 ($3.50)-acetate-c.						3.50

DOORWAY TO NIGHTMARE (See Cancelled Comic Cavalcade and Madame Xanadu)
DC Comics: Jan-Feb, 1978 - No. 5, Sept-Oct, 1978

1-Madame Xanadu in all	2	4	6	10	14	18
2-5: 4-Craig-a	2	4	6	8	10	12

NOTE: ***Kaluta** covers on all. Merged into The Unexpected with No. 190.*

DOPEY DUCK COMICS (Wacky Duck No. 3) (See Super Funnies)
Timely Comics (NPP): Fall, 1945 - No. 2, Apr, 1946

1,2-Casper Cat, Krazy Krow	24	48	72	140	230	320

DORK
Slave Labor: June, 1993 - Present ($2.50-$3.50, B&W, mature)

1-7,9-11: Evan Dorkin-c/a/scripts in all. 1(8/95),2(1/96)-(2nd printings). 1(3/97) (3rd printing). 1-Milk & Cheese app. 3-Eltingville Club starts. 6-Reprints 1st Eltingville Club app. from Instant Piano #1						3.00
8-($3.50)						3.50
Who's Laughing Now? TPB (2001, $11.95) reprints most of #1-5						12.00
The Collected Dork, Vol. 2: Circling the Drain (6/03, $13.95) r/most of #7-10 & other-s						14.00

DOROTHY LAMOUR (Formerly Jungle Lil)(Stage, screen, radio)
Fox Features Syndicate: No. 2, June, 1950 - No. 3, Aug, 1950

2,3-Wood-a(3) each, photo-c	27	54	81	158	259	360

DOT DOTLAND (Formerly Little Dot Dotland)
Harvey Publications: No. 62, Sept, 1974 - No. 63, Nov, 1974

62,63	2	4	6	9	12	15

DOTTY (...& Her Boy Friends)(Formerly Four Teeners; Glamorous Romances No. 41 on)
Ace Magazines (A. A. Wyn): No. 35, June, 1948 - No. 40, May, 1949

35-Teen-age	9	18	27	47	61	75
36-40: 37-Transvestism story	6	12	18	31	38	45

DOTTY DRIPPLE (Horace & Dotty Dripple No. 25 on)
Magazine Ent.(Life's Romances)/Harvey No. 3 on: 1946 - No. 24, June, 1952 (Also see A-1 No. 1, 3-8, 10)

1 (nd) (10¢)	11	22	33	62	86	110
2	7	14	21	37	46	55
3-10: 3,4-Powell-a	6	12	18	31	38	45
11-24	6	12	18	27	33	38

DOTTY DRIPPLE AND TAFFY
Dell Publishing Co.: No. 646, Sept, 1955 - No. 903, May, 1958

Four Color 646 (#1)	5	10	15	32	51	70
Four Color 691,718,746,801,903	4	8	12	22	34	45

DOUBLE ACTION COMICS
National Periodical Publications: No. 2, Jan, 1940 (68 pgs., B&W)

Double Dragon #1 © Technos

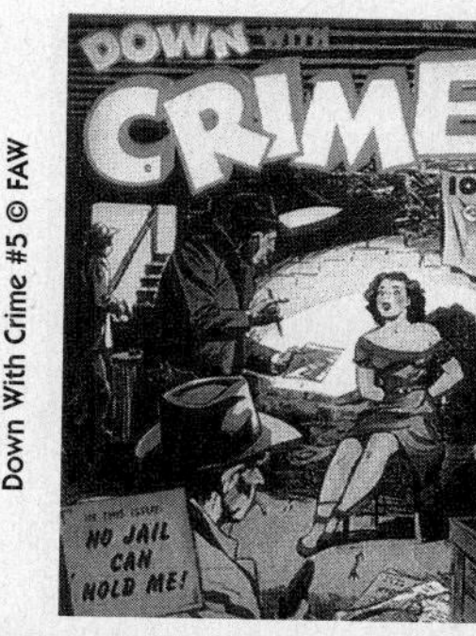

Down With Crime #5 © FAW

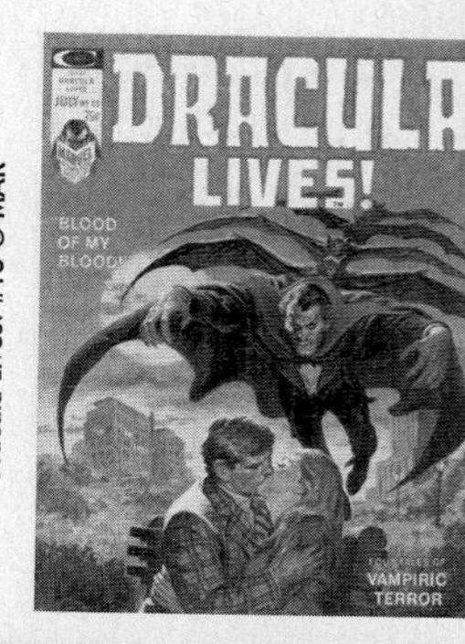

Dracula Lives! #13 © MAR

GD VG FN VF VF/NM NM-
2.0 4.0 6.0 8.0 9.0 9.2

2-Contains original stories(?); pre-hero DC contents; same cover as Adventure No. 37. (seven known copies, five in high grade) (not an ashcan) 2000 4000 6000 12,250 16,250 20,000

NOTE: *The cover to this book was probably reprinted from Adventure #37. #1 exists as an ash can copy with B&W cover; contains a coverless comic on inside with 1st & last page missing. There is proof of at least limited newsstand distribution. #2 cover proof only sold in 2005 for $4,000.*

DOUBLE COMICS
Elliot Publications: 1940 - 1944 (132 pgs.)

1940 issues; Masked Marvel-c & The Mad Mong vs. The White Flash covers known 248 496 744 1575 2713 3850
1941 issues; Tornado Tim-c, Nordac-c, & Green Light covers known 165 330 495 1048 1799 2550
1942 issues 118 236 354 749 1287 1825
1943,1944 issues 97 194 291 621 1061 1500

NOTE: *Double Comics consisted of an almost endless combination of pairs of remaindered, unsold issues of comics representing most publishers and usually mixed publishers in the same book; e.g., a Captain America with a Silver Streak, or a Feature with a Detective, etc., could appear inside the same cover. The actual contents would have to determine its price. Prices listed are for average contents. Any containing rare origin or first issues are worth much more. Covers also vary in same year. Value would be approximately 50 percent of contents.*

DOUBLE-CROSS (See The Crusaders)

DOUBLE-DARE ADVENTURES
Harvey Publications: Dec, 1966 - No. 2, Mar, 1967 (35¢/25¢, 68 pgs.)

1-Origin Bee-Man, Glowing Gladiator, & Magic-Master; Simon/Kirby-a (last S&K art as a team?) 6 12 18 43 69 95
2-Torres-a; r/Alarming Adv. #3('63) 5 10 15 30 48 65

NOTE: ***Powell** a-1. **Simon/Sparling** c-1, 2.*

DOUBLE DRAGON
Marvel Comics: July, 1991 - No. 6, Dec, 1991 ($1.00, limited series)

1-6: Based on video game. 2-Art Adams-c 2.50

DOUBLE EDGE
Marvel Comics: Alpha, 1995; Omega, 1995 ($4.95, limited series)

Alpha ($4.95)- Punisher story, Nick Fury app. 5.00
Omega ($4.95)-Punisher, Daredevil, Ghost Rider app. Death of Nick Fury 5.00

DOUBLE IMAGE
Image Comics: Feb, 2001 - No. 5, July, 2001 ($2.95)

1-5: 1-Flip covers of Codeflesh (Casey-s/Adlard-a) and The Bod (Young-s). 2-Two covers. 5-"Trust in Me" begins; Chaudhary-a 3.00

DOUBLE LIFE OF PRIVATE STRONG, THE
Archie Publications/Radio Comics: June, 1959 - No. 2, Aug, 1959

1-Origin & re-intro The Shield; Simon & Kirby-c/a, their re-entry into the super-hero genre; intro./1st app. The Fly; 1st S.A. super-hero for Archie Publ. 45 90 135 360 673 985
2-S&K-c/a; Tuska-a; The Fly app. (2nd or 3rd?) 28 56 84 207 384 560

DOUBLE TROUBLE
St. John Publishing Co.: Nov, 1957 - No. 2, Jan-Feb, 1958

1,2: Tuffy & Snuffy by Frank Johnson; dubbed "World's Funniest Kids" 6 12 18 31 38 45

DOUBLE TROUBLE WITH GOOBER
Dell Publishing Co.: No. 417, Aug, 1952 - No. 556, May, 1954

Four Color 417 4 8 12 28 44 60
Four Color 471,516,556 4 8 12 22 34 45

DOUBLE UP
Elliott Publications: 1941 (Pocket size, 200 pgs.)

1-Contains rebound copies of digest sized issues of Pocket Comics, Speed Comics, & Spitfire Comics 81 162 243 518 884 1250

DOVER & CLOVER (See All Funny & More Fun Comics #93)

DOVER BOYS (See Adventures of the...)

DOVER THE BIRD
Famous Funnies Publishing Co.: Spring, 1955

1-Funny animal; code approved 7 14 21 35 43 50

DOWN
Image Comics (Top Cow): Dec, 2005 - No. 4, Mar, 2006 ($2.99)

1-4-Warren Ellis-s. 1-Tony Harris-a/c. 2-4-Cully Hamner-a 3.00
Down & Top Cow's Best of Warren Ellis TPB (6/06, $15.99) r/#1-4 & Tales of the Witchblade #3,4; Ellis-s; script for Down #1 with Harris sketch pages 16.00

DOWN WITH CRIME
Fawcett Publications: Nov, 1952 - No. 7, Nov, 1953

GD VG FN VF VF/NM NM-
2.0 4.0 6.0 8.0 9.0 9.2

1 37 74 111 218 354 490
2,4,5: 2,4-Powell-a in each. 5-Bondage-c 19 38 57 111 176 240
3-Used in **POP**, pg. 106; "H is for Heroin" drug story 21 42 63 122 199 275
6,7: 6-Used in **POP**, pg. 80 15 30 45 90 140 190

DO YOU BELIEVE IN NIGHTMARES?
St. John Publishing Co.: Nov, 1957 - No. 2, Jan, 1958

1-Mostly Ditko-c/a 50 100 150 315 533 750
2-Ayers-a 28 56 84 168 274 380

D.P. 7
Marvel Comics Group (New Universe): Nov, 1986 - No. 32, June, 1989

1-20, Annual #1 (11/87)-Intro. The Witness 2.50
21-32-Low print 4.00
... Classic Vol. 1 TPB (2007, $24.99) r/#1-9; Mark Gruenwald-s/Paul Ryan-a in all 25.00

NOTE: ***Williamson** a-9i, 11i; c-9i.*

DRACULA (See Bram Stoker's Dracula, Giant-Size..., Little Dracula, Marvel Graphic Novel, Requiem for Dracula, Spider-Man Vs...., Stoker's..., Tomb of... & Wedding of...; also see Movie Classics under Universal Presents as well as Dracula)

DRACULA (See Movie Classics for #1)(Also see Frankenstein & Werewolf)
Dell Publ. Co.: No. 2, 11/66 - No. 4, 3/67; No. 6, 7/72 - No. 8, 7/73 (No #5)

2-Origin & 1st app. Dracula (11/66) (super hero) 5 10 15 30 48 65
3,4: 4-Intro. Fleeta ('67) 3 6 9 20 30 40
6-('72)-r/#2 w/origin 3 6 9 15 21 26
7,8-r/#3, #4 2 4 6 11 16 20

DRACULA (Magazine)
Warren Publishing Co.: 1979 (120 pgs., full color)

Book 1-Maroto art; Spanish material translated into English (mail order only) 6 12 18 41 66 90

DRACULA CHRONICLES
Topps Comics: Apr, 1995 - No. 3, June, 1995 ($2.50, limited series)

1-3-Linsner-c 3.00

DRACULA LIVES! (Magazine)(Also see Tomb of Dracula) (Reprinted in Stoker's Dracula)
Marvel Comics Group: 1973(no month) - No. 13, July, 1975 (75¢, B&W) (76 pgs.)

1-Boris painted-c 7 14 21 50 83 115
2 (7/73)-1st time origin Dracula; Adams, Starlin-a 5 10 15 32 51 70
3-1st app. Robert E. Howard's Soloman Kane; Adams-c/a 5 10 15 32 51 70
4,5: 4-Ploog-a. 5(V2#1)-Bram Stoker's Classic Dracula adapt. begins 4 8 12 24 37 50
6-9: 6-8-Bram Stoker adapt. 9-Bondage-c 4 8 12 24 37 50
10 (1/75)-16 pg. Lilith solo (1st?) 4 8 12 28 44 60
11-13: 11-21 pg. Lilith solo sty. 12-31 pg. Dracula sty 4 8 12 24 37 50
Annual 1(Summer, 1975, $1.25, 92 pgs.)-Morrow painted-c; 6 Dracula stys. 25 pgs. Adams-a(r) 4 8 12 26 41 55

NOTE: ***N. Adams** a-2, 3i, 10i, Annual 1r(2, 3i). **Alcala** a-9. **Buscema** a-3p, 6p, Annual 1p. **Colan** a(p)-1, 2, 5, 6, 8. **Evans** a-7. **Gulacy** a-9. **Heath** a-1r, 13. **Pakula** a-6r. Sutton a-13.**Weiss** r-Annual 1p. 4 **Dracula** stories each in 1, 609; 3 **Dracula** stories each in 2, 4, 5,, 13.*

DRACULA: LORD OF THE UNDEAD
Marvel Comics: Dec, 1998 - No. 3, Dec, 1998 ($2.99, limited series)

1-3-Olliffe & Palmer-a 3.00

DRACULA: RETURN OF THE IMPALER
Slave Labor Graphics: July, 1993 - No. 4, Oct, 1994 ($2.95, limited series)

1-4 3.00

DRACULA'S REVENGE
IDW Publishing: Apr, 2004 - No. 3 ($3.99, limited series)

1,2-Forbeck-s/Kudranski-a 4.00

DRACULA VERSUS ZORRO
Topps Comics: Oct, 1993 - No. 2, Nov, 1993 ($2.95, limited series)

1,2: 1-Spot varnish & red foil-c. 2-Polybagged w/16 pg. Zorro #0 3.00

DRACULA VERSUS ZORRO
Dark Horse Comics: Sept, 1998 - No. 2, Oct, 1998 ($2.95, limited series)

1,2 3.00

DRACULA: VLAD THE IMPALER (Also see Bram Stoker's Dracula)
Topps Comics: Feb, 1993 - No. 3, Apr, 1993 ($2.95, limited series)

1-3-Polybagged with 3 trading cards each; Maroto-c/a 3.00

DRAFT, THE
Marvel Comics: 1988 ($3.50, one-shot, squarebound)

Drafted: One Hundred Days #1 © Devil's Due

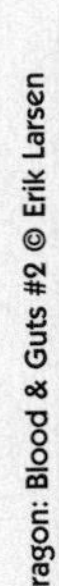
Dragon: Blood & Guts #2 © Erik Larsen

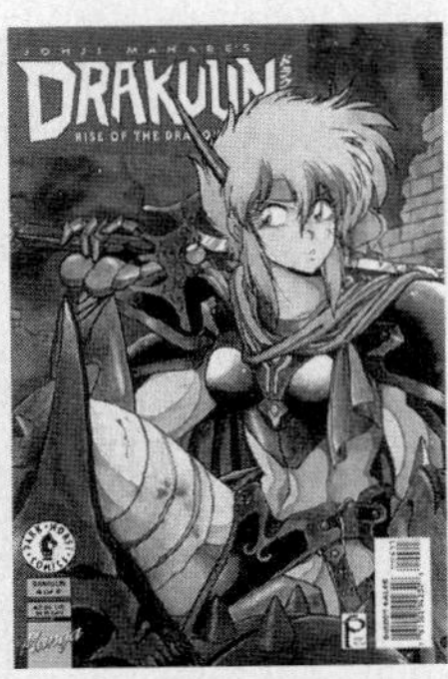

Drakuun #4 © Johji Manabe

GD VG FN VF VF/NM NM-
2.0 4.0 6.0 8.0 9.0 9.2

1-Sequel to "The Pitt" 3.50

DRAFTED: ONE HUNDRED DAYS
Devil's Due Publishing: June, 2009 ($5.99, one-shot)

1-Barack Obama on a post-galactic-war Earth; Powers-s 6.00

DRAG 'N' WHEELS (Formerly Top Eliminator)
Charlton Comics: No. 30, Sept, 1968 - No. 59, May, 1973

	GD	VG	FN	VF	VF/NM	NM-
30	4	8	12	28	44	60
31-40-Scot Jackson begins	3	6	9	19	29	38
41-50	3	6	9	17	25	32
51-59: Scot Jackson	2	4	6	13	18	22
Modern Comics Reprint 58('78)						5.00

DRAGON, THE (Also see The Savage Dragon)
Image Comics (Highbrow Ent.): Mar, 1996 - No. 5, July, 1996 (99¢, lim. series)

1-5: Reprints Savage Dragon limited series w/new story & art. 5-Youngblood app; includes 5 pg. Savage Dragon story from 1984 2.50

DRAGON ARCHIVES, THE (Also see The Savage Dragon)
Image Comics: Jun, 1998 - No. 4, Jan, 1999 ($2.95, B&W)

1-4: Reprints early Savage Dragon app. 3.00

DRAGON, THE: BLOOD & GUTS (Also see The Savage Dragon)
Image Comics (Highbrow Entertainment): Mar, 1995 - No. 3, May, 1995 ($2.50, lim. series)

1-3: Jason Pearson-c/a/scripts 2.50

DRAGON BALL
Viz Comics: Mar, 1998 - Part 6: #2, Feb, 2003($2.95, B&W, Manga reprints read right to left)

Part 1: 1-Akira Toriyama-s/a 6.00
2-12 5.00
1-12 (2nd & 3rd printings) 3.00
Part 2: 1-15: 15-($3.50-c) 4.00
Part 3: 1-14 3.00
Part 4: 1-10 3.00
Part 5: 1-7 3.00
Part 6: 1,2 3.50

DRAGON BALL Z
Viz Comics: Mar, 1998 - Part 5: #10, Oct, 2002 ($2.95, B&W, Manga reprints read right to left)

Part 1: 1-Akira Toriyama-s/a 2 4 6 8 10 12
2-9 5.00
1-9 (2nd & 3rd printings) 3.00
Part 2: 1-14 4.00
Part 3: 1-10 3.00
Part 4: 1-15 3.00
Part 5: 1-10 3.00

DRAGON CHIANG
Eclipse Books: 1991 ($3.95, B&W, squarebound, 52 pgs.)

nn-Timothy Truman-c/a(p) 4.00

DRAGONFLIGHT
Eclipse Books: Feb, 1991 - No. 3, 1991 ($4.95, 52 pgs.)

Book One - Three: Adapts 1968 novel 5.00

DRAGONFLY (See Americomics #4)
Americomics: Sum, 1985 - No. 8, 1986 ($1.75/$1.95)

1 3.50
2-8 2.50

DRAGONFORCE
Aircel Publishing: 1988 - No. 13, 1989 ($2.00)

1-Dale Keown-c/a/scripts in #1-12 3.00
2-13: 13-No Keown-a 2.50
...Chronicles Book 1-5 ($2.95, B&W, 60 pgs.): Dale Keown-r/Dragonring & Dragonforce 3.00

DRAGONHEART (Movie)
Topps Comics: May, 1996 - No. 2, June, 1996 ($2.95/$4.95, limited series)

1-($2.95, 24 pgs.)-Adaptation of the film; Hildebrandt Bros-c; Lim-a. 3.00
2-($4.95, 64 pgs.) 5.00

DRAGONLANCE (Also see TSR Worlds)
DC Comics: Dec, 1988 - No. 34, Sept, 1991 ($1.25/$1.50, Mando paper)

1-Based on TSR game 4.00
2-34: Based on TSR game. 30-32-Kaluta-c 3.00

DRAGONLANCE: CHRONICLES
Devil's Due Publ.: Aug, 2005 - No. 8, Mar, 2006 ($2.95)

1-8-Dabb-s/Kurth-a 3.00
...: Dragons of Autumn Twilight TPB (2006, $17.95) r/#1-8 18.00

DRAGONLANCE: CHRONICLES (Volume 2)
Devil's Due Publ.: July, 2006 - No. 4, Jan, 2007 ($4.95/$4.99, 48 pgs.)

1-4-Dragons of Winter Night; Dabb-s/Kurth-a 5.00
...: Dragons of Winter Night TPB (3/07, $18.99) r/#1-4; cover gallery 19.00

DRAGONLANCE: CHRONICLES (Volume 3)
Devil's Due Publ.: Mar, 2007 - No. 12, ($3.50)

1-11-Dragons of Spring Dawning; Dabb-s/Cope-a 3.50

DRAGONLANCE: THE LEGEND OF HUMA
Devil's Due Publ.: Jan, 2004 - No. 6, Oct, 2005 ($2.95)

1-6-Mike Miller & Rael-a 3.00

DRAGON LINES
Marvel Comics (Epic Comics/Heavy Hitters): May, 1993 - No. 4, Aug, 1993 ($1.95, limited series)

1-($2.50)-Embossed-c; Ron Lim-c/a in all 3.00
2-4 2.50

DRAGON LINES: WAY OF THE WARRIOR
Marvel Comics (Epic Comics/ Heavy Hitters): Nov, 1993 - No. 2, Jan, 1994 ($2.25, limited series)

1,2-Ron Lim-c/a(p) 2.50

DRAGON PRINCE
Image Comics (Top Cow): Sept, 2008 - No. 4, Jan, 2009 ($2.99)

1-4-Marz-s/Moder-a; two covers 3.00

DRAGONQUEST
Silverwolf Comics: Dec, 1986 - No. 2, 1987 ($1.50, B&W, 28 pgs.)

1,2-Tim Vigil-c/a in all 5.00

DRAGONRING
Aircel Publishing: 1986 - V2#15, 1988 ($1.70/$2.00, B&W/color)

1-6: 6-Last B&W issue, V2#1-15($2.00, color) 2.50

DRAGON'S CLAWS
Marvel UK, Ltd.: July, 1988 - No. 10, Apr, 1989 ($1.25/$1.50/$1.75, British)

1-10: 3-Death's Head 1 pg. strip on back-c (1st app.). 4-Silhouette of Death's Head on last pg. 5-1st full app. new Death's Head 2.50

DRAGON'S LAIR: SINGE'S REVENGE (Based on the Don Bluth video game)
CrossGen Comics: Sept, 2003 - No. 3 ($2.95, limited series)

1-3-Mangels-s/Laguna-a 3.00

DRAGONSLAYER (Movie)
Marvel Comics Group: October, 1981 - No. 2, Nov, 1981

1,2-Paramount Disney movie adaptation 3.00

DRAGOON WELLS MASSACRE
Dell Publishing Co.: No. 815, June, 1957

	GD	VG	FN	VF	VF/NM	NM-
Four Color 815-Movie, photo-c	7	14	21	50	83	115

DRAGSTRIP HOTRODDERS (World of Wheels No. 17 on)
Charlton Comics: Sum, 1963; No. 2, Jan, 1965 - No. 16, Aug, 1967

	GD	VG	FN	VF	VF/NM	NM-
1	7	14	21	49	80	110
2-5	4	8	12	26	41	55
6-16	4	8	12	22	34	45

DRAIN
Image Comics: Nov, 2006 - No. 6, Mar, 2008 ($2.99)

1-6: 1-Cebulski-s/Takeda-a; two covers by Takeda and Finch 3.00
Vol. 1 TPB (2008, $16.99) r/#1-6; cover gallery and Takeda sketch art gallery 17.00

DRAKUUN
Dark Horse Comics: Feb, 1997 - No. 25, Mar, 1999 ($2.95, B&W, manga)

1-25; 1-6- Johji Manabe-s/a in all. Rise of the Dragon Princess series. 7-12-Revenge of Gustav. 13-18-Shadow of the Warlock. 19-25-The Hidden War 3.00

DRAMA
Sirius: June, 1994 ($2.95, mature)

	GD	VG	FN	VF	VF/NM	NM-
1-1st full color Dawn app. in comics	2	4	6	11	16	20
1-Limited edition (1400 copies); signed & numbered; fingerprint authenticity	4	8	12	24	37	50

NOTE: *Dawn's 1st full color app. was a pin-up in Amazing Heroes' Swimsuit Special #5.*

DRAMA OF AMERICA, THE

The Dreaming #33 © DC

Druid #3 © MAR

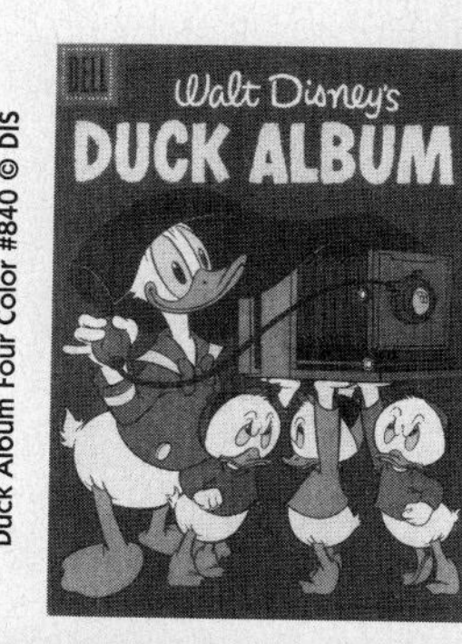

Duck Album Four Color #840 © DIS

GD 2.0 | VG 4.0 | FN 6.0 | VF 8.0 | VF/NM 9.0 | NM- 9.2

Action Text: 1973 ($1.95, 224 pgs.)
1- "Students' Supplement to History" 5.00

DRAWING ON YOUR NIGHTMARES
Dark Horse Comics: Oct, 2003 ($2.99, one-shot)
1-Short stories; The Goon, Criminal Macabre, Tales of the Vampires; Templesmith-c 3.00

DRAX THE DESTROYER
Marvel Comics: Nov, 2005 - No. 4, Feb, 2006 ($2.99, limited series)
1-4-Giffen-s/Breitweiser-a 3.00
...: Earthfall TPB (2006, $10.99) r/#1-4; character design page 11.00

DREADLANDS (Also see Epic)
Marvel Comics (Epic Comics): 1992 - No. 4, 1992 ($3.95, lim. series, 52 pgs.)
1-4: Stiff-c 4.00

DREADSTAR
Marvel Comics (Epic Comics)/First Comics No. 27 on: Nov, 1982 - No. 64, Mar, 1991
1 4.00
2-5,8-49 3.00
6,7,51-64: 6,7-1st app. Interstellar Toybox; 8pgs. ea.; Wrightson-a. 51-64-Lower print run 4.00
50 5.00
Annual 1 (12/83)-r/The Price 4.00

DREADSTAR
Malibu Comics (Bravura): Apr, 1994 - No. 6, Jan, 1995 ($2.50, limited series)
1-6-Peter David scripts: 1,2-Starlin-c 2.50
NOTE: *Issues 1-6 contain Bravura stamps.*

DREADSTAR AND COMPANY
Marvel Comics (Epic Comics): July, 1985 - No. 6, Dec, 1985
1-6: 1,3,6-New Starlin-a: 2-New Wrightson-c; reprints of Dreadstar series 2.50

DREAM BOOK OF LOVE (Also see A-1 Comics)
Magazine Enterprises: No. 106, June-July, 1954 - No. 123, Oct-Nov, 1954
A-1 106 (#1)-Powell, Bolle-a; Montgomery Clift, Donna Reed photo-c 14 28 42 80 115 150
A-1-114 (#2)-Guardineer, Bolle-a; Piper Laurie, Victor Mature photo-c 10 20 30 58 79 100
A-1 123 (#3)-Movie photo-c 10 20 30 54 72 90

DREAM BOOK OF ROMANCE (Also see A-1 Comics)
Magazine Enterprises: No. 92, 1954 - No. 124, Oct-Nov, 1954
A-1 92 (#5)-Guardineer-a; photo-c 14 28 42 76 108 140
A-1 101 (#6)(4-6/54)-Marlon Brando photo-c; Powell, Bolle, Guardineer-a 21 42 63 124 202 280
A-1 109,110,124: 109 (#7)(7-8/54)-Powell-a; movie photo-c. 110 (#8)(1/54)-Movie photo-c. 124 (#8)(10-11/54) 11 22 33 60 83 105

DREAMER, THE
Kitchen Sink Press: 1986 ($6.95, B&W, graphic novel)
nn-Will Eisner-s/a 12.00
DC Comics Reprint ($7.95, 6/00) 8.00

DREAMERY, THE
Eclipse Comics: Dec, 1986 - No. 14, Feb, 1989 ($2.00, B&W, Baxter paper)
1-14: 2-7-Alice In Wonderland adapt. 2.50

DREAMING, THE (See Sandman, 2nd Series)
DC Comics (Vertigo): June, 1996 - No. 60, May, 2001 ($2.50)
1-McKean-c on all.; LaBan scripts & Snejbjerg-a 4.00
2-30,32-60: 2,3-LaBan scripts & Snejbjerg-a. 4-7-Hogan scripts; Parkhouse-a. 8-Zulli-a. 9-11-Talbot-s/Taylor-a(p). 41-Previews Sandman: The Dream Hunters. 50-Hempel, Fegredo, McManus, Totleben-a 2.50
31-($3.95) Art by various 4.00
...Beyond The Shores of Night TPB ('97, $19.95) r/#1-8 20.00
...Special (7/98, $5.95, one-shot) Trial of Cain 6.00
...Through The Gates of Horn and Ivory TPB ('99, $19.95) r/#15-19,22-25 20.00

DREAM OF LOVE
I. W. Enterprises: 1958 (Reprints)
1,2,8: 1-r/Dream Book of Love #1; Bob Powell-a. 2-r/Great Lover's Romances #10. 8-Great Lover's Romances #1; also contains 2 Jon Juan stories by Siegel & Schomburg; Kinstler-c. 2 4 6 10 14 18
9-Kinstler-c; 1pg. John Wayne interview & Frazetta illo from John Wayne Adv. Comics #2 2 4 6 10 14 18

DREAM POLICE
Marvel Comics (Icon): Aug, 2005 ($3.99)
1-Straczynski-s/Deodato-a/c 4.00

DREAMS OF THE DARKCHYLDE
Darkchylde Entertainment: Oct, 2000 - No. 6, Sept, 2001 ($2.95)
1-6-Randy Queen-s in all. 1-Brandon Peterson-c/a 3.00

DREAM TEAM (See Battlezones: Dream Team 2)
Malibu Comics (Ultraverse): July, 1995 ($4.95, one-shot)
1-Pin-ups teaming up Marvel & Ultraverse characters by various artists including Allred, Romita, Darrow, Balent, Quesada & Palmiotti 5.00

DREAMWAVE PRODUCTIONS PREVIEW
Dreamwave Productions: May, 2002 ($1.00, one-shot)
nn-Previews Arkanium, Transformers: The War Within and other series 2.50

DRESDEN FILES (See Jim Butcher's...)

DRIFT FENCE (See Zane Grey 4-Color 270)

DRIFT MARLO
Dell Publishing Co.: May-July, 1962 - No. 2, Oct-Dec, 1962
01-232-207 (#1) 5 10 15 32 51 70
2 (12-232-212) 4 8 12 28 44 60

DRISCOLL'S BOOK OF PIRATES
David McKay Publ. (Not reprints): 1934 (B&W, hardcover; 124 pgs, 7x9")
nn-By Montford Amory 25 50 75 144 222 300

DROIDS (Based on Saturday morning cartoon) (Also see Dark Horse Comics)
Marvel Comics (Star Comics): April, 1986 - No. 8, June, 1987
1-R2D2 & C-3PO from Star Wars app. in all 2 4 6 11 16 20
2-8: 2,5,7,8-Williamson-a(i) 2 4 6 8 10 12
NOTE: ***Romita** a-3p. **Sinnott** a-3i.*

DROOPY (see Tom & Jerry #60)

DROOPY (Tex Avery's...)
Dark Horse Comics: Oct, 1995 - No. 3, Dec, 1995 ($2.50, limited series)
1-3: Characters created by Tex Avery; painted-c 2.50

DROPSIE AVENUE: THE NEIGHBORHOOD
Kitchen Sink Press: June, 1995 ($15.95/$24.95, B&W)
nn-Will Eisner (softcover) 16.00
nn-Will Eisner (hardcover) 25.00

DROWNED GIRL, THE
DC Comics (Piranha Press): 1990 ($5.95, 52 pgs, mature)
nn 6.00

DRUG WARS
Pioneer Comics: 1989 ($1.95)
1-Grell-c 2.50

DRUID
Marvel Comics: May, 1995 - No. 4, Aug, 1995 ($2.50, limited series)
1-4: Warren Ellis scripts. 3.00

DRUM BEAT
Dell Publishing Co.: No. 610, Jan, 1955
Four Color 610-Movie, Alan Ladd photo-c 8 16 24 56 93 130

DRUMS OF DOOM
United Features Syndicate: 1937 (25¢)(Indian)(Text w/color illos.)
nn-By Lt. F.A. Methot; Golden Thunder app.; Tip Top Comics ad in comic; nice-c 36 72 108 211 343 475

DRUNKEN FIST
Jademan Comics: Aug, 1988 - No. 54, Jan, 1993 ($1.50/$1.95, 68 pgs.)
1 4.00
2-50 3.00
51-54 2.50

DUCK ALBUM (See Donald Duck Album)
Dell Publishing Co.: No. 353, Oct, 1951 - No. 840, Sept, 1957
Four Color 353 (#1)-Barks-c; 1st Uncle Scrooge-c (also appears on back-c). 10 20 30 70 123 175
Four Color 450-Barks-c 7 14 21 49 80 110
Four Color 492,531,560,586,611,649,686, 6 12 18 41 66 90
Four Color 726,782,840 5 10 15 35 55 75

DUCKMAN
Dark Horse Comics: Sept, 1990 ($1.95, B&W, one-shot)

Duck Tales #1 © DIS

DV8 #24 © WSP

Dynamic Comics #17 © CHES

GD VG FN VF VF/NM NM-
2.0 4.0 6.0 8.0 9.0 9.2

GD VG FN VF VF/NM NM-
2.0 4.0 6.0 8.0 9.0 9.2

1-Story & art by Everett Peck 4.00

DUCKMAN
Topps Comics: Nov, 1994 - No. 5, May, 1995; No. 0, Feb, 1996 ($2.50)

0 (2/96, $2.95, B&W)-r/Duckman #1 from Dark Horse Comics 4.00
1-5: 1-w/ coupon #A for Duckman trading card. 2-w/Duckman 1st season episode guide 3.00

DUCKMAN: THE MOB FROG SAGA
Topps Comics: Nov, 1994 - No. 3, Feb, 1995 ($2.50, limited series)

1-3: 1-w/coupon #B for Duckman trading card, S. Shaw!-c 2.50

DUCKTALES
Gladstone Publ.: Oct, 1988 - No. 13, May, 1990 (1,2,9-11: $1.50; 3-8: 95¢)

1-Barks-r 6.00
2-11: 2-7,9-11-Barks-r 4.00
12,13 ($1.95, 68 pgs.)-Barks-r; 12-r/F.C. #495 5.00
Disney Presents Carl Barks' Greatest DuckTales Stories Vol. 1 (Gemstone Publ., 2006, $10.95) r/stories adapted for the animated TV series including "Back to the Klondike" 11.00
Disney Presents Carl Barks' Greatest DuckTales Stories Vol. 2 (Gemstone Publ., 2006, $10.95) r/stories adapted for the animated TV series; "Robot Robbers" app. 11.00

DUCKTALES (TV)
Disney Comics: June, 1990 - No. 18, Nov, 1991 ($1.50)

1-All new stories; Marv Wolfman-s 3.00
2-18 2.50
Disney's DuckTales by Marv Wolfman: Scrooge's Quest TPB (Gemstone, 9/07, $15.99) r/#1-7; intro. by Wolfman 16.00
Disney's DuckTales: The Gold Odyssey TPB (Gemstone, 10/08, $15.99) 16.00
The Movie nn (1990, $7.95, 68 pgs.)-Graphic novel adapting animated movie 9.00

DUDLEY (Teen-age)
Feature/Prize Publications: Nov-Dec, 1949 - No. 3, Mar-Apr, 1950

1-By Boody Rogers 15 30 45 83 124 165
2,3 10 20 30 54 72 90

DUDLEY DO-RIGHT (TV)
Charlton Comics: Aug, 1970 - No. 7, Aug, 1971 (Jay Ward)

1 9 18 27 61 103 145
2-7 6 12 18 43 69 95

DUEL MASTERS (Based on a trading card game) (Also see Free Comic Book Day Edition in the Promotional Comics section)
Dreamwave Productions: Nov, 2003 - Present ($2.95)

1-8: 1-Bagged with card; Augustyn-s 3.00

DUKE OF THE K-9 PATROL
Gold Key: Apr, 1963

1 (10052-304) 4 8 12 24 37 50

DUMBO (Disney; see Movie Comics, & Walt Disney Showcase #12)
Dell Publishing Co.: No. 17, 1941 - No. 668, Jan, 1958

Four Color 17 (#1)-Mickey Mouse, Donald Duck, Pluto app. 261 522 783 1657 2854 4050
Large Feature Comic 19 ('41)-Part-r 4-Color 17 294 588 882 1882 3216 4550
Four Color 234 ('49) 13 26 39 95 178 260
Four Color 668 (12/55)-1st of two printings. Dumbo on-c with starry sky. Same-c as #234 10 20 30 70 123 175
Four Color 668 (1/58)-2nd printing. Same cover altered with Timothy Mouse added. Same contents 7 14 21 45 73 100

DUMBO COMIC PAINT BOOK (See Dumbo, Large Feature Comic No. 19)

DUNC AND LOO (#1-3 titled "Around the Block with Dunc and Loo")
Dell Publishing Co.: Oct-Dec, 1961 - No. 8, Oct-Dec, 1963

1 8 16 24 58 97 135
2 6 12 18 41 66 90
3-8 5 10 15 32 51 70

NOTE: *Written by* ***John Stanley; Bill Williams*** *art.*

DUNE (Movie)
Marvel Comics: Apr, 1985 - No. 3, June, 1985

1-3-r/Marvel Super Special; movie adaptation 3.00

DURANGO KID, THE (Also see Best of the West, Great Western & White Indian)
(Charles Starrett starred in Columbia's Durango Kid movies)
Magazine Enterprises: Oct-Nov, 1949 - No. 41, Oct-Nov, 1955 (All 36 pgs.)

1-Charles Starrett photo-c; Durango Kid & his horse Raider begin; Dan Brand & Tipi (origin) begin by Frazetta & continue through #16 72 144 216 454 770 1085
2-Starrett photo-c. 35 70 105 203 327 450
3-5-All have Starrett photo-c. 30 60 90 176 283 390
6-10: 7-Atomic weapon-c/story 15 30 45 90 140 195
11-16-Last Frazetta issue 14 28 42 76 108 145
17-Origin Durango Kid 15 30 45 92 144 195
18-30: 18-Fred Meagher-a on Dan Brand begins.19-Guardineer-c/a(3) begins, end #41. 23-Intro. The Red Scorpion 10 20 30 54 72 90
31-Red Scorpion returns 9 18 27 52 69 85
32-41-Bolle/Frazetta*ish*-a (Dan Brand; true in later issues?) 9 18 27 50 65 80

NOTE: *#6, 8, 14, 15 contain* ***Frazetta*** *art not reprinted in White Indian.* ***Ayers*** *c-18.* ***Guardineer*** *a(3)-19-41; c-19-41.* ***Fred Meagher*** *a-18-29 at least.*

DURANGO KID, THE
AC Comics: 1990 - #2, 1990 ($2.50,$2.75, half-color)

1,2: 1-Starrett photo front/back-c; Guardineer-r. 2-B&W)-Starrett photo-c; White Indian-r by Frazetta; Guardineer-r (50th anniversary of films) 3.00

DUSTCOVERS: THE COLLECTED SANDMAN COVERS 1989-1997
DC Comics (Vertigo): 1997 ($39.95, Hardcover)

Reprints Dave McKean's Sandman covers with Gaiman text 40.00
Softcover (1998, $24.95) 25.00

DUSTY STAR
Image Comics (Desperado Studios): No. 0, Apr, 1997 - No. 1 ($2.95, B&W)

0,1-Pruett-s/Robinson-a 3.00

DUSTY STAR
Image Comics (Desperado Publishing): June, 2006 ($3.50)

1-Pruett-s/Robinson-s/a 3.50

DV8 (See Gen 13)
Image Comics (WildStorm Productions): Aug, 1996 - No. 25, Dec, 1998;
DC Comics (WildStorm Prod.): No. 0, Apr, 1999 - No. 32, Nov, 1999 ($2.50)

1/2 6.00
1-Warren Ellis scripts & Humberto Ramos-c/a(p) 4.00
1-(7-variant covers, w/1 by Jim Lee) ...each 4.00
2-4: 3-No Ramos-a 3.00
5-32: 14-Regular-c, 14-Variant-c by Charest. 26-(5/99)-McGuinness-c 2.50
14-($3.50) Voyager Pack w/Danger Girl preview 5.00
0-(4/99, $2.95) Two covers (Rio and McGuinness) 3.00
Annual 1 (1/98, $2.95) 3.00
Annual 1999 ($3.50) Slipstream x-over with Gen13 3.50
Rave-(7/96, $1.75)-Ramos-c; pinups & interviews 3.00
...: Neighborhood Threat TPB (2002, $14.95) r/#1-6 & #1/2; Ellis intro.; Ramos-c 15.00

DV8 VS. BLACK OPS
Image Comics (WildStorm): Oct, 1997 - No. 3, Dec, 1997 ($2.50, lim. series)

1-3-Bury-s/Norton-a 3.00

DWIGHT D. EISENHOWER
Dell Publishing Co.: December, 1969

01-237-912 - Life story 5 10 15 30 48 65

DYNABRITE COMICS
Whitman Publishing Co.: 1978 - 1979 (69¢, 10x7-1/8", 48 pgs., cardboard-c)
(Blank inside covers)

11350 - Walt Disney's Mickey Mouse & the Beanstalk (4-C 157). 11350-1 - Mickey Mouse Album (4-C 1057, 1151,1246). 11351 - Mickey Mouse & His Sky Adventure (4-C 214, 343). 11354 - Goofy: A Gaggle of Giggles. 11354-1 - Super Goof Meets Super Thief. 11356 - (?). 11359 - Bugs Bunny-r. 11360 - Winnie the Pooh Fun and Fantasy (Disney-r).
each.... 2 4 6 9 12 15

11352 - Donald Duck (4-C 408, Donald Duck 45,52)-Barks-a. 11352-1 - Donald Duck (4-C 318, 10 pg. Barks/ WDC&S 125,128)-Barks-c(r). 11353 - Daisy Duck's Diary (4-C 1055,1150) Barks-a. 11355 - Uncle Scrooge (Barks-a/U.S. 12,33). 11355-1 - Uncle Scrooge (Barks-a/U.S. 13,16) - Barks-c(r). 11357 - Star Trek (r/-Star Trek 33,41). 11358 - Star Trek (r/-Star Trek 34,36). 11361 - Gyro Gearloose & the Disney Ducks (r/4-C 1047,1184)-Barks-c(r)
each.... 2 4 6 10 14 18

DYNAMIC ADVENTURES
I. W. Enterprises: No. 8, 1964 - No. 9, 1964

8-Kayo Kirby-r by Baker?/Fight Comics 53. 3 6 9 14 20 25
9-Reprints Avon's "Escape From Devil's Island"; Kinstler-c 3 6 9 16 23 30
nn (no date)-Reprints Risks Unlimited with Rip Carson, Senorita Rio; r/Fight #53 3 6 9 16 22 28

DYNAMIC CLASSICS (See Cancelled Comic Cavalcade)
DC Comics: Sept-Oct, 1978 (44 pgs.)

1-Neal Adams Batman, Simonson Manhunter-r 2 4 6 8 10 12

Dynamo 5 #10 © Faerber & Asrar

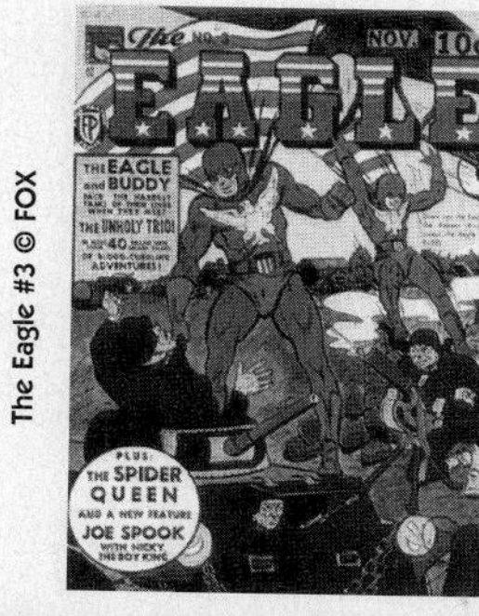

The Eagle #3 © FOX

Earth X #9 © MAR

GD VG FN VF VF/NM NM-
2.0 4.0 6.0 8.0 9.0 9.2

DYNAMIC COMICS (No #4-7)
Harry 'A' Chesler: Oct, 1941 - No. 3, Feb, 1942; No. 8, Mar, 1944 - No. 25, May, 1948

1-Origin Major Victory by Charles Sultan (reprinted in Major Victory #1), Dynamic Man & Hale the Magician; The Black Cobra only app.; Major Victory & Dynamic Man begin 206 412 618 1318 2259 3200
2-Origin Dynamic Boy & Lady Satan; intro. The Green Knight & sidekick Lance Cooper 92 184 276 584 1005 1425
3-1st small logo, resumes with #10 90 180 270 576 988 1400
8-Classic-c; Dan Hastings, The Echo, The Master Key, Yankee Boy begin; Yankee Doodle Jones app.; hypo story 110 220 330 704 1202 1700
9-Mr. E begins; Mac Raboy-c 76 152 228 486 831 1175
10-Small logo begins 58 116 174 371 636 900
11-16: 15-The Sky Chief app. 16-Marijuana story 50 100 150 315 533 750
17(1/46)-Illustrated in **SOTI**, "The children told me what the man was going to do with the hot poker," but Wertham saw this in Crime Reporter #2 65 130 195 416 708 1000
18-Classic Airplanehead monster-c 54 108 162 348 594 840
19-Classic puppeteer-c by Gattuso 54 108 162 348 594 840
20-Bare-breasted woman-c 79 158 237 502 864 1225
21,22,25: 21-Dinosaur-c; new logo 41 82 123 260 435 610
23,24-(68 pgs.): 23-Yankee Girl app. 40 80 120 246 411 575
I.W. Reprint #1,8('64): 1-r/#23. 8-Exist? 3 7 10 18 27 35
NOTE: *Kinstler c-IW #1. Tuska art in many issues, #3, 9, 11, 12, 16, 19. Bondage c-16.*

DYNAMITE (Becomes Johnny Dynamite No. 10 on)
Comic Media/Allen Hardy Publ.: May, 1953 - No. 9, Sept, 1954

1-Pete Morisi-a; Don Heck-c; r-as Danger #6 34 68 102 199 325 450
2 18 36 54 105 165 225
3-Marijuana story; Johnny Dynamite (1st app.) begins by Pete Morisi(c/a); Heck text-a; man shot in face at close range 21 42 63 126 206 285
4-Injury-to-eye, prostitution; Morisi-c/a 21 42 63 122 199 275
5-9-Morisi-c/a in all. 7-Prostitute story & reprints 17 34 51 98 154 210

DYNAMO (Also see Tales of Thunder & T.H.U.N.D.E.R. Agents)
Tower Comics: Aug, 1966 - No. 4, June, 1967 (25¢)

1-Crandall/Wood, Ditko/Wood-a; Weed series begins; NoMan & Lightning cameos; Wood-c/a 9 18 27 63 107 150
2-4: Wood-c/a in all 6 12 18 39 62 85
NOTE: *Adkins/Wood a-2. Ditko a-4?. Tuska a-2, 3.*

DYNAMO 5 (See Noble Causes: Extended Family #2 for debut of Captain Dynamo)
Image Comics: Jan, 2007 - No. 25, Oct, 2009 ($3.50/$2.99)

1-Intro. the offspring of Captain Dynamo; Faerber-s/Asrar-a 8.00
2 5.00
3-7,11-24 : 5-Intro. Synergy. 13-Origin of Myriad. 21-Firebird app. 3.50
8-10-($2.99) 3.00
25-($4.99) Back-up short stories of team members 5.00
Annual #1 (4/08, $5.99) r/Captain Dynamo app. in Nobel Causes: Extended Family #2 and three new stories by Faerber & various; pin-up gallery 6.00
#0 (2/09, 99¢) short story leading into #20; text synopsis of story so far 2.00
... Vol. 1: Post-Nuclear Family TPB (2007, $9.99) r/#1-7; Kirkman intro. 10.00
... Vol. 2: Moments of Truth TPB (2008, $14.99) r/#8-13 15.00

DYNAMO JOE (Also see First Adventures & Mars)
First Comics: May, 1986 - No. 15, Jan, 1988 (#12-15: $1.75)

1-15: 4-Cargonauts begin, Special 1(1/87)-Mostly-r/Mars 2.50

DYNOMUTT (TV)(See Scooby-Doo (3rd series))
Marvel Comics Group: Nov, 1977 - No. 6, Sept, 1978 (Hanna-Barbera)

1-The Blue Falcon, Scooby Doo in all 4 8 12 26 41 55
2-6-All newsstand only 3 6 9 18 27 35

EAGLE, THE (1st Series) (See Science Comics & Weird Comics #8)
Fox Features Syndicate: July, 1941 - No. 4, Jan, 1942

1-The Eagle begins; Rex Dexter of Mars app. by Briefer; all issues feature German war covers 181 362 543 1158 1979 2800
2-The Spider Queen begins (origin) 86 172 258 546 936 1325
3,4: 3-Joe Spook begins (origin) 67 134 201 426 731 1035

EAGLE (2nd Series)
Rural Home Publ.: Feb-Mar, 1945 - No. 2, Apr-May, 1945

1-Aviation stories 48 96 144 302 514 725
2-Lucky Aces 26 52 78 154 252 350
NOTE: *L. B. Cole c/a in each.*

EAGLE

GD VG FN VF VF/NM NM-
2.0 4.0 6.0 8.0 9.0 9.2

Crystal Comics/Apple Comics #17 on: Sept, 1986 - No. 23, 1989 ($1.50/1.75/1.95, B&W)

1-23: 12-Double size origin issue ($2.50) 2.50
1-Signed and limited 4.00

EARTH 4 (Also see Urth 4)
Continuity Comics: Dec, 1993 - No. 4, Jan, 1994 ($2.50)

1-4: 1-3 all listed as Dec, 1993 in indicia 2.50

EARTH 4 DEATHWATCH 2000
Continuity Comics: Apr, 1993 - No. 3, Aug, 1993 ($2.50)

1-3 2.50

EARTH MAN ON VENUS (An...) (Also see Strange Planets)
Avon Periodicals: 1951

nn-Wood-a (26 pgs.); Fawcette-c 135 270 405 864 1482 2100

EARTHWORM JIM (TV, cartoon)
Marvel Comics: Dec, 1995 - No. 3, Feb, 1996 ($2.25)

1-3: Based on video game and toys 3.00

EARTH X
Marvel Comics: No. 0, Mar, 1999 - No. 12, Apr, 2000 ($3.99/$2.99, lim. series)

nn- (Wizard supplement) Alex Ross sketchbook; painted-c 6.00
Sketchbook (2/99) New sketches and previews 6.00
0-(3/99)-Prelude; Leon-a(p)/Ross-c 1 2 3 4 5 7
1-(4/99)-Leon-a(p)/Ross-c 1 2 3 4 5 7
1-2nd printing 3.00
2-12 3.50
#1/2 (Wizard) Nick Fury on cover; Reinhold-a 6.00
#X (6/00, $3.99) 4.00
... Trilogy Companion TPB (2008, $29.99) r/#1/2; artwork and content from the Earth X, Paradise X and Universe X series; gallery of variant covers and promotional art 30.00
HC (2005, $49.99) r/#0,1-12, #1/2, X; foreward by Joss Whedon; Ross sketch pages 50.00
TPB (12/00, $24.95) r/#0,1-12, X; foreward by Joss Whedon 25.00

EASTER BONNET SHOP (See March of Comics No. 29)

EASTER WITH MOTHER GOOSE
Dell Publishing Co.: No. 103, 1946 - No. 220, Mar, 1949

Four Color 103 (#1)-Walt Kelly-a 17 34 51 119 230 340
Four Color 140 ('47)-Kelly-a 14 28 42 98 184 270
Four Color 185 ('48), 220-Kelly-a 13 26 39 90 165 240

EAST MEETS WEST
Innovation Publishing: Apr, 1990 - No. 2, 1990 ($2.50, limited series, mature)

1,2: 1-Stevens part-i; Redondo-c(i). 2-Stevens-c(i); 1st app. Cheech & Chong in comics 2.50

EC ARCHIVES (Also see EC Sampler in the Promotional Comics section)
Gemstone Publishing: 2006 - Present ($49.95, hardcover with dustjacket)

Crime SuspenStories Vol. 1 - Recolored reprints of #1-6; foreward by Max Allan Collins 50.00
Frontline Combat Vol. 1 - Recolored reprints of #1-6; foreward by Henry G. Franke III 50.00
Shock SuspenStories Vol. 1 - Recolored reprints of #1-6; foreward by Steven Spielberg 50.00
Shock SuspenStories Vol. 2 - Recolored reprints of #7-12; foreward by Dean Kamen 50.00
Tales From the Crypt Vol. 1 - Recolored reprints of Crypt of Terror #17-19 and Tales From the Crypt #20-22; foreward by John Carpenter; Al Feldstein behind-the-scenes info 50.00
Tales From the Crypt Vol. 2 - Recolored reprints of #23-28; foreward by Joe Dante 50.00
Tales From the Crypt Vol. 3 - Recolored reprints of #29-34; foreward by Bob Overstreet 50.00
Two-Fisted Tales Vol. 1 - Recolored reprints of #18-23; foreward by Stephen Geppi 50.00
Two-Fisted Tales Vol. 2 - Recolored reprints of #24-29; foreward by Rocco Versaci, Ph.D.50.00
Vault of Horror Vol. 1 - Recolored reprints of #12-17; foreward by R.L. Stine 50.00
Weird Science Vol. 1 - Recolored reprints of #1-6; foreward by George Lucas 50.00
Weird Science Vol. 2 - Recolored reprints of #7-12; foreward by Paul Levitz 50.00
Weird Science Vol. 3 - Recolored reprints of #13-18; foreward by Jerry Weist 50.00

E. C. CLASSIC REPRINTS
East Coast Comix Co.: May, 1973 - No. 12, 1976 (E. C. Comics reprinted in color minus ads)

1-The Crypt of Terror #1 (Tales from the Crypt #46) 2 4 6 11 16 20
2-12: 2-Weird Science #15('52). 3-Shock SuspenStories #12. 4-Haunt of Fear #12. 5-Weird Fantasy #13('52). 6-Crime SuspenStories #25. 7-Vault of Horror #26. 8-Shock SuspenStories #6. 9-Two-Fisted Tales #34. 10-Haunt of Fear #23. 11-Weird Science 12(#1). 12-Shock SuspenStories #2 2 4 6 8 11 14

EC CLASSICS
Russ Cochran: Aug, 1985 - No. 12, 1986? (High quality paper; each-r 8 stories in color) (#2-12 were resolicited in 1990)($4.95, 56 pgs., 8x11")

1-12: 1-Tales From the Crypt. 2-Weird Science. 3-Two-Fisted Tales (r/31); Frontline Combat (r/9). 4-Shock SuspenStories. 5-Weird Fantasy. 6-Vault of Horror. 7-Weird Science-Fantasy (r/23,24). 8-Crime SuspenStories (r/17,18). 9-Haunt of Fear (r/14,15). 10-Panic (r/1,2).

Echo #2 © Terry Moore

Eclipse Graphic Album #14 © MAR

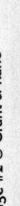

Edge #2 © Grant & Kane

11-Tales From the Crypt (r/23,24). 12-Weird Science (r/20,22) — 1 2 3 4 5 7

ECHO
Image Comics (Dreamwave Prod.): Mar, 2000 - No. 5, Sept, 2000 ($2.50)

1-5: 1-3-Pat Lee-c — 2.50
0-(7/00) — 2.50

ECHO
Abstract Studio: Mar, 2008 - Present ($3.50)

1-Terry Moore-s/a/c — 8.00
2-20 — 3.50
Terry Moore's Echo: Moon Lake TPB (2008, $15.95) r/#1-5; Moore sketch pages — 16.00

ECHO OF FUTUREPAST
Pacific Comics/Continuity Com.: May, 1984 - No. 9, Jan, 1986 ($2.95, 52 pgs.)

1-9: Neal Adams-c/a in all? — 6.00
NOTE: ***N. Adams** a-1-6,7i,9i; c-1-3, 5p,7i,8,9i. **Golden** a-1-6 (Bucky O'Hare); c-6. **Toth** a-6,7.*

ECLIPSE GRAPHIC ALBUM SERIES
Eclipse Comics: Oct, 1978 - 1989 (8-1/2x11") (B&W #1-5)

1-Sabre (10/78, B&W, 1st print.); Gulacy-a; 1st direct sale graphic novel — 16.00
1-Sabre (2nd printing, 1/79) — 8.00
1-Sabre (3rd printing, $5.95) — 6.00
1-Sabre 30th Anniversary Edition (2008, $14.99, 9x6" HC) new McGregor & Gulacy intros. original script with sketch art — 15.00
3,4: 3-Detectives, Inc. (5/80, B&W, $6.95)-Rogers-a. 4-Stewart The Rat (1980, B&W) -G. Colan-a — 10.00
5-The Price (10/81, B&W)-Starlin-a — 16.00
2,6,7,13: 2-Night Music (11/79, B&W)-Russell-a. 6-I Am Coyote (11/84, color)-Rogers-c/a. 7-The Rocketeer (2nd print, $7.95). 7-The Rocketeer (3rd print, 1991, $8.95). 13-The Sisterhood of Steel ('87, $8.95, color) — 10.00
7-The Rocketeer (9/85, color)-Dave Stevens-a (r/chapters 1-5)(see Pacific Presents & Starslayer); has 7 pgs. new-a — 14.00
7-The Rocketeer, signed & limited HC — 60.00
7-The Rocketeer, hardcover (1986, $19.95) — 20.00
7-The Rocketeer, unsigned HC (3rd, $32.95) — 33.00
8-Zorro In Old California ('86, color) — 14.00
8,12-Hardcover — 18.00
9,10: 9-Sacred And The Profane ('86)-Steacy-a. 10-Somerset Holmes ('86, $15.95)-Adults, soft-c — 16.00
9,10,12-Hardcover ($24.95). 12-signed & #'d — 25.00
11-Floyd Farland, Citizen of the Future ('87, $2.95, B&W) Chris Ware-s/a — 7.00
12,28,31,35: 12-Silverheels ('87, $7.95, color). 28-Miracleman Book I ($5.95). 31-Pigeons From Hell by R. E. Howard (11/88). 35-Rael: Into The Shadow of the Sun ('88, $7.95) — 10.00
14,16,18,20,23,24: 14-Samurai, Son of Death ('87, $4.95, B&W). 16,18,20,23-See Airfighters Classics #1-4. 24-Heartbreak ($4.95, B&W) — 7.00
14 (2nd pr.),17,21: 14-Samurai, Son of Death ($3.95, 2nd printing). 17-Valkyrie, Prisoner of the Past SC ('88, $3.95, color). 21-XYR-Multiple ending comic ('88, $3.95, B&W) — 6.00
15,22,27: 15-Twisted Tales (11/87, color)-Dave Stevens-c. 22-Alien Worlds #1 (5/88, $3.95, 52 pgs.)-Nudity. 27-Fast Fiction (She) ($5.95, B&W) — 8.00
17-Valkyrie, Prisoner of the Past S&N Hardcover ('88, $19.95) — 20.00
19-Scout: The Four Monsters ('88, $14.95, color)-r/Scout #1-7; soft-c — 15.00
25,30,32-34: 25-Alex Toth's Zorro Vol. 1 ,2($10.95, B&W). 30-Brought To Light; Alan Moore scripts ('89). 32-Teenaged Dope Slaves and Reform School Girls. 33-Bogie. 34-Air Fighters Classics #5 — 12.00
29-Real Love: Best of Simon & Kirby Romance Comics(10/88, $12.95) — 15.00
30,31: Limited hardcover ed. ($29.95). 31-signed — 30.00
36-Dr. Watchstop: Adventures in Time and Space ('89, $8.95) — 10.00

ECLIPSE MAGAZINE (Becomes Eclipse Monthly)
Eclipse Publishing: May, 1981 - No. 8, Jan, 1983 ($2.95, B&W, magazine)

1-8: 1-1st app. Cap'n Quick and a Foozle by Rogers, Ms. Tree by Beatty, and Dope by Trina Robbins. 2-1st app. I Am Coyote by Rogers. 7-1st app. Masked Man by Boyer — 3.00
NOTE: ***Colan** a-3, 5, 8. **Golden** c/a-2. **Gulacy** a-6, c-1, 6. **Kaluta** c/a-5. **Mayerik** a-2, 3. **Rogers** a-1-8. **Starlin** a-1. **Sutton** a-6.*

ECLIPSE MONTHLY
Eclipse Comics: Aug, 1983 - No. 10, Jul, 1984 (Baxter paper, $2.00/$1.50/$1.75)

1-10: ($2.00, 52 pgs.)-Cap'n Quick and a Foozle by Rogers, Static by Ditko, Dope by Trina Robbins, Rio by Wildey, The Masked Man by Boyer begin. 3-Ragamuffins begins — 2.50
NOTE: ***Boyer** c-6. **Ditko** a-1-3. **Rogers** a-1-4; c-2, 4, 7. **Wildey** a-1, 2, 5, 9, 10; c-5, 10.*

ECLIPSO (See Brave and the Bold #64, House of Secrets #61 & Phantom Stranger, 1987)
DC Comics: Nov, 1992 - No. 18, Apr, 1994 ($1.25)

1-18: 1-Giffen plots/breakdowns begin. 10-Darkseid app. Creeper in #3-6,9,11-13. 18-Spectre-c/s — 2.50
Annual 1 (1993, $2.50, 68 pgs.)-Intro Prism — 2.50
...: The Music of the Spheres TPB (2009, $19.99) r/stories from Countdown to Mystery #1-8 — 20.00

ECLIPSO: THE DARKNESS WITHIN
DC Comics: July, 1992 - No. 2, Oct, 1992 ($2.50, 68 pgs.)

1,2: 1-With purple gem attached to-c, 1-Without gem; Superman, Creeper app., 2-Concludes Eclipso storyline from annuals — 2.50

E. C. 3-D CLASSICS (See Three Dimensional...)

ECTOKID (See Razorline)
Marvel Comics: Sept, 1993 - No. 9, May, 1994 ($1.75/$1.95)

1-($2.50)-Foil embossed-c; created by C. Barker — 3.00
2-9: 2-Origin. 5-Saint Sinner x-over — 2.50
...: Unleashed! 1 (10/94, $2.95, 52 pgs.) — 3.00

ED "BIG DADDY" ROTH'S RATFINK COMIX (Also see Ratfink)
World of Fandom/ Ed Roth: 1991 - No. 3, 1991 ($2.50)

1-3: Regular Ed., 1-Limited double cover — 1 3 4 6 8 10

EDDIE CAMPBELL'S BACCHUS
Eddie Campbell Comics: May, 1995 - Present ($2.95, B&W)

1-Cerebus app. — 1 2 3 5 6 8
1-2nd printing (5/97) — 3.00
2-10: 9-Alex Ross back-c — 5.00
11-60 — 3.00
Doing The Islands With Bacchus ('97, $17.95) — 18.00
Earth, Water, Air & Fire ('98, $9.95) — 10.00
King Bacchus ('99, $12.95) — 13.00
The Eyeball Kid ('98, $8.50) — 8.50

EDDIE STANKY (Baseball Hero)
Fawcett Publications: 1951 (New York Giants)

nn-Photo-c — 34 68 102 199 325 450

EDEN'S TRAIL
Marvel Comics: Jan, 2003 - No. 6 ($2.99, limited series, Marvelscope-printed sideways)

1-5-Chuck Austen-s/Steve Uy-a — 3.00

EDGAR ALLAN POE'S - THE FALL OF THE HOUSE OF USHER AND OTHER TALES OF HORROR
Catlan Communications Pub.: Sept. 1985 (hardcover graphic novel)

nn-Reprints of Poe story issues from Warren comic mags; all Richard Corben-a; numbered edition of 350 signed by Corben; 60 pgs. — 130.00
nn-Softcover edition — 60.00

EDGAR BERGEN PRESENTS CHARLIE McCARTHY
Whitman Publishing Co. (Charlie McCarthy Co.): No. 764, 1938 (36 pgs.; 15x10-1/2"; color)

764 — 75 150 225 476 818 1160

EDGAR RICE BURROUGHS' TARZAN: A TALE OF MUGAMBI
Dark Horse Comics: 1995 ($2.95, one-shot)

1 — 3.00

EDGAR RICE BURROUGHS' TARZAN: IN THE LAND THAT TIME FORGOT AND THE POOL OF TIME
Dark Horse Comics: 1996 ($12.95, trade paperback)

nn-r/Russ Manning-a — 13.00

EDGAR RICE BURROUGHS' TARZAN OF THE APES
Dark Horse Comics: May, 1999 ($12.95, trade paperback)

nn-reprints — 13.00

EDGAR RICE BURROUGHS' TARZAN: THE LOST ADVENTURE
Dark Horse Comics: Jan, 1995 - No. 4, Apr, 1995 ($2.95, B&W, limited series)

1-4: ERB's last Tarzan story, adapted by Joe Lansdale — 3.00
Hardcover (12/95, $19.95) — 20.00
Limited Edition Hardcover ($99.95)-signed & numbered — 100.00

EDGAR RICE BURROUGHS' TARZAN: THE RETURN OF TARZAN
Dark Horse Comics: May, 1997 - No. 3, July, 1997 ($2.95, limited series)

1-3 — 3.00

EDGAR RICE BURROUGHS' TARZAN: THE RIVERS OF BLOOD
Dark Horse Comics: Nov, 1999 - No. 4, Feb, 2000 ($2.95, limited series)

1-4-Kordey-c/a — 3.00

EDGE
Malibu Comics (Bravura): July, 1994 - No. 3, Apr, 1995 ($2.50/$2.95, unfinished lim.series)

Eerie #17 © AVON

Eerie #21 © WP

Egbert #12 © QUA

GD 2.0 | VG 4.0 | FN 6.0 | VF 8.0 | VF/NM 9.0 | NM- 9.2

1,2-S. Grant-story & Gil Kane-c/a; w/Bravura stamp 2.50
3-($2.95-c) 3.00

EDGE (Re-titled as Vector starting with #13)
CrossGeneration Comics: May, 2002 - No. 12, Apr, 2003 ($9.95/$11.95/$7.95, TPB)
1-3: Reprints from various CrossGen titles 10.00
4-8-($11.95) 12.00
9-12-($7.95, 8-1/4" x 5-1/2") digest-sized reprints 8.00

EDGE OF CHAOS
Pacific Comics: July, 1983 - No. 3, Jan, 1984 (Limited series)
1-3-Morrow c/a; all contain nudity 2.50

ED WHEELAN'S JOKE BOOK STARRING FAT & SLAT (See Fat & Slat)

EERIE (Strange Worlds No. 18 on)
Avon Per.: No. 1, Jan, 1947; No. 1, May-June, 1951 - No. 17, Aug-Sept, 1954
1(1947)-1st supernatural comic; Kubert, Fugitani-a; bondage-c
443 886 1329 3234 5717 8200
1(1951)-Reprints story from 1947 #1 74 148 222 470 810 1150
2-Wood-c/a; bondage-c 76 152 228 486 831 1175
3-Wood-c; Kubert, Wood/Orlando-a 76 152 228 486 831 1175
4,5-Wood-c 60 120 180 381 658 935
6,8,13,14: 8-Kinstler-a; bondage-c; Phantom Witch Doctor story
36 72 108 211 343 475
7-Wood/Orlando-c; Kubert-a 46 92 138 290 488 685
9-Kubert-a; Check-c 39 78 117 231 378 525
10,11: 10-Kinstler-a. 11-Kinstlerish-a by McCann 36 72 108 211 343 475
12-Dracula story from novel, 25 pgs. 39 78 117 240 395 550
15-Reprints No. 1('51) minus-c(bondage) 23 46 69 136 223 320
16-Wood-a r-/No. 2 23 46 69 136 223 320
17-Wood/Orlando & Kubert-a; reprints #3 minus inside & outside Wood-c
23 46 69 136 223 320
NOTE: *Hollingsworth a-9-11; c-10, 11.*

EERIE
I. W. Enterprises: 1964
I.W. Reprint #1('64)-Wood-c(r); r-story/Spook #1 4 8 12 22 34 45
I.W. Reprint #2,6,8: 8-Dr. Drew by Grandenetti from Ghost #9
3 6 9 20 30 40
I.W. Reprint #9-r/Tales of Terror #1(Toby); Wood-c 4 8 12 24 37 50

EERIE (Magazine)(See Warren Presents)
Warren Publ. Co.: No. 1, Sept, 1965; No. 2, Mar, 1966 - No. 139, Feb, 1983
1-24 pgs., black & white, small size (5-1/4x7-1/4"), low distribution; cover from inside back cover of Creepy No. 2; stories reprinted from Creepy No. 7, 8. At least three different versions exist.
First Printing - B&W, 5-1/4" wide x 7-1/4" high, evenly trimmed. On page 18, panel 5, in the upper left-hand corner, the large rear view of a bald headed man blends into solid black and is unrecognizable. Overall printing quality is poor.
43 86 129 344 672 1000
Second Printing - B&W, 5-1/4x7-1/4", with uneven, untrimmed edges (if one of these were trimmed evenly, the size would be less than as indicated). The figure of the bald headed man on page 18, panel 5 is clear and discernible. The staples have a 1/4" blue stripe.
16 32 48 113 217 320
Other unauthorized reproductions for comparison's sake would be practically worthless. One known version was probably shot off a first printing copy with some loss of detail; the finer lines tend to disappear in this version which can be determined by looking at the lower right-hand corner of page one, first story. The roof of the house is shaded with straight lines. These lines are sharp and distinct on original, but broken on this version.
NOTE: ***The Overstreet Comic Book Price Guide*** *recommends that, before buying a 1st issue, you consult an expert.*
2-Frazetta-c; Toth-a; 1st app. host Cousin Eerie 10 20 30 73 129 185
3-Frazetta-c & half pg. ad (rerun in #4); Toth, Williamson, Ditko-a
8 16 24 58 97 135
4-7: 4-Frazetta-a (1/2 pg. ad). 5,7-Frazetta-c. Ditko-a in all.
6 12 18 37 59 80
8-Frazetta-c; Ditko-a 6 12 18 41 66 90
9-11,25: 9,10-Neal Adams-a, Ditko-a. 11-Karloff Mummy adapt.-Wood-s/a. 25-Steranko-c
6 12 18 39 62 85
12-16,18-22,24,32-35,40,45: 12,13,20-Poe-s. 12-Bloch-s. 12,15-Jones-a. 13-Lovecraft-s. 14,16-Toth-a. 16,19,24-Stoker-s. 16,32,33,43-Corben-a. 34-Early Boris-c. 35-Early Brunner-a. 35,40-Early Ploog-a. 40-Frankenstein; Ploog-a (6/72, 6 months before Marvel's series)
4 8 12 26 41 55
17-(low distribution) 17 34 51 122 236 350
23-Frazetta-c; Adams-a(reprint) 7 14 21 45 73 100
26-31,36-38,43,44 4 8 12 22 34 45
39,41: 39-1st Dax the Warrior; Maroto-a. 41-(low distribution)
4 8 12 28 44 60
42,51: 42-('73 Annual, 84 pgs.) Spooktacular; Williamson-a. 51-('74 Annual, 76 pgs.) Color poster insert; Toth-a 4 8 12 26 41 55
46,48: 46-Dracula series by Sutton begins; 2pgs. Vampirella. 48-Begin "Mummy Walks" and "Curse of the Werewolf" series (both continue in #49,50,52,53)
4 8 12 22 34 45
47,49,50,52,53: 47-Lilith. 49-Marvin the Dead Thing. 50-Satanna, Daughter of Satan. 52-Hunter by Neary begins. 53-Adams-a 3 6 9 21 32 42
54,55-Color insert Spirit story by Eisner, reprints sections 12/21/47 & 6/16/46
54-Dr. Archaeus series begins 3 6 9 19 29 38
56,57,59,63,69,77,78: All have 8 pg. slick color insert. 56,57,77-Corben-a. 59-(100 pgs.) Summer Special, all Dax issue. 69-Summer Special, all Hunter issue, Neary-a. 78-All Mummy issue 3 6 9 19 29 38
58,60,62,68,72,: 8 pg. slick color insert & Wrightson-a in all. 58,60,62-Corben-a. 60-Summer Giant (9/74, $1.25) 1st Exterminator One; Wood-a. 62-Mummies Walk. 68-Summer Special (84 pgs.) 3 6 9 21 32 42
61,64-67,71: 61-Mummies Walk-s, Wood-a. 64-Corben-a. 64,65,67-Toth-a. 65,66-El Cid. 67-Hunter II. 71-Goblin-c/1st app. 3 6 9 17 25 32
70,73-75 3 6 9 14 19 24
76-1st app. Darklon the Mystic by Starlin-s/a 3 6 9 20 30 40
79,80-Origin Darklon the Mystic by Starlin 3 6 9 17 25 32
81,86,97: 81-Frazetta-c, King Kong; Corben-a. 86-(92 pgs.) All Corben issue. 97-Time Travel/Dinosaur issue; Corben,Adams-a 3 6 9 16 22 28
82-Origin/1st app. The Rook 3 6 9 18 27 35
83,85,88,89,91-93,98,99: 98-Rook (31 pgs.). 99-1st Horizon Seekers.
2 4 6 9 13 16
84,87,90,96,100: 84,100-Starlin-a. 87-Hunter 3; Nino-a. 87,90-Corben-a. 96-Summer Special (92 pgs.). 100-(92 pgs.) Anniversary issue; Rook (30 pgs.)
2 4 6 11 16 20
94,95-The Rook & Vampirella team-up. 95-Vampirella-c; 1st MacTavish
3 6 9 16 23 30
101,106,112,115,118,120,121,128: 101-Return of Hunter II, Starlin-a. 106-Hard John Nuclear Hit Parade Special, Corben-a. 112-All Maroto issue, Luana-s. 115-All José Ortiz issues. 118-1st Haggarth. 120-1st Zud Kamish. 121-Hunter/Darklon. 128-Starlin-a, Hsu-a
2 4 6 9 13 16
102-105,107-111,113,114,116,117,119,122-124,126,127,129: 103-105,109-111-Gulacy-a. 104-Beast World. 2 4 6 8 11 14
125-(10/81, 84 pgs.) all Neal Adams issue 2 4 6 13 18 22
130-(76 pgs.) Vampirella-c/sty (54 pgs.); Pantha, Van Helsing, Huntress, Dax, Schreck, Hunter, Exterminator One, Rook app. 3 6 9 16 22 28
131-(Lower distr.); all Wood issue 3 6 9 14 19 24
132-134,136: 132-Rook returns. 133-All Ramon Torrents-a issue. 134,136-Color comic insert
2 4 6 9 13 16
135-(Lower distr., 10/82, 100 pgs.) All Ditko issue 3 6 9 14 19 24
137-139 (lower distr.):137-All Super-Hero issue. 138-Sherlock Holmes. 138,139-Color comic insert 2 4 6 11 16 20
Yearbook '70-Frazetta-c 6 12 18 37 59 80
Annual '71, '72-Reprints in both 4 8 12 26 41 55
... Archives - Volume One HC (Dark Horse, 3/09, $49.95, dustjacket) r/#1-5 50.00
... Archives - Volume Two HC (Dark Horse, 9/09, $49.95, dustjacket) r/#6-10; interview with Frank Frazetta from 1985 50.00
NOTE: *The above books contain art by many good artists:* ***N. Adams, Brunner, Corben, Craig (Taycee), Crandall, Ditko, Eisner, Evans, Jeff Jones, Krenkel, McWilliams, Morrow, Orlando, Ploog, Severin, Starlin, Torres, Toth, Williamson, Wood,*** *and* ***Wrightson****; covers by* ***Bode', Corben, Davis, Frazetta, Morrow,*** *and* ***Orlando. Frazetta*** *c-2, 3, 7, 8, 23. Annuals from 1973-on are included in regular numbering. 1970-74 Annuals are complete reprints. Annuals from 1975-on are in the format of the regular issues.*

EERIE ADVENTURES (Also see Weird Adventures)
Ziff-Davis Publ. Co.: Winter, 1951 (Painted-c)
1-Powell-a(2), McCann-a; used in **SOTI;** bondage-c; Krigstein back-c
47 94 141 296 498 700
NOTE: *Title dropped due to similarity to Avon's Eerie & legal action.*

EERIE TALES (Magazine)
Hastings Associates: 1959 (Black & White)
1-Williamson, Torres, Tuska-a, Powell(2), & Morrow(2)-a
15 30 45 86 133 180

EERIE TALES
Super Comics: 1963-1964
Super Reprint No. 10,11,12,18: 10('63)-r/Spook #27. Purple Claw in #11,12 ('63); #12-r/Avon's Eerie #1('51)-Kida-r 3 6 9 17 25 32
15-Wolverton-a, Spacehawk-r/Blue Bolt Weird Tales #113; Disbrow-a
5 10 15 30 48 65

EGBERT
Arnold Publications/Quality Comics Group: Spring, 1946 - No. 20, 1950
1-Funny animal; intro Egbert & The Count 20 40 60 114 180 245
2 11 22 33 62 86 110
3-10 9 18 27 47 61 75

Eightball #18 © Fantagraphics

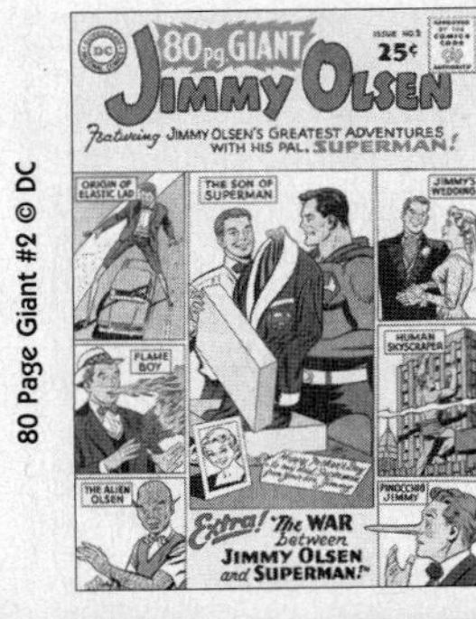

80 Page Giant #2 © DC

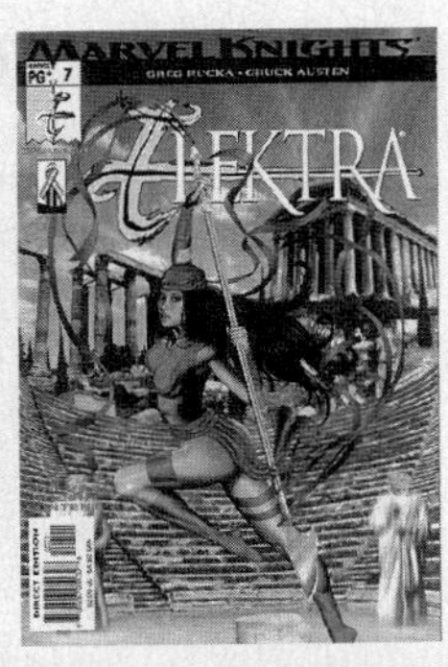

Elektra V2 #7 © MAR

GD 2.0 VG 4.0 FN 6.0 VF 8.0 VF/NM 9.0 NM- 9.2

11-20 7 14 21 37 46 55

EGON
Dark Horse Comics: Jan, 1998 - No.2, Feb, 1998 ($2.95, limited series)
1,2-Horley-painted-c 3.00

EGYPT
DC Comics (Vertigo): Aug, 1995 - No.7, Feb, 1996 ($2.50, lim. series, mature)
1-7: Milligan scripts in all. 3.00

EH! (...Dig This Crazy Comic) (From Here to Insanity No. 8 on)
Charlton Comics: Dec, 1953 - No. 7, Nov-Dec, 1954 (Satire)
1-Davis-*ish*-c/a by Ayers, Wood-*ish*-a by Giordano; Atomic Mouse app.
37 74 111 222 361 500
2-Ayers-c/a 21 42 63 124 202 280
3,5,7 19 38 57 112 179 245
4,6: Sexual innuendo-c. 6-Ayers-a 20 40 60 117 189 260

EIGHTBALL (Also see David Boring)
Fantagraphics Books: Oct, 1989 - Present ($2.75/$2.95/$3.95, semi-annually, mature)
1 (1st printing) Daniel Clowes-s/a in all 2 4 6 8 10 12
2,3 1 2 3 5 6 8
4-8 6.00
9-19: 17-(8/96) 4.00
20-($4.50) 4.50
21-($4.95) Concludes David Boring 3-parter 5.00
22-($5.95) 29 short stories 6.00
23-($7.00, 9" x 12") The Death Ray 7.00
Twentieth Century Eightball (2002, $19.00) r/Clowes strips 19.00

EIGHTH WONDER, THE
Dark Horse Comics: Nov, 1997 ($2.95, one-shot)
nn-Reprints stories from Dark Horse Presents #85-87 3.00

EIGHT IS ENOUGH KITE FUN BOOK (See Kite Fun Book 1979 in the Promotional Comics section)

EIGHT LEGGED FREAKS
DC Comics (WildStorm): 2002 ($6.95, one-shot, squarebound)
nn-Adaptation of 2002 mutant spider movie; Joe Phillips-a; intro by Dean Devlin 7.00

80 PAGE GIANT (...Magazine No. 2-15)
National Periodical Publications: 8/64 - No. 15, 10/65; No. 16, 11/65 - No. 89, 7/71 (25¢)
(All reprints) (#1-56: 84 pgs.; #57-89: 68 pgs.)
1-Superman Annual; originally planned as Superman Annual #9 (8/64)
38 76 114 294 567 840
2-Jimmy Olsen 21 42 63 148 287 425
3,4: 3-Lois Lane. 4-Flash-G.A.-r; Infantino-a 17 34 51 119 230 340
5-Batman; has Sunday newspaper strip; Catwoman-r; Batman's Life Story-r
(25th anniversary special) 17 34 51 119 230 340
6-Superman 15 30 45 105 200 295
7-Sgt. Rock's Prize Battle Tales; Kubert-c/a 22 44 66 157 304 450
8-More Secret Origins-origins of JLA, Aquaman, Robin, Atom, & Superman;
Infantino-a 30 60 90 218 422 625
9-15: 9-Flash (r/Flash #106,117,123 & Showcase #14); Infantino-a. 10-Superboy.
11-Superman; all Luthor issue. 12-Batman; has Sunday newspaper strip. 13-Jimmy Olsen.
14-Lois Lane. 15-Superman and Batman; Joker-c/story
14 28 42 100 188 275

Continued as part of regular series under each title in which that particular book came out, a Giant being published instead of the regular size. Issues No. 16 to No. 89 are listed for your information. See individual titles for prices.
16-JLA #39 (11/65), 17-Batman #176, 18-Superman #183, 19-Our Army at War #164, 20-Action #334, 21-Flash #160, 22-Superboy #129, 23-Superman #187, 24-Batman #182, 25-Jimmy Olsen #95, 26-Lois Lane #68, 27-Batman #185, 28-World's Finest #161, 29-JLA #48, 30-Batman #187, 31-Superman #193, 32-Our Army at War #177, 33-Action #347, 34-Flash #169, 35-Superboy #138, 36-Superman #197, 37-Batman #193, 38-Jimmy Olsen #104, 39-Lois Lane #77, 40-World's Finest #170, 41-JLA #58, 42-Superman #202, 43-Batman #198, 44-Our Army at War #190, 45-Action #360, 46-Flash #178, 47-Superboy #147, 48-Superman #207, 49-Batman #203, 50-Jimmy Olsen #113, 51-Lois Lane #86, 52-World's Finest #179, 53-JLA #67, 54-Superman #212, 55-Batman #208, 56-Our Army at War #203, 57-Action #373, 58-Flash #187, 59-Superboy #156, 60-Superman #217, 61-Batman #213, 62-Jimmy Olsen #122, 63-Lois Lane #95, 64-World's Finest #188, 65-JLA #76, 66-Superman #222, 67-Batman #218, 68-Our Army at War #216, 69-Adventure #390, 70-Flash #196, 71-Superboy #165, 72-Superman #227, 73-Batman #223, 74-Jimmy Olsen #131, 75-Lois Lane #104, 76-World's Finest #197, 77-JLA #85, 78-Superman #232, 79-Batman #228, 80-Our Army at War #229, 81-Adventure #403, 82-Flash #205, 83-Superboy #174, 84-Superman #239, 85-Batman #233, 86-Jimmy Olsen #140, 87-Lois Lane #113, 88-World's Finest #206, 89-JLA #93.

87TH PRECINCT (TV) (Based on the Ed McBain novels)
Dell Publishing Co.: Apr-June, 1962 - No. 2, July-Sept, 1962
Four Color 1309(#1)-Krigstein-a 9 18 27 65 113 160
2 8 16 24 56 93 130

EL BOMBO COMICS
Standard Comics/Frances M. McQueeny: 1946
nn(1946), 1(no date) 14 28 42 80 115 150

EL CAZADOR
CrossGen Comics: Oct, 2003 - No. 6, Jun, 2004 ($2.95)
1-Dixon-s/Epting-a 5.00
2-6: 5-Lady Death preview 3.00
Collected Edition (2003, $5.95) r/#1-3 6.00
...: The Bloody Ballad of Blackjack Tom 1 (4/04, $2.95, one-shot) Cariello-a 3.00

EL CID
Dell Publishing Co.: No. 1259, 1961
Four Color 1259-Movie, photo-c 7 14 21 47 76 105

EL DIABLO (See All-Star Western #2 & Weird Western Tales #12)
DC Comics: Aug, 1989 - No. 16, Jan, 1991 ($1.50-$1.75, color)
1 ($2.50, 52pgs.)-Masked hero 3.00
2-16 2.50

EL DIABLO
DC Comics (Vertigo): Mar, 2001 - No. 4, Jun, 2001 ($2.50, limited series)
1-4-Azzarello-s/Zezelj-a/Sale-c 2.50
TPB (2008, $12.99) r/#1-4 13.00

EL DIABLO
DC Comics: Nov, 2008 - No. 6, Apr, 2009 ($2.99, limited series)
1-6-Nitz-s/Hester-a/c. 4,5-Freedom Fighters app. 3.00
...: The Haunted Horseman TPB (2009, $17.99) r/#1-6 18.00

EL DORADO (See Movie Classics)

ELECTRIC UNDERTOW (See Strikeforce Morituri: Electric Undertow)

ELECTRIC WARRIOR
DC Comics: May, 1986 - No. 18, Oct, 1987 ($1.50, Baxter paper)
1-18 2.50

ELECTROPOLIS
Image Comics: May, 2001 - No. 4, Jan, 2003 ($2.95/$5.95)
1-3-Dean Motter-s/a. 3-(12/01) 3.00
4-(1/03, $5.95, 72 pages) The Infernal Machine pts. 4-6 6.00

ELEKTRA (Also see Daredevil #319-325)
Marvel Comics: Mar, 1995 - No. 4, June, 1995 ($2.95, limited series)
1-4-Embossed-c; Scott McDaniel-a 3.00

ELEKTRA (Also see Daredevil)
Marvel Comics: Nov, 1996 - No. 19, Jun, 1998 ($1.95)
1-Peter Milligan scripts; Deodato-c/a 3.00
1-Variant-c 5.00
2-19: 4-Dr. Strange-c/app. 10-Logan-c/app. 2.50
#(-1) Flashback (7/97) Matt Murdock-c/app.; Deodato-c/a 2.50
.../Cyblade (Image, 3/97,$2.95) Devil's Reign pt. 7 3.00

ELEKTRA (Vol. 2) (Marvel Knights)
Marvel Comics: Sept, 2001 - No. 35, Jun, 2004 ($3.50/$2.99)
1-Bendis-s/Austen-a/Horn-c 4.00
2-6: 2-Two covers (Sienkiewicz and Horn) 3,4-Silver Samurai app. 3.00
3-Initial printing with panel of nudity; most copies pulped 18.00
7-35: 7-Rucka-s begin. 9,10,17-Bennett-a. 19-Meglia-a. 23-25-Chen-a; Sienkiewicz-c 3.00
...Vol. 1: Introspect TPB (2002, $16.99) r/#10-15; Marvel Knights: Double Shot #3 17.00
...Vol. 2: Everything Old is New Again TPB (2003, $16.99) r/#16-22 17.00
...Vol. 3: Relentless TPB (2004, $14.99) r/#23-28 15.00
...Vol. 4: Frenzy TPB (2004, $17.99) r/#29-35 18.00

ELEKTRA & WOLVERINE: THE REDEEMER
Marvel Comics: Jan, 2002 - No. 3, Mar, 2002 ($5.95, square-bound, lim. series)
1-3-Greg Rucka-s/Yoshitaka Amano-a/c 6.00
HC (5/02, $29.95, with dustjacket) r/#1-3, interview with Greg Rucka 30.00

ELEKTRA: ASSASSIN (Also see Daredevil)
Marvel Comics (Epic Comics): Aug, 1986 - No. 8, June, 1987 (Limited series, mature)
1,8-Miller scripts in all; Sienkiewicz-c/a. 6.00
2-7 5.00
Signed & numbered hardcover (Graphitti Designs, $39.95, 2000 print run)- reprints 1-8 50.00
TPB (2000, $24.95) 25.00

ELEKTRA: GLIMPSE & ECHO
Marvel Comics: Sept, 2002 - No. 4, Dec, 2002 ($2.99, limited series)
1-4-Scott Morse-s/painted-a 3.00

Elektra: The Hand #1 © MAR

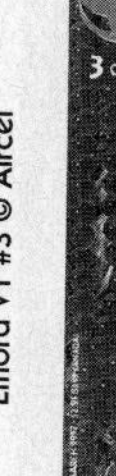

Elflord V1 #3 © Aircel

Elfquest V2 #15 © Warp Graphics

GD 2.0	VG 4.0	FN 6.0	VF 8.0	VF/NM 9.0	NM- 9.2

ELEKTRA LIVES AGAIN (Also see Daredevil)
Marvel Comics (Epic Comics): 1990 ($24.95, oversize, hardcover, 76 pgs.)(Produced by Graphitti Designs)
nn-Frank Miller-c/a/scripts; Lynn Varley painted-a; Matt Murdock & Bullseye app. 35.00
2nd printing (9/02, $24.99) 25.00

ELEKTRA MEGAZINE
Marvel Comics: Nov, 1996 - No. 2, Dec, 1996 ($3.95, 96 pgs., reprints, limited series)
1,2: Reprints Frank Miller's Elektra stories in Daredevil 4.00

ELEKTRA SAGA, THE
Marvel Comics Group: Feb, 1984 - No. 4, June, 1984 ($2.00, limited series, Baxter paper)
1-4-r/Daredevil 168-190; Miller-c/a 4.00

ELEKTRA: THE HAND
Marvel Comics: Nov, 2004 - No. 5, Feb, 2005 ($2.99, limited series)
1-5-Gossett-a/Sienkiewicz-c/Yoshida-s; origin of the Hand in the 16th century 3.00
TPB (2005, $13.99) r/#1-5 14.00

ELEKTRA: THE MOVIE
Marvel Comics: Feb, 2005 ($5.99)
1-Movie adaptation; McKeever-s/Perkins-a; photo-c 6.00
TPB (2005, $12.95) r/movie adaptation, Daredevil #168, 181 & Elektra #(-1) 13.00

ELEMENTALS, THE (See The Justice Machine & Morningstar Spec.)
Comico The Comic Co. : June, 1984 - No. 29, Sept, 1988; V2#1, Mar, 1989 - No. 28, 1994? ($1.50/$2.50, Baxter paper); V3#1, Dec, 1995 - No. 3 ($2.95)
1-Willingham-c/a, 1-8 5.00
2-29, V2#1-28: 9-Bissette-a(p). 10-Photo-c. V2#6-1st app. Strike Force America. 18-Prelude to Avalon mini-series. 27-Prequel to Strike Force America series 3.00
V3#1-3: 1-Daniel-a(p), bagged w/gaming card 3.00
Lingerie (5/96, $2.95) 3.00
Special 1,2 (3/86, 1/89)-1-Willingham-a(p) 3.00

ELEMENTALS: (Title series), **Comico**
--GHOST OF A CHANCE, 12/95 ($5.95)-graphic novel, nn-Ross-c. 6.00
--HOW THE WAR WAS WON, 6/96 - No. 2, 8/96 ($2.95) 1,2-Tony Daniel-a, & 1-Variant-c; no logo 3.00
--SEX SPECIAL, 1991 - No. 4, Feb, 1993 ($2.95, color) 2 covers for each 3.00
--SEX SPECIAL, 5/97 - No. 2, 6/97 ($2.95, B&W) 1-Tony Daniel, Jeff Moy-a, 2-Robb Phipps, Adam McDaniel-a 3.00
--SWIMSUIT SPECTACULAR 1996, 6/96 ($2.95), 1-pin-ups, 1-Variant-c; no logo 3.00
--THE VAMPIRE'S REVENGE, 6/96 - No. 2 8/96 ($2.95) 1,2-Willingham-s, 1-Variant-c; no logo 3.00

ELEPHANTMEN
Image Comics: July, 2006 - No. 11, Jul, 2007 ($2.99) (Flip covers on most)
1-23: 1-Starkings-s/Moritat-a/Ladronn-c. 6-Campbell flip-c. 15-Sale flip-c 3.00
...: The Pilot (5/07, $2.99) short stories and pin-ups by various incl. Sale, Jim Lee, Jae Lee 3.00
...: War Toys (11/07 - No. 3, 4/08, $2.99) 1-3-Mappo war; Starkings-s/Moritat-a/Ladronn-c 3.00
... War Toys: Yvette (7/09, $3.50) Starkings-s/Moritat-a 3.50

1111 (ELEVEN ELEVEN)
Crusade Entertainment: Oct, 1996 ($2.95, B&W, one-shot)
1-Wrightson-c/a 4.00

ELEVEN OR ONE
Sirius: Apr, 1995 ($2.95)
1-Linsner-c/a 1 3 4 6 8 10
1-(6/96) 2nd printing 3.50

ELFLORD
Nightwind Productions: Jun, 1980 - Vol. 2 #1, 1982 (B&W, magazine-size)
1-1st Barry Blair-s/c/a in comics; B&W-c; limited print run for all 11 22 33 79 140 200
2-5-B&W-c 5 10 15 35 55 75
6-14: 9-14-Color-c 4 8 12 28 44 60
Vol. 2 #1 (1982) 4 8 12 24 37 50

ELFLORD
Aircel Publ.: 1986 - No. 6, Oct, 1989 ($1.70, B&W); V2#1- V2#31, 1995 ($2.00)
1 3.00
2-4,V2#1-20,22-30: 4-6: Last B&W issue. V2#1-Color-a begin. 22-New cast. 25-Begin B&W 2.50
1,2-2nd printings 2.50
21-Double size ($4.95) 5.00

ELFLORD
Warp Graphics: Jan, 1997-No.4, Apr, 1997 ($2.95, B&W, mini-series)
1-4 3.00

ELFLORD (CUTS LOOSE) (Vol. 2)
Warp Graphics: Sept, 1997 - No. 7, Apr, 1998 ($2.95, B&W, mini-series)
1-7 3.00

ELFLORD: DRAGON'S EYE
Night Wynd Enterprises: 1993 ($2.50, B&W)
1 2.50

ELFLORD: THE RETURN
Mad Monkey Press: 1996 ($6.95, magazine size)
1 7.00

ELFQUEST (Also see Fantasy Quarterly & Warp Graphics Annual)
Warp Graphics, Inc.: No. 2, Aug, 1978 - No. 21, Feb, 1985 (All magazine size)
No. 1, Apr, 1979
NOTE: *Elfquest* was originally published as one of the stories in **Fantasy Quarterly** #1. When the publisher went out of business, the creative team, Wendy and Richard Pini, formed WaRP Graphics and continued the series, beginning with **Elfquest** #2. **Elfquest** #1, which reprinted the story from **Fantasy Quarterly**, was published about the same time **Elfquest** #4 was released. Thereafter, most issues were reprinted as demand warranted, until Marvel announced it would reprint the entire series under its Epic imprint (Aug., 1985).
1(4/79)-Reprints Elfquest story from Fantasy Quarterly No. 1
1st printing ($1.00-c) 4 8 12 22 34 45
2nd printing ($1.25-c) 1 3 4 6 8 10
3rd printings ($1.50-c) 3.00
4th printing; different-c ($1.50-c) 3.00
2(8/78) 1st printing ($1.00-c) 3 6 9 18 27 35
2nd printings ($1.25-c) 4.00
3rd & 4th printings ($1.50-c)(all 4th prints 1989) 3.00
3-5: 1st printings ($1.00-c) 3 6 9 14 20 25
6-9: 1st printings ($1.25-c) 2 4 6 8 11 14
2nd printings ($1.50-c) 3.50
3rd printings ($1.50-c) 3.00
10-21: ($1.50-c); 16-8pg. preview of A Distant Soil 1 2 3 5 7 9
10-14: 2nd printings ($1.50) 3.00

ELFQUEST
Marvel Comics (Epic Comics): Aug, 1985 - No. 32, Mar, 1988
1-Reprints in color the Elfquest epic by Warp Graphics 3.00
2-32 2.50

ELFQUEST
DC Comics: 2003 - 2005
Archives Vol. 1 (2003, $49.95, HC) r/#1-5 50.00
Archives Vol. 2 (2005, $49.95, HC) r/#6-10 & Epic Illustrated #1 50.00
25th Anniversary Special (2003, $2.95) r/Elfquest #1 (Apr, 1979); interview w/Pinis 3.00

ELFQUEST (Title series), Warp Graphics
'89 - No. 4, '89 ($1.50, B&W) 1-4: R-original Elfquest series 2.50

ELFQUEST (Volume 2),**Warp Graphics:** V2#1, 5/96 - No. 33, 2/99 ($4.95/$2.95, B&W)
V2#1-31: 1,3,5,8,10,12,13,18,21,23,25-Wendy Pini-c 5.00
32,33-($2.95-c) 3.00
--BLOOD OF TEN CHIEFS, 7/93 - No. 20, 9/95 ($2.00/$2.50) 1-20-By Richard & Wendy Pini 3.00
--HIDDEN YEARS, 5/92 - No. 29, 3/96 ($2.00/$2.25)1-9,9 1/2, 10-29 3.00
--JINK, 11/94 - No. 12, 2/6 ($2.25/$2.50) 1-12-W. Pini/John Byrne-back-c 3.00
--KAHVI, 10/95 - No. 6,3/96 ($2.25, B&W) 1-6 3.00
--KINGS CROSS, 11/97 - No. 2, 12/97 ($2.95, B&W) 1,2 3.00
--KINGS OF THE BROKEN WHEEL, 6/90 - No. 9, 2/92 ($2.00, B&W) (3rd Elfquest saga) 1-9: By R. & W. Pini; 1-Color insert 3.00
1-2nd printing 2.50
--METAMORPHOSIS, 4/96 ($2.95, B&W) 1 3.00
--NEW BLOOD (...Summer Special on-c #1 only), 8/92 - No. 35, 1/96 ($2.00-$2.50, color/ B&W) 1-($3.95, 68 pgs.,...Summer Special on-c)-Byrne-a/scripts (16 pgs.) 4.00
2-35: Barry Blair-a in all 3.00
1993 Summer Special ($3.95) Byrne-a/scripts 4.00
--SHARDS, 8/94 - No. 16, 3/96 ($2.25/$2.50) 1-16 3.00
--SIEGE AT BLUE MOUNTAIN, WaRP Graphics/Apple 3/87 - No. 8, 12/88 (1.75/ $1.95, B&W) 1-Staton-a(i) in all; 2nd Elfquest saga 4.00
1-3-2nd printing, 3-8 2.50
2 3.00

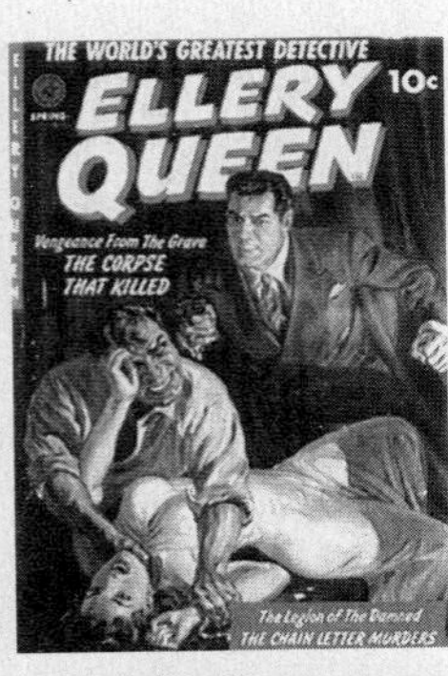

Ellery Queen #1 © Z-D

Elmer Fudd Four Color #470 © WB

Elric: The Vanishing Tower #1 © FC

GD 2.0 | VG 4.0 | FN 6.0 | VF 8.0 | VF/NM 9.0 | NM- 9.2

--THE REBELS, 11/94 - No. 12, 3/96 ($2.25/$2.50, B&W/color) 1-12 — 3.00

--TWO-SPEAR, 10/95 - No. 5, 2/96 ($2.25, B&W) 1-5 — 3.00

--WAVE DANCERS, 12/93 - No. 6, 3/96, 1-6: 1-Foil-c & poster — 3.00
Special 1 ($2.95) — 3.00

--WORLDPOOL, 7/97 ($2.95, B&W) 1-Richard Pini-s/Barry Blair-a — 3.00

ELFQUEST: THE DISCOVERY
DC Comics: March,2006 - No. 4, Sept, 2006 ($3.99, limited series)
1-4-Wendy Pini-a/Wendy & Richard Pini-s — 4.00
TPB (2006, $14.99) r/#1-4 — 15.00

ELFQUEST: THE GRAND QUEST
DC Comics: 2004 - Present ($9.95/$9.99, B&W, digest-size)
Vol. 1-6 ('04)1-r/Elfquest #1-5; new W. Pini-c. 2-r/#5-8. 3-r/#8-11. 4-r/#11-15. 5-r/#15-18 6-r/#18-20 — 10.00
Vol. 7-9 ('05) 1-r/Siege At Blue Mountain #1-3. 8-r/SABM #3-5. 9-r/SABM #6-8 — 10.00
Vol. 10-14 ('05) 10-r/Kings of the Broken Wheel #1-3. 11-KotBW #5-7 & Frazetta Fant. Ill. 12-r/Kings of the Broken Wheel #8&9. 13-r/Elfquest V2 #4-18. 14-r/Hidden Years #4-91/2 — 10.00

ELFQUEST: THE SEARCHER AND THE SWORD
DC Comics: 2004 ($24.95/$14.99, graphic novel)
HC (2004, $24.95, with dust jacket)-Wendy and Richard Pini-s/a/c — 25.00
SC (2004, $14.99) — 15.00

ELFQUEST: WOLFRIDER
DC Comics: 2003 - Present ($9.95, digest-size)
Volume 1 ('03, $9.95, digest-size) r/Elfquest V2#19,21,23,25,27,29,31; Blood of Ten Chiefs #2; Hidden Years #5; New Blood Special #1; New Blood 1993 Special #1; new W. Pini-c — 10.00
Volume 2 ('03, $9.95, digest-size) r/Elfquest V2#33; Blood of Ten Chiefs #10,11,19; Warp Graphics Annual #1 — 10.00

ELF-THING
Eclipse Comics: March, 1987 ($1.50, B&W, one-shot)
1 — 2.25

ELIMINATOR (Also see The Solution #16 & The Night Man #16)
Malibu Comics (Ultraverse): Apr, 1995 - No. 3, Jul, 1995 ($2.95/$2.50, lim. series)
0-Mike Zeck-a in all — 3.00
1-3-($2.50): 1-1st app. Siren — 2.50
1-($3.95)-Black cover edition — 4.00

ELIMINATOR FULL COLOR SPECIAL
Eternity Comics: Oct, 1991 ($2.95, one-shot)
1-Dave Dorman painted-c — 3.00

ELLA CINDERS (See Comics On Parade, Comics Revue #1,4, Famous Comics Cartoon Book, Giant Comics Editions, Sparkler Comics, Tip Top & Treasury of Comics)

ELLA CINDERS
United Features Syndicate: 1938 - 1940

	GD 2.0	VG 4.0	FN 6.0	VF 8.0	VF/NM 9.0	NM- 9.2
Single Series 3(1938)	40	80	120	246	411	575
Single Series 21(#2 on-c, #21 on inside), 28('40)	35	70	105	208	339	470

ELLA CINDERS
United Features Syndicate: Mar, 1948 - No. 5, Mar, 1949

	GD 2.0	VG 4.0	FN 6.0	VF 8.0	VF/NM 9.0	NM- 9.2
1-(#2 on cover)	14	28	42	80	115	150
2	10	20	30	54	72	90
3-5	8	16	24	40	50	60

ELLERY QUEEN
Superior Comics Ltd.: May, 1949 - No. 4, Nov, 1949

	GD 2.0	VG 4.0	FN 6.0	VF 8.0	VF/NM 9.0	NM- 9.2
1-Kamen-c; L.B. Cole-a; r-in Haunted Thrills	52	104	156	328	552	775
2-4: 3-Drug use stories(2)	39	78	117	236	388	540

NOTE: *Iger shop art in all issues.*

ELLERY QUEEN (TV)
Ziff-Davis Publishing Co.: 1-3/52 (Spring on-c) - No. 2, Summer/52 (Saunders painted-c)

	GD 2.0	VG 4.0	FN 6.0	VF 8.0	VF/NM 9.0	NM- 9.2
1-Saunders-c	46	92	138	290	488	685
2-Saunders bondage, torture-c	39	78	117	231	378	525

ELLERY QUEEN (Also see Crackajack Funnies No. 23)
Dell Publishing Co.: No. 1165, Mar-May, 1961 - No.1289, Apr, 1962

	GD 2.0	VG 4.0	FN 6.0	VF 8.0	VF/NM 9.0	NM- 9.2
Four Color 1165 (#1)	10	20	30	70	123	175
Four Color 1243 (11-1/61-61), 1289	8	16	24	56	93	130

ELMER FUDD (Also see Camp Comics, Daffy, Looney Tunes #1 & Super Book #10, 22)
Dell Publishing Co.: No. 470, May, 1953 - No. 1293, Mar-May, 1962

	GD 2.0	VG 4.0	FN 6.0	VF 8.0	VF/NM 9.0	NM- 9.2
Four Color 470 (#1)	8	16	24	56	93	130
Four Color 558,628,689('56)	5	10	15	30	48	65
Four Color 725,783,841,888,938,977,1032,1081,1131,1171,1222,1293('62)	4	8	12	26	41	55

ELMO COMICS
St. John Publishing Co.: Jan, 1948 (Daily strip-r)

	GD 2.0	VG 4.0	FN 6.0	VF 8.0	VF/NM 9.0	NM- 9.2
1-By Cecil Jensen	10	20	30	58	79	100

ELONGATED MAN (See Flash #112 & Justice League of America #105)
DC Comics: Jan, 1992 - No. 4, Apr, 1992 ($1.00, limited series)
1-4: 3-The Flash app. — 2.50

ELRIC (Of Melnibone)(See First Comics Graphic Novel #6 & Marvel Graphic Novel #2)
Pacific Comics: Apr, 1983 - No. 6, Apr, 1984 ($1.50, Baxter paper)
1-6: Russell-c/a(i) in all — 3.00

ELRIC
Topps Comics: 1996 ($2.95, one-shot)
0--One Life: Russell-c/a; adapts Neil Gaiman's short story "One Life--Furnished in Early Moorcock." — 3.00

ELRIC, SAILOR ON THE SEAS OF FATE
First Comics: June, 1985 - No. 7, June, 1986 ($1.75, limited series)
1-7: Adapts Michael Moorcock's novel — 3.00

ELRIC, STORMBRINGER
Dark Horse Comics/Topps Comics: 1997 - No. 7, 1997($2.95, limited series)
1-7: Russell-c/s/a; adapts Michael Moorcock's novel — 3.00

ELRIC: THE BANE OF THE BLACK SWORD
First Comics: Aug, 1988 - No. 6, June, 1989 ($1.75/$1.95, limited series)
1-6: Adapts Michael Moorcock's novel — 3.00

ELRIC: THE VANISHING TOWER
First Comics: Aug, 1987 - No. 6, June, 1988 ($1.75, limited series)
1-6: Adapts Michael Moorcock's novel — 3.00

ELRIC: WEIRD OF THE WHITE WOLF
First Comics: Oct, 1986 - No. 5, June, 1987 ($1.75, limited series)
1-5: Adapts Michael Moorcock's novel — 3.00

EL SALVADOR - A HOUSE DIVIDED
Eclipse Comics: March, 1989 ($2.50, B&W, Baxter paper, stiff-c, 52 pgs.)
1-Gives history of El Salvador — 2.50

ELSEWHERE PRINCE, THE (Moebius' Airtight Garage)
Marvel Comics (Epic): May, 1990 - No. 6, Oct, 1990 ($1.95, limited series)
1-6: Moebius scripts & back-up-a in all — 3.00

ELSEWORLDS 80-PAGE GIANT
DC Comics: Aug, 1999 ($5.95, one-shot)

	GD 2.0	VG 4.0	FN 6.0	VF 8.0	VF/NM 9.0	NM- 9.2
1-Most copies destroyed by DC over content of the "Superman's Babysitter" story; some UK shipments sold before recall	11	22	33	78	139	200

ELSEWORLD'S FINEST
DC Comics: 1997 - No. 2, 1997 ($4.95, limited series)
1,2: Elseworld's story-Superman & Batman in the 1920's — 5.00

ELSEWORLD'S FINEST: SUPERGIRL & BATGIRL
DC Comics: 1998 ($5.95, one-shot)
1-Haley-a — 6.00

ELSIE THE COW
D. S. Publishing Co.: Oct-Nov, 1949 - No. 3, July-Aug, 1950

	GD 2.0	VG 4.0	FN 6.0	VF 8.0	VF/NM 9.0	NM- 9.2
1-(36 pgs.)	25	50	75	147	241	335
2,3	18	36	54	105	165	225

ELSINORE
Alias Entertainment: Apr, 2005 - No. 5, Apr, 2006 (75¢/$2.99/$3.25)
1-5: 1-(75¢-c) Brian Denham-a/Kenneth Lillie-Paetz-s. 2-($2.99-c). 4-($3.25-c) 5-Sparacio-a — 3.25

ELSON'S PRESENTS
DC Comics: 1981 (100 pgs., no cover price)

	GD 2.0	VG 4.0	FN 6.0	VF 8.0	VF/NM 9.0	NM- 9.2
Series 1-6: Repackaged 1981 DC comics; 1-DC Comics Presents #29, Flash #303, Batman #331. 2-Superman #335, Ghosts #96, Justice League of America #186. 3-New Teen Titans #3, Secrets of Haunted House #32, Wonder Woman #275. 4-Secrets of the LSH #1, Brave & the Bold #170, New Adv. of Superboy #13. 5-LSH #271, Green Lantern #136, Super Friends #40. 6-Action #515, Mystery in Space #115, Detective #498	2	4	6	11	16	20

ELVEN (Also see Prime)

Elvira Mistress of the Dark #100 © Queen "B" Prods.

E-Man #5 © CC

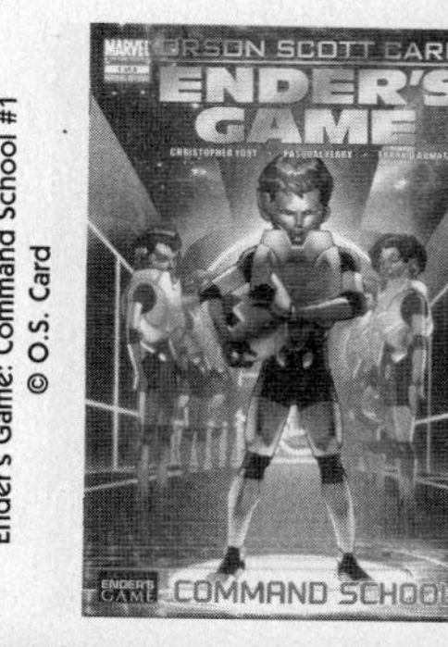

Ender's Game: Command School #1 © O.S. Card

	GD 2.0	VG 4.0	FN 6.0	VF 8.0	VF/NM 9.0	NM- 9.2

Malibu Comics (Ultraverse): Oct, 1994 - No. 4, Feb, 1995 ($2.50, lim. series)
0 ($2.95)-Prime app. 3.00
1-4: 2,4-Prime app. 3-Primevil app. 2.50
1-Limited Foil Edition- no price on cover 3.00

ELVIRA MISTRESS OF THE DARK
Marvel Comics: Oct, 1988 ($2.00, B&W, magazine size)
1-Movie adaptation 5.00

ELVIRA MISTRESS OF THE DARK
Claypool Comics (Eclipse): May, 1993 - No. 166, Feb, 2007 ($2.50, B&W)
1-Austin-a(i). Spiegle-a 6.00
2-6: Spiegle-a 4.00
7-99,101-166-Photo-c: 2.50
100-(8/01) Kurt Busiek back-up-s; art by DeCarlo and others 2.50
TPB ($12.95) 13.00

ELVIRA'S HOUSE OF MYSTERY
DC Comics: Jan, 1986 - No. 11, Jan, 1987
1,11: 11-Dave Stevens-c 6.00
2-10: 9-Photo-c, Special 1 (3/87, $1.25) 4.00

ELVIS MANDIBLE, THE
DC Comics (Piranha Press): 1990 ($3.50, 52 pgs., B&W, mature)
nn 3.50

ELVIS PRESLEY (See Career Girl Romances #32, Go-Go, Howard Chaykin's American Flagg #10, Humbug #8, I Love You #60 & Young Lovers #18)

EL ZOMBO FANTASMA
Dark Horse Comics (Rocket Comics): Apr, 2004 - No. 3, June, 2004 ($2.99)
1-3-Wilkins-s&a/Munroe-s 3.00

E-MAN
Charlton Comics: Oct, 1973 - No. 10, Sept, 1975 (Painted-c No. 7-10)
1-Origin & 1st app. E-Man; Staton c/a in all 3 6 9 16 23 30
2-5: 2,4,5-Ditko-a. 3-Howard-a. 5-Miss Liberty Belle app. by Ditko 2 4 6 9 12 15
6-10: 6,7,9,10-Early Byrne-a (#6 is 1/75). 6-Disney parody. 8-Full-length story; Nova begins as E-Man's partner 2 4 6 11 16 20
1-4,9,10 (Modern Comics reprints, '77) 4.00
NOTE: *Killjoy app.-No. 2, 4. Liberty Belle app.-No. 5. Rog 2000 app.-No. 6, 7, 9, 10. Travis app.-No. 3.* ***Sutton*** *a-1.*

E-MAN
Comico: Sept, 1989 ($2.75, one-shot, no ads, high quality paper)
1-Staton-c/a; Michael Mauser story 2.75

E-MAN
Comico: V4#1, Jan, 1990 - No. 3, Mar, 1990 ($2.50, limited series)
1-3: Staton-c/a 2.50

E-MAN
Alpha Productions: Oct, 1993 ($2.75)
V5#1-Staton-c/a; 20th anniversary issue 2.75

E-MAN COMICS (Also see Michael Mauser & The Original E-Man)
First Comics: Apr, 1983 - No. 25, Aug, 1985 ($1.00/$1.25, direct sales only)
1-25: 2-X-Men satire. 3-X-Men/Phoenix satire. 6-Origin retold. 8-Cutey Bunny app. 10-Origin Nova Kane. 24-Origin Michael Mauser 2.50
NOTE: ***Staton*** *a-1-5, 6-25p; c-1-25.*

E-MAN RETURNS
Alpha Productions: 1994 ($2.75, B&W)
1-Joe Staton-c/a(p) 2.75

EMERALD DAWN
DC Comics: 1991 ($4.95, trade paperback)
nn-Reprints Green Lantern: Emerald Dawn #1-6 5.00

EMERALD DAWN II (See Green Lantern...)

EMERGENCY (Magazine)
Charlton Comics: June, 1976 - No. 4, Jan, 1977 (B&W)
1-Neal Adams-c/a; Heath, Austin-a 4 8 12 24 37 50
2,3: 2-N. Adams-c. 3-N. Adams-a. 3 6 9 19 29 38
4-Alcala-a 3 6 9 14 20 25

EMERGENCY (TV)
Charlton Comics: June, 1976 - No. 4, Dec, 1976
1-Staton-c; early Byrne-a (22 pages) 3 6 9 20 30 40
2-4: 2-Staton-c. 2,3-Byrne text illos. 3 6 9 14 20 25

EMERGENCY DOCTOR
Charlton Comics: Summer, 1963 (one-shot)
1 3 6 9 19 29 38

EMIL & THE DETECTIVES (See Movie Comics)

EMISSARY (Jim Valentino's...)
Image Comics (Shadowline): May, 2006 - Present ($3.50)
1-6: 1-Rand-s/Ferreyra-a. 4-6-Long-s 3.50

EMMA FROST
Marvel Comics: Aug, 2003 - No. 18, Feb, 2005 ($2.50/$2.99)
1-7-Emma in high school; Bollers-s/Green-a/Horn-c 2.50
8-18-($2.99) 3.00
... Vol. 1: Higher Learning TPB (2004, $7.99, digest size) r/#1-6 8.00
... Vol. 2: Mind Games TPB (2005, $7.99, digest size) r/#7-12 8.00
... Vol. 3: Bloom TPB (2005, $7.99, digest size) r/#13-18 8.00

EMMA PEEL & JOHN STEED (See The Avengers)

EMPEROR'S NEW CLOTHES, THE
Dell Publishing Co.: 1950 (10¢, 68 pgs., 1/2 size, oblong)
nn - (Surprise Books series) 6 12 18 28 34 40

EMPIRE
Image Comics (Gorilla): May, 2000 - No. 2, Sept, 2000 ($2.50)
DC Comics: No. 0, Aug, 2003; Sept, 2003 - No. 6, Feb, 2004 ($4.95/$2.50, limited series)
1,2: 1 (5/00)-Waid-s/Kitson-a; w/Crimson Plague prologue 2.50
0-(8/03) reprints #1,2 5.00
1-6: 1-(9/03) new Waid-s/Kitson-a/c 2.50
TPB (DC, 2004, $14.95) r/series; Kitson sketch pages; Waid intro. 15.00

EMPIRE STRIKES BACK, THE (See Marvel Comics Super Special #16 & Marvel Special Edition)

EMPTY LOVE STORIES
Slave Labor #1 & 2/Funny Valentine Press: Nov, 1994 - Present ($2.95, B&W)
1,2: Steve Darnall scripts in all. 1-Alex Ross-c. 2-(8/96)-Mike Allred-c 4.00
1,2-2nd printing (Funny Valentine Press) 3.00
... 1999-Jeff Smith-c; Doran-a 3.00
..."Special" (2.95) Ty Templeton-c 3.00

ENCHANTED
Sirius Entertainment: 1997 - No. 3 ($2.50, B&W, limited series)
1-3-Robert Chang-s/a 2.50

ENCHANTED (Volume 2)
Sirius Entertainment: 1998 - No. 3 ($2.95, limited series)
1-Robert Chang-s/a 3.00

ENCHANTED APPLES OF OZ, THE (See First Comics Graphic Novel #5)

ENCHANTER
Eclipse Comics: Apr, 1987 - No. 3, Aug. 1987 ($2.00, B&W, limited series)
1-3 2.50

ENCHANTING LOVE
Kirby Publishing Co.: Oct, 1949 - No. 6, July, 1950 (All 52 pgs.)
1-Photo-c 15 30 45 90 140 190
2-Photo-c; Powell-a 10 20 30 56 76 95
3,4,6: 3-Jimmy Stewart photo-c 10 20 30 54 72 90
5-Ingels-a, 9 pgs.; photo-c 15 30 45 92 144 195

ENCHANTMENT VISUALETTES (Magazine)
World Editions: Dec, 1949 - No. 5, Apr, 1950 (Painted c-1)
1-Contains two romance comic strips each 15 30 45 88 137 185
2 12 24 36 67 94 120
3-5 10 20 30 56 76 95

ENDER'S GAME: BATTLE SCHOOL
Marvel Comics: Dec, 2008 - No. 5, Jun, 2009 ($3.99, limited series)
1-5-Adaptation of Orson Scott Card novel Ender's Game; Yost-s/Ferry-a. 1-Two covers 4.00
Ender's Game: Recruiting Valentine (8/09, $3.99) Timothy Green-a 4.00
Ender's Game: War of Gifts Special (2/10, $4.99) Timothy Green-a 5.00

ENDER'S GAME: COMMAND SCHOOL
Marvel Comics: Nov, 2009 - No. 5, Apr, 2010 ($3.99, limited series)
1-5-Adaptation of Orson Scott Card novel Ender's Game; Yost-s/Ferry-a 4.00

ENDER'S SHADOW: BATTLE SCHOOL
Marvel Comics: Feb, 2009 - No. 5, Jun, 2009 ($3.99, limited series)

The End League #3 © Remender & Broome

Epic Illustrated #15 © MAR

Espers V3 #3 © James Hudnall

GD VG FN VF VF/NM NM-
2.0 4.0 6.0 8.0 9.0 9.2

1-5-Adaptation of O.S. Card novel Ender's Shadow; Carey-s/Fiumara-a. 1-Two covers 4.00

ENDER'S SHADOW: COMMAND SCHOOL
Marvel Comics: Nov, 2009 - No. 5, Apr, 2010 ($3.99, limited series)

1-5-Adaptation of O.S. Card novel Ender's Shadow; Carey-s/Fiumara-a 4.00

END LEAGUE, THE
Dark Horse Comics: Dec, 2007 - No. 9, Nov, 2009 ($2.99/$3.99)

1-8: 1-Broome-c/a; Remender-s. 5,6-Canete-a 3.00
9-($3.99) MacDonald-a/Canete-c 4.00

ENEMY ACE SPECIAL (Also see Our Army at War #151, Showcase #57, 58 & Star Spangled War Stories #138)
DC Comics: 1990 ($1.00, one-shot)

1-Kubert-r/Our Army #151,153; c-r/Showcase 57 5.00

ENEMY ACE: WAR IDYLL
DC Comics: 1990 (Graphic novel)

Hardcover-George Pratt-s/painted-a/c 30.00
Softcover (1991, $14.95) 15.00

ENEMY ACE: WAR IN HEAVEN
DC Comics: 2001 - No. 2, 2001 ($5.95, squarebound, limited series)

1,2-Ennis-s; Von Hammer in WW2. 1-Weston & Alamy-a. 2-Heath-a 6.00
TPB (2003, $14.95) r/#1,2 & Star Spangled War Stories #139; Jim Dietz-painted-c 15.00

ENGINEHEAD
DC Comics: June, 2004 - No. 6, Nov, 2004 ($2.50, limited series)

1-6-Joe Kelly-s/Ted McKeever-a/c. 6-Metal Men app. 2.50

ENIGMA
DC Comics (Vertigo): Mar, 1993 - No. 8, Oct, 1993 ($2.50, limited series)

1-8: Milligan scripts 2.50
Trade paperback ($19.95)-reprints 20.00

ENO AND PLUM (Also see Cud Comics)
Oni Press: Mar, 1998 ($2.95, B&W)

1-Terry LaBan-s/c/a 3.00

ENSIGN O'TOOLE (TV)
Dell Publishing Co.: Aug-Oct, 1963

1 3 6 9 20 30 40

ENSIGN PULVER (See Movie Classics)

EPIC
Marvel Comics (Epic Comics): 1992 - Book 4, 1992 ($4.95, lim. series, 52 pgs.)

Book One-Four: 2-Dorman painted-c 5.00
NOTE: *Alien Legion in #3. Cholly & Flytrap by* ***Burden****(scripts) &* ***Suydam****(art) in 3, 4. Dinosaurs in #4. Dreadlands in #1. Hellraiser in #1. Nightbreed in #2. Sleeze Brothers in #2. Stalkers in #1-4. Wild Cards in #1-4.*

EPIC ANTHOLOGY
Marvel Comics (Epic Comics): Apr, 2004 ($5.99)

1-Short stories by various 6.00

EPIC ILLUSTRATED (Magazine)
Marvel Comics Group: Spring, 1980 - No. 34, Feb, 1986 ($2.00/$2.50, B&W/color, mature)

1-Frazetta-c; Silver Surfer/Galactus-sty; Wendy Pini-s/a; Suydam-s/a; Metamorphosis Odyssey begins (thru #9) Starlin-a 2 4 6 8 10 12
2-10: 2-Bissette/Veitch-a; Goodwin-s. 3-1st app. Dreadstar. 4-Ellison 15 pg. story w/Steacy-a; Hempel-s/a; Veitch-s/a. 5-Hildebrandts-c/interview; Jusko-a; Vess-s/a. 6-Ellison-s (26 pgs). 7-Adams-s/a(16 pgs.); BWS interview. 8-Suydam-s/a; Vess-s/a. 9-Conrad-c. 10-Marada the She-Wolf-c/sty(21 pgs.) by Claremont/Bolton 1 2 3 4 5 7
11-20: 11-Wood-a; Jusko-a. 12-Wolverton Spacehawk-r edited & recolored w/article on him; Muth-a. 13-Blade Runner preview by Williamson. 14-Elric of Melnibone by Russell; Revenge of the Jedi preview. 15-Vallejo-c & interview; 1st Dreadstar solo story (cont'd in Dreadstar #1). 16-B. Smith-c/a(2); Sim-s/a. 17-Starslammers preview. 18-Go Nagai; Williams-a. 19-Jabberwocky w/Hampton-a; Cheech Wizard-s. 20-The Sacred & the Profane begins by Ken Steacy; Elric by Gould; Williams-a 1 2 3 5 6 8
21-30: 21-Vess-s/a. 22-Frankenstein w/Wrightson-a. 26-Galactus series begins (thru #34); Cerebus the Aardvark story by Dave Sim. 27-Groo. 28-Cerebus. 29-1st Sheeva. 30-Cerebus; History of Dreadstar, Starlin-s/a; Williams-a; Vess-a 1 3 4 6 8 10
31-33: 31-Bolton-c/a. 32-Cerebus portfolio. 2 4 6 8 10 12
34-R.E.Howard tribute by Thomas-s/Plunkett-a; Moore-s/Veitch-a; Cerebus; Cholly & Flytrap w/Suydam-a; BWS-a 2 4 6 10 14 18
Sampler (early 1980 8 pg. preview giveaway) same cover as #1 with "Sampler" text 6.00
NOTE: ***N. Adams*** *a-7; c-6.* ***Austin*** *a-15-20i.* ***Bode*** *a-19, 23, 27r.* ***Bolton*** *a-7, 10-12, 15, 18, 22-25; c-10, 18, 22, 23.* ***Boris*** *c/a-15.* ***Brunner*** *c-12.* ***Buscema*** *a-1p, 9p, 11-13p.* ***Byrne/Austin*** *a-26-34.* ***Chaykin*** *a-2; c-8.* ***Conrad*** *a-2-5, 7-9, 25-34; c-17.* ***Corben*** *a-15; c-2.* ***Frazetta*** *c-1.* ***Golden*** *a-3r.* ***Gulacy*** *c/a-3.* ***Jeff Jones*** *c-25.* ***Kaluta*** *a-17r, 21, 24r, 26; c-4, 28.* ***Nebres*** *a-1.* ***Reese*** *a-12.* ***Russell*** *a-2-4, 9, 14, 33; c-14.* ***Simonson*** *a-17.* ***B. Smith*** *c/a-7, 16.* ***Starlin*** *a-1-9, 14, 15, 34.* ***Steranko*** *c-19.* ***Williamson*** *a-13, 27, 34.* ***Wrightson*** *a-13p, 22, 25, 27, 34; c-30.*

GD VG FN VF VF/NM NM-
2.0 4.0 6.0 8.0 9.0 9.2

EPIC LITE
Marvel Comics (Epic Comics): Sept, 1991 ($3.95, 52 pgs., one-shot)

1-Bob the Alien, Normalman by Valentino 4.00

EPICURUS THE SAGE
DC Comics (Piranha Press): Vol. 1, 1991 - Vol. 2, 1991 ($9.95, 8-1/8x10-7/8")

Volume 1,2-Sam Kieth-c/a; Messner-Loebs-s 10.00
TPB (2003, $19.95) r/ #1,2, Fast Forward Rising the Sun; new story 20.00

EPILOGUE
IDW Publishing: Sept, 2008 - No. 4, Dec, 2008 ($3.99)

1-4-Steve Niles-s/Kyle Hotz-a/c 4.00

ERADICATOR
DC Comics: Aug, 1996 - No. 3, Oct, 1996 ($1.75, limited series)

1-3: Superman app. 3.00

ERNIE COMICS (Formerly Andy Comics #21; All Love Romances #26 on)
Current Books/Ace Periodicals: No. 22, Sept, 1948 - No. 25, Mar, 1949

nn (9/48,11/48; #22,23)-Teenage humor 8 16 24 40 50 60
24,25 6 12 18 28 34 40

ESCAPADE IN FLORENCE (See Movie Comics)

ESCAPE FROM DEVIL'S ISLAND
Avon Periodicals: 1952

1-Kinstler-c; r/as Dynamic Adventures #9 39 78 117 240 395 550

ESCAPE FROM THE PLANET OF THE APES (See Power Record Comics)

ESCAPE TO WITCH MOUNTAIN (See Walt Disney Showcase No. 29)

ESCAPISTS, THE (See Michael Chabon Presents The Amazing Adventures of the Escapist)
Dark Horse Comics: July, 2006 - No. 6, Dec, 2006 ($1.00/$2.99, limited series)

1-($1.00) Frank Miller-c; r/Vaughan story from Michael Chabon... #8 2.50
2-6($2.99) Vaughan-s/Rolston & Alexander-a. 2-James Jean-c. 3-Cassaday-c 3.00

ESPERS (Also see Interface)
Eclipse Comics: July, 1986 - No. 5, Apr, 1987 ($1.25/$1.75, Mando paper)

1-5-James Hudnall story & David Lloyd-a. 3.00

ESPERS
Halloween Comics: V2#1, 1996 - No. 6, 1997 ($2.95, B&W) (1st Halloween Comics series)

V2#1-6: James D. Hudnall scripts 3.00
Undertow TPB ('98, $14.95) r/#1-6 15.00

ESPERS
Image Comics: V3#1, 1997 - Present ($2.95, B&W, limited series)

V3#1-7: James D. Hudnall scripts 3.00
Black Magic TPB ('98, $14.95) r/#1-4 15.00

ESPIONAGE (TV)
Dell Publishing Co.: May-July, 1964

1 3 6 9 20 30 40

ESSENTIAL (Title series), **Marvel Comics**

--ANT-MAN, '02 (B&W- r) V1-Reprints app. from Tales To Astonish #27, #35-69; Kirby-c 15.00

--AVENGERS, '98 (B&W- r) V1-R-Avengers #1-24; new Immonen-c 15.00
V2(6/00)-Reprints Avengers #25-46, King-Size Special #1; Immonen-c 15.00
V3(3/01)-Reprints Avengers #47-68, Annual #2; Immonen-c 15.00
V4('04)-Reprints Avengers #69-97, Incredible Hulk #140; Neal Adams-c 17.00
V5('06)-Reprints Avengers #98-119, Daredevil #99, Defenders #8-11 17.00
V6('08)-Reprints Avengers #120-140, Giant Size #1-4, Capt. Marvel #33 & FF #150 17.00

--CAPTAIN AMERICA, '00 (B&W- r) V1-Reprints stories from Tales of Suspense #59-99, Captain America #100-102; new Romita & Milgrom-c 15.00
V2(1/02)-Reprints #103-126; Steranko-c 15.00
V3('06)-Reprints #127-153 17.00
V4('07)-Reprints #157-186 17.00

--CLASSIC X-MEN, '06 - Present (B&W- r) (See Essential Uncanny X-Men for V1)
V2-($16.99) R-X-Men #25-53 & Avengers #53; Gil Kane-c 17.00

--CONAN, '00 (B&W- r) V1-R-Conan the Barbarian#1-25; new Buscema-c 15.00

--DAREDEVIL, '02 - Present (B&W-r)
V1-R-Daredevil #1-25 15.00
V2-($16.99) R-Daredevil #26-48, Special #1, Fantastic Four #73 17.00
V3-($16.99) R-Daredevil #49-74, Iron Man #35-38 17.00
V4-($16.99) R-Daredevil #75-101, Avengers #111 17.00

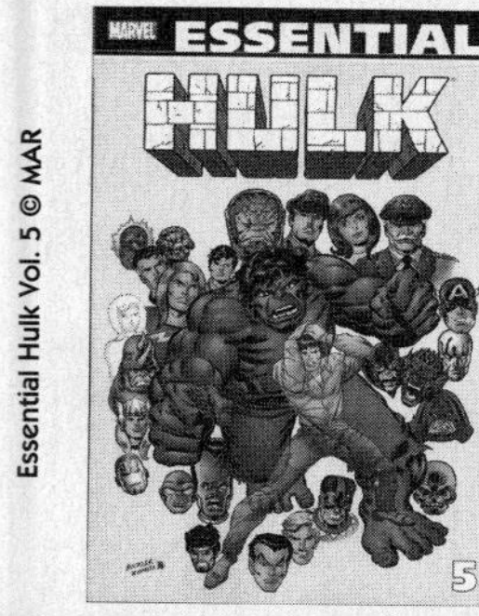

Essential Hulk Vol. 5 © MAR

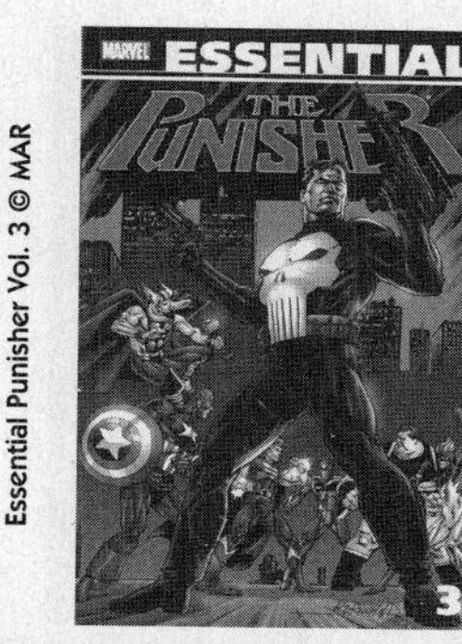

Essential Punisher Vol. 3 © MAR

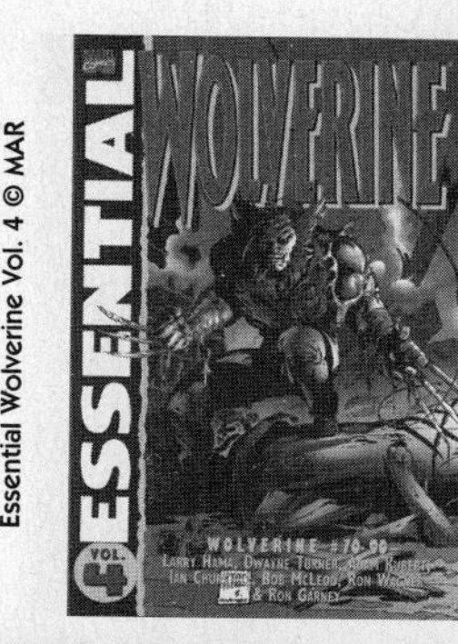

Essential Wolverine Vol. 4 © MAR

GD 2.0	VG 4.0	FN 6.0	VF 8.0	VF/NM 9.0	NM- 9.2

--DAZZLER, '07 (B&W- r) V1-R/#1-21, X-Men #130-131, Amaz. Spider-Man #203 17.00

--DEFENDERS, '05 (B&W-r) V1-Reprints Doctor Strange #183, Sub-Mariner #22,34,35, Incredible Hulk #126, Marvel Feature #1-3, Defenders #1-14, Avengers #115-118 17.00

V2-($16.99) R- Defenders #15-30, Giant-Size Defenders #1-4, Marvel Two-In-One #6,7, Marvel Team-Up #33-35 and Marvel Treasury Edition #12 17.00

V3-($16.99) R- Defenders #31-60 and Annual #1 17.00

--DOCTOR STRANGE, '04 - Present (B&W-r)

V1-($15.95) Reprints Strange Tales #110,111,114-168 16.00

V1 (2nd printing)-(2006, $16.99) Reprints Strange Tales #110,111,114-168 17.00

V2-($16.99) R-Doctor Strange #169-178,180-183; Avengers #61, Sub-Mariner #22 Marvel Feature #1, Incredible Hulk #126 and Marvel Premiere #3-14 17.00

V3-($16.99) R-Doctor Strange #1-29 & Annual #1;Tomb of Dracula #44,45 17.00

--FANTASTIC FOUR, '98 - Present (B&W-r)

V1-Reprints FF #1-20, Annual #1; new Alan Davis-c; multiple printings exist 17.00

V2-Reprints FF #21-40, Annual #2; Davis and Farmer-c 15.00

V3-Reprints FF #41-63, Annual #3,4; Davis-c 15.00

V4-Reprints FF #64-83, Annual #5,6 17.00

V5-Reprints FF #84-110 17.00

V6-Reprints FF #111-137 17.00

--GHOST RIDER, '05 (B&W-r) V1-Reprints Marvel Spotlight #5-12, Ghost Rider #1-20 and Daredevil #138 17.00

V2-Reprints Ghost Rider #21-50 17.00

--GODZILLA, '06 (B&W-r) V1-Godzilla #1-24 20.00

--HOWARD THE DUCK, '02 (B&W- r) V1-Reprints #1-27, Annual #1; plus stories from Marvel Treasury Ed. #12, Man-Thing #1, Giant-Size Man-Thing #4,5, Fear #19; Bolland-c 15.00

--HULK, '99 (B&W-r) V1-R-Incred. Hulk #1-6, Tales To Astonish stories; new Timm-c 15.00

V2-Reprints Tales To Astonish #102-117, Annual #1 15.00

V3-Reprints Incredible Hulk #118-142, Capt. Marvel #20&21, Avengers #88 17.00

V4-Reprints Incredible Hulk #143-170 17.00

V5-Reprints Incredible Hulk #171-200, Annual #5 17.00

--HUMAN TORCH, '03 (B&W-r) V1-Strange Tales #101-134 & Ann. 2; Kirby-c 15.00

--IRON MAN, '00 - Present (B&W-r)

V1-Reprints Tales Of Suspense #39-72; new Timm-c and back-c 15.00

V2-Reprints Tales Of Suspense #73-99, Tales To Astonish #82 & Iron Man #1-11 17.00

V3-Reprints Iron Man #12-38 & Daredevil #73 17.00

--KILLRAVEN, '05 (B&W-r) V1-Reprints Amazing Adventures V2 #18-39, Marvel Team-Up #45, Marvel Graphic Novel #7, Killraven #1 (2001) 17.00

--LUKE CAGE, POWER MAN, '05 (B&W-r) V1-Hero For Hire #1-16 & Power Man #17-27 17.00

V2-Reprints Power Man #28-49 & Annual #1 17.00

--MAN-THING, '06 (B&W-r) V1-Reprints Savage Tales #1, Astonishing Tales #12-13, Adventure Into Fear #10-19, Man-Thing #1-14, Giant-Size Man-Thing #1-2 & Monsters Unleashed #5,8,9 17.00

V2-R/Man-Thing #15-22 & #1-11 ('79 series), Giant-Size Man-Thing #3-5, Rampaging Hulk #7, Marvel Team-Up #68, Marvel Two-In-One #43 & Doctor Strange #41 17.00

--MARVEL HORROR, '06 (B&W-r) V1-R/#Ghost Rider #1-2, Marvel Spotlight #12-24, Son of Satan #1-8, Marvel Two-In-One #14, Marvel Team-Up #32,80,81, Vampire Tales #2-3, Haunt of Horror #2,4,5, Marvel Premiere #27, & Marvel Preview #7 17.00

--MARVEL SAGA, '08 (B&W-r) V1-R/#1-12 17.00

--MARVEL TEAM-UP, '02 - Present (B&W-r) V1('02, '06)-R/#1-24 17.00

V2-R/#25-51 and Marvel Two-In-One #17 17.00

--MARVEL TWO-IN-ONE, '05 - Present (B&W-r)

V1-Reprints Marvel Feature #11&12, Marvel Two-In-One #1-20,22-25 & Annual #1, Marvel Team-Up #47 and Fantastic Four Ann. #11 17.00

V2-R/#26-52 & Annual #2,3 17.00

--MONSTER OF FRANKENSTEIN, '04 (B&W-r) V1-Reprints Monster of Frankenstein #1-5, Frankenstein Monster #6-18, Giant-Size Werewolf #2, Monsters Unleashed #2,4-10 & Legion of Monsters #1 17.00

--MOON KNIGHT, '06 (B&W-r) V1-Reprints Moon Knight #1-10 and early apps. 17.00

V2-R/#11-30 17.00

--MS. MARVEL, '07 (B&W-r) V1-Reprints Ms. Marvel #1-23, Marvel Super-Heroes Magazine #10,11, and Avengers Annual #10 17.00

--NOVA, '06 (B&W-r) V1-Reprints Nova #1-25, AS-M #175, Marvel Two-In-One Ann. #3 17.00

--OFFICIAL HANDBOOK OF THE MARVEL UNIVERSE, '06 (B&W-r) V1-Reprints #1-15 profiling Abomination through Zzzax; dead and inactive characters; weapons & hardware; wraparound-c by Byrne 17.00

--OFFICIAL HANDBOOK OF THE MARVEL UNIVERSE - DELUXE EDITION, '06 (B&W-r)

V1-Reprints #1-7 profiling Abomination through Magneto; wraparound-c by Byrne 17.00

V2-Reprints #8-14 profiling Magus through Wolverine; wraparound-c by Byrne 17.00

V3-Reprints #15-20 profiling Wonder Man through Zzzax & Book of the Dead 17.00

--OFFICIAL HANDBOOK OF THE MARVEL UNIVERSE - MASTER EDITION, '08 (B&W-r)

V1-Reprints profiling Abomination through Gargoyle 17.00

V2-Reprints profiles 17.00

--OFFICIAL HANDBOOK OF THE MARVEL UNIVERSE - UPDATE '89, '06 (B&W-r)

V1-Reprints #1-8; wraparound-c by Frenz 17.00

--PETER PARKER, THE SPECTACULAR SPIDER-MAN, '05 (B&W-r) V1-Reprints #1-31 17.00

V2-Reprints #32-53 & Annual #1,2; Amazing Spider-Man Annual #13 17.00

V3-Reprints #54-74 & Annual #3; Frank Miller-c 17.00

--POWER MAN AND IRON FIST, '07 (B&W-r) V1-R/#50-72,74-75 17.00

--PUNISHER, '04, '06 - Present (B&W-r) V1-Reprints early app. in Amazing Spider-Man, Captain America, Daredevil, Marvel Preview and Punisher #1-5 (2 printings) 17.00

V2-Punisher #1-20, Annual #1 and Daredevil #257 17.00

V3-Punisher #21-40, Annual #2,3 17.00

--RAMPAGING HULK, '08 (B&W-r) V1-R/#1-9, The Hulk! #10-15 & Incredible Hulk #269 17.00

--SAVAGE SHE-HULK, '06 (B&W-r) V1-R/#1-25 17.00

--SILVER SURFER, '98 - Present (B&W-r)

V1-R-material from SS#1-18 and Fantastic Four Ann. #5 15.00

V2-R-SS#1(1982), SS#1-18 & Ann#1(1987), Epic Illustrated #1, Marvel Fanfare #51 17.00

--SPIDER-MAN, '96 - Present (B&W-r)

V1-R-AF #15, Amaz. S-M #1-20, Ann. #1 (2 printings) 15.00

V2-R-Amaz. Spider-Man #21-43, Annual #2,3 15.00

V3-R-Amaz. Spider-Man #44-68 15.00

V4-R-Amaz. Spider-Man #69-89; Annual #4,5; new Timm-f&b-c 15.00

V5-R-Amaz. Spider-Man #90-113; new Romita-c 15.00

V6-R-Amaz. Spider-Man #114-137, Giant-Size Super-Heroes #1 G-S S-M #1,2 17.00

V7-R-Amaz. Spider-Man #138-160, Annual #10; Giant-Size Spider-Man #3-5 17.00

V8-R-Amaz. Spider-Man #161-185, Annual #11; G-S Spider-Man #6; Nova #12 17.00

--SPIDER-WOMAN, '05 (B&W-r) V1-Reprints Marvel Spotlight #32, Marvel Two-In-One #29-33, Spider-Woman #1-25 17.00

V2-R-Spider-Woman #26-50, Marvel Team-Up #97 & Uncanny X-Men #148 17.00

--SUPER-VILLAIN TEAM-UP, '04 (B&W-r) V1-r/S-V T-U #1-14 & 16-17, Giant-Size S-V T-U #1,2; Avengers #154-156; Champions #16, & Astonishing Tales #1-8 17.00

--TALES OF THE ZOMBIE, '06 (B&W-r) V1-($16.99) r/#1-10 & Dracula Lives #1,2 17.00

--THOR, '01 (B&W-r) V1-R-Journey Into Mystery #83-112 15.00

V2-($16.99) R-Thor #113-136 & Annual #1,2 17.00

V3-($16.99) R-Thor #137-166 17.00

--TOMB OF DRACULA, '03 - Present (B&W-r) V1-R-Tomb of Dracula #1-25, Werewolf By Night #15, Giant-Size Chillers #1 15.00

V2-($16.99) R-Tomb of Dracula #26-49, Giant-Size Dracula #2-5, Dr. Strange #14 17.00

V3-($16.99) R-Tomb of Dracula #50-70, Tomb of Dracula Magazine #1-4 17.00

V4-($16.99) R/Stories from Tomb of Dracula Magazine #2-6, Dracula Lives! #1-13, and Frankenstein Monster #7-9 17.00

--UNCANNY X-MEN, '99 - Present (B&W reprints) (See Essential Classic X-Men for V2)

V1-Reprints X-Men (1st series) #1-24; Timm-c 15.00

ESSENTIAL VERTIGO: THE SANDMAN

DC Comics (Vertigo): Aug, 1996 - No. 32, Mar, 1999 ($1.95/$2.25, reprints)

1-13,15-31: Reprints Sandman, 2nd series 3.00

14-($2.95) 3.50

32-($4.50) Reprints Sandman Special #1 4.50

ESSENTIAL VERTIGO: SWAMP THING

DC Comics: Nov, 1996 - No. 24, Oct, 1998 ($1.95/$2.25,B&W, reprints)

1-11,13-24: 1-9-Reprints Alan Moore's Swamp Thing stories 3.00

12-($3.50) r/Annual #2 3.50

ESSENTIAL WEREWOLF BY NIGHT

Marvel Comics: 2005 - Present (B&W reprints)

V1-($16.99) r/Marvel Spotlight #2-4, Werewolf By Night 1-23, Marvel Team-Up #12, Tomb of Dracula #18, Giant-Size Creatures #1 17.00

V2-R/#22-43, Giant-Size Werewolf #2-5 and Marvel Premiere #28 17.00

ESSENTIAL WOLVERINE

Marvel Comics: 1999 - Present (B&W reprints)

V1-r/#1-23, V2-r/#24-47, V3-R/#48-69, V4-R/#70-90 17.00

ESSENTIAL X-FACTOR

Marvel Comics: 2005 - Present (B&W reprints)

V1-($16.99) r/X-Factor #1-16 & Annual #1, Avengers #262, Fantastic Four #286,

The Establishment #8 © DC

Eternals (2008 series) #6 © MAR

Everything Happens to Harvey #2 © DC

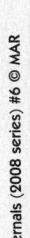

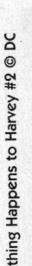

Thor #373&374 and Power Pack #27 — 17.00
V2-Reprints X-Factor #17-35 & Annual #2, Thor #378 — 17.00

ESSENTIAL X-MEN
Marvel Comics: 1996 - Present (B&W reprints)

V1-V4: V1-R/Giant Size X-Men #1, X-Men #94-119. V2-R-X-Men #120-144. V3-R-Uncanny X-Men #145-161, Ann. #3-5. V4-Uncanny X-Men #162-179, Ann. #6 — 15.00
V5-($16.99) R/Uncanny X-Men #180-198, Ann. #7-8 — 17.00
V6-($16.99) R/Uncanny X-Men #199-213, Ann. #9, New Mutants Special Edition #1, X-Factor #9-11, New Mutants #46, Thor #373-374 and Power Pack #27 — 17.00
V7-($16.99) R/Uncanny X-Men #214-228, Ann. #10,11, and F.F. vs. The X-Men #1-4 — 17.00
V8-($16.99) R/Uncanny X-Men #229-243, Ann. #12 & X-Factor #36-39 — 17.00

ESTABLISHMENT, THE (Also see The Authority and The Monarchy)
DC Comics (WildStorm): Nov, 2001 - No. 13, Nov, 2002 ($2.50)

1-13-Edginton-s/Adlard-a — 2.50

ETERNAL, THE
Marvel Comics (MAX): Aug, 2003 - No. 6, Jan, 2004 ($2.99, mature)

1-6-Austen-s/Walker-a — 3.00

ETERNAL BIBLE, THE
Authentic Publications: 1946 (Large size) (16 pgs. in color)

	GD	VG	FN	VF	VF/NM	NM-
1	15	30	45	84	127	170

ETERNALS, THE
Marvel Comics Group: July, 1976 - No. 19, Jan, 1978

	GD	VG	FN	VF	VF/NM	NM-
1-(Regular 25¢ edition)-Origin & 1st app. Eternals	3	6	9	16	22	28
1-(30¢-c variant, limited distribution)	3	6	9	21	32	42
2-(Reg. 25¢ edition)-1st app. Ajak & The Celestials	2	4	6	9	12	15
2-(30¢-c variant, limited distribution)	2	4	6	13	18	25
3-19: 14,15-Cosmic powered Hulk-c/story	2	4	6	8	10	12
12-16-(35¢-c variants, limited distribution)	2	4	6	10	14	18
Annual 1(10/77)	2	4	6	8	10	12

Eternals by Jack Kirby HC (2006, $75.00, dust jacket) r/#1-19 & Annual #1; intro by Royer; letter pages from #1,2,Annual #1; afterwords by Robert Greenberger — 75.00
NOTE: *Kirby c/a(p) in all.*

ETERNALS, THE
Marvel Comics: Oct, 1985 - No. 12, Sept, 1986 (Maxi-series, mando paper)

1,12 (52 pgs.): 12-Williamson-a(i) — 3.00
2-11 — 2.50

ETERNALS
Marvel Comics: Aug, 2006 - No. 7, Mar, 2007 ($3.99, limited series)

1-7-Neil Gaiman-s/John Romita Jr.-a/Rick Berry-c — 4.00
1-7-Variant covers by Romita Jr. — 4.00
1-Variant cover by Coipel — 4.00
... Sketchbook (2006, $1.99, B&W) character sketches and sketch pages from #1 — 2.25
HC (2007, $29.99, dustjacket) r/#1-7; gallery of variant covers; sketches, Gaiman interview, Gaiman's original proposal; background essay on Kirby's Eternals — 30.00

ETERNALS
Marvel Comics: Aug, 2008 - No. 9, May, 2009 ($2.99)

1-9: 1-6-Acuña-a/c; Knauf-s. 2,4-Iron Man app. 7,8-Nguyen-a; X-Men app. — 3.00
Annual 1 (1/09, $3.99) Alixe-a/McGuinness-c; & reprint from Eternals #7 ('77) Kirby-s/a — 4.00

ETERNALS: THE HEROD FACTOR
Marvel Comics: Nov, 1991 ($2.50, 68 pgs.)

1 — 2.50

ETERNAL WARRIOR (See Solar #10 & 11)
Valiant/Acclaim Comics (Valiant): Aug, 1992 - No. 50, Mar, 1996 ($2.25/$2.50)

1-Unity x-over; Miller-c; origin Eternal Warrior & Aram (Armstrong) — 4.00
1-($2.25-c) Gold logo — 5.00
1-Gold foil logo on embossed cover; no cover price — 6.00
2-8: 2-Unity x-over; Simonson-c. 3-Archer & Armstrong x-over. 4-1st brief app. Bloodshot (last pg.); see Rai #0 for 1st full app.; Cowan-c. 5-2nd full app. Bloodshot (12/92; see Rai #0). 6,7: 6-2nd app. Master Darque. 8-Flip book w/Archer & Armstrong #8 — 3.00
9-25,27-34: 9-1st Book of Geomancer. 14-16-Bloodshot app. 18-Doctor Mirage cameo. 19-Doctor Mirage app. 22-W/bound-in trading card. 25-Archer & Armstrong app.; cont'd from A&A #25 — 2.50
26-($2.75, 44 pgs.)-Flip book w/Archer & Armstrong — 2.75
35-50: 35-Double-c; $2.50-c begins. 50-Geomancer app. — 2.50
Special 1 (2/96, $2.50)-Wings of Justice; Art Holcomb script — 2.50
Yearbook 1 (1993, $3.95), 2(1994, $3.95) — 4.00

ETERNAL WARRIORS: BLACKWORKS
Acclaim Comics (Valiant Heroes): Mar, 1998 ($3.50, one-shot)

1 — 3.50

ETERNAL WARRIORS: DIGITAL ALCHEMY
Acclaim Comics (Valiant Heroes): Vol. 2, Sep, 1997 ($3.95, one-shot, 64 pgs.)

Vol. 2-Holcomb-s/Eaglesham-a(p) — 4.00

ETERNAL WARRIORS: FIST AND STEEL
Acclaim Comics (Valiant): May, 1996 - No. 2, June, 1996 ($2.50, lim. series)

1,2: Geomancer app. in both. 1-Indicia reads "June." 2-Bo Hampton-a — 2.50

ETERNAL WARRIORS: TIME AND TREACHERY
Acclaim Comics (Valiant Heroes): Vol. 1, Jun, 1997 ($3.95, one-shot, 48 pgs.)

Vol. 1-Reintro Aram, Archer, Ivar the Timewalker, & Gilad the Warmaster; 1st app. Shalla Redburn; Art Holcomb script — 4.00

ETERNITY SMITH
Renegade Press: Sept, 1986 - No. 5, May, 1987 ($1.25/$1.50, 36 pgs.)

1-5: 1st app. Eternity Smith. 5-Death of Jasmine — 2.50

ETERNITY SMITH
Hero Comics: Sept, 1987 - No. 9, 1988 ($1.95)

V2#1-9: 8-Indigo begins — 2.50

ETTA KETT
King Features Syndicate/Standard: No. 11, Dec, 1948 - No. 14, Sept, 1949

	GD	VG	FN	VF	VF/NM	NM-
11-Teenage	11	22	33	64	90	115
12-14	9	18	27	47	61	75

EVA: DAUGHTER OF THE DRAGON
Dynamite Entertainment: 2007 ($4.99, one-shot)

1-Two covers by Jo Chen and Edgar Salazar; Jerwa-s/Salazar-a — 5.00

EVANGELINE (Also see Primer)
Comico/First Comics V2#1 on/Lodestone Publ.: 1984 - #2, 6/84; V2#1, 5/87 - V2#12, Mar, 1989 (Baxter paper)

1,2, V2#1 (5/87) - 12, Special #1 (1986, $2.00)-Lodestone Publ. — 2.50

EVA THE IMP
Red Top Comic/Decker: 1957 - No. 2, Nov, 1957

	GD	VG	FN	VF	VF/NM	NM-
1,2	5	10	14	20	24	28

EVEN MORE FUND COMICS (Benefit book for the Comic Book Legal Defense Fund) (Also see More Fund Comics)
Sky Dog Press: Sept, 2004 ($10.00, B&W, trade paperback)

nn-Anthology of short stories and pin-ups by various; Spider-Man-c by Cho — 10.00

E.V.E. PROTOMECHA
Image Comics (Top Cow): Mar, 2000 - No. 6, Sept, 2000 ($2.50)

	GD	VG	FN	VF	VF/NM	NM-
Preview ($5.95) Flip book w/Soul Saga preview	2	4	6	8	10	12

1-6: 1-Covers by Finch, Madureira, Garza. 2-Turner var-c — 3.00
1-Another Universe variant-c — 5.00
TPB (5/01, $17.95) r/#1-6 plus cover galley and sketch pages — 18.00

EVERQUEST: ... (Based on online role-playing game)
DC Comics (WildStorm): 2002 ($5.95, one-shots)

The Ruins of Kunark - Jim Lee & Dan Norton-a; McQuaid & Lee-s; Lee-c — 6.00
Transformations - Philip Tan-a; Devin Grayson-s; Portacio-c — 6.00

EVERYBODY'S COMICS (See Fox Giants)

EVERYMAN, THE
Marvel Comics (Epic Comics): Nov, 1991 ($4.50, one-shot, 52 pgs.)

	GD	VG	FN	VF	VF/NM	NM-
1-Mike Allred-a	1	2	3	4	5	7

EVERYTHING HAPPENS TO HARVEY
National Periodical Publications: Sept-Oct, 1953 - No. 7, Sept-Oct, 1954

	GD	VG	FN	VF	VF/NM	NM-
1	28	56	84	168	274	380
2	16	32	48	94	147	200
3-7	14	28	42	82	121	160

EVERYTHING'S ARCHIE
Archie Publications: May, 1969 - No. 157, Sept, 1991 (Giant issues No. 1-20)

	GD	VG	FN	VF	VF/NM	NM-
1-(68 pages)	8	16	24	56	93	130
2-(68 pages)	5	10	15	30	48	65
3-5-(68 pages)	4	8	12	26	41	55
6-13-(68 pages)	3	6	9	18	27	35
14-31-(52 pages)	2	4	6	13	18	22
32 (7/74)-50 (8/76)	2	4	6	8	10	12
51-80 (12/79),100 (4/82)	1	2	3	5	6	8

Evil Ernie: Destroyer #7 © Chaos!

Ewoks #5 © Lucasfilm

Excalibur #125 © MAR

	GD 2.0	VG 4.0	FN 6.0	VF 8.0	VF/NM 9.0	NM- 9.2

81-99 6.00
101-120 5.00
121-156: 142,148-Gene Colan-a 4.00
157-Last issue 5.00

EVERYTHING'S DUCKY (Movie)
Dell Publishing Co.: No. 1251, 1961

Four Color 1251 5 10 15 30 48 65

EVIL DEAD, THE (Movie)
Dark Horse Comics: Jan, 2008 - No. 4, Apr, 2008 ($2.99, limited series)

1-4-Adaptation of the Sam Raimi/Bruce Campbell movie; Bolton painted-a/c 3.00

EVIL ERNIE
Eternity Comics: Dec, 1991 - No. 5, 1992 ($2.50, B&W, limited series)

1-1st app. Lady Death by Steven Hughes (12,000 print run); Lady Death app. in all issues 4 8 12 24 37 50
2,3: 2-1st Lady Death-c. 2,3-(7,000 print run) 3 6 9 14 20 25
4-(8,000 print run) 2 4 6 11 16 20
5 2 4 6 9 13 16
Special Edition 1 3 6 9 14 20 25
Youth Gone Wild! ($9.95, trade paperback)-r/#1-5 1 3 4 6 8 10
Youth Gone Wild! Director's Cut ($4.95)-Limited to 15,000, shows the making of the comic 5.00

EVIL ERNIE (Monthly series)
Chaos! Comics: July, 1998 - No. 10, Apr, 1999 ($2.95)

1-10-Pulido & Nutman-s/Brewer-a 3.00
1-($10.00) Premium Ed. 10.00
... Baddest Battles (1/97, $1.50) Pin-ups; 2 covers 2.50
... Pieces of Me (11/00, $2.95, B&W) Flashback story; Pulido-s/Beck-a 3.00
... Relentless (5/02, $4.99, B&W) Pulido-s/Beck, Bonk, & Brewer-a 5.00
... Returns (10/01, $3.99, B&W) Pulido-s/Beck-a 4.00

EVIL ERNIE: DEPRAVED
Chaos! Comics: Jul, 1999 - No. 3, Sept, 1999 ($2.95, limited series)

1-3-Pulido-s/Brewer-a 3.00

EVIL ERNIE: DESTROYER
Chaos! Comics: Oct, 1997 - No. 9, Jun, 1998 ($2.95, limited series)

Preview ($2.50), 1-9-Flip cover 3.00

EVIL ERNIE: IN SANTA FE
Devil's Due Publ.: Sept, 2005 - Mar, 2006 ($2.95, limited series)

1-4-Alan Grant-s/Tommy Castillo-a/Alex Horley-c 3.00

EVIL ERNIE: REVENGE
Chaos! Comics: Oct, 1994 - No. 4, Feb, 1995 ($2.95, limited series)

1-Glow-in-the-dark-c; Lady Death app. 1-3-flip book w. Kilzone Preview (series of 3) 5.00
1-Commemorative-(4000 print run) 1 3 4 6 8 10
2-4 4.00
Trade paperback (10/95, $12.95) 13.00

EVIL ERNIE: STRAIGHT TO HELL
Chaos! Comics: Oct, 1995 - No. 5, May, 1996 ($2.95, limited series)

1-5: 1-fold-out-c 3.00
1,3:1-($19.95) Chromium Ed. 3-Chastity Chase-c-(4000 printed) 20.00
Special Edition (10,000) 20.00

EVIL ERNIE: THE RESURRECTION
Chaos! Comics: 1993 - No. 4, 1994 (Limited series)

0 5.00
1 2 4 6 8 10 12
1A-Gold 3 6 9 16 23 30
2-4 1 2 3 5 6 8

EVIL ERNIE VS. THE MOVIE MONSTERS
Chaos! Comics: Mar, 1997 ($2.95, one-shot)

1 3.00
1-Variant-"Chaos-Scope•Terror Vision" card stock-c 5.00

EVIL ERNIE VS. THE SUPER HEROES
Chaos! Comics: Aug, 1995; Sept, 1998 ($2.95)

1-Lady Death poster 3.00
1-Foil-c variant (limited to 10,000) 2 4 6 11 16 20
1-Limited Edition (1000) 2 4 6 11 16 20
2-(9/98) Ernie vs. JLA and Marvel parodies 3.00

EVIL ERNIE: WAR OF THE DEAD
Chaos! Comics: Nov, 1999 - No. 3, Jan, 2000 ($2.95, limited series)

1-3-Pulido & Kaminski-s/Brewer-a. 3-End of Evil Ernie 3.00

EVIL EYE
Fantagraphics Books: June, 1998 - Present ($2.95/$3.50/$3.95, B&W)

1-7-Richard Sala-s/a 3.00
8-10-($3.50) 3.50
11,12-($3.95) 4.00

EVO (Crossover from Tomb Raider #25 & Witchblade #60)
Image Comics (Top Cow): Feb, 2003 ($2.99, one-shot)

1-Silvestri-c/a(p); Endgame x-over pt. 3; Sara Pezzini & Lara Croft app. 3.00

EWOKS (Star Wars) (TV) (See Star Comics Magazine)
Marvel Comics (Star Comics): June, 1985 - No. 14, Jul, 1987 (75¢/$1.00)

1,10: 10-Williamson-a (From Star Wars) 2 4 6 9 12 15
2-9 2 4 6 8 10 12
11-14: 14-($1.00-c) 2 4 6 8 11 14

EXCALIBUR (Also see Marvel Comics Presents #31)
Marvel Comics: Apr, 1988; Oct, 1988 - No. 125, Oct, 1998 ($1.50/$1.75/$1.99)

Special Edition nn (The Sword is Drawn)(4/88, $3.25)-1st Excalibur comic 6.00
Special Edition nn (4/88)-no price on-c 1 3 4 6 8 10
Special Edition nn (2nd & print, 10/88, 12/89) 3.00
...The Sword is Drawn (Apr, 1992, $4.95) 5.00
1($1.50, 10/88)-X-Men spin-off; Nightcrawler, Shadowcat(Kitty Pryde), Capt. Britain, Phoenix & Meggan begin 5.00
2-4 4.00
5-10 3.00
11-49,51-70,72-74,76: 10,11-Rogers/Austin-a. 21-Intro Crusader X. 22-Iron Man x-over. 24-John Byrne app. in story. 26-Ron Lim-c/a. 27-B. Smith-a(p). 37-Dr. Doom & Iron Man app. 41-X-Men (Wolverine) app.; Cable cameo. 49-Neal Adams c-swipe. 52,57-X-Men (Cyclops, Wolverine) app. 53-Spider-Man-c/story. 58-X-Men (Wolverine, Gambit, Cyclops, etc.)-c/story. 61-Phoenix returns. 68-Starjammers-c/story 2.50
50-($2.75, 56 pgs.)-New logo 3.00
71-($3.95, 52 pgs.)-Hologram on-c; 30th anniversary 5.00
75-($3.50, 52 pgs.)-Holo-grafx foil-c 4.00
75-($2.25, 52 pgs.)-Regular edition 2.50
77-81,83-86: 77-Begin $1.95-c; bound-in trading card sheet. 83-86-Deluxe Editions and Standard Editions. 86-1st app. Pete Wisdom 2.50
82-($2.50)-Newsstand edition 3.00
82-($3.50)-Enhanced edition 4.00
87-89,91-99,101-110: 87-Return from Age of Apocalypse. 92-Colossus-c/app. 94-Days of Future Tense 95-X-Man-c/app. 96-Sebastian Shaw & the Hellfire Club app. 99-Onslaught app. 101-Onslaught tie-in. 102-w/card insert. 103-Last Warren Ellis scripts; Belasco app. 104,105-Hitch & Neary-c/a. 109-Spiral-c/app. 2.50
90,100-($2.95)-double-sized. 100-Onslaught tie-in; wraparound-c 4.00
111-124: 111-Begin $1.99-c, wraparound-c. 119-Calafiore-a 2.50
125-($2.99) Wedding of Capt. Britain and Meggan 4.00
Annual 1,2 ('93, '94, 68 pgs.)-1st app. Khaos. 2-X-Men & Psylocke app. 3.00
#(-1) Flashback (7/97) 2.50
...Air Apparent nn (12/91, $4.95)-Simonson-c 5.00
...Mojo Mayhem nn (12/89, $4.50)-Art Adams/Austin-c/a 5.00
...: The Possession nn (7/91, $2.95, 52 pgs.) 3.00
...: XX Crossing (7/92, 5/92-inside, $2.50)-vs. The X-Men 2.50
...Classic Vol. 1: The Sword is Drawn TPB (2005, $19.99) r/#1-5 & Special Edition nn (The Sword is Drawn) 20.00
...Classic Vol. 2: Two-Edged Sword TPB (2006, $24.99) r/#6-11 25.00
...Classic Vol. 3: Cross-Time Caper Book 1 TPB (2007, $24.99) r/#12-20 25.00
...Classic Vol. 4: Cross-Time Caper Book 2 TPB (2007, $24.99) r/#21-28 25.00
...Classic Vol. 5 TPB (2008, $24.99) r/#29-34 & Marvel GN Excalibur: Weird War III 25.00

EXCALIBUR
Marvel Comics: Feb, 2001 - No. 4, May, 2001 ($2.99)

1-4-Return of Captain Britain; Raimondi-a 3.00

EXCALIBUR (X-Men Reloaded title) (Leads into House of M series, then New Excalibur)
Marvel Comics: July, 2004 - No. 14, July, 2005 ($2.99)

1-14: 1-Claremont-s/Lopresti-a/Park-c; Magneto returns. 6-11-Beast app. 13,14-Prelude to House of M; Dr. Strange app. 3.00
House of M Prelude: Excalibur TPB (2005, $11.99) r/#11-14 12.00
... Vol. 1: Forging the Sword (2004, $9.99) r/#1-4 10.00
... Vol. 2: Saturday Night Fever (2005, $14.99) r/#5-10 15.00

EXCITING COMICS
Nedor/Better Publications/Standard Comics: Apr, 1940 - No. 69, Sept, 1949

1-Origin & 1st app. The Mask, Jim Hatfield, Sgt. Bill King, Dan Williams begin; early Robot-c (see Smash #1) 411 822 1233 2877 5039 7200

Exciting Comics #13 © Nedor

Exiles #92 © MAR

Ex Machina #24 © Vaughan & Harris

	GD 2.0	VG 4.0	FN 6.0	VF 8.0	VF/NM 9.0	NM- 9.2
2-The Sphinx begins; The Masked Rider app.; Son of the Gods begins, ends #8	171	342	513	1086	1868	2650
3-Robot-c	123	246	369	787	1344	1900
4-6	77	154	231	493	847	1200
7,8	62	124	186	394	677	960
9-Origin/1st app. of The Black Terror & sidekick Tim, begin series (5/41) (Black Terror c-9-21,23-52,54,55)	1000	2000	3000	7400	13,200	19,000
10-2nd app. Black Terror	300	600	900	2010	3505	5000
11	155	310	465	992	1696	2400
12,13	103	206	309	659	1130	1600
14-Last Sphinx, Dan Williams	81	162	243	518	884	1250
15-The Liberator begins (origin)	116	232	348	742	1271	1800
16-20: 20-The Mask ends	61	122	183	390	670	950
21,23-25: 25-Robot-c	50	100	150	315	533	750
22-Origin The Eaglet; The American Eagle begins	61	122	183	390	670	950
26-Schomburg-c begin	84	168	252	538	919	1300
27,29,30	74	148	222	470	810	1150
28-(Scarce) Crime Crusader begins, ends #58	155	310	465	992	1696	2400
31-38: 35-Liberator ends, not in 31-33	63	126	189	403	689	975
39-Nazis giving poison candy to kids on cover; origin Kara, Jungle Princess	129	258	387	826	1413	2000
40-50: 42-The Scarab begins. 45-Schomburg Robot-c. 49-Last Kara, Jungle Princess. 50-Last American Eagle	61	122	183	390	670	950
51-Miss Masque begins (1st app.)	65	130	195	416	708	1000
52-54: Miss Masque ends. 53-Miss Masque-c	56	112	168	356	608	860
55-58: 55-Judy of the Jungle begins (origin), ends #69; 1 pg. Ingels-a; Judy of the Jungle c-56-66. 57,58-Airbrush-c	56	112	168	356	608	860
59-Frazetta art in Caniff style; signed Frank Frazeta (one t), 9 pgs.	56	112	168	356	613	870
60-66: 60-Rick Howard, the Mystery Rider begins. 66-Robinson/Meskin-a	52	102	156	328	552	775
67-69-All western covers	21	42	63	122	199	275

NOTE: ***Schomburg (Xela)** c-26-68; airbrush c-57-66. Black Terror by **R. Moreira**-#65. **Roussos** a-62. Bondage-c 9, 12, 13, 20, 23, 25, 30, 59.*

EXCITING ROMANCES
Fawcett Publications: 1949 (nd); No. 2, Spring, 1950 - No. 5, 10/50; No. 6 (1951, nd); No. 7, 9/51 -No. 12, 1/53

	GD	VG	FN	VF	VF/NM	NM-
1,3: 1(1949). 3-Wood-a	14	28	42	80	115	150
2,4,5-(1950)	10	20	30	54	72	90
6-12	9	18	27	47	61	75

NOTE: ***Powell** a-8-10. **Marcus Swayze** a-5, 6, 9. Photo c-1-7, 10-12.*

EXCITING ROMANCE STORIES (See Fox Giants)

EXCITING WAR (Korean War)
Standard Comics (Better Publ.): No. 5, Sept, 1952 - No. 8, May, 1953; No. 9, Nov, 1953

	GD	VG	FN	VF	VF/NM	NM-
5	10	20	30	58	79	100
6,7,9: 6-Flamethrower/burning body-c	8	16	24	40	50	60
8-Toth-a	9	18	27	47	61	75

EXCITING X-PATROL
Marvel Comics (Amalgam): June, 1997 ($1.95, one-shot)

	GD	VG	FN	VF	VF/NM	NM-
1-Barbara Kesel-s/ Bryan Hitch-a						2.50

EXECUTIONER, THE (Don Pendleton's...)
IDW Publishing: Apr, 2008 - No. 5, Aug, 2008 ($3.99)

	GD	VG	FN	VF	VF/NM	NM-
1-5-Mack Bolan origin re-told; Gallant-a/Wojtowicz-s						4.00

EXECUTIVE ASSISTANT: IRIS
Aspen MLT: No. 0, Apr, 2009 - Present ($2.50/$2.99)

	GD	VG	FN	VF	VF/NM	NM-
0-($2.50) Wohl-s/Francisco-a; 3 covers						2.50
1-4-($2.99) Multiple covers on each						3.00

EXILES (Also see Break-Thru)
Malibu Comics (Ultraverse): Aug, 1993 - No. 4, Nov, 1993 ($1.95)

	GD	VG	FN	VF	VF/NM	NM-
1,2,4: 1,2-Bagged copies of each exist. 4-Team dies; story cont'd in Break-Thru #1						2.50
3-($2.50, 40 pgs.)-Rune flip-c/story by B. Smith (3 pgs.)						2.50
1-Holographic-c edition	1	2	3	5	6	8

EXILES (All New, The) (2nd Series) (Also see Black September)
Malibu Comics (Ultraverse): Sept, 1995 - V2#11, Aug, 1996 ($1.50)

	GD	VG	FN	VF	VF/NM	NM-
Infinity (9/95, $1.50)-Intro new team including Marvel's Juggernaut & Reaper						2.50
Infinity (2000 signed), V2#1 (2000 signed)	1	3	4	6	8	10
V2#1-4,6-11: 1-(10/95, 64 pgs.)-Reprint of Ultraforce V2#1 follows lead story. 2-1st app. Hellblade. 8-Intro Maxis. 11-Vs. Maxis; Ripfire app.; cont'd in Ultraforce #12						2.50
V2#5-($2.50) Juggernaut returns to the Marvel Universe.						2.50

EXILES (Also see X-Men titles) (Leads into New Exiles series)
Marvel Comics: Aug, 2001 - No. 100, Feb, 2008 ($2.99/$2.25)

	GD	VG	FN	VF	VF/NM	NM-
1-($2.99) Blink and parallel world X-Men; Winick-s/McKone & McKenna-a	1	2	3	4	5	7
2-10-($2.25) 2-Two covers (McKone & JH Williams III). 5-Alpha Flight app.						3.00
11-24: 22-Blink leaves; Magik joins. 23,24-Walker-a; alternate Weapon-X app.						2.50
25-99: 25-Begin $2.99-c; Inhumans app.; Walker-a. 26-30-Austen-s. 33-Wolverine app. 35-37-Fantastic Four app. 37-Sunfire dies, Blink returns. 38-40-Hyperion app. 69-71-House of M. 77,78-Squadron Supreme app. 85,86-Multiple Wolverines. 90-Claremont-s begin; Psylocke app. 97-Shadowcat joins						3.00
100-($3.99) Last issue; Blink leaves; continues in Exiles (Days of Then and Now); r/#1						4.00
Annual 1 (2/07, $3.99) Bedard-s/Raney-a/c						4.00
Exiles #1 (Days of Then and Now) (3/08, $3.99) short stories by various						4.00
TPB (3/02, $12.95) r/#1-4						13.00
...: A World Apart TPB (7/02, $14.99) r/#5-11						15.00
...: Vol. 3: Out of Time TPB (2003, $17.99) r/#12-19						18.00
...: Vol. 4: Legacy TPB (2003, $12.99) r/#20-25						13.00
...: Vol. 5: Unnatural Instinct TPB (2003, $14.99) r/#26-30						15.00
...: Vol. 6: Fantastic Voyage TPB (2004, $17.99) r/#31-37						18.00
...: Vol. 7: A Blink in Time TPB (2004, $19.99) r/#38-45						20.00
...: Vol. 8: Earn Your Wings TPB (2004, $14.99) r/#46-51						15.00
...: Vol. 9: Bump in the Night TPB (2005, $17.99) r/#52-58						18.00
...: Vol. 10: Age of Apocalypse TPB ('05, $12.99) r/#59-61 & Official Handbook:AoA 2005						13.00
...: Vol. 11: Time Breakers TPB (2006, $17.99) r/#62-68						18.00
...: Vol. 12: World Tour Book 1 TPB (2006, $16.99) r/#69-74						17.00
...: Vol. 13: World Tour Book 2 TPB (2006, $23.99) r/#75-83						24.00
...: Vol. 14: The New Exiles TPB (2007, $14.99) r/#84-89 and Annual #1						15.00
...: Vol. 15: Enemy of the Stars TPB (2007, $13.99) r/#90-94						14.00
...: Vol. 16: Starting Over TPB (2008, $14.99) r/#95-100 & ...: Days of Then and Now						15.00

EXILES
Marvel Comics: Jun, 2009 - No. 6, Nov, 2009 ($2.99/$3.99)

	GD	VG	FN	VF	VF/NM	NM-
1,6-($3.99) Blink and parallel world Scarlet Witch Beast and others; Bullock-c						4.00
2-5-($2.99)						3.00

EXILES VS. THE X-MEN
Malibu Comics (Ultraverse): Oct, 1995 (one-shot)

	GD	VG	FN	VF	VF/NM	NM-
0-Limited Super Premium Edition; signed w/certificate; gold foil logo, 0-Limited Premium Edition	1	3	4	6	8	10

EX MACHINA
DC Comics: Aug, 2004 - Present ($2.95/$2.99)

	GD	VG	FN	VF	VF/NM	NM-
1-Intro. Mitchell Hundred; Vaughan-s/Harris-a/c						4.00
2-47: 12-Intro. Automaton. 33-Mitchell meets the Pope						3.00
...: The Deluxe Edition Book One HC (2008, $29.99, dustjacket) r/#1-11; Vaughan's original proposal, Harris sketch pages; Brad Meltzer intro.						30.00
...: The Deluxe Edition Book Two HC (2009, $29.99, dustjacket) r/#12-20; Special #1,2; script and pencil art for #20; Wachowski Bros. intro.						30.00
...: Inside the Machine (4/07, $2.99) script pages and Harris art and cover process						3.00
...: Masquerade Special (#3) (10/07, $3.50) John Paul Leon-a; Harris-c						3.50
... Special 1,2 (6/06 - No. 2, 8/06, $2.99) Sprouse-a; flashback to the Great Machine						3.00
... Special 4 (5/09, $3.99) Leon-a; Great Machine flashback; covers by Harris & Leon						4.00
...: Dirty Tricks TPB (2009, $12.99) r/#35-39 and Masquerade Special #3						13.00
...: Ex Cathedra TPB (2008, $12.99) r/#30-34						13.00
...: March To War TPB (2006, $12.99) r/#17-20 and Special #1,2						13.00
...: Power Down TPB (2008, $12.99) r/#26-29 & ...: Inside the Machine						13.00
...: Smoke Smoke TPB (2007, $12.99) r/#21-25						13.00
...: The First Hundred Days TPB ('05, $9.95) r/#1-5; photo reference and sketch pages						10.00
...: Tag TPB (2005, $12.99) r/#6-10; Harris sketch pages						13.00

EX-MUTANTS
Malibu Comics: Nov, 1992 - No. 18, Apr, 1994 ($1.95/$2.25/$2.50)

	GD	VG	FN	VF	VF/NM	NM-
1-18: 1-Polybagged w/Skycap; prismatic cover						2.50

EXORCISTS (See The Crusaders)

EXOSQUAD (TV)
Topps Comics: No. 0, Jan, 1994 ($1.25)

	GD	VG	FN	VF	VF/NM	NM-
0-($1.00, 20 pgs.)-1st app.; Staton-a(p); wraparound-c						2.25

EXOTIC ROMANCES (Formerly True War Romances)
Quality Comics Group (Comic Magazines): No. 22, Oct, 1955-No. 31, Nov, 1956

	GD	VG	FN	VF	VF/NM	NM-
22	13	26	39	72	101	130
23-26,29	8	16	24	44	57	70
27,31-Baker-c/a	15	30	45	86	133	180
28,30-Baker-a	13	26	39	74	105	135

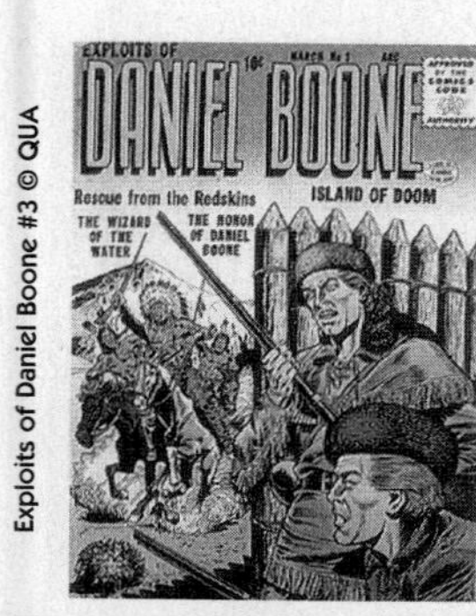

Exploits of Daniel Boone #3 © QUA

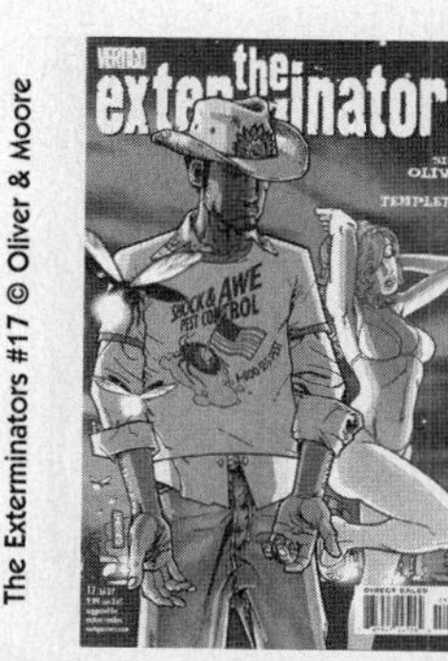

The Exterminators #17 © Oliver & Moore

Fables #64 © Bill Willingham & DC

	GD	VG	FN	VF	VF/NM	NM-
	2.0	4.0	6.0	8.0	9.0	9.2

EXPLOITS OF DANIEL BOONE
Quality Comics Group: Nov, 1955 - No. 6, Oct, 1956

1-All have Cuidera-c(i)	20	40	60	115	183	250
2	14	28	42	82	121	160
3-6	13	26	39	74	105	135

EXPLOITS OF DICK TRACY (See Dick Tracy)

EXPLORER JOE
Ziff-Davis Comic Group (Approved Comics): Win, 1951 - No. 2, Oct-Nov, 1952

1-2: Saunders painted covers; 2-Krigstein-a	14	28	42	76	108	140

EXPLORERS OF THE UNKNOWN (See Archie Giant Series #587, 599)
Archie Comics: June, 1990 - No. 6, Apr, 1991 ($1.00)

1-6: Featuring Archie and the gang 3.00

EXPOSED (...True Crime Cases; ...Cases in the Crusade Against Crime #5-9)
D. S. Publishing Co.: Mar-Apr, 1948 - No. 9, July-Aug, 1949

1	24	48	72	142	234	325
2-Giggling killer story with excessive blood; two injury-to-eye panels; electrocution panel	30	60	90	177	289	400
3,8,9	14	28	42	81	118	155
4-Orlando-a	15	30	45	83	124	165
5-Breeze Lawson, Sky Sheriff by E. Good	15	30	45	83	124	165
6,7: 6-Ingels-a; used in **SOTI**, illo. "How to prepare an alibi" 7-Illo. in **SOTI**, "Diagram for housebreakers;" used by N.Y. Legis. Committee	34	68	102	199	325	450

EXTERMINATORS, THE
DC Comics (Vertigo): Mar, 2006 - No. 30, Aug, 2008 ($2.99)

1-30: Simon Oliver-s/Tony Moore-a in most. 11,12-Hawthorne-a 3.00
...: Bug Brothers TPB (2006, $9.99) r/#1-5; intro. by screenwriter Josh Olson 10.00
...: Bug Brothers Forever TPB (2008, $14.99) r/#24-30; intro. by Simon Oliver 15.00
...: Crossfire and Collateral TPB (2008, $14.99) r/#17-23 15.00
...: Insurgency TPB (2007, $12.99) r/#6-10 13.00
...: Lies of Our Fathers TPB (2007, $14.99) r/#11-16 15.00

EXTINCT!
New England Comics Press: Wint, 1991-92 - No. 2, Fall, 1992 ($3.50, B&W)

1,2-Reprints and background info of "perfectly awful" Golden Age stories 3.50

EXTINCTION EVENT
DC Comics (WildStorm): Sept, 2003 - No. 5, Jan, 2004 ($2.50, limited series)

1-5-Booth-a/Weinberg-s 2.50

EXTRA!
E. C. Comics: Mar-Apr, 1955 - No. 5, Nov-Dec, 1955

1-Not code approved	20	40	60	160	255	350
2-5	13	26	39	104	165	225

NOTE: ***Craig, Crandall, Severin** art in all.*

EXTRA!
Gemstone Publishing: Jan, 2000 - No. 5, May, 2000 ($2.50)

1-5-Reprints E.C. series 2.50

EXTRA COMICS
Magazine Enterprises: 1948 (25¢, 3 comics in one)

1-Giant; consisting of rebound ME comics. Two versions known; (1)-Funnyman by Siegel & Shuster, Space Ace, Undercover Girl, Red Fox by L.B. Cole, Trail Colt & (2)-All Funnyman	54	108	162	343	584	825

EXTREME
Image Comics (Extreme Studios): Aug, 1993 (Giveaway)

0 3.00

EXTREME DESTROYER
Image Comics (Extreme Studios): Jan, 1996 ($2.50)

Prologue 1-Polybagged w/card; Liefeld-c, Epilogue 1-Liefeld-c 2.50

EXTREME JUSTICE
DC Comics: No. 0, Jan, 1995 - No. 18, July, 1996 ($1.50/$1.75)

0-18 3.00

EXTREMELY YOUNGBLOOD
Image Comics (Extreme Studios): Sept, 1996 ($3.50, one-shot)

1 3.50

EXTREME SACRIFICE
Image Comics (Extreme Studios): Jan, 1995 ($2.50, limited series)

Prelude (#1)-Liefeld wraparound-c; polybagged w/ trading card 2.50
Epilogue (#2)-Liefeld wraparound-c; polybagged w/trading card 2.50
Trade paperback (6/95, $16.95)-Platt-a 17.00

EXTREME SUPER CHRISTMAS SPECIAL
Image Comics (Extreme Studios): Dec, 1994 ($2.95, one-shot)

1 3.00

EXTREMIST, THE
DC Comics (Vertigo): Sept, 1993 - No. 4, Dec, 1993 ($1.95, limited series)

1-4-Peter Milligan scripts; McKeever-c/a 2.50
1-Platinum Edition 5.00

EYE OF THE STORM
Rival Productions: Dec, 1994 - No. 7, June, 1995? ($2.95)

1-7: Computer generated comic 3.00

EYE OF THE STORM
DC Comics (WildStorm): Sept, 2003 ($4.95)

Annual 1-Short stories by various incl. Portacio, Johns, Coker, Pearson, Arcudi 5.00

FABLES
DC Comics (Vertigo): July, 2002 - Present ($2.50/$2.75/$2.99)

1-Willingham-s/Medina-a; two covers by Maleev & Jean 8.00
#1: Special Edition (12/06, 25¢) r/#1 with preview of 1001 Nights of Snowfall 2.50
#1: Special Edition (9/09, $1.00) r/#1 with preview of Peter & Max 2.50
2-Medina-a 5.00
3-5 4.00
6-37: 6-10-Buckingham-a. 11-Talbot-a. 18-Medley-a. 26-Preview of The Witching 3.00
6-RRP Edition wraparound variant-c; promotional giveaway for retailers (200 printed) 50.00
38-49,51-74,76-92: 38-Begin $2.75-c. 49-Begin $2.99-c. 57,58,76-Allred-a. 83-85-Crossover with Jack of Fables and The Literals 3.00
50-($3.99) Wedding of Snow White and Bigby Wolf; preview of Jack of Fables series 4.00
75-($4.99) Geppetto surrenders; pin-up gallery by Powell, Nowlan, Cooke & others 5.00
Animal Farm (2003, $12.95, TPB) r/#6-10; sketch pages by Buckingham & Jean 13.00
...: Arabian Nights (And Days) (2006, $14.99, TPB) r/#42-47 15.00
...: Homelands (2005, $14.99, TPB) r/#34-41 15.00
Legends in Exile (2002, $9.95, TPB) r/#1-5; new short story Willingham-s/a 10.00
...: March of the Wooden Soldiers (2004, $17.95, TPB) r/#19-21 & ...: The Last Castle 18.00
...: 1001 Nights of Snowfall HC (2006, $19.99) short stories by Willingham with art by various incl. Bolton, Kaluta, Jean, McPherson, Thompson, Vess, Wheatley, Buckingham 20.00
...: 1001 Nights of Snowfall (2008, $14.99, TPB) short stories with art by various 15.00
...: Sons of Empire (2007, $17.99, TPB) r/#52-59 18.00
...: Storybook Love (2004, $14.95, TPB) r/#11-18 15.00
...: The Dark Ages (2009, $17.99, TPB) r/#76-82 18.00
...: The Deluxe Edition Book One HC (2009, $29.99, DJ) r/#1-10; character sketch-a 30.00
...: The Good Prince (2008, $17.99, TPB) r/#60-69 18.00
...: The Great Fables Crossover (2010, $17.99, TPB) r/#83-85, Jack of Fables #33-35 and The Literals #1-3; sneak preview of Peter & Max: A Fables Novel 18.00
...: The Last Castle (2003, $5.95) Hamilton-a/Willingham-s; prequel to title 6.00
...: The Mean Seasons (2005, $14.99, TPB) r/#22,28-33 15.00
...: War and Pieces (2008, $17.99, TPB) r/#70-75; sketch and pin-up pages 18.00
...: Wolves (2006, $17.99, TPB) r/#48-51; script to #50 18.00

FACE, THE (Tony Trent, the Face No. 3 on) (See Big Shot Comics)
Columbia Comics Group: 1941 - No. 2, 1943

1-The Face; Mart Bailey-c	87	174	261	553	952	1350
2-Bailey-c	50	100	150	315	533	750

FACES OF EVIL
DC Comics: Mar, 2009 ($2.99, series of one-shots)

...: Deathstroke 1 - Jeanty-a/Ladronn-c; Ravager app. 3.00
...: Kobra 1 - Jason Burr returns; Julian Lopez-a 3.00
...: Prometheus 1 - Gates-s/Dallacchio-a; origin re-told; Anima killed 3.00
...: Solomon Grundy 1 - Johns-s/Kolins-a; leads into Solomon Grundy mini-series 3.00

FACTOR X
Marvel Comics: Mar, 1995 - No. 4, July, 1995 ($1.95, limited series)

1-Age of Apocalypse 3.00
2-4 2.50

FACULTY FUNNIES
Archie Comics: June, 1989 - No. 5, May, 1990 (75¢/95¢ #2 on)

1-5: 1,2-The Awesome Four app. 3.00

FADE FROM GRACE
Beckett Comics: Aug, 2004 - No. 5, Mar, 2005 (99¢/$1.99)

1-(99¢) Jeff Amano-a/c; Gabriel Benson-s; origin of Fade 2.50
2-5-($1.99) 2.50

Faith #1 © Union City Inc.

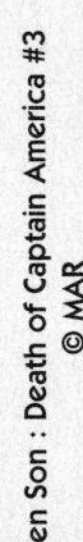

Fallen Son : Death of Captain America #3 © MAR

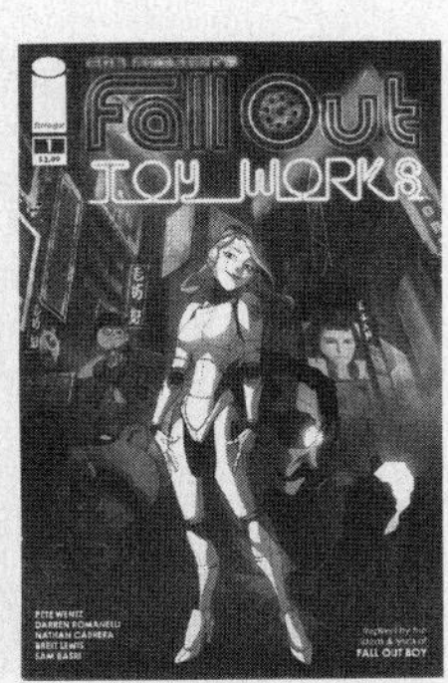

Fall Out Toy Works #1 © FOTW

	GD 2.0	VG 4.0	FN 6.0	VF 8.0	VF/NM 9.0	NM- 9.2

TPB (2005, $14.99) r/#1-5; cover gallery, afterword by David Mack 15.00

FAFHRD AND THE GREY MOUSER (Also see Sword of Sorcery & Wonder Woman #202)
Marvel Comics: Oct, 1990 - No. 4, 1991 ($4.50, 52 pgs., squarebound)

1-4: Mignola/Williamson-a; Chaykin scripts 4.50

FAGIN THE JAW
Doubleday: Oct, 2003 ($15.95, softcover graphic novel)

nn-Will Eisner-s/a; story of Fagin from Dickens' Oliver Twist 16.00

FAIRY TALE PARADE (See Famous Fairy Tales)
Dell Publishing Co.: June-July, 1942 - No. 121, Oct, 1946 (Most by Walt Kelly)

	GD	VG	FN	VF	VF/NM	NM-
1-Kelly-a begins	96	192	288	816	1608	2400
2(8-9/42)	43	86	129	344	672	1000
3-5 (10-11/42 - 2-4/43)	31	62	93	239	462	685
6-9 (5-7/43 - 11-1/43-44)	25	50	75	183	354	525
Four Color 50('44),69('45), 87('45)	24	48	72	175	338	500
Four Color 104,114('46)-Last Kelly issue	19	38	57	133	259	385
Four Color 121('46)-Not by Kelly	12	24	36	85	155	225

NOTE: *#1-9, 4-Color #50, 69 have* ***Kelly*** *c/a; 4-Color #87, 104, 114-****Kelly*** *art only. #9 has a redrawn version of The Reluctant Dragon. This series contains all the classic fairy tales from Jack In The Beanstalk to Cinderella.*

FAIRY TALES
Ziff-Davis Publ. Co. (Approved Comics): No. 10, Apr-May, 1951 - No. 11, June-July, 1951

	GD	VG	FN	VF	VF/NM	NM-
10,11-Painted-c	20	40	60	114	182	250

FAITH
DC Comics (Vertigo): Nov, 1999 - No. 5, Mar, 2000 ($2.50, limited series)

1-5-Ted McKeever-s/c/a 2.50

FAITHFUL
Marvel Comics/Lovers' Magazine: Nov, 1949 - No. 2, Feb, 1950 (52 pgs.)

	GD	VG	FN	VF	VF/NM	NM-
1,2-Photo-c	11	22	33	64	90	115

FAKER
DC Comics (Vertigo): Sept, 2007 - No. 6, Feb, 2008 ($2.99, limited series)

1-6-Mike Carey-s/Jock-a/c 3.00
TPB (2008, $14.99) r/#1-6; Jock sketch pages 15.00

FALCON (See Marvel Premiere #49, Avengers #181 & Captain America #117 & 133)
Marvel Comics Group: Nov, 1983 - No. 4, Feb, 1984 (Mini-series)

1-4: 1-Paul Smith-c/a(p). 2-Paul Smith-c/Mark Bright-a. 3-Kupperberg-c 3.00

FALLEN ANGEL
DC Comics: Sept, 2003 - No. 20, July, 2005 ($2.50/$2.95)

1-9-Peter David-s/David Lopez-a/Stelfreeze-c; intro. Lee 2.50
10-20: 10-Begin $2.95-c. 13,17-Kaluta-c. 20-Last issue; Pérez-c 3.00
TPB (2004, $12.95) r/#1-6; intro. by Harlan Ellison 13.00
Down to Earth TPB (2007, $14.99) r/#7-12 15.00

FALLEN ANGEL
IDW Publ.: Dec, 2005 - No. 33, Dec, 2008 ($3.99)

1-33: 1-14-Peter David-s/J.K Woodward-a. Retailer variant-c for each. 15-Donaldson-a. 17-Flip cover with Shi story; Tucci-a. 25-Wraparound-c; character gallery 4.00
... Reborn 1-4 (7/09 - No. 4, 10/09, $3.99) David-s/Woodward-a; Illyria (from Angel) app. 4.00
...: To Serve in Heaven TPB (8/06, $19.99) r/#1-5; gallery of reg & variant covers 20.00

FALLEN ANGEL ON THE WORLD OF MAGIC: THE GATHERING
Acclaim (Armada): May, 1996 ($5.95, one-shot)

1-Nancy Collins story 6.00

FALLEN ANGELS
Marvel Comics Group: April, 1987 - No. 8, Nov, 1987 (Limited series)

1-8 2.50

FALLEN SON: THE DEATH OF CAPTAIN AMERICA
Marvel Comics: June, 2007 - No. 5, Aug, 2007 ($2.99, limited series)

1-5: Loeb-s in all. 1-Wolverine; Yu-a/c. 2-Avengers; McGuinness-a/c. 3-Captain America; Romita Jr.-a/c; Hawkeye app. 4-Spider-Man; Finch-c/a. 5-Cassaday-c/a 3.00
1-5-Variant covers by Turner 3.00
HC (2007, $19.99, dustjacket) r/#1-5 20.00
TPB (2008, $13.99) r/#1-5 14.00

FALLING IN LOVE
Arleigh Pub. Co./National Per. Pub.: Sept-Oct, 1955 - No. 143, Oct-Nov, 1973

	GD	VG	FN	VF	VF/NM	NM-
1	39	78	117	240	395	550
2	20	40	60	120	195	270
3-10	14	28	42	80	115	150
11-20	12	24	36	67	94	120
21-40	10	20	30	54	72	90
41-47: 47-Last 10¢ issue	9	18	27	47	61	75
48-70	4	8	12	26	41	55
71-99,108: 108-Wood-a (4 pgs., 7/69)	3	6	9	18	27	35
100	4	8	12	23	36	48
101-107,109-124	3	6	9	14	19	24
134-143	2	4	6	11	16	20
125-133: 52 pgs.	3	6	9	20	30	40

NOTE: *Colan c/a-75, 81. 52 pgs.-#125-133.*

FALLING MAN, THE
Image Comics: Feb, 1998 ($2.95)

1-McCorkindale-s/Hester-a 3.00

FALL OF THE HOUSE OF USHER, THE (See A Corben Special & Spirit section 8/22/48)

FALL OF THE HULKS (Also see Hulk and Incredible Hulk)
Marvel Comics: Feb, 2010 - May, 2010 ($3.99, one-shots)

Alpha (2/10) Pelletier-a; The Leader, Dr. Doom, MODOK and The Thinker app. 4.00
Gamma (2/10) Romita Jr. -a; funeral for General Ross 4.00
Red Hulk 1,2: 1-(3/10) A-Bomb app. 4.00
Savage She-Hulks 1 (5/10) Two covers; Espin-a; Thundra and Lyra battle 4.00

FALL OF THE ROMAN EMPIRE (See Movie Comics)

FALL OUT TOY WORKS
Image Comics: Sept, 2009 - Present ($3.99)

1-3-Co-created by Pete Wentz of the band Fall Out Boy; Basri-a 4.00

FAMILY AFFAIR (TV)
Gold Key: Feb, 1970 - No. 4, Oct, 1970 (25¢)

	GD	VG	FN	VF	VF/NM	NM-
1-With pull-out poster; photo-c	6	12	18	39	62	85
1-With poster missing	3	6	9	18	27	35
2-4-Photo-c	3	6	9	21	32	42

FAMILY DYNAMIC, THE
DC Comics: Oct, 2008 - No. 3, Dec, 2008 ($2.25)

1-3-J. Torres-s/Tim Levins-a 2.25

FAMILY FUNNIES
Parents' Magazine Institute: No. 9, Aug-Sept, 1946

	GD	VG	FN	VF	VF/NM	NM-
9	5	10	15	24	30	35

FAMILY FUNNIES (Tiny Tot Funnies No. 9)
Harvey Publications: Sept, 1950 - No. 8, Apr, 1951

	GD	VG	FN	VF	VF/NM	NM-
1-Mandrake (has over 30 King Feature strips)	10	20	30	58	79	100
2-Flash Gordon, 1 pg.	8	16	24	40	50	60
3-8: 4,5,7-Flash Gordon, 1 pg.	6	12	18	31	38	45

FAMILY GUY (TV)
Devil's Due Publ.: 2006 ($6.95)

nn-101 Ways to Kill Lois; 2-Peter Griffin's Guide to Parenting; 3-Books Don't Taste Very Good 7.00
... A Big Book o' Crap TPB (10/06, $16.95) r/nn,2,3 17.00

FAMILY MATTER
Kitchen Sink Press: 1998 ($24.95/$15.95, graphic novel)

Hardcover ($24.95) Will Eisner-s/a 25.00
Softcover ($15.95) 16.00

FAMOUS AUTHORS ILLUSTRATED (See Stories by...)

FAMOUS CRIMES
Fox Features Syndicate/M.S. Dist. No. 51,52: June, 1948 - No. 19, Sept, 1950; No. 20, Aug, 1951; No. 51, 52, 1953

	GD	VG	FN	VF	VF/NM	NM-
1-Blue Beetle app. & crime story-r/Phantom Lady #16	50	100	150	315	533	750
2-Has woman dissolved in acid; lingerie-c/panels	40	80	120	246	411	575
3-Injury-to-eye story used in **SOTI**, pg. 112; has two electrocution stories	48	96	144	302	514	725
4-6	23	46	69	136	223	310
7- "Tarzan, the Wyoming Killer" (**SOTI**, pg. 44)	39	78	117	240	395	550
8-20: 17-Morisi-a. 20-Same cover as #15	18	36	54	107	169	230
51 (nd, 1953)	15	30	45	90	140	190
52 (Exist?)	15	30	45	90	140	190

FAMOUS FEATURE STORIES
Dell Publishing Co.: 1938 (7-1/2x11", 68 pgs.)

1-Tarzan, Terry & the Pirates, King of the Royal Mtd., Buck Jones, Dick Tracy, Smilin' Jack, Dan Dunn, Don Winslow, G-Man, Tailspin Tommy, Mutt & Jeff, Little Orphan Annie

Famous First Edition F-5 © DC

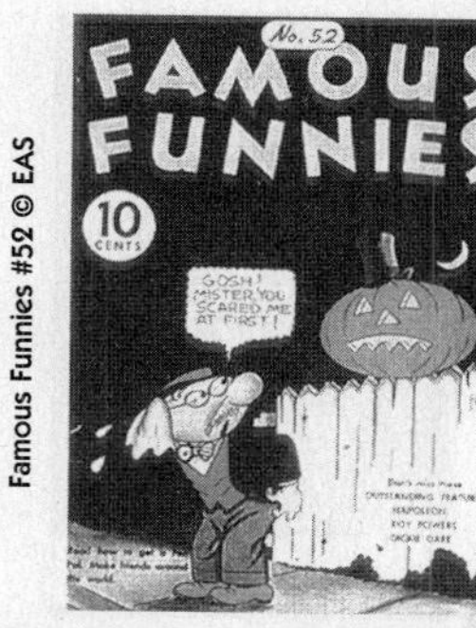

Famous Funnies #52 © EAS

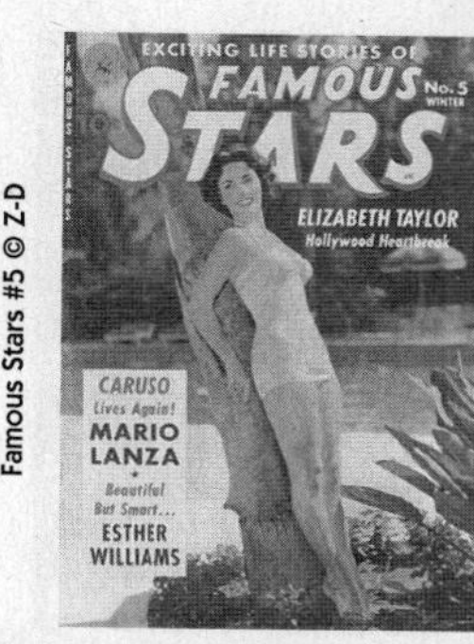

Famous Stars #5 © Z-D

	GD 2.0	VG 4.0	FN 6.0	VF 8.0	VF/NM 9.0	NM- 9.2

reprints - all illustrated text 75 140 210 455 710 965

FAMOUS FIRST EDITION (See Limited Collectors' Edition)
National Periodical Publications/DC Comics: ($1.00, 10x13-1/2", 72 pgs.) (No.6-8, 68 pgs.) 1974 - No. 8, Aug-Sept, 1975; C-61, 1979
(Hardbound editions with dust jackets are from Lyle Stuart, Inc.)

C-26-Action Comics #1; gold ink outer-c 6 12 18 41 66 90
C-26-Hardbound edition w/dust jacket 17 34 51 122 236 350
C-28-Detective #27; silver ink outer-c 6 12 18 41 66 90
C-28-Hardbound edition w/dust jacket 17 34 51 122 236 350
C-30-Sensation #1(1974); bronze ink outer-c 5 10 15 30 48 65
C-30-Hardbound edition w/dust jacket 15 30 45 104 197 290
F-4-Whiz Comics #2(#1)(10-11/74)-Cover not identical to original (dropped "Gangway for Captain Marvel" from cover); gold ink on outer-c 5 10 15 30 48 65
F-4-Hardbound edition w/dust jacket 15 30 45 104 197 290
F-5-Batman #1(F-6 inside); silver ink on outer-c 5 10 15 34 55 75
F-5-Hardbound edition w/dust jacket 15 30 45 104 197 290
V2#F-6-Wonder Woman #1 5 10 15 30 48 65
F-6-Wonder Woman #1 Hardbound w/dust jacket 15 30 45 104 197 290
F-7-All-Star Comics #3 5 10 15 30 48 65
F-8-Flash Comics #1(8-9/75) 5 10 15 30 48 65
V8#C-61-Superman #1(1979, $2.00) 4 8 12 26 41 55
V8#C-61 (Whitman variant) 4 8 12 28 44 60
V8#C-61 (SC in slipcase, edition of 250 copies) Each signed by Jerry Siegel and Joe Shuster 550.00

Warning: The above books are almost **exact** reprints of the originals that they represent except for the Giant-Size format. None of the originals are Giant-Size. The first five issues and C-61 were printed with two covers. Reprint information can be found on the outside cover, but not on the inside cover which was reprinted exactly like the original (inside and out).

FAMOUS FUNNIES
Eastern Color: 1934; July, 1934 - No. 218, July, 1955

A Carnival of Comics (See Promotional Comics section)

Series 1-(Very rare)(nd-early 1934)(68 pgs.) No publisher given (Eastern Color PrintingCo.); sold in chain stores for 10¢. 35,000 print run. Contains Sunday strip reprints of Mutt & Jeff, Reg'lar Fellers, Nipper, Hairbreadth Harry, Strange As It Seems, Joe Palooka, Dixie Dugan, The Nebbs, Keeping Up With the Jones, and others. Inside front and back covers and pages 1-16 of Famous Funnies Series 1, #s 49-64 reprinted from **Famous Funnies, A Carnival of Comics**, and most of pages 17-48 reprinted from **Funnies on Parade**. 4100 8200 12,300 30,000 - -

No. 1 (Rare)(7/34-on stands 5/34) - Eastern Color Printing Co. First monthly newsstand comic book. Contains Sunday strip reprints of Toonerville Folks, Mutt & Jeff, Hairbreadth Harry, S'Matter Pop, Nipper, Dixie Dugan, The Bungle Family, Connie, Ben Webster, Tailspin Tommy, The Nebbs, Joe Palooka, & others. 3050 6100 9150 22,500 - -
2 (Rare, 9/34) 640 1280 1920 4800 - -
3-Buck Rogers Sunday strip-r by Rick Yager begins, ends #218; not in #191-208; 1st comic book app. of Buck Rogers; the number of the 1st strip reprinted is pg. 190, Series No. 1 827 1654 2481 6200 - -
4 267 534 801 2000 - -
5-1st Christmas-c on a newsstand comic 267 534 801 2000 - -
6-10 177 354 531 1325 - -
11,12,18-Four pgs. of Buck Rogers in each issue, completes stories in Buck Rogers #1 which lacks these pages. 18-Two pgs. of Buck Rogers reprinted in Daisy Comics #1 102 204 306 612 969 1325
13-17,19,20: 14-Has two Buck Rogers panels missing. 17-2nd Christmas-c on a newsstand comic (12/35) 79 158 237 474 750 1025
21,23-30: 27-(10/36)-War on Crime begins (4 pgs.); 1st true crime in comics (reprints); part photo-c. 29-X-Mas-c (12/36) 60 120 180 360 580 800
22-Four pgs. of Buck Rogers needed to complete stories in Buck Rogers #1 63 126 189 378 602 825
31,33,34,36,37,39,40: 33-Careers of Baby Face Nelson & John Dillinger traced 42 84 126 252 406 560
32-(3/37) 1st app. the Phantom Magician (costume hero) in Advs. of Patsy 46 92 138 276 443 610
35-Two pgs. Buck Rogers omitted in Buck Rogers #2 46 92 138 276 443 610
38-Full color portrait of Buck Rogers 44 88 132 264 425 585
41-60: 41,53-X-Mas-c. 55-Last bottom panel, pg. 4 in Buck Rogers redrawn in Buck Rogers #3 31 62 93 182 296 410
61,63,64,66,67,69,70 23 46 69 136 223 310
62,65,68,73-78-Two pgs. Kirby-a "Lightnin' & the Lone Rider". 65,77-X-Mas-c 25 50 75 147 241 335
71,79,80: 80-(3/41)-Buck Rogers story continues from Buck Rogers #5 19 38 57 109 172 235
72-Speed Spaulding begins by Marvin Bradley (artist), ends #88. This series was written by Edwin Balmer & Philip Wylie (later appeared as film & book "When Worlds Collide") 20 40 60 120 195 270
81-Origin & 1st app. Invisible Scarlet O'Neil (4/41); strip begins #82, ends #167; 1st non-funny-c (Scarlet O'Neil) 21 42 63 126 206 285
82-Buck Rogers-c 22 44 66 132 216 300
83-87,90: 86-Connie vs. Monsters on the Moon-c (sci/fi). 87 has last Buck Rogers full page-r. 90-Bondage-c 17 34 51 98 154 210
88,89: 88-Buck Rogers in "Moon's End" by Calkins, 2 pgs.(not reprints). Beginning with #88, all Buck Rogers pgs. have rearranged panels. 89-Origin & 1st app. Fearless Flint, the Flint Man 18 36 54 103 162 220
91-93,95,96,98-99,101,103-110: 105-Series 2 begins (Strip Page #1) 15 30 45 84 127 170
94-Buck Rogers in "Solar Holocaust" by Calkins, 3 pgs.(not reprints) 15 30 45 90 140 190
97-War Bond promotion, Buck Rogers by Calkins, 2 pgs.(not reprints) 15 30 45 90 140 190
100-1st comic to reach #100; 100th Anniversary cover features 11 major Famous Funnies characters, including Buck Rogers 19 38 57 111 176 240
102-Chief Wahoo vs. Hitler,Tojo & Mussolini-c (1/43) 61 122 183 390 670 950
111-130 (5/45): 113-X-Mas-c 12 24 36 67 94 120
131-150 (1/47): 137-Strip page No. 110 omitted. 144-(7/46) 12th Anniversary cover 11 22 33 60 83 105
151-162,164-168 10 20 30 56 76 95
163-St. Valentine's Day-c 10 20 30 58 79 100
169,170-Two text illos. by Williamson, his 1st comic book work 13 26 39 72 101 130
171-190: 171-Strip pgs. 227,229,230, Series 2 omitted. 172-Strip Pg. 232 omitted. 190-Buck Rogers ends with start of strip pg. 302, Series 2; Oaky Doaks-c/story 9 18 27 52 69 85
191-197,199,201,203,206-208: No Buck Rogers. 191-Barney Carr, Space detective begins, ends #192. 9 18 27 50 65 80
198,200,202,205-One pg. Frazetta ads; no B. Rogers 9 18 27 52 69 85
204-Used in **POP**, pg. 79,99; war-c begin, end #208 10 20 30 54 72 90
209-216: Frazetta-c. 209-Buck Rogers begins (12/53) with strip pg. 480, Series 2; 211-Buck Rogers ads by Anderson begins, ends #217. #215-Contains B. Rogers strip pg. 515-518, series 2 followed by pgs.179-181, Series 3 118 236 354 749 1287 1825
217,218-B. Rogers ends with pg. 199, Series 3. 218-Wee Three-c/story 10 20 30 54 72 90

*NOTE: **Rick Yager** did the Buck Rogers Sunday strips reprinted in Famous Funnies. The Sundays were formerly done by Russ Keaton and Lt. Dick Calkins did the dailies, but would sometimes assist Yager on a panel or two from time to time. Strip No. 169 is Yager's first full Buck Rogers page. Yager did the strip until 1958 when **Murphy Anderson** took over. **Tuska** art from 4/26/59 - 1965. Virtually every panel was rewritten for Famous Funnies. Not identical to the original Sunday page. The Buck Rogers reprints run continuously through Famous Funnies issue No. 190 (Strip No. 302) with no break in story line. The story line has no continuity after No. 190. The Buck Rogers newspaper strips came out in four series: Series 1, 3/30/30 - 9/21/41 (No. 1 - 600); Series 2, 9/28/41 -10/21/51 (No. 1 -525)(Strip No. 110-1/2 (1/2 pg.) published in only a few newspapers); Series 3, 10/28/51 -2/9/58 (No. 100-428)(No No.1-99); Series 4, 2/16/58 - 6/13/65 (No numbers, dates only). **Everett** c-85, 86. **Moulton** a-100. Chief Wahoo c-93, 97, 102, 116, 136, 139, 151. Dickie Dare c-83, 88. Fearless Flint c-89. Invisible Scarlet O'Neil c-81, 87, 95, 121(part), 132. Scorchy Smith c-84, 90.*

FAMOUS FUNNIES
Super Comics: 1964

Super Reprint Nos. 15-18:17-r/Double Trouble #1. 18-Space Comics #? 2 4 6 9 12 15

FAMOUS GANGSTERS (Crime on the Waterfront No. 4)
Avon Periodicals/Realistic No. 3: Apr, 1951 - No. 3, Feb, 1952

1-3: 1-Capone, Dillinger; c-/Avon paperback #329. 2-Dillinger Machine Gun Killer; Wood-c/a (1 pg.); r/Saint #7 & retitled "Mike Strong". 3-Lucky Luciano & Murder, Inc; c-/Avon paperback #66 37 74 111 218 354 490

FAMOUS INDIAN TRIBES
Dell Publishing Co.: July-Sept, 1962; No. 2, July, 1972

12-264-209(#1) (The Sioux) 3 6 9 15 21 26
2(7/72)-Reprints above 1 3 4 6 8 10

FAMOUS STARS
Ziff-Davis Publ. Co.: Nov-Dec, 1950 - No. 6, Spring, 1952 (All have photo-c)

1-Shelley Winters, Susan Peters, Ava Gardner, Shirley Temple; Jimmy Stewart & Shelley Winters photo-c; Whitney-a 37 74 111 218 354 490
2-Betty Hutton, Bing Crosby, Colleen Townsend, Gloria Swanson; Betty Hutton photo-c; Everett-a(2) 23 46 69 136 223 310
3-Farley Granger, Judy Garland's ordeal (life story; she died 6/22/69 at the age of 47), Alan Ladd; Farley Granger photo-c; Whitney-a 29 58 87 172 281 390
4-Al Jolson, Bob Mitchum, Ella Raines, Richard Conte, Vic Damone; Jane Russell and Bob Mitchum photo-c; Crandall-a, 6pgs. 20 40 60 120 195 270
5-Liz Taylor, Betty Grable, Esther Williams, George Brent, Mario Lanza; Liz Taylor photo-c; Krigstein-a 43 86 129 271 461 650
6-Gene Kelly, Hedy Lamarr, June Allyson, William Boyd, Janet Leigh, Gary Cooper; Gene

Fanboy #2 © DC

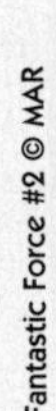

Fantastic Force #2 © MAR

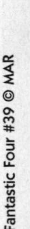

Fantastic Four #39 © MAR

	GD 2.0	VG 4.0	FN 6.0	VF 8.0	VF/NM 9.0	NM- 9.2

GD VG FN VF VF/NM NM- 2.0 4.0 6.0 8.0 9.0 9.2

Kelly photo-c 19 38 57 111 176 240

FAMOUS STORIES (...Book No. 2)
Dell Publishing Co.: 1942 - No. 2, 1942

1,2: 1-Treasure Island. 2-Tom Sawyer 30 60 90 177 289 400

FAMOUS TV FUNDAY FUNNIES
Harvey Publications: Sept, 1961 (25¢ Giant)

1-Casper the Ghost, Baby Huey, Little Audrey 6 12 18 39 62 85

FAMOUS WESTERN BADMEN (Formerly Redskin)
Youthful Magazines: No. 13, Dec, 1952 - No. 15, Apr, 1953

13-Redskin story 14 28 42 80 115 150
14,15: 15-The Dalton Boys story 10 20 30 58 79 100

FAN BOY
DC Comics: Mar, 1999 - No. 6, Aug, 1999 ($2.50, limited series)

1-6: 1-Art by Aragonés and various in all. 2-Green Lantern-c/a by Gil Kane. 3-JLA. 4-Sgt. Rock art by Heath, Marie Severin. 5-Batman art by Sprang, Adams, Miller, Timm. 6-Wonder Woman; art by Rude, Grell 2.50
TPB (2001, $12.95) r/#1-6 13.00

FANTASTIC (Formerly Captain Science; Beware No. 10 on)
Youthful Magazines: No. 8, Feb, 1952 - No. 9, Apr, 1952

8-Capt. Science by Harrison 42 84 126 265 445 625
9-Harrison-a; decapitation, shrunken head panels 34 68 102 204 332 460

FANTASTIC ADVENTURES
Super Comics: 1963 - 1964 (Reprints)

9,10,12,15,16,18: 9-r/? 10-r/He-Man #2(Toby). 11-Disbrow-a. 12-Unpublished Chesler material? 15-r/Spook #23. 16-r/Dark Shadows #2(Steinway); Briefer-a.18-r/Superior Stories #1 3 6 9 18 27 35
11-Wood-a; r/Blue Bolt #118 4 8 12 24 37 50
17-Baker-a(2) r/Seven Seas #6 4 8 12 24 37 50

FANTASTIC COMICS
Fox Features Syndicate: Dec, 1939 - No. 23, Nov, 1941

1-Intro/origin Samson; Stardust, The Super Wizard, Sub Saunders (by Kiefer), Space Smith, Capt. Kidd begin 486 972 1458 3550 6275 9000
2-Powell text illos 258 516 774 1651 2826 4000
3-Classic Lou Fine Robot-c; Powell text illos 1400 2800 4200 7000 10,500 14,000
4,5: Last Lou Fine-c 213 426 639 1363 2332 3300
6,7-Simon-c 145 290 435 919 1585 2250
8-10: 10-Intro/origin David, Samson's aide 97 194 291 621 1061 1500
11-17,19,20: 16-Stardust ends 79 178 237 502 864 1225
18,23: 18-1st app. Black Fury & sidekick Chuck; ends #23. 23-Origin The Gladiator 81 162 243 518 884 1250
21-The Banshee begins(origin); ends #23; Hitler-c 90 180 270 576 988 1400
22-Hitler-c (likeness of Hitler as furnace on cover) 100 200 300 635 1093 1550

*NOTE: **Lou Fine** c-1-5. **Tuska** a-3-5, 8. Bondage c-6, 8, 9. Issue #11 has indicia to Mystery Men Comics #15. All issues feature Samson covers.*

FANTASTIC COMICS (Imagining of a 1941 issue by modern creators in Golden Age style)
Image Comics: No. 24, Jan, 2008 ($5.99, Golden Age sized, one-shot)

24-Samson, Yank Wilson, Stardust, Sub Saunders, Space Smith, Capt. Kidd app.; Larsen-c/a; art by Allred, Sienkiewicz, Yeates, Scioli, Hembeck, Ashley Wood & others 6.00

FANTASTIC COMICS (Fantastic Fears #1-9; Becomes Samson #12)
Ajax/Farrell Publ.: No. 10, Nov-Dec, 1954 - No. 11, Jan-Feb, 1955

10 (#1) 21 42 63 124 202 280
11-Robot-c 26 52 78 154 252 350

FANTASTIC FABLES
Silverwolf Comics: Feb, 1987 - No. 2, 1987 ($1.50, 28 pgs., B&W)

1,2: 1-Tim Vigil-a (6 pgs.). 2-Tim Vigil-a (7 pgs.) 4.00

FANTASTIC FEARS (Formerly Captain Jet) (Fantastic Comics #10 on)
Ajax/Farrell Publ.: No. 7, May, 1953 - No. 9, Sept-Oct, 1954

7(#1, 5/53)-Tales of Stalking Terror 50 100 150 315 533 750
8(#2, 7/53) 37 74 111 222 361 500
3,4 29 58 87 170 278 385
5-(1-2/54)-Ditko story (1st drawn) is written by Bruce Hamilton; r-in Weird V2#8 (1st pro work for Ditko but Daring Love #1 was published 1st) 97 194 291 621 1061 1500
6-Decapitation-girl's head w/paper cutter (classic) 58 116 174 371 636 900
7(5-6/54), 9(9-10/54) 29 58 87 170 278 385
8(7-8/54)-Contains story intended for Jo-Jo; name changed to Kaza; decapitation story 29 58 87 172 281 390

FANTASTIC FIVE
Marvel Comics: Oct, 1999 - No. 5, Feb, 2000 ($1.99)

1-5: 1-M2 Universe; recaps origin; Ryan-a. 2-Two covers 2.50
Spider-Girl Presents Fantastic Five: In Search of Doom (2006, $7.99, digest) r/#1-5 8.00

FANTASTIC FIVE
Marvel Comics: Sept, 2007 - No. 5, Nov, 2007 ($2.99, limited series)

1-5-DeFalco-s/Lim-a; Dr. Doom returns vs. the future Fantastic Five 3.00
...: The Final Doom TPB (2007, $13.99) r/#1-5; cover sketches with inks 14.00

FANTASTIC FORCE
Marvel Comics: Nov, 1994 - No. 18, Apr, 1996 ($1.75)

1-($2.50)-Foil wraparound-c; intro Fantastic Force w/Huntara, Delvor, Psi-Lord & Vibraxas 3.00
2-18: 13-She-Hulk app. 2.50

FANTASTIC FORCE (See Fantastic Four #558, Nu-World heroes from 500 years in the future)
Marvel Comics: Jun, 2009 - No. 4, Sept, 2009 ($3.99/$2.99, limited series)

1-($3.99)-Ahearne-s/Kurth-a/Hitch-c; Fantastic Four app. 4.00
2-4-($2.99) 3,4-Ego the Living Planet app. 3.00

FANTASTIC FOUR (See America's Best TV..., Fireside Book Series, Giant-Size..., Giant Size Super-Stars, Marvel Age..., Marvel Collectors Item Classics, Marvel Knights 4, Marvel Milestone Edition, Marvel's Greatest, Marvel Treasury Edition, Marvel Triple Action, Official Marvel Index to..., Power Record Comics & Ultimate...)

FANTASTIC FOUR
Marvel Comics Group: Nov, 1961 - No. 416, Sept, 1996 (Created by Stan Lee & Jack Kirby)

1-Origin & 1st app. The Fantastic Four (Reed Richards: Mr. Fantastic, Johnny Storm: The Human Torch, Sue Storm: The Invisible Girl, & Ben Grimm: The Thing–Marvel's 1st super-hero group since the G.A.; 1st app. S.A. Human Torch); origin/1st app. The Mole Man. 2200 4400 6600 21,000 45,500 70,000
1-Golden Record Comic Set Reprint (1966)-cover not identical to original 19 38 57 139 270 400
with Golden Record 29 58 87 212 406 600
2-Vs. The Skrulls (last 10¢ issue) 389 778 1167 3500 7000 10,500
3-Fantastic Four don costumes & establish Headquarters; brief 1pg. origin; intro. The Fantasti-Car; Human Torch drawn w/two left hands on-c 326 652 978 2934 5867 8800
4-1st S. A. Sub-Mariner app. (5/62) 352 704 1056 3168 6334 9500
5-Origin & 1st app. Doctor Doom 481 962 1443 4330 8665 13,000
6-Sub-Mariner, Dr. Doom team up; 1st Marvel villain team-up (2nd S.A. Sub-Mariner app. 192 384 576 1680 3340 5000
7-10: 7-1st app. Kurrgo. 8-1st app. Puppet-Master & Alicia Masters. 9-3rd Sub-Mariner app. 10-Stan Lee & Jack Kirby app. in story 132 264 396 1122 2211 3300
11-Origin/1st app. The Impossible Man (2/63) 128 256 384 1088 2144 3200
12-Fantastic Four vs. The Hulk (1st meeting); 1st Hulk x-over & ties w/Amazing Spider-Man #1 as 1st Marvel x-over; (3/63) 333 666 1000 3000 6000 9000
13-Intro. The Watcher; 1st app. The Red Ghost 80 160 240 680 1340 2000
14,15,17,19: 14-Sub-Mariner x-over. 15-1st app. Mad Thinker. 19-Intro. Rama-Tut; Stan Lee & Jack Kirby cameo 50 100 150 413 807 1200
16-1st Ant-Man x-over (7/63); Wasp cameo 97 194 291 621 1061 1500
18-Origin/1st app. The Super Skrull 103 206 309 659 1130 1600
20-Origin/1st app. The Molecule Man 50 100 150 425 838 1250
21-Intro. The Hate Monger; 1st Sgt. Fury x-over (12/63) 48 96 144 384 742 1100
22-24: 22-Sue Storm gains more powers 32 64 96 245 473 700
25,26-The Hulk vs. The Thing (their 1st battle). 25-3rd Avengers x-over (1st time w/Captain America)(cameo, 4/64); 2nd S.A. app. Cap (takes place between Avengers #4 & 5.) 26-4th Avengers x-over 60 120 180 510 1005 1500
27-1st Doctor Strange x-over (6/64) 38 76 114 288 557 825
28-Early X-Men x-over (7/64); same date as X-Men #6 50 100 150 413 807 1200
29,30: 30-Intro. Diablo 26 52 78 190 370 550
31-40: 31-Early Avengers x-over (10/64). 33-1st app. Attuma; part photo-c. 35-Intro/1st app. Dragon Man. 36-Intro/1st app. Madam Medusa & the Frightful Four (Sandman, Wizard, Paste Pot Pete). 39-Wood inks on Daredevil (early x-over) 22 44 66 157 304 450
41-44,47: 41-43-Frightful Four app. 44-Intro. Gorgon 14 28 42 100 188 275
45-Intro/1st app. The Inhumans (c/story, 12/65); also see Incredible Hulk Special #1 & Thor #146, & 147 24 48 72 175 338 500
46-1st Black Bolt-c (Kirby) & 1st full app. 16 32 48 115 220 325
48-Partial origin/1st app. The Silver Surfer & Galactus (3/66) by Lee & Kirby; Galactus brief app. in last panel; 1st of 3 part story 56 112 168 476 938 1400
49-2nd app./1st cover Silver Surfer & Galactus 40 80 120 306 591 875
50-Silver Surfer battles Galactus; full S.S.-c 42 84 126 336 656 975
51-Classic "This Man...This Monster" story 19 38 57 139 270 400
52-1st app. The Black Panther (7/66) 30 60 90 228 439 650

Fantastic Four #202 © MAR

Fantastic Four #334 © MAR

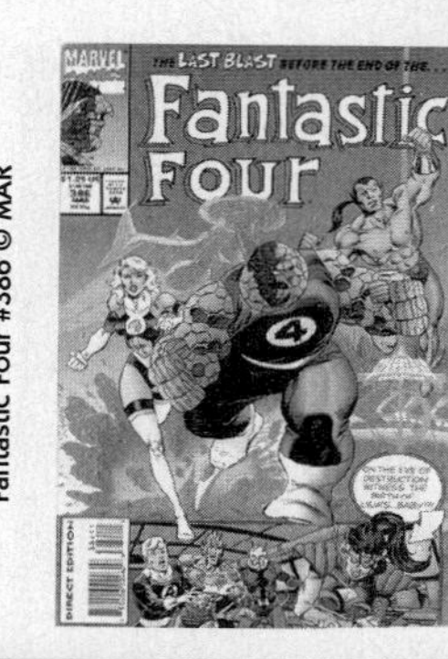

Fantastic Four #386 © MAR

	GD 2.0	VG 4.0	FN 6.0	VF 8.0	VF/NM 9.0	NM- 9.2
53-Origin & 2nd app. The Black Panther	17	34	51	122	236	350
54-Inhumans cameo	12	24	36	85	155	225
55-Thing battles Silver Surfer; 4th app. Silver Surfer	19	38	57	139	270	400
56-Silver Surfer cameo	12	24	36	85	155	225
57-60: Dr. Doom steals Silver Surfer's powers (also see Silver Surfer: Loftier Than Mortals). 59,60-Inhumans cameo	11	22	33	74	132	190
61-65,68-71: 61-Silver Surfer cameo; Sandman-c/s	9	18	27	60	100	140
66-Begin 2 part origin of Him (Warlock); does not app. (9/67)	12	24	36	86	158	230
66,67-2nd printings (1994)	2	4	6	8	10	12
67-Origin/1st brief app. Him (Warlock); 1 page; see Thor #165,166 for 1st full app.	12	24	36	86	158	230
72-Silver Surfer-c/story (pre-dates Silver Surfer #1)	12	24	36	85	155	225
73-Spider-Man, D.D., Thor x-over; cont'd from Daredevil #38	11	22	33	80	145	210
74-77: Silver Surfer app.(#77 is same date/S.S. #1)	10	20	30	70	123	175
78-80	7	14	21	45	73	100
81-88: 81-Crystal joins & dons costume. 82,83-Inhumans app. 84-87-Dr. Doom app. 88-Last 12¢ issue	6	12	18	41	66	90
89-99,101: 94-Intro. Agatha Harkness.	6	12	18	37	59	80
100 (7/70) F.F. vs Thinker and Puppet-Master	10	20	30	70	123	175
102-104: F.F. vs. Sub-Mariner. 104-Magneto-c/story	6	12	18	39	62	85
105-109,111: 108-Last Kirby issue (not in #103-107)	6	12	18	37	59	80
110-Initial version w/green Thing and blue faces and pink uniforms on-c	7	14	21	45	73	100
110-Corrected-c w/accurately colored faces and uniforms and orange Thing	6	12	18	39	62	85
112-Hulk Vs. Thing (7/71)	14	28	42	102	194	285
113-115: 115-Last 15¢ issue	4	8	12	28	44	60
116 (52 pgs.)	6	12	18	41	66	90
117-120	4	8	12	26	41	55
121-123-Silver Surfer-c/stories. 122,123-Galactus	5	10	15	30	48	65
124,125,127,129-149: 129-Intro. Thundra. 130-Sue leaves F.F. 131-Quicksilver app. 132-Medusa joins. 133-Thundra Vs. Thing. 142-Kirbyish-a by Buckler begins. 143-Dr. Doom-c/story. 147-Sub-Mariner	4	8	12	22	34	45
126-Origin F.F. retold; cover swipe of F.F. #1	4	8	12	24	37	50
128-Four pg. insert of F.F. Friends & Foes	4	8	12	24	37	50
150-Crystal & Quicksilver's wedding	4	8	12	24	37	50
151-154,158-160: 151-Origin Thundra. 159-Medusa leaves; Sue rejoins	3	6	9	14	20	25
155-157: Silver Surfer in all	3	6	9	18	27	35
161-165,168,174-180: 164-The Crusader (old Marvel Boy) revived (origin #165); 1st app. Frankie Raye. 168-170-Cage app. 176-Re-intro Impossible Man; Marvel artists app. 180-r/#101 by Kirby	2	4	6	9	12	15
166,167-vs. Hulk	3	6	9	16	23	30
169-173-(Regular 25¢ edition)(4-8/75)	2	4	6	9	12	15
169-173-(30¢-c, limited distribution)	3	6	9	14	19	30
181-199: 189-G.A. Human Torch app. & origin retold. 190,191-Fantastic Four break up	2	3	4	6	8	10
183-187-(35¢-c variants, limited dist.)(6-10/77)	4	8	12	24	37	50
200-(11/78, 52 pgs.)-F.F. re-united vs. Dr. Doom	2	4	6	9	13	16
201-208,219,222-231: 207-Human Torch vs. Spider-Man-c/story. 211-1st app. Terrax. 224-Contains unused alternate-c for FF #3 and pin-ups						5.00
209-216,218,220,221-Byrne-a. 209-1st Herbie the Robot. 220-Brief origin						6.00
217-Early app. Dazzler (4/80); by Byrne						6.00
232-Byrne-a begins						6.00
233-235,237-249,251-260: All Byrne-a. 238-Origin Frankie Raye. 244-Frankie Raye becomes Nova, Herald of Galactus. 252-Reads sideways; Annihilus app.; contains skin "Tattooz" decals						5.00
236-20th Anniversary issue(11/81, 68 pgs., $1.00)-Brief origin F.F.; Byrne-c/a(p); new Kirby-a(p)						6.00
250-(52 pgs)-Spider-Man x-over; Byrne-a; Skrulls impersonate New X-Men						6.00
261-285: 261-Silver Surfer. 262-Origin Galactus; Byrne writes & draws himself into story. 264-Swipes-c of F.F. #1. 274-Spider-Man's alien costume app. (4th app., 1/85, 2 pgs.)						4.00
286-2nd app. X-Factor continued from Avengers #263; story continues in X-Factor #1						5.00
287-295: 291-Action Comcis #1 cover swipe. 292-Nick Fury app. 293-Last Byrne-a						3.00
296-($1.50)-Barry Smith-c/a; Thing rejoins						4.00
297-318,321-330: 300-Johnny Storm & Alicia Masters wed. 306-New team begins (9/87). 311-Re-intro The Black Panther. 327-Mr. Fantastic & Invisible Girl return						3.00
319,320: 319-Double size. 320-Thing vs. Hulk						4.00
331-346,351-357,359,360: 334-Simonson-c/scripts begin. 337-Simonson-a begins. 342-Spider-Man cameo. 356-F.F. vs. The New Warriors; Paul Ryan-c/a begins. 360-Last $1.00-c						3.00
347-Ghost Rider, Wolverine, Spider-Man, Hulk-c/stories thru #349; Arthur Adams-c/a(p) in each						4.00
347,348-Gold 2nd printing						2.50
348-350: 350-($1.50, 52 pgs.)-Dr. Doom app.						3.00
358-(11/91, $2.25, 88 pgs.)-30th anniversary issue; gives history of F.F.; die cut-c; Art Adams back-up story-a						3.00
361-368,370,372-374,376-380,382-386: 362-Spider-Man app. 367-Wolverine app. (brief). 370-Infinity War x-over; Thanos & Magus app. 374-Secret Defenders (Ghost Rider, Hulk, Wolverine) x-over						2.50
369-Infinity War x-over; Thanos app.						2.50
371-All white embossed-c ($2.00)						4.00
371-All red 2nd printing ($2.00)						2.50
375-($2.95, 52 pgs.)-Holo-grafx foil-c; ann. issue						3.00
376-($2.95)-Variant polybagged w/Dirt Magazine #4 and music tape						5.00
381-Death of Reed Richards (Mister Fantastic) & Dr. Doom						4.00
387-Newsstand ed. ($1.25)						2.25
387-($2.95)-Collector's Ed. w/Die-cut foil-c						3.00
388-393,395-397: 388-bound-in trading card sheet. 394-($1.50-c)						2.50
394,398,399: 394 ($2.95)-Collector's Edition-polybagged w/16 pg. Marvel Action Hour book and acetate print; pink logo. 398,399-Rainbow Foil-c						3.00
400-Rainbow-Foil-c						4.00
401-415: 401,402-Atlantis Rising. 407,408-Return of Reed Richards. 411-Inhumans app. 414-Galactus vs. Hyperstorm. 415-Onslaught tie-in; X-Men app.						2.50
416-($2.50)-Onslaught tie-in; Dr. Doom app.; wraparound-c						3.00
#500-up (See Fantastic Four Vol. 3; series resumed original numbering after Vol. 3 #70)						
Annual 1('63)-Origin F.F.; Ditko-i; early Spidey app.	72	144	216	612	1206	1800
Annual 2('64)-Dr. Doom origin & c/story	39	78	117	297	574	850
Annual 3('65)-Reed & Sue wed; r/#6,11	19	38	57	133	259	385
Special 4(11/66)-G.A. Torch x-over (1st S.A. app.) & origin retold; r/#25,26 (Hulk vs. Thing); Torch vs. Torch battle	13	26	39	90	165	240
Special 5(11/67)-New art; Intro. Psycho-Man; early Black Panther, Inhumans & Silver Surfer (1st solo story) app.	13	26	39	93	172	250
Special 6(11/68)-Intro. Annihilus; birth of Franklin Richards; new 48 pg. movie length epic; last non-reprint annual	9	18	27	60	100	140
Special 7(11/69)-r/F.F. #1,2; Marvel staff photos	5	10	15	30	48	65
Special 8-10: All reprints. 8(12/70)-F.F. vs. Sub-Mariner plus gallery of F.F. foes. 9(12/71). 10('73)	3	6	9	17	25	32
Annual 11-14: 11(1976)-New art begins again. 12(1978). 13(1978). 14(1979)	2	3	4	6	8	10
Annual 15-17: 15('80, 68 pgs.). 17(1983)-Byrne-c/a						5.00
Annual 18-27: 21(1988)-Evolutionary War x-over. 22-Atlantis Attacks x-over; Sub-Mariner & The Avengers app.; Buckler-a. 23-Byrne-c; Guice-p. 24-2 pg. origin recap of Fantastic Four; Guardians of the Galaxy x-over. 25-Moondragon story. 26-Bagged w/card						3.00
Best of the Fantastic Four Vol. 1 HC (2005, $29.99) oversized reprints of classic stories from FF#1,39,40,51,100,116,176,236,267, Ann.2, V3#56,60 and more; Brevoort intro.						30.00
Maximum Fantastic Four HC (2005, $49.99, dust jacket) r/Fantastic Four #1 with super-sized art; historical background from Walter Mosley and Mark Evanier; dust jacket unfolds to a poster: giant FF#1 cover on one side, gallery of interior pages on other						50.00
...: Monsters Unleashed nn (1992, $5.95)-r/F.F. #347-349 w/new Arthur Adams-c						6.00
...: Nobody Gets Out Alive (1994, $15.95) TPB r/ #387-392						16.00
... Omnibus Vol. 1 HC (2005, $99.99) r/#1-30 & Annual 1 plus letter pages; 3 intros. and a 1974 essay by Stan Lee; original plot synopsis for FF #1; essays and Kirby art						100.00
... Omnibus Vol. 2 HC (2007, $99.99) r/#31-60, Annual 2-4 and Not Brand Echh #1 plus letter pages and essays by Stan Lee, Reginald Hudlin, Roy Thomas and others						100.00
Special Edition 1(5/84)-r/Annual #1; Byrne-c/a						3.00
...: The Lost Adventure (4/08, $4.99) Lee & Kirby story partially used in flashback in FF #108 completed with additional art by Frenz & Sinnott; plus reprint of FF #108						5.00
... Visionaries: George Pérez Vol. 1 (2005, $19.99) r/#164-167,170,176-178,184-186						20.00
... Visionaries: George Pérez Vol. 2 (2006, $19.99) r/#187-188,191-192, Annual #14-15, Marvel Two-In-One #60 and back-up story from Adventures of the Thing #3						20.00
... Visionaries (11/01, $19.95) r/#232-240 by John Byrne						20.00
... Visionaries Vol. 2 (2004, $24.99) r/#241-250 by John Byrne						25.00
... Visionaries John Byrne Vol. 3 (2004, $24.99) r/#251-257; Annual #17; Avengers #233 and Thing #2						25.00
... Visionaries John Byrne Vol. 4 (2005, $24.99) r/#258-267; Alpha Flight #4 & Thing #10						25.00
... Visionaries John Byrne Vol. 5 (2005, $24.99) r/#268-275; Annual #18 & Thing #19						25.00
... Visionaries John Byrne Vol. 6 ('06, $24.99) r/#276-284; Secret Wars II #2 & Thing #23						25.00
... Visionaries John Byrne Vol. 7 ('07, $24.99) r/#285,286, Ann. #19, Avengers #263 & Ann. #14, and X-Factor #1						25.00
... Visionaries John Byrne Vol. 8 ('07, $24.99) r/#287-295						25.00
... Visionaries: Walter Simonson Vol. 1 (2007, $19.99) r/#334-341						20.00

NOTE: ***Arthur Adams*** *c/a-347-349p.* ***Austin*** *c(i)-232-236, 238, 240-242, 250i, 286i.* ***Buckler*** *c-151, 168.* ***John Buscema*** *a(p)-107, 108(w/****Kirby, Sinnott*** *&* ***Romita****),109-130, 132, 134-141, 160, 173-175, 202, 296-309p, Annual 11, 13; c(p)-107-122, 124-129, 133-139, 202, Annual 12p, Special 10.* ***Byrne*** *a-209-218p, 220p, 221p, 232-265, 266i, 267-273, 274-293p, Annual 17, 19; c-211-214p, 220p, 232-236p, 237, 238p, 239, 240-242p, 243-249, 250p, 251-267, 269-277, 278-281p, 283p, 284, 285, 286p, 288-293, Annual 17, 18.* ***Ditko*** *a-13i, 14i(w/****Kirby****-p), Annual*

Fantastic Four V3 #32 © MAR

Fantastic Four #574 © MAR

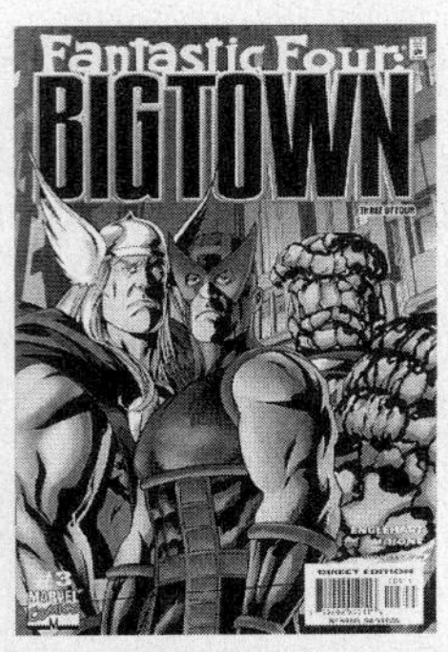
Fantastic Four: Bigtown #3 © MAR

GD 2.0	VG 4.0	FN 6.0	VF 8.0	VF/NM 9.0	NM- 9.2

*16. **G. Kane** c-145p, 146p, 150p, 160p. **Kirby** a-1-102p, 108p, 180r, 189r, 236p, Special 1-10; c-1-101, 164, 167, 171-177, 180, 181, 190, 200, Annual 11, Special 1-7, 9. **Marcos** a-Annual 14i. **Mooney** a-118i, 152i. **Perez** a(p)-164-167, 170-172, 176-178, 184-188, 191p, 192p. Annual 14p, 15p; c(p)-183-188, 191, 192, 194-197. **Simonson** a-337-341, 343, 344p, 345p, 346, 350p, 352-354; c-212, 334-341, 342p, 343-346, 350, 353, 354. **Steranko** c-130-132p. **Williamson** c-357i.*

FANTASTIC FOUR (Volume Two)
Marvel Comics: V2#1, Nov, 1996 - No. 13, Nov, 1997 ($2.95/$1.95/$1.99) (Produced by WildStorm Productions)

1-($2.95)-Reintro Fantastic Four; Jim Lee-c/a; Brandon Choi scripts; Mole Man app. 5.00
1-($2.95)-Variant-c 1 2 3 4 5 7
2-9: 2-Namor-c/app. 3-Avengers-c/app. 4-Two covers; Dr. Doom cameo 3.00
10,11,13: All $1.99-c. 13-"World War 3"-pt. 1, x-over w/Image 3.00
12-($2.99) "Heroes Reunited"-pt. 1 4.00
...: Heroes Reborn (7/00, $17.95, TPB) r/#1-6 18.00
Heroes Reborn: Fantastic Four (2006, $29.99, TPB) r/#1-12; Jim Lee intro.; pin-ups 30.00

FANTASTIC FOUR (Volume Three)
Marvel Comics: V3#1, Jan, 1998 - Present ($2.99/$1.99/$2.25)

1-($2.99)-Heroes Return; Lobdell-s/Davis & Farmer-a 6.00
1-Alternate Heroes Return-c 1 2 3 5 6 8
2-4,12: 2-2-covers. 4-Claremont-s/Larroca-a begin; Silver Surfer c/app. 12-($2.99) Wraparound-c by Larroca 4.00
5-11: 6-Heroes For Hire app. 9-Spider-Man-c/app. 3.50
13-24: 13,14-Ronan-c/app. 3.00
25-($2.99) Dr. Doom returns 3.50
26-49: 27-Dr. Doom marries Sue. 30-Begin $2.25-c. 32,42-Namor-c/app. 35-Regular cover; Pacheco-s/a begins. 37-Super-Skrull-c/app. 38-New Baxter Building 3.00
35-($3.25) Variant foil enhanced-c; Pacheco-s/a begins 3.50
50-($3.99, 64 pgs.) BWS-c; Grummett, Pacheco, Rude, Udon-a 4.00
51-53,55-59: 51-53-Bagley-a(p)/Wieringo-c; Inhumans app. 55,56-Immonen-a 57-59-Warren-s/Grant-a 3.00
54-($3.50, 100 pgs.) Birth of Valeria; r/Annual #6 birth of Franklin 4.00
60-(9¢-c) Waid-s/Wieringo-a begin 3.00
60-($2.25 newsstand edition)(also see Promotional Comics section) 3.00
61-70: 62-64-FF vs. Modulus. 65,66-Buckingham-a. 68-70-Dr. Doom app. 3.00
(After #70 [Aug, 2003] numbering reverted back to original Vol. 1 with #500, Sept, 2003)
500-($3.50) Regular edition; concludes Dr. Doom app.; Dr. Strange app.; Rivera painted-c 4.00
500-($4.99) Director's Cut Edition; chromium-c by Wieringo; sketch and script pages 8.00
501-516: 501,502-Casey Jones-a. 503-508-Porter-a. 509-Wieringo-c/a resumes. 512,513-Spider-Man app. 514-516-Ha-c/Medina-a 3.00
517-537: 517-Begin $2.99-c. 519-523-Galactus app. 527-Straczynski-s begins. 537-Dr. Doom. 3.00
527-Variant Edition with different McKone-c 3.00
527-Wizard World Philadelphia Edition with B&W McKone sketch-c 3.00
536-Variant cover by Bryan Hitch 5.00
537-B&W variant cover 5.00
538-542-Civil War. 538-Don Blake reclaims Thor's hammer 4.00
543-45th Anniversary; Black Panther and Storm replace Reed and Sue; Granov-c 4.00
544-553: 544-546-Silver Surfer app.; Turner-c 3.00
554-568-Millar-s/Hitch-a/c. 558-561-Dr. Doom-c/app. 562-Funeral & proposal 3.00
554-Variant-c by Bianchi 6.00
554-Variant Skrull-c by Suydam 30.00
569-($3.99) Wraparound-c; Immonen-a; Dr. Doom app. 4.00
570-576: 570-572,575,576-Eaglesham-a. 574-Spider-Man app. 3.00
...'98 Annual ($3.50) Immonen-a 3.50
...'99 Annual ($3.50) Ladronn-a 3.50
...'00 Annual ($3.50) Larocca-a; Marvel Girl back-up story 3.50
...'01 Annual ($2.99) Maguire-a; Thing back-up w/Yu-a 3.00
... : A Death in the Family (7/06, $3.99, one-shot) Weeks-a/c; and r/F.F. #245 4.00
... By J. Michael Straczynski Vol. 1 (2005, $19.99, HC) r/#527-532 20.00
Civil War: Fantastic Four TPB (2007, $17.99) r/#538-543; 45th Anniversary Toasts 18.00
... Cosmic-Size Special 1 (2/09, $4.99) Cary Bates-s/Bing Cansino-a; r/F.F. #237 5.00
Fantastic 4th Voyage of Sinbad (9/01, $5.95) Claremont-s/Ferry-a 6.00
Flesh and Stone (8/01, $12.95, TPB) r/#35-39 13.00
... Giant-Size Adventures 1 (8/09, $3.99) Cifuentes & Coover-a; Egghead app. 4.00
... /Inhumans TPB (2007, $19.99) r/#51-54 and Inhumans ('00) #1-4 20.00
...: Isla De La Muerte! (2/08, $3.99) English & Spanish editions; Beland-s/Doe-a 4.00
... Presents: Franklin Richards 1 (11/05, $2.99) r/back-up stories from Power Pack #1-4 plus new 5 pg. story; Sumerak-s/Eliopoulos-a (Also see Franklin Richards) 3.00
...Special (2/06, $2.99) McDuffie-s/Casey Jones-a; dinner with Dr. Doom 3.00
...Tales Vol. 1 (2005, $7.99, digest) r/Marvel Age: FF Tales #1, Tales of the Thing #1-3, and Spider-Man Team-Up Special 8.00
...: The New Fantastic Four HC (2007, $19.99) r/#544-550; variant covers & sketch pgs. 20.00
...: The New Fantastic Four SC (2008, $15.99) r/#544-550; variant covers & sketch pgs. 16.00
... : The Wedding Special 1 (1/06, $5.00) 40th Anniversary new story & r/FF Annual #3 5.00

GD 2.0	VG 4.0	FN 6.0	VF 8.0	VF/NM 9.0	NM- 9.2

... Vol. 1 HC (2004, $29.99, dust jacket) oversized reprint /#60-70, 500-502; Mark Waid intro and series proposal; cover gallery 30.00
... Vol. 2 HC (2005, $29.99, d.j.) oversized r/#503-513; Waid intro.; deleted scenes 30.00
... Vol. 3 HC (2005, $29.99, d.j.) oversized r/#514-524; Waid commentaries; cover sketches 30.00
... Vol. 1: Imaginauts (2003, $17.99, TPB) r/#56,60-66; Mark Waid's series proposal 18.00
... Vol. 2: Unthinkable (2003, $17.99, TPB) r/#67-70,500-502; #500 Director's Cut extras 18.00
... Vol. 3: Authoritative Action (2004, $12.99, TPB) r/#503-508 13.00
... Vol. 4: Hereafter (2004, $11.99, TPB) r/#509-513 12.00
... Vol. 5: Disassembled (2004, $14.99, TPB) r/#514-519 15.00
... Vol. 6: Rising Storm (2005, $13.99, TPB) r/#520-524 14.00
...: The Beginning of the End TPB (2008, $14.99) r/#525,526,551-553 & Fantastic Four: Isla De La Muerte! one-shot 15.00
...: The Life Fantastic TPB (2006, $16.99) r/#533-535; The Wedding Special, Special (2/06) and A Death in the Family one-shots 17.00
Wizard #1/2 -Lim-a 10.00

FANTASTIC FOUR AND POWER PACK
Marvel Comics: Sept, 2007 - No. 4, Dec, 2007 ($2.99, limited series)

1-4-Gurihiru-a/Van Lente-s; the Wizard app. 3.00
...: Favorite Son TPB (2008, $7.99, digest size) r/#1-4 8.00

FANTASTIC FOUR: ATLANTIS RISING
Marvel Comics: June, 1995 - No. 2, July, 1995 ($3.95, limited series)

1,2: Acetate-c 5.00
Collector's Preview (5/95, $2.25, 52 pgs.) 2.50

FANTASTIC FOUR: BIG TOWN
Marvel Comics: Jan, 2001 - No. 4, Apr, 2001 ($2.99, limited series)

1-4:"What If?" story; McKone-a/Englehart-s 3.00

FANTASTIC FOUR: FIREWORKS
Marvel Comics: Jan, 1999 - No. 3, Mar, 1999 ($2.99, limited series)

1-3-Remix; Jeff Johnson-a 3.00

FANTASTIC FOUR: FIRST FAMILY
Marvel Comics: May, 2006 - No. 6, Oct, 2006 ($2.99, limited series)

1-6-Casey-s/Weston-a; flashback to the days after the accident 3.00
TPB (2006, $15.99) r/#1-6 16.00

FANTASTIC FOUR: FOES
Marvel Comics: Mar, 2005 - No. 6, Aug, 2005 ($2.99, limited series)

1-6-Kirkman-s/Rathburn-a. 1-Puppet Master app. 3-Super-Skrull app. 4-Mole Man app. 3.00
TPB (2005, $16.99) r/#1-6 17.00

FANTASTIC FOUR: HOUSE OF M (Reprinted in House of M: Fantastic Four/ Iron Man TPB)
Marvel Comics: Sept, 2005 - No. 3, Nov, 2005 ($2.99, limited series)

1-3: Fearsome Four, led by Doom; Scot Eaton-a 3.00

FANTASTIC FOUR INDEX (See Official...)

FANTASTIC FOUR/ IRON MAN: BIG IN JAPAN
Marvel Comics: Dec, 2005 - No. 4, Mar, 2006 ($3.50, limited series)

1-4-Seth Fisher-a/c; Zeb Wells-s; wraparound-c on each 3.50
TPB (2006, $12.99) r/#1-4 and Seth Fisher illustrated story from Spider-Man Unlimited #8 13.00

FANTASTIC FOUR: 1 2 3 4
Marvel Comics: Oct, 2001 - No. 4, Jan, 2002 ($2.99, limited series)

1-4-Morrison-s/Jae Lee-a. 2-4-Namor-c/app. 3.00
TPB (2002, $9.99) r/#1-4 10.00

FANTASTIC FOUR ROAST
Marvel Comics Group: May, 1982 (75¢, one-shot, direct sales)

1-Celebrates 20th anniversary of F.F.#1; X-Men, Ghost Rider & many others cameo; Golden, Miller, Buscema, Rogers, Byrne, Anderson art; Hembeck/Austin-c 4.00

FANTASTIC FOUR: THE END
Marvel Comics: Jan, 2007 - No. 6, May, 2007 ($2.99, limited series)

1-6-Alan Davis-s/a; last adventure of the future FF. 1-Dr. Doom-c/app. 3.00
Roughcut #1 ($3.99) B&W pencil art for full story and text script; B&W sketch cover 4.00
HC (2007, $19.99, dustjacket) r/#1-6 20.00
SC (2008, $14.99) r/#1-6 15.00

FANTASTIC FOUR: THE LEGEND
Marvel Comics: Oct, 1996 ($3.95, one-shot)

1-Tribute issue 4.00

FANTASTIC FOUR: THE MOVIE
Marvel Comics: Aug, 2005 ($4.99/$12.99, one-shot)

1-($4.99) Movie adaptation; Jurgens-a; behind the scenes feature; Doom origin; photo-c 5.00

Fantastic Four: World's Greatest Comics Magazine #10 © MAR

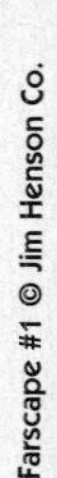

Farscape #1 © Jim Henson Co.

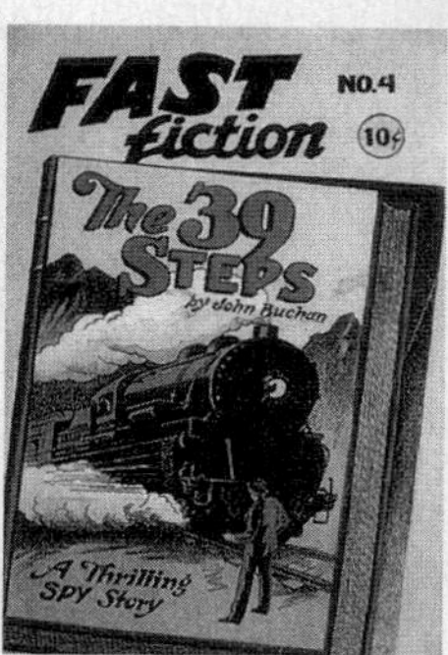

Fast Fiction #4 © Seaboard

GD VG FN VF VF/NM NM-
2.0 4.0 6.0 8.0 9.0 9.2

TPB-($12.99) Movie adaptation, r/Fantastic Four #5 & 190, and FF Vol. 3 #60, photo-c 13.00

FANTASTIC FOUR: TRUE STORY
Marvel Comics: Sept, 2008 - No. 4, Jan, 2009 ($2.99, limited series)
1-4-Cornell-s/Domingues-a/Henrichon-c 3.00

FANTASTIC FOUR 2099
Marvel Comics: Jan, 1996 - No. 8, Aug, 1996 ($3.95/$1.95)
1-($3.95)-Chromium-c; X-Nation preview 4.00
2-8: 4-Spider-Man 2099-c/app. 5-Doctor Strange app. 7-Thibert-c 2.50
NOTE: *Williamson a-1i; c-1i.*

FANTASTIC FOUR UNLIMITED
Marvel Comics: Mar, 1993 - No. 12, Dec, 1995 ($3.95, 68 pgs.)
1-12: 1-Black Panther app. 4-Thing vs. Hulk. 5-Vs. The Frightful Four. 6-Vs. Namor. 7, 9-12-Wraparound-c 4.00

FANTASTIC FOUR UNPLUGGED
Marvel Comics: Sept, 1995 - No. 6, Aug 1996 (99¢, bi-monthly)
1-6 2.50

FANTASTIC FOUR - UNSTABLE MOLECULES
(Indicia for #1 reads STARTLING STORIES: ... ; #2 reads UNSTABLE MOLECULES)
Marvel Comics: Mar, 2003 - No. 4, June, 2003 ($2.99, limited series)
1-4-Guy Davis-c/a 3.00
Fantastic Four Legends Vol. 1 TPB (2003, $13.99) r/#1-4, origin from FF #1 (1963) 14.00
TPB (2005, $13.99) r/#1-4 14.00

FANTASTIC FOUR VS. X-MEN
Marvel Comics: Feb, 1987 - No. 4, June, 1987 (Limited series)
1-4: 4-Austin-a(i) 4.00

FANTASTIC FOUR: WORLD'S GREATEST COMICS MAGAZINE
Marvel Comics: Feb, 2001 - No. 12 (Limited series)
1-12: Homage to Lee & Kirby era of F.F.; s/a by Larsen & various. 5-Hulk-c/app. 10-Thor app. 3.00

FANTASTIC GIANTS (Formerly Konga #1-23)
Charlton Comics: V2#24, Sept, 1966 (25¢, 68 pgs.)
V2#24-Special Ditko issue; origin Konga & Gorgo reprinted plus two new Ditko stories
6 12 18 43 69 95

FANTASTIC TALES
I. W. Enterprises: 1958 (no date) (Reprint, one-shot)
1-Reprints Avon's "City of the Living Dead" 3 6 9 20 30 40

FANTASTIC VOYAGE (See Movie Comics)
Gold Key: Aug, 1969 - No. 2, Dec, 1969
1 (TV) 4 8 12 28 44 60
2-Cover has the text "Civilian Miniaturized Defense Force" in yellow bar at top; back cover has painted art 3 6 9 20 30 40
2-Variant cover has text "In This Issue Sweepstakes..." along top; ad on back-c
4 8 12 24 37 50

FANTASTIC VOYAGES OF SINDBAD, THE
Gold Key: Oct, 1965 - No. 2, June, 1967
1-Painted-c on both 6 12 18 43 69 95
2 5 10 15 32 51 70

FANTASTIC WORLDS
Standard Comics: No. 5, Sept, 1952 - No. 7, Jan, 1953
5-Toth, Anderson-a 37 74 111 218 354 490
6-Toth-c/a 30 60 90 177 289 400
7 20 40 60 117 189 260

FANTASY FEATURES
Americomics: 1987 - No. 2, 1987 ($1.75)
1,2 3.00

FANTASY ILLUSTRATED
New Media Publ.: Spring 1982 ($2.95, B&W magazine)
1-P. Craig Russell-c/a; art by Ditko, Sekowsky, Sutton; Englehart-s
1 2 3 4 5 7

FANTASY MASTERPIECES (Marvel Super Heroes No. 12 on)
Marvel Comics Group: Feb, 1966 - No. 11, Oct, 1967; V2#1, Dec, 1979 - No. 14, Jan, 1981
1-Photo of Stan Lee (12¢-c #1,2) 8 16 24 52 86 120
2-r/1st Fin Fang Foom from Strange Tales #89 5 10 15 32 51 70
3-8: 3-G.A. Capt. America-r begin, end #11; 1st 25¢ Giant; Colan-r. 3-6-Kirby-c(p). 4-Kirby-c(p)(i). 7-Begin G.A. Sub-Mariner, Torch-r/M. Mystery. 8-Torch battles the Sub-Mariner-r/Marvel Mystery #9 5 10 15 34 55 75
9-Origin Human Torch-r/Marvel Comics #1 6 12 18 37 59 80
10,11: 10-r/origin & 1st app. All Winners Squad from All Winners #19. 11-r/origin of Toro (H.T. #1) & Black Knight #1 5 10 15 32 51 70
V2#1(12/79, 75¢, 52 pgs.)-r/origin Silver Surfer from Silver Surfer #1 with editing plus reprints cover; J. Buscema-a 1 2 3 5 6 8
2-14-Reprints Silver Surfer #2-14 w/covers 5.00
NOTE: ***Buscema** c-V2#7-9(in part). **Ditko** r-1-3, 7, 9. **Everett** r-1,7-9. **Matt Fox** r-9i. **Kirby** r-1-11; c(p)-3, 4i, 5, 6. **Starlin** r-8-13. Some direct sale V2#14's had a 50¢ cover price. #3-11 contain Capt. America-r/Capt. America #3-10. #7-11 contain G.A.Human Torch & Sub-Mariner-r.*

FANTASY QUARTERLY (Also see Elfquest)
Independent Publishers Syndicate: Spring, 1978 (B&W)
1-1st app. Elfquest; Dave Sim-a (6 pgs.) 7 14 21 49 80 110

FANTOMAN (Formerly Amazing Adventure Funnies)
Centaur Publications: No. 2, Aug, 1940 - No. 4, Dec, 1940
2-The Fantom of the Fair, The Arrow, Little Dynamite-r begin; origin The Ermine by Filchock; Fantoman app. in 2-4; Burgos, J. Cole, Ernst, Gustavson-a
110 220 330 704 1020 1700
3,4: Gustavson-r. 4-Red Blaze story 86 172 258 546 936 1325

FAREWELL MOONSHADOW (See Moonshadow)
DC Comics (Vertigo): Jan, 1997 ($7.95, one-shot)
nn-DeMatteis-s/Muth-c/a 8.00

FARGO KID (Formerly Justice Traps the Guilty)(See Feature Comics #47)
Prize Publications: V11#3(#1), June-July, 1958 - V11#5, Oct-Nov, 1958
V11#3(#1)-Origin Fargo Kid, Severin-c/a; Williamson-a(2); Heath-a
18 36 54 103 162 220
V11#4,5-Severin-c/a 13 26 39 74 105 135

FARMER'S DAUGHTER, THE
Stanhall Publ./Trojan Magazines: Feb-Mar, 1954 - No. 3, June-July, 1954; No. 4, Oct, 1954
1-Lingerie, nudity panel 39 78 117 240 395 550
2-4(Stanhall) 24 48 72 142 234 325

FARSCAPE (Based on TV series)
BOOM! Studios: Nov, 2008 - No. 4, Feb, 2009 ($3.99)
1-4-O'Bannon-s/Patterson-a; multiple covers 4.00

FARSCAPE (Based on TV series)
BOOM! Studios: Nov, 2009 - Present ($3.99)
1-5-O'Bannon-s/Sliney-a; multiple covers 4.00
...: D'Argo's Lament 1-4 (4/09 - No. 4, 7/09, $3.99) Edwards-a; three covers on each 4.00
...: D'Argo's Quest 1-4 (12/09 - No. 4, 3/10, $3.99) Cleveland-a; three covers on each 4.00
...: D'Argo's Trial 1-4 (8/09 - No. 4, 11/09, $3.99) Cleveland-a; multiple covers on each 4.00
...: Gone and Back 1-4 (7/09 - No. 4, 10/09, $3.99) Patterson-a; multiple covers on each 4.00
...: Strange Detractors 1-4 (3/09 - No. 4, 6/09, $3.99) Sliney-a; three covers on each 4.00

FARSCAPE: WAR TORN (Based on TV series)
DC Comics (WildStorm): Apr, 2002 - No. 2, May, 2002 ($4.95, limited series)
1,2-Teranishi-a/Wolfman-s; photo-c 5.00

FASHION IN ACTION
Eclipse Comics: Aug, 1986 - Feb, 1987 (Baxter paper)
Summer Special 1 , Winter Special 1, each Snyder III-c/a 2.50

FASTBALL EXPRESS (Major League Baseball)
Ultimate Sports Force: 2000 ($3.95, one-shot)
1-Polybagged with poster; Johnson, Maddux, Park, Nomo, Clemens app. 4.00

FASTEST GUN ALIVE, THE (Movie)
Dell Publishing Co.: No. 741, Sept, 1956 (one-shot)
Four Color 741-Photo-c 7 14 21 45 73 105

FAST FICTION (...Action) (Stories by Famous Authors Illustrated #6 on)
Seaboard Publ./Famous Authors Ill.: Oct, 1949 - No. 5, Mar, 1950
(All have Kiefer-c)(48 pgs.)
1-Scarlet Pimpernel; Jim Lavery-c/a 29 58 87 169 272 375
2-Captain Blood; H. C. Kiefer-c/a 25 50 75 147 236 325
3-She, by Rider Haggard; Vincent Napoli-a 31 62 93 181 291 400
4-(1/50, 52 pgs.)-The 39 Steps; Lavery-c/a 19 38 57 112 176 240
5-Beau Geste; Kiefer-c/a 19 38 57 112 176 240
NOTE: ***Kiefer** a-2, 5; c-2, 3,5. **Lavery** c/a-1, 4. **Napoli** a-3.*

FAST FORWARD
DC Comics (Piranha Press): 1992 - No. 3, 1993 ($4.95, 68 pgs.)

Fate #22 © DC

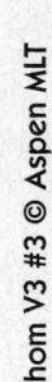

Fathom V3 #3 © Aspen MLT

Fawcett Movie Comic #10 © FAW

	GD 2.0	VG 4.0	FN 6.0	VF 8.0	VF/NM 9.0	NM- 9.2

1-3: 1-Morrison scripts; McKean-c/a. 3-Sam Kieth-a 5.00

FAST WILLIE JACKSON
Fitzgerald Periodicals, Inc.: Oct, 1976 - No. 7, 1977

1 3 6 9 16 22 28
2-7 2 4 6 10 14 18

FAT ALBERT (...& the Cosby Kids) (TV)
Gold Key: Mar, 1974 - No. 29, Feb, 1979

1 4 8 12 24 37 50
2-10 3 6 9 14 20 26
11-29 2 4 6 10 14 18

FATALE (Also see Powers That Be #1 & Shadow State #1,2)
Broadway Comics: Jan, 1996 - No. 6, Aug, 1996 ($2.50)

1-6: J.G. Jones-c/a in all, Preview Edition 1 (11/95, B&W) 2.50

FAT AND SLAT (Ed Wheelan) (Becomes Gunfighter No. 5 on)
E. C. Comics: Summer, 1947 - No. 4, Spring, 1948

1-Intro/origin Voltage, Man of Lightning; "Comics" McCormick, the World's No. 1 Comic Book Fan begins, ends #4 37 74 111 222 361 500
2-4: 4-Comics McCormick-c feature 24 48 72 142 234 325

FAT AND SLAT JOKE BOOK
All-American Comics (William H. Wise): Summer, 1944 (52 pgs., one-shot)

nn-by Ed Wheelan 28 56 84 165 270 375

FATE (See Hand of Fate & Thrill-O-Rama)

FATE
DC Comics: Oct, 1994 - No. 22, Sept, 1996 ($1.95/$2.25)

0,1-22: 8-Begin $2.25-c. 11-14-Alan Scott (Sentinel) app. 10,14-Zatanna app. 21-Phantom Stranger app. 22-Spectre app. 2.50

FATHOM
Comico: May, 1987 - No. 3, July, 1987 ($1.50, limited series)

1-3 2.50

FATHOM
Image Comics (Top Cow Prod.): Aug, 1998 - No. 14, May, 2002 ($2.50)

Preview 12.00
0-Wizard supplement 7.00
0-($6.95) DF Alternate 7.00
1/2 (Wizard) origin of Cannon; Turner-a 6.00
1/2 (3/03, $2.99) origin of Cannon 3.00
1-Turner-s/a; three covers; alternate story pages 6.00
1-Wizard World Ed. 9.00
2-14: 12-14-Witchblade app. 13,14-Tomb Raider app. 3.00
9-Green foil-c edition 15.00
9,12-Holofoil editions 18.00
12,13-DFE alternate-c 6.00
13,14-DFE Gold edition 8.00
14-DFE Blue 15.00
... Collected Edition 1 (3/99, $5.95) r/Preview & all three #1's 6.00
... Collected Edition 2-4 (3-12/99, $5.95) 2-r/#2,3. 3-r/#4,5. 4-r/#6,7 6.00
... Collected Edition 5 (4/00, $5.95) 5-r/#8,9 6.00
... Swimsuit Special (5/99, $2.95) Pin-ups by various 3.00
... Swimsuit Special 2000 (12/00, $2.95) Pin-ups by various; Turner-c 3.00
Michael Turner's Fathom HC ('01, $39.95) r/#1-9, black-c w/silver foil 40.00
Michael Turner's Fathom SC ('01, $24.95) r/#1-9, new Turner-c 25.00
Michael Turner's Fathom The Definitive Edition ('08, $49.95) r/Preview, #0,1/2,1-14, Swimsuit Special 1999 & 2000; cover gallery; foreword by Geoff Johns 50.00

FATHOM (MICHAEL TURNER'S...) (Volume 2)
Aspen MLT, Inc.: No. 0, Apr, 2005 - No. 11, Dec, 2006 ($2.50/$2.99)

0-($2.50) Turnbull-a/Turner-c 2.50
1-11-($2.99) 1-Five covers. 2-Two covers. 4-Six covers 3.00
... Beginnings (2005, $1.99) Two covers; Turnbull-a 2.50
...: Killian's Vessel 1 (7/07, $2.99) 3 covers; Odagawa-a 3.00
... Prelude (6/05, $2.99) Seven covers; Garza-a 3.00

FATHOM (MICHAEL TURNER'S...) (Volume 3)
Aspen MLT, Inc.: No. 0, Jun, 2008 - Present ($2.50/$2.99)

0-($2.50) Garza-a/c 2.50
1-9-($2.99) Garza-a; multiple covers on each 3.00

FATHOM: CANNON HAWKE (MICHAEL TURNER'S...)
Aspen MLT, Inc.: Nov, 2005 - No. 5, Feb, 2006 ($2.99)

1-5-To-a/Turner-c 3.00
... Prelude (11/05, $2.50) Turner-c 2.50

FATHOM: DAWN OF WAR (MICHAEL TURNER'S...)
Aspen MLT, Inc.: Oct, 2004 - No. 3, Dec, 2004 ($2.99, limited series)

0-Caldwell-a 2.50
1-3-Caldwell-a 3.00
...: Cannon Hawke #0 ('04, $2.50) Turner-c 2.50
... The Complete Saga Vol. 1 (2005, $9.99) r/series with cover gallery 10.00

FATHOM: KIANI (MICHAEL TURNER'S...)
Aspen MLT, Inc.: No. 0, Feb, 2007 - No. 4, Dec, 2007 ($2.99, limited series)

0-4-Marcus To-a. 1-Six covers 3.00

FATHOM: KILLIAN'S TIDE
Image Comics (Top Cow Prod.): Apr, 2001 - No. 4, Nov, 2001 ($2.95)

1-4-Caldwell-a(p); two covers by Caldwell and Turner. 2-Flip-book preview of Universe 3.00
1-DFE Blue, 1-Holographic logo 12.00
4-Foil-c 12.00

FATIMA...CHALLENGE TO THE WORLD
Catechetical Guild: 1951, 36 pgs. (15¢)

nn (not same as 'Challenge to the World') 5 10 15 24 30 35

FATMAN, THE HUMAN FLYING SAUCER
Lightning Comics(Milson Publ. Co.): April, 1967 - No. 3, Aug-Sept, 1967 (68 pgs.) (Written by Otto Binder)

1-Origin/1st app. Fatman & Tinman by Beck 6 12 18 41 66 90
2-C. C. Beck-a 4 8 12 26 41 55
3-(Scarce)-Beck-a 6 12 18 43 69 95

FAULTLINES
DC Comics (Vertigo): May, 1997 - No. 6, Oct, 1997 ($2.50, limited series)

1-6-Lee Marrs-s/Bill Koeb-a in all 2.50

FAUNTLEROY COMICS (Super Duck Presents...)
Close-Up/Archie Publications: 1950; No. 2, 1951; No. 3, 1952

1-Super Duck-c/stories by Al Fagaly in all 9 18 27 52 69 85
2,3 6 12 18 31 38 45

FAUST
Northstar Publishing/Rebel Studios #7 on: 1989 - No 11, 1997 ($2.00/$2.25, B&W, mature themes)

1-Decapitation-c; Tim Vigil-c/a in all 3 6 9 14 19 24
1-2nd - 4th printings 3.00
2 2 4 6 8 10 12
2-2nd & 3rd printings, 3,5-2nd printing 3.00
3 1 3 4 6 8 10
4-10: 7-Begin Rebel Studios series 5.00
11-($2.25) 3.00

FAWCETT MOTION PICTURE COMICS (See Motion Picture Comics)

FAWCETT MOVIE COMIC
Fawcett Publications: 1949 - No. 20, Dec, 1952 (All photo-c)

nn- "Dakota Lil"; George Montgomery & Rod Cameron (1949) 26 52 78 152 244 335
nn- "Copper Canyon"; Ray Milland & Hedy Lamarr (1950) 19 38 57 112 176 240
nn- "Destination Moon" (1950) 70 140 210 441 746 1050
nn- "Montana"; Errol Flynn & Alexis Smith (1950) 19 38 57 112 176 240
nn- "Pioneer Marshal"; Monte Hale (1950) 19 38 57 112 176 240
nn- "Powder River Rustlers"; Rocky Lane (1950) 27 54 81 158 254 350
nn- "Singing Guns"; Vaughn Monroe, Ella Raines & Walter Brennan (1950) 17 34 51 98 154 210
7- "Gunmen of Abilene"; Rocky Lane; Bob Powell-a (1950) 20 40 60 118 189 260
8- "King of the Bullwhip"; Lash LaRue; Bob Powell-a (1950) 30 60 90 174 280 385
9- "The Old Frontier"; Monte Hale; Bob Powell-a (2/51; mis-dated 2/50) 20 40 60 115 183 250
10- "The Missourians"; Monte Hale (4/51) 20 40 60 115 183 250
11- "The Thundering Trail"; Lash LaRue (6/51) 25 50 75 145 233 320
12- "Rustlers on Horseback"; Rocky Lane (8/51) 20 40 60 115 183 250
13- "Warpath"; Edmond O'Brien & Forrest Tucker (10/51) 15 30 45 88 137 185
14- "Last Outpost"; Ronald Reagan (12/51) 33 66 99 192 309 425
15-(Scarce)- "The Man From Planet X"; Robert Clark; Schaffenberger-a (2/52) 245 490 735 1568 2684 3800

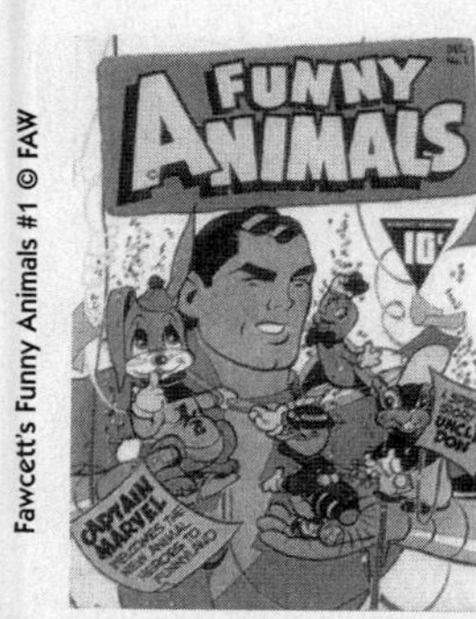

Fawcett's Funny Animals #1 © FAW

The F.B.I. #1 © DELL

Feature Comics #38 © QUA

	GD 2.0	VG 4.0	FN 6.0	VF 8.0	VF/NM 9.0	NM- 9.2
16- "10 Tall Men"; Burt Lancaster	14	28	42	78	112	145
17- "Rose of Cimarron"; Jack Buetel & Mala Powers	11	22	33	62	86	110
18- "The Brigand"; Anthony Dexter & Anthony Quinn; Schaffenberger-a	11	22	33	62	86	110
19- "Carbine Williams"; James Stewart; Costanza-a; James Stewart photo-c	12	24	36	69	97	125
20- "Ivanhoe"; Robert Taylor & Liz Taylor photo-c	18	36	54	105	165	225

FAWCETT'S FUNNY ANIMALS (No. 1-26, 80-on titled "Funny Animals"; becomes Li'l Tomboy No. 92 on?)
Fawcett Publications/Charlton Comics No. 84 on: 12/42 - #79, 4/53; #80, 6/53 - #83, 12?/53; #84, 4/54 - #91, 2/56

	GD	VG	FN	VF	VF/NM	NM-
1-Capt. Marvel on cover; intro. Hoppy The Captain Marvel Bunny, cloned from Capt. Marvel; Billy the Kid & Willie the Worm begin	58	116	174	371	636	900
2-Xmas-c	36	72	108	211	343	475
3-5: 3(2/43)-Spirit of '43-c	25	50	75	150	245	340
6,7,9,10	15	30	45	88	137	185
8-Flag-c	16	32	48	92	144	195
11-20: 14-Cover is a 1944 calendar	12	24	36	69	97	125
21-40: 25-Xmas-c. 26-St. Valentine's Day-c	10	20	30	54	72	90
41-86,90,91	9	18	27	47	61	75
87-89(10-54-2/55)-Merry Mailman ish (TV/Radio)-part photo-c	10	20	30	54	72	90

NOTE: *Marvel Bunny in all issues to at least No. 68 (not in 49-54).*

FAZE ONE FAZERS
AC Comics: 1986 - No. 4, Sept, 1986 (Limited series)

	GD	VG	FN	VF	VF/NM	NM-
1-4						2.50

F.B.I., THE
Dell Publishing Co.: Apr-June, 1965

	GD	VG	FN	VF	VF/NM	NM-
1-Sinnott-a	3	6	9	18	27	35

F.B.I. STORY, THE (Movie)
Dell Publishing Co.: No. 1069, Jan-Mar, 1960

	GD	VG	FN	VF	VF/NM	NM-
Four Color 1069-Toth-a; James Stewart photo-c	9	18	27	63	107	150

FEAR (Adventure into...)
Marvel Comics Group: Nov, 1970 - No. 31, Dec, 1975

	GD	VG	FN	VF	VF/NM	NM-
1-Fantasy & Sci-Fi-r in early issues; 68 pg. Giant size; Kirby-a(r)	6	12	18	37	59	80
2-6: 2-4-(68 pgs.). 5,6-(52 pgs.) Kirby-a(r)	4	8	12	22	34	45
7-9-Kirby-a(r)	3	6	9	14	20	25
10-Man-Thing begins (10/72, 4th app.), ends #19; see Savage Tales #1 for 1st app.; 1st solo series; Chaykin/Morrow-c/a;	5	10	15	30	48	65
11,12: 11-N. Adams-c. 12-Starlin/Buckler-a	3	6	9	14	20	26
13,14,16-18: 17-Origin/1st app. Wundarr	2	4	6	13	18	22
15-1st full-length Man-Thing story (8/73)	3	6	9	16	22	28
19-Intro. Howard the Duck; Val Mayerik-a (12/73)	5	10	15	30	48	65
20-Morbius, the Living Vampire begins, ends #31; has history recap of Morbius with X-Men & Spider-Man	5	10	15	30	48	65
21-23,25	2	4	6	13	18	22
24-Blade-c/sty	3	6	9	20	30	40
26-31	2	4	6	10	14	18

NOTE: ***Bolle** a-13i. **Brunner** c-15-17. **Buckler** a-11p, 12i. **Chaykin** a-10i. **Colan** a-23r. **Craig** a-10p. **Ditko** a-6-8r. **Evans** a-30. **Everett** a-9, 10i, 21r. **Gulacy** a-20p. **Heath** a-12r. **Heck** a-8r, 13r. **Gil Kane** a-21p; c(p)-20, 21, 23-28, 31. **Kirby** a-1-9r. **Maneely** a-24r. **Mooney** a-11i, 26r. **Morrow** a-11i. **Paul Reinman** a-14r. **Robbins** a(p)-25-27, 31. **Russell** a-23p, 24p. **Severin** c-8. **Starlin** c-12p.*

FEAR AGENT
Image Comics.: Oct, 2005 - Present ($2.99)

	NM-
1-11: 1-Remender-s/Moore-a. 5-Opeña-a begins. 11-Francavilla-a	3.00
... The Last Goodbye 1-4 (6/07 - No. 4, 9/07) (#12-15)	3.00
Tales of the Fear Agent: Twelve Steps in One (#16), 17-26	3.00
... Vol 1.: Re-Ignition TPB (2006, $9.99) r/#1-4	10.00
... Vol 2.: My War TPB (Dark Horse Books, 2007, $14.95) r/#5-10; Opeña sketch pages	15.00

FEARBOOK
Eclipse Comics: April, 1986 ($1.75, one-shot, mature)

	NM-
1-Scholastic Mag- r; Bissette-a	2.50

FEAR EFFECT (Based on the video game)
Image Comics (Top Cow): May, 2000; March, 2001 ($2.95)

	NM-
Retro Helix 1 (3/01), Special 1 (5/00)	3.00

FEAR IN THE NIGHT (See Complete Mystery No. 3)

FEARLESS FAGAN
Dell Publishing Co.: No. 441, Dec, 1952 (one-shot)

	GD 2.0	VG 4.0	FN 6.0	VF 8.0	VF/NM 9.0	NM- 9.2
Four Color 441	4	8	12	24	37	50

FEATURE BOOK (Dell) (See Large Feature Comic)

FEATURE BOOKS (Newspaper-r, early issues)
David McKay Publications: May, 1937 - No. 57, 1948 (B&W)
(Full color, 68 pgs. begin #26 on)

Note: See individual alphabetical listings for prices

- nn-Popeye & the Jeep (#1, 100 pgs.); reprinted as Feature Books #3(Very Rare; only 3 known copies, 1-VF, 2-in low grade)
- nn-Dick Tracy (#1)-Reprinted as Feature Book #4 (100 pgs.) & in part as 4-Color #1 (Rare, less than 10 known copies)

NOTE: *Above books were advertised together with different covers from Feat. Books #3 & 4.*

- 1-King of the Royal Mtd. (#1)
- 3-Popeye (7/37) by Segar;
- 4-Dick Tracy (8/37)-Same as nn issue but a new cover added
- 6-Dick Tracy (10/37)
- 8-Secret Agent X-9 (12/37) -Not by Raymond
- 9-Dick Tracy (1/38)
- 11-Little Annie Rooney (#1, 3/38)
- 13-Inspector Wade (5/38)
- 15-Barney Baxter (#1) (7/38)
- 17-Gangbusters (#1, 9/38) (1st app.)
- 20-Phantom (#1, 12/38)
- 22-Phantom
- 24-Lone Ranger (1941)
- 26-Prince Valiant (1941)-Hal Foster -c/a; newspaper strips reprinted, pgs. 1-28,30-63; color & 68 pg. issues begin; Foster cover is only original comic book artwork by him
- 36('43),38,40('44),42,43, 45,47-Blondie
- 39-Phantom
- 46-Mandrake in the Fire World-(58 pgs.)
- 48-Maltese Falcon by Dashiell Hammett('46)
- 51,54-Rip Kirby; Raymond-c/s; origin-#51
- 53,56,57-Phantom
- 2-Popeye (6/37) by Segar same as nn issue but a new cover added
- 5-Popeye (9/37) by Segar
- 7-Little Orphan Annie (#1, 11/37) (Rare)-Reprints strips from 12/31/34 to 7/17/35
- 10-Popeye (2/38)
- 12-Blondie (#1) (4/38) (Rare)
- 14-Popeye (6/38) by Segar
- 16-Red Eagle (8/38)
- 18,19-Mandrake
- 21-Lone Ranger
- 23-Mandrake
- 25-Flash Gordon (#1)-Reprints not by Raymond
- 27-29,31,34-Blondie
- 30-Katzenjammer Kids (#1, 1942)
- 32,35,41,44-Katzenjammer Kids
- 33(nn)-Romance of Flying; World War II photos
- 37-Katzenjammer Kids; has photo & biog. of Harold H. Knerr (1883-1949) who took over strip from Rudolph Dirks in 1914
- 49,50-Perry Mason; based on Gardner novels
- 52,55-Mandrake

NOTE: *All Feature Books through #25 are over-sized 8-1/2x11-3/8" comics with color covers and black and white interiors. The covers are rough, heavy stock. The page counts, including covers, are as follows: nn, #3, 4-100 pgs.; #1, 2-52 pgs.; #5-25 are all 76 pgs. #33 was found in bound set from publisher. Reprints from 1980s exist.*

FEATURE COMICS (Formerly Feature Funnies)
Quality Comics Group: No. 21, June, 1939 - No. 144, May, 1950

	GD	VG	FN	VF	VF/NM	NM-
21-The Clock, Jane Arden & Mickey Finn continue from Feature Funnies	66	132	198	363	582	800
22-26: 23-Charlie Chan begins (8/39, 1st app.)	46	92	138	253	402	550
26-(nn, nd)-Cover in one color, (10¢, 36 pgs.; issue No. blanked out. Two variations exist, each contain half of the regular #26)	46	92	138	253	402	550
27-(Rare)-Origin/1st app. Doll Man by Eisner (scripts) & Lou Fine (art); Doll Man begins, ends #139	497	994	1491	3628	6414	9200
28-2nd app. Doll Man by Lou Fine	194	388	582	1242	2121	3000
29	103	206	309	659	1130	1600
30-1st Doll Man-c	161	322	483	1030	1765	2500
31-Last Clock & Charlie Chan issue (4/40); Charlie Chan moves to Big Shot #1 following month (5/40)	71	142	213	454	777	1100
32,34,36: Dollman covers. 32-Rusty Ryan & Samar begin. 34-Captain Fortune app.	66	132	198	419	722	1025
33,35,37: 37-Last Fine Doll Man	47	94	141	296	498	700

NOTE: *A 15¢ Canadian version of Feature Comics #37, made in the US, exists.*

	GD	VG	FN	VF	VF/NM	NM-
38,40-Dollman covers. 38-Origin the Ace of Space. 40-Bruce Blackburn in costume	53	106	159	334	567	800
39,41: 39-Origin The Destroying Demon, ends #40; X-Mas-c.	39	78	117	240	395	550
42,46,48,50-Dollman covers. 42-USA, the Spirit of Old Glory begins. 46-Intro. Boyville Brigadiers in Rusty Ryan. 48-USA ends	40	80	120	246	411	575
43,45,47,49: 47-Fargo Kid begins	29	58	87	172	281	390
44-Doll Man by Crandall begins, ends #63; Crandall-a(2)	52	104	156	322	549	775
51,53,55,57,59: 57-Spider Widow begins	22	44	66	128	209	290
52,54,56,58,60-Dollman covers. 56-Marijuana story in Swing Sisson strip. 60-Raven begins, ends #71	31	62	93	186	303	420

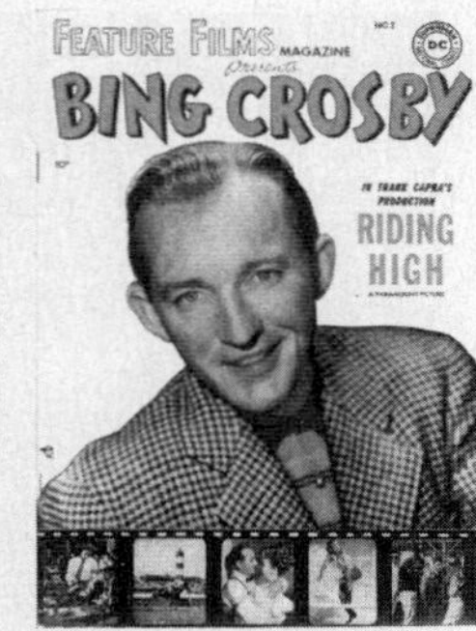

Feature Films #2 © DC

Felicia Hardy: The Black Cat #3 © MAR

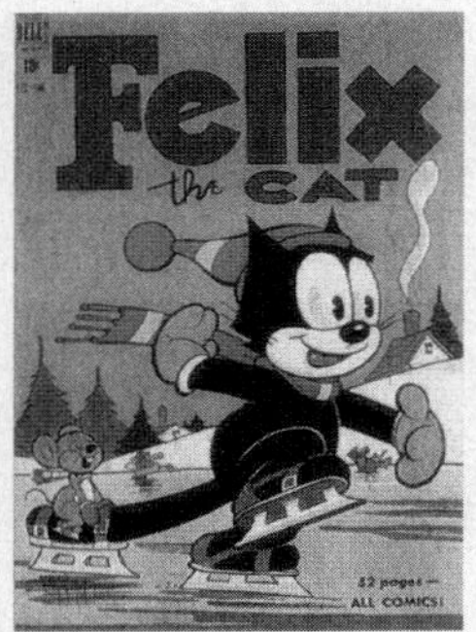

Felix the Cat #18 © KING

	GD 2.0	VG 4.0	FN 6.0	VF 8.0	VF/NM 9.0	NM- 9.2
61,63,65,67	20	40	60	114	182	250
62,64,66,68-Dollman covers. 68-(5/43)	27	54	81	160	263	365
69,71-Phantom Lady x-over in Spider Widow	22	44	66	128	209	290
70-Dollman-c; Phantom Lady x-over	30	60	90	177	289	400
72,74,77-80,100-Dollman covers. 72-Spider Widow ends	22	44	66	128	209	290
73,75,76	16	32	48	94	147	200
81-99-All Dollman covers	16	32	48	94	147	200
101-144: 139-Last Doll Man & last Doll Man cover. 140-Intro. Stuntman Stetson (Stuntman Stetson c-140-144)	14	28	42	82	121	160

NOTE: ***Celardo** a-37-43. **Crandall** a-44-60, 62, 63-on(most). **Gustavson** a-(Rusty Ryan)- 32-134. **Powell** a-34, 64-73. The Clock c-25, 28, 29. Doll Man c-30, 32, 34, 36, 38, 40, 42, 44, 46, 48, 50, 52, 54, 56, 58, 60, 62, 64, 66, 68, 70, 72, 74, 77-139. Joe Palooka c-21, 24, 27.*

FEATURE FILMS
National Periodical Publ.: Mar-Apr, 1950 - No. 4, Sept-Oct, 1950 (All photo-c)

	GD	VG	FN	VF	VF/NM	NM-
1- "Captain China" with John Payne, Gail Russell, Lon Chaney & Edgar Bergen	66	132	198	416	701	985
2- "Riding High" with Bing Crosby	69	138	207	435	735	1035
3- "The Eagle & the Hawk" with John Payne, Rhonda Fleming & D. O'Keefe	66	132	198	416	701	985
4- "Fancy Pants"; Bob Hope & Lucille Ball	72	144	216	454	770	1085

FEATURE FUNNIES (Feature Comics No. 21 on)
Harry 'A' Chesler: Oct, 1937 - No. 20, May, 1939

	GD	VG	FN	VF	VF/NM	NM-
1(V9#1-indicia)-Joe Palooka, Mickey Finn (1st app.), The Bungles, Jane Arden, Dixie Dugan (1st app.), Big Top, Ned Brant, Strange As It Seems, & Off the Record strip reprints begin	322	644	966	1770	2635	3500
2-The Hawk app. (11/37); Goldberg-c	150	300	450	825	1213	1600
3-Hawks of Seas begins by Eisner, ends #12; The Clock begins; Christmas-c	117	234	351	644	947	1250
4,5	86	172	258	473	699	925
6-12: 11-Archie O'Toole by Bud Thomas begins, ends #22	67	134	201	369	542	715
13-Espionage, Starring Black X begins by Eisner, ends #20	71	142	213	391	578	765
14-20	50	100	150	275	408	540

NOTE: *Joe Palooka covers 1, 6, 9, 12, 15, 18.*

FEATURE PRESENTATION, A (Feature Presentations Magazine #6)
(Formerly Women in Love) (Also see Startling Terror Tales #11)
Fox Features Syndicate: No. 5, April, 1950

	GD	VG	FN	VF	VF/NM	NM-
5(#1)-Black Tarantula	45	90	135	284	480	675

FEATURE PRESENTATIONS MAGAZINE (Formerly A Feature Presentation #5; becomes Feature Stories Magazine #3 on)
Fox Features Syndicate: No. 6, July, 1950

	GD	VG	FN	VF	VF/NM	NM-
6(#2)-Moby Dick; Wood-c	32	64	96	188	307	425

FEATURE STORIES MAGAZINE (Formerly Feature Presentations Mag. #6)
Fox Features Syndicate: No. 3, Aug, 1950

	GD	VG	FN	VF	VF/NM	NM-
3-Jungle Lil, Zegra stories; bondage-c	36	72	108	215	350	485

FEDERAL MEN COMICS
DC Comics: 1936

nn-Ashcan comic, not distributed to newsstands, only for in house use (no known sales)

FEDERAL MEN COMICS (See Adventure Comics #32, The Comics Magazine, New Adventure Comics, New Book of Comics, New Comics & Star Spangled Comics #91)
Gerard Publ. Co.: No. 2, 1945 (DC reprints from 1930's)

	GD	VG	FN	VF	VF/NM	NM-
2-Siegel/Shuster-a; cover redrawn from Det. #9	38	76	114	222	356	490

FELICIA HARDY: THE BLACK CAT
Marvel Comics: July, 1994 - No. 4, Oct, 1994 ($1.50, limited series)

1-4: 1,4-Spider-Man app. 2.50

FELIX'S NEPHEWS INKY & DINKY
Harvey Publications: Sept, 1957 - No. 7, Oct, 1958

	GD	VG	FN	VF	VF/NM	NM-
1-Cover shows Inky's left eye with 2 pupils	10	20	30	58	79	100
2-7	7	14	21	37	46	55

NOTE: ***Messmer** art in 1-6. **Oriolo** a-1-7.*

FELIX THE CAT (See Cat Tales 3-D, The Funnies, March of Comics #24,36,51, New Funnies & Popular Comics)
Dell Publ. No. 1-19/Toby No. 20-61/Harvey No. 62-118/Dell No. 1-12:
1943 - No. 118, Nov, 1961; Sept-Nov, 1962 - No. 12, July-Sept, 1965

	GD	VG	FN	VF	VF/NM	NM-
Four Color 15	74	148	222	629	1240	1850
Four Color 46('44)	40	80	120	314	607	900
Four Color 77('45)	38	76	114	294	567	840
Four Color 119('46)-All new stories begin	32	64	96	246	478	710
Four Color 135('46)	23	42	69	168	324	475
Four Color 162(9/47)	17	34	51	122	236	350
1(2-3/48)(Dell)	26	52	78	190	365	540
2	13	26	39	93	172	250
3-5	10	20	30	73	129	185
6-19(2-3/51-Dell)	8	16	24	58	97	135
20-30,32,33,36,38-61(6/55)-All Messmer issues.(Toby): 28-(2/52)-Some copies have #29 on cover, #28 on inside (Rare in high grade)	16	32	48	112	214	315
31,34,35-No Messmer-a; Messmer-c only 31,34	8	16	24	58	97	135
37-(100 pgs., 25 ¢, 1/15/53, X-Mas-c, Toby; daily & Sunday-r (rare)	38	76	114	294	567	840
62(8/55)-80,100 (Harvey)	4	8	12	28	44	60
81-99	4	8	12	24	37	50
101-118(11/61): 101-117-Reprints. 118-All new-a	3	6	9	18	27	35
12-269-211(#1, 9-11/62)(Dell)-No Messmer	5	10	15	30	48	65
2-12(7-9/65)(Dell, TV)-No Messmer	4	8	12	24	37	50
3-D Comic Book 1(1953-One Shot, 25¢)-w/glasses	22	44	66	157	304	450
Summer Annual nn ('53, 25¢, 100 pgs., Toby)-Daily & Sunday-r	31	62	93	236	456	675
Winter Annual 2 ('54, 25¢, 100 pgs., Toby)-Daily & Sunday-r	30	60	90	218	422	625

(Special note: Despite the covers on Toby 37 and the Summer Annual above proclaiming "all new stories," they were actually reformatted newspaper strips)

NOTE: ***Otto Messmer** went to work for Universal Film as an animator in 1915 and then worked for the Pat Sullivan animation studio in 1916. He created a black cat in the cartoon short, Feline Follies in 1919 that became known as Felix in the early 1920s. The Felix Sunday strip began Aug. 14, 1923 and continued until Sept. 19, 1943 whjen **Messmer** took the character to Dell (Western Publishing) and began doing Felix comic books, first adapting strips to the comic format. The first all new Felix comic was Four Color #119 in 1946 (#4 in the Dell run). The daily Felix was begun on May 9, 1927 by another artist, but by the following year, **Messmer** did it too. King Features took the daily away from **Messmer** in 1954 and he began to do some of his most dynamic art for Toby Press. The daily was continued by **Joe Oriolo** who drew it until it was discontinued Jan. 9, 1967. **Oriolo** was **Messmer's** assistant for many years and inked some of **Messmer's** pencils through the Toby run, as well as doing some of the stories by himself. Though **Messmer** continued to work for Harvey, his contirubitons were limited, and no all **Messmer** stories appeared after the Toby run until some early Toby reprints were published in the 1990s Harvey revival of the title. 4-Color No. 15, 46, 77 and the Toby Annuals are all daily or Sunday newspaper reprints from the 1930's-1940's drawn by **Otto Messmer**. #101-r/#64; 102-r/#65; 103-r/#67; 104-117-r/#68-81. **Messmer**-a in all Dell/Toby/Harvey issues except #31, 34, 35, 97, 98, 100, 118. **Oriolo** a-20, 31-on.*

FELIX THE CAT (Also see The Nine Lives of...)
Harvey Comics/Gladstone: Sept, 1991 - No. 7, Jan, 1993 ($1.25/$1.50, bi-monthly)

1: 1950s-r/Toby issues by Messmer begins. 1-Inky and Dinky back-up story (produced by Gladstone) 4.00
2-7, Big Book, V2#1 (9/92, $1.95, 52 pgs.) 3.00

FELIX THE CAT AND FRIENDS
Felix Comics: 1992 - No. 5, 1993 ($1.95)

1-5: 1-Contains Felix trading cards 3.00

FELIX THE CAT & HIS FRIENDS (Pat Sullivan's...)
Toby Press: Dec, 1953 - No. 3, 1954 (Indicia title for #2&3 as listed)

	GD	VG	FN	VF	VF/NM	NM-
1 (Indicia title, "Felix and His Friends," #1 only)	29	58	87	170	278	385
2-3	18	36	54	105	165	225

FELIX THE CAT DIGEST MAGAZINE
Harvey Comics: July, 1992 ($1.75, digest-size, 98 pgs.)

1-Felix, Richie Rich stories 6.00

FELIX THE CAT KEEPS ON WALKIN'
Hamilton Comics: 1991 ($15.95, 8-1/2"x11", 132 pgs.)

nn-Reprints 15 Toby Press Felix the Cat and Felix and His Friends stories in new color 16.00

FELL
Image Comics: Sept, 2005 - Present ($1.99)

1-9-Warren Ellis-s/Ben Templesmith-a 2.50
..., Vol. 1: Feral City TPB (2007, $14.99) r/#1-8 15.00

FELON
Image Comics (Minotaur Press): Nov, 2001 - No. 4, Apr, 2002 ($2.95, B&W)

1-4-Rucka-s/Clark-a/c 3.00

FEM FANTASTIQUE
AC Comics: Aug, 1988 ($1.95, B&W)

V2#1-By Bill Black; Betty Page pin-up 4.00

FEMFORCE (Also see Untold Origin of the Femforce)
Americomics: Apr, 1985 - No. 109 (1.75-/2.95, B&W #16-56)

	GD	VG	FN	VF	VF/NM	NM-
1-Black-a in most; Nightveil, Ms. Victory begin	1	3	4	6	8	10
2-10						4.00

Femforce #89 © AC Comics

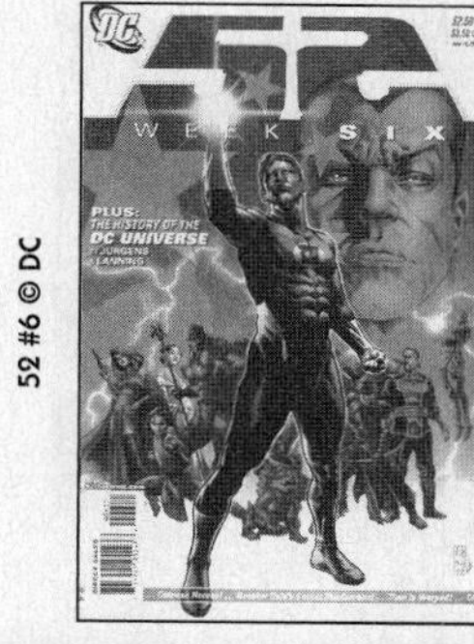

52 #6 © DC

Fight Comics #8 © FH

	GD 2.0	VG 4.0	FN 6.0	VF 8.0	VF/NM 9.0	NM- 9.2

11-43: 25-Origin/1st app. new Ms. Victory. 28-Colt leaves. 29,30-Camilla-r by Mayo from Jungle Comics. 36-(2.95, 52 pgs.) 4.00
44,64: 44-W/mini-comic, Catman & Kitten #0. 64-Re-intro Black Phantom 5.00
45-63,65-99: 50 (2.95, 52 pgs.)-Contains flexi-disc; origin retold; most AC characters app. 51-Photo-c from movie. 57-Begin color issues. 95-Photo-c 3.00
100-($3.95) 5.00
100-($6.90)-Polybagged 1 2 3 5 6 8
101-109-($4.95) 5.00
Special 1 (Fall, '84)(B&W, 52pgs.)-1st app. Ms. Victory, She-Cat, Blue Bulleteer, Rio Rita & Lady Luger 4.00
Bad Girl Backlash-(12/95, $5.00) 5.00
Frightbook 1 ('92, $2.95, B&W)-Halloween special, In the House of Horror 1 ('89, 2.50, B&W), Night of the Demon 1 ('90, 2.75, B&W), Out of the Asylum Special 1 ('87, B&W, $1.95), Pin-Up Portfolio 3.50
Pin-Up Portfolio (5 issues) 4.00

FEMFORCE UP CLOSE
AC Comics: Apr, 1992 - No. 11, 1995 ($2.75, quarterly)
1-11: 1-Stars Nightveil; inside f/c photo from Femforce movie. 2-Stars Stardust. 3-Stars Dragonfly. 4-Stars She-Cat 3.50

FERDINAND THE BULL (See Mickey Mouse Magazine V4#3)
Dell Publishing Co.: 1938 (10¢, large size, some color w/rest B&W)
nn 19 38 57 111 176 240

FERRET
Malibu Comics: Sept, 1992; May, 1993 - No. 10, Feb, 1994 ($1.95)
1-(1992, one-shot) 3.00
1-10: 1-Die-cut-c. 2-4-Collector's Ed. w/poster. 5-Polybagged w/Skycap 2.50
2-4-($1.95)-Newsstand Edition w/different-c 2.50

FERRYMAN
DC Comics (WildStorm): Early Dec, 2008 - No. 5, Mar, 2009 ($3.50)
1-5-Andreyko-s/Wayshak-a 3.50

F5
Image Comics/Dark Horse: Jan, 2000 - No. 4, Oct, 2000 ($2.50/$2.95)
Preview (1/00, $2.50) Character bios and b&w pages; Daniel-s/a 2.50
1-($2.95, 48 pages) Tony Daniel-s/a 3.00
1-($20.00) Variant bikini-c 20.00
2-4-($2.50) 2.50
F5 Origin (Dark Horse Comics, 11/01, $2.99) w/cove gallery & sketches 3.00

FIBBER McGEE & MOLLY (Radio)(Also see A-1 Comics)
Magazine Enterprises: No. 25, 1949 (one-shot)
A-1 25 11 22 33 64 90 115

FICTION ILLUSTRATED
Byron Preiss Visual Publ./Pyramid: No. 1, Jan, 1975 - No. 4, Jan, 1977 ($1.00, #1,2 are digest size, 132 pgs.; #3,4 are graphic novels for mail order and specialty bookstores only)
1,2: 1-Schlomo Raven; Sutton-a. 2-Starfawn; Stephen Fabian-a. 2 4 6 13 18 22
3-($1.00-c, 4 3/4 x 6 1/2" digest size) Chandler; new Steranko-a 3 6 9 14 20 26
3-($4.95-c, 8 1/2 x 11" graphic novel; low print) same contents and indicia, but "Chandler" is the cover feature title 5 10 15 34 55 75
4-($4.95-c, 8 1/2 x 11" graphic novel; low print) Son of Sherlock Holmes; Reese-a 4 8 12 28 44 60

FIERCE
Dark Horse Comics (Rocket Comics): July, 2004 - No. 4, Dec, 2004 ($2.99, limited series)
1-4-Jeremy Love-s/Robert Love-a 3.00

55 DAYS AT PEKING (See Movie Comics)

52 (Leads into Countdown series)
DC Comics: Week One, July, 2006 - Week Fifty-Two, Jul, 2007 ($2.50, weekly series)
1-Chronicles the year after Infinite Crisis; Johns, Morrison, Rucka & Waid-s; JG Jones-c 4.00
2-10: 2-History of the DC Universe back-up thru #11. 7-Intro. Kate Kane. 10-Supernova 3.00
11-Batwoman debut (single panel cameo in #9) 4.00
12-52: 12-Isis gains powers; back-up 2 pg. origins begin. 15-Booster Gold killed. 17-Lobo returns. 30-Batman-c/Robin & Nightwing app. 37-Booster Gold returns. 38-The Question dies. 42-Ralph Dibny dies. 44-Isis dies. 48-Renee becomes The Question. 50-World War III. 51-Mister Mind evolves. 52-The Multiverse is re-formed; wraparound-c 2.50
...: The Companion TPB (2007, $19.99) r/solo stories of series' prominent characters 20.00
...: Volume One TPB (2007, $19.99) r/#1-13; sample of page development; cover gallery 20.00
...: Volume Two TPB (2007, $19.99) r/#14-26; creator notes and sketches; cover gallery 20.00
...: Volume Three TPB (2007, $19.99) r/#27-39; notes and sketches; cover gallery 20.00
...: Volume Four TPB (2007, $19.99) r/#40-52; creator commentary; cover gallery 20.00

52 AFTERMATH: THE FOUR HORSEMEN (Takes place during 52 Week Fifty)
DC Comics: Oct, 2007 - No. 6, Mar, 2008 ($2.99, limited series)
1-6-Giffen-s/Olliffe-a; Superman, Batman & Wonder Woman app. 2-4,6-Van Sciver-c 3.00
TPB (2008, $19.99) r/#1-6 20.00

52/WWIII (Takes place during 52 Week Fifty)
DC Comics: Part One, Jun, 2007 - Part Four, Jun, 2007 ($2.50, 4 issues came out same day)
Part One - Part Four: Van Sciver-c; heroes vs. Black Adam. 3-Terra dies 2.50
DC: World War III TPB (2007, $17.99) r/Part One - Four and 52 Week 50 18.00

FIGHT AGAINST CRIME (Fight Against the Guilty #22, 23)
Story Comics: May, 1951 - No. 21, Sept, 1954
1-True crime stories #1-4 41 82 123 251 418 585
2 22 44 66 128 209 290
3,5: 5-Frazetta-a, 1 pg.; content change to horror & suspense 20 40 60 114 182 250
4-Drug story "Hopped Up Killers" 20 40 60 118 192 265
6,7: 6-Used in **POP**, pgs. 83,84 18 36 54 105 165 225
8-Last crime format issue 17 34 51 98 154 210

NOTE: *No. 9-21 contain violent, gruesome stories with blood, dismemberment, decapitation, E.C. style plot twists and several E.C. swipes. Bondage c-4, 6, 18, 19.*

9-11,13 39 78 117 240 395 550
12-Morphine drug story "The Big Dope" 41 82 123 256 428 600
14-Tothish art by Ross Andru; electrocution-c 41 82 123 251 418 585
15-B&W & color illos in **POP** 39 78 117 240 395 550
16-E.C. story swipe/Haunt of Fear #19; Tothish-a by Ross Andru; bondage-c 41 82 123 256 428 600
17-Wildey E.C. swipe/Shock SuspenStories #9; knife through neck-c (1/54) 42 84 126 265 445 625
18,19: 19-Bondage/torture-c 39 78 117 234 385 535
20-Decapitation cover; contains hanging, ax murder, blood & violence 81 162 243 518 884 1250
21-E.C. swipe 34 68 102 199 325 450

NOTE: ***Cameron** a-4, 5, 8. **Hollingsworth** a-3-7, 9, 10, 13. **Wildey** a-6, 15, 16.*

FIGHT AGAINST THE GUILTY (Formerly Fight Against Crime)
Story Comics: No. 22, Dec, 1954 - No. 23, Mar, 1955
22-Tothish-a by Ross Andru; Ditko-a; E.C. story swipe; electrocution-c (Last pre-code) 34 68 102 199 325 450
23-Hollingsworth-a 22 44 66 128 209 290

FIGHT COMICS
Fiction House Magazines: Jan, 1940 - No. 83, 11/52; No. 84, Wint, 1952-53; No. 85, Spring, 1953; No. 86, Summer, 1954
1-Origin Spy Fighter, Starring Saber; Jack Dempsey life story; Shark Brodie & Chip Collins begin; Fine-c; Eisner-a 337 674 1011 2359 4130 5900
2-Joe Louis life story; Fine/Eisner-c 123 246 369 787 1344 1900
3-Rip Regan, the Power Man begins (3/40) 110 220 330 704 1202 1700
4,5: 4-Fine-c 66 132 198 419 722 1025
6-10: 6,7-Powell-c 49 98 147 309 522 735
11-14: Rip Regan ends 46 92 138 290 488 685
15-1st app. Super American plus-c (10/41) 59 118 177 375 648 920
16-Captain Fight begins (12/41); Spy Fighter ends 59 118 177 375 648 920
17,18: Super American ends 46 92 138 290 488 685
19-Captain Fight ends; Senorita Rio begins (6/42, origin & 1st app.); Rip Carson, Chute Trooper begins 48 96 144 302 514 725
20 41 82 123 256 428 600
21-30 39 78 117 231 378 525
31-Classic decapitation-c 97 194 291 621 1061 1500
32-Tiger Girl begins (6/44, 1st app.?) 39 78 117 240 395 550
33-50: 44-Capt. Fight returns. 48-Used in Love and Death by Legman. 49-Jungle-c begin, end #81 31 62 93 186 303 420
51-Origin Tiger Girl; Patsy Pin-Up app. 38 76 114 226 368 510
52-60,62-64-Last Baker issue 22 44 66 132 216 300
61-Origin Tiger Girl retold 23 46 69 138 227 315
65-78: 78-Used in **POP**, pg. 99 19 38 57 111 176 240
79-The Space Rangers app. 20 40 60 114 182 250
80-85: 81-Last jungle-c. 82-85-War-c/stories 16 32 48 94 147 200
86-Two Tigerman stories by Evans-r/Rangers Comics #40,41; Moreira-r/Rangers Comics #45 16 32 48 94 147 200

NOTE: *Bondage covers, Lingerie, headlights panels are common. Captain Fight by **Kamen**-51-66. Kayo Kirby by **Baker**-#43-64, 67(not by Baker). Senorita Rio by **Kamen**-#57-64; by **Grandenetti**-#65, 66. Tiger Girl by **Baker**-#36-60, 62-64; **Eisner** c-1-3, 5, 10, 11. **Kamen** a-54?, 57? **Tuska** a-1, 5, 8, 10, 21, 29, 34. **Whitman** c-73-84. **Zolnerwich** c-16, 17, 22. Power Man c-5, 6, 9. Super American c-15-17. Tiger Girl c-49-81.*

FIGHT FOR LOVE

Fight For Tomorrow #2 © Wood & Cowan

Fighting American #5 © S&K

Fighting Man Annual #1 © AJAX

	GD 2.0	VG 4.0	FN 6.0	VF 8.0	VF/NM 9.0	NM- 9.2

United Features Syndicate: 1952 (no month)

nn-Abbie & Slats newspaper-r	9	18	27	47	61	75

FIGHT FOR TOMORROW
DC Comics (Vertigo): Nov, 2002 - No. 6, Apr, 2003 ($2.50, limited series)

1-6-Denys Cowan-a/Brian Wood-s. 1-Jim Lee-c. 5-Jo Chen-c						2.50
TPB (2008, $14.99) r/#1-6						15.00

FIGHTING AIR FORCE (See United States Fighting Air Force)

FIGHTIN' AIR FORCE (Formerly Sherlock Holmes?; Never Again? War and Attack #54 on)
Charlton Comics: No. 3, Feb, 1956 - No. 53, Feb-Mar, 1966

V1#3	9	18	27	50	65	80
4-10	7	14	21	35	43	50
11(3/58, 68 pgs.)	8	16	24	44	57	70
12 (100 pgs.)-U.S. Nukes Russia	12	24	36	69	97	125
13-30: 13,24-Glanzman-a. 24-Glanzman-c	3	6	9	19	29	38
31-50: 50-American Eagle begins	3	6	9	14	20	26
51-53	2	4	6	13	18	22

FIGHTING AMERICAN
Headline Publ./Prize (Crestwood): Apr-May, 1954 - No. 7, Apr-May, 1955

1-Origin & 1st app. Fighting American & Speedboy (Capt. America & Bucky clones); S&K-c/a(3); 1st super hero satire series	174	348	522	1114	1907	2700
2-S&K-a(3)	81	162	243	518	884	1250
3-5: 3,4-S&K-a(3). 5-S&K-a(2); Kirby/?-a	62	124	186	394	680	965
6-Origin-r (4 pgs.) plus 2 pgs. by S&K	59	118	177	375	643	910
7-Kirby-a	53	106	159	334	567	800

NOTE: ***Simon & Kirby*** *covers on all. 6 is last pre-code issue.*

FIGHTING AMERICAN
Harvey Publications: Oct, 1966 (25¢)

1-Origin Fighting American & Speedboy by S&K-r; S&K-c/a(3); 1 pg. Neal Adams ad	6	12	18	37	59	80

FIGHTING AMERICAN
DC Comics: Feb, 1994 - No. 6, 1994 ($1.50, limited series)

1-6						2.50

FIGHTING AMERICAN (Vol. 3)
Awesome Entertainment: Aug, 1997 - No. 2, Oct, 1997 ($2.50)

Preview-Agent America (pre-lawsuit)	1	2	3	5	6	7
1-Four covers by Liefeld, Churchill, Platt, McGuinness						2.50
1-Platinum Edition, 1-Gold foil Edition						10.00
1-Comic Cavalcade Edition, 2-American Ent. Spice Ed.						4.00
2-Platt-c, 2-Liefeld variant-c						2.50

FIGHTING AMERICAN: DOGS OF WAR
Awesome-Hyperwerks: Sept, 1998 - No. 3, May, 1999 ($2.50)

Limited Convention Special (7/98, B&W) Platt-a						2.50
1-3-Starlin-s/Platt-a/c						2.50

FIGHTING AMERICAN: RULES OF THE GAME
Awesome Entertainment: Nov, 1997 - No. 3, Mar, 1998 ($2.50, lim. series)

1-3: 1-Loeb-s/McGuinness-a/c. 2-Flip book with Swat! preview						2.50
1-Liefeld SPICE variant-c, 1-Dynamic Forces Ed.; McGuinness-c						2.50
1-Liefeld Fighting American & cast variant-c						2.50

FIGHTIN' ARMY (Formerly Soldier and Marine Comics) (See Captain Willy Schultz)
Charlton Comics: No. 16, 1/56 - No. 127, 12/76; No. 128, 9/77 - No. 172, 11/84

16	9	18	27	50	65	80
17-19,21-23,25-30	7	14	21	35	43	50
20-Ditko-a	9	18	27	50	65	80
24 (3/58, 68 pgs.)	8	16	24	42	54	65
31-45	3	6	9	19	28	38
46-60	3	6	9	16	23	30
61-74	3	6	9	14	19	24
75-1st The Lonely War of Willy Schultz	3	6	9	18	27	35
76-80: 76-92-The Lonely War of Willy Schultz. 79-Devil Brigade	3	6	9	14	19	24
81-88,91,93-99: 82,83-Devil Brigade	2	4	6	10	14	18
89,90,92-Ditko-a	3	6	9	14	20	26
100	2	4	6	13	18	22
101-127	2	4	6	8	11	14
128-140	1	2	3	5	7	9
141-165	1	2	3	4	5	7
166-172-Low print run	1	2	3	5	6	8
108(Modern Comics-1977)-Reprint						4.00

NOTE: ***Aparo*** *c-154.* ***Glanzman*** *a-77-88.* ***Montes/Bache*** *a-48, 49, 51, 69, 75, 76, 170r.*

FIGHTING CARAVANS (See Zane Grey 4-Color 632)

FIGHTING DANIEL BOONE
Avon Periodicals: 1953

nn-Kinstler-c/a, 22 pgs.	18	36	54	105	165	225
I.W. Reprint #1-Reprints #1 above; Kinstler-c/a; Lawrence/Alascia-a	3	6	9	14	19	24

FIGHTING DAVY CROCKETT (Formerly Kit Carson)
Avon Periodicals: No. 9, Oct-Nov, 1955

9-Kinstler-c	10	20	30	54	72	90

FIGHTIN' FIVE, THE (Formerly Space War) (Also see The Peacemaker)
Charlton Comics: July, 1964 - No. 41, Jan, 1967; No. 42, Oct, 1981 - No. 49, Dec, 1982

V2#28-Origin/1st app. Fightin' Five; Montes/Bache-a	6	12	18	41	66	90
29-39,41-Montes/Bache-a in all	4	8	12	22	34	45
40-Peacemaker begins (1st app.)	6	12	18	43	69	95
41-Peacemaker (2nd app.)	5	10	15	30	48	65
42-49: Reprints						5.00

FIGHTING FRONTS!
Harvey Publications: Aug, 1952 - No. 5, Jan, 1953

1	10	20	30	54	72	90
2-Extreme violence; Nostrand/Powell-a	11	22	33	60	83	105
3-5: 3-Powell-a	7	14	21	37	46	55

FIGHTING INDIAN STORIES (See Midget Comics)

FIGHTING INDIANS OF THE WILD WEST!
Avon Periodicals: Mar, 1952 - No. 2, Nov, 1952

1-Geronimo, Chief Crazy Horse, Chief Victorio, Black Hawk begin; Larsen-a; McCann-a(2)	17	34	51	98	154	210
2-Kinstler-c & inside-c only; Larsen, McCann-a	12	24	36	69	97	125
100 Pg. Annual (1952, 25¢)-Contains three comics rebound; Geronimo, Chief Crazy Horse, Chief Victorio; Kinstler-c	34	68	102	199	325	450

FIGHTING LEATHERNECKS
Toby Press: Feb, 1952 - No. 6, Dec, 1952

1- "Duke's Diary"; full pg. pin-ups by Sparling	14	28	42	80	115	150
2-5: 2- "Duke's Diary" full pg. pin-ups. 3-5- "Gil's Gals"; full pg. pin-ups	10	20	30	54	72	90
6-(Same as No. 3-5?)	10	20	30	54	72	90

FIGHTING MAN, THE (War)
Ajax/Farrell Publications(Excellent Publ.): May, 1952 - No. 8, July, 1953

1	14	28	42	80	115	150
2	9	18	27	47	61	75
3-8	8	16	24	40	50	60
Annual 1 (1952, 25¢, 100 pgs.)	24	48	72	140	230	320

FIGHTIN' MARINES (Formerly The Texan; also see Approved Comics)
St. John(Approved Comics)/Charlton Comics No. 14 on:
No. 15, 8/51 - No. 12, 3/53; No. 14, 5/55 - No. 132, 11/76; No. 133, 10/77 - No. 176, 9/84 (No #13?) (Korean War #1-3)

15(#1)-Matt Baker c/a "Leatherneck Jack"; slightly large size; Fightin' Texan No. 16 & 17?	43	86	129	271	461	650
2-1st Canteen Kate by Baker; slightly large size; partial Baker-c	52	104	156	322	549	775
3-9,11-Canteen Kate by Baker; Baker c-#2,3,5-11; 4-Partial Baker-c	30	60	90	177	289	400
10-Matt Baker-c	14	28	42	82	121	160
12-No Baker-a; Last St. John issue?	9	18	27	47	61	75
14 (5/55; 1st Charlton issue; formerly?)-Canteen Kate by Baker; all stories reprinted from #2	19	38	57	109	172	235
15-Baker-c	11	22	33	62	86	110
16,18-20-Not Baker-c	7	14	21	35	43	50
17-Canteen Kate by Baker	15	30	45	83	124	165
21-24	6	12	18	31	38	45
25-(68 pgs.)(3/58)-Check-a?	10	20	30	54	72	90
26-(100 pgs.)(8/58)-Check-a(5)	14	28	42	80	115	150
27-50	3	6	9	18	27	35
51-81: 78-Shotgun Harker & the Chicken series begin	3	6	9	16	22	28
82-85: 85-Last 12¢ issue	3	6	9	14	20	25
86-94: 94-Last 15¢ issue	2	4	6	10	14	18

95-100,122: 122-(1975) Pilot issue for "War" title (Fightin' Marines Presents War)

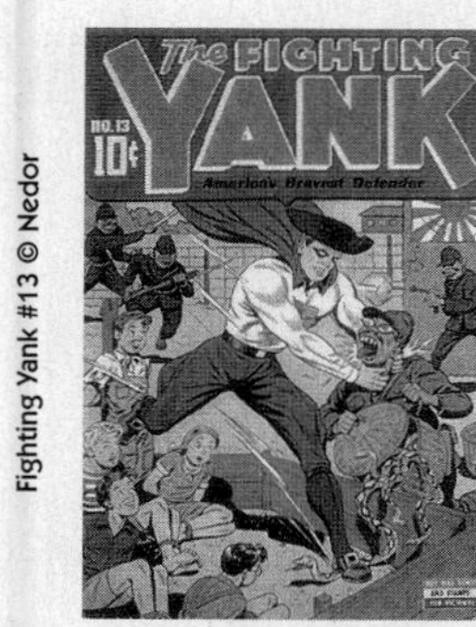

Fighting Yank #13 © Nedor

Fight the Enemy #3 © Tower

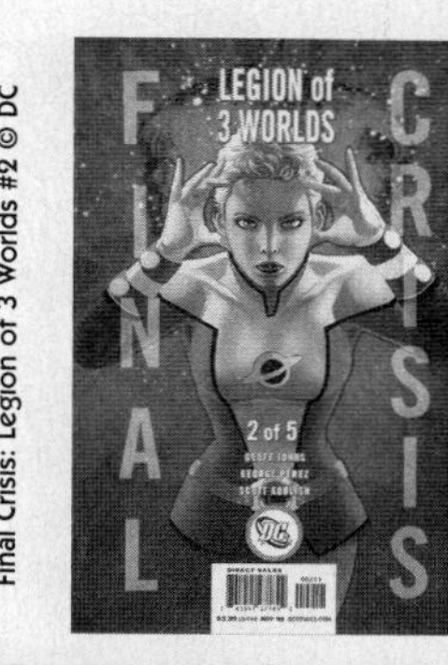

Final Crisis: Legion of 3 Worlds #2 © DC

	GD 2.0	VG 4.0	FN 6.0	VF 8.0	VF/NM 9.0	NM- 9.2
	2	4	6	9	13	16
101-121	2	4	6	8	10	12
123-140	1	2	3	5	7	9
141-170						6.00
171-176-Low print run	1	2	3	5	6	8
120(Modern Comics reprint, 1977)						4.00

NOTE: *No. 14 & 16 (CC) reprint St. John issues; No. 16 reprints St. John insignia on cover.* ***Colan*** *a-3, 7.* ***Glanzman*** *c/a-92, 94.* ***Montes/Bache*** *a-48, 53, 55, 64, 65, 72-74, 77-83, 176r.*

FIGHTING MARSHAL OF THE WILD WEST (See The Hawk)

FIGHTIN' NAVY (Formerly Don Winslow)
Charlton Comics: No. 74, 1/56 - No. 125, 4-5/66; No. 126, 8/83 - No. 133, 10/84

	GD	VG	FN	VF	VF/NM	NM-
74	6	12	18	37	59	80
75-81	4	8	12	22	34	45
82-Sam Glanzman-a (68 pg. Giant)	5	10	15	30	48	65
83-(100 pgs.)	6	12	18	41	66	90
84-99,101: 101-UFO-c/story	3	6	9	17	25	32
100	3	6	9	18	27	35
102-105,106-125('66)	3	6	9	14	19	24
126-133 (1984)-Low print run	1	2	3	5	6	8

NOTE: ***Montes/Bache*** *a-109.* ***Glanzman*** *a-82, 92, 96, 98, 100, 131r.*

FIGHTING PRINCE OF DONEGAL, THE (See Movie Comics)

FIGHTIN' TEXAN (Formerly The Texan & Fightin' Marines?)
St. John Publishing Co.: No. 16, Sept, 1952 - No. 17, Dec, 1952

	GD	VG	FN	VF	VF/NM	NM-
16,17: Tuska-a each. 17-Cameron-c/a	8	16	24	44	57	70

FIGHTING UNDERSEA COMMANDOS (See Undersea Fighting...)
Avon Periodicals: May, 1952 - No. 5, April, 1953 (U.S. Navy frogmen)

	GD	VG	FN	VF	VF/NM	NM-
1-Cover title is Undersea Fighting... #1 only	15	30	45	84	127	170
2	10	20	30	56	76	95
3-5: 1,3-Ravielli-c. 4-Kinstler-c	9	18	27	50	65	80

FIGHTING WAR STORIES
Men's Publications/Story Comics: Aug, 1952 - No. 5, 1953

	GD	VG	FN	VF	VF/NM	NM-
1	10	20	30	54	72	90
2-5	6	12	18	31	38	45

FIGHTING YANK (See America's Best Comics & Startling Comics)
Nedor/Better Publ./Standard: Sept, 1942 - No. 29, Aug, 1949

	GD	VG	FN	VF	VF/NM	NM-
1-The Fighting Yank begins; Mystico, the Wonder Man app; bondage-c	284	568	852	1818	3109	4400
2	116	232	348	742	1271	1800
3,4: 4-Schomburg-c begin	84	168	252	538	919	1300
5,6,8-10: 8,10-Bondage/torture-c	66	132	198	419	722	1025
7-Hitler special bomb-c; Grim Reaper app.	84	168	252	538	919	1300
11,13-20: 11-The Oracle app. 15-Bondage/torture-c. 18-The American Eagle app.	54	108	162	343	584	825
12-Hirohito bondage-c	81	162	243	518	884	1250
21,24: 21-Kara, Jungle Princess app.; lingerie-c. 24-Miss Masque app.	48	96	144	302	514	725
22-Miss Masque-c/story	54	108	162	343	584	825
23-Classic Schomburg hooded vigilante-c	77	154	231	493	847	1200
25-Robinson/Meskin-a; strangulation, lingerie panel; The Cavalier app.	53	106	159	334	567	800
26-29: All-Robinson/Meskin-a. 28-One pg. Williamson-a	43	86	129	271	461	650

NOTE: ***Schomburg (Xela)*** *c-4-29; airbrush-c 28, 29. Bondage c-1, 4, 8, 10, 11, 12, 15, 17.*

FIGHTMAN
Marvel Comics: June, 1993 ($2.00, one-shot, 52 pgs.)

	GD	VG	FN	VF	VF/NM	NM-
1						2.50

FIGHT THE ENEMY
Tower Comics: Aug, 1966 - No. 3, Mar, 1967 (25¢, 68 pgs.)

	GD	VG	FN	VF	VF/NM	NM-
1-Lucky 7 & Mike Manly begin	4	8	12	28	44	60
2-1st Boris Vallejo comic art; McWilliams-a	4	8	12	22	34	45
3-Wood-a (1/2 pg.); McWilliams, Bolle-a	4	8	12	22	34	45

FILM FUNNIES
Marvel Comics (CPC): Nov, 1949 - No. 2, Feb, 1950 (52 pgs.)

	GD	VG	FN	VF	VF/NM	NM-
1-Krazy Krow, Wacky Duck	20	40	60	114	182	250
2-Wacky Duck	15	30	45	83	124	165

FILM STARS ROMANCES
Star Publications: Jan-Feb, 1950 - No. 3, May-June, 1950 (True life stories of movie stars)

	GD	VG	FN	VF	VF/NM	NM-
1-Rudy Valentino & Gregory Peck stories; L. B. Cole-c; lingerie panels	43	86	129	271	461	650
2-Liz Taylor/Robert Taylor photo-c & true life story	55	110	165	352	601	850
3-Douglas Fairbanks story; photo-c	26	52	78	154	252	350

FILTH, THE
DC Comics (Vertigo): Aug, 2002 - No. 13, Oct, 2003 ($2.95, limited series)

1-13-Morrison-s/Weston & Erskine-a 3.00
TPB (2004, $19.95) r/#1-13 20.00

FINAL CRISIS
DC Comics: July, 2008 - No. 7, Mar, 2009 ($3.99, limited series)

1-Grant Morrison-s/J.G. Jones-a/c; Martian Manhunter killed; 2 covers 4.00
1-Director's Cut (10/08, $4.99) B&W printing of #1 with creator commentary 5.00
2-7: 2-Barry Allen-c/cameo; intro Big Science Action; two covers. 6-Batman zapped 4.00
...: Rage of the Red Lanterns (12/08, $3.99) Atrocitus app.; intro. Blue Lantern; 3 covers 4.00
...: Requiem (9/08, $3.99) History, death and funeral of the Martian Manhunter; 2 covers 4.00
...: Resist (12/08, $3.99) Checkmate app; Rucka & Trautman-s/Sook-a; 2 covers 4.00
...: Secret Files (2/09, $3.99) origin of Libra; Wein-s/Shasteen-a; JG Jones sketch-a 4.00
... Sketchbook (7/08, $2.99) Jones development sketches with Morrison commentary 3.00
...: Submit (12/08, $3.99) Black Lightning & Tattooed Man team up; Morrison-s; 2 covers 4.00

FINAL CRISIS: DANCE (Final Crisis Aftermath)
DC Comics: Jul, 2009 - No. 6, Dec, 2009 ($2.99, limited series)

1-6-Super Young Team; Joe Casey-s/Chriscross-a/Stanley Lau-c 3.00
TPB (2009, $17.99) r/#1-6 18.00

FINAL CRISIS: ESCAPE (Final Crisis Aftermath)
DC Comics: Jul, 2009 - No. 6, Dec, 2009 ($2.99, limited series)

1-6-Nemesis & Cameron Chase app.; Ivan Brandon-s/Marco Rudy-a/Scott Hampton-c 3.00
TPB (2010, $17.99) r/#1-6 18.00

FINAL CRISIS: INK (Final Crisis Aftermath)
DC Comics: Jul, 2009 - No. 6, Dec, 2009 ($2.99, limited series)

1-6-The Tattooed Man; Eric Wallace-s/Fabrizio Florentino-a/Brian Stelfreeze-c 3.00
TPB (2010, $17.99) r/#1-6 18.00

FINAL CRISIS: LEGION OF THREE WORLDS
DC Comics: Oct, 2008 - No. 5, Sept, 2009 ($3.99, limited series)

1-Johns-s/Pérez-a; R.J. Brande killed; Time Trapper app.; two covers on each issue 5.00
2-5-Three Legions meet; two covers. 3-Bart Allen returns. 4-Superboy (Conner) returns 4.00
HC (2009, $19.99) r/#1-5; variant covers 20.00

FINAL CRISIS: REVELATIONS
DC Comics: Oct, 2008 - No. 5, Feb, 2009 ($3.99, limited series)

1-5-Spectre and The Question; 2 covers on each. 1-Dr. Light killed; Rucka-s/Tan-a 4.00
HC (2009, $19.99, d.j.) r/#1-5; variant covers 20.00

FINAL CRISIS: ROGUE'S REVENGE
DC Comics: Sept, 2008 - No. 3, Nov, 2008 ($3.99, limited series)

1-3-Johns-s/Kolins-a; Flash's Rogues, Zoom and Inertia app. 4.00
HC (2009, $19.99, d.j.) r/#1-3 & Flash #182,197; variant covers 20.00

FINAL CRISIS: RUN (Final Crisis Aftermath)
DC Comics: Jul, 2009 - No. 6, Dec, 2009 ($2.99, limited series)

1-6-The Human Flame on the run; Sturges-s/Williams-a/Kako-c 3.00
TPB (2010, $17.99) r/#1-6 18.00

FINAL CRISIS: SUPERMAN BEYOND
DC Comics: Oct, 2008 - No. 2, Mar, 2009 ($4.50, limited series)

1,2-Morrison-s/Mahnke-a; parallel-Earth Supermen app.; 3-D pages and glasses 4.50

FINAL NIGHT, THE (See DC related titles and Parallax: Emerald Night)
DC Comics: Nov, 1996 - No. 4, Nov, 1996 ($1.95, weekly limited series)

1-4: Kesel-s/Immonen-a(p) in all. 4-Parallax's final acts 3.50
Preview 2.50
TPB-(1998, $12.95) r/#1-4, Parallax: Emerald Night #1, and preview 13.00

FINALS
DC Comics (Vertigo): Sept, 1999 - No. 4, Dec, 1999 ($2.95, limited series)

1-4-Will Pfeifer-s/Jill Thompson-a 3.00

FINDING NEMO: REEF RESCUE (Based on the Pixar movie)
BOOM! Studios: May, 2009 - No. 4, Aug, 2009 ($2.99, limited series)

1-4-Marie Croall-s/Erica Leigh Currey-a; 2 covers 3.00

FIN FANG FOUR RETURN!
Marvel Comics: Jul, 2009 ($3.99, one-shot)

1-Fin Fang Foom, Googam, Elektro, Gorgilla and Doc Samson app. 4.00

FIRE

Firehair Comics #7 © FH

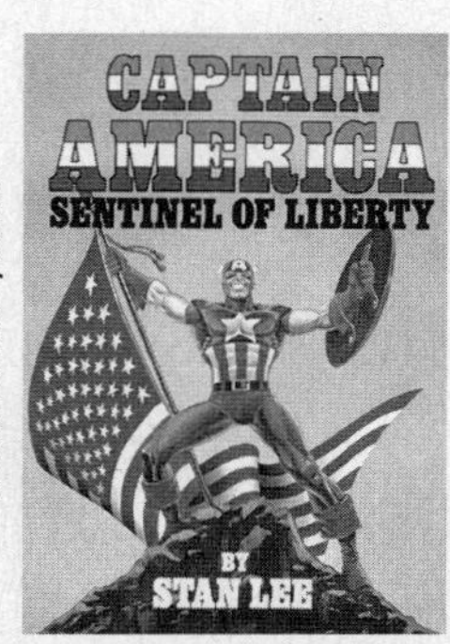

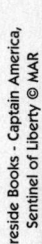

Fireside Books - Captain America, Sentinel of Liberty © MAR

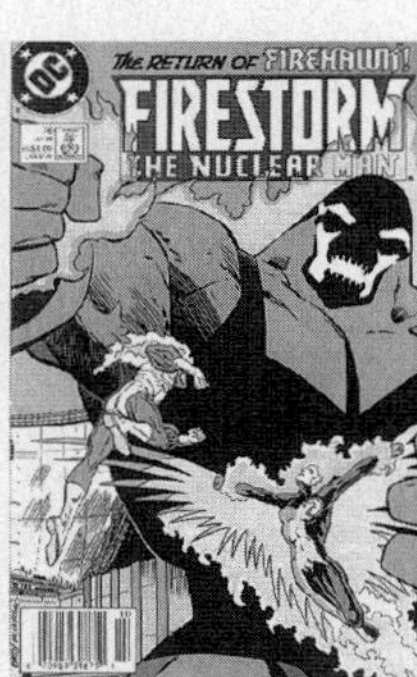

Firestorm, the Nuclear Man #76 © DC

	GD 2.0	VG 4.0	FN 6.0	VF 8.0	VF/NM 9.0	NM- 9.2

Caliber Press: 1993 - No. 2, 1993 ($2.95, B&W, limited series, 52 pgs.)

1,2-Brian Michael Bendis-s/a 3.00
TPB (1999, 2001, $9.95) Restored reprints of series 10.00

FIREARM (Also see Codename: Firearm, Freex #15, Night Man #4 & Prime #10)
Malibu Comics (Ultraverse): Sept, 1993 - No. 18, Mar, 1995 ($1.95/$2.50)

0 ($14.95)-Came w/ video containing 1st half of story (comic contains 2nd half); 1st app. Duet 15.00
1,3-6: 1-James Robinson scripts begin; Cully Hamner-a; Chaykin-c; 1st app. Alec Swan. 3-Intro The Sportsmen; Chaykin-c. 4-Break-Thru x-over; Chaykin-c. 5-1st app. Ellen (Swan's girlfriend); 2 pg. origin of Prime. 6-Prime app. (story cont'd in Prime #10); Brereton-c 2.50
1-($2.50)-Newsstand edition polybagged w/card 3.00
1-Ultra Limited silver foil-c 5.00
2 ($2.50, 44 pgs.)-Hardcase app.;Chaykin-c; Rune flip-c/story by B. Smith (3 pgs.) 3.00
7-10,12-17: 12-The Rafferty Saga begins, ends #18; 1st app. Rafferty. 15-Night Man & Freex app. 17-Swan marries Ellen 2.50
11-($3.50, 68 pgs.)-Flip book w/Ultraverse Premiere #5 3.50
18-Death of Rafferty; Chaykin-c 3.00

NOTE: *Brereton c-6. Chaykin c-1-4, 14, 16, 18. Hamner a-1-4. Herrera a-12. James Robinson scripts-0-18.*

FIRE BALL XL5 (See Steve Zodiac & The ...)

FIREBIRDS (See Noble Causes)
Image Comics: Nov, 2004 ($5.95)

1-Faerber-s/Ponce-a/c; intro. Firebird 6.00

FIREBRAND (Also see Showcase '96 #4)
DC Comics: Feb, 1996 - No. 9, Oct, 1996 ($1.75)

1-9: Brian Augustyn scripts; Velluto-c/a in all. 9-Daredevil #319-c/swipe 2.50

FIREBREATHER
Image Comics: Jan, 2003 - No. 4, Apr, 2003 ($2.95)

1-4-Hester-s/Kuhn-a 3.00
...: The Iron Saint (12/04, $6.95, squarebound) Hester-s/Kuhn-a 7.00
TPB (7/04, $13.95) r/#1-4; foreword by Brad Meltzer; gallery and sketch pages 14.00

FIREBREATHER
Image Comics: Jun, 2008 - No. 4, Feb, 2009 ($2.99)

1-4-Hester-s/Kuhn-a 3.00

FIRE FROM HEAVEN
Image Comics (WildStorm Productions): Mar, 1996 ($2.50)

1,2-Moore-s 2.50

FIREHAIR COMICS (Formerly Pioneer West Romances #3-6; also see Rangers Comics)
Fiction House Magazines (Flying Stories): Winter/48-49; No. 2, Wint/49-50; No. 7, Spr/51 - No. 11, Spr/52

	GD	VG	FN	VF	VF/NM	NM-
1-Origin Firehair	40	80	120	244	397	550
2-Continues as Pioneer West Romances for #3-6	20	40	60	118	189	260
7-11	15	30	45	85	130	175
I.W. Reprint 8-(nd)-Kinstler-c; reprints Rangers #57; Dr. Drew story by Grandenetti	3	6	9	18	24	30

FIRESIDE BOOK SERIES (Hard and soft cover editions)
Simon and Schuster: 1974 - 1980 (130-260 pgs.), Square bound, color

		GD	VG	FN	VF	VF/NM	NM-
Amazing Spider-Man, The, 1979,	HC	8	16	24	56	93	130
130 pgs., $3.95, Bob Larkin-c	SC	6	12	18	37	59	80
America At War–The Best of DC War	HC	11	22	33	78	139	200
Comics, 1979, $6.95, 260 pgs, Kubert-c	SC	7	14	21	50	83	115
Best of Spidey Super Stories (Electric Company) 1978, $3.95,	SC	6	12	18	43	69	95
Bring On The Bad Guys (Origins of the	HC	8	16	24	54	90	125
Marvel Comics Villains) 1976, $6.95, 260 pgs.; Romita-c	SC	5	10	15	34	55	75
Captain America, Sentinel of Liberty,1979,	HC	8	16	24	56	93	130
130 pgs., $12.95, Cockrum-c	SC	6	12	18	37	59	80
Doctor Strange Master of the Mystic	HC	8	16	24	56	93	130
Arts, 1980, 130 pgs.	SC	6	12	18	37	59	80
Fantastic Four, The, 1979, 130 pgs.	HC	8	16	24	54	90	125
	SC	5	10	15	34	55	75
Heart Throbs–The Best of DC Romance	HC	15	30	45	104	197	290
Comics, 1979, 260 pgs., $6.95	SC	9	18	27	65	113	160
Incredible Hulk, The, 1978, 260 pgs.	HC	8	16	24	54	90	125
(8 1/4" x 11")	SC	5	10	15	34	55	75
Marvel's Greatest Superhero Battles,	HC	10	20	30	67	116	165
1978, 260 pgs., $6.95, Romita-c	SC	6	12	18	43	69	95
Mysteries in Space, 1980, $7,95,	HC	9	18	27	61	103	145
Anderson-c. r-DC sci/fi stories	SC	6	12	18	39	62	85
Origins of Marvel Comics, 1974, 260 pgs., $5.95. r-covers & origins of Fantastic Four, Hulk, Spider-Man, Thor,	HC	8	16	24	54	90	125
& Doctor Strange	SC	5	10	15	34	55	75
Silver Surfer, The, 1978, 130 pgs.,	HC	8	16	24	56	93	130
$4.95, Norem-c	SC	6	12	18	39	62	85
Son of Origins of Marvel Comics, 1975, 260 pgs., $6.95, Romita-c. Reprints covers & origins of X-Men, Iron Man,	HC	8	16	24	54	90	125
Avengers, Daredevil, Silver Surfer	SC	5	10	15	34	55	75
Superhero Women, The–Featuring the	HC	10	20	30	67	116	165
Fabulous Females of Marvel Comics, 1977, 260 pgs., $6.95, Romita-c	SC	6	12	18	43	69	95

Note: Prices listed are for 1st printings. Later printings have lesser value.

FIRESTAR
Marvel Comics Group: Mar, 1986 - No. 4, June, 1986 (75¢)(From Spider-Man TV series)

1,2: 1-X-Men & New Mutants app. 2-Wolverine-c (not real Wolverine?); Art Adams-a(p) 6.00
3,4: 3-Art Adams/Sienkiewicz-c. 4-B. Smith-c 4.00
X-Men: Firestar Digest (2006, $7.99, digest-size) r/#1-4; profile pages 8.00

FIRESTONE (See Donald And Mickey Merry Christmas)

FIRESTORM (See Cancelled Comic Cavalcade, DC Comics Presents, Flash #289, The Fury of... & Justice League of America #179)
DC Comics: March, 1978 - No. 5, Oct-Nov, 1978

	GD	VG	FN	VF	VF/NM	NM-
1,5: 1-Origin & 1st app.	2	4	6	9	12	15
2-4: 2-Origin Multiplex. 3-Origin & 1st app. Killer Frost. 4-1st app. Hyena	1	2	3	5	7	9

FIRESTORM
DC Comics: July, 2004 - No. 35, June, 2007 ($2.50/$2.99)

1-24: 1-Intro. Jason Rusch; Jolley-s/ChrisCross-a. 6-Identity Crisis tie-in. 7-Bloodhound x-over. 8-Killer Frost returns. 9-Ronnie Raymond returns. 17-Villains United tie-in. 21-Infinite Crisis. 24-One Year Later; Killer Frost app. 2.50
25-35: 25-Begin $2.99-c; Mr. Freeze app. 33-35-Mister Miracle & Orion app. 3.00
...: Reborn TPB (2007, $14.99) r/#23-27 15.00

FIRESTORM, THE NUCLEAR MAN (Formerly Fury of Firestorm)
DC Comics: No. 65, Nov, 1987 - No. 100, Aug, 1990

65-99: 66-1st app. Zuggernaut; Firestorm vs. Green Lantern. 67,68-Millennium tie-ins. 71-Death of Capt. X. 83-1st new look 2.50
100-($2.95, 68 pgs.) 4.00
Annual 5 (10/87)-1st app. new Firestorm 3.00

FIRST, THE
CrossGeneration Comics: Jan, 2001 - No. 37, Jan, 2004 ($2.95)

1-3: 1-Barbara Kesel-s/Bart Sears & Andy Smith-a 5.00
4-10 4.00
11-37 3.00
Preview (11/00, free) 8 pg. intro 2.50
Two Houses Divided Vol. 1 TPB (11/01, $19.95) r/#1-7; new Moeller-c 20.00
Magnificent Tension Vol. 2 TPB (2002, $19.95) r/#8-13 20.00
Sinister Motives Vol. 3 TPB (2003, $15.95) r/#14-19 16.00
Vol. 4 Futile Endeavors (2003, $15.95) r/#20-25 16.00
Vol. 5 Liquid Alliances (2003, $15.95) r/#26-31 16.00
Vol. 6 Ragnarok (2004, $15.95) r/#32-37 16.00

FIRST ADVENTURES
First Comics: Dec, 1985 - No. 5, Apr, 1986 ($1.25)

1-5: Blaze Barlow, Whisper & Dynamo Joe in all 2.50

FIRST AMERICANS, THE
Dell Publishing Co.: No. 843, Sept, 1957

	GD	VG	FN	VF	VF/NM	NM-
Four Color 843-Marsh-a	8	16	24	56	93	130

FIRST BORN (See Witchblade and Darkness titles)
Image Comics (Top Cow): Aug, 2007 - No. 3 ($2.99, limited series)

... First Look (6/07, 99¢) Preview; The Darkness app.; Sejic-a; 2 covers (color & B&W) 2.25
1-3-($2.99) Two covers; Marz-s/Sejic-a. 3-Sara's baby is born 3.00
1-B&W variant Sejic cover 5.00
...: Aftermath (5/08, $3.99) short stories; Magdalena app.; two covers by Sook & Sejic 4.00

FIRST CHRISTMAS, THE (3-D)
Fiction House Magazines (Real Adv. Publ. Co.): 1953 (25¢, 8-1/4x10-1/4", oversize)(Came

First Issue Special #4 © DC

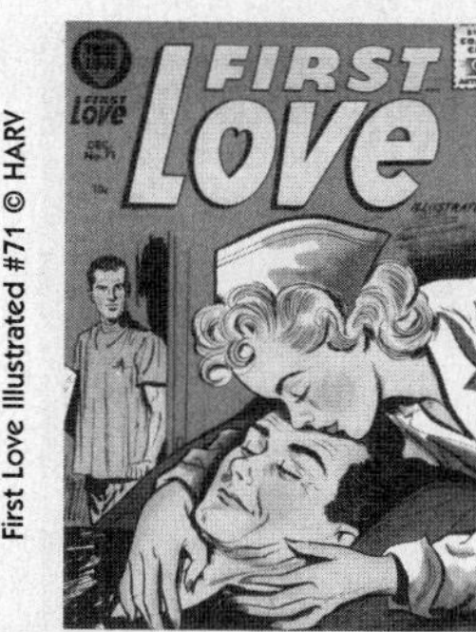

First Love Illustrated #71 © HARV

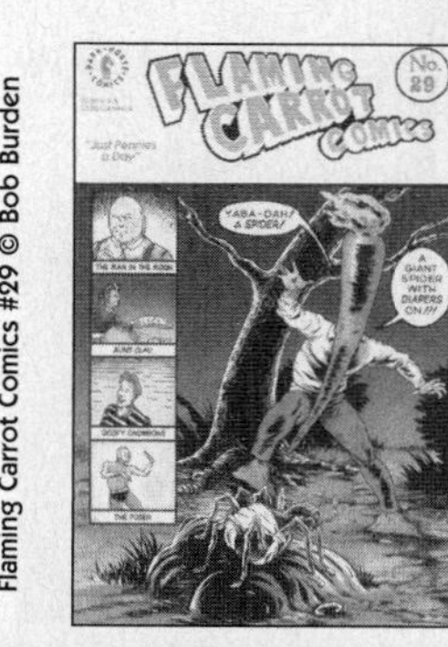

Flaming Carrot Comics #29 © Bob Burden

	GD 2.0	VG 4.0	FN 6.0	VF 8.0	VF/NM 9.0	NM- 9.2
w/glasses)						
nn-(Scarce)-Kelly Freas painted-c; Biblical theme, birth of Christ; Nativity-c	31	62	93	186	303	420

FIRST COMICS GRAPHIC NOVEL
First Comics: Jan, 1984 - No. 21? (52 pgs./176 pgs., high quality paper)

	GD	VG	FN	VF	VF/NM	NM-
1,2: 1-Beowulf ($5.95)(both printings). 2-Time Beavers						9.00
3($11.95, 100 pgs.)-American Flagg! Hard Times (2nd printing exists)						15.00
4-Nexus ($6.95)-r/B&W 1-3						12.00
5,7: 5-The Enchanted Apples of Oz ($7.95, 52 pgs.)-Intro by Harlan Ellison (1986). 7-The Secret Island Of Oz ($7.95)						10.00
6-Elric of Melnibone ($14.95, 176 pgs.)-Reprints with new color						18.00
8,10,14,18: Teenage Mutant Ninja Turtles Book I -IV ($9.95, 132 pgs.)-8-r/TMNT #1-3 in color w/12 pgs. new-a; origin. 10-r/TMNT #4-6 in color. 14-r/TMNT #7,8 in color plus new 12 pg. story. 18-r/TMNT #10,11 plus 3 pg. fold-out						11.00
9-Time 2: The Epiphany by Chaykin (11/86, $7.95, 52pgs. - indicia says #8)						10.00
11-Sailor On The Sea of Fate ($14.95)						16.00
nn-Time 2: The Satisfaction of Black Mariah (9/87)						10.00
12-American Flagg! Southern Comfort (10/87, $11.95)						14.00
13,16,17,21: 13-The Ice King Of Oz. 16-The Forgotten Forest of Oz ($8.95). 17-Mazinger (68 pgs., $8.95). 21-Elric, The Weird of the White Wolf; r/#1-5						10.00
15,19: 15-Hex Breaker: Badger ($7.95). 19-The Original Nexus Graphic Novel ($7.95, 104 pgs.)-Reprints First Comics Graphic Novel #4						12.00
20-American Flagg!: State of the Union ($11.95, 96 pgs.); r/A.F. #7-9						15.00

NOTE: *Most or all issues have been reprinted.*

1ST FOLIO (The Joe Kubert School Presents...)
Pacific Comics: Mar, 1984 ($1.50, one-shot)

	GD	VG	FN	VF	VF/NM	NM-
1-Joe Kubert-c/a(2 pgs.); Adam & Andy Kubert-a						3.00

1ST ISSUE SPECIAL
National Periodical Publications: Apr, 1975 - No. 13, Apr, 1976 (Tryout series)

	GD	VG	FN	VF	VF/NM	NM-
1,6: 1-Intro. Atlas; Kirby-c/a/script. 6-Dingbats	2	4	6	10	14	18
2,12: 2-Green Team (see Cancelled Comic Cavalcade). 12-Origin/1st app. "Blue" Starman (2nd app. in Starman, 2nd Series #3); Kubert-c	2	4	6	8	10	12
3-Metamorpho by Ramona Fradon	2	4	6	8	10	12
4,10,11: 4-Lady Cop. 10-The Outsiders. 11-Code Name: Assassin; Grell-c	1	2	3	5	7	9
5-Manhunter; Kirby-c/a/script	3	6	9	14	19	24
7,9: 7-The Creeper by Ditko (c/a). 9-Dr. Fate; Kubert-c/Simonson-a.	2	4	6	10	14	18
8-Origin/1st app. The Warlord; Grell-c/a (11/75)	4	8	12	22	34	45
13-Return of the New Gods; Darkseid app.; 1st new costume Orion; predates New Gods #12 by more than a year	3	6	9	17	25	32

FIRST KISS
Charlton Comics: Dec, 1957 - No. 40, Jan, 1965

	GD	VG	FN	VF	VF/NM	NM-
V1#1	4	8	12	28	44	60
V1#2-10	3	6	9	18	27	35
11-40	2	4	6	13	18	22

FIRST LOVE ILLUSTRATED
Harvey Publications(Home Comics)(True Love): 2/49 - No. 9, 6/50; No. 10, 1/51 - No. 86, 3/58; No. 87, 9/58 - No. 88, 11/58; No. 89, 11/62, No. 90, 2/63

	GD	VG	FN	VF	VF/NM	NM-
1-Powell-a(2)	19	38	57	111	176	240
2-Powell-a	12	24	36	67	94	120
3-"Was I Too Fat To Be Loved" story	14	28	42	80	115	150
4-10	9	18	27	50	65	80
11-30: 13-"I Joined a Teen-age Sex Club" story. 30-Lingerie panel	8	16	24	40	50	60
31-34,37,39-49: 49-Last pre-code (2/55)	7	14	21	35	43	50
35-Used in **SOTI**, illo "The title of this comic book is First Love"	20	40	60	114	182	250
36-Communism story, "Love Slaves"	12	24	36	67	94	120
38-Nostrand-a	8	16	24	44	57	70
50-66,71-90	6	12	18	28	34	40
67-70-Kirby-c	8	16	24	40	50	60

NOTE: ***Disbrow** a-13. **Orlando** c-87. **Powell** a-1, 3-5, 7, 10, 11, 13-17, 19-24, 26-29, 33,35-41, 43, 45, 46, 50, 54, 55, 57, 58, 61-63, 65, 71-73, 76, 79r, 82, 84, 88.*

FIRST MEN IN THE MOON (See Movie Comics)

FIRST ROMANCE MAGAZINE
Home Comics(Harvey Publ.)/True Love: 8/49 - #6, 6/50; #7, 6/51 - #50, 2/58; #51, 9/58 - #52, 11/58

	GD	VG	FN	VF	VF/NM	NM-
1	17	34	51	98	154	210
2	11	22	33	60	83	105
3-5	9	18	27	50	65	80
6-10,28: 28-Nostrand-a(Powell swipe)	8	16	24	40	50	60
11-20	7	14	21	35	43	50
21-27,29-32: 32-Last pre-code issue (2/55)	6	12	18	31	38	45
33-40,44-52	6	12	18	28	34	40
41-43-Kirby-c	8	16	24	40	50	60

NOTE: ***Powell** a-1-5, 8-10, 14, 18, 20-22, 24, 25, 28, 36, 46, 48, 51.*

FIRST TRIP TO THE MOON (See Space Adventures No. 20)

FIRST WAVE (Based on Sci-Fi Channel TV series)
Andromeda Entertainment: Dec, 2000 - No. 4, Jun, 2001 ($2.99)

	GD	VG	FN	VF	VF/NM	NM-
1-4-Kuhoric-s/Parsons-a/Busch-c						3.00

FISH POLICE (Inspector Gill of the...#2, 3)
Fishwrap Productions/Comico V2#5-17/Apple Comics #18 on: Dec, 1985 - No. 11, Nov, 1987 ($1.50, B&W); V2#5, April, 1988 - V2#17, May, 1989 ($1.75, color) No. 18, Aug, 1989 - No. 26, Dec, 1990 ($2.25, B&W)

	GD	VG	FN	VF	VF/NM	NM-
1-11, 1(5/86),2-2nd print, V2#5-17-(Color): V2#5-11. 12-17, new-a, 18-26 ($2.25-c, B&W). 18-Origin Inspector Gill						2.50
Special 1($2.50, 7/87, Comico)						2.50
Graphic Novel: Hairballs (1987, $9.95, TPB) r/#1-4 in color						10.00

FISH POLICE
Marvel Comics: V2#1, Oct, 1992 - No. 6, Mar, 1993 ($1.25)

	GD	VG	FN	VF	VF/NM	NM-
V2#1-6: 1-Hairballs Saga begins; r/#1 (1985)						2.50

5 CENT COMICS (Also see Whiz Comics)
Fawcett Publ.: Feb, 1940 (8 pgs., reg. size, B&W)

nn - 1st app. Dan Dare. Ashcan comic, not distributed to newsstands, only for in-house use. A CGC certified 9.6 copy sold for $10,800 in 2003.

5-STAR SUPER-HERO SPECTACULAR (See DC Special Series No. 1)

FLAME, THE (See Big 3 & Wonderworld Comics)
Fox Features Synd.: Sum, 1940 - No. 8, Jan, 1942 (#1,2: 68 pgs; #3-8: 44 pgs.)

	GD	VG	FN	VF	VF/NM	NM-
1-Flame stories reprinted from Wonderworld #5-9; origin The Flame; Lou Fine-a (36 pgs.),	300	600	900	2040	3570	5100
2-Fine-a(2); Wing Turner by Tuska; r/Wonderworld #3,10	121	242	363	768	1322	1875
3-8: 3-Powell-a	79	158	237	502	864	1225

FLAME, THE (Formerly Lone Eagle)
Ajax/Farrell Publications (Excellent Publ.): No. 5, Dec-Jan, 1954-55 - No. 3, April-May, 1955

	GD	VG	FN	VF	VF/NM	NM-
5(#1)-1st app. new Flame	45	90	135	284	480	675
2,3	29	58	87	172	281	390

FLAMING CARROT COMICS (Also see Junior Carrot Patrol)
Killian Barracks Press: Summer-Fall, 1981 ($1.95, one shot) (Lg size, 8-1/2x11")

	GD	VG	FN	VF	VF/NM	NM-
1-Bob Burden-c/a/scripts; serially #'ed to 6500	5	10	15	34	55	75

FLAMING CARROT COMICS (See Anything Goes, Cerebus, Teenage Mutant Ninja Turtles/Flaming Carrot Crossover & Visions)
Aardvark-Vanaheim/Renegade Press #6-17/Dark Horse #18-31: May, 1984 - No. 5, Jan, 1985; No. 6, Mar, 1985 - No. 31, Oct, 1994 ($1.70/$2.00, B&W)

	GD	VG	FN	VF	VF/NM	NM-
1-Bob Burden story/art	4	8	12	28	44	60
2	3	6	9	16	23	30
3	2	4	6	10	16	20
4-6	2	4	6	9	12	15
7-9	1	3	4	6	8	10
10-12						6.50
13-15						4.00
15-Variant without cover price						6.00
16-(6/87) 1st app. Mystery Men	1	2	3	5	6	8
17-20: 18-1st Dark Horse issue						4.00
21-23,25: 25-Contains trading cards; TMNT app.						3.00
24-(2.50, 52 pgs.)-10th anniversary issue						4.00
26-28: 26-Begin $2.25-c. 26,27-Teenage Mutant Ninja Turtles x-over. 27-McFarlane-c						3.00
29-31-(2.50-c)						3.00
Annual 1(1/97, $5.00)						5.00
... & Reid Fleming, World's Toughest Milkman (12/02, $3.99) listed as #32 in indicia						4.00
... :Fortune Favors the Bold (1998, $16.95, TPB) r/#19-24						17.00
... :Men of Mystery (7/97, $12.95, TPB) r/#1-3, + new material						13.00
... 's Greatest Hits (4/98, $17.95, TPB) r/#12-18, + new material						18.00
... :The Wild Shall Wild Remain (1997, $17.95, TPB) r/#4-11, + new s/a						18.00

FLAMING CARROT COMICS
Image Comics (Desperado): Dec, 2004 - Present ($2.95/$3.50, B&W)

	GD	VG	FN	VF	VF/NM	NM-
1-3-Bob Burden story/art						3.00

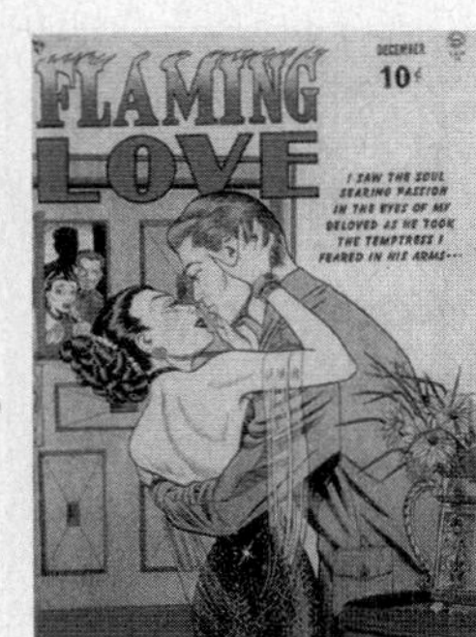

Flaming Love #1 © QUA

The Flash #171 © DC

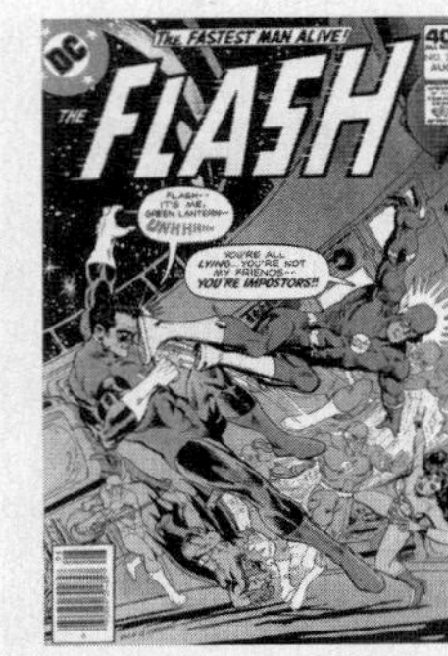

The Flash #276 © DC

	GD 2.0	VG 4.0	FN 6.0	VF 8.0	VF/NM 9.0	NM- 9.2
4-($3.50-c)						3.50
... Special #1 (3/06, $3.50) All Photo comic						3.50
... Vol. 6 (2006, $14.99) r/1-4 & Special #1; intro. by Brian Bolland						15.00

FLAMING LOVE
Quality Comics Group (Comic Magazines): Dec, 1949 - No. 6, Oct, 1950 (Photo covers #2-6) (52 pgs.)

	GD 2.0	VG 4.0	FN 6.0	VF 8.0	VF/NM 9.0	NM- 9.2
1-Ward-c/a (9 pgs.)	39	78	117	240	395	550
2	18	36	54	107	169	230
3-Ward-a (9 pgs.); Crandall-a	26	52	78	154	252	350
4-6: 4-Gustavson-a	15	30	45	90	140	190

FLAMING WESTERN ROMANCES (Formerly Target Western Romances)
Star Publications: No. 3, Mar-Apr, 1950

	GD 2.0	VG 4.0	FN 6.0	VF 8.0	VF/NM 9.0	NM- 9.2
3-Robert Taylor, Arlene Dahl photo on-c with biographies inside; L. B. Cole-c	35	70	105	203	327	450

FLARE (Also see Champions for 1st app. & League of Champions)
Hero Comics/Hero Graphics Vol. 2 on: Nov, 1988 - No. 3, Jan, 1989 ($2.75, color, 52 pgs); V2#1, Nov, 1990 - No. 7, Nov, 1991 ($2.95/$3.50, color, mature, 52 pgs.);V2#8, Oct, 1992 - No. 16, Feb, 1994 ($3.50/$3.95, B&W, 36 pgs.)

	GD 2.0	VG 4.0	FN 6.0	VF 8.0	VF/NM 9.0	NM- 9.2
V1#1-3, V2#1-16: 5-Eternity Smith returns. 6-Intro The Tigress						4.00
Annual 1(1992, $4.50, B&W, 52 pgs.)-Champions-r						4.50

FLARE ADVENTURES
Hero Graphics: Feb, 1992 - No. 12, 1993? ($3.50/$3.95)

	GD 2.0	VG 4.0	FN 6.0	VF 8.0	VF/NM 9.0	NM- 9.2
1 (90¢, color, 20 pgs.)						2.50
2-12-Flip books w/Champions Classics						4.00

FLASH, THE (See Adventure Comics, The Brave and the Bold, Crisis On Infinite Earths, DC Comics Presents, DC Special, DC Special Series, DC Super-Stars, The Greatest Flash Stories Ever Told, Green Lantern, Impulse, JLA, Justice League of America, Showcase, Speed Force, Super Team Family, Titans & World's Finest)

FLASH, THE (1st Series)(Formerly Flash Comics)(See Showcase #4,8,13,14)
National Periodical Publ./DC: No. 105, Feb-Mar, 1959 - No. 350, Oct, 1985

	GD 2.0	VG 4.0	FN 6.0	VF 8.0	VF/NM 9.0	NM- 9.2
105-(2-3/59)-Origin Flash(retold), & Mirror Master (1st app.)	533	1066	1600	4800	10,400	16,000
106-Origin Grodd & Pied Piper; Flash's 1st visit to Gorilla City; begin Grodd the Super Gorilla trilogy (Scarce)	185	370	555	1619	3210	4800
107-Grodd trilogy, part 2	106	212	318	901	1776	2650
108-Grodd trilogy ends	88	176	264	748	1474	2200
109-2nd app. Mirror Master	68	136	204	578	1139	1700
110-Intro/origin Kid Flash who later becomes Flash in Crisis On Infinite Earths #12; begin Kid Flash trilogy, ends #112 (also in #114,116,118); 1st app. & origin of The Weather Wizard	154	308	462	1348	2674	4000
111-2nd Kid Flash tryout; Cloud Creatures	50	100	150	413	807	1200
112-Origin & 1st app. Elongated Man (4-5/60); also apps. in #115,119,130	56	112	168	476	938	1400
113-Origin & 1st app. Trickster	49	98	147	392	759	1125
114-Captain Cold app. (see Showcase #8)	40	80	120	321	623	925
115,116,118-120: 119-Elongated Man marries Sue Dearborn. 120-Flash & Kid Flash team-up for 1st time	34	68	102	262	506	750
117-Origin & 1st app. Capt. Boomerang; 1st & only S.A. app. Winky Blinky & Noddy	38	76	114	288	557	825
121,122: 122-Origin & 1st app. The Top	27	54	81	197	386	575
123-(9/61)-Re-intro. Golden Age Flash; origins of both Flashes; 1st mention of an Earth II where DC G. A. heroes live	148	296	444	1258	2479	3700
124-Last 10¢ issue	21	42	63	153	297	440
125-128,130: 127-Return of Grodd-c/story. 128-Origin & 1st app. Abra Kadabra. 130-(7/62)-1st Gauntlet of Super-Villains (Mirror Master, Capt. Cold, The Top, Capt. Boomerang & Trickster)	20	40	60	142	276	410
129-2nd G.A. Flash x-over; J.S.A. cameo in flashback (1st S.A. app. G.A. Green Lantern, Hawkman, Atom, Black Canary & Dr. Mid-Nite. Wonder Woman (1st S.A. app.?) appears)	30	60	90	223	432	640
131-136,138,140: 131-Early Green Lantern x-over (9/62). 135-1st app. of Kid Flash's yellow costume (3/63). 136-1st Dexter Miles. 140-Origin & 1st app. Heat Wave	15	30	45	107	204	300
137-G.A. Flash x-over; J.S.A. cameo (1st S.A. app.)(1st real app. since 2-3/51); 1st S.A. app. Vandal Savage & Johnny Thunder; JSA team decides to re-form	39	78	117	297	574	850
139-Origin & 1st app. Prof. Zoom	16	32	48	113	217	320
141-150: 142-Trickster app. 147-2nd Prof. Zoom	12	24	36	85	155	225
151-Engagement of Barry Allen & Iris West; G.A. Flash vs. The Shade.	13	26	39	93	172	250
152-159: 159-Dr. Mid-Nite cameo	10	20	30	73	129	185
160-(80-Pg. Giant G-21); G.A. Flash & Johnny Quick-r	12	24	36	85	155	225
161-164,166,167: 167-New facts about Flash's origin	9	18	27	60	100	140
165-Barry Allen weds Iris West	9	18	27	63	107	150
168,170: 168-Green Lantern-c/app. 170-Dr. Mid-Nite, Dr. Fate, G.A. Flash x-over	9	18	27	60	100	140
169-(80-Pg. Giant G-34)-New facts about origin	9	18	27	64	110	155
171,172,174,176,177,179,180: 171-JLA, Green Lantern, Atom flashbacks. 174-Barry Allen reveals I.D. to wife. 179-(5/68)-Flash travels to Earth-Prime and meets DC editor Julie Schwartz; 1st unnamed app. Earth-Prime (See Justice League of America #123 for 1st named app. & 3rd app. overall)	8	16	24	52	86	120
173-G.A. Flash x-over	9	18	27	60	100	140
175-2nd Superman/Flash race (12/67) (See Superman #199 & World's Finest #198,199); JLA cameo; gold kryptonite used (on J'onn J'onzz impersonating Superman)	17	34	51	122	236	350
178-(80-Pg. Giant G-46)	9	18	27	60	100	140
181-186,188,189: 186-Re-intro. Sargon. 189-Last 12¢-c	6	12	18	37	59	80
187,196: (68-Pg. Giants G-58, G-70)	7	14	21	45	73	100
190-195,197-199	4	8	12	26	41	55
200	5	10	15	30	48	65
201-204,206,207: 201-New G.A. Flash story. 206-Elongated Man begins 207-Last 15¢ issue	3	6	9	21	32	42
205-(68-Pg. Giant G-82)	7	14	21	45	73	100
208-213-(52 pg.): 211-G.A. Flash origin-r/#104. 213-Reprints #137	4	8	12	24	37	50
214-DC 100 Page Super Spectacular DC-11; origin Metal Men-r/Showcase #37; never before published G.A. Flash story	9	18	27	60	100	140
215 (52 pgs.)-Flash-r/Showcase #4; G.A. Flash x-over, continued in #216	4	8	12	26	41	55
216,220: 220-1st app. Turtle since Showcase #4	3	6	9	17	25	32
217-219: Neal Adams-a in all. 217-Green Lantern/Green Arrow series begins (9/72); 2nd G.L. & G.A. team-up series (see Green Lantern #76). 219-Last Green Arrow	4	8	12	28	44	60
221-225,227,228,230,231,233: 222-G. Lantern x-over. 228-(7-8/74)-Flash writer Cary Bates travels to Earth-One & meets Flash, Iris Allen & Trickster; 2nd unnamed app. Earth-Prime (See Justice League of America #123 for 1st named app. & 3rd app. overall)	2	4	6	13	18	22
226-Neal Adams-p	3	6	9	16	23	30
229,232-(100 pg. issues)-G.A. Flash-r & new-a	4	8	12	28	44	60
234-250: 235-Green Lantern x-over. 243-Death of The Top. 245-Origin The Floronic Man in Green Lantern back-up, ends #246. 246-Last Green Lantern. 247-Jay Garrick app. 250-Intro Golden Glider	2	4	6	10	14	18
251-274: 256-Death of The Top retold. 265-267-(44 pgs.). 267-Origin of Flash's uniform. 270-Intro The Clown	2	4	6	8	10	12
268,273-276,278,283,286-(Whitman variants; low print run; no issue #s shown on covers	2	4	6	8	11	14
275,276-Iris Allen dies	2	4	6	9	12	15
277-288,290: 286-Intro/origin Rainbow Raider	1	2	3	5	6	8
289-1st Pérez DC art (Firestorm); new Firestorm back-up series begins (9/80), ends #304	2	3	4	6	8	10
291-299,301-305: 291-1st app. Saber-Tooth (villain). 295-Gorilla Grodd-c/story. 298-Intro & origin new Shade. 301-Atomic bomb-c. 303-The Top returns. 304-Intro/origin Colonel Computron; 305-G.A. Flash x-over						6.00
300-(52 pgs.)-Origin Flash retold; 25th ann. issue	1	2	3	5	6	8
306-313-Dr. Fate by Giffen. 309-Origin Flash retold						6.00
314-340: 318-323-Creeper back-ups. 323,324-Two part Flash vs. Flash story. 324-Death of Reverse Flash (Professor Zoom). 328-Iris West Allen's death retold. 329-JLA app. 340-Trial of the Flash begins						5.00
341-349: 344-Origin Kid Flash						6.00
350-Double size ($1.25) Final issue	1	2	3	4	5	7
Annual 1 (10-12/63, 84 pgs.)-Origin Elongated Man & Kid Flash-r; origin Grodd; G.A. Flash-r	36	72	108	277	531	785
Annual 1 Replica Edition (2001, $6.95)-Reprints the entire 1963 Annual						7.00
...Chronicles SC Vol. 1 (2009, $14.99)-r/Showcase #4,8,13,14 and Flash #105,106						15.00
The Flash Spectacular (See DC Special Series No. 11)						
The Flash vs. The Rogues TPB (2009, $14.99) r/1st app. of classic rogues in Showcase #8 and Flash #105,106,110,113,117,122,140,155; new Van Sciver-c						15.00
The Life Story of the Flash (1997, $19.95, Hardcover) "Iris Allen's" chronicle of Barry Allen's life; comic panels w/additional text; Waid & Augustyn-s/ Kane & Staton-a/Orbik painted-c						20.00
The Life Story of the Flash (1998, $12.95, Softcover) New Orbik-c						13.00

NOTE: ***N. Adams*** *c-194, 195, 203, 204, 206-208, 211, 213, 215, 226p, 246.* ***M. Anderson*** *c-165, a(i)-195, 200-204, 206-208.* ***Austin*** *a-233i, 234i, 246i.* ***Buckler*** *a-271p, 272p; c(p)-247-250, 252, 253p, 255, 256p, 258, 262, 265-267, 269-271.* ***Giffen*** *a-306-313p; c-310p, 315.* ***Giordano*** *a-226i.* ***Sid Greene*** *a-167-174i, 229i(r).* ***Grell*** *a-237p, 238p, 240-243p; c-236.* ***Heck*** *a-198p.* ***Infantino/Anderson*** *a-135. c-135, 170-174, 192, 200, 201, 328-330.* ***Infantino/Giella*** *c-105-112, 163, 164, 166-168.* ***G. Kane*** *a-195p, 197-199p, 229r, 232r; c-197-199, 312p.* ***Kubert*** *a-*

The Flash (2nd series) #231 © DC

The Flash: Rebirth #1 © DC

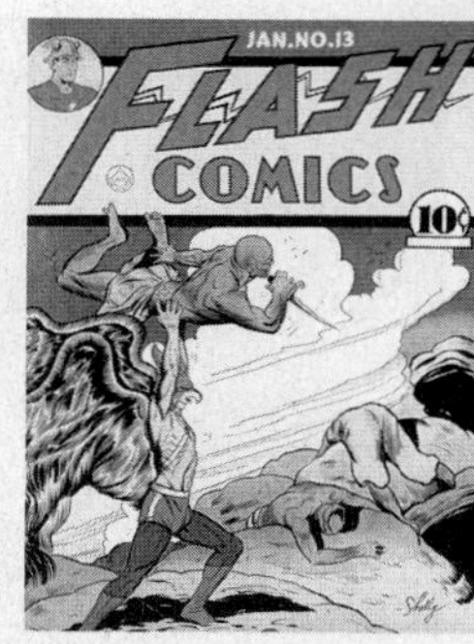

Flash Comics #13 © DC

GD 2.0 | VG 4.0 | FN 6.0 | VF 8.0 | VF/NM 9.0 | NM- 9.2

108p, 215i(r); c-189-191. ***Lopez*** *c-272.* ***Meskin*** *a-229r, 232r.* ***Perez*** *a-289-293p; c-293.* ***Starlin*** *a-294-296p.* ***Staton*** *c-263p, 264p. Green Lantern x-over-131, 143, 168, 171, 191.*

FLASH (2nd Series)(See Crisis on Infinite Earths #12 and All Flash #1)
DC Comics: June, 1987 - No. 230, Mar, 2006; No. 231, Oct, 2007 - No. 247, Feb, 2009

1-Guice-c/a begins; New Teen Titans app. 1 3 4 6 8 10
2-10: 3-Intro. Kilgore. 5-Intro. Speed McGee. 7-1st app. Blue Trinity. 8,9-Millennium tie-ins. 9-1st app. The Chunk 4.00
11-61: 12-Free extra 16 pg. Dr. Light story. 19-Free extra 16 pg. Flash story. 28-Capt. Cold app. 29-New Phantom Lady app. 40-Dr. Alchemy app. 50-($1.75, 52 pgs.) 3.00
62-78,80: 62-Flash: Year One begins, ends #65. 65-Last $1.00-c. 66-Aquaman app. 69,70-Green Lantern app. 70-Gorilla Grodd story ends. 73-Re-intro Barry Allen & begin saga ("Barry Allen's" true ID revealed in #78). 76-Re-intro of Max Mercury (Quality Comics' Quicksilver), not in uniform until #77. 80-($1.25-c) Regular Edition 4.00
79,80 ($2.50): 79-(68 pgs.) Barry Allen saga ends. 80-Foil-c 5.00
81-91,93,94,0,95-99,101: 81,82-Nightwing & Starfire app. 84-Razer app. 94-Zero Hour. 0-(10/94). 95-"Terminal Velocity" begins, ends #100. 96,98,99-Kobra app. 97-Origin Max Mercury; Chillblaine app. 4.00
92-1st Impulse 1 3 4 6 8 10
100 ($2.50)-Newstand edition; Kobra & JLA app. 4.00
100 ($3.50)-Foil-c edition; Kobra & JLA app. 5.00
102-131: 102-Mongul app.; begin-$1.75-c. 105-Mirror Master app. 107-Shazam app. 108-"Dead Heat" begins; 1st app. Savitar. 109-"Dead Heat" Pt. 2 (cont'd in Impulse #10). 110-"Dead Heat" Pt. 4 (cont'd in Impulse #11). 111-"Dead Heat" finale; Savitar disappears into the Speed Force; John Fox cameo (2nd app.). 112-"Race Against Time" begins, ends #118; re-intro John Fox. 113-Tornado Twins app. 119-Final Night x-over. 127-129-Rogue's Gallery & Neron. 128,129-JLA-app.130-Morrison & Millar-s begin 3.50
132-150: 135-GL & GA app. 142-Wally almost marries Linda; Waid-s return. 144-Cobalt Blue origin. 145-Chain Lightning begins.147-Professor Zoom app. 149-Barry Allen app. 150-($2.95) Final showdown with Cobalt Blue 3.00
151-162: 151-Casey-s. 152-New Flash-c. 154-New Flash ID revealed. 159-Wally marries Linda. 162-Last Waid-s. 3.00
163-187,189-196,198,199,201-206: 163-Begin $2.25-c. 164-186-Bolland-c. 183-New Trickster. 196-Winslade-a. 201-Dose-a begins. 205-Batman-c/app. 2.50
188-($2.95) Mirror Master, Weather Wizard, Trickster app. 3.00
197-Origin of Zoom (6/03) 6.00
200-($3.50) Flash vs. Zoom; Barry Allen & Hal Jordan app.; wraparound-c 3.50
207-230: 207-211-Turner-c/Porter-a. 209-JLA app. 210-Nightwing app. 212-Origin Mirror Master. 214-216-Identity Crisis x-over. 219-Wonder Woman app. 220-Rogue War 224-Zoom & Prof. Zoom app. 225-Twins born; Barry Allen app.; last Johns-s 2.50
231-247: 231-(10/07) Waid-s/Acuña-a. 240-Grodd app.; "Dark Side Club" 3.00
#1,000,000 (11/98) 853rd Century x-over 2.50
Annual 1-7,9: 2-('87-'94,'96, 68 pgs), 3-Gives history of G.A.,S.A., & Modern Age Flash in text. 4-Armaggedon 2001. 5-Eclipso-c/story. 7-Elseworlds story. 9-Legends of the Dead Earth story; J.H. Williams-a(p); Mick Gray-a(i) 3.00
Annual 8 (1995, $3.50)-Year One story 3.50
Annual 10 (1997, $3.95)-Pulp Heroes stories 4.00
Annual 11,12 ('98, '99)-11-Ghosts; Wrightson-c. 12-JLApe; Art Adams-c 3.00
Annual 13 ('00, $3.50) Planet DC; Alcatena-c/a 3.50
...: Blitz (2004, $19.95, TPB)-r/#192-200; Kolins-c 20.00
...: Blood Will Run (2002, 2008; $17.95, TPB)-r/#170-176, Secret Files #3, Iron Heights 18.00
...: Crossfire (2004, $17.95, TPB)-r/#183-191 & parts of Flash Secret Files #3 18.00
Dead Heat (2000, $14.95, TPB)-r/#108-111, Impulse #10,11 15.00
...80-Page Giant (8/98, $4.95) Flash family stories by Waid, Millar and others; Mhan-c 5.00
...80-Page Giant 2 (4/99, $4.95) Stories of Flash family, future Kid Flash, original Teen Titans and XS 5.00
...: Emergency Stop (2008, $12.99, TPB)-r/#130-135; Morrison & Millar-s 13.00
...: Ignition (2005, $14.95, TPB)-r/#201-206 15.00
...: Iron Heights (2001, $5.95)-Van Sciver-c/a; intro. Murmur 6.00
...: Mercury Falling (2009, $14.99, TPB)-r/Impulse #62-67 15.00
...: Our Worlds at War 1 (10/01, $2.95)-Jae Lee-c; Black Racer app. 3.00
...Plus 1 (1/1997, $2.95)-Nightwing-c/app. 3.00
Race Against Time (2001, $14.95, TPB)-r/#112-118 15.00
...: Rogues (2003, $14.95, TPB)-r/#177-182 15.00
...: Rogue War (2006, $17.99, TPB)-r/#1/2,212,218,220-225; cover gallery 18.00
...Secret Files 1 (11/97, $4.95) Origin-s & pin-ups 5.00
...Secret Files 2 (11/99, $4.95) Origin of Replicant 5.00
...Secret Files 3 (11/01; $4.95) Intro. Hunter Zolomon (who later becomes Zoom) 5.00
Special 1 (1990, $2.95, 84 pgs.)-50th anniversary issue; Kubert-c; 1st Flash story by Mark Waid; 1st app. John Fox (27th Century Flash) 3.00
Terminal Velocity (1996, $12.95, TPB)-r/#95-100. 13.00
...: The Greatest Stories Ever Told (2007, $19.99, TPB) reprints; Ross-c/Waid intro. 20.00
The Return of Barry Allen (1996, $12.95, TPB)-r/#74-79 13.00
The Secret of Barry Allen (2005, $19.99, TPB)-r/#207-211,213-217; Turner sketch page 20.00
...: The Wild Wests HC (2008, $24.99, dustjacket)-r/#231-237 25.00
...: Time Flies (2002, $5.95)-Seth Fisher-c/a; Rozum-s 6.00
TV Special 1 (1991, $3.95, 76 pgs.)-Photo-c plus behind the scenes photos of TV show; Saltares-a, Byrne scripts 4.00
Wizard #1/2 (2005) prelude to Rogue Wars; Justiano-a 10.00
...: Wonderland TPB (2007, $12.99, TPB)-r/#164-169 13.00
NOTE: ***Guice*** *a-1-9p, 11p, Annual 1p; c-1-9p, Annual 1p.* ***Perez*** *c-15-17, Annual 2i.* ***Charest*** *c/a-Annual 5p.*

FLASH: REBIRTH
DC Comics: Jun, 2009 - No. 6, Apr, 2010 ($3.99/$2.99, limited series)

1-($3.99) Barry Allen's return; Johns-s/Van Sciver-a; Flash-c by Van Sciver 4.00
1-Variant Barry Allen-c by Van Sciver 10.00
1-Second thru fourth printings 4.00
2-6-($2.99) 3-Max Mercury returns 3.00
2-6-Variant covers by Van Sciver 8.00

FLASH: THE FASTEST MAN ALIVE (3rd Series)(See Infinite Crisis)
DC Comics: Aug, 2006 - No. 13, Aug, 2007 ($2.99)

1-Bart Allen becomes the Flash; Lashley-a/Bilson & Demeo-s 3.00
1-Variant-c by Joe and Andy Kubert 5.00
2-12: 5-Cyborg app. 7-Inertia returns. 10-Zoom app. 3.00
13-Bart Allen dies; 2 covers 3.00
13-DC Nation Edition from the 2007 San Diego Comic-Con 8.00
...: Full Throttle TPB (2007, $12.99) r/#7-13, All-Flash #1, DCU Infinite Holiday Spec. story 13.00
...: Lightning in a Bottle TPB (2007, $12.99) r/#1-6 13.00

FLASH, THE (See Tangent Comics/ The Flash)

FLASH AND GREEN LANTERN: THE BRAVE AND THE BOLD
DC Comics: Oct, 1999 - No. 6, Mar, 2000 ($2.50, limited series)

1-6-Waid & Peyer-s/Kitson-a. 4-Green Arrow app.; Grindberg-a(p) 2.50
TPB (2001, $12.95) r/#1-6 13.00

FLASH COMICS
DC Comics:. Dec. 1939

1-Ashcan comic, not distributed to newsstands, only for in-house use. Cover art is Adventure Comics #41 and interior from All-American Comics #8. A CGC certified 9.6 sold for $11,500 in 2004. A CGC certified 9.4 sold for $6,572.50 in 2008.

FLASH COMICS (Whiz Comics No. 2 on)
Fawcett Publications: Jan, 1940 (12 pgs., B&W, regular size)
(Not distributed to newsstands; printed for in-house use)

NOTE: ***Whiz Comics*** *#2 was preceded by two books,* ***Flash Comics*** *and* ***Thrill Comics****, both dated Jan, 1940, (12 pgs, B&W, regular size) and were not distributed. These two books are identical except for the title, and were sent out to major distributors as ad copies to promote sales. It is believed that the complete 68 page issue of Fawcett's* ***Flash*** *and* ***Thrill Comics*** *#1 was finished and ready for publication with the January date. Since DC Comics was also about to publish a book with the same date and title, Fawcett hurriedly printed up the black and white version of* ***Flash Comics*** *to secure copyright before DC. The inside covers are blank, with the covers and inside pages printed on a high quality uncoated paper stock.The eight page origin story of Captain Thunder is composed of pages 1-7 and 13 of the Captain Marvel story essentially as they appeared in the first issue of* ***Whiz Comics****. The balloon dialogue on page thirteen was relettered to tie the story into the end of page seven in* ***Flash*** *and* ***Thrill Comics*** *to produce a shorter version of the origin story for copyright purposes. Obviously, DC acquired the copyright and Fawcett dropped* ***Flash*** *as well as* ***Thrill*** *and came out with* ***Whiz Comics*** *a month later. Fawcett never used the cover to* ***Flash*** *and* ***Thrill*** *#1, designing a new cover for* ***Whiz Comics****. Fawcett also must have discovered that Captain Thunder had already been used by another publisher (Captain Terry Thunder by Fiction House). All references to Captain Thunder were relettered to Captain Marvel before appearing in* ***Whiz****.*

1 (nn on-c, #1 on inside)-Origin & 1st app. Captain Thunder. Cover by C.C. Beck. Eight copies of Flash and three copies of Thrill exist. All 3 copies of Thrill sold in 1986 for between $4,000-$10,000 each. A NM copy of Thrill sold in 1987 for $12,000. A VG copy of Thrill sold in 1987 for $9000 cash. A VF(8.0) copy of Thrill sold in 2003 for $11,400. A CGC certified 9.0 copy of the Flash Comics version sold for $10,117.50 in 2006. A CGC certified 9.4 copy of the Flash Comics version sold for $14,340 in 2008. A CGC certified 9.0 copy of the Thrill Comics version sold for $8,000 in 2006. A CGC certified 9.0 copy of the Thrill Comics version sold for $20,315 in 2008.

FLASH COMICS (The Flash No. 105 on) (Also see All-Flash)
National Periodical Publ./All-American: Jan, 1940 - No. 104, Feb, 1949

1-The Flash (origin/1st app.) by Harry Lampert, Hawkman (origin/1st app.) by Gardner Fox, The Whip, & Johnny Thunder (origin/1st app.) by Stan Asch; Cliff Cornwall by Moldoff, Flash Picture Novelets (later Minute Movies w/#12) begin; Moldoff (Shelly) cover; 1st app. Shiera Sanders who later becomes Hawkgirl, #24; reprinted in Famous First Edition (on sale 11/10/39); The Flash-c 7500 15,000 22,500 56,250 100,625 145,000
1-Reprint, Oversize 13-1/2x10". **WARNING:** This comic is an exact reprint of the original except for its size. DC published it in 1974 with a second cover titling it as a Famous First Edition. There have been many reported cases of the outer cover being removed and the interior sold as the original edition. The reprint with the new outer cover removed is practically worthless. See Famous First Edition for value.
2-Rod Rian begins, ends #11; Hawkman-c 811 1622 2433 5920 10,460 15,000
3-King Standish begins (1st app.), ends #41 (called The King #16-37,39-41); E.E. Hibbard-a begins on Flash 541 1082 1623 3950 6975 10,000
4-Moldoff (Shelly) Hawkman begins; The Whip-c 423 846 1269 3046 5323 7600

Flash Comics #101 © DC

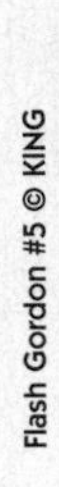

KING COMICS
FLASH GORDON
Flash is ambushed by the most terrifying creatures in all Mongo!

Flash Gordon #5 © KING

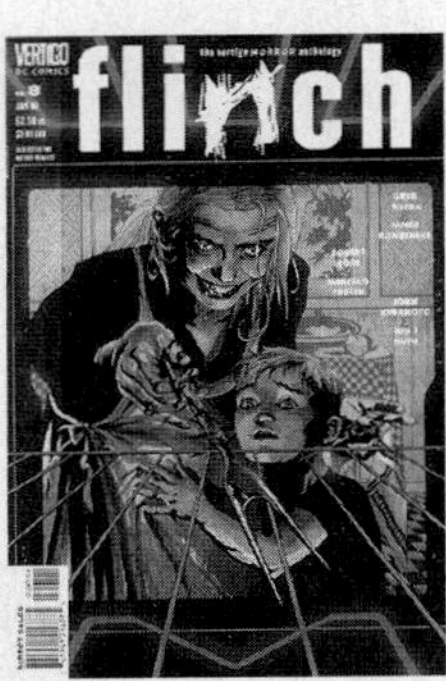

Flinch #8 © DC

	GD 2.0	VG 4.0	FN 6.0	VF 8.0	VF/NM 9.0	NM- 9.2
5-The King-c	354	708	1062	2478	4339	6200
6-2nd Flash-c (alternates w/Hawkman #6 on)	557	1114	1671	4066	7183	10,300
7-2nd Hawkman-c; 1st Moldoff Hawkman-c	541	1082	1623	3950	6975	10,000
8-New logo begins; classic Moldoff Flash-c	343	686	1029	2400	4200	6000
9,10: 9-Moldoff Hawkman-c; 10-Classic Moldoff Flash-c	354	708	1062	2478	4339	6200
11-13,15-20: 12-Les Watts begins; "Sparks" #16 on. 13-Has full page ad for All Star Comics #3. 17-Last Cliff Cornwall	232	464	696	1485	2543	3600
14-World War II cover	271	542	813	1734	2967	4200
21-Classic Hawkman-c	223	446	669	1416	2433	3450
22,23	200	400	600	1280	2190	3100
24-Shiera becomes Hawkgirl (12/41); see All-Star Comics #5 for 1st app.	242	484	726	1537	2644	3750
25-28,30: 28-Last Les Sparks.	126	252	378	806	1378	1950
29-Ghost Patrol begins (origin/1st app.), ends #104	129	258	387	826	1413	2000
31,33-Classic Hawkman-c. 33-Origin Shade	132	264	396	838	1444	2050
32,34-40: 36-1st app. Rag Doll	113	226	339	718	1234	1750
41-50	100	200	300	635	1093	1550
51-61: 52-1st computer in comics, c/s (4/44). 59-Last Minute Movies. 61-Last Moldoff Hawkman	89	178	267	565	970	1375
62-Hawkman by Kubert begins	115	230	345	730	1253	1775
63-85: 66-68-Hop Harrigan in all. 70-Mutt & Jeff app. 80-Atom begins, ends #104	79	158	237	502	864	1225
86-Intro. The Black Canary in Johnny Thunder (8/47); see All-Star #38.	300	600	900	1950	3375	4800
87,88,90: 87-Intro. The Foil. 88-Origin Ghost.	126	252	378	806	1378	1950
89-Intro villain The Thorn	187	374	561	1197	2049	2900
91,93-99: 98-Atom & Hawkman don new costumes	132	264	396	838	1444	2050
92-1st solo Black Canary plus-c; rare in Mint due to black ink smearing on white-c	349	698	1047	2443	4272	6100
100 (10/48),103(Scarce)-52 pgs. each	297	594	891	1900	3250	4600
101,102(Scarce)	258	516	774	1651	2826	4000
104-Origin The Flash retold (Scarce)	676	1352	2028	4935	8718	12,500

NOTE: ***Irwin Hasen** a-Wheaties Giveaway. c-97, Wheaties Giveaway. **E.E. Hibbard** c-6, 12, 20, 24, 26, 28, 30, 44, 46, 48, 50, 62, 66, 68, 69, 72, 74, 76, 78, 80, 82. **Infantino** a-86p, 90, 93-95, 99-104; c-90, 92, 93, 97, 99, 101, 103. **Kinstler** a-87, 89(Hawkman); c-87. **Chet Kozlak** c-77, 79, 81. **Krigstein** a-94. **Kubert** a-62-76, 83, 85, 86, 88-104; c-63, 65, 67, 70, 71, 73, 75, 83, 85, 86, 88, 89, 91, 94, 96, 98, 100, 104. **Moldoff** a-3; c-3, 7-11, 13-17, plus odd #'s 19-61. **Martin Naydell** c-52, 54, 56, 58, 60, 64, 84.*

FLASH DIGEST, THE (See DC Special Series #24)

FLASH GORDON (See Defenders Of The Earth, Eat Right to Work..., Giant Comic Album, King Classics, King Comics, March of Comics #118, 133, 142, The Phantom #18, Street Comix & Wow Comics, 1st series)

FLASH GORDON
Dell Publishing Co.: No. 25, 1941; No. 10, 1943 - No. 512, Nov, 1953

	GD	VG	FN	VF	VF/NM	NM-
Feature Books 25 (#1)(1941))-r-not by Raymond	123	246	369	787	1344	1900
Four Color 10(1942)-by Alex Raymond; reprints "The Ice Kingdom"	80	160	240	680	1340	2000
Four Color 84(1945)-by Alex Raymond; reprints "The Fiery Desert"	41	82	123	326	633	940
Four Color 173	19	38	57	133	259	385
Four Color 190-Bondage-c; "The Adventures of the Flying Saucers"; 5th Flying Saucer story (6/48)- see The Spirit 9/28/47(1st), Shadow Comics V7#10 (2nd, 1/48), Captain Midnight #60 (3rd, 2/48) & Boy Commandos #26 (4th, 3-4/48)	20	40	60	146	283	420
Four Color 204,247	15	30	45	104	197	290
Four Color 424-Painted-c	11	22	33	78	139	200
2(5-7/53-Dell)-Painted-c; Evans-a?	9	18	27	60	100	140
Four Color 512-Painted-c	9	18	27	60	100	140

FLASH GORDON (See Tiny Tot Funnies)
Harvey Publications: Oct, 1950 - No. 4, April, 1951

	GD	VG	FN	VF	VF/NM	NM-
1-Alex Raymond-a; bondage-c; reprints strips from 7/14/40 to 12/8/40	39	78	117	231	378	525
2-Alex Raymond-a; r/strips 12/15/40-4/27/41	23	46	69	136	223	310
3,4-Alex Raymond-a; 3-bondage-c; r/strips 5/4/41-9/21/41. 4-r/strips 10/24/37-3/27/38	21	42	63	126	206	285
5-(Rare)-Small size-5-1/2x8-1/2"; B&W; 32 pgs.; Distributed to some mail subscribers only	65	130	195	416	708	1000

(Also see All-New No. 15, Boy Explorers No. 2, and Stuntman No. 3)

FLASH GORDON
Gold Key: June, 1965

	GD	VG	FN	VF	VF/NM	NM-
1 (1947 reprint)-Painted-c	6	12	18	43	69	95

FLASH GORDON (Also see Comics Reading Libraries in the Promotional Comics section)

King #1-11/Charlton #12-18/Gold Key #19-23/Whitman #28 on:
9/66 - #11, 12/67; #12, 2/69 - #18, 1/70; #19, 9/78 - #37, 3/82 (Painted covers No. 19-30, 34)

	GD 2.0	VG 4.0	FN 6.0	VF 8.0	VF/NM 9.0	NM- 9.2
1-1st S.A. app Flash Gordon; Williamson c/a(2); E.C. swipe/Incredible S.F. #32; Mandrake story	8	16	24	52	86	120
1-Army giveaway(1968)("Complimentary" on cover)(Same as regular #1 minus Mandrake story & back-c)	4	8	12	28	44	60
2-8: 2-Bolle, Gil Kane-c; Mandrake story. 3-Williamson-c. 4-Secret Agent X-9 begins, Williamson-c/a(3). 5-Williamson-c/a(2). 6,8-Crandall-a. 7-Raboy-a (last in comics?). 8-Secret Agent X-9-r	4	8	12	28	44	60
9-13: 9,10-Raymond-r. 10-Buckler's 1st pro work (11/67). 11-Crandall-a. 12-Crandall-c/a. 13-Jeff Jones-a (15 pgs.)	4	8	12	26	41	55
14,15: 15-Last 12¢ issue	3	6	9	19	29	38
16,17: 17-Brick Bradford story	3	6	9	16	23	30
18-Kaluta-a (3rd pro work?)(see Teen Confessions)	3	6	9	20	30	40
19(9/78, G.K.), 20-26	1	3	4	6	8	10
27-29,34-37: 34-37-Movie adaptation	2	4	6	8	10	12
30 (10/80) (scarce, from Whitman 3-pack only)	3	6	9	18	27	35
30 (7/81; re-issue), 31-33-single issues	2	4	6	8	10	12
31-33 (Bagged 3-pack): Movie adaptation; Williamson-a.						36.00

NOTE: ***Aparo** a-8. **Bolle** a-21, 22. **Boyette** a-14-18. **Briggs** c-10. **Buckler** a-10. **Crandall** c-6. **Estrada** a-3. **Gene Fawcette** a-29, 30, 34, 37. **McWilliams** a-31-33, 36.*

FLASH GORDON
DC Comics: June, 1988 - No. 9, Holiday, 1988-'89 ($1.25, mini-series)

1-9: 1,5-Painted-c — 3.00

FLASH GORDON
Marvel Comics: June, 1995 - No. 2, July, 1995 ($2.95, limited series)

1,2: Schultz scripts; Williamson-a — 3.00

FLASH GORDON
Ardden Entertainment: Aug, 2008 - No. 6, Jul, 2009 ($3.99)

1-6: 1-Deneen-s/Green-a; two covers — 4.00

FLASH GORDON THE MOVIE
Western Publishing Co.: 1980 (8-1/4 x 11", $1.95, 68 pgs.)

	GD	VG	FN	VF	VF/NM	NM-
11294-Williamson-c/a; adapts movie	2	4	6	10	14	18
13743-Hardback edition	3	6	9	15	21	26

FLASH/ GREEN LANTERN: FASTER FRIENDS (See Green Lantern/Flash...)
DC Comics: No. 2, 1997 ($4.95, continuation of Green Lantern/Flash: Faster Friends #1)

2-Waid/Augustyn-s — 5.00

FLASHPOINT (Elseworlds Flash)
DC Comics: Dec, 1999 - No. 3, Feb, 2000 ($2.95, limited series)

1-3-Paralyzed Barry Allen; Breyfogle-a/McGreal-s — 3.00

FLAT-TOP
Mazie Comics/Harvey Publ.(Magazine Publ.) No. 4 on: 11/53 - No. 3, 5/54; No. 4, 3/55 - No. 7, 9/55

	GD	VG	FN	VF	VF/NM	NM-
1-Teenage; Flat-Top, Mazie, Mortie & Stevie begin	8	16	24	44	57	70
2,3	5	10	15	24	30	35
4-7	5	10	15	22	26	30

FLESH & BLOOD
Brainstorm Comics: Dec, 1995 ($2.95, B&W, mature)

1-Balent-c; foil-c. — 3.00

FLESH AND BONES
Upshot Graphics (Fantagraphics Books): June, 1986 - No. 4, Dec, 1986 (Limited series)

1-4: Alan Moore scripts (r) & Dalgoda by Fujitake — 3.00

FLESH CRAWLERS
Kitchen Sink Press: Aug, 1993 - No. 3, 1995 ($2.50, B&W, limited series, mature)

1-3 — 2.50

FLEX MENTALLO (Man of Muscle Mystery) (See Doom Patrol, 2nd Series)
DC Comics (Vertigo): Jun, 1996 - No. 4, Sept, 1996 ($2.50, lim. series, mature)

	GD	VG	FN	VF	VF/NM	NM-
1-4: Grant Morrison scripts & Frank Quitely-c/a in all; banned from reprints due to Charles Atlas legal action	2	4	6	9	13	16

FLINCH (Horror anthology)
DC Comics (Vertigo): Jun, 1999 - No. 16, Jan, 2001 ($2.50)

1-16: 1-Art by Jim Lee, Quitely, and Corben. 5-Sale-c. 11-Timm-a — 2.50

FLINTSTONE KIDS, THE (TV) (See Star Comics Digest)
Star Comics/Marvel Comics #5 on: Aug, 1987 - No. 11, Apr, 1989

1-11 — 4.50

Flintstones (1977 series) #4 © H-B

Flippity and Flop #41 © DC

Flying A's Range Rider #2 © DELL

FLINTSTONES, THE (TV)(See Dell Giant #48 for No. 1)
Dell Publ. Co./Gold Key No. 7 (10/62) on: No. 2, Nov-Dec, 1961 - No. 60, Sept, 1970 (Hanna-Barbera)

	GD 2.0	VG 4.0	FN 6.0	VF 8.0	VF/NM 9.0	NM- 9.2
2-2nd app. (TV show debuted on 9/30/60); 1st app. of Cave Kids; 15¢-c thru #5	10	20	30	70	123	175
3-6(7-8/62): 3-Perry Gunnite begins. 6-1st 12¢-c	7	14	21	45	73	100
7 (10/62; 1st GK)	7	14	21	45	73	100
8-10	6	12	18	37	59	80
11-1st app. Pebbles (6/63)	8	16	24	58	97	135
12-15,17-20	5	10	15	30	48	65
16-1st app. Bamm-Bamm (1/64)	8	16	24	54	90	125
21-23,25-30,33: 26,27-2nd & 3rd app. The Grusomes. 30-1st app. Martian Mopheads (10/65). 33-Meet Frankenstein & Dracula	4	8	12	28	44	60
24-1st app. The Grusomes	6	12	18	39	62	85
31,32,35-40: 31-Xmas-c. 36-Adaptation of "the Man Called Flintstone" movie. 39-Reprints	4	8	12	24	37	50
34-1st app. The Great Gazoo	6	12	18	39	62	85
41-60: 45-Last 12¢ issue	3	6	9	21	32	42
At N. Y. World's Fair ('64)-J.W. Books (25¢)-1st printing; no date on-c (29¢ version exists, 2nd print?) Most H-B characters app.; including Yogi Bear, Top Cat, Snagglepuss and the Jetsons	5	10	15	34	55	75
At N. Y. World's Fair (1965 on-c; re-issue; Warren Pub.) NOTE: Warehouse find in 1984	2	4	6	10	14	18
Bigger & Boulder 1(#30013-211) (Gold Key Giant, 11/62, 25¢, 84 pgs.)	8	16	24	54	90	125
Bigger & Boulder 2-(1966, 25¢)-Reprints B&B No. 1	5	10	15	32	51	70
...On the Rocks (9/61, $1.00, 6-1/4x9", cardboard-c, high quality paper,116 pgs.) B&W new material	9	18	27	63	107	150
...With Pebbles & Bamm Bamm (100 pgs., G.K.)-30028-511 (paper-c, 25¢) (11/65)	7	14	21	45	73	100

NOTE: *(See Comic Album #16, Bamm-Bamm & Pebbles Flintstone, Dell Giant 48, Golden Comics Digest, March of Comics #229, 243, 271, 289, 299, 317, 327, 341, Pebbles Flintstone, Top Comics #2-4, and Whitman Comic Book.)*

FLINTSTONES, THE (TV)(...& Pebbles)
Charlton Comics: Nov, 1970 - No. 50, Feb, 1977 (Hanna-Barbera)

	GD 2.0	VG 4.0	FN 6.0	VF 8.0	VF/NM 9.0	NM- 9.2
1	8	16	24	52	86	120
2	4	8	12	28	44	60
3-7,9,10	3	6	9	20	30	40
8- "Flintstones Summer Vacation" (Summer, 1971, 52 pgs.)	5	10	15	34	55	75
11-20,36: 36-Mike Zeck illos (early work)	3	6	9	16	23	30
21-35,38-41,43-45	3	6	9	14	19	24
37-Byrne text illos (early work; see Nightmare #20)	3	6	9	16	23	30
42-Byrne-a (2 pgs.)	3	6	9	16	23	30
46-50	2	4	6	13	18	22
Digest nn (1972, B&W, 100 pgs.) (low print run)	3	6	9	20	30	40

(Also see Barney & Betty Rubble, Dino, The Great Gazoo, & Pebbles & Bamm-Bamm)

FLINTSTONES, THE (TV)(See Yogi Bear, 3rd series) (Newsstand sales only)
Marvel Comics Group: October, 1977 - No. 9, Feb, 1979 (Hanna-Barbera)

	GD 2.0	VG 4.0	FN 6.0	VF 8.0	VF/NM 9.0	NM- 9.2
1,7-9: 1-(30¢-c). 7-9-Yogi Bear app.	3	6	9	20	30	40
1-(35¢-c variant, limited distribution)	9	18	27	60	100	140
2,3,5,6: Yogi Bear app.	3	6	9	16	22	28
4-The Jetsons app.	3	6	9	17	25	32

FLINTSTONES, THE (TV)
Harvey Comics: Sept, 1992 - No. 13, Jun, 1994 ($1.25/$1.50) (Hanna-Barbera)

	GD 2.0	VG 4.0	FN 6.0	VF 8.0	VF/NM 9.0	NM- 9.2
V2#1-13						4.00
...Big Book 1,2 (11/92, 3/93; both $1.95, 52 pgs.)						4.50
...Giant Size 1-3 (10/92, 4/93, 11/93; $2.25, 68 pgs.)						4.50

FLINTSTONES, THE (TV)
Archie Publications: Sept, 1995 - No. 22, June, 1997 ($1.50)

	GD 2.0	VG 4.0	FN 6.0	VF 8.0	VF/NM 9.0	NM- 9.2
1-22						3.00

FLINTSTONES AND THE JETSONS, THE (TV)
DC Comics: Aug, 1997 - No. 21, May, 1999 ($1.75/$1.95/$1.99)

	GD 2.0	VG 4.0	FN 6.0	VF 8.0	VF/NM 9.0	NM- 9.2
1						6.00
2-21: 19-Bizarro Elroy-c						3.00

FLINTSTONES CHRISTMAS PARTY, THE (See The Funtastic World of Hanna-Barbera No. 1)

FLIP
Harvey Publications: April, 1954 - No. 2, June, 1954 (Satire)

	GD 2.0	VG 4.0	FN 6.0	VF 8.0	VF/NM 9.0	NM- 9.2
1,2-Nostrand-a each. 2-Powell-a	22	44	66	128	209	290

FLIPPER (TV)
Gold Key: Apr, 1966 - No. 3, Nov, 1967 (All have photo-c)

	GD 2.0	VG 4.0	FN 6.0	VF 8.0	VF/NM 9.0	NM- 9.2
1	7	14	21	45	73	100
2,3	5	10	15	30	48	65

FLIPPITY & FLOP
National Per. Publ. (Signal Publ. Co.): 12-1/51-52 - No. 46, 8-10/59; No. 47, 9-11/60

	GD 2.0	VG 4.0	FN 6.0	VF 8.0	VF/NM 9.0	NM- 9.2
1-Sam dog & his pets Flippity The Bird and Flop The Cat begin; Twiddle and Twaddle begin	27	54	81	158	259	360
2	15	30	45	85	130	175
3-5	14	28	42	76	108	140
6-10	11	22	33	62	86	110
11-20: 20-Last precode (3/55)	10	20	30	56	76	95
21-47	9	18	27	50	65	80

FLOATERS
Dark Horse Comics: Sept, 1993 - No. 5, Jan, 1994 ($2.50, B&W, lim. series)

	GD 2.0	VG 4.0	FN 6.0	VF 8.0	VF/NM 9.0	NM- 9.2
1-5						2.50

FLOYD FARLAND (See Eclipse Graphic Album Series #11)

FLY, THE (Also see Adventures of..., Blue Ribbon Comics & Flyman)
Archie Enterprises, Inc.: May, 1983 - No. 9, Oct, 1984

	GD 2.0	VG 4.0	FN 6.0	VF 8.0	VF/NM 9.0	NM- 9.2
1,2: 1-Mr. Justice app; origin Shield; Kirby-a; Steranko-c. 2-Ditko-a; Flygirl app.						6.00
3-5: Ditko-a in all. 4,5-Ditko-c(p)						4.50
6-9: Ditko-a in all. 6-8-Ditko-c(p)						6.00

NOTE: *Ayers c-9. Buckler a-1, 2. Kirby a-1. Nebres c-3, 4, 5i, 6, 7i. Steranko c-1, 2.*

FLY, THE
Impact Comics (DC): Aug, 1991 - No. 17, Dec, 1992 ($1.00)

	GD 2.0	VG 4.0	FN 6.0	VF 8.0	VF/NM 9.0	NM- 9.2
1						3.00
2-17: 4-Vs. The Black Hood. 9-Trading card inside						2.50
Annual 1 ('92, $2.50, 68 pgs.)-Impact trading card						3.00

FLYBOY (Flying Cadets)(Also see Approved Comics #5)
Ziff-Davis Publ. Co. (Approved): Spring, 1952 - No. 2, Oct-Nov, 1952

	GD 2.0	VG 4.0	FN 6.0	VF 8.0	VF/NM 9.0	NM- 9.2
1-Saunders painted-c	20	40	60	114	182	250
2-(10-11/52)-Saunders painted-c	14	28	42	80	115	150

FLYING ACES (Aviation stories)
Key Publications: July, 1955 - No. 5, Mar, 1956

	GD 2.0	VG 4.0	FN 6.0	VF 8.0	VF/NM 9.0	NM- 9.2
1	8	16	24	44	57	70
2-5: 2-Trapani-a	5	10	15	24	30	35

FLYING A'S RANGE RIDER, THE (TV)(See Western Roundup under Dell Giants)
Dell Publishing Co.: #404, 6-7/52; #2, June-Aug, 1953 - #24, Aug, 1959 (All photo-c)

	GD 2.0	VG 4.0	FN 6.0	VF 8.0	VF/NM 9.0	NM- 9.2
Four Color 404(#1)-Titled "The Range Rider"	9	18	27	65	113	160
2	6	12	18	41	66	90
3-10	5	10	15	34	55	75
11-16,18-24	5	10	15	30	48	65
17-Toth-a	6	12	18	37	59	80

FLYING CADET (WW II Plane Photos)
Flying Cadet Publ. Co.; Jan, 1943 - V2#8, 1944 (Half photos, half comics)

	GD 2.0	VG 4.0	FN 6.0	VF 8.0	VF/NM 9.0	NM- 9.2
V1#1-Painted-c	15	30	45	85	130	175
2	9	18	27	52	69	85
3-9 (Two #6's, Sept. & Oct.): 5,6a,6b-Photo-c	9	18	27	47	61	75
V2#1-7(#10-16)	8	16	24	42	54	65
7(#17 on cover)-Bare-breasted woman-c	18	36	54	107	169	230

FLYING COLORS 10th ANNIVERSARY SPECIAL
Flying Colors Comics: Fall 1998 ($2.95, one-shot)

	GD 2.0	VG 4.0	FN 6.0	VF 8.0	VF/NM 9.0	NM- 9.2
1-Dan Brereton-c; pin-ups by Jim Lee and Jeff Johnson						3.00

FLYIN' JENNY
Pentagon Publ. Co./Leader Enterprises #2: 1946 - No. 2, 1947 (1945 strip-r)

	GD 2.0	VG 4.0	FN 6.0	VF 8.0	VF/NM 9.0	NM- 9.2
nn-Marcus Swayze strip-r (entire insides)	15	30	45	83	124	165
2-Baker-c; Swayze strip reprints	17	34	51	98	154	210

FLYING MODELS
H-K Publ. (Health-Knowledge Publs.): V61#3, May, 1954 (5¢, 16 pgs.)

	GD 2.0	VG 4.0	FN 6.0	VF 8.0	VF/NM 9.0	NM- 9.2
V61#3 (Rare)	9	18	27	50	65	80

FLYING NUN (TV)
Dell Publishing Co.: Feb, 1968 - No. 4, Nov, 1968

	GD 2.0	VG 4.0	FN 6.0	VF 8.0	VF/NM 9.0	NM- 9.2
1-Sally Field photo-c	7	14	21	45	73	100
2-4: 2-Sally Field photo-c	4	8	12	28	44	60

FLYING NURSES (See Sue & Sally Smith...)

FLYING SAUCERS (See The Spirit 9/28/47(1st app.), Shadow Comics V7#10 (2nd, 1/48), Captain Midnight #60 (3rd, 2/48), Boy Commandos #26 (4th, 3-4/48) & Flash Gordon Four Color 190 (5th, 6/48))

Fly Man #35 © AP

FOOM #15 © MAR

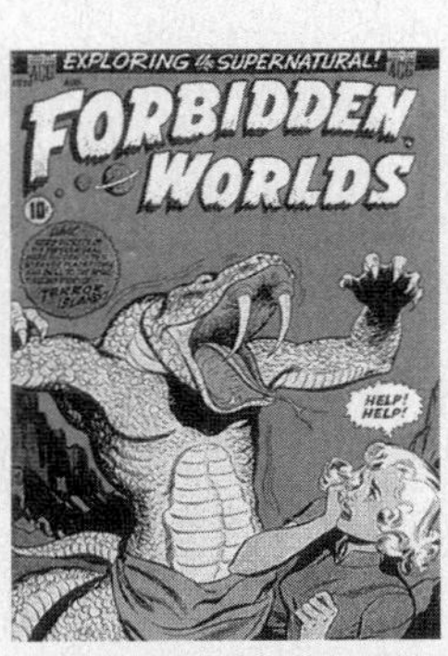

Forbidden Worlds #20 © ACG

	GD 2.0	VG 4.0	FN 6.0	VF 8.0	VF/NM 9.0	NM- 9.2

FLYING SAUCERS (See Out of This World Adventures #2)
Avon Periodicals/Realistic: 1950; 1952; 1953

	GD	VG	FN	VF	VF/NM	NM-
1(1950)-Wood-a, 21 pgs.; Fawcette-c	82	164	246	528	902	1275
nn(1952)-Cover altered plus 2 pgs. of Wood-a not in original	46	92	138	290	488	685
nn(1953)-Reprints above	35	70	105	208	339	470

FLYING SAUCERS (Comics)
Dell Publishing Co.: April, 1967 - No. 4, Nov, 1967; No. 5, Oct, 1969

	GD	VG	FN	VF	VF/NM	NM-
1-(12¢-c)	4	8	12	26	41	55
2-5: 5-Has same cover as #1, but with 15¢ price	3	6	9	19	29	38

FLY MAN (Formerly Adventures of The Fly; Mighty Comics #40 on)
Mighty Comics Group (Radio Comics) (Archie): No. 32, July, 1965 - No. 39, Sept, 1966 (Also see Mighty Crusaders)

	GD	VG	FN	VF	VF/NM	NM-
32,33-Comet, Shield, Black Hood, The Fly & Flygirl x-over. 33-Re-intro Wizard, Hangman (1st S.A. appearances)	6	12	18	39	62	85
34-39: 34-Shield begins. 35-Origin Black Hood. 36-Hangman x-over in Shield; re-intro. & origin of Web (1st S.A. app.). 37-Hangman, Wizard x-over in Flyman; last Shield issue. 38-Web story. 39-Steel Sterling (1st S.A. app.)	4	8	12	28	44	60

FOLLOW THE SUN (TV)
Dell Publishing Co.: May-July, 1962 - No. 2, Sept-Nov, 1962 (Photo-c)

	GD	VG	FN	VF	VF/NM	NM-
01-280-207(No.1)	5	10	15	30	48	65
12-280-211(No.2)	5	10	15	30	48	65

FOODANG
Continum Comics: July, 1994 ($1.95, B&W, bi-monthly)

	GD	VG	FN	VF	VF/NM	NM-
1						2.50

FOODINI (TV)(The Great...; see Jingle Dingle & Pinhead &...)
Continental Publ. (Holyoke): March, 1950 - No. 4, Aug, 1950 (All have 52 pgs.)

	GD	VG	FN	VF	VF/NM	NM-
1-Based on TV puppet show (very early TV comic)	22	44	66	128	209	290
2-Jingle Dingle begins	14	28	42	78	112	145
3,4	10	20	30	56	76	95

FOOEY (Magazine) (Satire)
Scoff Publishing Co.: Feb, 1961 - No. 4, May, 1961

	GD	VG	FN	VF	VF/NM	NM-
1	5	10	15	30	48	65
2-4	3	6	9	20	30	40

FOOFUR (TV)
Marvel Comics (Star Comics)/Marvel No. 5 on: Aug, 1987 - No. 6, Jun, 1988

	GD	VG	FN	VF	VF/NM	NM-
1-6						3.00

FOOLKILLER (Also see The Amazing Spider-Man #225, The Defenders #73, Man-Thing #3 & Omega the Unknown #8)
Marvel Comics: Oct, 1990 - No. 10, Oct, 1991 ($1.75, limited series)

	GD	VG	FN	VF	VF/NM	NM-
1-10: 1-Origin 3rd Foolkiller; Greg Salinger app; DeZuniga-a(i) in 1-4. 8-Spider-Man x-over						2.50

FOOLKILLER
Marvel Comics: Dec, 2007 - No. 5, Jul, 2008 ($3.99, limited series)

	GD	VG	FN	VF	VF/NM	NM-
1-5-Hurwitz-s/Medina-a. 2-Origin						4.00

FOOLKILLER: WHITE ANGELS
Marvel Comics: Sept, 2008 - No. 5, Jan, 2009 ($3.99, limited series)

	GD	VG	FN	VF	VF/NM	NM-
1-5-Hurwitz-s/Azaceta-a						4.00

FOOM (Friends Of Ol' Marvel)
Marvel Comics: 1973 - No. 22, 1979 (Marvel fan magazine)

	GD	VG	FN	VF	VF/NM	NM-
1	8	16	24	52	86	120
2-Hulk-c by Steranko	5	10	15	34	55	75
3,4	5	10	15	32	51	70
5-11: 11-Kirby-a and interview	4	8	12	28	44	60
12-15: 12-Vision-c. 13-Daredevil-c. 14-Conan. 15-Howard the Duck	4	8	12	28	44	60
16-20: 16-Marvel bullpen. 17-Stan Lee issue. 19-Defenders	4	8	12	24	37	50
21-Star Wars	4	8	12	26	41	55
22-Spider-Man-c; low print run final issue	6	12	18	39	62	85

FOOTBALL THRILLS (See Tops In Adventure)
Ziff-Davis Publ. Co.: Fall-Winter, 1951-52 - No. 2, Fall, 1952 (Edited by "Red" Grange)

	GD	VG	FN	VF	VF/NM	NM-
1-Powell a(2); Saunders painted-c; Red Grange, Jim Thorpe stories	27	54	81	158	259	360
2-Saunders painted-c	18	36	54	105	165	225

FOOT SOLDIERS, THE
Dark Horse Comics: Jan, 1996 - No. 4, Apr, 1996 ($2.95, limited series)

	GD	VG	FN	VF	VF/NM	NM-
1-4: Krueger story & Avon Oeming-a. in all. 1-Alex Ross-c. 4-John K. Snyder, III-c						3.00

FOOT SOLDIERS, THE (Volume Two)
Image Comics: Sept, 1997 - No. 5, May, 1998 ($2.95, limited series)

	GD	VG	FN	VF	VF/NM	NM-
1-5: 1-Yeowell-a. 2-McDaniel, Hester, Sienkiewicz, Giffen-a						3.00

FOR A NIGHT OF LOVE
Avon Periodicals: 1951

	GD	VG	FN	VF	VF/NM	NM-
nn-Two stories adapted from the works of Emile Zola; Astarita, Ravielli-a; Kinstler-c	31	62	93	182	296	410

FORBIDDEN KNOWLEDGE: ADVENTURE BEYOND THE DOORWAY TO SOULS WITH RADICAL DREAMER (Also see Radical Dreamer)
Mark's Giant Economy Size Comics: 1996 ($3.50, B&W, one-shot, 48 pgs.)

	GD	VG	FN	VF	VF/NM	NM-
nn-Max Wrighter app.; Wheatley-c/a/script; painted infinity-c						3.50

FORBIDDEN LOVE
Quality Comics Group: Mar, 1950 - No. 4, Sept, 1950 (52 pgs.)

	GD	VG	FN	VF	VF/NM	NM-
1-(Scarce)-Classic photo-c; Crandall-a	76	152	228	486	831	1175
2-(Scarce)-Classic photo-c	63	126	189	403	684	975
3-(Scarce)-Photo-c	40	80	120	243	402	560
4-(Scarce)-Ward/Cuidera-a; photo-c	40	80	120	246	411	575

FORBIDDEN LOVE (See Dark Mansion of...)

FORBIDDEN PLANET
Innovation Publishing: May, 1992 - No. 4, 1992 ($2.50, limited series)

	GD	VG	FN	VF	VF/NM	NM-
1-4: Adapts movie; painted-c						2.50

FORBIDDEN TALES OF DARK MANSION (Formerly Dark Mansion of Forbidden Love #1-4)
National Periodical Publ.: No. 5, May-June, 1972 - No. 15, Feb-Mar, 1974

	GD	VG	FN	VF	VF/NM	NM-
5-(52 pgs.)	6	12	18	39	62	85
6-15: 13-Kane/Howard-a	3	6	9	18	27	35

NOTE: ***N. Adams*** *c-9.* ***Alcala*** *a-9-11, 13.* ***Chaykin*** *a-7,15.* ***Evans*** *a-14.* ***Heck*** *a-5.* ***Kaluta*** *a-7i, 8-12; c-7, 8, 13.* ***G. Kane*** *a-13.* ***Kirby*** *a-6.* ***Nino*** *a-8, 12, 15.* ***Redondo*** *a-14.*

FORBIDDEN WORLDS
American Comics Group: 7-8/51 - No. 34, 10-11/54; No. 35, 8/55 - No. 145, 8/67 (No. 1-5: 52 pgs.; No. 6-8: 44 pgs.)

	GD	VG	FN	VF	VF/NM	NM-
1-Williamson/Frazetta-a (10 pgs.)	158	316	474	1003	1727	2450
2	66	132	198	419	722	1025
3-Williamson/Orlando-a (7 pgs.); Wood (2 panels); Frazetta (1 panel)	67	134	201	426	733	1040
4	43	86	129	269	455	640
5-Krenkel/Williamson-a (8 pgs.)	53	106	159	334	567	800
6-Harrison/Williamson-a (8 pgs.)	47	94	141	296	498	700
7,8,10: 7-1st monthly issue	32	64	96	188	307	425
9-A-Bomb explosion story	35	70	105	208	339	470
11-20	21	42	63	124	202	280
21-33: 24-E.C. swipe by Landau	17	34	51	100	158	215
34(10-11/54)(Scarce)(becomes Young Heroes #35 on)-Last pre-code issue; A-Bomb explosion story	19	38	57	112	179	245
35(8/55)-Scarce	19	38	57	109	172	235
36-62	13	26	39	74	105	135
63,69,76,78-Williamson-a in all; w/Krenkel #69	14	28	42	76	108	140
64,66-68,70-72,74,75,77,79-85,87-90	10	20	30	56	76	95
65- "There's a New Moon Tonight" listed in #114 as holding 1st record fan mail response	14	28	42	76	108	140
73-1st app. Herbie by Ogden Whitney	41	82	123	256	428	600
86-Flying saucer-c by Schaffenberger	11	22	33	62	86	110
91-93,95-100	5	10	15	34	55	75
94-Herbie (2nd app.)	11	22	33	74	132	190
101-109,111-113,115,117-120	4	8	12	28	44	60
110,116-Herbie app. 116-Herbie goes to Hell	7	14	21	49	80	110
114-1st Herbie-c; contains list of editor's top 20 ACG stories	9	18	27	63	107	150
121-123	4	8	12	22	34	45
124,126-130: 124-Magic Agent app. 126-Herbie	4	8	12	24	37	50
125-Magic Agent app.; intro. & origin Magicman series, ends #141; Herbie app.	5	10	15	34	55	75
131-139: 133-Origin/1st app. Dragonia in Magicman (1-2/66); returns in #138. 136-Nemesis x-over in Magicman	4	8	12	22	34	45
140-Mark Midnight app. by Ditko	4	8	12	24	37	50
141-145	3	6	9	20	30	40

NOTE: ***Buscema*** *a-75, 79, 81, 82, 140r.* ***Cameron*** *a-5.* ***Disbrow*** *a-10.* ***Ditko*** *a-137p, 138, 140.* ***Landau*** *a-24, 27-29, 31-34, 48, 86r, 96, 143-45.* ***Lazarus*** *a-18, 23, 24, 57.* ***Moldoff*** *a-27, 31, 139r.* ***Reinman*** *a-93.* ***Whitney*** *a-70, 115, 116, 137; c-40, 46, 57, 60, 68, 70, 78, 79, 90, 93, 94, 100, 102, 103, 106-108, 114, 129.*

FORCE, THE (See The Crusaders)

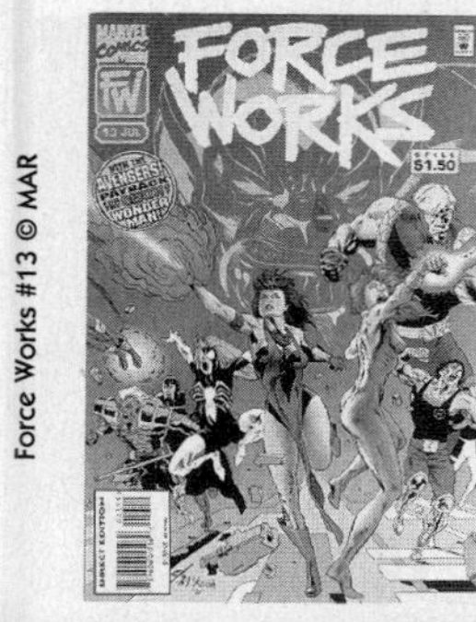

Force Works #13 © MAR

Formerly Known as the Justice League #1 © DC

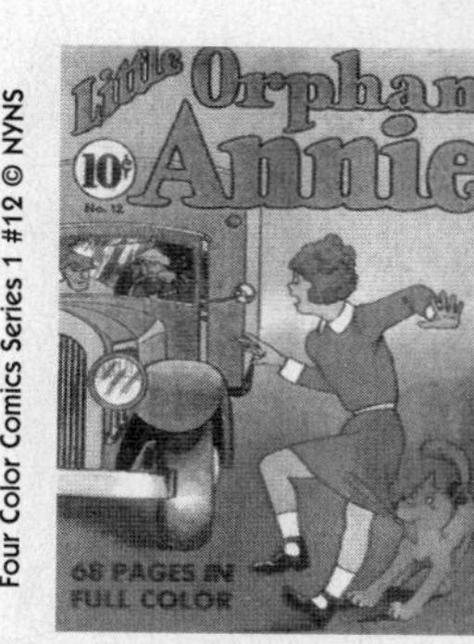

Four Color Comics Series 1 #12 © NYNS

GD 2.0 | VG 4.0 | FN 6.0 | VF 8.0 | VF/NM 9.0 | NM- 9.2

FORCE MAJEURE: PRAIRIE BAY (Also see Wild Stars)
Little Rocket Publications: May, 2002 ($2.95, B&W)

1-Tierney-s/Gil-c/a 3.00

FORCE OF BUDDHA'S PALM THE
Jademan Comics: Aug, 1988 - No. 55, Feb, 1993 ($1.50/$1.95, 68 pgs.)

1,55-Kung Fu stories in all 3.00
2-54 2.50

FORCE WORKS
Marvel Comics: July, 1994 - No. 22, Apr, 1996 ($1.50)

1-($3.95)-Fold-out pop-up-c; Iron Man, Wonder Man, Spider-Woman, U.S. Agent & Scarlet Witch (new costume) 4.00
2-11, 13-22: 5-Blue logo & pink logo versions. 9-Intro Dreamguard. 13-Avengers app. 2.50
5-Pink logo ($2.95)-polybagged w/ 16pg. Marvel Action Hour Preview & acetate print 3.00
12 ($2.50)-Flip book w/War Machine. 2.50

FORD ROTUNDA CHRISTMAS BOOK (See Christmas at the Rotunda)

FOREIGN INTRIGUES (Formerly Johnny Dynamite; becomes Battlefield Action #16 on)
Charlton Comics: No. 14, 1956 - No. 15, Aug, 1956

14,15-Johnny Dynamite continues 8 16 24 42 54 65

FOREMOST BOYS (See 4Most)

FOREVER AMBER
Image Comics: July, 1999 - Oct, 1999 ($2.95, B&W)

1-4-Don Hudson-s/a 3.00

FOREVER DARLING (Movie)
Dell Publishing Co.: No. 681, Feb, 1956

Four Color 681-w/Lucille Ball & Desi Arnaz; photo-c 11 22 33 80 145 210

FOREVER MAELSTROM
DC Comics: Jan, 2003 - No. 6, Jun, 2003 ($2.95, limited series)

1-6-Chaykin & Tischman-s/Lucas & Barreto-a 3.00

FOREVER PEOPLE, THE
National Periodical Publications: Feb-Mar, 1971 - No. 11, Oct-Nov, 1972 (Fourth World) (#1-3, 10-11 are 36 pgs; #4-9 are 52 pgs.)

1-1st app. Forever People; Superman x-over; Kirby-c/a begins; 1st full app. Darkseid (3rd anywhere, 3 weeks before New Gods #1); Darkseid storyline begins, ends #8 (app. in 1-4,6,8; cameos in 5,11) 7 14 21 49 80 110
2-9: 4-G.A. reprints thru #9. 9,10-Deadman app. 4 8 12 26 41 55
10,11 3 6 9 20 30 40
Jack Kirby's Forever People TPB ('99, $14.95, B&W&Grey) r/#1-11 plus cover gallery 15.00
NOTE: *Kirby c/a(p)-1-11; #4-9 contain Sandman reprints from Adventure #85, 84, 75, 80, 77, 74 in that order.*

FOREVER PEOPLE
DC Comics: Feb, 1988 - No. 6, July, 1988 ($1.25, limited series)

1-6 3.00

FORGE
CrossGeneration Comics: Feb, 2002 - No. 13, May, 2003 ($9.95/$11.95/$7.95, TPB)

1-3: Reprints from various CrossGen titles 10.00
4-8-($11.95) 12.00
9-13-($7.95, 8-1/4" x 5-1/2") digest-sized reprints 8.00

FOR GIRLS ONLY
Bernard Baily Enterprises: 11/53 - No. 2, 6/54 (100 pgs., digest size, 25¢)

1-25% comic book, 75% articles, illos, games 15 30 45 90 140 190
2-Eddie Fisher photo & story. 11 22 33 64 90 115

FORGOTTEN FOREST OF OZ, THE (See First Comics Graphic Novel #16)

FORGOTTEN REALMS (Also see Avatar & TSR Worlds)
DC Comics: Sept, 1989 - No. 25, Sept, 1991 ($1.50/$1.75)

1, Annual 1 (1990, $2.95, 68 pgs.) 3.00
2-25: Based on TSR role-playing game. 18-Avatar story 2.50

FORGOTTEN REALMS (Based on Wizards of the Coast game)
Devil's Due Publ.: June, 2005 - No. 3, Aug, 2005 ($4.95)

1-3-Salvatore-s/Seeley-a 5.00
...Exile (11/05 - No. 3, 1/06, $4.95) 1-3-Daab-s/Seeley-a. 1-Flip cover 5.00
...: Legacy (2/08 - No. 3, 6/08, $5.50) 1-3-Daab-s/Atkins-a 5.50
The Legend of Drizzt Book II: Exile (2006, $14.95, TPB) r/#1-3 15.00
...Sojourn (3/06 - No. 3, 6/06, $4.95) 1-3-Daab-s/Seeley-a 5.00
...: Streams of Silver (12/06 - No. 3, $5.50) 1-3-Daab-s/Semeiks-a 5.50
...The Crystal Shard (8/06 - No. 3, 12/06, $4.95) 1-3-Daab-s/Semeiks-a 5.00
...The Halfling's Gem (8/07 - No. 3, 12/07, $5.50) 1-3-Daab-s/Seeley-a; two covers 5.50

FORLORN RIVER (See Zane Grey Four Color 395)

FOR LOVERS ONLY (Formerly Hollywood Romances)
Charlton Comics: No. 60, Aug, 1971 - No. 87, Nov, 1976

60 3 6 9 20 30 40
61-80,82-87: 67-Morisi-a 2 4 6 11 16 20
81-Psychedelic cover 3 6 9 14 20 25

FORMERLY KNOWN AS THE JUSTICE LEAGUE
DC Comics: Sept, 2003 - No. 6, Feb, 2004 ($2.50, limited series)

1-Giffen & DeMatteis-s/Maguire-a; Booster Gold, Blue Beetle, Captain Atom, Mary Marvel, Fire, and Elongated Man app. 3.00
2-6: 3,4-Roulette app. 6-JLA app. 2.50
TPB (2004, $12.95) r/#1-6 13.00

FORT: PROPHET OF THE UNEXPLAINED
Dark Horse Comics: June, 2002 - No. 4, Sept, 2002 ($2.99, B&W, limited series)

1-4-Peter Lenkov-s/Frazer Irving-c/a 3.00
TPB (2003, $9.95) r/#1-4 10.00

FORTUNE AND GLORY
Oni Press: Dec, 1999 - No. 3, Apr, 2000 ($4.95, B&W, limited series)

1-3-Brian Michael Bendis in Hollywood 5.00
TPB ($14.95) 15.00

40 BIG PAGES OF MICKEY MOUSE
Whitman Publ. Co.: No. 945, Jan, 1936 (10-1/4x12-1/2", 44 pgs., cardboard-c)

945-Reprints Mickey Mouse Magazine #1, but with a different cover; ads were eliminated and some illustrated stories had expanded text. The book is 3/4" shorter than Mickey Mouse Mag. #1, but the reprints are same size (Rare) 164 328 492 1025 1663 2300

40 oz. COLLECTED
Image Comics: Nov, 2003 ($9.95, digest-size, B&W)

Vol. 1-Reprints Jim Mahfood's mini-comics plus 20 pgs. new material; Grrl Scouts app. 10.00

FOR YOUR EYES ONLY (See James Bond...)

FOUNTAIN, THE (Companion graphic novel to the Darren Aronofsky film)
DC Comics (Vertigo): 2005 ($39.99, hardcover with dust jacket)

1-Darren Aronofsky-s/Kent Williams-a 40.00

FOUR (Fantastic Four; See Marvel Knights 4 #28-30)

FOUR COLOR
Dell Publishing Co.: Sept?, 1939 - No. 1354, Apr-June, 1962 (Series I are all 68 pgs.)

NOTE: *Four Color only appears on issues #19-25, 1-99,101. Dell Publishing Co. filed these as Series I, #1-25, and Series II, #1-1354. Issues beginning with #710? were printed with and without ads on back cover. Issues without ads are worth more.*

SERIES I:
1(nn)-Dick Tracy 975 1950 2919 7100 12,550 18,000
2(nn)-Don Winslow of the Navy (#1) (Rare) (11/39?) 187 374 561 1197 2049 2900
3(nn)-Myra North (1/40) 95 190 285 603 1039 1475
4-Donald Duck by Al Taliaferro (1940)(Disney)(3/40?) 1500 3000 4500 11,250 17,625 24,000
(Prices vary widely on this book)
5-Smilin' Jack (#1) (5/40?) 71 142 213 454 777 1100
6-Dick Tracy (Scarce) 213 426 639 1363 2332 3300
7-Gang Busters 48 96 144 302 514 725
8-Dick Tracy 107 214 321 680 1165 1650
9-Terry and the Pirates-r/Super #9-29 67 134 201 426 731 1035
10-Smilin' Jack 61 122 183 387 664 940
11-Smitty (#1) 45 90 135 284 480 675
12-Little Orphan Annie; reprints strips from 12/19/37 to 6/4/38 57 114 171 362 624 885
13-Walt Disney's Reluctant Dragon('41)-Contains 2 pgs. of photos from film; 2 pg. foreword to Fantasia by Leopold Stokowski; Donald Duck, Goofy, Baby Weems & Mickey Mouse (as the Sorcerer's Apprentice) app. (Disney) 219 438 657 1402 2401 3400
14-Moon Mullins (#1) 45 90 135 284 480 675
15-Tillie the Toiler (#1) 45 90 135 284 480 675
16-Mickey Mouse (#1) (Disney) by Gottfredson 1250 2500 3750 15,500 - -
17-Walt Disney's Dumbo, the Flying Elephant (#1)(1941)-Mickey Mouse, Donald Duck, & Pluto app. (Disney) 261 522 783 1657 2854 4050
18-Jiggs and Maggie (#1)(1936-38-r) 48 96 144 300 510 720
19-Barney Google and Snuffy Smith (#1)-(1st issue with Four Color on the cover)

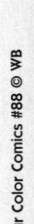

Four Color Comics Series 2 #29 © DIS

Four Color Comics #55 © KING

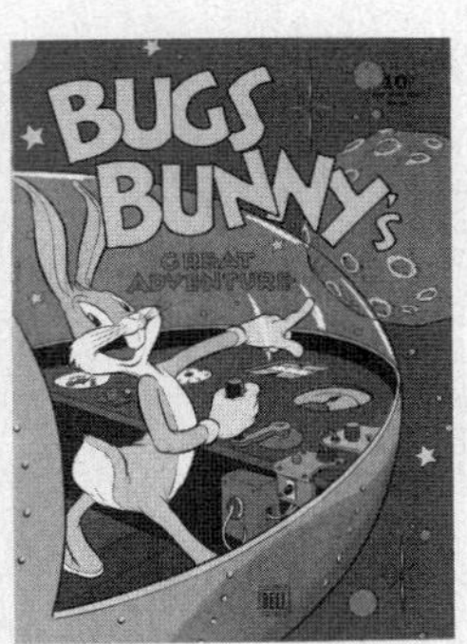

Four Color Comics #88 © WB

	GD 2.0	VG 4.0	FN 6.0	VF 8.0	VF/NM 9.0	NM- 9.2
	47	94	141	296	498	700
20-Tiny Tim	37	74	111	218	354	490
21-Dick Tracy	79	158	237	502	864	1225
22-Don Winslow	45	90	135	284	480	675
23-Gang Busters	39	78	117	240	395	550
24-Captain Easy	50	100	150	315	533	750
25-Popeye (1942)	84	168	252	538	919	1300
SERIES II:						
1-Little Joe (1942)	50	100	150	413	807	1200
2-Harold Teen	29	58	87	212	406	600
3-Alley Oop (#1)	42	84	126	336	656	975
4-Smilin' Jack	38	76	114	287	556	825
5-Raggedy Ann and Andy (#1)	46	92	138	368	709	1050
6-Smitty	21	42	63	149	290	430
7-Smokey Stover (#1)	27	54	81	194	377	560
8-Tillie the Toiler	23	46	69	163	314	465
9-Donald Duck Finds Pirate Gold, by Carl Barks & Jack Hannah (Disney) (© 8/17/42)	1000	2000	3000	7400	13,200	19,000
10-Flash Gordon by Alex Raymond; reprinted from "The Ice Kingdom"	80	160	240	680	1340	2000
11-Wash Tubbs	28	56	84	203	377	550
12-Walt Disney's Bambi (#1)	50	100	150	400	775	1150
13-Mr. District Attorney (#1)-See The Funnies #35 for 1st app.	27	54	81	194	377	560
14-Smilin' Jack	30	60	90	218	422	625
15-Felix the Cat (#1)	74	148	222	629	1240	1850
16-Porky Pig (#1)(1942)- "Secret of the Haunted House"	82	164	246	697	1374	2050
17-Popeye	42	84	126	336	648	960
18-Little Orphan Annie's Junior Commandos; Flag-c; reprints strips from 6/14/42 to 11/21/42	33	66	99	256	496	735
19-Walt Disney's Thumper Meets the Seven Dwarfs (Disney); reprinted in Silly Symphonies	46	92	138	368	709	1050
20-Barney Baxter	25	50	75	183	354	525
21-Oswald the Rabbit (#1)(1943)	42	84	126	336	651	965
22-Tillie the Toiler	17	34	51	119	230	340
23-Raggedy Ann and Andy	34	68	102	262	506	750
24-Gang Busters	26	52	78	185	360	535
25-Andy Panda (#1) (Walter Lantz)	50	100	150	413	807	1200
26-Popeye	42	84	126	336	648	960
27-Walt Disney's Mickey Mouse and the Seven Colored Terror	76	152	228	646	1273	1900
28-Wash Tubbs	19	38	57	135	250	365
29-Donald Duck and the Mummy's Ring, by Carl Barks (Disney) (9/43)	730	1460	2190	5329	9415	13,500
30-Bambi's Children (1943)-Disney	45	90	135	360	693	1025
31-Moon Mullins	17	34	51	119	230	340
32-Smitty	15	30	45	104	197	290
33-Bugs Bunny "Public Nuisance #1"	96	192	288	816	1608	2400
34-Dick Tracy	40	80	120	309	597	885
35-Smokey Stover	16	32	48	113	217	320
36-Smilin' Jack	22	44	66	155	300	445
37-Bringing Up Father	19	38	57	133	259	385
38-Roy Rogers (#1, © 4/44)-1st western comic with photo-c (see Movie Comics #3)	160	320	480	1400	2700	4000
39-Oswald the Rabbit (1944)	29	58	87	212	406	600
40-Barney Google and Snuffy Smith	21	42	63	148	287	425
41-Mother Goose and Nursery Rhyme Comics (#1)-All by Walt Kelly	22	44	66	157	304	450
42-Tiny Tim (1934-r)	16	32	48	112	214	315
43-Popeye (1938-'42-r)	30	60	90	218	422	625
44-Terry and the Pirates (1938-r)	34	68	102	260	500	740
45-Raggedy Ann	29	58	87	212	406	600
46-Felix the Cat and the Haunted Castle	40	80	120	314	607	900
47-Gene Autry (copyright 6/16/44)	33	66	99	254	477	700
48-Porky Pig of the Mounties by Carl Barks (7/44)	88	176	264	748	1474	2200
49-Snow White and the Seven Dwarfs (Disney)	50	100	150	400	775	1150
50-Fairy Tale Parade-Walt Kelly art (1944)	24	48	72	175	338	500
51-Bugs Bunny Finds the Lost Treasure	32	64	96	248	479	710
52-Little Orphan Annie; reprints strips from 6/18/38 to 11/19/38	26	52	78	186	361	535
53-Wash Tubbs	14	28	42	102	181	260
54-Andy Panda	29	58	87	212	406	600
55-Tillie the Toiler	13	26	39	91	168	245

	GD 2.0	VG 4.0	FN 6.0	VF 8.0	VF/NM 9.0	NM- 9.2
56-Dick Tracy	36	72	108	275	530	785
57-Gene Autry	31	62	93	239	445	650
58-Smilin' Jack	22	44	66	155	300	445
59-Mother Goose and Nursery Rhyme Comics-Kelly-c/a	18	36	54	126	246	365
60-Tiny Folks Funnies	15	30	45	104	197	290
61-Santa Claus Funnies(11/44)-Kelly art	23	46	69	163	314	465
62-Donald Duck in Frozen Gold, by Carl Barks (Disney) (1/45)	212	424	636	1855	3678	5500
63-Roy Rogers; color photo-all 4 covers	40	80	120	312	581	850
64-Smokey Stover	13	26	39	90	165	240
65-Smitty	12	24	36	86	158	230
66-Gene Autry	31	62	93	239	445	650
67-Oswald the Rabbit	17	34	51	119	230	340
68-Mother Goose and Nursery Rhyme Comics, by Walt Kelly	18	36	54	126	246	365
69-Fairy Tale Parade, by Walt Kelly	24	48	72	175	338	500
70-Popeye and Wimpy	22	44	66	155	300	445
71-Walt Disney's Three Caballeros, by Walt Kelly (© 4/45)-(Disney)	62	124	186	527	1039	1550
72-Raggedy Ann	23	46	69	170	328	485
73-The Gumps (#1)	12	24	36	83	152	220
74-Marge's Little Lulu (#1)	124	248	372	1054	2077	3100
75-Gene Autry and the Wildcat	25	50	75	185	343	500
76-Little Orphan Annie; reprints strips from 2/28/40 to 6/24/40	21	42	63	149	290	430
77-Felix the Cat	38	76	114	294	567	840
78-Porky Pig and the Bandit Twins	26	52	78	190	370	550
79-Walt Disney's Mickey Mouse in The Riddle of the Red Hat by Carl Barks (8/45)	92	184	276	782	1541	2300
80-Smilin' Jack	14	28	42	100	188	275
81-Moon Mullins	10	20	30	73	129	185
82-Lone Ranger	38	76	114	288	557	825
83-Gene Autry in Outlaw Trail	25	50	75	185	343	500
84-Flash Gordon by Alex Raymond-Reprints from "The Fiery Desert"	41	82	123	326	633	940
85-Andy Panda and the Mad Dog Mystery	16	32	48	115	220	325
86-Roy Rogers; photo-c	29	58	87	217	401	585
87-Fairy Tale Parade by Walt Kelly; Dan Noonan-c	24	48	72	175	338	500
88-Bugs Bunny's Great Adventure (Sci/fi)	23	46	69	163	314	465
89-Tillie the Toiler	13	26	39	91	168	245
90-Christmas with Mother Goose by Walt Kelly (11/45)	16	32	48	116	223	330
91-Santa Claus Funnies by Walt Kelly (11/45)	17	34	51	119	230	340
92-Walt Disney's The Wonderful Adventures Of Pinocchio (1945); Donald Duck by Kelly, 16 pgs. (Disney)	50	100	150	400	775	1150
93-Gene Autry in The Bandit of Black Rock	22	44	66	157	291	425
94-Winnie Winkle (1945)	12	24	36	85	155	225
95-Roy Rogers Comics; photo-c	29	58	87	217	401	585
96-Dick Tracy	24	48	72	175	338	500
97-Marge's Little Lulu (1946)	52	104	156	442	871	1300
98-Lone Ranger, The	29	58	87	212	406	600
99-Smitty	10	20	30	73	129	185
100-Gene Autry Comics; 1st Gene Autry photo-c	24	48	72	181	336	490
101-Terry and the Pirates	21	42	63	151	293	435

NOTE: *No. 101 is last issue to carry "Four Color" logo on cover; all issues beginning with No. 100 are marked "...O. S." (One Shot) which can be found in the bottom left-hand panel on the first page; the numbers following "O. S." relate to the year/month issued.*

	GD 2.0	VG 4.0	FN 6.0	VF 8.0	VF/NM 9.0	NM- 9.2
102-Oswald the Rabbit-Walt Kelly art, 1 pg.	14	28	42	100	188	275
103-Easter with Mother Goose by Walt Kelly	17	34	51	119	230	340
104-Fairy Tale Parade by Walt Kelly	19	38	57	133	259	385
105-Albert the Alligator and Pogo Possum (#1) by Kelly (4/46)	50	100	150	425	838	1250
106-Tillie the Toiler (5/46)	10	20	30	68	119	170
107-Little Orphan Annie; reprints strips from 11/16/42 to 3/24/43	18	36	54	127	249	370
108-Donald Duck in The Terror of the River, by Carl Barks (Disney) (© 4/16/46)	156	312	468	1326	2613	3900
109-Roy Rogers Comics; photo-c	22	44	66	163	302	440
110-Marge's Little Lulu	38	76	114	288	557	825
111-Captain Easy	13	26	39	93	172	250
112-Porky Pig's Adventure in Gopher Gulch	16	32	48	115	220	325
113-Popeye; all new Popeye stories begin	14	28	42	97	181	265
114-Fairy Tale Parade by Walt Kelly	19	38	57	133	259	385

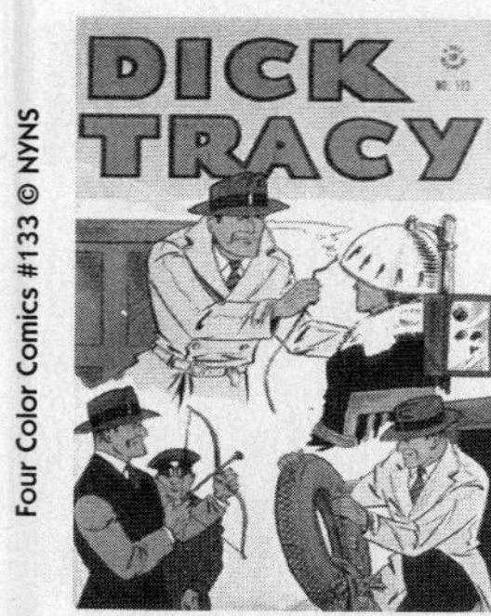

Four Color Comics #133 © NYNS

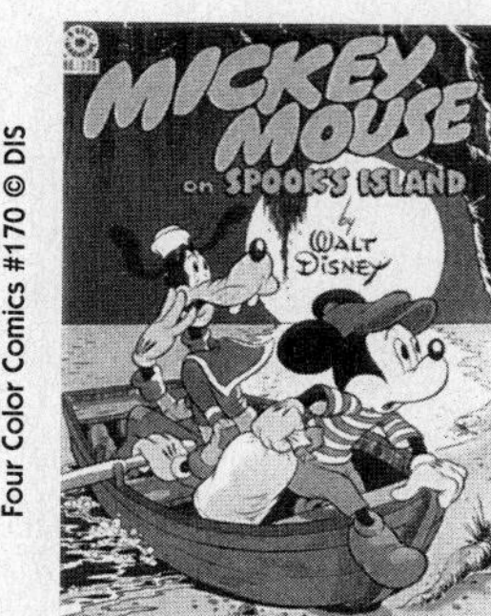

Four Color Comics #170 © DIS

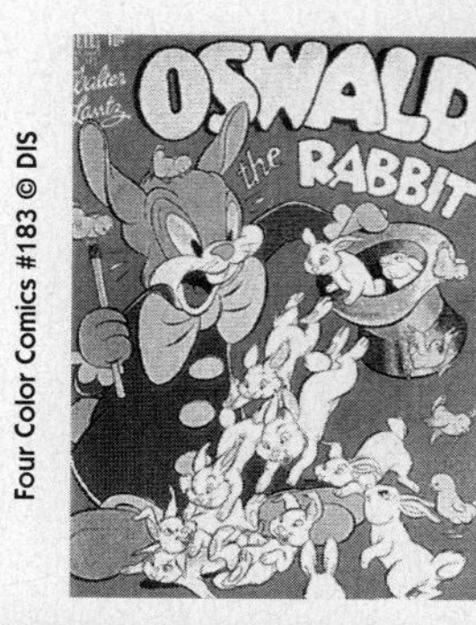

Four Color Comics #183 © DIS

	GD 2.0	VG 4.0	FN 6.0	VF 8.0	VF/NM 9.0	NM- 9.2
115-Marge's Little Lulu	36	72	108	280	540	800
116-Mickey Mouse and the House of Many Mysteries (Disney)	26	52	78	186	361	535
117-Roy Rogers Comics; photo-c	18	36	54	130	240	350
118-Lone Ranger, The	29	58	87	212	406	600
119-Felix the Cat; all new Felix stories begin	32	64	96	246	478	710
120-Marge's Little Lulu	31	62	93	236	456	675
121-Fairy Tale Parade-(not Kelly)	12	24	36	85	155	225
122-Henry (#1) (10/46)	14	28	42	100	188	275
123-Bugs Bunny's Dangerous Venture	15	30	45	110	210	310
124-Roy Rogers Comics; photo-c	18	36	54	130	240	350
125-Lone Ranger, The	19	38	57	139	270	400
126-Christmas with Mother Goose by Walt Kelly (1946)	13	26	39	90	165	240
127-Popeye	14	28	42	97	181	265
128-Santa Claus Funnies- "Santa & the Angel" by Gollub; "A Mouse in the House" by Kelly	14	28	42	100	188	275
129-Walt Disney's Uncle Remus and His Tales of Brer Rabbit (#1) (1946)-Adapted from Disney movie "Song of the South"	25	50	75	183	354	525
130-Andy Panda (Walter Lantz)	11	22	33	80	145	210
131-Marge's Little Lulu	31	62	93	236	456	675
132-Tillie the Toiler (1947)	10	20	30	68	119	170
133-Dick Tracy	19	38	57	133	259	385
134-Tarzan and the Devil Ogre; Marsh-c/a	52	104	156	442	871	1300
135-Felix the Cat	23	42	69	168	324	475
136-Lone Ranger, The	19	38	57	139	270	400
137-Roy Rogers Comics; photo-c	18	36	54	130	240	350
138-Smitty	9	18	27	64	110	155
139-Marge's Little Lulu (1947)	30	60	90	228	439	650
140-Easter with Mother Goose by Walt Kelly	14	28	42	98	184	270
141-Mickey Mouse and the Submarine Pirates (Disney)	21	42	63	151	293	435
142-Bugs Bunny and the Haunted Mountain	15	30	45	110	210	310
143-Oswald the Rabbit & the Prehistoric Egg	9	18	27	63	107	150
144-Roy Rogers Comics (1947)-Photo-c	18	36	54	130	240	350
145-Popeye	14	28	42	97	181	265
146-Marge's Little Lulu	30	60	90	228	439	650
147-Donald Duck in Volcano Valley, by Carl Barks (Disney) (5/47)	106	212	318	901	1776	2650
148-Albert the Alligator and Pogo Possum by Walt Kelly (5/47)	41	82	123	328	639	950
149-Smilin' Jack	10	20	30	70	123	175
150-Tillie the Toiler (6/47)	9	18	27	63	107	150
151-Lone Ranger, The	17	34	51	119	230	340
152-Little Orphan Annie; reprints strips from 1/2/44 to 5/6/44	12	24	36	87	158	230
153-Roy Rogers Comics; photo-c	16	32	48	116	216	315
154-Walter Lantz Andy Panda	11	22	33	80	145	210
155-Henry (7/47)	10	20	30	68	119	170
156-Porky Pig and the Phantom	12	24	36	85	155	225
157-Mickey Mouse & the Beanstalk (Disney)	21	42	63	151	293	435
158-Marge's Little Lulu	30	60	90	228	439	650
159-Donald Duck in the Ghost of the Grotto, by Carl Barks (Disney) (8/47)	90	180	270	765	1508	2250
160-Roy Rogers Comics; photo-c	16	32	48	116	216	315
161-Tarzan and the Fires Of Tohr; Marsh-c/a	48	96	144	384	742	1100
162-Felix the Cat (9/47)	17	34	51	122	236	350
163-Dick Tracy	17	34	51	119	230	340
164-Bugs Bunny Finds the Frozen Kingdom	15	30	45	110	210	310
165-Marge's Little Lulu	30	60	90	228	439	650
166-Roy Rogers Comics (52 pgs.)-Photo-c	16	32	48	116	216	315
167-Lone Ranger, The	17	34	51	119	230	340
168-Popeye (10/47)	14	28	42	97	181	265
169-Woody Woodpecker (#1)- "Manhunter in the North"; drug use story	17	34	51	119	230	340
170-Mickey Mouse on Spook's Island (11/47)(Disney)-reprinted in Mickey Mouse #103	18	36	54	127	249	370
171-Charlie McCarthy (#1) and the Twenty Thieves	24	48	72	175	338	500
172-Christmas with Mother Goose by Walt Kelly (11/47)	13	26	39	90	165	240
173-Flash Gordon	19	38	57	133	259	385
174-Winnie Winkle	8	16	24	58	97	135
175-Santa Claus Funnies by Walt Kelly (1947)	14	28	42	100	188	275
176-Tillie the Toiler (12/47)	9	18	27	63	107	150
177-Roy Rogers Comics-(36 pgs.); Photo-c	15	30	45	111	206	300
178-Donald Duck "Christmas on Bear Mountain" by Carl Barks; 1st app. Uncle Scrooge (Disney)(12/47)	122	244	366	1037	2044	3050
179-Uncle Wiggily (#1)-Walt Kelly-c	15	30	45	104	197	290
180-Ozark Ike (#1)	10	20	30	67	116	165
181-Walt Disney's Mickey Mouse in Jungle Magic	18	36	54	127	249	370
182-Porky Pig in Never-Never Land (2/48)	12	24	36	85	155	225
183-Oswald the Rabbit (Lantz)	9	18	27	63	107	150
184-Tillie the Toiler	9	18	27	63	107	150
185-Easter with Mother Goose by Walt Kelly (1948)	13	26	39	90	165	240
186-Walt Disney's Bambi (4/48)-Reprinted as Movie Classic Bambi #3 (1956)	16	32	48	115	220	325
187-Bugs Bunny and the Dreadful Dragon	12	24	36	83	152	220
188-Woody Woodpecker (Lantz, 5/48)	11	22	33	78	139	200
189-Donald Duck in The Old Castle's Secret, by Carl Barks (Disney) (6/48)	74	148	222	629	1240	1850
190-Flash Gordon (6/48); bondage-c; "The Adventures of the Flying Saucers"; 5th Flying Saucer story- see The Spirit 9/28/47(1st), Shadow Comics V7#10 (2nd, 1/48),Captain Midnight #60 (3rd, 2/48) & Boy Commandos #26 (4th, 3-4/48)	20	40	60	146	283	420
191-Porky Pig to the Rescue	12	24	36	85	155	225
192-The Brownies (#1)-by Walt Kelly (7/48)	13	26	39	93	172	250
193-M.G.M. Presents Tom and Jerry (#1)(1948)	22	44	66	157	304	450
194-Mickey Mouse in The World Under the Sea (Disney)-Reprinted in Mickey Mouse #101	18	36	54	127	249	370
195-Tillie the Toiler	7	14	21	50	83	115
196-Charlie McCarthy in The Haunted Hide-Out; part photo-c	15	30	45	107	204	300
197-Spirit of the Border (#1) (Zane Grey) (1948)	11	22	33	79	140	200
198-Andy Panda	11	22	33	80	145	210
199-Donald Duck in Sheriff of Bullet Valley, by Carl Barks; Barks draws himself on wanted poster, last page; used in Love & Death (Disney) (10/48)	80	160	240	680	1340	2000
200-Bugs Bunny, Super Sleuth (10/48)	12	24	36	83	152	220
201-Christmas with Mother Goose by W. Kelly	11	22	33	78	139	200
202-Woody Woodpecker	8	16	24	58	97	135
203-Donald Duck in the Golden Christmas Tree, by Carl Barks (Disney) (12/48)	56	112	168	476	938	1400
204-Flash Gordon (12/48)	15	30	45	104	197	290
205-Santa Claus Funnies by Walt Kelly	13	26	39	90	165	240
206-Little Orphan Annie; reprints strips from 11/10/40 to 1/11/41	8	16	24	54	90	125
207-King of the Royal Mounted (#1) (12/48)	13	26	39	93	172	250
208-Brer Rabbit Does It Again (Disney) (1/49)	11	22	33	78	139	200
209-Harold Teen	6	12	18	39	62	85
210-Tippie and Cap Stubbs	5	10	15	32	51	70
211-Little Beaver (#1)	8	16	24	56	93	130
212-Dr. Bobbs	6	12	18	37	59	80
213-Tillie the Toiler	7	14	21	50	83	115
214-Mickey Mouse and His Sky Adventure (2/49)(Disney)-Reprinted in Mickey Mouse #105	14	28	42	100	188	275
215-Sparkle Plenty (Dick Tracy-r by Gould)	11	22	33	80	145	210
216-Andy Panda and the Police Pup (Lantz)	8	16	24	58	97	135
217-Bugs Bunny in Court Jester	12	24	36	83	152	220
218-Three Little Pigs and the Wonderful Magic Lamp (Disney) (3/49)(#1)	10	20	30	71	126	180
219-Swee'pea	8	16	24	56	93	130
220-Easter with Mother Goose by Walt Kelly	13	26	39	90	165	240
221-Uncle Wiggily-Walt Kelly cover in part	9	18	27	63	107	150
222-West of the Pecos (Zane Grey)	7	14	21	47	76	105
223-Donald Duck "Lost in the Andes" by Carl Barks (Disney-4/49) (square egg story)	74	148	222	629	1240	1850
224-Little Iodine (#1), by Hatlo (4/49)	11	22	33	80	145	210
225-Oswald the Rabbit (Lantz)	7	14	21	45	73	100
226-Porky Pig and Spoofy, the Spook	10	20	30	70	123	175
227-Seven Dwarfs (Disney)	9	18	27	65	113	160
228-Mark of Zorro, The (#1) (1949)	19	38	57	139	270	400
229-Smokey Stover	6	12	18	41	66	90
230-Sunset Pass (Zane Grey)	7	14	21	47	76	105
231-Mickey Mouse and the Rajah's Treasure (Disney)	14	28	42	100	188	275
232-Woody Woodpecker (Lantz, 6/49)	8	16	24	58	97	135
233-Bugs Bunny, Sleepwalking Sleuth	12	24	36	83	152	220
234-Dumbo in Sky Voyage (Disney)	13	26	39	95	178	260

Four Color Comics #260 © WB

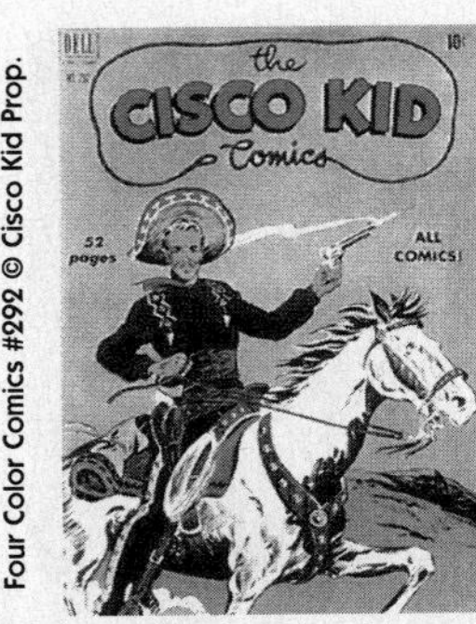

Four Color Comics #292 © Cisco Kid Prop.

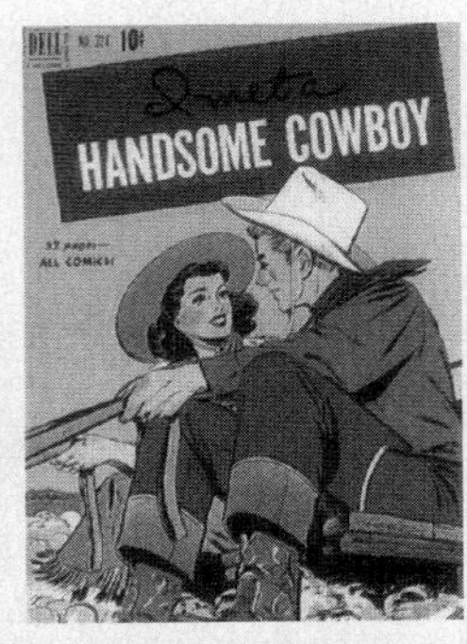

Four Color Comics #324 © WP

	GD 2.0	VG 4.0	FN 6.0	VF 8.0	VF/NM 9.0	NM- 9.2
235-Tiny Tim	6	12	18	37	59	80
236-Heritage of the Desert (Zane Grey) (1949)	7	14	21	47	76	105
237-Tillie the Toiler	7	14	21	50	83	115
238-Donald Duck in Voodoo Hoodoo, by Carl Barks (Disney) (8/49)	56	112	168	476	938	1400
239-Adventure Bound (8/49)	6	12	18	39	62	85
240-Andy Panda (Lantz)	8	16	24	58	97	135
241-Porky Pig, Mighty Hunter	10	20	30	70	123	175
242-Tippie and Cap Stubbs	4	8	12	26	41	55
243-Thumper Follows His Nose (Disney)	11	22	33	78	139	200
244-The Brownies by Walt Kelly	10	20	30	68	119	170
245-Dick's Adventures (9/49)	6	12	18	41	66	90
246-Thunder Mountain (Zane Grey)	5	10	15	32	51	70
247-Flash Gordon	15	30	45	104	197	290
248-Mickey Mouse and the Black Sorcerer (Disney)	14	28	42	100	188	275
249-Woody Woodpecker in the "Globetrotter" (10/49)	8	16	24	58	97	135
250-Bugs Bunny in Diamond Daze; used in **SOTI**, pg. 309	12	24	36	86	158	230
251-Hubert at Camp Moonbeam	7	14	21	45	73	100
252-Pinocchio (Disney)-not by Kelly; origin	10	20	30	73	129	185
253-Christmas with Mother Goose by W. Kelly	11	22	33	78	139	200
254-Santa Claus Funnies by Walt Kelly; Pogo & Albert story by Kelly (11/49)	13	26	39	90	165	240
255-The Ranger (Zane Grey) (1949)	5	10	15	32	51	70
256-Donald Duck in "Luck of the North" by Carl Barks (Disney) (12/49)-Shows #257 on inside	49	98	147	392	754	1125
257-Little Iodine	8	16	24	56	93	130
258-Andy Panda and the Balloon Race (Lantz)	8	16	24	58	97	135
259-Santa and the Angel (Gollub art-condensed from #128) & Santa at the Zoo (12/49) -two books in one	5	10	15	34	55	75
260-Porky Pig, Hero of the Wild West (12/49)	10	20	30	70	123	175
261-Mickey Mouse and the Missing Key (Disney)	14	28	42	100	188	275
262-Raggedy Ann and Andy	10	20	30	67	116	165
263-Donald Duck in "Land of the Totem Poles" by Carl Barks (Disney) (2/50)-Has two Barks stories	48	96	144	384	742	1100
264-Woody Woodpecker in the Magic Lantern (Lantz)	8	16	24	58	97	135
265-King of the Royal Mounted (Zane Grey)	8	16	24	58	97	135
266-Bugs Bunny on the "Isle of Hercules" (2/50)-Reprinted in Best of Bugs Bunny #1	10	20	30	67	116	165
267-Little Beaver; Harmon-c/a	5	10	15	34	55	75
268-Mickey Mouse's Surprise Visitor (1950)(Disney)	13	26	39	93	172	250
269-Johnny Mack Brown (#1)-Photo-c	21	42	63	148	287	425
270-Drift Fence (Zane Grey) (3/50)	5	10	15	32	51	70
271-Porky Pig in Phantom of the Plains	10	20	30	70	123	175
272-Cinderella (Disney) (4/50)	12	24	36	85	155	225
273-Oswald the Rabbit (Lantz)	7	14	21	45	73	100
274-Bugs Bunny, Hare-brained Reporter	10	20	30	67	116	165
275-Donald Duck in "Ancient Persia" by Carl Barks (Disney) (5/50)	47	94	141	376	726	1075
276-Uncle Wiggily	8	16	24	52	86	120
277-Porky Pig in Desert Adventure (5/50)	10	20	30	70	123	175
278-(Wild) Bill Elliott Comics (#1)-Photo-c	12	24	36	86	158	230
279-Mickey Mouse and Pluto Battle the Giant Ants (Disney); reprinted in Mickey Mouse #102 & 245	11	22	33	74	132	190
280-Andy Panda in The Isle Of Mechanical Men (Lantz)	8	16	24	58	97	135
281-Bugs Bunny in The Great Circus Mystery	10	20	30	67	116	165
282-Donald Duck and the Pixilated Parrot by Carl Barks (Disney) (© 5/23/50)	47	94	141	376	726	1075
283-King of the Royal Mounted (7/50)	8	16	24	58	97	135
284-Porky Pig in The Kingdom of Nowhere	10	20	30	70	123	175
285-Bozo the Clown & His Minikin Circus (#1) (TV)	18	36	54	126	246	365
286-Mickey Mouse in The Uninvited Guest (Disney	11	22	33	74	132	190
287-Gene Autry's Champion in The Ghost Of Black Mountain; photo-c	11	22	33	79	140	200
288-Woody Woodpecker in Klondike Gold (Lantz)	8	16	24	58	97	135
289-Bugs Bunny in "Indian Trouble"	10	20	30	67	116	165
290-The Chief (#1) (8/50)	7	14	21	49	80	110
291-Donald Duck in "The Magic Hourglass" by Carl Barks (Disney) (9/50)	47	94	141	376	726	1075
292-The Cisco Kid Comics (#1)	22	44	66	157	304	450
293-The Brownies-Kelly-c/a	10	20	30	68	119	170
294-Little Beaver	5	10	15	34	55	75

	GD 2.0	VG 4.0	FN 6.0	VF 8.0	VF/NM 9.0	NM- 9.2
295-Porky Pig in President Porky (9/50)	10	20	30	70	123	175
296-Mickey Mouse in Private Eye for Hire (Disney)	11	22	33	74	132	190
297-Andy Panda in The Haunted Inn (Lantz, 10/50)	8	16	24	58	97	135
298-Bugs Bunny in Sheik for a Day	10	20	30	67	116	165
299-Buck Jones & the Iron Horse Trail (#1)	13	26	39	90	165	240
300-Donald Duck in "Big-Top Bedlam" by Carl Barks (Disney) (11/50)	47	94	141	376	726	1075
301-The Mysterious Rider (Zane Grey)	5	10	15	32	51	70
302-Santa Claus Funnies (11/50)	7	14	21	45	73	100
303-Porky Pig in The Land of the Monstrous Flies	8	16	24	54	90	125
304-Mickey Mouse in Tom-Tom Island (Disney) (12/50)	10	20	30	67	116	165
305-Woody Woodpecker (Lantz)	6	12	18	41	66	90
306-Raggedy Ann	7	14	21	50	83	115
307-Bugs Bunny in Lumber Jack Rabbit	9	18	27	60	100	140
308-Donald Duck in "Dangerous Disguise" by Carl Barks (Disney) (1/51)	43	86	129	344	672	1000
309-Betty Betz' Dollface and Her Gang (1951)	5	10	15	35	55	75
310-King of the Royal Mounted (1/51)	6	12	18	43	69	95
311-Porky Pig in Midget Horses of Hidden Valley	8	16	24	54	90	125
312-Tonto (#1)	11	22	33	74	132	190
313-Mickey Mouse in The Mystery of the Double-Cross Ranch (#1) (Disney) (2/51)	10	20	30	67	116	165

Note: Beginning with the above comic in 1951 Dell/Western began adding #1 in small print on the covers of several long running titles with the evident intention of switching these titles to their own monthly numbers, but when the conversions were made, there was no connection. It is thought that the post office may have stepped in and decreed the sequences should commence as though the first four colors printed had each begun with number one, or the first issues sold by subscription. Since the regular series' numbers don't correctly match to the numbers of earlier issues published, it's not known whether or not the numbering was in error.

	GD 2.0	VG 4.0	FN 6.0	VF 8.0	VF/NM 9.0	NM- 9.2
314-Ambush (Zane Grey)	5	10	15	32	51	70
315-Oswald the Rabbit (Lantz)	6	12	18	39	62	85
316-Rex Allen (#1)-Photo-c; Marsh-a	14	28	42	97	181	265
317-Bugs Bunny in Hair Today Gone Tomorrow (#1)	9	18	27	60	100	140
318-Donald Duck in "No Such Varmint" by Carl Barks (#1)-Indicia shows #317 (Disney, © 1/23/51)	43	86	129	344	672	1000
319-Gene Autry's Champion; painted-c	7	14	21	45	73	90
320-Uncle Wiggily (#1)	8	16	24	52	86	120
321-Little Scouts (#1) (3/51)	5	10	15	30	48	65
322-Porky Pig in Roaring Rockets (#1 on-c)	8	16	24	54	90	125
323-Susie Q. Smith (#1) (3/51)	5	10	15	32	51	70
324-I Met a Handsome Cowboy (3/51)	8	16	24	56	93	130
325-Mickey Mouse in The Haunted Castle (#2) (Disney) (4/51)	10	20	30	67	116	165
326-Andy Panda (#1) (Lantz)	6	12	18	43	69	95
327-Bugs Bunny and the Rajah's Treasure (#2)	9	18	27	60	100	140
328-Donald Duck in Old California (#2) by Carl Barks-Peyote drug use issue (Disney) (5/51)	43	86	129	342	664	985
329-Roy Roger's Trigger (#1)(5/51)-Painted-c	14	28	42	103	184	265
330-Porky Pig Meets the Bristled Bruiser (#2)	8	16	24	54	90	125
331-Alice in Wonderland (Disney) (1951)	15	30	45	104	197	290
332-Little Beaver	5	10	15	34	55	75
333-Wilderness Trek (Zane Grey) (5/51)	5	10	15	32	51	70
334-Mickey Mouse and Yukon Gold (Disney) (6/51)	10	20	30	67	116	165
335-Francis the Famous Talking Mule (#1, 6/51)-1st Dell non animated movie comic (all issues based on movie)	10	20	30	71	126	180
336-Woody Woodpecker (Lantz)	6	12	18	41	66	90
337-The Brownies-not by Walt Kelly	6	12	18	37	59	80
338-Bugs Bunny and the Rocking Horse Thieves	9	18	27	60	100	140
339-Donald Duck and the Magic Fountain-not by Carl Barks (Disney) (7-8/51)	13	26	39	90	165	240
340-King of the Royal Mounted (7/51)	6	12	18	43	69	95
341-Unbirthday Party with Alice in Wonderland (Disney) (7/51)	15	30	45	104	197	290
342-Porky Pig the Lucky Peppermint Mine; r/in Porky Pig #3	6	12	18	43	69	95
343-Mickey Mouse in The Ruby Eye of Homar-Guy-Am (Disney)-Reprinted in Mickey Mouse #104	8	16	24	58	97	135
344-Sergeant Preston from Challenge of The Yukon (#1) (TV)	11	22	33	80	145	210
345-Andy Panda in Scotland Yard (8-10/51) (Lantz)	6	12	18	43	69	95
346-Hideout (Zane Grey)	5	10	15	32	51	70
347-Bugs Bunny the Frigid Hare (8-9/51)	9	18	27	60	100	140
348-Donald Duck "The Crocodile Collector"; Barks-c only (Disney) (9-10/51)						

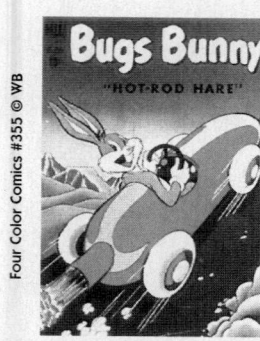

Four Color Comics #355 © WB

Four Color Comics #409 © W. Lantz

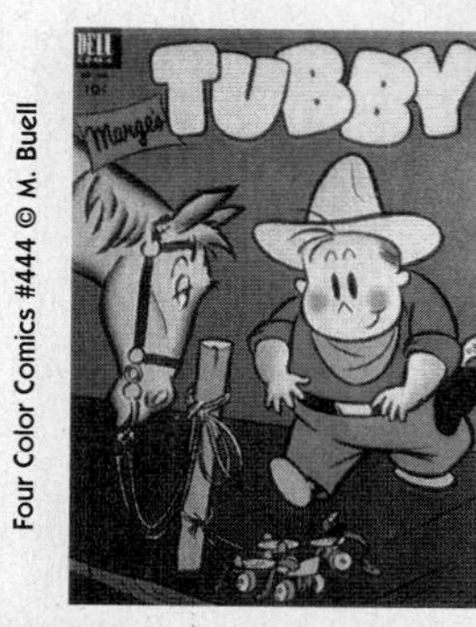

Four Color Comics #444 © M. Buell

	GD 2.0	VG 4.0	FN 6.0	VF 8.0	VF/NM 9.0	NM- 9.2
	21	42	63	148	287	425
349-Uncle Wiggily	6	12	18	43	69	95
350-Woody Woodpecker (Lantz)	6	12	18	41	66	90
351-Porky Pig & the Grand Canyon Giant (9-10/51)	6	12	18	43	69	95
352-Mickey Mouse in The Mystery of Painted Valley (Disney)	8	16	24	58	97	135
353-Duck Album (#1)-Barks-c (Disney)	10	20	30	70	123	175
354-Raggedy Ann & Andy	7	14	21	50	83	115
355-Bugs Bunny Hot-Rod Hare	9	18	27	60	100	140
356-Donald Duck in "Rags to Riches"; Barks-c only	21	42	63	148	287	425
357-Comeback (Zane Grey)	4	8	12	28	44	60
358-Andy Panda (Lantz) (11-1/52)	6	12	18	43	69	95
359-Frosty the Snowman (#1)	9	18	27	63	107	150
360-Porky Pig in Tree of Fortune (11-12/51)	6	12	18	43	69	95
361-Santa Claus Funnies	7	14	21	45	73	100
362-Mickey Mouse and the Smuggled Diamonds (Disney)	8	16	24	58	97	135
363-King of the Royal Mounted	6	12	18	39	62	85
364-Woody Woodpecker (Lantz)	5	10	15	34	55	75
365-The Brownies-not by Kelly	6	12	18	37	59	80
366-Bugs Bunny Uncle Buckskin Comes to Town (12-1/52)	9	18	27	60	100	140
367-Donald Duck in "A Christmas for Shacktown" by Carl Barks (Disney) (1-2/52)	34	68	102	262	506	750
368-Bob Clampett's Beany and Cecil (#1)	23	46	69	166	321	475
369-The Lone Ranger's Famous Horse Hi-Yo Silver (#1); Silver's origin	10	20	30	71	126	180
370-Porky Pig in Trouble in the Big Trees	6	12	18	43	69	95
371-Mickey Mouse in The Inca Idol Case (1952) (Disney)	8	16	24	58	97	135
372-Riders of the Purple Sage (Zane Grey)	4	8	12	28	44	60
373-Sergeant Preston (TV)	8	16	24	52	86	120
374-Woody Woodpecker (Lantz)	5	10	15	34	55	75
375-John Carter of Mars (E. R. Burroughs)-Jesse Marsh-a; origin	25	50	75	183	354	525
376-Bugs Bunny, "The Magic Sneeze"	9	18	27	60	100	140
377-Susie Q. Smith	4	8	12	26	41	55
378-Tom Corbett, Space Cadet (#1) (TV)-McWilliams-a	16	32	48	115	220	325
379-Donald Duck in "Southern Hospitality"; Not by Barks (Disney)	13	26	39	90	165	240
380-Raggedy Ann & Andy	7	14	21	50	83	115
381-Marge's Tubby (#1)	19	38	57	139	270	400
382-Snow White and the Seven Dwarfs (Disney)-origin; partial reprint of Four Color #49 (Movie)	9	18	27	65	113	160
383-Andy Panda (Lantz)	5	10	15	34	55	75
384-King of the Royal Mounted (3/52)(Zane Grey)	6	12	18	39	62	85
385-Porky Pig inThe Isle of Missing Ships (3-4/52)	6	12	18	43	69	95
386-Uncle Scrooge (#1)-by Carl Barks (Disney) in "Only a Poor Old Man" (3/52)	177	354	531	1549	3075	4600
387-Mickey Mouse in High Tibet (Disney) (4-5/52)	8	16	24	58	97	135
388-Oswald the Rabbit (Lantz)	6	12	18	39	62	85
389-Andy Hardy Comics (#1)	5	10	15	34	55	75
390-Woody Woodpecker (Lantz)	5	10	15	34	55	75
391-Uncle Wiggily	6	12	18	43	69	95
392-Hi-Yo Silver	6	12	18	41	66	90
393-Bugs Bunny	9	18	27	60	100	140
394-Donald Duck in Malayalaya-Barks-c only (Disney)	21	42	63	148	287	425
395-Forlorn River(Zane Grey)-First Nevada (5/52)	4	8	12	28	44	60
396-Tales of the Texas Rangers(#1)(TV)-Photo-c	10	20	30	73	129	185
397-Sergeant Preston of the Yukon (TV) (5/52)	8	16	24	52	86	120
398-The Brownies-not by Kelly	6	12	18	37	59	80
399-Porky Pig in The Lost Gold Mine	6	12	18	43	69	95
400-Tom Corbett, Space Cadet (TV)-McWilliams-c/a	10	20	30	70	123	175
401-Mickey Mouse and Goofy's Mechanical Wizard (Disney) (6-7/52)	7	14	21	47	76	105
402-Mary Jane and Sniffles	7	14	21	50	83	115
403-Li'l Bad Wolf (Disney) (6/52)(#1)	7	14	21	47	76	105
404-The Range Rider (#1) (Flying A's...)(TV)-Photo-c	9	18	27	65	113	160
405-Woody Woodpecker (Lantz) (6-7/52)	5	10	15	34	55	75
406-Tweety and Sylvester (#1)	10	20	30	71	126	180
407-Bugs Bunny, Foreign-Legion Hare	7	14	21	50	83	115
408-Donald Duck and the Golden Helmet by Carl Barks (Disney) (7-8/52)						

	GD 2.0	VG 4.0	FN 6.0	VF 8.0	VF/NM 9.0	NM- 9.2
	34	68	102	262	506	750
409-Andy Panda (7-9/52)	5	10	15	34	55	75
410-Porky Pig in The Water Wizard (7/52)	6	12	18	43	69	95
411-Mickey Mouse and the Old Sea Dog (Disney) (8-9/52)	7	14	21	47	76	105
412-Nevada (Zane Grey)	4	8	12	28	44	60
413-Robin Hood (Disney-Movie) (8/52)-Photo-c (1st Disney movie Four Color book)	9	18	27	65	113	160
414-Bob Clampett's Beany and Cecil (TV)	14	28	42	100	188	275
415-Rootie Kazootie (#1) (TV)	9	18	27	65	113	160
416-Woody Woodpecker (Lantz)	5	10	15	34	55	75
417-Double Trouble with Goober (#1) (8/52)	4	8	12	28	44	60
418-Rusty Riley, a Boy, a Horse, and a Dog (#1)-Frank Godwin-a (strip reprints) (8/52)	5	10	15	32	51	70
419-Sergeant Preston (TV)	8	16	24	52	86	120
420-Bugs Bunny in The Mysterious Buckaroo (8-9/52)	7	14	21	50	83	115
421-Tom Corbett, Space Cadet(TV)-McWilliams-a	10	20	30	70	123	175
422-Donald Duck and the Gilded Man, by Carl Barks (Disney) (9-10/52) (#423 on inside)	34	68	102	262	506	750
423-Rhubarb, Owner of the Brooklyn Ball Club (The Millionaire Cat) (#1)-Painted cover	6	12	18	39	62	85
424-Flash Gordon-Test Flight in Space (9/52)	11	22	33	78	139	200
425-Zorro, the Return of	11	22	33	80	145	210
426-Porky Pig in The Scalawag Leprechaun	6	12	18	43	69	95
427-Mickey Mouse and the Wonderful Whizzix (Disney) (10-11/52)-Reprinted in Mickey Mouse #100	7	14	21	47	76	105
428-Uncle Wiggily	5	10	15	34	55	75
429-Pluto in "Why Dogs Leave Home" (Disney) (10/52)(#1)	9	18	27	65	113	160
430-Marge's Tubby, the Shadow of a Man-Eater	12	24	36	83	152	220
431-Woody Woodpecker (10/52) (Lantz)	5	10	15	34	55	75
432-Bugs Bunny and the Rabbit Olympics	7	14	21	50	83	115
433-Wildfire (Zane Grey) (11-1/52-53)	4	8	12	28	44	60
434-Rin Tin Tin "In Dark Danger" (#1) (TV) (11/52)-Photo-c	14	28	42	97	181	265
435-Frosty the Snowman (11/52)	6	12	18	37	59	80
436-The Brownies-not by Kelly (11/52)	5	10	15	34	55	75
437-John Carter of Mars (E.R. Burroughs)-Marsh-a	15	30	45	107	204	300
438-Annie Oakley (#1) (TV)	14	28	42	103	184	265
439-Little Hiawatha (Disney) (12/52)j(#1)	6	12	18	39	62	85
440-Black Beauty (12/52)	5	10	15	30	48	65
441-Fearless Fagan	4	8	12	24	37	50
442-Peter Pan (Disney) (Movie)	10	20	30	70	123	175
443-Ben Bowie and His Mountain Men (#1)	9	18	27	60	100	140
444-Marge's Tubby	12	24	36	83	152	220
445-Charlie McCarthy	6	12	18	39	62	85
446-Captain Hook and Peter Pan (Disney)(Movie)(1/53)	9	18	27	60	100	140
447-Andy Hardy Comics	4	8	12	26	41	55
448-Bob Clampett's Beany and Cecil (TV)	14	28	42	100	188	275
449-Tappan's Burro (Zane Grey) (2-4/53)	4	8	12	28	44	60
450-Duck Album; Barks-c (Disney)	7	14	21	49	80	110
451-Rusty Riley-Frank Godwin-a (strip-r) (2/53)	4	8	12	26	41	50
452-Raggedy Ann & Andy (1953)	7	14	21	50	83	115
453-Susie Q. Smith (2/53)	4	8	12	26	41	55
454-Krazy Kat Comics; not by Herriman	5	10	15	32	51	70
455-Johnny Mack Brown Comics(3/53)-Photo-c	7	14	21	47	76	105
456-Uncle Scrooge Back to the Klondike (#2) by Barks (3/53) (Disney)	92	184	276	782	1541	2300
457-Daffy (#1)	10	20	30	71	126	180
458-Oswald the Rabbit (Lantz)	5	10	15	32	51	70
459-Rootie Kazootie (TV)	7	14	21	47	76	105
460-Buck Jones (4/53)	6	12	18	41	66	90
461-Marge's Tubby	11	22	33	74	132	190
462-Little Scouts	4	8	12	24	37	50
463-Petunia (4/53)	4	8	12	28	44	60
464-Bozo (4/53)	9	18	27	65	113	160
465-Francis the Famous Talking Mule	6	12	18	41	66	90
466-Rhubarb, the Millionaire Cat; painted-c	5	10	15	34	55	75
467-Desert Gold (Zane Grey) (5-7/53)	4	8	12	28	44	60
468-Goofy (#1) (Disney)	11	22	33	80	145	210
469-Beetle Bailey (#1) (5/53	11	22	33	78	139	200
470-Elmer Fudd	8	16	24	56	93	130
471-Double Trouble with Goober	4	8	12	22	34	45

Four Color Comics #519 © Field Ent.

Four Color Comics #567 © KING

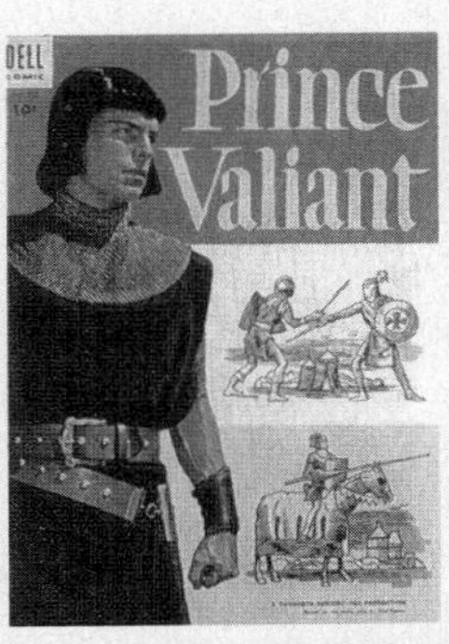

Four Color Comics #590 © DELL

	GD 2.0	VG 4.0	FN 6.0	VF 8.0	VF/NM 9.0	NM- 9.2
472-Wild Bill Elliott (6/53)-Photo-c	5	10	15	34	55	75
473-Li'l Bad Wolf (Disney) (6/53)(#2)	5	10	15	32	51	70
474-Mary Jane and Sniffles	7	14	21	47	76	105
475-M.G.M.'s The Two Mouseketeers (#1)	8	16	24	52	86	120
476-Rin Tin Tin (TV)-Photo-c	8	16	24	56	93	130
477-Bob Clampett's Beany and Cecil (TV)	14	28	42	100	188	275
478-Charlie McCarthy	6	12	18	39	62	85
479-Queen of the West Dale Evans (#1)-Photo-c	18	36	54	126	246	365
480-Andy Hardy Comics	4	8	12	26	41	55
481-Annie Oakley And Tagg (TV)	9	18	27	64	110	155
482-Brownies-not by Kelly	5	10	15	34	55	75
483-Little Beaver (7/53)	5	10	15	30	48	65
484-River Feud (Zane Grey) (8-10/53)	4	8	12	28	44	60
485-The Little People-Walt Scott (#1)	8	16	24	52	86	120
486-Rusty Riley-Frank Godwin strip-r	4	8	12	26	41	50
487-Mowgli, the Jungle Book (Rudyard Kipling's)	6	12	18	37	59	80
488-John Carter of Mars (Burroughs)-Marsh-a; painted-c	15	30	45	107	204	300
489-Tweety and Sylvester	6	12	18	41	66	90
490-Jungle Jim (#1)	7	14	21	49	80	110
491-Silvertip (#1) (Max Brand)-Kinstler-a (8/53)	8	16	24	52	86	120
492-Duck Album (Disney)	6	12	18	41	66	90
493-Johnny Mack Brown; photo-c	7	14	21	47	76	105
494-The Little King (#1)	9	18	27	60	100	140
495-Uncle Scrooge (#3) (Disney)-by Carl Barks (9/53)	62	124	186	527	1039	1550
496-The Green Hornet; painted-c	23	46	69	166	321	475
497-Zorro (Sword of...)-Kinstler-a	12	24	36	85	155	225
498-Bugs Bunny's Album (9/53)	6	12	18	41	66	90
499-M.G.M.'s Spike and Tyke (#1) (9/53)	7	14	21	45	73	100
500-Buck Jones	6	12	18	41	66	90
501-Francis the Famous Talking Mule	5	10	15	32	51	70
502-Rootie Kazootie (TV)	7	14	21	47	76	105
503-Uncle Wiggily (10/53)	5	10	15	34	55	75
504-Krazy Kat; not by Herriman	5	10	15	32	51	70
505-The Sword and the Rose (Disney) (10/53)(Movie)-Photo-c	8	16	24	56	93	130
506-The Little Scouts	4	8	12	24	37	50
507-Oswald the Rabbit (Lantz)	5	10	15	32	51	70
508-Bozo (10/53)	9	18	27	65	113	160
509-Pluto (Disney) (10/53)	6	12	18	41	66	90
510-Son of Black Beauty	4	8	12	26	41	55
511-Outlaw Trail (Zane Grey)-Kinstler-a	5	10	15	32	51	70
512-Flash Gordon (11/53)	9	18	27	60	100	140
513-Ben Bowie and His Mountain Men	5	10	15	32	51	70
514-Frosty the Snowman (11/53)	6	12	18	37	59	80
515-Andy Hardy	4	8	12	26	41	55
516-Double Trouble With Goober	4	8	12	22	34	45
517-Chip 'N' Dale (#1) (Disney)	10	20	30	73	129	185
518-Rivets (11/53)	4	8	12	24	37	50
519-Steve Canyon (#1)-Not by Milton Caniff	8	16	24	56	93	130
520-Wild Bill Elliott-Photo-c	5	10	15	34	55	75
521-Beetle Bailey (12/53)	7	14	21	45	73	100
522-The Brownies	5	10	15	34	55	75
523-Rin Tin Tin (TV)-Photo-c (12/53)	8	16	24	56	93	130
524-Tweety and Sylvester	6	12	18	41	66	90
525-Santa Claus Funnies	7	14	21	45	73	100
526-Napoleon	4	8	12	24	37	50
527-Charlie McCarthy	6	12	18	39	62	85
528-Queen of the West Dale Evans; photo-c	10	20	30	70	123	175
529-Little Beaver	5	10	15	30	48	65
530-Bob Clampett's Beany and Cecil (TV) (1/54)	14	28	42	100	188	275
531-Duck Album (Disney)	6	12	18	41	66	90
532-The Rustlers (Zane Grey) (2-4/54)	4	8	12	28	44	60
533-Raggedy Ann and Andy	7	14	21	50	83	115
534-Western Marshal(Ernest Haycox's)-Kinstler-a	6	12	18	39	62	85
535-I Love Lucy (#1) (TV) (2/54)-Photo-c	44	88	132	352	664	975
536-Daffy (3/54)	6	12	18	41	66	90
537-Stormy, the Thoroughbred... (Disney-Movie) on top 2/3 of each page; Pluto story on bottom 1/3 of each page (2/54)	5	10	15	30	48	65
538-The Mask of Zorro; Kinstler-a	12	24	36	85	155	225
539-Ben and Me (Disney) (3/54)	4	8	12	26	41	55
540-Knights of the Round Table (3/54) (Movie)-Photo-c	7	14	21	47	76	105

	GD 2.0	VG 4.0	FN 6.0	VF 8.0	VF/NM 9.0	NM- 9.2
541-Johnny Mack Brown; photo-c	7	14	21	47	76	105
542-Super Circus Featuring Mary Hartline (TV) (3/54)	7	14	21	47	76	105
543-Uncle Wiggily (3/54)	5	10	15	34	55	75
544-Rob Roy (Disney-Movie)-Manning-a; photo-c	7	14	21	50	83	115
545-The Wonderful Adventures of Pinocchio-Partial reprint of Four Color #92 (Disney-Movie)	7	14	21	47	76	105
546-Buck Jones	6	12	18	41	66	90
547-Francis the Famous Talking Mule	5	10	15	32	51	70
548-Krazy Kat; not by Herriman (4/54)	5	10	15	30	48	65
549-Oswald the Rabbit (Lantz)	5	10	15	32	51	70
550-The Little Scouts	4	8	12	24	37	50
551-Bozo (4/54)	9	18	27	65	113	160
552-Beetle Bailey	7	14	21	45	73	100
553-Susie Q. Smith	4	8	12	26	41	55
554-Rusty Riley (Frank Godwin strip-r)	4	8	12	26	41	50
555-Range War (Zane Grey)	4	8	12	28	44	60
556-Double Trouble With Goober (5/54)	4	8	12	22	34	45
557-Ben Bowie and His Mountain Men	5	10	15	32	51	70
558-Elmer Fudd (5/54)	5	10	15	30	48	65
559-I Love Lucy (#2) (TV)-Photo-c	29	58	87	213	394	575
560-Duck Album (Disney) (5/54)	6	12	18	41	66	90
561-Mr. Magoo (5/54)	10	20	30	68	119	170
562-Goofy (Disney)(#2)	7	14	21	47	76	105
563-Rhubarb, the Millionaire Cat (6/54)	5	10	15	34	55	75
564-Li'l Bad Wolf (Disney)(#3)	5	10	15	32	51	70
565-Jungle Jim	5	10	15	30	48	65
566-Son of Black Beauty	4	8	12	26	41	55
567-Prince Valiant (#1)-By Bob Fuje (Movie)-Photo-c	10	20	30	73	129	185
568-Gypsy Colt (Movie) (6/54)	5	10	15	32	51	70
569-Priscilla's Pop	4	8	12	26	41	55
570-Bob Clampett's Beany and Cecil (TV)	14	28	42	100	188	275
571-Charlie McCarthy	6	12	18	39	62	85
572-Silvertip (Max Brand) (7/54); Kinstler-a	5	10	15	30	48	65
573-The Little People by Walt Scott	5	10	15	32	51	70
574-The Hand of Zorro; Kinstler-a	12	24	36	85	155	225
575-Annie Oakley and Tagg (TV)-Photo-c	9	18	27	64	110	155
576-Angel (#1) (8/54)	4	8	12	26	41	55
577-M.G.M.'s Spike and Tyke	5	10	15	30	48	65
578-Steve Canyon (8/54)	5	10	15	34	55	75
579-Francis the Famous Talking Mule	5	10	15	32	51	70
580-Six Gun Ranch (Luke Short-8/54)	4	8	12	28	44	60
581-Chip 'N' Dale (#2) (Disney)	6	12	18	43	69	95
582-Mowgli Jungle Book (Kipling) (8/54)	5	10	15	30	48	65
583-The Lost Wagon Train (Zane Grey)	4	8	12	28	44	60
584-Johnny Mack Brown-Photo-c	7	14	21	47	76	105
585-Bugs Bunny's Album	6	12	18	41	66	90
586-Duck Album (Disney)	6	12	18	41	66	90
587-The Little Scouts	4	8	12	24	37	50
588-King Richard and the Crusaders (Movie) (10/54) Matt Baker-a; photo-c	9	18	27	63	107	150
589-Buck Jones	6	12	18	41	66	90
590-Hansel and Gretel; partial photo-c	6	12	18	43	69	95
591-Western Marshal(Ernest Haycox's)-Kinstler-a	5	10	15	34	55	75
592-Super Circus (TV)	6	12	18	43	69	95
593-Oswald the Rabbit (Lantz)	5	10	15	32	51	70
594-Bozo (10/54)	9	18	27	65	113	160
595-Pluto (Disney)	5	10	15	32	51	70
596-Turok, Son of Stone (#1)	50	100	150	425	838	1250
597-The Little King	5	10	15	34	55	75
598-Captain Davy Jones	5	10	15	30	48	65
599-Ben Bowie and His Mountain Men	5	10	15	32	51	70
600-Daisy Duck's Diary (#1) (Disney) (11/54)	7	14	21	47	76	105
601-Frosty the Snowman	6	12	18	37	59	80
602-Mr. Magoo and Gerald McBoing-Boing	10	20	30	68	119	170
603-M.G.M.'s The Two Mouseketeers	6	12	18	37	59	80
604-Shadow on the Trail (Zane Grey)	4	8	12	28	44	60
605-The Brownies-not by Kelly (12/54)	5	10	15	34	55	75
606-Sir Lancelot (not TV)	7	14	21	49	80	110
607-Santa Claus Funnies	7	14	21	45	73	100
608-Silvertip- "Valley of Vanishing Men" (Max Brand)-Kinstler-a	5	10	15	30	48	65
609-The Littlest Outlaw (Disney-Movie) (1/55)-Photo-c						

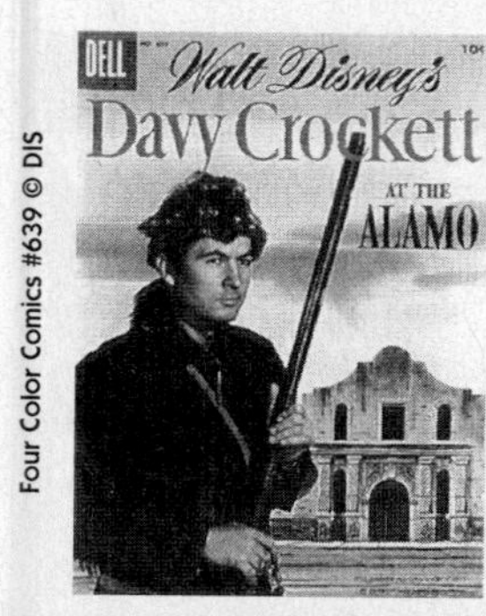

Four Color Comics #639 © DIS

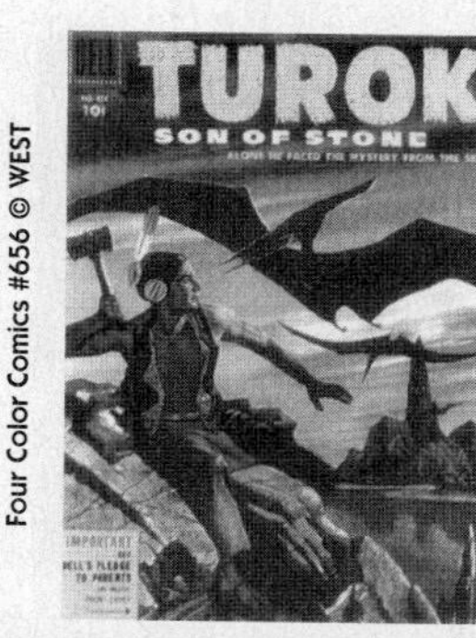

Four Color Comics #656 © WEST

Four Color Comics #691 © ME

	GD 2.0	VG 4.0	FN 6.0	VF 8.0	VF/NM 9.0	NM- 9.2
	6	12	18	43	69	95
610-Drum Beat (Movie); Alan Ladd photo-c	8	16	24	56	93	130
611-Duck Album (Disney)	6	12	18	41	66	90
612-Little Beaver (1/55)	5	10	15	30	48	65
613-Western Marshal (Ernest Haycox's) (2/55)-Kinstler-a	5	10	15	34	55	75
614-20,000 Leagues Under the Sea (Disney) (Movie) (2/55)-Painted-c	8	16	24	58	97	135
615-Daffy	6	12	18	41	66	90
616-To the Last Man (Zane Grey)	4	8	12	28	44	60
617-The Quest of Zorro	11	22	33	80	145	210
618-Johnny Mack Brown; photo-c	7	14	21	47	76	105
619-Krazy Kat; not by Herriman	5	10	15	30	48	65
620-Mowgli Jungle Book (Kipling)	5	10	15	30	48	65
621-Francis the Famous Talking Mule (4/55)	4	8	12	28	44	60
622-Beetle Bailey	7	14	21	45	73	100
623-Oswald the Rabbit (Lantz)	4	8	12	28	44	60
624-Treasure Island(Disney-Movie)(4/55)-Photo-c	8	16	24	54	90	125
625-Beaver Valley (Disney-Movie)	6	12	18	41	66	90
626-Ben Bowie and His Mountain Men	5	10	15	32	51	70
627-Goofy (Disney) (5/55)	7	14	21	47	76	105
628-Elmer Fudd	5	10	15	30	48	65
629-Lady and the Tramp with Jock (Disney)	7	14	21	47	76	105
630-Priscilla's Pop	4	8	12	26	41	55
631-Davy Crockett, Indian Fighter (#1) (Disney) (5/55) (TV)-Fess Parker photo-c	16	32	48	115	220	325
632-Fighting Caravans (Zane Grey)	4	8	12	28	44	60
633-The Little People by Walt Scott (6/55)	5	10	15	32	51	70
634-Lady and the Tramp Album (Disney) (6/55)	5	10	15	32	51	70
635-Bob Clampett's Beany and Cecil (TV)	14	28	42	100	188	275
636-Chip 'N' Dale (Disney)	6	12	18	43	69	95
637-Silvertip (Max Brand)-Kinstler-a	5	10	15	30	48	65
638-M.G.M.'s Spike and Tyke (8/55)	5	10	15	30	48	65
639-Davy Crockett at the Alamo (Disney) (7/55) (TV)-Fess Parker photo-c	13	26	39	95	178	260
640-Western Marshal(Ernest Haycox's)-Kinstler-a	5	10	15	34	55	75
641-Steve Canyon (1955)-by Caniff	5	10	15	34	55	75
642-M.G.M.'s The Two Mouseketeers	6	12	18	37	59	80
643-Wild Bill Elliott; photo-c	5	10	15	30	48	65
644-Sir Walter Raleigh (5/55)-Based on movie "The Virgin Queen"; photo-c	7	14	21	45	73	100
645-Johnny Mack Brown; photo-c	7	14	21	47	76	105
646-Dotty Dripple and Taffy (#1)	5	10	15	32	51	70
647-Bugs Bunny's Album (9/55)	6	12	18	41	66	90
648-Jace Pearson of the Texas Rangers (TV)-Photo-c	6	12	18	41	66	90
649-Duck Album (Disney)	6	12	18	41	66	90
650-Prince Valiant; by Bob Fuje	7	14	21	50	83	115
651-King Colt (Luke Short) (9/55)-Kinstler-a	4	8	12	28	44	60
652-Buck Jones	5	10	15	32	51	70
653-Smokey the Bear (#1) (10/55)	10	20	30	71	126	180
654-Pluto (Disney)	5	10	15	32	51	70
655-Francis the Famous Talking Mule	4	8	12	28	44	60
656-Turok, Son of Stone (#2) (10/55)	30	60	90	228	439	650
657-Ben Bowie and His Mountain Men	5	10	15	32	51	70
658-Goofy (Disney)	7	14	21	47	76	105
659-Daisy Duck's Diary (Disney)(#2)	6	12	18	37	59	80
660-Little Beaver	5	10	15	30	48	65
661-Frosty the Snowman	6	12	18	37	59	80
662-Zoo Parade (TV)-Marlin Perkins (11/55)	5	10	15	32	51	70
663-Winky Dink (TV)	8	16	24	52	86	120
664-Davy Crockett in the Great Keelboat Race (TV) (Disney) (11/55)-Fess Parker photo-c	13	26	39	91	168	245
665-The African Lion (Disney-Movie) (11/55)	6	12	18	37	59	80
666-Santa Claus Funnies	7	14	21	45	73	100
667-Silvertip and the Stolen Stallion (Max Brand) (12/55)-Kinstler-a	5	10	15	30	48	65
668-Dumbo (Disney) (12/55)-First of two printings. Dumbo on cover with starry sky. Reprints 4-Color #234?; same-c as #234	10	20	30	70	123	175
668-Dumbo (Disney) (1/58)-Second printing. Same cover altered, with Timothy Mouse added. Same contents as above	7	14	21	45	73	100
669-Robin Hood (Disney-Movie) (12/55)-Reprints #413 plus-c; photo-c	6	12	18	37	59	80
670-M.G.M's Mouse Musketeers (#1) (1/56)-Formerly the Two Mouseketeers	5	10	15	34	55	75

	GD 2.0	VG 4.0	FN 6.0	VF 8.0	VF/NM 9.0	NM- 9.2
671-Davy Crockett and the River Pirates (TV) (Disney) (12/55)-Jesse Marsh-a; Fess Parker photo-c	13	26	39	91	168	245
672-Quentin Durward (1/56) (Movie)-Photo-c	7	14	21	45	73	100
673-Buffalo Bill, Jr. (#1) (TV)-James Arness photo-c	9	18	27	60	100	140
674-The Little Rascals (#1) (TV)	9	18	27	60	100	140
675-Steve Donovan, Western Marshal (#1) (TV)-Kinstler-a; photo-c	8	16	24	52	86	120
676-Will-Yum!	4	8	12	26	41	55
677-Little King	5	10	15	34	55	75
678-The Last Hunt (Movie)-Photo-c	7	14	21	45	73	100
679-Gunsmoke (#1) (TV)-Photo-c	16	32	48	115	220	325
680-Out Our Way with the Worry Wart (2/56)	4	8	12	24	37	50
681-Forever Darling (Movie) with Lucille Ball & Desi Arnaz (2/56)-; photo-c	11	22	33	80	145	210
682-The Sword & the Rose (Disney-Movie)-Reprint of #505; Renamed When Knighthood Was in Flower for the novel; photo-c	7	14	21	47	76	105
683-Hi and Lois (3/56)	5	10	15	30	48	65
684-Helen of Troy (Movie)-Buscema-a; photo-c	9	18	27	65	113	160
685-Johnny Mack Brown; photo-c	7	14	21	47	76	105
686-Duck Album (Disney)	6	12	18	41	66	90
687-The Indian Fighter (Movie)-Kirk Douglas photo-c	7	14	21	50	83	115
688-Alexander the Great (Movie) (5/56)-Buscema-a; photo-c	7	14	21	49	80	110
689-Elmer Fudd (3/56)	5	10	15	30	48	65
690-The Conqueror (Movie) - John Wayne photo-c	15	30	45	107	204	300
691-Dotty Dripple and Taffy	4	8	12	22	34	45
692-The Little People-Walt Scott	5	10	15	32	51	70
693-Song of the South (Disney) (1956)-Partial reprint of #129	8	16	24	56	93	130
694-Super Circus (TV)-Photo-c	6	12	18	43	69	95
695-Little Beaver	5	10	15	30	48	65
696-Krazy Kat; not by Herriman (4/56)	5	10	15	30	48	65
697-Oswald the Rabbit (Lantz)	4	8	12	28	44	60
698-Francis the Famous Talking Mule (4/56)	4	8	12	28	44	60
699-Prince Valiant-by Bob Fuje	7	14	21	50	83	115
700-Water Birds and the Olympic Elk (Disney-Movie) (4/56)	5	10	15	34	55	75
701-Jiminy Cricket (#1) (Disney) (5/56)	8	16	24	56	93	130
702-The Goofy Success Story (Disney)	7	14	21	47	76	105
703-Scamp (#1) (Disney)	8	16	24	58	97	135
704-Priscilla's Pop (5/56)	4	8	12	26	41	55
705-Brave Eagle (#1) (TV)-Photo-c	6	12	18	43	69	95
706-Bongo and Lumpjaw (Disney) (6/56)	6	12	18	37	59	80
707-Corky and White Shadow (Disney) (5/56)-Mickey Mouse Club (TV); photo-c	7	14	21	47	76	105
708-Smokey the Bear	6	12	18	41	66	90
709-The Searchers (Movie) - John Wayne photo-c	22	44	66	157	304	450
710-Francis the Famous Talking Mule	4	8	12	28	44	60
711-M.G.M's Mouse Musketeers	4	8	12	26	41	55
712-The Great Locomotive Chase (Disney-Movie) (9/56)-Photo-c	7	14	21	47	76	105
713-The Animal World (Movie) (8/56)	4	8	12	26	41	55
714-Spin and Marty (#1) (TV) (Disney)-Mickey Mouse Club (6/56); photo-c	12	24	36	85	155	225
715-Timmy (8/56)	5	10	15	30	48	65
716-Man in Space (Disney)(A science feature from Tomorrowland)	8	16	24	56	93	130
717-Moby Dick (Movie)-Gregory Peck photo-c	8	16	24	56	93	130
718-Dotty Dripple and Taffy	4	8	12	22	34	45
719-Prince Valiant; by Bob Fuje (8/56)	7	14	21	50	83	115
720-Gunsmoke (TV)-James Arness photo-c	9	18	27	61	103	145
721-Captain Kangaroo (TV)-Photo-c	15	30	45	104	197	290
722-Johnny Mack Brown-Photo-c	7	14	21	47	76	105
723-Santiago (Movie)-Kinstler-a (9/56); Alan Ladd photo-c	9	18	27	63	107	150
724-Bugs Bunny's Album	5	10	15	34	55	75
725-Elmer Fudd (9/56)	4	8	12	26	41	55
726-Duck Album (Disney) (9/56)	5	10	15	35	55	75
727-The Nature of Things (TV) (Disney)-Jesse Marsh-a	5	10	15	34	55	75
728-M.G.M's Mouse Musketeers	4	8	12	26	41	55
729-Bob Son of Battle (11/56)	4	8	12	24	37	50
730-Smokey Stover	5	10	15	32	51	70

Four Color Comics #757 © 20th Cent. Fox

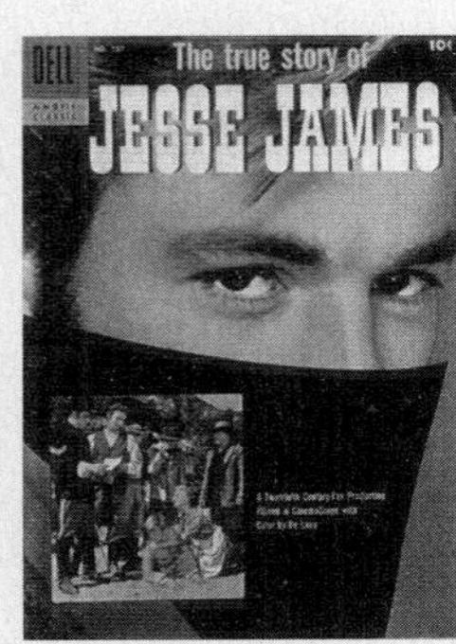

Four Color Comics #785 © Norbert

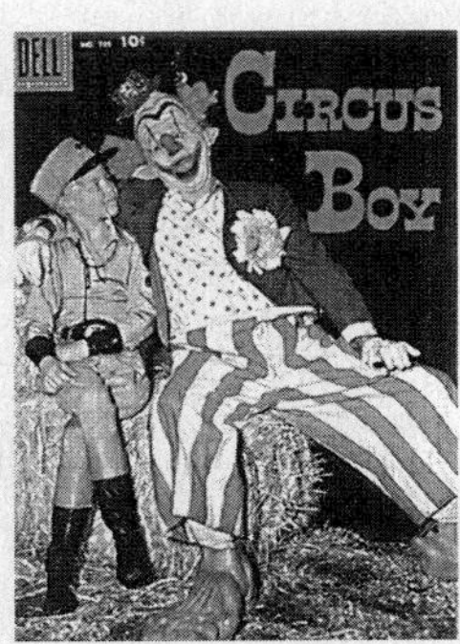

Four Color Comics #846 © Loew's Inc.

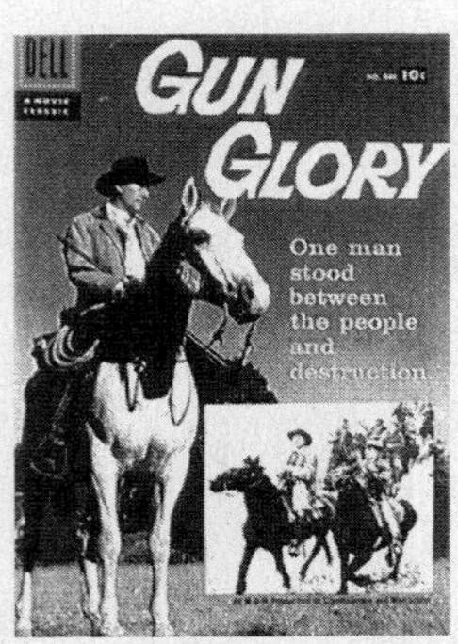

	GD 2.0	VG 4.0	FN 6.0	VF 8.0	VF/NM 9.0	NM- 9.2
731-Silvertip and The Fighting Four (Max Brand)-Kinstler-a	5	10	15	30	48	65
732-Zorro, the Challenge of (10/56)	11	22	33	80	145	210
733-Buck Jones	5	10	15	32	51	70
734-Cheyenne (#1) (TV) (10/56)-Clint Walker photo-c	14	28	42	102	194	285
735-Crusader Rabbit (#1) (TV)	24	48	72	175	338	500
736-Pluto (Disney)	5	10	15	32	51	70
737-Steve Canyon-Caniff-a	5	10	15	34	55	75
738-Westward Ho, the Wagons (Disney-Movie)-Fess Parker photo-c	9	18	27	63	107	150
739-Bounty Guns (Luke Short)-Drucker-a	4	8	12	26	41	55
740-Chilly Willy (#1) (Walter Lantz)	7	14	21	45	73	100
741-The Fastest Gun Alive (Movie)(9/56)-Photo-c	7	14	21	45	73	105
742-Buffalo Bill, Jr. (TV)-Photo-c	6	12	18	39	62	85
743-Daisy Duck's Diary (Disney) (11/56)	6	12	18	37	59	80
744-Little Beaver	5	10	15	30	48	65
745-Francis the Famous Talking Mule	4	8	12	28	44	60
746-Dotty Dripple and Taffy	4	8	12	22	34	45
747-Goofy (Disney)	7	14	21	47	76	105
748-Frosty the Snowman (11/56)	5	10	15	32	51	70
749-Secrets of Life (Disney-Movie)-Photo-c	5	10	15	32	51	70
750-The Great Cat Family (Disney-TV/Movie)-Pinocchio & Alice app.	6	12	18	43	69	95
751-Our Miss Brooks (TV)-Photo-c	7	14	21	50	83	115
752-Mandrake, the Magician	10	20	30	70	123	175
753-Walt Scott's Little People (11/56)	5	10	15	32	51	70
754-Smokey the Bear	6	12	18	41	66	90
755-The Littlest Snowman (12/56)	5	10	15	32	51	70
756-Santa Claus Funnies	7	14	21	45	73	100
757-The True Story of Jesse James (Movie)-Photo-c	8	16	24	58	97	135
758-Bear Country (Disney-Movie)	5	10	15	34	55	75
759-Circus Boy (TV)-The Monkees' Mickey Dolenz photo-c (12/56)	12	24	36	85	155	225
760-The Hardy Boys (#1) (TV) (Disney)-Mickey Mouse Club; photo-c	10	20	30	70	123	175
761-Howdy Doody (TV) (1/57)	10	20	30	73	129	185
762-The Sharkfighters (Movie) (1/57); Buscema-a; photo-c	7	14	21	50	83	115
763-Grandma Duck's Farm Friends (#1) (Disney)	8	16	24	52	86	120
764-M.G.M's Mouse Musketeers	4	8	12	26	41	55
765-Will-Yum!	4	8	12	26	41	55
766-Buffalo Bill, Jr. (TV)-Photo-c	6	12	18	39	62	85
767-Spin and Marty (TV) (Disney)-Mickey Mouse Club (2/57)	9	18	27	63	107	150
768-Steve Donovan, Western Marshal (TV)-Kinstler-a; photo-c	6	12	18	43	69	95
769-Gunsmoke (TV)-James Arness photo-c	9	18	27	61	103	145
770-Brave Eagle (TV)-Photo-c	4	8	12	26	41	55
771-Brand of Empire (Luke Short)(3/57)-Drucker-a	4	8	12	26	41	55
772-Cheyenne (TV)-Clint Walker photo-c	9	18	27	60	100	140
773-The Brave One (Movie)-Photo-c	5	10	15	34	55	75
774-Hi and Lois (3/57)	4	8	12	24	37	50
775-Sir Lancelot and Brian (TV)-Buscema-a; photo-c	9	18	27	65	113	160
776-Johnny Mack Brown; photo-c	7	14	21	47	76	105
777-Scamp (Disney) (3/57)	6	12	18	43	69	95
778-The Little Rascals (TV)	6	12	18	39	62	85
779-Lee Hunter, Indian Fighter (3/57)	5	10	15	34	55	75
780-Captain Kangaroo (TV)-Photo-c	12	24	36	88	162	235
781-Fury (#1) (TV) (3/57)-Photo-c	8	16	24	52	86	120
782-Duck Album (Disney)	5	10	15	35	55	75
783-Elmer Fudd	4	8	12	26	41	55
784-Around the World in 80 Days (Movie) (2/57)-Photo-c	7	14	21	50	83	115
785-Circus Boy (TV) (4/57)-The Monkees' Mickey Dolenz photo-c	10	20	30	70	123	175
786-Cinderella (Disney) (3/57)-Partial-r of #272	7	14	21	45	73	100
787-Little Hiawatha (Disney) (4/57)(#2)	5	10	15	30	48	65
788-Prince Valiant; by Bob Fuje	7	14	21	47	76	105
789-Silvertip-Valley Thieves (Max Brand) (4/57)-Kinstler-a	5	10	15	30	48	65
790-The Wings of Eagles (Movie) (John Wayne)-Toth-a; John Wayne photo-c; 10¢ & 15¢ editions exist	13	26	39	94	175	255
791-The 77th Bengal Lancers (TV)-Photo-c	7	14	21	47	76	105
792-Oswald the Rabbit (Lantz)	4	8	12	28	44	60
793-Morty Meekle	4	8	12	24	37	50
794-The Count of Monte Cristo (5/57) (Movie)-Buscema-a	8	16	24	56	93	130
795-Jiminy Cricket (Disney)(#2)	6	12	18	43	69	95
796-Ludwig Bemelman's Madeleine and Genevieve	4	8	12	24	37	50
797-Gunsmoke (TV)-Photo-c	9	18	27	61	103	145
798-Buffalo Bill, Jr. (TV)-Photo-c	6	12	18	39	62	85
799-Priscilla's Pop	4	8	12	26	41	55
800-The Buccaneers (TV)-Photo-c	7	14	21	47	76	105
801-Dotty Dripple and Taffy	4	8	12	22	34	45
802-Goofy (Disney) (5/57)	7	14	21	47	76	105
803-Cheyenne (TV)-Clint Walker photo-c	9	18	27	60	100	140
804-Steve Canyon-Caniff-a (1957)	5	10	15	34	55	75
805-Crusader Rabbit (TV)	18	36	54	131	256	380
806-Scamp (Disney) (6/57)	6	12	18	43	69	95
807-Savage Range (Luke Short)-Drucker-a	4	8	12	26	41	55
808-Spin and Marty (TV)(Disney)-Mickey Mouse Club; photo-c	9	18	27	63	107	150
809-The Little People (Walt Scott)	5	10	15	32	51	70
810-Francis the Famous Talking Mule	4	8	12	26	41	55
811-Howdy Doody (TV) (7/57)	10	20	30	73	129	185
812-The Big Land (Movie); Alan Ladd photo-c	9	18	27	60	100	140
813-Circus Boy (TV)-The Monkees' Mickey Dolenz photo-c	10	20	30	70	123	175
814-Covered Wagons, Ho! (Disney)-Donald Duck (TV) (6/57); Mickey Mouse app.	5	10	15	34	55	75
815-Dragoon Wells Massacre (Movie)-photo-c	7	14	21	50	83	115
816-Brave Eagle (TV)-photo-c	4	8	12	26	41	55
817-Little Beaver	5	10	15	30	48	65
818-Smokey the Bear (6/57)	6	12	18	41	66	90
819-Mickey Mouse in Magicland (Disney) (7/57)	6	12	18	39	62	85
820-The Oklahoman (Movie)-Photo-c	8	16	24	58	97	135
821-Wringle Wrangle (Disney)-Based on movie "Westward Ho, the Wagons"; Marsh-a; Fess Parker photo-c	8	16	24	52	86	120
822-Paul Revere's Ride with Johnny Tremain (TV) (Disney)-Toth-a	8	16	24	58	97	135
823-Timmy	4	8	12	26	41	55
824-The Pride and the Passion (Movie) (8/57)-Frank Sinatra & Cary Grant photo-c	9	18	27	63	107	150
825-The Little Rascals (TV)	6	12	18	39	62	85
826-Spin and Marty and Annette (TV) (Disney)-Mickey Mouse Club; Annette Funicello photo-c	21	42	63	148	287	425
827-Smokey Stover (8/57)	5	10	15	32	51	70
828-Buffalo Bill, Jr. (TV)-Photo-c	6	12	18	39	62	85
829-Tales of the Pony Express (TV) (8/57)-Painted-c	5	10	15	30	48	65
830-The Hardy Boys (TV) (Disney)-Mickey Mouse Club (8/57); photo-c	9	18	27	60	100	140
831-No Sleep 'Til Dawn (Movie)-Karl Malden photo-c	6	12	18	43	69	95
832-Lolly and Pepper (#1)	5	10	15	30	48	65
833-Scamp (Disney) (9/57)	6	12	18	43	69	95
834-Johnny Mack Brown; photo-c	7	14	21	47	76	105
835-Silvertip-The False Rider (Max Brand)	5	10	15	30	48	65
836-Man in Flight (Disney) (TV) (9/57)	7	14	21	47	76	105
837-All-American Athlete Cotton Woods	4	8	12	24	37	50
838-Bugs Bunny's Life Story Album (9/57)	5	10	15	34	55	75
839-The Vigilantes (Movie)	7	14	21	47	76	105
840-Duck Album (Disney) (9/57)	5	10	15	35	55	75
841-Elmer Fudd	4	8	12	26	41	55
842-The Nature of Things (Disney-Movie) ('57)-Jesse Marsh-a (TV series)	5	10	15	34	55	75
843-The First Americans (Disney) (TV)-Marsh-a	8	16	24	56	93	130
844-Gunsmoke (TV)-Photo-c	9	18	27	61	103	145
845-The Land Unknown (Movie)-Alex Toth-a	11	22	33	78	139	200
846-Gun Glory (Movie)-by Alex Toth; photo-c	8	16	24	58	97	135
847-Perri (squirrels) (Disney-Movie)-Two different covers published	5	10	15	35	55	75
848-Marauder's Moon (Luke Short)	4	8	12	26	41	55
849-Prince Valiant; by Bob Fuje	7	14	21	47	76	105
850-Buck Jones	5	10	15	32	51	70
851-The Story of Mankind (Movie) (1/58)-Hedy Lamarr & Vincent Price photo-c	7	14	21	47	76	105
852-Chilly Willy (2/58) (Lantz)	5	10	15	30	48	65
853-Pluto (Disney) (10/57)	5	10	15	32	51	70

DELL
10¢
TALES OF
WELLS
FARGO
"I've got a six-gun cure for strongbox fever."

Four Color Comics #876 © OV

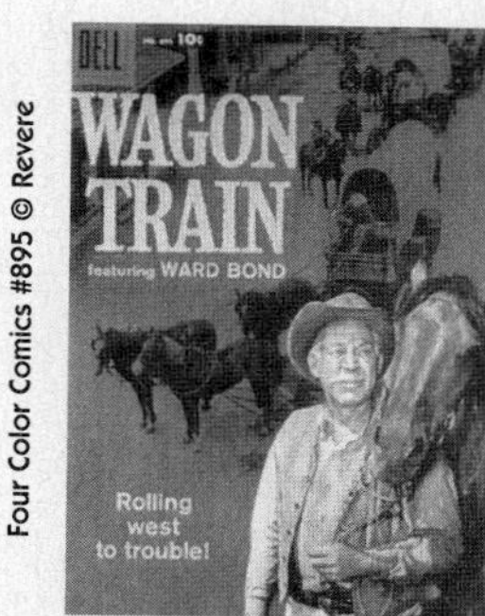

DELL
10¢
WAGON
TRAIN
featuring WARD BOND
Rolling west to trouble!

Four Color Comics #895 © Revere

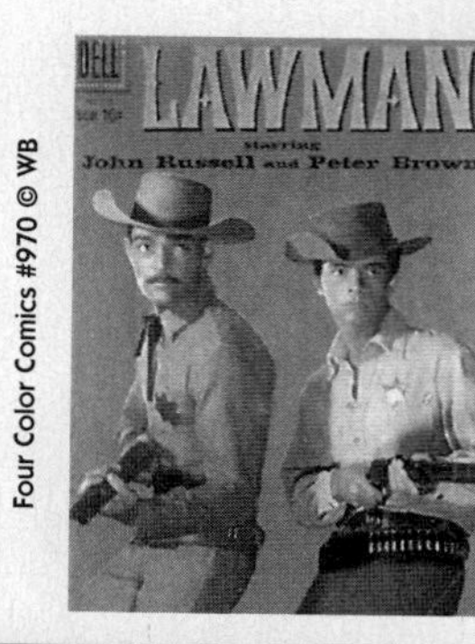

DELL
LAWMAN
starring
John Russell and Peter Brown

Four Color Comics #970 © WB

	GD 2.0	VG 4.0	FN 6.0	VF 8.0	VF/NM 9.0	NM- 9.2
854-The Hunchback of Notre Dame (Movie)-Photo-c	12	24	36	85	155	225
855-Broken Arrow (TV)-Photo-c	6	12	18	37	59	80
856-Buffalo Bill, Jr. (TV)-Photo-c	6	12	18	39	62	85
857-The Goofy Adventure Story (Disney) (11/57)	7	14	21	47	76	105
858-Daisy Duck's Diary (Disney) (11/57)	5	10	15	32	51	70
859-Topper and Neil (TV) (11/57)	5	10	15	30	48	65
860-Wyatt Earp (#1) (TV)-Manning-a; photo-c	9	18	27	65	113	160
861-Frosty the Snowman	5	10	15	32	51	70
862-The Truth About Mother Goose (Disney-Movie) (11/57)	7	14	21	49	80	110
863-Francis the Famous Talking Mule	4	8	12	26	41	55
864-The Littlest Snowman	5	10	15	32	51	70
865-Andy Burnett (TV) (Disney) (12/57)-Photo-c	8	16	24	58	97	135
866-Mars and Beyond (Disney-TV)(A science feature from Tomorrowland)	8	16	24	56	93	130
867-Santa Claus Funnies	7	14	21	45	73	100
868-The Little People (12/57)	5	10	15	32	51	70
869-Old Yeller (Disney-Movie)-Photo-c	5	10	15	34	55	75
870-Little Beaver (1/58)	5	10	15	30	48	65
871-Curly Kayoe	4	8	12	24	37	50
872-Captain Kangaroo (TV)-Photo-c	12	24	36	88	162	235
873-Grandma Duck's Farm Friends (Disney)	6	12	18	37	59	80
874-Old Ironsides (Disney-Movie with Johnny Tremain) (1/58)	6	12	18	43	69	95
875-Trumpets West (Luke Short) (2/58)	4	8	12	26	41	55
876-Tales of Wells Fargo (#1)(TV)(2/58)-Photo-c	9	18	27	60	100	140
877-Frontier Doctor with Rex Allen (TV)-Alex Toth-a; Rex Allen photo-c	9	18	27	63	107	150
878-Peanuts (#1)-Schulz-c only (2/58)	21	42	63	148	287	425
879-Brave Eagle (TV) (2/58)-Photo-c	4	8	12	26	41	55
880-Steve Donovan, Western Marshal-Drucker-a (TV)-Photo-c	5	10	15	30	48	65
881-The Captain and the Kids (2/58)	4	8	12	28	44	60
882-Zorro (Disney)-1st Disney issue; by Alex Toth (TV) (2/58); photo-c	14	28	42	102	194	285
883-The Little Rascals (TV)	6	12	18	37	59	80
884-Hawkeye and the Last of the Mohicans (TV) (3/58); photo-c	7	14	21	47	76	105
885-Fury (TV) (3/58)-Photo-c	6	12	18	41	66	90
886-Bongo and Lumpjaw (Disney) (3/58)	5	10	15	30	48	65
887-The Hardy Boys (Disney) (TV)-Mickey Mouse Club (1/58)-Photo-c	9	18	27	60	100	140
888-Elmer Fudd (3/58)	4	8	12	26	41	55
889-Clint and Mac (Disney) (TV) (3/58)-Alex Toth-a; photo-c	11	22	33	78	139	200
890-Wyatt Earp (TV)-by Russ Manning; photo-c	7	14	21	49	80	110
891-Light in the Forest (Disney-Movie) (3/58)-Fess Parker photo-c	7	14	21	50	83	115
892-Maverick (#1) (TV) (4/58)-James Garner photo-c	21	42	63	148	287	425
893-Jim Bowie (TV)-Photo-c	6	12	18	39	62	85
894-Oswald the Rabbit (Lantz)	4	8	12	28	44	60
895-Wagon Train (#1) (TV) (3/58)-Photo-c	10	20	30	71	126	180
896-The Adventures of Tinker Bell (Disney)	8	16	24	56	93	130
897-Jiminy Cricket (Disney)	6	12	18	43	69	95
898-Silvertip (Max Brand)-Kinstler-a (5/58)	5	10	15	30	48	65
899-Goofy (Disney) (5/58)	5	10	15	32	51	70
900-Prince Valiant; by Bob Fuje	7	14	21	47	76	105
901-Little Hiawatha (Disney)	5	10	15	30	48	65
902-Will-Yum!	4	8	12	26	41	55
903-Dotty Dripple and Taffy	4	8	12	22	34	45
904-Lee Hunter, Indian Fighter	4	8	12	26	41	55
905-Annette (Disney) (TV) (5/58)-Mickey Mouse Club; Annette Funicello photo-c	24	48	72	175	338	500
906-Francis the Famous Talking Mule	4	8	12	26	41	55
907-Sugarfoot (#1) (TV)Toth-a; photo-c	12	24	36	82	149	215
908-The Little People and the Giant-Walt Scott (5/58)	5	10	15	32	51	70
909-Smitty	4	8	12	24	37	50
910-The Vikings (Movie)-Buscema-a; Kirk Douglas photo-c	8	16	24	54	90	125
911-The Gray Ghost (TV)-Photo-c	8	16	24	56	93	130
912-Leave It to Beaver (#1) (TV)-Photo-c	15	30	45	104	197	290
913-The Left-Handed Gun (Movie) (7/58); Paul Newman photo-c	9	18	27	63	107	150

	GD 2.0	VG 4.0	FN 6.0	VF 8.0	VF/NM 9.0	NM- 9.2
914-No Time for Sergeants (Movie)-Andy Griffith photo-c; Toth-a	9	18	27	65	113	160
915-Casey Jones (TV)-Alan Hale photo-c	5	10	15	34	55	75
916-Red Ryder Ranch Comics (7/58)	5	10	15	30	48	65
917-The Life of Riley (TV)-Photo-c	10	20	30	70	123	175
918-Beep Beep, the Roadrunner (#1) (7/58)-Published with two different back covers	11	22	33	78	139	200
919-Boots and Saddles (#1) (TV)-Photo-c	7	14	21	50	83	115
920-Zorro (Disney) (TV) (6/58)Toth-a; photo-c	11	22	33	79	142	205
921-Wyatt Earp (TV)-Manning-a; photo-c	7	14	21	49	80	110
922-Johnny Mack Brown by Russ Manning; photo-c	7	14	21	45	73	100
923-Timmy	4	8	12	26	41	55
924-Colt .45 (#1) (TV) (8/58)-W. Preston photo-c	10	20	30	70	123	175
925-Last of the Fast Guns (Movie) (8/58)-Photo-c	6	12	18	43	69	95
926-Peter Pan (Disney)-Reprint of #442	4	8	12	28	44	60
927-Top Gun (Luke Short) Buscema-a	4	8	12	26	41	55
928-Sea Hunt (#1) (9/58) (TV)-Lloyd Bridges photo-c	11	22	33	78	139	200
929-Brave Eagle (TV)-Photo-c	4	8	12	26	41	55
930-Maverick (TV) (7/58)-James Garner photo-c	11	22	33	74	132	190
931-Have Gun, Will Travel (#1) (TV)-Photo-c	13	26	39	90	165	240
932-Smokey the Bear (His Life Story)	6	12	18	41	66	90
933-Zorro (Disney, 9/58) (TV)-Alex Toth-a; photo-c	11	22	33	79	142	205
934-Restless Gun (#1) (TV)-Photo-c	10	20	30	71	126	180
935-King of the Royal Mounted	4	8	12	28	44	60
936-The Little Rascals (TV)	6	12	18	37	59	80
937-Ruff and Reddy (#1) (9/58) (TV) (1st Hanna-Barbera comic book)	12	24	36	82	149	215
938-Elmer Fudd (9/58)	4	8	12	26	41	55
939-Steve Canyon - not by Caniff	5	10	15	34	55	75
940-Lolly and Pepper (10/58)	4	8	12	22	34	45
941-Pluto (Disney) (10/58)	4	8	12	28	44	60
942-Pony Express (Tales of the ...) (TV)	5	10	15	30	48	65
943-White Wilderness (Disney-Movie) (10/58)	6	12	18	43	69	95
944-The 7th Voyage of Sinbad (Movie) (9/58)-Buscema-a; photo-c	12	24	36	85	155	225
945-Maverick (TV)-James Garner/Jack Kelly photo-c	11	22	33	74	132	190
946-The Big Country (Movie)-Photo-c	7	14	21	47	76	105
947-Broken Arrow (TV)-Photo-c (11/58)	5	10	15	32	51	70
948-Daisy Duck's Diary (Disney) (11/58)	5	10	15	32	51	70
949-High Adventure(Lowell Thomas')(TV)-Photo-c	6	12	18	37	59	80
950-Frosty the Snowman	5	10	15	32	51	70
951-The Lennon Sisters Life Story (TV)-Toth-a, 32 pgs.; photo-c	13	26	39	90	165	240
952-Goofy (Disney) (11/58)	5	10	15	32	51	70
953-Francis the Famous Talking Mule	4	8	12	26	41	55
954-Man in Space-Satellites (TV)	7	14	21	47	76	105
955-Hi and Lois (11/58)	4	8	12	24	37	50
956-Ricky Nelson (#1) (TV)-Photo-c	17	34	51	119	230	340
957-Buffalo Bee (#1) (TV)	8	16	24	58	97	135
958-Santa Claus Funnies	6	12	18	41	66	90
959-Christmas Stories-(Walt Scott's Little People) (1951-56 strip reprints)	5	10	15	32	51	70
960-Zorro (Disney) (TV) (12/58)-Toth art; photo-c	11	22	33	79	142	205
961-Jace Pearson's Tales of the Texas Rangers (TV)-Spiegle-a; photo-c	6	12	18	37	59	80
962-Maverick (TV) (1/59)-James Garner/Jack Kelly photo-c	11	22	33	74	132	190
963-Johnny Mack Brown; photo-c	7	14	21	47	76	105
964-The Hardy Boys (TV) (Disney) (1/59)-Mickey Mouse Club; photo-c	9	18	27	60	100	140
965-Grandma Duck's Farm Friends (Disney)(1/59)	5	10	15	32	51	70
966-Tonka (starring Sal Mineo; Disney-Movie)-Photo-c	8	16	24	58	97	135
967-Chilly Willy (2/59) (Lantz)	5	10	15	30	48	65
968-Tales of Wells Fargo (TV)-Photo-c	8	16	24	56	93	130
969-Peanuts (2/59)	13	26	39	93	172	250
970-Lawman (#1) (TV)-Photo-c	12	24	36	85	155	225
971-Wagon Train (TV)-Photo-c	7	14	21	45	73	100
972-Tom Thumb (Movie)-George Pal (1/59)	8	16	24	58	97	135
973-Sleeping Beauty and the Prince(Disney)(5/59)	11	22	33	74	132	190
974-The Little Rascals (TV) (3/59)	6	12	18	37	59	80
975-Fury (TV)-Photo-c	6	12	18	41	66	90
976-Zorro (Disney) (TV)-Toth-a; photo-c	11	22	33	79	142	205

Four Color Comics #1010 © DIS

Four Color Comics #1038 © H-B

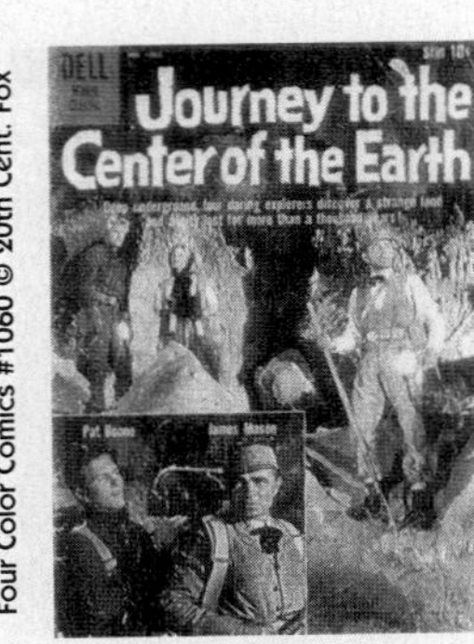

Four Color Comics #1060 © 20th Cent. Fox

	GD 2.0	VG 4.0	FN 6.0	VF 8.0	VF/NM 9.0	NM- 9.2
977-Elmer Fudd (3/59)	4	8	12	26	41	55
978-Lolly and Pepper	4	8	12	22	34	45
979-Oswald the Rabbit (Lantz)	4	8	12	28	44	60
980-Maverick (TV) (4-6/59)-James Garner/Jack Kelly photo-c	11	22	33	74	132	190
981-Ruff and Reddy (TV) (Hanna-Barbera)	8	16	24	52	86	120
982-The New Adventures of Tinker Bell (TV) (Disney)	8	16	24	52	86	120
983-Have Gun, Will Travel (TV) (4-6/59)-Photo-c	9	18	27	60	100	140
984-Sleeping Beauty's Fairy Godmothers (Disney)	9	18	27	61	103	145
985-Shaggy Dog (Disney-Movie)-Photo-all four covers; Annette on back-c(5/59)	7	14	21	50	83	115
986-Restless Gun (TV)-Photo-c	8	16	24	52	86	120
987-Goofy (Disney) (7/59)	5	10	15	32	51	70
988-Little Hiawatha (Disney)	5	10	15	30	48	65
989-Jiminy Cricket (Disney) (5-7/59)	6	12	18	43	69	95
990-Huckleberry Hound (#1)(TV)(Hanna-Barbera); 1st app. Huck, Yogi Bear, & Pixie & Dixie & Mr. Jinks	12	24	36	86	158	230
991-Francis the Famous Talking Mule	4	8	12	26	41	55
992-Sugarfoot (TV)-Toth-a; photo-c	11	22	33	76	136	195
993-Jim Bowie (TV)-Photo-c	5	10	15	35	55	75
994-Sea Hunt (TV)-Lloyd Bridges photo-c	8	16	24	54	90	125
995-Donald Duck Album (Disney) (5-7/59)(#1)	6	12	18	43	69	95
996-Nevada (Zane Grey)	4	8	12	28	44	60
997-Walt Disney Presents-Tales of Texas John Slaughter (#1) (TV) (Disney)-Photo-c; photo of W. Disney inside-c	7	14	21	49	80	110
998-Ricky Nelson (TV)-Photo-c	17	34	51	119	230	340
999-Leave It to Beaver (TV)-Photo-c	13	26	39	90	165	240
1000-The Gray Ghost (TV) (6-8/59)-Photo-c	8	16	24	56	93	130
1001-Lowell Thomas' High Adventure (TV) (8-10/59)-Photo-c	5	10	15	34	55	75
1002-Buffalo Bee (TV)	7	14	21	45	73	100
1003-Zorro (TV) (Disney)-Toth-a; photo-c	11	22	33	79	142	205
1004-Colt .45 (TV) (6-8/59)-Photo-c	8	16	24	56	93	130
1005-Maverick (TV)-James Garner/Jack Kelly photo-c	11	22	33	74	132	190
1006-Hercules (Movie)-Buscema-a; photo-c	9	18	27	60	100	140
1007-John Paul Jones (Movie)-Robert Stack photo-c	5	10	15	35	55	75
1008-Beep Beep, the Road Runner (7-9/59)	7	14	21	45	73	100
1009-The Rifleman (#1) (TV)-Photo-c	21	42	63	148	287	425
1010-Grandma Duck's Farm Friends (Disney)-by Carl Barks	12	24	36	85	155	225
1011-Buckskin (#1) (TV)-Photo-c	7	14	21	47	76	105
1012-Last Train from Gun Hill (Movie) (7/59)-Photo-c	8	16	24	56	93	130
1013-Bat Masterson (#1) (TV) (8/59)-Gene Barry photo-c	11	22	33	79	140	200
1014-The Lennon Sisters (TV)-Toth-a; photo-c	12	24	36	85	155	225
1015-Peanuts-Schulz-c	13	26	39	93	172	250
1016-Smokey the Bear Nature Stories	4	8	12	28	44	60
1017-Chilly Willy (Lantz)	5	10	15	30	48	65
1018-Rio Bravo (Movie)(6/59)-John Wayne; Toth-a; John Wayne, Dean Martin & Ricky Nelson photo-c	22	44	66	155	300	445
1019-Wagon Train (TV)-Photo-c	7	14	21	45	73	100
1020-Jungle Jim-McWilliams-a	4	8	12	26	41	55
1021-Jace Pearson's Tales of the Texas Rangers (TV)-Photo-c	6	12	18	37	59	80
1022-Timmy	4	8	12	26	41	55
1023-Tales of Wells Fargo (TV)-Photo-c	8	16	24	56	93	130
1024-Darby O'Gill and the Little People (Disney-Movie)-Toth-a; photo-c	9	18	27	65	113	160
1025-Vacation in Disneyland (8-10/59)-Carl Barks-a(24pgs.) (Disney)	16	32	48	112	214	315
1026-Spin and Marty (TV) (Disney) (9-11/59)-Mickey Mouse Club; photo-c	8	16	24	52	86	120
1027-The Texan (#1)(TV)-Photo-c	8	16	24	56	93	130
1028-Rawhide (#1) (TV) (9-11/59)-Clint Eastwood photo-c; Tufts-a	22	44	66	155	300	445
1029-Boots and Saddles (TV) (9/59)-Photo-c	5	10	15	34	55	75
1030-Spanky and Alfalfa, the Little Rascals (TV)	6	12	18	37	59	80
1031-Fury (TV)-Photo-c	6	12	18	41	66	90
1032-Elmer Fudd	4	8	12	26	41	55
1033-Steve Canyon-not by Caniff; photo-c	5	10	15	34	55	75
1034-Nancy and Sluggo Summer Camp (9-11/59)	5	10	15	32	51	70
1035-Lawman (TV)-Photo-c	8	16	24	54	90	125

	GD 2.0	VG 4.0	FN 6.0	VF 8.0	VF/NM 9.0	NM- 9.2
1036-The Big Circus (Movie)-Photo-c	6	12	18	43	69	95
1037-Zorro (Disney) (TV)-Tufts-a; Annette Funicello photo-c	14	28	42	97	181	265
1038-Ruff and Reddy (TV)(Hanna-Barbera)(1959)	8	16	24	52	86	120
1039-Pluto (Disney) (11-1/60)	4	8	12	28	44	60
1040-Quick Draw McGraw (#1) (TV) (Hanna-Barbera) (12-2/60)	13	26	39	90	165	240
1041-Sea Hunt (TV) (10-12/59)-Toth-a; Lloyd Bridges photo-c	8	16	24	54	90	125
1042-The Three Chipmunks (Alvin, Simon & Theodore) (#1) (TV) (10-12/59)	8	16	24	52	86	120
1043-The Three Stooges (#1)-Photo-c	23	46	69	168	324	480
1044-Have Gun, Will Travel (TV)-Photo-c	9	18	27	60	100	140
1045-Restless Gun (TV)-Photo-c	8	16	24	52	86	120
1046-Beep Beep, the Road Runner (11-1/60)	7	14	21	45	73	100
1047-Gyro Gearloose (#1) (Disney)-All Barks-c/a	16	32	48	116	223	330
1048-The Horse Soldiers (Movie) (John Wayne)-Sekowsky-a; painted cover featuring John Wayne	13	26	39	90	165	240
1049-Don't Give Up the Ship (Movie) (8/59)-Jerry Lewis photo-c	9	18	27	61	103	145
1050-Huckleberry Hound (TV) (Hanna-Barbera) (10-12/59)	8	16	24	58	97	135
1051-Donald in Mathmagic Land (Disney-Movie)	9	18	27	63	107	150
1052-Ben-Hur (Movie) (11/59)-Manning-a	10	20	30	67	116	165
1053-Goofy (Disney) (11-1/60)	5	10	15	32	51	70
1054-Huckleberry Hound Winter Fun (TV) (Hanna-Barbera) (12/59)	8	16	24	58	97	135
1055-Daisy Duck's Diary (Disney)-by Carl Barks (11-1/60)	9	18	27	60	100	140
1056-Yellowstone Kelly (Movie)-Clint Walker photo-c	6	12	18	37	59	80
1057-Mickey Mouse Album (Disney)	5	10	15	34	55	75
1058-Colt .45 (TV)-Photo-c	8	16	24	56	93	130
1059-Sugarfoot (TV)-Photo-c	8	16	24	58	97	135
1060-Journey to the Center of the Earth (Movie)-Pat Boone & James Mason photo-c	10	20	30	73	129	185
1061-Buffalo Bee (TV)	7	14	21	45	73	100
1062-Christmas Stories (Walt Scott's Little People strip-r)	5	10	15	32	51	70
1063-Santa Claus Funnies	6	12	18	41	66	90
1064-Bugs Bunny's Merry Christmas (12/59)	5	10	15	34	55	75
1065-Frosty the Snowman	5	10	15	32	51	70
1066-77 Sunset Strip (#1) (TV)-Toth-a (1-3/60)-Efrem Zimbalist, Jr. & Edd "Kookie" Byrnes photo-c	10	20	30	71	126	180
1067-Yogi Bear (#1) (TV) (Hanna-Barbera)	10	20	30	71	126	180
1068-Francis the Famous Talking Mule	4	8	12	26	41	55
1069-The FBI Story (Movie)-Toth-a; James Stewart photo on-c	9	18	27	63	107	150
1070-Solomon and Sheba (Movie)-Sekowsky-a; photo-c	8	16	24	58	97	135
1071-The Real McCoys (#1) (TV) (1-3/60)-Toth-a; Walter Brennan photo-c	9	18	27	60	100	140
1072-Blythe (Marge's)	6	12	18	37	59	80
1073-Grandma Duck's Farm Friends-Barks-c/a (Disney)	12	24	36	85	155	225
1074-Chilly Willy (Lantz)	5	10	15	30	48	65
1075-Tales of Wells Fargo (TV)-Photo-c	8	16	24	56	93	130
1076-The Rebel (#1) (TV)-Sekowsky-a; photo-c	9	18	27	65	113	160
1077-The Deputy (#1) (TV)-Buscema-a; Henry Fonda photo-c	11	22	33	79	140	200
1078-The Three Stooges (2-4/60)-Photo-c	12	24	36	86	158	230
1079-The Little Rascals (TV) (Spanky & Alfalfa)	6	12	18	37	59	80
1080-Fury (TV) (2-4/60)-Photo-c	6	12	18	41	66	90
1081-Elmer Fudd	4	8	12	26	41	55
1082-Spin and Marty (Disney) (TV)-Photo-c	8	16	24	52	86	120
1083-Men into Space (TV)-Anderson-a; photo-c	5	10	15	34	55	75
1084-Speedy Gonzales	5	10	15	34	55	75
1085-The Time Machine (H.G. Wells) (Movie) (3/60)-Alex Toth-a; Rod Taylor photo-c	14	28	42	97	181	265
1086-Lolly and Pepper	4	8	12	22	34	45
1087-Peter Gunn (TV)-Photo-c	8	16	24	58	97	135
1088-A Dog of Flanders (Movie)-Photo-c	5	10	15	30	48	65
1089-Restless Gun (TV)-Photo-c	8	16	24	52	86	120
1090-Francis the Famous Talking Mule	4	8	12	26	41	55
1091-Jacky's Diary (4-6/60)	5	10	15	30	48	65

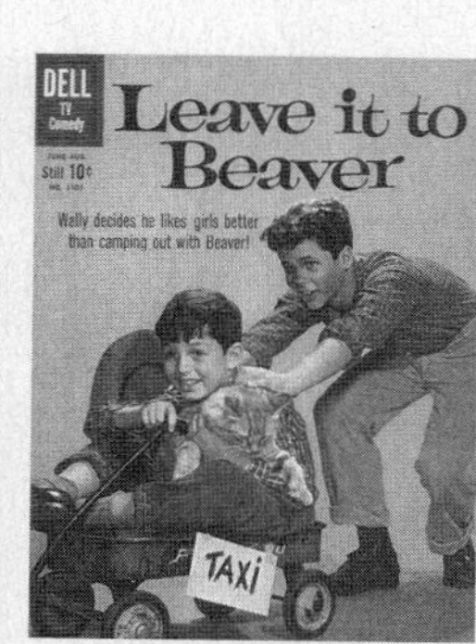

Four Color Comics #1103 © Gomalco

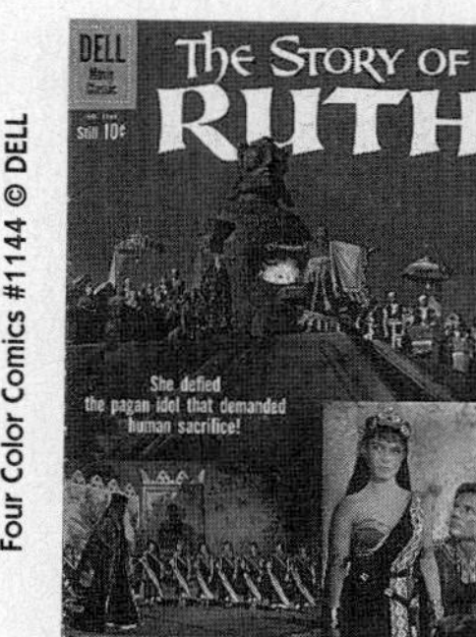

Four Color Comics #1144 © DELL

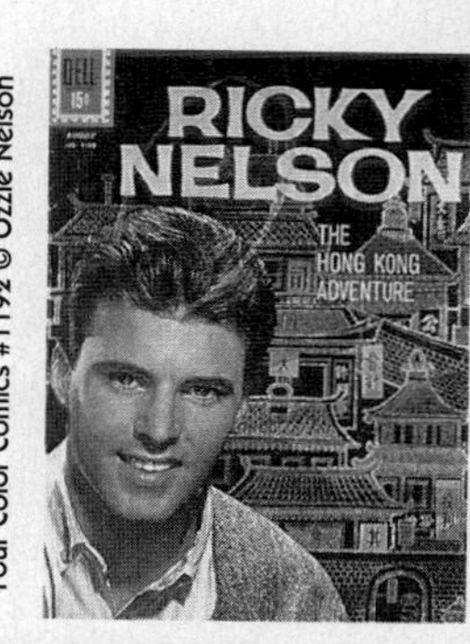

Four Color Comics #1192 © Ozzie Nelson

	GD 2.0	VG 4.0	FN 6.0	VF 8.0	VF/NM 9.0	NM- 9.2
1092-Toby Tyler (Disney-Movie)-Photo-c	6	12	18	43	69	95
1093-MacKenzie's Raiders (Movie/TV)-Richard Carlson photo-c from TV show	6	12	18	43	69	95
1094-Goofy (Disney)	5	10	15	32	51	70
1095-Gyro Gearloose (Disney)-All Barks-c/a	10	20	30	67	116	165
1096-The Texan (TV)-Rory Calhoun photo-c	8	16	24	52	86	120
1097-Rawhide (TV)-Manning-a; Clint Eastwood photo-c	14	28	42	97	181	265
1098-Sugarfoot (TV)-Photo-c	8	16	24	58	97	135
1099-Donald Duck Album (Disney) (5-7/60)-Barks-c	7	14	21	45	73	100
1100-Annette's Life Story (Disney-Movie) (5/60)-Annette Funicello photo-c	19	38	57	139	270	400
1101-Robert Louis Stevenson's Kidnapped (Disney-Movie) (5/60); photo-c	6	12	18	43	69	95
1102-Wanted: Dead or Alive (#1) (TV) (5-7/60); Steve McQueen photo-c	12	24	36	85	155	225
1103-Leave It to Beaver (TV)-Photo-c	13	26	39	90	165	240
1104-Yogi Bear Goes to College (TV) (Hanna-Barbera) (6-8/60)	7	14	21	49	80	110
1105-Gale Storm (Oh! Susanna) (TV)-Toth-a; photo-c	11	22	33	76	136	195
1106-77 Sunset Strip(TV)(6-8/60)-Toth-a; photo-c	8	16	24	58	97	135
1107-Buckskin (TV)-Photo-c	6	12	18	43	69	95
1108-The Troubleshooters (TV)-Keenan Wynn photo-c	5	10	15	34	55	75
1109-This Is Your Life, Donald Duck (Disney) (TV) (8-10/60)-Gyro flashback to WDC&S #141; origin Donald Duck (1st told)	13	26	39	95	178	260
1110-Bonanza (#1) (TV) (6-8/60)-Photo-c	31	62	93	236	456	675
1111-Shotgun Slade (TV)-Photo-c	6	12	18	41	66	90
1112-Pixie and Dixie and Mr. Jinks (#1) (TV) (Hanna-Barbera) (7-9/60)	7	14	21	50	83	115
1113-Tales of Wells Fargo (TV)-Photo-c	8	16	24	56	93	130
1114-Huckleberry Finn (Movie) (7/60)-Photo-c	5	10	15	34	55	75
1115-Ricky Nelson (TV)-Manning-a; photo-c	14	28	42	97	181	265
1116-Boots and Saddles (TV) (8/60)-Photo-c	5	10	15	34	55	75
1117-Boy and the Pirates (Movie)-Photo-c	6	12	18	43	69	95
1118-The Sword and the Dragon (Movie) (6/60)-Photo-c	7	14	21	50	83	115
1119-Smokey the Bear Nature Stories	4	8	12	28	44	60
1120-Dinosaurus (Movie)-Painted-c	8	16	24	56	93	130
1121-Hercules Unchained (Movie) (8/60)-Crandall/Evans-a	9	18	27	60	100	140
1122-Chilly Willy (Lantz)	5	10	15	30	48	65
1123-Tombstone Territory (TV)-Photo-c	8	16	24	56	93	130
1124-Whirlybirds (#1) (TV)-Photo-c	8	16	24	56	93	130
1125-Laramie (#1) (TV)-Photo-c; G. Kane/Heath-a	8	16	24	58	97	135
1126-Hotel Deparee - Sundance (TV) (8-10/60)-Earl Holliman photo-c	6	12	18	43	69	95
1127-The Three Stooges-Photo-c (8-10/60)	12	24	36	86	158	230
1128-Rocky and His Friends (#1) (TV) (Jay Ward) (8-10/60)	29	58	87	212	406	600
1129-Pollyanna (Disney-Movie)-Hayley Mills photo-c	7	14	21	50	83	115
1130-The Deputy (TV)-Buscema-a; Henry Fonda photo-c	9	18	27	63	107	150
1131-Elmer Fudd (9-11/60)	4	8	12	26	41	55
1132-Space Mouse (Lantz) (8-10/60)	4	8	12	28	44	60
1133-Fury (TV)-Photo-c	6	12	18	41	66	90
1134-Real McCoys (TV)-Toth-a; photo-c	9	18	27	60	100	140
1135-M.G.M.'s Mouse Musketeers (9-11/60)	4	8	12	24	37	50
1136-Jungle Cat (Disney-Movie)-Photo-c	6	12	18	43	69	95
1137-The Little Rascals (TV)	6	12	18	37	59	80
1138-The Rebel (TV)-Photo-c	8	16	24	56	93	130
1139-Spartacus (Movie) (11/60)-Buscema-a; Kirk Douglas photo-c	12	24	36	85	155	225
1140-Donald Duck Album (Disney)-Barks-c	7	14	21	45	73	100
1141-Huckleberry Hound for President (TV) (Hanna-Barbera) (10/60)	8	16	24	52	86	120
1142-Johnny Ringo (TV)-Photo-c	7	14	21	47	76	105
1143-Pluto (Disney) (11-1/61)	4	8	12	28	44	60
1144-The Story of Ruth (Movie)-Photo-c	8	16	24	58	97	135
1145-The Lost World (Movie)-Gil Kane-a; photo-c; 1 pg. Conan Doyle biography by Torres	9	18	27	64	110	155
1146-Restless Gun (TV)-Photo-c; Wildey-a	8	16	24	52	86	120
1147-Sugarfoot (TV)-Photo-c	8	16	24	58	97	135
1148-I Aim at the Stars-the Wernher Von Braun Story (Movie) (11-1/61)-Photo-c	7	14	21	47	76	105
1149-Goofy (Disney) (11-1/61)	5	10	15	32	51	70
1150-Daisy Duck's Diary (Disney) (12-1/61) by Carl Barks	9	18	27	60	100	140
1151-Mickey Mouse Album (Disney) (11-1/61)	5	10	15	34	55	75
1152-Rocky and His Friends (TV) (Jay Ward) (12-2/61)	18	36	54	126	246	365
1153-Frosty the Snowman	5	10	15	32	51	70
1154-Santa Claus Funnies	6	12	18	41	66	90
1155-North to Alaska (Movie)-John Wayne photo-c	16	32	48	112	214	315
1156-Walt Disney Swiss Family Robinson (Movie) (12/60)-Photo-c	7	14	21	49	80	110
1157-Master of the World (Movie) (7/61)	7	14	21	45	73	100
1158-Three Worlds of Gulliver (2 issues exist with different covers) (Movie)-Photo-c	7	14	21	45	73	100
1159-77 Sunset Strip (TV)-Toth-a; photo-c	8	16	24	58	97	135
1160-Rawhide (TV)-Clint Eastwood photo-c	14	28	42	97	181	265
1161-Grandma Duck's Farm Friends (Disney) by Carl Barks (2-4/61)	12	24	36	85	155	225
1162-Yogi Bear Joins the Marines (TV) (Hanna-Barbera) (5-7/61)	7	14	21	49	80	110
1163-Daniel Boone (3-5/61); Marsh-a	5	10	15	35	55	75
1164-Wanted: Dead or Alive (TV)-Steve McQueen photo-c	9	18	27	63	107	150
1165-Ellery Queen (#1) (3-5/61)	10	20	30	70	123	175
1166-Rocky and His Friends (TV) (Jay Ward)	18	36	54	126	246	365
1167-Tales of Wells Fargo (TV)-Photo-c	8	16	24	52	86	120
1168-The Detectives (TV)-Robert Taylor photo-c	9	18	27	65	113	160
1169-New Adventures of Sherlock Holmes	13	26	39	95	178	260
1170-The Three Stooges (3-5/61)-Photo-c	12	24	36	86	158	230
1171-Elmer Fudd	4	8	12	26	41	55
1172-Fury (TV)-Photo-c	6	12	18	41	66	90
1173-The Twilight Zone (#1) (TV) (5/61)-Crandall/Evans-c/a; Crandall tribute to Ingles	21	42	63	148	287	425
1174-The Little Rascals (TV)	5	10	15	30	48	65
1175-M.G.M.'s Mouse Musketeers (3-5/61)	4	8	12	24	37	50
1176-Dondi (Movie)-Origin; photo-c	5	10	15	35	55	75
1177-Chilly Willy (Lantz) (4-6/61)	5	10	15	30	48	65
1178-Ten Who Dared (Disney-Movie) (12/60)-Painted-c; cast member photo on back-c	7	14	21	49	80	110
1179-The Swamp Fox (TV) (Disney)-Leslie Nielsen photo-c	8	16	24	56	93	130
1180-The Danny Thomas Show (TV)-Toth-a; photo-c	14	28	42	100	188	275
1181-Texas John Slaughter (TV) (Walt Disney Presents...) (4-6/61)-Photo-c	7	14	21	47	76	105
1182-Donald Duck Album (Disney) (5-7/61)	5	10	15	32	51	70
1183-101 Dalmatians (Disney-Movie) (3/61)	9	18	27	65	113	160
1184-Gyro Gearloose; All Barks-c/a (Disney) (5-7/61) Two variations exist	10	20	30	67	116	165
1185-Sweetie Pie	5	10	15	30	48	65
1186-Yak Yak (#1) by Jack Davis (2 versions - one minus 3-pg. Davis-c/a)	8	16	24	58	97	135
1187-The Three Stooges (6-8/61)-Photo-c	12	24	36	86	158	230
1188-Atlantis, the Lost Continent (Movie) (5/61)-Photo-c	10	20	30	68	119	170
1189-Greyfriars Bobby (Disney-Movie) (11/61)-Photo-c (scarce)	7	14	21	47	76	105
1190-Donald and the Wheel (Disney-Movie) (11/61); Barks-c	8	16	24	54	90	125
1191-Leave It to Beaver (TV)-Photo-c	13	26	39	90	165	240
1192-Ricky Nelson (TV)-Manning-a; photo-c	14	28	42	97	181	265
1193-The Real McCoys (TV) (6-8/61)-Photo-c	8	16	24	56	93	130
1194-Pepe (Movie) (4/61)-Photo-c	4	8	12	24	37	50
1195-National Velvet (#1) (TV)-Photo-c	7	14	21	49	80	110
1196-Pixie and Dixie and Mr. Jinks (TV) (Hanna-Barbera) (7-9/61)	6	12	18	37	59	80
1197-The Aquanauts (TV) (5-7/61)-Photo-c	7	14	21	47	76	105
1198-Donald in Mathmagic Land (Disney-Movie)-Reprint of #1051	6	12	18	43	69	95
1199-The Absent-Minded Professor (Disney-Movie) (4/61)-Photo-c	8	16	24	56	93	130
1200-Hennessey (TV) (8-10/61)-Gil Kane-a; photo-c	7	14	21	47	76	105

Four Color Comics #1237 © Desilu

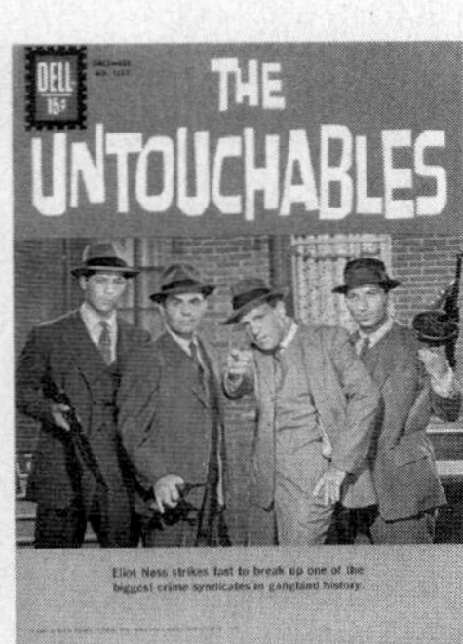

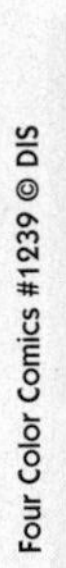
Four Color Comics #1239 © DIS

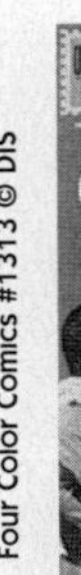
Four Color Comics #1313 © DIS

	GD 2.0	VG 4.0	FN 6.0	VF 8.0	VF/NM 9.0	NM- 9.2
1201-Goofy (Disney) (8-10/61)	5	10	15	32	51	70
1202-Rawhide (TV)-Clint Eastwood photo-c	14	28	42	97	181	265
1203-Pinocchio (Disney) (3/62)	5	10	15	34	55	75
1204-Scamp (Disney)	4	8	12	28	44	60
1205-David and Goliath (Movie) (7/61)-Photo-c	6	12	18	43	69	95
1206-Lolly and Pepper (9-11/61)	4	8	12	22	34	45
1207-The Rebel (TV)-Sekowsky-a; photo-c	8	16	24	56	93	130
1208-Rocky and His Friends (Jay Ward) (TV)	18	36	54	126	246	365
1209-Sugarfoot (TV)-Photo-c (10-12/61)	8	16	24	58	97	135
1210-The Parent Trap (Disney-Movie) (8/61)-Hayley Mills photo-c	9	18	27	60	100	140
1211-77 Sunset Strip (TV)-Manning-a; photo-c	8	16	24	54	90	125
1212-Chilly Willy (Lantz) (7-9/61)	5	10	15	30	48	65
1213-Mysterious Island (Movie)-Photo-c	8	16	24	56	93	130
1214-Smokey the Bear	4	8	12	28	44	60
1215-Tales of Wells Fargo (TV) (10-12/61)-Photo-c	8	16	24	52	86	120
1216-Whirlybirds (TV)-Photo-c	8	16	24	52	86	120
1218-Fury (TV)-Photo-c	6	12	18	41	66	90
1219-The Detectives (TV)-Robert Taylor & Adam West photo-c	8	16	24	56	93	130
1220-Gunslinger (TV)-Photo-c	8	16	24	56	93	130
1221-Bonanza (TV) (9-11/61)-Photo-c	17	34	51	119	230	340
1222-Elmer Fudd (9-11/61)	4	8	12	26	41	55
1223-Laramie (TV)-Gil Kane-a; photo-c	6	12	18	43	69	95
1224-The Little Rascals (TV) (10-12/61)	5	10	15	30	48	65
1225-The Deputy (TV)-Henry Fonda photo-c	9	18	27	63	107	150
1226-Nikki, Wild Dog of the North (Disney-Movie) (9/61)-Photo-c	5	10	15	34	55	75
1227-Morgan the Pirate (Movie)-Photo-c	7	14	21	50	83	115
1229-Thief of Baghdad (Movie)-Crandall/Evans-a; photo-c	7	14	21	45	73	100
1230-Voyage to the Bottom of the Sea (#1) (Movie)-Photo insert on-c	10	20	30	71	126	180
1231-Danger Man (TV) (9-11/61)-Patrick McGoohan photo-c	10	20	30	71	126	180
1232-On the Double (Movie)	5	10	15	30	48	65
1233-Tammy Tell Me True (Movie) (1961)	6	12	18	43	69	95
1234-The Phantom Planet (Movie) (1961)	7	14	21	47	76	105
1235-Mister Magoo (#1) (12-2/62)	8	16	24	56	93	130
1235-Mister Magoo (3-5/65) 2nd printing; reprint of 12-2/62 issue	6	12	18	41	66	90
1236-King of Kings (Movie)-Photo-c	7	14	21	50	83	115
1237-The Untouchables (#1) (TV)-Not by Toth; photo-c	19	38	57	135	263	390
1238-Deputy Dawg (TV)	10	20	30	73	129	185
1239-Donald Duck Album (Disney) (10-12/61)-Barks-c	7	14	21	45	73	100
1240-The Detectives (TV)-Tufts-a; Robert Taylor photo-c	8	16	24	56	93	130
1241-Sweetie Pie	4	8	12	24	37	50
1242-King Leonardo and His Short Subjects (#1) (TV) (11-1/62)	12	24	36	82	149	215
1243-Ellery Queen	8	16	24	56	93	130
1244-Space Mouse (Lantz) (11-1/62)	4	8	12	28	44	60
1245-New Adventures of Sherlock Holmes	12	24	36	86	158	230
1246-Mickey Mouse Album (Disney)	5	10	15	34	55	75
1247-Daisy Duck's Diary (Disney) (12-2/62)	5	10	15	32	51	70
1248-Pluto (Disney)	4	8	12	28	44	60
1249-The Danny Thomas Show (TV)-Manning-a; photo-c	13	26	39	93	172	250
1250-The Four Horsemen of the Apocalypse (Movie)-Photo-c	6	12	18	43	69	95
1251-Everything's Ducky (Movie) (1961)	5	10	15	30	48	65
1252-The Andy Griffith Show (TV)-Photo-c; 1st show aired 10/3/60	35	70	105	266	513	760
1253-Space Man (#1) (1-3/62)	7	14	21	49	80	110
1254- "Diver Dan" (#1) (TV) (2-4/62)-Photo-c	5	10	15	34	55	75
1255-The Wonders of Aladdin (Movie) (1961)	6	12	18	43	69	95
1256-Kona, Monarch of Monster Isle (#1) (2-4/62)-Glanzman-a	9	18	27	65	113	160
1257-Car 54, Where Are You? (#1) (TV) (3-5/62)-Photo-c	8	16	24	56	93	130
1258-The Frogmen (#1)-Evans-a	8	16	24	52	86	120
1259-El Cid (Movie) (1961)-Photo-c	7	14	21	47	76	105

	GD 2.0	VG 4.0	FN 6.0	VF 8.0	VF/NM 9.0	NM- 9.2
1260-The Horsemasters (TV, Movie) (Disney) (12-2/62)-Annette Funicello photo-c	12	24	36	85	155	225
1261-Rawhide (TV)-Clint Eastwood photo-c	14	28	42	97	181	265
1262-The Rebel (TV)-Photo-c	8	16	24	56	93	130
1263-77 Sunset Strip (TV) (12-2/62)-Manning-a; photo-c	8	16	24	54	90	125
1264-Pixie and Dixie and Mr. Jinks (TV) (Hanna-Barbera)	6	12	18	37	59	80
1265-The Real McCoys (TV)-Photo-c	8	16	24	56	93	130
1266-M.G.M.'s Spike and Tyke (12-2/62)	4	8	12	24	37	50
1267-Gyro Gearloose; Barks-c/a, 4 pgs. (Disney) (12-2/62)	8	16	24	54	90	125
1268-Oswald the Rabbit (Lantz)	4	8	12	28	44	60
1269-Rawhide (TV)-Clint Eastwood photo-c	14	28	42	97	181	265
1270-Bullwinkle and Rocky (#1) (TV) (Jay Ward) (3-5/62)	18	36	54	129	252	375
1271-Yogi Bear Birthday Party (TV) (Hanna-Barbera) (11/61) (Given away for 1 box top from Kellogg's Corn Flakes)	6	12	18	37	59	80
1272-Frosty the Snowman	5	10	15	32	51	70
1273-Hans Brinker (Disney-Movie)-Photo-c (2/62)	6	12	18	43	69	95
1274-Santa Claus Funnies (12/61)	6	12	18	41	66	90
1275-Rocky and His Friends (TV) (Jay Ward)	18	36	54	126	246	365
1276-Dondi	4	8	12	22	34	45
1278-King Leonardo and His Short Subjects (TV)	12	24	36	82	149	215
1279-Grandma Duck's Farm Friends (Disney)	5	10	15	32	51	70
1280-Hennesey (TV)-Photo-c	6	12	18	43	69	95
1281-Chilly Willy (Lantz) (4-6/62)	5	10	15	30	48	65
1282-Babes in Toyland (Disney-Movie) (1/62); Annette Funicello photo-c	13	26	39	95	178	260
1283-Bonanza (TV) (2-4/62)-Photo-c	17	34	51	119	230	340
1284-Laramie (TV)-Heath-a; photo-c	6	12	18	43	69	95
1285-Leave It to Beaver (TV)-Photo-c	13	26	39	90	165	240
1286-The Untouchables (TV)-Photo-c	14	28	42	97	181	265
1287-Man from Wells Fargo (TV)-Photo-c	6	12	18	37	59	80
1288-Twilight Zone (TV) (4/62)-Crandall/Evans-c/a	12	24	36	85	155	225
1289-Ellery Queen	8	16	24	56	93	130
1290-M.G.M.'s Mouse Musketeers	4	8	12	24	37	50
1291-77 Sunset Strip (TV)-Manning-a; photo-c	8	16	24	54	90	125
1293-Elmer Fudd (3-5/62)	4	8	12	26	41	55
1294-Ripcord (TV)	7	14	21	47	76	105
1295-Mister Ed, the Talking Horse (#1) (TV) (3-5/62)-Photo-c	12	24	36	85	155	225
1296-Fury (TV) (3-5/62)-Photo-c	6	12	18	41	66	90
1297-Spanky, Alfalfa and the Little Rascals (TV)	5	10	15	30	48	65
1298-The Hathaways (TV)-Photo-c	5	10	15	30	48	65
1299-Deputy Dawg (TV)	10	20	30	73	129	185
1300-The Comancheros (Movie) (1961)-John Wayne photo-c	14	28	42	101	191	280
1301-Adventures in Paradise (TV) (2-4/62)	6	12	18	39	62	85
1302-Johnny Jason, Teen Reporter (2-4/62)	4	8	12	24	37	50
1303-Lad: A Dog (Movie)-Photo-c	4	8	12	28	44	60
1304-Nellie the Nurse (3-5/62)-Stanley-a	7	14	21	47	76	105
1305-Mister Magoo (3-5/62)	8	16	24	56	93	130
1306-Target: The Corruptors (#1) (TV) (3-5/62)-Photo-c	6	12	18	37	59	80
1307-Margie (TV) (3-5/62)	6	12	18	37	59	80
1308-Tales of the Wizard of Oz (TV) (3-5/62)	11	22	33	78	139	200
1309-87th Precinct (#1) (TV) (4-6/62)-Krigstein-a; photo-c	9	18	27	65	113	160
1310-Huck and Yogi Winter Sports (TV) (Hanna-Barbera) (3/62)	8	16	24	56	93	130
1311-Rocky and His Friends (TV) (Jay Ward)	18	36	54	126	246	365
1312-National Velvet (TV)-Photo-c	4	8	12	28	44	60
1313-Moon Pilot (Disney-Movie)-Photo-c	7	14	21	47	76	105
1328-The Underwater City (Movie) (1961)-Evans-a; photo-c	7	14	21	47	76	105
1329-See Gyro Gearloose #01329-207						
1330-Brain Boy (#1)-Gil Kane-a	11	22	33	78	139	200
1332-Bachelor Father (TV)	7	14	21	50	83	115
1333-Short Ribs (4-6/62)	5	10	15	34	55	75
1335-Aggie Mack (4-6/62)	5	10	15	30	48	65
1336-On Stage; not by Leonard Starr	5	10	15	30	48	65
1337-Dr. Kildare (#1) (TV) (4-6/62)-Photo-c	8	16	24	58	97	135
1341-The Andy Griffith Show (TV) (4-6/62)-Photo-c	32	64	96	247	479	710

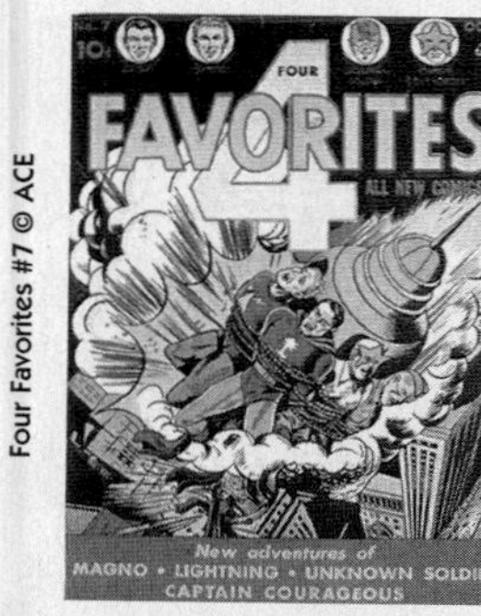

Four Favorites #7 © ACE

Four Women #1 © I Before E

Fox and the Crow #10 © DC

GD 2.0 | VG 4.0 | FN 6.0 | VF 8.0 | VF/NM 9.0 | NM- 9.2

1348-Yak Yak (#2)-Jack Davis-c/a 8 16 24 52 86 120
1349-Yogi Bear Visits the U.N. (TV) (Hanna-Barbera) (1/62)-Photo-c 8 16 24 58 97 135
1350-Comanche (Disney-Movie)(1962)-Reprints 4-Color #966 (title change from "Tonka" to "Comanche") (4-6/62)-Sal Mineo photo-c 5 10 15 35 55 75
1354-Calvin & the Colonel (#1) (TV) (4-6/62) 8 16 24 56 93 130
NOTE: *Missing numbers probably do not exist.*

4-D MONKEY, THE (Adventures of... #? on)
Leung's Publications: 1988 - No. 11, 1990 ($1.80/$2.00, 52 pgs.)
1-11: 1-Karate Pig, Ninja Flounder & 4-D Monkey (48 pgs., centerfold is a Christmas card). 2-4 (52 pgs.) 2.50

FOUR FAVORITES (Crime Must Pay the Penalty No. 33 on)
Ace Magazines: Sept, 1941 - No. 32, Dec, 1947
1-Vulcan, Lash Lightning (formerly Flash Lightning in Sure-Fire), Magno the Magnetic Man & The Raven begin; flag/Hitler-c 181 362 543 1158 1979 2800
2-The Black Ace only app. 63 126 189 403 689 975
3-Last Vulcan 52 104 156 322 549 775
4,5: 4-The Raven & Vulcan end; Unknown Soldier begins (see Our Flag), ends #28. 5-Captain Courageous begins (5/42), ends #28 (moves over from Captain Courageous #6); not in #6 45 90 135 284 480 675
6-8: 6-The Flag app.; Mr. Risk begins (7/42) 42 84 126 265 445 625
9-Kurtzman-a (Lash Lightning); robot-c 47 94 141 296 498 700
10-Classic Kurtzman-c/a (Magno & Davey) 57 114 171 362 619 875
11-Kurtzman-a; Hitler, Mussolini, Hirohito-c; L.B. Cole-a; Unknown Soldier by Kurtzman 84 168 252 538 919 1300
12-L.B. Cole-a 39 78 117 240 395 550
13-L.B. Cole-c (his first cover?) 57 114 171 362 619 875
14-20: 18,20-Palais-c/a 36 72 108 211 343 475
21-No Unknown Soldier; The Unknown app. 24 48 72 142 234 325
22-26: 22-Captain Courageous drops costume. 23-Unknown Soldier drops costume. 25-29-Hap Hazard app. 26-Last Magno 24 48 72 142 234 325
27-29: Hap Hazard app. in all 20 40 60 114 182 250
30-32: 30-Funny-c begin (teen humor), end #32 14 28 42 82 121 160
NOTE: ***Dave Berg** c-5. **Jim Mooney** a-6; c-1-3. **Palais** a-18-20; c-18-25. Torture chamber c-5.*

FOUR HORSEMEN, THE (See The Crusaders)

FOUR HORSEMEN
DC Comics (Vertigo): Feb, 2000 - No. 4, May, 2000 ($2.50, limited series)
1-4-Essad Ribic-c/a; Robert Rodi-s 2.50

FOUR HORSEMEN OF THE APOCALYPSE, THE (Movie)
Dell Publishing Co.: No. 1250, Jan-Mar, 1962 (one-shot)
Four Color 1250-Photo-c 6 12 18 43 69 95

4MOST (Foremost Boys No. 32-40; becomes Thrilling Crime Cases #41 on)
Novelty Publications/Star Publications No. 37-on:
Winter, 1941-42 - V8#5(#36), 9-10/49; #37, 11-12/49 - #40, 4-5/50
V1#1-The Target by Sid Greene, The Cadet & Dick Cole begin with origins retold; produced by Funnies Inc.; quarterly issues begin, end V6#3 152 304 456 965 1658 2350
2-Last Target (Spr/42); WWII cover 63 126 189 403 689 975
3-Dan'l Flannel begins; flag-c 47 94 141 296 498 700
4-1pg. Dr. Seuss (signed) (Aut/42); fish in the face-c 49 98 147 309 522 735
V2#1-3 20 40 60 114 182 250
4-Hitler, Tojo & Mussolini app. as pumpkins on-c 40 80 120 246 411 575
V3#1-4 15 30 45 88 137 185
V4#1-4: 2-Walter Johnson-c 13 26 39 74 105 135
V5#1-4: 1-The Target & Targeteers app. 11 22 33 64 90 115
V6#1-4 10 20 30 56 76 95
5-L. B. Cole-c 20 40 60 114 182 250
V7#1,3,5, V8#1, 37 10 20 30 56 76 95
2,4,6-L. B. Cole-c. 6-Last Dick Cole 20 40 60 114 182 250
V8#2,3,5-L. B. Cole-c/a 22 44 66 132 216 300
4-L. B. Cole-a 15 30 45 83 124 165
38-40: 38-Johnny Weismuller (Tarzan) life story & Jim Braddock (boxer) life story. 38-40-L.B. Cole-c. 40-Last White Rider 17 34 51 98 154 210
Accepted Reprint 38-40 (nd): 40-r/Johnny Weismuller life story; all have L.B. Cole-c 10 20 30 56 76 95

411
Marvel Comics: June, 2003 - No. 3 ($3.50, limited series)
1,2-Tributes to peacemakers; s/a by various. 1-Millar, Quitely, Mack, Winslade & others-s/a. 2-Harris, Phillips, Manco, Bruce Jones. 3.50

GD 2.0 | VG 4.0 | FN 6.0 | VF 8.0 | VF/NM 9.0 | NM- 9.2

FOUR-STAR BATTLE TALES
National Periodical Publications: Feb-Mar, 1973 - No. 5, Nov-Dec, 1973
1-Reprints begin 3 6 9 17 25 32
2-5 2 4 6 11 16 20
NOTE: ***Drucker** r-1, 3-5. **Heath** r-2, 5; c-1. **Krigstein** r-5. **Kubert** r-4; c-2.*

FOUR STAR SPECTACULAR
National Periodical Publications: Mar-Apr, 1976 - No. 6, Jan-Feb, 1977
1-Includes G.A. Flash story with new art 2 4 6 11 16 20
2-6: Reprints in all. 2-Infinity cover 2 4 6 8 10 12
NOTE: *All contain DC Superhero reprints. #1 has 68 pgs.; #2-6, 52 pgs.. #1, 4-Hawkman app.; #2-Kid Flash app.; #3-Green Lantern app; #2, 4, 5-Wonder Woman, Superboy app; #5-Green Arrow, Vigilante app; #6-Blackhawk G.A.-r.*

FOUR TEENERS (Formerly Crime Must Pay The Penalty; Dotty No. 35 on)
A. A. Wyn: No. 34, April, 1948 (52 pgs.)
34-Teen-age comic; Dotty app.; Curly & Jerry continue from Four Favorites 8 16 24 44 57 70

FOURTH WORLD GALLERY, THE (Jack Kirby's...)
DC Comics: 1996 (9/96) ($3.50, one-shot)
nn-Pin-ups of Jack Kirby's Fourth World characters (New Gods, Forever People & Mister Miracle) by John Byrne, Rick Burchett, Dan Jurgens, Walt Simonson & others 3.50

FOUR WOMEN
DC Comics (Homage): Dec, 2001 - No. 5, Apr, 2002 ($2.95, limited series)
1-5-Sam Kieth-s/a 3.00
TPB (2002, $17.95) r/series; foreward by Kieth 18.00

FOX AND THE CROW (Stanley & His Monster No. 109 on) (See Comic Cavalcade & Real Screen Comics)
National Periodical Publications: Dec-Jan, 1951-52 - No. 108, Feb-Mar, 1968
1 119 238 357 762 1306 1850
2(Scarce) 54 108 162 346 591 835
3-5 37 74 111 222 361 500
6-10 26 52 78 154 252 350
11-20 20 40 60 114 182 250
21-30: 22-Last precode issue (2/55) 15 30 45 83 124 165
31-40 12 24 36 69 97 125
41-60 6 12 18 43 69 95
61-80 5 10 15 34 55 75
81-94: 94-(11/65)-The Brat Finks begin 4 8 12 26 41 55
95-Stanley & His Monster begins (origin & 1st app) 6 12 18 37 59 80
96-99,101-108 3 6 9 20 30 40
100 (10-11/66) 4 8 12 22 34 45
NOTE: *Many later covers by **Mort Drucker.***

FOX AND THE HOUND, THE (Disney)(Movie)
Whitman Publishing Co.: Aug, 1981 - No. 3, Oct, 1981
11292- Golden Press Graphic Novel 2 4 6 8 10 12
1-3-Based on animated movie 1 2 3 5 7 9

FOXFIRE (See The Phoenix Resurrection)
Malibu Comics (Ultraverse): Feb, 1996 - No. 4, May, 1996 ($1.50)
1-4: Sludge, Ultraforce app. 4-Punisher app. 2.50

FOX GIANTS (Also see Giant Comics Edition)
Fox Features Syndicate: 1944 - 1950 (25¢, 132 - 196 pgs.)
Album of Crime nn(1949, 132p) 51 102 153 321 541 760
Album of Love nn(1949, 132p) 47 94 141 297 504 710
All Famous Crime Stories nn('49, 132p) 51 102 153 321 541 760
All Good Comics 1(1944, 132p)(R.W. Voigt)-The Bouncer, Purple Tigress, Rick Evans, Puppeteer, Green Mask; Infinity-c 47 94 141 296 498 700
All Great nn(1944, 132p)-Capt. Jack Terry, Rick Evans, Jaguar Man 41 82 123 249 417 585
All Great nn(Chicago Nite Life News)(1945, 132p)-Green Mask, Bouncer, Puppeteer, Rick Evans, Rocket Kelly 41 82 123 249 417 585
All-Great Confessions nn(1949, 132p) 46 92 138 290 488 685
All Great Crime Stories nn('49, 132p) 51 102 153 321 541 760
All Great Jungle Adventures nn('49, 132p) 54 108 162 346 591 835
All Real Confession Magazine 3 (3/49, 132p) 46 92 138 290 488 685
All Real Confession Magazine 4 (4/49, 132p) 46 92 138 290 488 685
All Your Comics 1(1944, 132p)-The Puppeteer, Red Robbins, & Merciless the Sorcerer 41 82 123 249 417 585
Almanac Of Crime nn(1948, 148p)-Phantom Lady 56 112 168 356 608 860
Almanac Of Crime 1(1950, 132p) 50 100 150 315 533 750

Fox Giant - Burning Romances © FOX

Foxhole #3 © Mainline

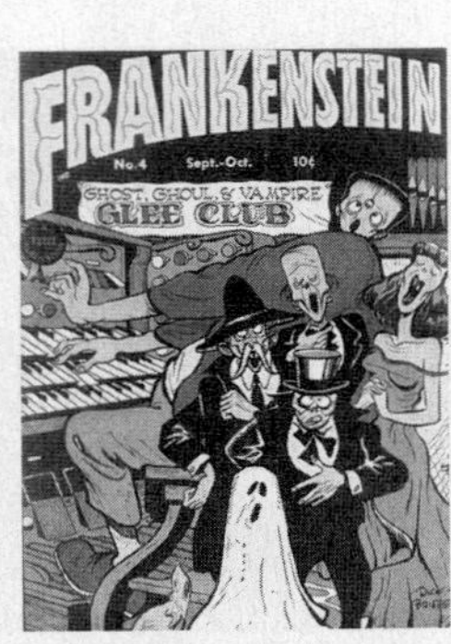

Frankenstein Comics #4 © PRIZE

	GD 2.0	VG 4.0	FN 6.0	VF 8.0	VF/NM 9.0	NM- 9.2
Book Of Love nn(1950, 132p)	44	88	132	277	469	660
Burning Romances 1(1949, 132p)	52	104	156	328	557	785
Crimes Incorporated nn(1950, 132p)	46	92	138	290	488	685
Daring Love Stories nn(1950, 132p)	44	88	132	277	469	660
Everybody's Comics 1(1944, 50¢, 196p)-The Green Mask, The Puppeteer, The Bouncer, Rocket Kelly, Rick Evans	46	92	138	290	488	685
Everybody's Comics 1(1946, 196p)-Green Lama, The Puppeteer	39	78	117	240	395	550
Everybody's Comics 1(1946, 196p)-Same as 1945 Ribtickler	31	62	93	182	296	410
Everybody's Comics nn(1947, 132p)-Jo-Jo, Purple Tigress, Cosmo Cat, Bronze Man	40	80	120	246	411	575
Exciting Romance Stories nn(1949, 132p)	47	94	141	297	504	710
Famous Love nn(1950, 132p)	44	88	132	277	469	660
Intimate Confessions nn(1950, 132p)	44	88	132	277	469	660
Journal Of Crime nn(1949, 132p)	51	102	153	321	541	760
Love Problems nn(1949, 132p)	46	92	138	290	488	685
Love Thrills nn(1950, 132p)	45	90	135	284	480	675
March of Crime nn('48, 132p)-Female w/rifle-c	50	100	150	315	533	750
March of Crime nn('49, 132p)-Cop w/pistol-c	47	94	141	297	504	710
March of Crime nn(1949, 132p)-Coffin & man w/machine-gun-c	47	94	141	297	504	710
Revealing Love Stories nn(1950, 132p)	44	88	132	277	469	660
Ribtickler nn(1945, 50¢, 196p)-Chicago Nite Life News; Marvel Mutt, Cosmo Cat, Flash Rabbit, The Nebbs app.	39	78	117	240	395	550
Romantic Thrills nn(1950, 132p)	44	88	132	277	469	660
Secret Love Stories nn(1949, 132p)	47	94	141	297	504	710
Strange Love nn(1950, 132p)-Photo-c	51	102	153	321	541	760
Sweetheart Scandals nn(1950, 132p)	44	88	132	277	469	660
Teen-Age Love nn(1950, 132p)	44	88	132	277	469	660
Throbbing Love nn(1950, 132p)-Photo-c; used in **POP**, pg. 107	52	104	156	322	549	775
Truth About Crime nn(1949, 132p)	51	102	153	321	541	760
Variety Comics 1(1946, 132p)-Blue Beetle, Jungle Jo	41	82	123	260	435	610
Variety Comics nn(1950, 132p)-Jungle Jo, My Secret Affair(w/Harrison/Wood-a), Crimes by Women & My Story	41	82	123	249	417	585
Western Roundup nn('50, 132p)-Hoot Gibson; Cody of the Pony Express app.	39	78	117	240	395	550

NOTE: *Each of the above usually contain four remaindered Fox books minus covers. Since these missing covers often had the first page of the first story, most Giants therefore are incomplete. Approximate values are listed. Books with appearances of Phantom Lady, Rulah, Jo-Jo, etc. could bring more.*

FOXHOLE (Becomes Never Again #8?)
Mainline/Charlton No. 5 on: 9-10/54 - No. 4, 3-4/55; No. 5, 7/55 - No. 7, 3/56

	GD 2.0	VG 4.0	FN 6.0	VF 8.0	VF/NM 9.0	NM- 9.2
1-Classic Kirby-c	50	100	150	315	533	750
2-Kirby-c/a(2); Kirby scripts based on his war time experiences	36	72	108	211	343	475
3-5-Kirby-c only	21	42	63	126	206	285
6-Kirby-c/a(2)	31	62	93	182	296	410
7	12	24	36	69	97	125
Super Reprints #10,15-17: 10-r/? 15,16-r/United States Marines #5,8. 17-r/Monty Hall #?	2	4	6	11	16	20
11,12,18-r/Foxhole #1,2,3; Kirby-c	3	6	9	17	25	32

NOTE: ***Kirby** a(r)-Super #11, 12. **Powell** a(r)-Super #15, 16. Stories by actual veterans.*

FOXY FAGAN COMICS (Funny Animal)
Dearfield Publishing Co.: Dec, 1946 - No. 7, Summer, 1948

	GD 2.0	VG 4.0	FN 6.0	VF 8.0	VF/NM 9.0	NM- 9.2
1-Foxy Fagan & Little Buck begin	13	26	39	72	101	130
2	8	16	24	42	54	65
3-7: 6-Rocket ship-c	7	14	21	37	46	55

FRACTION
DC Comics (Focus): June, 2004 - No. 6, Nov, 2004 ($2.50, limited series)

	GD 2.0	VG 4.0	FN 6.0	VF 8.0	VF/NM 9.0	NM- 9.2
1-6-David Tischman-s/Timothy Green II-a						2.50

FRACTURED FAIRY TALES (TV)
Gold Key: Oct, 1962 (Jay Ward)

	GD 2.0	VG 4.0	FN 6.0	VF 8.0	VF/NM 9.0	NM- 9.2
1 (10022-210)-From Bullwinkle TV show	10	20	30	71	126	180

FRAGGLE ROCK (TV)
Marvel Comics (Star Comics)/Marvel V2#1 on: Apr, 1985 - No. 8, Sept, 1986; V2#1, Apr, 1988 - No. 5, Aug, 1988

	GD 2.0	VG 4.0	FN 6.0	VF 8.0	VF/NM 9.0	NM- 9.2
1-6 (75¢-c)						5.00
7,8						6.00
V2#1-5-($1.00): Reprints 1st series						2.50

FRANCIS, BROTHER OF THE UNIVERSE
Marvel Comics Group: 1980 (75¢, 52 pgs., one-shot)

	GD 2.0	VG 4.0	FN 6.0	VF 8.0	VF/NM 9.0	NM- 9.2
nn-John Buscema/Marie Severin-a; story of Francis Bernadone celebrating his 800th birthday in 1982						4.00

FRANCIS THE FAMOUS TALKING MULE (All based on movie)
Dell Publishing Co.: No. 335 (#1), June, 1951 - No. 1090, March, 1960

	GD 2.0	VG 4.0	FN 6.0	VF 8.0	VF/NM 9.0	NM- 9.2
Four Color 335 (#1)	10	20	30	71	126	180
Four Color 465	6	12	18	41	66	90
Four Color 501,547,579	5	10	15	32	51	70
Four Color 621,655,698,710,745	4	8	12	28	44	60
Four Color 810,863,906,953,991,1068,1090	4	8	12	26	41	55

FRANK
Nemesis Comics (Harvey): Apr (Mar inside), 1994 - No. 4, 1994 ($1.75/$2.50, limited series)

	GD 2.0	VG 4.0	FN 6.0	VF 8.0	VF/NM 9.0	NM- 9.2
1-4-($2.50, direct sale): 1-Foil-c Edition						3.00
1-4-($1.75)-Newsstand Editions; Cowan-a in all						2.50

FRANK
Fantagraphics Books: Sept, 1996 ($2.95, B&W)

	GD 2.0	VG 4.0	FN 6.0	VF 8.0	VF/NM 9.0	NM- 9.2
1-Woodring-c/a/scripts						3.00

FRANK BUCK (Formerly My True Love)
Fox Features Syndicate: No. 70, May, 1950 - No. 3, Sept, 1950

	GD 2.0	VG 4.0	FN 6.0	VF 8.0	VF/NM 9.0	NM- 9.2
70-Wood a(p)(3 stories)-Photo-c	32	64	96	188	307	425
71-Wood-a (9 pgs.); photo/painted-c	18	36	54	105	165	225
3: 3-Photo/painted-c	14	28	42	80	115	150

NOTE: *Based on "Bring 'Em Back Alive" TV show.*

FRANKENSTEIN (See Dracula, Movie Classics & Werewolf)
Dell Publishing Co.: Aug-Oct, 1964; No. 2, Sept, 1966 - No. 4, Mar, 1967

	GD 2.0	VG 4.0	FN 6.0	VF 8.0	VF/NM 9.0	NM- 9.2
1(12-283-410)(1964)(2nd printing; see Movie Classics for 1st printing)	5	10	15	34	55	75
2-Intro. & origin super-hero character (9/66)	4	8	12	28	44	60
3,4	3	6	9	20	30	40

FRANKENSTEIN (The Monster of...; also see Monsters Unleashed #2, Power Record Comics, Psycho & Silver Surfer #7)
Marvel Comics Group: Jan, 1973 - No. 18, Sept, 1975

	GD 2.0	VG 4.0	FN 6.0	VF 8.0	VF/NM 9.0	NM- 9.2
1-Ploog-c/a begins, ends #6	7	14	21	49	80	110
2	4	8	12	26	41	55
3-5	3	6	9	20	30	40
6,7,10: 7-Dracula cameo	3	6	9	17	25	32
8,9-Dracula c/sty. 9-Death of Dracula	4	8	12	28	44	60
11-17	3	6	9	14	20	25
18-Wrightson-c(i)	3	6	9	16	23	30

NOTE: ***Adkins** c-17i. **Buscema** a-7-10p. **Ditko** a-12r. **G. Kane** c-15p. **Orlando** a-8r. **Ploog** a-1-3, 4p, 5p, 6; c-1-6. **Wrightson** c-18i.*

FRANKENSTEIN (Mary Wollstonecraft Shelley's...; A Marvel Illustrated Novel)
Marvel Pub.: 1983 ($8.95, B&W, 196 pgs., 8x11" TPB)

	GD 2.0	VG 4.0	FN 6.0	VF 8.0	VF/NM 9.0	NM- 9.2
nn-Wrightson-a; 4 pg. intro. by Stephen King	5	10	15	30	48	65
Limited HC Edition						175.00

FRANKENSTEIN COMICS (Also See Prize Comics)
Prize Publ. (Crestwood/Feature): Sum, 1945 - V5#5(#33), Oct-Nov, 1954

	GD 2.0	VG 4.0	FN 6.0	VF 8.0	VF/NM 9.0	NM- 9.2
1-Frankenstein begins by Dick Briefer (origin); Frank Sinatra parody	123	246	369	787	1344	1900
2	56	112	168	356	608	860
3-5	42	84	126	265	445	625
6-10: 7-S&K a(r)/Headline Comics. 8(7-8/47)-Superman satire	39	78	117	231	378	525
11-17(1-2/49)-11-Boris Karloff parody-c/story. 17-Last humor issue	34	68	102	199	325	450
18(3/52)-New origin, horror series begins	43	86	129	271	461	650
19,20(V3#4, 8-9/52)	29	58	87	170	278	385
21(V3#5), 22(V3#6), 23(V4#1) - #28(V4#6)	27	54	81	158	259	360
29(V5#1) - #33(V5#5)	26	52	78	154	252	350

NOTE: ***Briefer** c/a-all. **Meskin** a-21, 29.*

FRANKENSTEIN/DRACULA WAR, THE
Topps Comics: Feb, 1995 - No. 3, May, 1995 ($2.50, limited series)

	GD 2.0	VG 4.0	FN 6.0	VF 8.0	VF/NM 9.0	NM- 9.2
1-3						3.00

FRANKENSTEIN, JR. (...& the Impossibles) (TV)
Gold Key: Jan, 1966 (Hanna-Barbera)

	GD 2.0	VG 4.0	FN 6.0	VF 8.0	VF/NM 9.0	NM- 9.2
1-Super hero (scarce)	11	22	33	76	136	195

FRANKENSTEIN MOBSTER

Frankie Comics #4 © MAR

Fray #8 © Joss Whedon

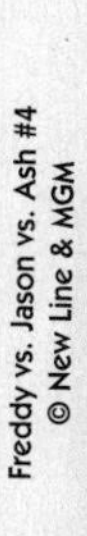
Freddy vs. Jason vs. Ash #4 © New Line & MGM

GD 2.0 | VG 4.0 | FN 6.0 | VF 8.0 | VF/NM 9.0 | NM- 9.2

Image Comics: No. 0, Oct, 2003 - No. 7, Dec, 2004 ($2.95)
0-7: 0-Two covers by Wheatley and Hughes; Wheatley-s/a. 1-Variant-c by Wieringo 3.00

FRANKENSTEIN: OR THE MODERN PROMETHEUS
Caliber Press: 1994 ($2.95, one-shot)
1 3.00

FRANK FRAZETTA FANTASY ILLUSTRATED (Magazine)
Quantum Cat Entertainment: Spring 1998 - No. 8 ($5.95, quarterly)
1-Anthology; art by Corben, Horley, Jusko 1 2 3 4 5 7
1-Linsner variant-c 10.00
2-Battle Chasers by Madureira; Harris-a 8.00
2-Madureira Battle Chasers variant-c 12.00
3-8-Frazetta-c 6.00
3-Tony Daniel variant-c 15.00
5,6-Portacio variant-c, 7,8-Alex Nino variant-c 10.00
8-Alex Ross Chicago Comicon variant-c 10.00

FRANK FRAZETTA'S DEATH DEALER
Image Comics: Mar, 2007 - No. 6, Jan, 2008 ($3.99)
1-6-Nat Jones-a; 3 covers (Frazetta, Jones, Jones sketch) 4.00

FRANK FRAZETTA'S...
Fantagraphics Books/Image Comics: one-shots
... Creatures 1 (Image Comics, 7/08, $3.99) Bergting-a; covers by Frazetta & Bergting 4.00
... Dark Kingdom 1-4 (Image, 4/08 - No. 4, 1/10, $3.99) Vigil-a; covers by Frazetta & Vigil 4.00
... Dracula Meets the Wolfman 1 (Image, 8/08, $3.99) Francavilla-a; 2 covers 4.00
... Moon Maid 1 (Image, 1/09, $3.99) Tim Vigil-a; covers by Frazetta & Vigil 4.00
... Neanderthal 1 (Image, 4/09, $3.99) Fotos & Vigil-a; covers by Frazetta & Fotos 4.00
... Sorcerer 1 (Image, 8/09, $3.99) Medors-a; covers by Frazetta & Medors 4.00
... Swamp Demon 1 (Image, 7/08, $3.99) Medors-a; covers by Frazetta & Medors 4.00
... Thun'da Tales 1 (Fantagraphics Books, 1987, $2.00) Frazetta-r 6.00
... Untamed Love 1 (Fantagraphics Books, 11/87, $2.00) r/1950's romance comics 6.00

FRANKIE COMICS (...& Lana No. 13-15) (Formerly Movie Tunes; becomes Frankie Fuddle No. 16 on)
Marvel Comics (MgPC): No. 4, Wint, 1946-47 - No. 15, June, 1949
4-Mitzi, Margie, Daisy app. 15 30 45 88 137 185
5-9 10 20 30 58 79 100
10-15: 13-Anti-Wertham editorial 10 20 30 54 72 90

FRANKIE DOODLE (See Sparkler, both series)
United Features Syndicate: No. 7, 1939
Single Series 7 33 66 99 194 317 440

FRANKIE FUDDLE (Formerly Frankie & Lana)
Marvel Comics: No. 16, Aug, 1949 - No. 17, Nov, 1949
16,17 10 20 30 54 72 90

FRANKLIN RICHARDS (Fantastic Four)
Marvel Comics: April, 2006 - Present ($2.99/$3.99, one-shots)
...: April Fools (6/09, $3.99) Eliopoulos-s/a 4.00
...: Collected Chaos (2008, $8.99, digest) reprints various one-shots 8.00
...: Fall Football Fiasco (1/08, $2.99) Eliopoulos-a/Sumerak-s 3.00
...: Happy Franksgiving (1/07, $2.99) Thanksgiving stories by Eliopoulos-a/Sumerak-s 3.00
...: It's Dark Reigning Cats & Dogs (4/09, $3.99) Eliopoulos-s/a 4.00
...: Lab Brat (2007, $7.99, digest) reprints one-shots and Masked Marvel back-ups 8.00
...: March Madness (5/07, $2.99) More science gone wrong by Eliopoulos-a/Sumerak-s 3.00
...: Monster Mash (11/07, $2.99) Science mishaps by Eliopoulos-a/Sumerak-s 3.00
...: Not-So-Secret Invasion (7/08, $2.99) Skrull cover; The Wizard app. 3.00
... One Shot (4/06, $2.99) short stories by Eliopoulos-a/Sumerak-s 3.00
...: School's Out (4/09, $3.99) Eliopoulos-s/a; Katie Power app. 4.00
...: Sons of Geniuses (1/09, $3.99) parallel dimension alternate version hijinks 4.00
...: Spring Break (5/08, $2.99) short stories by Eliopoulos-a/Sumerak-s 3.00
...: Summer Smackdown (10/08, $2.99) short stories by Eliopoulos-a/Sumerak-s 3.00
...: Super Summer Spectacular (9/06, $2.99) short stories by Eliopoulos-a/Sumerak-s 3.00
...: World Be Warned (8/07, $2.99) short stories by Eliopoulos-a/Sumerak-s; Hulk app. 3.00

FRANK LUTHER'S SILLY PILLY COMICS (See Jingle Dingle...)
Children's Comics (Maltex Cereal): 1950 (10¢)
1-Characters from radio, records, & TV 8 16 24 44 57 70

FRANK MERRIWELL AT YALE (Speed Demons No. 5 on?)
Charlton Comics: June, 1955 - No. 4, Jan, 1956 (Also see Shadow Comics)
1 7 14 21 37 46 55
2-4 5 10 15 24 30 35

FRANTIC (Magazine) (See Ratfink & Zany)

GD 2.0 | VG 4.0 | FN 6.0 | VF 8.0 | VF/NM 9.0 | NM- 9.2

Pierce Publishing Co.: Oct, 1958 - V2#2, Apr, 1959 (Satire)
V1#1 12 24 36 69 97 125
2 9 18 27 52 69 85
V2#1,2: 1-Burgos-a, Severin-c/a; Powell-a? 8 16 24 42 54 65

FRAY (Also see Buffy the Vampire Slayer "season eight" #16-19)
Dark Horse Comics: June, 2001 - No. 8, July, 2003 ($2.99, limited series)
1-Joss Whedon-s/Moline & Owens-a 1 2 3 5 6 8
1-DF Gold edition 2 4 6 9 12 15
2-8: 6-(3/02). 7-(4/03) 4.00
TPB (11/03, $19.95) r/#1-8; intros by Whedon & Loeb; Moline sketch pages 20.00

FREAK FORCE (Also see Savage Dragon)
Image Comics (Highbrow Ent.): Dec, 1993 - No. 18, July, 1995 ($1.95/$2.50)
1-18-Superpatriot & Mighty Man in all; Erik Larsen scripts in all. 4-Vanguard app. 8-Begin $2.50-c. 9-Cyberforce-c & app. 13-Variant-c 3.00

FREAK FORCE (Also see Savage Dragon)
Image Comics: Apr, 1997 - No. 3, July, 1997 ($2.95)
1-3-Larsen-s 3.00

FREAK OUT, USA (See On the Scene Presents...)

FREAK SHOW
Image Comics (Desperado): 2006 ($5.99, B&W, one-shot)
nn-Bruce Jones-s/Bernie Wrightson-c/a 6.00

FREAKS OF THE HEARTLAND
Dark Horse Comics: Jan, 2004 - No. 6, Nov, 2004 ($2.99)
1-6-Steve Niles-s/Greg Ruth-a 3.00

FRECKLES AND HIS FRIENDS (See Crackajack Funnies, Famous Comics Cartoon Book, Honeybee Birdwhistle... & Red Ryder)

FRECKLES AND HIS FRIENDS
Standard Comics/Argo: No. 5, 11/47 - No. 12, 8/49; 11/55 - No. 4, 6/56
5-Reprints 9 18 27 50 65 80
6-12-Reprints. 7-9-Airbrush-c (by Schomburg?). 11-Lingerie panels 7 14 21 35 43 50
NOTE: *Some copies of No. 8 & 9 contain a printing oddity. The negatives were elongated in the engraving process, probably to conform to page dimensions on the filler pages. Those pages only look normal when viewed at a 45 degree angle.*
1(Argo,'55)-Reprints (NEA Service) 6 12 18 28 34 40
2-4 4 8 12 18 22 25

FREDDY (Formerly My Little Margie's Boy Friends) (Also see Blue Bird)
Charlton Comics: V2#12, June, 1958 - No. 47, Feb, 1965
V2#12 4 8 12 22 34 45
13-15 3 6 9 16 22 28
16-47 2 4 6 11 16 20

FREDDY
Dell Publishing Co.: May-July, 1963 - No. 3, Oct-Dec, 1964
1 3 6 9 19 29 38
2,3 3 6 9 14 20 26

FREDDY KRUEGER'S A NIGHTMARE ON ELM STREET
Marvel Comics: Oct, 1989 - No. 2, Dec, 1989 ($2.25, B&W, movie adaptation, magazine)
1,2: Origin Freddy Krueger; Buckler/Alcala-a 1 2 3 4 5 7

FREDDY'S DEAD: THE FINAL NIGHTMARE
Innovation Publishing: Oct, 1991 - No. 3, Dec 1991 ($2.50, color mini-series, adapts movie)
1-3: Dismukes (film poster artist) painted-c 3.00

FREDDY VS. JASON VS. ASH (Freddy Krueger, Friday the 13th, Army of Darkness)
DC Comics (WildStorm): Early Jan, 2008 - No. 6, May, 2008 ($2.99, limited series)
1-Three covers by J. Scott Campbell; Kuhoric-s/Craig-a 5.00
1-Second printing with 3 covers combined sideways 4.00
2-6: 2-4-Eric Powell-c. 5,6-Richard Friend-c 3.00
2-4-Second printings with B&W covers 3.00
TPB (2008, $17.99) r/#1-6; creators' interview afterword 18.00

FREDDY VS. JASON VS. ASH: THE NIGHTMARE WARRIORS
DC Comics (WildStorm): Aug, 2009 - No. 6, Jan, 2010 ($3.99, limited series)
1-6-Katz & Kuhoric-s/Craig-a. 1-Suydam-c 4.00

FRED HEMBECK DESTROYS THE MARVEL UNIVERSE
Marvel Comics: July, 1989 ($1.50, one-shot)
1-Punisher app.; Staton-i (5 pgs.) 3.00

FRED HEMBECK SELLS THE MARVEL UNIVERSE

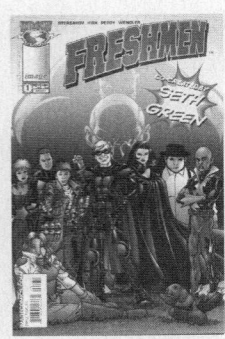

Freshmen #1 © TCOW

Friendly Ghost, Casper #1 © HARV

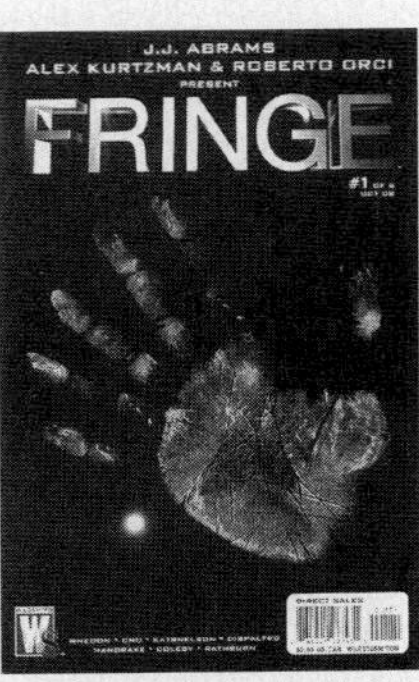
Fringe #1 © WB

	GD 2.0	VG 4.0	FN 6.0	VF 8.0	VF/NM 9.0	NM- 9.2
Marvel Comics: Oct, 1990 ($1.25, one-shot)						
1-Punisher, Wolverine parodies; Hembeck/Austin-c						3.00
FREEDOM AGENT (Also see John Steele)						
Gold Key: Apr, 1963 (12¢)						
1 (10054-304)-Painted-c	4	8	12	26	41	55
FREEDOM FIGHTERS (See Justice League of America #107,108)						
National Periodical Publ./DC Comics: Mar-Apr, 1976 - No. 15, July-Aug, 1978						
1-Uncle Sam, The Ray, Black Condor, Doll Man, Human Bomb, & Phantom Lady begin (all former Quality characters)	3	6	9	14	19	24
2-9: 4,5-Wonder Woman x-over. 7-1st app. Crusaders	2	4	6	9	12	15
10-15: 10-Origin Doll Man; Cat-Man-c/story (4th app; 1st revival since Detective #325). 11-Origin The Ray. 12-Origin Firebrand. 13-Origin Black Condor. 14-Batgirl & Batwoman app. 15-Batgirl & Batwoman app.; origin Phantom Lady	2	4	6	9	13	16
NOTE: *Buckler c-5-11p, 13p, 14p.*						
FREEDOM FORCE						
Image Comics: Jan, 2005 - No. 6, June, 2005 ($2.95)						
1-6-Eric Dieter-s/Tom Scioli-a						3.00
FREEMIND						
Future Comics: No. 0, Aug, 2002; Nov, 2002 - No. 7, June, 2003 ($3.50)						
0-($2.25) Giordano-c						2.50
0-($2.25) Variant-c by Layton						2.50
1-7 ($3.50) 1-Two covers by Giordano & Layton; Giordano-a thru #3. 4,5-Leeke-a						3.50
FREEREALMS						
DC Comics (WildStorm): Sept, 2009 - No. 12 ($3.99, limited series)						
1-5-Based on the online game; Jon Buran-a						4.00
FREEX						
Malibu Comics (Ultraverse): July, 1993 - No. 18, Mar, 1995 ($1.95)						
1-3,5-14,16-18: 1-Polybagged w/trading card. 2-Some were polybagged w/card. 6-Nightman-c/story. 7-2 pg. origin Hardcase by Zeck. 17-Rune app.						2.50
1-Holographic-c edition						6.00
1-Ultra 5,000 limited silver ink-c						3.00
4-($2.50, 48 pgs.)-Rune flip-c/story by B. Smith (3 pgs.); 3 pg. Night Man preview						2.50
15 ($3.50)-w/Ultraverse Premiere #9 flip book; Alec Swan & Rafferty app.						3.50
Giant Size 1 (1994, $2.50)-Prime app.						2.50
NOTE: *Simonson c-1.*						
FRENZY (Magazine) (Satire)						
Picture Magazine: Apr, 1958 - No. 6, Mar, 1959						
1	13	26	39	72	101	130
2-6	8	16	24	44	57	70
FRESHMEN						
Image Comics: Jul, 2005 - No. 6, Mar, 2006 ($2.99)						
1-Sterbakov-s/Kirk-a; co-created by Seth Green; covers by Pérez, Migliari, Linsner						3.00
2-6-Migliari-c						3.00
... Yearbook (1/06, $2.99) profile pages of characters; art by various incl. Chaykin, Kirk						3.00
... Vol. 1 (3/06, $16.99, TPB) r/#1-6 & Yearbook; cover gallery with concept art						17.00
FRESHMEN (Volume 2)						
Image Comics: Nov, 2006 - No. 6, Aug, 2007 ($2.99)						
1-6: 1-Sterbakov-s/Conrad-a; 4 covers						3.00
...: Summer Vacation Special (7/08, $4.99) Sterbakov-s; bonus pin-ups by various						5.00
... Vol. 2 Fundamentals of Fear (6/07, $16.99, TPB) r/#1-6; cover gallery, journals						17.00
FRIDAY FOSTER						
Dell Publishing Co.: October, 1972						
1	4	8	12	22	34	45
FRIDAY THE 13TH (Based on the horror movie franchise)						
DC Comics (WildStorm): Feb, 2007 - No. 6, July, 2007 ($2.99, mature)						
1-6: 1-Two covers by Sook and Bradstreet; Gray & Palmiotti-s						3.00
...: Abuser and The Abused (6/08, $3.50) Fialkov-s/Andy B. -a						3.50
...: Bad Land 1,2 (3/08 - No. 2, 4/08, $2.99) Marz-s/Huddleston-a/McKone-c						3.00
...: How I Spent My Summer Vacation 1,2 (11/07 - No. 2, 12/07, $2.99) Aaron-s/Archer-a						3.00
...: Pamela's Tale 1,2 (9/07 - No. 2, 10/07, $2.99) Andreyko-s/Moll-a/Nguyen-c						3.00
FRIENDLY GHOST, CASPER, THE (Becomes Casper... #254 on)						
Harvey Publications: Aug, 1958 - No. 224, Oct, 1982; No. 225, Oct, 1986 - No. 253, June, 1990						
1-Infinity-c	34	68	102	262	506	750
2	16	32	48	113	217	320

	GD 2.0	VG 4.0	FN 6.0	VF 8.0	VF/NM 9.0	NM- 9.2
3-10: 6-X-Mas-c	10	20	30	67	116	165
11-20: 18-X-Mas-c	7	14	21	50	83	115
21-30	5	10	15	34	55	75
31-50	4	8	12	24	37	50
51-70,100: 54-X-Mas-c	3	6	9	20	30	40
71-99	3	6	9	16	23	30
101-131: 131-Last 12¢ issue	3	6	9	14	20	26
132-159	2	4	6	11	16	20
160-163: All 52 pg. Giants	3	6	9	14	20	26
164-199: 173,179,185-Cub Scout Specials	2	4	6	8	10	12
200	2	4	6	8	11	14
201-224	1	2	3	5	7	9
225-237: 230-X-mas-c. 232-Valentine's-c						5.00
238-253: 238-Begin $1.00-c. 238,244-Halloween-c. 243-Last new material						4.00
FRIENDLY NEIGHBORHOOD SPIDER-MAN						
Marvel Comics: Dec, 2005 - No. 24, Nov, 2007 ($2.99)						
1-Evolve or Die pt. 1; Peter David-s/Mike Wieringo-a; Morlun app.						4.00
1-Variant Wieringo-c with regular costume						3.00
2-4: 2-New Avengers app. 3-Spider-Man dies						3.00
2-4-var-c: 2-Bag-Head Fantastic Four costume. 3-Captain Universe. 4-Wrestler						5.00
5-10: 6-Red & gold costume. 8-10-Uncle Ben app.						3.00
11-23: 17-Black costume; Sandman app.						3.00
24-($3.99) "One More Day" part 2; Quesada-a; covers by Quesada & Djurdjevic						4.00
Annual 1 (7/07, $3.99) Origin of The Sandman; back-up w/Doran-a						4.00
... Vol. 1: Derailed (2006, $14.99) r/#5-10; Wieringo sketch pages						15.00
... Vol. 2: Mystery Date (2007, $13.99) r/#11-16						14.00
FRIENDS OF MAXX (Also see Maxx)						
Image Comics (I Before E): Apr, 1996 - No. 3, Mar, 1997 ($2.95)						
1-3: Sam Kieth-c/a/scripts. 1-Featuring Dude Japan						3.00
FRIGHT						
Atlas/Seaboard Periodicals: June, 1975 (Aug. on inside)						
1-Origin/1st app. The Son of Dracula; Frank Thorne-c/a	2	4	6	9	12	15
FRIGHT NIGHT						
Now Comics: Oct, 1988 - No. 22, 1990 ($1.75)						
1-22: 1,2 Adapts movie. 8, 9-Evil Ed horror photo-c from movie						2.50
FRIGHT NIGHT II						
Now Comics: 1989 ($3.95, 52 pgs.)						
1-Adapts movie sequel						4.00
FRINGE (Based on the 2008 FOX television series)						
DC Comics (WildStorm): Oct, 2008 - No. 6, Aug, 2009 ($2.99, limited series)						
1-6-Anthology by various. 1-Mandrake & Coleby-a						3.00
TPB (2009, $19.99) r/#1-6; intro. by TV series co-creators Kurtzman & Orci						20.00
FRISKY ANIMALS (Formerly Frisky Fables; Super Cat #56 on)						
Star Publications: No. 44, Jan, 1951 - No. 55, Sept, 1953						
44-Super Cat; L.B. Cole	20	40	60	115	183	250
45-Classic L. B. Cole-c	29	58	87	169	272	375
46-51,53-55: Super Cat. 54-Super Cat-c begin	19	38	57	109	172	235
52-L. B. Cole-c/a, 3 1/2 pgs.; X-Mas-c	20	40	60	115	183	250
NOTE: *All have **L. B. Cole**-c. No. 47-No Super Cat. **Disbrow** a-49, 52. **Fago** a-51.*						
FRISKY ANIMALS ON PARADE (Formerly Parade Comics; becomes Superspook)						
Ajax-Farrell Publ. (Four Star Comic Corp.): Sept, 1957 - No. 3, Dec-Jan, 1957-1958						
1-L. B. Cole-c	17	34	51	98	154	210
2-No L. B. Cole-c	10	20	30	56	76	95
3-L. B. Cole-c	15	30	45	85	130	175
FRISKY FABLES (Frisky Animals No. 44 on)						
Premium Group/Novelty Publ./Star Publ. V5#4 on: Spring, 1945 - No. 43, Oct, 1950						
V1#1-Funny animal; Al Fago-c/a #1-38	22	44	66	128	209	290
2,3(Fall & Winter, 1945)	13	26	39	74	105	135
V2#1(#4, 4/46) - 9,11,12(#15, 3/47): 4-Flag-c	10	20	30	56	76	95
10-Christmas-c. 12-Valentine's-c	10	20	30	58	79	100
V3#1(#16, 4/47) - 12(#27, 3/48): 4-Flag-c. 7,9-Infinity-c. 10-X-Mas-c. 12-Washington crossing the Delaware parody-c	9	18	27	47	61	75
V4#1(#28, 4/48) - 7(#34, 2-3/49)	8	16	24	44	57	70
V5#1(#35, 4-5/49) - 4(#38, 10-11/49)	8	16	24	44	57	70
39-43-L. B. Cole-c; 40-Xmas-c	20	40	60	114	182	250
Accepted Reprint No. 43 (nd); L.B. Cole-c	10	20	30	54	72	90

FRITZI RITZ (See Comics On Parade, Single Series #5, 1(reprint), Tip Top & United Comics)

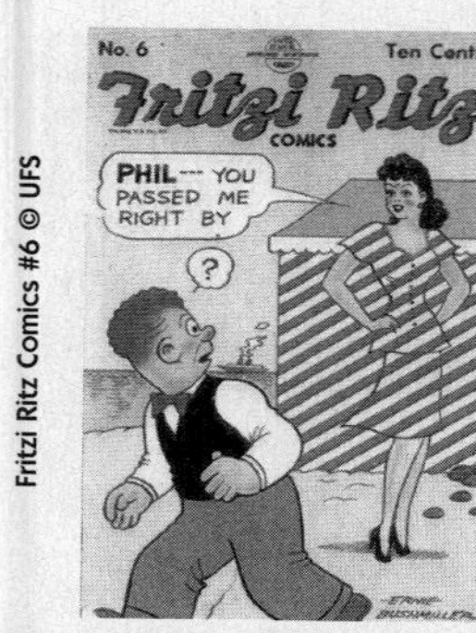

Fritzi Ritz Comics #6 © UFS

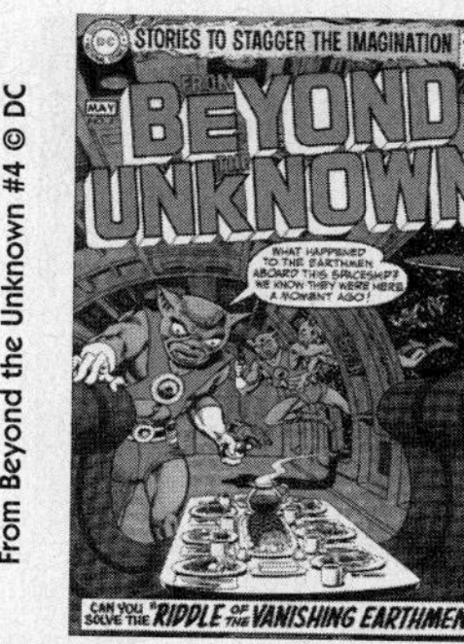

From Beyond the Unknown #4 © DC

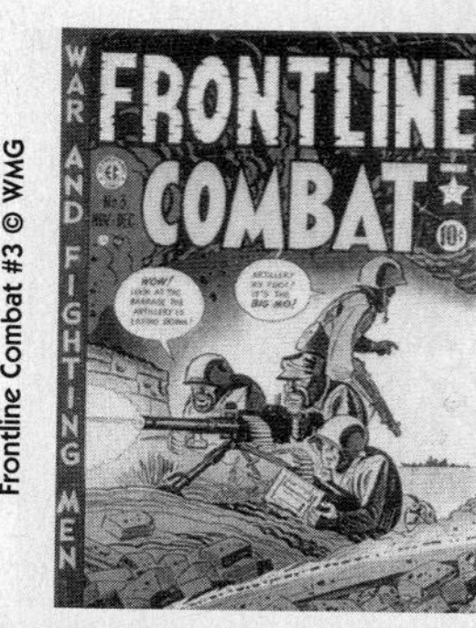

Frontline Combat #3 © WMG

GD VG FN VF VF/NM NM-
2.0 4.0 6.0 8.0 9.0 9.2

FRITZI RITZ (United Comics No. 8-26) (Also see Tip Topper for early Peanuts by Schulz)
United Features Synd./St. John No. 37-55/Dell No. 56 on:
1939; Fall, 1948; No. 3, 1949 - No. 7, 1949; No. 27, 3-4/53 - No. 36, 9-10/54; No. 37 - No. 55, 9-11/57; No. 56, 12-2/57-58 - No. 59, 9-11/58

Single Series #5 (1939) 32 64 96 188 307 425
nn(1948)-Special Fall issue; by Ernie Bushmiller 18 36 54 105 165 225
3(#1) 13 26 39 74 105 135
4-7(1949): 6-Abbie & Slats app. 10 20 30 54 72 90
27(1953)-33,37-50,57-59-Early Peanuts (1-4 pgs.) by Schulz. 29-Five pg. Abbie & Slats; 1 pg. Mamie by Russell Patterson. 38(9/55)-41(4/56)-Low print run
10 20 30 58 79 100
34-36,51-56: 36-1 pg. Mamie by Patterson 8 16 24 44 57 70

NOTE: *Abbie & Slats in #6,7, 27-31. Li'l Abner in #32-36.*

FROGMAN COMICS
Hillman Periodicals: Jan-Feb, 1952 - No. 11, May, 1953

1 15 30 45 86 133 180
2 10 20 30 54 72 90
3,4,6-11: 4-Meskin-a 8 16 24 42 54 65
5-Krigstein-a 9 18 27 47 61 75

FROGMEN, THE
Dell Publishing Co.: No. 1258, Feb-Apr, 1962 - No. 11, Nov-Jan, 1964-65 (Painted-c)

Four Color 1258(#1)-Evans-a 8 16 24 52 86 120
2,3-Evans-a; part Frazetta inks in #2,3 6 12 18 37 59 80
4,6-11 4 8 12 24 37 50
5-Toth-a 4 8 12 28 44 60

FROM BEYOND THE UNKNOWN
National Periodical Publications: 10-11/69 - No. 25, 11-12/73

1 6 12 18 37 59 80
2-6 3 6 9 20 30 40
7-11: (64 pgs.) 7-Intro Col. Glenn Merrit 4 8 12 22 34 45
12-17: (52 pgs.) 13-Wood-a(i)(r). 17-Pres. Nixon-c 3 6 9 18 27 35
18-25: Star Rovers-r begin #18,19. Space Museum in #23-25
2 4 6 13 18 22

NOTE: ***N. Adams** c-3, 6, 8, 9. **Anderson** c-2, 4, 5, 10, 11i, 15-17, 22; reprints-3, 4, 6-8, 10, 11, 13-16, 24, 25. **Infantino** r-1-5, 7-19, 23-25; c-11p. **Kaluta** c-18, 19. **Gil Kane** a-9r. **Kubert** c-1, 7, 12-14. **Toth** a-2r. **Wood** a-13i. Photo c-22.*

FROM DUSK TILL DAWN (Movie)
Big Entertainment: 1996 ($4.95, one-shot)

nn-Adaptation of the film; Brereton-c 5.00
nn-($9.95)Deluxe Ed. w/ new material 10.00

FROM HELL
Mad Love/Tundra Publishing/Kitchen Sink: 1991 - No. 11, Sept, 1998 (B&W)

1-Alan Moore and Eddie Campbell's Jack The Ripper story collected from the Taboo anthology series 2 4 6 11 16 20
1-(2nd printing) 2 4 6 8 10 12
1-(3rd printing) 1 2 3 4 5 7
2 1 2 3 5 6 8
2-(2nd printing) 6.00
2-(3rd printing) 4.00
3-1st Kitchen Sink Press issue 1 2 3 5 6 8
3-(2nd printing) 5.00
4-10: 10-(8/96) 1 2 3 4 5 7
11-Dance of the Gull Catchers (9/98, $4.95) Epilogue 2 4 6 9 12 15
Tundra Publishing reprintings 1-5 ('92) 1 2 3 4 5 7
HC 125.00
HC Ltd. Edition of 1,000 (signed and numbered) 225.00
TPB-1st printing (11/99) 60.00
TPB-2nd printing (3/00) 50.00
TPB-3rd printing (11/00) 40.00
TPB-4th printing (7/01) Regular and movie covers 35.00
TPB-5th printing - Regular and movie covers 35.00

FROM HERE TO INSANITY (Satire) (Formerly Eh! #1-7) (See Frantic & Frenzy)
Charlton Comics: No. 8, Feb, 1955 - V3#1, 1956

8 18 36 54 105 165 225
9 16 32 48 94 147 200
10-Ditko-c/a (3 pgs.) 24 48 72 140 230 320
11,12-All Kirby except 4 pgs. 34 68 102 199 325 450
V3#1(1956)-Ward-c/a(2) (signed McCartney); 5 pgs. Wolverton-a; 3 pgs. Ditko-a; magazine format (cover says "Crazy, Man, Crazy" and becomes Crazy, Man, Crazy with V2#2)
40 80 120 246 411 575

GD VG FN VF VF/NM NM-
2.0 4.0 6.0 8.0 9.0 9.2

FROM THE PIT
Fantagor Press: 1994 ($4.95, one-shot, mature)

1-R. Corben-a; HP Lovecraft back-up story 1 2 3 5 6 8

FRONTIER DOCTOR (TV)
Dell Publishing Co.: No. 877, Feb, 1958 (one-shot)

Four Color 877-Toth-a, Rex Allen photo-c 9 18 27 63 107 150

FRONTIER FIGHTERS
National Periodical Publications: Sept-Oct, 1955 - No. 8, Nov-Dec, 1956

1-Davy Crockett, Buffalo Bill (by Kubert), Kit Carson begin (Scarce)
55 110 165 352 601 850
2 37 74 111 222 361 500
3-8 34 68 102 199 325 450

NOTE: *Buffalo Bill by **Kubert** in all.*

FRONTIER ROMANCES
Avon Periodicals/I. W.: Nov-Dec, 1949 - No. 2, Feb-Mar, 1950 (Painted-c)

1-Used in **SOTI**, pg. 180 (General reference) & illo. "Erotic spanking in a western comic book" 48 96 144 302 514 725
2 (Scarce)-Woodish-a by Stallman 37 74 111 218 354 490
I.W. Reprint #1-Reprints Avon's #1 4 8 12 22 34 45
I.W. Reprint #9-Reprints ? 3 6 9 16 22 28

FRONTIER SCOUT: DAN'L BOONE (Formerly Death Valley; The Masked Raider No. 14 on)
Charlton Comics: No. 10, Jan, 1956 - No. 13, Aug, 1956; V2#14, Mar, 1965

10 10 20 30 54 72 90
11-13(1956) 6 12 18 31 38 45
V2#14(3/65) 5 10 14 20 24 28

FRONTIER TRAIL (The Rider No. 1-5)
Ajax/Farrell Publ.: No. 6, May, 1958

6 6 12 18 28 34 40

FRONTIER WESTERN
Atlas Comics (PrPl): Feb, 1956 - No. 10, Aug, 1957

1 19 38 57 111 176 240
2,3,6-Williamson-a, 4 pgs. each 14 28 42 80 115 150
4,7,9,10: 10-Check-a 10 20 30 56 76 95
5-Crandall, Baker, Davis-a; Williamson text illos 14 28 42 76 108 140
8-Crandall, Morrow, & Wildey-a 10 20 30 58 79 100

NOTE: ***Baker** a-9. **Colan** a-2, 6. **Drucker** a-3, 4. **Heath** c-5. **Maneely** c/a-2, 7, 9. **Maurera** a-2. **Romita** a-7. **Severin** c-6, 8, 10. **Tuska** a-2. **Wildey** a-5, 8. Ringo Kid in No. 4.*

FRONTLINE COMBAT
E. C. Comics: July-Aug, 1951 - No. 15, Jan, 1954

1-Severin/Kurtzman-a 69 138 207 552 876 1200
2 37 74 111 296 473 650
3 29 58 87 232 366 500
4-Used in **SOTI**, pg. 257; contains "Airburst" by Kurtzman which is his personal all-time favorite story 27 54 81 216 341 465
5-John Severin and Bill Elder bios. 23 46 69 184 292 400
6-10: 6-Kurtzman bio. 9-Civil War issue 20 40 60 160 255 350
11-15: 11-Civil War issue 15 30 45 120 193 265

NOTE: ***Davis** a-in all; c-11, 12. **Evans** a-10-15. **Heath** a-1. **Kubert** a-14. **Kurtzman** a-1-5; c-1-9. **Severin** a-5-7, 9, 13, 15. **Severin/Elder** a-2-11; c-10. **Toth** a-8, 12. **Wood** a-1-4, 6-10, 12-15; c-13-15. Special issues: No. 7 (Iwo Jima), No. 9 (Civil War), No. 12 (Air Force).*
(Canadian reprints known; see Table of Contents.)

FRONTLINE COMBAT
Russ Cochran/Gemstone Publishing: Aug, 1995 - No. 14 ($2.00/$2.50)

1-14-E.C. reprints in all 3.00

FRONT PAGE COMIC BOOK
Front Page Comics (Harvey): 1945

1-Kubert-a; intro. & 1st app. Man in Black by Powell; Fuje-c
40 80 120 243 404 565

FROST AND FIRE (See DC Science Fiction Graphic Novel)

FROSTY THE SNOWMAN
Dell Publishing Co.: No. 359, Nov, 1951 - No. 1272, Dec-Feb?/1961-62

Four Color 359 (#1) 9 18 27 63 107 150
Four Color 435,514,601,661 6 12 18 37 59 80
Four Color 748,861,950,1065,1153,1272 5 10 15 32 51 70

FRUITMAN SPECIAL
Harvey Publications: Dec, 1969 (68 pgs.)

1-Funny super hero 4 8 12 24 37 50

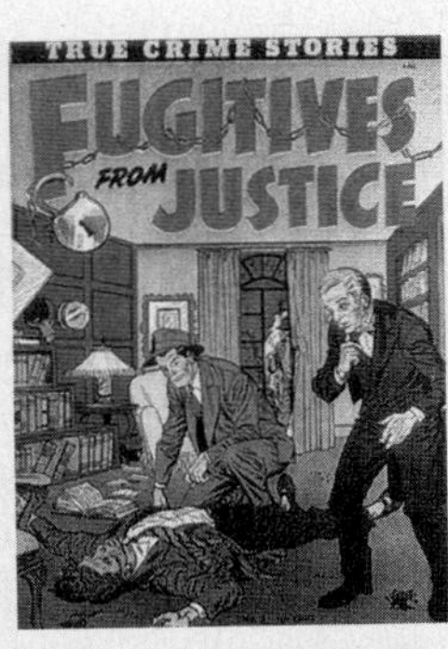

Fugitives From Justice #3 © STJ

Funky Phantom #12 © H-B

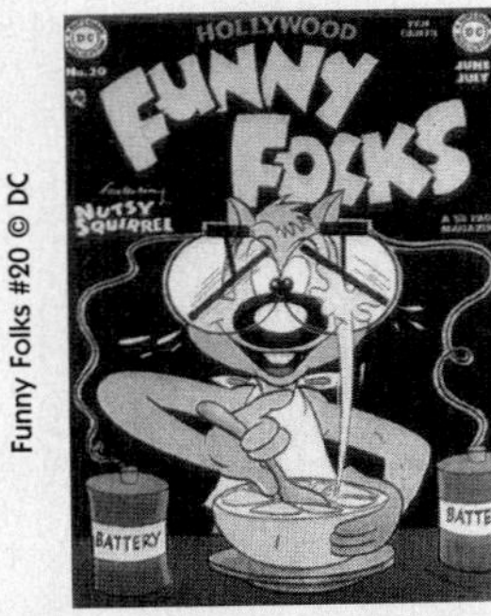

Funny Folks #20 © DC

	GD 2.0	VG 4.0	FN 6.0	VF 8.0	VF/NM 9.0	NM- 9.2

F-TROOP (TV)
Dell Publishing Co.: Aug, 1966 - No. 7, Aug, 1967 (All have photo-c)

1 9 18 27 64 110 155
2-7 6 12 18 39 62 85

FUGITIVES FROM JUSTICE
St. John Publishing Co.: Feb, 1952 - No. 5, Oct, 1952

1 22 44 66 132 216 300
2-Matt Baker-r/Northwest Mounties #2; Vic Flint strip reprints begin
22 44 66 128 209 290
3-Reprints panel from Authentic Police Cases that was used in **SOTI** with changes; Tuska-a
21 42 63 124 202 280
4 13 26 39 74 105 135
5-Last Vic Flint-r; bondage-c 14 28 42 81 118 155

FUGITOID
Mirage Studios: 1985 (B&W, magazine size, one-shot)

1-Ties into Teenage Mutant Ninja Turtles #5 2 3 4 6 8 10

FULL OF FUN
Red Top (Decker Publ.)(Farrell)/I. W. Enterprises: Aug, 1957 - No. 2, Nov, 1957; 1964

1(1957)-Funny animal; Dave Berg-a 7 14 21 37 46 55
2-Reprints Bingo, the Monkey Doodle Boy 5 10 15 22 26 30
8-I.W. Reprint('64) 2 4 6 9 12 15

FUN AT CHRISTMAS (See March of Comics No. 138)

FUN CLUB COMICS (See Interstate Theatres...)

FUN COMICS (Formerly Holiday Comics #1-8; Mighty Bear #13 on)
Star Publications: No. 9, Jan, 1953 - No. 12, Oct, 1953

9-(25¢ Giant)-L. B. Cole X-Mas-c; X-Mas issue 22 44 66 132 216 300
10-12-L. B. Cole-c. 12-Mighty Bear-c/story 18 36 54 105 165 225

FUNDAY FUNNIES (See Famous TV..., and Harvey Hits No. 35,40)

FUN-IN (TV)(Hanna-Barbera)
Gold Key: Feb, 1970 - No. 10, Jan, 1972; No. 11, 4/74 - No. 15, 12/74

1-Dastardly & Muttley in Their Flying Machines; Perils of Penelope Pitstop in #1-4; It's the Wolf in all 7 14 21 49 80 110
2-4,6-Cattanooga Cats in 2-4 4 8 12 22 34 45
5,7-Motormouse & Autocat, Dastardly & Muttley in both; It's the Wolf in #7
4 8 12 24 37 50
8,10-The Harlem Globetrotters, Dastardly & Muttley in #10
4 8 12 24 37 50
9-Where's Huddles?, Dastardly & Muttley, Motormouse & Autocat app.
4 8 12 24 37 50
11-Butch Cassidy 3 6 9 20 30 40
12-15: 12,15-Speed Buggy. 13-Hair Bear Bunch. 14-Inch High Private Eye
3 6 9 20 30 40

FUNKY PHANTOM, THE (TV)
Gold Key: Mar, 1972 - No. 13, Mar, 1975 (Hanna-Barbera)

1 5 10 15 32 51 75
2-5 3 6 9 18 27 38
6-13 3 6 9 15 21 28

FUNLAND
Ziff-Davis (Approved Comics): No date (1940s) (25¢)

nn-Contains games, puzzles, cut-outs, etc. 18 36 54 107 169 230

FUNLAND COMICS
Croyden Publishers: 1945

1-Funny animal 15 30 45 86 133 180

FUNNIES, THE (New Funnies No. 65 on)
Dell Publishing Co.: Oct, 1936 - No. 64, May, 1942

1-Tailspin Tommy, Mutt & Jeff, Alley Oop (1st app?), Capt. Easy (1st app.), Don Dixon begin
400 800 1200 2300 3650 5000
2 (11/36)-Scribbly by Mayer begins (see Popular Comics #6 for 1st app.)
180 360 540 1035 1643 2250
3 124 248 372 713 1132 1550
4,5: 4(1/37)-Christmas-c 92 184 276 529 840 1150
6-10 70 140 210 403 639 875
11-20: 16-Christmas-c 65 130 195 374 597 820
21-29: 25-Crime Busters by McWilliams(4pgs.) 52 104 156 299 475 650
30-John Carter of Mars (origin/1st app.) begins by Edgar Rice Burroughs; Jim Gary-a Warner Bros.' Bosko-c (4/39) 148 296 444 947 1624 2300
31-34,36-44: 31,32-Gary-a. 33-John Coleman Burroughs art begins on John Carter.
34-Last funny-c 79 158 237 502 864 1225
35-(9/39)-Mr. District Attorney begins; based on radio show; 1st cover app. John Carter of Mars 86 172 258 546 936 1325
45-Origin/1st app. Phantasmo, the Master of the World (Dell's 1st super-hero, 7/40) & his sidekick Whizzer McGee 92 184 276 584 1005 1425
46-50: 46-The Black Knight begins, ends #62 57 114 171 362 619 875
51-56-Last ERB John Carter of Mars 47 94 141 296 498 700
57-Intro. & origin Captain Midnight (7/41) 349 698 1047 2443 4272 6100
58-60: 58-Captain Midnight-c begin, end #63 87 174 261 553 952 1350
61-Andy Panda begins by Walter Lantz 97 194 291 621 1061 1500
62,63: 63-Last Captain Midnight-c; bondage-c 67 134 201 425 730 1035
64-Format change; Oswald the Rabbit, Felix the Cat, Li'l Eight Ball app.; origin & 1st app. Woody Woodpecker in Oswald; last Capt. Midnight; Oswald, Andy Panda, Li'l Eight Ball-c
142 284 426 909 1555 2200

NOTE: *Mayer c-26, 48.* ***McWilliams*** *art in many issues on "Rex King of the Deep". Alley Oop c-17, 20. Captain Midnight c-57(i/2), 58-63. John Carter c-35-37, 40. Phantasmo c-45-56, 57(1/2), 58-61(part). Rex King c-38, 39, 42. Tailspin Tommy c-41.*

FUNNIES ANNUAL, THE
Avon Periodicals: 1959 ($1.00, approx. 7x10", B&W; tabloid-size)

1-(Rare)-Features the best newspaper comic strips of the year: Archie, Snuffy Smith, Beetle Bailey, Henry, Blondie, Steve Canyon, Buz Sawyer, The Little King, Hi & Lois, Popeye, & others. Also has a chronological history of the comics from 2000 B.C. to 1959.
43 86 129 271 461 650

FUNNIES ON PARADE (See Promotional Comics section)

FUNNY ANIMALS (See Fawcett's Funny Animals)
Charlton Comics: Sept, 1984 - No. 2, Nov, 1984

1,2-Atomic Mouse-r; low print 6.00

FUNNYBONE (... The Laugh-Book of Comical Comics)
La Salle Publishing Co.: 1944 (25¢, 132 pgs.)

nn 29 58 87 172 281 390

FUNNY BOOK (...Magazine for Young Folks) (Hocus Pocus No. 9)
Parents' Magazine Press (Funny Book Publishing Corp.):
Dec, 1942 - No. 9, Aug-Sept, 1946 (Comics, stories, puzzles, games)

1-Funny animal; Alice In Wonderland app. 15 30 45 84 127 170
2-Gulliver in Giant-Land 10 20 30 54 72 90
3-9: 4-Advs. of Robin Hood. 9-Hocus-Pocus strip 8 16 24 44 57 70

FUNNY COMICS
Modern Store Publ.: 1955 (7¢, 5x7", 36 pgs.)

1-Funny animal 4 8 12 22 34 45

FUNNY COMIC TUNES (See Funny Tunes)

FUNNY FABLES
Decker Publications (Red Top Comics): Aug, 1957 - V2#2, Nov, 1957

V1#1 6 12 18 31 38 45
V1#2,V2#1,2: V1#2 (11/57)-Reissue of V1#1 5 10 14 20 24 28

FUNNY FILMS (Features funny animal characters from films)
American Comics Group(Michel Publ./Titan Publ.): Sept-Oct, 1949 - No. 29, May-June, 1954 (No. 1-4: 52 pgs.)

1-Puss An' Boots, Blunderbunny begin 18 36 54 105 165 225
2 11 22 33 62 86 110
3-10: 3-X-Mas-c 9 18 27 47 61 75
11-20 7 14 21 35 43 50
21-29 6 12 18 28 34 40

FUNNY FOLKS
DC Comics: Feb, 1946

nn-Ashcan comic, not distributed to newsstands, only for in house use (no known sales)

FUNNY FOLKS (Hollywood... on cover only No. 16-26; becomes Hollywood Funny Folks No. 27 on)
National Periodical Publ.: April-May, 1946 - No. 26, June-July, 1950 (52 pgs., #15 on)

1-Nutsy Squirrel begins (1st app.) by Rube Grossman; Grossman-a in most issues 39 78 117 240 395 550
2 20 40 60 114 182 250
3-5: 4-1st Nutsy Squirrel-c 15 30 45 84 127 170
6-10: 6,9-Nutsy Squirrel-c begin 11 22 33 62 86 110
11-26: 15-Begin 52 pg. issues (8-9/48) 10 20 30 54 72 90

NOTE: ***Sheldon Mayer*** *a-in some issues.* ***Post*** *a-18. Christmas c-12.*

FUNNY FROLICS
Timely/Marvel Comics (SPI): Summer, 1945 - No. 5, Dec, 1946

1-Sharpy Fox, Puffy Pig, Krazy Krow 25 50 75 150 245 340

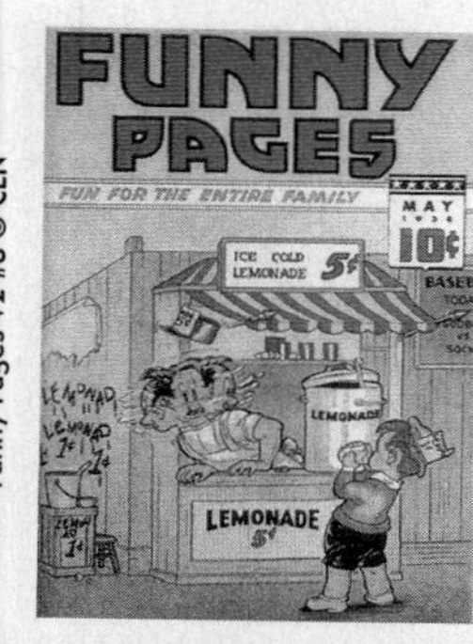

Funny Pages V2 #8 © CEN

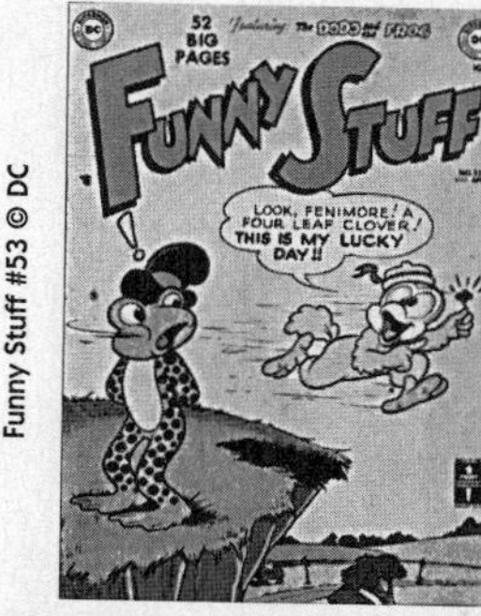

Funny Stuff #53 © DC

Further Adventures of Indiana Jones #12 © Lucasfilm

GD 2.0 VG 4.0 FN 6.0 VF 8.0 VF/NM 9.0 NM- 9.2

2 15 30 45 84 127 170
3,4 12 24 36 69 97 125
5-Kurtzman-a 14 28 42 76 108 140

FUNNY FUNNIES
Nedor Publishing Co.: April, 1943 (68 pgs.)

1-Funny animals; Peter Porker app. 19 38 57 109 172 235

FUNNYMAN (Also see Cisco Kid Comics & Extra Comics)
Magazine Enterprises: Dec, 1947; No. 1, Jan, 1948 - No. 6, Aug, 1948

nn(12/47)-Prepublication B&W undistributed copy by Siegel & Shuster-(5-3/4x8"), 16 pgs.; Sold at auction in 1997 for $575.00
1-Siegel & Shuster-a in all; Dick Ayers 1st pro work (as assistant) on 1st few issues 45 90 135 284 480 675
2 27 54 81 160 263 365
3-6 23 46 69 136 223 310

FUNNY MOVIES (See 3-D Funny Movies)

FUNNY PAGES (Formerly The Comics Magazine)
Comics Magazine Co./Ultem Publ.(Chesler)/Centaur Publications:
No. 6, Nov, 1936 - No. 42, Oct, 1940

V1#6 (nn, nd)-The Clock begins (2 pgs., 1st app.), ends #11; The Clock is the 1st masked comic book hero 265 530 795 1694 2897 4100
7-11 100 200 300 635 1093 1550
V2#1-V2#3: V2#1 (9/37)(V2#2 on-c; V2#1 in indicia). V2#2 (10/37)(V2#3 on-c; V2#2 in indicia). V2#3(11/37)-5 69 138 207 442 759 1075
6(1st Centaur, 3/38) 92 184 276 588 1007 1425
7-9 69 138 207 442 759 1075
10(Scarce, 9/38)-1st app. of The Arrow by Gustavson (Blue costume) 354 708 1062 2478 4339 6200
11,12 126 252 378 806 1378 1950
V3#1-Bruce Wayne prototype in "Case of the Missing Heir," by Bob Kane, 3 months before app. Batman (See Det. Pic. Stories #5) 132 264 396 838 1444 2050
2-6,8: 6,8-Last funny covers 111 222 333 705 1215 1725
7-1st Arrow-c (9/39) 300 600 900 1950 3375 4800
9-Tarpe Mills jungle-c 126 252 378 806 1378 1950
10-2nd Arrow-c 258 516 774 1651 2826 4000
V4#1(1/40, Arrow-c)-(Rare)-The Owl & The Phantom Rider app.; origin Mantoka, Maker of Magic by Jack Cole. Mad Ming begins, ends #42; Tarpe Mills-a 297 594 891 1901 3251 4600
35-Classic Arrow-c 297 594 891 1901 3251 4600
36-38-Mad Ming-c 123 246 369 787 1344 1900
39-41-Arrow-c 213 426 639 1363 2332 3300
42 (Scarce,10/40)-Last Arrow; Arrow-c 219 438 657 1402 2401 3400
NOTE: ***Biro*** *c-V2#9.* ***Burgos*** *c-V3#10.* ***Jack Cole*** *a-V2#3, 7, 8, 10, 11, V3#2, 6, 9, 10, V4#1, 37; c-V3#2, 4.* ***Eisner*** *a-V1#7, 8?, 10.* ***Ken Ernst*** *a-V1#7, 8.* ***Everett*** *a-V2#11 (illos).* ***Filchock*** *c-V2#10, V3#6.* ***Gill Fox*** *a-V2#11.* ***Sid Greene*** *a-39.* ***Guardineer*** *a-V2#2, 3, 5.* ***Gustavson*** *a-V2#5, 11, 12, V3#1-10, 35, 38-42; c-V3#7, 35, 39-42.* ***Bob Kane*** *a-V3#1.* ***McWilliams*** *a-V2#12, V3#1, 3-6.* ***Tarpe Mills*** *a-V3#8-10, V4#1; c-V3#9.* ***Ed Moore Jr.*** *a-V2#12.* ***Schwab*** *c-V3#1.* ***Bob Wood*** *a-V2#2, 3, 8, 11, V3#6, 9, 10; c-V2#6, 7. Arrow c-V3#7, 10, V4#1, 35, 40-42.*

FUNNY PICTURE STORIES (Comic Pages V3#4 on)
Comics Magazine Co./Centaur Publications: Nov, 1936 - V3#3, May, 1939

V1#1-The Clock begins (c-feature)(see Funny Pages for 1st app.) 349 698 1047 2443 4272 6100
2 129 258 387 826 1413 2000
3-6(4/37): 4-Eisner-a; X-Mas-c. 84 168 252 538 919 1300
7-(6/37) (Rare) Racial humor-c 129 258 387 826 1413 2000
V2#1 (9/37; V1#10 on-c; V2#1 in indicia)-Jack Strand begins 54 108 162 340 588 835
2 (10/37; V1#11 on-c; V2#2 in indicia) 54 108 162 340 588 835
3-5,7-11(11/38): 4-Xmas-c 49 98 147 309 522 735
6-(1st Centaur, 3/38) 79 158 237 505 865 1225
V3#1(1/39)-3 47 94 141 298 504 710
NOTE: ***Biro*** *c-V2#1, 8, 9, 11.* ***Guardineer*** *a-V1#11; c-V2#6, V3#5.* ***Bob Wood*** *c/a-V1#11, V2#2; c-V2#3, 5.*

FUNNY STUFF (Becomes The Dodo & the Frog No. 80)
All-American/National Periodical Publications No. 7 on: Summer, 1944 - No. 79, July-Aug, 1954 (#1-7 are quarterly)

1-The Three Mouseketeers (ends #28) & The "Terrific Whatzit" begin; Sheldon Mayer-a; Grossman-a in most issues 89 178 267 565 970 1375
2-Sheldon Mayer-a 42 84 126 265 445 625
3-5: 3-Flash parody. 5-All Mayer-a/scripts issue 30 60 90 177 289 400
6-10 10-(6/46) 20 40 60 114 182 250
11-17,19 15 30 45 90 140 190
18-The Dodo & the Frog (2/47, 1st app?) begin?; X-Mas-c 27 54 81 160 263 365
19-1st Dodo & the Frog-c (3/47) 18 36 54 105 165 225
20-2nd Dodo & the Frog-c (4/47) 14 28 42 80 115 150
21,23-30: 24-Infinity-c. 30-Christmas-c 11 22 33 62 86 110
22-Superman cameo 37 74 111 222 361 500
31-79: 70-1st Bo Bunny by Mayer & begins 10 20 30 56 76 95
NOTE: ***Mayer*** *a-1-8, 55, ,57, 58, 61, 62, 64, 65, 68, 70, 72, 74-79; c-2, 5, 6, 8.*

FUNNY STUFF STOCKING STUFFER
DC Comics: Mar, 1985 ($1.25, 52 pgs.)

1-Almost every DC funny animal featured 4.00

FUNNY 3-D
Harvey Publications: December, 1953 (25¢, came with 2 pair of glasses)

1-Shows cover in 3-D on inside 11 22 33 62 86 110

FUNNY TUNES (Animated Funny Comic Tunes No. 16-22; Funny Comic Tunes No. 23, on covers only; Oscar No. 24 on)
U.S.A. Comics Magazine Corp. (Timely): No. 16, Summer, 1944 - No. 23, Fall, 1946

16-Silly Seal, Ziggy Pig, Krazy Krow begin 17 34 51 100 158 210
17 (Fall/44)-Becomes Gay Comics #18 on? 14 28 42 81 118 150
18-22: 21-Super Rabbit app. 12 24 36 69 97 125
23-Kurtzman-a 14 28 42 76 108 140

FUNNY TUNES (Becomes Space Comics #4 on)
Avon Periodicals: July, 1953 - No. 3, Dec-Jan, 1953-54

1-Space Mouse, Peter Rabbit, Merry Mouse, Spotty the Pup, Cicero the Cat begin; all continue in Space Comics 11 22 33 60 83 105
2,3 8 16 24 44 57 70

FUNNY WORLD
Marbak Press: 1947 - No. 3, 1948

1-The Berrys, The Toodles & other strip-r begin 9 18 27 47 61 75
2,3 6 12 18 31 38 45

FUNTASTIC WORLD OF HANNA-BARBERA, THE (TV)
Marvel Comics Group: Dec, 1977 - No. 3, June, 1978 ($1.25, oversized)

1-3: 1-The Flintstones Christmas Party(12/77). 2-Yogi Bear's Easter Parade(3/78). 3-Laff-a-lympics(6/78) 4 8 12 26 41 55

FUN TIME
Ace Periodicals: Spring, 1953; No. 2, Sum, 1953; No. 3(nn), Fall, 1953; No. 4, Wint, 1953-54

1-(25¢, 100 pgs.)-Funny animal 18 36 54 105 165 225
2-4 (All 25¢, 100 pgs.) 15 30 45 85 130 175

FUN WITH SANTA CLAUS (See March of Comics No. 11, 108, 325)

FURTHER ADVENTURES OF CYCLOPS AND PHOENIX (Also see Adventures of Cyclops and Phoenix, Uncanny X-Men & X-Men)
Marvel Comics: June, 1996 - No. 4, Sept, 1996 ($1.95, limited series)

1-4: Origin of Mr. Sinister; Milligan scripts; John Paul Leon-c/a(p). 2-4-Apocalypse app. 3.00
Trade Paperback (1997, $14.99) r/1-4 15.00

FURTHER ADVENTURES OF INDIANA JONES, THE (Movie) (Also see Indiana Jones and the Last Crusade & Indiana Jones and the Temple of Doom)
Marvel Comics Group: Jan, 1983 - No. 34, Mar, 1986

1-Byrne/Austin-a; Austin-c 5.00
2-34: 2-Byrne/Austin-c/a 3.00
NOTE: ***Austin*** *a-1i, 2i, 6i, 9i; c-1, 2i, 6i, 9i.* ***Byrne*** *a-1p, 2p; c-2p.* ***Chaykin*** *a-6p; c-6p, 8p-10p.* ***Ditko*** *a-21p, 25-28, 34.* ***Golden*** *c-24, 25.* ***Simonson*** *c-9. Painted c-14.*

FURTHER ADVENTURES OF NYOKA, THE JUNGLE GIRL, THE (See Nyoka)
AC Comics: 1988 - No. 5, 1989 ($1.95, color; $2.25/$2.50, B&W)

1-5 : 1,2-Bill Black-a plus reprints. 3-Photo-c. 5-(B&W)-Reprints plus movie photos 2.50

FURY (Straight Arrow's Horse...) (See A-1 No. 119)

FURY (TV) (See March Of Comics #200)
Dell Publishing Co./Gold Key: No. 781, Mar, 1957 - Nov, 1962 (All photo-c)

Four Color 781 8 16 24 52 86 120
Four Color 885,975,1031,1080,1133,1172,1218,1296 6 12 18 41 66 90
01292-208(#1-'62), 10020-211(11/62-G.K.) 6 12 18 37 59 80

FURY
Marvel Comics: May, 1994 ($2.95, one-shot)

1-Iron Man, Red Skull, FF, Hatemonger, Logan app.; Origin Nick Fury 3.00

FURY (Volume 3)
Marvel Comics (MAX): Nov, 2001 - No. 6, Apr, 2002 ($2.99, mature content)

1-6-Ennis-s/Robertson-a 3.00

FURY/ AGENT 13

Fury of Firestorm #4 © DC

Futurama Comics #47 © Bongo

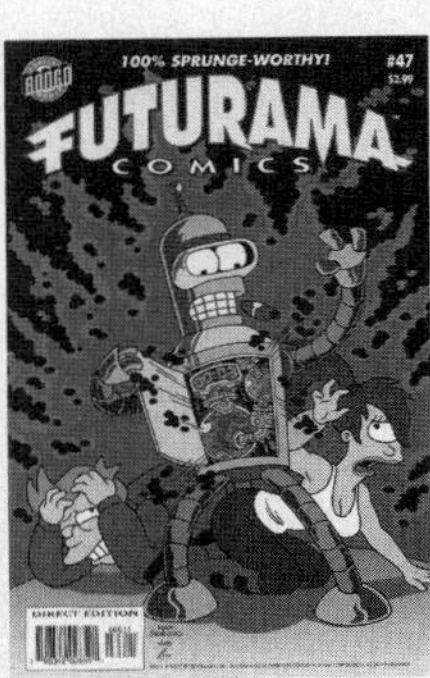

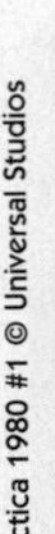
Galactica 1980 #1 © Universal Studios

GD VG FN VF VF/NM NM-
2.0 4.0 6.0 8.0 9.0 9.2

Marvel Comics: June, 1998 - No. 2, July, 1998 ($2.99, limited series)
1,2-Nick Fury returns 3.00

FURY OF FIRESTORM, THE (Becomes Firestorm The Nuclear Man on cover with #50, in indicia with #65) (Also see Firestorm)
DC Comics: June, 1982 - No. 64, Oct, 1987 (75¢ on)
1-Intro The Black Bison; brief origin 6.00
2-40,43-64: 4-JLA x-over. 17-1st app. Firehawk. 21-Death of Killer Frost. 22-Origin. 23-Intro. Byte. 24-(6/84)-1st app. Blue Devil & Bug (origin); origin Byte. 34-1st app./origin Killer Frost II. 39-Weasel's ID revealed. 48-Intro. Moonbow. 53-Origin/1st app. Silver Shade. 55,56-Legends x-over. 58-1st app./origin new Parasite 2.50
41,42-Crisis x-over 3.00
61-Test cover variant; Superman logo 4 8 12 22 34 45
Annual 1-4: 1(1983), 2(1984), 3(1985), 4(1986) 3.00
NOTE: *Colan a-19p, Annual 4p.* ***Giffen*** *a-Annual 4p.* ***Gil Kane*** *c-30.* ***Nino*** *a-37.* ***Tuska*** *a-(p)-17, 18, 32, 45.*

FURY OF SHIELD
Marvel Comics: Apr, 1995 - No. 4, July, 1995 ($2.50/$1.95, limited series)
1 ($2.50)-Foil-c 3.00
2-4: 4-Bagged w/ decoder 2.50

FURY: PEACEMAKER
Marvel Comics: Apr, 2006 - No. 6, Sept, 2006 ($3.50, limited series)
1-6-Flashback to WW2; Ennis-s/Robertson-a. 1-Deodato-c. 2-Texeira-c. 5-Dillon-c 3.50
TPB (2006, $17.99) r/#1-6 18.00

FUSED
Image Comics: Mar, 2002 - No. 4, Jan, 2003 ($2.95)
1-4-Steve Niles-s. 1,2-Paul Lee-a. 3-Brad Rader-a. 4-Templesmith-a 3.00
Canned Heat TPB (Dark Horse, 6/04, $12.95) r/series; Dan Wickline intro. 13.00

FUSED
Dark Horse Comics: Dec, 2003 - No. 4, Mar, 2004 ($2.95)
1-4-Steve Niles-s/Josh Medors-a. 1-Powell-c 3.00

FUSION
Eclipse Comics: Jan, 1987 - No. 17, Oct, 1989 ($2.00, B&W, Baxter paper)
1-17: 11-The Weasel Patrol begins (1st app.?) 2.50

FUSION
Image Comics (Top Cow): May, 2009 - No. 3, Jul, 2009 ($2.99, limited series)
1-3-Avengers, Thunderbolts, Cyberforce and Hunter-Killer meet; Kirkham-a 3.00

FUTURAMA (TV)
Bongo Comics: 2000 - Present ($2.50/$2.99, bi-monthly)
1-Based on the FOX-TV animated series; Groening/Morrison-c 3.50
1-San Diego Comic-Con Premiere Edition 5.00
2-47: 8-CGC cover spoof; X-Men parody. 40-Santa app. 3.00
Futurama Adventures TPB (2004, $14.95) r/#5-9 15.00
Futurama Conquers the Universe TPB (2007, $14.95) r/#10-13 15.00
Futurama-O-Rama TPB (2002, $12.95) r/#1-4; sketch pages of Fry's development 13.00
...: The Time Bender Trilogy TPB (2006, $14.95) r/#16-19; cover gallery 15.00

FUTURAMA/SIMPSONS INFINITELY SECRET CROSSOVER CRISIS (TV) (See Simpsons/Futurama Crossover Crisis II for sequel)
Bongo Comics: 2002 - No. 2, 2002 ($2.50, limited series)
1,2-Evil Brain Spawns put Futurama crew into the Simpsons' Springfield 2.50

FUTURE COMICS
David McKay Publications: June, 1940 - No. 4, Sept, 1940
1-(6/40, 64 pgs.)-Origin The Phantom (1st in comics) (4 pgs.); The Lone Ranger (8 pgs.) & Saturn Against the Earth (4 pgs.) begin 297 594 891 1901 3251 4600
2 123 246 369 787 1344 1900
3,4 87 174 261 553 952 1350

FUTURE COP L.A.P.D. (Electronic Arts video game) (Also see Promotional Comics section)
DC Comics (WildStorm): Jan, 1999 ($4.95, magazine sized)
1-Stories & art by various 5.00

FUTURE WORLD COMICS
George W. Dougherty: Summer, 1946 - No. 2, Fall, 1946
1,2: H. C. Kiefer-c; preview of the World of Tomorrow 30 60 90 174 280 385

FUTURE WORLD COMIX (Warren Presents...)
Warren Publications: Sept, 1978 (B&W magazine, 84 pgs.)
1-Corben, Maroto, Morrow, Nino, Sutton-a; Todd-c/a; contains nudity panels 2 4 6 8 11 14

FUTURIANS, THE (See Marvel Graphic Novel #9)
Lodestone Publishing/Eternity Comics: Sept, 1985 - No. 3, 1985 ($1.50)
1-3: Indicia title "Dave Cockrum's..." 2.25
Graphic Novel 1 ($9.95, Eternity)-r/#1-3, plus never published #4 issue 10.00

FX
IDW Publishing: Mar, 2008 - No. 6, Aug, 2008 ($3.99)
1-6-John Byrne-a/c; Wayne Osborne-s 4.00

G-8 (Listed at G-Eight)

GABBY (Formerly Ken Shannon) (Teen humor)
Quality Comics Group: No. 11, Jul, 1953; No. 2, Sep, 1953 - No. 9, Sep, 1954
11(#1)(7/53) 9 18 27 47 61 75
2 6 12 18 31 38 45
3-9 5 10 15 24 30 35

GABBY GOB (See Harvey Hits No. 85, 90, 94, 97, 100, 103, 106, 109)

GABBY HAYES ADVENTURE COMICS
Toby Press: Dec, 1953
1-Photo-c 15 30 45 88 137 185

GABBY HAYES WESTERN (Movie star)(See Monte Hale, Real Western Hero & Western Hero)
Fawcett Publications/Charlton Comics No. 51 on: Nov, 1948 - No. 50, Jan, 1953; No. 51, Dec, 1954 - No. 59, Jan, 1957
1-Gabby & his horse Corker begin; photo front/back-c begin 41 82 123 250 413 575
2 20 40 60 120 193 265
3-5 15 30 45 88 137 185
6-10: 9-Young Falcon begins 14 28 42 78 112 145
11-20: 19-Last photo back-c 11 22 33 64 90 115
21-49: 20,22,24,26,28,29-(52 pgs.) 9 18 27 52 69 85
50-(1/53)-Last Fawcett issue; last photo-c? 10 20 30 58 79 100
51-(12/54)-1st Charlton issue; photo-c 11 22 33 60 83 105
52-59(1955-57): 53,55-Photo-c. 58-Swayze-a 8 16 24 42 54 65

GAGS
United Features Synd./Triangle Publ. No. 9 on: Jul, 1937 - V3#10, Oct, 1944 (13-3/4x10-3/4")
1(7/37)-52 pgs.; 20 pgs. Grin & Bear It, Fellow Citizen 10 20 30 58 79 100
V1#9 (36 pgs.) (7/42) 6 12 18 31 38 45
V3#10 6 12 18 28 34 40

GALACTICA 1980 (Based on the Battlestar Galactica TV series)
Dynamite Entertainment: 2009 - No. 4, 2009 ($3.50)
1-4-Guggenheim-s/Razek-a 3.50

GALACTICA: THE NEW MILLENNIUM
Realm Press: Sept, 1999 ($2.99)
1-Stories by Shooter, Braden, Kuhoric 3.00

GALACTIC GUARDIANS
Marvel Comics: July, 1994 - No. 4, Oct, 1994 ($1.50, limited series)
1-4 2.50

GALACTIC WARS COMIX (Warren Presents... on cover)
Warren Publications: Dec, 1978 (B&W magazine, 84 pgs.)
nn-Wood, Williamson-r; Battlestar Galactica/Flash Gordon photo/text stories 2 4 6 8 11 14

GALACTUS THE DEVOURER
Marvel Comics: Sept, 1999 - No. 6, Mar, 2000 ($3.50/$2.50, limited series)
1-($3.50) L. Simonson-s/Muth & Sienkiewicz-a 3.50
2-5-($2.50) Buscema & Sienkiewicz-a 2.50
6-($3.50) Death of Galactus; Buscema & Sienkiewicz-a 3.50

GALAXIA (Magazine)
Astral Publ.: 1981 ($2.50, B&W, 52 pgs.)
1-Buckler/Giordano-c; Texeira/Guice-a; 1st app. Astron, Sojourner, Bloodwing, Warlords; Buckler-s/a 2 4 6 9 13 16

GALAXY QUEST: GLOBAL WARNING! (Based on the 1999 movie)
IDW Publishing: Aug, 2008 - No. 5, Dec, 2008 ($3.99)
1-5-Lobdell-s/Kyriazis-a 4.00

GALLANT MEN, THE (TV)
Gold Key: Oct, 1963 (Photo-c)
1(1008-310)-Manning-a 4 8 12 22 34 45

Gambit #2 © MAR

Gang Busters #2 © DC

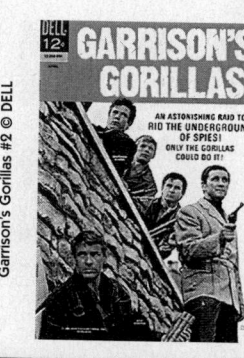

Garrison's Gorillas #2 © DELL

GALLEGHER, BOY REPORTER (Disney, TV)
Gold Key: May, 1965

	GD 2.0	VG 4.0	FN 6.0	VF 8.0	VF/NM 9.0	NM- 9.2
1(10149-505)-Photo-c	3	6	9	18	27	35

GAMBIT (See X-Men #266 & X-Men Annual #14)
Marvel Comics: Dec, 1993 - No. 4, Mar, 1994 ($2.00, limited series)

	GD 2.0	VG 4.0	FN 6.0	VF 8.0	VF/NM 9.0	NM- 9.2
1-($2.50)-Lee Weeks-c/a in all; gold foil stamped-c.						5.00
1 (Gold)	2	4	6	9	12	15
2-4						3.00

GAMBIT
Marvel Comics: Sept, 1997 - No. 4, Dec, 1997 ($2.50, limited series)

	GD 2.0	VG 4.0	FN 6.0	VF 8.0	VF/NM 9.0	NM- 9.2
1-4-Janson-a/Mackie & Kavanagh-s						3.00

GAMBIT
Marvel Comics: Feb, 1999 - No. 25, Feb, 2001 ($2.99/$1.99)

	GD 2.0	VG 4.0	FN 6.0	VF 8.0	VF/NM 9.0	NM- 9.2
1-($2.99) Five covers; Nicieza-a/Skroce-a						4.00
2-11,13-16-($1.99): 2-Two covers (Skroce & Adam Kubert)						2.50
12-($2.99)						3.50
17-24: 17-Begin $2.25-c. 21-Mystique-c/app.						2.50
25-($2.99) Leads into "Gambit & Bishop"						3.00
...1999 Annual ($3.50) Nicieza-s/McDaniel-a						3.50
...2000 Annual ($3.50) Nicieza-s/Derenick & Smith-a						3.50

GAMBIT
Marvel Comics: Nov, 2004 - No. 12, Aug, 2005 ($2.99)

	GD 2.0	VG 4.0	FN 6.0	VF 8.0	VF/NM 9.0	NM- 9.2
1-12: 1-Jeanty-a/Land-c/Layman-s. 5-Wolverine-c/app. 9-Brother Voodoo-c/app.						3.00
...: Hath No Fury TPB (2005, $14.99) r/#7-12						15.00
...: House of Cards TPB (2005, $14.99) r/#1-6; Land cover sketches; unused covers						15.00

GAMBIT & BISHOP (... : Sons of the Atom on cover)
Marvel Comics: Feb, 2001 - No. 6, May, 2001 ($2.25, bi-weekly limited series)

	GD 2.0	VG 4.0	FN 6.0	VF 8.0	VF/NM 9.0	NM- 9.2
Alpha (2/01) Prelude to series; Nord-a						2.50
1-6-Jeanty-a/Williams-c						2.50
Genesis (3/01, $3.50) reprints their first apps. and first meeting						3.50

GAMBIT AND THE X-TERNALS
Marvel Comics: Mar, 1995 - No. 4, July, 1995 ($1.95, limited series)

	GD 2.0	VG 4.0	FN 6.0	VF 8.0	VF/NM 9.0	NM- 9.2
1-4-Age of Apocalypse						2.50

GAMEBOY (Super Mario covers on all)
Valiant: 1990 - No. 5 ($1.95, coated-c)

	GD 2.0	VG 4.0	FN 6.0	VF 8.0	VF/NM 9.0	NM- 9.2
1-5: 3,4-Layton-c. 4-Morrow-a. 5-Layton-c(i)						4.00

GAMEKEEPER (Guy Ritchie's...)
Virgin Comics: Mar, 2007 - No. 5, Sept, 2007; Mar, 2008 - Present ($2.99)

	GD 2.0	VG 4.0	FN 6.0	VF 8.0	VF/NM 9.0	NM- 9.2
1-5-Andy Diggle-s/Mukesh Singh-a; 2 covers on each						3.00
1-Extended Edition (6/07, $2.99) r/#1 with script excerpt and sketch art						3.00
Series 2 (3/08 - Present) 1-5-Parker-s/Randle-a						3.00
Vol. 1 TPB (10/07, $14.99) r/#1-5; script and sketch pages; Guy Ritchie intro.						15.00

GAMERA
Dark Horse Comics: Aug, 1996 - No. 4, Nov, 1996 ($2.95, limited series)

	GD 2.0	VG 4.0	FN 6.0	VF 8.0	VF/NM 9.0	NM- 9.2
1-4						3.00

GAMMARAUDERS
DC Comics: Jan, 1989 - No. 10, Dec, 1989 ($1.25/$1.50/$2.00)

	GD 2.0	VG 4.0	FN 6.0	VF 8.0	VF/NM 9.0	NM- 9.2
1-10-Based on TSR game						2.50

GAMORRA SWIMSUIT SPECIAL
Image Comics (WildStorm Productions): June, 1996 ($2.50, one-shot)

	GD 2.0	VG 4.0	FN 6.0	VF 8.0	VF/NM 9.0	NM- 9.2
1-Campbell wraparound-c; pinups						2.50

GANDY GOOSE (Movies/TV)(See All Surprise, Giant Comics Edition #5A &10, Paul Terry's Comics & Terry-Toons)
St. John Publ. Co./Pines No. 5,6: Mar, 1953 - No. 5, Nov, 1953; No. 5, Fall, 1956 - No. 6, Sum/58

	GD 2.0	VG 4.0	FN 6.0	VF 8.0	VF/NM 9.0	NM- 9.2
1-All St. John issues are pre-code	10	20	30	58	79	100
2	7	14	21	35	43	50
3-5(1953)(St. John)	6	12	18	31	38	45
5,6(1956-58)(Pines)-CBS Television Presents...	5	10	15	24	30	35

GANG BUSTERS (See Popular Comics #38)
David McKay/Dell Publishing Co.: 1938 - 1943

	GD 2.0	VG 4.0	FN 6.0	VF 8.0	VF/NM 9.0	NM- 9.2
Feature Books 17(McKay)('38)-1st app.	65	130	195	416	708	1000
Large Feature Comic 10('39)-(Scarce)	65	130	195	416	708	1000
Large Feature Comic 17('41)	45	90	135	284	480	675
Four Color 7(1940)	48	96	144	302	514	725
Four Color 23('42)	39	78	117	240	395	550
Four Color 24('43)	26	52	78	185	360	535

GANG BUSTERS (Radio/TV)(Gangbusters #14 on)
National Periodical Publ.: Dec-Jan, 1947-48 - No. 67, Dec-Jan, 1958-59 (No. 1-23: 52 pgs.)

	GD 2.0	VG 4.0	FN 6.0	VF 8.0	VF/NM 9.0	NM- 9.2
1	84	168	252	538	919	1300
2	39	78	117	240	395	550
3-5	28	56	84	165	270	375
6-10: 9-Dan Barry-a. 9,10-Photo-c	21	42	63	122	199	275
11-13-Photo-c	17	34	51	100	158	215
14,17-Frazetta-a, 8 pgs. each. 14-Photo-c	36	72	108	211	343	475
15,16,18-20,26: 26-Kirby-a	15	30	45	85	130	175
21-25,27-30	14	28	42	76	108	140
31-44: 44-Last Pre-code (2-3/55)	12	24	36	67	94	120
45-67	10	20	30	54	72	90

NOTE: ***Barry** a-6, 8, 10. **Drucker** a-51. **Moreira** a-48, 50, 59. **Roussos** a-8.*

GANGLAND
DC Comics (Vertigo): Jun, 1998 - No. 4, Sept, 1998 ($2.95, limited series)

	GD 2.0	VG 4.0	FN 6.0	VF 8.0	VF/NM 9.0	NM- 9.2
1-4:Crime anthology by various. 2-Corben-a						3.00
TPB-(2000, $12.95) r/#1-4; Bradstreet-c						13.00

GANGSTERS AND GUN MOLLS
Avon Per./Realistic Comics: Sept, 1951 - No. 4, June, 1952 (Painted c-1-3)

	GD 2.0	VG 4.0	FN 6.0	VF 8.0	VF/NM 9.0	NM- 9.2
1-Wood-a, 1 pg; c-/Avon paperback #292	49	98	147	309	522	735
2-Check-a, 8 pgs.; Kamen-a; Bonnie Parker story	39	78	117	240	395	550
3-Marijuana mentioned; used in **POP**, pg. 84,85	38	76	114	226	368	510
4-Syd Shores-c	29	58	87	172	281	390

GANGSTERS CAN'T WIN
D. S. Publishing Co.: Feb-Mar, 1948 - No. 9, June-July, 1949 (All 52 pgs?)

	GD 2.0	VG 4.0	FN 6.0	VF 8.0	VF/NM 9.0	NM- 9.2
1-True crime stories	36	72	108	214	347	480
2	19	38	57	111	176	240
3,5,6	17	34	51	98	154	210
4-Acid in face story	21	42	63	124	202	280
7-9	14	28	42	82	121	160

NOTE: ***Ingles** a-5, 6. **McWilliams** a-5, 7, 8. **Reinman** c-6.*

GANG WORLD
Standard Comics: No. 5, Nov, 1952 - No. 6, Jan, 1953

	GD 2.0	VG 4.0	FN 6.0	VF 8.0	VF/NM 9.0	NM- 9.2
5-Bondage-c	19	38	57	109	172	235
6	15	30	45	83	124	165

GARGOYLE (See The Defenders #94)
Marvel Comics Group: June, 1985 - No. 4, Sept, 1985 (75¢, limited series)

	GD 2.0	VG 4.0	FN 6.0	VF 8.0	VF/NM 9.0	NM- 9.2
1-Wrightson-c; character from Defenders						3.50
2-4						2.50

GARGOYLES (TV cartoon)
Marvel Comics: Feb, 1995 - No. 11, Dec, 1995 ($2.50)

	GD 2.0	VG 4.0	FN 6.0	VF 8.0	VF/NM 9.0	NM- 9.2
1-11: Based on animated series						3.00

GARRISON'S GORILLAS (TV)
Dell Publishing Co.: Jan, 1968 - No. 4, Oct, 1968; No. 5, Oct, 1969 (Photo-c)

	GD 2.0	VG 4.0	FN 6.0	VF 8.0	VF/NM 9.0	NM- 9.2
1	5	10	15	30	48	65
2-5: 5-Reprints #1	3	6	9	20	30	40

GARY GIANNI'S THE MONSTERMEN
Dark Horse Comics: Aug, 1999 ($2.95, one-shot)

	GD 2.0	VG 4.0	FN 6.0	VF 8.0	VF/NM 9.0	NM- 9.2
1-Gianni-s/c/a; back-up Hellboy story by Mignola						3.00

GASM (Sci-Fi, Horror, Fantasy comics magazine)(Mature content)
Stories, Layouts & Press, Inc.: Nov, 1977 - nn (No. 5), Jun, 1978 (B&W/color)

	GD 2.0	VG 4.0	FN 6.0	VF 8.0	VF/NM 9.0	NM- 9.2
1-Mark Wheatley-s/a; Gene Day-s/a; Workman-a	3	6	9	14	19	24
2 (12/77) Wheatley-a; Winnick-s/a; Workman-a	2	4	6	11	16	20
nn(#3, 2/78) Day-s/a; Wheatley-a; Workman-a	2	4	6	10	14	18
nn(#4, 4/78) Day-s/a; Wheatley-a; Corben-a	3	6	9	14	20	26
nn(#5, 6/78) Hempel-a; Howarth-a; Corben-a	3	6	9	16	22	28

GASOLINE ALLEY (Top Love Stories No. 3 on?)
Star Publications: Sept-Oct, 1950 - No. 2, Dec, 1950 (Newspaper-r)

	GD 2.0	VG 4.0	FN 6.0	VF 8.0	VF/NM 9.0	NM- 9.2
1-Contains 1 pg. intro. history of the strip (The Life of Skeezix); reprints 15 scenes of highlights from 1921-1935, plus an adventure from 1935 and 1936 strips; a 2-pg. filler is included on the life of the creator Frank King, with photo of the cartoonist.	20	40	60	117	186	255
2-(1936-37 reprints)-L. B. Cole-c	22	44	66	131	211	290

(See Super Book No. 21)

GASP!
American Comics Group: Mar, 1967 - No. 4, Aug, 1967 (12¢)

Gay Comics #27 © MAR

Gears of War #1 © Epic Comics

Gene Autry Comics #52 © Gene Autry

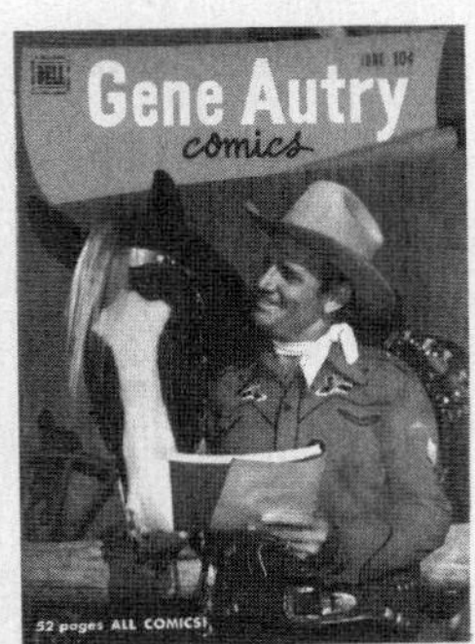

	GD 2.0	VG 4.0	FN 6.0	VF 8.0	VF/NM 9.0	NM- 9.2
1	5	10	15	32	51	70
2-4	4	8	12	22	34	45

GATECRASHER
Black Bull Entertainment: Mar, 2000 - No. 4, Jun, 2000 ($2.50, limited series)

1,2-Waid-s/Conner & Palmiotti-c/a; 1,2-variant-c by J.G. Jones 2.50
3,4: 3-Jusko var-c. 4-Linsner-c 2.50
... Ring of Fire TPB (11/00, $12.95) r/#1-4; Hughes-c; Ennis intro. 13.00

GATECRASHER (Regular series)
Black Bull Entertainment: Aug, 2000 - No. 6, Jan, 2001 ($2.50, limited series)

1-6-Waid-s/Conner & Palmiotti-c/a; 1-3-Variant-c by Fabry. 4-Hildebrandts variant-c. 5-Art Adams var-c. 6-Texeira var-c 2.50

GAY COMICS (Honeymoon No. 41)
Timely Comics/USA Comic Mag. Co. No. 18-24: Mar, 1944 (no month); No. 18, Fall, 1944 - No. 40, Oct, 1949

1-Wolverton's Powerhouse Pepper; Tessie the Typist begins; 1st app. Willie (one shot)
55 110 165 352 601 850
18-(Formerly Funny Tunes #17?)-Wolverton-a 37 74 111 222 361 500
19-29: Wolverton-a in all. 21,24-6 pg., 7 pg. Powerhouse Pepper; additional 2 pg. story in 24). 23-7 pg Wolverton story & 2 two pg stories(total of 11pgs.).
24,29-Kurtzman-a (24-"Hey Look"(2)) 34 68 102 199 325 450
30,33,36,37-Kurtzman's "Hey Look" 15 30 45 83 124 165
31-Kurtzman's "Hey Look" (1), Giggles 'N' Grins (1-1/2)
15 30 45 83 124 165
32,35,38-40: 35-Nellie The Nurse begins? 14 28 42 80 115 150
34-Three Kurtzman's "Hey Look" 15 30 45 85 130 175

GAY COMICS (Also see Smile, Tickle, & Whee Comics)
Modern Store Publ.: 1955 (7¢, 5x7-1/4", 52 pgs.)

1 4 8 12 22 34 45

GAY PURR-EE (See Movie Comics)

GAZILLION
Image Comics: Nov, 1998 ($2.50, one-shot)

1-Howard Shum-s/ Keron Grant-a 2.50

GEARS OF WAR (Based on the video game)
DC Comics (WildStorm): Dec, 2008 - Present ($3.99)

1-11: 1-Liam Sharp-a/Joshua Ortega-s. 1-Two covers 4.00
... Reader (4/09, $3.99) r/#1 & 2 in flipbook 4.00
... Sourcebook (8/09, $3.99) character pin-ups by various; Platt-c 4.00
Book One HC (2009, $19.99, dustjacket) r/#1-6 & Sourcebook 20.00

GEAR STATION, THE
Image Comics: Mar, 2000 - No. 5, Nov, 2000 ($2.50)

1-Four covers by Ross, Turner, Pat Lee, Fraga 2.50
1-($6.95) DF Cover 7.00
2-5: 2-Two covers by Fraga and Art Adams 2.50

GEEK, THE (See Brother Power... & Vertigo Visions)

GEEKSVILLE (Also see 3 Geeks, The)
3 Finger Prints/ Image: Aug, 1999 - No. 6, Mar, 2001 ($2.75/$2.95, B&W)

1,2,4-6-The 3 Geeks by Koslowski; Innocent Bystander by Sassaman 3.00
3-Includes "Babes & Blades" mini-comic 5.00
0-(3/00) First Image issue 3.00
(Vol. 2) 1-4-($2.95) 3-Mini-comic insert by the Geeks. 4-Steve Borock app. 3.00

G-8 AND HIS BATTLE ACES (Based on pulps)
Gold Key: Oct, 1966

1 (10184-610)-Painted-c 4 8 12 26 41 55

G-8 AND HIS BATTLE ACES
Blazing Comics: 1991 ($1.50, one-shot)

1-Glanzman-a; Truman-c 2.50
NOTE: *Flip book format with "The Spider's Web" #1 on other side w/**Glanzman**-a, **Truman**-c.*

GEISHA (Also see Oni Press Summer Vacation Supercolor Fun Special)
Oni Press: Sept, 1998 - No. 4, Dec, 1998 ($2.95, limited series)

1-4-Andi Watson-s/a. 2-Adam Warren-c 3.00
...One Shot (5/00, $4.50) 4.50
The Complete Geisha TPB (5/03, $15.95, digest size) r/#1-4, One Shot & story from Oni Press Summer Vacation Supercolor Fun Special 16.00

GEM COMICS
Spotlight Publishers: Apr, 1945 (52 pgs)

1-Little Mohee, Steve Strong app.; Jungle bondage-c

	GD 2.0	VG 4.0	FN 6.0	VF 8.0	VF/NM 9.0	NM- 9.2
	50	100	150	315	533	750

GEMINAR
Image Comics: July, 2000 ($4.95, B&W)

1-(72-Page Special) Terry Collins-s/Al Bigley-a 5.00

GEMINI BLOOD
DC Comics (Helix): Sept, 1996 - No. 9, May, 1997 ($2.25, limited series)

1-9: 5-Simonson-c 2.50

GEN ACTIVE
DC Comics (WildStorm): May, 2000 - No. 6, Aug, 2001 ($3.95)

1-6: 1-Covers by Campbell and Madureira; Gen 13 & DV8 app. 5-Mahfood-a; Quitely and Stelfreeze-c. 6-Portacio-a/c 4.00

GENE AUTRY (See March of Comics No. 25, 28, 39, 54, 78, 90, 104, 120, 135, 150 in the Promotional Comics section & Western Roundup under Dell Giants)

GENE AUTRY COMICS (Movie, Radio star; singing cowboy)
Fawcett Publications: Jan, 1942 (On sale 12/17/41) - No. 10, 1943 (68 pgs.)
(Dell takes over with No. 11)

1 (Rare)-Gene Autry & his horse Champion begin; photo back-c
556 1112 1668 4003 7002 10,000
2-(1942) 127 254 381 800 1350 1900
3-5: 3-(11/1/42) 67 134 201 422 711 1000
6-10 53 106 159 334 567 800

GENE AUTRY COMICS (...& Champion No. 102 on)
Dell Publishing Co.: No. 11, 1943 - No. 121, Jan-Mar, 1959 (TV - later issues)

11 (1943, 60 pgs.)-Continuation of Fawcett series; photo back-c; first Dell issue
38 76 114 293 547 800
12 (2/44, 60 pgs.) 33 66 99 254 477 700
Four Color 47 (1944, 60 pgs.) 33 66 99 254 477 700
Four Color 57 (11/44),66('45)(52 pgs. each) 31 62 93 239 445 650
Four Color 75,83 ('45, 36 pgs. each) 25 50 75 185 343 500
Four Color 93 ('45, 36 pgs.) 22 44 66 157 291 425
Four Color 100 ('46, 36 pgs.) First Gene Autry photo-c
24 48 72 181 336 490
1 (5-6/46, 52 pgs.) 33 66 99 254 477 700
2 (7-8/46)-Photo-c begin, end #111 17 34 51 120 223 325
3-5: 4-Intro Flapjack Hobbs 14 28 42 99 175 250
6-10 11 22 33 79 140 200
11-20: 20-Panhandle Pete begins 10 20 30 71 126 180
21-29 (36 pgs.) 9 18 27 61 103 145
30-40 (52 pgs.) 8 16 24 52 86 120
41-56 (52 pgs.) 7 14 21 45 73 100
57-66 (36 pgs.): 58-X-mas-c 6 12 18 39 62 85
67-80 (52 pgs.): 70-X-mas-c 6 12 18 39 62 85
81-90 (52 pgs.): 82-X-mas-c. 87-Blank inside-c 5 10 15 34 55 75
91-99 (36 pgs. No. 91-on). 94-X-mas-c 5 10 15 30 48 65
100 5 10 15 32 51 70
101-111-Last Gene Autry photo-c 4 8 12 28 44 60
112-121-All Champion painted-c, most by Savitt 4 8 12 26 41 55
NOTE: *Photo back covers 4-18, 20-45, 48-65.* **Manning** *a-118.* **Jesse Marsh** *art: 4-Color No. 66, 75, 93, 100, No. 1-25, 27-37, 39, 40.*

GENE AUTRY'S CHAMPION (TV)
Dell Publ. Co.: No. 287, 8/50; No. 319, 2/51; No. 3, 8-10/51 - No. 19, 8-10/55

Four Color 287(#1)('50, 52 pgs.)-Photo-c 11 22 33 79 140 200
Four Color 319(#2, '51), 3: 2-Painted-c begin, most by Sam Savitt
7 14 21 45 73 90
4-19: 19-Last painted-c 5 10 15 30 48 65

GENE COLAN TRIBUTE BOOK (Produced for The Hero Initiative)
Marvel Comics: 2008 ($9.99, one-shot)

1-Spotlighted stories from Tales of Suspense #89,90, Doctor Strange #174 and others 10.00

GENE DOGS
Marvel Comics UK: Oct, 1993 - No. 4, Jan, 1994 ($1.75, limited series)

1-($2.75)-Polybagged w/4 trading cards 3.00
2-4: 2-Vs. Genetix 2.50

GENE POOL
IDW Publishing: Oct, 2003 ($6.99, squarebound)

nn-Wein & Wolfman-s/Cummings-a 7.00

GENERAL DOUGLAS MACARTHUR
Fox Features Syndicate: 1951

nn-True life story 20 40 60 114 182 250

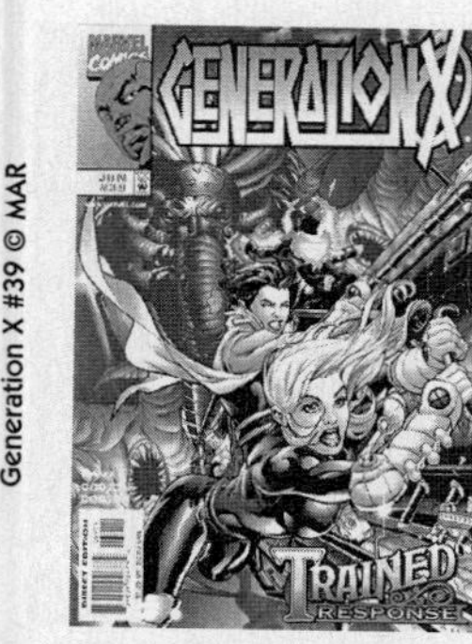

Generation X #39 © MAR

Genesis #4 © DC

Gen 13 #77 © WSP

GD VG FN VF VF/NM NM-
2.0 4.0 6.0 8.0 9.0 9.2

GENERIC COMIC, THE
Marvel Comics Group: Apr, 1984 (one-shot)

1 3.00

GENERATION HEX
DC Comics (Amalgam): June, 1997 ($1.95, one-shot)

1-Milligan-s/ Pollina & Morales-a 2.50

GENERATION M (Follows House of M x-over)
Marvel Comics: Jan, 2006 - No. 5, May, 2006 ($2.99, limited series)

1-5-Jenkins-s/Bachs-a. 1-Chamber app. 2-Jubilee app. 3-Blob-c. 4-Angel-c 3.00
Decimation: Generation M TPB (2006, $13.99) r/#1-5 14.00

GENERATION NEXT
Marvel Comics: Mar, 1995 - No. 4, June, 1995 ($1.95, limited series)

1-4-Age of Apocalypse; Scott Lobdell scripts & Chris Bachalo-c/a 2.50

GENERATION X (See Gen ^{13}/ Generation X)
Marvel Comics: Oct, 1994 - No. 75, June, 2001 ($1.50/$1.95/$1.99/$2.25)

Collectors Preview ($1.75), "Ashcan" Edition 2.25
-1(7/97) Flashback story 3.00
1/2 (San Diego giveaway) 2 4 6 8 10 12
1-($3.95)-Wraparound chromium-c; Scott Lobdell scripts & Chris Bachalo-a begins 6.00
2-($1.95)-Deluxe edition, Bachalo-a 4.00
3,4-($1.95)-Deluxe Edition; Bachalo-a 3.00
2-10: 2-4-Standard Edition. 5-Returns from "Age of Apocalypse," begin $1.95-c. 6-Bachalo-a(p) ends, returns #17. 7-Roger Cruz-a(p). 10-Omega Red-c/app. 3.00
11-24, 26-28: 13,14-Bishop-app. 17-Stan Lee app. (Stan Lee scripts own dialogue); Bachalo/Buckingham-a; Onslaught update. 18-Toad cameo. 20-Franklin Richards app; Howard the Duck cameo. 21-Howard the Duck app. 22-Nightmare app. 2.50
25-($2.99)-Wraparound-c. Black Tom, Howard the Duck app. 3.50
29-37: 29-Begin $1.99-c, "Operation Zero Tolerance". 33-Hama-s 2.50
38-49: 38-Dodson-a begins. 40-Penance ID revealed. 49-Maggott app. 2.50
50,57-($2.99): 50-Crossover w/X-Man #50 3.50
51-56, 58-62: 59-Avengers & Spider-Man app. 2.50
63-74: 63-Ellis-s begin. 64-Begin $2.25-c. 69-71-Art Adams-c 2.50
75-($2.99) Final issue; Chamber joins the X-Men; Lim-a 3.00
'95 Special-($3.95) 4.00
'96 Special-($2.95)-Wraparound-c; Jeff Johnson-c/a 3.50
'97 Special-($2.99)-Wraparound-c; 3.50
'98 Annual-($3.50)-vs. Dracula 3.50
'99 Annual-($3.50)-Monet leaves 3.50
75¢ Ashcan Edition 3.00
...Holiday Special 1 (2/99, $3.50) Pollina-a 3.50
...Underground Special 1 (5/98, $2.50, B&W) Mahfood-a 2.50

GENERATION X/ GEN ^{13} (Also see Gen ^{13}/ Generation X)
Marvel Comics: 1997 ($3.99, one-shot)

1-Robinson-s/Larroca-a(p) 4.00

GENE RODDENBERRY'S LOST UNIVERSE
Tekno Comix: Apr, 1995 - No. 7, Oct, 1995 ($1.95)

1-7: 1-3-w/ bound-in game piece & trading card. 4-w/bound-in trading card 2.50

GENE RODDENBERRY'S XANDER IN LOST UNIVERSE
Tekno Comix: No. 0, Nov, 1995; No. 1, Dec, 1995 - No. 8, July, 1996 ($2.25)

0,1-8: 1-5-Jae Lee-c. 4-Polybagged. 8-Pt. 5 of The Big Bang x-over 2.50

GENESIS (See DC related titles)
DC Comics: Oct, 1997 - No. 4, Oct, 1997 ($1.95, weekly limited series)

1-4: Byrne-s/Wagner-a(p) in all. 3.00

GENESIS: THE #1 COLLECTION (WildStorm Archives)
WildStorm Productions: 1998 ($9.99, TPB, B&W)

nn-Reprints #1 issues of WildStorm titles and pin-ups 10.00

GENETIX
Marvel Comics UK: Oct, 1993 - No. 6, Mar, 1994 ($1.75, limited series)

1-($2.75)-Polybagged w/4 cards; Dark Guard app. 3.00
2-6: 2-Intro Tektos. 4-Vs. Gene Dogs 2.50

GENEXT (Next generation of X-Men)
Marvel Comics: July, 2008 - No. 5, Nov, 2008 ($3.99, limited series)

1-5: 1-Claremont-s/Scherberger-a; character profile pages 4.00

GENEXT: UNITED
Marvel Comics: July, 2009 - No. 5, Dec, 2009 ($3.99, limited series)

1-5: 1-Claremont-s/Meyers-a; Beast app. 4.00

GD VG FN VF VF/NM NM-
2.0 4.0 6.0 8.0 9.0 9.2

GEN ^{12} (Also see Gen^{13} and Team 7)
Image Comics (WildStorm Productions): Feb, 1998 - No. 5, June, 1998 ($2.50, lim. series)

1-5: 1-Team 7 & Gen^{13} app.; wraparound-c 3.00

GEN ^{13} (Also see Wild C.A.T.S. #1 & Deathmate Black #2)
Image Comics (WildStorm Productions): Feb, 1994 - No. 5, July 1994 ($1.95, limited series)

0 (8/95, $2.50)-Ch. 1 w/Jim Lee-p; Ch.4 w/Charest-p 3.00
1/2 1 2 3 4 5 7
1-($2.50)-Created by Jim Lee 1 3 4 6 8 10
1-2nd printing 2.50
1-"3-D" Edition (9/97, $4.95)-w/glasses 5.00
2-($2.50) 1 2 3 4 5 7
3-Pitt-c & story 4.00
4-Pitt-c & story; wraparound-c 3.00
5 4.00
5-Alternate Portacio-c; see Deathblow #5 6.00
...Collected Edition ('94, $12.95)-r/#1-5 13.00
...Rave ($1.50, 3/95)-wraparound-c 3.00
...: Who They Are And How They Came To Be... (2006, $14.99) r/#1-5; sketch gallery 15.00

NOTE: *Issues 1-4 contain coupons redeemable for the ashcan edition of Gen 13 #0. Price listed is for a complete book.*

GEN ^{13}
Image Comics (WildStorm Productions): Mar, 1995 - No. 36, Dec, 1998;
DC Comics (WildStorm): No. 37, Mar, 1999 - No. 77, Jul, 2002 ($2.95/$2.50)

1-A (Charge)-Campbell/Garner-c 4.50
1-B (Thumbs Up)-Campbell/Garner-c 4.50
1-C-1-F,1-I-1-M: 1-C (Lil' GEN 13)-Art Adams-c. 1-D (Barbari-GEN)-Simon Bisley-c. 1-E (Your Friendly Neighborhood Grunge)-Cleary-c. 1-F (GEN 13 Goes Madison Ave.)-Golden-c. 1-I (That's the way we became GEN 13)-Campbell/Gibson-c. 1-J (All Dolled Up)-Campbell/ McWeeney-c. 1-K (Verti-GEN)-Dunn-c. 1-L (Picto-Fiction). 1-M (Do it Yourself Cover) 1 2 3 4 5 7
1-G (Lin-GEN-re)-Michael Lopez-c 2 4 6 8 10 12
1-H (GEN-et Jackson)-Jason Pearson-c 2 4 6 8 10 12
1-Chromium-c by Campbell 4 8 12 28 44 60
1-Chromium-c by Jim Lee 6 12 18 37 59 80
1-"3-D" Edition (2/98, $4.95)-w/glasses 5.00
2 ($1.95, Newsstand)-WildStorm Rising Pt. 4; bound-in card 2.50
2-12: 2-($2.50, Direct Market)-WildStorm Rising Pt. 4, bound-in card. 6,7-Jim Lee-c/a(p). 9-Ramos-a. 10,11-Fire From Heaven Pt. 3. & Pt.9 3.00
11-($4.95)-Special European Tour Edition; chromium-c 2 4 6 10 14 18
13A,13B,13C-($1.30, 13 pgs.): 13A-Archie & Friends app. 13B-Bone-c/app.; Teenage Mutant Ninja Turtles, Madman, Spawn & Jim Lee app. 3.00
14-24: 20-Last Campbell-a 2.50
25-($3.50)-Two covers by Campbell and Charest 3.50
25-($3.50)-Voyager Pack w/Danger Girl preview 4.50
25-Foil-c 10.00
26-32,34: 26-Arcudi-s/Frank-a begins. 34-Back-up story by Art Adams 2.50
33-Flip book w/Planetary preview 4.00
35-49: 35,36,38,40-Two covers. 37-First DC issue. 41-Last Frank-a 2.50
50-($3.95) Two covers by Lee and Benes; art by various 4.00
51-76: 51-Moy-a; Fairchild loses her powers. 60-Warren-s/a. 66-Art by various incl. Campbell (3 pgs.). 70,75,76-Mays-a. 76-Original team dies 2.50
77-($3.50) Mays, Andrews, Warren-a 3.50
Annual 1 (1997, $2.95) Ellis-s/ Dillon-c/a. 3.50
Annual 1999 ($3.50, DC) Slipstream x-over w/ DV8 3.50
Annual 2000 ($3.50) Devil's Night x-over w/WildStorm titles; Bermejo-c 3.50
...: A Christmas Caper (1/00, $5.95, one-shot) McWeeney-s/a 6.00
... Archives (4/98, $12.99) B&W reprints of mini-series, #0,1/2,1-13ABC; includes cover gallery and sourcebook 13.00
...: Carny Folk (2/00, $3.50) Collect back-up stories 3.50
... European Vacation TPB ($6.95) r/#6,7 7.00
.../ Fantastic Four (2001, $5.95) Maguire-s/c/a(p) 6.00
...: Going West (6/99, $2.50, one-shot) Pruett-s 2.50
...: Grunge Saves the World (5/99, $5.95, one-shot) Altieri-c/a 6.00
... I Love New York TPB ($9.95) r/part #25, 26-29; Frank-c 10.00
... London, New York, Hell TPB ($6.95) r/Annual #1 & Bootleg Ann. #1 7.00
... Lost in Paradise TPB ($6.95) r/#3-5 7.00
.../ Maxx (12/95, $3.50, one-shot) Messner-Loebs-s, 1st Coker-c/a. 3.50
...: Meanwhile (2003, $17.95) r/#43,44,66-70; all Warren-s; art by various 18.00
...: Medicine Song (2001, $5.95) Brent Anderson-c/a(p)/Raab-s 6.00
... Science Friction (2001, $5.95) Haley & Lopresti-a 6.00
... Starting Over TPB ($14.95) r/#1-7 15.00
... Superhuman Like You TPB ($12.95) r/#60-65; Warren-c 13.00

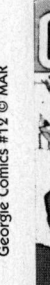

Gen 13 V4 #31 © WSP

Georgie Comics #12 © MAR

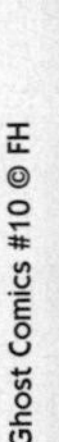
Ghost Comics #10 © FH

	GD 2.0	VG 4.0	FN 6.0	VF 8.0	VF/NM 9.0	NM- 9.2

... #13 A,B&C Collected Edition ($6.95, TPB) r/#13A,B&C 7.00
... 3-D Special (1997, $4.95, one-shot) Art Adams-s/a(p) 5.00
...: The Unreal World (7/96, $2.95, one-shot) Humberto Ramos-c/a 3.00
... We'll Take Manhattan TPB ($14.95) r/#45-50; new Benes-c 15.00
...: Wired (4/99, $2.50, one-shot) Richard Bennett-c/a 2.50
... Yearbook 1997 (6/97, $2.50) College-themed stories and pin-ups by various 2.50
...: 'Zine (12/96, $1.95, B&W, digest size) Campbell/Garner-c 2.50
Variant Collection-Four editions (all 13 variants w/Chromium variant-limited, signed) 100.00

GEN 13
DC Comics (WildStorm): No. 0, Sept, 2002 - No. 16, Feb, 2004 ($2.95)
0-(13¢-c) Intro. new team; includes previews of 21 Down & The Resistance 2.50
1-Claremont-s/Garza-c/a; Fairchild app. 3.00
2-16: 8-13-Bachs-a. 16-Original team returns 3.00
...: September Song TPB (2003, $19.95) r/#0-6; Garza sketch pages 20.00

GEN 13 (Volume 4)
DC Comics (WildStorm): Dec, 2006 - Present ($2.99)
1-33: 1-Simone-s/Caldwell-a; re-intro the original team; Caldwell-c. 8-The Authority app. 3.00
1-Variant-c by J. Scott Campbell 5.00
...: Armageddon (1/08, $2.99) Gage-s/Meyers-a; future Gen13 app. 3.00
...: Best of a Bad Lot TPB (2007, $14.99) r/#1-6 15.00
...: 15 Minutes TPB (2008, $14.99) r/#14-20 15.00
...: Road Trip TPB (2008, $14.99) r/#7-13 15.00
...: World's End TPB (2009, $17.99) r/#21-26 18.00

GEN 13 BOOTLEG
Image Comics (WildStorm): Nov, 1996 - No. 20, Jul, 1998 ($2.50)
1-Alan Davis-a; alternate costumes-c 2.50
1-Team falling variant-c 3.00
2-7: 2-Alan Davis-a. 5,6-Terry Moore-s. 7-Robinson-s/Scott Hampton-a 2.50
8-10-Adam Warren-s/a 4.00
11-20: 11,12-Lopresti-s/a & Simonson-s. 13-Wieringo-s/a. 14-Mariotte-s/Phillips-a. 15,16-Strnad-s/Shaw-a. 18-Altieri-s/a(p)/c, 18-Variant-c by Bruce Timm 2.50
Annual 1 (2/98, $2.95) Ellis-s/Dillon-c/a 3.00
... Grunge: The Movie (12/97, $9.95) r/#8-10, Warren-c 10.00
...Vol. 1 TPB (10/98, $11.95) r/#1-4 12.00

GEN 13/ GENERATION X (Also see Generation X / Gen 13)
Image Comics (WildStorm Publications): July, 1997 ($2.95, one-shot)
1-Choi-s/ Art Adams-p/Garner-i. Variant covers by Adams/Garner and Campbell/McWeeney 3.00
1-($4.95) 3-D Edition w/glasses; Campbell-c 5.00

GEN 13 INTERACTIVE
Image Comics (WildStorm): Oct, 1997 - No. 3, Dec, 1997 ($2.50, lim. series)
1-3-Internet voting used to determine storyline 2.50
... Plus! (7/98, $11.95) r/series & 3-D Special (in 2-D) 12.00

GEN 13 : MAGICAL DRAMA QUEEN ROXY
Image Comics (WildStorm): Oct, 1998 - No. 3, Dec, 1998 ($3.50, lim. series)
1-3-Adam Warren-s/c/a; manga style, 2-Variant-c by Hiroyuki Utatane 3.50
1-($6.95) Dynamic Forces Ed. w/Variant Warren-c 7.00

GEN 13 /MONKEYMAN & O'BRIEN
Image Comics (WildStorm): Jun, 1998 - No. 2, July, 1998 ($2.50, lim. series)
1,2-Art Adams-s/a(p); 1-Two covers 2.50
1-($4.95) Chromium-c 5.00
1-($6.95) Dynamic Forces Ed. 7.00

GEN 13: ORDINARY HEROES
Image Comics (WildStorm Publications): Feb, 1996 - No. 2, July, 1996 ($2.50, lim. series)
1,2-Adam Hughes-c/a/scripts 3.00
TPB (2004, $14.95) r/series, Gen13 Bootleg #1&2 and Wildstorm Thunderbook; new Hughes-c and art pages 15.00

GENTLE BEN (TV)
Dell Publishing Co.: Feb, 1968 - No. 5, Oct, 1969 (All photo-c)
1 4 8 12 26 41 55
2-5: 5-Reprints #1 3 6 9 16 23 30

GEOMANCER (Also see Eternal Warrior: Fist & Steel)
Valiant: Nov, 1994 - No. 8, June, 1995 ($3.75/$2.25)
1 ($3.75)-Chromium wraparound-c; Eternal Warrior app. 3.75
2-8 2.50

GEORGE OF THE JUNGLE (TV)(See America's Best TV Comics)
Gold Key: Feb, 1969 - No. 2, Oct, 1969 (Jay Ward)
1 9 18 27 65 113 160
2 6 12 18 41 66 90

GEORGE PAL'S PUPPETOONS (Funny animal puppets)
Fawcett Publications: Dec, 1945 - No. 18, Dec, 1947; No. 19, 1950
1-Captain Marvel-c 42 84 126 265 445 625
2 23 46 69 136 223 310
3-10 15 30 45 86 133 180
11-19 13 26 39 74 105 135

GEORGIE COMICS (...& Judy Comics #20-35?; see All Teen & Teen Comics)
Timely Comics/GPI No. 1-34: Spr, 1945 - No. 39, Oct, 1952 (#1-3 are quarterly)
1-Dave Berg-a 30 60 90 177 289 400
2 16 32 48 94 147 200
3-5,7,8 15 30 45 84 127 170
6-Georgie visits Timely Comics 16 32 48 94 147 200
9,10-Kurtzman's "Hey Look" (1 & ?); Millie the Model & Margie app. 15 30 45 85 130 175
11,12: 11-Margie, Millie app. 12 24 36 69 97 125
13-Kurtzman's "Hey Look", 3 pgs. 13 26 39 74 105 135
14-Wolverton-a(1 pg.); Kurtzman's "Hey Look" 14 28 42 78 112 145
15,16,18-20 11 22 33 64 90 115
17,29-Kurtzman's "Hey Look", 1 pg. 12 24 36 69 97 125
21-24,27,28,30-39: 21-Anti-Wertham editorial. 33-38-Hy Rosen-c 11 22 33 60 83 105
25-Painted-c by classic pin-up artist Peter Driben 14 28 42 78 112 145
26-Logo design swipe from Archie Comics 11 22 33 62 86 110

GERALD McBOING-BOING AND THE NEARSIGHTED MR. MAGOO (TV)
(Mr. Magoo No. 6 on)
Dell Publishing Co.: Aug-Oct, 1952 - No. 5, Aug-Oct, 1953
1 11 22 33 74 132 190
2-5 9 18 27 63 107 150

GERONIMO (See Fighting Indians of the Wild West!)
Avon Periodicals: 1950 - No. 4, Feb, 1952
1-Indian Fighter; Maneely-a; Texas Rangers-r/Cowpuncher #1; Fawcette-c 19 38 57 109 172 235
2-On the Warpath; Kit West app.; Kinstler-c/a 13 26 39 74 105 135
3-And His Apache Murderers; Kinstler-c/a(2); Kit West-r/Cowpuncher #6 13 26 39 74 105 135
4-Savage Raids of; Kinstler-c & inside front-c; Kinstlerish-a by McCann(3) 12 24 36 69 97 125

GERONIMO JONES
Charlton Comics: Sept, 1971 - No. 9, Jan, 1973
1 2 4 6 13 18 22
2-9 2 4 6 8 10 12
Modern Comics Reprint #7('78) 4.00

GETALONG GANG, THE (TV)
Marvel Comics (Star Comics): May, 1985 - No. 6, Mar, 1986
1-6: Saturday morning TV stars 3.00

GET LOST
Mikeross Publications/New Comics: Feb-Mar, 1954 - No. 3, June-July, 1954 (Satire)
1-Andru/Esposito-a in all? 31 62 93 182 296 410
2-Andru/Esposito-c; has 4 pg. E.C. parody featuring "The Sewer Keeper" 21 42 63 122 199 275
3-John Wayne 'Hondo' parody 17 34 51 100 158 215
1,2 (10,12/87-New Comics)-B&W r-original 2.50

GET SMART (TV)
Dell Publ. Co.: June, 1966 - No. 8, Sept, 1967 (All have Don Adams photo-c)
1 10 20 30 70 123 175
2,3-Ditko-a 7 14 21 47 76 105
4-8: 8-Reprints #1 (cover and insides) 6 12 18 37 59 80

GHOST (...Comics #9)
Fiction House Magazines: 1951(Winter) - No. 11, Summer, 1954
1-Most covers by Whitman 77 154 231 493 847 1200
2-Ghost Gallery & Werewolf Hunter stories 40 80 120 246 411 575
3-9: 3,6,7,9-Bondage-c. 9-Abel, Discount-a 34 68 102 206 336 465
10,11-Dr. Drew by Grandenetti in each, reprinted from Rangers; 11-Evans-r/ Rangers #39; Grandenetti-r/Rangers #49 29 58 87 170 278 385

GHOST (See Comic's Greatest World)
Dark Horse Comics: Apr, 1995 - No. 36, Apr, 1998 ($2.50/$2.95)

Ghost/Batgirl #2 © DC & DH

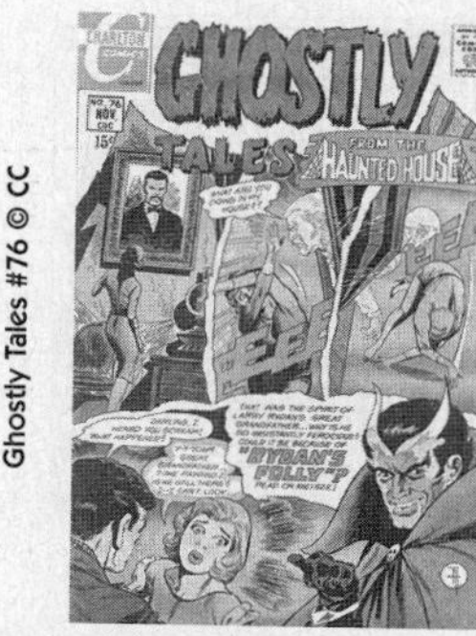

Ghostly Tales #76 © CC

Ghost Manor #19 © CC

	GD 2.0	VG 4.0	FN 6.0	VF 8.0	VF/NM 9.0	NM- 9.2
1-Adam Hughes-a	1	2	3	5	6	8
2,3-Hughes-a						4.00
4-24: 4-Barb Wire app. 5,6-Hughes-c. 12-Ghost/Hellboy preview. 15,21-X app. 18,19-Barb Wire app.						3.00
25-($3.50)-48 pgs. special						3.50
26-36: 26-Begin $2.95-c. 29-Flip book w/Timecop. 33-36-Jade Cathedral; Harris painted-c						3.00
Special 1 (7/94, $3.95, 48 pgs.)	1	2	3	4	5	7
Special 2 (6/98, $3.95) Barb Wire app.						4.00
... Black October (1/99, $14.95, trade paperback)-r/#6-9,26,27						15.00
... Nocturnes (1996, $9.95, trade paperback)-r/#1-3 & 5						10.00
... Omnibus Vol. 1 (10/08, $24.95, 9x6") r/#1-12; Special 1 and Decade of Dark Horse #2						25.00
...Stories (1995, $9.95, trade paperback)-r/Early Ghost app.						10.00

GHOST (Volume 2)
Dark Horse Comics: Sept, 1998 - No. 22, Aug, 2000 ($2.95)

1-22: 1-4-Ryan Benjamin-c/Zanier-a						3.00
Handbook (8/99, $2.95) guide to issues and characters						3.00
Special 3 (12/98, $3.95)						4.00

GHOST AND THE SHADOW
Dark Horse Comics: Dec, 1995 ($2.95, one-shot)

1-Moench scripts — 3.00

GHOST/BATGIRL
Dark Horse Comics: Aug, 2000 - No. 4, Dec, 2000 ($2.95, limited series)

1-4-New Batgirl; Oracle & Bruce Wayne app.; Benjamin-c/a — 3.00

GHOST/HELLBOY
Dark Horse Comics: May, 1996 - No. 2, June, 1996 ($2.50, limited series)

1,2: Mike Mignola-c/scripts & breakdowns; Scott Benefiel finished-a — 3.00

GHOST BREAKERS (Also see Racket Squad in Action, Red Dragon & (CC) Sherlock Holmes Comics)
Street & Smith Publications: Sept, 1948 - No. 2, Dec, 1948 (52 pgs.)

1-Powell-c/a(3); Dr. Neff (magician) app.	42	84	126	265	445	625
2-Powell-c/a(2); Maneely-a	34	68	102	206	336	465

GHOSTBUSTERS (TV) (Also, see Real...and Slimer)
First Comics: Feb, 1987 - No. 6, Aug, 1987 ($1.25)

1-6: Based on new animated TV series — 3.00

GHOSTBUSTERS: DISPLACED AGGRESSION
IDW Publishing: Sept, 2009 - No. 4, Dec, 2009 ($3.99)

1-3-Lobdell-s/Kyriazis-a — 4.00

GHOSTBUSTERS: LEGION (Movie)
88 MPH Studios: Feb, 2004 - No. 4, May, 2004 ($2.95/$3.50)

1-4-Steve Kurth-a/Andrew Dabb-s						3.00
1-3-($3.50) Brereton variant-c						3.50

GHOSTBUSTERS: THE OTHER SIDE
IDW Publishing: Oct, 2008 - No. 4, Jan, 2009 ($3.99)

1-4-Champagne-s/Nguyen-a — 4.00

GHOSTBUSTERS II
Now Comics: Oct, 1989 - No. 3, Dec, 1989 ($1.95, mini-series)

1-3: Movie Adaptation — 3.00

GHOST CASTLE (See Tales of...)

GHOSTING
Platinum Studios: 2007 - No. 5 ($2.99, limited series)

1-3-Van Lente-s/Carvalho-a/Wolfe-c — 3.00

GHOST IN THE SHELL (Manga)
Dark Horse: Mar, 1995 - No. 8, Oct, 1995 ($3.95, B&W/color, lim. series)

1,2	2	4	6	13	18	22
3	2	4	6	8	10	12
4-8	1	2	3	5	6	8

GHOST IN THE SHELL 2: MAN-MADE INTERFACE (Manga)
Dark Horse Comics: Jan, 2003 - No. 11, Dec, 2003 ($3.50, color/B&W, lim. series)

1-11-Masamune Shirow-s/a. 5-B&W — 3.50

GHOSTLY HAUNTS (Formerly Ghost Manor)
Charlton Comics: #20, 9/71 - #53, 12/76; #54, 9/77 - #55, 10/77; #56, 1/78 - #58, 4/78

20	3	6	9	18	27	35
21	2	4	6	11	16	20
22-25,27,31-34,36,37-Ditko-c/a. 27-Dr. Graves x-over. 32-New logo. 33-Back to old logo	3	6	9	14	19	24
26,29,30,35-Ditko-c	2	4	6	10	14	18
28,38-40-Ditko-a. 39-Origin & 1st app. Destiny Fox	2	4	6	10	14	18
41,42: 41-Sutton-c; Ditko-a. 42-Newton-c/a	2	4	6	11	16	20
43-46,48,50,52-Ditko-a	2	4	6	9	13	16
47,54,56-Ditko-c/a. 56-Ditko-a(r).	2	4	6	11	16	20
49,51,53,55,57	1	3	4	6	8	10
58 (4/78) Last issue	2	4	6	11	16	20
40,41(Modern Comics-r, 1977, 1978)						4.00

NOTE: ***Ditko*** *a-22-25, 27, 28, 31-34, 36-41, 43-48, 50, 52, 54, 56r; c-22-27, 29, 30, 33-37, 47, 54, 56.* ***Glanzman*** *a-20.* ***Howard*** *a-27, 30, 35, 40-43, 48, 54, 57.* ***Kim*** *a-38, 41, 57.* ***Larson*** *a-48, 50.* ***Newton*** *c/a-42.* ***Staton*** *a-32, 35; c-28, 46.* ***Sutton*** *c-33, 37, 39, 41.*

GHOSTLY TALES (Formerly Blue Beetle No. 50-54)
Charlton Comics: No. 55, 4-5/66 - No. 124, 12/76; No. 125, 9/77 - No. 169, 10/84

55-Intro. & origin Dr. Graves; Ditko-a	7	14	21	45	73	100
56-58,60,61,70,71-Ditko-a. 70-Dr. Graves ends. 71-Last 12¢ issue	4	8	12	24	37	50
59,62-66,68	3	6	9	17	25	32
67,69-Ditko-c/a	4	8	12	26	41	55
72,75,76,79-82,85-Ditko-a	3	6	9	14	19	24
73,77,78,83,84,86-90,92-95,97,99-Ditko-c/a	3	6	9	17	25	32
74,91,98,119,123,124,127-130: 127,130-Sutton-a	2	4	6	9	12	15
96-Ditko-c	3	6	9	14	19	24
100-Ditko-c; Sutton-a	3	6	9	14	19	24
101,103-105-Ditko-a	2	4	6	11	16	20
102,109-Ditko-c/a	3	6	9	14	20	26
110,113-Sutton-c; Ditko-a	2	4	6	11	16	20
106-Ditko & Sutton-a; Sutton-c	2	4	6	11	16	20
107-Ditko, Wood, Sutton-a	2	4	6	13	18	22
108,116,117,126-Ditko-a	2	4	6	11	16	20
111,118,120-122,125-Ditko-c/a	3	6	9	14	20	26
112,114,115: 112,114-Ditko, Sutton-a. 114-Newton-a. 115-Newton, Ditko-a.	2	4	6	11	16	20
131-134,151,157,163-Ditko-c/a	2	4	6	11	16	20
135,142,145-150,153,154,156,158-160	1	2	3	5	7	9
136-141,143,144,152,155-Ditko-a	2	4	6	8	10	12
161,162,164-168-Lower print run. 162-Nudity panel	2	4	6	9	12	15
169 (10/84) Last issue; lower print run	2	4	6	11	16	20

NOTE: ***Aparo*** *a-65, 66, 68, 72, 137, 141r, 142r; c-71, 72, 74-76, 81, 146r, 149.* ***Ditko*** *a-55-58, 60, 61, 67, 69-73, 75-90, 92-95, 97, 99-118, 120-122, 125r, 126r, 131-141r, 143r, 144r, 146, 147, 149-152, 154-157, 159-161, 163; c-67, 69, 73, 77, 78, 83, 84, 86-90, 92-97, 99, 102, 109, 111, 118, 120-122, 125, 131-133, 147, 148, 151, 157-160, 163.* ***Glanzman*** *a-167.* ***Howard*** *a-95, 98, 99, 108, 117, 129, 131; c-98, 107, 120, 121, 161.* ***Larson*** *a-117, 119, 136, 159; c-136.* ***Morisi*** *a-83, 84, 86.* ***Newton*** *a-114; c-115(painted).* ***Palais*** *a-61.* ***Staton*** *a-161; c-117.* ***Sutton*** *a-106, 107, 111-114, 127, 130, 162; c-100, 106, 110, 113(painted).* ***Wood*** *a-107.*

GHOSTLY WEIRD STORIES (Formerly Blue Bolt Weird)
Star Publications: No. 120, Sept, 1953 - No. 124, Sept, 1954

120-Jo-Jo-r	40	80	120	242	401	560
121-124: 121-Jo-Jo-r. 122-The Mask-r/Capt. Flight #5; Rulah-r; has 1pg. story 'Death and the Devil Pills'-r/Western Outlaws #17. 123-Jo-Jo; Disbrow-a(2). 124-Torpedo Man	37	74	111	218	354	490

NOTE: ***Disbrow*** *a-120-124.* ***L. B. Cole*** *covers-all issues (#122 is a sci-fi cover).*

GHOST MANOR (Ghostly Haunts No. 20 on)
Charlton Comics: July, 1968 - No. 19, July, 1971

1	6	12	18	37	59	80
2-6: 6-Last 12¢ issue	3	6	9	20	30	40
7-12,17: 17-Morisi-a	3	6	9	17	25	32
13,14,16-Ditko-a	3	6	9	20	30	40
15,18,19-Ditko-c/a	4	8	12	24	37	50

GHOST MANOR (2nd Series)
Charlton Comics: Oct, 1971-No. 32, Dec, 1976; No. 33, Sept, 1977-No. 77, 11/84

1	5	10	15	30	48	65
2,3,5-7,9-Ditko-c	3	6	9	17	25	32
4,10-Ditko-c/a	3	6	9	20	30	40
8-Wood, Ditko-a; Sutton-c	3	6	9	19	29	38
11,14-Ditko-c/a	3	6	9	16	23	30
12,17,27,30	2	4	6	9	12	15
13,15,16,23-26,29: 13-Ditko-a. 15,16-Ditko-c. 23-Sutton-a. 24-26,29-Ditko-a. 26-Early Zeck-a; Boyette-c	2	4	6	11	16	20
18-(3/74) Newton 1st pro art; Ditko-a; Sutton-c	3	6	9	14	20	26
19-21: 19-Newton, Sutton-a; nudity panels. 20-Ditko-a. 21-E-Man, Blue Beetle, Capt. Atom cameos; Ditko-a.	2	4	6	11	16	20
22-Newton-c/a; Ditko-a	2	4	6	13	18	22
25,28,31,37,38-Ditko-c/a: 28-Nudity panels	2	4	6	13	18	22
32-36,39,41,45,48-50,53: 34-Black Cat by Kim	2	3	4	6	8	10

Ghost Rider #5 © ME

Ghost Rider #7 © MAR

Ghost Rider (2006 series) #14 © MAR

	GD 2.0	VG 4.0	FN 6.0	VF 8.0	VF/NM 9.0	NM- 9.2
40-Ditko-a; torture & drug use	2	4	6	11	16	20
42,43,46,47,51,52,60,62,69-Ditko-c/a	2	4	6	10	14	18
44,54,71-Ditko-a	2	4	6	8	11	14
55,56,58,59,61,63,65-68,70	1	2	3	5	6	8
57-Wood, Ditko, Howard-a	2	4	6	9	12	15
64-Ditko & Newton-a	2	4	6	8	11	14
71-76 (low print)	2	3	4	6	8	10
77-(11/84) Last issue Aparo-r/Space Adventures V3#60 (Paul Mann)	2	4	6	9	13	16
19 (Modern Comics reprint, 1977)						4.00

NOTE: ***Ditko** a-4, 8, 10, 11(2), 13, 14, 18, 20-22, 24-26, 28, 29, 31, 37r, 38r, 40r, 42-44r, 46r, 47, 51r, 52r, 54r, 57, 60, 62(4), 64r, 69, 71; c-2-7, 9-11, 14-16, 28, 31, 37, 38, 42, 43, 46, 47, 51, 52, 60, 62, 64. **Howard** a-4, 8, 12, 17, 19-21, 31, 41, 45, 57. **Newton** a-18-20, 22, 64; c-22. **Staton** a-13, 38, 44, 45. **Sutton** a-19, 23, 25, 45;c-8, 18.*

GHOST RIDER (See A-1 Comics, Best of the West, Black Phantom, Bobby Benson, Great Western, Red Mask & Tim Holt)
Magazine Enterprises: 1950 - No. 14, 1954

NOTE: *The character was inspired by Vaughn Monroe's "Ghost Riders in the Sky", and Disney's movie "The Headless Horseman".*

	GD	VG	FN	VF	VF/NM	NM-
1(A-1 #27)-Origin Ghost Rider	113	226	339	718	1234	1750
2-5: 2(A-1 #29), 3(A-1 #31), 4(A-1 #34), 5(A-1 #37)-All Frazetta-c only	73	146	219	467	796	1125
6,7: 6(A-1 #44)-Loco weed story, 7(A-1 #51)	33	66	99	194	317	440
8,9: 8(A-1 #57)-Drug use story, 9(A-1 #69)	28	56	84	165	270	375
10(A-1 #71)-Vs. Frankenstein	30	60	90	177	289	400
11-14: 11(A-1 #75). 12(A-1 #80)-Bondage-c; one-eyed Devil-c. 13(A-1 #84). 14(A-1 #112)	24	48	72	142	234	325

NOTE: ***Dick Ayers** art in all; c-1, 6-14.*

GHOST RIDER, THE (See Night Rider & Western Gunfighters)
Marvel Comics Group: Feb, 1967 - No. 7, Nov, 1967 (Western hero)(12¢)

	GD	VG	FN	VF	VF/NM	NM-
1-Origin & 1st app. Ghost Rider; Kid Colt-reprints begin	9	18	27	61	103	145
2	5	10	15	34	55	75
3-7: 6-Last Kid Colt-r; All Ayers-c/a(p)	5	10	15	30	48	65

GHOST RIDER (See The Champions, Marvel Spotlight #5, Marvel Team-Up #15, 58, Marvel Treasury Edition #18, Marvel Two-In-One #8, The Original Ghost Rider & The Original Ghost Rider Rides Again)
Marvel Comics Group: Sept, 1973 - No. 81, June, 1983 (Super-hero)

	GD	VG	FN	VF	VF/NM	NM-
1-Johnny Blaze, the Ghost Rider begins; 1st brief app. Daimon Hellstrom (Son of Satan)	15	30	45	107	204	300
2-1st full app. Daimon Hellstrom; gives glimpse of costume (1 panel); story continues in Marvel Spotlight #12	7	14	21	45	73	100
3-5: 3-Ghost Rider gains power to make cycle of fire; Son of Satan app.	5	10	15	30	48	65
6-10: 10-Hulk on cover; reprints origin/1st app. from Marvel Spotlight #5; Ploog-a	4	8	12	22	34	45
11-16: 11-Hulk app.	3	6	9	14	20	25
17,19-(Reg. 25¢ editions)(4,8/76)	3	6	9	14	20	25
17,19-(30¢-c variants, limited distribution)	4	8	12	28	44	60
18-(Reg. 25¢ edition)(6/76). Spider-Man-c & app.	3	6	9	16	22	28
18-(30¢-c variant, limited distribution)	5	10	15	32	51	70
20-Daredevil x-over; ties into D.D. #138; Byrne-a	3	6	9	18	27	35
21-30: 22-1st app. Enforcer. 29,30-Vs. Dr. Strange	2	4	6	9	12	15
24-26-(35¢-c variants, limited distribution)	4	8	12	26	41	55
31-34,36-49	2	3	4	6	8	10
35-Death Race classic; Starlin-c/a/sty	2	4	6	9	13	16
50-Double size	2	4	6	8	10	12
51-76: 68-Origin retold						6.00
77-80: 77-Origin retold. 80-Brief origin recap	1	2	3	5	6	8
81-Death of Ghost Rider (Demon leaves Blaze)	3	6	9	16	23	30
... Team Up TPB (2007, $15.99) r/#27, 50, Marvel Team-Up #91, Marvel Two-In-One #80, Avengers #214 and Marvel Premiere #28; Night Rider app.; cover gallery						16.00

NOTE: ***Anderson** c-64p. **Infantino** a(p)-43, 44, 51. **G. Kane** a-21p; c(p)-1, 2, 4, 5, 8, 9, 11-13, 19, 20, 24, 25. **Kirby** c-21-23. **Mooney** a-2-9p, 30i. **Nebres** c-26i. **Newton** a-23i. **Perez** c-26p. **Shores** a-2i. J. **Sparling** a-62p, 64p, 65p. **Starlin** a(p)-35. **Sutton** a-1p, 44i, 64i, 65i, 66, 67i. **Tuska** a-13p, 14p, 16p.*

GHOST RIDER (Volume 2) (Also see Doctor Strange/Ghost Rider Special, Marvel Comics Presents & Midnight Sons Unlimited)
Marvel Comics (Midnight Sons imprint #44 on): V2#1, May, 1990 - No. 93, Feb, 1998 ($1.50/$1.75/$1.95)

	GD	VG	FN	VF	VF/NM	NM-
1-($1.95, 52 pgs.)-Origin/1st app. new Ghost Rider; Kingpin app.						6.00
1-2nd printing (not gold)						2.50
2-5: 3-Kingpin app. 5-Punisher app.; Jim Lee-c						3.00
5-Gold background 2nd printing						2.50
6-14,16-24,29,30,32-39: 6-Punisher app. 6,17-Spider-Man/Hobgoblin-c/story. 9-X-Factor app. 10-Reintro Johnny Blaze on the last pg. 11-Stroman-c/a(p). 12,13-Dr. Strange x-over cont'd in D.S. #28. 13-Painted-c. 14-Johnny Blaze vs. Ghost Rider; origin recap 1st Ghost Rider (Blaze). 18-Painted-c by Nelson. 29-Wolverine-c/story. 32-Dr. Strange x-over; Johnny Blaze app. 34-Williamson-a(i). 36-Daredevil app. 37-Archangel app.						3.00
15-Glow in the dark-c						3.00
25-27: 25-($2.75)-Contains pop-up scene insert. 26,27-X-Men x-over; Lee/Williams-c on both						3.00
28,31-($2.50, 52 pgs.)-Polybagged w/poster; part 1 & part 6 of Rise of the Midnight Sons storyline (see Ghost Rider/Blaze #1)						3.00
40-Outer-c is Darkhold envelope made of black parchment w/gold ink; Midnight Massacre; Demogoblin app.						3.00
41-48: 41-Lilith & Centurious app.; begin $1.75-c. 41-43-Neon ink-c. 43-Has free extra 16 pg. insert on Siege of Darkness. 44,45-Siege of Darkness parts 2 & 10. 44-Spot varnish-c. 46-Intro new Ghost Rider. 48-Spider-Man app.						2.50
49,51-60,62-74: 49-Begin $1.95-c; bound-in trading card sheet; Hulk app. 55-Werewolf by Night app. 65-Punisher app. 67,68-Gambit app. 68-Wolverine app. 73,74-Blaze, Vengeance app.						2.50
50,61: 50-($2.50, 52 pgs.)-Regular edition						3.00
50-($2.95, 52 pgs.)-Collectors Ed. die cut foil-c						3.00
75-89: 76-Vs. Vengeance. 77,78-Dr. Strange-app. 78-New costume						2.50
90-92						6.00
93-($2.99)-Last issue; Saltares & Texeira-a	2	4	6	8	10	12
(#94, see Ghost Rider Finale for unpublished story)						
#(-1) Flashback (7/97) Saltares-a						2.50
Annual 1,2 ('93, '94, $2.95, 68 pgs.) 1-Bagged w/card						3.00
...And Cable 1 (9/92, $3.95, stiff-c, 68 pgs.)-Reprints Marvel Comics Presents #90-98 w/new Kieth-c						4.00
...:Crossroads (11/95, $3.95) Die cut cover; Nord-a						5.00
... Finale (2007, $3.99) r/#93 and the story meant for the unpublished #94; Saltares-a						4.00
Highway to Hell (2001, $3.50) Reprints origin from Marvel Spotlight #5						3.50
...: Resurrected TPB (2001, $12.95) r/#1-7						13.00

NOTE: ***Andy & Joe Kubert** c/a-28-31. **Quesada** c-21. **Williamson** a(i)-33-35; c-33i.*

GHOST RIDER (Volume 3)
Marvel Comics: Aug, 2001 - No. 6, Jan, 2002 ($2.99, limited series)

1-6-Grayson-s/Kaniuga-a/c 3.00
...: The Hammer Lane TPB (6/02, $15.95) r/#1-6 16.00

GHOST RIDER
Marvel Comics: Nov, 2005 - No. 6, Apr, 2006 ($2.99, limited series)

1-6-Garth Ennis-s/Clayton Crain-a/c. 1-Origin retold 3.00
1 (Director's Cut) (2005, $3.99) r/#1 with Ennis pitch and script and Crain art process 4.00
...: Road to Damnation HC (2006, $19.99, dust jacket) r/#1-6; variant covers & concept-a 20.00
...: Road to Damnation SC (2007, $14.99) r/#1-6; variant covers & concept-a 15.00

GHOST RIDER
Marvel Comics: Sept, 2006 - Present ($2.99)

1-11: 1-Daniel Way-s/Saltares & Texeira-a. 2-4-Dr. Strange app. 6,7-Corben-a 3.00
12-27,29-35: 12,13-World War Hulk; Saltares-a/Dell'Otto-c. 23-Danny Ketch returns 3.00
28-($3.99) Silvestri-c/Huat-a; back-up history of Danny Ketch 4.00
Annual 1 (1/08, $3.99) Ben Oliver-a/c/Stuart Moore-s 4.00
Annual 2 (10/08, $3.99) Spurrier-s/Robinson-a; r/Ghost Rider #35 (1979) 4.00
... Vol. 1: Vicious Cycle TPB (2007, $13.99) r/#1-5 14.00
... Vol. 2: The Life and Death of Johnny Blaze TPB (2007, $13.99) r/#6-11 14.00
... Vol. 3: Apocalypse Soon TPB (2008, $10.99) r/#12,13 & Annual #1 11.00
... Vol. 4: Revelations TPB (2008, $14.99) r/#14-19 15.00

GHOST RIDER/BALLISTIC
Marvel Comics: Feb, 1997 ($2.95, one-shot)

1-Devil's Reign pt. 3 3.00

GHOST RIDER/BLAZE: SPIRITS OF VENGEANCE (Also see Blaze)
Marvel Comics (Midnight Sons imprint #17 on): Aug, 1992 - No. 23, June, 1994 ($1.75)

1-($2.75, 52 pgs.)-Polybagged w/poster; part 2 of Rise of the Midnight Sons storyline; Adam Kubert-c/a begins 3.00
2-11,14-21: 4-Art Adams & Joe Kubert-p. 5,6-Spirits of Venom parts 2 & 4 cont'd from Web of Spider-Man #95,96 w/Demogoblin. 14-17-Neon ink-c. 15-Intro Blaze's new costume & power. 17,18-Siege of Darkness parts 8 & 13. 17-Spot varnish-c 2.50
12-($2.95)-Glow-in-the-dark-c 3.00
13-($2.25)-Outer-c is Darkhold envelope made of black parchment w/gold ink; Midnight Massacre x-over 3.00
22,23: 22-Begin $1.95-c; bound-in trading card sheet 2.50

NOTE: ***Adam & Joe Kubert** c-7, 8. **Adam Kubert/Steacy** c-6. **J. Kubert** a-13p(6 pgs.)*

GHOST RIDER/CAPTAIN AMERICA: FEAR
Marvel Comics: Oct, 1992 ($5.95, 52 pgs.)

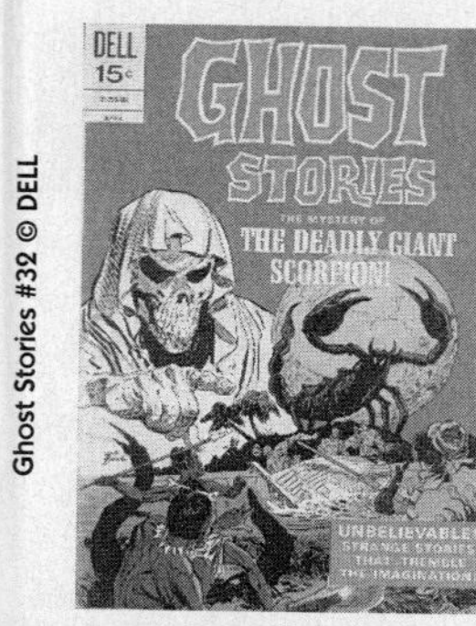

Ghost Stories #32 © DELL

Ghost Whisperer #1 © CBS Studios

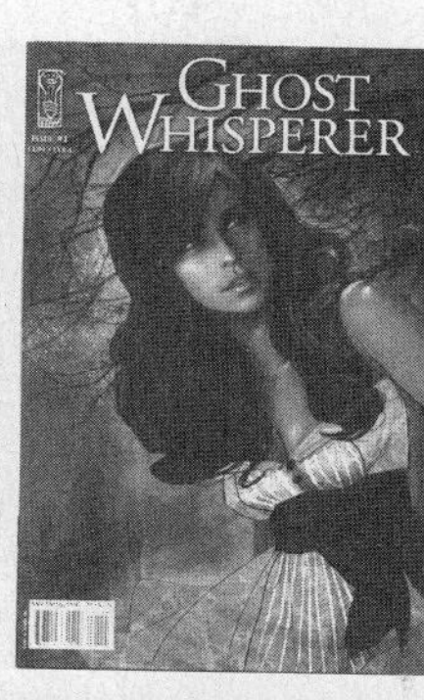

Giant Comics Edition #11 © STJ

	GD 2.0	VG 4.0	FN 6.0	VF 8.0	VF/NM 9.0	NM- 9.2
nn-Wraparound gatefold-c; Williamson inks						6.00

GHOST RIDER: DANNY KETCH
Marvel Comics: Dec, 2008 - No. 5, Apr, 2009 ($3.99, limited series)

	GD 2.0	VG 4.0	FN 6.0	VF 8.0	VF/NM 9.0	NM- 9.2
1-5-Saltares-a						4.00

GHOST RIDER: HEAVEN'S ON FIRE
Marvel Comics: Oct, 2009 - No. 6, Mar, 2010 ($3.99, limited series)

	GD 2.0	VG 4.0	FN 6.0	VF 8.0	VF/NM 9.0	NM- 9.2
1-6: 1-Jae Lee-c/Boschi-a/Aaron-s; Hellstorm app.; r/pages from Ghost Rider #1 ('73)						4.00

GHOST RIDER: TRAIL OF TEARS
Marvel Comics: Apr, 2007 - No. 6, Sept, 2007 ($2.99, limited series)

	GD 2.0	VG 4.0	FN 6.0	VF 8.0	VF/NM 9.0	NM- 9.2
1-6-Garth Ennis-s/Clayton Crain-a/c; Civil War era tale						3.00
HC (2007, $19.99) r/series						20.00
SC (2008, $14.99) r/series						15.00

GHOST RIDER 2099
Marvel Comics: May, 1994 - No. 25, May, 1996 ($1.50/$1.95)

	GD 2.0	VG 4.0	FN 6.0	VF 8.0	VF/NM 9.0	NM- 9.2
1 ($2.25)-Collector's Edition w/prismatic foil-c						3.00
1 ($1.50)-Regular Edition; bound-in trading card sheet						2.50
2-24: 7-Spider-Man 2099 app.						2.50
2-(Variant; polybagged with Sega Sub-Terrania poster)						5.00
25 ($2.95)						3.00

GHOST RIDER, WOLVERINE, PUNISHER: THE DARK DESIGN
Marvel Comics: Dec, 1994 ($5.95, one-shot)

	GD 2.0	VG 4.0	FN 6.0	VF 8.0	VF/NM 9.0	NM- 9.2
nn-Gatefold-c						6.00

GHOST RIDER; WOLVERINE; PUNISHER: HEARTS OF DARKNESS
Marvel Comics: Dec, 1991 ($4.95, one-shot, 52 pgs.)

	GD 2.0	VG 4.0	FN 6.0	VF 8.0	VF/NM 9.0	NM- 9.2
1-Double gatefold-c; John Romita, Jr.-c/a(p)						5.00

GHOSTS (Ghost No. 1)
National Periodical Publications/DC Comics: Sept-Oct, 1971 - No. 112, May, 1982 (No. 1-5: 52 pgs.)

	GD 2.0	VG 4.0	FN 6.0	VF 8.0	VF/NM 9.0	NM- 9.2
1-Aparo-a	13	26	39	93	172	250
2-Wood-a(i)	8	16	24	52	86	120
3-5-(52 pgs.)	7	14	21	45	73	100
6-10	3	6	9	20	40	60
11-20	3	6	9	14	20	25
21-39	2	4	6	9	13	16
40-(68 pgs.)	3	6	9	16	23	30
41-60	2	4	6	8	10	12
61-96	1	2	3	5	6	8
97-99-The Spectre vs. Dr. 13 by Aparo. 97,98-Spectre-c by Aparo.	2	4	6	10	14	18
100-Infinity-c	2	3	4	6	8	10
101-112	1	2	3	5	6	8

NOTE: *B. Baily a-77. Buckler c-99, 100. J. Craig a-108. Ditko a-77, 111. Giffen a-104p, 106p, 111p. Glanzman a-2. Golden a-88. Infantino a-8. Kaluta c-7, 93, 101. Kubert a-8; c-89, 105-108, 111. Mayer a-111. McWilliams a-99. Win Mortimer a-89, 91, 94. Nasser/Netzer a-97. Newton a-92p, 94p. Nino a-35, 37, 57. Orlando a-74i; c-80. Redondo a-8, 13, 45. Sparling a(p)-90, 93, 94. Spiegle a-103, 105. Tuska a-2i. Dr. 13, the Ghostbreaker back-ups in 95-99, 101.*

GHOSTS SPECIAL (See DC Special Series No. 7)

GHOST STORIES (See Amazing Ghost Stories)

GHOST STORIES
Dell Publ. Co.: Sept-Nov, 1962; No. 2, Apr-June, 1963 - No. 37, Oct, 1973

	GD 2.0	VG 4.0	FN 6.0	VF 8.0	VF/NM 9.0	NM- 9.2
12-295-211(#1)-Written by John Stanley	7	14	21	45	73	100
2	4	8	12	24	37	50
3-10: Two No. 6's exist with different c/a(12-295-406 & 12-295-503) #12-295-503 is actually #9 with indicia to #6	3	6	9	20	30	40
11-21: 21-Last 12¢ issue	3	6	9	16	23	30
22-37	2	4	6	13	18	22

NOTE: *#21-34, 36, 37 all reprint earlier issues.*

GHOST WHISPERER (Based on the CBS television series)
IDW Publishing: Mar, 2008 - No. 5, July, 2008 ($3.99)

	GD 2.0	VG 4.0	FN 6.0	VF 8.0	VF/NM 9.0	NM- 9.2
1-5: 1-Two covers by Casagrande & Ho; Casagrande-a						4.00

GHOST WHISPERER: THE MUSE
IDW Publishing: Dec, 2008 - No. 5 ($3.99)

	GD 2.0	VG 4.0	FN 6.0	VF 8.0	VF/NM 9.0	NM- 9.2
1-4-Two covers (photo & art) for each; Barbara Kesel-s/ Adriano Loyola-a						4.00

GHOUL, THE
IDW Publishing: Nov, 2009 - Present ($3.99)

	GD 2.0	VG 4.0	FN 6.0	VF 8.0	VF/NM 9.0	NM- 9.2
1,2-Niles-s/Wrightson-a						4.00

GHOUL TALES (Magazine)
Stanley Publications: Nov, 1970 - No. 5, July, 1971 (52 pgs.) (B&W)

	GD 2.0	VG 4.0	FN 6.0	VF 8.0	VF/NM 9.0	NM- 9.2
1-Aragon pre-code reprints; Mr. Mystery as host; bondage-c	8	16	24	52	86	120
2,3: 2-(1/71)Reprint/Climax #1. 3-(3/71)	4	8	12	28	44	60
4-(5/71)Reprints story "The Way to a Man's Heart" used in **SOTI**	5	10	15	32	51	70
5-ACG reprints	4	8	12	22	34	45

NOTE: *No. 1-4 contain pre-code Aragon reprints.*

GIANT BOY BOOK OF COMICS (Also see Boy Comics)
Newsbook Publications (Gleason): 1945 (240 pgs., hard-c)

	GD 2.0	VG 4.0	FN 6.0	VF 8.0	VF/NM 9.0	NM- 9.2
1-Crimebuster & Young Robin Hood; Biro-c	94	188	282	597	1024	1450

GIANT COMIC ALBUM
King Features Syndicate: 1972 (59¢, 11x14", 52 pgs., B&W, cardboard-c)

	GD 2.0	VG 4.0	FN 6.0	VF 8.0	VF/NM 9.0	NM- 9.2
Newspaper reprints: Barney Google, Little Iodine, Katzenjammer Kids, Henry, Beetle Bailey, Blondie, & Snuffy Smith each...	3	6	9	20	30	40
Flash Gordon ('68-69 Dan Barry)	4	8	12	26	41	55
Mandrake the Magician ('59 Falk), Popeye	4	8	12	24	37	50

GIANT COMICS
Charlton Comics: Summer, 1957 - No. 3, Winter, 1957 (25¢, 100 pgs.)

	GD 2.0	VG 4.0	FN 6.0	VF 8.0	VF/NM 9.0	NM- 9.2
1-Atomic Mouse, Hoppy app.	21	42	63	122	199	275
2,3: 2-Romance. 3-Christmas Book; Atomic Mouse, Atomic Rabbit, Li'l Genius, Li'l Tomboy & Atom the Cat stories	15	30	45	88	137	185

NOTE: *The above may be rebound comics; contents could vary.*

GIANT COMICS (See Wham-O Giant Comics)

GIANT COMICS EDITION (See Terry-Toons) (Also see Fox Giants)
St. John Publishing Co.: 1947 - No. 17, 1950 (25¢, 100-164 pgs.)

	GD 2.0	VG 4.0	FN 6.0	VF 8.0	VF/NM 9.0	NM- 9.2
1-Mighty Mouse	50	100	150	315	533	750
2-Abbie & Slats	27	54	81	158	259	360
3-Terry-Toons Album; 100 pgs.	40	80	120	243	402	560
4-Crime comics; contains Red Seal No. 16, used & illo. in **SOTI**	55	110	165	352	601	850
5-Police Case Book (4/49, 132 pgs.)-Contents varies; contains remaindered St. John books - some volumes contain 5 copies rather than 4, with 160 pages; Matt Baker-c	55	110	165	352	601	850
5A-Terry-Toons Album (132 pgs.)-Mighty Mouse, Heckle & Jeckle, Gandy Goose & Dinky stories	37	74	111	218	354	490
6-Western Picture Stories; Baker-c/a(3); Tuska-a; The Sky Chief, Blue Monk, Ventrilo app., 132 pgs.	52	104	156	328	552	775
7-Contains a teen-age romance plus 3 Mopsy comics	34	68	102	199	325	450
8-The Adventures of Mighty Mouse (10/49)	37	74	111	218	354	490
9-Romance and Confession Stories; Kubert-a(4); Baker-a; photo-c (132 pgs.)	81	162	243	518	884	1250
10-Terry-Toons Album (132 pgs.)-Mighty Mouse, Heckle & Jeckle, Gandy Goose stories	37	74	111	218	354	490
11-Western Picture Stories-Baker-c/a(4); The Sky Chief, Desperado, & Blue Monk app.; another version with Son of Sinbad by Kubert (132 pgs.)	52	104	156	328	552	775
12-Diary Secrets; Baker prostitute-c; 4 St. John romance comics; Baker-a	258	516	774	1651	2826	4000
13-Romances; Baker, Kubert-a	65	130	195	416	708	1000
14-Mighty Mouse Album (132 pgs.)	36	72	108	211	343	475
15-Romances (4 love comics)-Baker-c	71	142	213	454	777	1100
16-Little Audrey; Abbott & Costello, Casper	39	78	117	240	395	550
17(nn)-Mighty Mouse Album (nn, no date, but did follow No. 16); 100 pgs. on cover but has 148 pgs.	36	72	108	211	343	475

NOTE: *The above books contain remaindered comics and contents could vary with each issue. No. 11, 12 have part photo magazine insides.*

GIANT COMICS EDITIONS
United Features Syndicate: 1940's (132 pgs.)

	GD 2.0	VG 4.0	FN 6.0	VF 8.0	VF/NM 9.0	NM- 9.2
1-Abbie & Slats, Abbott & Costello, Jim Hardy, Ella Cinders, Iron Vic, Gordo, & Bill Bumlin	39	78	117	236	388	540
2-Jim Hardy, Ella Cinders, Elmo & Gordo	27	54	81	158	259	360

NOTE: *Above books contain rebound copies; contents can vary.*

GIANT GRAB BAG OF COMICS (See Archie All-Star Specials under Archie Comics)

GIANTKILLER
DC Comics: Aug, 1999 - No. 6, Jan, 2000 ($2.50, limited series)

	GD 2.0	VG 4.0	FN 6.0	VF 8.0	VF/NM 9.0	NM- 9.2
1-6-Story and painted art by Dan Brereton						2.50
...A to Z: A Field Guide to Big Monsters (8/99)						2.50
...Vol. 1 TPB (Image Comics, 2006, $14.99) r/#1-6 & A-Z; gallery of concept art						15.00

Giant-Size Captain Marvel #1 © MAR

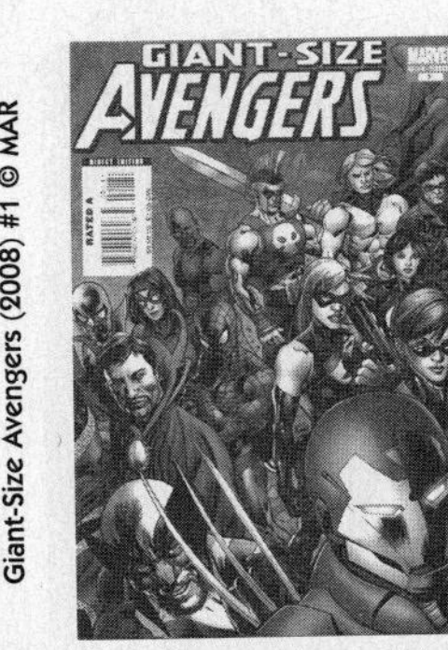

Giant-Size Avengers (2008) #1 © MAR

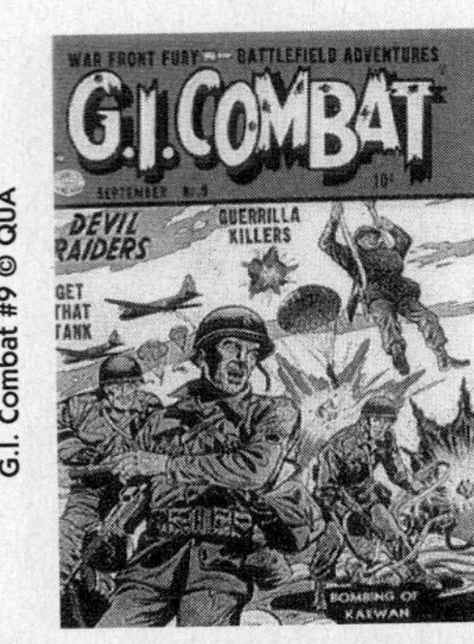

G.I. Combat #9 © QUA

GD VG FN VF VF/NM NM-
2.0 4.0 6.0 8.0 9.0 9.2

GIANTS (See Thrilling True Story of the Baseball...)

GIANT-SIZE...

Marvel Comics Group: May, 1974 - Dec, 1975 (35/50¢, 52/68 pgs.)
(Some titles quarterly) (Scarce in strict NM or better due to defective cutting, gluing and binding; warping, splitting and off-center pages are common)

Avengers 1(8/74)-New-a plus G.A. H. Torch-r; 1st modern app. The Whizzer; 1st & only modern app. Miss America; 2nd app. Invaders; Kang, Rama-Tut, Mantis app. 6 12 18 41 66 90

Avengers 2,3,5: 2(11/74)-Death of the Swordsman; origin of Rama-Tut. 3(2/75). 5(12/75)-Reprints Avengers Special #1 4 8 12 24 37 50

Avengers 4 (6/75)-Vision marries Scarlet Witch. 5 10 15 30 48 65

Captain America 1(12/75)-r/stories T.O.S. 59-63 by Kirby (#63 reprints origin) 4 8 12 26 41 55

Captain Marvel 1(12/75)-r/Capt. Marvel #17, 20, 21 by Gil Kane (p) 4 8 12 22 34 45

Chillers 1(6/74, 52 pgs)-Curse of Dracula; origin/1st app. Lilith, Dracula's daughter; Heath-r, Colan-c/a(p); becomes Giant-Size Dracula #2 on 6 12 18 39 62 85

Chillers 1(2/75, 50¢, 68 pgs.)-Alcala-a 4 8 12 22 34 45

Chillers 2(5/75)-All-r; Everett-r from Advs. into Weird Worlds 3 6 9 18 27 35

Chillers 3(8/75)-Wrightson-c(new)/a(r); Colan, Kirby, Smith-r 4 8 12 22 34 45

Conan 1(9/74)-B. Smith-r/#3; start adaptation of Howard's "Hour of the Dragon" (ends #4); 1st app. Belit; new-a begins 4 8 12 22 34 45

Conan 2(12/74)-B. Smith-r/#5; Sutton-a(i)(#1 also); Buscema-c 3 6 9 18 27 35

Conan 3-5: 3(4/75)-B. Smith-r/#6; Sutton-a(i). 4(6/75)-B. Smith-r/#7. 5(1975)-B. Smith-r/#14,15; Kirby-c 3 6 9 16 23 30

Creatures 1(5/74, 52 pgs.)-Werewolf app; 1st app. Tigra (formerly Cat); Crandall-r; becomes Giant-Size Werewolf w/#2 4 8 12 28 44 60

Daredevil 1(1975)-Reprints Daredevil Annual #1 3 6 9 20 30 40

Defenders 1(7/74)-Silver Surfer app.; Starlin-a; Ditko, Everett & Kirby reprints 5 10 15 30 48 65

Defenders 2(10/74, 68 pgs.)-New G. Kane-c/a(p); Son of Satan app.; Sub-Mariner-r by Everett; Ditko-r/Strange Tales #119 (Dr. Strange); Maneely-r 4 8 12 22 34 45

Defenders 3-5: 3(1/75)-1st app. Korvac.; Newton, Starlin-a; Ditko, Everett-r. 4(4/75)-Ditko, Everett-r; G. Kane-c. 5-(7/75)-Guardians app. 3 6 9 20 30 40

Doc Savage 1(1975, 68 pgs.)-r/#1,2; Mooney-r 3 6 9 16 23 30

Doctor Strange 1(11/75)-Reprints stories from Strange Tales #164-168; Lawrence, Tuska-r 3 6 9 18 27 35

Dracula 2(9/74, 50¢)-Formerly Giant-Size Chillers 4 8 12 22 34 45

Dracula 3(12/74)-Fox-r/Uncanny Tales #6 3 6 9 20 30 40

Dracula 4(3/75)-Ditko-r(2) 3 6 9 20 30 40

Dracula 5(6/75)-1st Byrne art at Marvel 5 10 15 34 55 75

Fantastic Four 2-4: 2(8/74)-Formerly Giant-Size Super-Stars; Ditko-r. 2,4-Buscema-a. 3(11/74)-Buckler-a. 4(2/75)-1st Madrox. 4 8 12 24 37 50

Fantastic Four 5,6: 5(5/75)-All-r; Kirby, G. Kane-r. 6(10/75)-All-r; Kirby-r 3 6 9 20 30 40

Hulk 1(1975) r/Hulk Special #1 4 8 12 22 34 45

Invaders 1(6/75, 50¢, 68 pgs.)-Origin; G.A. Sub-Mariner-r/Sub-Mariner #1; intro Master Man 4 8 12 26 41 55

Iron Man 1(1975)-Ditko reprint 4 8 12 22 34 45

Kid Colt 1-3: 1(1/75). 2(4/75). 3(7/75)-new Ayers-a 8 16 24 52 86 120

Man-Thing 1(8/74)-New Ploog-c/a (25 pgs.); Ditko-r/Amazing Adv. #11; Kirby-r/Strange Tales Ann. #2 & T.O.S. #15; (#1-5 all have new Man-Thing stories, pre-hero-r & are 68 pgs.) 4 8 12 26 41 55

Man-Thing 2,3: 2(11/74)-Buscema-c/a(p); Kirby, Powell-r. 3(2/75)-Alcala-a; Ditko, Kirby, Sutton-r; Gil Kane-c 3 6 9 20 30 40

Man-Thing 4,5: 4(5/75)-Howard the Duck by Brunner-c/a; Ditko-r. 5(8/75)-Howard the Duck by Brunner (p); Dracula cameo in Howard the Duck; Buscema-a(p); Sutton-a(i); G. Kane-c 4 8 12 26 41 55

Marvel Triple Action 1,2: 1(5/75). 2(7/75) 3 6 9 16 23 30

Master of Kung Fu 1(9/74)-Russell-a; Yellow Claw-r in #1-4; Gulacy-a in #1,2 4 8 12 24 37 50

Master of Kung Fu 2-4: 2-(12/74)-r/Yellow Claw #1. 3(3/75)-Gulacy-a; Kirby-a. 4(6/75)-Kirby-a 3 6 9 20 30 40

Power Man 1(1975) 3 6 9 18 27 35

Spider-Man 1(7/74)-Spider-Man /Human Torch-r by Kirby/Ditko; Byrne-r plus new-a (Dracula-c/story) 7 14 21 45 73 100

Spider-Man 2,3: 2(10/74)-Shang-Chi-c/app. 3(1/75)-Doc Savage-c/app.; Daredevil/Spider-Man-r w/Ditko-a 4 8 12 28 44 60

Spider-Man 4(4/75)-3rd Punisher app.; Byrne, Ditko-r 11 22 33 78 139 200

GD VG FN VF VF/NM NM-
2.0 4.0 6.0 8.0 9.0 9.2

Spider-Man 5,6: 5(7/75)-Man-Thing/Lizard-c. 6(9/75) 4 8 12 24 37 50

Super-Heroes Featuring Spider-Man 1(6/74, 35¢, 52 pgs.)-Spider-Man vs. Man-Wolf; Morbius, the Living Vampire app.; Ditko-r; G. Kane-a(p); Spidey villains app. 6 12 18 43 69 95

Super-Stars 1(5/74, 35¢, 52 pgs.)-Fantastic Four; Thing vs. Hulk; Kirbyish-c/a by Buckler/Sinnott; F.F. villains profiled; becomes Giant-Size Fantastic Four #2 on 6 12 18 39 62 85

Super-Villain Team-Up 1(3/75, 68 pgs.)-Craig-r(i) (Also see Fantastic Four #6 for 1st super-villain team-up) 3 6 9 21 32 42

Super-Villain Team-Up 2(6/75, 68 pgs.)-Dr. Doom, Sub-Mariner app.; Spider-Man-r from Amazing Spider-Man #8 by Ditko; Sekowsky-a(p) 3 6 9 18 27 35

Thor 1(7/75) 4 8 12 24 37 50

Werewolf 2(10/74, 68 pgs.)-Formerly Giant-Size Creatures; Ditko-r; Frankenstein app. 3 6 9 20 30 40

Werewolf 3,5: 3(1/75, 68 pgs.). 5(7/75, 68 pgs.) 3 6 9 20 30 40

Werewolf 4(4/75, 68 pgs.)-Morbius the Living Vampire app. 4 8 12 22 34 45

X-Men 1(Summer, 1975, 50¢, 68 pgs.)-1st app. new X-Men; intro. Nightcrawler, Storm, Colossus & Thunderbird; 2nd full app. Wolverine after Incredible Hulk #181 52 104 156 442 871 1300

X-Men 2 (11/75)-N. Adams-r (51 pgs) 9 18 27 61 103 145

Giant Size Marvel TPB (2005, $24.99) reprints stories from Giant-Size Avengers #1, G-S Fantastic Four #4, G-S Defenders #4, G-S Super-Heroes #1, G-S Invaders #1, G-S X-Men #1 and Giant-Size Creatures #1 25.00

GIANT-SIZE...

Marvel Comics: 2005 - Present ($4.99/$3.99)

Astonishing X-Men 1 (7/08, $4.99) Concludes story from Astonishing X-Men #24; Whedon-s/Cassaday-a/wraparound-c; Spider-Man, FF, Dr. Strange app.; variant cover gallery 5.00
Astonishing X-Men 1 (7/08, $4.99) Variant B&W cover 5.00
Avengers 1 (2/08, $4.99) new short stories and r/Avengers #58, 201; Hitch-c 5.00
Avengers/Invaders 1 ('08, $3.99) r/Avengers #71; Invaders #10, Ann. 1 & G-S #2 4.00
Hulk 1 (8/06, $4.99)-2 new stories; Planet Hulk (David-s/Santacruz-a) & Hulk vs. The Champions (Pak-s/Lopresti-a); r/Incredible Hulk: The End) 5.00
Incredible Hulk 1 (7/08, $3.99)-1 new story; r/Incredible Hulk Annual #7; Frank-c 4.00
Invaders 2 ('05, $4.99)-new Thomas-s/Weeks-a; r/Invaders #1&2 & All-Winners #1&2 5.00
Marvel Adventures The Avengers (9/07, $3.99) Agents of Atlas and Kang app.; Kirk-a: reprint of 1st Namora app. from Marvel Mystery Comics #82; reprint from Venus #1 4.00
Spider-Woman ('05, $4.99)-new Bendis-s/Mays-a; r/Marvel Spotlight #32 & S-W #1,37,38 5.00
Wolverine (12/06, $4.99)-new Lapham-s/Aja-a; r/X-Men #6,7 5.00
X-Men 3 ('05, $4.99)-new Whedon-s/N. Adams-a; r/team-ups; Cockrum & Cassaday-c 5.00

GIANT SPECTACULAR COMICS (See Archie All-Star Special under Archie Comics)

GIANT SUMMER FUN BOOK (See Terry-Toons...)

G. I. COMBAT

Quality Comics Group: Oct, 1952 - No. 43, Dec, 1956

1-Crandall-c; Cuidera a-1-43i 81 162 243 518 884 1250
2 39 78 117 240 395 550
3-5,10-Crandall-c/a 36 72 108 211 343 475
6-Crandall-a 31 62 93 186 303 420
7-9 27 54 81 162 266 370
11-20 21 42 63 122 199 275
21-31,33,35-43: 41-1st S.A. issue 20 40 60 114 182 250
32-Nuclear attack-c/story "Atomic Rocket Assault" 21 42 63 126 206 285
34-Crandall-a 20 40 60 118 192 265

G. I. COMBAT (See DC Special Series #22)

National Periodical Publ./DC Comics: No. 44, Jan, 1957 - No. 288, Mar, 1987

44-Grey tone-c 64 128 192 544 1072 1600
45 32 64 96 245 473 700
46-50 27 54 81 197 386 575
51-Grey tone-c 36 72 108 280 540 800
52-54,59,60 25 50 75 183 354 525
55-Minor Sgt. Rock prototype by Finger 26 52 78 190 370 550
56-Sgt. Rock prototype by Kanigher/Kubert 30 60 90 228 439 650
57,58-Pre-Sgt. Rock Easy Co. stories 30 60 90 218 422 625
61-65,70-73 18 36 54 129 252 375
66-Pre-Sgt. Rock Easy Co. story 27 54 81 197 386 575
67-1st Tank Killer 34 68 102 262 506 750
68-(1/59) Introduces "The Rock", Sgt. Rock prototype by Kanigher/Kubert; once considered his actual 1st app. (see Our Army at War #82,83) 92 184 276 782 1541 2300
69-Grey tone-c 31 62 93 236 456 675
74-American flag-c 19 38 57 139 270 400
75-80: 75-Grey tone-c begin, end #109 29 58 87 212 406 600
81,82,84-86 24 48 72 175 338 500

G.I. Combat #246 © DC

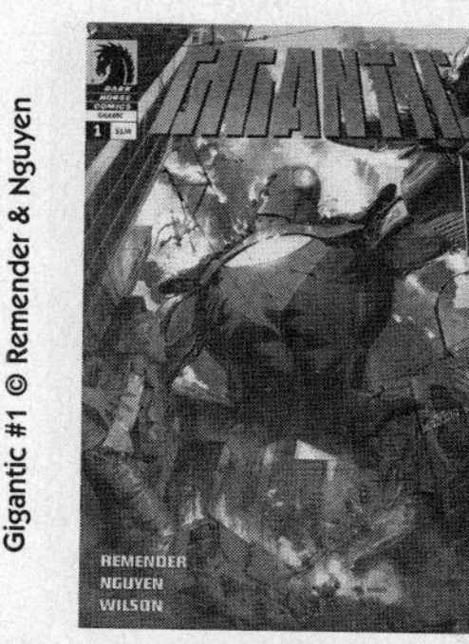

Gigantic #1 © Remender & Nguyen

G.I. Joe V2 #36 © Hasbro

	GD 2.0	VG 4.0	FN 6.0	VF 8.0	VF/NM 9.0	NM- 9.2
83-1st Big Al, Little Al, & Charlie Cigar; grey tone-c	30	60	90	228	439	650
87-(4-5/61) 1st Haunted Tank; series begins; classic Heath washtone-c	100	200	300	850	1675	2500
88-(6-7/61) 2nd Haunted Tank	36	72	108	280	540	800
89,90: 90-Last 10¢ issue	25	50	75	183	354	525
91-(12/61-1/62)1st Haunted Tank-c	43	86	129	344	672	1000
92-95,99-Grey tone-c	22	44	66	157	304	450
96-98	17	34	51	122	236	350
100,108: 100-(6-7/63). 108-1st Sgt. Rock x-over	19	38	57	139	270	400
101-103,105-107	15	30	45	107	204	300
104,109-Grey tone-c	17	34	51	122	236	350
110-112,115-118,120	12	24	36	85	155	225
113-Grey tone-c	15	30	45	107	204	300
114-Origin Haunted Tank	29	58	87	212	406	600
119-Grey tone-c	14	28	42	100	188	275
121-136: 121-1st app. Sgt. Rock's father. 125-Sgt. Rock app. 136-Last 12¢ issue	8	16	24	58	97	135
137,139,140	5	10	15	34	55	75
138-Intro. The Losers (Capt. Storm, Gunner/Sarge, Johnny Cloud) in Haunted Tank (10-11/69)	11	22	33	78	139	200
141-143	4	8	12	22	34	45
144-148 (68 pgs.)	4	8	12	28	44	60
149,151-154 (52 pgs.): 151-Capt. Storm story. 151,153-Medal of Honor series by Maurer	4	8	12	22	34	45
150- (52 pgs.) Ice Cream Soldier story (tells how he got his name); Death of Haunted Tank-c/s	4	8	12	28	44	60
155-167,169,170	2	4	6	13	18	22
168-Neal Adams-c	3	6	9	17	25	32
171-192,194-199: 195-Haunted Tank & War That Time Forgot	2	4	6	10	14	18
193-(10/76) Haunted Tank meets War That Time Forgot; Dinosaur-c/s; Kubert-a	2	4	6	13	18	22
200-(3/77) Haunted Tank-c/s; Sgt. Rock and the Losers app.; Kubert-c	3	6	9	14	20	26
201,202 ($1.00 size) Neal Adams-c	3	6	9	14	20	26
203-210 ($1.00 size)	2	4	6	13	18	22
211-230 ($1.00 size)	2	4	6	10	14	18
231-259 ($1.00 size).232-Origin Kana the Ninja. 244-Death of Slim Stryker; 1st app. The Mercenaries. 246-(76 pgs., $1.50)-30th Anniversary issue. 257-Intro. Stuart's Raiders	2	4	6	8	11	14
260-281: 260-Begin $1.25, 52 pg. issues, end #281. 264-Intro Sgt. Bullet; origin Kana. 269-Intro. The Bravos of Vietnam. 274-Cameo of Monitor from Crisis on Infinite Earths	2	3	4	6	8	10
282-288 (75¢): 282-New advs. begin	1	2	3	5	6	8

NOTE: ***N. Adams** c-168, 201, 202. **Check** a-168, 173. **Drucker** a-48, 61, 63, 66, 71, 72, 76, 134, 140, 141, 144, 147, 148, 153. **Evans** a-135, 138, 158, 164, 166, 201, 202, 204, 205, 215, 256. Giffen a-267. **Glanzman** a-most issues. **Kubert/Heath** a-most issues; **Kubert** covers most issues. **Morrow** a-159-161(2 pgs.). **Redondo** a-189, 240i, 243i. **Sekowsky** a-162p. **Severin** a-147, 152, 154. **Simonson** c-169. **Thorne** a-152, 156. **Wildey** a-153. Johnny Cloud app.-112, 115, 120. Mlle. Marie app.-123, 132, 200. Sgt. Rock app.-111-113, 115, 120, 125, 141, 146, 147, 149, 200. USS Stevens by **Glanzman**-145, 150-153, 157. **Grandenetti** c-44-48.*

GIDGET (TV)
Dell Publishing Co.: Apr, 1966 - No. 2, Dec, 1966

	GD 2.0	VG 4.0	FN 6.0	VF 8.0	VF/NM 9.0	NM- 9.2
1-Sally Field photo-c	9	18	27	60	100	140
2	6	12	18	43	69	95

GIFT COMICS
Fawcett Publications: 1942 - No. 4, 1949 (50¢/25¢, 324 pgs./152 pgs.)

	GD 2.0	VG 4.0	FN 6.0	VF 8.0	VF/NM 9.0	NM- 9.2
1-Captain Marvel, Bulletman, Golden Arrow, Ibis the Invincible, Mr. Scarlet, & Spy Smasher begin; not rebound, remaindered comics, printed at same time as originals; 50¢-c & 324 pgs. begin, end #3.	284	568	852	1818	3109	4400
2-Commando Yank, Phantom Eagle, others app.	168	336	504	1075	1838	2600
3-(50¢, 324 pgs.)	115	230	345	730	1253	1775
4-(25¢, 152 pgs.)-The Marvel Family, Captain Marvel, etc.; each issue can vary in contents	70	140	210	451	768	1085

GIFTS FROM SANTA (See March of Comics No. 137)

GIFTS OF THE NIGHT
DC Comics (Vertigo): Feb, 1999 - No. 4, May, 1999 ($2.95, limited series)

	GD 2.0	VG 4.0	FN 6.0	VF 8.0	VF/NM 9.0	NM- 9.2
1-4-Bolton-c/a; Chadwick-s						3.00

GIGANTIC
Dark Horse Comics: Nov, 2008 - No. 5, Jan, 2010 ($3.50, limited series)

	GD 2.0	VG 4.0	FN 6.0	VF 8.0	VF/NM 9.0	NM- 9.2
1-5-Remender-s/Nguyen-a; Earth as a reality show						3.50

GIGGLE COMICS (Spencer Spook No. 100) (Also see Ha Ha Comics)
Creston No.1-63/American Comics Group No. 64 on; Oct, 1943 - No. 99, Jan-Feb, 1955

	GD 2.0	VG 4.0	FN 6.0	VF 8.0	VF/NM 9.0	NM- 9.2
1-Funny animal	34	68	102	204	332	460
2	18	36	54	103	162	220
3-5: Ken Hultgren-a begins?	14	28	42	80	115	150
6-10: 9-1st Superkatt (6/44)	11	22	33	64	90	115
11-20	10	20	30	56	76	95
21-40: 32-Patriotic-c. 37,61-X-Mas-c	9	18	27	50	65	80
41-54,56-59,61-99: Spencer Spook app. in many	8	16	24	44	57	70
55,60-Milt Gross-a	10	20	30	56	76	95

G-I IN BATTLE (G-I No. 1 only)
Ajax-Farrell Publ./Four Star: Aug, 1952 - No. 9, July, 1953; Mar, 1957 - No. 6, May, 1958

	GD 2.0	VG 4.0	FN 6.0	VF 8.0	VF/NM 9.0	NM- 9.2
1	13	26	39	72	101	130
2	8	16	24	42	54	65
3-9	7	14	21	37	46	55
Annual 1(1952, 25¢, 100 pgs.)	25	50	75	147	241	335
1(1957-Ajax)	8	16	24	42	54	65
2-6	6	12	18	28	34	40

G. I. JANE
Stanhall/Merit No. 11: May, 1953 - No. 11, Mar, 1955 (Misdated 3/54)

	GD 2.0	VG 4.0	FN 6.0	VF 8.0	VF/NM 9.0	NM- 9.2
1-PX Pete begins; Bill Williams-c/a	14	28	42	82	121	160
2-7(5/54)	9	18	27	50	65	80
8-10(12/54, Stanhall)	8	16	24	44	57	70
11 (3/55, Merit)	8	16	24	42	54	65

G. I. JOE (Also see Advs. of..., Showcase #53, 54 & The Yardbirds)
Ziff-Davis Publ. Co. (Korean War): No. 10, 1950; No. 11, 4-5/51 - No. 51, 6/57(52pgs.: 10-14,6-17?)

	GD 2.0	VG 4.0	FN 6.0	VF 8.0	VF/NM 9.0	NM- 9.2
10(#1, 1950)-Saunders painted-c begin	17	34	51	98	154	210
11-14(#2-5, 10/51): 11-New logo. 12-New logo	12	24	36	67	94	120
V2#6(12/51)-17-(11/52; Last 52 pgs.?)	10	20	30	58	79	100
18-(25¢, 100 pg. Giant, 12-1/52-53)	25	50	75	147	241	335
19-30: 20-22,24,28-31-The Yardbirds app.	9	18	27	52	69	85
31-47,49-51	9	18	27	50	65	80
48-Atom bomb story	9	18	27	52	69	85

NOTE: ***Powell** a-V2#7, 8, 11. **Norman Saunders** painted c-10-14, V2#6-14, 26, 30, 31, 35, 38, 39. **Tuska** a-7. Bondage c-29, 35, 38.*

G. I. JOE (America's Movable Fighting Man)
Custom Comics: 1967 (5-1/8x8-3/8", 36 pgs.)

	GD 2.0	VG 4.0	FN 6.0	VF 8.0	VF/NM 9.0	NM- 9.2
nn-Schaffenberger-a; based on Hasbro toy	4	8	12	22	34	45

G.I. JOE
Dark Horse Comics: Dec, 1995 - No. 4, Apr, 1996 ($1.95, limited series)

	GD 2.0	VG 4.0	FN 6.0	VF 8.0	VF/NM 9.0	NM- 9.2
1-4: Mike W. Barr scripts. 1-Three Frank Miller covers with title logos in red, white and blue. 2-Breyfogle-c. 3-Simonson-c						3.00

G.I. JOE
Dark Horse Comics: V2#1, June, 1996 - V2#4, Sept, 1996 ($2.50)

	GD 2.0	VG 4.0	FN 6.0	VF 8.0	VF/NM 9.0	NM- 9.2
V2#1-4: Mike W. Barr scripts. 4-Painted-c						3.00

G.I. JOE
Image Comics/Devil's Due Publishing: 2001 - No. 43, May, 2005 ($2.95)

	GD 2.0	VG 4.0	FN 6.0	VF 8.0	VF/NM 9.0	NM- 9.2
1-Campbell-c; back-c painted by Beck; Blaylock-s	2	4	6	8	10	12
1-2nd printing with front & back covers switched						6.00
2,3						5.00
4-($3.50)						4.00
5-20,22-41: 6-SuperPatriot preview. 18-Brereton-c. 31-33-Wraith back-up; Caldwell-a						3.00
21-Silent issue; Zeck-a; two covers by Campbell and Zeck						3.00
42,43-($4.50)-Dawn of the Red Shadows; leads into G.I. Joe Vol. 2						4.50
...:Cobra Reborn (1/04, $4.95) Bradstreet-c/Jenkins-s						5.00
...:G.I. Joe Reborn (2/04, $4.95) Bradstreet-c/Bennett & Saltares-a						5.00
...: Malfunction (2003, $15.95) r/#11-15						16.00
... M. I. A. (2002, $4.95) r/#1&2; Beck back-c from #1 on cover						5.00
...: Players & Pawns (11/04, $12.95) r/#28-33; cover gallery						13.00
...: Reborn (2004, $9.95) r/Cobra Reborn & G.I. Joe Reborn						10.00
...: Reckonings (2002, $12.95) r/#6-9; Zeck-c						13.00
...: Reinstated (2002, $14.95) r/#1-4						15.00
...: The Return of Serpentor (9/04, $12.95) r/#16,22-25; cover gallery						13.00
...Vol. 8: The Rise of the Red Shadows (1/06, $14.95) r/#42,43 & prologue pgs. from #37-41						15.00

G.I. JOE (Volume 2) (Also see Snake Eyes: Declassified)
Devil's Due Publishing: No. 0, June, 2005 - No. 36, June, 2008 (25¢/$2.95/$3.50/$4.50)

	GD 2.0	VG 4.0	FN 6.0	VF 8.0	VF/NM 9.0	NM- 9.2
0-(25¢-c) Casey-s/Caselli-a						2.50
1-4,7-19 ($2.95): 1-Four covers; Casey-s/Caselli-a. 4-R. Black-c						3.00
5,6-($4.50) 6-Wraparound-c						4.50
20-29,31-35-($3.50) 25-Wraparound-c World War III part 1						3.50

G.I. Joe, A Real American Hero #94 © Hasbro

G.I. Joe: Frontline #1 © Hasbro

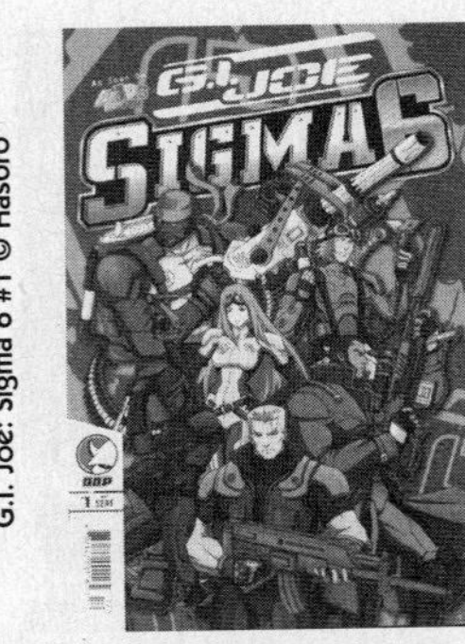

G.I. Joe: Sigma 6 #1 © Hasbro

GD VG FN VF VF/NM NM-
2.0 4.0 6.0 8.0 9.0 9.2

30,36-($5.50) 30-Double-sized World War III part 6. 36-Double-sized WW III part 12 5.50
...America's Elite Vol. 1: The Newest War TPB ('06, $14.95) r/#0-5; cover gallery 15.00
...America's Elite Vol. 2: The Ties That Bind TPB (8/06, $15.95) r/#6-12; cover gallery 16.00
...America's Elite Vol. 3: In Sheep's Clothing TPB (2007, $18.99) r/#13-18; cover gallery 19.00
...America's Elite Vol. 4: Truth and Consequences TPB (9/07, $18.99) r/#19-24; covers 19.00
... Data Desk Handbook (10/05, $2.95) character profile pages 3.00
... Data Desk Handbook A-M (10/07, $5.50) character profile pages 5.50
... Data Desk Handbook N-Z (11/07, $3.50) character profile pages 3.50
... :Scarlett: Declassified (7/06, $4.95) Scarlett's childhood and training; Noto-c/a 5.00
... Special Missions (2/06, $4.95) short stories and profile pages by various 5.00
... Special Missions Antarctica (12/06, $4.95) short stories and profile pages by various 5.00
... Special Missions Brazil (4/07, $5.50) short stories and profile pages by various 5.50
... Special Missions: The Enemy (9/07, $5.50) two stories and profile pages by various 5.50
... Special Missions Tokyo (9/06, $4.95) short stories and profile pages by various 5.00
...: The Hunt For Cobra Commander (5/06, 25¢) short story and character profiles 2.50

G.I. JOE
IDW Publishing: No. 0, Oct, 2008; No. 1, Jan, 2009 - Present ($1.00/$3.99)

0-($1.00) Short stories by Dixon & Hama; creator interviews and character sketches 2.25
1-14-($3.99) 1-Dixon-s/Atkins-a; covers by Johnson, Atkins and Dell'Otto 4.00
...: Special - Helix (8/09, $3.99) Reed-s/Suitor-a 4.00

G. I. JOE AND THE TRANSFORMERS
Marvel Comics Group: Jan, 1987 - No. 4, Apr, 1987 (Limited series)

1-4 6.00

G. I. JOE, A REAL AMERICAN HERO (...Starring Snake-Eyes on-c #135 on)
Marvel Comics Group: June, 1982 - No. 155, Dec, 1994

1-Printed on Baxter paper; based on Hasbro toy 3 6 9 20 30 40
2-Printed on regular paper; 1st app. Kwinn 3 6 9 18 27 35
3-10: 6-1st app. Oktober Guard 3 6 9 14 20 25
11-20: 11-Intro Airborne. 13-1st Destro (cameo). 14-1st full app. Destro. 15-1st app. Major Blood. 16-1st app. Cover Girl and Trip-Wire 2 4 6 10 14 18
21-1st app. Storm Shadow; silent issue 4 8 12 22 34 45
22-1st app. Duke and Roadblock 2 4 6 10 14 18
23-25,28-30,60: 25-1st full app. Zartan, 1st app of Cutter, Deep Six, Mutt and Junkyard, and The Dreadnoks. 60-Todd McFarlane-a 2 3 4 6 8 10
26,27-Origin Snake-Eyes parts 1 & 2 3 6 9 14 19 24
31-50: 31-1st Spirit Iron-Knife. 32-1st Blowtorch, Lady J, Recondo, Ripcord. 33-New headquarters. 40-1st app. of Shipwreck, Barbecue. 48-1st app. Sgt. Slaughter. 49-1st app. of Lift-Ticket, Slipstream, Leatherneck, Serpentor 6.00
51-59,61-90 5.00
91,92,94-99: 94-96-Snake Eyes Trilogy 6.00
93-Snake-Eyes' face first revealed 2 4 6 11 16 20
100,135-138: 135-138-($1.75)-Bagged w/trading card. 138-Transformers app. 2 4 6 9 13 16
101-134: 101-New Oktober Guard app. 110-1st Garney-a. 117- Debut G.I. Joe Ninja Force 2 3 4 6 8 10
139-142-New Transformers app. 2 4 6 13 18 22
143,145-149: 145-Intro. G.I. Joe Star Brigade 2 4 6 9 13 16
144-Origin Snake-Eyes 3 6 9 14 19 24
150-Low print thru #155 3 6 9 19 29 38
151-154: 152-30th Anniversary (of doll) issue, original G.I. Joe General Joseph Colton app. (also app. in #151) 3 6 9 18 27 35
155-Last issue 5 10 15 30 48 65
All 2nd printings 2.50
Special #1 (2/95, $1.50) r/#60 w/McFarlane-a. Cover swipe from Spider-Man #1 4 8 12 26 41 55
Special Treasury Edition (1982)-r/#1 3 6 9 20 30 40
Volume 1 TPB (4/02, $24.95) r/#1-10; new cover by Michael Golden 25.00
Volume 2 TPB (6/02, $24.95) r/#11-20; new cover by J. Scott Campbell 25.00
Volume 3 TPB (2002, $24.99) r/#21-30; new cover by J. Scott Campbell 25.00
Volume 4 TPB (2002, $25.99) r/#31-40; new cover by J. Scott Campbell 26.00
Volume 5 TPB (2002, $24.99) r/#42-50; new cover by J. Scott Campbell 25.00
Yearbook 1-4: (3/85-3/88)-r/#1; Golden-c. 2-Golden-c/a 5.00
NOTE: ***Garney** a(p)-110. **Golden** c-23, 29, 34, 36. **Heath** a-24. **Rogers** a(p)-75, 77-82, 84, 86; c-77.*

G.I. JOE: BATTLE FILES
Image Comics: 2002 - No. 3, 2002 ($5.95)

1-3-Profile pages of characters and history; Beck-c 6.00

G.I. JOE: COBRA
IDW Publishing: Mar, 2009 - No. 4, June, 2009 ($3.99, limited series)

1-4-Gage & Costa-s/Fuso-a/covers by Chaykin & Fuso 4.00
... Special (9/09, $3.99) Costa-s/Fuso-a 4.00
... II (1/10, $3.99) Gage & Costa-s/Fuso-a/covers by Chaykin & Fuso 4.00

G. I. JOE COMICS MAGAZINE
Marvel Comics Group: Dec, 1986 - No. 13, 1988 ($1.50, digest-size)

1-13: G.I. Joe-r 2 4 6 8 10 12

G.I. JOE DECLASSIFIED
Devil's Due Publishing: June, 2006 - No. 3 ($4.95, bi-monthly)

1-3-New "early" adventures of the team; Hama-s; Quinn & DeLandro-a; var-c for each 5.00
TPB (1/07, $18.99) r/#1-3; cover gallery 19.00

G.I. JOE DREADNOKS: DECLASSIFIED
Devil's Due Publishing: Nov, 2006 - No. 3, Mar, 2007 ($4.95/$4.99/$5.50, bi-monthly)

1,2-Secret history of the team; Blaylock-s; var-c for each 5.00
3-($5.50) 5.50

G.I. JOE EUROPEAN MISSIONS (Action Force in indicia) (Series reprints Action Force)
Marvel Comics Ltd. (British): Jun, 1988 - No. 15, Dec, 1989 ($1.50/$1.75)

1,3-Snake Eyes & Storm Shadow-c/s 1 2 3 5 7 9
2,4-15 6.00

G.I. JOE: FRONT LINE
Image Comics: 2002 - No. 18, Dec, 2003 ($2.95)

1-18: 1-Jurgens-a/Hama-s. 1-Two covers by Dorman & Sharpe. 7,8-Harris-c 3.00
...Vol. 1 - The Mission That Never Was TPB (2003, $14.95) r/ #1-4; script pages 15.00
...Vol. 2 - Icebound TPB (3/04, $12.95) r/ #5-8 13.00
...Vol. 3 - History Repeating TPB (4/04, $9.95) r/#11-14 10.00
...Vol. 4 - One-Shots TPB (5/04, $15.95) r/#9,10,15-18 16.00

G.I. JOE: MASTER & APPRENTICE
Image Comics: May, 2004 - No. 4, Aug, 2004 ($2.95)

1-4-Caselli-a/Jerwa-s 3.00

G.I. JOE: MASTER & APPRENTICE 2
Image Comics: Feb, 2005 - No. 4, May, 2005 ($2.95, limited series)

1-4: Stevens & Vedder-a/Jerwa-s 3.00

G.I. JOE MOVIE PREQUEL...
IDW Publishing: Mar, 2009 - No. 4, June, 2009 ($3.99, limited series)

1-3-Two covers on each: 1-Duke. 2-Destro. 3-The Baroness. 4-SnakeEyes 4.00

G. I. JOE ORDER OF BATTLE, THE
Marvel Comics Group: Dec, 1986 - No. 4, Mar, 1987 (limited series)

1-4 6.00

G.I. JOE: ORIGINS
IDW Publishing: Feb, 2009 - Present ($3.99, limited series)

1-12: 1-Origin of Snake Eyes; Hama-s. 12-Templesmith-a 4.00

G.I. JOE: RELOADED
Image Comics: Mar, 2004 -No. 14, Apr, 2005 ($2.95)

1-14: 1-3-Granov-c/Ney Rieber-s. 5,6-Rieber-s/Saltares-a. 8-Origin of the Baroness 3.00
Vol. 1 In the Name of Patriotism (11/04, $12.95) r/#1-6; cover gallery 13.00

G.I. JOE: RISE OF COBRA MOVIE ADAPTATION
IDW Publishing: July, 2009 - No. 4, July, 2009 ($3.99, weekly limited series)

1-4-Tipton-s/Maloney-a; two covers 4.00

G.I. JOE SIGMA 6 (Based on the cartoon TV series)
Devil's Due Publishing: Dec, 2005 - No. 6, May, 2006 ($2.95, limited series)

1-6-Andrew Daab-s 3.00
TPB Vol. 1 (10/06, $10.95, 8-1/4" x 5-3/4") r/#1-6; cover gallery 11.00

G.I. JOE: SNAKE EYES
IDW Publishing: Oct, 2009 - No. 4, Jan, 2010 ($3.99, limited series)

1-4-Ray Park & Kevin VanHook-s/Lee Ferguson-a; two covers 4.00

G. I. JOE SPECIAL MISSIONS (Indicia title: Special Missions)
Marvel Comics Group: Oct, 1986 - No. 28, Dec, 1989 ($1.00)

1-20 4.00
21-28 5.00

G.I. JOE VS. THE TRANSFORMERS
Image Comics: Jun, 2003 - No. 6, Nov, 2003 ($2.95, limited series)

1-Blaylock-s/Mike Miller-a; three covers by Miller, Campbell & Andrews 3.00
1-2nd printing; black cover with logo; back-c by Campbell 3.00
2-6: 2-Two covers by Miller & Brooks 3.00
TPB (3/04, $15.95) r/series; sketch pages 16.00

G.I. Joe vs. The Transformers #1 © Hasbro

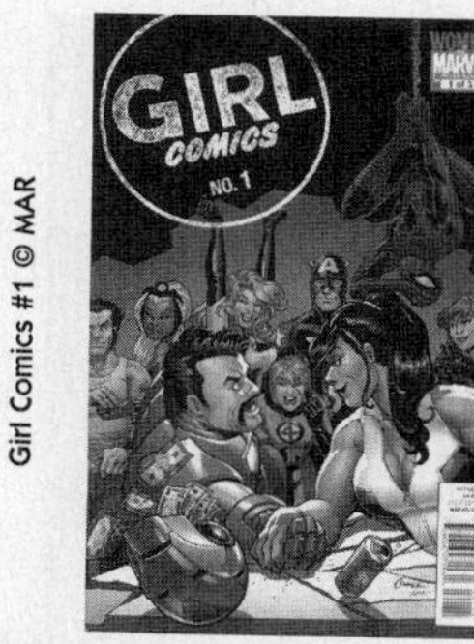

Girl Comics #1 © MAR

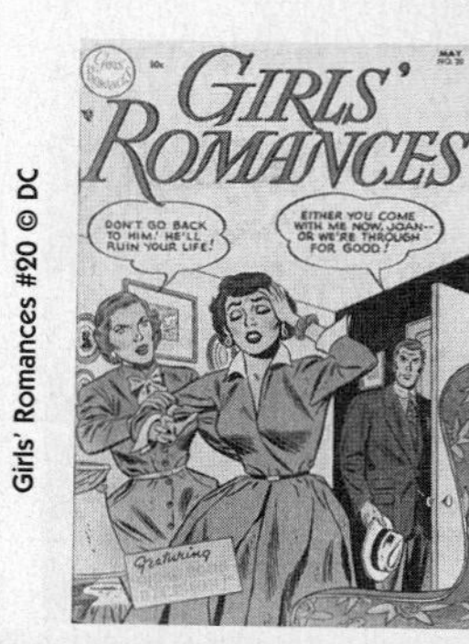

Girls' Romances #20 © DC

G.I. JOE VS. THE TRANSFORMERS (Volume 2)
Devil's Due Publ.: Sept, 2004 - No. 4, Dec, 2004 ($4.95/$2.95, limited series)

	GD 2.0	VG 4.0	FN 6.0	VF 8.0	VF/NM 9.0	NM- 9.2
1-($4.95) Three covers; Jolley-s/Su & Seeley-a						5.00
2-4-($2.95) Two covers by Su & Pollina						3.00
Vol. 2 TPB (4/05, $14.95) r/series; interview with creators; sketch pages and covers						15.00

G.I. JOE VS. THE TRANSFORMERS (Volume 3) THE ART OF WAR
Devil's Due Publ.: Mar, 2006 - No. 5, July, 2006 ($2.95, limited series)

	GD 2.0	VG 4.0	FN 6.0	VF 8.0	VF/NM 9.0	NM- 9.2
1-5: 1-Three covers; Seeley-s/Ng-a						3.00
TPB (8/06, $14.95) r/series; cover gallery						15.00

G.I. JOE VS. THE TRANSFORMERS (Volume 4) BLACK HORIZON
Devil's Due Publ.: Jan, 2007 - No. 2, July, 2006 ($5.50, limited series)

	GD 2.0	VG 4.0	FN 6.0	VF 8.0	VF/NM 9.0	NM- 9.2
1,2: 1-Three covers; Seeley-s/Wildman-a. 2-Two covers						5.50

G. I. JUNIORS (See Harvey Hits No. 86,91,95,98,101,104,107,110,112,114,116,118,120,122)

GILGAMESH II
DC Comics: 1989 - No. 4, 1989 ($3.95, limited series, prestige format, mature)

	GD 2.0	VG 4.0	FN 6.0	VF 8.0	VF/NM 9.0	NM- 9.2
1-4: Starlin-c/a/scripts						4.00

GIL THORP
Dell Publishing Co.: May-July, 1963

	GD 2.0	VG 4.0	FN 6.0	VF 8.0	VF/NM 9.0	NM- 9.2
1-Caniff-*ish* art	4	8	12	24	37	50

GINGER
Archie Publications: 1951 - No. 10, Summer, 1954

	GD 2.0	VG 4.0	FN 6.0	VF 8.0	VF/NM 9.0	NM- 9.2
1-Teenage humor	15	30	45	84	127	170
2-(1952)	9	18	27	52	69	85
3-6: 6-(Sum/53)	8	16	24	44	57	70
7-10-Katy Keene app.	10	20	30	56	76	95

GINGER FOX (Also see The World of Ginger Fox)
Comico: Sept, 1988 - No. 4, Dec, 1988 ($1.75, limited series)

	GD 2.0	VG 4.0	FN 6.0	VF 8.0	VF/NM 9.0	NM- 9.2
1-4: Part photo-c on all						2.50

G.I. R.A.M.B.O.T.
Wonder Color Comics/Pied Piper #2: Apr, 1987 - No. 2? ($1.95)

	GD 2.0	VG 4.0	FN 6.0	VF 8.0	VF/NM 9.0	NM- 9.2
1,2: 2-Exist?						2.50

GIRL
DC Comics (Vertigo Verite): Jul, 1996 - No. 3, 1996 ($2.50, lim. series, mature)

	GD 2.0	VG 4.0	FN 6.0	VF 8.0	VF/NM 9.0	NM- 9.2
1-3: Peter Milligan scripts; Fegredo-c/a						2.50

GIRL COMICS (Becomes Girl Confessions No. 13 on)
Marvel/Atlas Comics(CnPC): Oct, 1949 - No. 12, Jan, 1952 (#1-4: 52 pgs.)

	GD 2.0	VG 4.0	FN 6.0	VF 8.0	VF/NM 9.0	NM- 9.2
1-Photo-c	23	46	69	136	223	310
2-Kubert-a; photo-c	14	28	42	81	118	155
3-Everett-a; Liz Taylor photo-c	30	60	90	177	289	400
4-11: 4-Photo-c. 10-12-Sol Brodsky-c	12	24	36	67	94	120
12-Krigstein-a; Al Hartley-c	13	26	39	72	101	130

GIRL COMICS
Marvel Comics: May, 2010 - No. 3 ($4.99, limited series)

	GD 2.0	VG 4.0	FN 6.0	VF 8.0	VF/NM 9.0	NM- 9.2
1-Anthology of short stories by women creators; Conner-c						5.00

GIRL CONFESSIONS (Formerly Girl Comics)
Atlas Comics (CnPC/ZPC): No. 13, Mar, 1952 - No. 35, Aug, 1954

	GD 2.0	VG 4.0	FN 6.0	VF 8.0	VF/NM 9.0	NM- 9.2
13-Everett-a	14	28	42	78	112	145
14,15,19,20	10	20	30	58	79	100
16-18-Everett-a	12	24	36	67	94	120
21-35: Robinson-a	9	18	27	50	65	80

GIRL CRAZY
Dark Horse Comics: May, 1996 - No. 3, July, 1996 ($2.95, B&W, limited series)

	GD 2.0	VG 4.0	FN 6.0	VF 8.0	VF/NM 9.0	NM- 9.2
1-3: Gilbert Hernandez-a/scripts.						3.00

GIRL FROM U.N.C.L.E., THE (TV) (Also see The Man From...)
Gold Key: Jan, 1967 - No. 5, Oct, 1967

	GD 2.0	VG 4.0	FN 6.0	VF 8.0	VF/NM 9.0	NM- 9.2
1-McWilliams-a; Stephanie Powers photo front/back-c & pin-ups (no ads, 12¢)	8	16	24	52	86	120
2-5-Leonard Swift-Courier No. 5. 4-Back-c pin-up	6	12	18	37	59	80

GIRLS
Image Comics: May, 2005 - No. 24, Apr, 2007 ($2.95/$2.99)

	GD 2.0	VG 4.0	FN 6.0	VF 8.0	VF/NM 9.0	NM- 9.2
1-Luna Brothers-s/a/c						4.00
2-24						3.00
... Vol. 1: Conception TPB (2005, $14.99) r/#1-6						15.00
... Vol. 2: Emergence TPB (2006, $14.99) r/#7-12						15.00
... Vol. 3: Survival TPB (2006, $14.99) r/#13-18						15.00
... Vol. 4: Extinction TPB (2007, $14.99) r/#19-24						15.00

GIRLS' FUN & FASHION MAGAZINE (Formerly Polly Pigtails)
Parents' Magazine Institute: V5#44, Jan, 1950 - V5#48, Sept., 1950

	GD 2.0	VG 4.0	FN 6.0	VF 8.0	VF/NM 9.0	NM- 9.2
V5#44	7	14	21	37	46	55
45-48	6	12	18	27	33	38

GIRLS IN LOVE
Fawcett Publications: May, 1950 - No. 2, July, 1950

	GD 2.0	VG 4.0	FN 6.0	VF 8.0	VF/NM 9.0	NM- 9.2
1-Photo-c	12	24	36	69	97	125
2-Photo-c	10	20	30	54	72	90

GIRLS IN LOVE (Formerly G. I. Sweethearts No. 45)
Quality Comics Group: No. 46, Sept, 1955 - No. 57, Dec, 1956

	GD 2.0	VG 4.0	FN 6.0	VF 8.0	VF/NM 9.0	NM- 9.2
46	10	20	30	54	72	90
47-53,55,56	8	16	24	40	50	60
54- 'Commie' story	9	18	27	52	69	85
57-Matt Baker-c/a	14	28	42	76	108	140

GIRLS IN WHITE (See Harvey Comics Hits No. 58)

GIRLS' LIFE (Patsy Walker's Own Magazine For Girls!)
Atlas Comics (BFP): Jan, 1954 - No. 6, Nov, 1954

	GD 2.0	VG 4.0	FN 6.0	VF 8.0	VF/NM 9.0	NM- 9.2
1	14	28	42	80	115	150
2-Al Hartley-c	9	18	27	47	61	75
3-6	8	16	24	42	54	65

GIRLS' LOVE STORIES
National Comics(Signal Publ. No. 9-65/Arleigh No. 83-117): Aug-Sept, 1949 - No. 180, Nov-Dec, 1973 (No. 1-13: 52 pgs.)

	GD 2.0	VG 4.0	FN 6.0	VF 8.0	VF/NM 9.0	NM- 9.2
1-Toth, Kinstler-a, 8 pgs. each; photo-c	56	112	168	350	595	840
2-Kinstler-a?	31	62	93	182	296	410
3-10: 1-9-Photo-c	21	42	63	122	199	275
11-20	16	32	48	94	147	200
21-33: 21-Kinstler-a. 33-Last pre-code (1-2/55)	13	26	39	72	101	130
34-50	11	22	33	60	83	105
51-70	10	20	30	54	72	90
71-99: 83-Last 10¢ issue	5	10	15	32	51	70
100	5	10	15	34	55	75
101-146: 113-117-April O'Day app.	3	6	9	20	30	40
147-151- "Confessions" serial. 150-Wood-a	3	6	9	21	32	42
152-160,171-179	3	6	9	16	22	28
161-170 (52 pgs.)	4	8	12	22	34	45
180 Last issue	3	6	9	20	30	40
Ashcan (8-9/49) not distributed to newsstands, only for in house use						(no known sales)

GIRLS' ROMANCES
National Periodical Publ.(Signal Publ. No. 7-79/Arleigh No. 84): Feb-Mar, 1950 - No. 160, Oct, 1971 (No. 1-11: 52 pgs.)

	GD 2.0	VG 4.0	FN 6.0	VF 8.0	VF/NM 9.0	NM- 9.2
1-Photo-c	53	106	159	334	567	800
2-Photo-c; Toth-a	30	60	90	177	289	400
3-10: 3-6-Photo-c	21	42	63	122	199	275
11,12,14-20	15	30	45	86	133	180
13-Toth-c	15	30	45	90	140	190
21-31: 31-Last pre-code (2-3/55)	13	26	39	72	101	130
32-50	7	14	21	45	73	100
51-99: 80-Last 10¢ issue	5	10	15	32	51	70
100	5	10	15	34	55	75
101-108,110-120	3	6	9	20	30	40
109-Beatles-c/story	13	26	39	90	165	240
121-133,135-140	3	6	9	18	27	35
134-Neal Adams-c (splash pg. is same as-c)	5	10	15	34	55	75
141-158	3	6	9	16	22	28
159,160-52 pgs.	4	8	12	22	34	45

GIRL WHO WOULD BE DEATH, THE
DC Comics (Vertigo): Dec, 1998 - No. 4, March, 1999 ($2.50, lim. series)

	GD 2.0	VG 4.0	FN 6.0	VF 8.0	VF/NM 9.0	NM- 9.2
1-4-Kiernan-s/Ormston-a						2.50

G. I. SWEETHEARTS (Formerly Diary Loves; Girls In Love #46 on)
Quality Comics Group: No. 32, June, 1953 - No. 45, May, 1955

	GD 2.0	VG 4.0	FN 6.0	VF 8.0	VF/NM 9.0	NM- 9.2
32	10	20	30	58	79	100
33-45: 44-Last pre-code (3/55)	8	16	24	42	54	65

G.I. TALES (Formerly Sgt. Barney Barker No. 1-3)
Atlas Comics (MCI): No. 4, Feb, 1957 - No. 6, July, 1957

	GD 2.0	VG 4.0	FN 6.0	VF 8.0	VF/NM 9.0	NM- 9.2
4-Severin-a(4)	10	20	30	54	72	90

Gizmo #1 © MS

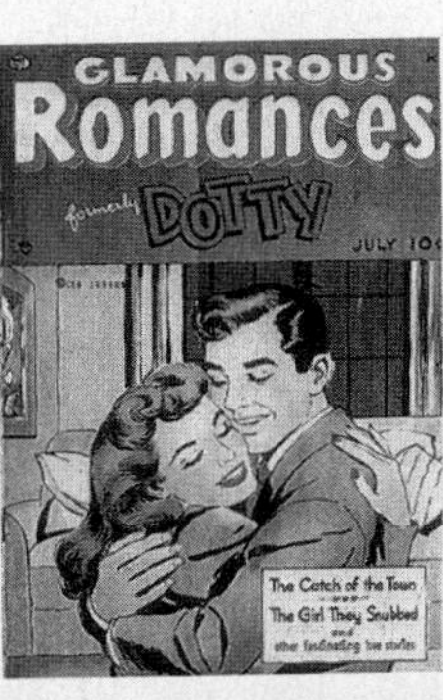

Glamorous Romances #41 © ACE

God Complex #1 © Berman & Oeming

	GD 2.0	VG 4.0	FN 6.0	VF 8.0	VF/NM 9.0	NM- 9.2
5	8	16	24	40	50	60
6-Orlando, Powell, & Woodbridge-a	8	16	24	42	54	65

GIVE ME LIBERTY (Also see Dark Horse Presents Fifth Anniversary Special, Dark Horse Presents #100-4, Happy Birthday Martha Washington, Martha Washington Goes to War, Martha Washington Stranded In Space & San Diego Comicon Comics #2)
Dark Horse Comics: June, 1990 - No. 4, 1991 ($4.95, limited series, 52 pgs.)

1-4: 1st app. Martha Washington; Frank Miller scripts, Dave Gibbons-c/a in all 5.00

G. I. WAR BRIDES
Superior Publishers Ltd.: Apr, 1954 - No. 8, June, 1955

	GD	VG	FN	VF	VF/NM	NM-
1	10	20	30	58	79	100
2	8	16	24	40	50	60
3-8: 4-Kamen*esque*-a; lingerie panels	7	14	21	35	43	50

G. I. WAR TALES
National Periodical Publications: Mar-Apr, 1973 - No. 4, Oct-Nov, 1973

	GD	VG	FN	VF	VF/NM	NM-
1-Reprints in all; dinosaur-c/s	3	6	9	18	27	35
2-N. Adams-a(r)	2	4	6	13	18	22
3,4: 4-Krigstein-a(r)	2	4	6	11	16	20

NOTE: ***Drucker** a-3r, 4r. **Heath** a-4r. **Kubert** a-2, 3; c-4r.*

GIZMO (Also see Domino Chance)
Chance Ent.: May-June, 1985 (B&W, one-shot)

1 6.00

GIZMO
Mirage Studios: 1986 - No. 6, July, 1987 ($1.50, B&W)

1-6 2.50

G.L.A. (Great Lakes Avengers)(Also see GLX-Mas Special)
Marvel Comics: June, 2005 - No. 4, Sept, 2005 ($2.99, limited series)

1-4-Slott-s/Pelletier-a 3.00
...: Misassembled TPB (2005, $14.99) r/#1-4, West Coast Avengers #46 (1st app.) and Marvel Super-Heroes #8 (1st app. Squirrel Girl; Ditko-a) 15.00

GLADSTONE COMIC ALBUM
Gladstone: 1987 - No. 28, 1990 ($5.95/$9.95, 8-1/2x11")(All Mickey Mouse albums are by Gottfredson)

1-10: 1-Uncle Scrooge; Barks-r; Beck-c. 2-Donald Duck; r/F.C. #108 by Barks. 3-Mickey Mouse-r by Gottfredson. 4-Uncle Scrooge; r/F.C. #456 by Barks w/unedited story. 5-Donald Duck Advs.; r/F.C. #199. 6-Uncle Scrooge-r by Barks. 7-Donald Duck-r by Barks. 8-Mickey Mouse-r. 9-Bambi; r/F.C. #186? 10-Donald Duck Advs.; r/F.C. #275
1 3 4 6 8 10

11-20: 11-Uncle Scrooge; r/U.S. #4. 12-Donald And Daisy; r/F.C. #1055, WDC&S. 13-Donald Duck Advs.; r/F.C. #408. 14-Uncle Scrooge; Barks-r/U.S #21. 15-Donald And Gladstone; Barks-r. 16-Donald Duck Advs.; r/F.C. #238. 17-Mickey Mouse strip-r (The World of Tomorrow, The Pirate Ghost Ship). 18-Donald Duck and the Junior Woodchucks; Barks-r. 19-Uncle Scrooge; r/U.S. #12; Rosa-c. 20-Uncle Scrooge; r/F.C. #386; Barks-c/a(r)
1 3 4 6 8 10

21-25: 21-Donald Duck Family; Barks-c/a(r). 22-Mickey Mouse strip-r. 23-Donald Duck; Barks-r/D.D. #26 w/unedited story. 24-Uncle Scrooge; Barks-r; Rosa-c. 25-D. Duck; Barks-c/a-r/F.C. #367
1 3 4 6 8 10

26-28: All have $9.95-c. 26-Mickey & Donald; Gottfredson-c/a(r). 27-Donald Duck; r/WDC&S by Barks; Barks painted-c. 28-Uncle Scrooge & Donald Duck; Rosa-c/a (4 stories)
1 3 4 6 8 10

Special 1-7: 1 ('89-'90, $9.95/13.95)-1-Donald Duck Finds Pirate Gold; r/F.C. #9. 2 ('89, $8.95)-Uncle Scrooge and Donald Duck; Barks-r/Uncle Scrooge #5; Rosa-c. 3 ('89, $8.95)-Mickey Mouse strip-r. 4 ('89, $11.95)-Uncle Scrooge; Rosa-c/a-r/Son of the Sun from U.S. #219 plus Barks-r/U.S. 5 ('90, $11.95)-Donald Duck Advs.; Barks-r/F.C. #282 & 422 plus Barks painted-c. 6 ('90, $12.95)-Uncle Scrooge; Barks-c/a-r/Uncle Scrooge. 7 ('90, $13.95)-Mickey Mouse; Gottfredson strip-r
2 4 6 9 11 14

GLADSTONE COMIC ALBUM (2nd Series)(Also see The Original Dick Tracy)
Gladstone Publishing: 1990 ($5.95, 8-1/2 x 11," stiff-c, 52 pgs.)

1,2-The Original Dick Tracy. 2-Origin of the 2-way wrist radio 6.00
3-D Tracy Meets the Mole-r by Gould ($6.95). 1 2 3 5 6 8

GLAMOROUS ROMANCES (Formerly Dotty)
Ace Magazines (A. A. Wyn): No. 41, July, 1949 - No. 90, Oct, 1956 (Photo-c 68-90)

	GD	VG	FN	VF	VF/NM	NM-
41-Dotty app.	11	22	33	62	86	110
42-72,74-80: 44-Begin 52 pg. issues. 45,50-61-Painted-c. 80-Last pre-code (2/55)	9	18	27	47	61	75
73-L.B. Cole-r/All Love #27	9	18	27	50	65	80
81-90	8	16	24	44	57	70

GLAMOURPUSS
Aardvark-Vanaheim Inc.: Apr, 2008 - Present ($3.00, B&W)

1-11: 1-Two covers; Dave Sim-s/a/c. 9,10-Gene Colan-c. 1-Heath-c 3.00
1-Comics Industry Preview Edition (Diamond Dateline supplement) 5.00

GLOBAL FREQUENCY
DC Comics (WildStorm): Dec, 2002 - No. 12, Aug, 2004 ($2.95, limited series)

1-12-Warren Ellis-s. 1-Leach-a. 2-Fabry-a. 3-Dillon-a. 5-Muth-a. 7-Bisley-a. 12-Ha-a 3.00
1-RRP Edition variant-c; promotional giveaway for retailers (200 printed) 10.00
...: Detonation Radio TPB (2005, $14.95) r/#7-12 15.00
...: Planet Ablaze TPB (2003, $14.95) r/#1-6 15.00

GLORY
Image Comics (Extreme Studios)/Maximum Press: Mar, 1995 - No. 22, Apr, 1997 ($2.50)

0-Deodato-c/a, 1-(3/95)-Deodato-a 2.50
1A-Variant-c 4.00
2-11,13-22: 4-Variant-c by Quesada & Palmiotti. 5-Bagged w/Youngblood gaming card. 7,8-Deodato-c/a(p). 8-Babewatch x-over. 9-Cruz-c; Extreme Destroyer Pt. 5; polybagged w/card. 10-Angela-c/app. 11-Deodato-c. 2.50
12-($3.50)-Photo-c 3.50
... & Friends Christmas Special (12/95, $2.50) Deodato-c 2.50
... & Friends Lingerie Special (9/95, $2.95) Pin-ups w/photos; photo-c; varant-c exists 3.00
... /Angela: Angels in Hell (4/96, $2.50) Flip book w/Darkchylde #1 2.50
... /Avengelyne (10/95, $3.95) 1-Chromium-c, 1-Regular-c 4.00
Trade Paperback (1995, $9.95)-r/#1-4 10.00

GLORY
Awesome Comics: Mar, 1999 ($2.50)

0-Liefeld-c; story and sketch pages 2.50

GLORY (ALAN MOORE'S...)
Avatar Press: Dec, 2001 - No. 2 ($3.50)

Preview-(9/01, $1.99) B&W pages and cover art; Alan Moore-s 2.50
0-Four regular covers 3.50
1,2: 1-Alan Moore-s/Mychaels & Gebbie-a; nine covers by various. 2-Five covers 3.50

GLORY & FRIENDS BIKINI FEST
Image Comics (Extreme): Sept, 1995 - No. 2, Oct, 1995 ($2.50, limited series)

1,2: 1-Photo-c; centerfold photo; pin-ups 2.50

GLORY/CELESTINE: DARK ANGEL
Image Comics/Maximum Press (Extreme Studios): Sept, 1996 - No. 3, Nov, 1996 ($2.50, limited series)

1-3 2.50

GLX-MAS SPECIAL (Great Lakes Avengers)
Marvel Comics: Feb, 2006 ($3.99, one-shot)

1-Christmas themed stories by various incl. Haley, Templeton, Grist, Wieringo 4.00

G-MAN: CAPE CRISIS
Image Comics: Aug, 2009 - No. 5, Jan, 2010 ($2.99, limited series)

1-5-Chris Giarrusso-s/a; back-up short strips by various 3.00

GNOME MOBILE, THE (See Movie Comics)

GOBBLEDYGOOK
Mirage Studios: 1984 - No. 2, 1984 (B&W)(1st Mirage comics, published at same time)

1-(24 pgs.)-(distribution of approx. 50) Teenage Mutant Ninja Turtles app. on full page back-c ad; Teenage Mutant Ninja Turtles do not appear inside. 1st app of Fugitoid
50 100 150 413 807 1200
2-(24 pgs.)-Teenage Mutant Ninja Turtles on full page back-c ad
34 68 102 262 506 750

NOTE: Counterfeit copies exist. Originals feature both black & white covers and interiors. Signed and numbered copies do not exist.

GOBBLEDYGOOK
Mirage Studios: Dec, 1986 ($3.50, B&W, one-shot, 100 pgs.)

1-New 8 pg. TMNT story plus a Donatello/Michaelangelo 7 pg. story & a Gizmo story; Corben-i(r)/TMNT #7
1 2 3 5 6 8

GOBLIN, THE
Warren Publishing Co.: June, 1982 - No. 3, Dec, 1982 ($2.25, B&W magazine with 8 pg. color insert comic in all)

1-The Gremlin app. Philo Photon & the Troll Patrol, Micro-Buccaneers & Wizard Wormglow begin & app. in all. Tin Man app. Golden-a(p). Nebres-c/a in all
2 4 6 13 18 22
2,3: 2-1st Hobgoblin. 3-Tin Man app. 2 4 6 9 12 15

NOTE: ***Bermejo** a-1-3. **Elias** a-1-3. **Laxamana** a-1-3. **Nino** a-3.*

GOD COMPLEX
Image Comics: Dec, 2009 - Present ($2.99)

Godzilla #12 © Toho Co.

Go Girl! #4 © Trina Robbins

Golden Age Secret Files #1 © DC

	GD	VG	FN	VF	VF/NM	NM-
	2.0	4.0	6.0	8.0	9.0	9.2

1-4-Oeming & Berman-s/Broglia-a/Oeming-c 3.00

GODDESS
DC Comics (Vertigo): June, 1995 - No. 8, Jan, 1996 ($2.95, limited series)

1-Garth Ennis scripts; Phil Winslade-c/a in all 5.00
2-8 4.00
TPB (2002, $19.95) r/#1-8; foreword and sketch pages by Winslade 20.00

GODFATHERS, THE (See The Crusaders)

GOD IS
Spire Christian Comics (Fleming H. Revell Co.): 1973, 1975 (35-49¢)

nn-(1973) By Al Hartley 2 4 6 9 12 15
nn-(1975) 1 3 4 6 8 10

GODLAND
Image Comics: July, 2005 - Present ($2.99)

1-15,17-30-Joe Casey-s; Kirby-esque art by Tom Scioli. 13-Var-c by Giffen & Larsen 3.00
16-(60¢-c) Re-cap/origin issue 2.25
...: Celestial Edition One HC (2007, $34.99) r/#1-12 and story from Image Holiday Special; intro. by Grant Morrison; cover gallery, developmental art and original story pitches 35.00
... Vol. 1: Hello Cosmic! TPB (1/06, $14.99) r/#1-6; sketch development pages 15.00
... Vol. 2: Another Sunny Delight TPB (8/06, $14.99) r/#7-12; early Christmas story 15.00
... Vol. 3: Proto-Plastic Party TPB (2007, $14.99) r/#13-18 15.00
... Vol. 4: Amplified Now TPB (2008, $14.99) r/#19-24 15.00

GOD SAVE THE QUEEN
DC Comics (Vertigo): 2007 ($19.99, hardcover with dustjacket, graphic novel)

HC-Mike Carey-s/John Bolton-painted art 20.00
SC-(2008, $12.99) Different Bolton painted-c 13.00

GOD'S COUNTRY (Also see Marvel Comics Presents)
Marvel Comics: 1994 ($6.95)

nn-P. Craig Russell-a; Colossus story; r/Marvel Comics Presents #10-17 7.00

GOD'S HEROES IN AMERICA
Catechetical Guild Educational Society: 1956 (nn) (25¢/35¢, 68 pgs.)

307 3 6 9 16 23 30

GOD'S SMUGGLER (Religious)
Spire Christian Comics/Fleming H. Revell Co.: 1972 (35¢/39¢/40¢)

1-Three variations exist 2 4 6 9 12 15

GODWHEEL
Malibu Comics (Ultraverse): No. 0, Jan, 1995 - No. 3, Feb, 1995 ($2.50, limited series)

0-3: 0-Flip-c. 1-1st app. of Primevil; Thor cameo (1 panel). 3-Perez-a in Chapter 3, Thor app. 2.50

GODZILLA (Movie)
Marvel Comics : August, 1977 - No. 24, July, 1979 (Based on movie series)

1-(Regular 30¢ edition)-Mooney-i 3 6 9 20 30 40
1-(35¢-c variant, limited distribution) 6 12 18 37 59 80
2-(Regular 30¢ edition)-Tuska-i. 2 4 6 9 13 16
2,3-(35¢-c variant, limited distribution) 3 6 9 20 30 40
3-(30¢-c) Champions app.(w/o Ghost Rider) 2 4 6 10 14 18
4-10: 4,5-Sutton-a 2 4 6 8 11 14
11-23: 14-Shield app. 20-F.F. app. 21,22-Devil Dinosaur app. 2 4 6 8 10 12
24-Last issue 2 4 6 9 13 16

GODZILLA (Movie)
Dark Horse Comics: May, 1988 - No. 6, 1988 ($1.95, B&W, limited series) (Based on movie series)

1 6.00
2-6 4.00
...Collection (1990, $10.95)-r/1-6 with new-c 11.00
...Color Special 1 (Sum, 1992, $3.50, color, 44 pgs.)-Arthur Adams wraparound-c/a & part scripts 5.00
...King Of The Monsters Special (8/87, $1.50)-Origin; Bissette-c/a 4.00
...Vs. Barkley nn (12/93, $2.95, color)-Dorman painted-c 4.00

GODZILLA (King of the Monsters) (Movie)
Dark Horse Comics: May, 1995 - No. 16, Sept, 1996 ($2.50) (Based on movies)

0-16: 0-r/Dark Horse Comics #10,11. 1-3-Kevin Maguire scripts. 3-8-Art Adams-c 4.00
...Vs. Hero Zero ($2.50) 3.00

GOG (VILLAINS) (See Kingdom Come)
DC Comics: Feb, 1998 ($1.95, one-shot)

1-Waid-s/Ordway-a(p)/Pearson-c 3.00

	GD	VG	FN	VF	VF/NM	NM-
	2.0	4.0	6.0	8.0	9.0	9.2

GO GIRL!
Image Comics: Aug, 2000 - No. 5 ($3.50, B&W, quarterly)

1-5-Trina Robbins-s/Anne Timmons-a; pin-up gallery 3.50

GO-GO
Charlton Comics: June, 1966 - No. 9, Oct, 1967

1-Miss Bikini Luv begins w/Jim Aparo's 1st published work; Rolling Stones, Beatles, Elvis, Sonny & Cher, Bob Dylan, Sinatra, parody; Herman's Hermits pin-ups; D'Agostino-c/a in #1-8 8 16 24 54 90 125
2-Ringo Starr, David McCallum & Beatles photos on cover; Beatles story and photos 8 16 24 54 90 125
3,4: 3-Blooperman begins, ends #6; 1 pg. Batman & Robin satire; full pg. photo pin-ups Lovin' Spoonful & The Byrds 5 10 15 32 51 70
5,7,9: 5 (2/67)-Super Hero & TV satire by Jim Aparo & Grass Green begins. 6-8-Aparo-a. 7-Photo of Brian Wilson of Beach Boys on-c & Beach Boys photo inside f/b-c. 9-Aparo-c/a 5 10 15 32 51 70
6-Parody of JLA & DC heroes vs. Marvel heroes; Aparo-a; Elvis parody; Petula Clark photo-c 6 12 18 37 59 80
8-Monkees photo on-c & photo inside f/b-c 6 12 18 41 66 90

GO-GO AND ANIMAL (See Tippy's Friends...)

GOING STEADY (Formerly Teen-Age Temptations)
St. John Publ. Co.: No. 10, Dec, 1954 - No. 13, June, 1955; No. 14, Oct, 1955

10(1954)-Matt Baker-c/a 28 56 84 165 270 375
11(2/55, last precode), 12(4/55)-Baker-c 18 36 54 105 165 225
13(6/55)-Baker-c/a 22 44 66 132 216 300
14(10/55)-Matt Baker-c/a, 25 pgs. 26 52 78 154 252 350

GOING STEADY (Formerly Personal Love)
Prize Publications/Headline: V3#3, Feb, 1960 - V3#6, Aug, 1960; V4#1, Sept-Oct, 1960

V3#3-6, V4#1 3 6 9 18 27 35

GOING STEADY WITH BETTY (Becomes Betty & Her Steady No. 2)
Avon Periodicals: Nov-Dec, 1949 (Teen-age)

1-Partial photo-c 15 30 45 88 137 185

GOLDEN AGE, THE (TPB also reprinted in 2005 as JSA: The Golden Age)
DC Comics (Elseworlds): 1993 - No. 4, 1994 ($4.95, limited series)

1-4: James Robinson scripts; Paul Smith-c/a; gold foil embossed-c 6.00
Trade Paperback (1995, $19.95) intro by Howard Chaykin 20.00

GOLDEN AGE SECRET FILES
DC Comics: Feb, 2001 ($4.95, one-shot)

1-Origins and profiles of JSA members and other G.A. heroes; Lark-c 5.00

GOLDEN ARROW (See Fawcett Miniatures, Mighty Midget & Whiz Comics)

GOLDEN ARROW (...Western No. 6)
Fawcett Publications: Spring, 1942 - No. 6, Spring, 1947 (68 pgs.)

1-Golden Arrow begins 60 120 180 378 639 900
2-(1943) 31 62 93 181 291 400
3-5: 3-(Win/45-46). 4-(Spr/46). 5-(Fall/46) 21 42 63 125 200 275
6-Krigstein-a 22 44 66 129 207 285
Ashcan (1942) not distributed to newsstands, only for in house use. A CGC certified 9.0 sold for $3,734.38 in 2008.

GOLDEN COMICS DIGEST
Gold Key: May, 1969 - No. 48, Jan, 1976

NOTE: *Whitman editions exist of many titles and are generally valued the same.*

1-Tom & Jerry, Woody Woodpecker, Bugs Bunny 6 12 18 37 59 80
2-Hanna-Barbera TV Fun Favorites; Space Ghost, Flintstones, Atom Ant, Jetsons, Yogi Bear, Banana Splits, others app. 7 14 21 49 80 110
3-Tom & Jerry, Woody Woodpecker 3 6 9 17 25 32
4-Tarzan; Manning & Marsh-a 5 10 15 30 48 65
5,8-Tom & Jerry, W. Woodpecker, Bugs Bunny 3 6 9 16 23 30
6-Bugs Bunny 3 6 9 16 23 30
7-Hanna-Barbera TV Fun Favorites 6 12 18 37 59 80
9-Tarzan 5 10 15 30 48 65
10,12-17: 10-Bugs Bunny. 12-Tom & Jerry, Bugs Bunny, W. Woodpecker Journey to the Sun. 13-Tom & Jerry. 14-Bugs Bunny Fun Packed Funnies. 15-Tom & Jerry, Woody Woodpecker, Bugs Bunny. 16-Woody Woodpecker Cartoon Special. 17-Bugs Bunny 3 6 9 16 23 30
11-Hanna-Barbera TV Fun Favorites 6 12 18 39 62 85
18-Tom & Jerry; Barney Bear-r by Barks 3 6 9 17 25 32
19-Little Lulu 4 8 12 26 41 55
20-22: 20-Woody Woodpecker Falltime Funtime. 21-Bugs Bunny Showtime. 22-Tom & Jerry Winter Wingding 3 6 9 16 23 30

Golden Lad #1 © Spark

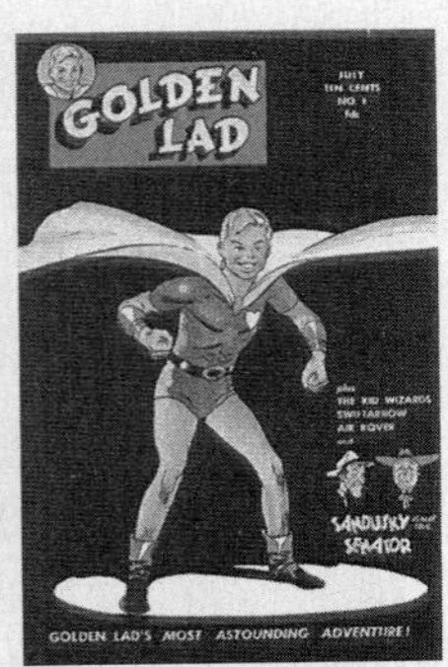

Golden West Love #1 © Kirby Publ.

Gold Key Spotlight #6 © GK

GD 2.0 | VG 4.0 | FN 6.0 | VF 8.0 | VF/NM 9.0 | NM- 9.2

23-Little Lulu & Tubby Fun Fling 4 8 12 26 41 55
24-26,28: 24-Woody Woodpecker Fun Festival. 25-Tom & Jerry. 26-Bugs Bunny Halloween Hulla-Boo-Loo; Dr. Spektor article, also #25. 28-Tom & Jerry
3 6 9 14 20 26
27-Little Lulu & Tubby in Hawaii 4 8 12 25 39 52
29-Little Lulu & Tubby 4 8 12 25 39 52
30-Bugs Bunny Vacation Funnies 3 6 9 14 20 26
31-Turok, Son of Stone; r/4-Color #596,656; c-r/#9 4 8 12 28 44 60
32-Woody Woodpecker Summer Fun 3 6 9 14 20 26
33,36: 33-Little Lulu & Tubby Halloween Fun; Dr. Spektor app. 36-Little Lulu & Her Friends
4 8 12 25 39 52
34,35,37-39: 34-Bugs Bunny Winter Funnies. 35-Tom & Jerry Snowtime Funtime. 37-Woody Woodpecker County Fair. 39-Bugs Bunny Summer Fun
3 6 9 14 20 26
38-The Pink Panther 3 6 9 17 25 32
40,43: 40-Little Lulu & Tubby Trick or Treat; all by Stanley. 43-Little Lulu in Paris
4 8 12 25 39 52
41,42,44,47: 41-Tom & Jerry Winter Carnival. 42-Bugs Bunny. 44-Woody Woodpecker Family Fun Festival. 47-Bugs Bunny 3 6 9 14 20 25
45-The Pink Panther 3 6 9 17 25 32
46-Little Lulu & Tubby 4 8 12 22 34 45
48-The Lone Ranger 3 6 9 18 27 35
NOTE: *#1-30, 164 pgs.; #31 on, 132 pgs..*

GOLDEN LAD
Spark/Fact & Fiction Publ.: July, 1945 - No. 5, June, 1946 (#4, 5: 52 pgs.)
1-Origin & 1st app. Golden Lad & Swift Arrow; Sandusky and the Senator begins
62 124 186 391 658 925
2-Mort Meskin-c/a 31 62 93 181 291 400
3,4-Mort Meskin-c/a 28 56 84 162 261 360
5-Origin & 1st app. Golden Girl; Shaman & Flame app.
31 62 93 181 291 400
NOTE: *All have **Robinson,** and **Roussos** art plus **Meskin** covers and art.*

GOLDEN LEGACY
Fitzgerald Publishing Co.: 1966 - 1972 (Black History) (25¢)
1-12,14-16: 1-Toussaint L'Ouverture (1966), 2-Harriet Tubman (1967), 3-Crispus Attucks & the Minutemen (1967), 4-Benjamin Banneker (1968), 5-Matthew Henson (1969), 6-Alexander Dumas & Family (1969), 7-Frederick Douglass, Part 1 (1969), 8-Frederick Douglass, Part 2 (1970), 9-Robert Smalls (1970), 10-J. Cinque & the Amistad Mutiny (1970), 11-Men in Action: White, Marshall J. Wilkins (1970), 12-Black Cowboys (1972), 14-The Life of Alexander Pushkin (1971), 15-Ancient African Kingdoms (1972), 16-Black Inventors (1972) each.... 3 6 9 17 25 32
13-The Life of Martin Luther King, Jr. (1972) 3 6 9 21 32 42
1-10,12,13,15,16(1976)-Reprints 2 3 4 6 8 10

GOLDEN LOVE STORIES (Formerly Golden West Love)
Kirby Publishing Co.: No. 4, April, 1950
4-Powell-a; Glenn Ford/Janet Leigh photo-c 17 34 51 98 154 210

GOLDEN PICTURE CLASSIC, A
Western Printing Co. (Simon & Shuster): 1956-1957 (Text stories w/illustrations in color; 100 pgs. each)
CL-401: Treasure Island 11 22 33 64 90 115
CL-402,403: 402: Tom Sawyer. 403: Black Beauty 10 20 30 54 72 90
CL-404, 405: CL-404: Little Women. CL-405: Heidi 10 20 30 54 72 90
CL-406: Ben Hur 8 16 24 44 57 70
CL-407: Around the World in 80 Days 8 16 24 44 57 70
CL-408: Sherlock Holmes 9 18 27 50 65 80
CL-409: The Three Musketeers 8 16 24 44 57 70
CL-410: The Merry Advs. of Robin Hood 8 16 24 44 57 70
CL-411,412: 411: Hans Brinker. 412: The Count of Monte Cristo
9 18 27 50 65 80
(Both soft & hardcover editions are valued the same)
NOTE: *Recent research has uncovered new information. Apparently #s 1-6 were issued in 1956 and #7-12 in 1957. But they can be found in five different series listings: CL-1 to CL-12 (softbound); CL-401 to CL-412 (also softbound); CL-101 to CL-112 (hardbound); plus two new series discoveries: A Golden Reading Adventure, publ. by Golden Press; edited down to 60 pages and reduced in size to 6x9"; only #s discovered so far are #381 (CL-4), #382 (CL-6) & #387 (CL-3). They have no reorder list and some have covers different from GPC. There have also been found British hardbound editions of GPC with dust jackets. Copies of all five listed series vary from scarce to very rare. Some editions of some series have not yet been found at all.*

GOLDEN PICTURE STORY BOOK
Racine Press (Western): Dec, 1961 (50¢, Treasury size, 52 pgs.) (All are scarce)
ST-1-Huckleberry Hound (TV); Hokey Wolf, Pixie & Dixie, Quick Draw McGraw, Snooper and Blabber, Augie Doggie app. 17 34 51 122 236 350
ST-2-Yogi Bear (TV); Snagglepuss, Yakky Doodle, Quick Draw McGraw, Snooper and Blabber, Augie Doggie app. 17 34 51 122 236 350
ST-3-Babes in Toyland (Walt Disney's...)-Annette Funicello photo-c
22 44 66 157 304 450
ST-4-(...of Disney Ducks)-Walt Disney's Wonderful World of Ducks (Donald Duck, Uncle Scrooge, Donald's Nephews, Grandma Duck, Ludwig Von Drake, & Gyro Gearloose stories) 22 44 66 157 304 450

GOLDEN RECORD COMIC (See Amazing Spider-Man #1, Avengers #4, Fantastic Four #1, Journey Into Mystery #83)

GOLDEN STORY BOOKS
Western Printing Co. (Simon & Shuster): 1949-1950 (Heavy covers, digest size, 128 pgs.) (Illustrated text in color)
7-Walt Disney's Mystery in Disneyville, a book-length adventure starring Donald and Nephews, Mickey and Nephews, and with Minnie, Daisy and Goofy. Art by Dick Moores & Manuel Gonzales (scarce) 30 60 90 177 289 400
10-Bugs Bunny's Treasure Hunt, a book-length adventure starring Bugs & Porky Pig, with Petunia Pig & Nephew, Cicero. Art by Tom McKimson (scarce)
21 42 63 122 199 275
11,12 ('50): 11-M-G-M's Tom & Jerry. 12-Walt Disney's "So Dear My Heart"
20 40 60 114 182 250

GOLDEN WEST LOVE (Golden Love Stories No. 4)
Kirby Publishing Co.: Sept-Oct, 1949 - No. 3, Feb, 1950 (All 52 pgs.)
1-Powell-a in all; Roussos-a; painted-c 22 44 66 128 209 290
2,3: Photo-c 17 34 51 98 154 210

GOLDEN WEST RODEO TREASURY (See Dell Giants)

GOLDFISH (See A.K.A. Goldfish)

GOLDILOCKS (See March of Comics No. 1)

GOLD KEY CHAMPION
Gold Key: Mar, 1978 - No. 2, May, 1978 (50¢, 52pgs.)
1,2: 1-Space Family Robinson; half-r. 2-Mighty Samson; half-r
1 3 4 6 8 10

GOLD KEY SPOTLIGHT
Gold Key: May, 1976 - No. 11, Feb, 1978
1-Tom, Dick & Harriet 2 4 6 8 11 14
2-11: 2-Wacky Advs. of Cracky. 3-Wacky Witch. 4-Tom, Dick & Harriet. 5-Wacky Advs. of Cracky. 6-Dagar the Invincible; Santos-a; origin Demonomicon. 7-Wacky Witch & Greta Ghost. 8-The Occult Files of Dr. Spektor, Simbar, Lu-sai; Santos-a. 9-Tragg. 10-O. G. Whiz. 11-Tom, Dick & Harriet 2 4 6 8 10 12

GOLD MEDAL COMICS
Cambridge House: 1945 (25¢, one-shot, 132 pgs.)
nn-Captain Truth by Fugitani as well as Stallman and Howie Post, Crime Detector, The Witch of Salem, Luckyman, others app. 30 60 90 177 289 400

GOMER PYLE (TV)
Gold Key: July, 1966 - No. 3, Oct, 1967
1-Photo front/back-c 8 16 24 54 90 125
2,3 6 12 18 39 62 85

GON
DC Comics (Paradox Press): July, 1996 - No. 4, Oct, 1996; No. 5, 1997 ($5.95, B&W, digest-size, limited series)
1-5: Misadventures of baby dinosaur; 1-Gon. 2-Gon Again. 3-Gon: Here Today, Gone Tomorrow. 4-Gon: Going, Going...Gon. 5-Gon Swimmin'. Tanaka-c/a/scripts in all
1 2 3 5 6 8

GON COLOR SPECTACULAR
DC Comics (Paradox Press): 1998 ($5.95, square-bound)
nn-Tanaka-c/a/scripts 1 2 3 5 6 8

GON ON SAFARI
DC Comics (Paradox Press): 2000 ($7.95, B&W, digest-size)
nn-Tanaka-c/a/scripts 1 2 3 5 6 8

GON UNDERGROUND
DC Comics (Paradox Press): 1999 ($7.95, B&W, digest-size)
nn-Tanaka-c/a/scripts 1 2 3 5 6 8

GON WILD
DC Comics (Paradox Press): 1997 ($9.95, B&W, digest-size)
nn-Tanaka-c/a/scripts in all. (Rep. Gon #3,4) 1 3 4 6 8 10

GOODBYE, MR. CHIPS (See Movie Comics)

GOOD GIRL ART QUARTERLY
AC Comics: Summer, 1990 - No. 15, Spring, 1994 (B&W/color, 52 pgs.)

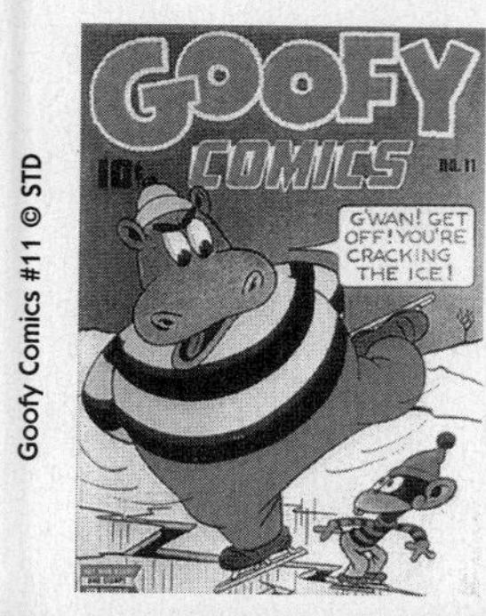

Goofy Comics #11 © STD

The Goon #26 © Eric Powell

Gotham City Sirens #1 © DC

	GD 2.0	VG 4.0	FN 6.0	VF 8.0	VF/NM 9.0	NM- 9.2

1,3-15 ($3.50)-All have one new story (often FemForce) & rest reprints by Baker, Ward & other "good girl" artists 4.00
2 ($3.95) 4.00

GOOD GIRL COMICS (Formerly Good Girl Art Quarterly)
AC Comics: No. 16, Summer, 1994 - No. 18, 1995 (B&W)

16-18 4.00

GOOD GUYS, THE
Defiant: Nov, 1993 - No. 9, July, 1994 ($2.50/$3.25/$3.50)

1-($3.50, 52 pgs.)-Glory x-over from Plasm 3.50
2,3,5-9: 9-Pre-Schism issue 2.50
4-($3.25, 52 pgs.) 3.25

GOOD, THE BAD AND THE UGLY, THE (Also see Man With No Name)
Dynamite Entertainment: 2009 - Present ($3.50)

1-8:1-Character from the 1966 Clint Eastwood movie; Dixon-s/Polls-a; three covers 3.50

GOOD TRIUMPHS OVER EVIL! (Also see Narrative Illustration)
M.C. Gaines: 1943 (12 pgs., 7-1/4"x10", B&W) (not a comic book) (Rare)

	GD	VG	FN	VF	VF/NM	NM-
nn-A pamphlet, sequel to Narrative Illustration	103	206	309	659	1130	1600

NOTE: *Print, A Quarterly Journal of the Graphic Arts Vol. 3 No. 3 (64 pg. square bound) features 1st printing of Good Triumphs Over Evil! A VG copy sold for $350 in 2005.*

GOOFY (Disney)(See Dynabrite Comics, Mickey Mouse Magazine V4#7, Walt Disney Showcase #35 & Wheaties)
Dell Publishing Co.: No. 468, May, 1953 - Sept-Nov, 1962

	GD	VG	FN	VF	VF/NM	NM-
Four Color 468 (#1)	11	22	33	80	145	210
Four Color 562,627,658,702,747,802,857	7	14	21	47	76	105
Four Color 899,952,987,1053,1094,1149,1201	5	10	15	32	51	70
12-308-211(Dell, 9-11/62)	5	10	15	32	51	70

GOOFY ADVENTURES
Disney Comics: June, 1990 - No. 17, 1991 ($1.50)

1-17: Most new stories. 2-Joshua Quagmire-a w/free poster. 7-WDC&S-r plus new-a. 9-Gottfredson-r. 14-Super Goof story. 15-All Super Goof issue. 17-Gene Colan-a(p) 3.00

GOOFY ADVENTURE STORY (See Goofy No. 857)

GOOFY COMICS (Companion to Happy Comics)(Not Disney)
Nedor Publ. Co. No. 1-14/Standard No. 14-48: June, 1943 - No. 48, 1953 (Animated Cartoons)

	GD	VG	FN	VF	VF/NM	NM-
1-Funny animal; Oriolo-c	29	58	87	170	278	385
2	15	30	45	90	140	190
3-10	14	28	42	76	108	140
11-19	10	20	30	58	79	100
20-35-Frazetta text illos in all	11	22	33	64	90	115
36-48	9	18	27	50	65	80

GOOFY SUCCESS STORY (See Goofy No. 702)

GOON, THE
Avatar Press: Mar, 1999 - No. 3, July, 1999 ($3.00, B&W)

1-Eric Powell-s/a 20.00
2 12.00
3 8.00
...: Rough Stuff (Albatross, 1/03, $15.95) r/Avatar Press series #1-3 16.00
...: Rough Stuff (Dark Horse, 2/04, $12.95) r/Avatar Press series #1-3 newly colored 13.00

GOON, THE (2nd series)
Albatross Exploding Funny Books: Oct, 2002 - No. 4, Feb, 2003 ($2.95)

1-Eric Powell-s/a 10.00
2-4 6.00
...Color Special 1 (8/02) 10.00
...: Nothin' But Misery Vol. 1 (Dark Horse, 7/03, $15.95, TPB) - Reprints The Goon #1-4 (Albatross series), Color Special, and story from DHP #157 16.00

GOON, THE (3rd series) (Also see Dethklok Versus the Goon)
Dark Horse Comics: June, 2003 - Present ($2.99)

1-Eric Powell-s/a in all 6.00
2-4 4.00
5-31: 7-Hellboy-c/app; framing seq. by Mignola 14-Two covers 3.00
32-($3.99, 3/09) Tenth Anniversary issue; with sketch pages and pin-ups 4.00
33-($3.50) Silent issue 3.50
... 25¢ Edition (9/05, 25¢) 2.50
...: Chinatown and the Mystery of Mr. Wicker HC (11/07, $19.95) original GN; Powell-s/a 20.00
...: Fancy Pants Edition HC (10/05, $24.95, dust jacket) r/#1,2 of 2nd series & #1,3,5,9 of 3rd series; Powell intro.; sketch pages and cover gallery 25.00
...: Heaps of Ruination (5/05, $12.95, TPB) r/#5-8; intro. by Frank Darabont 13.00
...: My Murderous Childhood (And Other Grievous Yarns) (5/04, $13.95, TPB) r/#1-4 and short story from Drawing on Your Nightmares one-shot; intro. by Frank Cho 14.00
...: Virtue and the Grim Consequences Thereof (2/06, $16.95) r/#9-13 17.00
...: Wicked Inclinations (12/06, $14.95) r/#14-18; intro. by Mike Allred 15.00

GOON NOIR, THE (Dwight T. Albatross's...)
Dark Horse Comics: Sept, 2006 - No. 3, Jan, 2007 ($2.99, B&W, limited series)

1-3-Anthology 1-Oswalt-s/Ploog-a; Sniegoski-s/Powell-a; Morrison-s/a; Niles-s/Sook-a. 2-Nowlan, Barta-a. 3-Ramos, Guy Davis-a; Nelson, Posehn, Thomas Lennon-s 3.00
TPB (7/07, $12.95) r/#1-3; sketch pages; intros by "Dwight" 13.00

GOOSE (Humor magazine)
Cousins Publ. (Fawcett): Sept, 1976 - No. 3, 1976 (75¢, 52 pgs., B&W)

	GD	VG	FN	VF	VF/NM	NM-
1-Nudity in all	3	6	9	16	23	30
2,3: 2-(10/76) Fonz-c/s; Lone Ranger story. 3-Wonder Woman, King Kong, Six Million Dollar Man stories	2	4	6	11	16	20

GORDO (See Comics Revue No. 5 & Giant Comics Edition)

GORGO (Based on M.G.M. movie) (See Return of...)
Charlton Comics: May, 1961 - No. 23, Sept, 1965

	GD	VG	FN	VF	VF/NM	NM-
1-Ditko-a, 22 pgs.	22	44	66	157	304	450
2,3-Ditko-c/a	12	24	36	88	162	235
4-Ditko-c	9	18	27	63	107	150
5-11,13-16: 11,13-16-Ditko-a	8	16	24	54	90	125
12,17-23: 12-Reptisaurus x-over; Montes/Bache-a-No. 17-23. 20-Giordano-c	5	10	15	34	55	75
Gorgo's Revenge('62)-Becomes Return of...	7	14	21	45	73	100

GOSPEL BLIMP, THE
Spire Christian Comics (Fleming H. Revell Co.): 1973,1975 (35¢/39¢, 36 pgs.)

	GD	VG	FN	VF	VF/NM	NM-
nn-(1973)	2	4	6	10	14	18
nn-(1975)	2	4	6	8	10	12

GOTHAM BY GASLIGHT (A Tale of the Batman)(See Batman: Master of...)
DC Comics: 1989 ($3.95, one-shot, squarebound, 52 pgs.)

nn-Mignola/Russell-a; intro by Robert Bloch 4.00

GOTHAM CENTRAL
DC Comics: Early Feb, 2003 - No. 40, Apr, 2006 ($2.50)

1-40-Stories of Gotham City Police. 1-Brubaker & Rucka-s/Lark-c/a. 10-Two-Face app. 13,15-Joker-c. 18-Huntress app. 27-Catwoman-c. 32-Poison Ivy app. 34-Teen Titans-c/app. 38-Crispus Allen killed (becomes The Spectre in Infinite Crisis #5) 2.50
... Book One: In the Line of Duty HC (2008, $29.99, dustjacket) r/#1-10; sketchpages 30.00
... Book Two: Jokers and Madmen HC (2009, $29.99, dustjacket) r/#11-22 30.00
...: Dead Robin (2007, $17.99, TPB) r/#33-40; cover gallery 18.00
...: Half a Life (2005, $14.99, TPB) r/#6-10, Batman Chronicles #16 and Detective #747 15.00
...: In The Line of Duty (2004, $9.95, TPB) r/#1-5, cover gallery & sketch pages 10.00
...: The Quick and the Dead TPB (2006, $14.99) r/#23-25,28-31 15.00
...: Unresolved Targets (2006, $14.99, TPB) r/#12-15,19-22, cover gallery 15.00

GOTHAM CITY SIRENS (Batman:Reborn)
DC Comics: Aug, 2009 - Present ($2.99)

1-7: 1-Catwoman, Harley Quinn and Poison Ivy; Dini-s/March-a/c 3.00
1-Variant-c by JG Jones 5.00

GOTHAM GAZETTE (Battle For The Cowl crossover in Batman titles)
DC Comics: May, 2009; Jul, 2009 ($2.99, one-shots)

1-Short stories of Gotham without Batman; Nguyen, March, ChrisCross & others-a 3.00
...: Batman Alive? (7/09) Vicki Vale app.; Nguyen, March, ChrisCross & others-a 3.00

GOTHAM GIRLS
DC Comics: Oct, 2002 - No. 5, Feb, 2003 ($2.25, limited series)

1-5-Catwoman, Batgirl, Poison Ivy, Harley Quinn from animated series 2.50

GOTHAM NIGHTS (See Batman: Gotham Nights II)
DC Comics: Mar, 1992 - No. 4, June, 1992 ($1.25, limited series)

1-4: Featuring Batman 2.50

GOTHAM UNDERGROUND
DC Comics: Dec, 2007 - No. 9, Aug, 2008 ($2.99, limited series)

1-9-Nine covers interlock for single image; Tieri-s/Calafiore-a/c. 7,8-Vigilante app. 3.00
Batman: Gotham Underground TPB (2008, $19.99) r/#1-9; interlocked image cover 20.00

GOTHIC ROMANCES
Atlas/Seaboard Publ.: Dec, 1974 (75¢, B&W, magazine, 76 pgs.)

	GD	VG	FN	VF	VF/NM	NM-
1-Text w/ illos by N. Adams, Chaykin, Heath (2 pgs. ea.); painted cover from Ravenwood Gothic paperback "The Conservatory"(scarce)	21	42	63	148	287	425

GOTHIC TALES OF LOVE (Magazine)

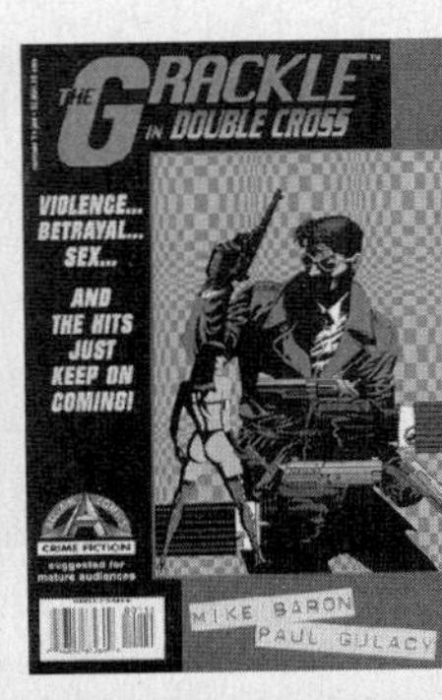

The Grackle #1 © Acclaim

Grand Prix #16 © CC

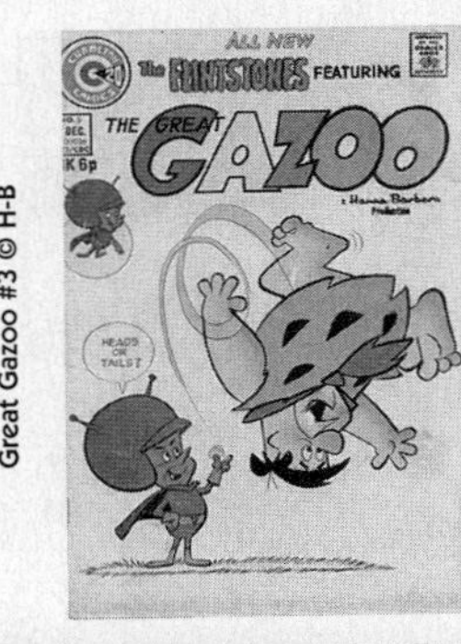

Great Gazoo #3 © H-B

	GD 2.0	VG 4.0	FN 6.0	VF 8.0	VF/NM 9.0	NM- 9.2
Marvel Comics: Apr, 1975 - No. 3, 1975 (B&W, 76 pgs.)						
1-3-Painted-c/a (scarce)	24	48	72	175	338	500
GOVERNOR & J. J., THE (TV)						
Gold Key: Feb, 1970 - No. 3, Aug, 1970 (Photo-c)						
1	4	8	12	26	41	55
2,3	3	6	9	19	29	38
GRACKLE, THE						
Acclaim Comics: Jan, 1997 - No. 4, Apr, 1997 ($2.95, B&W)						
1-4: Mike Baron scripts & Paul Gulacy-c/a. 1-4-Doublecross						3.00
GRAFIK MUSIK						
Caliber Press: Nov, 1990 - No. 4, Aug, 1991 ($3.50/$2.50)						
1-($3.50, 48 pgs., color) Mike Allred-c/a/scripts-1st app. in color of Frank Einstein (Madman)	3	6	9	14	20	25
2-($2.50, 24 pgs., color)	2	4	6	9	12	15
3,4-($2.50, 24 pgs., B&W)	2	4	6	8	10	12
GRANDMA DUCK'S FARM FRIENDS(See Walt Disney's C&S 293 & Wheaties)						
Dell Publishing Co.: No. 763, Jan, 1957 - No. 1279, Feb, 1962 (Disney)						
Four Color 763 (#1)	8	16	24	52	86	120
Four Color 873	6	12	18	37	59	80
Four Color 965,1279	5	10	15	32	51	70
Four Color 1010,1073,1161-Barks-a; 1073,1161-Barks c/a	12	24	36	85	155	225
GRAND PRIX (Formerly Hot Rod Racers)						
Charlton Comics: No. 16, Sept, 1967 - No. 31, May, 1970						
16-Features Rick Roberts	4	8	12	22	34	45
17-20	3	6	9	17	26	34
21-31	3	6	9	16	23	30
GRAPHIQUE MUSIQUE						
Slave Labor Graphics: Dec, 1989 - No. 3, May, 1990 ($2.95, 52 pgs.)						
1-Mike Allred-c/a/scripts	3	6	9	20	30	40
2,3	3	6	9	16	23	30
GRAVESLINGER						
Image Comics (Shadowline): Oct, 2007 - No. 4, Mar, 2008 ($3.50, limited series)						
1-4-Denton & Mariotte-s/Cboins-a						3.50
GRAVE TALES						
Hamilton Comics: Oct, 1991 - No. 3, Feb, 1992 ($3.95, B&W, mag., 52 pgs.)						
1-Staton-c/a	2	3	4	6	8	10
2,3: 2-Staton-a; Morrow-c	1	2	3	5	6	8
GRAVITY (Also see Beyond! limited series)						
Marvel Comics: Aug, 2005 - No. 5, Dec, 2005 ($2.99, limited series)						
1-5: 1-Intro. Gravity; McKeever-s/Norton-a. 2-Rhino-c/app. 5-Spider-Man app.						3.00
...: Big-City Super Hero (2005, $7.99, digest) r/#1-5						8.00
GRAY AREA, THE						
Image Comics: Jun, 2004 - No. 3, Oct, 2004 ($5.95/$3.95, limited series)						
1,3-($5.95) Romita, Jr.-a/Brunswick-s; sketch pages and script pages. 3-Pin-up pages						6.00
2-($3.95)						4.00
...Vol. 1: All Of This Can Be Yours (2005, $14.95) r/series & sketch,script & pin-up pages						15.00
GRAY GHOST, THE						
Dell Publishing Co.: No. 911, July, 1958; No. 1000, June-Aug, 1959						
Four Color 911 (#1), 1000-Photo-c each	8	16	24	56	93	130
GREAT ACTION COMICS						
I. W. Enterprises: 1958 (Reprints with new covers)						
1-Captain Truth reprinted from Gold Medal #1	3	6	9	16	23	30
8,9-Reprints Phantom Lady #15 & 23	7	14	21	49	80	110
GREAT AMERICAN COMICS PRESENTS - THE SECRET VOICE						
Peter George 4-Star Publ./American Features Syndicate: 1945 (10¢)						
1-Anti-Nazi; "What Really Happened to Hitler"	39	78	117	231	378	525
GREAT AMERICAN WESTERN, THE						
AC Comics: 1987 - No. 4, 1990? ($1.75/$2.95/$3.50, B&W with some color)						
1-4: 1-Western-r plus Bill Black-a. 2-Tribute to ME comics; Durango Kid photo-c 3-Tribute to Tom Mix plus Roy Rogers, Durango Kid; Billy the Kid-r by Severin; photo-c. 4- ($3.50, 52 pgs., 16 pgs. color)-Tribute to Lash LaRue; photo-c & interior photos; Fawcett-r						4.00
...Presents 1 (1991, $5.00) New Sunset Carson; film history						5.00
GREAT CAT FAMILY, THE (Disney-TV/Movie)						
Dell Publishing Co.: No. 750, Nov, 1956 (one-shot)						
Four Color 750-Pinocchio & Alice app.	6	12	18	43	69	95
GREAT COMICS						
Great Comics Publications: Nov, 1941 - No. 3, Jan, 1942						
1-Origin/1st app. The Great Zarro; Madame Strange & Guy Gorham, Wizard of Science & The Great Zarro begin	129	258	387	826	1413	2000
2-Buck Johnson, Jungle Explorer app.; X-Mas-c	65	130	195	416	708	1000
3-Futuro Takes Hitler to Hell-c/s; "The Lost City" movie story (starring William Boyd); continues in Choice Comics #3	500	1000	1500	3500	5750	8000
GREAT COMICS						
Novack Publishing Co./Jubilee Comics/Knockout/Barrel O' Fun: 1945						
1-(Four publ. variations: Barrel O-Fun, Jubilee, Knockout & Novack)-The Defenders, Capt. Power app.; L. B. Cole-c	32	64	96	188	307	425
1-(Jubilee)-Same cover; Boogey Man, Satanas, & The Sorcerer & His Apprentice	26	52	78	152	249	345
1-(Barrel O' Fun)-L. B. Cole-c; Barrel O' Fun overprinted in indicia; Li'l Cactus, Cuckoo Sheriff (humorous)	18	36	54	105	165	225
GREAT DOGPATCH MYSTERY (See Mammy Yokum & the...)						
GREATEST AMERICAN HERO (Based on the 1981-1986 TV series)						
Catastrophic Comics: Dec, 2008 - Present ($3.50/$3.95)						
1,3-Origin re-told; William Katt and others-s. 3-Obama-c/app.						3.50
GREATEST BATMAN STORIES EVER TOLD, THE						
DC Comics						
Hardcover ($24.95)						50.00
Softcover ($15.95) "Greatest DC Stories Vol. 2" on spine						20.00
Vol. 2 softcover (1992, $16.95) "Greatest DC Stories Vol. 7" on spine						20.00
GREATEST FLASH STORIES EVER TOLD, THE						
DC Comics: 1991						
nn-Hardcover ($29.95); Infantino-c						45.00
nn-Softcover ($14.95)						20.00
GREATEST GOLDEN AGE STORIES EVER TOLD, THE						
DC Comics: 1990 ($24.95, hardcover)						
nn-Ordway-c						60.00
GREATEST HITS						
DC Comics (Vertigo): Dec, 2008 - No. 6, Apr, 2009 ($2.99, limited series)						
1-6-Intro. The Mates superhero team in 1967 England; Tischman-s/Fabry-a/c						3.00
GREATEST JOKER STORIES EVER TOLD, THE (See Batman)						
DC Comics: 1983						
Hardcover ($19.95)-Kyle Baker painted-c						45.00
Softcover ($14.95)						20.00
Stacked Deck...Expanded Edition (1992, $29.95)-Longmeadow Press Publ.						32.00
GREATEST 1950s STORIES EVER TOLD, THE						
DC Comics: 1990						
Hardcover ($29.95)-Kubert-c						55.00
Softcover ($14.95) "Greatest DC Stories Vol. 5" on spine						22.00
GREATEST TEAM-UP STORIES EVER TOLD, THE						
DC Comics: 1989						
Hardcover ($24.95)-DeVries and Infantino painted-c						55.00
Softcover ($14.95) "Greatest DC Stories Vol. 4" on spine; Adams-c						22.00
GREATEST SUPERMAN STORIES EVER TOLD, THE						
DC Comics: 1987						
Hardcover ($24.95)						50.00
Softcover ($15.95)						22.00
GREAT EXPLOITS						
Decker Publ./Red Top: Oct, 1957						
1-Krigstein-a(2) (re-issue on cover); reprints Daring Advs. #6 by Approved Comics	6	12	18	31	38	45
GREAT FOODINI, THE (See Foodini)						
GREAT GAZOO, THE (The Flintstones)(TV)						
Charlton Comics: Aug, 1973 - No. 20, Jan, 1977 (Hanna-Barbera)						
1	4	8	12	24	37	50
2-10	3	6	9	14	19	24
11-20	2	4	6	10	14	18
GREAT GRAPE APE, THE (TV)(See TV Stars #1)						

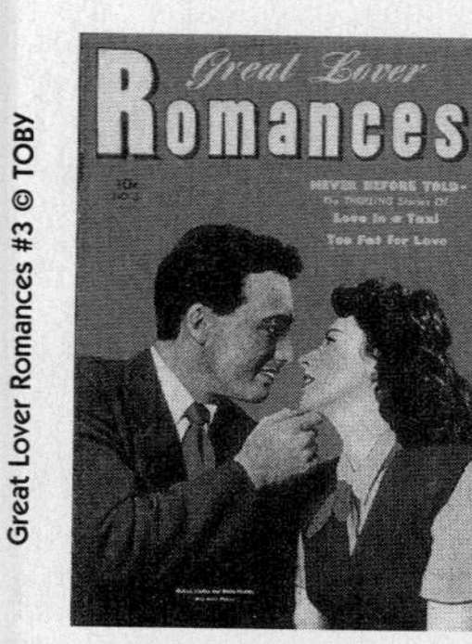

Great Lover Romances #3 © TOBY

Green Arrow #45 © DC

Green Arrow/Black Canary #5 © DC

Charlton Comics: Sept, 1976 - No. 2, Nov, 1976 (Hanna-Barbera)
1 4 8 12 22 34 45
2 3 6 9 14 20 25

GREAT LOCOMOTIVE CHASE, THE (Disney)
Dell Publishing Co.: No. 712, Sept, 1956 (one-shot)
Four Color 712-Movie, photo-c 7 14 21 47 76 105

GREAT LOVER ROMANCES (Young Lover Romances #4,5)
Toby Press: 3/51; #2, 1951(nd); #3, 1952 (nd); #6, Oct?, 1952 - No. 22, May, 1955 (Photo-c #1-5, 10 ,13, 15, 17) (no #4, 5)
1-Jon Juan story-r/Jon Juan #1 by Schomburg; Dr. Anthony King app.
18 36 54 107 169 230
2-Jon Juan, Dr. Anthony King app. 11 22 33 64 90 115
3,7,9-14,16-22: 10-Rita Hayworth photo-c. 17-Rita Hayworth & Aldo Ray photo-c
9 18 27 50 65 80
6-Kurtzman-a (10/52) 11 22 33 62 86 110
8-Five pgs. of "Pin-Up Pete" by Sparling 11 22 33 62 86 110
15-Liz Taylor photo-c (scarce) 37 74 111 222 361 500

GREAT RACE, THE (See Movie Classics)

GREAT SCOTT SHOE STORE (See Bulls-Eye)

GREAT SOCIETY COMIC BOOK, THE (Political parody)
Pocket Books Inc./Parallax Pub.: 1966 ($1.00, 36 pgs., 7"x10", one-shot)
nn-Super-LBJ-c/story; 60s politicians app. as super-heroes; Tallarico-a
3 6 9 18 27 35

GREAT TEN, THE (Characters from Final Crisis)
DC Comics: Jan, 2010 - No. 10 ($2.99, limited series)
1-4-Super team of China; Bedard-s/McDaniel-a/Stanley Lau-c 3.00

GREAT WEST (Magazine)
M. F. Enterprises: 1969 (B&W, 52 pgs.)
V1#1 2 4 6 10 14 18

GREAT WESTERN
Magazine Enterprises: No. 8, Jan-Mar, 1954 - No. 11, Oct-Dec, 1954
8(A-1 93)-Trail Colt by Guardineer; Powell Red Hawk-r/Straight Arrow begins, ends #11; Durango Kid story 18 36 54 103 162 220
9(A-1 105), 11(A-1 127)-Ghost Rider, Durango Kid app. in each. 9-Red Mask-c, but no app.
15 30 45 83 124 165
10(A-1 113)-The Calico Kid by Guardineer-r/Tim Holt #8; Straight Arrow, Durango Kid app.
12 24 36 69 97 125
I.W. Reprint #1,2 9: 1,2-r/Straight Arrow #36,42. 9-r/Straight Arrow #?
3 6 9 16 22 28
I.W. Reprint #8-Origin Ghost Rider(r/Tim Holt #11); Tim Holt app.; Bolle-a
3 6 9 17 25 32
NOTE: *Guardineer c-8. Powell a(r)-8-11 (from Straight Arrow).*

GREEK STREET
DC Comics (Vertigo): Sept, 2009 - Present ($1.00/$2.99)
1-8: 1-($1.00) Milligan-s/Gianfelice-a. 2,3-($2.99) 3.00

GREEN ARROW (See Action #440, Adventure, Brave & the Bold, DC Super Stars #17, Detective #521, Flash #217, Green Lantern #76, Justice League of America #4, Leading Comics, More Fun #73 (1st app.), Showcase '95 #9 & World's Finest Comics)

GREEN ARROW
DC Comics: May, 1983 - No. 4, Aug, 1983 (limited series)
1-Origin; Speedy cameo; Mike W. Barr scripts, Trevor Von Eeden-c/a 5.00
2-4 4.00

GREEN ARROW
DC Comics: Feb, 1988 - No. 137, Oct, 1998 ($1.00-$2.50) (Painted-c #1-3)
1-Mike Grell scripts begin, ends #80 5.00
2-49,51-74,76-86: 27,28-Warlord app. 35-38-Co-stars Black Canary; Bill Wray-i. 40-Grell-a. 47-Begin $1.50-c. 63-No longer has mature readers on-c. 63-66-Shado app. 81-Aparo-a begins, ends #100; Nuklon app. 82-Intro & death of Rival. 83-Huntress-c/story. 84, 85-Deathstroke app. 86-Catwoman-c/story w/Jim Balent layouts 2.50
50,75-($2.50, 52 pgs.): Anniversary issues. 75-Arsenal (Roy Harper) & Shado app. 3.00
0,87-96: 87-$1.95-c begins. 88-Guy Gardner, Martian Manhunter, & Wonder Woman-c/app.; Flash-c. 89-Anarky app. 90-(9/94)-Zero Hour tie-in. 0-(10/94)-1st app. Connor Hawke; Aparo-a(p). 91-(11/94). 93-1st app. Camorouge. 95-Hal Jordan cameo. 96-Intro new Force of July; Hal Jordan (Parallax) app; Oliver Queen learns that Connor Hawke is his son 2.50
97-99,102-109: 97-Begin $2.25-c; no Aparo-a. 97-99-Arsenal app. 102,103-Underworld Unleashed x-over. 104-GL(Kyle Rayner)-c/app. 105-Robin-c/app. 107-109-Thorn app. 109-Lois Lane cameo; Weeks-c. 2.50
100-($3.95)-Foil-c; Superman app. 1 3 4 6 8 10
101-Death of Oliver Queen; Superman app. 3 6 9 16 23 30
110,111-124: 110,111-GL x-over. 110-Intro Hatchet. 114-Final Night. 115-117-Black Canary & Oracle app. 2.50
125-($3.50, 48 pgs)-GL x-over cont. in GL #92 3.50
126-136: 126-Begin $2.50-c. 130-GL & Flash x-over. 132,133-JLA app. 134,135-Brotherhood of the Fist pts. 1,5. 136-Hal Jordan-c/app. 2.50
137-Last issue; Superman app.; last panel cameo of Oliver Queen
2 4 6 9 12 15
#1,000,000 (11/98) 853rd Century x-over 2.50
Annual 1-6 ('88-'94, 68 pgs.)-1-No Grell scripts. 2-No Grell scripts; recaps origin Green Arrow, Speedy, Black Canary & others. 3-Bill Wray-a. 4-50th anniversary issue. 5-Batman, Eclipso app. 6-Bloodlines; Hook app. 3.50
Annual 7-('95, $3.95)-Year One story 4.00
NOTE: ***Aparo** a-0, 81-85, 86 (partial),87p, 88p, 91-95, 96i, 98-100p, 109p; c-81,98-100p. **Austin** c-96i. **Balent** layouts-86. **Burchett** c-91-95. **Campanella** a-100-108i, 110-113i; c-99i, 101-108i,110-113i. **Denys Cowan** a-39p, 41-43p, 47p, 48p, 60p; c-41-43. **Damaggio** a(p)-97p, 100-108p, 110-112p; c-97-99p, 101-108p, 110-113p. **Mike Grell** c-1-4, 10p, 11, 39, 40, 44, 45, 47-80, Annual 4, 5. **Nasser/Netzer** a-89, 96. **Sienkiewicz** a-109i. **Springer** a-67, 68. **Weeks** c-109.*

GREEN ARROW
DC Comics: Apr, 2001 - No. 75, Aug, 2007 ($2.50/$2.99)
1-Oliver Queen returns; Kevin Smith-s/Hester-a/Wagner-painted-c
2 4 6 9 13 16
1-2nd-4th printings 3.00
2-Batman cameo 1 2 3 4 5 7
2-2nd printing 2.50
3-5: 4-JLA app. 5.00
6-15: 7-Barry Allen & Hal Jordan app. 9,10-Stanley & his Monster app. 10-Oliver regains his soul. 12-Hawkman-c/app. 3.00
16-25: 16-Brad Meltzer-s begin; The Shade app. 18-Solomon Grundy-c/app. 19-JLA app. 22-Beatty-s; Count Vertigo app. 23-25-Green Lantern app.; Raab-s/Adlard-a 2.50
26-49: 26-Winick-s begin. 35-37-Riddler app. 43-Mia learns she's HIV+. 45-Mia becomes the new Speedy. 46-Teen Titans app. 49-The Outsiders app. 2.50
50-($3.50) Green Arrow's team and the Outsiders vs. The Riddler and Drakon 3.50
51-59: 51-Anarky app. 52-Zatanna-c/app. 55-59-Dr. Light app. 2.50
60-74: 60-One Year Later starts. 62-Begin $2.99-c; Deathstroke app. 69-Batman app. 3.00
75-($3.50) Ollie proposes to Dinah (see Black Canary mini-series); JLA app. 3.50
...: City Walls SC (2005, $17.95) r/#32, 34-39 18.00
...: Crawling Through the Wreckage SC (2007, $12.99) r/#60-65 13.00
...: Heading Into the Light SC (2006, $12.99) r/#52,54-59 13.00
...: Moving Targets SC (2006, $17.99) r/#40-50 18.00
...: Quiver HC (2002, $24.95) r/#1-10; Smith intro. 25.00
...: Quiver SC (2003, $17.95) r/#1-10; Smith intro. 18.00
...: Road to Jericho SC (2007, $17.99) r/#66-75 18.00
...Secret Files & Origins 1-(12/02, $4.95) Origin stories & profiles; Wagner-c 5.00
...: Sounds of Violence HC (2003, $19.95) r/#11-15; Hester intro. & sketch pages 20.00
...: Sounds of Violence SC (2003, $12.95) r/#11-15; Hester intro. & sketch pages 13.00
...: Straight Shooter SC (2004, $12.95) r/#26-31 13.00
...: The Archer's Quest HC (2003, $19.95) r/#16-21; pitch, script and sketch pages 20.00
...: The Archer's Quest SC (2004, $14.95) r/#16-21; pitch, script and sketch pages 15.00

GREEN ARROW/BLACK CANARY
DC Comics: Dec, 2007 - Present ($3.50/$2.99)
1-($3.50) Connor Hawke & Black Canary; follows Wedding Special; Winick-s/Chang-a 3.50
2-21-($2.99) 3-Two covers; Connor shot. 5-Dinah & Ollie's real wedding 3.00
22-28-($3.99) Back-up stories begin. 28-Origin of Cupid 4.00
...: A League of Their Own TPB (2009, $17.99) r/#11-14 & G.A. Secret Files & Origins 18.00
...: Enemies List TPB (2009, $17.99) r/#15-20 18.00
...: Family Business TPB (2008, $17.99) r/#5-10 18.00
...: Road To The Altar TPB (2008, $17.99) r/proposal pages from Green Arrow #75, Birds of Prey #109, Black Canary #1-4 and Black Canary Wedding Planner #1 18.00
...: The Wedding Album HC (2008, $19.99, dustjacket) r/#1-5 & Wedding Special #1 20.00
...: The Wedding Album SC (2009, $17.99) r/#1-5 & Wedding Special #1 18.00
... Wedding Special 1 (11/07, $3.99) Winick-s/Conner-a/c; Dinah & Ollie's "wedding" 4.00
... Wedding Special 1 (11/07, $3.99) 2nd printing with Ryan Sook variant-c 4.00

GREEN ARROW: THE LONG BOW HUNTERS
DC Comics: Aug, 1987 - No. 3, Oct, 1987 ($2.95, limited series, mature)
1-Grell-c/a in all 6.00
1,2-2nd printings 3.00
2,3 4.00
Trade paperback (1989, $12.95)-r/#1-3 13.00

GREEN ARROW: THE WONDER YEAR
DC Comics: Feb, 1993 - No. 4, May, 1993 ($1.75, limited series)

Green Hornet #1 © Green Hornet Inc.

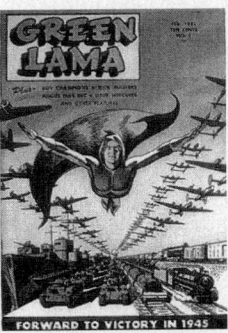

Green Lama #2 © Spark

Green Lantern #19 © DC

GD VG FN VF VF/NM NM-
2.0 4.0 6.0 8.0 9.0 9.2

1-4: Mike Grell-a(p)/scripts & Gray Morrow-a(i) 2.50

GREEN ARROW: YEAR ONE
DC Comics: Early Sept, 2007 - No. 6, Late Nov, 2007 ($2.99, bi-weekly limited series)

1-6-Origin re-told; Diggle-s/Jock-a 3.00
HC (2008, $24.99) r/#1-6; intro. by Brian K. Vaughan; script and sketch pages 25.00
SC (2009, $14.99) r/#1-6; intro. by Brian K. Vaughan; script and sketch pages 15.00

GREEN BERET, THE (See Tales of...)

GREEN GIANT COMICS (Also see Colossus Comics)
Pelican Publ. (Funnies, Inc.): 1940 (No price on cover; distributed in New York City only)

1-Dr. Nerod, Green Giant, Black Arrow, Mundoo & Master Mystic app.; origin Colossus (Rare)
1100 2200 3300 8400 15,200 22,000

NOTE: *The idea for this book came from George Kapitan. Printed by Moreau Publ. of Orange, N.J. as an experiment to see if they could profitably use the idle time of their 40-page Hoe color press. The experiment failed due to the difficulty of obtaining good quality color registration and Mr. Moreau believes the book never reached the stands. The book has no price or date which lends credence to this. Contains five pages reprinted from Motion Picture Funnies Weekly.*

GREEN GOBLIN
Marvel Comics: Oct, 1995 - No. 13, Oct, 1996 ($2.95/$1.95)

1-($2.95)-Scott McDaniel-c/a begins, ends #7; foil-c 3.50
2-13: 2-Begin $1.95-c. 4-Hobgoblin-c/app; Thing app. 6-Daredevil-c/app. 8-Robertson-a; McDaniel-c. 12,13-Onslaught x-over. 13-Green Goblin quits; Spider-Man app. 2.50

GREENHAVEN
Aircel Publishing: 1988 - No. 3, 1988 ($2.00, limited series, 28 pgs.)

1-3 2.50

GREEN HORNET, THE (TV)
Dell Publishing Co./Gold Key: Sept, 1953; Feb, 1967 - No. 3, Aug, 1967

Four Color 496-Painted-c. 23 46 69 166 321 475
1-Bruce Lee photo-c and back-c pin-up 17 34 51 119 230 340
2,3-Bruce Lee photo-c 12 24 36 82 149 215

GREEN HORNET, THE (Also see Kato of the... & Tales of the...)
Now Comics: Nov, 1989 - No. 14, Feb, 1991 ($1.75)
V2#1, Sept, 1991 - V2#40, Jan, 1995 ($1.95)

1 ($2.95, double-size)-Steranko painted-c; G.A. Green Hornet 5.00
1,2: 1-2nd printing ('90, $3.95)-New Butler-c 4.00
3-14: 5-Death of original ('30s) Green Hornet. 6-Dave Dorman painted-c. 11-Snyder-c 3.00
V2#1-11,13-21,24-26,28-30,32-37: 1-Butler painted-c. 9-Mayerik-c 2.50
12-($2.50)-Color Green Hornet button polybagged inside 4.00
22,23-($2.95)-Bagged w/color hologravure card 4.00
27-($2.95)-Newsstand ed. polybagged w/multi-dimensional card (1993 Anniversary Special on cover), 27-($2.95)-Direct Sale ed. polybagged w/multi-dimensional card; cover variations 3.00
31,38: 31-($2.50)-Polybagged w/trading card 2.50
39,40-Low print run 6.00
1-($2.50)-Polybagged w/button (same as #12) 3.00
2,3-($1.95)-Same as #13 & 14 2.50
Annual 1 (12/92, $2.50), Annual 1994 (10/94, $2.95) 3.50

GREEN HORNET (Also see FCBD Edition in the Promotional Comics section)
Dynamite Entertainment: 2010 - Present ($3.99)

1-Kevin Smith-s/Jonathan Lau-a; covers by Ross, Cassaday, Campbell and Segovia 4.00

GREEN HORNET: DARK TOMORROW
Now Comics: Jun, 1993 - No. 3, Aug, 1993 ($2.50, limited series)

1-3: Future Green Hornet 3.00

GREEN HORNET: SOLITARY SENTINEL, THE
Now Comics: Dec, 1992 - No. 3, 1993 ($2.50, limited series)

1-3 3.00

GREEN HORNET COMICS (...Racket Buster #44) (Radio, movies)
Helnit Publ. Co.(Holyoke) No. 1-6/Family Comics(Harvey) No. 7-on:
Dec, 1940 - No. 47, Sept, 1949 (See All New #13,14)(Early issues: 68 pgs.)

1-1st app. Green Hornet & Kato; origin of Green Hornet on inside front-c; intro the Black Beauty (Green Hornet's car); painted-c 541 1082 1623 3950 6975 10,000
2-Early issues based on radio adventures 219 438 657 1402 2401 3400
3 155 310 465 992 1696 2400
4-6: 6-(8/41) 126 252 378 806 1378 1950
7 (6/42)-Origin The Zebra & begins; Robin Hood, Spirit of '76, Blonde Bomber & Mighty Midgets begin; new logo 103 206 309 659 1130 1600
8,10 89 178 267 565 970 1375
9-Kirby-c 110 220 330 704 1202 1700
11,12-Mr. Q in both 84 168 252 538 919 1300

GD VG FN VF VF/NM NM-
2.0 4.0 6.0 8.0 9.0 9.2

13-1st Nazi-c; shows Hitler poster on-c 97 194 291 621 1061 1500
14-19 66 132 198 419 722 1025
20-Classic-c 81 162 243 518 884 1250
21-23,25-30 47 94 141 296 498 700
24-Sci-Fi-c 53 106 159 334 567 800
31-The Man in Black Called Fate begins (11-12/45, early app.)
49 98 147 308 522 735
32-36 36 72 108 211 343 475
37,38: Shock Gibson app. by Powell. 37-S&K Kid Adonis reprinted from Stuntman #3. 38-Kid Adonis app. 36 72 108 211 343 475
39-Stuntman story by S&K 39 78 117 236 388 540
40-47: 42-47-Kerry Drake in all. 45-Boy Explorers on-c only. 46- "Case of the Marijuana Racket" cover/story; Kerry Drake app. 27 51 81 158 259 360

NOTE: ***Fuje*** *a-23, 24, 26.* ***Henkle*** *c-7-9.* ***Kubert*** *a-20, 30.* ***Powell*** *a-7-10, 12, 14, 16-21, 30, 31(2), 32(3), 33, 34(3), 35, 36, 37(2), 38.* ***Robinson*** *a-27.* ***Schomburg*** *c-15, 17-23. Kirbyish c-7, 15. Bondage c-8, 14, 18, 26, 36.*

GREEN JET COMICS, THE (See Comic Books, Series 1 in the Promotional Comics section)

GREEN LAMA (Also see Comic Books, Series 1, Daring Adventures #17 & Prize Comics #7)
Spark Publications/Prize No. 7 on: Dec, 1944 - No. 8, Mar, 1946

1-Intro. Lt. Hercules & The Boy Champions; Mac Raboy-c/a #1-8
116 232 348 742 1271 1800
2-Lt. Hercules borrows the Human Torch's powers for one panel
62 124 186 394 680 965
3-5,8: 4-Dick Tracy take-off in Lt. Hercules story by H. L. Gold (science fiction writer). 5-Lt. Hercules story; Little Orphan Annie, Smilin' Jack & Snuffy Smith take-off (5/45) 50 100 150 315 533 750
6-Classic Raboy swastica-c 52 104 156 322 549 775
7-X-mas-c; Raboy craft tint-c/a (note: a small quantity of NM copies surfaced)
34 68 102 199 325 450
... Archives Featuring the Art of Mac Raboy Vol. 1 HC (Dark Horse Books, 4/08, $49.95) r/#1-4 including back-up features; foreward by Chuck Rozanski 50.00
... Archives Featuring the Art of Mac Raboy Vol. 2 HC (Dark Horse Books, 1/09, $49.95) r/#5-8; foreward by Chuck Rozanski 50.00

NOTE: ***Robinson*** *a-3-5, 8. Roussos a-8. Formerly a pulp hero who began in 1940.*

GREEN LANTERN (1st Series) (See All-American, All Flash Quarterly, All Star Comics, The Big All-American & Comic Cavalcade)
National Periodical Publications/All-American: Fall, 1941 - No. 38, May-June, 1949 (#1-18 are quarterly)

1-Origin retold; classic Purcell-c 3000 6000 9000 22,000 38,000 62,000
2-1st book-length story 676 1352 2028 4935 8718 12,500
3-Classic German war-c by Mart Nodell 541 1082 1623 3950 6975 10,000
4-Green Lantern & Doiby Dickles join the Army 394 788 1182 2758 4829 6900
5 300 600 900 2010 3505 5000
6,8: 8-Hop Harrigan begins; classic-c 245 490 735 1568 2684 3800
7-Robot-c. 258 516 774 1651 2826 4000
9,10: 10-Origin/1st app. Vandal Savage 219 438 657 1402 2401 3400
11-15: 12-Origin/1st app. Gambler 158 316 474 1003 1727 2450
16-Classic jungle-c (scarce in high grade) 165 330 495 1048 1799 2550
17,19,20 132 264 396 838 1444 2050
18-Christmas-c 181 362 543 1158 1979 2800
21-26,28 123 246 369 787 1344 1900
27-Origin/1st app. Sky Pirate 129 258 387 826 1413 2000
29-All Harlequin issue; classic Harlequin-c 142 284 426 909 1555 2200
30-Origin/1st app. Streak the Wonder Dog by Toth (2-3/48) (Rare)
290 580 870 1856 3178 4500
31-35: 35-Kubert-c. 35-38-New logo 110 220 330 704 1202 1700
36-38: 37-Sargon the Sorcerer app. 124 248 372 787 1356 1925

NOTE: *Book-length stories #2-7.* ***Mayer/Moldoff*** *c-9.* ***Mayer/Purcell*** *c-8.* ***Purcell*** *c-1.* ***Mart Nodell*** *c-2, 3, 7.* ***Paul Reinman*** *c-11, 12, 15-22.* ***Toth*** *a-28, 30, 31, 34-38; c-28, 30, 34p, 36-38p. Cover to #8 says Fall while the indicia says Summer Issue. Streak the Wonder Dog c-30 (w/Green Lantern), 34, 36, 38.*

GREEN LANTERN (See Action Comics Weekly, Adventure Comics, Brave & the Bold, Day of Judgment, DC Special, DC Special Series, Flash, Guy Gardner, Guy Gardner Reborn, JLA, JSA, Justice League of America, Parallax: Emerald Night, Showcase, Showcase '93 #12 & Tales of The...Corps)

GREEN LANTERN (2nd Series)(Green Lantern Corps #206 on) (See Showcase #22-24)
National Periodical Publ./DC Comics: Jul/Aug. 1960 - No. 89, Apr/May 1972;
No. 90, Aug/Sept. 1976 - No. 205, Oct, 1986

1-(7-8/60)-Origin retold; Gil Kane-c/a continues; 1st app. Guardians of the Universe
407 814 1221 3650 7325 11,000
2-1st Pieface 80 160 240 680 1340 2000
3-Contains readers poll 48 96 144 384 742 1100
4,5: 5-Origin/1st app. Hector Hammond 39 78 117 297 574 850
6-Intro Tomar-Re the alien G.L. 35 70 105 268 517 765
7-Origin/1st app. Sinestro (7-8/61) 40 80 120 314 607 900
8-1st 5700 A.D. story; grey tone-c 31 62 93 236 456 675

Green Lantern #67 © DC

Green Lantern #185 © DC

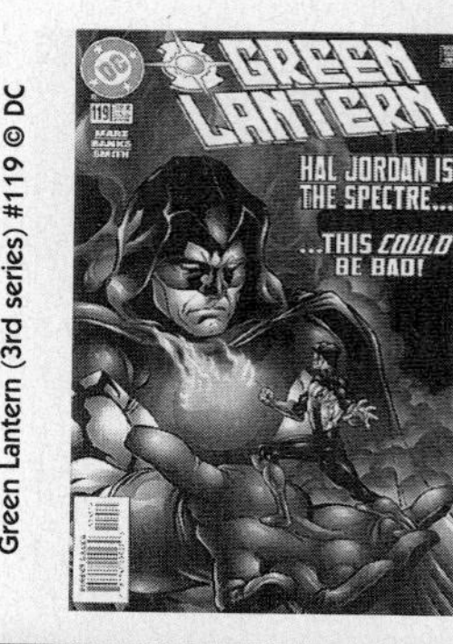

Green Lantern (3rd series) #119 © DC

GD 2.0 VG 4.0 FN 6.0 VF 8.0 VF/NM 9.0 NM- 9.2

9,10: 9-1st Jordan Brothers; last 10¢ issue 27 54 81 197 386 575
11,12 19 38 57 139 270 400
13-Flash x-over 32 64 96 245 473 700
14-20: 14-Origin/1st app. Sonar. 16-Origin & 1st app. (Silver Age) Star Sapphire. 20-Flash x-over 16 32 48 117 226 335
21-30: 21-Origin & 1st app. Dr. Polaris. 23-1st Tattooed Man. 24-Origin & 1st app. Shark. 29-JLA cameo; 1st Blackhand 13 26 39 93 172 250
31-39: 37-1st app. Evil Star (villain) 11 22 33 80 145 210
40-Origin of Infinite Earths (10/65); 2nd solo G.A. Green Lantern in Silver Age (see Showcase #55); origin The Guardians; Doiby Dickles app. 46 92 138 368 709 1050
41-44,46-50: 42-Zatanna x-over. 43-Flash x-over 10 20 30 68 119 170
45-2nd S.A. app. G.A. Green Lantern in title (6/66) 14 28 42 102 194 285
51,53-58 8 16 24 58 97 135
52-G.A. Green Lantern x-over; Sinestro app. 10 20 30 70 123 175
59-1st app. Guy Gardner (3/68) 16 32 48 115 220 325
60,62-69: 69-Wood inks; last 12¢ issue 6 12 18 43 69 95
61-G.A. Green Lantern x-over 7 14 21 50 83 115
70-75 6 12 18 37 59 80
76-(4/70)-Begin Green Lantern/Green Arrow series (by Neal Adams #76-89) ends #122 (see Flash #217 for 2nd series) 80 160 240 680 1340 2000
77 11 22 33 80 145 210
78-80 10 20 30 70 123 175
81-84: 82-Wrightson-i(1 pg.). 83-G.L. reveals i.d. to Carol Ferris. 84-N. Adams/Wrightson-a (22 pgs.); last 15¢-c; partial photo-c 9 18 27 63 107 150
85,86-(52 pgs.)-Anti-drug issues. 86-G.A. Green Lantern-r; Toth-a 11 22 33 78 139 200
87-(52 pgs.): 2nd app. Guy Gardner (cameo); 1st app. John Stewart (12-1/71-72) (becomes 3rd Green Lantern in #182) 9 18 27 60 100 140
88-(2-3/72, 52 pgs.)-Unpubbed G.A. Green Lantern story; Green Lantern-r/Showcase #23. N. Adams-c/a (1 pg.) 7 14 21 45 73 100
89-(4-5/72, 52 pgs.)-G.A. Green Lantern-r; Green Lantern & Green Arrow move to Flash #217 (2nd team-up series) 8 16 24 56 93 130
90 (8-9/76)-Begin 3rd Green Lantern/Green Arrow team-up series; Mike Grell-c/a begins, ends #111 3 6 9 14 20 26
91-99 2 4 6 9 12 15
100-(1/78, Giant)-1st app. Air Wave II 3 6 9 14 19 24
101-107,111,113-115,117-119: 107-1st Tales of the G.L. Corps story 2 3 4 6 8 10
108-110-(44 pgs)-G.A. Green Lantern back-ups in each. 111-Origin retold; G.A. Green Lantern app. 2 4 6 8 10 12
112-G.A. Green Lantern origin retold 2 4 6 10 14 18
116-1st app. Guy Gardner as a G.L. (5/79) 4 8 12 24 37 50
116-Whitman variant; issue # on cover 5 10 15 30 48 65
117-119,121-(Whitman variants; low print run; none have issue # on cover) 2 4 6 9 12 15
120-122,124-150: 122-Last Green Lantern/Green Arrow team-up. 130-132-Tales of the G.L. Corps. 132-Adam Strange series begins, ends147. 136,137-1st app. Citadel; Space Ranger app. 141-1st app. Omega Men (6/81). 142,143-Omega Men app.;Perez-c. 144-Omega Men cameo. 148-Tales of the G.L. Corps begins, ends #173. 150-Anniversary issue, 52 pgs.; no G.L. Corps 1 2 3 4 5 7
123-Green Lantern back to solo action; 2nd app. Guy Gardner as Green Lantern 2 4 6 8 10 12
151-180,183,184,186,187: 159-Origin Evil Star. 160,161-Omega Men app. 5.00
181,182,185,188: 181-Hal Jordan resigns as G.L. 182-John Stewart becomes new G.L.; origin recap of Hal Jordan as G.L. 185-Origin new G.L. (John Stewart).188-I.D. revealed; Alan Moore back-up scripts. 6.00
189-193,196-199,201-205: 191-Re-intro Star Sapphire (cameo). 192-Re-intro & origin of Star Sapphire (1st full app.). 194,198-Crisis x-over. 199-Hal Jordan returns as a member of G.L. Corps (3 G.L.s now). 201-Green Lantern Corps begins (is cover title, says premiere issue); intro. Kilowog 4.00
194-Hal Jordan/Guy Gardner battle; Guardians choose Guy Gardner to become new Green Lantern 1 2 3 4 5 7
195-Guy Gardner becomes Green Lantern; Crisis on Infinite Earths x-over 2 4 6 8 11 14
200-Double-size 5.00
Annual 1 (Listed as Tales Of The Green Lantern Corps Annual 1)
Annual 2,3 (See Green Lantern Corps Annual #2,3) 4.00
Special 1 (1988), 2 (1989)-(Both $1.50, 52 pgs.) 4.00
... Chronicles TPB (2009, $14.99) r/Showcase #22-24 & Green Lantern #1-3 15.00
... Chronicles Vol. 2 TPB (2009, $14.99) r/Green Lantern #4-9 15.00

NOTE: ***N. Adams*** *a-76, 77-87p, 89; c-63, 76-89.* ***M. Anderson*** *a-137i.* ***Austin*** *a-93i, 94i, 171i.* ***Chaykin*** *c-196.* ***Greene*** *a-39-49i, 58-63i; c-54-58i.* ***Grell*** *a-90-100, 106, 108-111; c-90-106, 108-112.* ***Heck*** *a-120-122p.* ***Infantino*** *a-137p, 145-147p, 151, 152p.* ***Gil Kane*** *a-1-49p, 50-57, 58-61p, 68-75p, 85p(r), 87p(r), 88p(r), 156, 177, 184p; c-1-52, 54-61p, 67-75, 123, 154, 156, 165-171, 177, 184.* ***Newton*** *a-148p, 149p, 181.* ***Perez*** *c-132p, 141-144.* ***Sekowsky*** *a-65p, 170p.* ***Simonson*** *c-200.* ***Sparling*** *a-63p.* ***Starlin*** *c-129, 133.* ***Staton*** *a-117p, 123-127p, 128, 129-131p, 132-139, 140p, 141-146, 147p, 148-150, 151-155p; c-107p, 117p, 135(i), 136p, 145p, 146, 147, 148-152p, 155p.* ***Toth*** *a-86r, 171p.* ***Tuska*** *a-166-168p, 170p.*

GD 2.0 VG 4.0 FN 6.0 VF 8.0 VF/NM 9.0 NM- 9.2

GREEN LANTERN (3rd Series)
DC Comics: June, 1990 - No. 181, Nov, 2004 ($1.00/$1.25/$1.50/$1.75/$1.95/$1.99/$2.25)

1-Hal Jordan, John Stewart & Guy Gardner return; Batman & JLA app. 5.00
2-26: 9-12-Guy Gardner solo story. 13-(52 pgs.). 18-Guy Gardner solo story. 19-($1.75, 52 pgs.)-50th anniversary issue; Mart Nodell (original G.A. artist) part-p on G.A. Gr.Lantern; G. Kane-c. 25-($1.75, 52 pgs.)-Hal Jordan/Guy Gardner battle 4.00
27-45,47: 30,31-Gorilla Grodd-c/story(see Flash #69). 38,39-Adam Strange-c/story. 42-Deathstroke-c/s. 47-Green Arrow x-over 3.00
46,48,49,50: 46-Superman app. cont'd in Superman #82. 48-Emerald Twilight part 1. 50-($2.95, 52 pgs.)-Glow-in-the-dark-c 6.00
0, 51-62: 51-1st app. New Green Lantern (Kyle Rayner) with new costume. 53-Superman-c/story. 55-(9/94)-Zero Hour. 0-(10/94). 56-(11/94) 4.00
63,64-Kyle Rayner vs. Hal Jordan. 4.00
65-80,82-92: 63-Begin $1.75-c. 65-New Titans app. 66,67-Flash app. 71-Batman & Robin app. 72-Shazam!-c/app. 73-Wonder Woman-c/app. 73-75-Adam Strange app. 76,77-Green Arrow x-over. 80-Final Night. 87-JLA app. 91-Genesis x-over. 92-Green Arrow x-over 3.00
81-(Regular Ed.)-Memorial for Hal Jordan (Parallax); most DC heroes app. 5.00
81-($3.95, Deluxe Edition)-Embossed prism-c 6.00
93-99: 93-Begin $1.95-c; Deadman app. 94-Superboy app. 95-Starlin-a(p). 98,99-Legion of Super-Heroes-c/app. 2.50
100-($2.95) Two covers (Jordan & Rayner); vs. Sinestro 5.00
101-106: 101-106-Hal Jordan-c/app. 103-JLA-c/app. 104-Green Arrow app. 105,106-Parallax app. 3.00
107-126: 107-Jade becomes a Green Lantern. 119-Hal Jordan/Spectre app. 125-JLA app. 2.50
127-149: 127-Begin $2.25-c. 129-Winick-s begin. 134-136-JLA-c/app. 143-Joker: Last Laugh; Lee-c. 145-Kyle becomes The Ion. 149-Superman-c/app. 2.50
150-($3.50) Jim Lee-c; Kyle becomes Green Lantern again; new costume 3.50
151-181: 151-155-Jim Lee-c: 154-Terry attacked. 155-Spectre-c/app. 162-164-Crossover with Green Arrow #23-25. 165-Raab-s begin. 169-Kilowog returns 2.50
#1,000,000 (11/98) 853rd Century x-over; Hitch & Neary-a/c 3.00
Annual 1-3: ('92-'94, 68 pgs.)-1-Eclipso app. 2 -Intro Nightblade. 3-Elseworlds story 3.50
Annual 4 (1995, $3.50)-Year One story 4.00
Annual 5,7,8 ('96, '98, '99, $2.95): 5-Legends of the Dead Earth. 7-Ghosts; Wrightson-c. 8-JLApe; Art Adams-c 3.00
Annual 6 (1997, $3.95)-Pulp Heroes story 5.00
Annual 9 (2000, $3.50) Planet DC 3.50
...80 Page Giant (12/98, $4.95) Stories by various 5.00
...80 Page Giant 2 (6/99, $4.95) Team-ups 5.00
...80 Page Giant 3 (8/00, $5.95) Darkseid vs. the GL Corps 6.00
...: 1001 Emerald Nights (2001, $6.95) Elseworlds; Guay-a/c; LaBan-s 7.00
...3-D #1 (12/98, $3.95) Jeanty-a 4.00
...: A New Dawn TPB (1998, $9.95)-r/#50-55 10.00
...: Baptism of Fire TPB (1999, $12.95)-r/#59,66,67,70-75 13.00
...: Brother's Keeper (2003, $12.95)-r/#151-155; Green Lantern Secret Files #3 13.00
...: Emerald Allies TPB (2000, $14.95)-r/GL/GA team-ups 15.00
...: Emerald Knights TPB (1998, $12.95)-r/Hal Jordan's return 13.00
...: Emerald Twilight nn (1994, $5.95)-r/#48-50 6.00
...: Emerald Twilight/New Dawn TPB (2003, $19.95)-r/#48-55 20.00
...: Ganthet's Tale nn (1992, $5.95, 68 pgs.)-Silver foil logo; Niven scripts; Byrne-c/a 6.00
.../Green Arrow Vol. 1 (2004, $12.95) -r/GL #76-82; intro. by O'Neil 13.00
.../Green Arrow Vol. 2 (2004, $12.95) -r/GL #83-87,89 & Flash #217-219, 226; cover gallery with 1983-84 GL/GA covers #1-7; intro. by Giordano 13.00
.../Green Arrow Collection, Vol. 2-r/GL #84-87,89 & Flash #217-219 & GL/GA #5-7 by O'Neil/Adams/Wrightson 13.00
...: New Journey, Old Path TPB (2001, $12.95)-r/#129-136 13.00
... : Our Worlds at War (8/01, $2.95) Jae Lee-c; prelude to x-over 3.00
...: Passing The Torch (2004, $12.95, TPB) r/#156,158-161 & GL Secret Files #2 13.00
...Plus 1 (12/1996, $2.95)-The Ray & Polaris-c/app. 3.00
...Secret Files 1-3 (7/98-7/02, $4.95)1-Origin stories & profiles. 2-Grell-c 5.00
.../Superman: Legend of the Green Flame (2000, $5.95) 1988 unpub. Neil Gaiman story of Hal Jordan with new art by various; Frank Miller-c 6.00
...: The Power of Ion (2003, $14.95, TPB) r/#142-150 15.00
...The Road Back nn (1992, $8.95)-r/1-8 w/covers 9.00
...: Traitor TPB (2001, $12.95) r/Legends of the DCU #20,21,28,29,37,38 13.00
...: Willworld (2001, $24.95, HC) Seth Fisher-a/J.M. DeMatteis-s; Hal Jordan 25.00
...: Willworld (2003, $17.95, SC) Seth Fisher-a/J.M. DeMatteis-s; Hal Jordan 18.00

NOTE: ***Staton*** *a(p)-9-12; c-9-12.*

GREEN LANTERN (See Tangent Comics/ Green Lantern)

GREEN LANTERN (4th Series) (Follows Hal Jordan's return in Green Lantern: Rebirth)
DC Comics: July, 2005 - Present ($3.50/$2.99)

1-($3.50) Two covers by Pacheco and Ross; Johns-s/Van Sciver and Pacheco-a 5.00

Green Lantern (4th series) #46 © DC

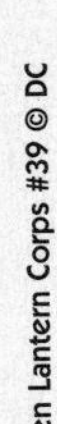
Green Lantern Corps #39 © DC

Green Lantern: Rebirth #3 © DC

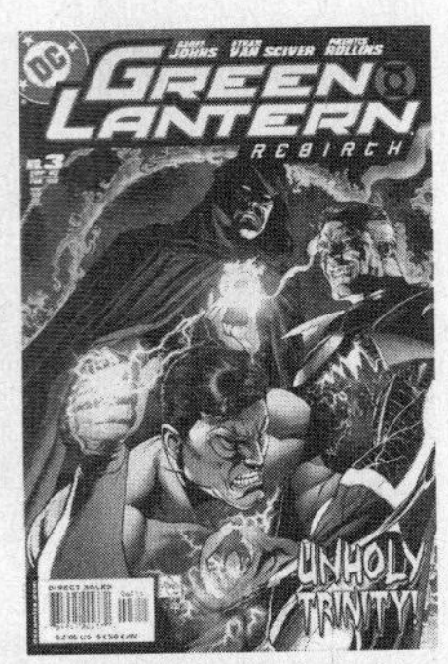

2-20-($2.99) 2-4-Manhunters app. 6-Bianchi-a. 7,8-Green Arrow app. 8-Bianchi-c. 9-Batman app.; two covers by Bianchi and Van Sciver. 10,11-Reis-a. 17-19-Star Sapphire returns. 18-Acuna-a; Sinestro Corps back-ups begin 3.00
8-Variant-c by Neal Adams 8.00
21-Sinestro Corps War pt. 2 5.00
21-2nd printing with variant green hued background-c 3.00
22-24: 22-Sinestro Corps War pt. 4; green hued-c. 23-Part 6. 24-Part 8 4.00
22,23-2nd printings. 22-Yellow hued-c. 23-B&W Hal Jordan with colored rings 3.00
25-($4.99) Sinestro Corps War conclusion; Ivan Reis-c 6.00
25-($4.99) Variant cover by Gary Frank; Sinestro Corps War conclusion 8.00
26-43: 26-Alpha Lanterns. 29-35-Childhood & origin re-told; Sinestro app. 41-Origin Larfleeze. 43-Prologue to Blackest Night, origin of Black Hand; Mahnke-a 3.00
39-43-Variant covers: 39,40-Migliari. 41-42-Barrows 12.00
44-49,51-Blackest Night. 44-Flash app. 46-Sinestro vs. Mongul. 47-Black Lantern Abin Sur. 49-Art by Benes & Ordway; Atom and Mera app. 51-Nekron app. 3.00
44-49,51-Variant covers: 44-Tan. 45-Manapul. 46. Andy Kubert. 47-Benes. 48-Morales. 49-Migliari. 51-Horn 10.00
50-($3.99)-Black Lantern Spectre & Parallax app.; Mahnke-a/c 4.00
50-Variant-c by Jim Lee 12.00
...Secret Files and Origins 2005 (6/05, $4.99) Johns-s/Cooke & Van Sciver-a; profiles with art by various incl. Chaykin, Gibbons, Gleason, Igle; Pacheco-c 5.00
.../Sinestro Corps: Secret Files 1 (2/08, $4.99) Profiles of Green Lanterns and Corps info 5.00
...: Agent Orange HC (2009, $19.99) r/#38-42 & Blackest Night #0; sketch art 20.00
...: In Brightest Day SC (2008, $19.99) r/stories selected by Geoff Johns w/commentary 20.00
...: No Fear HC (2006, $24.99) r/#1-6 & Secret Files and Origins 25.00
...: No Fear SC (2008, $12.99) r/#1-6 & Secret Files and Origins 13.00
...: Rage of the Red Lanterns HC (2009, $24.99) r/#26-28,36-38 & Final Crisis: Rage... 25.00
...: Revenge of the Green Lanterns HC (2006, $19.99) r/#7-13; variant cover gallery 20.00
...: Revenge of the Green Lanterns SC (2008, $12.99) r/#7-13; variant cover gallery 13.00
...: Secret Origin HC (2008, $19.99) r/#29-35 20.00
...: Secret Origin SC (2008, $14.99) r/#29-35 15.00
...: Tales of the Sinestro Corps HC (2008, $29.99, d.j.) r/back-up stories from #18-20, Tales of the Sinestro Corps series, Green Lantern: Sinestro Corps Special and Sinestro Corps: Secret Files 30.00
...: Tales of the Sinestro Corps SC (2009, $14.99) same contents as HC 15.00
...: The Sinestro Corps War Vol. 1 HC (2008, $24.99, d.j.) r/#21-23, Green Lantern Corps #14-15 and Green Lantern: Sinestro Corps Special 25.00
...: The Sinestro Corps War Vol. 1 SC (2009, $14.99) same contents as HC 15.00
...: The Sinestro Corps War Vol. 2 HC (2008, $24.99, d.j.) r/#24,25, Green Lantern Corps #16-19; interview with the creators and sketch art 25.00
... - Wanted: Hal Jordan HC (2007, $19.99) r/#14-20 without Sinestro Corps back-ups 20.00
... - Wanted: Hal Jordan SC (2008, $14.99) r/#14-20 without Sinestro Corps back-ups 15.00

GREEN LANTERN ANNUAL NO. 1, 1963
DC Comics: 1998 ($4.95, one-shot)

1-Reprints Golden Age & Silver Age stories in 1963-style 80 pg. Giant format; new Gil Kane sketch art 5.00

GREEN LANTERN: BRIGHTEST DAY; BLACKEST NIGHT
DC Comics: 2002 ($5.95, squarebound, one-shot)

nn-Alan Scott vs. Solomon Grundy in 1944; Snyder III-c/a; Seagle-s 6.00

GREEN LANTERN: CIRCLE OF FIRE
DC Comics: Early Oct, 2000 - No. 2, Late Oct, 2000 (limited series)

1-($4.95) Intro. other Green Lanterns 5.00
2-($3.75) 4.00
Green Lantern (x-overs)- .../Adam Strange; .../Atom; .../Firestorm; ... /Green Lantern, Winick-s; .../Power Girl (all $2.50-c) 2.50
TPB (2002, $17.95) r/#1,2 & x-overs 18.00

GREEN LANTERN CORPS, THE (Formerly Green Lantern; see Tales of...)
DC Comics: No. 206, Nov, 1986 - No. 224, May, 1988

206-223: 212-John Stewart marries Katma Tui. 220,221-Millennium tie-ins 3.00
224-Double-size last issue 4.00
...Corps Annual 2,3- (12/86,8/87) 1-Formerly Tales of ...Annual #1; Alan Moore scripts. 3-Indicia says Green Lantern Annual #3; Moore scripts; Byrne-a 3.00
NOTE: ***Austin** a-Annual 3i. **Gil Kane** a-223, 224p; c-223, 224, Annual 2. **Russell** a-Annual 3i. **Staton** a-207-213p, 217p, 221p, 222p, Annual 3; c-207-213p, 217p, 221p, 222p. **Willingham** a-213p, 219p, 220p, 218p, 219p, Annual 2, 3p; c-218p, 219p.*

GREEN LANTERN CORPS
DC Comics: Aug, 2006 - Present ($2.99)

1-13: 1-6,10,11-Gibbons-s. 9-Darkseid app. 3.00
14-19-Sinestro Corps War pts. 3,5,7,9,10, Epilogue 3.00
20-38: 20-Mongul app. 3.00
20-Second printing with sketch-c 3.00
34-38: 34-37-Variant covers by Migliari. 38-Fabry var-c 10.00
39-45-Blackest Night. 43-45-Red Lantern Guy Gardner 3.00
39-45-Variant covers: 39-Jusko. 40-Tucci. 41,42,44-Horn. 43-Ladronn. 45 Bolland 8.00
...: Emerald Eclipse HC (2009, $24.99) r/#33-39; gallery of variant covers 25.00
...: Ring Quest TPB (2008, $14.99) r/#19,20,23-26 15.00
...: The Dark Side of Green TPB (2007, $12.99) r/#7-13 13.00
...: To Be a Lantern TPB (2007, $12.99) r/#1-6 13.00

GREEN LANTERN CORPS QUARTERLY
DC Comics: Summer, 1992 - No. 8, Spring, 1994 ($2.50/$2.95, 68 pgs.)

1,7,8: 1-G.A. Green Lantern story; Staton-a(p). 7-Painted-c; Tim Vigil-a. 8-Lobo-c/s 3.50
2-6: 2-G.A. G.L.-c/story; Austin-c(i); Gulacy-a(p). 3-G.A. G.L. story. 4-Austin-i 3.00

GREEN LANTERN CORPS: RECHARGE
DC Comics: Nov, 2005 - No. 5, Mar, 2006 ($3.50/$2.99, limited series)

1-($3.50) Kyle Rayner, Guy Gardner & Kilowog app.; Gleason-a 3.50
2-5-($2.99) 3.00
TPB (2006, $12.99) r/series 13.00

GREEN LANTERN: DRAGON LORD
DC Comics: 2001 - No. 3, 2001 ($4.95, squarebound, limited series)

1-3: A G.L. in ancient China; Moench-s/Gulacy-c/a 5.00

GREEN LANTERN: EMERALD DAWN (Also see Emerald Dawn)
DC Comics: Dec, 1989 - No. 6, May, 1990 ($1.00, limited series)

1-Origin retold; Giffen plots in all 5.00
2-6: 4-Re-intro. Tomar-Re 4.00

GREEN LANTERN: EMERALD DAWN II (Emerald Dawn II #1 & 2)
DC Comics: Apr, 1991 - No. 6, Sept, 1991 ($1.00, limited series)

1-6 2.50
TPB (2003, $12.95) r/#1-6; Alan Davis-c 13.00

GREEN LANTERN: EVIL'S MIGHT (Elseworlds)
DC Comics: 2002 - No. 3 ($5.95, squarebound, limited series)

1-3-Kyle Rayner in 19th century NYC; Rogers-a; Chaykin & Tischman-s 6.00

GREEN LANTERN: FEAR ITSELF
DC Comics: 1999 (Graphic novel)

Hardcover ($24.95) Ron Marz-s/Brad Parker painted-a 25.00
Softcover ($14.95) 15.00

GREEN LANTERN/FLASH: FASTER FRIENDS (See Flash/Green Lantern...)
DC Comics: 1997 ($4.95, limited series)

1-Marz-s 5.00

GREEN LANTERN GALLERY
DC Comics: Dec, 1996 ($3.50, one-shot)

1-Wraparound-c; pin-ups by various 3.50

GREEN LANTERN/GREEN ARROW (Also see The Flash #217)
DC Comics: Oct, 1983 - No. 7, April, 1984 (52-60 pgs.)

1-7- r-Green Lantern #76-89 4.00
NOTE: ***Neal Adams** r-1-7; c-1-4. **Wrightson** r-4, 5.*

GREEN LANTERN • LEGACY: THE LAST WILL & TESTAMENT OF HAL JORDAN
DC Comics: 2002 ($24.95, hardcover graphic novel)

Hardcover-Anderson & Sienkiewicz-a/c; Kelly-s; Return of Oa 25.00
Softcover (2004, $17.95) 18.00

GREEN LANTERN: MOSAIC (Also see Cosmic Odyssey #2)
DC Comics: June, 1992 - No. 18, Nov, 1993 ($1.25)

1-18: Featuring John Stewart. 1-Painted-c by Cully Hamner 2.50

GREEN LANTERN: REBIRTH
DC Comics: Dec, 2004 - No. 6, May, 2005 ($2.95, limited series)

1-Johns-s/Van Sciver-a; Hal Jordan as The Spectre on-c 8.00
1-2nd printing; Hal Jordan as Green Lantern on-c 4.00
1-3rd printing; B&W-c version of 1st printing 3.00
1 Special Edition (9/09, $1.00) r/#1 with "After Watchmen" cover frame 1.00
2-Guy Gardner becomes a Green Lantern again; JLA app. 5.00
2-2nd & 3rd printings 3.00
3-6: 3-Sinestro returns. 4-6-JLA & JSA app. 3.00
HC (2005, $24.99, dust jacket) r/series & Wizard preview; intro. by Brad Meltzer 25.00
SC (2007, $14.99) r/series & Wizard preview; intro. by Brad Meltzer 15.00

GREEN LANTERN/SENTINEL: HEART OF DARKNESS
DC Comics: Mar, 1998 - No. 3, May, 1998 ($1.95, limited series)

1-3-Marz-s/Pelletier-a 3.00

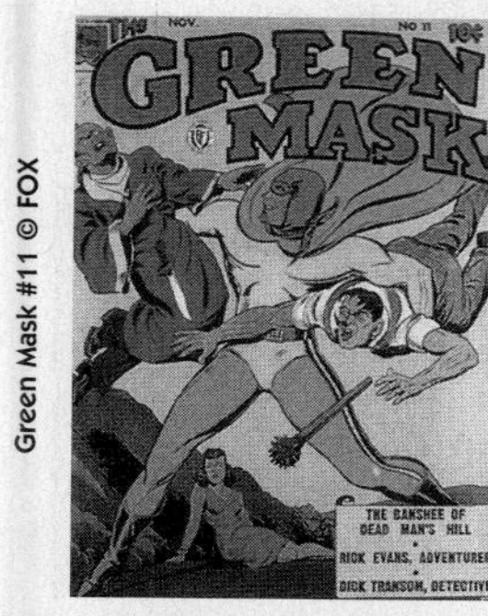

Green Mask #11 © FOX

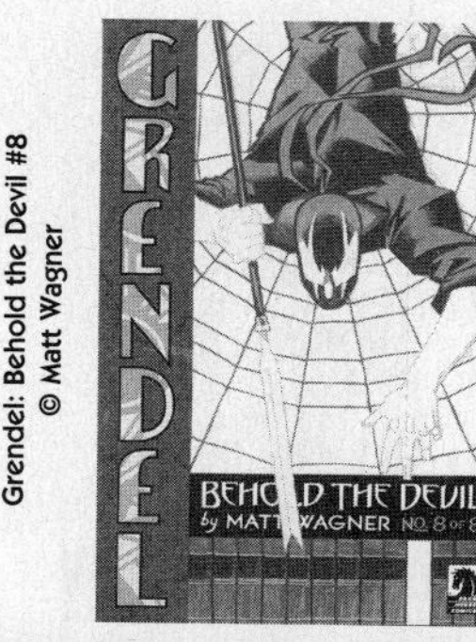

Grendel: Behold the Devil #8 © Matt Wagner

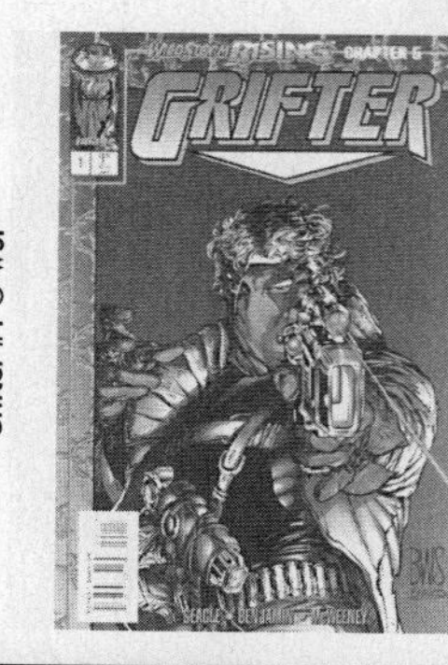

Grifter #1 © WSP

GD 2.0 | VG 4.0 | FN 6.0 | VF 8.0 | VF/NM 9.0 | NM- 9.2

GREEN LANTERN/SILVER SURFER: UNHOLY ALLIANCES
DC Comics: 1995 ($4.95, one-shot)(Prelude to DC Versus Marvel)
nn-Hal Jordan app. 5.00

GREEN LANTERN SINESTRO CORPS SPECIAL (Continues in Green Lantern #21)
DC Comics: Aug, 2007 ($4.99, one-shot)
1-Kyle Rayner becomes Parallax; Cyborg Superman & Earth-Prime Superboy app.; Johns-s; Van Sciver-a/c; back-up story origin of Sinestro; Gibbons-a; Sinestro on cover 8.00
1-(2nd printing) Kyle Rayner as Parallax on cover 6.00
1-(3rd printing) Sinestro cover with muted colors 5.00

GREEN LANTERN: THE GREATEST STORIES EVER TOLD
DC Comics: 2006 ($19.99, TPB)
SC-Reprints Showcase #22; G.L. #1,31,74,87,172; ('90 series) #3, and others; Ross-c 20.00

GREEN LANTERN: THE NEW CORPS
DC Comics:1999 - No. 2, 1999 ($4.95, limited series)
1,2-Kyle recruits new GLs; Eaton-a 5.00

GREEN LANTERN VS. ALIENS
Dark Horse Comics: Sept, 2000 - No. 4, Dec, 2000 ($2.95, limited series)
1-4: 1-Hal Jordan and GL Corps vs. Aliens; Leonardi-p. 2-4-Kyle Rayner 3.00

GREEN MASK, THE (See Mystery Men)
Summer, 1940 - No. 9, 2/42; No. 10, 8/44 - No. 11, 11/44;
Fox Features Syndicate: V2#1, Spring, 1945 - No. 6, 10-11/46

	GD 2.0	VG 4.0	FN 6.0	VF 8.0	VF/NM 9.0	NM- 9.2
V1#1-Origin The Green Mask & Domino; reprints/Mystery Men #1-3,5-7; Lou Fine-c	337	674	1011	2359	4130	5900
2-Zanzibar The Magician by Tuska	132	264	396	838	1444	2050
3-Powell-a; Marijuana story	84	168	252	538	919	1300
4-Navy Jones begins, ends #6	65	130	195	416	708	1000
5	53	106	159	334	567	800
6-The Nightbird begins, ends #9; bondage/torture-c	45	90	135	284	480	675
7-9: 9(2/42)-Becomes The Bouncer #10(nn) on? & Green Mask #10 on	39	78	117	231	378	525
10,11: 10-Origin One Round Hogan & Rocket Kelly	30	60	90	177	289	400
V2#1	23	46	69	136	223	310
2-6	19	38	57	112	179	245

GREEN PLANET, THE
Charlton Comics: 1962 (one-shot) (12¢)

	GD 2.0	VG 4.0	FN 6.0	VF 8.0	VF/NM 9.0	NM- 9.2
nn-Giordano-c; sci-fi	6	12	18	43	69	95

GREEN TEAM (See Cancelled Comic Cavalcade & 1st Issue Special)

GREETINGS FROM SANTA (See March of Comics No. 48)

GRENDEL (Also see Primer #2, Mage and Comico Collection)
Comico: Mar, 1983 - No. 3, Feb, 1984 ($1.50, B&W)(#1 has indicia to Skrog #1)

	GD 2.0	VG 4.0	FN 6.0	VF 8.0	VF/NM 9.0	NM- 9.2
1-Origin Hunter Rose	11	22	33	74	132	190
2,3: 2-Origin Argent	8	16	24	54	90	125

GRENDEL
Comico: Oct, 1986 - No. 40, Feb, 1990 ($1.50/$1.95/$2.50, mature)

	GD 2.0	VG 4.0	FN 6.0	VF 8.0	VF/NM 9.0	NM- 9.2
1	1	2	3	5	7	9
1,2: 2nd printings						3.00
2,3,5-15: 13-15-Ken Steacy-c.						4.00
4,16: 4-Dave Stevens-c(i). 16-Re-intro Mage (series begins, ends #19)						6.00
17-40: 24-25,27-28,30-31-Snyder-c/a						3.00
Devil by the Deed (Graphic Novel, 10/86, $5.95, 52 pgs.)-r/Grendel back-ups/ Mage 6-14; Alan Moore intro.	1	2	3	4	5	7
Devil's Legacy ($14.95, 1988, Graphic Novel)	2	4	6	9	12	15
Devil's Vagary (10/87, B&W & red)-No price; included in Comico Collection	2	4	6	8	10	12

GRENDEL (Title series): **Dark Horse Comics**

--ARCHIVES, 5/07 ($14.95, HC) r/1st apps. in Primer #2 and Grendel #1-3; Wagner intro. 15.00

--BEHOLD THE DEVIL, No. 0, 7/07 - No. 8, 6/08 ($3.50/50¢, B&W&Red)
0-(50¢-c) Prelude to series; Matt Wagner-s/a; interview with Wagner 2.25
1-8-Matt Wagner-s/a/c in all 3.50

--BLACK, WHITE, AND RED, 11/98 - No. 4, 2/99 ($3.95, anthology)
1-Wagner-s in all. Art by Sale, Leon and others 5.00
2-4: 2-Mack, Chadwick-a. 3-Allred, Kristensen-a. 4-Pearson, Sprouse-a 4.00

--CLASSICS, 7/95 - 8/95 ($3.95, mature) 1,2-reprints; new Wagner-c 4.00

--CYCLE, 10/95 ($5.95) 1-nn-history of Grendel by M. Wagner & others 6.00

--DEVIL BY THE DEED, 7/93 ($3.95, varnish-c) 1-nn-M. Wagner-c/a/scripts; r/Grendel back-ups from Mage #6-14 4.00
Reprint (12/97, $3.95) w/pin-ups by various 4.00
Hardcover (2007, $12.95) reprint recolored to B&W&red; includes covers and intros from previously reprinted editions 13.00

--DEVIL CHILD, 6/99 - No. 2, 7/99 ($2.95, mature) 1,2-Sale & Kristiansen-a/Schutz-s 3.00

--DEVIL QUEST, 11/95 ($4.95) 1-nn-Prequel to Batman/Grendel II; M. Wagner story & art; r/back-up story from Grendel Tales series. 5.00

--DEVILS AND DEATHS, 10/94 - 11/94 ($2.95, mature) 1,2 3.00

: DEVIL'S LEGACY, 3/00 - No. 12, 2/01 ($2.95, reprints 1986 series, recolored)
1-12-Wagner-s/c; Pander Bros.-a 3.00

: DEVIL'S REIGN, 5/04 - No. 7, 12/04 ($3.50, repr. 1989 series #34-40, recolored)
1-7-Sale-c/a. 3.50

: GOD AND THE DEVIL, No. 0, 1/03 - No. 10, 12/03 ($3.50/$4.99, repr. 1986 series, recolored)
0-9: 0-Sale-c/a; r/#23. 1-9-Snyder-c 3.50
10-($4.99) Double-sized; Snyder-c 5.00

--RED, WHITE & BLACK, 9/02 - No. 4, 12/02 ($4.99, anthology)
1-4-Wagner-s in all. 1-Art by Thompson, Sakai, Mahfood and others. 2-Kelley Jones, Watson, Brereton, Hester & Parks-a. 3-Oeming, Noto, Cannon, Ashley Wood, Huddleston-a 4-Chiang, Dalrymple, Robertson, Snyder III and Zulli-a 5.00
TPB (2005, $19.95) r/#1-4; cover gallery, artist bios 20.00

--TALES: DEVIL'S CHOICES, 3/95 - 6/95 ($2.95, mature) 1-4 3.00

--TALES: FOUR DEVILS, ONE HELL, 8/93 - 1/94 ($2.95, mature)
1-6-Wagner painted-c 3.00
TPB (12/94, $17.95) r/#1-6 18.00

--TALES: HOMECOMING, 12/94 - 2/95 ($2.95, mature) 1-3 3.00

--TALES: THE DEVIL IN OUR MIDST, 5/94 - 9/95 ($2.95, mature) 1-5-Wagner painted-c 3.00

--TALES: THE DEVIL MAY CARE, 12/95 - No. 6, 5/96 ($2.95, mature)
1-6-Terry LaBan scripts. 5-Batman/Grendel II preview 3.00

--TALES: THE DEVIL'S APPRENTICE, 9/97 - No. 3, 11/97 ($2.95, mature)
1-3 3.00

: THE DEVIL INSIDE, 9/01 - No. 3, 11/01 ($2.99)
1-3-r/#13-15 with new Wagner-c 3.00

: WAR CHILD, 8/92 - No. 10, 6/93 ($2.50, lim. series, mature)
1-9: 1-4-Bisley painted-c; Wagner-i & scripts in all 3.00
10-($3.50, 52 pgs.) Wagner-c 4.00
Limited Edition Hardcover ($99.95) 100.00

GREYFRIARS BOBBY (Disney)(Movie)
Dell Publishing Co.: No. 1189, Nov, 1961 (one-shot)

	GD 2.0	VG 4.0	FN 6.0	VF 8.0	VF/NM 9.0	NM- 9.2
Four Color 1189-Photo-c (scarce)	7	14	21	47	76	105

GREYLORE
Sirius: 12/85 - No. 5, Sept, 1986 ($1.50/$1.75, high quality paper)
1-5: Bo Hampton-a in all 2.50

GREYSHIRT: INDIGO SUNSET (Also see Tomorrow Stories)
America's Best Comics: Dec, 2001 - No. 6, Aug, 2002 ($3.50, limited series)
1-6-Veitch-s/a. 4-Back-up w/John Severin-a. 6-Cho-a 3.50
TPB (2002, $19.95) r/#1-6; preface by Alan Moore 20.00

GRIDIRON GIANTS
Ultimate Sports Ent.: 2000 - No. 2 ($3.95, cardstock covers)
1,2-NFL players Sanders, Marino, Plummer, T. Davis battle evil 4.00

GRIFFIN, THE
DC Comics: 1991 - No. 6, 1991 ($4.95, limited series, 52 pgs.)
Book 1-6: Matt Wagner painted-c 5.00

GRIFTER (Also see Team 7 & WildC.A.T.S)
Image Comics (WildStorm Prod.): May, 1995 - No. 10, Mar, 1996 ($1.95)
1 ($1.95, Newsstand)-WildStorm Rising Pt. 5 2.50
1-10:1 ($2.50, Direct)-WildStorm Rising Pt. 5, bound-in trading card 3.00
...: One Shot (1/95, $4.95) Flip-c 5.00

GRIFTER
Image Comics (WildStorm Prod.): V2#1, July, 1996 - No. 14, Aug, 1997 ($2.50)
V2#1-14: Steven Grant scripts 3.00

GRIFTER & MIDNIGHTER
DC Comics (WildStorm Prod.): May, 2007 - No. 6, Oct, 2007 ($2.99, limited series)
1-6-Dixon-s/Benjamin-a/c. 1,3-The Authority app. 3.00

Grimm's Ghost Stories #6 © WEST

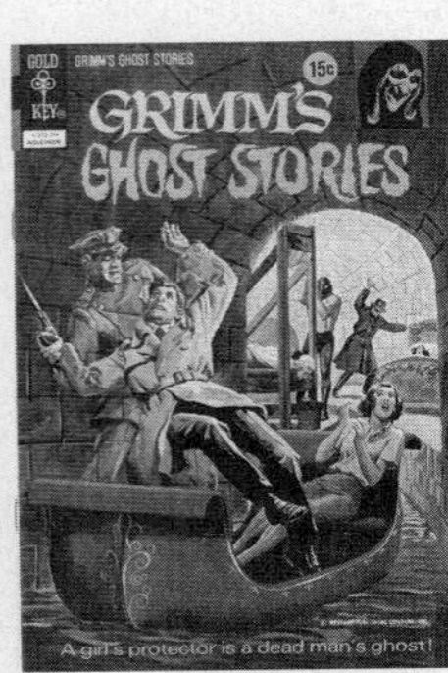

Grip: The Strange World of Men #1 © Gilbert Hernandez

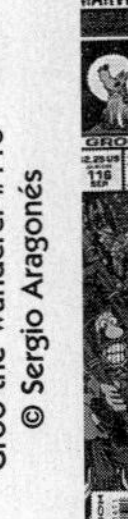
Groo the Wanderer #116 © Sergio Aragonés

	GD 2.0	VG 4.0	FN 6.0	VF 8.0	VF/NM 9.0	NM- 9.2

TPB (2008, $17.99) r/#1-6 18.00

GRIFTER AND THE MASK
Dark Horse Comics: Sept, 1996 - No. 2, Oct, 1996 ($2.50, limited series)
(1st Dark Horse Comics/Image x-over)
1,2: Steve Seagle scripts 3.00

GRIFTER/BADROCK (Also see WildC.A.T.S & Youngblood)
Image Comics (Extreme Studios): Oct, 1995 - No.2, Nov, 1995 ($2.50, unfinished lim. series)
1,2: 2-Flip book w/Badrock #2 2.50

GRIFTER/SHI
Image Comics (WildStorm Productions): Apr, 1996 - No. 2, May, 1996 ($2.95, limited series)
1,2: 1-Jim Lee-c/a(p); Travis Charest-a(p). 2-Billy Tucci-c/a(p); Travis Charest-a(p) 3.00

GRIM GHOST, THE
Atlas/Seaboard Publ.: Jan, 1975 - No. 3, July, 1975
1-3: Fleisher-s in all. 1-Origin. 2-Son of Satan; Colan-a. 3-Heath-c 2 4 6 8 10 12

GRIMJACK (Also see Demon Knight & Starslayer)
First Comics: Aug, 1984 - No. 81, Apr, 1991 ($1.00/$1.95/$2.25)
1-John Ostrander scripts & Tim Truman-c/a begins. 3.00
2-25: 20-Sutton-c/a begins. 22-Bolland-a. 2.50
26-2nd color Teenage Mutant Ninja Turtles 4.00
27-74,76-81 (Later issues $1.95, $2.25): 30-Dynamo Joe x-over; 31-Mandrake-c/a begins. 73,74-Kelley Jones-a 2.50
75-($5.95, 52 pgs.)-Fold-out map; coated stock 6.00
The Legend of Grimjack Vol. 1 (IDW Publishing, 2004, $19.99) r/Starslayer #10-18; 8 new pages & art 20.00
The Legend of Grimjack Vol. 2 (IDW, 2005, $19.99) r/#1-7; unpublished art 20.00
The Legend of Grimjack Vol. 3 (IDW, 2005, $19.99) r/#8-14; cover gallery 20.00
The Legend of Grimjack Vol. 4 (IDW, 2005, $24.99) r/#15-21; cover gallery 25.00
The Legend of Grimjack Vol. 5 (IDW, 5/06, $24.99) r/#22-30; cover gallery 25.00
The Legend of Grimjack Vol. 6 (IDW, 1/07, $24.99) r/#31-37; cover gallery 25.00
The Legend of Grimjack Vol. 7 (IDW, 4/07, $24.99) r/#38-46; covers; "Rough Trade" 25.00
NOTE: *Truman c/a-1-17.*

GRIMJACK CASEFILES
First Comics: Nov, 1990 - No. 5, Mar, 1991 ($1.95, limited series)
1-5 Reprints 1st stories from Starslayer #10 on 2.50

GRIMJACK: KILLER INSTINCT
IDW Publ.: Jan, 2005 - No. 6, June, 2005 ($3.99, limited series)
1-6-Ostrander-s/Truman-a 4.00

GRIMJACK: THE MANX CAT
IDW Publ.: Aug, 2009 - No. 6, Jan, 2010 ($3.99, limited series)
1-6-Ostrander-s/Truman-a 4.00

GRIMM'S GHOST STORIES (See Dan Curtis)
Gold Key/Whitman No. 55 on: Jan, 1972 - No. 60, June, 1982 (Painted-c #1-42,44,46-56)
1 4 8 12 22 34 45
2-5,8: 5,8-Williamson-a 2 4 6 13 18 22
6,7,9,10 2 4 6 11 16 20
11-20 2 4 6 8 11 14
21-42,45-54: 32,34-Reprints. 45-Photo-c 1 3 4 6 8 10
43,44,55-60: 43,44-(52 pgs.). 43-Photo-c. 58(2/82). 59(4/82)-Williamson-a(r/#8). 60(6/82) 2 4 6 8 11 14
Mini-Comic No. 1 (3-1/4x6-1/2", 1976) 1 3 4 6 8 10
NOTE: *Reprints-#32?, 34?, 39, 43, 44, 47?, 53; 56-60(1/3).* ***Bolle*** *a-8, 17, 22-25, 27, 29(2), 33, 35, 41, 43r, 45(2), 48(2), 50, 52, 57.* ***Celardo*** *a-17, 26, 28p, 30, 31, 43(2), 45.* ***Lopez*** *a-24, 25.* ***McWilliams*** *a-33, 44r, 48, 54(2), 57, 58.* ***Win Mortimer*** *a-31, 33, 49, 51, 55, 56, 58(2), 59, 60.* ***Roussos*** *a-25, 30.* ***Sparling*** *a-23, 24, 28, 30, 31, 33, 43r, 44, 45, 51(2), 52, 56-58, 59(2), 60.* ***Spiegle*** *a-44.*

GRIN (The American Funny Book) (Satire)
APAG House Pubs: Nov, 1972 - No. 3, April, 1973 (Magazine, 52 pgs.)
1-Parodies-Godfather, All in the Family 3 6 9 17 25 32
2,3 2 4 6 11 16 20

GRIN & BEAR IT (See Gags)
Dell Publishing Co.: No. 28, 1941
Large Feature Comic 28 16 32 48 94 147 200

GRIPS (Extreme violence)
Silverwolf Comics: Sept, 1986 - No. 4, Dec, 1986 ($1.50, B&W, mature)
1-Tim Vigil-c/a in all 6.00
2-4 4.00

GRIP: THE STRANGE WORLD OF MEN
DC Comics (Vertigo): Jan, 2002 - No. 5, May, 2002 ($2.50, limited series)
1-4-Gilbert Hernandez-s/a 2.50

GRIT GRADY (See Holyoke One-Shot No. 1)

GROO (Also see Sergio Aragonés' Groo...)

GROO (Sergio Aragonés'...)
Image Comics: Dec, 1994 - No. 12, Dec, 1995 ($1.95)
1-12: 2-Indicia reads #1, Jan, 1995; Aragonés-c/a in all 3.50

GROO (Sergio Aragonés'...)
Dark Horse Comics: Jan, 1998 - No. 4, Apr, 1998 ($2.95)
1-4: Aragonés-c/a in all 4.00

GROO CHRONICLES, THE (Sergio Aragonés)
Marvel Comics (Epic Comics): June, 1989 - No. 6, Feb, 1990 ($3.50)
Book 1-6: Reprints early Pacific issues 3.50

GROO SPECIAL
Eclipse Comics: Oct, 1984 ($2.00, 52 pgs., Baxter paper)
1-Aragonés-c/a 3 6 9 16 22 28

GROO THE WANDERER (See Destroyer Duck #1 & Starslayer #5)
Pacific Comics: Dec, 1982 - No. 8, Apr, 1984
1-Aragonés-c/a(p) in all; Aragonés bio., photo 2 4 6 13 18 22
2-5: 5-Deluxe paper (1.00-c) 2 4 6 9 12 15
6-8 2 4 6 10 14 18

GROO THE WANDERER (Sergio Aragonés'...) (See Marvel Graphic Novel #32)
Marvel Comics (Epic Comics): March, 1985 - No. 120, Jan, 1995
1-Aragonés-c/a in all 2 4 6 9 13 16
2-10 1 2 3 5 6 8
11-20,50-($1.50, double size) 5.00
21-49,51-99: 87-direct sale only, high quality paper 3.00
100-($2.95, 52 pgs.) 5.00
101-120 4.00
Groo Carnival, The (12/91, $8.95)-r/#9-12 11.00
Groo Garden, The (4/94, $10.95)-r/#25-28 11.00

GROOVY (Cartoon Comics - not CCA approved)
Marvel Comics Group: March, 1968 - No. 3, July, 1968
1-Monkees, Ringo Starr, Sonny & Cher, Mamas & Papas photos 9 18 27 60 100 140
2,3 6 12 18 41 66 90

GROSS POINT
DC Comics: Aug, 1997 - No. 14, Aug, 1998 ($2.50)
1-14: 1-Waid/Augustyn-s 2.50

GROUNDED
Image Comics: July, 2005 - No. 6, May, 2006 ($2.95/$2.99, limited series)
1-6-Mark Sable-s/Paul Azaceta-a. 1-Mike Oeming-c 3.00
Vol. 1: Powerless TPB (2006, $14.99) r/#1-6; sketch pages and creator bios 15.00

GRRL SCOUTS (Jim Mahfood's...) (Also see 40 oz. Collected)
Oni Press: Mar,1999 - No. 4, Dec, 1999 ($2.95, B&W, limited series)
1-4-Mahfood-s/c/a 3.00
TPB (2003, $12.95) r/#1-4; pin-ups by Warren, Winick, Allred, Fegredo and others 13.00

GRRL SCOUTS: WORK SUCKS
Image Comics: Feb, 2003 - No. 4, May, 2003 ($2.95, B&W, limited series)
1-4-Mahfood-s/c/a 3.00
TPB (2004, $12.95) r/#1-4; pin-ups by Oeming, Dwyer, Tennapel and others 13.00

GUADALCANAL DIARY (See American Library)

GUARDIAN ANGEL
Image Comics: May, 2002 - No. 2, July, 2002 ($2.95)
1,2-Peterson-s/Wiesenfeld-a 3.00

GUARDIANS
Marvel Comics: Sept, 2004 - No. 5, Dec, 2004 ($2.99, limited series)
1-5-Sumerak-s/Casey Jones-a 3.00

GUARDIANS OF METROPOLIS
DC Comics: Nov, 1995 - Feb, 1995 ($1.50, limited series)
1-4: 1-Superman & Granny Goodness app. 2.50

GUARDIANS OF THE GALAXY (Also see The Defenders #26, Marvel Presents #3, Marvel Super-Heroes #18, Marvel Two-In-One #5)

Guardians of the Galaxy #15 © MAR

Gunfire #5 © DC

Gunsmoke Four Color #720 © DELL

	GD 2.0	VG 4.0	FN 6.0	VF 8.0	VF/NM 9.0	NM- 9.2

Marvel Comics: June, 1990 - No. 62, July, 1995 ($1.00/$1.25)

1-Valentino-c/a(p) begin. 3.00
2-16: 2-Zeck-c(i). 5-McFarlane-c(i). 7-Intro Malevolence (Mephisto's daughter); Perez-c(i). 8-Intro Rancor (descendant of Wolverine) in cameo. 9-1st full app. Rancor; Rob Liefeld-c(i). 10-Jim Lee-c(i). 13,14-1st app. Spirit of Vengeance (futuristic Ghost Rider). 14-Spirit of Vengeance vs. The Guardians. 15-Starlin-c(i). 16-($1.50, 52 pgs.)-Starlin-c(i) 2.50
17-24,26-38,40-47: 17-20-31st century Punishers storyline. 20-Last $1.00-c. 21-Rancor app. 22-Reintro Starhawk. 24-Silver Surfer-c/story; Ron Lim-c. 26-Origin retold. 27-28-Infinity War x-over; 27-Inhumans app. 43-Intro Wooden (son of Thor) 2.50
25-($2.50)-Prism foil-c; Silver Surfer/Galactus-c/s 3.00
25-($2.50)-Without foil-c; newsstand edition 2.50
39-($2.95, 52 pgs.)-Embossed & holo-grafx foil-c; Dr. Doom vs. Rancor 3.00
48,49,51-62: 48-bound-in trading card sheet 2.50
50-($2.00, 52 pgs.)-Newsstand edition 2.75
50-($2.95, 52 pgs.)-Collectors ed. w/foil embossed-c 3.00
Annual 1-4: ('91-'94, 68 pgs.)-1-Origin. 2-Spirit of Vengeance-c/story. 3,4-Bagged w/card 3.00

GUARDIANS OF THE GALAXY (See Annihilation series)
Marvel Comics: July, 2008 - Present ($2.99)

1-24: 1-Pelletier-a/Abnett & Lanning-s; 2nd printing exists. 24-Thanos returns 3.00

GUERRILLA WAR (Formerly Jungle War Stories)
Dell Publishing Co.: No. 12, July-Sept, 1965 - No. 14, Mar, 1966

12-14 3 6 9 16 22 28

GUILTY (See Justice Traps the Guilty)

GULLIVER'S TRAVELS (See Dell Jr. Treasury No. 3)
Dell Publishing Co.: Sept-Nov, 1965

1 5 10 15 34 55 75

GUMBY
Wildcard Ink: July, 2006 - No. 3 ($3.99)

1-3-Bob Burden & Rick Geary-s&a 4.00

GUMBY'S SUMMER FUN SPECIAL
Comico: July, 1987 ($2.50)

1-Art Adams-c/a; B. Burden scripts 3.00

GUMBY'S WINTER FUN SPECIAL
Comico: Dec, 1988 ($2.50, 44 pgs.)

1-Art Adams-c/a 3.00

GUMPS, THE (See Merry Christmas..., Popular & Super Comics)
Dell Publ. Co./Bridgeport Herald Corp.: No. 73, 1945; Mar-Apr, 1947 - No. 5, Nov-Dec, 1947

Four Color 73 (Dell)(1945) 12 24 36 83 152 220
1 (3-4/47) 15 30 45 88 137 185
2-5 11 22 33 60 83 105

GUN CANDY (Also see The Ride)
Image Comics: July, 2005 - Present ($5.99)

1,2-Stelfreeze-c/a; flip book with The Ride (1-Pearson-c. 2-Noto-c) 6.00

GUNFIGHTER (Fat & Slat #1-4) (Becomes Haunt of Fear #15 on)
E. C. Comics (Fables Publ. Co.): No. 5, Sum, 1948 - No. 14, Mar-Apr, 1950

5,6-Moon Girl in each 55 110 165 347 586 825
7-14: 14-Bondage-c 40 80 120 246 411 575

NOTE: *Craig & H. C. Kiefer art in most issues. Craig c-5, 6, 13, 14. Feldstein/Craig a-10. Feldstein a-7-11. Harrison/Wood a-13, 14. Ingels a-5-14; c-7-12.*

GUNFIGHTERS, THE
Super Comics (Reprints): 1963 - 1964

10-12,15,16,18: 10,11-r/Billy the Kid #s? 12-r/The Rider #5(Swift Arrow). 15-r/Straight Arrow #42; Powell-r. 16-r/Billy the Kid #?(Toby). 18-r/The Rider #3; Severin-c
2 4 6 10 14 18

GUNFIGHTERS, THE (Formerly Kid Montana)
Charlton Comics: No. 51, 10/66 - No. 52, 10/67; No. 53, 6/79 - No. 85, 7/84

51,52 2 4 6 11 16 20
53,54,56:53,54-Williamson/Torres-r/Six Gun Heroes #47,49. 56-Williamson/Severin-c; Severin-r/Sheriff of Tombstone #1 1 3 4 6 8 10
55,57-80 6.00
81-84-Lower print run 1 2 3 5 6 8
85-S&K-r/1955 Bullseye 1 3 4 6 8 10

GUNFIRE (See Deathstroke Annual #2 & Showcase 94 #1,2)
DC Comics: May, 1994 - No. 13, June, 1995 ($1.75/$2.25)

1-5,0,6-13: 2-Ricochet-c/story. 5-(9/94). 0-(10/94). 6-(11/94) 2.50

GUN GLORY (Movie)
Dell Publishing Co.: No. 846, Oct, 1957 (one-shot)

Four Color 846-Toth-a, photo-c. 8 16 24 58 97 135

GUNHAWK, THE (Formerly Whip Wilson)(See Wild Western)
Marvel Comics/Atlas (MCI): No. 12, Nov, 1950 - No. 18, Dec, 1951
(Also see Two-Gun Western #5)

12 18 36 54 105 165 225
13-18: 13-Tuska-a. 16-Colan-a. 18-Maneely-c 14 28 42 76 108 140

GUNHAWKS (Gunhawk No. 7)
Marvel Comics Group: Oct, 1972 - No. 7, October, 1973

1,6: 1-Reno Jones, Kid Cassidy; Shores-c/a(p). 6-Kid Cassidy dies
3 6 9 16 23 30
2-5,7: 7-Reno Jones solo 2 4 6 11 16 20

GUNMASTER (Becomes Judo Master #89 on)
Charlton Comics: 9/64 - No. 4, 1965; No. 84, 7/65 - No. 88, 3-4/66; No. 89, 10/67

V1#1 4 8 12 22 34 45
2,4, V5#84-86: 84-Formerly Six-Gun Heroes 3 6 9 16 22 28
V5#87-89 2 4 6 11 16 20

NOTE: *Vol. 5 was originally cancelled with #88 (3-4/66). #89 on, became Judo Master, then later in 1967, Charlton issued #89 as a Gunmaster one-shot.*

GUN RUNNER
Marvel Comics UK: Oct, 1993 - No. 6, Mar, 1994 ($1.75, limited series)

1-($2.75)-Polybagged w/4 trading cards; Spirits of Vengeance app. 3.00
2-6: 2-Ghost Rider & Blaze app. 2.50

GUNS AGAINST GANGSTERS (True-To-Life Romances #8 on)
Curtis Publications/Novelty Press: Sept-Oct, 1948 - No. 6, July-Aug, 1949; V2#1, Sept-Oct, 1949

1-Toni & Greg Gayle begins by Schomburg; L.B. Cole-c
39 78 117 240 395 550
2-L.B. Cole-c 28 56 84 165 270 375
3-6, V2#1: 6-Toni Gayle-c by Cole 25 50 75 147 241 335

NOTE: *L. B. Cole c-1-6, V2#1, 2; a-1, 2, 3(2), 4-6.*

GUNSLINGER
Dell Publishing Co.: No. 1220, Oct-Dec, 1961 (one-shot)

Four Color 1220-Photo-c 8 16 24 56 93 130

GUNSLINGER (Formerly Tex Dawson...)
Marvel Comics Group: No. 2, Apr, 1973 - No. 3, June, 1973

2,3 2 4 6 13 18 22

GUNSLINGERS
Marvel Comics: Feb, 2000 ($2.99)

1-Reprints stories of Two-Gun Kid, Rawhide Kid and Caleb Hammer 3.00

GUNSMITH CATS: (Title series), **Dark Horse Comics**

--BAD TRIP (Manga), 6/98 - No. 6, 11/98 ($2.95, B&W) 1-6 3.00
--BEAN BANDIT (Manga), 1/99 - No. 9 ($2.95, B&W, limited series) 1-9 3.00
--GOLDIE VS. MISTY (Manga), 11/97 - No. 7, 5/98 ($2.95, B&W) 1-7 3.00
--KIDNAPPED (Manga), 11/99 - No. 10, 8/00 ($2.95, B&W) 1-10 3.00
--MISTER V (Manga), 10/00 - No. 11, 8/01 ($3.50/$2.99), B&W) 1-7,9-11 3.50
8-($2.99) 3.00
--THE RETURN OF GRAY (Manga), 8/96 - No. 7, 2/97 ($2.95, B&W) 1-7 3.00
--SHADES OF GRAY (Manga), 5/97 - No. 5, 9/97 ($2.95, B&W) 1-5 3.00
--SPECIAL (Manga) Nov, 2001 ($2.99, B&W, one-shot) 3.00

GUNSMOKE (Blazing Stories of the West)
Western Comics (Youthful Magazines): Apr-May, 1949 - No. 16, Jan, 1952

1-Gunsmoke & Masked Marvel begin by Ingels; Ingels bondage-c
45 90 135 284 480 675
2-Ingels-c/a(2) 30 60 90 177 289 400
3-Ingels bondage-c/a 25 50 75 150 245 340
4-6: Ingels-c 20 40 60 117 189 260
7-10 14 28 42 76 108 140
11-16: 15,16-Western/horror stories 13 26 39 72 101 130

NOTE: *Stallman a-11, 14. Wildey a-15, 16.*

GUNSMOKE (TV)
Dell Publishing Co./Gold Key (All have James Arness photo-c): No. 679, Feb, 1956 - No. 27, Feb, 1969 - No. 6, Feb, 1970

Guy Gardner: Warrior #21 © DC

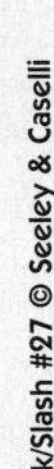
Hack/Slash #27 © Seeley & Caselli

Halloween II #1 © New Line

	GD 2.0	VG 4.0	FN 6.0	VF 8.0	VF/NM 9.0	NM- 9.2
Four Color 679(#1)	16	32	48	115	220	325
Four Color 720,769,797,844 (#2-5),6(11-1/57-58)	9	18	27	61	103	145
7,8,9,11,12-Williamson-a in all, 4 pgs. each	9	18	27	63	107	150
10-Williamson/Crandall-a, 4 pgs.	9	18	27	63	107	150
13-27	8	16	24	52	86	120
1 (Gold Key)	6	12	18	41	66	90
2-6('69-70)	4	8	12	22	34	45

GUNSMOKE TRAIL
Ajax-Farrell Publ./Four Star Comic Corp.: June, 1957 - No. 4, Dec, 1957

	GD 2.0	VG 4.0	FN 6.0	VF 8.0	VF/NM 9.0	NM- 9.2
1	11	22	33	60	83	105
2-4	7	14	21	35	43	50

GUNSMOKE WESTERN (Formerly Western Tales of Black Rider)
Atlas Comics No. 32-35(CPS/NPI); Marvel No. 36 on: No. 32, Dec, 1955 - No. 77, July, 1963

	GD 2.0	VG 4.0	FN 6.0	VF 8.0	VF/NM 9.0	NM- 9.2
32-Baker & Drucker-a	18	36	54	105	165	225
33,35,36-Williamson-a in each: 5,6 & 4 pgs. plus Drucker-a #33. 33-Kinstler-a?	14	28	42	82	121	160
34-Baker-a, 4 pgs.; Severin-c	14	28	42	82	121	160
37-Davis-a(2); Williamson text illo	12	24	36	67	94	120
38,39: 39-Williamson text illo (unsigned)	10	20	30	54	72	90
40-Williamson/Mayo-a (4 pgs.)	10	20	30	58	79	100
41,42,45,46,48,49,52-54,57,58,60: 49,52-Kid from Texas story. 57-1st Two Gun Kid by Severin. 60-Sam Hawk app. in Kid Colt	8	16	24	44	57	70
43,44-Torres-a	8	16	24	44	57	70
47,51,59,61: 47,51,59-Kirby-a. 61-Crandall-a	9	18	27	52	69	85
50-Kirby, Crandall-a	10	20	30	58	79	100
55,56-Matt Baker-a	10	20	30	58	79	100
62-67,69,71-73,77-Kirby-a. 72-Origin Kid Colt	5	10	15	35	55	75
68,70,74-76: 68-(10¢-c)	4	8	12	28	44	60
68-(10¢ cover price blacked out, 12¢ printed on)	9	18	27	60	100	140

NOTE: ***Colan*** *a-35-37, 39, 72, 76.* ***Davis*** *a-37, 52, 54, 55; c-50, 54.* ***Ditko*** *a-66; c-56p.* ***Drucker*** *a-32-34.* ***Heath*** *c-33.* ***Jack Keller*** *a-34, 35, 40, 55, 56, 60, 61, 65, 68, 72, 74, 75, 77; c-72.* ***Kirby*** *a-47, 50, 51, 59, 62(3), 63-67, 69, 71, 73, 77; c-56(w/****Ditko****), 57, 58, 60, 61(w/****Ayers****), 62, 63, 65, 66, 68, 69, 71-77.* ***Maleely*** *c-455.* ***Robinson*** *a-35.* ***Severin*** *a-35, 59-61; c-34, 35, 39, 42, 43.* ***Tuska*** *a-34.* ***Wildey*** *a-10, 37, 42, 56, 57. Kid Colt in all. Two-Gun Kid in No. 57, 59, 60-63. Wyatt Earp in No. 45, 48, 49, 52, 54, 55, 56, 58.*

GUNS OF FACT & FICTION (Also see A-1 Comics)
Magazine Enterprises: No. 13, 1948 (one-shot)

	GD 2.0	VG 4.0	FN 6.0	VF 8.0	VF/NM 9.0	NM- 9.2
A-1 13-Used in **SOTI**, pg. 19; Ingels & J. Craig-a	27	54	81	158	259	360

GUNS OF THE DRAGON
DC Comics: Oct, 1998 - No. 4, Jan, 1999 ($2.50, limited series)

1-4-DCU in the 1920's; Enemy Ace & Bat Lash app. 2.50

GUN THEORY
Marvel Comics (Epic): Oct, 2003 - No. 4 ($2.50, limited series)

1,2-Daniel Way-s/Jon Proctor-a 2.50

GUNWITCH, THE : OUTSKIRTS OF DOOM (See The Nocturnals)
Oni Press: June, 2001 - No. 3, Oct, 2001 ($2.95, B&W, limited series)

1-3-Brereton-s/painted-c/Naifeh-s 3.00

GUY GARDNER (Guy Gardner: Warrior #17 on)(Also see Green Lantern #59)
DC Comics: Oct, 1992 - No. 44, July, 1996 ($1.25/$1.50/$1.75)

	NM- 9.2
1-24,0,26-30: 1-Staton-c/a(p) begins. 6-Guy vs. Hal Jordan. 8-Vs. Lobo-c/story. 15-JLA x-over, begin $1.50-c. 18-Begin 4-part Emerald Fallout story; splash page x-over GL #50. 18-21-Vs. Hal Jordan. 24-(9/94)-Zero Hour. 0-(10/94)	2.50
25 (11/94, $2.50, 52 pgs.)	3.00
29 ($2.95)-Gatefold-c	3.50
29-Variant-c (Edward Hopper's Nighthawks)	2.50
31-44: 31-$1.75-c begins. 40-Gorilla Grodd-c/app. 44-Parallax-app. (1 pg.)	2.50
Annual 1 (1995, $3.50)-Year One story	4.00
Annual 2 (1996, $2.95)-Legends of the Dead Earth story	3.00

GUY GARDNER: COLLATERAL DAMAGE
DC Comics: 2006 - No. 2 ($5.99, square-bound, limited series)

1,2-Howard Chaykin-s/a 6.00

GUY GARDNER REBORN
DC Comics: 1992 - Book 3, 1992 ($4.95, limited series)

1-3: Staton-c/a(p). 1-Lobo-c/cameo. 2,3-Lobo-c/s 5.00

GYPSY COLT
Dell Publishing Co.: No. 568, June, 1954 (one-shot)

	GD 2.0	VG 4.0	FN 6.0	VF 8.0	VF/NM 9.0	NM- 9.2
Four Color 568--Movie	5	10	15	32	51	70

GYRO GEARLOOSE (See Dynabrite Comics, Walt Disney's C&S #140 &Walt Disney Showcase #18)
Dell Publishing Co.: No. 1047, Nov-Jan/1959-60 - May-July, 1962 (Disney)

	GD 2.0	VG 4.0	FN 6.0	VF 8.0	VF/NM 9.0	NM- 9.2
Four Color 1047 (No. 1)-All Barks-c/a	16	32	48	116	223	330
Four Color 1095,1184-All by Carl Barks	10	20	30	67	116	165
Four Color 1267-Barks c/a, 4 pgs.	8	16	24	54	90	125
01329-207 (#1, 5-7/62)-Barks-c only (intended as 4-Color 1329?)	6	12	18	41	66	90

HACKER FILES, THE
DC Comics: Aug, 1992 - No. 12, July, 1993 ($1.95)

1-12: 1-Sutton-a(p) begins; computer generated-c 2.50

HACK/SLASH
Devil's Due Publishing: Apr. 2004 - Present ($3.25/$4.95)

	NM- 9.2
1-Seeley-s/Caselli-a/c	5.00
...: (The Series) 1-24,26-29 (5/07-Present, $3.50) Flashack to Cassie's childhood and origin. 12-Milk & Cheese cameo. 15-Re-Animator app.	3.50
25-($5.50) Double sized issue; Baugh-a; two covers	5.50
...: Comic Book Carnage (3/05) Manfredi-a/Seeley-s; Robert Kirkman & Steve Niles app.	5.00
...: First Cut TPB (10/05, $14.95) r/one-shots with sketch pages , designs, interviews	15.00
...: Girls Gone Dead (10/04, $4.95) Manfredi-a/Seeley-s	5.00
...: Land of Lost Toys 1-3 (11/05 - No. 3, 1/06, $3.25) Crossland-a/Seeley-s	3.25
...: New Reader Halloween Treat #1 (10/08, $3.50) origin retold; Cassie's diary pages	3.50
...: The Final Revenge of Evil Ernie (6/05, $4.95) Salman-a/Seeley-s; two covers	5.00
...: Trailers (2/05, $3.25) short stories by Seeley; art by various; three covers	3.25
...: Slice Hard (12/05, $4.95) Seeley-s	5.00
...: Slice Hard Pre-Sliced 25¢ Special (2/06, 25¢) origin story by Seeley; sketch pages	2.25
...: Vs Chucky (3/07, $5.50) Seeley-s/Merhoff-a; 3 covers	5.50
...: Vol. 2 Death By Sequel TPB (1/07, $18.99) r/Land of Lost Toys #1-3, Trailers, Slice Hard	19.00
...: Vol. 3 Friday the 31st TPB (10/07, $18.99) r/The Series #1-4 & ... Vs Chucky	19.00

HAGAR THE HORRIBLE (See Comics Reading Libraries in the Promotional Comics section)

HA HA COMICS (Teepee Tim No. 100 on; also see Giggle Comics)
Scope Mag.(Creston Publ.) No. 1-80/American Comics Group: Oct, 1943 - No. 99, Jan, 1955

	GD 2.0	VG 4.0	FN 6.0	VF 8.0	VF/NM 9.0	NM- 9.2
1-Funny animal	34	68	102	204	332	460
2	18	36	54	103	162	220
3-5: Ken Hultgren-a begins?	14	28	42	80	115	150
6-10	11	22	33	64	90	115
11-20: 14-Infinity-c	10	20	30	56	76	95
21-40	9	18	27	50	65	80
41-94,96-99: 49,61-X-Mas-c	8	16	24	44	57	70
95-3-D effect-c	15	30	45	90	140	190

HAIR BEAR BUNCH, THE (TV) (See Fun-In No. 13)
Gold Key: Feb, 1972 - No. 9, Feb, 1974 (Hanna-Barbera)

	GD 2.0	VG 4.0	FN 6.0	VF 8.0	VF/NM 9.0	NM- 9.2
1	4	8	12	24	37	50
2-9	3	6	9	17	25	32

HALF DEAD
Marvel Comics (Dabel Brothers Prods.): March, 2007 ($10.99, softcover, graphic novel)

SC-Barb Lien-Cooper & Park Cooper-s/Jimmy Bott-a 11.00

HALLELUJAH TRAIL, THE (See Movie Classics)

HALL OF FAME FEATURING THE T.H.U.N.D.E.R. AGENTS
JC Productions(Archie Comics Group): May, 1983 - No. 3, Dec, 1983

1-3: Thunder Agents-r(Crandall, Kane, Tuska, Wood-a). 2-New Ditko-c 3.00

HALLOWEEN (Movie)
Chaos! Comics: Nov, 2000; Apr, 2001 ($2.95/$2.99, one-shots)

	NM- 9.2
1-Brewer-a; Michael Myers childhood at the Sanitarium	3.00
...II: The Blackest Eyes (4/01, $2.99) Beck-a	3.00
...III: The Devil's Eyes (11/01, $2.99) Justiniano-a	3.00

HALLOWEEN (Halloween Nightdance on cover)(Movie)
Devils Due Publishing: Mar, 2008 - No. 4, May, 2008 ($3.50, limited series)

	NM- 9.2
1-4-Seeley-a/Hutchinson-s; multiple covers on each	3.50
...: 30 Years of Terror (8/08, $5.50) short stories by various incl. Seeley	5.50

HALLOWEEN HORROR
Eclipse Comics: Oct, 1987 (Seduction of the Innocent #7)($1.75)

1-Pre-code horror-r 3.00

HALLOWEEN MEGAZINE
Marvel Comics: Dec, 1996 ($3.95, one-shot, 96 pgs.)

1-Reprints Tomb of Dracula 4.00

HALO GRAPHIC NOVEL (Based on video game)

Halo: Uprising #3 © Microsoft

Hangman Comics #3 © MLJ

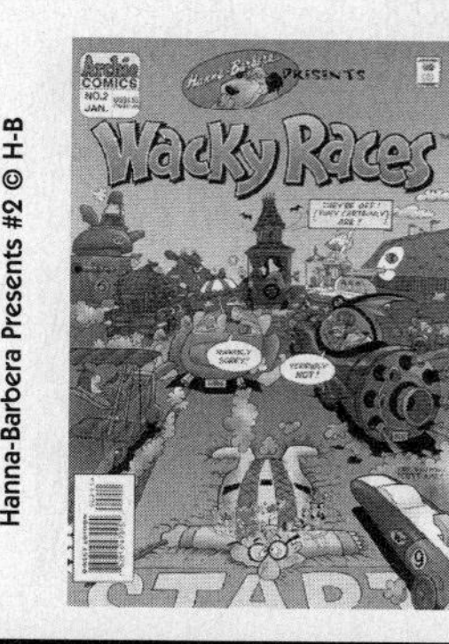

Hanna-Barbera Presents #2 © H-B

	GD 2.0	VG 4.0	FN 6.0	VF 8.0	VF/NM 9.0	NM- 9.2

Marvel Publishing Inc.: 2006 ($24.99, hardcover with dust jacket)
HC-Anthology set in the Halo universe; art by Bisley, Moebius and others; pin-up gallery by various incl. Darrow, Pratt, Williams and Van Fleet; Phil Hale painted-c 25.00

HALO: BLOOD LINE (Based on video game)
Marvel Comics: Feb, 2010 - No. 5 ($3.99, limited series)
1-4-Van Lente-s/Portela-a 4.00

HALO: HELLJUMPER (Based on video game)
Marvel Comics: Sept, 2009 - No. 5, Jan, 2010 ($3.99, limited series)
1-5-Peter David-s/Eric Nguyen-a 4.00

HALO: UPRISING (Based on video game) (Also see Marvel Spotlight: Halo)
Marvel Comics: Oct, 2007 - No. 4, Jun, 2009 ($3.99, limited series)
1-4-Bendis-s/Maleev-a; takes pllace between the *Halo 2* and *Halo 3* video games 4.00

HALO JONES (See The Ballad of...)

HAMMER, THE
Dark Horse Comics: Oct, 1997 - No. 4, Jan, 1998 ($2.95, limited series)
1-4-Kelley Jones-s/c/a, ...: Uncle Alex (8/98, $2.95) 3.00

HAMMER, THE: THE OUTSIDER
Dark Horse Comics: Feb, 1999 - No. 3, Apr, 1999 ($2.95, limited series)
1-3-Kelley Jones-s/c/a 3.00

HAMMERLOCKE
DC Comics: Sept, 1992 - No. 9, May, 1993 ($1.75, limited series)
1-($2.50, 52 pgs.)-Chris Sprouse-c/a in all 3.00
2-9 2.50

HAMMER OF GOD (Also see Nexus)
First Comics: Feb, 1990 - No. 4, May, 1990 ($1.95, limited series)
1-4 2.50

HAMMER OF GOD: BUTCH
Dark Horse Comics: May, 1994 - No. 4, Aug, 1994 ($2.50, limited series)
1-3 2.50

HAMMER OF GOD: PENTATHLON
Dark Horse Comics: Jan, 1994 ($2.50, one shot)
1-Character from Nexus 2.50

HAMMER OF GOD: SWORD OF JUSTICE
First Comics: Feb 1991 - Mar 1991 ($4.95, lim. series, squarebound, 52 pgs.)
V2#1,2 5.00

HAMMER OF THE GODS
Insight Studio Groups: 2001 - No. 5, 2001 ($2.95, limited series)
1-Michael Oeming & Mark Wheatley-s/a; Frank Cho-c 6.00
2-5: 3-Hughes-c. 5-Dave Johnson-c 3.00
The ColorSaga (2002, $4.95) r/"Enemy of the Gods" internet strip 5.00
Mortal Enemy TPB (2002, $18.95) r/#1-5; intro. by Peter David; afterword by Raven 19.00

HAMMER OF THE GODS: HAMMER HITS CHINA
Image Comics: Feb, 2003 - No. 3, Sept, 2003 ($2.95, limited series)
1-3-Oeming & Wheatley-s/a; Oeming-c. 2-Frankenstein Mobster by Wheatley 3.00

HANDBOOK OF THE CONAN UNIVERSE, THE
Marvel Comics: June, 1985; Jan, 1986 ($1.25, one-shot)
1-(6/85) Kaluta-c (2 printings) 4.00
1-(1/86) Kaluta-c 6.00
nn-(no date, circa '87-88, B&W, 36 pgs.) reprints '86 with changes; new painted cover

	1	2	3	5	6	8

HAND OF FATE (Formerly Men Against Crime)
Ace Magazines: No. 8, Dec, 1951 - No. 25, Dec, 1954 (Weird/horror stories) (Two #25's)

	GD	VG	FN	VF	VF/NM	NM-
8-Surrealistic text story	42	84	126	265	445	625
9,10,21-Necronomicon sty; drug belladonna used	25	50	75	150	245	340
11-18,20,22,23	21	42	63	126	206	285
19-Bondage, hypo needle scenes	22	44	66	132	216	300
24-Electric chair-c	31	62	93	186	303	420
25a(11/54), 25b(12/54)-Both have Cameron-a	18	36	54	103	162	220

NOTE: ***Cameron** a-9, 10, 19-25a, 25b; c-13. **Sekowsky** a-8, 9, 13, 14.*

HAND OF FATE
Eclipse Comics: Feb, 1988 - No. 3, Apr, 1988 ($1.75/$2.00, Baxter paper)
1-3; 3-B&W 2.50

HANDS OF THE DRAGON
Seaboard Periodicals (Atlas): June, 1975

	GD	VG	FN	VF	VF/NM	NM-
1-Origin/1st app.; Craig-a(p)/Mooney inks	2	4	6	8	11	14

HANGMAN COMICS (Special Comics No. 1; Black Hood No. 9 on)
(Also see Flyman, Mighty Comics, Mighty Crusaders & Pep Comics)
MLJ Magazines: No. 2, Spring, 1942 - No. 8, Fall, 1943

	GD	VG	FN	VF	VF/NM	NM-
2-The Hangman, Boy Buddies begin	200	400	600	1280	2190	3100
3-Beheading splash pg.; 1st Nazi war-c	135	270	405	864	1482	2100
4-8: 5-1st Japan war-c. 8-2nd app. Super Duck (ties w/Jolly Jingles #11)	116	232	348	742	1271	1800

NOTE: ***Fuje** a-7(3), 8(3); c-3. **Reinman** c/a-3. Bondage c-3. **Sahle** c-6.*

HANK
Pentagon Publishing Co.: 1946

	GD	VG	FN	VF	VF/NM	NM-
nn-Coulton Waugh's newspaper reprint	8	16	24	44	57	70

HANNA-BARBERA (See Golden Comics Digest No. 2, 7, 11)

HANNA-BARBERA ALL-STARS
Archie Publications: Oct, 1995 - No. 4, Apr, 1996 ($1.50, bi-monthly)
1-4 4.00

HANNA-BARBERA BANDWAGON (TV)
Gold Key: Oct, 1962 - No. 3, Apr, 1963

	GD	VG	FN	VF	VF/NM	NM-
1-Giant, 84 pgs. 1-Augie Doggie app.; 1st app. Lippy the Lion, Touché Turtle & Dum Dum, Wally Gator, Loopy de Loop,	12	24	36	85	155	225
2-Giant, 84 pgs.; Mr. & Mrs. J. Evil Scientist (1st app.) in Snagglepuss story; Yakky Doodle, Ruff and Reddy and others app.	9	18	27	60	100	140
3-Regular size; Mr. & Mrs. J. Evil Scientist app. (pre-#1), Snagglepuss, Wally Gator and others app.	7	14	21	47	76	105

HANNA-BARBERA GIANT SIZE
Harvey Comics: Oct, 1992 - No. 3 ($2.25, 68 pgs.)
V2#1-3:Flintstones, Yogi Bear, Magilla Gorilla, Huckleberry Hound, Quick Draw McGraw, Yakky Doodle & Chopper, Jetsons & others 6.00

HANNA-BARBERA HI-ADVENTURE HEROES (See Hi-Adventure...)

HANNA-BARBERA PARADE (TV)
Charlton Comics: Sept, 1971 - No. 10, Dec, 1972

	GD	VG	FN	VF	VF/NM	NM-
1	7	14	21	49	80	110
2,4-10	4	8	12	26	41	55
3-(52 pgs.)- "Summer Picnic"	6	12	18	37	59	80

NOTE: *No. 4 (1/72) went on sale late in 1972 with the January 1973 issues.*

HANNA-BARBERA PRESENTS
Archie Publications: Nov, 1995 - No. 6 ($1.50, bi-monthly)
1-8: 1-Atom Ant & Secret Squirrel. 2-Wacky Races. 3-Yogi Bear. 4-Quick Draw McGraw & Magilla Gorilla. 5-A Pup Named Scooby-Doo. 6-Superstar Olympics. 7-Wacky Races. 8-Frankenstein Jr. & the Impossibles 3.00

HANNA-BARBERA SPOTLIGHT (See Spotlight)

HANNA-BARBERA SUPER TV HEROES (TV)
Gold Key: Apr, 1968 - No. 7, Oct, 1969 (Hanna-Barbera)

	GD	VG	FN	VF	VF/NM	NM-
1-The Birdman, The Herculoids(ends #6; not in #3), Moby Dick, Young Samson & Goliath (ends #2,4), and The Mighty Mightor begin; Spiegle-a in all	13	26	39	93	172	250
2-The Galaxy Trio app.; Shazzan begins; 12¢ & 15¢ versions exist	9	18	27	65	113	160
3,6,7-The Space Ghost app.	9	18	27	60	100	140
4,5	8	16	24	52	86	120

NOTE: *Birdman in #1,2,4,5. Herculoids in #2,4-7. Mighty Mightor in #1,2,4-7. Moby Dick in all. Shazzan in #2-5. Young Samson & Goliath in #1,3.*

HANNA-BARBERA TV FUN FAVORITES (See Golden Comics Digest #2,7,11)

HANNA-BARBERA (TV STARS) (See TV Stars)

HANS BRINKER (Disney)
Dell Publishing Co.: No. 1273, Feb, 1962 (one-shot)

	GD	VG	FN	VF	VF/NM	NM-
Four Color 1273-Movie, photo-c	6	12	18	43	69	95

HANS CHRISTIAN ANDERSEN
Ziff-Davis Publ. Co.: 1953 (100 pgs., Special Issue)

	GD	VG	FN	VF	VF/NM	NM-
nn-Danny Kaye (movie)-Photo-c; fairy tales	16	32	48	94	147	200

HANSEL & GRETEL
Dell Publishing Co.: No. 590, Oct, 1954 (one-shot)

	GD	VG	FN	VF	VF/NM	NM-
Four Color 590-Partial photo-c	6	12	18	43	69	95

HANSI, THE GIRL WHO LOVED THE SWASTIKA

Hap Hazard Comics #6 © ACE

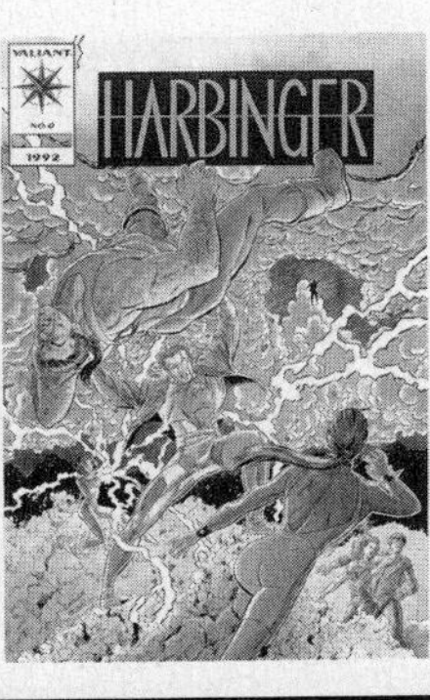

Harbinger #0 © Voyager Comm.

Hardware #17 © Milestone

	GD 2.0	VG 4.0	FN 6.0	VF 8.0	VF/NM 9.0	NM- 9.2

Spire Christian Comics (Fleming H. Revell Co.): 1973, 1976 (39¢/49¢)

1973 edition with 39¢-c	6	12	18	37	59	80
1976 edition with 49¢-c	4	8	12	22	34	45

HAP HAZARD COMICS (Real Love No. 25 on)
Ace Magazines (Readers' Research): Summer, 1944 - No. 24, Feb, 1949
(#1-6 are quarterly issues)

1	15	30	45	84	127	170
2	9	18	27	52	69	85
3-10	8	16	24	44	57	70
11-13,15-24	8	16	24	40	50	60
14-Feldstein-c (4/47)	10	20	30	56	76	95

HAP HOPPER (See Comics Revue No. 2)

HAPPIEST MILLIONAIRE, THE (See Movie Comics)

HAPPI TIM (See March of Comics No. 182)

HAPPY BIRTHDAY MARTHA WASHINGTON (Also see Give Me Liberty, Martha Washington Goes To War, & Martha Washington Stranded In Space)
Dark Horse Comics: Mar, 1995 ($2.95, one-shot)

1-Miller script; Gibbons-c/a 3.00

HAPPY COMICS (Happy Rabbit No. 41 on)
Nedor Publ./Standard Comics (Animated Cartoons): Aug, 1943 - No. 40, Dec, 1950
(Companion to Goofy Comics)

1-Funny animal	27	54	81	158	259	360
2	15	30	45	86	133	180
3-10	12	24	36	67	94	120
11-19	10	20	30	54	72	90
20-31,34-37-Frazetta text illos in all (2 in #34&35, 3 in #27,28,30). 27-Al Fago-a	11	22	33	64	90	115
32-Frazetta-a, 7 pgs. plus 2 text illos; Roussos-a	20	40	60	120	195	270
33-Frazetta-a(2), 6 pgs. each (Scarce)	28	56	84	165	270	375
38-40	9	18	27	47	61	75

HAPPYDALE: DEVILS IN THE DESERT
DC Comics (Vertigo): 1999 - No. 2, 1999 ($6.95, limited series)

1,2-Andrew Dabb-s/Seth Fisher-a 7.00

HAPPY DAYS (TV)(See Kite Fun Book)
Gold Key: Mar, 1979 - No. 6, Feb, 1980

1-Photo-c of TV cast; 35¢-c	3	6	9	16	23	30
2-6-(40¢-c)	2	4	6	9	12	15

HAPPY HOLIDAY (See March of Comics No. 181)

HAPPY HOULIHANS (Saddle Justice No. 3 on; see Blackstone, The Magician Detective)
E. C. Comics: Fall, 1947 - No. 2, Winter, 1947-48

1-Origin Moon Girl (same date as Moon Girl #1)	56	112	168	353	597	840
2	31	62	93	186	303	420

HAPPY JACK
Red Top (Decker): Aug, 1957 - No. 2, Nov, 1957

V1#1,2	5	10	15	22	26	30

HAPPY JACK HOWARD
Red Top (Farrell)/Decker: 1957

nn-Reprints Handy Andy story from E. C. Dandy Comics #5, renamed "Happy Jack"	5	10	15	22	26	30

HAPPY RABBIT (Formerly Happy Comics)
Standard Comics (Animated Cartoons): No. 41, Feb, 1951 - No. 48, Apr, 1952

41-Funny animal	8	16	24	44	57	70
42-48	7	14	21	35	43	50

HARBINGER (Also see Unity)
Valiant: Jan, 1992 - No. 41, June, 1995 ($1.95/$2.50)

0-Prequel to the series; available by redeeming coupons in #1-6; cover image has pink sky; title logo is blue	4	8	12	24	37	50
0-(2nd printing) cover has blue sky & red logo						5.00
1-1st app.	2	4	6	8	10	12
2-4: 4-Low print run	1	2	3	5	7	9
5,6: 5-Solar app. 6-Torque dies	1	2	3	4	5	7
7-10: 8,9-Unity x-overs. 8-Miller-c. 9-Simonson-c. 10-1st app. H.A.R.D Corps (10/92)						5.00
11-24,26-41: 14-1st app. Stronghold. 18-Intro Screen. 19-1st app. Stunner. 22-Archer & Armstrong app. 24-Cover similar to #1. 26-Intro New Harbingers. 29-Bound-in trading card. 30-H.A.R.D. Corps app. 32-Eternal Warrior app. 33-Dr. Eclipse app.						2.50
25-($3.50, 52 pgs.)-Harada vs. Sting						3.50
...Files 1,2 (8/94,2/95 $2.50)						2.50
...: The Beginning HC (2007, $24.95) recolored reprints #0-7 and Story of Harada from coupons from #1-6; new "Origin of Harada" story by Shooter and Bob Hall						25.00
Trade paperback nn (11/92, $9.95)-Reprints #1-4 & comes polybagged with a copy of Harbinger #0 w/new-c. Price for TPB only						10.00

NOTE: *Issues 1-6 have coupons with origin of Harada and are redeemable for Harbinger #0.*

HARD BOILED
Dark Horse Comics: Sept, 1990 - No. 3, Mar, 1992 ($4.95/$5.95, 8 1/2x11", lim. series)

1-3-Miller-s; Darrow-c/a; sexually explicit & violent	1	2	3	4	5	7
TPB (5/93, $15.95)						16.00
Big Damn Hard Boiled (12/97, $29.95, B&W) r/#1-3						30.00

HARDCASE (See Break Thru, Flood Relief & Ultraforce, 1st Series)
Malibu Comics (Ultraverse): June, 1993 - No. 26, Aug, 1995 ($1.95/$2.50)

1-Intro Hardcase; Dave Gibbons-c; has coupon for Ultraverse Premiere #0; Jim Callahan-a(p) begin, ends #3	3.00
1-With coupon missing	2.25
1-Platinum Edition	4.00
1-Holographic Cover Edition; 1st full-c holograph tied w/Prime 1 & Strangers 1	7.00
1-Ultra Limited silver foil-c	4.00
2,3-Callahan-a, 2-($2.50)-Newsstand edition bagged w/trading card	2.50
4,6-15, 17-19: 4-Strangers app. 7-Break-Thru x-over. 8-Solution app. 9-Vs. Turf. 12-Silver foil logo, wraparound-c. 17-Prime app.	2.50
5-($2.50, 48 pgs.)-Rune flip-c/story by B. Smith (3 pgs.)	2.50
16 ($3.50, 68 pgs.)-Rune pin-up	3.50
20-26: 23-Loki app.	2.50

NOTE: ***Perez** a-8(2); c-20i.*

HARDCORE STATION
DC Comics: July, 1998 - No. 6, Dec, 1998 ($2.50, limited series)

1-6-Starlin-s/a(p). 3-Green Lantern-c/app. 5,6-JLA-c/app. 3.00

H.A.R.D. CORPS, THE (See Harbinger #10)
Valiant: Dec, 1992 - No. 30, Feb, 1995 ($2.25) (Harbinger spin-off)

1-($2.50)-Gatefold-c by Jim Lee & Bob Layton	3.00
1-Gold variant	5.00
2-30: 5-Bloodshot-c/story cont'd from Bloodshot #3. 5-Variant edition; came w/Comic Defense System. 10-Turok app. 17-vs. Armorines. 18-Bound-in trading card. 20-Harbinger app.	2.50

HARD TIME
DC Comics (Focus): Apr, 2004 - No. 12, Mar, 2005 ($2.50)

1-12-Gerber-s/Hurtt-a; 1-Includes previews of other DC Focus series	2.50
...: 50 to Life (2004, $9.95, TPB) r/#1-6; cover gallery with sketches	10.00

HARD TIME: SEASON TWO
DC Comics: Feb, 2006 - No. 7, Aug, 2006 ($2.50/$2.99)

1-5-Gerber-s/Hurtt-a	2.50
6,7-($2.99) 7-Ethan paroled in 2053	3.00

HARDWARE
DC Comics (Milestone): Apr, 1993 - No. 50, Apr, 1997 ($1.50/$1.75/$2.50)

1-($2.95)-Collector's Edition polybagged w/poster & trading card (direct sale only)	4.00
1-Platinum Edition	6.00
1-15,17-19: 11-Shadow War x-over. 11,14-Simonson-c. 12-Buckler-a(p). 17-Worlds Collide Pt. 2. 18-Simonson-c; Worlds Collide Pt. 9. 15-1st Humberto Ramos DC work	2.50
16,50-($3.95, 52 pgs.)-16-Collector's Edition w/gatefold 2nd cover by Byrne; new armor; Icon app.	4.00
16,20-24,26-49: 16-($2.50, 52 pgs.)-Newsstand Ed. 49-Moebius-c	2.50
25-($2.95, 52 pgs.)	3.00

HARDY BOYS, THE (Disney
Dell Publ. Co.: No. 760, Dec, 1956 - No. 964, Jan, 1959 (Mickey Mouse Club)

Four Color 760 (#1)-Photo-c	10	20	30	70	123	175
Four Color 830(8/57), 887(1/58), 964-Photo-c	9	18	27	60	100	140

HARDY BOYS, THE (TV)
Gold Key: Apr, 1970 - No. 4, Jan, 1971

1	4	8	12	28	44	60
2-4	3	6	9	18	27	35

HARLAN ELLISON'S DREAM CORRIDOR
Dark Horse Comics: Mar, 1995 - No. 5, July, 1995 ($2.95, anthology)

1-5: Adaptation of Ellison stories. 1-4-Byrne-a.	3.00
Special (1/95, $4.95)	5.00
Trade paperback-(1996, $18.95, 192 pgs)-r/#1-5 & Special #1	19.00

HARLAN ELLISON'S DREAM CORRIDOR QUARTERLY

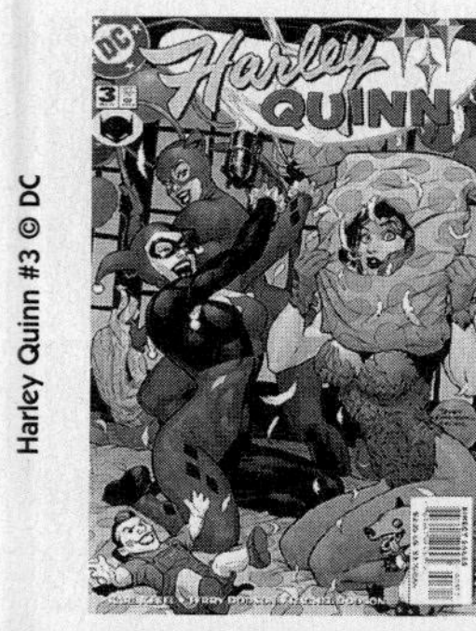

Harley Quinn #3 © DC

Harvey Comics Hits #52 © HARV

Harvey Hits #5 © HARV

	GD 2.0	VG 4.0	FN 6.0	VF 8.0	VF/NM 9.0	NM- 9.2

Dark Horse Comics: V2#1, Aug, 1996 ($5.95, anthology, squarebound)

V2#1-Adaptations of Ellison's stories w/new material; Neal Adams-a						6.00
Volume 2 TPB (3/07, $19.95) r/V2#1 and unpublished material incl. last Swan-a						20.00

HARLEM GLOBETROTTERS (TV) (See Fun-In No. 8, 10)
Gold Key: Apr, 1972 - No. 12, Jan, 1975 (Hanna-Barbera)

	GD	VG	FN	VF	VF/NM	NM-
1	4	8	12	26	41	55
2-5	3	6	9	16	22	28
6-12	2	4	6	13	18	22

NOTE: *#4, 8, and 12 contain 16 extra pages of advertising.*

HARLEQUIN ROMANCE
Dark Horse Comics: Nov, 2001 ($10.95, hardcover, one-shot)

nn-Neil Gaiman-s; painted-a/c by John Bolton						11.00

HARLEY QUINN (Also see Gotham City Sirens)
DC Comics: Dec, 2000 - No. 38, Jan, 2004 ($2.95/$2.25/$2.50)

1-Joker and Poison Ivy app.; Terry & Rachel Dodson-a/c						6.00
2-11-($2.25). 2-Two-Face-c/app. 3-Slumber party. 6,7-Riddler app.						2.50
12-($2.95) Batman app.						3.00
13-38: 13-Joker: Last Laugh. 17,18-Bizarro-c/app. 23-Begin $2.50-c. 23,24-Martian Manhunter app. 25,32-Joker-c/app.						2.50
Harley & Ivy: Love on the Lam (2001, $5.95) Winick-s/Chiodo-c/a						6.00
...: Our Worlds at War (10/01, $2.95) Jae Lee-c; art by various						3.00

HAROLD TEEN (See Popular Comics, & Super Comics)
Dell Publishing Co.: No. 2, 1942 - No. 209, Jan, 1949

	GD	VG	FN	VF	VF/NM	NM-
Four Color 2	29	58	87	212	406	600
Four Color 209	6	12	18	39	62	85

HARROWERS, THE (See Clive Barker's...)

HARSH REALM (Inspired 1999 TV series)
Harris Comics: 1993- No. 6, 1994 ($2.95, limited series)

1-6: Painted-c. Hudnall-s/Paquette & Ridgway-a						3.50
TPB (2000, $14.95) r/series						15.00

HARVEY
Marvel Comics: Oct, 1970; No. 2, 12/70; No. 3, 6/72 - No. 6, 12/72

	GD	VG	FN	VF	VF/NM	NM-
1	10	20	30	67	116	165
2-6	7	14	21	45	73	100

HARVEY COLLECTORS COMICS (Titled Richie Rich Collectors Comics on cover of #6-on)
Harvey Publ.: Sept, 1975 - No. 15, Jan, 1978; No. 16, Oct, 1979 (52 pgs.)

	GD	VG	FN	VF	VF/NM	NM-
1-Reprints Richie Rich #1,2	2	4	6	13	18	22
2-10: 7-Splash pg. shows cover to Friendly Ghost Casper #1	2	4	6	8	11	14
11-16: 16-Sad Sack-r	1	2	3	5	7	9

NOTE: *All reprints: Casper-#2, 7, Richie Rich-#1, 3, 5, 6, 8-15, Sad Sack-#16. Wendy-#4.*

HARVEY COMICS HITS (Formerly Joe Palooka #50)
Harvey Publications: No. 51, Oct, 1951 - No. 62, Apr, 1953

	GD	VG	FN	VF	VF/NM	NM-
51-The Phantom	31	62	93	184	300	415
52-Steve Canyon's Air Power(Air Force sponsored)	13	26	39	72	101	130
53-Mandrake the Magician	20	40	60	114	182	250
54-Tim Tyler's Tales of Jungle Terror	13	26	39	74	105	135
55-Love Stories of Mary Worth	11	22	33	62	86	110
56-The Phantom; bondage-c	26	52	78	154	252	350
57-Rip Kirby Exposes the Kidnap Racket; entire book by Alex Raymond	15	30	45	85	130	175
58-Girls in White (nurses stories)	11	22	33	62	86	110
59-Tales of the Invisible featuring Scarlet O'Neil	12	24	36	67	94	120
60-Paramount Animated Comics #1 (9/52) (3rd app. Baby Huey); 2nd Harvey app. Baby Huey & Casper the Friendly Ghost (1st in Little Audrey #25 (8/52)); 1st app. Herman & Catnip (c/story) & Buzzy the Crow	43	86	129	271	461	650
61-Casper the Friendly Ghost #6 (3rd Harvey Casper, 10/52)-Casper-c	47	94	141	296	498	700
62-Paramount Animated Comics #2; Herman & Catnip, Baby Huey & Buzzy the Crow	17	34	51	98	154	210

HARVEY COMICS LIBRARY
Harvey Publications: Apr, 1952 - No. 2, 1952

	GD	VG	FN	VF	VF/NM	NM-
1-Teen-Age Dope Slaves as exposed by Rex Morgan, M.D.; drug propaganda story; used in **SOTI**, pg. 27	161	322	483	1030	1765	2500
2-Dick Tracy Presents Sparkle Plenty in "Blackmail Terror"	20	40	60	114	182	250

HARVEY COMICS SPOTLIGHT
Harvey Comics: Sept, 1987 - No. 4, Mar, 1988 (75¢/$1.00)

1-New material; begin 75¢, ends #3; Sand Sack						5.00
2-4: 2,4-All new material. 2-Baby Huey. 3-Little Dot; contains reprints w/5 pg. new story. 4-$1.00-c; Little Audrey						4.00

NOTE: No. 5 was advertised but not published.

HARVEY HITS (Also see Tastee-Freez Comics in the Promotional Comics section)
Harvey Publications: Sept, 1957 - No. 122, Nov, 1967

	GD	VG	FN	VF	VF/NM	NM-
1-The Phantom	25	50	75	183	354	525
2-Rags Rabbit (10/57)	5	10	15	34	55	75
3-Richie Rich (11/57)-r/Little Dot; 1st book devoted to Richie Rich; see Little Dot for 1st app.	128	256	384	1088	2144	3200
4-Little Dot's Uncles (12/57)	16	32	48	115	220	325
5-Stevie Mazie's Boy Friend (1/58)	4	8	12	28	44	60
6-The Phantom (2/58); Kirby-c; 2pg. Powell-a	17	34	51	119	230	340
7-Wendy the Good Little Witch (3/58, pre-dates Wendy #1; 1st book devoted to Wendy)	27	54	81	197	386	575
8-Sad Sack's Army Life; George Baker-c	7	14	21	50	83	115
9-Richie Rich's Golden Deeds; (2nd book devoted to Richie Rich) reprints Richie Rich story from Tastee-Freez #1	50	100	150	425	838	1250
10-Little Lotta's Lunch Box	11	22	33	78	139	200
11-Little Audrey Summer Fun (7/58)	9	18	27	60	100	140
12-The Phantom; Kirby-c; 2pg. Powell-a (8/58)	14	28	42	100	188	275
13-Little Dot's Uncles (9/58); Richie Rich 1pg.	11	22	33	78	139	200
14-Herman & Katnip (10/58, TV/movies)	4	8	12	28	44	60
15-The Phantom (12/58)-1 pg. origin	14	28	42	100	188	275
16-Wendy the Good Little Witch (1/59); Casper app.	11	22	33	80	145	210
17-Sad Sack's Army Life (2/59)	6	12	18	39	62	85
18-Buzzy & the Crow	4	8	12	26	41	55
19-Little Audrey (4/59)	6	12	18	37	59	80
20-Casper & Spooky	8	16	24	52	86	120
21-Wendy the Witch	8	16	24	52	86	120
22-Sad Sack's Army Life	5	10	15	30	48	65
23-Wendy the Witch (8/59)	8	16	24	52	86	120
24-Little Dot's Uncles (9/59); Richie Rich 1pg.	9	18	27	60	100	140
25-Herman & Katnip (10/59)	4	8	12	22	34	45
26-The Phantom (11/59)	10	20	30	73	129	185
27-Wendy the Good Little Witch (12/59)	7	14	21	50	83	115
28-Sad Sack's Army Life (1/60)	4	8	12	26	41	55
29-Harvey-Toon (No.1)('60); Casper, Buzzy	5	10	15	34	55	75
30-Wendy the Witch (3/60)	7	14	21	50	83	115
31-Herman & Katnip (4/60)	3	6	9	20	30	40
32-Sad Sack's Army Life (5/60)	4	8	12	22	34	45
33-Wendy the Witch (6/60)	7	14	21	47	76	105
34-Harvey-Toon (7/60)	4	8	12	24	37	50
35-Funday Funnies (8/60)	3	6	9	20	30	40
36-The Phantom (1960)	10	20	30	68	119	170
37-Casper & Nightmare	6	12	18	37	59	80
38-Harvey-Toon	4	8	12	24	37	50
39-Sad Sack's Army Life (12/60)	3	6	9	21	32	42
40-Funday Funnies (1/61)	3	6	9	17	25	32
41-Herman & Katnip	3	6	9	17	25	32
42-Harvey-Toon (3/61)	3	6	9	19	29	38
43-Sad Sack's Army Life (4/61)	3	6	9	19	29	38
44-The Phantom (5/61)	9	18	27	65	113	160
45-Casper & Nightmare	5	10	15	30	48	65
46-Harvey-Toon (7/61)	3	6	9	17	25	32
47-Sad Sack's Army Life (8/61)	3	6	9	17	25	32
48-The Phantom (9/61)	9	18	27	65	113	160
49-Stumbo the Giant (1st app. in Hot Stuff)	9	18	27	65	113	160
50-Harvey-Toon (11/61)	3	6	9	16	23	30
51-Sad Sack's Army Life (12/61)	3	6	9	16	23	30
52-Casper & Nightmare	4	8	12	28	44	60
53-Harvey-Toons (2/62)	3	6	9	16	23	30
54-Stumbo the Giant	5	10	15	34	55	75
55-Sad Sack's Army Life (4/62)	3	6	9	16	23	30
56-Casper & Nightmare	4	8	12	26	41	55
57-Stumbo the Giant	5	10	15	34	55	75
58-Sad Sack's Army Life	3	6	9	16	23	30
59-Casper & Nightmare (7/62)	4	8	12	26	41	55
60-Stumbo the Giant (9/62)	5	10	15	34	55	75
61-Sad Sack's Army Life	3	6	9	16	22	28
62-Casper & Nightmare	4	8	12	23	36	48
63-Stumbo the Giant	4	8	12	28	44	60
64-Sad Sack's Army Life (1/63)	3	6	9	16	22	28
65-Casper & Nightmare	4	8	12	23	36	48

Harvey Hits #95 © HARV

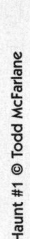

Haunt #1 © Todd McFarlane

Haunt of Fear #19 © WMG

	GD 2.0	VG 4.0	FN 6.0	VF 8.0	VF/NM 9.0	NM- 9.2
66-Stumbo The Giant (3/63)	4	8	12	28	44	60
67-Sad Sack's Army Life (4/63)	3	6	9	16	22	28
68-Casper & Nightmare	4	8	12	23	36	48
69-Stumbo the Giant (6/63)	4	8	12	28	44	60
70-Sad Sack's Army Life (7/63)	3	6	9	16	22	28
71-Casper & Nightmare (8/63)	3	6	9	21	32	42
72-Stumbo the Giant	4	8	12	28	44	60
73-Little Sad Sack (10/63)	3	6	9	16	22	28
74-Sad Sack's Muttsy... (11/63)	3	6	9	16	22	28
75-Casper & Nightmare	3	6	9	19	29	38
76-Little Sad Sack	3	6	9	16	22	28
77-Sad Sack's Muttsy...	3	6	9	16	22	28
78-Stumbo the Giant (3/64); JFK caricature	4	8	12	28	44	60
79-87: 79-Little Sad Sack (4/64). 80-Sad Sack's Muttsy... (5/64). 81-Little Sad Sack. 82-Sad Sack's Muttsy... 83-Little Sad Sack(8/64). 84-Sad Sack's Muttsy... 85-Gabby Gob (#1) (10/64). 86-G. I. Juniors (#1)(11/64). 87-Sad Sack's Muttsy... (12/64)	3	6	9	16	22	28
88-Stumbo the Giant (1/65)	4	8	12	28	44	60
89-122: 89-Sad Sack's Muttsy... 90-Gabby Gob. 91-G. I. Juniors. 92-Sad Sack's Muttsy... (5/65). 93-Sadie Sack (6/65). 94-Gabby Gob. 95-G. I. Juniors (8/65). 96-Sad Sack's Muttsy... (9/65). 97-Gabby Gob (10/65). 98-G. I. Juniors (11/65). 99-Sad Sack's Muttsy... (12/65). 100-Gabby Gob(1/66). 101-G. I. Juniors (2/66). 102-Sad Sack's Muttsy... (3/66). 103-Gabby Gob. 104- G. I. Juniors. 105-Sad Sack's Muttsy... 106-Gabby Gob (7/66). 107-G. I. Juniors (8/66). 108-Sad Sack's Muttsy...109-Gabby Gob. 110-G. I. Juniors (11/66). 111-Sad Sack's Muttsy... (12/66). 112-G. I. Juniors. 113-Sad Sack's Muttsy... 114-G. I. Juniors. 115-Sad Sack's Muttsy... 116-G. I. Juniors (5/67). 117-Sad Sack's Muttsy... 118-G. I. Juniors. 119-Sad Sack's Muttsy... (8/67). 120-G. I. Juniors (9/67). 121-Sad Sack's Muttsy... (10/67). 122-G. I. Juniors (11/67)	2	4	6	10	14	18

HARVEY HITS COMICS
Harvey Publications: Nov, 1986 - No. 6, Oct, 1987

	GD	VG	FN	VF	VF/NM	NM-
1-Little Lotta, Little Dot, Wendy & Baby Huey	1	2	3	4	5	7
2-6: 3-Xmas-c						4.50

HARVEY POP COMICS (Rock Happening) (Teen Humor)
Harvey Publications: Oct, 1968 - No. 2, Nov, 1969 (Both are 68 pg. Giants)

	GD	VG	FN	VF	VF/NM	NM-
1-The Cowsills	6	12	18	39	62	85
2-Bunny	5	10	15	34	55	75

HARVEY 3-D HITS (See Sad Sack)

HARVEY-TOON (...S) (See Harvey Hits No. 29, 34, 38, 42, 46, 50, 53)

HARVEY WISEGUYS (...Digest #? on)
Harvey Comics: Nov, 1987; #2, Nov, 1988; #3, Apr, 1989 - No. 4, Nov, 1989 (98 pgs., digest-size, $1.25/$1.75)

	GD	VG	FN	VF	VF/NM	NM-
1-Hot Stuff, Spooky, etc.	2	3	4	6	8	10
2-4: 2 (68 pgs.)	1	2	3	4	5	7

HATARI (See Movie Classics)

HATE
Fantagraphics Books: Spr, 1990 - No. 30, 1998 ($2.50/$2.95, B&W/color)

	GD	VG	FN	VF	VF/NM	NM-
1	2	4	6	10	12	15
2-3	1	2	3	5	6	8
4-10						5.00
11-20: 16- color begins						4.00
21-29						3.00
30-($3.95) Last issue						4.00
Annual 1 (2/01, $3.95) Peter Bagge-s/a						4.00
Annual 2-7 (12/01-Present; $4.95) Peter Bagge-s/a						5.00
Buddy Bites the Bullet! (2001, $16.95) r/Buddy stories in color						17.00
Buddy Go Home! (1997, $16.95) r/Buddy stories in color						17.00
Hate-Ball Special Edition ($3.95, giveaway)-reprints						4.00
Hate Jamboree (10/98, $4.50) old & new cartoons						4.50

HATHAWAYS, THE (TV)
Dell Publishing Co.: No. 1298, Feb-Apr, 1962 (one-shot)

	GD	VG	FN	VF	VF/NM	NM-
Four Color 1298-Photo-c	5	10	15	30	48	65

HAUNTED (See This Magazine Is Haunted)

HAUNT
Image Comics: Oct, 2009 - Present ($2.99)

	GD	VG	FN	VF	VF/NM	NM-
1-McFarlane & Kirkman-s/Capullo & Ottley-a/McFarlane-a(i)/c; two variant-c						3.00
2-5: 2-Two covers						3.00

HAUNTED (Baron Weirwulf's Haunted Library on-c #21 on)
Charlton Comics: 9/71 - No. 30, 11/76; No. 31, 9/77 - No. 75, 9/84

	GD 2.0	VG 4.0	FN 6.0	VF 8.0	VF/NM 9.0	NM- 9.2
1-All Ditko issue	5	10	15	32	51	70
2-7-Ditko-c/a	3	6	9	18	27	35
8,12,28-Ditko-a	2	4	6	11	16	20
9,19	2	4	6	8	11	14
10,20,15,18: 10,20-Sutton-a. 15-Sutton-c	2	4	6	8	11	14
11,13,14,16-Ditko-c/a	2	4	6	13	18	22
17-Sutton-c/a; Newton-a	2	4	6	9	12	15
21-Newton-c/a; Sutton-a; 1st Baron Weirwulf	3	6	9	16	22	28
22-Newton-c/a; Sutton-a	2	4	6	9	13	16
23,24-Sutton-c; Ditko-a	2	4	6	9	13	16
25-27,29,32,33	1	3	4	6	8	10
30,41,47,49-52,60,74-Ditko-c/a: 51-Reprints #1	2	4	6	10	14	18
31,35,37,38-Sutton-a	1	3	4	6	8	10
34,36,39,40,42,57-Ditko-a	2	4	6	8	10	12
43-46,48,53-56,58,59,61-73: 59-Newton-a. 64-Sutton-c. 71-73-Low print	1	2	3	5	6	8
75-(9/84) Last issue; low print	2	4	6	9	13	16

NOTE: ***Aparo** c-45. **Ditko** a-1-8, 11-16, 18, 23, 24, 28, 30, 34r, 36r, 39-42r, 47r, 49-52r, 57, 60, 74. c-1-7, 11, 13, 14, 16, 30, 41, 47, 49-52; 74. **Howard** a-6, 9, 18, 22, 25, 32. **Kim** a-9, 19. **Morisi** a-13. **Newton** a-17, 21, 59r; c-21, 22(painted). **Staton** a-11, 12, 18, 21, 22, 30, 33, 35, 38; c-18, 33, 38. **Sutton** a-10, 17, 20-22, 31, 35, 37, 38; c-15, 17, 18, 23(painted), 24(painted), 27, 64r. #49 reprints Tales of the Mysterious Traveler #4.*

HAUNTED, THE
Chaos! Comics: Jan, 2002 - No. 4, Apr, 2002 ($2.99, limited series)

	GD	VG	FN	VF	VF/NM	NM-
1-4-Peter David-s/Nat Jones-a						3.00
...: Gray Matters (7/02, $2.99) David-s/Jones-a						3.00

HAUNTED LOVE
Charlton Comics: Apr, 1973 - No. 11, Sept, 1975

	GD	VG	FN	VF	VF/NM	NM-
1-Tom Sutton-a (16 pgs.)	5	10	15	34	55	75
2,3,6,7,10,11	3	6	9	17	25	32
4,5-Ditko-a	3	6	9	21	32	42
8,9-Newton-c	3	6	9	18	27	35
Modern Comics #1(1978)	2	3	4	6	8	10

NOTE: ***Howard** a-8i. **Kim** a-7-9. **Newton** c-8, 9. **Staton** a-1-6. **Sutton** a-1, 3-5, 10, 11.*

HAUNTED TANK, THE
DC Comics (Vertigo): Feb, 2009 - No. 5, June, 2009 ($2.99, limited series)

	GD	VG	FN	VF	VF/NM	NM-
1-5-Marraffino-s/Flint-a. 1-Two covers by Flint and Joe Kubert						3.00

HAUNTED THRILLS (Tales of Horror and Terror)
Ajax/Farrell Publications: June, 1952 - No. 18, Nov-Dec, 1954

	GD	VG	FN	VF	VF/NM	NM-
1-r/Ellery Queen #1	58	116	174	371	636	900
2-L. B. Cole-a r-/Ellery Queen #1	39	78	117	240	395	550
3-5: 3-Drug use story	35	70	105	208	339	470
6-10,12: 7-Hitler story.	31	62	93	182	296	410
11-Nazi death camp story	32	64	96	190	310	430
13-18: 18-Lingerie panels. 14-Jesus Christ apps. in story by Webb. 15-Jo-Jo-r	25	50	75	150	245	340

NOTE: ***Kamenish** art in most issues. **Webb** a-12.*

HAUNT OF FEAR (Formerly Gunfighter)
E. C. Comics: No. 15, May-June, 1950 - No. 28, Nov-Dec, 1954

	GD	VG	FN	VF	VF/NM	NM-
15(#1, 1950)(Scarce)	291	582	873	2328	3714	5100
16-1st app. "The Witches Cauldron" & the Old Witch (by Kamen); begin series as hostess of Haunt of Fear	120	240	360	960	1530	2100
17-Origin of Crypt of Terror, Vault of Horror, & Haunt of Fear; used in **SOTI**, pg. 43; last pg. Ingels-a used by N.Y. Legis. Comm.; story "Monster Maker" based on Frankenstein. Old Witch by Feldstein	120	240	360	960	1530	2100
4-Ingles becomes regular artist for Old Witch. 1st Vault Keeper & Crypt Keeper app. in HOF; begin series	77	154	231	616	983	1350
5-Injury-to-eye panel, pg. 4 of Wood story	61	122	183	488	774	1060
6,7,9,10: 6-Crypt Keeper by Feldstein begins. 9-Crypt Keeper by Davis begins. 10-Ingels biog.	46	92	138	368	584	800
8-Classic Feldstein Shrunken Head-c	50	100	150	400	638	875
11,12: Classic Ingels-c; 11-Kamen biog. 12-Feldstein biog.	39	78	117	312	494	675
13,15,16,20: 16-Ray Bradbury adaptation. 20-Feldstein-r/Vault of Horror #12	36	72	108	288	457	625
14-Origin Old Witch by Ingels; classic-Ingels-c	50	100	150	400	638	875
17-Classic Ingels-c	39	78	117	312	494	675
18-Old Witch-c; Ray Bradbury adaptation & biography	38	76	114	304	482	660
19-Used in **SOTI**, ill. "A comic book baseball game" & Senate investigation on juvenile delinq. bondage/decapitation-c	46	92	138	368	584	800

21-27: 23-EC version of the Hansel and Gretel story; **SOTI**, pg. 241 discusses the original Grimm tale in relation to comics. 24-Used in Senate Investigative Report, pg.8. 26-Contains

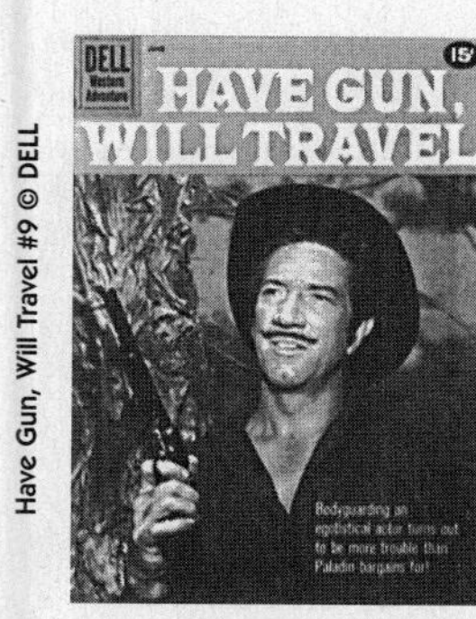

Have Gun, Will Travel #9 © DELL

Hawkeye V2 #2 © MAR

Hawkman #5 © DC

	GD 2.0	VG 4.0	FN 6.0	VF 8.0	VF/NM 9.0	NM- 9.2

anti-censorship editorial, 'Are you a Red Dupe?' 27-Cannibalism story; Vault Keeper shown reading **SOTI** 26 52 78 208 329 450
28-Low distribution 33 66 99 264 425 585

NOTE: *(Canadian reprints known; see Table of Contents).* ***Craig*** *a-15-17, 5, 7, 10, 12, 13; c-15-17, 5-7.* ***Crandall*** *a-20, 21, 26, 27.* ***Davis*** *a-4-26, 28.* ***Evans*** *a-15-19, 22-25, 27.* ***Feldstein*** *a-15-17, 20; c-4, 8-10.* ***Ingels*** *a-16, 17, 4-28; c-11-28.* ***Kamen*** *a-16, 4, 6, 7, 9-11, 13-19, 21-28.* ***Krigstein*** *a-28.* ***Kurtzman*** *a-15(#1), 17(#3).* ***Orlando*** *a-9, 12.* ***Wood*** *a-15, 16, 4-6.*

HAUNT OF FEAR, THE
Gladstone Publishing: May, 1991 - No. 2, July, 1991 ($2.00, 68 pgs.)

1,2: 1-Ghastly Ingels-c(r); 2-Craig-c(r) 3.00

HAUNT OF FEAR
Russ Cochran/Gemstone Publ.: Sept, 1991 - No. 5, 1992 ($2.00, 68 pgs.); Nov, 1992 - No. 28, Aug, 1998 ($1.50/$2.00/$2.50)

1-28: 1-Ingels-c(r). 1-3-r/HOF #15-17 with original-c. 4,5-r/HOF #4,5 with original-c 2.50
Annual 1-5: 1- r/#1-5. 2- r/#6-10. 3- r/#11-15. 4- r/#16-20. 5- r/#21-25 14.00
Annual 6-r/#26-28 9.00

HAUNT OF HORROR, THE (Digest)
Marvel Comics: Jun, 1973 - No. 2, Aug, 1973 (164 pgs.; text and art)

1-Morrow painted skull-c; stories by Ellison, Howard, and Leiber; Brunner-a 4 8 12 24 37 50
2-Kelly Freas painted bondage-c; stories by McCaffrey, Goulart, Leiber, Ellison; art by Simonson, Brunner, and Buscema 3 6 9 17 25 32

HAUNT OF HORROR, THE (Magazine)
Cadence Comics Publ. (Marvel): May, 1974 - No. 5, Jan, 1975 (75¢) (B&W).

1,2: 2-Origin & 1st app. Gabriel the Devil Hunter; Satana begins 3 6 9 14 20 26
3-5: 4-Neal Adams-a. 5-Evans-a(2) 3 6 9 18 27 35

NOTE: ***Alcala*** *a-2.* ***Colan*** *a-2p.* ***Heath*** *r-1.* ***Krigstein*** *r-3.* ***Reese*** *a-1.* ***Simonson*** *a-1.*

HAUNT OF HORROR: EDGAR ALLAN POE
Marvel Comics (MAX): July, 2006 - No. 3, Sept, 2006 ($3.99, B&W, limited series)

1-3- Poe-inspired/adapted stories with Richard Corben-a 4.00
HC (2006, $19.99) r/series; cover sketches 20.00

HAUNT OF HORROR: LOVECRAFT
Marvel Comics (MAX): Aug, 2008 - No. 3, Oct, 2008 ($3.99, B&W, limited series)

1-3-Lovecraft-inspired/adapted stories with Richard Corben-a 4.00

HAVE GUN, WILL TRAVEL (TV)
Dell Publishing Co.: No. 931, 8/58 - No. 14, 7-9/62 (All Richard Boone photo-c)

Four Color 931 (#1) 13 26 39 90 165 240
Four Color 983,1044 (#2,3) 9 18 27 60 100 140
4 (1-3/60) - 10 8 16 24 54 90 125
11-14 8 16 24 52 86 120

HAVEN: THE BROKEN CITY (See JLA/Haven: Arrival and JLA/Haven: Anathema)
DC Comics: Feb, 2002 - No. 9, Oct, 2002 ($2.50, limited series)

1-9-Olivetti-c/a: 1- JLA app. Series concludes in JLA/Haven: Anathema 2.50

HAVOK & WOLVERINE - MELTDOWN (See Marvel Comics Presents #24)
Marvel Comics (Epic Comics): Mar, 1989 - No. 4, Oct, 1989 ($3.50, mini-series, square-bound, mature)

1-4: Art by Kent Williams & Jon J. Muth; story by Walt & Louise Simonson 4.00

HAWAIIAN DICK
Image Comics: Dec, 2002 - No. 3, Feb, 2003 ($2.95, limited series)

1-3-B. Clay Moore-s/Steven Griffin-a 3.00
...: Byrd of Paradise TPB (8/03, $14.95) r/#1-3, script & sketch pages 15.00

HAWAIIAN DICK: SCREAMING BLACK THUNDER
Image Comics: Nov, 2007 - No. 5, Oct, 2008 ($2.99, limited series)

1-5-B. Clay Moore-s/Scott Chantler-a 3.00

HAWAIIAN DICK: THE LAST RESORT
Image Comics: Aug, 2004 - No. 4, June, 2006 ($2.95/$2.99, limited series)

1-4-B. Clay Moore-s/Steven Griffin-a 3.00
Vol. 2 TPB (10/06, $14.99) r/#1-4 & the original series pitch 15.00

HAWAIIAN EYE (TV)
Gold Key: July, 1963 (Troy Donahue, Connie Stevens photo-c)

1 (10073-307) 5 10 15 34 55 75

HAWAIIAN ILLUSTRATED LEGENDS SERIES
Hogarth Press: 1975 (B&W)(Cover printed w/blue, yellow, and green)

1-Kalelealuaka, the Mysterious Warrior 5.00

HAWK, THE (Also see Approved Comics #1, 7 & Tops In Adventure)
Ziff-Davis/St. John Publ. Co. No. 4 on: Wint/51 - No. 3, 11-12/52; No. 4, 1-2/53; No. 8, 9/54 - No. 12, 5/55 (Painted c-1-4)(#5-7 don't exist)

1-Anderson-a 20 40 60 114 182 250
2 (Sum, '52)-Kubert, Infantino-a 12 24 36 69 97 125
3-4,11: 10 20 30 56 76 95
8-12: 8(9/54)-Reprints #3 w/different-c by Baker. 9-Baker-c/a; Kubert-a(r)/#2. 10-Baker-c/a; r/one story from #2. 11-Baker-c; Buckskin Belle & The Texan app. 12-Baker-c/a; Buckskin Belle app. 15 30 45 85 130 175
3-D 1(11/53, 25¢)-Came w/glasses; Baker-c 32 64 96 188 307 425

NOTE: ***Baker*** *c-8-12.* ***Larsen*** *a-10.* ***Tuska*** *a-1, 9, 12. Painted c-1, 4, 7.*

HAWK AND THE DOVE, THE (See Showcase #75 & Teen Titans) (1st series)
National Periodical Publications: Aug-Sept, 1968 - No. 6, June-July, 1969

1-Ditko-c/a 8 16 24 54 90 125
2-6: 5-Teen Titans cameo 5 10 15 32 51 70

NOTE: ***Ditko*** *c/a-1, 2.* ***Gil Kane*** *a-3p, 4p, 5, 6p; c-3-6.*

HAWK AND DOVE (2nd Series)
DC Comics: Oct, 1988 - No. 5, Feb, 1989 ($1.00, limited series)

1-Rob Liefeld-c/a(p) in all 4.00
2-5 3.00
Trade paperback ('93, $9.95)-Reprints #1-5 10.00

HAWK AND DOVE
DC Comics: June, 1989 - No. 28, Oct, 1991 ($1.00)

1-28 2.50
Annual 1,2 ('90, '91; $2.00) 1-Liefeld pin-up. 2-Armageddon 2001 x-over 3.00

HAWK AND DOVE
DC Comics: Nov, 1997 - No. 5, Mar, 1998 ($2.50, limited series)

1-5-Baron-s/Zachary & Giordano-a 2.50

HAWK AND WINDBLADE (See Elflord)
Warp Graphics: Aug, 1997 - No.2, Sept, 1997 ($2.95, limited series)

1,2-Blair-s/Chan-c/a 3.00

HAWKEYE (See The Avengers #16 & Tales Of Suspense #57)
Marvel Comics Group: Sept, 1983 - No. 4, Dec, 1983 (limited series)

1-4: Mark Gruenwald-a/scripts. 1-Origin Hawkeye. 3-Origin Mockingbird. 4-Hawkeye & Mockingbird elope 3.00

HAWKEYE
Marvel Comics: Jan, 1994 - No. 4, Apr, 1994 ($1.75, limited series)

1-4 2.50

HAWKEYE (Volume 2)
Marvel Comics: Dec, 2003 - No. 8, Aug, 2004 ($2.99)

1-8: 1-6-Nicieza-s/Raffaele-a. 7,8-Bennett-a; Black Widow app. 3.00

HAWKEYE & THE LAST OF THE MOHICANS (TV)
Dell Publishing Co.: No. 884, Mar, 1958 (one-shot)

Four Color 884-Photo-c 7 14 21 47 76 105

HAWKEYE: EARTH'S MIGHTIEST MARKSMAN
Marvel Comics: Oct, 1998 ($2.99, one-shot)

1-Justice and Firestar app.; DeFalco-s 3.00

HAWKGIRL (Title continued from Hawkman #49, Apr, 2006)
DC Comics: No. 50, May, 2006 - No. 66, Sept, 2007 ($2.50/$2.99)

50-66: 50-Chaykin-a/Simonson-s begin; One Year Later. 52-Begin $2.99-c. 57,58-Bennett-a. 59-Blackfire app. 63-Batman app. 64-Superman app. 3.00
...: Hath-Set TPB (2008, $17.99) r/#61-66 18.00
...: Hawkman Returns TPB (2007, $17.99) r/#57-60 & JSA Classified #21,22 18.00
...: The Maw TPB (2007, $17.99) r/#50-56 18.00

HAWKMAN (See Atom & Hawkman, The Brave & the Bold, DC Comics Presents, Detective Comics, Flash Comics, Hawkworld, JSA, Justice League of America #31, Legend of the Hawkman, Mystery in Space, Shadow War Of..., Showcase, & World's Finest #256)

HAWKMAN (1st Series) (Also see The Atom #7 & Brave & the Bold #34-36, 42-44, 51)
National Periodical Publications: Apr-May, 1964 - No. 27, Aug-Sept, 1968

1-(4-5/64)-Anderson-c/a begins, ends #21 54 108 162 459 905 1350
2 22 44 66 161 311 460
3,5: 5-2nd app. Shadow Thief 15 30 45 104 197 290
4-Origin & 1st app. Zatanna (10-11/64) 17 34 51 124 242 360
6 11 22 33 82 149 210
7 10 20 30 71 126 180
8-10: 9-Atom cameo; Hawkman & Atom learn each other's I.D.; 3rd app. Shadow Thief

Hawkman (2002 series) #1 © DC

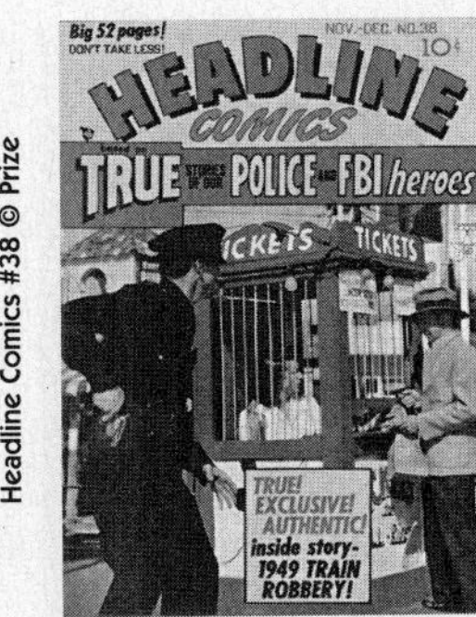

Headline Comics #38 © Prize

Heart Throbs #9 © QUA

	GD 2.0	VG 4.0	FN 6.0	VF 8.0	VF/NM 9.0	NM- 9.2
	9	18	27	63	107	150
11-15	7	14	21	47	76	105
16-27: 18-Adam Strange x-over (cameo #19). 25-G.A. Hawkman-r by Moldoff. 26-Kirby-a(r). 27-Kubert-c	6	12	18	37	59	80

HAWKMAN (2nd Series)
DC Comics: Aug, 1986 - No. 17, Dec, 1987

1-17: 10-Byrne-c, Special #1 (1986, $1.25) 2.50
Trade paperback (1989, $19.95)-r/Brave and the Bold #34-36,42-44 by Kubert; Kubert-c 20.00

HAWKMAN (4th Series)(See both Hawkworld limited & ongoing series)
DC Comics: Sept, 1993 - No. 33, July, 1996 ($1.75/$1.95/$2.25)

1-($2.50)-Gold foil embossed-c; storyline cont'd from Hawkworld ongoing series; new costume & powers. 3.00
2-13,0,14-33: 2-Green Lantern x-over. 3-Airstryke app. 4,6-Wonder Woman app. 13-(9/94)-Zero Hour. 0-(10/94). 14-(11/94). 15-Aquaman-c & app. 23-Wonder Woman app. 25-Kent Williams-c. 29,30-Chaykin-c. 32-Breyfogle-c 2.50
Annual 1 (1993, $2.50, 68 pgs.)-Bloodlines Earthplague 3.00
Annual 2 (1995, $3.95)-Year One story 4.00

HAWKMAN (Title continues as Hawkgirl #50-on) (See JSA #23 for return)
DC Comics: May, 2002 - No. 49, Apr, 2006 ($2.50)

1-Johns & Robinson-s/Morales-a 5.00
1-2nd printing 2.50
2-40: 2-4-Shadow Thief app. 5,6-Green Arrow-c/app. 8-Atom-c/app. 13-Van Sciver-a. 14-Gentleman Ghost app. 15-Hawkwoman app. 16-Byth returns. 23-25-Black Reign x-over with JSA #56-58. 26-Byrne-c/a. 29,30-Land-c. 37-Golden Eagle returns 2.50
41-49: 41-Hawkman killed. 43-Golden Eagle origin. 46-49-Adam Kubert-c 2.50
...: Allies & Enemies TPB (2004, $14.95) r/#7-14 & pages from Secret Files and Origins 15.00
...: Endless Flight TPB (2003, $12.95) r/#1-6 & Secret Files and Origins 13.00
...: Rise of the Golden Eagle TPB (2006, $17.99) r/#37-45 18.00
... Secret Files and Origins (10/02, $4.95) profiles and pin-ups by various 5.00
... Special 1 (10/08, $3.50) Tie-in to Rann-Thanagar Holy War series; Starlin-s/a(p) 3.50
...: Wings of Fury TPB (2005, $17.99) r/#15-22 18.00

HAWKMOON: THE JEWEL IN THE SKULL
First Comics: May, 1986 - No. 4, Nov, 1986 ($1.75, limited series, Baxter paper)

1-4: Adapts novel by Michael Moorcock 2.50

HAWKMOON: THE MAD GOD'S AMULET
First Comics: Jan, 1987 - No. 4, July, 1987 ($1.75, limited series, Baxter paper)

1-4: Adapts novel by Michael Moorcock 2.50

HAWKMOON: THE RUNESTAFF
First Comics: Jun, 1988 -No. 4, Dec, 1988 ($1.75-$1.95, lim. series, Baxter paper)

1-4: ($1.75) Adapts novel by Michael Moorcock. 3,4 ($1.95) 2.50

HAWKMOON: THE SWORD OF DAWN
First Comics: Sept, 1987 - No. 4, Mar, 1988 ($1.75, lim. series, Baxter paper)

1-4: Dorman painted-c; adapts Moorcock novel 2.50

HAWKS OF THE SEAS (WILL EISNER'S...)
Dark Horse Comics: July, 2003 ($19.95, B&W, hardcover)

nn-Reprints 1937-1939 weekly Pirate serial by Will Eisner; Williamson intro. 20.00

HAWKWORLD
DC Comics: 1989 - No. 3, 1989 ($3.95, prestige format, limited series)

Book 1-3: 1-Tim Truman story & art in all; Hawkman dons new costume; reintro Byth 4.00
TPB (1991, $16.95) r/#1-3 17.00

HAWKWORLD (3rd Series)
DC Comics: June, 1990 - No. 32, Mar, 1993 ($1.50/$1.75)

1-Hawkman spin-off; story cont'd from limited series. 3.00
2-32: 15,16-War of the Gods x-over. 22-J'onn J'onzz app. 2.50
Annual 1-3 ('90-'92, $2.95, 68 pgs.), 2-2nd printing with silver ink-c 3.00
NOTE: *Truman a-30-32; c-27-32, Annual 1.*

HAYWIRE
DC Comics: Oct, 1988 - No. 13, Sept, 1989 ($1.25, mature)

1-13 2.50

HAZARD
Image Comics (WildStorm Prod.): June, 1996 - No. 7, Nov, 1996 ($1.75)

1-7: 1-Intro Hazard; Jeff Mariotte scripts begin; Jim Lee-c(p) 3.00

HEADHUNTERS
Image Comics: Apr, 1997 - No. 3, June, 1997 ($2.95, B&W)

1-3: Chris Marrinan-s/a 3.00

HEADLINE COMICS
DC Comics: Jan. 1942

nn - Ashcan comic, not distributed to newsstands, only for in-house use. Cover art is More Fun Comics #73 with interior being Star Spangled Comics #2 (no known sales)

HEADLINE COMICS (...For the American Boy) (...Crime No. 32-39)
Prize Publ./American Boys' Comics: Feb, 1943 - No. 22, Nov-Dec, 1946; No. 23, 1947 - No. 77, Oct, 1956

	GD 2.0	VG 4.0	FN 6.0	VF 8.0	VF/NM 9.0	NM- 9.2
1-Junior Rangers-c/stories begin; Yank & Doodle x-over in Junior Rangers (Junior Rangers are Uncle Sam's nephews)	58	116	174	371	636	900
2	34	68	102	199	325	450
3-Used in **POP**, pg. 84	23	46	69	136	223	310
4-7,9,10: 4,9,10-Hitler stories in each	20	40	60	117	189	260
8-Classic Hitler-c	116	232	348	742	1271	1800
11,12	18	36	54	107	169	230
13-15-Blue Streak in all	19	38	57	112	179	245
16-Origin & 1st app. Atomic Man (11-12/45)	30	60	90	177	289	400
17,18,20,21: 21-Atomic Man ends (9-10/46)	16	32	48	94	147	200
19-S&K-a	32	64	96	188	307	425
22-Last Junior Rangers; Kiefer-c	14	28	42	82	121	160
23,24: (All S&K-a). 23-Valentine's Day Massacre story; content changes to true crime. 24-Dope-crazy killer story	32	64	96	188	307	425
25-35-S&K-c/a. 25-Powell-a	29	58	87	170	278	385
36-S&K-a; photo-c begin	21	42	63	124	202	280
37-1 pg. S&K, Severin-a; rare Kirby photo-c app.	22	44	66	128	209	290
38,40-Meskin-a	11	22	33	60	83	105
39,41-43,46-50,52-55: 41-J. Edgar Hoover 26th Anniversary Issue with photo on-c. 43,49-Meskin-a	9	18	27	52	69	85
44-S&K-c; Severin/Elder, Meskin-a	15	30	45	84	127	170
45-Kirby-a	13	26	39	72	101	130
51-Kirby-c	13	26	39	72	101	130
56-S&K-a	14	28	42	81	118	155
57-77: 72-Meskin-c/a(i)	8	16	24	44	57	70

NOTE: ***Hollingsworth** a-30. Photo c-36-43. **H. C. Kiefer** c-12-16, 22. Atomic Man c-17-19.*

HEADMAN
Innovation Publishing: 1990 ($2.50, mature)

1-Sci/fi 2.50

HEAP, THE
Skywald Publications: Sept, 1971 (52 pgs.)

1-Kinstler-r/Strange Worlds #8; new-s w/Sutton-a 4 8 12 22 34 45

HEART AND SOUL
Mikeross Publications: April-May, 1954 - No. 2, June-July, 1954

1,2 9 18 27 47 61 75

HEARTBREAKERS (Also see Dark Horse Presents)
Dark Horse Comics: Apr, 1996 - No. 4, July, 1996 ($2.95, limited series)

1-4: 1-W/paper doll & pin-up. 2-Alex Ross pin-up. 3-Evan Dorkin pin-ups. 4-Brereton-c; Matt Wagner pin-up 3.00
...Superdigest (7/98, $9.95, digest-size) new stories 10.00

HEARTLAND (See Hellblazer)
DC Comics (Vertigo): Mar, 1997 ($4.95, one-shot, mature)

1-Garth Ennis-s/Steve Dillon-c/a 5.00

HEART OF DARKNESS
Hardline Studios: 1994 ($2.95)

1-Brereton-c 3.00

HEART OF EMPIRE
Dark Horse Comics: Apr, 1999 - No. 9, Dec, 1999 ($2.95, limited series)

1-9-Bryan Talbot-s/a 3.00

HEART OF THE BEAST, THE
DC Comics (Vertigo): 1994 ($19.95, hardcover, mature)

1-Dean Motter scripts 20.00

HEARTS OF DARKNESS (See Ghost Rider; Wolverine; Punisher: Hearts of...)

HEART THROBS (Love Stories No. 147 on)
Quality Comics/National Periodical #47(4-5/57) on (Arleigh #48-101): 8/49 - No. 8, 10/50; No. 9, 3/52 - No. 146, Oct, 1972

	GD 2.0	VG 4.0	FN 6.0	VF 8.0	VF/NM 9.0	NM- 9.2
1-Classic Ward-c, Gustavson-a, 9 pgs.	42	84	126	265	450	635
2-Ward-c/a (9 pgs); Gustavson-a	26	52	78	154	252	350
3-Gustavson-a	14	28	42	76	108	140
4,6,8-Ward-a, 8-9 pgs.	16	32	48	94	147	200

Heckle and Jeckle #8 © CBS

Hedy Devine Comics #38 © MAR

Hellblazer #125 © DC

	GD 2.0	VG 4.0	FN 6.0	VF 8.0	VF/NM 9.0	NM- 9.2
5,7	11	22	33	62	86	110
9-Robert Mitchum, Jane Russell photo-c	14	28	42	80	115	150
10,15-Ward-a	14	28	42	80	115	150
11-14,16-20: 12 (7/52)	10	20	30	54	72	90
21-Ward-c	14	28	42	76	108	140
22,23-Ward-a(p)	10	20	30	58	79	100
24-33: 33-Last pre-code (3/55)	9	18	27	52	69	85
34-39,41-44,46 (12/56; last Quality issue)	9	18	27	50	65	80
40-Ward-a; r-7 pgs./#21	10	20	30	54	72	90
45-Baker-a	6	12	18	43	69	95
47-(4-5/57; 1st DC issue)	21	42	63	148	287	425
48-60, 100	9	18	27	63	107	150
61-70	7	14	21	45	73	100
71-99: 74-Last 10 cent issue	6	12	18	39	62	85
101-The Beatles app. on-c	13	26	39	95	178	260
102-120: 102-123-(Serial)-Three Girls, Their Lives, Their Loves	4	8	12	24	37	50
121-132,143-146	3	6	9	21	32	42
133-142-(52 pgs.)	4	8	12	26	41	55

NOTE: ***Gustavson** a-8. **Tuska** a-128. Photo c-4, 5, 8-10, 15, 17.*

HEART THROBS - THE BEST OF DC ROMANCE COMICS (See Fireside Book Series)

HEART THROBS
DC Comics (Vertigo): Jan, 1999 - No. 4, Apr, 1999 ($2.95, lim. series)

	GD 2.0	VG 4.0	FN 6.0	VF 8.0	VF/NM 9.0	NM- 9.2
1-4-Romance anthology. 1-Timm-c. 3-Corben-a						3.00

HEATHCLIFF (See Star Comics Magazine)
Marvel Comics (Star Comics)/Marvel Comics No. 23 on: Apr, 1985 - No. 56, Feb, 1991 (#16-on, $1.00)

	GD 2.0	VG 4.0	FN 6.0	VF 8.0	VF/NM 9.0	NM- 9.2
1-Post-a most issues	1	2	3	4	5	7
2-10,47: 47-Batman parody (Catman vs. the Soaker)						5.00
11-46,48-56: 43-X-Mas issue						4.00
Annual 1 ('87)						4.00

HEATHCLIFF'S FUNHOUSE
Marvel Comics (Star Comics)/Marvel No. 6 on: May, 1987 - No. 10, 1988

	GD 2.0	VG 4.0	FN 6.0	VF 8.0	VF/NM 9.0	NM- 9.2
1						5.00
2-10						4.00

HEAVEN'S DEVILS
Image Comics: Sept, 2003 - No. 4, July, 2004 ($2.95/$3.50, B&W, limited series)

	GD 2.0	VG 4.0	FN 6.0	VF 8.0	VF/NM 9.0	NM- 9.2
1-3-($2.95) Jai Nitz-s/Zach Howard-a						3.00
4-($3.50) Kevin Sharpe-a						3.50

HEAVY HITTERS
Marvel Comics (Epic Comics): 1993 ($3.75, 68 pgs.)

	GD 2.0	VG 4.0	FN 6.0	VF 8.0	VF/NM 9.0	NM- 9.2
1-Bound w/trading card; Lawdog, Feud, Alien Legion, Trouble With Girls, & Spyke						3.75

HEAVY LIQUID
DC Comics (Vertigo): Oct, 1999 - No. 5, Feb, 2000 ($5.95, limited series)

	GD 2.0	VG 4.0	FN 6.0	VF 8.0	VF/NM 9.0	NM- 9.2
1-5-Paul Pope-s/a; flip covers						6.00
TPB (2001, $29.95) r/#1-5						30.00
TPB (2009, $24.95) r/#1-5; development sketches and cover gallery; new cover						25.00
HC (2008, $39.99, dustjacket) r/#1-5; development sketches and cover gallery						40.00

HECKLE AND JECKLE (Paul Terry's...)(See Blue Ribbon, Giant Comics Edition #5A & 10, Paul Terry's, Terry-Toons Comics)
St. John Publ. Co. No. 1-24/Pines No. 25 on: No. 3, 2/52 - No. 24, 10/55; No. 25, Fall/56 - No. 34, 6/59

	GD 2.0	VG 4.0	FN 6.0	VF 8.0	VF/NM 9.0	NM- 9.2
3(#1)-Funny animal	24	48	72	140	230	320
4(6/52), 5	13	26	39	74	105	135
6-10(4/53)	9	18	27	50	65	80
11-20	8	16	24	40	50	60
21-34: 25-Begin CBS Television Presents on-c	7	14	21	35	43	50

HECKLE AND JECKLE (TV) (See New Terrytoons)
Gold Key/Dell Publ. Co.: 11/62 - No. 4, 8/63; 5/66; No. 2, 10/66; No. 3, 8/67

	GD 2.0	VG 4.0	FN 6.0	VF 8.0	VF/NM 9.0	NM- 9.2
1 (11/62; Gold Key)	6	12	18	43	69	95
2-4	4	8	12	22	34	45
1 (5/66; Dell)	4	8	12	26	41	55
2,3	3	6	9	19	29	38

(See March of Comics No. 379, 472, 484)

HECKLE AND JECKLE 3-D
Spotlight Comics: 1987 - No. 2?, 1987 ($2.50)

	GD 2.0	VG 4.0	FN 6.0	VF 8.0	VF/NM 9.0	NM- 9.2
1,2						5.00

HECKLER, THE
DC Comics: Sept, 1992 - No. 6, Feb, 1993 ($1.25)

	GD 2.0	VG 4.0	FN 6.0	VF 8.0	VF/NM 9.0	NM- 9.2
1-6-T&M Bierbaum-s/Keith Giffen-c/a						2.50

HECTIC PLANET
Slave Labor Graphics 1998 ($12.95/$14.95)

	GD 2.0	VG 4.0	FN 6.0	VF 8.0	VF/NM 9.0	NM- 9.2
Book 1,2-r-Dorkin-s/a from Pirate Corp$ Vol. 1 & 2						15.00

HECTOR COMICS (The Keenest Teen in Town)
Key Publications: Nov, 1953 - No. 3, 1954

	GD 2.0	VG 4.0	FN 6.0	VF 8.0	VF/NM 9.0	NM- 9.2
1-Teen humor	7	14	21	35	43	50
2,3	5	10	14	20	24	28

HECTOR HEATHCOTE (TV)
Gold Key: Mar, 1964

	GD 2.0	VG 4.0	FN 6.0	VF 8.0	VF/NM 9.0	NM- 9.2
1 (10111-403)	7	14	21	47	76	105

HECTOR THE INSPECTOR (See Top Flight Comics)

HEDGE KNIGHT, THE
Image Comics: Aug, 2003 - No. 6, Apr, 2004 ($2.95, limited series)

	GD 2.0	VG 4.0	FN 6.0	VF 8.0	VF/NM 9.0	NM- 9.2
1-6-George R.R. Martin-s/Mike S. Miller-a. 1-Two covers by Kaluta and Miller						3.00
George R.R. Martin's The Hedge Knight HC (Marvel, 2006, $19.99) r/series; 2 covers						20.00
George R.R. Martin's The Hedge Knight SC (Marvel, 2007, $14.99) r/series						15.00
TPB (2004, $14.95) r/series plus new short story						15.00

HEDGE KNIGHT II: SWORN SWORD
Marvel Comics (Dabel Brothers): Jun, 2007 - No. 6, Jun, 2008 ($2.99, limited series)

	GD 2.0	VG 4.0	FN 6.0	VF 8.0	VF/NM 9.0	NM- 9.2
1-6-George R.R. Martin-s/Mike Miller-a. 1-Two covers by Yu & Miller, plus Miller B&W-c						3.00
... HC (2008, $19.99) r/series; 2 covers						20.00

HEDY DEVINE COMICS (Formerly All Winners #21? or Teen #22?(6/47); Hedy of Hollywood #36 on; also see Annie Oakley, Comedy & Venus)
Marvel Comics (RCM)/Atlas #50: No. 22, Aug, 1947 - No. 50, Sept, 1952

	GD 2.0	VG 4.0	FN 6.0	VF 8.0	VF/NM 9.0	NM- 9.2
22-1st app. Hedy Devine (also see Joker #32)	32	64	96	188	307	425
23,24,27-30: 23-Wolverton-a, 1 pg; Kurtzman's "Hey Look", 2 pgs. 24,27-30- "Hey Look" by Kurtzman, 1-3 pgs.	20	40	60	114	182	250
25-Classic "Hey Look" by Kurtzman, "Optical Illusion"	21	42	63	122	199	275
26- "Giggles 'n' Grins" by Kurtzman	17	34	51	98	154	210
31-34,36-50: 32-Anti-Wertham editorial	13	26	39	74	105	135
35-Four pgs. "Rusty" by Kurtzman	17	34	51	98	154	210

HEDY-MILLIE-TESSIE COMEDY (See Comedy Comics)

HEDY WOLFE (Also see Patsy & Hedy & Miss America Magazine V1#2)
Atlas Publishing Co. (Emgee): Aug, 1957

	GD 2.0	VG 4.0	FN 6.0	VF 8.0	VF/NM 9.0	NM- 9.2
1-Patsy Walker's rival; Al Hartley-c	12	24	36	69	97	125

HEE HAW (TV)
Charlton Press: July, 1970 - No. 7, Aug, 1971

	GD 2.0	VG 4.0	FN 6.0	VF 8.0	VF/NM 9.0	NM- 9.2
1	4	8	12	28	44	60
2-7	3	6	9	19	29	38

HEIDI (See Dell Jr. Treasury No. 6)

HELEN OF TROY (Movie)
Dell Publishing Co.: No. 684, Mar, 1956 (one-shot)

	GD 2.0	VG 4.0	FN 6.0	VF 8.0	VF/NM 9.0	NM- 9.2
Four Color 684-Buscema-a, photo-c	9	18	27	65	113	160

HELL
Dark Horse Comics: July, 2003 - No. 4, Mar, 2004 ($2.99, limited series)

	GD 2.0	VG 4.0	FN 6.0	VF 8.0	VF/NM 9.0	NM- 9.2
1-4-Augustyn-s/Demong-a/Meglia-c						3.00

HELLBLAZER (John Constantine) (See Saga of Swamp Thing #37) (Also see Books of Magic limited series)
DC Comics (Vertigo #63 on): Jan, 1988 - Present ($1.25-$2.99)

	GD 2.0	VG 4.0	FN 6.0	VF 8.0	VF/NM 9.0	NM- 9.2
1-(44 pgs.)-John Constantine; McKean-c thru #21	2	4	6	8	10	12
2-5	1	2	3	4	5	7
6-8,10: 10-Swamp Thing cameo						5.00
9,19: 9-X-over w/Swamp Thing #76. 19-Sandman app.						6.00
11-18,20						5.00
21-26,28-30: 22-Williams-c. 24-Contains bound-in Shocker movie poster. 25,26-Grant Morrison scripts.						5.00
27-Gaiman scripts; Dave McKean-a; low print run	2	4	6	10	12	15
31-39: 36-Preview of World Without End.						4.00
40-($2.25, 52 pgs.)-Dave McKean-a & colors; preview of Kid Eternity						4.00
41-Ennis scripts begin; ends #83						5.00
42-120: 44,45-Sutton-a(i). 50-($3.00, 52 pgs.). 52-Glenn Fabry painted-c begin. 62-Special Death insert by McKean. 63-Silver metallic ink on-c. 77-Totleben-c. 84-Sean Phillips-c/a						

Hellblazer #258 © DC

Hellboy: Seed of Destruction #2 © M. Mignola

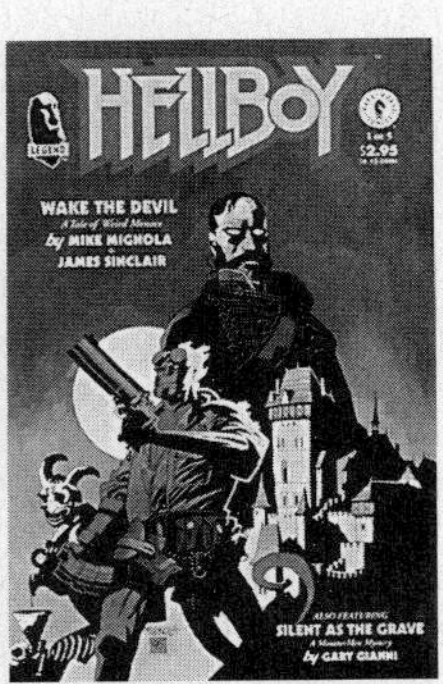

Hellboy: Wake the Devil #1 © M. Mignola

	GD 2.0	VG 4.0	FN 6.0	VF 8.0	VF/NM 9.0	NM- 9.2

begins; Delano story. 85-88-Eddie Campbell story. 75-($2.95, 52 pgs.). 89-Paul Jenkins scripts begin. 100,120 ($3.50,48 pgs.). 108-Adlard-a. 3.50
121-199, 201-249, 251-263: 129-Ennis-s. 141-Bradstreet-a. 146-150-Corben-a. 151-Azzarello-s begin. 175-Carey-s begin; Dillon-a. 176-Begin $2.75-c. 182,183-Bermejo-a. 216-Mina-s begins. 220-Begin $2.99-c. 229-Carey-s/Leon-a. 234-Initial printing (white title logo) has missing text; corrected printing has lt. blue title logo 3.00
200-($4.50) Carey-s/Dillon, Frusin, Manco-a 4.50
250-($3.99) Short stories by various; art by Lloyd, Phillips, Milligan; Bermejo-c 4.00
Annual 1 (1989, $2.95, 68 pgs.)-Bryan Talbot's 1st work in American comics 5.00
Special 1 (1993, $3.95, 68 pgs.)-Ennis story; w/pin-ups. 4.00
...Black Flowers (2005, $14.99, TPB) r/#181-186 15.00
...Bloodlines (2007, $19.99, TPB) r/#47-50,52-55,59-61 20.00
...Damnation's Flame (1999, $16.95, TPB) r/#72-77 17.00
...Dangerous Habits (1997, $14.95, TPB) r/#41-46 15.00
...Fear and Loathing (1997, $14.95, TPB) r/#62-67 18.00
...Fear and Loathing (2nd printing, $17.95) 18.00
...: Freezes Over (2003, $14.95, TPB) r/#157-163 15.00
...Good Intentions (2002, $12.95, TPB) r/#151-156 13.00
...Hard Time (2001, $9.95, TPB) r/#146-150 10.00
...Haunting (2003, $12.95, TPB) r/#134-139 13.00
...Highwater (2004, $19.95, TPB) r/#164-174 20.00
John Constantine Hellblazer: All His Engines HC (2005, $24.95, with dustjacket) new graphic novel; Mike Carey-s/Leonardo Manco-a 25.00
John Constantine Hellblazer: All His Engines SC (2006, $14.99) new graphic novel 15.00
John Constantine Hellblazer: Empathy is the Enemy SC (2006, $14.99) r/#216-222 15.00
John Constantine Hellblazer: Joyride SC (2008, $14.99) r/#230-237 15.00
John Constantine Hellblazer: Pandemonium HC (2010, $24.99,with dustjacket) new graphic novel; Jamie Delano-s/Jock-a 25.00
John Constantine Hellblazer: Scab SC (2009, $14.99) r/#250-255 15.00
John Constantine Hellblazer: The Devil You Know SC (2007, $19.99) r/#10-13, Annual #1 and The Horrorist miniseries #1,2 20.00
John Constantine Hellblazer: The Family Man SC (2008, $19.99, TPB) r/#23,24,28-33 20.00
John Constantine Hellblazer: The Fear Machine SC (2008, $19.99, TPB) r/#14-22 20.00
John Constantine Hellblazer: The Red Right Hand SC (2007, $14.99) r/#223-228 15.00
John Const. Hellblazer: The Roots of Coincidence SC ('09, $14.99) r/#243,244,247-249 15.00
...Original Sins (1993, $19.95, TPB) r/#1-9 20.00
...Rake at the Gates of Hell (2003, $19.95, TPB) r/#78-83; Heartland #1 20.00
...: Rare Cuts (2005, $14.95, TPB) r/#11,25,26,35,56,84 & Vertigo Secret Files: Hellblazer 15.00
...: Reasons To Be Cheerful (2007, $14.99, TPB) r/#201-206 15.00
...: Red Sepulchre (2005, $12.99, TPB) r/#175-180 13.00
...: Setting Sun (2004, $12.95, TPB) r/#140-143 13.00
...: Son of Man (2004, $12.95, TPB) r/#129-133 13.00
...: Stations of the Cross (2006, $14.99, TPB) r/#194-200 15.00
...: Staring At The Wall (2005, $14.99, TPB) r/#187-193 15.00
...Tainted Love (1998, $16.95, TPB) r/#68-71, Vertigo Jam #1 and Hellblazer Special #1 17.00
NOTE: ***Alcala** a-8i, 9i, 18-22i. **Gaiman** scripts-27. **McKean** a-27,40; c-1-21. **Sutton** a-44i, 45i. **Talbot** a-Annual 1.*

HELLBLAZER SPECIAL: BAD BLOOD
DC Comics (Vertigo): Sept, 2000 - No. 4, Dec, 2000 ($2.95, mini-series)
1-4-Delano-s/Bond-a; Constantine in 2025 London 3.00

HELLBLAZER SPECIAL: CHAS
DC Comics (Vertigo): Sept, 2008 - No. 5, Jan, 2009 ($2.99, mini-series)
1-5-Story of Constantine's cab driver; Oliver-s/Sudzuka-a/Fabry-c 3.00
... - The Knowledge TPB (2009, $14.99) r/#1-5 15.00

HELLBLAZER SPECIAL: LADY CONSTANTINE
DC Comics (Vertigo): Feb, 2003 - No. 4, May, 2003 ($2.95, mini-series)
1-4-Story of Johanna Constantine in 1785; Diggle-s/Sudzuka-a/Noto-c 3.00

HELLBLAZER/THE BOOKS OF MAGIC
DC Comics (Vertigo): Dec, 1997 - No. 2, Jan, 1998 ($2.50, mini-series)
1,2-John Constantine and Tim Hunter 2.50

HELLBOY (Also see Batman/Hellboy/Starman, Danger Unlimited #4, Dark Horse Presents, Free Comic Book Day edition in the Promotional section, Gen[13] #13B, Ghost/Hellboy, John Byrne's Next Men, San Diego Comic Con #2, & Savage Dragon)

HELLBOY: ALMOST COLOSSUS
Dark Horse Comics (Legend): Jun, 1997 - No. 2, Jul, 1997 ($2.95, lim. series)
1,2-Mignola-s/a 3.50

HELLBOY: BOX FULL OF EVIL
Dark Horse Comics: Aug, 1999 - No. 2, Sept, 1999 ($2.95, lim. series)
1,2-Mignola-s/a; back-up story w/ Matt Smith-a 3.50

HELLBOY CHRISTMAS SPECIAL
Dark Horse Comics: Dec, 1997 ($3.95, one-shot)
nn-Christmas stories by Mignola, Gianni, Darrow, Purcell 4.50

HELLBOY: CONQUEROR WORM
Dark Horse Comics: May, 2001 - No. 4, Aug, 2001 ($2.99, lim. series)
1-4-Mignola-s/a/c 3.00

HELLBOY: DARKNESS CALLS
Dark Horse Comics: Apr, 2007 - No. 6, Nov, 2007 ($2.99, lim. series)
1-6-Mignola-s/Fegredo-a 3.00

HELLBOY: IN THE CHAPEL OF MOLOCH
Dark Horse Comics: Oct, 2008 ($2.99, one-shot)
nn-Mignola-s/a/c 3.00

HELLBOY, JR.
Dark Horse Comics: Oct, 1999 - No. 2, Nov, 1999 ($2.95, limited series)
1,2-Stories and art by various 3.50
TPB (1/04, $14.95) r/#1&2, Halloween; sketch pages; intro. by Steve Niles; Bill Wray-c 15.00

HELLBOY, JR., HALLOWEEN SPECIAL
Dark Horse Comics: Oct, 1997 ($3.95, one-shot)
nn-"Harvey" style renditions of Hellboy characters; Bill Wray, Mike Mignola & various-s/a; wraparound-c by Wray 4.50

HELLBOY: MAKOMA, OR A TALE TOLD...
Dark Horse Comics: Feb, 2006 - No. 2, Mar, 2006 ($2.99, lim. series)
1,2-Mignola-s/c; Mignola & Corben-a 3.00

HELLBOY PREMIERE EDITION
Dark Horse Comics (Wizard): 2004 (no price, one-shot)
nn- Two covers by Mignola & Davis; Mignola-s/a; BPRD story w/Arcudi-s/Davis-a 5.00
Wizard World Los Angeles-Movie photo-c; Mignola-s/a; BPRD story w/Arcudi-s/Davis-a 10.00

HELLBOY: SEED OF DESTRUCTION
Dark Horse Comics (Legend): Mar, 1994 - No. 4, Jun, 1994 ($2.50, lim. series)
1-4-Mignola-c/a w/Byrne scripts; Monkeyman & O'Brien back-up story (origin) by Art Adams. 5.00
Trade paperback (1994, $17.95)-collects all four issues plus r/Hellboy's 1st app. in San Diego Comic Con #2 & pin-ups 18.00
Limited edition hardcover (1995, $99.95)-includes everything in trade paperback plus additional material. 100.00

HELLBOY STRANGE PLACES
Dark Horse Books: Apr, 2006 ($17.95, TPB)
SC - Reprints Hellboy: The Third Wish #1,2 and Hellboy: The Island #1,2; sketch pages 18.00

HELLBOY: THE BRIDE OF HELL
Dark Horse Comics: Dec, 2009 ($3.50, one-shot)
1-Mignola-s/c; Corben-a; preview of The Marquis: Inferno 3.50

HELLBOY: THE CHAINED COFFIN AND OTHERS
Dark Horse Comics (Legend): Aug, 1998 ($17.95, TPB)
nn-Mignola-c/a/s; reprints out-of-print one shots; pin-up gallery 18.00

HELLBOY: THE COMPANION
Dark Horse Books: May, 2008 ($14.95, 9"x6", TPB)
nn-Overview of Hellboy history, characters, stories, mythology; text with Mignola panels 15.00

HELLBOY: THE CORPSE
Dark Horse Comics: Mar, 2004 (25¢, one-shot)
nn-Mignola-c/a/scripts; reprints "The Corpse" serial from Capitol City's Advance Comics catalog; development sketches and photos of the Corpse from the Hellboy movie 2.50

HELLBOY: THE CORPSE AND THE IRON SHOES
Dark Horse Comics (Legend): Jan, 1996 ($2.95, one-shot)
nn-Mignola-c/a/scripts; reprints "The Corpse" serial w/new story 3.50

HELLBOY: THE CROOKED MAN
Dark Horse Comics: Jul, 2008 - No. 3, Sept, 2008 ($2.99, lim. series)
1-3-Mignola-s/Corben-a/c 3.00

HELLBOY: THE GOLDEN ARMY
Dark Horse Comics: Jan, 2008 (no cover price)
nn-Prelude to the 2008 movie; Del Toro & Mignola-s/Velasco-a; 3 photo covers 2.25

HELLBOY: THE ISLAND
Dark Horse Comics: June, 2005 - No. 2, July, 2005 ($2.99, lim. series)
1,2: Mignola-c/a & scripts 3.00

HELLBOY: THE RIGHT HAND OF DOOM
Dark Horse Comics (Legend): Apr, 2000 ($17.95, TPB)

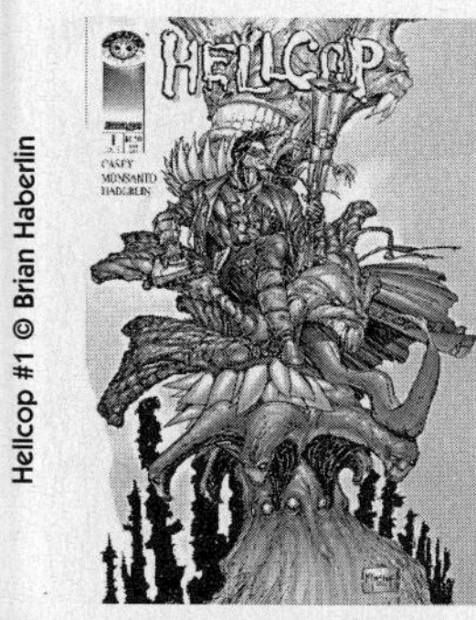

Hellcop #1 © Brian Haberlin

Hell's Angel #4 © MAR

Henry #1 © DELL

GD VG FN VF VF/NM NM-
2.0 4.0 6.0 8.0 9.0 9.2

nn-Mignola-c/a/s; reprints 18.00

HELLBOY: THE THIRD WISH
Dark Horse Comics (Maverick): July, 2002 - No. 2, Aug, 2002 ($2.99, limited series)
1,2-Mignola-c/a/s 3.00

HELLBOY THE TROLL WITCH AND OTHERS
Dark Horse Books: Nov, 2007 ($17.95, TPB)
SC - Reprints Hellboy: Makoma, Hellboy Premiere Edition and stories from Dark Horse Book of Hauntings, DHB of Witchcraft, DHB of the Dead, DHB of Monsters 18.00

HELLBOY: THE WILD HUNT
Dark Horse Comics: Dec, 2008 - No. 8, Nov, 2009 ($2.99, lim. series)
1-8: Mignola-c/s; Fegredo-a 3.00

HELLBOY: THE WOLVES OF ST. AUGUST
Dark Horse Comics (Legend): 1995 ($4.95, squarebound, one-shot)
nn-Mignola--c/a/scripts; r/Dark Horse Presents #88-91 with additional story 5.00

HELLBOY: WAKE THE DEVIL (Sequel to Seed of Destruction)
Dark Horse Comics (Legend): Jun, 1996 - No. 5, Oct, 1996 ($2.95, lim. series)
1-5: Mignola-c/a & scripts; The Monstermen back-up story by Gary Gianni 4.00
TPB (1997, $17.95) r/#1-5 18.00

HELLBOY: WEIRD TALES
Dark Horse Comics: Feb, 2003 - No. 8, Apr, 2004 ($2.99, limited series, anthology)
1-8-Hellboy stories from other creators. 1-Cassaday-c/s/a; Watson-s/a. 6-Cho-c 3.00
... Vol. 1 (2004, 17.95) r/#1-4 18.00
... Vol. 2 (2004, 17.95) r/#5-8 and Lobster Johnson serial from #1-8 18.00

HELLCAT
Marvel Comics: Sept, 2000 - No. 3, Nov, 2000 ($2.99)
1-3-Englehart-s/Breyfogle-a; Hedy Wolfe app. 3.00

HELLCOP
Image Comics (Avalon Studios): Aug, 1998 - No. 4, Mar, 1999 ($2.50)
1-4: 1-(Oct. on-c) Casey-s 2.50

HELL ETERNAL
DC Comics (Vertigo Verité): 1998 ($6.95, squarebound, one-shot)
1-Delano-s/Phillips-a 7.00

HELLGATE: LONDON (Based on the video game)
Dark Horse Comics: No. 0, May 2006 - No. 3, Mar, 2007 ($2.99)
0-3-Edginton-s/Pugh-a/Briclot-c 3.00

HELLHOUNDS (...: Panzer Cops #3-6)
Dark Horse Comics: 1994 - No. 6, July, 1994 ($2.50, B&W, limited series)
1-6: 1-Hamner-c. 3-(4/94). 2-Joe Phillips-c 3.00

HELLHOUND, THE REDEMPTION QUEST
Marvel Comics (Epic Comics): Dec, 1993 - No. 4, Mar, 1994 ($2.25, lim. series, coated stock)
1-4 2.50

HELLO BUDDIES
Harvey Publications: 1953 (25¢, small size)
1 2 4 6 11 16 20

HELLO, I'M JOHNNY CASH
Spire Christian Comics (Fleming H. Revell Co.): 1976 (39¢/49¢)
nn-(39¢-c) 3 6 9 14 19 24
nn-(49¢-c) 2 4 6 9 13 16

HELL ON EARTH (See DC Science Fiction Graphic Novel)

HELLO PAL COMICS (Short Story Comics)
Harvey Publications: Jan, 1943 - No. 3, May, 1943 (Photo-c)
1-Rocketman & Rocketgirl begin; Yankee Doodle Jones app.; Mickey Rooney photo-c 63 126 189 403 689 975
2-Charlie McCarthy photo-c (scarce) 56 112 168 349 595 840
3-Bob Hope photo-c (scarce) 60 120 180 384 660 935

HELLRAISER/NIGHTBREED – JIHAD (Also see Clive Barker's...)
Epic Comics (Marvel Comics): 1991 - Book 2, 1991 ($4.50, 52 pgs.)
Book 1,2 4.50

HELL-RIDER (Motorcycle themed magazine)
Skywald Publications: Aug, 1971 - No. 2, Oct, 1971 (B&W, 68 pgs.)
1-Origin & 1st app.; Butterfly & the Wild Bunch begin; 1st Hell-Rider by Andru, Esposito and Friedrich 6 12 18 41 66 90
2-Andru, Ayers, Buckler, Shores-a 4 8 12 28 44 60
NOTE: *#3 advertised in Psycho #5 but did not come out.* ***Buckler*** *a-1, 2.* ***Rosenbaum*** *c-1,2.*

GD VG FN VF VF/NM NM-
2.0 4.0 6.0 8.0 9.0 9.2

HELL'S ANGEL (Becomes Dark Angel #6 on)
Marvel Comics UK: July, 1992 - No. 5, Nov, 1993 ($1.75)
1-5: X-Men (Wolverine, Cyclops)-c/stories. 1-Origin. 3-Jim Lee cover swipe 2.50

HELLSHOCK
Image Comics: July, 1994 - No. 4, Nov, 1994 ($1.95, limited series)
1-4-Jae Lee-c/a & scripts. 4-Variant-c. 2.50

HELLSHOCK
Image Comics: Jan, 1997 - No. 3, Jan, 1998 ($2.95/$2.50, limited series)
1-($2.95)-Jae Lee-c/s/a, Villarrubia-painted-a 4.00
2-($2.50) 2.50
Book 3: The Science of Faith (1/98, $2.50) Jae Lee-c/s/a, Villarrubia-painted-a 2.50
Vol. 1 HC (2006, $49.99) r/#1-3 re-colored, with unpublished 22 pg. conclusion; cover gallery and sketches; alternate opening art; intro. by Jim Lee 50.00

HELLSPAWN
Image Comics: Aug, 2000 - No. 16, Apr, 2003 ($2.50)
1-Bendis-s/Ashley Wood-c/a; Spawn and Clown app. 2.50
2-9: 6-Last Bendis-s; Mike Moran (Miracleman app.). 7-Niles-s 2.50
10-16-Templesmith-a 2.50
...: The Ashley Wood Collection Vol. 1 (4/06, $24.95, TPB) r/#1-10; sketch & cover gallery 25.00

HELLSTORM: PRINCE OF LIES (See Ghost Rider #1 & Marvel Spotlight #12)
Marvel Comics: Apr, 1993 - No. 21, Dec, 1994 ($2.00)
1-($2.95)-Parchment-c w/red thermographic ink 3.00
2-21: 14-Bound-in trading card sheet. 18-P. Craig Russell-c 2.50

HELLSTORM: SON OF SATAN
Marvel Comics (MAX): Dec, 2006 - No. 5, Apr, 2007 ($3.99, limited series)
1-5-Suydam-c/Irvine-s/Braun & Janson-a 4.00
... - Equinox TPB (2007, $17.99) r/#1-5; interviews with the creators 18.00

HELMET OF FATE, THE (Series of one-shots following Doctor Fate's helmet)
DC Comics: Mar, 2007 - May 2007 ($2.99, one-shots)
...: Black Alice (5/07) Simone-s/Rouleau-a/c 3.00
...: Detective Chimp (3/07) Willingham-s/McManus-a/Bolland-c 3.00
...: Ibis the Invincible (3/07) Williams-s/Winslade-a; the Ibistick returns 3.00
...: Sargon the Sorcerer (4/07) Niles-s/Scott Hampton-s; debut new Sargon 3.00
...: Zauriel (4/07) Gerber-s/Snejbjerg-a/Kaluta-c; leads into new Doctor Fate series 3.00
TPB (2007, $14.99) r/one-shots 15.00

HE-MAN (See Masters Of The Universe)

HE-MAN (Also see Tops In Adventure)
Ziff-Davis Publ. Co. (Approved Comics): Fall, 1952
1-Kinstler painted-c; Powell-a 16 32 48 94 147 200

HE-MAN
Toby Press: May, 1954 - No. 2, July, 1954 (Painted-c by B. Safran)
1 15 30 45 88 137 185
2-Shark-c 15 30 45 85 130 175

HENNESSEY (TV)
Dell Publishing Co.: No. 1200, Aug-Oct, 1961 - No. 1280, Mar-May, 1962
Four Color 1200-Gil Kane-a, photo-c 7 14 21 47 76 105
Four Color 1280-Photo-c 6 12 18 43 69 95

HENRY (Also see Little Annie Rooney)
David McKay Publications: 1935 (52 pgs.) (Daily B&W strip reprints)(10"x10" cardboard-c)
1-By Carl Anderson 39 78 117 240 395 550

HENRY (See King Comics & Magic Comics)
Dell Publishing Co.: No. 122, Oct, 1946 - No. 65, Apr-June, 1961
Four Color 122-All new stories begin 14 28 42 100 188 275
Four Color 155 (7/47), 1 (1-3/48)-All new stories 10 20 30 68 119 170
2 6 12 18 41 66 90
3-10 5 10 15 34 55 75
11-20: 20-Infinity-c 4 8 12 28 44 60
21-30 4 8 12 22 34 45
31-40 3 6 9 19 29 38
41-65 3 6 9 16 23 30

HENRY (See Giant Comic Album and March of Comics No. 43, 58, 84, 101, 112, 129, 147, 162, 178, 189)

HENRY ALDRICH COMICS (TV)
Dell Publishing Co.: Aug-Sept, 1950 - No. 22, Sept-Nov, 1954

Herbie #2 © ACG

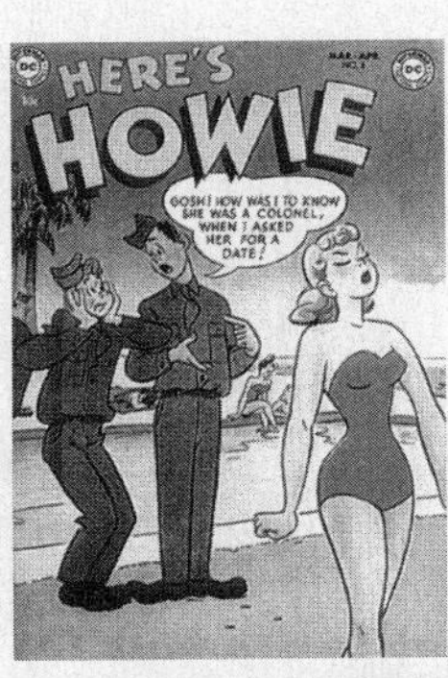

Here's Howie Comics #8 © DC

H-E-R-O #1 © DC

	GD 2.0	VG 4.0	FN 6.0	VF 8.0	VF/NM 9.0	NM- 9.2
1-Part series written by John Stanley; Bill Williams-a	9	18	27	65	113	160
2	6	12	18	37	59	80
3-5	5	10	15	30	48	65
6-10	4	8	12	26	41	55
11-22	4	8	12	22	34	45

HENRY BREWSTER
Country Wide (M.F. Ent.): Feb, 1966 - V2#7, Sept, 1967 (All 25¢ Giants)

	GD 2.0	VG 4.0	FN 6.0	VF 8.0	VF/NM 9.0	NM- 9.2
1	3	6	9	19	29	38
2-6(12/66), V2#7-Powell-a in most	2	4	6	13	18	22

HEPCATS
Antarctic Press: Nov, 1996 - No. 12 ($2.95, B&W)

	GD 2.0	VG 4.0	FN 6.0	VF 8.0	VF/NM 9.0	NM- 9.2
0-12-Martin Wagner-c/s/a: 0-color						3.00
0-($9.95) CD Edition						10.00

HERBIE (See Forbidden Worlds #73,94,110,114,116 & Unknown Worlds #20)
American Comics Group: April-May, 1964 - No. 23, Feb, 1967 (All 12¢)

	GD 2.0	VG 4.0	FN 6.0	VF 8.0	VF/NM 9.0	NM- 9.2
1-Whitney-c/a in most issues	16	32	48	115	220	325
2-4	9	18	27	65	113	160
5-Beatles parody (10 pgs.), Dean Martin, Frank Sinatra app. (10-11/64)	10	20	30	73	129	185
6,7,9,10	8	16	24	56	93	130
8-Origin & 1st app. The Fat Fury	9	18	27	64	110	155
11-23: 14-Nemesis & Magicman app. 17-r/2nd Herbie from Forbidden Worlds #94. 23-r/1st Herbie from F.W. #73	6	12	18	43	69	95
... Archives Volume One HC (Dark Horse, 8/08, $49.95, dust jacket) r/earliest apps. in Forbidden Worlds, Unknown Worlds, and Herbie #1-5; Scott Shaw intro.						50.00

HERBIE
Dark Horse Comics: Oct, 1992 - No. 12, 1993 ($2.50, limited series)

	GD 2.0	VG 4.0	FN 6.0	VF 8.0	VF/NM 9.0	NM- 9.2
1-Whitney-r plus new-c/a in all; Byrne-c/a & scripts						3.00
2-6: 3-Bob Burden-c/a. 4-Art Adams-c						2.50

HERBIE GOES TO MONTE CARLO, HERBIE RIDES AGAIN (See Walt Disney Showcase No. 24, 41)

HERCULES (See Hit Comics #1-21, Journey Into Mystery Annual, Marvel Graphic Novel #37, Marvel Premiere #26 & The Mighty...)

HERCULES (See Charlton Classics)
Charlton Comics: Oct, 1967 - No. 13, Sept, 1969; Dec, 1968

	GD 2.0	VG 4.0	FN 6.0	VF 8.0	VF/NM 9.0	NM- 9.2
1-Thane of Bagarth begins; Glanzman-a in all	4	8	12	26	41	55
2-13: 1-5,7-10-Aparo-a. 8-(12¢-c)	3	6	9	16	23	50
8-(Low distribution)(12/68, 35¢, B&W); magazine format; new Hercules story plus-r story/#1; Thane-r/#1-3	6	12	18	37	59	80
Modern Comics reprint 10('77), 11('78)						6.00

HERCULES (Prince of Power) (Also see The Champions)
Marvel Comics Group: V1#1, Sept, 1982 - V1#4, Dec, 1982; V2#1, Mar, 1984 - V2#4, Jun, 1984 (color, both limited series)

	GD 2.0	VG 4.0	FN 6.0	VF 8.0	VF/NM 9.0	NM- 9.2
1-4, V2#1-4: Layton-c/a. 4-Death of Zeus.						3.00

NOTE: *Layton a-1, 2, 3p, 4p, V2#1-4; c-1-4, V2#1-4.*

HERCULES
Marvel Comics: Jun, 2005 - No. 5, Sept, 2005 ($2.99, limited series)

	GD 2.0	VG 4.0	FN 6.0	VF 8.0	VF/NM 9.0	NM- 9.2
1-5-Texeira-a/c; Tieri-s. 4-Capt. America, Wolverine and New Avengers app.						3.00
...: New Labors of Hercules TPB (2005, $13.99) r/#1-5						14.00

HERCULES: HEART OF CHAOS
Marvel Comics: Aug, 1997 - No. 3, Oct, 1997 ($2.50, limited series)

	GD 2.0	VG 4.0	FN 6.0	VF 8.0	VF/NM 9.0	NM- 9.2
1-3-DeFalco-s, Frenz-a						2.50

HERCULES: OFFICIAL COMICS MOVIE ADAPTION
Acclaim Books: 1997 ($4.50, digest size)

	GD 2.0	VG 4.0	FN 6.0	VF 8.0	VF/NM 9.0	NM- 9.2
nn-Adaption of the Disney animated movie						4.50

HERCULES: THE LEGENDARY JOURNEYS (TV)
Topps Comics: June, 1996 - No. 5, Oct, 1996 ($2.95)

	GD 2.0	VG 4.0	FN 6.0	VF 8.0	VF/NM 9.0	NM- 9.2
1-2: 1-Golden-c.						3.00
3-Xena-c/app.	1	2	3	4	5	7
3-Variant-c	2	4	6	9	12	15
4,5: Xena-c/app.						5.00

HERCULES UNBOUND
National Periodical Publications: Oct-Nov, 1975 - No. 12, Aug-Sept, 1977

	GD 2.0	VG 4.0	FN 6.0	VF 8.0	VF/NM 9.0	NM- 9.2
1-Wood-i begins	2	4	6	9	13	16
2-12: 7-Adams ad. 10-Atomic Knights x-over	2	3	4	6	8	10

NOTE: ***Buckler** c-7p. **Layton** inks-No. 9, 10. **Simonson** a-7-10p, 11, 12; c- 8p, 9-12. **Wood** a-1-8i; c-7i, 8i.*

HERCULES (...Unchained #1121) (Movie)
Dell Publishing Co.: No. 1006, June-Aug, 1959 - No.1121, Aug, 1960

	GD 2.0	VG 4.0	FN 6.0	VF 8.0	VF/NM 9.0	NM- 9.2
Four Color 1006-Buscema-a, photo-c	9	18	27	60	100	140
Four Color 1121-Crandall/Evans-a	9	18	27	60	100	140

HERE COMES SANTA (See March of Comics No. 30, 213, 340)

HERE'S HOWIE COMICS
National Periodical Publications: Jan-Feb, 1952 - No. 18, Nov-Dec, 1954

	GD 2.0	VG 4.0	FN 6.0	VF 8.0	VF/NM 9.0	NM- 9.2
1	27	54	81	160	263	365
2	15	30	45	86	133	180
3-5: 5-Howie in the Army issues begin (9-10/52)	13	26	39	74	105	135
6-10	11	22	33	62	86	110
11-18	10	20	30	58	79	100

Ashcan (1,2/51) not distributed to newsstands, only for in house use (no known sales)

HERETIC, THE
Dark Horse (Blanc Noir): Nov, 1996 - No. 4, Mar, 1997 ($2.95, lim. series)

	GD 2.0	VG 4.0	FN 6.0	VF 8.0	VF/NM 9.0	NM- 9.2
1-4:-w/back-up story						3.00

HERITAGE OF THE DESERT (See Zane Grey, 4-Color 236)

HERMAN & KATNIP (See Harvey Comics Hits #60 & 62, Harvey Hits #14,25,31,41 & Paramount Animated Comics #1)

HERMES VS. THE EYEBALL KID
Dark Horse Comics: Dec, 1994 - No. 3,Feb, 1995 ($2.95, B&W, limited series)

	GD 2.0	VG 4.0	FN 6.0	VF 8.0	VF/NM 9.0	NM- 9.2
1-3: Eddie Campbell-c/a/scripts						3.00

H-E-R-O (Dial H For HERO)
DC Comics: Apr, 2003 - No. 22, Jan, 2005 ($2.50)

	GD 2.0	VG 4.0	FN 6.0	VF 8.0	VF/NM 9.0	NM- 9.2
1-Will Pfeiffer-s/Kano-a/Van Fleet-c						3.00
2-22: 2-6-Kano-a. 7,8-Gleason-a. 12-14-Kirk-a. 15-22-Robby Reed app.						2.50
...: Double Feature (6/03, $4.95) r/#1&2						5.00
...: Powers and Abilities (2003, $9.95) r/#1-6; intro. by Geoff Johns						10.00

HERO (Warrior of the Mystic Realms)
Marvel Comics: May, 1990 - No. 6, Oct, 1990 ($1.50, limited series)

	GD 2.0	VG 4.0	FN 6.0	VF 8.0	VF/NM 9.0	NM- 9.2
1-6: 1-Portacio-i						2.50

HERO ALLIANCE, THE
Sirius Comics: Dec, 1985 - No. 2, Sept, 1986 (B&W)

	GD 2.0	VG 4.0	FN 6.0	VF 8.0	VF/NM 9.0	NM- 9.2
1,2: 2-($1.50), Special Edition 1 (7/86, color)						2.50

HERO ALLIANCE
Wonder Color Comics: May, 1987 ($1.95)

	GD 2.0	VG 4.0	FN 6.0	VF 8.0	VF/NM 9.0	NM- 9.2
1-Ron Lim-a						2.50

HERO ALLIANCE
Innovation Publishing: V2#1, Sept, 1989 - V2#17, Nov, 1991 ($1.95, 28 pgs.)

	GD 2.0	VG 4.0	FN 6.0	VF 8.0	VF/NM 9.0	NM- 9.2
V2#1-17: 1,2-Ron Lim-a						2.50
Annual 1 (1990, $2.75, 36 pgs.)-Paul Smith-c/a						2.75
Special 1 (1992, $2.50, 32 pgs.)-Stuart Immonen-a (10 pgs.)						2.50

HERO ALLIANCE: END OF THE GOLDEN AGE
Innovation Publ.: July, 1989 - No. 3, Aug, 1989 ($1.75, bi-weekly lim. series)

	GD 2.0	VG 4.0	FN 6.0	VF 8.0	VF/NM 9.0	NM- 9.2
1-3: Bart Sears & Ron Lim-c/a; reprints & new-a						2.50

HERO COMICS (Hero Initiative benefit book)
IDW Publishing: 2009 ($3.99)

	GD 2.0	VG 4.0	FN 6.0	VF 8.0	VF/NM 9.0	NM- 9.2
1-Short story anthology by various incl. Colan, Chaykin; covers by Wagner & Campbell						4.00

HEROES
Marvel Comics: Dec, 2001 ($3.50, magazine-size, one-shot)

	GD 2.0	VG 4.0	FN 6.0	VF 8.0	VF/NM 9.0	NM- 9.2
1-Pin-up tributes to the rescue workers of the Sept. 11 tragedy; art and text by various; cover by Alex Ross						3.50
1-2nd and 3rd printings						3.50

HEROES (Also see Shadow Cabinet & Static)
DC Comics (Milestone): May, 1996 - No. 6, Nov, 1996 ($2.50, limited series)

	GD 2.0	VG 4.0	FN 6.0	VF 8.0	VF/NM 9.0	NM- 9.2
1-6: 1-Intro Heroes (Iota, Donner, Blitzen, Starlight, Payback & Static)						2.50

HEROES (Based on the NBC TV series)
DC Comics (WildStorm): 2007; 2009 ($29.99, hardcover with dustjacket)

	GD 2.0	VG 4.0	FN 6.0	VF 8.0	VF/NM 9.0	NM- 9.2
Vol. 1 - Collects 34 installments of the online graphic novel; art by various; two covers by Jim Lee and Alex Ross; intro. by Masi Oka; Jeph Loeb interview						30.00
Vol. 2 - (2009) Collects 46 installments of the online graphic novel; art by various incl. Gaydos, Grummett, Gunnell, Odagawa; two covers by Tim Sale and Gene Ha						30.00

HEROES AGAINST HUNGER
DC Comics: 1986 ($1.50; one-shot for famine relief)

Heroes For Hire (2006 series) #8 © MAR

Heroic Comics #4 © EAS

Hex #1 © DC

	GD 2.0	VG 4.0	FN 6.0	VF 8.0	VF/NM 9.0	NM- 9.2

1-Superman, Batman app.; Neal Adams-c(p); includes many artists work; Jeff Jones assist (2 pg.) on B. Smith-a; Kirby-a 5.00

HEROES ALL CATHOLIC ACTION ILLUSTRATED
Heroes All Co.: 1943 - V6#5, Mar 10, 1948 (paper covers)

	GD	VG	FN	VF	VF/NM	NM-
V1#1-(16 pgs., 8x11")	24	48	72	142	234	325
V1#2-(16 pgs., 8x11")	19	38	57	111	176	240
V2#1(1/44)-3(3/44)-(16 pgs., 8x11")	15	30	45	94	147	200
V3#1(1/45)-10(12/45)-(16 pgs., 8x11")	15	30	45	85	130	175
V4#1-35 (12/20/46)-(16 pgs.)	14	28	42	80	115	150
V5#1(1/10/47)-8(2/28/47)-(16 pgs.), V5#9(3/7/47)-20(11/25/47)-(32 pgs.), V6#1(1/10/48)-5(3/10/48)-(32 pgs.)	12	24	36	69	97	125

HEROES ANONYMOUS
Bongo Comics: 2003 - No. 6, 2004 ($2.99, limited series)

1-6-($2.99)-Bill Morrison-c. 2-Guerra-a. 3-Pepoy-a 3.00

HEROES FOR HIRE
Marvel Comics: July, 1997 - No. 19, Jan, 1999 ($2.99/$1.99)

1-($2.99)-Wraparound cover 5.00
2-19: 2-Variant cover. 7-Thunderbolts app. 9-Punisher-c/app. 10,11-Deadpool-c/app. 18,19-Wolverine-c/app. 3.00
.../Quicksilver '98 Annual ($2.99) Siege of Wundagore pt.5 3.00

HEROES FOR HIRE
Marvel Comics: Oct, 2006 - No. 15, Dec, 2007 ($2.99)

1-5-Tucci-a/c; Black Cat, Shang-Chi, Tarantula, Humbug & Daughters of the Dragon app. 3.00
6-15: 6-8-Sparacio-c. 9,10-Golden-c. 11-13-World War Hulk x-over. 13-Takeda-c 3.00
... Vol. 1: Civil War (2007, $13.99) r/#1-5 14.00
... Vol. 2: Ahead of the Curve (2007, $13.99) r/#6-10 14.00
... Vol. 3: World War Hulk (2008, $13.99) r/#11-15 14.00

HEROES FOR HOPE STARRING THE X-MEN
Marvel Comics Group: Dec, 1985 ($1.50, one-shot, 52 pgs., proceeds donated to famine relief)

1-Stephen King scripts; Byrne, Miller, Corben-a; Wrightson/J. Jones-a (3 pgs.); Art Adams-c; Starlin back-c 5.00

HEROES, INC. PRESENTS CANNON
Wally Wood/CPL/Gang Publ.:1969 - No. 2, 1976 (Sold at Army PX's)

	GD	VG	FN	VF	VF/NM	NM-
nn-Ditko, Wood-a; Wood-c; Reese-a(p)	2	4	6	9	12	15
2-Wood-c; Ditko, Byrne, Wood-a; 8-1/2x10-1/2"; B&W; $2.00	3	6	9	16	23	30

NOTE: *First issue not distributed by publisher; 1,800 copies were stored and 900 copies were stolen from warehouse. Many copies have surfaced in recent years.*

HEROES OF THE WILD FRONTIER (Formerly Baffling Mysteries)
Ace Periodicals: No. 27, Jan, 1956 - No. 2, Apr, 1956

	GD	VG	FN	VF	VF/NM	NM-
27(#1),2-Davy Crockett, Daniel Boone, Buffalo Bill	6	12	18	29	36	42

HEROES REBORN (one-shots)
Marvel Comics: Jan, 2000 ($1.99)

...:Ashema; ...:Doom; ...:Doomsday; ...:Masters of Evil; ...:Rebel; ...:Remnants; ...:Young Allies 2.50

HEROES REBORN: THE RETURN (Also see Avengers, Fantastic Four, Iron Man & Captain America titles for issues and TPBs)
Marvel Comics: Dec, 1997 - No. 4 ($2.50, weekly mini-series)

1-4-Avengers, Fantastic Four, Iron Man & Captain America rejoin regular Marvel Universe; Peter David-s/Larocca-c/a 4.00
1-4-Variant-c for each 6.00

	GD	VG	FN	VF	VF/NM	NM-
Wizard 1/2	1	2	3	5	7	9

Return of the Heroes TPB ('98, $14.95) r/#1-4 15.00

HERO FOR HIRE (Power Man No. 17 on; also see Cage)
Marvel Comics Group: June, 1972 - No. 16, Dec, 1973

	GD	VG	FN	VF	VF/NM	NM-
1-Origin & 1st app. Luke Cage; Tuska-a(p)	11	22	33	78	139	200
2-Tuska-a(p)	6	12	18	37	59	80
3-5: 3-1st app. Mace. 4-1st app. Phil Fox of the Bugle	4	8	12	24	37	50
6-10: 8,9-Dr. Doom app. 9-F.F. app.	3	6	9	16	23	30
11-16: 14-Origin retold. 15-Everett Sub-Mariner-r('53). 16-Origin Stilletto; death of Rackham	2	4	6	11	16	20

HERO HOTLINE (1st app. in Action Comics Weekly #637)
DC Comics: April, 1989 - No. 6, Sept, 1989 ($1.75, limited series)

1-6: Super-hero humor; Schaffenberger-i 2.50

HEROIC ADVENTURES (See Adventures)

HEROIC COMICS (Reg'lar Fellers...#1-15; New Heroic #41 on)
Eastern Color Printing Co./Famous Funnies(Funnies, Inc. No. 1): Aug, 1940 - No. 97, June, 1955

	GD	VG	FN	VF	VF/NM	NM-
1-Hydroman (origin) by Bill Everett, The Purple Zombie (origin) & Mann of India by Tarpe Mills begins (all 1st apps.)	194	388	582	1242	2121	3000
2	81	162	243	518	884	1250
3,4	52	104	156	328	552	775
5,6	43	86	129	271	461	650
7-Origin & 1st app. Man O'Metal (1 pg.)	46	92	138	290	488	685
8-10: 10-Lingerie panels	35	70	105	208	339	470
11,13	32	64	96	192	314	435
12-Music Master (origin/1st app.) begins by Everett, ends No. 31; last Purple Zombie & Mann of India	37	74	111	218	354	490
14,15-Hydroman x-over in Rainbow Boy. 14-Origin & 1st app. Rainbow Boy (super hero). 15-1st app. Downbeat	35	70	105	208	339	470
16-20: 16-New logo. 17-Rainbow Boy x-over in Hydroman. 19-Rainbow Boy x-over in Hydroman & vice versa	24	48	72	142	234	325
21-30:25-Rainbow Boy x-over in Hydroman. 28-Last Man O'Metal. 29-Last Hydroman	18	36	54	107	169	230
31,34,38	9	18	27	47	61	75
32,36,37-Toth-a (3-4 pgs. each)	10	20	30	54	72	90
33,35-Toth-a (8 & 9 pgs.)	10	20	30	56	76	95
39-42-Toth, Ingels-a	10	20	30	56	76	95
43,46,47,49-Toth-a (2-4 pgs.). 47-Ingels-a	9	18	27	52	69	85
44,45,50-Toth-a (6-9 pgs.)	10	20	30	54	72	90
48,53,54	8	16	24	44	57	70
51-Williamson-a	10	20	30	54	72	90
52-Williamson-a (3 pg. story)	9	18	27	47	61	75
55-Toth-a	9	18	27	52	69	85
56-60: 60-Everett-a	9	18	27	47	61	75
61-Everett-a	8	16	24	44	57	70
62,64-Everett-c/a	9	18	27	52	69	85
63-Everett-c	9	18	27	50	65	80
65-Williamson/Frazetta-a; Evans-a (2 pgs.)	12	24	36	69	97	125
66,75,94-Frazetta-a (2 pgs. each)	9	18	27	50	65	80
67,73-Frazetta-a (4 pgs. each)	10	20	30	58	79	100
68,74,76-80,84,85,88-93,95-97: 95-Last pre-code	8	16	24	44	57	70
69,72-Frazetta-a (6 & 8 pgs. each); 1st (?) app. Frazetta Red Cross ad	12	24	36	69	97	125
70,71,86,87-Frazetta, 3-4 pgs. each; 1 pg. ad by Frazetta in #70	10	20	30	54	72	90
81,82-Frazetta art (1 pg. each): 81-1st (?) app. Frazetta Boy Scout ad (tied w/ Buster Crabbe #9	9	18	27	47	61	75
83-Frazetta-a (1/2 pg.)	9	18	27	47	61	75

NOTE: ***Evans*** *a-64, 65.* ***Everett*** *a-(Hydroman-c/a-No. 1-9), 44, 60-64; c-1-9, 62-64.* ***Harvey Fuller*** *c-28-35.* ***Sid Greene*** *a-38-43, 46.* ***Guardineer*** *a-42(3), 43, 44, 45(2), 49(3), 50, 60, 61(2), 65, 67(2) 70-72.* ***Ingels*** *c-41.* ***Kiefer*** *a-46, 48; c-19-22, 24, 44, 46, 48, 51-53, 65, 67-69, 71-74, 76, 77, 79, 80, 82, 85, 86, 88, 89, 94, 95.* ***Mort Lawrence*** *a-45.* ***Tarpe Mills*** *a-2(2), 3(2), 10.* ***Ed Moore*** *a-49, 52-54, 56-63, 65-69, 72-74, 76, 77.* ***H.G. Peter*** *a-58-74, 76, 77, 87.* ***Paul Reinman*** *a-49.* ***Rico*** *a-31. Captain Tootsie by* ***Beck****-31, 32. Painted-c #16 on. Hydroman c-1-11. Music Master c-12, 13, 15. Rainbow Boy c-14.*

HERO INITIATIVE: MIKE WIERINGO BOOK (Also see Hero Comics)
Marvel Comics: Aug, 2008 ($4.99)

1-The "What If" Fantastic Four story with Wieringo-a (7 pgs.) finished by other artists after his passing; art by Davis, Immonen, Ramos, Kitson and others; written tributes 5.00

HERO ZERO (Also see Comics' Greatest World & Godzilla Versus Hero Zero)
Dark Horse Comics: Sept, 1994 ($2.50)

0 2.50

HEX (Replaces Jonah Hex)
DC Comics: Sept, 1985 - No. 18, Feb, 1987 (Story cont'd from Jonah Hex # 92)

	GD	VG	FN	VF	VF/NM	NM-
1-Hex in post-atomic war world; origin	2	3	4	6	8	10

2-18: 6-Origin Stiletta. 11-13: All contain future Batman storyline. 13-Intro The Dogs of War (origin #15) 6.00

NOTE: ***Giffen*** *a(p)-15-18; c(p)-15,17,18.* ***Texeira*** *a-1, 2p, 3p, 5-7p, 9p, 11-14p; c(p)-1, 2, 4-7, 12.*

HEXBREAKER (See First Comics Graphic Novel #15)

HEY THERE, IT'S YOGI BEAR (See Movie Comics)

HI-ADVENTURE HEROES (TV)
Gold Key: May, 1969 - No. 2, Aug, 1969 (Hanna-Barbera)

	GD	VG	FN	VF	VF/NM	NM-
1-Three Musketeers, Gulliver, Arabian Knights	5	10	15	32	51	70
2-Three Musketeers, Micro-Venture, Arabian Knights	4	8	12	28	44	60

HI AND LOIS

High Roads #1 © Leinil Yu

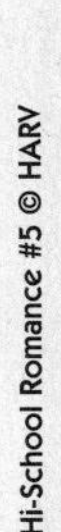
Hi-School Romance #5 © HARV

Hit Comics #26 © QUA

GD VG FN VF VF/NM NM-
2.0 4.0 6.0 8.0 9.0 9.2

Dell Publishing Co.: No. 683, Mar, 1956 - No. 955, Nov, 1958

Four Color 683 (#1) 5 10 15 30 48 65
Four Color 774(3/57),955 4 8 12 24 37 50

HI AND LOIS
Charlton Comics: Nov, 1969 - No. 11, July, 1971

1 3 6 9 14 20 25
2-11 2 4 6 9 12 15

HICKORY (See All Humor Comics)
Quality Comics Group: Oct, 1949 - No. 6, Aug, 1950

1-Sahl-c/a in all; Feldstein?-a 19 38 57 112 176 240
2 12 24 36 67 94 120
3-6 10 20 30 56 76 95

HIDDEN CREW, THE (See The United States Air Force Presents:...)

HIDE-OUT (See Zane Grey, Four Color No. 346)

HIDING PLACE, THE
Spire Christian Comics (Fleming H. Revell Co.): 1973 (39¢/49¢)

nn 2 4 6 8 11 14

HIGH ADVENTURE
Red Top(Decker) Comics (Farrell): Oct, 1957

1-Krigstein-r from Explorer Joe (re-issue on-c) 5 10 15 23 28 32

HIGH ADVENTURE (TV)
Dell Publishing Co.: No. 949, Nov, 1958 - No. 1001, Aug-Oct, 1959 (Lowell Thomas)

Four Color 949 (#1)-Photo-c 6 12 18 37 59 80
Four Color 1001-Lowell Thomas'...(#2) 5 10 15 34 55 75

HIGH CHAPPARAL (TV)
Gold Key: Aug, 1968 (Photo-c)

1 (10226-808)-Tufts-a 5 10 15 32 51 70

HIGHLANDER
Dynamite Entertainment: No. 0, 2006 - No. 12, 2007 (25¢/$2.99)

0-(25¢-c) Takes place after the first movie; photo-c and Dell'Otto painted-c 2.25
1-12: 1-($2.99) Three covers; Moder-a/Jerwa & Oeming-s. 2-Three covers 3.00
... Origins: The Kurgan 1,2 (2009 - No. 2, 2009, $4.99) Three covers; Rafael-a 5.00
...: Way of the Sword (2007 - No. 4, 2008, $3.50) Two interlocking covers for each 3.50

HIGH ROADS
DC Comics (Cliffhanger): June, 2002 - No. 6, Nov, 2002 ($2.95, limited series)

1-6-Leinil Yu-c/a; Lobdell-s 3.00
TPB (2003, $14.95) r/#1-6; sketch pages 15.00

HIGH SCHOOL CONFIDENTIAL DIARY (Confidential Diary #12 on)
Charlton Comics: June, 1960 - No. 11, Mar, 1962

1 4 8 12 26 41 55
2-11 3 6 9 17 25 32

HIGHWAYMEN
DC Comics (WildStorm): Aug, 2007 - No. 5, Dec, 2007 ($2.99)

1-5-Bernardin & Freeman-s/Garbett-a 3.00
TPB (2008, $17.99) r/#1-5 18.00

HI HI PUFFY AMIYUMI (Based on Cartoon Network animated series)
DC Comics: Apr, 2006 - No. 3, June, 2006 ($2.25, limited series)

1-3-Phil Moy-a 2.50

HI-HO COMICS
Four Star Publications: nd (2/46?) - No. 3, 1946

1-Funny Animal; L. B. Cole-c 37 74 111 222 361 500
2,3: 2-L. B. Cole-c 21 42 63 122 199 275

HI-JINX (Teen-age Animal Funnies)
La Salle Publ. Co./B&I Publ. Co. (American Comics Group)/Creston: 1945; July-Aug, 1947 - No. 7, July-Aug, 1948

nn-(© 1945, 25 cents, 132 Pgs.)(La Salle) 24 48 72 140 230 320
1-Teen-age, funny animal 17 34 51 100 158 215
2,3 12 24 36 67 94 120
4-7-Milt Gross. 4-X-Mas-c 16 32 48 94 147 200

HI-LITE COMICS
E. R. Ross Publishing Co.: Fall, 1945

1-Miss Shady 20 40 60 114 182 250

HILLBILLY COMICS
Charlton Comics: Aug, 1955 - No. 4, July, 1956 (Satire)

1-By Art Gates 9 18 27 52 69 85
2-4 7 14 21 35 43 50

HILLY ROSE'S SPACE ADVENTURES
Astro Comics: May, 1995 - No. 9 ($2.95, B&W)

1 1 2 3 5 7 9
2-5 5.00
6-9 3.00
Trade Paperback (1996, $12.95)-r/#1-5 13.00

HIP FLASK UNNATURAL SELECTION
Active Images: Sept, 2002 ($2.99)

1-Casey & Starkings-s/Ladronn-a; var.-c by Madureira, Campbell, Churchill 3.00

HIP-IT-TY HOP (See March of Comics No. 15)

HIRE, THE (BMWfilms.com's...)
Dark Horse Comics: July, 2004 - No. 6 ($2.99)

1-4: 1-Matt Wagner-s/Wagner & Velasco-a. 2-Bruce Campbell-s/Plunkett-a. 3-Waid-s 3.00
TPB (4/06, $17.95) r/#1-4 18.00

HI-SCHOOL ROMANCE (...Romances No. 41 on)
Harvey Publ./True Love(Home Comics): Oct, 1949 - No. 5, June, 1950; No. 6, Dec, 1950 - No. 73, Mar, 1958; No. 74, Sept, 1958 - No. 75, Nov, 1958

1-Photo-c 15 30 45 90 140 190
2-Photo-c 10 20 30 56 76 95
3-9: 3-5-Photo-c 9 18 27 47 61 75
10-Rape story 10 20 30 56 76 95
11-20 8 16 24 40 50 60
21-31 6 12 18 31 38 45
32- "Unholy passion" story 9 18 27 50 65 80
33-36: 36-Last pre-code (2/55) 6 12 18 29 36 42
37-53,59-72,74,75 5 10 15 24 30 35
54-58,73-Kirby-c 6 12 18 31 38 45

NOTE: ***Powell** a-1-3, 5, 8, 12-16, 18, 21-23, 25-27, 30-34, 36, 37, 39, 45-48, 50-52, 57, 58, 60, 64, 65, 67, 69.*

HI-SCHOOL ROMANCE DATE BOOK
Harvey Publications: Nov, 1962 - No. 3, Mar, 1963 (25¢ Giants)

1-Powell, Baker-a 6 12 18 41 66 90
2,3 4 8 12 22 34 45

HIS NAME IS SAVAGE (Magazine format)
Adventure House Press: June, 1968 (35¢, 52 pgs.)

1-Gil Kane-a 5 10 15 34 55 75

HI-SPOT COMICS (Red Ryder No. 1 & No. 3 on)
Hawley Publications: No. 2, Nov, 1940

2-David Innes of Pellucidar; art by J. C. Burroughs; written by Edgar Rice Burroughs
129 258 387 826 1413 2000

HISTORY OF THE DC UNIVERSE (Also see Crisis on Infinite Earths)
DC Comics: Sept, 1986 - No. 2, Nov, 1986 ($2.95, limited series)

1,2: 1-Perez-c/a 3.00
Limited Edition hardcover 4 8 12 26 41 55
Softcover (2002, $9.95) new Alex Ross wraparound-c 10.00
Softcover (2009, $12.99) Alex Ross wraparound-c 13.00

HISTORY OF VIOLENCE, A (Inspired the 2005 movie)
DC Comics (Paradox Press) 1997 ($9.95, B&W graphic novel)

nn-Paperback ($9.95) John Wagner-s/Vince Locke-a 10.00

HITCHHIKERS GUIDE TO THE GALAXY (See Life, the Universe and Everything & Restaurant at the End of the Universe)
DC Comics: 1993 - No. 3, 1993 ($4.95, limited series)

1-3: Adaptation of Douglas Adams book 5.00
TPB (1997, $14.95) r/#1-3 15.00

HIT COMICS
Quality Comics Group: July, 1940 - No. 65, July, 1950

1-Origin/1st app. Neon, the Unknown & Hercules; intro. The Red Bee; Bob & Swab, Blaze Barton, the Strange Twins, X-5 Super Agent, Casey Jones & Jack & Jill (ends #7) begin
757 1514 2271 5526 9763 14,000
2-The Old Witch begins, ends #14 284 568 852 1818 3109 4400
3-Casey Jones ends; transvestism story "Jack & Jill"
271 542 813 1734 2967 4200
4-Super Agent (ends #17), & Betty Bates (ends #65) begin; X-5 ends
232 464 696 1485 2543 3600
5-Classic Lou Fine cover 649 1298 1947 4738 8369 12,000
6-10: 10-Old Witch by Crandall (4 pgs.); 1st work in comics (4/41)

Hitman #21 © DC

Hollywood Diary #1 © QUA

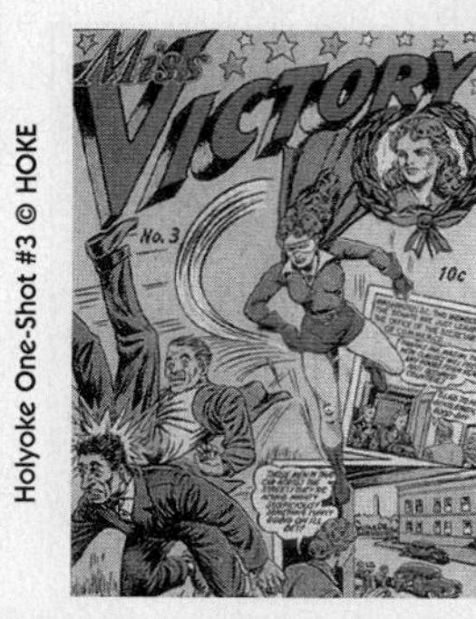

Holyoke One-Shot #3 © HOKE

	GD 2.0	VG 4.0	FN 6.0	VF 8.0	VF/NM 9.0	NM- 9.2
	194	388	582	1242	2121	3000
11-Classic cover	206	412	618	1318	2259	3200
12-17: 13-Blaze Barton ends. 17-Last Neon; Crandall Hercules in all; Last Lou Fine-c	123	246	369	787	1344	1900
18-Origin & 1st app. Stormy Foster, the Great Defender (12/41); The Ghost of Flanders begins; Crandall-c	127	254	381	807	1391	1975
19,20	100	200	300	635	1093	1550
21-24: 21-Last Hercules. 24-Last Red Bee & Strange Twins	97	194	291	621	1061	1500
25-Origin & 1st app. Kid Eternity and begins by Moldoff (12/42); 1st app. The Keeper (Kid Eternity's aide)	184	368	552	1168	2009	2850
26-Blackhawk x-over in Kid Eternity	97	194	291	621	1061	1500
27-29	49	98	147	309	522	735
30,31- "Bill the Magnificent" by Kurtzman, 11 pgs. in each	45	90	135	284	480	675
32-40: 32-Plastic Man x-over. 34-Last Stormy Foster	30	60	90	177	289	400
41-50	21	42	63	126	206	285
51-60-Last Kid Eternity	20	40	60	120	195	270
61-63-Crandall-c/a; 61-Jeb Rivers begins	21	42	63	124	202	280
64,65-Crandall-a	20	40	60	120	195	270

NOTE: ***Crandall** a-11-17(Hercules), 23, 24(Stormy Foster); c-18-20, 23, 24. **Fine** c-1-14, 16, 17(most). **Ward** c-33. Bondage c-7, 64. Hercules c-3, 10-17. Jeb Rivers c-61-65. Kid Eternity c-25-60 (w/Keeper-28-34, 36, 39-43, 45-55). Neon the Unknown c-2, 4, 8, 9. Red Bee c-1, 5-7. Stormy Foster c-18-24.*

HITLER'S ASTROLOGER (See Marvel Graphic Novel #35)

HITMAN (Also see Bloodbath #2, Batman Chronicles #4, Demon #43-45 & Demon Annual #2)
DC Comics: May, 1996 - No. 60, Apr, 2001 ($2.25/$2.50)

1-Garth Ennis-s & John McCrea-c/a begin; Batman app.	1	2	3	5	7	9
2-Joker-c;Two Face, Mad Hatter, Batman app.						6.00
3-5: 3-Batman-c/app.; Joker app. 4-1st app. Nightfist						4.00
6-20: 8-Final Night x-over. 10-GL cameo. 11-20: 11,12-GL-c/app. 15-20-"Ace of Killers". 16-18-Catwoman app. 17-19-Demon-app.						3.00
21-59: 34-Superman-c/app.						2.50
60-($3.95) Final issue; includes pin-ups by various						4.00
#1,000,000 (11/98) Hitman goes to the 853rd Century						2.50
Annual 1 (1997, $3.95) Pulp Heroes						4.00
.../Lobo: That Stupid Bastich (7/00, $3.95) Ennis-s/Mahnke-a						4.00
TPB-(1997, $9.95) r/#1-3, Demon Ann. #2, Batman Chronicles #4						10.00
Ace of Killers TPB ('00, $17.95) r/#15-22						18.00
Local Heroes TPB ('99, $17.95) r/#9-14 & Annual #1						18.00
10,000 Bullets TPB ('98, $9.95) r/#4-8						10.00
Who Dares Wins TPB ('01, $12.95) r/#23-28						13.00

HIT-MONKEY (See Deadpool)
Marvel Comics: Apr, 2010 ($3.99, one-shot)

1-Printing of story from Marvel Digital Comics; Frank Cho-c; origin revealed 4.00

HI-YO SILVER (See Lone Ranger's Famous Horse... and The Lone Ranger; and March of Comics No. 215 in the Promotional Comics section)

HOBBIT, THE
Eclipse Comics: 1989 - No. 3, 1990 ($4.95, squarebound, 52 pgs.)

Book 1-3: Adapts novel; Wenzel-a	8.00
Book 1-Second printing	5.00
Graphic Novel (1990, Ballantine)-r/#1-3	25.00

HOCUS POCUS (See Funny Book #9)

HOGAN'S HEROES (TV) (Also see Wild!)
Dell Publishing Co.: June, 1966 - No. 8, Sept, 1967; No. 9, Oct, 1969

1: #1-7 photo-c	8	16	24	56	93	130
2,3-Ditko-a(p)	6	12	18	37	59	80
4-9: 9-Reprints #1	5	10	15	30	48	65

HOKUM & HEX (See Razorline)
Marvel Comics (Razorline): Sept, 1993 - No. 9, May, 1994 ($1.75/$1.95)

1-($2.50)-Foil embossed-c; by Clive Barker	3.00
2-9: 5-Hyperkind x-over	2.50

HOLIDAY COMICS
Fawcett Publications: 1942 (25¢, 196 pgs.)

1-Contains three Fawcett comics plus two page portrait of Captain Marvel; Capt. Marvel, Jungle Girl #1, & Whiz. Not rebound, remaindered comics; printed at the same time as originals	226	452	678	1446	2473	3500

HOLIDAY COMICS (Becomes Fun Comics #9-12)
Star Publications: Jan, 1951 - No. 8, Oct, 1952

1-Funny animal contents (Frisky Fables) in all; L. B. Cole X-Mas-c	30	60	90	174	280	385
2-Classic L. B. Cole-c	32	64	96	190	305	420
3-8: 5,8-X-Mas-c; all L.B. Cole-c	19	38	57	109	172	235
Accepted Reprint 4 (nd)-L.B. Cole-c	10	20	30	58	79	100

HOLIDAY DIGEST
Harvey Comics: 1988 ($1.25, digest-size)

1	1	2	3	5	7	9

HOLIDAY PARADE (Walt Disney's...)
W. D. Publications (Disney): Winter, 1990-91(no year given) - No. 2, Winter, 1990-91 ($2.95, 68 pgs.)

1-Reprints 1947 Firestone by Barks plus new-a	4.00
2-Barks-r plus other stories	4.00

HOLI-DAY SURPRISE (Formerly Summer Fun)
Charlton Comics: V2#55, Mar, 1967 (25¢ Giant)

V2#55	4	8	12	24	37	50

HOLLYWOOD COMICS
New Age Publishers: Winter, 1944 (52 pgs.)

1-Funny animal	18	36	54	105	165	225

HOLLYWOOD CONFESSIONS
St. John Publishing Co.: Oct, 1949 - No. 2, Dec, 1949

1-Kubert-c/a (entire book)	32	64	96	192	314	435
2-Kubert-c/a (entire book) (Scarce)	34	68	102	204	332	460

HOLLYWOOD DIARY
Quality Comics Group: Dec, 1949 - No. 5, July-Aug, 1950

1-No photo-c	21	42	63	124	202	280
2-Photo-c	14	28	42	82	121	160
3-5-Photo-c. 5-June Allyson/Peter Lawford photo-c	13	26	39	74	105	135

HOLLYWOOD FILM STORIES
Feature Publications/Prize: April, 1950 - No. 4, Oct, 1950 (All photo-c; "Fumetti" type movie comic)

1-June Allyson photo-c	20	40	60	114	182	250
2-4: 2-Lizabeth Scott photo-c. 3-Barbara Stanwick photo-c. 4-Betty Hutton photo-c	15	30	45	83	124	165

HOLLYWOOD FUNNY FOLKS (Formerly Funny Folks; Becomes Nutsy Squirrel #61 on)
National Periodical Publ.: No. 27, Aug-Sept, 1950 - No. 60, July-Aug, 1954

27	14	28	42	76	108	140
28-40	10	20	30	54	72	90
41-60	9	18	27	47	61	75

NOTE: ***Rube Grossman** a-most issues. **Sheldon Mayer** a-27-35, 37-40, 43-46, 48-51, 53, 56, 57, 60.*

HOLLYWOOD LOVE DOCTOR (See Doctor Anthony King...)

HOLLYWOOD PICTORIAL (...Romances on cover)
St. John Publishing Co.: No. 3, Jan, 1950

3-Matt Baker-a; photo-c	27	54	81	160	263	365

(Becomes a movie magazine - Hollywood Pictorial Western with No. 4.)

HOLLYWOOD ROMANCES (Formerly Brides In Love; becomes For Lovers Only #60 on)
Charlton Comics: V2#46, 11/66; #47, 10/67; #48, 11/68;V3#49,11/69-V3#59, 6/71

V2#46-Rolling Stones-c/story	9	18	27	65	113	160
V2#47-V3#59: 56- "Born to Heart Break" begins	3	6	9	14	19	24

HOLLYWOOD SECRETS
Quality Comics Group: Nov, 1949 - No. 6, Sept, 1950

1-Ward-c/a (9 pgs.)	34	68	102	204	332	460
2-Crandall-a, Ward-c/a (9 pgs.)	23	46	69	136	223	310
3-6: All photo-c. 5-Lex Barker (Tarzan)-c	14	28	42	78	112	145
...of Romance, I.W. Reprint #9; r/#2 above w/Kinstler-c	2	4	6	10	14	18

HOLLYWOOD SUPERSTARS
Marvel Comics (Epic Comics): Nov, 1990 - No. 5, Apr, 1991 ($2.25)

1-($2.95, 52 pgs.)-Spiegle-c/a in all; Aragones-a, inside front-c plus 2-4 pgs.	3.00
2-5 ($2.25)	2.50

HOLO-MAN (See Power Record Comics)

HOLYOKE ONE-SHOT
Holyoke Publishing Co. (Tem Publ.): 1944 - No. 10, 1945 (All reprints)

1,2: 1-Grit Grady (on cover only), Miss Victory, Alias X (origin)-All reprints from Captain Fearless. 2-Rusty Dugan (Corporal); Capt. Fearless (origin), Mr. Miracle (origin) app.

Homer, The Happy Ghost #16 © MAR

Hook #1 © MAR

Hopalong Cassidy #20 © FAW

GD VG FN VF VF/NM NM-
2.0 4.0 6.0 8.0 9.0 9.2

21 42 63 122 199 275

3-Miss Victory; r/Crash #4; Cat Man (origin), Solar Legion by Kirby app.; Miss Victory on cover only (1945) 32 64 96 192 314 435

4,6,8: 4-Mr. Miracle; The Blue Streak app. 6-Capt. Fearless, Alias X, Capt. Stone (splash used as-c to #10); Diamond Jim & Rusty Dugan (splash from cover of #2). 8-Blue Streak, Strong Man (story matches cover to #7)-Crash reprints
19 38 57 111 176 240

5,7: 5-U.S. Border Patrol Comics (Sgt. Dick Carter of the...), Miss Victory (story matches cover to #3), Citizen Smith, & Mr. Miracle app. 7-Secret Agent Z-2, Strong Man, Blue Streak (story matches cover to #8); Reprints from Crash #2
20 40 60 118 192 265

9-Citizen Smith, The Blue Streak, Solar Legion by Kirby & Strongman, the Perfect Human app.; reprints from Crash #4 & 5; Citizen Smith on cover only-from story in #5 (1944-before #3) 22 44 66 132 216 300

10-Captain Stone; r/Crash; Solar Legion by S&K 22 44 66 132 216 300

HOMER COBB (See Adventures of...)

HOMER HOOPER
Atlas Comics: July, 1953 - No. 4, Dec, 1953

1-Teenage humor 10 20 30 58 79 100
2-4 8 16 24 40 50 60

HOMER, THE HAPPY GHOST (See Adventures of...)
Atlas(ACI/PPI/WPI)/Marvel: 3/55 - No. 22, 11/58; V2#1, 11/69 - V2#4, 5/70

V1#1-Dan DeCarlo-c/a begins, ends #22 22 44 66 128 209 290
2-1st code approved issue 14 28 42 78 112 145
3-10 12 24 36 69 97 125
11-22 11 22 33 60 83 105
V2#1 (11/69) 11 22 33 74 132 190
2-4 6 12 18 43 69 95

HOME RUN (Also see A-1 Comics)
Magazine Enterprises: No. 89, 1953 (one-shot)

A-1 89 (#3)-Powell-a; Stan Musial photo-c 14 28 42 80 115 150

HOMICIDE (Also see Dark Horse Presents)
Dark Horse Comics: Apr, 1990 ($1.95, B&W, one-shot)

1-Detective story 2.50

HONEYMOON (Formerly Gay Comics)
A Lover's Magazine(USA) (Marvel): No. 41, Jan, 1950

41-Photo-c; article by Betty Grable 12 24 36 67 94 120

HONEYMOONERS, THE (TV)
Lodestone: Oct, 1986 ($1.50)

1-Photo-c 4.00

HONEYMOONERS, THE (TV)
Triad Publications: Sept, 1987 - No. 13? ($2.00)

1-13 4.00

HONEYMOON ROMANCE
Artful Publications (Canadian): Apr, 1950 - No. 2, July, 1950 (25¢, digest size)

1,2-(Rare) 40 80 120 246 411 575

HONEY WEST (TV)
Gold Key: Sept, 1966 (Photo-c)

1 (10186-609) 9 18 27 60 100 140

HONG KONG PHOOEY (TV)
Charlton Comics: June, 1975 - No. 9, Nov, 1976 (Hanna-Barbera)

1 5 10 15 34 55 75
2 3 6 9 19 29 38
3-9 3 6 9 16 22 28

HONG ON THE RANGE
Image/Flypaper Press: Dec, 1997 - No. 3, Feb, 1998 ($2.50, lim. series)

1-3: Wu-s/Lafferty-a 2.50

HOOD, THE
Marvel Comics (MAX): Jul, 2002 - No. 6, Dec, 2002 ($2.99, limited series)

1-6-Vaughan-s/Hotz-c/a 3.00
Vol. 1 Blood From Stones HC (2007, $19.99, dustjacket) r/#1-6; production sketch art 20.00
Vol. 1 Blood From Stones TPB (2003, $14.99) r/#1-6 15.00

HOODED HORSEMAN, THE (Formerly Blazing West)
American Comics Group (Michel Publ.): No. 21, 1-2/52 - No. 27, 1-2/54; No. 18, 12-1/54-55 - No. 22, 8-9/55

GD VG FN VF VF/NM NM-
2.0 4.0 6.0 8.0 9.0 9.2

21(1-2/52)-Hooded Horseman, Injun Jones cont. 15 30 45 83 124 165
22 10 20 30 56 76 95
23,24,27(1-2/54) 9 18 27 50 65 80
25 (9-10/53)-Cowboy Sahib on cover only; Hooded Horseman i.d. revealed
9 18 27 52 69 85
26-Origin/1st app. Cowboy Sahib by L. Starr 11 22 33 62 86 110
18(12-1/54-55)(Formerly Out of the Night) 10 20 30 54 72 90
19,21,22: 19-Last precode (1-2/55) 8 16 24 44 57 70
20-Origin Johnny Injun 9 18 27 50 65 80

NOTE: *Whitney c/a-21('52), 20-22.*

HOODED MENACE, THE (Also see Daring Adventures)
Realistic/Avon Periodicals: 1951 (one-shot)

nn-Based on a band of hooded outlaws in the Pacific Northwest, 1900-1906; reprinted in Daring Advs. #15 48 96 144 302 514 725

HOODS UP (See the Promotional Comics section)

HOOK (Movie)
Marvel Comics: Early Feb, 1992 - No. 4, Late Mar, 1992 ($1.00, limited series)

1-4: Adapts movie; Vess-c; 1-Morrow-a(p) 2.50
nn (1991, $5.95, 84 pgs.)-Contains #1-4; Vess-c 6.00
1 (1991, $2.95, magazine, 84 pgs.)-Contains #1-4; Vess-c (same cover as nn issue) 3.00

HOOT GIBSON'S WESTERN ROUNDUP (See Western Roundup under Fox Giants)

HOOT GIBSON WESTERN (Formerly My Love Story)
Fox Features Syndicate: No. 5, May, 1950 - No. 3, Sept, 1950

5,6(#1,2): 5-Photo-c. 6-Photo/painted-c 21 42 63 123 197 270
3-Wood-a; painted-c 22 44 66 131 211 290

HOPALONG CASSIDY (Also see Bill Boyd Western, Master Comics, Real Western Hero, Six Gun Heroes & Western Hero; Bill Boyd starred as Hopalong Cassidy in movies, radio & TV)
Fawcett Publications: Feb, 1943; No. 2, Summer, 1946 - No. 85, Nov, 1953

1 (1943, 68 pgs.)-H. Cassidy & his horse Topper begin (on sale 1/8/43)-Captain Marvel app. on-c 423 846 1269 3000 5250 7500
2-(Sum, '46) 63 126 189 397 674 950
3,4: 3-(Fall, '46, 52 pgs. begin) 33 66 99 192 309 425
5- "Mad Barber" story mentioned in **SOTI**, pgs. 308,309; photo-c
25 50 75 147 236 325
6-10: 8-Photo-c 19 38 57 112 176 240
11-19: 11,13-19-Photo-c 15 30 45 85 130 175
20-29 (52 pgs.)-Painted/photo-c 14 28 42 76 108 140
30,31,33,34,37-39,41 (52 pgs.)-Painted-c 11 22 33 64 90 115
32,40 (36pgs.)-Painted-c 10 20 30 58 79 100
35,42,43,45-47,49-51,53,54,56 (52 pgs.)-Photo-c 11 22 33 60 83 105
36,44,48 (36 pgs.)-Photo-c 10 20 30 56 76 95
52,55,57-70 (36 pgs.)-Photo-c 9 18 27 52 69 85
71-84-Photo-c 8 16 24 44 57 70
85-Last Fawcett issue; photo-c 10 20 30 54 72 90

NOTE: *Line-drawn c-1-4, 6, 7, 9, 10, 12.*

... & The 5 Men of Evil (AC Comics, 1991, $12.95) r/newspaper strips and Fawcett story "Signature of Death" 13.00

HOPALONG CASSIDY
National Periodical Publications: No. 86, Feb, 1954 - No. 135, May-June, 1959 (All-36 pgs.)

86-Gene Colan-a begins, ends #117; photo covers continue
37 74 111 220 353 485
87 20 40 60 118 189 260
88-91: 91-1 pg. Superboy-sty (7/54) 15 30 45 83 124 165
92-99 (98 has #93 on-c; last precode issue, 2/55). 95-Reversed photo-c to #52. 98-Reversed photo-c to #61. 99-Reversed photo-c to #60 14 28 42 76 108 140
100-Same cover as #50 15 30 45 83 124 165
101-108: 105-Same photo-c as #54. 107-Same photo-c as #51. 108-Last photo-c
7 14 21 45 73 100
109-130: 118-Gil Kane-a begins. 123-Kubert-a (2 pgs.). 124-Painted-c
6 12 18 41 66 90
131-135 6 12 18 43 69 95

HOPELESS SAVAGES (Also see Too Much Hopeless Savages; and the Promotional Comics section for Free Comic Book Day edition)
Oni Press: Aug, 2001 - No. 4, Nov, 2001 ($2.95, B&W, limited series)

1-4-Van Meter-s/Norrie-a/Clugston-Major-a/Watson-c 3.00
TPB (2002, $13.95, 8" x 5.75") r/#1-4; plus color stories; Watson-c 14.00

HOPELESS SAVAGES: GROUND ZERO
Oni Press: June, 2002 - No. 4, Oct, 2002 ($2.95, B&W, limited series)

Horrific #7 © Comic Media

Hot Rod and Speedway Comics #1 © HILL

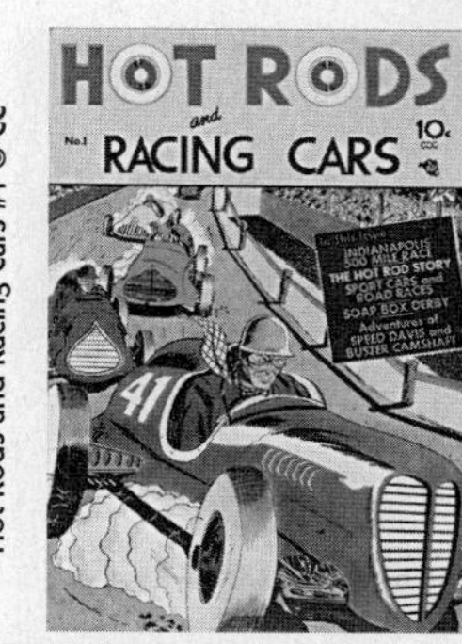

Hot Rods and Racing Cars #1 © CC

	GD 2.0	VG 4.0	FN 6.0	VF 8.0	VF/NM 9.0	NM- 9.2
1-4-Van Meter-s/O'Malley-a/Dodson-c. 1-Watson-a						3.00
TPB (2003, $11.95, 8" x 5.75") r/#1-4; Dodson-c						12.00

HOPE SHIP
Dell Publishing Co.: June-Aug, 1963

1	3	6	9	16	22	28

HOPPY THE MARVEL BUNNY (See Fawcett's Funny Animals)
Fawcett Publications: Dec, 1945 - No. 15, Sept, 1947

1	28	56	84	165	270	375
2	14	28	42	82	121	160
3-15: 7-Xmas-c	12	24	36	67	94	120

HORACE & DOTTY DRIPPLE (Dotty Dripple No. 1-24)
Harvey Publications: No. 25, Aug, 1952 - No. 43, Oct, 1955

25-43	4	9	13	18	22	26

HORIZONTAL LIEUTENANT, THE (See Movie Classics)

HOROBI
Viz Premiere Comics: 1990 - No. 8, 1990 ($3.75, B&W, mature readers, 84 pgs.) V2#1, 1990 - No. 7, 1991 ($4.25, B&W, 68 pgs.)

1-8: Japanese manga, Part Two, #1-7						4.50

HORRIFIC (Terrific No. 14 on)
Artful/Comic Media/Harwell/Mystery: Sept, 1952 - No. 13, Sept, 1954

1	60	120	180	381	653	925
2	39	78	117	231	378	525
3-Bullet in head-c	71	142	213	454	777	1100
4,5,7,9,10: 4-Shrunken head-c. 7-Guillotine-c	34	68	102	199	325	450
6-Jack The Ripper story	34	68	102	206	336	465
8-Origin & 1st app. The Teller (E.C. parody)	39	78	117	231	378	525
11-13: 11-Swipe/Witches Tales #6,27; Devil-c	27	54	81	160	263	365

NOTE: *Don Heck a-8; c-3-13.* ***Hollingsworth** a-4.* ***Morisi** a-8.* ***Palais** a-5, 7-12.*

HORRORCIDE
IDW Publishing: Sept, 2004 ($6.99)

1-Steve Niles short stories; art by Templesmith, Medors and Chee						7.00

HORROR FROM THE TOMB (Mysterious Stories No. 2 on)
Premier Magazine Co.: Sept, 1954

1-Woodbridge/Torres, Check-a; The Keeper of the Graveyard is host	42	84	126	265	445	625

HORRORIST, THE (Also see Hellblazer)
DC Comics (Vertigo): Dec, 1995 - No. 2, Jan, 1996 ($5.95, lim. series, mature)

1,2: Jamie Delano scripts, David Lloyd-c/a; John Constantine (Hellblazer) app.						6.00

HORROR OF COLLIER COUNTY
Dark Horse Comics: Oct, 1999 - No. 5, Feb, 2000 ($2.95, B&W, limited series)

1-5-Rich Tommaso-s/a						3.00

HORRORS, THE (Formerly Startling Terror Tales #10)
Star Publications: No. 11, Jan, 1953 - No. 15, Apr, 1954

11-Horrors of War; Disbrow-a(2)	30	60	90	177	289	400
12-Horrors of War; color illo in **POP**	28	56	84	165	270	375
13-Horrors of Mystery; crime stories	26	52	78	154	252	350
14,15-Horrors of the Underworld; crime stories	28	56	84	165	270	375

NOTE: *All have* ***L. B. Cole** covers; a-12.* ***Hollingsworth** a-13.* ***Palais** a-13r.*

HORROR TALES (Magazine)
Eerie Publications: V1#7, 6/69 - V6#6, 12/74; V7#1, 2/75; V7#2, 5/76 - V8#5, 1977; V9#1-3, 8/78; V10#1(2/79) (V1-V6: 52 pgs.; V7, V8#2: 112 pgs.; V8#4 on: 68 pgs.) (No V5#3, V8#1,3)

V1#7	6	12	18	41	66	90
V1#8,9	4	8	12	28	44	60
V2#1-6('70), V3#1-6('71), V4#1-3,5-7('72)	4	8	12	24	37	50
V4#4-LSD story reprint/Weird V3#5	5	10	15	32	51	70
V5#1,2,4,5(6/73),5(10/73),6(12/73),V6#1-6('74),V7#1,2,4('76),V7#3('76)-Giant issue, V8#2,4,5('77)	4	8	12	24	37	50
V9#1-3(11/78, $1.50), V10#1(2/79)	4	8	12	26	41	55

NOTE: *Bondage-c-V6#1, 3, V7#2.*

HORSE FEATHERS COMICS
Lev Gleason Publ.: Nov, 1945 - No. 4, July(Summer on-c), 1948 (52 pgs.) (#2,3 are oversized)

1-Wolverton's Scoop Scuttle, 2 pgs.	19	38	57	109	172	235
2	11	22	33	60	83	105
3,4: 3-(5/48)	9	18	27	47	61	75

HORSEMAN
Crusade Comics/Kevlar Studios: Mar, 1996 - No. 3, Nov, 1997 ($2.95)

0-1st Kevlar Studios issue, 1-(3/96)-Crusade issue; Shi-c/app., 1-(11/96)-3-(11/97)-Kevlar Studios						3.00

HORSEMASTERS, THE (Disney)(TV, Movie)
Dell Publishing Co.: No. 1260, Dec-Feb, 1961/62

Four Color 1260-Annette Funicello photo-c	12	24	36	85	155	225

HORSE SOLDIERS, THE
Dell Publishing Co.: No. 1048, Nov-Jan, 1959/60 (John Wayne movie)

Four Color 1048-Painted-c, Sekowsky-a	13	26	39	90	165	240

HORSE WITHOUT A HEAD, THE (See Movie Comics)

HOT DOG
Magazine Enterprises: June-July, 1954 - No. 4, Dec-Jan, 1954-55

1(A-1 #107)	9	18	27	47	61	75
2,3(A-1 #115),4(A-1 #136)	6	12	18	31	38	45

HOT DOG (See Jughead's Pal, Hotdog)

HOTEL DEPAREE - SUNDANCE (TV)
Dell Publishing Co.: No. 1126, Aug-Oct, 1960 (one-shot)

Four Color 1126-Earl Holliman photo-c	6	12	18	43	69	95

HOT ROD AND SPEEDWAY COMICS
Hillman Periodicals: Feb-Mar, 1952 - No. 5, Apr-May, 1953

1	27	54	81	158	259	360
2-Krigstein-a	18	36	54	105	165	225
3-5	13	26	39	72	101	130

HOT ROD COMICS (...Featuring Clint Curtis) (See XMas Comics)
Fawcett Publications: Nov, 1951 (no month given) - V2#7, Feb, 1953

nn (V1#1)-Powell-c/a in all	29	58	87	170	278	385
2 (4/52)	15	30	45	90	140	190
3-6, V2#7	13	26	39	72	101	130

HOT ROD KING (Also see Speed Smith the Hot Rod King)
Ziff-Davis Publ. Co.: Fall, 1952

1-Giacoia-a; Saunders painted-c	25	50	75	147	241	335

HOT ROD RACERS (Grand Prix No. 16 on)
Charlton Comics: Dec, 1964 - No. 15, July, 1967

1	8	16	24	54	90	125
2-5	5	10	15	32	51	70
6-15	4	8	12	24	37	50

HOT RODS AND RACING CARS
Charlton Comics (Motor Mag. No. 1): Nov, 1951 - No. 120, June, 1973

1-Speed Davis begins; Indianapolis 500 story	28	56	84	165	270	375
2	15	30	45	86	133	180
3-10	12	24	36	67	94	120
11-20	10	20	30	54	72	90
21-33,36-40	8	16	24	44	57	70
34, 35 (? & 6/58, 68 pgs.)	11	22	33	60	83	105
41-60	7	14	21	37	46	55
61-80	3	6	9	20	30	40
81-100	3	6	9	16	23	30
101-120	3	6	9	14	19	24

HOT SHOT CHARLIE
Hillman Periodicals: 1947 (Lee Elias)

1	11	22	33	62	86	110

HOT SHOTS: AVENGERS
Marvel Comics: Oct, 1995 ($2.95, one-shot)

nn-pin-ups						3.00

HOTSPUR
Eclipse Comics: Jun, 1987 - No. 3, Sep, 1987 ($1.75, lim. series, Baxter paper)

1-3						3.00

HOT STUFF (See Stumbo Tinytown)
Harvey Comics: V2#1, Sept, 1991 - No. 12, June, 1994 ($1.00)

V2#1-Stumbo back-up story						5.00
2-12 ($1.50)						4.00
...Big Book 1 (11/92), 2 (6/93) (Both $1.95, 52 pgs.)						5.00

HOT STUFF CREEPY CAVES
Harvey Publications: Nov, 1974 - No. 7, Nov, 1975

1	4	8	12	22	34	45

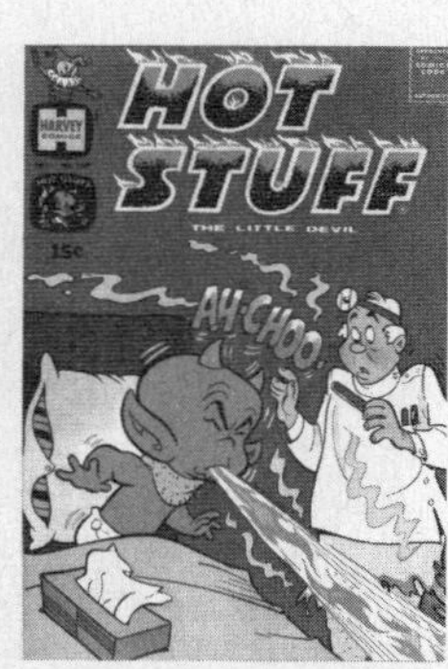

Hot Stuff, The Little Devil #100 © HARV

Hourman #25 © DC

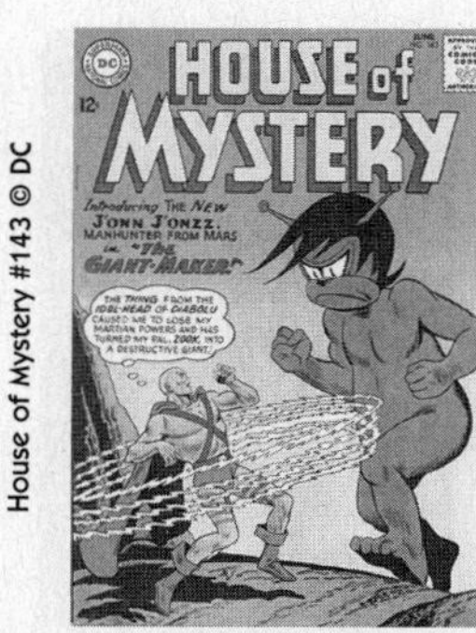

House of Mystery #143 © DC

	GD 2.0	VG 4.0	FN 6.0	VF 8.0	VF/NM 9.0	NM- 9.2
2-7	3	6	9	15	21	26

HOT STUFF DIGEST
Harvey Comics: July, 1992 - No. 5, Nov, 1993 ($1.75, digest-size)

	GD 2.0	VG 4.0	FN 6.0	VF 8.0	VF/NM 9.0	NM- 9.2
V2#1-Hot Stuff, Stumbo, Richie Rich stories						6.00
2-5						4.00

HOT STUFF GIANT SIZE
Harvey Comics: Oct, 1992 - No. 3, Oct, 1993 ($2.25, 68 pgs.)

	GD 2.0	VG 4.0	FN 6.0	VF 8.0	VF/NM 9.0	NM- 9.2
V2#1-Hot Stuff & Stumbo stories						4.50
2,3						3.50

HOT STUFF SIZZLERS
Harvey Publications: July, 1960 - No. 59, Mar, 1974; V2#1, Aug, 1992

	GD 2.0	VG 4.0	FN 6.0	VF 8.0	VF/NM 9.0	NM- 9.2
1- 84 pgs. begin, ends #5; Hot Stuff, Stumbo begin	15	30	45	107	204	300
2-5	8	16	24	58	97	135
6-10: 6-68 pgs. begin, ends #45	6	12	18	41	66	90
11-20	4	8	12	28	44	60
21-45	3	6	9	20	30	40
46-52: 52 pgs. begin	3	6	9	16	23	30
53-59	2	4	6	10	14	18
V2#1-(8/92, $1.25)-Stumbo back-up						5.00

HOT STUFF, THE LITTLE DEVIL (Also see Devil Kids & Harvey Hits)
Harvey Publications (Illustrated Humor): 10/57 - No. 141, 7/77; No. 142, 2/78 - No. 164, 8/82; No. 165, 10/86 - No. 171, 11/87; No. 172, 11/88; No. 173, Sept, 1990 - No. 177, 1/91

	GD 2.0	VG 4.0	FN 6.0	VF 8.0	VF/NM 9.0	NM- 9.2
1	50	100	150	413	807	1200
2-Stumbo-like giant 1st app. (12/57)	24	48	72	175	338	500
3-5: 3-Stumbo the Giant debut (2/58)	18	36	54	126	246	365
6-10	11	22	33	78	139	200
11-20	9	18	27	60	100	140
21-40	6	12	18	39	62	85
41-60	4	8	12	26	41	55
61-80	3	6	9	20	30	40
81-105	3	6	9	16	22	28
106-112: All 52 pg. Giants	3	6	9	18	27	35
113-125	2	4	6	9	12	15
126-141	1	2	3	5	7	9
142-177: 172-177-($1.00)						6.00
Harvey Comics Classics Vol. 3 TPB (Dark Horse Books, 3/08, $19.95) Reprints Hot Stuff's earliest appearances in this title and Devil Kids, mostly B&W with some color stories; history, early concept drawings; foreword by Mark Arnold						20.00

HOT WHEELS (TV)
National Periodical Publications: Mar-Apr, 1970 - No. 6, Jan-Feb, 1971

	GD 2.0	VG 4.0	FN 6.0	VF 8.0	VF/NM 9.0	NM- 9.2
1	9	18	27	65	113	160
2,4,5	6	12	18	37	59	80
3-Neal Adams-c	7	14	21	45	73	100
6-Neal Adams-c/a	8	16	24	54	90	125

NOTE: *Toth a-1p, 2-5; c-1p, 5.*

HOURMAN (Justice Society member, see Adventure Comics #48)

HOURMAN (See JLA and DC One Million)
DC Comics: Apr, 1999 - No. 25, Apr, 2001 ($2.50)

	GD 2.0	VG 4.0	FN 6.0	VF 8.0	VF/NM 9.0	NM- 9.2
1-25: 1-JLA app.; McDaniel-c. 2-Tomorrow Woman-c/app. 6,7-Amazo app. 11-13-Justice Legion A app. 16-Silver Age flashback. 18,19-JSA-c/app. 22-Harris-c/a. 24-Hourman Vs. Rex Tyler						2.50

HOUSE OF M (Also see miniseries with Fantastic Four, Iron Man and Spider-Man)
Marvel Comics: Aug, 2005 - No. 8, Dec, 2005 ($2.99, limited series)

	GD 2.0	VG 4.0	FN 6.0	VF 8.0	VF/NM 9.0	NM- 9.2
1-Bendis-s/Coipel-a/Ribic-c; Scarlet Witch changes reality; Quesada variant-c						3.00
2-8-Variant covers for each. 3-Hawkeye returns						3.00
Secrets Of The House Of M (2005, $3.99, one-shot) profile pages and background info						4.00
... Sketchbook (6/05) B&W preview sketches by Coipel, Davis, Hairsine, Quesada						2.50
TPB (2006, $24.99) r/#1-8 and The Pulse: House of M Special Edition newspaper						25.00
...: Fantastic Four/ Iron Man TPB (2006, $13.99) r/ both House of M mini-series						14.00
...: World of M Featuring Wolverine TPB (2006, $13.99) r/2005 x-over issues Wolverine #33-35, Black Panther #7, Captain America #10 and The Pulse #10						14.00
HC (2008, $29.99, oversized with d.j.) r/#1-8, The Pulse: House of M Special Edition newspaper and Secrets Of The House Of M one-shot; script pages; cover gallery						30.00

HOUSE OF M: AVENGERS
Marvel Comics: Jan, 2008 - No. 5, Apr, 2008 ($2.99, limited series)

	GD 2.0	VG 4.0	FN 6.0	VF 8.0	VF/NM 9.0	NM- 9.2
1-5-Gage-s/Perkins-a; Luke Cage, Iron Fist, Hawkeye, Tigra, Misty Knight, Shang-Chi						3.00

HOUSE OF M: MASTERS OF EVIL
Marvel Comics: Oct, 2009 - No. 4, Jan, 2010 ($3.99, limited series)

	GD 2.0	VG 4.0	FN 6.0	VF 8.0	VF/NM 9.0	NM- 9.2
1-4-Gage-s/Garcia-a/Perkins-c; The Hood app.						4.00

HOUSE OF MYSTERY
DC Comics: Dec/Jan. 1951

nn - Ashcan comic, not distributed to newsstands, only for in-house use. Cover art is Danger Trail #3 with interior being Star Spangled Comics #109. A VG+ copy sold for $2,357.50 in 2002.

HOUSE OF MYSTERY (See Brave and the Bold #93, Elvira's House of Mystery, Limited Collectors' Edition & Super DC Giant)

HOUSE OF MYSTERY, THE
National Periodical Publications/DC Comics: Dec-Jan, 1951-52 - No. 321, Oct, 1983 (No. 194-203: 52 pgs.)

	GD 2.0	VG 4.0	FN 6.0	VF 8.0	VF/NM 9.0	NM- 9.2
1-DC's first horror comic	245	490	735	1568	2684	3800
2	94	188	282	597	1024	1450
3	65	130	195	416	708	1000
4,5	52	104	156	324	550	775
6-10	45	90	135	284	480	675
11-15	39	78	117	240	395	550
16(7/53)-25	32	64	96	188	307	425
26-35(2/55)-Last pre-code issue; 30-Woodish-a	24	48	72	142	234	325
36-50: 50-Text story of Orson Welles' War of the Worlds broadcast	14	28	42	97	181	265
51-60: 55-1st S.A. issue	12	24	36	82	149	215
61,63,65,66,69,70,72,76,85-Kirby-a	13	26	39	91	168	245
62,64,67,68,71,73-75,77-83,86-99	10	20	30	73	129	185
84-Prototype of Negative Man (Doom Patrol)	13	26	39	91	168	245
100 (7/60)	11	22	33	78	139	200
101-116: 109-Toth, Kubert-a. 116-Last 10¢ issue	10	20	30	67	116	165
117-130: 117-Swipes-c to HOS #20. 120-Toth-a	9	18	27	61	103	145
131-142	8	16	24	54	90	125
143-J'onn J'onzz, Manhunter begins (6/64), ends #173; story continues from Detective #326; intro. Idol-Head of Diabolu	19	38	57	133	259	385
144	9	18	27	60	100	140
145-155,157-159: 149-Toth-a. 155-The Human Hurricane app. (12/65), Red Tornado prototype. 158-Origin Diabolu Idol-Head	6	12	18	41	66	90
156-Robby Reed begins (origin/1st app.), ends #173	8	16	24	52	86	120
160-(7/66)-Robby Reed becomes Plastic Man in this issue only; 1st S.A. app. Plastic Man; intro Marco Xavier (Martian Manhunter) & Vulture Crime Organization; ends #173	9	18	27	65	113	160
161-173: 169-Origin/1st app. Gem Girl	5	10	15	30	48	65
174-Mystery format begins.	11	22	33	78	139	200
175-1st app. Cain (House of Mystery host)	8	16	24	56	93	130
176,177	8	16	24	52	86	120
178-Neal Adams-a (2/69)	8	16	24	58	97	135
179-N. Adams/Orlando, Wrightson-a (1st pro work, 3 pgs.)	10	20	30	70	123	175
180,181,183: Wrightson-a (3,10, & 3 pgs.). 180-Last 12¢ issue; Kane/Wood-a(2). 183-Wood-a	8	16	24	52	86	120
182,184: 182-Toth-a. 184-Kane/Wood, Toth-a	6	12	18	37	59	80
185-Williamson/Kaluta-a; Howard-a (3 pgs.)	6	12	18	41	66	90
186-N. Adams-c/a; Wrightson-a (10 pgs.)	8	16	24	58	97	135
187,190: Adams-c. 187-Toth-a. 190-Toth-a(r)	5	10	15	34	55	75
188-Wrightson-a (8 & 3pgs.); Adams-c	7	14	21	45	73	100
189,192,197: Adams-c on all. 189-Wood-a(i). 192-Last 15¢-c	5	10	15	34	55	75
191-Wrightson-a (8 & 3pgs.); Adams-c	7	14	21	45	73	100
193-Wrightson-c	5	10	15	34	55	75
194-Wrightson-c; 52 pgs begin, end #203; Toth,Kirby-a	7	14	21	45	73	100
195: Wrightson-c. Swamp creature story by Wrightson similar to Swamp Thing (10 pgs.)(10/71)	9	18	27	60	100	140
196,198	5	10	15	30	48	65
199-Adams-c; Wood-a(8pgs.); Kirby-a	6	12	18	39	62	85
200-(25¢, 52 pgs.)-One third-r (3/72)	6	12	18	37	59	80
201-203-(25¢, 52 pgs.)-One third-r	4	8	12	26	41	55
204-Wrightson-c/a, 9 pgs.	4	8	12	28	44	60
205,206,208,210,212,215,216,218	3	6	9	18	27	35
207-Wrightson-c/a; Starlin, Redondo-a	4	8	12	28	44	60
209,211,213,214,217,219-Wrightson-c	4	8	12	24	37	50
220,222,223	3	6	9	16	23	30
221-Wrightson/Kaluta-a(8 pgs.)	4	8	12	26	41	55
224-229: 224-Wrightson-r from Spectre #9; Dillin/Adams-r from House of Secrets #82; begin 100 pg. issues; Phantom Stranger-r. 225,227-(100 pgs.): 225-Spectre app. 226-Wrightson/Redondo-a Phantom Stranger-r. 228-N. Adams inks; Wrightson-r. 229-Wrightson-a(r); Toth-r; last 100 pg. issue	6	12	18	37	59	80

House of Mystery (2008 series) #12 © DC

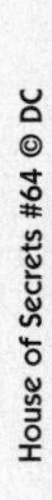
House of Secrets #64 © DC

Howard the Duck #11 © MAR

	GD 2.0	VG 4.0	FN 6.0	VF 8.0	VF/NM 9.0	NM- 9.2
230,232-235,237-250	2	4	6	11	16	20
231-Classic Wrightson-c	4	8	12	28	44	60
236-Wrightson-c; Ditko-a(p); N. Adams-i	3	6	9	20	30	40
251-254-(84 pgs.)-Adams-c. 251-Wood-a	4	8	12	22	34	45
255,256-(84 pgs.)-Wrightson-c	4	8	12	22	34	45
257-259-(84 pgs.)	3	6	9	16	23	30
260-289: 282-(68 pgs.)-Has extra story "The Computers That Saved Metropolis" Radio Shack giveaway by Jim Starlin	2	3	4	6	8	10
290-1st "I, Vampire"	3	6	9	16	22	28
291-299: 291,293,295-299- "I, Vampire"	2	4	6	9	13	16
300,319,321: Death of "I, Vampire"	2	4	6	10	14	18
301-318,320: 301-318-"I, Vampire"	2	4	6	9	13	16
Welcome to the House of Mystery (7/98, $5.95) reprints stories with new framing story by Gaiman and Aragonés						6.00

NOTE: ***Neal Adams*** *a-236i; c-175-192, 197, 199, 251-254.* ***Alcala*** *a-209, 217, 219, 224, 227.* ***M. Anderson*** *a-212; c/a-37.* ***Aparo*** *a-209.* ***Aragones*** *a-185, 186, 194, 196, 200, 202, 229, 251.* ***Baily*** *a-279p.* ***Cameron*** *a-76, 79.* ***Colan*** *a-202r.* ***Craig*** *a-263, 275, 295, 300.* ***Dillin/Adams*** *r-224.* ***Ditko*** *a-236p, 247, 254, 258, 276; c-277.* ***Drucker*** *a-37.* ***Evans*** *c-218.* ***Fradon*** *a-251.* ***Giffen*** *a-284.* ***Giunta*** *a-199, 227r.* ***Golden*** *a-257, 259.* ***Heath*** *a-194r; c-203.* ***Howard*** *a-182, 185, 187, 196, 229r, 247i, 254, 279i.* ***Kaluta*** *a-195, 200, 250r; c-200-202, 210, 212, 233, 260, 261, 263, 265, 267, 268, 273, 276, 284, 287, 288, 293-295, 300, 302, 304, 305, 309-319, 321.* ***Bob Kane*** *a-84.* ***Gil Kane*** *a-196p, 253p, 300p.* ***Kirby*** *a-194r, 199r; c-65, 76, 78, 79, 85.* ***Kubert*** *c-282, 283, 285, 286, 289-292, 297-299, 301, 303, 306-308.* ***Maneely*** *a-68, 227r.* ***Mayer*** *a-317p.* ***Meskin*** *a-52-144 (most), 195r, 224r, 229r; c-63, 66, 124, 127.* ***Mooney*** *a-24, 159, 160.* ***Moreira*** *a-3, 4, 20-50, 58, 59, 62, 68, 77, 79, 90, 108, 113, 123, 201r, 228; c-4-28, 44, 47, 50, 54, 59, 62, 64, 68, 70, 73.* ***Morrow*** *a-192, 196, 255, 320i.* ***Mortimer*** *a-204(3 pgs.).* ***Nasser*** *a-276.* ***Newton*** *a-259, 272.* ***Nino*** *a-204, 212, 213, 220, 224, 225, 245, 250, 252-256, 283.* ***Orlando*** *a-175(2 pgs.), 178, 240i; c-240, 258p, 262, 264p, 270p, 271, 272, 274, 275, 278, 296i.* ***Redondo*** *a-194, 195, 197, 202, 203, 207, 211, 214, 217, 219, 226, 227, 229, 235, 241, 287(layout), 302p, 303i, 308; c-229.* ***Reese*** *a-195, 200, 205i.* ***Rogers*** *a-254, 274, 277.* ***Roussos*** *a-65, 84, 224i.* ***Sekowsky*** *a-282p.* ***Sparling*** *a-203.* ***Starlin*** *a-207(2 pgs.), 282p; c-281.* ***Leonard Starr*** *a-9.* ***Staton*** *a-300p.* ***Sutton*** *a-189, 271, 290, 291, 293, 295, 297-299, 302, 303, 306-309, 310-313i, 314.* ***Tuska*** *a-293p, 294p, 316p.* ***Wrightson*** *c-193-195, 204, 207, 209, 211, 213, 214, 217, 219, 221, 231, 236, 255, 256; r-224.*

HOUSE OF MYSTERY
DC Comics (Vertigo): Jul, 2008 - Present ($2.99)

	GD 2.0	VG 4.0	FN 6.0	VF 8.0	VF/NM 9.0	NM- 9.2
1-12,14-22: 1-Cain & Abel app.; Rossi-a/Weber-c. 9-Wrightson-a (6 pgs.). 16-Corben-a						3.00
1-Variant-c by Bernie Wrightson						5.00
13-Art by Neal Adams, Ralph Reese, Eric Powell, Sergio Aragonés						3.00
13-Variant-c by Neal Adams						5.00
... Halloween Annual #1 (12/09, $4.99) short stories by various incl. Hadley, Allred Nowlan						5.00
...: Love Stories for Dead People TPB (2009, $14.99) r/#6-10						15.00
...: Room and Boredom TPB (2008, $9.99) r/#1-5						10.00
...: The Space Between TPB (2010, $14.99) r/#11-15; sketch pages						15.00

HOUSE OF SECRETS (Combined with The Unexpected after #154)
National Periodical Publications/DC Comics: 11-12/56 - No. 80, 9-10/66; No. 81, 8-9/69 - No. 140, 2-3/76; No. 141, 8-9/76 - No. 154, 10-11/78

	GD 2.0	VG 4.0	FN 6.0	VF 8.0	VF/NM 9.0	NM- 9.2
1-Drucker-a; Moreira-c	112	224	336	952	1876	2800
2-Moreira-a	40	80	120	321	623	925
3-Kirby-c/a	35	70	105	267	514	760
4-Kirby-a	25	50	75	183	354	525
5-7	18	36	54	127	249	370
8-Kirby-a	20	40	60	142	276	410
9-11: 11-Lou Cameron-a (unsigned)	16	32	48	115	220	325
12-Kirby-c/a; Lou Cameron-a	17	34	51	122	236	350
13-15: 14-Flying saucer-c	13	26	39	90	165	240
16-20	12	24	36	82	149	215
21,22,24-30	10	20	30	73	129	185
23-1st app. Mark Merlin & begin series (8/59)	11	22	33	78	139	200
31-50: 48-Toth-a. 50-Last 10¢ issue	10	20	30	67	116	165
51-60: 58-Origin Mark Merlin	8	16	24	56	93	130
61-First Eclipso (7-8/63) and begin series	15	30	45	104	197	290
62	8	16	24	54	90	125
63-65-Toth-a on Eclipso (see Brave and the Bold #64)	6	12	18	43	69	95
66-1st Eclipso-c (also #67,70,78,79); Toth-a	8	16	24	54	90	125
67,73: 67-Toth-a on Eclipso. 73-Mark Merlin becomes Prince Ra-Man (1st app.)	6	12	18	43	69	95
68-72,74-80: 76-Prince Ra-Man vs. Eclipso. 80-Eclipso, Prince Ra-Man end	6	12	18	39	62	85
81-Mystery format begins; 1st app. Abel (House Of Secrets host); (cameo in DC Special #4)	11	22	33	78	139	200
82-84: 82-Neal Adams-c(i)	7	14	21	45	73	100
85,90: 85-N. Adams-a(i). 90-Buckler (early work)/N. Adams-a(i)	7	14	21	47	76	105
86,88,89,91	6	12	18	39	62	85
87-Wrightson & Kaluta-a	7	14	21	49	80	110
92-1st app. Swamp Thing-c/story (8 pgs.)(6-7/71) by Berni Wrightson(p) w/JeffJones/Kaluta/Weiss ink assists; classic-c.	48	96	144	384	742	1100
93,94,96-(52 pgs.)-Wrightson-c. 94-Wrightson-a(i); 96-Wood-a	6	12	18	41	66	90
95,97,98-(52 pgs.)	5	10	15	32	51	70
99-Wrightson splash pg.	4	8	12	28	44	60
100-Classic Wrightson-c	7	14	21	45	73	100
101,102,104,105,108-111,113-120	3	6	9	16	23	30
103,106,107-Wrightson-c	4	8	12	26	41	55
112-Grey tone-c	3	6	9	18	27	35
121-133	2	4	6	10	14	18
134-136,139-Wrightson-a	3	6	9	16	23	30
137,138,141-153	2	4	6	8	10	12
140-1st solo origin of the Patchworkman (see Swamp Thing #3)	3	6	9	16	23	30
154 (10-11/78, 44 pgs.) Last issue	2	4	6	9	13	16

NOTE: ***Neal Adams*** *c-81, 82, 84-88, 90, 91.* ***Alcala*** *a-104-107.* ***Anderson*** *a-91. Aparo a-93, 97, 105.* ***B. Bailey*** *a-107.* ***Cameron*** *a-13, 15.* ***Colan*** *a-63.* ***Ditko*** *a-139p, 148.* ***Elias*** *a-58.* ***Evans*** *a-118.* ***Finlay*** *a-7r(Real Fact?).* ***Glanzman*** *a-91.* ***Golden*** *a-151.* ***Heath*** *a-31.* ***Heck*** *a-85.* ***Kaluta*** *a-87, 98, 99; c-98, 99, 101, 102, 105, 149, 151, 154.* ***Bob Kane*** *a-18, 21.* ***G. Kane*** *a-85p.* ***Kirby*** *c-3, 11, 12.* ***Kubert*** *a-39.* ***Meskin*** *a-2-68 (most), 94r; c-55-60.* ***Moreira*** *a-7, 8, 51, 54, 102-104, 106, 108, 113, 116, 118, 121, 123, 127; c-1, 2, 4-10, 13-20.* ***Morrow*** *a-86, 89, 90; c-89, 146-148.* ***Nino*** *a-101, 103, 106, 109, 115, 117, 126, 128, 131, 147, 153.* ***Redondo*** *a-95, 99, 102, 104p, 113, 116, 134, 136, 139, 140.* ***Reese*** *a-85.* ***Severin*** *a-91.* ***Starlin*** *c-150.* ***Sutton*** *a-154.* ***Toth*** *a-63-67, 83, 93r, 94r, 96r-98r, 123.* ***Tuska*** *a-90, 104.* ***Wrightson*** *a-134; c-92-94, 96, 100, 103, 106, 107, 135, 136, 139.*

HOUSE OF SECRETS
DC Comics (Vertigo): Oct, 1996 - No. 25, Dec, 1998 ($2.50) (Creator-owned series)

	GD 2.0	VG 4.0	FN 6.0	VF 8.0	VF/NM 9.0	NM- 9.2
1-Steven Seagle-s/Kristiansen-c/a.						3.50
2-25: 5,7-Kristiansen-c/a. 6-Fegrado-a						3.00
TPB-(1997, $14.95) r/1-5						15.00

HOUSE OF SECRETS: FACADE
DC Comics (Vertigo): 2001 - No. 2, 2001 ($5.95, limited series)

	GD 2.0	VG 4.0	FN 6.0	VF 8.0	VF/NM 9.0	NM- 9.2
1,2-Steven Seagle-s/Teddy Kristiansen-c/a.						6.00

HOUSE OF TERROR (3-D)
St. John Publishing Co.: Oct, 1953 (25¢, came w/glasses)

	GD 2.0	VG 4.0	FN 6.0	VF 8.0	VF/NM 9.0	NM- 9.2
1-Kubert, Baker-a	27	54	81	158	259	360

HOUSE OF YANG, THE (See Yang)
Charlton Comics: July, 1975 - No. 6, June, 1976; 1978

	GD 2.0	VG 4.0	FN 6.0	VF 8.0	VF/NM 9.0	NM- 9.2
1-Sanho Kim-a in all	2	4	6	13	18	22
2-6	2	4	6	8	10	12
Modern Comics #1,2(1978)						4.00

HOUSE ON THE BORDERLAND
DC Comics (Vertigo): 2000 ($29.95, hardcover, one-shot)

	GD 2.0	VG 4.0	FN 6.0	VF 8.0	VF/NM 9.0	NM- 9.2
HC-Adaptation of William Hope Hodgson book; Corben-a						30.00
SC (2003, $19.95)						20.00

HOUSE II: THE SECOND STORY
Marvel Comics: Oct, 1987 (One-shot)

	GD 2.0	VG 4.0	FN 6.0	VF 8.0	VF/NM 9.0	NM- 9.2
1-Adapts movie						2.50

HOWARD CHAYKIN'S AMERICAN FLAGG (See American Flagg!)
First Comics: V2#1, May, 1988 - V2#12, Apr, 1989 ($1.75/$1.95, Baxter paper)

	GD 2.0	VG 4.0	FN 6.0	VF 8.0	VF/NM 9.0	NM- 9.2
V2#1-9,11,12-Chaykin-c(p) in all						2.50
10-Elvis Presley photo-c						3.00

HOWARD THE DUCK (See Bizarre Adventures #34, Crazy Magazine, Fear, Man-Thing, Marvel Treasury Edition & Sensational She-Hulk #14-17)
Marvel Comics Group: Jan, 1976 - No. 31, May, 1979; No. 32, Jan, 1986; No. 33, Sept, 1986

	GD 2.0	VG 4.0	FN 6.0	VF 8.0	VF/NM 9.0	NM- 9.2
1-Brunner-c/a; Spider-Man x-over (low distr.)	4	8	12	22	34	45
2-Brunner-c/a	2	4	6	11	16	20
3,4-(Regular 25¢ edition). 3-Buscema-a(p), (7/76)	2	4	6	8	11	14
3,4-(30¢-c, limited distribution)	3	6	9	16	22	28
5	2	4	6	8	11	14
6-11: 8-Howard The Duck for president. 9-1st Sgt. Preston Dudley of RCMP. 10-Spider-Man-c/sty	1	2	3	5	7	9
12-1st brief app. Kiss (3/77)	4	8	12	22	34	45
13-(30¢-c) 1st full app. Kiss (6/77); Daimon Hellstrom app. plus cameo of Howard as Son of Satan	4	8	12	24	37	50
13-(35¢-c, limited distribution)	9	18	27	65	113	160
14-32: 14-17-(Regular 30¢-c). 14-Howard as Son of Satan-c/story; Son of Satan app. 16-Album issue; 3 pgs. comics. 22,23-Man-Thing-c/stories; Star Wars parody. 30,32-P. Smith-a						6.00
14-17-(35¢-c, limited distribution)	3	6	9	14	20	25
33-Last issue; low print run	1	2	3	5	6	8
Annual 1(1977, 52 pgs.)-Mayerik-a	2	3	4	6	8	10
... Omnibus HC (2008, $99.99, dustjacket) r/#1-33 & Annual #1, Adventure Into Fear #19,						

Howdy Doody #3 © Cal. Nat. Prods.

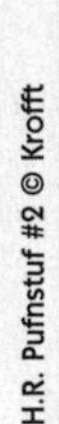
H.R. Pufnstuf #2 © Krofft

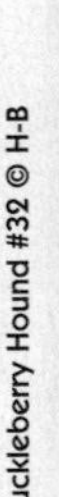
Huckleberry Hound #32 © H-B

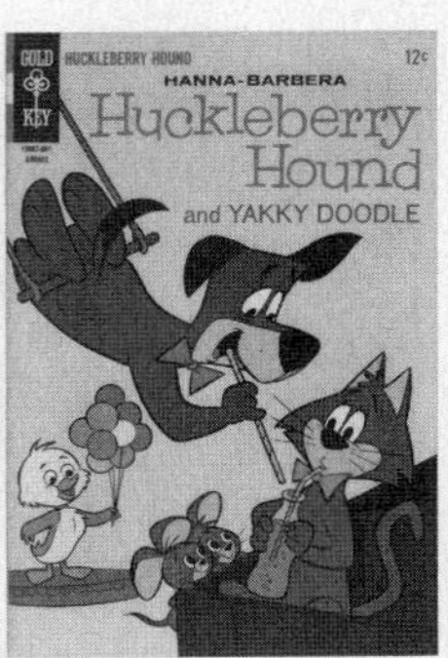

	GD 2.0	VG 4.0	FN 6.0	VF 8.0	VF/NM 9.0	NM- 9.2

Man-Thing #1, Giant-Size Man-Thing #4&5, Marvel Treasury Ed. #12, Marvel Team-Up #96 and FOOM #15; Gerber foreword; creator interviews; bonus art; 2 covers 100.00

NOTE: ***Austin** c-29i. **Bolland** c-33. **Brunner** a-1p, 2p; c-1, 2. **Buckler** c-3p. **Buscema** a-3p. **Colan** a(p)-4-15, 17-20, 24-27, 30, 31; c(p)-4-31, Annual 1p. **Leialoha** a-1-13i; c(i)-3-5, 8-11. **Mayerik** a-22, 23, 33. **Paul Smith** a-30p, 32. Man-Thing app. in #22, 23.*

HOWARD THE DUCK (Magazine)
Marvel Comics Group: Oct, 1979 - No. 9, Mar, 1981 (B&W, 68 pgs.)

	GD	VG	FN	VF	VF/NM	NM-
1-Art by Colan, Janson, Golden. Kidney Lady app.	2	4	6	8	10	12
2,3,5-9 (nudity in most): 2-Mayerick-c. 3-Xmas issue; Jack Davis-c; Duck World flashback. 5-Dracula app. 6-1st Street People back-up story. 7-Has pin-up by Byrne; Man-Thing-c/s (46 pgs.). 8-Batman parody w/Marshall Rogers-a; Dave Sim-a (1 pg.). 9-Marie Severin-a; John Pound painted-c						6.00
4-Beatles, John Lennon, Elvis, Kiss & Devo cameos; Hitler app.	2	4	6	9	12	15

NOTE: ***Buscema** a-4p. **Colan** a-1-5p, 7-9p. **Jack Davis** c-3. **Golden** a(p)-1, 5, 6(51pgs.). **Rogers** a-7, 8. **Simonson** a-7.*

HOWARD THE DUCK (Volume 2)
Marvel Comics: Mar, 2002 - No. 6, Aug, 2002 ($2.99)

1-Gerber-s/Winslade-a/Fabry-c 4.00
2-6: 2,4-6-Gerber-s/Winslade-a/Fabry-c. 3-Fabry-a/c 3.00
TPB (9/02, $14.99) r/#1-6 15.00

HOWARD THE DUCK (Volume 3)
Marvel Comics: Dec, 2007 - No. 4, Feb, 2008 ($2.99, limited series)

1-4-Templeton-s/Bobillo-a/c; She-Hulk app. 3.00
...: Media Duckling TPB (2008, $11.99) r/#1-4; Howard the Duck #1 (1/76) and pages from Civil War: Choosing Sides 12.00

HOWARD THE DUCK HOLIDAY SPECIAL
Marvel Comics: Feb, 1997 ($2.50, one-shot)

1-Wraparound-c; Hama-s 2.50

HOWARD THE DUCK: THE MOVIE
Marvel Comics Group: Dec, 1986 - No. 3, Feb, 1987 (Limited series)

1-3: Movie adaptation; r/Marvel Super Special 2.50

HOW BOYS AND GIRLS CAN HELP WIN THE WAR
The Parents' Magazine Institute: 1942 (10¢, one-shot)

	GD	VG	FN	VF	VF/NM	NM-
1-All proceeds used to buy war bonds	26	52	78	154	252	350

HOWDY DOODY (TV)(See Jackpot of Fun-- & Poll Parrot)
Dell Publishing Co.: 1/50 - No. 38, 7-9/56; No. 761, 1/57; No. 811, 7/57

	GD	VG	FN	VF	VF/NM	NM-
1-(Scarce)-Photo-c; 1st TV comic	80	160	240	680	1340	2000
2-Photo-c	38	76	114	294	567	840
3-5: All photo-c	22	44	66	161	311	460
6-Used in **SOTI**, pg. 309; classic-c; painted covers begin	24	48	72	175	338	500
7-10	14	28	42	102	194	285
11-20: 13-X-Mas-c	12	24	36	86	158	230
21-38, Four Color 761,811	10	20	30	73	129	185

HOW IT BEGAN
United Features Syndicate: No. 15, 1939 (one-shot)

	GD	VG	FN	VF	VF/NM	NM-
Single Series 15	34	68	102	199	325	450

HOW SANTA GOT HIS RED SUIT (See March of Comics No. 2)

HOW THE WEST WAS WON (See Movie Comics)

HOW TO DRAW FOR THE COMICS
Street and Smith: No date (1942?) (10¢, 64 pgs., B&W & color, no ads)

	GD	VG	FN	VF	VF/NM	NM-
nn-Art by Robert Winsor McCay (recreating his father's art), George Marcoux (Supersnipe artist), Vernon Greene (The Shadow artist), Jack Binder (with biog.), Thorton Fisher, Jon Small, & Jack Farr; has biographies of each artist	29	58	87	170	278	385

H. P. LOVECRAFT'S CTHULHU
Millennium Publications: Dec, 1991 - No. 3, May, 1992 ($2.50, limited series)

1-3: 1-Contains trading cards on thin stock 3.00

H. R. PUFNSTUF (TV) (See March of Comics #360)
Gold Key: Oct, 1970 - No. 8, July, 1972

	GD	VG	FN	VF	VF/NM	NM-
1-Photo-c	11	22	33	78	139	200
2-8-Photo-c on all. 6-8-Both Gold Key and Whitman editions exist	8	16	24	54	90	125

HUBERT AT CAMP MOONBEAM
Dell Publishing Co.: No. 251, Oct, 1949 (one shot)

	GD	VG	FN	VF	VF/NM	NM-
Four Color 251	7	14	21	45	73	100

HUCK & YOGI JAMBOREE (TV)
Dell Publishing Co.: Mar, 1961 ($1.00, 6-1/4x9", 116 pgs., cardboard-c, high quality paper) (B&W original material)

	GD	VG	FN	VF	VF/NM	NM-
nn (scarce)	9	18	27	63	107	150

HUCK & YOGI WINTER SPORTS (TV)
Dell Publishing Co.: No. 1310, Mar, 1962 (Hanna-Barbara) (one-shot)

	GD	VG	FN	VF	VF/NM	NM-
Four Color 1310	8	16	24	56	93	130

HUCK FINN (See The New Adventures of... & Power Record Comics)

HUCKLEBERRY FINN (Movie)
Dell Publishing Co.: No. 1114, July, 1960

	GD	VG	FN	VF	VF/NM	NM-
Four Color 1114-Photo-c	5	10	15	34	55	75

HUCKLEBERRY HOUND (See Dell Giant #31,44, Golden Picture Story Book, Kite Fun Book, March of Comics #199, 214, 235, Spotlight #1 & Whitman Comic Books)

HUCKLEBERRY HOUND (TV)
Dell/Gold Key No. 18 (10/62) on: No. 990, 5-7/59 - No. 43, 10/70 (Hanna-Barbera)

	GD	VG	FN	VF	VF/NM	NM-
Four Color 990(#1)-1st app. Huckleberry Hound, Yogi Bear, & Pixie & Dixie & Mr. Jinks	12	24	36	86	158	230
Four Color 1050,1054 (12/59)	8	16	24	58	97	135
3(1-2/60) - 7 (9-10/60), Four Color 1141 (10/60)	8	16	24	52	86	120
8-10	6	12	18	43	69	95
11,13-17 (6-8/62)	5	10	15	32	51	70
12-1st Hokey Wolf & Ding-a-Ling	6	12	18	37	59	80
18,19 (84pgs.; 18-20 titled ...Chuckleberry Tales)	8	16	24	52	86	120
20-Titled Chuckleberry Tales	5	10	15	30	48	65
21-30: 28-30-Reprints	4	8	12	24	37	50
31-43: 31,32,35,37-43-Reprints	3	6	9	20	30	40

HUCKLEBERRY HOUND (TV)
Charlton Comics: Nov, 1970 - No. 8, Jan, 1972 (Hanna-Barbera)

	GD	VG	FN	VF	VF/NM	NM-
1	5	10	15	32	51	70
2-8	3	6	9	18	27	35

HUEY, DEWEY, & LOUIE (See Donald Duck, 1938 for 1st app. Also see Mickey Mouse Magazine V4#2, V5#7 & Walt Disney's Junior Woodchucks Limited Series)

HUEY, DEWEY, & LOUIE BACK TO SCHOOL (See Dell Giant #22, 35, 49 & Dell Giants)

HUEY, DEWEY, AND LOUIE JUNIOR WOODCHUCKS (Disney)
Gold Key No. 1-61/Whitman No. 62 on: Aug, 1966 - No. 81, July, 1984
(See Walt Disney's Comics & Stories #125)

	GD	VG	FN	VF	VF/NM	NM-
1	6	12	18	41	66	90
2,3(12/68)	4	8	12	22	34	45
4,5(4/70)-r/two WDC&S D.Duck stories by Barks	3	6	9	20	30	40
6-17	3	6	9	18	27	35
18,27-30	3	6	9	15	21	26
19-23,25-New storyboarded scripts by Barks, 13-25 pgs. per issue	3	6	9	19	29	38
24,26: 26-r/Barks Donald Duck WDC&S stories	3	6	9	16	23	30
31-57,60,61: 35,41-r/Barks J.W. scripts	2	4	6	8	11	14
58,59: 58-r/Barks Donald Duck WDC&S stories	2	4	6	9	13	16
62-64 (Whitman)	2	4	6	9	13	16
65-(9/80), 66 (Pre-pack? scarce)	4	8	12	22	34	45
67 (1/81),68	2	4	6	9	13	16
67-40¢ cover variant	4	8	12	17	21	24
69-74: 72(2/82), 73(2-3/82), 74(3/82)	2	4	6	8	11	14
75-81 (all #90183; pre-pack; nd, nd code; scarce): 75(4/83), 76(5/83), 77(7/83), 78(8/83), 79(4/84), 80(5/84), 81(7/84)	3	6	9	14	20	25

HUGGA BUNCH (TV)
Marvel Comics (Star Comics): Oct, 1986 - No. 6, Aug, 1987

1-6 4.00

HULK (Magazine)(Formerly The Rampaging Hulk)(Also see The Incredible Hulk)
Marvel Comics: No. 10, Aug., 1978 - No. 27, June, 1981 ($1.50)

	GD	VG	FN	VF	VF/NM	NM-
10-18: 10-Bill Bixby interview. 11-Moon Knight begins. 12-15,17,18-Moon Knight stories. 12-Lou Ferrigno interview.	2	4	6	10	14	18
19-27: 20-Moon Knight story. 23-Last full color issue; Banner is attacked. 24-Part color, Lou Ferrigno interview. 25-Part color. 26,27-are B&W	2	4	6	9	12	15

NOTE: *#10-20 have fragile spines which split easily. **Alcala** a(i)-15, 17-20, 22, 24-27. **Buscema** a-23; c-26. **Chaykin** a-21-25. **Colan** a(p)-11, 19, 24-27. **Jusko** painted c-12. **Nebres** a-16. **Severin** a-19i. Moon Knight by **Sienkiewicz** in 13-15, 17, 18, 20. **Simonson** a-27; c-23. Dominic Fortune appears in #21-24.*

HULK (Becomes Incredible Hulk Vol. 2 with issue #12) (Also see Marvel Age Hulk)

Hulk (2008 series) #13 © MAR

Hulk: The Movie Adaptation © MAR

Human Target #4 © DC

	GD	VG	FN	VF	VF/NM	NM-
	2.0	4.0	6.0	8.0	9.0	9.2

Marvel Comics: Apr, 1999 - No. 11, Feb, 2000 ($2.99/$1.99)

1-($2.99) Byrne-s/Garney-a 5.00
1-Variant-c 9.00
1-DFE Remarked-c 50.00
1-Gold foil variant 10.00
2-7-($1.99): 2-Two covers. 5-Art by Jurgens, Buscema & Texeira. 7-Avengers app. 4.00
8-Hulk battles Wolverine 7.00
9-11: 11-She-Hulk app. 3.00
1999 Annual ($3.50) Chapter One story; Byrne-s/Weeks-a 3.50
Hulk Vs. The Thing (12/99, $3.99, TPB) reprints their notable battles 4.00

HULK (Also see Fall of the Hulks and King-Size Hulk)
Marvel Comics: Mar, 2008 - Present ($2.99)

1-Red Hulk app.; Abomination killed; Loeb-s/McGuinness-a/c 5.00
1-Variant-c by Acuña 10.00
1-Variant-c with Incredible Hulk #1 cover swipe by McGuinness 20.00
1,2-2nd printings with wraparound McGuinness variant-c 3.00
2-20: 2-Iron Man app.; Rick Jones becomes the new Abomination. 4,6-Red Hulk vs. green Hulk; two covers (each Hulk); Thor app. 7-9-Art Adams & Cho-a (2 covers) 10-Defenders re-form. 14,15-X-Force, Elektra & Deadpool app. 15-Red She-Hulk app. 19,20-Fall of the Hulks x-over. 199-FF app. 4.00
2-9: 2-Variant-c by Djurdjevic. 3-Var-c by Finch. 5-Var-c by Coipel. 6,7-Var-c by Turner 8-Var-c by Sal Buscema. 9-Two covers w/Hulks as Santa 6.00
... Family: Green Genes 1 (2/09, $4.99) new She-Hulk, Scorpion, Skaar & Mr. Fixit stories 5.00
... Monster-Size Special (12/08, $3.99) monster-themed stories by Niles, David & others 4.00
...: Raging Thunder 1 (8/08, $3.99) Hulk vs. Thundra; Breitweiser-a; r/FF #133; Land-c 4.00
... Vs. Fin Fang Foom (2/08, $3.99) new re-telling of first meeting; r/Strange Tales #89 4.00
... Vs. Hercules (6/08, $3.99) Djurdjevic-c; new story w/art by various; r/Tales To Ast. #79 4.00
...: Winter Guard (2/10, $3.99) Darkstar, Crimson Dynamo app. Steve Ellis-a/c 4.00
Hulk 100 Project (2008, $10.00, SC, charity book for the HERO Initiative) collection of 100 variant covers by Adams, Romita Sr. & Jr., Cho, McGuinness and more 10.00

HULK AND POWER PACK (All ages series)
Marvel Comics: May, 2007 - No. 4, Aug, 2007 ($2.99, limited series)

1-4-Sumerak-s. 1,2,4-Williams-a. 1-Absorbing Man app. 3-Kuhn-a; Abomination app. 3.00
...: Pack Smash! (2007, $6.99, digest) r/#1-4 7.00

HULK & THING: HARD KNOCKS
Marvel Comics: Nov, 2004 - No. 4, Feb, 2005 ($3.50, limited series)

1-4-Bruce Jones-s/Jae Lee-a/c 3.50
TPB (2005, $13.99) r/#1-4 and Giant-Size Super-Stars #1 14.00

HULK: BROKEN WORLDS
Marvel Comics: May, 2009 -No. 2, July, 2009 ($3.99, limited series)

1,2-Short stories of alternate world Hulks by various, incl. Trimpe, David, Warren 4.00

HULK CHRONICLES: WWH
Marvel Comics: Oct, 2008 - No. 6, Mar, 2009 ($4.99, limited series)

1-6-Reprints stories from World War Hulk x-over. 1-R/Inc. Hulk #106 & WWH Prologue 5.00

HULK: DESTRUCTION
Marvel Comics: Sept, 2005 - No. 4, Dec, 2005 ($2.99, limited series)

1-4-Origin of the Abomination; Peter David-s/Jim Muniz-a 3.00

HULK: FUTURE IMPERFECT
Marvel Comics: Jan, 1993 - No. 2, Dec, 1992 (In error) ($5.95, 52 pgs., squarebound, limited series)

1,2: Embossed-c; Peter David story & George Perez-c/a. 1-1st app. Maestro.
1 2 3 5 6 8

HULK: GRAY
Marvel Comics: Dec, 2003 - No. 6, Apr, 2004 ($3.50, limited series)

1-6-Hulk's origin & early days; Loeb-s/Sale-a/c 3.50
HC (2004, $21.99, with dust jacket) oversized r/#1-6 22.00
SC (2005, $19.99) r/#1-6 20.00

HULK: NIGHTMERICA
Marvel Comics: Aug, 2003 - No. 6, May, 2004 ($2.99, limited series)

1-6-Brian Ashmore painted-a/c 3.00

HULK/ PITT
Marvel Comics: 1997 ($5.99, one-shot)

1-David-s/Keown-c/a 6.00

HULK SMASH
Marvel Comics: Mar, 2001 - No. 2, Apr, 2001 ($2.99, limited series)

1,2-Ennis-s/McCrea & Janson-a/Nowlan painted-c 3.00

	GD	VG	FN	VF	VF/NM	NM-
	2.0	4.0	6.0	8.0	9.0	9.2

HULK: THE MOVIE
Marvel Comics

...Adaptation (8/03, $3.50) Bruce Jones-s/Bagley-a/Keown-c 3.50
TPB (2003, $12.99) r/Adaptation, Ultimates #5, Inc. Hulk #34, Ult. Marvel Team-Up #2&3 13.00

HULK 2099
Marvel Comics: Dec, 1994 - No. 10, Sept, 1995 ($1.50/$1.95)

1-($2.50)-Green foil-c 3.00
2-10: 2-A. Kubert-c 2.50

HULK/WOLVERINE: 6 HOURS
Marvel Comics: Mar, 2003 - No. 4, May, 2003 ($2.99, limited series)

1-4-Bruce Jones-s/Scott Kolins-a; Bisley-c 3.00
Hulk Legends Vol. 1: Hulk/Wolverine: 6 Hours (2003, $13.99, TPB) r/#1-4 & 1st Wolverine app. from Incredible Hulk #181 14.00

HUMAN DEFENSE CORPS
DC Comics: Jul, 2003 - No. 6, Dec, 2003 ($2.50, limited series)

1-6-Ty Templeton-s/Sauve, Jr & Vlasco-a. 1-Lois Lane app. 2.50

HUMAN FLY
I.W. Enterprises/Super: 1963 - 1964 (Reprints)

I.W. Reprint #1-Reprints Blue Beetle #44('46) 2 4 6 13 18 22
Super Reprint #10-R/Blue Beetle #46('47) 2 4 6 13 18 22

HUMAN FLY, THE
Marvel Comics Group: Sept, 1977 - No. 19, Mar, 1979

1,2,9,19: 1,2-(Regular 30¢-c). 1-Origin; Spider-Man x-over. 2-Ghost Rider app. 9-Daredevil x-over; Byrne-c(p). 19-Last issue 2 3 4 6 8 10
1,2-(35¢-c, limited distribution) 3 6 9 20 30 40
3-8,10-18 5.00
NOTE: *Austin c-4i, 9i.* ***Elias*** *a-1, 3p, 4p, 7p, 10-12p, 15p, 18p, 19p.* ***Layton*** *c-19.*

HUMANKIND
Image Comics (Top Cow): Sept, 2004 - No. 5, Mar, 2005 ($2.99, limited series)

1-5-Tony Daniel-a. 1-Three covers by Daniel, Silvestri, and Land 3.00

HUMAN RACE, THE
DC Comics: May, 2005 - No. 7, Nov, 2005 ($2.99, limited series)

1-7-Raab-s/Justiniano-a/c 3.00

HUMAN TARGET
DC Comics (Vertigo): Apr, 1999 - No. 4, July, 1999 ($2.95, limited series)

1-4-Milligan-s/Bradstreet-c/Biukovic-a 3.00
TPB (2000, $12.95) new Bradstreet-c 13.00
...: Chance Meetings TPB (2010, $14.99) r/#1-4 and Human Target: Final Cut GN 15.00

HUMAN TARGET
DC Comics (Vertigo): Oct, 2003 - No. 21, June, 2005 ($2.95)

1-21: 1-5-Milligan-s/Pulido-a/c. 6-Chiang-a 3.00
...: Living in Amerika TPB (2004, $14.95) r/#6-10; Chiang sketch pages 15.00
...: Strike Zones TPB (2004, $9.95) r/#1-5 10.00

HUMAN TARGET: FINAL CUT
DC Comics (Vertigo): 2002 ($29.95/$19.95, graphic novel)

Hardcover (2002, $29.95) Milligan-s/Pulido-a/c 30.00
Softcover (2003, $19.95) 20.00

HUMAN TARGET SPECIAL (TV)
DC Comics: Nov, 1991 ($2.00, 52 pgs., one-shot)

1 3.00

HUMAN TORCH, THE (Red Raven #1)(See All-Select, All Winners, Marvel Mystery, Men's Adventures, Mystic Comics (2nd series), Sub-Mariner, USA & Young Men)
Timely/Marvel Comics (TP 2,3/TCI 4-9/SePI 10/SnPC 11-25/CnPC 26-35/Atlas Comics (CPC 36-38)): No. 2, Fall, 1940 - No. 15, Spring, 1944; No. 16, Fall, 1944 - No. 35, Mar, 1949 (Becomes Love Tales #36 on); No. 36, April, 1954 - No. 38, Aug, 1954

2(#1)-Intro & Origin Toro; The Falcon, The Fiery Mask, Mantor the Magician, & Microman only app.; Human Torch by Burgos, Sub-Mariner by Everett begin (origin of each in text)
3200 6400 9600 24,000 44,000 64,000
3(#2)-40 pg. H.T. story; H.T. & S.M. battle over who is best artist in text-Everett or Burgos
568 1136 1704 4146 7323 10,500
4(#3)-Origin The Patriot in text; last Everett Sub-Mariner; Sid Greene-a
438 876 1314 3197 5649 8100
5(#4)-The Patriot app; Angel x-over in Sub-Mariner (Summer, 1941); 1st Nazi war-c this title
377 754 1131 2639 4620 6600
5-Human Torch battles Sub-Mariner (Fall, '41); 60 pg. story
595 1190 1785 4350 7675 11,000

Human Torch #28 © MAR

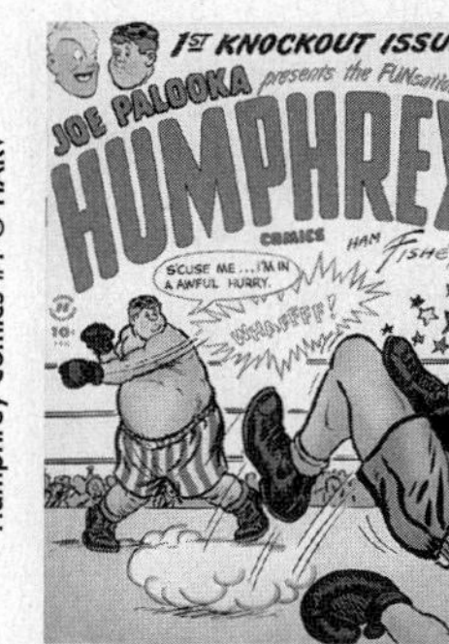

Humphrey Comics #1 © HARV

Huntress #4 © DC

	GD 2.0	VG 4.0	FN 6.0	VF 8.0	VF/NM 9.0	NM- 9.2
6,9	300	600	900	1950	3375	4800
7-1st Japanese war-c	300	600	900	1980	3440	4900
8-Human Torch battles Sub-Mariner; 52 pg. story; Wolverton-a, 1 pg.	400	800	1200	2800	4900	7000
10-Human Torch battles Sub-Mariner, 45 pg. story; Wolverton-a, 1 pg.	320	640	960	2244	3920	5600
11,13-15: 14-1st Atlas Globe logo (Winter, 1943-44; see All Winners #11 also)	239	478	717	1530	2615	3700
12-Classic-c	371	742	1113	2600	4550	6500
16-20: 20-Last War issue	161	322	483	1030	1765	2500
21,22,24-30: 27-2nd app. (1st-c) Asbestos Lady (see Capt. America Comics #63 for 1st app.)	139	278	417	883	1517	2150
23 (Sum/46)-Becomes Junior Miss 24? Classic Schomburg Robot-c	168	338	504	1075	1838	2600
31,32: 31-Namora x-over in Sub-Mariner (also #30); last Toro. 32-Sungirl, Namora app.; Sungirl-c	123	246	369	787	1344	1900
33-Capt. America x-over	127	254	381	807	1391	1975
34-Sungirl solo	116	232	348	742	1271	1800
35-Captain America & Sungirl app. (1949)	123	246	369	787	1344	1900
36-38(1954)-Sub-Mariner in all	103	206	309	659	1130	1600

NOTE: ***Ayers*** *Human Torch in 36(3).* ***Brodsky*** *c-25, 31-33?, 37, 38.* ***Burgos*** *c-36.* ***Everett*** *a-1-3, 27, 28, 30, 37, 38.* ***Powell*** *a-36(Sub-Mariner).* ***Schomburg*** *c-1-3, 5-8, 10-23.* ***Sekowsky*** *c-28, 34?, 35?* ***Shores*** *c-24, 26, 27, 29, 30.* ***Mickey Spillane*** *text 4-6. Bondage c-2, 12, 19.*

HUMAN TORCH, THE (Also see Avengers West Coast, Fantastic Four, The Invaders, Saga of the Original... & Strange Tales #101)
Marvel Comics Group: Sept, 1974 - No. 8, Nov, 1975

	GD	VG	FN	VF	VF/NM	NM-
1: 1-8-r/stories from Strange Tales #101-108	3	6	9	14	20	25
2-8: 1st H.T. title since G.A. 7-vs. Sub-Mariner	2	4	6	9	12	15

NOTE: *Golden Age & Silver Age Human Torch-r #1-8.* ***Ayers*** *r-6, 7.* ***Kirby/Ayers*** *r-1-5, 8.*

HUMAN TORCH (From the Fantastic Four)
Marvel Comics: June, 2003 - No. 12, Jun, 2004 ($2.50/$2.99)

	GD	VG	FN	VF	VF/NM	NM-
1-7-Skottie Young-c/a; Karl Kesel-s						2.50
8-12-($2.99) 8,10-Dodd-a. 9-Young-a. 11-Porter-a. 12-Medina-a						3.00
... Vol. 1: Burn TPB (2005, $7.99, digest size) r/#1-6						8.00

HUMAN TORCH COMICS 70TH ANNIVERSARY SPECIAL
Marvel Comics: July, 2009 ($3.99, one-shot)

	GD	VG	FN	VF	VF/NM	NM-
1-Covers by Granov and Martin; new story and r/1st app Toro from Human Torch #2						4.00

HUMBUG (Satire by Harvey Kurtzman)
Humbug Publications: Aug, 1957 - No. 9, May, 1958; No. 10, June, 1958; No. 11, Oct, 1958

	GD	VG	FN	VF	VF/NM	NM-
1-Wood-a (intro pgs. only)	27	54	81	158	259	360
2	15	30	45	85	130	175
3-9: 8-Elvis in Jailbreak Rock	14	28	42	76	108	140
10,11-Magazine format. 10-Photo-c	15	30	45	90	140	190
Bound Volume(#1-9)(extremely rare)	65	130	195	416	708	1000

NOTE: ***Davis*** *a-1-11.* ***Elder*** *a-2-4, 6-9, 11.* ***Heath*** *a-2, 4-8, 10.* ***Jaffee*** *a-2, 4-9.* ***Kurtzman*** *a-11.*

HUMDINGER (Becomes White Rider and Super Horse #3 on?)
Novelty Press/Premium Group: May-June, 1946 - V2#2, July-Aug, 1947

	GD	VG	FN	VF	VF/NM	NM-
1-Jerkwater Line, Mickey Starlight by Don Rico, Dink begin	36	72	108	211	343	475
2	16	32	48	94	147	200
3-6, V2#1,2	12	24	36	69	97	125

HUMONGOUS MAN
Alternative Press (Ikon Press): Sept, 1997 -No. 3 ($2.25, B&W)

	GD	VG	FN	VF	VF/NM	NM-
1-3-Stepp & Harrison-c/s/a.						2.50

HUMOR (See All Humor Comics)

HUMPHREY COMICS (Joe Palooka Presents...; also see Joe Palooka)
Harvey Publications: Oct, 1948 - No. 22, Apr, 1952

	GD	VG	FN	VF	VF/NM	NM-
1-Joe Palooka's pal (r); (52 pgs.)-Powell-a	14	28	42	80	115	150
2,3: Powell-a	9	18	27	47	61	75
4-Boy Heroes app.; Powell-a	9	18	27	50	65	80
5-8,10: 5,6-Powell-a. 7-Little Dot app.	8	16	24	40	50	60
9-Origin Humphrey	9	18	27	47	61	75
11-22	7	14	21	37	46	55

HUNCHBACK OF NOTRE DAME, THE
Dell Publishing Co.: No. 854, Oct, 1957 (one shot)

	GD	VG	FN	VF	VF/NM	NM-
Four Color 854-Movie, photo-c	12	24	36	85	155	225

HUNGER, THE
Speakeasy Comics: May, 2005 - Present ($2.99)

	GD	VG	FN	VF	VF/NM	NM-
1-Andy Bradshaw-s/a; Eric Powell-c						3.00

HUNGER DOGS, THE (See DC Graphic Novel #4)

HUNK
Charlton Comics: Aug, 1961 - No. 11, 1963

	GD	VG	FN	VF	VF/NM	NM-
1	4	8	12	24	37	50
2-11	3	6	9	14	20	25

HUNTED (Formerly My Love Memoirs)
Fox Features Syndicate: No. 13, July, 1950; No. 2, Sept, 1950

	GD	VG	FN	VF	VF/NM	NM-
13(#1)-Used in **SOTI**, pg. 42 & illo. "Treating police contemptuously" (lower left); Hollingsworth bondage-c	36	72	108	214	347	480
2	17	34	51	100	158	215

HUNTER-KILLER
Image Comics (Top Cow): Nov, 2004 - No. 12, Mar, 2007 ($2.99)

	GD	VG	FN	VF	VF/NM	NM-
0-(11/04, 25¢) Prelude with Silvestri sketch page and Waid afterword						2.25
1-12: 1-(3/05, $2.99) Waid-s/Silvestri-a; four covers. 2-Linsner variant-c						3.00
... Collected Edition Vol. 1 (9/05, $4.99) r/#0-3						5.00
...Dossier 1 (9/05, $2.99) character profiles with art by various; Migliari-c						3.00
... Volume 1 TPB (1/08, $24.99) r/#0-12; Dossier and Script Book; variant covers						25.00

HUNTER: THE AGE OF MAGIC (See Books of Magic)
DC Comics (Vertigo): Sept, 2001 - No. 25, Sept, 2003 ($2.50/$2.75)

	GD	VG	FN	VF	VF/NM	NM-
1-25: Horrocks-s/Case-a. 1-8-Bolton-c. 14-Begin $2.75-c. 19-Bachalo-c						2.75

HUNTRESS, THE (See All-Star Comics #69, Batman Family, DC Super Stars #17, Detective #652, Infinity, Inc. #1 & Wonder Woman #271)
DC Comics: Apr, 1989 - No. 19, Oct, 1990 ($1.00, mature)

	GD	VG	FN	VF	VF/NM	NM-
1-16: Staton-c/a(p) in all						2.50
17-19-Batman-c/stories						3.00
...: Darknight Daughter TPB (2006, $19.99) r/origin & early apps. in DC Super Stars #17, Batman Family #18-20 & Wonder Woman #271-287,289,290,294,295; Bolland-c						20.00

HUNTRESS, THE
DC Comics: June, 1994 - No. 4, Sept, 1994 ($1.50, limited series)

	GD	VG	FN	VF	VF/NM	NM-
1-4-Netzer-c/a: 2-Batman app.						2.50

HUNTRESS: YEAR ONE
DC Comics: Early July, 2008 - No. 6, Late Sept, 2008 ($2.99, limited series)

	GD	VG	FN	VF	VF/NM	NM-
1-6-Origin re-told; Cliff Richards-a/Ivory Madison-s						3.00
TPB (2009, $17.99) r/#1-6; intro. by Paul Levitz						18.00

HURRICANE COMICS
Cambridge House: 1945 (52 pgs.)

	GD	VG	FN	VF	VF/NM	NM-
1-(Humor, funny animal)	23	46	69	136	223	310

HYBRIDS
Continunity Comics: Jan, 1994 ($2.50, one-shot)

	GD	VG	FN	VF	VF/NM	NM-
1-Neal Adams-c(p) & part-a(i); embossed-c.						3.50

HYBRIDS DEATHWATCH 2000
Continuity Comics: Apr, 1993 - No. 3, Aug, 1993 ($2.50)

	GD	VG	FN	VF	VF/NM	NM-
0-(Giveaway)-Foil-c; Neal Adams-c(i) & plots (also #1,2)						3.50
1-3: 1-Polybagged w/card; die-cut-c. 2-Thermal-c. 3-Polybagged w/card; indestructible-c; Adams plot						3.00

HYBRIDS ORIGIN
Continunity Comics: 1993 - No. 5, Jan, 1994 ($2.50)

	GD	VG	FN	VF	VF/NM	NM-
1-5: 2,3-Neal Adams-c. 4,5-Valeria the She-Bat app. Adams-c(i)						3.25

HYDE
IDW Publ.: Oct, 2004 ($7.49, one-shot)

	GD	VG	FN	VF	VF/NM	NM-
1-Steve Niles-s/Nick Stakal						7.50

HYDE-25
Harris Publications: Apr, 1995 ($2.95, one-shot)

	GD	VG	FN	VF	VF/NM	NM-
0-coupon for poster; r/Vampirella's 1st app.						3.00

HYDROMAN (See Heroic Comics)

HYPERKIND (See Razorline)
Marvel Comics: Sept, 1993 - No. 9, May, 1994 ($1.75/$1.95)

	GD	VG	FN	VF	VF/NM	NM-
1-($2.50)-Foil embossed-c; by Clive Barker						3.00
2-9						2.50

HYPERKIND UNLEASED
Marvel Comics: Aug, 1994 ($2.95, 52 pgs., one-shot)

	GD	VG	FN	VF	VF/NM	NM-
1						3.00

HYPER MYSTERY COMICS
Hyper Publications: May, 1940 - No. 2, June, 1940 (68 pgs.)

I Am Legion #1 © Humanoids

Icon #15 © Milestone Media

Identity Crisis #2 © DC

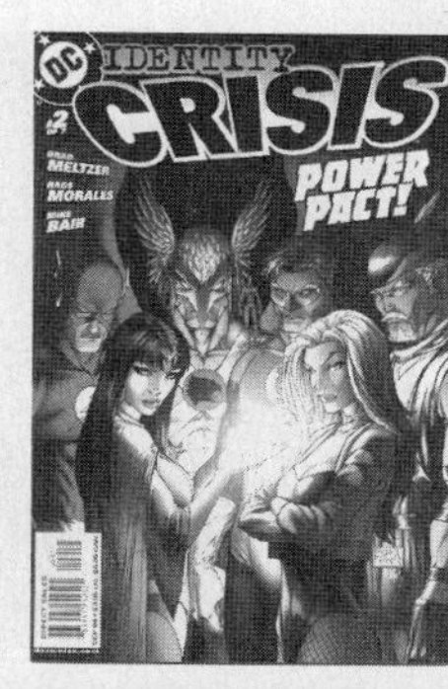

	GD 2.0	VG 4.0	FN 6.0	VF 8.0	VF/NM 9.0	NM- 9.2
1-Hyper, the Phenomenal begins; Calkins-a	206	412	618	1318	2259	3200
2	103	206	309	659	1130	1600

HYPERSONIC
Dark Horse Comics: Nov, 1997 - No. 4, Feb, 1998 ($2.95, limited series)

	GD	VG	FN	VF	VF/NM	NM-
1-4: Abnett & White/Erskine-a						3.00

I AIM AT THE STARS (Movie)
Dell Publishing Co.: No. 1148, Nov-Jan/1960-61 (one-shot)

	GD	VG	FN	VF	VF/NM	NM-
Four Color 1148-The Werner Von Braun Sty-photo-c	7	14	21	47	76	105

I AM COYOTE (See Eclipse Graphic Album Series & Eclipse Magazine #2)

I AM LEGEND
Eclipse Books: 1991 - No. 4, 1991 ($5.95, B&W, squarebound, 68 pgs.)

	GD	VG	FN	VF	VF/NM	NM-
1-4: Based on 1954 novel by Richard Matheson						6.00

I AM LEGION (English version of French graphic novel Je Suis Légion)
Devils Due Publishing: Jan, 2009 - No. 6, July, 2009 ($3.50)

	GD	VG	FN	VF	VF/NM	NM-
1-6-John Cassaday-a/Fabien Nury-s; two covers						3.50

IBIS, THE INVINCIBLE (See Fawcett Miniatures, Mighty Midget & Whiz)
Fawcett Publications: 1942 (Fall?); #2, Mar.,1943; #3, Wint, 1945 - #5, Fall, 1946; #6, Spring, 1948

	GD	VG	FN	VF	VF/NM	NM-
1-Origin Ibis; Raboy-c; on sale 1/2/43	232	464	696	1485	2543	3600
2-Bondage-c (on sale 2/5/43)	100	200	300	635	1093	1550
3-Wolverton-a #3-6 (4 pgs. each)	73	146	219	464	800	1135
4-6: 5-Bondage-c	49	98	147	309	522	735

NOTE: ***Mac Raboy c(p)-3-5. Schaffenberger c-6.***

I-BOTS (See Isaac Asimov's I-BOTS)

ICE AGE ON THE WORLD OF MAGIC: THE GATHERING (See Magic The Gathering)

ICE KING OF OZ, THE (See First Comics Graphic Novel #13)

ICEMAN (Also see The Champions & X-Men #94)
Marvel Comics Group: Dec, 1984 - No. 4, June, 1985 (Limited series)

	GD	VG	FN	VF	VF/NM	NM-
1,2,4: Zeck covers on all						4.00
3-The Defenders, Champions (Ghost Rider) & the original X-Men x-over						5.00

ICEMAN (X-Men)
Marvel Comics: Dec, 2001 - No. 4, Mar, 2002 ($2.50, limited series)

	GD	VG	FN	VF	VF/NM	NM-
1-4-Abnett & Lanning-s/Kerschl-a						3.00

ICON
DC Comics (Milestone): May, 1993 - No. 42, Feb, 1997($1.50/$1.75/$2.50)

	GD	VG	FN	VF	VF/NM	NM-
1-($2.95)-Collector's Edition polybagged w/poster & trading card (direct sale only)						3.00
1-24,30-42: 9-Simonson-c. 15,16-Worlds Collide Pt. 4 & 11. 15-Superboy app. 16-Superman-c/story. 40-Vs. Blood Syndicate						2.50
25-($2.95, 52 pgs.)						3.00
...A Hero's Welcome SC (2009, $19.99) r/#1-8; intro. by Reginald Hudlin						20.00

IDAHO
Dell Publishing Co.: June-Aug, 1963 - No. 8, July-Sept, 1965

	GD	VG	FN	VF	VF/NM	NM-
1	3	6	9	17	25	32
2-8: 5-7-Painted-c	2	4	6	9	13	16

IDEAL (... a Classical Comic) (2nd Series) (Love Romances No. 6 on)
Timely Comics: July, 1948 - No. 5, March, 1949 (Feature length stories)

	GD	VG	FN	VF	VF/NM	NM-
1-Antony & Cleopatra	37	74	111	222	361	500
2-The Corpses of Dr. Sacotti	31	62	93	186	303	420
3-Joan of Arc; used in **SOTI**, pg. 310 'Boer War'	29	58	87	172	281	390
4-Richard the Lion-hearted; titled "...the World's Greatest Comics"; The Witness story	40	80	120	246	411	575
5-Ideal Love & Romance; change to love; photo-c	20	40	60	117	189	260

IDEAL COMICS (1st Series) (Willie Comics No. 5 on)
Timely Comics (MgPC): Fall, 1944 - No. 4, Spring, 1946

	GD	VG	FN	VF	VF/NM	NM-
1-Funny animal; Super Rabbit in all	26	52	78	154	252	350
2	15	30	45	85	130	175
3,4	15	30	45	83	124	165

IDEAL LOVE & ROMANCE (See Ideal, A Classical Comic)

IDEAL ROMANCE (Formerly Tender Romance)
Key Publ.: No. 3, April, 1954 - No. 8, Feb, 1955 (Diary Confessions No. 9 on)

	GD	VG	FN	VF	VF/NM	NM-
3-Bernard Baily-c	10	20	30	54	72	90
4-8: 4-6-B. Baily-c	7	14	21	37	46	55

IDEALS (Secret Stories)
Ideals Publ., USA: 1981 (68 pgs, graphic novels, 7x10", stiff-c)

	GD	VG	FN	VF	VF/NM	NM-
Captain America - Star Spangled Super Hero	3	6	9	18	27	35
Fantastic Four - Cosmic Quartet	3	6	9	18	27	35
Incredible Hulk - Gamma Powered Goliath	3	6	9	18	27	35
Spider-Man - World Famous Wall Crawler	4	8	12	22	34	45

IDENTITY CRISIS
DC Comics: Aug, 2004 - No. 7, Feb, 2005 ($3.95, limited series)

	GD	VG	FN	VF	VF/NM	NM-
1-Meltzer-s/Morales-a/Turner-c in all; Sue Dibny murdered						5.00
1-(Second printing) black-c with white sketch lines						5.00
1-(3rd & 4th) 3rd-Bloody broken photo glass image-c by Morales. 4th-Turner red-c						4.00
1-Diamond Retailer Summit Edition with sketch-c						30.00
1-Special Edition (6/09, $1.00) r/#1 with "After Watchmen" cover frame						1.00
2-7: 2-4-Deathstroke app. 5-Firestorm, Jack Drake, Capt. Boomerang killed						4.00
2-(Second printing) new Morales sketch-c						4.00
Final printings for all issues with red background variant covers						4.00
HC (2005, $24.99, dust jacket) r/series; Director's Cut extras; cover gallery; Whedon intro.; 2 covers: Direct Market-c by Turner, Bookstore-c with Morales-a						25.00
SC (2006, $14.99) r/series; Director's Cut extras; cover gallery; Whedon intro						15.00

IDENTITY DISC
Marvel Comics: Aug, 2004 - No. 5, Dec, 2004 ($2.99, limited series)

	GD	VG	FN	VF	VF/NM	NM-
1-5-Sabretooth, Bullseye, Sandman, Vulture, Deadpool, Juggernaut app.; Higgins-a						4.00
TPB (2004, $13.99) r/#1-5						14.00

I DIE AT MIDNIGHT (Vertigo V2K)
DC Comics (Vertigo): 2000 ($6.95, prestige format, one-shot)

	GD	VG	FN	VF	VF/NM	NM-
1-Kyle Baker-s/a						7.00

IDOL
Marvel Comics (Epic Comics): 1992 - No. 3, 1992 ($2.95, mini-series, 52 pgs.)

	GD	VG	FN	VF	VF/NM	NM-
Book 1-3						3.00

I DREAM OF JEANNIE (TV)
Dell Publishing Co.: Apr, 1965 - No. 2, Dec, 1966 (Photo-c)

	GD	VG	FN	VF	VF/NM	NM-
1-Barbara Eden photo-c, each	13	26	39	95	178	260
2	11	22	33	76	136	195

I FEEL SICK
Slave Labor Graphics: Aug, 1999 - No. 2, May, 2000 ($3.95, limited series)

	GD	VG	FN	VF	VF/NM	NM-
1,2-Jhonen Vasquez-s/a						4.00

I HATE GALLANT GIRL
Image Comics (Shadowline): Nov, 2008 - No. 3, Jan, 2009 ($3.50, limited series)

	GD	VG	FN	VF	VF/NM	NM-
1-3-Kat Cahill-s/Seth Damoose-a						3.50

I (heart) MARVEL
Marvel Comics: Apr, 2006; May, 2006 ($2.99, one-shots)

	GD	VG	FN	VF	VF/NM	NM-
...: Marvel AI 1 (4/06) Cebulski-s; manga art by various; Vision, Daredevil, Elektra app.						3.00
...: Masked Intentions 1 (5/06) Squirrel Girl, Speedball, Firestar, Justice app.; Nicieza-s						3.00
...: My Mutant Heart 1 (4/06) Wolverine, Cannonball, Doop app.						3.00
...: Outlaw Love 1 (4/06) Bullseye, The Answer, Ruby Thursday app.; Nicieza-s						3.00
...: Web of Romance 1 (4/06) Spider-Man, Mary Jane, The Avengers app.						3.00

ILLUMINATOR
Marvel Comics/Nelson Publ.: 1993 - No. 4, 1993 ($4.99/$2.95, 52 pgs.)

	GD	VG	FN	VF	VF/NM	NM-
1,2-($4.99) Religious themed						5.00
3,4						3.00

ILLUSTRATED GAGS
United Features Syndicate: No. 16, 1940

	GD	VG	FN	VF	VF/NM	NM-
Single Series 16	16	32	48	94	147	200

ILLUSTRATED LIBRARY OF..., AN (See Classics Illustrated Giants)

ILLUSTRATED STORIES OF THE OPERAS
Baily (Bernard) Publ. Co.: 1943 (16 pgs.; B&W) (25 cents) (cover-B&W & red)

	GD	VG	FN	VF	VF/NM	NM-
nn-(Rare)(4 diff. issues)-Faust (part-r in Cisco Kid #1), nn-Aida, nn-Carmen; Baily-a, nn-Rigoleito	55	110	165	352	601	850

ILLUSTRATED STORY OF ROBIN HOOD & HIS MERRY MEN, THE (See Classics Giveaways, 12/44)

ILLUSTRATED TARZAN BOOK, THE (See Tarzan Book)

I LOVED (Formerly Rulah; Colossal Features Magazine No. 33 on)
Fox Features Syndicate: No. 28, July, 1949 - No. 32, Mar, 1950

	GD	VG	FN	VF	VF/NM	NM-
28	14	28	42	76	108	140
29-32	10	20	30	56	76	95

I LOVE LUCY
Eternity Comics : 6/90 - No. 6, 1990;V2#1, 11/90 - No. 6, 1991 ($2.95, B&W, mini-series)

	GD	VG	FN	VF	VF/NM	NM-
1-6: Reprints 1950s comic strip; photo-c						4.00

Image United #1 © Image

I'm Dickens - He's Fenster #2 © DELL

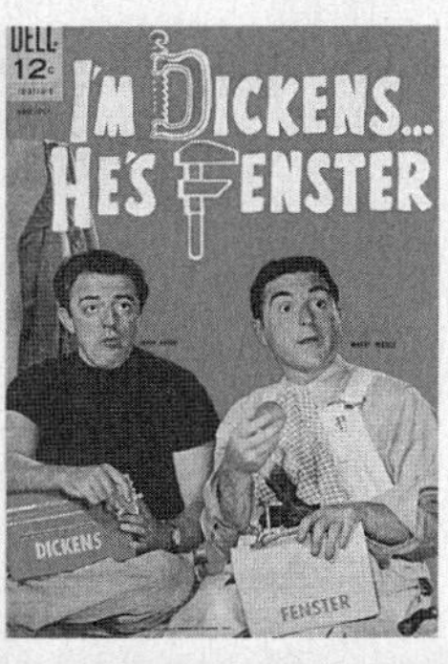

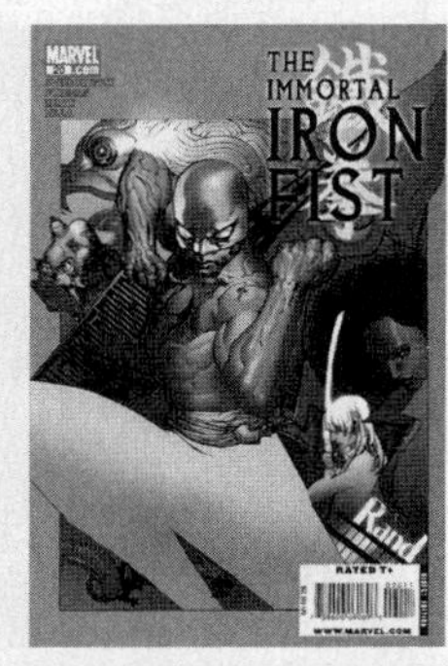

Immortal Iron Fist #20 © MAR

	GD 2.0	VG 4.0	FN 6.0	VF 8.0	VF/NM 9.0	NM- 9.2

Book II #1-6: Reprints comic strip; photo-c 4.00

...In Full Color 1 (1991, $5.95, 52 pgs.)-Reprints I Love Lucy Comics #4,5,8,16; photo-c with embossed logo (2 versions exist, one with pgs. 18 & 19 reversed, the other corrected)	1	2	3	5	6	8

...In 3-D 1 (1991, $3.95, w/glasses)-Reprints I Love Lucy Comics; photo-c; bagged 6.00

I LOVE LUCY COMICS (TV) (Also see The Lucy Show)
Dell Publishing Co.: No. 535, Feb, 1954 - No. 35, Apr-June, 1962 (Lucille Ball photo-c on all)

Four Color 535(#1)	44	88	132	352	664	975
Four Color 559(#2, 5/54)	29	58	87	213	394	575
3 (8-10/54) - 5	17	34	51	120	223	325
6-10	14	28	42	102	181	260
11-20	10	20	30	73	129	185
21-35	9	18	27	63	107	150

I LOVE NEW YORK
Linsner.com: 2002 ($2.95, B&W, one-shot)

1-Linsner-s/a; benefit book for the Sept. 11 charities 3.00

I LOVE YOU
Fawcett Publications: June, 1950 (one-shot)

1-Photo-c	15	30	45	83	124	165

I LOVE YOU (Formerly In Love)
Charlton Comics: No. 7, 9/55 - No. 121, 12/76; No. 122, 3/79 - No. 130, 5/80

7-Kirby-c; Powell-a	9	18	27	63	107	150
8-10	5	10	15	32	51	70
11-16,18-20	4	8	12	28	44	60
17-(68 pg. Giant)	7	14	21	49	80	110
21-50: 26-No Torres-a	3	6	9	21	32	42
51-59	3	6	9	16	23	30
60-(1/66)-Elvis Presley line drawn c/story	15	30	45	107	204	300
61-85	2	4	6	11	16	20
86-90,92-110: 99-David Cassidy pin-up	2	4	6	8	10	12
91-(5/71) Ditko-a (5 pgs.)	2	4	6	11	16	20
111-113,115-130	1	2	3	5	7	9
114-Psychedelic cover	2	4	6	11	16	20

I, LUSIPHUR (Becomes Poison Elves, 1st series #8 on)
Mulehide Graphics: 1991 - No. 7, 1992 (B&W, magazine size)

1-Drew Hayes-c/a/scripts	4	8	12	26	41	55
2,4,5	3	6	9	14	20	25
3-Low print run	4	8	12	28	44	60
6,7	2	4	6	8	11	14

Poison Elves: Requiem For An Elf (Sirius Ent., 6/96, $14.95, trade paperback) -Reprints I, Lusiphur #1,2 as text, and 3-6 15.00

I'M A COP
Magazine Enterprises: 1954 - No. 3, 1954

1(A-1 #111)-Powell-c/a in all	15	30	45	88	137	185
2(A-1 #126), 3(A-1 #128)	10	20	30	56	76	95

IMAGE COMICS HARDCOVER
Image Comics: 2005 ($24.99, hardcover with dust jacket)

Vol. 1-New Spawn by McFarlane-s/a; Savage Dragon origin by Larsen; CyberForce by Silvestri; ShadowHawk by Valentino; intro by Marder; Image timeline 25.00

IMAGE FIRST
Image Comics: 2005 ($6.99, TPB)

Vol. 1 (2005) r/Strange Girl #1, Sea of Red #1, The Walking Dead #1 and Girls #1 7.00

IMAGE GRAPHIC NOVEL
Image Int.: 1984 ($6.95)(Advertised as Pacific Comics Graphic Novel #1)

1-The Seven Samuroid; Brunner-c/a 7.00

IMAGE HOLIDAY SPECIAL 2005
Image Comics: 2005 ($9.99, TPB)

nn-Holiday-themed short stories by various incl. Larsen, Kurtz, Kirkman, Valentino 10.00

IMAGE INTRODUCES...
Image Comics: Oct, 2001 - June, 2002 ($2.95, anthology)

Believer #1-Schamberger-s/Thurman & Molder-a; Legend of Isis preview 3.00
Cryptopia #1-Raab-s/Quinn-a 3.00
Dog Soldiers #1-Hunter-s/Pachoumis-a 3.00
Legend of Isis #1-Valdez-a 3.00
Primate #1-Two covers; Beau Smith & Bernhardt-s/Byrd-a 3.00

IMAGES OF A DISTANT SOIL
Image Comics: Feb, 1997 ($2.95, B&W, one-shot)

GD VG FN VF VF/NM NM-
2.0 4.0 6.0 8.0 9.0 9.2

1-Sketches by various 3.00

IMAGES OF SHADOWHAWK (Also see Shadowhawk)
Image Comics: Sept, 1993 - No. 3, 1994 ($1.95, limited series)

1-3: Keith Giffen-c/a; Trencher app. 2.50

IMAGE TWO-IN-ONE
Image Comics: Mar, 2001 ($2.95, 48 pgs., B&W, one-shot)

1-Two stories; 24 pages produced in 24 hrs. by Larsen and Eliopoulos 3.00

IMAGE UNITED
Image Comics: No. 0, Mar, 2010; Nov, 2009 - No. 6 ($3.99, limited series)

0-(3/10, $2.99) Fortress and Savage Dragon app. 3.00
1,2-($3.99) Image character crossover; Kirkman-s; art by Larsen, Liefeld, McFarlane, Portacio, Silvestri and Valentino; Spawn, Witchblade, Savage Dragon, Youngblood, Cyberforce and Shadowhawk app. Multiple covers on each 4.00
1-Jim Lee variant-c 8.00

IMAGE ZERO
Image Comics: 1993 (Received through mail w/coupons from Image books)

0-Savage Dragon, StormWatch, Shadowhawk, Strykeforce; 1st app. Troll; 1st app. McFarlane's Freak, Blotch, Sweat and Bludd 5.00

IMAGINARIES, THE
Image Comics: Mar, 2005 - No. 4, June, 2005 ($2.95, limited series)

1-4-Mike S. Miller & Ben Avery-s; Miller & Titus-a 3.00

I'M DICKENS - HE'S FENSTER (TV)
Dell Publishing Co.: May-July, 1963 - No. 2, Aug-Oct, 1963 (Photo-c)

1	6	12	18	37	59	80
2	5	10	15	32	51	70

I MET A HANDSOME COWBOY
Dell Publishing Co.: No. 324, Mar, 1951

Four Color 324	8	16	24	56	93	130

IMMORTAL DOCTOR FATE, THE
DC Comics: Jan, 1985 - No. 3, Mar, 1985 ($1.25, limited series)

1-3: 1-Simonson-c/a. 2-Giffen-c/a(p) 4.00

IMMORTAL IRON FIST, THE (Also see Iron Fist)
Marvel Comics: Jan, 2007 - No. 27, Aug, 2009 ($2.99/$3.99)

1-Brubaker & Fraction-s/Aja-c/a; origin retold; intro. Orson Randall 5.00
1-Variant-c by Dell'Otto 8.00
1-Director's Cut ($3.99) r/#1 and 8-page story from Civil War: Choosing Sides; script excerpt; character designs; sketch and inks art; cover variant and concepts 4.00
2-13,15-26: 6,17-20-Flashback-a by Heath. 21-Green-a 3.00
14,27: 14-($3.99) Heroes For Hire app. 27-Last issue; 2 covers; Foreman & Lapham-a 4.00
Annual 1 (11/07, $3.99) Brubaker & Fraction-s/Chaykin, Brereton & J. Djurdjevic-a 4.00
... Orson Randall and the Death Queen of California (11/08, $3.99) art by Camuncoli 4.00
... Orson Randall and the Green Mist of Death (4/08, $3.99) art by Heath and various 4.00
...: The Origin of Danny Rand (2008, $3.99) r/Marvel Premiere #15-16 recolored 4.00
... Vol. 1: The Last Iron Fist Story HC (2007, $19.99, dustjacket) r/#1-6, story from Civil War: Choosing Sides; sketch pages 20.00
... Vol. 1: The Last Iron Fist Story SC (2007, $14.99) same content as HC 15.00
... Vol. 2: The Seven Capital Cities HC (2008, $24.99, dustjacket) r/#8-14 & Annual #1 25.00

IMMORTALIS (See Mortigan Goth: Immortalis)

IMMORTAL II
Image Comics: Apr, 1997 - No. 5, Feb, 1998 ($2.50, B&W&Grey, limited series)

1-5: 1-B&W w/ color pull-out poster 2.50

IMMORTAL WEAPONS (Also see Immortal Iron Fist)
Marvel Comics: Sept, 2009 - No. 5, Jan, 2010 ($3.99, limited series)

1-5: Back-up Iron Fist stories in all. 1-Origin of Fat Cobra. 2-Brereton-a 4.00

IMPACT
E. C. Comics: Mar-Apr, 1955 - No. 5, Nov-Dec, 1955

1-Not code approved	18	36	54	144	227	310
2	11	22	33	88	137	185
3-5: 4-Crandall-a	9	18	27	72	119	165

NOTE: ***Crandall** a-1-4. **Davis** a-2-4; c-1-5. **Evans** a-1, 4, 5. **Ingels** a-in all. **Kamen** a-3. **Krigstein** a-1, 5. **Orlando** a-2, 5.*

IMPACT
Gemstone Publishing: Apr, 1999 - No. 5, Aug, 1999 ($2.50)

1-5-Reprints E.C. series 2.50

IMPACT CHRISTMAS SPECIAL

Impulse #85 © DC

Incredible Hercules #116 © MAR

Incredible Hulk #141 © MAR

GD 2.0 | VG 4.0 | FN 6.0 | VF 8.0 | VF/NM 9.0 | NM- 9.2

DC Comics (Impact Comics): 1991 ($2.50, 68 pgs.)
1-Gift of the Magi by Infantino/Rogers; The Black Hood, The Fly, The Jaguar, & The Shield stories 2.50

IMPERIAL GUARD
Marvel Comics: Jan, 1997 - No. 3, Mar, 1997 ($1.95, limited series)
1-3: Augustyn-s in all; 1-Wraparound-c 2.50

IMPOSSIBLE MAN SUMMER VACATION SPECTACULAR, THE
Marvel Comics: Aug, 1990; No. 2, Sept, 1991 ($2.00, 68 pgs.) (See Fantastic Four#11)
1-Spider Man, Quasar, Dr. Strange, She-Hulk, Punisher & Dr. Doom stories; Barry Crain, Guice-a; Art Adams-c(i) 2.50
2-Ka Zar & Thor app.; Cable Wolverine-c app. 2.50

IMPULSE (See Flash #92, 2nd Series for 1st app.) (Also see Young Justice)
DC Comics: Apr, 1995 - No. 89, Oct, 2002 ($1.50/$1.75/$1.95/$2.25/$2.50)
1-Mark Waid scripts & Humberto Ramos-c/a(p) begin; brief retelling of origin 6.00
2-12: 9-XS from Legion (Impulse's cousin) comes to the 20th Century, returns to the 30th Century in #12. 10-Dead Heat Pt. 3 (cont'd in Flash #110). 11-Dead Heat Pt. 4 (cont'd in Flash #111); Johnny Quick dies. 3.00
13-25: 14-Trickster app. 17-Zatanna-c/app. 21-Legion-c/app. 22-Jesse Quick-c/app. 24-Origin; Flash app. 25-Last Ramos-a. 2.50
26-55: 26-Rousseau-a begins. 28-1st new Arrowette (see World's Finest #113). 30-Genesis x-over. 47-Superman-c/app. 50-Batman & Joker-c/app. Van Sciver-a begins 2.50
56-62: 56-Young Justice app. 2.50
63-89: 63-Begin $2.50-c. 66-JLA,JSA-c/app. 68,69-Adam Strange, GL app. 77-Our Worlds at War x-over; Young Justice-c/app. 85-World Without Young Justice x-over pt. 2. 2.50
#1,000,000 (11/98) John Fox app. 2.50
Annual 1 (1996, $2.95)-Legends of the Dead Earth; Parobeck-a 4.00
Annual 2 (1997, $3.95)-Pulp Heroes stories; Orbik painted-c 4.00
.../Atom Double-Shot 1(2/98, $1.95) Jurgens-s/Mhan-a 3.00
...: Bart Saves the Universe (4/99, $5.95) JSA app. 6.00
...Plus(9/97, $2.95) w/Gross Out (Scare Tactics)-c/app. 3.00
...Reckless Youth (1997, $14.95, TPB) r/Flash #92-94, Impulse #1-6 15.00

INCAL, THE
Marvel Comics (Epic): Nov, 1988 - No. 3, Jan, 1989 ($10.95/$12.95, mature)
1-3: Moebius-c/a in all; sexual content 16.00

INCOGNEGRO
DC Comics (Vertigo): 2008 ($19.99, B&W, hardcover graphic novel with dustjacket)
HC-Mat Johnson-s/Warren Pleece-a 20.00

INCOGNITO
Marvel Comics (Icon): Dec, 2008 - No. 6, Aug, 2009 ($3.50/$3.99, limited series)
1-5-Brubaker-s/Phillips-a/c; pulp noir-style 3.50
6-($3.99) Bonus history of the Zeppelin pulps 4.00

INCOMPLETE DEATH'S HEAD (Also see Death's Head)
Marvel Comics UK: Jan, 1993 - No. 12, Dec, 1993 ($1.75, limited series)
1-($2.95, 56 pgs.)-Die-cut cover 3.00
2-11: 2-Re-intro original Death's Head. 3-Original Death's Head vs. Dragon's Claws 2.50
12-($2.50, 52 pgs.)-She Hulk app. 2.50

INCORRUPTIBLE (Also see Irredeemable)
BOOM! Studios: Dec, 2000 - Present ($3.99)
1-3: 1-Waid-s/Diaz-a; 3 covers 4.00

INCREDIBLE HERCULES (Continued from Incredible Hulk #112, Jan, 2008)
Marvel Comics: No. 113, Feb, 2008 - Present ($2.99)
113-125: 113-Ares and Wonder Man app.; Art Adams-c. 116-Romita Jr-c; Eternals app. 3.00
113-Variant-c by Pham 5.00
126-($3.99) Hercules origin retold; back-up story w/Miyazawa-a 4.00
127-137: 128-Dark Avengers app. 132-Replacement Thor. 136-Thor app. 3.00
138-141-($3.99) Assault on New Olympus; Avengers app. 4.00

INCREDIBLE HULK, THE (See Aurora, The Avengers #1, The Defenders #1, Giant-Size..., Hulk, Marvel Collectors Item Classics, Marvel Comics Presents #26, Marvel Fanfare, Marvel Treasury Edition, Power Record Comics, Rampaging Hulk, She-Hulk, 2099 Unlimited & World War Hulk)

INCREDIBLE HULK, THE
Marvel Comics: May, 1962 - No. 6, Mar, 1963; No. 102, Apr, 1968 - No. 474, Mar, 1999
1-Origin & 1st app. (skin is grey colored); Kirby pencils begin, end #5
1400 2800 4200 16,800 40,900 65,000
2-1st green skinned Hulk; Kirby/Ditko-a 288 576 864 2520 5010 7500
3-Origin retold; 1st app. Ringmaster (9/62) 173 346 519 1514 3007 4500
4,5: 4-Brief origin retold 158 316 474 1383 2742 4100
6-(3/63) Intro. Teen Brigade; all Ditko-a 173 346 519 1514 3007 4500
102-(4/68) (Formerly Tales to Astonish)-Origin retold; story continued from Tales to Astonish #101 22 44 66 157 304 450
103 10 20 30 68 119 170
104-Rhino app. 10 20 30 68 119 170
105-108: 105-1st Missing Link. 107-Mandarin app.(9/68). 108-Mandarin & Nick Fury app. (10/68) 7 14 21 49 80 110
109,110: 109-Ka-Zar app. 6 12 18 41 66 90
111-117: 117-Last 12¢ issue 5 10 15 34 55 75
118-Hulk vs. Sub-Mariner 7 14 21 45 73 100
119-121,123-125 4 8 12 26 41 55
122-Hulk battles Thing (12/69) 8 16 24 56 93 130
126-1st Barbara Norriss (Valkyrie) 4 8 12 28 44 60
127-139: 131-Hulk vs. Iron Man; 1st Jim Wilson, Hulk's new sidekick. 136-1st Xeron, The Star-Slayer 3 6 9 19 29 38
140-Written by Harlan Ellison; 1st Jarella, Hulk's love 3 6 9 21 32 42
140-2nd printing (1994) 2 4 6 8 10 12
141-1st app. Doc Samson (7/71) 9 18 27 64 110 155
142-144: 144-Last 15¢ issue 3 6 9 18 27 35
145-(52 pgs.)-Origin retold 4 8 12 28 44 60
146-160: 149-1st app. The Inheritor. 155-1st app. Shaper. 158-Warlock cameo(12/72) 3 6 9 16 23 30
161-The Mimic dies; Beast app. 4 8 12 28 44 60
162-1st app. The Wendigo (4/73); Beast app. 7 14 21 47 76 105
163-171,173-176: 163-1st app. The Gremlin. 164-1st Capt. Omen & Colonel John D. Armbruster. 166-1st Zzzax. 168-1st The Harpy; nudity panels of Betty Ross. 169-1st app. Bi-Beast.176-Warlock cameo (2 panels only); same date as Strange Tales #178 (6/74) 3 6 9 14 19 24
172-X-Men cameo; origin Juggernaut retold 4 8 12 26 41 55
177-1st actual death of Warlock (last panel only) 3 6 9 14 20 26
178-Rebirth of Warlock 3 6 9 14 20 26
179 2 4 6 13 18 22
180-(10/74)-1st brief app. Wolverine (last pg.) 16 32 48 115 220 325
181-(11/74)-1st full Wolverine story; Trimpe-a 90 180 270 700 1175 1650
182-Wolverine cameo; see Giant-Size X-Men #1 for next app.; 1st Crackajack Jackson 11 22 33 78 139 200
183-199: 185-Death of Col. Armbruster. 195,196-Abomination app. 197,198-Man-Thing-c/s 2 4 6 9 12 15
198,199, 201,202-(30¢-c variants, lim. distribution) 3 6 9 18 27 35
200-(25¢-c) Silver Surfer app.; anniversary issue 3 6 9 19 29 38
200-(30¢-c variant, limited distribution)(6/76) 6 12 18 39 62 85
201-220: 201-Conan swipe-c/sty. 212-1st app. The Constrictor 1 2 3 5 6 8
212-216-(35¢-c variant, limited distribution) 4 8 12 24 37 50
221-249: 227-Original Avengers app. 232-Capt. America x-over from C.A. #230. 233-Marvel Man app. 234-(4/79)-1st app. Quasar (formerly called Marvel Man. 243-Cage app. 1 2 3 4 5 7
250-Giant size; Silver Surfer app. 2 4 6 9 12 15
251-277,280-299: 271-Rocket Raccoon app. 272-Sasquatch & Wendigo app.; Wolverine & Alpha Flight cameo in flashback. 282-284-She-Hulk app. 293-F.F. app. 5.00
278,279-Most Marvel characters app. (Wolverine in both). 279-X-Men & Alpha Flight cameos 6.00
300-(11/84, 52 pgs.)-Spider-Man app in new black costume on-c & 2 pg. cameo 1 2 3 4 5 7
301-313: 312-Origin Hulk retold 4.00
314-Byrne-c/a begins, ends #319 6.00
315-319: 319-Bruce Banner & Betty Talbot wed 5.00
320-323,325,327-329 4.00
324-1st app. Grey Hulk since #1 (c-swipe of #1) 2 4 6 8 10 12
326-Grey vs. Green Hulk 6.00
330,331: 330-1st McFarlane ish (4/87); Thunderbolt Ross dies. 331-Grey Hulk series begins 3 6 9 16 22 28
332-334,336-339: 336,337-X-Factor app. 2 4 6 9 12 15
335-No McFarlane-a 6.00
340-Hulk battles Wolverine by McFarlane 4 8 12 24 37 50
341-346: 345-($1.50, 52 pgs.). 346-Last McFarlane issue 1 2 3 5 7 9
347-349,351-358,360-366: 347-1st app. Marlo 3.00
350-Hulk/Thing battle 6.00
359-Wolverine app. (illusion only) 3.00
367,372,377: 367-1st Dale Keown-a on Hulk (3/90). 372-Green Hulk app.;Keown-c/a. 377-1st all new Hulk; fluorescent-c; Keown-c/a 1 2 3 5 6 8
368-371,373-376: 368-Sam Kieth-c/a, 1st app. Pantheon. 369,370-Dale Keown-c/a. 370,371-Original Defenders app. 371,373-376: Keown-c/a. 376-Green vs. Grey Hulk 5.00
377-Fluorescent green logo 2nd printing 3.00

Incredible Hulk #468 © MAR

Incredible Hulk (2nd series) #12 © MAR

Incredibles: City of Incredibles #3 © DIS/Pixar

GD 2.0 | VG 4.0 | FN 6.0 | VF 8.0 | VF/NM 9.0 | NM- 9.2

378,380,389: No Keown-a. 380-Doc Samson app. 3.00
379,381-388,390-392-Keown-a. 385-Infinity Gauntlet x-over. 389-Last $1.00-c. 392-X-Factor app. 4.00
393-($2.50, 72 pgs.)-30th anniversary issue; green foil stamped-c; swipes-c to #1; has pin-ups of classic battles; Keown-c/a 5.00
393-2nd printing 2.50
394-399: 394-No Keown-c/a; intro Trauma. 395,396-Punisher-c/stories; Keown-c/a. 397-Begin "Ghost of the Past" 4-part sty; Keown c/a. 398-Last Keown-c/a 2.50
400-($2.50, 68 pgs.)-Holo-grafx foil-c & r/TTA #63 3.00
400-416: 400-2nd print-Diff. color foil-c. 402-Return of Doc Samson 2.50
417-424: 417-Begin $1.50-c; Rick Jones' bachelor party; Hulk returns from "Future Imperfect"; bound-in trading card sheet. 418-(Regular edition)-Rick Jones marries Marlo; includes cameo apps of various Marvel characters as well as DC's Death & Peter David. 420-Death of Jim Wilson 2.50
418-($2.50)-Collector's Edition w/gatefold die-cut-c 3.00
425 ($2.25, 52 pgs.) 2.50
425 ($3.50, 52 pgs.)-Holographic-c 4.00
426-434, 436-442: 426-Begin $1.95-c. 427, 428-Man-Thing app. 431,432-Abomination app. 434-Funeral for Nick Fury. 436-Ghosts of the Future begins, ends #440. 439-Hulk becomes Maestro, Avengers app. 440-Thor-c/app. 441,442-She-Hulk-c/app. 2.50
435 ($2.50)-Rhino-app; excerpt from "What Savage Beast" 3.00
443,446-448: 443-Begin $1.50-c; re-app. of Hulk. 446-w/card insert. 447-Begin Deodato-c/a(p) 2.50
444,445: 444-Cable-c/app.; "Onslaught". 445-"Onslaught" 4.00
447-Variant cover 4.00
449-1st app. Thunderbolts 6.00
450-($2.95)-Thunderbolts app.; 2 stories; Heroes Reborn-c/app. 5.00
451-470: 455-X-Men-c/app. 460-Bruce Banner returns. 464-Silver Surfer-c/app. 466,467: Betty dies. 467-Last Peter David-s/Kubert-a. 468-Casey-s/Pulido-a begin 2.50
471-473 3.00
474-($2.99) Last issue; Abomination app. 4.00
#(-1) Flashback (7/97) Kubert-a 2.50
Special 1 (10/68, 25¢, 68 pg.)-New 51 pg. story, Hulk battles The Inhumans (early app.); Steranko-c. 10 20 30 73 129 185
Special 2 (10/69, 25¢, 68 pg.)-Origin retold 6 12 18 41 66 90
Special 3,4: 3-(1/71, 25¢, 68 pg.). 4-(1/72, 52pgs.) 3 6 9 20 30 40
Annual 5 (1976) 2 4 6 10 14 18
Annual 6-8 ('77-79): 7-Byrne/Layton-c/a; Iceman & Angel app. in book-length story. 8-Book-length Sasquatch-c/sty 2 4 6 8 10 12
Annual 9,10: 9('80). 10 ('81) 6.00
Annual 11('82)-Doc Samson back-up by Miller(p)(5 pgs.); Spider-Man & Avengers app. Buckler-a(p) 6.00
Annual 12-17: 12 ('83). 13('84). 14('85). 15('86). 16('90, $2.00, 68 pgs.)-She-Hulk app. 17(1991, $2.00)-Origin retold 3.50
Annual 18-20 ('92-'94 68 pgs.)-18-Return of the Defenders, Pt. I; no Keown-c/a 19-Bagged w/card 3.00
...'97 ($2.99) Pollina-c 3.00
...And Wolverine 1 (10/86, $2.50)-r/1st app. (#180-181) 1 3 4 6 8 10
...: Beauty and the Behemoth ('98, $19.95, TPB) r/Bruce & Betty stories 20.00
...Ground Zero ('95, $12.95) r/#340-346 13.00
...Hercules Unleashed (10/96, $2.50) David-s/Deodato-c/a 2.50
... Omnibus Vol. 1 HC (2008, $99.99, dustjacket) r/#1-6 & 102, Tales To Astonish #59-101 bonus art, cover reprints; afterword by Peter David; 2 covers (Kirby & Ross swipe) 100.00
.../Sub-Mariner '98 Annual ($2.99) 3.00
...Versus Quasimodo 1 (3/83, one-shot)-Based on Saturday morning cartoon 4.00
...Vs. Superman 1 (7/99, $5.95, one-shot)-painted-c by Rude 6.00
...Versus Venom 1 (4/94, $2.50, one-shot)-Embossed-c; red foil logo 3.00
... Visionaries: Peter David Vol. 1 (2005, $19.99) r/#331-339 written by Peter David 20.00
... Visionaries: Peter David Vol. 2 (2005, $19.99) r/#340-348 20.00
... Visionaries: Peter David Vol. 3 (2006, $19.99) r/#349-354, Web of Spider-Man #44, and Fantastic Four #320 20.00
... Visionaries: Peter David Vol. 4 (2007, $19.99) r/#355-363 and Marvel Comics Presents #26,45 20.00
... Visionaries: Peter David Vol. 5 (2008, $19.99) r/#364-372 and Annual #16 20.00
Wizard #1 Ace Edition - Reprints #1 with new Andy Kubert-c 14.00
Wizard #181 Ace Edition - Reprints #181 with new Chen-c 14.00

(Also see titles listed under **Hulk**)

NOTE: **Adkins** *a-111-116i.* **Austin** *a(i)-350, 351, 353, 354; c-302i, 350i.* **Ayers** *a-3-5i.* **Buckler** *a-Annual 5; c-252.* **John Buscema** *c-202p.* **Byrne** *a-314-319p; c-314-316, 318, 319, 359, Annual 14i.* **Colan** *c-363.* **Ditko** *a-2i, 6, 249, Annual 2r(5), 3r, 9p; c-2i, 6, 235, 249.* **Everett** *c-133i.* **Golden** *c-248, 251.* **Kane** *c(p)-193, 194, 196, 198.* **Dale Keown** *a(p)-367, 369-377, 379, 381-388, 390-393, 395-398; c-369-377p, 381, 382p, 384, 385, 386, 387p, 388, 390p, 391-393, 395p, 396, 397p, 398.* **Kirby** *a-1-5p, Special 2, 3p, Annual 5p; c-1-5, Annual 5.* **McFarlane** *a-330-334p, 336-339p, 340-343, 344-346p; c-330p, 340p, 341-343, 344p, 345, 346p.* **Mignola** *c-302, 305, 313.* **Miller** *c-258p, 261, 264, 268.* **Mooney** *a-230p, 287i, 288i.* **Powell** *a-Special 3r(2).* **Romita** *a-Annual 17p.* **Severin** *a(i)-108-110, 131-133, 141-151, 153-155; c(i)-109, 110, 132, 142, 144-155.* **Simonson** *c-283, 364-367.* **Starlin** *a-222p; c-217.* **Staton** *a(i)-187-189, 191-209.* **Tuska** *a-102i, 105i, 106i, 218p.* **Williamson** *a-310i; c-310i, 311i.*

Wrightson *c-197.*

INCREDIBLE HULK (Vol. 2) (Formerly Hulk #1-11; becomes Incredible Hercules with #113) (Also see World War Hulk)
Marvel Comics: No. 12, Mar, 2000 - No. 112, Jan, 2008 ($1.99-$3.50)
No. 600, Sept, 2009 - Present ($3.99/$4.99)

12-Jenkins-s/Garney & McKone-a 3.00
13,14-($1.99) Garney & Buscema-a 2.50
15-24,26-32: 15-Begin $2.25-c. 21-Maximum Security x-over. 24-($1.99-c) 2.50
25-($2.99) Hulk vs. The Abomination; Romita Jr.-a 3.00
33-($3.50, 100 pgs.) new Bogdanove-a/Priest-s; reprints 3.50
34-Bruce Jones-s begin; Romita Jr.-a 5.00
35-49,51-54: 35-39-Jones-s/Romita Jr.-a. 40-43-Weeks-a. 44-49-Immonen-a 3.00
50-($3.50) Deodato-a begins; Abomination app. thru #54 3.50
55-74,77-91: 55(25¢-c) Absorbing Man returns; Fernandez-a. 60-65,70-72-Deodato-a. 66-69-Braithwaite-a. 71-74-Iron Man app. 77-($2.99-c) Peter David-s begin/Weeks-a. 80-Wolverine-c. 82-Jae Lee-c/a. 83-86-House of M x-over. 87-Scorpion app. 3.00
75,76-($3.50) The Leader app. 75-Robertson-a/Frank-c. 76-Braithwaite-a 3.50
92-Planet Hulk begins; Ladronn-c 5.00
92-2nd printing with variant-c by Bryan Hitch 4.00
93-99,101-105 Planet Hulk; Ladronn-c 3.00
100-($3.99) Planet Hulk continues; back-up w/Frank-a; r/#152,153; Ladronn-c 4.00
100-($3.99) Green Hulk variant-c by Michael Turner 10.00
100-($3.99) Gray Hulk variant-c by Michael Turner 30.00
106-World War Hulk begins; Gary Frank-a/c 5.00
106-2nd printing with new cover of Hercules and Angel 3.00
107-112: 107-Hercules vs. Hulk. 108-Rick Jones app. 112-Art Adams-c 3.00
600-(9/09, $4.99) Covers by Ross, Sale and wraparound-c by McGuinness; back-up with Stan Lee-s; r/Hulk: Gray #1; cover gallery 5.00
601-607-($3.99): 601-605-Olivetti-a. 603-Wolverine app. 606,607-Fall of the Hulks 4.00
Annual 2000 ($3.50) Texeira-a/Jenkins-s; Avengers app. 3.50
Annual 2001 ($2.99) Thor-c/app.; Larsen-s/Williams III-c 3.00
... : Boiling Point (Volume 2, 2002, $8.99, TPB) r/#40-43; Andrews-c 9.00
Dogs of War (6/01, $19.95, TPB) r/#12-20 20.00
House of M (2006, $13.99) r/House of M tie-in issues Incredible Hulk #83-87 14.00
Hulk: Planet Hulk HC (2007, $39.99, dustjacket) oversized r/#92-105, Planet Hulk: Gladiator Guidebook, stories from Amazing Fantasy (2004) #15 and Giant-Size Hulk #1 40.00
Hulk: Planet Hulk SC (2008, $34.99) same content as HC 35.00
Planet Hulk: Gladiator Guidebook (2006, $3.99) bios of combatants and planet history 4.00
...: Prelude to Planet Hulk (2006, $13.99, TPB) r/#88-91 & Official Handbook: Hulk 2004 14.00
...: Return of the Monster (7/02, $12.99, TPB) r/#34-39 13.00
...: The End (8/02, $5.95) David-s/Keown-a; Hulk in the far future 6.00
...: The End HC (2008, $19.99, dustjacket) r/The End and Hulk: Future Imperfect #1-2 20.00
...Volume 1 HC (2002, $29.99, oversized) r/#34-43 & Startling Stories: Banner #1-4 30.00
...Volume 2 HC (2003, $29.99, oversized) r/#44-54; sketch pages and cover gallery 30.00
Volume 3: Transfer of Power (2003, $12.99, TPB) r/#44-49 13.00
Volume 4: Abominable (2003, $11.99, TPB) r/#50-54; Abomination app.; Deodato-a 12.00
Volume 5: Hide in Plain Sight (2003, $11.99, TPB) r/#55-59; Fernandez-a 12.00
Volume 6: Split Decisions (2004, $12.99, TPB) r/#60-65; Deodato-a 13.00
Volume 7: Dead Like Me (2004, $12.99, TPB) r/#66-69 & Hulk Smash #1&2 13.00
Volume 8: Big Things (2004, $17.99, TPB) r/#70-76; Iron Man app. 18.00
Volume 9: Tempest Fugit (2005, $14.99, TPB) r/#77-82 15.00

INCREDIBLE MR. LIMPET, THE (See Movie Classics)

INCREDIBLES, THE
Image Comics: Nov, 2004 - No. 4, Feb, 2005 ($2.99, limited series)

1-4-Adaptation of 2004 Pixar movie; Ricardo Curtis-a 3.00
TPB (2005, $12.95) r/#1-4; cover gallery 13.00

INCREDIBLES, THE (Pixar characters)
BOOM! Studios

...: City of Incredibles 0-6 (No. 0, 7/09 - Present) Waid & Walker-s. 0,1-Wagner-c 3.00
...: Family Matters 1-4 (3/09 - No. 4, 6/09) Waid-s/Takara-a. 1-Five covers 3.00

INCREDIBLE SCIENCE FICTION (Formerly Weird Science-Fantasy)
E. C. Comics: No. 30, July-Aug, 1955 - No. 33, Jan-Feb, 1956

30-Davis-c begin, end #32 39 78 117 312 499 685
31-Williamson/Krenkel-a, Wood-a(2) 40 80 120 320 510 700
32-Williamson/Krenkel-a 40 80 120 320 510 700
33-Classic Wood-c; "Judgment Day" story-r/Weird Fantasy #18; final issue & last E.C. comic book 41 82 123 328 524 720

NOTE: **Davis** *a-30, 32, 33; c-30-32.* **Krigstein** *a-in all.* **Orlando** *a-30, 32, 33.* **Wood** *a-30, 31, 33; c-33.*

INCREDIBLE SCIENCE FICTION (Formerly Weird Science-Fantasy)
Russ Cochran/Gemstone Publ.: No. 8, Aug, 1994 - No. 11, May, 1995 ($2.00)

8-11: Reprints #30-33 of E.C. series 2.50

Indiana Jones and the Kingdom of the Crystal Skull #2 © Lucasfilm

Indians #12 © FH

Infinite Crisis #7 © DC

	GD 2.0	VG 4.0	FN 6.0	VF 8.0	VF/NM 9.0	NM- 9.2

INDEPENDENCE DAY (Movie)
Marvel Comics: No. 0, June, 1996 - No. 2, Aug, 1996 ($1.95, limited series)
0-Special Edition; photo-c 5.00
0-2 2.50

INDIANA JONES (Title series), **Dark Horse Comics**
--ADVENTURES, 6/08 ($6.95, digest-sized) Vol. 1 - new all-ages adventures; Beavers-a 7.00
--AND THE ARMS OF GOLD, 2/94 - 5/94 ($2.50) 1-4 2.50
--AND THE FATE OF ATLANTIS, 3/91 - 9/91 ($2.50) 1-4-Dorman painted-c on all; contain trading cards (#1 has a 2nd printing, 10/91) 2.50
--AND THE GOLDEN FLEECE, 6/94 - 7/94 ($2.50) 1,2 2.50
--AND THE IRON PHOENIX, 12/94 - 3/95 ($2.50) 1-4 2.50

INDIANA JONES AND THE KINGDOM OF THE CRYSTAL SKULL
Dark Horse Comics: May, 2008 - No. 2, May, 2008 ($5.99, limited series, movie adaptation)
1,2-Luke Ross-a/John Jackson Miller-adapted-s; two covers by Struzan & Fleming 6.00
TPB (5/08, $12.95) r/#1,2; Struzan-c 13.00

INDIANA JONES AND THE LAST CRUSADE
Marvel Comics: 1989 - No. 4, 1989 ($1.00, limited series, movie adaptation)
1-4: Williamson-i assist 3.00
1-(1989, $2.95, B&W mag., 80 pgs.) 4.00
--AND THE SHRINE OF THE SEA DEVIL: Dark Horse, 9/94 ($2.50, one shot)
1-Gary Gianni-a 2.50
--AND THE SARGASSO PIRATES: Dark Horse, 12/95 - 3/96 ($2.50) 1-4: 1,2-Ross-c 2.50
--AND THE SPEAR OF DESTINY: Dark Horse, 4/95 - 8/95 ($2.50) 1-4 2.50
--AND THE TOMB OF THE GODS, 6/08 - No. 4, 3/09 ($2.99) 1-4: 1-Tony Harris-c 3.00
--THUNDER IN THE ORIENT: Dark Horse, 9/93 - '94 ($2.50)
1-6: Dan Barry story & art in all; 1-Dorman painted-c 2.50

INDIANA JONES AND THE TEMPLE OF DOOM
Marvel Comics Group: Sept, 1984 - No. 3, Nov, 1984 (Movie adaptation)
1-3-r/Marvel Super Special; Guice-a 3.00

INDIANA JONES OMNIBUS
Dark Horse Books: Feb, 2008; June 2008; Feb, 2009 ($24.95, digest-size)
Volume One - Reprints Indiana Jones and the Fate of Atlantis, Indiana Jones: Thunder in the Orient; and Indiana Jones and the Arms of Gold mini-series 25.00
Volume Two - Reprints I.J. and the Golden Fleece, I.J. and the Shrine of the Sea Devil, I.J. and the Iron Phoenix, I.J. and the Spear of Destiny, I.J. and the Sargasso Pirates 25.00
The Further Adventures Volume One - (2/09) r/Raiders of the Lost Ark #1-3 & The Further Adventures of Indiana Jones #1-12 25.00

INDIAN BRAVES (Baffling Mysteries No. 5 on)
Ace Magazines: March, 1951 - No. 4, Sept, 1951
1-Green Arrowhead begins, ends #3 15 30 45 84 127 170
2 9 18 27 52 69 85
3,4 8 16 24 44 57 70
I.W. Reprint #1 (nd)-r/Indian Braves #4 2 4 6 9 13 16

INDIAN CHIEF (White Eagle...) (Formerly The Chief, Four Color 290)
Dell Publ. Co.: No. 3, July-Sept, 1951 - No. 33, Jan-Mar, 1959 (All painted-c)
3 5 10 15 34 55 75
4-11: 6-White Eagle app. 4 8 12 28 44 60
12-1st White Eagle(10-12/53)-Not same as earlier character
5 10 15 34 55 75
13-29 4 8 12 23 36 48
30-33-Buscema-a 4 8 12 24 37 50

INDIAN CHIEF (See March of Comics No. 94, 110, 127, 140, 159, 170, 187)

INDIAN FIGHTER, THE (Movie)
Dell Publishing Co.: No. 687, May, 1956 (one-shot)
Four Color 687-Kirk Douglas photo-c 7 14 21 50 83 115

INDIAN FIGHTER
Youthful Magazines: May, 1950 - No. 11, Jan, 1952
1 14 28 42 82 121 160
2-Wildey-a/c(bondage) 10 20 30 58 79 100
3-11: 3,4-Wildey-a 8 16 24 44 57 70
NOTE: ***Hollingsworth** a-5. **Walter Johnson** c-1, 3, 4, 6. **Palais** a-10. **Stallman** a-5-8. **Wildey** a-2-4; c-2, 5.*

INDIAN LEGENDS OF THE NIAGARA (See American Graphics)

INDIANS
Fiction House Magazines (Wings Publ. Co.): Spring, 1950 - No. 17, Spr, 1953 (1-8: 52 pgs.)
1-Manzar The White Indian, Long Bow & Orphan of the Storm begin
30 60 90 177 289 400
2-Starlight begins 15 30 45 90 140 190
3-5: 5-17-Most-c by Whitman 14 28 42 81 118 155
6-10 13 26 39 72 101 130
11-17 11 22 33 64 90 115

INDIANS OF THE WILD WEST
I. W. Enterprises: Circa 1958? (no date) (Reprints)
9-Kinstler-c; Whitman-a; r/Indians #? 2 4 6 10 14 18

INDIANS ON THE WARPATH
St. John Publishing Co.: No date (Late 40s, early 50s) (132 pgs.)
nn-Matt Baker-c; contains St. John comics rebound. Many combinations possible
38 76 114 228 369 510

INDIAN TRIBES (See Famous Indian Tribes)

INDIAN WARRIORS (Formerly White Rider and Super Horse; becomes Western Crime Cases #9)
Star Publications: No. 7, June, 1951 - No. 8, Sept, 1951
7-White Rider & Superhorse continue; "Last of the Mohicans" serial begins;
L.B. Cole-c 18 36 54 105 165 225
8-L. B. Cole-c 17 34 51 98 154 210
3-D 1(12/53, 25¢)-Came w/glasses; L. B. Cole-c 34 68 102 199 325 450
Accepted Reprint(nn)(inside cover shows White Rider & Superhorse #11)-r/cover to #7; origin White Rider &...; L. B. Cole-c 8 16 24 40 50 60
Accepted Reprint #8 (nd); L.B. Cole-c (r-cover to #8) 8 16 24 40 50 60

INDOORS-OUTDOORS (See Wisco)

INDOOR SPORTS
National Specials Co.: nd (6x9", 64 pgs., B&W-r, hard-c)
nn-By Tad 5 10 15 24 30 35

INDUSTRIAL GOTHIC
DC Comics (Vertigo): Dec, 1995 - No. 5, Apr, 1996 ($2.50, limited series)
1-5: Ted McKeever-c/a/scripts 2.50

INFERIOR FIVE, THE (Inferior 5 #11, 12) (See Showcase #62, 63, 65)
National Periodical Publications (#1-10: 12¢): 3-4/67 - No. 10, 9-10/68; No. 11, 8-9/72 - No. 12, 10-11/72
1-(3-4/67)-Sekowsky-a(p); 4th app. 6 12 18 37 59 80
2-5: 2-Plastic Man, F.F. app. 4-Thor app. 3 6 9 20 30 40
6-9: 6-Stars DC staff 3 6 9 16 23 30
10-Superman x-over; F.F., Spider-Man & Sub-Mariner app.
3 6 9 19 29 38
11,12: Orlando-c/a; both r/Showcase #62,63 2 4 6 11 16 20

INFERNO
Caliber Comics: 1995 - No. 5 ($2.95, B&W)
1-5 3.00

INFERNO (See Legion of Super-Heroes)
DC Comics: Oct, 1997 - No. 4, Feb, 1998 ($2.50, limited series)
1-Immonen-s/c/a in all 4.00
2-4 3.00

INFERNO: HELLBOUND
Image Comics (Top Cow): Jan, 2002 - No. 3 ($2.50/$2.99)
1,2: 1-Seven covers; Silvestri-a/Silvestri and Wohl-s 2.50
3-($2.99) Tan-a 3.00
#0 (7/02, $3.00) Tan-a 3.00
Wizard #0- Previews series; bagged with Wizard Top Cow Special mag 2.25

INFINITE CRISIS
DC Comics: Dec, 2005 - No. 7, Jun, 2006 ($3.99, limited series)
1-Johns-s/Jimenez-a; two covers by Jim Lee and George Pérez 5.00
1-RRP Edition with Jim Lee sketch-c 275.00
2-7: 4-New Spectre; Earth-2 returns. 5-Earth-2 Lois dies; new Blue Beetle debut. 6-Superboy killed, new Earth formed. 7-Earth-2 Superman dies 4.00
HC (2006, $24.99, dustjacket) r/#1-7; DiDio intro.; sketch cover gallery; interview/commentary with Johns, Jimenez and editors; sketch art 25.00
... Companion TPB (2006, $14.99) r/Day of Vengeance: Infinite Crisis Special #1, Rann-Thanagar War: ICS #1, The Omac Project: ICS #1, Villains United: ICS #1 15.00
... Secret Files 2006 (4/06, $5.99) tie-in story with Earth-2 Lois and Superman, Earth-Prime Superboy and Alexander Luthor; art by various; profile pages 6.00

INFINITE CRISIS AFTERMATH (See Crisis Aftermath:...)

INFINITE HORIZON

Infinity Inc. #3 © DC

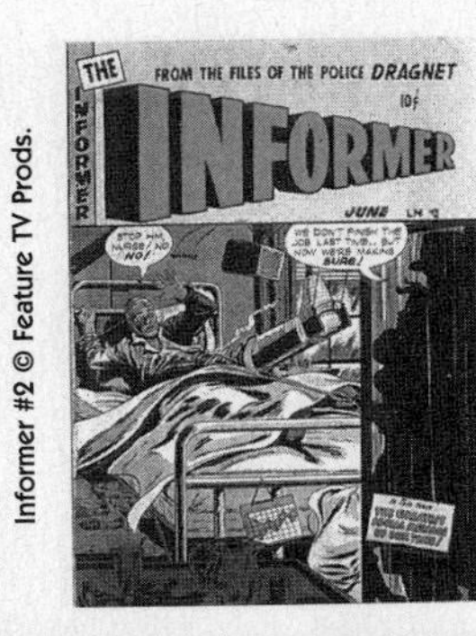

Informer #2 © Feature TV Prods.

Inhumans V3 #1 © MAR

	GD 2.0	VG 4.0	FN 6.0	VF 8.0	VF/NM 9.0	NM- 9.2

Image Comics: Dec, 2007 - No. 6 ($2.99)

1-4-Re-imagining of Homer's The Odyssey in modern times; Noto-a/Duggan-s						3.00

INFINITY ABYSS (Also see Marvel Universe: The End)
Marvel Comics: Aug, 2002 - No. 6 ($2.99, limited series)

1-5-Starlin-s/a; Thanos, Captain Marvel, Spider-Man, Dr. Strange app.						3.00
6-($3.50)						3.50
Thanos Vol. 2: Infinity Abyss TPB (2003, $17.99) r/ #1-6						18.00

INFINITY CRUSADE
Marvel Comics: June, 1993 - No. 6, Nov, 1993 ($2.50, limited series, 52 pgs.)

1-6: By Jim Starlin & Ron Lim						2.50

INFINITY GAUNTLET (The... #2 on; see Infinity Crusade, The Infinity War & Warlock & the Infinity Watch)
Marvel Comics: July, 1991 - No. 6, Dec, 1991 ($2.50, limited series)

1-6:Thanos-c/stories in all; Starlin scripts in all; 5,6-Ron Lim-c/a						3.00
TPB (4/99, $24.95) r/#1-6						25.00

NOTE: ***Lim*** *a-3p(part), 5p, 6p; c-5i, 6i.* ***Perez*** *a-1-3p, 4p(part); c-1(painted), 2-4, 5i, 6i.*

INFINITY, INC. (See All-Star Squadron #25)
DC Comics: Mar, 1984 - No. 53, Aug, 1988 ($1.25, Baxter paper, 36 pgs.)

1-Brainwave, Jr., Fury, The Huntress, Jade, Northwind, Nuklon, Obsidian, Power Girl, Silver Scarab & Star Spangled Kid begin						4.00
2-13,38-49,51-53: 2-Dr. Midnite, G.A. Flash, W. Woman, Dr. Fate, Hourman, Green Lantern, Wildcat app. 5-Nudity panels. 46,47-Millennium tie-ins						3.00
14-Todd McFarlane-a (5/85, 2nd full story)	1	2	3	6	8	9
15-37-McFarlane-a (20,23,24: 5 pgs. only; 33: 2 pgs.); 18-24-Crisis x-over. 21-Intro new Hourman & Dr. Midnight. 26-New Wildcat app. 31-Star Spangled Kid becomes Skyman. 32-Green Fury becomes Green Flame. 33-Origin Obsidian. 35-1st modern app. G.A. Fury						4.00
50 ($2.50, 52 pgs.)						3.00
Annual 1,2: 1(12/85)-Crisis x-over. 2('88, $2.00), Special 1 ('87, $1.50)						3.00

NOTE: ***Kubert*** *r-4.* ***McFarlane*** *a-14-37p, Annual 1p; c(p)-14-19, 22, 25, 26, 31-33, 37, Annual 1.* ***Newton*** *a-12p, 13p(last work 4/85).* ***Tuska*** *a-11p. JSA app. 3-10.*

INFINITY, INC. (See 52)
DC Comics: Nov, 2007 - No. 12, Oct, 2008 ($2.99)

1-12: 1-Milligan-s; Steel app.						3.00
...: Luthor's Monsters TPB (2008, $14.99) r/#1-5						15.00
...: The Bogeyman TPB (2008, $14.99) r/#6-10						15.00

INFINITY WAR, THE (Also see Infinity Gauntlet & Warlock and the Infinity...)
Marvel Comics: June, 1992 - No. 6, Nov, 1992 ($2.50, mini-series)

1-Starlin scripts, Lim-c/a(p), Thanos app. in all						2.50
2-6: All have wraparound gatefold covers						2.50
TPB (2006, $29.99) r/#1-6, Marvel Comics Presents #108-111, Warlock and the Infinity Watch #7-10; cover gallery and synopses of Infinity War crossovers						30.00

INFORMER, THE
Feature Television Productions: April, 1954 - No. 5, Dec, 1954

1-Sekowsky-a begins	12	24	36	69	97	125
2	9	18	27	47	61	75
3-5	8	16	24	42	54	65

IN HIS STEPS
Spire Christian Comics (Fleming H. Revell Co.): 1973, 1977 (39/49¢)

nn	2	4	6	8	11	14

INHUMANOIDS, THE (TV)
Marvel Comics (Star Comics): Jan, 1987 - No. 4, July 1987

1-4: Based on Hasbro toys						3.00

INHUMANS, THE (See Amazing Adventures, Fantastic Four #54 & Special #5, Incredible Hulk Special #1, Marvel Graphic Novel & Thor #146)
Marvel Comics Group: Oct, 1975 - No. 12, Aug, 1977

1: #1-4,6 are 25¢ issues	3	6	9	14	19	24
2-4-Peréz-a	2	4	6	8	10	12
5-12: 9-Reprints Amazing Adventures #1,2('70). 12-Hulk app.	1	3	4	6	8	10
4-(30¢-c variant, limited distribution)(4/76) Peréz-a	3	6	9	16	23	30
6-(30¢-c variant, limited distribution)(8/76)	3	6	9	16	23	30
11,12-(35¢-c variants, limited distribution)	4	8	12	24	37	50
Special 1(4/90, $1.50, 52 pgs.)-F.F. cameo						3.00
...: The Great Refuge (5/95, $2.95)						3.00

NOTE: ***Buckler*** *c-2-4p, 5.* ***Gil Kane*** *a-5-7p; c-1p, 7p, 8p.* ***Kirby*** *a-9r.* ***Mooney*** *a-11i.* ***Perez*** *a-1-4p, 8p.*

INHUMANS (Marvel Knights)
Marvel Comics: Nov, 1998 - No. 12, Oct, 1999 ($2.99, limited series)

1-Jae Lee-c/a; Paul Jenkins-s						10.00
1-($6.95) DF Edition; Jae Lee variant-c						7.00
2-Two covers by Lee and Darrow						4.00
3-12						3.00
TPB (10/00, $24.95) r/#1-12						25.00

INHUMANS (Volume 3)
Marvel Comics: Jun, 2000 - No. 4, Oct, 2000 ($2.99, limited series)

1-4-Ladronn-c/Pacheco & Marin-s. 1-3-Ladronn-a. 4-Lucas-a						3.00

INHUMANS (Volume 6)
Marvel Comics: Jun, 2003 - No. 12, Jun, 2004 ($2.50/$2.99)

1-12: 1-6-McKeever-s/Clark-a/JH Williams III-c. 7-Begin $2.99-c. 7,8-Teranishi-a						3.00
Vol. 1: Culture Shock (2005, $7.99, digest) r/#1-6; story pitch and sketch pages						8.00

INHUMANS 2099
Marvel Comics: Nov, 2004 ($2.99, one-shot)

1-Kirkman-s/Rathburn-a/Pat Lee-c						3.00

INKY & DINKY (See Felix's Nephews...)

IN LOVE (...Magazine on-c; I Love You No. 7 on)
Mainline/Charlton No. 5 (5/55)-on: Aug-Sept, 1954 - No. 6, July, 1955 ('Adult Reading' on-c)

1-Simon & Kirby-a; book-length novel in all issues	39	78	117	240	395	550
2,3-S&K-a. 3-Last pre-code (12-1/54-55)	23	46	69	136	223	310
4-S&K-a.(Rare)	26	52	78	152	249	345
5-S&K-c only	14	28	42	78	112	145
6-No S&K-a	9	18	27	52	69	85

INNOVATION SPECTACULAR
Innovation Publishing: 1991 - No. 2, 1991 ($2.95, squarebound, 100 pgs.)

1,2: Contains rebound comics w/o covers						3.00

INNOVATION SUMMER FUN SPECIAL
Innovation Publishing: 1991 ($3.50, B&W/color, squarebound)

1-Contains rebound comics (Power Factory)						3.50

IN SEARCH OF THE CASTAWAYS (See Movie Comics)

INSIDE CRIME (Formerly My Intimate Affair)
Fox Features Syndicate (Hero Books): No. 3, July, 1950 - No. 2, Sept, 1950

3-Wood-a (10 pgs.); L. B. Cole-c	30	60	90	177	289	400
2-Used in **SOTI**, pg. 182,183; r/Spook #24	23	46	69	136	223	310
nn(no publ. listed, nd)	11	22	33	62	86	110

INSPECTOR, THE (TV) (Also see The Pink Panther)
Gold Key: July, 1974 - No. 19, Feb, 1978

1	3	6	9	19	29	38
2-5	2	4	6	13	18	22
6-9	2	4	6	10	14	18
10-19: 11-Reprints	2	4	6	8	10	12

INSPECTOR GILL OF THE FISH POLICE (See Fish Police)

INSPECTOR WADE
David McKay Publications: No. 13, May, 1938

Feature Books 13	29	58	87	170	278	385

INSTANT PIANO
Dark Horse Comics: Aug, 1994 - No. 4, Feb, 1995 ($3.95, B&W, bimonthly, mature)

1-4						4.00

INTERFACE
Marvel Comics (Epic Comics): Dec, 1989 - No. 8, Dec, 1990 ($1.95, mature, coated paper)

1-8: Cont. from 1st ESPers series; painted-c/a						2.50
Espers: Interface TPB ('98, $16.95) r/#1-6						17.00

INTERNATIONAL COMICS (...Crime Patrol No. 6)
E. C. Comics: Spring, 1947 - No. 5, Nov-Dec, 1947

1-Schaffenberger-a begins, ends #4	62	124	186	394	677	960
2	43	86	129	271	461	650
3-5	40	80	120	243	402	560

INTERNATIONAL CRIME PATROL (Formerly International Comics #1-5; becomes Crime Patrol No. 7 on)
E. C. Comics: No. 6, Spring, 1948

6-Moon Girl app.	62	124	186	394	677	960

IN THE DAYS OF THE MOB (Magazine)
Hampshire Dist. Ltd. (National): Fall, 1971 (B&W)

1-Kirby-a; John Dillinger wanted poster inside (1/2 value if poster is missing)

Intimate Confessions #2 © Realistic

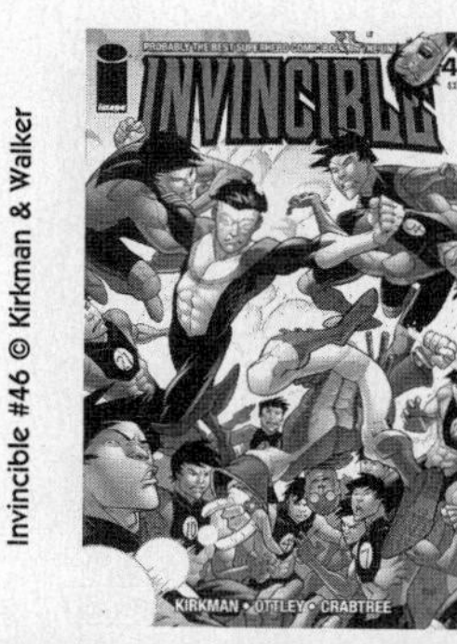

Invincible #46 © Kirkman & Walker

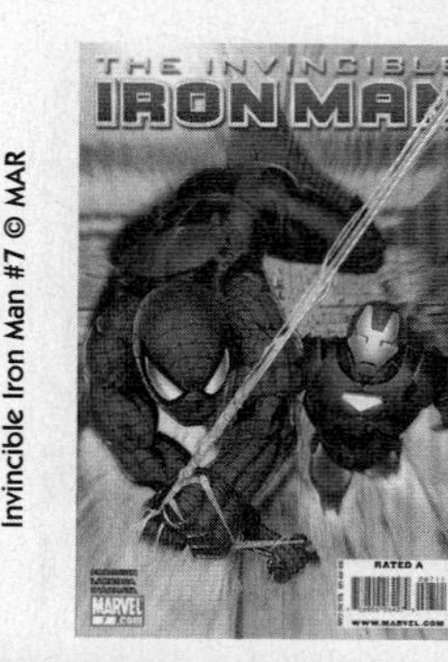

Invincible Iron Man #7 © MAR

	GD 2.0	VG 4.0	FN 6.0	VF 8.0	VF/NM 9.0	NM- 9.2
	8	16	24	52	86	120

IN THE PRESENCE OF MINE ENEMIES
Spire Christian Comics/Fleming H. Revell Co.: 1973 (35/49¢)

nn	2	4	6	8	10	12

IN THE SHADOW OF EDGAR ALLAN POE
DC Comics (Vertigo): 2002 (Graphic novel)

Hardcover (2002, $24.95) Fuqua-s/Phillips and Parke photo-a 25.00
Softcover (2003, $17.95) 18.00

INTIMATE
Charlton Comics: Dec, 1957 - No. 3, May, 1958

1	6	12	18	28	34	40
2,3	4	8	12	18	22	25

INTIMATE CONFESSIONS (See Fox Giants)

INTIMATE CONFESSIONS
Country Press Inc.: 1942

nn-Ashcan comic, not distributed to newsstands, only for in house use. A VF copy sold for $1,000 in 2007, and a VF+ copy sold for $1,525 in 2007.

INTIMATE CONFESSIONS
Realistic Comics: July-Aug, 1951 - No. 7, Aug, 1952; No. 8, Mar, 1953 (All painted-c)

1-Kinstler-c/a; c/Avon paperback #222	90	180	270	576	988	1400
2	24	48	72	140	230	320
3-c/Avon paperback #250; Kinstler-c/a	27	54	81	162	266	370
4-8: 4-c/Avon paperback #304; Kinstler-c. 6-c/Avon paperback #120. 8-c/Avon paperback #375; Kinstler-a	23	46	69	138	227	315

INTIMATE CONFESSIONS
I. W. Enterprises/Super Comics: 1964

I.W. Reprint #9,10, Super Reprint #10,12,18	2	4	6	10	14	18

INTIMATE LOVE
Standard Comics: No. 5, 1950 - No. 28, Aug, 1954

5-8: 6-8-Severin/Elder-a	10	20	30	54	72	90
9	8	16	24	40	50	60
10-Jane Russell, Robert Mitchum photo-c	14	28	42	76	108	140
11-18,20,23,25,27,28	7	14	21	37	46	55
19,21,22,24,26-Toth-a	8	16	24	44	57	70

NOTE: ***Celardo** a-8, 10. **Colletta** a-23. **Moreira** a-13(2). Photo-c-6, 7, 10, 12, 14, 15, 18-20, 24, 26, 27.*

INTIMATES, THE
DC Comics (WildStorm): Jan, 2005 - No. 12, Dec, 2005 ($2.95/$2.99)

1-12: 1-Joe Casey-s/Jim Lee-c/Lee and Giuseppe Camuncoli-a 3.00

INTIMATE SECRETS OF ROMANCE
Star Publications: Sept, 1953 - No. 2, Apr, 1954

1,2-L. B. Cole-c	19	38	57	109	172	235

INTRIGUE
Quality Comics Group: Jan, 1955

1-Horror; Jack Cole reprint/Web of Evil	34	68	102	199	325	450

INTRIGUE
Image Comics: Aug, 1999 - No. 3, Feb, 2000 ($2.50/$2.95)

1,2: 1-Two covers (Andrews, Wieringo); Shum-s/Andrews-a 2.50
3-($2.95) 3.00

INTRUDER
TSR, Inc.: 1990 - No. 10, 1991 ($2.95, 44 pgs.)

1-10 3.00

INVADERS, THE (TV)
Gold Key: Oct, 1967 - No. 4, Oct, 1968 (All have photo-c)

1-Spiegle-a in all	9	18	27	60	100	140
2-4: 2-Pin-up on back-c	6	12	18	41	66	90

INVADERS, THE (Also see The Avengers #71 & Giant-Size Invaders)
Marvel Comics Group: August, 1975 - No. 40, May, 1979; No. 41, Sept, 1979

1-Captain America & Bucky, Human Torch & Toro, & Sub-Mariner begin; cont'd. from Giant Size Invaders #1; #1-7 are 25¢ issues	6	12	18	39	62	85
2-5: 2-1st app. Brain-Drain. 3-Battle issue; Cap vs. Namor vs. Torch; intro U-Man	3	6	9	16	23	30
6-10: 6,7-(Regular 25¢ edition). 6-(7/76) Liberty Legion app. 7-Intro Baron Blood & intro/1st app. Union Jack; Human Torch origin retold. 8-Union Jack-c/story. 9-Origin Baron Blood. 10-G.A. Capt. America-r/C.A #22	2	4	6	9	13	16
6,7-(30¢-c variants, limited distribution)	4	8	12	24	37	50
11-19: 11-Origin Spitfire; intro The Blue Bullet. 14-1st app. The Crusaders. 16-Re-intro The Destroyer. 17-Intro Warrior Woman. 18-Re-intro The Destroyer w/new origin. 19-Hitler-c/story	2	4	6	8	10	12
17-19,21-(35¢-c variants, limited distribution)	4	8	12	28	44	60
20-(Regular 30¢-c) Reprints origin/1st app. Sub-Mariner from Motion Picture Funnies Weekly with color added & brief write-up about MPFW; 1st app. new Union Jack II	2	4	6	9	13	16
20-(35¢-c variant, limited distribution)	5	10	15	32	51	70
21-(Regular 30¢ edition)-r/Marvel Mystery #10 (battle issue)	2	4	6	8	11	14
22-30,34-40: 22-New origin Toro. 24-r/Marvel Mystery #17 (team-up issue; all-r). 25-All new-a begins. 28-Intro new Human Top & Golden Girl. 29-Intro Teutonic Knight. 34-Mighty Destroyer joins. 35-The Whizzer app.	1	2	3	5	6	8
31-33: 31-Frankenstein-c/sty. 32,33-Thor app.	2	4	6	8	10	12
41-Double size last issue	2	4	6	13	18	22
Annual 1 (9/77)-Schomburg, Rico stories (new); Schomburg-c/a (1st for Marvel in 30 years); Avengers app.; re-intro The Shark & The Hyena	5	10	15	30	48	65

... Classic Vol. 1 TPB (2007, $24.99) r/#1-9, Giant-Size Invaders #1 and Marvel Premiere #29,30; cover pencils and cover inks 25.00

NOTE: ***Buckler** a-5. **Everett** r-20('39), 21(1940), 24, Annual 1. **Gil Kane** c(p)-13, 17, 18, 20-27. **Kirby** c(p)-3-12, 14-16, 32, 33. **Mooney** a-5i, 16, 22. **Robbins** a-1-4, 6-9, 10(3 pg.), 11-15, 17-21, 23, 25-28; c-28.*

INVADERS (See Namor, the Sub-Mariner #12)
Marvel Comics Group: May, 1993 - No. 4, Aug, 1993 ($1.75, limited series)

1-4 2.50

INVADERS (2004 title - see New Invaders)

INVADERS FROM HOME
DC Comics (Piranha Press): 1990 - No. 6, 1990 ($2.50, mature)

1-6 2.50

INVASION
DC Comics: Holiday, 1988-'89 - No. 3, Jan, 1989 ($2.95, lim. series, 84 pgs.)

1-3:1-McFarlane/Russell-a. 2-McFarlane/Russell & Giffen/Gordon-a 3.00
Invasion! TPB (2008, $24.99) r/#1-3 25.00

INVINCIBLE (Also see The Pact #4)
Image Comics: Jan, 2003 - Present ($2.95/$2.99)

1-Kirkman-s/Walker-a 40.00
2-8-Kirkman-s/Walker-a. 4-Preview of The Moth 12.00
9-14: 11-Origin of Omni-Man. 14-Cho-c 6.00
15-24,26-41,43-49: 33-Tie-in w/Marvel Team-Up #14 3.00
25-($4.95) Science Dog app.; back-up stories w/origins of Science Dog and teammates 5.00
42-($1.99) Includes re-cap of the entire series 2.25
50-(6/08, $4.99) Two covers; back-up origin of Cecil Stedman; Science Dog app. 5.00
51-59,61-70: 51-Jim Lee-c; new costumes. 57-Continues in Astounding Wolf-Man #11 3.00
60-($3.99) Invincible War; Witchblade, Savage Dragon, Spawn, Youngblood app. 4.00
#0-(4/05, 50¢) Origin of Invincible; Ottley-a 2.25
Official Handbook of the Invincible Universe 1,2 (11/06, 1/07, $4.99) profile pages 5.00
Official Handbook of the Invincible Universe Vol. 1 (2007, $12.99) r/#1-2; sketch pages 13.00
... Presents Atom Eve 1,2 (12/07, 3/08, $2.99) origin of Atom Eve; Bellegarde-a 3.00
... Presents Atom Eve & Rex Splode 1-3 (10/09 - 2/10, $2.99) origin of Rex 3.00
... Universe Primer 1 (5/08, $5.99) r/Invincible #1, Brit #1, Astounding Wolf-Man #1 6.00
The Complete Invincible Library Vol. 1 Slipcase HC (2006, $125.00) oversized r/#1-24, #0 and story from Image Comics Summer Special (FCBD 2004); sketch pages; script for #1 125.00
..., Ultimate Collection Vol. 1 HC (2005, $34.95) oversized r/#1-13; sketch pages 35.00
..., Ultimate Collection Vol. 2 HC (2006, $34.99) oversized r/#14-24, #0 and story from Image Comics Summer Special (FCBD 2004); sketch pages and script for #23; intro by Damon Lindelof; afterword by Robert Kirkman 35.00
..., Ultimate Collection Vol. 3 HC (2007, $34.95) oversized r/#25-35 & The Pact #4; sketch pages and script for #28; afterword by Robert Kirkman 35.00
..., Ultimate Collection Vol. 4 HC (2008, $34.99) oversized r/#36-47; sketch & script pgs. 35.00
Vol. 1: Family Matters TPB (8/03, $12.95) r/#1-4; intro. by Busiek; sketch pages 13.00
Vol. 2: Eight in Enough TPB (3/04, $12.95) r/#5-8; intro. by Larsen; sketch pages 13.00
Vol. 3: Perfect Strangers TPB (2004, $12.95) r/#9-12; intro. by Brevoort; sketch pages 13.00
Vol. 4: Head of the Class TPB (1/05, $14.95) r/#14-19; intro. by Waid; sketch pages 15.00
Vol. 5: The Facts of Life TPB (2005, $14.99) r/#0,20-24; intro. by Wieringo; sketch pages 15.00
Vol. 6: A Different World TPB (2006, $14.99) r/#25-30; intro. by Brubaker; sketch pages 15.00
Vol. 7: Three's Company TPB (2006, $14.99) r/#31-35 & The Pact #4; sketch pages 15.00
Vol. 8: My Favorite Martian TPB (2007, $14.99) r/#36-41; sketch pages 15.00
Vol. 9: Out of This World TPB (2008, $14.99) r/#42-47; sketch pages 15.00

INVINCIBLE FOUR OF KUNG FU & NINJA
Leung Publications: April, 1988 - No. 6, 1989 ($2.00)

1-($2.75) 3.00
2-6: 2-Begin $2.00-c 2.50

Invisibles #8 © Grant Morrison

Iron Fist #14 © MAR

Iron Man #109 © MAR

	GD 2.0	VG 4.0	FN 6.0	VF 8.0	VF/NM 9.0	NM- 9.2

INVINCIBLE IRON MAN
Marvel Comics: July, 2008 - Present ($2.99)

1-Fraction-s/Larroca-a; covers by Larroca & Quesada 3.00
1-Downey movie photo wraparound 5.00
1-Secret Movie Variant white-c with movie cast 30.00
2-18: 2-War Machine and Thor app. 7-Spider-Man app. 8-10-Dark Reign. 11-War Machine app.; Pepper gets her armor suit. 12-Namor app. 3.00
19,20-($3.99) 20-Stark Disassembled starts; back-up synopsis of recent storylines 4.00
21-24-Covers by Larocca and Zircher: 21-Thor & Capt. America app. 22-Dr. Strange app. 3.00

INVISIBLE BOY (See Approved Comics)

INVISIBLE MAN, THE (See Superior Stories #1 & Supernatural Thrillers #2)

INVISIBLE PEOPLE
Kitchen Sink Press: 1992 (B&W, lim. series)

Book One: Sanctum; Book Two: "The Power": Will Eisner-s/a in all 2.50
Book Three: "Mortal Combat" 4.00
Hardcover ($34.95) 35.00
TPB (DC Comics, 9/00, $12.95) reprints series 13.00

INVISIBLES, THE (1st Series)
DC Comics (Vertigo): Sept, 1994 - No. 25, Oct, 1996 ($1.95/$2.50, mature)

1-($2.95, 52 pgs.)-Intro King Mob, Ragged Robin, Boy, Lord Fanny & Dane (Jack Frost); Grant Morrison scripts in all 6.00
2-8: 4-Includes bound-in trading cards. 5-1st app. Orlando; brown paper-c 4.00
9-25: 10-Intro Jim Crow. 13-15-Origin Lord Fanny. 19-Origin King Mob; polybagged. 20-Origin Boy. 21-Mister Six revealed. 25-Intro Division X 2.50
Apocalipstick (2001, $19.95, TPB)-r/#9-16; Bolland-c 20.00
Entropy in the U.K. (2001, $19.95, TPB)-r/#17-25; Bolland-c 20.00
Say You Want A Revolution (1996, $17.50, TPB)-r/#1-8 18.00

NOTE: ***Buckingham** a-25p. **Rian Hughes** c-1, 5. **Phil Jimenez** a-17p-19p. **Paul Johnson** a-16, 21. **Sean Phillips** c-2-4, 6-25. **Weston** a-10p. **Yeowell** a-1p-4p, 22p-24p.*

INVISIBLES, THE (2nd Series)
DC Comics (Vertigo): V2#1, Feb, 1997 - No. 22, Feb, 1999 ($2.50, mature)

1-Intro Jolly Roger; Grant Morrison scripts, Phil Jimenez-a, & Brian Bolland-c begins 4.00
2-22: 9,14-Weston-a 2.50
Bloody Hell in America TPB ('98, $12.95) r/#1-4 13.00
Counting to None TPB ('99, $19.95) r/#5-13 20.00
Kissing Mr. Quimper TPB ('00, $19.95) r/#14-22 20.00

INVISIBLES, THE (3rd Series) (Issue #'s go in reverse from #12 to #1)
DC Comics (Vertigo): V3#12, Apr, 1999 - No. 1, June, 2000 ($2.95, mature)

1-12-Bolland-c; Morrison-s on all. 1-Quitely-a. 2-4-Art by various. 5-8-Phillips-a. 9-12-Phillip Bond-a. 3.00
The Invisible Kingdom TPB ('02, $19.95) r/#12-1; new Bolland-c 20.00

INVISIBLE SCARLET O'NEIL (Also see Famous Funnies #81 & Harvey Comics Hits #59)
Famous Funnies (Harvey): Dec, 1950 - No. 3, Apr, 1951 (2-3 pgs. of Powell-a in each issue.)

	GD	VG	FN	VF	VF/NM	NM-
1	15	30	45	86	133	180
2,3	12	24	36	67	94	120

ION (Green Lantern Kyle Rayner) (See Countdown)
DC Comics: Jun, 2006 - No. 12, May, 2007 ($2.99)

1-12: 1-Marz-s/Tocchini-a. 3-Mogo app. 9,10-Tangent Green Lantern app. 12-Monitor app. 3.00
...: The Torchbearer TPB (2007, $14.99) r/#1-6 15.00

I, PAPARAZZI
DC Comics (Vertigo): 2001 ($29.95, HC, digitally manipulated photographic art)

nn-Pat McGreal-s/Steven Parke-digital-a/Stephen John Phillips-photos 30.00

IRON AND THE MAIDEN
Aspen MLT: Sept, 2007 - No. 4, Dec, 2007 ($3.99)

1-4: 1-Two covers by Manapul and Madureira/Matsuda; Jason Rubin-s 4.00
...: Brutes, Bims and the City (2/08, $2.99) character backgrounds/development art 3.00

IRON CORPORAL, THE (See Army War Heroes #22)
Charlton Comics: No. 23, Oct, 1985 - No. 25, Feb, 1986

23-25: Glanzman-a(r); low print 6.00

IRON FIST (See Immortal Iron Fist, Deadly Hands of Kung Fu, Marvel Premiere & Power Man)
Marvel Comics: Nov, 1975 - No. 15, Sept, 1977

	GD	VG	FN	VF	VF/NM	NM-
1-Iron Fist battles Iron Man (#1-6: 25¢)	6	12	18	43	69	95
2	4	8	12	22	34	45
3-10: 4-6-(Regular 25¢ edition)(4-6/76). 8-Origin retold	3	6	9	18	27	35
4-6-(30¢-c variant, limited distribution)	6	12	18	37	59	80
11,13: 13-(30¢-c)	3	6	9	16	22	28
12-Capt. America app.	3	6	9	18	27	35
13-(35¢-c variant, limited distribution)	7	14	21	49	80	110
14-1st app. Sabretooth (8/77)(see Power Man)	14	28	42	100	188	275
14-(35¢-c variant, limited distribution)	64	128	192	544	1072	1600
15-(Regular 30¢ ed.) X-Men app., Byrne-a	7	14	21	45	73	100
15-(35¢-c variant, limited distribution)	18	36	54	129	252	375

NOTE: ***Adkins** a-8p, 10i, 13i; c-8i. **Byrne** a-1-15p; c-8p, 15p. **G. Kane** c-4-6p. **McWilliams** a-1i.*

IRON FIST
Marvel Comics: Sept, 1996 - No. 2, Oct, 1996 ($1.50, limited series)

1,2 3.00

IRON FIST
Marvel Comics: Jul, 1998 - No. 3, Sept, 1998 ($2.50, limited series)

1-3: Jurgens-s/Guice-a 2.50

IRON FIST (Also see Immortal Iron Fist)
Marvel Comics: May, 2004 - No. 6, Oct, 2004 ($2.99)

1-6: 1-4,6-Kevin Lau-c/a. 5-Mays-c/a 3.00

IRON FIST: WOLVERINE
Marvel Comics: Nov, 2000 - No. 4, Feb, 2001 ($2.99, limited series)

1-4-Igle-c/a; Kingpin app. 2-Iron Man app. 3,4-Capt. America app. 3.00

IRON GHOST
Image Comics: Apr, 2005 - No. 6, Mar, 2006 ($2.95/$2.99, limited series)

1-6-Chuck Dixon-s/Sergio Cariello-a; flip cover on each 3.00

IRONHAND OF ALMURIC (Robert E. Howard's...)
Dark Horse Comics: Aug, 1991 - No. 4, 1991 ($2.00, B&W, mini-series)

1-4: 1-Conrad painted-c 2.25

IRON HORSE (TV)
Dell Publishing Co.: March, 1967 - No. 2, June, 1967

	GD	VG	FN	VF	VF/NM	NM-
1-Dale Robertson photo covers on both	3	6	9	18	27	35
2	3	6	9	15	21	26

IRONJAW (Also see The Barbarians)
Atlas/Seaboard Publ.: Jan, 1975 - No. 4, July, 1975

	GD	VG	FN	VF	VF/NM	NM-
1,2-Neal Adams-c. 1-1st app. Iron Jaw; Sekowsky-a(p); Fleisher-s	2	4	6	9	12	15
3,4-Marcos. 4-Origin	2	3	4	6	8	10

IRON LANTERN
Marvel Comics (Amalgam): June, 1997 ($1.95, one-shot)

1-Kurt Busiek-s/Paul Smith & Al Williamson-a 2.50

IRON MAN (Also see The Avengers #1, Giant-Size..., Marvel Collectors Item Classics, Marvel Double Feature, Marvel Fanfare, Tales of Suspense #39 & Uncanny Tales #52)
Marvel Comics: May, 1968 - No. 332, Sept, 1996

	GD	VG	FN	VF	VF/NM	NM-
1-Origin; Colan-c/a(p); story continued from Iron Man & Sub-Mariner #1	36	72	108	280	540	800
2	14	28	42	97	181	265
3	10	20	30	67	116	165
4,5	8	16	24	58	97	135
6-10: 9-Iron Man battles green Hulk-like android	7	14	21	45	73	100
11-15: 15-Last 12¢ issue	6	12	18	37	59	80
16-20	5	10	15	30	48	65
21-24,26-30: 22-Death of Janice Cord. 27-Intro Firebrand	4	8	12	22	34	45
25-Iron Man battles Sub-Mariner	4	8	12	26	41	55
31-42: 33-1st app. Spymaster. 35-Nick Fury & Daredevil x-over. 42-Last 15¢ issue	3	6	9	16	23	30
43-Intro The Guardsman; 25¢ giant (52 pgs.)	4	8	12	26	41	55
44-46,48-50: 43-Giant-Man back-up by Ayers. 44-Ant-Man by Tuska. 46-The Guardsman dies. 50-Princess Python app.	3	6	9	14	20	25
47-Origin retold; Barry Smith-a(p)	3	6	9	19	29	38
51-53: 53-Starlin part pencils	2	4	6	11	16	20
54-Iron Man battles Sub-Mariner; 1st app. Moondragon (1/73) as Madame MacEvil; Everett part-c	4	8	12	28	44	60
55-1st app. Thanos, Drax the Destroyer, Mentor, Starfox & Kronos (2/73); Starlin-c/a	14	28	42	102	194	285
56-Starlin-a	4	8	12	28	44	60
57-65,67-70: 59-Firebrand returns. 65-Origin Dr. Spectrum. 67-Last 20¢ issue. 68-Sunfire & Unicorn app.; origin retold; Starlin-c	2	4	6	10	14	18
66-Iron Man vs. Thor.	3	6	9	18	27	35
71-84: 72-Cameo portraits of N. Adams. 73-Rename Stark Industries to Stark International; Brunner. 76-r/#9.	2	4	6	8	11	14

Iron Man #306 © MAR

Iron Man V3 #87 © MAR

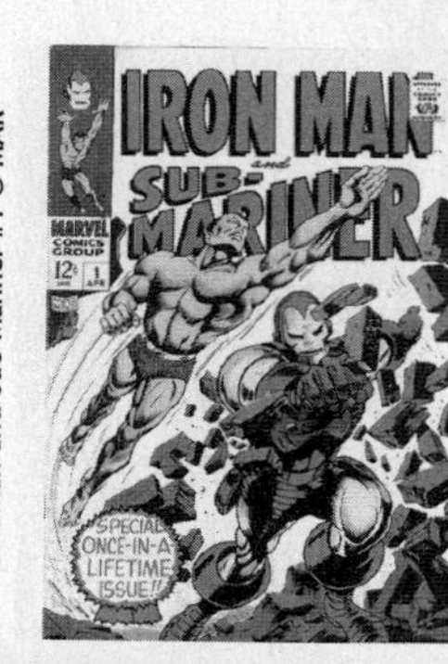
Iron Man and Sub-Mariner #1 © MAR

	GD 2.0	VG 4.0	FN 6.0	VF 8.0	VF/NM 9.0	NM- 9.2
85-89-(Regular 25¢ editions): 86-1st app. Blizzard. 87-Origin Blizzard. 88-Thanos app. 89-Daredevil app.; last 25¢-c	2	4	6	8	11	14
85-89-(30¢-c variants, limited distribution)(4-8/76)	4	8	12	22	34	45
90-99: 96-1st app. new Guardsman	2	4	6	8	10	12
99,101-103-(35¢-c variants, limited dist.)	4	8	12	28	44	60
100-(7/77)-Starlin-c	3	6	9	19	29	38
100-(35¢-c variant, limited dist.)	9	18	27	60	100	140
101-117: 101-Intro DreadKnight. 109-1st app. new Crimson Dynamo; 1st app. Vanguard. 110-Origin Jack of Hearts retold; death of Count Nefaria. 114-Avengers app.	2	3	4	6	8	10
118-Byrne-a(p); 1st app. Jim Rhodes	2	4	6	11	16	20
119-127: 120,121-Sub-Mariner x-over. 122-Origin. 123-128-Tony Stark treated for alcohol problem. 125-Ant-Man app.	2	4	6	10	14	18
128-(11/79) Classic Tony Stark alcoholism cover	3	6	9	16	23	30
129,130,134-149	1	2	3	4	5	7
131-133: 131,132-Hulk x-over. 133-Hulk/Ant Man-c	1	2	3	5	7	9
150-Double size	2	3	4	6	8	10
151-168: 152-New armor. 161-Moon Knight app. 167-Tony Stark alcohol problem resurfaces						5.00
169-New Iron Man (Jim Rhodes replaces Tony Stark)	1	2	3	5	6	8
170,171						5.00
172-199: 172-Captain America x-over. 186-Intro Vibro. 190-Scarlet Witch app. 191-198-Tony Stark returns as original Iron Man. 192-Both Iron Men battle						3.50
200-(11/85, $1.25, 52 pgs.)-Tony Stark returns as new Iron Man (red & white armor) thru #230						6.00
201-213,215-224: 213-Intro new Dominic Fortune						3.50
214,225,228,231,234,247: 214-Spider-Woman app. in new black costume (1/87). 225-Double size ($1.25). 228-vs. Capt. America. 231-Intro new Iron Man. 234-Spider-Man x-over. 247-Hulk x-over						4.50
226,227,229,230,232,233,235-243,245,246,248,249: 233-Ant-Man app. 243-Tony Stark loses use of legs						2.75
244-($1.50, 52 pgs.)-New Armor makes him walk						3.25
250-($1.50, 52 pgs.)-Dr. Doom-c/story						3.25
251-274,276-281,283,285-287,289,291-299: 258-277-Byrne scripts. 271-Fin Fang Foom app. 276-Black Widow-c/story; last $1.00-c. 281-1st brief app. War Machine. 283-2nd full app. War Machine						2.50
275-($1.50, 52 pgs.)						3.00
282-1st full app. War Machine (7/92)						4.00
284-Death of Iron Man (Tony Stark)						4.00
288-($2.50, 52pg.)-Silver foil stamped-c; Iron Man's 350th app. in comics						3.00
290-($2.95, 52pg.)-Gold foil stamped-c; 30th ann.						3.00
300-($3.95, 68 pgs.)-Collector's Edition w/embossed foil-c; anniversary issue; War Machine-c/story						4.00
300-($2.50, 68 pgs.)-Newsstand Edition						2.50
301-303: 302-Venom-c/story (cameo #301)						2.50
304-316,318-324,326-331: 304-Begin $1.50-c; bound-in trading card sheet; Thunderstrike-c/story. 310-Orange logo. 312-w/bound-in Power Ranger Card. 319-Prologue to "The Crossing." 326-New Tony Stark; Pratt-c. 330-War Machine & Stockpile app; return of Morgan Stark						2.50
310,325: 310 ($2.95)-Polybagged w/ 16 pg. Marvel Action Hour preview & acetate print; white logo. 325-($2.95)-Wraparound-c						3.00
317-($2.50)-Flip book						2.50
332-Onslaught x-over						4.00
Special 1 (8/70)-Sub-Mariner x-over; Everett-c	5	10	15	30	48	65
Special 2 (11/71, 52 pgs.)-r/TOS #81,82,91 (all-r)	3	6	9	18	27	35
Annual 3 (1976)-Man-Thing app.	2	4	6	13	18	22
King Size 4 (8/77)-The Champions (w/Ghost Rider) app.; Newton-a(i)	2	4	6	10	14	18
Annual 5 ('82) New-a	1	2	3	5	6	8
Annual 6-8: ('83-'85) 6-New Iron Man (J. Rhodes) app. 8-X-Factor app.						5.00
Annual 9-15: ('86-'94) 10-Atlantis Attacks x-over; P. Smith-a; Layton/Guice-a; Sub-Mariner app. 11-(1990)-Origin of Mrs. Arbogast by Ditko (p&i). 12-1 pg. origin recap; Ant-Man back-up-s. 13-Darkhawk & Avengers West Coast app.; Colan/Williamson-a. 14-Bagged w/card						3.00
...: Armor Wars TPB (2007, $24.99) r/#225-232; Michelinie intro.						25.00
Manual 1 (1993, $1.75)-Operations handbook						2.50
Graphic Novel: Crash (1988, $12.95, Adults, 72 pgs.)-Computer generated art & color; violence & nudity						13.00
...Collector's Preview 1(11/94, $1.95)-wraparound-c; text & illos-no comics						2.50
...: Demon in a Bottle HC (2008, $24.99) r/#120-128; two covers						25.00
...: Demon in a Bottle TPB (2006, $24.99) r/#120-128						25.00
...: Many Armors of Iron Man (2008, $24.99) r/#47, 142-144, 152-153, 200, 218						25.00
...Vs. Dr. Doom (12/94, $12.95)-r/#149-150, 249,250. Julie Bell-c						13.00
...Vs. Dr. Doom: Doomquest HC (2008, $19.99, dustjacket)-r/#149-150, 249,250; new Michelinie intro.; bonus art						20.00
...: War Machine TPB (2008, $29.99) r/#280-291						30.00
The Invincible Iron Man Omnibus Vol. 1 HC (2008, $99.99, dustjacket) r/Iron Man stories from Tales of Suspense #39-83 & Tales To Astonish #82; 1992 intro. by Stan Lee; 1975 essay by Lee; 2008 essay by Layton; gallery of original art and covers; creator bios						100.00

NOTE: **Austin** *c-105i, 109-111i, 151i.* **Byrne** *a-118p; c-109p, 197, 253.* **Colan** *a-1p, 253, Special 1p(3); c-1p.* **Craig** *a-1i, 2-4, 5-13i, 14, 15-19i, 24p, 25p, 26-28i; c-2-4.* **Ditko** *a-160p.* **Everett** *c-29.* **Guice** *a-233-241p.* **G. Kane** *c(p)-52-54, 63, 67, 72-75, 77-79, 88, 98.* **Kirby** *a-Special 1p; c-13, 80p, 90, 92-95.* **Mooney** *a-40i, 43i, 47i.* **Perez** *c-103p.* **Simonson** *c-Annual 8.* **B. Smith** *a-232p, 243i; c-232.* **P. Smith** *a-159p, 245p, Annual 10p; c-159.* **Starlin** *a-53p(part), 55p, 56p; c-55p, 160, 163.* **Tuska** *a-5-13p, 15-23p, 24i, 32p, 38-46p, 48-54p, 57-61p, 63-69p, 70-72p, 78p, 86-92p, 95-106p, Annual 4p.* **Wood** *a-Special 1i.*

IRON MAN (The Invincible...) (Volume Two)
Marvel Comics: Nov, 1996 - No. 13, Nov, 1997 ($2.95/$1.95/$1.99)
(Produced by WildStorm Productions)

	GD 2.0	VG 4.0	FN 6.0	VF 8.0	VF/NM 9.0	NM- 9.2
V2#1-3-Heroes Reborn begins; Scott Lobdell scripts & Whilce Portacio-c/a begin; new origin Iron Man & Hulk. 2-Hulk app. 3-Fantastic Four app.						4.00
1-Variant-c						5.00
4-11: 4-Two covers. 6-Fantastic Four app.; Industrial Revolution; Hulk app. 7-Return of Rebel. 11-($1.99) Dr. Doom-c/app.						3.00
12-($2.99) "Heroes Reunited"-pt. 3; Hulk-c/app.						3.50
13-($1.99) "World War 3"-pt. 3, x-over w/Image						3.00
Heroes Reborn: Iron Man (2006, $29.99, TPB) r/#1-12; Heroes Reborn #1/2; pin-ups						30.00

IRON MAN (The Invincible...) (Volume Three)
Marvel Comics: Feb, 1998 - No. 89, Dec, 2004 ($2.99/$1.99/$2.25)

	GD 2.0	VG 4.0	FN 6.0	VF 8.0	VF/NM 9.0	NM- 9.2
V3#1-($2.99)-Follows Heroes Return; Busiek scripts & Chen-c/a begin; Deathsquad app.						5.00
1-Alternate Ed.	1	2	3	5	6	8
2-12: 2-Two covers. 6-Black Widow-c/app. 7-Warbird-c/app. 8-Black Widow app. 9-Mandarin returns						3.00
13-($2.99) battles the Controller						3.50
14-24: 14-Fantastic Four-c/app.						3.00
25-($2.99) Iron Man and Warbird battle Ultimo; Avengers app.						3.00
26-30-Quesada-s. 28-Whiplash killed. 29-Begin $2.25-c.						2.50
31-45,47-49,51-54: 35-Maximum Security x-over; FF-c/app. 41-Grant-a begins. 44-New armor debut. 48-Ultron-c/app.						2.50
46-($3.50, 100 pgs.) Sentient armor returns; r/V1#78,140,141						3.50
50-($3.50) Grell-s begins; Black Widow app.						3.50
55-($3.50) 400th issue; Asamiya-c; back-up story Stark reveals ID; Grell-a						3.50
56-66: 56-Reis-a. 57,58-Ryan-a. 59-61-Grell-c/a. 62,63-Ryan-a. 64-Davis-a; Thor-c/app.						2.50
67-89: 67-Begin $2.99-c; Gene Ha-c. 75-83-Granov-c. 84-Avengers Disassembled prologue 85-89-Avengers Disassembled. 85-88-Harris-a. 86-89-Pat Lee-c. 87-Rumiko killed						3.00
.../Captain America '98 Annual ($3.50) vs. Modok						3.50
1999, 2000 Annual ($3.50)						3.50
2001 Annual ($2.99) Claremont-s/Ryan-a						3.00
Avengers Disassembled: Iron Man TPB (2004, $14.99) r/#84-89						15.00
Mask in the Iron Man (5/01, $14.95, TPB) r/#26-30, #1/2						15.00

IRON MAN (The Invincible...)
Marvel Comics: Jan, 2005 - No. 35, Jan, 2009 ($3.50/$2.99)

	GD 2.0	VG 4.0	FN 6.0	VF 8.0	VF/NM 9.0	NM- 9.2
1-($3.50-c) Warren Ellis-s/Adi Granov-c/a						3.50
2-14-($2.99) 5-Flashback to origin; Stark gets new abilities. 7-Knauf-s/Zircher-a 13,14-Civil War						3.00
15-24,26,27,29-35: 15-Stark becomes Director of S.H.I.E.L.D. 19,20-World War Hulk. 33-Secret Invasion; War Machine app. 34,35-War Machine title logo						3.00
25,28-($3.99) 25-Includes movie preview & armor showcase. 28-Red & white armor						4.00
All-New Iron Manual (2/08, $4.99) Handbook-style guide to characters & armor suits						5.00
...: Director of S.H.I.E.L.D. Annual 1 (1/08, $3.99) Madame Hydra app.; Cheung-c						4.00
...Golden Avenger 1 (11/08, $2.99) Santacruz-a; movie photo-c						3.00
.../Hulk/Fury 1 (2/09, $3.99) crossover of movie-version characters						4.00
Indomitable Iron Man (4/10, $3.99) B&W stories; Chaykin-s/a; Rosado-a; Parrillo-c						4.00
...: Iron Protocols (12/09, $3.99) Olivetti-c/Nelson-a						4.00
...: Requiem (2009, $4.99) r/TOS #39, Iron Man #144 (1981); armor profiles						5.00
...: The End (1/09, $4.99) future Tony Stark retires; Michelinie-s/Chang & Layton-a						5.00
Civil War: Iron Man TPB (2007, $11.99) r/#13,14, .../Captain America: Casualities of War, and Civil War: The Confession						12.00
.../Captain America: Casualities of War (2/07, $3.99) two covers; flashbacks						4.00
HC (2006, $19.99, dust jacket) r/#1-6 and Granov covers from Iron Man V3 #75-83						20.00
...: Director of S.H.I.E.L.D. TPB (2007, $14.99) r/#15-18; Strange Tales #135 (1965) and Iron Man #129; profile pages for Iron Man and S.H.I.E.L.D.; creator interviews						15.00
...: Extremis SC (2007, $14.99) r/#1-6 and Granov covers from Iron Man V3 #75-83						15.00
...: Execute Program SC (2007, $14.99) r/#7-12; cover layouts and sketches						15.00

IRON MAN AND POWER PACK
Marvel Comics: Jan, 2008 - No. 4, Apr, 2008 ($2.99, limited series)

	GD 2.0	VG 4.0	FN 6.0	VF 8.0	VF/NM 9.0	NM- 9.2
1-4-Gurihiru-c/Sumerak-s; Puppet Master app.; Mini Marvels back-ups in each						3.00
...: Armored and Dangerous TPB (2008, $7.99, digest size) r/series						8.00

Iron Man: Enter the Mandarin #2 © MAR

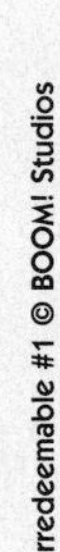

Irredeemable #1 © BOOM! Studios

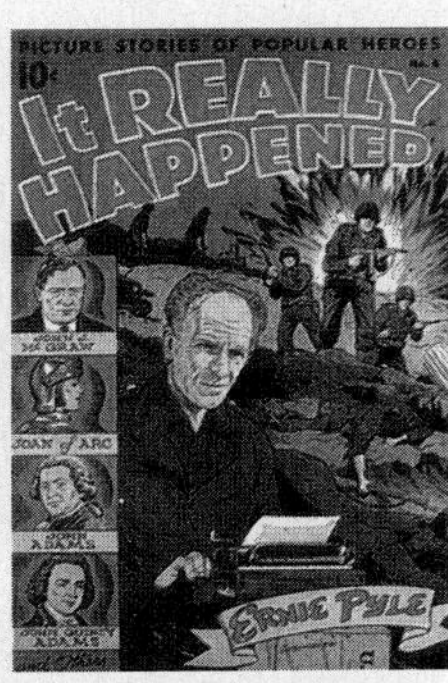

It Really Happened #6 © STD

GD 2.0 | VG 4.0 | FN 6.0 | VF 8.0 | VF/NM 9.0 | NM- 9.2

GD 2.0 | VG 4.0 | FN 6.0 | VF 8.0 | VF/NM 9.0 | NM- 9.2

IRON MAN & SUB-MARINER
Marvel Comics Group: Apr, 1968 (12¢, one-shot) (Pre-dates Iron Man #1 & Sub-Mariner #1)
1-Iron Man story by Colan/Craig continued from Tales of Suspense #99 & continued in Iron Man #1; Sub-Mariner story by Colan continued from Tales to Astonish #101 & continued in Sub-Mariner #1; Colan/Everett-c 15 30 45 107 204 300

IRON MAN AND THE ARMOR WARS
Marvel Comics: Oct, 2009 - No. 4, Jan, 2010 ($2.99, limited series)
1-4-Rousseau-a; Crimson Dynamo & Omega Red app. 3.00

IRON MAN: ARMORED ADVENTURES
Marvel Comics: Sept, 2009 ($3.99, one-shot)
1-Based on the 2009 cartoon; Brizuela-a; Nick Fury & Living Laser app. 4.00

IRON MAN: BAD BLOOD
Marvel Comics: Sept, 2000 - No. 4, Dec, 2000 ($2.99, limited series)
1-4-Micheline-s/Layton-a 3.00

IRON MAN: ENTER THE MANDARIN
Marvel Comics: Nov, 2007 - No. 6, Apr, 2008 ($2.99, limited series)
1-6-Casey-s/Canete-a; retells first meeting 3.00
TPB (2008, $14.99) r/#1-6 15.00

IRON MAN: HOUSE OF M (Also see House of M and related x-overs)
(Reprinted in House of M: Fantastic Four/ Iron Man TPB)
Marvel Comics: Sept, 2005 - No. 3, Nov, 2005 ($2.99, limited series)
1-3-Pat Lee-a/c; Greg Pak-s 3.00

IRON MAN: HYPERVELOCITY
Marvel Comics: Mar, 2007 - No. 6, Aug, 2007 ($2.99, limited series)
1-6-Adam Warren-s/Brian Denham-a/c 3.00
TPB (2007, $14.99) r/#1-6; layout pages and armor design sketches 15.00

IRON MAN: I AM IRON MAN
Marvel Comics: Mar, 2010 - No. 2, Apr, 2010 ($3.99, limited series)
1,2-Adaptation of the first movie; Peter David-s/Sean Chen-a/Adi Granov-c 4.00

IRON MAN: INEVITABLE
Marvel Comics: Feb, 2006 - No. 6, July, 2006 ($2.99, limited series)
1-6-Joe Casey-s/Frazer Irving; Spymaster and the Living Laser app. 3.00
TPB (2006, $14.99) r/#1-6; cover sketches 15.00

IRON MAN: LEGACY OF DOOM
Marvel Comics: Jun, 2008 - No. 4, Sept, 2008 ($2.99, limited series)
1-4-Michelinie-s/Lim & Layton-a; Dr. Doom app. 3.00

IRON MAN: THE IRON AGE
Marvel Comics: Aug, 1998 - No. 2, Sept, 1998 ($5.99, limited series)
1,2-Busiek-s; flashback story from gold armor days 6.00

IRON MAN: THE LEGEND
Marvel Comics: Sept, 1996 ($3.95, one-shot)
1-Tribute issue 4.50

IRON MAN 2020 (Also see Machine Man limited series)
Marvel Comics: June, 1994 ($5.95, one-shot)
nn 6.00

IRON MAN: VIVA LAS VEGAS
Marvel Comics: Jul, 2008 - No. 4 ($3.99, limited series)
1,2-Jon Favreau-s/Adi Granov-a/c 4.00

IRON MAN VS WHIPLASH
Marvel Comics: Jan, 2010 - No. 4, Apr, 2010 ($3.99, limited series)
1-4-Briones-a/Peterson-c; origin of new Whiplash 4.00

IRON MAN/X-O MANOWAR: HEAVY METAL (See X-O Manowar/Iron Man: In Heavy Metal)
Marvel Comics: Sept, 1996 ($2.50, one-shot) (1st Marvel/Valiant x-over)
1-Pt. II of Iron Man/X-O Manowar x-over; Fabian Nicieza scripts; 1st app. Rand Banion 2.50

IRON MARSHALL
Jademan Comics: July, 1990 - No. 32, Feb, 1993 ($1.75, plastic coated-c)
1,32: Kung Fu stories. 1-Poster centerfold 2.50
2-31-Kung Fu stories in all 2.50

IRON VIC (See Comics Revue No. 3 & Giant Comics Editions)
United Features Syndicate/St. John Publ. Co.: 1940
Single Series 22 34 68 102 199 325 450

IRONWOLF
DC Comics: 1986 ($2.00, one shot)
1-r/Weird Worlds 8-10; Chaykin story & art 2.50

IRONWOLF: FIRES OF THE REVOLUTION (See Weird Worlds #8-10)
DC Comics: 1992 ($29.95, hardcover)
nn-Chaykin/Moore story, Mignola-a w/Russell inks. 30.00

IRREDEEMABLE (Also see Incorruptible)
Marvel Comics: Apr, 2009 - Present ($3.99)
1-12: 1-Waid-s/Krause-a; 3 covers; Grant Morrison afterword. 2-12-Three covers 4.00

IRREDEEMABLE ANT-MAN, THE
Marvel Comics: Dec, 2006 - No. 12, Nov, 2007 ($2.99)
1-12-Kirkman-s/Hester-a/c; intro. Eric O'Grady as the new Ant-Man. 7-Ms. Marvel app. 10-World War Hulk x-over 3.00
... Vol. 1: Lowlife (2007, $9.99, digest) r/#1-6 10.00
... Vol. 2: Small-Minded (2007, $9.99, digest) r/#7-12 10.00

ISAAC ASIMOV'S I-BOTS
Tekno Comix: Dec, 1995 - No. 7, May, 1996 ($1.95)
1-7: 1-6-Perez-c/a. 2-Chaykin variant-c exists. 3-Polybagged. 7-Lady Justice-c/app. 2.50

ISAAC ASIMOV'S I-BOTS
BIG Entertainment: V2#1, June, 1996 - No. 9, Feb, 1997 ($2.25)
V2#1-9: 1-Lady Justice-c/app. 6-Gil Kane-c 2.50

ISIS (TV) (Also see Shazam)
National Per.l Publ./DC Comics: Oct-Nov, 1976 - No. 8, Dec-Jan, 1977-78
1-Wood inks 2 4 6 10 14 18
2-8: 5-Isis new look. 7-Origin 2 3 4 6 8 10

ISLAND AT THE TOP OF THE WORLD (See Walt Disney Showcase #27)

ISLAND OF DR. MOREAU, THE (Movie)
Marvel Comics Group: Oct, 1977 (52 pgs.)
1-Gil Kane-c 1 2 3 5 6 8

I SPY (TV)
Gold Key: Aug, 1966 - No. 6, Sept, 1968 (All have photo-c)
1-Bill Cosby, Robert Culp photo covers 14 28 42 99 175 250
2-6: 3,4-McWilliams-a. 5-Last 12¢-c 9 18 27 60 100 140

IT! (See Astonishing Tales No. 21-24 & Supernatural Thrillers No. 1)

ITCHY & SCRATCHY COMICS (The Simpsons TV show)
Bongo Comics: 1993 - No. 3, 1993 ($1.95)
1-3: 1-Bound-in jumbo poster. 3-w/decoder screen trading card 4.00
Holiday Special ('94, $1.95) 4.00

IT GIRL (Also see Atomics, and Madman Comics)
Oni Press: May, 2002 ($2.95, one-shot)
1-Allred-s/Clugston-Major-c/a; Atomics and Madman app. 3.00

IT REALLY HAPPENED
William H. Wise No. 1,2/Standard (Visual Editions): 1944 - No. 11, Oct, 1947
1-Kit Carson & Ben Franklin stories 23 46 69 136 223 310
2 14 28 42 81 118 155
3,4,6,9,11: 4-D-Day story. 6-Joan of Arc story. 9-Captain Kidd & Frank Buck stories 12 24 36 69 97 125
5-Lou Gehrig & Lewis Carroll stories 17 34 51 100 158 215
7-Teddy Roosevelt story 14 28 42 80 115 150
8-Story of Roy Rogers 17 34 51 98 154 210
10-Honus Wagner & Mark Twain stories 15 30 45 85 130 175
NOTE: *Guardineer a-7(2), 8(2), 10, 11.* ***Schomburg*** *c-1-7, 9-11.*

IT RHYMES WITH LUST (Also see Bold Stories & Candid Tales)
St. John Publishing Co.: 1950 (Digest size, 128 pgs., 25¢)
nn (Rare)-Matt Baker & Ray Osrin-a 110 220 330 704 1202 1700

IT'S A BIRD...
DC Comics: 2004 ($24.95, hardcover with dust jacket)
HC-Semi-autobiographical story of Steven Seagle writing Superman; Kristiansen-a 25.00
SC-($17.95) 18.00

IT'S ABOUT TIME (TV)
Gold Key: Jan, 1967
1 (10195-701)-Photo-c 4 8 12 28 44 60

IT'S A DUCK'S LIFE
Marvel Comics/Atlas(MMC): Feb, 1950 - No. 11, Feb, 1952

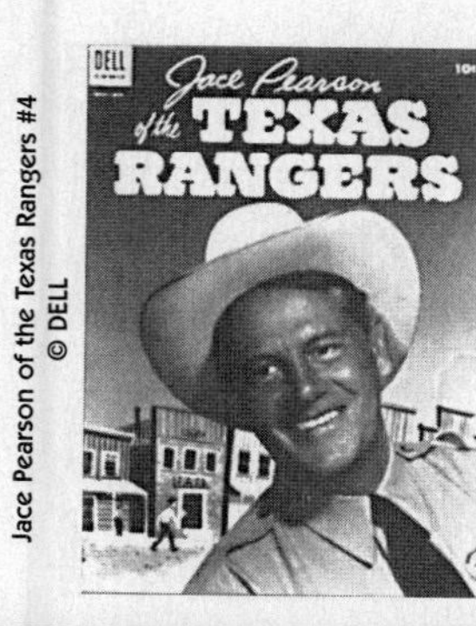

Jace Pearson of the Texas Rangers #4 © DELL

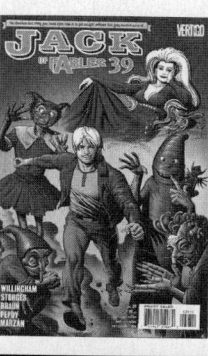

Jack of Fables #39 © Bill Willingham & DC

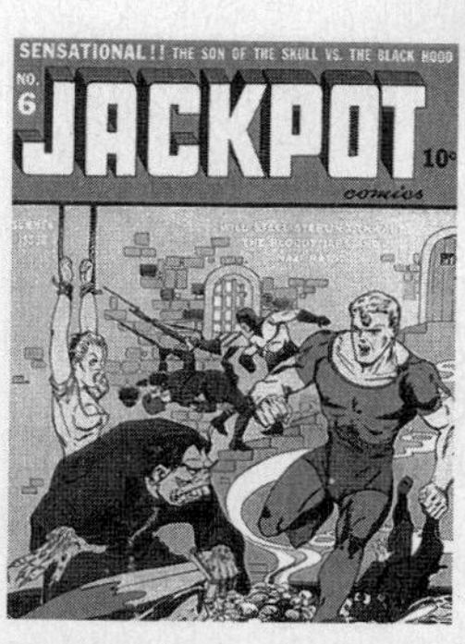

Jackpot Comics #6 © MLJ

	GD 2.0	VG 4.0	FN 6.0	VF 8.0	VF/NM 9.0	NM- 9.2
1-Buck Duck, Super Rabbit begin	15	30	45	90	140	190
2	10	20	30	56	76	95
3-11	9	18	27	52	69	85

IT'S GAMETIME
National Periodical Publications: Sept-Oct, 1955 - No. 4, Mar-Apr, 1956

1-(Scarce)-Infinity-c; Davy Crockett app. in puzzle	81	162	243	518	884	1250
2,3 (Scarce): 2-Dodo & The Frog	60	120	180	380	653	925
4 (Rare)	63	126	189	403	689	975

IT'S LOVE, LOVE, LOVE
St. John Publishing Co.: Nov, 1957 - No. 2, Jan, 1958 (10¢)

1,2	6	12	18	31	38	45

IVANHOE (See Fawcett Movie Comics No. 20)

IVANHOE
Dell Publishing Co.: July-Sept, 1963

1 (12-372-309)	3	6	9	21	32	42

IWO JIMA (See Spectacular Features Magazine)

JACE PEARSON OF THE TEXAS RANGERS (Radio/TV)(4-Color #396 is titled Tales of the Texas Rangers; ...'s Tales of ... #11-on)(See Western Roundup under Dell Giants)
Dell Publishing Co.: No. 396, 5/52 - No. 1021, 8-10/59 (No #10) (All-Photo-c)

Four Color 396 (#1)	10	20	30	73	129	185
2(5-7/53) - 9(2-4/55)	7	14	21	47	76	105
Four Color 648(#10, 9/55)	6	12	18	41	66	90
11(11-2/55-56) - 14,17-20(6-8/58)	6	12	18	37	59	80
15,16-Toth-a	6	12	18	39	62	85
Four Color 961,1021: 961-Spiegle-a	6	12	18	37	59	80

NOTE: *Joel McCrea photo c-1-9, F.C. 648 (starred on radio show only); Willard Parker photo c-11-on (starred on TV series).*

JACK ARMSTRONG (Radio)(See True Comics)
Parents' Institute: Nov, 1947 - No. 9, Sept, 1948; No. 10, Mar, 1949 - No. 13, Sept, 1949

1-(Scarce) (odd size) Cast intro. inside front-c; Vic Hardy's Crime Lab begins	43	86	129	271	461	650
2	20	40	60	114	182	250
3-5	15	30	45	83	124	165
6-13	13	26	39	72	101	130

JACK CROSS
DC Comics: Oct, 2005 - No. 4, Jan, 2006 ($2.50)

1-4-Warren Ellis-s/Gary Erskine-a 2.50

JACK HUNTER
Blackthorne Publishing: July, 1987 - No. 3 ($1.25)

1-3 2.50

JACKIE CHAN'S SPARTAN X
Topps Comics: May, 1997 - No. 3 ($2.95, limited series)

1-3-Michael Golden-s/a; variant photo-c 3.00

JACKIE CHAN'S SPARTAN X: HELL BENT HERO FOR HIRE
Image Comics (Little Eva Ink): Mar, 1998 - No. 3 ($2.95, B&W)

1-3-Michael Golden-s/a: 1-variant photo-c 3.00

JACKIE GLEASON (TV) (Also see The Honeymooners)
St. John Publishing Co.: Sept, 1955 - No. 4, Dec, 1955?

1(1955)(TV)-Photo-c	62	124	186	394	680	965
2-4	42	84	126	265	445	625

JACKIE GLEASON AND THE HONEYMOONERS (TV)
National Periodical Publications: June-July, 1956 - No. 12, Apr-May, 1958

1-1st app. Ralph Kramden	90	180	270	576	988	1400
2	53	106	159	334	567	800
3-11	42	84	126	265	445	625
12 (Scarce)	60	120	180	380	653	925

JACKIE JOKERS (Became Richie Rich &...)
Harvey Publications: March, 1973 - No. 4, Sept, 1973 (#5 was advertised, but not published)

1-1st app.	3	6	9	16	22	28
2-4: 2-President Nixon app.	2	4	6	8	11	14

JACKIE ROBINSON (Famous Plays of...) (Also see Negro Heroes #2 & Picture News #4)
Fawcett Publications: May, 1950 - No. 6, 1952 (Baseball hero) (All photo-c)

nn	97	194	291	621	1061	1500
2	55	110	165	352	601	850
3-6	47	94	141	296	498	700

JACK IN THE BOX (Formerly Yellowjacket Comics #1-10; becomes Cowboy Western Comics #17 on)
Frank Comunale/Charlton Comics No. 11 on: Feb, 1946; No. 11, Oct, 1946 - No. 16, Nov-Dec, 1947

	GD 2.0	VG 4.0	FN 6.0	VF 8.0	VF/NM 9.0	NM- 9.2
1-Stitches, Marty Mouse & Nutsy McKrow	18	36	54	105	165	225
11-Yellowjacket (early Charlton comic)	20	40	60	120	195	270
12,14,15	12	24	36	69	97	125
13-Wolverton-a	21	42	63	122	199	275
16-12 pg. adapt. of Silas Marner; Kiefer-a	14	28	42	76	108	140

JACK KIRBY'S FOURTH WORLD (See Mister Miracle & New Gods, 3rd Series)
DC Comics: Mar, 1997 - No. 20, Oct, 1998 ($1.95/$2.25)

1-20: 1-Byrne-a/scripts & Simonson-c begin; story cont'd from New Gods, 3rd Series #15; retells "The Pact" (New Gods, 1st Series #7); 1st brief DC app. Thor. 2-Thor vs. Big Barda; "Apokolips Then" back-up begins; Kirby-c/swipe (Thor #126) 8-Genesis x-over. 10-Simonson-s/a 13-Simonson back-up story. 20-Superman-c/app. 2.50

JACK KIRBY'S FOURTH WORLD OMNIBUS
DC Comics: 2007 - Vol. 4, 2008 ($49.99, hardcovers with dustjackets)

Vol. 1 ('07) Recolored reprints in chronological order of Superman's Pal, Jimmy Olsen #133-139, Forever People #1-3, New Gods #1-3, and Mister Miracle #1-3; Morrison intro, bonus art 50.00
Vol. 2 ('07) r/Jimmy Olsen #141-145, F.P. #4-6, N.G. #4-6 & M.M. #4-6; bonus art 50.00
Vol. 3 ('07) r/Jimmy Olsen #146-148, F.P. #7-10, N.G. #7-10 & M.M. #7-9; bonus art 50.00
Vol. 4 ('08) r/F.P. #11, M.M. #10-18, N.G. #11 & reprint series #6, & DC Graphic Novel #6 (The Hunger Dogs); Levitz intro.; Evanier afterword; character profile pages 50.00

JACK KIRBY'S GALACTIC BOUNTY HUNTERS
Marvel Comics (Icon): July, 2006 - No. 6, Nov, 2007 ($3.99)

1-6-Based on a Kirby concept; Mike Thibodeaux-a; Lisa Kirby, Thibodeaux and others-s 4.00
HC (2007, $24.99) r/series; pin-ups and supplemental art and interviews 25.00

JACK KIRBY'S SECRET CITY SAGA
Topps Comics (Kirbyverse): No. 0, Apr, 1993; No. 1, May, 1993 - No. 4, Aug, 1993 ($2.95, limited series)

0-(No cover price, 20 pgs.)-Simonson-c/a 3.00
0-Red embossed-c (limited ed.) 5.00
1-4-Bagged w/3 trading cards; Ditko-c/a: 1-Ditko/Art Adams-c. 2-Ditko/Byrne-c; has coupon for Pres. Clinton holo-foil trading card. 3-Dorman poster; has coupon for Gore holo-foil trading card. 4-Ditko/Perez-c 3.00
NOTE: *Issues #1-4 contain coupons redeemable for Kirbychrome version of #1*

JACK KIRBY'S SILVER STAR (Also see Silver Star)
Topps Comics (Kirbyverse): Oct, 1993 ($2.95)(Intended as a 4-issue limited series)

1-Silver ink-c; Austin-c/a(i); polybagged w/3 cards 3.00

JACK KIRBY'S TEENAGENTS (See Satan's Six)
Topps Comics (Kirbyverse): Aug, 1993 - No. 4, Nov, 1993 ($2.95, limited series)

1-4: Bagged with/3 trading cards; Busiek-s/Austin-c(i): 3-Liberty Project app. 3.00

JACK OF FABLES (See Fables)
DC Comics (Vertigo): Sept, 2006 - Present ($2.99)

1-42: 1-Willingham & Sturges-s/Akins-a. 33-35-Crossover with Fables and The Literals 3.00
...: Americana TPB (2008, $14.99) r/#17-21 15.00
...: Jack of Hearts TPB (2007, $14.99) r/#6-11 15.00
...: The Bad Prince TPB (2008, $14.99) r/#12-16 15.00
...: The Big Book of War TPB (2009, $14.99) r/#28-32 15.00
...: The (Nearly) Great Escape TPB (2007, $14.99) r/#1-5; Akins sketch pages 15.00
...: Turning Pages TPB (2009, $14.99) r/#22-27 15.00

JACK OF HEARTS (Also see The Deadly Hands of Kung Fu #22 & Marvel Premiere #44)
Marvel Comics Group: Jan, 1984 - No. 4, Apr, 1984 (60¢, limited series)

1-4 3.00

JACKPOT COMICS (Jolly Jingles #10 on)
MLJ Magazines: Spring, 1941 - No. 9, Spring, 1943

1-The Black Hood, Mr. Justice, Steel Sterling & Sgt. Boyle begin; Biro-c	326	652	978	2282	3991	5700
2-S. Cooper-c	148	296	444	947	1624	2300
3-Hubbell-c	110	220	330	704	1202	1700
4-Archie begins (Win/41; on sale 12/41)-(also see Pep Comics #22); 1st app. Mrs. Grundy, the principal; Novick-c	459	918	1377	3350	5925	8500
5-Hitler, Tojo, Mussolini-c by Montana; 1st definitive Mr. Weatherbee; 1st brief app. Reggie in 1 panel	194	388	582	1242	2121	3000
6-9: 6,7-Bondage-c by Novick. 8,9-Sahle-c	110	220	330	704	1202	1700

JACK Q FROST (See Unearthly Spectaculars)

JACK STAFF (Vol. 2; previously published in Britain)

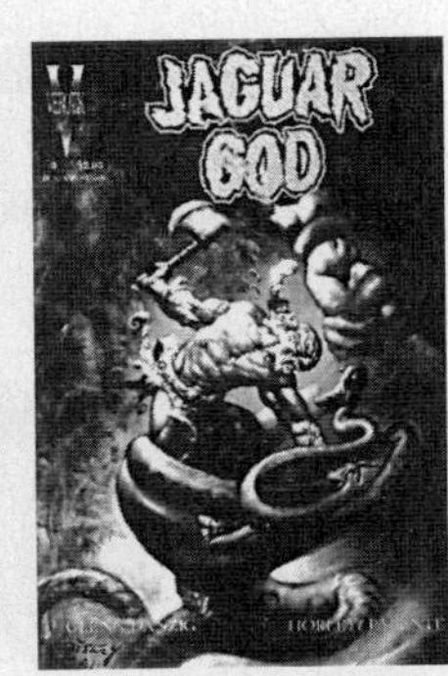

Jaguar God #3 © Verotik

James Bond Jr. #1 © Eon Prods.

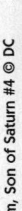

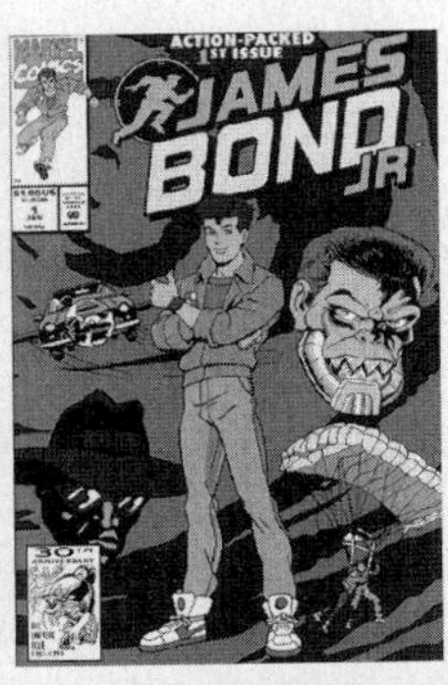

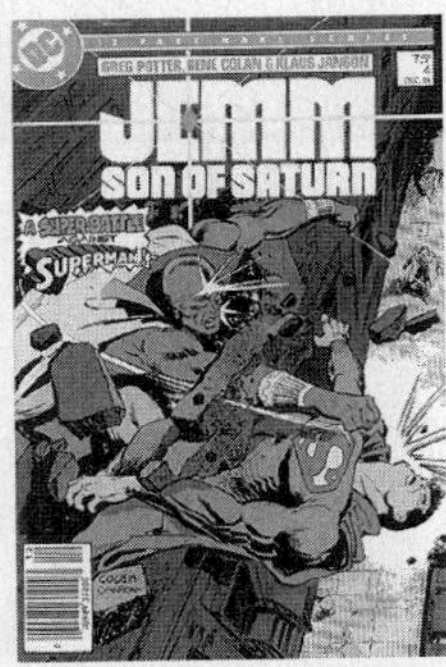

Jemm, Son of Saturn #4 © DC

	GD 2.0	VG 4.0	FN 6.0	VF 8.0	VF/NM 9.0	NM- 9.2

Image Comics: Feb, 2003 - No. 20, May, 2009 ($2.95/$3.50)

Issue	GD	VG	FN	VF	VF/NM	NM-
1-5-Paul Grist-s/a						3.00
6-20-($3.50) 6-Flashback to the WW2 Freedom Fighters						3.50
... Special 1 (1/08, $3.50) Molachi the Immortal app.						3.50
The Weird World of Jack Staff King Size Special 1 (7/07, $5.99, B&W) r/story serialized in Comics International magazine; afterword by Grist						6.00
Vol. 1: Everything Used to Be Black and White TPB (12/03, $19.95) r/British issues						20.00
Vol. 2: Soldiers TPB (2005, $15.95) r/#1-5; cover gallery						16.00
Vol. 3: Echoes of Tomorrow TPB (2006, $16.99) r/#6-12; cover gallery						17.00

JACK THE GIANT KILLER (See Movie Classics)

JACK THE GIANT KILLER (New Adventures of...)
Bimfort & Co.: Aug-Sept, 1953

Issue	GD	VG	FN	VF	VF/NM	NM-
V1#1-H. C. Kiefer-c/a	24	48	72	140	230	320

JACKY'S DIARY
Dell Publishing Co.: No. 1091, Apr-June, 1960 (one-shot)

Issue	GD	VG	FN	VF	VF/NM	NM-
Four Color 1091	5	10	15	30	48	65

JADEMAN COLLECTION
Jademan Comics: Dec, 1989 - No. 3, 1990 ($2.50, plastic coated-c, 68 pgs.)

Issue	GD	VG	FN	VF	VF/NM	NM-
1-3: 1-Wraparound-c w/fold-out poster						2.50

JADEMAN KUNG FU SPECIAL
Jademan Comics: 1988 ($1.50, 64 pgs.)

Issue	GD	VG	FN	VF	VF/NM	NM-
1						2.50

JADE WARRIORS (Mike Deodato's...)
Image Comics (Glass House Graphics): Nov, 1999 - No. 3, 2000 ($2.50)

Issue	GD	VG	FN	VF	VF/NM	NM-
1-3-Deodato-a						2.50
1-Variant-c						2.50

JAGUAR, THE (Also see The Adventures of...)
Impact Comics (DC): Aug, 1991 - No. 14, Oct, 1992 ($1.00)

Issue	GD	VG	FN	VF	VF/NM	NM-
1-14: 4-The Black Hood x-over. 7-Sienkiewicz-c. 9-Contains Crusaders trading card						2.50
Annual 1 (1992, $2.50, 68 pgs.)-With trading card						2.50

JAGUAR GOD
Verotik: Mar, 1995 - No. 7, June, 1997 ($2.95, mature)

Issue	GD	VG	FN	VF	VF/NM	NM-
0 (2/96, $3.50)-Embossed Frazetta-c; Bisley-a; w/pin-ups.						5.00
1-Frazetta-c.						5.00
2-7: 2-Frazetta-c. 3-Bisley-c. 4-Emond-c. 7-($2.95)-Frazetta-c						4.00

JAKE THRASH
Aircel Publishing: 1988 - No. 3, 1988 ($2.00)

Issue	GD	VG	FN	VF	VF/NM	NM-
1-3						2.50

JAM, THE (...Urban Adventure)
Slave Labor Nos. 1-5/Dark Horse Comics Nos. 6-8/Caliber Comics No. 9 on: Nov, 1989 - No. 14, 1997 ($1.95/$2.50/$2.95, B&W)

Issue	GD	VG	FN	VF	VF/NM	NM-
1-14: Bernie Mireault-c/a/scripts. 6-1st Dark Horse issue. 9-1st Caliber issue						3.00

JAMBOREE
Round Publishing Co.: Feb, 1946(no month given) - No. 3, Apr, 1946

Issue	GD	VG	FN	VF	VF/NM	NM-
1-Funny animal	21	42	63	122	199	275
2,3	15	30	45	85	130	175

JAMES BOND 007: A SILENT ARMAGEDDON
Dark Horse Comics/Acme Press: Mar, 1993 - Apr 1993 (limited series)

Issue	GD	VG	FN	VF	VF/NM	NM-
1,2						3.50

JAMES BOND 007: GOLDENEYE (Movie)
Topps Comics: Jan, 1996 ($2.95, unfinished limited series of 3)

Issue	GD	VG	FN	VF	VF/NM	NM-
1-Movie adaptation; Stelfreeze-c						3.00

JAMES BOND 007: SERPENT'S TOOTH
Dark Horse Comics/Acme Press: July 1992 - Aug 1992 ($4.95, limited series)

Issue	GD	VG	FN	VF	VF/NM	NM-
1-3-Paul Gulacy-c/a						5.00

JAMES BOND 007: SHATTERED HELIX
Dark Horse Comics: Jun 1994 - July 1994 ($2.50, limited series)

Issue	GD	VG	FN	VF	VF/NM	NM-
1,2						3.00

JAMES BOND 007: THE QUASIMODO GAMBIT
Dark Horse Comics: Jan 1995 - May 1995 ($3.95, limited series)

Issue	GD	VG	FN	VF	VF/NM	NM-
1-3						4.50

JAMES BOND FOR YOUR EYES ONLY
Marvel Comics Group: Oct, 1981 - No. 2, Nov, 1981

Issue	GD	VG	FN	VF	VF/NM	NM-
1,2-Movie adapt.; r/Marvel Super Special #19						3.00

JAMES BOND JR. (TV)
Marvel Comics: Jan, 1992 - No. 12, Dec, 1992 (#1: $1.00, #2-on: $1.25)

Issue	GD	VG	FN	VF	VF/NM	NM-
1-12: Based on animated TV show						2.50

JAMES BOND: LICENCE TO KILL (See Licence To Kill)

JAMES BOND: PERMISSION TO DIE
Eclipse Comics/ACME Press: 1989 - No. 3, 1991 ($3.95, lim. series, squarebound, 52 pgs.)

Issue	GD	VG	FN	VF	VF/NM	NM-
1-3: Mike Grell-c/a/scripts in all. 3-($4.95)						5.00

JAM, THE: SUPER COOL COLOR INJECTED TURBO ADVENTURE #1 FROM HELL!
Comico: May, 1988 ($2.50, 44 pgs., one-shot)

Issue	GD	VG	FN	VF	VF/NM	NM-
1						2.50

JANE ARDEN (See Feature Funnies & Pageant of Comics)
St. John (United Features Syndicate): Mar, 1948 - No. 2, June, 1948

Issue	GD	VG	FN	VF	VF/NM	NM-
1-Newspaper reprints	15	30	45	88	137	185
2	12	24	36	67	94	120

JANN OF THE JUNGLE (Jungle Tales No. 1-7)
Atlas Comics (CSI): No. 8, Nov, 1955 - No. 17, June, 1957

Issue	GD	VG	FN	VF	VF/NM	NM-
8(#1)	36	72	108	211	343	475
9,11-15	20	40	60	117	189	260
10-Williamson/Colletta-c	20	40	60	118	192	265
16,17-Williamson/Mayo-a(3), 5 pgs. each	21	42	63	122	199	275

NOTE: *Everett c-15-17. **Heck** a-8, 15, 17. **Maneely** c-11. **Shores** a-8.*

JASON & THE ARGOBOTS
Oni Press: Aug, 2002 - No. 4, Dec, 2002 ($2.95, B&W, limited series)

Issue	GD	VG	FN	VF	VF/NM	NM-
1-4-Torres-s/Norton-c/a						3.00
Vol. 1 Birthquake TPB (6/03, $11.95, digest size) r/#1-4, Sunday comic strips						12.00
Vol. 2 Machina Ex Deus TPB (9/03, $11.95, digest size) new story						12.00

JASON & THE ARGONAUTS (See Movie Classics)

JASON GOES TO HELL: THE FINAL FRIDAY (Movie)
Topps Comics: July, 1993 - No. 3, Sept, 1993 ($2.95, limited series)

Issue	GD	VG	FN	VF	VF/NM	NM-
1-3: Adaptation of film. 1-Glow-in-the-dark-c						3.00

JASON'S QUEST (See Showcase #88-90)

JASON VS. LEATHERFACE
Topps Comics: Oct, 1995 - No. 3, Jan, 1996 ($2.95, limited series)

Issue	GD	VG	FN	VF	VF/NM	NM-
1-3: Collins scripts; Bisley-c						5.00

JAWS 2 (See Marvel Comics Super Special, A)

JAY & SILENT BOB (See Clerks, Oni Double Feature, and Tales From the Clerks)
Oni Press: July, 1998 - No. 4, Oct, 1999 ($2.95, B&W, limited series)

Issue	GD	VG	FN	VF	VF/NM	NM-
1-Kevin Smith-s/Fegredo-a; photo-c & Quesada/Palmiotti-c						8.00
1-San Diego Comic Con variant covers (2 different covers, came packaged with action figures)						10.00
1-2nd & 3rd printings, 2-4: 2-Allred-c. 3-Flip-c by Jaime Hernandez						3.00
Chasing Dogma TPB (1999, $11.95) r/#1-4; Alanis Morissette intro.						12.00
Chasing Dogma TPB (2001, $12.95) r/#1-4 in color; Morissette intro.						13.00
Chasing Dogma HC (1999, $69.95, S&N) r/#1-4 in color; Morissette intro.						70.00

JCP FEATURES
J.C. Productions (Archie): Feb, 1982-c; Dec, 1981-indicia ($2.00, one-shot, B&W magazine)

Issue	GD	VG	FN	VF	VF/NM	NM-
1-T.H.U.N.D.E.R. Agents; Black Hood by Morrow & Neal Adams; Texeira-a; 2 pgs. S&K-a from Fly #1	2	4	6	8	10	12

JEANIE COMICS (Formerly All Surprise; Cowgirl Romances #28)
Marvel Comics/Atlas(CPC): No. 13, April, 1947 - No. 27, Oct, 1949

Issue	GD	VG	FN	VF	VF/NM	NM-
13-Mitzi, Willie begin	21	42	63	124	202	280
14,15	15	30	45	86	133	180
16-Used in Love and Death by Legman; Kurtzman's "Hey Look"	17	34	51	100	158	215
17-19,21,22-Kurtzman's "Hey Look" (1-3 pgs. each)	14	28	42	80	115	150
20,23-27	13	26	39	74	105	135

JEEP COMICS (Also see G.I. Comics and Overseas Comics)
R. B. Leffingwell & Co.: Winter, 1944, No. 2, Spring, 1945 - No. 3, Mar-Apr, 1948

Issue	GD	VG	FN	VF	VF/NM	NM-
1-Capt. Power, Criss Cross & Jeep & Peep (costumed) begin	60	120	180	381	658	935
2	39	78	117	240	395	550
3-L. B. Cole dinosaur-c	48	96	144	302	514	725

Jersey Gods #6 © Glen Brunswick

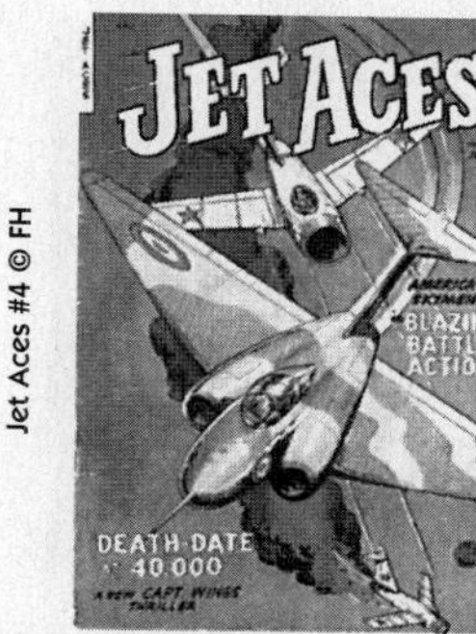

Jet Aces #4 © FH

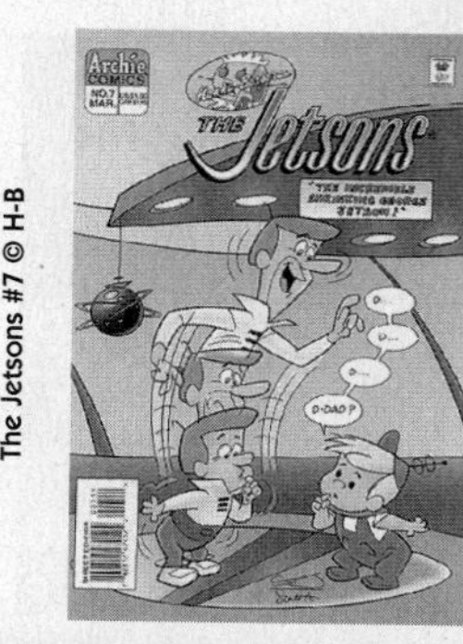

The Jetsons #7 © H-B

JEFF JORDAN, U.S. AGENT
D. S. Publishing Co.: Dec, 1947 - Jan, 1948

	GD 2.0	VG 4.0	FN 6.0	VF 8.0	VF/NM 9.0	NM- 9.2
1	15	30	45	85	130	175

JEMM, SON OF SATURN
DC Comics: Sept, 1984 - No. 12, Aug, 1985 (Maxi-series, mando paper)

	GD 2.0	VG 4.0	FN 6.0	VF 8.0	VF/NM 9.0	NM- 9.2
1-12: 3-Origin						2.50

NOTE: *Colan a-1-12p; c-1-5, 7-12p.*

JENNY FINN
Oni Press: June, 1999 - No. 2, Sept, 1999 ($2.95, B&W, unfinished lim. series)

	GD 2.0	VG 4.0	FN 6.0	VF 8.0	VF/NM 9.0	NM- 9.2
1,2-Mignola & Nixey-s/Nixey-a/Mignola-c						3.00
...: Doom (Atomeka, 2005, $6.99, TPB) r/#1 & 2 with new supplemental material						7.00

JENNY SPARKS: THE SECRET HISTORY OF THE AUTHORITY
DC Comics (WildStorm): Aug, 2000 - No. 5, Mar, 2001 ($2.50, limited series)

	GD 2.0	VG 4.0	FN 6.0	VF 8.0	VF/NM 9.0	NM- 9.2
1-Millar-s/McCrea & Hodgkins-a/Hitch & Neary-c						3.50
1-Variant-c by McCrea	1	3	4	6	8	10
2-5: 2-Apollo & Midnighter. 3-Jack Hawksmoor. 4-Shen. 5-Engineer						3.00
TPB (2001, $14.95) r/#1-5; Ellis intro.						15.00

JERICHO (Based on the TV series)
Devil's Due Publishing: Oct, 2009 - Present ($3.99)

	GD 2.0	VG 4.0	FN 6.0	VF 8.0	VF/NM 9.0	NM- 9.2
... Season 3: Civil War 1,2: 1-Story by the show's writing staff						4.00

JERRY DRUMMER (Formerly Soldier & Marine V2#9)
Charlton Comics: V2#10, Apr, 1957 - V3#12, Oct, 1957

	GD 2.0	VG 4.0	FN 6.0	VF 8.0	VF/NM 9.0	NM- 9.2
V2#10, V3#11,12: 11-Whitman-c/a	6	12	18	29	36	42

JERRY IGER'S... (All titles, Blackthorne/First)(Value: cover or less)

JERRY LEWIS (See The Adventures of...)

JERSEY GODS
Image Comics: Feb, 2009 - Present ($3.50)

	GD 2.0	VG 4.0	FN 6.0	VF 8.0	VF/NM 9.0	NM- 9.2
1-10: 1-Brunswick-s/McDaid-a; two covers by McDaid and Allred						3.50

JESSE JAMES (The True Story Of..., also seeThe Legend of...)
Dell Publishing Co.: No. 757, Dec, 1956 (one shot)

	GD 2.0	VG 4.0	FN 6.0	VF 8.0	VF/NM 9.0	NM- 9.2
Four Color 757-Movie, photo-c	8	16	24	58	97	135

JESSE JAMES (See Badmen of the West & Blazing Sixguns)
Avon Periodicals: 8/50 - No. 9, 11/52; No. 15, 10/53 - No. 29, 8-9/56

	GD 2.0	VG 4.0	FN 6.0	VF 8.0	VF/NM 9.0	NM- 9.2
1-Kubert Alabam-r/Cowpuncher #1	17	34	51	98	154	210
2-Kubert-a(3)	14	28	42	80	115	150
3-Kubert Alabam-r/Cowpuncher #2	14	28	42	76	108	140
4,9-No Kubert	8	16	24	44	57	70
5,6-Kubert Jesse James-a(3); 5-Wood-a(1pg.)	14	28	42	76	108	140
7-Kubert Jesse James-a(2)	12	24	36	67	94	120
8-Kinstler-a(3)	9	18	27	50	65	80
15-Kinstler-r/#3	8	16	24	40	50	60
16-Kinstler-r/#3 & story-r/Butch Cassidy #1	8	16	24	42	54	65
17-19,21: 17-Jesse James-r/#4; Kinstler-c idea from Kubert splash in #6. 18-Kubert Jesse James-r/#5. 19-Kubert Jesse James-r/#6. 21-Two Jesse James-r/#4, Kinstler-r/#4	7	14	21	37	46	55
20-Williamson/Frazetta-a; r/Chief Vic. Apache Massacre; Kubert Jesse James-r/#6; Kit West story by Larsen	14	28	42	80	115	150
22-29: 22,23-No Kubert. 24-New McCarty strip by Kinstler; Kinstler-r. 25-New McCarty Jesse James strip by Kinstler; Jesse James-r/#7,9. 26,27-New McCarty Jesse James strip plus a Kinstler/McCann Jesse James-r. 28-Reprints most of Red Mountain, Featuring Quantrells Raiders	7	14	21	37	46	55
Annual nn (1952; 25¢, 100 pgs.)- "...Brings Six-Gun Justice to the West"- 3 earlier issues rebound; Kubert, Kinstler-a(3)	28	56	84	165	270	375

NOTE: *Mostly reprints #10 on.* **Fawcette** *c-1, 2.* **Kida** *a-5.* **Kinstler** *a-3, 4, 7-9, 15r, 16r(2), 21-27; c-3, 4, 9, 17-27. Painted c-5-8. 22 has 2 stories r/Sheriff Bob Dixon's Chuck Wagon #1 with name changed to Sheriff Bob Trent.*

JESSE JAMES
Realistic Publications: July, 1953

	GD 2.0	VG 4.0	FN 6.0	VF 8.0	VF/NM 9.0	NM- 9.2
nn-Reprints Avon's #1; same-c, colors different	9	18	27	52	69	85

JEST (Formerly Snap; becomes Kayo #12)
Harry 'A' Chesler: No. 10, 1944; No. 11, 1944

	GD 2.0	VG 4.0	FN 6.0	VF 8.0	VF/NM 9.0	NM- 9.2
10-Johnny Rebel & Yankee Boy app. in text	17	34	51	100	158	215
11-Little Nemo in Adventure Land	17	34	51	100	158	215

JESTER
Harry 'A' Chesler: No. 10, 1945

	GD 2.0	VG 4.0	FN 6.0	VF 8.0	VF/NM 9.0	NM- 9.2
10	15	30	45	88	137	185

JESUS
Spire Christian Comics (Fleming H. Revell Co.): 1979 (49¢)

	GD 2.0	VG 4.0	FN 6.0	VF 8.0	VF/NM 9.0	NM- 9.2
nn	2	4	6	9	13	16

JET (See Jet Powers)

JET (Crimson from Wildcore & Backlash)
DC Comics (WildStorm): Nov, 2000 - No. 4, Feb, 2001 ($2.50, limited series)

	GD 2.0	VG 4.0	FN 6.0	VF 8.0	VF/NM 9.0	NM- 9.2
1-4-Nguyen-a/Abnett & Lanning-s						2.50

JET ACES
Fiction House Magazines: 1952 - No. 4, 1953

	GD 2.0	VG 4.0	FN 6.0	VF 8.0	VF/NM 9.0	NM- 9.2
1	16	32	48	94	147	200
2-4	11	22	33	60	83	105

JETCAT CLUBHOUSE (Also see Land of Nod, The)
Oni Press: Apr, 2001 - No. 3, Aug, 2001 ($3.25)

	GD 2.0	VG 4.0	FN 6.0	VF 8.0	VF/NM 9.0	NM- 9.2
1-3-Jay Stephens-s/a. 1-Wraparound-c						3.25
TPB (8/02, $10.95, 8 3/4" x 5 3/4") r/#1-3 & stories from Nickelodeon mag. & other						11.00

JET DREAM (...and Her Stunt-Girl Counterspies)(See The Man from Uncle #7)
Gold Key: June, 1968 (12¢)

	GD 2.0	VG 4.0	FN 6.0	VF 8.0	VF/NM 9.0	NM- 9.2
1-Painted-c	4	8	12	22	34	45

JET FIGHTERS (Korean War)
Standard Magazines: No. 5, Nov, 1952 - No. 7, Mar, 1953

	GD 2.0	VG 4.0	FN 6.0	VF 8.0	VF/NM 9.0	NM- 9.2
5,7-Toth-a. 5-Toth-c	12	24	36	69	97	125
6-Celardo-a	8	16	24	44	57	70

JET POWER
I.W. Enterprises: 1963

	GD 2.0	VG 4.0	FN 6.0	VF 8.0	VF/NM 9.0	NM- 9.2
I.W. Reprint 1,2-r/Jet Powers #1,2	3	6	9	17	25	32

JET POWERS (American Air Forces No. 5 on)
Magazine Enterprises: 1950 - No. 4, 1951

	GD 2.0	VG 4.0	FN 6.0	VF 8.0	VF/NM 9.0	NM- 9.2
1(A-1 #30)-Powell-c/a begins	38	76	114	226	368	510
2(A-1 #32) Classic Powell dinosaur-c/a	38	76	114	226	368	510
3(A-1 #35)-Williamson/Evans-a	40	80	120	244	407	570
4(A-1 #38)-Williamson/Wood-a; "The Rain of Sleep" drug story	40	80	120	244	407	570

JET PUP (See 3-D Features)

JETSONS, THE (TV) (See March of Comics #276, 330, 348 & Spotlight #3)
Gold Key: Jan, 1963 - No. 36, Oct, 1970 (Hanna-Barbera)

	GD 2.0	VG 4.0	FN 6.0	VF 8.0	VF/NM 9.0	NM- 9.2
1-1st comic book app.	22	44	66	157	304	450
2	11	22	33	80	145	210
3-10	9	18	27	60	100	140
11-22	7	14	21	47	76	105
23-36-Reprints	4	8	12	28	44	60

JETSONS, THE (TV) (Also see Golden Comics Digest)
Charlton Comics: Nov, 1970 - No. 20, Dec, 1973 (Hanna-Barbera)

	GD 2.0	VG 4.0	FN 6.0	VF 8.0	VF/NM 9.0	NM- 9.2
1	8	16	24	56	93	130
2	5	10	15	30	48	65
3-10	3	6	9	21	32	42
11-20	3	6	9	17	25	32
nn (1973, digest, 60¢, 100 pgs.) B&W one page gags	4	8	12	24	37	50

JETSONS, THE (TV)
Harvey Comics: V2#1, Sept, 1992 - No. 5, Nov, 1993 ($1.25/$1.50) (Hanna-Barbera)

	GD 2.0	VG 4.0	FN 6.0	VF 8.0	VF/NM 9.0	NM- 9.2
V2#1-5						5.00
...Big Book V2#1,2,3 ($1.95, 52 pgs.): 1-(11/92). 2-(4/93). 3-(7/93)						5.00
...Giant Size 1,2,3 ($2.25, 68 pgs): 1-(10/92). 2-(4/93). 3-(10/93)						5.00

JETSONS, THE (TV)
Archie Comics: Sept, 1995 - No. 8, Apr, 1996 ($1.50)

	GD 2.0	VG 4.0	FN 6.0	VF 8.0	VF/NM 9.0	NM- 9.2
1-8						3.00

JETTA OF THE 21ST CENTURY
Standard Comics: No. 5, Dec, 1952 - No. 7, Apr, 1953 (Teen-age Archie type)

	GD 2.0	VG 4.0	FN 6.0	VF 8.0	VF/NM 9.0	NM- 9.2
5-Dan DeCarlo-a	23	46	69	136	223	310
6,7: 6-Robot-c	15	30	45	84	127	170
TPB (Airwave Publ., 2006, $9.99) B&W reprint of series; Bill Morrison intro./back-c						10.00

JEZEBEL JADE (Hanna-Barbera)
Comico: Oct, 1988 - No. 3, Dec, 1988 ($2.00, mini-series)

	GD 2.0	VG 4.0	FN 6.0	VF 8.0	VF/NM 9.0	NM- 9.2
1-3: Johnny Quest spin-off						3.00

JEZEBELLE (See Wildstorm 2000 Annuals)
DC Comics (WildStorm): Mar, 2001 - No. 6, Aug, 2001 ($2.50, limited series)

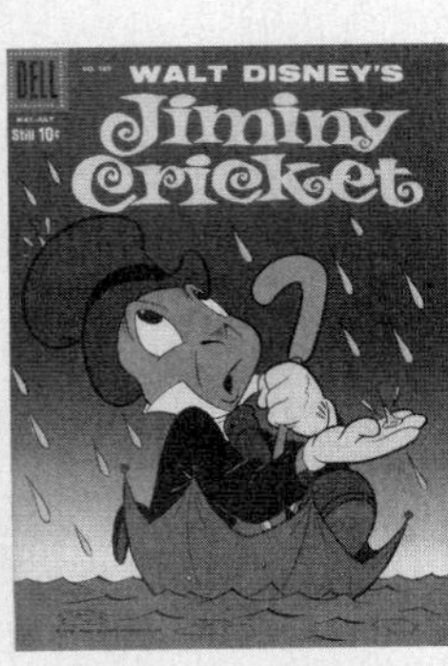

Jiminy Cricket Four Color #989 © DIS

Jimmy Olsen: Adventures By Jack Kirby Vol. 1 TPB © DC

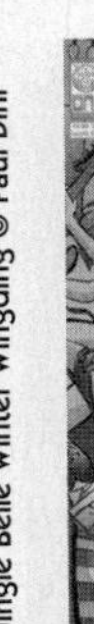
Jingle Belle Winter Wingding © Paul Dini

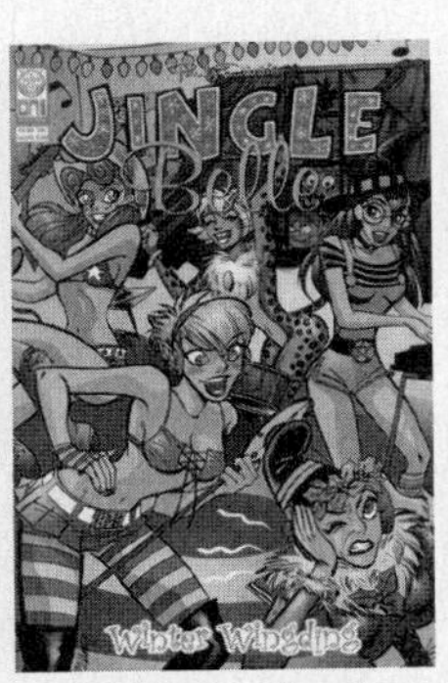

	GD 2.0	VG 4.0	FN 6.0	VF 8.0	VF/NM 9.0	NM- 9.2
1-6-Ben Raab-s/Steve Ellis-a						2.50

JIGGS & MAGGIE
Dell Publishing Co.: No. 18, 1941 (one shot)

	GD 2.0	VG 4.0	FN 6.0	VF 8.0	VF/NM 9.0	NM- 9.2
Four Color 18 (#1)-(1936-38-r)	48	96	144	300	510	720

JIGGS & MAGGIE
Standard Comics/Harvey Publications No. 22 on: No. 11, 1949 (June) - No. 21, 2/53; No. 22, 4/53 - No. 27, 2-3/54

	GD 2.0	VG 4.0	FN 6.0	VF 8.0	VF/NM 9.0	NM- 9.2
11	15	30	45	84	127	170
12-15,17-21	10	20	30	54	72	90
16-Wood text illos.	10	20	30	56	76	95
22-24-Little Dot app.	10	20	30	58	79	100
25,27	10	20	30	54	72	90
26-Four pgs. partially in 3-D	14	28	42	80	115	150

NOTE: *Sunday page reprints by McManus loosely blended into story continuity. Based on Bringing Up Father strip. Advertised on covers as "All New."*

JIGSAW (Big Hero Adventures)
Harvey Publ. (Funday Funnies): Sept, 1966 - No. 2, Dec, 1966 (36 pgs.)

	GD 2.0	VG 4.0	FN 6.0	VF 8.0	VF/NM 9.0	NM- 9.2
1-Origin & 1st app.; Crandall-a (5 pgs.)	4	8	12	22	34	45
2-Man From S.R.A.M.	3	6	9	16	22	28

JIGSAW OF DOOM (See Complete Mystery No. 2)

JIM BOWIE (Formerly Danger?; Black Jack No. 20 on)
Charlton Comics: No. 16, Mar, 1956 - No. 19, Apr, 1957

	GD 2.0	VG 4.0	FN 6.0	VF 8.0	VF/NM 9.0	NM- 9.2
16	8	16	24	42	54	65
17-19: 18-Giordano-c	6	12	18	29	36	42

JIM BOWIE (TV, see Western Tales)
Dell Publishing Co.: No. 893, Mar, 1958 - No. 993, May-July, 1959

	GD 2.0	VG 4.0	FN 6.0	VF 8.0	VF/NM 9.0	NM- 9.2
Four Color 893 (#1)	6	12	18	39	62	85
Four Color 993-Photo-c	5	10	15	35	55	75

JIM BUTCHER'S THE DRESDEN FILES: STORM FRONT (Based on the Dresden Files novels)
Dabel Bros. Productions: Oct, 2008 (Nov. on-c) - No. 4, Apr, 2009 ($3.99, limited series)

	GD 2.0	VG 4.0	FN 6.0	VF 8.0	VF/NM 9.0	NM- 9.2
1-4-Jim Butcher & Mark Powers-s/Ardian Syaf-a; covers by Syaf & Tsai						4.00
Vol. 2: 1 (7/09 - No. 4)						4.00

JIM BUTCHER'S THE DRESDEN FILES: WELCOME TO THE JUNGLE
Dabel Bros. Productions: Mar, 2008 (Apr. on-c) - No. 4, Jul, 2008 ($3.99, limited series)

	GD 2.0	VG 4.0	FN 6.0	VF 8.0	VF/NM 9.0	NM- 9.2
1-Jim Butcher-s/Ardian Syaf-a; Ardian Syaf-c						5.00
1-Variant-c by Chris McGrath						8.00
1-New York Comic-Con 2008 variant-c						15.00
1-Second printing						4.00
2-4-Two covers on each						4.00
HC (2008, $19.95, dustjacket) r/#1-4; Butcher intro.; concept art pages						20.00

JIM DANDY
Dandy Magazine (Lev Gleason): May, 1956 - No. 3, Sept, 1956 (Charles Biro)

	GD 2.0	VG 4.0	FN 6.0	VF 8.0	VF/NM 9.0	NM- 9.2
1-Biro-c	9	18	27	47	61	75
2,3	6	12	18	29	36	42

JIM HARDY (See Giant Comics Eds., Sparkler & Treasury of Comics #2 & 5)
United Features Syndicate/Spotlight Publ.: 1939; 1942; 1947 - No. 2, 1947

	GD 2.0	VG 4.0	FN 6.0	VF 8.0	VF/NM 9.0	NM- 9.2
Single Series 6 ('39)	41	82	123	256	428	600
Single Series 27('42)	36	72	108	211	343	475
1('47)-Spotlight Publ.	15	30	45	85	130	175
2	10	20	30	54	72	90

JIM HARDY
Spotlight/United Features Synd.: 1944 (25¢, 132 pgs.) (Tip Top, Sparkler-r)

	GD 2.0	VG 4.0	FN 6.0	VF 8.0	VF/NM 9.0	NM- 9.2
nn-Origin Mirror Man; Triple Terror app.	40	80	120	231	378	525

JIMINY CRICKET (Disney,, see Mickey Mouse Mag. V5#3 & Walt Disney Showcase #37)
Dell Publishing Co.: No. 701, May, 1956 - No. 989, May-July, 1959

	GD 2.0	VG 4.0	FN 6.0	VF 8.0	VF/NM 9.0	NM- 9.2
Four Color 701	8	16	24	56	93	130
Four Color 795, 897, 989	6	12	18	43	69	95

JIM LEE SKETCHBOOK
DC Comics (WildStorm): 2002 (no price, 16 pgs.)

	GD 2.0	VG 4.0	FN 6.0	VF 8.0	VF/NM 9.0	NM- 9.2
nn-Various DC and WildStorm character sketches by Lee						2.50

JIMMY CORRIGAN (See Acme Novelty Library)

JIMMY DURANTE (Also see A-1 Comics)
Magazine Enterprises: No. 18, 1949 - No. 20, 1949

	GD 2.0	VG 4.0	FN 6.0	VF 8.0	VF/NM 9.0	NM- 9.2
A-1 18,20-Photo-c	43	86	129	271	461	650

JIMMY OLSEN (See Superman's Pal...)

JIMMY OLSEN: ADVENTURES BY JACK KIRBY
DC Comics: 2003, 2004 ($19.95, TPB)

	GD 2.0	VG 4.0	FN 6.0	VF 8.0	VF/NM 9.0	NM- 9.2
nn-(2003) Reprints Jack Kirby's early issues of Superman's Pal Jimmy Olsen #133-139,141; Mark Evanier intro.; cover by Kirby and Steve Rude						20.00
Vol. 2 (2004) Reprints #142-148; Evanier intro.; cover gallery and sketch pages						20.00

JIMMY WAKELY (Cowboy movie star)
National Per. Publ.: Sept-Oct, 1949 - No. 18, July-Aug, 1952 (1-13: 52pgs.)

	GD 2.0	VG 4.0	FN 6.0	VF 8.0	VF/NM 9.0	NM- 9.2
1-Photo-c, 52 pgs. begin; Alex Toth-a; Kit Colby Girl Sheriff begins	80	160	240	504	852	1200
2-Toth-a	35	70	105	203	327	450
3,4,6,7-Frazetta-a in all, 3 pgs. each; Toth-a in all. 7-Last photo-c. 4-Kurtzman "Pot-Shot Pete", 1 pg; Toth-a	40	80	120	235	380	525
5,8-15-Toth-a; 12,14-Kubert-a (3 & 2 pgs.)	27	54	81	158	254	350
16-18	23	46	69	135	218	300

NOTE: *Gil Kane c-10-19p.*

JIM RAY'S AVIATION SKETCH BOOK
Vital Publishers: Mar-Apr, 1946 - No. 2, May-June, 1946 (15¢)

	GD 2.0	VG 4.0	FN 6.0	VF 8.0	VF/NM 9.0	NM- 9.2
1-Picture stories of planes and pilots	39	78	117	231	378	525
2-Story of General "Nap" Arnold	25	50	75	147	241	335

JIM SOLAR (See Wisco/Klarer in the Promotional Comics section)

JINGLE BELLE (Paul Dini's...)
Oni Press/Top Cow: Nov, 1999 - No. 2, Dec, 1999 ($2.95, B&W, limited series)

	GD 2.0	VG 4.0	FN 6.0	VF 8.0	VF/NM 9.0	NM- 9.2
1,2-Paul Dini-s. 2-Alex Ross flip-c						3.00
Jingle Belle: Dash Away All (12/03, $11.95, digest-size) Dini-s/Garibaldi-a						12.00
Jingle Belle: Santa Claus vs. Frankenstein (Top Cow, 12/08, $2.99) Dini-s/Gladden-a						3.00
Jingle Belle's Cool Yule (11/02, $13.95,TPB) r/All-Star Holiday Hullabaloo, The Mighty Elves, and Jubilee; internet strips and a color section w/DeStefano-a						14.00
Paul Dini's Jingle Belle Jubilee (11/01, $2.95) Dini-s; art by Rolston, DeCarlo, Morrison and Bone; pin-ups by Thompson and Aragonés						3.00
Paul Dini's Jingle Belle's All-Star Holiday Hullabaloo (11/00, $4.95) stories by various including Dini, Aragonés, Jeff Smith, Bill Morrison; Frank Cho-c						5.00
Paul Dini's Jingle Belle: The Fight Before Christmas (12/05, $2.99) Dini-s/Bone & others-a						3.00
Paul Dini's Jingle Belle: The Mighty Elves (7/01, $2.95) Dini-s/Bone-a						3.00
Paul Dini's Jingle Belle Winter Wingding (11/02, $2.95) Dini-s/Clugston-Major-c						3.00
The Bakers Meet Jingle Belle (12/06, $2.99) Dini-s/Kyle Baker-a						3.00
TPB (10/00, $8.95) r/#1&2, and app. from Oni Double Feature #13						9.00

JINGLE BELLE (Paul Dini's...)
Dark Horse Comics: Nov, 2004 - No. 4, Apr, 2005 ($2.99, limited series)

	GD 2.0	VG 4.0	FN 6.0	VF 8.0	VF/NM 9.0	NM- 9.2
1-4-Paul Dini-s/Jose Garibaldi-a						3.00
TPB (9/05, $12.95) r/#1-4						13.00

JINGLE BELLS (See March of Comics No. 65)

JINGLE DINGLE CHRISTMAS STOCKING COMICS (See Foodini #2)
Stanhall Publications: V2#1, 1951 (no date listed) (25¢, 100 pgs.; giant-size) (Publ. annually)

	GD 2.0	VG 4.0	FN 6.0	VF 8.0	VF/NM 9.0	NM- 9.2
V2#1-Foodini & Pinhead, Silly Pilly plus games & puzzles	19	38	57	109	172	235

JINGLE JANGLE COMICS (Also see Puzzle Fun Comics)
Eastern Color Printing Co.: Feb, 1942 - No. 42, Dec, 1949

	GD 2.0	VG 4.0	FN 6.0	VF 8.0	VF/NM 9.0	NM- 9.2
1-Pie-Face Prince of Old Pretzleburg, Jingle Jangle Tales by George Carlson, Hortense, & Benny Bear begin	44	88	132	277	469	660
2-4: 2,3-No Pie-Face Prince. 4-Pie-Face Prince-c	20	40	60	120	195	270
5	19	38	57	111	176	240
6-10: 8-No Pie-Face Prince	15	30	45	85	130	175
11-15	12	24	36	69	97	125
16-30: 17,18-No Pie-Face Prince. 24,30-XMas-c	10	20	30	56	76	95
31-42: 36,42-Xmas-c	9	18	27	52	69	85

NOTE: ***George Carlson** a-(2) in all except No. 2, 3, 8; c-1-6. **Carlson** 1 pg. puzzles in 9, 10, 12-15, 18, 20. **Carlson** illustrated a series of Uncle Wiggily books in 1930's.*

JING PALS
Victory Publishing Corp.: Feb, 1946 - No. 4, Aug?, 1946 (Funny animal)

	GD 2.0	VG 4.0	FN 6.0	VF 8.0	VF/NM 9.0	NM- 9.2
1-Wishing Willie, Puggy Panda & Johnny Rabbit begin	15	30	45	84	127	170
2-4	9	18	27	52	69	85

JINKS, PIXIE, AND DIXIE (See Kite Fun Book & Whitman Comic Books)

JINX
Caliber Press: 1996 - No. 7, 1996 ($2.95, B&W, 32 pgs.)

	GD 2.0	VG 4.0	FN 6.0	VF 8.0	VF/NM 9.0	NM- 9.2
1-7: Brian Michael Bendis-c/a/scripts. 2-Photo-c						3.00

JINX (Volume 2)

JLA #18 © DC

JLA #50 © DC

JLA / Avengers #1 © DC & MAR

	GD 2.0	VG 4.0	FN 6.0	VF 8.0	VF/NM 9.0	NM- 9.2

Image Comics: 1997 - No. 5, 1998 ($2.95, B&W, bi-monthly)

1-4: Brian Michael Bendis-c/a/scripts. 3.00
5-($3.95) Brereton-c 4.00
...Buried Treasures ('98, $3.95) short stories, ...Confessions ('98, $3.95) short stories, ...Pop Culture Hoo-Hah ('98, $3.95) humor shorts 4.00
TPB (1997, $10.95) r/Vol 1,#1-4 11.00
...: The Definitive Collection ('01, $24.95) remastered #1-5, sketch pages, art gallery, script excerpts, Mack intro. 25.00

JINX: TORSO
Image Comics: 1998 - No. 6, 1999 ($3.95/$4.95, B&W)

1-6-Based on Eliot Ness' pursuit of America's first serial killer; Brian Michael Bendis & Marc Andreyko-s/Bendis-a. 3-6-($4.95) 5.00
Softcover (2000, $24.95) r/#1-6; intro. by Greg Rucka; photo essay of the actual murders and police documents 25.00
Hardcover (2000, $49.95) signed & numbered 50.00

JLA (See Justice League of America and Justice Leagues)
DC Comics: Jan, 1997 - No. 125, Apr, 2006 ($1.95/$1.99/$2.25/$2.50)

	GD	VG	FN	VF	VF/NM	NM-
1-Morrison-s/Porter & Dell-a. The Hyperclan app.	2	4	6	9	12	15
2	1	3	4	6	8	10
3,4	1	2	3	5	7	9

5-Membership drive; Tomorrow Woman app. 6.00
6-9: 8-Green Arrow joins. 6.00
10-21: 10-Rock of Ages begins. 11-Joker and Luthor-c/app. 15-($2.95) Rock of Ages concludes. 16-New members join; Prometheus app. 17,20-Jorgensen-a. 18-21-Waid-s. 20,21-Adam Strange c/app. 5.00
22-40: 22-Begin $1.99-c; Sandman (Daniel) app. 27-Amazo app. 28-31-JSA app. 35-Hal Jordan/Spectre app. 36-40-World War 3 2.50
41-($2.99) Conclusion of World War 3; last Morrison-s 3.00
42-46: 43-Waid-s; Ra's al Ghul app. 44-Begin $2.25-c. 46-Batman leaves 2.50
47-49: 47-Hitch & Neary-a begins; JLA battles Queen of Fables 2.50
50-($3.75) JLA vs. Dr. Destiny; art by Hitch & various 3.75
51-74: 52-55-Hitch-a. 59-Joker: Last Laugh. 61-68-Kelly-s/Mahnke-a. 69-73-Hunt for Aquaman; bi-monthly with alternating art by Mahnke and Guichet 2.50
75-(1/03, $3.95) leads into Aquaman (4th series) #1 4.00
76-93: 76-Firestorm app. 77-Banks-a. 79-Kanjar Ro app. 91-93-O'Neil-s/Huat-a 2.50
94-99-Byrne & Ordway-a/Claremont-s; Doom Patrol app. 2.50
100-($3.50) Intro. Vera Black; leads into Justice League Elite #1 3.50
101-114: 101-106-Austen-s/Garney-a/c. 107-114-Crime Syndicate app.; Busiek-s 2.50
115-125: 115-Begin $2.50-c; Johns & Heinberg-s;Secret Society of Super-Villains app. 2.50
#1,000,000 (11/98) 853rd Century x-over 2.50
Annual 1 (1997, $3.95) Pulp Heroes; Augustyn-s/Olivetti & Ha-a 4.00
Annual 2 (1998, $2.95) Ghosts; Wrightson-c 4.00
Annual 3 (1999, $2.95) JLApe; Art Adams-c 3.00
Annual 4 (2000, $3.50) Planet DC x-over; Steve Scott-c/a 3.50
... American Dreams (1998, $7.95, TPB) r/#5-9 8.00
...: Crisis of Conscience TPB (2006, $12.99) r/#115-119 13.00
.../ Cyberforce (DC/Top Cow, 2005, $5.99) Kelly-s/Mahnke-a/Silvestri-c 6.00
Divided We Fall (2001, $17.95, TPB) r/#47-54 18.00
...80-Page Giant 1 (7/98, $4.95) stories & art by various 6.00
...80-Page Giant 2 (11/99, $4.95) Green Arrow & Hawkman app. Hitch-c 6.00
...80-Page Giant 3 (10/00, $5.95) Pariah & Harbinger; intro. Moon Maiden 6.00
...Foreign Bodies (1999, $5.95, one-shot) Kobra app.; Semeiks-a 6.00
...Gallery (1997, $2.95) pin-ups by various; Quitely-c 3.00
...God & Monsters (2001, $6.95, one-shot) Benefiel-a/c 7.00
Golden Perfect (2003, $12.95, TPB) r/#61-65 13.00
.../ Haven: Anathema (2002, $6.95) Concludes the Haven: The Broken City series 7.00
.../ Haven: Arrival (2001, $6.95) Leads into the Haven: The Broken City series 7.00
...In Crisis Secret Files 1 (11/98, $4.95) recap of JLA in DC x-overs 5.00
...: Island of Dr. Moreau, The (2002, $6.95, one-shot) Elseworlds; Pugh-c/a; Thomas-s 7.00
.../ JSA Secret Files & Origins (1/03, $4.95) prelude to JLA/JSA: Virtue & Vice; short stories and pin-ups by various; Pacheco-c 5.00
.../ JSA: Virtue and Vice HC (2002, $24.95) Teams battle Despero & Johnny Sorrow; Goyer & Johns-s/Pacheco-a/c 25.00
.../ JSA: Virtue and Vice SC (2003, $17.95) 18.00
Justice For All (1999, $14.95, TPB) r/#24-33 15.00
New World Order (1997, $5.95, TPB) r/#1-4 6.00
...: Obsidian Age Book One, The (2003, $12.95) r/#66-71 13.00
...: Obsidian Age Book Two, The (2003, $12.95) r/#72-76 13.00
One Million (2004, $19.95, TPB) r/#DC One Million #1-4 and other #1,000,000 x-overs 20.00
...: Our Worlds at War (9/01, $2.95) Jae Lee-c; Aquaman presumed dead 3.00
...: Pain of the Gods (2005, $12.99) r/#101-106 13.00
...Primeval (1999, $5.95, one-shot) Abnett & Lanning-s/Olivetti-a 6.00
...: Riddle of the Beast HC (2001, $24.95) Grant-s/painted-a by various; Sweet-c 25.00

	GD 2.0	VG 4.0	FN 6.0	VF 8.0	VF/NM 9.0	NM- 9.2

...: Riddle of the Beast SC (2003, $14.95) Grant-s/painted-a by various; Kaluta-c 15.00
Rock of Ages (1998, $9.95, TPB) r/#10-15 10.00
Rules of Engagement (2004, $12.95, TPB) r/#77-82 13.00
...: Seven Caskets (2000, $5.95, one-shot) Brereton-s/painted-c/a 6.00
...: Shogun of Steel (2002, $6.95, one-shot) Elseworlds; Justiniano-c/a 7.00
...Showcase 80-Page Giant (2/00, $4.95) Hitch-c 5.00
Strength in Numbers (1998, $12.95, TPB) r/#16-23, Secret Files #2 and Prometheus #1 13.00
...Superpower (1999, $5.95, one-shot) Arcudi-s/Eaton-a; Mark Antaeus joins 6.00
Syndicate Rules (2005, $17.99, TPB) r/#107-114, Secret Files #4 18.00
Terror Incognita (2002, $12.95, TPB) r/#55-60 13.00
...: The Deluxe Edition Vol. 1 HC (2008, $29.99, dustjacket) oversized r/#1-9 and JLA Secret Files #1 30.00
The Tenth Circle (2004, $12.95, TPB) r/#94-99 13.00
...: The Greatest Stories Ever Told TPB (2006, $19.99) r/Justice League of America #19,71,122, 166-168,200, Justice League #1, JLA Secret Files #1 and JLA #61; Alex Ross-c 20.00
Tower of Babel (2001, $12.95, TPB) r/#42-46, Secret Files #3, 80-Page Giant #1 13.00
Trial By Fire (2004, $12.95, TPB) r/#84-89 13.00
...Vs. Predator (DC/Dark Horse, 2000, $5.95, one-shot) Nolan-c/a 6.00
...: Welcome to the Working Week (2003, $6.95, one-shot) Patton Oswalt-s 7.00
...: World War III (2000, $12.95, TPB) r/#34-41 13.00
...: World Without a Justice League (2006, $12.99, TPB) r/#120-125 13.00
...: Zatanna's Search (2003, $12.95, TPB) rep. Zatanna's early app. & origin; Bolland-c 13.00

JLA: ACT OF GOD
DC Comics: 2000 - No. 3, 2001 ($4.95, limited series)

1-3-Elseworlds; metahumans lose their powers; Moench-s/Dave Ross-a 5.00

JLA: AGE OF WONDER
DC Comics: 2003 - No. 2, 2003 ($5.95, limited series)

1,2-Elseworlds; Superman and the League of Science during the Industrial Revolution 6.00

JLA: A LEAGUE OF ONE
DC Comics: 2000 (Graphic novel)

Hardcover ($24.95) Christopher Moeller-s/painted-a 25.00
Softcover (2002, $14.95) 15.00

JLA/AVENGERS (See Avengers/JLA for #2 & #4)
Marvel Comics: Sept, 2003; No. 3, Dec, 2003 ($5.95, limited series)

1-Busiek-s/Pérez-a; wraparound-c; Krona, Starro, Grandmaster, Terminus app. 6.00
3-Busiek-s/Pérez-a; wraparound-c; Phantom Stranger app. 6.00
SC (2008, $19.99) r/4-issue series; cover gallery; intros by Stan Lee & Julius Schwartz 20.00

JLA: BLACK BAPTISM
DC Comics: May, 2001 - No. 4, Aug, 2001 ($2.50, limited series)

1-4-Saiz-a(p)/Bradstreet-c; Zatanna app. 2.50

JLA: CLASSIFIED
DC Comics: Jan, 2005 - No. 54, May, 2008 ($2.95/$2.99)

1-3-Morrison-s/McGuinness-a/c; Ultramarines app. 3.00
4-9-"I Can't Believe It's Not The Justice League," Giffen & DeMatteis-s/Maguire-a 3.00
10-31,33-54: 10-15-New Maps of Hell; Ellis-s/Guice-a. 16-21-Garcia-Lopez-a. 22-25-Detroit League & Royal Flush Gang app.; Englehart-s. 26-28-Chaykin-s. 37-41-Kid Amazo. 50-54-Byrne-a/Middleston-c 3.00
32-($3.99) Dr. Destiny app.; Jurgens-a 4.00
I Can't Believe It's Not The Justice League TPB (2005, $12.99) r/#4-9 13.00
...: Kid Amazo TPB (2007, $12.99) r/#37-41 13.00
...: New Maps of Hell TPB (2006, $12.99) r/#10-15 13.00
...: That Was Now, This Is Then TPB (2008, $14.99) r/#50-54 15.00
...: The Hypothetical Woman TPB (2008, $12.99) r/#16-21 13.00
...: Ultramarine Corps TPB (2007, $14.99) r/#1-3, JLA/WildC.A.T.s #1 and JLA Secret Files 2004 #1 15.00

JLA CLASSIFIED: COLD STEEL
DC Comics: 2005 - No. 2, 2006 ($5.99, limited series, prestige format)

1,2-Chris Moeller-s/a; giant robot Justice League 6.00

JLA: CREATED EQUAL
DC Comics: 2000 - No. 2, 2000 ($5.95, limited series, prestige format)

1,2-Nicieza-s/Maguire-a; Elseworlds-Superman as the last man on Earth 6.00

JLA: DESTINY
DC Comics: 2002 - No. 4, 2002 ($5.95, prestige format, limited series)

1-4-Elseworlds; Arcudi-s/Mandrake-a 6.00

JLA: EARTH 2
DC Comics: 2000 (Graphic novel)

Hardcover ($24.95) Morrison-s/Quitely-a; Crime Syndicate app. 25.00
Softcover ($14.95) 15.00

JLA Paradise Lost #1 © DC

JLA: Year One #12 © DC

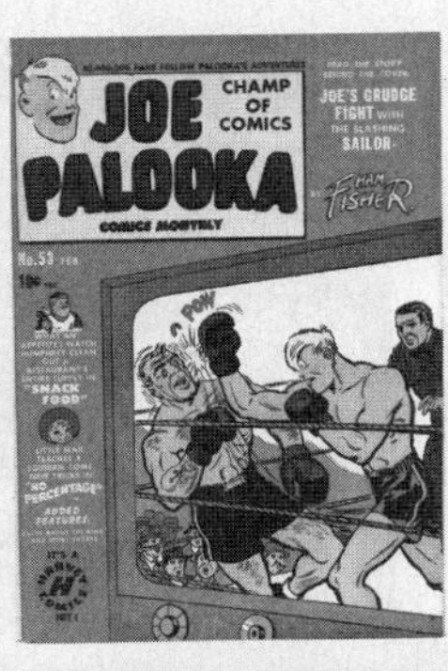

Joe Palooka #53 © HARV

GD 2.0 | VG 4.0 | FN 6.0 | VF 8.0 | VF/NM 9.0 | NM- 9.2

JLA: GATEKEEPER
DC Comics: 2001 - No. 3, 2001 ($4.95, prestige format, limited series)
1-3-Truman-s/a 5.00

JLA: HEAVEN'S LADDER
DC Comics: 2000 ($9.95, Treasury-size one-shot)
nn-Bryan Hitch & Paul Neary-c/a; Mark Waid-s 10.00

JLA/HITMAN (Justice League/Hitman in indicia)
DC Comics: Nov, 2007 - No. 2, Dec, 2007 ($3.99, limited series)
1,2-Ennis-s/McCrea-a; Bloodlines creatures return 4.00

JLA: INCARNATIONS
DC Comics: Jul, 2001 - No. 7, Feb, 2002 ($3.50, limited series)
1-7-Ostrander-s/Semeiks-a; different eras of the Justice League 3.50

JLA: LIBERTY AND JUSTICE
DC Comics: Nov, 2003 ($9.95, Treasury-size one-shot)
nn-Alex Ross-c/a; Paul Dini-s; story of the classic Justice League 10.00

JLA PARADISE LOST
DC Comics: Jan, 1998 - No. 3, Mar, 1998 ($1.95, limited series)
1-3-Millar-s/Olivetti-a 2.50

JLA: SCARY MONSTERS
DC Comics: May, 2003 - No. 6, Oct, 2003 ($2.50, limited series)
1-6-Claremont-s/Art Adams-c 2.50

JLA SECRET FILES
DC Comics: Sept, 1997 - 2004 ($4.95)
1-Standard Ed. w/origin-s & pin-ups 5.00
1-Collector's Ed. w/origin-s & pin-ups; cardstock-c 6.00
2,3: 2-(8/98) origin-s of JLA #16's newer members. 3-(12/00) 5.00
... 2004 (11/04) Justice League Elite app.; Mahnke & Byrne-a; Crime Syndicate app. 5.00

JLA: SECRET ORIGINS
DC Comics: Nov, 2002 ($7.95, Treasury-size one-shot)
nn-Alex Ross 2-page origins of Justice League members; text by Paul Dini 8.00

JLA: SECRET SOCIETY OF SUPER-HEROES
DC Comics: 2000 - No. 2, 2000 ($5.95, limited series, prestige format)
1,2-Elseworlds JLA; Chaykin and Tischman-s/McKone-a 6.00

JLA /SPECTRE: SOUL WAR
DC Comics: 2003 - No. 2, 2003 ($5.95, limited series, prestige format)
1,2-DeMatteis-s/Banks & Neary-a 6.00

JLA: THE NAIL (Elseworlds) (Also see Justice League of America: Another Nail)
DC Comics: Aug, 1998 - No. 3, Oct, 1998 ($4.95, prestige format)
1-3-JLA in a world without Superman; Alan Davis-s/a(p) 5.00
TPB ('98, $12.95) r/series w/new Davis-c 13.00

JLA / TITANS
DC Comics: Dec, 1998 - No. 3, Feb, 1999 ($2.95, limited series)
1-3-Grayson-s; P. Jimenez-c/a 3.00
...:The Technis Imperative ('99, $12.95, TPB) r/#1-3; Titans Secret Files 13.00

JLA: TOMORROW WOMAN (Girlfrenzy)
DC Comics: June, 1998 ($1.95, one-shot)
1-Peyer-s; story takes place during JLA #5 2.50

JLA / WILDC.A.T.S
DC Comics: 1997 ($5.95, one-shot, prestige format)
1-Morrison-s/Semeiks & Conrad-a 6.00

JLA /WITCHBLADE
DC Comics/Top Cow: 2000 ($5.95, prestige format, one-shot)
1-Pararillo-c/a 6.00

JLA / WORLD WITHOUT GROWN-UPS (See Young Justice)
DC Comics: Aug, 1998 - No. 2, Sept, 1998 ($4.95, prestige format)
1,2-JLA, Robin, Impulse & Superboy app.; Ramos & McKone-a 6.00
TPB ('98, $9.95) r/series & Young Justice: The Secret #1 10.00

JLA: YEAR ONE
DC Comics: Jan, 1998 - No. 12, Dec, 1998 ($2.95/$1.95, limited series)
1-($2.95)-Waid & Augustyn-s/Kitson-a 5.00
1-Platinum Edition 10.00
2-8-($1.95): 5-Doom Patrol-c/app. 7-Superman app. 4.00
9-12 3.00
TPB ('99,'09; $19.95/$19.99) r/#1-12; Busiek intro. 20.00

JLA-Z
DC Comics: Nov, 2003 - No. 3, Jan, 2004 ($2.50, limited series)
1-3-Pin-ups and info on current and former JLA members and villains; art by various 2.50

JLX
DC Comics (Amalgam): Apr, 1996 ($1.95, one-shot)
1-Mark Waid scripts 2.50

JLX UNLEASHED
DC Comics (Amalgam): June, 1997 ($1.95, one-shot)
1-Priest-s/ Oscar Jimenez & Rodriquez/a 2.50

JOAN OF ARC (Also see A-1 Comics & Ideal a Classical Comic)
Magazine Enterprises: No. 21, 1949 (one shot)
A-1 21-Movie adaptation; Ingrid Bergman photo-covers & interior photos; Whitney-a 29 58 87 170 278 385

JOE COLLEGE
Hillman Periodicals: Fall, 1949 - No. 2, Wint, 1950 (Teen-age humor, 52 pgs.)
1-Powell-a; Briefer-a 12 24 36 67 94 120
2-Powell-a 10 20 30 54 72 90

JOE JINKS
United Features Syndicate: No. 12, 1939
Single Series 12 31 62 93 182 296 410

JOE LOUIS (See Fight Comics #2, Picture News #6 & True Comics #5)
Fawcett Publications: Sept, 1950 - No. 2, Nov, 1950 (Photo-c) (Boxing champ) (See Dick Cole #10)
1-Photo-c; life story 55 110 165 352 601 850
2-Photo-c 39 78 117 240 395 550

JOE PALOOKA (1st Series)(Also see Big Shot Comics, Columbia Comics & Feature Funnies)
Columbia Comic Corp. (Publication Enterprises): 1942 - No. 4, 1944
1-1st to portray American president; gov't permission required 98 196 294 622 1074 1525
2 (1943)-Hitler-c 58 116 174 371 636 900
3-Nazi Sub-c 39 78 117 240 395 550
4 34 68 102 199 325 450

JOE PALOOKA (2nd Series) (Battle Adv. #68-74; ...Advs. #75, 77-81, 83-85, 87; Champ of the Comics #76, 82, 86, 89-93) (See All-New)
Harvey Publications: Nov, 1945 - No. 118, Mar, 1961
1 48 96 144 302 514 725
2 24 48 72 142 234 325
3,4,6,7-1st Flyin' Fool, ends #25 16 32 48 94 147 200
5-Boy Explorers by S&K (7-8/46) 21 42 63 122 199 275
8-10 14 28 42 80 115 150
11-14,16,18-20: 14-Black Cat text-s(2). 18-Powell-a.; Little Max app. 19-Freedom Train-c 11 22 33 64 90 115
15-Origin & 1st app. Humphrey (12/47); Super-heroine Atoma app. by Powell 15 30 45 90 140 190
17-Humphrey vs. Palooka-c/s; 1st app. Little Max 15 30 45 90 140 190
21-26,29,30: 22-Powell-a. 30-Nude female painting 10 20 30 56 76 95
27-Little Max app.; Howie Morenz-s 10 20 30 58 79 100
28-Babe Ruth 4 pg. sty. 10 20 30 58 79 100
31,39,51: 31-Dizzy Dean 4 pg. sty. 39-(12/49) Humphrey & Little Max begin; Sonny Baugh football-s; Sherlock Max-s. 51-Babe Ruth 2 pg. sty; Jake Lamotta 1/2 pg. sty 9 18 27 50 65 80
32-38,40-50,52-61: 35-Little Max-c/story(4 pgs.); Joe Louis 1 pg. sty. 36-Humphrey story. 41-Bing Crosby photo on-c. 44-Palooka marries Ann Howe. 50-(11/51)-Becomes Harvey Comics Hits #51 8 16 24 44 57 70
62-S&K Boy Explorers-r 9 18 27 50 65 80
63-65,73-80,100: 79-Story of 1st meeting with Ann 8 16 24 40 50 60
66,67-'Commie' torture story "Drug-Diet Horror" 10 20 30 56 76 95
68,70-72: 68,70-Joe vs. "Gooks"-c. 71-Bloody bayonets-c. 72-Tank-c 10 20 30 54 72 90
69-1st "Battle Adventures" issue; torture & bondage 10 20 30 56 76 95
81-99,101-115: 104,107-Humphrey & Little Max-s 7 14 21 37 46 55
116-S&K Boy Explorers-r (Giant, '60) 9 18 27 47 61 75
117-(84 pg. Giant) r/Commie issues #66,67; Powell-a 9 18 27 50 65 80
118-(84 pg. Giant) Jack Dempsey 2 pg. sty, Powell-a 9 18 27 47 61 75
...**Visits the Lost City** nn (1945)(One Shot)(50¢)-164 page continuous story strip reprint. Has biography & photo of Ham Fisher; possibly the single longest comic book story published in that era (159 pgs.?) 187 374 561 1197 2049 2900

John Byrne's Next Men #13 © John Byrne

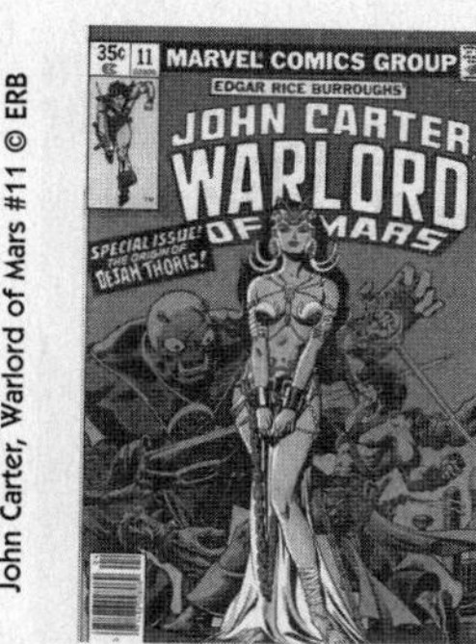

John Carter, Warlord of Mars #11 © ERB

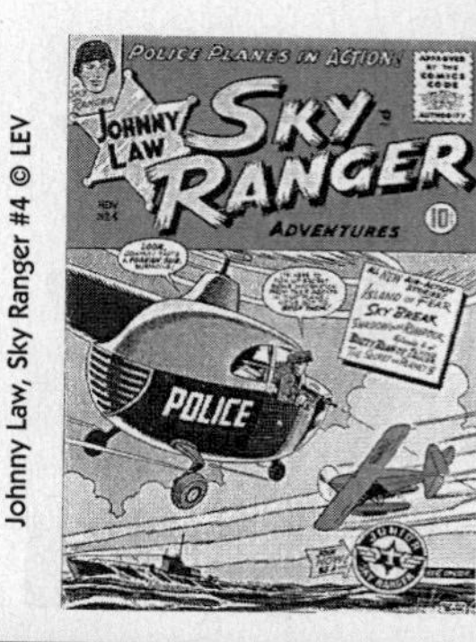

Johnny Law, Sky Ranger #4 © LEV

	GD	VG	FN	VF	VF/NM	NM-
	2.0	4.0	6.0	8.0	9.0	9.2

NOTE: *Nostrand/Powell a-73. Powell a-7, 8, 10, 12, 14, 17, 19, 26-45, 47-53, 70, 73 at least. Black Cat text stories #8, 12, 13, 19.*

JOE PSYCHO & MOO FROG
Goblin Studios: 1996 - No. 5, 1997 ($2.50, B&W)
1-5: 4-Two covers 2.50
...Full Color Extravagarbonzo ($2.95, color) 3.00

JOE THE BARBARIAN
DC Comics (Vertigo): Mar, 2010 - Present ($1.00)
1-Grant Morrison-s/Sean Murphy-a 1.00

JOE YANK (Korean War)
Standard Comics (Visual Editions): No. 5, Mar, 1952 - No. 16, 1954
5-Toth, Celardo, Tuska-a 10 20 30 54 72 90
6-Toth, Severin/Elder-a 9 18 27 52 69 85
7-Pinhead Perkins by Dan DeCarlo (in all?) 8 16 24 40 50 60
8-Toth-c 8 16 24 44 57 70
9-16: 9-Andru-c. 12-Andru-a 7 14 21 37 46 55

JOHN BOLTON'S HALLS OF HORROR
Eclipse Comics: June, 1985 - No. 2, June, 1985 ($1.75, limited series)
1,2-British-r; Bolton-c/a 3.00

JOHN BOLTON'S STRANGE WINK
Dark Horse Comics: Mar, 1998 - No. 3, May, 1998 ($2.95, B&W, limited series)
1-3-Anthology; Bolton-s/c/a 3.00

JOHN BYRNE'S NEXT MEN (See Dark Horse Presents #54)
Dark Horse Comics (Legend imprint #19 on): Jan, 1992 - No. 30, Dec, 1994 ($2.50, mature)
1-Silver foil embossed-c; Byrne-c/a/scripts in all 4.00
1-4: 1-2nd printing with gold ink logo 2.50
0-(2/92)-r/chapters 1-4 from DHP w/new Byrne-c 2.50
5-20,22-30: 7-10-MA #1-4 mini-series on flip side. 16-Origin of Mark IV. 17-Miller-c. 19-22-Faith storyline. 23-26-Power storyline. 27-30-Lies storyline Pt. 1-4 2.50
21-(12/93) 1st Hellboy; cover and Hellboy pages by Mike Mignola; Byrne other pages 3 6 9 18 27 35
...Parallel, Book 2 ($16.95)-TPB; r/#7-12 17.00
...Fame, Book 3($16.95)-TPB r/#13-18 17.00
...Faith, Book 4($14.95)-TPB r/#19-22 15.00
NOTE: *Issues 1 through 6 contain certificates redeemable for an exclusive Next Men trading card set by Byrne. Prices are for complete books.* ***Cody*** *painted c-23-26.* ***Mignola*** *a-21(part); c-21.*

JOHN BYRNE'S 2112
Dark Horse Comics (Legend): Oct, 1994 ($9.95, TPB)
1-Byrne-c/a/s 10.00

JOHN CARTER OF MARS (See The Funnies & Tarzan #207)
Dell Publishing Co.: No. 375, Mar-May, 1952 - No. 488, Aug-Oct, 1953 (Edgar Rice Burroughs)
Four Color 375 (#1)-Origin; Jesse Marsh-a 25 50 75 183 354 525
Four Color 437, 488-Painted-c 15 30 45 107 204 300

JOHN CARTER OF MARS
Gold Key: Apr, 1964 - No. 3, Oct, 1964
1(10104-404)-r/4-Color #375; Jesse Marsh-a 6 12 18 41 66 90
2(407), 3(410)-r/4-Color #437 & 488; Marsh-a 4 8 12 28 44 60

JOHN CARTER OF MARS
House of Greystroke: 1970 (10-1/2x16-1/2", 72 pgs., B&W, paper-c)
1941-42 Sunday strip-r; John Coleman Burroughs-a 4 8 12 22 34 45

JOHN CARTER, WARLORD OF MARS (Also see Weird Worlds)
Marvel Comics: June, 1977 - No. 28, Oct, 1979
1,18: 1-Origin. 18-Frank Miller-a(p)(1st publ. Marvel work) 2 4 6 8 10 12
1-(35¢-c variant, limited dist.) 4 8 12 22 34 45
2-5-(35¢-c variants, limited dist.) 3 6 9 18 27 35
2-17,19-28: 11-Origin Dejah Thoris 6.00
Annuals 1-3: 1(1977). 2(1978). 3(1979)-All 52 pgs. with new book-length stories 6.00
NOTE: ***Austin*** *c-24i.* ***Gil Kane*** *a-1-10p; c-1p, 2p, 3, 4-9p, 10, 15p, Annual 1p.* ***Layton*** *a-17i.* ***Miller*** *c-25, 26p.* ***Nebres*** *a-2-4i, 8-16i; c(i)-6-9, 11-22, 25, Annual 1.* ***Perez*** *c-24p.* ***Simonson*** *a-15p.* ***Sutton*** *a-7i.*

JOHN CONSTANTINE - HELLBLAZER SPECIAL: PAPA MIDNITE
DC Comics (Vertigo): April, 2005 - No. 5, Aug, 2005 ($2.95/$2.99, limited series)
1-5-Origin of Papa Midnite; Akins-a/Johnson-s 3.00

JOHN F. KENNEDY, CHAMPION OF FREEDOM
Worden & Childs: 1964 (no month) (25¢)
nn-Photo-c 7 14 21 49 80 110

JOHN F. KENNEDY LIFE STORY
Dell Publishing Co.: Aug-Oct, 1964; Nov, 1965; June, 1966 (12¢)
12-378-410-Photo-c 6 12 18 43 69 95
12-378-511 (reprint, 11/65) 4 8 12 22 34 45
12-378-606 (reprint, 6/66) 3 6 9 20 30 40

JOHN FORCE (See Magic Agent)

JOHN HIX SCRAP BOOK, THE
Eastern Color Printing Co. (McNaught Synd.): Late 1930's (no date) (10¢, 68 pgs., regular size)
1-Strange As It Seems (resembles Single Series books) 39 78 117 231 378 525
2-Strange As It Seems 25 50 75 147 241 335

JOHN JAKES' MULLKON EMPIRE
Tekno Comix: Sept, 1995 - No. 6, Feb, 1996 ($1.95)
1-6 2.50

JOHN LAW DETECTIVE (See Smash Comics #3)
Eclipse Comics: April, 1983 ($1.50, Baxter paper)
1-Three Eisner stories originally drawn in 1948 for the never published John Law #1; original cover pencilled in 1948 & inked in 1982 by Eisner 3.00

JOHN McCAIN (See Presidential Material: John McCain)

JOHNNY APPLESEED (See Story Hour Series)

JOHNNY CASH (See Hello, I'm...)

JOHNNY DANGER (See Movie Comics, 1946)
Toby Press: 1950 (Based on movie serial)
1-Photo-c; Sparling-a 18 36 54 105 165 225

JOHNNY DANGER PRIVATE DETECTIVE
Toby Press: Aug, 1954 (Reprinted in Danger #11 by Super)
1-Photo-c; Opium den story 14 28 42 81 118 155

JOHNNY DELGADO IS DEAD
Image Comics: Sept, 2007 - Present ($3.99)
1,2-Chris Moreno-a/John Leekley & Michael D. Olmos-s 4.00

JOHNNY DYNAMITE (Formerly Dynamite #1-9; Foreign Intrigues #14 on)
Charlton Comics: No. 10, June, 1955 - No. 12, Oct, 1955
10-12 11 22 33 62 86 110

JOHNNY DYNAMITE
Dark Horse Comics: Sept, 1994 - Dec, 1994 ($2.95, B&W & red, limited series)
1-4: Max Allan Collins scripts in all; Terry Beatty-a 3.00
...: Underworld GN (AiT/Planet Lar, 3/03, $12.95, B&W) r/#1-4 in B&W without red 13.00

JOHNNY HAZARD
Best Books (Standard Comics) (King Features): No. 5, Aug, 1948 - No. 8, May, 1949; No. 35, date?
5-Strip reprints by Frank Robbins (c/a) 18 36 54 105 165 225
6,8-Strip reprints by Frank Robbins 15 30 45 88 137 185
7,35: 7-New art, not Robbins 12 24 36 67 94 120

JOHNNY JASON (...Teen Reporter)
Dell Publishing Co.: Feb-Apr, 1962 - No. 2, June-Aug, 1962
Four Color 1302, 2(01380-208) 4 8 12 24 37 50

JOHNNY LAW, SKY RANGER
Good Comics (Lev Gleason): Apr, 1955 - No. 3, Aug, 1955; No. 4, Nov, 1955
1-Edmond Good-c/a 10 20 30 56 76 95
2-4 7 14 21 35 43 50

JOHNNY MACK BROWN (Western star; see Western Roundup under Dell Giants)
Dell Publishing Co.: No. 269, Mar, 1950 - No. 963, Feb, 1959 (All Photo-c)
Four Color 269(#1)(3/50, 52pgs.)-Johnny Mack Brown & his horse Rebel begin; photo front/back-c begin; Marsh-a in #1-9 21 42 63 148 287 425
2(10-12/50, 52pgs.) 11 22 33 78 139 200
3(1-3/51, 52pgs.) 9 18 27 63 107 150
4-10 (9-11/52)(36pgs.), Four Color 455,493,541,584,618,645,685,722,776,834,963 7 14 21 47 76 105
Four Color 922-Manning-a 7 14 21 45 73 100

JOHNNY NEMO
Eclipse Comics: Sept, 1985 - No. 3, Feb, 1986 (Mini-series)
1-3 2.50

JOHNNY PERIL (See Comic Cavalcade #15, Danger Trail #5, Sensation Comics #107 & Sensation Mystery)

John Wayne Adventure Comics #6 © TOBY

Joker HC © DC

Joker Comics #14 © MAR

GD 2.0 | VG 4.0 | FN 6.0 | VF 8.0 | VF/NM 9.0 | NM- 9.2

JOHNNY RINGO (TV)
Dell Publishing Co.: No. 1142, Nov-Jan, 1960/61 (one shot)
Four Color 1142-Photo-c 7 14 21 47 76 105

JOHNNY STARBOARD (See Wisco)

JOHNNY THE HOMICIDAL MANIAC (Also see Squee)
Slave Labor Graphics: Aug, 1995 - No. 7, Jan, 1997 ($2.95, B&W, lim. series)
1-Jhonen Vasquez-c/s/a 1 3 4 6 8 10
1-Signed & numbered edition 2 4 6 9 12 15
2,3: 2-(11/95). 3-(2/96) 6.00
4-7: 4-(5-96). 5-(8/96) 4.00
Hardcover-($29.95) r/#1-7 30.00
TPB-($19.95) 20.00

JOHNNY THUNDER
National Periodical Publications: Feb-Mar, 1973 - No. 3, July-Aug, 1973
1-Johnny Thunder & Nighthawk-r. in all 2 4 6 13 18 22
2,3: 2-Trigger Twins app. 2 4 6 8 11 14
NOTE: *All contain 1950s DC reprints from All-American Western.* ***Drucker*** *r-2, 3.* ***G. Kane*** *r-2, 3.* ***Moreira*** *r-1.* ***Toth*** *r-1, 3; c-1r, 3r. Also see All-American, All-Star Western, Flash Comics, Western Comics, World's Best & World's Finest.*

JOHN PAUL JONES
Dell Publishing Co.: No. 1007, July-Sept, 1959 (one-shot)
Four Color 1007-Movie, Robert Stack photo-c 5 10 15 35 55 75

JOHN ROMITA JR. 30TH ANNIVERSARY SPECIAL
Marvel Comics: 2006 ($3.99, one-shot)
nn-r/1st story in Amazing Spider-Man Annual #11; timeline, sketch pages, interviews 4.00

JOHN STEED & EMMA PEEL (See The Avengers, Gold Key series)

JOHN STEELE SECRET AGENT (Also see Freedom Agent)
Gold Key: Dec, 1964
1-Freedom Agent 6 12 18 37 59 80

JOHN WAYNE ADVENTURE COMICS (Movie star; See Big Tex, Oxydol-Dreft, Tim McCoy, & With The Marines...#1)
Toby Press: Winter, 1949-50 - No. 31, May, 1955 (Photo-c: 1-12,17,25-on)
1 (36pgs.)-Photo-c begin (1st time in comics on-c) 161 322 483 1030 1765 2500
2-4: 2-(4/50, 36pgs.)-Williamson/Frazetta-a(2) 6 & 2 pgs. (one story-r/Billy the Kid #1); photo back-c. 3-(36pgs.)-Williamson/Frazetta-a(2), 16 pgs. total; photo back-c. 4-(52pgs.)-Williamson/Frazetta-a(2), 16 pgs. total 69 138 207 442 759 1075
5 (52pgs.)-Kurtzman-a-(Alfred "L" Newman in Potshot Pete) 51 102 153 321 541 760
6 (52pgs.)-Williamson/Frazetta-a (10 pgs.); Kurtzman-a "Pot-Shot Pete", (5 pgs.); & "Genius Jones", (1 pg.) 60 120 180 381 653 925
7 (52pgs.)-Williamson/Frazetta-a (10 pgs.) 52 104 156 328 557 785
8 (36pgs.)-Williamson/Frazetta-a(2) (12 & 9 pgs.) 64 128 192 406 696 985
9-11: Photo western-c 39 78 117 230 375 520
12,14-Photo war-c. 12-Kurtzman-a(2 pg.) "Genius" 39 78 117 230 375 520
13,15: 13,15-Line-drawn-c begin, end #24 32 64 96 192 314 435
16-Williamson/Frazetta-r/Billy the Kid #1 36 72 108 211 343 475
17-Photo-c 36 72 108 211 343 475
18-Williamson/Frazetta-a (r/#4 & 8, 19 pgs.) 39 78 117 234 385 535
19-24: 23-Evans-a? 28 56 84 168 274 380
25-Photo-c resume; end #31; Williamson/Frazetta-r/Billy the Kid #3 39 78 117 234 385 535
26-28,30-Photo-c 32 64 96 192 314 435
29,31-Williamson/Frazetta-a in each (r/#4, 2) 37 74 111 222 361 500
NOTE: *Williamsonish art in later issues by* ***Gerald McCann.***

JO-JO COMICS (...Congo King #7-29; My Desire #30 on)(Also see Fantastic Fears and Jungle Jo)
Fox Feature Syndicate: 1945 - No. 29, July, 1949 (Two No.7's; no #13)
nn(1945)-Funny animal, humor 17 34 51 98 154 210
2(Sum,'46)-6(4-5/47): Funny animal. 2-Ten pg. Electro story (Fall/46) 11 22 33 60 83 105
7(7/47)-Jo-Jo, Congo King begins (1st app.); Bronze Man & Purple Tigress app. 90 180 270 576 988 1400
7(#8) (9/47) 66 132 198 419 722 1025
8-10(#9-11): 8-Tanee begins 55 110 165 352 601 850
11,12(#12,13),14,16: 11,16-Kamen bondage-c 48 96 144 302 514 725
15,17: 15-Cited by Dr. Wertham in 5/47 Saturday Review of Literature. 17-Kamen bondage-c 50 100 150 315 533 750
18-20 48 96 144 302 514 725
21-29: 21-Hollingsworth-a(4 pgs.; 23-1 pg.) 40 80 120 246 411 575
NOTE: *Many bondage-c/a by* ***Baker/Kamen/Feldstein/Good.*** *No. 7's have Princesses Gwenna, Geesa, Yolda, & Safra before settling down on Tanee.*

JOKEBOOK COMICS DIGEST ANNUAL (...Magazine No. 5 on)
Archie Publications: Oct, 1977 - No. 13, Oct, 1983 (Digest Size)
1(10/77)-Reprints; Neal Adams-a 2 4 6 13 18 22
2(4/78)-5 2 4 6 9 12 15
6-13 1 3 4 6 8 10

JOKER
DC Comics: 2008 ($19.99, hardcover graphic novel with dustjacket)
HC-Joker is released from Arkham; Azzarello-s/Bermejo-a 20.00

JOKER, THE (See Batman #1, Batman: The Killing Joke, Brave & the Bold, Detective, Greatest Joker Stories & Justice League Annual #2)
National Periodical Publications: May, 1975 - No. 9, Sept-Oct, 1976
1-Two-Face app. 6 12 18 37 59 80
2,3: 3-The Creeper app. 3 6 9 20 30 40
4-9: 4-Green Arrow-c/sty. 6-Sherlock Holmes-c/sty. 7-Lex Luthor-c/story. 8-Scarecrow-c/story. 9-Catwoman-c/story 3 6 9 16 23 30
...: The Greatest Stories Ever Told TPB (2008, $19.99) r/Batman #1 and other apps. 20.00

JOKER, THE (See Tangent Comics/ The Joker)

JOKER COMICS (Adventures Into Terror No. 43 on)
Timely/Marvel Comics No. 36 on (TCI/CDS): Apr, 1942 - No. 42, Aug, 1950
1-(Rare)-Powerhouse Pepper (1st app.) begins by Wolverton; Stuporman app. from Daring Comics 300 600 900 1920 3310 4700
2-Wolverton-a; 1st app. Tessie the Typist & begin series 97 194 291 621 1061 1500
3-5-Wolverton-a 54 108 162 346 591 835
6-10-Wolverton-a. 6-Tessie-c begin 42 84 126 265 445 625
11-20-Wolverton-a 39 78 117 240 395 550
21,22,24-27,29,30-Wolverton cont'd. & Kurtzman's "Hey Look" in #23-27 34 68 102 204 332 460
23-1st "Hey Look" by Kurtzman; Wolverton-a 37 74 111 218 354 490
28,32,34,37-41: 28-Millie the Model begins. 32-Hedy begins. 41-Nellie the Nurse app. 15 30 45 86 133 180
31-Last Powerhouse Pepper; not in #28 28 56 84 165 270 375
33,35,36-Kurtzman's "Hey Look" 15 30 45 90 140 190
42-Only app. 'Patty Pinup,' clone of Millie the Model 15 30 45 88 137 185

JOKER: DEVIL'S ADVOCATE
DC Comics: 1996 ($24.95/$12.95, one-shot)
nn-(Hardcover)-Dixon scripts/Nolan & Hanna-a 25.00
nn-(Softcover) 13.00

JOKER: LAST LAUGH (See Batman: The Joker's Last Laugh for TPB)
DC Comics: Dec, 2001 - No. 6, Jan, 2002 ($2.95, weekly limited series)
1-6: 1,6-Bolland-c 3.00
...Secret Files (12/01, $5.95) Short stories by various; Simonson-c 6.00

JOKER / MASK
Dark Horse Comics: May, 2000 - No. 4, Aug, 2000 ($2.95, limited series)
1-4-Batman, Harley Quinn, Poison Ivy app. 3.00

JOKER'S ASYLUM
DC Comics: Sept, 2008 ($2.99, weekly limited series of one-shots)
...: Joker - Andy Kubert-c, Sanchez-a; ...: Penguin - Pearson-c/a; ...: Poison Ivy - Guillem March-c/a; ...: Scarecrow - Juan Doe-c/a; ...: Two-Face - Andy Clarke-c/a 3.00
Batman: The Joker's Asylum TPB (2008, $14.99) r/one-shots 15.00

JOLLY CHRISTMAS, A (See March of Comics No. 269)

JOLLY COMICS: **Four Star Publishing Co.:** 1947 (Advertised, not published)

JOLLY JINGLES (Formerly Jackpot Comics)
MLJ Magazines: No. 10, Sum, 1943 - No. 16, Wint, 1944/45
10-Super Duck begins (origin & 1st app.); Woody The Woodpecker begins (not same as Lantz character) 39 78 117 240 395 550
11 (Fall, '43)-2nd Super Duck(see Hangman #8) 20 40 60 120 195 270
12-Hitler-c 34 68 102 199 325 450
13-16: 13-Sahle-c. 15,16-Vigoda-c 14 28 42 82 121 160

JONAH HEX (See All-Star Western, Hex and Weird Western Tales)
National Periodical Pub./DC Comics: Mar-Apr, 1977 - No. 92, Aug, 1985
1 10 20 30 70 123 175
2 6 12 18 39 62 85
3,4,9: 9-Wrightson-c. 5 10 15 32 51 70
5,6,10: 5-Rep 1st app. from All-Star Western #10 4 8 12 28 44 60

Jonah Hex (2006 series) #6 © DC

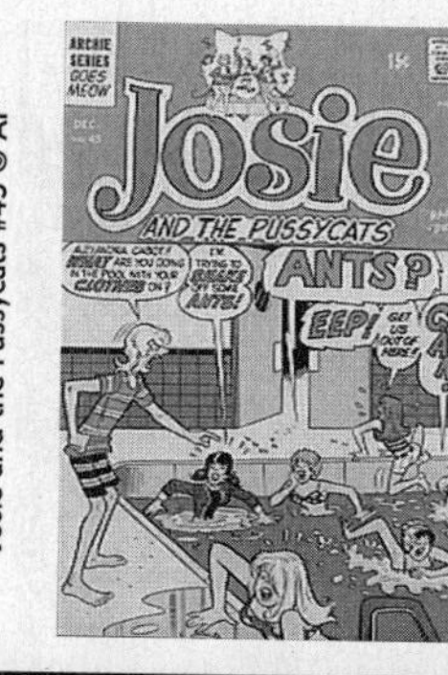

Josie and the Pussycats #45 © AP

Journey Into Fear #11 © SUPR

	GD 2.0	VG 4.0	FN 6.0	VF 8.0	VF/NM 9.0	NM- 9.2
7,8-Explains Hex's face disfigurement (origin)	5	10	15	34	55	75
11-20: 12-Starlin-c	3	6	9	18	27	35
21-32: 31,32-Origin retold	2	4	6	11	16	20
33-50	2	4	6	8	10	12
51-80	1	2	3	5	6	8
81-91: 89-Mark Texeira-a. 91-Cover swipe from Superman #243 (hugging a mystery woman)	1	2	3	5	7	9
92-Story cont'd in Hex #1	3	6	9	16	23	30

NOTE: ***Ayers** a(p)-35-37, 40, 41, 44-53, 56, 58-82. **Buckler** a-11; c-11, 13-16. **Kubert** c-43-46. **Morrow** a-90-92; c-10. **Spiegle(Tothish)** a-34, 38, 40, 49, 52. **Texeira** a-89p. Batlash back-ups in 49, 52. El Diablo back-ups in 48, 56-60, 73-75. Scalphunter back-ups in 40, 41, 45-47.*

JONAH HEX
DC Comics: Jan, 2006 - Present ($2.99)

1-Justin Gray & Jimmy Palmiotti-s/Luke Ross-a/Quitely-c 5.00
2-49,51,52: 3-Bat Lash app. 10,16,17,19,20,22-Noto-a. 11-El Diablo app.; Beck-a. 13-15-Origin retold. 21,23,27,30,32,37,38,42,52-Bernet-a. 33-Darwyn Cooke-a/c. 34-Sparacio-a. 51-Giordano-c 3.00
50-($3.99) Darwayn Cooke-a/c 4.00
...: Bullets Don't Lie TPB (2009, $14.99) r/#31-36 15.00
...: Face Full of Violence TPB (2006, $12.99) r/#1-6 13.00
...: Guns of Vengeance TPB (2007, $12.99) r/#7-12 13.00
...: Lead Poisoning TPB (2009, $14.99) r/#37-42 15.00
...: Luck Runs Out TPB (2008, $12.99) r/#25-30 13.00
...: Only the Good Die Young TPB (2008, $12.99) r/#19-24 13.00
...: Origins TPB (2007, $12.99) r/#13-18 13.00

JONAH HEX AND OTHER WESTERN TALES (Blue Ribbon Digest)
DC Comics: Sept-Oct, 1979 - No. 3, Jan-Feb, 1980 (100 pgs.)

1-3: 1-Origin Scalphunter-r, Ayers/Evans, Neal Adams-a.; painted-c. 2-Weird Western Tales-r; Neal Adams, Toth, Aragones-a. 3-Outlaw-r, Scalphunter-r; Gil Kane, Wildey-a
2 4 6 11 16 20

JONAH HEX: RIDERS OF THE WORM AND SUCH
DC Comics (Vertigo): Mar, 1995 - No. 5, July, 1995 ($2.95, limited series)

1-5-Lansdale story, Truman -a 4.00

JONAH HEX: SHADOWS WEST
DC Comics (Vertigo): Feb, 1999 - No. 3, Apr, 1999 ($2.95, limited series)

1-3-Lansdale-s/Truman -a 4.00

JONAH HEX SPECTACULAR (See DC Special Series No. 16)

JONAH HEX: TWO-GUN MOJO
DC Comics (Vertigo): Aug, 1993 - No. 5, Dec, 1993 ($2.95, limited series)

1-Lansdale scripts in all; Truman/Glanzman-a in all w/Truman-c 6.00
1-Platinum edition with no price on cover 20.00
2-5 4.00
TPB-(1994, $12.95) r/#1-5 13.00

JONESY (Formerly Crack Western)
Comic Favorite/Quality Comics Group: No. 85, Aug, 1953; No. 2, Oct, 1953 - No. 8, Oct, 1954

	GD	VG	FN	VF	VF/NM	NM-
85(#1)-Teen-age humor	8	16	24	44	57	70
2	6	12	18	27	33	38
3-8	5	10	15	23	28	32

JON JUAN (Also see Great Lover Romances)
Toby Press: Spring, 1950

1-All Schomburg-a (signed Al Reid on-c); written by Siegel; used in **SOTI**, pg. 38 (Scarce)
64 128 192 406 696 985

JONNI THUNDER (...A.K.A. Thunderbolt)
DC Comics: Feb, 1985 - No. 4, Aug, 1985 (75¢, limited series)

1-4: 1-Origin & 1st app. 2.50

JONNY DOUBLE
DC Comics (Vertigo): Sept, 1998 - No. 4, Dec, 1998 ($2.95, limited series)

1-4-Azzarello-s 3.00
TPB (2002, $12.95) r/#1-4; Chiarello-c 13.00

JONNY QUEST (TV)
Gold Key: Dec, 1964 (Hanna-Barbera)

1 (10139-412) 32 64 96 246 461 675

JONNY QUEST (TV)
Comico: June 1986 - No. 31, Dec, 1988 ($1.50/$1.75)(Hanna-Barbera)

1 5.00
2,3,5: 3,5-Dave Stevens-c 4.00
4,6-31: 30-Adapts TV episode 3.00
Special 1(9/88, $1.75), 2(10/88, $1.75) 4.00

NOTE: ***M. Anderson** a-9. **Mooney** a-Special 1. **Pini** a-2. **Quagmire** a-31p. **Rude** a-1; c-2i. **Sienkiewicz** c-11. **Spiegle** a-7, 12, 21; c-21 **Staton** a-2i, 11p. **Steacy** c-8. **Stevens** a-4i; c-3,5. **Wildey** a-1, c-1, 7, 12. **Williamson** a-4i; c-4i.*

JONNY QUEST CLASSICS (TV)
Comico: May, 1987 - No. 3, July, 1987 ($2.00) (Hanna-Barbera)

1-3: Wildey-c/a; 3-Based on TV episode 3.00

JON SABLE, FREELANCE (Also see Mike Grell's Sable & Sable)
First Comics: 6/83 - No. 56, 2/88 (#1-17, $1; #18-33, $1.25, #34-on, $1.75)

1-Mike Grell-c/a/scripts 3.00
2-56: 3-5-Origin, parts 1-3. 6-Origin, part 4. 11-1st app. of Maggie the Cat. 14-Mando paper begins. 16-Maggie the Cat. app. 25-30-Shatter app. 34-Deluxe format begins ($1.75) 2.50
The Complete Jon Sable, Freelance: Vol. 1 (IDW, 2005, $19.99) r/#1-6 20.00
The Complete Jon Sable, Freelance: Vol. 2 (IDW, 2005, $19.99) r/#7-11 20.00
The Complete Jon Sable, Freelance: Vol. 3 (IDW, 2005, $19.99) r/#12-16 20.00
The Complete Jon Sable, Freelance: Vol. 4 (IDW, 2005, $19.99) r/#17-21 20.00

NOTE: ***Aragones** a-33; c-33(part). **Grell** a-1-43;c-1-52, 53p, 54-56.*

JON SABLE, FREELANCE
IDW Publ.: (Limited series)

...: Ashes of Eden 1-5 (2009 - No. 5, 2/10, $3.99) Mike Grell-c/a/scripts 4.00
...: Bloodtrail 1-6 (4/05 - No. 6, 11/05, $3.99) Mike Grell-c/a/scripts 4.00
...: Bloodtrail TPB (4/06, $19.99) r/#1-6; cover gallery 20.00

JOSEPH & HIS BRETHREN (See The Living Bible)

JOSIE (She's... #1-16) (...& the Pussycats #45 on) (See Archie's Pals 'n' Gals #23 for 1st app.) (Also see Archie Giant Series Magazine #528, 540, 551, 562, 571, 584, 597, 610, 622)
Archie Publ./Radio Comics: Feb, 1963; No. 2, Aug, 1963 - No. 106, Oct, 1982

	GD	VG	FN	VF	VF/NM	NM-
1	15	30	45	104	197	290
2	9	18	27	61	103	145
3-5	7	14	21	45	73	100
6-10: 6-(5/64) Book length Haunted Mansion-c/s. 7-(8/64) 1st app. Alexandra Cabot?	5	10	15	30	48	65
11-20	4	8	12	22	34	45
21, 23-30	3	6	9	18	27	35
22 (9/66)-Mighty Man & Mighty (Josie Girl) app.	4	8	12	24	37	50
31-44	3	6	9	16	22	28
45 (12/69)-Josie and the Pussycats begins (Hanna Barbera TV cartoon); 1st app. of the Pussycats	10	20	30	73	129	185
46-2nd app./1st cover Pussycats	7	14	21	50	83	115
47-3rd app. of the Pussycats	5	10	15	34	55	75
48,49-Pussycats band-c/s	6	12	18	39	62	85
50-J&P-c; go to Hollywood, meet Hanna & Barbera	7	14	21	45	73	100
51-54	3	6	9	19	29	38
55-74 (2/74)(52 pg. issues)	3	6	9	19	29	38
75-90(8/76)	2	4	6	13	18	22
91-99	2	4	6	10	14	18
100 (10/79)	2	4	6	13	18	22
101-106	2	4	6	11	16	20

JOSIE & THE PUSSYCATS (TV)
Archie Comics: 1993 - No. 2, 1994 ($2.00, 52 pgs.)(Published annually)

1,2-Bound-in pull-out poster in each. 2-(Spr/94) 5.00

JOURNAL OF CRIME (See Fox Giants)

JOURNEY
Aardvark-Vanaheim #1-14/Fantagraphics Books #15-on: 1983 - No. 14, Sept, 1984; No. 15, Apr, 1985 - No. 27, July, 1986 (B&W)

1 3.00
2-27: 20-Sam Kieth-a 2.50

JOURNEY INTO FEAR
Superior-Dynamic Publications: May, 1951 - No. 21, Sept, 1954

	GD	VG	FN	VF	VF/NM	NM-
1-Baker-r(2)	66	132	198	419	722	1025
2-Classic horror-c	47	94	141	296	498	700
3,4	39	78	117	240	395	550
5-10,15: 15-Used in **SOTI**, pg. 389	30	60	90	177	289	400
11-14,16-21	27	54	81	160	263	365

NOTE: *Kamenish 'headlight'-a most issues. **Robinson** a-10.*

JOURNEY INTO MYSTERY (1st Series) (Thor Nos. 126-502)
Atlas(CPS No. 1-48/AMI No. 49-68/Marvel No. 69 (6/61) on): 6/52 - No. 48, 8/57; No. 49, 11/58 - No. 125, 2/66; 503, 11/96 - No. 521, June, 1998

1-Weird/horror stories begin 314 628 942 2198 3849 5500

Journey Into Mystery #86 © MAR

Journey Into Unknown Worlds #36 © MAR

JSA #78 © DC

GD VG FN VF VF/NM NM-
2.0 4.0 6.0 8.0 9.0 9.2

2 110 220 330 704 1202 1700
3,4 82 164 246 528 902 1275
5-11 56 112 168 356 608 860
12-20,22: 15-Atomic explosion panel. 22-Davis*esque*-a; last pre-code issue (2/55)
45 90 135 284 480 675
21-Kubert-a; Tothish-a by Andru 46 92 138 290 488 685
23-32,35-38,40: 24-Torres?-a. 38-Ditko-a 35 70 105 208 339 470
33-Williamson-a; Ditko-a (his 1st for Atlas?) 37 74 111 222 361 500
34,39: 34-Krigstein-a. 39-1st S.A. issue; Wood-a 36 72 108 211 343 475
41-Crandall-a; Frazetta*esque*-a by Morrow 19 38 57 139 270 400
42,46,48: 42,48-Torres-a. 46-Torres & Krigstein-a 19 38 57 135 263 390
43,44-Williamson/Mayo-a in both. 43-Invisible Woman prototype
19 38 57 139 270 400
45,47 18 36 54 131 256 380
49-Matt Fox, Check-a 19 38 57 135 263 390
50,52-54: Ditko/Kirby-a. 50-Davis-a. 54-Williamson-a
32 64 96 188 307 425
51-Kirby/Wood-a 21 42 63 153 297 440
55-61,63-65,67-69,71,72,74,75: 74-Contents change to Fantasy. 75-Last 10¢ issue
21 42 63 148 287 425
62-Prototype ish. (The Hulk); 1st app. Xemnu (Titan) called "The Hulk"
30 60 90 220 428 635
66-Prototype ish. (The Hulk)-Return of Xemnu "The Hulk"
27 54 81 194 377 560
70-Prototype ish. (The Sandman)(7/61); similar to Spidey villain
25 50 75 183 354 525
73-Story titled "The Spider" where a spider is exposed to radiation & gets powers of a human and shoots webbing; a reverse prototype of Spider-Man's origin
38 76 114 288 557 825
76,77,80-82: 80-Anti-communist propaganda story 17 34 51 122 236 350
76-(10¢ cover price blacked out, 12¢ printed on) 39 78 117 297 574 850
78-The Sorceror (Dr. Strange prototype) app. (3/62) 25 50 75 183 354 525
79-Prototype issue. (Mr. Hyde) 22 44 66 157 304 450
83-Origin & 1st app. The Mighty Thor by Kirby (8/62) and begin series; Thor-c also begin
850 1700 2550 8500 16,250 24,000
83-Reprint from the Golden Record Comic Set 16 32 48 113 217 320
With the record (1966) 23 46 69 168 324 480
84-2nd app. Thor 192 384 576 1680 3340 5000
85-1st app. Loki & Heimdall; 1st brief app. Odin (1 panel); 1st app. Asgard
124 248 372 1054 2077 3100
86-1st full app. Odin 76 152 228 646 1273 1900
87-89: 89-Origin Thor retold 60 120 180 510 1005 1500
90-No Kirby-a 50 100 150 400 775 1150
91,92,94,96-Sinnott-a 40 80 120 314 607 900
93,97-Kirby-a; Tales of Asgard series begins #97 (origin which concludes in #99); origin/1st app. Lava Man 45 90 135 360 693 1025
95-Sinnott-a 43 86 129 344 672 1000
98,99-Kirby/Heck-a. 98-Origin/1st app. The Human Cobra. 99-1st app. Surtur & Mr. Hyde
33 66 99 254 490 725
100-Kirby/Heck-a; Thor battles Mr. Hyde 33 66 99 254 490 725
101,108: 101-(2/64)-2nd Avengers x-over (w/o Capt. America); see Tales Of Suspense #49 for 1st x-over. 108-(9/64)-Early Dr. Strange & Avengers x-over; ten extra pgs. Kirby-a
22 44 66 161 311 460
102,104-107,110: 102-Intro Sif. 105-109-Ten extra pgs. Kirby-a in each.
107-1st app. Grey Gargoyle 21 42 63 153 297 440
103-1st app. Enchantress 25 50 75 183 354 525
109-Magneto-c & app. (1st x-over, 10/64) 40 80 120 321 623 925
111,113: 113-Origin Loki 17 34 51 122 236 350
112-Thor Vs. Hulk (1/65); Origin Loki 50 100 150 425 838 1250
114-Origin/1st app. Absorbing Man 23 46 69 166 321 475
115-Detailed origin of Loki 21 42 63 148 287 425
116-123,125: 118-1st app. Destroyer. 119-Intro Hogun, Fandral, Volstagg
15 30 45 107 204 300
124-Hercules-c/story 16 32 48 112 214 315
503-521: 503-(11/96, $1.50)-The Lost Gods begin; Tom DeFalco scripts & Deodato Studios-c/a. 505-Spider-Man-c/app. 509-Loki-c/app. 514-516-Shang-Chi 2.50
#(-1) Flashback (7/97) Tales of Asgard Donald Blake app. 2.50
Annual 1(1965, 25¢, 72 pgs.)-New Thor vs. Hercules(1st app.)-c/story (see Incredible Hulk #3); Kirby-c/a; r/#85,93,95,97 23 46 69 166 321 475

NOTE: ***Ayers*** *a-14, 39, 64i, 71i, 74i, 80i.* ***Bailey*** *a-43.* ***Briefer*** *a-5, 12.* ***Cameron*** *a-35.* ***Check*** *a-17.* ***Colan*** *a-23, 81; c-14.* ***Ditko*** *a-33, 38, 50-96; c-58, 67, 71, 88i.* ***Kirby/Ditko*** *a-50-83.* ***Everett*** *a-20, 48; c-4-7, 9, 36, 37, 39-42, 44, 45, 47.* ***Forte*** *a-19, 35, 40, 53.* ***Heath*** *a-4-6, 11, 14; c-1, 8, 11, 15, 51.* ***Heck*** *a-53, 73.* ***Kirby*** *a(p)-51, 52, 56, 57-60, 62-64, 66, 67, 69-89, 93, 97, 98, 100(w/****Heck****), 101-125; c-50-57, 59-66, 68-70, 72-82, 88(w/****Ditko****), 83 & 84(w/****Sinnott****), 85-96(w/****Ayers****), 97-125p.* ***Leiber/Fox*** *a-93, 98-102.* ***Maneely*** *c-20-22.* ***Morisi*** *a-42.* ***Morrow*** *a-41, 42.* ***Orlando*** *a-30, 45, 57.* ***Mac Pakula*** *(Tothish) a-9, 35, 41.* ***Powell*** *a-20, 27, 34.* ***Reinman*** *a-39, 87, 92, 96i.*

GD VG FN VF VF/NM NM-
2.0 4.0 6.0 8.0 9.0 9.2

Robinson *a-9.* ***Roussos*** *a-39.* ***Robert Sale*** *a-14.* ***Severin*** *a-27; c-30.* ***Sinnott*** *a-41; c-50.* ***Tuska*** *a-11.* ***Wildey*** *a-16.*

JOURNEY INTO MYSTERY (2nd Series)
Marvel Comics: Oct, 1972 - No. 19, Oct, 1975

1-Robert Howard adaptation; Starlin/Ploog-a 3 6 9 20 30 40
2-5: 2,3,5-Bloch adapt. 4-H. P. Lovecraft adapt. 3 6 9 14 20 26
6-19: Reprints 2 4 6 11 16 20

NOTE: ***N. Adams*** *a-2i.* ***Ditko*** *r-7, 10, 12, 14, 15, 19; c-10.* ***Everett*** *r-9, 14.* ***G. Kane*** *a-1p, 2p; c-1-3p.* ***Kirby*** *r-7, 13, 15, 18, 19; c-7.* ***Mort Lawrence*** *r-2.* ***Maneely*** *r-3.* ***Orlando*** *r-16.* ***Reese*** *a-1, 2i.* ***Starlin*** *a-1p, 3p.* ***Torres*** *r-16.* ***Wildey*** *r-9, 14.*

JOURNEY INTO UNKNOWN WORLDS (Formerly Teen)
Atlas Comics (WFP): No. 36, Sept, 1950 - No. 38, Feb, 1951;
No. 4, Apr, 1951 - No. 59, Aug, 1957

36(#1)-Science fiction/weird; "End Of The Earth" c/story
258 516 774 1651 2826 4000
37(#2)-Science fiction; "When Worlds Collide" c/story; Everett-c/a; Hitler story
105 210 315 667 1146 1625
38(#3)-Science fiction 89 178 267 565 970 1375
4-6,8,10-Science fiction/weird 54 108 162 346 591 835
7-Wolverton-a "Planet of Terror", 6 pgs; electric chair c-inset/story
90 180 270 576 988 1400
9-Giant eyeball story 68 136 204 435 743 1050
11,12-Krigstein-a 41 82 123 250 418 585
13,16,17,20 37 74 111 218 354 490
14-Wolverton-a "One of Our Graveyards Is Missing", 4 pgs; Tuska-a
66 132 198 419 722 1025
15-Wolverton-a "They Crawl by Night", 5 pgs.; 2 pg. Maneely s/f story
66 132 198 419 722 1025
18,19-Matt Fox-a 41 82 123 250 418 585
21-33: 21-Decapitation-c. 24-Sci/fic story. 26-Atom bomb panel. 27-Sid Check-a.
33-Last pre-code (2/55) 27 54 81 158 259 360
34-Kubert, Torres-a 21 42 63 124 202 280
35-Torres-a 20 40 60 114 182 250
36-45,48,50,53,55,59: 43-Krigstein-a. 44-Davis-a. 45,55,59-Williamson-a in all; with Mayo #55,59. 55-Crandall-a. 48,53-Crandall-a (4 pgs. #48). 48-Check-a. 50-Davis, Crandall-a
19 38 57 111 176 240
46,47,49,52,54,56-58: 54-Torres-a 17 34 51 100 158 215
51-Ditko, Wood-a 20 40 60 118 192 265

NOTE: ***Ayers*** *a-24, 43,* ***Berg*** *a-38(#3), 43.* ***Lou Cameron*** *a-33.* ***Colan*** *a-37(#2), 6, 17, 19, 20, 23, 39.* ***Ditko*** *a-45, 51.* ***Drucker*** *a-35, 58.* ***Everett*** *a-37(#2), 11, 14, 41, 55, 56; c-37(#2), 11, 13, 14, 17, 22, 47, 48, 50, 53-55, 59.* ***Forte*** *a-49.* ***Fox*** *a-21i.* ***Heath*** *a-36(#1), 4, 6-8, 17, 20, 22, 36i; c-18.* ***Keller*** *a-15.* ***Mort Lawrence*** *a-38, 39.* ***Maneely*** *a-7, 8, 15, 16, 22, 49, 58; c-19, 25, 52.* ***Morrow*** *a-48.* ***Orlando*** *a-44, 57.* ***Pakula*** *a-36.* ***Powell*** *a-42, 53, 54.* ***Reinman*** *a-8.* ***Rico*** *a-21.* ***Robert Sale*** *a-24, 49.* ***Sekowsky*** *a-4, 5, 9.* ***Severin*** *a-38, 51; c-38, 48i, 56.* ***Sinnott*** *a-9, 21, 24.* ***Tuska*** *a-38(#3), 14.* ***Wildey*** *a-25, 43, 44.*

JOURNEYMAN
Image Comics: Aug, 1999 - No. 3, Oct, 1999 ($2.95, B&W, limited series)

1-3-Brandon McKinney-s/a 3.00

JOURNEY TO THE CENTER OF THE EARTH (Movie)
Dell Publishing Co.: No. 1060, Nov-Jan, 1959/60 (one-shot)

Four Color 1060-Pat Boone & James Mason photo-c 10 20 30 73 129 185

JSA (Justice Society of America) (Also see All Star Comics)
DC Comics: Aug, 1999 - No. 87, Sept, 2006 ($2.50/$2.99)

1-Robinson and Goyer-s; funeral of Wesley Dodds 2 4 6 8 10 12
2-5: 4-Return of Dr. Fate 6.00
6-24: 6-Black Adam-c/app. 11,12-Kobra. 16-20-JSA vs. Johnny Sorrow. 19,20-Spectre app. 22-Hawkgirl origin. 23-Hawkman returns 4.00
25-($3.75) Hawkman rejoins the JSA 1 2 3 5 7 9
26-36, 38-49: 27-Capt. Marvel app. 29-Joker: Last Laugh. 31,32-Snejbjerg-a. 33-Ultra-Humanite. 34-Intro. new Crimson Avenger and Hourman. 42-G.A. Mr. Terrific and the Freedom Fighters app. 46-Eclipso returns 3.00
37-($3.50) Johnny Thunder merges with the Thunderbolt; origin new Crimson Avenger 3.50
50-($3.95) Wraparound-c by Pacheco; Sentinel becomes Green Lantern again 4.00
51-74,76-82: 51-Kobra killed. 54-JLA app. 55-Ma Hunkle (Red Tornado) app. 56-58-Black Reign x-over with Hawkman #23-25. 64-Sand returns. 67-Identity Crisis tie-in; Gibbons-a. 68,69,72-81-Ross-c. 73,74-Day of Vengeance tie-in. 76-OMAC tie-in. 82-Infinite Crisis x-over; Levitz-s/Perez-a 2.50
75-($2.99) Day of Vengeance tie-in; Alex Ross Spectre-c 3.00
83-87: One Year Later; Pérez-c. 83-85,87-Morales-a; Gentleman Ghost app. 85-Begin $2.99-c; Earth-2 Batman, Atom, Sandman, Mr. Terrific app. 86,87-Ordway-a. 3.00
Annual 1 (10/00, $3.50) Planet DC; intro. Nemesis 3.50
...: Black Reign TPB (2005, $12.99) r/#56-58, Hawkman #23-25; Watson cover gallery 13.00
...: Black Vengeance TPB (2006, $19.99) r/#66-75 20.00
...: Darkness Falls TPB (2002, $19.95) r/#6-15 20.00

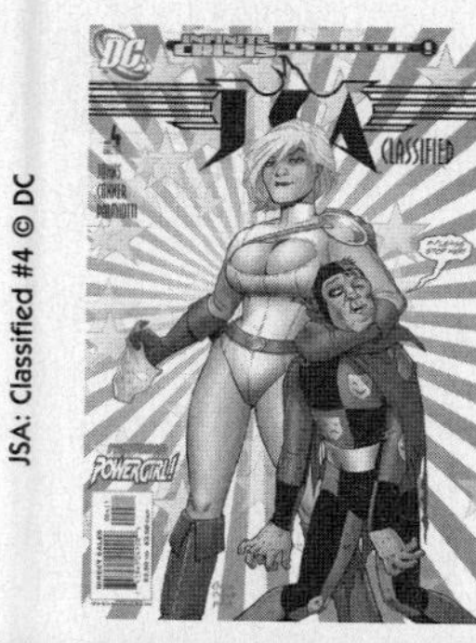

JSA: Classified #4 © DC

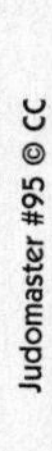
Judomaster #95 © CC

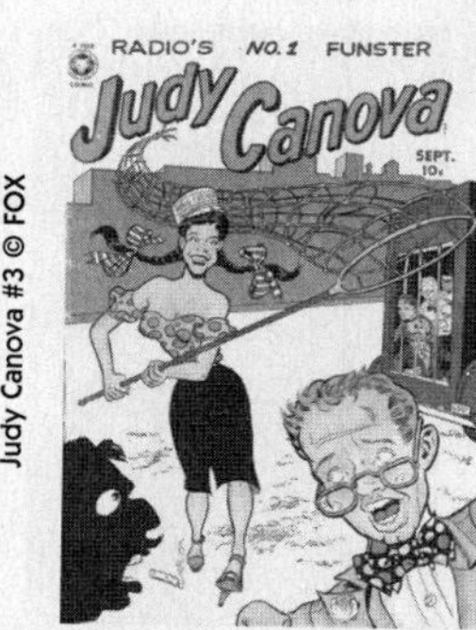

Judy Canova #3 © FOX

GD 2.0 | VG 4.0 | FN 6.0 | VF 8.0 | VF/NM 9.0 | NM- 9.2

...: Fair Play TPB (2003, $14.95) r/#26-31 & Secret Files #2 15.00
...: Ghost Stories TPB (2006, $14.99) r/#82-87 15.00
...: Justice Be Done TPB (2000, $14.95) r/Secret Files & #1-5 15.00
...: Lost TPB (2005, $19.99) r/#59-67 20.00
...: Mixed Signals TPB (2006, $14.99) r/#76-81 15.00
...: Our Worlds at War 1 (9/01, $2.95) Jae Lee-c; Saltares-a 3.00
... Presents Green Lantern TPB (2008, $14.99) r/JSA Classified #25,32,33 and Green Lantern: Brightest Day, Blackest Night 15.00
...: Princes of Darkness TPB (2005, $19.95) r/#46-55 20.00
...: Savage Times TPB (2004, $14.95) r/#39-45 15.00
... Secret Files 1 (8/99, $4.95) Origin stories and pin-ups; death of Wesley Dodds (G.A. Sandman); intro new Hawkgirl 5.00
... Secret Files 2 (9/01, $4.95) Short stories and profile pages 5.00
...: Stealing Thunder TPB (2003, $14.95) r/#32-38; JSA vs. The Ultra-Humanite 15.00
...: The Golden Age TPB (2005, $19.99) r/"The Golden Age" Elseworlds mini-series 20.00
...: The Return of Hawkman TPB (2002, $19.95) r/#16-26 & Secret Files #1 20.00

JSA: ALL STARS
DC Comics: July, 2003 - No. 8, Feb, 2004 ($2.50/$3.50, limited series, back-up stories in Golden Age style)
1-6,8-Goyer & Johns-s/Cassaday-c. 1-Velluto-a; intro. Legacy. 2-Hawkman by Loeb/Sale 3-Dr. Fate by Cooke. 4-Starman by Robinson/Harris. 5-Hourman by Chaykin. 6-Dr. Mid-nite by Azzarello/Risso 2.50
7-($3.50) Mr. Terrific back-up story by Chabon; Lark-a 3.50
TPB (2004, $14.95) r/#1-8 15.00

JSA: ALL STARS
DC Comics: Feb, 2010 - Present ($3.99)
1,2-Younger JSA members from team. 1-Covers by Williams and Sook 4.00

JSA: CLASSIFIED (Issues #1-4 reprinted in Power Girl TPB)
DC Comics: Sept, 2005 - No. 39, Aug, 2008 ($2.50/$2.99)
1-(1st printing) Conner-c/a; origin of Power Girl 3.00
1-(1st printing) Adam Hughes variant-c 5.00
1-(2nd & 3rd printings) 2nd-Hughes B&W sketch-c. 3rd-Close-up of Conner-c 2.50
2-11: 2-LSH app. 4-Leads into Infinite Crisis #2. 5-7-Injustice Society app. 10-13-Vandal Savage origin retold; Gulacy-a/c 2.50
12-39: 12-Begin $2.99-c. 17,18-Bane app. 19,20-Morales-a. 21,22-Simonson-s/a 3.00
...: Honor Among Thieves TPB (2007, $14.99) r/#5-9 15.00

JSA STRANGE ADVENTURES
DC Comics: Oct, 2004 - No. 6, Mar, 2005 ($3.50, limited series)
1-6-Johnny Thunder as pulp writer; Kitson-a/Watson-c/ Kevin Anderson-s 3.50
TPB (2010, $14.99) r/#1-6 15.00

JSA: THE LIBERTY FILE (Elseworlds)
DC Comics: Feb, 2000 - No. 2, Mar, 2000 ($6.95, limited series)
1,2-Batman, Dr. Mid-Nite and Hourman vs. WW2 Joker; Tony Harris-c/a 7.00
JSA: The Liberty Files TPB (2004, $19.95) r/The Liberty File and The Unholy Three series 20.00

JSA: THE UNHOLY THREE (Elseworlds)(Sequel to JSA: The Liberty File)
DC Comics: 2003 - No. 2, 2003 ($6.95, limited series)
1,2-Batman, Superman and Hourman; Tony Harris-c/a 7.00

JSA VS. KOBRA
DC Comics: Aug, 2009 - No. 6, Jan, 2010 ($2.99, limited series)
1-6-Kramer-a/Ha-c; Jason Burr app. 3.00

J2 (Also see A-Next and Juggernaut)
Marvel Comics: Oct, 1998 - No. 12, Sept, 1999 ($1.99)
1-12:1-Juggernaut's son; Lim-a. 2-Two covers; X-People app. 3-J2 battles the Hulk 2.50
Spider-Girl Presents Juggernaut Jr. Vol.1: Secrets & Lies (2006, $7.99, digest) r/#1-6 8.00

JUBILEE (X-Men)
Marvel Comics: Nov, 2004 - No. 6, Apr, 2005 ($2.99)
1-6: 1-Jubilee in a Los Angeles high school; Kirkman-s; Casey Jones-c 3.00

JUDENHASS
Aardvark-Vanaheim Press: 2008 ($4.00, B&W, squarebound)
nn-Dave Sim-writer/artist; The Shoah and Jewish persecution through history 4.00

JUDE, THE FORGOTTEN SAINT
Catechetical Guild Education Soc.: 1954 (16 pgs.; 8x11"; full color; paper-c)
nn 5 10 15 24 30 35

J.U.D.G.E.: THE SECRET RAGE
Image Comics: Mar, 2000 - No. 3, May, 2000 ($2.95)
1-3-Greg Horn-s/c/a 3.00

JUDGE COLT
Gold Key: Oct, 1969 - No. 4, Sept, 1970
1 3 6 9 16 23 30
2-4 2 4 6 9 13 16

JUDGE DREDD (...Classics #62 on; also see Batman - Judge Dredd, The Law of Dredd & 2000 A.D. Monthly)
Eagle Comics/IPC Magazines Ltd./Quality Comics #34-35, V2#1-37/ Fleetway #38 on: Nov, 1983 - No. 35, 1986; V2#1, Oct, 1986 - No. 77, 1993
1-Bolland-c/a 6.00
2-35 3.00
V2#1-77: 1-('86)-New look begins. 20-Begin $1.50-c. 21/22, 23/24-Two issue numbers in one. 28-1st app. Megaman (super-hero). 39-Begin $1.75-c. 51-Begin $1.95-c. 53-Bolland-a. 57-Reprints 1st published Judge Dredd story 2.50
Special 1 2.50
NOTE: *Bolland* a-1-6, 8, 10; c-1-10, 15. *Guice* c-V2#23/24, 26, 27.

JUDGE DREDD (3rd Series)
DC Comics: Aug, 1994 - No. 18, Jan, 1996 ($1.95)
1-18: 12-Begin $2.25-c 2.50
nn ($5.95)-Movie adaptation, Sienkiewicz-c 6.00

JUDGE DREDD'S CRIME FILE
Eagle Comics: Aug, 1989 - No. 6, Feb, 1986 ($1.25, limited series)
1-6: 1-Byrne-a 2.50

JUDGE DREDD: LEGENDS OF THE LAW
DC Comics: Dec, 1994 - No. 13, Dec, 1995 ($1.95)
1-13: 1-5-Dorman-c 2.50

JUDGE DREDD: THE EARLY CASES
Eagle Comics: Feb, 1986 - No. 6, Jul, 1986 ($1.25, Mega-series, Mando paper)
1-6: 2000 A.D.-r 2.50

JUDGE DREDD: THE JUDGE CHILD QUEST (Judge Child in indicia)
Eagle Comics: Aug, 1984 - No. 5, Oct, 1984 ($1.25, Lim. series, Baxter paper)
1-5: 2000A.D.-r; Bolland-c/a 2.50

JUDGE DREDD: THE MEGAZINE
Fleetway/Quality: 1991 - Present ($4.95, stiff-c, squarebound, 52 pgs.)
1-3 5.00

JUDGE DREDD VS. ALIENS: INCUBUS
Dark Horse Comics: March, 2003 - No. 4, June, 2003 ($2.99, limited series)
1-4-Flint-a/Wagner & Diggle-s 3.00

JUDGE PARKER
Argo: Feb, 1956 - No. 2, 1956
1-Newspaper strip reprints 7 14 21 35 43 50
2 5 10 15 24 30 35

JUDGMENT DAY
Awesome Entertainment: June, 1997 - No. 3, Oct, 1997 ($2.50, limited series)
1-3: 1 Alpha-Moore-s/Liefeld-c/a(p) flashback art by various in all. 2 Omega. 3 Final Judgment. All have a variant cover by Dave Gibbons 2.50
...Aftermath-($3.50) Moore-s/Kane-a; Youngblood, Glory, New Men, Maximage, Allies and Spacehunter short stories. Also has a variant cover by Dave Gibbons 3.50
TPB (Checker Books, 2003, $16.95) r/series 17.00

JUDO JOE
Jay-Jay Corp.: Aug, 1953 - No. 3, Dec, 1953 (Judo lessons in each issue)
1-Drug ring story 10 20 30 58 79 100
2,3: 3-Hypo needle story 8 16 24 40 50 60

JUDOMASTER (Gun Master #84-89) (Also see Crisis on Infinite Earths, Sarge Steel #6 & Special War Series)
Charlton Comics: No. 89, May-June, 1966 - No. 98, Dec, 1967 (Two No. 89's)
89-3rd app. Judomaster 4 8 12 26 41 55
90-Origin of Thunderbolt 4 8 12 24 37 50
91-Sarge Steel begins 4 8 12 22 34 45
92-98: 93-Intro. Tiger 3 6 9 21 32 42
93,94,96,98 (Modern Comics reprint, 1977) 4.00
NOTE: *Morisi* Thunderbolt #90. #91 has 1 pg. biography on writer/artist Frank McLaughlin.

JUDY CANOVA (Formerly My Experience) (Stage, screen, radio)
Fox Features Syndicate: No. 23, May, 1950 - No. 3, Sept, 1950
23(#1)-Wood-c,a(p)? 23 46 69 136 223 310
24-Wood-a(p) 22 44 66 132 216 300
3-Wood-c; Wood/Orlando-a 24 48 72 144 237 330

Juggernaut #1 © MAR

Jughead's Diner #1 © AP

Jughead With Archie Digest #177 © AP

	GD 2.0	VG 4.0	FN 6.0	VF 8.0	VF/NM 9.0	NM- 9.2

JUDY GARLAND (See Famous Stars)

JUDY JOINS THE WAVES
Toby Press: 1951 (For U.S. Navy)

nn 7 14 21 35 43 50

JUGGERNAUT (See X-Men)
Marvel Comics: Apr, 1997, Nov, 1999 ($2.99, one-shots)

1-(4/97) Kelly-s/ Rouleau-a 3.00
1-(11/99) Casey-s; Eighth Day x-over; Thor, Iron Man, Spidey app. 3.00

JUGHEAD (Formerly Archie's Pal...)
Archie Publications: No. 127, Dec, 1965 - No. 352, June, 1987

127-130: 129-LBJ on cover 3 6 9 17 25 32
131,133,135-160(9/68) 3 6 9 14 20 26
132,134: 132-Shield-c; The Fly & Black Hood app.; Shield cameo.
134-Shield-c 4 8 12 24 37 50
161-180 2 4 6 11 16 20
181-199 2 4 6 9 12 15
200(1/'72) 2 4 6 10 14 18
201-240(5/75) 2 4 6 8 10 12
241-270(11/77) 1 2 3 5 7 9
271-299 1 2 3 4 5 7
300(5/80)-Anniversary issue; infinity-c 1 2 3 5 6 8
301-320(1/82) 5.00
321-324,326-352 4.00
325-(10/82) Cheryl Blossom app. (not on cover); same month as intro. (cover & story) in Archie's Girls, Betty & Veronica #320; Jason Blossom app.; DeCarlo-a
3 6 9 18 27 35

JUGHEAD (2nd Series)(Becomes Archie's Pal Jughead Comics #46 on)
Archie Enterprises: Aug, 1987 - No. 45, May, 1993 (.75/$1.00/$1.25)

1 1 2 3 4 5 7
2-10 4.00
11-45: 4-X-Mas issue. 17-Colan-c/a 3.00

JUGHEAD & FRIENDS DIGEST MAGAZINE
Archie Publ.: June, 2005 - Present ($2.39/$2.49/$2.69, digest-size)

1-37: 1-That Wilkin Boy app. 2.75

JUGHEAD AS CAPTAIN HERO (See Archie as Pureheart the Powerful, Archie Giant Series Magazine #142 & Life With Archie)
Archie Publications: Oct, 1966 - No. 7, Nov, 1967

1-Super hero parody 7 14 21 47 76 105
2 5 10 15 30 48 65
3-7 4 8 12 26 41 55

JUGHEAD JONES COMICS DIGEST, THE (...Magazine No. 10-64; Jughead Jones Digest Magazine #65)
Archie Publ.: June, 1977 - No. 100, May, 1996 ($1.35/$1.50/$1.75, digest-size, 128 pgs.)

1-Neal Adams-a; Capt. Hero-r 3 6 9 21 32 42
2(9/77)-Neal Adams-a 3 6 9 16 22 28
3-6,8-10 2 4 6 11 16 20
7-Origin Jaguar-r; N. Adams-a. 2 4 6 13 18 22
11-20: 13-r/1957 Jughead's Folly 2 4 6 8 10 12
21-50 1 2 3 4 5 7
51-70 5.00
71-100 3.00

JUGHEAD'S BABY TALES
Archie Comics: Spring, 1994 - No. 2, Wint. 1994 ($2.00, 52 pgs.)

1,2: 1-Bound-in pull-out poster 4.00

JUGHEAD'S DINER
Archie Comics: Apr, 1990 - No. 7, Apr, 1991 ($1.00)

1 4.00
2-7 2.50

JUGHEAD'S DOUBLE DIGEST (...Magazine #5)
Archie Comics: Oct, 1989 - Present ($2.25 - $3.69)

1 2 4 6 8 10 12
2-10: 2,5-Capt. Hero stories 1 2 3 5 6 8
11-25 5.00
26-160: 58-Begin $2.99-c. 66-Begin $3.19-c. 91-Begin $3.59-c. 138-Reprints entire Jughead #1 (1949). 139-142-"New Look" Jughead; Staton-a. 148-Begin $3.99-c 4.00
Archie New Look Series Book 2, Jughead "The Matchmakers" TPB (2009, $10.95) r/new look series in #139-142; new cover by Staton & Milgrom 11.00

JUGHEAD'S EAT-OUT COMIC BOOK MAGAZINE (See Archie Giant Series Magazine No. 170)

JUGHEAD'S FANTASY
Archie Publications: Aug, 1960 - No. 3, Dec, 1960

1 16 32 48 113 217 320
2 11 22 33 74 132 190
3 9 18 27 61 103 145

JUGHEAD'S FOLLY
Archie Publications (Close-Up): 1957 (36 pgs.)(one-shot)

1-Jughead a la Elvis (Rare) (1st reference to Elvis in comics?)
52 104 156 323 549 775

JUGHEAD'S JOKES
Archie Publications: Aug, 1967 - No. 78, Sept, 1982
(No. 1-8, 38 on: reg. size; No. 9-23: 68 pgs.; No. 24-37: 52 pgs.)

1 6 12 18 43 69 95
2 4 8 12 24 37 50
3-8 3 6 9 17 25 32
9,10 (68 pgs.) 3 6 9 19 29 38
11-23(4/71) (68 pgs.) 3 6 9 16 23 30
24-37(1/74) (52 pgs.) 2 4 6 11 16 20
38-50(9/76) 1 3 4 6 8 10
51-78 6.00

JUGHEAD'S PAL HOT DOG (See Laugh #14 for 1st app.)
Archie Comics: Jan, 1990 - No. 5, Oct, 1990 ($1.00)

1 4.00
2-5 2.50

JUGHEAD'S SOUL FOOD
Spire Christian Comics (Fleming H. Revell Co.): 1979 (49¢/59¢)

nn-Low print run 2 4 6 11 16 20

JUGHEAD'S TIME POLICE
Archie Comics: July, 1990 - No. 6, May, 1991 ($1.00, bi-monthly)

1 4.00
2-6: Colan a-3-6p; c-3-6 2.50

JUGHEAD WITH ARCHIE DIGEST (...Plus Betty & Veronica & Reggie Too No. 1,2; ...Magazine #33-?, 101-on; ...Comics Digest Mag.)
Archie Pub.: Mar, 1974 - No. 200, May, 2005 ($1.00-$2.39)

1 5 10 15 34 55 75
2 4 8 12 22 34 45
3-10 3 6 9 18 27 35
11-13,15-17,19,20: Capt. Hero-r in #14-16; Capt. Pureheart #17,19
2 4 6 10 14 18
14,18,21,22-Pureheart the Powerful in #18,21,22 2 4 6 11 16 20
23-30: 29-The Shield-r. 30-The Fly-r 1 3 4 6 8 10
31-50,100 1 2 3 5 6 8
51-99 1 2 3 4 5 7
101-121 4.00
122-200: 156-Begin $2.19-c. 180-Begin $2.39-c 2.50

JUKE BOX COMICS
Famous Funnies: Mar, 1948 - No. 6, Jan, 1949

1-Toth-c/a; Hollingsworth-a 38 76 114 226 363 500
2-Transvestism story 23 46 69 135 218 300
3-6: 3-Peggy Lee story. 4-Jimmy Durante line drawn-c. 6-Features Desi Arnaz plus Arnaz line drawn-c 18 36 54 105 165 225

JUMBO COMICS (Created by S.M. Iger)
Fiction House Magazines (Real Adv. Publ. Co.): Sept, 1938 - No. 167, Mar, 1953 (No. 1-3: 68 pgs.; No. 4-8: 52 pgs.)(No. 1-8 oversized-10-1/2x14-1/2"; black & white)

1-(Rare)-Sheena Queen of the Jungle(1st app.) by Meskin, Hawks of the Seas (The Hawk #10 on; see Feature Funnies #3) by Eisner, The Hunchback by Dick Briefer (ends #8), Wilton of the West (ends #24), Inspector Dayton (ends #67) & ZX-5 (ends #140) begin; 1st comic art by Jack Kirby (Count of Monte Cristo & Wilton of the West); Mickey Mouse appears (1 panel) with brief biography of Walt Disney; 1st app. Peter Pupp by Bob Kane. Note: Sheena was created by Iger for publication in England as a newspaper strip. The early issues of Jumbo contain Sheena strip-r; multiple panel-c 1,2,7
2150 4300 6450 21,500 - -
2-(Rare)-Origin Sheena. Diary of Dr. Hayward by Kirby (also #3) plus 2 other stories; contains strip from Universal Film featuring Edgar Bergen & Charlie McCarthy plus-c (preview of film) 700 1400 2100 7000 - -
3-Last Kirby issue 500 1000 1500 5000 - -
4-(Scarce)-Origin The Hawk by Eisner; Wilton of the West by Fine (ends #14)(1st comic

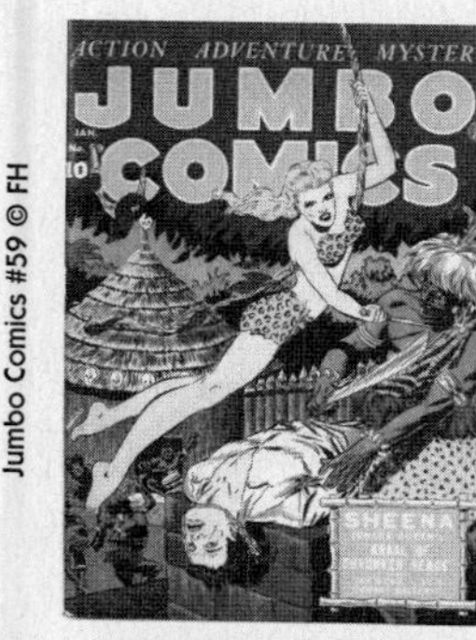

Jumbo Comics #59 © FH

Jungle Action #7 © MAR

Jungle Girl #5 © Jungle Girl LLC

	GD	VG	FN	VF	VF/NM	NM-
	2.0	4.0	6.0	8.0	9.0	9.2
work); Count of Monte Cristo by Fine (ends #15); The Diary of Dr. Hayward by Fine (cont'd #8,9)	460	920	1380	4600	-	-
5-Christmas-c	395	790	1185	3950	-	-
6-8-Last B&W issue. #8 was a 1939 N. Y. World's Fair Special Edition; Frank Buck's Jungleland story	355	710	1065	3550	-	-
9-Stuart Taylor begins by Fine (ends #140); Fine-c; 1st color issue (8-9/39)-1st Sheena (jungle) cover; 8-1/4x10-1/4" (oversized in width only)	335	670	1005	3350	-	-
10-Regular size 68 pg. issues begin; Sheena dons new costume w/origin costume; Stuart Taylor sci/fi-c; classic Lou Fine-c.	206	412	618	1318	2259	3200
11-13: 12-The Hawk-c by Eisner. 13-Eisner-c	132	264	396	838	1444	2050
14-Intro. Lightning (super-hero) on-c only	135	270	405	864	1482	2100
15,17-20: 15-1st Lightning story and begins, ends #41. 17-Lightning part-c	84	168	252	538	919	1300
16-Lightning-c	98	196	294	622	1074	1525
21-30: 22-1st Tom, Dick & Harry; origin The Hawk retold. 25-Midnight the Black Stallion begins, ends #65	62	124	186	394	680	965
31-40: 31-(9/41)-1st app. Mars God of War in Stuart Taylor story (see Planet Comics #15. 35-Shows V2#11 (correct number does not appear)	52	104	156	323	549	775
41-50: 42-Ghost Gallery begins, ends #167	41	82	123	250	418	585
51-60: 52-Last Tom, Dick & Harry	37	74	111	218	354	490
61-70: 68-Sky Girl begins, ends #130; not in #79	28	56	84	168	274	380
71-93,95-99: 89-ZX5 becomes a private eye.	23	46	69	136	223	310
94-Used in Love and Death by Legman	25	50	75	147	241	335
100	25	50	75	147	241	335
101-121	21	42	63	124	202	280
121-140,150-158: 155-Used in **POP**, pg. 98	19	38	57	112	179	245
141-149-Two Sheena stories. 141-Long Bow, Indian Boy begins, ends #160	20	40	60	115	185	255
159-163: Space Scouts serial in all. 160-Last jungle-c (6/52). 161-Ghost Gallery covers begin, end #167. 163-Suicide Smith app.	18	36	54	103	162	220
164-The Star Pirate begins, ends #165	18	36	54	103	162	220
165-167: 165,167-Space Rangers app.	18	36	54	103	162	220

NOTE: *Bondage covers, negligee panels, torture, etc. are common in this series. Hawks of the Seas, Inspector Dayton, Spies in Action, Sports Shorts, & Uncle Otto by Eisner, #1-7. Hawk by* **Eisner**-*#10-15.* **Eisner** *c-1-8, 12-14. 1pg. Patsy pin-ups in 92-97, 99-101. Sheena by* **Meskin**-*#1, 4; by* **Powell**-*#2, 3, 5-28;* **Powell** *c-14, 16, 17, 19.* **Powell/Eisner** *c-15. Sky Girl by* **Matt Baker**-*#69-78, 80-130. ZX-5 & Ghost Gallery by* **Kamen**-*#90-130.* **Bailey** *a-3-8.* **Briefer** *a-1-8, 10.* **Fine** *a-14; c-9-11.* **Kamen** *a-101, 105, 123, 132; c-105, 121-145.* **Bob Kane** *a-1-8.* **Whitman** *c-146-167(most). Jungle c-9, 13, 15, 17 on.*

JUMPER: JUMPSCARS
Oni Press: Jan, 2008 ($14.95, graphic novel)

SC-Prelude to 2008 movie Jumper; Brian Hurtt-a/c 15.00

JUNGLE ACTION
Atlas Comics (IPC): Oct, 1954 - No. 6, Aug, 1955

	GD	VG	FN	VF	VF/NM	NM-
1-Leopard Girl begins by Al Hartley (#1,3); Jungle Boy by Forte; Maneely-a in all	37	74	111	218	354	490
2-(3-D effect cover)	37	74	111	218	354	490
3-6: 3-Last precode (2/55)	23	46	69	136	223	310

NOTE: **Maneely** *c-1, 2, 5, 6.* **Romita** *a-3, 6.* **Shores** *a-3, 6; c-3, 4?.*

JUNGLE ACTION (...& Black Panther #18-21?)
Marvel Comics Group: Oct, 1972 - No. 24, Nov, 1976

	GD	VG	FN	VF	VF/NM	NM-
1-Lorna, Jann-r (All reprints in 1-4)	2	4	6	13	18	22
2-4	2	4	6	8	11	14
5-Black Panther begins (r/Avengers #62)	3	6	9	18	27	35
6-New solo Black Panther stories begin	3	6	9	16	23	30
7,9,10: 9-Contains pull-out centerfold ad by Mark Jewelers	2	4	6	10	14	18
8-Origin Black Panther	3	6	9	14	19	24
11-20,23,24: 19-23-KKK x-over. 23-r/#22. 24-1st Wind Eagle; story contd in Marvel Premiere #51-#53	2	4	6	8	10	12
21,22-(Regular 25¢ edition)(5,7/76)	2	4	6	8	10	12
21,22-(30¢-c variant, limited distribution)	3	6	9	18	27	35

NOTE: **Buckler** *a-6-9p, 22; c-8p, 12p.* **Buscema** *a-5p; c-22.* **Byrne** *c-23.* **Gil Kane** *a-8p; c-2, 4, 10p, 11p, 13-17, 19, 24.* **Kirby** *c-18.* **Maneely** *r-1.* **Russell** *a-13i.* **Starlin** *c-3p.*

JUNGLE ADVENTURES
Super Comics: 1963 - 1964 (Reprints)

	GD	VG	FN	VF	VF/NM	NM-
10,12,15,17,18: 10-r/Terrors of the Jungle #4 & #10(Rulah). 12-r/Zoot #14(Rulah).15-r/Kaanga from Jungle #152 & Tiger Girl. 17-All Jo-Jo-r. 18-Reprints/White Princess of the Jungle #1; no Kinstler-a; origin of both White Princess & Cap'n Courage	3	6	9	19	29	38

JUNGLE ADVENTURES
Skywald Comics: Mar, 1971 - No. 3, June, 1971 (25¢, 52 pgs.) (Pre-code reprints & new-s)

	GD	VG	FN	VF	VF/NM	NM-
	2.0	4.0	6.0	8.0	9.0	9.2
1-Zangar origin; reprints of Jo-Jo, Blue Gorilla(origin)/White Princess #3, Kinstler-r/White Princess #2	3	6	9	17	25	32
2,3: 2-Zangar, Sheena-r/Sheena #17 & Jumbo #162, Jo-Jo, origin Slave Girl-r. 3-Zangar, Jo-Jo, White Princess, Rulah-r	2	4	6	13	18	22

JUNGLE BOOK (See King Louie and Mowgli, Movie Comics, Mowgli..., Walt Disney Showcase #45 & Walt Disney's The Jungle Book)

JUNGLE CAT (Disney)
Dell Publishing Co.: No. 1136, Sept-Nov, 1960 (one shot)

	GD	VG	FN	VF	VF/NM	NM-
Four Color 1136-Movie, photo-c	6	12	18	43	69	95

JUNGLE COMICS
Fiction House Magazines: 1/40 - No. 157, 3/53; No. 158, Spr, 1953 - No. 163, Summer, 1954

	GD	VG	FN	VF	VF/NM	NM-
1-Origin The White Panther, Kaanga, Lord of the Jungle, Tabu, Wizard of the Jungle; Wambi, the Jungle Boy, Camilla & Capt. Terry Thunder begin (all 1st app.). Lou Fine-c	459	918	1377	3350	5925	8500
2-Fantomah, Mystery Woman of the Jungle begins, ends #51; The Red Panther begins, ends #26	168	336	504	1075	1838	2600
3,4	135	270	405	864	1482	2100
5-Classic Eisner-c	150	300	450	953	1639	2325
6-10: 7,8-Powell-c	79	158	237	502	864	1225
11-20: 13-Tuska-c	54	108	162	346	591	835
21-30: 25-Shows V2#1 (correct number does not appear). #27-New origin Fantomah, Daughter of the Pharoahs; Camilla dons new costume	46	92	138	290	488	685
31-40	37	74	111	222	361	500
41,43-50	33	66	99	194	317	440
42-Kaanga by Crandall, 12 pgs.	34	68	102	204	332	460
51-60	28	56	84	168	274	380
61-70: 67-Cover swipes Crandall splash pg. in #42	25	50	75	147	241	335
71-80: 79-New origin Tabu	22	44	66	132	216	300
81-97,99	21	42	63	124	202	280
98-Used in **SOTI**, pg. 185 & illo "In ordinary comic books, there are pictures within pictures for children who know how to look;" used by N.Y. Legis. Comm.	33	66	99	194	317	440
100	25	50	75	147	241	335
101-110: 104-In Camilla story, villain is Dr. Wertham	20	40	60	120	195	270
111-120: 118-Clyde Beatty app.	20	40	60	117	189	260
121-130	19	38	57	112	179	245
131-163: 135-Desert Panther begins in Terry Thunder (origin), not in #137; ends (dies) #138. 139-Last 52 pg. issue. 141-Last Tabu. 143,145-Used in **POP**, pg. 99. 151-Last Camilla & Terry Thunder. 152-Tiger Girl begins. 158-Last Wambi; Sheena app.	18	36	54	103	162	220
I.W. Reprint #1,9: 1-r/? 9-r/#151	3	6	9	17	25	32

NOTE: *Bondage covers, negligee panels, torture, etc. are common to this series. Camilla by* **Fran Hopper**-*#70-92; by* **Baker**-*#69, 100-113, 115, 116; by* **Lubbers**-*#97-99 by* **Tuska**-*#63, 65. Kaanga by* **John Celardo**-*#80-113; by* **Larsen**-*#71, 75-79; by* **Moreira**-*#58, 60, 61, 63-70, 72-74; by* **Tuska**-*#37, 62; by* **Whitman**-*#114-163. Tabu by* **Larsen**-*#59-75, 82-92; by* **Whitman**-*#93-115. Terry Thunder by* **Hopper**-*#71, 72; by* **Celardo**-*#78, 79; by* **Lubbers**-*#80-85. Tiger Girl-r by* **Baker**-*#152, 153, 155-157, 159. Wambi by* **Baker**-*#62-67, 74.* **Astarita** *c-45, 46.* **Celardo** *a-78; c-98-113.* **Crandall** *c-67 from splash pg.* **Eisner** *c-2, 5, 6.* **Fine** *c-1.* **Larsen** *a-65, 66, 71, 72, 74, 75, 79, 83, 84, 87-90.* **Moreira** *c-43, 44.* **Morisi** *a-51.* **Powell** *c-7, 8.* **Sultan** *c-3, 4.* **Tuska** *c-13.* **Whitman** *c-132-163(most).* **Zolnerowich** *c-11, 12, 18-41.*

JUNGLE COMICS
Blackthorne Publishing: May, 1988 - No. 4 ($2.00, B&W/color)

1-Dave Stevens-c; B. Jones scripts in all. 3.00
2-4: 2-B&W-a begins 2.50

JUNGLE GIRL (See Lorna, the...)

JUNGLE GIRL (Nyoka, Jungle Girl No. 2 on)
Fawcett Publications: Fall, 1942 (one-shot)(No month listed)

	GD	VG	FN	VF	VF/NM	NM-
1-Bondage-c; photo of Kay Aldridge who played Nyoka in movie serial app. on-c. Adaptation of the classic Republic movie serial Perils of Nyoka. 1st comic to devote entire contents to a movie serial adaptation	124	248	372	787	1356	1925

JUNGLE GIRL
Dynamite Entertainment: No. 0, 2007 - 2009 (25¢/$2.99/$3.50)

0-(25¢-c) Eight page preview; preview of Superpowers w/Alex Ross-a 2.25
1-5-Frank Cho-plot/cover; Batista-a/variant-c 3.00
... Season 2 ($3.50) 1-5-Two covers by Cho & Batista 3.50

JUNGLE GIRLS
AC Comics: 1989 - No. 16, 1993 (B&W)

1-16: 1-4,10,13-16-New story & "good girl" reprints. 5-9,11,12-All g.g. reprints (Baker, Powell, Lubbers, others) 3.00

JUNGLE JIM (Also see Ace Comics)

Jungle Jo #2 © FOX

Jungle Tales #5 © ATLAS

Jurassic Park: Raptors Hijack #2 © Univ.

	GD 2.0	VG 4.0	FN 6.0	VF 8.0	VF/NM 9.0	NM- 9.2

Standard Comics (Best Books): No. 11, Jan, 1949 - No. 20, Apr, 1951

11	11	22	33	62	86	110
12-20	8	16	24	42	54	65

JUNGLE JIM
Dell Publishing Co.: No. 490, 8/53 - No. 1020, 8-10/59 (Painted-c)

Four Color 490(#1)	7	14	21	49	80	110
Four Color 565(#2, 6/54)	5	10	15	30	48	65
3(10-12/54)-5	4	8	12	28	44	60
6-19(1-3/59), Four Color 1020(#20)	4	8	12	26	41	55

JUNGLE JIM
King Features Syndicate: No. 5, Dec, 1967

5-Reprints Dell #5; Wood-c	2	4	6	10	14	18

JUNGLE JIM (Continued from Dell series)
Charlton Comics: No. 22, Feb, 1969 - No. 28, Feb, 1970 (#21 was an overseas edition only)

22-Dan Flagg begins; Ditko/Wood-a	3	6	9	21	32	42
23-26: 23-Last Dan Flagg; Howard-c. 24-Jungle People begin	3	6	9	15	21	26
27,28: 27-Ditko/Howard-a. 28-Ditko-a	3	6	9	17	25	32

NOTE: *Ditko cover of #22 reprints story panels*

JUNGLE JO
Fox Feature Syndicate (Hero Books): Mar, 1950 - No. 3, Sept, 1950

nn-Jo-Jo blanked out in titles of interior stories, leaving Congo King; came out after Jo-Jo #29 (intended as Jo-Jo #30?)	50	100	150	315	533	750
1-Tangi begins; part Wood-a	52	104	156	323	549	775
2,3	40	80	120	246	411	575

JUNGLE LIL (Dorothy Lamour #2 on; also see Feature Stories Magazine)
Fox Feature Syndicate (Hero Books): April, 1950

1	41	82	123	256	428	600

JUNGLE TALES (Jann of the Jungle No. 8 on)
Atlas Comics (CSI): Sept, 1954 - No. 7, Sept, 1955

1-Jann of the Jungle	39	78	117	233	382	530
2-7: 3-Last precode (1/55)	26	52	78	154	252	350

NOTE: *Heath c-5.* ***Heck*** *a-6, 7.* ***Maneely*** *a-2; c-1, 3.* ***Shores*** *a-5-7; c-4, 6.* ***Tuska*** *a-2.*

JUNGLE TALES OF TARZAN
Charlton Comics: Dec, 1964 - No. 4, July, 1965

1	6	12	18	37	59	80
2-4	4	8	12	24	37	50

NOTE: ***Giordano*** *c-3p.* ***Glanzman*** *a-1-3.* ***Montes/Bache*** *a-4.*

JUNGLE TERROR (See Harvey Comics Hits No. 54)

JUNGLE THRILLS (Formerly Sports Thrills; Terrors of the Jungle #17 on)
Star Publications: No. 16, Feb, 1952; Dec, 1953; No. 7, 1954

16-Phantom Lady & Rulah story-reprint/All Top No. 15; used in **POP**, pg. 98,99; L. B. Cole-c	49	98	147	309	522	735
3-D 1(12/53, 25¢)-Came w/glasses; Jungle Lil & Jungle Jo appear; L. B. Cole-c	49	98	147	309	522	735
7-Titled 'Picture Scope Jungle Adventures;' (1954, 36 pgs, 15¢)-3-D effect c/stories; story & coloring book; Disbrow-a/script; L.B. Cole-c	49	98	147	309	522	735

JUNGLE TWINS, THE (Tono & Kono)
Gold Key/Whitman No. 18: Apr, 1972 - No. 17, Nov, 1975; No. 18, May, 1982

1	3	6	9	16	22	28
2-5	2	4	6	8	11	14
6-18: 18(Whitman, 5/82)-Reprints	1	2	3	5	7	9

NOTE: *UFO c/story No. 13. Painted-c No. 1-17.* ***Spiegle*** *c-18.*

JUNGLE WAR STORIES (Guerrilla War No. 12 on)
Dell Publishing Co.: July-Sept, 1962 - No. 11, Apr-June, 1965 (Painted-c)

01-384-209 (#1)	4	8	12	22	34	45
2-11	3	6	9	16	23	30

JUNIE PROM (Also see Dexter Comics)
Dearfield Publishing Co.: Winter, 1947-48 - No. 7, Aug, 1949

1-Teen-age	14	28	42	80	115	150
2	9	18	27	47	61	75
3-7	8	16	24	40	50	60

JUNIOR
Fantagraphics Books: June, 2000 - No. 5, Jan, 2001 ($2.95, B&W)

1-5-Peter Bagge-s/a						3.00

JUNIOR CARROT PATROL (Jr. Carrot Patrol #2)
Dark Horse Comics: May, 1989; No. 2, Nov, 1990 ($2.00, B&W)

1,2-Flaming Carrot spin-off. 1-Bob Burden-c(i)						2.50

JUNIOR COMICS (Formerly Li'l Pan; becomes Western Outlaws with #17)
Fox Feature Syndicate: No. 9, Sept, 1947 - No. 16, July, 1948

9-Feldstein-c/a; headlights-c	123	246	369	787	1344	1900
10-16-Feldstein-c/a; headlights-c on all	113	226	339	718	1234	1750

JUNIOR FUNNIES (Formerly Tiny Tot Funnies No. 9)
Harvey Publ. (King Features Synd.): No. 10, Aug, 1951 - No. 13, Feb, 1952

10-Partial reprints in all; Blondie, Dagwood, Daisy, Henry, Popeye, Felix, Katzenjammer Kids	6	12	18	28	34	40
11-13	5	10	15	24	30	35

JUNIOR HOPP COMICS
Stanmor Publ.: Feb, 1952 - No. 3, July, 1952

1-Teenage humor	10	20	30	58	79	100
2,3: 3-Dave Berg-a	7	14	21	35	43	50

JUNIOR MEDICS OF AMERICA, THE
E. R. Squire & Sons: No. 1359, 1957 (15¢)

1359	4	8	12	17	21	24

JUNIOR MISS
Timely/Marvel (CnPC): Wint, 1944; No. 24, Apr, 1947 - No. 39, Aug, 1950

1-Frank Sinatra & June Allyson life story	31	62	93	182	296	410
24-Formerly The Human Torch #23?	15	30	45	88	137	185
25-38: 29,31,34-Cindy-c/stories (others?)	10	20	30	56	76	95
39-Kurtzman-a	11	22	33	64	90	115

NOTE: *Painted-c 35-37. 35, 37-all romance. 36, 38-mostly teen humor.* ***Louise Alston*** *c-36.*

JUNIOR PARTNERS (Formerly Oral Roberts' True Stories)
Oral Roberts Evangelistic Assn.: No. 120, Aug, 1959 - V3#12, Dec, 1961

120(#1)	4	8	12	24	37	50
2(9/59)	3	6	9	17	25	32
3-12(7/60)	2	4	6	13	18	22
V2#1(8/60)-5(12/60)	2	4	6	9	13	16
V3#1(1/61)-12	2	4	6	8	10	12

JUNIOR TREASURY (See Dell Junior...)

JUNIOR WOODCHUCKS GUIDE (Walt Disney's...)
Danbury Press: 1973 (8-3/4"x5-3/4", 214 pgs., hardcover)

nn-Illustrated text based on the long-standing J.W. Guide used by Donald Duck's nephews Huey, Dewey & Louie by Carl Barks. The guidebook was a popular plot device to enable the nephews to solve problems facing their uncle or Scrooge McDuck (scarce)	5	10	15	35	55	75

JUNIOR WOODCHUCKS LIMITED SERIES (Walt Disney's...)
W. D. Publications (Disney): July, 1991 - No. 4, Oct, 1991 ($1.50, limited series; new & reprint-a)

1-4: 1-The Beagle Boys app.; Barks-r						2.50

JUNIOR WOODCHUCKS (See Huey, Dewey & Louie...)

JURASSIC PARK
Topps Comics: June, 1993 - No. 4, Aug, 1993; No. 5, Oct, 1994 - No. 10, Feb, 1995

1-($2.50)-Newsstand Edition; Kane/Perez-a in all; 1-4: movie adaptation						2.50
1-($2.95)-Collector's Ed.; polybagged w/3 cards						4.00
1-Amberchrome Edition w/no price or ads	1	2	3	4	5	7
2-4-($2.50)-Newsstand Edition						2.50
2,3-($2.95)-Collector's Ed.; polybagged w/3 cards						3.00
4-10: 4-($2.95)-Collector's Ed.; polybagged w/1 of 4 different action hologram trading card; Gil Kane/Perez-a. 5-becomes Advs. of						3.00
Annual 1 ($3.95, 5/95)						4.00
Trade paperback (1993, $9.95)-r/#1-4; bagged w/#0						10.00

JURASSIC PARK: RAPTOR
Topps Comics: Nov, 1993 - No. 2, Dec, 1993 ($2.95, limited series)

1,2: 1-Bagged w/3 trading cards & Zorro #0; Golden c-1,2						3.00

JURASSIC PARK: RAPTORS ATTACK
Topps Comics: Mar, 1994 - No. 4, June, 1994 ($2.50, limited series)

1-4-Michael Golden-c/frontispiece						2.50

JURASSIC PARK: RAPTORS HIJACK
Topps Comics: July, 1994 - No. 4, Oct, 1994 ($2.50, limited series)

1-4: Michael Golden-c/front piece						2.50

Justice #9 © DC

Justice Comics #7(#1) © MAR

Justice League Europe #32 © DC

GD 2.0 | VG 4.0 | FN 6.0 | VF 8.0 | VF/NM 9.0 | NM- 9.2

JUST A PILGRIM
Black Bull Entertainment: May, 2001 - No. 5, Sept, 2001 ($2.99)

Limited Preview Edition (12/00, $7.00) Ennis & Ezquerra interviews 7.00
1-Ennis-s/Ezquerra-a; two covers by Texeira & JG Jones 3.00
2-5: 2-Fabry-c. 3-Nowlan-c. 4-Sienkiewicz-c 3.00
TPB (11/01, $12.99) r/#1-5; Waid intro. 13.00

JUST A PILGRIM: GARDEN OF EDEN
Black Bull Entertainment: May, 2002 - No. 4, Aug, 2002 ($2.99, limited series)

Limited Preview Ed. (1/02, $7.00) Ennis & Ezquerra interviews; Jones-c 7.00
1-4-Ennis-s/Ezquerra-a 3.00
TPB (11/02, $12.99) r/#1-4; Gareb Shamus intro. 13.00

JUSTICE
Marvel Comics Group (New Universe): Nov, 1986 - No. 32, June, 1989

1-32: 26-32-$1.50-c (low print run) 2.50

JUSTICE
DC Comics: Oct, 2005 - No. 12, Aug, 2007 ($2.99/$3.50/$3.99, bi-monthly maxi-series)

1-Classic Justice League vs. The Legion of Doom; Alex Ross & Doug Braithwaite-a; Jim Krueger-s; two covers by Ross; Ross sketch pages 5.00
1-2nd & 3rd printings 4.00
2-($3.50) 4.00
2 (2nd printing), 3-11-($3.50) 3.50
12-($3.99) Two covers (Heroes & Villains) 4.00
Absolute Justice HC (2009, $99.99, slipcased book with dustjacket) oversized r/#1-12; afterwords by creators; Ross sketch and design art; photo gallery of action figures 100.00
... Volume One HC (2006, $19.99, dustjacket) r/#1-4; Krueger intro.; sketch pages 20.00
... Volume One SC (2008, $14.99) r/#1-4; Krueger intro.; sketch pages 15.00
... Volume Two HC (2007, $19.99, dustjacket) r/#5-8; Krueger intro.; sketch pages 20.00
... Volume Two SC (2008, $14.99) r/#5-8; Krueger intro.; sketch pages 15.00
... Volume Three HC (2007, $19.99, dustjacket) r/#9-12; Ross intro.; sketch pages 20.00
... Volume Three SC (2007, $14.99) r/#9-12; Ross intro.; sketch pages 15.00

JUSTICE COMICS (Formerly Wacky Duck; Tales of Justice #53 on)
Marvel/Atlas Comics (NPP 7-9,4-19/CnPC 20-23/MjMC 24-38/Male 39-52:
No. 7, Fall/47 - No. 9, 6/48; No. 4, 8/48 - No. 52, 3/55

7(#1, 1947) 30 60 90 177 289 400
8(#2)-Kurtzman-a "Giggles 'n' Grins" (3) 20 40 60 117 189 260
9(#3, 6/48) 18 36 54 105 165 225
4 16 32 48 94 147 200
5(9/48)-9: 8-Anti-Wertham editorial 15 30 45 83 124 165
10-15-Photo-c 13 26 39 72 101 130
16-30 11 22 33 62 86 110
31-40,42-52: 35-Gene Colan-a. 48-Last precode; Pakula & Tuska-a.
10 20 30 58 79 100
41-Electrocution-c 17 34 51 98 154 210
NOTE: *Hartley a-48. Heath a-24. Maneely c-44, 52. Pakula a-43, 45, 47, 48. Louis Ravielli a-39, 47. Robinson a-22, 25, 41. Sale c-45. Shores c-7(#1), 8(#2)? Tuska a-41, 48. Wildey a-52.*

JUSTICE: FOUR BALANCE
Marvel Comics: Sept, 1994 - No. 4, Dec, 1994 ($1.75, limited series)

1-4: 1-Thing & Firestar app. 2.50

JUSTICE, INC. (The Avenger) (Pulp)
National Periodical Publications: May-June, 1975 - No. 4, Nov-Dec, 1975

1-McWilliams-a, Kubert-c; origin 2 4 6 10 14 18
2-4: 2-4-Kirby-a(p), c-2,3p. 4-Kubert-c 2 4 6 10 14 18
NOTE: *Adapted from Kenneth Robeson novel, creator of Doc Savage.*

JUSTICE, INC. (Pulp)
DC Comics: 1989 - No. 2, 1989 ($3.95, 52 pgs., squarebound, mature)

1,2: Re-intro The Avenger; Andrew Helfer scripts & Kyle Baker-c/a 4.00

JUSTICE LEAGUE (...International #7-25; ...America #26 on)
DC Comics: May, 1987 - No. 113, Aug, 1996 (Also see Legends #6)

1-Batman, Green Lantern (Guy Gardner), Blue Beetle, Mr. Miracle, Capt. Marvel & Martian Manhunter begin 1 2 3 4 5 7
2,3: 3-Regular-c (white background) 5.00
3-Limited-c (yellow background, Superman logo) 4 8 12 24 37 50
4-10: 4-Booster Gold joins. 5-Origin Gray Man; Batman vs. Guy Gardner; Creeper app. 7-($1.25, 52 pgs.)-Capt. Marvel & Dr. Fate resign; Capt. Atom & Rocket Red join. 9,10-Millennium x-over 3.00
11-17,22,23,25-49,51-68,71-82: 16-Bruce Wayne-c/story. 31,32-J. L. Europe x-over. 58-Lobo app. 61-New team begins; swipes-c to J.L. of A. #1('60). 70-Newsstand version w/o outer-c. 71-Direct sales version w/black outer-c. 71-Newsstand version w/o outer-c. 80-Intro new Booster Gold. 82,83-Guy Gardner-c/stories 2.50
18-21,24,50: 18-21-Lobo app. 24-($1.50)-1st app. Justice League Europe. 50-($1.75, 52 pgs.) 3.00
69-Doomsday tie-in; takes place between Superman: The Man of Steel #18 & Superman #74 5.00
69,70-2nd printings 2.50
70-Funeral for a Friend part 1; red 3/4 outer-c 4.00
83-99,101-113: 92-(9/94)-Zero Hour x-over; Triumph app. 113-Green Lantern, Flash & Hawkman app. 2.50
100 ($3.95)-Foil-c; 52 pgs. 4.00
100 ($2.95)-Newstand 3.00
#0-(10/94) Zero Hour (publ between #92 & #93); new team begins (Hawkman, Flash, Wonder Woman, Metamorpho, Nuklon, Crimson Fox, Obsidian & Fire) 2.50
Annual 1-8,10 ('87-'94, '96, 68 pgs.): 2-Joker-c/story; Batman cameo. 5-Armageddon 2001 x-over; Silver ink 2nd print. 7-Bloodlines x-over. 8-Elseworlds story. 10-Legends of the Dead Earth 3.00
Annual 9 (1995, $3.50)-Year One story 3.50
Special 1,2 ('90,'91, 52 pgs.): 1-Giffen plots. 2-Staton-a(p) 3.00
Spectacular 1 (1992, $1.50, 52 pgs.)-Intro new JLI & JLE teams; ties into JLI #61 & JLE #37; two interlocking covers by Jurgens 3.00
A New Beginning Trade Paperback (1989, $12.95)-r/#1-7 13.00
... International Vol. 1 HC (2008, $24.99) r/#1-7; new intro. by Giffen 25.00
... International Vol. 1 SC (2009, $17.99) r/#1-7; new intro. by Giffen 18.00
... International Vol. 2 HC (2008, $24.99) r/#8-13, Annual #1 and Suicide Squad #13 25.00
... International Vol. 2 SC (2009, $17.99) r/#8-13, Annual #1 and Suicide Squad #13 18.00
... International Vol. 3 SC (2009, $19.99) r/#14-22 20.00
NOTE: *Anderson c-61i. Austin a-1i, 60i; c-1i. Giffen a-13; c-21p. Guice a-62i. Maguire a-1-12, 16-19, 22, 23. Russell a-Annual 1i; c-54i. Willingham a-30p, Annual 2.*

JUSTICE LEAGUE ADVENTURES (Based on Cartoon Network series)
DC Comics: Jan, 2002 - No. 34, Oct, 2004 ($1.99/$2.25)

1-Timm & Ross-c 3.00
2-32: 3-Nicieza-s. 5-Starro app. 10-Begin $2.25-c. 14-Includes 16 pg. insert for VERB with Haberlin CG-art. 15,29-Amancio-a. 16-McCloud-s. 20-Psycho Pirate app. 25,26-Adam Strange-c/app. 28-Legion of Super-Heroes app. 30-Kamandi app. 2.50
Free Comic Book Day giveaway - (See Promotional Comics section)
TPB (2003, $9.95) r/#1,3,6,10-13; Timm/Ross-c from #1 10.00
...Vol. 1: The Magnificent Seven (2004, $6.95) digest-size reprints #3,6,10-12 7.00
...Vol. 2: Friends and Foes (2004, $6.95) digest-size reprints #13,14,16,19,20 7.00

JUSTICE LEAGUE: A MIDSUMMER'S NIGHTMARE
DC Comics: Sept, 1996 - No. 3, Nov, 1996 ($2.95, limited series, 38 pgs.)

1-3: Re-establishes Superman, Batman, Green Lantern, The Martian Manhunter, Flash, Aquaman & Wonder Woman as the Justice League; Mark Waid & Fabian Nicieza co-scripts; Jeff Johnson & Darick Robertson-a(p); Kevin Maguire-c 5.00
TPB-(1997, $8.95) r/1-3 9.00

JUSTICE LEAGUE: CRY FOR JUSTICE
DC Comics: Sept, 2009 - No. 7 ($3.99, limited series)

1-6-James Robinson-s/Mauro Cascioli-a/c. 1-Two covers; Congorilla origin 4.00

JUSTICE LEAGUE ELITE (See JLA #100 and JLA Secret Files 2004)
DC Comics: Sept, 2004 - No. 12, Aug, 2005 ($2.50)

1-12-Flash, Green Arrow, Vera Black and others; Kelly-s/Mahnke-a. 5,6-JSA app. 2.50
JL Elite TPB (2005, $19.99) r/#1-4, Action #775, JLA #100, JLA Secret Files 2004 20.00
... Vol. 2 TPB (2007, $19.99) r/#5-12 20.00

JUSTICE LEAGUE EUROPE (Justice League International #51 on)
DC Comics: Apr, 1989 - No. 68, Sept., 1994 (75¢/ $1.00/$1.25/$1.50)

1-Giffen plots in all, breakdowns in #1-8,13-30; Justice League #1-c/swipe 3.00
2-10: 7-9-Batman app. 7,8-JLA x-over. 8,9-Superman app. 2.50
11-49: 12-Metal Men app. 20-22-Rogers-c/a(p). 33,34-Lobo vs. Despero. 37-New team begins; swipes-c to JLA #9; see JLA Spectacular 2.50
50-($2.50, 68 pgs.)-Battles Sonar 3.00
51-68: 68-Zero Hour x-over; Triumph joins Justice League Task Force (See JLTF #17) 2.50
Annual 1-5 ('90-'94, 68 pgs.)-1-Return of the Global Guardians; Giffen plots/breakdowns. 2-Armageddon 2001; Giffen-a(p); Rogers-a(p); Golden-a(i). 5-Elseworlds story 3.00
NOTE: *Phil Jimenez a-68p. Rogers c/a-20-22. Sears a-1-12, 14-19, 23-29; c-1-10, 12, 14-19, 23-29.*

JUSTICE LEAGUE INTERNATIONAL (See Justice League Europe)

JUSTICE LEAGUE OF AMERICA (See Brave & the Bold #28-30, Mystery In Space #75 & Official... Index) (See Crisis on Multiple Earths TPBs for reprints of JLA/JSA crossovers)
National Periodical Publ./DC Comics: Oct-Nov, 1960 - No. 261, Apr, 1987 (#91-99,139-157: 52 pgs.)

1-(10-11/60)-Origin & 1st app. Despero; Aquaman, Batman, Flash, Green Lantern, J'onn J'onzz, Superman & Wonder Woman continue from Brave and the Bold
500 1000 1500 4500 9250 14,000

Justice League of America #25 © DC

Justice League of America #148 © DC

Justice League of America (2006 series) #19 © DC

	GD 2.0	VG 4.0	FN 6.0	VF 8.0	VF/NM 9.0	NM- 9.2
2	112	224	336	952	1876	2800
3-Origin/1st app. Kanjar Ro (see Mystery in Space #75)(scarce in high grade due to black-c)	96	192	288	816	1608	2400
4-Green Arrow joins JLA	64	128	192	544	1072	1600
5-Origin & 1st app. Dr. Destiny	52	104	156	442	871	1300
6-8,10: 6-Origin & 1st app. Prof. Amos Fortune. 7-(10-11/61)-Last 10¢ issue. 10-(3/62)-Origin & 1st app. Felix Faust; 1st app. Lord of Time	42	84	126	336	656	975
9-(2/62)-Origin JLA (1st origin)	50	100	150	413	807	1200
11-15: 12-(6/62)-Origin & 1st app. Dr. Light. 13-(8/62)-Speedy app. 14-(9/62)-Atom joins JLA.	29	58	87	212	406	600
16-20: 17-Adam Strange flashback	24	48	72	175	338	500
21-(8/63)-"Crisis on Earth-One"; re-intro. of JSA in this title (see Flash #129) (1st S.A. app. Hourman & Dr. Fate)	39	78	117	297	574	850
22- "Crisis on Earth-Two"; JSA x-over (story continued from #21)	33	66	99	254	490	725
23-28: 24-Adam Strange app. 27-Robin app.	17	34	51	124	242	360
29-JSA x-over; 1st S.A. app. Starman; "Crisis on Earth-Three"	21	42	63	148	287	425
30-JSA x-over	19	38	57	139	270	400
31-Hawkman joins JLA, Hawkgirl cameo (11/64)	14	28	48	100	188	275
32,34: 32-Intro & Origin Brain Storm. 34-Joker-c/sty	11	22	33	80	145	210
33,35,36,40,41: 40-3rd S.A. Penguin app. 41-Intro & origin The Key	11	22	33	76	136	195
37-39: 37,38-JSA x-over. 37-1st S.A. app. Mr. Terrific; Batman cameo. 38-"Crisis on Earth-A". 39-Giant G-16; r/B&B #28,30 & JLA #5	13	26	39	93	172	250
42-45: 42-Metamorpho app. 43-Intro. Royal Flush Gang	9	18	27	63	107	150
46-JSA x-over; 1st S.A. app. Sandman; 3rd S.A. app. of G.A. Spectre (8/66)	13	26	39	90	165	240
47-JSA x-over; 4th S.A. app of G.A. Spectre.	10	20	30	68	119	170
48-Giant G-29; r/JLA #2,3 & B&B #29	9	18	27	65	113	160
49-54,57,59,60	8	16	24	52	86	120
55-Intro. Earth 2 Robin (1st G.A. Robin in S.A.)	9	18	27	65	113	160
56-JLA vs. JSA (1st G.A. Wonder Woman in S.A.)	9	18	27	60	100	140
58-Giant G-41; r/JLA #6,8,1	9	18	27	60	100	140
61-63,66,68-72: 69-Wonder Woman quits. 71-Manhunter leaves. 72-Last 12¢ issue	6	12	18	39	62	85
64,65-JSA story. 64-(8/68)-Origin/1st app. S.A. Red Tornado	6	12	18	43	69	85
67-Giant G-53; r/JLA #4,14,31	8	16	24	52	86	120
73-1st S.A. app. of G.A. Superman	7	14	21	45	73	100
74-Black Canary joins; Larry Lance dies; 1st meeting of G.A. & S.A. Superman; Neal Adams-c	7	14	21	47	76	105
75-2nd app. Green Arrow in new costume (see Brave & the Bold #85)	6	12	18	43	69	95
76-Giant G-65	6	12	18	43	69	95
77-80: 78-Re-intro Vigilante (1st S.A. app?)	4	8	12	26	41	55
81-84,86-90: 82-1st S.A. app. of G.A. Batman (cameo). 83-Apparent death of The Spectre. 90-Last 15¢ issue	4	8	12	24	37	50
85,93-(Giant G-77,G-89; 68 pgs.)	5	10	15	32	51	70
91,92: 91-1st meeting of the G.A. & S.A. Robin; begin 25¢, 52 pgs. issues, ends #99. 92-S.A. Robin tries on costume that is similar to that of G.A. Robin in All Star Comics #58	4	8	12	28	44	60
94-Reprints 1st Sandman story (Adv. #40) & origin/1st app. Starman (Adventure #61); Deadman x-over; N. Adams-a (4 pgs.)	9	18	27	60	100	140
95,96: 95-Origin Dr. Fate & Dr. Midnight -r/ More Fun #67, All-American #25). 96-Origin Hourman (Adv. #48); Wildcat-r	5	10	15	30	48	65
97-99: 97-Origin JLA retold; Sargon, Starman-r. 98-G.A. Sargon, Starman-r. 99-G.A. Sandman, Atom-r; last 52 pg. issue	4	8	12	26	41	55
100-(8/72)-1st meeting of G.A. & S.A. W. Woman	5	10	15	30	48	65
101,102: JSA x-overs. 102-Red Tornado dies	4	8	12	24	37	50
103-106,109: 103-Rutland Vermont Halloween x-over; Phantom Stranger joins. 105-Elongated Man joins. 106-New Red Tornado joins. 109-Hawkman resigns	3	6	9	17	25	32
107,108-JSA x-over; 1st revival app. of G.A. Uncle Sam, Black Condor, The Ray, Dollman, Phantom Lady & The Human Bomb	3	6	9	19	29	38
110,112-116: All 100 pgs. 112-Amazo app; Crimson Avenger, Vigilante-r; origin Starman-r/ Adv. #81. 115-Martian Manhunter app.	5	10	15	30	48	65
111-JLA vs. Injustice Gang; intro. Libra (re-appears in 2008's Final Crisis); Shining Knight, Green Arrow-r	5	10	15	32	51	70
117-122,125-134: 117-Hawkman rejoins. 120,121-Adam Strange app. 125,126-Two-Face-app. 128-Wonder Woman rejoins. 129-Destruction of Red Tornado	3	6	9	14	20	26
123-(10/75),124: JLA/JSA x-over. DC editor Julie Schwartz & JLA writers Cary Bates & Elliot S! Maggin appear in story as themselves. 1st named app. Earth-Prime (3rd app. after Flash; 1st Series #179 & 228)	3	6	9	16	23	30
135-136: 135-137-G.A. Bulletman, Bulletgirl, Spy Smasher, Mr. Scarlet, Pinky & Ibis x-over, 1st appearances since G.A.	3	6	9	16	23	30
137-Superman battles G.A. Capt. Marvel	3	6	9	18	27	35
138-Adam Strange app. w/c by Neal Adams; 1st app. Green Lantern of the 73rd Century	3	6	9	16	22	28
139-157: 139-157-(52 pgs.): 139-Adam Strange app. 144-Origin retold; origin J'onn J'onzz. 145-Red Tornado resurrected. 147,148-Legion of Super-Heroes x-over	2	4	6	9	13	16
158-160-(44 pgs.)	2	4	6	8	10	12
158,160-162,169,171,172,173,176-179,181-(Whitman variants; low print run, none show issue # on cover)	2	4	6	9	13	16
161-165,169-182: 161-Zatanna joins & new costume. 171,172-JSA x-over. 171-Mr. Terrific murdered. 178-Cover similar to #1; J'onn J'onzz app. 179-Firestorm joins. 181-Green Arrow leaves JLA	1	2	3	4	5	7
166-168- "Identity Crisis (2004)" precursor; JSA app. vs. Secret Society of Super-Villains	2	4	6	13	18	22
166-168-Whitman variants (no issue # on covers)	4	8	12	22	34	45
183-185-JSA/New Gods/Darkseid/Mr. Miracle x-over	1	3	4	6	8	10
186-194,198,199: 192,193-Real origin Red Tornado. 193-1st app. All-Star Squadron as free 16 pg. insert						6.00
195-197-JSA app. vs. Secret Society of Super-Villains	1	2	3	5	6	8
200 ($1.50, Anniversary issue, 76 pgs.)-JLA origin retold; Green Arrow rejoins; Bolland, Aparo, Giordano, Gil Kane, Infantino, Kubert-a; Perez-c/a	1	2	3	5	6	8
201-206,209-243,246-259: 203-Intro/origin new Royal Flush Gang. 219,220-True origin Black Canary. 228-Re-intro Martian Manhunter. 228-230-War of the Worlds storyline; JLA Satellite destroyed by Martians. 233-Story cont'd from Annual #2. 243-Aquaman leaves. 250-Batman rejoins. 253-Origin Despero. 258-Death of Vibe. 258-261-Legends x-over						5.00
207,208-JSA, JLA, & All-Star Squadron team-up	1	2	3	4	5	7
244,245-Crisis x-over						6.00
260-Death of Steel	1	2	3	4	5	7
261-Last issue	1	3	4	6	8	10
Annual 1-3 ('83-'85), 2-Intro new J.L.A. (Aquaman, Martian Manhunter, Steel, Gypsy, Vixen, Vibe, Elongated Man & Zatanna). 3-Crisis x-over						4.00
... Hereby Elects (2006, $14.99, TPB) reprints issues where new members joined; JLofA #4,75,105,106,146,161,173&174; roster of various incarnations; Ordway-c						15.00

NOTE: ***Neal Adams** c-63, 66, 67, 70, 74, 79, 81, 82, 86-89, 91, 92, 94, 96-98, 138, 139. **M. Anderson** c-1-4, 6, 7, 10, 12-14. **Aparo** a-200. **Austin** a-200i. **Baily** a-96r. **Bolland** a-200. **Buckler** c-158, 163, 164. **Burnley** r-94, 98, 99. **Greene** a-46-61i, 64-73i, 110i(r). **Grell** c-117, 122. **Kaluta** c-154p. **Gil Kane** a-200. **Krigstein** a-96(r/Sensation #84). **Kubert** a-200; c-72, 73. **Nino** a-228i, 230i. **Orlando** c-151i. **Perez** a-184-186p, 192-197p, 200p; c-184p, 186, 192-195, 196p, 197p, 199, 200, 201p, 202, 203-205p, 207-209, 212-215, 217, 219, 220. **Reinman** r-97. **Roussos** a-62i. **Sekowsky** a-37, 38, 44-63p, 110-112p(r); c-46-48p, 51p. **Sekowsky/Anderson** c-5, 8, 9, 11, 15. **B. Smith** c-185i. **Starlin** c-178-180, 183, 185p. **Staton** a-244p; c-157p, 244p. **Toth** r-110. **Tuska** a-153, 228p, 241-243p. JSA x-overs-21, 22, 29, 30, 37, 38, 46, 47, 55, 56, 64, 65, 73, 74, 82, 83, 91, 92, 100, 101, 102, 107, 108, 110, 113, 115, 123, 124, 135-137, 147, 148, 159, 160, 171, 172, 183-185, 195-197, 207-209, 219, 220, 231, 232, 244.*

JUSTICE LEAGUE OF AMERICA

DC Comics: No. 0, Sept, 2006 - Present ($2.99/$3.99)

	NM- 9.2
0-Meltzer-s; history of the JLA; art by various incl. Lee, Giordano, Benes; Turner-c	5.00
0-Variant-c by Campbell	12.00
1-($3.99) Two interlocking covers by Benes; Benes-a	5.00
1-Variant-c by Turner	8.00
1-RRP Edition; sideways composite of both Benes covers	80.00
1-Second printing; Benes cover image between black bars	4.00
2-5-($2.99) Turner-c	3.00
2-5: Variant-c: 2-Jimenez. 3-Sprouse. 4-JG Jones. 5-Art Adams	5.00
6,7-($3.50) 6-JLA vs. Amazo; covers by Turner and Hughes. 7-Roster picked, new HQs; two Benes covers and Turner cover.	3.50
8-11,13-24,26-38-($2.99) 8-11-JLA/JSA team-up; covers by Turner & Jimenez. 10-Wally West returns. 13-Two covers. 13-15-Injustice Gang. 16-Tangent Flash. 20-Queen Bee app. 21-Libra app.; leads into Final Crisis #1. 35,36-Royal Flush Gang app. 38-Bagley-a begins	3.00
12-($3.50) Two Ross covers; origin retold with Wight-a; Benes-a	3.50
25-($3.99) McDuffie-s/art by various; Benes-c	4.00
39-41-($3.99) 39,40-Blackest Night. 41-New team; 2 covers	4.00
... 80 Page Giant (11/09, $5.99) Anacleto-c; short stories by various; Ra's al Ghul app.	6.00
Justice League Wedding Special 1 (11/07, $3.99) McKone-a; Injustice League forms	4.00
...: The Injustice Gang HC (2008, $19.99, dustjacket) r/#13-16; Wedding Special	20.00
...: The Lightning Saga HC (2008, $24.99, dustjacket) r/#0,8-12 & Justice Society of America #5,6; intro. by Patton Oswalt	25.00
...: The Lightning Saga SC (2008, $17.99) r/#0,8-12 & J.S.A. #5,6; intro. by Oswalt	18.00
...: Sanctuary SC (2009, $14.99) r/#17-21	15.00
...: Second Coming HC (2009, $19.99, dustjacket) r/#22-26	20.00

Justice League Unlimited #21 © DC

Justice Society of America (2007 series) #13 © DC

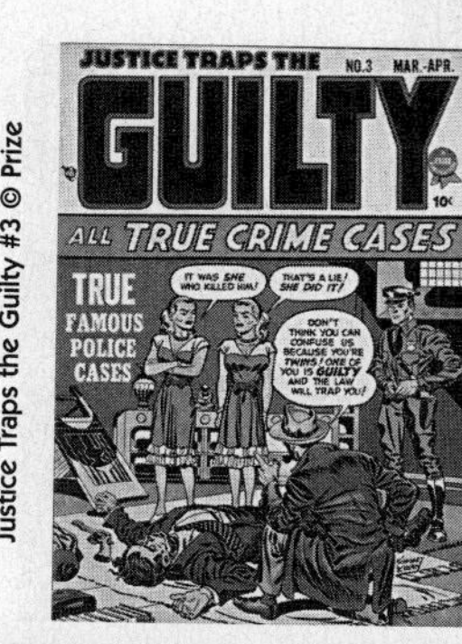

Justice Traps the Guilty #3 © Prize

GD 2.0 | VG 4.0 | FN 6.0 | VF 8.0 | VF/NM 9.0 | NM- 9.2

GD 2.0 | VG 4.0 | FN 6.0 | VF 8.0 | VF/NM 9.0 | NM- 9.2

...: The Tornado's Path HC (2007, $24.99, dustjacket) r/#1-7; variant cover gallery; Lindelof intro.; commentary by Meltzer & Benes 25.00
...: The Tornado's Path SC (2008, $17.99) r/#1-7; variant cover gallery; Lindelof intro.; commentary by Meltzer & Benes 25.00
...: When Worlds Collide HC (2009, $24.99, dustjacket) r/#27,28,30-34 25.00

JUSTICE LEAGUE OF AMERICA : ANOTHER NAIL (Elseworlds) (Also see JLA: The Nail)
DC Comics: 2004 - No. 3, 2004 ($5.95, prestige format)

1-3-Sequel to JLA: The Nail; Alan Davis-s/a(p) 6.00
TPB (2004, $12.95) r/series 13.00

JUSTICE LEAGUE OF AMERICA SUPER SPECTACULAR
DC Comics: 1999 ($5.95, mimics format of DC 100 Page Super Spectaculars)

1-Reprints Silver Age JLA and Golden Age JSA 6.00

JUSTICE LEAGUE QUARTERLY (...International Quarterly #6 on)
DC Comics: Winter, 1990-91 - No. 17, Winter, 1994 ($2.95/$3.50, 84 pgs.)

1-12,14-17: 1-Intro The Conglomerate (Booster Gold, Praxis, Gypsy, Vapor, Echo, Maxi-Man, & Reverb); Justice League #1-c/swipe. 1,2-Keith Giffen plots/breakdowns. 3-Giffen plot; 72 pg. story. 4-Rogers/Russell-a in back-up. 5,6-Mark Waid scripts. 8,17-Global Guardians app. 3.50
13-Linsner-c 6.00
NOTE: ***Phil Jimenez** a-17p. **Sprouse** a-1p.*

JUSTICE LEAGUES...
DC Comics: Mar, 2001 ($2.50, limited series)

JL?, Justice League of Amazons, Justice League of Atlantis, Justice League of Arkham, Justice League of Aliens, JLA: JLA split by the Advance Man; Perez-c in all; s&a by various 2.50

JUSTICE LEAGUE TASK FORCE
DC Comics: June, 1993 - No. 37, Aug, 1996 ($1.25/$1.50/$1.75)

1-16,0,17-37: Aquaman, Nightwing, Flash, J'onn J'onzz, & Gypsy form team. 5,6-Knight-quest tie-ins (new Batman cameo #5, 1 pg.). 15-Triumph cameo. 16-(9/94)-Zero Hour x-over; Triumph app. 0-(10/94). 17-(11/94)-Triumph becomes part of Justice League Task Force (See JLE #68). 26-Impulse app. 35-Warlord app. 37-Triumph quits team 2.50

JUSTICE LEAGUE: THE NEW FRONTIER SPECIAL (Also see DC: The New Frontier)
DC Comics: May, 2008 ($4.99, one-shot)

1-Short stories by Darwyn Cooke, J.Bone and Dave Bullock; bonus storyboards from the movie 5.00

JUSTICE LEAGUE UNLIMITED (Based on Cartoon Network animated series) (Also see Free Comic Book Day Edition in the Promotional Comics section)
DC Comics: Nov, 2004 - No. 46, Aug, 2008 ($2.25)

1-46: 1-Zatanna app. 2,23,42-Royal Flush Gang app. 4-Adam Strange app. 10-Creeper app. 17-Freedom Fighters app. 18-Space Cabby app. 27-Black Lightning app. 34-Zod app. 2.50
Jam Packed Action (2005, $7.99, digest) adaptations of two TV episodes 8.00
... Vol. 1: United They Stand (2005, $6.99, digest) r/#1-5 7.00
... Vol. 2: World's Greatest Heroes (2006, $6.99, digest) r/#6-10 7.00
... Vol. 3: Champions of Justice (2006, $6.99, digest) r/#11-15 7.00
...: Heroes (2009, $12.99, full-size) r/#23-29 13.00
...: The Ties That Bind (2008, $12.99, full-size) r/#16-22 13.00

JUSTICE MACHINE, THE
Noble Comics: June, 1981 - No. 5, Nov, 1983 ($2.00, nos. 1-3 are mag. size)

	GD	VG	FN	VF	VF/NM	NM-
1-Byrne-c(p)	3	6	9	15	21	26
2-Austin-c(i)	2	4	6	9	12	15
3	1	3	4	6	8	10

4,5, Annual 1: Ann. 1-(1/84, 68 pgs.)(published by Texas Comics); 1st app. The Elementals; Golden-c(p); new Thunder Agents story (43 pgs.) 6.00

JUSTICE MACHINE (Also see The New Justice Machine)
Comico/Innovation Publishing: Jan, 1987 - No. 29, May 1989 ($1.50/$1.75)

1-29 2.50
Annual 1(6/89, $2.50, 36 pgs.)-Last Comico ish. 3.00
Summer Spectacular 1 ('89, $2.75)-Innovation Publ.; Byrne/Gustovich-c 3.00

JUSTICE MACHINE, THE
Innovation Publishing: 1990 - No. 4, 1990 ($1.95/$2.25, deluxe format, mature)

1-4: Gustovich-c/a in all 2.50

JUSTICE MACHINE FEATURING THE ELEMENTALS
Comico: May, 1986 - No. 4, Aug, 1986 ($1.50, limited series)

1-4 2.50

JUSTICE RIDERS
DC Comics: 1997 ($5.95, one-shot, prestige format)

1-Elseworlds; Dixon-s/Williams & Gray-a 6.00

JUSTICE SOCIETY
DC Comics: 2006; 2007 ($14.99, TPB)

Vol. 1 - Rep. from 1976 revival in All Star Comics #58-67 & DC Special #29; Bolland-c 15.00
Vol. 2 - R/All Star Comics #68-74 & Adventure Comics #461-466; new Bolland-c 15.00

JUSTICE SOCIETY OF AMERICA (See Adventure #461 & All-Star #3)
DC Comics: April, 1991 - No. 8, Nov, 1991 ($1.00, limited series)

1-8: 1-Flash. 2-Black Canary. 3-Green Lantern. 4-Hawkman. 5-Flash/Hawkman. 6-Green Lantern/Black Canary. 7-JSA 2.50

JUSTICE SOCIETY OF AMERICA (Also see Last Days of the... Special)
DC Comics: Aug, 1992 - No. 10, May, 1993 ($1.25)

1-10 2.50

JUSTICE SOCIETY OF AMERICA (Follows JSA series)
DC Comics: Feb, 2007 - Present ($3.99/$2.99)

1-($3.99) New team selected; intro. Maxine Hunkle; Alex Ross-c 4.00
1-Variant-c by Eaglesham 6.00
2-35: 1-Covers by Ross and Eaglesham. 3,4-Vandal Savage app. 5,6-JLA/JSA team-up. 9-22-Kingdom Come Superman app.18-Magog app. 22-Superman returns to Kingdom Come Earth; Ross partial art. 23-25-Ordway-a. 26-Triptych cover by Ross. 33-Team splits. 34,35-Mordru app. 3.00
JSA Annual 1 (9/08, $3.99) Power Girl on Earth-2; Ross-c/Ordway-a 4.00
JSA Annual 2 (4/10, $4.99) All Star team app.; Magog quits; Williams-a 5.00
... 80 Page Giant (1/10, $5.99) short stories by various incl. Ordway, S. Hampton 6.00
...: Black Adam and Isis HC (2009, $19.99, d.j.) r/#23-28 20.00
... Kingdom Come Special: Magog (1/09, $3.99) Pasarin-a; origin re-told; 2 covers 4.00
... Kingdom Come Special: Superman (1/09, $3.99) Lois' death re-told; Alex Ross-s/a/c; thumbnails, photo references, sketch art 4.00
... Kingdom Come Special: Superman (1/09, $3.99) Eaglesham variant cover 8.00
... Kingdom Come Special: The Kingdom (1/09, $3.99) Pasarin-a; 2 covers 4.00
...: The Next Age SC (2008, $14.99) r/#1-4; Ross and Eaglesham sketch pages 15.00
...: Thy Kingdom Come Part One HC (2008, $19.99, d.j.) r/#7-12; Ross sketch pages 20.00
...: Thy Kingdom Come Part One SC (2009, $14.99) r/#7-12; Ross sketch pages 15.00
...: Thy Kingdom Come Part Two HC (2008, $24.99, d.j.) r/#13-18 & Annual #1; Ross sketch pages 25.00
...: Thy Kingdom Come Part Two SC (2009, $19.99) r/#13-18 & Ann. #1; Ross sketch-a 20.00
...: Thy Kingdom Come Part Three HC (2009, $24.99, d.j.) r/#19-22 & K.C. Specials - Superman, Magog and The Kingdom; Ross sketch pages 25.00

JUSTICE SOCIETY OF AMERICA 100-PAGE SUPER SPECTACULAR
DC Comics: 2000 ($6.95, mimics format of DC 100 Page Super Spectaculars)

1-"1975 Issue" reprints Flash team-up and Golden Age JSA 7.00

JUSTICE SOCIETY RETURNS, THE (See All Star Comics (1999) for related titles)
DC Comics: 2003 ($19.95, TPB)

TPB-Reprints 1999 JSA x-over from All-Star Comics #1,2 and related one-shots 20.00

JUSTICE TRAPS THE GUILTY (Fargo Kid V11#3 on)
Prize/Headline Publications: Oct-Nov, 1947 - V11#2(#92), Apr-May, 1958 (True FBI Cases)

	GD	VG	FN	VF	VF/NM	NM-
V2#1-S&K-c/a; electrocution-c	58	116	174	371	636	900
2-S&K-c/a	35	70	105	208	339	470
3-5-S&K-c/a	32	64	96	192	314	435
6-S&K-c/a; Feldstein-a	34	68	102	204	332	460
7,9-S&K-c/a. 7-9-V2#1-3 in indicia; #7-9 on-c	28	56	84	168	274	380
8-Krigstein-a; S&K-c	27	54	81	158	259	360
10-Krigstein-a; S&K-c/a	28	56	84	168	274	380
11,18,19-S&K-c	16	32	48	94	147	200
12,14-17,20-No S&K. 14-Severin/Elder-a (8pg.)	11	22	33	60	83	105
13-Used in **SOTI**, pg. 110-111	13	26	39	72	101	130
21,30-S&K-c/a	17	34	51	98	154	210
22,23-S&K-c	14	28	42	76	108	140
24-26,27,29,31-50: 32-Meskin story	10	20	30	58	79	100
28-Kirby-c	13	26	39	72	101	130
51-55,57,59-70	9	18	27	52	69	85
56-Ben Oda, Joe Simon, Joe Genola, Mort Meskin & Jack Kirby app. in police line-up on classic-c	14	28	42	80	115	150
58-Illo. in **SOTI**, "Treating police contemptuously" (top left); text on heroin	25	50	75	150	245	340
71-92: 76-Orlando-a	8	16	24	44	57	70

NOTE: ***Bailey** a-12, 13. **Elder** a-8. **Kirby** a-19p. **Meskin** a-22, 27, 63, 64; c-45, 46. **Robinson/Meskin** a-5, 19. **Severin** a-8, 11p. Photo c-12, 15-17.*

JUST IMAGINE STAN LEE WITH... (Stan Lee re-invents DC icons)
DC Comics: 2001 - 2002 ($5.95, prestige format, one-shots)
(Adam Hughes back-c on all)(Michael Uslan back-up stories in all, diff. artists)

Ka'a'nga Comics #4 © FH

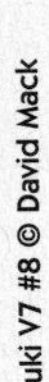
Kabuki V7 #8 © David Mack

Kamandi, The Last Boy on Earth #3 © DC

GD 2.0 | VG 4.0 | FN 6.0 | VF 8.0 | VF/NM 9.0 | NM- 9.2

Scott McDaniel Creating **Aquaman**- Back-up w/Fradon-a 6.00
Joe Kubert Creating **Batman**- Back-up w/Kaluta-a 6.00
Chris Bachalo Creating **Catwoman**- Back-up w/Cooke & Allred-a 6.00
John Cassaday Creating **Crisis**- no back-up story 6.00
Kevin Maguire Creating **The Flash**- Back-up w/Aragonés-a 6.00
Dave Gibbons Creating **Green Lantern**- Back-up w/Giordano-a 6.00
Jerry Ordway Creating **JLA** 6.00
John Byrne Creating **Robin**- Back-up w/John Severin-a 6.00
Walter Simonson Creating **Sandman**- Back-up w/Corben-a 6.00
Gary Frank Creating **Shazam!**- Back-up w/Kano-a 6.00
John Buscema Creating **Superman**- Back-up w/Kyle Baker-a 6.00
Jim Lee Creating **Wonder Woman**- Back-up w/Gene Colan-a 6.00
Secret Files and Origins #1 (3/02, $4.95) Crisis prologue; Jurgens-a 5.00
TPB -Just Imagine Stan Lee Creating the DC Universe: Book One (2002, $19.95) r/Batman, Wonder Woman, Superman, Green Lantern 20.00
TPB -Just Imagine Stan Lee Creating the DC Universe: Book Two (2003, $19.95) r/Flash, JLA, Secret Files and Origins, Robin, Shazam; sketch pages 20.00
TPB -Just Imagine Stan Lee Creating the DC Universe: Book Three (2004, $19.95) r/Aquaman, Catwoman, Sandman, Crisis; profile pages 20.00

JUST MARRIED
Charlton Comics: January, 1958 - No. 114, Dec, 1976

	GD	VG	FN	VF	VF/NM	NM-
1	6	12	18	39	62	85
2	3	6	9	21	32	42
3-10	3	6	9	17	25	32
11-30	3	6	9	14	19	24
31-50	2	4	6	10	14	18
51-70	2	4	6	9	12	15
71-78,80-89	2	4	6	8	10	12
79-Ditko-a (7 pages)	2	4	6	9	13	16
90-Susan Dey and David Cassidy full page poster	2	4	6	10	14	18
91-114	1	3	4	6	8	10

KA'A'NGA COMICS (...Jungle King)(See Jungle Comics)
Fiction House Magazines (Glen-Kel Publ. Co.): Spring, 1949 - No. 20, Summer, 1954

	GD	VG	FN	VF	VF/NM	NM-
1-Ka'a'nga, Lord of the Jungle begins	52	104	156	323	549	775
2 (Winter, '49-'50)	30	60	90	177	289	400
3,4	22	44	66	132	216	300
5-Camilla app.	21	42	63	122	199	275
6-10: 7-Tuska-a. 9-Tabu, Wizard of the Jungle app. 10-Used in **POP**, pg. 99	15	30	45	88	137	185
11-15: 15-Camilla-r by Baker/Jungle #106	14	28	42	78	112	145
16-Sheena app.	14	28	42	81	118	155
17-20	13	26	39	72	101	130
I.W. Reprint #1,8: 1-r/#18; Kinstler-c. 8-r/#10	3	6	9	14	20	25

NOTE: *Celardo c-1.* ***Whitman*** *c-8-20(most).*

KABOOM
Awesome Entertainment: Sept, 1997 - No. 3, Nov, 1997 ($2.50)
1-3: 1-Matsuda-a/Loeb-s; 4 covers exist (Matsuda, Sale, Pollina and McGuinness), 1-Dynamic Forces Edition, 2-Regular, 2-Alicia Watcher variant-c, 2-Gold logo variant-c, 3-Two covers by Liefeld & Matsuda, 3-Dynamic Forces Ed., Prelude Ed. 2.50
Prelude Gold Edition 4.00

KABOOM (2nd series)
Awesome Entertainment: July, 1999 - No. 3, Dec, 1999 ($2.50)
1-3: 1-Grant-a(p); at least 4 variant covers 2.50

KABUKI
Caliber: Nov, 1994 ($3.50, B&W, one-shot)
nn-(Fear The Reaper) 1st app.; David Mack-c/a/s 1 2 3 5 6 8
Color Special (1/96, $2.95)-Mack-c/a/scripts; pin-ups by Tucci, Harris & Quesada 4.00
Gallery (8/95, $2.95)- pinups from Mack, Bradstreet, Paul Pope & others 3.00

KABUKI
Image Comics: Oct, 1997 - No. 9, Mar, 2000 ($2.95, color)
1-David Mack-c/s/a 5.00
1-($10.00)-Dynamic Forces Edition 1 3 4 6 8 10
2-5 4.00
6-9 3.00
#1/2 (9/01, $2.95) r/Wizard 1/2; Eklipse Mag. article; bio 3.00
...Classics (2/99, $3.95) Reprints Fear the Reaper 4.00
...Classics 2 (3/99, $3.95) Reprints Dance of Dance 4.00
...Classics 3-5 (3-6/99, $4.95) Reprints Circle of Blood-Acts 1-3 5.00
...Classics 6-12 (7/99-3/00, $3.25) Various reprints 3.25
...Images (6/98, $4.95) r/#1 with new pin-ups 5.00
...Images 2 (1/99, $4.95) r/#1 with new pin-ups 5.00
...Metamorphosis TPB (10/00, $24.95) r/#1-9; Sienkiewicz intro.; 2nd printing exists 25.00
...Reflections 1-4 (7/98-5/02; $4.95) new story plus art techniques 5.00
... The Ghost Play (11/02, $2.95) new story plus interview 3.00

KABUKI
Marvel Comics (Icon): July, 2004 - Present ($2.99, color)
1-9: 1-David Mack-c/s/a in all; variant-c by Alex Maleev. 4-Variant-c by Adam Hughes. 6-Variant-c by Mignola. 8-Variant-c by Kent Williams. 9-Allred var-c 3.00
...: The Alchemy HC (2008, $29.99, dust jacket) oversized r/#1-9; bonus art & content 30.00
... Reflections 5-15 (7/05-10/09, $5.99) paintings & sketches of recent work; photos 6.00

KABUKI AGENTS (SCARAB)
Image Comics: Aug, 1999 - No. 8, Aug, 2001 ($2.95, B&W)
1-8-David Mack-s/Rick Mays-a 3.00
Lost in Translation HC (3/02, $29.95) r/#1-8; intro. by Paul Pope 30.00
Lost in Translation SC (3/02, $19.95) r/#1-8; intro. by Paul Pope 20.00

KABUKI: CIRCLE OF BLOOD
Caliber Press: Jan, 1995 - No. 6, Nov, 1995 ($2.95, B&W)
1-David Mack story/a in all 5.00
2-6: 3-#1 on inside indicia. 3.00
6-Variant-c 3.00
TPB ($16.95) r/#1-6, intro. by Steranko 17.00
TPB (1997, $17.95) Image Edition-r/#1-6, intro. by Steranko 18.00
TPB ($24.95) Deluxe Edition 25.00

KABUKI: DANCE OF DEATH
London Night Studios: Jan, 1995 ($3.00, B&W, one-shot)
1-David Mack-c/a/scripts 1 2 3 5 6 8

KABUKI: DREAMS
Image Comics: Jan, 1998 ($4.95, TPB)
nn-Reprints Color Special & Dreams of the Dead 5.00

KABUKI: DREAMS OF THE DEAD
Caliber: July, 1996 ($2.95, one-shot)
nn-David Mack-c/a/scripts 3.00

KABUKI FAN EDITION
Gemstone Publ./Caliber: Feb, 1997 (mail-in offer, one-shot)
nn-David Mack-c/a/scripts 4.00

KABUKI: MASKS OF THE NOH
Caliber: May, 1996 - No. 4, Feb, 1997 ($2.95, limited series)
1-4: 1-Three-c (1A-Quesada, 1B-Buzz, &1C-Mack). 3-Terry Moore pin-up 3.00
TPB-(4/98, $10.95) r/#1-4; intro by Terry Moore 11.00

KABUKI: SKIN DEEP
Caliber Comics: Oct, 1996 - No. 3, May, 1997 ($2.95)
1-3:David Mack-c/a/scripts. 2-Two-c (1-Mack, 1-Ross) 3.00
TPB-(5/98, $9.95) r/#1-3; intro by Alex Ross 10.00

KAMANDI: AT EARTH'S END
DC Comics: June, 1993 - No. 6, Nov, 1993 ($1.75, limited series)
1-6: Elseworlds storyline 2.50

KAMANDI, THE LAST BOY ON EARTH (Also see Alarming Tales #1, Brave and the Bold #120 & 157 & Cancelled Comic Cavalcade)
National Periodical Publ./DC Comics: Oct-Nov, 1972 - No. 59, Sept-Oct, 1978

	GD	VG	FN	VF	VF/NM	NM-
1-Origin & 1st app. Kamandi	7	14	21	49	80	110
2,3	4	8	12	28	44	60
4,5: 4-Intro. Prince Tuftan of the Tigers	4	8	12	24	37	50
6-10	3	6	9	18	27	35
11-20	3	6	9	14	20	25
21-28,30,31,33-40: 24-Last 20¢ issue. 31-Intro Pyra.	2	4	6	11	16	20
29,32: 29-Superman x-over. 32-(68 pgs.)-r/origin from #1 plus one new story; 4 pg. biog. of Jack Kirby with B&W photos	3	6	9	14	19	24
41-57	2	4	6	9	13	16
58-(44 pgs.)-Karate Kid x-over from LSH	2	4	6	13	18	22
59-(44 pgs.)-Cont'd in B&B #157; The Return of Omac back-up by Starlin-c/a(p)	2	4	6	13	18	22

NOTE: ***Ayers*** *a(p)-48-59 (most).* ***Giffen*** *a-44p, 45p.* ***Kirby*** *a-1-40p; c-1-33.* ***Kubert*** *c-34-41.* ***Nasser*** *a-45p, 46p.* ***Starlin*** *a-59p; c-57, 59p.*

KAMUI (Legend Of...#2 on)
Eclipse Comics/Viz Comics: May 12, 1987 - No. 37, Nov. 15, 1988 ($1.50, B&W, bi-weekly)
1-37: 1-3 have 2nd printings 2.50

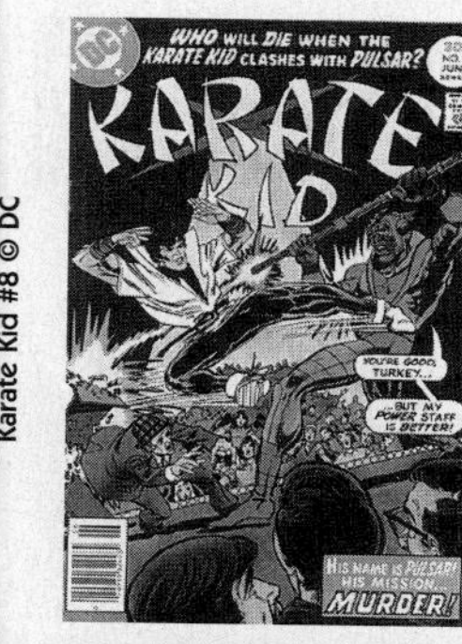

Karate Kid #8 © DC

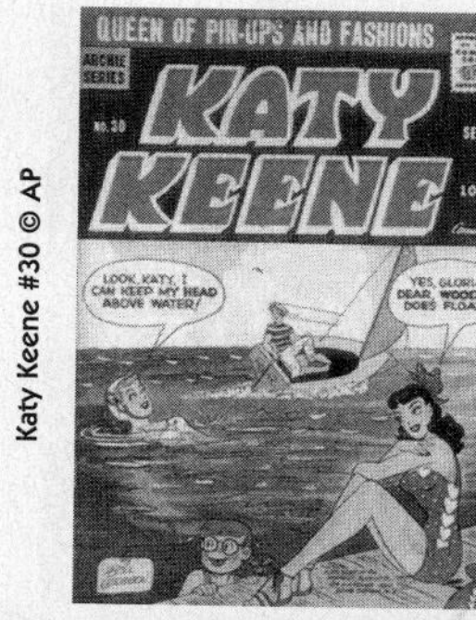

Katy Keene #30 © AP

Ka-Zar (2nd series) #5 © MAR

KAOS MOON (Also see Negative Burn #34)
Caliber Comics: 1996 - No. 4, 1997 ($2.95, B&W)

	GD 2.0	VG 4.0	FN 6.0	VF 8.0	VF/NM 9.0	NM- 9.2
1-4-David Boller-s/a						3.00
3,4-Limited Alternate-c						4.00
3,4-Gold Alternate-c, Full Circle TPB ($5.95) r/#1,2						6.00

KARATE KID (See Action, Adventure, Legion of Super-Heroes, & Superboy)
National Periodical Publications/DC Comics: Mar-Apr, 1976 - No. 15, July-Aug, 1978 (Legion of Super-Heroes spin-off)

	GD 2.0	VG 4.0	FN 6.0	VF 8.0	VF/NM 9.0	NM- 9.2
1,15: 1-Meets Iris Jacobs; Estrada/Staton-a. 15-Continued into Kamandi #58	2	4	6	10	14	18
2-14: 2-Major Disaster app. 14-Robin x-over	2	3	4	6	8	10

NOTE: *Grell c-1-4, 5p, 6p, 7, 8. Staton a-1-9i. Legion x-over-No. 1, 2, 4, 6, 10, 12, 13. Princess Projectra x-over-#8, 9.*

KATHY
Standard Comics: Sept, 1949 - No. 17, Sept, 1955

	GD 2.0	VG 4.0	FN 6.0	VF 8.0	VF/NM 9.0	NM- 9.2
1-Teen-age	14	28	42	82	121	160
2-Schomburg-c	11	22	33	60	83	105
3-5	8	16	24	44	57	70
6-17: 17-Code approved	8	16	24	40	50	60

KATHY (The Teenage Tornado)
Atlas Comics/Marvel (ZPC): Oct, 1959 - No. 27, Feb, 1964 (most issues contain paper dolls and pin-up pages)

	GD 2.0	VG 4.0	FN 6.0	VF 8.0	VF/NM 9.0	NM- 9.2
1-The Teen-age Tornado; Goldberg-c/a in all	8	16	24	56	93	130
2	5	10	15	32	51	70
3-15	4	8	12	26	41	55
16-23,25,27	3	6	9	19	29	38
24-(8/63) Frank Sinatra, Cary Grant, Ed Sullivan & Liz Taylor-c	4	8	12	24	37	50
26-(12/63) Kathy becomes a model; Millie app.	3	6	9	21	32	42

KAT KARSON
I. W. Enterprises: No date (Reprint)

	GD 2.0	VG 4.0	FN 6.0	VF 8.0	VF/NM 9.0	NM- 9.2
1-Funny animals	2	4	6	10	12	15

KATO OF THE GREEN HORNET (Also see The Green Hornet)
Now Comics: Nov, 1991 - No. 4, Feb, 1992 ($2.50, mini-series)

	GD 2.0	VG 4.0	FN 6.0	VF 8.0	VF/NM 9.0	NM- 9.2
1-4: Brent Anderson-c/a						2.50

KATO OF THE GREEN HORNET II (Also see The Green Hornet)
Now Comics: Nov, 1992 - No. 2, Dec, 1993 ($2.50, mini-series)

	GD 2.0	VG 4.0	FN 6.0	VF 8.0	VF/NM 9.0	NM- 9.2
1,2-Baron-s/Mayerik & Sherman-a						2.50

KATY KEENE (Also see Kasco Komics, Laugh, Pep, Suzie, & Wilbur)
Archie Publ./Close-Up/Radio Comics: 1949 - No. 4, 1951; No. 5, 3/52 - No. 62, Oct, 1961 (50-53-Adventures of...on-c) (Cut and missing pages are common)

	GD 2.0	VG 4.0	FN 6.0	VF 8.0	VF/NM 9.0	NM- 9.2
1-Bill Woggon-c/a begins; swipes-c to Mopsy #1	161	322	483	1030	1765	2500
2-(1950)	60	120	180	381	653	925
3-5: 3-(1951). 4-(1951)	47	94	141	296	498	700
6-10	37	74	111	218	354	490
11,13-21: 21-Last pre-code issue (3/55)	30	60	90	177	289	400
12-(Scarce)	36	72	108	216	351	485
22-40	21	42	63	124	202	280
41-60: 54-Wedding Album plus wedding pin-up	17	34	51	100	158	215
61,62: 62-Robot-c	19	38	57	111	176	240
Annual 1('54, 25¢)-All new stories; last pre-code	55	110	165	347	586	825
Annual 2-6('55-59, 25¢)-All new stories	31	62	93	182	296	410
3-D 1(1953, 25¢, large size)-Came w/glasses	39	78	117	231	378	525
Charm 1(9/58)-Woggon-c/a; new stories, and cut-outs	29	58	87	170	278	385
Glamour 1(1957)-Puzzles, games, cut-outs	29	58	87	170	278	385
Spectacular 1('56)	30	60	90	177	289	400

NOTE: *Debby's Diary in #45, 47-49, 52, 57.*

KATY KEENE COMICS DIGEST MAGAZINE
Close-Up, Inc. (Archie Ent.): 1987 - No. 10, July, 1990 ($1.25/$1.35/$1.50, digest size)

	GD 2.0	VG 4.0	FN 6.0	VF 8.0	VF/NM 9.0	NM- 9.2
1	2	4	6	10	14	18
2-10	1	3	4	6	8	10

NOTE: *Many used copies are cut-up inside.*

KATY KEENE FASHION BOOK MAGAZINE
Radio Comics/Archie Publications: 1955 - No. 13, Sum, '56 - N. 23, Wint, '58-59 (nn 3-10)

	GD 2.0	VG 4.0	FN 6.0	VF 8.0	VF/NM 9.0	NM- 9.2
1-Bill Woggon-c/a	53	106	159	334	567	800
2	30	60	90	177	289	400
11-18: 18-Photo Bill Woggon	22	44	66	130	213	295
19-23	19	38	57	111	176	240

KATY KEENE HOLIDAY FUN (See Archie Giant Series Magazine No. 7, 12)

KATY KEENE MODEL BEHAVIOR
Archie Comic Publications: 2008 ($10.95, TPB)

	GD 2.0	VG 4.0	FN 6.0	VF 8.0	VF/NM 9.0	NM- 9.2
Vol. 1 - New story and reprinted apps./pin-ups from Archie & Friends #101-112						11.00

KATY KEENE PINUP PARADE
Radio Comics/Archie Publications: 1955 - No. 15, Summer, 1961 (25¢) (Cut-out & missing pages are common)

	GD 2.0	VG 4.0	FN 6.0	VF 8.0	VF/NM 9.0	NM- 9.2
1-Cut-outs in all?; last pre-code issue	53	106	159	334	567	800
2-(1956)	30	60	90	177	289	400
3-5: 3-(1957)	26	52	78	152	249	345
6-10,12-14: 8-Mad parody. 10-Bill Woggon photo	21	42	63	126	206	285
11-Story of how comics get CCA approved, narrated by Katy	26	52	78	154	252	350
15(Rare)-Photo artist & family	40	80	120	246	411	575

KATY KEENE SPECIAL (Katy Keene #7 on; see Laugh Comics Digest)
Archie Ent.: Sept, 1983 - No. 33, 1990 (Later issues published quarterly)

	GD 2.0	VG 4.0	FN 6.0	VF 8.0	VF/NM 9.0	NM- 9.2
1-10: 1-Woggon-r; new Woggon-c. 3-Woggon-r						5.00
11-25: 12-Spider-Man parody						6.00
26-32-(Low print run)	1	2	3	5	7	9
33	2	4	6	8	10	12

KATZENJAMMER KIDS, THE (See Captain & the Kids & Giant Comic Album)
David McKay Publ./Standard No. 12-21(Spring/'50 - 53)/Harvey No. 22, 4/53 on: 1945-1946; Summer, 1947 - No. 27, Feb-Mar, 1954

	GD 2.0	VG 4.0	FN 6.0	VF 8.0	VF/NM 9.0	NM- 9.2
Feature Books 30	20	40	60	114	182	250
Feature Books 32,35('45),41,44('46)	18	36	54	103	162	220
Feature Book 37-Has photos & biography of Harold Knerr	19	38	57	109	172	235
1(1947)-All new stories begin	19	38	57	109	172	235
2	11	22	33	64	90	115
3-11	9	18	27	52	69	85
12-14(Standard)	8	16	24	42	54	65
15-21(Standard)	8	16	24	40	50	60
22-25,27(Harvey): 22-24-Henry app.	7	14	21	35	43	50
26-Half in 3-D	16	32	48	94	147	200

KAYO (Formerly Bullseye & Jest; becomes Carnival Comics)
Harry 'A' Chesler: No. 12, Mar, 1945

	GD 2.0	VG 4.0	FN 6.0	VF 8.0	VF/NM 9.0	NM- 9.2
12-Green Knight, Capt. Glory, Little Nemo (not by McCay)	18	36	54	105	165	225

KA-ZAR (Also see Marvel Comics #1, Savage Tales #6 & X-Men #10)
Marvel Comics Group: Aug, 1970 - No. 3, Mar, 1971 (Giant-Size, 68 pgs.)

	GD 2.0	VG 4.0	FN 6.0	VF 8.0	VF/NM 9.0	NM- 9.2
1-Reprints earlier Ka-Zar stories; Avengers x-over in Hercules; Daredevil, X-Men app.; hidden profanity-c	4	8	12	24	37	50
2,3-Daredevil-r. 2-r/Daredevil #13 w/Kirby layouts; Ka-Zar origin, Angel-r from X-Men by Tuska. 3-Romita & Heck-a (no Kirby)	3	6	9	17	25	32

NOTE: *Buscema r-2. Colan a-1p(r). Kirby c/a-1, 2. #1-Reprints X-Men #10 & Daredevil #24*

KA-ZAR
Marvel Comics Group: Jan, 1974 - No. 20, Feb, 1977 (Regular Size)

	GD 2.0	VG 4.0	FN 6.0	VF 8.0	VF/NM 9.0	NM- 9.2
1	3	6	9	14	19	24
2-10	2	4	6	8	10	12
11-14,16,18-20: 16-Only a 30 ¢ edition exists	1	2	3	5	6	8
15,17-(Regular 25¢ edition)(8/76)	1	2	3	5	6	8
15,17-(30¢-c variants, limited distribution)	3	6	9	14	20	25

NOTE: *Alcala a-6i, 8i. Brunner c-4. J. Buscema a-6-10p; c-1, 5, 7. Heath a-12. G. Kane c(p)-3, 5, 8-11, 15, 20. Kirby c-12p. Reinman a-1p.*

KA-ZAR (Volume 2)
Marvel Comics: May, 1997 - No. 20, Dec, 1998 ($1.95/$1.99)

	GD 2.0	VG 4.0	FN 6.0	VF 8.0	VF/NM 9.0	NM- 9.2
1-Waid-s/Andy Kubert-c/a. thru #4						3.00
1-2nd printing; new cover						2.50
2,4: 2-Two-c						2.50
3-Alpha Flight #1 preview						3.00
5-13,15-20: 8-Includes Spider-Man Cybercomic CD-ROM. 9-11-Thanos app. 15-Priest-s/Martinez & Rodriguez-a begin; Punisher app.						2.50
14-($2.99) Last Waid/Kubert issue; flip book with 2nd story previewing new creative team of Priest-s/Martinez & Rodriguez-a						3.00
'97 Annual ($2.99)-Wraparound-c						3.00

KA-ZAR OF THE SAVAGE LAND
Marvel Comics: Feb, 1997 ($2.50, one-shot)

	GD 2.0	VG 4.0	FN 6.0	VF 8.0	VF/NM 9.0	NM- 9.2
1-Wraparound-c						2.50

Keen Detective Funnies #23 © CEN

Ken Maynard Western #5 © FAW

Kick-Ass #4 © Mark Millar & John Romita Jr.

KA-ZAR: SIBLING RIVALRY
Marvel Comics: July, 1997 ($1.95, one-shot)

	GD 2.0	VG 4.0	FN 6.0	VF 8.0	VF/NM 9.0	NM- 9.2
(# -1) Flashback story w/Alpha Flight #1 preview						2.50

KA-ZAR THE SAVAGE (See Marvel Fanfare)
Marvel Comics Group: Apr, 1981 - No. 34, Oct, 1984 (Regular size)(Mando paper #10 on)

	GD 2.0	VG 4.0	FN 6.0	VF 8.0	VF/NM 9.0	NM- 9.2
1						4.00
2-20,24,27,28,30-34: 11-Origin Zabu. 12-One of two versions with panel missing on pg. 10. 20-Kraven the Hunter-c/story (also apps. in #21)						2.50
12-Version with panel on pg. 10 (1600 printed)						6.00
21-23, 25,26-Spider-Man app. 26-Photo-c.						3.00
29-Double size; Ka-Zar & Shanna wed						3.00

NOTE: *B. Anderson a-1-15p, 18, 19; c-1-17, 18p, 20(back). G. Kane a(back-up)-11, 12, 14.*

KEEN DETECTIVE FUNNIES (Formerly Detective Picture Stories?)
Centaur Publications: No. 8, July, 1938 - No. 24, Sept, 1940

	GD 2.0	VG 4.0	FN 6.0	VF 8.0	VF/NM 9.0	NM- 9.2
V1#8-The Clock continues-r/Funny Picture Stories #1; Roy Crane-a (1st?)	245	490	735	1568	2684	3800
9-Tex Martin by Eisner; The Gang Buster app.	89	178	267	565	970	1375
10,11: 11-Dean Denton story (begins?)	81	162	243	518	884	1250
V2#1,2-The Eye Sees by Frank Thomas begins; ends #23(Not in V2#3&5). 2-Jack Cole-a	74	148	222	470	810	1150
3-6: 3-TNT Todd begins. 4-Gabby Flynn begins. 5,6-Dean Denton story	70	140	210	445	765	1085
7-The Masked Marvel by Ben Thompson begins (7/39, 1st app.)(scarce)	252	504	756	1613	2757	3900
8-Nudist ranch panel w/four girls	89	178	267	565	970	1375
9-11	79	158	237	502	864	1225
12(12/39)-Origin The Eye Sees by Frank Thomas; death of Masked Marvel's sidekick ZL	95	190	285	603	1039	1475
V3#1,2	70	140	210	445	765	1085
18,19,21,22: 18-Bondage/torture-c	70	140	210	445	765	1085
20-Classic Eye Sees-c by Thomas	107	214	321	680	1165	1650
23-Air Man begins (intro); Air Man-c	97	194	291	621	1061	1500
24-(scarce) Air Man-c	103	206	309	659	1130	1600

NOTE: *Burgos a-V2#2. Jack Cole a-V2#2. Eisner a-10, V2#6r. Ken Ernst a-V2#4-7, 9, 10, 19, 21; c-V2#4. Everett a-V2#6, 7, 9, 11, 12, 20. Guardineer a-V2#5, 66. Gustavson a-V2#4-6. Simon c-V3#1. Thompson c-V2#7, 9, 10, 22.*

KEEN KOMICS
Centaur Publications: V2#1, May, 1939 - V2#3, Nov, 1939

	GD 2.0	VG 4.0	FN 6.0	VF 8.0	VF/NM 9.0	NM- 9.2
V2#1(Large size)-Dan Hastings (s/f), The Big Top, Bob Phantom the Magician, The Mad Goddess app.	98	196	294	622	1074	1525
V2#2(Reg. size)-The Forbidden Idol of Machu Picchu; Cut Carson by Burgos begins	62	124	186	394	680	965
V2#3-Saddle Sniffl by Jack Cole, Circus Pays, Kings Revenge app.	62	124	186	394	680	965

NOTE: *Binder a-V2#2. Burgos a-V2#2, 3. Ken Ernst a-V2#3. Gustavson a-V2#2. Jack Cole a-V2#3.*

KEEN TEENS (Girls magazine)
Life's Romances Publ./Leader/Magazine Ent.: 1945 - No. 6, Aug-Sept, 1947

	GD 2.0	VG 4.0	FN 6.0	VF 8.0	VF/NM 9.0	NM- 9.2
nn (#1)-14 pgs. Claire Voyant (cont'd. in other nn issue) movie photos, Dotty Dripple, Gertie O'Grady & Sissy; Van Johnson, Frank Sinatra photo-c	39	78	117	240	395	550
nn (#2, 1946)-16 pgs. Claire Voyant & 16 pgs. movie photos	28	56	84	165	270	375
3-6: 4-Glenn Ford photo-c. 5-Perry Como-c	15	30	45	84	127	170

KELLYS, THE (Formerly Rusty Comics; Spy Cases No. 26 on)
Marvel Comics (HPC): No. 23, Jan, 1950 - No. 25, June, 1950 (52 pgs.)

	GD 2.0	VG 4.0	FN 6.0	VF 8.0	VF/NM 9.0	NM- 9.2
23-Teenage	14	28	42	76	108	140
24,25: 24-Margie app.	9	18	27	52	69	85

KEN MAYNARD WESTERN (Movie star)(See Wow Comics, 1936)
Fawcett Publ.: Sept, 1950 - No. 8, Feb, 1952 (All 36 pgs; photo front/back-c)

	GD 2.0	VG 4.0	FN 6.0	VF 8.0	VF/NM 9.0	NM- 9.2
1-Ken Maynard & his horse Tarzan begin	43	86	129	267	446	625
2	26	52	78	152	244	335
3-8: 6-Atomic bomb explosion panel	19	38	57	109	172	235

KEN SHANNON (Becomes Gabby #11 on) (Also see Police Comics #103)
Quality Comics Group: Oct, 1951 - No. 10, Apr, 1953 (A private eye)

	GD 2.0	VG 4.0	FN 6.0	VF 8.0	VF/NM 9.0	NM- 9.2
1-Crandall-a	39	78	117	240	395	550
2-Crandall c/a(2)	29	58	87	172	281	390
3-Horror-c; Crandall-a	25	50	75	147	241	335
4,5-Crandall-a	21	42	63	124	202	280
6-Crandall-c/a; "The Weird Vampire Mob"-c/s	24	48	72	142	234	325
7,10: 7-Crandall-a. 10-Crandall-c	18	36	54	107	169	230
8,9: 8-Opium den drug use story	18	36	54	103	162	220

NOTE: *Crandall/Cuidera c-1-10. Jack Cole a-1-9. #1-15 published after title change to Gabby.*

KEN STUART
Publication Enterprises: Jan, 1949 (Sea Adventures)

	GD 2.0	VG 4.0	FN 6.0	VF 8.0	VF/NM 9.0	NM- 9.2
1-Frank Borth-c/a	10	20	30	54	72	90

KENT BLAKE OF THE SECRET SERVICE (Spy)
Marvel/Atlas Comics (20CC): May, 1951 - No. 14, July, 1953

	GD 2.0	VG 4.0	FN 6.0	VF 8.0	VF/NM 9.0	NM- 9.2
1-Injury to eye, bondage, torture; Brodsky-c	21	42	63	122	199	275
2-Drug use w/hypo scenes; Brodsky-c	15	30	45	86	133	180
3-14: 8-R.Q. Sale-a (2 pgs.)	10	20	30	56	76	95

NOTE: *Heath c-5, 7, 8. Infantino c-12. Maneely c-3. Sinnott a-2(3). Tuska a-8(3pg.).*

KENTS, THE
DC Comics: Aug, 1997 - No. 12, July, 1998 ($2.50, limited series)

	GD 2.0	VG 4.0	FN 6.0	VF 8.0	VF/NM 9.0	NM- 9.2
1-12-Ostrander-s/art by Truman and Bair (#1-8), Mandrake (#9-12)						3.00
TPB ($19.95) r/#1-12						20.00

KERRY DRAKE (Also see A-1 Comics)
Argo: Jan, 1956 - No. 2, March, 1956

	GD 2.0	VG 4.0	FN 6.0	VF 8.0	VF/NM 9.0	NM- 9.2
1,2-Newspaper-r	8	16	24	44	57	70

KERRY DRAKE DETECTIVE CASES (...Racket Buster No. 32,33)
(Also see Chamber of Clues & Green Hornet Comics #42-47)
Life's Romances/Com/Magazine Ent. No.1-5/Harvey No.6 on: 1944 - No. 5, 1944; No. 6, Jan, 1948 - No. 33, Aug, 1952

	GD 2.0	VG 4.0	FN 6.0	VF 8.0	VF/NM 9.0	NM- 9.2
nn(1944)(A-1 Comics)(slightly over-size)	30	60	90	177	289	400
2	18	36	54	107	169	230
3-5(1944)	15	30	45	90	140	190
6,8(1948): Lady Crime by Powell. 8-Bondage-c	12	24	36	67	94	120
7-Kubert-a; biog of Andriola (artist)	13	26	39	74	105	135
9,10-Two-part marijuana story; Kerry smokes marijuana in #10	15	30	45	88	137	185
11-15	10	20	30	58	79	100
16-33	9	18	27	50	65	80

NOTE: *Andiola c-6-9. Berg a-5. Powell a-10-23, 28, 29.*

KEWPIES
Will Eisner Publications: Spring, 1949

	GD 2.0	VG 4.0	FN 6.0	VF 8.0	VF/NM 9.0	NM- 9.2
1-Feiffer-a; Kewpie Doll ad on back cover; used in **SOTI**, pg. 35	47	94	141	296	498	700

KEY COMICS
Consolidated Magazines: Jan, 1944 - No. 5, Aug, 1946

	GD 2.0	VG 4.0	FN 6.0	VF 8.0	VF/NM 9.0	NM- 9.2
1-The Key, Will-O-The-Wisp begin	42	84	126	265	445	625
2 (3/44)	23	46	69	136	223	310
3,4: 4-(5/46)-Origin John Quincy The Atom (begins); Walter Johnson c-3-5	20	40	60	118	192	265
5-4pg. Faust Opera adaptation; Kiefer-a; back-c advertises "Masterpieces Illustrated" by Lloyd Jacquet after he left Classic Comics (no copies of Masterpieces Illustrated known)	25	50	75	147	241	335

KEY RING COMICS
Dell Publishing Co.: 1941 (16 pgs.; two colors) (sold 5 for 10¢)

	GD 2.0	VG 4.0	FN 6.0	VF 8.0	VF/NM 9.0	NM- 9.2
1-Sky Hawk, 1-Viking Carter, 1-Features Sleepy Samson, 1-Origin Greg Gilday; r/War Comics #2	9	18	27	47	61	75
1-Radior (Super hero)	10	20	30	54	72	90

NOTE: *Each book has two holes in spine to put in binder.*

KICK-ASS
Marvel Comics (Icon): April, 2008 - No. 8, Mar, 2010 ($2.99)

	GD 2.0	VG 4.0	FN 6.0	VF 8.0	VF/NM 9.0	NM- 9.2
1-Mark Millar-s/John Romita Jr.-a/c						15.00
1-Red variant cover by McNiven						20.00
1-2nd printing						4.00
1-Director's Cut (8/08, $3.99) r/#1 with script and sketch pages; Millar afterword						4.00
2						8.00
3-8: 5-Intro. Red Mist						4.00

NOTE: *Multiple printings exist for most issues.*

KID CARROTS
St. John Publishing Co.: September, 1953

	GD 2.0	VG 4.0	FN 6.0	VF 8.0	VF/NM 9.0	NM- 9.2
1-Funny animal	8	16	24	42	54	65

KID COLT ONE-SHOT
Marvel Comics: Sept, 2009 ($3.99)

	GD 2.0	VG 4.0	FN 6.0	VF 8.0	VF/NM 9.0	NM- 9.2
1-DeFalco-s/Burchett-a/Luke Ross-c						4.00

Kid Colt Outlaw #5 © MAR

Kiddie Kapers #1 © Decker Publ.

Kid Montana V2 #21 © CC

GD VG FN VF VF/NM NM-
2.0 4.0 6.0 8.0 9.0 9.2

KID COLT OUTLAW (Kid Colt #1-4; ...Outlaw #5-on)(Also see All Western Winners, Best Western, Black Rider, Giant-Size..., Two-Gun Kid, Two-Gun Western, Western Winners, Wild Western, Wisco)
Marvel Comics(LCC) 1-16; Atlas(LMC) 17-102; Marvel 103-on: 8/48 - No. 139, 3/68; No. 140, 11/69 - No. 229, 4/79

1-Kid Colt & his horse Steel begin. 116 232 348 742 1271 1800
2 54 108 162 343 584 825
3-5: 4-Anti-Wertham editorial; Tex Taylor app. 5-Blaze Carson app.
42 84 126 266 451 635
6-8: 6-Tex Taylor app; 7-Nimo the Lion begins, ends #10
30 60 90 177 289 400
9,10 (52 pgs.) 30 60 90 177 289 400
11-Origin 35 70 105 208 339 470
12-20 20 40 60 120 195 270
21-32 17 34 51 100 158 215
33-45: Black Rider in all 14 28 42 82 121 160
46,47,49,50 13 26 39 72 101 130
48-Kubert-a 13 26 39 74 105 135
51-53,55,56 11 22 33 60 83 105
54-Williamson/Maneely-c 11 22 33 64 90 115
57-60,66: 4-pg. Williamson-a in all 8 16 24 52 86 120
61-63,67-78,80-86: 70-Severin-c. 69,73-Maneely-c. 86-Kirby-a(r).
6 12 18 41 66 90
64,65-Crandall-a 6 12 18 43 69 95
79,87: 79-Origin retold. 87-Davis-a(r) 6 12 18 43 69 95
88,89-Williamson-a in both (4 pgs.). 89-Redrawn Matt Slade #2
7 14 21 45 73 100
90-99,101-106,108,109: 91-Kirby/Ayers-c. 95-Kirby/Ayers-c/story. 102-Last 10¢ issue
6 12 18 37 59 80
100 6 12 18 39 62 85
107-Only Kirby sci-fi cover of title; Kirby -a. 7 14 21 49 80 110
110-(5/63)-1st app. Iron Mask (Iron Man type villain) 6 12 18 43 69 95
111-120: 114-(1/64)-2nd app. Iron Mask 5 10 15 30 48 65
121-129,133-139: 121-Rawhide Kid x-over. 125-Two-Gun Kid x-over. 139-Last 12¢ issue
4 8 12 24 37 50
130-132 (68 pgs.)-one new story each. 130-Origin 5 10 15 32 51 70
140-155: 140-Reprints begin (later issues mostly-r). 155-Last 15¢ issue
3 6 9 14 19 24
156-Giant; reprints (52 pgs.) 3 6 9 18 27 35
157-180,200: 170-Origin retold. 2 4 6 11 16 20
181-199 2 4 6 9 13 16
201-229: 201-New material w/Rawhide Kid app; Kane-c. 229-Rawhide Kid-r
2 4 6 8 11 14
205-209-(30¢-c variants, limited dist.) 6 12 18 37 59 80
218-220-(35¢-c variants, limited dist.) 9 18 27 60 100 140
...Album (no date; 1950's; Atlas Comics)-132 pgs.; random binding, cardboard cover, B&W stories; contents can vary (Rare) 90 180 270 576 988 1400

NOTE: ***Ayers** a-many. **Colan** a-52, 53; c(p)-223, 228, 229. **Crandall** a-140r, 167r. **Everett** a-90, 137i, 225i(r). **Heath** a-8(2); c-34, 35, 39, 44, 46, 48, 49, 57, 64. **Heck** a-135, 139. **Jack Keller** a-25(2), 26-68(3-4), 78, 94p, 98, 99, 108, 110, 130, 132, 140-150r. **Kirby** a-86r, 93, 96, 107, 119, 176(part); c-87, 92-95, 97, 99-112, 114-117, 121-123, 197r; w/**Ditko** c-89. **Maneely** a-12, 68, 81; c-17, 19, 40-43, 47, 52, 53, 62, 65, 68, 78, 81, 142r, 150r. **Morrow** a-173r, 216r. **Rico** a-13, 18. **Severin** c-58, 59, 143, 148, 149i. **Shores** a-39, 41-43, 143r; c-1-10(most), 24. **Sutton** a-136, 137p, 225p(r). **Wildey** a-47, 54, 82, 144r. **Williamson** r-147, 170, 172, 216. **Woodbridge** a-64, 81. Black Rider in #33-45, 74, 86. Iron Mask in #110, 114, 121, 127. Sam Hawk in #80, 84, 101, 111, 121, 146, 174, 181, 188.*

KID COWBOY (Also see Approved Comics #4 & Boy Cowboy)
Ziff-Davis Publ./St. John (Approved Comics) #11,14: 1950 - No. 11, Wint, '52-'53; No. 13, April 1953; No. 14, June, 1954 (No #12) (Painted covers #1-10,13,14)

1-Lucy Belle & Red Feather begin 16 32 48 94 147 200
2-Maneely-c 11 22 33 62 86 110
3-11,13,14: (#3, spr. '51). 5-Berg-a. 14-Code approved
10 20 30 56 76 95

KID DEATH & FLUFFY HALLOWEEN SPECIAL
Event Comics: Oct, 1997 ($2.95, B&W, one-shot)

1-Variant-c by Cebollero & Quesada/Palmiotti 3.00

KID DEATH & FLUFFY SPRING BREAK SPECIAL
Event Comics: July, 1996 ($2.50, B&W, one-shot)

1-Quesada & Palmiotti-c/scripts 2.50

KIDDIE KAPERS
Kiddie Kapers Co., 1945/Decker Publ. (Red Top-Farrell): 1945?(nd); Oct, 1957; 1963 - 1964

1(nd, 1945-46?, 36 pgs.)-Infinity-c; funny animal 10 20 30 54 72 90
1(10/57)(Decker)-Little Bit-r from Kiddie Karnival 5 10 15 22 26 30

GD VG FN VF VF/NM NM-
2.0 4.0 6.0 8.0 9.0 9.2

Super Reprint #7, 10('63), 12, 14('63), 15,17('64), 18('64): 10, 14-r/Animal Adventures #1. 15-Animal Advs. #? 17-Cowboys 'N' Injuns #? 2 4 6 8 11 14

KIDDIE KARNIVAL
Ziff-Davis Publ. Co. (Approved Comics): 1952 (25¢, 100 pgs.) (One Shot)

nn-Rebound Little Bit #1,2; painted-c 36 72 108 211 343 475

KID ETERNITY (Becomes Buccaneers) (See Hit Comics)
Quality Comics Group: Spring, 1946 - No. 18, Nov, 1949

1 110 220 330 704 1202 1700
2 41 82 123 256 428 600
3-Mac Raboy-a 41 82 123 260 438 615
4-10 25 50 75 147 241 335
11-18 19 38 57 112 179 245

KID ETERNITY
DC Comics: 1991 - No. 3, Nov, 1991 ($4.95, limited series)

1-3: Grant Morrison scripts/Duncan Fegredo-a/c 6.00
TPB (2006, $14.99) r/#1-3 15.00

KID ETERNITY
DC Comics (Vertigo): May, 1993 - No. 16, Sept, 1994 ($1.95, mature)

1-16: 1-Gold ink-c. 6-Photo-c. All Sean Phillips-c/a except #15 (Phillips-c/i only) 2.50

KID FROM DODGE CITY, THE
Atlas Comics (MMC): July, 1957 - No. 2, Sept, 1957

1-Don Heck-c 10 20 30 56 76 95
2-Everett-c 7 14 21 37 46 55

KID FROM TEXAS, THE (A Texas Ranger)
Atlas Comics (CSI): June, 1957 - No. 2, Aug, 1957

1-Powell-a; Severin-c 10 20 30 56 76 95
2 7 14 21 37 46 55

KID KOKO
I. W. Enterprises: 1958

Reprint #1,2-(r/M.E.'s Koko & Kola #4, 1947) 2 4 6 8 11 14

KID KOMICS (Kid Movie Komics No. 11)
Timely Comics (USA 1,2/FCI 3-10): Feb, 1943 - No. 10, Spring, 1946

1-Origin Captain Wonder & sidekick Tim Mullrooney, & Subbie; intro the Sea-Going Lad, Pinto Pete, & Trixie Trouble; Knuckles & Whitewash Jones (from Young Allies) app.; Wolverton-a (7 pgs.) 423 846 1269 3046 5323 7600
2-The Young Allies, Red Hawk, & Tommy Tyme begin; last Captain Wonder & Subbie
200 400 600 1280 2190 3100
3-The Vision, Daredevils & Red Hawk app. 152 304 456 965 1658 2350
4-The Destroyer begins; Sub-Mariner app.; Red Hawk & Tommy Tyme end
129 258 387 826 1413 2000
5,6: 5-Tommy Tyme begins, ends #10 97 194 291 621 1061 1500
7-10: 7,10-The Whizzer app. Destroyer not in #7,8. 10-Last Destroyer, Young Allies & Whizzer 87 174 261 553 952 1350

NOTE: ***Brodsky** c-5. **Schomburg** c-2-4, 6-10. **Shores** c-1. Captain Wonder c-1, 2. The Young Allies c-3-10.*

KID MONTANA (Formerly Davy Crockett Frontier Fighter; The Gunfighters No. 51 on)
Charlton Comics: V2#9, Nov, 1957 - No. 50, Mar, 1965

V2#9 (#1) 4 8 12 28 44 60
10 3 6 9 20 30 40
11,12,14-20 3 6 9 16 22 28
13-Williamson-a 3 6 9 20 30 40
21-35: 25,31-Giordano-c. 32-Origin Kid Montana. 34-Geronimo-c/s. 35-Snow Monster-c/s
2 4 6 11 16 20
36-50: 36-Dinosaur-c/s. 37,48-Giordano-c 2 4 6 9 12 15

NOTE: *Title change to Montana Kid on cover only #44 & 45; remained Kid Montana on inside. **Chasal** a-29,30. **Giordano** c-25,31,37,48. **Giordano/Alascia** c-12. **Mastroserio** a-9,11,13,14,22; c-11,14. **Masulli/Mastroserio** c-13. **Montes/Bache** c-42. **Morisi** c-16,32-34,36?,40,41,44,46; a-13,15;16,31-50. **Nicholas/Alascia** a-44,48.*

KID MOVIE KOMICS (Formerly Kid Komics; Rusty Comics #12 on)
Timely Comics: No. 11, Summer, 1946

11-Silly Seal & Ziggy Pig; 2 pgs. Kurtzman "Hey Look" plus 6 pg. "Pigtales" story 27 54 81 158 259 360

KIDNAPPED (See Marvel Illustrated: Kidnapped)

KIDNAPPED (Robert Louis Stevenson's...also see Movie Comics)(Disney)
Dell Publishing Co.: No. 1101, May, 1960

Four Color 1101-Movie, photo-c 6 12 18 43 69 95

KIDNAP RACKET (See Harvey Comics Hits No. 57)

KID SLADE GUNFIGHTER (Formerly Matt Slade...)
Atlas Comics (SPI): No. 5, Jan, 1957 - No. 8, July, 1957

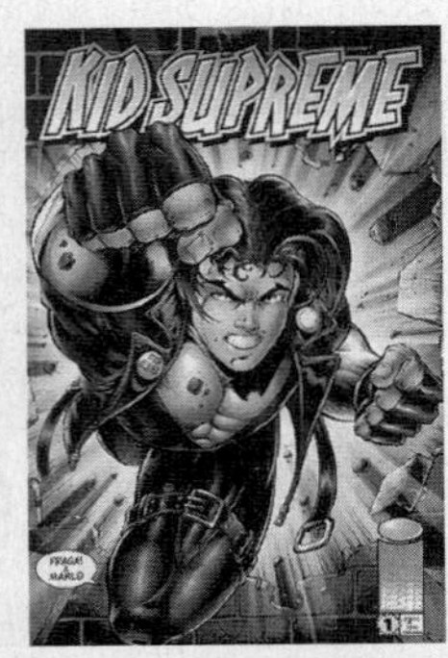

Kid Supreme #1 © Liefeld

The Kilroys #6 © ACG

King Comics #17 © DMP

	GD 2.0	VG 4.0	FN 6.0	VF 8.0	VF/NM 9.0	NM- 9.2
5-Maneely, Roth, Severin-a in all; Maneely-c	13	26	39	72	101	130
6,8-Severin-c	8	16	24	44	57	70
7-Williamson/Mayo-a, 4 pgs.	10	20	30	56	76	95

KID SUPREME (See Supreme)
Image Comics (Extreme Studios): Mar, 1996 - No. 3, July, 1996 ($2.50)
1-3: Fraga-a/scripts. 3-Glory-c/app. 2.50

KID TERRIFIC
Image Comics: Nov, 1998 ($2.95, B&W)
1-Snyder & Diliberto-s/a 3.00

KID ZOO COMICS
Street & Smith Publications: July, 1948 (52 pgs.)
1-Funny Animal 30 60 90 177 289 400

KILL ALL PARENTS
Image Comics: June, 2008 ($3.99, one-shot)
1-Marcelo Di Chiara-a/Mark Andrew Smith-s 4.00

KILLAPALOOZA
DC Comics (WildStorm): July, 2009 - No. 6, Dec, 2009 ($2.99, limited series)
1-6: 1-Beechen-s/Hairsine-a/c 3.00

KILLER (...Tales By Timothy Truman)
Eclipse Comics: March, 1985 ($1.75, one-shot, Baxter paper)
1-Timothy Truman-c/a 2.50

KILLER INSTINCT (Video game)
Acclaim Comics: June, 1996 - No. 6 ($2.50, limited series)
1-6: 1-Bart Sears-a(p). 4-Special #1. 5-Special #2. 6-Special #3 3.00

KILLERS, THE
Magazine Enterprises: 1947 - No. 2, 1948 (No month)
1-Mr. Zin, the Hatchet Killer; mentioned in **SOTI**, pgs. 179,180; used by N.Y. Legis. Comm.; L. B. Cole-c 119 238 357 762 1306 1850
2-(Scarce)-Hashish smoking story; "Dying, Dying, Dead" drug story; Whitney, Ingels-a; Whitney hanging-c 97 194 291 621 1061 1500

KILLING GIRL
Image Comics: Aug, 2007 - No. 5, Dec, 2007 ($2.99, limited series)
1-5: 1-Frank Espinosa-a/Glen Brunswick-s; covers by Espinosa and Frank Cho 3.00

KILLING JOKE, THE (See Batman: The Killing Joke under Batman one-shots)

KILLPOWER: THE EARLY YEARS
Marvel Comics UK: Sept, 1993 - No. 4, Dec, 1993 ($1.75, mini-series)
1-($2.95)-Foil embossed-c 3.00
2-4: 2-Genetix app. 3-Punisher app. 2.25

KILLRAVEN (See Amazing Adventures #18 (5/73))
Marvel Comics: Feb, 2001 ($2.99, one-shot)
1-Linsner-s/a/c 3.00

KILLRAVEN
Marvel Comics: Dec, 2002 - No. 6, May, 2003 ($2.99, limited series)
1-6-Alan Davis-s/a(p)/Mark Farmer-i 3.00
HC (2007, $19.99) r/#1-6; cover gallery, pencil art; foreward by Alan Davis 20.00

KILLRAZOR
Image Comics (Top Cow Productions): Aug, 1995 ($2.50, one-shot)
1 2.50

KILL YOUR BOYFRIEND
DC Comics (Vertigo): June, 1995 ($4.95, one-shot)
1-Grant Morrison story 6.00
1 ($5.95, 1998) 2nd printing 6.00

KILROY (Volume 2)
Caliber Press: 1998 ($2.95, B&W)
1-Pruett-s 3.00

KILROY IS HERE
Caliber Press: 1995 ($2.95, B&W)
1-10 3.00

KILROYS, THE
B&I Publ. Co. No. 1-19/American Comics Group: June-July, 1947 - No. 54, June-July, 1955

	GD 2.0	VG 4.0	FN 6.0	VF 8.0	VF/NM 9.0	NM- 9.2
1	22	44	66	128	209	290
2	14	28	42	78	112	145
3-5: 5-Gross-a	12	24	36	69	97	125
6-10: 8-Milt Gross's Moronica	10	20	30	54	72	90
11-20: 14-Gross-a	9	18	27	47	61	75
21-30	8	16	24	42	54	65
31-47,50-54	8	16	24	40	50	60
48,49-(3-D effect-c/stories)	17	34	51	98	154	210

KILROY: THE SHORT STORIES
Caliber Press: 1995 ($2.95, B&W)
1 3.00

KIN
Image Comics (Top Cow): Mar, 2000 - No. 6, Sept, 2000 ($2.95)
1-5-Gary Frank-s/c/a 3.00
1-($6.95) DF Alternate footprint cover 7.00
6-($3.95) 4.00
... Descent of Man TPB (2002, $19.95) r/ #1-6 20.00

KINDRED, THE
Image Comics (WildStorm Productions): Mar, 1994 - No. 4, July, 1995 ($1.95, lim. series)
1-($2.50)-Grifter & Backlash app. in all; bound-in trading card 2.50
2-4 2.50
2,3: 2-Variant-c. 3-Alternate-c by Portacio, see Deathblow #5 4.00
Trade paperback (2/95, $9.95) 10.00
NOTE: *Booth c/a-1-4. The first four issues contain coupons redeemable for a Jim Lee Grifter/Backlash print.*

KINDRED II, THE
DC Comics (WildStorm): Mar, 2002 - No. 4, June, 2002 ($2.50, limited series)
1-4-Booth-s/Booth & Regla-a 2.50

KINETIC
DC Comics (Focus): May, 2004 - No. 8, Dec, 2004 ($2.50)
1-8-Puckett-s/Pleece-a/c 2.50
TPB (2005, $9.99) r/#1-8; cover gallery and sketch pages 10.00

KING (Magazine)
Skywald Publ.: Mar, 1971 - No. 2, July, 1971
1-Violence; semi-nudity; Boris Vallejo-a (2 pgs.) 5 10 15 32 51 70
2-Photo-c 3 6 9 20 30 40

KING ARTHUR AND THE KNIGHTS OF JUSTICE
Marvel Comics UK: Dec, 1993 - No. 3, Feb, 1994 ($1.25, limited series)
1-3: TV adaptation 2.50

KING CLASSICS
King Features : 1977 (36 pgs., cardboard-c) (Printed in Spain for U.S. distr.)
1-Connecticut Yankee, 2-Last of the Mohicans, 3-Moby Dick, 4-Robin Hood, 5-Swiss Family Robinson, 6-Robinson Crusoe, 7-Treasure Island, 8-20,000 Leagues, 9-Christmas Carol, 10-Huck Finn, 11-Around the World in 80 Days, 12-Davy Crockett, 13-Don Quixote, 14-Gold Bug, 15-Ivanhoe, 16-Three Musketeers, 17-Baron Munchausen, 18-Alice in Wonderland, 19-Black Arrow, 20-Five Weeks in a Balloon, 21-Great Expectations, 22-Gulliver's Travels, 23-Prince & Pauper, 24-Lawrence of Arabia (Originals, 1977-78)
each.... 2 4 6 10 14 18
Reprints (1979; HRN-24) 2 4 6 8 10 12
NOTE: *The first eight issues were not numbered. Issues No. 25-32 were advertised but not published. The 1977 originals have HRN 32a; the 1978 originals have HRN 32b.*

KING COLT (See Luke Short's Western Stories)

KING COMICS (Strip reprints)
David McKay Publications/Standard #156-on: 4/36 - No. 155, 11-12/49; No. 156, Spr/50 - No. 159, 2/52 (Winter on-c)

	GD 2.0	VG 4.0	FN 6.0	VF 8.0	VF/NM 9.0	NM- 9.2
1-1st app. Flash Gordon by Alex Raymond; Brick Bradford (1st app.), Popeye, Henry (1st app.) & Mandrake the Magician (1st app.) begin; Popeye-c begin	1250	2500	3750	10,000	-	-
2	360	720	1080	1980	2790	3600
3	245	490	735	1348	1899	2450
4	190	380	570	1045	1473	1900
5	140	280	420	770	1085	1400
6-10: 9-X-Mas-c	95	190	285	523	737	950
11-20	75	150	225	413	582	750
21-30: 21-X-Mas-c	55	110	165	303	427	550
31-40: 33-Last Segar Popeye	45	90	135	248	349	450
41-50: 46-Text illos by Marge Buell contain characters similar to Lulu, Alvin & Tubby. 50-The Lone Ranger begins	32	64	96	186	298	410
51-60: 52-Barney Baxter begins?	23	46	69	133	214	295
61-The Phantom begins	24	48	72	140	225	310
62-80: 76-Flag-c. 79-Blondie begins	17	34	51	98	154	210
81-99	14	28	42	81	118	155
100	16	32	48	92	144	195

101-114: 114-Last Raymond issue (1 pg.); Flash Gordon by Austin Briggs begins, ends #155

Kingdom Come SC (2008) © DC

Kingpin #1 © MAR

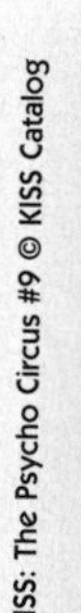
KISS: The Psycho Circus #9 © KISS Catalog

	GD 2.0	VG 4.0	FN 6.0	VF 8.0	VF/NM 9.0	NM- 9.2
115-145: 117-Phantom origin retold	14	28	42	76	108	140
146,147-Prince Valiant in both	10	20	30	56	76	95
148-155: 155-Flash Gordon ends (11-12/49)	9	18	27	50	65	80
156-159: 156-New logo begins (Standard)	9	18	27	50	65	80
	9	18	27	47	61	75

NOTE: *Marge Buell text illos in No. 24-46 at least.*

KING CONAN (Conan The King No. 20 on)
Marvel Comics Group: Mar, 1980 - No. 19, Nov, 1983 (52 pgs.)

1	1	2	3	5	6	8
2-19: 4-Death of Thoth Amon. 7-1st Paul Smith-a, 1 pg. pin-up (9/81)						5.00

NOTE: ***J. Buscema*** *a-1-9p, 17p; c(p)-1-5, 7-9, 14, 17.* ***Kaluta*** *c-19.* ***Nebres*** *a-17i, 18, 19i.* ***Severin*** *c-18.* ***Simonson*** *c-6.*

KING DAVID
DC Comics (Vertigo): 2002 ($19.95, 8 1/2" x 11")

nn-Story of King David; Kyle Baker-s/a 20.00

KINGDOM, THE
DC Comics: Feb, 1999 - No. 2, Feb, 1999 ($2.95/$1.99, limited series)

1,2-Waid-s; sequel to Kingdom Come; introduces Hypertime 4.00
...: Kid Flash 1 (2/99, $1.99) Waid-s/Pararillo-a, ...: Nightstar 1 (2/99, $1.99) Waid-s/Haley-a, ...: Offspring 1 (2/99, $1.99) Waid-s/Quitely-a, ...: Planet Krypton 1 (2/99, $1.99) Waid-s/ Kitson-a, ...: Son of the Bat 1 (2/99, $1.99) Waid-s/Apthorp-a 2.50

KINGDOM COME (Also see Justice Society of America #9-22)
DC Comics: 1996 - No. 4, 1996 ($4.95, painted limited series)

1-Mark Waid scripts & Alex Ross-painted c/a in all; tells the last days of the DC Universe; 1st app. Magog	1	2	3	5	6	8
2-Superman forms new Justice League	1	2	3	4	5	7
3-Return of Captain Marvel						5.00
4-Final battle of Superman and Captain Marvel	1	2	3	4	5	7
Deluxe Slipcase Edition-($89.95) w/Revelations companion book, 12 new story pages, foil stamped covers, signed and numbered						120.00
Hardcover Edition-($29.95)-Includes 12 new story pages and artwork from Revelations, new cover artwork with gold foil inlay						35.00
Hardcover 2nd printing						30.00
Softcover Ed.-($14.95)-Includes 12 new story pgs. & artwork from Revelations, new c-artwork						15.00
Softcover Ed.-(2008, $17.99)-New wraparound gatefold cover by Ross						18.00

KING KONG (See Movie Comics)

KING KONG: THE 8TH WONDER OF THE WORLD (Adaptation of 2005 movie)
Dark Horse Comics: Dec, 2005 ($3.99, planned limited series completed in TPB)

1-Photo-c; Dustin Weaver-a/Christian Gossett-s 4.00
TPB (11/06, $12.95) r/#1 and unpublished parts 2&3; photo-c; Dorman paintings 13.00

KING LEONARDO & HIS SHORT SUBJECTS (TV)
Dell Publishing Co./Gold Key: Nov-Jan, 1961-62 - No. 4, Sept, 1963

Four Color 1242,1278	12	24	36	82	149	215
01390-207(5-7/62)(Dell)	9	18	27	61	103	145
1 (10/62)	10	20	30	71	126	180
2-4	8	16	24	56	93	130

KING LOUIE & MOWGLI (See Jungle Book under Movie Comics)
Gold Key: May, 1968 (Disney)

1 (#10223-805)-Characters from Jungle Book	3	6	9	20	30	40

KING OF DIAMONDS (TV)
Dell Publishing Co.: July-Sept, 1962

01-391-209-Photo-c	4	8	12	26	41	55

KING OF KINGS (Movie)
Dell Publishing Co.: No. 1236, Oct-Nov, 1961

Four Color 1236-Photo-c	7	14	21	50	83	115

KING OF THE BAD MEN OF DEADWOOD
Avon Periodicals: 1950 (See Wild Bill Hickok #16)

nn-Kinstler-c; Kamen/Feldstein-r/Cowpuncher #2	15	30	45	94	147	200

KING OF THE ROYAL MOUNTED (See Famous Feature Stories, King Comics, Red Ryder #3 & Super Book #2, 6)

KING OF THE ROYAL MOUNTED (Zane Grey's...)
David McKay/Dell Publishing Co.: No. 1, May, 1937; No. 9, 1940; No. 207, Dec, 1948 - No. 935, Sept-Nov, 1958

Feature Books 1 (5/37)(McKay)	87	174	261	553	952	1350
Large Feature Comic 9 (1940)	47	94	141	296	498	700
Four Color 207(#1, 12/48)	13	26	39	93	172	250

	GD 2.0	VG 4.0	FN 6.0	VF 8.0	VF/NM 9.0	NM- 9.2
Four Color 265,283	8	16	24	58	97	135
Four Color 310,340	6	12	18	43	69	95
Four Color 363,384, 8(6-8/52)-10	6	12	18	39	62	85
11-20	5	10	15	34	55	75
21-28(3-5/58), Four Color 935(9-11/58)	4	8	12	28	44	60

NOTE: *4-Color No. 207, 265, 283, 310, 340, 363, 384 are all newspaper reprints with* ***Jim Gary*** *art. No. 8 on are all Dell originals. Painted c-No. 9-on.*

KINGPIN
Marvel Comics: Nov, 1997 ($5.99, squarebound, one-shot)

nn-Spider-Man & Daredevil vs. Kingpin; Stan Lee-s/ John Romita Sr.-a 6.00

KINGPIN
Marvel Comics: Aug, 2003 - No. 7, Jan, 2004 ($2.50/$2.99, limited series)

1-6-Bruce Jones-s/Sean Phillips & Klaus Janson-a 2.50
7-($2.99) 3.00

KING RICHARD & THE CRUSADERS
Dell Publishing Co.: No. 588, Oct, 1954

Four Color 588-Movie, Matt Baker-a, photo-c	9	18	27	63	107	150

KING-SIZE CABLE SPECTACULAR (Takes place between Cable (2008 series) #6 & #7)
Marvel Comics: Nov, 2008 ($4.99, one-shot)

1-Lashley-a; Deadpool #1 preview; cover gallery of variants from 2008 series 5.00

KING-SIZE HULK (Takes place between Hulk (2008 series) #3 & #4)
Marvel Comics: July, 2008 ($4.99, one-shot)

1-Art Adams, Frank Cho, & Herb Trimpe-a; double-c by Cho & Adams; Red Hulk, She-Hulk & Wendigo app.; origin Abomination; r/Incr. Hulk #180,181 & Avengers #83 5.00

KING-SIZE SPIDER-MAN SUMMER SPECIAL
Marvel Comics: Oct, 2008 ($4.99, one-shot)

1-Short stories by various; Falcon app.; Burchett, Giarrusso & Coover-a 5.00

KINGS OF THE NIGHT
Dark Horse Comics: 1990 - No. 2, 1990 ($2.25, limited series)

1,2-Robert E. Howard adaptation; Bolton-c 2.50

KING SOLOMON'S MINES (Movie)
Avon Periodicals: 1951

nn (#1 on 1st page)	39	78	117	240	395	550

KIPLING, RUDYARD (See Mowgli, The Jungle Book)

KISS (See Crazy Magazine, Howard the Duck #12, 13, Marvel Comics Super Special #1, 5, Rock Fantasy Comics #10 & Rock N' Roll Comics #9)

KISS
Dark Horse Comics: June, 2002 - No. 13, Sept, 2003 ($2.99, limited series)

1-Photo-c and J. Scott Campbell-c; Casey-s 4.00
2-13: 2-Photo-c and J. Scott Campbell-c. 3-Photo-c and Leinil Yu-c 3.00
...: Men and Monsters TPB (9/03, $12.95) r/#7-10 13.00
...: Rediscovery TPB (2003, $9.95) r/#1-3 10.00
...: Return of the Phantom TPB (2003, $9.95) r/#4-6 10.00
...: Unholy War TPB (2004, $9.95) r/#11-13 10.00

KISS 4K
Platinum Studios Comics: May, 2007 - No. 6, Apr, 2008 ($3.99/$2.99)

1-Sprague-s/Crossley & Campos-a/Migliari-c 4.00
1-B&W sketch-c 6.00
1-Destroyer Edition ($50.00, 30"x18", edition of 5000) 50.00
2-6-($2.99) 3.00
KISSMAS (12/07, $4.99) Christmas-themed issue; re-cap of issues #1-4 5.00

KISS: THE PSYCHO CIRCUS
Image Comics: Aug, 1997 - No. 31, June, 2000 ($1.95/$2.25/$2.50)

1-Holguin-s/Medina-a(p)	1	2	3	5	6	8
1-2nd & 3rd printings						2.50
2						5.00
3,4: 4-Photo-c						4.00
5-8: 5-Begin $2.25-c						3.00
9-29						2.50
30,31: 30-Begin $2.50-c						2.50
Book 1 TPB ('98, $12.95) r/#1-6						13.00
Book 2 Destroyer TPB (8/99, $9.95) r/#10-13						10.00
Book 3 Whispered Scream TPB ('00, $9.95) r/#7-9,18						10.00
...Magazine 1 ($6.95) r/#1-3 plus interviews						7.00
...Magazine 2-5 ($4.95) 2-r/#4,5 plus interviews. 3-r/#6,7. 4-r/#8,9						5.00
Wizard Edition ('98, supplement) Bios, tour preview and interviews						2.50

Kit Carson #6 © AVON

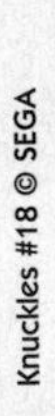

Knuckles #18 © SEGA

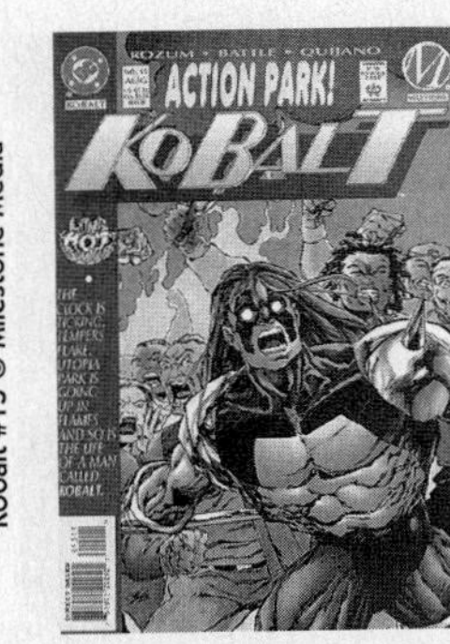

Kobalt #15 © Milestone Media

	GD 2.0	VG 4.0	FN 6.0	VF 8.0	VF/NM 9.0	NM- 9.2

KISSING CHAOS
Oni Press: Sept, 2001 - No. 8, Mar, 2002 ($2.25, B&W, 6" x 9", limited series)

1-8-Arthur Dela Cruz-s/a						2.50
...: Nine Lives (12/03, $2.99, regular comic-sized)						3.00
...: 1000 Words (7/03, $2.99, regular comic-sized)						3.00
TPB (9/02, $17.95) r/#1-8						18.00

KISSING CHAOS: NONSTOP BEAUTY
Oni Press: Oct, 2002 - No. 4, March, 2003 ($2.95, B&W, 6" x 9", limited series)

1-4-Arthur Dela Cruz-s/a						3.00
TPB (9/03, $11.95) r/#1-4						12.00

KISS KISS BANG BANG
CrossGen Comics: Feb, 2004 - No. 5, Jun, 2004 ($2.95)

1-5-Bedard-s/Perkins-a						3.00

KISSYFUR (TV)
DC Comics: 1989 (Sept.) ($2.00, 52 pgs., one-shot)

1-Based on Saturday morning cartoon						4.00

KIT CARSON (Formerly All True Detective Cases No. 4; Fighting Davy Crockett No. 9; see Blazing Sixguns & Frontier Fighters)
Avon Periodicals: 1950; No. 2, 8/51 - No. 3, 12/51; No. 5, 11-12/54 - No. 8, 9/55 (No #4)

nn(#1) (1950)- "...Indian Scout" ; r-Cowboys 'N' Injuns #?	14	28	42	76	108	140
2(8/51)	10	20	30	56	76	95
3(12/51)- "...Fights the Comanche Raiders"	9	18	27	50	65	80
5-6,8(11-12/54-9/55): 5-Formerly All True Detective Cases (last pre-code); titled "...and the Trail of Doom"	9	18	27	47	61	75
7-McCann-a?	9	18	27	47	61	75
I.W. Reprint #10('63)-r/Kit Carson #1; Severin-c	2	4	6	11	16	20

NOTE: *Kinstler c-1-3, 5-8.*

KIT CARSON & THE BLACKFEET WARRIORS
Realistic: 1953

nn-Reprint; Kinstler-c	9	18	27	52	69	85

KIT KARTER
Dell Publishing Co.: May-July, 1962

1	3	6	9	19	29	38

KITTY
St. John Publishing Co.: Oct, 1948

1-Teenage; Lily Renee-c/a	8	16	24	44	57	70

KITTY PRYDE, AGENT OF S.H.I.E.L.D. (Also see Excalibur and Mekanix)
Marvel Comics: Dec, 1997 - No. 3, Feb, 1998 ($2.50, limited series)

1-3-Hama-s						2.50

KITTY PRYDE AND WOLVERINE (Also see Uncanny X-Men & X-Men)
Marvel Comics Group: Nov, 1984 - No. 6, Apr, 1985 (Limited series)

1-6: Characters from X-Men						4.50
X-Men: Kitty Pryde and Wolverine HC (2008, $19.99) r/series						20.00

KLARER GIVEAWAYS (See Wisco in the Promotional Comics section)

KNIGHTHAWK
Acclaim Comics (Windjammer): Sept, 1995 - No. 6, Nov, 1995 ($2.50, lim. series)

1-6: 6-origin						2.50

KNIGHTMARE
Antarctic Press: July, 1994 - May, 1995 ($2.75, B&W, mature readers)

1-6						2.75

KNIGHTMARE
Image Comics (Extreme Studios): Feb, 1995 - No. 5, June, 1995 ($2.50)

0 ($3.50)						3.50
1-5: 4-Quesada & Palmiotti variant-c, 5-Flip book w/Warcry						2.50

KNIGHTS 4 (See Marvel Knights 4)

KNIGHTS OF PENDRAGON, THE (Also see Pendragon)
Marvel Comics Ltd.: July, 1990 - No. 18, Dec, 1991 ($1.95)

1-18: 1-Capt. Britain app. 2,8-Free poster inside. 9,10-Bolton-c. 11,18-Iron Man app.						2.50

KNIGHTS OF THE ROUND TABLE
Dell Publishing Co.: No. 540, Mar, 1954

Four Color 540-Movie, photo-c	7	14	21	47	76	105

KNIGHTS OF THE ROUND TABLE
Pines Comics: No. 10, April, 1957

10	5	10	15	24	30	35

KNIGHTS OF THE ROUND TABLE
Dell Publishing Co.: Nov-Jan, 1963-64

1 (12-397-401)-Painted-c	3	6	9	21	32	42

KNIGHTSTRIKE (Also see Operation: Knightstrike)
Image Comics (Extreme Studios): Jan, 1996 ($2.50)

1-Rob Liefeld & Eric Stephenson story; Extreme Destroyer Part 6.						2.50

KNIGHT WATCHMAN (See Big Bang Comics & Dr. Weird)
Image Comics: June, 1998 - No. 4, Oct, 1998 ($2.95/$3.50, B&W, lim. series)

1-3-Ben Torres-c/a in all						3.00
4-($3.50)						3.50

KNIGHT WATCHMAN: GRAVEYARD SHIFT
Caliber Press: 1994 ($2.95, B&W)

1,2-Ben Torres-a						3.00

KNOCK KNOCK (...Who's There?)
Dell Publ./Gerona Publications: No. 801, 1936 (52 pgs.) (8x9", B&W)

801-Joke book; Bob Dunn-a	10	20	30	56	76	95

KNOCKOUT ADVENTURES
Fiction House Magazines: Winter, 1953-54

1-Reprints Fight Comics #53 w/Rip Carson-c/s	14	28	42	76	108	140

KNUCKLES (Spin-off of Sonic the Hedgehog)
Archie Publications: Apr, 1997 - No. 32, Feb, 2000 ($1.50/$1.75/$1.79)

1-32						3.00

KNUCKLES' CHAOTIX
Archie Publications: Jan, 1996 ($2.00, annual)

1						3.00

KOBALT
DC Comics (Milestone): June, 1994 - No. 16, Sept, 1995 ($1.75/$2.50)

1-16: 1-Byrne-c. 4-Intro Page. 16-Kent Williams-c						2.50

KOBRA (Unpublished #8 appears in DC Special Series No. 1)
National Periodical Publications: Feb-Mar, 1976 - No. 7, Mar-Apr, 1977

1-1st app.; Kirby-a redrawn by Marcos; only 25¢-c	2	4	6	8	11	14
2-7: (All 30¢ issues) 3-Giffen-a	1	2	3	5	6	8
...: Resurrection TPB (2010, $19.99) r/#1, DC Special Series No. 1 and later apps. in Checkmate #23-25, Faces of Evil: Kobra #1 and various Who's Who issues						20.00

NOTE: *Austin a-3i. Buckler a-5p; c-5p. Kubert c-4. Nasser a-6p, 7; c-7.*

KOKEY KOALA (...and the Magic Button)
Toby Press: May, 1952

1-Funny animal	11	22	33	62	86	110

KOKO AND KOLA (Also see A-1 Comics #16 & Tick Tock Tales)
Com/Magazine Enterprises: Fall, 1946 - No. 5, May, 1947; No. 6, 1950

1-Funny animal	12	24	36	67	94	120
2-X-Mas-c	8	16	24	44	57	70
3-6: 6(A-1 28)	8	16	24	40	50	60

KO KOMICS
Gerona Publications: Oct, 1945 (scarce)

1-The Duke of Darkness & The Menace (hero)	74	148	222	470	810	1150

KOLCHAK: THE NIGHT STALKER (TV)
Moonstone: 2002 - Present ($6.50/$6.95)

1-($6.50) Jeff Rice-s/Gordon Purcell-a						6.50
... Black & White & Read All Over (2005, $4.95) short stories by various; 2 covers						5.00
... Devil in the Details (2003, $6.95) Trevor Von Eeden-a						7.00
... Eve of Terror (2005, $5.95) Gentile-s/Figueroa-a/ Beck-c						6.00
... Fever Pitch (2002, $6.95) Christopher Jones-a						7.00
... Get of Belial (2002, $6.95) Art Nichols-a						7.00
... Lambs to the Slaughter (2003, $6.95) Trevor Von Eeden-a						7.00
... Pain Most Human (2004, $6.95) Greg Scott-a						7.00
... Tales: The Frankenstein Agenda 1 (2007 - No. 3, $3.50) Michelinie-s						3.50
... Tales of the Night Stalker 1-7 (2003-Present, $3.50) two covers by Moore & Ulanski						3.50
TPB (2004, $17.95) r/#1, Get of Belial & Fever Pitch						18.00
Vol. 2: Terror Within TPB (2006, $16.95) r/Pain Most Human, Pain Without Tears & Devil in the Details						17.00

KOMIC KARTOONS
Timely Comics (EPC): Fall, 1945 - No. 2, Winter, 1945

Kookaburra K #1 © MAR

Krazy Komics #1 © MAR

Krypton Chronicles #1 © DC

GD 2.0 | VG 4.0 | FN 6.0 | VF 8.0 | VF/NM 9.0 | NM- 9.2

1,2-Andy Wolf, Bertie Mouse 21 42 63 122 199 275

KOMIK PAGES (Formerly Snap; becomes Bullseye #11)
Harry 'A' Chesler, Jr. (Our Army, Inc.): Apr, 1945 (All reprints)
10(#1 on inside)-Land O' Nod by Rick Yager (2 pgs.), Animal Crackers, Foxy GrandPa, Tom, Dick & Mary, Cheerio Minstrels, Red Starr plus other 1-2 pg. strips; Cole-a
23 46 69 136 223 310

KONA (...Monarch of Monster Isle)
Dell Publishing Co.: Feb-Apr, 1962 - No. 21, Jan-Mar, 1967 (Painted-c)
Four Color 1256 (#1) 9 18 27 65 113 160
2-10: 4-Anak begins. 6-Gil Kane-c 6 12 18 37 59 80
11-21 5 10 15 30 48 65
NOTE: *Glanzman a-all issues.*

KONGA (Fantastic Giants No. 24) (See Return of...)
Charlton Comics: 1960; No. 2, Aug, 1961 - No. 23, Nov, 1965
1(1960)-Based on movie; Giordano-c 23 46 69 166 321 475
2-5: 2-Giordano-c; no Ditko-a 11 22 33 78 139 200
6-9-Ditko-c/a 9 18 27 65 113 160
10-15 9 18 27 61 103 145
16-23 6 12 18 41 66 90
NOTE: *Ditko a-1, 3-15; c-4, 6-9. Glanzman a-12. Montes & Bache a-16-23.*

KONGA'S REVENGE (Formerly Return of...)
Charlton Comics: No. 2, Summer, 1963 - No. 3, Fall, 1964; Dec, 1968
2,3: 2-Ditko-c/a 7 14 21 45 73 100
1(12/68)-Reprints Konga's Revenge #3 3 6 9 17 25 32

KONG THE UNTAMED
National Periodical Publications: June-July, 1975 - V2#5, Feb-Mar, 1976
1-1st app. Kong; Wrightson-c; Alcala-a 2 4 6 10 14 18
2-Wrightson-c; Alcala-a 2 4 6 8 11 14
3-5: 3-Alcala-a 1 2 3 5 6 8

KOOKABURRA K
Marvel Comics (Soleil): 2009 - No. 3, 2010 ($5.99, limited series)
1-3-Humbertos Ramos-a/c 6.00

KOOKIE
Dell Publishing Co.: Feb-Apr, 1962 - No. 2, May-July, 1962 (15 cents)
1-Written by John Stanley; Bill Williams-a 8 16 24 54 90 125
2 7 14 21 49 80 110

KOOSH KINS
Archie Comics: Oct, 1991 - No. 3, Feb, 1992 ($1.00, bi-monthly, limited series)
1-3 2.50
NOTE: *No. 4 was planned, but cancelled.*

KORAK, SON OF TARZAN (Edgar Rice Burroughs)(See Tarzan #139)
Gold Key: Jan, 1964 - No. 45, Jan, 1972 (Painted-c No. 1-?)
1-Russ Manning-a 9 18 27 65 113 160
2-5-Russ Manning-a 6 12 18 37 59 80
6-11-Russ Manning-a 5 10 15 32 51 70
12-23: 12,13-Warren Tufts-a. 14-Jon of the Kalahari ends. 15-Mabu, Jungle Boy begins. 21-Manning-a. 23-Last 12¢ issue 4 8 12 28 44 60
24-30 4 8 12 22 34 45
31-45 3 6 9 18 27 35

KORAK, SON OF TARZAN (Tarzan Family #60 on; see Tarzan #230)
National Periodical Publications: V9#46, May-June, 1972 - V12#56, Feb-Mar, 1974; No. 57, May-June, 1975 - No. 59, Sept-Oct, 1975 (Edgar Rice Burroughs)
46-(52 pgs.)-Carson of Venus begins (origin), ends #56; Pellucidar feature; Weiss-a
3 6 9 16 22 28
47-59: 49-Origin Korak retold 2 4 6 8 11 14
NOTE: *All have covers by* ***Joe Kubert. Manning*** *strip reprints-No. 57-59.* ***Murphy Anderson*** *a-52.* ***Michael Kaluta*** *a-46-56.* ***Frank Thorne*** *a-46-51.*

KORE
Image Comics: Apr, 2003 - No. 5, Sept, 2003 ($2.95)
1-5: 1-Two covers by Capullo and Seeley; Seeley-a (p) 3.00

KORG: 70,000 B. C. (TV)
Charlton Publications: May, 1975 - No. 9, Nov, 1976 (Hanna-Barbera)
1,2: 1-Boyette-c/a. 2-Painted-c; Byrne text illos 2 4 6 11 16 20
3-9 2 4 6 8 11 14

KORNER KID COMICS: Four Star Publications: 1947 (Advertised, not pub.)

KOSMIC KAT ACTIVITY BOOK (See Deity)

GD 2.0 | VG 4.0 | FN 6.0 | VF 8.0 | VF/NM 9.0 | NM- 9.2

Image Comics: Aug, 1999 ($2.95, one-shot)
1-Stories and games by various 3.00

KRAZY KAT
Holt: 1946 (Hardcover)
Reprints daily & Sunday strips by Herriman 56 112 168 353 597 840
dust jacket only 43 86 129 267 446 625

KRAZY KAT (See Ace Comics & March of Comics No. 72, 87)

KRAZY KAT COMICS (...& Ignatz the Mouse early issues)
Dell Publ. Co./Gold Key: May-June, 1951 - F.C. #696, Apr, 1956; Jan, 1964 (None by Herriman)
1(1951) 9 18 27 61 103 145
2-5 (#5, 8-10/52) 5 10 15 35 55 75
Four Color 454,504 5 10 15 32 51 70
Four Color 548,619,696 (4/56) 5 10 15 30 48 65
1(10098-401)(1/64-Gold Key)(TV) 4 8 12 26 41 55

KRAZY KOMICS (1st Series) (Cindy Comics No. 27 on) (Also see Ziggy Pig)
Timely Comics (USA No. 1-21/JPC No. 22-26): July, 1942 - No. 26, Spr, 1947
1-Toughy Tomcat, Ziggy Pig (by Jaffee) & Silly Seal begin
71 142 213 454 777 1100
2 32 64 96 192 314 435
3-8,10 22 44 66 132 216 300
9-Hitler parody 23 46 69 136 223 310
11,13,14 17 34 51 100 158 215
12-Timely's entire art staff drew themselves into a Creeper story
27 54 81 160 263 365
15-(8-9/44)-Has "Super Soldier" by Pfc. Stan Lee 18 36 54 105 165 225
16-24,26: 16-(10-11/44). 26-Super Rabbit-c/story 15 30 45 85 130 175
25-Wacky Duck-c/story & begin; Kurtzman-a (6pgs.) 17 34 51 100 158 215

KRAZY KOMICS (2nd Series)
Timely/Marvel Comics: Aug, 1948 - No. 2, Nov, 1948
1-Wolverton (10 pgs.) & Kurtzman (8 pgs.)-a; Eustice Hayseed begins (Li'l Abner swipe)
43 86 129 271 461 650
2-Wolverton-a (10 pgs.); Powerhouse Pepper cameo
32 64 96 188 307 425

KRAZY KROW (Also see Dopey Duck, Film Funnies, Funny Frolics & Movie Tunes)
Marvel Comics (ZPC): Summer, 1945 - No. 3, Wint, 1945/46
1 22 44 66 128 209 290
2,3 15 30 45 84 127 170
I.W. Reprint #1('57), 2('58), 7 2 4 6 11 16 20

KRAZYLIFE (Becomes Nutty Life #2)
Fox Feature Syndicate: 1945 (no month)
1-Funny animal 20 40 60 117 189 260

KREE/SKRULL WAR STARRING THE AVENGERS, THE
Marvel Comics: Sept, 1983 - No. 2, Oct, 1983 ($2.50, 68 pgs., Baxter paper)
1,2 4.00
NOTE: ***Neal Adams*** *p-1r, 2.* ***Buscema*** *a-1r, 2r.* ***Simonson*** *a-1p; c-1p.*

KROFFT SUPERSHOW (TV)
Gold Key: Apr, 1978 - No. 6, Jan, 1979
1-Photo-c 3 6 9 18 27 35
2-6: 6-Photo-c 3 6 9 14 19 24

KRULL
Marvel Comics Group: Nov, 1983 - No. 2, Dec, 1983
1,2-Adaptation of film; r/Marvel Super Special. 1-Photo-c from movie 2.50

KRUSTY COMICS (TV)(See Simpsons Comics)
Bongo Comics: 1995 - No. 3, 1995 ($2.25, limited series)
1-3 2.50

KRYPTON CHRONICLES
DC Comics: Sept, 1981 - No. 3, Nov, 1981
1-3: 1-Buckler-c(p) 4.00

KRYPTO THE SUPERDOG (TV)
DC Comics: Nov, 2006 - No. 6, Apr, 2007 ($2.25)
1-6-Based on Cartoon Network series. 1-Origin retold 2.50

KULL
Dark Horse Comics: Nov, 2008 - No. 6, May, 2009 ($2.99)
1-6: 1-Nelson-s/Conrad-a; two covers by Andy Brase and Joe Kubert 3.00

Kull and the Barbarians #1 © Kull Prods.

Kurt Busiek's Astro City #4 © Jukebox

Lady Death #6 © Chaos!

GD 2.0 | VG 4.0 | FN 6.0 | VF 8.0 | VF/NM 9.0 | NM- 9.2

KULL AND THE BARBARIANS
Marvel Comics: May, 1975 - No. 3, Sept, 1975 ($1.00, B&W, magazine)
1-(84 pgs.) Andru/Wood-r/Kull #1; 2 pgs. Neal Adams; Gil Kane(p), Marie & John Severin-a(r); Krenkel text illo. 3 6 9 17 25 32
2,3: 2-(84 pgs.) Red Sonja by Chaykin begins; Solomon Kane by Weiss/Adams; Gil Kane-a; Solomon Kane pin-up by Wrightson. 3-(76 pgs.) Origin Red Sonja by Chaykin; Adams-a; Solomon Kane app. 3 6 9 14 19 24

KULL THE CONQUEROR (...the Destroyer #11 on; see Conan #1, Creatures on the Loose #10, Marvel Preview, Monsters on the Prowl)
Marvel Comics Group: June, 1971 - No. 2, Sept, 1971; No. 3, July, 1972 - No. 15, Aug, 1974; No. 16, Aug, 1976 - No. 29, Oct, 1978
1-Andru/Wood-a; 2nd app. & origin Kull; 15¢ issue 6 12 18 39 62 85
2-5: 2-3rd Kull app. Last 15¢ iss. 3-13: 20¢ issues. 3-Thulsa Doom-c/app. 3 6 9 18 27 35
6-10: 7-Thulsa Doom-c/app 2 4 6 10 14 18
11-15: 11-15-Ploog-a. 14,15: 25¢ issues 2 4 6 8 11 14
16-(Regular 25¢ edition)(8/76) 2 3 4 6 8 10
16-(30¢-c variant, limited distribution) 3 6 9 14 20 25
17-29: 21-23-(Reg. 30¢ editions) 2 3 4 6 8 10
21-23-(35¢-c variants, limited distribution) 3 6 9 20 40 60
NOTE: *No. 1, 2, 7-9, 11 are based on Robert E. Howard stories.* ***Alcala*** *a-17p, 18-20i; c-24.* ***Ditko*** *a-12r, 15r.* ***Gil Kane*** *c-15p, 21.* ***Nebres*** *a-22i-27i; c-25i, 27i.* ***Ploog*** *c-11, 12p, 13.* ***Severin*** *a-2-9i; c-2-10i, 19.* ***Starlin*** *c-14.*

KULL THE CONQUEROR
Marvel Comics Group: Dec, 1982 - No. 2, Mar, 1983 (52 pgs., Baxter paper)
1,2: 1-Buscema-a(p) 4.00

KULL THE CONQUEROR (No. 9,10 titled "Kull")
Marvel Comics Group: 5/83 - No. 10, 6/85 (52 pgs., Baxter paper)
V3#1-10: Buscema-a in #1-3,5-10 3.00
NOTE: *Bolton a-4. Golden painted c-3-8. Guice a-4p. Sienkiewicz a-4; c-2.*

KUNG FU (See Deadly Hands of..., & Master of...)

KUNG FU FIGHTER (See Richard Dragon...)

KURT BUSIEK'S ASTRO CITY (Limited series) (Also see Astro City: Local Heroes)
Image Comics (Juke Box Productions): Aug, 1995 - No. 6, Jan, 1996 ($2.25)
1-Kurt Busiek scripts, Brent Anderson-a & Alex Ross front & back-c begins; 1st app. Samaritan & Honor Guard (Cleopatra, MHP, Beautie, The Black Rapier, Quarrel & N-Forcer) 2 4 6 8 10 12
2-6: 2-1st app. The Silver Agent, The Old Soldier, & the "original" Honor Guard (Max O'Millions, Starwoman, the "original" Cleopatra, the "original" N-Forcer, the Bouncing Beatnik, Leopardman & Kitkat). 3-1st app. Jack-in-the-Box & The Deacon. 4-1st app. Winged Victory (cameo), The Hanged Man & The First Family. 5-1st app. Crackerjack, The Astro City Irregulars, Nightingale & Sunbird. 6-Origin Samaritan; 1st full app. Winged Victory 1 3 4 6 8 10
Life In The Big City-(8/96, $19.95, trade paperback)-r/Image Comics limited series w/sketchbook & cover gallery; Ross-c 20.00
Life In The Big City-(8/96, $49.95, hardcover, 1000 print run)-r/Image Comics limited series w/sketchbook & cover gallery; Ross-c 50.00

KURT BUSIEK'S ASTRO CITY (1st Homage Comics series)
Image Comics (Homage Comics): V2#1, Sept, 1996 - No. 15, Dec, 1998;
DC Comics (Homage Comics): No. 16, Mar, 1999 - No. 22, Aug, 2000 ($2.50)
1/2-(10/96)-The Hanged Man story; 1st app. The All-American & Slugger, The Lamplighter, The Time-Keeper & Eterneon 1 3 4 6 8 10
1/2-(1/98) 2nd printing w/new cover 2.50
1- Kurt Busiek scripts, Alex Ross-c, Brent Anderson-p & Will Blyberg-i begin; intro The Gentleman, Thunderhead & Helia. 1 2 3 5 6 8
1-(12/97, $4.95) "3-D Edition" w/glasses 5.00
2-Origin The First Family; Astra story 1 2 3 4 5 7
3-5: 4-1st app. The Crossbreed, Ironhorse, Glue Gun & The Confessor (cameo) 6.00
6-10 5.00
11-22: 14-20-Steeljack story arc. 16-(3/99) First DC issue 2.50
TPB-($19.95) Ross-c, r/#4-9, #1/2 w/sketchbook 20.00
Family Album TPB ($19.95) r/#1-3,10-13 20.00
The Tarnished Angel HC ($29.95) r/#14-20; new Ross dust jacket; sketch pages by Anderson & Ross; cover gallery with reference photos 30.00
The Tarnished Angel SC ($19.95) r/#14-20; new Ross-c 20.00

LABMAN
Image Comics: Nov, 1996 ($3.50, one-shot)
1-Allred-c 4.00

LAB RATS
DC Comics: June, 2002 - No. 8, Jan, 2003 ($2.50)

GD 2.0 | VG 4.0 | FN 6.0 | VF 8.0 | VF/NM 9.0 | NM- 9.2

1-8-John Byrne-s/a. 5,6-Superman app. 2.50

LABYRINTH
Marvel Comics Group: Nov, 1986 - No. 3, Jan, 1987 (Limited series)
1-3: David Bowie movie adaptation; r/Marvel Super Special #40 5.00

LA COSA NOSTROID (See Scud: The Disposible Assassin)
Fireman Press: Mar, 1996 - No. 9, 1998 ($2.95, B&W)
1-9-Dan Harmon-s/Rob Schrab-c/a 3.00

LAD: A DOG (Movie)
Dell Publishing Co.: 1961 - No. 2, July-Sept, 1962
Four Color 1303 4 8 12 28 44 60
2 4 8 12 24 37 50

LADY AND THE TRAMP (Disney, See Dell Giants & Movie Comics)
Dell Publishing Co.: No. 629, May, 1955 - No. 634, June, 1955
Four Color 629 (#1)-..with Jock 7 14 21 47 76 105
Four Color 634-...Album 5 10 15 32 51 70

LADY COP (See 1st Issue Special)

LADY DEATH (See Evil Ernie)
Chaos! Comics: Jan, 1994 - No. 3, Mar, 1994 ($2.75, limited series)
1/2-S. Hughes-c/a in all, 1/2 Velvet 1 2 3 4 5 7
1/2 Gold 1 3 4 6 8 10
1/2 Signed Limited Edition 2 4 6 8 10 12
1-($3.50)-Chromium-c 2 4 6 10 14 18
1-Commemorative 2 4 6 9 13 16
1-(9/96, $2.95) "Encore Presentation"; r/#1 3.00
2 1 2 3 5 6 8
3 5.00
... And Jade (4/02, $2.99) Augustyn-s/Reis-a 3.00
...And The Women of Chaos! Gallery #1 (11/96, $2.25) pin-ups by various 3.00
.../Bad Kitty (9/01, $2.99) Mota-c/a 3.00
.../Bedlam (6/02, $2.99) Augustyn-s/Reis-c 3.00
...By Steven Hughes (6/00, $2.95) Tribute issue to Steven Hughes 3.00
...By Steven Hughes Deluxe Edition(6/00, $15.95) 16.00
.../Chastity (1/02, $2.99) Mota-c/a; Augustyn-s 3.00
...Death Becomes Her #0 (11/97, $2.95) Hughes-c/a 3.00
...FAN Edition: All Hallow's Eve #1 (1/97, mail-in) 5.00
...In Lingerie #1 (8/95, $2.95) pin-ups, wraparound-c 3.00
...In Lingerie #1-Leather Edition (10,000) 12.00
...In Lingerie #1-Micro Premium Edition; Lady Demon-c (2,000) 35.00
...: Love Bites (3/01, $2.99) Kaminski-s/Luke Ross-a 3.00
.../Medieval Witchblade (8/01, $3.50) covers by Molenaar and Silvestri 3.50
.../Medieval Witchblade Preview Ed. (8/01, $1.99) Molenaar-c 2.50
...: Mischief Night (11/01, $2.99) Ostrander-s/Reis-a 3.00
...: Re-Imagined (7/02, $2.99) Gossett-c 3.00
...: River of Fear (4/01, $2.99) Bennett-a(p)/Cleavenger-c 3.00
...Swimsuit Special #1-($2.50)-Wraparound-c 3.00
...Swimsuit Special #1-Red velvet-c 14.00
...Swimsuit 2001 #1-(2/01, $2.99)-Reis-c; art by various 3.00
...: The Reckoning (7/94, $6.95)-r/#1-3 7.00
...: The Reckoning (8/95, $12.95)- new printing including Lady Death 1/2 & Swimsuit Special #1 13.00
.../Vampirella (3/99, $3.50) Hughes-c/a 3.50
.../Vampirella 2 (3/00, $3.50) Deodato-c/a 3.50
... Vs. Purgatori (12/99, $3.50) Deodato-a 3.50
... Vs. Vampirella Preview (2/00, $1.00) Deodato-a/c 2.50

LADY DEATH (Ongoing series)
Chaos! Comics: Feb, 1998 - No. 16, May, 1999 ($2.95)
1-16: 1-4: Pulido-s/Hughes-c/a. 5-8,13-16-Deodato-a. 9-11-Hughes-a 3.00
...Retribution (8/98, $2.95) Jadsen-a 3.00
...Retribution Premium Ed. 6.00

LADY DEATH: ALIVE
Chaos! Comics: May, 2001 - No. 4, Aug, 2001 ($2.99, limited series)
1-4-Ivan Reis-a; Lady Death becomes mortal 3.00

LADY DEATH: A MEDIEVAL TALE (Brian Pulido's...)
CG Entertainment: Mar, 2003 - No. 12, Apr, 2004 ($2.95)
1-12: 1-Brian Pulido-s/Ivan Reis-a; Lady Death in the CrossGen Universe 3.00
Vol.1 TPB (2003, $9.95) digest-sized reprint of #1-6 10.00

LADY DEATH: DARK ALLIANCE
Chaos! Comics: July, 2002 - No. 5, ($2.99, limited series)

Lady Death: The Gauntlet #1 © Chaos!

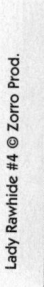

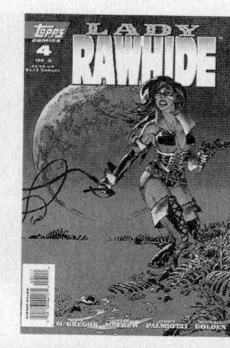

Lady Rawhide #4 © Zorro Prod.

Lance O'Casey #4 © FAW

GD 2.0 | VG 4.0 | FN 6.0 | VF 8.0 | VF/NM 9.0 | NM- 9.2

1-3-Reis-a/Ostrander-s 3.00

LADY DEATH: DARK MILLENNIUM
Chaos! Comics: Feb, 2000 - No. 3, Apr, 2000 ($2.95, limited series)
Preview (6/00, $5.00) 5.00
1-3-Ivan Reis-a 3.00

LADY DEATH: GODDESS RETURNS
Chaos! Comics: Jun, 2002 - No. 2, Aug, 2002 ($2.99, limited series)
1,2-Mota-a/Ostrander-s 3.00

LADY DEATH: HEARTBREAKER
Chaos! Comics: Mar, 2002 - No. 4, ($2.99, limited series)
1-Molenaar-a/Ostrander-s 3.00

LADY DEATH: JUDGEMENT WAR
Chaos! Comics: Nov, 1999 - No. 3, Jan, 2000 ($2.95, limited series)
Prelude (10/99) two covers 3.00
1-3-Ivan Reis-a 3.00

LADY DEATH: LAST RITES
Chaos! Comics: Oct, 2001 - No. 4, Feb, 2001 ($2.99, limited series)
1-4-Ivan Reis-a/Ostrander-s 3.00

LADY DEATH: THE CRUCIBLE
Chaos! Comics: Nov, 1996 - No. 6, Oct, 1997 ($3.50/$2.95, limited series)
1/2 4.00
1/2 Cloth Edition 8.00
1-Wraparound silver foil embossed-c 4.00
2-6-($2.95) 3.00

LADY DEATH: THE GAUNTLET
Chaos! Comics: Apr, 2002 - No. 2, May, 2002 ($2.99, limited series)
1,2: 1-J. Scott Campbell-c/redesign of Lady Death's outfit; Mota-a 3.00

LADY DEATH: THE ODYSSEY
Chaos! Comics: Apr, 1996 - No. 4, Aug, 1996 ($3.50/$2.95)
1-($1.50)-Sneak Peek Preview 2.50
1-($1.50)-Sneak Peek Preview Micro Premium Edition (2500 print run) 2 4 6 8 10 12
1-($3.50)-Embossed, wraparound goil foil-c 5.00
1-Black Onyx Edition (200 print run) 6 12 18 37 59 80
1-($19.95)-Premium Edition (10,000 print run) 20.00
2-4-($2.95) 3.00

LADY DEATH: THE RAPTURE
Chaos! Comics: Jun, 1999 - No. 4, Sept, 1999 ($2.95, limited series)
1-4-Ivan Reis-c/a; Pulido-s 3.00

LADY DEATH: THE WILD HUNT (Brian Pulido's...)
CG Entertainment: Apr, 2004 - No. 2, May, 2005 ($2.95)
1-2: 1-Brian Pulido-s/Jim Cheung-a 3.00

LADY DEATH: TRIBULATION
Chaos! Comics: Dec, 2000 - No. 4, Mar, 2001 ($2.95, limited series)
1-4-Ivan Reis-a; Kaminski-s 3.00

LADY DEATH II: BETWEEN HEAVEN & HELL
Chaos! Comics: Mar, 1995 - No. 4, July, 1995 ($3.50, limited series)
1-Chromium wraparound-c; Evil Ernie cameo 5.00
1-Commemorative (4,000), 1-Black Velvet-c 2 4 6 10 14 18
1-Gold 1 3 4 6 8 10
1-"Refractor" edition (5,000) 2 4 6 11 16 20
2-4 3.50
4-Lady Demon variant-c 1 2 3 5 7 9
Trade paperback-($12.95)-r/#1-4 13.00

LADY DEMON
Chaos! Comics: Mar, 2000 - No. 3, May, 2000 ($2.95, limited series)
1-3-Kaminski-s/Brewer-a 3.00
1-Premium Edition 10.00

LADY FOR A NIGHT (See Cinema Comics Herald)

LADY JUSTICE (See Neil Gaiman's...)

LADY LUCK (Formerly Smash #1-85) (Also see Spirit Sections #1)
Quality Comics Group: No. 86, Dec, 1949 - No. 90, Aug, 1950
86(#1) 92 184 276 584 1005 1425
87-90 65 130 195 416 708 1000

LADY PENDRAGON
Maximum Press: Mar, 1996 ($2.50)
1-Matt Hawkins script 2.50

LADY PENDRAGON
Image Comics: Nov, 1998 - No. 3, Jan, 1999 ($2.50, mini-series)
Preview (6/98) Flip book w/ Deity preview 3.00
1-3: 1-Matt Hawkins-s/Stinsman-a 3.00
1-($6.95) DF Ed. with variant-c by Jusko 7.00
2-($4.95)Variant edition 5.00
0-(3/99) Origin; flip book 2.50

LADY PENDRAGON (Volume 3)
Image Comics: Apr, 1999 - No. 9, Mar, 2000 ($2.50, mini-series)
1,2,4-6,8-10: 1-Matt Hawkins-s/Stinsman-a. 2-Peterson-c 2.50
3-Flip book w/Alley Cat preview (1st app.) 3.00
7-($3.95) Flip book; Stinsman-a/Cleavenger painted-a 4.00
Gallery Edition (10/99, $2.95) pin-ups 3.00
...Merlin (1/00, $2.95) Stinsman-a 3.00
.../ More Than Mortal (5/99, $2.50) Scott-s/Norton-a; 2 covers by Norton & Finch 2.50
.../ More Than Mortal Preview (2/99) Diamond Dateline supplement 2.50
Pilot Season: Lady Pendragon (5/08, $3.99) Hawkins-s/Eru-a; wraparound-c by Struzan 4.00

LADY RAWHIDE
Topps Comics: July, 1995 - No. 5, Mar, 1996 ($2.95, bi-monthly, limited series)
1-5: Don McGregor scripts & Mayhew-a. in all. 2-Stelfreeze-c. 3-Hughes-c. 4-Golden-c. 5-Julie Bell-c. 3.00
It Can't Happen Here TPB (8/99, $16.95) r/#1-5 17.00
Mini Comic 1 (7/95) Maroto-a; Zorro app. 2.50
Special Edition 1 (6/95, $3.95)-Reprints 4.00

LADY RAWHIDE (Volume 2)
Topps Comics: Oct, 1996 -No. 5, June, 1997 ($2.95, limited series)
1-5: 1-Julie Bell-c. 3.00

LADY RAWHIDE OTHER PEOPLE'S BLOOD (ZORRO'S ...)
Image Comics: Mar, 1999 - No. 5, July, 1999 ($2.95, B&W)
1-5-Reprints Lady Rawhide series in B&W 3.00

LADY SUPREME (See Asylum)(Also see Supreme & Kid Supreme)
Image Comics (Extreme): May, 1996 - No. 2, June, 1996 ($2.50, limited series)
1,2-Terry Moore -s: 1-Terry Moore-c. 2-Flip book w/Newmen preview 2.50

LAFF-A-LYMPICS (TV)(See The Funtastic World of Hanna-Barbera)
Marvel Comics: Mar, 1978 - No. 13, Mar, 1979 (Newsstand sales only)
1-Yogi Bear, Scooby Doo, Pixie & Dixie, etc. 3 6 9 18 27 35
2-8 3 6 9 14 19 24
9-13: 11-Jetsons x-over; 1 pg. illustrated bio of Mighty Mightor, Herculoids, Shazzan, Galaxy Trio & Space Ghost 3 6 9 16 23 30

LAFFY-DAFFY COMICS
Rural Home Publ. Co.: Feb, 1945 - No. 2, Mar, 1945
1,2-Funny animal 10 20 30 56 76 95

LANA (Little Lana No. 8 on)
Marvel Comics (MjMC): Aug, 1948 - No. 7, Aug, 1949 (Also see Annie Oakley)
1-Rusty, Millie begin 22 44 66 132 216 300
2-Kurtzman's "Hey Look" (1); last Rusty 14 28 42 82 121 160
3-7: 3-Nellie begins 11 22 33 64 90 115

LANCELOT & GUINEVERE (See Movie Classics)

LANCELOT LINK, SECRET CHIMP (TV)
Gold Key: Apr, 1971 - No. 8, Feb, 1973
1-Photo-c 6 12 18 41 66 90
2-8: 2-Photo-c 4 8 12 24 37 50

LANCELOT STRONG (See The Shield)

LANCE O'CASEY (See Mighty Midget & Whiz Comics)
Fawcett Publications: Spring, 1946 - No. 3, Fall, 1946; No. 4, Summer, 1948
1-Captain Marvel app. on-c 30 60 90 174 280 385
2 19 38 57 112 176 240
3,4 15 30 45 86 133 180

NOTE: *The cover for the 1st issue was done in 1942 but was not published until 1946. The cover shows 68 pages but actually has only 36 pages.*

LANCER (TV)(Western)
Gold Key: Feb, 1969 - No. 3, Sept, 1969 (All photo-c)
1 4 8 12 24 37 50

Land of Nod #3 © Jay Stephens

Large Feature Comic #29 © NYNS

Lassie #17 © MGM

	GD 2.0	VG 4.0	FN 6.0	VF 8.0	VF/NM 9.0	NM- 9.2
2,3	3	6	9	18	27	35

LAND OF NOD, THE
Dark Horse Comics: July, 1997 - No. 3, Feb, 1998 ($2.95, B&W)

	GD 2.0	VG 4.0	FN 6.0	VF 8.0	VF/NM 9.0	NM- 9.2
1-3-Jetcat; Jay Stephens-s/a						3.00

LAND OF OZ
Arrow Comics: 1998 - No. 9 ($2.95, B&W)

	GD 2.0	VG 4.0	FN 6.0	VF 8.0	VF/NM 9.0	NM- 9.2
1-9-Bishop-s/Bryan-s/a						3.00

LAND OF THE DEAD (George A. Romaro's...)
IDW Publishing: Aug, 2005 - No. 5 ($3.99, limited series)

	GD 2.0	VG 4.0	FN 6.0	VF 8.0	VF/NM 9.0	NM- 9.2
1-4-Adaptation of 2005 movie; Ryall-s/Rodriguez-a						4.00
TPB (3/06, $19.99) r/#1-5; cover gallery						20.00

LAND OF THE GIANTS (TV)
Gold Key: Nov, 1968 - No. 5, Sept, 1969 (All have photo-c)

	GD 2.0	VG 4.0	FN 6.0	VF 8.0	VF/NM 9.0	NM- 9.2
1	6	12	18	43	69	95
2-5	4	8	12	26	41	55

LAND OF THE LOST COMICS (Radio)
E. C. Comics: July-Aug, 1946 - No. 9, Spring, 1948

	GD 2.0	VG 4.0	FN 6.0	VF 8.0	VF/NM 9.0	NM- 9.2
1	39	78	117	232	381	530
2	24	48	72	140	230	320
3-9	20	40	60	120	195	270

LAND UNKNOWN, THE (Movie)
Dell Publishing Co.: No. 845, Sept, 1957

	GD 2.0	VG 4.0	FN 6.0	VF 8.0	VF/NM 9.0	NM- 9.2
Four Color 845-Alex Toth-a	11	22	33	78	139	200

LA PACIFICA
DC Comics (Paradox Press): 1994/1995 ($4.95, B&W, limited series, digest size, mature)

	GD 2.0	VG 4.0	FN 6.0	VF 8.0	VF/NM 9.0	NM- 9.2
1-3						5.00

LARAMIE (TV)
Dell Publishing Co.: Aug, 1960 - July, 1962 (All photo-c)

	GD 2.0	VG 4.0	FN 6.0	VF 8.0	VF/NM 9.0	NM- 9.2
Four Color 1125-Gil Kane/Heath-a	8	16	24	58	97	135
Four Color 1223,1284, 01-418-207 (7/62)	6	12	18	43	69	95

LAREDO (TV)
Gold Key: June, 1966

	GD 2.0	VG 4.0	FN 6.0	VF 8.0	VF/NM 9.0	NM- 9.2
1 (10179-606)-Photo-c	4	8	12	22	34	45

LARGE FEATURE COMIC (Formerly called Black & White in previous guides)
Dell Publishing Co.: 1939 - No. 13, 1943

Note: See individual alphabetical listings for prices

1 (Series I)-Dick Tracy Meets the Blank
3-Heigh-Yo Silver! The Lone Ranger (text & ill.)(76 pgs.); also exists as a Whitman #710; based on radio
6-Terry & the Pirates & The Dragon Lady; reprints dailies from 1936
8-Dick Tracy the Racket Buster
9-King of the Royal Mounted (Zane Grey's...)
10-(Scarce)-Gang Busters (No. appears on inside front cover); first slick cover (based on radio program)
13-Dick Tracy and Scottie of Scotland Yard
15-Dick Tracy and the Kidnapped Princes
17-Gang Busters (1941)
18-Phantasmo (see The Funnies #45)
20-Donald Duck Comic Paint Book (rarer than #16) (Disney)
21,22: 21-Private Buck. 22-Nuts & Jolts
24-Popeye in "Thimble Theatre" by Segar
26-Smitty
28-Grin and Bear It
30-Tillie the Toiler
2-Winnie Winkle (#1)
3-Dick Tracy
4-Tiny Tim (#1)
6-Terry and the Pirates; Caniff-a
8-Bugs Bunny (#1)('42)
9-Bringing Up Father
10-Popeye (Thimble Theatre)
2-Terry and the Pirates (#1)
4-Dick Tracy Gets His Man
5-Tarzan of the Apes (#1) by Harold Foster (origin); reprints 1st Tarzan dailies from 1929
7-(Scarce, 52 pgs.)-Hi-Yo Silver the Lone Ranger to the Rescue; also exists as a Whitman #715, based on radio program
11-Dick Tracy Foils the Mad Doc Hump
12-Smilin' Jack; no number on-c
14-Smilin' Jack Helps G-Men Solve a Case!
16-Donald Duck; 1st app. Daisy Duck on back cover (6/41-Disney)
19-Dumbo Comic Paint Book (Disney); partial-r from 4-Color #17
23-The Nebbs
25-Smilin' Jack-1st issue to show title on-c
27-Terry and the Pirates; Caniff-c/a
29-Moon Mullins
1 (Series II)-Peter Rabbit by Harrison Cady; arrival date-3/27/42
5-Toots and Casper
7-Pluto Saves the Ship (#1) (Disney)-Written by Carl Barks, Jack Hannah, & Nick George (Barks' 1st comic book work)
11-Barney Google and Snuffy Smith
13-(nn)-1001 Hours Of Fun; puzzles & games; by A. W. Nugent. This book was bound as #13 with Large Feature Comics in publisher's files
12-Private Buck

NOTE: *The Black & White Feature Books are oversized 8-1/2x11-3/8" comics with color covers and black and white interiors. The first nine issues all have rough, heavy stock covers and, except for #7, all have 76 pages, including covers. #7 and #10-on all have 52 pages. Beginning with #10 the covers are slick and thin and, because of their size, are difficult to handle without damaging. For this reason, they are seldom found in fine to mint condition. The paper stock, unlike Wow #1 and Capt. Marvel #1, is itself not unstable ...just thin. Issues #2,6, and 27 were reprinted in the early 1980s, identical except for the copyright notice on the first page.*

LARRY DOBY, BASEBALL HERO
Fawcett Publications: 1950 (Cleveland Indians)

	GD 2.0	VG 4.0	FN 6.0	VF 8.0	VF/NM 9.0	NM- 9.2
nn-Bill Ward-a; photo-c	77	154	231	489	837	1185

LARRY HARMON'S LAUREL AND HARDY (...Comics)
National Periodical Publ.: July-Aug, 1972 (Digest advertised, not published)

	GD 2.0	VG 4.0	FN 6.0	VF 8.0	VF/NM 9.0	NM- 9.2
1-Low print run	8	16	24	58	97	135

LARS OF MARS
Ziff-Davis Publishing Co.: No. 10, Apr-May, 1951 - No. 11, July-Aug, 1951 (Painted-c)
(Created by Jerry Siegel, editor)

	GD 2.0	VG 4.0	FN 6.0	VF 8.0	VF/NM 9.0	NM- 9.2
10-Origin; Anderson-a(3) in each; classic robot-c	87	174	261	553	952	1350
11-Gene Colan-a; classic-c	66	132	198	419	722	1025

LARS OF MARS 3-D
Eclipse Comics: Apr, 1987 ($2.50)

	GD 2.0	VG 4.0	FN 6.0	VF 8.0	VF/NM 9.0	NM- 9.2
1-r/Lars of Mars #10,11 in 3-D plus new story						4.00
2-D limited edition (B&W, 100 copies)						6.00

LASER ERASER & PRESSBUTTON (See Axel Pressbutton & Miracle Man 9)
Eclipse Comics: Nov, 1985 - No. 6, 1987 (95¢/$2.50, limited series)

	GD 2.0	VG 4.0	FN 6.0	VF 8.0	VF/NM 9.0	NM- 9.2
1-6: 5,6-(95¢)						2.50
...In 3-D 1 (8/86, $2.50)						4.00
2-D 1 (B&W, limited to 100 copies signed & numbered)						8.00

LASH LARUE WESTERN (Movie star; King of the bullwhip)(See Fawcett Movie Comic, Motion Picture Comics & Six-Gun Heroes)
Fawcett Publications: Sum, 1949 - No. 46, Jan, 1954 (36 pgs., 1-6,9,13,16-on)

	GD 2.0	VG 4.0	FN 6.0	VF 8.0	VF/NM 9.0	NM- 9.2
1-Lash & his horse Black Diamond begin; photo front/back-c begin	73	146	219	460	780	1100
2(11/49)	35	70	105	203	327	450
3-5	27	54	81	158	254	350
6,9: 6-Last photo back-c; intro. Frontier Phantom (Lash's twin brother)	22	44	66	129	207	285
7,8,10 (52pgs.)	23	46	69	135	218	300
11,12,14,15 (52pgs.)	15	30	45	94	147	200
13,16-20 (36pgs.)	15	30	45	86	133	180
21-30: 21-The Frontier Phantom app.	14	28	42	80	115	150
31-45	12	24	36	69	97	125
46-Last Fawcett issue & photo-c	13	26	39	74	105	135

LASH LARUE WESTERN (Continues from Fawcett series)
Charlton Comics: No. 47, Mar-Apr, 1954 - No. 84, June, 1961

	GD 2.0	VG 4.0	FN 6.0	VF 8.0	VF/NM 9.0	NM- 9.2
47-Photo-c	15	30	45	85	130	175
48	12	24	36	69	97	125
49-60, 67,68-(68 pgs.). 68-Check-a	10	20	30	54	72	90
61-66,69,70: 52-r/#8; 53-r/#22	9	18	27	50	65	80
71-83	8	16	24	40	50	60
84-Last issue	9	18	27	50	65	80

LASH LARUE WESTERN
AC Comics: 1990 ($3.50, 44 pgs) (24 pgs. of color, 16 pgs. of B&W)

	GD 2.0	VG 4.0	FN 6.0	VF 8.0	VF/NM 9.0	NM- 9.2
1-Photo covers; r/Lash #6; r/old movie posters						3.50
Annual 1 (1990, $2.95, B&W, 44 pgs.)-Photo covers						3.00

LASSIE (TV)(M-G-M's... #1-36; see Kite Fun Book)
Dell Publ. Co./Gold Key No. 59 (10/62) on: June, 1950 - No. 70, July, 1969

	GD 2.0	VG 4.0	FN 6.0	VF 8.0	VF/NM 9.0	NM- 9.2
1 (52 pgs.)-Photo-c; inside lists One Shot #282 in error	15	30	45	107	204	300
2-Painted-c begin	8	16	24	58	97	135
3-10	6	12	18	39	62	85
11-19: 12-Rocky Langford (Lassie's master) marries Gerry Lawrence. 15-1st app. Timbu	5	10	15	30	48	65
20-22-Matt Baker-a	5	10	15	34	55	75
23-38: 33-Robinson-a.	4	8	12	28	44	60

39-1st app. Timmy as Lassie picks up her TV family; photo-c

Last American #4 © MAR

Last Days of Animal Man #1 © DC

Last Temptation #2 © MAR

	GD 2.0	VG 4.0	FN 6.0	VF 8.0	VF/NM 9.0	NM- 9.2
40-50-Photo-c on all	6	12	18	39	62	85
51-58-Photo-c on all	4	8	12	28	44	60
59 (10/62)-1st Gold Key	4	8	12	26	41	55
60-70: 63-Last Timmy (10/63). 64-r/#19. 65-Forest Ranger Corey Stuart begins, ends #69. 70-Forest Rangers Bob Ericson & Scott Turner app. (Lassie's new masters)	4	8	12	28	44	60
	4	8	12	24	37	50
11193(1978, $1.95, 224 pgs., Golden Press)-Baker-r (92 pgs.)	4	8	12	26	41	55

NOTE: *Also see March of Comics #210, 217, 230, 254, 266, 278, 296, 308, 324,334, 346, 358, 370, 381, 394, 411, 432.*

LAST AMERICAN, THE
Marvel Comics (Epic): Dec, 1990 - No. 4, March, 1991 ($2.25, mini-series)
1-4: Alan Grant scripts 2.50

LAST AVENGERS STORY, THE (Last Avengers #1)
Marvel Comics: Nov, 1995 - No. 2, Dec, 1995 ($5.95, painted, limited series) (Alterniverse)
1,2: Peter David story; acetate-c in all. 1-New team (Hank Pym, Wasp, Human Torch, Cannonball, She-Hulk, Hotshot, Bombshell, Tommy Maximoff, Hawkeye & Mockingbird) forms to battle Ultron 59, Kang the Conqueror, The Grim Reaper & Oddball 6.00

LAST CHRISTMAS, THE
Image Comics: May, 2006 - No. 5, Oct, 2006 ($2.99, limited series)
1-5-Gerry Duggan & Brian Posehn-s/Rick Remender & Hilary Barta-a 3.00
TPB (2006, $14.99) r/#1-5; Patton Oswalt intro.; sketch pages and art 15.00

LAST DAY IN VIETNAM
Dark Horse Books: July, 2000 ($10.95, graphic novel)
nn-Will Eisner-s/a/c 11.00

LAST DAYS OF ANIMAL MAN, THE
DC Comics: July, 2009 - No. 6, Dec, 2009 ($2.99, limited series)
1-6: 1-Conway-s/Batista-a/Bolland-c. 3,4-Starfire app. 5,6-Future Justice League app. 3.00

LAST DAYS OF THE JUSTICE SOCIETY SPECIAL
DC Comics: 1986 ($2.50, one-shot, 68 pgs.)
1-62 pg. JSA story plus unpubbed G.A. pg. 2 4 6 8 10 12

LAST DEFENDERS, THE
Marvel Comics: May, 2008 - No. 6, Oct, 2008 ($2.99, limited series)
1-6-Nighthawk, She-Hulk, Colossus, and Blazing Skull; Muniz-a. 2-Deodato-c 3.00

LAST FANTASTIC FOUR STORY, THE
Marvel Comics: Oct, 2007 ($4.99, one-shot)
1-Stan Lee-s/John Romita, Jr.-a/c; Galactus app. 5.00

LAST GENERATION, THE
Black Tie Studios: 1986 - No. 5, 1989 ($1.95, B&W, high quality paper)
1-5 2.50
Book 1 (1989, $6.95)-By Caliber Press 7.00

LAST HERO STANDING (Characters from Spider-Girl's M2 universe)
Marvel Comics: Aug, 2005 - No. 5, Aug, 2005 ($2.99, weekly limited series)
1-5: 1-DeFalco-s/Olliffe-a. 4-Thor app. 5-Capt. America dies 3.00
TPB (2005, $13.99) r/#1-5 14.00

LAST HUNT, THE
Dell Publishing Co.: No. 678, Feb, 1956
Four Color 678-Movie, photo-c 7 14 21 45 73 100

LAST KISS
ACME Press (Eclipse): 1988 ($3.95, B&W, squarebound, 52 pgs.)
1-One story adapts E.A. Poe's The Black Cat 4.00

LAST OF THE COMANCHES (Movie) (See Wild Bill Hickok #28)
Avon Periodicals: 1953
nn-Kinstler-c/a, 21pgs.; Ravielli-a 15 30 45 88 137 185

LAST OF THE ERIES, THE (See American Graphics)

LAST OF THE FAST GUNS, THE
Dell Publishing Co.: No. 925, Aug, 1958
Four Color 925-Movie, photo-c 6 12 18 43 69 95

LAST OF THE MOHICANS (See King Classics & White Rider and...)

LAST OF THE VIKING HEROES, THE (Also see Silver Star #1)
Genesis West Comics: Mar, 1987 - No. 12 ($1.50/$1.95)
1-4,5A,5B,6-12: 4-Intro The Phantom Force, 1-Signed edition ($1.50), 5A-Kirby/Stevens-c. 5B,6 ($1.95). 7-Art Adams-c. 8-Kirby back-c. 4.00

Summer Special 1-3: 1-(1988)-Frazetta-c & illos. 2 (1990, $2.50)-A TMNT app. 3 (1991, $2.50)-Teenage Mutant Ninja Turtles 4.00
Summer Special 1-Signed edition (sold for $1.95) 4.00
NOTE: *Art Adams* c-7. *Byrne* c-3. *Kirby* c-1p, 5p. *Perez* c-2i. *Stevens* c-5Ai.

LAST ONE, THE
DC Comics (Vertigo): July, 1993 - No. 6, Dec, 1993 ($2.50, lim. series, mature)
1-6 2.50

LAST PLANET STANDING
Marvel Comics: July, 2006 - No. 5, Sept, 2006 ($2.99, limited series)
1-5-Galactus threatens Spider-Girl & Fantastic Five's M2 Earth; Avengers app.; Olliffe-a 3.00
TPB (2006, $13.99) r/series 14.00

LAST SHOT
Image Comics: Aug, 2001 - No. 4, Mar, 2002 ($2.95, limited series)
1-4: 1-Wraparound-c; by Studio XD 3.00
...: First Draw (5/01, $2.95) Introductory one-shot 3.00

LAST STARFIGHTER, THE
Marvel Comics Group: Oct, 1984 - No. 3, Dec, 1984 (75¢, movie adaptation)
1-3: r/Marvel Super Special; Guice-c 2.50

LAST TEMPTATION, THE
Marvel Comics: 1994 - No. 3, 1994 ($4.95, limited series)
1-3-Alice Cooper story; Neil Gaiman scripts; McKean-c; Zulli-a: 1-Two covers 5.00
HC (Dark Horse Comics, 2005, $14.95) r/#1-3; Gaiman intro. 15.00

LAST TRAIN FROM GUN HILL
Dell Publishing Co.: No. 1012, July, 1959
Four Color 1012-Movie, photo-c 8 16 24 56 93 130

LAST TRAIN TO DEADSVILLE: A CAL McDONALD MYSTERY (See Criminal Macabre)
Dark Horse Comics: May, 2004 - No. 4, Sept, 2004 ($2.99, limited series)
1-4-Steve Niles-s/Kelley Jones-a/c 3.00
TPB (2005, $14.95) r/series 15.00

LATEST ADVENTURES OF FOXY GRANDPA (See Foxy Grandpa)

LATEST COMICS (Super Duper No. 3?)
Spotlight Publ./Palace Promotions (Jubilee): Mar, 1945 - No. 2, 1945?
1-Super Duper 16 32 48 94 147 200
2-Bee-29 (nd); Jubilee in indicia blacked out 14 28 42 76 108 140

LAUGH
Archie Enterprises: June, 1987 - No. 29, Aug, 1991 (75¢/$1.00)
V2#1 5.00
2-10,14,24: 5-X-Mas issue. 14-1st app. Hot Dog. 24-Re-intro Super Duck 4.00
11-13,15-23,25-29: 19-X-Mas issue 3.00

LAUGH COMICS (Teenage) (Formerly Black Hood #9-19) (Laugh #226 on)
Archie Publications (Close-Up): No. 20, Fall, 1946 - No. 400, Apr, 1987

	GD 2.0	VG 4.0	FN 6.0	VF 8.0	VF/NM 9.0	NM- 9.2
20-Archie begins; Katy Keene & Taffy begin by Woggon; Suzie & Wilbur also begin; Archie covers begin	77	154	231	493	847	1200
21-23,25	39	78	117	236	388	540
24- "Pipsy" by Kirby (6 pgs.)	39	78	117	240	395	550
26-30	24	48	72	142	234	325
31-40	18	36	54	105	165	225
41-60: 41,54-Debbi by Woggon	14	28	42	80	115	150
61-80: 67-Debbi by Woggon	10	20	30	58	79	100
81-99	6	12	18	37	59	80
100	6	12	18	39	62	85
101-105,110,112,114-126: 125-Debbi app.	4	8	12	28	44	60
106-109,111,113-Neal Adams-a (1 pg.) in each	5	10	15	30	48	65
127-144: Super-hero app. in all (see note)	5	10	15	34	55	75
145-(4/63) Josie by DeCarlo begins	6	12	18	37	59	80
146-149-early Josie app. by DeCarlo	4	8	12	26	41	55
150,162,163,165,167,169,170-No Josie	3	6	9	18	27	35
151-161,164,168-Josie app. by DeCarlo	4	8	12	23	36	48
166-Beatles-c (1/65)	6	12	18	37	59	80
171-180, 200 (12/67)	3	6	9	16	23	30
181-199	3	6	9	14	19	24
201-240(3/71)	2	4	6	10	14	18
241-280(7/74)	2	4	6	9	12	15
281-299	2	4	6	8	10	12
300(3/76)	2	4	6	8	11	14
301-340 (7/79)	1	2	3	5	7	9
341-370 (1/82)	1	2	3	4	5	7

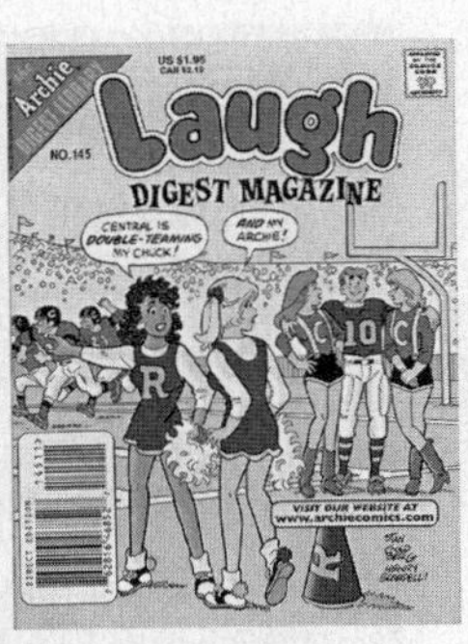

Laugh Digest Magazine #145 © AP

Lawbreakers Suspense Stories #15 © CC

Leading Comics #8 © DC

	GD 2.0	VG 4.0	FN 6.0	VF 8.0	VF/NM 9.0	NM- 9.2

371-380,385-399: 380-Cheryl Blossom app. 5.00
381-384,400: 381-384-Katy Keene app.; by Woggon-381,382 6.00

NOTE: *The Fly app. in 128, 129, 132, 134, 138, 139. Flygirl app. in 136, 137, 143. Flyman app. in 137. The Jaguar app. in 127, 130, 131, 133, 135, 140-142, 144. Josie app. in 145-149, 151-161, 164, 168. Katy Keene app. in 20-125, 129, 130, 133. Horror/Sci-Fi covers on 128-135, 137, 139. Many issues contain paper dolls. **Al Fagaly** c-20-29. **Montana** c-33, 36, 37, 42. **Bill Vigoda** c-30, 50.*

LAUGH COMICS DIGEST (...Magazine #23-89; Laugh Digest Mag. #90 on)
Archie Publ. (Close-Up No. 1, 3 on): 8/74; No. 2, 9/75; No. 3, 3/76 - No. 200, Apr, 2005
(Digest-size) (Josie and Sabrina app. in most issues)

1-Neal Adams-a 5 10 15 34 55 75
2,7,8,19-Neal Adams-a 3 6 9 20 30 40
3-6,9,10 3 6 9 16 22 28
11-18,20 2 4 6 11 16 20
21-40 2 4 6 9 13 16
41-60 1 3 4 6 8 10
61-80 1 2 3 5 6 8
81-99 5.00
100 6.00
101-138 3.00
139-200: 139-Begin $1.95-c. 148-Begin $1.99-c. 156-Begin $2.19-c. 180-Begin $2.39-c 2.50

NOTE: *Katy Keene in 23, 25, 27, 32-38, 40, 45-48, 50. The Fly-r in 19, 20. The Jaguar-r in 25, 27. Mr. Justice-r in 21. The Web-r in 23.*

LAUGH COMIX (Laugh Comics inside)(Formerly Top Notch Laugh; Suzie Comics No. 49 on)
MLJ Magazines: No. 46, Summer, 1944 - No. 48, Winter, 1944-45

46-Wilbur & Suzie in all; Harry Sahle-c 23 46 69 136 223 310
47,48: 47-Sahle-c. 48-Bill Vigoda-c 16 32 48 94 147 200

LAUGH-IN MAGAZINE (TV)(Magazine)
Laufer Publ. Co.: Oct, 1968 - No. 12, Oct, 1969 (50¢) (Satire)

V1#1 5 10 15 32 51 70
2-12 4 8 12 22 34 45

LAUREL & HARDY (See Larry Harmon's... & March of Comics No. 302, 314)

LAUREL AND HARDY (...Comics)
St. John Publ. Co.: 3/49 - No. 3, 9/49; No. 26, 11/55 - No. 28, 3/56 (No #4-25)

1 73 146 219 467 796 1125
2 40 80 120 242 401 560
3 31 62 93 182 296 410
26-28 (Reprints) 15 30 45 92 144 195

LAUREL AND HARDY (TV)
Dell Publishing Co.: Oct, 1962 - No. 4, Sept-Nov, 1963

12-423-210 (8-10/62) 6 12 18 43 69 95
2-4 (Dell) 4 8 12 28 44 60

LAUREL AND HARDY (Larry Harmon's...)
Gold Key: Jan, 1967 - No. 2, Oct, 1967

1-Photo back-c 4 8 12 28 44 60
2 4 8 12 22 34 45

LAUREL AND HARDY DIGEST: DC Comics. 1972 (Advertised, not published)

L.A.W., THE (LIVING ASSAULT WEAPONS)
DC Comics: Sept, 1999 - No. 6, Feb, 2000 ($2.50, limited series)

1-6-Blue Beetle, Question, Judomaster, Capt. Atom app.; Giordano-a. 5-JLA app. 2.50

LAW AGAINST CRIME (Law-Crime on cover)
Essenkay Publishing Co.: April, 1948 - No. 3, Aug, 1948 (Real Stories from Police Files)

1-(#1-3 are half funny animal, half crime stories)-L. B. Cole-c/a in all; electrocution-c
73 146 219 464 800 1135
2-L. B. Cole-c/a 54 108 162 346 591 835
3-Used in **SOTI**, pg. 180,181 & illo "The wish to hurt or kill couples in lovers' lanes;" reprinted in All-Famous Crime #9 68 136 204 432 746 1060

LAW AND ORDER
Maximum Press: Sept, 1995 - No. 2, 1995 ($2.50, unfinished limited series)

1,2 2.50

LAWBREAKERS (...Suspense Stories No. 10 on)
Law and Order Magazines (Charlton): Mar, 1951 - No. 9, Oct-Nov, 1952

1 41 82 123 251 418 585
2 23 46 69 136 223 310
3,5,6,8,9 20 40 60 115 185 255
4- "White Death" junkie story 25 50 75 147 241 335
7- "The Deadly Dopesters" drug story 25 50 75 147 241 335

LAWBREAKERS ALWAYS LOSE!
Marvel Comics (CBS): Spring, 1948 - No. 10, Oct, 1949

1-2pg. Kurtzman-a, "Giggles 'n' Grins" 36 72 108 216 351 485
2 20 40 60 114 182 250
3-5: 4-Vampire story 15 30 45 90 140 190
6(2/49)-Has editorial defense against charges of Dr. Wertham
17 34 51 100 158 215
7-Used in **SOTI**, illo "Comic-book philosophy" 31 62 93 182 296 410
8-10: 9,10-Photo-c 15 30 45 83 124 165

NOTE: ***Brodsky** c-4, 5. **Shores** c-1-3, 6-8.*

LAWBREAKERS SUSPENSE STORIES (Formerly Lawbreakers; Strange Suspense Stories No. 16 on)
Capitol Stories/Charlton Comics: No. 10, Jan, 1953 - No. 15, Nov, 1953

10 41 82 123 251 418 585
11 (3/53)-Severed tongues-c/story & woman negligee scene
148 296 444 947 1624 2300
12-14: 13-Giordano-c begin, end #15 27 54 81 160 263 365
15-Acid-in-face-c/story; hands dissolved in acid story
57 114 171 362 619 875

LAW-CRIME (See Law Against Crime)

LAWDOG
Marvel Comics (Epic Comics): May, 1993 - No. 10, Feb, 1993

1-10 2.50

LAWDOG/GRIMROD: TERROR AT THE CROSSROADS
Marvel Comics (Epic Comics): Sept, 1993 ($3.50)

1 3.50

LAWMAN (TV)
Dell Publishing Co.: No. 970, Feb, 1959 - No. 11, Apr-June, 1962 (All photo-c)

Four Color 970(#1) 12 24 36 85 155 225
Four Color 1035('60), 3(2-4/60)-Toth-a 8 16 24 54 90 125
4-11 6 12 18 43 69 95

LAW OF DREDD, THE (Also see Judge Dredd)
Quality Comics/Fleetway #8 on: 1989 - No. 33, 1992 ($1.50/$1.75)

1-33: Bolland a-1-6,8,10-12,14(2 pg),15,19 2.50

LAWRENCE (See Movie Classics)

LAZARUS CHURCHYARD
Tundra Publishing: June, 1992 - No. 3, 1992 ($3.95, 44 pgs., coated stock)

1-3 4.00
The Final Cut (Image, 1/01, $14.95, TPB) Reprints Ellis/D'Israeli strips 15.00

LAZARUS FIVE
DC Comics: July, 2000 - No. 5, Nov, 2000 ($2.50, limited series)

1-5-Harris-c/Abell-a(p) 2.50

LEADING COMICS
DC Comics: Jan. 1942

nn - Ashcan comic, not distributed to newsstands, only for in-house use. Cover art is Detective Comics #57 with interior being Star Spangled Comics #2 (no known sales)

LEADING COMICS (...Screen Comics No. 42 on)
National Periodical Publications: Winter, 1941-42 - No. 41, Feb-Mar, 1950

1-Origin The Seven Soldiers of Victory; Crimson Avenger, Green Arrow & Speedy, Shining Knight, The Vigilante, Star Spangled Kid & Stripesy begin; The Dummy (Vigilante villain) 1st app. 423 846 1269 3000 5250 7500
2-Meskin-a; Fred Ray-c 133 266 399 838 1419 2000
3 100 200 300 630 1065 1500
4,5 73 146 219 460 780 1100
6-10 57 114 171 359 605 850
11,12,14(Spring, 1945) 41 82 123 256 428 600
13-Classic robot-c 90 180 270 567 959 1350
15-(Sum,'45)-Contents change to funny animal 27 54 81 158 254 350
16-22,24-30: 16-Nero Fox-c begin, end #22 14 28 42 80 115 150
23-1st app. Peter Porkchops by Otto Feuer & begins 27 54 81 158 254 350
31,32,34-41: 34-41-Leading Screen... on-c only 12 24 36 67 94 120
33-(Scarce) 20 40 60 115 183 250

NOTE: ***Otto Feuer**-a most #15-on; **Rube Grossman**-a most #15-on;c-15-41. **Post** a-23-37, 39, 41.*

LEADING MAN
Image Comics: June, 2006 - No. 5, Feb, 2007 ($3.50, limited series)

1-5-B. Clay Moore-s/Jeremy Haun-a 3.50
TPB (2/07, $14.95) r/#1-5; sketch gallery 15.00

LEADING SCREEN COMICS (Formerly Leading Comics)
National Periodical Publ.: No. 42, Apr-May, 1950 - No. 77, Aug-Sept, 1955

League of Extraordinary Gentlemen #2 © Moore & O'Neill

Leave It to Chance #6 © Robinson & Smith

Legend of the Shield #7 © AP

	GD 2.0	VG 4.0	FN 6.0	VF 8.0	VF/NM 9.0	NM- 9.2
42-Peter Porkchops-c/stories continue	12	24	36	67	94	120
43-77	11	22	33	60	83	105

NOTE: *Grossman a-most. Mayer a-45-48, 50, 54-57, 60, 62-74, 75(3), 76, 77.*

LEAGUE OF CHAMPIONS, THE (Also see The Champions)
Hero Graphics: Dec, 1990 - No. 12, 1992 ($2.95, 52 pgs.)

1-12: 1-Flare app. 2-Origin Malice 3.00

LEAGUE OF EXTRAORDINARY GENTLEMEN, THE
America's Best Comics: Mar, 1999 - No. 6, Sept, 2000 ($2.95, limited series)

	GD	VG	FN	VF	VF/NM	NM-
1-Alan Moore-s/Kevin O'Neill-a	2	4	6	8	10	12
1-DF Edition ($10.00) O'Neill-c	2	4	6	9	12	15
2,3						6.00
4-6: 5-Revised printing with "Amaze 'Whirling Spray' Syringe" parody ad						4.00
5-Initial printing recalled because of "Marvel Co. Syringe" parody ad						270.00
... Compendium 1,2: 1-r/#1,2. 2-r/#3,4						6.00
Hardcover (2000, $24.95) r/#1-6 plus cover gallery						25.00

LEAGUE OF EXTRAORDINARY GENTLEMEN, THE (Volume 2)
America's Best Comics: Sept, 2002 - No. 6, Nov, 2003 ($3.50, limited series)

1-6-Alan Moore-s/Kevin O'Neill-a 4.00
... Bumper Compendium 1,2: 1-r/#1,2. 2-r/#3,4 6.00
... Black Dossier (HC, 2007, $29.99) new graphic novel; 3-D section with glasses; extras 30.00

LEAGUE OF EXTRAORDINARY GENTLEMEN CENTURY: 1910
Top Shelf Productions/Knockabout Comics: 2009 ($7.95, squarebound one-shot)

1-Alan Moore-s/Kevin O'Neill-a 8.00

LEAGUE OF JUSTICE
DC Comics (Elseworlds): 1996 - No. 2, 1996 ($5.95, 48 pgs., squarebound)

1,2: Magic-based alternate DC Universe story; Giordano-i 6.00

LEATHERFACE
Arpad Publishing: May (April on-c), 1991 - No. 4, May, 1992 ($2.75, painted-c)

1-4-Based on Texas Chainsaw movie; Dorman-c 1 2 3 5 7 9

LEATHERNECK THE MARINE (See Mighty Midget Comics)

LEAVE IT TO BEAVER (TV)
Dell Publishing Co.: No. 912, June, 1958; May-July, 1962 (All photo-c)

	GD	VG	FN	VF	VF/NM	NM-
Four Color 912	15	30	45	104	197	290
Four Color 999,1103,1191,1285, 01-428-207	13	26	39	90	165	240

LEAVE IT TO BINKY (Binky No. 72 on) (Super DC Giant) (No. 1-22: 52 pgs.)
National Periodical Publications: 2-3/48 - #60, 10/58; #61, 6-7/68 - #71, 2-3/70 (Teen-age humor)

	GD	VG	FN	VF	VF/NM	NM-
1-Lucy wears Superman costume	36	72	108	211	343	475
2	19	38	57	111	176	240
3,4	14	28	42	76	108	140
5-Superman cameo	18	36	54	105	165	225
6-10	12	24	36	67	94	120
11-14,16-22: Last 52 pg. issue	10	20	30	58	79	100
15-Scribbly story by Mayer	12	24	36	67	94	120
23-28,30-45: 45-Last pre-code (2/55)	9	18	27	50	65	80
29-Used in **POP**, pg. 78	9	18	27	52	69	85
46-60: 60-(10/58)	5	10	15	34	55	75
61 (6-7/68) 1950's reprints with art changes	6	12	18	39	62	85
62-69: 67-Last 12¢ issue	4	8	12	28	44	60
70-7pg. app. Bus Driver who looks like Ralph from Honeymooners	5	10	15	32	51	70
71-Last issue	5	10	15	30	48	65

NOTE: *Aragones-a-61, 62, 67. Drucker a-28. Mayer a-1, 2, 15. Created by Mayer.*

LEAVE IT TO CHANCE (Also see Promotional Comics section for FCBD Ed.)
Image Comics (Homage Comics): Sept, 1996 - No. 11, Sept, 1998; No. 13, July, 2002
DC Comics (Homage Comics): No. 12, Jun, 1999 ($2.50/$2.95/$4.95)

1-3: 1-Intro Chance Falconer & St. George; James Robinson scripts & Paul Smith-c/a 5.00
4-12: 12-(6/99) 3.00
13-(7/02, $4.95) includes sketch pages and pin-ups 5.00
Shaman's Rain TPB (1997, $9.95) r/#1-4 10.00
Shaman's Rain HC (2002, $14.95, over-sized 8 1/4" x 12") r/#1-4 15.00
Trick or Threat TPB (1997, $12.95) r/#5-8 13.00
Trick or Threat HC (2002, $14.95, over-sized 8 1/4" x 12") r/#5-8 15.00
Vol. 3: Monster Madness and Other Stories HC (2003, $14.95, 8 1/4" x 12") r/#9-11 15.00

LEE HUNTER, INDIAN FIGHTER
Dell Publishing Co.: No. 779, Mar, 1957; No. 904, May, 1958

	GD	VG	FN	VF	VF/NM	NM-
Four Color 779 (#1)	5	10	15	34	55	75
Four Color 904	4	8	12	26	41	55

LEFT-HANDED GUN, THE (Movie)
Dell Publishing Co.: No. 913, July, 1958

Four Color 913-Paul Newman photo-c 9 18 27 63 107 150

LEGACY
Majestic Entertainment: Oct, 1993 - No. 2, Nov, 1993; No. 0, 1994 ($2.25)

1-2,0: 1-Glow-in-the-dark-c. 0-Platinum 2.50

LEGACY
Image Comics: May, 2003 - No. 4, Feb, 2004 ($2.95)

1-4: 1-Francisco-a/Treffiletti-s 3.00

LEGACY OF KAIN (Based on the Eidos video game)
Top Cow Productions: Oct, 1999; Jan, 2004 ($2.99)

...Defiance 1 (1/04, $2.99) Cha-c; Kirkham-a 3.00
...Soul Reaver 1 (10/99, Diamond Dateline supplement) Benitez-c 2.50

LEGEND
DC Comics (WildStorm): Apr, 2005 - No. 4, July, 2005 ($5.95/$5.99, limited series)

1-4-Howard Chaykin-s/Russ Heath-a; inspired by Philip Wylie's novel "Gladiator" 6.00

LEGENDARY TALESPINNERS
Dynamite Entertainment: 2010 - Present ($3.99)

1-Kuhoric-s/Bond-a; two covers 4.00

LEGEND OF CUSTER, THE (TV)
Dell Publishing Co.: Jan, 1968

1-Wayne Maunder photo-c 3 6 9 18 27 35

LEGEND OF ISIS
Alias Entertainment: May, 2005 - Present ($2.99)

1-5: 1-Three covers; Ottney-s/Fontana-a 3.00
...: Beginnings TPB (5/05, $9.99) Ottney-s 10.00

LEGEND OF JESSE JAMES, THE (TV)
Gold Key: Feb, 1966

10172-602-Photo-c 3 6 9 18 27 35

LEGEND OF KAMUI, THE (See Kamui)

LEGEND OF LOBO, THE (See Movie Comics)

LEGEND OF MOTHER SARAH (Manga)
Dark Horse Comics: Apr, 1995 - No. 8, Nov, 1995 ($2.50, limited series)

1-8: Katsuhiro Otomo scripts 4.00

LEGEND OF MOTHER SARAH: CITY OF THE ANGELS (Manga)
Dark Horse Comics: Oct, 1996 - No. 9 ($3.95, B&W, limited series)

1(10/96), 2(12/97),3-9: Otomo scripts 4.00

LEGEND OF MOTHER SARAH: CITY OF THE CHILDREN (Manga)
Dark Horse Comics: Jan, 1996 - No. 7, July, 1996 ($3.95, B&W, limited series)

1-7:Otomo scripts 4.00

LEGEND OF SUPREME
Image Comics (Extreme): Dec, 1994 - No. 3, Feb, 1995 ($2.50, limited series)

1-3 2.50

LEGEND OF THE ELFLORD
DavDez Arts: July, 1998 - No. 2, Sept, 1998 ($2.95)

1,2-Barry Blair & Colin Chin-s/a 3.00

LEGEND OF THE HAWKMAN
DC Comics: 2000 - No. 3, 2000 ($4.95, limited series)

1-3-Raab-s/Lark-c/a 5.00

LEGEND OF THE SHIELD, THE
DC Comics (Impact Comics): July, 1991 - No. 16, Oct, 1992 ($1.00)

1-16: 6,7-The Fly x-over. 12-Contains trading card 2.50
Annual 1 (1992, $2.50, 68 pgs.)-Snyder-a; w/trading card 2.50

LEGEND OF WONDER WOMAN, THE
DC Comics: May, 1986 - No. 4, Aug, 1986 (75¢, limited series)

1-4 4.00

LEGEND OF YOUNG DICK TURPIN, THE (Disney)(TV)
Gold Key: May, 1966

1 (10176-605)-Photo/painted-c 3 6 9 18 27 35

LEGEND OF ZELDA, THE (Link: The Legend... in indicia)
Valiant Comics: 1990 - No. 4, 1990 ($1.95, coated stiff-c) V2#1, 1990 - No. 5, 1990 ($1.50)

Legends of Daniel Boone #5 © DC

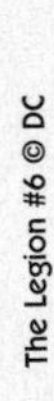
The Legion #6 © DC

Legionnaires #14 © DC

GD 2.0 | VG 4.0 | FN 6.0 | VF 8.0 | VF/NM 9.0 | NM- 9.2

GD 2.0 | VG 4.0 | FN 6.0 | VF 8.0 | VF/NM 9.0 | NM- 9.2

1-4: 4-Layton-c(i) 3.00
V2#1-5 3.00

LEGENDS
DC Comics: Nov, 1986 - No. 6, Apr, 1987 (75¢, limited series)
1-5: 1-Byrne-c/a(p) in all; 1st app. new Capt. Marvel. 3-1st app. new Suicide Squad; death of Blockbuster 5.00
6-1st app. new Justice League 1 2 3 4 5 7

LEGENDS OF DANIEL BOONE, THE (...Frontier Scout)
National Periodical Publications: Oct-Nov, 1955 - No. 8, Dec-Jan, 1956-57
1 (Scarce)-Nick Cardy c-1-8 56 112 168 353 594 835
2 (Scarce) 41 82 123 250 413 575
3-8 (Scarce) 35 70 105 203 327 450

LEGENDS OF NASCAR, THE
Vortex Comics: Nov, 1990 - No. 14, 1992? (#1 3rd printing (1/91) says 2nd printing inside)
1-Bill Elliott biog.; Trimpe-a ($1.50) 5.00
1-2nd printing (11/90, $2.00) 2.50
1-3rd print; contains Maxx racecards ($3.00) 3.00
2-14: 2-Richard Petty. 3-Ken Schrader (7/91). 4-Bobby Allison; Spiegle-a(p); Adkins part-i. 5-Sterling Marlin. 6-Bill Elliott. 7-Junior Johnson; Spiegle-c/a. 8-Benny Parsons; Heck-a 3.00
1-13-Hologram cover versions. 2-Hologram shows Bill Elliott's car by mistake (all are numbered & limited) 5.00
2-Hologram corrected version 5.00
Christmas Special ($5.95) 6.00

LEGENDS OF THE DARK CLAW
DC Comics (Amalgam): Apr, 1996 ($1.95)
1-Jim Balent-c/a 3.00

LEGENDS OF THE DARK KNIGHT (See Batman: ...)

LEGENDS OF THE DC UNIVERSE
DC Comics: Feb, 1998 - No. 41, June, 2001 ($1.95/$1.99/$2.50)
1-13,15-21: 1-3-Superman; Robinson-s/Semeiks-a/Orbik-painted-c. 4,5-Wonder Woman; Deodato-a/Rude painted-c. 8-GL/GA, O'Neil-s. 10,11-Batgirl; Dodson-a. 12,13-Justice League. 15-17-Flash. 18-Kid Flash; Guice-a. 19-Impulse; prelude to JLApe Annuals. 20,21-Abin Sur 3.00
14-($3.95) Jimmy Olsen; Kirby-esque-c by Rude 4.00
22-27,30: 22,23-Superman; Rude-c/Ladronn-a. 26,27-Aquaman/Joker 2.50
28,29: Green Lantern & the Atom; Gil Kane-a; covers by Kane and Ross 2.50
31,32: 32-Begin $2.50-c; Wonder Woman; Texeira-c 2.50
33-36-Hal Jordan as The Spectre; DeMatteis-s/Zulli-a; Hale painted-c 2.50
37-41: 37,38-Kyle Rayner. 39-Superman. 40,41-Atom; Harris-c 2.50
... Crisis on Infinite Earths 1 (2/99, $4.95) Untold story during and after Crisis on Infinite Earths #4; Wolfman-s/Ryan-a/Orbik-c 5.00
... 80 Page Giant 1 (9/98, $4.95) Stories and art by various incl. Ditko, Perez, Gibbons, Mumy; Joe Kubert-c 5.00
... 80 Page Giant 2 (1/00, $4.95) Stories and art by various incl. Challengers by Art Adams; Sean Phillips-c 5.00
... 3-D Gallery (12/98, $2.95) Pin-ups w/glasses 3.00

LEGENDS OF THE LEGION (See Legion of Super-Heroes)
DC Comics: Feb, 1998 - No. 4, May, 1998 ($2.25, limited series)
1-4:1-Origin-s of Ultra Boy. 2-Spark. 3-Umbra. 4-Star Boy 3.00

LEGENDS OF THE STARGRAZERS (See Vanguard Illustrated #2)
Innovation Publishing: Aug, 1989 - No. 6, 1990 ($1.95, limited series, mature)
1-6: 1-Redondo part inks 2.50

LEGENDS OF THE WORLD'S FINEST (See World's Finest)
DC Comics: 1994 - No. 3, 1994 ($4.95, squarebound, limited series)
1-3: Simonson scripts; Brereton-c/a; embossed foil logos 6.00
TPB-(1995, $14.95) r/#1-3 15.00

L.E.G.I.O.N. (The # to right of title represents year of print)(Also see Lobo & R.E.B.E.L.S.)
DC Comics: Feb, 1989 - No. 70, Sept, 1994 ($1.50/$1.75)
1-Giffen plots/breakdowns in #1-12,28 5.00
2-22,24-47: 3-Lobo app. #3 on. 4-1st Lobo-c this title. 5-Lobo joins L.E.G.I.O.N. 13-Lar Gand app. 16-Lar Gand joins L.E.G.I.O.N., leaves #19. 31-Capt. Marvel app. 35-L.E.G.I.O.N. '92 begins 3.00
23,70-($2.50, 52 pgs.)-L.E.G.I.O.N. '91 begins. 70-Zero Hour 4.00
48,49,51-69: 48-Begin $1.75-c. 63-L.E.G.I.O.N. '94 begins; Superman x-over 3.00
50-($3.50, 68 pgs.) 4.00
Annual 1-5 ('90-94, 68 pgs.): 1-Lobo, Superman app. 2-Alan Grant scripts. 5-Elseworlds story; Lobo app. 4.00
NOTE: *Alan Grant scripts in #1-39, 51, Annual 1, 2.*

LEGION, THE (Continued from Legion Lost & Legion Worlds)
DC Comics: Dec, 2001 - No. 38, Oct, 2004 ($2.50)
1-Abnett & Lanning-s; Coipel & Lanning-c/a 4.00
2-24: 3-8-Ra's al Ghul app. 5-Snejbjerg-a. 9-DeStefano-a. 12-Legion vs. JLA. 16-Fatal Five app.; Walker-a 17,18-Ra's al Ghul app. 20-23-Universo app. 2.50
25-($3.95) Art by Harris, Cockrum, Rivoche; teenage Clark Kent app.; Harris-c 4.00
26-38-Superboy in classic costume. 26-30-Darkseid app. 31-Giffen-a. 35-38-Jurgens-a 2.50
...Secret Files 3003 (1/04, $4.95) Kirk-a, Harris-c/a; Superboy app. 5.00
...Foundations TPB (2004, $19.95) r/#25-30 & Secret Files 3003; Harris-c 20.00

LEGION LOST (Continued from Legion of Super-Heroes [4th series] #125)
DC Comics: May, 2000 - No. 12, Apr, 2001 ($2.50, limited series)
1-Abnett & Lanning-s. Coipel & Lanning-c/a 1 2 3 4 5 7
2-12-Abnett & Lanning-s. Coipel & Lanning-c/a in most. 4,9-Alixe-a 3.00

LEGIONNAIRES (See Legion of Super-Heroes #40, 41 & Showcase 95 #6)
DC Comics: Apr, 1992 - No. 81, Mar, 2000 ($1.25/$1.50/$2.25)
0-(10/94)-Zero Hour restart of Legion; released between #18 & #19 2.50
1-49,51-77: 1-(4/92)-Chris Sprouse-c/a; polybagged w/SkyBox trading card. 11-Kid Quantum joins. 18-(9/94)-Zero Hour. 19(11/94). 37-Valor (Lar Gand) becomes M'onel (5/96). 43-Legion tryouts; reintro Princess Projectra, Shadow Lass & others. 47-Forms one cover image with LSH #91. 60-Karate Kid & Kid Quantum join. 61-Silver Age & 70's Legion app. 76-Return of Wildfire. 79,80-Coipel-c/a; Legion vs. the Blight 2.50
50-($3.95) Pullout poster by Davis/Farmer 4.00
#1,000,000 (11/98) Sean Phillips-a 2.50
Annual 1,3 ('94,'96 $2.95)-1-Elseworlds-s. 3-Legends of the Dead Earth-s 3.00
Annual 2 (1995, $3.95)-Year One-s 4.50

LEGIONNAIRES THREE
DC Comics: Jan, 1986 - No. 4, May, 1986 (75¢, limited series)
1-4 3.00

LEGION OF MONSTERS (Also see Marvel Premiere #28 & Marvel Preview #8)
Marvel Comics Group: Sept, 1975 ($1.00, B&W, magazine, 76 pgs.)
1-Origin & 1st app. Legion of Monsters; Neal Adams-c; Morrow-a; origin & only app. The Manphibian; Frankenstein by Mayerik; Bram Stoker's Dracula adaptation; Reese-a; painted-c (#2 was advertised with Morbius & Satana, but was never published) 5 10 15 34 55 75

LEGION OF MONSTERS (One-shots)
Marvel Comics: Apr, 2007 - Sept, 2007 ($2.99)
... Man-Thing (5/07) Huston-s/Janson-a/Land-c; Simon Garth: Zombie by Ted McKeever 3.00
... Morbius (9/07) Cahill-s/Gaydos-a/Land-c; Dracula w/Finch-a/Cebulski-s 3.00
... Satana (8/07) Furth-s/Andrasofszky-a/Land-c; Living Mummy by Hickman 3.00
... Werewolf By Night (4/07) Carey-s/Land-a/c; Monster of Frankenstein by Skottie Young 3.00
HC (2007, $24.99, dustjacket) oversized r/series and classic stories; sketch pages 25.00

LEGION OF NIGHT, THE
Marvel Comics: Oct, 1991 - No. 2, Oct, 1991 ($4.95, 52 pgs.)
1,2-Whilce Portacio-c/a(p) 5.00

LEGION OF SUBSTITUTE HEROES SPECIAL (See Adventure Comics #306)
DC Comics: July, 1985 ($1.25, one-shot, 52 pgs.)
1-Giffen-c/a(p) 3.00

LEGION OF SUPER-HEROES (See Action Comics, Adventure, All New Collectors Edition, Legionnaires, Legends of the Legion, Limited Collectors Edition, Secrets of the..., Superboy & Superman)
National Periodical Publications: Feb, 1973 - No. 4, July-Aug, 1973
1-Legion & Tommy Tomorrow reprints begin 3 6 9 18 27 35
2-4: 2-Forte-r. 3-r/Adv. #340. Action #240. 4-r/Adv. #341, Action #233; Mooney-r 2 4 6 11 16 20

LEGION OF SUPER-HEROES, THE (Formerly Superboy and...; Tales of The Legion No. 314 on)
DC Comics: No. 259, Jan, 1980 - No. 313, July, 1984
259(#1)-Superboy leaves Legion 2 4 6 8 11 14
260-270,285-289: 265-Contains 28 pg. insert "Superman & the TRS-80 computer"; origin Tyroc; Tyroc leaves Legion 6.00
261,263,264,266-(Whitman variants; low print run; no cover #'s) 2 4 6 8 11 14
271-284: 272-Blok joins; origin; 20 pg. insert-Dial 'H' For Hero. 277-Intro. Reflecto. 280-Superboy re-joins Legion. 282-Origin Reflecto. 283-Origin Wildfire 6.00
290-294-Great Darkness saga. 294-Double size (52 pgs.) 1 2 3 5 7 9
295-299,301-313: 297-Origin retold. 298-Free 16 pg. Amethyst preview. 306-Brief origin Star Boy (Swan art). 311-Colan-a 3.00

Legion of Super-Heroes #269 © DC

Legion of Super-Heroes (5th series) #37 © DC

Legion of Super-Heroes in the 31st Century #15 © DC

GD 2.0 | VG 4.0 | FN 6.0 | VF 8.0 | VF/NM 9.0 | NM- 9.2

300-(68 pgs., Mando paper)-Anniversary issue; has c/a by almost everyone at DC 5.00
Annual 1-3(82-84, 52 pgs.)-1-Giffen-c/a; 1st app./origin new Invisible Kid who joins Legion. 2-Karate Kid & Princess Projectra wed & resign 3.00
...The Great Darkness Saga (1989, $17.95, 196 pgs.)-r/LSH #287,290-294 & Annual #3; Giffen-c/a 2 4 6 10 14 18

NOTE: ***Aparo** c-282, 283, 300(part). **Austin** c-268i. **Buckler** c-273p, 274p, 276p. **Colan** a-311p. **Ditko** a(p)-267, 268, 272, 274, 276, 281. **Giffen** a-285-313p, Annual 1p; c-287p, 288p, 289, 290p, 291p, 292, 293, 294-299p, 300, 301-313p, Annual 1p, 2p. **Perez** c-268p, 277-280, 281p. **Starlin** a-265. **Staton** a-259p, 260p, 280. **Tuska** a-308p.*

LEGION OF SUPER-HEROES (3rd Series) (Reprinted in Tales of the Legion)
DC Comics: Aug, 1984 - No. 63, Aug, 1989 ($1.25/$1.75, deluxe format)

1-Silver ink logo 5.00
2-36,39-44,46-49,51-62: 4-Death of Karate Kid. 5-Death of Nemesis Kid. 12-Cosmic Boy, Lightning Lad, & Saturn Girl resign. 14-Intro new members: Tellus, Sensor Girl, Quislet. 15-17-Crisis tie-ins. 18-Crisis x-over. 25-Sensor Girl i.d. revealed as Princess Projectra. 35-Saturn Girl rejoins. 42,43-Millennium tie-ins. 44-Origin Quislet 3.00
37,38-Death of Superboy 2 4 6 8 11 14
45,50: 45 ($2.95, 68 pgs.)-Anniversary ish. 50-Double size ($2.50-c) 4.00
63-Final issue 4.00
Annual 1-4 (10/85-'88, 52 pgs.)-1-Crisis tie-in 3.00
...: An Eye For An Eye TPB (2007, $17.99)-r/#1-6; intro by Paul Levitz; cover gallery 18.00
...: The More Things Change TPB (2008, $17.99)-r/#7-13; cover gallery 18.00

NOTE: ***Byrne** c-36p. **Giffen** a(p)-1, 2, 50-55, 57-63, Annual 1p, 2; c-1-5p, 54p, Annual 1. **Orlando** a-6p. **Steacy** c-45-50, Annual 3.*

LEGION OF SUPER-HEROES (4th Series)
DC Comics: Nov, 1989 - No. 125, Mar, 2000 ($1.75/$1.95/$2.25)

0-(10/94)-Zero Hour restart of Legion; released between #61 & #62 2.50
1-Giffen-c/a(p)/scripts begin (4 pg.-a only #18) 4.00
2-20,26-49,51-53,55-58: 4-Mon-El (Lar Gand) destroys Time Trapper, changes reality. 5-Alt. reality story where Mordru rules all; Ferro Lad app. 6-1st app. of Laurel Gand (Lar Gand's cousin). 8-Origin. 13-Free poster by Giffen showing new costumes. 15-(2/91)-1st reference of Lar Gand as Valor. 26-New map of headquarters. 34-Six pg. preview of Timber Wolf mini-series. 40-Minor Legionnaires app. 41-(3/93)-SW6 Legion renamed Legionnaires w/new costumes and some new code-names 3.00
21-25: 21-24-Lobo & Darkseid storyline. 24-Cameo SW6 younger Legion duplicates. 25-SW6 Legion full intro. 3.50
50-($3.50, 68 pgs.) 4.00
54-($2.95)-Die-cut & foil stamped-c 4.00
59-99: 61-(9/94)-Zero Hour. 62-(11/94). 75-XS travels back to the 20th Century (cont'd in Impulse #9). 77-Origin of Brainiac 5. 81-Reintro Sun Boy. 85-Half of the Legion sent to the 20th century, Superman-c/app. 86-Final Night. 87-Deadman-c/app. 88-Impulse-c/app. Adventure Comics #247 cover swipe. 91-Forms one cover image with Legionnaires #47. 96-Wedding of Ultra Boy and Apparition. 99-Robin, Impulse, Superboy app. 2.50
100-($5.95, 96 pgs.)-Legionnaires return to the 30th Century; gatefold-c; 5 stories-art by Simonson, Davis and others 1 2 3 4 5 7
101-121: 101-Armstrong-a(p) begins. 105-Legion past & present vs. Time Trapper. 109-Moder-a. 110-Thunder joins. 114,115-Bizarro Legion. 120,121-Fatal Five. 2.50
122-124: 122,123-Coipel-c/a. 124-Coipel-c 3.00
125-Leads into "Legion Lost" maxi-series; Coipel-c 5.00
#1,000,000 (11/98) Giffen-a 2.50
Annual 1-5 (1990-1994, $3.50, 68 pgs.): 4-Bloodlines. 5-Elseworlds story 3.50
Annual 6 (1995,$3.95)-Year One story 4.00
Annual 7 (1996, $3.50, 48 pgs.)-Legends of the Dead Earth story; intro 75th Century Legion of Super-Heroes; Wildfire app. 3.50
Legion: Secret Files 1 (1/98, $4.95) Retold origin & pin-ups 5.00
Legion: Secret Files 2 (6/99, $4.95) Story and profile pages 5.00
The Beginning of Tomorrow TPB ('99, $17.95) r/post-Zero Hour reboot 18.00

NOTE: ***Giffen** a-1-24; breakdowns-26-32, 34-36; c-1-7, 8(part), 9-24. **Brandon Peterson** a(p)-15(1st for DC), 16, 18, Annual 2(54 pgs.); c-Annual 2p. **Swan/Anderson** c-8(part).*

LEGION OF SUPER-HEROES (5th Series) (Title becomes Supergirl and the Legion of Super-Heroes #16-36) (Intro. in Teen Titans/Legion Special)
DC Comics: Feb, 2005 - No. 15, Apr, 2006; No. 37, Feb, 2008 - No. 50, Mar, 2009 ($2.95/$2.99)

1-15: 1-Waid-s/Kitson-a/c. 4-Kirk & Gibbons-a. 9-Jeanty-a. 15-Dawnstar, Tyroc, Blok-c 3.00
37-50: 37-Shooter-s/Manapul-a begin; two interlocking covers. 50-Wraparound cover 3.00
44-Variant-c by Neal Adams 5.00
... Death of a Dream TPB ('06, $14.99) r/#7-13 15.00
... Enemy Manifest HC ('09, $24.99, dustjacket) r/#45-50 25.00
... Enemy Rising HC ('08, $19.99, dustjacket) r/#37-44 20.00
... Enemy Rising SC ('09, $14.99) r/#37-44 15.00
...: 1050 Years of the Future TPB ('08, $19.99) r/greatest tales of their 50 year history 20.00
... Teenage Revolution TPB ('05, $14.99) r/#1-6 & Teen Titans/Legion Spec.; sketch pages 15.00

LEGION OF SUPER-HEROES IN THE 31ST CENTURY (Based on the animated series)

GD 2.0 | VG 4.0 | FN 6.0 | VF 8.0 | VF/NM 9.0 | NM- 9.2

DC Comics: June, 2007 - No. 20, Jan, 2009 ($2.25)

1-20: 1-Chynna Clugston-a; Fatal Five app. 6-Green Lantern Corps app. 15-Impulse app. 2.25
...: Tomorrow's Heroes (2008, $14.99) r/#1-7; cover gallery 15.00

LEGION: PROPHETS (Prelude to 2010 movie)
IDW Publishing: Nov, 2009 - No. 4, Dec, 2009 ($3.99, limited series)

1-4: Stewart & Waltz-s. 1-Muriel-a. 2-Holder-a. 3-Paronzini-a. 4-Gaydos-a 4.00

LEGION: SCIENCE POLICE (See Legion of Super-Heroes)
DC Comics: Aug, 1998 - No. 4, Nov, 1998 ($2.25, limited series)

1-4-Ryan-a 2.50

LEGION WORLDS (Follows Legion Lost series)
DC Comics: Jun, 2001 - No. 6, Nov, 2001 ($3.95, limited series)

1-6-Abnett & Lanning-s; art by various. 5-Dillon-a. 6-Timber Wolf app. 4.00

LEMONADE KID, THE (See Bobby Benson's B-Bar-B Riders)
AC Comics: 1990 ($2.50, 28 pgs.)

1-Powell-c(r); Red Hawk-r by Powell; Lemonade Kid-r/Bobby Benson by Powell (2 stories) 2.50

LENNON SISTERS LIFE STORY, THE
Dell Publishing Co.: No. 951, Nov, 1958 - No. 1014, Aug, 1959

Four Color 951 (#1)-Toth-a, 32pgs, photo-c 13 26 39 90 165 240
Four Color 1014-Toth-a, photo-c 12 24 36 85 155 225

LENORE
Slave Labor Graphics: Feb, 1998 - Present ($2.95/$3.95, B&W, color #13-on)

1-12: 1-Roman Dirge-s/a, 1,2-2nd printing 3.00
13-($3.95, color) 4.00
...: Noogies TPB ($11.95) r/#1-4 12.00
...: Wedgies TPB (2000, $13.95) r/#5-8 14.00
...: Cooties TPB (3/06, $13.95) r/#9-12; pin-ups by various 14.00

LEONARD NIMOY'S PRIMORTALS
Tekno Comix: Mar, 1995 - No. 15, May, 1996 ($1.95)

1-15: Concept by Leonard Nimoy & Isaac Asimov 1-3-w/bound-in game piece & trading card. 4-w/Teknophage Steel Edition coupon. 13,14-Art Adams-c. 15-Simonson-c 2.50

LEONARD NIMOY'S PRIMORTALS
BIG Entertainment: V2#0, June, 1996 - No. 8, Feb, 1997 ($2.25)

V2#0-8: 0-Includes Pt. 9 of "The Big Bang" x-over. 0,1-Simonson-c. 3-Kelley Jones-c 2.50

LEONARD NIMOY'S PRIMORTALS ORIGINS
Tekno Comix: Nov, 1995 - No. 2, Dec, 1995 ($2.95, limited series)

1,2: Nimoy scripts; Art Adams-c; polybagged 3.00

LEONARDO (Also see Teenage Mutant Ninja Turtles)
Mirage Studios: Dec, 1986 ($1.50, B&W, one-shot)

1 6.00

LEO THE LION
I. W. Enterprises: No date(1960s) (10¢)

1-Reprint 2 4 6 9 13 16

LEROY (Teen-age)
Standard Comics: Nov, 1949 - No. 6, Nov, 1950

1 14 28 42 80 115 150
2-Frazetta text illo. 10 20 30 56 76 95
3-6: 3-Lubbers-a 9 18 27 50 65 80

LETHAL (Also see Brigade)
Image Comics (Extreme Studios): Feb, 1996 ($2.50, unfinished limited series)

1-Marat Mychaels-c/a. 2.50

LETHAL FOES OF SPIDER-MAN (Sequel to Deadly Foes of Spider-Man)
Marvel Comics: Sept, 1993 - No. 4, Dec, 1993 ($1.75, limited series)

1-4 2.50

LETHARGIC LAD
Crusade Ent.: June, 1996 - No. 3, Sept, 1996 ($2.95, B&W, limited series)

1,2 3.00
3-Alex Ross-c/swipe (Kingdom Come) 4.00
...Jumbo Sized Annual #1 (Summer 2002, $3.99) prints comic stories from internet 4.00

LETHARGIC LAD ADVENTURES
Crusade Ent./Destination Ent.#3 on: Oct, 1997 - No. 12, Sept./Oct. 1999 ($2.95, B&W)

1-12-Hyland-s/a. 9-Alex Ross sketch page & back-c 3.00

LET'S PRETEND (CBS radio)

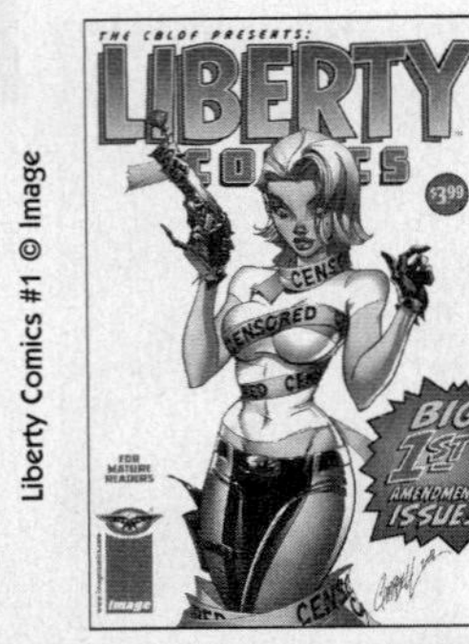

Liberty Comics #1 © Image

Liberty Meadows #18 © Creators Synd.

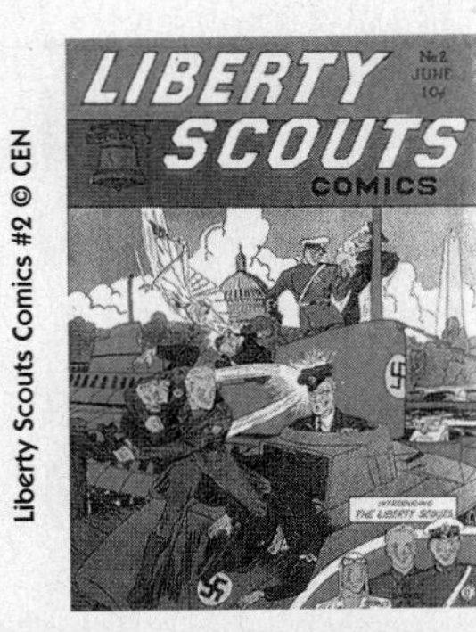

Liberty Scouts Comics #2 © CEN

D. S. Publishing Co.: May-June, 1950 - No. 3, Sept-Oct, 1950

	GD 2.0	VG 4.0	FN 6.0	VF 8.0	VF/NM 9.0	NM- 9.2
1	18	36	54	105	165	225
2,3	14	28	42	82	121	160

LET'S READ THE NEWSPAPER
Charlton Press: 1974

	GD 2.0	VG 4.0	FN 6.0	VF 8.0	VF/NM 9.0	NM- 9.2
nn-Features Quincy by Ted Sheares	1	3	4	6	8	10

LET'S TAKE A TRIP (TV) (CBS Television Presents)
Pines Comics: Spring, 1958

	GD 2.0	VG 4.0	FN 6.0	VF 8.0	VF/NM 9.0	NM- 9.2
1-Marv Levy-c/a	5	10	15	23	28	32

LETTERS TO SANTA (See March of Comics No. 228)

LEX LUTHOR: MAN OF STEEL
DC Comics: May, 2005 - No. 5, Sept, 2005 ($2.99, limited series)

	GD 2.0	VG 4.0	FN 6.0	VF 8.0	VF/NM 9.0	NM- 9.2
1-5: 1-Azzarello-s/Bermejo-a/c in all. 3-Batman-c/app.						3.00
TPB (2005, $12.99) r/series						13.00

LEX LUTHOR: THE UNAUTHORIZED BIOGRAPHY
DC Comics: 1989 ($3.95, 52 pgs., one-shot, squarebound)

	GD 2.0	VG 4.0	FN 6.0	VF 8.0	VF/NM 9.0	NM- 9.2
1-Painted-c; Clark Kent app.						4.00

LIBERTY COMICS (Miss Liberty No. 1)
Green Publishing Co.: No. 5, May, '46 - No. 15, July, 1946 (MLJ & other-r)

	GD 2.0	VG 4.0	FN 6.0	VF 8.0	VF/NM 9.0	NM- 9.2
5 (5/46)-The Prankster app; Starr-a	21	42	63	122	199	275
10-Hangman & Boy Buddies app.; reprints 3 Hangman stories, incl. Hangman #8	22	44	66	128	209	290
11 (V2#2, 1/46)-Wilbur in women's clothes	17	34	51	100	158	215
12 (V2#4)-Black Hood & Suzie app.; classic Skull-c	58	116	174	371	636	900
14,15-Patty of Airliner; Starr-a in both	16	32	48	94	147	200

LIBERTY COMICS (The CBLDF Presents...)
Image Comics: July, 2008; Oct, 2009 ($3.99/$4.99, Comic Book Legal Defense Fund benefit)

	GD 2.0	VG 4.0	FN 6.0	VF 8.0	VF/NM 9.0	NM- 9.2
1-Two covers by Campbell & Mignola; art by Cooke, Aragones, A. Adams & others						4.00
1-(12/08) Second printing with Thor-c by Simonson						4.00
2-(10/09, $4.99) two covers by Romita Jr. & Sale; art by Allred, Templesmith, Jim Lee						5.00

LIBERTY COMICS
Heroic Publishing: Sept, 2007 ($4.50)

	GD 2.0	VG 4.0	FN 6.0	VF 8.0	VF/NM 9.0	NM- 9.2
1-Mark Sparacio-c						4.50

LIBERTY GIRL
Heroic Publishing: Aug, 2006 - No. 3, May, 2007 ($3.25/$2.99)

	GD 2.0	VG 4.0	FN 6.0	VF 8.0	VF/NM 9.0	NM- 9.2
1-3-Mark Sparacio-c/a						3.25

LIBERTY GUARDS
Chicago Mail Order: No date (1946?)

	GD 2.0	VG 4.0	FN 6.0	VF 8.0	VF/NM 9.0	NM- 9.2
nn-Reprints Man of War #1 with cover of Liberty Scouts #1; Gustavson-c	34	68	102	199	325	450

LIBERTY MEADOWS
Insight Studios Group/Image Comics #27 on: 1999 - Present ($2.95, B&W)

	GD 2.0	VG 4.0	FN 6.0	VF 8.0	VF/NM 9.0	NM- 9.2
1-Frank Cho-s/a; reprints newspaper strips	3	6	9	14	20	25
1-2nd & 3rd printings	1	2	3	4	5	7
2,3	2	4	6	8	11	14
4-10	1	2	3	4	5	7
11-25,27-37: 20-Adam Hughes-c. 22-Evil Brandy vs. Brandy. 27-1st Image issue, printed sideways						3.00
..., Cover Girl HC (Image, 2006, $24.99, with dustjacket) r/color covers of #1-19,21-37 along with B&W inked versions, sketches and pin-up art						25.00
...: Eden Book 1 SC (Image, 2002, $14.95) r/#1-9; sketch gallery						15.00
...: Eden Book 1 SC 2nd printing (Image, 2004, $19.95) r/#1-9; sketch gallery						20.00
...: Eden Book 1 HC (Image, 2003, $24.95, with dustjacket) r/#1-9; sketch gallery						25.00
...: Creature Comforts Book 2 HC (Image, 2004, $24.95, with d.j.) r/#10-18; sketch gallery						25.00
...: Creature Comforts Book 2 SC (Image, 12/04, $14.95) r/#10-18; sketch gallery						15.00
...Book 3: Summer of Love HC (Image, 12/04, $24.95) r/#19-27; sketch gallery						25.00
...Book 3: Summer of Love SC (Image, 7/05, $14.95) r/#19-27; sketch gallery						15.00
...Book 4: Cold, Cold Heart HC (Image, 9/05, $24.95) r/#28-36; sketch gallery						25.00
...Book 4: Cold, Cold Heart SC (Image, 2006, $14.99) r/#28-36; sketch gallery						15.00
... Sourcebook (5/04, $4.95) character info and unpublished strips						5.00
... Wedding Album (#26) (2002, $2.95)						3.00

LIBERTY PROJECT, THE
Eclipse Comics: June, 1987 - No. 8, May, 1988 ($1.75, color, Baxter paper)

	GD 2.0	VG 4.0	FN 6.0	VF 8.0	VF/NM 9.0	NM- 9.2
1-8: 6-Valkyrie app.						2.50

LIBERTY SCOUTS (See Liberty Guards & Man of War)
Centaur Publications: No. 2, June, 1941 - No. 3, Aug, 1941

GD VG FN VF VF/NM NM-
2.0 4.0 6.0 8.0 9.0 9.2

	GD 2.0	VG 4.0	FN 6.0	VF 8.0	VF/NM 9.0	NM- 9.2
2(#1)-Origin The Fire-Man, Man of War; Vapo-Man & Liberty Scouts begin; intro Liberty Scouts; Gustavson-c/a in both	129	258	387	826	1413	2000
3(#2)-Origin & 1st app. The Sentinel	90	180	270	576	988	1400

LICENCE TO KILL (James Bond 007) (Movie)
Eclipse Comics: 1989 ($7.95, slick paper, 52 pgs.)

	GD 2.0	VG 4.0	FN 6.0	VF 8.0	VF/NM 9.0	NM- 9.2
nn-Movie adaptation; Timothy Dalton photo-c	1	2	3	5	6	8
Limited Hardcover ($24.95)						25.00

LIDSVILLE (TV)
Gold Key: Oct, 1972 - No. 5, Oct, 1973

	GD 2.0	VG 4.0	FN 6.0	VF 8.0	VF/NM 9.0	NM- 9.2
1-Photo-c	5	10	15	35	55	75
2-5	4	8	12	22	34	45

LIEUTENANT, THE (TV)
Dell Publishing Co.: April-June, 1964

	GD 2.0	VG 4.0	FN 6.0	VF 8.0	VF/NM 9.0	NM- 9.2
1-Photo-c	3	6	9	18	27	35

LIEUTENANT BLUEBERRY (Also see Blueberry)
Marvel Comics (Epic Comics): 1991 - No. 3, 1991 (Graphic novel)

	GD 2.0	VG 4.0	FN 6.0	VF 8.0	VF/NM 9.0	NM- 9.2
1,2 ($8.95)-Moebius-a in all	2	4	6	11	16	20
3 ($14.95)	3	6	9	16	22	28

LT. ROBIN CRUSOE, U.S.N. (See Movie Comics & Walt Disney Showcase #26)

LIFE EATERS, THE
DC Comics (WildStorm): 2003 ($29.95, hardcover with dust jacket)

	GD 2.0	VG 4.0	FN 6.0	VF 8.0	VF/NM 9.0	NM- 9.2
HC-David Brin-s; Scott Hampton-painted-a/c; Norse Gods team with the Nazis						30.00
SC-(2004, $19.95)						20.00

LIFE OF CAPTAIN MARVEL, THE
Marvel Comics Group: Aug, 1985 - No. 5, Dec, 1985 ($2.00, Baxter paper)

	GD 2.0	VG 4.0	FN 6.0	VF 8.0	VF/NM 9.0	NM- 9.2
1-5: 1-All reprint Starlin issues of Iron Man #55, Capt. Marvel #25-34 plus Marvel Feature #12 (all with Thanos). 4-New Thanos back-c by Starlin						3.00

LIFE OF CHRIST, THE
Catechetical Guild Educational Society: No. 301, 1949 (35¢, 100 pgs.)

	GD 2.0	VG 4.0	FN 6.0	VF 8.0	VF/NM 9.0	NM- 9.2
301-Reprints from Topix(1949)-V5#11,12	9	18	27	50	65	80

LIFE OF CHRIST: THE CHRISTMAS STORY, THE
Marvel Comics/Nelson: Feb, 1993 ($2.99, slick stock)

	GD 2.0	VG 4.0	FN 6.0	VF 8.0	VF/NM 9.0	NM- 9.2
nn						5.00

LIFE OF CHRIST: THE EASTER STORY, THE
Marvel Comics/Nelson: 1993 ($2.99, slick stock)

	GD 2.0	VG 4.0	FN 6.0	VF 8.0	VF/NM 9.0	NM- 9.2
nn						5.00

LIFE OF CHRIST VISUALIZED
Standard Publishers: 1942 - No. 3, 1943

	GD 2.0	VG 4.0	FN 6.0	VF 8.0	VF/NM 9.0	NM- 9.2
1-3: All came in cardboard case, each...	9	18	27	47	61	75
Case only.....	10	20	30	54	72	90

LIFE OF CHRIST VISUALIZED
The Standard Publ. Co.: 1946? (48 pgs. in color)

	GD 2.0	VG 4.0	FN 6.0	VF 8.0	VF/NM 9.0	NM- 9.2
nn	7	14	21	35	43	50

LIFE OF ESTHER VISUALIZED
The Standard Publ. Co.: No. 2062, 1947 (48 pgs. in color)

	GD 2.0	VG 4.0	FN 6.0	VF 8.0	VF/NM 9.0	NM- 9.2
2062	7	14	21	35	43	50

LIFE OF JOSEPH VISUALIZED
The Standard Publ. Co.: No. 1054, 1946 (48 pgs. in color)

	GD 2.0	VG 4.0	FN 6.0	VF 8.0	VF/NM 9.0	NM- 9.2
1054	7	14	21	35	43	50

LIFE OF PAUL (See The Living Bible)

LIFE OF POPE JOHN PAUL II, THE
Marvel Comics Group: Jan, 1983 ($1.50/$1.75)

	GD 2.0	VG 4.0	FN 6.0	VF 8.0	VF/NM 9.0	NM- 9.2
1	1	3	4	6	8	10

LIFE OF RILEY, THE (TV)
Dell Publishing Co.: No. 917, July, 1958

	GD 2.0	VG 4.0	FN 6.0	VF 8.0	VF/NM 9.0	NM- 9.2
Four Color 917-Photo-c	10	20	30	70	123	175

LIFE ON ANOTHER PLANET
Kitchen Sink Press: 1978 (B&W, graphic novel, magazine size)

	GD 2.0	VG 4.0	FN 6.0	VF 8.0	VF/NM 9.0	NM- 9.2
nn-Will Eisner-s/a						13.00
Reprint (DC Comics, 5/00, $12.95)						13.00

LIFE'S LIKE THAT
Croyden Publ. Co.: 1945 (25¢, B&W, 68 pgs.)

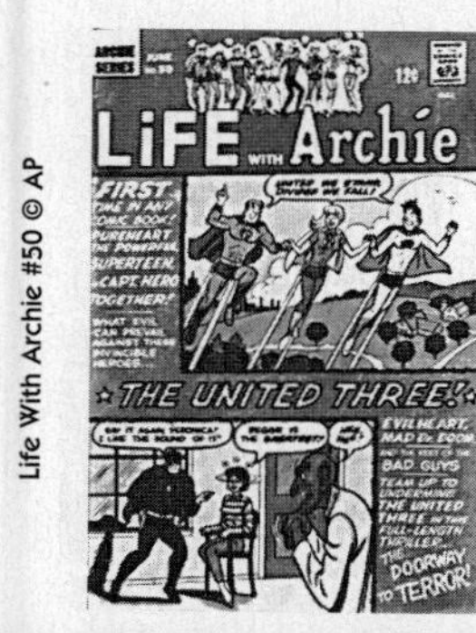

Life With Archie #50 © AP

Lightning Comics Presents #1 © LC

Limited Collectors' Edition C-35 © DC

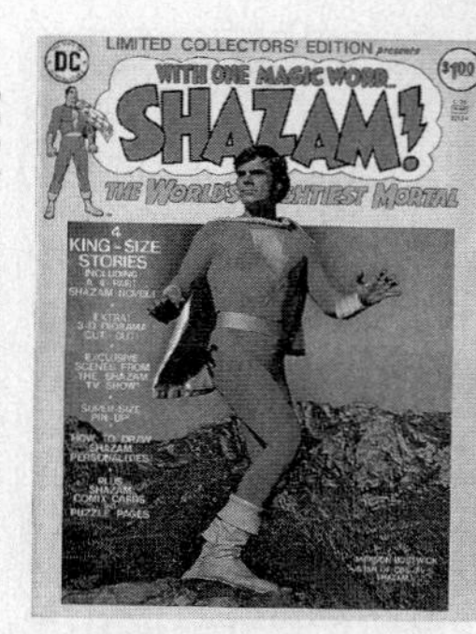

	GD 2.0	VG 4.0	FN 6.0	VF 8.0	VF/NM 9.0	NM- 9.2
nn-Newspaper Sunday strip-r by Neher	7	14	21	35	43	50

LIFE STORIES OF AMERICAN PRESIDENTS (See Dell Giants)

LIFE STORY
Fawcett Publications: Apr, 1949 - V8#46, Jan, 1953; V8#47, Apr, 1953 (All have photo-c?)

	GD 2.0	VG 4.0	FN 6.0	VF 8.0	VF/NM 9.0	NM- 9.2
V1#1	15	30	45	84	127	170
2	9	18	27	52	69	85
3-6, V2#7-12	8	16	24	44	57	70
V3#13-Wood-a	15	30	45	84	127	170
V3#14-18, V4#19-24, V5#25-30, V6#31-35	8	16	24	40	50	60
V6#36- "I sold drugs" on-c	11	22	33	60	83	105
V7#37,40-42, V8#44,45	7	14	21	37	46	55
V7#38, V8#43-Evans-a	8	16	24	40	50	60
V7#39-Drug Smuggling & Junkie story	10	20	30	54	72	90
V8#46,47 (Scarce)	9	18	27	50	65	80

NOTE: ***Powell** a-13, 23, 24, 26, 28, 30, 32, 39. **Marcus Swayze** a-1-3, 10-12, 15, 16, 20, 21, 23-25, 31, 35, 37, 40, 44, 46.*

LIFE, THE UNIVERSE AND EVERYTHING (See Hitchhikers Guide to the Galaxy & Restaurant at the End of the Universe)
DC Comics: 1996 - No. 3, 1996 ($6.95, squarebound, limited series)

	GD 2.0	VG 4.0	FN 6.0	VF 8.0	VF/NM 9.0	NM- 9.2
1-3: Adaptation of novel by Douglas Adams.	1	2	3	4	5	7

LIFE WITH ARCHIE
Archie Publications: Sept, 1958 - No. 286, Sept, 1991

	GD 2.0	VG 4.0	FN 6.0	VF 8.0	VF/NM 9.0	NM- 9.2
1	25	50	75	183	354	525
2-(9/59)	13	26	39	93	172	250
3-5: 3-(7/60)	9	18	27	65	113	160
6-8,10	8	16	24	52	86	120
9,11-Horror/SciFi-c	9	18	27	60	100	140
12-20	6	12	18	41	66	90
21(7/63)-30	5	10	15	32	51	70
31-34,36-38,40,41	4	8	12	26	41	55
35,39-Horror/Sci-Fi-c	5	10	15	32	51	70
42-Pureheart begins (1st app.-c/s, 10/65)	8	16	24	52	86	120
43,44	5	10	15	34	55	75
45(1/66) 1st Man From R.I.V.E.R.D.A.L.E.	6	12	18	43	69	95
46-Origin Pureheart	5	10	15	34	55	75
47-49	4	8	12	26	41	55
50-United Three begin: Pureheart (Archie), Superteen (Betty), Captain Hero (Jughead)	6	12	18	37	59	80
51-59: 59-Pureheart ends	4	8	12	26	41	55
60-Archie band begins, ends #66	5	10	15	34	55	75
61-66: 61-Man From R.I.V.E.R.D.A.L.E.-c/s	4	8	12	24	37	50
67-80	3	6	9	16	23	30
81-99	3	6	9	16	22	28
100 (8/70), 113-Sabrina & Salem app.	3	6	9	19	29	38
101-112, 114-130(2/73), 139(11/73)-Archie Band c/s	2	4	6	11	16	20
131,134-138,140-146,148-161,164-170(6/76)	2	4	6	9	12	15
132,133,147,163-all horror-c/s	3	6	9	14	19	24
162-UFO c/s	3	6	9	14	19	24
171,173-175,177-184,186,189,191-194,196	2	3	4	6	8	10
172,185,197 : 172-(9/77)-Bi-Cent. spec. ish, 185-2nd 24th cent.-c/s, 197-Time machine/SF-c/s	2	4	6	8	10	12
176(12/76)-1st app. Capt. Archie of Starship Rivda, in 24th century c/s; 1st app. Stella the Robot	3	6	9	14	19	24
187,188,195,198,199-all horror-c/s	2	4	6	9	13	16
190-1st Dr. Doom-c/s	2	4	6	9	13	16
200 (12/78) Maltese Pigeon-s	2	4	6	8	11	14
201-203,205-237,239,240(1/84): 208-Reintro Veronica	1	2	3	5	6	8
204-Flying saucer-c/s	2	3	4	6	8	10
238-(9/83)-25th anniversary issue; Ol' Betsy (jalopy) replaced	1	2	3	5	7	9
241-278,280-285: 250-Comic book convention-s						5.00
279,286: 279-Intro Mustang Sally ($1.00, 7/90)						6.00

NOTE: ***Gene Colan** a-272-279, 285, 286. Horror/Sci-Fi-c 9, 11, 35, 39, 162.*

LIFE WITH MILLIE (Formerly A Date With Millie) (Modeling With Millie #21 on)
Atlas/Marvel Comics Group: No. 8, Dec, 1960 - No. 20, Dec, 1962

	GD 2.0	VG 4.0	FN 6.0	VF 8.0	VF/NM 9.0	NM- 9.2
8-Teenage	8	16	24	56	93	130
9-11	6	12	18	41	66	90
12-20	6	12	18	37	59	80

LIFE WITH SNARKY PARKER (TV)
Fox Feature Syndicate: Aug, 1950

	GD 2.0	VG 4.0	FN 6.0	VF 8.0	VF/NM 9.0	NM- 9.2
1-Early TV comic; photo-c from TV puppet show	27	54	81	158	259	360

LIGHT AND DARKNESS WAR, THE
Marvel Comics (Epic Comics): Oct, 1988 - No. 6, Dec, 1989 ($1.95, lim. series)

	GD 2.0	VG 4.0	FN 6.0	VF 8.0	VF/NM 9.0	NM- 9.2
1-6						2.50

LIGHT BRIGADE, THE
DC Comics: 2004 - No. 4, 2004 ($5.95, limited series)

	GD 2.0	VG 4.0	FN 6.0	VF 8.0	VF/NM 9.0	NM- 9.2
1-4-Archangels in World War II; Tomasi-s/Snejbjerg-a						6.00
TPB (2005, 2009, $19.99) r/series; cover galery						20.00

LIGHT FANTASTIC, THE (Terry Pratchett's)
Innovation Publishing: June, 1992 - No. 4, Sept, 1992 ($2.50, mini-series)

	GD 2.0	VG 4.0	FN 6.0	VF 8.0	VF/NM 9.0	NM- 9.2
1-4: Adapts 2nd novel in Discworld series						2.50

LIGHT IN THE FOREST (Disney)
Dell Publishing Co.: No. 891, Mar, 1958

	GD 2.0	VG 4.0	FN 6.0	VF 8.0	VF/NM 9.0	NM- 9.2
Four Color 891-Movie, Fess Parker photo-c	7	14	21	50	83	115

LIGHTNING COMICS (Formerly Sure-Fire No. 1-3)
Ace Magazines: No. 4, Dec, 1940 - No. 13(V3#1), June, 1942

	GD 2.0	VG 4.0	FN 6.0	VF 8.0	VF/NM 9.0	NM- 9.2
4-Characters continue from Sure-Fire	100	200	300	635	1093	1550
5,6: 6-Dr. Nemesis begins	68	136	204	432	746	1060
V2#1-6: 2- "Flash Lightning" becomes "Lash..."	54	108	162	346	591	835
V3#1-Intro. Lightning Girl & The Sword	54	108	162	346	591	835

NOTE: ***Anderson** a-V2#6. **Mooney** c-V1#5, 6, V2#1-6, V3#1. Bondage c-V2#6. Lightning-c on all.*

LIGHTNING COMICS PRESENTS
Lightning Comics: May, 1994 ($3.50)

	GD 2.0	VG 4.0	FN 6.0	VF 8.0	VF/NM 9.0	NM- 9.2
1-Red foil-c distr. by Diamond Distr., 1-Black/yellow/blue-c distrib. by Capital Distr., 1-Red/yellow-c distributed by H. World, 1-Platinum						3.50

LI'L ... (See Little ...)

LILI
Image Comics: No. 0, 1999 ($4.95, B&W)

	GD 2.0	VG 4.0	FN 6.0	VF 8.0	VF/NM 9.0	NM- 9.2
0-Bendis & Yanover-s						5.00

LILLITH (See Warrior Nun...)
Antarctic Press: Sept, 1996 - No. 3, Feb, 1997 ($2.95, limited series)

	GD 2.0	VG 4.0	FN 6.0	VF 8.0	VF/NM 9.0	NM- 9.2
1-3: 1-Variant-c						3.00

LIMITED COLLECTORS' EDITION (See Famous First Edition, Marvel Treasury #28, Rudolph The Red-Nosed Reindeer, & Superman Vs. The Amazing Spider-Man; becomes All-New Collectors' Edition)
National Periodical Publications/DC Comics:
(#21-34,51-59: 84 pgs.; #35-41: 68 pgs.; #42-50: 60 pgs.)
C-21, Summer, 1973 - No. C-59, 1978 ($1.00) (10x13-1/2")

	GD 2.0	VG 4.0	FN 6.0	VF 8.0	VF/NM 9.0	NM- 9.2
(Rudolph...C-20 (implied), 12/72)-See Rudolph The Red-Nosed Reindeer						
C-21: Shazam (TV); r/Captain Marvel Jr. #11 by Raboy; C.C. Beck-c, biog. & photo	3	6	9	20	30	40
C-22: Tarzan; complete origin reprinted from #207-210; all Kubert-c/a; Joe Kubert biography & photo inside	3	6	9	17	25	32
C-23: House of Mystery; Wrightson, N. Adams/Orlando, G. Kane/Wood, Toth, Aragones, Sparling reprints	4	8	12	24	37	50
C-24: Rudolph The Red-Nosed Reindeer	7	14	21	45	73	100
C-25: Batman; Neal Adams-c/a(r); G.A. Joker-r; Batman/Enemy Ace-r; Novick-a(r); has photos from TV show	4	8	12	26	41	55
C-26: See Famous First Edition C-26 (same contents)						
C-27,C-29,C-31: C-27: Shazam (TV); G.A. Capt. Marvel & Mary Marvel-r; Beck-r. C-29: Tarzan; reprints "Return of Tarzan" from #219-223 by Kubert; Kubert-c. C-31: Superman; origin-r; Giordano-a; photos of George Reeves from 1950s TV show on inside b/c; Burnley, Boring-r	3	6	9	16	23	30
C-32: Ghosts (new-a)	4	8	12	22	34	45
C-33: Rudolph The Red-Nosed Reindeer(new-a)	6	12	18	41	66	90
C-34: Christmas with the Super-Heroes; unpublished Angel & Ape story by Oksner & Wood; Batman & Teen Titans-r	3	6	9	16	23	30
C-35: Shazam (TV); photo cover features TV's Captain Marvel, Jackson Bostwick; Beck-r; TV photos inside b/c	3	6	9	16	22	28
C-36: The Bible; all new adaptation beginning with Genesis by Kubert, Redondo & Mayer; Kubert-c	3	6	9	16	22	28
C-37: Batman; r-1946 Sundays; inside b/c photos of Batman TV show villains (all villain issue; r/G.A. Joker, Catwoman, Penguin, Two-Face, & Scarecrow stories plus 1946 Sundays-r)	3	6	9	18	27	35
C-38: Superman; 1 pg. N. Adams; part photo-c; photos from TV show on inside back-c	3	6	9	16	22	28
C-39: Secret Origins of Super-Villains; N. Adams-i(r); collection reprints 1950's Joker origin, Luthor origin from Adv. Comics #271, Captain Cold origin from Showcase #8 among others; G.A. Batman-r; Beck-r	3	6	9	16	22	28

Linda #2 © AJAX

Li'l Abner #65 © TOBY

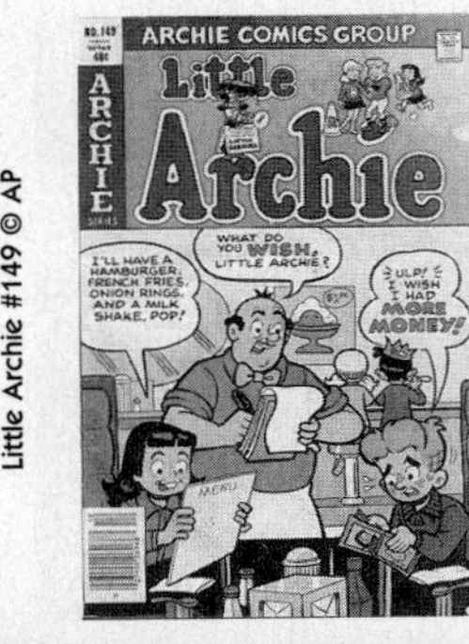

Little Archie #149 © AP

	GD 2.0	VG 4.0	FN 6.0	VF 8.0	VF/NM 9.0	NM- 9.2
C-40: Dick Tracy by Gould featuring Flattop; newspaper-r from 12/21/43 - 5/17/44; biog. of Chester Gould	3	6	9	16	22	28
C-41: Super Friends (TV); JLA-r(1965); Toth-c/a	3	6	9	16	23	30
C-42: Rudolph	4	8	12	28	44	60
C-43-C-47: C-43: Christmas with the Super-Heroes; Wrightson, S&K, Neal Adams-a. C-44: Batman; N. Adams-p(r) & G.A.-r; painted-c. C-45: More Secret Origins of Super-Villains; Flash-r/#105; G.A. Wonder Woman & Batman/Catwoman-r. C-46: Justice League of America(1963-r); 3 pgs. Toth-a C-47: Superman Salutes the Bicentennial (Tomahawk interior); 2 pgs. new-a	3	6	9	14	20	26
C-48,C-49: C-48: Superman Vs. The Flash (Superman/Flash race); swipes-c to Superman #199; r/Superman #199 & Flash #175; 6 pgs. Neal Adams-a. C-49: Superboy & the Legion of Super-Heroes	3	6	9	16	23	30
C-50: Rudolph The Red-Nosed Reindeer; contains poster (1/2 price if poster is missing)	4	8	12	28	44	60
C-51: Batman; Neal Adams-c/a	3	6	9	17	25	32
C-52,C-57: C-52: The Best of DC; Neal Adams-c/a; Toth, Kubert-a. C-57: Welcome Back, Kotter-r(TV)(5/78) includes unpublished #11	3	6	9	16	22	28
C-53 thru C-56, C-58, C-60 thru C-62 (See All-New Collectors' Edition)						
C-59: Batman's Strangest Cases; N. Adams-r; Wrightson-r/Swamp Thing #7; N. Adams/Wrightson-c	3	6	9	16	22	28

NOTE: *All-r with exception of some special features and covers.* ***Aparo*** *a-52r; c-37.* ***Grell*** *c-49.* ***Infantino*** *a-25, 39, 44, 45, 52.* ***Bob Kane*** *r-25.* ***Robinson*** *r-25, 44.* ***Sprang*** *r-44. Issues #21-31, 35-39, 45, 48 have back cover cut-outs.*

LINDA (Everybody Loves...) (Phantom Lady No. 5 on)
Ajax-Farrell Publ. Co.: Apr-May, 1954 - No. 4, Oct-Nov, 1954

	GD	VG	FN	VF	VF/NM	NM-
1-Kamenish-a	15	30	45	85	130	175
2-Lingerie panel	13	26	39	72	101	130
3,4	10	20	30	56	76	95

LINDA CARTER, STUDENT NURSE
Atlas Comics (AMI): Sept, 1961 - No. 9, Jan, 1963

	GD	VG	FN	VF	VF/NM	NM-
1-Al Hartley-c	6	12	18	41	66	90
2-9	4	8	12	28	44	60

LINDA LARK
Dell Publishing Co.: Oct-Dec, 1961 - No. 8, Aug-Oct, 1963

	GD	VG	FN	VF	VF/NM	NM-
1	3	6	9	19	29	38
2-8	3	6	9	14	19	24

LINUS, THE LIONHEARTED (TV)
Gold Key: Sept, 1965

	GD	VG	FN	VF	VF/NM	NM-
1 (10155-509)	7	14	21	45	73	100

LION, THE (See Movie Comics)

LIONHEART
Awesome Comics: Sept, 1999 - No. 2, Dec, 1999 ($2.99/$2.50)

	GD	VG	FN	VF	VF/NM	NM-
1-Ian Churchill-story/a, Jeph Loeb-s; Coven app.						3.00
2-Flip book w/Coven #4						2.50

LION OF SPARTA (See Movie Classics)

LIPPY THE LION AND HARDY HAR HAR (TV)
Gold Key: Mar, 1963 (12¢) (See Hanna-Barbera Band Wagon #1)

	GD	VG	FN	VF	VF/NM	NM-
1 (10049-303)	8	16	24	54	90	125

LISA COMICS (TV)(See Simpsons Comics)
Bongo Comics: 1995 ($2.25)

	GD	VG	FN	VF	VF/NM	NM-
1-Lisa in Wonderland						3.00

LITERALS, THE (See Fables and Jack of Fables)
DC Comics (Vertigo): June, 2009 - No. 3, Aug, 2009 ($2.99)

	GD	VG	FN	VF	VF/NM	NM-
1-3-Crossover with Fables #83-85 and Jack of Fables #33-35; Buckingham-c/a						3.00

LI'L ABNER (See Comics on Parade, Sparkle, Sparkler Comics, Tip Top Comics & Tip Topper)
United Features Syndicate: 1939 - 1940

	GD	VG	FN	VF	VF/NM	NM-
Single Series 4 ('39)	76	152	228	486	831	1175
Single Series 18 ('40) (#18 on inside, #2 on-c)	59	118	177	375	643	910

LI'L ABNER (Al Capp's; continued from Comics on Parade #58)
Harvey Publ. No. 61-69 (2/49)/Toby Press No. 70 on: No. 61, Dec, 1947 - No. 97, Jan, 1955
(See Oxydol-Dreft in Promotional Comics section)

	GD	VG	FN	VF	VF/NM	NM-
61(#1)-Wolverton & Powell-a	30	60	90	174	280	385
62-65: 63-The Wolf Girl app. 65-Powell-a	17	34	51	98	154	210
66,67,69,70	15	30	45	90	140	190
68-Full length Fearless Fosdick-c/story	16	32	48	94	147	200
71-74,76,80	14	28	42	80	115	150
75,77-79,86,91-All with Kurtzman art; 86-Sadie Hawkins Day. 91-r/#77	15	30	45	90	140	190
81-85,87-90,92-94,96,97: 83-Evil-Eye Fleegle & Double Whammy app. 88-Cousin Weakeyes goes hunting. 94-Six lessons from Adam Lazonga. 96-Football issue	14	28	42	76	108	140
95-Full length Fearless Fosdick story	14	28	42	82	121	160

LI'L ABNER
Toby Press: 1951

	GD	VG	FN	VF	VF/NM	NM-
1	18	36	54	103	162	220

LI'L ABNER'S DOGPATCH (See Al Capp's...)

LITTLE AL OF THE F.B.I.
Ziff-Davis Publications: No. 10, 1950 (no month) - No. 11, Apr-May, 1951 (Saunders painted-c)

	GD	VG	FN	VF	VF/NM	NM-
10(1950)	16	32	48	94	147	200
11(1951)	14	28	42	78	112	145

LITTLE AL OF THE SECRET SERVICE
Ziff-Davis Publications: No. 10, 7-8/51; No. 2, 9-10/51; No. 3, Winter, 1951 (Saunders painted-c)

	GD	VG	FN	VF	VF/NM	NM-
10(#1)	16	32	48	92	144	195
2,3	14	28	42	76	108	140

LITTLE AMBROSE
Archie Publications: September, 1958

	GD	VG	FN	VF	VF/NM	NM-
1-Bob Bolling-c	15	30	45	84	127	170

LITTLE ANGEL
Standard (Visual Editions)/Pines: No. 5, Sept, 1954; No. 6, Sept, 1955 - No. 16, Sept, 1959

	GD	VG	FN	VF	VF/NM	NM-
5-Last pre-code issue	8	16	24	40	50	60
6-16	5	10	15	24	30	35

LITTLE ANNIE ROONEY (Also see Henry)
David McKay Publ.: 1935 (25¢, B&W dailies, 48 pgs.)(10"x10", cardboard-c)

	GD	VG	FN	VF	VF/NM	NM-
Book 1-Daily strip-r by Darrell McClure	38	76	114	226	368	510

LITTLE ANNIE ROONEY (See King Comics & Treasury of Comics)
David McKay/St. John/Standard: 1938; Aug, 1948 - No. 3, Oct, 1948

	GD	VG	FN	VF	VF/NM	NM-
Feature Books 11 (McKay, 1938)	39	78	117	231	378	525
1 (St. John)	15	30	45	88	137	185
2,3	10	20	30	54	72	90

LITTLE ARCHIE (The Adventures of... #13-on) (See Archie Giant Series Mag. #527, 534, 538, 545, 549, 556, 560, 566, 570, 583, 594, 596, 607, 609, 619)
Archie Publications: 1956 - No. 180, Feb, 1983 (Giants No. 3-84)

	GD	VG	FN	VF	VF/NM	NM-
1-(Scarce)	56	112	168	476	938	1400
2 (1957)	24	48	72	175	338	500
3-5: 3-(1958)-Bob Bolling-c & giant issues begin	14	28	42	102	194	285
6-10	11	22	33	78	139	200
11-17,19,21 (84 pgs.)	8	16	24	58	97	135
18,20,22 (84 pgs.)-Horror/Sci-Fi-c	10	20	30	67	116	165
23-39 (68 pgs.)	6	12	18	43	69	95
40 (Fall/66)-Intro. Little Pureheart-c/s (68 pgs.)	7	14	21	47	76	105
41,44-Little Pureheart (68 pgs.)	6	12	18	41	66	90
42-Intro The Little Archies Band, ends #66 (68 pgs.)	7	14	21	45	73	100
43-1st Boy From R.I.V.E.R.D.A.L.E. (68 pgs.)	6	12	18	43	69	95
45-58 (68 pgs.)	5	10	15	32	51	70
59 (68 pgs.)-Little Sabrina begins	8	16	24	54	90	125
60-66 (68 pgs.)	4	8	12	26	41	55
67(9/71)-84: 84-Last 52pg. Giant-Size (2/74)	3	6	9	17	25	32
85-99	2	4	6	9	13	16
100	2	4	6	11	16	20
101-112,114-116,118-129	2	4	6	8	10	12
113,117,130: 113-Halloween Special issue(12/76). 117-Donny Osmond-c cameo 130-UFO cover (5/78)	2	4	6	9	13	16
131-150(1/80), 180(Last issue, 2/83)	1	2	3	5	7	9
151-179						5.00
...In Animal Land 1 (1957)	13	26	39	93	172	250
...In Animal Land 17 (Winter, 1957-58)-19 (Summer,1958)-Formerly Li'l Jinx	8	16	24	54	90	125
Archie Classics - The Adventures of Little Archie Vol. 1 TPB (2004, $10.95) reprints						11.00
Vol. 2 TPB (2008, $9.95) reprints plus new 22 pg. story with Bolling-s/a						10.00

NOTE: *Little Archie Band app. 42-66. Little Sabrina in 59-78,80-180*

LITTLE ARCHIE CHRISTMAS SPECIAL (See Archie Giant Series #581)

LITTLE ARCHIE COMICS DIGEST ANNUAL (...Magazine #5 on)
Archie Publications: 10/77 - No. 48, 5/91 (Digest-size, 128 pgs., later issues $1.35-$1.50)

	GD	VG	FN	VF	VF/NM	NM-
1(10/77)-Reprints	3	6	9	20	30	40

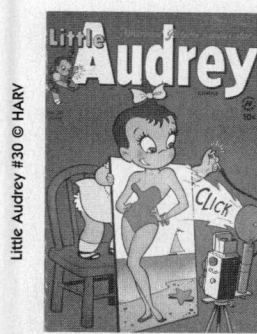

Little Audrey #30 © HARV

Little Dot #10 © HARV

Little Dot Dotland #3 © HARV

	GD 2.0	VG 4.0	FN 6.0	VF 8.0	VF/NM 9.0	NM- 9.2
2(4/78,3(11/78)-Neal Adams-a. 3-The Fly-r by S&K	3	6	9	14	20	26
4(4/79) - 10	2	4	6	10	14	18
11-20	2	4	6	8	10	12
21-30: 28-Christmas-c	1	2	3	5	6	8
31-48: 40,46-Christmas-c						5.00

NOTE: *Little Archie, Little Jinx, Little Jughead & Little Sabrina in most issues.*

LITTLE ARCHIE DIGEST MAGAZINE
Archie Comics: July, 1991 - No. 21, Mar, 1998 ($1.50/$1.79/$1.89, digest size, bi-annual)

	GD	VG	FN	VF	VF/NM	NM-
V2#1						6.00
2-10						3.50
11-21						2.50

LITTLE ARCHIE MYSTERY
Archie Publications: Aug, 1963 - No. 2, Oct, 1963 (12¢ issues)

	GD	VG	FN	VF	VF/NM	NM-
1	11	22	33	74	132	190
2	6	12	18	43	69	95

LITTLE ASPIRIN (See Little Lenny & Wisco)
Marvel Comics (CnPC): July, 1949 - No. 3, Dec, 1949 (52 pgs.)

	GD	VG	FN	VF	VF/NM	NM-
1-Oscar app.; Kurtzman-a (4 pgs.)	17	34	51	98	154	210
2-Kurtzman-a (4 pgs.)	11	22	33	60	83	105
3-No Kurtzman-a	9	18	27	47	61	75

LITTLE AUDREY (Also see Playful...)
St. John Publ.: Apr, 1948 - No. 24, May, 1952

	GD	VG	FN	VF	VF/NM	NM-
1-1st app. Little Audrey	53	106	159	334	567	800
2	26	52	78	154	252	350
3-5	18	36	54	105	165	225
6-10	14	28	42	80	115	150
11-20: 16-X-Mas-c	10	20	30	58	79	100
21-24	9	18	27	52	69	85

LITTLE AUDREY (See Harvey Hits #11, 19)
Harvey Publications: No. 25, Aug, 1952 - No. 53, April, 1957

	GD	VG	FN	VF	VF/NM	NM-
25-(Paramount Pictures Famous Star... on-c); 1st Harvey Casper and Baby Huey (1 month earlier than Harvey Comic Hits #60(9/52))	13	26	39	93	172	250
26-30: 26-28-Casper app.	8	16	24	52	86	120
31-40: 32-35-Casper app.	7	14	21	45	73	100
41-53	5	10	15	34	55	75
...Clubhouse 1 (9/61, 68 pg. Giant)-New stories & reprints	9	18	27	60	100	140

LITTLE AUDREY
Harvey Comics: Aug, 1992 - No. 8, July, 1994 ($1.25/$1.50)

	GD	VG	FN	VF	VF/NM	NM-
V2#1						3.00
2-8						2.50

LITTLE AUDREY (...Yearbook)
St. John Publishing Co.: 1950 (50¢, 260 pgs.)

Contains 8 complete 1949 comics rebound; Casper, Alice in Wonderland, Little Audrey, Abbott & Costello, Pinocchio, Moon Mullins, Three Stooges (from Jubilee), Little Annie Rooney app. (Rare)

	GD	VG	FN	VF	VF/NM	NM-
	84	168	252	538	919	1300

(Also see All Good & Treasury of Comics)

NOTE: *This book contains remaindered St. John comics; many variations possible.*

LITTLE AUDREY & MELVIN (Audrey & Melvin No. 62)
Harvey Publications: May, 1962 - No. 61, Dec, 1973

	GD	VG	FN	VF	VF/NM	NM-
1	10	20	30	68	119	170
2-5	6	12	18	39	62	85
6-10	5	10	15	30	48	65
11-20	3	6	9	19	29	38
21-40: 22-Richie Rich app.	3	6	9	14	20	26
41-50,55-61	2	4	6	11	16	20
51-54: All 52 pg. Giants	3	6	9	14	20	26

LITTLE AUDREY TV FUNTIME
Harvey Publ.: Sept, 1962 - No. 33, Oct, 1971 (#1-31: 68 pgs.; #32,33: 52 pgs.)

	GD	VG	FN	VF	VF/NM	NM-
1-Richie Rich app.	10	20	30	68	119	170
2,3: Richie Rich app.	6	12	18	39	62	85
4,5: 5-25¢ & 35¢ issues exist	5	10	15	32	51	70
6-10	3	6	9	21	32	42
11-20	3	6	9	16	23	28
21-33	3	6	9	14	19	24

LITTLE BAD WOLF (Disney; seeWalt Disney's C&S #52, Walt Disney Showcase #21 & Wheaties)
Dell Publishing Co.: No. 403, June, 1952 - No. 564, June, 1954

	GD 2.0	VG 4.0	FN 6.0	VF 8.0	VF/NM 9.0	NM- 9.2
Four Color 403 (#1)	7	14	21	47	76	105
Four Color 473 (6/53), 564	5	10	15	32	51	70

LITTLE BEAVER
Dell Publishing Co.: No. 211, Jan, 1949 - No. 870, Jan, 1958 (All painted-c)

	GD	VG	FN	VF	VF/NM	NM-
Four Color 211('49)-All Harman-a	8	16	24	56	93	130
Four Color 267,294,332(5/51)	5	10	15	34	55	75
3(10-12/51)-8(1-3/53)	5	10	15	32	51	70
Four Color 483(8-10/53),529	5	10	15	30	48	65
Four Color 612,660,695,744,817,870	5	10	15	30	48	65

LITTLE BIT
Jubilee/St. John Publishing Co.: Mar, 1949 - No. 2, June, 1949

	GD	VG	FN	VF	VF/NM	NM-
1	9	18	27	52	69	85
2	7	14	21	37	46	55

LITTLE DOT (See Humphrey, Li'l Max, Sad Sack, and Tastee-Freez Comics)
Harvey Publications: Sept, 1953 - No. 164, Apr, 1976

	GD	VG	FN	VF	VF/NM	NM-
1-Intro./1st app. Richie Rich & Little Lotta	300	600	900	1950	3375	4800
2-1st app. Freckles & Pee Wee (Richie Rich's poor friends)	97	194	291	621	1061	1500
3	58	116	174	371	636	900
4	53	106	159	334	567	800
5-Origin dots on Little Dot's dress	58	116	174	371	636	900
6-Richie Rich, Little Lotta, & Little Dot all on cover; 1st Richie Rich cover featured	58	116	174	371	636	900
7-10: 9-Last pre-code issue (1/55)	37	74	111	222	361	500
11-20	25	50	75	150	245	340
21-30	17	34	51	98	154	210
31-40	14	28	42	76	108	140
41-50	10	20	30	58	79	100
51-60	9	18	27	47	61	75
61-80	4	8	12	26	41	55
81-100	3	6	9	19	29	38
101-141	3	6	9	16	22	28
142-145: All 52 pg. Giants	3	6	9	17	25	32
146-164	2	4	6	11	16	20

NOTE: *Richie Rich & Little Lotta in all.*

LITTLE DOT
Harvey Comics: Sept, 1992 - No. 7, June, 1994 ($1.25/$1.50)

	GD	VG	FN	VF	VF/NM	NM-
V2#1-Little Dot, Little Lotta, Richie Rich in all						3.00
2-7 ($1.50)						2.50

LITTLE DOT DOTLAND (Dot Dotland No. 62, 63)
Harvey Publications: July, 1962 - No. 61, Dec, 1973

	GD	VG	FN	VF	VF/NM	NM-
1-Richie Rich begins	12	24	36	86	158	230
2,3	7	14	21	50	83	115
4,5	6	12	18	41	66	90
6-10	5	10	15	32	51	70
11-20	4	8	12	24	37	50
21-30	3	6	9	18	27	35
31-50	3	6	9	16	23	30
51-54: All 52 pg. Giants	3	6	9	18	27	35
55-61	2	4	6	11	16	20

LITTLE DOT'S UNCLES & AUNTS (See Harvey Hits No. 4, 13, 24)
Harvey Enterprises: Oct, 1961; No. 2, Aug, 1962 - No. 52, Apr, 1974

	GD	VG	FN	VF	VF/NM	NM-
1-Richie Rich begins; 68 pgs. begin	14	28	42	100	188	275
2,3	8	16	24	58	97	135
4,5	6	12	18	41	66	90
6-10	5	10	15	34	55	75
11-20	4	8	12	24	37	50
21-37: Last 68 pg. issue	3	6	9	19	29	38
38-52: All 52 pg. Giants	3	6	9	16	23	30

LITTLE DRACULA
Harvey Comics: Jan, 1992 - No. 3, May, 1992 ($1.25, quarterly, mini-series)

	GD	VG	FN	VF	VF/NM	NM-
1-3						3.00

LITTLE ENDLESS STORYBOOK, THE (See The Sandman titles)
DC Comics: 2001 ($5.95, Prestige format, one-shot)

	GD	VG	FN	VF	VF/NM	NM-
nn-Jill Thompson-s/painted-a/c; puppy Barnabas searches for Delirium						20.00

LITTLE EVA
St. John Publishing Co.: May, 1952 - No. 31, Nov, 1956

	GD	VG	FN	VF	VF/NM	NM-
1	16	32	48	94	147	200

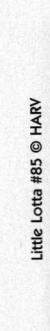

Li'l Ghost #2 © Fago

Little Lenny #1 © MAR

Little Lotta #85 © HARV

	GD 2.0	VG 4.0	FN 6.0	VF 8.0	VF/NM 9.0	NM- 9.2
2	10	20	30	58	79	100
3-5	9	18	27	47	61	75
6-10	8	16	24	42	54	65
11-31	7	14	21	37	46	55
3-D 1,2(10/53, 11/53, 25¢)-Both came w/glasses. 1-Infinity-c	18	36	54	107	169	230
I.W. Reprint #1-3,6-8: 1-r/Little Eva #28. 2-r/Little Eva #29. 3-r/Little Eva #24	2	4	6	8	11	14
Super Reprint #10,12('63),14,16,18('64): 18-r/Little Eva #25.	2	4	6	8	11	14
LI'L GENIUS (Formerly Super Brat; Summer Fun No. 54) (See Blue Bird & Giant Comics #3) **Charlton Comics:** 1954 - No. 52, 1/65; No. 53, 10/65; No. 54, 10/85 - No. 55, 1/86						
5(#1?)	11	22	33	62	86	110
6-10	7	14	21	37	46	55
11-15,19,20	6	12	18	29	36	42
16,17-(68 pgs.)	8	16	24	40	50	60
18-(100 pgs., 10/58)	11	22	33	60	83	105
21-35	3	6	9	16	22	28
36-53	2	4	6	10	14	18
54,55 (Low print)						5.00
LI'L GHOST **St. John Publ. Co./Fago No. 1 on:** 2/58; No. 2,1/59 - No. 3, Mar, 1959						
1(St. John)	9	18	27	50	65	80
2,3	6	12	18	28	34	40
LITTLE GIANT COMICS **Centaur Publications:** 7/38 - No. 3, 10/38; No. 4, 2/39 (132 pgs.) (6-3/4x4-1/2")						
1-B&W with color-c; stories, puzzles, magic	100	200	300	635	1093	1550
2,3-B&W with color-c	65	130	195	416	708	1000
4 (6-5/8x9-3/8")(68 pgs., B&W inside)	65	130	195	416	708	1000
NOTE: *Filchock c-2, 4.* ***Gustavson*** *a-1.* ***Pinajian*** *a-4.* ***Bob Wood*** *a-1.*						
LITTLE GIANT DETECTIVE FUNNIES **Centaur Publ.:** Oct, 1938; No. 4, Jan, 1939 (6-3/4x4-1/2", 132 pgs., B&W)						
1-B&W with color-c	100	200	300	65	1093	1550
4(1/39, B&W; color-c; 68 pgs., 6-1/2x9-1/2")-Eisner-r	65	130	195	416	708	1000
LITTLE GIANT MOVIE FUNNIES **Centaur Publ.:** Aug, 1938 - No. 2, Oct, 1938 (6-3/4x4-1/2", 132 pgs., B&W)						
1-Ed Wheelan's "Minute Movies" reprints	100	200	300	635	1093	1550
2-Ed Wheelan's "Minute Movies" reprints	65	130	195	416	708	1000
LITTLE GROUCHO (...the Red-Headed Tornado; ...Grouchy No. 2) **Reston Publ. Co.:** No. 16; Feb-Mar, 1955 - No. 2, June-July, 1955 (See Tippy Terry)						
16, 1 (2-3/55)	8	16	24	42	54	65
2(6-7/55)	6	12	18	27	33	38
LITTLE HIAWATHA (Disney; see Walt Disney's C&S #143) **Dell Publishing Co.:** No. 439, Dec, 1952 - No. 988, May-July, 1959						
Four Color 439 (#1)	6	12	18	39	62	85
Four Color 787 (4/57), 901 (5/58), 988	5	10	15	30	48	65
LITTLE IKE **St. John Publishing Co.:** April, 1953 - No. 4, Oct, 1953						
1	10	20	30	54	72	90
2	6	12	18	31	38	45
3,4	5	10	15	24	30	35
LITTLE IODINE (See Giant Comic Album) **Dell Publ. Co.:** No. 224, 4/49 - No. 257, 1949; 3-5/50 - No. 56, 4-6/62 (1-4-52pgs.)						
Four Color 224-By Jimmy Hatlo	11	22	33	80	145	210
Four Color 257	8	16	24	56	93	130
1(3-5/50)	9	18	27	65	113	160
2-5	6	12	18	37	59	80
6-10	4	8	12	28	44	60
11-20	4	8	12	22	34	45
21-30: 27-Xmas-c	3	6	9	20	30	40
31-40	3	6	9	18	27	35
41-56	3	6	9	16	23	30
LITTLE JACK FROST **Avon Periodicals:** 1951						
1	11	22	33	62	86	110
LI'L JINX (Little Archie in Animal Land #17) (Also see Pep Comics #62)						

	GD 2.0	VG 4.0	FN 6.0	VF 8.0	VF/NM 9.0	NM- 9.2
Archie Publications: No. 1(#11), Nov, 1956 - No. 16, Sept, 1957						
1(#11)-By Joe Edwards; "First Issue" on cover	14	28	42	76	108	140
12(1/57)-16	10	20	30	54	72	90
LI'L JINX (See Archie Giant Series Magazine No. 223)						
LI'L JINX CHRISTMAS BAG (See Archie Giant Series Mag. No. 195, 206, 219)						
LI'L JINX GIANT LAUGH-OUT (See Archie Giant Series Mag. No. 176, 185) **Archie Publications:** No. 33, Sept, 1971 - No. 43, Nov, 1973 (52 pgs.)						
33-43 (52 pgs.)	2	4	6	13	18	22
LITTLE JOE (See Popular Comics & Super Comics) **Dell Publishing Co.:** No. 1, 1942						
Four Color 1	50	100	150	413	807	1200
LITTLE JOE **St. John Publishing Co.:** Apr, 1953						
1	5	10	15	24	30	35
LI'L KIDS (Also see Li'l Pals) **Marvel Comics Group:** 8/70 - No. 2, 10/70; No. 3, 11/71 - No. 12, 6/73						
1	7	14	21	49	80	110
2-9	4	8	12	26	41	55
10-12-Calvin app.	4	8	12	28	44	60
LITTLE KING **Dell Publishing Co.:** No. 494, Aug, 1953 - No. 677, Feb, 1956						
Four Color 494 (#1)	9	18	27	60	100	140
Four Color 597, 677	5	10	15	34	55	75
LITTLE LANA (Formerly Lana) **Marvel Comics (MjMC):** No. 8, Nov, 1949; No. 9, Mar, 1950						
8,9	11	22	33	64	90	115
LITTLE LENNY **Marvel Comics (CDS):** June, 1949 - No. 3, Nov, 1949						
1-Little Aspirin app.	13	26	39	74	105	135
2,3	9	18	27	47	61	75
LITTLE LIZZIE **Marvel Comics (PrPI)/Atlas (OMC):** 6/49 - No. 5, 4/50; 9/53 - No. 3, Jan, 1954						
1	14	28	42	82	121	160
2-5	9	18	27	50	65	80
1 (9/53, 2nd series by Atlas)-Howie Post-c	10	20	30	56	76	95
2,3	8	16	24	42	54	65
LITTLE LOTTA (See Harvey Hits No. 10) **Harvey Publications:** 11/55 - No. 110, 11/73; No. 111, 9/74 - No. 120, 5/76 V2#1, Oct, 1992 - No. 4, July, 1993 ($1.25)						
1-Richie Rich (r) & Little Dot begin	36	72	108	280	540	800
2,3	16	32	48	117	226	335
4,5	11	22	33	78	139	200
6-10	8	16	24	54	90	125
11-20	6	12	18	41	66	90
21-40	4	8	12	24	37	50
41-60	3	6	9	19	29	38
61-80: 62-1st app. Nurse Jenny	3	6	9	16	22	28
81-99	2	4	6	11	16	20
100-103: All 52 pg. Giants	3	6	9	14	19	24
104-120	2	4	6	8	10	12
V2#1-4 (1992-93)						3.00
NOTE: *No. 121 was advertised, but never released.*						
LITTLE LOTTA FOODLAND **Harvey Publications:** 9/63 - No. 14, 10/67; No. 15, 10/68 - No. 29, Oct, 1972						
1-Little Lotta, Little Dot, Richie Rich, 68 pgs. begin	13	26	39	90	165	240
2,3	9	18	27	60	100	140
4,5	7	14	21	45	73	100
6-10	5	10	15	32	51	70
11-20	3	6	9	20	30	40
21-26: 26-Last 68 pg. issue	3	6	9	16	23	30
27,28: Both 52 pgs.	3	6	9	14	19	24
29-(36 pgs.)	2	4	6	9	13	16
LITTLE LULU (Formerly Marge's Little Lulu) **Gold Key 207-257/Whitman 258 on:** No. 207, Sept, 1972 - No. 268, Mar, 1984						
207,209,220-Stanley-r. 207-1st app. Henrietta	2	4	6	11	16	20
208,210-219: 208-1st app. Snobbly, Wilbur's butler	2	4	6	9	12	15

Lilte Lulu #215 © M. Buell

Little Max Comics #50 © HARV

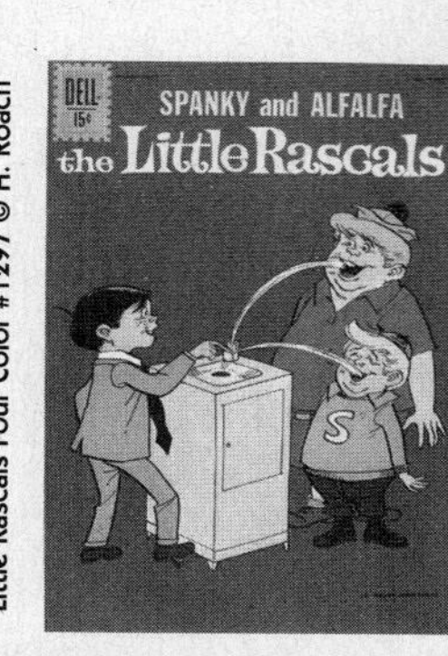

Little Rascals Four Color #1297 © H. Roach

	GD 2.0	VG 4.0	FN 6.0	VF 8.0	VF/NM 9.0	NM- 9.2
221-240,242-249, 250(r/#166), 251-254(r/#206)	1	3	4	6	8	10
241,263-Stanley-r	2	4	6	8	10	12
255-257(Gold Key): 256-r/#212	1	2	3	5	7	9
258,259,262(50¢-c),264(2/82),265(3/82) (Whitman)	2	4	6	8	11	14
260-(9/80)(Whitman pre-pack only - low distribution)	13	26	39	93	172	250
261-(11/80)(Whitman pre-pack only)	4	8	12	24	37	50
262-(1/81) Variant 40¢-c price error (reg. ed. 50¢-c)	2	4	6	11	16	20
266-268 (All #90028 on-c; no date, no date code; 3-pack): 266(7/83). 267(8/83). 268(3/84)-Stanley-r	3	6	9	15	21	26

LITTLE LULU
Dark Horse Books: Nov, 2004 - Present ($9.95/$10.95, B&W, digest-size TPB)

	GD 2.0	VG 4.0	FN 6.0	VF 8.0	VF/NM 9.0	NM- 9.2
Vol. 1 -B&W reprints of Marge's Little Lulu #6-12; John Stanley-s/a & Irving Tripp-a						10.00
...: (Vol. 2) Lulu Takes a Trip (2/05) -B&W r/Marge's Little Lulu #13-16						10.00
...: (Vol. 3) My Dinner With Lulu (4/05) -B&W r/Four Color #74,97,110,115,120						10.00
...: (Vol. 4) Sunday Afternoon (6/05) -B&W r/Four Color #131,139,146,158						10.00
...: (Vol. 5) Lulu in the Doghouse (8/05) -B&W r/Four Color #165 & Marge's Little Lulu #1-5						10.00
...: (Vol. 6) Letters to Santa (10/05) -B&W r/Marge's Little Lulu #18-22						10.00
...: (Vol. 7) Lulu's Umbrella Service (12/05) -B&W r/Marge's Little Lulu #23-27						10.00
...: (Vol. 8) Late For School (2/06) -B&W r/Marge's Little Lulu #28-32						10.00
...: (Vol. 9) Lucky Lulu (4/06) -B&W r/Marge's Little Lulu #33-37						10.00
...: (Vol. 10) All Dressed Up (6/06) -B&W r/Marge's Little Lulu #38-42						10.00
...: (Vol. 11) April Fools (8/06) -B&W r/Marge's Little Lulu #43-48						10.00
...: (Vol. 12) Leave It to Lulu (10/06) -B&W r/Marge's Little Lulu #49-53						10.00
...: (Vol. 13) Too Much Fun (12/06) -B&W r/Marge's Little Lulu #54-58						10.00
...: (Vol. 14) Queen Lulu (2/07) -B&W r/Marge's Little Lulu #59-63						10.00
...: (Vol. 15) The Explorers (4/07) -B&W r/Marge's Little Lulu #64-68						10.00
...: (Vol. 16) A Handy Kid (7/07, $10.95) -B&W r/Marge's Little Lulu #69-74						11.00
...: (Vol. 17) The Valentine (10/07, $10.95) -B&W r/Marge's Little Lulu #75-81						11.00
...: (Vol. 18) The Expert (1/08, $10.95) -B&W r/Marge's Little Lulu #82-87						11.00
Color Special (9/06, $13.95, standard size) r/various stories from Marge's Little Lulu						14.00

LITTLE MARY MIXUP (See Comics On Parade)
United Features Syndicate: No. 10, 1939, - No. 26, 1940

	GD 2.0	VG 4.0	FN 6.0	VF 8.0	VF/NM 9.0	NM- 9.2
Single Series 10, 26	34	68	102	199	325	450

LITTLE MAX COMICS (Joe Palooka's Pal; see Joe Palooka)
Harvey Publications: Oct, 1949 - No. 73, Nov, 1961

	GD 2.0	VG 4.0	FN 6.0	VF 8.0	VF/NM 9.0	NM- 9.2
1-Infinity-c; Little Dot begins; Joe Palooka on-c	22	44	66	128	209	290
2-Little Dot app.; Joe Palooka on-c	14	28	42	78	112	145
3-Little Dot app.; Joe Palooka on-c	10	20	30	58	79	100
4-10: 5-Little Dot app., 1pg.	9	18	27	47	61	75
11-20	8	16	24	40	50	60
21-40: 23-Little Dot app. 38-r/#20	6	12	18	31	38	45
41-62,66	3	6	9	18	27	35
63-65,67-73-Include new five pg. Richie Rich stories. 70-73-Little Lotta app.	3	6	9	19	29	38

LI'L MENACE
Fago Magazine Co.: Dec, 1958 - No. 3, May, 1959

	GD 2.0	VG 4.0	FN 6.0	VF 8.0	VF/NM 9.0	NM- 9.2
1-Peter Rabbit app.	8	16	24	44	57	70
2-Peter Rabbit (Vincent Fago's)	7	14	21	35	43	50
3	6	12	18	28	34	40

LITTLE MERMAID, THE (Walt Disney's...; also see Disney's...)
W. D. Publications (Disney): 1990 (no date given)($5.95, no ads, 52 pgs.)

	GD 2.0	VG 4.0	FN 6.0	VF 8.0	VF/NM 9.0	NM- 9.2
nn-Adapts animated movie	1	2	3	4	5	7
nn-Comic version ($2.50)						3.00

LITTLE MERMAID, THE
Disney Comics: 1992 - No. 4, 1992 ($1.50, mini-series)

	GD 2.0	VG 4.0	FN 6.0	VF 8.0	VF/NM 9.0	NM- 9.2
1-4: Based on movie						3.00
1-4: 2nd printings sold at Wal-Mart w/different-c						2.25

LITTLE MISS MUFFET
Best Books (Standard Comics)/King Features Synd.: No. 11, Dec, 1948 - No. 13, March, 1949

	GD 2.0	VG 4.0	FN 6.0	VF 8.0	VF/NM 9.0	NM- 9.2
11-Strip reprints; Fanny Cory-c/a	9	18	27	50	65	80
12,13-Strip reprints; Fanny Cory-c/a	7	14	21	35	43	50

LITTLE MISS SUNBEAM COMICS
Magazine Enterprises/Quality Bakers of America: June-July, 1950 - No. 4, Dec-Jan, 1950-51

	GD 2.0	VG 4.0	FN 6.0	VF 8.0	VF/NM 9.0	NM- 9.2
1	15	30	45	94	147	200
2-4	10	20	30	56	76	95
...Advs. In Space ('55)	7	14	21	35	43	50

LITTLE MONSTERS, THE (See March of Comics #423, Three Stooges #17)
Gold Key: Nov, 1964 - No. 44, Feb, 1978

	GD 2.0	VG 4.0	FN 6.0	VF 8.0	VF/NM 9.0	NM- 9.2
1	6	12	18	37	59	80
2	3	6	9	20	30	40
3-10	3	6	9	17	25	32
11-20	3	6	9	15	21	26
21-30: 19-21-Reprints	2	4	6	11	16	20
31-44: 34-39,43-Reprints	2	4	6	8	11	14

LITTLE MONSTERS (Movie)
Now Comics: 1989 - No. 6, June, 1990 ($1.75)

	GD 2.0	VG 4.0	FN 6.0	VF 8.0	VF/NM 9.0	NM- 9.2
1-6: Photo-c from movie						2.50

LITTLE NEMO (See Cocomalt, Future Comics, Help, Jest, Kayo, Punch, Red Seal, & Superworld; most by Winsor McCay Jr., son of famous artist) (Other McCay books: see Little Sammy Sneeze & Dreams of the Rarebit Fiend)

LITTLE NEMO (...in Slumberland)
McCay Features/Nostalgia Press('69): 1945 (11x7-1/4", 28 pgs., B&W)

	GD 2.0	VG 4.0	FN 6.0	VF 8.0	VF/NM 9.0	NM- 9.2
1905 & 1911 reprints by Winsor McCay	10	20	30	56	76	95
1969-70 (Exact reprint)	2	4	6	9	12	15

LITTLE ORPHAN ANNIE (See Annie, Famous Feature Stories, Marvel Super Special, Merry Christmas..., Popular Comics, Super Book #7, 11, 23 & Super Comics)

LITTLE ORPHAN ANNIE
David McKay Publ./Dell Publishing Co.: No. 7, 1937 - No. 3, Sept-Nov, 1948; No. 206, Dec, 1948

	GD 2.0	VG 4.0	FN 6.0	VF 8.0	VF/NM 9.0	NM- 9.2
Feature Books(McKay) 7-(1937) (Rare)	97	194	291	621	1061	1500
Four Color 12(1941)	57	114	171	362	624	885
Four Color 18(1943)-Flag-c	33	66	99	256	496	735
Four Color 52(1944)	26	52	78	186	361	535
Four Color 76(1945)	21	42	63	149	290	430
Four Color 107(1946)	18	36	54	127	249	370
Four Color 152(1947)	12	24	36	87	158	230
1(3-5/48)-r/strips from 5/7/44 to 7/30/44	12	24	36	85	155	225
2-r/strips from 7/21/40 to 9/9/40	9	18	27	60	100	140
3-r/strips from 9/10/40 to 11/9/40	9	18	27	60	100	140
Four Color 206(12/48)	8	16	24	54	90	125

LI'L PALS (Also see Li'l Kids)
Marvel Comics Group: Sept, 1972 - No. 5, May, 1973

	GD 2.0	VG 4.0	FN 6.0	VF 8.0	VF/NM 9.0	NM- 9.2
1	6	12	18	41	66	90
2-5	4	8	12	26	41	55

LI'L PAN (Formerly Rocket Kelly; becomes Junior Comics with #9)
Fox Features Syndicate: No. 6, Dec-Jan, 1946-47 - No. 8, Apr-May, 1947
(Also see Wotalife Comics)

	GD 2.0	VG 4.0	FN 6.0	VF 8.0	VF/NM 9.0	NM- 9.2
6	10	20	30	58	79	100
7,8: 7-Atomic bomb story; robot-c	8	16	24	44	57	70

LITTLE PEOPLE (Also see Darby O'Gill & the...)
Dell Publishing Co.: No. 485, Aug-Oct, 1953 - No. 1062, Dec, 1959 (Walt Scott's)

	GD 2.0	VG 4.0	FN 6.0	VF 8.0	VF/NM 9.0	NM- 9.2
Four Color 485 (#1)	8	16	24	52	86	120
Four Color 573(7/54), 633(6/55)	5	10	15	32	51	70
Four Color 692(3/56),753(11/56),809(7/57),868(12/57),908(5/58), 959(12/58), 1062	5	10	15	32	51	70

LITTLE RASCALS
Dell Publishing Co.: No. 674, Jan, 1956 - No. 1297, Mar-May, 1962

	GD 2.0	VG 4.0	FN 6.0	VF 8.0	VF/NM 9.0	NM- 9.2
Four Color 674 (#1)	9	18	27	60	100	140
Four Color 778(3/57),825(8/57)	6	12	18	39	62	85
Four Color 883(3/58),936(9/58),974(3/59),1030(9/59),1079(2-4/60),1137(9-11/60)	6	12	18	37	59	80
Four Color 1174(3-5/61),1224(10-12/61),1297	5	10	15	30	48	65

LI'L RASCAL TWINS (Formerly Nature Boy)
Charlton Comics: No. 6, 1957 - No. 18, Jan, 1960

	GD 2.0	VG 4.0	FN 6.0	VF 8.0	VF/NM 9.0	NM- 9.2
6-Li'l Genius & Tomboy in all	6	12	18	29	36	42
7-18: 7-Timmy the Timid Ghost app.	4	8	12	18	22	25

LITTLE RED HOT: (CHANE OF FOOLS)
Image Comics: Feb, 1999 - No. 3, Apr, 1999 ($2.95/$3.50, B&W, limited series)

	GD 2.0	VG 4.0	FN 6.0	VF 8.0	VF/NM 9.0	NM- 9.2
1-3-Dawn Brown-s/a. 2,3-($3.50-c)						3.50
The Foolish Collection TPB ($12.95) r/#1-3						13.00

LITTLE RED HOT: BOUND
Image Comics: July, 2001 - No. 3, Nov, 2001 ($2.95, color, limited series)

	GD 2.0	VG 4.0	FN 6.0	VF 8.0	VF/NM 9.0	NM- 9.2
1-3-Dawn Brown-s/a.						3.00

LITTLE ROQUEFORT COMICS (See Paul Terry's Comics #105)
St. John Publishing Co.(all pre-code)/Pines No. 10: June, 1952 - No. 9, Oct, 1953; No. 10,

Little Sad Sack #14 © HARV

Lobo #15 © DC

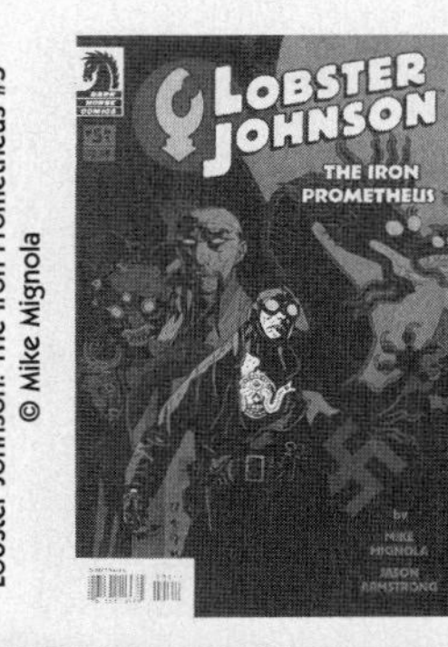

Lobster Johnson: The Iron Prometheus #5 © Mike Mignola

	GD 2.0	VG 4.0	FN 6.0	VF 8.0	VF/NM 9.0	NM- 9.2
Summer, 1958						
1-By Paul Terry	10	20	30	54	72	90
2	6	12	18	31	38	45
3-10: 10-CBS Television Presents on-c	5	10	15	24	30	35
LITTLE SAD SACK (See Harvey Hits No. 73, 76, 79, 81, 83)						
Harvey Publications: Oct, 1964 - No. 19, Nov, 1967						
1-Richie Rich app. on cover only	5	10	15	32	51	70
2-10	3	6	9	18	27	35
11-19	3	6	9	16	22	28
LITTLE SCOUTS						
Dell Publishing Co.: No. 321, Mar, 1951 - No. 587, Oct, 1954						
Four Color 321 (#1, 3/51)	5	10	15	30	48	65
2(10-12/51) - 6(10-12/52)	4	8	12	24	37	50
Four Color 462,506,550,587	4	8	12	24	37	50
LITTLE SHOP OF HORRORS SPECIAL (Movie)						
DC Comics: Feb, 1987 ($2.00, 68 pgs.)						
1-Colan-c/a						4.00
LITTLE SPUNKY						
I. W. Enterprises: No date (1963?) (10¢)						
1-r/Frisky Fables #1	2	4	6	8	11	14
LITTLE STAR						
Oni Press: Feb, 2005 - No. 6, Dec, 2005 ($2.99, B&W, limited series)						
1-6-Andi Watson-s/a						3.00
TPB (4/06, $19.95) r/#1-6						20.00
LITTLE STOOGES, THE (The Three Stooges' Sons)						
Gold Key: Sept, 1972 - No. 7, Mar, 1974						
1-Norman Maurer cover/stories in all	3	6	9	19	29	38
2-7	2	4	6	13	18	22
LITTLEST OUTLAW (Disney)						
Dell Publishing Co.: No. 609, Jan, 1955						
Four Color 609-Movie, photo-c	6	12	18	43	69	95
LITTLEST SNOWMAN, THE						
Dell Publishing Co.: No. 755, 12/56; No. 864, 12/57; 12-2/1963-64						
Four Color 755,864, 1(1964)	5	10	15	32	51	70
LI'L TOMBOY (Formerly Fawcett's Funny Animals; see Giant Comics #3)						
Charlton Comics: V14#92, Oct, 1956; No. 93, Mar, 1957 - No. 107, Feb, 1960						
V14#92	6	12	18	27	33	38
93-107: 97-Atomic Bunny app.	5	10	14	20	24	28
LI'L WILLIE COMICS (Formerly & becomes Willie Comics #22 on)						
Marvel Comics (MgPC): No. 20, July, 1949 - No. 21, Sept, 1949						
20,21: 20-Little Aspirin app.	14	28	42	76	108	140
LITTLE WOMEN (See Power Record Comics)						
LIVE IT UP						
Spire Christian Comics (Fleming H. Revell Co.): 1973, 1974 (39-49 cents)						
nn-1973 Edition	2	4	6	9	12	15
nn-1974 Edition	1	3	4	6	8	10
LIVEWIRES						
Marvel Comics: Apr, 2005 - No. 6, Sept, 2005 ($2.99, limited series)						
1-6-Adam Warren-s/c; Rick Mays-a						3.00
...: Clockwork Thugs, Yo (2005, $7.99, digest) r/#1-6						8.00
LIVING BIBLE, THE						
Living Bible Corp.: Fall, 1945 - No. 3, Spring, 1946						
1-The Life of Paul; all have L. B. Cole-c	39	78	117	231	378	525
2-Joseph & His Brethren; Jonah & the Whale	27	54	81	158	259	360
3-Chaplains At War (classic-c)	40	80	120	246	411	575
LIVING WITH THE DEAD						
Dark Horse Comics: Oct, 2007 - No. 3, Nov, 2007 ($2.99, limited series)						
1-3-Zombies; Mike Richardson-s/Ben Stenbeck-a/Richard Corben-c						3.00
LOADED BIBLE						
Image Comics: Apr, 2006; May, 2007; Feb, 2008 ($4.99)						
...: Jesus vs. Vampires (4/06) Tim Seeley-s/Nate Bellegarde-a						5.00
...2: Blood of Christ (5/07) Seeley-s/Mike Norton-a. ...3: Communion (2/08)						5.00
LOBO						

	GD 2.0	VG 4.0	FN 6.0	VF 8.0	VF/NM 9.0	NM- 9.2
Dell Publishing Co.: Dec, 1965; No. 2, Oct, 1966						
1-1st black character to have his own title	4	8	12	28	44	60
2	3	6	9	20	30	40
LOBO (Also see Action #650, Adventures of Superman, Demon (2nd series), Justice League, L.E.G.I.O.N., Mister Miracle, Omega Men #3 & Superman #41)						
DC Comics: Nov, 1990 - No. 4, Feb, 1991 ($1.50, color, limited series)						
1-(99¢)-Giffen plots/Breakdowns in all						4.00
1-2nd printing						2.50
2-4: 2-Legion '89 spin-off. 1-4 have Bisley painted covers & art						2.50
...: Blazing Chain of Love 1 (9/92, $1.50)-Denys Cowan-c/a; Alan Grant scripts, ...Convention Special 1 (1993, $1.75), ...Paramilitary Christmas Special 1 (1991, $2.39, 52 pgs.) -Bisley-c/a, ...: Portrait of a Victim 1 (1993, $1.75)						2.50
...: Portrait of a Bastich TPB (2008, $19.99) r/#1-4 & Lobo's Back #1-4						20.00
LOBO (Also see Showcase '95 #9)						
DC Comics: Dec, 1993 - No. 64, Jul, 1999 ($1.75/$1.95/$2.25/$2.50, mature)						
1 ($2.95)-Foil enhanced-c; Alan Grant scripts begin						3.00
2-9,0,10-64: 2-7-Alan Grant scripts. 9-(9/94). 0-(10/94)-Origin retold. 50-Lobo vs. the DCU. 58-Giffen-a						2.50
#1,000,000 (11/98) 853rd Century x-over						2.50
Annual 1 (1993, $3.50, 68 pgs.)-Bloodlines x-over						3.50
Annual 2 (1994, $3.50)-21 artists (20 listed on-c); Alan Grant script; Elseworlds story						3.50
Annual 3 (1995, $3.95)-Year One story						4.00
.../Authority: Holiday Hell TPB (2006, $17.99) r/Lobo Paramilitary Christmas Special; Authority/Lobo: Jingle Hell and Spring Break Massacre; WildStorm Winter Special						18.00
...Big Babe Spring Break Special (Spr, '95, $1.95)-Balent-a						2.50
...Bounty Hunting for Fun and Profit ('95)-Bisley-c						5.00
... Chained (5/97, $2.50)-Alan Grant story						2.50
.../Deadman: The Brave And The Bald (2/95, $3.50)						3.50
.../Demon: Helloween (12/96, $2.25)-Giarrano-a						2.50
...Fragtastic Voyage 1 ('97, $5.95)-Mejia painted-c/a						6.00
...Gallery (9/95, $3.50)-pin-ups.						3.50
...In the Chair 1 (8/94, $1.95, 36 pgs.), ...I Quit-(12/95, $2.25)						2.50
.../Judge Dredd ('95, $4.95).						5.00
...Lobocop 1 (2/94, $1.95)-Alan Grant scripts; painted-c						2.50
LOBO: (Title Series), DC Comics						
--A CONTRACT ON GAWD, 4/94 - 7/94 (mature) 1-4: Alan Grant scripts. 3-Groo cameo						2.50
--DEATH AND TAXES, 10/96 - No. 4, 1/97, 1-4-Giffen/Grant scripts						2.50
--GOES TO HOLLYWOOD, 8/96 ($2.25), 1-Grant scripts						2.50
--HIGHWAY TO HELL, 1/10 - No. 2, 2/10 ($6.99), 1,2-Scott Ian-s/Sam Kieth-a/c						7.00
--INFANTICIDE, 10/92 - 1/93 ($1.50, mature), 1-4-Giffen-c/a; Grant scripts						2.50
--/ MASK, 2/97 - No. 2, 3/97 ($5.95), 1,2						6.00
--'S BACK, 5/92 - No. 4, 11/92 ($1.50, mature), 1-4: 1-Has 3 outer covers. Bisley painted-c 1,2; a-1-3. 3-Sam Kieth-c; all have Giffen plots/breakdown & Grant scripts						2.50
Trade paperback (1993, $9.95)-r/1-4						10.00
--THE DUCK, 6/97 ($1.95), 1-A. Grant-s/V. Semeiks & R. Kryssing-a						2.50
--UNAMERICAN GLADIATORS, 6/93 - No. 4, 9/93 ($1.75, mature), 1-4-Mignola-c; Grant/Wagner scripts						2.50
--UNBOUND, 8/03 - No. 6, 5/04 ($2.95), 1-6-Giffen-s/Horley-c/a. 4-6-Ambush Bug app.						3.00
LOBSTER JOHNSON: THE IRON PROMETHEUS (See B.P.R.D. and Hellboy titles)						
Dark Horse Comics: Sept, 2007 - No. 5, Jan, 2008 ($2.99, limited series)						
1-5-Mignola-s/c; Armstrong-a						3.00
LOCKE & KEY						
IDW Publ.: Feb, 2008 - No. 6, July, 2008 ($3.99, limited series)						
1-Joe Hill-s/Gabriel Rodriguez-a						10.00
1-Second printing						4.00
2-6						4.00
...: Welcome to Lovecraft Special Edition #1 SC (9/09, $5.99) Hill-s/Rodriguez-a; script; back-up story with final art from Seth Fisher						6.00
LOCKE & KEY: CROWN OF SHADOWS						
IDW Publ.: Nov, 2009 - Present ($3.99, limited series)						
1-Joe Hill-s/Gabriel Rodriguez-a						4.00
LOCKE & KEY: HEAD GAMES						
IDW Publ.: Jan, 2009 - No. 6, Jun, 2009 ($3.99, limited series)						
1-6-Joe Hill-s/Gabriel Rodriguez-a. 3-EC style-c						4.00
LOCKJAW AND THE PET AVENGERS (Also see Tails of the Pet Avengers)						
Marvel Comics: July, 2009 - No. 4, Oct, 2009 ($2.99, limited series)						

Logan's Run #1 © MAR

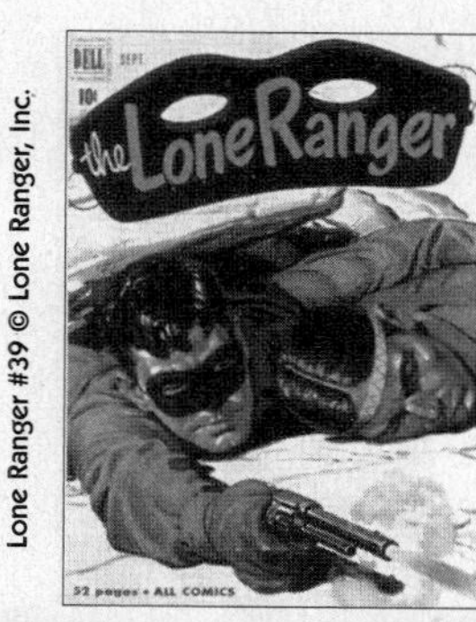

Lone Ranger #39 © Lone Ranger, Inc.

Lone Ranger (2006 series) #9 © Classic Media

	GD 2.0	VG 4.0	FN 6.0	VF 8.0	VF/NM 9.0	NM- 9.2
1-4-Lockheed, Frog Thor, Zabu, Lockjaw and Redwing team up; 2 covers on each						3.00

LOCO (Magazine) (Satire)
Satire Publications: Aug, 1958 - V1#3, Jan, 1959

	GD	VG	FN	VF	VF/NM	NM-
V1#1-Chic Stone-a	9	18	27	47	61	75
V1#2,3-Severin-a, 2 pgs. Davis; 3-Heath-a	7	14	21	35	43	50

LOGAN (Wolverine)
Marvel Comics: May, 2008 - No. 3, Jul, 2008 ($3.99, limited series)

	GD	VG	FN	VF	VF/NM	NM-
1-3-Vaughan-s/Risso-a/c; regular & B&W editions for each						4.00

LOGAN: PATH OF THE WARLORD
Marvel Comics: Feb, 1996 ($5.95, one-shot)

	GD	VG	FN	VF	VF/NM	NM-
1-John Paul Leon-a						6.00

LOGAN: SHADOW SOCIETY
Marvel Comics: 1996 ($5.95, one-shot)

	GD	VG	FN	VF	VF/NM	NM-
1						6.00

LOGAN'S RUN
Marvel Comics Group: Jan, 1977 - No. 7, July, 1977

	GD	VG	FN	VF	VF/NM	NM-
1: 1-5-Based on novel & movie	2	4	6	8	10	12
2-5,7: 6,7-New stories adapted from novel	1	2	3	5	6	8
6-1st Thanos (also see Iron Man #55) solo story (back-up) by Zeck (6/77)	3	6	9	20	30	40
6-(35¢-c variant, limited distribution)	8	16	24	52	86	120
7-(35¢-c variant, limited distribution)	3	6	9	20	30	40

NOTE: ***Austin** a-6i. **Gulacy** c-6. **Kane** c-7p. **Perez** a-1-5p; c-1-5p. **Sutton** a-6p, 7p.*

LOIS & CLARK, THE NEW ADVENTURES OF SUPERMAN
DC Comics: 1994 ($9.95, one-shot)

	GD	VG	FN	VF	VF/NM	NM-
1-r/Man of Steel #2, Superman Ann. 1, Superman #9 & 11, Action #600 & 655, Adventures of Superman #445, 462 & 466	1	3	4	6	8	10

LOIS LANE (Also see Daring New Adventures of Supergirl, Showcase #9,10 & Superman's Girlfriend...)
DC Comics: Aug, 1986 - No. 2, Sept, 1986 ($1.50, 52 pgs.)

	GD	VG	FN	VF	VF/NM	NM-
1,2-Morrow-c/a in each						4.00

LOKI (Thor)
Marvel Comics: Sept, 2004 - No. 4, Nov, 2004 ($3.50)

	GD	VG	FN	VF	VF/NM	NM-
1-4-Rodi-s/Ribic-a/c						3.50
HC (2005, $17.99, with dustjacket) oversized r/#1-4; original proposal and sketch pages						18.00
SC (2007, $12.99) r/#1-4; original proposal and sketch pages						13.00

LOLLY AND PEPPER
Dell Publishing Co.: No. 832, Sept, 1957 - July, 1962

	GD	VG	FN	VF	VF/NM	NM-
Four Color 832(#1)	5	10	15	30	48	65
Four Color 940,978,1086,1206	4	8	12	22	34	45
01-459-207 (7/62)	3	6	9	18	27	35

LOMAX (See Police Action)

LONDON'S DARK
Escape/Titan: 1989 ($8.95, B&W, graphic novel)

	GD	VG	FN	VF	VF/NM	NM-
nn-James Robinson script; Paul Johnson-c/a	1	2	3	5	7	9

LONE
Dark Horse Comics: Sept, 2003 - No. 6, Mar, 2004 ($2.99)

	GD	VG	FN	VF	VF/NM	NM-
1-6-Stuart Moore-s/Jerome Opeña-a/Templesmith-c						3.00

LONE EAGLE (The Flame No. 5 on)
Ajax/Farrell Publications: Apr-May, 1954 - No. 4, Oct-Nov, 1954

	GD	VG	FN	VF	VF/NM	NM-
1	13	26	39	74	105	135
2-4: 3-Bondage-c	9	18	27	50	65	80

LONE GUNMEN, THE (From the X-Files)
Dark Horse Comics: June, 2001 ($2.99, one-shot)

	GD	VG	FN	VF	VF/NM	NM-
1-Paul Lee-a; photo-c						3.00

LONELY HEART (Formerly Dear Lonely Hearts; Dear Heart #15 on)
Ajax/Farrell Publ. (Excellent Publ.): No. 9, Mar, 1955 - No. 14, Feb, 1956

	GD	VG	FN	VF	VF/NM	NM-
9-Kamenesque-a; (Last precode)	10	20	30	54	72	90
10-14	7	14	21	37	46	55

LONE RANGER, THE (See Ace Comics, Aurora, Dell Giants,Future Comics, Golden Comics Digest #48, King Comics, Magic Comics & March of Comics #165, 174, 193, 208, 225, 238, 310, 322, 338, 350)

LONE RANGER, THE
Dell Publishing Co.: No. 3, 1939 - No. 167, Feb, 1947

	GD	VG	FN	VF	VF/NM	NM-
Large Feature Comic 3(1939)-Heigh-Yo Silver; text with illus. by Robert Weisman; also exists as a Whitman #710	174	348	522	1114	1907	2700
Large Feature Comic 7(1939)-Illustr. by Henry Vallely; Hi-Yo Silver the Lone Ranger to the Rescue; also exists as a Whitman #715	161	322	483	1030	1765	2500
Feature Book 21(1940), 24(1941)	87	174	261	553	952	1350
Four Color 82(1945)	38	76	114	288	557	825
Four Color 98(1945),118(1946)	29	58	87	212	406	600
Four Color 125(1946),136(1947)	19	38	57	139	270	400
Four Color 151,167(1947)	17	34	51	119	230	340

LONE RANGER, THE (Movie, radio & TV; Clayton Moore starred as Lone Ranger in the movies; No. 1-37: strip reprints)(See Dell Giants)
Dell Publishing Co.: Jan-Feb, 1948 - No. 145, May-July, 1962

	GD	VG	FN	VF	VF/NM	NM-
1 (36 pgs.)-The Lone Ranger, his horse Silver, companion Tonto & his horse Scout begin	52	104	156	442	871	1300
2 (52 pgs. begin, end #41)	27	54	81	196	381	565
3-5	20	40	60	146	283	420
6,7,9,10	17	34	51	122	236	350
8-Origin retold; Indian back-c begin, end #35	20	40	60	142	276	410
11-20: 11- "Young Hawk" Indian boy serial begins, ends #145	13	26	39	90	165	240
21,22,24-31: 51-Reprint. 31-1st Mask logo	10	20	30	73	129	185
23-Origin retold	13	26	39	91	168	245
32-37: 32-Painted-c begin. 36-Animal photo back-c begin, end #49. 37-Last newspaper-r issue; new outfit; red shirt becomes blue; most known copies show the blue shirt on-c & inside	9	18	27	64	110	155
37-Variant issue; Long Ranger wears a red shirt on-c and inside. A few copies of the red shirt outfit were printed before catching the mistake and changing the color to blue (rare)	16	32	48	115	220	325
38-41 (All 52 pgs.) 38-Paul S. Newman-s (wrote most of the stories #38-on)	9	18	27	61	103	145
42-50 (36 pgs.)	8	16	24	52	86	120
51-74 (52 pgs.): 56-One pg. origin story of Lone Ranger & Tonto. 71-Blank inside-c	7	14	21	49	80	110
75,77-99: 79-X-mas-c	7	14	21	45	73	100
76-Classic flag-c	7	14	21	49	80	110
100	8	16	24	52	86	120
101-111: Last painted-c	6	12	18	43	69	95
112-Clayton Moore photo-c begin, end #145	17	34	51	119	230	340
113-117: 117-10¢ &15¢-c exist	10	20	30	70	123	175
118-Origin Lone Ranger, Tonto, & Silver retold; Special anniversary issue	22	44	66	155	300	445
119-140: 139-Fran Striker-s	9	18	27	64	110	155
141-145	10	20	30	67	116	165

NOTE: ***Hank Hartman** painted c(signed)-65, 66, 70, 75, 82; unsigned-64?, 67-69?, 71, 72, 73?, 74?, 76-78, 80, 81, 83-91, 92?, 93-111. **Ernest Nordli** painted c(signed)-42, 50, 52, 53, 56, 59, 60; unsigned-39-41, 44-49, 51, 54, 55, 57, 58, 61-63?*

LONE RANGER, THE
Gold Key (Reprints in #13-20): 9/64 - No. 16, 12/69; No. 17, 11/72; No. 18, 9/74 - No. 28, 3/77

	GD	VG	FN	VF	VF/NM	NM-
1-Retells origin	6	12	18	41	66	90
2	4	8	12	22	34	45
3-10: Small Bear-r in #6-12. 10-Last 12¢ issue	3	6	9	20	30	40
11-17	3	6	9	16	22	28
18-28	2	4	6	11	16	20
Golden West 1(30029-610, 10/66)-Giant; r/most Golden West #3 including Clayton Moore photo front/back-c	7	14	21	45	73	100

LONE RANGER
Dynamite Entertainment: 2006 - Present ($2.99/$3.50)

	GD	VG	FN	VF	VF/NM	NM-
1-Retells origin; Carriello-a/Matthews-s; badge cover by Cassaday						3.00
1-Variant mask cover by Cassaday						5.00
1-Baltimore Comic-Con 2006 variant cover with masked face and horse silhouette						12.00
1-Directors' Cut ($4.99) r/#1 with comments at page bottoms, script and sketches						5.00
2-20: 2-Origin continues; Tonto app.						3.50
... and Tonto 1-3 (2008, 2009, $4.99) Cassaday-c						5.00
... Volume 1: Now and Forever TPB (2007, $19.99) r/#1-6; sketch pages						20.00

LONE RANGER AND TONTO, THE
Topps Comics: Aug, 1994 - No. 4, Nov, 1994 ($2.50, limited series)

	GD	VG	FN	VF	VF/NM	NM-
1-4: 3-Origin of Lone Ranger; Tonto leaves; Lansdale story, Truman-c/a in all.						2.50
1-4: Silver logo. 1-Signed by Lansdale and Truman						6.00
Trade paperback (1/95, $9.95)						10.00

LONE RANGER'S COMPANION TONTO, THE (TV)
Dell Publishing Co.: No. 312, Jan, 1951 - No. 33, Nov-Jan/58-59 (All painted-c)

	GD	VG	FN	VF	VF/NM	NM-
Four Color 312(#1, 1/51)	11	22	33	74	132	190

Lone Rider #4 © Farrell

Looney Tunes #142 © WB

Looney Tunes and Merrie Melodies #95 © WB

	GD 2.0	VG 4.0	FN 6.0	VF 8.0	VF/NM 9.0	NM- 9.2
2(8-10/51),3: (#2 titled "Tonto")	6	12	18	43	69	95
4-10	6	12	18	37	59	80
11-20	5	10	15	32	51	70
21-33	4	8	12	28	44	60

NOTE: ***Ernest Nordli*** *painted c(signed)-2, 7; unsigned-3-6, 8-11, 12?, 13, 14, 18?, 22-24? See Aurora Comic Booklets.*

LONE RANGER'S FAMOUS HORSE HI-YO SILVER, THE (TV)
Dell Publishing Co.: No. 369, Jan, 1952 - No. 36, Oct-Dec, 1960 (All painted-c, most by Sam Savitt) (Lone Ranger appears in most issues)

	GD	VG	FN	VF	VF/NM	NM-
Four Color 369(#1)-Silver's origin as told by The Lone Ranger	10	20	30	71	126	180
Four Color 392(#2, 4/52)	6	12	18	41	66	90
3(7-9/52)-10(4-6/52)	5	10	15	35	55	75
11-36	4	8	12	28	44	60

LONE RIDER (Also see The Rider)
Superior Comics(Farrell Publ.): Apr, 1951 - No. 26, Jul, 1955 (#3-on: 36 pgs.)

	GD	VG	FN	VF	VF/NM	NM-
1 (52 pgs.)-The Lone Rider & his horse Lightnin' begin; Kamenish-a begins	31	62	93	182	296	410
2 (52 pgs.)-The Golden Arrow begins (origin)	17	34	51	98	154	210
3-6: 6-Last Golden Arrow	16	32	48	94	147	200
7-Golden Arrow becomes Swift Arrow; origin of his shield	17	34	51	98	154	210
8-Origin Swift Arrow	18	36	54	103	162	220
9,10	12	24	36	67	94	120
11-14	10	20	30	54	72	90
15-Golden Arrow origin-r from #2, changing name to Swift Arrow	10	20	30	58	79	100
16-20,22-26: 23-Apache Kid app.	9	18	27	50	65	80
21-3-D effect-c	16	32	48	94	147	200

LONERS, THE
Marvel Comics: June, 2007 - No. 6, Jan, 2008 ($2.99, limited series)

	GD	VG	FN	VF	VF/NM	NM-
1-6-Cebulski-s/Moline-a/Pearson-c; Lightspeed, Spider-Woman, Ricochet app.						3.00
...: The Secret Lives of Super Heroes TPB (2008, $14.99) r/#1-6; sketch pages						15.00

LONE WOLF AND CUB
First Comics: May, 1987 - No. 45, Apr, 1991 ($1.95-$3.25, B&W, deluxe size)

	GD	VG	FN	VF	VF/NM	NM-
1-Frank Miller-c & intro.; reprints manga series by Koike & Kojima	1	2	3	6	8	10
1-2nd print, 3rd print, 2-2nd print						3.25
2-12: 6-72 pgs. origin issue						5.50
13-38,40: 40-Ploog-c						4.00
39-($5.95, 120 pgs.)-Ploog-c						6.50
41-44: 41-($3.95, 84 pgs.)-Ploog-c. 42-Ploog-c						6.00
45-Last issue; low print	2	4	6	8	10	12
Deluxe Edition ($19.95, B&W)						20.00

NOTE: ***Sienkiewicz*** *c-13-24.* ***Matt Wagner*** *c-25-30.*

LONE WOLF AND CUB (Trade paperbacks)
Dark Horse Comics: Aug, 2000 - No. 28 ($9.95, B&W, 4" x 6", approx. 300 pgs.)

	GD	VG	FN	VF	VF/NM	NM-
1-Collects First Comics reprint series; Frank Miller-c						18.00
1-(2nd printing)						12.00
1-(3rd-5th printings)						10.00
2,3-(1st printings)						12.00
2,3-(2nd printings)						10.00
4-28						10.00

LONE WOLF 2100 (Also see Reveal)
Dark Horse Comics: May, 2002 - No. 11, Dec, 2003 ($2.99, color)

	GD	VG	FN	VF	VF/NM	NM-
1-New homage to Lone Wolf and Cub; Kennedy-s/Velasco-a						4.00
2-11						3.00
...: The Red File (1/03, $2.99) character and story background files						3.00
... Vol. 1 - Shadows on Saplings TPB (2003, $12.95, 6" x 9") r/#1-4						13.00
... Vol. 2 - The Language of Chaos TPB (2003, $12.95, 6" x 9") r/#5-8, Dirty Tricks short story from Reveal						13.00

LONG BOW (...Indian Boy)(See Indians & Jumbo Comics #141)
Fiction House Mag. (Real Adventures Publ.): 1951 - No. 9, Wint, 1952/53

	GD	VG	FN	VF	VF/NM	NM-
1-Most covers by Maurice Whitman	17	34	51	98	154	210
2	11	22	33	60	83	105
3-9	10	20	30	54	72	90

LONG HOT SUMMER, THE
DC Comics (Milestone): Jul, 1995 - No. 3, Sept, 1995 ($2.95/$2.50, lim. series)

	GD	VG	FN	VF	VF/NM	NM-
1-3: 1-($2.95-c). 2,3-($2.50-c)						3.00

LONG JOHN SILVER & THE PIRATES (Formerly Terry & the Pirates)
Charlton Comics: No. 30, Aug, 1956 - No. 32, March, 1957 (TV)

	GD	VG	FN	VF	VF/NM	NM-
30-32: Whitman-c	10	20	30	54	72	90

LONGSHOT (Also see X-Men, 2nd Series #10)
Marvel Comics: Sept, 1985 - No. 6, Feb, 1986 (60¢, limited series)

	GD	VG	FN	VF	VF/NM	NM-
1-6: 1-Art Adams/Whilce Portacio-c/a in all. 4-Spider-Man app. 6-Double size	1	2	3	4	5	7
Trade Paperback (1989, $16.95)-r/#1-6						17.00

LONGSHOT
Marvel Comics: Feb, 1998 ($3.99, one-shot)

	GD	VG	FN	VF	VF/NM	NM-
1-DeMatteis-s/Zulli-a						4.00

LOOKING GLASS WARS: HATTER M
Image Comics (Desperado): Dec, 2005 - No. 4, Nov, 2006 ($3.99)

	GD	VG	FN	VF	VF/NM	NM-
1-4-Templesmith-a/c						4.00

LOONEY TUNES (2nd Series) (TV)
Gold Key/Whitman: April, 1975 - No. 47, June, 1984

	GD	VG	FN	VF	VF/NM	NM-
1-Reprints	4	8	12	22	34	45
2-10: 2,4-reprints	2	4	6	13	18	22
11-20: 16-reprints	2	4	6	9	12	15
21-30	2	3	4	6	8	10
31,32,36-42(2/82)	1	2	3	5	6	8
33-(8/80)-35 (Whitman pre-pack only, scarce)	3	6	9	17	25	32
43(4/82),44(6/83) (low distribution)	2	4	6	9	13	16
45-47 (All #90296 on-c; nd, nd code, pre-pack) 45(8/83), 46(3/84), 47(6/84)	3	6	9	14	20	26

LOONEY TUNES (3rd Series) (TV)
DC Comics: Apr, 1994 - Present ($1.50/$1.75/$1.95/$1.99/$2.25/$2.50)

	GD	VG	FN	VF	VF/NM	NM-
1-10,120: 1-Marvin Martian-c/sty; Bugs Bunny, Roadrunner, Daffy begin. 120-($2.95-C)						3.00
11-119,121-183: 23-34-($1.75-c). 35-43-($1.95-c). 44-Begin $1.99-c. 93-Begin $2.25-c. 100-Art by various incl. Kyle Baker, Marie Severin, Darwyn Cooke, Jill Thompson						2.50
...Back In Action Movie Adaptation (12/03, $3.95) photo-c						4.00

LOONEY TUNES AND MERRIE MELODIES COMICS ("Looney Tunes" #166(8/55) on) (Also see Porky's Duck Hunt)
Dell Publishing Co.: 1941 - No. 246, July-Sept, 1962

	GD	VG	FN	VF	VF/NM	NM-
1-Porky Pig, Bugs Bunny, Daffy Duck, Elmer Fudd, Mary Jane & Sniffles, Pat Patsy and Pete begin (1st comic book app. of each). Bugs Bunny story by Win Smith (early Mickey Mouse artist)	1100	2200	3300	8400	15,200	22,000
2 (11/41)	154	308	462	1348	2674	4000
3-Kandi the Cave Kid begins by Walt Kelly; also in #4-6,8,11,15	112	224	336	952	1876	2800
4-Kelly-a	112	224	336	952	1876	2800
5-Bugs Bunny The Super-Duper Rabbit story (1st funny animal super hero, 3/42; also see Coo Coo); Kelly-a	84	168	252	714	1407	2100
6,8-Kelly-a	65	130	195	553	1089	1625
7,9,10: 9-Painted-c. 10-Flag-c	50	100	150	413	807	1200
11,15-Kelly-a; 15-X-Mas-c	53	106	159	419	822	1225
12-14,16-19	40	80	120	306	591	875
20-25: Pat, Patsy & Pete by Walt Kelly in all. 20-War Bonds-c	33	66	99	254	490	725
26-30	25	50	75	183	354	525
31-40: 33-War Bonds-c. 39-X-Mas-c	21	42	63	148	287	425
41-50: 45-War Bonds-c	16	32	48	113	217	320
51-60	13	26	39	93	172	250
61-80	9	18	27	65	113	160
81-99: 87-X-Mas-c	8	16	24	58	97	135
100	9	18	27	61	103	145
101-120	7	14	21	47	76	105
121-150	6	12	18	41	67	90
151-200: 159-X-Mas-c	6	12	18	37	59	80
201-240	5	10	15	34	55	75
241-246	6	12	18	37	59	80

LOONY SPORTS (Magazine)
3-Strikes Publishing Co.: Spring, 1975 (68 pgs.)

	GD	VG	FN	VF	VF/NM	NM-
1-Sports satire	2	4	6	8	11	14

LOOSE CANNON (Also see Action Comics Annual #5 & Showcase '94 #5)
DC Comics: June, 1995 - No. 4, Sept, 1995 ($1.75, limited series)

	GD	VG	FN	VF	VF/NM	NM-
1-4: Adam Pollina-a. 1-Superman app.						2.50

LOOY DOT DOPE

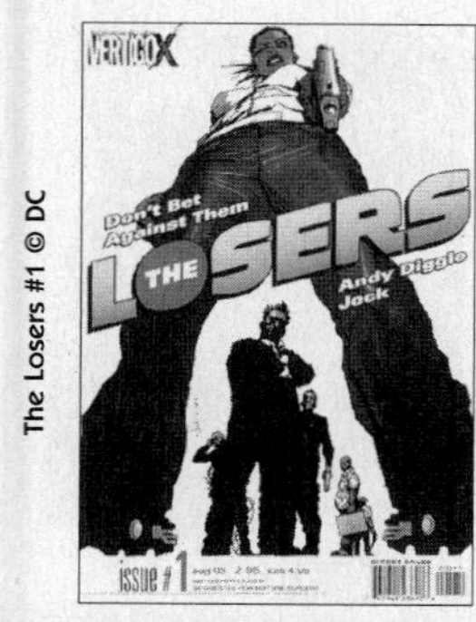

The Losers #1 © DC

Love Adventures #2 © MAR

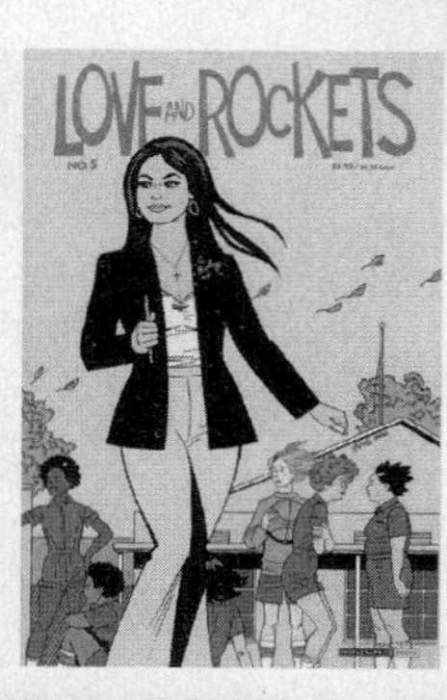

Love and Rockets V2 #5 © Fantagraphics

	GD	VG	FN	VF	VF/NM	NM-
	2.0	4.0	6.0	8.0	9.0	9.2

United Features Syndicate: No. 13, 1939
Single Series 13 — 30 60 90 177 289 400

LORD JIM (See Movie Comics)

LORD PUMPKIN
Malibu Comics (Ultraverse): Oct, 1994 ($2.50, one-shot)
0-Two covers — 2.50

LORD PUMPKIN/NECROMANTRA
Malibu Comics (Ultraverse): Apr, 1995 - No. 4, July, 1995 ($2.95, limited series, flip book)
1-4 — 3.00

LORDS OF AVALON: KNIGHT OF DARKNESS
Marvel Comics: Jan, 2008 - No. 6, July, 2009 ($3.99, limited series)
1-6-($3.99)-Kenyon & Furth-s; Ohtsuka-a/c — 4.00

LORDS OF AVALON: SWORD OF DARKNESS
Marvel Comics: Apr, 2008 - No. 6, Sept, 2006 ($3.99/$2.99, limited series)
1-($3.99)-Adaptation of Sherrilyn Kenyon's Arthurian fantasy; Ohtsuka-a/c — 4.00
2-6-($2.99) — 3.00
HC (2008, $19.99) r/#1-6; two covers — 20.00

LORNA THE JUNGLE GIRL (...Jungle Queen #1-5)
Atlas Comics (NPI 1/OMC 2-11/NPI 12-26): July, 1953 - No. 26, Aug, 1957

	GD	VG	FN	VF	VF/NM	NM-
1-Origin & 1st app.	39	78	117	240	395	550
2-Intro. & 1st app. Greg Knight	20	40	60	117	189	260
3-5	18	36	54	103	162	220
6-11: 11-Last pre-code (1/55)	15	30	45	85	130	175
12-17,19-26: 14-Colletta & Maneely-c	14	28	42	78	112	145
18-Williamson/Colletta-c	14	28	42	81	118	155

NOTE: ***Brodsky** c-1-3, 5, 9. **Everett** c-21, 23-26. **Heath** c-6, 7. **Maneely** c-12, 15. **Romita** a-20, 22, 24, 26. **Shores** a-14-16, 24, 26; c-11, 13, 16. **Tuska** a-6.*

LOSERS (Inspired the 2010 movie)
DC Comics (Vertigo): Aug, 2003 - No. 32, Mar, 2006 ($2.95/$2.99)
1-Andy Diggle-s/Jock-a — 4.00
2-32: 15-Bagged with Sky Captain CD. 20-Oliver-a. 27-Wilson-a — 3.00
...: Ante Up TPB (2004, $9.95) r/#1-6 — 10.00
...: Close Quarters TPB (2005, $14.99) r/#20-25 — 15.00
...: Double Down TPB (2004, $12.95) r/#7-12 — 13.00
...: Endgame TPB (2006, $14.99) r/#26-32 — 15.00
...: Trifecta TPB (2005, $14.99) r/#13-19 — 15.00
...: Volumes One and Two TPB (2010, $19.99) r/#1-12; new intro. by Diggle — 20.00

LOSERS SPECIAL (See Our Fighting Forces #123)(Also see G.I. Combat & Our Fighting Forces)
DC Comics: Sept, 1985 ($1.25, one-shot)
1-Capt. Storm, Gunner & Sarge; Crisis on Infinite Earths x-over — 6.00

LOST, THE
Chaos! Comics: Dec, 1997 - No. 3 ($2.95, B&W, unfinished limited series)
1-3-Andreyko-script: 1-Russell back-c — 3.00

LOST BOYS: REIGN OF FROGS (Based on the 1987 vampire movie)
DC Comics (WildStorm): Jul, 2008 - No. 4, Oct, 2008 ($3.50, limited series)
1-4-Rodionoff-s/Gomez-a; Edgar Frog app. — 3.50
TPB (2009, $12.99) r/#1-4 — 13.00

LOST CONTINENT
Eclipse Int'l: Sept, 1990 - No. 6, 1991 ($3.50, B&W, squarebound, 60 pgs.)
1-6: Japanese story translated to English — 3.50

LOST IN SPACE (Movie)
Dark Horse Comics: Apr, 1998 - No. 3, July, 1998 ($2.95, limited series)
1-3-Continuation of 1998 movie; Erskine-c — 3.00

LOST IN SPACE (TV)(Also see Space Family Robinson)
Innovation Publishing: Aug, 1991 - No. 12, Jan, 1993 ($2.50, limited series)
1-12: Bill Mumy (Will Robinson) scripts in #1-9. 9-Perez-c — 3.00
1,2-Special Ed.; r/#1,2 plus new art & new-c — 3.00
Annual 1,2 (1991, 1992, $2.95, 52 pgs.) — 3.00
...: Project Robinson (11/93, $2.50) 1st & only part of intended series — 3.00

LOST IN SPACE: VOYAGE TO THE BOTTOM OF THE SOUL
Innovation Publishing: No. 13, Aug, 1993 - No. 18, 1994 ($2.50, limited series)
13(V1#1, $2.95)-Embossed silver logo edition; Bill Mumy scripts begin; painted-c — 3.00
13(V1#1, $4.95)-Embossed gold logo edition bagged w/poster — 5.00
14-18: Painted-c — 3.00

NOTE: *Originally intended to be a 12 issue limited series.*

LOST ONES, THE
Image Comics: Mar, 2000 ($2.95)
1-Ken Penders-s/a — 3.00

LOST PLANET
Eclipse Comics: 5/87 - No. 5, 2/88; No. 6, 3/89 (Mini-series, Baxter paper)
1-6-Bo Hampton-c/a in all — 2.50

LOST WAGON TRAIN, THE (See Zane Grey Four Color 583)

LOST WORLD, THE
Dell Publishing Co.: No. 1145, Nov-Jan, 1960-61
Four Color 1145-Movie, Gil Kane-a, photo-c; 1pg. Conan Doyle biography by Torres — 9 18 27 64 110 155

LOST WORLD, THE (See Jurassic Park)
Topps Comics: May, 1997 - No. 4, Aug, 1997 ($2.95, limited series)
1-4-Movie adaption — 3.00

LOST WORLDS (Weird Tales of the Past and Future)
Standard Comics: No. 5, Oct, 1952 - No. 6, Dec, 1952

	GD	VG	FN	VF	VF/NM	NM-
5- "Alice in Terrorland" by Alex Toth; J. Katz-a	43	86	129	271	461	650
6-Toth-a	36	72	108	211	343	475

LOTS 'O' FUN COMICS
Robert Allen Co.: 1940's? (5¢, heavy stock, blue covers)
nn-Contents can vary; Felix, Planet Comics known; contents would determine value. Similar to Up-To-Date Comics. Remainders - re-packaged.

LOU GEHRIG (See The Pride of the Yankees)

LOVE ADVENTURES (Actual Confessions #13)
Marvel (IPS)/Atlas Comics (MPI): Oct, 1949; No. 2, Jan, 1950; No. 3, Feb, 1951 - No. 12, Aug, 1952

	GD	VG	FN	VF	VF/NM	NM-
1-Photo-c	17	34	51	100	158	215
2-Powell-a; Tyrone Power, Gene Tierney photo-c	15	30	45	85	130	175
3-8,10-12: 8-Robinson-a	10	20	30	56	76	95
9-Everett-a	10	20	30	58	79	100

LOVE AND MARRIAGE
Superior Comics Ltd. (Canada): Mar, 1952 - No. 16, Sept, 1954

	GD	VG	FN	VF	VF/NM	NM-
1	15	30	45	83	124	165
2	9	18	27	50	65	80
3-10	8	16	24	44	57	70
11-16	8	16	24	40	50	60
I.W. Reprint #1,2,8,11,14: 8-r/Love and Marriage #3. 11-r/Love and Marriage #11	2	4	6	9	13	16
Super Reprint #10('63),15,17('64):15-Love and Marriage #?	2	4	6	9	13	16

NOTE: *All issues have **Kamenish** art.*

LOVE AND ROCKETS
Fantagraphics Books: July, 1982 - No. 50, May, 1996 ($2.95/$2.50/$4.95, B&W, mature)

	GD	VG	FN	VF	VF/NM	NM-
1-B&W-c (6/82, $2.95; small size, publ. by Hernandez Bros.)(800 printed)	6	12	18	39	62	85
1 (Fall, '82; color-c)	4	8	12	22	34	45
1-2nd & 3rd printing, 2-11,29-31: 2nd printings						3.00
2	2	4	6	10	14	18
3-10	1	3	4	6	8	10
11-49: 30 ($2.95, 52 pgs.)						5.00
50-($4.95)						6.00

LOVE AND ROCKETS (Volume 2)
Fantagraphics Books: Spring, 2001 - Present ($3.95-$7.99, B&W, mature)
1-9-Gilbert, Jaime and Mario Hernandez-s/a — 4.00
10-($5.95) — 6.00
11-19-($4.50) — 4.50
20-($7.99) — 8.00

LOVE AND ROMANCE
Charlton Comics: Sept, 1971 - No. 24, Sept, 1975

	GD	VG	FN	VF	VF/NM	NM-
1	3	6	9	18	27	35
2-5,7-10	2	4	6	10	14	18
6-David Cassidy pin-up; grey-tone cover	3	6	9	14	19	24
11,13-24	2	4	6	8	10	12
12-Susan Dey poster	2	4	6	10	14	18

LOVE AT FIRST SIGHT

Love Diary #42 © Our Publ. Co.

Loveless #24 © Azzarello & Frusin

Lovelorn #11 © ACG

	GD 2.0	VG 4.0	FN 6.0	VF 8.0	VF/NM 9.0	NM- 9.2

Ace Magazines (RAR Publ. Co./Periodical House): Oct, 1949 - No. 43, Nov, 1956 (Photo-c: 18-42)

	GD	VG	FN	VF	VF/NM	NM-
1-Painted-c	16	32	48	94	147	200
2-Painted-c	10	20	30	58	79	100
3-10: 4,7-Painted-c	9	18	27	50	65	80
11-20	9	18	27	47	61	75
21-33: 33-Last pre-code	8	16	24	44	57	70
34-43	8	16	24	42	54	65

LOVE BUG, THE (See Movie Comics)

LOVEBUNNY AND MR. HELL
Devil's Due Publ./Image Comics: 2002 - 2004 ($2.95, B&W, one-shots)

	GD	VG	FN	VF	VF/NM	NM-
1-Tim Seeley-s						3.00
...: A Day in the Lovelife (Image, 2003) Blaylock-a						3.00
...: Savage Love (Image, 2003) Seeley-s/a; Savage Dragon app.; Seeley & Larsen-c						3.00
TPB (4/04, $9.95, digest-sized) reprints						10.00

LOVE CLASSICS
A Lover's Magazine/Marvel: Nov, 1949 - No. 2, Feb, 1950 (Photo-c, 52 pgs.)

	GD	VG	FN	VF	VF/NM	NM-
1,2: 2-Virginia Mayo photo-c; 30 pg. story "I Turned Into a Small-Town Flirt"	15	30	45	88	137	185

LOVE CONFESSIONS
Quality Comics: Oct, 1949 - No. 54, Dec, 1956 (Photo-c: 3,4,6,7,9,11-18,21,24,25)

	GD	VG	FN	VF	VF/NM	NM-
1-Ward-c/a, 9 pgs; Gustavson-a	31	62	93	182	296	410
2-Gustavson-a; Ward-c	15	30	45	90	140	190
3	11	22	33	62	86	110
4-Crandall-a	12	24	36	69	97	125
5-Ward-a, 7 pgs.	14	28	42	78	112	145
6,7,9,11-13,15,16,18: 7-Van Johnson photo-c. 8-Robert Mitchum & Jane Russell photo-c	9	18	27	52	69	85
8,10-Ward-a (2 stories in #10)	14	28	42	78	112	145
14,17,19,22-Ward-a; 17-Faith Domerque photo-c	13	26	39	74	105	135
20-Ward-a(2)	14	28	42	78	112	145
21,23-28,30-38,40-42: Last precode, 4/55	8	16	24	44	57	70
29-Ward-a	12	24	36	69	97	125
39,53-Matt Baker-a	11	22	33	60	83	105
43,44,46,47,50-52,54: 47-Ward-c?	8	16	24	42	54	65
45,48-Ward-a	9	18	27	52	69	85
49-Baker-c/a	13	26	39	72	101	130

LOVECRAFT
DC Comics: 2003 (graphic novel)

	GD	VG	FN	VF	VF/NM	NM-
Hardcover ($24.95) Rodionoff & Giffen-s/Breccia-a; intro. by John Carpenter						25.00
Softcover ($17.95)						18.00

LOVE DIARY
Our Publishing Co./Toytown/Patches: July, 1949 - No. 48, Oct, 1955 (Photo-c: 1-24,27-29) (52 pgs. #1-11?)

	GD	VG	FN	VF	VF/NM	NM-
1-Krigstein-a	20	40	60	120	195	270
2,3-Krigstein & Mort Leav-a in each	14	28	42	82	121	160
4-8	10	20	30	58	79	100
9,10-Everett-a	11	22	33	62	86	110
11-15,17-20	9	18	27	52	69	85
16- Mort Leav-a, 3 pg. Baker-sty. Leav-a	10	20	30	54	72	90
21-30,32-48: 45-Leav-a. 47-Last precode(12/54)	9	18	27	47	61	75
31-John Buscema headlights-c	10	20	30	58	79	100

LOVE DIARY (Diary Loves #2 on; title change due to previously published title)
Quality Comics Group: Sept, 1949

	GD	VG	FN	VF	VF/NM	NM-
1-Ward-c/a, 9 pgs.	31	62	93	182	296	410

LOVE DIARY
Charlton Comics: July, 1958 - No. 102, Dec, 1976

	GD	VG	FN	VF	VF/NM	NM-
1	11	22	33	60	83	105
2	7	14	21	37	46	55
3-5,7-10: 10-Photo-c	6	12	18	31	38	45
6-Torres-a	7	14	21	35	43	50
11-20: 20-Photo-c	3	6	9	17	25	32
21-40	3	6	9	14	20	25
41-60	2	4	6	11	16	20
61-78,80,100-102	2	4	6	9	12	15
79-David Cassidy pin-up	2	4	6	11	16	20
81,83,84,86-99	1	3	4	6	8	10
82,85: 82-Partridge Family poster. 85-Danny poster	2	4	6	9	12	15

LOVE DOCTOR (See Dr. Anthony King...)

LOVE DRAMAS (True Secrets No. 3 on?)
Marvel Comics (IPS): Oct, 1949 - No. 2, Jan, 1950

	GD	VG	FN	VF	VF/NM	NM-
1-Jack Kamen-a; photo-c	19	38	57	111	176	240
2-Photo-c	14	28	42	80	115	150

LOVE EXPERIENCES (Challenge of the Unknown No. 6)
Ace Periodicals (A.A. Wyn/Periodical House): Oct, 1949 - No. 5, June, 1950; No. 6, Apr, 1951 - No. 38, June, 1956

	GD	VG	FN	VF	VF/NM	NM-
1-Painted-c	15	30	45	90	140	190
2	10	20	30	56	76	95
3-5: 5-Painted-c	9	18	27	52	69	85
6-10	9	18	27	47	61	75
11-30: 30-Last pre-code (2/55)	8	16	24	42	54	65
31-38: 38-Indicia date-6/56; c-date-8/56	7	14	21	37	46	55

NOTE: ***Anne Brewster** a-15. Photo c-4, 15-35, 38.*

LOVE FIGHTS (Also see Free Comic Book Day Edition in the Promotional Comics section)
Oni Press: June, 2003 - No. 12, Aug, 2004 ($2.99, B&W)

	GD	VG	FN	VF	VF/NM	NM-
1-12-Andi Watson-s/a						3.00
Vol. 1 TPB (4/04, $14.95, digest-size) r/#1-6						15.00

LOVE JOURNAL
Our Publishing Co.: No. 10, Oct, 1951 - No. 25, July, 1954

	GD	VG	FN	VF	VF/NM	NM-
10	14	28	42	80	115	150
11-15,17-25: 19-Mort Leav-a	9	18	27	52	69	85
16-Buscema headlight-c	10	20	30	58	79	100

LOVELAND
Mutual Mag./Eye Publ. (Marvel): Nov, 1949 - No. 2, Feb, 1950 (52 pgs.)

	GD	VG	FN	VF	VF/NM	NM-
1,2-Photo-c	14	28	42	76	108	140

LOVELESS
DC Comics: Dec, 2005 - No. 24, Jun, 2008 ($2.99)

	GD	VG	FN	VF	VF/NM	NM-
1-24: 1-Azzarello-s/Frusin-a. 6-8,15,22,23,24-Zezelj-a. 11,12,16-21-Dell'Edera-a						3.00
...: A Kin of Homecoming TPB (2006, $9.99) r/#1-5						10.00
...: Blackwater Falls TPB (2008, $19.99) r/#13-24						20.00
...: Thicker Than Blackwater TPB (2007, $14.99) r/#6-12						15.00

LOVE LESSONS
Harvey Comics/Key Publ. No. 5: Oct, 1949 - No. 5, June, 1950

	GD	VG	FN	VF	VF/NM	NM-
1-Metallic silver-c printed over the cancelled covers of Love Letters #1; indicia title is "Love Letters"	15	30	45	85	130	175
2-Powell-a; photo-c	9	18	27	52	69	85
3-5: 3,4-Photo-c	8	16	24	42	54	65

LOVE LETTERS (10/49, Harvey; advertised but never published; covers were printed before cancellation and were used as the cover to Love Lessions #1)

LOVE LETTERS (Love Secrets No. 32 on)
Quality Comics: 11/49 - #6, 9/50; #7, 3/51 - #31, 6/53; #32, 2/54 - #51, 12/56

	GD	VG	FN	VF	VF/NM	NM-
1-Ward-c, Gustavson-a	25	50	75	147	241	335
2-Ward-c, Gustavson-a	20	40	60	118	192	265
3-Gustavson-a	15	30	45	84	127	170
4-Ward-a, 9 pgs.; photo-c	19	38	57	111	176	240
5-8,10	10	20	30	58	79	100
9-One pg. Ward "Be Popular with the Opposite Sex"; Robert Mitchum photo-c	11	22	33	64	90	115
11-Ward-r/Broadway Romances #2 & retitled	11	22	33	64	90	115
12-15,18-20	9	18	27	52	69	85
16,17-Ward-a; 16-Anthony Quinn photo-c. 17-Jane Russell photo-c	14	28	42	82	121	160
21-29	9	18	27	50	65	80
30,31(6/53)-Ward-a	10	20	30	58	79	100
32(2/54)-39: 37-Ward-a. 38-Crandall-a. 39-Last precode (4/55)	8	16	24	44	57	70
40-48	8	16	24	42	54	65
49,50-Baker-a	12	24	36	69	97	125
51-Baker-c	12	24	36	67	94	120

NOTE: *Photo-c on most 3-28.*

LOVE LIFE
P. L. Publishing Co.: Nov, 1951

	GD	VG	FN	VF	VF/NM	NM-
1	10	20	30	58	79	100

LOVELORN (Confessions of the Lovelorn #52 on)
American Comics Group (Michel Publ./Regis Publ.): Aug-Sept, 1949 - No. 51, July, 1954 (No. 1-26: 52 pgs.)

	GD	VG	FN	VF	VF/NM	NM-
1	16	32	48	94	147	200

Lovers #52 © MAR

Love Scandals #2 © QUA

Lucifer #6 © DC

	GD 2.0	VG 4.0	FN 6.0	VF 8.0	VF/NM 9.0	NM- 9.2
2	10	20	30	58	79	100
3-10	9	18	27	50	65	80
11-20,22-48: 18-Drucker-a(2 pgs.). 46-Lazarus-a	8	16	24	42	54	65
21-Prostitution story	10	20	30	54	72	90
49-51-Has 3-D effect-c/stories	16	32	48	94	147	200

LOVE MEMORIES
Fawcett Publications: 1949 (no month) - No. 4, July, 1950 (All photo-c)

	GD	VG	FN	VF	VF/NM	NM-
1	15	30	45	88	137	185
2-4: 2-(Win/49-50)	10	20	30	56	76	95

LOVE ME TENDERLOIN: A CAL McDONALD MYSTERY
Dark Horse Comics: Jan, 2004 ($2.99, one-shot)

	GD	VG	FN	VF	VF/NM	NM-
1-Niles-s/Templesmith-a/c						3.00

LOVE MYSTERY
Fawcett Publications: June, 1950 - No. 3, Oct, 1950 (All photo-c)

	GD	VG	FN	VF	VF/NM	NM-
1-George Evans-a	21	42	63	124	202	280
2,3-Evans-a. 3-Powell-a	16	32	48	92	144	195

LOVE PROBLEMS (See Fox Giants)

LOVE PROBLEMS AND ADVICE ILLUSTRATED (see True Love...)

LOVE ROMANCES (Formerly Ideal #5)
Timely/Marvel/Atlas(TCI No. 7-71/Male No. 72-106): No. 6, May, 1949 - No. 106, July, 1963

	GD	VG	FN	VF	VF/NM	NM-
6-Photo-c	18	36	54	103	162	220
7-Photo-c; Kamen-a	12	24	36	67	94	120
8-Kubert-a; photo-c	12	24	36	67	94	120
9-20: 9-12-Photo-c	11	22	33	60	83	105
21,24-Krigstein-a	11	22	33	62	86	110
22,23,25-35,37,39,40	10	20	30	58	79	100
36,38-Krigstein-a	11	22	33	60	83	105
41-44,46,47: Last precode (2/55)	10	20	30	56	76	95
45,57-Matt Baker-a	12	24	36	67	94	120
48,50-52,54-56,58-74	6	12	18	37	59	80
49,53-Toth-a, 6 & ? pgs.	6	12	18	41	66	90
75,77,82-Matt Baker-a	7	14	21	49	80	110
76,78-81,86,88-90,92-95: 80-Heath-c. 95-Last 10¢-c?	5	10	15	34	55	75
83,84,87,91-Kirby-c. 83-Severin-a	7	14	21	45	73	100
85,96,97,99-106-Kirby-c/a. 97-10¢ cover price blacked out, 12¢ printed on cover	8	16	24	52	86	120
98-Kirby-c/a	8	16	24	54	90	125

NOTE: ***Anne Brewster** a-67, 72. **Colletta** a-37, 40, 42, 44, 67(2); c-42, 44, 49, 54, 80. **Everett** c-70. **Hartley** c-20, 21, 30, 31. **Heath** a-87. **Kirby** c-80, 85, 88. **Robinson** a-29.*

LOVERS (Formerly Blonde Phantom)
Marvel Comics No. 23,24/Atlas No. 25 on (ANC): No. 23, May, 1949 - No. 86, Aug?, 1957

	GD	VG	FN	VF	VF/NM	NM-
23-Photo-c begin, end #29	18	36	54	107	169	230
24-Toth-*ish* plus Robinson-a	11	22	33	64	90	115
25,30-Kubert-a; 7, 10 pgs.	12	24	36	67	94	120
26-29,31-36,39,40: 35-Maneely-c	10	20	30	58	79	100
37,38-Krigstein-a	11	22	33	64	90	115
41-Everett-a(2)	11	22	33	64	90	115
42,44-65: 65-Last pre-code (1/55)	9	18	27	50	65	80
43-Frazetta 1 pg. ad	9	18	27	52	69	85
66,68-80,82-86	8	16	24	47	61	75
67-Toth-a	9	18	27	52	69	85
81-Baker-a	10	20	30	54	72	90

NOTE: ***Anne Brewster** a-86. **Colletta** a-54, 59, 62, 64, 65, 69, 85; c-61, 64, 65, 75. **Hartley** c-37, 53, 54. **Heath** a-61. **Maneely** a-57. **Powell** a-27, 30. **Robinson** a-42, 54, 56.*

LOVERS' LANE
Lev Gleason Publications: Oct, 1949 - No. 41, June, 1954 (No. 1-18: 52 pgs.)

	GD	VG	FN	VF	VF/NM	NM-
1-Biro-c	15	30	45	84	127	170
2-Biro-c	10	20	30	54	72	90
3-20: 3,4-Painted-c. 20-Frazetta 1 pg. ad	9	18	27	50	65	80
21-38,40,41	8	16	24	42	54	65
39-Story narrated by Frank Sinatra	10	20	30	54	72	90

NOTE: ***Briefer** a-6, 13, 21. **Esposito** a-5. **Fuje** a-4, 16; c-many. **Guardineer** a-1, 3. **Kinstler** c-41. **Sparling** a-3. **Tuska** a-6. Painted c-3-18. Photo c-19-22, 26-28.*

LOVE SCANDALS
Quality Comics: Feb, 1950 - No. 5, Oct, 1950 (Photo-c #2-5) (All 52 pgs.)

	GD	VG	FN	VF	VF/NM	NM-
1-Ward-c/a, 9 pgs.	26	52	78	154	252	350
2,3: 2-Gustavson-a	14	28	42	76	108	140
4-Ward-a, 18 pgs; Gil Fox-a	20	40	60	120	195	270
5-C. Cuidera-a; tomboy story "I Hated Being a Woman"	14	28	42	80	115	150

LOVE SECRETS
Marvel Comics(IPC): Oct, 1949 - No. 2, Jan, 1950 (52 pgs., photo-c)

	GD	VG	FN	VF	VF/NM	NM-
1	16	32	48	94	147	200
2	11	22	33	64	90	115

LOVE SECRETS (Formerly Love Letters #31)
Quality Comics Group: No. 32, Aug, 1953 - No. 56, Dec, 1956

	GD	VG	FN	VF	VF/NM	NM-
32	13	26	39	72	101	130
33,35-39	9	18	27	50	65	80
34-Ward-a	13	26	39	72	101	130
40-Matt Baker-c	12	24	36	69	97	125
41-43: 43-Last precode (3/55)	9	18	27	50	65	80
44,47-50,53,54	8	16	24	42	54	65
45-Ward-a	10	20	30	58	79	100
46-Ward-a; Baker-a	11	22	33	64	90	115
51,52-Ward(r). 52-r/Love Confessions #17	9	18	27	50	65	80
55,56: 55-Baker-a. 56-Baker-c	11	22	33	60	83	105

LOVE STORIES (See Top Love Stories)

LOVE STORIES (Formerly Heart Throbs)
National Periodical Publ.: No. 147, Nov, 1972 - No. 152, Oct-Nov, 1973

	GD	VG	FN	VF	VF/NM	NM-
147-152	3	6	9	14	20	26

LOVE STORIES OF MARY WORTH (See Harvey Comics Hits #55 & Mary Worth)
Harvey Publications: Sept, 1949 - No. 5, May, 1950

	GD	VG	FN	VF	VF/NM	NM-
1-1940's newspaper reprints-#1-4	9	18	27	47	61	75
2-5: 3-Kamen/Baker-a?	6	12	18	31	38	45

LOVE TALES (Formerly The Human Torch #35)
Marvel/Atlas Comics (ZPC No. 36-50/MMC No. 67-75): No. 36, 5/49 - No. 58, 8/52; No. 59, date? - No. 75, Sept, 1957

	GD	VG	FN	VF	VF/NM	NM-
36-Photo-c	17	34	51	98	154	210
37	11	22	33	60	83	105
38-44,46-50: 39-41-Photo-c	10	20	30	56	76	95
45,51,52,69: 45-Powell-a. 51,69-Everett-a. 52-Krigstein-a	10	20	30	58	79	100
53-60: 60-Last pre-code (2/55)	9	18	27	47	61	75
61-68,70-75: 75-Brewster, Cameron, Colletta-a	8	16	24	44	57	70

LOVE THRILLS (See Fox Giants)

LOVE TRAILS (Western romance)
A Lover's Magazine (CDS)(Marvel): Dec, 1949 - No. 2, Mar, 1950 (52 pgs.)

	GD	VG	FN	VF	VF/NM	NM-
1,2: 1-Photo-c	15	30	45	85	130	175

LOWELL THOMAS' HIGH ADVENTURE (See High Adventure)

LT. (See Lieutenant)

LUCIFER (See The Sandman #4)
DC Comics (Vertigo): Jun, 2000 - No. 75, Aug, 2006 ($2.50/$2.75)

	GD	VG	FN	VF	VF/NM	NM-
1-Carey-s/Weston-a/Fegredo-c						8.00
2,3-Carey-s/Weston-a/Fegredo-c						5.00
4-10: 4-Pleece-a. 5-Gross-a						4.00
11-49,51-73: 16-Moeller-c begin. 25,26-Death app. 45-Naifeh-a. 53-Kaluta-c begin. 62-Doran-a. 63-Begin $2.75-c						2.75
50-($3.50) P. Craig Russell-a; Mazikeen app.						3.50
74-($2.99) Kaluta-c						3.00
75-($3.99) Last issue; Lucifer's origins retold; Morpheus app.; Gross-a/Moeller-c						4.00
Preview-16 pg. flip book w/Swamp Thing Preview						3.00
...: A Dalliance With the Damned TPB ('02, $14.95) r/#14-20						15.00
...: Children and Monsters TPB ('01, $17.95) r/#5-13						18.00
...: Crux TPB (2006, $14.99) r/#55-61						15.00
...: Devil in the Gateway TPB ('01, $14.95) r/#1-4 & Sandman Presents:..#1-3						15.00
...: Evensong TPB (2007, $14.99) r/#70-75 & Lucifer: Nirvana one-shot						15.00
...: Exodus TPB (2005, $14.95) r/#42-44,46-49						15.00
...: Inferno TPB (2003, $14.95) r/#29-35						15.00
...: Mansions of the Silence TPB (2004, $14.95) r/#36-41						15.00
...: Morningstar TPB (2006, $14.99) r/#62-69						15.00
...: Nirvana (2002, $5.95) Carey-s/Muth-painted-c/a; Daniel app.						6.00
...: The Divine Comedy TPB (2003, $17.95) r/#21-28						18.00
...: The Wolf Beneath the Tree TPB (2005, $14.99) r/#45,50-54						15.00

LUCIFER'S HAMMER (Larry Niven & Jerry Pournelle's...)
Innovation Publishing: Nov, 1993 - No. 6, 1994 ($2.50, painted, limited series)

	GD	VG	FN	VF	VF/NM	NM-
1-6: Adaptatin of novel, painted-c & art						2.50

Lucky Duck #7 © STD

Luke Cage Noir #3 © MAR

Machine Man #7 © MAR

	GD 2.0	VG 4.0	FN 6.0	VF 8.0	VF/NM 9.0	NM- 9.2
LUCKY COMICS						
Consolidated Magazines: Jan, 1944; No. 2, Sum, 1945 - No. 5, Sum, 1946						
1-Lucky Starr & Bobbie begin	22	44	66	128	209	290
2-5: 5-Devil-c by Walter Johnson	14	28	42	80	115	150
LUCKY DUCK						
Standard Comics (Literary Ent.): No. 5, Jan, 1953 - No. 8, Sept, 1953						
5-Funny animal; Irving Spector-a	11	22	33	60	83	105
6-8-Irving Spector-a	10	20	30	54	72	90
NOTE: *Harvey Kurtzman tried to hire Spector for Mad #1.*						
LUCKY "7" COMICS						
Howard Publishers Ltd.: 1944 (No date listed)						
1-Pioneer, Sir Gallagher, Dick Royce, Congo Raider, Punch Powers; bondage-c	39	78	117	240	395	550
LUCKY STAR (Western)						
Nation Wide Publ. Co.: 1950 - No. 7, 1951; No. 8, 1953 - No. 14, 1955 (5x7-1/4"; full color, 5¢)						
nn (#1)-(5¢, 52 pgs.)-Davis-a	18	36	54	105	165	225
2,3-(5¢, 52 pgs.)-Davis-a	12	24	36	67	94	120
4-7-(5¢, 52 pgs.)-Davis-a	11	22	33	60	83	105
8-14-(36 pgs.)(Exist?)	9	18	27	50	65	80
Given away with Lucky Star Western Wear by the Juvenile Mfg. Co.	7	14	21	35	43	50
LUCY SHOW, THE (TV) (Also see I Love Lucy)						
Gold Key: June, 1963 - No. 5, June, 1964 (Photo-c: 1,2)						
1	12	24	36	85	155	225
2	7	14	21	49	80	110
3-5: Photo back c-1,2,4,5	6	12	18	43	69	95
LUCY, THE REAL GONE GAL (Meet Miss Pepper #5 on)						
St. John Publishing Co.: June, 1953 - No. 4, Dec, 1953						
1-Negligee panels	15	30	45	84	127	170
2	9	18	27	52	69	85
3,4: 3-Drucker-a	9	18	27	47	61	75
LUDWIG BEMELMAN'S MADELEINE & GENEVIEVE						
Dell Publishing Co.: No. 796, May, 1957						
Four Color 796	4	8	12	24	37	50
LUDWIG VON DRAKE (TV)(Disney)(See Walt Disney's C&S #256)						
Dell Publishing Co.: Nov-Dec, 1961 - No. 4, June-Aug, 1962						
1	7	14	21	45	73	100
2-4	5	10	15	32	51	70
LUFTWAFFE: 1946 (Volume 1)						
Antarctic Press: July, 1996 - No. 4, Jan, 1997 ($2.95, B&W, limited series)						
1-4-Ben Dunn & Ted Nomura-s/a, ...Special Ed.						3.00
LUFTWAFFE: 1946 (Volume 2)						
Antarctic Press: Mar, 1997 - No. 18 ($2.95/$2.99, B&W, limited series)						
1-18: 8-Reviews Tigers of Terra series						3.00
Annual 1 (4/98, $2.95)-Reprints early Nomura pages						3.00
...Color Special (4/98)						3.00
...Technical Manual 1,2 (2/98, 4/99)						4.00
LUGER						
Eclipse Comics: Oct, 1986 - No. 3, Feb, 1987 ($1.75, miniseries, Baxter paper)						
1-3: Bruce Jones scripts; Yeates-c/a						2.50
LUKE CAGE (See Cage & Hero for Hire)						
LUKE CAGE NOIR						
Marvel Comics: Oct, 2009 - No. 4, Jan, 2010 ($3.99, limited series)						
1-4-Glass & Benson-a/Martinbrough-a; covers by Bradstreet and Calero						4.00
LUKE SHORT'S WESTERN STORIES						
Dell Publishing Co.: No. 580, Aug, 1954 - No. 927, Aug, 1958						
Four Color 580(8/54), 651(9/55)-Kinstler-a	4	8	12	28	44	60
Four Color 739,771,807,848,875,927	4	8	12	26	41	55
LUNATIC FRINGE, THE						
Innovation Publishing: July, 1989 - No. 2, 1989 ($1.75, deluxe format)						
1,2						2.50
LUNATICKLE (Magazine) (Satire)						
Whitstone Publ.: Feb, 1956 - No. 2, Apr, 1956						
1,2-Kubert-a (scarce)	9	18	27	47	61	75

	GD 2.0	VG 4.0	FN 6.0	VF 8.0	VF/NM 9.0	NM- 9.2
LUNATIK						
Marvel Comics: Dec, 1995 - No. 3, Feb, 1996 ($1.95, limited series)						
1-3						2.50
LURKERS, THE						
IDW Publ.: Oct, 2004 - No. 4, Jan, 2005 ($3.99)						
1-4-Niles-s/Casanova-a						4.00
LUST FOR LIFE						
Slave Labor Graphics: Feb, 1997 - No. 4, Jan, 1998 ($2.95, B&W)						
1-4: 1-Jeff Levin-s/a						3.00
LYCANTHROPE LEO						
Viz Communications: 1994 - No. 7($2.95, B&W, limited series, 44 pgs.)						
1-7						3.00
LYNCH (See Gen [13])						
Image Comics (WildStorm Productions): May, 1997 ($2.50, one-shot)						
1-Helmut-c/app.						2.50
LYNCH MOB						
Chaos! Comics: June, 1994 - No. 4, Sept, 1994 ($2.50, limited series)						
1-4						5.00
1-Special edition full foil-c	1	2	3	5	6	8
LYNDON B. JOHNSON						
Dell Publishing Co.: Mar, 1965						
12-445-503-Photo-c	3	6	9	20	30	40
M						
Eclipse Books: 1990 - No. 4, 1991 ($4.95, painted, 52 pgs.)						
1-Adapts movie; contains flexi-disc ($5.95)						6.00
2-4						5.00
MACE GRIFFIN BOUNTY HUNTER (Based on video game)						
Image Comics (Top Cow): May, 2003 ($2.99, one-shot)						
1-Nocon-a						3.00
MACHINE, THE						
Dark Horse Comics: Nov, 1994 - No. 4, Feb, 1995 ($2.50, limited series)						
1-4						2.50
MACHINE MAN (Also see 2001, A Space Odyssey)						
Marvel Comics Group: Apr, 1978 - No. 9, Dec, 1978; No. 10, Aug, 1979 - No. 19, Feb, 1981						
1-Jack Kirby-c/a/scripts begin; end #9	3	6	9	14	19	24
2-9-Kirby-c/a/s. 9-(12/78)	2	4	6	8	10	12
10-17: 10-(8/79) Marv Wolfman scripts & Ditko-a begins	1	2	3	5	6	8
18-Wendigo, Alpha Flight-ties into X-Men #140	3	6	9	14	19	24
19-Intro/1st app. Jack O'Lantern (Macendale), later becomes 2nd Hobgoblin	2	4	6	11	16	20
NOTE: ***Austin** c-7i, 19i. **Buckler** c-17p, 18p. **Byrne** c-14p. **Ditko** a-10-19; c-10-13, 14i, 15, 16. **Kirby** a-1-9p; c-1-5, 7-9p. **Layton** c-7i. **Miller** c-19p. **Simonson** c-6.*						
MACHINE MAN (Also see X-51)						
Marvel Comics Group: Oct, 1984 - No. 4, Jan, 1985 (limited series)						
1-4-Barry Smith-c/a(i) & colors in all						5.00
TPB (1988, $6.95) r/ #1-4; Barry Smith-c						7.00
.../Bastion '98 Annual ($2.99) wraparound-c						3.00
MACHINE MAN 2020						
Marvel Comics: Aug, 1994 - Nov, 1994 ($2.00, 52 pgs., limited series)						
1-4: Reprints Machine Man limited series; Barry Windsor-Smith-c/i(r)						2.50
MACHINE TEEN						
Marvel Comics: July, 2005 - No. 5, Nov, 2005 ($2.99, limited series)						
1-5-Sumerak-s/Hawthorne-a. 1-James Jean-c						3.00
...: History (2005, $7.99, digest) r/#1-5						8.00
MACK BOLAN: THE EXECUTIONER (Don Pendleton's...)						
Innovation Publishing: July, 1993 ($2.50)						
1-3-($2.50)						2.50
1-($3.95)-Indestructible Cover Edition						4.00
1-($2.95)-Collector's Gold Edition; foil stamped						3.00
1-($3.50)-Double Cover Edition; red foil outer-c						3.50
MACKENZIE'S RAIDERS (Movie, TV)						
Dell Publishing Co.: No. 1093, Apr-June, 1960						
Four Color 1093-Richard Carlson photo-c from TV show						

Mad #64 © EC

Mad #343 © EC

Mad About Millie #1 © MAR

GD 2.0 | VG 4.0 | FN 6.0 | VF 8.0 | VF/NM 9.0 | NM- 9.2

6 12 18 43 69 95

MACROSS (Becomes Robotech: The Macross Saga #2 on)
Comico: Dec, 1984 ($1.50)(Low print run)
1-Early manga app. 3 6 9 14 20 25

MACROSS II
Viz Select Comics: 1992 - No. 10, 1993 ($2.75, B&W, limited series)
1-10: Based on video series 2.75

MAD (Tales Calculated to Drive You...)
E. C. Comics (Educational Comics): Oct-Nov, 1952 - Present (No. 24-on are magazine format) (Kurtzman editor No. 1-28, Feldstein No. 29 - No. ?)
1-Wood, Davis, Elder start as regulars 417 834 1251 3336 5318 7300
2-Dick Tracy cameo 110 220 330 880 1403 1925
3,4: 3-Stan Lee mentioned. 4-Reefer mention story "Flob Was a Slob" by Davis; Superman parody 77 154 231 616 983 1350
5-Low distr.; W.M. Gaines biog. 157 314 471 1256 2003 2750
6-11: 6-Popeye cameo. 7,8- "Hey Look" reprints by Kurtzman. 11-Wolverton-a; Davis story was-r/Crime Suspenstories #12 w/new Kurtzman dialogue 60 120 180 480 765 1050
12-15: 15,18-Pot Shot Pete-r by Kurtzman 48 96 144 384 612 840
16-23(5/55): 18-Alice in Wonderland by Jack Davis. 21-1st app. Alfred E. Neuman on-c in fake ad. 22-All by Elder plus photo-montages by Kurtzman.
23-Special cancel announcement 40 80 120 320 510 700
24(7/55)-1st magazine issue (25¢); Kurtzman logo & border on-c; 1st "What? Me Worry?" on-c; 2nd printing exists 94 188 282 752 1201 1650
25-Jaffee starts as regular writer 44 88 132 352 564 775
26,27: 27-Jaffee starts as story artist; new logo 39 78 117 312 499 685
28-Last issue edited by Kurtzman; (three cover variations exist with different wording on contents banner on lower right of cover; value of each the same) 37 74 111 231 358 485
29-Kamen-a; Don Martin starts as regular; Feldstein editing begins 37 74 111 231 358 485
30-1st A. E. Neuman cover by Mingo; last Elder-a; Bob Clarke starts as regular; Disneyland & Elvis Presley spoof 58 116 174 363 557 750
31-Freas starts as regular; last Davis-a until #99 34 68 102 213 324 435
32,33: 32-Orlando, Drucker, Woodbridge start as regulars; Wood back-c. 33-Orlando back-c 29 58 87 181 276 370
34-Berg starts as regular 23 46 69 144 222 300
35-Mingo wraparound-c; Crandall-a 23 46 69 144 222 300
36-40 (7/58): 39-Beall-c 17 34 51 106 166 225
41-50: 42-Danny Kaye-s. 44-Xmas-c. 47-49-Sid Caesar-s. 48-Uncle Sam-c.
50 (10/59)-Peter Gunn-s 15 30 45 94 142 190
51-59: 52-Xmas-c; 77 Sunset Strip. 53-Rifleman-s. 54-Jaffee-a begins. 55-Sid Caesar-s. 59-Strips of Superman, Flash Gordon, Donald Duck & others. 59-Halloween/Headless Horseman-c 12 24 36 75 113 150
60 (1/61)-JFK/Nixon flip-c; 1st Spy vs. Spy by Prohias, who starts as regular 14 28 42 88 134 180
61-70: 64-Rickard starts as regular. 65-JFK-s. 66-JFK-c. 68-Xmas-c by Martin. 70-Route 66-s 9 18 27 56 83 110
71-75,77-80 (7/63): 72-10th Anniv. special; 1/3 pg. strips of Superman, Tarzan & others.
73-Bonanza-s. 74-Dr. Kildare-s 5 10 15 34 55 75
76-Aragonés starts as regular 6 12 18 39 62 85
81-85: 81-Superman strip. 82-Castro-c. 85-Lincoln-c 5 10 15 30 48 65
86-1st Fold-in; commonly creased back covers makes these and later issues scarcer in NM 6 12 18 37 59 80
87,88 5 10 15 34 55 75
89,90: 89-One strip by Walt Kelly; Frankenstein-c; Fugitive-s. 90-Ringo back-c by Frazetta; Beatles app. 6 12 18 37 59 80
91,94,96,100: 94-King Kong-c. 96-Man From U.N.C.L.E. 100-(1/66)-Anniversary issue 5 10 15 30 48 65
92,93,95,97-99: 99-Davis-a resumes 4 8 12 28 44 60
101,104,106,108,114,115,119,121: 101-Infinity-c; Voyage to the Bottom of the Sea-s. 104-Lost in Space-s. 106-Tarzan back-c by Frazetta; 2 pg. Batman by Aragonés. 108-Hogan's Heroes by Davis. 114-Rat Patrol-s. 115-Star Trek. 119-Invaders (TV). 121-Beatles-c; Ringo pin-up; flip-c of Sik-Teen; Flying Nun-s 3 6 9 21 32 42
102,103,107,109-113,116-118,120(7/68): 118-Beatles cameo 3 6 9 19 29 38
105-Batman-c/s, TV show parody (9/66) 4 8 12 24 37 50
122,124,126,128,129,131-134,136,137,139,140: 122-Ronald Reagan photo inside; Drucker & Mingo-c. 126-Family Affair-s. 128-Last Orlando. 131-Reagan photo back-c. 132-Xmas-c. 133-John Wayne/True Grit. 136-Room 222 3 6 9 16 22 28
123-Four different covers 3 6 9 16 23 30
125,127,130,135,138: 125-2001 Space Odyssey; Hitler back-c. 127-Mod Squad-c/s. 130-Land of the Giants-s; Torres begins as reg. 135-Easy Rider-c by Davis. 138-Snoopy-c; MASH-s 3 6 9 17 25 32
141-149,151-156,158-165,167-170: 141-Hawaii Five-0. 147-All in the Family-s. 153-Dirty Harry-s. 155-Godfather-c/s. 156-Columbo-s. 159-Clockwork Orange-c/s. 161-Tarzan-s. 164-Kung Fu (TV)-s. 165-James Bond-s; Dean Martin-c. 169-Drucker-c; McCloud-s. 170-Exorcist-s 3 6 9 14 19 24
150-(4/72) Partridge Family-s 3 6 9 15 21 26
157-(3/73) Planet of the Apes-c/s 3 6 9 16 23 30
166-(4/74) Classic finger-c 3 6 9 16 23 30
171-185,187,189-192,194,195,198,199: 172-Six Million Dollar Man-s; Hitler back-c. 178-Godfather II-c/s. 180-Jaws-c/s (1/76). 182-Bob Jones starts as regular.185-Starsky & Hutch-s. 187-Fonz/Happy Days-c/s; Harry North starts as regular. 189-Travolta/Kotter-c/s. 190-John Wayne-c/s. 192-King Kong-c/s. 194-Rocky-c/s; Laverne & Shirley-s. 199-James Bond-s 2 4 6 10 14 18
186,188,197,200: 186-Star Trek-c/s. 188-Six Million Dollar Man/ Bionic Woman. 197-Spock-s; Star Wars-s. 200-Close Encounters 2 4 6 13 18 22
193,196: 193-Farrah/Charlie's Angels-c/s. 196-Star Wars-c/s 3 6 9 14 19 24
201,203,205,220: 201-Sat. Night Fever-c/s. 203-Star Wars. 205-Travolta/Grease. 220-Yoda-c, Empire Strikes Back-s 2 4 6 9 13 16
202,204,206,207,209,211-219,221-227,229,230: 204-Hulk TV show. 206-Tarzan. 208-Superman movie. 209-Mork & Mindy. 212-Spider-Man-s; Alien (movie)-s. 213-James Bond, Dracula, Rocky II-s 216-Star Trek. 219-Martin-c. 221-Shining-s. 223-Dallas-c/s. 225-Popeye. 226-Superman II. 229-James Bond. 230-Star Wars 1 3 4 6 8 10
208,228: 208-Superman movie-c/s; Battlestar Galactica-s. 228-Raiders of the Lost Ark-c/s 2 4 6 9 12 15
210-Lord of the Rings 2 4 6 9 13 16
231-235,237-241,243-249,251-260: 233-Pac-Man-c. 234-MASH-c/s. 235-Flip-c with Rocky III & Conan; Boris-a. 239-Mickey Mouse-c. 241-Knight Rider-s. 243-Superman III. 245- Last Rickard-a. 247-Seven Dwarfs-c. 253-Supergirl movie-s; Prince/Purple Rain-s. 254-Rock stars-s. 255-Reagan-c; Cosby-s. 256-Last issue edited by Feldstein; Dynasty, Bev. Hills Cop. 259-Rambo. 260-Back to the Future-c/s; Honeymooners-s 1 2 3 5 6 8
236,242,250: 236-E.T.-c/s;Star Trek II-s. 242-Star Wars/A-Team-c/s. 250-Temple of Doom-c/s; Tarzan-s 1 2 3 5 7 9
261-267,269-276,278-288,290-297: 261-Miami Vice. 262-Rocky IV-c/s, Leave It To Beaver-s. 263-Young Sherlock Holmes-s. 264-Hulk Hogan-c; Rambo-s. 267-Top Gun. 271-Star Trek IV-c/s. 272-ALF-c; Get Smart-s. 273-Pee Wee Herman-c/s. 274-Last Martin-a. 281-California Raisins-c. 282-Star Trek:TNG-s; ALF-s. 283-Rambo III-c/s. 284-Roger Rabbit-c/s. 285-Hulk Hogan-c. 287-3 pgs. Eisner-a. 291-TMNT-c; Indiana Jones-s. 292-Super Mario Bros.-c; Married with Children-s. 295-Back to the Future II. 297-Mike Tyson-c 1 2 3 4 5 7
268,277,289,298-300: 268-Aliens-c/s. 277-Michael Jackson-c/s; Robocop-s. 289-Batman movie parody. 298-Gremlins II-c/s; Robocop II. Batman-s. 299-Simpsons-c/story; Total Recall-s. 300(1/91) Casablanca-s, Dick Tracy-s, Wizard of Oz-s, Gone With The Wind-s 1 2 3 5 6 8
300-303 (1/91-6/91)-Special Hussein Asylum Editions; only distributed to the troops in the Middle East (see Mad Super Spec.) 2 4 6 13 18 22
301-310,312,313,315-320,322,324,326-334,337-349: 303-Home Alone-c/s. 305-Simpsons-s. 306-TMNT II movie. 308-Terminator II. 315-Tribute to William Gaines. 316-Photo-c. 319-Dracula-c/s. 320-Disney's Aladdin-s. 322-Batman Animated series. 327-Seinfeld-s; X-Men-s. 331-Flintstones-c/s. 332-O.J. Simpson-c/s; Simpsons app. in Lion King. 334-Frankenstein-c/s. 338-Judge Dredd-c by Frazetta. 341-Pocahontas-s. 345-Beatles app. (1 pg.) 347-Broken Arrow & Mission Impossible 5.00
311,314,321,323,325,335,336,350,354,358: 311-Addams Family-c/story, Home Improvement-s. 314-Batman Returns-c/story. 321-Star Trek DS9-c/s. 323-Jurassic Park-c/s. 325,336-Beavis & Butthead-c/s. 335-X-Files-s; Pulp Fiction-s; Interview with the Vampire-s. 336-Lois & Clark-s. 350-Polybagged w/CD Rom. 354-Star Wars; Beavis & Butthead-s. 358-X-Files 6.00
351-353,355-357,359-500 5.00
501-503-($5.99) 6.00
Mad About Super Heroes (2002, $9.95) r/super hero app.; Alex Ross-c 10.00

NOTE: ***Aragones*** *c-210, 293.* ***Beall*** *c-39.* ***Davis*** *c-2, 27, 135, 139, 173, 178, 212, 213, 219, 246, 260, 296, 308.* ***Drucker*** *a-35-62; c-122, 169, 176, 225, 234, 264, 266, 274, 280, 285, 297, 299, 303, 314, 315, 321.* ***Elder*** *c-5, 259, 261, 268.* ***Elder/Kurtzman*** *a-258-274.* ***Jules Feiffer*** *a(r)-42.* ***Freas*** *c-40-59, 62-67, 69-70, 72, 74.* ***Heath*** *a-14, 27.* ***Jaffee*** *c-199, 217, 224, 258.* ***Kamen*** *a-29.* ***Krigstein*** *a-12, 17, 24, 26.* ***Kurtzman*** *c-1, 3, 4, 6-10, 13, 16, 18.* ***Martin*** *a-29-62; c-68, 165, 229.* ***Mingo*** *c-30-37, 61, 71, 75-80, 82-114, 117-124, 126, 129, 131, 133, 134, 136, 140, 143-148, 150-162, 164, 166-168, 171, 172, 174, 175, 177, 179, 181, 183, 185, 198, 206, 209, 211, 214, 218, 221, 222, 300.* ***John Severin*** *a-1-6, 9, 10.* ***Wolverton*** *c-11; a-11, 17, 29, 31, 36, 40, 82, 137.* ***Wood*** *a-1-21, 23-62; c-26, 28, 29.* ***Woodbridge*** *a-35-62. Issues 1-23 are 36 pgs.; 24-28 are 58 pgs.; 29 on are 52 pgs.*

MAD (See Mad Follies, ...Special, More Trash from..., and The Worst from...)

MAD ABOUT MILLIE (Also see Millie the Model)
Marvel Comics Group: April, 1969 - No. 16, Nov, 1970
1-Giant issue 9 18 27 63 107 150
2,3 (Giants) 6 12 18 41 66 90

Madame Xanadu #6 © DC

Mad Follies #1 © EC

Madman Atomic Comics #14 © Mike Allred

	GD 2.0	VG 4.0	FN 6.0	VF 8.0	VF/NM 9.0	NM- 9.2
4-10	4	8	12	28	44	60
11-16: 16-r	4	8	12	26	41	55
Annual 1(11/71, 52 pgs.)	4	8	12	28	44	60

MADAME MIRAGE
Image Comics (Top Cow): June, 2007 - No. 6, May, 2008 ($2.99)

1-6: 1-Paul Dini-s/Kenneth Rocafort-a; two covers by Horn and Rocafort 3.00
... First Look (5/07, 99¢) preview of series; Dini interview; cover gallery 2.25
Volume 1 TPB (7/08, $14.99) r/#1-6; cover gallery; cover and design sketches 15.00

MADAME XANADU
DC Comics: July, 1981 ($1.00, no ads, 36 pgs.)

1-Marshall Rogers-a (25 pgs.); Kaluta-c/a (2pgs.); pin-up 6.00

MADAME XANADU (Also see Doorway to Nightmare)
DC Comics (Vertigo): Aug, 2008 - Present ($2.99)

1-Matt Wagner-s/Amy Reeder Hadley-a/c; Phantom Stranger app. 4.00
1,2-Variant covers. 1-Wagner. 2-Kaluta 5.00
2-19: 2-10-Amy Reeder Hadley-a/c; Phantom Stranger app. 6-Death (from The Sandman) app.; covers by Hadley & Quitely. 9-Zatara app. 10-Jim Corrigan becomes The Spectre. 11-15-Kaluta-a. 14,15-Sandman (Wesley Dodds) app. 16-18-Hadley-a; Det. Jones app. 3.00
...: Disenchanted TPB (2009, $12.99) r/#1-10; James Robinson intro.; Hadley sketch-a 13.00
...: Exodus TPB (2010, $12.99) r/#11-15; Chris Roberson intro. 13.00

MADBALLS
Star Comics/Marvel Comics #9 on: Sept, 1986 - No. 3, Nov, 1986; No. 4, June, 1987 - No. 10, June, 1988

1-10: Based on toys. 9-Post-a 4.00

MAD DISCO
E.C. Comics: 1980 (one-shot, 36 pgs.)

1-Includes 30 minute flexi-disc of Mad disco music 2 4 6 11 16 20

MAD-DOG
Marvel Comics: May, 1993 - No. 6, Oct, 1993 ($1.25)

1-6-Flip book w/2nd story "created" by Bob Newhart's character from his TV show "Bob" set at a comic book company; actual s/a-Ty Templeton 2.50

MAD DOGS
Eclipse Comics: Feb, 1992 - No. 3, July, 1992 ($2.50, B&W, limited series)

1-3 2.50

MAD 84 (Mad Extra)
E.C. Comics: 1984 (84 pgs.)

1 1 3 4 6 8 10

MAD FOLLIES (Special)
E. C. Comics: 1963 - No. 7, 1969

	GD	VG	FN	VF	VF/NM	NM-
nn(1963)-Paperback book covers	22	44	66	155	300	445
2(1964)-Calendar	17	34	51	119	230	340
3(1965)-Mischief Stickers	13	26	39	93	172	250
4(1966)-Mobile; Frazetta-r/back-c Mad #90	10	20	30	67	116	165
5,6: 5(1967)-Stencils. 6(1968)-Mischief Stickers	8	16	24	52	86	120
7(1969)-Nasty Cards	8	16	24	52	86	120

(If bonus is missing, issue is half price)
NOTE: ***Clarke** c-4. **Frazetta** r-4, 6 (1 pg. ea.). **Mingo** c-1-3. **Orlando** a-5.*

MAD HATTER, THE (Costumed Hero)
O. W. Comics Corp.: Jan-Feb, 1946; No. 2, Sept-Oct, 1946

	GD	VG	FN	VF	VF/NM	NM-
1-Freddy the Firefly begins; Giunta-c/a	77	154	231	493	847	1200
2-Has ad for E.C.'s Animal Fables #1	40	80	120	246	411	575

MADHOUSE
Ajax/Farrell Publ. (Excellent Publ./4-Star): 3-4/54 - No. 4, 9-10/54; 6/57 - No. 4, Dec?, 1957

	GD	VG	FN	VF	VF/NM	NM-
1(1954)	31	62	93	182	296	410
2,3	17	34	51	100	158	215
4-Surrealistic-c	23	46	69	136	223	310
1(1957, 2nd series)	14	28	42	80	115	150
2-4 (#4 exist?)	10	20	30	54	72	90

MAD HOUSE (Formerly Madhouse Glads; ...Comics #104? on)
Red Circle Productions/Archie Publications: No. 95, 9/74 - No. 97, 1/75; No. 98, 8/75 - No. 130, 10/82

	GD	VG	FN	VF	VF/NM	NM-
95,96-Horror stories through #97; Morrow-c	2	4	6	11	16	20
97-Intro. Henry Hobson; Morrow-a/c, Thorne-a	2	4	6	10	14	18
98,99,101-120-Satire/humor stories. 110-Sabrina app.,1pg.	1	3	4	6	8	10
100	2	4	6	8	10	12
121-129	2	4	6	8	10	12
130	2	4	6	9	13	16
Annual 8(1970-71)-Formerly Madhouse Ma-ad Annual; Sabrina app. (6 pgs.)	4	8	12	24	37	50
Annual 9-12(1974-75): 11-Wood-a(r)	2	4	6	13	18	22
...Comics Digest 1('75-76)	2	4	6	10	14	18
2-8(8/82)(...Mag. #5 on)-Sabrina in many	2	4	6	8	11	14

NOTE: ***B. Jones** a-96. **McWilliams** a-97. **Wildey** a-95, 96. See Archie Comics Digest #1, 13.*

MADHOUSE GLADS (Formerly ...Ma-ad; Madhouse #95 on)
Archie Publ.: No. 73, May, 1970 - No. 94, Aug, 1974 (No. 78-92: 52 pgs.)

	GD	VG	FN	VF	VF/NM	NM-
73-77,93,94: 74-1 pg. Sabrina	2	4	6	9	13	16
78-92 (52 pgs.)	2	4	6	11	16	20

MADHOUSE MA-AD (...Jokes #67-70; ...Freak-Out #71-74)
(Formerly Archie's Madhouse) (Becomes Madhouse Glads #73 on)
Archie Publications: No. 67, April, 1969 - No. 72, Jan, 1970

	GD	VG	FN	VF	VF/NM	NM-
67-71: 70-1 pg. Sabrina	2	4	6	14	20	25
72-6 pgs. Sabrina	4	8	12	24	37	50
...Annual 7(1969-70)-Formerly Archie's Madhouse Annual; becomes Madhouse Annual; 6 pgs. Sabrina	4	8	12	24	37	50

MADMAN (See Creatures of the Id #1)
Tundra Publishing: Mar, 1992 - No. 3, 1992 ($3.95, duotone, high quality, lim. series, 52 pgs.)

1-Mike Allred-c/a in all 2 4 6 8 10 12
1-2nd printing 4.00
2,3 6.00

MADMAN ADVENTURES
Tundra Publishing: 1992 - No. 3, 1993 ($2.95, limited series)

1-Mike Allred-c/a in all 1 2 3 5 7 9
2,3 5.00
TPB (Oni Press, 2002, $14.95) r/#1-3 & first app. of Frank Einstein from Creatures of the Id in color; gallery pages 15.00

MADMAN ATOMIC COMICS (Also see The Atomics)
Image Comics: Apr, 2007 - Present ($2.99/$3.50)

1-12-Mike Allred-s/c/a. 1-Origin re-told; pin-ups by Rivoche and Powell. 3-Sale back-c 3.00
13-17-($3.50) Wraparound-c. 14-Back up w/Darwyn Cooke-a 3.50
... Vol. 1 (2008, $19.99) r/#1-7; bonus art; Jamie Rich intro. 20.00

MADMAN COMICS (Also see The Atomics)
Dark Horse Comics (Legend No. 2 on): Apr, 1994 - No. 20, Dec, 2000 ($2.95/$2.99)

1-Allred-c/a; F. Miller back-c. 1 2 3 5 6 8
2-3: 3-Alex Toth back-c. 5.00
4-11: 4-Dave Stevens back-c. 6,7-Miller/Darrow's Big Guy app. 6-Bruce Timm back-c. 7-Darrow back-c. 8-Origin?; Bagge back-c. 10-Allred/Ross-c; Ross back-c. 11-Frazetta back-c 4.00
12-16: 12-(4/99) 3.00
17-20: 17-The G-Men From Hell #1 on cover; Brereton back-c. 18-(#2). 19,20-($2.99-c). 20-Clowes back-c 3.00
... Boogaloo TPB (6/99, $8.95) r/Nexus Meets Madman & Madman/The Jam 9.00
... Gargantua! (2007, $125.00, HC with dustjacket) r/Madman#1-3, Madman Adventures #1-3, Madman Comics #1-20 and Madman King-Size Super Groovy Special; pin-ups 125.00
Ltd. Ed. Slipcover (1997, $99.95, signed and numbered) w/Vol.1 & Vol. 2. Vol.1- reprints #1-5; Vol. 2- reprints #6-10 100.00
The Complete Madman Comics: Vol. 2 (11/96, $17.95, TPB) r/#6-10 plus new material 18.00
Madman King-Size Super Groovy Special (Oni Press, 7/03, $6.95) new short stories by Allred, Derington, Krall and Weissman 7.00
Madman Picture Exhibition No. 1-4 (4-7/02, $3.95) pin-ups by various 4.00
Madman Picture Exhibition Limited Edition (10/02, $29.95) Hardcover collects MPE #1-4 30.00
... Volume 2 SC (2007, $17.99) r/#1-11; Erik Larsen intro. 18.00
... Volume 3 SC (2007, $17.99) r/#12-20 and story from King-Size Groovy; Allred intro. 18.00
Yearbook '95 (1996, $17.95, TPB)-r/#1-5, intro by Teller 18.00

MADMAN / THE JAM
Dark Horse Comics: Jul, 1998 - No. 2, Aug, 1998 ($2.95, mini-series)

1,2-Allred & Mireault-s/a 3.00

MAD MONSTER PARTY (See Movie Classics)

MADNESS IN MURDERWORLD
Marvel Comics: 1989 (Came with computer game from Paragon Software)

V1#1-Starring The X-Men 2.50

MADRAVEN HALLOWEEN SPECIAL
Hamilton Comics: Oct, 1995 ($2.95, one-shot)

nn-Morrow-a 3.00

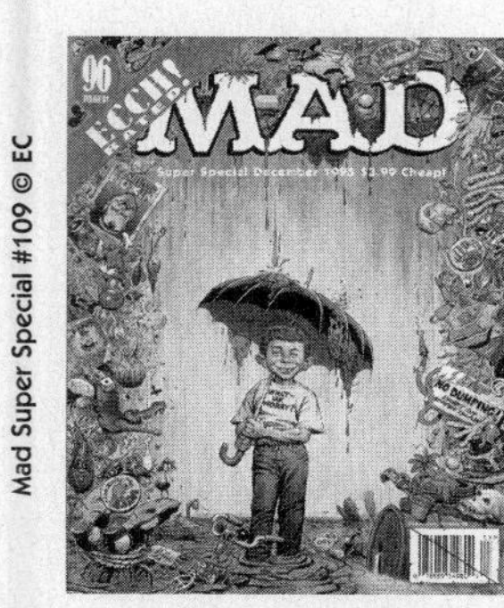

Mad Super Special #109 © EC

Magic Comics #43 © DMP

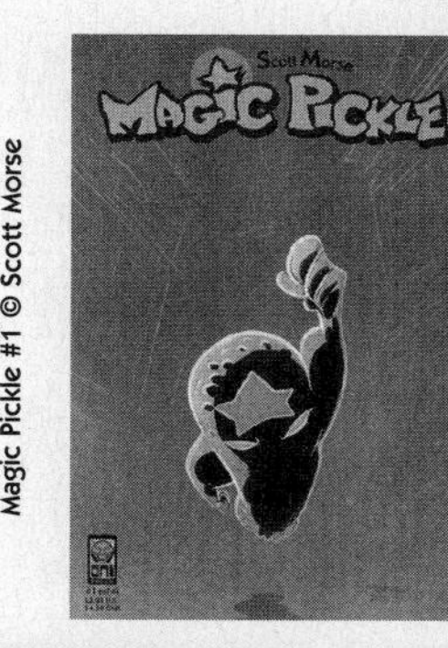

Magic Pickle #1 © Scott Morse

GD VG FN VF VF/NM NM-
2.0 4.0 6.0 8.0 9.0 9.2

MADROX (from X-Factor)
Marvel Comics (Marvel Knights): Nov, 2004 - No. 5, Mar, 2005 ($2.99)

1-5-Peter David-s/Pablo Raimondi-a; Strong Guy app. 3.00
...: Multiple Choice TPB (2005, $13.99) r/#1-5 14.00
X-Factor: Madrox - Multiple Choice HC (2008, $19.99) r/#1-5 20.00

MAD SPECIAL (...Super Special)
E. C. Publications, Inc.: Fall, 1970 - Present (84 - 116 pgs.)
(If bonus is missing, issue is one half price)

Fall 1970(#1)-Bonus-Voodoo Doll; contains 17 pgs. new material
10 20 30 68 119 170
Spring 1971(#2)-Wall Nuts; 17 pgs. new material 6 12 18 37 59 80
3-Protest Stickers 6 12 18 37 59 80
4-8: 4-Mini Posters. 5-Mad Flag. 6-Mad Mischief Stickers. 7-Presidential candidate posters, Wild Shocking Message posters. 8-TV Guise 5 10 15 32 51 70
9(1972)-Contains Nostalgic Mad #1 (28 pgs.) 4 8 12 26 41 55
10-13: 10-Nonsense Stickers (Don Martin). 13-Sickie Stickers; 3 pgs. Wolverton-r/Mad #137. 11-Contains 33-1/3 RPM record. 12-Contains Nostalgic Mad #2 (36 pgs.); Davis, Wolverton-a 3 6 9 20 30 40
14,16-21,24: 4-Vital Message posters & Art Depreciation paintings. 16-Mad-hesive Stickers. 17-Don Martin posters. 20-Martin Stickers. 18-Contains Nostalgic Mad #4 (36 pgs.). 21,24-Contains Nostalgic Mad #5 (28 pgs.) & #6 (28 pgs.)
3 6 9 16 23 30
15-Contains Nostalgic Mad #3 (28 pgs.) 3 6 9 17 25 32
22,23,25,27-29,30: 22-Diplomas. 23-Martin Stickers. 25-Martin Posters. 27-Mad Shock-Sticks. 28-Contains Nostalgic Mad #7 (36 pgs.). 29-Mad Collectable-Connectables Posters. 30-The Movies 2 4 6 9 13 16
26-Has 33-1/3 RPM record 2 4 6 13 18 22
31,33-35,37-50 2 4 6 8 11 14
32-Contains Nostalgic Mad #8. 36-Has 96 pgs. of comic book & comic strip spoofs: titles "The Comics" on-c 2 4 6 9 13 16
51-70 1 3 4 6 8 10
71-88,90-100: 71-Batman parodies-r by Wood, Drucker. 72-Wolverton-c r-from 1st panel in Mad #11; Wolverton-s r/new dialogue. 83-All Star Trek spoof issue
1 2 3 5 6 8
76-(Fall, 1991)-Special Hussein Asylum Edition; distributed only to the troops in the Middle East (see Mad #300-303) 2 4 6 13 18 22
89-($3.95)-Polybagged w/1st of 3 Spy vs. Spy hologram trading cards (direct sale only issue) (other cards came w/card set) 1 3 4 6 8 10
101-135: 117-Sci-Fi parodies-r. 4.00
NOTE: *#28-30 have no number on cover.* ***Freas*** *c-76.* ***Mingo*** *c-9, 11, 15, 19, 23.*

MAGDALENA, THE (See The Darkness #15-18)
Image Comics (Top Cow): Apr, 2000 - No. 3, Jan, 2001 ($2.50)

Preview Special ('00, $4.95) Flip book w/Blood Legacy preview 5.00
1-Benitez-c/a; variant covers by Silvestri & Turner 2.50
2,3: 2-Two covers 2.50
.../Angelus #1/2 (11/01, $2.95) Benitez-c/Ching-a 3.00
...Blood Divine (2002, $9.95) r/#1-3 & #1/2; cover gallery 10.00
.../Vampirella (7/03, $2.99) Wohl-s/Benitez-a; two covers 3.00

MAGDALENA, THE (Volume 2)
Image Comics (Top Cow): Aug, 2003 - No. 4 ($2.99)

Preview (6/03) B&W preview; Wizard World East logo on cover 2.50
1-4-Holguin-s/Basaldua-a 3.00
1-Variant-c by Jim Silke benefitting ACTOR charity 5.00
TPB Volume 1 (12/06, $19.99) r/both series, Darkness #15-18 & Magdalena/Angelus 20.00
.../Daredevil (5/08, $3.99) Phil Hester-s/a; Hester & Sejic-c 4.00
.../Vampirella (12/04, $2.99) Kirkman-s/Manapul-a; two covers by Manapul and Bachalo 3.00
... Vs. Dracula Monster War 2005 (6/05, $2.99) four covers; Joyce Chin-a 3.00

MAGE (The Hero Discovered...; also see Grendel #16)
Comico: Feb, 1984 (no month) - No. 15, Dec, 1986 ($1.50, Mando paper)

1-Comico's 1st color comic 2 4 6 8 11 14
2-5: 3-Intro Edsel 6.00
6-Grendel begins (1st in color) 3 6 9 14 20 25
7-1st new Grendel story 2 4 6 8 10 12
8-14: 13-Grendel dies. 14-Grendel story ends 6.00
15-($2.95) Double size w/pullout poster 1 2 3 5 6 8
TPB Volume 1-4 (Image, $5.95) 1- r/#1,2. 2- r/#3,4. 3- r/#5,6. 4- r/#7,8 7.00
TPB Volume 5-7 (Image, $6.95) 5- r/#9,10. 6- r/#11,12. 7- r/#13,14 7.00
TPB Volume 8 (Image, 9/99, $7.50) r/#15 7.50
..., Vol. 1 TPB (Image, 2004, $29.99) r/#1-15; cover gallery, promo artwork, bonus art 30.00

MAGE (The Hero Defined) (Volume 2)
Image Comics: July, 1997 - No. 15, Oct, 1999 ($2.50)

GD VG FN VF VF/NM NM-
2.0 4.0 6.0 8.0 9.0 9.2

0-(7/97, $5.00) American Ent. Ed. 5.00
1-14:Matt Wagner-c/s/a in all. 13-Three covers 2.50
1-"3-D Edition" (2/98, $4.95) w/glasses 5.00
15-($5.95) Acetate cover 6.00
Volume 1,2 TPB ('98,'99, $9.95) 1- r/#1-4. 2-r/#5-8 10.00
Volume 3 TPB ('00, $12.95) r/#9-12 13.00
Volume 4 TPB ('01, $14.95) r/#13-15 15.00
Hardcover Vol. 2 (2005, $49.95) r/#1-15; cover gallery, character design & sketch pages 50.00

MAGE KNIGHT: STOLEN DESTINY (Based on the fantasy game Mage Knight)
Idea + Design Works: Oct, 2002 - No. 5, Feb, 2003 ($3.50, limited series)

1-5: 1-J. Scott Campbell-c; Cabrera-a/Dezago-s, 2-Dave Johnson-c 3.50

MAGGIE AND HOPEY COLOR SPECIAL (See Love and Rockets)
Fantagraphics Books: May, 1997 ($3.50, one-shot)

1 3.50

MAGGIE THE CAT (Also see Jon Sable, Freelance #11 & Shaman's Tears #12)
Image Comics (Creative Fire Studio): Jan, 1996 - No. 2, Feb, 1996 ($2.50, unfinished limited series)

1,2: Mike Grell-c/a/scripts 2.50

MAGICA DE SPELL (See Walt Disney Showcase #30)

MAGIC AGENT (See Forbidden Worlds & Unknown Worlds)
American Comics Group: Jan-Feb, 1962 - No. 3, May-June, 1962

1-Origin & 1st app. John Force 4 8 12 26 41 55
2,3 3 6 9 19 29 38

MAGICAL POKÉMON JOURNEY
Viz Comics: 2000 - Present ($4.95, B&W, magazine-size)

1-4 5.00
Part 2: 1-3; Part 3: 1-4: 1-Includes color poster; Part 4: 1-4; Part 5: 1-4; Part 6: 1-4 5.00

MAGIC COMICS
David McKay Publications: Aug, 1939 - No. 123, Nov-Dec, 1949

1-Mandrake the Magician, Henry, Popeye , Blondie, Barney Baxter, Secret Agent X-9 (not by Raymond), Bunky by Billy DeBeck & Thornton Burgess text stories illustrated by Harrison Cady begin; Henry covers begin 349 698 1047 1989 3045 4100
2 124 248 372 707 1084 1460
3 91 182 273 519 797 1075
4 72 144 216 410 630 850
5 60 120 180 342 521 700
6-10: 8-11,21-Mandrake/Henry-c 48 96 144 274 417 560
11-16,18,20: 12-Mandrake-c begin. 39 78 117 222 341 460
17-The Lone Ranger begins 44 88 132 251 386 520
19-Classic robot-c (scarce) 89 178 267 507 779 1050
21-30: 25-Only Blondie-c. 26-Dagwood-c begin 26 52 78 154 252 350
31-40: 36-Flag-c 18 36 54 107 169 230
41-50 15 30 45 84 127 170
51-60 13 26 39 74 105 135
61-70 11 22 33 62 86 110
71-99, 107,108-Flash Gordon app; not by Raymond 9 18 27 52 69 85
100 10 20 30 56 76 95
101-106,109-123: 123-Last Dagwood-c 9 18 27 47 61 75

MAGIC FLUTE, THE (See Night Music #9-11)

MAGICIAN: APPRENTICE
Dabel Brothers/Marvel Comics (Dabel Brothers) #3 on: Mar, 2007 - No. 12, Dec, 2007 ($2.95/$2.99)

1-12-Adaptation of the Raymond E. Feist Riftwar Saga series 3.00
1,2-($5.95) 1-Wraparound variant-c by Maitz. 2-Wraparound variant-c by Booth 6.00
Collected Edition (10/06, $3.99) r/#1&2 4.00
Vol. 1 HC (2007, $19.99, dustjacket) r/#1-6; foreword by Feist 20.00
Vol. 1 SC (2007, $15.99) r/#1-6; foreword by Feist 16.00
Vol. 2 HC (2008, $19.99, dustjacket) r/#7-12 20.00

MAGIC PICKLE
Oni Press: Sept, 2001 - No. 4, Dec, 2001 ($2.95, limited series)

1-4-Scott Morse-s/a; Mahfood-a (2 pgs.) 3.00

MAGIC SWORD, THE (See Movie Classics)

MAGIC THE GATHERING (Title Series), **Acclaim Comics (Armada)**

...ANTIQUITIES WAR,11/95 - 2/96 ($2.50), 1-4-Paul Smith-a(p) 2.50
...ARABIAN NIGHTS, 12/95 - 1/96 ($2.50), 1,2 2.50
...COLLECTION ,'95 ($4.95), 1,2-polybagged 5.00

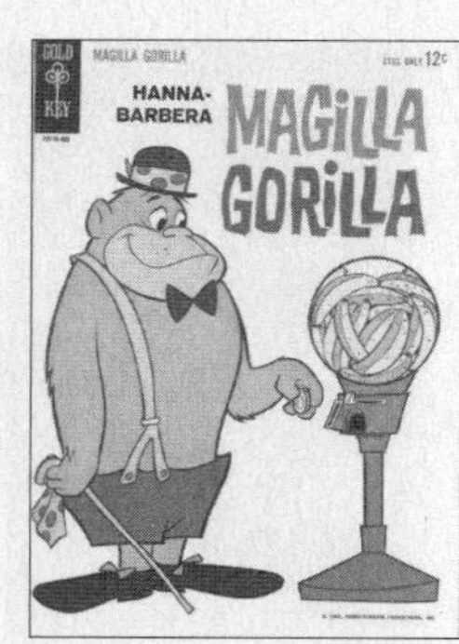

Magilla Gorilla #1 © H-B

Magnus, Robot Fighter #37 © GK

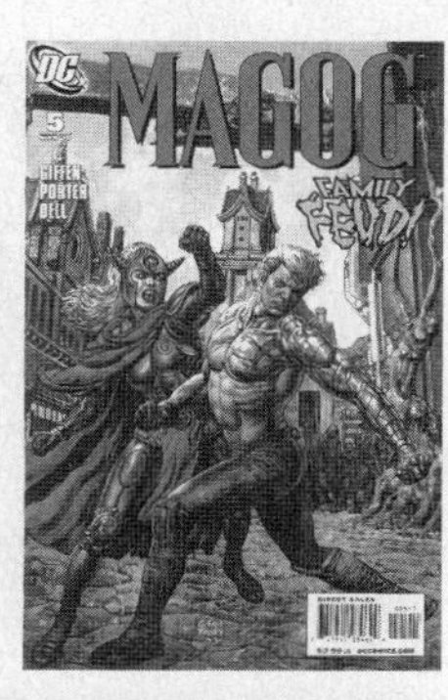

Magog #5 © DC

	GD 2.0	VG 4.0	FN 6.0	VF 8.0	VF/NM 9.0	NM- 9.2

...CONVOCATIONS, '95 ($2.50), 1-nn-pin-ups 2.50
...ELDER DRAGONS ,'95 ($2.50), 1,2-Doug Wheatley-a 2.50
...FALLEN ANGEL ,'95 ($5.95), nn 6.00
...FALLEN EMPIRES ,9/95 - 10/95 ($2.75), 1,2 3.00
...Collection ($4.95)-polybagged 5.00
...HOMELANDS ,'95 ($5.95), nn-polybagged w/card; Hildebrandts-c 6.00
... ICE AGE (On The World of...) ,7/5 -11/95 ($2.50), 1-4: 1,2-bound-in Magic Card. 3,4-bound-in insert 2.50
...LEGEND OF JEDIT OJANEN, '96 ($2.50), 1,2 2.50
...NIGHTMARE, '95 ($2.50, one shot), 1 2.50
...THE SHADOW MAGE, 7/95 - 10/95 ($2.50), 1-4-bagged w/Magic The Gathering card 2.50
...Collection 1,2 (1995, $4.95)-Trade paperback; polybagged 5.00
...SHANDALAR ,'96 ($2.50), 1,2 2.50
...WAYFARER ,11/95 - 2/96 ($2.50), 1-5 2.50

MAGIC: THE GATHERING: GERRARD'S QUEST
Dark Horse Comics: Mar, 1998 - No. 4, June, 1998 ($2.95, limited series)
1-4: Grell-s/Mhan-a 3.00

MAGIK (Illyana and Storm Limited Series)
Marvel Comics Group: Dec, 1983 - No. 4, Mar, 1984 (60¢, limited series)
1-4: 1-Characters from X-Men; Inferno begins; X-Men cameo (Buscema pencils in #1,2; c-1p. 2-4: 2-Nightcrawler app. & X-Men cameo 3.00

MAGIK (See Black Sun mini-series)
Marvel Comics: Dec, 2000 - No. 4, Mar, 2001 ($2.99, limited series)
1-4-Liam Sharp-a/Abnett & Lanning-s; Nightcrawler app. 3.00

MAGILLA GORILLA (TV) (See Kite Fun Book)
Gold Key: May, 1964 - No. 10, Dec, 1968 (Hanna-Barbera)
1-1st comic app. 9 18 27 65 113 160
2-4: 3-Vs. Yogi Bear for President. 4-1st Punkin Puss & Mushmouse, Ricochet Rabbit & Droop-a-Long 6 12 18 37 59 80
5-10: 10-Reprints 5 10 15 30 48 65

MAGILLA GORILLA (TV)(See Spotlight #4)
Charlton Comics: Nov, 1970 - No. 5, July, 1971 (Hanna-Barbera)
1 5 10 15 34 55 75
2-5 4 8 12 22 34 45

MAGNETIC MEN FEATURING MAGNETO
Marvel Comics (Amalgam): June, 1997 ($1.95, one-shot)
1-Tom Peyer-s/Barry Kitson & Dan Panosian-a 2.50

MAGNETO (See X-Men #1)
Marvel Comics: nd (Sept, 1993) (Giveaway) (one-shot)
0-Embossed foil-c by Sienkiewicz; r/Classic X-Men #19 & 12 by Bolton 5.00

MAGNETO
Marvel Comics: Nov, 1996 - No. 4, Feb, 1997 ($1.95, limited series)
1-4: Peter Milligan scripts & Kelley Jones-a(p) 2.50

MAGNETO AND THE MAGNETIC MEN
Marvel Comics (Amalgam): Apr, 1996 ($1.95, one-shot)
1-Jeff Matsuda-a(p) 2.50

MAGNETO ASCENDANT
Marvel Comics: May, 1999 ($3.99, squarebound one-shot)
1-Reprints early Magneto appearances 4.00

MAGNETO: DARK SEDUCTION
Marvel Comics: Jun, 2000 - No. 4, Sept, 2000 ($2.99, limited series)
1-4: Nicieza-s/Cruz-a. 3,4-Avengers-c/app. 3.00

MAGNETO REX
Marvel Comics: Apr, 1999 - No. 3, July, 1999 ($2.50, limited series)
1-3-Rogue, Quicksilver app.; Peterson-a(p) 2.50

MAGNUS, ROBOT FIGHTER (...4000 A.D.)(See Doctor Solar)
Gold Key: Feb, 1963 - No. 46, Jan, 1977 (All painted covers except #5,30,31)
1-Origin & 1st app. Magnus; Aliens (1st app.) series begins 22 44 66 157 304 450
2,3 10 20 30 73 129 185
4-10: 10-Simonson fan club illo (5/65, 1st-a?) 7 14 21 47 76 105
11-20 5 10 15 32 51 70
21,24-28: 28-Aliens ends 4 8 12 22 34 45
22,23: 22-Origin-r/#1; last 12¢ issue 4 8 12 23 36 48
29-46-Mostly reprints 2 4 6 11 16 20
Russ Manning's Magnus Robot Fighter - Vol. 1 HC (Dark Horse, 2004, $49.95) r/#1-7 70.00
Russ Manning's Magnus Robot Fighter - Vol. 2 HC (DH, 6/05, $49.95) r/#8-14; forward by Steve Rude 50.00
Russ Manning's Magnus Robot Fighter - Vol. 3 HC (Dark Horse, 10/06, $49.95) r/#15-21 50.00
NOTE: *Manning a-1-22, 28-43(r). Spiegle a-23, 44r.*

MAGNUS ROBOT FIGHTER (Also see Vintage Magnus)
Valiant/Acclaim Comics: May, 1991 - No. 64, Feb, 1996 ($1.75/$1.95/$2.25/$2.50)
1-Nichols/Layton-c/a; 1-8 have trading cards 1 2 3 5 6 8
2-8: 4-Rai cameo. 5-Origin & 1st full app. Rai (10/91); 5-8 are in flip book format and back-c & half of book are Rai #1-4 mini-series. 6-1st Solar x-over. 7-Magnus vs. Rai-c/story; 1st X-O Armor 6.00
0-Origin issue; Layton-a; ordered through mail w/coupons from 1st 8 issues plus 50¢; B. Smith trading card 2 4 6 11 16 20
0-Sold thru comic shops without trading card 2 4 6 8 10 12
9-11 3.00
12-(3.25, 44 pgs.)-Turok-c/story (1st app. in Valiant universe, 5/92); has 8 pg. Magnus story insert 1 3 4 6 8 10
13-24,26-48: 14-1st app. Isak. 15,16-Unity x-overs. 15-Miller-c. 16-Birth of Magnus. 21-New direction & new logo. 21-Gold ink variant. 24-Story cont'd in Rai & the Future Force #9. 33-Timewalker app.36-Bound-in trading cards. 37-Rai & Starwatchers app. 44-Bound-in sneak peek card. 2.50
25-($2.95)-Embossed silver foil-c; new costume 3.00
49-63 3.00
64-($2.50): 64-Magnus dies? 4.00
...Invasion (1994, $9.95)-r/Rai #1-4 & Magnus #5-8 10.00
Magnus Steel Nation (1994, $9.95) r/#1-4 10.00
Yearbook (1994, $3.95, 52 pgs.) 4.00
NOTE: ***Ditko/Reese** a-18. **Layton** a(i)-5; c-6-9i, 25; back(i)-5-8. **Reese** a(i)-22, 25, 28; c(i)-22, 24, 28. **Simonson** c-16. Prices for issues 1-8 are for trading cards and coupons intact.*

MAGNUS ROBOT FIGHTER
Acclaim Comics (Valiant Heroes): V2#1, May, 1997 - No. 18, Jun, 1998 ($2.50)
1-18: 1-Reintro Magnus; Donavon Wylie (X-O Manowar) cameo; Tom Peyer scripts & Mike McKone-c/a begin; painted variant-c exists 2.50

MAGNUS ROBOT FIGHTER/NEXUS
Valiant/Dark Horse Comics: Dec, 1993 - No. 2, Apr, 1994 ($2.95, lim. series)
1,2: Steve Rude painted-c & pencils in all 3.00

MAGOG (See Justice Society of America 2007 series)
DCComics: Nov, 2009 - Present ($2.99)
1-5: 1-Giffen-s/Porter-a/Fabry-c; variant-c by Porter 3.00

MAID OF THE MIST (See American Graphics)

MAI, THE PSYCHIC GIRL
Eclipse Comics: May, 1987 - No. 28, July, 1989 ($1.50, B&W, bi-weekly, 44pgs.)
1-28, 1,2-2nd print 2.50

MAJESTIC (Mr. Majestic from WildCATS)
DC Comics: Oct, 2004 - No. 4, Jan, 2005 ($2.95, limited series)
1-4-Kerschl-a/Abnett & Lanning-s. 1-Superman app.; Superman #1 cover swipe 3.00
...: Strange New Visitor TPB (2005, $14.99) r/#1-4 & Action #811, Advs. of Superman #624 & Superman #201 15.00

MAJESTIC (Mr. Majestic from WildCATS)
DC Comics (WildStorm): Mar, 2005 - No. 17, July, 2006 ($2.95/$2.99)
1-17: 1-Googe-a/Abnett & Lanning-s; Superman app. 9-Jeanty-a; Zealot app. 3.00
...: Meanwhile, Back on Earth... TPB (2006, $14.99) r/#8-12 13.00
...: The Final Cut TPB (2007, $14.99) r/#13-17 & story fro WildStorm Winter Special 15.00
...: While You Were Out TPB (2006, $12.99) r/#1-7 13.00

MAJOR BUMMER
DC Comics: Aug, 1997 - No. 15, Oct, 1998 ($2.50)
1-15: 1-Origin and 1st app. Major Bummer 2.50

MAJOR HOOPLE COMICS (See Crackajack Funnies)
Nedor Publications: nd (Jan, 1943)
1-Mary Worth, Phantom Soldier app. by Moldoff 38 76 114 219 352 485

MAJOR VICTORY COMICS (Also see Dynamic Comics)
H. Clay Glover/Service Publ./Harry 'A' Chesler: 1944 - No. 3, Summer, 1945
1-Origin Major Victory (patriotic hero) by C. Sultan (reprint from Dynamic #1); 1st app. Spider Woman 64 128 192 406 696 985
2-Dynamic Boy app. 39 78 117 240 395 550

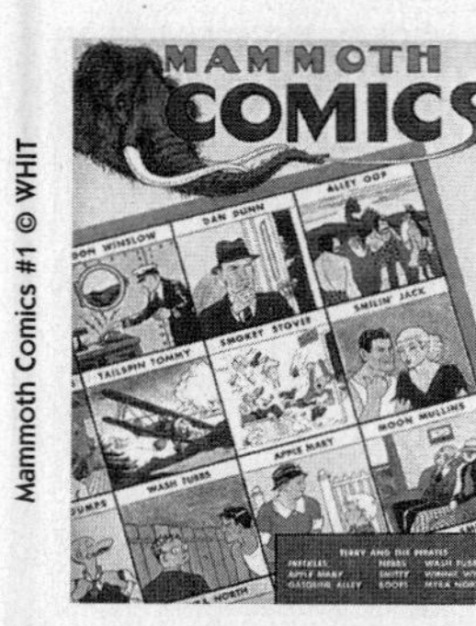

Mammoth Comics #1 © WHIT

Man Comics #3 © MAR

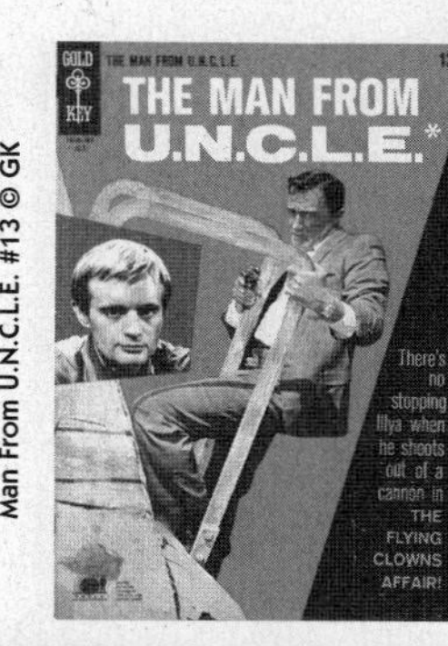

Man From U.N.C.L.E. #13 © GK

	GD	VG	FN	VF	VF/NM	NM-
	2.0	4.0	6.0	8.0	9.0	9.2

3-Rocket Boy app. 37 74 111 218 354 490

MALIBU ASHCAN: RAFFERTY (See Firearm #12)
Malibu Comics (Ultraverse): Nov, 1994 (99¢, B&W w/color-c; one-shot)
1-Previews "The Rafferty Saga" storyline in Firearm; Chaykin-c 2.50

MALTESE FALCON
David McKay Publications: No. 48, 1946
Feature Books 48-by Dashiell Hammett 82 164 246 528 902 1275

MALU IN THE LAND OF ADVENTURE
I. W. Enterprises: 1964 (See White Princess of Jungle #2)
1-r/Avon's Slave Girl Comics #1; Severin-c 5 10 15 30 48 65

MAMMOTH COMICS
Whitman Publishing Co.(K. K. Publ.): 1938 (84 pgs.) (B&W, 8-1/2x11-1/2")
1-Alley Oop, Terry & the Pirates, Dick Tracy, Little Orphan Annie, Wash Tubbs, Moon Mullins, Smilin' Jack, Tailspin Tommy, Don Winslow, Dan Dunn, Smokey Stover & other reprints (scarce) 200 400 600 1280 2190 3100

MAN AGAINST TIME
Image Comics (Motown Machineworks): May, 1996 - No. 4, Aug, 1996 ($2.25, lim. series)
1-4: 1-Simonson-c. 2,3-Leon-c. 4-Barreto & Leon-c 2.50

MAN-BAT (See Batman Family, Brave & the Bold, & Detective #400)
National Periodical Publ./DC Comics: Dec-Jan, 1975-76 - No. 2, Feb-Mar, 1976; Dec, 1984
1-Ditko-a(p); Aparo-c; Batman app.; 1st app. She-Bat? 3 6 9 14 20 25
2-Aparo-c 2 4 6 9 12 15
1 (12/84)-N. Adams-r(3)/Det.(Vs. Batman on-c) 4.00

MAN-BAT
DC Comics: Feb, 1996 - No. 3, Apr, 1996 ($2.25, limited series)
1-3: Dixon scripts in all. 2-Killer Croc-c/app. 2.50

MAN-BAT
DC Comics: Jun, 2006 - No. 5, Oct, 2006 ($2.99, limited series)
1-5: Bruce Jones-s/Mike Huddleston-a/c. 1-Hush app. 3.00

MAN CALLED A-X, THE
Malibu Comics (Bravura): Nov, 1994 - No. 4, Jun, 1995 ($2.95, limited series)
0-4: Marv Wolfman scripts & Shawn McManus-c/a. 0-(2/95). 1-"1A" on cover 3.00

MAN CALLED A-X, THE
DC Comics: Oct, 1997 - No. 8, May, 1998 ($2.50)
1-8: Marv Wolfman scripts & Shawn McManus-c/a. 2.50

MAN CALLED KEV, A (See The Authority)
DC Comics (WildStorm): Sept, 2006 - No. 5, Feb, 2007 ($2.99, limited series)
1-5-Ennis-s/Ezquerra-a/Fabry-c 3.00
TPB (2007, $14.99) r/#1-5; cover gallery 15.00

MAN COMICS
Marvel/Atlas Comics (NPI): Dec, 1949 - No. 28, Sept, 1953 (#1-6: 52 pgs.)
1-Tuska-a 23 46 69 136 223 310
2-Tuska-a 14 28 42 82 121 160
3-6 12 24 36 67 94 120
7,8 11 22 33 62 86 110
9-13,15: 9-Format changes to war 9 18 27 52 69 85
14-Henkel (3 pgs.); Pakula-a 10 20 30 54 72 90
16-21,23-28: 28-Crime issue (Bob Brant) 9 18 27 47 61 75
22-Krigstein-a, 5 pgs. 10 20 30 56 76 95
NOTE: ***Berg** a-14, 15, 19. **Colan** a-9, 21, 23. **Everett** a-8, 22; c-22, 25. **Heath** a-11, 13, 17, 21. **Kubertish** a-by **Bob Brown**-3. **Maneely** a-11-13; c-10, 11. **Reinman** a-11. **Robinson** a-7, 10, 14. **Robert Sale** a-9, 11. **Sinnott** a-22, 23. **Tuska** a-14, 23.*

MANDRAKE THE MAGICIAN (See Defenders Of The Earth, 123, 46, 52, 55, Giant Comic Album, King Comics, Magic Comics, The Phantom #21, Tiny Tot Funnies & Wow Comics, '36)

MANDRAKE THE MAGICIAN (See Harvey Comics Hits #53)
David McKay Publ./Dell/King Comics (All 12¢): 1938 - 1948; Sept, 1966 - No. 10, Nov, 1967
Feature Books 18,19,23 (1938) 68 136 204 435 743 1050
Feature Books 46 45 90 135 284 480 675
Feature Books 52,55 39 78 117 231 378 525
Four Color 752 (11/56) 10 20 30 70 123 175
1-Begin S.O.S. Phantom, ends #3 6 12 18 37 59 80
2-7,9: 4-Girl Phantom app. 5-Flying Saucer-c/story. 5,6-Brick Bradford app. 7-Origin Lothar. 9-Brick Bradford app. 4 8 12 22 34 45
8-Jeff Jones-a (4 pgs.) 4 8 12 24 37 50
10-Rip Kirby app.; Raymond-a (14 pgs.) 4 8 12 28 44 60

MANDRAKE THE MAGICIAN
Marvel Comics: Apr, 1995 - No. 2, May, 1995 ($2.95, unfinished limited series)
1,2: Mike Barr scripts 3.00

MAN-EATING COW (See Tick #7,8)
New England Comics: July, 1992 - No. 10, 1994? ($2.75, B&W, limited series)
1-10 3.00
Man-Eating Cow Bonanza (6/96, $4.95, 128 pgs.)-r/#1-4. 5.00

MAN FROM ATLANTIS (TV)
Marvel Comics: Feb, 1978 - No. 7, Aug, 1978
1-(84 pgs.)-Sutton-a(p), Buscema-c; origin & cast photos 2 4 6 8 12 12
2-7 6.00

MAN FROM PLANET X, THE
Planet X Productions: 1987 (no price; probably unlicensed)
1-Reprints Fawcett Movie Comic 2.50

MAN FROM U.N.C.L.E., THE (TV) (Also see The Girl From Uncle)
Gold Key: Feb, 1965 - No. 22, Apr, 1969 (All photo-c)
1 13 26 39 90 165 240
2-Photo back c-2-8 7 14 21 50 83 115
3-10: 7-Jet Dream begins (1st app., also see Jet Dream) (all new stories) 6 12 18 37 59 80
11-22: 19-Last 12¢ issue. 21,22-Reprint #10 & 7 5 10 15 32 51 70

MAN FROM U.N.C.L.E., THE (TV)
Entertainment Publishing: 1987 - No. 11 ($1.50/$1.75, B&W)
1-7 ($1.50), 8-11 ($1.75) 4.00

MAN FROM WELLS FARGO (TV)
Dell Publishing Co.: No. 1287, Feb-Apr, 1962 - May-July, 1962 (Photo-c)
Four Color 1287, #01-495-207 6 12 18 37 59 80

MANGA DARKCHYLDE (Also see Darkchylde titles)
Dark Horse Comics: Feb, 2005 - No. 5 ($2.99, limited series)
1,2-Randy Queen-s/a; manga-style pre-teen Ariel Chylde 3.00

MANGA SHI (See Tomoe)
Crusade Entertainment: Aug, 1996 ($2.95)
1-Printed backwards (manga-style) 3.00

MANGA SHI 2000
Crusade Entertainment: Feb, 1997 - No. 3, June, 1997 ($2.95, mini-series)
1-3: 1-Two covers 3.00

MANGA ZEN (Also see Zen Intergalactic Ninja)
Zen Comics (Fusion Studios): 1996 - No. 3, 1996 ($2.50, B&W)
1-3 2.50

MANGAZINE
Antarctic Press: Aug, 1985 - No. 4, Sept, 1986 (B&W)
1-Soft paper-c 2 4 6 11 16 20
2-4 2 4 6 8 11 14

MANGLE TANGLE TALES
Innovation Publishing: 1990 ($2.95, deluxe format)
1-Intro by Harlan Ellison 3.00

MANHUNT! (Becomes Red Fox #15 on)
Magazine Enterprises: 10/47 - No. 11, 8/48; #13,14, 1953 (no #12)
1-Red Fox by L. B. Cole, Undercover Girl by Whitney, Space Ace begin (1st app.); negligee panels 50 100 150 315 533 750
2-Electrocution-c 39 78 117 240 395 550
3-6: 6-Bondage-c 32 64 96 188 307 425
7-10: 7-Space Ace ends. 8-Trail Colt begins (intro/1st app., 5/48) by Guardineer; Trail Colt-c. 10-G. Ingels-a 28 56 84 165 270 375
11(8/48)-Frazetta-a, 7 pgs.; The Duke, Scotland Yard begin 40 80 120 246 411 575
13(A-1 #63)-Frazetta, r-/Trail Colt #1, 7 pgs. 39 78 117 231 378 525
14(A-1 #77)-Bondage/hypo-c; last L. B. Cole Red Fox; Ingels-a 39 78 117 240 395 550
NOTE: ***Guardineer** a-1-5; c-8. **Whitney** a-2-14; c-1-6, 10. Red Fox by **L. B. Cole**-#1-14. #15 was advertised but came out as Red Fox #15.*

MANHUNTER (See Adventure #58, 73, Brave & the Bold, Detective Comics, 1st Issue Special, House of Mystery #143 and Justice League of America)
DC Comics: 1984 ($2.50, 76 pgs; high quality paper)
1-Simonson-c/a(r)/Detective; Batman app. 3.50

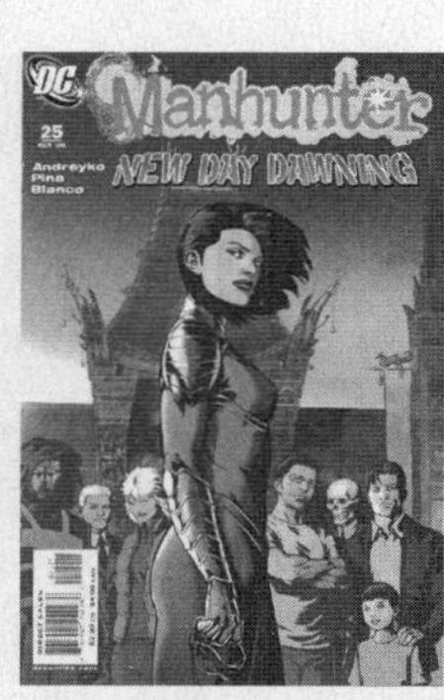

Manhunter (2004 series) #25 © DC

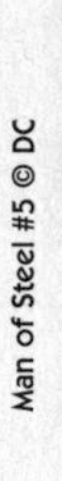
Man of Steel #5 © DC

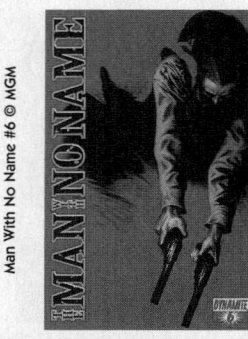

Man With No Name #6 © MGM

GD VG FN VF VF/NM NM-
2.0 4.0 6.0 8.0 9.0 9.2

GD VG FN VF VF/NM NM-
2.0 4.0 6.0 8.0 9.0 9.2

MANHUNTER
DC Comics: July, 1988 - No. 24, Apr, 1990 ($1.00)
1-24: 8,9-Flash app. 9-Invasion. 17-Batman-c/sty 2.50

MANHUNTER
DC Comics: No. 0, Nov, 1994 - No. 12, Nov, 1995 ($1.95/$2.25)
0-12 2.50

MANHUNTER (Also see Batman: Streets of Gotham)
DC Comics: Oct, 2004 - No. 38, Mar, 2009 ($2.50/$2.99)
1-21: 1-Intro. Kate Spencer; Saiz-a/Jae Lee-c/Andreyko-s. 2,3 Shadow Thief app. 13,14-Omac x-over. 20-One Year Later 2.50
22-30: 22-Begin $2.99-c. 23-Sandra Knight app. 27-Chaykin-c. 28-Batman app. 3.00
31-38: 31-(8/08) Gaydos-a. 33,34-Suicide Squad app. 3.00
...: Forgotten (2009, $17.99) r/#31-38 18.00
...: Origins (2007, $17.99) r/#15-23 18.00
...: Street Justice (2005, $12.99) r/#1-5; Andreyko intro. 13.00
...: Trial By Fire (2007, $17.99) r/#6-14 18.00
...: Unleashed (2008, $17.99) r/#24-30 18.00

MANHUNTER: ...
DC Comics: 1979, 1999
The Complete Saga TPB (1979) Reprints stories from Detective Comics #437-443 by Goodwin and Simonson 40.00
The Special Edition TPB (1999, $9.95) r/stories from Detective Comics #437-443 10.00

MANIFEST ETERNITY
DC Comics: Aug, 2006 - No. 6, Jan, 2007 ($2.99)
1-6-Lobdell-s/Nguyen-a/c 3.00

MAN IN BLACK (See Thrill-O-Rama) (Also see All New Comics, Front Page, Green Hornet #31, Strange Story & Tally-Ho Comics)
Harvey Publications: Sept, 1957 - No. 4, Mar, 1958
1-Bob Powell-c/a 18 36 54 105 165 225
2-4: Powell-c/a 14 28 42 80 115 150

MAN IN BLACK
Lorne-Harvey Publications (Recollections): 1990 - No. 2, July, 1991 (B&W)
1,2 4.00

MAN IN FLIGHT (Disney, TV)
Dell Publishing Co.: No. 836, Sept, 1957
Four Color 836 7 14 21 47 76 105

MAN IN SPACE (Disney, TV, see Dell Giant #27)
Dell Publishing Co.: No. 716, Aug, 1956 - No. 954, Nov, 1958
Four Color 716-A science feat. from Tomorrowland 8 16 24 56 93 130
Four Color 954-Satellites 7 14 21 47 76 105

MANKIND (WWF Wrestling)
Chaos Comics: Sept, 1999 ($2.95, one-shot)
1-Regular and photo-c 3.00
1-Premium Edition ($10.00) Dwayne Turner & Danny Miki-c 10.00

MANN AND SUPERMAN
DC Comics: 2000 ($5.95, prestige format, one-shot)
nn-Michael T. Gilbert-s/a 6.00

MAN OF STEEL, THE (Also see Superman: The Man of Steel)
DC Comics: 1986 (June release) - No. 6, 1986 (75¢, limited series)
1-6: 1-Silver logo; Byrne-c/a/scripts in all; origin, 1-Alternate-c for newsstand sales,1-Distr. to toy stores by So Much Fun, 2-6: 2-Intro. Lois Lane, Jimmy Olsen. 3-Intro/origin Magpie; Batman-c/story. 4-Intro. new Lex Luthor 4.00
1-6-Silver Editions (1993, $1.95)-r/1-6 3.00
...The Complete Saga nn-Contains #1-6, given away in contest 35.00
Limited Edition, softcover 4 8 12 28 44 60
NOTE: *Issues 1-6 were released between Action #583 (9/86) & Action #584 (1/87) plus Superman #423 (9/86) & Advs. of Superman #424 (1/87).*

MAN OF THE ATOM (See Solar, Man of the Atom Vol. 2)

MAN OF WAR (See Liberty Guards & Liberty Scouts)
Centaur Publications: Nov, 1941 - No. 2, Jan, 1942
1-The Fire-Man, Man of War, The Sentinel, Liberty Guards, & Vapo-Man begin; Gustavson-c/a; Flag-c 168 336 504 1075 1838 2600
2-Intro The Ferret; Gustavson-c/a 123 246 369 787 1344 1900

MAN OF WAR
Eclipse Comics: Aug, 1987 - No. 3, Feb, 1988 ($1.75, Baxter paper)
1-3: Bruce Jones scripts 2.50

MAN OF WAR (See The Protectors)
Malibu Comics: 1993 - No, 8, Feb, 1994 ($1.95/$2.50/$2.25)
1-5 ($1.95)-Newsstand Editions w/different-c 2.50
1-8: 1-5-Collector's Edi. w/poster. 6-8 ($2.25): 6-Polybagged w/Skycap. 8-Vs. Rocket Rangers 3.00

MAN O' MARS
Fiction House Magazines: 1953; 1964
1-Space Rangers; Whitman-c 45 90 135 284 480 675
I.W. Reprint #1-r/Man O'Mars #1 & Star Pirate; Murphy Anderson-a 6 12 18 37 59 80

MANTECH ROBOT WARRIORS
Archie Enterprises, Inc.: Sept, 1984 - No. 4, Apr, 1985 (75¢)
1-4: Ayers-c/a(p). 1-Buckler-c(i) 3.00

MAN-THING (See Fear, Giant-Size..., Marvel Comics Presents, Marvel Fanfare, Monsters Unleashed, Power Record Comics & Savage Tales)
Marvel Comics Group: Jan, 1974 - No. 22, Oct, 1975; V2#1, Nov, 1979 - V2#11, July, 1981
1-Howard the Duck(2nd app.) cont'd/Fear #19 6 12 18 39 62 85
2 3 6 9 17 25 32
3-1st app. original Foolkiller 3 6 9 14 20 26
4-Origin Foolkiller; last app. 1st Foolkiller 3 6 9 14 19 24
5-11-Ploog-a. 11-Foolkiller cameo (flashback) 3 6 9 14 19 24
12-22: 19-1st app. Scavenger. 20-Spidey cameo. 21-Origin Scavenger, Man-Thing. 22-Howard the Duck cameo 2 4 6 9 12 15
V2#1(1979) 2 3 4 6 8 10
V2#2-11: 4-Dr. Strange-c/app. 11-Mayerik-a 5.00
NOTE: ***Alcala** a-14. **Brunner** c-1. J. **Buscema** a-12p, 13p, 16p. **Gil Kane** c-4p, 10p, 12-20p, 21. **Mooney** a-17, 18, 19p, 20-22, V2#1-3p. **Ploog** Man-Thing-5p, 6p, 7, 8, 9-11p; c-5, 6, 8, 9, 11. **Sutton** a-13i. No. 19 says #10 in indicia.*

MAN-THING (Volume Three, continues in Strange Tales #1 (9/98))
Marvel Comics: Dec, 1997 - No. 8, July, 1998 ($2.99)
1-8-DeMatteis-s/Sharp-a. 2-Two covers. 6-Howard the Duck-c/app. 3.00

MAN-THING (Prequel to 2005 movie)
Marvel Comics: Sept, 2004 - No. 3, Nov, 2004 ($2.99, limited series)
1-3-Hans Rodionoff-s/Kyle Hotz-a 3.00
...: Whatever Knows Fear... (2005, $12.99, TPB) r/#1-3, Savage Tales #1, Adv. Into Fear #16 13.00

MANTRA
Malibu Comics (Ultraverse): July, 1993 - No. 24, Aug, 1995 ($1.95/$2.50)
1-Polybagged w/trading card & coupon 3.00
1-Newsstand edition w/o trading card or coupon 2.50
1-Full cover holographic edition 1 3 4 6 8 10
1-Ultra-limited silver foil-c 5.00
2-9,11-24: 3-Intro Warstrike & Kismet. 6-Break-Thru x-over. 2-($2.50-Newsstand edition bagged w/card. 4-($2.50, 48 pgs.)-Rune flip-c/story by B. Smith (3 pgs.). 7-Prime app.; origin Prototype by Jurgens/Austin (2 pgs.). 11-New costume. 17-Intro NecroMantra & Pinnacle; prelude to Godwheel 2.50
10-($3.50, 68 pgs.)-Flip-c w/Ultraverse Premiere #2 3.50
Giant Size 1 (7/94, $2.50, 44 pgs.) 2.50
...Spear of Destiny 1,2 (4/95, $2.50, 36pgs.) 2.50

MANTRA (2nd Series) (Also See Black September)
Malibu Comics (Ultraverse): Infinity, Sept, 1995 - No. 7, Apr, 1996 ($1.50)
Infinity (9/95, $1.50)-Black September x-over, Intro new Mantra 2.50
1-7: 1-(10/95). 5-Return of Eden (original Mantra). 6,7-Rush app. 2.50

MAN WITH NO NAME, THE (Based on the Clint Eastwood gunslinger character)
Dynamite Entertainment: 2008 - No. 11, 2009 ($3.50)
1-11:1-Gage-s/Dias-a/Isanove-c. 7-Bernard-a 3.50

MAN WITH THE SCREAMING BRAIN (Based on screenplay by Bruce Campbell & David Goodman)
Dark Horse Comics: Apr, 2005 - No. 4, July, 2005 ($2.99, limited series)
1-4-Campbell & Goodman-s; Remender-a/c. 1-Variant-c by Noto. 3-Powell var-c. 4-Mignola var-c 3.00
TPB (11/05, $13.95) r/#1-4; David Goodman intro.; cover gallery 14.00

MAN WITH THE X-RAY EYES, THE (See X,... under Movie Comics)

MANY GHOSTS OF DR. GRAVES, THE (Doctor Graves #73 on)
Charlton Comics: 5/67 - No. 60, 12/76; No. 61, 9/77 - No. 62, 10/77; No. 63, 2/78 - No. 65, 4/78; No. 66, 6/81 - No. 72, 5/82
1-Ditko-a; Palais-a; early issues 12¢-c 6 12 18 41 66 90

Many Ghost of Doctor Graves #42 © CC

Marc Spector: Moon Knight #20 © MAR

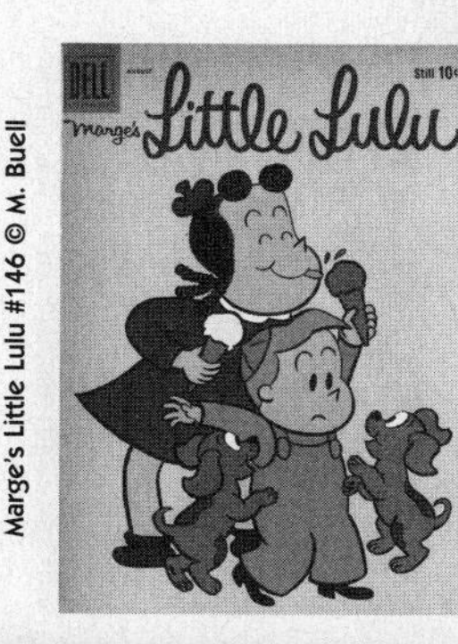

Marge's Little Lulu #146 © M. Buell

	GD 2.0	VG 4.0	FN 6.0	VF 8.0	VF/NM 9.0	NM- 9.2
2-6,8,10	3	6	9	20	30	40
7,9-Ditko-a	4	8	12	22	34	45
11-13,16-18-Ditko-c/a	3	6	9	18	27	35
14,19,23,25	2	4	6	9	13	16
15,20,21-Ditko-a	2	4	6	13	18	22
22,24,26,27,29-35,38,40-Ditko-c/a	3	6	9	14	20	25
28-Ditko-c	2	4	6	13	18	22
36,46,56,57,59,61,66,67,69,71	2	3	4	6	8	10
37,41,43,51,60-Ditko-a	2	4	6	8	11	14
39,58-Ditko-c. 39-Sutton-a. 58-Ditko-a	2	4	6	8	11	14
42,44,53-Sutton-c; Ditko-a. 42-Sutton-a	2	4	6	8	11	14
45-(5/74) 2nd Newton comic work (8 pgs.); new logo; Sutton-c	2	4	6	10	14	18
47-Newton, Sutton, Ditko-a	2	4	6	9	13	16
48-Ditko, Sutton-a	2	4	6	8	11	14
49-Newton-c/a; Sutton-a.	2	4	6	8	10	12
50-Sutton-a	2	3	4	6	8	10
52-Newton-c; Ditko-a	2	4	6	8	11	14
54-Early Byrne-c; Ditko-a	2	4	6	9	13	16
55-Ditko-c; Sutton-a	2	4	6	8	11	14
62-65,68-Ditko-c/a. 65-Sutton-a	2	4	6	10	14	18
70,72-Ditko-a	2	4	6	9	13	16
Modern Comics Reprint 12,25 (1978)						4.00

NOTE: ***Aparo** a-4, 5, 7, 8, 66r, 69r; c-8, 14, 19, 66r, 67r. **Byrne** c-54. **Ditko** a-1, 7, 9, 11-13, 15-18, 20-22, 24, 26, 27, 29, 30-35, 37, 38, 40-44, 47, 48, 51-54, 58, 60r-65r, 70, 72; c-11-13, 16-18, 22, 24, 26-35, 38, 40, 55, 58, 62-65. **Howard** a-38, 39, 45i, 65; c-48. **Kim** a-36, 46, 52. **Larson** a-58. **Morisi** a-13, 14, 23, 26. **Newton** a-45, 47p, 49p; c-49, 52. **Staton** a-36, 37, 41, 43. **Sutton** a-39, 42, 47-50, 55, 65; c-42, 44, 45; painted c-53. **Zeck** a-56, 59.*

MANY LOVES OF DOBIE GILLIS (TV)
National Periodical Publications: May-June, 1960 - No. 26, Oct, 1964

	GD	VG	FN	VF	VF/NM	NM-
1-Most covers by Bob Oskner	22	44	66	155	300	445
2-5	12	24	36	85	155	225
6-10: 10-Last 10¢-c	9	18	27	60	100	140
11-26: 20-Drucker-a. 24-(3-4/64). 25-(9/64)	8	16	24	54	90	125

MANY WORLDS OF TESLA STRONG, THE (Also see Tom Strong)
America's Best Comics: July, 2003 ($5.95, one-shot)

1-Two covers by Timm & Art Adams; art by various incl. Campbell, Cho, Noto, Hughes 6.00

MARAUDER'S MOON (See Luke Short, Four Color #848)

MARCH OF COMICS (See Promotional Comics section)

MARCH OF CRIME (Formerly My Love Affair #1-6) (See Fox Giants)
Fox Features Synd.: No. 7, July, 1950 - No. 2, Sept, 1950; No. 3, Sept, 1951

	GD	VG	FN	VF	VF/NM	NM-
7(#1)(7/50)-True crime stories; Wood-a	40	80	120	246	411	575
2(9/50)-Wood-a (exceptional)	39	78	117	240	395	550
3(9/51)	20	40	60	114	182	250

MARCO POLO
Charlton Comics Group: 1962 (Movie classic)

	GD	VG	FN	VF	VF/NM	NM-
nn (Scarce)-Glanzman-c/a (25 pgs.)	10	20	30	67	116	165

MARC SILVESTRI SKETCHBOOK
Image Comics (Top Cow): Jan, 2004 ($2.99, one-shot)

1-Character sketches, concept artwork, storyboards of Witchblade, Darkness & others 3.00

MARC SPECTOR: MOON KNIGHT (Also see Moon Knight)
Marvel Comics: June, 1989 - No. 60, Mar, 1994 ($1.50/$1.75, direct sales)

	NM-
1-24,26-49,51-54,58,59: 4-Intro new Midnight. 8,9-Punisher app. 15-Silver Sable app. 19-21-Spider-Man & Punisher app. 25-(52 pgs.)-Ghost Rider app. 32,33-Hobgoblin II (Macendale) & Spider-Man (in black costume) app. 35-38-Punisher story. 42-44-Infinity War x-over. 46-Demogoblin app. 51,53-Gambit app. 55-New look. 57-Spider-Man-c/story. 60-Moon Knight dies	2.50
50-(56 pgs.)-Special die-cut-c	3.00
55-57,60-Platt a	3.50
...: Divided We Fall ($4.95, 52 pgs.)	5.00
Special 1 (1992, $2.50)	2.50

NOTE: *Cowan c(p) 20-23. Guice c-20. Heath c/a-4. Platt -a 55-57,60; c-55-60.*

MARGARET O'BRIEN (See The Adventures of...)

MARGE'S LITTLE LULU (Continues as Little Lulu from #207 on)
Dell Publishing Co./Gold Key #165-206: No. 74, 6/45 - No. 164, 7-9/62; No. 165, 10/62 - No. 206, 8/72

Marjorie Henderson Buell, born in Philadelphia, Pa., in 1904, created Little Lulu, a cartoon character that appeared weekly in the Saturday Evening Post from Feb. 23, 1935 through Dec. 30, 1944. She was not responsible for any of the comic books. **John Stanley** did pencils only on all Little Lulu comics through at least #135 (1959). He did pencils and inks on Four Color #74 & 97. **Irving Tripp** began inking stories from #1 on, and remained the comic's illustrator throughout its entire run. **Stanley** did storyboards (layouts), pencils, and scripts in all cases and inking only on covers. His word balloons were written in cursive. **Tripp** and occasionally other artists at Western Publ. in Poughkeepsie, N.Y. blew up the pencilled pages, inked the blowups, and lettered them. **Arnold Drake** did storyboards, pencils and scripts starting with #197 (1970) on, amidst reprinted issues. **Buell** sold her rights exclusively to Western Publ. in Dec., 1971. The earlier issues had to be approved by **Buell** prior to publication.

	GD	VG	FN	VF	VF/NM	NM-
Four Color 74('45)-Intro Lulu, Tubby & Alvin	124	248	372	1054	2077	3100
Four Color 97(2/46)	52	104	156	442	871	1300
(Above two books are all John Stanley - cover, pencils, and inks.)						
Four Color 110('46)-1st Alvin Story Telling Time; 1st app. Willy; variant cover exists	38	76	114	288	557	825
Four Color 115-1st app. Boys' Clubhouse	36	72	108	280	540	800
Four Color 120, 131: 120-1st app. Eddie	31	62	93	236	456	675
Four Color 139('47),146,158	30	60	90	228	439	650
Four Color 165 (10/47)-Smokes doll hair & has wild hallucinations. 1st Tubby detective story	30	60	90	228	439	650
1(1-2/48)-Lulu's Diary feature begins	64	128	192	544	1072	1600
2-1st app. Gloria; 1st app. Miss Feeny	30	60	90	231	446	660
3-5	28	56	84	205	395	585
6-10: 7-1st app. Annie; Xmas-c	23	46	69	166	321	475
11-20: 18-X-Mas-c. 19-1st app. Wilbur. 20-1st app. Mr. McNabbem	18	36	54	127	249	370
21-30: 26-r/F.C. 110. 30-Xmas-c	16	32	48	113	217	320
31-38,40: 35-1st Mumday story	13	26	39	93	172	250
39-Intro. Witch Hazel in "That Awful Witch Hazel"	13	26	39	94	175	255
41-60: 42-Xmas-c. 45-2nd Witch Hazel app. 49-Gives Stanley & others credit	11	22	33	80	145	210
61-80: 63-1st app. Chubby (Tubby's cousin). 68-1st app. Prof. Cleff. 78-Xmas-c. 80-Intro. Little Itch (2/55)	9	18	27	65	113	160
81-99: 90-Xmas-c	8	16	24	54	90	125
100	8	16	24	58	97	135
101-130: 123-1st app. Fifi	6	12	18	43	69	95
131-164: 135-Last Stanley-p	6	12	18	37	59	80
165-Giant; ...in Paris ('62)	10	20	30	73	129	185
166-Giant; ...Christmas Diary (1962 - '63)	10	20	30	73	129	185
167-169	5	10	15	30	48	65
170,172,175,176,178-196,198-200-Stanley-r. 182-1st app. Little Scarecrow Boy	3	6	9	18	27	35
171,173,174,177,197	3	6	9	16	23	30
201,203,206-Last issue to carry Marge's name	3	6	9	14	20	26
202,204,205-Stanley-r	3	6	9	16	23	30
...& Tubby in Japan (12¢)(5-7/62) 01476-207	8	16	24	52	86	120
...Summer Camp 1(8/67-G.K.-Giant) '57-58-r	6	12	18	41	66	90
...Trick 'N' Treat 1(12¢)(12/62-Gold Key)	7	14	21	47	76	105

NOTE: *See Dell Giant Comics #23, 29, 36, 42, 50, & Dell Giants for annuals. All Giants not by Stanley from L.L. on Vacation (7/54) on. Irving Tripp a-#1-on. Christmas c-7, 18, 30, 42, 78, 90, 126, 166, 250. Summer Camp issues #173, 177, 181, 189, 197, 201, 206.*

MARGE'S LITTLE LULU (See Golden Comics Digest #19, 23, 27, 29, 33, 36, 40, 43, 46, & March of Comics #251, 267, 275, 293, 307, 323, 335, 349, 355, 369, 385, 406, 417, 427, 439, 456, 468, 475, 488)

MARGE'S TUBBY (Little Lulu)(See Dell Giants)
Dell Publishing Co./Gold Key: No. 381, Aug, 1952 - No. 49, Dec-Feb, 1961-62

	GD	VG	FN	VF	VF/NM	NM-
Four Color 381(#1)-Stanley script; Irving Tripp-a	19	38	57	139	270	400
Four Color 430,444-Stanley-a	12	24	36	83	152	220
Four Color 461 (4/53)-1st Tubby & Men From Mars story; Stanley-a	11	22	33	74	132	190
5 (7-9/53)-Stanley-a	9	18	27	61	103	145
6-10	8	16	24	52	86	120
11-20	6	12	18	39	62	85
21-30	5	10	15	32	51	70
31-49	4	8	12	28	44	60
...& the Little Men From Mars No. 30020-410(10/64-G.K.)-25¢, 68 pgs.	8	16	24	52	86	120

NOTE: ***John Stanley** did all storyboards & scripts through at least #35 (1959). **Lloyd White** did all art except F.C. 381, 430, 444, 461 & #5.*

MARGIE (See My Little...)

MARGIE (TV)
Dell Publ. Co.: No. 1307, Mar-May, 1962 - No. 2, July-Sept, 1962 (Photo-c)

	GD	VG	FN	VF	VF/NM	NM-
Four Color 1307(#1)	6	12	18	37	59	80
2	5	10	15	30	48	65

MARGIE COMICS (Formerly Comedy Comics; Reno Browne #50 on)
(Also see Cindy Comics & Teen Comics)
Marvel Comics (ACI): No. 35, Winter, 1946-47 - No. 49, Dec, 1949

	GD	VG	FN	VF	VF/NM	NM-
35	18	36	54	107	169	230
36-38,42,45,47-49	11	22	33	64	90	115
39,41,43(2),44,46-Kurtzman's "Hey Look"	13	26	39	72	101	130
40-Three "Hey Looks", three "Giggles 'n' Grins" by Kurtzman						

Marines in Battle #2 © MAR

The Mark #1 © DH

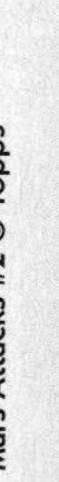

Mars Attacks #2 © Topps

GD VG FN VF VF/NM NM-
2.0 4.0 6.0 8.0 9.0 9.2

GD VG FN VF VF/NM NM-
2.0 4.0 6.0 8.0 9.0 9.2

14 28 42 80 115 150

MARINES (See Tell It to the...)

MARINES ATTACK
Charlton Comics: Aug, 1964 - No. 9, Feb-Mar, 1966

1-Glanzman-a begins 4 8 12 22 34 45
2-9 3 6 9 14 19 24

MARINES AT WAR (Formerly Tales of the Marines #4)
Atlas Comics (OPI): No. 5, Apr, 1957 - No. 7, Aug, 1957

5-7 10 20 30 54 72 90
NOTE: *Colan a-5. Drucker a-5. Everett a-5. Maneely a-5. Orlando a-7. Severin c-5.*

MARINES IN ACTION
Atlas News Co.: June, 1955 - No. 14, Sept, 1957

1-Rock Murdock, Boot Camp Brady begin 13 26 39 74 105 135
2-14 10 20 30 54 72 90
NOTE: *Berg a-2, 8, 9, 11, 14. Heath c-2, 9. Maneely c-1, 3. Severin a-4; c-7-11, 14.*

MARINES IN BATTLE
Atlas Comics (ACI No. 1-12/WPI No. 13-25): Aug, 1954 - No. 25, Sept, 1958

1-Heath-c; Iron Mike McGraw by Heath; history of U.S. Marine Corps. begins
21 42 63 124 202 280
2-Heath-c 14 28 42 76 108 140
3-6,8-10: 4-Last precode (2/55); Romita-a 10 20 30 58 79 100
7-Kubert/Moskowitz-a (6 pgs.) 11 22 33 60 83 105
11-16,18-21,24 10 20 30 54 72 90
17-Williamson-a (3 pgs.) 11 22 33 62 86 110
22,25-Torres-a 10 20 30 56 76 95
23-Crandall-a; Mark Murdock app. 10 20 30 58 79 100
NOTE: *Berg a-22. G. Colan a-22, 23. Drucker a-6. Everett a-4, 15; c-21. Heath c-1, 2, 4. Maneely c-23, 24. Orlando a-14. Pakula a-6, 23. Powell a-16. Severin a-22; c-12. Sinnott a-23. Tuska a-15.*

MARINE WAR HEROES (Charlton Premiere #19 on)
Charlton Comics: Jan, 1964 - No. 18, Mar, 1967

1-Montes/Bache-c/a 4 8 12 23 36 48
2-18: 14,18-Montes/Bache-a 3 6 9 14 20 26

MARK, THE (Also see Mayhem)
Dark Horse Comics: Dec, 1993 - No. 4, Mar, 1994 ($2.50, limited series)

1-4 2.50

MARK HAZZARD: MERC
Marvel Comics Group: Nov, 1986 - No. 12, Oct, 1987 (75¢)

1-12: Morrow-a, Annual 1 (11/87, $1.25) 2.50

MARK OF CHARON (See Negation)
CG Entertainment: Apr, 2003 - No. 5, Aug, 2003 ($2.95, limited series)

1-5-Bedard-s/Bennett-a 3.00

MARK OF ZORRO (See Zorro, Four Color #228)

MARK 1 COMICS (Also see Shaloman)
Mark 1 Comics: Apr, 1988 - No. 3, Mar, 1989 ($1.50)

1-3: Early Shaloman app. 2-Origin 2.50

MARKSMAN, THE (Also see Champions)
Hero Comics: Jan, 1988 - No. 5, 1988 ($1.95)

1-5: 1-Rose begins. 1-3-Origin The Marksman 2.50
Annual 1 ('88, $2.75, 52pgs)-Champions app. 2.75

MARK TRAIL
Standard Magazines (Hall Syndicate)/Fawcett Publ. No. 5: Oct, 1955; No. 5, Summer, 1959

1(1955)-Sunday strip-r 7 14 21 37 46 55
5(1959) 5 10 15 22 26 30
...Adventure Book of Nature 1 (Summer, 1958, 25¢, Pines)-100 pg. Giant; Special Camp Issue; contains 78 Sunday strip-r 9 18 27 52 69 85

MARMADUKE MONK
I. W. Enterprises/Super Comics: No date; 1963 (10¢)

I.W. Reprint 1 (nd) 2 4 6 8 11 14
Super Reprint 14 (1963)-r/Monkeyshines Comics #? 2 4 6 8 10 12

MARMADUKE MOUSE
Quality Comics Group (Arnold Publ.): Spring, 1946 - No. 65, Dec, 1956 (Early issues: 52 pgs.)

1-Funny animal 17 34 51 98 154 210
2 11 22 33 60 83 105
3-10 9 18 27 47 61 75
11-30 7 14 21 35 43 50
31-65: Later issues are 36 pgs. 6 12 18 28 34 40
Super Reprint #14(1963) 2 4 6 9 12 15

MARQUIS, THE
Oni Press

...: A Sin of One ($2.99, 5/03) Guy Davis-s/a; Michael Gaydos-c 3.00
...: Intermezzo TPB ($11.95, 12/03) r/A Sin of One and Hell's Courtesan #1,2 12.00

MARQUIS, THE: DANSE MACABRE
Oni Press: May, 2000 - No. 5, Feb, 2001 ($2.95, B&W, limited series)

1-5-Guy Davis-s/a. 1-Wagner-c. 2-Mignola-c. 3-Vess-c. 5-K. Jones-c 3.00
TPB (8/2001, $18.95) r/1-5 & Les Preludes; Seagle intro. 19.00

MARQUIS, THE: DEVIL'S REIGN: HELL'S COURTESAN
Oni Press: Feb, 2002 - No. 2, Apr, 2002 ($2.95, B&W, limited series)

1,2-Guy Davis-s/a 3.00

MARRIAGE OF HERCULES AND XENA, THE
Topps Comics: July, 1998 ($2.95, one-shot)

1-Photo-c; Lopresti-a; Alex Ross pin-up, 1-Alex Ross painted-c 3.00
1-Gold foil logo-c 5.00

MARRIED ... WITH CHILDREN (TV)(Based on Fox TV show)
Now Comics: June, 1990 - No. 7, Feb, 1991(12/90 inside) ($1.75)
V2#1, Sept, 1991 - No. 12, 1992 ($1.95)

1-7: 2-Photo-c, 1,2-2nd printing, V2#1-12: 1,4,5,9-Photo-c 2.50
...Buck's Tale (6/94, $1.95) 2.50
...1994 Annual nn (2/94, $2.50, 52 pgs.)-Flip book format 3.00
Special 1 (7/92, $1.95)-Kelly Bundy photo-c/poster 2.50

MARRIED ... WITH CHILDREN: KELLY BUNDY
Now Comics: Aug, 1992 - No. 3, Oct, 1992 ($1.95, limited series)

1-3: Kelly Bundy photo-c & poster in each 2.50

MARRIED ... WITH CHILDREN: QUANTUM QUARTET
Now Comics: Oct, 1993 - No. 4, 1994, ($1.95, limited series)

1-4: Fantastic Four parody 2.50

MARRIED ... WITH CHILDREN: 2099
Now Comics: June, 1993 - No. 3, Aug, 1993 ($1.95, limited series)

1-3 2.50

MARS
First Comics: Jan, 1984 - No. 12, Jan, 1985 ($1.00, Mando paper)

1-12: Marc Hempel & Mark Wheatley story & art. 2-The Black Flame begins. 10-Dynamo Joe begins 2.50
TPB (IDW Publ., 8/05, $39.99) r/#1-12, creator commentary; bonus art; new Hempel-c 40.00

MARS & BEYOND (Disney, TV)
Dell Publishing Co.: No. 866, Dec, 1957

Four Color 866-A Science feat. from Tomorrowland 8 16 24 56 93 130

MARS ATTACKS
Topps Comics: May, 1994 - No. 5, Sept, 1994 ($2.95, limited series)

1-5-Giffen story; flip books 4.50
Special Edition 2 4 6 8 10 12
Trade paperback (12/94, $12.95)-r/limited series plus new 8 pg. story 13.00

MARS ATTACKS
Topps Comics: V2#1, 8/95 - V2#3, 10/95; V2#4, 1/96 - No. 7, 5/96($2.95, bi-monthly #6 on)

V2#1-7: 1-Counterstrike storyline begins. 4-(1/96). 5-(1/96). 5,7-Brereton-c. 6-(3/96)-Simonson-c. 7-Story leads into Baseball Special #1 3.00
Baseball Special 1 (6/96, $2.95)-Bisley-c. 3.00

MARS ATTACKS HIGH SCHOOL
Topps Comics: May, 1997 - No. 2, Sept, 1997 ($2.95, B&W, limited series)

1,2-Stelfreeze-c 3.00

MARS ATTACKS IMAGE
Topps Comics: Dec, 1996 - No. 4, Mar, 1997 ($2.50, limited series)

1-4-Giffen-s/Smith/Sienkiewicz-a 3.00

MARS ATTACKS THE SAVAGE DRAGON
Topps Comics: Dec, 1996 - No. 4, Mar, 1997 ($2.95, limited series)

1-4: 1-w/bound-in card 3.00

MARSHAL BLUEBERRY (See Blueberry)
Marvel Comics (Epic Comics): 1991 ($14.95, graphic novel)

1-Moebius-a 3 6 9 14 19 24

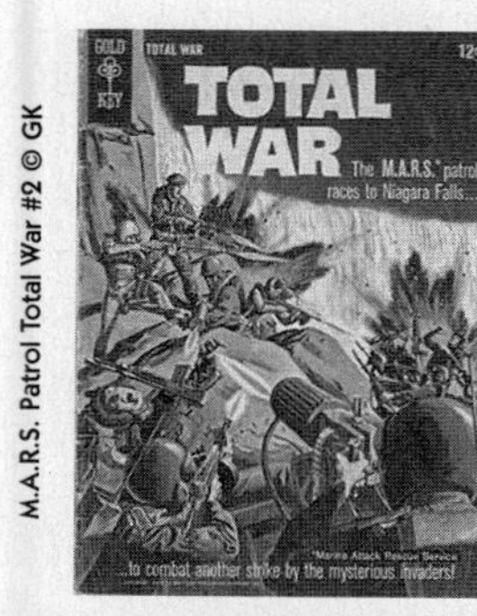

M.A.R.S. Patrol Total War #2 © GK

Marvel Adventures Hulk #14 © MAR

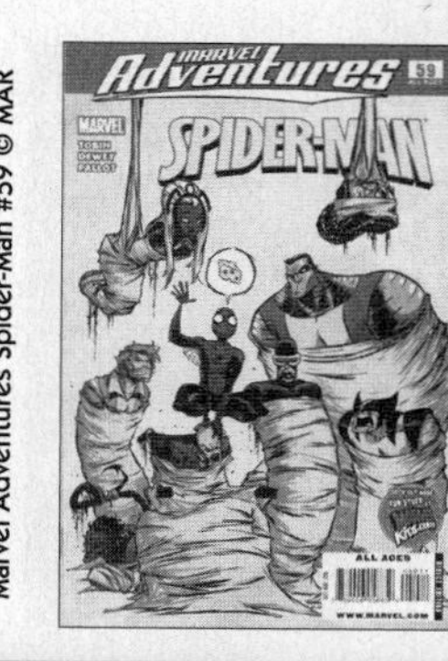

Marvel Adventures Spider-Man #59 © MAR

	GD 2.0	VG 4.0	FN 6.0	VF 8.0	VF/NM 9.0	NM- 9.2

MARSHAL LAW (Also see Crime And Punishment: Marshall Law...)
Marvel Comics (Epic Comics): Oct, 1987 - No. 6, May, 1989 ($1.95, mature)

1-6 — 2.50

M.A.R.S. PATROL TOTAL WAR (Formerly Total War #1,2)
Gold Key: No. 3, Sept, 1966 - No. 10, Aug, 1969 (All-Painted-c except #7)

	GD	VG	FN	VF	VF/NM	NM-
3-Wood-a; aliens invade USA	6	12	18	41	66	90
4-10	4	8	12	24	37	50

Wally Wood's M.A.R.S. Patrol Total War TPB (Dark Horse, 9/04, $12.95) r/#3 & Total War #1&2; foreward by Batton Lash; afterword by Dan Adkins — 13.00

MARTHA WASHINGTON (Also see Dark Horse Presents Fifth Anniversary Special, Dark Horse Presents #100-4, Give Me Liberty, Happy Birthday Martha Washington & San Diego Comicon Comics #2)

MARTHA WASHINGTON... (one-shots)
Dark Horse Comics (Legend): ($2.95/$3.50, one-shots)

... Dies (7/07, $3.50) Miller-s/Gibbons-a; r/Miller's original outline for Give Me Liberty — 3.50
... Stranded in Space (11/95, $2.95) Miller-s/Gibbons-a; Big Guy app. — 3.00

MARTHA WASHINGTON GOES TO WAR
Dark Horse Comics (Legend): May, 1994 - No. 5, Sep, 1994 ($2.95, lim. series)

1-5-Miller scripts; Gibbons-c/a — 3.00
TPB ($17.95) r/#1-5 — 18.00

MARTHA WASHINGTON SAVES THE WORLD
Dark Horse Comics: Dec, 1997 - No. 3, Feb, 1998 ($2.95/$3.95, lim. series)

1,2-Miller scripts; Gibbons-c/a in all — 3.00
3-($3.95) — 4.00

MARTHA WAYNE (See The Story of...)

MARTIAN MANHUNTER (See Detective Comics & Showcase '95 #9)
DC Comics: May, 1988 - No. 4, Aug,. 1988 ($1.25, limited series)

1-4: 1,4-Batman app. 2-Batman cameo — 2.50
Special 1-(1996, $3.50) — 3.50

MARTIAN MANHUNTER (See JLA)
DC Comics: No. 0, Oct, 1998 - No. 36, Nov, 2001 ($1.99)

0-(10/98) Origin retold; Ostrander-s/Mandrake-c/a — 3.00
1-36: 1-(12/98). 6-9-JLA app. 18,19-JSA app. 24-Mahnke-a — 2.50
#1,000,000 (11/98) 853rd Century x-over — 2.50
Annual 1,2 (1998,1999; $2.95) 1-Ghosts; Wrightson-c. 2-JLApe — 3.00

MARTIAN MANHUNTER (See DCU Brave New World)
DC Comics: Oct, 2006 - No. 8, May, 2007 ($2.99, limited series)

1-8-Lieberman-s/Barrionuevo-a/c — 3.00
...: The Others Among Us TPB (2007, $19.99) r/#1-8 & story from DCU Brave New World — 20.00

MARTIAN MANHUNTER: AMERICAN SECRETS
DC Comics: 1992 - Book Three, 1992 ($4.95, limited series, prestige format)

1-3: Barreto-a — 5.00

MARTIN KANE (William Gargan as... Private Eye)(Stage/Screen/Radio/TV)
Fox Features Syndicate (Hero Books): No. 4, June, 1950 - No. 2, Aug, 1950 (Formerly My Secret Affair)

	GD	VG	FN	VF	VF/NM	NM-
4(#1)-True crime stories; Wood-c/a(2); used in **SOTI**, pg. 160; photo back-c	31	62	93	182	296	410
2-Wood/Orlando story, 5 pgs; Wood-a(2)	23	46	69	136	223	310

MARTIN MYSTERY
Dark Horse (Bonelli Comics): Mar, 1999 - No. 6, Aug, 1999 ($4.95, B&W, digest size)

1-6-Reprints Italian series in English; Gibbons-c on #1-3 — 5.00

MARTY MOUSE
I. W. Enterprises: No date (1958?) (10¢)

	GD	VG	FN	VF	VF/NM	NM-
1-Reprint	2	4	6	9	12	15

MARVEL ACTION HOUR FEATURING IRON MAN (TV cartoon)
Marvel Comics: Nov, 1994 - No. 8, June, 1995 ($1.50/$2.95)

1-8: Based on cartoon series — 2.50
1 ($2.95)-Polybagged w/16 pg Marvel Action Hour Preview & acetate print — 3.00

MARVEL ACTION HOUR FEATURING THE FANTASTIC FOUR (TV cartoon)
Marvel Comics: Nov, 1994 - No. 8, June, 1995 ($1.50/$2.95)

1-8: Based on cartoon series — 2.50
1-($2.95)-Polybagged w/ 16 pg. Marvel Action Hour Preview & acetate print — 3.00

MARVEL ACTION UNIVERSE (TV cartoon)
Marvel Comics: Jan, 1989 ($1.00, one-shot)

1-r/Spider-Man And His Amazing Friends — 4.00

	GD 2.0	VG 4.0	FN 6.0	VF 8.0	VF/NM 9.0	NM- 9.2

MARVEL ADVENTURES
Marvel Comics: Apr, 1997 - No. 18, Sept, 1998 ($1.50)

1-18-"Animated style": 1,4,7-Hulk-c/app. 2,11-Spider-Man. 3,8,15-X-Men. 5-Spider-Man & X-Men. 6-Spider-Man & Human Torch. 9,12-Fantastic Four. 10,16-Silver Surfer. 13-Spider-Man & Silver Surfer. 14-Hulk & Dr. Strange. 18-Capt. America — 2.50

MARVEL ADVENTURES FANTASTIC FOUR (All ages title)
Marvel Comics: No. 0, July, 2005 - No. 48, July, 2009 ($1.99/$2.50/$2.99)

0-($1.99) Movie version characters; Dr. Doom app.; Eaton-a — 2.50
1-10-($2.50) 1-Skrulls app.; Pagulayan-a. 7-Namor app. — 2.50
11-48-($2.99) 12,42-Dr. Doom app. 24-Namor app. 26,28-Silver Surfer app. — 3.00
... Vol. 1: Family of Heroes (2005, $6.99, digest) r/#1-4 — 7.00
... Vol. 2: Fantastic Voyages (2006, $6.99, digest) r/#5-8 — 7.00
... Vol. 3: World's Greatest (2006, $6.99, digest) r/#9-12 — 7.00
... Vol. 4: Cosmic Threats (2006, $6.99, digest) r/#13-16 — 7.00
... Vol. 5: All 4 One, 4 For All (2007, $6.99, digest) r/#17-20 — 7.00
... Vol. 6: Monsters & Mysteries (2007, $6.99, digest) r/#21-24 — 7.00
... Vol. 7: The Silver Surfer (2007, $6.99, digest) r/#25-28 — 7.00
... Vol. 8: Monsters, Moles, Cowboys & Coupons (2008, $7.99, digest) r/#29-32 — 8.00

MARVEL ADVENTURES FLIP MAGAZINE (All ages title)
Marvel Comics: Aug, 2005 - Present ($3.99/$4.99)

1-11: 1-10-Rep. Marvel Advs. Fantastic Four and Marvel Advs. Spider-Man in flip format — 4.00
12-14-($4.99) Reprints Marvel Advs. Spider-Man & X-Men/Power Pack in flip format — 5.00
15-26-Rep. Marvel Advs. Fantastic Four and Marvel Advs. Spider-Man in flip format — 5.00

MARVEL ADVENTURES HULK (All ages title)
Marvel Comics: Sept, 2007 - No. 16, Dec, 2008 ($2.99)

1-16: 1-New version of Hulk's origin; Pagulayan-c. 2-Jamie Madrox app. 13-Mummies — 3.00
... Vol. 1: Misunderstood Monster (2007, $6.99, digest) r/#1-4 — 7.00

MARVEL ADVENTURES IRON MAN (All ages title)
Marvel Comics: July, 2007 - Present ($2.99)

1-13: 1-4-Michael Golden-c. 1-New version of Iron Man's origin. 2-Intro. the Mandarin — 3.00
... Vol. 1: Heart of Steel (2007, $6.99, digest) r/#1-4 — 7.00
... Vol. 2: Iron Armory (2008, $7.99, digest) r/#5-8 — 8.00

MARVEL ADVENTURES SPIDER-MAN (All ages title)
Marvel Comics: May, 2005 - No. 61, May, 2010 ($2.50/$2.99)

1-13-Lee & Ditko stories retold with new art. 13-Conner-c — 2.50
14-48: 14-Begin $2.99-c. 14-16-Conner-c. 22,23-Black costume. 35-Venom app. — 3.00
50-($3.99) Sinister Six app.; back-up w/Sonny Liew-a — 4.00
51-61: 53-Emma Frost becomes a regular; intro. Chat; Skottie Young-c begin — 3.00
... Vol. 1 HC (2006, $19.99, with dustjacket) r/#1-8; plot for #7; sketch pages from #6,8 — 20.00
... Vol. 1: The Sinister Six (2005, $6.99, digest) r/#1-4 — 7.00
... Vol. 2: Power Struggle (2005, $6.99, digest) r/#5-8 — 7.00
... Vol. 3: Doom With a View (2006, $6.99, digest) r/#9-12 — 7.00
... Vol. 4: Concrete Jungle (2006, $6.99, digest) r/#13-16 — 7.00
... Vol. 5: Monsters on the Prowl (2007, $6.99, digest) r/#17-20 — 7.00
... Vol. 6: The Black Costume (2007, $6.99, digest) r/#21-24 — 7.00
... Vol. 7: Secret Identity (2007, $6.99, digest) r/#25-28 — 7.00
... Vol. 8: Forces of Nature (2008, $7.99, digest) r/#29-32 — 8.00
... Vol. 9: Fiercest Foes (2008, $7.99, digest) r/#33-36 — 8.00

MARVEL ADVENTURES STARRING DAREDEVIL (...Adventure #3 on)
Marvel Comics Group: Dec, 1975 - No. 6, Oct, 1976

	GD	VG	FN	VF	VF/NM	NM-
1	2	4	6	8	10	12
2-6-r/Daredevil #22-27 by Colan. 3-5-(25¢-c)	1	2	3	5	6	8
3-5-(30¢-c variants, limited distribution)(4,6,8/76)	2	4	6	11	16	20

MARVEL ADVENTURES SUPER HEROES (All ages title)
Marvel Comics: Sept, 2008 - No. 21, May, 2010 ($2.99)

1-21: 1-4: Spider-Man, Hulk and Iron Man team-ups. 1-Hercules app. 5-Dr. Strange app. 6-Ant-Man origin re-told. 7-Thor. 8,12-Capt. America. 17-Avengers begin — 3.00

MARVEL ADVENTURES THE AVENGERS (All ages title)
Marvel Comics: July, 2006 - No. 39, Oct, 2009 ($2.99)

1-39-Spider-Man, Wolverine, Hulk, Iron Man, Capt. America, Storm, Giant-Girl app. — 3.00
... Vol. 1: Heroes Assembled (2006, $6.99, digest) r/#1-4 — 7.00
... Vol. 2: Mischief (2007, $6.99, digest) r/#5-8 — 7.00
... Vol. 3: Bizarre Adventures (2007, $6.99, digest) r/#9-12 — 7.00
... Vol. 4: The Dream Team (2007, $6.99, digest) r/#13-15 & Giant-Size #1 — 7.00
... Vol. 5: Some Assembling Required (2008, $7.99, digest) r/#16-19 — 8.00

MARVEL ADVENTURES TWO-IN-ONE
Marvel Comics: Oct, 2007 - Present ($4.99, bi-weekly)

1-18: 1-9-Reprints Marvel Adventures Spider-Man and Fantastic Four stories. 10-Hulk — 5.00

Marvel Age Fantastic Four #2 © MAR

Marvel Classic Comics #24 © MAR

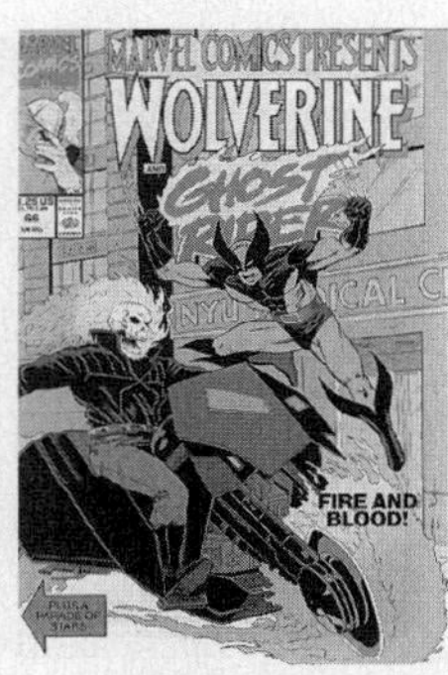

Marvel Comics Presents #66 © MAR

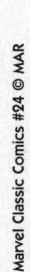

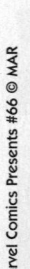

GD	VG	FN	VF	VF/NM	NM-
2.0	4.0	6.0	8.0	9.0	9.2

MARVEL AGE FANTASTIC FOUR (All ages title)
Marvel Comics: Jun, 2004 - No. 12, Mar, 2005 ($2.25)

1-12-Lee & Kirby stories retold with new art by various. 11-Impossible Man app. 2.50
...Tales (4/05, $2.25) retells first meeting with the Black Panther; O'Hare & Lim-a 2.50
Vol. 1: All For One TPB (2004, $5.99, digest size) r/#1-4 6.00
Vol. 2: Doom TPB (2004, $5.99, digest size) r/#5-8 6.00
Vol. 3: The Return of Doctor Doom TPB (2005, $5.99, digest size) r/#9-12 6.00

MARVEL AGE HULK (All ages title)
Marvel Comics: Nov, 2004 - No. 4, Feb, 2005 ($1.75)

1-3-Lee & Kirby stories retold with new art by various 2.50
Vol. 1: Incredible TPB (2005, $5.99, digest size) r/#1-4 6.00
Vol. 2: Defenders (2008, $7.99, digest) r/#5-8 8.00

MARVEL AGE SPIDER-MAN (All ages title) (Also see Free Comic Book Day edition in the Promotional Comics section)
Marvel Comics: May, 2004 - No. 20, Mar, 2005 ($2.25)

1-20-Lee & Ditko stories retold with new art. 4-Doctor Doom app. 5-Lizard app. 2.50
Vol. 1 TPB (2004, $5.99, digest) 1-r/#1-4 6.00
Vol. 2: Everyday Hero TPB (2004, $5.99, digest) r/#5-8 6.00
Vol. 3: Swingtime TPB (2004, $5.99, digest) r/#9-12 6.00
Spidey Strikes Back TPB (2005, 5.99, digest) r/#17-20 6.00

MARVEL AGE TEAM-UP (All ages Spider-Man team-ups) (Also see Free Comic Book Day edition in the Promotional Comics section)
Marvel Comics: Nov, 2004 - No. 5, Apr, 2005 ($1.75)

1-5-Stories retold with new art by various. 1-Fantastic Four app. 3-Kitty Pryde app. 2.50
... Vol. 1: A Little Help From My Friends (2005, $7.99, digest) r/#1-5 8.00

MARVEL AND DC PRESENT FEATURING THE UNCANNY X-MEN AND THE NEW TEEN TITANS
Marvel Comics/DC Comics: 1982 ($2.00, 68 pgs., one-shot, Baxter paper)

1-3rd app. Deathstroke the Terminator; Darkseid app.; Simonson/Austin-c/a
2 4 6 11 16 20

MARVEL APES
Marvel Comics: Nov, 2008 - No. 4, Dec, 2008 ($3.99, limited series)

1-4: 1-Kesel-s/Bachs-a; back-up history story with Peyer-s/Kitson-a; two covers 4.00
1-($10.00) Hero Initiative edition with Daredevil gorilla cover by Mike Wieringo 10.00
#0-(2008, $3.99) r/Amazing Spider-Man #110,111; gallery of Marvel Apes variant covers 4.00
...: Amazing Spider-Monkey Special1 (6/09, $3.99) Sandmonk and the Apevengers app. 4.00
...: Grunt Line 1 (7/09, $3.99) Kesel-s; Charles Darwin app. 4.00
...: Speedball Special 1 (5/09, $3.99) Bachs & Hardin-a 4.00

MARVEL ASSISTANT-SIZED SPECTACULAR
Marvel Comics: Jun, 2009 - No. 2, Jun, 2009 ($3.99, limited series)

1,2-Short stories by various incl. Isanove, Giarrusso, Nauck, Wyatt Cenak, Warren 4.00

MARVEL ATLAS (Styled after the Official Marvel Handbooks)
Marvel Comics: 2007 - No. 2, 2008 ($3.99, limited series)

1,2-Profiles and maps of countries in the Marvel Universe 4.00

MARVEL BOY (Astonishing #3 on; see Marvel Super Action #4)
Marvel Comics (MPC): Dec, 1950 - No. 2, Feb, 1951

1-Origin Marvel Boy by Russ Heath 113 226 339 718 1234 1750
2-Everett-a 79 158 237 502 864 1225

MARVEL BOY (Marvel Knights)
Marvel Comics: Aug, 2000 - No. 6, Mar, 2001 ($2.99, limited series)

1-Intro. Marvel Boy; Morrison-s/J.G. Jones-c/a 3.50
1-DF Variant-c 5.00
2-6 3.00
TPB (6/01, $15.95) 16.00

MARVEL BOY: THE URANIAN (Agents of Atlas)
Marvel Comics: Mar, 2010 - No. 3, May, 2010 ($2.99, limited series)

1-3-Origin re-told; back-up reprints from 1950s; Heath & Everett-a 3.00

MARVEL CHILLERS (Also see Giant-Size Chillers)
Marvel Comics Group: Oct, 1975 - No. 7, Oct, 1976 (All 25¢ issues)

1-Intro. Modred the Mystic, ends #2; Kane-c(p) 2 4 6 11 16 20
2,4,5,7: 4-Kraven app. 5,6-Red Wolf app. 7-Kirby-c; Tuska-p
2 4 6 8 10 12
3-Tigra, the Were-Woman begins (origin), ends #7 (see Giant-Size Creatures #1). Chaykin/Wrightson-c. 3 6 9 16 23 30
4-6-(30¢-c variants, limited distribution)(4-8/76) 3 6 9 18 27 35
6-Byrne-a(p); Buckler-c(p) 2 4 6 10 14 18
NOTE: *Bolle a-1. Buckler c-2. Kirby c-7.*

MARVEL CLASSICS COMICS SERIES FEATURING...
(Also see Pendulum Illustrated Classics)
Marvel Comics Group: 1976 - No. 36, Dec, 1978 (52 pgs., no ads)

1-Dr. Jekyll and Mr. Hyde 2 4 6 10 14 18
2-10,28: 28-1st Golden-c/a; Pit and the Pendulum 2 4 6 8 10 12
11-27,29-36 1 2 3 5 7 9
NOTE: ***Adkins** c-1i, 4i, 12i. **Alcala** a-34i; c-34. **Bolle** a-35. **Buscema** c-17p, 19p, 26p. **Golden** c/a-28. **Gil Kane** c-1-16p, 21p, 22p, 24p, 32p. **Nebres** a-5; c-24i. **Nino** a-2, 8, 12. **Redondo** a-1, 9. No. 1-12 were reprinted from Pendulum Illustrated Classics.*

MARVEL COLLECTIBLE CLASSICS: AVENGERS
Marvel Comics: 1998 ($10.00, reprints with chromium wraparound-c)

1-Reprints Avengers Vol.3, #1; Perez-c 10.00

MARVEL COLLECTIBLE CLASSICS: SPIDER-MAN
Marvel Comics: 1998 ($10.00, reprints with chromium wraparound-c)

1-Reprints Amazing Spider-Man #300; McFarlane-c 10.00
2-Reprints Spider-Man #1; McFarlane-c 10.00

MARVEL COLLECTIBLE CLASSICS: X-MEN
Marvel Comics: 1998 ($10.00, reprints with chromium wraparound-c)

1-6: 1-Reprints (Uncanny) X-Men #1 & 2; Adam Kubert-c. 2-Reprints Uncanny X-Men #141 & 142; Byrne-c. 3-Reprints (Uncanny) X-Men #137; Larroca-c. 4-Reprints X-Men #25; Andy Kubert-c. 5-Reprints Giant Size X-Men #1; Gary Frank-c. 6-Reprints X-Men V2#1; Ramos-c 10.00

MARVEL COLLECTOR'S EDITION
Marvel Comics: 1992 (Ordered thru mail with Charleston Chew candy wrapper)

1-Flip-book format; Spider-Man, Silver Surfer, Wolverine (by Sam Kieth), & Ghost Rider stories; Wolverine back-c by Kieth 3.00

MARVEL COLLECTORS' ITEM CLASSICS (Marvel's Greatest #23 on)
Marvel Comics Group(ATF): Feb, 1965 - No. 22, Aug, 1969 (25¢, 68 pgs.)

1-Fantastic Four, Spider-Man, Thor, Hulk, Iron Man-r begin
11 22 33 74 132 190
2 (4/66) 6 12 18 43 69 95
3,4 5 10 15 34 55 75
5-10 5 10 15 30 48 65
11-22: 22-r/The Man in the Ant Hill/TTA #27 4 8 12 26 41 55
NOTE: *All reprints; **Ditko, Kirby** art in all.*

MARVEL COMICS (Marvel Mystery Comics #2 on)
Timely Comics (Funnies, Inc.): Oct, Nov, 1939

NOTE: The first issue was originally dated October 1939. Most copies have a black circle stamped over the date (on cover and inside) with "November" printed over it. However, some copies do not have the November overprint and could have a higher value. Most No. 1's have printing defects, i.e., tilted pages which caused trimming into the panels usually on right side and bottom. Covers exist with and without gloss finish.

1-Origin Sub-Mariner by Bill Everett(1st newsstand app.); 1st 8 pgs. were produced for Motion Picture Funnies Weekly #1 which was probably not distributed outside of advance copies; intro Human Torch by Carl Burgos, Kazar the Great (1st Tarzan clone), & Jungle Terror(only app.); intro. The Angel by Gustavson, The Masked Raider & his horse Lightning (ends #12); cover by sci/fi pulp illustrator Frank R. Paul
20,000 40,000 60,000 134,000 235,000 450,000

MARVEL COMICS 70th ANNIVERARY SPECIAL
Marvel Comics: Oct, 2009 ($3.99, one-shot)

1-Re-colored reprint of entire Marvel Comics #1; cover swipe by Jelena Djurdjevic 4.00

MARVEL COMICS PRESENTS
Marvel Comics (Midnight Sons imprint #143 on): Early Sept, 1988 - No. 175, Feb, 1995 ($1.25/$1.50/$1.75, bi-weekly)

1-Wolverine by Buscema in #1-10 6.00
2-5 4.00
6-10: 6-Sub-Mariner app. 10-Colossus begins 3.00
11-47,51-71: 17-Cyclops begins. 19-1st app. Damage Control. 24-Havok begins. 25-Origin/1st app. Nth Man. 26-Hulk begins by Rogers. 29-Quasar app. 31-Excalibur begins by Austin (i). 32-McFarlane-a(p). 33-Capt. America; Jim Lee-a. 37-Devil-Slayer app. 38-Wolverine begins by Buscema; Hulk app. 39-Spider-Man app. 46-Liefeld Wolverine-c. 51-53-Wolverine by Rob Liefeld. 54-61-Wolverine/Hulk story: 54-Werewolf by Night begins; The Shroud by Ditko. 58-Iron Man by Ditko. 59-Punisher. 62-Deathlok & Wolverine stories 63-Wolverine. 64-71-Wolverine/Ghost Rider 8-part story. 70-Liefeld Ghost Rider/ Wolverine-c 2.50
48-50-Wolverine & Spider-Man team-up by Erik Larsen-c/a. 48-Wasp app. 49,50-Savage Dragon prototype app. by Larsen. 50-Silver Surfer. 50-53-Comet Man; Mumy scripts 4.00
72-Begin 13-part Weapon-X story (Wolverine origin) by B. Windsor-Smith (prologue) 5.00
73-Weapon-X part 1; Black Knight, Sub-Mariner 4.00
74-84: 74-Weapon-X part 2; Black Knight, Sub-Mariner. 76-Death's Head story.

Marvel Comics Presents (2007 series) #2 © MAR

Marvel Double Feature #4 © MAR

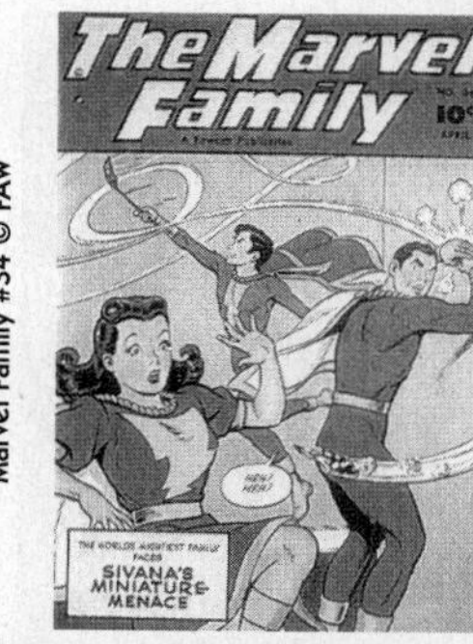

Marvel Family #34 © FAW

GD VG FN VF VF/NM NM-
2.0 4.0 6.0 8.0 9.0 9.2

77-Mr. Fantastic story. 78-Iron Man by Steacy. 80,81-Capt. America by Ditko/Austin. 81-Daredevil by Rogers/Williamson. 82-Power Man. 83-Human Torch by Ditko(a&scripts); $1.00-c direct, $1.25 newsstand. 84-Last Weapon-X (24 pg. conclusion) 3.00
85-Begin 8-part Wolverine story by Sam Kieth (c/a); 1st Kieth-a on Wolverine; begin 8-part Beast story by Jae Lee(p) with Liefeld part pencils #85,86; 1st Jae Lee-a (assisted w/Liefeld, 1991) 4.00
86-90: 86-89-Wolverine, Beast stories continue. 90-Begin 8-part Ghost Rider & Cable story, ends #97; begin flip book format w/two-c 3.00
91-175: 93-Begin 6-part Wolverine story, ends #98. 98-Begin 2-part Ghost Rider story. 99-Spider-Man story. 100-Full-length Ghost Rider/Wolverine story by Sam Kieth w/Tim Vigil assists; anniversary issue, non flip-book. 101-Begin 6-part Ghost Rider/Dr. Strange story & begin 8-part Wolverine/Nightcrawler story by Colan/Williamson; Punisher story. 107-Begin 6-part Ghost Rider/Werewolf by Night story. 109-Begin 8 part Wolverine/Typhoid Mary story. 111-Iron Fist. 113-Begin 6-part Giant-Man & begin 6-part Ghost Rider/Iron Fist stories. 117-Preview of Ravage 2099 (1st app.); begin 6 part Wolverine/Venom story w/Kieth-a. 118-Preview of Doom 2099 (1st app.). 119-Begin Ghost Rider/Cloak & Dagger by Colan. 120,136,138-Spider-Man. 123-Begin 8-part Ghost Rider/Typhoid Mary story; begin 4-part She Hulk story; begin 8-part Wolverine/Lynx story. 125-Begin 6-part Iron Fist story. 130-Begin 6-part Ghost Rider/ Cage story. 136-Daredevil. 137-Begin 6-part Wolverine story & 6-part Ghost Rider story. 147-Begin 2-part Vengeance-c/story w/new Ghost Rider. 149-Vengeance-c/story w/new Ghost Rider. 150-Silver ink-c; begin 2-part Bloody Mary story w/Typhoid Mary,Wolverine, Daredevil, new Ghost Rider; intro Steel Raven. 152-Begin 4-part Wolverine, 4-part War Machine, 4-part Vengeance, 3-part Moon Knight stories; same date as War Machine #1. 143-146: Siege of Darkness parts 3,6,11,14; all have spot-varnished-c. 143-Ghost Rider/Scarlet Witch; intro new Werewolf. 144-Begin 2-part Morbius story. 145-Begin 2-part Nightstalkers story. 153-155-Bound-in Spider-Man trading card sheet 2.50
...Colossus: God's Country (1994, $6.95) r/#10-17 1 2 3 4 5 7
...: Wolverine Vol. 1 TPB (2005, $12.99) r/Wolverine stories from #1-10 13.00
...: Wolverine Vol. 2 TPB (2006, $12.99) r/from #39-50 and Marvel Age Annual #4 13.00
...: Wolverine Vol. 3 TPB (2006, $12.99) r/from #51-61 13.00
...: Wolverine Vol. 4 TPB (2006, $12.99) r/from #62-71 13.00

NOTE: ***Austin** a-31-37i; c(i)-48, 50, 99, 122. **Buscema** a-1-10, 38-47; c-6. **Byrne** a-79; c-71. **Colan** a(p)-36, 37. **Colan/Williamson** a-101-108. **Ditko** a-7p, 10, 56p, 58, 80, 81, 83. **Guice** a-62. **Sam Kieth** a-85-92, 117-122; c-85-98, 99p, 100-108, 117, 118, 120-122; back c-109-113, 117. **Jae Lee** c-129(back). **Liefeld** a-51, 52, 53p(2), 85p; c-46, 70. **McFarlane** c-32. **Mooney** a-73. **Rogers** a-26, 38, 46i, 81p. **Russell** a-10-14,16,17i; c-4,19, 30,31i. **Saltares** a-8p(early), 38-45p. **Simonson** c-1. **B. Smith** a-72-84; c-72-84. **P. Smith** c-34. **Sparling** a-33. **Starlin** a-89i. **Staton** a-74. **Steacy** a-78. **Sutton** a-101-105. **Williamson** c-62i. Two Gun Kid by **Gil Kane** in #116, 122.*

MARVEL COMICS PRESENTS
Marvel Comics: Nov, 2007 - No. 12, Oct, 2008 ($3.99)

1-12-Short stories by various. 1-Wraparound-c by Campbell 4.00

MARVEL COMICS SUPER SPECIAL, A (Marvel Super Special #5 on)
Marvel Comics: Sept, 1977 - No. 41(?), Nov, 1986 (nn 7) ($1.50, magazine)

1-Kiss, 40 pgs. comics plus photos & features; John Buscema-a(p); also see Howard the Duck #12; ink contains real KISS blood; Dr. Doom, Spider-Man, Avengers, Fantastic Four, Mephisto app. 11 22 33 80 145 210
2-Conan (1978) 3 6 9 14 19 24
3-Close Encounters of the Third Kind (1978); Simonson-a 2 4 6 9 13 16
4-The Beatles Story (1978)-Perez/Janson-a; has photos & articles 5 10 15 30 48 65
5-Kiss (1978)-Includes poster 11 22 33 80 145 210
6-Jaws II (1978) 2 4 6 9 13 16
7-Sgt. Pepper; Beatles movie adaptation; withdrawn from U.S. distribution (French ed. exists)
8-Battlestar Galactica; tabloid size ($1.50, 1978); adapts TV show 2 4 6 13 18 20
8-Modern-r of tabloid size 2 4 6 10 14 18
8-Battlestar Galactica; publ. in regular magazine format; low distribution ($1.50, 8-1/2x11") 3 6 9 14 19 24
9-Conan 2 4 6 11 16 20
10-Star-Lord 2 4 6 9 13 16
11-13-Weirdworld begins #11; 25 copy special press run of each with gold seal and signed by artists (Proof quality), Spring-June, 1979 8 16 24 54 90 125
11-15: 11-13-Weirdworld (regular issues): 11-Fold-out centerfold. 14-Miller-c(p); adapts movie "Meteor." 15-Star Trek with photos & pin-ups ($1.50-c) 1 3 4 6 8 10
15-With $2.00 price; the price was changed at tail end of a 200,000 press run 2 4 6 8 10 12
16-Empire Strikes Back adaption; Williamson-a 2 4 6 9 12 15
17-20 (Movie adaptations):17-Xanadu. 18-Raiders of the Lost Ark. 19-For Your Eyes Only (James Bond). 20-Dragonslayer 6.00
21-26,28-30 (Movie adaptations): 21-Conan. 22-Blade Runner; Williamson-a; Steranko-c. 23-Annie. 24-The Dark Crystal. 25-Rock and Rule-w/photos; artwork is from movie. 26-Octopussy (James Bond). 28-Krull; photo-c. 29-Tarzan of the Apes (Greystoke movie). 30-Indiana Jones and the Temple of Doom 1 2 3 4 5 7
27,31-41: 27-Return of the Jedi. 31-The Last Star Fighter. 32-The Muppets Take Manhattan. 33-Buckaroo Banzai. 34-Sheena. 35-Conan The Destroyer. 36-Dune. 37-2010. 38-Red Sonja. 39-Santa Claus:The Movie. 40-Labyrinth. 41-Howard The Duck 1 2 3 5 7 9

NOTE: ***J. Buscema** a-1, 2, 9, 11-13, 18p, 21, 35, 40; c-11(part), 12. **Chaykin** a-9, 19p; c-18, 19. **Colan** a(p)-6, 10, 14. **Morrow** a-34; c-1i, 34. **Nebres** a-11. **Spiegle** a-29. **Stevens** a-27. **Williamson** a-27. #22-28 contain photos from movies.*

MARVEL COMICS: 2001
Marvel Comics: 2001 (no cover price, one-shot)

1-Previews new titles for Fall 2001; Wolverine-c 2.50

MARVEL DABEL BROTHERS SAMPLER
Marvel Comics: Dec, 2006 (no cover price, one-shot)

1-Profiles and sample pages of Anita Blake, Magician: Apprentice, Red Prophet, Ptolus 2.50

MARVEL DIVAS
Marvel Comics: Sept, 2009 - No. 4, Dec, 2009 ($3.99, limited series)

1-4-Black Cat, Firestar, Hellcat and Photon app.. 1-Campbell-c 4.00

MARVEL DOUBLE FEATURE
Marvel Comics Group: Dec, 1973 - No. 21, Mar, 1977

1-Capt. America, Iron Man-r/T.O.S. begin 2 4 6 11 16 20
2-10: 3-Last 20¢ issue 2 4 6 8 10 12
11-17,20,21:17-Story-r/Iron Man & Sub-Mariner #1; last 25¢ issue 1 2 3 5 6 8
15-17-(30¢-c variants, limited distribution)(4,6,8/76) 2 4 6 9 13 16
18,19-Colan/Craig-r from Iron Man #1 in both 2 3 4 6 8 10

NOTE: ***Colan** r-1-19p. **Craig** r-17-19i. **G. Kane** r-15p; c-15p. **Kirby** r-1-16p, 20, 21; c-17-20.*

MARVEL DOUBLE SHOT
Marvel Comics: Jan, 2003 - No. 4, April, 2003 ($2.99, limited series)

1-4: 1-Hulk by Haynes; Thor w/Asamiya-a; Jusko-c. 2-Dr. Doom by Rivera; Simpsons-style Avengers by Bill Morrison 3.00

MARVEL FAMILY (Also see Captain Marvel Adventures No. 18)
Fawcett Publications: Dec, 1945 - No. 89, Jan, 1954

1-Origin Captain Marvel, Captain Marvel Jr., Mary Marvel, & Uncle Marvel retold; origin/1st app. Black Adam 181 362 543 1158 1979 2800
2-The 3 Lt. Marvels & Uncle Marvel app. 77 154 231 493 847 1200
3 54 108 162 343 584 825
4,5 44 88 132 277 469 660
6-10: 7-Shazam app. 39 78 117 230 375 520
11-20 29 58 87 170 278 385
21-30 24 48 72 144 237 330
31-40 20 40 60 120 195 270
41-46,48-50 18 36 54 103 162 220
47-Flying Saucer-c/story (5/50) 23 46 69 136 223 310
51-76 16 32 48 94 147 200
77-Communist Threat-c 26 52 78 154 252 350
78,81-Used in **POP**, pg. 92,93. 19 38 57 111 176 240
79,80,82-88: 79-Horror satire-c 18 36 54 107 169 230
89-Last issue; last Fawcett Captain Marvel app. (low distribution) 21 42 63 122 199 275

MARVEL FANFARE (1st Series)
Marvel Comics Group: Mar, 1982 - No. 60, Jan, 1992 ($1.25/$2.25, slick paper, direct sales)

1-Spider-Man/Angel team-up; 1st Paul Smith-a (1st full story; see King Conan #7); Daredevil app. (many copies were printed missing the centerfold) 1 2 3 5 6 8
2-Spider-Man, Ka-Zar, The Angel. F.F. origin retold 6.00
3,4-X-Men & Ka-Zar. 4-Deathlok, Spidey app. 5.00
5-14: 5-Dr. Strange, Capt. America. 6-Spider-Man, Scarlet Witch. 7-Incredible Hulk; D.D. back-up(also 15). 8-Dr. Strange; Wolf Boy begins. 9-Man-Thing. 10-13-Black Widow. 14-The Vision 3.00
15,24,33: 15-The Thing by Barry Smith, c/a. 24-Weirdworld; Wolverine back-up. 33-X-Men, Wolverine app.; Punisher pin-up 4.00
16-23,25-32,34-44,46-50: 16,17-Skywolf. 16-Sub-Mariner back-up. 17-Hulk back-up. 18-Capt. America by Miller. 19-Cloak and Dagger. 20-Thing/Dr. Strange. 21-Thing/Dr. Strange /Hulk. 22,23-Iron Man vs. Dr. Octopus. 25,26-Weirdworld. 27-Daredevil/Spider-Man. 28-Alpha Flight. 29-Hulk. 30-Moon Knight. 31,32-Captain America. 34-37-Warriors Three. 38-Moon Knight/Dazzler. 39-Moon Knight/Hawkeye. 40-Angel/Rogue & Storm. 41-Dr. Strange. 42-Spider-Man. 43-Sub-Mariner/Human Torch. 44-Iron Man vs. Dr. Doom by Ken Steacy. 46-Fantastic Four. 47-Hulk. 48-She-Hulk/Vision. 49-Dr. Strange/Nick Fury. 50-X-Factor 2.50
45-All pin-up issue by Steacy, Art Adams & others 5.00

Marvel Fanfare (2nd series) #4 © MAR

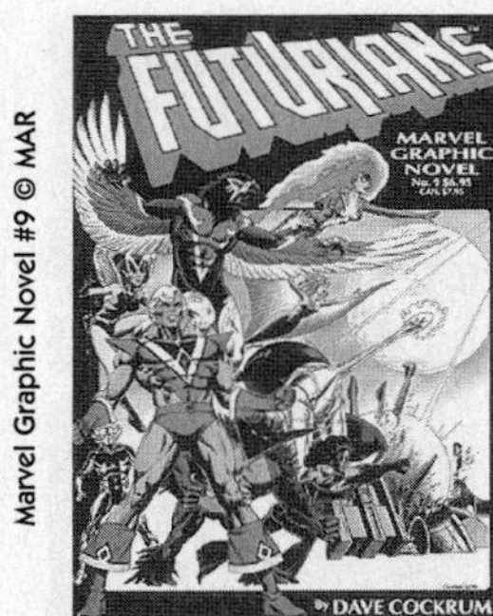

Marvel Graphic Novel #9 © MAR

Marvel Holiday Special 1993 © MAR

GD 2.0 | VG 4.0 | FN 6.0 | VF 8.0 | VF/NM 9.0 | NM- 9.2

51-($2.95, 52 pgs.)-Silver Surfer; Fantastic Four & Capt. Marvel app.; 51,52-Colan/Williamson back-up (Dr. Strange) 3.00
52,53,56-60: 52,53-Black Knight; 53-Iron Man back up. 56-59-Shanna the She-Devil. 58-Vision & Scarlet Witch back-up. 60-Black Panther/Rogue/Daredevil stories 2.50
54,55-Wolverine back-ups. 54-Black Knight. 55-Power Pack 4.00
... Vol. 1 TPB (2008, $24.99) r/#1-7 25.00

NOTE: ***Art Adams*** *c-13.* ***Austin*** *a-1i, 4i, 33i, 38i; c-8i, 33i.* ***Buscema*** *a-51p.* ***Byrne*** *a-1p, 29, 48; c-29.* ***Chiodo*** *painted c-56-59.* ***Colan*** *a-51p.* ***Cowan/Simonson*** *c/a-60.* ***Golden*** *a-1, 2, 4p, 47; c-1, 2, 47.* ***Infantino*** *c/a(p)-8.* ***Gil Kane*** *a-8-11p.* ***Miller*** *a-18; c-1(Back-c), 18.* ***Perez*** *a-10, 11p, 12, 13p; c-10-13p.* ***Rogers*** *a-5p; c-5p.* ***Russell*** *a-5i, 6i, 8-11i, 43i; c-5i, 6.* ***Paul Smith*** *a-1p, 4p, 32, 60; c-4p. Staton c/a-50(p).* ***Williamson*** *a-30i, 51i.*

MARVEL FANFARE (2nd Series)
Marvel Comics: Sept, 1996 - No. 6, Feb, 1997 (99¢)

1-6: 1-Capt. America & The Falcon-c/story; Deathlok app. 2-Wolverine & Hulk-c/app. 3-Ghost Rider & Spider-Man-c/app. 5-Longshot-c/app. 6-Sabretooth, Power Man, & Iron Fist-c/app 2.50

MARVEL FEATURE (See Marvel Two-In-One)
Marvel Comics Group: Dec, 1971 - No. 12, Nov, 1973 (1,2: 25¢, 52 pg. giants) (#1-3: quarterly)

1-Origin/1st app. The Defenders (Sub-Mariner, Hulk & Dr. Strange); see Sub-Mariner #34,35 for prequel; Dr. Strange solo story (predates Dr.Strange #1) plus 1950s Sub-Mariner-r; Neal Adams-c 16 32 48 115 220 325
2-2nd app. Defenders; 1950s Sub-Mariner-r. Rutland, Vermont Halloween x-over 9 18 27 63 107 150
3-Defenders ends 7 14 21 45 73 100
4-Re-intro Antman (1st app. since 1960s), begin series; brief origin; Spider-Man app. 4 8 12 28 44 60
5-7,9,10: 6-Wasp app. & begins team-ups. 9-Iron Man app. 10-Last Antman 3 6 9 18 27 35
8-Origin Antman & Wasp-r/TTA #44; Kirby-a 3 6 9 20 30 40
11-Thing vs. Hulk; 1st Thing solo book (9/73); origin Fantastic Four retold 8 16 24 52 86 120
12-Thing/Iron Man; early Thanos app.; occurs after Capt. Marvel #33; Starlin-a(p) 5 10 15 32 51 70

NOTE: ***Bolle*** *a-9i.* ***Everett*** *a-1i, 3i.* ***Hartley*** *r-10.* ***Kane*** *c-3p, 7p.* ***Russell*** *a-7-10p.* ***Starlin*** *a-8, 11, 12; c-8.*

MARVEL FEATURE (Also see Red Sonja)
Marvel Comics: Nov, 1975 - No. 7, Nov, 1976 (Story cont'd in Conan #68)

1,7: 1-Red Sonja begins (pre-dates Red Sonja #1); adapts Howard short story; Adams-r/Savage Sword of Conan #1. 7-Battles Conan 2 4 6 8 11 14
2-6: Thorne-c/a in #2-7. 4,5-(Regular 25¢ edition)(5,7/76) 1 2 3 5 6 8
4,5-(30¢-c variants, limited distribution) 3 6 9 14 20 25

MARVEL FRONTIER COMICS UNLIMITED
Marvel Frontier Comics: Jan, 1994 ($2.95, 68 pgs.)

1-Dances with Demons, Immortalis, Children of the Voyager, Evil Eye, The Fallen stories 3.00

MARVEL FUMETTI BOOK
Marvel Comics Group: Apr, 1984 ($1.00, one-shot)

1-All photos; Stan Lee photo-c; Art Adams touch-ups 5.00

MARVEL FUN & GAMES
Marvel Comics Group: 1979/80 (color comic for kids)

1,11: 1-Games, puzzles, etc. 11-X-Men-c 2 3 4 6 8 10
2-10,12,13: (beware marked pages) 1 2 3 4 5 7

MARVEL GRAPHIC NOVEL
Marvel Comics Group (Epic Comics): 1982 - No. 38, 1990? ($5.95/$6.95)

1-Death of Captain Marvel (2nd Marvel graphic novel); Capt. Marvel battles Thanos by Jim Starlin (c/a/scripts) 3 6 9 14 19 24
1 (2nd & 3rd printings) 1 2 3 5 6 8
2-Elric: The Dreaming City 2 4 6 8 10 12
3-Dreadstar; Starlin-c/a, 52 pgs. 2 4 6 8 11 14
4-Origin/1st app. The New Mutants (1982) 2 4 6 8 11 14
4,5-2nd printings 1 2 3 4 5 7
5-X-Men; book-length story (1982) 3 6 9 14 20 25
6-15,20,23,25,30,31: 6-The Star Slammers. 7-Killraven. 8-Super Boxers; Byrne scripts. 9-The Futurians. 10-Heartburst. 11-Void Indigo. 12-Dazzler. 13-Starstruck. 14-The Swords Of The Swashbucklers. 15-The Raven Banner (a Tale of Asgard). 20-Greenberg the Vampire. 23-Dr. Strange. 25-Alien Legion. 30-A Sailor's Story. 31-Wolfpack 1 2 3 5 7 9
16,17,21,29: 16-The Aladdin Effect (Storm, Tigra, Wasp, She-Hulk). 17-Revenge Of The Living Monolith (Spider-Man, Avengers, FF app.). 21-Marada the She-Wolf. 29-The Big Chance (Thing vs. Hulk) 1 2 3 5 7 9
18,19,26-28: 18-She Hulk. 19-Witch Queen of Acheron (Conan). 26-Dracula. 27-Avengers (Emperor Doom). 28-Conan the Reaver 2 4 6 9 11 13
22-Amaz. Spider-Man in Hooky by Wrightson 2 4 6 9 12 15
24-Love and War (Daredevil); Miller scripts 2 4 6 8 11 14
32-Death of Groo 2 4 6 9 12 15
32-2nd printing ($5.95) 1 2 3 5 6 8
33,34,36,37: 33-Thor. 34-Predator & Prey (Cloak & Dagger). 36-Willow (movie adapt.). 37-Hercules 1 3 4 6 8 10
35-Hitler's Astrologer (The Shadow, $12.95, HC) 2 4 6 9 13 16
35-Soft-c reprint (1990, $10.95) 2 4 6 8 10 12
38-Silver Surfer (Judgement Day)($14.95, HC) 2 4 6 10 14 18
38-Soft-c reprint (1990, $10.95) 2 4 6 8 11 14
nn-Abslom Daak: Dalak Killer (1990, $8.95) Dr. Who 1 3 4 6 8 10
nn-Arena by Bruce Jones (1989, $5.95) Dinosaurs 1 2 3 5 6 8
nn- A-Team Storybook Comics Illustrated (1983) r/ A-Team mini-series #1-3 1 3 4 6 8 10
nn-Ax (1988, $5.95) Ernie Colan-s/a 1 3 4 6 8 10
nn-Black Widow Coldest War (4/90, $9.95) 2 4 6 8 10 12
nn-Chronicles of Genghis Grimtoad (1990, $8.95)-Alan Grant-s 1 3 4 6 8 10
nn-Conan the Barbarian in the Horn of Azoth (1990, $8.95) 2 4 6 8 11 16
nn-Conan of Isles ($8.95) 2 4 6 8 11 16
nn-Conan Ravagers of Time (1992, $9.95) Kull & Red Sonja app. 2 4 6 8 11 16
nn-Conan -The Skull of Set 2 4 6 8 11 16
nn-Doctor Strange and Doctor Doom Triumph and Torment (1989, $17.95, HC) 2 4 6 13 18 22
nn-Dreamwalker (1989, $6.95)-Morrow-a 1 2 3 5 7 9
nn-Excalibur Weird War III (1990, $9.95) 2 4 6 8 10 12
nn-G.I. Joe - The Trojan Gambit (1983, 68 pgs.) 2 4 6 8 10 12
nn-Harvey Kurtzman Strange Adventures (Epic, $19.95, HC) Aragonés, Crumb 3 6 9 14 20 25
nn-Hearts and Minds (1990, $8.95) Heath-a 1 3 4 6 8 10
nn-Inhumans (1988, $7.95)-Williamson-i 1 2 3 5 7 9
nn-Jhereg (Epic, 1990, $8.95) 1 3 4 6 8 10
nn-Kazar-Guns of the Savage Land (7/90, $8.95) 1 3 4 6 8 10
nn-Kull-The Vale of Shadow ('89, $6.95) 2 4 6 8 10 12
nn-Last of the Dragons (1988, $6.95) Austin-a(i) 1 2 3 4 5 7
nn-Nightraven: House of Cards (1991, $14.95) 2 4 6 9 12 15
nn-Nightraven: The Collected Stories (1990, $9.95) Bolton-r/British Hulk mag.; David Lloyd-c/a 2 4 6 8 10 12
nn-Original Adventures of Cholly and Flytrap (Epic, 1991, $9.95) Suydam-s/c/a 2 4 6 9 12 15
nn-Rick Mason Agent (1989, $9.95) 1 3 4 6 8 10
nn-Roger Rabbit In The Resurrection Of Doom (1989, $8.95) 1 3 4 6 8 10
nn-A Sailor's Story Book II: Winds, Dreams and Dragons ('86, $6.95, softcover) Glansman-s/c/a 1 3 4 6 8 10
nn-Squadron Supreme: Death of a Universe (1989, $9.95) Gruenwald-s; Ryan & Williamson-a 3 6 9 14 20 25
nn-Who Framed Roger Rabbit (1989, $6.95) 1 3 4 6 8 10

NOTE: ***Aragones*** *a-27, 32.* ***Buscema*** *a-38.* ***Byrne*** *c/a-18.* ***Heath*** *a-35i.* ***Kaluta*** *a-13, 35p; c-13.* ***Miller*** *a-24p.* ***Simonson*** *a-6; c-6.* ***Starlin*** *c/a-1,3.* ***Williamson*** *a-34.* ***Wrightson*** *c-29i.*

MARVEL HEARTBREAKERS
Marvel Comics: Apr, 2010 ($3.99, one-shot)

1-Romance short stories; Spider-Man, MJ & Gwen app.; Casagrande-a; Beast app. 4.00

MARVEL-HEROES & LEGENDS
Marvel Comics: Oct, 1996; 1997 ($2.95)

nn-Wraparound-c, ...1997 ($2.99) -Original Avengers story 3.00

MARVEL HEROES FLIP MAGAZINE
Marvel Comics: Aug, 2005 - No. 26, Sept, 2007 ($3.99/$4.99)

1-11-Reprints New Avengers and Captain America (2005 series) in flip format thru #13 4.00
12-26: 14-19-Reprints New Avengers and Young Avengers in flip format. 20-Ghost Rider 5.00

MARVEL HOLIDAY SPECIAL
Marvel Comics: No. 1, 1991 ($2.25, 84 pgs.) - Present

1-X-Men, Fantastic Four, Punisher, Thor, Capt. America, Ghost Rider, Capt. Ultra, Spidey stories; Art Adams-c/a 3.00
nn (1/93)-Wolverine, Thanos (by Starlin/Lim/Austin) 3.00
nn (1994)-Capt. America, X-Men, Silver Surfer 3.00
...1996-Spider-Man by Waid & Olliffe; X-Men, Silver Surfer 3.00
...2004-Spider-Man by DeFalco & Miyazawa; X-Men, Fantastic Four 3.00
...2004 TPB ($15.99) r/M.H.S. 2004 & past Christmas-themed stories 16.00

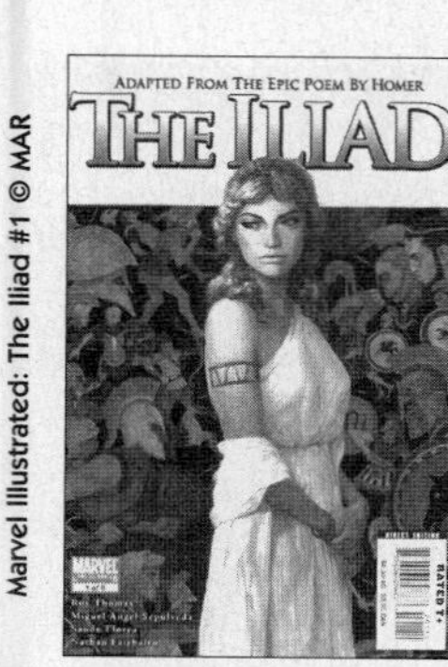
Marvel Illustrated: The Iliad #1 © MAR

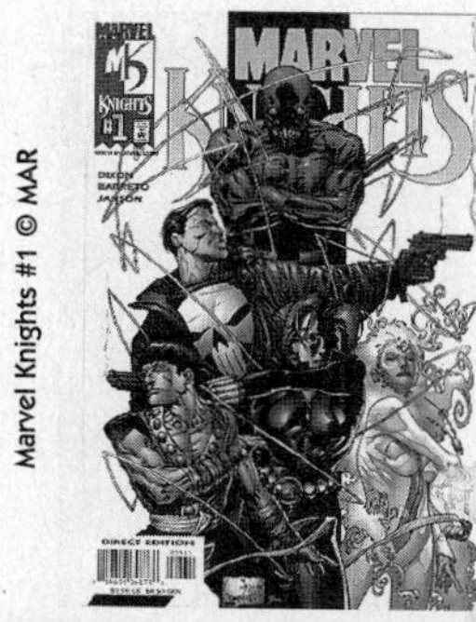
Marvel Knights #1 © MAR

Marvel Masterpieces Collection #4 © MAR

GD VG FN VF VF/NM NM-
2.0 4.0 6.0 8.0 9.0 9.2

1 (1/06, $3.99) new Christmas-themed stories by various; Immonen-c 4.00
....2006 (2/07, $3.99) Fin Fang Foom, Hydra, AIM app.; gallery of past covers; Irving-c 4.00
....2007 (2/08, $3.99) Spider-Man & Wolverine stories; Hembeck-a 4.00
Marvel Holiday (2006, $7.99, digest) reprints from M.H.S. 2004, 2006 & TPB 8.00
Marvel Holiday Spectacular Magazine (2009, $9.99, magazine) reprints from M.H.S. '93, '94, & Amazing Spider-Man #166; and new material w/Doe, Semeiks & Nauck-a 10.00
NOTE: ***Art Adams** c-'93. **Golden** a-'93. **Perez** c-'94.*

MARVEL ILLUSTRATED...
Marvel Comics: 2007 ($2.99)

...Jungle Book - reprints from Marvel Fanfare #8-11; Gil Kane-s/a(p); P. Craig Russell-i 3.00

MARVEL ILLUSTRATED: KIDNAPPED (Title changes to Kidnapped with #5)
Marvel Comics: Jan, 2009 - No. 5, May, 2009 ($3.99, limited series)

1-5-Adaptation of the Stevenson novel; Roy Thomas-s/Mario Gully-a/Parel-c 4.00

MARVEL ILLUSTRATED: LAST OF THE MOHICANS
Marvel Comics: July, 2007 - No. 6, Dec, 2007 ($2.99, limited series)

1-6-Adaptation of the Cooper novel; Roy Thomas-s/Steve Kurth-a. 1-Jo Chen-c 3.00
HC (2008, $19.99) r/#1-6 20.00

MARVEL ILLUSTRATED: MOBY DICK
Marvel Comics: Apr, 2008 - No. 6, Sept, 2008 ($2.99, limited series)

1-6-Adaptation of the Melville novel; Roy Thomas-s/Alixe-a/Watson-c 3.00

MARVEL ILLUSTRATED: PICTURE OF DORIAN GRAY
Marvel Comics: Jan, 2008 - No. 6, July, 2008 ($2.99, limited series)

1-6-Adaptation of the Wilde novel; Roy Thomas-s/Fiumara-a. 1-Parel-c 3.00

MARVEL ILLUSTRATED: SWIMSUIT ISSUE (Also see Marvel Swimsuit Special)
Marvel Comics: 1991 ($3.95, magazine, 52 pgs.)

V1#1-Parody of Sports Illustrated swimsuit issue; Mary Jane Parker centerfold pin-up by Jusko; 2nd print exists 1 3 4 6 8 10

MARVEL ILLUSTRATED: THE ILIAD
Marvel Comics: Feb, 2008 - No. 8, Sept, 2008 ($2.99, limited series)

1-8-Adaptation of Homer's Epic Poem; Roy Thomas-s/Sepulveda-a/Rivera-c 3.00

MARVEL ILLUSTRATED: THE MAN IN THE IRON MASK
Marvel Comics: Sept, 2007 - No. 6, Feb, 2008 ($2.99, limited series)

1-6-Adaptation of the Dumas novel; Roy Thomas-s/Hugo Petrus-a. 1-Djurdjevic-c 3.00
HC (2008, $19.99) r/#1-6 20.00

MARVEL ILLUSTRATED: THE ODYSSEY (Title changes to The Odyssey with #7)
Marvel Comics: Nov, 2008 - No. 8, June, 2009 ($3.99, limited series)

1-8-Adaptation of Homer's Epic Poem; Roy Thomas-s/Greg Tocchini-a/c 4.00

MARVEL ILLUSTRATED: THE THREE MUSKETEERS
Marvel Comics: Aug, 2008 - No. 6, Jan, 2009 ($3.99, limited series)

1-6-Adaptation of the Dumas novel; Roy Thomas-s/Hugo Petrus-a/Parel-c 4.00

MARVEL ILLUSTRATED: TREASURE ISLAND
Marvel Comics: Aug, 2007 - No. 6, Jan, 2008 ($2.99, limited series)

1-6-Adaptation of the Stevenson novel; Roy Thomas-s/Mario Gully-a/Greg Hildebrandt-c 3.00
HC (2008, $19.99) r/#1-6 20.00

MARVEL KNIGHTS (See Black Panther, Daredevil, Inhumans, & Punisher)
Marvel Comics: 1998 (Previews for upcoming series)

Sketchbook-Wizard suppl.; Quesada & Palmiotti-c 3.00
Tourbook-($2.99) Interviews and art previews 3.00

MARVEL KNIGHTS
Marvel Comics: July, 2000 - No. 15, Sept, 2001 ($2.99)

1-Daredevil, Punisher, Black Widow, Shang-Chi, Dagger app. 4.00
2-15: 2-Two covers by Barreto & Quesada 3.00
.../Marvel Boy Genesis Edition (6/00) Sketchbook preview 2.50
...: Millennial Visions (2/02, $3.99) Pin-ups by various; Harris-c 4.00

MARVEL KNIGHTS (Volume 2)
Marvel Comics: May, 2002 - No. 6, Oct, 2002 ($2.99)

1-6-Daredevil, Punisher, Black Widow app.; Ponticelli-a 3.00

MARVEL KNIGHTS: DOUBLE SHOT
Marvel Comics: June, 2002 - No. 4, Sept, 2002 ($2.99, limited series)

1-4: 1-Punisher by Ennis & Quesada; Daredevil by Haynes; Fabry-c 3.00

MARVEL KNIGHTS 4 (Fantastic Four) (Issues #1&2 are titled **Knights 4**) (#28-30 titled **Four**)
Marvel Comics: Apr, 2004 - No. 30, July, 2006 ($2.99)

1-30: 1-7-McNiven-c/a; Aguirre-Sacasa-a. 8,9-Namor app. 13-Cho-c. 14-Land-c. 21-Flashback meeting with Black Panther. 30-Namor app. 3.00

GD VG FN VF VF/NM NM-
2.0 4.0 6.0 8.0 9.0 9.2

...Vol. 1: The Wolf at the Door (2004, $16.99, TPB) r/#1-7 17.00
...Vol. 2: The Stuff of Nightmares (2005, $13.99, TPB) r/#8-12 14.00
...Vol. 3: Divine Time (2005, $14.99, TPB) r/#13-18 15.00
...Vol. 4: Impossible Things Happen Every Day (2006, $14.99, TPB) r/#19-24 15.00
Fantastic Four: The Resurrection of Nicholas Scratch TPB (2006, $14.99) r/#25-30 15.00

MARVEL KNIGHTS MAGAZINE
Marvel Comics: May, 2001 - No. 6, Oct, 2001 ($3.99, magazine size)

1-6-Reprints of recent Daredevil, Punisher, Black Widow, Inhumans 4.00

MARVEL KNIGHTS SPIDER-MAN (Title continues in Sensational Spider-Man #23)
Marvel Comics: Jun, 2004 - No. 22, Mar, 2006 ($2.99)

1-Wraparound-c by Dodson; Millar-s/Dodson-a; Green Goblin app. 3.00
2-12: 2-Avengers app. 2,3-Vulture & Electro app. 5,8-Cho-c/a. 6-8-Venom app. 3.00
13-18-Reginald Hudlin-s/Billy Tan-a. 13,14,18-New Avengers app. 15-Punisher app. 3.00
19-22-The Other x-over pts. 2,5,8,11; Pat Lee-a 3.00
19-22-var-c: 19-Black costume. 20-Scarlet Spider. 21-Spider-Armor. 22-Peter Parker 5.00
... Vol. 1 HC (2005, $29.99, over-sized with d.j.) r/#1-12; Stan Lee intro.; Dodson & Cho sketch pages 30.00
... Vol. 1: Down Among the Dead Men (2004, $9.99, TPB) r/#1-4 10.00
... Vol. 2: Venomous (2005, $9.99, TPB) r/#5-8 10.00
... Vol. 3: The Last Stand (2005, $9.99, TPB) r/#9-12 10.00
... Vol. 4: Wild Blue Yonder (2005, $14.99, TPB) r/#13-18 15.00

MARVEL KNIGHTS 2099
Marvel Comics: 2005 ($13.99, TPB)

nn-Reprints one shots: Daredevil 2099, Punisher 2099, Black Panther 2099, Inhumans 2099 and Mutant 2099; Pat Lee-c 14.00

MARVEL LEGACY: ...
Marvel Comics: 2006, 2007 ($4.99, one-shots)

... The 1960s Handbook - Profiles of 1960s iconic and minor characters; info thru 1969 5.00
... The 1970s Handbook - Profiles of 1970s iconic and minor characters; info thru 1979 5.00
... The 1980s Handbook - Profiles of 1980s iconic and minor characters; info thru 1989 5.00
... The 1990s Handbook - Profiles of 1990s iconic and minor characters; Lim-c 5.00
...: The 1960s-1990s Handbook TPB (207, $19.99) r/one-shots 20.00

MARVEL MANGAVERSE:... (one-shots)
Marvel Comics: March, 2002 ($2.25, manga-inspired one-shots)

Avengers Assemble! - Udon Studio-s/a 2.50
Eternity Twilight ($3.50) - Ben Dunn-s/a/wrap-around-c 3.50
Fantastic Four - Adam Warren-s/Keron Grant-a 2.50
Ghost Riders - Chuck Austen-s/a 2.50
Punisher - Peter David-s/Lea Hernandez-a 2.50
Spider-Man - Kaare Andrews-s/a 2.50
X-Men - C.B. Cebulski-s/Jeff Matsuda-a 2.50

MARVEL MANGAVERSE (Manga series)
Marvel Comics: June, 2002 - No. 6, Nov., 2002 ($2.25)

1-6: 1-Ben Dunn-s/a; intro. manga Captain Marvel 2.50
Vol. 1 TPB (2002, $24.95) r/one-shots 25.00
Vol. 2 TPB (2002, $12.99) r/#1-6 13.00
Vol. 3: Spider-Man-Legend of the Spider-Clan (2003, $11.99, TPB) r/series 12.00

MARVEL MASTERPIECES COLLECTION, THE
Marvel Comics: May, 1993 - No. 4, Aug, 1993 ($2.95, coated paper, lim. series)

1-4-Reprints Marvel Masterpieces trading cards w/ new Jusko paintings in each; Jusko painted-c/a 3.00

MARVEL MASTERPIECES 2 COLLECTION, THE
Marvel Comics: July, 1994 - No. 3, Sept, 1994 ($2.95, limited series)

1-3: 1-Kaluta-c; r/trading cards; new Steranko centerfold 3.00

MARVEL MILESTONE EDITION
Marvel Comics: 1991 - 1999 ($2.95, coated stock)(r/originals with original ads w/silver ink-c)

...: X-Men #1-Reprints X-Men #1 (1991) 3.00
...: Giant Size X-Men #1-(1991, $3.95, 68 pgs.) 4.00
...: Fantastic Four #1 (11/91), ...: Incredible Hulk #1 (3/92, says 3/91 by error), ...: Amazing Fantasy #15 (3/92), ...: Fantastic Four #5 (11/92), ...: Amazing Spider-Man #129 (11/92), ...: Iron Man #55 (11/92), ...: Iron Fist #14 (11/92), ...: Amazing Spider-Man #1 (1/93), ...: Amazing Spider-Man #1 (1/93) variation- no price on-c, ...: Tales of Suspense #39 (3/93), ...: Avengers #1 (9/93), ...: X-Men #9 (10/93), ...: Avengers #16 (10/93), ...:Amazing Spider-Man #149 (11/94, $2.95), ...:X-Men #28 (11/94, $2.95) 3.00
...:Captain America #1 (3/95, $3.95) 4.00
...:Amazing Spider-Man #3 (3/95, $2.95), ...:Avengers #4 (3/95, $2.95), ...:Strange Tales-r/Dr. Strange stories from #110, 111, 114, & 115 3.00
....:Hulk #181 (8/99, $2.99) 3.00

Marvel Milestones : Iron Man, Ant-Man and Captain America © MAR

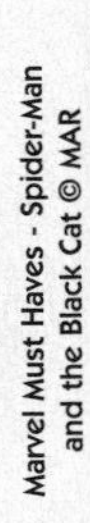
Marvel Must Haves - Spider-Man and the Black Cat © MAR

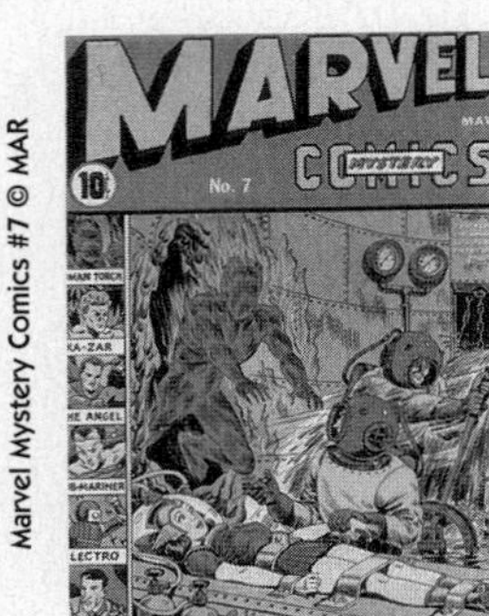

Marvel Mystery Comics #7 © MAR

GD 2.0 | VG 4.0 | FN 6.0 | VF 8.0 | VF/NM 9.0 | NM- 9.2

GD 2.0 | VG 4.0 | FN 6.0 | VF 8.0 | VF/NM 9.0 | NM- 9.2

MARVEL MILESTONES
Marvel Comics: 2005 - Present ($3.99, coated stock)(r/originals w/silver ink-c)

...: Beast & Kitty Pryde-r/from Amazing Adventures #11 & Uncanny X-Men #153 4.00
...: Black Panther, Storm & Ka-Zar-r/from Black Panther #26, Marvel Team-Up #100 and Marvel Mystery Comics #7 4.00
...: Blade, Man-Thing & Satana-r/from Tomb of Dracula #10, Adv. Into Fear #16 and Vampire Tales #2 4.00
...: Captain Britain, Psylocke & Sub-Mariner-r/from Spect. Spidey #114, Uncanny X-Men #213 and Human Torch #2 4.00
...: Doom, Sub-Mariner & Red Skull -r/from FF Ann. #2, Sub-Mariner Comics #1, Captain America Comics #1 4.00
...: Dragon Lord, Speedball and The Man in the Sky -r/from Marvel Spotlight #5, Speedball #1 and Amazing Adult Fantasy #14; Ditko-a on all 4.00
...: Dr. Strange, Silver Surfer, Sub-Mariner, & Hulk -r/from Marvel Premiere #3, FF Ann. #5, Marvel Comics #1, Incredible Hulk #3 4.00
...: Ghost Rider, Black Widow & Iceman -r/from Marvel Spotlight #5, Daredevil #81, X-Men #47 4.00
...: Iron Man, Ant-Man & Captain America -r/from TOS #39,40, TTA #27, Capt. America #1 4.00
...: Legion of Monsters, Spider-Man and Brother Voodoo -r/Marvel Premiere #28 & others 4.00
...: Millie the Model & Patsy Walker-r/from Millie the Model #100, Defenders #65 4.00
...: Onslaught -r/Onslaught: Marvel; wraparound-c 4.00
...: Rawhide Kid & Two-Gun Kid-r/Two-Gun Kid #60 and Rawhide Kid #17 4.00
...: Special: Bloodstone, X-51 & Captain Marvel II ($4.99) -r/from Marvel Presents #1, Machine Man #1, Amazing Spider-Man Ann. #19, and Bloodstone #1 5.00
...: Star Brand & Quasar -r/from Star Brand #1 & Quasar #1 4.00
...: Ultimate Spider-Man, Ult. X-Men, Microman & Mantor -r/from Ultimate Spider-Man #1/2, Ultimate X-Men #1/2 and Human Torch #2 4.00
...: Venom & Hercules -r/Marvel S-H Secret Wars #8, Journey Into Mystery Ann. #1 4.00
...: Wolverine, X-Men & Tuk: Caveboy -r/from Marvel Comics Presents #1, Uncanny X-Men #201, Capt. America Comics #1,2 4.00
...: (Jim Lee and Chris Claremont) X-Men and the Starjammers Pt. 1 -r/Unc. X-Men #275 4.00
...: X-Men and the Starjammers Pt. 2 -r/Unc. X-Men #276,277 4.00

MARVEL MINI-BOOKS (See Promotional Comics section)

MARVEL MONSTERS:... (one-shots)
Marvel Comics: Dec, 2005 ($3.99)

...Devil Dinosaur 1 - Hulk app.; Eric Powell-c/a; Sniegoski-s; r/Journey Into Mystery #62 4.00
...Fin Fang Four 1 - FF app.; Powell-c; Langridge-s/Gray-a; r/Strange Tales #89 4.00
...From the Files of Ulysses Bloodstone 1 - Guide to classic Marvel monsters; Powell-c 4.00
...Monsters on the Prowl 1 - Niles-s/Fegredo-a/Powell-c; Thing, Hulk, Giant-Man & Beast app. 4.00
...Where Monsters Dwell 1 - Giffen-s/a; David-s/Pander-a; Parker-s/Braun-s; Powell-c 4.00
HC (2006, $20.99, dust jacket) r/one-shots 21.00

MARVEL MOVIE PREMIERE (Magazine)
Marvel Comics Group: Sept, 1975 (B&W, one-shot)

1-Burroughs' "The Land That Time Forgot" adapt. 2 4 6 9 13 16

MARVEL MOVIE SHOWCASE FEATURING STAR WARS
Marvel Comics Group: Nov, 1982 - No. 2, Dec, 1982 ($1.25, 68 pgs.)

1,2-Star Wars movie adaptation; reprints Star Wars #1-6 by Chaykin; 1-Reprints-c to Star Wars #1. 2-Stevens-r 4.00

MARVEL MOVIE SPOTLIGHT FEATURING RAIDERS OF THE LOST ARK
Marvel Comics Group: Nov, 1982 ($1.25, 68 pgs.)

1-Edited-r/Raiders of the Lost Ark #1-3; Buscema-c/a(p); movie adapt. 3.00

MARVEL MUST HAVES (Reprints of recent sold-out issues)
Marvel Comics: Dec, 2001 - Present ($2.99/$3.99/$4.99)

1,2,4-6: 1-r/Wolverine: Origin #1, Startling Stories: Banner #1, Tangled Web #4 and Cable #97. 2-Amazing Spider-Man #36 and others. 4-Truth #1, Capt. America V4 #1, and The Ultimates #1. 5-r/Ultimate War #1, Ult. X-Men #26, Ult Spider-Man #33. 6-Ult. Spider-Man #33-36 4.00
3-r/Call of Duty: The Brotherhood #1 & Daredevil #32,33 3.00
Amazing Spider-Man #30-32; Incredible Hulk #34-36; The Ultimates #1-3; Ultimate Spider-Man #1-3; Ultimate X-Men #1-3; (New) X-Men #114-116 each.... 4.00
NYX #1-3; NYX #4-5 with sketch & cover gallery; Ultimates 2 #1-3 each... 5.00
Spider-Man and the Black Cat #1-3; preview of #4 5.00

MARVEL MYSTERY COMICS (Formerly Marvel Comics) (Becomes Marvel Tales No. 93 on)
Timely /Marvel Comics (TP #2-17/TCI #18-54/MCI #55-92): No. 2, Dec, 1939 - No. 92, June, 1949 (Some material from #8-10 reprinted in 2004's Marvel 65th Anniversary Special #1)

2-(Rare)-American Ace begins, ends #3; Human Torch (blue costume) by Burgos, Sub-Mariner by Everett continue; 2 pg. origin recap of Human Torch 3150 6300 9450 23,600 44,300 65,000
3-New logo from Marvel pulp begins; 1st app. of television in comics? in Human Torch story (1/40) 1800 3600 5400 13,500 24,750 36,000
4-Intro. Electro, the Marvel of the Age (ends #19), The Ferret, Mystery Detective (ends #9); 1st Sub-Mariner-c by Schomburg; 2nd German swastika on-c of a comic (2/40); one month after Top-Notch Comics #2 1450 2900 4350 11,000 20,000 29,000
5 Classic Schomburg-c (Scarce) 2625 5250 7875 19,600 36,800 54,000
6,7: 6-Gustavson Angel story 919 1838 2757 6709 11,855 17,000
8-1st Human Torch & Sub-Mariner battle(6/40) 1300 2600 3900 9500 17,250 25,000
9-(Scarce)-Human Torch & Sub-Mariner battle (cover/story); classic-c 3600 7200 10,800 27,000 48,500 70,000
10-Human Torch & Sub-Mariner battle, conclusion; Terry Vance, the Schoolboy Sleuth begins, ends #57 1150 2300 3450 9000 16,000 23,000
11 411 822 1233 2877 5039 7200
12-Classic Kirby-c 443 886 1329 3234 5717 8200
13-Intro. & 1st app. The Vision by S&K (11/40); Sub-Mariner dons new costume, ends #15 595 1190 1785 4350 7675 11,000
14-16: 14-Shows-c to Human Torch #1 on-c (12/40). 15-S&K Vision, Gustavson Angel story 309 618 927 2163 3782 5400
17-Human Torch/Sub-Mariner team-up by Burgos/Everett; pin-up on back-c; shows-c to Human Torch #2 on-c 337 674 1011 2359 4130 5900
18 300 600 900 2010 3505 5000
19,20: 19-Origin Toro in text; shows-c to Sub-Mariner #1 on-c. 20-Origin The Angel in text 300 600 900 2040 3570 5100
21-The Patriot begins, (intro. in Human Torch #4 (#3)); not in #46-48; pin-up on back-c (7/41) 300 600 900 2010 3505 5000
22-25: 23-Last Gustavson Angel; origin The Vision in text. 24-Injury-to-eye story 300 600 900 1950 3375 4800
26-30: 27-Ka-Zar ends; last S&K Vision who battles Satan. 28-Jimmy Jupiter in the Land of Nowhere begins, ends #48; Sub-Mariner vs. The Flying Dutchman. 30-1st Japanese war-c 290 580 870 1856 3178 4500
31-33,35,36,38,39: 31-Sub-Mariner by Everett ends, resumes #84. 32-1st app. The Boboes 258 516 774 1651 2826 4000
34-Everett, Burgos, Martin Goodman, Funnies, Inc. office appear in story & battles Hitler; last Burgos Human Torch 284 568 852 1818 3109 4400
37-Classic Hitler-c 297 594 891 1901 3251 4600
40-Classic Zeppelin-c 290 580 870 1856 3178 4500
41-43,45,47 226 452 678 1446 2473 3500
44-Classic Super Plane-c 271 542 813 1734 2967 4200
46-Classic Hitler-c 265 530 795 1694 2897 4100
48-Last Vision; flag-c 232 464 696 1485 2543 3600
49-Origin Miss America 239 478 717 1530 2615 3700
50-Mary becomes Miss Patriot (origin) 226 452 678 1446 2473 3500
51-60: 54-Bondage-c 194 388 582 1242 2121 3000
61,62,64-Last German war-c 174 348 522 1114 1907 2700
63-Classic Hitler War-c; The Villainess Cat-Woman only app. 219 438 657 1402 2401 3400
65,66-Last Japanese War-c 174 348 522 1114 1907 2700
67-78: 74-Last Patriot. 75-Young Allies begin. 76-Ten Chapter Miss America serial begins, ends #85 127 254 381 807 1391 1975
79-New cover format; Super Villains begin on cover; last Angel 135 270 405 864 1482 2100
80-1st app. Capt. America in Marvel Comics 153 306 459 972 1674 2375
81-Captain America app. 126 252 378 806 1378 1950
82-Origin & 1st app. Namora (5/47); 1st Sub-Mariner/Namora team-up; Captain America app. 297 594 891 1901 3251 4600
83,85: 83-Last Young Allies. 85-Last Miss America; Blonde Phantom app. 115 230 345 730 1253 1775
84-Blonde Phantom begins (on-c of #84,88,89); Sub-Mariner by Everett begins; Captain America app. 153 306 459 972 1674 2375
86-Blonde Phantom i.d. revealed; Captain America app.; last Bucky app. 121 242 363 768 1322 1875
87-1st Capt. America/Golden Girl team-up; last Toro app. (8/48) 131 262 393 832 1429 2025
88-Golden Girl, Namora, & Sun Girl (1st in Marvel Comics) x-over; Captain America, Blonde Phantom app. 123 246 369 787 1344 1900
89-1st Human Torch/Sun Girl team-up; 1st Captain America solo; Blonde Phantom app. 121 242 363 768 1322 1875
90,91: 90-Blonde Phantom un-masked; Captain America app. 91-Capt. America app.; Blonde Phantom & Sub-Mariner end; early Venus app. (4/49) (scarce) 168 336 504 1075 1838 2600
92-Feature story on the birth of the Human Torch and the death of Professor Horton (his creator); 1st app. The Witness in Marvel Comics; Captain America app. (scarce) 331 662 993 2317 4059 5800
132 Pg. issue, B&W, 25¢ (1943-44)-printed in N. Y.; square binding, blank inside covers); has Marvel No. 33-c in color; contains Capt. America #18 & Marvel Mystery Comics #33; same contents as Captain America Annual (Less than 5 copies known to exist) 6000 12,000 18,000 36,000 - -

Marvel 1985 #2 © MAR

Marvel Premiere #32 © MAR

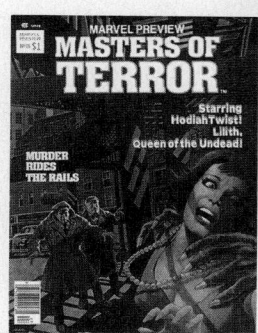

Marvel Preview #16 © MAR

GD 2.0 VG 4.0 FN 6.0 VF 8.0 VF/NM 9.0 NM- 9.2

132 Pg. issue (with variant contents), B&W, 25¢ (1942-'43)- square binding, blank inside covers; has same Marvel No. 33-c in color but contains Capt. America #22 & Marvel Mystery Comics #41 instead (possibly scarcer than other version)
(a VG+ copy sold in 2007 for $28,680 and a VG copy sold in 2009 for $19,120)

NOTE: **Brodsky** c-49, 72, 86, 88-92. **Crandall** a-26i. **Everett** c-7-9, 27, 84. **Gabrielle** c-30-32. **Schomburg** c-3-11, 13-29, 33-36, 39-48, 50-59, 63-69, 74, 76, 132 pg. issue. **Shores** c-37, 38, 75p, 77, 78p, 79p, 80, 81p, 82-84, 85p, 87p. **Sekowsky** c-73. Bondage covers-3, 4, 7, 12, 28, 29, 49, 50, 52, 56, 57, 58, 59, 65. Angel c-2, 3, 8, 12. Remember Pearl Harbor issues-#30-32.

MARVEL MYSTERY COMICS
Marvel Comics: Dec, 1999 ($3.95, reprints)

1-Reprints original 1940s stories; Schomburg-c from #74 — 4.00

MARVEL MYSTERY COMICS 70th ANNIVERARY SPECIAL
Marvel Comics: Jul, 2009 ($3.99, one-shot)

1-Rivera-c; new Sub-Mariner/Human Torch team-up set in 1941; reps. from #4 & 5 — 4.00

MARVEL MYSTERY HANDBOOK: 70th ANNIVERARY SPECIAL
Marvel Comics: 2009 ($4.99, one-shot)

1-Official Handbook-style profile pages of characters from Marvel's first year — 5.00

MARVEL NEMESIS: THE IMPERFECTS (EA Games characters)
Marvel Comics: July, 2005 - No. 6, Dec, 2005 ($2.99, limited series)

1-6-Jae Lee-c/Greg Pak-s/Renato Arlem-a; Spider-Man, Thing, Wolverine, Elektra app — 3.00
Digest (2005, $7.99) r/#1-6 — 3.00

MARVEL 1985
Marvel Comics: July, 2008 - No. 6, Dec, 2008 ($3.99, limited series)

1-6: 1-Marvel villains come to the real world; Millar-s/Edwards-a; three covers — 4.00
HC (2009, $24.99) r/#1-6; intro. by Lindelof; Edwards production art — 25.00

MARVEL NO-PRIZE BOOK, THE (The Official... on-c)
Marvel Comics Group: Jan, 1983 (one-shot, direct sales only)

1-Golden-c; Kirby-a — 4.00

MARVELOUS ADVENTURES OF GUS BEEZER
Marvel Comics: May, 2003; Feb, 2004 ($2.99, one-shots)

...: Gus Beezer & Spider-Man 1 - (5/03) Gurihiru-a — 3.00
...: Hulk 1 - (5/03) Simone-s/Lethcoe-a; She-Hulk app. — 3.00
...: Spider-Man 1 - (5/03) Simone-s/Lethcoe-a; The Lizard & Dr. Doom app. — 3.00
...: X-Men 1 - (5/03) Simone-s/Lethcoe-a — 3.00

MARVELOUS LAND OF OZ (Sequel to Wonderful Wizard of Oz)
Marvel Comics: Jan, 2010 - No. 8 ($3.99, limited series)

1-4-Eric Shanower-a/Skottie Young-a/c. 1-Two covers by Young — 4.00
1-Variant Pumpkinhead/Saw-Horse cover by McGuinness — 6.00

MARVEL PETS HANDBOOK (Also see "Lockjaw and the Pet Avengers")
Marvel Comics: 2009 ($3.99, one-shot)

1-Official Handbook-style profile pages of animal characters — 4.00

MARVEL PREMIERE
Marvel Comics Group: April, 1972 - No. 61, Aug, 1981 (A tryout book for new characters)

Issue	GD 2.0	VG 4.0	FN 6.0	VF 8.0	VF/NM 9.0	NM- 9.2
1-Origin Warlock (pre-#1) by Gil Kane/Adkins; origin Counter-Earth; Hulk & Thor cameo (#1-14 are 20¢-c)	7	14	21	49	80	110
2-Warlock ends; Kirby Yellow Claw-r	4	8	12	24	37	50
3-Dr. Strange series begins (pre #1, 7/72), B. Smith-c/a(p)	7	14	21	49	80	110
4-Smith/Brunner-a	4	8	12	22	34	45
5-9: 8-Starlin-c/a(p)	3	6	9	16	23	30
10-Death of the Ancient One	3	6	9	18	27	35
11-14: 11-Dr. Strange origin-r by Ditko. 14-Last Dr. Strange (3/74), gets own title 3 months later	2	4	6	11	16	20
15-Origin/1st app. Iron Fist (5/74), ends #25	9	18	27	63	107	150
16,25: 16-2nd app. Iron Fist; origin cont'd from #15; Hama's 1st Marvel-a. 25-1st Byrne Iron Fist (moves to own title next)	4	8	12	28	44	60
17-24: Iron Fist in all	3	6	9	20	30	40
26-Hercules.	2	4	6	8	10	12
27-Satana	2	4	6	9	12	15
28-Legion of Monsters (Ghost Rider, Man-Thing, Morbius, Werewolf)	3	6	9	18	27	35
29-46,49: 29,30-The Liberty Legion. 29-1st modern app. Patriot. 31-1st app. Woodgod; last 25¢ issue. 32-1st app. Monark Starstalker. 33,34-1st color app. Solomon Kane (Robert E. Howard adaptation "Red Shadows".) 35-Origin/1st app. 3-D Man. 36,37-3-D Man. 38-1st Weirdworld. 39,40-Torpedo. 41-1st Seeker 3000! 42-Tigra. 43-Paladin. 44-Jack of Hearts (1st solo book, 10/78). 45,46-Man-Wolf. 49-The Falcon (1st solo book, 8/79)						6.00
29-31-(30¢-c variants, limited distribution)(4,6,8/76)	2	4	6	11	16	20
36-38-(35¢-c variants, limited distribution)(6,8,10/77)	3	6	9	18	27	35
47,48-Byrne-a: 47-Origin/1st app. new Ant-Man. 48-Ant-Man	2	4	6	10	14	18
50-1st app. Alice Cooper; co-plotted by Alice	2	4	6	9	13	16
51-56,58-61: 51-53-Black Panther. 54-1st Caleb Hammer. 55-Wonder Man. 56-1st color app. Dominic Fortune. 58-60-Dr. Who. 61-Star Lord						5.00
57-Dr. Who (2nd U.S. app.-see Movie Classics)	1	2	3	5	6	8

NOTE: **N. Adams** (Crusty Bunkers) part inks-10, 12, 13. **Austin** a-50i, 56i; c-46i, 50i, 56i, 58. **Brunner** a-4i, 6p, 9-14p; c-9-14. **Byrne** a-47p, 48p. **Chaykin** a-32-34; c-32, 33, 56. **Giffen** a-31p, 44p; c-44. **Gil Kane** a(p)-1, 2, 15; c(p)-1, 2, 15, 16, 22-24, 27, 36, 37. **Kirby** c-26, 29-31, 35. **Layton** a-47i, 48i; c-47. **McWilliams** a-25i. **Miller** c-49p, 53p, 58p. **Nebres** a-44i; c-38i. **Nino** a-38i. **Perez** c/a-38p, 45p, 46p. **Ploog** a-38; c-5-7. **Russell** a-7p. **Simonson** a-60(2pgs.); c-57. **Starlin** a-8p; c-8. **Sutton** a-41, 43, 50p, 61; c-50p, 61. #57-60 publ'd w/two different prices on-c.

MARVEL PRESENTS
Marvel Comics: October, 1975 - No. 12, Aug, 1977 (#1-6 are 25¢ issues)

Issue	GD 2.0	VG 4.0	FN 6.0	VF 8.0	VF/NM 9.0	NM- 9.2
1-Origin & 1st app. Bloodstone	2	4	6	9	13	16
2-Origin Bloodstone continued; Kirby-c	2	3	4	6	8	10
3-Guardians of the Galaxy (1st solo book, 2/76) begins, ends #12	2	4	6	11	16	20
4-7,9-12: 9,10-Origin Starhawk	2	3	4	6	8	10
4-6-(30¢-c variants, limited distribution)(4-8/76)	3	6	9	16	23	30
8-r/story from Silver Surfer #2 plus 4 pgs. new-a	2	3	4	6	8	10
11,12-(35¢-c variants, limited distribution)(6,8/77)	4	8	12	24	37	50

NOTE: **Austin** a-6i. **Buscema** r-8p. **Chaykin** a-5p. **Kane** c-1p. **Starlin** layouts-10.

MARVEL PREVIEW (Magazine) (Bizarre Adventures #25 on)
Marvel Comics: Feb (no month), 1975 - No. 24, Winter, 1980 (B&W) ($1.00)

Issue	GD 2.0	VG 4.0	FN 6.0	VF 8.0	VF/NM 9.0	NM- 9.2
1-Man-Gods From Beyond the Stars; Crusty Bunkers (Neal Adams)-a(i) & cover; Nino-a	3	6	9	16	22	28
2-1st origin The Punisher (see Amaz. Spider-Man #129 & Classic Punisher); 1st app. Dominic Fortune; Morrow-c	10	20	30	73	129	185
3,8,10: 3-Blade the Vampire Slayer. 8-Legion of Monsters; Morbius app. 10-Thor the Mighty; Starlin frontispiece	3	6	9	17	25	32
4,5: 4-Star-Lord & Sword in the Star (origins & 1st app.). 5,6-Sherlock Holmes.	2	4	6	13	18	22
6,9: 6-Sherlock Holmes; N. Adams frontispiece. 9-Man-God; origin Star Hawk, ends #20	2	4	6	10	14	18
7-Satana, Sword in the Star app.	2	4	6	11	16	20
11,12,16,19: 11-Star-Lord; Byrne-a; Starlin frontispiece. 12-Haunt of Horror. 16-Masters of Terror. 19-Kull	2	4	6	8	10	12
13-15,17,18,20-24: 14,15-Star-Lord. 14-Starlin painted-c. 17-Blackmark by G. Kane (see SSOC #1-3). 18-Star-Lord; Sienkiewicz-a; Veitch & Bissette-a. 20-Bizarre Advs. 21-Moon Knight (Spr/80)-Predates Moon Knight #1; The Shroud by Ditko. 22-King Arthur. 23-Bizarre Advs.; Miller-a. 24-Debut Paradox	1	2	3	5	6	8

NOTE: **N. Adams** (C. Bunkers) r-20i. **Buscema** a-22, 23. **Byrne** a-11. **Chaykin** a-20r; c-20 (new). **Colan** a-8, 16p(3), 18p, 23p; c-16p. **Elias** a-18. **Giffen** a-7. **Infantino** a-14p. **Kaluta** a-12; c-15. **Miller** a-23. **Morrow** a-8i; c-2-4. **Perez** a-20p. **Ploog** a-8. **Starlin** c-13, 14. Nudity in some issues

MARVEL RIOT
Marvel Comics: Dec, 1995 ($1.95, one-shot)

1-"Age of Apocalypse" spoof; Lobdell script — 2.50

MARVEL ROMANCE
Marvel Comics: 2006 ($19.99, TPB)

nn-Reprints romance stories from 1960-1972; art by Kirby, Buscema, Colan, Romita — 20.00

MARVEL ROMANCE REDUX (Humor stories using art reprinted from Marvel romance comics)
Marvel Comics: Apr, 2006 - Aug, 2006 ($2.99, one-shots)

...: But I Thought He Loved Me Too (4/06) art by Kirby, Colan, Buscema & Romita; Giffen-c — 3.00
...: Guys & Dolls (5/06) art by Starlin, Heck, Colan & Buscema; Conner-c — 3.00
...: I Should Have Been a Blonde (7/06) art by Brodsky Colletta & Colan; Cho-c — 3.00
...: Love is a Four Letter Word (8/06) art by Kirby, Buscema, Colan & Heck; Land-c — 3.00
...: Restraining Orders are For Other Girls (6/06) art by Giordano, Kirby; Baker-c — 3.00
...: Another Kind of Love TPB (2007, $13.99) r/one-shots — 14.00

MARVELS (Also see Marvels: Eye of the Camera)
Marvel Comics: Jan, 1994 - No. 4, Apr, 1994 ($5.95, painted lim. series)
No. 1 (2nd Printing), Apr, 1996 - No. 4 (2nd Printing), July, 1996 ($2.95)

Issue	GD 2.0	VG 4.0	FN 6.0	VF 8.0	VF/NM 9.0	NM- 9.2
1-4: Kurt Busiek scripts & Alex Ross painted-c/a in all; double-c w/acetate overlay	1	2	3	5	6	8
Marvel Classic Collectors Pack ($11.90)-Issues #1 & 2 boxed (1st printings).	2	4	6	9	13	16
0-(8/94, $2.95)-no acetate overlay.						4.00
1-4-(2nd printing): r/original limited series w/o acetate overlay						3.00
Hardcover (1994, $59.95)-r/#0-4; w/intros by Stan Lee, John Romita, Sr., Kurt Busiek & Scott McCloud.						60.00
...: 10th Anniversary Edition (2004, $49.99, hardcover w/dustjacket) r/#0-4; scripts and commentaries; Ross sketch pages, cover gallery, behind the scenes art						50.00

Marvel Selects: Fantastic Four #6 © MAR

Marvel 1602: New World #1 © MAR

Marvel Spotlight: Captain America #1 © MAR

GD 2.0 | VG 4.0 | FN 6.0 | VF 8.0 | VF/NM 9.0 | NM- 9.2

Trade paperback ($19.95) 20.00

MARVEL SAGA, THE
Marvel Comics Group: Dec, 1985 - No. 25, Dec, 1987
1,21-25 2.50
2-20 2.50
NOTE: ***Williamson*** *a(i)-9, 10; c(i)-7, 10-12, 14, 16.*

MARVELS COMICS: ... (Marvel-type comics read in the Marvel Universe)
Marvel Comics: Jul, 2000 ($2.25, one-shots)
...Captain America #1 -Frenz & Sinnott-a; ...Daredevil #1 -Isabella-s/Newell-a; ...Fantastic Four #1 -Kesel-s/Paul Smith-a; Spider-Man #1 -Oliff-a; ...Thor #1 -Templeton-s/Aucoin-a 2.50
...X-Men #1 -Millar-s/ Sean Phillips & Duncan Fegredo-a 2.50
The History of Marvels Comics (no cover price)-Faux history; previews titles 2.50

MARVEL SELECT FLIP MAGAZINE
Marvel Comics: Aug, 2005 - Present ($3.99/$4.99)
1-11-Reprints Astonishing X-Men and New X-Men: Academy X in flip format 4.00
12-24-($4.99) Reprints recent X-Men mini-series in flip format 5.00

MARVEL SELECTS:
Marvel Comics: Jan, 2000 - No. 6, June, 2000 ($2.75/$2.99, reprints)
...Fantastic Four 1-6: Reprints F.F. #107-112; new Davis-c 2.75
...Spider-Man 1,2,4-6: Reprints AS-M #100,101,103,104,93; Wieringo-c 2.75
...Spider-Man 3 ($2.99): Reprints AS-M #102; new Wieringo-c 3.00

MARVELS: EYE OF THE CAMERA (Sequel to Marvels)
Marvel Comics: Feb, 2009 - No. 6, Apr, 2010 ($3.99, limited series)
1-6-Kurt Busiek-s/Jay Anacleto-a; continuing story of photographer Phil Sheldon 4.00
1-6-B&W edition 4.00

MARVEL'S GREATEST COMICS (Marvel Collectors' Item Classics #1-22)
Marvel Comics Group: No. 23, Oct, 1969 - No. 96, Jan, 1981
23-34 (Giants). Begin Fantastic Four-r/#30s?-116 3 6 9 17 25 32
35-37-Silver Surfer-r/Fantastic Four #48-50 2 4 6 8 11 14
38-50: 42-Silver Surfer-r/F.F.(others?) 1 2 3 5 7 9
51-70: 63,64-(25¢ editions) 6.00
63,64-(30¢-c variants, limited distribution)(5,7/76) 2 4 6 11 16 20
71-96: 71-73-(30¢ editions) 5.00
71-73-(35¢-c variants, limited distribution)(7,9-10/77) 3 6 9 18 27 35
...: Fantastic Four #52 (2006, $2.99) reprints entire comic with ads and letter column 3.00
NOTE: *Dr. Strange, Fantastic Four, Iron Man, Watcher-#23, 24. Capt. America, Dr. Strange, Iron Man, Fantastic Four-#25-28. Fantastic Four-#38-96.* ***Buscema*** *r-85-92; c-87-92r.* ***Ditko*** *r-23-28.* ***Kirby*** *r-23-82; c-75, 77p, 80p. #81 reprints Fantastic Four #100.*

MARVEL'S GREATEST SUPERHERO BATTLES (See Fireside Book Series)

MARVEL: SHADOWS AND LIGHT
Marvel Comics: Feb, 1997 ($2.95, B&W, one-shot)
1-Tony Daniel-c 3.00

MARVEL 1602
Marvel Comics: Nov, 2003 - No. 8, June, 2004 ($3.50, limited series)
1-8-Neil Gaiman-s; Andy Kubert & Richard Isanove-a 3.50
HC (2004, $24.99) r/series; script pages for #1, sketch pages and Gaiman afterword 25.00
SC (2005, $19.99) 20.00

MARVEL 1602: FANTASTICK FOUR
Marvel Comics: Nov, 2006 - No. 5, Mar, 2007s ($3.50, limited series)
1-5-Peter David-s/Pascal Alixe-a/Leinil Yu-c 3.50
TPB (2007, $14.99) r/#1-5; sketch page 15.00

MARVEL 1602: NEW WORLD
Marvel Comics: Oct, 2005 - No. 5, Jan, 2006 ($3.50, limited series)
1-5-Greg Pak-s/Greg Tocchini-a; "Hulk" and "Iron Man" app. 3.50
TPB (2006, $14.99) r/#1-5 15.00

MARVEL 65TH ANNIVERSARY SPECIAL
Marvel Comics: 2004 ($4.99, one-shot)
1-Reprints Sub-Mariner & Human Torch battle from Marvel Mystery Comics #8-10 5.00

MARVELS OF SCIENCE
Charlton Comics: March, 1946 - No. 4, June, 1946
1-A-Bomb story 23 46 69 136 223 310
2-4 14 28 42 80 115 150

MARVEL SPECIAL EDITION FEATURING... (Also see Special Collectors' Ed.)
Marvel Comics Group: 1975 - 1978 (84 pgs.) (Oversized)
1-The Spectacular Spider-Man ($1.50); r/Amazing Spider-Man #6,35, Annual 1; Ditko-a(r) 3 6 9 20 30 40
1,2-Star Wars ('77,'78; r/Star Wars #1-3 & #4-6; regular edition and Whitman variant exist 2 4 6 11 16 20
3-Star Wars ('78, $2.50, 116 pgs.); r/S. Wars #1-6; regular edition and Whitman variant exist 3 6 9 14 20 26
3-Close Encounters of the Third Kind (1978, $1.50, 56 pgs.)-Movie adaptation; Simonson-a(p) 2 4 6 10 14 18
V2#2(Spring, 1980, $2.00, oversized)- "Star Wars: The Empire Strikes Back"; r/Marvel Comics Super Special #16 3 6 9 16 23 30
NOTE: ***Chaykin*** *c/a(r)-1(1977), 2, 3.* ***Stevens*** *a(r)-2i, 3i.* ***Williamson*** *a(r)-V2#2.*

MARVEL SPECTACULAR
Marvel Comics Group: Aug, 1973 - No. 19, Nov, 1975
1-Thor-r from mid-sixties begin by Kirby 2 4 6 8 11 14
2-19 1 2 3 5 6 8

MARVELS: PORTRAITS
Marvel Comics: Mar, 1995 - No. 4, June, 1995 ($2.95, limited series)
1-4:Different artists renditions of Marvel characters 3.00

MARVEL SPOTLIGHT (...& Son of Satan #19, 20, 23, 24)
Marvel Comics Group: Nov, 1971 - No. 33, Apr, 1977; V2#1, July, 1979 - V2#11, Mar, 1981
(A try-out book for new characters)
1-Origin Red Wolf (western hero)(1st solo book, pre-#1); Wood inks, Neal Adams-c; only 15¢ issue 6 12 18 37 59 80
2-(25¢, 52 pgs.)-Venus-r by Everett; origin/1st app. Werewolf By Night (begins) by Ploog; N. Adams-c 19 38 57 139 270 400
3,4: 4-Werewolf By Night ends (6/72); gets own title 9/72 7 14 21 45 73 100
5-Origin/1st app. Ghost Rider (8/72) & begins 24 48 72 175 338 500
6-8: 6-Origin G.R. retold. 8-Last Ploog issue 8 16 24 52 86 120
9-11-Last Ghost Rider (gets own title next mo.) 6 12 18 41 66 90
12-Origin & 2nd full app. The Son of Satan (10/73); story cont'd from Ghost Rider #2 & into #3; series begins, ends #24 4 8 12 26 41 55
13-24: 13-Partial origin Son of Satan. 14-Last 20¢ issue. 22-Ghost Rider-c & cameo (5 panels). 24-Last Son of Satan (10/75); gets own title 12/75 2 4 6 9 12 15
25,27,30,31: 27-(Regular 25¢-c), Sub-Mariner app. 30-The Warriors Three. 31-Nick Fury 6.00
26-Scarecrow 1 3 4 6 8 10
27-(30¢-c variant, limited distribution) 2 4 6 13 18 22
28-(Regular 25¢-c) 1st solo Moon Knight app. 3 6 9 20 30 40
28-(30¢-c variant, limited distribution) 8 16 24 54 90 125
29,32: 29-(Regular 25¢-c) (8/76) Moon Knight app.; last 25¢ issue. 32-1st app./partial origin Spider-Woman (2/77); Nick Fury app. 3 6 9 16 22 28
29-(30¢-c variant, limited distribution) 6 12 18 41 66 90
33-Deathlok; 1st app. Devil-Slayer 2 3 4 6 8 10
V2#1-7,9-11: 1-4-Capt. Marvel. 5-Dragon Lord. 6,7-StarLord; origin #6. 9-11-Capt. Universe (see Micronauts #8) 4.00
1-Variant copy missing issue #1 on cover 2 4 6 9 12 15
8-Capt. Marvel; Miller-c/a(p) 1 2 3 5 6 8
NOTE: ***Austin*** *c-V2#2i, 8.* ***J. Buscema*** *c/a-30p.* ***Chaykin*** *a-31; c-26, 31.* ***Colan*** *a-18p, 19p.* ***Ditko*** *a-V2#4, 5, 9-11; c-V2#4, 9-11.* ***Kane*** *c-21p, 32p.* ***Kirby*** *c-29p.* ***McWilliams*** *a-20i.* ***Miller*** *a-V2#8p; c(p)-V2#2, 5, 7, 8.* ***Mooney*** *a-8i, 10i, 14p, 15, 16p, 17p, 24p, 27, 32i.* ***Nasser*** *a-33p.* ***Ploog*** *a-2-5, 6-8p; c-3-9.* ***Romita*** *c-13.* ***Sutton*** *a-9-11p, V2#6, 7. #29-25¢ & 30¢ issues exist.*

MARVEL SPOTLIGHT (Most issues spotlight one Marvel artist and one Marvel writer)
Marvel Comics: 2005 - Present ($2.99/$3.99)
...Brian Bendis/Mark Bagley; Daniel Way/Olivier Coipel; David Finch/Roberto Aguirre-Sacasa; Ed Brubaker/Billy Tan; John Cassaday/Sean McKeever; Joss Whedon/Michael Lark; Laurell K. Hamilton/George R.R. Martin; Neil Gaiman/Salvador Larroca; Robert Kirkman/Greg Land; Stan Lee/Jack Kirby; Warren Ellis/Jim Cheung each... 3.00
...Steve McNiven/Mark Millar - Civil War 10.00
...: Captain America (2009) interviews with Brubaker & Hitch; Reborn preview 3.00
...: Captain America Remembered (2007) character features; creator interviews 3.00
...: Civil War Aftermath (2007) Top 10 Moments, casualty list, previews of upcoming series 3.00
...: Dark Reign (2009) features on the Avengers, Fury and others; creator interview 4.00
...: Dark Tower (2007) previews the Stephen King adaptation; creator interviews 5.00
...: Deadpool (2009) character features; interviews with Kelly, Way, Medina & Benson 3.00
...: Fantastic Four and Silver Surfer (2007) character features; creator interviews 3.00
...: Ghost Rider (2007) character and movie features; creator interviews 3.00
...: Halo (2007) a World of Halo feature; Bendis & Maleev interviews 3.00
...: Heroes Reborn/Onslaught Reborn (2006) 3.00
...: Hulk Movie (2008) character and movie features; comic & movie creator interviews 3.00
...: Iron Man Movie (2008) character and movie features; Terrence Howard interview 3.00
...: Iron Man 2 (4/10) movie preview; Granov, Fraction interviews; Whiplash profile 4.00
...: Marvel Knights 10th Anniversary (2008) Quesada interview; series synopsies 3.00
...: Marvel Zombies/Mystic Arcana (2008) character features; creator interviews 3.00
...: Marvel Zombies Return (2009) character features; creator interviews 3.00

Marvel Super-Heroes #71 © MAR

Marvel Super Hero Squad #1 © MAR

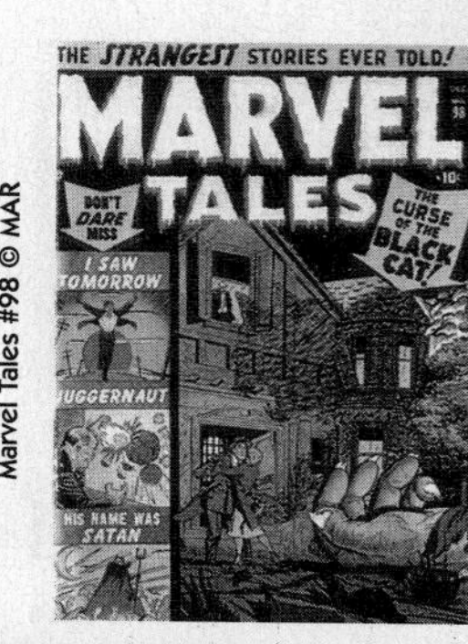

Marvel Tales #98 © MAR

GD VG FN VF VF/NM NM-
2.0 4.0 6.0 8.0 9.0 9.2

...: New Mutants (2009) character features; Claremont & McLeod interviews 3.00
...: Punisher Movie (2008) character and movie features; creator interviews 3.00
...: Secret Invasion (2008) features on the Skrulls; Bendis, Reed & Yu interviews 3.00
...: Secret Invasion Aftermath (2008) Skrull profiles; Bendis, Reed & Diggle interviews 4.00
...: Spider-Man (2007) character features; creator interviews; Ditko art showcase 3.00
...: Spider-Man - Brand New Day (2008) storyline features; Romitas interviews 3.00
...: Spider-Man-One More Day/Brand New Day (2008) storyline features; interviews 3.00
...: Summer Events (2009, $3.99) 2009 title previews; creator interviews 4.00
...: Thor (2007) character features; Straczynski interview; Romita Jr. art showcase 3.00
...: Ultimates 3 (2008) character features; Loeb & Madureira interviews 3.00
...: Ultimatum (2008) previews the limited series; Loeb & Bendis interviews 3.00
...: Uncanny X-Men 500 Issues Celebration (2008) creator interviews; timeline 3.00
...: War of Kings (2009) character features; Abnett, Lanning, Pelletier interviews 3.00
...: Wolverine (2009, $3.99) preview of 2009 Wolverine stories; creator interviews 4.00
...: World War Hulk (2007) character features; creator interviews; early art showcase 3.00
...: X-Men: Messiah Complex (2008) X-Men crossover features; creator interviews 3.00

MARVELS PROJECT, THE
Marvel Comics: Oct, 2009 - No. 8 ($3.99, limited series)

1-7-Emergence of Marvel heroes in 1939-40; Brubaker-s/Epting-a; Epting & McNiven-c 4.00
1-7-Variant covers by Parel 10.00

MARVEL SUPER ACTION (Magazine)
Marvel Comics Group: Jan, 1976 (B&W, 76 pgs.)

1-2nd app. Dominic Fortune (see Marvel Preview); early Punisher app.; Weird World & The Huntress; Evans, Ploog-a 8 16 24 54 90 125

MARVEL SUPER ACTION
Marvel Comics Group: May, 1977 - No. 37, Nov, 1981

1-Reprints Capt. America #100 by Kirby 2 4 6 8 11 14
2-13: 2,3,5-13 reprint Capt. America #101,102,103-111. 4-Marvel Boy-r(origin)/M. Boy #1. 11-Origin-r. 12,13-Classic Steranko-c/a(r). 1 2 3 5 7 9
2,3-(35¢-c variants, limited distribution)(6,8/77) 4 8 12 22 34 45
14-20: r/Avengers #55,56, Annual 2, others 6.00
21-37: 30-r/Hulk #6 from U.K. 5.00

NOTE: ***Buscema*** *a(r)-14p, 15p; c-18-20, 22, 35r-37.* ***Everett*** *a-4.* ***Heath*** *a-4r.* ***Kirby*** *r-1-3, 5-11.* ***B. Smith*** *a-27r, 28r.* ***Steranko*** *a(r)-12p, 13p; c-12r, 13r.*

MARVEL SUPER HERO CONTEST OF CHAMPIONS
Marvel Comics Group: June, 1982 - No. 3, Aug, 1982 (Limited series)

1-3: Features nearly all Marvel characters currently appearing in their comics; 1st Marvel limited series 1 2 3 5 6 8

MARVEL SUPER HEROES
Marvel Comics Group: October, 1966 (25¢, 68 pgs.) (1st Marvel one-shot)

1-r/origin Daredevil from D.D. #1; r/Avengers #2; G.A. Sub-Mariner-r/Marvel Mystery #8 (Human Torch app.). Kirby-a 11 22 33 78 139 200

MARVEL SUPER-HEROES (Formerly Fantasy Masterpieces #1-11)
(Also see Giant-Size Super Heroes) (#12-20: 25¢, 68 pgs.)
Marvel Comics: No. 12, 12/67 - No. 31, 11/71; No. 32, 9/72 - No. 105, 1/82

12-Origin & 1st app. Capt. Marvel of the Kree; G.A. Human Torch, Destroyer, Capt. America, Black Knight, Sub-Mariner-r (#12-20 all contain new stories and reprints) 13 26 39 90 165 240
13-2nd app. Capt. Marvel; G.A. Black Knight, Torch, Vision, Capt. America, Sub-Mariner-r 8 16 24 52 86 120
14-Amazing Spider-Man (5/68, new-a by Andru/Everett); G.A. Sub-Mariner, Torch, Mercury (1st Kirby-a at Marvel), Black Knight, Capt. America reprints 10 20 30 70 123 175
15-17: 15-Black Bolt cameo in Medusa (new-a); Black Knight, Sub-Mariner, Black Marvel, Capt. America-r. 16-Origin & 1st app. S. A. Phantom Eagle; G.A. Torch, Capt. America, Black Knight, Patriot, Sub-Mariner-r. 17-Origin Black Knight (new-a); G.A. Torch, Sub-Mariner-r; reprint from All-Winners Squad #21 (cover & story) 5 10 15 30 48 65
18-Origin/1st app. Guardians of the Galaxy (1/69); G.A. Sub-Mariner, All-Winners Squad-r 7 14 21 47 76 105
19-Ka-Zar (new-a); G.A. Torch, Marvel Boy, Black Knight, Sub-Mariner reprints; Smith-c(p); Tuska-a(r) 4 8 12 24 37 50
20-Doctor Doom (5/69); r/Young Men #24 w/-c 4 8 12 28 44 60
21-31: All-r issues. 21-X-Men, Daredevil, Iron Man-r begin, end #31. 31-Last Giant issue 3 6 9 16 22 28
32-50: 32-Hulk/Sub-Mariner-r begin from TTA. 1 2 3 5 7 9
51-70,100: 56-r/origin Hulk/Inc. Hulk #102; Hulk-r begin 6.00
57,58-(30¢-c variants, limited distribution)(5,7/76) 2 4 6 11 16 20
65,66-(35¢-c variants, limited distribution)(7,9/77) 3 6 9 17 25 32
71-99,101-105 4.00

NOTE: ***Austin*** *a-104.* ***Colan*** *a(p)-12, 13, 15, 18; c-12, 13, 15, 18.* ***Everett*** *a-14i(new); r-14, 15i, 18, 19, 33; c-85(r). New* ***Kirby*** *c-22, 27, 54.* ***Maneely*** *r-14, 15, 19.* ***Severin*** *r-83-85i, 100-102; c-100-102r.* ***Starlin*** *c-47.* ***Tuska*** *a-19p. Black Knight-r by* ***Maneely*** *in 12-16, 19. Sub-Mariner-r by* ***Everett*** *in 12-20.*

GD VG FN VF VF/NM NM-
2.0 4.0 6.0 8.0 9.0 9.2

MARVEL SUPER-HEROES
Marvel Comics: May, 1990 - V2#15, Oct, 1993 ($2.95/$2.50, quart., 68-84 pgs.)

1-Moon Knight, Hercules, Black Panther, Magik, Brother Voodoo, Speedball (by Ditko) & Hellcat; Hembeck-a 3.00
2,4,5,V2#3,6-15: 2-Summer Special(7/90); Rogue, Speedball (by Ditko), Iron Man, Falcon, Tigra & Daredevil. 4-Spider-Man/Nick Fury, Daredevil,Speedball, Wonder Man, Spitfire & Black Knight; Byrne-c. 5-Thor, Dr. Strange, Thing & She-Hulk; Speedball by Ditko(p). V2#3-Retells origin Capt. America w/new facts; Blue Shield, Capt. Marvel,Speedball, Wasp; Hulk by Ditko/Rogers V2#6-9: 6-8-$2.25-c. 6,7-X-Men, Cloak & Dagger, The Shroud (by Ditko) & Marvel Boy in each. 8-X-Men, Namor & Iron Man (by Ditko); Larsen-c. 9-West Coast Avengers, Iron Man app.; Kieth-c(p). V2#10-Ms. Marvel/Sabretooth-c/story (intended for Ms. Marvel #24; shows-c to #24); Namor, Vision, Scarlet Witch stories. V2#11,12 :11-Original Ghost Rider-c/story; Giant-Man, Ms. Marvel stories. 12-Dr. Strange, Falcon, Iron Man. V2#13-15 ($2.75, 84 pgs.): 13-All Iron Man 30th anniversary. 15-Iron Man/Thor/Volstagg/Dr. Druid 2.75

MARVEL SUPER-HEROES MEGAZINE
Marvel Comics: Oct, 1994 - No. 6, Mar, 1995 ($2.95, 100 pgs.)

1-6: 1-r/FF #232, DD #159, Iron Man #115, Incred. Hulk #314 3.00

MARVEL SUPER-HEROES SECRET WARS (See Secret Wars II)
Marvel Comics Group: May, 1984 - No. 12, Apr, 1985 (limited series)

1 1 2 3 5 6 8
1-3-(2nd printings, sold in multi-packs) 2.50
2-6,9-11: 6-The Wasp dies 6.00
7,12: 7-Intro. new Spider-Woman. 12-($1.00, 52 pgs.) 1 2 3 4 5 7
8-Spider-Man's new black costume explained as alien costume (1st app. Venom as alien costume) 3 6 9 17 25 32
Secret Wars Omnibus HC (2008, $99.99, dustjacket) r/#1-12, Thor #383, She-Hulk (2004) #10 and What If? (1989) #4 & #114; photo gallery of related toys; pencil-a from #1 100.00

NOTE: ***Zeck*** *a-1-12; c-1,3,8-12. Additional artists (John Romita Sr., Art Adams and others) had uncredditted art in #12.*

MARVEL SUPER HERO SQUAD (All ages)
Marvel Comics: Mar, 2009; Nov, 2009 - No. 4, Feb, 2010 ($3.99/$2.99)

1-4-Based on the animated series; back-up humor strips and pin-ups 3.00
...Hero Up! (3/09, $3.99) Collects humor strips from MarvelKids.com; 2 covers 4.00

MARVEL SUPER HERO SQUAD (All ages)
Marvel Comics: Mar, 2010 - Present ($2.99)

1-3-Based on the animated series. 1-Wraparound-c 3.00

MARVEL SUPER SPECIAL, A (See Marvel Comics Super...)

MARVEL SWIMSUIT SPECIAL (Also see Marvel Illustrated...)
Marvel Comics: 1992 - No. 4, 1995 ($3.95/$4.50, magazine, 52 pgs.)

1-4-Silvestri-c; pin-ups by diff. artists. 2-Jusko-c. 3-Hughes-c 1 3 4 6 8 10

MARVEL TAILS STARRING PETER PORKER THE SPECTACULAR SPIDER-HAM
(Also see Peter Porker...)
Marvel Comics Group: Nov, 1983 (one-shot)

1-Peter Porker, the Spectacular Spider-Ham, Captain Americat, Goose Rider, Hulk Bunny app. 4.00

MARVEL TALES (Formerly Marvel Mystery Comics #1-92)
Marvel/Atlas Comics (MCI): No. 93, Aug, 1949 - No. 159, Aug, 1957

93-Horror/weird stories begin 148 296 444 947 1624 2300
94-Everett-a 94 188 282 597 1024 1450
95-New logo 69 138 207 442 759 1075
96,99,101,103,105 59 118 177 375 648 920
97-Sun Girl, 2 pgs; Kirbyish-a; one story used in N.Y. State Legislative document 77 154 231 443 847 1200
98,100: 98-Krigstein-a 60 120 180 381 658 935
102-Wolverton-a "The End of the World", (6 pgs.) 84 168 252 538 919 1300
104-Wolverton-a "Gateway to Horror", (6 pgs.) 84 168 252 538 919 1300
106,107-Krigstein-a. 106-Decapitation story 48 96 144 302 514 725
108-120: 116-(7/53) Werewolf By Night story. 118-Hypo-c/panels in End of World story. 120-Jack Katz-a 37 74 111 218 354 490
121,123-131: 128-Flying Saucer-c. 131-Last precode (2/55) 28 56 84 168 274 380
122-Kubert-a 29 58 87 172 281 390
132,133,135-141,143,145 21 42 63 126 206 285
134-Krigstein, Kubert-a; flying saucer-c 23 46 69 136 223 310
142-Krigstein-a 22 44 66 130 213 295

Marvel Tales (2nd series) #155 © MAR

Marvel Tales (2nd series) #266 © MAR

Marvel Team-Up #131 © MAR

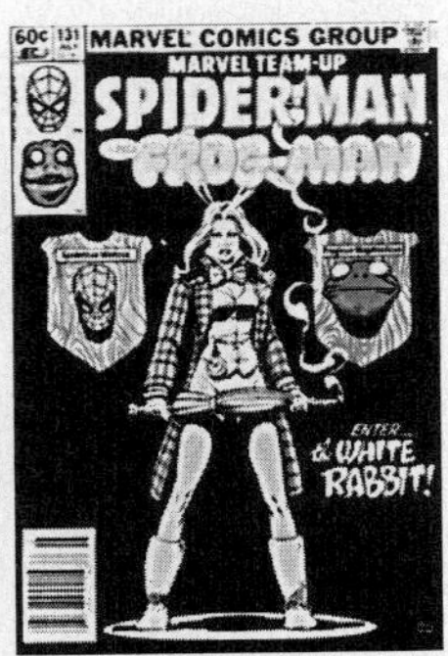

GD VG FN VF VF/NM NM-
2.0 4.0 6.0 8.0 9.0 9.2

144-Williamson/Krenkel-a, 3 pgs. 22 44 66 130 213 295
146,148-151,154-156,158: 150-1st S.A. issue. 156-Torres-a
18 36 54 103 162 220
147,152: 147-Ditko-a. 152-Wood, Morrow-a 20 40 60 115 185 255
153-Everett End of World c/story 21 42 63 126 206 285
157,159-Krigstein-a 19 38 57 109 172 235

NOTE: *Andru a-103. Briefer a-118. Check a-147. Colan a-102, 105, 107, 118, 120, 121, 127, 131. Drucker a-127, 135, 141, 146, 150. Everett a-98, 104, 106(2), 108(2), 131, 148, 151, 153, 155; c-107, 109, 111, 112, 114, 117, 127, 143, 147-151, 153, 155, 156. Forte a-119, 125, 130, 158. Heath a-110, 113, 118, 119; c-104-106, 110, 130. Gil Kane a-117. Lawrence a-130. Maneely a-111, 126, 129; c-108, 116, 120, 129, 152. Mooney a-114. Morisi a-153. Morrow a-150, 152, 156. Orlando a-149, 151, 157. Pakula a-119, 121, 133, 135, 144, 150, 152, 156. Powell a-136, 137, 150, 154. Ravielli a-117, 123. Rico a-97, 99. Romita a-108. Sekowsky a-96-98. Shores a-110; c-96. Sinnott a-105, 116, 144. Tuska a-114. Whitney a-107. Wildey a-126, 138.*

MARVEL TALES (...Annual #1,2; ...Starring Spider-Man #123 on)
Marvel Comics Group (NPP earlier issues): 1964 - No. 291, Nov, 1994 (No. 1-32: 72 pgs.)
(#1-3 have Canadian variants; back & inside-c are blank, same value)

1-Reprints origins of Spider-Man/Amazing Fantasy #15, Hulk/Inc. Hulk#1, Ant-Man/T.T.A. #35, Giant Man/T.T.A. #49, Iron Man/T.O.S. #39,48, Thor/J.I.M. #83 & r/Sgt. Fury #1
30 60 90 218 422 625
2 ('65)-r/X-Men #1(origin), Avengers #1(origin), origin Dr. Strange-r/Strange Tales #115 & origin Hulk(Hulk #3) 11 22 33 78 139 200
3 (7/66)-Spider-Man, Strange Tales (H. Torch), Journey into Mystery (Thor), Tales to Astonish (Ant-Man)-r begin (r/Strange Tales #101) 7 14 21 45 73 100
4,5 5 10 15 32 51 70
6-8,10: 10-Reprints 1st Kraven/Amaz. S-M #15 4 8 12 22 34 45
9-r/Amazing Spider-Man #14 w/cover 4 8 12 24 37 50
11-33: 11-Spider-Man battles Daredevil-r/Amaz. Spider-Man #16. 13-Origin Marvel Boy-r from M. Boy #1. 22-Green Goblin-c/story-r/Amaz. Spider-Man #27. 30-New Angel story (x-over w/Ka-Zar #2,3). 32-Last 72 pg. iss. 33-(52 pgs.) Kraven-r
3 6 9 16 23 30
34-50: 34-Begin regular size issues 2 3 4 6 8 10
51-65 6.00
66-70-(Regular 25¢ editions)(4-8/76) 5.00
66-70-(30¢-c variants, limited distribution) 2 4 6 11 16 20
71-105: 75-Origin Spider-Man-r. 77-79-Drug issues-r/Amaz. Spider-Man #96-98. 98-Death of Gwen Stacy-r/Amaz. Spider-Man #121 (Green Goblin). 99-Death Green Goblin-r/Amaz. Spider-Man #122. 100-(52 pgs.)-New Hawkeye/Two Gun Kid story. 101-105-All Spider-Man-r 4.00
80-84-(35¢-c variants, limited distribution)(6-10/77) 3 6 9 16 23 30
106-r/1st Punisher-Amazing Spider-Man #129 1 2 3 5 7 9
107-136: 107-133-All Spider-Man-r. 111,112-r/Spider-Man #134,135 (Punisher). 113,114-r/Spider-Man #136,137(Green Goblin). 126-128-r/clone story from Amazing Spider-Man #149-151. 134-136-Dr. Strange-r begin; SpM stories continue. 134-Dr. Strange-r/Strange Tales #110 4.00
137-Origin-r Dr. Strange; shows original unprinted-c & origin Spider-Man/Amazing Fantasy #15
1 2 3 4 5 7
137-Nabisco giveaway 1 2 3 5 6 8
138-Reprints all Amazing Spider-Man #1; begin reprints of Spider-Man with covers similar to originals 6.00
139-144: r/Amazing Spider-Man #2-7 4.00
145-149,151-190,193-199: Spider-Man-r continue w/#8 on. 149-Contains skin "Tattooz" decals. 153-r/1st Kraven/Spider-Man #15. 155-r/2nd Green Goblin/Spider-Man #17. 161,164,165-Gr. Goblin-c/stories-r/Spider-Man #23,26,27. 178,179-Green Goblin-c/story-r/ Spider-Man #39,40. 187,189-Kraven-r. 193-Byrne-r/Marvel Team-Up begin w/scripts 3.00
150,191,192,200: 150-($1.00, 52pgs.)-r/Spider-Man Annual #1(Kraven app.). 191-($1.50, 68 pgs.)-r/Spider-Man #96-98. 192-($1.25, 52 pgs.)-r/Spider-Man #121,122. 200-Double size ($1.25)-Miller-c & r/Annual #14 4.00
201-257: 208-Last Byrne-r. 210,211-r/Spidey #134,135. 212,213-r/Giant-Size Spidey #4. 213-r/1st solo Silver Surfer story/F.F. Annual #5. 214,215-r/Spidey #161,162. 222-Reprints origin Punisher/Spectacular Spider-Man #83; last Punisher reprint. 209-Reprints 1st app. The Punisher/Amazing Spider-Man #129; Punisher reprints begin, end #222. 223-McFarlane-c begins, end #239. 233-Spider-Man/X-Men team-ups begin; r/X-Men #35. 234-r/Marvel Team-Up #4. 235,236-r/M. Team-Up Annual #1. 237,238-r/M. Team-Up #150. 239,240-r/M. Team-Up #38,90(Beast). 242-r/M.Team-Up #89. 243-r/M. Team-Up #117 (Wolverine). 250-($1.50, 52pgs.)-r/1st Karma/M. Team-Up #100. 251-r/Spider-Man #100 (Green Goblin-c/story). 252-r/1st app. Morbius/Amaz. Spider-Man #101. 253-($1.50, 52 pgs.) -r/Amaz. S-M #102254-r/M. Team-Up #15(Ghost Rider); new painted-c. 255,256-Spider-Man & Ghost Rider-r/Marvel Team-Up #58,91. 257-Hobgoblin-r begin (r/Amazing Spider-Man #238) 2.50
258-291: 258-261-r/A. Spider-Man #239,249-251(Hobgoblin). 262,263-r/Marv. Team-Up #53,54. 262-New X-Men vs. Sunstroke story. 263-New Woodgod origin story. 264,265-r/Amazing Spider-Man Annual 5. 266-273-Reprints alien costume stories/A. S-M 252-259. 277-r/1st Silver Sable/A. S-M 265. 283-r/A. S-M 275 (Hobgoblin). 284-r/A. S-M 276 (Hobgoblin) 2.50
285-variant w/Wonder-Con logo on c-no price-giveaway 2.50
286-($2.95)-p/bagged w/16 page insert & animation print 3.00

GD VG FN VF VF/NM NM-
2.0 4.0 6.0 8.0 9.0 9.2

NOTE: *All contain reprints; some have new art. #89-97-r/Amazing Spider-Man #110-118; #98-136-r/#121-159; #137-150-r/Amazing Fantasy #15, #1-12 & Annual 1; #151-167-r/#13-28 & Annual 2; #168-186-r/#29-46. Austin a-100i; c-272i, 273i. Byrne a(r)-193-198p, 201-208p. Ditko a-1-30, 83, 100, 137-155. G. Kane a-71, 81, 98-101p, 249r; c-125-127p, 130p, 137-155. Sam Kieth c-255, 262, 263. Ron Lim c-266p-281p, 283p-285p. McFarlane c-223-239. Mooney a-63, 95-97i, 103(i). Nasser a-100p. Nebres a-242i. Perez c-259-261. Rogers c-240, 241, 243-252.*

MARVEL TALES FLIP MAGAZINE
Marvel Comics: Sept, 2005 - No. 25, Sept, 2007 ($3.99/$4.99)

1-6-Reprints Amazing Spider-Man #30-up and Amazing Fantasy (2004) in flip format 4.00
7-10-Reprints Amazing Spider-Man #36-up and Runaways Vol. 2 in flip format 4.00
11-25-($4.99) Reprints Amazing Spider-Man #36-up and Runaways Vol. 2 in flip format 5.00

MARVEL TAROT, THE
Marvel Comics: 2007 ($3.99, one-shot)

1-Marvel characters featured in Tarot deck images; Djurdjevic-c 4.00

MARVEL TEAM-UP (See Marvel Treasury Edition #18 & Official Marvel Index To...)
(Replaced by Web of Spider-Man)
Marvel Comics Group: March, 1972 - No. 150, Feb, 1985
NOTE: *Spider-Man team-ups in all but Nos. 18, 23, 26, 29, 32, 35, 97, 104, 105, 137.*

1-Human Torch 13 26 39 93 172 250
2-Human Torch 6 12 18 39 62 85
3-Spider-Man/Human Torch vs. Morbius (part 1); 3rd app. of Morbius (7/72)
7 14 21 45 73 100
4-Spider-Man/X-Men vs. Morbius (part 2 of story); 4th app. of Morbius
7 14 21 45 73 100
5-10: 5-Vision. 6-Thing. 7-Thor. 8-The Cat (4/73, came out between The Cat #3 & 4). 9-Iron Man. 10-H-T 3 6 9 20 30 40
11,13,14,16-20: 11-Inhumans. 13-Capt. America. 14-Sub-Mariner. 16-Capt. Marvel. 17-Mr. Fantastic. 18-H-T/Hulk. 19-Ka-Zar. 20-Black Panther; last 20¢ issue
2 4 6 11 16 20
12-Werewolf (By Night) (8/73) 3 6 9 19 29 38
15-1st Spider-Man/Ghost Rider team-up (11/73) 3 6 9 20 30 40
21-30: 21-Dr. Strange. 22-Hawkeye. 23-H-T/Iceman (X-Men cameo). 24-Brother Voodoo. 25-Daredevil. 26-H-T/Thor. 27-Hulk. 28-Hercules. 29-H-T/Iron Man. 30-Falcon
2 4 6 8 10 12
31-45,47-50: 31-Iron Fist. 32-H-T/Son of Satan. 33-Nighthawk. 34-Valkyrie. 35-H-T/Dr. Strange. 36-Frankenstein. 37-Man-Wolf. 38-Beast. 39-H-T. 40-Sons of the Tiger/H-T. 41-Scarlet Witch. 42-The Vision. 43-Dr. Doom; retells origin. 44-Moondragon. 45-Killraven. 47-Thing. 48-Iron Man; last 25¢ issue. 49-Dr. Strange; Iron Man app. 50-Iron Man; Dr. Strange app.
1 2 3 5 6 8
44-48-(30¢-c variants, limited distribution)(4-8/76) 3 6 9 20 30 40
46-Spider-Man/Deathlok team-up 1 2 3 5 7 9
51,52,56,57: 51-Iron Man; Dr. Strange app. 52-Capt. America. 56-Daredevil. 57-Black Widow
1 2 3 4 5 7
53-Hulk; Woodgod & X-Men app., 1st Byrne-a on X-Men (1/77)
3 6 9 20 30 40
54,55,58-60: 54,59,60: 54-Hulk; Woodgod app. 59-Yellowjacket/The Wasp. 60-The Wasp (Byrne-a in all). 55-Warlock-c/story; Byrne-a. 58-Ghost Rider
2 3 4 6 8 10
58-62-(35¢-c variants, limited distribution)(6-10/77) 5 10 15 30 48 65
61-70: All Byrne-a; 61-H-T. 62-Ms. Marvel; last 30¢ issue. 63-Iron Fist. 64-Daughters of the Dragon. 65-Capt. Britain (1st U.S. app.). 66-Capt. Britain; 1st app. Arcade. 67-Tigra; Kraven the Hunter app. 68-Man-Thing. 69-Havok (from X-Men). 70-Thor
1 2 3 5 7 9
71-74,76-78,80: 71-Falcon. 72-Iron Man. 73-Daredevil. 74-Not Ready for Prime Time Players (Belushi). 76-Dr. Strange. 77-Ms. Marvel. 78-Wonder Man. 80-Dr. Strange/Clea; last 35¢ issue 5.00
75,79,81: Byrne-a(p). 75-Power Man; Cage app. 79-Mary Jane Watson as Red Sonja; Clark Kent cameo (1 panel, 3/79). 81-Death of Satana
1 2 3 4 5 7
82-99: 82-Black Widow. 83-Nick Fury. 84-Shang-Chi. 86-Guardians of the Galaxy. 89-Nightcrawler (from X-Men). 91-Ghost Rider. 92-Hawkeye. 93-Werewolf by Night. 94-Spider-Man vs. The Shroud. 95-Mockingbird (intro.); Nick Fury app. 96-Howard the Duck; last 40¢ issue. 97-Spider-Woman/ Hulk. 98-Black Widow. 99-Machine Man. 85-Shang-Chi/ Black Widow/Nick Fury. 87-Black Panther. 88-Invisible Girl. 90-Beast 4.00
100-(Double-size)-Fantastic Four/Storm/Black Panther; origin/1st app. Karma, one of the New Mutants; origin Storm; X-Men x-over; Miller-c/a(p); Byrne-a (on X-Men app. only)
1 2 3 5 7 9
101-116: 101-Nighthawk(Ditko-a). 102-Doc Samson. 103-Ant-Man. 104-Hulk/Ka-Zar. 105-Hulk/Powerman/Iron Fist. 106-Capt. America. 107-She-Hulk. 108-Paladin; Dazzler cameo. 109-Dazzler; Paladin app. 110-Iron Man. 111-Devil-Slayer. 112-King Kull; last 50¢ issue. 113-Quasar. 114-Falcon. 115-Thor. 116-Valkyrie 4.00
117-Wolverine-c/story 2 4 6 8 10 12
118-140,142-149: 118-Professor X; Wolverine app. (4 pgs.); X-Men cameo. 119-Gargoyle.

Marvel Team-Up #148 © MAR

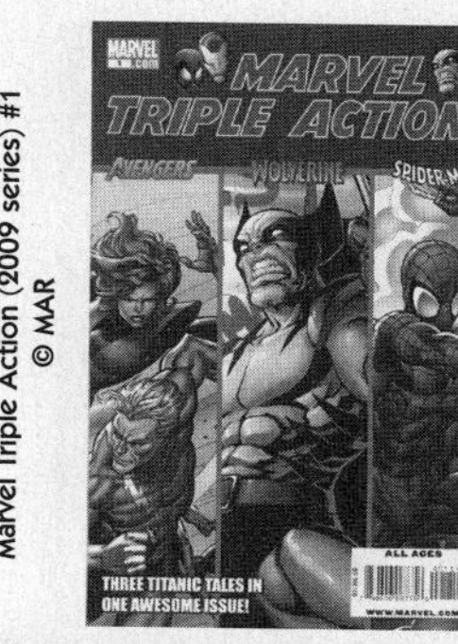

Marvel Triple Action (2009 series) #1 © MAR

Marvel Two-In-One #42 © MAR

GD 2.0 | VG 4.0 | FN 6.0 | VF 8.0 | VF/NM 9.0 | NM- 9.2

120-Dominic Fortune. 121-Human Torch. 122-Man-Thing. 123-Daredevil. 124-The Beast. 125-Tigra. 126-Hulk & Powerman/Son of Satan. 127-The Watcher. 128-Capt. America; Spider-Man/Capt. America photo-c. 129-The Vision. 130-Scarlet Witch. 131-Frogman. 132-Mr. Fantastic. 133-Fantastic Four. 134-Jack of Hearts. 135-Kitty Pryde; X-Men cameo. 136-Wonder Man. 137-Aunt May/Franklin Richards. 138-Sandman. 139-Nick Fury. 140-Black Widow. 142-Capt. Marvel. 143-Starfox. 144-Moon Knight. 145-Iron Man. 146-Nomad. 147-Human Torch; Spider-Man back to old costume. 148-Thor. 149-Cannonball 3.00

141-Daredevil; SpM/Black Widow app. (Spidey in new black costume; ties w/ Amazing Spider-Man #252 for 1st black costume) 2 4 6 8 12 15

150-X-Men ($1.00, double-size); B. Smith-c 6.00

Annual 1 (1976)-Spider-Man/X-Men (early app.) 3 6 9 20 30 40

Annual 2 (1979)-Spider-Man/Hulk 1 3 4 6 8 10

Annuals 3,4: 3 (1980)-Hulk/Power Man/Machine Man/Iron Fist; Miller-c(p). 4 (1981)-Spider-Man /Daredevil/Moon Knight/Power Man/Iron Fist; brief origins of each; Miller-c; Miller scripts on Daredevil 1 2 3 4 5 7

Annuals 5-7: 5 (1982)-SpM/The Thing/Scarlet Witch/Dr. Strange/Quasar. 6 (1983)-Spider-Man/ New Mutants (early app.), Cloak & Dagger. 7(1984)-Alpha Flight; Byrne-c(i) 6.00

NOTE: ***Art Adams*** *c-141p.* ***Austin*** *a-79i; c-76i, 79i, 96i, 101i, 112i, 130i.* ***Bolle*** *a-9i.* ***Byrne*** *a(p)-53-55, 59-70, 75, 79, 100; c-68p, 70p, 72p, 75, 76p, 79p, 129i, 133i.* ***Colan*** *a-87p.* ***Ditko*** *a-101.* ***Kane*** *a(p)-4-6, 13, 14, 16-19, 23; c(p)-4, 13, 14, 17-19, 23, 25, 26, 32-35, 37, 41, 44, 45, 47, 53, 54.* ***Miller*** *a-100p; c-95p, 99p, 100p, 102p, 106.* ***Mooney*** *a-2i, 7i, 8, 10p, 11p, 16i, 24-31p, 72, 93i, Annual 5i.* ***Nasser*** *a-89p; c-101p.* ***Simonson*** *c-99i, 148.* ***Paul Smith*** *c-131, 132.* ***Starlin*** *c-27.* ***Sutton*** *a-93p. "H-T" means Human Torch; "SpM" means Spider-Man; "S-M" means Sub-Mariner.*

MARVEL TEAM-UP (2nd Series)
Marvel Comics: Sept, 1997 - No. 11, July, 1998 ($1.99)

1-11: 1-Spider-Man team-ups begin, Generation x-app. 2-Hercules-c/app.; two covers. 3-Sandman. 4-Man-Thing. 7-Blade. 8-Namor team-ups begin, Dr. Strange app. 9-Capt. America. 10-Thing. 11-Iron Man 2.50

MARVEL TEAM-UP
Marvel Comics: Jan, 2005 - No. 25, Dec, 2006 ($2.25/$2.99)

1-7,9: 1,2-Spider-Man & Wolverine; Kirkman-s/Kolins-a. 5,6-X-23 app. 2.50
8,10-25 ($2.99-c) 10-Spider-Man & Daredevil. 12-Origin of Titannus. 14-Invincible app. 3.00
... Vol. 1: The Golden Child TPB (2005, $12.99) r/#1-6 13.00
... Vol. 2: Master of the Ring TPB (2005, $17.99) r/#7-13 18.00
... Vol. 3: League of Losers TPB (2006, $13.99) r/#14-18 14.00
... Vol. 4: Freedom Ring TPB (2007, $17.99) r/#19-25 18.00

MARVEL: THE LOST GENERATION
Marvel Comics: No. 12, Mar, 2000 - No. 1, Feb, 2001 ($2.99, issue #s go in reverse)

1-12-Stern-s/Byrne-s/a; untold story of The First Line. 5-Thor app. 3.00

MARVEL/ TOP COW CROSSOVERS
Image Comics (Top Cow): Nov, 2005 ($24.99, TPB)

Vol. 1-Reprints crossovers with Wolverine, Witchblade, Hulk, Darkness; Devil's Reign 25.00

MARVEL TREASURY EDITION
Marvel Comics Group/Whitman #17,18: 1974; #2, Dec, 1974 - #28, 1981 ($1.50/$2.50, 100 pgs., oversized, new-a &-r)(Also see Amazing Spider-Man, The, Marvel Spec. Ed. Feat.--, Savage Fists of Kung Fu, Superman Vs., & 2001, A Space Odyssey)

1-Spectacular Spider-Man; story-r/Marvel Super-Heroes #14; Romita-c/a(r); G. Kane, Ditko-r; Green Goblin/Hulk-r 6 12 18 37 59 80

1-1,000 numbered copies signed by Stan Lee & John Romita on front-c & sold thru mail for $5.00; these were the1st 1,000 copies off the press 11 22 33 78 139 200

2-10: 2-Fantastic Four-r/F.F. 6,11,48-50(Silver Surfer). 3-The Mighty Thor-r/Thor #125-130. 4-Conan the Barbarian; Barry Smith-c/a(r)/Conan #11. 5-The Hulk (origin-r/Hulk #3). 6-Dr. Strange. 7-Mighty Avengers. 8-Giant Superhero Holiday Grab-Bag; Spider-Man, Hulk, Nick Fury. 9-Giant; Super-hero Team-up. 10-Thor; r/Thor #154-157 3 6 9 18 27 35

11-20: 11-Fantastic Four. 12-Howard the Duck (r/#H. the Duck #1 & G.S. Man-Thing #4,5) plus new Defenders story. 13-Giant Super-Hero Holiday Grab-Bag. 14-The Sensational Spider-Man; r/1st Morbius from Amazing S-M #101,102 plus #100 & r/Not Brand Echh #6. 15-Conan; B. Smith, Neal Adams-i; r/Conan #24. 16-The Defenders (origin) & Valkyrie; r/Defenders #1;4,13,14. 17-Incredible Hulk; Blob, Havok, Rhino and The Leader app. 18-The Astonishing Spider-Man; r/Spider-Man's 1st team-ups with Iron Fist, The X-Men, Ghost Rider & Werewolf by Night; inside back-c has photos from 1978 Spider-Man TV show. 19-Conan the Barbarian. 20-Hulk 3 6 9 14 20 25

21-24,27: 21-Fantastic Four. 22-Spider-Man. 23-Conan. 24-Rampaging Hulk. 27-Spider-Man 3 6 9 14 20 25

25-Spider-Man vs. The Hulk new story 3 6 9 16 23 30
26-The Hulk; 6 pg. new Wolverine/Hercules-s 3 6 9 16 22 28
28-Spider-Man/Superman; (origin of each) 5 10 15 32 51 70

NOTE: *Reprints-2, 3, 5, 7-9, 13, 14, 16, 17.* ***Neal Adams*** *a(i)-6, 15.* ***Brunner*** *a-6, 12; c-6.* ***Buscema*** *a-15, 19, 28; c-28.* ***Colan*** *a-6r; c-12p.* ***Ditko*** *a-1, 6.* ***Gil Kane*** *c-16p.* ***Kirby*** *a-1-3, 5, 7, 9-11; c-7.* ***Perez*** *a-26.* ***Romita*** *c-1, 5.* ***B. Smith*** *a-4, 15, 19; c-4, 19.*

GD 2.0 | VG 4.0 | FN 6.0 | VF 8.0 | VF/NM 9.0 | NM- 9.2

MARVEL TREASURY OF OZ FEATURING THE MARVELOUS LAND OF OZ
Marvel Comics Group: 1975 ($1.50, oversized) (See MGM's Marvelous...)

1-Roy Thomas-s/Alfredo Alcala-a; Romita-c & bk-c 3 6 9 16 23 30

MARVEL TREASURY SPECIAL (Also see 2001: A Space Odyssey)
Marvel Comics Group: 1974; 1976 ($1.50, oversized, 84 pgs.)

Vol. 1-Spider-Man, Torch, Sub-Mariner, Avengers "Giant Superhero Holiday Grab-Bag"; Wood, Colan/Everett, plus 2 Kirby-r; reprints Hulk vs. Thing from Fantastic Four #25,26 3 6 9 17 25 32

Vol. 1-... Featuring Captain America's Bicentennial Battles (6/76)-Kirby-a; B. Smith inks, 11 pgs. 3 6 9 18 27 35

MARVEL TRIPLE ACTION (See Giant-Size...)
Marvel Comics Group: Feb, 1972 - No. 24, Mar, 1975; No. 25, Aug, 1975 - No. 47, Apr, 1979

1-(25¢ giant, 52 pgs.)-Dr. Doom, Silver Surfer, The Thing begin, end #4 ('66 reprints from Fantastic Four) 4 8 12 22 34 45
2-5 2 4 6 10 14 18
6-10 1 2 3 5 6 8
11-47: 45-r/X-Men #45. 46-r/Avengers #53(X-Men) 6.00
29,30-(30¢-c variants, limited distribution)(5,7/76) 3 6 9 14 20 25
36,37-(35¢-c variants, limited distribution)(7,9/77) 3 6 9 20 30 40

NOTE: *#5-44, 46, 47 reprint Avengers #11 thru ?. #40-r/Avengers #48(1st Black Knight).* ***Buscema*** *a(r)-35p, 36p, 38p, 39p, 41, 42, 43p, 44p, 46p, 47p.* ***Ditko*** *a-2r; c-47.* ***Kirby*** *a(r)-1-4p; c-1-4, 9-19, 22, 24, 29.* ***Starlin*** *c-7.* ***Tuska*** *a(r)-40p, 43i, 46i, 47i. #2 through #17 are 20¢-c.*

MARVEL TRIPLE ACTION
Marvel Comics: May, 2009 - No. 2, Jun, 2009 ($5.99, limited series)

1,2-Reprints stories from Wolverine First Class, Marvel Adventures Avengers & Marvel Super Heroes 6.00

MARVEL TV: GALACTUS - THE REAL STORY
Marvel Comics: Apr, 2009 ($3.99, one-shot)

1-The "hoax" of Galactus, Tieri-s/Santacruz-a; r/Fantastic Four #50 4.00

MARVEL TWO-IN-ONE (...Featuring ... #82 on; also see The Thing)
Marvel Comics Group: January, 1974 - No. 100, June, 1983

1-Thing team-ups begin; Man-Thing 7 14 21 45 73 100
2,3: 2-Sub-Mariner; last 20¢ issue. 3-Daredevil 3 6 9 20 30 40
4-6: 4-Capt. America. 5-Guardians of the Galaxy (9/74, 2nd app.?). 6-Dr. Strange (11/74) 3 6 9 16 22 28
7,9,10 2 4 6 10 14 18
8-Early Ghost Rider app. (3/75) 3 6 9 16 22 28
11-14,19,20: 13-Power Man. 14-Son of Satan (early app.) 1 3 4 6 8 10
15-18-(Regular 25¢ editions)(5-7/76) 17-Spider-Man. 1 3 4 6 8 10
15-18-(30¢-c variants, limited distribution) 3 6 9 18 27 35
21-29: 27-Deathlok. 29-Master of Kung Fu; Spider-Woman cameo 1 2 3 4 5 7
28,29,31-(35¢-c variants, limited distribution) 4 8 12 24 37 50
30-2nd full app. Spider-Woman (see Marvel Spotlight #32 for 1st app.) 2 4 6 8 10 12
30-(35¢-c variant, limited distribution)(8/77) 5 10 15 32 51 70
31-33-Spider-Woman app. 1 3 4 6 8 10
34-40: 39-Vision 1 2 3 4 5 7
41,42,44,45,47-49: 42-Capt. America. 45-Capt. Marvel 5.00
43,50,53,55-Byrne-a(p). 53-Quasar(7/79, 2nd app.) 1 2 3 5 7 9
46-Thing battles Hulk-c/story 2 4 6 8 10 12
51-The Beast, Nick Fury, Ms. Marvel; Miller-p 1 2 3 5 7 9
52-Moon Knight app. 5.00
54-Death of Deathlok: Byrne-a 2 4 6 8 10 12
56-60,64-74,76-79,81,82: 60-Intro. Impossible Woman. 68-Angel. 69-Guardians of the Galaxy. 71-1st app. Maelstrom. 76-Iceman 4.00
61-63: 61-Starhawk (from Guardians); "The Coming of Her" storyline begins, ends #63; cover similar to F.F. #67 (Him-c). 62-Moondragon; Thanos & Warlock cameo in flashback; Starhawk app. 63-Warlock revived shortly; Starhawk & Moondragon app. 5.00
75-Avengers (52 pgs.) 5.00
80,90,100: 80-Ghost Rider. 90-Spider-Man. 100-Double size, Byrne-s 5.00
83-89,91-99: 83-Sasquatch. 84-Alpha Flight app. 93-Jocasta dies. 96-X-Men-c & cameo 4.00
Annual 1(1976, 52 pgs.)-Thing/Liberty Legion; Kirby-c 2 4 6 9 13 16
Annual 2(1977, 52 pgs.)-Thing/Spider-Man; 2nd death of Thanos; end of Thanos saga; Warlock app.; Starlin-c/a 5 10 15 32 51 70
Annual 3,4 (1978-79, 52 pgs.): 3-Nova. 4-Black Bolt 1 2 3 4 5 7
Annual 5-7 (1980-82, 52 pgs.): 5-Hulk. 6-1st app. American Eagle. 7-The Thing/Champion; Sasquatch, Colossus app.; X-Men cameo (1 pg.) 5.00

NOTE: ***Austin*** *c(i)-42, 54, 56, 58, 61, 63, 66.* ***John Buscema*** *a-30p, 45; c-30p.* ***Byrne*** *(p)-43, 50, 53-55; c-43,*

Marvel Universe #1 © MAR

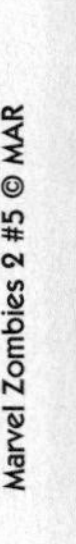
Marvel Zombies 2 #5 © MAR

Mary Marvel Comics #13 © FAW

GD VG FN VF VF/NM NM-
2.0 4.0 6.0 8.0 9.0 9.2

53p, 56p, 98i, 99i. ***Gil Kane*** *a-1p, 2p; c(p)-1-3, 9, 11, 14, 28.* ***Kirby*** *c-10, 12, 19p, 20, 25, 27.* ***Mooney*** *a-18i, 38i, 90i.* ***Nasser*** *a-70p.* ***Perez*** *a(p)-56-58, 60, 64, 65; c(p)-32, 33, 42, 50-52, 54, 55, 57, 58, 61-66, 70.* ***Roussos*** *a-Annual 1i.* ***Simonson*** *c-43i, 97p, Annual 6i.* ***Starlin*** *c-6, Annual 1.* ***Tuska*** *a-6p.*

MARVEL TWO-IN-ONE
Marvel Comics: Sept, 2007 - Present ($4.99, 64 pgs.)
1-8,13-16-Reprints Marvel Adventures Avengers and X-Men: First Class stories 5.00
9-12,17-Reprints Marvel Adventures Iron Man and Avengers stories 5.00

MARVEL UNIVERSE (See Official Handbook Of The...)

MARVEL UNIVERSE (Title on variant covers for newsstand editions of some 2001 Marvel titles. See indicia for actual titles and issue numbers)

MARVEL UNIVERSE
Marvel Comics: June, 1998 - No. 7, Dec, 1998 ($2.99/$1.99)
1-($2.99)-Invaders stories from WW2; Stern-s 3.00
2-7-($1.99): 2-Two covers. 4-7-Monster Hunters; Manley-a/Stern-s 2.50

MARVEL UNIVERSE: MILLENNIAL VISIONS
Marvel Comics: Feb, 2002 ($3.99, one-shot)
1-Pin-ups by various; wraparound-c by JH Williams & Gray 4.00

MARVEL UNIVERSE: THE END (Also see Infinity Abyss)
Marvel Comics: May, 2003 - No. 6, Aug, 2003 ($3.50/$2.99, limited series)
1-($3.50)-Thanos, X-Men, FF, Avengers, Spider-Man, Daredevil app.; Starlin-s/a(p) 3.50
2-6-($2.99) Akhenaten, Eternity, Living Tribunal app. 3.00
Thanos Vol. 3: Marvel Universe - The End (2003, $16.99) r/#1-6 17.00

MARVEL UNLIMITED (Title on variant covers for newsstand editions of some 2001 Daredevil issues. See indicia for actual titles and issue numbers)

MARVEL VALENTINE SPECIAL
Marvel Comics: Mar, 1997 ($2.99, one-shot)
1-Valentine stories w/Spider-Man, Daredevil, Cyclops, Phoenix 3.00

MARVEL VERSUS DC (See DC Versus Marvel) (Also see Amazon, Assassins, Bruce Wayne: Agent of S.H.I.E.L.D., Bullets & Bracelets, Doctor Strangefate, JLX, Legend of the Dark Claw, Magneto & The Magnetic Men, Speed Demon, Spider-Boy, Super Soldier, & X-Patrol)
Marvel Comics: No. 2, 1996 - No. 3, 1996 ($3.95, limited series)
2,3: 2-Peter David script. 3-Ron Marz script; Dan Jurgens-a(p). 1st app. of Super Soldier, Spider-Boy, Dr. Doomsday, Doctor Strangefate, The Dark Claw, Nightcreeper, Amazon, Wraith & others. Storyline continues in Amalgam books. 4.00

MARVEL VISIONARIES
Marvel Comics: 2002 - Present (various prices, HC and TPB)
...: Chris Claremont (2005, $29.99) r/X-Men #137, Uncanny X-Men #153,205,268 & Ann. #12, Iron Fist #14, Wolverine #3, New Mutants #21 and other highlights 30.00
...: Gil Kane (8/02, $24.95) r/Amazing Spider-Man #99, Marvel Premiere #1,#15, TOA #76 & others; plus sketch pages and a cover gallery 25.00
...: Jack Kirby HC (2004, $29.99) r/career highlights- Red Raven Comics #1 (1st work), Captain America Comics #1, Avengers #4, Fantastic Four #48-50 and more 30.00
...: Jack Kirby Vol. 2 HC (2006, $34.99) r/career highlights- Captain America, Two-Gun Kid, Fantastic Four, Thor, Fin Fang Foom, Devil Dinosaur, romance and more 35.00
...: Jim Steranko (9/02, $14.95) r/Captain America #110,111,113; X-Men #50,51 and stories from Tower of Shadows #1 and Our Love Story #5; plus a cover gallery 15.00
...: John Buscema (2007, $34.99) r/career highlights-Avengers, Silver Surfer, Thor, FF, Hulk, Wolverine and others; Roy Thomas intro.; sketch pages and pin-up art 35.00
...: John Romita Jr. (2005, $29.99) r/various stories 1977-2002; debut in AS-M Ann. #11; Iron Man #128, AS-M V2 #36, issues of Hulk, Daredevil: The Man Without Fear, Punisher; sketch pages; intro. by John Romita Sr. 30.00
...: John Romita Sr. (2005, $29.99) r/various stories 1951-1997 including Young Men #24&26, Daredevil #16, ASM #39,42,50; sketch pages; intro. by John Romita Jr. 30.00
...: Roy Thomas (2006, $34.99) r/career highlights; intro. by Stan Lee 35.00
...: Steve Ditko (2005, $29.99) r/various stories 1961-1992; intro. by Blake Bell 30.00
...: Stan Lee HC (2005, $29.99) r/career highlights- Captain America Comics #3 (1st work), and various Spider-Man, FF, Thor, Daredevil stories; 1940-1995; Roy Thomas intro. 30.00

MARVEL WEDDINGS
Marvel Comics: 2005 ($19.99, TPB)
TPB-Reprints weddings of Peter & Mary Jane, Reed & Sue, Scott & Jean, and others 20.00

MARVEL WESTERNS: ...
Marvel Comics: 2006 ($3.99, one-shots)
... Kid Colt and the Arizona Girl 1 (9/06) 2 short stories & 3 Kirby/Ayers reps.; Powell-c 4.00
... Outlaw Files-Profiles and essays about Marvel western characters 4.00
... Strange Westerns Starring The Black Rider 1 (10/06) Englehart-s/Rogers-a & 2 Kirby Rawhide Kid reprints; Rogers-c 4.00
... The Two-Gun Kid 1 (8/06) 2 short stories & a Kirby/Ayers reprint; Powell-c 4.00
... Western Legends 1 (9/06) 2 short stories & r/Rawhide Kid origin by Kirby; Powell-c 4.00

HC (2006, $20.99, dustjacket) r/one-shots 21.00

MARVEL X-MEN COLLECTION, THE
Marvel Comics: Jan, 1994 - No. 3, Mar, 1994 ($2.95, limited series)
1-3-r/X-Men trading cards by Jim Lee 3.00

MARVEL - YEAR IN REVIEW (Magazine)
Marvel Comics: 1989 - No. 3, 1991 (52 pgs.)
1-3: 1-Spider-Man-c by McFarlane. 2-Capt. America-c. 3-X-Men/Wolverine-c 5.00

MARVEL: YOUR UNIVERSE
Marvel Comics: 2008; May, 2009 - No. 3, July, 2009 ($5.99)
1-3-Reprints of 5 recent comics (Ms. Marvel, Nova, Immortal Iron Fist & others) 6.00
...Saga (2008, no cover price) - Re-caps of crossovers (Secret War thru Secret Invasion) 2.25

MARVEL ZOMBIES (See Ultimate Fantastic Four #21-23, 30-32)
Marvel Comics: Feb, 2006 - No. 5, June, 2006 ($2.99, limited series)
1-Zombies vs. Magneto; Kirkman-s/Phillips-a/Suydam-c swipe of A.F. #15 15.00
1-(2nd-4th printings) Variant Suydam-c swipes of Spider-Man #1, Amazing Spider-Man #50 and Incredible Hulk #1 5.00
2-Avengers #4 cover swipe by Suydam 8.00
3-5: 3-Inc. Hulk #340 c-swipe. 4-X-Men #1 c-swipe. 5-AS-M Ann. #21 c-swipe 5.00
3-5-(2nd printings) 3-Daredevil #179 c-swipe. 4-AS-M #39 c-swipe. 5-Silver Surfer #1 3.00
...: Dead Days (7/07, $3.99) Early days of the plaque; Kirkman-s/Phillips-a/Suydam-c 4.00
...: Dead Days HC (2008, $29.99, oversized) r/Dead Days one-shot, Ultimate Fantastic Four #21-23, 30-32, and Black Panther #28-30 30.00
...: Evil Evolution (1/10, $4.99) Apes vs. Zombies; Marcos Martin-c 5.00
...: The Book of Angels, Demons and Various Monstrosities (2007, $3.99) profile pages 4.00
...: The Covers HC (2007, $19.99, d.j.) Suydam's covers with originals and commentary 20.00
HC (2006, $19.99) r/#1-5; Kirkman foreword; cover gallery with variants 20.00

MARVEL ZOMBIES 2
Marvel Comics: Dec, 2007 - No. 5, Apr, 2008 ($2.99, limited series)
1-5-Kirkman-s/Phillips-a/Suydam zombie-fied cover swipes 3.00
HC (2008, $19.99) r/#1-5; cover swipe gallery 20.00

MARVEL ZOMBIES 3
Marvel Comics: Dec, 2008 - No. 4, Mar, 2009 ($3.99, limited series)
1-4-Van Lente-s/Walker-a/Land-c; Machine Man, Jocasta and Morbius app. 4.00

MARVEL ZOMBIES 4
Marvel Comics: Jun, 2009 - No. 4, Sept, 2009 ($3.99, limited series)
1-4-Van Lente-s/Walker-a/Land-c; Zombie Deadpool head app. 4.00

MARVEL ZOMBIES / ARMY OF DARKNESS
Marvel Comics/Dynamite Entertainment: May, 2007 - No. 5, Aug, 2007($2.99, limited series)
1-Zombies vs. Ash during the start of the plaque; Layman-s/Neves-a/Suydam-c 5.00
1-Second printing with Suydam zombie-fied Captain America Comics #1 cover swipe 3.00
2-5-Suydam zombie-fied cover swipes on all 3.00
HC (2007, $19.99) r/#1-5; cover gallery with variants and non-zombied original covers 20.00

MARVEL ZOMBIES RETURN
Marvel Comics: Nov, 2009 - No. 5, Nov, 2009 ($3.99, weekly limited series)
1-5-Suydam-c. 1-Zombie Spider-Man eats the Earth-Z Sinister Six; Dragotta-a. 4.00

MARVILLE
Marvel Comics: Nov, 2002 - No. 7, Jul, 2003 ($2.25, limited series)
1-6-Satire on DC/AOL-Time-Warner; Jemas-a/Bright-a/Horn-c 2.50
1-($3.95) Variant foil cover by Udon Studios; bonus sketch pages and Jemas afterword 4.00
7-($2.99) Intro. to Epic Comics line with submission guidelines 3.00

MARVIN MOUSE
Atlas Comics (BPC): September, 1957
1-Everett-c/a; Maneely-a 14 28 42 80 115 150

MARY JANE (Spider-Man) (Also see Spider-Man Loves Mary Jane)
Marvel Comics: Aug, 2004 - No. 4, Nov, 2004 ($2.25, limited series)
1-4-Marvel Age series with teen-age MJ Watson; Miyazawa-c/a; McKeever-s 2.50
... Vol. 1: Circle of Friends (2004, $5.99, digest-size) r/#1-4 6.00

MARY JANE & SNIFFLES (See Looney Tunes)
Dell Publishing Co.: No. 402, June, 1952 - No. 474, June, 1953
Four Color 402 (#1) 7 14 21 50 83 115
Four Color 474 7 14 21 47 76 105

MARY JANE: HOMECOMING (Spider-Man)
Marvel Comics: May, 2005 - No. 4, Aug, 2005 ($2.99, limited series)
1-4-Teen-age MJ Watson in high school; Miyazawa-c/a; McKeever-s 3.00
... Vol. 2 (2005, $6.99, digest-size) r/#1-4 7.00

The Masked Man #11 © ECL

Masquerade #3 © SPH

Master Comics #12 © FAW

	GD 2.0	VG 4.0	FN 6.0	VF 8.0	VF/NM 9.0	NM- 9.2

MARY MARVEL COMICS (Monte Hale #29 on) (Also see Captain Marvel #18, Marvel Family, Shazam, & Wow Comics)
Fawcett Publications: Dec, 1945 - No. 28, Sept, 1948

	GD	VG	FN	VF	VF/NM	NM-
1-Captain Marvel introduces Mary on-c; intro/origin Georgia Sivana	219	438	657	1402	2401	3400
2	80	160	240	508	874	1240
3,4: 3-New logo	53	106	159	334	567	800
5-8: 8-Bulletgirl x-over in Mary Marvel; X-Mas-c	40	80	120	244	402	560
9,10	37	74	111	218	354	490
11-20	25	50	75	147	241	335
21-28: 28-Western-c	21	42	63	124	202	280

MARY POPPINS (See Movie Comics & Walt Disney Showcase No. 17)

MARY SHELLEY'S FRANKENSTEIN
Topps Comics: Oct, 1994 - Jan, 1995 ($2.95, limited series)

1-4-polybagged w/3 trading cards 3.00
1-4 ($2.50)-Newstand ed. 2.50

MARY WORTH (See Harvey Comics Hits #55 & Love Stories of...)
Argo: March, 1956 (Also see Romantic Picture Novelettes)

	GD	VG	FN	VF	VF/NM	NM-
1	8	16	24	42	54	65

MASK (TV)
DC Comics: Dec, 1985 - No. 4, Mar, 1986; Feb, 1987 - No. 9, Oct, 1987

1-4; 1-9 (2nd series)-Sat. morning TV show. 2.50

MASK, THE (Also see Mayhem)
Dark Horse Comics: Aug, 1991 - No. 4, Oct, 1991; No. 0, Dec, 1991 ($2.50, 36 pgs., limited series)

1-4: 1-1st app. Lt. Kellaway as The Mask (see Dark Horse Presents #10 for 1st app.) 5.00
0-(12/91, B&W, 56 pgs.)-r/Mayhem #1-4 4.00
...Omnibus Vol. 1 (8/08, $24.95) r/#1-4, Mask Returns and Mask Strikes Back series 25.00
...Omnibus Vol. 2 (4/09, $24.95) r/#1-4, The Hunt For Green October, World Tour, Southern Discomfort, Toys in the Attic series and short stories from DHP 25.00

...: HUNT FOR GREEN OCTOBER July, 1995 - Oct, 1995 ($2.50, lim. series)
1-4-Evan Dorkin scripts 2.50

.../ MARSHALL LAW Feb, 1998 - No. 2, Mar, 1998 ($2.95, lim. series)
1,2-Mills-s/O'Neill-a 3.00

...: OFFICIAL MOVIE ADAPTATION July, 1994 - Aug, 1994 ($2.50, lim. series)
1,2 2.50

... RETURNS Oct, 1992 - No. 4, Mar, 1993 ($2.50, limited series)
1-4 4.00

... SOUTHERN DISCOMFORT Mar, 1996 - No. 4, July, 1996 ($2.50, lim. series)
1-4 2.50

... STRIKES BACK Feb, 1995 - No. 5, Jun, 1995 ($2.50, limited series)
1-5 2.50

... SUMMER VACATION July, 1995 ($10.95, one shot, hard-c)
1-nn-Rick Geary-c/a 11.00

... TOYS IN THE ATTIC Aug, 1998 - No. 4, Nov, 1998 ($2.95, limited series)
1-4-Fingerman-s 3.00

... VIRTUAL SURREALITY July, 1997 ($2.95, one shot)
nn-Mignola, Aragonés, and others-s/a 3.00

... WORLD TOUR Dec, 1995 - No. 4, Mar, 1996 ($2.50, limited series)
1-4: 3-X & Ghost-c/app. 2.50

MASK COMICS
Rural Home Publ.: Feb-Mar, 1945 - No. 2, Apr-May, 1945; No. 2, Fall, 1945

	GD	VG	FN	VF	VF/NM	NM-
1-Classic L. B. Cole Satan-c/a; Palais-a	300	600	900	1950	3375	4800
2-(Scarce)-Classic L. B. Cole Satan-c; Black Rider, The Boy Magician, & The Collector app.	194	388	582	1242	2121	3000
2-(Fall, 1945)-No publ.-same as regular #2; L. B. Cole-c	150	300	450	953	1639	2325

MASKED BANDIT, THE
Avon Periodicals: 1952

	GD	VG	FN	VF	VF/NM	NM-
nn-Kinstler-a	16	32	48	94	147	200

MASKED MAN, THE
Eclipse Comics: 12/84 - #10, 4/86; #11, 10/87; #12, 4/88 ($1.75/$2.00, color/B&W #9 on, Baxter paper)

1-12: 1-Origin retold. 3-Origin Aphid-Man; begin $2.00-c 2.50

MASKED MARVEL (See Keen Detective Funnies)
Centaur Publications: Sept, 1940 - No. 3, Dec, 1940

	GD	VG	FN	VF	VF/NM	NM-
1-The Masked Marvel begins	168	336	504	1075	1838	2600
2,3: 2-Gustavson, Tarpe Mills-a	110	220	330	704	1202	1700

MASKED RAIDER, THE (Billy The Kid #9 on; Frontier Scout, Daniel Boone #10-13) (Also see Blue Bird)
Charlton Comics: June, 1955 - No. 8, July, 1957; No. 14, Aug, 1958 - No. 30, June, 1961

	GD	VG	FN	VF	VF/NM	NM-
1-Masked Raider & Talon the Golden Eagle begin; painted-c	13	26	39	72	101	130
2	8	16	24	42	54	65
3-8,15: 8-Billy The Kid app. 15-Williamson-a, 7 pgs.	6	12	18	31	38	45
14,16-30: 22-Rocky Lane app.	5	10	15	24	30	35

MASKED RANGER
Premier Magazines: Apr, 1954 - No. 9, Aug, 1955

	GD	VG	FN	VF	VF/NM	NM-
1-The Masked Ranger, his horse Streak, & The Crimson Avenger (origin) begin, end #9; Woodbridge/Frazetta-a	40	80	120	240	390	540
2,3	15	30	45	85	130	175
4-8-All Woodbridge-a. 5-Jesse James by Woodbridge. 6-Billy The Kid by Woodbridge. 7-Wild Bill Hickok by Woodbridge. 8-Jim Bowie's Life Story	15	30	45	86	133	180
9-Torres-a; Wyatt Earp by Woodbridge; Says Death of Masked Ranger on-c	16	32	48	92	144	195

NOTE: *Check a-1. Woodbridge c/a-1, 4-9.*

MASK OF DR. FU MANCHU, THE (See Dr. Fu Manchu)
Avon Periodicals: 1951

	GD	VG	FN	VF	VF/NM	NM-
1-Sax Rohmer adapt.; Wood-c/a (26 pgs.); Hollingsworth-a	94	188	282	597	1024	1450

MASK OF ZORRO, THE
Image Comics: Aug, 1998 - No. 4, Dec, 1998 ($2.95, limited series)

1-4-Movie adapt. Photo variant-c 3.00

MASKS: TOO HOT FOR TV!
DC Comics (WildStorm): Feb, 2004 ($4.95)

1-Short stories by various incl. Thompson, Brubaker, Mahnke, Conner; Fabry-c 5.00

MASQUE OF THE RED DEATH (See Movie Classics)

MASQUERADE (See Project Superpowers)
Dynamite Entertainment: 2009 - No. 4, 2009 ($3.50, limited series)

1-4-Alex Ross & Phil Hester-s/Carlos Paul-a; covers by Ross & others 3.50

MASS EFFECT: REDEMPTION (Based on the EA video game)
Dark Horse Comics: Jan, 2010 - No. 4 ($3.50, limited series)

1-3-Walters & Jackson Miller-s/Francia-a 3.50

MASTER COMICS (Combined with Slam Bang Comics #7 on)
Fawcett Publications: Mar, 1940 - No. 133, Apr, 1953 (No. 1-6: oversized issues) (#1-3: 15¢, 52 pgs.; #4-6: 10¢, 36 pgs.; #7-Begin 68 pg. issues)

	GD	VG	FN	VF	VF/NM	NM-
1-Origin & 1st app. Master Man; The Devil's Dagger, El Carim, Master of Magic, Rick O'Say, Morton Murch, White Rajah, Shipwreck Roberts, Frontier Marshal, Streak Sloan, Mr. Clue begin (all features end #6)	784	1568	2352	5723	10,112	14,500
2	245	490	735	1568	2684	3800
3-6: 6-Last Master Man	174	348	522	1114	1907	2700

NOTE: *#1-6 rarely found in near mint or very fine condition due to large-size format.*

	GD	VG	FN	VF	VF/NM	NM-
7-(10/40)-Bulletman, Zoro, the Mystery Man (ends #22), Lee Granger, Jungle King, & Buck Jones begin; only app. The War Bird & Mark Swift & the Time Retarder; Zoro, Lee Granger, Jungle King & Mark Swift all continue from Slam Bang; Bulletman moves from Nickel	297	594	891	1900	3250	4600
8-The Red Gaucho (ends #13), Captain Venture (ends #22) & The Planet Princess begin	157	314	471	997	1711	2425
9,10: 10-Lee Granger ends	123	246	369	787	1344	1900
11-Origin & 1st app. Minute-Man (2/41)	265	530	795	1694	2897	4100
12	129	258	387	826	1413	2000
13-Origin & 1st app. Bulletgirl; Hitler-c	206	412	618	1318	2259	3200
14-16: 14-Companions Three begins, ends #31	110	220	330	704	1202	1700
17-20: 17-Raboy-a on Bulletman begins. 20-Captain Marvel cameo app. in Bulletman	100	200	300	635	1093	1550
21-(12/41; Scarce)-Captain Marvel & Bulletman team up against Capt. Nazi; origin & 1st app. Capt. Marvel Jr's most famous nemesis Captain Nazi who will cause creation of Capt. Marvel Jr. in Whiz #25. Part I of trilogy origin of Capt. Marvel Jr.; 1st Mac Raboy-c for Fawcett; Capt. Nazi-c	541	1082	1623	3950	6975	10,000
22-(1/42)-Captain Marvel Jr. moves over from Whiz #25 & teams up with Bulletman against Captain Nazi; part III of trilogy origin of Capt. Marvel Jr. & his 1st cover and adventure	486	972	1458	3550	6275	9000

23-Capt. Marvel Jr. c/stories begin (1st solo story); fights Capt. Nazi by himself.

Master Comics #107 © FAW

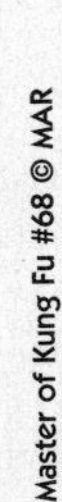

Master of Kung Fu #68 © MAR

Matrix Comics TPB © WB

GD VG FN VF VF/NM NM-
2.0 4.0 6.0 8.0 9.0 9.2

300 600 900 1920 3310 4700
24,25 103 206 309 659 1130 1600
26-28,30-Captain Marvel Jr. vs. Capt. Nazi. 28-Liberty Bell-c. 30-Flag-c
95 190 285 603 1039 1475
29-Hitler & Hirohito-c 135 270 405 864 1482 2100
31-33,35: 32-Last El Carim & Buck Jones; intro Balbo, the Boy Magician in El Carim story; classic Eagle-c by Raboy. 33-Balbo, the Boy Magician (ends #47), Hopalong Cassidy (ends #49) begins 77 154 231 493 847 1200
34-Capt. Marvel Jr. vs. Capt. Nazi-c/story; 1st mention of Capt. Nippon
84 168 252 538 919 1300
36-40: 40-Flag-c 61 122 183 390 670 950
41-(8/43)-Bulletman, Capt. Marvel Jr. & Bulletgirl x-over in Minute-Man; only app. Crime Crusaders Club (Capt. Marvel Jr., Minute-Man, Bulletman & Bulletgirl)
65 130 195 416 708 1000
42-47,49: 47-Hitler becomes Corpl. Hitler Jr. 49-Last Minute-Man
41 82 123 256 428 600
48-Intro. Bulletboy; Capt. Marvel cameo in Minute-Man
47 94 171 296 498 700
50-Intro Radar & Nyoka the Jungle Girl & begin series (5/44); Radar also intro in Captain Marvel #35 (same date); Capt. Marvel x-over in Radar; origin Radar; Capt. Marvel & Capt. Marvel, Jr. introduce Radar on-c 41 82 123 258 434 610
51-58 25 50 75 147 241 335
59-62: Nyoka serial "Terrible Tiara" in all; 61-Capt. Marvel Jr. 1st meets Uncle Marvel
27 54 81 158 259 360
63-80 20 40 60 114 182 250
81,83-87,89-91,95-99: 88-Hopalong Cassidy begins (ends #94). 95-Tom Mix begins (cover only in #123, ends #133) 18 36 54 103 162 220
82,88,92-94-Krigstein-a 18 36 54 107 169 230
100 18 36 54 107 169 230
101-106-Last Bulletman (not in #104) 17 34 51 98 154 210
107-120: 118-Mary Marvel 16 32 48 94 147 200
121-131-(lower print run): 123-Tom Mix-c only 18 36 54 103 162 220
132-B&W and color illos in **POP**; last Nyoka 18 36 54 105 165 225
133-Bill Battle app. 22 44 66 132 216 300

NOTE: ***Mac Raboy*** *a-15-39, 40(part), 42, 58. c-21-49, 51, 52, 54, 56, 58, 68(part), 69(part).* ***Bulletman*** *c-7-11, 13(half), 15, 18(part), 19, 20, 21(w/Capt. Marvel & Capt. Nazi), 22(w/Capt. Marvel, Jr.). Capt. Marvel, Jr. c-23-133. Master Man c-1-6. Minute Man c-12, 13(half), 14, 16, 17, 18(part).*

MASTER DARQUE
Acclaim Comics (Valiant): Feb, 1998 ($3.95)
1-Manco-a/Christina Z.-s 4.00

MASTER DETECTIVE
Super Comics: 1964 (Reprints)
17-r/Criminals on the Loose V4 #2; r/Young King Cole #?; McWilliams-r
2 4 6 8 11 14

MASTER OF KUNG FU (Formerly Special Marvel Edition; see Deadly Hands of Kung Fu & Giant-Size...)
Marvel Comics Group: No. 17, April, 1974 - No. 125, June, 1983
17-Starlin-a; intro Black Jack Tarr; 3rd Shang-Chi (ties w/Deadly Hands #1)
4 8 12 24 37 50
18,20 3 6 9 14 20 25
19-Man-Thing-c/story 3 6 9 16 23 30
21-23,25-30 2 4 6 9 13 16
24-Starlin, Simonson-a 2 4 6 10 14 18
31-50: 33-1st Leiko Wu. 43-Last 25¢ issue 1 2 3 5 7 9
39-43-(30¢-c variants, limited distribution)(5-7/76) 3 6 9 16 22 28
51-99 5.00
53-57-(35¢-c variants, limited distribution)(6-10/77) 3 6 9 18 27 35
100,118,125-Double size 6.00
101-117,119-124 4.00
Annual 1(4/76)-Iron Fist app. 3 6 9 17 25 32

NOTE: ***Austin*** *c-63i, 74i.* ***Buscema*** *c-44p.* ***Gulacy*** *a(p)-18-20, 22, 25, 29-31, 33-35, 38, 39, 40(p&i), 42-50, 53r(#20); c-51, 55, 64, 67.* ***Gil Kane*** *c(p)-20, 38, 39, 42, 45, 59, 63.* ***Nebres*** *c-73i.* ***Starlin*** *a-17p, 24; c-54.* ***Sutton*** *a-42i. #53 reprints #20.*

MASTER OF KUNG-FU, SHANG-CHI:... (2002 series, see Shang Chi:...)

MASTER OF KUNG-FU: BLEEDING BLACK
Marvel Comics: Feb, 1991 ($2.95, 84 pgs., one-shot)
1-The Return of Shang-Chi 3.00

MASTER OF THE WORLD
Dell Publishing Co.: No. 1157, July, 1961
Four Color 1157-Movie based on Jules Verne's "Master of the World" and "Robur the Conqueror" novels; with Vincent Price & Charles Bronson 7 14 21 45 73 100

MASTERS OF TERROR (Magazine)
Marvel Comics Group: July, 1975 - No. 2, Sept, 1975 (B&W) (All reprints)
1-Brunner, Barry Smith-a; Morrow/Steranko-c; Starlin-a(p); Gil Kane-a
3 6 9 18 27 35
2-Reese, Kane, Mayerik-a; Adkins/Steranko-c 2 4 6 13 18 22

MASTERS OF THE UNIVERSE (See DC Comics Presents #47 for 1st app.)
DC Comics: Dec, 1982 - No. 3, Feb, 1983 (Mini-series)
1 6.00
2,3: 2-Origin He-Man & Ceril 4.00

NOTE: ***Alcala*** *a-1i,, 2i.* ***Tuska*** *a-1-3p; c-1-3p. #2 has 75 & 95 cent cover price.*

MASTERS OF THE UNIVERSE (Comic Album)
Western Publishing Co.: 1984 (8-1/2x11", $2.95, 64 pgs.)
11362-Based on Mattel toy & cartoon 2 4 6 11 16 20

MASTERS OF THE UNIVERSE
Star Comics/Marvel #7 on: May 1986 - No. 13, May, 1988 (75¢/$1.00)
1 1 2 3 5 6 8
2-11: 8-Begin $1.00-c 6.00
12-Death of He-Man (1st Marvel app.) 2 4 6 8 11 14
13-Return of He-Man & death of Skeletor 2 4 6 8 11 14
The Motion Picture (11/87, $2.00)-Tuska-p 1 2 3 4 5 7

MASTERS OF THE UNIVERSE
Image Comics: Nov, 2002 - No. 4, March, 2003 ($2.95, limited series)
1-($2.95) Two covers by Santalucia and Campbell; Santalucia-a 3.00
1-($5.95) Variant-c by Norem w/gold foil logo 6.00
2-4($2.95) 2-Two covers by Santalucia and Manapul. 3,4-Two covers 3.00
TPB (CrossGen, 2003, $9.95, 8-1/4" x 5-1/2") digest-sized reprints #1-4 10.00

MASTERS OF THE UNIVERSE (Volume 2)
Image Comics: March, 2003 - No. 6, Aug, 2003 ($2.95)
1-6-($2.95) 1-Santalucia-c. 2-Two covers by Santalucia & JJ Kirby 3.00
1-($5.95) Wraparound variant-c by Struzan w/silver foil logo 6.00
3,4-($5.95) Wraparound variant holofoil-c. 3-By Edwards 4-By Boris Vallejo & Julie Bell 6.00
Volume 2 Dark Reflections TPB (2004, $18.95) r/#1-6 19.00

MASTERS OF THE UNIVERSE (Volume 3)
MVCreations: Apr, 2004 - No. 8, Dec, 2004 ($2.95)
1-8: 1-Santalucia-c 3.00

MASTERS OF THE UNIVERSE...
CrossGen Comics
...Rise of the Snake-Men (Nov, 2003 - No. 3, $2.95) Meyers-a 3.00
...The Power of Fear (12/03, $2.95, one-shot) Santalucia-a 3.00

MASTERS OF THE UNIVERSE, ICONS OF EVIL
Image Comics/CrossGen Comics: 2003 ($4.95, one-shots)
...Beastman -(Image) Origin of Beast Man; Tony Moore-a 5.00
...Mer-Man -(CrossGen) 5.00
...Trapjaw -(CrossGen) 5.00
...Tri-Klops -(CrossGen) Walker-c 5.00
TPB (3/04, $18.95, MVCreations) r/one-shots; sketch pages 19.00

MASTERWORKS SERIES OF GREAT COMIC BOOK ARTISTS, THE
Sea Gate Dist./DC Comics: May, 1983 - No. 3, Dec, 1983 (Baxter paper)
1-3: 1,2-Shining Knight by Frazetta r-/Adventure. 2-Tomahawk by Frazetta-r. 3-Wrightson-c/a(r) 6.00

MATADOR
DC Comics (WildStorm): July, 2005 - No. 6, May, 2006 ($2.99, limited series)
1-6-Devin Grayson-s/Brian Stelfreeze-a/c 3.00

MATRIX COMICS, THE (Movie)
Burlyman Entertainment: 2003; 2004 ($21.95, trade paperback)
nn-Short stories by various incl. Wachowskis, Darrow, Gaiman, Sienkiewicz, Bagge 22.00
...Volume One Preview (7/03, no cover price) bios of creators; Chadwick-s/a 2.50
Volume 2-(2004) Short stories by various incl. Wachowskis, Sale, McKeever, Dorman 22.00

MATT SLADE GUNFIGHTER (Kid Slade Gunfighter #5 on; See Western Gunfighters)
Atlas Comics (SPI): May, 1956 - No. 4, Nov, 1956
1-Intro Matt & horse Eagle; Williamson/Torres-a 18 36 54 107 169 230
2-Williamson-a 13 26 39 74 105 135
3,4 10 20 30 56 76 95

NOTE: ***Maneely*** *a-1, 3, 4; c-1, 2, 4.* ***Roth*** *a-2-4.* ***Severin*** *a-1, 3, 4.* ***Maneely*** *c/a-1. Issue #s stamped on cover after printing.*

MAUS: A SURVIVOR'S TALE (First graphic novel to win a Pulitzer Prize)

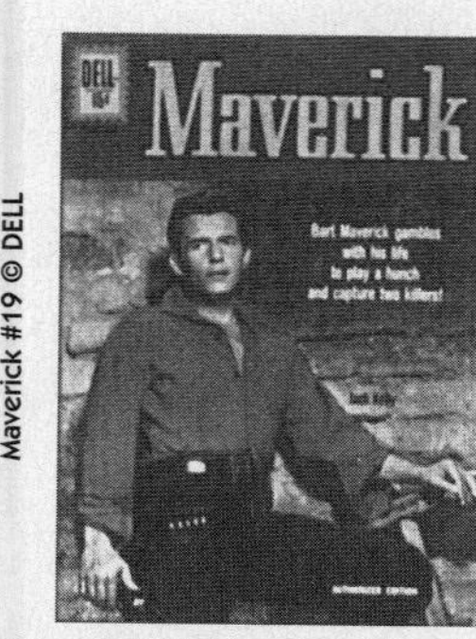

Maverick #19 © DELL

Mayhem #1 © Gibson

MD #5 © WMG

GD VG FN VF VF/NM NM-
2.0 4.0 6.0 8.0 9.0 9.2

Pantheon Books: 1986, 1991 (B&W)
Vol. 1-(...: My Father Bleeds History)(1986) Art Spiegelman-s/a; recounts stories of Spiegelman's father in 1930s-40s Nazi-occupied Poland; collects first six stories serialized in Raw Magazine from 1980-1985 20.00
Vol. 2-(...: And Here My Troubles Began)(1991) 20.00
Complete Maus Survivor's Tale -HC Vols. 1& 2 w/slipcase 35.00
Hardcover Vol. 1 (1991) 24.00
Hardcover Vol. 2 (1991) 24.00
TPB (1992, $14.00) Vols. 1& 2 14.00

MAVERICK (TV)
Dell Publishing Co.: No. 892, 4/58 - No. 19, 4-6/62 (All have photo-c)
Four Color 892 (#1)-James Garner photo-c begin 21 42 63 148 287 425
Four Color 930,945,962,980,1005 (6-8/59): 945-James Garner/Jack Kelly photo-c begin
11 22 33 74 132 190
7 (10-12/59) - 14: 11-Variant edition has "Time For Change" comic strip on back-c. 14-Last Garner/Kelly-c 9 18 27 63 109 150
15-18: Jack Kelly/Roger Moore photo-c 8 16 24 52 86 120
19-Jack Kelly photo-c (last issue) 8 16 24 54 90 125

MAVERICK (See X-Men)
Marvel Comics: Jan, 1997 ($2.95, one-shot)
1-Hama-s 3.00

MAVERICK (See X-Men)
Marvel Comics: Sept, 1997 - No. 12, Aug, 1998 ($2.99/$1.99)
1,12: 1-($2.99)-Wraparound-c. 12-($2.99) Battles Omega Red 4.00
2-11: 2-Two covers. 4-Wolverine app. 6,7-Sabretooth app. 3.00

MAVERICK MARSHAL
Charlton Comics: Nov, 1958 - No. 7, May, 1960
1 6 12 18 33 41 48
2-7 5 10 15 23 28 32

MAVERICKS
Daggar Comics Group: Jan, 1994 - No. 5, 1994 (#1-$2.75, #2-5-$2.50)
1-5: 1-Bronze. 1-Gold. 1-Silver 2.75

MAX BRAND (See Silvertip)

MAX HAMM FAIRY TALE DETECTIVE
Nite Owl Comix: 2002 - 2004 ($4.95, B&W, 6 1/2" x 8")
1-(2002) Frank Cammuso-s/a 5.00
Vol. 2 #1-3 (2003-2004) Frank Cammuso-s/a 5.00

MAXIMAGE
Image Comics (Extreme Studios): Dec, 1995 - No. 7, June 1996 ($2.50)
1-7: 1-Liefeld-c. 2-Extreme Destroyer Pt. 2; polybagged w/card. 4-Angela & Glory-c/app. 2.50

MAXIMO
Dreamwave Prods.: Jan, 2004 ($3.95, one-shot)
1-Based on the Capcom video game 4.00

MAXIMUM SECURITY (Crossover)
Marvel Comics: Oct, 2000 - No. 3, Jan, 2001 ($2.99)
1-3-Busiek-s/Ordway-a; Ronan the Accuser, Avengers app. 3.00
...Dangerous Planet 1: Busiek-s/Ordway-a; Ego, the Living Planet 3.00
Thor vs. Ego (11/00, $2.99) Reprints Thor #133,160,161; Kirby-a 3.00

MAXX (Also see Darker Image, Primer #5, & Friends of Maxx)
Image Comics (I Before E): Mar, 1993 - No. 35, Feb, 1998 ($1.95)
1/2 1 3 4 6 8 10
1/2 (Gold) 20.00
1-Sam Kieth-c/a/scripts 4.00
1-Glow-in-the-dark variant 2 4 6 8 10 12
1-"3-D Edition" (1/98, $4.95) plus new back-up story 5.00
2-12: 6-Savage Dragon cameo(1 pg.). 7,8-Pitt-c & story 2.50
13-16 2.50
17-35: 21-Alan Moore-s 2.50
Volume 1 TPB (DC/WildStorm, 2003, $17.95) r/#1-6 18.00
Volume 2 TPB (DC/WildStorm, 2004, $17.95) r/#7-13 18.00
Volume 3 TPB (DC/WildStorm, 2004, $17.95) r/#14-20 18.00
Volume 4 TPB (DC/WildStorm, 2005, $17.95) r/#21-27 18.00
Volume 5 TPB (DC/WildStorm, 2005, $19.99) r/#28-35 20.00
Volume 6 TPB (DC/WildStorm, 2006, $19.99) r/Friends of Maxx #1-3 & The Maxx 3-D 20.00

MAYA (See Movie Classics)
Gold Key: Mar, 1968

GD VG FN VF VF/NM NM-
2.0 4.0 6.0 8.0 9.0 9.2

1 (10218-803)(TV) 3 6 9 17 25 32

MAYHEM
Dark Horse Comics: May, 1989 - No. 4, Sept, 1989 ($2.50, B&W, 52 pgs.)
1- Four part Stanley Ipkiss/Mask story begins; Mask-c
1 3 4 6 8 10
2-4: 2-Mask 1/2 back-c. 4-Mask-c 1 2 3 5 7 9

MAYHEM (Tyrese Gibson's...)
Image Comics: Aug, 2009 - No. 3, Oct, 2009 ($2.99, limited series)
1-3-Tyrese Gibson co-writer; Tone Rodriguez-a/c 3.00

MAZE AGENCY, THE
Comico/Innovation Publ. #8 on: Dec, 1988 - No. 20, 1991 ($1.95-$2.50, color)
1-20: 9-Ellery Queen app. 7 ($2.50)-Last Comico issue 2.50
Annual 1 (1990, $2.75)-Ploog-c; Spirit tribute ish 2.75
Special 1 (1989, $2.75)-Staton-p (Innovation) 2.75
TPB (IDW Publ., 11/05, $24.99) r/#1-5 25.00

MAZE AGENCY, THE (Vol. 2)
Caliber Comics: July, 1997 - No. 3, 1998 ($2.95, B&W)
1-3: 1-Barr-s/Gonzales-a(p). 3-Hughes-c 3.00

MAZE AGENCY, THE
Caliber Comics: Nov, 2005 - No. 3, Jan, 2006 ($3.99, limited series)
1-3-Barr-s/Padilla-a(p)/c 4.00

MAZIE (...& Her Friends) (See Flat-Top, Mortie, Stevie & Tastee-Freez)
Mazie Comics(Magazine Publ.)/Harvey Publ. No. 13-on: 1953 - #12, 1954; #13, 12/54 - #22, 9/56; #23, 9/57 - #28, 8/58
1-(Teen-age)-Stevie's girlfriend 10 20 30 58 79 100
2 7 14 21 35 43 50
3-10 6 12 18 31 38 45
11-28 5 10 15 24 30 35

MAZIE
Nation Wide Publishers: 1950 - No. 7, 1951 (5¢) (5x7-1/4"-miniature)(52 pgs.)
1-Teen-age 15 30 45 94 147 200
2-7 10 20 30 58 79 100

MAZINGER (See First Comics Graphic Novel #17)

'MAZING MAN
DC Comics: Jan, 1986 - No. 12, Dec, 1986
1-11: 7,8-Hembeck-a 2.50
12-Dark Knight part-c by Miller 3.00
Special 1 ('87), 2 (4/88), 3 ('90)-All $2.00, 52pgs. 2.50

McCANDLESS & COMPANY
Mandalay Books: 2001 ($7.95)
...: Dead Razor - J.C. Vaughn-s/Busch & Sheehan-a; 3 covers 8.00
Crime Scenes: A McCandless & Company Reader TPB (Spring 2006, $17.95) Vaughn-s 18.00

McHALE'S NAVY (TV) (See Movie Classics)
Dell Publ. Co.: May-July, 1963 - No. 3, Nov-Jan, 1963-64 (All have photo-c)
1 7 14 21 45 73 100
2,3 5 10 15 32 51 70

McKEEVER & THE COLONEL (TV)
Dell Publishing Co.: Feb-Apr, 1963 - No. 3, Aug-Oct, 1963
1-Photo-c 6 12 18 39 62 85
2,3 5 10 15 30 48 65

McLINTOCK (See Movie Comics)

MD
E. C. Comics: Apr-May, 1955 - No. 5, Dec-Jan, 1955-56
1-Not approved by code; Craig-c 15 30 45 120 190 260
2-5 10 20 30 80 125 170
NOTE: ***Crandall, Evans, Ingels, Orlando*** *art in all issues;* ***Craig*** *c-1-5.*

MD
Russ Cochran/Gemstone Publishing: Sept, 1999 - No. 5, Jan, 2000 ($2.50)
1-5-Reprints original EC series 2.50
Annual 1 (1999, $13.50) r/#1-5 14.00

MEASLES
Fantagraphics Books: Christmas 1998 - No. 8 ($2.95, B&W, quarterly)
1-8-Anthology: 1-Venus-s by Hernandez 3.00

MECHA (Also see Mayhem)

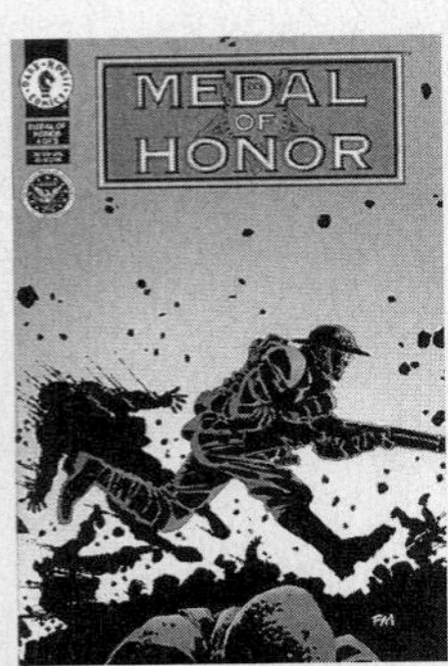

Medal of Honor #4 © DH

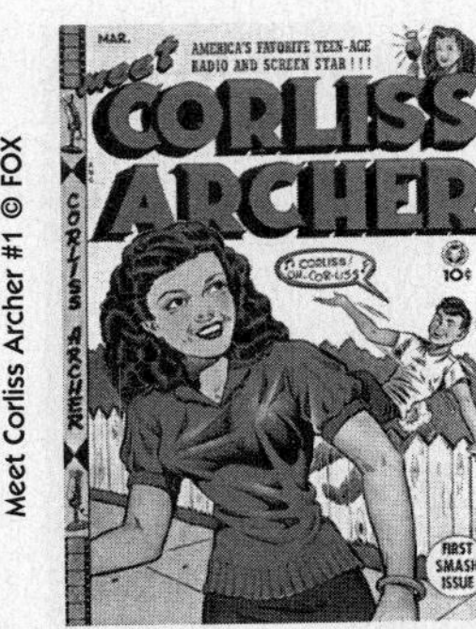

Meet Corliss Archer #1 © FOX

Mekanix #1 © MAR

GD VG FN VF VF/NM NM-
2.0 4.0 6.0 8.0 9.0 9.2

Dark Horse Comics: June, 1987 - No. 6, 1988 ($1.50/$1.95, color/B&W)
1-6: 1,2 ($1.95, color), 3,4-($1.75, B&W), 5,6-($1.50, B&W) 2.50

MECHANIC, THE
Image Comics: 1998 ($5.95, one-shot, squarebound)
1-Chiodo-painted art; Peterson-s 6.00
1-($10.00) DF Alternate Cover Ed. 10.00

MECHA SPECIAL
Dark Horse Comics: May, 1995 ($2.95, one-shot)
1 3.00

MECH DESTROYER
Image Comics: Apr, 2001 - No. 4, Sept, 2001 ($2.95, limited series)
1-4-Jae Kim-c/a; Robert Chong-s 3.00

MEDAL FOR BOWZER, A (See Promotional Comics section)

MEDAL OF HONOR COMICS
A. S. Curtis: Spring, 1946
1-War stories 13 26 39 74 105 135

MEDAL OF HONOR SPECIAL
Dark Horse Comics: 1994 ($2.50, one-shot)
1-Kubert-c/a (first story) 2.50

MEDIA STARR
Innovation Publ.: July, 1989 - No. 3, Sept, 1989 ($1.95, mini-series, 28 pgs.)
1-3: Deluxe format 2.50

MEDIEVAL SPAWN/WITCHBLADE
Image Comics (Top Cow Productions): May, 1996 - No. 3, June, 1996 ($2.95, limited series)
1-3-Garth Ennis scripts in all 6.00
1-Platinum foil-c (500 copies from Pittsburgh Con) 35.00
1-Gold 10.00
1-ETM Exclusive Edition; gold foil logo 7.00
TPB ($9.95) r/#1-3 10.00

MEET ANGEL (Formerly Angel & the Ape)
National Periodical Publications: No. 7, Nov-Dec, 1969
7-Wood-a(i) 3 6 9 20 30 40

MEET CORLISS ARCHER (Radio/Movie)(My Life #4 on)
Fox Features Syndicate: Mar, 1948 - No. 3, July, 1948
1-(Teen-age)-Feldstein-c/a; headlight-c 110 220 330 704 1202 1700
2 55 110 165 352 601 850
3-Part Feldstein-c only 52 104 156 323 549 775
NOTE: *No. 1-3 used in Seduction of the Innocent, pg. 39.*

MEET HERCULES (See Three Stooges)

MEET MERTON
Toby Press: Dec, 1953 - No. 4, June, 1954
1-(Teen-age)-Dave Berg-c/a 9 18 27 52 69 85
2-Dave Berg-c/a 6 12 18 29 36 42
3,4-Dave Berg-c/a 6 12 18 27 33 38
I.W. Reprint #9, Super Reprint #11('63), 18 2 4 6 8 11 14

MEET MISS BLISS (Becomes Stories Of Romance #5 on)
Atlas Comics (LMC): May, 1955 - No. 4, Nov, 1955
1-Al Hartley-c/a 14 28 42 80 115 150
2-4 9 18 27 52 69 85

MEET MISS PEPPER (Formerly Lucy, The Real Gone Gal)
St. John Publishing Co.: No. 5, April, 1954 - No. 6, June, 1954
5-Kubert/Maurer-a 21 42 63 122 199 275
6-Kubert/Maurer-a; Kubert-c 18 36 54 105 165 225

MEGACITY909
Devil's Due Publ.: Sept, 2004 - No. 8, Aug, 2005 ($2.95)
1-8-Kano Kang & Zack Suh-a 3.00

MEGA DRAGON & TIGER
Image Comics: Mar, 1999 - No. 5 ($2.95)
1-5-Tony Wong-s/a 3.00

MEGAHURTZ
Image Comics: Aug, 1997 - No. 3, Oct, 1997 ($2.95, B&W)
1-3-St. Pierre-s 3.00

MEGALITH (Megalith Deathwatch 2000 #1,2 of second series)

GD VG FN VF VF/NM NM-
2.0 4.0 6.0 8.0 9.0 9.2

Continuity: 1989 - No. 9, Mar, 1992; No, 0, Apr, 1993 - No. 7, Jan, 1994
1-9-($2.00-c) 1-Neal Adams & Mark Texiera-c/Texiera & Nebres-a 3.00
2nd series: 0-(4/93)-Foil-c; no c-price, giveaway; Adams plot 3.00
1-7: 1-3-Bagged w/card: 1-Gatefold-c by Nebres; Adams plot. 2-Fold-out-c; Adams plot. 3-Indestructible-c. 4-7-Embossed-c: 4-Adams/Nebres-c; Adams part-i. 5-Sienkiewicz-i. 6-Adams part-i. 7-Adams-c(p); Adams plot 3.00

MEGAMAN
Dreamwave Productions: Sept, 2003 - No. 4, Dec, 2003 ($2.95)
1-4-Brian Augustyn-s/Mic Fong-a 3.00
1-($5.95) Chromium wraparound variant-c 6.00

MEGA MORPHS
Marvel Comics: Oct, 2005 - No. 4, Dec, 2005 ($2.99, limited series)
1-4-Giant robots based on action figures; McKeever-s; Kang-a 3.00
Digest (2006, $7.99) r/#1-4 plus mini-comics 8.00

MEGATON (A super hero)
Megaton Publ.: Nov, 1983; No. 2, Oct, 1985 - No. 8, Aug, 1987 (B&W)
1-($2.00, 68 pgs.)-Erik Larsen's 1st pro work; Vanguard by Larsen begins (1st app.), ends #4; 1st app. Megaton, Berzerker, & Ethrian; Guice-c/a(p); Gustovich-a(p) in #1,2 2 4 6 10 14 18
2-($2.00, 68 pgs.)-1st brief app. The Dragon (1 pg.) by Larsen (later The Savage Dragon in Image Comics); Guice-c/a(p) 2 4 6 9 12 15
3-(44 pgs.)-1st full app. Savage Dragon-c/story by Larsen; 1st comic book work by Angel Medina (pin-up) 2 4 6 13 18 22
4-(52 pgs.)-2nd full app. Savage Dragon by Larsen; 4,5-Wildman by Grass Green 2 4 6 8 10 12
5-1st Liefeld published-a (inside f/c, 6/86) 1 2 3 5 7 9
6,7: 6-Larsen-c 1 2 3 4 5 7
8-1st Liefeld story-a (7 pg. super hero story) plus 1 pg. Youngblood ad 1 3 4 6 8 10
...Explosion (6/87, 16 pg. color giveaway)-1st app. Youngblood by Rob Liefeld (2 pg. spread); shows Megaton heroes 3 6 9 14 20 25
...Holiday Special 1 (1994, $2.95, color, 40 pgs., publ. by Entity Comics)-Gold foil logo; bagged w/Kelley Jones card; Vanguard, Megaton plus shows unpublished-c to 1987 Youngblood #1 by Liefeld/Ordway 5.00
NOTE: *Copies of Megaton Explosion were also released in early 1992 all signed by Rob Liefeld and were made available to retailers.*

MEGATON MAN (See Don Simpson's Bizarre Heroes)
Kitchen Sink Enterprises: Nov, 1984 - No. 10, 1986
1-10, 1-2nd printing (1989) 3.00
...Meets The Uncategorizable X-Thems 1 (4/89, $2.00) 3.00

MEGATON MAN: BOMB SHELL
Image Comics: Jul, 1999 - No. 2 ($2.95, B&W, mini-series)
1-Reprints stories from Megaton Man internet site 3.00

MEGATON MAN: HARD COPY
Image Comics: Feb, 1999 - No. 2, Apr, 1999 ($2.95, B&W, mini-series)
1,2-Reprints stories from Megaton Man internet site 3.00

MEGATON MAN VS. FORBIDDEN FRANKENSTEIN
Fiasco Comics: Apr, 1996 ($2.95, B&W, one-shot)
1-Intro The Tomb Team (Forbidden Frankenstein, Drekula, Bride of the Monster, & Moon Wolf). 3.00

MEK (See Reload/Mek flipbook for TPB reprint)
DC Comics (Homage): Jan, 2003 - No. 3, Mar, 2003 ($2.95, limited series)
1-3-Warren Ellis-s/Steve Rolston-a 3.00

MEKANIX (See X-Men titles) (See X-Treme X-Men Vol. 4 for TPB)
Marvel Comics: Dec, 2002 - No. 6, May, 2003 ($2.99, limited series)
1-6-Kitty Pryde in college; Claremont-s/Bobillo & Sosa-a 3.00

MEL ALLEN SPORTS COMICS (The Voice of the Yankees)
Standard Comics: No. 5, Nov, 1949; No. 6, June, 1950
5(#1 on inside)-Tuska-a 23 46 69 136 223 310
6(#2)-Lou Gehrig story 16 32 48 94 147 200

MELTDOWN
Image Comics: Dec, 2006 - No. 2, Jan, 2007 ($5.95, squarebound, limited series)
1,2-Schwartz-s/Wang-a. 1-Bachalo-c. 2-Horn-c 6.00

MELVIN MONSTER
Dell Publishing Co.: Apr-June, 1965 - No. 10, Oct, 1969
1-By John Stanley 8 16 24 58 97 135

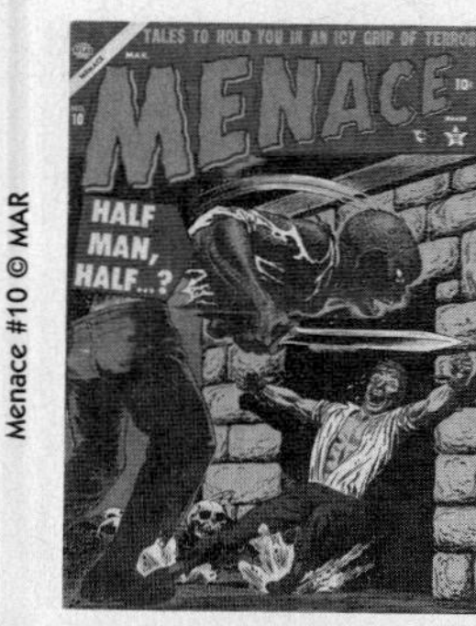

Menace #10 © MAR

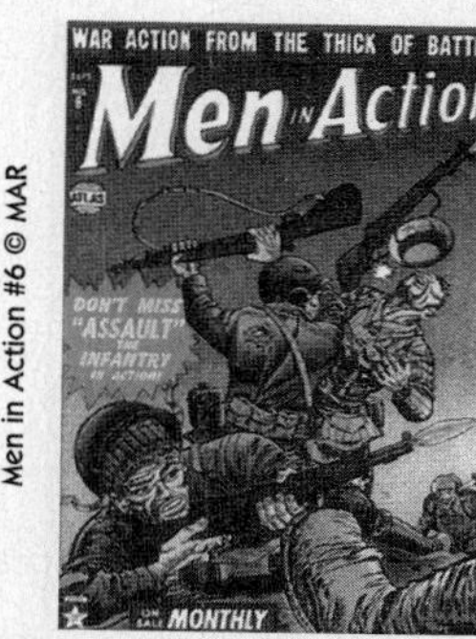

Men in Action #6 © MAR

Men's Adventures #14 © MAR

GD 2.0 | VG 4.0 | FN 6.0 | VF 8.0 | VF/NM 9.0 | NM- 9.2

2-10-All by Stanley. #10-r/#1 6 12 18 41 66 90

MELVIN THE MONSTER (See Peter, the Little Pest & Dexter The Demon #7)
Atlas Comics (HPC): July, 1956 - No. 6, July, 1957

1-Maneely-c/a 14 28 42 80 115 150
2-6: 4-Maneely-c/a 10 20 30 54 72 90

MENACE
Atlas Comics (HPC): Mar, 1953 - No. 11, May, 1954

1-Horror & sci/fi stories begin; Everett-c/a 74 148 222 470 810 1150
2-Post-atom bomb disaster by Everett; anti-Communist propaganda/torture scenes; Sinnott sci/fi story "Rocket to the Moon" 50 100 150 315 533 750
3,4,6-Everett-a. 4-Sci/fi story "Escape to the Moon". 6-Romita sci/fi story "Science Fiction" 41 82 123 256 428 600
5-Origin & 1st app. The Zombie by Everett (reprinted in Tales of the Zombie #1)(7/53); 5-Sci/fi story "Rocket Ship" 58 116 174 371 636 900
7,8,10,11: 7-Frankenstein story. 8-End of world story; Heath 3-D art(3 pgs.). 10-H-Bomb panels 34 68 102 199 325 450
9-Everett-a r-in Vampire Tales #1 37 74 111 222 361 500

NOTE: ***Brodsky*** *c-7, 8, 11.* ***Colan*** *a-6; c-9.* ***Everett*** *a-1-6, 9; c-1-6.* ***Heath*** *a-1-8; c-10.* ***Katz*** *a-11.* ***Maneely*** *a-3, 5, 7-9.* ***Powell*** *a-11.* ***Romita*** *a-3, 6, 8, 11.* ***Shelly*** *a-10.* ***Shores*** *a-7.* ***Sinnott*** *a-2, 7.* ***Tuska*** *a-1, 2, 5.*

MENACE
Awesome-Hyperwerks: Nov, 1998 ($2.50)

1-Jada Pinkett Smith-s/Fraga-a 2.50

MEN AGAINST CRIME (Formerly Mr. Risk; Hand of Fate #8 on)
Ace Magazines: No. 3, Feb, 1951 - No. 7, Oct, 1951

3-Mr. Risk app. 11 22 33 60 83 105
4-7: 4-Colan-a; entire book-r as Trapped! #4. 5-Meskin-a 8 16 24 44 57 70

MEN, GUNS, & CATTLE (See Classics Illustrated Special Issue)

MEN IN ACTION (Battle Brady #10 on)
Atlas Comics (IPS): April, 1952 - No. 9, Dec, 1952 (War stories)

1-Berg, Reinman-a 17 34 51 98 154 210
2,3: 3-Heath-c/a 11 22 33 60 83 105
4-6,8,9 10 20 30 54 72 90
7-Krigstein-a; Heath-c 11 22 33 60 83 105

NOTE: ***Brodsky*** *a-3; c-1, 4-6.* ***Maneely*** *c-5.* ***Pakula*** *a-1, 6.* ***Robinson*** *c-8.* ***Shores*** *c-9.* ***Sinnott*** *a-6.*

MEN IN ACTION
Ajax/Farrell Publications: April, 1957 - No. 6, 1958

1 10 20 30 54 72 90
2 7 14 21 35 43 50
3-6 6 12 18 29 36 42

MEN IN BLACK, THE (1st series)
Aircel Comics (Malibu): Jan, 1990 - No. 3 Mar, 1990 ($2.25, B&W, lim. series)

1-Cunningham-s/a in all 4 8 12 28 44 60
2,3 3 6 9 17 25 32
Graphic Novel (Jan, 1991) r/#1-3 3 6 9 16 22 28

MEN IN BLACK (2nd series)
Aircel Comics (Malibu): May, 1991 - No. 3, Jul, 1991 ($2.50, B&W, lim. series)

1-Cunningham-s/a in all 3 6 9 17 25 32
2,3 2 4 6 9 13 16

MEN IN BLACK: FAR CRY
Marvel Comics: Aug, 1997 ($3.99, color, one-shot)

1-Cunningham-s 4.00

MEN IN BLACK: RETRIBUTION
Marvel Comics: Dec, 1997 ($3.99, color, one-shot)

1-Cunningham-s; continuation of the movie 4.00

MEN IN BLACK: THE MOVIE
Marvel Comics: Oct, 1997 ($3.99, one-shot, movie adaptation)

1-Cunningham-s 4.00

MEN INTO SPACE
Dell Publishing Co.: No. 1083, Feb-Apr, 1960

Four Color 1083-Anderson-a, photo-c 5 10 15 34 55 75

MEN OF BATTLE (Also see New Men of Battle)
Catechetical Guild: V1#5, March, 1943 (Hardcover)

V1#5-Topix reprints 6 12 18 28 34 40

MEN OF WAR

GD 2.0 | VG 4.0 | FN 6.0 | VF 8.0 | VF/NM 9.0 | NM- 9.2

DC Comics, Inc.: August, 1977 - No. 26, March, 1980 (#9,10: 44 pgs.)

1-Enemy Ace, Gravedigger (origin #1,2) begin 3 6 9 16 22 28
2-4,8-10,12-14,19,20: All Enemy Ace stories. 4-1st Dateline Frontline. 9-Unknown Soldier app. 2 4 6 9 13 16
5-7,11,15-18,21-25: 17-1st app. Rosa 2 4 6 8 10 12
26-Sgt. Rock & Easy Co.-c/s 2 4 6 13 18 22

NOTE: ***Chaykin*** *a-9, 10, 12-14, 19, 20.* ***Evans*** *c-25.* ***Kubert*** *c-2-23, 24p, 26.*

MEN'S ADVENTURES (Formerly True Adventures)
Marvel/Atlas Comics (CCC): No. 4, Aug, 1950 - No. 28, July, 1954

4(#1)(52 pgs.) 33 66 99 194 317 440
5-Flying Saucer story 21 42 63 124 202 280
6-8: 7-Buried alive story. 8-Sci/fic story 20 40 60 114 182 250
9-20: All war format 14 28 42 80 115 150
21,22,24,26: All horror format 22 44 66 132 216 300
23-Crandall-a; Fox-a(i); horror format 23 46 69 136 223 310
25-Shrunken head-c 36 72 108 216 351 485
27,28-Human Torch & Toro-c/stories; Captain America & Sub-Mariner stories in each (also see Young Men #24-28) 119 238 357 762 1306 1850

NOTE: ***Ayers*** *a-20, 27(H. Torch).* ***Berg*** *a-15, 16.* ***Brodsky*** *c-4-9, 11, 12, 16-18, 24.* ***Burgos*** *c-27, 28(Human Torch).* ***Colan*** *a-13, 14, 19.* ***Everett*** *a-10, 14, 22, 25, 28; c-14, 21-23.* ***Hartley*** *a-12.* ***Heath*** *a-8, 11, 24; c-13, 20, 26.* ***Lawrence*** *a-23; 27(Captain America).* ***Maneely*** *a-24; c-10, 15.* ***Mac Pakula*** *a-15, 25.* ***Post*** *a-23.* ***Powell*** *a-27(Sub-Mariner).* ***Reinman*** *a-11, 12.* ***Robinson*** *c-19.* ***Romita*** *a-22.* ***Sale*** *a-12.* ***Shores*** *c-25.* ***Sinnott*** *a-13, 21.* ***Tuska*** *a-24. Adventure-#4-8; War-#9-20; Weird/Horror-#21-26.*

MENZ INSANA
DC Comics (Vertigo): 1997 ($7.95, one-shot)

nn-Fowler-s/Bolton painted art 1 2 3 5 6 8

MEPHISTO VS... (See Silver Surfer #3)
Marvel Comics Group: Apr, 1987 - No. 4, July, 1987 ($1.50, mini-series)

1-4: 1-Fantastic Four; Austin-i. 2-X-Factor. 3-X-Men. 4-Avengers 3.00

MERC (See Mark Hazzard: Merc)

MERCENARIES (Based on the Pandemic video game)
Dynamite Entertainment: 2007 - No. 3, 2008 ($3.99, limited series)

1-3-Michael Turner-c; Brian Reed-s/Edgar Salazar-a 4.00

MERCHANTS OF DEATH
Acme Press (Eclipse): Jul, 1988 - No. 4, Nov, 1988 ($3.50, B&W/16 pgs. color, 44 pg. mag.)

1-4: 4-Toth-c 3.50

MERCY THOMPSON: HOMECOMING (Patricia Briggs'...)
Dabel Brothers Prods.: Oct, 2008 (Nov. on-c) - No. 4 ($3.99, limited series)

1-Characters from the Patricia Briggs werewolf novels; Francis Tsai-a 4.00

MERIDIAN
CrossGeneration Comics: Jul, 2000 - No. 44, Apr, 2004 ($2.95)

1-44: Barbara Kesel-s 3.00
Flying Solo Vol. 1 TPB (2001, $19.95) r/#1-7; cover by Steve Rude 20.00
Going to Ground Vol. 2 TPB (2002, $19.95) r/#8-14 20.00
Taking the Skies Vol. 3 TPB (2002, $15.95) r/#15-20 16.00
Vol. 4: Coming Home (12/02, $15.95) r/#21-26 16.00
Vol. 5: Minister of Cadador (7/03, $15.95) r/#27-32 16.00
Vol. 6: Changing Course (1/04, $15.95) r/#33-38 16.00
Traveler Vol. 1-4 ($9.95): Digest-size reprints of TPBs 10.00

MERLIN JONES AS THE MONKEY'S UNCLE (See Movie Comics and The Misadventures of... under Movie Comics)

MERRILL'S MARAUDERS (See Movie Classics)

MERRY CHRISTMAS (See A Christmas Adventure, Donald Duck..., Dell Giant #39, & March of Comics #153 in the Promotional Comics section)

MERRY COMICS
Carlton Publishing Co.: Dec, 1945 (10¢)

nn-Boogeyman app. 20 40 60 114 182 250

MERRY COMICS: Four Star Publications: 1947 (Advertised, not published)

MERRY-GO-ROUND COMICS
LaSalle Publ. Co./Croyden Publ./Rotary Litho.: 1944 (25¢, 132 pgs.); 1946; 9-10/47 - No. 2, 1948

nn(1944)(LaSalle)-Funny animal; 29 new features 18 36 54 105 165 225
21 (Publisher?) 9 18 27 47 61 75
1(1946)(Croyden)-Al Fago-c; funny animal 11 22 33 60 83 105
V1#1,2(1947-48; 52 pgs.)(Rotary Litho. Co. Ltd., Canada); Ken Hultgren-a 9 18 27 47 61 75

MERRY MAILMAN (See Fawcett's Funny Animals #87-89)

Metal Men #5 © DC

Metamorpho: Year One #6 © DC

Mice Templar V2 #1 © Oeming & Glass

	GD 2.0	VG 4.0	FN 6.0	VF 8.0	VF/NM 9.0	NM- 9.2

MERRY MOUSE (Also see Funny Tunes & Space Comics)
Avon Periodicals: June, 1953 - No. 4, Jan-Feb, 1954

	GD	VG	FN	VF	VF/NM	NM-
1-1st app.; funny animal; Frank Carin-c/a	10	20	30	54	72	90
2-4	7	14	21	35	43	50

MERV PUMPKINHEAD, AGENT OF D.R.E.A.M. (See The Sandman)
DC Comics (Vertigo): 2000 ($5.95, one-shot)

	GD	VG	FN	VF	VF/NM	NM-
1-Buckingham-a(p); Nowlan painted-c						6.00

META-4
First Comics: Feb, 1991 - No. 4, 1991 ($2.25)

	GD	VG	FN	VF	VF/NM	NM-
1-($3.95, 52pgs.)						4.00
2-4						2.50

METAL GEAR SOLID (Based on the video game)
IDW Publ.: Sept, 2004 - No. 12, Aug, 2005 ($3.99)

	GD	VG	FN	VF	VF/NM	NM-
1-12: 1-Two covers; Ashley Wood-a/Kris Oprisko-s						4.00
1-Retailer edition with foil cover						20.00

METAL GEAR SOLID: SONS OF LIBERTY
IDW Publ.: Sept, 2005 - Present ($3.99)

	GD	VG	FN	VF	VF/NM	NM-
#0 (9/05) profile pages on characters; Ashley Wood-a						4.00
1-9: 1-Two covers; Ashley Wood-a/Alex Garner-s						4.00

METALLIX
Future Comics: Dec, 2002 - No. 6, June, 2003 ($3.50)

	GD	VG	FN	VF	VF/NM	NM-
0-6-Ron Lim-a. 0-(6/03) Origin. 1-Layton-c						3.50
1-Collector's Edition with variant cover by Lim						3.50
1-Free Comic Book Day Edition (4/03) Layton-c						2.50

METAL MEN (See Brave & the Bold, DC Comics Presents, and Showcase #37-40)
National Periodical Publications/DC Comics: 4-5/63 - No. 41, 12-1/69-70; No. 42, 2-3/73 - No. 44, 7-8/73; No. 45, 4-5/76 - No. 56, 2-3/78

	GD	VG	FN	VF	VF/NM	NM-
1-(4-5/63)-5th app. Metal Men	54	108	162	459	905	1350
2	22	44	66	157	304	450
3-5	14	28	42	102	194	285
6-10	10	20	30	68	119	170
11-20: 12-Beatles cameo (2-3/65)	8	16	24	54	90	125
21-Batman, Robin & Flash x-over	6	12	18	43	69	95
22-26,28-30	6	12	18	39	62	85
27-Origin Metal Men retold	7	14	21	50	83	115
31-41(1968-70): 38-Last 12¢ issue. 41-Last 15¢	5	10	15	34	55	75
42-44(1973)-Reprints	2	4	6	10	14	18
45('76)-49-Simonson-a in all: 48,49-Re-intro Eclipso	2	4	6	10	14	18
50-56: 50-Part-r. 54,55-Green Lantern x-over	2	4	6	9	12	15

NOTE: ***Andru/Esposito** c-1-30. **Aparo** c-53-56. **Giordano** c-45, 46. **Kane/Esposito** a-30, 31; c-31. **Simonson** a-45-49; c-47-52. **Staton** a-50-56.*

METAL MEN (Also see Tangent Comics/ Metal Men)
DC Comics: Oct, 1993 - No. 4, Jan, 1994 ($1.25, mini-series)

	GD	VG	FN	VF	VF/NM	NM-
1-($2.50)-Multi-colored foil-c						4.00
2-4: 2-Origin						2.50

METAL MEN (Also see 52)
DC Comics: Oct, 2007 - No. 8, Jul, 2008 ($2.99, limited series)

	GD	VG	FN	VF	VF/NM	NM-
1-8-Duncan Rouleau-s/a; origin re-told. 3-Chemo returns						3.00
HC (2008, $24.99, dustjacket) r/#1-8; cover gallery and sketch pages						25.00
SC (2009, $14.99) r/#1-8; cover gallery and sketch pages						15.00

METAMORPHO (See Action Comics #413, Brave & the Bold #57,58, 1st Issue Special, & World's Finest #217)
National Periodical Publications: July-Aug, 1965 - No. 17, Mar-Apr, 1968 (All 12¢ issues)

	GD	VG	FN	VF	VF/NM	NM-
1-(7-8/65)-3rd app. Metamorpho	13	26	39	93	172	250
2,3	7	14	21	50	83	115
4-6,10:10-Origin & 1st app. Element Girl (1-2/67)	6	12	18	43	69	95
7-9	6	12	18	37	59	80
11-17: 17-Sparling-c/a	5	10	15	32	51	70

NOTE: ***Ramona Fradon** a-B&B 57, 58, 1-4. **Orlando** a-5, 6; c-5-9, 11. **Trapani** a(p)-7-16; i-16.*

METAMORPHO
DC Comics: Aug, 1993 - No. 4, Nov, 1993 ($1.50, mini-series)

	GD	VG	FN	VF	VF/NM	NM-
1-4						2.50

METAMORPHO: YEAR ONE
DC Comics: Early Dec, 2007 - No. 6, Late Feb, 2008 ($2.99, limited series)

	GD	VG	FN	VF	VF/NM	NM-
1-6-Origin re-told; Jurgens-s/Jurgens & Delperdang-a/Nowlan-c. 6-Justice League app.						3.00
TPB ('08, $14.99) r/#1-6						15.00

METAPHYSIQUE
Malibu Comics (Bravura): Apr, 1995 - No. 6, Oct, 1995 ($2.95, limited series)

	GD	VG	FN	VF	VF/NM	NM-
1-6: Norm Breyfogle-c/a/scripts						3.00

METEOR COMICS
L. L. Baird (Croyden): Nov, 1945

	GD	VG	FN	VF	VF/NM	NM-
1-Captain Wizard, Impossible Man, Race Wilkins app.; origin Baldy Bean, Capt. Wizard's sidekick; bare-breasted mermaids story	39	78	117	240	395	550

METEOR MAN
Marvel Comics: Aug, 1993 - No. 6, Jan, 1994 ($1.25, limited series)

	GD	VG	FN	VF	VF/NM	NM-
1-6: 1-Regular unbagged. 4-Night Thrasher-c/story. 6-Terry Austin-c(i)						2.50
1-Polybagged w/button & rap newspaper						4.00
...: The Movie (4/93 [7/93 on cover], $2.25) movie adaptation						2.50

METROPOL (See Ted McKeever's...)

METROPOL A.D. (See Ted McKeever's...)

METROPOLIS S.C.U. (Also see Showcase '96 #1)
DC Comics: Nov, 1995 - No. 4, Feb, 1996 ($1.50, limited series)

	GD	VG	FN	VF	VF/NM	NM-
1-4:1-Superman-c & app.						2.50

MEZZ: GALACTIC TOUR 2494 (Also See Nexus)
Dark Horse Comics: May, 1994 ($2.50, one-shot)

	GD	VG	FN	VF	VF/NM	NM-
1						2.50

MGM'S MARVELOUS WIZARD OF OZ (See Marvel Treasury of Oz)
Marvel Comics Group/National Periodical Publications: 1975 ($1.50, 84 pgs.; oversize)

	GD	VG	FN	VF	VF/NM	NM-
1-Adaptation of MGM's movie; J. Buscema-a	3	6	9	16	23	30

M.G.M'S MOUSE MUSKETEERS (Formerly M.G.M.'s The Two Mouseketeers)
Dell Publishing Co.: No. 670, Jan, 1956 - No. 1290, Mar-May, 1962

	GD	VG	FN	VF	VF/NM	NM-
Four Color 670 (#4)	5	10	15	34	55	75
Four Color 711,728,764	4	8	12	26	41	55
8 (4-6/57) - 21 (3-5/60)	4	8	12	24	37	50
Four Color 1135,1175,1290	4	8	12	24	37	50

M.G.M.'S SPIKE AND TYKE (also see Tom & Jerry #79)
Dell Publishing Co.: No. 499, Sept, 1953 - No. 1266, Dec-Feb, 1961-62

	GD	VG	FN	VF	VF/NM	NM-
Four Color 499 (#1)	7	14	21	45	73	100
Four Color 577,638	5	10	15	30	48	65
4(12-2/55-56)-10	4	8	12	26	41	55
11-24(12-2/60-61)	4	8	12	22	34	45
Four Color 1266	4	8	12	24	37	50

M.G.M.'S THE TWO MOUSKETEERS
Dell Publishing Co.: No. 475, June, 1953 - No. 642, July, 1955

	GD	VG	FN	VF	VF/NM	NM-
Four Color 475 (#1)	8	16	24	52	86	120
Four Color 603 (11/54), 642	6	12	18	37	59	80

MICE TEMPLAR, THE
Image Comics: Sept, 2007 - No. 6, Oct, 2008 ($3.99/$2.99)

	GD	VG	FN	VF	VF/NM	NM-
1-($3.99)-Bryan Glass-s/Michael Avon Oeming-a/c						4.00
2-6-($2.99)						3.00

MICE TEMPLAR, THE , VOLUME 2: DESTINY
Image Comics: July, 2009 - Present ($3.99/$2.99)

	GD	VG	FN	VF	VF/NM	NM-
1,2-($3.99) 1-Bryan Glass-s/Oeming & Santos-a; 2 covers. 2-Santos-a						4.00
3-7-($2.99)-Santos-a; 2 covers by Oeming & Santos						3.00

MICHAELANGELO CHRISTMAS SPECIAL (See Teenage Mutant Ninja Turtles Christmas Special)

MICHAELANGELO, TEENAGE MUTANT NINJA TURTLE
Mirage Studios: 1986 (One shot) ($1.50, B&W)

	GD	VG	FN	VF	VF/NM	NM-
1						5.00
1-2nd printing ('89, $1.75)-Reprint plus new-a						2.50

MICHAEL CHABON PRESENTS THE AMAZING ADVENTURES OF THE ESCAPIST
Dark Horse Comics: Feb, 2004 - Present ($8.95, squarebound)

	GD	VG	FN	VF	VF/NM	NM-
1-5,7,8-Short stories by Chabon and various incl. Chaykin, Starlin, Brereton, Baker						9.00
6-Includes 6 pg. Spirit & Escapist story (Will Eisner's last work); Spirit on cover						9.00
... Vol. 1 (5/04, $17.95, digest-size) r/#1&2; wraparound-c by Chris Ware						18.00
... Vol. 2 (11/04, $17.95, digest-size) r/#3&4; wraparound-c by Matt Kindt						18.00
... Vol. 3 (4/06, $14.95, digest-size) r/#5&6; Tim Sale-c						15.00

MICHAEL MOORCOCK'S ELRIC: THE MAKING OF A SORCEROR
DC Comics: 2004 - No. 4, 2006 ($5.95, prestige format, limited series)

	GD	VG	FN	VF	VF/NM	NM-
1-4-Moorcock-s/Simonson-a						6.00
TPB (2007, $19.99) r/#1-4						20.00

MICHAEL MOORCOCK'S MULTIVERSE

Mickey Mouse #30 © DIS

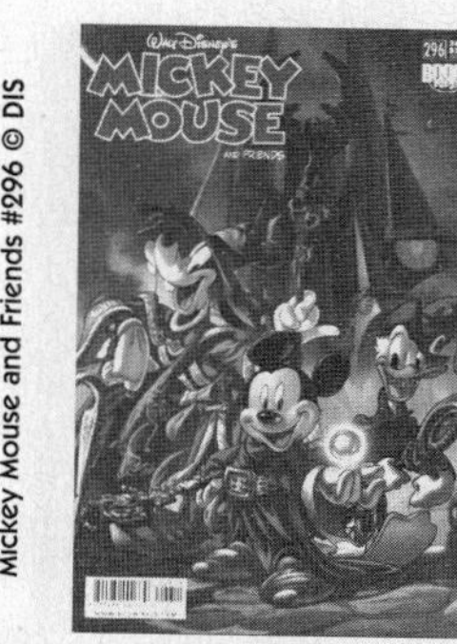

Mickey Mouse and Friends #296 © DIS

Mickey Mouse Magazine V1 #2 © DIS

	GD 2.0	VG 4.0	FN 6.0	VF 8.0	VF/NM 9.0	NM- 9.2

DC Comics (Helix): Nov, 1997 - No. 12, Oct, 1998 ($2.50, limited series)

1-12: Simonson, Reeve & Ridgway-a 2.50
TPB (1999, $19.95) r/#1-12 20.00

MICHAEL TURNER, A TRIBUTE TO...
Aspen MLT: 2008 ($8.99, squarebound)

nn-Pin-ups and tributes from Turner's colleagues and friends; Turner & Ross-c 9.00

MICHAEL TURNER PRESENTS: ASPEN (See Aspen)

MICKEY AND DONALD (See Walt Disney's...)

MICKEY AND DONALD IN VACATIONLAND (See Dell Giant No. 47)

MICKEY & THE BEANSTALK (See Story Hour Series)

MICKEY & THE SLEUTH (See Walt Disney Showcase #38, 39, 42)

MICKEY FINN (Also see Big Shot Comics #74 & Feature Funnies)
Eastern Color 1-4/McNaught Synd. #5 on (Columbia)/Headline V3#2:
Nov?, 1942 - V3#2, May, 1952

	GD	VG	FN	VF	VF/NM	NM-
1	30	60	90	177	289	400
2	15	30	45	90	140	190
3-Charlie Chan story	12	24	36	69	97	125
4	10	20	30	56	76	95
5-10	9	18	27	47	61	75
11-15(1949): 12-Sparky Watts app.	8	16	24	40	50	60
V3#1,2(1952)	6	12	18	31	38	45

MICKEY MALONE
Hale Nass Corp.: 1936 (Color, punchout-c) (B&W-a on back)

	GD	VG	FN	VF	VF/NM	NM-
nn-1pg. of comics	200	400	800	-	-	-

MICKEY MANTLE (See Baseball's Greatest Heroes #1)

MICKEY MOUSE (See Adventures of Mickey Mouse, The Best of Walt Disney Comics, Cheerios giveaways, Donald and ..., Dynabrite Comics, 40 Big Pages..., Gladstone Comic Album, Merry Christmas From..., Walt Disney's Mickey and Donald, Walt Disney's Comics & Stories, Walt Disney's..., & Wheaties)

MICKEY MOUSE (...Secret Agent #107-109; Walt Disney's... #148-205?)
(See Dell Giants for annuals) (#204 exists from both G.K. & Whitman)
Dell Publ. Co./Gold Key #85-204/Whitman #204-218/Gladstone #219 on:
#16, 1941 - #84, 7-9/62; #85, 11/62 - #218, 6/84; #219, 10/86 - #256, 4/90

	GD	VG	FN	VF	VF/NM	NM-
Four Color 16(1941)-1st Mickey Mouse comic book; "...vs. the Phantom Blot" by Gottfredson	1250	2500	3750	15,500	-	-
Four Color 27(1943)- "7 Colored Terror"	76	152	228	646	1273	1900
Four Color 79(1945)-By Carl Barks (1 story)	92	184	276	782	1541	2300
Four Color 116(1946)	26	52	78	186	361	535
Four Color 141,157(1947)	21	42	63	151	293	435
Four Color 170,181,194('48)	18	36	54	127	249	370
Four Color 214('49),231,248,261	14	28	42	100	188	275
Four Color 268-Reprints/WDC&S #22-24 by Gottfredson ("Surprise Visitor")	13	26	39	93	172	250
Four Color 279,286,296	11	22	33	74	132	190
Four Color 304,313(#1),325(#2),334	10	20	30	67	116	165
Four Color 343,352,362,371,387	8	16	24	58	97	135
Four Color 401,411,427(10-11/52)	7	14	21	47	76	105
Four Color 819-Mickey Mouse in Magicland	6	12	18	39	62	85
Four Color 1057,1151,1246(1959-61)-Album; #1057 has 10¢ & 12¢ editions; back covers are different	5	10	15	34	55	75
28(12-1/52-53)-32,34	6	12	18	41	66	90
33-(Exists with 2 dates, 10-11/53 & 12-1/54)	6	12	18	41	66	90
35-50	6	12	18	37	59	80
51-73,75-80	5	10	15	30	48	65
74-Story swipe "The Rare Stamp Search" from 4-Color #422- "The Gilded Man"	5	10	15	32	51	70
81-105: 93,95-titled "Mickey Mouse Club Album". 100-105: Reprint 4-Color #427,194,279, 170,343,214 in that order	4	8	12	24	37	50
106-120	3	6	9	18	27	35
121-130	3	6	9	14	20	25
131-146	2	4	6	13	18	22
147,148: 147-Reprints "The Phantom Fires" from WDC&S #200-202.148-Reprints "The Mystery of Lonely Valley" from WDC&S #208-210	2	4	6	13	18	22
149-158	2	4	6	9	13	16
159-Reprints "The Sunken City" from WDC&S #205-207	2	4	6	9	13	16
160-178: 162-165,167-170-r	2	4	6	9	13	16
179-(52 pgs.)	2	4	6	10	14	18
180-203: 200-r/Four Color #371	2	3	4	6	8	10
204-(Whitman or G.K.), 205,206	2	4	6	9	12	15
207(8/80), 209(pre-pack?)	4	8	12	24	37	50
208-(8-12/80)-Only distr. in Whitman 3-pack	9	18	27	63	107	150
210(2/81),211-214	2	4	6	9	12	15
215-218: 215(2/82), 216(4/82), 217(3/84), 218(misdated 8/82; actual date 7/84)	2	4	6	10	14	18
219-1st Gladstone issue; The Seven Ghosts serial-r begins by Gottfredson	2	4	6	11	16	20
220,221	2	3	4	6	8	10
222-225: 222-Editor-in Grief strip-r						5.00
226-230						5.00
231-243,246-254: 240-r/March of Comics #27. 245-r/F.C. #279. 250-r/F.C. #248						4.00
244 (1/89, $2.95, 100 pgs.)-Squarebound 60th anniversary issue; gives history of Mickey						5.00
245, 256: 245-r/F.C. #279. 256-$1.95, 68 pgs.						5.00
255 ($1.95, 68 pgs.)						5.00

NOTE: *Reprints #195-197, 198(2/3), 199(1/3), 200-208, 211(1/2), 212, 213, 215(1/3), 216-on.* ***Gottfredson*** *Mickey Mouse serials in #219-239, 241-244, 246-249, 251-253, 255.*

	GD	VG	FN	VF	VF/NM	NM-
Album 01-518-210(Dell), 1(10082-309)(9/63-Gold Key)	3	6	9	21	32	42
...Club 1(1/64-Gold Key)(TV)	4	8	12	22	34	45
Mini Comic 1(1976)(3-1/4x6-1/2")-Reprints 158	1	2	3	5	6	8
Surprise Party 1(30037-901, G.K.)(1/69)-40th Anniversary (see Walt Disney Showcase #47)	3	6	9	21	32	42
Surprise Party 1(1979)-r/1969 issue	1	2	3	5	6	8

MICKEY MOUSE ADVENTURES
Disney Comics: June, 1990 - No. 18, Nov, 1991 ($1.50)

1,8,9: 1-Bradbury, Murry-r/M.M. #45,73 plus new-a. 8-Byrne-c. 9-Fantasia 50th ann. issue w/new adapt. of movie 3.00
2-7,10-18: 2-Begin all new stories. 10-r/F.C. #214 2.50

MICKEY MOUSE AND FRIENDS (Continued from Walt Disney's Mickey Mouse and Friends)
BOOM! Studios: No. 296, Sept, 2009 - Present ($2.99)

296-299-Wizards of Mickey stories 3.00

MICKEY MOUSE CLUB FUN BOOK
Golden Press: 1977 (1.95, 228 pgs.)(square bound)

	GD	VG	FN	VF	VF/NM	NM-
11190-1950s-r; 20,000 Leagues, M. Mouse Silly Symphonys, The Reluctant Dragon, etc.	4	8	12	28	44	60

MICKEY MOUSE CLUB MAGAZINE (See Walt Disney...)

MICKEY MOUSE COMICS DIGEST
Gladstone: 1986 - No. 5, 1987 (96 pgs.)

	GD	VG	FN	VF	VF/NM	NM-
1 ($1.25-c)	1	2	3	5	6	8
2-5: 3-5 ($1.50-c)						5.00

MICKEY MOUSE IN COLOR
Another Rainbow/Pantheon: 1988 (Deluxe, 13"x17", hard-c, $250.00)
(Trade, 9-7/8"x11-1/2", hard-c, $39.95)

	GD	VG	FN	VF	VF/NM	NM-
Deluxe limited edition of 3,000 copies signed by Floyd Gottfredson and Carl Barks, designated as the "Official Mickey Mouse 60th Anniversary" book. Mickey Sunday and daily reprints, plus Barks "Riddle of the Red Hat" from Four Color #79. Comes with 45 r.p.m. record interview with Gottfredson and Barks. 240 pgs.	14	28	42	100	188	275
Deluxe, limited to 100 copies, as above, but with a unique colored pencil original drawing of Mickey Mouse by Carl Barks.						800.00
Pantheon trade edition, edited down & without Barks, 192 pgs.	3	6	9	20	30	40

MICKEY MOUSE MAGAZINE (Becomes Walt Disney's Comics & Stories)(Also see 40 Big Pages of Mickey Mouse)
K. K. Publ./Western Publishing Co.: Summer, 1935 (June-Aug, indicia) - V5#12, Sept, 1940; V1#1-5, V3#11,12, V4#1-3 are 44 pgs; V2#3-100 pgs; V5#12-68 pgs; rest are 36 pgs.(No V3#1, V4#6)

	GD	VG	FN	VF	VF/NM	NM-
V1#1 (Large size, 13-1/4x10-1/4"; 25¢)-Contains puzzles, games, cels, stories & comics of Disney characters. Promotional magazine for Disney cartoon movies and paraphernalia	1425	2850	4275	9200	19,000	-

Note: *Some copies were autographed by the editors & given away with all early one year subscriptions.*

	GD	VG	FN	VF	VF/NM	NM-
2 (Size change, 11-1/2x8-1/2"; 10/35; 10¢)-High quality paper begins; Messmer-a	282	564	846	2400	-	-
3,4: 3-Messmer-a	153	306	459	1300	-	-
5-1st Donald Duck solo-c; 2nd cover app. ever; last 44 pg. & high quality paper issue	271	542	813	2300	-	-
6-9: 6-36 pg. issues begin; Donald becomes editor. 8-2nd Donald solo-c. 9-1st Mickey/Minnie-c	141	282	423	1200	-	-
10-12, V2#1,2: 11-1st Pluto/Mickey-c; Donald fires himself and appoints Mickey as editor	135	270	405	1150	-	-

V2#3-Special 100 pg. Christmas issue (25¢); Messmer-a; Donald becomes editor of

Mickey Mouse Magazine V5 #6 © DIS

Micronauts #1 © Takara Ltd.

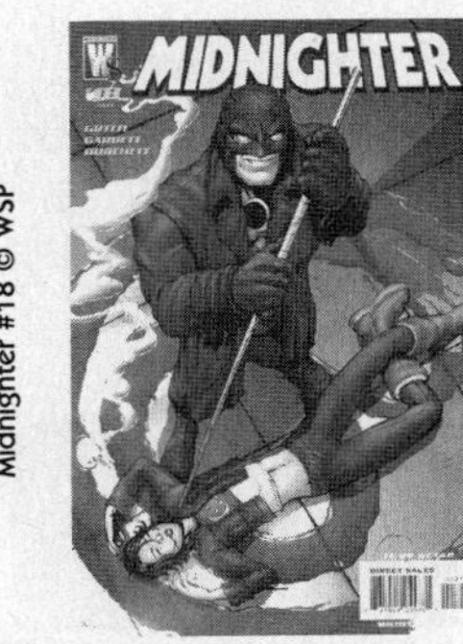

Midnighter #18 © WSP

GD VG FN VF VF/NM NM-
2.0 4.0 6.0 8.0 9.0 9.2

Wise Quacks 447 894 1341 3800 - -
4-Mickey Mouse Comics & Roy Ranger (adventure strip) begin; both end V2#9; Messmer-a 115 230 345 975 - -
5-9: 5-Ted True (adventure strip, ends V2#9) & Silly Symphony Comics (ends V3#3) begin. 6-1st solo Minnie-c. 6-9-Mickey Mouse Movies cut-out in each 54 108 162 343 584 825
10-1st full color issue; Mickey Mouse (by Gottfredson; ends V3#12) & Silly Symphony (ends V3#3) full color Sunday-r, Peter The Farm Detective (ends V5#8) & Ole Of The North (ends V3#3) begins 81 162 243 518 884 1250
11-13: 12-Hiawatha-c & feature story 53 106 159 334 567 800
V3#2-Big Bad Wolf Halloween-c 60 120 180 381 653 925
3 (12/37)-1st app. Snow White & The Seven Dwarfs (before release of movie) (possibly 1st in print); Mickey X-Mas-c 107 214 321 680 1165 1650
4 (1/38)-Snow White & The Seven Dwarfs serial begins (on stands before release of movie); Ducky Symphony (ends V3#11) begins 89 178 267 565 970 1375
5-1st Snow White & Seven Dwarfs-c (St. Valentine's Day) 107 214 321 680 1165 1650
6-Snow White serial ends; Lonesome Ghosts app. (2 pp.) 60 120 180 381 658 935
7-Seven Dwarfs Easter-c 56 112 168 355 615 875
8-10: 9-Dopey-c. 10-1st solo Goofy-c 48 96 144 302 514 725
11,12 (44 pgs; 8 more pgs. color added). 11-Mickey the Sheriff serial (ends V4#3) & Donald Duck strip-r (ends V3#12) begin. Color feature on Snow White's Forest Friends 52 104 156 328 552 775
V4#1 (10/38; 44 pgs.)-Brave Little Tailor-c/feature story, nominated for Academy Award; Bobby & Chip by Otto Messmer (ends V4#2) & The Practical Pig (ends V4#2) begin 52 104 156 328 552 775
2 (44 pgs.)-1st Huey, Dewey & Louie-c 53 106 159 334 567 800
3 (12/38, 44 pgs.)-Ferdinand The Bull-c/feature story, Academy Award winner; Mickey Mouse & The Whalers serial begins, ends V4#12 52 104 156 328 552 775
4-Spotty, Mother Pluto strip-r begin, end V4#8 48 96 144 302 514 725
5-St. Valentine's day-c. 1st Pluto solo-c 54 108 162 343 584 825
7 (3/39)-The Ugly Duckling-c/feature story, Academy Award winner 52 104 156 328 552 775
7 (4/39)-Goofy & Wilbur The Grasshopper classic-c/feature story from 1st Goofy solo cartoon movie; Timid Elmer begins, ends V5#5 52 104 156 328 552 775
8-Big Bad Wolf-c from Practical Pig movie poster; Practical Pig feature story 52 104 156 328 552 775
9-Donald Duck & Mickey Mouse Sunday-r begin; The Pointer feature story, nominated for Academy Award 52 104 156 328 552 775
10-Classic July 4th drum & fife-c; last Donald Sunday-r 62 124 186 394 680 965
11-1st slick-c; last over-sized issue 48 96 144 302 514 725
12 (9/39; format change, 10-1/4x8-1/4")-1st full color, cover to cover issue; Donald's Penguin-c/feature story 55 110 165 352 601 850
V5#1-Black Pete-c; Officer Duck-c/feature story; Autograph Hound feature story; Robinson Crusoe serial begins 54 108 162 346 591 835
2-Goofy-c; 1st brief app. Pinocchio 71 142 213 454 777 1100
3 (12/39)-Pinocchio Christmas-c (Before movie release). 1st app. Jiminy Cricket; Pinocchio serial begins 84 168 252 538 919 1300
4,5: 5-Jiminy Cricket-c; Pinocchio serial ends; Donald's Dog Laundry feature story 56 112 168 348 594 840
6,7: 6-Tugboat Mickey feature story; Rip Van Winkle feature begins, ends V5#8. 7-2nd Huey, Dewey & Louie-c 54 108 162 336 573 810
8-Last magazine size issue; 2nd solo Pluto-c; Figaro & Cleo feature story 56 112 168 348 594 840
9-11: 9 (6/40; change to comic book size)-Jiminy Cricket feature story; Donald-c & Sunday-r begin. 10-Special Independence Day issue. 11-Hawaiian Holiday & Mickey's Trailer feature stories; last 36 pg. issue 60 120 180 381 653 925
12 (Format change)-The transition issue (68 pgs.) becoming a comic book. With only a title change to follow, becomes Walt Disney's Comics & Stories #1 with the next issue 465 930 1395 3395 5998 8600

NOTE: ***Otto Messmer**-a is in many issues of the first two-three years. The following story titles and issues have gags created by **Carl Barks**: V4#3(12/38)-'Donald's Better Self' & 'Donald's Golf Game;' V4#4(1/39)-'Donald's Lucky Day;' V4#7(3/39)-'Hockey Champ;' V4#7(4/39)-'Donald's Cousin Gus;' V4#9(6/39)-'Sea Scouts;' V4#12(9/39)-'Donald's Penguin;' V5#9 (6/40)-'Donald's Vacation;' V5#10(7/40)-'Bone Trouble;' V5#12(9/40)-'Window Cleaners.'*

MICKEY MOUSE MAGAZINE (Russian Version)
May 16, 1991 (1st Russian printing of a modern comic book)
1-Bagged w/gold label commemoration in English 10.00

MICKEY MOUSE MARCH OF COMICS (See March of Comics #8,27,45,60,74)

MICKEY MOUSE'S SUMMER VACATION (See Story Hour Series)

MICKEY MOUSE SUMMER FUN (See Dell Giants)

MICKEY SPILLANE'S MIKE DANGER
Tekno Comix: Sept, 1995 - No. 11, May, 1996 ($1.95)
1-11: 1-Frank Miller-c. 7-polybagged; Simonson-c. 8,9-Simonson-c 2.50

MICKEY SPILLANE'S MIKE DANGER
Big Entertainment: V2#1, June, 1996 - No. 10, Apr, 1997 ($2.25)
V2#1-10: Max Allan Collins scripts 2.50

MICKEY'S TWICE UPON A CHRISTMAS (Disney)
Gemstone Publishing: 2004 ($3.95, square-bound, one-shot)
nn-Christmas short stories with Mickey, Minnie, Donald, Uncle Scrooge, Goofy and others 4.00

MICROBOTS, THE
Gold Key: Dec, 1971 (one-shot)
1 (10271-112) 3 6 9 16 22 28

MICRONAUTS (Toys)
Marvel Comics Group: Jan, 1979 - No. 59, Aug, 1984 (Mando paper #53 on)
1-Intro/1st app. Baron Karza 1 2 3 4 5 7
2-10,35,37,57: 7-Man-Thing app. 8-1st app. Capt. Universe (8/79). 9-1st app. Cilicia. 35-Double size; origin Microverse; intro Death Squad; Dr. Strange app. 37-Nightcrawler app.; X-Men cameo (2 pgs.). 57-(52 pgs.) 4.00
11-34,36,38-56,58,59: 13-1st app. Jasmine. 15-Death of Microtron. 15-17-Fantastic Four app. 17-Death of Jasmine. 20-Ant-Man app. 21-Microverse series begins. 25-Origin Baron Karza. 25-29-Nick Fury app. 27-Death of Biotron. 34-Dr. Strange app. 38-First direct sale. 40-Fantastic Four app. 48-Early Guice-a begins. 59-Golden painted-c 3.00
nn-Blank UPC; diamond on top 2.50
Annual 1,2 (12/79,10/80)-Ditko-c/a 4.00

NOTE: *#38-on distributed only through comic shops. **N. Adams** c-7i. **Chaykin** a-13-18p. **Ditko** a-39p. **Giffen** a-36p, 37p(part). **Golden** a-1-12p; c-2-7p, 8-23, 24p, 38, 39, 59. **Guice** a-48-58p; c-49-58. **Gil Kane** a-38, 40-45p; c-40-45. **Layton** c-33-37. **Miller** c-31.*

MICRONAUTS (Micronauts: The New Voyages on cover)
Marvel Comics Group: Oct, 1984 - No. 20, May, 1986
V2#1-20 2.50
NOTE: ***Kelley Jones** a-1; c-1, 6. **Guice** a-4p; c-2p.*

MICRONAUTS
Image Comics: 2002 - No. 11, Sept, 2003 ($2.95)
2002 Convention Special (no cover price, B&W) previews series 2.50
1-11: 1-3-Hanson-a; Dave Johnson-c. 4-Su-a; 2 covers by Linsner & Hanson 3.00
...Vol. 1: Revolution (2003, $12.95, digest size) r/#1-5 13.00

MICRONAUTS (Volume 2)
Devil's Due Publishing: Mar, 2004 - No. 3, May, 2004 ($2.95)
1-3-Jolley-s/Broderick-a 3.00

MICRONAUTS: KARZA
Image Comics: Feb, 2003 - No. 4, May, 2003 ($2.95)
1-4-Krueger-s/Kurth-a 3.00

MICRONAUTS SPECIAL EDITION
Marvel Comics Group: Dec, 1983 - No. 5, Apr, 1984 ($2.00, limited series, Baxter paper)
1-5: r-/original series 1-12; Guice-c(p)-all 3.00

MIDGET COMICS (Fighting Indian Stories)
St. John Publishng Co.: Feb, 1950 - No. 2, Apr, 1950 (5-3/8x7-3/8", 68 pgs.)
1-Fighting Indian Stories; Matt Baker-c 19 38 57 111 176 240
2-Tex West, Cowboy Marshal (also in #1) 10 20 30 58 79 100

MIDNIGHT (See Smash Comics #18)

MIDNIGHT
Ajax/Farrell Publ. (Four Star Comic Corp.): Apr, 1957 - No. 6, June, 1958
1-Reprints from Voodoo & Strange Fantasy with some changes 15 30 45 88 137 185
2-6 10 20 30 58 79 100

MIDNIGHTER (See The Authority)
DC Comics (WildStorm): Jan, 2007 - No. 20, Aug, 2008 ($2.99)
1-20: 1-Ennis-s/Sprouse-a/c. 6-Fabry-a. 7-Vaughan-s. 8-Gage-s. 9-Stelfreeze-a 3.00
1-4-Variant covers. 1-Michael Golden. 2-Art Adams 3-Jason Pearson. 4-Glenn Fabry 4.00
...: Anthem TPB (2008, $14.99) r/#7,10-15 15.00
...: Armageddon (12/07, $2.99) Gage-s/Coleby-a/McKone-c 3.00
...: Assassin8 TPB (2009, $14.99) r/#16-20 15.00
...: Killing Machine TPB (2008, $14.99) r/#1-6 15.00

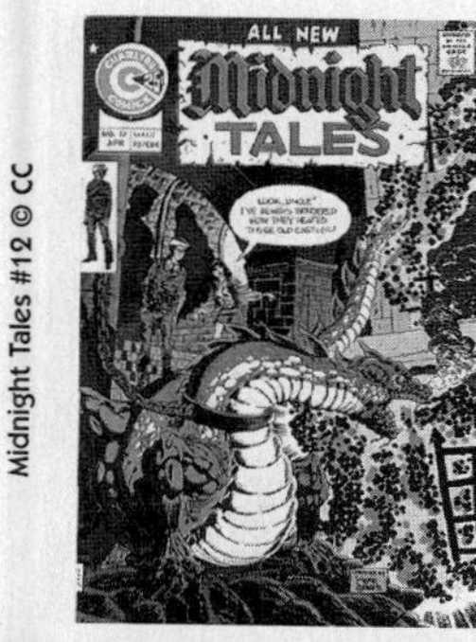

Midnight Tales #12 © CC

Mighty Avengers #13 © MAR

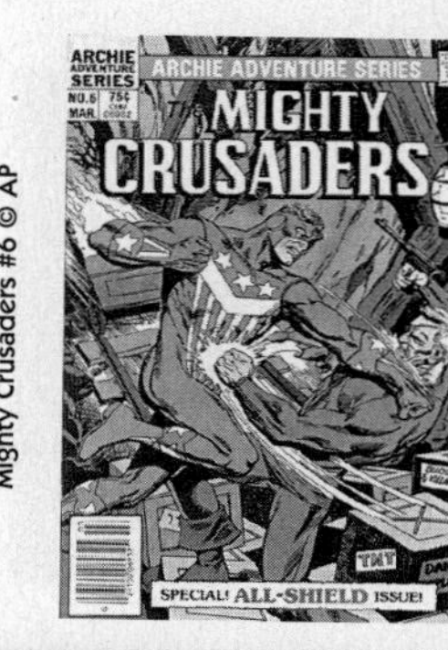

Mighty Crusaders #6 © AP

MIDNIGHT MASS
DC Comics (Vertigo): Jun, 2002 - No. 8, Jan, 2003 ($2.50)

	GD 2.0	VG 4.0	FN 6.0	VF 8.0	VF/NM 9.0	NM- 9.2
1-8-Rozum-s/Saiz & Palmiotti-a						2.50

MIDNIGHT MASS: HERE THERE BE MONSTERS
DC Comics (Vertigo): March, 2004 - No. 6, Aug, 2004 ($2.95, limited series)

	GD 2.0	VG 4.0	FN 6.0	VF 8.0	VF/NM 9.0	NM- 9.2
1-6-Rozum-s/Paul Lee-a						3.00

MIDNIGHT MEN
Marvel Comics (Epic Comics/Heavy Hitters): June, 1993 - No. 4, Sept, 1993 ($2.50/$1.95, limited series)

	GD 2.0	VG 4.0	FN 6.0	VF 8.0	VF/NM 9.0	NM- 9.2
1-($2.50)-Embossed-c; Chaykin-c/a & scripts in all						3.00
2-4						2.50

MIDNIGHT MYSTERY
American Comics Group: Jan-Feb, 1961 - No. 7, Oct, 1961

	GD 2.0	VG 4.0	FN 6.0	VF 8.0	VF/NM 9.0	NM- 9.2
1-Sci/Fi story	8	16	24	52	86	120
2-7: 7-Gustavson-a	4	8	12	28	44	60

NOTE: ***Reinman** a-1, 3. **Whitney** a-1, 4-6; c-1-3, 5, 7.*

MIDNIGHT NATION
Image Comics (Top Cow): Oct, 2000 - No. 12, July, 2002 ($2.50/$2.95)

	GD 2.0	VG 4.0	FN 6.0	VF 8.0	VF/NM 9.0	NM- 9.2
1-Straczynski-s/Frank-a; 2 covers						3.00
2-11: 9-Twin Towers cover						2.50
12-($2.95)Last issue						3.00
Wizard #1/2 (2001) Michael Zulli-a; two covers by Frank						3.00
Vol. 1 ('03, $29.99, TPB) r/#1-12 & Wizard #1/2; cover gallery; afterword by Straczynski						30.00

MIDNIGHT SONS UNLIMITED
Marvel Comics (Midnight Sons imprint #4 on): Apr, 1993 - No. 9, May, 1995 ($3.95, 68 pgs.)

	GD 2.0	VG 4.0	FN 6.0	VF 8.0	VF/NM 9.0	NM- 9.2
1-9: Blaze, Darkhold (by Quesada #1), Ghost Rider, Morbius & Nightstalkers in all. 1-Painted-c. 3-Spider-Man app. 4-Siege of Darkness part 17; new Dr. Strange & new Ghost Rider app.; spot varnish-c						4.00

NOTE: ***Sears** a-2.*

MIDNIGHT TALES
Charlton Press: Dec, 1972 - No. 18, May, 1976

	GD 2.0	VG 4.0	FN 6.0	VF 8.0	VF/NM 9.0	NM- 9.2
V1#1	3	6	9	14	20	26
2-10	2	4	6	9	13	16
11-18: 11-14-Newton-a(p)	2	4	6	8	10	12
12,17(Modern Comics reprint, 1977)						5.00

NOTE: ***Adkins** a-12i, 13i. **Ditko** a-12. **Howard** (Wood imitator) a-1-15, 17, 18; c-1-18. **Don Newton** a-11-14p. **Staton** a-1, 3-11, 13. **Sutton** a-3-10.*

MIGHTY, THE
DC Comics: Apr, 2009 - No. 12, Mar, 2010 ($2.99)

	GD 2.0	VG 4.0	FN 6.0	VF 8.0	VF/NM 9.0	NM- 9.2
1-12: Tomasi & Champagne-s/Dave Johnson-c. 1-4-Snejbjerg-a. 5-12-Samnee-a						3.00
...: Volume 1 TPB (2009, $17.99) r/#1-6						18.00

MIGHTY ATOM, THE (...& the Pixies #6) (Formerly The Pixies #1-5)
Magazine Enterprises: No. 6, 1949; Nov, 1957 - No. 6, Aug-Sept, 1958

	GD 2.0	VG 4.0	FN 6.0	VF 8.0	VF/NM 9.0	NM- 9.2
6(1949-M.E.)-no month (1st Series)	7	14	21	35	43	50
1-6(2nd Series)-Pixies-r	4	8	12	18	22	25
I.W. Reprint #1(nd)	2	4	6	8	11	14

MIGHTY AVENGERS
Marvel Comics: May, 2007 - Present ($3.99/$2.99)

	GD 2.0	VG 4.0	FN 6.0	VF 8.0	VF/NM 9.0	NM- 9.2
1-($3.99) Iron Man, Ms. Marvel select new team; Bendis-s/Cho-a/c; Mole Man app.						5.00
2-6-($2.99) Ultron returns						3.00
7-15: 7-Bagley-a begins; Venom on-c. 9-11-Dr. Doom app.						3.00
12-20-Secret Invasion: 12,13-Maleev-a. 15-Romita Jr.-a. 16-Elektra. 20-Wasp funeral						3.00
21-($3.99) Dark Reign; Scarlet Witch returns; new team assembled; Pham-a						4.00
22-35: 25,26-Fantastic Four app. 35-Siege						3.00
...: Most Wanted Files (2007, $3.99) profiles of members, accomplices & adversaries						4.00
... Vol. 1: The Ultron Initiative HC (2008, $19.99) r/#1-6; variant covers and sketch art						20.00
... Vol. 2: Venom Bomb HC (2008, $19.99) r/#7-11; B&W cover art						20.00

MIGHTY BEAR (Formerly Fun Comics; becomes Unsane #15)
Star Publ. No. 13,14/Ajax-Farrell (Four Star): No. 13, Jan, 1954 - No. 14, Mar, 1954; 9/57 - No. 3, 2/58

	GD 2.0	VG 4.0	FN 6.0	VF 8.0	VF/NM 9.0	NM- 9.2
13,14-L. B. Cole-c	18	36	54	103	162	220
1-3('57-58)Four Star; becomes Mighty Ghost #4	7	14	21	35	43	50

MIGHTY COMICS (...Presents) (Formerly Flyman)
Radio Comics (Archie): No. 40, Nov, 1966 - No. 50, Oct, 1967 (All 12¢ issues)

	GD 2.0	VG 4.0	FN 6.0	VF 8.0	VF/NM 9.0	NM- 9.2
40-Web	4	8	12	28	44	60
41-50: 41-Shield, Black Hood. 42-Black Hood. 43-Shield, Web & Black Hood. 44-Black Hood, Steel Sterling & The Shield. 45-Shield & Hangman; origin Web retold. 46-Steel Sterling, Web & Black Hood. 47-Black Hood & Mr. Justice. 48-Shield & Hangman; Wizard x-over in Shield. 49-Steel Sterling & Fox; Black Hood x-over in Steel Sterling. 50-Black Hood & Web; Inferno x-over in Web	4	8	12	26	41	55

NOTE: ***Paul Reinman** a-40-50.*

MIGHTY CRUSADERS, THE (Also see Adventures of the Fly, The Crusaders & Fly Man)
Mighty Comics Group (Radio Comics): Nov, 1965 - No. 7, Oct, 1966 (All 12¢)

	GD 2.0	VG 4.0	FN 6.0	VF 8.0	VF/NM 9.0	NM- 9.2
1-Origin The Shield	7	14	21	49	80	110
2-Origin Comet	4	8	12	28	44	60
3,5-7: 3-Origin Fly-Man. 5-Intro. Ultra-Men (Fox, Web, Capt. Flag) & Terrific Three (Jaguar, Mr. Justice, Steel Sterling). 7-Steel Sterling feature; origin Fly-Girl	4	8	12	26	41	55
4-1st S.A. app. Fireball, Inferno & Fox; Firefly, Web, Bob Phantom, Blackjack, Hangman, Zambini, Kardak, Steel Sterling, Mr. Justice, Wizard, Capt. Flag, Jaguar x-over	4	8	12	28	44	60
Volume 1: Origin of a Super Team TPB (2003, $12.95) r/#1 & Fly Man #31-33						13.00

NOTE: ***Reinman** a-6.*

MIGHTY CRUSADERS, THE (All New Advs. of...#2)
Red Circle Prod./Archie Ent. No. 6 on: Mar, 1983 - No. 13, Sept, 1985 ($1.00, 36 pgs, Mando paper)

	GD 2.0	VG 4.0	FN 6.0	VF 8.0	VF/NM 9.0	NM- 9.2
1-Origin Black Hood, The Fly, Fly Girl, The Shield, The Wizard, The Jaguar, Pvt. Strong & The Web.	1	2	3	4	5	7
2-10: 2-Mister Midnight begins. 4-Darkling replaces Shield. 5-Origin Jaguar, Shield begins. 7-Untold origin Jaguar. 10-Veitch-a						5.00
11-13-Lower print run						6.00

NOTE: ***Buckler** a-1-3, 4i, 5p, 7p, 8i, 9i; c-1-10p.*

MIGHTY GHOST (Formerly Mighty Bear #1-3)
Ajax/Farrell Publ.: No. 4, June, 1958

	GD 2.0	VG 4.0	FN 6.0	VF 8.0	VF/NM 9.0	NM- 9.2
4	7	14	21	35	43	50

MIGHTY HERCULES, THE (TV)
Gold Key: July, 1963 - No. 2, Nov, 1963

	GD 2.0	VG 4.0	FN 6.0	VF 8.0	VF/NM 9.0	NM- 9.2
1 (10072-307)	13	26	39	94	175	255
2 (10072-311)	13	26	39	90	165	240

MIGHTY HEROES, THE (TV) (Funny)
Dell Publishing Co.: Mar, 1967 - No. 4, July, 1967

	GD 2.0	VG 4.0	FN 6.0	VF 8.0	VF/NM 9.0	NM- 9.2
1-Also has a 1957 Heckle & Jeckle-r	11	22	33	78	139	200
2-4: 4-Has two 1958 Mighty Mouse-r	8	16	24	52	86	120

MIGHTY HEROES
Spotlight Comics: 1987 (B&W, one-shot)

	GD 2.0	VG 4.0	FN 6.0	VF 8.0	VF/NM 9.0	NM- 9.2
1-Heckle & Jeckle backup						5.00

MIGHTY HEROES
Marvel Comics: Jan, 1998 ($2.99, one-shot)

	GD 2.0	VG 4.0	FN 6.0	VF 8.0	VF/NM 9.0	NM- 9.2
1-Origin of the Mighty Heroes						3.00

MIGHTY LOVE
DC Comics: 2003 ($24.99/$17.95, graphic novel)

	GD 2.0	VG 4.0	FN 6.0	VF 8.0	VF/NM 9.0	NM- 9.2
HC-($24.95) Howard Chaykin-s/a; intro. Skylark and the Iron Angel						25.00
SC-($17.95)						18.00

MIGHTY MAN (From Savage Dragon titles)
Image Comics: Dec, 2004 ($7.95, one-shot)

	GD 2.0	VG 4.0	FN 6.0	VF 8.0	VF/NM 9.0	NM- 9.2
1-Reprints seriaizedl back-up from Savage Dragon #109-118						8.00

MIGHTY MARVEL TEAM-UP THRILLERS
Marvel Comics: 1983 ($5.95, trade paperback)

	GD 2.0	VG 4.0	FN 6.0	VF 8.0	VF/NM 9.0	NM- 9.2
1-Reprints team-up stories						38.00

MIGHTY MARVEL WESTERN, THE
Marvel Comics Group (LMC earlier issues): Oct, 1968 - No. 46, Sept, 1976 (#1-14: 68 pgs.; #15,16: 52 pgs.)

	GD 2.0	VG 4.0	FN 6.0	VF 8.0	VF/NM 9.0	NM- 9.2
1-Begin Kid Colt, Rawhide Kid, Two-Gun Kid-r	6	12	18	37	59	80
2-5: (2-14 are 68 pgs.)	4	8	12	26	41	55
6-16: (15,16 are 52 pgs.)	4	8	12	22	34	45
17-20	2	4	6	13	18	22
21-30,32,37: 24-Kid Colt-r end. 25-Matt Slade-r begin. 32-Origin-r/Rawhide Kid #23; Williamson-r/Kid Slade #7. 37-Williamson, Kirby-r/Two-Gun Kid 51	2	4	6	9	13	16
31,33-36,38-46: 31-Baker-r.	2	4	6	8	11	14
45-(30¢-c variant, limited distribution)(6/76)	4	8	12	26	41	55

NOTE: ***Jack Davis** a(r)-21-24. **Keller** r-1-13, 22. **Kirby** a(r)-1-3, 6, 9, 12-14, 16, 25-29, 32-38, 40, 41, 43-46; c-29. **Maneely** a(r)-22. **Severin** c-3i, 9. No Matt Slade-#43.*

MIGHTY MIDGET COMICS, THE (Miniature)

Mighty Midget Comics - Balbo #12 © FAW

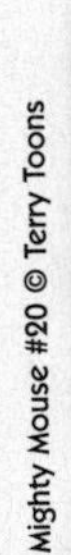

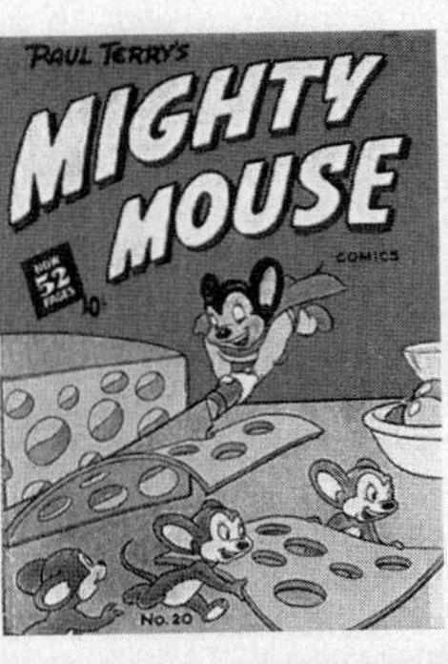

Mighty Mouse #20 © Terry Toons

Miek Grell's Sable #2 © FC

	GD 2.0	VG 4.0	FN 6.0	VF 8.0	VF/NM 9.0	NM- 9.2
Samuel E. Lowe & Co.: No date; circa 1942-1943 (Sold 2 for 5¢, B&W and red, 36 pgs, approx. 5x4")						
Bulletman #11(1943)-r/cover/Bulletman #3	16	32	48	94	147	200
Captain Marvel Adventures #11	16	32	48	94	147	200
Captain Marvel #11 (Same as above except for full color ad on back cover; this issue was glued to cover of Captain Marvel #20 and is not found in fine-mint condition)	340	680	1020	-	-	-
Captain Marvel Jr. #11 (Same-c as Master #27	16	32	48	94	147	200
Captain Marvel Jr. #11 (Same as above except for full color ad on back-c; this issue was glued to cover of Captain Marvel #21 and is not found in fine-mint condition)	340	680	1020	-	-	-
Golden Arrow #11	15	30	45	86	133	180
Golden Arrow #11 (Same as above except for full color ad on back-c; this issue was glued to cover of Captain Marvel #21 and is not found in fine-mint condition)	280	560	840	-	-	-
Ibis the Invincible #11(1942)-Origin; reprints cover to Ibis #1 (Predates Fawcett's Ibis the Invincible #1).	16	32	48	94	147	200
Spy Smasher #11(1942)	16	32	48	94	147	200

NOTE: *The above books came in a box called "box full of books" and was distributed with other Samuel Lowe puzzles, paper dolls, coloring books, etc. They are not titled Mighty Midget Comics. All have a war bond seal on back cover which is otherwise blank. These books came in a "Mighty Midget" flat cardboard counter display rack.*

	GD	VG	FN	VF	VF/NM	NM-
Balbo, the Boy Magician #12 (1943)-1st book devoted entirely to character.	10	20	30	54	72	90
Bulletman #12	12	24	36	69	97	125
Commando Yank #12 (1943)-Only comic devoted entirely to character.	10	20	30	56	76	95
Dr. Voltz the Human Generator (1943)-Only comic devoted entirely to character.	10	20	30	54	72	90
Lance O'Casey #12 (1943)-1st comic devoted entirely to character (Predates Fawcett's Lance O'Casey #1).	10	20	30	54	72	90
Leatherneck the Marine (1943)-Only comic devoted entirely to character.	10	20	30	54	72	90
Minute Man #12	12	24	36	67	94	120
Mister "Q" (1943)-Only comic devoted entirely to character.	10	20	30	54	72	90
Mr. Scarlet and Pinky #12 (1943)-Only comic devoted entirely to character.	10	20	30	58	79	100
Pat Wilton and His Flying Fortress (1943)-1st comic devoted entirely to character.	10	20	30	54	72	90
The Phantom Eagle #12 (1943)-Only comic devoted entirely to character.	10	20	30	54	72	90
State Trooper Stops Crime (1943)-Only comic devoted entirely to character.	10	20	30	54	72	90
Tornado Tom (1943)-Origin, r/from Cyclone #1-3; only comic devoted entirely to character.	10	20	30	54	72	90

MIGHTY MORPHIN' POWER RANGERS: THE MOVIE (Also see Saban's Mighty Morphin' Power Rangers)
Marvel Comics: Sept, 1995 ($3.95, one-shot)

	GD	VG	FN	VF	VF/NM	NM-
nn-Adaptation of movie						4.00

MIGHTY MOUSE (See Adventures of..., Dell Giant #43, Giant Comics Edition, March of Comics #205, 237, 247, 257, 447, 459, 471, 483, Oxydol-Dreft, Paul Terry's, & Terry-Toons Comics)

MIGHTY MOUSE (1st Series)
Timely/Marvel Comics (20th Century Fox): Fall, 1946 - No. 4, Summer, 1947

	GD	VG	FN	VF	VF/NM	NM-
1	168	336	504	1075	1838	2600
2	66	132	198	419	722	1025
3,4	42	84	126	265	445	625

MIGHTY MOUSE (2nd Series) (Paul Terry's... #62-71)
St. John Publishing Co./Pines No. 68 (3/56) on (TV issues #72 on):
Aug, 1947 - No. 67, 11/55; No. 68, 3/56 - No. 83, 6/59

	GD	VG	FN	VF	VF/NM	NM-
5(#1)	39	78	117	240	395	550
6-10: 10-Over-sized issue	20	40	60	117	189	260
11-19	14	28	42	80	115	150
20 (11/50) - 25-(52 pg. editions)	11	22	33	62	86	110
20-25-(36 pg. editions)	10	20	30	54	72	90
26-37: 35-Flying saucer-c	9	18	27	50	65	80
38-45-(100 pgs.)	18	36	54	107	169	230
46-83: 62-64,67-Painted-c. 82-Infinity-c	9	18	27	47	61	75
Album nn (nd, 1952/53?, St. John)(100 pgs.)(Rebound issues w/new cover)	22	44	66	128	209	290
Album 1(10/52, 25¢, 100 pgs., St. John)-Gandy Goose app.	28	56	84	165	270	375
Album 2,3(11/52 & 12/52, St. John) (100 pgs.)	22	44	66	128	209	290
Fun Club Magazine 1(Fall, 1957-Pines, 25¢, 100 pgs.) (CBS TV)-Tom Terrific, Heckle & Jeckle, Dinky Duck, Gandy Goose	15	30	45	90	140	190
Fun Club Magazine 2-6(Winter, 1958-Pines)	11	22	33	62	86	110
3-D 1-(1st printing-9/53, 25¢)(St. John)-Came w/glasses; stiff covers; says World's First! on-c; 1st 3-D comic	28	56	84	165	270	375
3-D 1-(2nd printing-10/53, 25¢)-Came w/glasses; slick, glossy covers, slightly smaller	20	40	60	114	182	250
3-D 2,3(11/53, 12/53, 25¢)-(St. John)-With glasses	20	40	60	114	182	250

MIGHTY MOUSE (TV)(3rd Series)(Formerly Adventures of Mighty Mouse)
Gold Key/Dell Publ. Co. No. 166-on: No. 161, Oct, 1964 - No. 172, Oct, 1968

	GD	VG	FN	VF	VF/NM	NM-
161(10/64)-165(9/65)-(Becomes Adventures of... No. 166 on)	5	10	15	30	48	65
166(3/66), 167(6/66)-172	3	6	9	21	32	42

MIGHTY MOUSE (TV)
Spotlight Comics: 1987 - No. 2, 1987 ($1.50, color)

	GD	VG	FN	VF	VF/NM	NM-
1,2-New stories						3.00
...And Friends Holiday Special (11/87, $1.75)						3.00

MIGHTY MOUSE (TV)
Marvel Comics: Oct, 1990 - No. 10, July, 1991 ($1.00)(Based on Sat. cartoon)

	GD	VG	FN	VF	VF/NM	NM-
1-10: 1-Dark Knight-c parody. 2-10: 3-Intro Bat-Bat; Byrne-c. 4,5-Crisis-c/story parodies w/Perez-c. 6-Spider-Man-c parody. 7-Origin Bat-Bat						2.50

MIGHTY MOUSE ADVENTURE MAGAZINE
Spotlight Comics: 1987 ($2.00, B&W, 52 pgs., magazine size, one-shot)

	GD	VG	FN	VF	VF/NM	NM-
1-Deputy Dawg, Heckle & Jeckle backup stories						5.00

MIGHTY MOUSE ADVENTURES (Adventures of... #2 on)
St. John Publishing Co.: November, 1951

	GD	VG	FN	VF	VF/NM	NM-
1	34	68	102	199	325	450

MIGHTY MOUSE ADVENTURE STORIES (Paul Terry's... on-c only)
St. John Publishing Co.: 1953 (50¢, 384 pgs.)

	GD	VG	FN	VF	VF/NM	NM-
nn-Rebound issues	45	90	135	284	480	675

MIGHTY MUTANIMALS (See Teenage Mutant Ninja Turtles Adventures #19)
May, 1991 - No. 3, July, 1991 ($1.00, limited series)
Archie Comics: Apr, 1992 - No. 8, June, 1993 ($1.25)

	GD	VG	FN	VF	VF/NM	NM-
1-3: 1-Story cont'd from TMNT Advs. #19.						6.00
1-4 (1992)						6.00
5-8: 7-1st app. Merdude	1	2	3	5	7	9

MIGHTY SAMSON (Also see Gold Key Champion)
Gold Key/Whitman #32: July, 1964 - No. 20, Nov, 1969; No. 21, Aug, 1972; No. 22, Dec, 1973 - No. 31, Mar, 1976; No. 32, Aug, 1982 (Painted-c #1-31)

	GD	VG	FN	VF	VF/NM	NM-
1-Origin/1st app.; Thorne-a begins	8	16	24	54	90	125
2-5	5	10	15	30	48	65
6-10: 7-Tom Morrow begins, ends #20	3	6	9	20	30	40
11-20	3	6	9	16	23	30
21-31: 21,22-r	2	4	6	11	16	20
32(Whitman, 8/82)-r	2	4	6	8	10	12

MIGHTY THOR (See Thor)

MIKE BARNETT, MAN AGAINST CRIME (TV)
Fawcett Publications: Dec, 1951 - No. 6, Oct, 1952

	GD	VG	FN	VF	VF/NM	NM-
1	19	38	57	109	172	235
2	13	26	39	72	101	130
3,4,6	10	20	30	58	79	100
5- "Market for Morphine" cover/story	14	28	42	80	115	150

MIKE DANGER (See Mickey Spillane's...)

MIKE DEODATO'S...
Caliber Comics: 1996, ($2.95, B&W)

	GD	VG	FN	VF	VF/NM	NM-
...FALLOUT 3000 #1, **...JONAS** (mag. size) #1,**...PRIME CUTS** (mag. size) #1, **...PROTHEUS** #1,2, **...RAMTHAR** #1,**...RAZOR NIGHTS** #1						3.00

MIKE GRELL'S SABLE (Also see Jon Sable & Sable)
First Comics: Mar, 1990 - No. 10, Dec, 1990 ($1.75)

	GD	VG	FN	VF	VF/NM	NM-
1-10: r/Jon Sable Freelance #1-10 by Grell						2.50

MIKE MIST MINUTE MIST-ERIES (See Ms. Tree/Mike Mist in 3-D)
Eclipse Comics: April, 1981 ($1.25, B&W, one-shot)

	GD	VG	FN	VF	VF/NM	NM-
1						2.50

MIKE SHAYNE PRIVATE EYE
Dell Publishing Co.: Nov-Jan, 1962 - No. 3, Sept-Nov, 1962

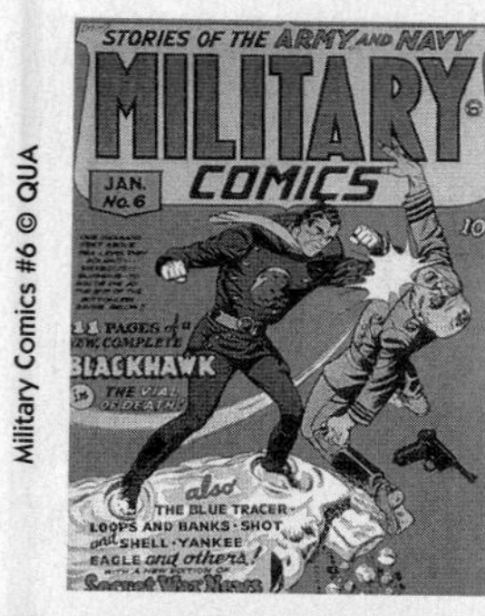

Military Comics #6 © QUA

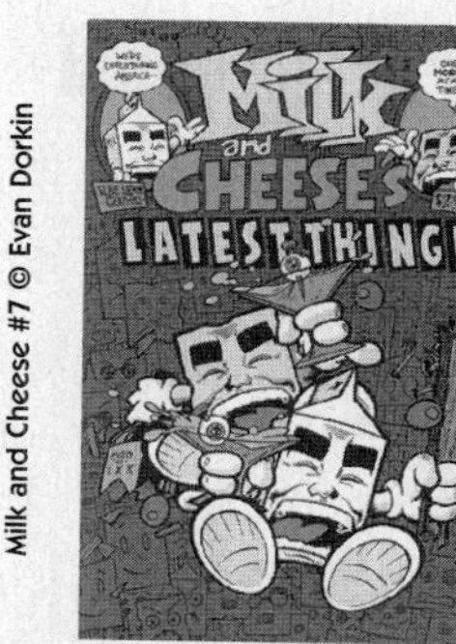

Milk and Cheese #7 © Evan Dorkin

Millie the Model #7 © MAR

	GD 2.0	VG 4.0	FN 6.0	VF 8.0	VF/NM 9.0	NM- 9.2
1	4	8	12	24	37	50
2,3	3	6	9	17	25	32

MILESTONE FOREVER
DC Comics: Apr, 2010 - No. 2 ($5.99, squarebound, limites series)

	GD	VG	FN	VF	VF/NM	NM-
1-McDuffie-s/Leon & Bright-a; Icon, Blood Syndicate, Hardware and Static app.						6.00

MILITARY COMICS (Becomes Modern Comics #44 on)
Quality Comics Group: Aug, 1941 - No. 43, Oct, 1945

	GD	VG	FN	VF	VF/NM	NM-
1-Origin/1st app. Blackhawk by C. Cuidera (Eisner scripts); Miss America, The Death Patrol by Jack Cole (also #2-7,27-30), & The Blue Tracer by Guardineer; X of the Underground, The Yankee Eagle, Q-Boat & Shot & Shell, Archie Atkins, Loops & Banks by Bud Ernest (Bob Powell)(ends #13) begin	667	1334	2001	4802	8401	12,000
2-Secret War News begins (by McWilliams #2-16); Cole-a; new uniform with yellow circle & hawk's head for Blackhawk	200	400	600	1260	2130	3000
3-Origin/1st app. Chop Chop (9/41)	173	346	519	1090	1845	2600
4	140	280	420	882	1491	2100
5-The Sniper begins; Miss America in costume #4-7	113	226	339	712	1231	1750
6-9: 8-X of the Underground begins (ends #13). 9-The Phantom Clipper begins (ends #16)	80	160	240	504	852	1200
10-Classic Eisner-c	93	186	279	586	993	1400
11-Flag-c	73	146	219	460	780	1100
12-Blackhawk by Crandall begins, ends #22	80	160	240	504	852	1200
13-15: 14-Private Dogtag begins (ends #83)	60	120	180	378	639	900
16-20: 16-Blue Tracer ends. 17-P.T. Boat begins	53	106	159	334	567	800
21-31: 22-Last Crandall Blackhawk. 23-Shrunken head-c. 27-Death Patrol revived	48	96	144	298	499	700
32-43	41	82	123	256	428	600

NOTE: *Berg a-6.* ***Al Bryant*** *c-31-34, 38, 40-43.* ***J. Cole*** *a-1-3, 27-32.* ***Crandall*** *a-12-22; c-13-20.* ***Cuidera*** *c-2-9.* ***Eisner*** *c-1, 2(part), 9, 10.* ***Kotsky*** *c-21-29, 35, 37, 39.* ***McWilliams*** *a-2-16.* ***Powell*** *a-1-13.* ***Ward*** *Blackhawk-30, 31(15 pgs. each); c-30.*

MILK AND CHEESE (Also see Cerebus Bi-Weekly #20)
Slave Labor: 1991 - Present ($2.50, B&W)

	GD	VG	FN	VF	VF/NM	NM-
1-Evan Dorkin story & art in all	4	8	12	24	37	50
1-2nd-6th printings						4.00
2-"Other #1"	3	6	9	16	23	30
2-reprint						3.00
3-"Third #1"	2	4	6	11	16	20
4-"Fourth #1", 5-"First Second Issue"	1	3	4	6	8	10
6,7: 6-"#666"						5.00

NOTE: *Multiple printings of all issues exist and are worth cover price unless listed here.*

MILKMAN MURDERS, THE
Dark Horse Comics: Jun, 2004 - No. 4, Aug, 2004 ($2.99, limited series)

	GD	VG	FN	VF	VF/NM	NM-
1-4-Casey-s/Parkhouse-a						3.00

MILLENNIUM
DC Comics: Jan, 1988 - No. 8, Feb, 1988 (Weekly limited series)

	GD	VG	FN	VF	VF/NM	NM-
1-Englehart-s/Staton c/a(p)						3.00
2-8						2.50
TPB (2008, $19.99) r/#1-8						20.00

MILLENNIUM EDITION:... (Reprints of classic DC issues)
DC Comics: Feb, 2000 - Feb, 2001 (gold foil cover stamps)

	GD	VG	FN	VF	VF/NM	NM-
Action Comics #1, Adventure Comics #61, All Star Comics #3, All Star Comics #8, Batman #1, Detective Comics #1, Detective Comics #27, Detective Comics #38, Flash Comics #1, Military Comics #1, More Fun Comics #73, Police Comics #1, Sensation Comics #1, Superman #1, Whiz Comics #2, Wonder Woman #1 -($3.95-c)						4.00
Action Comics #252, Adventure Comics #247, Brave and the Bold #28, Brave and the Bold #85, Crisis on Infinte Earths #1, Detective #225, Detective #327, Detective #359, Detective #395, Flash #123, Gen13 #1, Green Lantern #76, House of Mystery #1, House of Secrets #92, JLA #1, Justice League #1, Mad #1, Man of Steel #1, Mysterious Suspense #1, New Gods, #1, New Teen Titans #1, Our Army at War #81, Plop! #1, Saga of the Swamp Thing #21, Shadow #1, Showcase #4, Showcase #9, Showcase #22, Superman #233, Superman (2nd) #75, Superman's Pal Jimmy Olsen #1, Watchmen #1, WildC.A.T.s #1, Wonder Woman (2nd) #1, World's Finest #71 -($2.50-c)						2.50
All-Star Western #10, Hellblazer #1, More Fun Comics #101, Preacher #1, Sandman #1, Spirit #1, Superboy #1, Superman #76, Young Romance #1-($2.95-c)						3.00
Batman: The Dark Knight Returns #1, Kingdom Come #1 -($5.95-c)						6.00
All Star Comics #3, Batman #1, Justice League #1: Chromium cover						10.00
Crisis on Infinite Earths #1 Chromium cover						20.00

MILLENNIUM FEVER
DC Comics (Vertigo): Oct, 1995 - No.4, Jan, 1996 ($2.50, limited series)

	GD	VG	FN	VF	VF/NM	NM-
1-4: Duncan Fegredo-c/a						2.50

MILLENNIUM INDEX
Independent Comics Group: Mar, 1988 - No. 2, Mar, 1988 ($2.00)

	GD	VG	FN	VF	VF/NM	NM-
1,2						2.50

MILLENNIUM 2.5 A.D.
ACG Comics: No. 1, 2000 ($2.95)

	GD	VG	FN	VF	VF/NM	NM-
1-Reprints 1934 Buck Rogers daily strips #1-48						3.00

MILLIE, THE LOVABLE MONSTER
Dell Publishing Co.: Sept-Nov, 1962 - No. 6, Jan, 1973

	GD	VG	FN	VF	VF/NM	NM-
12-523-211-Bill Woggon c/a in all	5	10	15	34	55	75
2(8-10/63)	5	10	15	30	48	65
3(8-10/64)	4	8	12	26	41	55
4(7/72), 5(10/72), 6(1/73)	3	6	9	14	19	24

NOTE: ***Woggon*** *a-3-6; c-3-6. 4 reprints 1; 5 reprints 2; 6 reprints 3.*

MILLIE THE MODEL (See Comedy Comics, A Date With..., Joker Comics #28, Life With..., Mad About..., Marvel Mini-Books, Misty & Modeling With...)
Marvel/Atlas/Marvel Comics(CnPC #1)(SPI/Male/VPI):1945 - No. 207, Dec, 1973

	GD	VG	FN	VF	VF/NM	NM-
1-Origin	94	188	282	597	1024	1450
2 (10/46)-Millie becomes The Blonde Phantom to sell Blonde Phantom perfume; a pre-Blonde Phantom app. (see All-Select #11, Fall, 1946)	43	86	129	271	461	650
3-8,10: 4-7-Willie app. 7-Willie smokes extra strong tobacco. 8,10-Kurtzman's "Hey Look". 8-Willie & Rusty app.	32	64	96	192	314	435
9-Powerhouse Pepper by Wolverton, 4 pgs.	36	72	108	216	351	485
11-Kurtzman-a, "Giggles 'n' Grins"	21	42	63	126	206	285
12,15,17,19,20: 12-Rusty & Hedy Devine app.	17	34	51	100	158	215
13,14,16,18: 13,14,16-Kurtzman's "Hey Look". 13-Hedy Devine app. 18-Dan DeCarlo-a begins	18	36	54	105	165	225
21-30	14	28	42	80	115	150
31-40	8	16	24	54	90	125
41-60	7	14	21	45	73	100
61-99	6	12	18	37	59	80
100	6	12	18	41	66	90
101-130: 107-Jack Kirby app. in story	5	10	15	32	51	70
131-134,136,138-153: 141-Groovy Gears-c/s	4	8	12	26	41	55
135-(2/66) 1st app. Groovy Gears	5	10	15	32	51	70
137-2nd app. Groovy Gears	4	8	12	28	44	60
154-New Millie begins (10/67)	6	12	18	39	62	85
155-190	4	8	12	26	41	55
191,193-199,201-206	4	8	12	22	34	45
192-(52 pgs.)	4	8	12	26	41	55
200,207(Last issue)	4	8	12	26	41	55
(Beware: cut-up pages are common in all Annuals)						
Annual 1(1962)-Early Marvel annual (2nd?)	19	38	57	133	259	385
Annual 2(1963)	13	26	39	90	165	240
Annual 3-5 (1964-1966)	9	18	27	60	100	140
Annual 6-10(1967-11/71)	7	14	21	47	76	105
Queen-Size 11(9/74), 12(1975)	6	12	18	41	66	90

NOTE: ***Dan DeCarlo*** *a-18-93.*

MILLION DOLLAR DIGEST (Richie Rich... #23 on; also see Richie Rich...)
Harvey Publications: 11/86 - No. 7, 11/87; No. 8, 4/88 - No. 34, Nov, 1994 ($1.25/$1.75, digest size)

	GD	VG	FN	VF	VF/NM	NM-
1	1	2	3	5	6	8
2-8: 8-(68 pgs.)						6.00
9-20: 9-Begin $1.75-c. 14-May not exist	1	2	3	4	5	7
21-34	1	3	4	6	8	10

MILT GROSS FUNNIES (Also see Picture News #1)
Milt Gross, Inc. (ACG?): Aug, 1947 - No. 2, Sept, 1947

	GD	VG	FN	VF	VF/NM	NM-
1	21	42	63	124	202	280
2	15	30	45	86	133	180

MILTON THE MONSTER & FEARLESS FLY (TV)
Gold Key: May, 1966

	GD	VG	FN	VF	VF/NM	NM-
1 (10175-605)	9	18	27	63	107	150

MINIMUM WAGE
Fantagraphics Books: V1#1, July, 1995 ($9.95, B&W, graphic novel, mature)
V2#1, 1995 - Present ($2.95, B&W, mature)

	GD	VG	FN	VF	VF/NM	NM-
V1#1-Bob Fingerman story & art	1	3	4	6	8	10
V2#1-9($2.95): Bob Fingerman story & art. 2-Kevin Nowlan back-c. 4-w/pin-ups. 5-Mignola back-c						3.00
Book Two TPB ('97, $12.95) r/V2#1-5						13.00

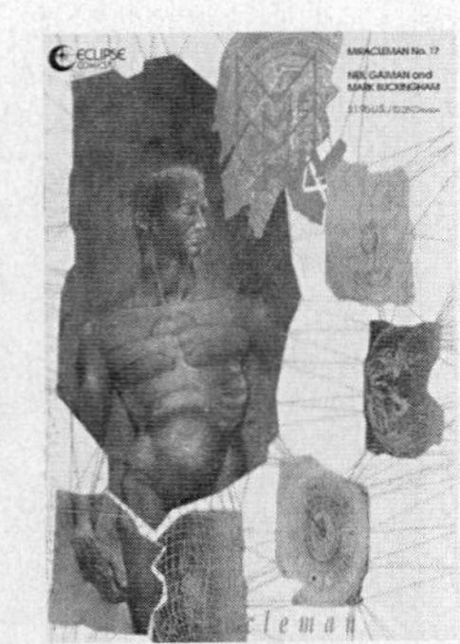

Miracleman #17 © ECL

Mirror's Edge #1 © EA Digital

Miss America Magazine #6 © MAR

GD VG FN VF VF/NM NM-
2.0 4.0 6.0 8.0 9.0 9.2

GD VG FN VF VF/NM NM-
2.0 4.0 6.0 8.0 9.0 9.2

MINISTRY OF SPACE
Image Comics: Apr, 2001 - No. 3, Apr, 2004 ($2.95, limited series)
1-3-Warren Ellis-s/Chris Weston-a 3.00
...Vol. 1 Omnibus (3/04, $4.95) r/1&2 5.00
TPB (12/04, $12.95) r/series; sketch & design pages; intro by Mark Millar 13.00

MINOR MIRACLES
DC Comics: 2000 ($12.95, B&W, squarebound)
nn-Will Eisner-s/a 13.00

MINUTE MAN (See Master Comics & Mighty Midget Comics)
Fawcett Publications: Summer, 1941 - No. 3, Spring, 1942 (68 pgs.)
1 206 412 618 1318 2259 3200
2,3 123 246 369 787 1344 1900

MINX, THE
DC Comics (Vertigo): Oct, 1998 - No. 8, May, 1999 ($2.50, limited series)
1-8-Milligan-s/Phillips-c/a 3.00

MIRACLE COMICS
Hillman Periodicals: Feb, 1940 - No. 4, Mar, 1941
1-Sky Wizard Master of Space, Dash Dixon, Man of Might, Pinkie Parker, Dusty Doyle, The Kid Cop, K-7, Secret Agent, The Scorpion, & Blandu, Jungle Queen begin; Masked Angel only app. (all 1st app.) 187 374 561 1197 2049 2900
2 94 188 282 597 1024 1450
3,4: 3-Bill Colt, the Ghost Rider begins. 4-The Veiled Prophet & Bullet Bob (by Burnley) app. 81 162 243 518 884 1250

MIRACLEMAN
Eclipse Comics: Aug, 1985 - No. 15, Nov, 1988; No. 16, Dec, 1989 - No. 24, Aug, 1993
1-r/British Marvelman series; Alan Moore scripts in #1-16 2 3 4 6 8 10
1-Gold variant (edition of 400, signed by Alan Moore, came with signed & #'d certificate of authenticity) 60 120 180 510 1005 1500
1-Blue variant (edition of 600, came with signed certificate of authenticity) 36 72 108 280 540 800
2-10: 8-Airboy preview. 6,9,10-Origin Miracleman. 9-Shows graphic scenes of childbirth. 10-Snyder-c 1 2 3 5 6 8
11-14(5/87-4/88) Totleben-a 2 4 6 11 16 20
15-($1.75-c, scarce) end of Kid Miracleman 6 12 18 41 66 90
16-Last Alan Moore-s; 1st $1.95-c (low print) 3 6 9 16 23 30
17-22: 17-"The Golden Age" begins, ends #22. Dave McKean-c begins, end #22; Neil Gaiman scripts in #17-24 2 4 6 10 14 18
23-"The Silver Age" begins; Barry W. Smith-c 2 4 6 11 16 20
24-Last issue; Smith-c 3 6 9 14 20 25
3-D #1 (12/85) 1 2 3 5 7 9
3-D #1 Blue variant (edition of 99) 3 6 9 16 23 30
3-D #1 Gold variant (edition of 199) 2 4 6 11 16 20
NOTE: *Miracleman 3-D #1 (12/85) (2D edition) Interior is the same as the 3-D version except in non 3-D format. Indicia are the same for both versions of the book with only the non 3-D art distinguishing this book from the standard 3-D version. Standard 3-D edition has house ad mentioning the non 3-D edition. Two known copies exist, one in the Michigan State University Special Collection Department. (No known sales)*
Book One: A Dream of Flying (1988, $9.95, TPB) r/#1-5; Leach-c 22.00
Book One: A Dream of Flying-Hardcover (1988, $29.95) r/#1-5 70.00
Book Two: The Red King Syndrome (1990, $12.95, TPB) r/#6-10; Bolton-c 30.00
Book Two: The Red King Syndrome-Hardcover (1990, $30.95) r/#6-10 85.00
Book Three: Olympus (1990, $12.95, TPB) r/#11-16 130.00
Book Three: Olympus-Hardcover (1990, $30.95) r/#11-16 250.00
Book Four: The Golden Age (1992, $15.95, TPB) r/#17-22 30.00
Book Four: The Golden Age Hardcover (1992, $33.95) r/#17-22 50.00
Book Four: The Golden Age (1993, $12.99, TPB) new McKean-c 15.00
NOTE: *Eclipse archive copies exist for #4,5,8,17,23. Each has a small Miracleman image foil-stamped on the cover.* ***Chaykin*** *c-3.* ***Gulacy*** *c-7.* ***McKean*** *c-17-22.* ***B. Smith*** *c-23, 24.* ***Starlin*** *c-4.* ***Totleben*** *a-11-13; c-9, 11-13.* ***Truman*** *c-6.*

MIRACLEMAN: APOCRYPHA
Eclipse Comics: Nov, 1991 - No. 3, Feb, 1992 ($2.50, limited series)
1-3: 1-Stories by Neil Gaiman, Mark Buckingham, Alex Ross & others. 3-Stories by James Robinson, Kelley Jones, Matt Wagner, Neil Gaiman, Mark Buckingham & others 1 2 3 4 5 7
TPB (12/92, $15.95) r/#1-3; Buckingham-c 20.00

MIRACLEMAN FAMILY
Eclipse Comics: May, 1988 - No. 2, Sept, 1988 ($1.95, lim. series, Baxter paper)
1,2: 2-Gulacy-c 5.00

MIRACLE OF THE WHITE STALLIONS, THE (See Movie Comics)

MIRROR'S EDGE (Based on the EA video game)
DC Comics (WildStorm): Dec, 2008 - No. 6, Jun, 2009 ($3.99, limited series)
1-6: 1-Origin of Faith; Rhianna Pratchett-s/Matthew Dow Smith-a 4.00
TPB (2009, $19.99) r/#1-6 20.00

MISADVENTURES OF MERLIN JONES, THE (See Movie Comics & Merlin Jones as the Monkey's Uncle under Movie Comics)

MISPLACED
Image Comics: May, 2003 - No. 4, Dec, 2004 ($2.95)
1-4: 1-Three covers by Blaylock, Green and Clugston-Major; Blaylock-s/a 3.00
... @17 (12/04, $4.95) Nara from "Dead @17" app.; Blaylock-s/a 5.00

MISS AMERICA COMICS (Miss America Magazine #2 on; also see Blonde Phantom & Marvel Mystery Comics)
Marvel Comics (20CC): 1944 (one-shot)
1-2 pgs. pin-ups 187 374 561 1197 2049 2900

MISS AMERICA COMICS 70th ANNIVERARY SPECIAL
Marvel Comics: Aug, 2009 ($3.99, one-shot)
1-Eaglesham-c; new Miss America & Whizzer story; reps. from All Winners #9-11 4.00

MISS AMERICA MAGAZINE (Formerly Miss America; Miss America #51 on)
Miss America Publ. Corp./Marvel/Atlas (MAP): V1#2, Nov, 1944 - No. 93, Nov, 1958
V1#2-Photo-c of teenage girl in Miss America costume; Miss America, Patsy Walker (intro.) comic stories plus movie reviews & stories; intro. Buzz Baxter & Hedy Wolfe; 1 pg. origin Miss America 142 284 426 909 1555 2200
3-5-Miss America & Patsy Walker stories 58 116 174 371 636 900
6-Patsy Walker only 34 68 102 199 325 450
V2#1(4/45)-6(9/45)-Patsy Walker continues 14 28 42 82 121 160
V3#1(10/45)-6(4/46) 13 26 39 74 105 135
V4#1(5/46),2,5(9/46) 12 24 36 67 94 120
V4#3(7/46)-Liz Taylor photo-c 30 60 90 177 289 400
V4#4 (8/46; 68 pgs.), V4#6 (10/46; 92 pgs.) 11 22 33 62 86 110
V5#1(11/46)-6(4/47), V6#1(5/47)-3(7/47) 11 22 33 60 83 105
V7#1(8/47)-23(#56, 6/49) 10 20 30 58 79 100
V7#24(#57, 7/49)-Kamen-a (becomes Best Western #58 on?) 11 22 33 60 83 105
V7#25(8/49), 27-44(3/52), VII,nn(5/52) 10 20 30 56 76 95
V7#26(9/49)-All comics 11 22 33 60 83 105
V1,nn(7/52)-V1,nn(1/53)(#46-49), V7#50(Spring '53), V1#51-V7?#54(7/53), 55-93 10 20 30 54 72 90
NOTE: *Photo-c #1, 4, V2#1, 4, 5, V3#5, V4#3, 4, 6, V7#15, 16, 24, 26, 34, 37, 38. Painted c-3.* ***Powell*** *a-V7#31.*

MISS BEVERLY HILLS OF HOLLYWOOD (See Adventures of Bob Hope)
National Periodical Publ.: Mar-Apr, 1949 - No. 9, July-Aug, 1950 (52 pgs.)
1 (Meets Alan Ladd) 60 120 180 378 639 900
2-William Holden photo on-c 44 88 132 273 454 635
3-5: 2-9-Part photo-c. 5-Bob Hope photo on-c 40 80 120 236 383 530
6,7,9: 6-Lucille Ball photo on-c 36 72 108 212 341 470
8-Reagan photo on-c 40 80 120 244 397 550
NOTE: *Beverly meets Alan Ladd in #1, Eve Arden #2, Betty Hutton #4, Bob Hope #5.*

MISS CAIRO JONES
Croyden Publishers: 1945
1-Bob Oksner daily newspaper-r (1st strip story); lingerie panels 19 38 57 112 179 245

MISS FURY COMICS (Newspaper strip reprints)
Timely Comics (NPI 1/CmPI 2/MPC 3-8): Winter, 1942-43 - No. 8, Winter, 1946 (Published twice a year)
1-Origin Miss Fury by Tarpe' Mills (68 pgs.) in costume w/paper dolls with cut-out costumes 394 788 1182 2758 4829 6900
2-(60 pgs.)-In costume w/paper dolls 203 406 609 1289 2220 3150
3-(60 pgs.)-In costume w/paper dolls; Hitler-c 158 316 474 1003 1727 2450
4-(52 pgs.)-Classic Nazi WWII-c with giant swastika, Tojo & Hitler photo on wall; in costume, 2 pgs. w/paper dolls 135 270 405 864 1482 2100
5-(52 pgs.)-In costume w/paper dolls 103 206 309 659 1130 1600
6-(52 pgs.)-Not in costume in inside stories, w/paper dolls 94 188 282 597 1024 1450
7,8-(36 pgs.)-In costume 1 pg. each; no paper dolls 82 164 246 528 902 1275
NOTE: ***Schomburg*** *c-1, 5, 6.*

MISS FURY
Adventure Comics: 1991 - No. 4, 1991 ($2.50, limited series)
1-4: 1-Origin; granddaughter of original Miss Fury 3.00
1-Limited ed. ($4.95) 5.00

MISSION IMPOSSIBLE (TV) (Also see Wild!)
Dell Publ. Co.: May, 1967 - No. 4, Oct, 1968; No. 5, Oct, 1969 (All have photo-c)

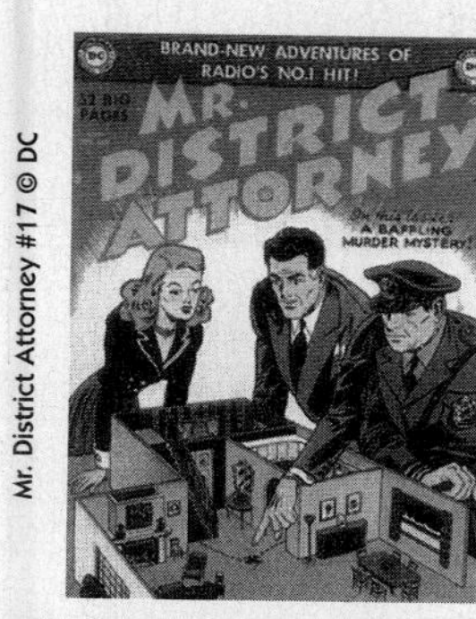

Mr. District Attorney #17 © DC

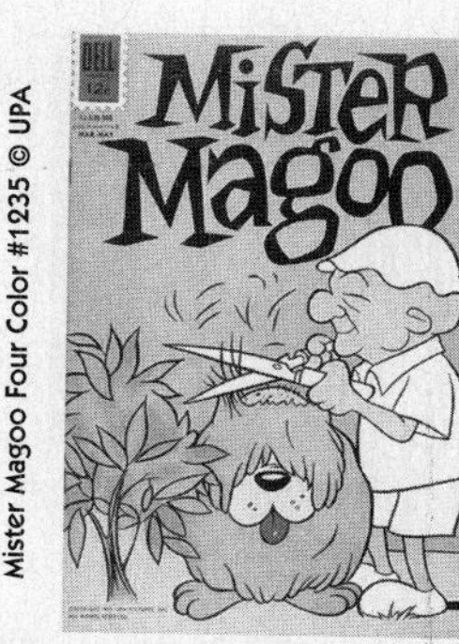

Mister Magoo Four Color #1235 © UPA

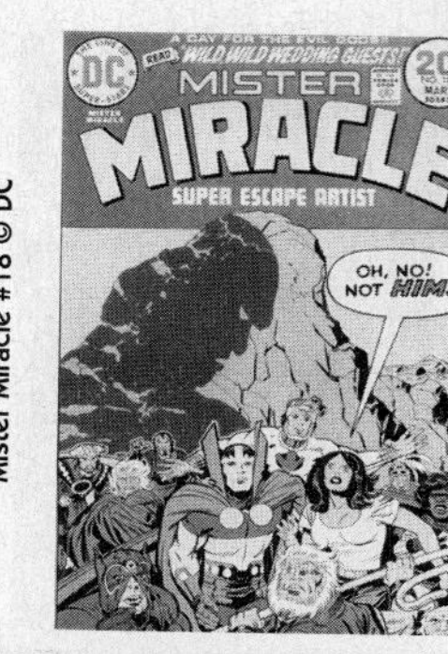

Mister Miracle #18 © DC

	GD 2.0	VG 4.0	FN 6.0	VF 8.0	VF/NM 9.0	NM- 9.2
1	8	16	24	58	97	135
2-5: 5-Reprints #1	6	12	18	41	66	90

MISSION IMPOSSIBLE (Movie) (1st Paramount Comics book)
Marvel Comics (Paramount Comics): May, 1996 ($2.95, one-shot)

	GD	VG	FN	VF	VF/NM	NM-
1-Liefeld-c & back-up story						3.00

MISS LIBERTY (Becomes Liberty Comics)
Burten Publishing Co.: 1945 (MLJ reprints)

	GD	VG	FN	VF	VF/NM	NM-
1-The Shield & Dusty, The Wizard, & Roy, the Super Boy app.; r/Shield-Wizard #13	28	56	84	165	270	375

MISS MELODY LANE OF BROADWAY (See The Adventures of Bob Hope)
National Periodical Publ.: Feb-Mar, 1950 - No. 3, June-July, 1950 (52 pgs.)

	GD	VG	FN	VF	VF/NM	NM-
1-Movie stars photos app. on all-c.	60	120	180	378	639	900
2,3: 3-Ed Sullivan photo on-c.	40	80	120	235	380	525

MISS PEACH
Dell Publishing Co.: Oct-Dec, 1963; 1969

	GD	VG	FN	VF	VF/NM	NM-
1-Jack Mendelsohn-a/script	8	16	24	52	86	120
...Tells You How to Grow (1969; 25¢)-Mel Lazarus-a; also given away (36 pgs.)	5	10	15	32	51	70

MISS PEPPER (See Meet Miss Pepper)

MISS SUNBEAM (See Little Miss...)

MISS VICTORY (See Captain Fearless #1,2, Holyoke One-Shot #3, Veri Best Sure Fire & Veri Best Sure Shot Comics)

MISTER AMERICA
Endeavor Comics: Apr, 1994 - No. 2, May, 1994 ($2.95, limited series)

	GD	VG	FN	VF	VF/NM	NM-
1,2						3.00

MR. & MRS. BEANS
United Features Syndicate: No. 11, 1939

	GD	VG	FN	VF	VF/NM	NM-
Single Series 11	34	68	102	199	325	450

MR. & MRS. J. EVIL SCIENTIST (TV)(See The Flintstones & Hanna-Barbera Band Wagon #3)
Gold Key: Nov, 1963 - No. 4, Sept, 1966 (Hanna-Barbera, all 12¢)

	GD	VG	FN	VF	VF/NM	NM-
1	6	12	18	41	66	90
2-4	4	8	12	24	37	50

MR. ANTHONY'S LOVE CLINIC (Based on radio show)
Hillman Periodicals: Nov, 1949 - No. 5, Apr-May, 1950 (52 pgs.)

	GD	VG	FN	VF	VF/NM	NM-
1-Photo-c on all	15	30	45	88	137	185
2	10	20	30	58	79	100
3-5	10	20	30	54	72	90

MISTER BLANK
Amaze Ink: No. 0, Jan, 1996 - No. 14, May, 2000 ($1.75/$2.95, B&W)

	GD	VG	FN	VF	VF/NM	NM-
0-($1.75, 16 pgs.) Origin of Mr. Blank						2.25
1-14-($2.95) Chris Hicks-s/a						3.00

MR. DISTRICT ATTORNEY (Radio/TV)
National Per. Publ.: Jan-Feb, 1948 - No. 67, Jan-Feb, 1959 (1-23: 52 pgs.)

	GD	VG	FN	VF	VF/NM	NM-
1-Howard Purcell c-5-23 (most)	87	174	261	553	952	1350
2	41	82	123	256	428	600
3-5	29	58	87	170	278	385
6-10	22	44	66	132	216	300
11-20	17	34	51	98	154	210
21-43: 43-Last pre-code (1-2/55)	14	28	42	76	108	140
44-67	11	22	33	62	86	110

MR. DISTRICT ATTORNEY (SeeThe Funnies #35)
Dell Publishing Co.: No. 13, 1942

	GD	VG	FN	VF	VF/NM	NM-
Four Color 13-See The Funnies #35 for 1st app.	27	54	81	194	377	560

MISTER E (Also see Books of Magic limited series)
DC Comics: Jun, 1991- No. 4, Sept, 1991($1.75, limited series)

	GD	VG	FN	VF	VF/NM	NM-
1-4-Snyder III-c/a; follow-up to Books of Magic limited series						3.00

MISTER ED, THE TALKING HORSE (TV)
Dell Publishing Co./Gold Key: Mar-May, 1962 - No. 6, Feb, 1964 (All photo-c; photo back-c: 1-6)

	GD	VG	FN	VF	VF/NM	NM-
Four Color 1295	12	24	36	85	155	225
1(11/62) (Gold Key)-Photo-c	9	18	27	60	100	140
2-6: Photo-c	6	12	18	37	59	80

(See March of Comics #244, 260, 282, 290)

MR. GUM (From The Atomics)
Oni Press: April, 2003 ($2.99, one-shot)

	GD	VG	FN	VF	VF/NM	NM-
1-Mike Allred-s/J. Bone-a; Madman & The Atomics app.						3.00

MR. HERO, THE NEWMATIC MAN (See Neil Gaiman's...)

MR. MAGOO (TV) (The Nearsighted..., ...& Gerald McBoing Boing 1954 issues; formerly Gerald McBoing-Boing And ...)
Dell Publishing Co.: No. 6, Nov-Jan, 1953-54; 5/54 - 3-5/62; 9-11/63 - 3-5/65

	GD	VG	FN	VF	VF/NM	NM-
6	10	20	30	68	119	170
Four Color 561(5/54),602(11/54)	10	20	30	68	119	170
Four Color 1235(#1, 12-2/62),1305(#2, 3-5/62)	8	16	24	56	93	130
3(9-11/63) - 5	7	14	21	50	83	115
Four Color 1235(12-536-505)(3-5/65)-2nd Printing	6	12	18	41	66	90

MR. MAJESTIC (See WildC.A.T.S.)
DC Comics (WildStorm): Sept, 1999 - No. 9, May, 2000 ($2.50)

	GD	VG	FN	VF	VF/NM	NM-
1-9: 1-McGuinness-a/Casey & Holguin-s. 2-Two covers						2.50
TPB (2002, $14.95) r/#1-6 & Wildstorm Spotlight #1						

MISTER MIRACLE (1st series) (See Cancelled Comic Cavalcade)
National Periodical Publications/DC Comics: 3-4/71 - V4#18, 2-3/74; V5#19, 9/77 - V6#25, 8-9/78; 1987 (Fourth World)

	GD	VG	FN	VF	VF/NM	NM-
1-1st app. Mr. Miracle (#1-3 are 15¢)	8	16	24	56	93	130
2,3: 2-Intro. Granny Goodness. 3-Last 15¢ issue	5	10	15	30	48	65
4-8: 4-Intro. Barda; Boy Commandos-r begin; all 52 pgs.	5	10	15	30	48	65
9-18: 9-Origin Mr. Miracle; Darkseid cameo. 15-Intro/1st app. Shilo Norman. 18-Barda & Scott Free wed; New Gods app. & Darkseid cameo; Last Kirby issue.	3	6	9	16	23	30
19-25 (1977-78)	2	4	6	8	10	12
Special 1(1987, $1.25, 52 pgs.)						4.00
Jack Kirby's Fourth World TPB ('01, $12.95) B&W&Grey-toned reprint of #11-18; Mark Evanier intro.						13.00
Jack Kirby's Mister Miracle TPB ('98, $12.95) B&W&Grey-toned reprint of #1-10; David Copperfield intro.						13.00

NOTE: ***Austin** a-19i. **Ditko** a-6r. **Golden** a-23-25p; c-25p. **Heath** a-24i, 25i; c-25i. **Kirby** a(p)/c-1-18. **Nasser** a-19i. **Rogers** a-19-22p; c-19, 20p, 21p, 22-24. 4-8 contain **Simon & Kirby** Boy Commandos reprints from Detective 82,76, Boy Commandos 1, 3 & Detective 64 in that order.*

MISTER MIRACLE (2nd Series) (See Justice League)
DC Comics: Jan, 1989 - No. 28, June, 1991 ($1.00/$1.25)

	GD	VG	FN	VF	VF/NM	NM-
1-28: 13,14-Lobo app. 22-1st new Mr. Miracle w/new costume						2.50

MISTER MIRACLE (3rd Series)
DC Comics: Apr, 1996 - No. 7, Oct, 1996 ($1.95)

	GD	VG	FN	VF	VF/NM	NM-
1-7: 2-Vs. JLA. 6-Simonson-c						2.50

MR. MIRACLE (See Capt. Fearless #1 & Holyoke One-Shot #4)

MR. MONSTER (1st Series)(Doc Stearn... #7 on; See Airboy-Mr. Monster Special, Dark Horse Presents, Super Duper Comics & Vanguard Illustrated #7)
Eclipse Comics: Jan, 1985 - No. 10, June, 1987 ($1.75, Baxter paper)

	GD	VG	FN	VF	VF/NM	NM-
1-3: 1-1st story-r from Vanguard Ill. #7(1st app.). 2-Dave Stevens-c. 3-Alan Moore scripts; Wolverton-r/Weird Mysteries #5.						5.00
4-10: 6-Ditko-r/Fantastic Fears #5 plus new Giffen-a. 10- "6-D" issue						4.00

MR. MONSTER
Dark Horse Comics: Feb, 1988 - No. 8, July, 1991 ($1.75, B&W)

	GD	VG	FN	VF	VF/NM	NM-
1-7						3.00
8-($4.95, 60 pgs.)-Origins conclusion						5.00

MR. MONSTER ATTACKS! (Doc Stearn...)
Tundra Publ.: Aug, 1992 - No. 3, Oct, 1992 ($3.95, limited series, 32 pgs.)

	GD	VG	FN	VF	VF/NM	NM-
1-3: Michael T. Gilbert-a/scripts; Gilbert/Dorman painted-c						4.00

MR. MONSTER PRESENTS (CRACK-A-BOOM!)
Caliber Comics: 1997 - No. 3, 1997 ($2.95, B&W&Red, limited series)

	GD	VG	FN	VF	VF/NM	NM-
1-3: Michael T. Gilbert-a/scripts: 1-Wraparound-c						3.00

MR. MONSTER'S GAL FRIDAY...KELLY!
Image Comics: Jan, 2000 - No. 3, May, 2004 ($3.50, B&W)

	GD	VG	FN	VF	VF/NM	NM-
1-3-Michael T. Gilbert-c; story & art by various. 3-Alan Moore-s						3.50

MR. MONSTER'S SUPER-DUPER SPECIAL
Eclipse Comics: May, 1986 - No. 8, July, 1987

	GD	VG	FN	VF	VF/NM	NM-
1-(5/86)...3-D High Octane Horror #1						5.00
1-(5/86)...2-D version, 100 copies	2	4	6	9	13	16

2-(8/86)...High Octane Horror #1, 3-(9/86)...True Crime #1, 4-(11/86)...True Crime #2, 5-(1/87)...Hi-Voltage Super Science #1, 6-(3/87)...High Shock Schlock #1, 7-(5/87)...High

Mister Mystery #6 © Media Pub,

Mister X V2 #10 © Dean Motter

Models, Inc. #3 © MAR

	GD 2.0	VG 4.0	FN 6.0	VF 8.0	VF/NM 9.0	NM- 9.2

Shock Schlock #2, 8-(7/87)...Weird Tales Of The Future #1 — 4.00

NOTE: ***Jack Cole** r-3, 4. **Evans** a-2r. **Kubert** a-1r. **Powell** a-5r. **Wolverton** a-2r, 7r, 8r.*

MR. MONSTER VS. GORZILLA
Image Comics: July, 1998 ($2.95, one-shot)

1-Michael T. Gilbert-a — 3.00

MR. MONSTER: WORLDS WAR TWO
Atomeka Press: 2004 ($6.99, one-shot)

nn-Michael T. Gilbert-s/George Freeman-a; two covers by Horley & Dorman — 7.00

MR. MUSCLES (Formerly Blue Beetle #18-21)
Charlton Comics: No. 22, Mar, 1956; No. 23, Aug, 1956

	GD	VG	FN	VF	VF/NM	NM-
22,23	9	18	27	47	61	75

MR. MXYZPTLK (VILLAINS)
DC Comics: Feb, 1998 ($1.95, one-shot)

1-Grant-s/Morgan-a/Pearson-c — 2.50

MISTER MYSTERY (Tales of Horror and Suspense)
Mr. Publ. (Media Publ.) No. 1-3/SPM Publ./Stanmore (Aragon): Sept, 1951 - No. 19, Oct, 1954

	GD	VG	FN	VF	VF/NM	NM-
1-Kurtzman*esque* horror story	94	188	282	597	1024	1450
2,3-Kurtzman*esque* story. 3-Anti-Wertham edit.	63	126	189	403	689	975
4-Bondage-c	63	126	189	403	689	975
5,8,10	56	112	168	356	611	865
6-Classic torture-c	76	152	228	486	831	1175
7- "The Brain Bats of Venus" by Wolverton; partially re-used in Weird Tales of the Future #7	126	252	378	806	1378	1950
9-Nostrand-a	56	112	168	356	611	865
11-Wolverton "Robot Woman" story/Weird Mysteries #2, cut up, rewritten & partially redrawn	87	174	261	553	952	1350
12-Classic injury to eye-c	142	284	426	909	1555	2200
13-17,19: 15- "Living Dead" junkie story. 16-Bondage-c. 17-Severed heads-c. 19-Reprints	44	88	132	277	469	660
18- "Robot Woman" by Wolverton reprinted from Weird Mysteries #2; decapitation, bondage-c	64	128	192	406	696	985

NOTE: ***Andru** a-1, 2p, 3p. **Andru/Esposito** c-1-3. **Baily** c-10-18(most). **Mortellaro** c-5-7. Bondage c-7, 16. Some issues have graphic dismemberment scenes.*

MR. PUNCH
DC Comics (Vertigo): 1994 ($24.95, one-shot)

nn (Hard-c)-Gaiman scripts; McKean-c/a — 40.00
nn (Soft-c) — 15.00

MISTER Q (See Mighty Midget Comics & Our Flag Comics #5)

MR. RISK (Formerly All Romances; Men Against Crime #3 on)(Also see Our Flag Comics & Super-Mystery Comics)
Ace Magazines: No. 7, Oct, 1950; No. 2, Dec, 1950

	GD	VG	FN	VF	VF/NM	NM-
7,2	11	22	33	62	86	110

MR. SCARLET & PINKY (See Mighty Midget Comics)

MR. T
APComics: May, 2005 ($3.50)

1-Chris Bunting-s/Neil Edwards-a — 3.50

MR. T AND THE T-FORCE
Now Comics: June, 1993 - No. 10, May, 1994 ($1.95, color)

1-10-Newsstand editions: 1-7-polybagged with photo trading card in each. 1,2-Neal Adams-c/a(p). 3-Dave Dorman painted-c — 2.50
1-10-Direct Sale editions polybagged w/line drawn trading cards. 1-Contains gold foil trading card by Neal Adams — 2.50

MISTER UNIVERSE (Professional wrestler)
Mr. Publications Media Publ. (Stanmor, Aragon): July, 1951; No. 2, Oct, 1951 - No. 5, April, 1952

	GD	VG	FN	VF	VF/NM	NM-
1	22	44	66	128	209	290
2- "Jungle That Time Forgot", (24 pg. story); Andru/Esposito-c	14	28	42	81	118	155
3-Marijuana story	14	28	42	81	118	155
4,5- "Goes to War" cover/stories	11	22	33	62	86	110

MISTER X (See Vortex)
Mr. Publications/Vortex Comics/Caliber V3#1 on: 6/84 - No. 14, 8/88 ($1.50/$2.25, direct sales, coated paper);V2#1, Apr, 1989 - V2#12, Mar, 1990 ($2.00/$2.50, B&W, newsprint) V3#1, 1996 - Present ($2.95, B&W)

1-14: 11-Dave McKean story & art (6 pgs.) — 4.00
V2 #1-12: 1-11 (Second Coming, B&W): 1-Four diff.-c. 10-Photo-c — 3.00
V3 #1-4 — 3.00
Return of... ($11.95, graphic novel)-r/V1#1-4 — 12.00
Return of... ($34.95, hardcover limited edition)-r/1-4 — 35.00
Special (no date, 1990?) — 3.00

MISTER X: CONDEMNED
Dark Horse Comics: Dec, 2008 - No. 4, Mar, 2009 ($3.50, limited series)

1-4-Dean Motter-s/a — 3.50

MISTY
Marvel Comics (Star Comics): Dec, 1985 - No. 6, May, 1986 (Limited series)

1-6: Millie The Model's niece — 4.00

MITZI COMICS (Becomes Mitzi's Boy Friend #2-7)(See All Teen)
Timely Comics: Spring, 1948 (one-shot)

	GD	VG	FN	VF	VF/NM	NM-
1-Kurtzman's "Hey Look" plus 3 pgs. "Giggles 'n' Grins"	26	52	78	154	252	350

MITZI'S BOY FRIEND (Formerly Mitzi Comics; becomes Mitzi's Romances)
Marvel Comics (TCI): No. 2, June, 1948 - No. 7, April, 1949

	GD	VG	FN	VF	VF/NM	NM-
2	15	30	45	84	127	170
3-7	13	26	39	74	105	135

MITZI'S ROMANCES (Formerly Mitzi's Boy Friend)
Timely/Marvel Comics (TCI): No. 8, June, 1949 - No. 10, Dec, 1949

	GD	VG	FN	VF	VF/NM	NM-
8-Becomes True Life Tales #8 (10/49) on?	14	28	42	78	112	145
9,10: 10-Painted-c	11	22	33	64	90	115

MNEMOVORE
DC Comics (Vertigo): Jun, 2005 - No. 6, Nov, 2005 ($2.99, limited series)

1-6-Rodionoff & Fawkes-s/Huddleston-a/c — 3.00

MOBY DICK (See Feature Presentations #6, and King Classics)
Dell Publishing Co.: No. 717, Aug, 1956

	GD	VG	FN	VF	VF/NM	NM-
Four Color 717-Movie, Gregory Peck photo-c	8	16	24	56	93	130

MOBY DUCK (See Donald Duck #112 & Walt Disney Showcase #2,11)
Gold Key (Disney): Oct, 1967 - No. 11, Oct, 1970; No. 12, Jan, 1974 - No. 30, Feb, 1978

	GD	VG	FN	VF	VF/NM	NM-
1	3	6	9	21	32	42
2-5	2	4	6	11	16	20
6-11	2	4	6	9	13	16
12-30: 21,30-r	1	3	4	6	8	10

MODEL FUN (With Bobby Benson)
Harle Publications: No. 2, Fall, 1954 - No. 5, July, 1955

	GD	VG	FN	VF	VF/NM	NM-
2-Bobby Benson	7	14	21	35	43	50
3-5-Bobby Benson	5	10	15	23	28	32

MODELING WITH MILLIE (Formerly Life With Millie)
Atlas/Marvel Comics (Male Publ.): No. 21, Feb, 1963 - No. 54, June, 1967

	GD	VG	FN	VF	VF/NM	NM-
21	9	18	27	60	100	140
22-30	5	10	15	34	55	75
31-53	4	8	12	28	44	60
54-Last issue; Gears-c & 6 pg. story; Beatles swipe imitators; FF #63 comic appears in story; "Millie the Marvel" 6 pg. story as super-hero	5	10	15	32	51	70

MODELS, INC.
Marvel Comics: Oct, 2009 - No. 4, Jan, 2010 ($3.99, limited series)

1-4-Millie the Model, Patsy Walker, Mary Jane Watson app.; Land-c. 1-Tim Gunn app. — 4.00

MODERN COMICS (Formerly Military Comics #1-43)
Quality Comics Group: No. 44, Nov, 1945 - No. 102, Oct, 1950

	GD	VG	FN	VF	VF/NM	NM-
44-Blackhawk continues	53	106	159	332	559	785
45-52: 49-1st app. Fear, Lady Adventuress	39	78	117	230	370	510
53-Torchy by Ward begins (9/46)	41	82	123	253	419	585
54-60: 55-J. Cole-a	33	66	99	196	316	435
61-Classic-c	37	74	111	222	356	485
62-64,66-77,79,80: 73-J. Cole-a	32	64	96	186	298	410
65-Classic Grim Reaper Skull-c	41	82	123	250	413	575
78-1st app. Madame Butterfly	35	70	105	203	327	450
81-99,101: 82,83-One pg. J. Cole-a. 83-Last 52 pg. issue	30	60	90	174	280	385
99-Blackhawks on the moon-c/story	32	64	96	190	305	420
100						
102-(Scarce)-J. Cole-a; Spirit by Eisner app.	40	80	120	234	377	520

NOTE: ***Al Bryant** c-44-51, 54, 55, 66, 69. **Jack Cole** a-55, 73. **Crandall** Blackhawk-#46, 47, 50, 51, 54, 56, 58-60, 64, 67-70, 73, 74, 76-78, 80-83; c-60-65, 67, 68, 70-95. **Crandall/Cuidera** c-56-59, 96-102. **Gustavson** a-47, 49. **Ward** Blackhawk-#52, 53, 55 (15 pgs. each). Torchy in #53-102; by **Ward** only in #53-89(9/49); by **Gil Fox** #92, 93, 102.*

Modern Love #2 © WMG

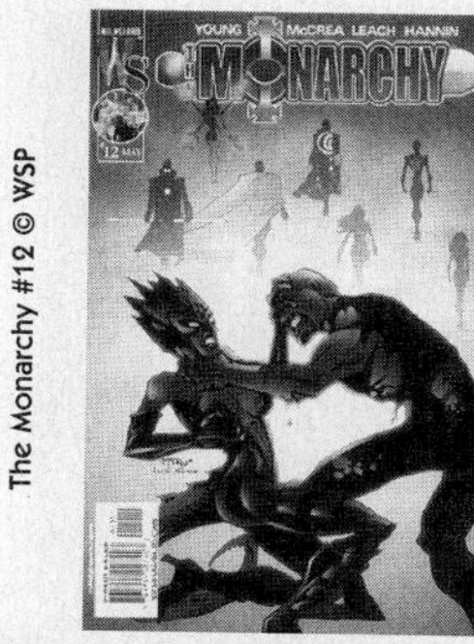

The Monarchy #12 © WSP

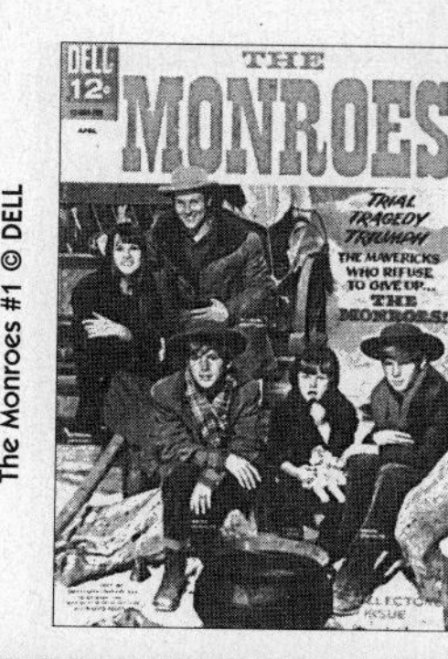

The Monroes #1 © DELL

MODERN LOVE
E. C. Comics: June-July, 1949 - No. 8, Aug-Sept, 1950

	GD 2.0	VG 4.0	FN 6.0	VF 8.0	VF/NM 9.0	NM- 9.2
1-Feldstein, Ingels-a	80	162	243	518	884	1250
2-Craig/Feldstein-c/s	52	104	156	323	549	775
3	46	92	138	290	488	685
4-6 (Scarce): 4-Bra/panties panels	57	114	171	362	619	875
7,8	46	92	138	290	488	685

NOTE: ***Craig** a-3. **Feldstein** a-in most issues; c-1, 2i, 3-8. **Harrison** a-4. **Iger** a-6-8. **Ingels** a-1, 2, 4-7. **Palais** a-5. **Wood** a-7. **Wood/Harrison** a-5-7. (Canadian reprints known; see Table of Contents.)*

MODERN WARFARE 2: GHOST (Based on the videogame)
DC Comics (WildStorm): Jan, 2010 - No. 6 ($3.99, limited series)

	GD 2.0	VG 4.0	FN 6.0	VF 8.0	VF/NM 9.0	NM- 9.2
1,2: 1-Two covers; Lapham-s/West-a						4.00

MOD LOVE
Western Publishing Co.: 1967 (50¢, 36 pgs.)

	GD 2.0	VG 4.0	FN 6.0	VF 8.0	VF/NM 9.0	NM- 9.2
1-(Low print)	6	12	18	39	62	85

MODNIKS, THE
Gold Key: Aug, 1967 - No. 2, Aug, 1970

	GD 2.0	VG 4.0	FN 6.0	VF 8.0	VF/NM 9.0	NM- 9.2
10206-708(#1)	4	8	12	22	34	45
2	3	6	9	16	22	28

M.O.D.O.K.: REIGN DELAY
Marvel Comics: Nov, 2009 ($3.99, one-shot)

	GD 2.0	VG 4.0	FN 6.0	VF 8.0	VF/NM 9.0	NM- 9.2
1-M.O.D.O.K. cartoony humor stories from Marvel Digital Comics; Ryan Dunlavey-s/a						4.00

MOD SQUAD (TV)
Dell Publishing Co.: Jan, 1969 - No. 3, Oct, 1969 - No. 8, April, 1971

	GD 2.0	VG 4.0	FN 6.0	VF 8.0	VF/NM 9.0	NM- 9.2
1-Photo-c	7	14	21	45	73	100
2-4: 2-4-Photo-c	4	8	12	28	44	60
5-8: 8-Photo-c; Reprints #2	4	8	12	24	37	50

MOD WHEELS
Gold Key: Mar, 1971 - No. 19, Jan, 1976

	GD 2.0	VG 4.0	FN 6.0	VF 8.0	VF/NM 9.0	NM- 9.2
1	4	8	12	26	41	55
2-9	3	6	9	16	23	30
10-19: 11,15-Extra 16 pgs. ads	3	6	9	14	19	24

MOE & SHMOE COMICS
O. S. Publ. Co.: Spring, 1948 - No. 2, Summer, 1948

	GD 2.0	VG 4.0	FN 6.0	VF 8.0	VF/NM 9.0	NM- 9.2
1	9	18	27	47	61	75
2	6	12	18	31	38	45

MOEBIUS (Graphic novel)
Marvel Comics (Epic Comics): Oct, 1987 - No. 6, 1988; No. 7, 1990; No. 8, 1991 ($9.95, 8x11", mature)

	GD 2.0	VG 4.0	FN 6.0	VF 8.0	VF/NM 9.0	NM- 9.2
1,2,4-6,8: (#2, 2nd printing, $9.95)	3	6	9	16	22	28
3,7,0: 3-(1st & 2nd printings, $12.95). 0 (1990, $12.95)	3	6	9	17	25	32
Moebius I-Signed & #'d hard-c ($45.95, Graphitti Designs, 1,500 copies printed)-r/#1-3	5	10	15	32	51	70

MOEBIUS COMICS
Caliber: May, 1996 - No. 6 ($2.95, B&W)

	GD 2.0	VG 4.0	FN 6.0	VF 8.0	VF/NM 9.0	NM- 9.2
1-6: Moebius-c/a. 1-William Stout-a						4.00

MOEBIUS: THE MAN FROM CIGURI
Dark Horse Comics: 1996 ($7.95, digest-size)

	GD 2.0	VG 4.0	FN 6.0	VF 8.0	VF/NM 9.0	NM- 9.2
nn-Moebius-c/a	1	2	3	5	7	9

MOLLY MANTON'S ROMANCES (Romantic Affairs #3)
Marvel Comics (SePI): Sept, 1949 - No. 2, Dec, 1949 (52 pgs.)

	GD 2.0	VG 4.0	FN 6.0	VF 8.0	VF/NM 9.0	NM- 9.2
1-Photo-c (becomes Blaze the Wonder Collie #2 (10/49) on? & Molly Manton's Romances #2	18	36	54	105	165	225
2-Titled "Romances of..."; photo-c	14	28	42	76	108	140

MOLLY O'DAY (Super Sleuth)
Avon Periodicals: February, 1945 (1st Avon comic)

	GD 2.0	VG 4.0	FN 6.0	VF 8.0	VF/NM 9.0	NM- 9.2
1-Molly O'Day, The Enchanted Dagger by Tuska (r/Yankee #1), Capt'n Courage, Corporal Grant app.	57	114	171	362	619	875

MOMENT OF SILENCE
Marvel Comics: Feb, 2002 ($3.50, one-shot)

	GD 2.0	VG 4.0	FN 6.0	VF 8.0	VF/NM 9.0	NM- 9.2
1-Tributes to the heroes and victims of Sept. 11; s/a by various						3.50

MONARCHY, THE (Also see The Authority and StormWatch)
DC Comics (WildStorm): Apr, 2001 - No. 12, May, 2002 ($2.50)

	GD 2.0	VG 4.0	FN 6.0	VF 8.0	VF/NM 9.0	NM- 9.2
1-12: 1-McCrea & Leach-a/Young-s						2.50
Bullets Over Babylon TPB (2001, $12.95) r/#1-4, Authority #21						13.00

MONKEES, THE (TV)(Also see Circus Boy, Groovy, Not Brand Echh #3, Teen-Age Talk, Teen Beam & Teen Beat)
Dell Publishing Co.: March, 1967 - No. 17, Oct, 1969

	GD 2.0	VG 4.0	FN 6.0	VF 8.0	VF/NM 9.0	NM- 9.2
1-Photo-c	10	20	30	68	119	170
2-17: All photo-c. 17-Reprints #1	6	12	18	41	66	90

MONKEY AND THE BEAR, THE
Atlas Comics (ZPC): Sept, 1953 - No. 3, Jan, 1954

	GD 2.0	VG 4.0	FN 6.0	VF 8.0	VF/NM 9.0	NM- 9.2
1-Howie Post-c/a in all; funny animal	10	20	30	54	72	90
2,3	8	16	24	40	50	60

MONKEYMAN AND O'BRIEN (Also see Dark Horse Presents #80, 100-5, Gen^{13}/..., Hellboy: Seed of Destruction, & San Diego Comic Con #2)
Dark Horse Comics (Legend): Jul, 1996 - No. 3, Sept, 1996 ($2.95, lim. series)

	GD 2.0	VG 4.0	FN 6.0	VF 8.0	VF/NM 9.0	NM- 9.2
1-3: New stories; Art Adams-c/a/scripts						3.50
nn-(2/96, $2.95)-r/back-up stories from Hellboy: Seed of Destruction; Adams-c/a/scripts						3.50

MONKEYSHINES COMICS
Ace Periodicals/Publishers Specialists/Current Books/Unity Publ.: Summer, 1944 - No. 27, July, 1949

	GD 2.0	VG 4.0	FN 6.0	VF 8.0	VF/NM 9.0	NM- 9.2
1-Funny animal	14	28	42	82	121	160
2-(Aut/44)	9	18	27	50	65	80
3-10: 3-(Win/44)	8	16	24	44	57	70
11-18,20-27: 23,24-Fago-c/a	8	16	24	40	50	60
19-Frazetta-a	9	18	27	50	65	80

MONKEY'S UNCLE, THE (See Merlin Jones As... under Movie Comics)

MONOLITH, THE
DC Comics: Apr, 2004 - No. 12, Mar, 2005 ($3.50/$2.95)

	GD 2.0	VG 4.0	FN 6.0	VF 8.0	VF/NM 9.0	NM- 9.2
1-($3.50) Palmiotti & Gray-s/Winslade-a						3.50
2-12-($2.95): 6-8-Batman app.; Coker-a						3.00

MONROES, THE (TV)
Dell Publishing Co.: Apr, 1967

	GD 2.0	VG 4.0	FN 6.0	VF 8.0	VF/NM 9.0	NM- 9.2
1-Photo-c	3	6	9	18	27	35

MONSTER
Fiction House Magazines: 1953 - No. 2, 1953

	GD 2.0	VG 4.0	FN 6.0	VF 8.0	VF/NM 9.0	NM- 9.2
1-Dr. Drew by Grandenetti; reprint from Rangers Comics #48; Whitman-c	52	104	156	325	550	775
2-Whitman-c	39	78	117	240	395	550

MONSTER CRIME COMICS (Also see Crime Must Stop)
Hillman Periodicals: Oct, 1952 (15¢, 52 pgs.)

	GD 2.0	VG 4.0	FN 6.0	VF 8.0	VF/NM 9.0	NM- 9.2
1 (Scarce)	161	322	483	1030	1765	2500

MONSTER HOUSE (Companion to the 2006 movie)
IDW Publishing: June, 2006 ($7.99, one-shot)

	GD 2.0	VG 4.0	FN 6.0	VF 8.0	VF/NM 9.0	NM- 9.2
nn-Two stories about Bones and Skull by Joshua Dysart and Simeon Wilkins						8.00

MONSTER HOWLS (Magazine)
Humor-Vision: December, 1966 (Satire) (35¢, 68 pgs.)

	GD 2.0	VG 4.0	FN 6.0	VF 8.0	VF/NM 9.0	NM- 9.2
1	6	12	18	39	62	85

MONSTER HUNTERS
Charlton Comics: Aug, 1975 - No. 9, Jan, 1977; No. 10, Oct, 1977 - No. 18, Feb, 1979

	GD 2.0	VG 4.0	FN 6.0	VF 8.0	VF/NM 9.0	NM- 9.2
1-Howard-a; Newton-c; 1st Countess Von Bludd and Colonel Whiteshroud	3	6	9	18	27	35
2-Sutton-c/a; Ditko-a	3	6	9	14	19	24
3,4,5,7: 4-Sutton-c/a	2	4	6	9	12	15
6,8,10: 6,8,10-Ditko-a	2	4	6	10	14	18
9,11,12	1	3	4	6	8	10
13,15,18-Ditko-c/a. 18-Sutton-a	2	4	6	10	14	18
14-Special all-Ditko issue	3	6	9	17	25	32
16,17-Sutton-a	2	3	4	6	8	10
1,2 (Modern Comics reprints, 1977)						4.00

NOTE: ***Ditko** a-2, 6, 8, 10, 13-15r, 18r; c-13-15, 18. **Howard** a-1, 3, 17; r-13. **Morisi** a-1. **Staton** a-1, 13. **Sutton** a-2, 4; c-2, 4; r-16-18. **Zeck** a-4-9. Reprints in #12-18.*

MONSTER MADNESS (Magazine)
Marvel Comics: 1972 - No. 3, 1973 (60¢, B&W)

	GD 2.0	VG 4.0	FN 6.0	VF 8.0	VF/NM 9.0	NM- 9.2
1-3: Stories by "Sinister" Stan Lee	4	8	12	26	41	55

MONSTER MAN
Image Comics (Action Planet): Sept, 1997 ($2.95, B&W)

	GD 2.0	VG 4.0	FN 6.0	VF 8.0	VF/NM 9.0	NM- 9.2
1-Mike Manley-c/s/a						3.00

Monsters, Inc.: Laugh Factory #1 © DIS/Pixar

Monte Hale Western #82 © FAW

Moon Knight V3 #1 © MAR

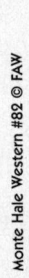

GD 2.0 | VG 4.0 | FN 6.0 | VF 8.0 | VF/NM 9.0 | NM- 9.2

MONSTER MASTERWORKS
Marvel Comics: 1989 ($12.95, TPB)

nn-Reprints 1960's monster stories; art by Kirby, Ditko, Ayers, Everett 20.00

MONSTER MATINEE
Chaos! Comics: Oct, 1997 - No. 3, Oct, 1997 ($2.50, limited series)

1-3: pin-ups 2.50

MONSTER MENACE
Marvel Comics: Dec, 1993 - No. 4, Mar, 1994 ($1.25, limited series)

1-4: Pre-code Atlas horror reprints. 6.00
NOTE: ***Ditko**-r & **Kirby**-r in all.*

MONSTER OF FRANKENSTEIN (See Frankenstein and Essential Monster of Frankenstein)

MONSTER PILE-UP
Image Comics: Aug, 2008 ($1.99)

1-New short stories of Astounding Wolf-Man, Firebreather, Perhapanauts, Proof 2.25

MONSTERS ATTACK (Magazine)
Globe Communications Corpse: Sept, 1989 - No. 5, Dec, 1990 (B&W)

1-5-Ditko, Morrow, J. Severin-a. 5-Toth, Morrow-a 1 2 3 4 5 7

MONSTERS, INC. (Based on the Disney/Pixar movie)
BOOM! Studios: Jun, 2009 - No. 4, Nov, 2009 ($2.99, limited series)

...: Laugh Factory 1-4: 1,3-Three covers. 2,4-Two covers 3.00

MONSTERS ON THE PROWL (Chamber of Darkness #1-8)
Marvel Comics Group (No. 13,14: 52 pgs.): No. 9, 2/71 - No. 27, 11/73; No. 28, 6/74 - No. 30, 10/74

9-Barry Smith inks 4 8 12 24 37 50
10-12,15: 12-Last 15¢ issue 3 6 9 16 22 28
13,14-(52 pgs.) 3 6 9 18 27 35
16-(4/72)-King Kull 4th app.; Severin-c 3 6 9 18 27 35
17-30 2 4 6 13 18 22
NOTE: ***Ditko** r-9, 14, 16. **Kirby** r-10-17, 21, 23, 25, 27, 28, 30; c-9, 25. **Kirby/Ditko** r-14, 17-20, 22, 24, 26, 29. **Marie/John Severin** a-16(Kull). 9-13, 15 contain one new story. Woodish art by **Reese**-11. King Kull created by Robert E. Howard.*

MONSTERS TO LAUGH WITH (Magazine) (Becomes Monsters Unlimited #4)
Marvel Comics Group: 1964 - No. 3, 1965 (B&W)

1-Humor by Stan Lee 7 14 21 49 80 110
2,3 5 10 15 30 48 65

MONSTERS UNLEASHED (Magazine)
Marvel Comics Group: July, 1973 - No. 11, Apr, 1975; Summer, 1975 (B&W)

1-Soloman Kane sty; Werewolf app. 5 10 15 30 48 65
2-4: 2-The Frankenstein Monster begins, ends #10. 3-Neal Adams-c/a; The Man-Thing begins (origin-r); Son of Satan preview. 4-Werewolf app. 4 8 12 24 37 50
5-7: Werewolf in all. 5-Man-Thing. 7-Williamson-a(r) 3 6 9 18 27 35
8-11: 8-Man-Thing; N. Adams-r. 9-Man-Thing; Wendigo app. 10-Origin Tigra
3 6 9 19 29 38
Annual 1 (Summer,1975, 92 pgs.)-Kane-a 3 6 9 18 27 35
NOTE: ***Boris** c-2, 6. **Brunner** a-2; c-11. **J. Buscema** a-2p, 4p, 5p. **Colan** a-1, 4r. **Davis** a-3r. **Everett** a-2r. **G. Kane** a-3. **Krigstein** r-4. **Morrow** a-3; c-1. **Perez** a-8. **Ploog** a-6. **Reese** a-1, 2. **Tuska** a-3p. **Wildey** a-1r.*

MONSTERS UNLIMITED (Magazine) (Formerly Monsters To Laugh With)
Marvel Comics Group: No. 4, 1965 - No. 7, 1966 (B&W)

4-7 5 10 15 30 48 65

MONSTER WORLD
DC Comics (WildStorm): Jul, 2001 - No. 4, Oct, 2001 ($2.50, limited series)

1-4-Lobdell-s/Meglia-c/a 2.50

MONTANA KID, THE (See Kid Montana)

MONTE HALE WESTERN (Movie star; Formerly Mary Marvel #1-28; also see Fawcett Movie Comic, Motion Picture Comics, Picture News #8, Real Western Hero, Six-Gun Heroes, Western Hero & XMas Comics)
Fawcett Publ./Charlton No. 83 on: No. 29, Oct, 1948 - No. 88, Jan, 1956

29-(#1, 52 pgs.)-Photo-c begin, end #82; Monte Hale & his horse Pardner begin
32 64 96 190 305 420
30-(52 pgs.)-Big Bow and Little Arrow begin, end #34; Captain Tootsie by Beck
15 30 45 86 133 180
31-36,38-40-(52 pgs.): 34-Gabby Hayes begins, ends #80. 39-Captain Tootsie by Beck
14 28 42 78 112 145
37,41,45,49-(36 pgs.) 11 22 33 60 83 105
42-44,46-48,50-(52 pgs.): 47-Big Bow & Little Arrow app.
12 24 36 67 94 120
51,52,54-56,58,59-(52 pgs.) 10 20 30 58 79 100
53,57-(36 pgs.): 53-Slim Pickens app. 9 18 27 52 69 85
60-81: 36 pgs. #60-on. 80-Gabby Hayes ends 9 18 27 50 65 80
82-Last Fawcett issue (6/53) 10 20 30 58 79 100
83-1st Charlton issue (2/55); B&W photo back-c begin. Gabby Hayes returns, ends #86
11 22 33 64 90 115
84 (4/55) 9 18 27 52 69 85
85-86 9 18 27 50 65 80
87,88: 87-Wolverton-r, 1/2 pg. 88-Last issue 9 18 27 52 69 85
NOTE: ***Gil Kane** a-33?, 34? Rocky Lane -1 pg. (Carnation ad)-38, 40, 41, 43, 44, 46, 55.*

MONTY HALL OF THE U.S. MARINES (See With the Marines...)
Toby Press: Aug, 1951 - No. 11, Apr, 1953

1 12 24 36 69 97 125
2 8 16 24 42 54 65
3-5 8 16 24 40 50 60
6-11 7 14 21 37 46 55
NOTE: *Full page pin-ups (Pin-Up Pete) by **Jack Sparling** in #1-9.*

MOON, A GIRL...ROMANCE, A (Becomes Weird Fantasy #13 on; formerly Moon Girl #1-8)
E. C. Comics: No. 9, Sept-Oct, 1949 - No. 12, Mar-Apr, 1950

9-Moon Girl cameo 81 162 243 518 884 1250
10,11 66 132 198 419 722 1025
12-(Scarce) 81 162 243 518 884 1250
NOTE: ***Feldstein, Ingels** art in all. **Feldstein** c-9-12. **Wood/Harrison** a-10-12. Canadian reprints known; see Table of Contents.*

MOON GIRL AND THE PRINCE (#1) (Moon Girl #2-6; Moon Girl Fights Crime #7, 8; becomes A Moon, A Girl, Romance #9 on)(Also see Animal Fables #7, Int. Crime Patrol #6, Happy Houlihans & Tales From The Crypt #22)
E. C. Comics: Fall, 1947 - No. 8, Summer, 1949

1-Origin Moon Girl (see Happy Houlihans #1). Intro Santana, Queen of the Underworld
107 214 321 680 1165 1650
2-Moon Girl battles Futureman 61 122 183 390 670 950
3,4: 3-Santana, Queen of the Underworld returns. 4-Moon Girl vs. a vampire
54 108 162 343 577 810
5-E.C.'s 1st horror story, "Zombie Terror" 116 232 348 742 1271 1800
6-8 (Scarce): 7-Origin Star (Moongirl's sidekick) 61 122 183 390 670 950
NOTE: ***Craig** a-2, 5; c-1, 2. **Moldoff** a-1-8; c-3-8 (Shelly). **Wheelan's** Fat and Slat app. in #3, 4, 6. #2 & #3 are 52 pgs., #4 on, 36 pgs. Canadian reprints known; (see Table of Contents.)*

MOON KNIGHT (Also see The Hulk, Marc Spector..., Marvel Preview #21, Marvel Spotlight & Werewolf by Night #32)
Marvel Comics Group: Nov, 1980 - No. 38, Jul, 1984 (Mando paper #33 on)

1-Origin resumed in #4 5.00
2-15,25,35: 4-Intro Midnight Man. 25-Double size. 35-($1.00, 52 pgs.)-X-Men app.; F.F. cameo 3.00
16-24,26-28,30-34,36-38: 16-The Thing app. 2.50
29,30-Werewolf By Night app. 4.00
NOTE: ***Austin** c-27i, 31i. **Cowan** a-16; c-16, 17. **Kaluta** c-36-38; back c-35. **Miller** c-9, 12p, 13p, 15p, 27p. **Ploog** back c-35. **Sienkiewicz** a-1-15, 17-20, 22-26, 28-30, 33i, 36(4), 37; c-1-5, 7, 8, 10, 11, 14-16, 18-26, 28-30, 31p, 33, 34.*

MOON KNIGHT
Marvel Comics Group: June, 1985 - V2#6, Dec, 1985

V2#1-6: 1-Double size; new costume. 6-Sienkiewicz painted-c 2.50

MOON KNIGHT
Marvel Comics: Jan, 1998 - No. 4, Apr, 1998 ($2.50, limited series)

1-4-Moench-s/Edwards-c/a 2.50

MOON KNIGHT (Volume 3)
Marvel Comics: Jan, 1999 - No. 4, Feb, 1999 ($2.99, limited series)

1-4-Moench-s/Texeira-a(p) 3.00

MOON KNIGHT (Fourth series) (Leads into Vengeance of the Moon Knight)
Marvel Comics: June, 2006 - No. 30, Jul, 2009 ($2.99, limited series)

1-Finch-a/c; Huston-s 4.00
1-B&W sketch variant-c 6.00
2-19,21-26: 7-Spider-Man app. 9,10-Punisher app. 13-Suydam-c begin. 23-25-Bullseye 3.00
20-($3.99) Deodato-a; back-up r/1st app. in Werewolf By Night #32,33 4.00
Annual 1 (1/08, $3.99) Swierczynski-s/Palo-a 4.00
... Saga (2009, free) synopsis of origin and major storylines 2.00
...: Silent Knight 1 (1/09, $3.99) Milligan-s/Laurence Campbell-a/Crain-c 4.00
... Vol. 1: The Bottom HC (2006, $19.99) r/#1-6; Huston afterword; 2 covers 20.00
... Vol. 1: The Bottom SC (2007, $14.99) r/#1-6; Huston afterword 15.00
... Vol. 2: Midnight Sun HC (2008, $19.99) r/#7-13 & Annual #1 20.00
... Vol. 2: Midnight Sun SC (2008, $14.99) r/#7-13 & Annual #1 15.00

MOON KNIGHT: DIVIDED WE FALL

Moonshadow #12 © DeMatteis & Muth

Morbius: The Living Vampire #25 © MAR

More Fun Comics #80 © DC

	GD 2.0	VG 4.0	FN 6.0	VF 8.0	VF/NM 9.0	NM- 9.2

Marvel Comics: 1992 ($4.95, 52 pgs.)
nn-Denys Cowan-c/a(p) 5.00

MOON KNIGHT SPECIAL
Marvel Comics: Oct, 1992 ($2.50, 52 pgs.)
1-Shang Chi, Master of Kung Fu-c/story 2.50

MOON KNIGHT SPECIAL EDITION
Marvel Comics Group: Nov, 1983 - No. 3, Jan, 1984 ($2.00, limited series, Baxter paper)
1-3: Reprints from Hulk mag. by Sienkiewicz 3.00

MOON MULLINS (See Popular Comics, Super Book #3 & Super Comics)
Dell Publishing Co.: 1941 - 1945

	GD	VG	FN	VF	VF/NM	NM-
Four Color 14(1941)	45	90	135	284	480	675
Large Feature Comic 29(1941)	36	72	108	211	343	475
Four Color 31(1943)	17	34	51	119	230	340
Four Color 81(1945)	10	20	30	73	129	185

MOON MULLINS
Michel Publ. (American Comics Group)#1-6/St. John #7,8: Dec-Jan, 1947-48 - No. 8, 1949 (52 pgs)

	GD	VG	FN	VF	VF/NM	NM-
1-Alternating Sunday & daily strip-r	22	44	66	128	209	290
2	14	28	42	78	112	145
3-8: 7,8-St. John Publ. 8-...Featuring Kayo on-c	13	26	39	74	105	135

NOTE: *Milt Gross a-2-6, 8. Frank Willard r-all.*

MOON PILOT
Dell Publishing Co.: No. 1313, Mar-May, 1962

	GD	VG	FN	VF	VF/NM	NM-
Four Color 1313-Movie, photo-c	7	14	21	47	76	105

MOONSHADOW (Also see Farewell, Moonshadow)
Marvel Comics (Epic Comics): 5/85 - #12, 2/87 ($1.50/$1.75, mature)
(1st fully painted comic book)
1-Origin; J. M. DeMatteis scripts & Jon J. Muth painted-c/a. 6.00
2-12: 11-Origin 4.00
Trade paperback (1987?)-r/#1-12 14.00
Signed & numbered hard-c ($39.95, 1,200 copies)-r/#1-12

	GD	VG	FN	VF	VF/NM	NM-
	4	8	12	28	44	60

MOONSHADOW
DC Comics (Vertigo): Oct, 1994 - No. 12, Aug, 1995 ($2.25/$2.95)
1-11: Reprints Epic series. 2.50
12 ($2.95)-w/expanded ending 3.00
The Complete Moonshadow TPB ('98, $39.95) r/#1-12 and Farewell Moonshadow; new Muth painted-c 40.00

MOON-SPINNERS, THE (See Movie Comics)

MOONSTONE MONSTERS
Moonstone: 2003 - 2005 ($2.95, B&W)
...: Demons ($2.95) - Short stories by various; Frenz-c 3.00
...: Ghosts ($2.95) - Short stories by various; Frenz-c 3.00
...: Sea Creatures ($2.95) - Short stories by various; Frenz-c 3.00
...: Witches ($2.95) - Short stories by various; Frenz-c 3.00
...: Zombies ($2.95) - Short stories by various; Frenz-c 3.00
Volume 1 (2004, $16.95, TPB) r/short stories from series; Wolak-c 17.00

MOONSTONE NOIR
Moonstone: 2003 - Present ($2.95/$4.95/$5.50, B&W)
...: Bulldog Drummond (2004, $4.95) - Messner-Loebs-s/Barkley-a 5.00
...: Johnny Dollar ($4.95) - Gallaher-s/Theriault-a 5.00
...: Mr. Keen, Tracer of Lost Persons 1,2 ($2.95, limited series) - Ferguson-a 3.00
...: Mysterious Traveler (2003, $5.50) - Trevor Von Eeden-a/Joe Gentile-s 5.50
...: Mysterious Traveler Returns (2004, $4.95) - Trevor Von Eeden-a/Joe Gentile-s 5.00
...: The Lone Wolf ($4.95) - Jolley-s/Croall-a 5.00

MOPSY (See Pageant of Comics & TV Teens)
St. John Publ. Co.: Feb, 1948 - No. 19, Sept, 1953

	GD	VG	FN	VF	VF/NM	NM-
1-Part-r; reprints "Some Punkins" by Neher	18	36	54	103	162	220
2	11	22	33	62	86	110
3-10(1953): 8-Lingerie panels	10	20	30	56	76	95
11-19: 19-Lingerie-c	9	18	27	52	69	85

NOTE: *#1-7, 13, 18, 19 have paper dolls.*

MORBIUS REVISITED
Marvel Comic: Aug, 1993 - No. 5, Dec, 1993 ($1.95, mini-series)
1-5-Reprints Fear #27-31 2.50

MORBIUS: THE LIVING VAMPIRE (Also see Amazing Spider-Man #101,102, Fear #20, Marvel Team-Up #3, 4, Midnight Sons Unl. & Vampire Tales)
Marvel Comics (Midnight Sons imprint #16 on): Sep, 1992 - No. 32, Apr, 1995 ($1.75/$1.95)
1-($2.75, 52 pgs.)-Polybagged w/poster; Ghost Rider & Johnny Blaze x-over (part 3 of Rise of the Midnight Sons) 3.00
2-11,13-24,26-32: 3,4-Vs. Spider-Man-c/s.15-Ghost Rider app. 16-Spot varnish-c. 16,17-Siege of Darkness,parts 5 &13. 18-Deathlok app. 21-Bound-in Spider-Man trading card sheet; Spider-Man app. 2.50
12-($2.25)-Outer-c is a Darkhold envelope made of black parchment w/gold ink; Midnight Massacre x-over 2.50
25-($2.50, 52 pgs.)-Gold foil logo 2.50

MORE FUN COMICS (Formerly New Fun Comics #1-6)
National Periodical Publications: No. 7, Jan, 1936 - No. 127, Nov-Dec, 1947 (No. 7,9-11: paper-c)

	GD	VG	FN	VF	VF/NM	NM-
7(1/36)-Oversized, paper-c; 1 pg. Kelly-a	800	1600	2400	6400	-	-
8(2/36)-Oversized (10x12"), paper-c; 1 pg. Kelly-a; Sullivan-c	800	1600	2400	6400	-	-
9(3-4/36)(Very rare, 1st standard-sized comic book with original material)-Last multiple panel-c	963	1926	2889	7700	-	-
10,11(7/36): 10-Last Henri Duval by Siegel & Shuster. 11-1st "Calling All Cars" by Siegel & Shuster; new classic logo begins	563	1126	1689	4500	-	-
12(8/36)-Slick-c begin	444	888	1332	3550	-	-
V2#1(9/36, #13) 1 pg. Fred Astaire photo/bio	406	812	1218	3250	-	-
2(10/36, #14)-Dr. Occult in costume (1st in color)(Superman proto-type; 1st DC appearance) continues from The Comics Magazine, ends #17	1875	3750	5625	15,000	-	-
V2#3(11/36, #15), 17(V2#5)	763	1526	2289	6100	-	-
16(V2#4)-Cover numbering begins; ties with New Comics #11 as 1st DC Christmas-c; last Superman tryout issue	788	1576	2364	6300	-	-
18-20(V2#8, 5/37)	325	650	975	2600	-	-
21(V2#9)-24(V2#12, 9/37)	276	552	828	1518	2259	3000
25(V3#1, 10/37)-27(V3#3, 12/37): 27-Xmas-c	276	552	828	1518	2259	3000
28-30: 30-1st non-funny cover	250	500	750	1375	2038	2700
31-Has ad for Action Comics #1	265	530	795	1458	2154	2850
32-35: 32-Last Dr. Occult	250	500	750	1375	2038	2700
36-40: 36-(10/38)-The Masked Ranger & sidekick Pedro begins; Ginger Snap by Bob Kane (2 pgs.; 1st-a?). 39-Xmas-c	250	500	750	1375	2038	2700
41-50: 41-Last Masked Ranger	212	424	636	1166	1783	2400
51-The Spectre app. (in costume) in one panel ad at end of Buccaneer story	741	1482	2223	4076	5938	7800
52-(2/40)-Origin/1st app. The Spectre (in costume splash panel only), part 1 by Bernard Baily (parts 1 & 2 written by Jerry Siegel; Spectre's costume changes color from purple & blue to green & grey; last Wing Brady; Spectre-c	7000	14,000	21,000	52,500	93,750	135,000
53-Origin The Spectre (in costume at end of story), part 2; Capt. Desmo begins; Spectre-c	3150	6300	9450	22,365	46,183	70,000
54-The Spectre in costume; last King Carter; classic-Spectre-c	1650	3300	4950	12,375	22,188	32,000
55-(Scarce, 5/40)-Dr. Fate begins (1st app.); last Bulldog Martin; Spectre-c	1575	3150	4725	11,815	21,408	31,000
56-1st Dr. Fate-c (classic), origin continues. Congo Bill begins (6/40), 1st app.;	811	1622	2433	5920	10,460	15,000
57-60-All Spectre-c	423	846	1269	3046	5323	7600
61,65: 61-Classic Dr. Fate-c. 65-Classic Spectre-c	400	800	1200	2800	4900	7000
62-64,66: 63-Last Lt. Bob Neal. 64-Lance Larkin begins; all Spectre-c	320	640	960	2240	3920	5600
67-(5/41)-Origin (1st) Dr. Fate; last Congo Bill & Biff Bronson (Congo Bill continues in Action Comics #37, 6/41)-Spectre-c	784	1568	2352	5723	10,112	14,500
68-70: 68-Clip Carson begins. 70-Last Lance Larkin; all Dr. Fate-c	284	568	852	1818	3109	4400
71-Origin & 1st app. Johnny Quick by Mort Weisinger (9/41); classic sci/fi Dr. Fate-c	524	1048	1572	3825	6763	9700
72-Dr. Fate's new helmet; last Sgt. Carey, Sgt. O'Malley & Captain Desmo; German submarine-c (Nazi war-c)	277	554	831	1759	3030	4300
73-Origin & 1st app. Aquaman (11/41) by Paul Norris; intro. Green Arrow & Speedy; Dr. Fate-c	1575	3150	4725	11,815	20,908	30,000
74-2nd Aquaman; 1st Percival Popp, Supercop; Dr. Fate-c	297	594	891	1990	3445	4900
75,76: 75-New origin Spectre; Nazi spy ring cover w/Hitler's photo. 76-Last Dr. Fate-c; Johnny Quick (by Meskin #76-97) begins, ends #107; last Clip Carson	255	310	765	1619	2785	3950
77-80: 77-Green Arrow-c begin	194	388	582	1242	2121	3000
81-83,85,88,90: 81-Last large logo. 82-1st small logo.	132	264	396	838	1444	2050

More Than Mortal: Otherworlds #4 © Image

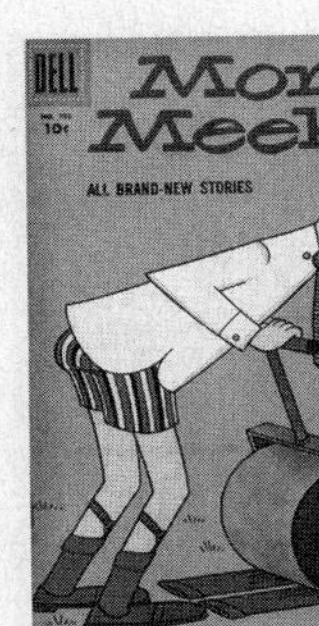
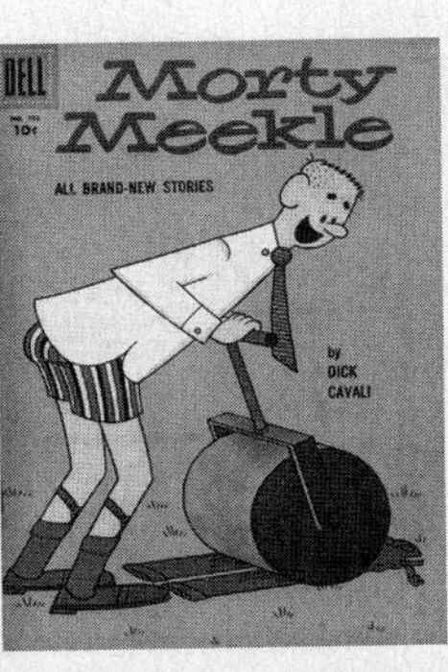

Morty Meekle Four Color #793 © DELL

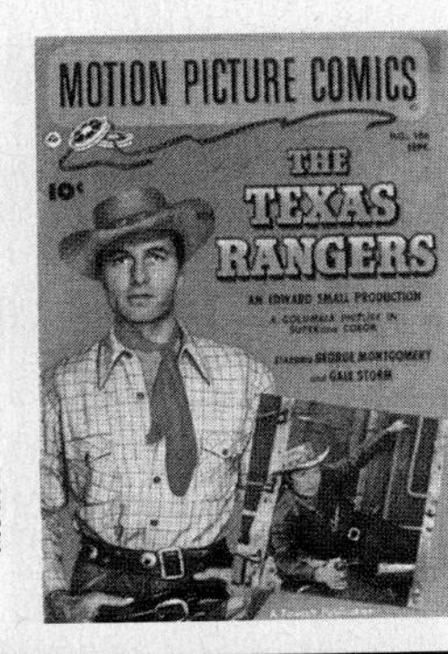

Motion Picture Comics #106 © FAW

GD VG FN VF VF/NM NM-
2.0 4.0 6.0 8.0 9.0 9.2

84-Green Arrow Japanese war-c 135 270 405 864 1482 2100
86,87-Johnny Quick-c. 87-Last Radio Squad 132 264 396 838 1444 2050
89-Origin Green Arrow & Speedy Team-up 139 278 417 883 1517 2150
91-97,99: 91-1st bi-monthly issue. 93-Dover & Clover begin (1st app., 9-10/43).
97-Kubert-a 87 174 261 553 952 1350
98-Last Dr. Fate (scarce) 107 214 321 680 1165 1650
100 (11-12/44)-Johnny Quick-c 118 236 354 749 1287 1825
101-Origin & 1st app. Superboy (1-2/45)(not by Siegel & Shuster); last Spectre issue; Green Arrow-c 892 1784 2676 6512 11,506 16,500
102-2nd Superboy app; 1st Dover & Clover-c 140 280 420 889 1532 2175
103-3rd Superboy app; last Green Arrow-c 100 200 300 635 1093 1550
104-1st Superboy-c w/Dover & Clover 87 174 261 553 952 1350
105,106-Superboy-c 80 160 240 508 874 1240
107-Last Johnny Quick & Superboy 80 160 240 508 874 1240
108-120: 108-Genius Jones begins; 1st c-app. (3-4/46; cont'd from Adventure Comics #102) 25 50 75 147 241 335
121-124,126: 121-123,126-Post funny animal (Jimminy & the Magic Book)-c 23 46 69 136 223 310
125-Superman c-app.w/Jimminy 80 160 240 508 874 1240
127-(Scarce)-Post-c/a 38 76 114 228 369 510

NOTE: *All issues are scarce to rare. Cover features: The Spectre-#52-55, 57-60, 62-67. Dr. Fate-#56, 61, 68-76. The Green Arrow & Speedy-#77-85, 88-97, 99, 101 (w/Dover & Clover-#98, 103). Johnny Quick-#86, 87, 100. Dover & Clover-#102, (104, 106 w/Superboy), 107, 108(w/Genius Jones), 110, 112, 114, 117, 119. Genius Jones-#109, 111, 113, 115, 116, 118, 120.* ***Baily*** *a-45, 52-on; c-52-55, 57-60, 62-67.* ***Al Capp*** *a-45(signed Koppy).* ***Ellsworth*** *c-7.* ***Craig Flessel*** *c-30, 31, 35-48(most).* ***Guardineer*** *c-47, 49, 50.* ***Kiefer*** *a-20.* ***Meskin*** *c-86, 87, 100?* ***Moldoff*** *c-51.* ***George Papp*** *c-77-85.* ***Post*** *c-121-127.* ***Vincent Sullivan*** *c-8-28, 32-34.*

MORE FUND COMICS (Benefit book for the Comic Book Legal Defense Fund)
(Also see Even More Fund Comics)
Sky Dog Press: Sept, 2003 ($10.00, B&W, trade paperback)
nn-Anthology of short stories and pin-ups by various; Hulk-c by Pérez 10.00

MORE SEYMOUR (See Seymour My Son)
Archie Publications: Oct, 1963
1-DeCarlo-a? 3 6 9 20 30 40

MORE THAN MORTAL (Also see Lady Pendragon/...)
Liar Comics: June, 1997 - No. 4, Apr, 1998 ($2.95, limited series)
Image Comics: No. 5, Dec, 1999 - Present ($2.95)
1-Blue forest background-c, 1-Variant-c 4.00
1-White-c 6.00
1-2nd printing; purple sky cover 3.00
2-4: 3-Silvestri-c, 4-Two-c, one by Randy Queen 3.00
5,6: 5-1st Image Comics issue 3.00

MORE THAN MORTAL: OTHERWORLDS
Image Comics: July, 1999 - No. 4, Dec, 1999 ($2.95, limited series)
1-4-Firchow-a. 1-Two covers 3.00

MORE THAN MORTAL SAGAS
Liar Comics: Jun, 1998 - No. 3, Dec, 1998 ($2.95, limited series)
1,2-Painted art by Romano. 2-Two-c, one by Firchow 3.00
1-Variant-c by Linsner 5.00

MORE THAN MORTAL TRUTHS AND LEGENDS
Liar Comics: Aug, 1998 - No. 6, Apr, 1999 ($2.95)
1-6-Firchow-a(p) 3.00
1-Variant-c by Dan Norton 4.50

MORE TRASH FROM MAD (Annual)
E. C. Comics: 1958 - No. 12, 1969
(Note: Bonus missing = half price)
nn(1958)-8 pgs. color Mad reprint from #20 19 38 57 133 259 385
2(1959)-Market Product Labels 13 26 39 93 172 250
3(1960)-Text book covers 12 24 36 85 155 225
4(1961)-Sing Along with Mad booklet 12 24 36 85 155 225
5(1962)-Window Stickers; r/from Mad #39 9 18 27 63 107 150
6(1963)-TV Guise booklet 9 18 27 63 107 150
7(1964)-Alfred E. Neuman commemorative stamps 8 16 24 52 86 120
8(1965)-Life size poster-Alfred E. Neuman 6 12 18 41 66 90
9-12: 9,10(1966-67)-Mischief Sticker. 11(1968)-Campaign poster & bumper sticker. 12(1969)-Pocket medals 6 12 18 41 66 90

NOTE: ***Kelly Freas*** *c-1, 2, 4.* ***Mingo*** *c-3, 5-9, 12.*

MORGAN THE PIRATE (Movie)
Dell Publishing Co.: No. 1227, Sept-Nov, 1961
Four Color 1227-Photo-c 7 14 21 50 83 115

MORLOCKS
Marvel Comics: June, 2002 - No. 4, Sept, 2002 ($2.50, limited series)
1-4-Johns-s/Martinbrough-c/a 2.50

MORLOCK 2001
Atlas/Seaboard Publ.: Feb, 1975 - No. 3, July, 1975
1,2: 1-(Super-hero)-Origin & 1st app.; Milgrom-c 2 4 6 8 10 12
3-Ditko/Wrightson-a; origin The Midnight Man & The Mystery Men 2 4 6 11 16 20

MORNINGSTAR SPECIAL
Comico: Apr, 1990 ($2.50)
1-From the Elementals; Willingham-c/a/scripts 3.00

MORTAL KOMBAT
Malibu Comics: July, 1994 - No. 6, Dec, 1994 ($2.95)
1-6: 1-Two diff. covers exist 3.00
1-Limited edition gold foil embossed-c 4.00
0 (12/94), Special Edition 1 (11/94) 3.00
Tournament Edition I12/94, $3.95), II('95)($3.95) 4.00
...: **BARAKA** ,June, 1995 ($2.95, one-shot) #1; ...**BATTLEWAVE** ,2/95 - No. 6, 7/95 , #1-6; ...**GORO, PRINCE OF PAIN** ,9/94 - No. 3, 11/94, #1-3; ...**KITANA AND MILEENA** ,8/95 , ...**KUNG LAO** ,7/95 , #1; ... **RAYDON & KANO** ,3/95 - No. 3, 5/95, #1-3: ...(all $2.95-c) 3.00
...: **U.S. SPECIAL FORCES** ,1/95 - No. 2, ($3.50), #1,2 3.50

MORTIE (Mazie's Friend; also see Flat-Top)
Magazine Publishers: Dec, 1952 - No. 4, June, 1953?
1 9 18 27 50 65 80
2-4 6 12 18 28 34 40

MORTIGAN GOTH: IMMORTALIS (See Marvel Frontier Comics Unlimited)
Marvel Comics: Sept, 1993 - No. 4, Mar, 1994 ($1.95, mini-series)
1-($2.95)-Foil-c 3.00
2-4 2.50

MORT THE DEAD TEENAGER
Marvel Comics: Nov, 1993 - No. 4, Mar, 1994 ($1.75, mini-series)
1-4 3.00

MORTY MEEKLE
Dell Publishing Co.: No. 793, May, 1957
Four Color 793 4 8 12 24 37 50

MOSES & THE TEN COMMANDMENTS (See Dell Giants)

MOSTLY WANTED
DC Comics (WildStorm): Jul, 2000 - No. 4, Nov, 2000 ($2.50, limited series)
1-4-Lobdell-s/Flores-a 2.50

MOTH, THE (Also see Promotional Comics section for Free Comic Book Day edition)
Dark Horse Comics: Apr, 2004 - No. 4 ($2.99)
1-4-Steve Rude-c/a; Gary Martin-s 3.00
... Special (3/04, $4.95) 5.00
TPB (5/05, $12.95) r/#1-4 and Special; gallery of extras 13.00

MOTHER GOOSE AND NURSERY RHYME COMICS (See Christmas With Mother Goose)
Dell Publishing Co.: No. 41, 1944 - No. 862, Nov, 1957
Four Color 41-Walt Kelly-c/a 22 44 66 157 304 450
Four Color 59, 68-Kelly c/a 18 36 54 126 246 365
Four Color 862-The Truth About..., Movie (Disney) 7 14 21 49 80 110

MOTHER TERESA OF CALCUTTA
Marvel Comics Group: 1984
1-(52 pgs.) No ads 5.00

MOTION PICTURE COMICS (See Fawcett Movie Comics)
Fawcett Publications: No. 101, 1950 - No. 114, Jan, 1953 (All-photo-c)
101- "Vanishing Westerner"; Monte Hale (1950) 20 40 60 115 183 250
102- "Code of the Silver Sage"; Rocky Lane (1/51) 17 34 51 100 158 215
103- "Covered Wagon Raid"; Rocky Lane (3/51) 17 34 51 100 158 215
104- "Vigilante Hideout"; Rocky Lane (5/51)-Book length Powell-a 17 34 51 100 158 215
105- "Red Badge of Courage"; Audie Murphy; Bob Powell-a (7/51) 22 44 66 131 211 290
106- "The Texas Rangers"; George Montgomery (9/51) 17 34 51 100 158 215
107- "Frisco Tornado"; Rocky Lane (11/51) 15 30 45 94 147 200
108- "Mask of the Avenger"; John Derek 14 28 42 82 121 160

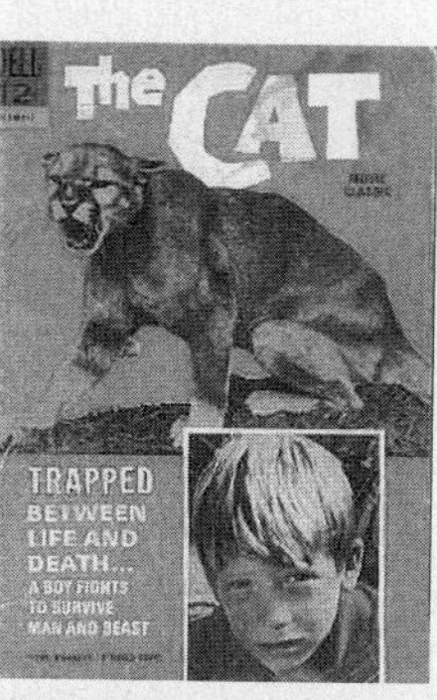

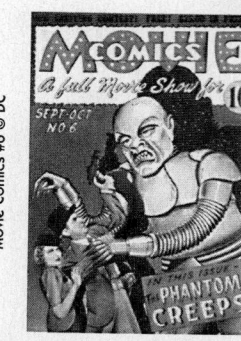

Movie Classics - The Cat © DELL

Movie Classics - Sons of Katie Elder © DELL

Movie Comics #6 © DC

GD 2.0 | VG 4.0 | FN 6.0 | VF 8.0 | VF/NM 9.0 | NM- 9.2

109- "Rough Rider of Durango"; Rocky Lane 15 30 45 94 147 200
110- "When Worlds Collide"; George Evans-a (5/52); Williamson & Evans drew themselves in story; (also see Famous Funnies No. 72-88) 90 180 270 567 959 1350
111- "The Vanishing Outpost"; Lash LaRue 20 40 60 115 183 250
112- "Brave Warrior"; Jon Hall & Jay Silverheels 14 28 42 80 115 150
113- "Walk East on Beacon"; George Murphy; Schaffenberger-a 11 22 33 62 86 110
114- "Cripple Creek"; George Montgomery (1/53) 12 24 36 67 94 120

MOTION PICTURE FUNNIES WEEKLY (See Promotional Comics section)

MOTORHEAD (See Comic's Greatest World)
Dark Horse Comics: Aug, 1995 - No. 6, Jan, 1996 ($2.50)
1-6: Bisley-c on all. 1-Predator app. 2.50
Special 1 (3/94, $3.95, 52pgs.)-Jae Lee-c; Barb Wire, The Machine & Wolf Gang app. 4.00

MOTORMOUTH (... & Killpower #7? on)
Marvel Comics UK: June, 1992 - No. 12, May, 1993 ($1.75)
1-13: 1,2-Nick Fury app. 3-Punisher-c/story. 5,6-Nick Fury & Punisher app. 6-Cable cameo. 7-9-Cable app. 2.50

MOUNTAIN MEN (See Ben Bowie)

MOUSE MUSKETEERS (See M.G.M.'s...)

MOUSE ON THE MOON, THE (See Movie Classics)

MOVIE CARTOONS
DC Comics: Dec, 1944 (cover only ashcan)
nn-Ashcan comic, not distributed to newsstands, only for in house use. Covers were produced, but not the rest of the book. A copy sold in 2006 for $500.

MOVIE CLASSICS
Dell Publishing Co.: Apr, 1956; May-Jul, 1962 - Dec, 1969
(Before 1963, most movie adaptations were part of the 4-Color series)
(Disney movie adaptations after 1970 are in Walt Disney Showcase)
Around the World Under the Sea 12-030-612 (12/66) 3 6 9 20 30 40
Bambi 3(4/56)-Disney; r/4-Color #186 4 8 12 24 37 50
Battle of the Bulge 12-056-606 (6/66) 3 6 9 21 32 42
Beach Blanket Bingo 12-058-509 7 14 21 47 76 105
Bon Voyage 01-068-212 (12/62)-Disney; photo-c 4 8 12 22 34 45
Castilian, The 12-110-401 3 6 9 20 30 40
Cat, The 12-109-612 (12/66) 3 6 9 19 29 38
Cheyenne Autumn 12-112-506 (4-6/65) 5 10 15 34 55 75
Circus World, Samuel Bronston's 12-115-411; John Wayne app.; John Wayne photo-c 9 18 27 65 113 160
Countdown 12-150-710 (10/67)-James Caan photo-c 3 6 9 21 32 42
Creature, The 1 (12-142-302) (12-2/62-63) 8 16 24 58 97 135
Creature, The 12-142-410 (10/64) 5 10 15 32 51 70
David Ladd's Life Story 12-173-212 (10-12/62)-Photo-c 7 14 21 47 76 105
Die, Monster, Die 12-175-603 (3/66)-Photo-c 5 10 15 34 55 75
Dirty Dozen 12-180-710 (10/67) 4 8 12 28 44 60
Dr. Who & the Daleks 12-190-612 (12/66)-Peter Cushing photo-c; 1st U.S. app. of Dr. Who 10 20 30 73 129 185
Dracula 12-231-212 (10-12/62) 8 16 24 52 86 120
El Dorado 12-240-710 (10/67)-John Wayne; photo-c 11 22 33 78 139 200
Ensign Pulver 12-257-410 (8-10/64) 3 6 9 19 29 38
Frankenstein 12-283-305 (3-5/63)(see Frankenstein 8-10/64 for 2nd printing) 8 16 24 54 90 125
Great Race, The 12-299-603 (3/66)-Natallie Wood, Tony Curtis photo-c 4 8 12 28 44 60
Hallelujah Trail, The 12-307-602 (2/66) (Shows 1/66 inside); Burt Lancaster, Lee Remick photo-c 5 10 15 30 48 65
Hatari 12-340-301 (1/63)-John Wayne 8 16 24 52 86 120
Horizontal Lieutenant, The 01-348-210 (10/62) 3 6 9 19 29 38
Incredible Mr. Limpet, The 12-370-408; Don Knotts photo-c 5 10 15 30 48 65
Jack the Giant Killer 12-374-301 (1/63) 8 16 24 52 86 120
Jason & the Argonauts 12-376-310 (8-10/63)-Photo-c 9 18 27 61 103 145
Lancelot & Guinevere 12-416-310 (10/63) 5 10 15 32 51 70
Lawrence 12-426-308 (8/63)-Story of Lawrence of Arabia; movie ad on back-c; not exactly like movie 5 10 15 32 51 70
Lion of Sparta 12-439-301 (1/63) 4 8 12 22 34 45
Mad Monster Party 12-460-801 (9/67)-Based on Kurtzman's screenplay 8 16 24 58 97 135
Magic Sword, The 01-496-209 (9/62) 5 10 15 35 55 75

GD 2.0 | VG 4.0 | FN 6.0 | VF 8.0 | VF/NM 9.0 | NM- 9.2

Masque of the Red Death 12-490-410 (8-10/64)-Vincent Price photo-c 6 12 18 41 66 90
Maya 12-495-612 (12/66)-Clint Walker & Jay North part photo-c 4 8 12 24 37 50
McHale's Navy 12-500-412 (10-12/64) 4 8 12 28 44 60
Merrill's Marauders 12-510-301 (1/63)-Photo-c 3 6 9 19 29 38
Mouse on the Moon, The 12-530-312 (10/12/63)-Photo-c 4 8 12 22 34 45
Mummy, The 12-537-211 (9-11/62) 2 versions with different back-c 8 16 24 56 93 130
Music Man, The 12-538-301 (1/63) 3 6 9 20 30 40
Naked Prey, The 12-545-612 (12/66)-Photo-c 5 10 15 34 55 75
Night of the Grizzly, The 12-558-612 (12/66)-Photo-c 4 8 12 22 34 45
None But the Brave 12-565-506 (4-6/65) 5 10 15 34 55 75
Operation Bikini 12-597-310 (10/63)-Photo-c 3 6 9 20 30 40
Operation Crossbow 12-590-512 (10-12/65) 3 6 9 20 30 40
Prince & the Pauper, The 01-654-207 (5-7/62)-Disney 4 8 12 22 34 45
Raven, The 12-680-309 (9/63)-Vincent Price photo-c 6 12 18 39 62 85
Ring of Bright Water 01-701-910 (10/69) (inside shows #12-701-909) 4 8 12 22 34 45
Runaway, The 12-707-412 (10-12/64) 3 6 9 19 29 38
Santa Claus Conquers the Martians #? (1964)-Photo-c 9 18 27 65 113 160
Santa Claus Conquers the Martians 12-725-603 (3/66, 12¢)-Reprints 1964 issue; photo-c 7 14 21 47 76 105
Another version given away with a Golden Record, SLP 170, nn, no price (3/66)-Complete with record 12 24 36 85 155 225
Six Black Horses 12-750-301 (1/63)-Photo-c 3 6 9 20 30 40
Ski Party 12-743-511 (9-11/65)-Frankie Avalon photo-c; photo inside-c; Adkins-a 5 10 15 30 48 65
Smoky 12-746-702 (2/67) 3 6 9 19 29 38
Sons of Katie Elder 12-748-511 (9-11/65); John Wayne app.; photo-c 11 22 33 78 139 200
Tales of Terror 12-793-302 (2/63)-Evans-a 5 10 15 34 55 75
Three Stooges Meet Hercules 01-828-208 (8/62)-Photo-c 9 18 27 60 100 140
Tomb of Ligeia 12-830-506 (4-6/65) 5 10 15 34 55 75
Treasure Island 01-845-211 (7-9/62)-Disney; r/4-Color #624 3 6 9 20 30 40
Twice Told Tales (Nathaniel Hawthorne) 12-840-401 (11-1/63-64); Vincent Price photo-c 6 12 18 37 59 80
Two on a Guillotine 12-850-506 (4-6/65) 4 8 12 22 34 45
Valley of Gwangi 01-880-912 (12/69) 9 18 27 60 100 140
War Gods of the Deep 12-900-509 (7-9/65) 3 6 9 20 30 40
War Wagon, The 12-533-709 (9/67); John Wayne app. 8 16 24 54 90 125
Who's Minding the Mint? 12-924-708 (8/67) 3 6 9 19 29 38
Wolfman, The 12-922-308 (6-8/63) 8 16 24 54 90 125
Wolfman, The 1(12-922-410)(8-10/64)-2nd printing; r/#12-922-308 4 8 12 23 36 48
Zulu 12-950-410 (8-10/64)-Photo-c 7 14 21 49 80 110

MOVIE COMICS (See Cinema Comics Herald & Fawcett Movie Comics)

MOVIE COMICS
National Periodical Publications/Picture Comics: April, 1939 - No. 6, Sept-Oct, 1939 (Most all photo-c)
1- "Gunga Din", "Son of Frankenstein", "The Great Man Votes", "Fisherman's Wharf", & "Scouts to the Rescue" part 1; Wheelan "Minute Movies" begin 354 708 1062 2478 4339 6200
2- "Stagecoach", "The Saint Strikes Back", "King of the Turf", "Scouts to the Rescue" part 2, "Arizona Legion", Andy Devine photo-c 245 490 735 1568 2684 3800
3- "East Side of Heaven", "Mystery in the White Room", "Four Feathers", "Mexican Rose" with Gene Autry, "Spirit of Culver", "Many Secrets", "The Mikado" (1st Gene Autry photo cover) 174 348 522 1114 1907 2700
4- "Captain Fury", Gene Autry in "Blue Montana Skies", "Streets of N.Y." with Jackie Cooper, "Oregon Trail" part 1 with Johnny Mack Brown, "Big Town Czar" with Barton MacLane, & "Star Reporter" with Warren Hull 147 294 441 934 1605 2275
5- "The Man in the Iron Mask", "Five Came Back", "Wolf Call", "The Girl & the Gambler", "The House of Fear", "The Family Next Door", "Oregon Trail" part 2 160 320 480 1016 1746 2475
6- "The Phantom Creeps", "Chumps at Oxford", & "The Oregon Trail" part 3; 2nd Robot-c 200 400 600 1280 2190 3100

NOTE: *Above books contain many original movie stills with dialogue from movie scripts. All issues are scarce.*

Movie Comics #2 © FH

Movie Comics - Bambi #1 © DIS

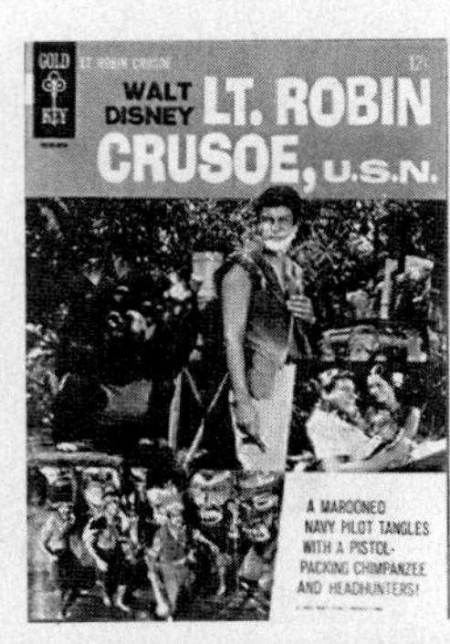

Movie Comics - Lt. Robin Crusoe © DIS

MOVIE COMICS
Fiction House Magazines: Dec, 1946 - No. 4, 1947

	GD 2.0	VG 4.0	FN 6.0	VF 8.0	VF/NM 9.0	NM- 9.2
1-Big Town (by Lubbers), Johnny Danger begin; Celardo-a; Mitzi of the Movies by Fran Hopper	41	82	123	256	428	600
2-(2/47)- "White Tie & Tails" with William Bendix; Mitzi of the Movies begins	32	64	96	190	305	420
3-(6/47)-Andy Hardy starring Mickey Rooney	32	64	96	190	305	420
4-Mitzi In Hollywood by Matt Baker; Merton of the Movies with Red Skelton; Yvonne DeCarlo & George Brent in "Slave Girl"	40	80	120	235	380	525

MOVIE COMICS
Gold Key/Whitman: Oct, 1962 - 1984

	GD 2.0	VG 4.0	FN 6.0	VF 8.0	VF/NM 9.0	NM- 9.2
Alice in Wonderland 10144-503 (3/65)-Disney; partial reprint of 4-Color #331	4	8	12	22	34	45
Alice In Wonderland #1 (Whitman pre-pack, 3/84)	2	4	6	10	14	18
Aristocats, The 1 (30045-103)(3/71)-Disney; with pull-out poster (25¢) (No poster = half price)	7	14	21	47	76	105
Bambi 1 (10087-309)(9/63)-Disney; r/4-C #186	4	8	12	24	37	50
Bambi 2 (10087-607)(7/66)-Disney; r/4-C #186	3	6	9	20	30	40
Beneath the Planet of the Apes 30044-012 (12/70)-with pull-out poster; photo-c (No poster = half price)	9	18	27	61	103	145
Big Red 10026-211 (11/62)-Disney; photo-c	3	6	9	20	30	40
Big Red 10026-503 (3/65)-Disney; reprints 10026-211; photo-c	3	6	9	16	23	30
Blackbeard's Ghost 10222-806 (6/68)-Disney	3	6	9	19	29	38
Bullwhip Griffin 10181-706 (6/67)-Disney; Spiegle-a; photo-c	4	8	12	22	34	45
Captain Sindbad 10077-309 (9/63)-Manning-a; photo-c	6	12	18	41	66	90
Chitty Chitty Bang Bang 1 (30038-902)(2/69)-with pull-out poster; Disney; photo-c (No poster = half price)	6	12	18	43	69	95
Cinderella 10152-508 (8/65)-Disney; r/4-C #786	4	8	12	26	41	55
Darby O'Gill & the Little People 10251-001(1/70)-Disney; reprints 4-Color #1024 (Toth-a); photo-c	5	10	15	30	48	65
Dumbo 1 (10090-310)(10/63)-Disney; r/4-C #668	3	6	9	21	32	42
Emil & the Detectives 10120-502 (11/64)-Disney; photo-c & back-c photo pin-up	3	6	9	20	30	40
Escapade in Florence 1 (10043-301)(1/63)-Disney; starring Annette Funicello	8	16	24	52	86	120
Fall of the Roman Empire 10118-407 (7/64); Sophia Loren photo-c	4	8	12	24	37	50
Fantastic Voyage 10178-702 (2/67)-Wood/Adkins-a; photo-c	6	12	18	37	59	80
55 Days at Peking 10081-309 (9/63)-Photo-c	3	6	9	20	30	40
Fighting Prince of Donegal, The 10193-701 (1/67)-Disney	3	6	9	19	29	38
First Men in the Moon 10132-503 (3/65)-Fred Fredericks-a; photo-c	4	8	12	24	37	50
Gay Purr-ee 30017-301(1/63, 84 pgs.)	5	10	15	32	51	70
Gnome Mobile, The 10207-710 (10/67)-Disney; Walter Brennan photo-c & back-c photo pin-up	4	8	12	22	34	45
Goodbye, Mr. Chips 10246-006 (6/70)-Peter O'Toole photo-c	3	6	9	20	30	40
Happiest Millionaire, The 10221-804 (4/68)-Disney	4	8	12	22	34	45
Hey There, It's Yogi Bear 10122-409 (9/64)-Hanna-Barbera	6	12	18	43	69	95
Horse Without a Head, The 10109-401 (1/64)-Disney	3	6	9	19	29	38
How the West Was Won 10074-307 (7/63)-Based on the L'Amour novel; Tufts-a	4	8	12	28	44	60
In Search of the Castaways 10048-303 (3/63)-Disney; Hayley Mills photo-c	6	12	18	43	69	95
Jungle Book, The 1 (6022-801)(1/68-Whitman)-Disney; large size (10x13-1/2"); 59¢	6	12	18	43	69	95
Jungle Book, The 1 (30033-803)(3/68, 68 pgs.)-Disney; same contents as Whitman #1	4	8	12	24	37	50
Jungle Book, The 1 (6/78, $1.00 tabloid)	3	6	9	16	23	30
Jungle Book (7/84)-r/Giant; Whitman pre-pack	2	4	6	10	14	18
Kidnapped 10080-306 (6/63)-Disney; reprints 4-Color #1101; photo-c	3	6	9	20	30	40
King Kong 30036-809(9/68-68 pgs.)-painted-c	4	8	12	26	41	55
King Kong nn-Whitman Treasury($1.00, 68 pgs.,1968), same cover as Gold Key issue	5	10	15	34	55	75
King Kong 11299(#1-786, 10x13-1/4", 68 pgs., $1.00, 1978)	3	6	9	18	27	35
Lady and the Tramp 10042-301 (1/63)-Disney; r/4-Color #629	3	6	9	21	32	42
Lady and the Tramp 1 (1967-Giant; 25¢)-Disney; reprints part of Dell #1	5	10	15	34	55	75
Lady and the Tramp 2 (10042-203)(3/72)-Disney; r/4-Color #629	3	6	9	16	23	30
Legend of Lobo, The 1 (10059-303)(3/63)-Disney; photo-c	3	6	9	16	23	30
Lt. Robin Crusoe, U.S.N. 10191-610 (10/66)-Disney; Dick Van Dyke photo-c & back-c photo pin-up	3	6	9	18	27	35
Lion, The 10035-301 (1/63)-Photo-c	3	6	9	17	25	32
Lord Jim 10156-509 (9/65)-Photo-c	3	6	9	17	25	32
Love Bug, The 10237-906 (6/69)-Disney; Buddy Hackett photo-c	4	8	12	22	34	45
Mary Poppins 10136-501 (1/65)-Disney; photo-c	5	10	15	30	48	65
Mary Poppins 30023-501 (1/65-68 pgs.)-Disney; photo-c	7	14	21	47	76	105
McLintock 10110-403 (3/64); John Wayne app.; John Wayne & Maureen O'Hara photo-c	11	22	33	80	145	210
Merlin Jones as the Monkey's Uncle 10115-510 (10/65)-Disney; Annette Funicello front/back photo-c	6	12	18	39	62	85
Miracle of the White Stallions, The 10065-306 (6/63)-Disney	3	6	9	19	29	38
Misadventures of Merlin Jones, The 10115-405 (5/64)-Disney; Annette Funicello photo front/back-c	6	12	18	39	62	85
Moon-Spinners, The 10124-410 (10/64)-Disney; Hayley Mills photo-c	6	12	18	43	69	95
Mutiny on the Bounty 1 (10040-302)(2/63)-Marlon Brando photo-c	4	8	12	22	34	45
Nikki, Wild Dog of the North 10141-412 (12/64)-Disney; reprints 4-Color #1226	3	6	9	16	23	30
Old Yeller 10168-601 (1/66)-Disney; reprints 4-Color #869; photo-c	3	6	9	16	23	30
One Hundred & One Dalmations 1 (10247-002) (2/70)-Disney; reprints Four Color #1183	3	6	9	18	27	35
Peter Pan 1 (10086-309)(9/63)-Disney; reprints Four Color #442	3	6	9	21	32	42
Peter Pan 2 (10086-909)(9/69)-Disney; reprints Four Color #442	3	6	9	16	23	30
Peter Pan 1 (3/84)-r/4-Color #442; Whitman pre-pack	2	4	6	11	16	20
P.T. 109 10123-409 (9/64)-John F. Kennedy	5	10	15	30	48	65
Rio Conchos 10143-503(3/65)	4	8	12	22	34	45
Robin Hood 10163-506 (6/65)-Disney; reprints Four Color #413	3	6	9	17	25	32
Shaggy Dog & the Absent-Minded Professor 30032-708 (8/67-Giant, 68 pgs.) Disney; reprints 4-Color #985,1199	5	10	15	32	51	70
Sleeping Beauty 1 (30042-009)(9/70)-Disney; reprints Four Color #973; with pull-out poster (No poster = half price)	6	12	18	43	69	95
Snow White & the Seven Dwarfs 1 (10091-310)(10/63)-Disney; reprints Four Color #382	3	6	9	20	30	40
Snow White & the Seven Dwarfs 10091-709 (9/67)-Disney; reprints Four Color #382	3	6	9	16	23	30
Snow White & the Seven Dwarfs 90091-204 (2/84)-Reprints Four Color #382; Whitman pre-pack	2	4	6	11	16	20
Son of Flubber 1 (10057-304)(4/63)-Disney; sequel to "The Absent-Minded Professor"	4	8	12	22	34	45
Summer Magic 10076-309 (9/63)-Disney; Hayley Mills photo-c; Manning-a	6	12	18	43	69	95
Swiss Family Robinson 10236-904 (4/69)-Disney; reprints Four Color #1156; photo-c	3	6	9	18	27	35
Sword in the Stone, The 30019-402 (2/64-Giant, 68 pgs.)-Disney (see March of Comics #258 & Wart and the Wizard	6	12	18	43	69	95
That Darn Cat 10171-602 (2/66)-Disney; Hayley Mills photo-c	6	12	18	43	69	95
Those Magnificent Men in Their Flying Machines 10162-510 (10/65); photo-c	3	6	9	20	30	40
Three Stooges in Orbit 30016-211 (11/62-Giant, 32 pgs.)-All photos from movie; stiff-photo-c	9	18	27	65	113	160
Tiger Walks, A 10117-406 (6/64)-Disney; Torres?, Tufts-a; photo-c	4	8	12	24	37	50
Toby Tyler 10142-502 (2/65)-Disney; reprints Four Color #1092; photo-c	3	6	9	18	27	35
Treasure Island 1 (10200-703)(3/67)-Disney; reprints Four Color #624; photo-c	3	6	9	16	23	30

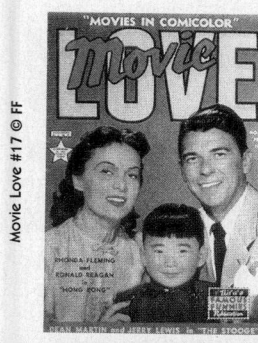

Movie Love #17 © FF

Ms. Marvel (2006 series) #13 © MAR

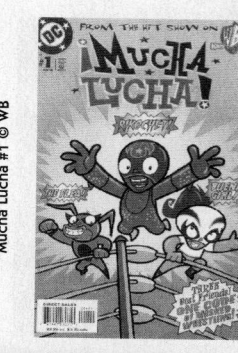

Mucha Lucha #1 © WB

	GD 2.0	VG 4.0	FN 6.0	VF 8.0	VF/NM 9.0	NM- 9.2

20,000 Leagues Under the Sea 1 (10095-312)(12/63)-Disney; reprints Four Color #614
3 6 9 18 27 35

Wonderful Adventures of Pinocchio, The 1 (10089-310)(10/63)-Disney; reprints Four Color #545 (see Wonderful Advs. of...) 3 6 9 21 32 42

Wonderful Adventures of Pinocchio, The 10089-109 (9/71)-Disney; reprints Four Color #545
3 6 9 16 23 30

Wonderful World of the Brothers Grimm 1 (10008-210)(10/62)
4 8 12 28 44 60

X, the Man with the X-Ray Eyes 10083-309 (9/63)-Ray Milland photo on-c
7 14 21 49 80 110

Yellow Submarine 35000-902 (2/69-Giant, 68 pgs.)-With pull-out poster;
The Beatles cartoon movie; Paul S. Newman-s 21 42 63 148 287 425
Without poster 9 18 27 64 110 155

MOVIE FABLES
DC Comics: Dec, 1944 (cover only ashcan)

nn-Ashcan comic, not distributed to newsstands, only for in house use. Covers were produced, but not the rest of the book. A copy sold in 2006 for $500.

MOVIE GEMS
DC Comics: Dec, 1944 (cover only ashcan)

nn-Ashcan comic, not distributed to newsstands, only for in house use. Covers were produced, but not the rest of the book. A copy sold in 2006 for $500.

MOVIE LOVE (Also see Personal Love)
Famous Funnies: Feb, 1950 - No. 22, Aug, 1953 (All photo-c)

1-Dick Powell, Evelyn Keyes, & Mickey Rooney photo-c
18 36 54 103 162 220
2-Myrna Loy photo-c 11 22 33 62 86 110
3-7,9: 6-Ricardo Montalban photo-c. 9-Gene Tierney, John Lund, Glenn Ford, & Rhonda Fleming photo-c. 10 20 30 58 79 100
8-Williamson/Frazetta-a, 6 pgs. 45 90 135 284 480 675
10-Frazetta-a, 6 pgs. 46 92 138 290 488 685
11,14-16: 14-Janet Leigh photo-c 10 20 30 56 76 95
12-Dean Martin & Jerry Lewis photo-c (12/51, pre-dates Advs. of Dean Martin & Jerry Lewis comic) 19 38 57 111 176 240
13-Ronald Reagan photo-c with 1 pg. biog. 25 50 75 147 241 335
17-Leslie Caron & Ralph Meeker photo-c; 1 pg. Frazetta ad
10 20 30 58 79 100
18-22: 19-John Derek photo-c. 20-Donald O'Connor & Debbie Reynolds photo-c. 21-Paul Henreid & Patricia Medina photo-c. 22-John Payne & Coleen Gray photo-c
10 20 30 54 72 90

NOTE: *Each issue has a full-length movie adaptation with photo covers.*

MOVIE THRILLERS (Movie)
Magazine Enterprises: 1949

1-Adaptation of "Rope of Sand" w/Burt Lancaster; Burt Lancaster photo-c
28 56 84 165 270 375

MOVIE TOWN ANIMAL ANTICS (Formerly Animal Antics; becomes Raccoon Kids #52 on)
National Periodical Publ.: No. 24, Jan-Feb, 1950 - No. 51, July-Aug, 1954

24-Raccoon Kids continue 12 24 36 67 94 120
25-51 10 20 30 54 72 90

NOTE: ***Sheldon Mayer** a-28-33, 35, 37-41, 43, 44, 47, 49-51.*

MOVIE TUNES COMICS (Formerly Animated...; Frankie No. 4 on)
Marvel Comics (MgPC): No. 3, Fall, 1946

3-Super Rabbit, Krazy Krow, Silly Seal & Ziggy Pig 15 30 45 85 130 175

MOWGLI JUNGLE BOOK (Rudyard Kipling's...)
Dell Publ. Co.: No. 487, Aug-Oct, 1953 - No. 620, Apr, 1955

Four Color 487 (#1) 6 12 18 37 59 80
Four Color 582 (8/54), 620 5 10 15 30 48 65

MR. (See Mister)

M. REX
Image Comics: July, 1999 - No. 2, Dec, 1999 ($2.95)

Preview ($5.00) B&W pages and sketchbook; Rouleau-a 5.00
1,2-($2.95) 1-Joe Kelly-s/Rouleau-a/Anacleto-c. 2-Rouleau-c 3.00

MS. MARVEL (Also see The Avengers #183)
Marvel Comics Group: Jan, 1977 - No. 23, Apr, 1979

1-1st app. Ms. Marvel; Scorpion app. in #1,2 2 4 6 10 14 18
2-10: 2-Origin. 5-Vision app. 6-10-(Reg. 30¢-c). 10-Last 30¢ issue
1 2 3 5 7 9
6-10-(35¢-c variants, limited dist.)(6/77) 4 8 12 22 34 45
11-15,19-23: 19-Capt. Marvel app. 20-New costume. 23-Vance Astro (leader of the Guardians) app. 6.00
16,17-1st brief app. Mystique 3 6 9 14 20 25
18-1st full app. Mystique; Avengers x-over 4 8 12 28 44 60

NOTE: ***Austin** c-14i, 16i, 17i, 22i. **Buscema** a-1-3p; c(p)-2, 4, 6, 7, 15. **Infantino** a-14p, 19p. **Gil Kane** c-8. **Mooney** a-4-8p, 13p, 15-18p. **Starlin** c-12.*

MS. MARVEL (Also see New Avengers)
Marvel Comics: May, 2006 - Present ($2.99)

1-24: 1-Cho-c/Reed-s/De La Torre-a; Stilt-Man app. 4,5-Dr. Strange app. 6,7-Araña app. 3.00
1-Variant cover by Michael Turner 5.00
25-($3.99) Two covers by Horn and Dodson; Secret Invasion 4.00
26-49: 26-31-Secret Invasion. 34-Spider-Man app. 35-Dark Reign. 37-Carol explodes. 39,40,46,48,49-Takeda-a. 41-Carol returns. 47-Spider-Man app. 3.00
50-($3.99) Mystique and Captain Marvel app.; Takeda & Oliver-a 4.00
... Annual 1 (11/08, $3.99) Spider-Man app.; Horn-c 3.00
... Special (3/07, $2.99) Reed-s/Camuncoli-a/c 3.00
... Storyteller (1/09, $2.99) Reed-s/Camuncoli-a/c 3.00
... Vol. 1: Best of the Best HC (2006, $19.99) r/#1-5 & Giant-Size Ms. Marvel #1 20.00
... Vol. 1: Best of the Best SC (2007, $14.99) r/#1-5 & Giant-Size Ms. Marvel #1 15.00
... Vol. 2: Civil War HC (2007, $19.99) r/#6-10 & Ms. Marvel Special #1 20.00
... Vol. 2: Civil War SC (2007, $14.99) r/#6-10 & Ms. Marvel Special #1 15.00
... Vol. 3: Operation Lightning Storm HC (2007, $19.99) r/#11-17 20.00
... Vol. 4: Monster Smash HC (2008, $19.99) r/#18-24 20.00

MS. MYSTIC
Pacific Comics: Oct, 1982 - No. 2, Feb, 1984 ($1.00/$1.50)

1,2: Neal Adams-c/a/script. 1-Origin; intro Erth, Ayre, Fyre & Watr 4.00

MS. MYSTIC
Continuity Comics: 1988 - No. 9, May, 1992 ($2.00)

1-9: 1,2-Reprint Pacific Comics issues 3.00

MS. MYSTIC
Continunity Comics: V2#1, Oct, 1993 - V2#4, Jan, 1994 ($2.50)

V2#1-4: 1-Adams-c(i)/part-i. 2-4-Embossed-c. 2-Nebres part-i. 3-Adams-c(i)/plot. 4-Adams-c(p)/plot 2.50

MS. MYSTIC DEATHWATCH 2000 (Ms. Mystic #3)
Continuity: May, 1993 - No. 3, Aug, 1993 ($2.50)

1-3-Bagged w/card; Adams plots 2.50

MS. TREE QUARTERLY / SPECIAL
DC Comics: Summer, 1990 -No. 10, 1992 ($3.95/$3.50, 84 pgs, mature)

1-10: 1-Midnight story; Batman text story, Grell-a. 2,3-Midnight stories; The Butcher text stories 4.00

NOTE: ***Cowan** c-2. **Grell** c-1, 6. **Infantino** a-8.*

MS. TREE'S THRILLING DETECTIVE ADVS (Ms. Tree #4 on; also see The Best of Ms. Tree) (Baxter paper #4-9)
Eclipse Comics/Aardvark-Vanaheim 10-18/Renegade Press 19 on:
2/83 - #9, 7/84; #10, 8/84 - #18, 5/85; #19, 6/85 - #50, 6/89

1 3.00
2-49: 2-Schythe begins. 9-Last Eclipse & last color issue. 10,11-two-tone 2.50
50-Contains flexi-disc ($3.95, 52 pgs.) 4.00
Summer Special 1 (8/86) 3.00
1950s 3-D Crime (7/87, no glasses)-Johnny Dynamite in 3-D 3.00
Mike Mist in 3-D (8/85)-With glasses 3.00

NOTE: ***Miller** pin-up 1-4. Johnny Dynamite-r begin #36 by **Morisi**.*

MS. VICTORY SPECIAL(Also see Capt. Paragon & Femforce)
Americomics: Jan, 1985 (nd)

1 2.50

MUCHA LUCHA (Based on Kids WB animated TV show)
DC Comics: Jun, 2003 - No. 3, Aug, 2003 ($2.25, limited series)

1-3-Rikochet, Buena Girl and The Flea app. 2.50

MUGGSY MOUSE (Also see Tick Tock Tales)
Magazine Enterprises: 1951 - No. 3, 1951; No. 4, 1954 - No. 5, 1954; 1963

1(A-1 #33) 9 18 27 50 65 80
2(A-1 #36)-Racist-c 13 26 39 72 101 130
3(A-1 #39), 4(A-1 #95), 5(A-1 #99) 7 14 21 37 46 55
Super Reprint #14(1963), I.W. Reprint #1,2 (nd) 2 4 6 8 11 14

MUGGY-DOO, BOY CAT
Stanhall Publ.: July, 1953 - No. 4, Jan, 1954

1-Funny animal; Irving Spector-a 9 18 27 47 61 75
2-4 6 12 18 27 33 38

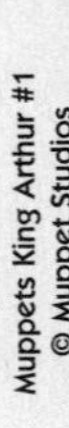
Muppets King Arthur #1 © Muppet Studios

Murder Incorporated #14 © FOX

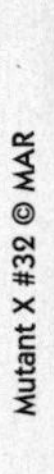
Mutant X #32 © MAR

	GD 2.0	VG 4.0	FN 6.0	VF 8.0	VF/NM 9.0	NM- 9.2

Super Reprint #12('63), 16('64) 2 4 6 8 11 14

MULLKON EMPIRE (See John Jake's...)

MUMMY, THE (See Universal Presents... under Dell Giants & Movie Classics)

MUMMY, THE: THE RISE AND FALL OF XANGO'S AX (Based on the Brendan Fraser movies)
IDW Publishing: Apr, 2008 - No. 4, July, 2008 ($3.99, limited series)

1-4-Prequel to '08 movie The Mummy: Tomb of the Dragon Emperor; Stephen Mooney-a 4.00

MUNDEN'S BAR ANNUAL
First Comics: Apr, 1988; 1989 ($2.95/$5.95)

1-($2.95)-r/from Grimjack; Fish Police story; Ordway-c 3.00
2-($5.95)-Teenage Mutant Ninja Turtles app. 6.00

MUNSTERS, THE (TV)
Gold Key: Jan, 1965 - No. 16, Jan, 1968 (All photo-c)

1 (10134-501) 17 34 51 119 230 340
2 9 18 27 65 113 160
3-5 8 16 24 54 90 125
6-16 7 14 21 47 76 105

MUNSTERS, THE (TV)
TV Comics!: Aug, 1997 - No. 4 ($2.95, B&W)

1-4-All have photo-c 3.00
1,4-($7.95)-Variant-c 8.00
2-Variant-c w/Beverly Owens as Marilyn 3.00
Special Comic Con Ed. (7/97, $9.95) 10.00

MUPPET... (TV)
BOOM! Studios

... King Arthur 1-3 (12/09 - No. 4, $2.99) Benjamin & Storck-s/Alvarez-a; 2 covers 3.00
... Peter Pan 1-4 (8/09 - No. 4, 11/09, $2.99) Randolph-s/Mebberson-a; multiple covers 3.00
... Robin Hood 1-4 (4/09 - No. 4, 7/09, $2.99) Beedle-s/Villavert Jr.-a; multiple covers 3.00

MUPPET BABIES, THE (TV)(See Star Comics Magazine)
Marvel Comics (Star Comics)/Marvel #18 on: Aug, 1985 - No. 26, July, 1989 (Children's book)

1-26 3.00

MUPPET SHOW, THE (TV)
BOOM! Studios: Mar, 2009 - No. 4, Jun, 2009 ($2.99, limited series)

1-4-Roger Landridge-s/a; multiple covers 3.00
...: The Treasure of Peg Leg Wilson (7/09 - No. 4, 10/09) 1-4-Landridge-s/a; multiple-c 3.00

MUPPET SHOW COMIC BOOK, THE (TV)
BOOM! Studios: No. 0, Nov, 2009 - Present ($2.99)

0-3-Roger Landridge-s/a; multiple covers. 0-Paroline-a; Pigs in Space 3.00

MUPPETS TAKE MANHATTAN, THE
Marvel Comics (Star Comics): Nov, 1984 - No. 3, Jan, 1985

1-3-Movie adapt. r-/Marvel Super Special 3.00

MURCIELAGA, SHE-BAT
Heroic Publishing: Jan, 1993 - No. 2, 1993 (B&W)

1-($1.50, 28 pgs.) 2.50
2-($2.95, 36 pgs.)-Coated-c 3.00

MURDER CAN BE FUN
Slave Labor Graphics: Feb, 1996 - No. 12 ($2.95, B&W)

1-12: 1-Dorkin-c. 2-Vasquez-c. 3.00

MURDER INCORPORATED (My Private Life #16 on)
Fox Feature Syndicate: 1/48 - No. 15, 12/49; (2 No.9's); 6/50 - No. 3, 8/51

1 (1st Series); 1,2 have 'For Adults Only' on-c 50 100 150 315 533 750
2-Electrocution story 39 78 117 240 395 550
3-7,9(4/49),10(5/49),11-15 23 46 69 136 223 310
8-Used in **SOTI**, pg. 160 25 50 75 150 245 340
9(3/49)-Possible use in **SOTI**, pg. 145; r/Blue Beetle #56('48)
23 46 69 136 223 310
5(#1, 6/50)(2nd Series)-Formerly My Desire #4; bondage-c.
20 40 60 114 182 250
2(8/50)-Morisi-a 18 36 54 103 162 220
3(8/51)-Used in **POP**, pg. 81; Rico-a; lingerie-c/panels
20 40 60 114 182 250

MURDER ME DEAD
El Capitán Books: July, 2000 - No. 9, Oct, 2001 ($2.95/$4.95, B&W)

1-8-David Lapham-s/a 3.00
9-($4.95) 5.00

MURDEROUS GANGSTERS
Avon Per./Realistic No. 3 on: Jul, 1951; No. 2, Dec, 1951 - No. 4, Jun, 1952

1-Pretty Boy Floyd, Leggs Diamond; 1 pg. Wood-a 45 90 135 284 480 675
2-Baby-Face Nelson; 1 pg. Wood-a; painted-c 29 58 87 170 278 385
3-Painted-c 24 48 72 140 230 320
4- "Murder by Needle" drug story; Mort Lawrence-a; Kinstler-c
30 60 90 177 289 400

MURDER MYSTERIES (Neil Gaiman's...)
Dark Horse Comics: 2002 ($13.95, HC, one-shot)

HC-Adapts Gaiman story; P. Craig Russell-script/art 14.00

MURDER TALES (Magazine)
World Famous Publications: V1#10, Nov, 1970 - V1#11, Jan, 1971 (52 pgs.)

V1#10-One pg. Frazetta ad 4 8 12 28 44 60
11-Guardineer-r; bondage-c 4 8 12 24 37 50

MUSHMOUSE AND PUNKIN PUSS (TV)
Gold Key: September, 1965 (Hanna-Barbera)

1 (10153-509) 8 16 24 58 97 135

MUSIC MAN, THE (See Movie Classics)

MUTANT CHRONICLES (Video game)
Acclaim Comics (Armada): May, 1996 - No. 4, Aug, 1996 ($2.95, lim. series)

1-4: Simon Bisley-c on all, Sourcebook (#5) 3.00

MUTANT EARTH (Stan Winston's...)
Image Comics: April, 2002 - No. 4, Jan, 2003 ($2.95)

1-4-Flip book w/Realm of the Claw 3.00
Trakk...His Adventures in Mutant Earth TPB (2003, $16.95) r/#1-4; Winston interview 17.00

MUTANT MISADVENTURES OF CLOAK AND DAGGER, THE
(Becomes Cloak and Dagger #14 on)
Marvel Comics: Oct, 1988 - No. 19, Aug, 1991 ($1.25/$1.50)

1-8,10-15: 1-X-Factor app. 10-Painted-c. 12-Dr. Doom app. 14-Begin new direction 2.50
9,16-19: 9-(52 pgs.) The Avengers x-over; painted-c. 16-18-Spider-Man x-over. 18-Infinity Gauntlet x-over; Thanos cameo; Ghost Rider app. 19-(52 pgs.) Origin Cloak & Dagger 3.00
NOTE: ***Austin** a-12i; c(i)-4, 12, 13; scripts-all. **Russell** a-2i. **Williamson** a-14i-16i; c-15i.*

MUTANTS & MISFITS
Silverline Comics (Solson): 1987 - No. 3, 1987 ($1.95)

1-3 2.50

MUTANTS VS. ULTRAS
Malibu Comics (Ultraverse): Nov, 1995 ($6.95, one-shot)

1-r/Exiles vs. X-Men, Night Man vs. Wolverine, Prime vs. Hulk 7.00

MUTANT, TEXAS: TALES OF SHERIFF IDA RED (Also see Jingle Belle)
Oni Press: May, 2002 - No. 4, Nov, 2002 ($2.95, B&W, limited series)

1-4-Paul Dini-s/J. Bone-c/a 3.00
TPB (2003, $11.95) r/#1-4; intro. by Joe Lansdale 12.00

MUTANT 2099
Marvel Comics (Marvel Knights): Nov, 2004 ($2.99, one-shot)

1-Kirkman-s/Pat Lee-c 3.00

MUTANT X (See X-Factor)
Marvel Comics: Nov, 1998 - No. 32, June, 2001 ($2.99/$1.99/$2.25)

1-($2.99) Alex Summers with alternate world's X-Men 3.00
2-11,13-19-($1.99): 2-Two covers. 5-Man-Spider-c/app. 2.50
12,25-($2.99): 12-Pin-up gallery by Kaluta, Romita, Byrne 3.00
20-24,26-32: 20-Begin $2.25-c. 28-31-Logan-c/app. 32-Last issue 2.50
Annual '99, '00 (5/99,'00, $3.50) '00-Doran-a(p) 3.50
Annual 2001 ($2.99) Story occurs between #31 & #32; Dracula app. 3.00

MUTANT X (Based on TV show)
Marvel Comics: May, 2002 - Present ($3.50)

...: Dangerous Decisions (6/02) -Kuder-s/Immonen-a 3.50
...: Origin (5/02) -Tischman & Chaykin-s/Ferguson-a 3.50

MUTATIS
Marvel Comics (Epic Comics): 1992 - No. 3, 1992 ($2.25, mini-series)

1-3: Painted-c 2.50

MUTIES
Marvel Comics: Apr, 2002 - No. 6, Sept, 2002 ($2.50)

1-6: 1-Bollars-s/Ferguson-a. 2-Spaziante-a. 3-Haspiel-a. 4-Kanuiga-a 2.50

MUTINY (Stormy Tales of the Seven Seas)

Mutt & Jeff #49 © DC

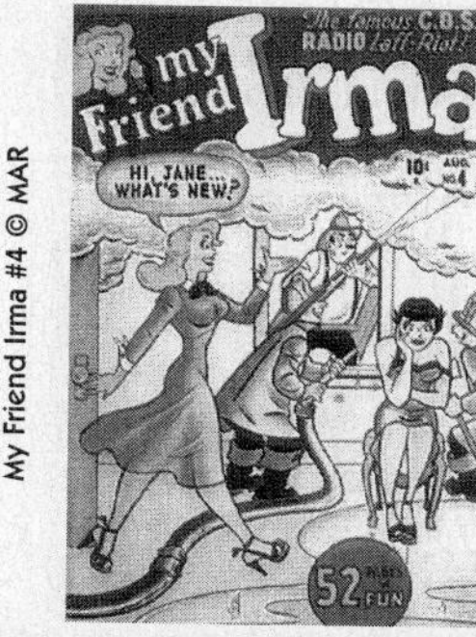

My Friend Irma #4 © MAR

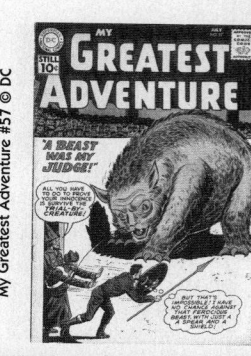

My Greatest Adventure #57 © DC

Aragon Magazines: Oct, 1954 - No. 3, Feb, 1955

	GD 2.0	VG 4.0	FN 6.0	VF 8.0	VF/NM 9.0	NM- 9.2
1	16	32	48	92	144	195
2,3: 2-Capt. Mutiny. 3-Bondage-c	14	28	42	76	108	140

MUTINY ON THE BOUNTY (See Classics Illustrated #100 & Movie Comics)

MUTOPIA X (Also see House of M and related titles)
Marvel Comics: Sept, 2005 - No. 5, Jan, 2006 ($2.99, limited series)

	GD 2.0	VG 4.0	FN 6.0	VF 8.0	VF/NM 9.0	NM- 9.2
1-5-Medina-a/Hine-s						3.00
House of M: Mutopia X (2006, $13.99, TPB) r/series						14.00

MUTT AND JEFF (See All-American, All-Flash #18, Cicero's Cat, Comic Cavalcade, Famous Feature Stories, The Funnies, Popular & Xmas Comics)
All American/National 1-103(6/58)/Dell 104(10/58)-115 (10-12/59)/ Harvey 116(2/60)-148: Summer, 1939 (nd) - No. 148, Nov, 1965

	GD 2.0	VG 4.0	FN 6.0	VF 8.0	VF/NM 9.0	NM- 9.2
1(nn)-Lost Wheels	142	284	426	909	1555	2200
2(nn)-Charging Bull (Summer, 1940, nd; on sale 6/20/40)	68	136	204	432	746	1060
3(nn)-Bucking Broncos (Summer, 1941, nd)	49	98	147	309	522	735
4(Winter, '41), 5(Summer, '42)	45	90	135	284	480	675
6-10: 6-Includes Minute Man Answers the Call	26	52	78	154	252	350
11-20: 20-X-Mas-c	19	38	57	111	176	240
21-30	15	30	45	84	127	170
31-50: 32-X-Mas-c	13	26	39	72	101	130
51-75-Last Fisher issue. 53-Last 52 pgs.	10	20	30	56	76	95
76-99,101-103: 76-Last pre-code issue(1/55)	5	10	15	34	55	75
100	6	12	18	37	59	80
104-115,132-148	4	8	12	24	44	60
116-131-Richie Rich app.	5	10	15	30	48	65
...Jokes 1-3(8/60-61, Harvey)-84 pgs.; Richie Rich in all; Little Dot in #2,3; Lotta in #2	5	10	15	30	48	65
...New Jokes 1-4(10/63-11/65, Harvey)-68 pgs.; Richie Rich in #1-3; Stumbo in #1	4	8	12	24	37	50

NOTE: *Most all issues by* ***Al Smith****. Issues from 1963 on have* ***Fisher*** *reprints. Clarification: early issues signed by Fisher are mostly drawn by Smith.*

MY BROTHERS' KEEPER
Spire Christian Comics (Fleming H. Revell Co.): 1973 (35/49¢, 36 pgs.)

	GD 2.0	VG 4.0	FN 6.0	VF 8.0	VF/NM 9.0	NM- 9.2
nn	2	4	6	8	11	14

MY CONFESSIONS (My Confession #7&8; formerly Western True Crime; A Spectacular Feature Magazine #11)
Fox Feature Syndicate: No. 7, Aug, 1949 - No. 10, Jan-Feb, 1950

	GD 2.0	VG 4.0	FN 6.0	VF 8.0	VF/NM 9.0	NM- 9.2
7-Wood-a (10 pgs.)	24	48	72	140	230	320
8,9: 8-Harrison/Wood-a (19 pgs.). 9-Wood-a	22	44	66	128	209	290
10	13	26	39	72	101	130

MY DATE COMICS (Teen-age)
Hillman Periodicals: July, 1947 - V1#4, Jan, 1948 (2nd Romance comic; see Young Romance)

	GD 2.0	VG 4.0	FN 6.0	VF 8.0	VF/NM 9.0	NM- 9.2
1-S&K-c/a	39	78	117	231	378	525
2-4-S&K-c/a; Dan Barry-a	26	52	78	154	252	350

MY DESIRE (Formerly Jo-Jo Comics; becomes Murder, Inc. #5 on)
Fox Feature Syndicate: No. 30, Aug, 1949 - No. 4, April, 1950

	GD 2.0	VG 4.0	FN 6.0	VF 8.0	VF/NM 9.0	NM- 9.2
30(#1)	18	36	54	105	165	225
31 (#2, 10/49),3(2/50),4	14	28	42	80	115	150
31 (Canadian edition)	9	18	27	47	61	75
32(12/49)-Wood-a	21	42	63	124	202	280

MY DIARY (Becomes My Friend Irma #3 on?)
Marvel Comics (A Lovers Mag.): Dec, 1949 - No. 2, Mar, 1950

	GD 2.0	VG 4.0	FN 6.0	VF 8.0	VF/NM 9.0	NM- 9.2
1,2-Photo-c	15	30	45	86	133	180

MY EXPERIENCE (Formerly All Top; becomes Judy Canova #23 on)
Fox Feature Syndicate: No. 19, Sept, 1949 - No. 22, Mar, 1950

	GD 2.0	VG 4.0	FN 6.0	VF 8.0	VF/NM 9.0	NM- 9.2
19,21: 19-Wood-a. 21-Wood-a(2)	26	52	78	152	249	345
20	14	28	42	80	115	150
22-Wood-a (9 pgs.)	22	44	66	128	209	290

MY FAITH IN FRANKIE
DC Comics (Vertigo): March, 2004 - No. 4, June, 2004 ($2.95, limited series)

	GD 2.0	VG 4.0	FN 6.0	VF 8.0	VF/NM 9.0	NM- 9.2
1-4-Mike Carey-s/Sonny Liew & Marc Hempel-a						3.00
TPB (2004, $6.95, digest-size) r/series in B&W; Dead Boy Detectives preview						7.00

MY FAVORITE MARTIAN (TV)
Gold Key: 1/64; No.2, 7/64 - No. 9, 10/66 (No. 1,3-9 have photo-c)

	GD 2.0	VG 4.0	FN 6.0	VF 8.0	VF/NM 9.0	NM- 9.2
1-Russ Manning-a	12	24	36	85	155	225
2	7	14	21	49	80	110
3-9	6	12	18	41	66	90

MY FRIEND IRMA (Radio/TV) (Formerly My Diary? and/or Western Life Romances?)
Marvel/Atlas Comics (BFP): No. 3, June, 1950 - No. 47, Dec, 1954; No. 48, Feb, 1955

	GD 2.0	VG 4.0	FN 6.0	VF 8.0	VF/NM 9.0	NM- 9.2
3-Dan DeCarlo-a in all; 52 pgs. begin, end ?	20	40	60	114	182	250
4-Kurtzman-a (10 pgs.)	19	38	57	111	176	240
5- "Egghead Doodle" by Kurtzman (4 pgs.)	15	30	45	86	133	180
6,8-10: 9-Paper dolls, 1 pg; Millie app. (5 pgs.)	13	26	39	72	101	130
7-One pg. Kurtzman-a	13	26	39	74	105	135
11-23: 23-One pg. Frazetta-a	10	20	30	54	72	90
24-48: 41,48-Stan Lee & Dan DeCarlo app.	9	18	27	47	61	75

MY GIRL PEARL
Atlas Comics: 4/55 - #4, 10/55; #5, 7/57 - #6, 9/57; #7, 8/60 - #11, ?/61

	GD 2.0	VG 4.0	FN 6.0	VF 8.0	VF/NM 9.0	NM- 9.2
1-Dan DeCarlo-c/a in #1-6	15	30	45	90	140	190
2	10	20	30	56	76	95
3-6	9	18	27	47	61	75
7-11	5	10	15	30	48	65

MY GREATEST ADVENTURE (Doom Patrol #86 on)
National Periodical Publications: Jan-Feb, 1955 - No. 85, Feb, 1964

	GD 2.0	VG 4.0	FN 6.0	VF 8.0	VF/NM 9.0	NM- 9.2
1-Before CCA	124	248	372	1054	2077	3100
2	47	94	141	376	726	1075
3-5	34	68	102	262	506	750
6-10: 6-Science fiction format begins	28	56	84	204	395	585
11-14: 12-1st S.A. issue	21	42	63	148	287	425
15-17: Kirby-a in all	22	44	66	161	311	460
18-Kirby-c/a	25	50	75	183	354	525
19,22-25	17	34	51	122	236	350
20,21,28-Kirby-a	20	40	60	146	283	420
26,27,29,30	14	28	42	97	181	265
31-40	11	22	33	80	145	210
41,42,44-57,59	10	20	30	68	119	170
43-Kirby-a	10	20	30	73	129	185
58,60,61-Toth-a; Last 10¢ issue	10	20	30	70	123	175
62-76,78,79: 79-Promotes "Legion of the Strange" for next issue; renamed Doom Patrol for #80	8	16	24	54	90	125
77-Toth-a; Robotman prototype	8	16	24	56	93	130
80-(6/63)-Intro/origin Doom Patrol and begin series; origin & 1st app. Negative Man, Elasti-Girl & S.A. Robotman	50	100	150	400	775	1150
81,85-Toth-a	18	36	54	129	252	375
82-84	17	34	51	122	236	350

NOTE: ***Anderson*** *a-42.* ***Cameron*** *a-24.* ***Colan*** *a-77.* ***Meskin*** *a-25, 26, 32, 39, 45, 50, 56, 57, 61, 64, 70, 73, 74, 76, 79; c-76.* ***Moreira*** *a-11, 12, 15, 17, 20, 23, 25, 27, 37, 40-43, 46, 48, 55-57, 59, 60, 62-65, 67, 69, 70; c-1-4, 7-10.* ***Roussos*** *c/a-71-73.* ***Wildey*** *a-32.*

MY GREAT LOVE (Becomes Will Rogers Western #5)
Fox Feature Syndicate: Oct, 1949 - No. 4, Apr, 1950

	GD 2.0	VG 4.0	FN 6.0	VF 8.0	VF/NM 9.0	NM- 9.2
1	15	30	45	90	140	190
2-4	10	20	30	56	76	95

MY INTIMATE AFFAIR (Inside Crime #3)
Fox Feature Syndicate: Mar, 1950 - No. 2, May, 1950

	GD 2.0	VG 4.0	FN 6.0	VF 8.0	VF/NM 9.0	NM- 9.2
1	15	30	45	90	140	190
2	10	20	30	56	76	95

MY LIFE (Formerly Meet Corliss Archer)
Fox Feature Syndicate: No. 4, Sept, 1948 - No. 15, July, 1950

	GD 2.0	VG 4.0	FN 6.0	VF 8.0	VF/NM 9.0	NM- 9.2
4-Used in SOTI, pg. 39; Kamen/Feldstein-a	40	80	120	246	411	575
5-Kamen-a	24	48	72	142	234	325
6-Kamen/Feldstein-a	27	54	81	158	259	360
7-Wood-a; wash cover	21	42	63	124	202	280
8,9,11-15	13	26	39	72	101	130
10-Wood-a	19	38	57	112	179	245

MY LITTLE MARGIE (TV)
Charlton Comics: July, 1954 - No. 54, Nov, 1964

	GD 2.0	VG 4.0	FN 6.0	VF 8.0	VF/NM 9.0	NM- 9.2
1-Photo front/back-c	37	74	111	218	354	490
2-Photo front/back-c	18	36	54	107	169	230
3-7,10	12	24	36	69	97	125
8,9-Infinity-c	13	26	39	72	101	130
11-14: Part-photo-c (#13, 8/56)	10	20	30	58	79	100
15-19	10	20	30	54	72	90
20-(25¢, 100 pg. issue)	15	30	45	86	133	180
21-40: 40-Last 10¢ issue	5	10	15	32	51	70
41-53	4	8	12	28	44	60

54-(11/64) Beatles on cover; lead story spoofs the Beatle haircut craze of the 1960's;

My Love Life #11 © FOX

My Name is Bruce #1 © My Name is Bruce

My Only Love #8 © CC

	GD 2.0	VG 4.0	FN 6.0	VF 8.0	VF/NM 9.0	NM- 9.2
Beatles app. (scarce)	16	32	48	115	220	325

NOTE: *Doll cut-outs in 32, 33, 40, 45, 50.*

MY LITTLE MARGIE'S BOY FRIENDS (TV) (Freddy V2#12 on)
Charlton Comics: Aug, 1955 - No. 11, Apr?, 1958

	GD	VG	FN	VF	VF/NM	NM-
1-Has several Archie swipes	15	30	45	84	127	170
2	9	18	27	52	69	85
3-11	8	16	24	44	57	70

MY LITTLE MARGIE'S FASHIONS (TV)
Charlton Comics: Feb, 1959 - No. 5, Nov, 1959

	GD	VG	FN	VF	VF/NM	NM-
1	14	28	42	76	108	140
2-5	8	16	24	44	57	70

MY LOVE (Becomes Two Gun Western #5 (11/50) on?)
Marvel Comics (CLDS): July, 1949 - No. 4, Apr, 1950 (All photo-c)

	GD	VG	FN	VF	VF/NM	NM-
1	16	32	48	94	147	200
2,3	11	22	33	62	86	110
4-Bettie Page photo-c (see Cupid #2)	40	80	120	246	411	575

MY LOVE
Marvel Comics Group: Sept, 1969 - No. 39, Mar, 1976

	GD	VG	FN	VF	VF/NM	NM-
1	7	14	21	49	80	110
2-9: 4-6-Colan-a	4	8	12	26	41	55
10-Williamson-r/My Own Romance #71; Kirby-a	4	8	12	28	44	60
11-13,15-19	4	8	12	22	34	45
14-(52 pgs.)-Woodstock-c/sty; Morrow-c/a; Kirby/Colletta-r	6	12	18	37	59	80
20-Starlin-a	4	8	12	24	37	50
21,22,24-27,29-38: 38-Reprints	3	6	9	20	30	40
23-Steranko-r/Our Love Story #5	4	8	12	24	37	50
28-Kirby-a	3	6	9	21	32	42
39-Last issue; reprints	3	6	9	21	32	42
Special 1 (12/71)(52 pgs.)	5	10	15	32	51	70

NOTE: ***John Buscema** a-1-7, 10, 18-21, 22r(2), 24r, 25r, 29r, 34r, 36r, 37r, Spec. (r)(4); c-13, 15, 25, 27, Spec. **Colan** a-4, 5, 6, 8, 9, 16, 17, 20, 21, 22, 24r, 27r, 30r, 35r, 39r. **Colan/Everett** a-13, 15, 16, 27(r/#13). **Kirby** a-(r)-10, 14, 26, 28. **Romita** a-1-3, 19, 20, 25, 34, 38; c-1-3, 15.*

MY LOVE AFFAIR (March of Crime #7 on)
Fox Feature Syndicate: July, 1949 - No. 6, May, 1950

	GD	VG	FN	VF	VF/NM	NM-
1	15	30	45	90	140	190
2	10	20	30	56	76	95
3-6-Wood-a. 5-(3/50)-Becomes Love Stories #6	19	38	57	109	172	235

MY LOVE LIFE (Formerly Zegra)
Fox Feature Synd.: No. 6, June, 1949 - No. 13, Aug, 1950; No. 13, Sept, 1951

	GD	VG	FN	VF	VF/NM	NM-
6-Kamenish-a	15	30	45	90	140	190
7-13	10	20	30	58	79	100
13 (9/51)(Formerly My Story #12)	10	20	30	54	72	90

MY LOVE MEMOIRS (Formerly Women Outlaws; Hunted #13 on)
Fox Feature Syndicate: No. 9, Nov, 1949 - No. 12, May, 1950

	GD	VG	FN	VF	VF/NM	NM-
9,11,12-Wood-a	19	38	57	109	172	235
10	10	20	30	58	79	100

MY LOVE SECRET (Formerly Phantom Lady; Animal Crackers #31)
Fox Feature Syndicate/M. S. Distr.: No. 24, June, 1949 - No. 30, June, 1950; No. 53, 1954

	GD	VG	FN	VF	VF/NM	NM-
24-Kamen/Feldstein-a	19	38	57	112	179	245
25-Possible caricature of Wood on-c?	14	28	42	76	108	140
26,28-Wood-a	19	38	57	109	172	235
27,29,30: 30-Photo-c	11	22	33	64	90	115
53-(Reprint, M.S. Distr.) 1954? nd given; formerly Western Thrillers; becomes Crimes by Women #54; photo-c	7	14	21	37	46	55

MY LOVE STORY (Hoot Gibson Western #5 on)
Fox Feature Syndicate: Sept, 1949 - No. 4, Mar, 1950

	GD	VG	FN	VF	VF/NM	NM-
1	15	30	45	90	140	190
2	10	20	30	56	76	95
3,4-Wood-a	19	38	57	109	172	235

MY LOVE STORY
Atlas Comics (GPS): April, 1956 - No. 9, Aug, 1957

	GD	VG	FN	VF	VF/NM	NM-
1	14	28	42	76	108	140
2	8	16	24	44	57	70
3,7: Matt Baker-a. 7-Toth-a	11	22	33	60	83	105
4-6,8,9	8	16	24	42	54	65

NOTE: ***Brewster** a-3. **Colletta** a-1(2), 3, 4(2), 5; c-3.*

MY NAME IS BRUCE
Dark Horse Comics: Sept, 2008 ($3.50, one-shot)

	GD	VG	FN	VF	VF/NM	NM-
nn-Adaptation of the Bruce Campbell movie; Cliff Richards-a/Bart Sears-c						3.50

MY NAME IS HOLOCAUST
DC Comics: May, 1995 - No. 5, Sept, 1995 ($2.50, limited series)

	GD	VG	FN	VF	VF/NM	NM-
1-5						2.50

MY ONLY LOVE
Charlton Comics: July, 1975 - No. 9, Nov, 1976

	GD	VG	FN	VF	VF/NM	NM-
1	3	6	9	14	19	24
2,4-9	2	4	6	9	13	16
3-Toth-a	2	4	6	11	16	20

MY OWN ROMANCE (Formerly My Romance; Teen-Age Romance #77 on)
Marvel/Atlas (MjPC/RCM No. 4-59/ZPC No. 60-76): No. 4, Mar, 1949 - No. 76, July, 1960

	GD	VG	FN	VF	VF/NM	NM-
4-Photo-c	16	32	48	94	147	200
5-10: 5,6,8-10-Photo-c	11	22	33	62	86	110
11-20: 14-Powell-a	10	20	30	56	76	95
21-42,55: 42-Last precode (2/55). 55-Toth-a	9	18	27	52	69	85
43-54,56-60	5	10	15	32	51	70
61-70,72,73,75,76	4	8	12	28	44	60
71-Williamson-a	5	10	15	34	55	75
74-Kirby-a	5	10	15	34	55	75

NOTE: ***Brewster** a-59. **Colletta** a-45(2), 48, 50, 55, 57(2), 59; c-58i, 59, 61. **Everett** a-25; c-58p. **Kirby** c-71, 75, 76. **Morisi** a-18. **Orlando** a-61. **Romita** a-36. **Tuska** a-10.*

MY PAL DIZZY (See Comic Books, Series I)

MY PAST (...Confessions) (Formerly Western Thrillers)
Fox Feature Syndicate: No. 7, Aug, 1949 - No. 11, Apr, 1950 (Crimes Inc. #12)

	GD	VG	FN	VF	VF/NM	NM-
7	15	30	45	90	140	190
8-10	10	20	30	56	76	95
11-Wood-a	19	38	57	109	172	235

MY PERSONAL PROBLEM
Ajax/Farrell/Steinway Comic: 11/55; No. 2, 2/56; No. 3, 9/56 - No. 4, 11/56; 10/57 - No. 3, 5/58

	GD	VG	FN	VF	VF/NM	NM-
1	9	18	27	52	69	85
2-4	7	14	21	35	43	50
1-3('57-'58)-Steinway	6	12	18	28	34	40

MY PRIVATE LIFE (Formerly Murder, Inc.; becomes Pedro #18)
Fox Feature Syndicate: No. 16, Feb, 1950 - No. 17, April, 1950

	GD	VG	FN	VF	VF/NM	NM-
16,17	14	28	42	80	115	150

MYRA NORTH (See The Comics, Crackajack Funnies & Red Ryder)
Dell Publishing Co.: No. 3, Jan, 1940

	GD	VG	FN	VF	VF/NM	NM-
Four Color 3	95	190	285	603	1039	1475

MY REAL LOVE
Standard Comics: No. 5, June, 1952 (Photo-c)

	GD	VG	FN	VF	VF/NM	NM-
5-Toth-a, 3 pgs.; Tuska, Cardy, Vern Greene-a	14	28	42	76	108	140

MY ROMANCE (Becomes My Own Romance #4 on)
Marvel Comics (RCM): Sept, 1948 - No. 3, Jan, 1949

	GD	VG	FN	VF	VF/NM	NM-
1	19	38	57	111	176	240
2,3: 2-Anti-Wertham editorial (11/48)	13	26	39	74	105	135

MY ROMANTIC ADVENTURES (Formerly Romantic Adventures)
American Comics Group: No. 68, 8/56 - No. 115, 12/60; No. 116, 7/61 - No. 138, 3/64

	GD	VG	FN	VF	VF/NM	NM-
68	8	16	24	40	50	60
69-85	6	12	18	31	38	45
86-Three pg. Williamson-a (2/58)	8	16	24	42	54	65
87-100	3	6	9	18	27	35
101-138	3	6	9	16	22	28

NOTE: ***Whitney** art in most issues.*

MY SECRET (Becomes Our Secret #4 on)
Superior Comics, Ltd.: Aug, 1949 - No. 3, Oct, 1949

	GD	VG	FN	VF	VF/NM	NM-
1	16	32	48	94	147	200
2,3	13	26	39	72	101	130

MY SECRET AFFAIR (Becomes Martin Kane #4)
Hero Book (Fox Feature Syndicate): Dec, 1949 - No. 3, April, 1950

	GD	VG	FN	VF	VF/NM	NM-
1-Harrison/Wood-a (10 pgs.)	23	46	69	136	223	310
2,3-Wood-a	19	38	57	109	172	235

MY SECRET CONFESSION
Sterling Comics: September, 1955

My Secret Marriage #3 © SUPR

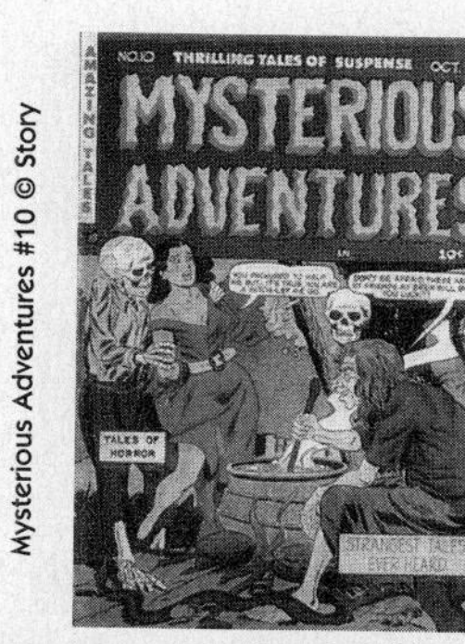

Mysterious Adventures #10 © Story

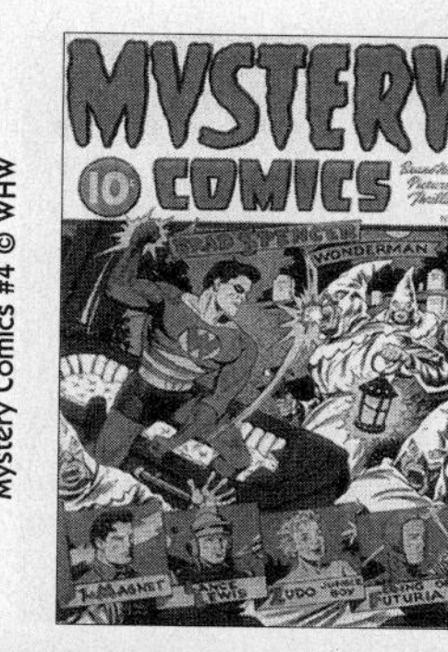

Mystery Comics #4 © WHW

GD 2.0 | VG 4.0 | FN 6.0 | VF 8.0 | VF/NM 9.0 | NM- 9.2

1-Sekowsky-a 9 18 27 52 69 85

MY SECRET LIFE (Formerly Western Outlaws; Romeo Tubbs #26 on)
Fox Feature Syndicate: No. 22, July, 1949 - No. 27, July, 1950; No. 27, 9/51
22 13 26 39 74 105 135
23,26-Wood-a, 6 pgs. 19 38 57 109 172 235
24,25,27 11 22 33 64 90 115
27 (9/51) 10 20 30 56 76 95
NOTE: *The title was changed to Romeo Tubbs after #25 even though #26 & 27 did come out.*

MY SECRET LIFE (Formerly Young Lovers; Sue & Sally Smith #48)
Charlton Comics: No. 19, Aug, 1957 - No. 47, Sept, 1962
19 4 8 12 26 41 55
20-35 3 6 9 16 23 30
36-47: 44-Last 10¢ issue 3 6 9 14 20 26

MY SECRET MARRIAGE
Superior Comics, Ltd.: May, 1953 - No. 24, July, 1956 (Canadian)
1 14 28 42 80 115 150
2 9 18 27 47 61 75
3-24 8 16 24 40 50 60
I.W. Reprint #9 2 4 6 8 11 14
NOTE: *Many issues contain* ***Kamen-ish*** *art.*

MY SECRET ROMANCE (Becomes A Star Presentation #3)
Hero Book (Fox Feature Syndicate): Jan, 1950 - No. 2, March, 1950
1 15 30 45 88 137 185
2-Wood-a 19 38 57 109 172 235

MY SECRETS (Magazine)
Atlas/Seaboard: Feb, 1975 (B&W, 68 pgs.)
Vol. 1 #1 7 14 21 45 73 100

MY SECRET STORY (Formerly Captain Kidd #25; Sabu #30 on)
Fox Feature Syndicate: No. 26, Oct, 1949 - No. 29, April, 1950
26 15 30 45 84 127 170
27-29 10 20 30 56 76 95

MYSPACE DARK HORSE PRESENTS
Dark Horse Books: Sept, 2008; Feb, 2009; Aug, 2009 ($19.95, TPB)
Vol. 1 - Short stories previously appearing on Dark Horse's MySpace.com webpage; s/a by various incl. Whedon, Bá, Bagge, Mignola, Moon, Nord, Trimpe, Warren, Way 20.00
Vol. 2 - Collects stories from online #7-12; s/a by Way, Niles, Dorkin, Hotz & others 20.00
Vol. 3 - Collects stories from online #13-19; s/a by Mignola, Cloonan & others 20.00

MYSTERIES (...Weird & Strange)
Superior/Dynamic Publ. (Randall Publ. Ltd.): May, 1953 - No. 11, Jan, 1955
1-All horror stories 41 82 123 256 428 600
2-A-Bomb blast story 26 52 78 154 252 350
3-11: 10-Kamenish-c/a reprinted from Strange Mysteries #2; cover is from a panel in Strange Mysteries #2 23 46 69 136 223 310

MYSTERIES IN SPACE (See Fireside Book Series)

MYSTERIES OF SCOTLAND YARD (Also see A-1 Comics)
Magazine Enterprises: No. 121, 1954 (one shot)
A-1 121-Reprinted from Manhunt (5 stories) 15 30 45 85 130 175

MYSTERIES OF UNEXPLORED WORLDS (See Blue Bird)(Becomes Son of Vulcan V2#49 on)
Charlton Comics: Aug, 1956; No. 2, Jan, 1957 - No. 48, Sept, 1965
1 37 74 111 222 361 500
2-No Ditko 16 32 48 94 147 200
3,4,8,9 Ditko-a. 3-Diko c/a (4). 4-Ditko c/a (2). 30 60 90 177 289 400
5,6,10,11: 5,6-Ditko-c/a (all). 10-Ditko-c/a(4). 11-Ditko-c/a(3); signed J. Kotdi 31 62 93 186 303 420
7-(2/58, 68 pgs.) 4 stories w/Ditko-a 34 68 102 204 332 460
12-Ditko sty (3); Baker story "The Charm Bracelet" 30 60 90 177 289 400
13-18,20 10 20 30 56 76 95
19,21-24,26-Ditko-a 23 46 69 136 223 310
25,27-30 5 10 15 34 55 75
31-45 4 8 12 26 41 55
46(5/65)-Son of Vulcan begins (origin/1st app.) 4 8 12 28 44 60
47,48 4 8 12 23 34 45
NOTE: ***Ditko*** *c-3-6, 10, 11, 19, 21-24. Covers to #19, 21-24 reprint story panels.*

MYSTERIOUS ADVENTURES
Story Comics: Mar, 1951 - No. 24, Mar, 1955; No. 25, Aug, 1955
1-All horror stories 71 142 213 454 777 1100
2-(6/51) 40 80 120 246 411 575
3,4,6,10 39 78 117 236 388 540
5-Bondage-c 40 80 120 246 411 575
7-Dagger in eye panel; dismemberment stories 44 88 132 277 469 660
8-Eyeball story 51 102 153 318 539 760
9-Extreme violence (8/52) 41 82 123 256 428 600
11-(12/52)-Used in **SOTI**, pg. 84 41 82 123 256 428 600
12,14: 14-E.C. Old Witch swipe 39 78 117 236 388 540
13-Classic skull-c 47 94 141 296 498 700
15-21: 18-Used in Senate Investigative report, pgs. 5,6; E.C. swipe/TFTC #35; The Coffin-Keeper & Corpse (hosts). 20-Used by Wertham in the Senate hearings. 21-Bondage/beheading-c 42 84 126 265 445 625
22- "Cinderella" parody 39 78 117 236 388 540
23-Disbrow-a (6 pgs.); E.C. swipe "The Mystery Keeper's Tale" (host) and "Mother Ghoul's Nursery Tale" 39 78 117 236 388 540
24,25 28 56 84 165 270 375
NOTE: ***Tothish*** *art by* ***Ross Andru****-#22, 23.* ***Bache*** *a-8.* ***Cameron*** *a-5-7.* ***Harrison*** *a-12.* ***Hollingsworth*** *a-3-8, 12.* ***Schaffenberger*** *a-24, 25.* ***Wildey*** *a-15, 17.*

MYSTERIOUS ISLAND
Dell Publishing Co.: No. 1213, July-Sept, 1961
Four Color 1213-Movie, photo-c 8 16 24 56 93 130

MYSTERIOUS ISLE
Dell Publishing Co.: Nov-Jan, 1963/64 (Jules Verne)
1 4 8 12 22 34 45

MYSTERIOUS RIDER, THE (See Zane Grey, 4-Color 301)

MYSTERIOUS STORIES (Formerly Horror From the Tomb #1)
Premier Magazines: No. 2, Dec-Jan, 1954-1955 - No. 7, Dec, 1955
2-Woodbridge-c; last pre-code issue 48 96 144 302 514 725
3-Woodbridge-c/a 34 68 102 204 332 460
4-7: 5-Cinderella parody. 6-Woodbridge-c 31 62 93 186 303 420
NOTE: ***Hollingsworth*** *a-2, 4.*

MYSTERIOUS STRANGER
DC Comics: Aug/Sept. 1952
nn-Ashcan comic, not distributed to newsstands, only for in-house use. Cover art is All Star Western #60 with interior being Sensation Comics #100. A FN/VF copy sold for $2,357.50 in 2002.

MYSTERIOUS SUSPENSE (Also see Blue Beetle #1 (1967))
Charlton Comics: Oct, 1968 (12¢)
1-Return of the Question by Ditko (c/a) 7 14 21 47 76 105

MYSTERIOUS TRAVELER (See Tales of the...)

MYSTERIOUS TRAVELER COMICS (Radio)
Trans-World Publications: Nov, 1948
1-Powell-c/a(2); Poe adaptation, "Tell Tale Heart" 58 116 174 371 636 900

MYSTERIUS
DC Comics (WildStorm): Mar, 2009 - No. 6, Aug, 2009 ($2.99, limited series)
1-6-Jeff Parker-a/Tom Fowler-a 3.00

MYSTERY COMICS
William H. Wise & Co.: 1944 - No. 4, 1944 (No months given)
1-The Magnet, The Silver Knight, Brad Spencer, Wonderman, Dick Devins, King of Futuria, & Zudo the Jungle Boy begin (all 1st app.); Schomburg-c on all 123 246 369 787 1344 1900
2-Bondage-c 69 138 207 442 759 1075
3,4: 3-Lance Lewis, Space Detective begins (1st app.); Robot-c. 4(V2#1 inside) 63 126 189 403 689 975

MYSTERY COMICS DIGEST
Gold Key/Whitman?: Mar, 1972 - No. 26, Oct, 1975
1-Ripley's Believe It or Not; reprint of Ripley's #1 origin Ra-Ka-Tep the Mummy; Wood-a 4 8 12 26 41 55
2-9: 2-Boris Karloff Tales of Mystery; Wood-a; 1st app. Werewolf Count Wulfstein. 3-Twilight Zone (TV); Crandall, Toth & George Evans-a; 1st app. Tragg & Simbar the Lion Lord; (2) Crandall/Frazetta-r/Twilight Zone #1 4-Ripley's Believe It or Not; 1st app. Baron Tibor, the Vampire. 5-Boris Karloff Tales of Mystery; 1st app. Dr. Spektor. 6-Twilight Zone (TV); 1st app. U.S. Marshal Reid & Sir Duane; Evans-r. 7-Ripley's Believe It or Not; origin The Lurker in the Swamp; 1st app. Duroc. 8-Boris Karloff Tales of Mystery; McWilliams-r; Orlando-r. 9-Twilight Zone (TV); Williamson, Crandall, McWilliams-a; 2nd Tragg app.;Torres, Evans, Heck/Tuska-r 3 6 9 20 30 40
10-26: 10,13-Ripley's Believe It or Not: 13-Orlando-r. 11,14-Boris Karloff Tales of Mystery. 14-1st app. Xorkon. 12,15-Twilight Zone (TV). 16,19,22,25-Ripley's Believe It or Not. 17-Boris Karloff Tales of Mystery; Williamson-r; Orlando-r. 18,21,24-Twilight Zone (TV). 20,23,26-Boris Karloff Tales of Mystery 3 6 9 16 23 30

Mystery in Space #24 © DC

Mystery Men Comics #15 © FOX

Mystic #1 © CRO

NOTE: Dr. Spektor app.-#5, 10-12, 21. Durak app.-#15. Duroc app.-#14 (later called Durak). King George 1st app.-#8.

MYSTERY IN SPACE (Also see Fireside Book Series and Pulp Fiction Library: ...)
National Periodical Pub.: 4-5/51 - No. 110, 9/66; No. 111, 9/80 - No. 117, 3/81 (#1-3: 52 pgs.)

	GD 2.0	VG 4.0	FN 6.0	VF 8.0	VF/NM 9.0	NM- 9.2
1-Frazetta-a, 8 pgs.; Knights of the Galaxy begins, ends #8	242	484	726	2118	4209	6300
2	86	172	258	731	1441	2150
3	67	134	201	570	1123	1675
4,5	55	110	165	468	922	1375
6-10: 7-Toth-a	43	86	129	344	672	1000
11-15	35	70	105	266	516	765
16-18,20-25: Interplanetary Insurance feature by Infantino in all. 21-1st app. Space Cabbie. 24-Last pre-code issue	30	60	90	233	449	665
19-Virgil Finlay-a	33	66	99	252	486	720
26-40: 26-Space Cabbie feature begins. 34-1st S.A. issue	25	50	75	183	354	525
41-52: 47-Space Cabbie feature ends	19	38	57	133	259	385
53-Adam Strange begins (8/59, 10pg. sty); robot-c	154	308	462	1348	2674	4000
54	45	90	135	360	693	1025
55-Grey tone-c	41	82	123	328	639	950
56-60: 59-Kane/Anderson-a	23	46	69	169	327	485
61-71: 61-1st app. Adam Strange foe Ulthoon. 62-1st app. A.S. foe Mortan. 63-Origin Vandor. 66-Star Rovers begin (1st app.). 68-1st app. Dust Devils (6/61). 69-1st Mailbag. 70-2nd app. Dust Devils. 71-Last 10¢ issue	19	38	57	133	259	385
72-74,76-80	13	26	39	95	178	260
75-JLA x-over in Adam Strange (5/62)(sequel to J.L.A. #3, 2nd app. of Kanjar Ro)	23	46	69	169	327	485
81-86	11	22	33	76	136	195
87-(11/63)-Adam Strange/Hawkman double feat begins; 3rd Hawkman tryout series	17	34	51	119	230	340
88-Adam Strange & Hawkman stories	15	30	45	107	204	300
89-Adam Strange & Hawkman stories	15	30	45	104	197	290
90-Book-length Adam Strange & Hawkman story; 1st team-up (3/64); Hawkman moves to own title next month; classic-c	17	34	51	119	230	340
91-102: 91-End Infantino art on Adam Strange; double-length Adam Strange story. 92-Space Ranger begins (6/64), ends #103. 92-94,96,98-Space Ranger-c. 94,98-Adam Strange/Space Ranger team-up. 102-Adam Strange ends (no Space Ranger)	7	14	21	49	80	110
103-Origin Ultra, the Multi-Alien; last Space Ranger	6	12	18	41	66	90
104-110: 110-(9/66)-Last 12¢ issue	5	10	15	32	51	70
V17#111(9/80)-117: 117-Newton-a(3 pgs.)	2	4	6	8	10	12

NOTE: ***Anderson** a-2, 4, 8-10, 12-17, 19, 45-48, 51, 57, 59i, 61-64, 70, 76, 87-91; c-9, 10, 15-25, 87, 89, 105-108, 110. **Aparo** a-111. **Austin** a-112i. **Bolland** a-115. **Craig** a-114, 116. **Ditko** a-111, 114-116. **Drucker** a-13, 14. **Elias** a-98, 102, 103. **Golden** a-113p. **Sid Greene** a-78, 91. **Infantino** a-1-8, 11, 14-25, 27-46, 48, 49, 51, 53-91, 103, 117; c-60-86, 88, 90, 91, 105, 107. **Gil Kane** a-14p, 15p, 18p, 19p, 26p, 29-59p(most), 100-102; c-52, 101. **Kubert** a-113; c-111-115. **Moreira** c-27, 28. **Rogers** a-111. **Sekowsky** a-52. **Simon & Kirby** a-4(2 pgs.). **Spiegle** a-111, 114. **Starlin** c-116. **Sutton** a-112. **Tuska** a-115p, 117p.*

MYSTERY IN SPACE
DC Comics: Nov, 2006 - No. 8, Jul, 2007 ($3.99, limited series)

	GD 2.0	VG 4.0	FN 6.0	VF 8.0	VF/NM 9.0	NM- 9.2
1-8: 1-Captain Comet's rebirth; Starlin-s/Shane Davis-a; The Weird by Starlin						4.00
1-Variant cover by Neal Adams						10.00
Volume One TPB (2007, $17.99) r/#1-5						18.00
Volume Two TPB (2007, $17.99) r/#6-8 and The Weird #1-4						18.00

MYSTERY MEN COMICS
Fox Features Syndicate: Aug, 1939 - No. 31, Feb, 1942

	GD 2.0	VG 4.0	FN 6.0	VF 8.0	VF/NM 9.0	NM- 9.2
1-Intro. & 1st app. The Blue Beetle, The Green Mask, Rex Dexter of Mars by Briefer, Zanzibar by Tuska, Lt. Drake, D-13-Secret Agent by Powell, Chen Chang, Wing Turner, & Captain Denny Scott	1000	2000	3000	7300	12,900	18,500
2-Robot & sci/fi-c (2nd Robot-c w/Movie #6)	337	674	1011	2359	4130	5900
3 (10/39)-Classic Lou Fine-c	432	864	1296	3154	5577	8000
4,5: 4-Capt. Savage begins (11/39)	271	542	813	1734	2967	4200
6-Tuska-c	226	452	678	1446	2473	3500
7-1st Blue Beetle-c app.	284	568	852	1818	3109	4400
8-Lou Fine bondage-c	258	516	774	1651	2826	4000
9-The Moth begins; Lou Fine-c	129	258	387	826	1413	2000
10-12: All Joe Simon-c. 10-Wing Turner by Kirby; Simon bondage-c. 11-Intro. Domino	107	214	321	680	1165	1650
13-Intro. Lynx & sidekick Blackie (8/40)	66	132	198	419	722	1025
14-18	63	126	189	403	689	975
19-Intro. & 1st app. Miss X (ends #21)	66	132	198	419	722	1025
20-31: 26-The Wraith begins	60	120	180	381	658	935

NOTE: ***Briefer** a-1-15, 20, 24; c-9. **Cuidera** a-22. **Lou Fine** c-1-5,8,9. **Powell** a-1-15, 24. **Simon** c-10-12. **Tuska** a-1-16, 22, 24, 27; c-6. Bondage-c 1, 3, 7, 8, 10, 25, 27-29, 31. Blue Beetle c-7, 8, 10-31. D-13 Secret Agent c-6. Green Mask c-1, 3-5. Rex Dexter of Mars c-2, 9.*

MYSTERY MEN MOVIE ADAPTION
Dark Horse Comics: July, 1999 - No. 2, Aug, 1999 ($2.95, mini-series)

	GD 2.0	VG 4.0	FN 6.0	VF 8.0	VF/NM 9.0	NM- 9.2
1,2-Fingerman-s; photo-c						3.00

MYSTERY PLAY, THE
DC Comics (Vertigo): 1994 ($19.95, one-shot)

	GD 2.0	VG 4.0	FN 6.0	VF 8.0	VF/NM 9.0	NM- 9.2
nn-Hardcover-Morrison-s/Muth-painted art						25.00
Softcover ($9.95)-New Muth cover						10.00

MYSTERY TALES
Atlas Comics (20CC): Mar, 1952 - No. 54, Aug, 1957

	GD 2.0	VG 4.0	FN 6.0	VF 8.0	VF/NM 9.0	NM- 9.2
1-Horror/weird stories in all	89	178	267	565	970	1375
2-Krigstein-a	47	94	141	296	498	700
3-10: 6-A-Bomb panel. 10-Story similar to "The Assassin" from Shock SuspenStories	42	84	126	265	445	625
11,13-21: 14-Maneely s/f story. 20-Electric chair issue. 21-Matt Fox-a; decapitation story	30	60	90	177	289	400
12,22: 12-Matt Fox-a. 22-Forte/Matt Fox-c; a(i)	34	68	102	199	325	450
23-26 (2/55)-Last precode issue	24	48	72	142	234	325
27,29-35,37,38,41-43,48,49: 43-Morisi story contains Frazetta art swipes from Untamed Love	20	40	60	115	185	255
28,36,39,40,45: 28-Jack Katz-a. 36,39-Krigstein-a. 40,45-Ditko-a (#45 is 3 pgs. only)	20	40	60	118	192	265
44,51-Williamson/Krenkel-a	21	42	63	124	202	280
46-Williamson/Krenkel-a; Crandall text illos	21	42	63	124	202	280
47-Crandall, Ditko, Powell-a	21	42	63	124	202	280
50,52,53: 50-Torres, Morrow-a	20	40	60	115	185	255
54-Crandall, Check-a	20	40	60	118	192	265

NOTE: ***Ayers** a-18, 49, 52. **Berg** a-17, 51. **Colan** a-1, 3, 18, 35, 43. **Colletta** a-18. **Drucker** a-41. **Everett** a-2, 29, 33, 35, 41; c-8-11, 14, 38, 39, 41, 43, 44, 46, 48-51, 53. **Fass** a-16. **Forte** a-21, 22, 45, 46. **Matt Fox** a-12?, 21, 22; c-22. **Heath** a-3; c-3, 15, 17, 26. **Heck** a-25. **Kinstler** a-15. **Mort Lawrence** a-26, 32, 34. **Maneely** a-1, 9, 14, 22; c-12, 23, 24, 27. **Mooney** a-3, 40. **Morisi** a-43, 49, 52. **Morrow** a-50. **Orlando** a-51. **Pakula** a-16. **Powell** a-21, 29, 37, 38, 47. **Reinman** a-1, 14, 17. **Robinson** a-7p, 42. **Romita** a-37. **Roussos** a-4, 44. **R.Q. Sale** a-45, 46, 49. **Severin** c-52. **Shores** a-17, 45. **Tuska** a-10, 12, 14. **Whitney** a-2. **Wildey** a-37.*

MYSTERY TALES
Super Comics: 1964

	GD 2.0	VG 4.0	FN 6.0	VF 8.0	VF/NM 9.0	NM- 9.2
Super Reprint #16,17('64): 16-r/Tales of Horror #2. 17-r/Eerie #14(Avon), 18-Kubert-r/Strange Terrors #4	3	6	9	14	20	25

MYSTERY TRAIL
DC Comics: Feb/Mar 1950

nn - Ashcan comic, not distributed to newsstands, only for in-house use. Cover art is Danger Trail #3 with interior being Star Spangled Comics #109. A FN/VF copy sold for $2,357.50 in 2002.

MYSTIC (3rd Series)
Marvel/Atlas Comics (CLDS 1/CSI 2-21/OMC 22-35/CSI 35-61): March, 1951 - No. 61, Aug, 1957

	GD 2.0	VG 4.0	FN 6.0	VF 8.0	VF/NM 9.0	NM- 9.2
1-Atom bomb panels; horror/weird stories in all	94	188	282	597	1024	1450
2	50	100	150	315	533	750
3-Eyes torn out	45	90	135	284	480	675
4- "The Devil Birds" by Wolverton (6 pgs.)	81	162	243	518	884	1250
5,7-10	37	74	111	222	361	500
6- "The Eye of Doom" by Wolverton (7 pgs.)	81	162	243	518	884	1250
11-20: 16-Bondage/torture c/story	30	60	90	177	289	400
21-25,27-36-Last precode (3/55). 25-E.C. swipe	24	48	72	142	234	325
26-Atomic War story; severed head story/cover	28	56	84	165	270	375
37-51,53-56,61	20	40	60	118	192	265
52-Wood-a; Crandall-a?	22	44	66	128	209	290
57-Story "Trapped in the Ant-Hill" (1957) is very similar to "The Man in the Ant Hill" in TTA #27	24	48	72	140	230	320
58,59-Krigstein-a	20	40	60	120	195	270
60-Williamson/Mayo-a (4 pgs.)	20	40	60	120	195	270

NOTE: ***Andru** a-23, 25. **Ayers** a-35, 53; c-8. **Berg** a-49. **Cameron** a-49, 51. **Check** a-31, 60. **Colan** a-3, 7, 12, 21, 37, 60. **Colletta** a-29. **Drucker** a-46, 52, 56. **Everett** a-8, 9, 17, 40, 44, 57; c-13, 18, 21, 42, 47, 49, 51-55, 57-59, 61. **Forte** a-35, 52, 58. **Fox** a-24i. **Al Hartley** a-35. **Heath** a-10; c-10, 20, 22, 23, 25, 30. **Infantino** a-12. **Kane** a-8, 24p. **Jack Katz** a-31, 33. **Mort Law.rence** a-19, 37. **Maneely** a-22, 24, 58; c-7, 15, 28, 29, 31. **Moldoff** a-29. **Morisi** a-48, 49, 52. **Morrow** a-51. **Orlando** a-57, 61. **Pakula** a-52, 57, 59. **Powell** a-52, 54-56. **Robinson** a-5. **Romita** a-11, 15. **R.Q. Sale** a-35, 53, 58. **Sekowsky** a-1, 2, 4, 5. **Severin** c-56, 60. **Tuska** a-15. **Whitney** a-33. **Wildey** a-28, 30. **Ed Win** a-17, 20. Canadian reprints known-title 'Startling.'*

MYSTIC (Also see CrossGen Chronicles)
CrossGeneration Comics: Jul, 2000 - No. 43, Jan, 2004 ($2.95)

	GD 2.0	VG 4.0	FN 6.0	VF 8.0	VF/NM 9.0	NM- 9.2
1-43: 1-Marz-s/Peterson & Dell-a. 15-Cameos by DC & Marvel characters						3.00
...: Rite of Passage Vol. 1 TPB (5/01, $19.95) r/#1-7; Linsner-c						20.00
...: The Demon Queen Vol. 2 TPB (2002, $19.95) r/#8-14						20.00
...: Siege of Scales Vol. 3 TPB (2002, $15.95) r/#15-20						16.00

Mystic Arcana #3 © MAR

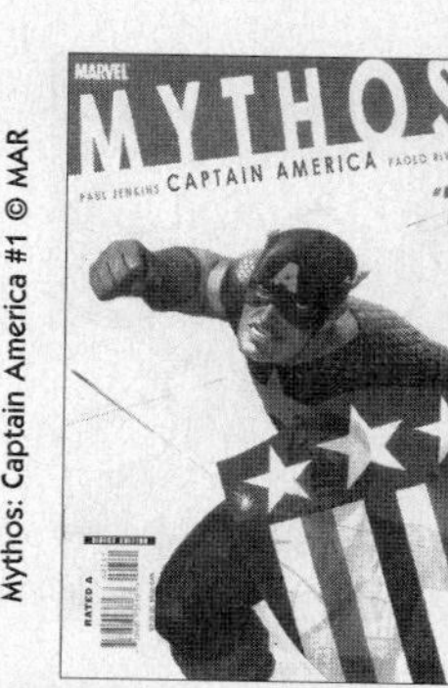

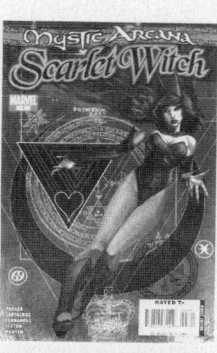

Mythos: Captain America #1 © MAR

The Names of Magic #1 © DC

GD VG FN VF VF/NM NM-
2.0 4.0 6.0 8.0 9.0 9.2

...: Out All Night Vol.4 TPB (2003, $15.95) r/#21-26 16.00
Vol. 5: Master Class (2003, $15.95) r/#27-32 16.00

MYSTICAL TALES
Atlas Comics (CCC 1/EPI 2-8): June, 1956 - No. 8, Aug, 1957

1-Everett-c/a 48 96 144 302 514 725
2-4: 2-Berg-a. 3,4-Crandall-a. 26 52 78 154 252 350
5-Williamson-a (4 pgs.) 28 56 84 165 270 375
6-Torres, Krigstein-a 25 50 75 147 241 335
7-Bolle, Forte, Torres, Orlando-a 24 48 72 142 234 325
8-Krigstein, Check-a 25 50 75 147 241 335
NOTE: ***Everett** a-1; c-1-4, 6, 7. **Orlando** a-1, 2, 7. **Pakula** a-3. **Powell** a-1, 4.*

MYSTIC ARCANA
Marvel Comics: Aug, 2007 - Jan, 2008 ($2.99)

1-Magik on-c; art by Scott and Nguyen; Ian McNee and Dani Moonstar app. 3.00
(#2)...: Black Knight 1 (9/07, $2.99) Djurdjevic-c/Grummett & Hanna-a; origin retold 3.00
3-("Scarlet Witch" on cover)(10/07, $2.99) Djurdjevic-c/Santacruz-a; childhood 3.00
(#4)...: Sister Grimm 1 (1/08, $2.99) Nico Minoru from Runaways; Djurdjevic-c/Noto-a 3.00
...: The Book of Marvel Magic ('07, $3.99) Official Handbook profiles of the magic-related 4.00
HC (2007, $24.99, d.j.) r/series and ...: The Book of Marvel Magic 25.00

MYSTIC COMICS (1st Series)
Timely Comics (TPI 1-5/TCI 8-10): March, 1940 - No. 10, Aug, 1942

1-Origin The Blue Blaze, The Dynamic Man, & Flexo the Rubber Robot; Zephyr Jones, 3X's & Deep Sea Demon app.; The Magician begins (all 1st app.); c-from Spider pulp V18#1, 6/39 1385 2770 4155 10,500 18,750 27,000
2-The Invisible Man & Master Mind Excello begin; Space Rangers, Zara of the Jungle, Taxi Taylor app. (scarce) 497 994 1491 3628 6414 9200
3-Origin Hercules, who last appears in #4 349 698 1047 2443 4272 6100
4-Origin The Thin Man & The Black Widow; Merzak the Mystic app.; last Flexo, Dynamic Man, Invisible Man & Blue Blaze (some issues have date sticker on cover; others have July w/August overprint in silver color); Roosevelt assassination-c 389 778 1167 2723 4762 6800
5-(3/41)-Origin The Black Marvel, The Blazing Skull, The Sub-Earth Man, Super Slave & The Terror; The Moon Man & Black Widow app.; 5-German war-c begin, end #10 360 720 1080 2520 4410 6300
6-(10/41)-Origin The Challenger & The Destroyer (1st app.?; also see All-Winners #2, Fall, 1941) 423 846 1269 3067 5384 7700
7-The Witness begins (12/41, origin & 1st app.); origin Davey & the Demon; last Black Widow; Hitler opens his trunk of terror-c by Simon & Kirby (classic-c) 454 908 1362 3314 5857 8400
8,10: 10-Father Time, World of Wonder, & Red Skeleton app.; last Challenger & Terror 290 580 870 1856 3178 4500
9-Gary Gaunt app.; last Black Marvel, Mystic & Blazing Skull; Hitler-c 300 600 900 2010 3505 5000
NOTE: ***Gabrielle** c-8-10. **Kirby/Schomburg** c-6. **Rico** a-9(2). **Schomburg** a-1-4; c-1-5. **Sekowsky** a-9. **Sekowsky/Klein** a-8(Challenger). Bondage c-1, 2, 9.*

MYSTIC COMICS (2nd Series)
Timely Comics (ANC): Oct, 1944 - No. 3, Win, 1944-45; No. 4, Mar, 1945

1-The Angel, The Destroyer, The Human Torch, Terry Vance the Schoolboy Sleuth, & Tommy Tyme begin 277 554 831 1759 3030 4300
2-(Fall/44)-Last Human Torch & Terry Vance; bondage/hypo-c 142 284 426 909 1555 2200
3-Last Angel (two stories) & Tommy Tyme 127 254 381 807 1391 1975
4-The Young Allies-c & app.; Schomburg-c 116 232 348 742 1271 1800

MYSTIC COMICS 70th ANNIVERARY SPECIAL
Marvel Comics: Oct, 2009 ($3.99, one-shot)

1-New story of The Vision; r/G.A. Vision app. from Marvel Myst. Comics #13 & 16 4.00

MYSTIC EDGE (Manga)
Antarctic Press: Oct, 1998 ($2.95, one-shot)

1-Ryan Kinnaird-s/a/c 3.00

MYSTIC HANDS OF DR. STRANGE
Marvel Comics: May, 2010 ($3.99, B&W, one-shot)

1-Short stories; art by Irving, Brunner, McKeever & Marcos Martin; Parrillo-c 4.00

MYSTIQUE (See X-Men titles)
Marvel Comics: June, 2003 - No. 24, Apr, 2005 ($2.99)

1-24: 1-6-Linsner-c/Vaughan-s/Lucas-a. 7-Ryan-a begins. 8-Horn-c. 9-24-Mayhew-c 23-Wolverine & Rogue app. 3.00
... Vol. 1: Drop Dead Gorgeous TPB (2004, $14.99) r/#1-6 15.00
... Vol. 2: Tinker, Tailor, Mutant, Spy TPB (2004, $17.99) r/#7-13 18.00
... Vol. 3: Unnatural TPB (2004, $13.99) r/#14-18 14.00

GD VG FN VF VF/NM NM-
2.0 4.0 6.0 8.0 9.0 9.2

MYSTIQUE & SABRETOOTH (Sabretooth and Mystique on-c)
Marvel Comics: Dec, 1996 - No. 4, Mar, 1997 ($1.95, limited series)

1-4: Characters from X-Men 3.00

MY STORY (...True Romances in Pictures #5,6; becomes My Love Life #13) (Formerly Zago)
Hero Books (Fox Features Syndicate): No. 5, May, 1949 - No. 12, Aug, 1950

5-Kamen/Feldstein-a 21 42 63 122 199 275
6-8,11,12: 12-Photo-c 12 24 36 69 97 125
9,10-Wood-a 19 38 57 109 172 235

MYTHOS
Marvel Comics: Mar, 2006 - Dec, 2007 ($3.99)

1-Retelling of X-Men #1 with painted-a by Paolo Rivera; Paul Jenkins-s 4.00
...: Captain America 1 (8/08) Retelling of origin; painted-a by Rivera; Jenkins-s 4.00
...: Fantastic Four 1 (12/07) Retelling of Fantastic Four #1; painted-a by Rivera; Jenkins-s 4.00
...: Ghost Rider 1 (3/07) Retelling of Marvel Spotlight #5; painted-a by Rivera; Jenkins-s 4.00
...: Hulk 1 (10/06) Retelling of Incredible Hulk #1; painted-a by Rivera; Jenkins-s 4.00
...: Spider-Man 1 (8/07) Retelling of Amazing Fantasy #15; painted-a by Rivera; Jenkins-s 4.00

MYTHOS: THE FINAL TOUR
DC Comics/Vertigo: Dec, 1996 - No. 3, Feb, 1997 ($5.95, limited series)

1-3: 1-Ney Rieber-s/Amaro-a. 2-Snejbjerg-a; Constantine-app. 3-Kristiansen-a; Black Orchid-app. 6.00

MYTHSTALKERS
Image Comics: Mar, 2003 - No. 8, Mar, 2004 ($2.95)

1-8-Jiro-a 3.00

MY TRUE LOVE (Formerly Western Killers #64; Frank Buck #70 on)
Fox Features Syndicate: No. 65, July, 1949 - No. 69, March, 1950

65 16 32 48 94 147 200
66,68,69: 69-Morisi-a 12 24 36 67 94 120
67-Wood-a 19 38 57 109 172 235

NAIL, THE
Dark Horse Comics: June, 2004 - No. 4, Oct, 2004 ($2.99, limited series)

1-4-Rob Zombie & Steve Niles-s/Nat Jones-a/Simon Bisley-c 3.00
TPB (2005, $12.95) r/series 13.00

NAKED BRAIN (Marc Hempel's...)
Insight Studios Group: 2002 - No. 3, 2002 ($2.95, B&W, limited series)

1-3-Marc Hempel cartoons and sketches; Tug & Buster app. 3.00

NAKED PREY, THE (See Movie Classics)

'NAM, THE (See Savage Tales #1, 2nd series & Punisher Invades...)
Marvel Comics Group: Dec, 1986 - No. 84, Sept, 1993

1-Golden a(p)/c begins, ends #13 5.00
1 (2nd printing) 2.50
2-7,9-19,21-66,70-74: 7-Golden-a (2 pgs.). 32-Death R. Kennedy. 52,53-Frank Castle (The Punisher) app. 52,53-Gold 2nd printings. 58-Silver logo. 65-Heath-c/a. 70-Lomax scripts begin 3.00
8-1st app. Fudd Verzyl, Tunnel Rat 4.00
20-2nd app. Fudd Verzyl, Tunnel Rat 3.50
67-69,76-84: 67-69-Punisher 3 part story 3.00
75-($2.25, 52 pgs.) 6.00
Trade Paperback 1,2: 1-r/#1-4. 2-r/#5-8 5.00
TPB ('99, $14.95) r/#1-4; recolored 15.00

'NAM MAGAZINE, THE
Marvel Comics: Aug, 1988 - No. 10, May, 1989 ($2.00, B&W, 52pgs.)

1-10: Each issue reprints 2 issues of the comic 3.00

NAMELESS, THE
Image Comics: May, 1997 - No. 5, Sept, 1997 ($2.95, B&W)

1-5: Pruett/Hester-s/a 3.00
...: The Director's Cut TPB (2006, $15.99) r/#1-5; original proposal by Pruett 16.00

NAMES OF MAGIC, THE (Also see Books of Magic)
DC Comics (Vertigo): Feb, 2001 - No. 5, June, 2001 ($2.50, limited series)

1-5: Bolton painted-c on all; Case-a; leads into Hunter: The Age of Magic 2.50
TPB (2002, $14.95) r/#1-5 15.00

NAME OF THE GAME, THE
DC Comics: 2001 ($29.95, graphic novel)

Hardcover ($29.95) Will Eisner-s/a 30.00

NAMOR (Volume 2)
Marvel Comics: June, 2003 - No. 12, May, 2004 (25¢/$2.25/$2.99)

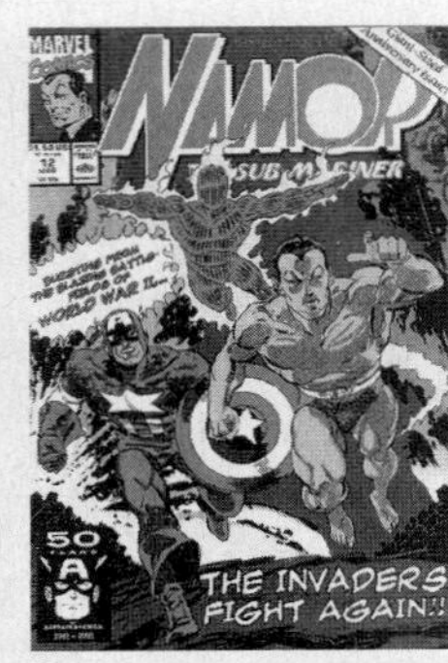

Namor, The Sub-Mariner #12 © MAR

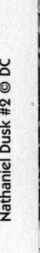

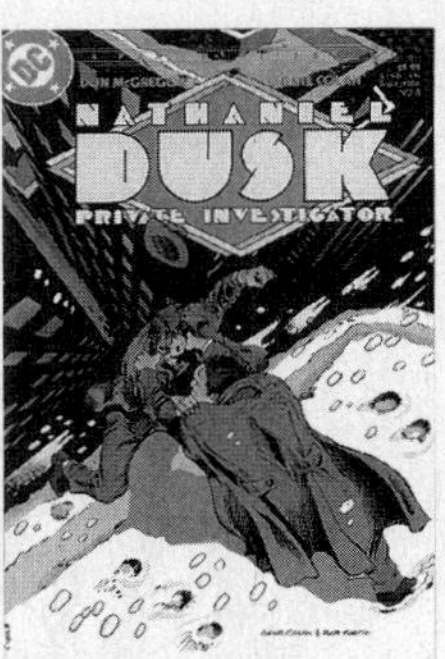

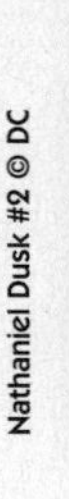
Nathaniel Dusk #2 © DC

National Comics #29 © QUA

GD 2.0 | VG 4.0 | FN 6.0 | VF 8.0 | VF/NM 9.0 | NM- 9.2

GD 2.0 | VG 4.0 | FN 6.0 | VF 8.0 | VF/NM 9.0 | NM- 9.2

1-(25¢-c)Young Namor in the 1920s; Larroca-c/a 2.50
2-6-($2.25) Larroca-a 2.50
7-12-($2.99): 7-Olliffe-a begins 3.00

NAMORA (See Marvel Mystery Comics #82 & Sub-Mariner Comics)
Marvel Comics (PrPI): Fall, 1948 - No. 3, Dec, 1948

1-Sub-Mariner x-over in Namora; Namora by Everett(2), Sub-Mariner by Rico (10 pgs.) 274 548 822 1740 2995 4250
2-The Blonde Phantom & Sub-Mariner story; Everett-a 148 296 444 947 1624 2300
3-(Scarce)-Sub-Mariner app.; Everett-a 155 310 465 992 1696 2400

NAMOR, THE SUB-MARINER (See Prince Namor & Sub-Mariner)
Marvel Comics: Apr, 1990 - No. 62, May, 1995 ($1.00/$1.25/$1.50)

1-Byrne-c/a/scripts in 1-25 (scripts only #26-32) 4.00
2-5: 5-Iron Man app. 3.00
6-11,13-23,25,27-49,51-62: 16-Re-intro Iron Fist (8-cameo only). 18-Punisher cameo (1 panel); 21-23,25-Wolverine cameos. 22,23-Iron Fist app. 28-Iron Fist-c/story. 31-Dr. Doom-c/story. 33,34-Iron Fist cameo. 35-New Tiger Shark-c/story. 37-Aqua holografx foil-c. 48-The Thing app. 2.50
12,24: 12-(52pgs.)-Re-intro. The Invaders. 24-Namor vs. Wolverine 3.00
26-Namor w/new costume; 1st Jae Lee-c/a this title (5/92) & begins 3.50
50-($1.75, 52 pgs.)-Newsstand ed.; w/bound-in S-M trading card sheet (both versions) 2.50
50-($2.95, 52 pgs.)-Collector edition w/foil-c 3.00
Annual 1-4 ('91-94, 68 pgs.): 1-3 pg. origin recap. 2-Return/Defenders. 3-Bagged w/card. 4-Painted-c 3.00

NOTE: ***Jae Lee** a-26-30p, 31-37, 38p, 39, 40; c-26-40.*

NANCY AND SLUGGO (See Comics On Parade & Sparkle Comics)
United Features Syndicate: No. 16, 1949 - No. 23, 1954

16(#1) 10 20 30 58 79 100
17-23 8 16 24 40 50 60

NANCY & SLUGGO (Nancy #146-173; formerly Sparkler Comics)
St. John/Dell #146-187/Gold Key #188 on: No. 121, Apr, 1955-No. 192, Oct, 1963

121(4/55)(St. John) 10 20 30 54 72 90
122-145(7/57)(St. John) 8 16 24 44 57 70
146(9/57)-Peanuts begins, ends #192 (Dell) 9 18 27 60 100 140
147-161 (Dell) Peanuts in all 7 14 21 47 76 105
162-165,177-180-John Stanley-a 8 16 24 52 86 120
166-176-Oona & Her Haunted House series; Stanley-a 8 16 24 58 97 135
181-187(3-5/62)(Dell) 6 12 18 41 66 90
188(10/62)-192 (Gold Key) 6 12 18 41 66 90
Four Color 1034(9-11/59)-Summer Camp 5 10 15 32 51 70
(See Dell Giant #34, 45 & Dell Giants)

NANNY AND THE PROFESSOR (TV)
Dell Publishing Co.: Aug, 1970 - No. 2, Oct, 1970 (Photo-c)

1-(01-546-008) 5 10 15 32 51 70
2 4 8 12 26 41 55

NAPOLEON
Dell Publishing Co.: No. 526, Dec, 1953

Four Color 526 4 8 12 24 37 50

NAPOLEON & SAMANTHA (See Walt Disney Showcase No. 10)

NAPOLEON & UNCLE ELBY (See Clifford McBride's...)
Eastern Color Printing Co.: July, 1942 (68 pgs.) (One Shot)

1 43 86 129 268 454 640
1945-American Book-Strafford Press (128 pgs.) (8x10-1/2"; B&W reprints; hardcover) 15 30 45 83 124 165

NARRATIVE ILLUSTRATION, THE STORY OF THE COMICS (Also see Good Triumphs Over Evil!)
M.C. Gaines: Summer, 1942 (32 pgs., 7-1/4"x10", B&W w/color inserts)

nn-16 pgs. text with illustrations of ancient art, strips and comic covers; 4 pg. WWII War Bond promo, "The Minute Man Answers the Call" color comic drawn by Shelly and a special 8-page color comic insert of "The Story of Saul" (from Picture Stories from the Bible #10 or soon to appear in PS #10) or "Noah and His Ark" or "The Story of Ruth". Insert has special title page indicating it was part of a Sunday newspaper supplement insert series that had already run in a New England "Sunday Herald." Another version exists with insert from Picture Stories from the Bible #7.
(very rare) Estimated value... 1500.00

NOTE: ***Print, A Quarterly Journal of the Graphic Arts** Vol. 3 No. 2 (88 pg., square bound) features the 1st printing of Narrative Illustration, The Story of The Comics. A VG+ copy sold for $750 in 2005.*

NASCAR HEROES (Also see Promotional Comics section for Free Comic Book Day edition)
Starbridge Media: 2007 - Present ($3.95)

1-3: 1-Origin of fictional racer Jimmy Dash. 3-Origin of the Daytona 500; DeStefano-s 4.00

NASH (WCW Wrestling)
Image Comics: July, 1999 - No. 2, July, 1999 ($2.95)

1,2-Regular and photo-c 3.00
1-($6.95) Photo-split-cover Edition 7.00

NATHANIEL DUSK
DC Comics: Feb, 1984 - No. 4, May, 1984 ($1.25, mini-series, direct sales, Baxter paper)

1-4: 1-Intro/origin; Gene Colan-c/a in all 2.50

NATHANIEL DUSK II
DC Comics: Oct, 1985 - No. 4, Jan, 1986 ($2.00, mini-series, Baxter paper)

1-4: Gene Colan-c/a in all 2.50

NATIONAL COMICS
Quality Comics Group: July, 1940 - No. 75, Nov, 1949

1-Uncle Sam begins (1st app.); origin sidekick Buddy by Eisner; origin Wonder Boy & Kid Dixon; Merlin the Magician (ends #45); Cyclone, Kid Patrol, Sally O'Neil Policewoman, Pen Miller (by Klaus Nordling; ends #22), Prop Powers (ends #26), & Paul Bunyan (ends #22) begin 519 1038 1557 3789 6695 9600
2 242 484 726 1537 2644 3750
3-Last Eisner Uncle Sam 168 336 504 1075 1838 2600
4-Last Cyclone 132 264 396 838 1444 2050
5-(11/40)-Quicksilver begins (1st app.; 3rd w/lightning speed?; re-intro'd by DC in 1993 as Max Mercury in Flash #76, 2nd series); origin Uncle Sam; bondage-c 150 300 450 953 1639 2325
6,8-11: 8-Jack & Jill begins (ends #22). 9-Flag-c 126 252 378 806 1378 1950
7-Classic Lou Fine-c 248 496 744 1575 2713 3850
12 86 172 258 546 936 1325
13-16-Lou Fine-a 87 174 261 552 951 1350
17,19-22: 21-Classic Nazi swastika cover. 22-Last Pen Miller (moves to Crack #23) 68 136 204 435 743 1050
18-(12/41)-Shows Asians attacking Pearl Harbor; on stands one month before actual event 132 264 396 838 1444 2050
23-The Unknown & Destroyer 171 begin 69 138 207 442 759 1075
24-Japanese War-c 69 138 207 442 759 1075
25-30: 25-Nazi drug usage/hypodermic needle in story. 26-Wonder Boy ends. 27- G-2 the Unknown begins (ends #46). 29-Origin The Unknown 48 96 144 302 514 725
31-33: 33-Chic Carter begins (ends #47) 43 86 129 271 461 650
34-37,40: 35-Last Kid Patrol 39 78 117 234 385 535
38-Hitler, Tojo, Mussolini-c 57 114 171 362 619 875
39-Hitler-c 58 116 174 371 636 900
41,43-50: 48-Origin The Whistler 26 52 78 154 252 350
42-The Barker begins (1st app?, 5/44); The Barker covers begin 39 78 117 240 395 550
51-Sally O'Neil by Ward, 8 pgs. (12/45) 30 60 90 117 289 400
52-60 20 40 60 117 189 260
61-67: 67-Format change; Quicksilver app. 15 30 45 88 137 185
68-75: The Barker ends 14 28 42 81 118 155

NOTE: ***Cole** Quicksilver-13; Barker-43; c-43, 46, 47, 49-51. **Crandall** Uncle Sam-11-13 (with **Fine**), 25, 26; c-24-26, 30-33, 43. **Crandall** Paul Bunyan-10-13. **Fine** Uncle Sam-13 (w/**Crandall**), 17, 18; c-1-14, 16, 18, 21. **Gill Fox** c-69-74. **Guardineer** Quicksilver-27, 35. **Gustavson** Quicksilver-14-26. **McWilliams** a-23-28, 55, 57. Uncle Sam c-1-41. Barker c-42-75.*

NATIONAL COMICS (Also see All Star Comics 1999 crossover titles)
DC Comics: May, 1999 ($1.99, one-shot)

1-Golden Age Flash and Mr. Terrific; Waid-s/Lopresti-a 2.50

NATIONAL CRUMB, THE (Magazine-Size)
Mayfair Publications: August, 1975 (52 pgs., B&W) (Satire)

1-Grandenetti-c/a, Ayers-a 2 4 6 11 16 20

NATIONAL VELVET (TV)
Dell Publishing Co./Gold Key: May-July, 1961 - No. 2, Mar, 1963 (All photo-c)

Four Color 1195 (#1) 7 14 21 49 80 110
Four Color 1312, 01-556-207, 12-556-210 (Dell) 4 8 12 28 44 60
1,2: 1(12/62) (Gold Key). 2(3/63) 4 8 12 28 44 60

NATION OF SNITCHES
Piranha Press (DC): 1990 ($4.95, color, 52 pgs.)

nn 5.00

NATION X (X-Men on the Utopia island)
Marvel Comics: Feb, 2010 - No. 4, May, 2010 ($3.99, limited series)

1-4-Short stories by various. 1,4-Allred-a. 2-Choi, Cloonan-a. 4-Doop app. 4.00

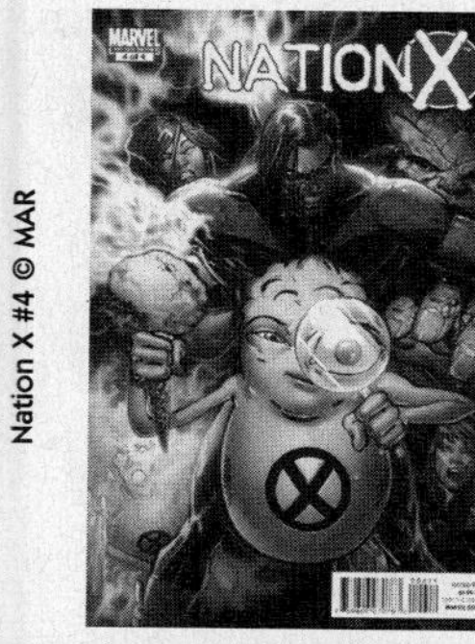
Nation X #4 © MAR

Nature Boy #5 © CC

Negative Burn #48 © Caliber

	GD 2.0	VG 4.0	FN 6.0	VF 8.0	VF/NM 9.0	NM- 9.2
...: X-Factor (3/10, $3.99) David-s/DeLandro-a						4.00

NATURE BOY (Formerly Danny Blaze; Li'l Rascal Twins #6 on)
Charlton Comics: No. 3, March, 1956 - No. 5, Feb, 1957

	GD 2.0	VG 4.0	FN 6.0	VF 8.0	VF/NM 9.0	NM- 9.2
3-Origin; Blue Beetle story; Buscema-c/a	22	44	66	130	213	295
4,5	15	30	45	92	144	195

NOTE: *John Buscema a-3, 4p, 5; c-3. Powell a-4.*

NATURE OF THINGS (Disney, TV/Movie)
Dell Publishing Co.: No. 727, Sept, 1956 - No. 842, Sept, 1957

	GD 2.0	VG 4.0	FN 6.0	VF 8.0	VF/NM 9.0	NM- 9.2
Four Color 727 (#1), 842-Jesse Marsh-a	5	10	15	34	55	75

NAUSICAA OF THE VALLEY OF WIND
Viz Comics: 1988 - No. 7, 1989; 1989 - No. 4, 1990 ($2.50, B&W, 68pgs.)

	GD 2.0	VG 4.0	FN 6.0	VF 8.0	VF/NM 9.0	NM- 9.2
Book 1-7: 1-Contains Moebius poster						3.25
Part II, Book 1-4 ($2.95)						3.25

NAVY ACTION (Sailor Sweeney #12-14)
Atlas Comics (CDS): Aug, 1954 - No. 11, Apr, 1956; No. 15, 1/57 - No. 18, 8/57

	GD 2.0	VG 4.0	FN 6.0	VF 8.0	VF/NM 9.0	NM- 9.2
1-Powell-a	20	40	60	114	182	250
2-Lawrence-a; RQ Sale-a	12	24	36	69	97	125
3-11: 4-Last precode (2/55)	10	20	30	56	76	95
15-18	10	20	30	54	72	90

NOTE: *Berg a-7, 9. Colan a-8. Drucker a-7, 17. Everett a-3, 7, 16; c-16, 17. Heath c-1, 2, 5, 6. Maneely a-5, 7, 8, 18; c-9, 11. Pakula a-2, 3, 9. Reinman a-17.*

NAVY COMBAT
Atlas Comics (MPI): June, 1955 - No. 20, Oct, 1958

	GD 2.0	VG 4.0	FN 6.0	VF 8.0	VF/NM 9.0	NM- 9.2
1-Torpedo Taylor begins by Don Heck	20	40	60	114	182	250
2	12	24	36	69	97	125
3-10	10	20	30	56	76	95
11,13-16,18-20: 14-Torres-a	10	20	30	54	72	90
12-Crandall-a	11	22	33	60	83	105
17-Williamson-a, 4 pgs.; Torres-a	10	20	30	58	79	100

NOTE: *Ayers a-15. Berg a-10, 11. Colan a-11. Drucker a-7. Everett a-3, 20; c-8 & 9 w/Tuska, 10, 13-16. Forte a-15, 18. Heck a-11(2), 15, 19. Maneely c-1, 6, 11, 17. Morisi a-8. Pakula a-7, 18. Powell a-20. Reinman a-18.*

NAVY HEROES
Almanac Publishing Co.: 1945

	GD 2.0	VG 4.0	FN 6.0	VF 8.0	VF/NM 9.0	NM- 9.2
1-Heavy in propaganda	14	28	42	80	115	150

NAVY PATROL
Key Publications: May, 1955 - No. 4, Nov, 1955

	GD 2.0	VG 4.0	FN 6.0	VF 8.0	VF/NM 9.0	NM- 9.2
1	8	16	24	44	57	70
2-4	6	12	18	28	34	40

NAVY TALES
Atlas Comics (CDS): Jan, 1957 - No. 4, July, 1957

	GD 2.0	VG 4.0	FN 6.0	VF 8.0	VF/NM 9.0	NM- 9.2
1-Everett-c; Berg, Powell-a	17	34	51	98	154	210
2-Williamson/Mayo-a(5 pgs); Crandall-a	14	28	42	80	115	150
3,4-Reinman-a; Severin-c. 4-Crandall-a	12	24	36	69	97	125

NOTE: *Colan a-4. Maneely c-2. Reinman a-2-4. Sinnott a-4.*

NAVY TASK FORCE
Stanmor Publications/Aragon Mag. No. 4-8: Feb, 1954 - No. 8, April, 1956

	GD 2.0	VG 4.0	FN 6.0	VF 8.0	VF/NM 9.0	NM- 9.2
1	9	18	27	50	65	80
2	6	12	18	31	38	45
3-8: #8-r/Navy Patrol #1	6	12	18	28	34	40

NAVY WAR HEROES
Charlton Comics: Jan, 1964 - No. 7, Mar-Apr, 1965

	GD 2.0	VG 4.0	FN 6.0	VF 8.0	VF/NM 9.0	NM- 9.2
1	3	6	9	20	30	40
2-7	3	6	9	14	19	24

NAZA (Stone Age Warrior)
Dell Publishing Co.: Nov-Jan, 1963-64 - No. 9, March, 1966

	GD 2.0	VG 4.0	FN 6.0	VF 8.0	VF/NM 9.0	NM- 9.2
12-555-401 (#1)-Painted-c	5	10	15	34	55	75
2-9: 2-4-Painted-c	4	8	12	24	37	50

NEBBS, THE (Also see Crackajack Funnies)
Dell Publishing Co./Croydon Publishing Co.: 1941; 1945

	GD 2.0	VG 4.0	FN 6.0	VF 8.0	VF/NM 9.0	NM- 9.2
Large Feature Comic 23(1941)	21	42	63	122	199	275
1(1945, 36 pgs.)-Reprints	13	26	39	74	105	135

NECESSARY EVIL
Desperado Publishing: Oct, 2007 - No. 9, Nov, 2008 ($3.99)

	GD 2.0	VG 4.0	FN 6.0	VF 8.0	VF/NM 9.0	NM- 9.2
1-9: 1-Joshua Williamson-s/Marcus Harris-a/Dustin Nguyen-c						4.00

NECROMANCER
Image Comics (Top Cow): Sept, 2005 - No. 6, July 2006 ($2.99)

	GD 2.0	VG 4.0	FN 6.0	VF 8.0	VF/NM 9.0	NM- 9.2
1-6: 1-Manapul-a/Ortega-s; three covers by Manapul, Horn & Bachalo						3.00
... Pilot Season Vol. 1 #1 (11/07, $2.99) Ortega-s/Meyers-a/Manapul-c						3.00

NECROMANCER: THE GRAPHIC NOVEL
Marvel Comics (Epic Comics): 1989 ($8.95)

	GD 2.0	VG 4.0	FN 6.0	VF 8.0	VF/NM 9.0	NM- 9.2
nn						9.00

NECROWAR
Dreamwave Productions: July, 2003 - No. 3, Sept, 2003 ($2.95)

	GD 2.0	VG 4.0	FN 6.0	VF 8.0	VF/NM 9.0	NM- 9.2
1-3-Furman-s/Granov-digital art						3.00

NEGATION
CrossGeneration Comics: Dec, 2001 - No. 27, Mar, 2004 ($2.95)

	GD 2.0	VG 4.0	FN 6.0	VF 8.0	VF/NM 9.0	NM- 9.2
Prequel (12/01)						3.00
1-27: 1-(1/02) Pelletier-a/Bedard & Waid-s						3.00
... Lawbringer (11/02, $2.95) Nebres-a						3.00
Vol. 1: Bohica! (10/02, $19.95, TPB) r/ Prequel & #1-6						20.00
Vol. 2: Baptism of Fire (5/03, $15.95, TPB) r/#7-12						16.00
Vol. 3: Hounded (12/03, $15.95, TPB) r/#13-18						16.00

NEGATION WAR
CrossGeneration Comics: Apr, 2004 - No. 6 ($2.95)

	GD 2.0	VG 4.0	FN 6.0	VF 8.0	VF/NM 9.0	NM- 9.2
1-4-Bedard-s/Pelletier-a						3.00

NEGATIVE BURN
Caliber: 1993 - No. 50, 1997 ($2.95, B&W, anthology)

	GD 2.0	VG 4.0	FN 6.0	VF 8.0	VF/NM 9.0	NM- 9.2
1,2,4-12,14-47: Anthology by various including Bolland, Burden, Doran, Gaiman, Moebius, Moore, & Pope						4.00
3,13: 3-Bone story. 13-Strangers in Paradise story	2	4	6	8	10	12
48,49-($4.95)						5.00
50-($6.95, 96 pgs.)-Gaiman, Robinson, Bolland						7.00
...Summer Special 2005 (Image, 2005, $9.99) new short stories by various						10.00
...: The Best From 1993-1998 (Image, 1/05, $19.95) r/short stories by various						20.00
...Winter Special 2005 (Image, 2005, $9.95) new short stories by various						10.00

NEGATIVE BURN
Image Comics (Desperado): May, 2006 - Present ($5.99, B&W, anthology)

	GD 2.0	VG 4.0	FN 6.0	VF 8.0	VF/NM 9.0	NM- 9.2
1-21: 1-Art by Bolland, Powell, Luna, Smith, Hester. 2-Milk & Cheese by Dorkin						6.00

NEGRO (See All-Negro)

NEGRO HEROES (Calling All Girls, Real Heroes, & True Comics reprints)
Parents' Magazine Institute: Spring, 1947 - No. 2, Summer, 1948

	GD 2.0	VG 4.0	FN 6.0	VF 8.0	VF/NM 9.0	NM- 9.2
1	103	206	309	659	1130	1600
2-Jackie Robinson-c/story	116	232	348	742	1271	1800

NEGRO ROMANCE (Negro Romances #4)
Fawcett Publications: June, 1950 - No. 3, Oct, 1950 (All photo-c)

	GD 2.0	VG 4.0	FN 6.0	VF 8.0	VF/NM 9.0	NM- 9.2
1-Evans-a (scarce)	129	258	387	826	1413	2000
2,3 (scarce)	103	206	309	659	1130	1600

NEGRO ROMANCES (Formerly Negro Romance; Romantic Secrets #5 on)
Charlton Comics: No. 4, May, 1955

	GD 2.0	VG 4.0	FN 6.0	VF 8.0	VF/NM 9.0	NM- 9.2
4-Reprints Fawcett #2 (scarce)	68	136	204	435	743	1050

NEIL GAIMAN AND CHARLES VESS' STARDUST
DC Comics (Vertigo): 1997 - No. 4, 1998 ($5.95/$6.95, square-bound, lim. series)

	GD 2.0	VG 4.0	FN 6.0	VF 8.0	VF/NM 9.0	NM- 9.2
1-4: Gaiman text with Vess paintings in all						7.00
Hardcover (1998, $29.95) r/series with new sketches						35.00
Softcover (1999, $19.95) oversized; new Vess-c						20.00

NEIL GAIMAN'S LADY JUSTICE
Tekno Comix: Sept, 1995 - No. 11, May, 1996 ($1.95/$2.25)

	GD 2.0	VG 4.0	FN 6.0	VF 8.0	VF/NM 9.0	NM- 9.2
1-11: 1-Sienkiewicz-c; pin-ups. 1-5-Brereton-c. 7-Polybagged. 11-The Big Bang Pt. 7						2.50

NEIL GAIMAN'S LADY JUSTICE
BIG Entertainment: V2#1, June, 1996 - No. 9, Feb, 1997 ($2.25)

	GD 2.0	VG 4.0	FN 6.0	VF 8.0	VF/NM 9.0	NM- 9.2
V2#1-9: Dan Brereton-c on all. 6-8-Dan Brereton script						2.50

NEIL GAIMAN'S MIDNIGHT DAYS
DC Comics (Vertigo): 1999 ($17.95, trade paperback)

	GD 2.0	VG 4.0	FN 6.0	VF 8.0	VF/NM 9.0	NM- 9.2
nn-Reprints Gaiman's short stories; new Swamp Thing w/ Bissette-a						18.00

NEIL GAIMAN'S MR. HERO-THE NEWMATIC MAN
Tekno Comix: Mar, 1995 - No. 17, May, 1996 ($1.95/$2.25)

	GD 2.0	VG 4.0	FN 6.0	VF 8.0	VF/NM 9.0	NM- 9.2
1-17: 1-Intro Mr. Hero & Teknophage; bound-in game piece and trading card. 4-w/Steel edition Neil Gaiman's Teknophage #1 coupon. 13-Polybagged						2.50

NEIL GAIMAN'S MR. HERO-THE NEWMATIC MAN
BIG Entertainment: V2#1, June, 1996 ($2.25)

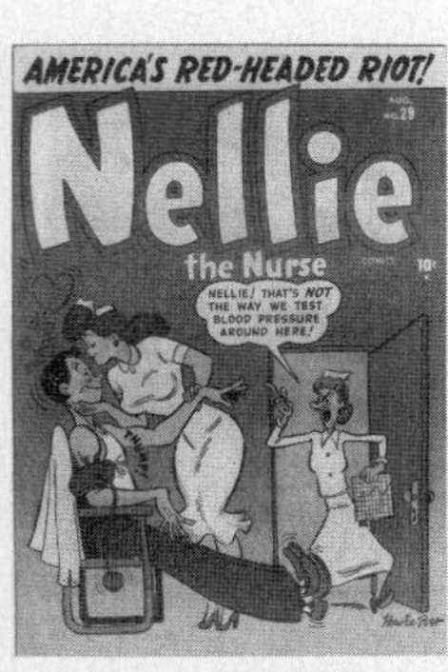

Nellie the Nurse #29 © MAR

Nevermore #1 © Dean Koontz

New Adventure Comics #26 © DC

	GD 2.0	VG 4.0	FN 6.0	VF 8.0	VF/NM 9.0	NM- 9.2

V2#1-Teknophage destroys Mr. Hero; includes The Big Bang Pt. 10 — 2.50

NEIL GAIMAN'S NEVERWHERE
DC Comics (Vertigo): Aug, 2005 - No. 9, Sept, 2006 ($2.99, limited series)

1-9-Adaptation of Gaiman novel; Carey-s/Fabry-a/c — 3.00
TPB (2007, $19.99) r/series; intro. by Carey — 20.00

NEIL GAIMAN'S PHAGE-SHADOWDEATH
BIG Entertainment: June, 1996 - No. 6, Nov, 1996 ($2.25, limited series)

1-6: Bryan Talbot-c & scripts in all. 1-1st app. Orlando Holmes — 2.50

NEIL GAIMAN'S TEKNOPHAGE
Tekno Comix: Aug, 1995 - No. 10, Mar, 1996 ($1.95/$2.25)

1-6-Rick Veitch scripts & Bryan Talbot-c/a. — 2.50
1-Steel Edition — 4.00
7-10: Paul Jenkins scripts in all. 8-polybagged — 2.50

NEIL GAIMAN'S WHEEL OF WORLDS
Tekno Comix: Apr, 1995 - No. 1, May, 1996 ($2.95/$3.25)

0-1st app. Lady Justice; 48 pgs.; bound-in poster — 3.25
0-Regular edition — 2.50
1 ($3.25, 5/96)-Bruce Jones scripts; Lady Justice & Teknophage app.; CGI photo-c — 3.25

NEIL THE HORSE (See Charlton Bullseye #2)
Aardvark-Vanaheim #1-10/Renegade Press #11 on: 2/83 - No. 10, 12/84; No. 11, 4/85 - #15, 1985 (B&W)

1($1.40) — 4.00
1-2nd print — 2.50
2-13: 13-Double size; 11,13-w/paperdolls — 2.50
14,15: Double size ($3.00). 15 is a flip book(2-c) — 3.00

NELLIE THE NURSE (Also see Gay Comics & Joker Comics)
Marvel/Atlas Comics (SPI/LMC): 1945 - No. 36, Oct, 1952; 1957

	GD	VG	FN	VF	VF/NM	NM-
1-(1945)	43	86	129	271	461	650
2-(Spring/46)	22	44	66	132	216	300
3,4: 3-New logo (9/46)	18	36	54	105	165	225
5-Kurtzman's "Hey Look" (3); Georgie app.	19	38	57	111	176	240
6-8,10: 7,8-Georgie app. 10-Millie app.	17	34	51	98	154	210
9-Wolverton-a (1 pg.); Mille the Model app.	17	34	51	100	158	215
11,14-16,18-Kurtzman's "Hey Look"	18	36	54	103	162	220
12- "Giggles 'n' Grins" by Kurtzman	17	34	51	98	154	210
13,17,19,20: 17-Annie Oakley app.	14	28	42	80	115	150
21-30: 28-Mr. Nexdoor-r (3 pgs.) by Kurtzman/Rusty #22	12	24	36	69	97	125
31-36: 36-Post-c	11	22	33	60	83	105
1('57)-Leading Mag. (Atlas)-Everett-a, 20 pgs	11	22	33	64	90	115

NELLIE THE NURSE
Dell Publishing Co.: No. 1304, Mar-May, 1962

	GD	VG	FN	VF	VF/NM	NM-
Four Color 1304-Stanley-a	7	14	21	47	76	105

NEMESIS (Millar & McNiven's...)
Marvel Comics (Icon): May, 2010 - Present ($2.99)

1-Millar-s/McNiven-a — 3.00

NEMESIS ARCHIVES (Listed with Adventures Into the Unknown)

NEMESIS THE WARLOCK (Also see Spellbinders)
Eagle Comics: Sept, 1984 - No. 7, Mar, 1985 (limited series, Baxter paper)

1-7: 2000 A.D. reprints — 2.50

NEMESIS THE WARLOCK
Quality Comics/Fleetway Quality #2 on: 1989 - No. 19, 1991 ($1.95, B&W)

1-19 — 2.50

NEUTRO
Dell Publishing Co.: Jan, 1967

	GD	VG	FN	VF	VF/NM	NM-
1-Jack Sparling-c/a (super hero); UFO-s	4	8	12	26	41	55

NEVADA (See Zane Grey's Four Color 412, 996 & Zane Grey's Stories of the West #1)

NEVADA (Also see Vertigo Winter's Edge #1)
DC Comics (Vertigo): May, 1998 - No. 6, Oct, 1998 ($2.50, limited series)

1-6-Gerber-s/Winslade-c/a — 2.50
TPB-(1999, $14.95) r/#1-6 & Vertigo Winter's Edge preview — 15.00

NEVER AGAIN (War stories; becomes Soldier & Marine V2#9)
Charlton Comics: Aug, 1955; No. 8, July, 1956 (No #2-7)

	GD	VG	FN	VF	VF/NM	NM-
1	9	18	27	52	69	85
8-(Formerly Foxhole?)	6	12	18	29	36	42

NEVERMEN, THE (See Dark Horse Presents #148-150)
Dark Horse Comics: May, 2000 - No. 4, Aug, 2000 ($2.95, limited series)

1-4-Phil Amara-s/Guy Davis-a — 3.00

NEVERMEN, THE: STREETS OF BLOOD
Dark Horse Comics: Jan, 2003 - No. 3, Apr, 2003 ($2.99, limited series)

1-3-Phil Amara-s/Guy Davis-a — 3.00
TPB (7/03, $9.95) r/#1-3; Paul Jenkins intro.; Davis sketch pages — 10.00

NEVERMORE (DEAN KOONTZ'S:...)
Dabel Brothers Prods.: Mar, 2009 - No. 5 ($3.99, limited series)

1-Keith Champagne-s/Andy Smith-a — 4.00

NEW ADVENTURE COMICS (Formerly New Comics; becomes Adventure Comics #32 on; V1#12 indicia says NEW COMICS #12)
National Periodical Publications: V1#12, Jan, 1937 - No. 31, Oct, 1938

	GD	VG	FN	VF	VF/NM	NM-
V1#12-Federal Men by Siegel & Shuster continues; Jor-L mentioned; Whitney Ellsworth-c begin, end #14	533	1066	1600	4200	–	–
V2#1(2/37, #13)-(Rare)	507	1014	1521	4000	–	–
V2#2 (#14)	450	900	1350	3600	–	–
15(V2#3)-20(V2#8): 15-1st Adventure logo; Creig Flessel-c begin, end #31. 16-1st non-funny cover. 17-Nadir, Master of Magic begins, ends #30	360	720	1080	1980	3090	4200
21(V2#9),22(V2#10, 2/37): 22-X-Mas-c	320	640	960	1760	2780	3800
23-25,28-31	270	540	810	1485	2393	3300
26(5/38) (scarce) has house ad for Action Comics #1 showing B&W image of cover (early published image of Superman)(prices vary widely on this book) (A CGC 5.0 sold in 2006 for $5377.50)						
27(6/38) has house ad for Action Comics #1 showing B&W image of cover (scarce) (early published image of Superman)	400	800	1200	2400	3200	4000

NEW ADVENTURES OF ABRAHAM LINCOLN, THE
Image Comics (Homage): 1998 ($19.95, one-shot)

1-Scott McCloud-s/computer art — 20.00

NEW ADVENTURES OF CHARLIE CHAN, THE (TV)
National Periodical Publications: May-June, 1958 - No. 6, Mar-Apr, 1959

	GD	VG	FN	VF	VF/NM	NM-
1 (Scarce)-John Broome-s/Sid Greene-a in all	73	146	219	467	796	1125
2 (Scarce)	46	92	138	290	488	685
3-6 (Scarce)-Greene/Giella-a	40	80	120	242	401	560

NEW ADVENTURES OF HUCK FINN, THE (TV)
Gold Key: December, 1968 (Hanna-Barbera)

	GD	VG	FN	VF	VF/NM	NM-
1- "The Curse of Thut"; part photo-c	4	8	12	22	34	45

NEW ADVENTURES OF PINOCCHIO (TV)
Dell Publishing Co.: Oct-Dec, 1962 - No. 3, Sept-Nov, 1963

	GD	VG	FN	VF	VF/NM	NM-
12-562-212(#1)	8	16	24	56	93	130
2,3	7	14	21	45	73	100

NEW ADVENTURES OF ROBIN HOOD (See Robin Hood)

NEW ADVENTURES OF SHERLOCK HOLMES (Also see Sherlock Holmes)
Dell Publishing Co.: No. 1169, Mar-May, 1961 - No. 1245, Nov-Jan, 1961/62

	GD	VG	FN	VF	VF/NM	NM-
Four Color 1169(#1)	13	26	39	95	178	260
Four Color 1245	12	24	36	86	158	230

NEW ADVENTURES OF SPEED RACER
Now Comics: Dec, 1993 - No. 7, 1994? ($1.95)

1-7 — 2.50
0-(Premiere)-3-D cover — 3.00

NEW ADVENTURES OF SUPERBOY, THE (Also see Superboy)
DC Comics: Jan, 1980 - No. 54, June, 1984

1 — 5.00
2-6,8-10 — 4.00
11-49,51-54: 11-Superboy gets new power. 14-Lex Luthor app. 15-Superboy gets new parents. 28-Dial "H" For Hero begins, ends #49. 45-47-1st app. Sunburst. 48-Begin 75¢-c. — 3.00

	GD	VG	FN	VF	VF/NM	NM-
1,2,5,6,8 (Whitman variants; low print run; no issue # shown on cover)	2	4	6	8	10	12

7,50: 7-Has extra story "The Computers That Saved Metropolis" by Starlin (Radio Shack giveaway w/indicia). 50-Legion app. — 5.00

NOTE: *Buckler a-9p; c-36p. Giffen a-50; c-50. 40i. Gil Kane c-32p, 33p, 35, 39, 41-49. Miller c-51. Starlin a-7. Krypto back-ups in 17, 22. Superbaby in 11, 14, 19, 24.*

NEW ADVENTURES OF THE PHANTOM BLOT, THE (See The Phantom Blot)

NEW AMERICA
Eclipse Comics: Nov, 1987 - No. 4, Feb, 1988 ($1.75, Baxter paper)

New Avengers #35 © MAR

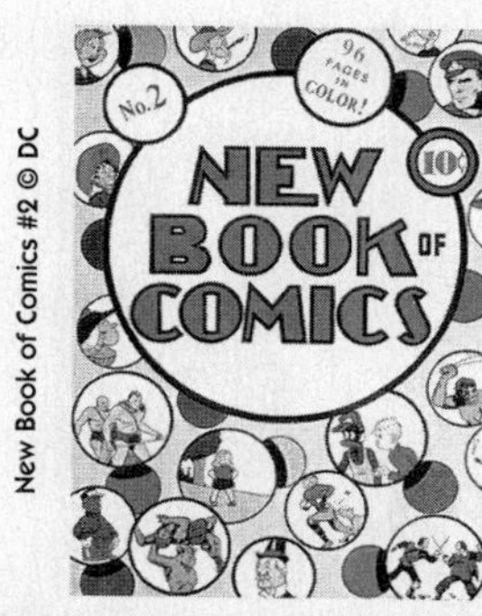

New Book of Comics #2 © DC

New Excalibur #18 © MAR

GD 2.0 | VG 4.0 | FN 6.0 | VF 8.0 | VF/NM 9.0 | NM- 9.2

1-4: Scout limited series 2.50

NEW ARCHIES, THE (TV)
Archie Comic Publications: Oct, 1987 - No. 22, May, 1990 (75¢)

1 5.00
2-10: 3-Xmas issue 4.00
11-22: 17-22 (95¢-$1.00): 21-Xmas issue 3.00

NEW ARCHIES DIGEST (TV)(...Comics Digest Magazine #4?-10; ...Digest Magazine #11 on)
Archie Comics: May, 1988 - No. 14, July, 1991 ($1.35/$1.50, quarterly)

1 6.00
2-14: 6-Begin $1.50-c 3.50

NEW AVENGERS, THE (Also see Promotional section for military giveaway)
Marvel Comics: Jan, 2005 - Present ($2.25/$2.50/$2.99/$3.99)

1-Bendis-s/Finch-a; Spider-Man app.; re-intro The Sentry; 4 covers by McNiven, Quesada & Finch; variants from #1-6 combine for one team image 5.00
1-Director's Cut ($3.99) includes alternate covers, script, villain gallery 4.00
2-20: 2-6-Finch-a. 5-Wolverine app. 7-10-Origin of the Sentry; McNiven-a. 11-Debut of Ronin. 14,15-Cho-c/a. 17-20-Deodato-a 3.00
21-48: 21-26-Civil War. 21-Chaykin-a/c. 26-Maleev-a. 27-31-Yu-a; Echo & "Elektra" app. 33-37-The Hood app. 38-Gaydos-a. 39-Mack-a. 40-47-Secret Invasion 3.00
49-($3.99) Dark Reign 4.00
50-($4.99) Dark Reign; Tan, Hitch, McNiven, Yu, Horn & others-a; Tan wraparound-c 5.00
50-($4.99) Adam Kubert variant-c 6.00
51-63-($3.99) Dark Reign. 51,52-Tan & Bachalo-a. 54-Brother Voodoo becomes Sorceror Supreme. 56-Wrecking Crew app. 61-63-Siege; Steve Rogers app. 4.00
51-54-Variant covers by Bachalo 7.00
56, 57-Variant covers. 56-70th Anniversary frame. 57-Super Hero Squad 6.00
Annual 1 (6/06, $3.99) Wedding of Luke Cage and Jessica Jones; Bendis-s/Coipel-a 4.00
Annual 2 (2/08, $3.99) Avengers vs. The Hood's gang; Bendis-s/Pagulayan-a 4.00
Annual 3 (2/10, $4.99) Mayhew-c/a; Dark Avengers app.; Siege preview 5.00
...: Illuminati (5/06, $3.99) Bendis-s/Maleev-a; leads into Planet Hulk; Civil War preview 4.00
... Most Wanted Files (2006, $3.99) profile pages of Avenger villains 4.00
... Vol. 1: Breakout HC (2005, $19.99) r/#1-6; gallery of variant covers 20.00
... Vol. 1: Breakout SC (2006, $14.99) r/#1-6; gallery of variant covers 15.00
... Vol. 2: Sentry HC (2006, $19.99) r/#7-10 & ... Most Wanted Files 20.00
... Vol. 2: Sentry SC (2006, $14.99) r/#7-10 & ... Most Wanted Files 15.00
... Vol. 3: Secrets and Lies HC (2006, $19.99) r/#11-15 & Giant-Size Spider-Woman #1 20.00
... Vol. 3: Secrets and Lies SC (2006, $14.99) r/#11-15 & Giant-Size Spider-Woman #1 15.00
... Vol. 4: The Collective HC (2006, $19.99) r/#16-20 20.00
... Vol. 4: The Collective SC (2007, $14.99) r/#16-20 15.00
... Vol. 5: Civil War HC (2007, $19.99) r/#21-25 20.00
... Vol. 5: Civil War SC (2007, $14.99) r/#21-25 15.00
... Vol. 6: Revolution HC (2007, $19.99) r/#26-31 20.00
... Vol. 6: Revolution SC (2007, $14.99) r/#26-31 15.00
... Volume 1 HC (2007, $29.99) oversized r/#1-10, ... Most Wanted Files, and ... Guest Starring the Fantastic Four (militiary giveaway); new intro. by Bendis; script & sketch pages 30.00
... Volume 2 HC (2008, $29.99) oversized r/#11-20, ... Annual #1, and story from Giant-Size Spider-Woman; variant covers & sketch pages 30.00

NEW AVENGERS: ILLUMINATI (Also see Civil War and Secret Invasion)
Marvel Comics: Feb, 2007 - No. 5, Jan, 2008 ($2.99, limited series)

1-5-Bendis & Reed-s/Cheung-a. 3-Origin of The Beyonder. 5-Secret Invasion 3.00
HC (2008, $19.99, dustjacket) r/#1-5; cover sketch art 20.00
SC (2008, $14.99) r/#1-5; cover sketch art 15.00

NEW AVENGERS: THE REUNION
Marvel Comics: May, 2009 - No. 4, Aug, 2009 ($3.99, limited series)

1-4-Mockingbird and Ronin (Hawkeye); McCann-s/López-a/Jo Chen-c 4.00

NEW AVENGERS/TRANSFORMERS
Marvel Comics: Sept, 2007 - No. 4, Dec, 2007 ($2.99, limited series)

1-4-Kirkham-a; Capt. America app. 1-Cheung-c. 2-Pearson-c 3.00
TPB (2008, $10.99) r/#1-4 11.00

NEW BOOK OF COMICS (Also see Big Book Of Fun)
National Periodical Publ.: 1937; No. 2, Spring, 1938 (100 pgs. each) (Reprints)

1(Rare)-1st regular size comic annual; 2nd DC annual; contains r/New Comics #1-4 & More Fun #9; r/Federal Men (8 pgs.), Henri Duval (1 pg.), & Dr. Occult in costume (1 pg.) by Siegel & Shuster; Moldoff, Sheldon Mayer (15 pgs.)-a
1850 3700 5550 12,000 21,000 30,000
2-Contains-r/More Fun #15 & 16; r/Dr. Occult in costume (a Superman prototype), & Calling All Cars (4 pgs.) by Siegel & Shuster 950 1900 2850 6175 11,088 16,000

NEW COMICS (New Adventure #12 on)
National Periodical Publ.: 12/35 - No. 11, 12/36 (No. 1-6: paper cover) (No. 1-5: 84 pgs.)

V1#1-Billy the Kid, Sagebrush 'n' Cactus, Jibby Jones, Needles, The Vikings, Sir Loin of Beef, Now-When I Was a Boy, & other 1-2 pg. strips; 2 pgs. Kelly art(1st)-(Gulliver's Travels); Sheldon Mayer-a(1st)(2 2pg. strips); Vincent Sullivan-c(1st)
2857 5714 8571 20,000 – –
2-1st app. Federal Men by Siegel & Shuster & begins (also see The Comics Magazine #2); Mayer, Kelly-a (Rare)(1/36) 1200 2400 3600 8400 – –
3-6: 3,4-Sheldon Mayer-a which continues in The Comics Magazine #1. 3-Vincent Sullivan-c. 4-Dickens' "A Tale of Two Cities" adaptation begins. 5-Junior Federal Men Club; Kiefer-a. 6- "She" adaptation begins 857 1714 2571 6000 – –
7-10 614 1228 1842 4300 – –
11-Ties with More Fun #16 as DC's 1st Christmas-c 643 1286 1929 4500 – –
NOTE: *#1-6 rarely occur in mint condition.* ***Whitney Ellsworth*** *c-4-11.*

NEW DEFENDERS (See Defenders)

NEW DNAGENTS, THE (Formerly DNAgents)
Eclipse Comics: V2#1, Oct, 1985 - V2#17, Mar, 1987 (Whole #s 25-40; Mando paper)

V2#1-17: 1-Origin recap. 7-Begin 95 cent-c. 9,10-Airboy preview 2.50
3-D 1 (1/86, $2.25) 2.50
2-D 1 (1/86)-Limited ed. (100 copies) 10.00

NEW DYNAMIX
DC Comics (WildStorm): May, 2008 - No. 5, Sept, 2008 ($2.99, limited series)

1-5-Warner-s/J.J. Kirby-a/c. 1-Variant-c by Jim Lee. 1-Convention Ed. with Lee-c 3.00

NEW ETERNALS: APOCALYPSE NOW (Also see Eternals, The)
Marvel Comics: Feb, 2000 ($3.99, one-shot)

1-Bennett & Hanna-a; Ladronn-c 4.00

NEW EXCALIBUR
Marvel Comics: Jan, 2006 - No. 24, Dec, 2007 ($2.99)

1-24: 1-Claremont-s/Ryan-a; Dazzler app. 3-Juggernaut app. 4-Lionheart app. 3.00
... Vol. 1: Defenders of the Realm TPB (2006, $17.99) r/#1-7 18.00
... Vol. 2: Last Days of Camelot TPB (2007, $19.99) r/#8-15 20.00
... Vol. 3: Battle for Eternity TPB (2007, $24.99) r/#16-24; sketch pages 25.00

NEW EXILES (Continued from Exiles #100 and Exiles - Days of Then and Now)
Marvel Comics: Mar, 2008 - No. 18, Apr, 2009 ($2.99)

1-18: 1-Claremont-s/Grummett-a; 2 covers by Land & Golden; new team 3.00
1-2nd printing with Grummett-c 3.00
Annual 1 (2/09, $3.99) Claremont-s/Grummett-a 4.00

NEWFORCE (Also see Newmen)
Image Comics (Extreme Studios): Jan, 1996-No. 4, Apr, 1996 ($2.50, lim. series)

1-4: 1-"Extreme Destroyer" Pt. 8; polybagged w/gaming card. 4-Newforce disbands 2.50

NEW FUN COMICS (More Fun #7 on; see Big Book of Fun Comics)
National Periodical Publications: Feb, 1935 - No. 6, Oct, 1935 (10x15", No. 1-4,: slick-c) (No. 1-5: 36 pgs; 40 pgs. No. 6)

V1#1 (1st DC comic); 1st app. Oswald The Rabbit; Jack Woods (cowboy) begins
7286 14,572 21,858 51,000 – –
2(3/35)-(Very Rare) 3143 6286 9429 22,000 – –
3-5(8/35): 3-Don Drake on the Planet Soro-c/story (sci/fi, 4/35); early (maybe 1st) DC letter column. 5-Soft-c 1786 3572 5358 12,500 – –
6(10/35)-1st Dr. Occult by Siegel & Shuster (Leger & Reuths); last "New Fun" title. "New Comics" #1 begins in Dec. which is reason for title change to More Fun; Henri Duval (ends #10) by Siegel & Shuster begins; paper-c
3429 6858 10,287 24,000 – –

NEW FUNNIES (The Funnies #1-64; Walter Lantz...#109 on; New TV... #259, 260, 272, 273; TV Funnies #261-271)
Dell Publishing Co.: No. 65, July, 1942 - No. 288, Mar-Apr, 1962

65(#1)-Andy Panda in a world of real people, Raggedy Ann & Andy, Oswald the Rabbit (with Woody Woodpecker x-overs), Li'l Eight Ball & Peter Rabbit begin; Bugs Bunny and Elmer app. 70 140 210 595 1173 1750
66-70: 66-Felix the Cat begins. 67-Billy & Bonny Bee by Frank Thomas begins. 69-Kelly-a (2 pgs.); The Brownies begin (not by Kelly) 32 64 96 246 478 710
71-75: 72-Kelly illos. 75-Brownies by Kelly? 23 46 69 166 321 475
76-Andy Panda (Carl Barks & Pabian-a); Woody Woodpecker x-over in Oswald ends
74 148 222 629 1240 1850
77,78: 77-Kelly-c. 78-Andy Panda in a world with real people ends
22 44 66 157 304 450
79-81 15 30 45 104 197 290
82-Brownies by Kelly begins; Homer Pigeon begins 15 30 45 110 210 310
83-85-Brownies by Kelly in ea. 83-X-mas-c; Homer Pigeon begins. 85-Woody Woodpecker, 1 pg. strip begins 15 30 45 108 207 305
86-90: 87-Woody Woodpecker stories begin 12 24 36 83 152 220
91-99 10 20 30 67 116 165

New Gods (2nd series) #12 © DC

New Guardians #7 © DC

New Mutants #98 © MAR

	GD 2.0	VG 4.0	FN 6.0	VF 8.0	VF/NM 9.0	NM- 9.2

100 (6/45) 10 20 30 70 123 175
101-120: 119-X-Mas-c 8 16 24 54 90 125
121-150: 131,143-X-Mas-c 7 14 21 47 76 105
151-200: 155-X-Mas-c. 167-X-Mas-c. 182-Origin & 1st app. Knothead & Splinter. 191-X-Mas-c 6 12 18 41 66 90
201-240 6 12 18 37 59 80
241-288: 270,271-Walter Lantz c-app. 281-1st story swipes/WDC&S #100 5 10 15 32 51 70

NOTE: *Early issues written by* **John Stanley.**

NEW GODS, THE (1st Series)(New Gods #12 on)(See Adventure #459, DC Graphic Novel #4, 1st Issue Special #13 & Super-Team Family)
National Periodical Publications/DC Comics: 2-3/71 - V2#11, 10-11/72; V3#12, 7/77 - V3#19, 7-8/78 (Fourth World)

1-Intro/1st app. Orion; 4th app. Darkseid (cameo; 3 weeks after Forever People #1) (#1-3 are 15¢ issues) 9 18 27 63 107 150
2-Darkseid-c/story (2nd full app., 4-5/71) 5 10 15 32 51 70
3-1st app. Black Racer; last 15¢ issue 4 8 12 24 37 50
4-9: (25¢, 52 pg. giants): 4-Darkseid cameo; origin Manhunter-r. 5,7,8-Young Gods feature. 7-Darkseid app. (2-3/72); origin Orion; 1st origin of all New Gods as a group. 9-1st app. Forager 4 8 12 24 37 50
10,11: 11-Last Kirby issue. 3 6 9 20 30 40
12-19: Darkseid storyline w/minor apps. 12-New costume Orion (see 1st Issue Special #13 for 1st new costume). 19-Story continued in Adventure Comics #459,460 2 4 6 8 10 12
Jack Kirby's New Gods TPB ('98, $11.95, B&W&Grey) r/#1-11 plus cover gallery of original series and "84 reprints 12.00

NOTE: *#4-9(25¢, 52 pgs.) contain Manhunter-r by* **Simon & Kirby** *from Adventure #73, 74, 75, 76, 77, 78 with covers in that order.* **Adkins** *i-12-14, 17-19.* **Buckler** *a(p)-15.* **Kirby** *c/a-1-11p.* **Newton** *a(p)-12-14, 16-19.* **Starlin** *c-17.* **Staton** *c-19p.*

NEW GODS (Also see DC Graphic Novel #4)
DC Comics: June, 1984 - No. 6, Nov, 1984 ($2.00, Baxter paper)

1-5: New Kirby-c; r/New Gods #1-10. 4.00
6-Reprints New Gods #11 w/48 pgs of new Kirby story & art; leads into DC Graphic Novel #4 2 4 6 8 10 12

NEW GODS (2nd Series)
DC Comics: Feb, 1989 - No. 28, Aug, 1991 ($1.50)

1-28 2.50

NEW GODS (3rd Series) (Becomes Jack Kirby's Fourth World) (Also see Showcase '94 #1 & Showcase '95 #7)
DC Comics: Oct, 1995 - No. 15, Feb, 1997 ($1.95)

1-11,13-15: 9-Giffen-a(p). 10,11-Superman app. 13-Takion, Mr. Miracle & Big Barda app. 13-15-Byrne-a(p)/scripts & Simonson-c. 15-Apokolips merged w/ New Genesis; story cont'd in Jack Kirby's Fourth World 2.50
12-(11/96, 99¢)-Byrne-a(p)/scripts & Simonson-c begin; Takion cameo; indicia reads October 1996 2.50
...Secret Files 1 (9/98, $4.95) Origin-s 5.00

NEW GUARDIANS, THE
DC Comics: Sept, 1988 - No. 12, Sept, 1989 ($1.25)

1-($2.00, 52 pgs)-Staton-c/a in #1-9 3.00
2-12 2.50

NEW HEROIC (See Heroic)

NEW INVADERS (Titled Invaders for #0 & #1) (See Avengers V3#83,84)
Marvel Comics: No. 0, Aug, 2004 - No. 9, June, 2005 ($2.99)

0-9-Roster of U.S. Agent, Sub-Mariner, Blazing Skull and others. 0-Avengers app. 3.00

NEW JUSTICE MACHINE, THE (Also see The Justice Machine)
Innovation Publishing: 1989 - No. 3, 1989 ($1.95, limited series)

1-3 2.50

NEW KIDS ON THE BLOCK, THE (Also see Richie Rich and...)
Harvey Comics: Dec, 1990 - No. 8, Dec, 1991 ($1.25)

1-8 2.50
...**Back Stage Pass** 1(12/90) - 7(11/91) **Chillin'** 1(12/90) - 7(12/91): 1-Photo-c ...**Comic Tour** '90/91 1 (12/90) - 7(12/91) **Digest** 1(1/91) - 5(1/92) **Hanging Tough** 1 (2/91) **Magic Summer Tour** 1 (Fall/90) **Magic Summer Tour** nn (Fall/90, sold at concerts) **Step By Step** 1 (Fall/90, one-shot) **Valentine Girl** 1 (Fall/90, one-shot)-Photo-c 2.50

NEW LINE CINEMA'S TALES OF HORROR (Anthology)
DC Comics (WildStorm): Nov, 2007 ($2.99, one-shot)

1-Freddy Krueger and Leatherface app.; Darick Robertson-c 3.00

NEW LOVE (See Love & Rockets)

Fantagraphics Books: Aug, 1996 - No. 6, Dec, 1997 ($2.95, B&W, lim. series)

1-6: Gilbert Hernandez-s/a 3.00

NEWMAN
Image Comics (Extreme Studios): Jan, 1996 - No. 4, Apr, 1996 ($2.50, lim. series)

1-4: 1-Extreme Destroyer Pt. 3; polybagged w/card. 4-Shadowhunt tie-in; Eddie Collins becomes new Shadowhawk 2.50

NEW MANGVERSE (Also see Marvel Mangaverse)
Marvel Comics: Mar, 2006 - No. 5, July, 2006 ($2.99, lim. series)

1-5: Cebulski-s/Ohtsuka-a; The Hand and Elektra app. 3.00
...: The Rings of Fate (2006, $7.99, digest) r/#1-5 8.00

NEWMEN (becomes The Adventures Of The...#22)
Image Comics (Extreme Studios): Apr, 1994 - No. 20, Nov, 1995; No. 21, Nov, 1996 ($1.95/$2.50)

1-21: 1-5: Matsuda-c/a. 10-Polybagged w/trading card. 11-Polybagged. 20-Has a variant-c; Babewatch! x-over. 21-(11/96)-Series relaunch; Chris Sprouse-a begins; pin-up. 16-Has a variant-c by Quesada & Palmiotti 2.50
TPB-(1996, $12.95) r/#1-4 w/pin-ups 13.00

NEW MEN OF BATTLE, THE
Catechetical Guild: 1949 (nn) (Carboard-c)

nn(V8#1-3,5,6)-192 pgs.; contains 5 issues of Topix rebound 9 18 27 47 61 75
nn(V8#7-V8#11)-160 pgs.; contains 5 iss. of Topix 9 18 27 47 61 75

NEW MUTANTS, THE (See Marvel Graphic Novel #4 for 1st app.)(Also see X-Force & Uncanny X-Men #167)
Marvel Comics Group: Mar, 1983 - No. 100, Apr, 1991

1 5.00
2-10: 3,4-Ties into X-Men #167. 10-1st app. Magma 3.00
11-17,19,20: 13-Kitty Pryde app. 16-1st app. Warpath (w/out costume); see X-Men #193 2.50
18,21: 18-Intro. new Warlock. 21-Double size; origin new Warlock; newsstand version has cover price written in by Sienkiewicz 3.00
22-24,27-30: 23-25-Cloak & Dagger app. 2.50
25,26: 25-1st brief app. Legion. 26-1st full Legion app. 4.00
31-58: 35-Magneto intro'd as new headmaster. 43-Portacio-i. 50-Double size. 58-Contains pull-out mutant registration form 2.50
59-61: Fall of The Mutants series. 60(52 pgs.) 3.00
62-85: 68-Intro Spyder. 63-X-Men & Wolverine clones app. 73-(52 pgs.). 76-X-Factor & X-Terminator app. 85-Liefeld-c begin 2.50
86-Rob Liefeld-a begins; McFarlane-c(i) swiped from Ditko splash pg.; 1st brief app. Cable (last page teaser) 6.00
87-1st full app. Cable (3/90) 2 4 6 11 16 20
87-2nd printing; gold metallic ink-c ($1.00) 2.50
88-2nd app. Cable 1 2 3 4 5 7
92-No Liefeld-a; Liefeld-c 4.00
89,90,91,93-97,99,100: 89-3rd app. Cable. 90-New costumes. 90,91-Sabretooth app. 93,94-Cable vs. Wolverine. 95-97-X-Tinction Agenda x-over. 95-Death of new Warlock. 97-Wolverine & Cable-c, but no app. 99-1st app. of Feral (of X-Force); Byrne-c/swipe (X-Men, 1st Series #138). 100-(52 pgs.)-1st brief app. X-Force 5.00
95,100-Gold 2nd printing. 100-Silver ink 3rd printing 2.50
98-1st app. Deadpool, Gideon & Domino (2/91); 2nd Shatterstar (cameo); Liefeld-c/a 3 6 9 14 20 25
Annual 1 (1984) 4.00
Annual 2 (1986, $1.25)-1st Psylocke 1 2 3 5 6 8
Annual 3,4,6,7 ('87, '88,'90,'91, 68 pgs.): 4-Evolutionary War x-over. 6-1st new costumes by Liefeld (3 pgs.); 1st brief app. Shatterstar (of X-Force). 7-Liefeld pin-up only; X-Terminators back-up story; 2nd app. X-Force (cont'd in New Warriors Annual #1) 3.00
Annual 5 (1989, $2.00, 68 pgs.)-Atlantis Attacks; 1st Liefeld-a on New Mutants 4.00
... Classic Vol. 1 TPB (2006, $24.99) r/#1-7, Marvel Graphic Novel #4, Uncanny X-Men #167 25.00
... Classic Vol. 2 TPB (2007, $24.99) r/#8-17 25.00
... Classic Vol. 3 TPB (2008, $24.99) r/#18-25 & Annual #1 25.00
Special 1-Special Edition ('85, 68 pgs.)-Ties in w/X-Men Alpha Flight limited series; cont'd in X-Men Annual #9; Art Adams/Austin-a 5.00
Summer Special 1(Sum/90, $2.95, 84 pgs.) 3.00

NOTE: **Art Adams** *c-38, 39.* **Austin** *c-57i.* **Byrne** *c/a-75p.* **Liefeld** *a-86-91p, 93-96p, 98-100, Annual 5p, 6(3 pgs.); c-85-91p, 92, 93p, 94, 95, 96p, 97-100, Annual 5, 6p.* **McFarlane** *c-85-89i, 93i.* **Portacio** *a(i)-43.* **Russell** *a-48i.* **Sienkiewicz** *a-18-31, 35-38i; c-17-31, 35i, 37i, Annual 1.* **Simonson** *c-11p.* **B. Smith** *c-36, 40-48.* **Williamson** *a(i)-69, 71-73, 78-80, 82, 83; c(i)-69, 72, 73, 78i.*

NEW MUTANTS (Continues as New X-Men (Academy X))
Marvel Comics: July, 2003 - No. 13, June, 2004 ($2.50/$2.99)

1-7: 1-6-Josh Middleton-c. 7-Bachalo-c 2.50
8-13 ($2.99) 8-11-Bachalo-c 3.00

New People #1 © T/S Prods.

New Teen Titans #10 © DC

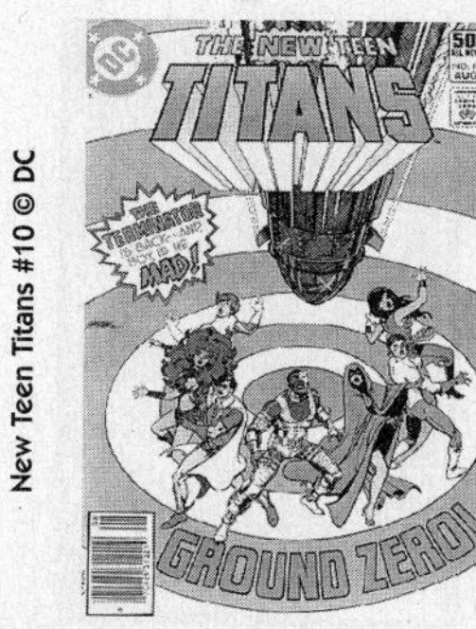

New Titans #120 © DC

GD VG FN VF VF/NM NM-
2.0 4.0 6.0 8.0 9.0 9.2

... Vol. 1: Back To School TPB (2005, $16.99) r/#1-6; new Middleton-c 17.00

NEW MUTANTS
Marvel Comics: July, 2009 - Present ($3.99/$2.99)

1-($3.99) Neves-a; Legion app.; covers by Ross, Adam Kubert, McLeod, Benjamin 4.00
2-11-($2.99) 2-10-Adam Kubert-c. 11-Siege; Dodson-c 3.00
... Saga (2009, giveaway) New Mutants character profiles and story synopsies; Neves-c 2.50

NEW MUTANTS, THE: TRUTH OR DEATH
Marvel Comics: Nov, 1997 - No. 3, Jan, 1998 ($2.50, limited series)

1-3-Raab-s/Chang-a(p) 2.50

NEW ORDER, THE
CFD Publishing: Nov, 1994 ($2.95)

1 3.00

NEW PEOPLE, THE (TV)
Dell Publishing Co.: Jan, 1970 - No. 2, May, 1970

1 3 6 9 17 25 32
2-Photo-c 3 6 9 15 21 26

NEW ROMANCES
Standard Comics: No. 5, May, 1951 - No. 21, May, 1954

5-Photo-c 15 30 45 85 130 175
6-9: 6-Barbara Bel Geddes, Richard Basehart "Fourteen Hours" photo-c. 7-Ray Milland & Joan Fontaine photo-c. 9-Photo-c from '50s movie 10 20 30 56 76 95
10,14,16,17-Toth-a 11 22 33 60 83 105
11-Toth-a; Liz Taylor, Montgomery Cliff photo-c 28 56 84 165 270 375
12,13,15,18-21 9 18 27 52 69 85

NOTE: *Celardo a-9. Moreira a-6. Tuska a-7, 20. Photo c-5-16.*

NEW SHADOWHAWK, THE (Also see Shadowhawk & Shadowhunt)
Image Comics (Shadowline Ink): June, 1995 - No. 7, Mar, 1996 ($2.50)

1-7: Kurt Busiek scripts in all 3.00

NEW STATESMEN, THE
Fleetway Publications (Quality Comics): 1989 - No. 5, 1990 ($3.95, limited series, mature readers, 52pgs.)

1-5: Futuristic; squarebound; 3-Photo-c 4.00

NEWSTRALIA
Innovation Publ.: July, 1989 - No. 5, 1989 ($1.75, color)(#2 on, $2.25, B&W)

1-5: 1,2: Timothy Truman-c/a; Gustovich-i 2.50

NEW TALENT SHOWCASE (Talent Showcase #16 on)
DC Comics: Jan, 1984 - No. 19, Oct, 1985 (Direct sales only)

1-19: Features new strips & artists. 18-Williamson-c(i) 2.50

NEW TEEN TITANS, THE (See DC Comics Presents #26, Marvel and DC Present & Teen Titans; Tales of the Teen Titans #41 on)
DC Comics: Nov, 1980 - No. 40, Mar, 1984

1-Robin, Kid Flash, Wonder Girl, The Changeling (1st app.), Starfire, The Raven, Cyborg begin; partial origin 3 6 9 14 20 25
2-1st app. Deathstroke the Terminator 3 6 9 20 30 40
3-10: 3-Origin Starfire; Intro The Fearsome Five. 4-Origin continues; J.L.A. app. 6-Origin Raven. 7-Cyborg origin. 8-Origin Kid Flash retold. 9-Minor app. Deathstroke on last pg. 10-2nd app. Deathstroke the Terminator (see Marvel & DC Present for 3rd app.); origin Changeling retold 1 2 3 5 7 9
11-20: 13-Return of Madame Rouge & Capt. Zahl; Robotman revived. 14-Return of Mento; origin Doom Patrol. 15-Death of Madame Rouge & Capt. Zahl; intro. new Brotherhood of Evil. 16-1st app. Captain Carrot (free 16 pg. preview). 18-Return of Starfire. 19-Hawkman teams-up 6.00
21-40: 21-Intro Night Force in free 16 pg. insert; intro Brother Blood. 23-1st app. Vigilante (not in costume), & Blackfire. 24-Omega Men app. 25-Omega Men cameo; free 16 pg. preview Masters of the Universe. 26-1st app. Terra. 27-Free 16 pg. preview Atari Force. 29-The New Brotherhood of Evil & Speedy app. 30-Terra joins the Titans. 34-4th app. Deathstroke the Terminator.37-Batman & The Outsiders x-over. 38-Origin Wonder Girl. 39-Last Dick Grayson as Robin; Kid Flash quits 5.00
Annual 1(11/82)-Omega Men app. 6.00
Annual V2#2(9/83)-1st app. Vigilante in costume; 1st app. Lyla 6.00
Annual 3 (See Tales of the Teen Titans Annual #3)
...: Terra Incognito TPB (2006, $19.99) r/#26,28-34 & Annual #2 20.00
...: The Judas Contract TPB (2003, $19.95) r/#39,40 plus Tales of the Teen Titans #41-44 & Annual #3 20.00
...: Who is Donna Troy? TPB (2005, $19.99) r/#38,Tales of the Teen Titans #50, New Titans #50-55 and Teen Titans/Outsiders Secret Files 2003 20.00

NOTE: *Perez a-1-4p, 6-34p, 37-40p, Annual 1p, 2p; c-1-12, 13-17p, 18-21, 22p, 23p, 24-37, 38, 39(painted), 40, Annual 1, 2.*

NEW TEEN TITANS, THE (Becomes The New Titans #50 on)
DC Comics: Aug, 1984 - No. 49, Nov, 1988 ($1.25/$1.75; deluxe format)

1-New storyline; Perez-c/a begins 1 2 3 5 6 8
2,3: 2-Re-intro Lilith 6.00
4-10: 5-Death of Trigon. 7-9-Origin Lilith. 8-Intro Kole. 10-Kole joins 5.00
11-49: 13,14-Crisis x-over. 20-Robin (Jason Todd) joins; original Teen Titans return. 38-Infinity, Inc. x-over. 47-Origin of all Titans; Titans (East & West) pin-up by Perez 4.00
Annual 1-4 (9/85-'88): 1-Intro. Vanguard. 2-Byrne c/a(p); origin Brother Blood; intro new Dr. Light. 3-Intro. Danny Chase. 4-Perez-c 4.00
...: The Terror of Trigon TPB (2003, $17.95) r/#1-5; new cover by Phil Jimenez 18.00

NOTE: *Buckler c-10. Kelley Jones a-47, Annual 4. Erik Larsen a-33. Orlando c-33p. Perez a-1-5; c-1-7, 19-23, 43. Steacy c-47.*

NEW TERRYTOONS (TV)
Dell Publishing Co./Gold Key: 6-8/60 - No. 8, 3-5/62; 10/62 - No. 54, 1/79

1(1960-Dell)-Deputy Dawg, Dinky Duck & Hashimoto-San begin (1st app. of each) 9 18 27 65 113 160
2-8(1962) 6 12 18 41 66 90
1(30010-210)(10/62-Gold Key, 84 pgs.)-Heckle & Jeckle begins 9 18 27 65 113 160
2(30010-301)-84 pgs. 8 16 24 58 97 135
3-5 4 8 12 28 44 60
6-10 4 8 12 22 34 45
11-20 3 6 9 16 22 28
21-30 2 4 6 9 13 16
31-43 1 3 4 6 8 10
44-54: Mighty Mouse-c/s in all 2 4 6 8 11 14

NOTE: *Reprints: #4-12, 38, 40, 47. (See March of Comics #379, 393, 412, 435)*

NEW TESTAMENT STORIES VISUALIZED
Standard Publishing Co.: 1946 - 1947

"New Testament Heroes–Acts of Apostles Visualized, Book I"
"New Testament Heroes–Acts of Apostles Visualized, Book II"
"Parables Jesus Told" Set.... 17 34 51 98 154 210

NOTE: *All three are contained in a cardboard case, illustrated on front and info about the set.*

NEW THUNDERBOLTS (Continues in Thunderbolts #100)
Marvel Comics: Jan, 2005 - No. 18, Apr, 2006 ($2.99)

1-18: 1-Grummett-a/Nicieza-s. 1-Captain Marvel app. 2-Namor app. 4-Wolverine app. 3.00
... Vol. 1: One Step Forward (2005, $14.99) r/#1-6 15.00
... Vol. 2: Modern Marvels (2005, $14.99) r/#7-12 15.00
... Vol. 3: Right of Power (2006, $17.99) r/#13-18 & Thunderbolts #100 18.00

NEW TITANS, THE (Formerly The New Teen Titans)
DC Comics: No. 50, Dec, 1988 - No. 130, Feb, 1996 ($1.75/$2.25)

50-Perez-c/a begins; new origin Wonder Girl 6.00
51-59: 50-55-Painted-c. 55-Nightwing (Dick Grayson) forces Danny Chase to resign; Batman app. in flashback, Wonder Girl becomes Troia 3.00
60,61: 60-A Lonely Place of Dying Part 2 continues from Batman #440; new Robin tie-in; Timothy Drake app. 61-A Lonely Place of Dying Part 4 3.00
62-99,101-124,126-130: 62-65: Deathstroke the Terminator app. 65-Tim Drake (Robin) app. 70-1st Deathstroke solo cover/sty. 71-(44 pgs.)-10th anniversary issue; Deathstroke cameo. 72-79-Deathstroke in all: 74-Intro. Pantha. 79-Terra brought back to life; 1 panel cameo Team Titans (1st app.). Deathstroke in #80-84,86. 80-2nd full app. Team Titans. 83,84-Deathstroke kills his son, Jericho. 85-Team Titans app. 86-Deathstroke vs. Nightwing-c/story; last Deathstroke app. 87-New costume Nightwing. 90-92-Parts 2,5,8 Total Chaos (Team Titans). 115-(11/94) 2.50
100-($3.50, 52 pgs.)-Holo-grafx foil-c 3.50
125 (3.50)-wraparound-c 3.50
#0-(10/94) Zero Hour, released between #114 & 115 2.50
Annual 5-10 ('89-'94, 68 pgs.. 7-Armaggedon 2001 x-over; 1st full app. Teen (Team) Titans (new group). 8-Deathstroke app.; Eclipso app. (minor). 10-Elseworlds story 3.50
Annual 11 (1995, $3.95)-Year One story 4.00

NOTE: *Perez a-50-55p, 57,60p, 58,59,61(layouts); c-50-61, 62-67i, Annual 5i; co-plots-66.*

NEW TV FUNNIES (See New Funnies)

NEW TWO-FISTED TALES, THE
Dark Horse Comics/Byron Preiss:1993 ($4.95, limited series, 52 pgs.)

1-Kurtzman-r & new-a 5.00

NOTE: *Eisner c-1i. Kurtzman c-1p, 2.*

NEWUNIVERSAL
Marvel Comics: Feb, 2007 - No. 6, July, 2007 ($2.99)

1-6-Warren Ellis-s/Salvador Larroca-a. 1,2-Variant covers by Ribic 3.00
...: 1959 (9/08, $3.99) Aftermath of the White Event of 1953; Tony Stark app. 4.00

New Warriors #10 © MAR

New X-Men #45 © MAR

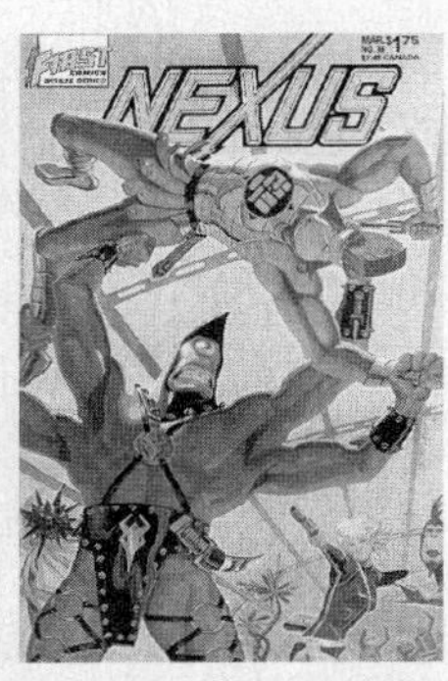

Nexus #18 © FC

GD 2.0 | VG 4.0 | FN 6.0 | VF 8.0 | VF/NM 9.0 | NM- 9.2

...: Conqueror (10/08, $3.99) The White Event of 2689 B.C.; Eric Nguyen-a 4.00
... : Everything Went White HC (2007, $19.99) r/#1-6; sketch pages 20.00
... : Everything Went White SC (2008, $14.99) r/#1-6; sketch pages 15.00

NEWUNIVERSAL: SHOCKFRONT
Marvel Comics: Jul, 2008 - Present ($2.99)

1,2-Warren Ellis-s/Steve Kurth-a 3.00

NEW WARRIORS, THE (See Thor #411,412)
Marvel Comics: July, 1990 - No. 75, 1996 ($1.00/$1.25/$1.50)

1-Williamson-i; Bagley-c/a(p) in 1-13, Annual 1 5.00
1-Gold 2nd printing (7/91) 2.50
2-5: 1,3-Guice-c(i). 2-Williamson-c/a(i). 3.00
6-24,26-49,51-75: 7-Punisher cameo (last pg.). 8,9-Punisher app. 14-Darkhawk & Namor x-over. 17-Fantastic Four & Silver Surfer x-over. 19-Gideon (of X-Force) app. 28-Intro Turbo & Cardinal. 31-Cannonball & Warpath app. 42-Nova vs. Firelord. 46-Photo-c. 47-Bound-in S-M trading card sheet. 52-12 pg. ad insert. 62-Scarlet Spider-c/app. 70-Spider-Man-c/app. 72-Avengers-c/app. 2.50
25-($2.50, 52 pgs.)-Die-cut cover 3.00
40,60: 40-($2.25)-Gold foil collector's edition 3.00
50-($2.95, 52 pgs.)-Glow in the dark-c 3.00
Annual 1-4('91-'94,68 pgs.)-1-Origins all members; 3rd app. X-Force (cont'd from New Mutants Ann. #7 & cont'd in X-Men Ann. #15); x-over before X-Force #1. 3-Bagged w/card 3.00

NEW WARRIORS, THE
Marvel Comics: Oct, 1999 - No. 10, July, 2000 ($2.99/$2.50)

0-Wizard supplement; short story and preview sketchbook 2.25
1-($2.99) 3.00
2-11: 2-Two covers. 5-Generation X app. 9-Iron Man-c 2.50

NEW WARRIORS (See Civil War #1)
Marvel Comics: Aug, 2005 - No. 6, Feb, 2006 ($2.99, limited series)

1-6-Scottie Young-a 3.00
...: Reality Check TPB (2006, $14.99) r/#1-6 15.00

NEW WARRIORS (The Initiative)
Marvel Comics: Aug, 2007 - No. 20, Mar, 2009 ($2.99)

1-19: 1-Medina-a; new team is formed. 2-Jubilee app. 14-16-Secret Invasion 3.00
20-($3.99) 4.00
...: Defiant TPB (2008, $14.99) r/#1-6 15.00

NEW WAVE, THE
Eclipse Comics: 6/10/86 - No. 13, 3/87 (#1-8: bi-weekly, 20pgs; #9-13: monthly)

1-13:1-Origin, concludes #5. 6-Origin Megabyte. 8,9-The Heap returns. 13-Snyder-c 2.50
...Versus the Volunteers 3-D #1,2(4/87): 1-Snyder-c 3.00

NEW WEST, THE
Black Bull Comics: Mar, 2005 - No. 2, Jun, 2005 ($4.99, limited series)

1,2-Phil Noto-a/c; Jimmy Palmiotti-s 5.00

NEW WORLD (See Comic Books, series I)

NEW WORLDS
Caliber: 1996 - No. 6 ($2.95/$3.95, 80 pgs., B&W, anthology)

1-6: 1-Mister X & other stories 4.00

NEW X-MEN (See X-Men *2nd series* #114-156)

NEW X-MEN (Academy X) (Continued from New Mutants)
Marvel Comics: July, 2004 - Present ($2.99)

1-46: 1,2-Green-c/a. 16-19-House of M. 20,21-Decimation. 40-Endangered Species back-ups begin. 44-46-Messiah Complex x-over; Ramos-a 3.00
Yearbook 1 (12/05, $3.99) new story and profile pages 4.00
...: Childhood's End Vol. 1 TPB (2006, $10.99) r/#20-23 11.00
...: Childhood's End Vol. 2 TPB (2006, $10.99) r/#24-27 11.00
...: Childhood's End Vol. 3 TPB (2006, $10.99) r/#28-32 11.00
...: Childhood's End Vol. 4 TPB (2007, $10.99) r/#33-36 11.00
...: Childhood's End Vol. 5 TPB (2007, $17.99) r/#37-43 18.00
House of M: New X-Men TPB (2006, $13.99) r/#16-19 and selections from Secrets Of The House of M one-shot 14.00
... Vol. 1: Choosing Sides TPB (2004, $14.99) r/#1-6 15.00
... Vol. 2: Haunted TPB (2005, $14.99) r/#7-12 15.00
... Vol. 3: X-Posed TPB (2006, $14.99) r/#12-15 & Yearbook Special 15.00

NEW X-MEN: HELLIONS
Marvel Comics: July, 2005 - No. 4, Oct, 2005 ($2.99, limited series)

1-4-Henry-a/Weir & DeFilippis-s 3.00
TPB (2006, $9.99) r/#1-4 10.00

NEW YORK GIANTS (See Thrilling True Story of the Baseball Giants)

NEW YORK STATE JOINT LEGISLATIVE COMMITTEE TO STUDY THE PUBLICATION OF COMICS, THE
N.Y. State Legislative Document: 1951, 1955

This document was referenced by Wertham for **Seduction of the Innocent.** Contains numerous repros from comics showing violence, sadism, torture, and sex. 1955 version (196p, No. 37, 2/23/55) - Sold for $180 in 1986.

NEW YORK, THE BIG CITY
Kitchen Sink Press: 1986 ($10.95, B&W); **DC Comics:** July, 2000 ($12.95, B&W)

nn-Will Eisner-s/a 13.00

NEW YORK WORLD'S FAIR (Also see Big Book of Fun & New Book of Fun)
National Periodical Publ.: 1939, 1940 (100 pgs.; cardboard covers)
(DC's 4th & 5th annuals)

1939-Scoop Scanlon, Superman (blond haired Superman on-c), Sandman, Zatara, Slam Bradley, Ginger Snap by Bob Kane begin; 1st published app. The Sandman (see Adventure #40 for his 1st drawn story); Vincent Sullivan-c; cover background by Guardineer 1700 3400 5100 12,750 29,000 –
1940-Batman, Hourman, Johnny Thunderbolt, Red, White & Blue & Hanko (by Creig Flessel) app.; Superman, Batman & Robin-c (1st time they all appear together); early Robin app.; 1st Burnley-c/a (per Burnley) 922 1844 2766 6915 15,500 –

NOTE: *The 1939 edition was published 4/29/39 and released 4/30/39, the day the fair opened, at 25¢, and was first sold only at the fair. Since all other comics were 10¢, it didn't sell. Remaining copies were advertised beginning in the August issues of most DC comics for 25¢, but soon the price was dropped to 15¢. Everyone that sent a quarter through the mail for it received a free Superman #1 or a #2 to make up the dime difference. 15¢ stickers were placed over the 25¢ price. Four variations on the 15¢ stickers are known. The 1940 edition was published 5/11/40 and was priced at 15¢. It was a precursor to World's Best #1.*

NEW YORK: YEAR ZERO
Eclipse Comics: July, 1988 - No. 4, Oct, 1988 ($2.00, B&W, limited series)

1-4 2.50

NEXT, THE
DC Comics: Sept, 2006 - No. 6, Feb, 2007 ($2.99, limited series)

1-6-Tad Williams-s/Dietrich Smith-a; Superman app. 3.00

NEXT MEN (See John Byrne's...)

NEXT NEXUS, THE
First Comics: Jan, 1989 - No. 4, April, 1989 ($1.95, limited series, Baxter paper)

1-4: Mike Baron scripts & Steve Rude-c/a. 2.50
TPB (10/89, $9.95) r/series 10.00

NEXTWAVE: AGENTS OF H.A.T.E
Marvel Comics: Mar, 2006 - No. 12, Mar, 2007 ($2.99)

1-12-Warren Ellis-s/Stuart Immonen-a. 2-Fin Fang Foom app. 12-Devil Dinosaur app. 3.00
Vol. 1 - This Is What They Want HC (2006, $19.99) r/#1-6; Ellis original pitch 20.00
Vol. 1 - This Is What They Want SC (2007, $14.99) r/#1-6; Ellis original pitch 15.00
Vol. 2 - I Kick Your Face HC (2007, $19.99) r/#7-12 20.00
Vol. 2 - I Kick Your Face SC (2008, $14.99) r/#7-12 15.00

NEXUS (See First Comics Graphic Novel #4, 19 & The Next Nexus)
Capital Comics/First Comics No. 7 on: June, 1981 - No. 6, Mar, 1984; No. 7, Apr, 1985 - No. 80?, May, 1991 (Direct sales only, 36 pgs.; V2#1('83)-printed on Baxter paper)

1-B&W version; mag. size; w/double size poster 3 6 9 14 20 26
1-B&W 1981 limited edition; 500 copies printed and signed; same as above except this version has a 2-pg. poster & a pencil sketch on paperboard by Steve Rude 4 8 12 24 37 50
2-B&W, magazine size 2 4 6 11 16 20
3-B&W, magazine size; Brunner back-c; contains 33-1/3 rpm record ($2.95 price) 2 4 6 9 13 16
V2#1-Color version 4.00
2-49,51-80: 2-Nexus' origin begins. 67-Snyder-c/a 2.50
50-($3.50, 52 pgs.) 3.50
Hardcover Volume One (Dark Horse Books, 11/05, $49.95) r/#1-3 & V2 #1-4; creator bios 50.00
HC Volume Two (Dark Horse Books, 3/06, $49.95) r/V2 #5-11; creator bios 50.00
HC Volume Three (Dark Horse Books, 5/06, $49.95) r/V2 #12-18; Marz forward 50.00
HC Volume Four (Dark Horse Books, 8/06, $49.95) r/V2 #19-25; Powell forward 50.00
HC Volume Five (Dark Horse Books, 2/07, $49.95) r/V2 #26-32; Brubaker forward 50.00
HC Volume Six (Dark Horse Books, 2/07, $49.95) r/V2 #33-39; Evanier forward 50.00
HC Volume Seven (Dark Horse Books, 2/08, $49.95) r/V2 #40-46; Brunning forward 50.00
HC Volume Eight (Dark Horse Books, 1/09, $49.95) r/V2 #47-52 and The Next Nexus #1; interview with original publishers John Davis and Milton Griepp 50.00

NOTE: ***Bissette*** *c-V2#29.* ***Giffen*** *c/a-V2#23.* ***Gulacy*** *c-1 (B&W), 2(B&W).* ***Mignola*** *c/a-V2#28.* ***Rude*** *c-3(B&W), V2#1-22, 24-27, 33-36, 39-42, 45-48, 50, 58-60, 75; a-1-3, V2#1-7, 8-16p, 18-22p, 24-27p, 33-36p, 39-42p, 45-48p, 50, 58, 59p, 60.* ***Paul Smith*** *a-V2#37, 38, 43, 44, 51-55p; c-V2#37, 38, 43, 44, 51-55.*

NEXUS
Rude Dude Productions: No. 99, July, 2007 - Present ($2.99)

99-Mike Baron scripts & Steve Rude-c/a 3.00

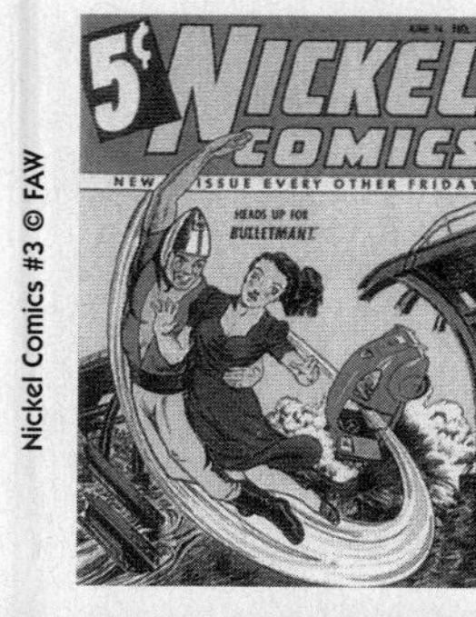

Nickel Comics #3 © FAW

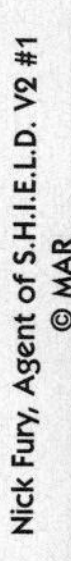

Nick Fury, Agent of S.H.I.E.L.D. V2 #1 © MAR

Nightcrawler V2 #4 © MAR

GD VG FN VF VF/NM NM-
2.0 4.0 6.0 8.0 9.0 9.2

100-($4.99) Part 2 of Space Opera; back-up feature: History of Nexus 5.00
101/102-(6/09, $4.95) Combined issue 5.00
... Greatest Hits (8/07, $1.99) Excerpts from previous issues and preview of #99 2.25
...: The Origin (11/07, $3.99) reprints the 7/96 one-shot 4.00

NEXUS: ALIEN JUSTICE
Dark Horse Comics: Dec, 1992 - No. 3, Feb, 1993 ($3.95, limited series)
1-3: Mike Baron scripts & Steve Rude-c/a 4.00

NEXUS: EXECUTIONER'S SONG
Dark Horse Comics: June, 1996 - No. 4, Sept, 1996 ($2.95, limited series)
1-4: Mike Baron scripts & Steve Rude-c/a 3.00

NEXUS FILES
First Comics: 1989 ($4.50, color/16pgs. B&W, one-shot, squarebound, 52 pgs.)
1-New Rude-a; info on Nexus 4.50

NEXUS: GOD CON
Dark Horse Comics: Apr, 1997 - No. 2, May, 1997 ($2.95, limited series)
1,2-Baron-s/Rude-c/a 3.00

NEXUS LEGENDS
First Comics: May, 1989 - No. 23, Mar, 1991 ($1.50, Baxter paper)\
1-23: R/1-3(Capital) & early First Comics issues w/new Rude covers #1-6,9,10 2.50

NEXUS MEETS MADMAN (...Special)
Dark Horse Comics: May, 1996 ($2.95, one-shot)
nn-Mike Baron & Mike Allred scripts, Steve Rude-c/a. 3.00

NEXUS: NIGHTMARE IN BLUE
Dark Horse Comics: July, 1997 - No. 4, Oct, 1997 ($2.95, limited series)
1-4: 1,2,4-Adam Hughes-c 3.00

NEXUS: THE LIBERATOR
Dark Horse Comics: Aug, 1992 - No. 4, Nov, 1992 ($2.95, limited series)
1-4 3.00

NEXUS: THE ORIGIN
Dark Horse Comics: July, 1996 ($3.95, one-shot)
nn-Mike Baron- scripts, Steve Rude-c/a. 4.00

NEXUS: THE WAGES OF SIN
Dark Horse Comics: Mar, 1995 - No. 4, June, 1995 ($2.95, limited series)
1-4 3.00

NFL SUPERPRO
Marvel Comics: Oct, 1991 - No. 12, Sept, 1992 ($1.00)
1-12: 1-Spider-Man-c/app. 2.50
Special Edition (9/91, $2.00) Jusko painted-c 3.00
Super Bowl Edition (3/91, squarebound) Jusko painted-c 4.00

NICKEL COMICS
Dell Publishing Co.: 1938 (Pocket size - 7-1/2x5-1/2")(68 pgs.)
1- "Bobby & Chip" by Otto Messmer, Felix the Cat artist. Contains some English reprints
81 162 243 518 884 1250

NICKEL COMICS
Fawcett Publications: Feb 1940
nn - Ashcan comic, not distributed to newsstands, only for in-house use. A CGC certified 9.6 copy sold for $7,200 in 2003. In 2008, a CGC certified 8.5 sold for $2,390 and an uncertified Near Mint copy sold for $3,100.

NICKEL COMICS
Fawcett Publications: May, 1940 - No. 8, Aug, 1940 (36 pgs.; Bi-Weekly; 5¢)
1-Origin/1st app. Bulletman 366 732 1098 2562 4481 6400
2 116 232 348 742 1271 1800
3 84 168 252 538 919 1300
4-The Red Gaucho begins 67 134 201 426 733 1040
5-7 66 132 198 425 725 1025
8-World's Fair-c; Bulletman moved to Master Comics #7 in October (scarce)
87 174 261 553 952 1350
NOTE: ***Beck** c-5-8. **Jack Binder** c-1-4. Bondage c-5. Bulletman c-1-8.*

NICK FURY, AGENT OF SHIELD (See Fury, Marvel Spotlight #31 & Shield)
Marvel Comics Group: 6/68 - No. 15, 11/69; No. 16, 11/70 - No. 18, 3/71
1 13 26 39 90 165 240
2-4: 4-Origin retold 8 16 24 52 86 120
5-Classic-c 8 16 24 56 93 130
6,7: 7-Salvador Dali painting swipe 7 14 21 49 80 110
8-11,13: 9-Hate Monger begins, ends #11. 10-Smith layouts/pencil. 11-Smith-c. 13-1st app. Super-Patriot; last 12¢ issue 4 8 12 28 44 60
12-Smith-c/a 5 10 15 30 48 65
14-Begin 15¢ issues 4 8 12 24 37 50
15-1st app. & death of Bullseye-c/story(11/69); Nick Fury shot & killed; last 15¢ issue
8 16 24 54 90 125
16-18-(25¢, 52 pgs.)-r/Str. Tales #135-143 3 6 9 20 30 40
TPB (May 2000, $19.95) r/ Strange Tales #150-168 20.00
...: Who is Scorpio? TPB (11/00, $12.95) r/#1-3,5; Steranko-c 13.00
NOTE: ***Adkins** a-3i. **Craig** a-10i. **Sid Greene** a-12i. **Kirby** a-16-18r. **Springer** a-4, 6, 7, 8p, 9, 10p, 11; c-8, 9. **Steranko** a(p)-1-3, 5; c-1-7.*

NICK FURY AGENT OF SHIELD (Also see Strange Tales #135)
Marvel Comics: Dec, 1983 - No. 2, Jan, 1984 (2.00, 52 pgs., Baxter paper)
1,2-r/Nick Fury #1-4; new Steranko-c 3.50

NICK FURY, AGENT OF S.H.I.E.L.D.
Marvel Comics: Sept, 1989 - No. 47, May, 1993 ($1.50/$1.75)
V2#1-26,30-47: 10-Capt. America app. 13-Return of The Yellow Claw. 15-Fantastic Four app. 30,31-Deathlok app. 36-Cage app. 37-Woodgod c/story. 38-41-Flashes back to pre-Shield days after WWII. 44-Capt. America-c/s. 45-Viper-c/s. 46-Gideon x-over 2.50
27-29-Wolverine-c/stories 3.00
NOTE: ***Alan Grant** scripts-11. **Guice** a(p)-20-23, 25, 26; c-20-28.*

NICK FURY'S HOWLING COMMANDOS
Marvel Comics: Dec, 2005 - No. 6, May, 2006 ($2.99)
1-6: 1-Giffen-s/Francisco-a 3.00
1-Director's Cut ($3.99) r/#1 with original script and sketch design pages 4.00

NICK FURY VS. S.H.I.E.L.D.
Marvel Comics: June, 1988 - No. 6, Nov, 1988 ($3.50, 52 pgs, deluxe format)
1,2: 1-Steranko-c. 2-(Low print run) Sienkiewicz-c 5.00
3-6 4.00

NICK HALIDAY (Thrill of the Sea)
Argo: May, 1956
1-Daily & Sunday strip-r by Petree 8 16 24 44 57 70

NIGHT AND THE ENEMY (Graphic Novel)
Comico: 1988 (8-1/2x11") ($11.95, color, 80 pgs.)
1-Harlan Ellison scripts/Ken Steacy-c/a; r/Epic Illustrated & new-a (1st & 2nd printings) 12.00
1-Limited edition ($39.95) 40.00

NIGHT BEFORE CHRISTMAS, THE (See March of Comics No. 152 in the Promotional Comics section)

NIGHT BEFORE CHRISTMASK, THE
Dark Horse Comics: Nov, 1994 ($9.95, one-shot)
nn-Hardcover book; The Mask; Rick Geary-c/a 10.00

NIGHTBREED (See Clive Barker's Nightbreed)

NIGHT CLUB
Image Comics: Apr, 2005 - No. 4, Dec, 2006 ($2.95/$2.99, limited series)
1-4: 1-Mike Baron-s/Mike Norton-a 3.00

NIGHTCRAWLER (X-Men)
Marvel Comics Group: Nov, 1985 - No. 4, Feb, 1986 (Mini-series from X-Men)
1-4: 1-Cockrum-c/a 4.00

NIGHTCRAWLER (Volume 2)
Marvel Comics: Feb, 2002 - No. 4, May, 2002 ($2.50, limited series)
1-4-Matt Smith-a 2.50

NIGHTCRAWLER
Marvel Comics: Nov, 2004 - No. 12, Jan, 2006 ($2.99)
1-12: 1-6-Robertson-a/Land-c. 2-Magik app. 8-Wolverine app. 10-Man-Thing app. 3.00
...: The Devil Inside TPB (2005, $14.99) r/#1-6 15.00
...: The Winding Way TPB (2006, $14.99) r/#7-12 15.00

NIGHTFALL: THE BLACK CHRONICLES
DC Comics (Homage): Dec, 1999 - No. 3, Feb, 2000 ($2.95, limited series)
1-3-Coker-a/Gilmore-s 3.00

NIGHT FORCE, THE (See New Teen Titans #21)
DC Comics: Aug, 1982 - No. 14, Sept, 1983 (60¢)
1 4.00
2-14: 13-Origin Baron Winter. 14-Nudity panels 3.00
NOTE: ***Colan** c/a-1-14p. **Giordano** c-1i, 2i, 4i, 5i, 7i, 12i.*

NIGHT FORCE
DC Comics: Dec, 1996 - No. 12, Nov, 1997 ($2.25)

Nightmare #1 © Skywald

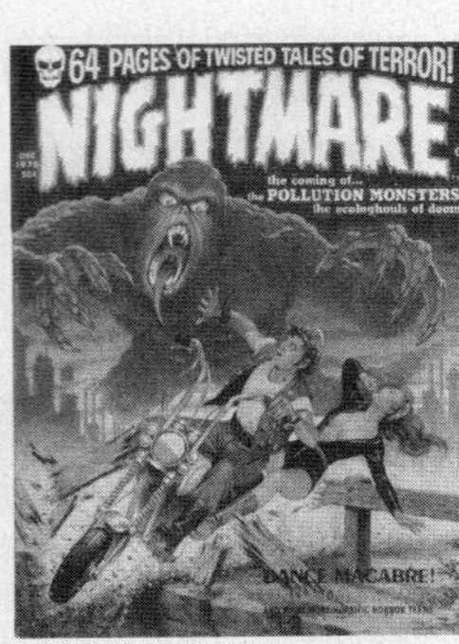

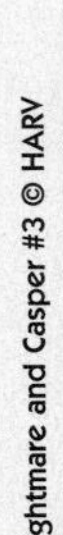
Nightmare and Casper #3 © HARV

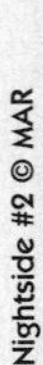
Nightside #2 © MAR

	GD 2.0	VG 4.0	FN 6.0	VF 8.0	VF/NM 9.0	NM- 9.2

1-12: 1-3-Wolfman-s/Anderson-a(p). 8-"Convergence" part 2 — 2.50

NIGHT GLIDER
Topps Comics (Kirbyverse): April, 1993 ($2.95, one-shot)

1-Kirby c-1, Heck-a; polybagged w/Kirbychrome trading card — 3.00

NIGHTHAWK
Marvel Comics: Sept, 1998 - No. 3, Nov, 1998 ($2.99, mini-series)

1-3-Krueger-s; Daredevil app. — 3.00

NIGHTINGALE, THE
Henry H. Stansbury Once-Upon-A-Time Press, Inc.: 1948 (10¢, 7-1/4x10-1/4", 14 pgs., 1/2 B&W)

(Very Rare)-Low distribution; distributed to Westchester County & Bronx, N.Y. only; used in **Seduction of the Innocent**, pg. 312,313 as the 1st and only "good" comic book ever published. Ill. by Dong Kingman; 1,500 words of text, printed on high quality paper & no word balloons. Copyright registered 10/22/48, distributed week of 12/5/48. (By Hans Christian Andersen)
Estimated value........ — 250.00

NIGHT MAN, THE (See Sludge #1)
Malibu Comics (Ultraverse): Oct, 1993 - No. 23, Aug, 1995 ($1.95/$2.50)

	GD	VG	FN	VF	VF/NM	NM-
1-($2.50, 48 pgs.)-Rune flip-c/story by B. Smith (3 pgs.)						2.50
1-Ultra-Limited silver foil-c						6.00
2-15, 17: 3-Break-Thru x-over; Freex app. 4-Origin Firearm (2 pgs.) by Chaykin. 6-TNTNT app. 8-1st app. Teknight						2.50
16 ($3.50)-flip book (Ultraverse Premiere #11)						3.50
...:The Pilgrim Conundrum Saga (1/95, $3.95, 68 pgs.)-Strangers app.						4.00
18-23: 22-Loki-c/a						2.50
Infinity ($1.50)						2.50
...Vs. Wolverine #0-Kelley Jones-c; mail in offer	1	3	4	6	8	10

NOTE: Zeck a-16.

NIGHT MAN, THE
Malibu Comics (Ultraverse): Sept, 1995 - No.4, Dec, 1995 ($1.50, lim. series)

1-4: Post Black September storyline — 2.50

NIGHT MAN, THE /GAMBIT
Malibu Comics (Ultraverse): Mar, 1996 - No. 3, May, 1996 ($1.95, lim. series)

0-Limited Premium Edition — 4.00
1-3: David Quinn scripts in all. 3-Rhiannon discovered to be The Night Man's mother — 2.50

NIGHTMARE
Ziff-Davis (Approved Comics)/St. John No. 3: Summer, 1952 - No. 3, Winter, 1952, 53 (Painted-c)

	GD	VG	FN	VF	VF/NM	NM-
1-1 pg. Kinstler-a; Tuska-a(2)	55	110	165	352	601	850
2-Kinstler-a-Poe's "Pit & the Pendulum"	39	78	117	240	395	550
3-Kinstler-a	36	72	108	211	343	475

NIGHTMARE (Weird Horrors #1-9) (Amazing Ghost Stories #14 on)
St. John Publishing Co.: No. 10, Dec, 1953 - No. 13, Aug, 1954

	GD	VG	FN	VF	VF/NM	NM-
10-Reprints Ziff-Davis Weird Thrillers #2 w/new Kubert-c plus 2 pgs. Kinstler-a; Anderson, Colan & Toth-a	53	106	159	334	567	800
11-Krigstein-a; painted-c; Poe adapt., "Hop Frog"	39	78	117	240	395	550
12-Kubert bondage-c; adaptation of Poe's "The Black Cat"; Cannibalism story	39	78	117	231	378	525
13-Reprints Z-D Weird Thrillers #3 with new cover; Powell-a(2), Tuska-a; Baker-c	28	56	84	165	270	375

NIGHTMARE (Magazine) (Also see Psycho)
Skywald Publishing Corp.: Dec, 1970 - No. 23, Feb, 1975 (B&W, 68 pgs.)

	GD	VG	FN	VF	VF/NM	NM-
1-Everett-a; Heck-a; Shores-a	9	18	27	65	113	160
2-5,8,9: 2,4-Decapitation story. 5-Nazi-s; Boris Karloff 4 pg. photo/text-s. 8-Features E.C. movie "Tales From the Crypt"; reprints some E.C. comics panels. 9-Wrightson-a; bondage-c; 1st Lovecraft Saggoth Chronicles/Cthulhu	6	12	18	37	59	80
6-Kaluta-a; Jeff Jones-c, photo & interview; 1st Living Gargoyle; Love Witch-s w/nudity; Boris Karloff-s	6	12	18	39	62	85
7	5	10	15	30	48	65
10-Wrightson-a (1 pg.); Princess of Earth-c/s; Edward & Mina Sartyros, the Human Gargoyles series continues from Psycho #8	6	12	18	39	62	85
11-19: 12-Excessive gore, severed heads. 13-Lovecraft-s. 15-Dracula-c/s. 17-Vampires issue; Autobiography of a Vampire series begins	4	8	12	24	37	50
20-John Byrne's 1st artwork (2 pgs.)(8/74); severed head-c; Hitler app.	8	16	24	52	86	120
21-23: 21-(1974 Summer Special)-Kaluta-a. 22-Tomb of Horror issue. 23-(1975 Winter Special)	4	8	12	28	44	60
Annual 1(1972)-Squarebound; B. Jones-a	4	8	12	28	44	60
Winter Special 1(1973)-All new material	4	8	12	24	37	50
Yearbook nn(1974)-B. Jones, Reese, Wildey-a	4	8	12	24	37	50

NOTE: ***Adkins** a-5. **Boris** c-2, 3, 5 (#4 is not by Boris). **Buckler** a-3, 15. **Byrne** a-20p. **Everett** a-1, 2, 4, 5, 12. **Jeff Jones** a-6, 21r(Psycho #6); c-6. **Katz** a-3, 5, 21. **Reese** a-4, 5. **Wildey** a-4, 5, 6, 21, '74 Yearbook. **Wrightson** a-9, 10.*

NIGHTMARE (Alex Nino's)
Innovation Publishing: 1989 ($1.95)

1-Alex Nino-a — 2.50

NIGHTMARE
Marvel Comics: Dec, 1994 - No. 4, Mar, 1995 ($1.95, limited series)

1-4 — 2.50

NIGHTMARE & CASPER (See Harvey Hits #71) (Casper & Nightmare #6 on) (See Casper The Friendly Ghost #19)
Harvey Publications: Aug, 1963 - No. 5, Aug, 1964 (25¢)

	GD	VG	FN	VF	VF/NM	NM-
1-All reprints?	8	16	24	54	90	125
2-5: All reprints?	5	10	15	32	51	70

NIGHTMARE ON ELM STREET, A (Also see Freddy Krueger's...)
DC Comics (WildStorm): Dec, 2006 - Present ($2.99)

1-8: 1-Two covers by Harris & Bradstreet; Dixon-s/West-a — 3.00

NIGHTMARES (See Do You Believe in Nightmares)

NIGHTMARES
Eclipse Comics: May, 1985 - No. 2, May, 1985 ($1.75, Baxter paper)

1,2 — 3.00

NIGHTMARE THEATER
Chaos! Comics: Nov, 1997 - No. 4, Nov, 1997 ($2.50, mini-series)

1-4-Horror stories by various; Wrightson-a — 2.50

NIGHTMARK: BLOOD & HONOR
Alpha Productions: 1994 - No. 3, 1994 ($2.50, B&W, mini-series)

1,2 — 2.50

NIGHTMARK MYSTERY SPECIAL
Alpha Productions: Jan, 1994 ($2.50, B&W)

1 — 2.50

NIGHTMASK
Marvel Comics Group: Nov, 1986 - No. 12, Oct, 1987

1-12 — 2.50

NIGHT MASTER
Silverwolf: Feb, 1987 ($1.50, B&W)

1-Tim Vigil-c/a — 3.00

NIGHT MUSIC (See Eclipse Graphic Album Series, The Magic Flute)
Eclipse Comics: Dec, 1984 - No. 11, 1990 ($1.75/$3.95/$4.95, Baxter paper)

1-7: 3-Russell's Jungle Book adapt. 4,5-Pelleas And Melisande (double titled) 6-Salomé (double titled). 7-Red Dog #1 — 2.50
8-($3.95) Ariane and Bluebeard — 4.00
9-11-($4.95) The Magic Flute; Russell adapt. — 5.00

NIGHT NURSE
Marvel Comics Group: Nov, 1972 - No. 4, May, 1973

	GD	VG	FN	VF	VF/NM	NM-
1	11	22	33	78	139	200
2-4	8	16	24	58	97	135

NIGHT OF MYSTERY
Avon Periodicals: 1953 (no month) (one-shot)

	GD	VG	FN	VF	VF/NM	NM-
nn-1 pg. Kinstler-a, Hollingsworth-c	45	90	135	284	480	675

NIGHT OF THE GRIZZLY, THE (See Movie Classics)

NIGHTRAVEN (See Marvel Graphic Novel)

NIGHT RIDER (Western)
Marvel Comics Group: Oct, 1974 - No. 6, Aug, 1975

	GD	VG	FN	VF	VF/NM	NM-
1: 1-6 reprint Ghost Rider #1-6 (#1-origin)	2	4	6	10	14	18
2-6	2	4	6	8	10	12

NIGHT'S CHILDREN: THE VAMPIRE
Millenium: July, 1995 - No. 2, Aug, 1995 ($2.95, B&W)

1,2: Wendy Snow-Lang story & art — 3.00

NIGHTSIDE
Marvel Comics: Dec, 2001 - No. 4, Mar, 2002 ($2.99)

1-4: 1-Weinberg-s/Derenick-a; intro Sydney Taine — 3.00

NIGHTS INTO DREAMS (Based on video game)
Archie Comics: Feb, 1998 -No. 6, Oct, 1998 ($1.75, limited series)

Night Terrors #1 © Wrightson & Monks

Nightwing #141 © DC

9-11 - The World's Finest... © DC

GD 2.0 | VG 4.0 | FN 6.0 | VF 8.0 | VF/NM 9.0 | NM- 9.2

1-6 2.50

NIGHTSTALKERS (Also see Midnight Sons Unlimited)
Marvel Comics (Midnight Sons #14 on): Nov, 1992 - No. 18, Apr, 1994 ($1.75)

1-($2.75, 52 pgs.)-Polybagged w/poster; part 5 of Rise of the Midnight Sons storyline; Garney/Palmer-c/a begins; Hannibal King, Blade & Frank Drake begin (see Tomb of Dracula for & Dr. Strange) 3.00
2-9,11-18: 5-Punisher app. 7-Ghost Rider app. 8,9-Morbius app. 14-Spot varnish-c. 14,15-Siege of Darkness Pts 1 & 9 2.50
10-($2.25)-Outer-c is a Darkhold envelope made of black parchment w/gold ink; Midnight Massacre part 1 2.75

NIGHT TERRORS,THE
Chanting Monks Studios: 2000 ($2.75, B&W)

1-Bernie Wrightson-c; short stories, one by Wrightson-s/a 2.75

NIGHT THRASHER (Also see The New Warriors)
Marvel Comics: Aug, 1993 - No. 21, Apr, 1995 ($1.75/$1.95)

1-($2.95, 52 pgs.)-Red holo-grafx foil-c; origin 3.00
2-21: 2-Intro Tantrum. 3-Gideon (of X-Force) app. 10-Bound-in trading card sheet; Iron Man app. 15-Hulk app. 2.50

NIGHT THRASHER: FOUR CONTROL
Marvel Comics: Oct, 1992 - No. 4, Jan, 1993 ($2.00, limited series)

1-4: 2-Intro Tantrum. 3-Gideon (of X-Force) app. 2.50

NIGHT TRIBES
DC Comics (WildStorm): July, 1999 ($4.95, one-shot)

1-Golden & Sniegoski-s/Chin-a 5.00

NIGHTVEIL (Also see Femforce)
Americomics/AC Comics: Nov, 1984 - No. 7, 1987 ($1.75)

1-7 2.50
...'s Cauldron Of Horror 1 (1989, B&W)-Kubert, Powell, Wood-r plus new Nightveil story 3.00
...'s Cauldron Of Horror 2 (1990, $2.95, B&W)-Pre-code horror-r by Kubert & Powell 3.00
...'s Cauldron Of Horror 3 (1991) 3.00
Special 1 ('88, $1.95)-Kaluta-c 2.50
One Shot ('96, $5.95)-Flip book w/ Colt 6.00

NIGHTWATCH
Marvel Comics: Apr, 1994 - No. 12, Mar, 1995 ($1.50)

1-($2.95)-Collectors edition; foil-c; Ron Lim-c/a begins; Spider-Man app. 3.00
1-12-Regular edition. 2-Bound-in S-M trading card sheet; 5,6-Venom-c & app. 7,11-Cardiac app. 2.50

NIGHTWING (Also see New Teen Titans, New Titans, Showcase '93 #11,12, Tales of the New Teen Titans & Teen Titans Spotlight)
DC Comics: Sept, 1995 - No. 4, Dec, 1995 ($2.25, limited series)

1-Dennis O'Neil story/Greg Land-a in all 5.00
2-4 4.00
...: Alfred's Return (7/95, $3.50) Giordano-a 4.00
...Ties That Bind (1997, $12.95, TPB) r/mini-series & Alfred's Return 13.00

NIGHTWING
DC Comics: Oct, 1996 - No. 153, Apr, 2009 ($1.95/$1.99/$2.25/$2.50/$2.99)

1-Chuck Dixon scripts & Scott McDaniel-c/a 2 4 6 9 11 12
2,3 6.00
4-10: 6-Robin-c/app. 4.00
11-20: 13-15-Batman app. 19,20-Cataclysm pts. 2,11 3.00
21-49,51-64: 23-Green Arrow app. 26-29-Huntress-c/app. 30-Superman-c/app. 35-39-No Man's Land. 41-Land/Geraci-a begins. 46-Begin $2.25-c. 47-Texiera-c. 52-Catwoman-c/app. 54-Shrike app. 2.50
50-($3.50) Nightwing battles Torque 3.50
65-74,76-99: 65,66-Bruce Wayne: Murderer x-over pt. 3,9. 68,69: B.W.: Fugitive pt. 6,9. 70-Last Dixon-s. 71-Devin Grayson-s begin. 81-Batgirl vs. Deathstroke. 93-Blockbuster killed. 94-Copperhead app. 96-Bagged w/CD. 96-98-War Games 2.50
75-(1/03, $2.95) Intro. Tarantula 3.00
100-(2/05, $2.95) Tarantula app. 3.00
101-117: 101-Year One begins. 103-Jason Todd & Deadman app. 107-110-Hester-a. 109-Begin $2.50-c. 109,110-Villains United tie-ins. 112-Deathstroke app. 2.50
118-149,151-153: 118-One Year Later; Jason Todd as 2nd Nightwing. 120-Begin $2.99-c. 138,139-Resurrection of Ra's al Ghul x-over. 138-2nd printing. 147-Two-Face app. 3.00
150-($3.99) Batman R.I.P. x-over; Nightwing vs. Two-Face; Tan-c 4.00
#1,000,000 (11/98) teams with future Batman 2.50
Annual 1(1997, $3.95) Pulp Heroes 4.00
Annual 2 (6/07, $3.99) Dick Grayson and Barbara Gordon's shared history 4.00
...Eighty Page Giant 1 (12/00, $5.95) Intro. of Hella; Dixon-s/Haley-c 6.00
...: Big Guns (2004, $14.95, TPB) r/#47-50; Secret Files 1, Eighty Page Giant 1 15.00
...: Brothers in Blood (2007, $14.99, TPB) r/#118-124 15.00
...: A Darker Shade of Justice (2001, $19.95, TPB) r/#30-39, Secret Files #1 20.00
...: Freefall (2008, $17.99, TPB) r/#140-146 18.00
...: A Knight in Blüdhaven (1998, $14.95, TPB) r/#1-8 15.00
...: Love and Bullets (2000, $17.95, TPB) r/#1/2, 19,21,22,24-29 18.00
...: Love and War (2007, $14.99, TPB) r/#125-132 15.00
...: On the Razor's Edge (2005, $14.99, TPB) r/#52,54-60 15.00
...: Our Worlds at War (9/01, $2.95) Jae Lee-c 3.00
...: Renegade TPB (2006, $17.95) r/#112-117 18.00
...: Rough Justice (1999, $17.95, TPB) r/#9-18 18.00
Secret Files 1 (10/99, $4.95) Origin-s and pin-ups 5.00
...: The Great Leap (2009, $19.99) r/#147-153 20.00
...: The Hunt for Oracle (2003, $14.95, TPB) r/#41-46 & Birds of Prey #20,21 15.00
...: The Lost Year (2008, $14.99) r/#133-137 & Annual #2 15.00
...: The Target (2001, $5.95) McDaniel-c/a 6.00
Wizard 1/2 (Mail offer) 5.00
...: Year One (2005, $14.99) r/#101-106 15.00

NIGHTWING (See Tangent Comics/ Nightwing)

NIGHTWING AND HUNTRESS
DC Comics: May, 1998 - No. 4, Aug, 1998 ($1.95, limited series)

1-4-Grayson-s/Land & Sienkiewicz-a 2.50
TPB (2003, $9.95) r/#1/4; cover gallery 10.00

NIGHTWINGS (See DC Science Fiction Graphic Novel)

NIKKI, WILD DOG OF THE NORTH (Disney, see Movie Comics)
Dell Publishing Co.: No. 1226, Sept, 1961

Four Color 1226-Movie, photo-c 5 10 15 34 55 75

9-11 - ARTISTS RESPOND
Dark Horse Comics: 2002 ($9.95, TPB, proceeds donated to charities)

Volume 1-Short stories about the September 11 tragedies by various Dark Horse, Chaos! and Image writers and artists; Eric Drooker-c 10.00

9-11: EMERGENCY RELIEF
Alternative Comics: 2002 ($14.95, TPB, proceeds donated to the Red Cross)

nn-Short stories by various inc. Pekar, Eisner, Hester, Oeming, Noto; Cho-c 15.00

9-11 - THE WORLD'S FINEST COMIC BOOK WRITERS AND ARTISTS TELL STORIES TO REMEMBER
DC Comics: 2002 ($9.95, TPB, proceeds donated to charities)

Volume 2-Short stories about the September 11 tragedies by various DC, MAD, and WildStorm writers and artists ; Alex Ross-c 10.00

NINE RINGS OF WU-TANG
Image Comics: July, 1999 - No. 5, July, 2000 ($2.95)

Preview (7/99, $5.00, B&W) 5.00
1-5: 1-(11/99, $2.95) Clayton Henry-a 3.00
Tower Records Variant-c 5.00
Wizard #0 Prelude 2.50
TPB (1/01, $19.95) r/#1-5, Preview & Prelude; sketchbook & cover gallery 20.00

1963
Image Comics (Shadowline Ink): Apr, 1993 - No. 6, Oct, 1993 ($1.95, lim. series)

1-6: Alan Moore scripts; Veitch, Bissette & Gibbons-a(p) 2.50
1-Gold 3.00

*NOTE: **Bissette** a-2-4; **Gibbons** a-1i, 2i, 6i; c-2.*

1984 (Magazine) (1994 #11 on)
Warren Publishing Co.: June, 1978 - No. 10, Jan, 1980 ($1.50, B&W with color inserts, mature content with nudity; 84 pgs. except #4 has 92 pgs.)

1-Nino-a in all; Mutant World begins by Corben 3 6 9 14 19 24
2-10: 4-Rex Havoc begins. 7-1st Ghita of Alizarr by Thorne. 9-1st Starfire 2 4 6 9 13 16

NOTE: ***Alcala** a-1-3,5,7i. **Corben** a-1-8; c-1,2. **Nebres** a-1-8,10. **Thorne** a-7,8,10. **Wood** a-1,2,5i.*

1994 (Formerly 1984) (Magazine)
Warren Publishing Co.: No. 11, Feb, 1980 - No. 29, Feb, 1983 (B&W with color; mature; #11-(84 pgs.); #12-16,18-21,24-(76 pgs.); #17,22,23,25-29-(68 pgs.)

11,17,18,20,22,23,29: 11,17-8 pgs. color insert. 18-Giger-c. 20-1st Diana Jacklighter Manhuntress by Maroto. 22-1st Sigmund Pavlov by Nino; 1st Ariel Hart by Hsu. 23-All Nino issue 2 4 6 8 11 14
12-16,19,21,24-28: 21-1st app. Angel by Nebres. 27-The Warhawks return 1 3 4 6 8 10

NOTE: ***Corben** c-26. **Maroto** a-20, 21, 24-28. **Nebres** a-11-13, 15, 16, 18, 21, 22, 25, 28. **Nino** a-11-19, 20(2), 21, 25, 26, 28; c-21. **Redondo** c-20. **Thorne** a-11-14, 17-21, 24-26, 28, 29.*

Ninja Boy #3 © Ale Garza

Noble Causes #37 © Jay Faerber

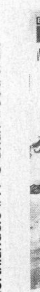

Northlanders #19 © Brian Wood & DC

	GD 2.0	VG 4.0	FN 6.0	VF 8.0	VF/NM 9.0	NM- 9.2

NINJA BOY
DC Comics (WildStorm): Oct, 2001 - No. 6, Mar, 2002 ($3.50/$2.95)

1-($3.50) Ale Garza-a/c 3.50
2-6-($2.95) 3.00
...: Faded Dreams TPB (2003, $14.95) r/#1-6; sketch pages 15.00

NINJA HIGH SCHOOL (1st series)
Antarctic Press: 1986 - No. 3, Aug, 1987 (B&W)

1-Ben Dunn-s/c/a; early Manga series 2 4 6 9 12 15
2,3 1 3 4 6 8 10

NINJAK (See Bloodshot #6, 7 & Deathmate)
Valiant/Acclaim Comics (Valiant) No. 16 on: Feb, 1994 - No. 26, Nov. 1995 ($2.25/$2.50)

1 ($3.50)-Chromium-c; Quesada-c/a(p) in #1-3 3.50
1-Gold 5.00
2-13: 3-Batman, Spawn & Random (from X-Factor) app. as costumes at party (cameo). 4-w/bound-in trading card. 5,6-X-O app. 2.50
0,00,14-26: 14-(4/95)-Begin $2.50-c. 0-(6/95, $2.50). 00-(6/95, $2.50) 2.50
Yearbook 1 (1994, $3.95) 4.00

NINJAK
Acclaim Comics (Valiant Heroes): V2#1, Mar, 1997 -No. 12, Feb, 1998 ($2.50)

V2#1-12: 1-Intro new Ninjak; 1st app. Brutakon; Kurt Busiek scripts begin; painted variant-c exists. 2-1st app. Karnivor & Zeer. 3-1st app. Gigantik, Shurikai, & Nixie. 4-Origin; 1st app. Yasuiti Motomiya; intro The Dark Dozen; Colin King cameo. 9-Copycat-c 2.50

NINJA SCROLL
DC Comics (WildStorm): Nov, 2006 - Present ($2.99)

1-12: 1-J. Torres-s/Michael Chang Ting Yu-a/c. 11-Puckett-s/Meyers-a 3.00
1-3-Variant covers by Jim Lee 5.00
TPB (2007, $19.99) r/#1-3,5-7 20.00

NINTENDO COMICS SYSTEM (Also see Adv. of Super Mario Brothers)
Valiant Comics: Feb, 1990 - No. 9, Oct, 1991 ($4.95, card stock-c, 68pgs.)

1-9: 1-Featuring Game Boy, Super Mario, Clappwall. 3-Layton-c. 5-8-Super Mario Bros. 9-Dr. Mario 1st app. 5.00

NOAH'S ARK
Spire Christian Comics/Fleming H. Revell Co.: 1973 (35/49¢)

nn-By Al Hartley 2 4 6 8 11 14

NOBLE CAUSES
Image Comics: July, 2001; Jan, 2002 - No. 4, May, 2002 ($2.95)

...First Impressions (7/01) Intro. the Noble family; Faerber-s 3.00
1-4: 1-(1/02) Back-up-s with Conner-a. 2-Igle back-up-a. 2-4-Two covers 3.00
...: Extended Family (5/03, $6.95) short stories by various 7.00
...: Extended Family 2 (6/04, $7.95) short stories by various 8.00
Vol. 1: In Sickness and in Health (2003, $12.95) r/#1-4 & ...First Impresssions 13.00

NOBLE CAUSES (Volume 3)
Image Comics: July, 2004 - No. 40, Mar, 2009 ($3.50)

1-24,26-40-Faerber-s. 1-Two covers. 2-Venture app. 5-Invincible app. 3.50
25-($4.99) Art by various; Randolph-c 5.00
Vol. 4: Blood and Water (2005, $14.95) r/#1-6 15.00
Vol. 5: Betrayals (2006, $14.99) r/#7-12 & The Pact V2 #2 15.00
Vol. 6: Hidden Agendas (2006, $15.99) r/#13-18 and Image Holiday Spec. 2005 story 16.00
Vol. 7: Powerless (2007, $15.99) r/#19-25; Wieringo sketch page 16.00

NOBLE CAUSES: DISTANT RELATIVES
Image Comics: Jul, 2003 - No. 4, Oct, 2003 ($2.95, B&W, limited series)

1-4-Faerber-s/Richardson & Ponce-a 3.00
Vol. 3: Distant Relatives (1/05, $12.95) r/#1-4; intro. by Joe Casey 13.00

NOBLE CAUSES: FAMILY SECRETS
Image Comics: Oct, 2002 - No. 4, Jan, 2003 ($2.95, limited series)

1-4-Faerber-s/Oeming-c. 1-Variant cover by Walker. 2,3-Valentino var-c. 4-Hester var-c 3.00
Vol. 2: Family Secrets (2004, $12.95) r/#1-4; sketch pages 13.00

NOBODY (Amado, Cho & Adlard's...)
Oni Press: Nov, 1998 - No. 4, Feb, 1999 ($2.95, B&W, mini-series)

1-4 3.00

NOCTURNALS, THE
Malibu Comics (Bravura): Jan, 1995 - No. 6, Aug, 1995 ($2.95, limited series)

1-6: Dan Brereton painted-c/a & scripts 3.00
1-Glow-in-the-Dark premium edition 5.00

NOCTURNALS, THE
Dark Horse Comics/Image Comics/Oni Press: one-shots and trade paperbacks

Black Planet TPB (Oni Press, 1998, $19.95) r/#1-6 (Malibu Comics series) 20.00
Black Planet and Other Stories HC (Olympian Publ.; 7/07, $39.95) r/Black Planet & Witching Hour contents; cover & sketch gallery with Brereton interviews 40.00
Carnival of Beasts (Image, 7/08, $6.99) short stories; Brereton-s/Brereton & others-a 7.00
Troll Bridge (Oni Press, 2000, $4.95, B&W & orange) Brereton-s/painted-c; art by Brereton, Chin, Art Adams, Sakai, Timm, Warren, Thompson, Purcell, Stephens and others 5.00
Unhallowed Eve TPB (Oni Press, 10/02, $9.95) r/Witching Hour & Troll Bridge one-shots 10.00
Witching Hour (Dark Horse, 5/98, $4.95) Brereton-s/a; reprints DHP stories + 8 new pgs. 5.00

NOCTURNALS: THE DARK FOREVER
Oni Press: Jul, 2001 -No. 3, Feb, 2002 ($2.95, limited series)

1-3-Brereton-s/painted-a/c 3.00
TPB (5/02, $9.95) r/#1-3; afterword & pin-ups by Alex Ross 10.00

NOCTURNE
Marvel Comics: June, 1995 - No. 4, Sept. 1995 ($1.50, limited series)

1-4 2.50

NO ESCAPE (Movie)
Marvel Comics: June, 1994 - No. 3, Aug, 1994 ($1.50)

1-3: Based on movie 2.50

NO HONOR
Image Comics (Top Cow): Feb, 2001 - No. 4, July, 2001 ($2.50)

Preview (12/00, B&W) Silvestri-c 2.50
1-4-Avery-s/Crain-a 2.50
TPB (8/03, $12.99) r/#1-4; intro. by Straczynski 13.00

NOMAD (See Captain America #180)
Marvel Comics: Nov, 1990 - No. 4, Feb, 1991 ($1.50, limited series)

1-4: 1,4-Captain America app. 2.50

NOMAD
Marvel Comics: V2#1, May, 1992 - No. 25, May, 1994 ($1.75)

V2#1-25: 1-Has gatefold-c w/map/wanted poster. 4-Deadpool x-over. 5-Punisher vs. Nomad-c/story. 6-Punisher & Daredevil-c/story cont'd in Punisher War Journal #48. 7-Gambit-c/story. 10-Red Wolf app. 21-Man-Thing-c/story. 25-Bound-in trading card sheet 2.50

NOMAD: GIRL WITHOUT A WORLD (Rikki Barnes from Captain America V2 Heroes Reborn)
Marvel Comics: Nov, 2009 - No. 4, Feb, 2010 ($3.99, limited series)

1-4-McKeever-s. 2-Falcon app. 4-Young Avengers app. 4.00

NOMAN (See Thunder Agents)
Tower Comics: Nov, 1966 - No. 2, March, 1967 (25¢, 68 pgs.)

1-Wood/Williamson-c; Lightning begins; Dynamo cameo; Kane-a(p) & Whitney-a 9 18 27 63 107 150
2-Wood-c only; Dynamo x-over; Whitney-a 6 12 18 39 62 85

NONE BUT THE BRAVE (See Movie Classics)

NOODNIK COMICS (See Pinky the Egghead)
Comic Media/Mystery/Biltmore: Dec, 1953; No. 2, Feb, 1954 - No. 5, Aug, 1954

3-D(1953, 25¢; Comic Media)(#1)-Came w/glasses 29 58 87 170 278 385
2-5 9 18 27 52 69 85

NORMALMAN (See Cerebus the Aardvark #55, 56)
Aardvark-Vanaheim/Renegade Press #6 on: Jan, 1984 - No. 12, Dec, 1985 ($1.70/$2.00)

1-12: 1-Jim Valentino-c/a in all. 6-12 ($2.00, B&W): 10-Cerebus cameo; Sim-a (2 pgs.) 2.50
...- Megaton Man Special 1 (Image Comics, 8/94, $2.50) 3.00
...3-D 1 (Annual, 1986, $2.25) 2.50
...Twentieth Anniversary Special (7/04, $2.95) 3.00

NORTH AVENUE IRREGULARS (See Walt Disney Showcase #49)

NORTH 40
DC Comics (WildStorm): Sept, 2009 - No. 6, Feb, 2010 ($2.99)

1-6-Aaron Williams-s/Fiona Staples-a 3.00

NORTHLANDERS
DC Comics (Vertigo): Feb, 2008 - Present ($2.99)

1-24: 1-Vikings in 980 A.D.; Wood-s/Gianfelice-a; covers by Carnivale 3.00
1-3-Variant covers. 1-Adam Kubert. 2-Andy Kubert. 3-Dave Gibbons 5.00
...: Sven the Returned TPB (2008, $9.99) r/#1-8; cover gallery 10.00
...: The Cross + The Hammer TPB (2009, $14.99) r/#11-16 15.00

NORTHSTAR
Marvel Comics: Apr, 1994 - No. 4, July, 1994 ($1.75, mini-series)

1-4: Character from Alpha Flight 2.50

NORTH TO ALASKA
Dell Publishing Co.: No. 1155, Dec, 1960

Nova (2007 series) #26 © MAR

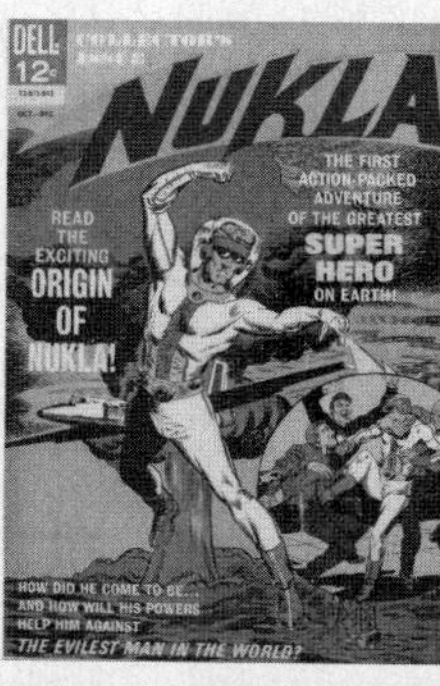

Nukla #1 © DELL

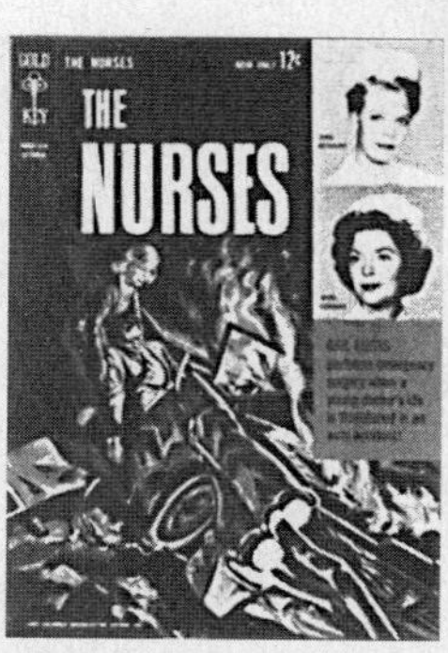

The Nurses #3 © GK

GD 2.0 | VG 4.0 | FN 6.0 | VF 8.0 | VF/NM 9.0 | NM- 9.2

Four Color 1155-Movie, John Wayne photo-c 16 32 48 112 214 315

NORTHWEST MOUNTIES (Also see Approved Comics #12)
Jubilee Publications/St. John: Oct, 1948 - No. 4, July, 1949

1-Rose of the Yukon by Matt Baker; Walter Johnson-a; Lubbers-c
47 94 141 296 498 700
2-Baker-a; Lubbers-c. Ventrilo app. 39 78 117 231 378 525
3-Bondage-c, Baker-a; Sky Chief, K-9 app. 39 78 117 240 395 550
4-Baker-c/a(2 pgs.); Blue Monk & The Desperado app.
41 82 123 250 418 585

NO SLEEP 'TIL DAWN
Dell Publishing Co.: No. 831, Aug, 1957

Four Color 831-Movie, Karl Malden photo-c 6 12 18 43 69 95

NOSTALGIA ILLUSTRATED
Marvel Comics: Nov, 1974 - V2#8, Aug, 1975 (B&W, 76 pgs.)

V1#1 4 8 12 22 34 45
V1#2, V2#1-8 3 6 9 16 22 28

NOT BRAND ECHH (Brand Echh #1-4; See Crazy, 1973)
Marvel Comics Group (LMC): Aug, 1967 - No. 13, May, 1969
(1st Marvel parody book)

1: 1-8 are 12¢ issues 7 14 21 47 76 105
2-8: 3-Origin Thor, Hulk & Capt. America; Monkees, Alfred E. Neuman cameo. 4-X-Men app. 5-Origin/intro. Forbush Man. 7-Origin Fantastical-4 & Stuporman. 8-Beatles cameo; X-Men satire; last 12¢-c 4 8 12 26 41 55
9-13 (25¢, 68 pgs., all Giants) 9-Beatles cameo. 10-All-r; The Old Witch, Crypt Keeper & Vault Keeper cameos. 12,13-Beatles cameo 5 10 15 32 51 70

NOTE: ***Colan** a(p)-4, 5, 8, 9, 13. **Everett** a-1i. **Kirby** a(p)-1, 3, 5-7, 10r; c-1p. **J. Severin** a-1; c-3, 6-8, 11. **M. Severin** a-1-13; c-2, 9, 10, 12, 13. **Sutton** a-3, 4, 5i, 6i, 8, 9, 10r, 11-13; c-5. Archie satire in #9. Avengers satire in #8, 12.*

NOTHING CAN STOP THE JUGGERNAUT
Marvel Comics: 1989 ($3.95)

1-r/Amazing Spider-Man #229 & 230 4.00

NO TIME FOR SERGEANTS (TV)
Dell Publ. Co.: No. 914, July, 1958; Feb-Apr, 1965 - No. 3, Aug-Oct, 1965

Four Color 914 (Movie)-Toth-a; Andy Griffith photo-c 9 18 27 65 113 160
1(2-4/65) (TV): Photo-c 6 12 18 39 62 85
2,3 (TV): Photo-c 5 10 15 30 48 65

NOVA (The Man Called... No. 22-25)(See New Warriors)
Marvel Comics Group: Sept, 1976 - No. 25, May, 1979

1-Origin/1st app. Nova 3 6 9 14 20 25
2-4,12: 4-Thor x-over. 12-Spider-Man x-over 2 4 6 8 10 12
5-11 1 2 3 5 7 9
10,11-(35¢-c variants, limited distribution)(6,7/77) 4 8 12 26 41 55
12-(35¢-c variant, limited distribution)(8/77) 5 10 15 32 51 70
13,14-(Regular 30¢ editions)(9/77) 13-Intro Crime-Buster
1 2 3 5 6 8
13,14-(35¢-c variants, limited distribution) 4 8 12 24 37 50
15-24: 18-Yellow Claw app. 19-Wally West (Kid Flash) cameo
1 2 3 5 6 8
25-Last issue 2 3 4 6 8 10

NOTE: ***Austin** c-21i, 23i. **John Buscema** a(p)-1-3, 8, 21; c-1p, 2, 15. **Infantino** a(p)-15-20, 22-25; c-17-20, 21p, 23p, 24p. **Kirby** c-4p, 5, 7. **Nebres** c-25i. **Simonson** a-23i.*

NOVA
Marvel Comics: Jan, 1994 - June, 1995 ($1.75/$1.95) (Started as 4-part mini-series)

1-($2.95, 52 pgs.)-Collector's Edition w/gold foil-c; new Nova costume 3.00
1-($2.25, 52 pgs.)-Newsstand Edition w/o foil-c 2.50
2-18: 3-Spider-Man-c/story. 5-Stan Lee app. 5-Bound-in card sheet. 13-Firestar & Night Thrasher app.14-Darkhawk 2.50

NOVA
Marvel Comics: May, 1999 - No. 7, Nov, 1999 ($2.99/$1.99)

1-($2.99) Larsen-s/Bennett-a; wraparound-c by Larsen 3.00
2-7-($1.99): 2-Two covers; Capt. America app. 5-Spider-Man. 7-Venom 2.50

NOVA
Marvel Comics: June, 2007 - Present ($2.99)

1-35: 1-Sean Chen-a/Granov-c. 2,3-Iron Man app. 3-Thunderbolts app. 14,15-Silver Surfer & Galacus app. 16-18-Secret Invasion. 21-Fantastic Four app. 23-28-War of Kings 3.00
... Annual 1 (4/08, $3.99) Origin retold; Annihilation: Conquest tie-in 4.00
...: Origin of Richard Rider (2009, $4.99) origin retold from Nova #1 & 4 ('76) 5.00
... Vol. 1: Annihilation - Conquest TPB (2007, $17.99) r/#1-7; cover sketches 18.00

NOW AGE ILLUSTRATED (See Pendulum Illustrated Classics)

NOW AGE BOOKS ILLUSTRATED (See Pendulum Illustrated Classics)

NTH MAN THE ULTIMATE NINJA (See Marvel Comics Presents #25)
Marvel Comics: Aug, 1989 - No. 16, Sept, 1990 ($1.00)

1-16-Ninja mercenary. 8-Dale Keown's 1st Marvel work (1/90, pencils) 2.50

NUCLEUS (Also see Cerebus)
Heiro-Graphic Publications: May, 1979 ($1.50, B&W, adult fanzine)

1-Contains "Demonhorn" by Dave Sim; early app. of Cerebus The Aardvark (4 pg. story)
5 10 15 34 55 75

NUKLA
Dell Publishing Co.: Oct-Dec, 1965 - No. 4, Sept, 1966

1-Origin & 1st app. Nukla (super hero) 5 10 15 30 48 65
2,3 3 6 9 20 30 40
4-Ditko-a, c(p) 4 8 12 24 37 50

NUMBER OF THE BEAST
DC Comics (WildStorm): June, 2008 - No. 8, Sept, 2008 ($2.99, limited series)

1-8-Beatty-s/Sprouse-a/c. 1-Variant-c by Mahnke. 6-The Authority app. 3.00
TPB (2008, $19.99) r/#1-8; character dossiers 20.00

NURSE BETSY CRANE (Formerly Teen Secret Diary) (Also see Registered Nurse for reprints)
Charlton Comics: V2#12, Aug, 1961 - V2#27, Mar, 1964 (See Soap Opera Romances)

V2#12-27 3 6 9 16 23 30

NURSE HELEN GRANT (See The Romances of...)

NURSE LINDA LARK (See Linda Lark)

NURSERY RHYMES
Ziff-Davis Publ. Co. (Approved Comics): No. 10, July-Aug, 1951 - No. 2, Winter, 1951 (Painted-c)

10 (#1), 2: 10-Howie Post-a 16 32 48 94 147 200

NURSES, THE (TV)
Gold Key: April, 1963 - No. 3, Oct, 1963 (Photo-c: #1,2)

1 4 8 12 24 37 50
2,3 3 6 9 18 27 35

NUTS! (Satire)
Premiere Comics Group: March, 1954 - No. 5, Nov, 1954

1-Hollingsworth-a 30 60 90 177 289 400
2,4,5: 5-Capt. Marvel parody 20 40 60 117 189 260
3-Drug "reefers" mentioned 20 40 60 118 192 265

NUTS (Magazine) (Satire)
Health Knowledge: Feb, 1958 - No. 2, April, 1958

1 10 20 30 54 72 90
2 7 14 21 37 46 55

NUTS & JOLTS
Dell Publishing Co.: No. 22, 1941

Large Feature Comic 22 18 36 54 103 162 220

NUTSY SQUIRREL (Formerly Hollywood Funny Folks)(See Comic Cavalcade)
National Periodical Publications: #61, 9-10/54 - #69, 1-2/56; #70, 8-9/56 - #71, 10-11/56; #72, 11/57

61-Mayer-a; Grossman-a in all 14 28 42 76 108 140
62-72: Mayer a-62,65,67-72 10 20 30 54 72 90

NUTTY COMICS
Fawcett Publications: Winter, 1946

1-Capt. Kidd story; 1 pg. Wolverton-a 14 28 42 80 115 150

NUTTY COMICS
Home Comics (Harvey Publications): 1945; No. 4, May-June, 1946 - No. 8, June-July, 1947 (No #2,3)

nn-Helpful Hank, Bozo Bear & others (funny animal) 9 18 27 50 65 80
4 7 14 21 37 46 55
5-Rags Rabbit begins(1st app.); infinity-c 8 16 24 40 50 60
6-8 6 12 18 31 38 45

NUTTY LIFE (Formerly Krazy Life #1; becomes Wotalife Comics #3 on)
Fox Features Syndicate: No. 2, Summer, 1946

2 15 30 45 88 137 185

NYOKA, THE JUNGLE GIRL (Formerly Jungle Girl; see The Further Adventures of..., Master Comics #50 & XMas Comics)
Fawcett Publications: No. 2, Winter, 1945 - No. 77, June, 1953 (Movie serial)

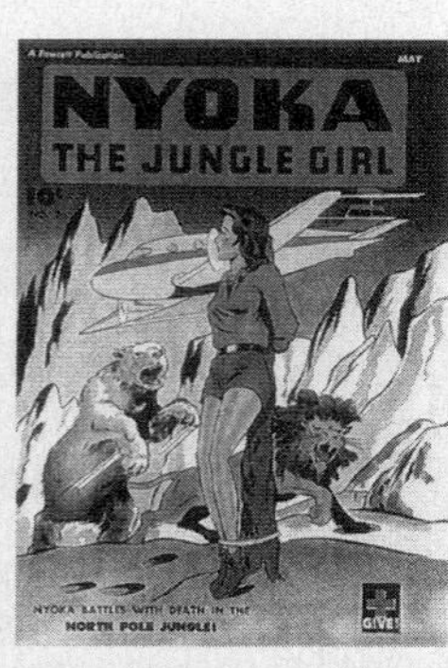

Nyoka, The Jungle Girl #7 © FAW

NYX #1 © MAR

Offcastes #3 © Mike Vosburg

	GD 2.0	VG 4.0	FN 6.0	VF 8.0	VF/NM 9.0	NM- 9.2
2	58	116	174	371	636	900
3	32	64	96	192	314	435
4,5	27	54	81	158	259	360
6-11,13,14,16-18-Krigstein-a: 17-Sam Spade ad by Lou Fine	19	38	57	112	179	245
12,15,19,20	18	36	54	103	162	220
21-30: 25-Clayton Moore photo-c?	14	28	42	76	108	140
31-40	11	22	33	62	86	110
41-50	10	20	30	56	76	95
51-60	9	18	27	50	65	80
61-77	8	16	24	44	57	70

NOTE: *Photo-c from movies 25, 30-70, 72, 75-77. Bondage c-4, 5, 7, 8, 14, 24.*

NYOKA, THE JUNGLE GIRL (Formerly Zoo Funnies; Space Adventures #23 on)
Charlton Comics: No. 14, Nov, 1955 - No. 22, Nov, 1957

	GD	VG	FN	VF	VF/NM	NM-
14	11	22	33	62	86	110
15-22	9	18	27	52	69	85

NYX (Also see X-23 title)
Marvel Comics: Nov, 2003 - No. 7, Oct, 2005 ($2.99)

	GD	VG	FN	VF	VF/NM	NM-
1,2: 1-Quesada-s/Middleton-a/c; intro. Kiden Nixon						3.00
3-1st app. X-23	1	3	4	6	8	10
4-6: 5,6-Teranishi-a						3.00
7-($3.99) Teranishi-a						4.00
NYX X-23 (2005, $34.99, oversized with d.j.) r/X-23 #1-6 & NYX #1-7; intro by Craig Kyle; sketch pages, development art and unused covers						35.00
...: Wannabe TPB (2006, $19.99) r/#1-7; development art and unused covers						20.00

NYX: NO WAY HOME
Marvel Comics: Oct, 2008 - No. 6, Apr, 2009 ($3.99)

1-6: 1-Andrasofszky-a/Liu-s/Urusov-c; sketch pages, character and cover design art 4.00

OAKLAND PRESS FUNNYBOOK, THE
The Oakland Press: 9/17/78 - 4/13/80 (16 pgs.) (Weekly)
Full color in comic book form; changes to tabloid size 4/20/80-on

Contains Tarzan by Manning, Marmaduke, Bugs Bunny, etc. (low distribution); 9/23/79 - 4/13/80 contain Buck Rogers by Gray Morrow & Jim Lawrence 2.50

OAKY DOAKS (See Famous Funnies #190)
Eastern Color Printing Co.: July, 1942 (One Shot)

	GD	VG	FN	VF	VF/NM	NM-
1	34	68	102	199	325	450

OBERGEIST: RAGNAROK HIGHWAY
Image Comics (Top Cow/Minotaur): May, 2001 - No. 6, Nov, 2001 ($2.95, limited series)

Preview ('01, B&W, 16 pgs.) Harris painted-c 2.25
1-6-Harris-c/a/Jolley-s. 1-Three covers 3.00
... :The Directors' Cut (2002, $19.95, TPB) r/#1-6; Bruce Campbell intro. 20.00
... :The Empty Locket (3/02, $2.95, B&W) Harris & Snyder-a 3.00

OBIE
Store Comics: 1953 (6¢)

	GD	VG	FN	VF	VF/NM	NM-
1	6	12	18	28	34	40

OBJECTIVE FIVE
Image Comics: July, 2000 - No. 6, Jan, 2001($2.95)

1-6-Lizalde-a 3.00

OBLIVION
Comico: Aug, 1995 - No. 3, May, 1996 ($2.50)

1-3: 1-Art Adams-c. 2-(1/96)-Bagged w/gaming card. 3-(5/96)-Darrow-c 2.50

OBNOXIO THE CLOWN (Character from Crazy Magazine)
Marvel Comics Group: April, 1983 (one-shot)

1-Vs. the X-Men 4.00

OCCULT CRIMES TASKFORCE
Image Comics: July, 2006 - No. 4, May, 2007 ($2.99, limited series)

1-4-Rosario Dawson & David Atchison-s/Tony Shasteen-a 3.00
... Vol. 1 TPB (2007, $14.99) r/#1-4; sketch and cover development art 15.00

OCCULT FILES OF DR. SPEKTOR, THE
Gold Key/Whitman No. 25: Apr, 1973 - No. 24, Feb, 1977; No. 25, May, 1982 (Painted-c #1-24)

	GD	VG	FN	VF	VF/NM	NM-
1-1st app. Lakota; Baron Tibor begins	5	10	15	32	51	70
2-5: 3-Mummy-c/s. 5-Jekyll & Hyde-c/s	3	6	9	18	27	35
6-10: 6,9-Frankenstein. 8,9-Dracula c/s. 9.-Jekyll & Hyde c/s. 9,10-Mummy-c/s	3	6	9	14	20	25
11-13,15-17,19-22,24: 11-1st app. Spektor as Werewolf. 11-13-Werewolf-c/s. 12,16-Frankenstein c/s. 17-Zombie/Voodoo-c. 19-Sea monster-c/s. 20-Mummy-s. 21-Swamp monster-c/s. 24-Dragon-c/s	2	4	6	10	14	18
14-Dr. Solar app.	3	6	9	16	23	30
18,23-Dr. Solar cameo	2	4	6	11	16	20
22-Return of the Owl c/s	2	4	6	11	16	20
25(Whitman, 5/82)-r/#1 with line drawn-c	2	4	6	8	11	14

NOTE: *Also see Dan Curtis, Golden Comics Digest 33, Gold Key Spotlight, Mystery Comics Digest 5, & Spine Tingling Tales.*

OCEAN
DC Comics (WildStorm): Dec, 2005 - No. 6, Sept, 2005 ($2.95/$2.99/$3.99, limited series)

1-5-Warren Ellis-s/Chris Sprouse-a 3.00
6-($3.99) Conclusion 4.00

ODELL'S ADVENTURES IN 3-D (See Adventures in 3-D)

ODYSSEY, THE (See Marvel Illustrated: The Odyssey)

OFFCASTES
Marvel Comics (Epic Comics/Heavy Hitters): July, 1993 - No. 3, Sept, 1993 ($1.95, limited series)

1-3: Mike Vosburg-c/a/scripts in all 2.50

OFFICIAL CRISIS ON INFINITE EARTHS INDEX, THE
Independent Comics Group (Eclipse): Mar, 1986 ($1.75)

1 5.00

OFFICIAL CRISIS ON INFINITE EARTHS CROSSOVER INDEX, THE
Independent Comics Group (Eclipse): July, 1986 ($1.75)

1-Perez-c. 5.00

OFFICIAL DOOM PATROL INDEX, THE
Independent Comics Group (Eclipse): Feb, 1986 - No. 2, Mar, 1986 ($1.50, limited series)

1,2: Byrne-c. 4.00

OFFICIAL HANDBOOK OF THE CONAN UNIVERSE (See Handbook of...)

OFFICIAL HANDBOOK OF THE MARVEL UNIVERSE, THE
Marvel Comics Group: Jan, 1983 - No. 15, May, 1984 (Limited series)

1-Lists Marvel heroes & villains (letter A) 5.00
2-15: 2 (B-C, 3-(C-D). 4-(D-G). 5-(H-J), 6-(K-L). 7-(M). 8-(N-P); Punisher-c. 9-(Q-S), 10-(S). 11-(S-U). 12-(V-Z); Wolverine-c. 13,14-Book of the Dead. 15-Weaponry catalogue 4.00

NOTE: ***Bolland** a-8. **Byrne** c/a(p)-1-14; c-15p. **Grell** a-6, 9. **Kirby** a-1, 3. **Layton** a-2, 5, 7. **Mignola** a-3, 4, 5, 6, 8, 12. **Miller** a-4-6, 8, 10. **Nebres** a-3, 4, 8. **Redondo** a-3, 4, 8, 13, 14. **Simonson** a-1, 4, 6-13. **Paul Smith** a-1-12. **Starlin** a-5, 7, 8, 10, 13, 14. **Steranko** a-8p. **Zeck**-2-14.*

OFFICIAL HANDBOOK OF THE MARVEL UNIVERSE, THE
Marvel Comics Group: Dec, 1985 - No. 20, Feb, 1988 ($1.50, maxi-series)

	GD	VG	FN	VF	VF/NM	NM-
V2#1-Byrne-c						4.00
2-20: 2,3-Byrne-c						3.00
Trade paperback Vol. 1-10 ($6.95)	1	3	4	6	8	10

NOTE: ***Art Adams** a-7, 8, 11, 12, 14. **Bolland** a-8, 10, 13. **Buckler** a-1, 3, 5, 10. **Buscema** a-1, 5, 8, 9, 10, 13, 14. **Byrne** a-1-14; c-1-11. **Ditko** a-1, 2, 4, 6, 7, 11, 13. a-7, 11. **Mignola** a-2, 4, 9, 11, 13. **Miller** a-2, 4, 12. **Simonson** a-1, 2, 4-13, 15. **Paul Smith** a-1-5, 7-12, 14. **Starlin** a-6, 8, 9, 12, 16. **Zeck** a-1-4, 6, 7, 9-14, 16.*

OFFICIAL HANDBOOK OF THE MARVEL UNIVERSE, THE
Marvel Comics: July, 1989 - No. 8, Mid-Dec, 1990 ($1.50, lim. series, 52 pgs.)

V3#1-8: 1-McFarlane-a (2 pgs.) 3.00

OFFICIAL HANDBOOK OF THE MARVEL UNIVERSE, THE (Also see Spider-Man)
Marvel Comics: 2004 - Present ($3.99, one-shots)

...: Alternate Universes 2005 - Profile pages of 1602, MC2, 2099, Earth X, Mangaverse, Days of Future Past, Squadron Supreme, Spider-Ham's Larval Earth and others 4.00
...: Avengers 2004 - Profile pages; art by various; lists of character origins and 1st apps. 4.00
...: Avengers 2005 - Profile pages and info for New Avengers, Young Avengers & others 4.00
...: Book of the Dead 2004 - Profile pages of deceased Marvel characters; art by various; 4.00
...: Daredevil 2004 - Profile pages; art by various; lists of character origins and 1st apps. 4.00
...: Fantastic Four 2005 - Profile pages of members, friends & enemies 4.00
...: Golden Age 2005 - Profile pages; art by various; lists of character origins and 1st apps. 4.00
...: Horror 2005 - Profile pages; art by various; lists of character origins and 1st apps. 4.00
...: Hulk 2004 - Profile pages; art by various; lists of character origins and 1st apps. 4.00
...: Marvel Knights 2005 - Profile pages of characters from Marvel Knights line 4.00
...: Spider-Man 2004 - Profile pages; art by various; lists of character origins and 1st apps. 4.00
...: Spider-Man 2005 - Profile pages of Spidey's friends and foes, emphasizing the recent 4.00
...: Wolverine 2004 - Profile pages; art by various; lists of character origins and 1st apps. 4.00
...: Teams 2005 - Profile pages of Avengers, X-Men and other teams 4.00
...: Women of Marvel 2005 - Profile pages; art by various; Greg Land-c 4.00
...: X-Men 2004 - Profile pages; art by various; lists of character origins and 1st apps. 4.00
...: X-Men 2005 - Profile pages; art by various; lists of character origins and 1st apps. 4.00
...: X-Men - The Age of Apocalypse 2005 - Profile pages of characters plus Exiles 4.00
HC A-Z Vol. 1 (2008, $24.99, dustjacket) editied & updated pages for characters A-B 25.00
HC A-Z Vol. 2 (2008, $24.99, dustjacket) editied & updated pages for characters B-C 25.00

Official Marvel Index to the Avengers #2 © MAR

Oh My Goddess #93 © Kosuke Fujishima

Oklahoma Kid #1 © AJAX

	GD 2.0	VG 4.0	FN 6.0	VF 8.0	VF/NM 9.0	NM- 9.2
HC A-Z Vol. 3 (2008, $24.99, dustjacket) editied & updated pages for characters C-E						25.00
OFFICIAL HANDBOOK OF THE ULTIMATE MARVEL UNIVERSE, THE						
Marvel Comics: 2005 ($3.99, one-shots)						
... 2005: The Fantastic Four and Spider-Man - Profile pages; art by various						4.00
... The Ultimates and X-Men 2005 - Profile pages; art by various; Bagley-c						4.00
OFFICIAL HAWKMAN INDEX, THE						
Independent Comics Group: Nov, 1986 - No. 2, Dec, 1986 ($2.00)						
1,2						4.00
OFFICIAL INDEX TO THE MARVEL UNIVERSE						
Marvel Comics: 2009 - Present ($3.99)						
1-14-Each issue has chronological synopsies, creator credits, character lists for 40-50 issues of apps. for Iron Man, Spider-Man and the X-Men starting with 1st apps. in issue #1						4.00
OFFICIAL JUSTICE LEAGUE OF AMERICA INDEX, THE						
Independent Comics Group (Eclipse): April, 1986 - No. 8, Mar, 1987 ($2.00, Baxter paper)						
1-8: 1,2-Perez-c.						6.00
OFFICIAL LEGION OF SUPER-HEROES INDEX, THE						
Independent Comics Group (Eclipse): Dec, 1986 - No. 5, 1987 ($2.00, limited series) (No Official in Title #2 on)						
1-5: 4-Mooney-c						6.00
OFFICIAL MARVEL INDEX TO MARVEL TEAM-UP						
Marvel Comics Group: Jan, 1986 - No. 6, 1987 ($1.25, limited series)						
1-6						4.00
OFFICIAL MARVEL INDEX TO THE AMAZING SPIDER-MAN						
Marvel Comics Group: Apr, 1985 - No. 9, Dec, 1985 ($1.25, limited series)						
1 ($1.00)-Byrne-c.						4.00
2-9: 5,6,8,9-Punisher-c.						3.00
OFFICIAL MARVEL INDEX TO THE AVENGERS, THE						
Marvel Comics: Jun, 1987 - No. 7, Aug, 1988 ($2.95, limited series)						
1-7						5.00
OFFICIAL MARVEL INDEX TO THE AVENGERS, THE						
Marvel Comics: V2#1, Oct, 1994 - V2#6, 1995 ($1.95, limited series)						
V2#1-#6						3.00
OFFICIAL MARVEL INDEX TO THE FANTASTIC FOUR						
Marvel Comics Group: Dec, 1985 - No. 12, Jan, 1987 ($1.25, limited series)						
1-12: 1-Byrne-c. 1,2-Kirby back-c (unpub. art)						3.00
OFFICIAL MARVEL INDEX TO THE X-MEN, THE						
Marvel Comics: May, 1987 - No. 7, July, 1988 ($2.95, limited series)						
1-7						5.00
OFFICIAL MARVEL INDEX TO THE X-MEN, THE						
Marvel Comics: V2#1, Apr, 1994 - V2#5, 1994 ($1.95, limited series)						
V2#1-5: 1-Covers X-Men #1-51. 2-Covers #52-122,Special #1,2,Giant-Size #1,2. 3-Byrne-c; covers #123-177, Annuals 3-7, Spec. Ed. #1. 4-Covers Uncanny X-Men #178-234, Annuals 8-12. 5-Covers #235-287, Annuals 13-15						3.00
OFFICIAL SOUPY SALES COMIC (See Soupy Sales)						
OFFICIAL TEEN TITANS INDEX, THE						
Indep. Comics Group (Eclipse): Aug, 1985 - No. 5, 1986 ($1.50, lim. series)						
1-5						4.00
OFFICIAL TRUE CRIME CASES (Formerly Sub-Mariner #23; All-True Crime Cases #26 on)						
Marvel Comics (OCI): No. 24, Fall, 1947 - No. 25, Winter, 1947-48						
24(#1)-Burgos-a; Syd Shores-c	23	46	69	136	223	310
25-Syd Shores-c; Kurtzman's "Hey Look"	18	36	54	107	169	230
OF SUCH IS THE KINGDOM						
George A. Pflaum: 1955 (15¢, 36 pgs.)						
nn-Reprints from 1951 Treasure Chest	4	7	10	14	17	20
O.G. WHIZ (See Gold Key Spotlight #10)						
Gold Key: 2/71 - No. 6, 5/72; No. 7, 5/78 - No. 11, 1/79 (No. 7: 52 pgs.)						
1-John Stanley script	5	10	15	34	55	75
2-John Stanley script	4	8	12	24	37	50
3-6(1972)	3	6	9	18	27	35
7-11(1978-79)-Part-r: 9-Tubby issue	2	4	6	9	12	15
OH, BROTHER! (Teen Comedy)						
Stanhall Publ.: Jan, 1953 - No. 5, Oct, 1953						
1-By Bill Williams	9	18	27	47	61	75

	GD 2.0	VG 4.0	FN 6.0	VF 8.0	VF/NM 9.0	NM- 9.2
2-5	6	12	18	31	38	45
OH MY GODDESS! (Manga)						
Dark Horse Comics: Aug, 1994 - Present ($2.50-$3.99, B&W)						
1-6-Kosuke Fujishima-s/a in all						3.00
... PART II 2/95 - No. 9, 9/95 ($2.50, B&W, lim.series) #1-9						3.00
... PART III 11/95 - No. 11, 9/96 ($2.95, B&W, lim. series) #1-11						3.00
... PART IV 12/96 - No. 8, 7/97 ($2.95, B&W, lim. series) #1-8						3.00
... PART V 9/97 - Np. 12, 8/98 ($2.95, B&W, lim. series)						
1,2,5,8: 5-Ninja Master pt. 1						3.00
3,4,6,7,10-12-($3.95, 48 pgs.) 10-Fallen Angel. 11-Play The Game						4.00
9-($3.50) "It's Lonely At The Top"						3.50
... PART VI 10/98 - No. 5, 3/99 ($3.50/$2.95, B&W, lim. series)						
1-($3.50)						3.50
2-6-($2.95)-6-Super Urd one-shot						3.00
... PART VII 5/99 - No. 8, 12/99 ($2.95, B&W, lim. series) #1-3						3.00
4-8-($3.50)						3.50
... PART VIII 1/00 - No. 6, 6/00 ($3.50, B&W, lim. series) #1-3,5,7						3.50
4-($2.95) "Hail To The Chief" begins						3.00
... PART IX 7/00 - No. 7, 1/01 ($3.50/$2.99) #1-4: 3-Queen Sayoko						3.50
5-7-($2.99)						3.00
... PART X 2/01 - No. 5, 6/01 ($3.50) #1-5						3.50
... PART XI 10/01 - No. 10, 3/02 ($3.50) #1,2,7,8						3.50
3-6,9-($2.99) Mystery Child						3.00
10-($3.99)						4.00
(Series adapts new numbering) 88-90-($3.50) Learning to Love						3.50
91-94,96-103,105,107-110: 91-94 ($2.99) Traveler. 96-98-The Phantom Racer						3.00
95,104,106-($3.50) 95-Traveler pt. 5						3.50
111,112-($3.99)						4.00
OH SUSANNA (TV)						
Dell Publishing Co.: No. 1105, June-Aug, 1960 (Gale Storm)						
Four Color 1105-Toth-a, photo-c	11	22	33	76	136	195
OKAY COMICS						
United Features Syndicate: July, 1940						
1-Captain & the Kids & Hawkshaw the Detective reprints	45	90	135	279	465	650
O.K. COMICS						
Hit Publications: May, 1940 (ashcan)						
nn-Ashcan comic, not distributed to newsstands, only for in house use. A CGC certified 8.0 copy sold in 2003 for $1,000.						
O.K. COMICS						
United Features Syndicate/Hit Publications: July, 1940 - No. 2, Oct, 1940						
1-Little Giant (w/super powers), Phantom Knight, Sunset Smith, & The Teller Twins begin	74	148	222	470	810	1150
2 (Rare)-Origin Mister Mist by Chas. Quinlan	76	152	228	486	831	1175
OKLAHOMA KID						
Ajax/Farrell Publ.: June, 1957 - No. 4, 1958						
1	11	22	33	60	83	105
2-4	7	14	21	37	46	55
OKLAHOMAN, THE						
Dell Publishing Co.: No. 820, July, 1957						
Four Color 820-Movie, photo-c	8	16	24	58	97	135
OKTANE						
Dark Horse Comics: Aug, 1995 - Nov, 1995 ($2.50, color, limited series)						
1-4-Gene Ha-a						2.50
OKTOBERFEST COMICS						
Now & Then Publ.: Fall 1976 (75¢, Canadian, B&W, one-shot)						
1-Dave Sim-s/a; Gene Day-a; 1st app. Uncle Hans & Natter P. Bombast; The Beavers sty; 1st Cap'n Riverrat, Sim-s/Day-a	3	6	9	16	23	30
OLD GLORY COMICS						
DC Comics: 1941						
nn - Ashcan comic, not distributed to newsstands, only for in-house use. Cover art is Flash Comics #12 with interior being Action Comics #37 (no known sales)						
OLD IRONSIDES (Disney)						
Dell Publishing Co.: No. 874, Jan, 1958						
Four Color 874-Movie w/Johnny Tremain	6	12	18	43	69	95
OLD YELLER (Disney, see Movie Comics, and Walt Disney Showcase #25)						
Dell Publishing Co.: No. 869, Jan, 1958						

Omac #6 © DC

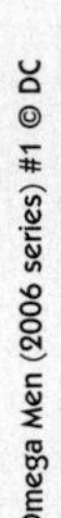
Omega Men (2006 series) #1 © DC

100 Bullets #94 © Azzarello, Risso & DC

	GD 2.0	VG 4.0	FN 6.0	VF 8.0	VF/NM 9.0	NM- 9.2
Four Color 869-Movie, photo-c	5	10	15	34	55	75
OMAC (One Man Army; ...Corps. #4 on; also see Kamandi #59 & Warlord) (See Cancelled Comic Cavalcade)						
National Periodical Publications: Sept-Oct, 1974 - No. 8, Nov-Dec, 1975						
1-Origin	5	10	15	34	55	75
2-8: 8-2 pg. Neal Adams ad	3	6	9	18	27	35
Jack Kirby's Omac: One Man Army Corps HC (2008, $24.99, d.j.) r/#1-8; Evanier intro.						25.00
NOTE: *Kirby a-1-8p; c-1-7p. Kubert c-8.*						
OMAC (See DCU Brave New World)						
DC Comics: Sept, 2006 - No. 8, Apr, 2007 ($2.99, limited series)						
1-8: 1-Bruce Jones-s/Renato Guedes-a. 1-3-Firestorm & Cyborg app. 8-Superman app.						3.00
OMAC: ONE MAN ARMY CORPS						
DC Comics: 1991 - No. 4, 1991 ($3.95, B&W, mini-series, mature, 52 pgs.)						
Book One - Four: John Byrne-c/a & scripts						4.00
OMAC PROJECT, THE						
DC Comics: June, 2005 - No. 6, Nov, 2005 ($2.50, limited series)						
1-6-Prelude to Infinite Crisis x-over; Rucka-s/Saiz-a						2.50
...: Infinite Crisis Special 1 (5/06, $4.99) Rucka-s/Saiz-a; follows destruction of satellite						5.00
TPB (2005, $14.99) r/#1-6, Countdown to Infinite Crisis, Wonder Woman #219						15.00
O'MALLEY AND THE ALLEY CATS						
Gold Key: April, 1971 - No. 9, Jan, 1974 (Disney)						
1	3	6	9	16	23	30
2-9	2	4	6	9	13	16
OMEGA ELITE						
Blackthorne Publishing: 1987 ($1.25)						
1-Starlin-c						3.00
OMEGA FLIGHT						
Marvel Comics: Jun, 2007 - No. 5, Oct, 2007 ($2.99, limited series)						
1-Oeming-s/Kolins-a; Wrecking Crew app.						4.00
1-Second printing with Sasquatch variant-c						3.00
2-5: 5-Beta Ray Bill app.						3.00
...: Alpha to Omega TPB ('07, $13.99) r/#1-5, USAgent story/Civil War: Choosing Sides						14.00
OMEGA MEN, THE (See Green Lantern #141)						
DC Comics: Dec, 1982 - No. 38, May, 1986 ($1.00/$1.25/$1.50; Baxter paper)						
1,20: 20-2nd full Lobo story						3.00
2,4-9,11-19,21-25,28-30,32,33,36,38: 2-Origin Broot. 5,9-2nd & 3rd app. Lobo (cameo, 2 pgs. each). 7-Origin The Citadel. 19-Lobo cameo. 30-Intro new Primus						2.50
3-1st app. Lobo (5 pgs.)(6/83); Lobo-c	1	2	3	4	5	7
10-1st full Lobo story						5.00
26,27,31,34,35: 26,27-Alan Moore scripts. 31-Crisis x-over. 34,35-Teen Titans x-over						3.00
37-1st solo Lobo story (8 pg. back-up by Giffen)						4.00
Annual 1(11/84, 52 pgs.), 2(11/85)						3.00
NOTE: *Giffen c/a-1-6p. Morrow a-24r. Nino c/a-16, 21; a-Annual 1i.*						
OMEGA MEN, THE						
DC Comics: Dec, 2006 - No. 6, May, 2007 ($2.99, limited series)						
1-6: 1-Superman, Wonder Girl, Green Lantern app.; Flint-a/Gabrych-s						3.00
OMEGA THE UNKNOWN						
Marvel Comics Group: March, 1976 - No. 10, Oct, 1977						
1-1st app. Omega	2	4	6	10	14	18
2,3-(Regular 25¢ editions). 2-Hulk-c/story. 3-Electro-c/story.	2	3	4	6	8	10
2,3-(30¢-c variants, limited distribution)	3	6	9	18	27	35
4-10: 8-1st brief app. 2nd Foolkiller (Greg Salinger), 1 panel only. 9,10-(Reg. 30¢ editions). 9-1st full app. 2nd Foolkiller	1	2	3	5	6	8
9,10-(35¢-c variants, limited distribution)	4	8	12	22	34	45
... Classic TPB (2005, $29.99) r/#1-10						30.00
NOTE: *Kane c(p)-3, 5, 8, 9. Mooney a-1-3, 4p, 5, 6p, 7, 8i, 9, 10.*						
OMEGA: THE UNKNOWN						
Marvel Comics: Dec, 2007 - No. 10, Sept, 2008 ($2.99, limited series)						
1-10-Jonathan Lethem-s/Farel Dalrymple-a						3.00
OMEN						
Northstar Publishing: 1989 - No. 3, 1989 ($2.00, B&W, mature)						
1-Tim Vigil-c/a in all	1	2	3	5	7	9
1, (2nd printing)						3.00
2,3						6.00
OMEN, THE						

	GD 2.0	VG 4.0	FN 6.0	VF 8.0	VF/NM 9.0	NM- 9.2
Chaos! Comics: May, 1998 - No. 5, Sept, 1998 ($2.95, limited series)						
1-5: 1-Six covers, ...: Vexed (10/98, $2.95) Chaos! characters appear						3.00
OMNI MEN						
Blackthorne Publishing: 1987 - No. 3, 1987 ($1.25)						
1-3						2.50
Graphic Novel (1989, $3.50)						3.50
ONE, THE						
Marvel Comics (Epic Comics): July, 1985 - No. 6, Feb, 1986 (Limited series, mature)						
1-6: Post nuclear holocaust super-hero. 2-Intro The Other						2.50
ONE-ARM SWORDSMAN, THE						
Victory Prod./Lueng's Publ. #4 on: 1987 - No. 12, 1990 ($2.75/$1.80, 52 pgs.)						
1-3 ($2.75)						2.75
4-12: 4-6-$1.80-c. 7-12-$2.00-c						2.50
ONE HUNDRED AND ONE DALMATIANS (Disney, see Cartoon Tales, Movie Comics, and Walt Disney Showcase #9, 51)						
Dell Publishing Co.: No. 1183, Mar, 1961						
Four Color 1183-Movie	9	18	27	65	113	160
101 DALMATIONS (Movie)						
Disney Comics: 1991 (52 pgs., graphic novel)						
nn-($4.95, direct sales)-r/movie adaptation & more						5.00
1-($2.95, newsstand edition)						3.00
101 WAYS TO END THE CLONE SAGA (See Spider-Man)						
Marvel Comics: Jan, 1997 ($2.50, one-shot)						
1						2.50
100 BULLETS						
DC Comics (Vertigo): Aug, 1999 - No. 100, Jun, 2009 ($2.50/$2.75/$2.99)						
1-Azzarello-s/Risso-a/Dave Johnson-c						4.00
2-5						3.00
6-49,51-61: 26-Series summary; art by various. 45-Preview of Losers						2.50
50-($3.50) History of the Trust						3.50
62-71: 62-Begin $2.75-c. 64-Preview of Loveless						2.75
72-99: 72-Begin $2.99-c						3.00
100-($4.99) Final issue						5.00
...#1/Crime Line Sampler Flip-Book (9/09, $1.00) r/#1 with previews of upcoming GNs						1.00
...: A Foregone Tomorrow TPB (2002, $17.95) r/#20-30						18.00
...: Decayed TPB (2006, $14.99) r/#68-75; Darwyn Cooke intro.						15.00
...: First Shot, Last Call TPB (2000, $9.95) r/#1-5, Vertigo Winter's Edge #3						10.00
...: Hang Up on the Hang Low TPB (2001, $9.95) r/#15-19; Jim Lee intro.						10.00
...: Once Upon a Crime TPB (2007, $12.99) r/#76-83						13.00
...: Samurai TPB (2003, $12.95) r/#43-49						13.00
...: Six Feet Under the Gun TPB (2003, $12.95) r/#37-42						13.00
...: Split Second Chance TPB (2001, $14.95) r/#6-14						15.00
...: Strychnine Lives TPB (2006, $14.99) r/#59-67; Manuel Ramos intro.						15.00
...: The Counterfifth Detective TPB (2003, $12.95) r/#31-36						13.00
...: The Hard Way TPB (2005, $14.99) r/#50-58						15.00
...: Wilt TPB (2009, $19.99) r/#89-100; Azzarello intro.						20.00
100 GREATEST MARVELS OF ALL TIME						
Marvel Comics: Dec, 2001 ($7.50/$3.50, limited series)						
1-5-Reprints top #6-#25 stories voted by poll for Marvel's 40th ann.						7.50
6-($3.50) (#5 on-c) Reprints X-Men (2nd series) #1						3.50
7-($3.50) (#4 on-c) Reprints Giant-Size X-Men #1						3.50
8-($3.50) (#3 on-c) Reprints (Uncanny) X-Men #137 (Death of Jean Grey)						3.50
9-($3.50) (#2 on-c) Reprints Fantastic Four #1						3.50
10-($3.50) (#1 on-c) Reprints Amazing Fantasy #15 (1st app. Spider-Man)						3.50
100 PAGES OF COMICS						
Dell Publishing Co.: 1937 (Stiff covers, square binding)						
101(Found on back cover)-Alley Oop, Wash Tubbs, Capt. Easy, Og Son of Fire, Apple Mary, Tom Mix, Dan Dunn, Tailspin Tommy, Doctor Doom	145	290	435	921	1586	2250
100 PAGE SUPER SPECTACULAR (See DC 100 Page Super Spectacular)						
100%						
DC Comics (Vertigo): Aug, 2002 - No. 5, July, 2003 ($5.95, B&W, limited series)						
1-5-Paul Pope-s/a						6.00
HC (2009, $39.99, dustjacket) r/#1-5; sketch pages and background info						40.00
TPB (2005, $24.99) r/#1-5; sketch pages and background info						25.00
100% TRUE?						
DC Comics (Paradox Press): Summer 1996 - No. 2 ($4.95, B&W)						

Onslaught Reborn #2 © MAR

Operation Peril #5 © ACG

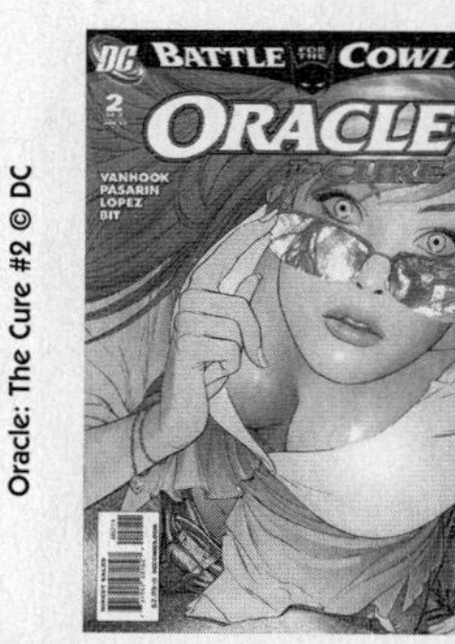

Oracle: The Cure #2 © DC

	GD 2.0	VG 4.0	FN 6.0	VF 8.0	VF/NM 9.0	NM- 9.2

1,2-Reprints stories from various Paradox Press books. 5.00

$1,000,000 DUCK (See Walt Disney Showcase #5)

ONE MILLION YEARS AGO (Tor #2 on)
St. John Publishing Co.: Sept, 1953

1-Origin & 1st app. Tor; Kubert-c/a; Kubert photo inside front cover 18 36 54 105 165 225

ONE PLUS ONE
Oni Press: Sept, 2002 - No. 5, March, 2003 ($2.95, B&W, limited series)

1-5-Shaffer-s/Krall-a 3.00
TPB (9/03, $14.95, digest-size) r/#1-5 & story from Oni Press Color Special 2002 15.00

ONE SHOT (See Four Color...)

1001 HOURS OF FUN
Dell Publishing Co.: No. 13, 1943

Large Feature Comic 13 (nn)-Puzzles & games; by A.W. Nugent. This book was bound as #13 w/Large Feature Comics in publisher's files 28 56 84 165 270 375

ONE TRICK RIP OFF, THE (See Dark Horse Presents)

ONI (Adaption of video game)
Dark Horse Comics: Feb, 2001 - No. 3, Apr, 2001 ($2.99, limited series)

1-3-Sunny Lee-a(p) 3.00

ONI DOUBLE FEATURE (See Clerks: The Comic Book and Jay & Silent Bob)
Oni Press: Jan, 1998 - No. 13, Sept, 1999 ($2.95, B&W)

1-Jay & Silent Bob; Kevin Smith-s/Matt Wagner-a 1 3 4 6 8 10
1-2nd printing 3.00
2-11,13: 2,3-Paul Pope-s/a. 3,4-Nixey-s/a. 4,5-Sienkewicz-s/a. 6,7-Gaiman-s. 9-Bagge-c. 13-All Paul Dini-s; Jingle Belle 3.00
12-Jay & Silent Bob as Bluntman & Chronic; Smith-s/Allred-a 5.00

ONI PRESS COLOR SPECIAL
Oni Press: Jun, 2001; Jul, 2002 ($5.95, annual)

...2001-Oeming "Who Killed Madman?" cover; stories & art by various 6.00
...2002-Allred wraparound-c; stories & art by various 6.00

ONSLAUGHT: EPILOGUE
Marvel Comics: Feb, 1997 ($2.95, one-shot)

1-Hama-s/Green-a; Xavier-c; Bastion-app. 3.00

ONSLAUGHT: MARVEL
Marvel Comics: Oct, 1996 ($3.95, one-shot)

1-Conclusion to Onslaught x-over; wraparound-c 1 2 3 4 5 7

ONSLAUGHT REBORN
Marvel Comics: Jan, 2007 - No. 5, Feb, 2008 ($2.99, limited series)

1-5-Loeb-s/Liefeld-a; female Bucky app. 2-Variant-c by Joe Madureira. 3-McGuiness var-c. 4-Campbell var-c. 5-Bianchi var-c; female Bucky goes to regular Marvel Universe 3.00
1-Variant-c by Michael Turner 4.00
HC (2008, $19.99) r/#1-5; sketch pages; foreword by Liefeld 20.00

ONSLAUGHT: X-MEN
Marvel Comics: Aug, 1996 ($3.95, one-shot)

1-Waid & Lobdell script; Fantastic Four & Avengers app.; Xavier as Onslaught 5.00
1-Variant-c 2 4 6 8 10 12

ON STAGE
Dell Publishing Co.: No. 1336, Apr-June, 1962

Four Color 1336-Not by Leonard Starr 5 10 15 30 48 65

ON THE DOUBLE (Movie)
Dell Publishing Co.: No. 1232, Sept-Nov, 1961

Four Color 1232 5 10 15 30 48 65

ON THE ROAD TO PERDITION (Movie)
DC Comics (Paradox Press): 2003 - Book 3, 2004 ($7.95, 8"x5 1/2", B&W, limited series)

...: Oasis, Book 1-Max Allan Collins-s/José Luis García-López-a/David Beck-c 8.00
...: Sanctuary, Book 2-Max Allan Collins-s/Steve Lieber-a/José Luis García-López-c 8.00
...: Detour, Book 3-Max Allan Collins-s/José Luis García-López-a/Steve Lieber-c/a(i) 8.00
Road to Perdition 2: On the Road (2004, $14.95) r/series; Collins intro. 15.00

ON THE ROAD WITH ANDRAE CROUCH
Spire Christian Comics (Fleming H. Revell): 1973, 1974 (39¢)

nn-1973 Edition 2 4 6 9 12 15
nn-1974 Edition 1 3 4 6 8 10

ON THE SCENE PRESENTS:...
Warren Publishing Co.: Oct, 1966 - No. 2, 1967 (B&W magazine, two #1 issues)

#1 "Super Heroes" (68 pgs.) Batman 1966 movie photo-c/s; has articles/photos/comic art from serials on Superman, Flash Gordon, Capt. America, Capt. Marvel and The Phantom 5 10 15 30 48 65
#1 "Freak Out, USA" (Fall/1966, 60 pgs.) (lower print run) articles on musicians like Zappa, Jefferson Airplane, Supremes 5 10 15 32 51 70
#2 "Freak Out, USA" (2/67, 52 pgs.) Beatles, Country Joe, Doors/Jim Morrison, Bee Gees 5 10 15 32 51 70

ON THE SPOT (Pretty Boy Floyd...)
Fawcett Publications: Fall, 1948

nn-Pretty Boy Floyd photo on-c; bondage-c 34 68 102 199 325 450

ONYX OVERLORD
Marvel Comics (Epic): Oct, 1992 - No. 4, Jan, 1993 ($2.75, mini-series)

1-4: Moebius scripts 2.75

OPEN SPACE
Marvel Comics: Mid-Dec, 1989 - No. 4, Aug, 1990 ($4.95, bi-monthly, 68 pgs.)

1-4: 1-Bill Wray-a; Freas-c 5.00
0-(1999) Wizard supplement; unpubl. early Alex Ross-a; new Ross-c 2.50

OPERATION BIKINI (See Movie Classics)

OPERATION BUCHAREST (See The Crusaders)

OPERATION CROSSBOW (See Movie Classics)

OPERATION: KNIGHTSTRIKE (See Knightstrike)
Image Comics (Extreme Studios): May, 1995 - No.3, July, 1995 ($2.50)

1-3 2.50

OPERATION PERIL
American Comics Group (Michel Publ.): Oct-Nov, 1950 - No. 16, Apr-May, 1953 (#1-5: 52 pgs.)

1-Time Travelers, Danny Danger (by Leonard Starr) & Typhoon Tyler (by Ogden Whitney) begin 39 78 117 240 395 550
2-War-c 23 46 69 136 223 310
3-War-c; horror story 21 42 63 122 199 275
4,5-Sci/fi-c/story 23 46 69 136 223 310
6-10: 6,8,9,10-Sci/fi-c. 6-Dinosaur-c. 7-Sabretooth-c 20 40 60 118 192 265
11,12-War-c; last Time Travelers 14 28 42 80 115 150
13-16: All war format 10 20 30 56 76 95

NOTE: *Starr a-2, 5. Whitney a-1, 2, 5-10, 12; c-1, 3, 5, 8, 9.*

OPERATION: STORMBREAKER
Acclaim Comics (Valiant Heroes): Aug, 1997 ($3.95, one-shot)

1-Waid/Augustyn-s, Braithwaite-a 4.00

OPTIC NERVE
Drawn and Quarterly: Apr, 1995 - Present ($2.95-$3.95, bi-annual)

1-7: Adrian Tomine-c/a/scripts in all 3.00
8-11: 8-($3.50). 9-11-($3.95) 4.00
32 Stories-($9.95, trade paperback)-r/Optic Nerve mini-comics 10.00
32 Stories-($29.95, hardcover)-r/Optic Nerve mini-comics; signed & numbered 30.00

ORACLE: THE CURE
DC Comics: May, 2009 - No. 3, Jul, 2009 ($2.99, limited series)

1-3-Guillem March-c; Calculator app. 3.00

ORAL ROBERTS' TRUE STORIES (Junior Partners #120 on)
TelePix Publ. (Oral Roberts' Evangelistic Assoc./Healing Waters): 1956 (no month) - No. 119, 7/59 (15¢)(No. 102: 25¢)

V1#1(1956)-(Not code approved)- "The Miracle Touch" 19 38 57 109 172 235
102-(Only issue approved by code, 10/56) "Now I See" 13 26 39 74 105 135
103-119: 115-(114 on inside) 10 20 30 54 72 90

NOTE: *Also see Happiness & Healing For You.*

ORANGE BIRD, THE
Walt Disney Educational Media Co.: No date (1980) (36 pgs.; in color; slick cover)

nn-Included with educational kit on foods, ...in Nutrition Adventures nn (1980) ...and the Nutrition Know-How Revue nn (1983) 3.00

ORB (Magazine)
Orb Publishing: 1974 - No. 6, Mar/Apr 1976 (B&W/color)

1-1st app. Northern Light & Kadaver, both series begin 5 10 15 32 51 70
2,3 (72 pgs.) 3 6 9 16 23 30
4-6 (60 pgs.): 4,5-origin Northern Light 2 4 6 10 14 18

NOTE: *Allison a-1-3. Gene Day a-1-6. P. Hsu a-4-6. Steacy s/a-3,4.*

Orbiter HC © Ellis & Doran

Orion #13 © DC

Oscar Comics #3 © MAR

	GD 2.0	VG 4.0	FN 6.0	VF 8.0	VF/NM 9.0	NM- 9.2

GD 2.0 VG 4.0 FN 6.0 VF 8.0 VF/NM 9.0 NM- 9.2

ORBIT
Eclipse Books: 1990 - No. 3, 1990 ($4.95, 52 pgs., squarebound)

1-3: Reprints from Isaac Asimov's Science Fiction Magazine; 1-Dave Stevens-c, Bolton-a. 3-Bolton-c/a, Yeates-a 5.00

ORBITER
DC Comics (Vertigo): 2003 ($24.95, hardcover with dust jacket)

HC-Warren Ellis-s/Colleen Doran-a 25.00
SC-(2004, $17.95) Warren Ellis-s/Colleen Doran-a 18.00

ORDER, THE (cont'd from Defenders V2#12)
Marvel Comics: Apr, 2002 - No. 6, Sept, 2002 ($2.25, limited series)

1-6: 1-Haley-a/Duffy & Busiek-s. 3-Avengers-c/app. 4-Jurgens-a 2.50

ORDER, THE (The Initiative following Civil War)
Marvel Comics: Sept, 2007 - No. 10, Jun, 2008 ($2.99)

1-10-California's Initiative team; Fraction-s/Kitson-a/c 3.00
... Vol. 1: The Next Right Thing TPB (2008, $14.99) r/#1-7 15.00

ORIENTAL HEROES
Jademan Comics: Aug, 1988 - No. 55, Feb, 1993 ($1.50/$1.95, 68 pgs.)

1,55 2.50
2-54 2.50

ORIGINAL ADVENTURES OF CHOLLY & FLYTRAP, THE
Image Comics: Feb, 2006 - No. 2, June, 2006 ($5.99, limited series)

1,2-Arthur Suydam-s/a; interview with Suydam and art pages 6.00

ORIGINAL ASTRO BOY, THE
Now Comics: Sept, 1987 - No. 20, Jun, 1989 ($1.50/$1.75)

1-20-All have Ken Steacy painted-c/a 3.00

ORIGINAL BLACK CAT, THE
Recollections: Oct. 6, 1988 - No. 9, 1992 ($2.00, limited series)

1-9: Elias-r; 1-Bondage-c. 2-Murphy Anderson-c 4.00

ORIGINAL DICK TRACY, THE
Gladstone Publishing: Sept, 1990 - No. 5, 1991 ($1.95, bi-monthly, 68pgs.)

1-5: 1-Vs. Pruneface. 2-& the Evil influence; begin $2.00-c 2.50
NOTE: *#1 reprints strips 7/16/43 - 9/30/43. #2 reprints strips 12/1/46 - 2/2/47. #3 reprints 8/31/46 - 11/14/46. #4 reprints 9/17/45 - 12/23/45. #5 reprints 6/10/46 - 8/28/46.*

ORIGINAL DOCTOR SOLAR, MAN OF THE ATOM, THE
Valiant: Apr, 1995 ($2.95, one-shot)

1-Reprints Doctor Solar, Man of the Atom #1,5; Bob Fugitani-r; Paul Smith-c; afterword by Seaborn Adamson 4.00

ORIGINAL E-MAN AND MICHAEL MAUSER, THE
First Comics: Oct, 1985 - No. 7, April, 1986 ($1.75, Baxter paper)

1-7: 1-Has r-/Charlton's E-Man, Vengeance Squad. 2-Shows #4 in indicia by mistake. 7-($2.00, 44pgs.)-Staton-a 2.50

ORIGINAL GHOST RIDER, THE
Marvel Comics: July, 1992 - No. 20, Feb, 1994 ($1.75)

1-20: 1-7-r/Marvel Spotlight #5-11 by Ploog w/new-c. 3-New Phantom Rider (former Night Rider) back-ups begin by Ayers. 4-Quesada-c(p). 8-Ploog-c. 8,9-r/Ghost Rider #1,2. 10-r/Marvel Spotlight #12. 11-18,20-r/Ghost Rider #3-12. 19-r/Marvel Two-in-One #8 2.50

ORIGINAL GHOST RIDER RIDES AGAIN, THE
Marvel Comics: July, 1991 - No. 7, Jan, 1992, ($1.50, limited series, 52 pgs.)

1-7: 1-r/Ghost Rider #68(origin),69 w/covers. 2-7: R/ G.R. #70-81 w/covers 2.50

ORIGINAL MAGNUS ROBOT FIGHTER, THE
Valiant: Apr, 1995 ($2.95, one-shot)

1-Reprints Magnus, Robot Fighter 4000 #2; Russ Manning-r; Rick Leonardi-c; afterword by Seaborn Adamson 4.00

ORIGINAL NEXUS GRAPHIC NOVEL (See First Comics Graphic Novel #19)

ORIGINALS, THE
DC Comics (Vertigo): 2004 ($24.95/$17.99, B&W graphic novel)

HC (2004, $24.95) Dave Gibbons-s/a 25.00
SC (2005, $17.99) 18.00

ORIGINAL SHIELD, THE
Archie Enterprises, Inc.: Apr, 1984 - No. 4, Oct, 1984

1-4: 1,2-Origin Shield; Ayers p-1-4, Nebres c-1,2 4.00

ORIGINAL SWAMP THING SAGA, THE (See DC Special Series #2, 14, 17, 20)

ORIGINAL TUROK, SON OF STONE, THE
Valiant: Apr, 1995 - No. 2, May, 1995 ($2.95, limited series)

1,2: 1-Reprints Turok, Son of Stone #24,25,42; Alberto Gioletti-r; Rags Morales-c; afterword by Seaborn Adamson. 2-Reprints Turok, Son of Stone #24,33; Gioletti-r; McKone-c 4.00

ORIGIN OF GALACTUS (See Fantastic Four #48-50)
Marvel Comics: Feb, 1996 ($2.50, one-shot)

1-Lee & Kirby reprints w/pin-ups 2.50

ORIGIN OF THE DEFIANT UNIVERSE, THE
Defiant Comics: Feb, 1994 ($1.50, 20 pgs., one-shot)

1-David Lapham, Adam Pollina & Alan Weiss-a; Weiss-c 5.00
NOTE: *The comic was originally published as Defiant Genesis and was distributed at the 1994 Philadelphia ComicCon.*

ORIGINS OF MARVEL COMICS (See Fireside Book Series)

ORION (Manga)
Dark Horse Comics: Sept, 1992 - No. 6, July, 1993 ($2.95/$3.95, B&W, bimonthly, lim. series)

1-6:1,2,6-Squarebound): 1-Masamune Shirow-c/a/s in all 4.00

ORION (See New Gods)
DC Comics: June, 2000 - No. 25, June, 2002 ($2.50)

1-14-Simonson-s/a. 3-Back-up story w/Miller-a. 4-Gibbons-a back-up. 7-Chaykin back-up. 8-Loeb/Liefeld back-up. 10-A. Adams back-up-a 12-Jim Lee back-up-a. 13-JLA-c/app.; Byrne-a 2.50
15-($3.95) Black Racer app.; back-up story w/J.P. Leon-a 4.00
16-24-Simonson-s/a: 19-Joker: Last Laugh x-over 2.50
25-($3.95) Last issue; Mister Miracle-c/app. 4.00
The Gates of Apocalypse (2001, $12.95, TPB) r/#1-5 & various short-s 13.00

ORORO: BEFORE THE STORM (Storm from X-Men)
Marvel Comics: Aug, 2005 - No. 4, Nov, 2005 ($2.99, limited series)

1-4-Barberi-a/Sumerak-s; young Storm in Egypt 3.00
... Digest (2006, $6.99) r/#1-4 7.00

OSBORNE JOURNALS (See Spider-Man titles)
Marvel Comics: Feb, 1997 ($2.95, one-shot)

1-Hotz-c/a 3.00

OSCAR COMICS (Formerly Funny Tunes; Awful...#11 & 12) (Also see Cindy Comics)
Marvel Comics: No. 24, Spring, 1947 - No. 10, Apr, 1949; No. 13, Oct, 1949

	GD	VG	FN	VF	VF/NM	NM-
24(#1, Spring, 1947)	18	36	54	107	169	230
25(#2, Sum, 1947)-Wolverton-a plus Kurtzman's "Hey Look"	20	40	60	114	182	250
26(#3)-Same as regular #3 except #26 was printed over in black ink with #3 appearing on-c below the over print	14	28	42	76	108	140
3-9,13: 8-Margie app.	14	28	42	76	108	140
10-Kurtzman's "Hey Look"	14	28	42	82	121	160

OSWALD THE RABBIT (Also see New Fun Comics #1)
Dell Publishing Co.: No. 21, 1943 - No. 1268, 12-2/61-62 (Walter Lantz)

	GD	VG	FN	VF	VF/NM	NM-
Four Color 21(1943)	42	84	126	336	651	965
Four Color 39(1943)	29	58	87	212	406	600
Four Color 67(1944)	17	34	51	119	230	340
Four Color 102(1946)-Kelly-a, 1 pg.	14	28	42	100	188	275
Four Color 143,183	9	18	27	63	107	150
Four Color 225,273	7	14	21	45	73	100
Four Color 315,388	6	12	18	39	62	85
Four Color 458,507,549,593	5	10	15	32	51	70
Four Color 623,697,792,894,979,1268	4	8	12	28	44	60

OSWALD THE RABBIT (See The Funnies, March of Comics #7, 38, 53, 67, 81, 95, 111, 126, 141, 156, 171, 186, New Funnies & Super Book #8, 20)

OTHER SIDE, THE
DC Comics (Vertigo): Dec, 2006 - No. 5, Apr, 2007 ($2.99, limited series)

1-5-Soldiers from both sides of the Vietnam War; Aaron-s/Stewart-a/c 3.00
TPB (2007, $12.99) r/#1-5; sketch pages, Stewart's travelogue to Saigon 13.00

OTHERWORLD
DC Comics (Vertigo): May, 2005 - No. 7, Nov, 2005 ($2.99)

1-7-Phil Jimenez-s/a(p) 3.00
...: Book One TPB (2006, $19.99) r/#1-7; cover gallery 20.00

OUR ARMY AT WAR (Becomes Sgt. Rock #302 on; also see Army At War)
National Periodical Publications: Aug, 1952 - No. 301, Feb, 1977

	GD	VG	FN	VF	VF/NM	NM-
1	173	346	519	1514	3007	4500
2	76	152	228	646	1273	1900
3,4: 4-Krigstein-a	56	112	168	476	938	1400

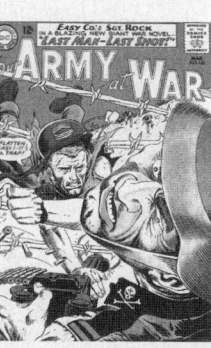

Our Army at War #152 © DC

Our Fighting Forces #96 © DC

Our Flag Comics #4 © ACE

	GD 2.0	VG 4.0	FN 6.0	VF 8.0	VF/NM 9.0	NM- 9.2
5-7	48	96	144	384	742	1100
8-11,14-Krigstein-a	45	90	135	360	693	1025
12,15-20	40	80	120	306	591	875
13-Krigstein-c/a; flag-c	47	94	141	376	726	1075
21-31: Last precode (2/55)	27	54	81	197	386	575
32-40	23	46	69	166	321	475
41-60: 51-1st S.A. issue	21	42	63	148	287	425
61-70: 61-(8/57) Pre-Sgt. Rock Easy Co.-c/s. 67-Minor Sgt. Rock prototype	18	36	54	129	252	375
71-80	16	32	48	115	220	325
81-(4/59)-Sgt. Rocky of Easy Co. app. by Andru & Esposito-a/ Haney-s; (the last Sgt. Rock prototype)	250	500	750	2188	4344	6500
82-1st Sgt. Rock app., in name only, in Easy Co. story (6 panels) by Kanigher & Drucker	66	132	198	561	1106	1650
83-(6/59)-1st true Sgt. Rock app. in "The Rock and the Wall" by Kubert & Kanigher; (most similar to prototype in G.I. Combat #68)	212	424	636	1855	3678	5500
84-Kubert-c	41	82	123	328	639	950
85-Origin & 1st app. Ice Cream Soldier	50	100	150	400	775	1150
86,87-Early Sgt. Rock; Kubert-a	40	80	120	314	607	900
88-1st Sgt. Rock-c; Kubert-c/a	50	100	150	413	807	1200
89	35	70	105	271	523	775
90-Kubert-c/a; How Rock got his stripes	46	92	138	368	709	1050
91-All-Sgt. Rock issue; Grandenetti-c/Kubert-a	88	176	264	748	1474	2200
92,94,96-99: 97-Regular Kubert-c begin	25	50	75	183	354	525
93-1st Zack Nolan	26	52	78	190	370	550
95,100: 95-1st app. Bulldozer	27	54	81	194	377	560
101,105,108,113,114: 101-1st app. Buster. 105-1st app. Junior. 113-1st app. Wildman & Jackie Johnson	20	40	60	146	283	420
102-104,106,107,109,110,114,116-120: 104-Nurse Jane-c/s. 109-Pre Easy Co. Sgt. Rock-s. 118-Sunny injured	18	36	54	129	252	375
111-1st app. Wee Willie & Sunny	23	46	69	170	328	485
112-Classic Easy Co. roster-c	26	52	78	190	370	550
115-Rock revealed as orphan; 1st x-over Mlle. Marie. 1st Sgt. Rock's battle family	23	46	69	166	321	475
121-125,129-139,141-150: 138-1st Sparrow. 141-1st Shaker. 147,148-Rock becomes a General	13	26	39	93	172	250
126-1st app. Canary; grey tone-c	16	32	48	115	220	325
127-2nd all-Sgt. Rock issue; 1st app. Little Sure Shot	18	36	54	129	252	375
128-Training & origin Sgt. Rock; 1st Sgt. Krupp	34	68	102	262	506	750
140-3rd all-Sgt. Rock issue	15	30	45	107	204	300
151-Intro. Enemy Ace by Kubert (2/65), black-c	42	84	126	336	656	975
152-4th all-Sgt. Rock issue	14	28	42	100	188	275
153-2nd app. Enemy Ace (4/65)	21	42	63	148	287	425
154,156,157,159-161,165-167: 157-2 pg. pin-up: 159-1st Nurse Wendy Winston-c/s. 165-2nd Iron Major	10	20	30	70	123	175
155-3rd app. Enemy Ace (6/65)(see Showcase)	15	30	45	107	204	300
158-Origin & 1st app. Iron Major(9/65), formerly Iron Captain	11	22	33	80	145	210
162,163-Viking Prince x-over in Sgt. Rock	11	22	33	78	139	200
164-Giant G-19	16	32	48	115	220	325
168-1st Unknown Soldier app.; referenced in Star-Spangled War Stories #157; (Sgt. Rock x-over) (6/66)	15	30	45	110	210	310
169,170	9	18	27	60	100	140
171-176,178-181: 171-1st Mad Emperor	8	16	24	54	90	125
177-(80 pg. Giant G-32)	10	20	30	73	129	185
182,183,186-Neal Adams-a. 186-Origin retold	9	18	27	63	107	150
184-Wee Willie dies	10	20	30	67	116	165
185,187,188,193-195,197-199	7	14	21	45	73	100
189,191,192,196: 189-Intro. The Teen-age Underground Fighters of Unit 3. 196-Hitler cameo	7	14	21	47	76	105
190-(80 pg. Giant G-44)	9	18	27	60	100	140
200-12 pg. Rock story told in verse; Evans-a	7	14	21	49	80	110
201,202,204-207: 201-Krigstein-r/#14. 204,205-All reprints; no Sgt. Rock. 207-Last 12¢ cover	5	10	15	34	55	75
203-(80 pg. Giant G-56)-All-r, Sgt. Rock story	8	16	24	52	86	120
208-215	4	8	12	26	41	55
216,229-(80 pg. Giants G-68, G-80): 216-Has G-58 on-c by mistake	7	14	21	45	73	100
217-219: 218-1st U.S.S. Stevens	4	8	12	24	37	50
220-Classic dinosaur/Sgt. Rock-c/s	4	8	12	28	44	60
221-228,230-234: 231-Intro/death Rock's brother. 234-Last 15¢ issue	3	6	9	20	30	40
235-239,241: 52 pg. Giants	4	8	12	26	41	55
240-Neal Adams-a; 52 pg. Giant	5	10	15	32	51	70
242-Also listed as DC 100 Page Super Spectacular #9	9	18	27	65	113	160
243-246: (All 52 pgs.) 244-No Adams-a	4	8	12	24	37	50
247-250,254-268,270: 247-Joan of Arc	3	6	9	14	20	25
251-253-Return of Iron Major	3	6	9	16	23	30
269,275-(100 pgs.)	5	10	15	32	51	70
271,272,274,276-279	2	4	6	13	18	22
273-Crucifixion-c	3	6	9	16	23	30
280-(68 pgs.)-200th app. Sgt. Rock; reprints Our Army at War #81,83	4	8	12	22	34	45
281-299,301: 295-Bicentennial cover	2	4	6	11	16	20
300-Sgt. Rock-s by Kubert (2/77)	3	6	9	14	20	25

NOTE ***Alcala*** *a-251.* ***Drucker*** *a-27, 67, 68, 79, 82, 83, 96, 164, 177, 203, 212, 243r, 244, 269r, 275r, 280r.* ***Evans*** *a-165-175, 200, 266, 269, 270, 274, 276, 278, 280.* ***Glanzman*** *a-218, 220, 222, 223, 225, 227, 230-232, 238-241, 244, 247, 248, 256-259, 261, 265-267, 271, 282, 283, 298.* ***Grandenetti*** *c-91,120.* ***Grell*** *a-287.* ***Heath*** *a-50, 164, & most 176-281.* ***Kubert*** *a-38, 59, 67, 68 & most issues from 83-165, 171, 233, 236, 267, 275, 300; c-84, 280.* ***Maurer*** *a-233, 237, 239, 240, 45, 280, 284, 288, 290, 291, 295.* ***Severin*** *a-236, 252, 265, 267, 269r, 272.* ***Toth*** *a-235, 241, 254.* ***Wildey*** *a-283-285, 287p.* ***Wood*** *a-249.*

OUR FIGHTING FORCES

National Per. Publ./DC Comics: Oct-Nov, 1954 - No. 181, Sept-Oct, 1978

	GD 2.0	VG 4.0	FN 6.0	VF 8.0	VF/NM 9.0	NM- 9.2
1-Grandenetti-c/a	120	240	360	1020	2010	3000
2	48	96	144	384	742	1100
3-Kubert-c; last precode issue (3/55)	40	80	120	314	607	900
4,5	33	66	99	254	490	725
6-9: 7-1st S.A. issue	28	56	84	204	395	585
10-Wood-a	29	58	87	212	406	600
11-19	24	48	72	175	338	500
20-Grey tone-c (4/57)	31	62	93	236	456	675
21-30	19	38	57	139	270	400
31-40	17	34	51	122	236	350
41-Unknown Soldier tryout	21	42	63	148	287	425
42-44	16	32	48	115	220	325
45-1st app. of Gunner & Sarge, app. thru #94	50	100	150	413	807	1200
46	22	44	66	157	304	450
47	17	34	51	122	236	350
48,50	15	30	45	107	204	300
49-1st Pooch	19	38	57	139	270	400
51-Grey tone-c	18	36	54	129	252	375
52-64: 64-Last 10¢ issue	12	24	36	85	155	225
65-70	9	18	27	65	113	160
71-Grey tone-c	13	26	39	93	172	250
72-80	8	16	24	56	93	130
81-90	7	14	21	45	73	100
91-98: 95-Devil-Dog begins, ends #98.	6	12	18	37	59	80
99-Capt. Hunter begins, ends #106	6	12	18	39	62	85
100	6	12	18	39	62	85
101-105,107-120: 116-Mlle. Marie app. 120-Last 12¢ issue	4	8	12	28	44	60
106-Hunters Hellcats begin	5	10	15	30	48	65
121,122: 121-Intro. Heller	4	8	12	24	37	50
123-The Losers (Capt. Storm, Gunner & Sarge, Johnny Cloud) begin	8	16	24	54	90	125
124-132: 132-Last 15¢ issue	3	6	9	20	30	40
133-137 (Giants). 134-Toth-a	4	8	12	24	37	50
138-145,147-150	3	6	9	14	20	25
146-Classic "Burma Sky" story; Toth-a/Goodwin-s	3	6	9	16	23	30
151-162-Kirby a(p)	3	6	9	17	25	32
163-180	2	4	6	9	16	20
181-Last issue	3	6	9	14	20	25

NOTE: ***N. Adams*** *c-147.* ***Drucker*** *a-28, 37, 39, 42-44, 49, 53, 133r.* ***Evans*** *a-149, 164-174, 177-181.* ***Glanzman*** *a-125-128, 132, 134, 138-141, 143, 144.* ***Heath*** *a-2, 16, 18, 28, 41, 44, 49, 114, 135-138r; c-51.* ***Kirby*** *a-151-162p; c-152-159.* ***Kubert*** *c/a in many issues.* ***Maurer*** *a-135.* ***Redondo*** *a-166.* ***Severin*** *a-123-130, 131i, 132-150.*

OUR FIGHTING MEN IN ACTION (See Men In Action)

OUR FLAG COMICS

Ace Magazines: Aug, 1941 - No. 5, April, 1942

	GD 2.0	VG 4.0	FN 6.0	VF 8.0	VF/NM 9.0	NM- 9.2
1-Captain Victory, The Unknown Soldier (intro.) & The Three Cheers begin	258	516	774	1651	2826	4000
2-Origin The Flag (patriotic hero); 1st app?	110	220	330	704	1202	1700
3-5: 5-Intro & 1st app. Mr. Risk	84	168	252	538	919	1300

NOTE: ***Anderson*** *a-1, 4.* ***Mooney*** *a-1, 2; c-2.*

OUR GANG COMICS (With Tom & Jerry #39-59; becomes Tom & Jerry #60 on; based on film characters)

Dell Publishing Co.: Sept-Oct, 1942 - No. 59, June, 1949

1-Our Gang & Barney Bear by Kelly, Tom & Jerry, Pete Smith, Flip & Dip, The Milky Way

Our Love Story #33 © MAR

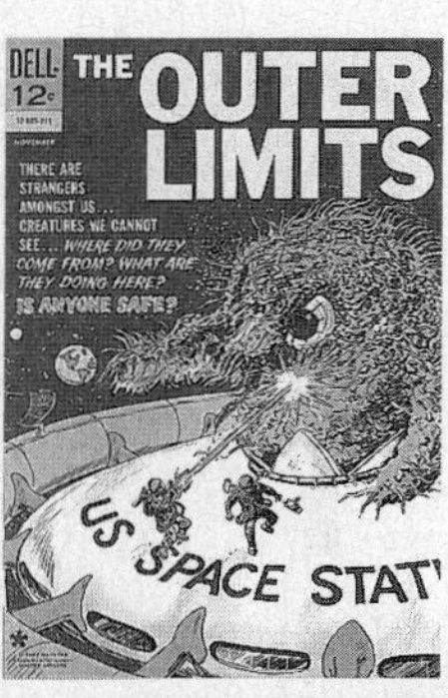

Outer Limits #16 © DELL

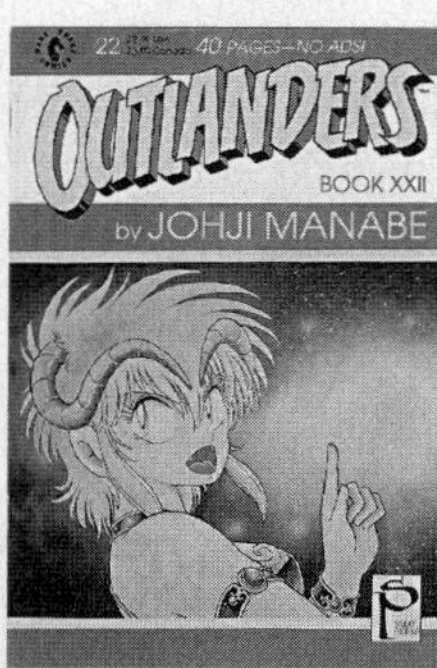

Outlanders #22 © DH

	GD 2.0	VG 4.0	FN 6.0	VF 8.0	VF/NM 9.0	NM- 9.2
begin (all 1st app.)	70	140	210	595	1135	1675
2-Benny Burro begins (#2 by Kelly)	37	74	111	284	530	775
3-5	26	52	78	187	349	510
6-Bumbazine & Albert only app. by Kelly	34	68	102	260	485	710
7-No Kelly story	19	38	57	139	257	375
8-Benny Burro begins by Barks	43	86	129	344	647	950
9-Barks-a(2): Benny Burro & Happy Hound; no Kelly story	40	80	120	308	574	840
10-Benny Burro by Barks	30	60	90	222	411	600
11-1st Barney Bear & Benny Burro by Barks (5-6/44); Happy Hound by Barks	40	80	120	308	574	840
12-20	19	38	57	135	250	365
21-30: 30-X-Mas-c	14	28	42	100	178	255
31-36-Last Barks issue	11	22	33	77	136	195
37-40	8	16	24	52	86	120
41-50	7	14	21	45	73	100
51-57	6	12	18	41	66	90
58,59-No Kelly art or Our Gang stories	6	12	18	37	59	80

Our Gang Volume 1 (Fantagraphics Books, 2006, $12.95, TPB) r/Our Gang stories written and by Walt Kelly from #1-8; Leonard Maltin intro.; Jeff Smith-c 13.00
Our Gang Volume 2 (Fantagraphics Books, 2007, $12.95, TPB) r/Our Gang stories written and by Walt Kelly from #9-15; Steve Thompson intro.; Jeff Smith-c 13.00
Our Gang Volume 3 (Fantagraphics Books, 2008, $14.99, TPB) r/Our Gang stories written and by Walt Kelly from #16-23; Steve Thompson intro.; Jeff Smith-c 15.00

NOTE: ***Barks** art in part only. **Barks** did not write Barney Bear stories #30-34. (See March of Comics #3, 26). Early issues have photo back-c.*

OUR LADY OF FATIMA
Catechetical Guild Educational Society: 3/11/55 (15¢) (36 pgs.)

	GD	VG	FN	VF	VF/NM	NM-
395	6	12	18	28	34	40

OUR LOVE (True Secrets #3 on? or Romantic Affairs #3 on?)
Marvel Comics (SPC): Sept, 1949 - No. 2, Jan, 1950

	GD	VG	FN	VF	VF/NM	NM-
1-Photo-c	16	32	48	94	147	200
2-Photo-c	11	22	33	64	90	115

OUR LOVE STORY
Marvel Comics Group: Oct, 1969 - No. 38, Feb, 1976

	GD	VG	FN	VF	VF/NM	NM-
1	8	16	24	52	86	120
2-4,6-8,10,11	4	8	12	26	41	55
5-Steranko-a	10	20	30	73	129	185
9,12-Kirby-a	4	8	12	28	44	60
13-(10/71, 52 pgs.)	5	10	15	32	51	70
14-New story by Gary Fredrich & Tarpe' Mills	4	8	12	28	44	60
15-20,27:27-Colan/Everett-a(r?); Kirby/Colletta-r	3	6	9	20	30	40
21-26,28-37	3	6	9	18	27	35
38-Last issue	4	8	12	22	34	45

NOTE: ***J. Buscema** a-1-3, 5-7, 9, 13r, 16r, 19r(2), 21r, 22r(2), 23r, 34r, 35r; c-11, 13, 16, 22, 23, 24, 27, 35. **Colan** a-3-6, 21r(#6), 22r, 23r(#3), 24r(#4), 27; c-19. **Katz** a-17. **Maneely** a-13r. **Romita** a-13r; c-1, 2, 4-6. **Weiss** a-16, 17, 29r(#17).*

OUR MEN AT WAR
DC Comics: Aug/Sept 1952

nn - Ashcan comic, not distributed to newsstands, only for in-house use. Cover art is All Star Western #60 with interior being Detective Comics #181 (no known sales)

OUR MISS BROOKS
Dell Publishing Co.: No. 751, Nov, 1956

	GD	VG	FN	VF	VF/NM	NM-
Four Color 751-Photo-c	7	14	21	50	83	115

OUR SECRET (Exciting Love Stories)(Formerly My Secret)
Superior Comics Ltd.: No. 4, Nov, 1949 - No. 8, Jun, 1950

	GD	VG	FN	VF	VF/NM	NM-
4-Kamen-a; spanking scene	19	38	57	111	176	240
5,6,8	12	24	36	67	94	120
7-Contains 9 pg. story intended for unpublished Ellery Queen #5; lingerie panels	13	26	39	72	101	130

OUTBREED 999
Blackout Comics: May, 1994 - No. 6, 1994 ($2.95)

1-6: 4-1st app. of Extreme Violet in 7 pg. backup story 3.00

OUTCAST, THE
Valiant: Dec, 1995 ($2.50, one-shot)

1-Breyfogle-a. 2.50

OUTCASTS
DC Comics: Oct, 1987 - No. 12, Sept, 1988 ($1.75, limited series)

1-12: John Wagner & Alan Grant scripts in all 2.50

OUTER LIMITS, THE (TV)
Dell Publishing Co.: Jan-Mar, 1964 - No. 18, Oct, 1969 (Most painted-c)

	GD	VG	FN	VF	VF/NM	NM-
1	12	24	36	83	152	220
2-5	7	14	21	49	80	110
6-10	6	12	18	41	66	90
11-18: 17-Reprints #1. 18-r/#2	5	10	15	34	55	75

OUTER SPACE (Formerly This Magazine Is Haunted, 2nd Series)
Charlton Comics: No. 17, May, 1958 - No. 25, Dec, 1959; Nov, 1968

	GD	VG	FN	VF	VF/NM	NM-
17-Williamson/Wood style art; not by them (Sid Check?)	14	28	42	80	115	150
18-20-Ditko-a	23	46	69	136	223	310
21-Ditko-c	20	40	60	114	182	250
22-25	14	28	42	80	115	150
V2#1(11/68)-Ditko-a, Boyette-c	5	10	15	32	51	70

OUT FOR BLOOD
Dark Horse: Sept, 1999 - No. 4, Dec, 1999 ($2.95, B&W, limited series)

1-4-Kelley Jones-c; Erskine-a 3.00

OUTLANDERS (Manga)
Dark Horse Comics: Dec, 1988 - No. 33, Sept,1991 ($2.00-$2.50, B&W, 44 pgs.)

1-33: Japanese Sci-fi manga 2.50

OUTLAW (See Return of the...)

OUTLAW FIGHTERS
Atlas Comics (IPC): Aug, 1954 - No. 5, Apr, 1955

	GD	VG	FN	VF	VF/NM	NM-
1-Tuska-a	14	28	42	76	108	140
2-5: 5-Heath-c/a, 7 pgs.	9	18	27	50	65	80

NOTE: ***Hartley** a-3. **Heath** c/a-5. **Maneely** c-2. **Pakula** a-2. **Reinman** a-2. **Tuska** a-1-3.*

OUTLAW KID, THE (1st Series; see Wild Western)
Atlas Comics (CCC No. 1-11/EPI No. 12-29): Sept, 1954 - No. 19, Sept, 1957

	GD	VG	FN	VF	VF/NM	NM-
1-Origin; The Outlaw Kid & his horse Thunder begin; Black Rider app.	27	54	81	158	259	360
2-Black Rider app.	14	28	42	80	115	150
3-7,9: 3-Wildey-a(3)	12	24	36	69	97	125
8-Williamson/Woodbridge-a, 4 pgs.	13	26	39	74	105	135
10-Williamson-a	13	26	39	74	105	135
11-17,19: 13-Baker text illo. 15-Williamson text illo (unsigned)	9	18	27	52	69	85
18-Williamson/Mayo-a	10	20	30	56	76	95

NOTE: ***Berg** a-4, 7, 13. **Maneely** c-1-3, 5-8, 11-13, 15, 16, 18. **Pakula** a-3. **Severin** c-10, 17, 19. **Shores** a-1. **Wildey** a-1(3), 2-8, 10, 11, 12(4), 13(4), 15-19(4 each); c-4.*

OUTLAW KID, THE (2nd Series)
Marvel Comics Group: Aug, 1970 - No. 30, Oct, 1975

	GD	VG	FN	VF	VF/NM	NM-
1-Reprints; 1-Orlando-r, Wildey-r(3)	3	6	9	20	30	40
2,3,9: 2-Reprints. 3,9-Williamson-a(r)	2	4	6	13	18	22
4-7: 7-Last 15¢ issue	2	4	6	11	16	20
8-Double size (52 pgs.); Crandall-r	3	6	9	17	25	32
10-Origin	3	6	9	20	30	40
11-20: new-a in #10-16	2	4	6	13	18	22
21-30: 27-Origin-r/#10	2	4	6	9	13	16

NOTE: ***Ayers** a-10, 27r. **Berg** a-7, 25r. **Everett** a-2(2 pgs.). **Gil Kane** c-10, 11, 15, 27r, 28. **Roussos** a-10i, 27i(r). **Severin** c-1, 9, 20, 25. **Wildey** r-1-4, 6-9, 19-22, 25, 26. **Williamson** a-28r. **Woodbridge/Williamson** a-9r.*

OUTLAW NATION
DC Comics (Vertigo): Nov, 2000 - No. 19, May, 2002 ($2.50)

1-19-Fabry painted-c/Delano-s/Sudzuka-a 2.50
TPB (Image Comics, 11/06, $15.99) B&W reprint of #1-19; Delano intro. 16.00

OUTLAWS
D. S. Publishing Co.: Feb-Mar, 1948 - No. 9, June-July, 1949

	GD	VG	FN	VF	VF/NM	NM-
1-Violent & suggestive stories	34	68	102	199	325	450
2-Ingels-a; Baker-a	34	68	102	199	325	450
3,5,6: 3-Not Frazetta. 5-Sky Sheriff by Good app. 6-McWilliams-a	16	32	48	94	147	200
4-Orlando-a	17	34	51	98	154	210
7,8-Ingels-a in each	24	48	72	140	230	320
9-(Scarce)-Frazetta-a (7 pgs.)	47	94	141	296	498	700

NOTE: *Another #3 was printed in Canada with **Frazetta** art "Prairie Jinx," 7 pgs.*

OUTLAWS, THE (Formerly Western Crime Cases)
Star Publishing Co.: No. 10, May, 1952 - No. 13, Sep, 1953; No. 14, Apr, 1954

	GD	VG	FN	VF	VF/NM	NM-
10-L. B. Cole-c	21	42	63	122	199	275
11-14-L. B. Cole-c. 14-Reprints Western Thrillers #4 (Fox) w/new L.B. Cole-c; Kamen, Feldstein-r	16	32	48	92	144	195

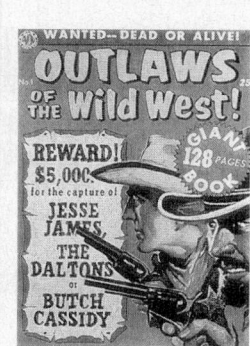

Outlaws of the Wild West #1 © AVON

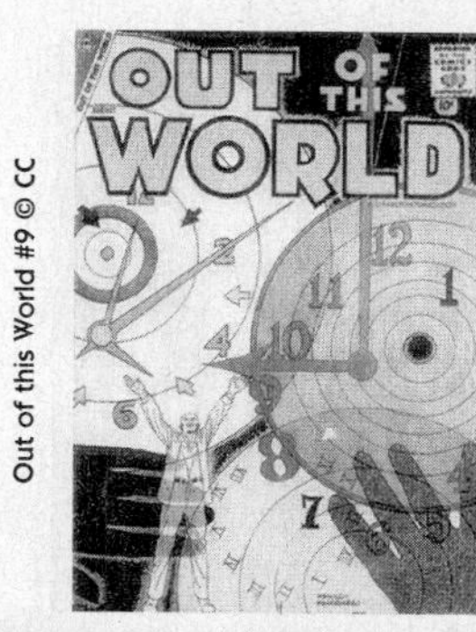

Out of this World #9 © CC

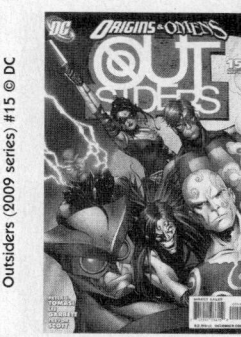

Outsiders (2009 series) #15 © DC

	GD 2.0	VG 4.0	FN 6.0	VF 8.0	VF/NM 9.0	NM- 9.2

OUTLAWS
DC Comics: Sept, 1991 - No. 8, Apr, 1992 ($1.95, limited series)

	GD	VG	FN	VF	VF/NM	NM-
1-8: Post-apocalyptic Robin Hood.						2.50

OUTLAWS OF THE WEST (Formerly Cody of the Pony Express #10)
Charlton Comics: No. 11, 7/57 - No. 81, 5/70; No. 82, 7/79 - No. 88, 4/80

	GD	VG	FN	VF	VF/NM	NM-
11	8	16	24	44	57	70
12,13,15-17,19,20	6	12	18	27	33	38
14-(68 pgs., 2/58)	9	18	27	50	65	80
18-Ditko-a	10	20	30	56	76	95
21-30	3	6	9	16	23	30
31-50: 34-Gunmaster app.	2	4	6	13	18	22
51-63,65,67-70: 54-Kid Montana app.	2	4	6	10	14	18
64,66: 64-Captain Doom begins (1st app.). 68-Kid Montana series begins	2	4	6	13	18	22
71-79: 73-Origin & 1st app. The Sharp Shooter, last app. #74. 75-Last Capt. Doom	2	4	6	9	12	15
80,81-Ditko-a	2	4	6	13	18	22
82-88						6.00
64,79(Modern Comics-r, 1977, '78)						4.00

OUTLAWS OF THE WILD WEST
Avon Periodicals: 1952 (25¢, 132 pgs.) (4 rebound comics)

	GD	VG	FN	VF	VF/NM	NM-
1-Wood back-c; Kubert-a (3 Jesse James-r)	34	68	102	199	325	450

OUTLAW TRAIL (See Zane Grey 4-Color 511)

OUT OF SANTA'S BAG (See March of Comics #10 in the Promotional Comics section)

OUT OF THE NIGHT (The Hooded Horseman #18 on)
Amer. Comics Group (Creston/Scope): Feb-Mar, 1952 - No. 17, Oct-Nov, 1954

	GD	VG	FN	VF	VF/NM	NM-
1-Williamson/LeDoux-a (9 pgs.)	66	132	198	419	722	1025
2-Williamson-a (5 pgs.)	47	94	141	296	498	700
3,5-10: 9-Sci/Fic story	29	58	87	172	281	390
4-Williamson-a (7 pgs.)	40	80	120	243	402	560
11-17: 13-Nostrand-a? 17-E.C. Wood swipe	22	44	66	128	209	290

NOTE: *Landau a-14, 16, 17. Shelly a-12.*

OUT OF THE SHADOWS
Standard Comics/Visual Editions: No. 5, July, 1952 - No. 14, Aug, 1954

	GD	VG	FN	VF	VF/NM	NM-
5-Toth-p; Moreira, Tuska-a; Roussos-c	56	112	168	348	594	840
6-Toth/Celardo-a; Katz-a(2)	39	78	117	240	395	550
7,9: 7-Jack Katz-c/a(2). 9-Crandall-a(2)	32	64	96	192	314	435
8-Katz shrunken head-c	53	106	159	334	567	800
10-Spider-c; Sekowsky-a	32	64	96	192	314	435
11-Toth-a, 2 pgs.; Katz-a; Andru-c	32	64	96	192	314	435
12-Toth/Peppe-a(2); Katz-a	39	78	117	240	395	550
13-Cannabalism story; Sekowsky-a; Roussos-c	38	76	114	228	369	510
14-Toth-a	32	64	96	192	314	435

OUT OF THE VORTEX (Comics' Greatest World:... #1-4)
Dark Horse Comics: Oct., 1993 - No. 12, Oct, 1994 ($2.00, limited series)

	GD	VG	FN	VF	VF/NM	NM-
1-11: 1-Foil logo. 4-Dorman-c(p). 6-Hero Zero x-over						2.50
12 ($2.50)						2.50

NOTE: *Art Adams c-7. Golden c-8. Mignola c-2. Simonson c-3. Zeck c-10.*

OUT OF THIS WORLD
Charlton Comics: Aug, 1956 - No. 16, Dec, 1959

	GD	VG	FN	VF	VF/NM	NM-
1	26	52	78	154	252	350
2	15	30	45	84	127	170
3-6-Ditko-c/a (3) each	31	62	93	184	300	415
7-(2/58, 15¢, 68 pgs.)-Ditko-c/a(4)	33	66	99	194	317	440
8-(5/58, 15¢, 68 pgs.)-Ditko-a(2)	29	58	87	172	281	390
9,10,12,16-Ditko-a	22	44	66	132	216	300
11-Ditko c/a (3)	26	52	78	154	252	350
13-15	12	24	36	69	97	125

NOTE: *Ditko c-3-12, 16. Reinman a-10.*

OUT OF THIS WORLD
Avon Periodicals: June, 1950; Aug, 1950

	GD	VG	FN	VF	VF/NM	NM-
1-Kubert-a(2) (one reprinted/Eerie #1, 1947) plus Crom the Barbarian by Gardner Fox & John Giunta (origin); Fawcette-c	74	148	222	470	810	1150
1-(8/50) Reprint; no month on cover	45	90	135	284	480	675

OUT OF THIS WORLD ADVENTURES
Avon Periodicals: July, 1950 - No. 2, Apr, 1951 (25¢ sci-fi pulp magazine with 32-page color comic insert)

	GD	VG	FN	VF	VF/NM	NM-
1-Kubert-a(2); Crom the Barbarian by Fox & Giunta; text stories by Cummings, Van Vogt, del Rey, Chandler	68	136	204	435	743	1050
2-Kubert-a plus The Spider God of Akka by Gardner Fox & John Giunta pulp magazine w/comic insert; Wood-a (21 pgs.); mentioned in **SOTI**, page 120	48	96	144	302	514	725

OUT OUR WAY WITH WORRY WART
Dell Publishing Co.: No. 680, Feb, 1956

	GD	VG	FN	VF	VF/NM	NM-
Four Color 680	4	8	12	24	37	50

OUTPOSTS
Blackthorne Publishing: June, 1987 - No. 4, 1987 ($1.25)

	GD	VG	FN	VF	VF/NM	NM-
1-4: 1-Kaluta-c(p)						2.50

OUTSIDERS, THE
DC Comics: Nov, 1985 - No. 28, Feb, 1988

	GD	VG	FN	VF	VF/NM	NM-
1						3.00
2-17						2.50
18-28: 18-26-Batman returns. 21-Intro. Strike Force Kobra; 1st app. Clayface IV 22-E.C. parody; Orlando-a. 21- 25-Atomic Knight app. 27,28-Millennium tie-ins						2.50
Annual 1 (12/86, $2.50), Special 1 (7/87, $1.50)						2.50

NOTE: *Aparo a-1-7, 9-14, 17-22, 25, 26; c-1-7, 9-14, 17, 19-26. Byrne a-11. Bolland a-6, 18; c-16. Ditko a-13p. Erik Larsen a-24, 27 28; c-27, 28. Morrow a-12.*

OUTSIDERS
DC Comics: Nov, 1993 - No. 24, Nov, 1995 ($1.75/$1.95/$2.25)

	GD	VG	FN	VF	VF/NM	NM-
1-11,0,12-24: 1-Alpha; Travis Charest-c. 1-Omega; Travis Charest-c. 5-Atomic Knight app. 8-New Batman-c/story. 11-(9/94)-Zero Hour. 0-(10/94).12-(11/94). 21-Darkseid cameo. 22-New Gods app.						2.50

OUTSIDERS (See Titans/Young Justice: Graduation Day)(Leads into Batman and the Outsiders)
DC Comics: Aug, 2003 - No. 50, Nov, 2007 ($2.50/$2.99)

	GD	VG	FN	VF	VF/NM	NM-
1-Nightwing, Arsenal, Metamorpho app.; Winick-s/Raney-a						5.00
2-Joker and Grodd app.						3.00
3-33: 3-Joker-c. 5,6-ChrisCross-a. 8-Huntress app. 9,10-Capt. Marvel Jr. app. 24,25-X-over with Teen Titans. 26,27-Batman & old Outsiders						2.50
34-50: 34-One Year Later. 36-Begin $2.99-c. 37-Superman app. 44-Red Hood app.						3.00
Annual 1 (6/07, $3.99) McDaniel-a; Black LIghtning app.						4.00
.../Checkmate: Checkout TPB (2008, $14.99) r/#47-49 & Checkmate #13-15						15.00
... Double Feature (10/03, $4.95) r/#1,2						5.00
...: Crisis Intervention TPB (2006, $12.99) r/#29-33						13.00
...: Looking For Trouble TPB (2004, $12.95) r/#1-7 & Teen Titans/Outsiders Secret Files & Origins 2003; intro. by Winick						13.00
...: Pay As You Go TPB (2007, $14.99) r/#42-46 & Annual #1						15.00
...: Sum of All Evil TPB (2004, $14.95) r/#8-15						15.00
...: The Good Fight TPB (2006, $14.99) r/#34-41						15.00
...: Wanted TPB (2005, $14.99) r/#16-23						15.00

OUTSIDERS, THE (Continued from Batman and the Outsiders #14)
DC Comics: No. 15, Apr, 2009 - Present ($2.99)

	GD	VG	FN	VF	VF/NM	NM-
15-23,26: 15-Alfred assembles a new team; Garbett-a. 17-19-Deathstroke app.						3.00
24,25-($3.99) Blackest Night; Terra rises as a Black Lantern						4.00
...: The Deep TPB (2009, $14.99) r/#15-20 & Batman and the Outsiders Special #1						15.00

OUTSIDERS: FIVE OF A KIND (Bridges Outsiders #49 & 50)
DC Comics: Oct, 2007 ($2.99, weekly limited series)

	GD	VG	FN	VF	VF/NM	NM-
...Katana/Shazam! (part 2 of 5) - Barr-s/Sharpe-a						3.00
...Metamorpho/Aquaman (part 4 of 5) - Wilson-s/Middleton-a						3.00
...Nightwing/Captain Boomerang (part 1 of 5) - DeFilippis & Weir-s/Willams-a						3.00
...Thunder/Martian Manhunter (part 3 of 5) - Bedard-s/Turnbull-a; Grayven app.						3.00
...Wonder Woman/Grace (part 5 of 5) - Andreyko-s/Richards-a						3.00
TPB (2008, $14.99) r/series & Outsiders #50						15.00

OUT THERE
DC Comics(Cliffhanger): July, 2001 - No. 18, Aug, 2003 ($2.50/$2.95)

	GD	VG	FN	VF	VF/NM	NM-
1-Humberto Ramos-c/a; Brian Augustyn-s						3.00
1-Variant-c by Carlos Meglia						4.00
2-8: 3-Variant-c by Bruce Timm						2.50
9-18: 9-Begin $2.95-c						3.00
...: The Evil Within TPB (2002, $12.95) r/#1-6; Ramos sketch pages						13.00

OVERKILL: WITCHBLADE/ ALIENS/ DARKNESS/ PREDATOR
Image Comics/Dark Horse Comics: Dec, 2000 - No. 2, 2001 ($5.95)

	GD	VG	FN	VF	VF/NM	NM-
1,2-Jenkins-s/Lansing, Ching & Benitez-a						6.00

OVER THE EDGE
Marvel Comics: Nov, 1995 - No. 10, Aug, 1996 (99¢)

	GD	VG	FN	VF	VF/NM	NM-
1-10: 1,6,10-Daredevil-c/story. 2,7-Dr. Strange-c/story. 3-Hulk-c/story. 4,9-Ghost Rider-c/story. 5-Punisher-c/story. 8-Elektra-c/story						2.50

OWL, THE (See Crackajack Funnies #25, Popular Comics #72 and Occult Files of

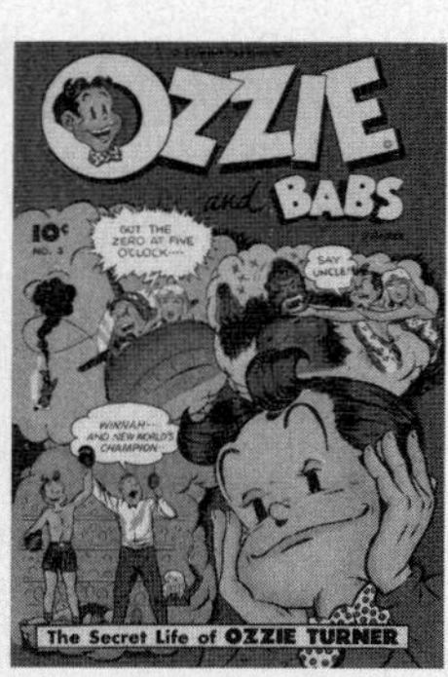

Ozzie and Babs #3 © FAW

Panhandle Pete and Jennifer #1 © JC

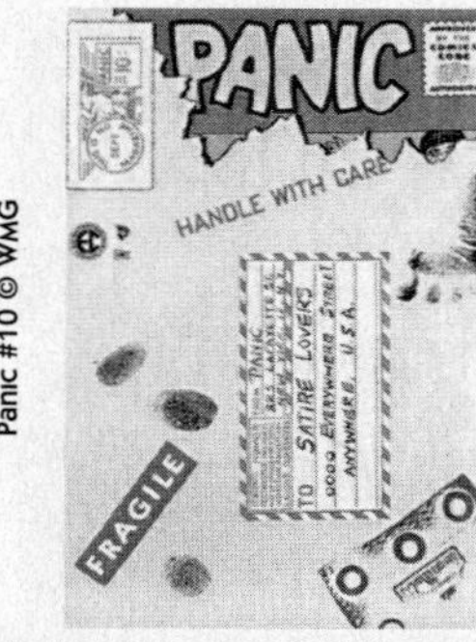

Panic #10 © WMG

	GD 2.0	VG 4.0	FN 6.0	VF 8.0	VF/NM 9.0	NM- 9.2

Dr. Spektor #22)
Gold Key: April, 1967; No. 2, April, 1968

	GD	VG	FN	VF	VF/NM	NM-
1-Written by Jerry Siegel; '40s super hero	6	12	18	39	62	85
2	5	10	15	30	48	65

OZ (See First Comics Graphic Novel, Marvel Treaury Of Oz & MGM's Marvelous...)

OZ
Caliber Press: 1994 - 1997 ($2.95, B&W)

	GD	VG	FN	VF	VF/NM	NM-
0-20: 0-Released between #10 & #11						3.00
1 ($5.95)-Limited Edition; double-c						6.00
...Specials: Freedom Fighters. Lion. Scarecrow. Tin Man						3.00

OZARK IKE
Dell Publishing Co./Standard Comics B11 on: Feb, 1948; Nov, 1948 - No. 24, Dec, 1951; No. 25, Sept, 1952

	GD	VG	FN	VF	VF/NM	NM-
Four Color 180(1948-Dell)	10	20	30	67	116	165
B11, B12, 13-15	10	20	30	54	72	90
16-25	9	18	27	47	61	75

OZ: DAEMONSTORM
Caliber Press: 1997 ($3.95, B&W, one-shot)

	GD	VG	FN	VF	VF/NM	NM-
1						4.00

OZ: ROMANCE IN RAGS
Caliber Press: 1996 ($2.95, B&W, limited series)

	GD	VG	FN	VF	VF/NM	NM-
1-3, ..Special						3.00

OZ SQUAD
Brave New Worlds/Patchwork Press: 1992 - No. 4, 1994 ($2.50/$2.75, B&W)

	GD	VG	FN	VF	VF/NM	NM-
1-4-Patchwork Press						3.00

OZ SQUAD
Patchwork Press: Dec, 1995 - No. 10, 1996 ($3.95/$2.95, B&W)

	GD	VG	FN	VF	VF/NM	NM-
1-($3.95)						4.00
2-10						3.00

OZ: STRAW AND SORCERY
Caliber Press: 1997 ($2.95, B&W, limited series)

	GD	VG	FN	VF	VF/NM	NM-
1-3						3.00

OZ-WONDERLAND WARS, THE
DC Comics: Jan, 1986 - No. 3, March, 1986 (Mini-series)(Giants)

	GD	VG	FN	VF	VF/NM	NM-
1-3-Capt. Carrot app.; funny animals						4.00

OZZIE & BABS (TV Teens #14 on)
Fawcett Publications: Dec, 1947 - No. 13, Fall, 1949

	GD	VG	FN	VF	VF/NM	NM-
1-Teen-age	10	20	30	54	72	90
2	6	12	18	31	38	45
3-13	6	12	18	27	33	38

OZZIE AND HARRIET (The Adventures of... on cover) (Radio)
National Periodical Publications: Oct-Nov, 1949 - No. 5, June-July, 1950

	GD	VG	FN	VF	VF/NM	NM-
1-Photo-c	94	188	282	597	1024	1450
2	47	94	141	296	498	700
3-5	39	78	117	240	395	550

OZZY OSBOURNE (Todd McFarlane Presents)
Image Comics (Todd McFarlane Prod.): June, 1999 ($4.95, magazine-sized)

	GD	VG	FN	VF	VF/NM	NM-
1-Bio, interview and comic story; Ormston painted-a; Ashley Wood-c						5.00

PACIFIC COMICS GRAPHIC NOVEL (See Image Graphic Novel)

PACIFIC PRESENTS (Also see Starslayer #2, 3)
Pacific Comics: Oct, 1982 - No. 2, Apr, 1983; No. 3, Mar, 1984 - No. 4, Jun, 1984

	GD	VG	FN	VF	VF/NM	NM-
1-Chapter 3 of The Rocketeer; Stevens-c/a; Bettie Page model	2	3	4	6	8	10
2-Chapter 4 of The Rocketeer (4th app.); nudity; Stevens-c/a	2	3	4	6	8	10
3,4: 3-1st app. Vanity						3.00

NOTE: ***Conrad** a-3, 4; c-3. **Ditko** a-1-3; c-1(1/2). **Dave Stevens** a-1, 2; c-1(1/2), 2.*

PACT, THE
Image Comics: Feb, 1994 - No. 3, June, 1994 ($1.95, limited series)

	GD	VG	FN	VF	VF/NM	NM-
1-3: Valentino co-scripts & layouts						2.50

PACT, THE
Image Comics: Apr, 2005 - No. 4, Jan, 2006 ($2.99/$2.95)

	GD	VG	FN	VF	VF/NM	NM-
1-4: Invincible, Shadowhawk, Firebreather & Zephyr team-up. 1-Valentino-s/a						3.00

PAGEANT OF COMICS (See Jane Arden & Mopsy)
Archer St. John: Sept, 1947 - No. 2, Oct, 1947

	GD	VG	FN	VF	VF/NM	NM-
1,2: 1-Mopsy strip-r. 2-Jane Arden strip-r	10	20	30	54	72	90

PAINKILLER JANE
Event Comics: June, 1997 - No. 5, Nov, 1997 ($3.95/$2.95)

	GD	VG	FN	VF	VF/NM	NM-
1-Augustyn/Waid-s/Leonardi/Palmiotti-a, variant-c						4.00
2-5: Two covers (Quesada, Leonardi)						3.00
0-(1/99, $3.95) Retells origin; two covers						4.00
Essential Painkiller Jane TPB (2007, $19.99) r/#0-5; cover gallery and pin-ups						20.00

PAINKILLER JANE
Dynamite Entertainment: 2006 - No. 3, 2006 ($2.99)

	GD	VG	FN	VF	VF/NM	NM-
1-3-Quesada & Palmiotti-s/Moder-a. 1-Four covers by Q&P, Moder, Tan and Conner						3.00
Volume #1 TPB (2007, $9.99) r/#1-3; cover gallery and Palmiotti interview						10.00

PAINKILLER JANE
Dynamite Entertainment: No. 0, 2007 - Present ($3.50)

	GD	VG	FN	VF	VF/NM	NM-
0-(25¢) Quesada & Palmiotti-s/Moder-a						2.25
1-5-($3.50) 1-Continued from #0; 5 covers. 4,5-Crossover with Terminator 2 #6,7						3.50
Volume #2 TPB (2007, $11.99) r/#0-3; cover gallery						12.00

PAINKILLER JANE / DARKCHYLDE
Event Comics: Oct, 1998 ($2.95, one-shot)

	GD	VG	FN	VF	VF/NM	NM-
Preview-($6.95) DF Edition, 1-($6.95) DF Edition						7.00
1-Three covers; J.G. Jones-a						3.00

PAINKILLER JANE / HELLBOY
Event Comics: Aug, 1998 ($2.95, one-shot)

	GD	VG	FN	VF	VF/NM	NM-
1-Leonardi & Palmiotti-a						3.00

PAINKILLER JANE VS. THE DARKNESS
Event Comics: Apr, 1997 ($2.95, one-shot)

	GD	VG	FN	VF	VF/NM	NM-
1-Ennis-s; four variant-c (Conner, Hildebrandts, Quesada, Silvestri)						3.50

PAKKINS' LAND
Caliber Comics (Tapestry): Oct, 1996 - No. 6, July, 1997 ($2.95, B&W)

	GD	VG	FN	VF	VF/NM	NM-
1-Gary and Rhoda Shipman-s/a						6.00
2,3						4.00
1-3-2nd printing						3.00
4-6						3.00
0-(6/97, $1.95)						3.00

PAKKINS' LAND
Alias Enterprises: Apr, 2005 - No. 2 ($2.99)

	GD	VG	FN	VF	VF/NM	NM-
1,2-Gary Shipman-s/a						3.00

PAKKINS' LAND: FORGOTTEN DREAMS
Caliber Comics/Image Comics #4: Apr, 1998 - No. 4, Mar, 2000 ($2.95, B&W)

	GD	VG	FN	VF	VF/NM	NM-
1-4-Gary and Rhoda Shipman-s/a						3.00

PAKKINS' LAND: QUEST FOR KINGS
Caliber Comics: Aug, 1997 - No. 6, Mar, 1998 ($2.95, B&W)

	GD	VG	FN	VF	VF/NM	NM-
1-6: 1-Gary and Rhoda Shipman-s/a; Jeff Smith var-c						3.00

PANCHO VILLA
Avon Periodicals: 1950

	GD	VG	FN	VF	VF/NM	NM-
nn-Kinstler-c	23	46	69	136	223	310

PANHANDLE PETE AND JENNIFER (TV) (See Gene Autry #20)
J. Charles Laue Publishing Co.: July, 1951 - No. 3, Nov, 1951

	GD	VG	FN	VF	VF/NM	NM-
1	10	20	30	54	72	90
2,3: 2-Interior photo-cvrs	7	14	21	37	46	55

PANIC (Companion to Mad)
E. C. Comics (Tiny Tot Comics): Feb-Mar, 1954 - No. 12, Dec-Jan, 1955-56

	GD	VG	FN	VF	VF/NM	NM-
1-Used in Senate Investigation hearings; Elder draws entire E. C. staff; Santa Claus & Mickey Spillane parody	33	66	99	264	420	575
2	16	32	48	128	202	275
3,4: 3-Senate Subcommittee parody; Davis draws Gaines, Feldstein & Kelly, 1 pg.; Old King Cole smokes marijuana. 4-Infinity-c; John Wayne parody	13	26	39	104	162	220
5-11: 8-Last pre-code issue (5/55). 9-Superman, Smilin' Jack & Dick Tracy app. on-c; has photo of Walter Winchell on-c. 11-Wheedies cereal box-c	11	22	33	88	144	200
12 (Low distribution; thousands were destroyed)	15	30	45	120	190	260

NOTE: ***Davis** a-1-12; c-12. **Elder** a-1-12. **Feldstein** c-1-3, 5. **Kamen** a-1. **Orlando** a-1-9. **Wolverton** c-4, panel-3. **Wood** a-2-9, 11, 12.*

PANIC (Magazine) (Satire)

Paradise X: Heralds #1 © MAR

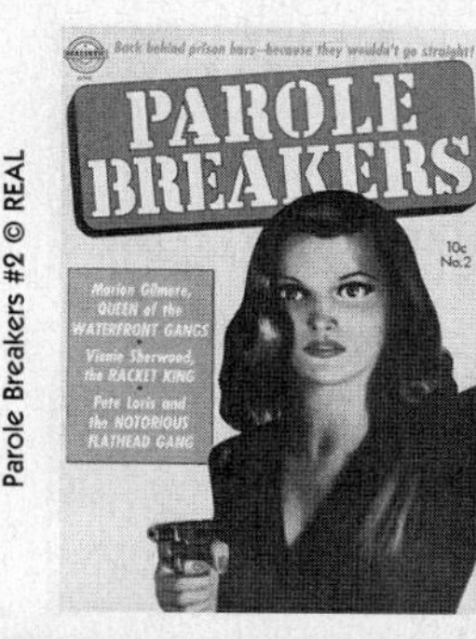

Parole Breakers #2 © REAL

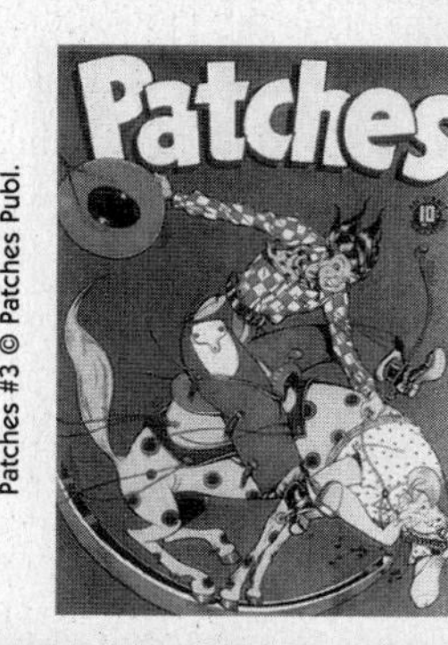

Patches #3 © Patches Publ.

	GD	VG	FN	VF	VF/NM	NM-
	2.0	4.0	6.0	8.0	9.0	9.2

Panic Publ.: July, 1958 - No. 6, July, 1959; V2#10, Dec, 1965 - V2#12, 1966
1 13 26 39 74 105 135
2-6 9 18 27 47 61 75
V2#10-12: Reprints earlier issues 3 6 9 18 27 35
NOTE: *Davis a-3(2 pgs.), 4, 5, 10; c-10.* ***Elder*** *a-5.* ***Powell*** *a-V2#10, 11.* ***Torres*** *a-1-5.* ***Tuska*** *a-V2#11.*

PANIC
Gemstone Publishing: March, 1997 - No. 12, Dec, 1999 ($2.50, quarterly)
1-12: E.C. reprints 2.50

PANTHA (See Vampirella-The New Monthly #16,17)

PANTHA: HAUNTED PASSION (Also see Vampirella Monthly #0)
Harris Comics: May, 1997 ($2.95, B&W, one-shot)
1-r/Vampirella #30,31 3.00

PAPA MIDNITE (See John Constantine - Hellblazer Special:...)

PARADE (See Hanna-Barbera...)

PARADE COMICS (See Frisky Animals on Parade)

PARADE OF PLEASURE
Derric Verschoyle Ltd., London, England: 1954 (192 pgs.) (Hardback book)
By Geoffrey Wagner. Contains section devoted to the censorship of American comic books with illustrations in color and black and white. (Also see **Seduction of the Innocent**).
Distributed in USA by Library Publishers, N. Y. 108 216 324 464 557 650
with dust jacket.... 105 210 315 578 889 1200

PARADISE TOO!
Abstract Studios: 2000 - No. 14, 2003 ($2.95, B&W)
1-14-Terry Moore's unpublished newspaper strips and sketches 3.00
...: Checking For Weirdos TPB (4/03, $14.95) r/#8-12 15.00
...: Drunk Ducks! TPB (7/02, $15.95) r/#1-7 16.00

PARADISE X (Also see Earth X and Universe X)
Marvel Comics: Apr, 2002 - No. 12, Aug, 2003 ($4.50/$2.99)
0-Ross-c; Braithwaite-a 4.50
1-12-($2.99) Ross-c; Braithwaite-a. 7-Punisher on-c. 10-Kingpin on-c 3.00
...:A (10/03, $2.99) Braithwaite-a; Ross-c 3.00
...:Devils (11/02, $4.50) Sadowski-a; Ross-c 4.50
...:Ragnarok 1,2 (3/02, 4/03; $2.99) Yeates-a; Ross-c 3.00
...:X (11/03, $2.99) Braithwaite-a; Ross-c; conclusion of story 3.00
...:Xen (7/02, $4.50) Yeowell & Sienkiewicz-a; Ross-c 4.50
Earth X Vol. 4: Paradise X Book 1 (2003, $29.99, TPB) r/#0,1-5, ...: Xen; Heralds #1-3 30.00
Vol. 5: Paradise X Book 2 (2004, $29.99, TPB) r/#6-12, Ragnarok #1&2; Devils, A & X 30.00

PARADISE X: HERALDS (Also see Earth X and Universe X)
Marvel Comics: Dec, 2001 - No. 3, Feb, 2002 ($3.50)
1-3-Prelude to Paradise X series; Ross-c; Pugh-a 3.50
Special Edition (Wizard preview) Ross-c 2.50

PARADOX
Dark Visions Publ: June, 1994 - No. 2, Aug, 1994 ($2.95, B&W, mature)
1,2: 1-Linsner-c. 2-Boris-c. 3.00

PARALLAX: EMERALD NIGHT (See Final Night)
DC Comics: Nov, 1996 ($2.95, one-shot, 48 pgs.)
1-Final Night tie-in; Green Lantern (Kyle Rayner) app. 4.00

PARAMOUNT ANIMATED COMICS (See Harvey Comics Hits #60, 62)
Harvey Publications: No. 3, Feb, 1953 - No. 22, July, 1956
3-Baby Huey, Herman & Katnip, Buzzy the Crow begin
23 46 69 136 223 310
4-6 13 26 39 74 105 135
7-Baby Huey becomes permanent cover feature; cover title becomes Baby Huey with #9
22 44 66 128 209 290
8-10: 9-Infinity-c 12 24 36 69 97 125
11-22 10 20 30 54 72 90

PARENT TRAP, THE (Disney)
Dell Publishing Co.: No. 1210, Oct-Dec, 1961
Four Color 1210-Movie, Hayley Mills photo-c 9 18 27 60 100 140

PARLIAMENT OF JUSTICE
Image Comics: Mar, 2003 ($5.95, B&W, one-shot, square-bound)
1-Michael Avon Oeming-c/s; Neil Vokes-a 6.00

PARODY
Armour Publishing: Mar, 1977 - No. 3, Aug, 1977 (B&W humor magazine)
1 3 6 9 14 19 24
2,3: 2-King Kong, Happy Days. 3-Charlie's Angels, Rocky
2 4 6 10 14 18

PAROLE BREAKERS
Avon Periodicals/Realistic #2 on: Dec, 1951 - No. 3, July, 1952
1(#2 on inside)-r-c/Avon paperback #283 (painted-c)
43 86 129 271 461 650
2-Kubert-a; r-c/Avon paperback #114 (photo-c) 30 60 90 177 289 400
3-Kinstler-c 27 54 81 158 259 360

PARTRIDGE FAMILY, THE (TV)(Also see David Cassidy)
Charlton Comics: Mar, 1971 - No. 21, Dec, 1973
1-(2 versions: B&W photo-c & tinted color photo-c) 7 14 21 45 73 100
2-4,6-10 4 8 12 24 37 50
5-Partridge Family Summer Special (52 pgs.); The Shadow, Lone Ranger, Charlie McCarthy, Flash Gordon, Hopalong Cassidy, Gene Autry & others app.
7 14 21 50 83 115
11-21 3 6 9 21 32 42

PARTS OF A HOLE
Caliber Press: 1991 ($2.50, B&W)
1-Short stories & cartoons by Brian Michael Bendis 3.00

PARTS UNKNOWN
Eclipse Comics/FX: July, 1992 - No. 4, Oct, 1992 ($2.50, B&W, mature)
1-4: All contain FX gaming cards 2.50

PARTS UNKNOWN
Image Comics: May, 2000 - Present ($2.95, B&W)
...: Killing Attractions 1 (5/00) Beau Smith-s/Brad Gorby-a 3.00
...: Hostile Takeover 1-4 (6-9/00) 3.00

PASSION, THE
Catechetical Guild: No. 394, 1955
394 6 12 18 28 34 40

PASSOVER (See Avengelyne)
Maximum Press: Dec, 1996 ($2.99, one-shot)
1 3.00

PAT BOONE (TV)(Also see Superman's Girlfriend Lois Lane #9)
National Per. Publ.: Sept-Oct, 1959 - No. 5, May-Jun, 1960 (All have photo-c)
1 43 86 129 267 446 625
2-5: 3-Fabian, Connie Francis & Paul Anka photos on-c. 4-Previews "Journey To The Center Of The Earth". 4-Johnny Mathis & Bobby Darin photos on-c. 5-Dick Clark & Frankie Avalon photos on-c 35 70 105 203 327 450

PATCHES
Rural Home/Patches Publ. (Orbit): Mar-Apr, 1945 - No. 11, Nov, 1947
1-L. B. Cole-c 40 80 120 244 397 550
2 15 30 45 88 137 185
3,4,6,8-11: 6-Henry Aldrich story. 8-Smiley Burnette-c/s (6/47); pre-dates Smiley Burnette #1. 9-Mr. District Attorney story (radio). Leav/Keigstein-a (16 pgs.). 9-11-Leav-c. 10-Jack Carson (radio) c/story; Leav-c. 11-Red Skelton story 15 30 45 85 130 175
5-Danny Kaye-c/story; L.B. Cole-c. 20 40 60 117 186 255
7-Hopalong Cassidy-c/story 18 36 54 103 162 220

PATH, THE (Also see Negation War)
CrossGeneration Comics: Apr, 2002 - No. 23, Apr, 2004 ($2.95)
1-23: 1-Ron Marz-s/Bart Sears-a. 13-Matthew Smith-a begins 3.00
Vol. 1: Crisis of Faith (2002, $15.95, TPB) r/#1-6 16.00
Vol. 2: Blood on Snow (5/03, $15.95, TPB) r/#7-12 16.00
Vol. 3: Death and Dishonor ('03, $15.95, TPB) r/#13-18 16.00

PATHWAYS TO FANTASY
Pacific Comics: July, 1984
1-Barry Smith-c/a; Jeff Jones-a (4 pgs.) 4.00

PATIENT ZERO
Image Comics: Mar, 2004 - No. 4, Jun, 2004 ($2.95, limited series)
1-4-Brent White-a/John McLean-Foreman-s 3.00

PATORUZU (See Adventures of...)

PATRIOTS, THE
DC Comics (WildStorm): Jan, 2000 - No. 10, Oct, 2000 ($2.50)
1-10-Choi and Peterson-s/Ryan-a 2.50

PATSY & HEDY (Teenage)(Also see Hedy Wolfe)
Atlas Comics/Marvel (GPI/Male): Feb, 1952 - No. 110, Feb, 1967

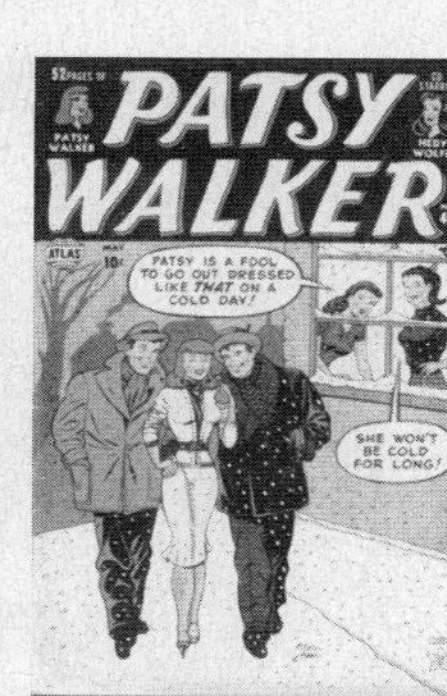

Patsy Walker #46 © MAR

Paul the Samurai #1 © NEC

Peanuts #2 © UFS

	GD 2.0	VG 4.0	FN 6.0	VF 8.0	VF/NM 9.0	NM- 9.2
1-Patsy Walker & Hedy Wolfe; Al Jaffee-c	24	48	72	142	234	325
2	14	28	42	82	121	160
3-10: 3,7,8,9-Al Jaffee-c	12	24	36	69	97	125
11-20: 17,19,20-Al Jaffee-c	11	22	33	60	83	105
21-40	9	18	27	52	69	85
41-50	5	10	15	34	55	75
51-60	5	10	15	32	51	70
61-80,100: 88-Lingerie panel	4	8	12	28	44	60
81-87,89-99,101-110	4	8	12	26	41	55
Annual 1(1963)-Early Marvel annual	9	18	27	63	107	150

PATSY & HER PALS (Teenage)
Atlas Comics (PPI): May, 1953 - No. 29, Aug, 1957

	GD 2.0	VG 4.0	FN 6.0	VF 8.0	VF/NM 9.0	NM- 9.2
1-Patsy Walker	18	36	54	105	165	240
2	12	24	36	67	94	120
3-10	11	22	33	60	83	105
11-29: 24-Everett-c	9	18	27	52	69	85

PATSY WALKER (See All Teen, A Date With Patsy, Girls' Life, Miss America Magazine, Patsy & Hedy, Patsy & Her Pals & Teen Comics)
Marvel/Atlas Comics (BPC): 1945 (no month) - No. 124, Dec, 1965

	GD 2.0	VG 4.0	FN 6.0	VF 8.0	VF/NM 9.0	NM- 9.2
1-Teenage	55	110	165	352	601	850
2	31	62	93	182	296	410
3,4,6-10	24	48	72	142	234	325
5-Injury-to-eye-c	27	54	81	160	263	365
11,12,15,16,18	15	30	45	88	137	185
13,14,17,19-22-Kurtzman's "Hey Look"	16	32	48	92	144	195
23,24	14	28	42	78	112	145
25-Rusty by Kurtzman; painted-c	16	32	48	92	144	195
26-29,31: 26-31: 52 pgs.	12	24	36	67	94	120
30(52 pgs.)-Egghead Doodle by Kurtzman (1 pg.)	13	26	39	72	101	130
32-57: Last precode (3/55)	10	20	30	56	76	95
58-80,100	5	10	15	34	55	75
81-99: 92,98-Millie x-over. 99-Linda Carter x-over	5	10	15	30	48	65
101-124	4	8	12	28	44	60
Fashion Parade 1(1966, 68 pgs.) (Beware cut-out & marked pages)	8	16	24	54	90	125

NOTE: *Painted c-25-28. Anti-Wertham editorial in #21. Georgie app. in #8, 11. Millie app. in #10, 92, 98. Mitzi app. in #11. Rusty app. in #12, 25. Willie app. in #12.* ***Al Jaffee*** *c-44, 47, 49, 57, 58.*

PATSY WALKER: HELLCAT
Marvel Comics: Sept, 2008 - No. 5, Feb, 2009 ($2.99, limited series)

	GD 2.0	VG 4.0	FN 6.0	VF 8.0	VF/NM 9.0	NM- 9.2
1-5-Lafuente-a/Kathryn Immonen-s/Stuart Immonen-c; Hellcat joins The Initiative						3.00

PAT THE BRAT (Adventures of Pipsqueak #34 on)
Archie Publications (Radio): June, 1953; Summer, 1955 - No. 4, 5/56; No. 15, 7/56 - No. 33, 7/59

	GD 2.0	VG 4.0	FN 6.0	VF 8.0	VF/NM 9.0	NM- 9.2
nn(6/53)	14	28	42	76	108	140
1(Summer, 1955)	10	20	30	54	72	90
2-4-(5/56) (#5-14 not published). 3-Early Bolling-a	7	14	21	37	46	55
15-(7/56)-33: 18-Early Bolling-a	4	8	12	22	34	45

PAT THE BRAT COMICS DIGEST MAGAZINE
Archie Publications: October, 1980

	GD 2.0	VG 4.0	FN 6.0	VF 8.0	VF/NM 9.0	NM- 9.2
1-Li'l Jinx & Super Duck app.	2	4	6	9	13	16

PATTY CAKE
Permanent Press: Mar, 1995 - No. 9, Jul, 1996 ($2.95, B&W)

	GD 2.0	VG 4.0	FN 6.0	VF 8.0	VF/NM 9.0	NM- 9.2
1-9: Scott Roberts-s/a						3.00

PATTY CAKE
Caliber Press (Tapestry): Oct, 1996 - No. 3, Apr, 1997 ($2.95, B&W)

	GD 2.0	VG 4.0	FN 6.0	VF 8.0	VF/NM 9.0	NM- 9.2
1-3: Scott Roberts-s/a, ...Christmas (12/96)						3.00

PATTY CAKE & FRIENDS
Slave Labor Graphics: Nov, 1997 - Present ($2.95, B&W)

	GD 2.0	VG 4.0	FN 6.0	VF 8.0	VF/NM 9.0	NM- 9.2
Here There Be Monsters (10/97), 1-14: Scott Roberts-s/a						3.00
Volume 2 #1 (11/00, $4.95)						5.00

PATTY POWERS (Formerly Della Vision #3)
Atlas Comics: No. 4, Oct, 1955 - No. 7, Oct, 1956

	GD 2.0	VG 4.0	FN 6.0	VF 8.0	VF/NM 9.0	NM- 9.2
4	11	22	33	60	83	105
5-7	7	14	21	37	46	55

PAT WILTON (See Mighty Midget Comics)

PAUL
Spire Christian Comics (Fleming H. Revell Co.): 1978 (49¢)

	GD 2.0	VG 4.0	FN 6.0	VF 8.0	VF/NM 9.0	NM- 9.2
nn	2	4	6	8	11	14

PAULINE PERIL (See The Close Shaves of...)

PAUL REVERE'S RIDE (TV, Disney, see Walt Disney Showcase #34)
Dell Publishing Co.: No. 822, July, 1957

	GD 2.0	VG 4.0	FN 6.0	VF 8.0	VF/NM 9.0	NM- 9.2
Four Color 822-w/Johnny Tremain, Toth-a	8	16	24	58	97	135

PAUL TERRY (See Heckle and Jeckle)

PAUL TERRY'S ADVENTURES OF MIGHTY MOUSE (See Adventures of...)

PAUL TERRY'S COMICS (Formerly Terry-Toons Comics; becomes Adventures of Mighty Mouse No. 126 on)
St. John Publishing Co.: No. 85, Mar, 1951 - No. 125, May, 1955

	GD 2.0	VG 4.0	FN 6.0	VF 8.0	VF/NM 9.0	NM- 9.2
85,86-Same as Terry-Toons #85, & 86 with only a title change; published at same time?; Mighty Mouse, Heckle & Jeckle & Gandy Goose continue from Terry-Toons	12	24	36	67	94	120
87-99	9	18	27	50	65	80
100	10	20	30	54	72	90
101-104,107-125: 121,122,125-Painted-c	9	18	27	47	61	75
105,106-Giant Comics Edition (25¢, 100 pgs.) (9/53 & ?). 105-Little Roquefort-c/story	18	36	54	105	165	225

PAUL TERRY'S MIGHTY MOUSE (See Mighty Mouse)

PAUL TERRY'S MIGHTY MOUSE ADVENTURE STORIES (See Mighty Mouse Adventure Stories)

PAUL THE SAMURAI (See The Tick #4)
New England Comics: July, 1992 - No. 6, July, 1993 ($2.75, B&W)

	GD 2.0	VG 4.0	FN 6.0	VF 8.0	VF/NM 9.0	NM- 9.2
1-6						2.75

PAWNEE BILL
Story Comics (Youthful Magazines?): Feb, 1951 - No. 3, July, 1951

	GD 2.0	VG 4.0	FN 6.0	VF 8.0	VF/NM 9.0	NM- 9.2
1-Bat Masterson, Wyatt Earp app.	13	26	39	72	101	130
2,3: 3-Origin Golden Warrior; Cameron-a	8	16	24	42	54	65

PAY-OFF (This Is the..., ...Crime, ...Detective Stories)
D. S. Publishing Co.: July-Aug, 1948 - No. 5, Mar-Apr, 1949 (52 pgs.)

	GD 2.0	VG 4.0	FN 6.0	VF 8.0	VF/NM 9.0	NM- 9.2
1-True Crime Cases #1,2	26	52	78	152	249	345
2	15	30	45	94	147	200
3-5-Thrilling Detective Stories	14	28	42	82	121	160

PEACEMAKER, THE (Also see Fightin' Five)
Charlton Comics: V3#1, Mar, 1967 - No. 5, Nov, 1967 (All 12¢ cover price)

	GD 2.0	VG 4.0	FN 6.0	VF 8.0	VF/NM 9.0	NM- 9.2
1-Fightin' Five begins	5	10	15	34	55	75
2,3,5	3	6	9	21	32	42
4-Origin The Peacemaker	4	8	12	26	41	55
1,2(Modern Comics reprint, 1978)						5.00

PEACEMAKER (Also see Crisis On Infinite Earths & Showcase '93 #7,9,10)
DC Comics: Jan, 1988 - No. 4, Apr, 1988 ($1.25, limited series)

	GD 2.0	VG 4.0	FN 6.0	VF 8.0	VF/NM 9.0	NM- 9.2
1-4						2.50

PEANUTS (Charlie Brown) (See Fritzi Ritz, Nancy & Sluggo, Sparkle & Sparkler, Tip Top, Tip Topper & United Comics)
United Features Syndicate/Dell Publishing Co./Gold Key: 1953-54; No. 878, 2/58 - No. 13, 5-7/62; 5/63 - No. 4, 2/64

	GD 2.0	VG 4.0	FN 6.0	VF 8.0	VF/NM 9.0	NM- 9.2
1(U.F.S.)(1953-54)-Reprints United Features' Strange As It Seems, Willie, Ferdnand	11	22	33	80	145	210
Four Color 878(#1) (Dell) Schulz-s/a, with assistance from Dale Hale and Jim Sasseville thru #4	21	42	63	148	287	425
Four Color 969,1015('59)	13	26	39	93	172	250
4(2-4/60) Schulz-s/a; one story by Anthony Pocrnich, Schulz's assistant cartoonist	11	22	33	80	145	210
5-13-Schulz-c only; s/a by Pocrnich	10	20	30	67	116	165
1(Gold Key, 5/63)	11	22	33	74	132	190
2-4	8	16	24	52	86	120

PEBBLES & BAMM BAMM (TV) (See Cave Kids #7, 12)
Charlton Comics: Jan, 1972 - No. 36, Dec, 1976 (Hanna-Barbera)

	GD 2.0	VG 4.0	FN 6.0	VF 8.0	VF/NM 9.0	NM- 9.2
1-From the Flintstones; "Teen Age..." on cover	5	10	15	30	48	65
2-10	3	6	9	17	25	32
11-20	2	4	6	13	18	22
21-36	2	4	6	9	13	16
nn (1973, digest, 100 pgs.) B&W one page gags	3	6	9	18	27	35

PEBBLES & BAMM BAMM (TV)
Harvey Comics: Nov, 1993 - No. 3, Mar, 1994 ($1.50) (Hanna-Barbera)

	GD 2.0	VG 4.0	FN 6.0	VF 8.0	VF/NM 9.0	NM- 9.2
V2#1-3						3.00
...Giant Size 1 (10/93, $2.25, 68 pgs.)("Summer Special" on-c)						4.00

PEBBLES FLINTSTONE (TV) (See The Flintstones #11)

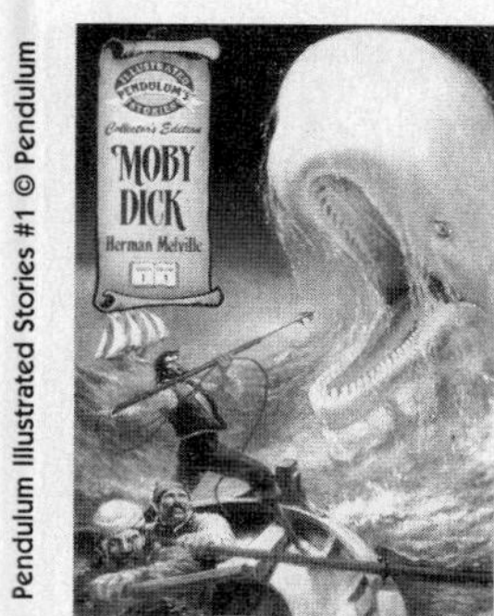

Pendulum Illustrated Stories #1 © Pendulum

Pep Comics #85 © AP

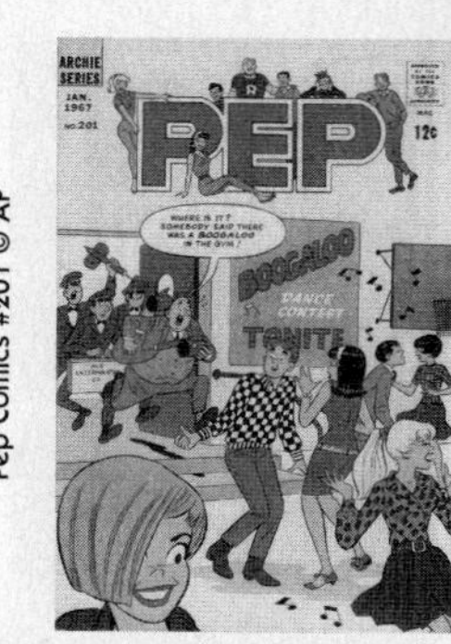

Pep Comics #201 © AP

	GD 2.0	VG 4.0	FN 6.0	VF 8.0	VF/NM 9.0	NM- 9.2

Gold Key: Sept, 1963 (Hanna-Barbera)

1 (10088-309)-Early Pebbles app. 9 18 27 60 100 140

PEDRO (Formerly My Private Life #17; also see Romeo Tubbs)
Fox Features Syndicate: No. 18, June, 1950 - No. 2, Aug, 1950?

18(#1)-Wood-c/a(p) 22 44 66 128 209 290
2-Wood-a? 15 30 45 88 137 185

PEE-WEE PIXIES (See The Pixies)

PELLEAS AND MELISANDE (See Night Music #4, 5)

PENALTY (See Crime Must Pay the...)

PENANCE: RELENTLESS (See Civil War, Thunderbolts and related titles)
Marvel Comics: Nov, 2007 - No. 5 ($2.99)

1-5-Speedball/Penance; Jenkins-s/Gulacy-a. 3-Wolverine app. 3.00
TPB (2008, $13.99) r/#1-5 14.00

PENDRAGON (Knights of... #5 on; also see Knights of...)
Marvel Comics UK, Ltd.: July, 1992 - No. 15, Sept, 1993 ($1.75)

1-15: 1-4-Iron Man app. 6-8-Spider-Man app. 2.50

PENDULUM ILLUSTRATED BIOGRAPHIES
Pendulum Press: 1979 (B&W)

19-355x-George Washington/Thomas Jefferson, 19-3495-Charles Lindbergh/Amelia Earhart, 19-3509-Harry Houdini/Walt Disney, 19-3517-Davy Crockett/Daniel Boone-Redondo-a, 19-3525-Elvis Presley/Beatles, 19-3533-Benjamin Franklin/Martin Luther King Jr, 19-3541-Abraham Lincoln/Franklin D. Roosevelt, 19-3568-Marie Curie/Albert Einstein-Redondo-a, 19-3576-Thomas Edison/Alexander Graham Bell-Redondo-a, 19-3584-Vince Lombardi/Pele, 19-3592-Babe Ruth/Jackie Robinson, 19-3606-Jim Thorpe/Althea Gibson
Softback 5.00
Hardback 1 2 3 4 5 7

PENDULUM ILLUSTRATED CLASSICS (Now Age Illustrated)
Pendulum Press: 1973 - 1978 (75¢, 62pp, B&W, 5-3/8x8")
(Also see Marvel Classics)

64-100x(1973)-Dracula-Redondo art, 64-131x-The Invisible Man-Nino art, 64-0968-Dr. Jekyll and Mr. Hyde-Redondo art, 64-1005-Black Beauty, 64-1010-Call of the Wild, 64-1020-Frankenstein, 64-1025-Hucklebury Finn, 64-1030-Moby Dick-Nino-a, 64-1040-Red Badge of Courage, 64-1045-The Time Machine-Nino-a, 64-1050-Tom Sawyer, 64-1055-Twenty Thousand Leagues Under the Sea, 64-1069-Treasure Island, 64-1328(1974)-Kidnapped, 64-1336-Three Musketeers-Nino art, 64-1344-A Tale of Two Cities, 64-1352-Journey to the Center of the Earth, 64-1360-The War of the Worlds-Nino-a, 64-1379-The Greatest Advs. of Sherlock Holmes-Redondo art, 64-1387-Mysterious Island, 64-1395-Hunchback of Notre Dame, 64-1409-Helen Keller-story of my life, 64-1417-Scarlet Letter, 64-1425-Gulliver's Travels, 64-2618(1977)-Around the World in Eighty Days, 64-2626-Captains Courageous, 64-2634-Connecticut Yankee, 64-2642-The Hound of the Baskervilles, 64-2650-The House of Seven Gables, 64-2669-Jane Eyre, 64-2677-The Last of the Mohicans, 64-2685-The Best of O'Henry, 64-2693-The Best of Poe-Redondo-a, 64-2707-Two Years Before the Mast, 64-2715-White Fang, 64-2723-Wuthering Heights, 64-3126(1978)-Ben Hur-Redondo art, 64-3134-A Christmas Carol, 64-3142-The Food of the Gods, 64-3150-Ivanhoe, 64-3169-The Man in the Iron Mask, 64-3177-The Prince and the Pauper, 64-3185-The Prisoner of Zenda, 64-3193-The Return of the Native, 64-3207-Robinson Crusoe, 64-3215-The Scarlet Pimpernel, 64-3223-The Sea Wolf, 64-3231-The Swiss Family Robinson, 64-3851-Billy Budd, 64-386x-Crime and Punishment, 64-3878-Don Quixote, 64-3886-Great Expectations, 64-3894-Heidi, 64-3908-The Iliad, 64-3916-Lord Jim, 64-3924-The Mutiny on Board H.M.S. Bounty, 64-3932-The Odyssey, 64-3940-Oliver Twist, 64-3959-Pride and Prejudice, 64-3967-The Turn of the Screw
Softback 6.00
Hardback 1 2 3 5 6 8

NOTE: *All of the above books can be ordered from the publisher; some were reprinted as Marvel Classic Comics #1-12. In 1972 there was another brief series of 12 titles which contained Classics Ill. artwork. They were entitled* ***Now Age Books*** *Illustrated, but can be easily distinguished from later series by the small Classics Illustrated logo at the top of the front cover. The format is the same as the later series. The 48 pg. C.I. art was stretched out to make 62 pgs. After Twin Circle Publ. terminated the Classics Ill. series in 1971, they made a one year contract with Pendulum Press to print these twelve titles of C.I. art. Pendulum was unhappy with the contract, and at the end of 1972 began their own art series, utilizing the talents of the Filipino artist group. One detail which makes this rather confusing is that when they redid the art in 1973, they gave it the same identifying no. as the 1972 series. All 12 of the 1972 C.I. editions have new covers, taken from internal art panels. In spite of their recent age, all of the 1972 C.I. series are very rare. Mint copies would fetch at least $50. Here is a list of the 1972 series, with C.I. title no. counterpart:*

64-1005 (CI#60-A2) 64-1010 (CI#91) 64-1015 (CI-Jr #503) 64-1020 (CI#26)
64-1025 (CI#19-A2) 64-1030 (CI#5-A2) 64-1035 (CI#169) 64-1040 (CI#98)
64-1045 (CI#133) 64-1050 (CI#50-A2) 64-1055 (CI#47) 64-1060 (CI-Jr#535)

PENDULUM ILLUSTRATED ORIGINALS
Pendulum Press: 1979 (In color)

94-4254-Solarman: The Beginning (See Solarman) 6.00

PENDULUM'S ILLUSTRATED STORIES
Pendulum Press: 1990 - No. 72, 1990? (No cover price ($4.95), squarebound, 68 pgs.)

1-72: Reprints Pendulum Ill. Classics series 5.00

PENNY
Avon Comics: 1947 - No. 6, Sept-Oct, 1949 (Newspaper reprints)

1-Photo & biography of creator 20 40 60 114 182 250
2-5 10 20 30 58 79 100
6-Perry Como photo on-c 11 22 33 62 86 110

PENNY CENTURY (See Love and Rockets)
Fantagraphics Books: Dec, 1997 - Present ($2.95, B&W, mini-series)

1-7-Jaime Hernandez-s/a 3.00

PEP COMICS (See Archie Giant Series #576, 589, 601, 614, 624)
MLJ Magazines/Archie Publications No. 56 (3/46) on: Jan, 1940 - No. 411, Mar, 1987

1-Intro. The Shield (1st patriotic hero) by Irving Novick; origin & 1st app. The Comet by Jack Cole, The Queen of Diamonds & Kayo Ward; The Rocket, The Press Guardian (The Falcon #1 only), Sergeant Boyle, Fu Chang, & Bentley of of Scotland Yard; Robot-c; Shield-c begin 892 1784 2676 6512 11,506 16,500
2-Origin The Rocket 265 530 795 1694 2897 4100
3 194 388 582 1242 2121 3000
4-Wizard cameo; early robot-s 155 310 465 992 1696 2400
5-Wizard cameo in Shield story 155 310 465 992 1696 2400
6-10: 8-Last Cole Comet; no Cole-a in #6,7 127 254 381 807 1391 1975
11-Dusty, Shield's sidekick begins (1st app.); last Press Guardian, Fu Chang 131 262 393 832 1429 2025
12-Origin & 1st app. Fireball (2/41); last Rocket & Queen of Diamonds; Danny in Wonderland begins 150 300 450 953 1639 2325
13-15 103 206 309 659 1130 1600
16-Origin Madam Satan; blood drainage-c 165 330 495 1048 1799 2550
17-Origin/1st app. The Hangman (7/41); death of The Comet; Comet is revealed as Hangman's brother 383 766 1149 2681 4691 6700
18,19,21: 21-Last Madam Satan 97 194 291 621 1061 1500
20-Classic Nazi swastika-c; last Fireball 142 284 426 909 1555 2200
22-Intro. & 1st app. Archie, Betty, & Jughead(12/41); (also see Jackpot) 3200 6400 9600 24,000 37,000 50,000
23 297 594 891 1900 3250 4600
24,25: 24-Coach Kleets app. (unnamed until Archie #94); bondage/torture-c. 25-1st app. Archie's jalopy; 1st skinny Mr. Weatherbee prototype 206 412 618 1318 2259 3200
26-1st app. Veronica Lodge (4/42); "Remember Pearl Harbor!" cover caption 300 600 900 1920 3310 4700
27,29,30: 27-Bill of Rights-c. 29-Origin Shield retold; 30-Capt. Commando begins; bondage/torture-c; 1st Miss Grundy (definitive version); see Jackpot #4 161 322 483 1030 1765 2500
28-Classic swastika/Hangman-c 174 348 522 1114 1907 2700
31-35: 31-MLJ offices & artists are visited in Sgt. Boyle story; 1st app. Mr. Lodge. 32-Shield dons new costume. 34-Bondage/Hypo-c. 33-Pre-Moose tryout (see Jughead #1) 129 258 387 826 1413 2000
36-1st Archie-c (2/43) w/Shield & Hangman 300 600 900 2010 3505 5000
37-40 81 162 243 518 884 1250
41-50: 41-Archie-c begin. 47-Last Hangman issue; infinity-c. 48-Black Hood begins (5/44); ends #51,59,60 58 116 174 371 636 900
51-60: 52-Suzie begins; 1st Mr Weatherbee-c. 56-Last Capt. Commando. 59-Black Hood not in costume; lingerie panels; Archie dresses as his aunt; Suzie ends. 60-Katy Keene begins(3/47), ends #154 37 74 111 222 361 500
61-65-Last Shield. 62-1st app. Li'l Jinx (7/47) 30 60 90 177 289 400
66-80: 66-G-Man Club becomes Archie Club (2/48); Nevada Jones by Bill Woggon. 78-1st app. Dilton 18 36 54 105 165 225
81-99 15 30 45 83 124 165
100 17 34 51 98 154 210
101-130 10 20 30 58 79 100
131(2/59)-137 5 10 15 34 55 75
138-140-Neal Adams-a (1 pg.) in each 6 12 18 39 62 85
141-149(9/61) 4 8 12 28 44 60
150-160-Super-heroes app. in each (see note). 150 (10/61?)-2nd or 3rd app. The Jaguar? 151-154,156-158-Horror/Sci/Fi-c. 157-Li'l Jinx. 159-Both 12¢ and 15¢ covers exist 6 12 18 41 66 90
161(3/63)-167,169-180: 161-3rd Josie app.; early Josie stories w/DeCarlo-a begin (see Note for others) 4 8 12 22 34 45
168,200: 168-(1/64)-Jaguar app. 200-(12/66) 4 8 12 24 37 50
181(5/65)-199: 187-Pureheart try-out story. 192-UFO-c. 198-Giantman-c(only) 3 6 9 17 25 32
201-217,219-226,228-240(4/70) 3 6 9 14 20 26
218,227-Archies Band-c only 3 6 9 16 23 30
241-270(10/72) 2 4 6 11 16 20
271-297,299 2 4 6 8 11 14
298, 300: 298-Josie and the Pussycats-c. 300(4/75) 2 4 6 11 16 20
301-340(8/78) 1 2 3 5 7 9
341-382 6.00
383(4/82),393(3/84): 383-Marvelous Maureen begins (Sci/fi). 393-Thunderbunny begins 1 2 3 4 5 7
384-392,394-399,401-410: 396-Early Cheryl Blossom-c 4.00
400(5/85),411: 400-Story featuring Archie staff (DeCarlo-a) 6.00

Perfect Love #3 © Z-D

Peter Panda #7 © DC

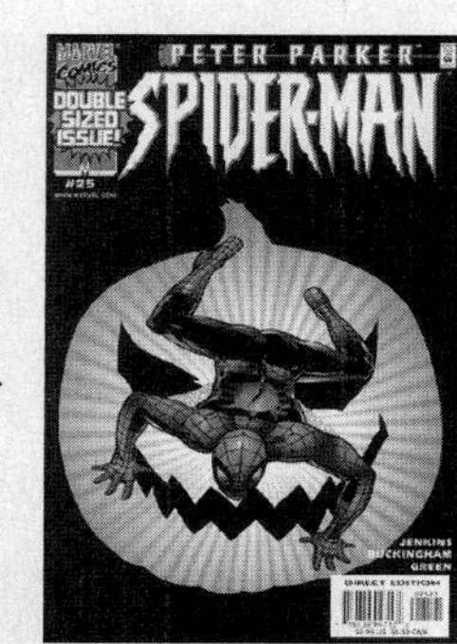

Peter Parker: Spider-Man #25 © MAR

NOTE: ***Biro** a-2, 4, 5. **Jack Cole** a-1-5, 8. **Al Fagaly** c-55-72. **Fuje** a-39, 45, 47; c-34. **Meskin** a-2, 4, 5, 11(2). **Montana** c-30, 32, 33, 36, 73-87(most). **Novick** c-1-28, 29(w/**Schomburg**), 31i. **Harry Sahle** c-35, 39-50. **Schomburg** c-38. **Bob Wood** a-2, 4-6, 11. The Fly app. in 151, 154, 160. Flygirl app. in 153, 155, 156, 158. Jaguar app. in 150, 152, 157, 159, 168. Josie by **DeCarlo** in 161-166, 168-171, 173, 175-177, 179, 181. Katy Keene by **Bill Woggon** in 73-126. Bondage c-7, 12, 13, 15, 18, 21, 31, 32. Cover features: Shield #1-16; Shield/Hangman #17-27, 29-41; Hangman #28. Archie #36, 41-on.*

PEPE
Dell Publishing Co.: No. 1194, Apr, 1961

	GD 2.0	VG 4.0	FN 6.0	VF 8.0	VF/NM 9.0	NM- 9.2
Four Color 1194-Movie, photo-c	4	8	12	24	37	50

PERFECT CRIME, THE
Cross Publications: Oct, 1949 - No. 33, May, 1953 (#2-12, 52 pgs.)

	GD 2.0	VG 4.0	FN 6.0	VF 8.0	VF/NM 9.0	NM- 9.2
1-Powell-a(2)	36	72	108	211	343	475
2 (4/50)	20	40	60	114	182	250
3-10: 7-Steve Duncan begins, ends #30. 10-Flag-c	17	34	51	98	154	210
11-Used in **SOTI**, pg. 159	19	38	57	111	176	240
12-14	16	32	48	92	144	195
15- "The Most Terrible Menace" 2 pg. drug editorial	17	34	51	100	158	215
16,17,19-25,27-29,31-33	14	28	42	76	108	140
18-Drug cover, heroin drug propaganda story, plus 2 pg. anti-drug editorial	26	52	78	154	252	350
26-Drug-c with hypodermic needle; drug propaganda story	27	54	81	160	263	365
30-Strangulation cover	26	52	78	156	256	355

NOTE: ***Powell** a-No. 1, 2, 4. **Wildey** a-1, 5. Bondage c-11.*

PERFECT LOVE
Ziff-Davis(Approved Comics)/St. John No. 9 on: #10, 8-9/51 (cover date; 5-6/51 indicia date); #2, 10-11/51 - #10, 12/53

	GD 2.0	VG 4.0	FN 6.0	VF 8.0	VF/NM 9.0	NM- 9.2
10(#1)(8-9/51)-Painted-c	21	42	63	122	199	275
2(10-11/51)	15	30	45	85	130	175
3,5-7: 3-Painted-c. 5-Photo-c	14	28	42	76	108	140
4,8 (Fall, 1952)-Kinstler-a; last Z-D issue	14	28	42	78	112	145
9,10 (10/53, 12/53, St. John): 9-Painted-c. 10-Photo-c	13	26	39	74	105	135

PERHAPANAUTS, THE
Dark Horse Comics: Nov, 2005 - No. 4, Feb, 2006 ($2.99, limited series)

	NM- 9.2
1-4-Todd Dezago-s/Craig Rousseau-a/c	3.00
... Annual #1 (2/08, $3.50) Two covers by Rousseau and Allred	3.50
... Halloween Spooktacular1 (10/09, $3.50) Hembeck, Rousseau and others-a	3.50
,,, - Molly's Story (2/10, $3.50) Copland-a	3.50
(2nd series) (4/08 - Present, $3.50) 1-6: 1-Two covers by Art Adams and Rousseau	3.50

PERHAPANAUTS: SECOND CHANCES, THE
Dark Horse Comics: Oct, 2006 - No. 4, Jan, 2007 ($2.99, limited series)

	NM- 9.2
1-4-Todd Dezago-s/Craig Rousseau-a/c	3.00

PERRI (Disney)
Dell Publishing Co.: No. 847, Jan, 1958

	GD 2.0	VG 4.0	FN 6.0	VF 8.0	VF/NM 9.0	NM- 9.2
Four Color 847-Movie, w/2 diff-c publ.	5	10	15	35	55	75

PERRY MASON
David McKay Publications: No. 49, 1946 - No. 50, 1946

	GD 2.0	VG 4.0	FN 6.0	VF 8.0	VF/NM 9.0	NM- 9.2
Feature Books 49, 50-Based on Gardner novels	31	62	93	182	296	410

PERRY MASON MYSTERY MAGAZINE (TV)
Dell Publishing Co.: June-Aug, 1964 - No. 2, Oct-Dec, 1964

	GD 2.0	VG 4.0	FN 6.0	VF 8.0	VF/NM 9.0	NM- 9.2
1	6	12	18	39	62	85
2-Raymond Burr photo-c	5	10	15	32	51	70

PERSONAL LOVE (Also see Movie Love)
Famous Funnies: Jan, 1950 - No. 33, June, 1955

	GD 2.0	VG 4.0	FN 6.0	VF 8.0	VF/NM 9.0	NM- 9.2
1-Photo-c	20	40	60	120	195	270
2-Kathryn Grayson & Mario Lanza photo-c	13	26	39	74	105	135
3-7,10: 7-Robert Walker & Joanne Dru photo-c. 10-Loretta Young & Joseph Cotton photo-c	12	24	36	67	94	120
8,9: 8-Esther Williams & Howard Keel photo-c. 9-Debra Paget & Louis Jourdan photo-c	12	24	36	69	97	125
11-Toth-a; Glenn Ford & Gene Tierney photo-c	14	28	42	80	115	150
12,16,17-One pg. Frazetta each. 17-Rock Hudson & Yvonne DeCarlo photo-c	12	24	36	67	94	120
13-15,18-23: 12-Jane Greer & William Lundigan photo-c. 14-Kirk Douglas photo-c. 15-Dale Robertson & Joanne Dru photo-c. 18-Gregory Peck & Susan Hayworth photo-c. 19-Anthony Quinn & Suzan Ball photo-c. 20-Robert Wagner & Kathleen Crowley photo-c. 21-Roberta Peters & Byron Palmer photo-c. 22-Dale Robertson photo-c. 23-Rhonda Fleming-c	11	22	33	62	86	110
24,27,28-Frazetta-a in each (8,8&6 pgs.). 27-Rhonda Fleming & Fernando Lamas photo-c. 28-Mitzi Gaynor photo-c	43	86	129	271	461	650
25-Frazetta-a (tribute to Bettie Page, 7 pg. story); Tyrone Power/Terry Moore photo-c from "King of the Khyber Rifles"	55	110	165	352	601	850
26,29,30,33: 26-Constance Smith & Byron Palmer photo-c. 29-Charlton Heston & Nicol Morey photo-c. 30-Johnny Ray & Mitzi Gaynor photo-c. 33-Dana Andrews & Piper Laurie photo-c	11	22	33	62	86	110
31-Marlon Brando & Jean Simmons photo-c; last pre-code (2/55)	14	28	42	76	108	140
32-Classic Frazetta-a (8 pgs.); Kirk Douglas & Bella Darvi photo-c	61	122	183	390	670	950

NOTE: *All have photo-c. Many feature movie stars. **Everett** a-5, 9, 10, 24.*

PERSONAL LOVE (Going Steady V3#3 on)
Prize Publ. (Headline): V1#1, Sept, 1957 - V3#2, Nov-Dec, 1959

	GD 2.0	VG 4.0	FN 6.0	VF 8.0	VF/NM 9.0	NM- 9.2
V1#1	10	20	30	56	76	95
2	7	14	21	37	46	55
3-6(7-8/58)	6	12	18	31	38	45
V2#1(9-10/58)-V2#6(7-8/59)	6	12	18	28	34	40
V3#1-Wood?/Orlando-a	6	12	18	31	38	45
2	6	12	18	27	33	38

PETER CANNON - THUNDERBOLT (See Crisis on Infinite Earths)(Also see Thunderbolt)
DC Comics: Sept, 1992 - No. 12, Aug, 1993 ($1.25)

	NM- 9.2
1-12	2.50

PETER COTTONTAIL
Key Publications: Jan, 1954; Feb, 1954 - No. 2, Mar, 1954 (Says 3/53 in error)

	GD 2.0	VG 4.0	FN 6.0	VF 8.0	VF/NM 9.0	NM- 9.2
1(1/54)-Not 3-D	9	18	27	50	65	80
1(2/54)-(3-D, 25¢)-Came w/glasses; written by Bruce Hamilton	21	42	63	122	199	275
2-Reprints 3-D #1 but not in 3-D	6	12	18	31	38	45

PETER GUNN (TV)
Dell Publishing Co.: No. 1087, Apr-June, 1960

	GD 2.0	VG 4.0	FN 6.0	VF 8.0	VF/NM 9.0	NM- 9.2
Four Color 1087-Photo-c	8	16	24	58	97	135

PETE ROSE: HIS INCREDIBLE BASEBALL CAREER
Masstar Creations Inc.: 1995

	NM- 9.2
1-John Tartaglione-a	2.50

PETER PAN (Disney) (See Hook, Movie Classics & Comics, New Adventures of... & Walt Disney Showcase #36)
Dell Publishing Co.: No. 442, Dec, 1952 - No. 926, Aug, 1958

	GD 2.0	VG 4.0	FN 6.0	VF 8.0	VF/NM 9.0	NM- 9.2
Four Color 442 (#1)-Movie	10	20	30	70	123	175
Four Color 926-Reprint of 442	4	8	12	28	44	60

PETER PAN
Disney Comics: 1991 ($5.95, graphic novel, 68 pgs.)(Celebrates video release)

	NM- 9.2
nn-r/Peter Pan Treasure Chest from 1953	7.00

PETER PANDA
National Periodical Publications: Aug-Sept, 1953 - No. 31, Aug-Sept, 1958

	GD 2.0	VG 4.0	FN 6.0	VF 8.0	VF/NM 9.0	NM- 9.2
1-Grossman-c/a in all	47	94	141	296	498	700
2	24	48	72	142	234	325
3,4,6-8,10	21	42	63	122	199	275
5-Classic-c (scarce)	65	130	195	416	708	1000
9-Robot-c	28	56	84	165	270	375
11-31	15	30	45	84	127	170

PETER PAN RECORDS (See Power Records)

PETER PAN TREASURE CHEST (See Dell Giants)

PETER PARKER (See The Spectacular Spider-Man)

PETER PARKER
Marvel Comics: May, 2010 - Present ($3.99)

	NM- 9.2
1-Prints material from Marvel Digital Comics; Olliffe-a; back-up w/Hembeck-s/a	4.00

PETER PARKER: SPIDER-MAN
Marvel Comics: Jan, 1999 - No. 57, Aug, 2003 ($2.99/$1.99/$2.25)

	NM- 9.2
1-Mackie-s/Romita Jr.-a; wraparound-c	3.00
1-($6.95) DF Edition w/variant cover by the Romitas	7.00
2-11,13-17-($1.99): 2-Two covers; Thor app. 3-Iceman-c/app. 4-Marrow-c/app. 5-Spider-Woman app. 7,8-Blade app. 9,10-Venom app. 11-Iron Man & Thor-c/app.	2.50
12-($2.99) Sinister Six and Venom app.	3.00
18-24,26-43: 18-Begin $2.25-c. 20-Jenkins-s/Buckingham-a start. 23-Intro Typeface. 24-Maximum Security x-over. 29-Rescue of MJ. 30-Ramos-c. 42,43-Mahfood-a	2.50
25-($2.99) Two covers; Spider-Man & Green Goblin	3.00

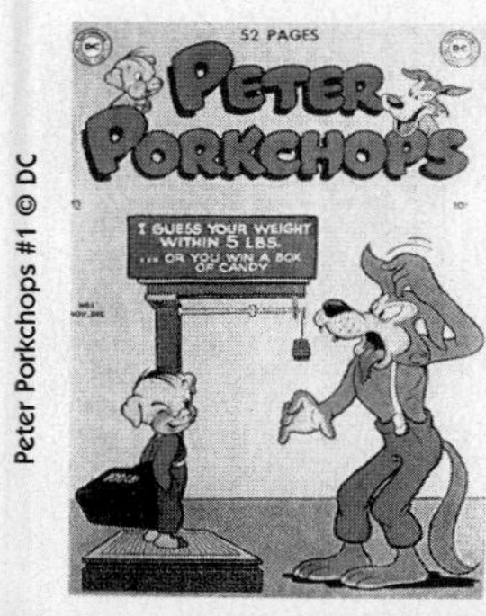

Peter Porkchops #1 © DC

Peter Rabbit #4 © AVON

Phantom #73 © KING

	GD 2.0	VG 4.0	FN 6.0	VF 8.0	VF/NM 9.0	NM- 9.2
44-47-Humberto Ramos-c/a; Green Goblin-c/app.						3.00
48,49,51-57: 48,49-Buckingham-c/a. 51,52-Herrera-a. 56,57-Kieth-a; Sandman returns						2.50
50-($3.50) Buckingham-c/a						3.50
...'99 Annual (8/99, $3.50) Man-Thing app.						3.50
...'00 Annual ($3.50) Bounty app.; Joe Bennett-a; Black Cat back-up story						3.50
...'01 Annual ($2.99) Avery-s						3.00
...: A Day in the Life TPB (5/01, $14.95) r/#20-22,26; Webspinners #10-12						15.00
...: One Small Break TPB (2002, $16.95) r/#27,28,30-34; Andrews-c						17.00
Spider-Man: Return of the Goblin TPB (2002, $8.99) r/#44-47; Ramos-c						9.00
...Vol. 4: Trials & Tribulations TPB (2003, $11.99) r/#35,37,48-50; Cho-c						12.00

PETER PAT
United Features Syndicate: No. 8, 1939

	GD 2.0	VG 4.0	FN 6.0	VF 8.0	VF/NM 9.0	NM- 9.2
Single Series 8	36	72	108	211	343	475

PETER PAUL'S 4 IN 1 JUMBO COMIC BOOK
Capitol Stories (Charlton): No date (1953)

	GD 2.0	VG 4.0	FN 6.0	VF 8.0	VF/NM 9.0	NM- 9.2
1-Contains 4 comics bound; Space Adventures, Space Western, Crime & Justice, Racket Squad in Action	39	78	117	240	395	550

PETER PIG
Standard Comics: No. 5, May, 1953 - No. 6, Aug, 1953

	GD 2.0	VG 4.0	FN 6.0	VF 8.0	VF/NM 9.0	NM- 9.2
5,6	7	14	21	35	43	50

PETER PORKCHOPS (See Leading Comics #23) (Also see Capt. Carrot)
National Periodical Publications: 11-12/49 - No. 61, 9-11/59; No. 62, 10-12/60 (1-11: 52 pgs.)

	GD 2.0	VG 4.0	FN 6.0	VF 8.0	VF/NM 9.0	NM- 9.2
1	34	68	102	199	325	450
2	15	30	45	90	140	190
3-10: 6- "Peter Rockets to Mars!" c/story	13	26	39	74	105	135
11-30	10	20	30	56	76	95
31-62	9	18	27	47	61	75

NOTE: ***Otto Feuer** a-all. **Rube Grossman**-a most issues. **Sheldon Mayer** a-30-38, 40-44, 46-52, 61.*

PETER PORKER, THE SPECTACULAR SPIDER-HAM
Star Comics (Marvel): May, 1985 - No. 17, Sept, 1987 (Also see Marvel Tails)

	GD 2.0	VG 4.0	FN 6.0	VF 8.0	VF/NM 9.0	NM- 9.2
1-Michael Golden-c						5.00
2-17: 12-Origin/1st app. Bizarro Phil. 13-Halloween issue						4.00

NOTE: *Back-up features: 2-X-Bugs. 3-Iron Mouse. 4-Croctor Strange. 5-Thrr, Dog of Thunder.*

PETER POTAMUS (TV)
Gold Key: Jan, 1965 (Hanna-Barbera)

	GD 2.0	VG 4.0	FN 6.0	VF 8.0	VF/NM 9.0	NM- 9.2
1-1st app. Peter Potamus & So-So, Breezly & Sneezly	9	18	27	63	107	150

PETER RABBIT (See New Funnies #65 & Space Comics)
Dell Publishing Co.: No. 1, 1942

	GD 2.0	VG 4.0	FN 6.0	VF 8.0	VF/NM 9.0	NM- 9.2
Large Feature Comic 1	60	120	180	381	653	925

PETER RABBIT (Adventures of...; New Advs. of... #9 on)(Also see Funny Tunes & Space Comics)
Avon Periodicals: 1947 - No. 34, Aug-Sept, 1956

	GD 2.0	VG 4.0	FN 6.0	VF 8.0	VF/NM 9.0	NM- 9.2
1(1947)-Reprints 1943-44 Sunday strips; contains a biography & drawing of Cady	35	70	105	208	339	470
2 (4/48)	24	48	72	140	230	320
3 ('48) - 6(7/49)-Last Cady issue	21	42	63	122	199	275
7-10(1950-8/51): 9-New logo	11	22	33	60	83	105
11(11/51)-34('56)-Avon's character	9	18	27	50	65	80
...Easter Parade (1952, 25¢, 132 pgs.)	20	40	60	114	182	250
...Jumbo Book (1954-Giant Size, 25¢)-Jesse James by Kinstler (6 pgs.); space ship-c	23	46	69	136	223	310

PETER RABBIT 3-D
Eternity Comics: April, 1990 ($2.95, with glasses; sealed in plastic bag)

	GD 2.0	VG 4.0	FN 6.0	VF 8.0	VF/NM 9.0	NM- 9.2
1-By Harrison Cady (reprints)						3.00

PETER, THE LITTLE PEST (#4 titled Petey)
Marvel Comics Group: Nov, 1969 - No. 4, May, 1970

	GD 2.0	VG 4.0	FN 6.0	VF 8.0	VF/NM 9.0	NM- 9.2
1	6	12	18	43	69	95
2-4-r-Dexter the Demon & Melvin the Monster	5	10	15	30	48	65

PETE'S DRAGON (See Walt Disney Showcase #43)

PETE THE PANIC
Stanmor Publications: November, 1955

	GD 2.0	VG 4.0	FN 6.0	VF 8.0	VF/NM 9.0	NM- 9.2
nn-Code approved	5	10	15	24	30	35

PETEY (See Peter, the Little Pest)

PETTICOAT JUNCTION (TV, inspired Green Acres)
Dell Publ. Co.: Oct-Dec, 1964 - No. 5, Oct-Dec, 1965 (#1-3, 5 have photo-c)

	GD 2.0	VG 4.0	FN 6.0	VF 8.0	VF/NM 9.0	NM- 9.2
1	7	14	21	47	76	105
2-5	5	10	15	32	51	70

PETUNIA (Also see Looney Tunes and Porky Pig)
Dell Publishing Co.: No. 463, Apr, 1953

	GD 2.0	VG 4.0	FN 6.0	VF 8.0	VF/NM 9.0	NM- 9.2
Four Color 463	4	8	12	28	44	60

PHAGE (See Neil Gaiman's Teknophage & Neil Gaiman's Phage-Shadowdeath)

PHANTACEA
McPherson Publishing Co.: Sept, 1977 - No. 6, Summer, 1980 (B&W)

	GD 2.0	VG 4.0	FN 6.0	VF 8.0	VF/NM 9.0	NM- 9.2
1-Early Dave Sim-a (32 pgs.)	5	10	15	30	48	65
2-Dave Sim-a(10 pgs.)	3	6	9	14	19	24
3-6: 3-Flip-c w/Damnation Bridge. 4-Gene Day-a	2	4	6	10	14	18

PHANTASMO (See The Funnies #45)
Dell Publishing Co.: No. 18, 1941

	GD 2.0	VG 4.0	FN 6.0	VF 8.0	VF/NM 9.0	NM- 9.2
Large Feature Comic 18	38	76	114	226	368	510

PHANTOM, THE
David McKay Publishing Co.: 1939 - 1949

	GD 2.0	VG 4.0	FN 6.0	VF 8.0	VF/NM 9.0	NM- 9.2
Feature Books 20	90	180	270	576	988	1400
Feature Books 22	65	130	195	416	708	1000
Feature Books 39	50	100	150	315	533	750
Feature Books 53,56,57	40	80	120	246	411	575

PHANTOM, THE (See Ace Comics, Defenders Of The Earth, Eat Right to Work and Win, Future Comics, Harvey Comics Hits #51,56, Harvey Hits #1, 6, 12, 15, 26, 36, 44, 48, & King Comics)

PHANTOM, THE (nn (#29)-Published overseas only) (Also see Comics Reading Libraries in the Promotional Comics section)
Gold Key(#1-17)/King(#18-28)/Charlton(#30 on): Nov, 1962 - No. 17, Jul, 1966; No. 18, Sept, 1966 - No. 28, Dec, 1967; No. 30, Feb, 1969 - No. 74, Jan, 1977

	GD 2.0	VG 4.0	FN 6.0	VF 8.0	VF/NM 9.0	NM- 9.2
1-Origin revealed on inside-c & back-c	16	32	48	115	220	325
2-King, Queen & Jack begins, ends #11	9	18	27	63	107	150
3-5	8	16	24	54	90	125
6-10	7	14	21	45	73	100
11-17: 12-Track Hunter begins	6	12	18	37	59	80
18-Flash Gordon begins; Wood-a	5	10	15	30	48	65
19-24: 20-Flash Gordon ends (both by Gil Kane). 21-Mandrake begins. 20,24-Girl Phantom app.	4	8	12	28	44	60
25-28: 25-Jeff Jones-a(4 pgs.); 1 pg. Williamson ad. 26-Brick Bradford app. 28(nn)-Brick Bradford app.	4	8	12	22	34	45
30-33: 33-Last 12¢ issue	3	6	9	17	25	32
34-40: 36,39-Ditko-a	3	6	9	16	23	30
41-66: 46-Intro. The Piranha. 62-Bolle-c	3	6	9	14	19	24
67-Origin retold; Newton-c/a	3	6	9	17	25	32
68-73-Newton-c/a	2	4	6	13	18	22
74-Classic flag-c by Newton; Newton-a;	3	6	9	16	23	30

NOTE: ***Aparo** a-31-34, 36-38; c-31-38, 60, 61. Painted c-1-17.*

PHANTOM, THE
DC Comics: May, 1988 - No. 4, Aug, 1988 ($1.25, mini-series)

	GD 2.0	VG 4.0	FN 6.0	VF 8.0	VF/NM 9.0	NM- 9.2
1-4: Orlando-c/a in all						3.00

PHANTOM, THE
DC Comics: Mar, 1989 - No. 13, Mar, 1990 ($1.50)

	GD 2.0	VG 4.0	FN 6.0	VF 8.0	VF/NM 9.0	NM- 9.2
1-13: 1-Brief origin						3.00

PHANTOM, THE
Wolf Publishing: 1992 - No. 8, 1993 ($2.25)

	GD 2.0	VG 4.0	FN 6.0	VF 8.0	VF/NM 9.0	NM- 9.2
1-8						2.50

PHANTOM, THE
Moonstone: 2003 - No. 26, Dec, 2008 ($3.50/$3.99)

	GD 2.0	VG 4.0	FN 6.0	VF 8.0	VF/NM 9.0	NM- 9.2
1-26: 1-Cassaday-c/Raab-s/Quinn-a						4.00
... Annual #1 (2007, $6.50) Blevins-c; story and art by various incl. Nolan						6.50

PHANTOM BLOT, THE (#1 titled New Adventures of...)
Gold Key: Oct, 1964 - No. 7, Nov, 1966 (Disney)

	GD 2.0	VG 4.0	FN 6.0	VF 8.0	VF/NM 9.0	NM- 9.2
1 (Meets The Mysterious Mr. X)	6	12	18	41	66	90
2-1st Super Goof	5	10	15	34	55	75
3-7	4	8	12	22	34	45

PHANTOM EAGLE (See Mighty Midget, Marvel Super Heroes #16 & Wow #6)

PHANTOM FORCE
Image Comics/Genesis West #0, 3-7: 12/93 - #2, 1994; #0, 3/94; #3, 5/94 - #8, 10/94 ($2.50/$3.50, limited series)

	GD 2.0	VG 4.0	FN 6.0	VF 8.0	VF/NM 9.0	NM- 9.2
0 (3/94, $2.50)-Kirby/Jim Lee-c; Kirby-p pgs. 1,5,24-29.						3.00

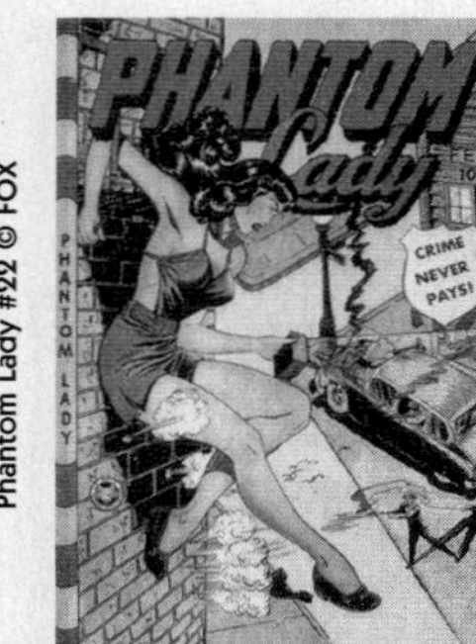

Phantom Lady #22 © FOX

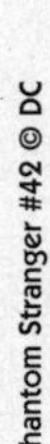

Phantom Stranger #42 © DC

Pictorial Confessions #1 © STJ

	GD 2.0	VG 4.0	FN 6.0	VF 8.0	VF/NM 9.0	NM- 9.2

1 (12/93, $2.50)-Polybagged w/trading card; Kirby Liefeld-c; Kirby plots/pencils w/inks by Liefeld, McFarlane, Jim Lee, Silvestri, Larsen, Williams, Ordway & Miki 3.00
2 ($3.50)-Kirby-a(p); Kirby/Larson-c 3.50
3-8: 3-(5/94, $2.50)-Kirby/McFarlane-c 4-(5/94)-Kirby-c(p). 5-(6/94) 3.00

PHANTOM GUARD
Image Comics (WildStorm Productions): Oct, 1997 - No. 6, Mar, 1998 ($2.50)

1-6: 1-Two covers 3.00
1-($3.50)-Voyager Pack w/Wildcore preview 3.50

PHANTOM JACK
Image Comics: Mar, 2004 - No. 5, July, 2004 ($2.95)

1-5-Mike San Giacomo-s/Mitchell Breitweiser-a. 4-Initial printings with errors exist 3.00
The Collected Edition (Speakeasy Comics, 2005, $17.99) r/series; Bendis intro 18.00

PHANTOM LADY (1st Series) (My Love Secret #24 on) (Also see All Top, Daring Adventures, Freedom Fighters, Jungle Thrills, & Wonder Boy)
Fox Features Syndicate: No. 13, Aug, 1947 - No. 23, Apr, 1949

13(#1)-Phantom Lady by Matt Baker begins (see Police Comics #1 for 1st app.); Blue Beetle story 423 846 1269 3088 5444 7800
14-16: 14(#2)-Not Baker-c. 15-P.L. injected with experimental drug. 16-Negligee-c, panels; true crime stories begin 265 530 795 1694 2897 4100
17-Classic bondage cover; used in **SOTI**, illo "Sexual stimulation by combining 'headlights' with the sadist's dream of tying up a woman" 676 1352 2028 4935 8718 12,500
18,19 184 368 552 1168 2009 2850
20-22 155 310 465 992 1696 2400
23-Bondage-c 184 368 552 1168 2009 2850
NOTE: ***Matt Baker** a-in all; c-13, 15-21. **Kamen** a-22, 23.*

PHANTOM LADY (2nd Series) (See Terrific Comics) (Formerly Linda)
Ajax/Farrell Publ.: V1#5, Dec-Jan, 1954/1955 - No. 4, June, 1955

V1#5(#1)-By Matt Baker 118 236 354 749 1287 1825
V1#2-Last pre-code 87 174 261 553 952 1350
3,4-Red Rocket. 3-Heroin story 69 138 207 442 759 1075

PHANTOM LADY
Verotik Publications: 1994 ($9.95)

1-Reprints G. A. stories from Phantom Lady and All Top Comics; Adam Hughes-c 10.00

PHANTOM PLANET, THE
Dell Publishing Co.: No. 1234, 1961

Four Color 1234-Movie 7 14 21 47 76 105

PHANTOM STRANGER, THE (1st Series)(See Saga of Swamp Thing)
National Periodical Publications: Aug-Sept, 1952 - No. 6, June-July, 1953

1(Scarce)-1st app. 200 400 600 1280 2190 3100
2 (Scarce) 110 220 330 704 1202 1700
3-6 (Scarce) 95 190 285 603 1039 1475
Ashcan (8,9/52) Not distributed to newsstands, only for in house use (no known sales)

PHANTOM STRANGER, THE (2nd Series) (See Showcase #80) (See Showcase Presents for B&W reprints)
National Periodical Publs.: May-June, 1969 - No. 41, Feb-Mar, 1976; No. 42, Mar, 2010

1-2nd S.A. app. P. Stranger; only 12¢ issue 11 22 33 80 145 210
2,3 6 12 18 43 69 95
4-1st new look Phantom Stranger; N. Adams-a 7 14 21 45 73 100
5-7 5 10 15 32 51 70
8-14: 14-Last 15¢ issue 4 8 12 22 34 45
15-19: All 25¢ giants (52 pgs.) 4 8 12 24 37 50
20-Dark Circle begins, ends #24. 3 6 9 16 23 30
21,22 3 6 9 14 19 24
23-Spawn of Frankenstein begins by Kaluta 4 8 12 24 37 50
24,25,27-30-Last Spawn of Frankenstein 3 6 9 19 29 38
26- Book-length story featuring Phantom Stranger, Dr. 13 & Spawn of Frankenstein 3 6 9 21 32 42
31-The Black Orchid begins (6-7/74). 3 6 9 19 29 38
32,34-38: 34-Last 20¢ issue (#35 on are 25¢) 2 4 6 11 16 20
33,39-41: 33-Deadman-c/story. 39-41-Deadman app. 3 6 9 14 19 24
42-(3/10, $2.99) Blackest Night one-shot; Syaf-a; Spectre, Deadman and Blue Devil app. 3.00
NOTE: ***N. Adams** a-4; c-3-19. **Anderson** a-4, 5i. **Aparo** a-7-17, 19-26; c-20-24, 33-41. **B. Bailey** a-27-30. **DeZuniga** a-12-16, 18, 19, 21, 22, 31, 34. **Grell** a-33. **Kaluta** a-23-25; c-26. **Meskin** r-15, 16, 18, 19. **Redondo** a-32, 35, 36. **Sparling** a-20. **Starr** a-17r. **Toth** a-15r. Black Orchid by **Carrilo**-38-41. Dr. 13 solo in-13, 18, 19, 20, 21, 34. Frankenstein by **Kaluta**-23-25; by **Baily**-27-30. No Black Orchid-33, 34, 37.*

PHANTOM STRANGER (See Justice League of America #103)
DC Comics: Oct, 1987 - No. 4, Jan, 1988 (75¢, limited series)

1-4-Mignola/Russell-c/a & Eclipso app. in all. 3,4-Eclipso-c 3.00

PHANTOM STRANGER (See Vertigo Visions-The Phantom Stranger)

PHANTOM: THE GHOST WHO WALKS
Marvel Comics: Feb, 1995 - No. 3, Apr, 1995 ($2.95, limited series)

1-3 4.00

PHANTOM: THE GHOST WHO WALKS
Moonstone: 2003 ($16.95, TPB)

nn-Three new stories by Raab, Goulart, Collins, Blanco and others; Klauba painted-c 17.00

PHANTOM 2040 (TV cartoon)
Marvel Comics: May, 1995 - No. 4, Aug, 1995 ($1.50)

1-4-Based on animated series; Ditko-a(p) in all 3.00

PHANTOM WITCH DOCTOR (Also see Durango Kid #8 & Eerie #8)
Avon Periodicals: 1952

1-Kinstler-c/a (7 pgs.) 47 94 141 298 504 710

PHANTOM ZONE, THE (See Adventure #283 & Superboy #100, 104)
DC Comics: January, 1982 - No. 4, April, 1982

1-4-Superman app. in all. 2-4: Batman, Green Lantern app. 3.00
NOTE: ***Colan** a-1-4p; c-1-4p. **Giordano** c-1-4i.*

PHAZE
Eclipse Comics: Apr, 1988 - No. 2, Oct, 1988 ($2.25)

1,2: 1-Sienkiewicz-c. 2-Gulacy painted-c 2.50

PHIL RIZZUTO (Baseball Hero)(See Sport Thrills, Accepted reprint)
Fawcett Publications: 1951 (New York Yankees)

nn-Photo-c 69 138 207 442 759 1075

PHOENIX
Atlas/Seaboard Publ.: Jan, 1975 - No. 4, Oct, 1975

1-Origin; Rovin-s/Amendola-a 2 4 6 8 10 12
2-4: 3-Origin & only app. The Dark Avenger. 4-New origin/costume The Protector (formerly Phoenix) 2 3 4 6 8 10
NOTE: ***Infantino** appears in #1, 2. **Austin** a-3i. **Thorne** c-3.*

PHOENIX (...The Untold Story)
Marvel Comics Group: April, 1984 ($2.00, one-shot)

1-Byrne/Austin-r/X-Men #137 with original unpublished ending 2 4 6 8 10 12

PHOENIX RESURRECTION, THE
Malibu Comics (Ultraverse): 1995 - 1996 ($3.95)

Genesis #1 (12/95)-X-Men app; wraparound-c, Revelations #1 (12/95)-X-Men app; wraparound-c, Aftermath #1 (1/96)-X-Men app. 4.00
0-($1.95)-r/series 2.50
0-American Entertainment Ed. 4.00

PICNIC PARTY (See Dell Giants)

PICTORIAL CONFESSIONS (Pictorial Romances #4 on)
St. John Publishing Co.: Sept, 1949 - No. 3, Dec, 1949

1-Baker-c/a(3) 47 94 141 296 498 700
2-Baker-a; photo-c 25 50 75 150 245 340
3-Kubert, Baker-a; part Kubert-c 27 54 81 160 263 365

PICTORIAL LOVE STORIES (Formerly Tim McCoy)
Charlton Comics: No. 22, Oct, 1949 - No. 26, July, 1950 (all photo-c)

22-26: All have "Me-Dan Cupid". 25-Fred Astaire-c 19 38 57 111 176 240

PICTORIAL LOVE STORIES
St. John Publishing Co.: October, 1952

1-Baker-c 32 64 96 188 307 425

PICTORIAL ROMANCES (Formerly Pictorial Confessions)
St. John Publ. Co.: No. 4, Jan, 1950; No. 5, Jan, 1951 - No. 24, Mar, 1954

4-Baker-a; photo-c 32 64 96 188 307 425
5,10-All Matt Baker issues. 5-Reprints all stories from #4 w/new Baker-c 28 56 84 165 270 375
6-9,12,13,15,16-Baker-c, 2-3 stories 24 48 72 142 234 325
11-Baker-c/a(3); Kubert-r/Hollywood Confessions #1 30 60 90 177 289 400
14,21-24: Baker-c/a each. 21,24-Each has signed story by Estrada 24 48 72 142 234 325
17-20(7/53, 25¢, 100 pgs.): Baker-c/a; each has two signed stories by Estrada 43 86 129 271 461 650
NOTE: ***Matt Baker** art in most issues. **Estrada** a-17-20(2), 21, 24.*

PICTURE NEWS
Lafayette Street Corp.: Jan, 1946 - No. 10, Jan-Feb, 1947

Picture Parade #2 © GIL

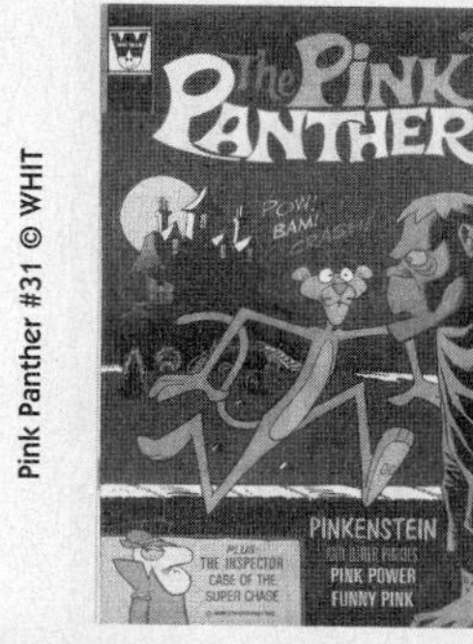

Pink Panther #31 © WHIT

Pinky and the Brain #5 © WB

	GD 2.0	VG 4.0	FN 6.0	VF 8.0	VF/NM 9.0	NM- 9.2

1-Milt Gross begins, ends No. 6; 4 pg. Kirby-a; A-Bomb-c/story 41 82 123 256 428 600
2-Atomic explosion panels; Frank Sinatra/Perry Como story 22 44 66 128 209 290
3-Atomic explosion panels; Frank Sinatra, June Allyson, Benny Goodman stories 20 40 60 114 182 250
4-Atomic explosion panels; "Caesar and Cleopatra" movie adapt. w/Claude Raines & Vivian Leigh; Jackie Robinson story 21 42 63 124 202 280
5-7: 5-Hank Greenberg story; Atomic explosion panel. 6-Joe Louis-c/story 15 30 45 94 147 200
8,10: 8-Monte Hale story (9-10/46; 1st?). 10-Dick Quick; A-Bomb story; Krigstein, Gross-a 17 34 51 98 154 210
9-A-Bomb story; "Crooked Mile" movie adaptation; Joe DiMaggio story. 19 38 57 111 176 240

PICTURE PARADE (Picture Progress #5 on)
Gilberton Company (Also see A Christmas Adventure): Sept, 1953 - V1#4, Dec, 1953 (28 pgs.)

V1#1-Andy's Atomic Adventures; A-bomb blast-c; (Teachers version distributed to schools exists) 20 40 60 114 182 250
2-Around the World with the United Nations 12 24 36 69 97 125
3-Adventures of the Lost One(The American Indian), 4-A Christmas Adventure (r-under same title in 1969) 12 24 36 69 97 125

PICTURE PROGRESS (Formerly Picture Parade)
Gilberton Corp.: V1#5, Jan, 1954 - V3#2, Oct, 1955 (28-36 pgs.)

V1#5-9,V2#1-9: 5-News in Review 1953. 6-The Birth of America. 7-The Four Seasons. 8-Paul Revere's Ride. 9-The Hawaiian Islands(5/54). V2#1-The Story of Flight(9/54). 2-Vote for Crazy River (The Meaning of Elections). 3-Louis Pasteur. 4-The Star Spangled Banner. 5-News in Review 1954. 6-Alaska: The Great Land. 7-Life in the Circus. 8-The Time of the Cave Man. 9-Summer Fun(5/55) 9 18 27 50 65 80
V3#1,2: 1-The Man Who Discovered America. 2-The Lewis & Clark Expedition 9 18 27 47 61 75

PICTURE SCOPE JUNGLE ADVENTURES (See Jungle Thrills)

PICTURE STORIES FROM AMERICAN HISTORY
National/All-American/E. C. Comics: 1945 - No. 4, Sum, 1947 (#1,2: 10¢, 56 pgs.; #3,4: 15¢, 52 pgs.)

1 30 60 90 177 289 400
2-4 24 48 72 140 230 320

PICTURE STORIES FROM SCIENCE
E.C. Comics: Spring, 1947 - No. 2, Fall, 1947

1-(15¢) 30 60 90 177 289 400
2-(10¢) 24 48 72 140 230 320

PICTURE STORIES FROM THE BIBLE (See Narrative Illustration, the Story of the Comics by M.C. Gaines)
National/All-American/E.C. Comics: 1942 - No. 4, Fall, 1943; 1944-46

1-4('42-Fall, '43)-Old Testament (DC) 24 48 72 140 230 320
Complete Old Testament Edition, (12/43-DC, 50¢, 232 pgs.);-1st printing; contains #1-4; 2nd - 8th (1/47) printings exist; later printings by E.C. some with 65¢-c 27 54 81 158 259 360
Complete Old Testament Edition (1945-publ. by Bible Pictures Ltd.)-232 pgs., hardbound, in color with dust jacket 27 54 81 158 259 360
NOTE: *Both Old and New Testaments published in England by Bible Pictures Ltd. in hardback, 1943, in color, 376 pgs. (2 vols.: O.T. 232 pgs. & N.T. 144 pgs.), and were also published by Scarf Press in 1979 (Old Test., $9.95) and in 1980 (New Test., $7.95)*
1-3(New Test.; 1944-46, DC)-52 pgs. ea. 19 38 57 112 179 245
The Complete Life of Christ Edition (1945, 25¢, 96 pgs.)-Contains #1&2 of the New Testament Edition 27 54 81 158 259 360
1,2(Old Testament-r in comic book form)(E.C., 1946; 52 pgs.) 19 38 57 112 179 245
1(DC),2(AA),3(EC)(New Testament-r in comic book form)(E.C., 1946; 52 pgs.) 19 38 57 112 179 245
Complete New Testament Edition (1945-E.C., 40¢, 144 pgs.)-Contains #1-3 1946 printing has 50¢-c 27 54 81 158 259 360
NOTE: *Another British series entitled* ***The Bible Illustrated*** *from 1947 has recently been discovered, with the same internal artwork. This eight edition series (5-OT, 3-NT) is of particular interest to Classics Ill. collectors because it exactly copied the C.I. logo format. The British publisher was Thorpe & Porter, who in 1951 began publishing the British Classics Ill. series. All editions of The Bible Ill. have new British painted covers. While this market is still new, and not all editions have as yet been found, current market value is about the same as the first U.S. editions of Picture Stories From The Bible.*

PICTURE STORIES FROM WORLD HISTORY
E.C. Comics: Spring, 1947 - No. 2, Summer, 1947 (52, 48 pgs.)

1-(15¢) 30 60 90 177 289 400
2-(10¢) 24 48 72 140 230 320

PILOT SEASON...
Image Comics (Top Cow): 2009 - 2010 ($1.00/$2.99, one-shots)

...: Declassified (10/09, $1.00) Preview of one-shots with covers, script and sketch pgs. 1.00
...: Demonic (1/10, $2.99) Kirkman-s/Benitez-a; two covers by Silvestri 3.00
...: Murdered (11/09, $2.99) Kirkman-s/Blake-a; two covers by Silvestri 3.00

PINHEAD
Marvel Comics (Epic Comics): Dec, 1993 - No. 6, May, 1994 ($2.50)

1-($2.95)-Embossed foil-c by Kelley Jones; Intro Pinhead & Disciples (Snakeoil, Hangman, Fan Dancer & Dixie) 3.00
2-6 2.50

PINHEAD & FOODINI (TV)(Also see Foodini & Jingle Dingle Christmas...)
Fawcett Publications: July, 1951 - No. 4, Jan, 1952 (Early TV comic)

1-(52 pgs.)-Photo-c; based on TV puppet show 31 62 93 186 303 425
2,3-Photo-c 16 32 48 96 151 200
4 14 28 42 80 115 150

PINHEAD VS. MARSHALL LAW (Law in Hell)
Marvel Comics (Epic): Nov, 1993 - No. 2, Dec, 1993 ($2.95, lim. series)

1,2: 1-Embossed red foil-c. 2-Embossed silver foil-c 3.00

PINK DUST
Kitchen Sink Press: 1998 ($3.50, B&W, mature)

1-J. O'Barr-s/a 3.50

PINK PANTHER, THE (TV)(See The Inspector & Kite Fun Book)
Gold Key #1-70/Whitman #71-87: April, 1971 - No. 87, Mar, 1984

1-The Inspector begins 5 10 15 34 55 75
2-5 3 6 9 18 27 35
6-10 3 6 9 14 19 24
11-30: Warren Tufts-a #16-on 2 4 6 9 13 16
31-60 2 4 6 8 11 14
61-70 1 2 3 5 7 9
71-74,81-83: 81(2/82), 82(3/82), 83(4/82) 2 4 6 8 10 12
75(8/80)-77 (Whitman pre-pack) (scarce) 3 6 9 19 29 38
78(1/81)-80 (Whitman pre-pack) (not as scarce) 2 4 6 10 14 18
78 (1/81, 40¢-c) Cover price error variant 3 6 9 14 20 26
84-87(All #90266 on-c, no date or date code): 84(6/83), 85(8/83), 87(3/84) 3 6 9 14 20 26
Mini-comic No. 1(1976)(3-1/4x6-1/2") 1 3 4 6 8 10
NOTE: *Pink Panther began as a movie cartoon. (See Golden Comics Digest #38, 45 and March of Comics #376, 384, 390, 409, 418, 429, 441, 449, 461, 473, 486); #37, 72, 80-85 contain reprints.*

PINK PANTHER SUPER SPECIAL (TV)
Harvey Comics: Oct, 1993 ($2.25, 68 pgs.)

V2#1-The Inspector & Wendy Witch stories also 4.00

PINK PANTHER, THE
Harvey Comics: Nov, 1993 - No. 9, July, 1994 ($1.50)

V2#1-9 3.00

PINKY & THE BRAIN (See Animaniacs)
DC Comics: July, 1996 - No. 27, Nov, 1998 ($1.75/$1.95/$1.99)

1-27, ...Christmas Special (1/96, $1.50) 3.00

PINKY LEE (See Adventures of...)

PINKY THE EGGHEAD
I.W./Super Comics: 1963 (Reprints from Noodnik)

I.W. Reprint #1,2(nd) 2 4 6 8 11 14
Super Reprint #14-r/Noodnik Comics #4 2 4 6 8 11 14

PINOCCHIO (See 4-Color #92, 252, 545, 1203, Mickey Mouse Mag. V5#3, Movie Comics under Wonderful Advs. of..., New Advs. of..., Thrilling Comics #2, Walt Disney Showcase, Walt Disney's..., Wonderful Advs. of..., & World's Greatest Stories #2)
Dell Publishing Co.: No. 92, 1945 - No. 1203, Mar, 1962 (Disney)

Four Color 92-The Wonderful Adventures of...; 16 pg. Donald Duck story ; entire book by Kelly 50 100 150 400 775 1150
Four Color 252 (10/49)-Origin, not by Kelly 10 20 30 73 129 185
Four Color 545 (3/54)-The Wonderful Advs. of...; part-r of 4-Color #92; Disney-movie 7 14 21 47 76 105
Four Color 1203 (3/62) 5 10 15 34 55 75

PINOCCHIO AND THE EMPEROR OF THE NIGHT
Marvel Comics: Mar, 1988 ($1.25, 52 pgs.)

1-Adapts film 3.00

Piracy #4 © WMG

Planetary #27 © WSP

Planet Comics #14 © FH

PINOCCHIO LEARNS ABOUT KITES (See Kite Fun Book)

PIN-UP PETE (Also see Great Lover Romances & Monty Hall...)
Toby Press: 1952

1-Jack Sparling pin-ups 18 36 54 105 165 225

PIONEER MARSHAL (See Fawcett Movie Comics)

PIONEER PICTURE STORIES
Street & Smith Publications: Dec, 1941 - No. 9, Dec, 1943

1-The Legless Air Ace begins 36 72 108 211 343 475
2 -True life story of Errol Flynn 18 36 54 105 165 225
3-9 15 30 45 86 133 180

PIONEER WEST ROMANCES (Firehair #1,2,7-11)
Fiction House Magazines: No. 3, Spring, 1950 - No. 6, Winter, 1950-51

3-(52 pgs.)-Firehair continues 19 38 57 109 172 235
4-6 19 38 57 109 172 235

PIPSQUEAK (See The Adventures of...)

PIRACY
E. C. Comics: Oct-Nov, 1954 - No. 7, Oct-Nov, 1955

1-Williamson/Torres-a 27 54 81 216 346 475
2-Williamson/Torres-a 17 34 51 136 218 300
3-7: 5-7-Comics Code symbol on cover 14 28 42 112 176 240

NOTE: *Crandall a-in all; c-2-4.* ***Davis*** *a-1, 2, 6.* ***Evans*** *a-3-7; c-7.* ***Ingels*** *a-3-7.* ***Krigstein*** *a-3-5, 7; c-5, 6.* ***Wood*** *a-1, 2; c-1.*

PIRACY
Gemstone Publishing: March, 1998 - No. 7, Sept, 1998 ($2.50)

1-7: E.C. reprints 2.50
Annual 1 ($10.95) Collects #1-4 11.00
Annual 2 ($7.95) Collects #5-7 8.00

PIRANA (See The Phantom #46 & Thrill-O-Rama #2, 3)

PIRATE CORP$, THE (See Hectic Planet)
Eternity Comics/Slave Labor Graphics: 1987 - No. 4, 1988 ($1.95)

1-4: 1,2-Color. 3,4-B&W 2.50
Special 1 ('89, B&W)-Slave Labor Publ. 2.50

PIRATE CORP$, THE (Volume 2)
Slave Labor Graphics: 1989 - No. 6, 1992 ($1.95)

1-6-Dorkin-s/a 2.50

PIRATE OF THE GULF, THE (See Superior Stories #2)

PIRATES COMICS
Hillman Periodicals: Feb-Mar, 1950 - No. 4, Aug-Sept, 1950 (All 52 pgs.)

1 24 48 72 140 230 320
2-Dave Berg-a 17 34 51 98 154 210
3,4-Berg-a 15 30 45 88 137 185

PIRATES OF CONEY ISLAND, THE
Image Comics: Oct, 2006 - No. 8 ($2.99)

1-6-Rick Spears-s/Vasilis Lolos-a; two covers. 2-Cloonan var-c 3.00

PIRATES OF DARK WATER, THE (Hanna Barbera)
Marvel Comics: Nov, 1991 - No. 9, Aug, 1992 ($1.95)

1-9: 9-Vess-c 3.00

P.I.'S: MICHAEL MAUSER AND MS. TREE, THE
First Comics: Jan, 1985 - No. 3, May, 1985 ($1.25, limited series)

1-3: Staton-c/a(p) 2.50

PITT, THE (Also see The Draft & The War)
Marvel Comics: Mar, 1988 ($3.25, 52 pgs., one-shot)

1-Ties into Starbrand, D.P.7 3.50

PITT (See Youngblood #4 & Gen 13 #3,#4)
Image Comics #1-9/Full Bleed #1/2,10-on: Jan, 1993 - No. 20 ($1.95, intended as a four part limited series)

1/2-(12/95)-1st Full Bleed issue 4.00
1-Dale Keown-c/a. 1-1st app. The Pitt 4.00
2-13: All Dale Keown-c/a. 3 (Low distribution). 10 (1/96)-Indicia reads "January 1995" 3.00
14-20: 14-Begin $2.50-c, pullout poster 2.50
TPB-(1997, $9.95) r/#1/2, 1-4 10.00
TPB 2-(1999, $11.95) r/#5-9 12.00

PITT CREW
Full Bleed Studios: Aug, 1998 - No. 5, Dec, 1999 ($2.50)

1-5: 1-Richard Pace-s/Ken Lashley-a. 2-4-Scott Lee-a 2.50

PITT IN THE BLOOD
Full Bleed Studios: Aug, 1996 ($2.50, one-shot)

nn-Richard Pace-a/script 2.50

PIXIE & DIXIE & MR. JINKS (TV)(See Jinks, Pixie, and Dixie & Whitman Comic Books)
Dell Publishing Co./Gold Key: July-Sept, 1960 - Feb, 1963 (Hanna-Barbera)

Four Color 1112 7 14 21 50 83 115
Four Color 1196,1264, 01-631-207 (Dell, 7/62) 6 12 18 37 59 80
1(2/63-Gold Key) 6 12 18 43 69 95

PIXIE PUZZLE ROCKET TO ADVENTURELAND
Avon Periodicals: Nov, 1952

1 14 28 42 80 115 150

PIXIES, THE (Advs. of...)(The Mighty Atom and ...#6 on)(See A-1 Comics #16)
Magazine Enterprises: Winter, 1946 - No. 4, Fall?, 1947; No. 5, 1948

1-Mighty Atom 9 18 27 50 65 80
2-5-Mighty Atom 6 12 18 28 34 40
I.W. Reprint #1(1958), 8-(Pee-Wee Pixies), 10-I.W. on cover, Super on inside
2 4 6 8 10 12

PIZZAZZ
Marvel Comics: Oct, 1977 - No. 16, Jan, 1979 (slick-color kids mag. w/puzzles, games, comics)

1-Star Wars photo-c/article; origin Tarzan; KISS photos/article; Iron-On bonus; 2 pg. pin-up calendars thru #8 3 6 9 20 30 40
2-Spider-Man-c; Beatles pin-up calendar 2 4 6 13 18 22
3-8: 3-Close Encounters-s; Bradbury-s. 4-Alice Cooper, Travolta; Charlie's Angels/Fonz/Hulk/ Spider-Man-c. 5-Star Trek quiz. 6-Asimov-s. 7-James Bond; Spock/Darth Vader-c. 8-TV Spider-Man photo-c/article 2 4 6 11 16 20
9-14: 9-Shaun Cassidy-c. 10-Sgt. Pepper-c/s. 12-Battlestar Galactica-s; Spider-Man app. 13-TV Hulk-c/s. 14-Meatloaf-c/s 2 4 6 10 14 18
15,16: 15-Battlestar Galactica-s. 16-Movie Superman photo-c/s, Hulk.
2 4 6 11 16 20

NOTE: ***Star Wars*** *comics in all (1-6:Chaykin-a, 7-9: DeZuniga-a, 10-13:Simonson/Janson-a. 14-16:Cockrum-a).* ***Tarzan*** *comics, 1pg.-#1-8. 1pg. "Hey Look" by Kurtzman #12-16.*

PLANETARY (See Preview in flip book Gen13 #33)
DC Comics (WildStorm Prod.): Apr, 1999 - No. 27, Dec, 2009 ($2.50/$2.95/$2.99)

1-Ellis-s/Cassaday-a/c 1 3 4 6 8 10
1-Special Edition (6/09, $1.00) r/#1 with "After Watchmen" cover frame 1.00
2-5 6.00
6-10 5.00
11-15: 12-Fourth Man revealed 4.00
16-26: 16-Begin $2.95-c. 23-Origin of The Drummer 3.00
27-($3.99) Wraparound gatefold-c 4.00
...: All Over the World and Other Stories (2000, $14.95) r/#1-6 & Preview 15.00
...: All Over the World and Other Stories-Hardcover (2000, $24.95) r/#1-6 & Preview; with dustjacket 25.00
.../Batman: Night on Earth 1 (8/03, $5.95) Ellis-s/Cassaday-a 6.00
...: Crossing Worlds (2004, $14.95) r/Batman, JLA, and The Authority x-overs 15.00
.../JLA: Terra Occulta (11/02, $5.95) Elseworlds; Ellis-s/Ordway-a 6.00
...: Leaving the 20th Century -HC (2004, $24.95) r/#13-18 25.00
...: Leaving the 20th Century -SC (2004, $14.99) r/#13-18 25.00
.../The Authority: Ruling the World (8/00, $5.95) Ellis-s/Phil Jimenez-a 6.00
...: The Fourth Man -Hardcover (2001, $24.95) r/#7-12 25.00
...: The Planetary Reader (8/03, $5.95) r/#13-15 6.00

PLANETARY BRIGADE (Also see Hero Squared)
Boom Studios: Feb, 2006 - Present ($2.99)

1,2-Giffen & DeMatteis-s/art by various; Haley-c 3.00
... Origins 1-3 (10/06-4/07, $3.99) Giffen & DeMatteis-s/Julia Bax-a 4.00

PLANET COMICS
Fiction House Magazines: 1/40 - No. 62, 9/49; No. 63, Wint, 1949-50; No. 64, Spring, 1950; No. 65, 1951(nd); No. 66-68, 1952(nd); No. 69, Wint, 1952-53; No. 70-72, 1953(nd); No. 73, Winter, 1953-54

1-Origin Auro, Lord of Jupiter by Briefer (ends #61); Flint Baker & The Red Comet begin; Eisner/Fine-c 1250 2500 3750 9400 16,700 24,000
2-Lou Fine-c (Scarce) 432 864 1296 3154 5577 8000
3-Eisner-c 300 600 900 2070 3635 5200
4-Gale Allen and the Girl Squadron begins 284 368 852 1818 3109 4400
5,6-(Scarce): 5-Eisner/Fine-c 274 548 822 1740 2995 4250
7-12: 8-Robot-c. 12-The Star Pirate begins 210 420 630 1334 2292 3250
13,14: 13-Reff Ryan begins 153 306 459 972 1674 2375

Planet of Vampires #2 © Seaboard

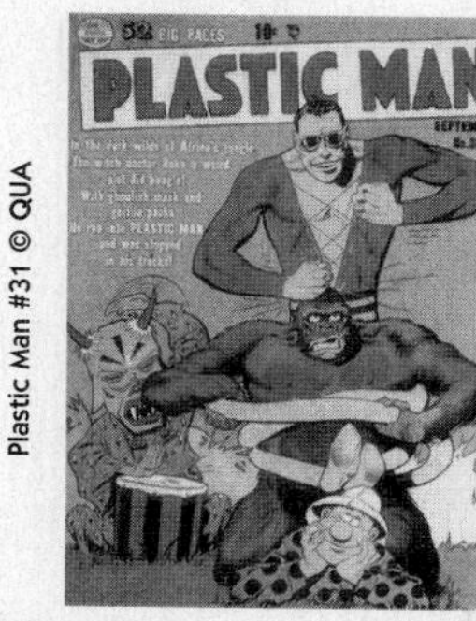

Plastic Man #31 © QUA

Plop #19 © DC

	GD 2.0	VG 4.0	FN 6.0	VF 8.0	VF/NM 9.0	NM- 9.2
15-(Scarce)-Mars, God of War begins (11/41); see Jumbo Comics #31 for 1st app.	300	600	900	2070	3635	5200
16-20,22	140	280	420	889	1532	2175
21-The Lost World & Hunt Bowman begin	147	294	441	934	1605	2275
23-26: 26-Space Rangers begin (9/43), end #71	129	258	387	826	1413	2000
27-30	103	206	309	659	1130	1600
31-35: 33-Origin Star Pirates Wonder Boots, reprinted in #52. 35-Mysta of the Moon begins, ends #62	89	178	267	565	970	1375
36-45: 38-1st Mysta of the Moon-c. 41-New origin of "Auro, Lord of Jupiter". 42-Last Gale Allen. 43-Futura begins	82	164	246	528	902	1275
46-60: 48-Robot-c. 53-Used in **SOTI**, pg. 32	64	128	192	406	696	985
61-68,70: 64,70-Robot-c. 65-70-All partial-r of earlier issues. 70-r/stories from #41	48	96	144	302	514	725
69-Used in **POP**, pgs. 101,102	49	98	147	309	522	735
71-73-No series stories. 71-Space Rangers strip	39	78	117	240	395	550
I.W. Reprint 1,8,9: 1(nd)-r/#70; cover-r from Attack on Planet Mars. 8 (r/#72), 9-r/#73	8	16	24	52	86	120

NOTE: ***Anderson*** *a-33-38, 40-51 (Star Pirate).* ***Matt Baker*** *a-53-59 (Mysta of the Moon).* ***Celardo*** *c-12.* ***Bill Discount*** *a-71 (Space Rangers).* ***Elias*** *c-70.* ***Evans*** *a-46-49 (Auro, Lord of Jupiter), 50-64 (Lost World).* ***Fine*** *c-2, 5.* ***Hopper*** *a-31, 35 (Gale Allen), 41, 42, 48, 49 (Mysta of the Moon).* ***Ingels*** *a-24-31 (Lost World), 56-61 (Auro, Lord of Jupiter).* ***Lubbers*** *a-44-47 (Space Rangers); c-40, 41.* ***Moreira*** *a-43, 44 (Mysta of the Moon).* ***Renee*** *a-40-49 (Lost World); c-33, 35, 39.* ***Tuska*** *a-30 (Star Pirate).* ***M. Whitman*** *a-50-52 (Mysta of the Moon), 53-58 (Star Pirate); c-71-73.* ***Starr*** *a-59.* ***Zolnerwich*** *c-10. 13-25. Bondage c-53.*

PLANET COMICS
Pacific Comics: 1984 ($5.95)

	GD	VG	FN	VF	VF/NM	NM-
1-Reprints Planet Comics #1(1940)	1	2	3	5	6	8

PLANET COMICS
Blackthorne Publishing: Apr, 1988 - No. 3 ($2.00, color/B&W #3)

	GD	VG	FN	VF	VF/NM	NM-
1-3: New stories. 1-Dave Stevens-c						3.00

PLANET HULK (See Incredible Hulk and Giant-Size Hulk #1 (2006))

PLANET OF THE APES (Magazine) (Also see Adventures on the... & Power Record Comics)
Marvel Comics Group: Aug, 1974 - No. 29, Feb, 1977 (B&W) (Based on movies)

	GD	VG	FN	VF	VF/NM	NM-
1-Ploog-a	4	8	12	24	37	50
2-Ploog-a	3	6	9	16	23	30
3-10	3	6	9	14	19	24
11-20	3	6	9	14	20	26
21-28 (low distribution)	3	6	9	16	23	30
29 (low distribution)	5	10	15	32	51	70

NOTE: ***Alcala*** *a-7-11, 17-22, 24.* ***Ploog*** *a-1-4, 6, 8, 11, 13, 14, 19.* ***Sutton*** *a-11, 12, 15, 17, 19, 20, 23, 24, 29.* ***Tuska*** *a-1-6.*

PLANET OF THE APES
Adventure Comics: Apr, 1990 - No. 24, 1992 ($2.50, B&W)

	GD	VG	FN	VF	VF/NM	NM-
1-New movie tie-in; comes w/outer-c (3 colors)						4.00
1-Limited serial numbered edition ($5.00)						5.00
1-2nd printing (no outer-c, $2.50)						2.50
2-24						3.00
Annual 1 ($3.50)						4.00
...Urchak's Folly 1-4 ($2.50, mini-series)						3.00

PLANET OF THE APES (The Human War)
Dark Horse Comics: Jun, 2001 - No. 3, Aug, 2001 ($2.99, limited series)

	GD	VG	FN	VF	VF/NM	NM-
1-3-Follows the 2001 movie; Edginton-s						3.00

PLANET OF THE APES
Dark Horse Comics: Sept, 2001 - No. 6, Feb, 2002 ($2.99, ongoing series)

	GD	VG	FN	VF	VF/NM	NM-
1-6: 1-3-Edginton-s. 1-Photo & Wagner covers. 2-Plunkett & photo-c						3.00

PLANET OF VAMPIRES
Seaboard Publications (Atlas): Feb, 1975 - No. 3, July, 1975

	GD	VG	FN	VF	VF/NM	NM-
1-Neal Adams-c(i); 1st Broderick-c/a(p); Hama-s	2	4	6	10	14	18
2,3: 2-Neal Adams-c. 3-Heath-c/a	2	4	6	8	10	12

PLANET TERRY
Marvel Comics (Star Comics)/Marvel: April, 1985 - No. 12, March, 1986 (Children's comic)

	GD	VG	FN	VF	VF/NM	NM-
1-12						3.00
1-Variant with "Star Chase" game on last page & inside back-c						10.00

PLASM (See Warriors of Plasm)
Defiant Comics: June, 1993

	GD	VG	FN	VF	VF/NM	NM-
0-Came bound into Diamond Previews V3#6 (6/93); price is for complete Previews with comic still attached						3.00
0-Comic only removed from Previews						2.50

PLASMER
Marvel Comics UK: Nov, 1993 - No. 4, Feb, 1994 ($1.95, limited series)

	GD 2.0	VG 4.0	FN 6.0	VF 8.0	VF/NM 9.0	NM- 9.2
1-($2.50)-Polybagged w/4 trading cards						2.75
2-4: Capt. America & Silver Surfer app.						2.50

PLASTIC FORKS
Marvel Comis (Epic Comics): 1990 - No. 5, 1990 ($4.95, 68 pgs., limited series, mature)

	GD	VG	FN	VF	VF/NM	NM-
Book 1-5: Squarebound						5.00

PLASTIC MAN (Also see Police Comics & Smash Comics #17)
Vital Publ. No. 1,2/Quality Comics No. 3 on: Sum, 1943 - No. 64, Nov, 1956

	GD	VG	FN	VF	VF/NM	NM-
nn(#1)- "In The Game of Death"; Skull-c; Jack Cole-c/a begins; ends-#64?	423	846	1269	3067	5384	7700
nn(#2, 2/44)- "The Gay Nineties Nightmare"	181	362	543	1158	1979	2800
3 (Spr, '46)	118	236	354	749	1287	1825
4 (Sum, '46)	89	178	267	565	970	1375
5 (Aut, '46)	73	146	219	467	796	1125
6-10	60	120	180	381	653	925
11-15,17-20	53	106	159	334	567	800
16-Classic-c	58	116	174	371	636	900
21-30: 26-Last non-r issue?	41	82	123	256	428	600
31-40: 40-Used in POP, pg. 91	34	68	102	199	325	450
41-64: 53-Last precode issue. 54-Robot-c	26	52	78	152	249	345
Super Reprint 11,16,18: 11('63)-r/#16. 16-r/#18 & #21; Cole-a. 18('64)-Spirit-r by Eisner from Police #95	4	8	12	24	37	50

NOTE: ***Cole*** *r-44, 49, 56, 58, 59 at least.* ***Cuidera*** *c-32-64i.*

PLASTIC MAN (See DC Special #15 & House of Mystery #160)
National Periodical Publications/DC Comics: 11-12/66 - No. 10, 5-6/68; V4#11, 2-3/76 - No. 20, 10-11/77

	GD	VG	FN	VF	VF/NM	NM-
1-Real 1st app. Silver Age Plastic Man (House of Mystery #160 is actually tryout); Gil Kane-c/a; 12¢ issues begin	10	20	30	68	119	170
2-5: 4-Infantino-c; Mortimer-a	5	10	15	34	55	75
6-10('68): 7-G.A. Plastic Man & Woozy Winks (1st S.A. app.) app.; origin retold. 10-Sparling-a; last 12¢ issue	4	8	12	28	44	60
V4#11('76)-20: 11-20-Fradon-p. 17-Origin retold	2	4	6	8	10	12
...80-Page Giant (2003, $6.95) reprints origin and other stories in 80-Pg. Giant format						7.00
...Special 1 (8/99, $3.95)						4.00

PLASTIC MAN
DC Comics: Nov, 1988 - No. 4, Feb, 1989 ($1.00, mini-series)

	GD	VG	FN	VF	VF/NM	NM-
1-4: 1-Origin; Woozy Winks app.						2.50

PLASTIC MAN
DC Comics: Feb, 2004 - No. 20, Mar, 2006 ($2.95/$2.99)

	GD	VG	FN	VF	VF/NM	NM-
1-20-Kyle Baker-s/a in most. 1-Retells origin. 7,12-Scott Morse-s/a. 8-JLA cameo						3.00
...: On the Lam TPB (2004, $14.95) r/#1-6						15.00
...: Rubber Bandits TPB (2005, $14.99) r/#8-11,13,14						15.00

PLASTRON CAFE
Mirage Studios: Dec, 1992 - No. 4, July, 1993 ($2.25, B&W)

	GD	VG	FN	VF	VF/NM	NM-
1-4: 1-Teenage Mutant Ninja Turtles app.; Kelly Freas-c. 2-Hildebrandt painted-c. 4-Spaced & Alien Fire stories						2.50

PLAYFUL LITTLE AUDREY (TV)(Also see Little Audrey #25)
Harvey Publications: 6/57 - No. 110, 11/73; No. 111, 8/74 - No. 121, 4/76

	GD	VG	FN	VF	VF/NM	NM-
1	23	46	69	166	321	475
2	12	24	36	83	152	220
3-5	9	18	27	63	107	150
6-10	7	14	21	47	76	105
11-20	5	10	15	34	55	75
21-40	4	8	12	26	41	55
41-60	3	6	9	20	30	40
61-84: 84-Last 12¢ issue	3	6	9	16	22	28
85-99	2	4	6	11	16	20
100-52 pg. Giant	3	6	9	16	23	30
101-103: 52 pg. Giants	3	6	9	14	20	25
104-121	1	3	4	6	8	10
...In 3-D (Spring, 1988, $2.25, Blackthorne #66)						4.00

PLOP! (Also see The Best of DC #60)
National Periodical Publications: Sept-Oct, 1973 - No. 24, Nov-Dec, 1976

	GD	VG	FN	VF	VF/NM	NM-
1-Sergio Aragonés-a begins; Wrightson-a	4	8	12	24	37	50
2-4,6-20	3	6	9	14	20	26
5-Wrightson-a	3	6	9	16	22	28
21-24 (52 pgs.). 23-No Aragonés-a	3	6	9	16	23	30

NOTE: ***Alcala*** *a-1-3.* ***Anderson*** *a-5.* ***Aragonés*** *a-1-22, 24.* ***Ditko*** *a-16p.* ***Evans*** *a-1.* ***Mayer*** *a-1.* ***Orlando*** *a-21, 22; c-21.* ***Sekowsky*** *a-5, 6p.* ***Toth*** *a-11.* ***Wolverton*** *r-4, 22-24(1 pg.ea.); c-1-12, 14, 17, 18.* ***Wood*** *a-14, 16i, 18-24; c-13, 15, 16, 19.*

Pogo Possum #2 © Oskar Lebeck

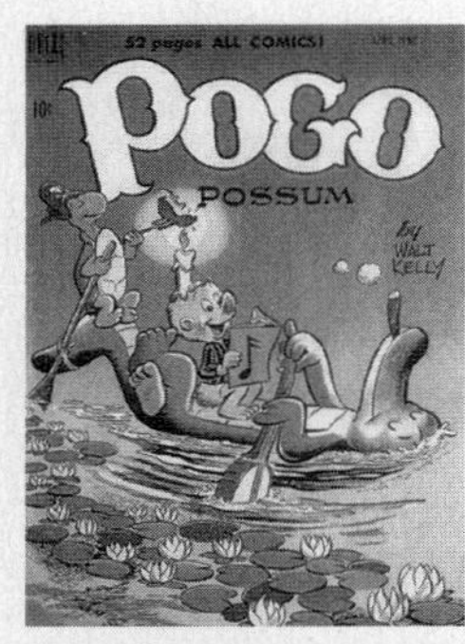

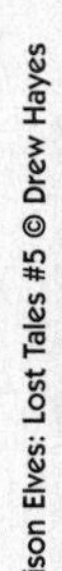

Poison Elves: Lost Tales #5 © Drew Hayes

Pokémon Adventures #4 © Nintendo

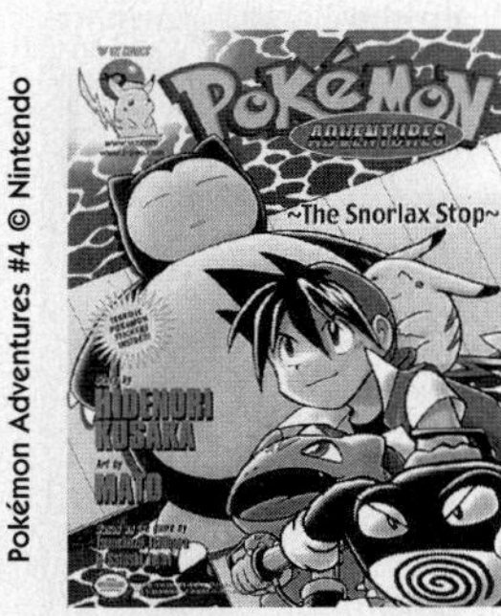

	GD	VG	FN	VF	VF/NM	NM-
	2.0	4.0	6.0	8.0	9.0	9.2

PLUTO (See Cheerios Premiums, Four Color #537, Mickey Mouse Magazine, Walt Disney Showcase #4, 7, 13, 20, 23, 33 & Wheaties)
Dell Publ. Co.: No. 7, 1942; No. 429, 10/52 - No. 1248, 11-1/61-62 (Disney)

	GD	VG	FN	VF	VF/NM	NM-
Large Feature Comic 7(1942)-Written by Carl Barks, Jack Hannah, & Nick George (Barks' 1st comic book work)	161	322	483	1030	1765	2500
Four Color 429 (#1)	9	18	27	65	113	160
Four Color 509	6	12	18	41	66	90
Four Color 595,654,736,853	5	10	15	32	51	70
Four Color 941,1039,1143,1248	4	8	12	28	44	60

POCKET CLASSICS
Academic Inc. Publications: 1984 (B&W, 4 1/4" x 6 3/4", 68 pages)

C1(Black Beauty. C2(The Call of the Wild). C3(Dr. Jekyll and Mr. Hyde). C4(Dracula). C5(Frankenstein). C6(Huckleberry Finn). C7(Moby Dick). C8(The Red Badge of Courage). C9(The Time Machine). C10(Tom Sawyer). C11(Treasure Island). C12(20,000 Leagues Under the Sea). C13(The Great Adventures of Sherlock Holmes). C14(Gulliver's Travels). C15(The Hunchback of Notre Dame). C16(The Invisible Man). C17(Journey to the Center of the Earth). C18(Kidnapped). C19(The Mysterious Island). C20(The Scarlet Letter). C21(The Story of My Life). C22(A Tale of Two Cities). C23(The Three Musketeers). C24(The War of the Worlds). C25(Around the World in Eighty Days). C26(Captains Courageous). C27(A Connecticut Yankee in King Arthur's Court). C28(Sherlock Holmes - The Hound of the Baskervilles). C29(The House of the Seven Gables). C30(Jane Eyre). C31(The Last of the Mohicans). C32(The Best of O. Henry). C33(The Best of Poe). C34(Two Years Before the Mast). C35(White Fang). C36(Wuthering Heights). C37(Ben Hur). C38(A Christmas Carol). C39(The Food of the Gods). C40(Ivanhoe). C41(The Man in the Iron Mask). C42(The Prince and the Pauper). C43(The Prisoner of Zenda). C44(The Return of the Native). C45(Robinson Crusoe). C46(The Scarlet Pimpernel). C47(The Sea Wolf). C48(The Swiss Family Robinson). C49(Billy Budd). C50(Crime and Punishment). C51(Don Quixote). C52(Great Expectations). C53(Heidi). C54(The Illiad). C55(Lord Jim). C56(The Mutiny on Board H.M.S. Bounty). C57(The Odyssey). C58(Oliver Twist). C59(Pride and Prejudice). C60(The Turn of the Screw) each... 8.00

Shakespeare Series:
S1(As You Like It). S2(Hamlet). S3(Julius Caesar). S4(King Lear). S5(Macbeth). S6(The Merchant of Venice). S7(A Midsummer Night's Dream). S8(Othello). S9(Romeo and Juliet). S10(The Taming of the Shrew). S11(The Tempest). S12(Twelfth Night) each... 9.00

POCKET COMICS (Also see Double Up)
Harvey Publications: Aug, 1941 - No. 4, Jan, 1942 (Pocket size; 100 pgs.) (1st Harvey comic)

	GD	VG	FN	VF	VF/NM	NM-
1-Origin & 1st app. The Black Cat, Cadet Blakey the Spirit of '76, The Red Blazer, The Phantom, Sphinx, & The Zebra; Phantom Ranger, British Agent #99, Spin Hawkins, Satan, Lord of Evil begin (1st app. of each); Simon-c/a in #1-3	100	200	300	635	1093	1550
2 (9/41)-Black Cat on-c #2-4	65	130	195	416	708	1000
3,4	50	100	150	315	533	750

POE
Cheese Comics: Sept, 1996 - No. 6, Apr, 1997 ($2.00, B&W)

1-6-Jason Asala-s/a 3.00

POE
Sirius Entertainment (Dogstar Press): Oct, 1997 - No. 24 ($2.50/$2.95, B&W)

1-24-Jason Asala-s/a. 20-24 ($2.95) 3.00
... Color Special (12/98, $2.95) Linsner-c 3.00

POGO PARADE (See Dell Giants)

POGO POSSUM (Also see Animal Comics & Special Delivery)
Dell Publishing Co.: No. 105, 4/46 - No. 148, 5/47; 10-12/49 - No. 16, 4-6/54

	GD	VG	FN	VF	VF/NM	NM-
Four Color 105(1946)-Kelly-c/a	50	100	150	425	838	1250
Four Color 148-Kelly-c/a	41	82	123	328	639	950
1-(10-12/49)-Kelly-c/a in all	36	72	108	280	540	800
2	25	50	75	183	354	525
3-5	17	34	51	124	242	360
6-10: 10-Infinity-c	15	30	45	110	210	310
11-16: 11-X-Mas-c	12	24	36	85	155	225

NOTE: *#1-4, 9-13: 52 pgs.; #5-8, 14-16: 36 pgs.*

POINT BLANK (See Wildcats)
DC Comics (WildStorm): Oct, 2002 - No. 5, Feb, 2003 ($2.95, limited series)

1-5-Brubaker-s/Wilson-a/Bisley-c. 1-Variant-c by Wilson; Grifter and John Lynch app. 3.00
TPB (2003, $14.95), (2009, $14.99) r/#1-5; afterword by Brubaker 15.00

POISON ELVES (Formerly I, Lusiphur)
Mulehide Graphics: No. 8, 1993- No. 20, 1995 (B&W, magazine/comic size, mature readers)

	GD	VG	FN	VF	VF/NM	NM-
8-Drew Hayes-c/a/scripts.	2	4	6	8	10	12
9-11: 11-1st comic size issue	2	4	6	8	10	12
12,14,16	1	2	3	5	6	8
13,15-(low print)	2	4	6	8	11	14
15-2nd print						4.00
17-20	1	2	3	5	6	8
...Desert of the Third Sin-(1997, $14.95, TPB)-r/#13-18						15.00
...Patrons-($4.95, TPB)-r/#19,20						5.00
...Traumatic Dogs-(1996, $14.95,TPB)-Reprints I, Lusiphur #7, Poison Elves #8-12						15.00

POISON ELVES (See I, Lusiphur)
Sirius Entertainment: June, 1995 - No. 79, Sept, 2004 ; No. 80, Nov, 2007 ($2.50/$2.95, B&W, mature readers)

	GD	VG	FN	VF	VF/NM	NM-
1-Linsner-c; Drew Hayes-a/scripts in all.						5.00
1-2nd print						2.50
2-25: 12-Purple Marauder-c/app.						3.00
26-45, 47-49						2.50
46,50-79: 61-Fillbäch Brothers-s/a. 74-Art by Crilley (3 pgs.)						3.00
80-($3.50) Tribute issue to Drew Hayes; sketchbook and notebook art with commentary						3.50
... Baptism By Fire-(2003, $19.95, TPB)-r/#48-59						20.00
... Color Special #1 (12/98, $2.95)						5.00
... Companion (12/02, $3.50) Back-story and character bios						3.50
... : Dark Wars TPB Vol. 1 (2005, $15.95) r/#60,62-68						16.00
... FAN Edition #1 mail-in offer; Drew Hayes-c/s/a	1	2	3	5	6	8
... Rogues-(2002, $15.95, TPB)-r/#40-47						16.00
...Salvation-(2001, $19.95, TPB)-r/#26-39						20.00
...Sanctuary-(1999, $14.95, TPB)-r/#1-12						15.00

POISON ELVES: DOMINION
Sirius Entertainment: Sept, 2005 - No. 6, Sept, 2006 ($3.50, B&W, limited series)

1-6-Keith Davidsen-s/Scott Lewis-a 3.50

POISON ELVES: HYENA
Sirius Entertainment: Sept, 2004 - No. 4, Feb, 2005 ($2.95, B&W, limited series)

1-4-Keith Davidsen-s/Scott Lewis-a 3.00
Ventures TPB Vol. 1: The Hyena Collection (2006, $14.95) r/#1-4 & 2 short stories 15.00

POISON ELVES: LOST TALES
Sirius Entertainment: Jan, 2006 - Present ($2.95, B&W, limited series)

1-11-Aaron Bordner-a; Bordner & Davidsen-s 3.00

POISON ELVES: LUSIPHUR & LIRILITH
Sirius Entertainment: 2001 - No. 4, 2001 ($2.95, B&W, limited series)

1-4-Drew Hayes-s/Jason Alexander-a 3.00
TPB (2002, $11.95) r/#1-4 12.00

POISON ELVES: PARINTACHIN
Sirius Entertainment: 2001 - No. 3, 2002 ($2.95, B&W, limited series)

1-3-Drew Hayes-c/Fillbäch Brothers-s/a 3.00
TPB (2003, $8.95) r/#1-3 9.00

POISON ELVES VENTURES
Sirius Entertainment: May, 2005 - No. 4, Apr, 2006 ($3.50, B&W, limited series)

... #1: Cassanova; ...#2: Lynn; ...#3: The Purple Marauder; #4: Jace - Bordner-a 3.50

POKÉMON (TV) (Also see Magical Pokémon Journey)
Viz Comics: Nov, 1998 - 2000 ($3.25/$3.50, B&W)

	GD	VG	FN	VF	VF/NM	NM-
...Part 1: The Electric Tale of Pikachu						
1-Toshiro Ono-s/a	1	3	4	6	8	10
1-4 (2nd through current printings)						3.50
2						6.00
3,4						4.00
TPB ($12.95)						13.00
...Part 2: Pikachu Strikes Back						
1						5.00
2-4						4.00
TPB						13.00
...Part 3: Electric Pikachu Boogaloo						
1						4.00
2-4 ($2.95-c)						3.50
TPB						13.00
...Part 4: Surf's Up Pikachu						
1,3,4						4.00
2 ($2.95-c)						3.50
TPB						13.00

NOTE: Multiple printings exist for most issues

POKÉMON ADVENTURES
Viz Comics: Sept, 1999 - No. 4 ($5.95, B&W, magazine-size)

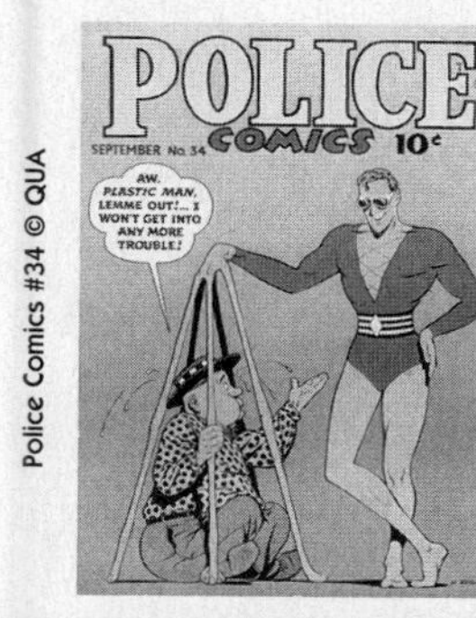

Police Comics #34 © QUA

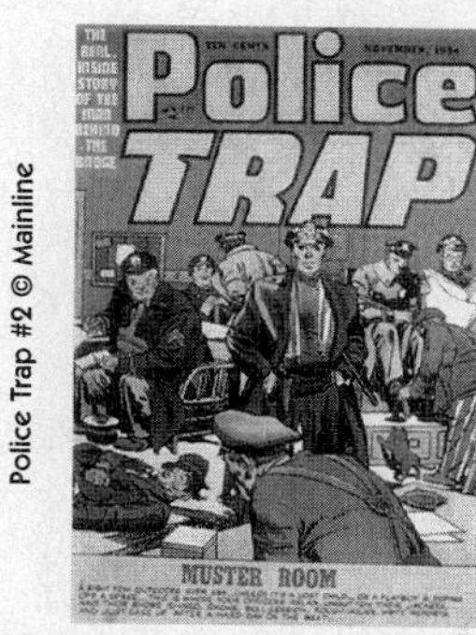

Police Trap #2 © Mainline

Polly Pigtales #36 © PMI

	GD 2.0	VG 4.0	FN 6.0	VF 8.0	VF/NM 9.0	NM- 9.2

1-4-Includes stickers bound in 6.00

POKÉMON ADVENTURES
Viz Comics: 2000 - Present ($2.95/$4.95, B&W)

Part 2 (2/00-7/00) 1-6-Includes stickers bound in 3.50
Part 3 (8/00-2/01) 1-7 3.50
Part 4 (3/00-6/01) 1-4 5.00
Part 5 (7/01-10/01) 1-4 5.00
Part 6: 1-4, Part 7 1-5 5.00

POKÉMON: THE FIRST MOVIE
Viz Comics: 1999 ($3.95)

Mewtwo Strikes Back 1-4 4.00
Pikachu's Vacation 4.00

POKÉMON: THE MOVIE 2000
Viz Comics: 2000 ($3.95)

1-Official movie adaption 4.00
Pikachu's Rescue Adventure 4.00
...:The Power of One (mini-series) 1-3 4.00

POLICE ACADEMY (TV)
Marvel Comics: Nov, 1989 - No. 6, Feb, 1990 ($1.00)

1-6: Based on TV cartoon; Post-c/a(p) in all 2.50

POLICE ACTION
Atlas News Co.: Jan, 1954 - No. 7, Nov, 1954

	GD	VG	FN	VF	VF/NM	NM-
1-Violent-a by Robert Q. Sale	21	42	63	124	202	280
2	13	26	39	72	101	130
3-7: 7-Powell-a	11	22	33	64	90	115

NOTE: ***Ayers** a-4, 5. **Colan** a-1. **Forte** a-1, 2. **Mort Lawrence** a-5. **Maneely** a-3; c-1, 5. **Reinman** a-6, 7.*

POLICE ACTION
Atlas/Seaboard Publ.: Feb, 1975 - No. 3, June, 1975

	GD	VG	FN	VF	VF/NM	NM-
1-3: 1-Lomax, N.Y.P.D., Luke Malone begin; McWilliams-a. 2-Origin Luke Malone, Manhunter; Ploog-a	2	4	6	8	10	12

NOTE: ***Ploog** art in all. **Sekowsky/McWilliams** a-1-3. **Thorne** c-3.*

POLICE AGAINST CRIME
Premiere Magazines: April, 1954 - No. 9, Aug, 1955

	GD	VG	FN	VF	VF/NM	NM-
1-Disbrow-a; extreme violence (man's face slashed with knife); Hollingsworth-a	28	56	84	165	270	375
2-Hollingsworth-a	15	30	45	90	140	190
3-9	14	28	42	80	115	150

POLICE BADGE #479 (Formerly Spy Thrillers #1-4)
Atlas Comics (PrPI): No. 5, Sept, 1955

	GD	VG	FN	VF	VF/NM	NM-
5-Maneely-c/a (6 pgs.); Heck-a	11	22	33	60	83	105

POLICE CASE BOOK (See Giant Comics Editions)

POLICE CASES (See Authentic... & Record Book of...)

POLICE COMICS
Quality Comics Group (Comic Magazines): Aug, 1941 - No. 127, Oct, 1953

	GD	VG	FN	VF	VF/NM	NM-
1-Origin/1st app. Plastic Man by Jack Cole (r-in DC Special #15), The Human Bomb by Gustavson, & No. 711; intro. The Firebrand by Reed Crandall, The Mouthpiece by Guardineer, Phantom Lady, & The Sword; Chic Carter by Eisner app.; Firebrand-c 1-4	784	1568	2352	5723	10,112	14,500
2-Plastic Man smuggles opium	309	618	927	2163	3782	5400
3	232	464	696	1485	2543	3600
4	194	388	582	1242	2121	3000
5-Plastic Man-c begin; Plastic Man forced to smoke marijuana; Plastic Man covers begin, end #102	290	580	870	1856	3178	4500
6,7	169	338	507	1073	1849	2625
8-Manhunter begins (origin/1st app.) (3/42)	194	388	582	1242	2121	3000
9,10	134	268	402	851	1463	2075
11-The Spirit strip reprints begin by Eisner (origin-strip #1); 1st comic book app. The Spirit & 1st cover app. (9/42)	290	580	870	1856	3178	4500
12-Intro. Ebony	155	310	465	992	1696	2400
13-Intro. Woozy Winks; last Firebrand	158	316	474	1003	1727	2450
14-19: 15-Last No. 711; Destiny begins	95	190	285	603	1039	1475
20-The Raven x-over in Phantom Lady; features Jack Cole himself	95	190	285	603	1039	1475
21,22: 21-Raven & Spider Widow x-over in Phantom Lady (cameo in #22)	80	160	240	508	874	1240
23-30: 23-Last Phantom Lady. 24-26-Flatfoot Burns by Kurtzman in all	75	150	225	476	818	1160
31-41: 37-1st app. Candy by Sahle & begins (12/44). 41-Last Spirit-r by Eisner	52	104	156	328	557	785
42,43-Spirit-r by Eisner/Fine	52	104	156	323	549	775
44-Fine Spirit-r begin, end #88,90,92	51	102	153	321	546	770
45-50: 50-(#50 on-c, #49 on inside, 1/46)	40	80	120	246	411	575
51-60: 58-Last Human Bomb	33	66	99	194	317	440
61-88,90,92: 63-(Some issues have #65 printed on cover, but #63 on inside) Kurtzman-a, 6 pgs. 90,92-Spirit by Fine	25	50	75	147	241	335
89,91,93-No Spirit stories	23	46	69	136	223	310
94-99,101,102: Spirit by Eisner in all; 101-Last Manhunter. 102-Last Spirit & Plastic Man by Jack Cole	32	64	96	188	307	425
100	38	76	114	228	369	510
103-Content change to crime; Ken Shannon & T-Man begin (1st app. of each, 12/50)	27	54	81	158	259	360
104-112,114-127: Crandall-a most issues (not in 104,105,122,125-127). 109-Atomic bomb story. 112-Crandall-a	19	38	57	112	176	240
113-Crandall-c/a(2), 9 pgs. each	21	42	63	122	199	275

NOTE: *Most Spirit stories signed by Eisner are not by him; all are reprints. **Crandall** Firebrand-1-8. Spirit by **Eisner** 1-41, 94-102; by **Eisner/Fine**-42, 43; by **Fine**-44-88, 90, 92. 103, 109. **Al Bryant** c-33, 34. **Cole** c-17-32, 35-102(most). **Crandall** c-13, 14. **Crandall/Cuidera** c-105-127. **Eisner** c-4i. **Gill Fox** c-1-3, 4p, 5-12, 15. Bondage c-103, 109, 125.*

POLICE LINE-UP
Avon Periodicals/Realistic Comics #3,4: Aug, 1951 - No. 4, July, 1952 (Painted-c #1-3)

	GD	VG	FN	VF	VF/NM	NM-
1-Wood-a, 1 pg. plus part-c; spanking panel-r/Saint #5	39	78	117	231	378	525
2-Classic story "The Religious Murder Cult", drugs, perversion; r/Saint #5; c-r/Avon paperback #329	27	54	81	158	259	360
3,4: 3-Kubert-a(r?)/part-c; Kinstler-a (inside-c only)	20	40	60	117	189	260

POLICE TRAP (Public Defender In Action #7 on)
Mainline #1-4/Charlton #5,6: 8-9/54 - No. 4, 2-3/55; No. 5, 7/55 - No. 6, 9/55

	GD	VG	FN	VF	VF/NM	NM-
1-S&K covers-all issues; Meskin-a; Kirby scripts	31	62	93	182	296	410
2-4	20	40	60	114	182	250
5,6-S&K-c/a	25	50	75	147	241	335

POLICE TRAP
Super Comics: No. 11, 1963; No. 16-18, 1964

	GD	VG	FN	VF	VF/NM	NM-
Reprint #11,16-18: 11-r/Police Trap #3. 16-r/Justice Traps the Guilty #? 17-r/Inside Crime #3 & r/Justice Traps The Guilty #83; 18-r/Inside Crime #3	2	4	6	9	13	16

POLLY & HER PALS (See Comic Monthly #1)

POLLY & THE PIRATES
Oni Press: Sept, 2005 - No. 6, June, 2006 ($2.99, B&W, limited series)

1-6-Ted Naifeh-s/a; Polly is shanghaied by the pirate ship Titania 3.00
TPB (7/06, $11.95, digest) r/#1-6 12.00

POLLYANNA (Disney)
Dell Publishing Co.: No. 1129, Aug-Oct, 1960

	GD	VG	FN	VF	VF/NM	NM-
Four Color 1129-Movie, Hayley Mills photo-c	7	14	21	50	83	115

POLLY PIGTAILS (Girls' Fun & Fashion Magazine #44 on)
Parents' Magazine Institute/Polly Pigtails: Jan, 1946 - V4#43, Oct-Nov, 1949

	GD	VG	FN	VF	VF/NM	NM-
1-Infinity-c; photo-c	15	30	45	86	113	180
2-Photo-c	10	20	30	54	72	90
3-5: 3,4-Photo-c	9	18	27	47	61	75
6-10: 7-Photo-c	8	16	24	42	54	65
11-30: 22-Photo-c	7	14	21	37	46	55
31-43	6	12	18	31	38	45

PONY EXPRESS (See Tales of the...)

PONYTAIL (Teen-age)
Dell Publishing Co./Charlton No. 13 on: 7-9/62 - No. 12, 10-12/65; No. 13, 11/69 - No. 20, 1/71

	GD	VG	FN	VF	VF/NM	NM-
12-641-209(#1)	4	8	12	24	37	50
2-12	3	6	9	18	27	35
13-20	3	6	9	14	19	24

POP COMICS
Modern Store Publ.: 1955 (36 pgs.; 5x7"; in color) (7¢)

	GD	VG	FN	VF	VF/NM	NM-
1-Funny animal	6	12	18	28	34	40

POPEYE (See Comic Album #7, 11, 15, Comics Reading Libraries *in the Promotional Comics section,* Eat Right to Work and Win, Giant Comic Album, King Comics, Kite Fun Book, Magic Comics, March of Comics #37,52, 66, 80, 96, 117, 134, 148, 157, 169, 194, 246, 264, 274, 294, 453, 465, 477 & Wow Comics, 1st series)

POPEYE
David McKay Publications: 1937 - 1939 (All by Segar)

Popeye #5 © KING

Popular Comics #5 © DELL

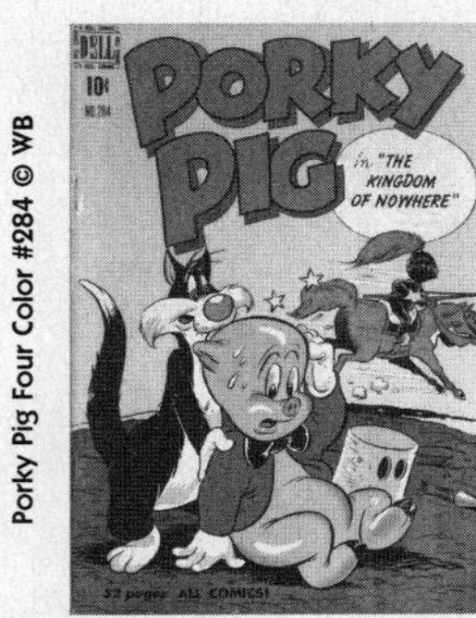

Porky Pig Four Color #284 © WB

	GD 2.0	VG 4.0	FN 6.0	VF 8.0	VF/NM 9.0	NM- 9.2
Feature Books nn (100 pgs.) (Very Rare)	750	1500	2250	5300	8400	11,500
Feature Books 2 (52 pgs.)	90	180	270	576	988	1400
Feature Books 3 (100 pgs.)-r/nn issue with a new-c	84	168	252	538	919	1300
Feature Books 5,10 (76 pgs.)	76	152	228	486	831	1175
Feature Books 14 (76 pgs.) (Scarce)	82	164	246	528	902	1275

POPEYE (Strip reprints through 4-Color #70)
Dell #1-65/Gold Key #66-80/King #81-92/Charlton #94-138/Gold Key #139-155/Whitman #156 on: 1941 - 1947; #1, 2-4/48 - #65, 7-9/62; #66, 10/62 - #80, 5/66; #81, 8/66 - #92, 12/67; #94, 2/69 - #138, 1/77; #139, 5/78 - #171, 6/84 (no #93,160,161)

	GD 2.0	VG 4.0	FN 6.0	VF 8.0	VF/NM 9.0	NM- 9.2
Large Feature Comic 24('41)-Half by Segar	69	138	207	442	759	1075
Four Color 25('41)-by Segar	84	168	252	538	919	1300
Large Feature Comic 10('43)	56	112	168	356	608	860
Four Color 17('43),26('43)-by Segar	42	84	126	336	648	960
Four Color 43('44)	30	60	90	218	422	625
Four Color 70('45)-Title: ...& Wimpy	22	44	66	155	300	445
Four Color 113('46-original strips begin),127,145('47),168	14	28	42	97	181	265
1(2-4/48)(Dell)-All new stories continue	26	52	78	190	370	550
2	14	28	42	97	181	265
3-10: 5-Popeye on moon w/rocket-c	11	22	33	78	139	200
11-20	9	18	27	63	107	150
21-40,46: 46-Origin Swee' Pee	8	16	24	52	86	120
41-45,47-50	6	12	18	43	69	95
51-60	6	12	18	37	59	80
61-65 (Last Dell issue)	5	10	15	32	51	70
66(10/62),67-Both 84 pgs. (Gold Key)	7	14	21	47	76	105
68-80	4	8	12	26	41	55
81-92,94-97 (no #93): 97-Last 12¢ issue	3	6	9	21	32	42
98,99,101-138	3	6	9	14	19	24
100	3	6	9	18	27	35
139-155: 144-50th Anniversary issue	2	4	6	8	10	12
156,157,162-167(Whitman)(no #160,161).167(3/82)	2	4	6	10	14	18
158(9/80),159(11/80)-pre-pack only	4	8	12	22	34	45
168-171:(All #90069 on-c; pre-pack) 168(6/83). 169(#168 on-c)(8/83). 170(3/84). 171(6/84)	3	6	9	16	22	28

NOTE: *Reprints-#145, 147, 149, 151, 153, 155, 157, 163-168(1/3), 170.*

POPEYE
Harvey Comics: Nov, 1993 - No. 7, Aug, 1994 ($1.50)

	GD 2.0	VG 4.0	FN 6.0	VF 8.0	VF/NM 9.0	NM- 9.2
V2#1-7						3.00
...Summer Special V2#1-(10/93, $2.25, 68 pgs.)-Sagendorf-r & others						4.00

POPEYE SPECIAL
Ocean Comics: Summer, 1987 - No. 2, Sept, 1988 ($1.75/$2.00)

	GD 2.0	VG 4.0	FN 6.0	VF 8.0	VF/NM 9.0	NM- 9.2
1,2: 1-Origin						4.00

POPPLES (TV, movie)
Star Comics (Marvel): Dec, 1986 - No. 4, Jun, 1987

	GD 2.0	VG 4.0	FN 6.0	VF 8.0	VF/NM 9.0	NM- 9.2
1-4-Based on toys						4.00

POPPO OF THE POPCORN THEATRE
Fuller Publishing Co. (Publishers Weekly): 10/29/55 - No. 13, 1956 (weekly)

	GD 2.0	VG 4.0	FN 6.0	VF 8.0	VF/NM 9.0	NM- 9.2
1	9	18	27	52	69	85
2-5	7	14	21	37	46	55
6-13	6	12	18	31	38	45

NOTE: *By* ***Charles Biro.*** *10¢ cover, given away by supermarkets such as IGA.*

POP-POP COMICS
R. B. Leffingwell Co.: No date (Circa 1945) (52 pgs.)

	GD 2.0	VG 4.0	FN 6.0	VF 8.0	VF/NM 9.0	NM- 9.2
1-Funny animal	13	26	39	74	105	135

POPULAR COMICS
Dell Publishing Co.: Feb, 1936 - No. 145, July-Sept, 1948

	GD 2.0	VG 4.0	FN 6.0	VF 8.0	VF/NM 9.0	NM- 9.2
1-Dick Tracy (1st comic book app.), Little Orphan Annie, Terry & the Pirates, Gasoline Alley, Don Winslow (1st app.), Harold Teen, Little Joe, Skippy, Moon Mullins, Mutt & Jeff, Tailspin Tommy, Smitty, Smokey Stover, Winnie Winkle & The Gumps begin (all strip-r)	771	1542	2313	5400	-	-
2	257	514	771	1800	-	-
3	193	386	579	1350	-	-
4-6(7/36): 5-Tom Mix begins. 6-1st app. Scribbly	150	300	450	1050	-	-
7-10: 8,9-Scribbly & Reglar Fellers app.	121	242	363	850	-	-
11-20: 12-X-Mas-c	83	166	249	477	739	1000
21-27: 27-Last Terry & the Pirates, Little Orphan Annie, & Dick Tracy	63	126	189	362	556	750
28-37: 28-Gene Autry app. 31,32-Tim McCoy app. 35-Christmas-c; Tex Ritter app.	49	98	147	282	434	585
38-43: Tarzan in text only. 38-(4/39)-Gang Busters (Radio, 2nd app.) & Zane Grey's Tex Thorne begins? 43-The Masked Pilot app.; 1st non-funny-c?	47	94	141	270	415	560
44,45: 45-Hurricane Kid-c	36	72	108	207	321	435
46-Origin/1st app. Martan, the Marvel Man(12/39)	46	92	138	265	408	550
47-50	35	70	105	201	311	420
51-Origin The Voice (The Invisible Detective) strip begins (5/40)	37	74	111	213	327	440
52-Robot-c	42	84	126	242	371	500
53-59: 55-End of World story	33	66	99	190	295	400
60-Origin/1st app. Professor Supermind and Son (2/41)	34	68	102	196	303	410
61-71: 63-Smilin' Jack begins	26	52	78	150	230	310
72-The Owl & Terry & the Pirates begin (2/42); Smokey Stover reprints begin	42	84	126	242	371	500
73-75	29	58	87	167	259	350
76-78-Capt. Midnight in all (see The Funnies #57)	40	80	120	230	358	485
79-85-Last Owl	27	54	81	155	238	320
86-99: 98-Felix the Cat, Smokey Stover-r begin	18	36	54	104	157	210
100	20	40	60	115	175	235
101-130	10	20	30	58	89	120
131-145: 142-Last Terry & the Pirates	9	18	27	52	79	105

NOTE: *Martan, the Marvel Man c-47-49, 52, 57-59. Professor Supermind c-60-63, 64(1/2), 65, 66. The Voice c-53.*

POPULAR FAIRY TALES (See March of Comics #6, 18)

POPULAR ROMANCE
Better-Standard Publications: No. 5, Dec, 1949 - No. 29, July, 1954

	GD 2.0	VG 4.0	FN 6.0	VF 8.0	VF/NM 9.0	NM- 9.2
5	14	28	42	80	115	150
6-9: 7-Palais-a; lingerie panels	10	20	30	58	79	100
10-Wood-a (2 pgs.)	12	24	36	69	97	125
11,12,14-16,18-21,28,29	9	18	27	50	65	80
13,17-Severin/Elder-a (3&8 pgs.)	10	20	30	54	72	90
22-27-Toth-a	11	22	33	60	83	105

NOTE: *All have photo-c.* ***Tuska*** *art in most issues.*

POPULAR TEEN-AGERS (Secrets of Love) (School Day Romances #1-4)
Star Publications: No. 5, Sept, 1950 - No. 23, Nov, 1954

	GD 2.0	VG 4.0	FN 6.0	VF 8.0	VF/NM 9.0	NM- 9.2
5-Toni Gay, Midge Martin & Eve Adams continue from School Day Romances; Ginger Bunn (formerly Ginger Snapp & becomes Honey Bunn #6 on) begins; all features end #8	27	54	81	158	259	360
6-8 (7/51)-Honey Bunn begins; all have L. B. Cole-c; 6-Negligee panels	22	44	66	128	209	290
9-(...Romances; 1st romance issue, 10/51)	18	36	54	105	165	225
10-(...Secrets of Love thru #23)	17	34	51	98	154	210
11,16,18,19,22,23	15	30	45	83	124	165
12,13,17,20,21-Disbrow-a	15	30	45	88	137	185
14-Harrison/Wood-a	21	42	63	122	199	275
15-Wood?, Disbrow-a	16	32	48	94	147	200
Accepted Reprint 5,6 (nd); L.B. Cole-c	9	18	27	47	61	75

NOTE: *All have* ***L. B. Cole*** *covers.*

PORKY PIG (See Bugs Bunny &..., Kite Fun Book, Looney Tunes, March of Comics #42, 57, 71, 89, 99, 113, 130, 143, 164, 175, 192, 209, 218, 367, and Super Book #6, 18, 30)

PORKY PIG (...& Bugs Bunny #40-69)
Dell Publishing Co./Gold Key No. 1-93/Whitman No. 94 on: No. 16, 1942 - No. 81, Mar-Apr, 1962; Jan, 1965 - No. 109, June, 1984

	GD 2.0	VG 4.0	FN 6.0	VF 8.0	VF/NM 9.0	NM- 9.2
Four Color 16(#1, 1942)	82	164	246	697	1374	2050
Four Color 48(1944)-Carl Barks-a	88	176	264	748	1474	2200
Four Color 78(1945)	26	52	78	190	370	550
Four Color 112(7/46)	16	32	48	115	220	325
Four Color 156,182,191('49)	12	24	36	85	155	225
Four Color 226,241('49),260,271,277,284,295	10	20	30	70	123	175
Four Color 303,311,322,330: 322-Sci/fi-c/story	8	16	24	54	90	125
Four Color 342,351,360,370,385,399,410,426	6	12	18	43	69	95
25 (11-12/52)-30	6	12	18	37	59	80
31-40	5	10	15	32	51	70
41-60	4	8	12	26	41	55
61-81(3-4/62)	4	8	12	22	34	45
1(1/65-Gold Key)(2nd Series)	5	10	15	34	55	75
2,4,5-r/4-Color 226,284 & 271 in that order	3	6	9	20	30	40
3,6-10: 3-r/Four Color #342	3	6	9	17	25	32
11-30	3	6	9	14	19	24
31-54	2	4	6	10	14	18
55-70	2	4	6	8	11	14

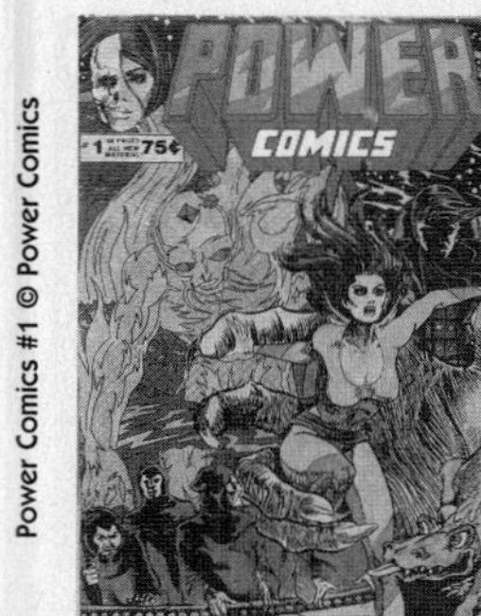

Power Comics #1 © Power Comics

Power Girl #8 © DC

Power Man #83 © MAR

	GD	VG	FN	VF	VF/NM	NM-
	2.0	4.0	6.0	8.0	9.0	9.2

71-93(Gold Key) 2 3 4 6 8 10
94-96 2 4 6 8 10 12
97(9/80),98-pre-pack only (99 known not to exist) 3 6 9 21 32 42
100 2 4 6 10 14 18
101-105: 104(2/82). 105(4/82) 2 4 6 8 11 14
106-109 (All #90140 on-c, no date or date code): 106(7/83), 107(8/83), 108(2/84), 109(6/84) low print run 3 6 9 14 20 26
NOTE: *Reprints-#1-8, 9-35(2/3); 36-46(1/4-1/2), 58, 67, 69-74, 76, 78, 102-109(1/3-1/2).*

PORKY PIG'S DUCK HUNT
Saalfield Publishing Co.: 1938 (12pgs.)(large size)(heavy linen-like paper)
2178-1st app. Porky Pig & Daffy Duck by Leon Schlesinger. Illustrated text story book written in verse. 1st book ever devoted to these characters. (see Looney Tunes #1 for their 1st comic book app.) 73 146 219 467 796 1125

PORTENT, THE
Image Comics: Feb, 2006 - No. 4, Aug, 2006 ($2.99)
1-4-Peter Bergting-s/a 3.00
Vol. 1: Duende TPB (2006, 12.99) r/#1-4; pin-up art; intro. by Kaluta 13.00

PORTIA PRINZ OF THE GLAMAZONS
Eclipse Comics: Dec, 1986 - No. 6, Oct, 1987 ($2.00, B&W, Baxter paper)
1-6 2.50

POSSESSED, THE
DC Comics (Cliffhanger): Sept, 2003 - No. 6, March, 2004 ($2.95, limited series)
1-6-Johns & Grimminger-s/Sharp-a 3.00
TPB (2004, $14.95) r/#1-6; promo art and sketch pages 15.00

POST GAZETTE (See Meet the New... in the Promotional Comics section)

POWDER RIVER RUSTLERS (See Fawcett Movie Comics)

POWER & GLORY (See American Flagg! & Howard Chaykin's American Flagg!
Malibu Comics (Bravura): Feb, 1994 - No. 4, May, 1994 ($2.50, limited series, mature)
1A, 1B-By Howard Chaykin; w/Bravura stamp 2.50
1-Newsstand ed. (polybagged w/children's warning on bag), Gold ed., Silver-foil ed., Blue-foil ed.(print run of 10,000), Serigraph ed. (print run of 3,000)($2.95)-Howard Chaykin-c/a begin 3.00
2-4-Contains Bravura stamp 2.50
Holiday Special (Win '94, $2.95) 3.00

POWER COMICS
Holyoke Publ. Co./Narrative Publ.: 1944 - No. 4, 1945
1-L. B. Cole-c 139 278 417 883 1517 2150
2-Hitler, Hirohito-c (scarce) 145 290 435 921 1586 2250
3-Classic L.B. Cole-c; Dr. Mephisto begins? 168 336 504 1075 1838 2600
4-L.B. Cole-c; Miss Espionage app. #3,4; Leav-a 139 278 417 883 1517 2150

POWER COMICS
Power Comics Co.: 1977 - No. 5, Dec, 1977 (B&W)
1- "A Boy And His Aardvark" by Dave Sim; first Dave Sim aardvark (not Cerebus) 3 6 9 14 20 25
1-Reprint (3/77, black-c) 1 2 3 5 6 8
2-Cobalt Blue by Gustovich 1 3 4 6 8 10
3-5: 3-Nightwitch. 4-Northern Light. 5-Bluebird 1 3 4 6 8 10

POWER COMICS
Eclipse Comics (Acme Press): Mar, 1988 - No. 4, Sept, 1988 ($2.00, B&W, mini-series)
1-4: Bolland, Gibbons-r in all 2.50

POWER COMPANY, THE
DC Comics: Apr, 2002 - No. 18, Sep, 2003 ($2.50/$2.75)
1-6-Busiek-s/Grummett-a. 6-Green Arrow & Black Canary-c/app. 2.50
7-18: 7:Begin $2.75-c. 8,9-Green Arrow app. 11-Firestorm joins. 15-Batman app. 2.75
...Bork (3/02) Busiek-s/Dwyer-a; Batman & Flash (Barry Allen) app. 2.50
...Josiah Power (3/02) Busiek-s/Giffen-a; Superman app. 2.50
...Manhunter (3/02) Busiek-s/Jurgens-a; Nightwing app. 2.50
...Sapphire (3/02) Busiek-s/Bagley-a; JLA & Kobra app. 2.50
...Skyrocket (3/02) Busiek-s/Staton-a; Green Lantern (Hal Jordan) app. 2.50
...Striker Z (3/02) Busiek-s/Bachs-a; Superboy app. 2.50
...Witchfire (3/02) Busiek-s/Haley-a; Wonder Woman app. 2.50

POWER FACTOR
Wonder Color Comics #1/Pied Piper #2: May, 1987 - No. 2, 1987 ($1.95)
1,2: Super team. 2-Infantino-c 2.50

POWER FACTOR
Innovation Publishing: Oct, 1990 - No. 3, 1991 ($1.95/$2.25)
1-3: 1-R-/1st story + new-a, 2-r/2nd story + new-a. 3-Infantino-a 2.50

POWER GIRL (See All-Star #58, Infinity, Inc., JSA Classified, Showcase #97-99)
DC Comics: June, 1988 - No. 4, Sept, 1988 ($1.00, color, limited series)
1-4 3.00
TPB (2006, $14.99) r/Showcase #97-99; Secret Origins #11; JSA Classified #1-4 and pages from JSA #32,39; cover gallery 15.00

POWER GIRL
DC Comics: Jul, 2009 - Present ($2.99)
1-8: 1,2-Amanda Conner-a; covers by Conner and Hughes; Ultra-Humanite app. 3-6-Covers by Conner and March 3.00

POWERHOUSE PEPPER COMICS (See Gay Comics, Joker Comics & Tessie the Typist)
Marvel Comics (20CC): No. 1, 1943; No. 2, May, 1948 - No. 5, Nov, 1948
1-(60 pgs.)-Wolverton-a in all; c-2,3 206 412 618 1318 2259 3200
2 89 178 267 565 970 1375
3,4 82 164 246 528 902 1275
5-(Scarce) 94 188 282 597 1024 1450

POWERLESS
Marvel Comics: Aug, 2004 - No. 6, Jan, 2005 ($2.99, limited series)
1-6-Peter Parker, Matt Murdock and Logan without powers; Gaydos-a 3.00
TPB (2005, $14.99) r/series; sketch page by Gaydos 15.00

POWER LINE
Marvel Comics (Epic Comics): May, 1988 - No. 8, Sept, 1989 ($1.25/$1.50)
1-8: 2-Williamson-i. 3-Dr. Zero app. 4-7-Morrow-a. 8-Williamson-i 2.50

POWER LORDS
DC Comics: Dec, 1983 - No. 3, Feb, 1984 (Limited series, Mando paper)
1-3: Based on Revell toys 2.50

POWER MAN (Formerly Hero for Hire; ...& Iron Fist #50 on; see Cage & Giant-Size...)
Marvel Comics Group: No. 17, Feb, 1974 - No. 125, Sept, 1986
17-Luke Cage continues; Iron Man app. 3 6 9 14 20 25
18-20: 18-Last 20¢ issue 2 4 6 9 13 16
21-30 2 3 4 6 8 10
30-(30¢-c variant, limited distribution)(4/76) 3 6 9 17 25 32
31-46: 31-Part Neal Adams-i. 34-Last 25¢ issue. 36-r/Hero For Hire #12. 41-1st app. Thunderbolt. 45-Starlin-c. 1 2 3 5 7 9
31-34-(30¢-c variants, limited distribution)(5-8/76) 3 6 9 17 25 32
44-46-(35¢-c variants, limited distribution)(6-8/77) 4 8 12 22 34 45
47-Barry Smith-a 2 4 6 8 10 12
47-(35¢-c variant, limited distribution)(10/77) 4 8 12 26 41 55
48-50-Byrne-a(p); 48-Power Man/Iron Fist 1st meet. 50-Iron Fist joins Cage 2 4 6 9 13 16
51-56,58-65,67-77: 58-Intro El Aguila. 75-Double size. 77-Daredevil app. 5.00
57-New X-Men app. (6/79) 4 8 12 24 37 50
66-2nd app. Sabretooth (see Iron Fist #14) 5 10 15 30 48 65
78,84: 78-3rd app. Sabretooth (cameo under cloak). 84-4th app. Sabretooth 3 6 9 20 30 40
79-83,85-99,101-124: 87-Moon Knight app. 109-The Reaper app. 4.00
100,125-Double size: 100-Origin K'un L'un. 125-Death of Iron Fist 5.00
Annual 1(1976)-Punisher cameo in flashback 2 4 6 11 16 20
NOTE: ***Austin*** *c-102i.* ***Byrne*** *a-48-50; c-102, 104, 106, 107, 112-116.* ***Kane*** *c(p)-24, 25, 28, 48.* ***Miller*** *a-68, 76(2 pgs.); c-66-68, 70-74, 80i.* ***Mooney*** *a-38i, 53i, 55i.* ***Nebres*** *a-76p.* ***Nino*** *a-42i, 43i.* ***Perez*** *a-27.* ***B. Smith*** *a-47i.* ***Tuska*** *a(p)-17, 20, 24, 26, 28, 29, 36, 47. Painted c-75, 100.*

POWER OF PRIME
Malibu Comics (Ultraverse): July, 1995 - No. 4, Nov, 1995 ($2.50, lim. series)
1-4 2.50

POWER OF SHAZAM!, THE (See SHAZAM!)
DC Comics: 1994 (Painted graphic novel) (Prequel to new series)
Hardcover-($19.95)-New origin of Shazam!; Ordway painted-c/a & script 3 6 9 14 20 25
Softcover-($7.50), Softcover-($9.95)-New-c. 2 4 6 8 10 12

POWER OF SHAZAM!, THE
DC Comics: Mar, 1995 - No. 47, Mar, 1999; No. 48, Mar, 2010 ($1.50/$1.75/$1.95/$2.50)
1-Jerry Ordway scripts begin 4.00
2-20: 4-Begin $1.75-c. 6:Re-intro of Capt. Nazi. 8-Re-intro of Spy Smasher, Bulletman & Minuteman; Swan-a (7 pgs.). 11-Re-intro of Ibis, Swan-a(2 pgs.). 14-Gil Kane-a(p). 20-Superman-c/app.; "Final Night" 3.00
21-47: 21-Plastic Man-c/app. 22-Batman-c/app. 35,36-X-over w/Starman #39,40. 38-41-Mr. Mind. 43-Bulletman app. 45-JLA-c/app. 2.50
48-(3/10, $2.99) Blackest Night one-shot; Osiris rises as a Black Lantern; Kramer-a 3.00

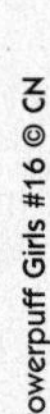
Power Pack: Day One #2 © MAR

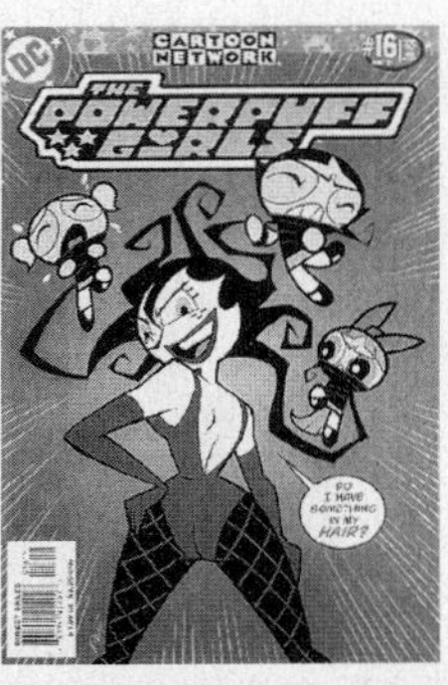

Powerpuff Girls #16 © CN

Powers V2 #17 © Jinxworld

GD 2.0 | VG 4.0 | FN 6.0 | VF 8.0 | VF/NM 9.0 | NM- 9.2

#1,000,000 (11/98) 853rd Century x-over; Ordway-c/s/a 3.00
Annual 1 (1996, $2.95)-Legends of the Dead Earth story; Jerry Ordway-c; Mike Manley-a 4.00

POWER OF STRONGMAN, THE (Also see Strongman)
AC Comics: 1989 ($2.95)
1-Powell G.A.-r 3.00

POWER OF THE ATOM (See Secret Origins #29)
DC Comics: Aug, 1988 - No. 18, Nov, 1989 ($1.00)
1-18: 6-Chronos returns; Byrne-p. 9-JLI app. 2.50

POWER PACHYDERMS
Marvel Comics: Sept, 1989 ($1.25, one-shot)
1-Elephant super-heroes; parody of X-Men, Elektra, & 3 Stooges 2.50

POWER PACK
Marvel Comics Group: Aug, 1984 - No. 62, Feb, 1991
1-($1.00, 52 pgs.)-Origin & 1st app. Power Pack 3.00
2-18,20-26,28,30-45,47-62 2.50
19-(52 pgs.)-Cloak & Dagger, Wolverine app. 3.00
27-Mutant massacre; Wolverine & Sabretooth app. 5.00
29,46: 29-Spider-Man & Hobgoblin app. 46-Punisher app. 2.75
Graphic Novel: Power Pack & Cloak & Dagger: Shelter From the Storm ('89, SC, $7.95) Velluto/Farmer-a 10.00
...Holiday Special 1 (2/92, $2.25, 68 pgs.) 2.50
NOTE: *Austin scripts-53. Mignola c-20. Morrow a-51. Spiegle a-55i. Williamson a(i)-43, 50, 52.*

POWER PACK (Volume 2)
Marvel Comics: Aug, 2000 - No. 4, Nov, 2000 ($2.99, limited series)
1-4-Doran & Austin-c/a 3.00

POWER PACK
Marvel Comics: June, 2005 - No. 4, Aug, 2005 ($2.99, limited series)
1-4-Sumerak-s/Gurihiru-a; back-up Franklin Richards story. 3-Fantastic Four app. 3.00
... Digest (2006, $6.99) r/#1-4 7.00

POWER PACK: DAY ONE
Marvel Comics: May, 2008 - No. 4, Aug, 2008($2.99, limited series)
1-4-Van Lente-s/Gurihiru-a; origin retold; Coover-a back-ups. 1-Fantastic Four cameo 3.00

POWERPUFF GIRLS, THE (Also see Cartoon Network Starring... #1)
DC Comics: May, 2000 - No. 70, Mar, 2006 ($1.99/$2.25)
1 4.00
2-55,57-70: 25-Pin-ups by Allred, Byrne, Baker, Mignola, Hernandez, Warren 2.50
56-($2.95) Bonus pages; Mojo Jojo-c 3.00
...Double Whammy (12/00, $3.95) r/#1,2 & a Dexter's Lab story 4.00
...Movie: The Comic (9/02, $2.95) Movie adaptation; Phil Moy & Chris Cook-a 3.00

POWER RANGERS ZEO (TV)(Saban's...)(Also see Saban's Mighty Morphin Power Rangers)
Image Comics (Extreme Studios): Aug, 1996 ($2.50)
1-Based on TV show 2.50

POWER RECORD COMICS (Named Peter Pan Record Comics for #34-47)
Marvel Comics/Power Records: 1974 - 1978 ($1.49, 7x10" comics, 20 pgs. with 45 R.P.M. record) (Clipped corners - reduce value 20%) (Comic alone - 50%; record alone - 50%)
PR10-Spider-Man-r/from #124,125; Man-Wolf app. PR18-Planet of the Apes-r. PR19-Escape From the Planet of the Apes-r. PR20-Beneath the Planet of the Apes-r. PR21-Battle for the Planet of the Apes-r. PR24-Spider-Man II-New-a begins. PR27-Batman "Stacked Cards"; N. Adams-a(p). PR30-Batman; N. Adams-r/Det.(7 pgs.).
With record; each... 5 10 15 34 55 75
PR11-Hulk-r. PR12-Captain America-r/#168. PR13-Fantastic Four-r/#126. PR14-Frankenstein -Ploog-r/#1. PR15-Tomb of Dracula-Colan-r/#2. PR16-Man-Thing-Ploog-r/#5. PR17-Werewolf By Night-Ploog-r/Marvel Spotlight #2. PR28-Superman "Alien Creatures". PR29-Space: 1999 "Breakaway". PR31-Conan-N. Adams-a; reprinted in Conan #116. PR32-Space: 1999 "Return to the Beginning". PR33-Superman-G.A. origin, Buckler-a(p). PR34-Superman. PR35-Wonder Woman-Buckler-a(p)
With record; each... 5 10 15 30 48 65
PR11-(1981 Peter Pan records re-issue) new Abomination & Rhino-c
With record 5 10 15 32 51 70
PR25-Star Trek "Passage to Moauv". PR26-Star Trek "Crier in Emptiness." PR36-Holo-Man. PR37-Robin Hood. PR39-Huckleberry Finn. PR40-Davy Crockett. PR41-Robinson Crusoe. PR42-20,000 Leagues Under the Sea. PR45-Star Trek "Dinosaur Planet". PR46-Star Trek "The Robot Masters". PR47-Little Women
With record; each... 4 8 12 26 41 55
NOTE: *Peter Pan re-issues exist for #25-34 and are valued the same.*

POWERS
Image Comics: 2000 - No. 37, Feb, 2004 ($2.95)
1-Bendis-s/Oeming-a; murder of Retro Girl 1 3 4 6 8 10
2-6: 6-End of Retro Girl arc. 5.00
7-14: 7-Warren Ellis app. 12-14-Death of Olympia 3.50
15-37: 31-36-Origin of the Powers 3.00
Annual 1 (2001, $3.95) 4.00
...: Anarchy TPB (11/03, $14.95) r/#21-24; interviews, sketchbook, cover gallery 15.00
...Coloring/Activity Book (2001, $1.50, B&W, 8 x 10.5") Oeming-a 2.50
...: Forever TPB (2005, $19.95) r/#31-37; script for #31, sketchbook, cover gallery 20.00
...: Little Deaths TPB (2002, $19.95) r/#7,12-14, Ann. #1, Coloring/Activity Book; sketch pages, cover gallery 20.00
...: Roleplay TPB (2001, $13.95) r/#8-11; sketchbook, cover gallery 14.00
... Scriptbook (2001, $19.95) scripts for #1-11; Oeming sketches 20.00
...: Supergroup TPB (2003, $19.95) r/#15-20; sketchbook, cover gallery 20.00
...: The Definitive Collection Vol. 1 HC (2006, $29.99, dust jacket) r/#1-11 & Coloring/Activity Book, script for #1, sketch pages and covers, interviews, letter column highlights 30.00
...: The Definitive Collection Vol. 2 HC (2009, $29.99, dust jacket) r/#12-24 & Annual #1; cover gallery; 1st Bendis/Oeming Jinx story; interviews, letter column highlights 30.00
...: Who Killed Retro Girl TPB (2000, $21.95) r/#1-6; sketchbook, cover gallery, and promotional strips from Comic Shop News 22.00

POWERS
Marvel Comics (Icon): Jul, 2004 - No. 30, Sept, 2008 ($2.95/$3.95)
1-11,13-24-Bendis-s/Oeming-a. 14-Cover price error 3.00
12-($3.95, 64 pages) 2 covers; Bendis & Oeming interview 4.00
25-30-($3.95, 40 pages) 25-Two covers; Bendis interview 4.00
Annual 2008 (5/08, $4.95) Bendis-s/Oeming-a; interview with Brubaker, Simone, others 5.00
...: Legends TPB (2005, $17.95) r/#1-6; sketchbook, cover gallery 18.00
...: Psychotic TPB (1/06, $19.95) r/#7-12; Bendis & Oeming interview, cover gallery 20.00
...: Cosmic TPB (10/07, $19.95) r/#13-18; script and sketch pages 20.00
...: Secret Identity TPB (12/07, $19.95) r/#19-24; script pages 20.00

POWERS (Volume 3)
Marvel Comics (Icon): Nov, 2009 - Present ($3.95)
1-3-Bendis-s/Oeming-a 4.00

POWERS THAT BE (Becomes Star Seed No.7 on)
Broadway Comics: Nov, 1995 - No. 6, June, 1996 ($2.50)
1-6: 1-Intro of Fatale & Star Seed. 6-Begin $2.95-c. 3.00
Preview Editions 1-3 (9/95 - 11/95, B&W) 2.50

POW MAGAZINE (Bob Sproul's) (Satire Magazine)
Humor-Vision: Aug, 1966 - No. 3, Feb, 1967 (30¢)
1,2: 2-Jones-a 5 10 15 30 48 65
3-Wrightson-a 6 12 18 39 62 85

PREACHER
DC Comics (Vertigo): Apr, 1995 - No. 66, Oct, 2000 ($2.50, mature)
nn-Preview 2 4 6 11 16 20
1 ($2.95)-Ennis scripts, Dillon-a & Fabry-c in all; 1st app. Jesse, Tulip, & Cassidy
2 4 6 8 11 14
1-Special Edition (6/09, $1.00) r/#1 with "After Watchmen" cover frame 1.00
2,3: 2-1st app. Saint of Killers. 1 2 3 5 7 9
4,5 1 2 3 4 5 7
6-10 5.00
11-20: 12-Polybagged w/videogame w/Ennis text. 13-Hunters storyline begins; ends #17. 19-Saint of Killers app.; begin "Crusaders", ends #24 4.00
21-25: 21-24-Saint of Killers app. 25-Origin of Cassidy. 3.00
26-49,52-64: 52-Tulip origin 2.50
50-($3.75) Pin-ups by Jim Lee, Bradstreet, Quesada and Palmiotti 3.75
51-Includes preview of 100 Bullets; Tulip origin 4.00
65,66-($3.75) 65-Almost everyone dies. 66-Final issue 5.00
Alamo (2001, $17.95, TPB) r/#59-66; Fabry-c 18.00
All Hell's a-Coming (2000, $17.95, TPB)-r/#51-58, ...:Tall in the Saddle 18.00
... Book One HC (2009, $39.99, d.j.) r/#1-12; new Ennis intro.; pin-ups from #50,66 40.00
... Book Two HC (2010, $39.99, d.j.) r/#13-26; new Stuart Moore intro. 40.00
...: Dead or Alive HC (2000, $29.95) Gallery of Glenn Fabry's cover paintings for every Preacher issue; commentary by Fabry & Ennis 30.00
...: Dead or Alive SC (2003, $19.95) 20.00
Dixie Fried (1998, $14.95, TPB)-r/#27-33, Special: Cassidy 15.00
Gone To Texas (1996, $14.95, TPB)-r/#1-7; Fabry-c 15.00
Proud Americans (1997, $14.95, TPB)-r/#18-26; Fabry-c 15.00
Salvation (1999, $14.95, TPB)-r/#41-50; Fabry-c 15.00
Until the End of the World (1996, $14.95, TPB)-r/#8-17; Fabry-c 15.00
War in the Sun (1999, $14.95, TPB)-r/#34-40 15.00

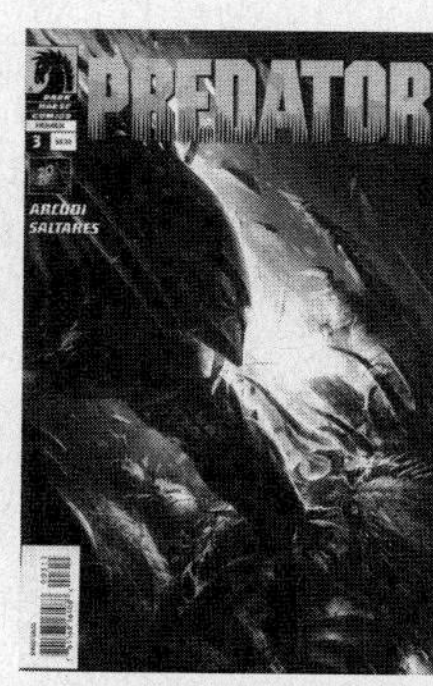

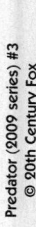

Predator (2009 series) #3 © 20th Century Fox

Prelude to Deadpool Corps #1 © MAR

Primal Force #7 © DC

	GD	VG	FN	VF	VF/NM	NM-
	2.0	4.0	6.0	8.0	9.0	9.2

PREACHER SPECIAL: CASSIDY: BLOOD & WHISKEY
DC Comics (Vertigo): 1998 ($5.95, one-shot)
1-Ennis-scripts/Fabry-c /Dillon-a 6.00

PREACHER SPECIAL: ONE MAN'S WAR
DC Comics (Vertigo): Mar, 1998 ($4.95, one-shot)
1-Ennis-scripts/Fabry-c /Snejbjerg-a 5.00

PREACHER SPECIAL: SAINT OF KILLERS
DC Comics (Vertigo): Aug, 1996 - No. 4, Nov, 1996 ($2.50, lim. series, mature)
1-4: Ennis-scripts/Fabry-c. 1,2-Pugh-a. 3,4-Ezquerra-a 3.00
1-Signed & numbered 20.00

PREACHER SPECIAL: THE GOOD OLD BOYS
DC Comics (Vertigo): Aug, 1997 ($4.95, one-shot, mature)
1-Ennis-scripts/Fabry-c /Esquerra-a 5.00

PREACHER SPECIAL: THE STORY OF YOU-KNOW-WHO
DC Comics (Vertigo): Dec, 1996 ($4.95, one-shot, mature)
1-Ennis-scripts/Fabry-c/Case-a 5.00

PREACHER: TALL IN THE SADDLE
DC Comics (Vertigo): 2000 ($5.95, one-shot)
1-Ennis-scripts/Fabry-c/Dillon-a; early romance of Tulip and Jesse 6.00

PREDATOR (Also see Aliens Vs. ..., Batman vs. ..., Dark Horse Comics, & Dark Horse Presents)
Dark Horse Comics: June, 1989 - No. 4, Mar, 1990 ($2.25, limited series)
1-Based on movie; 1st app. Predator 1 2 3 4 5 7
1-2nd printing 3.00
2 5.00
3,4 4.00
Trade paperback (1990, $12.95)-r/#1-4 13.00
... Omnibus Volume 1 (8/07, $24.95, 6" x 9") r/#1-4, ... Cold War, ... Dark River, ...Bloody Sands of Time mini-series and stories from Dark Horse Comics #1,2,4-7,10-12 25.00
... Omnibus Volume 2 (2/08, $24.95, 6" x 9") r/ ... Big Game, ... Race War, ...Invaders From The, Fourth Dimension mini-series and stories from Dark Horse Comics #16-18,20,21; Dark Horse Presents #46 and A Decade of Dark Horse 25.00
... Omnibus Volume 3 (6/08, $24.95, 6" x 9") r/ ... Bad Blood, ... Kindred, ...Hell and Hot Water, ... Strange Roux mini-series and stories from Dark Horse Comics #12-14 and Dark Horse Presents #119 & 124 25.00

PREDATOR
Dark Horse Comics: June, 2009 - No. 4, Jan, 2010 ($3.50, limited series)
1-4-Arcudi-s/Saltares-a/Swanland-c; variant-c by Warner 3.50

PREDATOR: (title series) **Dark Horse Comics**
--BAD BLOOD, 12/93 - No. 4, 1994 ($2.50) 1-4 3.00
--BIG GAME, 3/91 - No. 4, 6/91 ($2.50) 1-4: 1-3-Contain 2 Dark Horse trading cards 3.00
--BLOODY SANDS OF TIME, 2/92 - No. 2, 2/92 ($2.50) 1,2-Dan Barry-c/a(p)/scripts 3.00
--CAPTIVE, 4/98 ($2.95, one-shot) 1 3.00
--COLD WAR, 9/91 - No. 4, 12/91 ($2.50) 1-4: All have painted-c 3.00
--DARK RIVER, 7/96 - No.4, 10/96 ($2.95)1-4: Miran Kim-c 3.00
--HELL & HOT WATER, 4/97 - No. 3, 6/97 ($2.95) 1-3 3.00
--HELL COME A WALKIN', 2/98 - No. 2, 3/98 ($2.95) 1,2-In the Civil War 3.00
--HOMEWORLD, 3/99 - No. 4, 6/99 ($2.95) 1-4 3.00
--INVADERS FROM THE FOURTH DIMENSION, 7/94 ($3.95, one-shot, 52 pgs.) 1 4.00
--JUNGLE TALES. 3/95 ($2.95t) 1-r/Dark Horse Comics 3.00
--KINDRED, 12/96 - No. 4, 3/97 ($2.50) 1-4 3.00
--NEMESIS, 12/97 - No. 2, 1/98 ($2.95) 1,2-Predator in Victorian England; Taggart-c 3.00
--PRIMAL, 7/97 - No. 2, 8/97 ($2.95) 1,2 3.00
--RACE WAR (See Dark Horse Presents #67), 2/93 - No. 4,10/93 ($2.50, color)
1-4,0: 1-4-Dorman painted-c #1-4, 0(4/93) 3.00
--STRANGE ROUX, 11/96 ($2.95, one-shot) 1 3.00
--XENOGENESIS (Also see Aliens Xenogenesis), 8/99 - No. 4, 11/99 ($2.95)
1,2-Edginton-s 3.00

PREDATOR 2
Dark Horse Comics: Feb, 1991 - No. 2, June, 1991 ($2.50, limited series)
1,2: 1-Adapts movie; both w/trading cards & photo-c 3.00

PREDATOR VS. JUDGE DREDD
Dark Horse Comics: Oct, 1997 - No. 3 ($2.50, limited series)
1-3-Wagner-s/Alcatena-a/Bolland-c 3.00

PREDATOR VS. MAGNUS ROBOT FIGHTER
Dark Horse/Valiant: Oct, 1992 - No. 2, 1993 ($2.95, limited series)
(1st Dark Horse/Valiant x-over)
1,2: (Reg.)-Barry Smith-c; Lee Weeks-a. 2-w/trading cards 3.00
1 (Platinum edition, 11/92)-Barry Smith-c 10.00

PREHISTORIC WORLD (See Classics Illustrated Special Issue)

PRELUDE TO DEADPOOL CORPS (Leads into Deadpool Corps #1)
Marvel Comics: May, 2010 - No. 5, May, 2010 ($3.99/$2.99, weekly limited series)
1-($3.99) Deadpool & Lady Deadpool vs. alternate dimension Capt. America; Liefeld-a 4.00
2-5-($2.99) Alternate reality Deadpools team-up; Dave Johnson interlocking covers 3.00

PRELUDE TO INFINITE CRISIS
DC Comics: 2005 ($5.99, squarebound)
nn-Reprints stories and panels with commentary leading into Infinite Crisis series 6.00

PREMIERE (See Charlton Premiere)

PRESIDENTIAL MATERIAL
IDW Publishing: Oct, 2008 ($3.99/$7.99)
...: Barack Obama - Biography of the candidate; Mariotte-s/Morgan-a/Campbell-c 4.00
...: John McCain - Biography of the candidate; Helfer-s/Thompson-a/Campbell-c 4.00
Flipbook ($7.99) Both issues in flipbook format 8.00

PRESTO KID, THE (See Red Mask)

PRETTY BOY FLOYD (See On the Spot)

PREZ (See Cancelled Comic Cavalcade, Sandman #54 & Supergirl #10)
National Periodical Publications: Aug-Sept, 1973 - No. 4, Feb-Mar, 1974
1-Origin; Joe Simon scripts 3 6 9 18 27 35
2-4 2 4 6 13 18 22

PRICE, THE (See Eclipse Graphic Album Series)

PRIDE & JOY
DC Comics (Vertigo): July, 1997 - No. 4, Oct, 1997 ($2.50, limited series)
1-4-Ennis-s 2.50
TPB (2004, $14.95) r/#1-4 15.00

PRIDE & PREJUDICE
Marvel Comics: June, 2009 - No. 5, Oct, 2009 ($3.99, limited series)
1-5-Adaptation of the Jane Austen novel; Nancy Butler-s/Hugo Petrus-a 4.00

PRIDE AND THE PASSION, THE
Dell Publishing Co.: No. 824, Aug, 1957
Four Color 824-Movie, Frank Sinatra & Cary Grant photo-c
9 18 27 63 107 150

PRIDE OF BAGHDAD
DC Comics (Vertigo): 2006 ($19.99, hardcover with dustjacket)
HC-A pride of lions escaping from the Baghdad zoo in 2003; Vaughan-s/Henrichon-a 20.00
SC-(2007, $12.99) 13.00

PRIDE OF THE YANKEES, THE (See Real Heroes & Sport Comics)
Magazine Enterprises: 1949 (The Life of Lou Gehrig)
nn-Photo-c; Ogden Whitney-a 82 164 246 521 893 1265

PRIEST (Also see Asylum)
Maximum Press: Aug, 1996 - No. 2, Oct, 1996 ($2.99)
1,2 3.00

PRIMAL FORCE
DC Comics: No. 0, Oct, 1994 - No. 14, Dec, 1995 ($1.95/$2.25)
0-14: 0- Teams Red Tornado, Golem, Jack O'Lantern, Meridian & Silver Dragon. 9-begin $2.25-c 2.50

PRIMAL MAN (See The Crusaders)

PRIMAL RAGE
Sirius Entertainment: 1996 ($2.95)
1-Dark One-c; based of video game 3.00

PRIME (See Break-Thru, Flood Relief & Ultraforce)
Malibu Comics (Ultraverse): June, 1993 - No. 26, Aug, 1995 ($1.95/$2.50)
1-1st app. Prime; has coupon for Ultraverse Premiere #0 3.00
1-With coupon missing 2.00
1-Full cover holographic edition; 1st of kind w/Hardcase #1 & Strangers #1 6.00
1-Ultra 5,000 edition w/silver ink-c 4.00
2-11,14-26: 2-Polybagged w/card & coupon for U. Premiere #0. 3,4-Prototype app. 4-Direct

Primer #1 © Comico

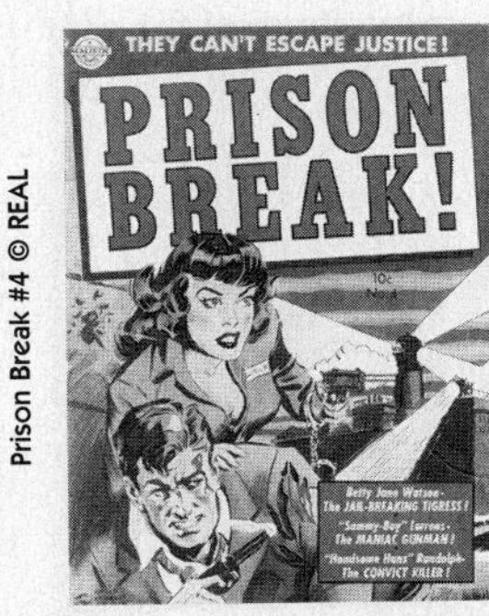

Prison Break #4 © REAL

Prize Comics #2 © PRIZE

GD VG FN VF VF/NM NM-
2.0 4.0 6.0 8.0 9.0 9.2

sale w/o card.4-($2.50)-Newsstand ed. polybagged w/card. 5-($2.50, 48 pgs.)-Rune flip-c/ story part B by Barry Smith; see Sludge #1 for 1st app. Rune; 3-pg. Night Man preview.
6-Bill & Chelsea Clinton app.115-Intro Papa Verite; Perez-c/a. 16-Intro Turbo Charge 2.50
12-($3.50, 68 pgs.)-Flip book w/Ultraverse Premiere #3; silver foil logo 3.50
13-($2.95, 52 pgs.)-Variant covers 3.00
...: Gross and Disgusting 1 (10/94, $3.95)-Boris-c; "Annual" on cover, published monthly in indicia 4.00
...Month "Ashcan" (8/94, 75¢)-Boris-c 2.50
... Time: A Prime Collection (1994, $9.95)-r/1-4 10.00
...Vs. The Incredible Hulk (1995)-mail away limited edition 10.00
...Vs. The Incredible Hulk Premium edition 10.00
...Vs. The Incredible Hulk Super Premium edition 15.00
NOTE: *Perez a-15; c-15, 16.*

PRIME (Also see Black September)
Malibu Comics (Ultraverse): Infinity, Sept, 1995 - V2#15, Dec, 1996 ($1.50)
Infinity, V2#1-8: Post Black September storyline. 6-8-Solitaire app. 9-Breyfogle-c/a. 10-12-Ramos-c. 15-Lord Pumpkin app. 2.50
Infinity Signed Edition (2,000 printed) 5.00

PRIME/CAPTAIN AMERICA
Malibu Comics: Mar, 1996 ($3.95, one-shot)
1-Norm Breyfogle-a 4.00

PRIME8: CREATION
Two Morrows Publishing: July, 2001 ($3.95, B&W)
1-Neal Adams-c 4.00

PRIMER (Comico...)
Comico: Oct (no month), 1982 - No. 6, Feb, 1984 (B&W)
1 (52 pgs.) 2 4 6 11 16 20
2-1st app. Grendel & Argent by Wagner 9 18 27 63 107 150
3,4 2 4 6 9 12 15
5-1st Sam Kieth art in comics ('83) & 1st The Maxx 4 8 12 24 37 50
6-Intro & 1st app. Evangeline 2 4 6 13 18 22

PRIMORTALS (Leonard Nimoy's...)

PRIMUS (TV)
Charlton Comics: Feb, 1972 - No. 7, Oct, 1972
1-Staton-a in all 2 4 6 11 16 20
2-7: 6-Drug propaganda story 2 4 6 8 11 14

PRINCE NAMOR, THE SUB-MARINER (Also see Namor ...)
Marvel Comics Group: Sept, 1984 - No. 4, Dec, 1984 (Limited-series)
1-4 2.50

PRINCESS SALLY (Video game)
Archie Publications: Apr, 1995 - No. 3, June, 1995 ($1.50, limited series)
1-3: Spin-off from Sonic the Hedgehog 4.00

PRINCE VALIANT (See Ace Comics, Comics Reading Libraries *in the Promotional Comics section*, & King Comics #146, 147)
David McKay Publ./Dell: No. 26, 1941; No. 67, June, 1954 - No. 900, May, 1958
Feature Books 26 ('41)-Harold Foster-c/a; newspaper strips reprinted, pgs. 1-28,30-63; color & 68 pgs; Foster cover is only original comic book artwork by him
100 200 300 635 1093 1550
Four Color 567 (6/54)(#1)-By Bob Fuje-Movie, photo-c
10 20 30 73 129 185
Four Color 650 (9/55), 699 (4/56), 719 (8/56),-Fuje-a 7 14 21 50 83 115
Four Color 788 (4/57), 849 (1/58), 900-Fuje-a 7 14 21 47 76 105

PRINCE VALIANT
Marvel Comics: Dec, 1994 - No. 4, Mar, 1995 ($3.95, limited series)
1-4; Kaluta-c in all. 4.00

PRINCE VANDAL
Triumphant Comics: Nov, 1993 - Apr?, 1994 ($2.50)
1-6: 1,2-Triumphant Unleashed x-over 2.50

PRIORITY: WHITE HEAT
AC Comics: 1986 - No. 2, 1986 ($1.75, mini-series)
1,2-Bill Black-a 3.00

PRISCILLA'S POP
Dell Publishing Co.: No. 569, June, 1954 - No. 799, May, 1957
Four Color 569 (#1), 630 (5/55), 704 (5/56),799 4 8 12 26 41 55

PRISON BARS (See Behind...)

PRISON BREAK!
Avon Per./Realistic No. 3 on: Sept, 1951 - No. 5, Sept, 1952 (Painted c-3)
1-Wood-c & 1 pg.; has-r/Saint #7 retitled Michael Strong Private Eye
41 82 123 256 428 600
2-Wood-c; Kubert-a; Kinstler inside front-c 30 60 90 177 289 400
3-Orlando, Check-a; c-/Avon paperback #179 24 48 72 140 230 320
4,5: 4-Kinstler-c & inside f/c; Lawrence, Lazarus-a. 5-Kinstler-c; Infantino-a
21 42 63 122 199 275

PRISONER, THE (TV)
DC Comics: 1988 - No. 4, 1989 ($3.50, squarebound, mini-series)
1-4 (Books a-d) 3.50

PRISON RIOT
Avon Periodicals: 1952
1-Marijuana Murders-1 pg. text; Kinstler-c; 2 Kubert illos on text pages
28 56 84 165 270 375

PRISON TO PRAISE
Logos International: 1974 (35¢) (Religious, Christian)
nn-True Story of Merlin R. Carothers 2 4 6 10 14 18

PRIVATE BUCK
Dell Publishing Co./Rand McNally: No. 21, 1941 - No. 12, 1942 (4-1/2" x 5-1/2", 1942)
Large Feature Comic 21 (#1)(1941)(Series I), 22 (1941)(Series I), 12 (1942)(Series II)
17 34 51 98 154 210
382-Rand McNally, one panel per page; small size 10 20 30 58 79 100

PRIVATE EYE (Cover title: Rocky Jorden...#6-8)
Atlas Comics (MCI): Jan, 1951 - No. 8, March, 1952
1-Cover title: Crime Cases... #1-5 21 42 63 122 199 275
2,3-Tuska c/a(3) 14 28 42 76 108 140
4-8 11 22 33 60 83 105
NOTE: *Henkel a-6(3), 7; c-7.* ***Sinnott*** *a-6.*

PRIVATE EYE (See Mike Shayne...)

PRIVATE SECRETARY
Dell Publishing Co.: Dec-Feb, 1962-63 - No. 2, Mar-May, 1963
1 3 6 9 21 32 42
2 3 6 9 17 25 32

PRIVATE STRONG (See The Double Life of...)

PRIZE COMICS (...Western #69 on) (Also see Treasure Comics)
Prize Publications: March, 1940 - No. 68, Feb-Mar, 1948
1-Origin Power Nelson, The Futureman & Jupiter, Master Magician; Ted O'Neil, Secret Agent M-11, Jaxon of the Jungle, Bucky Brady & Storm Curtis begin (1st app. of each)
274 548 822 1740 2995 4250
2-The Black Owl begins (1st app.) 119 238 357 762 1306 1850
3 103 206 309 659 1130 1600
4-Classic robot-c 119 238 357 762 1306 1850
5,6: Dr. Dekkar, Master of Monsters app. in each 95 190 285 603 1039 1475
7-(Scarce)-1st app. The Green Lama (12/40); Black Owl by S&K; origin/1st app. Dr. Frost & Frankenstein; Capt. Gallant, The Great Voodini & Twist Turner begin;
226 452 678 1446 2473 3500
8,9-Black Owl & Ted O'Neil by S&K 100 200 300 635 1093 1550
10-12,14,15: 11-Origin Bulldog Denny. 14-War-c 73 146 219 467 796 1125
13-Yank & Doodle begin (8/41, origin/1st app.) 79 158 237 502 864 1225
16-20: 16-Spike Mason begins 66 132 198 419 722 1025
21,25,27,28,31-All WWII covers 52 104 156 328 552 775
22-24,26: 22-Statue of Liberty Japanese attack war-c. 23-Uncle Sam patriotic war-c. 24-Lincoln statue patriotic-c. 26-Liberty Bell-c 57 114 171 362 619 875
29,30 41 82 123 256 428 600
32 36 72 108 211 343 475
33-Classic bondage/torture-c 43 86 129 271 461 650
34-Origin Airmale, Yank & Doodle; The Black Owl joins army, Yank & Doodle's father assumes Black Owl's role 37 74 111 222 361 500
35-36,38-40: 35-Flying Fist & Bingo begin 26 52 78 154 252 350
37-Intro. Stampy, Airmale's sidekick; Hitler-c 47 94 141 296 498 700
41-45,47-50: 45-Yank & Doodle learn Black Owl's I.D. (their father). 48-Prince Ra begins
21 42 63 122 199 275
46-Classic Zombie Horror-c/story 30 60 90 177 289 400
51-62,64,67,68: 53-Transvestism story. 55-No Frankenstein. 57-X-Mas-c. 64-Black Owl retires 16 32 48 94 147 200
63-Simon & Kirby c/a 20 40 60 114 182 250
65,66-Frankenstein-c by Briefer 18 36 54 103 162 220
NOTE: ***Briefer*** *a 7-on; c-65, 66.* ***J. Binder*** *a-16; c-21-29.* ***Guardineer*** *a-62.* ***Kiefer*** *c-62.* ***Palais*** *c-68.* ***Simon & Kirby*** *c-63, 75, 83.*

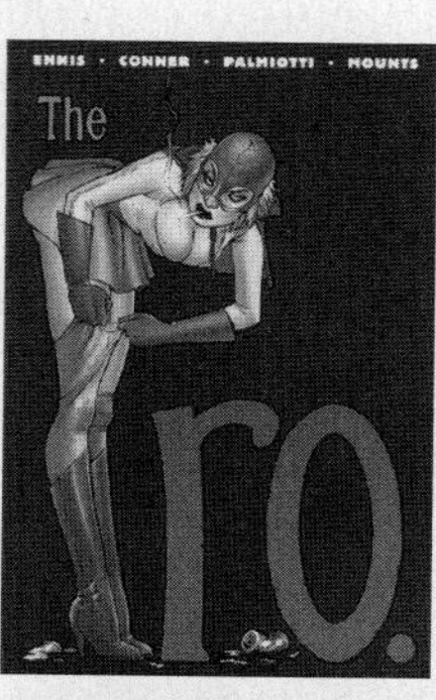

The Pro #1 © Ennis, Palmiotti & Conner

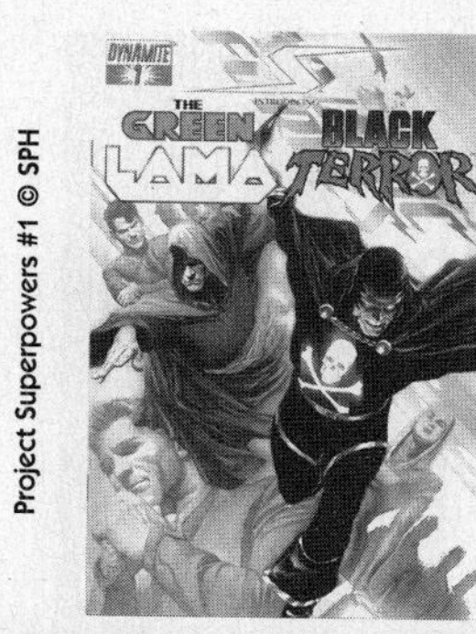

Project Superpowers #1 © SPH

Promethea #10 © ABC

	GD 2.0	VG 4.0	FN 6.0	VF 8.0	VF/NM 9.0	NM- 9.2

PRIZE COMICS WESTERN (Formerly Prize Comics #1-68)
Prize Publications (Feature): No. 69(V7#2), Apr-May, 1948 - No. 119, Nov-Dec, 1956 (No. 69-84: 52 pgs.)

69(V7#2) 14 28 42 80 115 150
70-75: 74-Kurtzman-a (8 pgs.) 12 24 36 67 94 120
76-Randolph Scott photo-c; "Canadian Pacific" movie adaptation 13 26 39 72 101 130
77-Photo-c; Severin/Elder, Mart Bailey-a; "Streets of Laredo" movie adaptation 12 24 36 67 94 120
78-Photo-c; S&K-a, 10 pgs.; Severin, Mart Bailey-a; "Bullet Code", & "Roughshod" movie adaptations 15 30 45 90 140 190
79-Photo-c; Kurtzman-a, 8 pgs.; Severin/Elder, Severin, Mart Bailey-a; "Stage To Chino" movie adaptation w/George O'Brien 15 30 45 90 140 190
80-82-Photo-c; 80,81-Severin/Elder-a(2). 82-1st app. The Preacher by Mart Bailey; Severin/Elder-a(3) 13 26 39 72 101 130
83,84 10 20 30 58 79 100
85-1st app. American Eagle by John Severin & begins (V9#6, 1-2/51) 19 38 57 111 176 240
86,101-105, 109-Severin/Williamson-a 11 22 33 64 90 115
87-99,110,111-Severin/Elder-a(2-3) each 12 24 36 69 97 125
100 13 26 39 74 105 135
106-108,112 9 18 27 47 61 75
113-Williamson/Severin-a(2)/Frazetta? 12 24 36 69 97 125
114-119: Drifter series in all; by Mort Meskin #114-118 8 16 24 42 54 65

NOTE: ***Fass** a-81. **Severin & Elder** c-84-99. **Severin** a-72, 75, 77-79, 83-86, 96, 97, 100-105; c-92,100-109(most), 110-119. **Simon & Kirby** c-75, 83.*

PRIZE MYSTERY
Key Publications: May, 1955 - No. 3, Sept, 1955

1 11 22 33 60 83 105
2,3 8 16 24 44 57 70

PRO, THE
Image Comics: July, 2002 ($5.95, squarebound, one-shot)

1-Ennis-s/Conner & Palmiotti-a; prostitute gets super-powers 8.00
1-Second printing with different cover 6.00
Hardcover Edition (10/04, $14.95) oversized reprint plus new 8 pg. story; sketch pages 15.00

PROFESSIONAL FOOTBALL (See Charlton Sport Library)

PROFESSOR COFFIN
Charlton Comics: No. 19, Oct, 1985 - No. 21, Feb, 1986

19-21: Wayne Howard-a(r); low print run 1 2 3 5 6 8

PROFESSOR OM
Innovation Publishing: May, 1990 - No. 2, 1990 ($2.50, limited series)

1,2-East Meets West spin-off 2.50

PROFESSOR XAVIER AND THE X-MEN (Also see X-Men, 1st series)
Marvel Comics: Nov, 1995 - No. 18 (99¢)

1-18: Stories featuring the Original X-Men. 2-vs. The Blob. 5-Vs. the Original Brotherhood of Evil Mutants. 10-Vs. The Avengers 2.50

PROGRAMME, THE
DC Comics (WildStorm): Sept, 2007 - No. 12, Aug, 2008 ($2.99, limited series)

1-12: 1-Milligan-s/C.P. Smith-a; covers by Smith & Van Sciver 3.00
Book One TPB (2008, $17.99) r/#1-6; cover sketches 18.00
Book Two TPB (2008, $17.99) r/#7-12; cover sketches 18.00

PROJECT A-KO (Manga)
Malibu Comics: Mar, 1994 - No. 4, June, 1994 ($2.95)

1-4-Based on anime film 3.00

PROJECT A-KO 2 (Manga)
CPM Comics: May, 1995 - No. 3, Aug, 1995 ($2.95, limited series)

1-3 3.00

PROJECT A-KO VERSUS THE UNIVERSE (Manga)
CPM Comics: Oct, 1995 - No. 5, June, 1996 ($2.95, limited series, bi-monthly)

1-5 3.00

PROJECT SUPERPOWERS
Dynamite Entertainment: 2008 - No. 7, 2008 ($1.00/$3.50/$2.99)

0-($1.00) Two connecting covers by Alex Ross; re-intro of Golden Age heroes 3.00
0-($1.00) Variant cover by Michael Turner 5.00
1-($3.50) Covers by Ross and Turner; Jim Krueger-s/Carlos Paul-a 3.50
2-7-($2.99) 3.00
... Chapter One HC (2008, $29.99, dustjacket) r/#0-7; Ross sketch pages; layout art 30.00

PROJECT SUPERPOWERS: CHAPTER TWO
Dynamite Entertainment: 2009 - Present ($1.00/$2.99)

... Chapter Two Prelude (2008, $1.00) Ross sketch pages and mini-series previews 2.50
0-($1.00) Three connecting covers by Alex Ross; The Inheritors assemble 2.50
1-7-($2.99) 1-Krueger & Ross-s/Salazar-a; Ross sketch pages; 2 Ross covers 3.00

PROJECT SUPERPOWERS: MEET THE BAD GUYS
Dynamite Entertainment: 2009 - No. 4, 2009 ($2.99)

1-4: Ross & Casey-s. 1-Bloodlust. 2-The Revolutionary. 3-Dagon. 4-Supremacy 3.00

PROMETHEA
America's Best Comics: Aug, 1999 - No. 32, Apr, 2005 ($3.50/$2.95)

1-Alan Moore-s/Williams III & Gray-a; Alex Ross painted-c 3.50
1-Variant-c by Williams III & Gray 3.50
2-31-($2.95): 7-Villarrubia photo-a. 10-"Sex, Stars & Serpents". 26-28-Tom Strong app. 27-Cover swipe of Superman vs. Spider-Man treasury ed. 3.00
32-($3.95) Final issue; pages can be cut & assembled into a 2-sided poster 4.00
32-Limited edition of 1000; variant issue printed as 2-sided poster, signed by Moore and Williams; each came with a 48 page book of Promethea covers 120.00
Book 1 Hardcover ($24.95, dust jacket) r/#1-6 25.00
Book 1 TPB ($14.95) r/#1-6 15.00
Book 2 Hardcover ($24.95, dust jacket) r/#7-12 25.00
Book 2 TPB ($14.95) r/#7-12 15.00
Book 3 Hardcover ($24.95, dust jacket) r/#13-18 25.00
Book 3 TPB ($14.95) r/#13-18 15.00
Book 4 Hardcover ($24.95, dust jacket) r/#19-25 25.00
Book 4 TPB ($14.99) r/#19-25 15.00
Book 5 Hardcover ($24.95, d.j.) r/#26-32; includes 2-sided poster image from #32 25.00
Book 5 TPB ($14.99) r/#26-32; includes 2-sided poster image from #32 15.00

PROMETHEUS (VILLAINS) (Leads into JLA #16,17)
DC Comics: Feb, 1998 ($1.95, one-shot)

1-Origin & 1st app.; Morrison-s/Pearson-c 3.00

PROPELLERMAN
Dark Horse Comics: Jan, 1993 - No. 8, Mar, 1994 ($2.95, limited series)

1-8: 2,4,8-Contain 2 trading cards 3.00

PROPHET (See Youngblood #2)
Image Comics (Extreme Studios): Oct, 1993 - No. 10, 1995 ($1.95)

1-($2.50)-Liefeld/Panosian-c/a; 1st app. Mary McCormick; Liefeld scripts in 1-4; #1-3 contain coupons for Prophet #0 2.50
1-Gold foil embossed-c edition rationed to dealers 4.00
2-10: 2-Liefeld-c(p). 3-1st app. Judas. 4-1st app. Omen; Black and White Pt. 3 by Thibert. 4-Alternate-c by Stephen Platt. 5,6-Platt-c/a. 7-(9/94, $2.50)-Platt-c/a. 8-Bloodstrike app. 10-Polybagged w/trading card; Platt-c. 2.50
0-(7/94, $2.50)-San Diego Comic Con ed. (2200 copies) 3.00

PROPHET
Image Comics (Extreme Studios): V2#1, Aug, 1995 - No. 8 ($3.50)

V2#1-8: Dixon scripts in all. 1-4-Platt-a. 1-Boris-c; F. Miller variant-c. 4-Newmen app. 5,6-Wraparound-c 3.50
Annual 1 (9/95, $2.50)-Bagged w/Youngblood gaming card; Quesada-c 2.50
Babewatch Special 1 (12/95, $2.50)-Babewatch tie-in 2.50
1995 San Diego Edition-B&W preview of V2#1. 3.00
TPB-(1996, $12.95) r/#1-7 13.00

PROPHET (Volume 3)
Awesome Comics: Mar, 2000 ($2.99)

1-Flip-c by Jim Lee and Liefeld 3.00

PROPHET/CABLE
Image Comics (Extreme): Jan, 1997 - No. 2, Mar, 1997 ($3.50, limited series)

1,2-Liefeld-c/a: 2-#1 listed on cover 3.50

PROPHET/CHAPEL: SUPER SOLDIERS
Image Comics (Extreme): May, 1996 - No. 2, June, 1996 ($2.50, limited series)

1,2: 1-Two covers exist 2.50
1-San Diego Edition; B&W-c 2.50

PROPOSITION PLAYER
DC Comics (Vertigo): Dec, 1999 - No. 6, May, 2000 ($2.50, limited series)

1-6-Willingham-s/Guinan-a/Bolton-c 2.50
TPB (2003, $14.95) r/#1-6; intro. by James McManus 15.00

PROTECTORS (Also see The Ferret)
Malibu Comics: Sept, 1992 - No. 20, May, 1994 ($1.95-$2.95)

Prototype #4 © Sierra Ent.

Psylocke #1 © MAR

Pudgy Pig #1 © CC

	GD 2.0	VG 4.0	FN 6.0	VF 8.0	VF/NM 9.0	NM- 9.2

1-20 ($2.50, direct sale)-With poster & diff-c: 1-Origin; has 3/4 outer-c. 3-Polybagged w/Skycap — 2.50
1-12 ($1.95, newsstand)-Without poster — 2.25

PROTOTYPE (Also see Flood Relief & Ultraforce)
Malibu Comics (Ultraverse): Aug, 1993 - No. 18, Feb, 1995 ($1.95/$2.50)

1-Holo-c — 6.00
1-Ultra Limited silver foil-c — 4.00
1-12,0,14-18: 3-($2.50, 48 pgs.)-Rune flip-c/story by B. Smith (3 pgs.). 4-Intro Wrath. 5-Break-Thru & Strangers x-over. 6-Arena cameo. 7,8-Arena-c/story. 12-(7/94). 0-(8/94, $2.50, 44 pgs.), 14(10/94) — 2.50
13 (8/94, $3.50)-Flip book(Ultraverse Premiere #6) — 3.50
Giant Size 1 (10/94, $2.50, 44 pgs.) — 2.50

PROTOTYPE (Based on the Activision video game)
DC Comics (WildStorm): Jun, 2009 - No. 6, Nov, 2009 ($3.99, limited series)

1-6-Darick Robertson-c/a — 4.00

PRUDENCE & CAUTION (Also see Dogs of War & Warriors of Plasm)
Defiant: May, 1994 - No. 2, June, 1994 ($3.50/$2.50)(Spanish versions exist)

1-($3.50, 52 pgs.)-Chris Claremont scripts in all — 3.50
2-($2.50) — 2.50

PRYDE AND WISDOM (Also see Excalibur)
Marvel Comics: Sept, 1996 - No. 3, Nov, 1996 ($1.95, limited series)

1-3: Warren Ellis scripts; Terry Dodson & Karl Story-c/a — 2.50

PSI-FORCE
Marvel Comics Group: Nov, 1986 - No. 32, June, 1989 (75¢/$1.50)

1-25: 11-13-Williamson-i — 2.50
26-32 — 2.50
Annual 1 (10/87) — 3.00
... Classic Vol. 1 TPB (2008, $24.99) r/#1-9 — 25.00

PSI-JUDGE ANDERSON
Fleetway Publications (Quality): 1989 - No. 15, 1990 ($1.95, B&W)

1-15 — 2.50

PSI-LORDS
Valiant: Sept, 1994 - No. 10, June, 1995 ($2.25)

1-($3.50)-Chromium wraparound-c — 3.50
1-Gold — 5.00
2-10: 3-Chaos Effect Epsilon Pt. 2 — 2.50

PSYBA-RATS (Also see Showcase '94 #3,4)
DC Comics: Apr, 1995-No. 3, June, 1995 ($2.50, limited series)

1-3 — 2.50

PSYCHO (Magazine) (Also see Nightmare)
Skywald Publ. Corp.: Jan, 1971 - No. 24, Mar, 1975 (68 pgs.; B&W)

	GD	VG	FN	VF	VF/NM	NM-
1-All reprints	9	18	27	60	100	140
2-Origin & 1st app. The Heap, series begins	6	12	18	41	66	90
3-Frankenstein series by Adkins begins	6	12	18	39	62	85
4,7,9,10: 4-7-Squarebound. 4-1st Out of Chaos/Satan-c/s	5	10	15	34	55	75
8-(Squarebound)1st app. Edward & Mina Sartyros, the Human Gargoyles	6	12	18	39	62	85
11-18: 13-Cannabalism; 3 pgs of Christopher Lee as Dracula photos. 18-Injury to eye-c.	4	8	12	26	41	55
19-Origin Dracula.	4	8	12	28	44	60
20-Severed Head-c	5	10	15	34	55	75
21-24: 22-1974 Fall Special; Reese, Wildey-a(r). 24-1975 Winter Special; Dave Sim scripts (1st pro work)	5	10	15	30	48	65
Annual 1 (1972)(68 pgs.) Dracula & the Heap app.	5	10	15	30	48	65
Yearbook (1974-nn)-Everett, Reese-a	4	8	12	26	41	55

NOTE: ***Boris** c-3, 5. **Buckler** a-2, 4, 5. **Gene Day** a-21, 23, 24. **Everett** a-3-6. **B. Jones** a-4. **Jeff Jones** a-6, 7, 9; c-12. **Kaluta** a-13. **Katz/Buckler** a-3. **Kim** a-24. **Morrow** a-1. **Reese** a-5. **Dave Sim** s-24. **Sutton** a-3. **Wildey** a-5.*

PSYCHO, THE
DC Comics: 1991 - No. 3, 1991 ($4.95, squarebound, limited series)

1-3-Hudnall-s/Brereton painted-a/c — 5.00
TPB (Image Comics, 2006, $17.99) r/series; Brereton sketch pages; Hudnall afterword — 18.00

PSYCHOANALYSIS
E. C. Comics: Mar-Apr, 1955 - No. 4, Sept-Oct, 1955

	GD	VG	FN	VF	VF/NM	NM-
1-All Kamen-c/a; not approved by code	20	40	60	160	255	350
2-4-Kamen-c/a in all	14	28	42	112	176	240

PSYCHOANALYSIS
Gemstone Publishing: Oct, 1999 - No. 4, Jan, 2000 ($2.50)

1-4-Reprints E.C. series — 2.50
Annual 1 (2000, $10.95) r/#1-4 — 11.00

PSYCHOBLAST
First Comics: Nov, 1987 - No. 9, July, 1988 ($1.75)

1-9 — 2.50

PSYCHONAUTS
Marvel Comics (Epic Comics): Oct, 1993 - No. 4, Jan, 1994 ($4.95, lim. series)

1-4: American/Japanese co-produced comic — 5.00

PSYLOCKE
Marvel Comics: Jan, 2010 - No. 4, Apr, 2010 ($3.99, limited series)

1-4-Finch-c/Yost-s/Tolibao-a. 3,4-Wolverine app. — 4.00

PSYLOCKE & ARCHANGEL CRIMSON DAWN
Marvel Comics: Aug, 1997 - No. 4, Nov, 1997 ($2.50, limited series)

1-4-Raab-s/Larroca-a(p) — 2.50

PTOLUS: CITY BY THE SPIRE
Dabel Brothers Productions/Marvel Comics (Dabel Brothers) #2 on: June, 2006 - No. 6, Mar, 2007 ($2.99)

1-(1st printing, Dabel) Adaptation of the Monte Cook novel; Cook-s — 3.00
1-(2nd printing, Marvel), 2-6 — 3.00
Monte Cooke's Ptolus: City By the Spire TPB (2007, $14.99) r/#1-6 — 15.00

P.T. 109 (See Movie Comics)

PUBLIC DEFENDER IN ACTION (Formerly Police Trap)
Charlton Comics: No. 7, Mar, 1956 - No. 12, Oct, 1957

	GD	VG	FN	VF	VF/NM	NM-
7	10	20	30	58	79	100
8-12	8	16	24	40	50	60

PUBLIC ENEMIES
D. S. Publishing Co.: 1948 - No. 9, June-July, 1949

	GD	VG	FN	VF	VF/NM	NM-
1-True Crime Stories	26	52	78	154	252	350
2-Used in **SOTI**, pg. 95	22	44	66	128	209	290
3-5: 5-Arrival date of 10/1/48	15	30	45	86	133	180
6,8,9	15	30	45	84	127	170
7-McWilliams-a; injury to eye panel	15	30	45	86	133	180

PUBO
Dark Horse Comics: Dec, 2002 - No. 3, Mar, 2003 ($3.50, B&W, limited series)

1-3-Leland Purvis-s/a — 3.50

PUDGY PIG
Charlton Comics: Sept, 1958 - No. 2, Nov, 1958

	GD	VG	FN	VF	VF/NM	NM-
1,2	3	6	9	17	25	32

PUFFED
Image Comics: Jul, 2003 - No. 3, Sept, 2003 ($2.95, B&W)

1-3-Layman-s/Crosland-a. 1-Two covers by Crosland & Quitely — 3.00

PULP FANTASTIC (Vertigo V2K)
DC Comics (Vertigo): Feb, 2000 - No. 3, Apr, 2000 ($2.50, limited series)

1-3-Chaykin & Tischman-s/Burchett-a — 2.50

PULP FICTION LIBRARY: MYSTERY IN SPACE
DC Comics: 1999 ($19.95, TPB)

nn-Reprints classic sci-fi stories from Mystery in Space, Strange Adventures, Real Fact Comics and My Greatest Adventure — 20.00

PULSE, THE (Also see Alias and Deadline)
Marvel Comics: Apr, 2004 - No. 14, May, 2006 ($2.99)

1-14: 1-5-Bendis-s/Bagley-a; Jessica Jones, Ben Urich, Kat Farrell app. 3-5-Green Goblin app. 6,7-Brent Anderson-a 9-Wolverine app. 10-House of M. 11-14-Gaydos-a — 3.00
...: House of M Special (9/05, 50¢) tabloid newspaper format; Mayhew- "photos" — 2.50
Vol. 1: Thin Air (2004, $13.99) r/#1-5, gallery of cover layouts and sketches — 14.00
Vol. 2: Secret War (2005, $11.99) r/#6-9 — 12.00
Vol. 3: Fear (2006, $14.99) r/#11-14 and New Avengers Annual #1 — 15.00

PUMA BLUES
Aardvark One International/Mirage Studios #21 on: 1986 - No. 26, 1990 ($1.70-$1.75, B&W)

1-19, 21-26: 1-1st & 2nd printings. 25,26-$1.75-c — 2.50
20 ($2.25)-By Alan Moore, Miller, Grell, others — 3.00
Trade Paperback (12/88, $14.95) — 15.00

PUMPKINHEAD: THE RITES OF EXORCISM (Movie)

Punch Comics #14 © CHES

Punisher #94 © MAR

Punisher (2004 series) #69 © MAR

	GD	VG	FN	VF	VF/NM	NM-
	2.0	4.0	6.0	8.0	9.0	9.2

Dark Horse Comics: 1993 - No. 2, 1993 ($2.50, limited series)

1,2: Based on movie; painted-c by McManus 2.50

PUNCH & JUDY COMICS
Hillman Per.: 1944; No. 2, Fall, 1944 - V3#2, 12/47; V3#3, 6/51 - V3#9, 12/51

	GD	VG	FN	VF	VF/NM	NM-
V1#1-(60 pgs.)	23	46	69	136	223	310
2	14	28	42	80	115	150
3-12(7/46)	11	22	33	64	90	115
V2#1(8/49),3-9	9	18	27	50	65	80
V2#2,10-12, V3#1-Kirby-a(2) each	21	42	63	122	199	275
V3#2-Kirby-a	19	38	57	112	179	245
3-9	9	18	27	47	61	75

PUNCH COMICS
Harry 'A' Chesler: 12/41; #2, 2/42; #9, 7/44 - #19, 10/46; #20, 7/47 - #23, 1/48

	GD	VG	FN	VF	VF/NM	NM-
1-Mr. E, The Sky Chief, Hale the Magician, Kitty Kelly begin	148	296	444	947	1624	2300
2-Captain Glory app.	90	180	270	576	988	1400
9-Rocketman & Rocket Girl & The Master Key begin	87	174	261	553	952	1350
10-Sky Chief app.; J. Cole-a; Master Key-r/Scoop #3	62	124	186	394	680	965
11-Origin Master Key-r/Scoop #1; Sky Chief, Little Nemo app.; Jack Cole-a; Fine-*ish* art by Sultan	57	114	171	362	624	885
12-Rocket Boy & Capt. Glory app; classic Skull-c	271	542	813	1734	2967	4200
13-Cover has list of 4 Chesler artists' names on tombstone	63	126	189	403	689	975
14,15,19,21: 21-Hypo needle story	54	108	162	346	591	835
16,17-Gag-c	42	84	126	265	445	625
18-Bondage-c; hypodermic panels	67	134	201	426	731	1035
20-Unique cover with bare-breasted women. Rocket Girl-c	110	220	330	704	1202	1700
22,23-Little Nemo-not by McCay. 22-Intro Baxter (teenage)(68 pgs.)	23	46	69	136	223	310

PUNCHY AND THE BLACK CROW
Charlton Comics: No. 10, Oct, 1985 - No. 12, Feb, 1986

10-12: Al Fago funny animal-r; low print run 6.00

PUNISHER (See Amazing Spider-Man #129, Blood and Glory, Born, Captain America #241, Classic Punisher, Daredevil #182-184, 257, Daredevil and the..., Ghost Rider V2#5, 6, Marc Spector #8 & 9, Marvel Preview #2, Marvel Super Action, Marvel Tales, Power Pack #46, Spectacular Spider-Man #81-83, 140, 141, 143 & new Strange Tales #13 & 14)

PUNISHER (The...)
Marvel Comics Group: Jan, 1986 - No. 5, May, 1986 (Limited series)

	GD	VG	FN	VF	VF/NM	NM-
1-Double size	3	6	9	14	20	25
2-5	2	4	6	8	11	14

Trade Paperback (1988)-r/#1-5 11.00
Circle of Blood TPB (8/01, $15.95) Zeck-c 16.00
Circle of Blood HC (2008, $19.99) two covers 20.00
NOTE: *Zeck a-1-4; c-1-5.*

PUNISHER (The...) (Volume 2)
Marvel Comics: July, 1987 - No. 104, July, 1995

	GD	VG	FN	VF	VF/NM	NM-
1	1	3	4	6	8	10
2-9: 8-Portacio/Williams-c/a begins, ends #18. 9-Scarcer, low dist.						6.00
10-Daredevil app; ties in w/Daredevil #257	1	3	4	6	8	10

11-74,76-85,87-89: 13-18-Kingpin app. 19-Stroman-c/a. 20-Portacio-c(p). 24-1st app. Shadowmasters. 25,50:($1.50,52 pgs.). 25-Shadowmasters app. 57-Photo-c; came w/outer-c (newsstand ed. w/o outer-c). 59-Punisher is severely cut & has skin grafts (has black skin). 60-62-Luke Cage app. 62-Punisher back to white skin. 68-Tarantula-c/story. 85-Prequel to Suicide Run Pt. 0. 87,88-Suicide Run Pt. 6 & 9 2.50
75-($2.75, 52 pgs.)-Embossed silver foil-c 3.00
86-($2.95, 52 pgs.)-Embossed & foil stamped-c; Suicide Run part 3 3.00
90-99: 90-bound-in cards. 99-Cringe app. 2.50
100,104: 100-($2.95, 68 pgs.). 104-Last issue 4.00
100-($3.95, 68 pgs.)-Foil cover 5.00
101-103: 102-Bullseye 3.50
"Ashcan" edition (75¢)-Joe Kubert-c 3.00
Annual 1-7 ('88-'94, 68 pgs.) 1-Evolutionary War x-over. 2-Atlantis Attacks x-over; Jim Lee-a(p) (back-up story, 6 pgs.); Moon Knight app. 4-Golden-c(p). 6-Bagged w/card. 3.00
...: A Man Named Frank (1994, $6.95, TPB) 7.00
...and Wolverine in African Saga nn (1989, $5.95, 52 pgs.)-Reprints Punisher War Journal #6 & 7; Jim Lee-c/a(r) 6.00
... Assassin Guild ('88, $6.95, graphic novel) 10.00
Back to School Special 1-3 (11/92-10/94, $2.95, 68 pgs.) 3.00

	GD	VG	FN	VF	VF/NM	NM-
	2.0	4.0	6.0	8.0	9.0	9.2

.../Batman: Deadly Knights (10/94, $4.95) 5.00
.../Black Widow: Spinning Doomsday's Web (1992, $9.95, graphic novel) 12.00
...Bloodlines nn (1991, $5.95, 68 pgs.) 6.00
...: Die Hard in the Big Easy nn ('92, $4.95, 52 pgs.) 5.00
...: Empty Quarter nn ('94, $6.95) 7.00
...G-Force nn (1992, $4.95, 52 pgs.)-Painted-c 5.00
...Holiday Special 1-3 (1/93-1/95,, 52 pgs.,68pgs.)-1-Foil-c 3.00
...Intruder Graphic Novel (1989, $14.95, hardcover) 20.00
...Intruder Graphic Novel (1991, $9.95, softcover) 12.00
...Invades the 'Nam: Final Invasion nn (2/94, $6.95)-J. Kubert-c & chapter break art; reprints The 'Nam #84 & unpublished #85,86 7.00
...Kingdom Gone Graphic Novel (1990, $16.95, hardcover) 20.00
...Meets Archie (8/94, $3.95, 52 pgs.)-Die cut-c; no ads; same contents as Archie Meets The Punisher 5.00
...Movie Special 1 (6/90, $5.95, squarebound, 68 pgs.) painted-c; Brent Anderson-a; contents intended for a 3 issue series which was advertised but not published 6.00
...: No Escape nn (1990, $4.95, 52 pgs.)-New-a 5.00
...Return to Big Nothing Graphic Novel (Epic, 1989, $16.95, hardcover) 25.00
...Return to Big Nothing Graphic Novel (Marvel, 1989, $12.95, softcover) 15.00
...The Prize nn (1990, $4.95, 68 pgs.)-New-a 5.00
Summer Special 1-4(8/91-7/94, 52 pgs.):1-No ads. 2-Bisley-c; Austin-a(i). 3-No ads 3.00
NOTE: ***Austin** c(i)-47, 48. **Cowan** c-39. **Golden** c-50, 85, 86, 100. **Heath** a-26, 27, 89, 90, 91; c-26, 27. **Quesada** c-56p, 62p. **Sienkiewicz** c-Back to School 1.**Stroman** a-76p(9 pgs.). **Williamson** a(i)-25, 60-62i, 64-70, 74, Annual 5; c(i)-62, 65-68.*

PUNISHER (Also see Double Edge)
Marvel Comics: Nov, 1995 - No. 18, Apr, 1997 ($2.95/$1.95/$1.50)

1 ($2.95)-Ostrander scripts begin; foil-c. 3.00
2-18: 7-Vs. S.H.I.E.L.D. 11-"Onslaught." 12-17-X-Cutioner-c/app. 17-Daredevil, Spider-Man-c/app. 2.50

PUNISHER (Marvel Knights)
Marvel Comics: Nov, 1998 - No. 4, Feb, 1999 ($2.99, limited series)

1-4: 1-Wrightson-a; Wrightson & Jusko-c 3.00
1-($6.95) DF Edition; Jae Lee variant-c 7.00

PUNISHER (Marvel Knights) (Volume 3)
Marvel Comics: Apr, 2000 - No. 12, Mar, 2001 ($2.99, limited series)

1-Ennis-s/Dillon & Palmiotti-a/Bradstreet-c 5.00
1-Bradstreet white variant-c 10.00
1-($6.95) DF Edition; Jurgens & Ordway variant-c 7.00
2-Two covers by Bradstreet & Dillon 3.00
3-($3.99) Bagged with Marvel Knights Genesis Edition; Daredevil app. 4.00
4-12: 9-11-The Russian app. 3.00
HC (6/02, $34.95) r/#1-12, Punisher Kills the Marvel Universe, and Marvel Knights Double Shot #1 35.00
... By Garth Ennis Omnibus (2008, $99.99) oversized r/#1-12, #1-7 & #13-37 of 2001 series, Punisher Kills the Marvel Universe, and Marvel Knights Double Shot #1; extras 100.00
.../Painkiller Jane (1/01, $3.50) Jusko-c; Ennis-s/Jusko and Dave Ross-a(p) 3.50
...: Welcome Back Frank TPB (4/01, $19.95) r/#1-12 20.00

PUNISHER (Marvel Knights) (Volume 4)
Marvel Comics: Aug, 2001 - No. 37, Feb, 2004 ($2.99)

1-Ennis-s/Dillon & Palmiotti-a/Bradstreet-c; The Russian app. 4.00
2-Two covers (Dillon & Bradstreet) Spider-Man-c/app. 3.00
3-37: 3-7-Ennis-s/Dillon-a. 9-12-Peyer-s/Gutierrez-a. 13,14-Ennis-s/Dilllon-a. 16,17-Wolverine app.; Robertson-a. 18-23,32-Dillon-a. 24-27-Mandrake-a. 27-Elektra app. 33-37-Spider-Man, Daredevil, & Wolverine app. 36,37-Hulk app. 3.00
...Army of One TPB (2/02, $15.95) r/#1-7; Bradstreet-c 16.00
Vol. 2 HC (2003, $29.95) r/#1-7,13-18; intro. by Mike Millar 30.00
Vol. 3 HC (2004, $29.95) r/#19-27; script pages for #19 30.00
Vol. 3: Business as Usual TPB (2003, $14.99) r/#13-18; Bradstreet-c 15.00
Vol. 4: Full Auto TPB (2003, $17.99) r/#20-26; Bradstreet-c 18.00
Vol. 5: Streets of Laredo TPB (2003, $17.99) r/#19,27-32 18.00
Vol. 6: Confederacy of Dunces TPB (2004, $13.99) r/#33-37 14.00

PUNISHER (Marvel MAX)(Title becomes "Punisher: Frank Castle MAX" with #66)
Marvel Comics: Mar, 2004 - No. 75, Dec, 2009 ($2.99/$3.99)

1-49,51-60: 1-Ennis-s/LaRosa-a/Bradstreet-c; flashback to his family's murder; Micro app. 6-Micro killed. 7-12,19-25-Fernandez-a. 13-18-Braithwaite-a. 31-36-Barracuda. 43-49-Medina-a. 51-54-Barracuda app. 60-Last Ennis-s/Bradstreet-c 3.00
50-($3.99) Barracuda returns; Chaykin-a 4.00
61-65-Gregg Hurwitz-s/Dave Johnson-c/Laurence Campbell-a 3.00
66-73-($3.99) 66-70-Six Hours to Kill; Swierczynski-s. 71-73-Parlov-a 4.00
74,75-($4.99) 74-Parlov-a. 75-Short stories; art by Lashley, Coker, Parlov & others 5.00
Annual (11/07, $3.99) Mike Benson-s/Laurence Campbell-a 4.00

Punisher (2009 series) #11 © MAR

Punisher Noir #4 © MAR

Punisher: War Zone (2009 series) #1 © MAR

	GD	VG	FN	VF	VF/NM	NM-
	2.0	4.0	6.0	8.0	9.0	9.2

...: Bloody Valentine (4/06, $3.99) Palmiotti & Gray-s/Gulacy & Palmiotti-a; Gulacy-c 4.00
...: Force of Nature (4/08, $3.99) Swierczynski-s/Lacombe-a/Deodato-c 4.00
...: MAX: Naked Kill (8/09, $3.99) Campbell-a/Bradstreet-c 4.00
...: MAX Special: Little Black Book (8/08, $3.99) Gischler-s/Palo-a/Johnson-c 4.00
...: MAX X-Mas Special (2/09, $3.99) Aaron-s/Boschi-a/Bachalo-c 4.00
...: Red X-Mas (2/05, $3.99) Palmiotti & Gray-s/Texeira & Palmiotti-a; Texeira-c 4.00
...: Silent Night (2/06, $3.99) Diggle-s/Hotz-a/Deodato-c 4.00
...: The Cell (7/05, $4.99) Ennis-s/LaRosa-a/Bradstreet-c 5.00
...: The Tyger (2/06, $4.99) Ennis-s/Severin-a/Bradstreet-c; Castle's childhood 5.00
...: Very Special Holidays TPB ('06, $12.99) r/Red X-Mas, Bloody Valentine and Silent Night 13.00
...: X-Mas Special (1/07, $3.99) Stuart Moore-s/CP Smith-a 4.00
... MAX: From First to Last HC (2006, $19.99) r/The Tyger, The Cell and The End 1-shots 20.00
... MAX Vol. 1 (2005, $29.99) oversized r/#1-12; gallery of Fernandez art from #7 shown from layout to colored pages 30.00
... MAX Vol. 2 (2006, $29.99) oversized r/#13-24; gallery of Fernandez pencil art 30.00
... MAX Vol. 3 (2007, $29.99) oversized r/#25-36; gallery of Fernandez & Parlov art 30.00
... MAX Vol. 4 (2008, $29.99) oversized r/#37-49; gallery of Fernandez & Medina art 30.00
Vol. 1: In the Beginning TPB (2004, $14.99) r/#1-6 15.00
Vol. 2: Kitchen Irish TPB (2004, $14.99) r/#7-12 15.00
Vol. 3: Mother Russia TPB (2005, $14.99) r/#13-18 15.00
Vol. 4: Up is Down and Black is White TPB (2005, $14.99) r/#19-24 15.00
Vol. 5: The Slavers TPB (2006, $15.99) r/#25-30; Fernandez pencil pages 16.00
Vol. 6: Barracuda TPB (2006, $15.99) r/#31-36; Parlov sketch page 16.00
Vol. 7: Man of Stone TPB (2007, $15.99) r/#37-42 16.00
Vol. 8: Widowmaker TPB (2007, $17.99) r/#43-49 18.00
Vol. 9: Long Cold Dark TPB (2008, $15.99) r/#50-54 16.00

PUNISHER (Frank Castle in the Marvel Universe after Secret Invasion)
Marvel Comics: Mar, 2009 - Present ($3.99/$2.99)

1-($3.99) Dark Reign; Sentry app.; Remender-s/Opena-a; character history; 2 covers 4.00
2-5,710($2.99) 2-7-The Hood app. 4-Microchip returns. 5-Daredevil #183 cover swipe 3.00
6-($3.99) Huat-a/McKone-c; profile pages of resurrected villains 4.00
11-Follows Dark Reign: The List - Punisher; Franken-Castle begins; Tony Moore-a 4.00
12-15-Franken-Castle; Legion of Monsters app. 14-Brereton & Moore-a 3.00
Annual 1 (11/09, $3.99) Pearson-a/c; Spider-Man app. 4.00

PUNISHER AND WOLVERINE: DAMAGING EVIDENCE (See Wolverine and...)

PUNISHER ARMORY, THE
Marvel Comics: 7/90 ($1.50); No. 2, 6/91; No. 3, 4/92 - 10/94($1.75/$2.00)

1-10: 1-r/weapons pgs. from War Journal. 1,2-Jim Lee-c. 3-10- All new material. 3-Jusko painted-c 2.50

PUNISHER KILLS THE MARVEL UNIVERSE
Marvel Comics: Nov, 1995 ($5.95, one-shot)

1-Garth Ennis script/Doug Braithwaite-a 7.00
1-2nd printing (3/00) Steve Dillon-c 6.00
1-3rd printing (2008, $4.99) original 1995 cover 5.00

PUNISHER MAGAZINE, THE
Marvel Comics: Oct, 1989 - No. 16, Nov, 1990 ($2.25, B&W, Magazine, 52 pgs.)

1-16: 1-r/Punisher #1('86). 2,3-r/Punisher 2-5. 4-16: 4-7-r/Punisher V2#1-8. 4-Chiodo-c. 8-r/Punisher #10 & Daredevil #257; Portacio & Lee-r. 14-r/Punisher War Journal #1,2 w/new Lee-c. 16-r/Punisher W. J. #3,8 3.00

NOTE: *Chiodo painted c-4, 7, 16.* ***Jusko*** *painted c-6, 8.* ***Jim Lee*** *r-8, 14-16; c-14.* ***Portacio/Williams*** *r-7-12.*

PUNISHERMAX
Marvel Comics (MAX): Jan, 2010 - Present ($3.99)

1-5-Aaron-s/Dillon-a/Johnson-c; rise of the Kingpin 4.00
...: Butterfly (5/10, $4.99) Valerie D'Orazio-s/Laurence Campbell-a/c 5.00
...: Get Castle (3/10, $4.99) Rob Williams-s/Laurence Campbell-a/Bradstreet-c 5.00

PUNISHER NOIR
Marvel Comics: Oct, 2009 - No. 4, Jan, 2010 ($3.99, limited series)

1-4-Pulp-style set in 1935; Tieri-s/Azaceta-a 4.00

PUNISHER: OFFICIAL MOVIE ADAPTATION
Marvel Comics: May, 2004 - No. 3, May, 2004 ($2.99, limited series)

1-3-Photo-c of Thomas Jane; Milligan-s/Olliffe-a 3.00

PUNISHER: ORIGIN OF MICRO CHIP, THE
Marvel Comics: July, 1993 - No. 2, Aug, 1993 ($1.75, limited series)

1,2 2.50

PUNISHER: P.O.V.
Marvel Comics: 1991 - No. 4, 1991 ($4.95, painted, limited series, 52 pgs.)

1-4: Starlin scripts & Wrightson painted-c/a in all. 2-Nick Fury app. 5.00

PUNISHER PRESENTS: BARRACUDA MAX
Marvel Comics (MAX): Apr, 2007 - No. 5, Aug, 2007 ($3.99, limited series)

1-5-Ennis-s/Parlov-a/c 4.00
SC (2007, $17.99) r/series; sketch pages 18.00

PUNISHER: THE END
Marvel Comics: June, 2004 ($4.50, one-shot)

1-Ennis-s/Corben-a/c 4.50

PUNISHER: THE GHOSTS OF INNOCENTS
Marvel Comics: Jan, 1993 - No. 2, Jan, 1993 ($5.95, 52 pgs.)

1,2-Starlin scripts 6.00

PUNISHER: THE MOVIE
Marvel Comics: 2004 ($12.99,TPB)

nn-Reprints Amazing Spider-Man #129; Official Movie Adaptation and Punisher V3 #1 13.00

PUNISHER 2099 (See Punisher War Journal #50)
Marvel Comics: Feb, 1993 - No. 34, Nov, 1995 ($1.25/$1.50/$1.95)

1-24,26-34: 1-Foil stamped-c. 1-Second printing. 13-Spider-Man 2099 x-over; Ron Lim-c(p). 16-bound-in card sheet 2.50
25 ($2.95, 52 pgs.)-Deluxe edition; embossed foil-cover 3.00
25 ($2.25, 52 pgs.) 2.50
(Marvel Knights) #1 (11/04, $2.99) Kirkman-s/Mhan-a/Pat Lee-c 3.00

PUNISHER VS. BULLSEYE
Marvel Comics: Jan, 2006 - No. 5, May, 2006 ($2.99, limited series)

1-5-Daniel Way-s/Steve Dillon-a 3.00
TPB (2006, $13.99) r/#1-5; cover sketch pages 14.00

PUNISHER VS. DAREDEVIL
Marvel Comics: Jun, 2000 ($3.50, one-shot)

1-Reprints Daredevil #183,#184 & #257 3.50

PUNISHER WAR JOURNAL, THE
Marvel Comics: Nov, 1988 - No. 80, July, 1995 ($1.50/$1.75/$1.95)

1-Origin The Punisher; Matt Murdock cameo; Jim Lee inks begin 5.00
2-7: 2,3-Daredevil x-over; Jim Lee-c(i). 4-Jim Lee c/a begins. 6-Two part Wolverine story begins. 7-Wolverine-c, story ends 4.00
8-49,51-60,62,63,65: 13-16,20-22: No Jim Lee-a. 13-Lee-c only. 13-15-Heath-i. 14,15-Spider-Man x-over. 19-Last Jim Lee-c/a.29,30-Ghost Rider app. 31-Andy & Joe Kubert art. 36-Photo-c. 47,48-Nomad/Daredevil-c/stories; see Nomad. 57,58-Daredevil & Ghost Rider-c/stories. 62,63-Suicide Run Pt. 4 & 7 3.00
50,61,64($2.95, 52 pgs.): 50-Preview of Punisher 2099 (1st app.); embossed-c. 61-Embossed foil cover; Suicide Run Pt. 1. 64-Die-cut-c; Suicide Run Pt. 10 3.00
64-($2.25, 52 pgs.)-Regular cover edition 2.50
66-74,76-80: 66-Bound-in card sheet 2.50
75 ($2.50, 52 pgs.) 2.75

NOTE: ***Golden*** *c-25-30, 40, 61, 62.* ***Jusko*** *painted c-31, 32.* ***Jim Lee*** *a-1i-3i, 4p-13p, 17p-19p; c-2i, 3i, 4p-15p, 17p, 18p, 19p. Painted c-40.*

PUNISHER WAR JOURNAL (Frank Castle back in the regular Marvel Universe)
Marvel Comics: Jan, 2007 - No. 26, Feb, 2009 ($2.99)

1-Civil War tie-in; Spider-Man app; Fraction-s/Olivetti-a 5.00
1-B&W edition (11/06) 5.00
2-5: 2,3-Civil War tie-in. 4-Deodato-a 4.00
6-11,13-24,26: 6-10-Punisher dons Captain America-*esque* outfit. 7-Two covers. 11-Winter Soldier app. 16-23-Chaykin-a. 18-23-Jigsaw app. 24-Secret Invasion 3.00
12,25-($3.99) 12-World War Hulk x-over; Fraction-s/Olivetti-a. 25-Secret Invasion 4.00
... Annual 1 (1/09, $3.99) Spurrier-s/Dell'edera-a 4.00
... Vol. 1: Civil War HC (2007, $19.99) r/#1-4 and #1 B&W edition; Olivetti sketch pages 20.00
... Vol. 1: Civil War SC (2007, $14.99) r/#1-4 and #1 B&W edition; Olivetti sketch pages 15.00
... Vol. 2: Goin' Out West HC (2007, $24.99) r/#5-11; Olivetti sketch page 25.00
... Vol. 2: Goin' Out West SC (2008, $17.99) r/#5-11; Olivetti sketch page 18.00
... Vol. 3: Hunter Hunted HC (2008, $19.99) r/#12-17 20.00

PUNISHER: WAR ZONE, THE
Marvel Comics: Mar, 1992 - No. 41, July, 1995 ($1.75/$1.95)

1-($2.25, 40 pgs.)-Die cut-c; Romita, Jr.-c/a begins 3.00
2-22,24,26,27-41: 8-Last Romita, Jr.-c/a. 19-Wolverine app. 24-Suicide Run Pt. 5. 27-Bound-in card sheet. 31-36-Joe Kubert-a 2.50
23-($2.95, 52 pgs.)-Embossed foil-c; Suicide Run part 2; Buscema-a(part) 3.00
25-($2.25, 52 pgs.)-Suicide Run part 8; painted-c 2.50
Annual 1,2 ('93, 94, $2.95, 68 pgs.)-1-Bagged w/card; John Buscema-a 3.00
...: River Of Blood TPB (2006, $15.99) r/#31-36; Joe Kubert-a 16.00

NOTE: ***Golden*** *c-23.* ***Romita, Jr.*** *c/a-1-8.*

PUNISHER: WAR ZONE
Marvel Comics: Feb, 2009 - No. 6, Mar, 2009 ($3.99, weekly limited series)

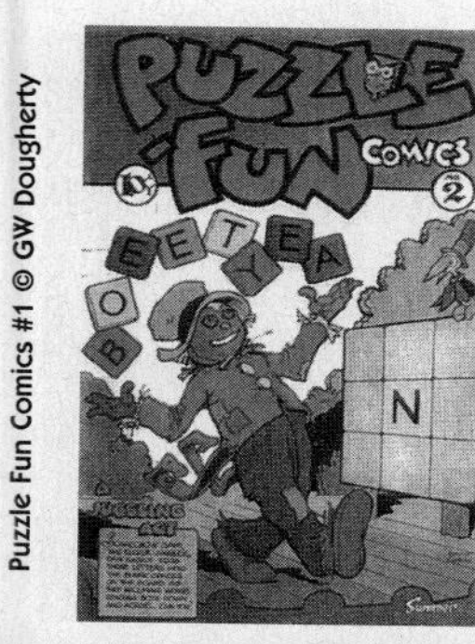

Puzzle Fun Comics #1 © GW Dougherty

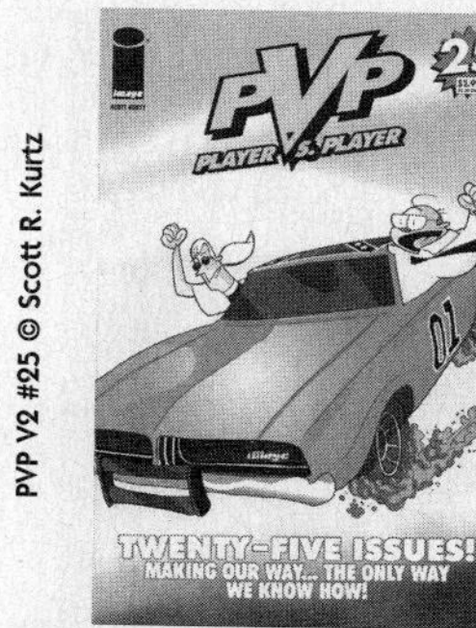

PVP V2 #25 © Scott R. Kurtz

Quasar #7 © MAR

GD 2.0 | VG 4.0 | FN 6.0 | VF 8.0 | VF/NM 9.0 | NM- 9.2

1-6-Ennis-s/Dillon-a/c; return of Ma Gnucci 4.00
1-Variant cover by John Romita, Jr. 6.00

PUNISHER: YEAR ONE
Marvel Comics: Dec, 1994 - No. 4, Apr, 1995 ($2.50, limited series)

1-4 2.50

PUNX
Acclaim (Valiant): Nov, 1995 - No. 3, Jan, 1996 ($2.50, unfinished lim. series)

1-3: Giffen story & art in all. 2-Satirizes Scott McCloud's Understanding Comics 2.50
(Manga) Special 1 (3/96, $2.50)-Giffen scripts 2.50

PUPPET COMICS
George W. Dougherty Co.: Spring, 1946 - No. 2, Summer, 1946

1-Funny animal in both 14 28 42 76 108 140
2 11 22 33 60 83 105

PUPPETOONS (See George Pal's...)

PUREHEART (See Archie as...)

PURGATORI
Chaos! Comics: Prelude #-1, 5/96 ($1.50, 16 pgs.); 1996 - No. 3 Dec, 1996 ($3.50/$2.95, limited series)

Prelude #-1-Pulido story; Balent-c/a; contains sketches & interviews 2.25
0-(2/01, $2.99) Prelude to "Love Bites"; Rio-c/a 3.00
1/2 (12/00, $2.95) Al Rio-c/a 3.00
1-($3.50)-Wraparound cover; red foil embossed-c; Jim Balent-a 5.00
1-($19.95)-Premium Edition (1000 print run) 20.00
2-($3.00)-Wraparound-c 3.00
2-Variant-c 5.00
...: Heartbreaker 1 (3/02, $2.99) Jolley-s 3.00
...: Love Bites 1 (3/01, $2.99) Turnbull-a/Kaminski-s 3.00
...: Mischief Night 1 (11/01, $2.99) 3.00
...: Re-Imagined 1 (7/02, $2.99) Jolley-s/Neves-a 3.00
...The Dracula Gambit-($2.95) 3.00
...The Dracula Gambit Sketchbook-($2.95) 3.00
...The Vampire's Myth 1-($19.95) Premium Ed. (10,000) 20.00
...Vs. Chastity (7/00, $2.95) Two versions (Alpha and Omega) with different endings; Rio-a 3.00
...Vs. Lady Death (1/01, $2.95) Kaminski-s 3.00
...Vs. Vampirella (4/00, $2.95) Zanier-a; Chastity app. 3.00

PURGATORI
Chaos! Comics: Oct, 1998 - No. 7, Apr, 1999 ($2.95)

1-7-Quinn-s/Rio-c/a. 2-Lady Death-c 3.00

PURGATORI: DARKEST HOUR
Chaos! Comics: Sept, 2001 - No. 2, Oct, 2001 ($2.99, limited series)

1,2 3.00

PURGATORI: EMPIRE
Chaos! Comics: May, 2000 - No. 3, July, 2000 ($2.95, limited series)

1-3-Cleavenger-c 3.00

PURGATORI: GODDESS RISING
Chaos! Comics: July, 1999 - No. 4, Oct, 1999 ($2.95, limited series)

1-4-Deodato-c/a 3.00

PURGATORI: GOD HUNTER
Chaos! Comics: Apr, 2002 - No. 2, May, 2002 ($2.99, limited series)

1,2-Molenaar-a/Jolley-s 3.00

PURGATORI: GOD KILLER
Chaos! Comics: Jun, 2002 - No. 2, July, 2002 ($2.99, limited series)

1,2-Molenaar-a/Jolley-s 3.00

PURGATORI: THE HUNTED
Chaos! Comics: Jun, 2001 - No. 2, Aug, 2001 ($2.99, limited series)

1,2 3.00

PURPLE CLAW, THE (Also see Tales of Horror)
Minoan Publishing Co./Toby Press: Jan, 1953 - No. 3, May, 1953

1-Origin; horror/weird stories in all 32 64 96 188 307 425
2,3: 1-3 r-in Tales of Horror #9-11 23 46 69 136 223 310
I.W. Reprint #8-Reprints #1 3 6 9 16 23 30

PUSH (Based on the 2009 movie)
DC Comics (WildStorm): Early Jan, 2009 - No. 6, Apr, 2009 ($3.50, limited series)

1-6-Movie prequel; Bruno Redondo-a. 1-Jock-c 3.50
TPB (2009, $19.99) r/#1-6 20.00

PUSSYCAT (Magazine)
Marvel Comics Group: Oct, 1968 (B&W reprints from Men's magazines)

1-(Scarce)-Ward, Everett, Wood-a; Everett-c 17 34 51 122 236 350

PUZZLE FUN COMICS (Also see Jingle Jangle)
George W. Dougherty Co.: Spring, 1946 - No. 2, Summer, 1946 (52 pgs.)

1-Gustavson-a 23 46 69 136 223 310
2 15 30 45 88 137 185

NOTE: *#1 & 2('46) each contain a* **George Carlson** *cover plus a 6 pg. story "Alec in Fumbleland"; also many puzzles in each.*

PvP (Player vs. Player)
Image Comics: Mar, 2003 - Present ($2.95/$2.99/$3.50, B&W, reads sideways)

1-34,36-Scott Kurtz-s/a in all. 1,16-Frank Cho-c. 11-Savage Dragon-c/app. 14-Invincible app. 19-Jonathan Luna-c. 25-Cho-a (2 pgs.) 3.00
35,37-45 ($3.50): 45-Brandy from Liberty Meadows app. 3.50
#0 (7/05, 50¢) Secret Origin of Skull 2.25
...: At Large TPB (7/04, $11.95) r/#1-6 12.00
... Vol. 2: Reloaded TPB (12/04, $11.95) r/#7-12 12.00
... Vol. 3: Rides Again TPB (2005, $11.99) r/#13-18 12.00
... Vol. 4: PVP Goes Bananas TPB (2007, $12.99) r/#19-24 13.00
... Vol. 5: PVP Treks On TPB (2008, $14.99) r/#25-31 15.00
...: The Dork Ages TPB (2/04, $11.95) r/#1-6 from Dork Storm Press 12.00

QUACK!
Star Reach Productions: July, 1976 - No. 6, 1977? ($1.25, B&W)

1-Brunner-c/a on Duckaneer (Howard the Duck clone); Dave Stevens, Gilbert, Shaw-a 2 4 6 10 14 18
1-2nd printing (10/76) 5.00
2-6: 2-Newton the Rabbit Wonder by Aragonés/Leialoha; Gilbert, Shaw-a; Leialoha-c. 3-The Beavers by Dave Sim begin, end #5; Gilbert, Shaw-a; Sim/Leialoha-c. 6-Brunner-a (Duckeneer); Gilbert-a 2 4 6 8 10 12

QUADRANT
Quadrant Publications: 1983 - No. 8, 1986 (B&W, nudity, adults)

1-Peter Hsu-c/a in all 2 4 6 10 14 18
2-8 2 3 4 6 8 10

QUANTUM & WOODY
Acclaim Comics: June, 1997 - No. 17, No. 32 (9/99), No. 18 - No. 21, Feb, 2000 ($2.50)

1-17: 1-1st app.; two covers. 6-Copycat-c. 9-Troublemakers app. 2.50
32-(9/99); 18-(10/99),19-21 2.50
The Director's Cut TPB ('97, $7.95) r/#1-4 plus extra pages 8.00

QUANTUM LEAP (TV) (See A Nightmare on Elm Street)
Innovation Publishing: Sept, 1991 - No. 12, Jun, 1993 ($2.50, painted-c)

1-12: Based on TV show; all have painted-c. 8-Has photo gallery 3.00
Special Edition 1 (10/92)-r/#1 w/8 extra pgs. of photos & articles 3.00
Time and Space Special 1 (#13) ($2.95)-Foil logo 3.00

QUANTUM TUNNELER, THE
Revolution Studio: Oct, 2001 (no cover price, one-shot)

1-Prequel to "The One" movie; Clayton Henry-a 2.50

QUASAR (See Avengers #302, Captain America #217, Incredible Hulk #234, Marvel Team-Up #113 & Marvel Two-in-One #53)
Marvel Comics: Oct, 1989 - No. 60, Jul, 1994 ($1.00/$1.25, Direct sales #17 on)

1-Origin; formerly Marvel Boy/Marvel Man 3.00
2-49,51-60: 3-Human Torch app. 6-Venom cameo (2 pgs.). 7-Cosmic Spidey. 11-Excalibur x-over. 14-McFarlane-c. 16-($1.50, 52 pgs.). 17-Flash parody (Buried Alien). 20-Fantastic Four app. 23-Ghost Rider x-over. 25-($1.50, 52 pgs.)-New costume Quasar. 26-Infinity Gauntlet x-over; Thanos-c/story. 27-Infinity Gauntlet x-over. 30-Thanos cameo in flashback; last $1.00-c. 31-Begin $1.25-c; D.P. 7 guest stars. 38-40-Infinity War x-overs. 38-Battles Warlock. 39-Thanos-c & cameo. 40-Thanos app. 42-Punisher-c/story. 53-Warlock & Moondragon app. 58-w/bound-in card sheet 2.50
50-($2.95, 52 pgs.)-Holo-grafx foil-c; Silver Surfer, Man-Thing, Ren & Stimpy app. 3.00
Special #1-3 ($1.25, newsstand)-Same as #32-34 2.50

QUEEN & COUNTRY (See Whiteout)
Oni Press: Mar, 2001 - No. 32, Aug, 2007 ($2.95/$2.99, B&W)

1-Rucka-s in all. Rolston-a/Sale-c 1 2 3 4 5 7
2-5: 2-4-Rolston-a/Sale-c. 5-Snyder-c/Hurtt-a 4.00
6-24,26-32: 6,7-Snyder-c/Hurtt-a. 13-15-Alexander-a. 16-20-McNeil-a. 21-24-Hawthorne-a 26-28-Norton-a 3.00
25-($5.99) Rolston-a 6.00
Free Comic Book Day giveaway (5/02) r/#1 with "Free Comic Book Day" banner on-c 2.25
Operation: Blackwall (10/03, $8.95, TPB) r/#13-15; John Rogers intro. 9.00

Queen Sonja #1 © Red Sonja LLC

The Question #37 © DC

Race For the Moon #1 © HARV

GD 2.0 | VG 4.0 | FN 6.0 | VF 8.0 | VF/NM 9.0 | NM- 9.2

Operation: Broken Ground (2002, $11.95, TPB) r/#1-4; Ellis intro. 12.00
Operation: Crystal Ball (1/03, $14.95, TPB) r/#8-12; Judd Winick intro. 15.00
Operation: Dandelion HC (8/04, $25.00) r/#21-24; Jamie S. Rich intro. 25.00
Operation: Dandelion (8/04, $11.95, TPB) r/#21-24; Jamie S. Rich intro. 12.00
Operation: Morningstar (9/02, $8.95, TPB) r/#5-7; Stuart Moore intro. 9.00
Operation: Storm Front (3/04, $14.95, TPB) r/#16-20; Geoff Johns intro. 15.00

QUEEN & COUNTRY: DECLASSIFIED
Oni Press: Nov, 2002 - No. 3, Jan, 2003 ($2.95, B&W, limited series)

1-3-Rucka-s/Hurtt-a/Morse-c 3.00
TPB (7/03, $8.95) r/#1-3; intro. by Micah Wright 9.00

QUEEN & COUNTRY: DECLASSIFIED (Volume 2)
Oni Press: Jan, 2005 - No. 3, Feb, 2006 ($2.95/$2.99, B&W, limited series)

1-3-Rucka-s/Burchett-a/c 3.00
TPB (3/06, $8.95) r/#1-3 9.00

QUEEN & COUNTRY: DECLASSIFIED (Volume 3)
Oni Press: Jun, 2005 - No. 3, Aug, 2005 ($2.95, B&W, limited series)

1-3- "Sons & Daughters;" Johnston-s/Mitten-a/c 3.00
TPB (3/06, $8.95) r/#1-3 9.00

QUEEN OF THE WEST, DALE EVANS (TV)(See Dale Evans Comics, Roy Rogers & Western Roundup under Dell Giants)
Dell Publ. Co.: No. 479, 7/53 - No. 22, 1-3/59 (All photo-c; photo back c-4-8,15)

Four Color 479(#1, '53) 18 36 54 126 246 365
Four Color 528(#2, '54) 10 20 30 70 123 175
3,4: 3(4-6/54)-Toth-a. 4-Toth, Manning-a 8 16 24 54 90 125
5-10-Manning-a. 5-Marsh-a 7 14 21 47 76 105
11,19,21-No Manning 21-Tufts-a 5 10 15 34 55 75
12-18,20,22-Manning-a 6 12 18 39 62 85

QUEEN SONJA (See Red Sonja)
Dynamite Entertainment: 2009 - Present ($2.99)

1-5: 1-Rubi-a/Ortega-s; 3 covers; back-up r/Marvel Feature #1 3.00

QUENTIN DURWARD
Dell Publishing Co.: No. 672, Jan, 1956

Four Color 672-Movie, photo-c 7 14 21 45 73 100

QUESTAR ILLUSTRATED SCIENCE FICTION CLASSICS
Golden Press: 1977 (224 pgs.) ($1.95)

11197-Stories by Asimov, Sturgeon, Silverberg & Niven; Starstream-r
3 6 9 20 30 40

QUEST FOR CAMELOT
DC Comics: July, 1998 ($4.95)

1-Movie adaption 5.00

QUEST FOR DREAMS LOST (Also see Word Warriors)
Literacy Volunteers of Chicago: July 4, 1987 ($2.00, B&W, 52 pgs.)(Proceeds donated to help fight illiteracy)

1-Teenage Mutant Ninja Turtles by Eastman/Laird, Trollords, Silent Invasion, The Realm, Wordsmith, Reacto Man, Eb'nn, Aniverse 2.50

QUESTION, THE (See Americomics, Blue Beetle (1967), Charlton Bullseye & Mysterious Suspense)

QUESTION, THE (Also see Showcase '95 #3)
DC Comics: Feb, 1987 - No. 36, Mar, 1990; No. 37, Mar, 2010 ($1.50)

1-36: Denny O'Neil scripts in all 2.50
37-(3/10, $2.99) Blackest Night one-shot; Victor Sage rises; Shiva app.; Cowan-a 3.00
Annual 1 (1988, $2.50) 2.50
Annual 2 (1989, $3.50) 3.50
...: Epitaph For a Hero TPB (2008, $19.99) r/#13-18 20.00
...: Poisoned Ground TPB (2008, $19.99) r/#7-12 20.00
...: Riddles TPB (2009, $19.99) r/#25-30 20.00
...: Welcome to Oz TPB (2009, $19.99) r/#19-24 20.00
...: Zen and Violence TPB (2007, $19.99) r/#1-6 20.00

QUESTION, THE (Also see Crime Bible and 52)
DC Comics: Jan, 2005 - No. 6, Jun, 2005 ($2.95, limited series)

1-6-Rick Veitch-s/Tommy Lee Edwards-a. 4,6-Superman app. 3.00

QUESTION QUARTERLY, THE
DC Comics: Summer, 1990 - No. 5, Spring, 1992 ($2.50, 52pgs.)

1-5 2.50
NOTE: ***Cowan** a-1, 2, 4, 5; c-1-3, 5. **Mignola** a-5i. **Quesada** a-3-5.*

QUESTION RETURNS, THE
DC Comics: Feb, 1997 ($3.50, one-shot)

1-Brereton-c 3.50

QUESTPROBE
Marvel Comics: 8/84; No. 2, 1/85; No. 3, 11/85 (lim. series)

1-3: 1-The Hulk app. by Romita. 2-Spider-Man; Mooney-a(i). 3-Human Torch & Thing 3.00

QUICK DRAW McGRAW (TV) (Hanna-Barbera)(See Whitman Comic Books)
Dell Publishing Co./Gold Key No. 12 on: No. 1040, 12-2/59-60 - No. 11, 7-9/62; No. 12, 11/62; No. 13, 2/63; No. 14, 4/63; No. 15, 6/69 (1st show aired 9/29/59)

Four Color 1040(#1) 1st app. Quick Draw & Baba Looey, Augie Doggie & Doggie Daddy and Snooper & Blabber 13 26 39 90 165 240
2(4-6/60)-4,6: 2-Augie Doggie & Snooper & Blabber stories (8 pgs. each); pre-dates both of their #1 issues. 4-Augie Doggie & Snooper & Blabber stories.
6 12 18 41 66 90
5-1st Snagglepuss app.; last 10¢ issue 7 14 21 45 73 100
7-11 5 10 15 32 51 70
12,13-Title change to ...Fun-Type Roundup (84pgs.) 7 14 21 45 73 100
14,15: 15-Reprints 4 8 12 28 44 60

QUICK DRAW McGRAW (TV)(See Spotlight #2)
Charlton Comics: Nov, 1970 - No. 8, Jan, 1972 (Hanna-Barbera)

1 5 10 15 32 51 70
2-8 3 6 9 19 29 38

QUICKSILVER (See Avengers)
Marvel Comics: Nov, 1997 - No. 13, Nov, 1998 ($2.99/$1.99)

1-($2.99)-Peyer-s/Casey Jones-a; wraparound-c 3.00
2-11: 2-Two covers-variant by Golden. 4-6-Inhumans app. 2.50
12-($2.99) Siege of Wundagore pt. 4 3.00
13-Magneto-c/app.; last issue 2.50

QUICK-TRIGGER WESTERN (...Action #12; Cowboy Action #5-11)
Atlas Comics (ACI #12/WPI #13-19): No. 12, May, 1956 - No. 19, Sept, 1957

12-Baker-a 15 30 45 90 140 190
13-Williamson-a, 5 pgs. 15 30 45 84 127 170
14-Everett, Crandall, Torres-a; Heath-c 14 28 42 81 118 155
15,16: 15-Torres, Crandall-a. 16-Orlando, Kirby-a 12 24 36 69 97 125
17,18: 18-Baker-a 12 24 36 67 94 120
19 10 20 30 54 72 90
NOTE: ***Ayers** a-17. **Colan** a-16. **Maneely** a-15, 17; c-15, 18. **Morrow** a-18. **Powell** a-14. **Severin** a-19; c-12, 13, 16, 17, 19. **Shores** a-16. **Tuska** a-17.*

QUINCY (See Comics Reading Libraries in the Promotional Comics section)

QUITTER, THE
DC Comics (Vertigo): 2005 ($19.99, B&W graphic novel)

HC ($19.99) Autobiography of Harvey Pekar; Pekar-s/Daen Haspiel-a 20.00
SC (2006, $12.99) 13.00

RACCOON KIDS, THE (Formerly Movietown Animal Antics)
National Periodical Publications (Arleigh No. 63,64): No. 52, Sept-Oct, 1954 - No. 62, Oct-Nov, 1956; No. 63, Sept, 1957; No. 64, Nov, 1957

52-Doodles Duck by Mayer 15 30 45 83 124 165
53-64: 53-62-Doodles Duck by Mayer 11 22 33 62 86 110
NOTE: ***Otto Feuer**-a most issues. **Rube Grossman**-a most issues.*

RACE FOR THE MOON
Harvey Publications: Mar, 1958 - No. 3, Nov, 1958

1-Powell-a(5); 1/2-pg. S&K-a; cover redrawn from Galaxy Science Fiction pulp (5/53)
18 36 54 103 162 220
2-Kirby/Williamson-c(r)/a(3); Kirby-p 7 more stys 26 52 78 154 252 350
3-Kirby/Williamson-c/a(4); Kirby-p 6 more stys 28 56 84 165 270 375

RACER-X
Now Comics: 8/88 - No. 11, 8/89; V2#1, 9/89 - V2#10, 1990 ($1.75)

0-Deluxe ($3.50) 3.50
1 (9/88) - 11, V2#1-10 2.50

RACER X (See Speed Racer)
DC Comics (WildStorm): Oct, 2000 - No. 3, Dec, 2000 ($2.95, limited series)

1-3: 1-Tommy Yune-s/Jo Chen-a; 2 covers by Yune. 2,3-Kabala app. 3.50

RACING PETTYS
STP Corp.: 1980 ($2.50, 68 pgs., 10 1/8" x 13 1/4")

1-Bob Kane-a. Kane bio on inside back-c. 10.00

RACK & PAIN
Dark Horse Comics: Mar, 1994 - No. 4, June, 1994 ($2.50, limited series)

1-4: Brian Pulido scripts in all. 1-Greg Capullo-c 3.00

Radioactive Man #4 (1953) © Bongo

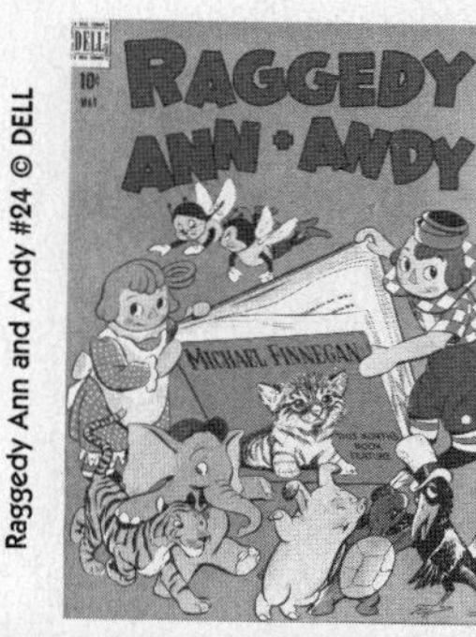

Raggedy Ann and Andy #24 © DELL

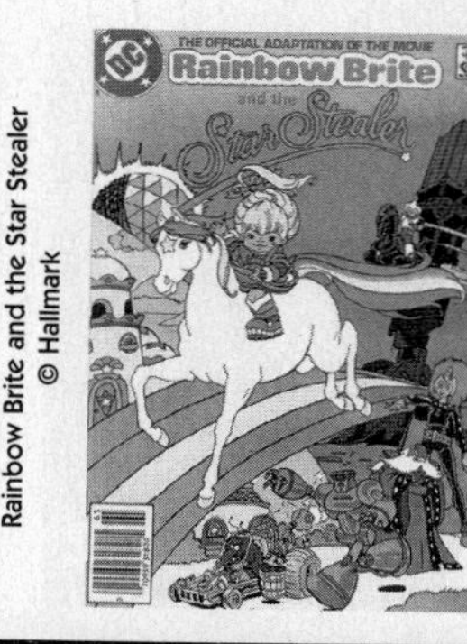

Rainbow Brite and the Star Stealer © Hallmark

	GD 2.0	VG 4.0	FN 6.0	VF 8.0	VF/NM 9.0	NM- 9.2

RACK & PAIN: KILLERS
Chaos! Comics: Sept, 1996 - No. 4, Jan, 1997 ($2.95, limited series)

	GD	VG	FN	VF	VF/NM	NM-
1-4: Reprints Dark Horse series; Jae Lee-c						3.00

RACKET SQUAD IN ACTION
Capitol Stories/Charlton Comics: May-June, 1952 - No. 29, Mar, 1958

	GD	VG	FN	VF	VF/NM	NM-
1	28	56	84	165	270	375
2-4,6: 3,4,6-Dr. Neff, Ghost Breaker app.	15	30	45	85	130	175
5-Dr. Neff, Ghost Breaker app; headlights-c	21	42	63	122	199	275
7-10: 10-Explosion-c	14	28	42	80	115	150
11-Ditko-c/a	30	60	90	177	289	400
12-Ditko explosion-c (classic); Shuster-a(2)	52	104	156	328	552	775
13-Shuster-c(p)/a.	12	24	36	69	97	125
14-Marijuana story "Shakedown"; Giordano-c	15	30	45	85	130	175
15-28: 15,20,22,23-Giordano-c	11	22	33	60	83	105
29-(15¢, 68 pgs.)	14	28	42	76	108	140

RADIANT LOVE (Formerly Daring Love #1)
Gilmor Magazines: No. 2, Dec, 1953 - No. 6, Aug, 1954

	GD	VG	FN	VF	VF/NM	NM-
2	12	24	36	67	94	120
3-6	8	16	24	44	57	70

RADICAL DREAMER
Blackball Comics: No. 0, May, 1994 - No. 4, Nov, 1994 ($1.99, bi-monthly) (1st poster format comic)

	GD	VG	FN	VF	VF/NM	NM-
0-4: 0-2-($1.99, poster format): 0-1st app. Max Wrighter. 3,4-($2.50-c)						3.00

RADICAL DREAMER
Mark's Giant Economy Size Comics: V2#1, June, 1995 - V2#6, Feb, 1996 ($2.95, B&W, limited series)

	GD	VG	FN	VF	VF/NM	NM-
V2#1-6						3.00
Prime (5/96, $2.95)						3.00
Dreams Cannot Die!-(1996, $20.00, softcover)-Collects V1#0-4 & V2#1-6; intro by Kurt Busiek; afterward by Mark Waid						20.00
Dreams Cannot Die!-(1996, $60.00, hardcover)-Signed & limited edition; collects V1#0-4 & V2#1-6; intro by Kurt Busiek; afterward by Mark Waid						60.00

RADIOACTIVE MAN (Simpsons TV show)
Bongo Comics: 1993 - No. 6, 1994 ($1.95/$2.25, limited series)

	GD	VG	FN	VF	VF/NM	NM-
1-($2.95)-Glow-in-the-dark-c; bound-in jumbo poster; origin Radioactive Man; (cover dated Nov. 1952)						5.00
2-6: 2-Says #88 on-c & inside & dated May 1962; cover parody of Atlas Kirby monster-c; Superior Squad app.; origin Fallout Boy. 3-($1.95)-Cover "dated" Aug 1972 #216. 4-($2.25)-Cover "dated" Oct 1980 #412; w/trading card. 5-Cover "dated" Jan 1986 #679; w/trading card. 6-(Jan 1995 #1000)						4.00
Colossal #1-($4.95)						7.00
#4 (2001, $2.50) Faux 1953 issue; Murphy Anderson-i (6 pgs.)						2.50
#100 (2000, $2.50) Comic Book Guy-c/app.; faux 1963 issue inside						2.50
#136 (2001, $2.50) Dan DeCarlo-c/a						2.50
#222 (2001, $2.50) Batton Lash-s; Radioactive Man in 1972-style						2.50
#575 (2002, $2.50) Chaykin-c; Radioactive Man in 1984-style						2.50
1963-106 (2002, $2.50) Radioactive Man in 1960s Gold Key-style; Groening-c						2.50
#7 Bongo Super Heroes Starring... (2003, $2.50) Marvel Silver Age-style Superior Squad						2.50
#8 Official Movie Adaptation (2004, $2.99) starring Rainier Wolfcastle and Milhouse						3.00
#9 (#197 on-c) (2004, $2.50) Kirby-esque New Gods spoof; Golden Age Radio Man app.						2.50

RADIO FUNNIES
DC Comics: Mar. 1939; undated variant

nn-(3/39) Ashcan comic, not distributed to newsstands, only for in-house use. Cover art is Adventure Comics #39 with interior being Detective Comics #19 (no known sales)
nn - Ashcan comic. No date. Cover art is Detective #26 with interior from Detective #17; the only known copy, graded at GD/VG, sold at auction for $4481.25 in Nov, 2009

RAGAMUFFINS
Eclipse Comics: Jan, 1985 ($1.75, one shot)

	GD	VG	FN	VF	VF/NM	NM-
1-Eclipse Magazine-r, w/color; Colan-a						2.50

RAGGEDY ANN AND ANDY (See Dell Giants, March of Comics #23 & New Funnies)
Dell Publishing Co.: No. 5, 1942 - No. 533, 2/54; 10-12/64 - No. 4, 3/66

	GD	VG	FN	VF	VF/NM	NM-
Four Color 5(1942)	46	92	138	368	709	1050
Four Color 23(1943)	34	68	102	262	506	750
Four Color 45(1943)	29	58	87	212	406	600
Four Color 72(1945)	23	46	69	170	328	485
1(6/46)-Billy & Bonnie Bee by Frank Thomas	32	64	96	245	473	700
2,3: 3-Egbert Elephant by Dan Noonan begins	17	34	51	119	230	340
4-Kelly-a, 16 pgs.	17	34	51	124	242	360
5,6,8-10	14	28	42	97	181	265
7-Little Black Sambo, Black Mumbo & Black Jumbo only app; Christmas-c	16	32	48	113	217	320
11-20	11	22	33	78	139	200
21-Alice In Wonderland cover/story	14	28	42	97	181	265
22-27,29-39(8/49), Four Color 262(1/50): 34-"...In Candyland"	10	20	30	67	116	165
28-Kelly-c	10	20	30	70	123	175
Four Color 306,354,380,452,533	7	14	21	50	83	115
1(10-12/64-Dell)	4	8	12	24	37	50
2,3(10-12/65), 4(3/66)	3	6	9	16	23	30

NOTE: ***Kelly** art ("Animal Mother Goose")-#1-34, 36, 37; c-28. Peterkin Pottle by **John Stanley** in 32-38.*

RAGGEDY ANN AND ANDY
Gold Key: Dec, 1971 - No. 6, Sept, 1973

	GD	VG	FN	VF	VF/NM	NM-
1	3	6	9	19	29	38
2-6	3	6	9	15	21	26

RAGGEDY ANN & THE CAMEL WITH THE WRINKLED KNEES (See Dell Jr. Treasury #8)

RAGMAN (See Batman Family #20, The Brave & The Bold #196 & Cancelled Comic Cavalcade)
National Per. Publ./DC Comics No. 5: Aug-Sept, 1976 - No. 5, Jun-Jul, 1977

	GD	VG	FN	VF	VF/NM	NM-
1-Origin & 1st app.	2	4	6	9	13	16
2-5: 2-Origin ends; Kubert-c. 4-Drug use story	2	3	4	6	8	10

NOTE: ***Kubert** a-4, 5; c-1-5. **Redondo** studios a-1-4.*

RAGMAN (2nd Series)
DC Comics: Oct, 1991 - No. 8, May, 1992 ($1.50, limited series)

	GD	VG	FN	VF	VF/NM	NM-
1-8: 1-Giffen plots/breakdowns. 3-Origin. 8-Batman-c/story						3.00

RAGMAN: CRY OF THE DEAD
DC Comics: Aug, 1993 - No. 6, Jan, 1994 ($1.75, limited series)

	GD	VG	FN	VF	VF/NM	NM-
1-6: Joe Kubert-c						3.00

RAGS RABBIT (Formerly Babe Ruth Sports #10 or Little Max #10?; also see Harvey Hits #2, Harvey Wiseguys & Tastee Freez)
Harvey Publications: No. 11, June, 1951 - No. 18, March, 1954 (Written & drawn for little folks)

	GD	VG	FN	VF	VF/NM	NM-
11-(See Nutty Comics #5 for 1st app.)	6	12	18	31	38	45
12-18	5	10	15	24	30	35

RAI (Rai and the Future Force #9-23) (See Magnus #5-8)
Valiant: Mar, 1992 - No. 0, Oct, 1992; No. 9, May, 1993 - No. 33, Jun, 1995 ($1.95/$2.25)

	GD	VG	FN	VF	VF/NM	NM-
1-Valiant's 1st original character	2	4	6	8	11	14
2-4,0: 4-Low print run. 0-(11/92)-Origin/1st app. new Rai (Rising Spirit) & 1st full app. & partial origin Bloodshot; also see Eternal Warrior #4; tells future of all characters	1	3	4	6	8	10
5-10: 6,7-Unity x-overs. 7-Death of Rai. 9-($2.50)-Gatefold-c; story cont'd from Magnus #24; Magnus, Eternal Warrior & X-O app.						5.00
11-33: 15-Manowar Armor app. 17-19-Magnus x-over. 21-1st app. The Starwatchers (cameo); trading card. 22-Death of Rai. 26-Chaos Effect Epsilon Pt. 3						2.50

NOTE: ***Layton** c-2i, 9i. **Miller** c-6. **Simonson** c-7.*

RAIDERS OF THE LOST ARK (Movie)
Marvel Comics Group: Sept, 1981 - No. 3, Nov, 1981 (Movie adaptation)

	GD	VG	FN	VF	VF/NM	NM-
1-3: 1-r/Marvel Comics Super Special #18						3.00

NOTE: ***Buscema** a(p)-1-3; c(p)-1. **Simonson** a-3i; scripts-1-3.*

RAINBOW BRITE AND THE STAR STEALER
DC Comics: 1985

	GD	VG	FN	VF	VF/NM	NM-
nn-Movie adaptation	2	4	6	8	10	12

RAISE THE DEAD
Dynamite Entertainment: 2007 - No. 4, Aug, 2007 ($3.50)

	GD	VG	FN	VF	VF/NM	NM-
1-4-Arthur Suydam-c/Leah Moore & John Reppion-s/Petrus-a; Phillips var-c on all						3.50
... Vol. 1 HC (2007, $19.99) r/#1-4; script, interview & sketch pages; cover gallery						20.00

RALPH KINER, HOME RUN KING
Fawcett Publications: 1950 (Pittsburgh Pirates)

	GD	VG	FN	VF	VF/NM	NM-
nn-Photo-c; life story	59	118	177	375	643	910

RALPH SNART ADVENTURES
Now Comics: June, 1986 - V2#9, 1987; V3#1 - #26, Feb, 1991; V4#1, 1992 - #4, 1992

	GD	VG	FN	VF	VF/NM	NM-
1-3, V2#1-7,V3#1-23,25,26:1-($1.00, B&W)-1(B&W),V2#1(11/86), B&W), 8,9-color. V3#1(9/88)-Color begins						2.50
V3#24-($2.50)-3-D issue, V4#1-3-Direct sale versions w/cards						2.50
V4#1-3-Newsstand versions w/random cards						2.50
Book 1	1	2	3	5	6	8
3-D Special (11/92, $3.50)-Complete 12-card set w/3-D glasses						3.50

RAMAR OF THE JUNGLE (TV)

Rangeland Love #2 © MAR

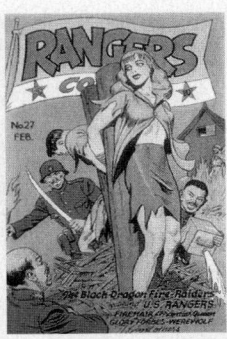

Rangers Comics #27 © FH

RASL #1 © Jeff Smith

	GD 2.0	VG 4.0	FN 6.0	VF 8.0	VF/NM 9.0	NM- 9.2

Toby Press No. 1/Charlton No. 2 on: 1954 (no month); No. 2, Sept, 1955 - No. 5, Sept, 1956

1-Jon Hall photo-c; last pre-code issue 21 42 63 122 199 275
2-5: 2-Jon Hall photo-c 15 30 45 85 130 175

RAMAYAN 3392 A.D.
Virgin Comics: Sept, 2006 - Present ($2.99)

1-8: 1-Alex Ross-c; re-imagining of the Indian myth of Ramayana; poster of cover inside 3.00
... Reloaded (8/07 - No. 7, 7/08, $2.99) 1-7: 1-Two covers by Kang and Oeming 3.00
... Reloaded Guidebook (4/08, $2.99) Profiles of characters and weapons 3.00

RAMM
Megaton Comics: May, 1987 - No. 2, Sept, 1987 ($1.50, B&W)

1,2-Both have 1 pg. Youngblood ad by Liefeld 2.50

RAMPAGING HULK (The Hulk #10 on; also see Marvel Treasury Edition)
Marvel Comics Group: Jan, 1977 - No. 9, June, 1978 ($1.00, B&W magazine)

1-Bloodstone story w/Buscema & Nebres-a. Origin re-cap w/Simonson-a; Gargoyle, UFO story; Ken Barr-c 3 6 9 19 29 38
2-Old X-Men app; origin old w/Simonson-a & new X-Men in text w/Cockrum illos; Bloodstone story w/Brown & Nebres-a 3 6 9 16 22 28
3-9: 3-Iron Man app.; Norem-c. 4-Gallery of villains w/Giffen-a. 5,6-Hulk vs. Sub-Mariner. 7-Man-Thing story. 8-Original Avengers app. 9-Thor vs. Hulk battle; Shanna the She-Devil story w/DeZuniga-a 2 4 6 13 18 22

NOTE: ***Alcala** a-1-3i, 5i, 8i. **Buscema** a-1. **Giffen** a-4. **Nino** a-4i. **Simonson** a-1-3p. **Starlin** a-4(w/Nino), 7; c-4, 5, 7.*

RAMPAGING HULK
Marvel Comics: Aug, 1998 - No. 6, Jan, 1999 ($2.99/$1.99)

1-($2.99) Flashback stories of Savage Hulk; Leonardi-a 3.00
2-6-($1.99): 2-Two covers 2.50

RAMPAGING WOLVERINE
Marvel Comics: June, 2009 ($3.99, B&W, one-shot)

1-Short stories by Fialkov, Luque, Ted McKeever, Yost, Santolouco, Firth, Nelson 4.00

RANDOLPH SCOTT (Movie star)(See Crack Western #67, Prize Comics Western #76, Western Hearts #8, Western Love #1 & Western Winners #7)

RANGE BUSTERS
Fox Features Syndicate: Sept, 1950 (One shot)

1 (Exist?) 19 38 57 112 179 245

RANGE BUSTERS (Formerly Cowboy Love?; Wyatt Earp, Frontier Marshall #11 on)
Charlton Comics: No. 8, May, 1955 - No. 10, Sept, 1955

8 8 16 24 42 54 65
9,10 6 12 18 28 34 40

RANGELAND LOVE
Atlas Comics (CDS): Dec, 1949 - No. 2, Mar, 1950 (52 pgs.)

1-Robert Taylor & Arlene Dahl photo-c 17 34 51 98 154 210
2-Photo-c 14 28 42 80 115 150

RANGER, THE (See Zane Grey, Four Color #255)

RANGE RIDER, THE (TV)(See Flying A's...)

RANGE ROMANCES
Comic Magazines (Quality Comics): Dec, 1949 - No. 5, Aug, 1950 (#5: 52 pg)

1-Gustavson-c/a 26 52 78 152 244 335
2-Crandall-c/a 26 52 78 152 244 335
3-Crandall, Gustavson-a; photo-c 22 44 66 127 204 280
4-Crandall-a; photo-c 19 38 57 112 176 240
5-Gustavson-a; Crandall-a(p); photo-c 19 38 57 112 176 240

RANGERS COMICS (...of Freedom #1-7)
Fiction House Magazines: 10/41 - No. 67, 10/52; No. 68, Fall, 1952; No. 69, Winter, 1952-53 (Flying stories)

1-Intro. Ranger Girl & The Rangers of Freedom; ends #7, cover app. only #5 320 640 960 2240 3920 5600
2 95 190 285 603 1039 1475
3 69 138 207 442 759 1075
4,5 62 124 186 394 680 965
6-10: 8-U.S. Rangers begin 50 100 150 315 533 750
11,12-Commando Rangers app. 47 94 141 296 498 700
13-Commando Ranger begins-not same as Commando Rangers 45 90 135 284 480 675
14-20 40 80 120 246 411 575
21-Intro/origin Firehair (begins, 2/45) 41 82 123 260 435 610
22-30: 23-Kazanda begins, ends #28. 28-Tiger Man begins (origin/1st app., 4/46), ends #46. 30-Crusoe Island begins, ends #40 31 62 93 182 296 410
31-40: 33-Hypodermic panels 26 52 78 154 252 350
41-46: 41-Last Werewolf Hunter 22 44 66 128 209 290
47-56- "Eisnerish" Dr. Drew by Grandenetti. 48-Last Glory Forbes. 53-Last 52 pg. issue. 55-Last Sky Rangers 21 42 63 124 202 280
57-60-Straight run of Dr. Drew by Grandenetti 16 32 48 94 147 200
61-69: 64-Suicide Smith begins. 63-Used in **POP**, pgs. 85, 99. 67-Space Rangers begin, end #69 15 30 45 83 124 165

NOTE: *Bondage, discipline covers, lingerie panels are common. Crusoe Island by **Larsen**-#30-36. Firehair by **Lubbers**-#30-49. Glory Forbes by **Baker**-#36-45, 47; by **Whitman**-#34, 35. I Confess in #41-53. Jan of the Jungle in #42-58. King of the Congo in #49-53. Tiger Man by **Celardo**-#30-39. **M. Anderson** a-30? **Baker** a-36-38, 42, 44. **John Celardo** a-34, 36-39. **Lee Elias** a-21-28. **Evans** a-19, 38-46, 48-52. **Hopper** a-25, 26. **Ingels** a-13-16. **Larsen** a-34. **Bob Lubbers** a-30-38, 40-44; c-40-45. **Moreira** a-41-47. **Tuska** a-16, 17, 19, 22. **M. Whitman** c-61-66. **Zolnerwich** c-1-17.*

RANGO (TV)
Dell Publishing Co.: Aug, 1967

1-Photo-c of comedian Tim Conway 4 8 12 24 37 50

RANN-THANAGAR HOLY WAR (Also see Hawkman Special #1)
DC Comics: July, 2008 - No. 8, Feb, 2009 ($3.50, limited series)

1-8-Adam Strange & Hawkman app.; Starlin-s/Lim-a. 1-Two covers by Starlin & Lim 3.50
Volume One TPB (2009, $19.99) r/#1-4 & Hawkman Special #1 20.00
Volume Two TPB (2009, $19.99) r/#5-8 & Adam Strange Special #1 20.00

RANN-THANAGAR WAR (See Adam Strange 2004 mini-series)(Prelude to Infinite Crisis)
DC Comics: July, 2005 - No. 6, Dec, 2005 ($2.50, limited series)

1-6-Adam Strange, Hawkman and Green Lantern (Kyle Rayner) app.; Gibbons-s/Reis-a 2.50
...: Infinite Crisis Special (4/06, $4.99) Kyle Rayner becomes Ion again; Jade dies 5.00
TPB (2005, $12.99) r/#1-6; cover gallery; new Bolland-c 13.00

RAPHAEL (See Teenage Mutant Ninja Turtles)
Mirage Studios: 1985 ($1.50, 7-1/2x11", B&W w/2 color cover, one-shot)

1-1st Turtles one-shot spin-off; contains 1st drawing of the Turtles as a group from 1983 6.00
1-2nd printing (11/87); new-c & 8 pgs. art 2.50

RAPHAEL BAD MOON RISING (See Teenage Mutant Ninja Turtles)
Mirage Publishing: July, 2007 - No. 4, Oct, 2007 ($3.25, B&W, limited series)

1-4-Continued from Tales of the TMNT #7; Lawson-a 3.25

RAPTURE
Dark Horse Comics: May, 2009 - No. 6, Jan, 2010 ($2.99, limited series)

1-6-Taki Soma & Michael Avon Oeming-s/a/c. 1-Maleev var-c. 2-Mack var-c 3.00

RASCALS IN PARADISE
Dark Horse Comics: Aug, 1994 - No. 3, Dec, 1994 ($3.95, magazine size)

1-3-Jim Silke-a/story 4.00
Trade paperback-($16.95)-r/#1-3 17.00

RASL
Cartoon Books: Mar, 2008 - Present ($3.50, B&W)

1-7-Jeff Smith-s/a/c 3.50

RATFINK (See Frantic, Zany, & Ed "Big Daddy" Roth's Ratfink Comix)
Canrom, Inc.: Oct, 1964

1-Woodbridge-a 7 14 21 49 80 110

RAT PATROL, THE (TV) (Also see Wild!)
Dell Publishing Co.: Mar, 1967 - No. 5, Nov, 1967; No. 6, Oct, 1969

1-Christopher George photo-c 7 14 21 47 76 105
2-6: 3-6-Photo-c 4 8 12 28 44 60

RAVAGE 2099 (See Marvel Comics Presents #117)
Marvel Comics: Dec, 1992 - No. 33, Aug, 1995($1.25/$1.50)

1-($1.75)-Gold foil stamped-c; Stan Lee scripts 3.00
1-($1.75)-2nd printing 2.50
2-24,26-33: 5-Last Ryan-c. 6-Last Ryan-a. 14-Punisher 2099 x-over. 15-Ron Lim-c(p). 18-Bound-in card sheet 2.50
25 ($2.25, 52 pgs.) 2.50
25 ($2.95, 52 pgs.)-Silver foil embossed-c 3.00

RAVEN (See DC Special: Raven and Teen Titans titles)

RAVEN, THE (See Movie Classics)

RAVEN CHRONICLES
Caliber (New Worlds): 1995 - No. 16 ($2.95, B&W)

1-16: 10-Flip book w/Wordsmith #6. 15-Flip book w/High Caliber #4 3.00

RAVENS AND RAINBOWS
Pacific Comics: Dec, 1983 (Baxter paper)(Reprints fanzine work in color)

1-Jeff Jones-c/a(r); nudity scenes 3.00

Rawhide Kid (2003 series) #5 © MAR

The Ray #19 © DC

Real Fact Comics #12 © DC

GD 2.0 | VG 4.0 | FN 6.0 | VF 8.0 | VF/NM 9.0 | NM- 9.2

RAWHIDE (TV)
Dell Publishing Co./Gold Key: Sept-Nov, 1959 - June-Aug, 1962; July, 1963 - No. 2, Jan, 1964
Four Color 1028 (#1) 22 44 66 155 300 445
Four Color 1097,1160,1202,1261,1269 14 28 42 97 181 265
01-684-208 (8/62, Dell) 12 24 36 85 155 225
1(10071-307) (7/63, Gold Key) 12 24 36 85 155 225
2-(12¢) 11 22 33 78 139 200
NOTE: *All have Clint Eastwood photo-c.* ***Tufts*** *a-1028.*

RAWHIDE KID
Atlas/Marvel Comics (CnPC No. 1-16/AMI No. 17-30): Mar, 1955 - No. 16, Sept, 1957; No. 17, Aug, 1960 - No. 151, May, 1979
1-Rawhide Kid, his horse Apache & sidekick Randy begin; Wyatt Earp app.; #1 was not code approved; Maneely splash pg. 92 184 276 584 1005 1425
2 39 78 117 240 395 550
3-5 30 60 90 177 289 400
6-10: 7-Williamson-a (4 pgs.) 23 46 69 136 223 310
11-16: 16-Torres-a 19 38 57 111 176 240
17-Origin by Jack Kirby; Kirby-a begins 42 84 126 265 450 635
18-21,24-30 11 22 33 80 145 210
22-Monster-c/story by Kirby/Ayers 14 28 42 100 188 275
23-Origin retold by Jack Kirby 17 34 51 120 233 345
31-35,40: 31,32-Kirby-a. 33-35-Davis-a. 34-Kirby-a. 35-Intro & death of The Raven. 40-Two-Gun Kid x-over. 10 20 30 71 126 180
36,37,39,41,42-No Kirby. 42-1st Larry Lieber issue 9 18 27 63 107 150
38-Red Raven-c/story; Kirby-c (2/64). 11 22 33 78 139 200
43-Kirby-a (beware: pin-up often missing) 11 22 33 78 139 200
44,46: 46-Toth-a. 46-Doc Holliday-c/s 9 18 27 60 100 140
45-Origin retold, 17 pgs. 10 20 30 71 126 180
47-49,51-60 6 12 18 39 62 85
50-Kid Colt x-over; vs. Rawhide Kid 6 12 18 43 69 95
61-70: 64-Kid Colt story. 66-Two-Gun Kid story. 67-Kid Colt story. 70-Last 12¢ issue 5 10 15 30 48 65
71-78,80-83,85 3 6 9 18 27 35
79,84,86,95: 79-Williamson-a(r). 84,86: Kirby-a. 86-Origin-r; Williamson-r/Ringo Kid #13 (4 pgs.) 3 6 9 19 29 38
87-91: 90-Kid Colt app. 91-Last 15¢ issue 3 6 9 16 23 30
92,93 (52 pg.Giants). 92-Kirby-a 4 8 12 22 34 45
94,96-99 3 6 9 14 20 26
100 (6/72)-Origin retold & expanded 3 6 9 19 29 38
101-120: 115-Last new story 2 4 6 11 16 20
121-151 2 4 6 8 11 14
133,134-(30¢-c variants, limited distribution)(5,7/76) 4 8 12 26 41 55
140,141-(35¢-c variants, limited distribution)(7,9/77) 6 12 18 39 62 85
Special 1(9/71, 25¢, 68 pgs.)-All Kirby/Ayers-r 4 8 12 28 44 60
NOTE: ***Ayers*** *a-13, 14, 16, 29, 37, 39, 61.* ***Colan*** *a-5, 35, 37; c-145p, 148p, 149p.* ***Davis*** *a-125r.* ***Everett*** *a-54i, 65, 66, 88, 96i, 148i(r).* ***Gulacy*** *c-147.* ***Heath*** *c-4.* ***G. Kane*** *c-101, 144.* ***Keller*** *a-5, 39, 41, 144r.* ***Kirby*** *a-17-32, 34, 42, 43, 84, 86, 92, 109r, 112r, 116r, 117r, 137r, Spec. 1; c-17-35, 37, 38, 40, 41, 43-47, 137r.* ***Maneely*** *c-1, 2, 5, 6, 14.* ***Morisi*** *a-13.* ***Morrow/Williamson*** *r-111.* ***Roussos*** *r-146i, 147i, 149-151i.* ***Severin*** *a-16; c-8, 13.* ***Sutton*** *a-61, 93.* ***Torres*** *a-99r.* ***Tuska*** *a-14.* ***Wildey*** *r-146-151(Outlaw Kid).* ***Williamson*** *r-79, 86, 95.*

RAWHIDE KID
Marvel Comics Group: Aug, 1985 - No. 4, Nov, 1985 (Mini-series)
1-4 5.00

RAWHIDE KID
Marvel Comics (MAX): Apr, 2003 - No. 5, June, 2003 ($2.99, limited series)
1-John Severin-a/Ron Zimmerman-s; Dave Johnson-c 3.00
2-5: 3-Dodson-c. 4-Darwyn Cooke-c. 5-J. Scott Campbell-c 3.00
Vol. 1: Slap Leather TPB (2003, $12.99) r/#1-5 13.00

RAY, THE (See Freedom Fighters & Smash Comics #14)
DC Comics: Feb, 1992 - No. 6, July, 1992 ($1.00, mini-series)
1-Sienkiewicz-c; Joe Quesada-a(p) in 1-5 5.00
2-6: 3-6-Quesada-c(p). 6-Quesada layouts only 3.00
...In a Blaze of Power (1994, $12.95)-r/#1-6 w/new Quesada-c 13.00

RAY, THE
DC Comics: May, 1994 - No. 28, Oct, 1996 ($1.75/$1.95/$2.25)
1-Quesada-c(p); Superboy app. 3.00
1-($2.95)-Collectors Edition w/diff. Quesada-c; embossed foil-c 4.00
2-5,0,6-24,26-28: 2-Quesada-c(p); Superboy app. 5-(9/94). 0-(10/94) 2.50
25-($3.50)-Future Flash (Bart Allen)-c/app; double size 3.50
Annual 1 ($3.95, 68 pgs.)-Superman app. 4.00

RAY BRADBURY COMICS
Topps Comics: Feb, 1993 - V4#1, June, 1994 ($2.95)
1-5-Polybagged w/3 trading cards each. 1-All dinosaur issue; Corben-a; Williamson/Torres/Krenkel-r/Weird Science-Fantasy #25. 3-All dinosaur issue; Steacy painted-c; Stout-a 3.00
Special Edition 1 (1994, $2.95)-The Illustrated Man 3.00
...Special: Tales of Horror #1 ($2.50), ...Trilogy of Terror V3#1 (5/94, $2.50), ...Martian Chronicles V4#1 (6/94, $2.50)-Steranko-c 2.50
NOTE: ***Kelley Jones*** *a-Trilogy of Terror V3#1.* ***Kaluta*** *a-Martian Chronicles V4#1.* ***Kurtzman/Matt Wagner*** *c-2.* ***McKean*** *c-4.* ***Mignola*** *a-4.* ***Wood*** *a-Trilogy of Terror V3#1r.*

RAZORLINE
Marvel Comics: Sept, 1993 (75¢, one-shot)
1-Clive Barker super-heroes: Ectokid, Hokum & Hex, Hyperkind & Saint Sinner 2.50

RAZOR'S EDGE, THE
DC Comics (WildStorm): Dec, 2004 - No. 5, Apr, 2005 ($2.95)
1-5-Warblade; Bisley-c/a; Ridley-s 3.00

REAL ADVENTURE COMICS (Action Adventure #2 on)
Gillmor Magazines: Apr, 1955
1 9 18 27 47 61 75

REAL ADVENTURES OF JONNY QUEST, THE
Dark Horse Comics: Sept, 1996 - No. 12, Sept, 1997 ($2.95)
1-12 3.00

REAL CLUE CRIME STORIES (Formerly Clue Comics)
Hillman Periodicals: V2#4, June, 1947 - V8#3, May, 1953
V2#4(#1)-S&K c/a(3); Dan Barry-a 48 96 144 302 514 725
5-7-S&K c/a(3-4). 7-Iron Lady app. 39 78 117 240 395 550
8-12 14 28 42 80 115 150
V3#1-8,10-12, V4#1-3,5-8,11,12 12 24 36 69 97 125
V3#9-Used in **SOTI**, pg. 102 14 28 42 81 118 155
V4#4-S&K-a 15 30 45 83 124 165
V4#9,10-Krigstein-a 13 26 39 72 101 130
V5#1-5,7,8,10,12 10 20 30 56 76 95
6,9,11(1/54)-Krigstein-a 11 22 33 60 83 105
V6#1-5,8,9,11 9 18 27 52 69 85
6,7,10,12-Krigstein-a. 10-Bondage-c 11 22 33 60 83 105
V7#1-3,5-11, V8#1-3: V7#6-1 pg. Frazetta ad "Prayer" - 1st app.? 10 20 30 56 76 95
4,12-Krigstein-a 11 22 33 60 83 105
NOTE: ***Barry*** *a-9, 10; c-V2#8.* ***Briefer*** *a-V6#6.* ***Fuje*** *a- V2#7(2), 8, 11.* ***Infantino*** *a-V2#8; c-V2#11.* ***Lawrence*** *a-V3#8, V5#7.* ***Powell*** *a-V4#11, 12. V5#4, 5, 7 are 68 pgs.*

REAL EXPERIENCES (Formerly Tiny Tessie)
Atlas Comics (20CC): No. 25, Jan, 1950
25-Virginia Mayo photo-c from movie "Red Light" 11 22 33 60 83 105

REAL FACT COMICS
National Periodical Publications: Mar-Apr, 1946 - No. 21, July-Aug, 1949
1-S&K-c/a; Harry Houdini story; Just Imagine begins (not by Finlay); Fred Ray-a 48 96 144 298 499 700
2-S&K-a; Rin-Tin-Tin & P. T. Barnum stories 29 58 87 169 272 375
3-H.G. Wells, Lon Chaney stories; early DC letter column (New Fun Comics #3 from 1935 may be the 1st) 27 54 81 158 254 350
4-Virgil Finlay-a on 'Just Imagine' begins, ends #12 (2 pgs. each); Jimmy Stewart & Jack London stories; Joe DiMaggio 1 pg. biography 30 60 90 176 283 390
5-Batman/Robin-c taken from cover of Batman #9; 5 pg. story about creation of Batman & Robin; Tom Mix story 160 320 480 1008 1704 2400
6-Origin & 1st app. Tommy Tomorrow by Weisinger and Sherman (1-2/47); Flag-c; 1st writing by Harlan Ellison (letter column, non-professional); "First Man to Reach Mars" epic-c/story 87 174 261 548 924 1300
7-(No. 6 on inside)-Roussos-a; D. Fairbanks sty. 15 30 45 94 147 200
8-2nd app. Tommy Tomorrow by Finlay (5-6/47) 50 100 150 310 518 725
9-S&K-a; Glenn Miller, Indianapolis 500 stories 21 42 63 125 200 275
10-Vigilante by Meskin (based on movie serial); 4 pg. Finlay s/f story 20 40 60 120 193 265
11,12: 11-Annie Oakley, G-Men stories; Kinstler-a 14 28 42 82 121 160
13-Dale Evans and Tommy Tomorrow-c/stories 38 76 114 226 363 500
14,17,18: 14-Will Rogers story 14 28 42 80 115 150
15-Nuclear explosion part-c ("Last War on Earth" story); Clyde Beatty story 15 30 45 94 147 200
16-Tommy Tomorrow app.; 1st Planeteers? 37 74 111 215 345 475
19-Sir Arthur Conan Doyle story 15 30 45 83 124 165
20-Kubert-a, 4 pgs; Daniel Boone story 15 30 45 88 137 185
21-Kubert-a, 2 pgs; Kit Carson story 14 28 42 80 115 150
Ashcan (2/46) nn-Not distributed to newsstands, only for in house use. Covers were produced, but not the rest of the book. A copy sold in 2008 for $500.

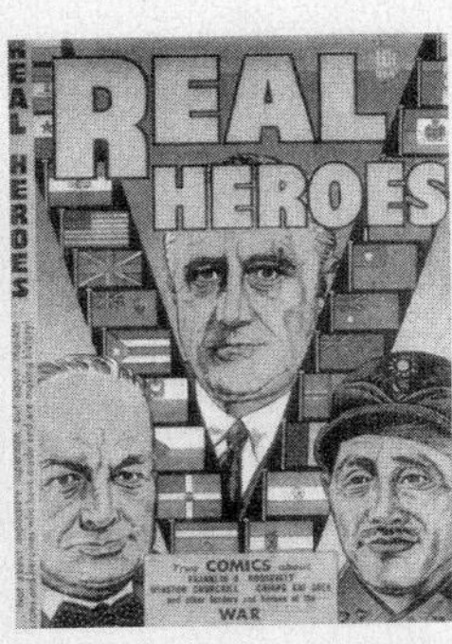

Real Heroes Comics #4 © PMI

Realm of Kings #1 © MAR

Real Screen Comics #6 © DC

	GD 2.0	VG 4.0	FN 6.0	VF 8.0	VF/NM 9.0	NM- 9.2

NOTE: *Barry c-16.* ***Virgil Finlay*** *c-6, 8.* ***Meskin*** *c-10.* ***Roussos*** *a-1-4, 6.*

REAL FUNNIES
Nedor Publishing Co.: Jan, 1943 - No. 3, June, 1943

	GD	VG	FN	VF	VF/NM	NM-
1-Funny animal, humor; Black Terrier app. (clone of The Black Terror)	32	64	96	188	307	425
2,3	15	30	45	94	147	200

REAL GHOSTBUSTERS, THE (Also see Slimer)
Now Comics: Aug, 1988 - No. 32, 1991 ($1.75/$1.95)

1-32: 1-Based on Ghostbusters movie. #29-32 exist? 3.00

REAL HEROES COMICS
Parents' Magazine Institute: Sept, 1941 - No. 16, Oct, 1946

	GD	VG	FN	VF	VF/NM	NM-
1-Roosevelt-c/story	32	64	96	188	307	425
2-J. Edgar Hoover-c/story	15	30	45	83	124	165
3-5,7-10: 4-Churchill, Roosevelt stories	14	28	42	76	108	140
6-Lou Gehrig-c/story	19	38	57	112	179	245
11-16: 13-Kiefer-a	10	20	30	54	72	90

REALISTIC ROMANCES
Realistic Comics/Avon Periodicals: July-Aug, 1951 - No. 17, Aug-Sept, 1954 (No #9-14)

	GD	VG	FN	VF	VF/NM	NM-
1-Kinstler-a; c-/Avon paperback #211	28	56	84	165	270	375
2	15	30	45	84	127	170
3,4	14	28	42	82	121	160
5,8-Kinstler-a	15	30	45	83	124	165
6-c-/Diversey Prize Novels #6; Kinstler-a	15	30	45	84	127	170
7-Evans-a?; c-/Avon paperback #360	15	30	45	84	127	170
15,17: 17-Kinstler-c	14	28	42	80	115	150
16-Kinstler marijuana story-r/Romantic Love #6	15	30	45	83	124	165
I.W. Reprint #1,8,9: #1-r/Realistic Romances #4; Astarita-a. 9-r/Women To Love #1	2	4	6	10	14	18

NOTE: ***Astarita*** *a-2-4, 7, 8, 17. Photo c-1, 2. Painted c-3, 4.*

REAL LIFE COMICS
Nedor/Better/Standard Publ./Pictorial Magazine No. 13: Sept, 1941 - No. 59, Sept, 1952

	GD	VG	FN	VF	VF/NM	NM-
1-Uncle Sam-c/story; Daniel Boone story	60	120	180	381	653	925
2	30	60	90	177	289	400
3-Hitler cover	161	322	483	1030	1765	2500
4,5: 4-Story of American flag "Old Glory"	19	38	57	112	179	245
6-10: 6-Wild Bill Hickok story	19	38	57	109	172	235
11-20: 17-Albert Einstein story	17	34	51	98	154	210
21-23,25,26,28-30: 29-A-Bomb story	15	30	45	86	133	180
24-Story of Baseball (Babe Ruth)	21	42	63	124	202	280
27-Schomburg A-Bomb-c; story of A-Bomb	20	40	60	118	192	265
31-33,35,36,42-44,48,49: 49-Baseball issue	14	28	42	82	121	160
34,37-41,45-47: 34-Jimmy Stewart story. 37-Story of motion pictures; Bing Crosby story. 38-Jane Froman story. 39- "1,000,000 A.D." story. 40-Bob Feller. 41-Jimmie Foxx story ("Jimmy" on-c); "Home Run" Baker story. 45-Story of Olympic games; Burl Ives & Kit Carson story. 46-Douglas Fairbanks Jr. & Sr. story. 47-George Gershwin story	15	30	45	86	133	180
50-Frazetta-a (5 pgs.)	30	60	90	177	289	400
51-Jules Verne "Journey to the Moon" by Evans; Severin/Elder-a	20	40	60	118	192	265
52-Frazetta-a (4 pgs.); Severin/Elder-a(2); Evans-a	33	66	99	194	317	440
53-57-Severin/Elder-a. 54-Bat Masterson-c/story	16	32	48	96	151	205
58-Severin/Elder-a(2)	17	34	51	98	154	210
59-1 pg. Frazetta; Severin/Elder-a	16	32	48	96	151	205

NOTE: *Some issues had two titles.* ***Guardineer*** *a-40(2), 44.* ***Meskin*** *a-52.* ***Roussos*** *a-50.* ***Schomburg*** *c-1, 2, 4, 5, 7, 11, 13-21, 23, 24, 26, 28, 30-32, 34-40, 42, 44-47, 55.* ***Tuska*** *a-53. Photo-c 5, 6.*

REAL LIFE SECRETS (Real Secrets #2 on)
Ace Periodicals: Sept, 1949 (one-shot)

	GD	VG	FN	VF	VF/NM	NM-
1-Painted-c	14	28	42	80	115	150

REAL LIFE STORY OF FESS PARKER (Magazine)
Dell Publishing Co.: 1955

	GD	VG	FN	VF	VF/NM	NM-
1	9	18	27	61	103	145

REAL LIFE TALES OF SUSPENSE (See Suspense)

REAL LOVE (Formerly Hap Hazard)
Ace Periodicals (A. A. Wyn): No. 25, April, 1949 - No. 76, Nov, 1956

	GD	VG	FN	VF	VF/NM	NM-
25	14	28	42	80	115	150
26	10	20	30	58	79	100
27-L. B. Cole-a	12	24	36	69	97	125
28-35	9	18	27	52	69	85
36-66: 66-Last pre-code (2/55)	9	18	27	47	61	75
67-76	8	16	24	40	50	60

NOTE: *Photo c-50-76. Painted c-46.*

REALM, THE
Arrow Comics/WeeBee Comics #13/Caliber Press #14 on: Feb, 1986 - No. 21, 1991 (B&W)

1-21: 4-1st app. Deadworld (9/86) 2.50
Book 1 ($4.95, B&W) 5.00

REAL McCOYS, THE (TV)
Dell Publ. Co.: No. 1071, 1-3/60 - 5-7/1962 (All have Walter Brennan photo-c)

	GD	VG	FN	VF	VF/NM	NM-
Four Color 1071,1134-Toth-a in both	9	18	27	60	100	140
Four Color 1193,1265	8	16	24	56	93	130
01-689-207 (5-7/62)	7	14	21	50	83	115

REALM OF KINGS (Also see Guardians of the Galaxy and Nova)
Marvel Comics: Jan, 2010 ($3.99, one-shot)

1-Abnett & Lanning-s/Manco & Asrar-a; Guardians of the Galaxy app. 4.00

REALM OF KINGS: IMPERIAL GUARD
Marvel Comics: Jan, 2010 - No. 5, May, 2010 ($3.99, limited series)

1-5-Abnett & Lanning-s/Walker-a; Starjammers app. 4.00

REALM OF KINGS: INHUMANS
Marvel Comics: Jan, 2010 - No. 5, May, 2010 ($3.99, limited series)

1-5-Abnett & Lanning-s/Raimondi-a; Mighty Avengers app. 4.00

REALM OF KINGS: SON OF HULK
Marvel Comics: Apr, 2010 - No. 4 ($3.99, limited series)

1,2-Reed-s/Munera-a 4.00

REALM OF THE CLAW (Also see Mutant Earth as part of a flipbook)
Image Comics: Oct, 2003 - No. 2 ($2.95)

0-(7/03, $5.95) Convention Special; cover has gold-foil title logo 6.00
1,2-Two covers by Yardin 3.00
Vol. 1 TPB (2006, $16.99) r/series; concept art & sketch pages 17.00

REAL SCREEN COMICS (#1 titled Real Screen Funnies; TV Screen Cartoons #129-138)
National Periodical Publications: Spring, 1945 - No. 128, May-June, 1959 (#1-40: 52 pgs.)

	GD	VG	FN	VF	VF/NM	NM-
1-The Fox & the Crow, Flippity & Flop, Tito & His Burrito begin	98	196	294	622	1074	1525
2	47	94	141	296	498	700
3-5	32	64	96	188	307	425
6-10 (2-3/47)	21	42	63	122	199	275
11-20 (10-11/48): 13-The Crow x-over in Flippity & Flop	16	32	48	94	147	200
21-30 (6-7/50)	14	28	42	76	108	140
31-50	11	22	33	60	83	105
51-99	10	20	30	54	72	90
100	10	20	30	56	76	95
101-128	8	16	24	44	57	70

REAL SCREEN FUNNIES
DC Comics: Spring 1945

1-Ashcan comic, not distributed to newsstands, only for in-house use. Cover art is Real Screen Funnies #1 with interior being Detective Comics #92. Only ashcan cover to be produced using the regular production first issue art and only using the color yellow. A copy sold in 2008 for $3,000.

REAL SECRETS (Formerly Real Life Secrets)
Ace Periodicals: No. 2, Nov, 1950 - No. 5, May, 1950

	GD	VG	FN	VF	VF/NM	NM-
2-Painted-c	10	20	30	58	79	100
3-5: 3-Photo-c	8	16	24	44	57	70

REAL SPORTS COMICS (All Sports Comics #2 on)
Hillman Periodicals: Oct-Nov, 1948 (52 pgs.)

	GD	VG	FN	VF	VF/NM	NM-
1-Powell-a (12 pgs.)	39	78	117	240	395	550

REAL WAR STORIES
Eclipse Comics: July, 1987; No. 2, Jan, 1991 ($2.00, 52 pgs.)

1-Bolland-a(p), Bissette-a, Totleben-a(i); Alan Moore scripts (2nd printing exists, 2/88) 3.00
2-($4.95) 5.00

REAL WESTERN HERO (Formerly Wow #1-69; Western Hero #76 on)
Fawcett Publications: No. 70, Sept, 1948 - No. 75, Feb, 1949 (All 52 pgs.)

	GD	VG	FN	VF	VF/NM	NM-
70(#1)-Tom Mix, Monte Hale, Hopalong Cassidy, Young Falcon begin	23	46	69	135	218	300
71-75: 71-Gabby Hayes begins. 71,72-Captain Tootsie by Beck. 75-Big Bow and Little Arrow app.	15	30	45	85	130	175

R.E.B.E.L.S. #1 © DC

Red Arrow #3 © P.L. Publ.

Red Herring #1 © Tischman & Bond

GD 2.0 | VG 4.0 | FN 6.0 | VF 8.0 | VF/NM 9.0 | NM- 9.2

NOTE: *Painted/photo c-70-73; painted c-74, 75.*

REAL WEST ROMANCES
Crestwood Publishing Co./Prize Publ.: 4-5/49 - V1#6, 3/50; V2#1, Apr-May, 1950 (All 52 pgs. & photo-c)

V1#1-S&K-a(p) 26 52 78 154 252 350
2-Gail Davis and Rocky Shahan photo-c 14 28 42 80 115 150
3-Kirby-a(p) only 14 28 42 82 121 160
4-S&K-a; Whip Wilson, Reno Browne photo-c 19 38 57 111 176 240
5-Audie Murphy, Gale Storm photo-c; S&K-a 17 34 51 98 154 210
6-Produced by S&K, no S&K-a; Robert Preston & Cathy Downs photo-c 13 26 39 74 105 135
V2#1-Kirby-a(p) 13 26 39 74 105 135

NOTE: ***Meskin** a-V1#5, 6. **Severin/Elder** a-V1#3-6, V2#1. **Meskin** a-V1#6. **Leonard Starr** a-1-3. Photo-c V1#1-6, V2#1.*

REALWORLDS :...
DC Comics: 2000 ($5.95, one-shots, prestige format)

Batman - Marshall Rogers-a/Golden & Sniegoski-s; Justice League of America -Dematteis-s/Barr-painted art; Superman - Vance-s/García-López & Rubenstein-a; Wonder Woman - Hanson & Neuwirth-s/Sam-a 6.00

RE-ANIMATOR IN FULL COLOR
Adventure Comics: Oct, 1991 - No. 3, 1992 ($2.95, mini-series)

1-3: Adapts horror movie. 1-Dorman painted-c 3.00

REAP THE WILD WIND (See Cinema Comics Herald)

REBEL, THE (TV)
Dell Publishing Co.: No. 1076, Feb-Apr, 1960 - No. 1262, Dec-Feb, 1961-62

Four Color 1076 (#1)-Sekowsky-a, photo-c 9 18 27 65 113 160
Four Color 1138 (9-11/60), 1207 (9-11/61), 1262-Photo-c 8 16 24 56 93 130

R.E.B.E.L.S.
DC Comics: Apr, 2009 - Present ($2.99)

1-9,12: 1-Bedard-s/Clarke-a; Vril Dox returns; Supergirl app.; 2 covers 3.00
10,11-($3.99) Blackest Night x-over; Vril Dox joins the Sinestro Corps 4.00
Annual 1 (12/09, $4.99) Origin on Starro the Conqueror; Despero app. 5.00
...: The Coming of Starro TPB (2010, $17.99) r/#1-6 18.00

R.E.B.E.L.S. '94 (Becomes R.E.B.E.L.S. '95 & R.E.B.E.L.S. '96)
DC Comics: No. 0, Oct, 1994 - No. 17, Mar, 1996 ($1.95/$2.25)

0-17: 8-$2.25-c begins. 15-R.E.B.E.L.S '96 begins. 2.50

RECORD BOOK OF FAMOUS POLICE CASES
St. John Publishing Co.: 1949 (25¢, 132 pgs.)

nn-Kubert-a(3); r/Son of Sinbad; Baker-c 40 80 120 246 411 575

RED
DC Comics (Homage): Sept, 2003 - No. 3, Feb, 2004 ($2.95, limited series)

1-3-Warren Ellis-s/Cully Hamner-a/c 3.00
Red/Tokyo Storm Warning TPB (2004, $14.95) Flip book r/both series 15.00

RED ARROW
P. L. Publishing Co.: May-June, 1951 - No. 3, Oct, 1951

1 11 22 33 60 83 105
2,3 9 18 27 47 61 75

RED BAND COMICS
Enwil Associates: Nov, 1944, No. 2, Jan, 1945 - No. 4, May, 1945

1-Bogeyman-c 39 78 117 240 395 550
2-Origin Bogeyman & Santanas; c-reprint/#1 28 56 84 165 270 375
3,4-Captain Wizard app. in both (1st app.); each has identical contents/cover 26 52 78 154 252 350

REDBLADE
Dark Horse Comics: Apr, 1993 - No. 3, July, 1993 ($2.50, mini-series)

1-3: 1-Double gatefold-c 3.00

RED CIRCLE, THE (Re-introduction of characters from MLJ/Archie publications)
DC Comics: Oct, 2009 ($2.99, series of one-shots)

...Inferno 1 - Hangman app.; Straczynski-s/Greg Scott-a 3.00
...The Hangman 1 - Origin retold; Straczynski-s/Derenick & Sienkiewicz-a 3.00
...The Shield 1 - Origin retold; Straczynski-s/McDaniel-a 3.00
...The Web 1 - Straczynski-s/Robinson-a 3.00

RED CIRCLE COMICS (Also see Blazing Comics & Blue Circle Comics)
Rural Home Publications (Enwil): Jan, 1945 - No. 4, April, 1945

1-The Prankster & Red Riot begin 40 80 120 246 411 575

GD 2.0 | VG 4.0 | FN 6.0 | VF 8.0 | VF/NM 9.0 | NM- 9.2

2-Starr-a; The Judge (costumed hero) app. 29 58 87 170 278 385
3,4-Starr-c/a. 3-The Prankster not in costume 23 46 69 136 223 310
4-(Dated 4/45)-Leftover covers to #4 were later restapled over early 1950s coverless comics; variations in the coverless comics used are endless; Woman Outlaws, Dorothy Lamour, Crime Does Not Pay, Sabu, Diary Loves, Love Confessions & Young Love V3#3 known 17 34 51 98 154 210

RED CIRCLE SORCERY (Chilling Adventures in Sorcery #1-5)
Red Circle Prod. (Archie): No. 6, Apr, 1974 - No. 11, Feb, 1975 (All 25¢ iss.)

6,8,9,11: 6-Early Chaykin-a. 7-Pino-a. 8-Only app. The Cobra 2 4 6 8 11 14
7-Bruce Jones-a with Wrightson, Kaluta, Jeff Jones 2 4 6 13 18 22
10-Wood-a(i) 2 4 6 9 13 16

NOTE: ***Chaykin** a-6, 10. **McWilliams** a-10(2 & 3 pgs.). **Mooney** a-11p. **Morrow** a-6-8, 9(text illos), 10, 11i; c-6-11. **Thorne** a-8, 10. **Toth** a-8, 9.*

RED DOG (See Night Music #7)

RED DRAGON
Comico: June, 1996 ($2.95)

1-Bisley-c 3.00

RED DRAGON COMICS (1st Series) (Formerly Trail Blazers; see Super Magician V5#7, 8)
Street & Smith Publications: No. 5, Jan, 1943 - No. 9, Jan, 1944

5-Origin Red Rover, the Crimson Crimebuster; Rex King, Man of Adventure, Captain Jack Commando, & The Minute Man begin; text origin Red Dragon; Binder-c 97 194 291 621 1061 1500
6-Origin The Black Crusader & Red Dragon (3/43); 1st story app. Red Dragon & 1st cover (classic-c) 252 504 756 1613 2757 3900
7-Classic-c 213 426 639 1363 2332 3300
8-The Red Knight app. 76 152 228 486 831 1175
9-Origin Chuck Magnon, Immortal Man 76 152 228 486 831 1175

RED DRAGON COMICS (2nd Series)(See Super Magician V2#8)
Street & Smith Publications: Nov, 1947 - No. 6, Jan, 1949; No. 7, July, 1949

1-Red Dragon begins; Elliman, Nigel app.; Edd Cartier-c/a 94 188 282 597 1024 1450
2-Cartier-c 65 130 195 416 708 1000
3-1st app. Dr. Neff Ghost Breaker by Powell; Elliman, Nigel app. 54 108 162 343 584 825
4-Cartier c/a 77 154 231 489 837 1185
5-7 40 80 120 246 411 575

NOTE: ***Maneely** a-5, 7. **Powell** a-2-7; c-3, 5, 7.*

RED EAGLE
David McKay Publications: No. 16, Aug, 1938

Feature Books 16 26 52 78 154 252 350

REDEYE (See Comics Reading Libraries in the Promotional Comics section)

RED FOX (Formerly Manhunt! #1-14; also see Extra Comics)
Magazine Enterprises: No. 15, 1954

15(A-1 #108)-Undercover Girl story; L.B. Cole-c/a (Red Fox); r-from Manhunt; Powell-a 19 38 57 109 172 235

RED GOOSE COMIC SELECTIONS (See Comic Selections)

RED HAWK (See A-1 Comics, Bobby Benson's ..#14-16 & Straight Arrow #2)
Magazine Enterprises: No. 90, 1953

11-(A-1 Comics #90)-Powell-c/a 13 26 39 72 101 130

RED HERRING
DC Comics (WildStorm): Oct, 2009 - No. 6, Mar, 2010 ($2.99, limited series)

1-6-Tischman-s/Bond-a 3.00

RED MASK (Formerly Tim Holt; see Best Comics, Blazing Six-Guns)
Magazine Enterprises No. 42-53/Sussex No. 54 (M.E. on-c): No. 42, June-July, 1954 - No. 53, May, 1956; No. 54, Sept, 1957

42-Ghost Rider by Ayers continues, ends #50; Black Phantom continues; 3-D effect c/stories begin 21 42 63 122 199 275
43- 3-D effect-c/stories 19 38 57 109 172 235
44-52: 3-D effect stories only. 47-Last pre-code issue. 50-Last Ghost Rider. 51-The Presto Kid begins by Ayers (1st app.); Presto Kid-c begins; last 3-D effect story.
52-Origin The Presto Kid 17 34 51 98 154 210
53,54-Last Black Phantom; last Presto Kid-c 15 30 45 83 124 165
I.W. Reprint #1 (r-/#52). 2 (nd, r/#51 w/diff.-c). 3, 8 (nd; Kinstler-c); 8-r/Red Mask #52 3 6 9 16 22 28

NOTE: ***Ayers** art on Ghost Rider & Presto Kid. **Bolle** art in all (Red Mask); c-43, 44, 49. **Guardineer** a-52. Black Phantom in #42-44, 47-50, 53, 54.*

REDMASK OF THE RIO GRANDE

Red Robin #4 © DC

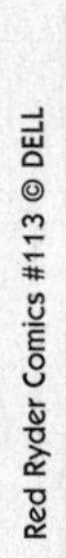

Red Ryder Comics #113 © DELL

Red Sonja (2005 series) #46 © Red Sonja LLC

	GD 2.0	VG 4.0	FN 6.0	VF 8.0	VF/NM 9.0	NM- 9.2

AC Comics: 1990 ($2.50, 28pgs.)(Has photos of movie posters)

	GD 2.0	VG 4.0	FN 6.0	VF 8.0	VF/NM 9.0	NM- 9.2
1-Bolle-c/a(r); photo inside-c						2.50

RED MENACE
DC Comics (WildStorm): Jan, 2007 - No. 6, Jun, 2007 ($2.99, limited series)

	GD 2.0	VG 4.0	FN 6.0	VF 8.0	VF/NM 9.0	NM- 9.2
1-6-Ordway-a/c; Bilson, DeMeo & Brody-s						3.00
TPB (2007, $17.99) r/series, sketch pages & variant covers						18.00

RED MOUNTAIN FEATURING QUANTRELL'S RAIDERS (Movie)(Also see Jesse James #28)
Avon Periodicals: 1952

	GD 2.0	VG 4.0	FN 6.0	VF 8.0	VF/NM 9.0	NM- 9.2
nn-Alan Ladd; Kinstler-c	27	54	81	158	259	360

RED PROPHET: THE TALES OF ALVIN MAKER
Dabel Brothers Prods./Marvel Comics (Dabel Brothers): Mar, 2006 - No. 12, Mar, 2008 ($2.99)

	GD 2.0	VG 4.0	FN 6.0	VF 8.0	VF/NM 9.0	NM- 9.2
1-12-Adaptation of Orson Scott Card novel. 1-Miguel Montenegro-a						3.00
... Vol. 1 HC (2007, $19.99, dustjacket) r/#1-6						20.00
... Vol. 1 SC (2007, $15.99) r/#1-6						16.00
... Vol. 2 HC (2008, $19.99, dustjacket) r/#7-12						20.00

"RED" RABBIT COMICS
Dearfield Comic/J. Charles Laue Publ. Co.: Jan, 1947 - No. 22, Aug-Sep, 1951

	GD 2.0	VG 4.0	FN 6.0	VF 8.0	VF/NM 9.0	NM- 9.2
1	14	28	42	76	108	140
2	8	16	24	44	57	70
3-10	7	14	21	37	46	55
11-17,19-22	7	14	21	35	43	50
18-Flying Saucer-c (1/51)	8	16	24	44	57	70

RED RAVEN COMICS (Human Torch #2 on)(Also see X-Men #44 & Sub-Mariner #26, 2nd series)
Timely Comics: August, 1940

	GD 2.0	VG 4.0	FN 6.0	VF 8.0	VF/NM 9.0	NM- 9.2
1-Origin & 1st app. Red Raven; Comet Pierce & Mercury by Kirby, The Human Top & The Eternal Brain; intro. Magar, the Mystic & only app.; Kirby-c (his 1st signed work)	1200	2400	3600	9000	16,250	23,500

RED ROBIN (Batman: Reborn)
DC Comics: Aug, 2009 - Present ($2.99)

	GD 2.0	VG 4.0	FN 6.0	VF 8.0	VF/NM 9.0	NM- 9.2
1-9-Tim (Drake) Wayne in the Kingdom Come costume; Bachs-a. 1-Two covers						3.00

RED ROCKET 7
Dark Horse Comics: Aug, 1997 - No. 7, June, 1998 ($3.95, square format, limited series)

	GD 2.0	VG 4.0	FN 6.0	VF 8.0	VF/NM 9.0	NM- 9.2
1-7-Mike Allred-c/s/a						4.00

RED RYDER COMICS (Hi Spot #2)(Movies, radio)(See Crackajack Funnies & Super Book of Comics)
Hawley Publ. No. 1/Dell Publishing Co.(K.K.) No. 3 on: 9/40; No. 3, 8/41 - No. 5, 12/41; No. 6, 4/42 - No. 151, 4-6/57

	GD 2.0	VG 4.0	FN 6.0	VF 8.0	VF/NM 9.0	NM- 9.2
1-Red Ryder, his horse Thunder, Little Beaver & his horse Papoose strip reprints begin by Fred Harman; 1st meeting of Red & Little Beaver; Harman line-drawn-c #1-85	253	506	759	1594	2697	3800
3-(Scarce)-Alley Oop, Capt. Easy, Dan Dunn, Freckles & His Friends, King of the Royal Mtd., Myra North strip-r begin	58	116	174	493	947	1400
4-6: 6-1st Dell issue (4/42)	30	60	90	222	411	600
7-10	25	50	75	185	343	500
11-20	18	36	54	130	240	350
21-32-Last Alley Oop, Dan Dunn, Capt. Easy, Freckles	12	24	36	87	156	225
33-40 (52 pgs.): 40-Photo back-c begin, end #57	10	20	30	68	119	170
41 (52 pgs.)-Rocky Lane photo back-c	10	20	30	71	126	180
42-46 (52 pgs.): 46-Last Red Ryder strip-r	8	16	24	58	97	135
47-53 (52 pgs.): 47-New stories on Red Ryder begin. 49,52-Harmon photo back-c	7	14	21	49	80	110
54-92: 54-73 (36 pgs.). 59-Harmon photo back-c. 73-Last King of the Royal Mtd; strip-r by Jim Gary. 74-85 (52 pgs.)-Harman line-drawn-c. 86-92 (52 pgs.)-Harman painted-c	6	12	18	43	69	95
93-99,101-106: 94-96 (36 pgs.)-Harman painted-c. 97,98,(36 pgs.)-Harman line-drawn-c. 99,101-106 (36 pgs.)-Jim Bannon Photo-c	6	12	18	37	59	80
100 (36 pgs.)-Bannon photo-c	6	12	18	39	62	85
107-118 (52 pgs.)-Harman line-drawn-c	5	10	15	34	55	75
119-129 (52 pgs.): 119-Painted-c begin, not by Harman, end #151	5	10	15	32	51	70
130-151 (36 pgs.): 145-Title change to Red Ryder Ranch Magazine 149-Title change to Red Ryder Ranch Comics	5	10	15	30	48	65
Four Color 916 (7/58)	5	10	15	30	48	65

NOTE: ***Fred Harman*** *a-1-99; c-1-98, 107-118. Don Red Barry, Allan Rocky Lane, Wild Bill Elliott & Jim Bannon starred as Red Ryder in the movies. Robert Blake starred as Little Beaver.*

RED RYDER PAINT BOOK
Whitman Publishing Co.: 1941 (8-1/2x11-1/2", 148 pgs.)

	GD 2.0	VG 4.0	FN 6.0	VF 8.0	VF/NM 9.0	NM- 9.2
nn-Reprints 1940 daily strips	76	152	228	479	810	1140

RED SEAL COMICS (Formerly Carnival Comics, and/or Spotlight Comics?)
Harry 'A' Chesler/Superior Publ. No. 19 on: No. 14, 10/45 - No. 18, 10/46; No. 19, 6/47 - No. 22, 12/47

	GD 2.0	VG 4.0	FN 6.0	VF 8.0	VF/NM 9.0	NM- 9.2
14-The Black Dwarf begins (continued from Spotlight?); Little Nemo app; bondage/hypo-c; Tuska-a	77	154	231	493	847	1200
15-Torture story; funny-c	41	82	123	256	428	600
16-Used in **SOTI**, pg. 181, illo "Outside the forbidden pages of de Sade, you find draining a girl's blood only in children's comics;" drug club story r-later in Crime Reporter #1; Veiled Avenger & Barry Kuda app; Tuska-a; funny-c	62	124	186	394	680	965
17,18,20: Lady Satan, Yankee Girl & Sky Chief app; 17-Tuska-a	49	98	147	309	522	735
19-No Black Dwarf (on-c only); Zor, El Tigre app.	43	86	129	271	461	650
21-Lady Satan & Black Dwarf app.	32	64	96	188	307	425
22-Zor, Rocketman app. (68 pgs.)	32	64	96	188	307	425

REDSKIN (Thrilling Indian Stories)(Famous Western Badmen #13 on)
Youthful Magazines: Sept, 1950 - No. 12, Oct, 1952

	GD 2.0	VG 4.0	FN 6.0	VF 8.0	VF/NM 9.0	NM- 9.2
1-Walter Johnson-a (7 pgs.)	17	34	51	98	154	210
2	11	22	33	62	86	110
3-12: 3-Daniel Boone story. 6-Geronimo story	10	20	30	54	72	90

NOTE: ***Walter Johnson*** *c-3, 4.* ***Palais*** *a-11.* ***Wildey*** *a-5, 11. Bondage c-6, 12.*

RED SONJA (Also see Conan #23, Kull & The Barbarians, Marvel Feature & Savage Sword Of Conan #1)
Marvel Comics Group: 1/77 - No. 15, 5/79; V1#1, 2/83 - V2#2, 3/83; V3#1, 8/83 - V3#4, 2/84; V3#5, 1/85 - V3#13, 5/86

	GD 2.0	VG 4.0	FN 6.0	VF 8.0	VF/NM 9.0	NM- 9.2
1-Created by Robert E. Howard	2	4	6	10	14	18
2-10: 5-Last 30¢ issue	1	2	3	5	7	9
4,5-(35¢-c variants, limited distribution)(7,9/77)	3	6	9	20	30	40
11-15, V1#1,V2#2: 14-Last 35¢ issue	1	2	3	4	5	7
V3#1-13: #1-4 ($1.00, 52 pgs.)						3.50

NOTE: ***Brunner*** *c-12-14.* ***J. Buscema*** *a(p)-12, 13, 15; c-V#1.* ***Nebres*** *a-V3#3i(part).* ***N. Redondo*** *a-8i, V3#2i, 3i.* ***Simonson*** *a-V3#1.* ***Thorne*** *c/a-1-11.*

RED SONJA (Continues in Queen Sonja)
Dynamite Entertainment: No. 0, Apr, 2005 - No. 49, 2009 (25¢/$2.99)

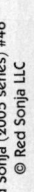

	GD 2.0	VG 4.0	FN 6.0	VF 8.0	VF/NM 9.0	NM- 9.2
0-(4/05, 25¢) Greg Land-c/Mel Rubi-a/Oeming & Carey-s						2.25
1-(6/05, $2.99) Five covers by Ross, Linsner, Cassaday, Turner, Rivera; Rubi-a						3.00
2-46-Multiple covers on all. 29-Sonja dies. 34-Sonja reborn						3.00
5-RRP Edition with Red Foil logo and Isonove-a						10.00
Annual #1 (2007, $3.50) Oeming-s/Sadowski-a; Red Sonja Comics Chronology						3.50
Annual #2 (2009, $3.99) Gage-s/Marcos-a; wraparound Prado-c & Marcos-c						4.00
... Cover Showcase Vol. 1 (2007, $5.99) gallery of variant covers; Cho sketches						6.00
Giant Size Red Sonja #1 (2007, $4.99) Chaykin-c; new story and reprints and pin-ups						5.00
Giant Size Red Sonja #2 (2008, $4.99) Segovia-c; new story and reprints and pin-ups						5.00
... Goes East ($4.99) three covers; Joe Ng-a						5.00
...: Monster Isle ($4.99) two covers; Pablo Marcos-a/Roy Thomas-s						5.00
... One More Day ($4.99) two covers; Liam Sharp-a						5.00
... Vacant Shell ($4.99) two covers; Remender-s/Renaud-a						5.00
...: Wrath of the Gods 1,2 (2010 - No. 5, $3.99) Geovani-a						4.00
The Adventures of Red Sonja TPB (2005, $19.99) r/Marvel Feature #1-7						20.00
The Adventures of Red Sonja Vol. 2 TPB (2007, $19.99) r/#1-7 of '77 Marvel series						20.00
... Vol. 1 TPB (2006, $19.99) r/#0-6; gallery of covers and variants; creators interview						20.00
... Vol. 2 Arrowsmith TPB (2007, $19.99) r/#7-12; gallery of covers and variants						20.00
... Vol. 3 The Rise of Gath TPB (2007, $19.99) r/#13-18; gallery of covers and variants						20.00
... Vol. 4 Animals & More TPB (2007, $24.99) r/#19-24; gallery of covers and variants						25.00

RED SONJA/CLAW: THE DEVIL'S HANDS (See Claw the Unconquered)
DC Comics (WildStorm)/Dynamite Ent.: May, 2006 - No. 4, Aug, 2006 ($2.99, limited series)

	GD 2.0	VG 4.0	FN 6.0	VF 8.0	VF/NM 9.0	NM- 9.2
1-4-Covers by Jim Lee & Dell'Otto.; Andy Smith-a 1-Alex Ross var-c. 2-Dell'Otto var-c. 3-Bermejo var-c. 4-Andy Smith var-c						3.00
TPB (2007, $12.99) r/#1-4; cover gallery						13.00

RED SONJA: SCAVENGER HUNT
Marvel Comics: Dec, 1995 ($2.95, one-shot)

	GD 2.0	VG 4.0	FN 6.0	VF 8.0	VF/NM 9.0	NM- 9.2
1						3.00

RED SONJA: THE MOVIE
Marvel Comics Group: Nov, 1985 - No. 2, Dec, 1985 (Limited series)

	GD 2.0	VG 4.0	FN 6.0	VF 8.0	VF/NM 9.0	NM- 9.2
1,2-Movie adapt-r/Marvel Super Spec. #38						3.00

RED SONJA VS. THULSA DOOM
Dynamite Entertainment: 2005 - No. 4, 2006 ($3.50)

	GD 2.0	VG 4.0	FN 6.0	VF 8.0	VF/NM 9.0	NM- 9.2
1-4-Conrad-a; Conrad & Dell'Otto covers						3.50
..., Volume 1 TPB (2006, $14.99) r/series; cover gallery						15.00

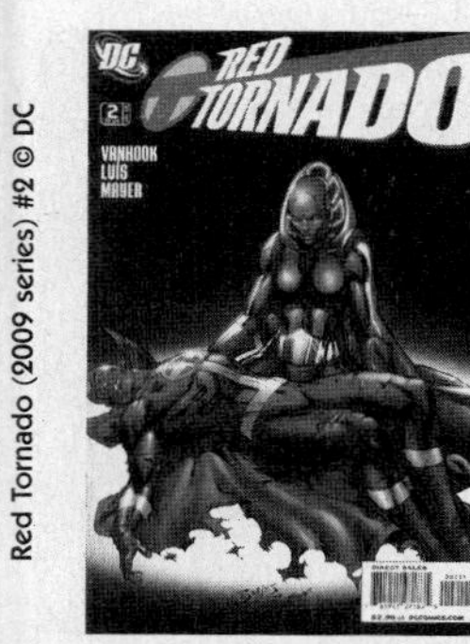

Red Tornado (2009 series) #2 © DC

Reggie and Me #19 © AP

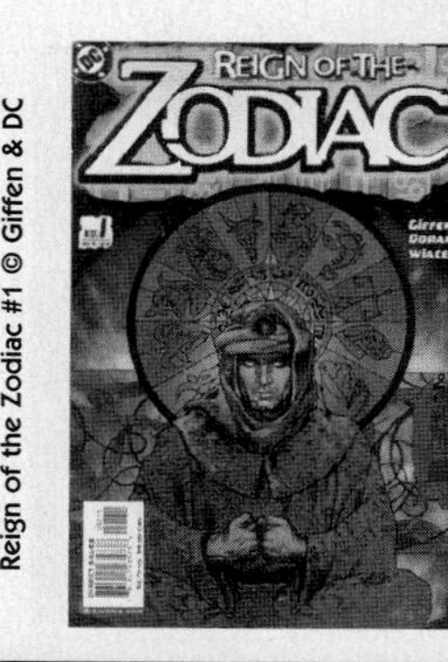

Reign of the Zodiac #1 © Giffen & DC

GD VG FN VF VF/NM NM-
2.0 4.0 6.0 8.0 9.0 9.2

RED STAR, THE
Image Comics/Archangel Studios: June, 2000 - No. 9, June, 2002 ($2.95)
1-Christian Gossett-s/a(p) 4.00
2-9: 9-Beck-c 3.00
#(7.5) Reprints Wizard #1/2 story with new pages 3.00
Annual 1 (Archangel Studios, 11/02, $3.50) "Run Makita Run" 3.50
TPB (4/01, $24.95, 9x12") oversized r/#1-4; intro. by Bendis 25.00
Nokgorka TPB (8/02, $24.95, 9x12") oversized r/#6-9; w/sketch pages 25.00
Wizard 1/2 (mail order) 10.00

RED STAR, THE (Volume 2)
CrossGen #1,2/Archangel Studios #3 on: Feb, 2003 - No. 5, July, 2004 ($2.95/$2.99)
1-5-Christian Gossett-s/a(p) 3.00
Prison of Souls TPB (8/04, $24.95, 9x12") oversized r/#1-5; w/sketch pages 25.00

RED STAR, THE: SWORD OF LIES
Archangel Studios: Aug, 2006 ($4.50)
1-Christian Gossett-s/a(p); origin of the Red Star team 4.50

RED TORNADO (See All-American #20 & Justice League of America #64)
DC Comics: July, 1985 - No. 4, Oct, 1985 (Limited series)
1-4: Kurt Busiek scripts in all. 1-3-Superman & Batman cameos 3.00

RED TORNADO
DC Comics: Nov, 2009 - No. 6 ($2.99, limited series)
1-6: 1-3-Benes-c. 5,6-Vixen app. 3.00

RED WARRIOR
Marvel/Atlas Comics (TCI): Jan, 1951 - No. 6, Dec, 1951
1-Red Warrior & his horse White Wing; Tuska-a 16 32 48 92 144 195
2-Tuska-c 10 20 30 56 76 95
3-6: 4-Origin White Wing. 6-Maneely-c 9 18 27 47 61 75

RED, WHITE & BLUE COMICS
DC Comics: 1941
nn - Ashcan comic, not distributed to newsstands, only for in-house use. Cover art is All-American Comics #20 with interior being Flash Comics #17 (no known sales)

RED WOLF (See Avengers #80 & Marvel Spotlight #1)
Marvel Comics Group: May, 1972 - No. 9, Sept, 1973
1-(Western hero); Gil Kane/Severin-c; Shores-a 3 6 9 18 27 35
2-9: 2-Kane-c; Shores-a. 6-Tuska-r in back-up. 7-Red Wolf as super hero begins. 9-Origin sidekick, Lobo (wolf) 2 4 6 13 18 22

REESE'S PIECES
Eclipse Comics: Oct, 1985 - No.2, Oct, 1985 ($1.75, Baxter paper)
1,2-B&W-r in color 2.50

REFORM SCHOOL GIRL!
Realistic Comics: 1951
nn-Used in **SOTI**, pg. 358, & cover ill. with caption "Comic books are supposed to be like fairy tales" 423 846 1269 3000 5250 7500
(Prices vary widely on this book)

NOTE: *The cover and title originated from a digest-sized book published by Diversey Publishing Co. of Chicago in 1948. The original book "House of Fury", Doubleday, came out in 1941. The girl's real name which appears on the cover of the digest and comic is Marty Collins, Canadian model and ice skating star who posed for this special color photograph for the Diversey novel.*

REGENTS ILLUSTRATED CLASSICS
Prentice Hall Regents, Englewood Cliffs, NJ 07632: 1981 (Plus more recent reprintings) (48 pgs., B&W-a with 14 pgs. of teaching helps)

NOTE: *This series contains Classics Ill. art, and was produced from the same illegal source as* **Cassette Books.** *But when Twin Circle sued to stop the sale of the Cassette Books, they decided to permit this series to continue. This series was produced as a teaching aid. The 20 title series is divided into four levels based upon number of basic words used therein. There is also a teacher's manual for each level. All of the titles are still available from the publisher for about $5 each retail. The number to call for mail order purchases is (201)767-5937. Almost all of the issues have new covers taken from some interior art panel. Here is a list of the series by Regents ident. no. and the Classics Ill. counterpart.*

16770(Cl#24-A2)18333(Cl#3-A2)21668(Cl#13-A2)32224(Cl#21)33051(Cl#26)35788(Cl#84)37153(Cl#16)44460(Cl#19-A2)44808(Cl#18-A2)52395(Cl#4-A2)58627(Cl#5-A2)60067(Cl#30)68405(Cl#23A1)70302(Cl#29)78192(Cl#7-A2)78193(Cl#10-A2)79679(Cl#85)92046(Cl#1-A2)93062(Cl#64)93512(Cl#25)

RE: GEX
Awesome-Hyperwerks: Jul, 1998 - No. 0, Dec, 1998; ($2.50)
Preview (7/98) Wizard Con Edition 3.00
0-(12/98) Loeb-s/Liefeld-a/Pat Lee-c, 1-(9/98) Loeb-s/Liefeld-a/c 2.50

REGGIE (Formerly Archie's Rival...; Reggie & Me #19 on)
Archie Publications: No. 15, Sept, 1963 - No. 18, Nov, 1965
15(9/63), 16(10/64), 17(8/65), 18(11/65) 5 10 15 32 51 70

NOTE: *Cover title No. 15 & 16 is Archie's Rival Reggie.*

REGGIE AND ME (Formerly Reggie)
Archie Publ.: No. 19, Aug, 1966 - No. 126, Sept, 1980 (No. 50-68: 52 pgs.)
19-Evilheart app. 4 8 12 24 37 50
20-23-Evilheart app.; with Pureheart #22 3 6 9 20 30 40
24-40(3/70) 3 6 9 14 20 26
41-49(7/71) 2 4 6 11 16 20
50(9/71)-68 (1/74, 52 pgs.) 3 6 9 14 19 24
69-99 2 4 6 8 10 12
100(10/77) 2 4 6 9 12 15
101-126 1 2 3 5 7 9

REGGIE'S JOKES (See Reggie's Wise Guy Jokes)

REGGIE'S REVENGE!
Archie Comic Publications, Inc.: Spring, 1994 - No. 3 ($2.00, 52 pgs.) (Published semi-annually)
1-Bound-in pull-out poster 3.00
2,3 2.50

REGGIE'S WISE GUY JOKES
Archie Publications: Aug, 1968 - No. 55, 1980 (#5-28 are Giants)
1 4 8 12 28 44 60
2-4 3 6 9 14 20 26
5-16 (1/71)(68 pg. Giants) 3 6 9 17 25 32
17-28 (52 pg. Giants) 2 4 6 13 18 22
29-40(1/77) 1 3 4 6 8 10
41-55 1 2 3 5 6 8

REGISTERED NURSE
Charlton Comics: Summer, 1963
1-r/Nurse Betsy Crane & Cynthia Doyle 3 6 9 17 25 32

REG'LAR FELLERS
Visual Editions (Standard): No. 5, Nov, 1947 - No. 6, Mar, 1948
5,6 9 18 27 47 61 75

REG'LAR FELLERS HEROIC (See Heroic Comics)

REID FLEMING, WORLD'S TOUGHEST MILKMAN
Eclipse Comics/ Deep Sea Comics: 8/86; V2#1, 12/86 - V2#3, 12/88; V2#4, 11/89; V2#5, 11/90 (B&W)
1 (3rd print, large size, 8/86, $2.50), 1-4th & 5th printings ($2.50) 3.00
V2#1 (10/86, regular size, $2.00), 1-2nd print, 3rd print ($2.00, 2/89) 2.50
2-8 , V2#2-2nd & 3rd printings, V2#4-2nd printing, V2#5 ($2.00) 2.50

REIGN IN HELL
DC Comics: Sept, 2008 - No. 8, Apr, 2009 ($3.50, limited series)
1-8-Neron, Shadowpact app.; Giffen-s; Dr. Occult back-up w/Segovia-a. 1-Two covers 3.50
TPB (2009, $19.99) r/#1-8 20.00

REIGN OF THE ZODIAC
DC Comics: Oct, 2003 - No. 8, May, 2004 ($2.75)
1-8: 1-6,8-Giffen-s/Doran-a/Harris-c. 7-Byrd-a 2.75

RELATIVE HEROES
DC Comics: Mar, 2000 - No. 6, Aug, 2000 ($2.50, limited series)
1-6-Grayson-s/Guichet & Sowd-a. 6-Superman-c/app. 2.50

RELOAD
DC Comics (Homage): May, 2003 - No. 3, Sept, 2003 ($2.95, limited series)
1-3-Warren Ellis-s/Paul Gulacy & Jimmy Palmiotti-a 3.00
.../Mek TPB (2004, $14.95, flip book) r/Reload #1-3 & Mek #1-3 15.00

RELUCTANT DRAGON, THE (Walt Disney's...)
Dell Publishing Co.: No. 13, 1940
Four Color 13-Contains 2 pgs. of photos from film; 2 pg. foreword to Fantasia by Leopold Stokowski; Donald Duck, Goofy, Baby Weems & Mickey Mouse (as the Sorcerer's Apprentice) app. 219 438 657 1402 2401 3400

REMAINS
IDW Publishing: May, 2004 - No. 5, Sept, 2004 ($3.99)
1-5-Steve Niles-s/Kieron Dwyer-a 4.00

REMARKABLE WORLDS OF PROFESSOR PHINEAS B. FUDDLE, THE
DC Comics (Paradox Press): 2000 - No. 4, 2000 ($5.95, limited series)
1-4-Boaz Yakin-s/Erez Yakin-a 6.00
TPB (2001, $19.95) r/series 20.00

REMEMBER PEARL HARBOR

Ren and Stimpy Show #35 © Nickelodeon

Reptisaurus #1 © CC

Resident Evil: Fire and Ice #1 © Capcom

GD 2.0 | VG 4.0 | FN 6.0 | VF 8.0 | VF/NM 9.0 | NM- 9.2

Street & Smith Publications: 1942 (68 pgs.) (Illustrated story of the battle)
nn-Uncle Sam-c; Jack Binder-a 48 96 144 302 514 725

REN & STIMPY SHOW, THE (TV) (Nicklodeon cartoon characters)
Marvel Comics: Dec, 1992 - No. 44, July, 1996 ($1.75/$1.95)
1-($2.25)-Polybagged w/scratch & sniff Ren or Stimpy air fowler (equal numbers of each were made) 6.00
1-2nd & 3rd printing; different dialogue on-c 2.50
2-6: 4-Muddy Mudskipper back-up. 5-Bill Wray painted-c. 6-Spider-Man vs. Powdered Toast Man 4.00
7-17: 12-1st solo back-up story w/Tank & Brenner 2.50
18-44: 18-Powered Toast Man app. 2.50
25 ($2.95) Deluxe edition w/die cut cover 3.00
...Don't Try This at Home (3/94, $12.95, TPB)-r/#9-12 13.00
...Eenteractive Special ('95, $2.95) 3.00
...Holiday Special 1994 (2/95, $2.95, 52 pgs.) 3.00
...Mini Comic (1995) 5.00
...Pick of the Litter nn (1993, $12.95, TPB)-r/#1-4 13.00
...Radio Daze (11/95, $1.95) 2.50
...Running Joke nn (1993, $12.95, TPB)-r/#1-4 plus new-a 13.00
...Seeck Little Monkeys (1/95, $12.95)-r/#17-20 13.00
...Special 2 (7/94, $2.95, 52 pgs.), ...Special 3 (10/94, $2.95, 52 pgs.)-Choose adventure, ...Special: Around the World in a Daze ($2.95), ...Special: Four Swerks (1/95, $2.95, 52 pgs.)-FF #1 cover swipe; cover reads "Four Swerks w/5 pg. coloring book.", ...Special: Powdered Toast Man 1 (4/94, $2.95, 52 pgs.), ...Special: Powdered Toast Man's Cereal Serial (4/95, $2.95), ...Special: Sports (10/95, $2.95) 3.00
...Tastes Like Chicken nn (11/93,$12.95,TPB)-r/#5-8 13.00
...Your Pals (1994, $12.95, TPB)-r/#13-16 13.00

RENFIELD
Caliber Press:1994 - No. 3, 1995 ($2.95, B&W, limited series)
1-3 3.00

RENO BROWNE, HOLLYWOOD'S GREATEST COWGIRL (Formerly Margie Comics; Apache Kid #53 on; also see Western Hearts, Western Life Romances & Western Love)
Marvel Comics (MPC): No. 50, April, 1950 - No. 52, Sept, 1950 (52 pgs.)
50-Reno Browne photo-c on all 30 60 90 174 280 385
51,52 25 50 75 147 236 325

REPLACEMENT GOD
Amaze Ink: June, 1995 - No. 8 ($2.95, B&W)
1-8-Zander Cannon-s/a 3.00

REPLACEMENT GOD
Image Comics: May, 1997 - No. 5 ($2.95, B&W)
1-5: 1-Flip book w/"Knute's Escapes", r/original series. 2-Flip book w/"Harris Thermidor". 3-5: 3-Flip book w/"Myth and Legend" 3.00

REPTILICUS (Becomes Reptisaurus #3 on)
Charlton Comics: Aug, 1961 - No. 2, Oct, 1961
1 (Movie) 19 38 57 133 259 385
2 11 22 33 74 132 190

REPTISAURUS (Reptilicus #1,2)
Charlton Comics: V2#3, Jan, 1962 - No. 8, Dec, 1962; Summer, 1963
V2#3-8: 3-Flying saucer-c/s. 8-Montes/Bache-c/a 6 12 18 41 66 90
Special Edition 1 (Summer, 1963) 6 12 18 39 62 85

REQUIEM FOR DRACULA
Marvel Comics: Feb, 1993 ($2.00, 52 pgs.)
nn-r/Tomb of Dracula #69,70 by Gene Colan 2.50

RESCUERS, THE (See Walt Disney Showcase #40)

RESIDENT EVIL (Based on video game)
Image Comics (WildStorm): Mar, 1998 - No. 5 ($4.95, quarterly magazine)
1 7.00
2-5 5.00
...Code: Veronica 1-4 (2002, $14.95) English reprint of Japanese comics 15.00
...Collection One ('99, $14.95, TPB) r/#1-4 15.00

RESIDENT EVIL (Volume 2)
DC Comics (WildStorm): May, 2009 - No. 3, Jan, 2010 ($3.99)
1-3: 1,2-Liam Sharpe-a. 1-Two covers 4.00

RESIDENT EVIL: FIRE AND ICE
DC Comics (WildStorm): Dec, 2000 - No. 4, May, 2001 ($2.50, limited series)
1-4-Bermejo-c 2.50
TPB (2009, $24.99) r/#1-4 plus short stories from Resident Evil magazine 25.00

RESISTANCE (Based on the video game)
DC Comics (WildStorm): Early Mar, 2009 - No. 6, Jul, 2009 ($3.99, limited series)
1-6-Ramón Pérez-a/C.P. Smith-c 4.00
TPB (2010, $19.99) r/#1-6 20.00

RESISTANCE, THE
DC Comics (WildStorm): Nov, 2002 - No. 8, June, 2003 ($2.95)
1-8-Palmiotti & Gray-s/Santacruz-a 3.00

REST (Milo Ventimiglia Presents...)
Devil's Due Publ.: No. 0, Aug, 2008 - Present (99¢/$3.50)
0-(99¢) Prelude to series; Powers-s/McManus-a 2.25
1,2-($3.50) 1-Two covers (Tim Sale art & Milo Ventimiglia photo) 3.50

RESTAURANT AT THE END OF THE UNIVERSE, THE (See Hitchhiker's Guide to the Galaxy & Life, the Universe & Everything)
DC Comics: 1994 - No. 3, 1994 ($6.95, limited series)
1-3 7.00

RESTLESS GUN (TV)
Dell Publishing Co.: No. 934, Sept, 1958 - No. 1146, Nov-Jan, 1960-61
Four Color 934 (#1)-Photo-c 10 20 30 71 126 180
Four Color 986 (5/59), 1045 (11-1/60), 1089 (3/60), 1146-Wildey-a; all photo-c 8 16 24 52 86 120

RESURRECTION MAN
DC Comics: May, 1997 - No. 27, Aug, 1999 ($2.50)
1-Lenticular disc on cover 5.00
2-5: 2-JLA app. 4.00
6-10: 6-Genesis-x-over. 7-Batman app. 10-Hitman-c/app. 3.00
11-27: 16,17-Supergirl x-over. 18-Deadman & Phantom Stranger-c/app. 21-JLA-c/app. 2.50
#1,000,000 (11/98) 853rd Century x-over 2.50

RETIEF (Keith Laumer's)
Adventure Comics (Malibu): Dec, 1989 - Vol. 2, No.6, ($2.25, B&W)
1-6,Vol. 2, #1-6,Vol. 3 (...of The CDT) #1-6 2.50
...and The Warlords #1-6, ...: Diplomatic Immunity #1 (4/91), ...: Giant Killer #1 (9/91), ...: Crime & Punishment #1 (11/91) 2.50

RETURN FROM WITCH MOUNTAIN (See Walt Disney Showcase #44)

RETURN OF ALISON DARE: LITTLE MISS ADVENTURES, THE (Also see Alison Dare: Little Miss Adventures)
Oni Press: Apr, 2001 - No. 3, Sept, 2001 ($2.95, B&W, limited series)
1-3-J. Torres-s/J.Bone-c/a 3.00

RETURN OF GORGO, THE (Formerly Gorgo's Revenge)
Charlton Comics: No. 2, Aug, 1963; No. 3, Fall, 1964 (12¢)
2,3-Ditko-c/a; based on M.G.M. movie 8 16 24 52 86 120

RETURN OF KONGA, THE (Konga's Revenge #2 on)
Charlton Comics: 1962
nn 8 16 24 52 86 120

RETURN OF MEGATON MAN
Kitchen Sink Press: July, 1988 - No. 3, 1988 ($2.00, limited series)
1-3: Simpson-c/a 2.50

RETURN OF THE GREMLINS (The Roald Dahl characters)
Dark Horse Comics: Mar, 2008 - No. 3, May, 2008 ($2.99, limited series)
1-3-Richardson-s/Yeagle-a. 1-Back-up reprint of intro. from 1943. 2-Back-up reprints of three Gremlin Gus 2-pagers from 1943. 3-Back-up reprints 3.00

RETURN OF THE OUTLAW
Toby Press (Minoan): Feb, 1953 - No. 11, 1955
1-Billy the Kid 10 20 30 54 72 90
2 7 14 21 35 43 50
3-11 6 12 18 31 38 45

RETURN TO JURASSIC PARK
Topps Comics: Apr, 1995 - No. 9, Feb, 1996 ($2.50/$2.95)
1-9: 3-Begin $2.95-c. 9-Artist's Jam issue 3.00

RETURN TO THE AMALGAM AGE OF COMICS: THE MARVEL COMICS COLLECTION
Marvel Comics: 1997 ($12.95, TPB)
nn-Reprints Amalgam one-shots: Challengers of the Fantastic #1, The Exciting X-Patrol #1, Iron Lantern #1, The Magnetic Men Featuring Magneto #1, Spider-Boy Team-Up #1 & Thorion of the New Asgods #1 13.00

Rex Allen Comics #5 © DELL

Ribtickler #9 © FOX

Richie Rich #154 © HARV

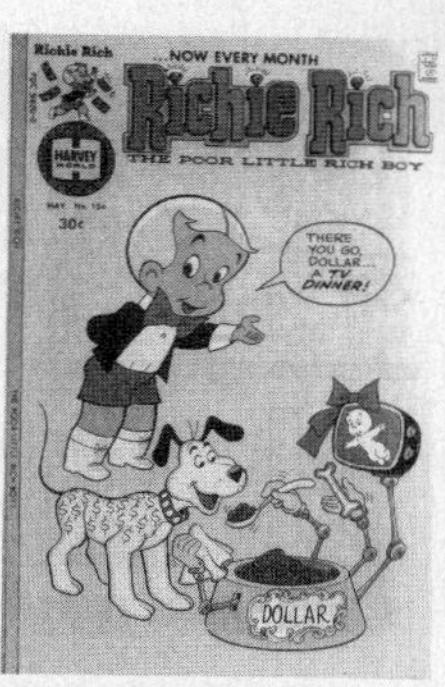

	GD 2.0	VG 4.0	FN 6.0	VF 8.0	VF/NM 9.0	NM- 9.2

REVEAL
Dark Horse Comics: Nov, 2002 ($6.95, squarebound)

1-Short stories of Dark Horse characters by various; Lone Wolf 2100, Buffy, Spyboy app. 7.00

REVEALING LOVE STORIES (See Fox Giants)

REVEALING ROMANCES
Ace Magazines: Sept, 1949 - No. 6, Aug, 1950

	GD	VG	FN	VF	VF/NM	NM-
1	14	28	42	82	121	160
2	9	18	27	50	65	80
3-6	8	16	24	44	57	70

REVELATIONS
Dark Horse Comics: Aug, 2005 - No. 6, Jan, 2006 ($2.99, limited series)

1-6-Paul Jenkins-s/Humberto Ramos-a/c 3.00

REVENGE OF THE PROWLER (Also see The Prowler)
Eclipse Comics: Feb, 1988 - No. 4, June, 1988 ($1.75/$1.95)

1,3,4: 1-$1.75. 3,4-$1.95-c; Snyder III-a(p) 2.50
2 ($2.50)-Contains flexi-disc 2.75

REVOLUTION ON THE PLANET OF THE APES
Mr. Comics: Dec, 2005 - No. 6, Aug, 2006 ($3.95)

1-6: 1,2-Salgood Sam-a 4.00

REX ALLEN COMICS (Movie star)(Also see Four Color #877 & Western Roundup under Dell Giants)
Dell Publ. Co.: No. 316, Feb, 1951 - No. 31, Dec-Feb, 1958-59 (All-photo-c)

	GD	VG	FN	VF	VF/NM	NM-
Four Color 316(#1)(52 pgs.)-Rex Allen & his horse Koko begin; Marsh-a	14	28	42	97	181	265
2 (9-11/51, 36 pgs.)	9	18	27	63	107	150
3-10	7	14	21	45	73	100
11-20	6	12	18	39	62	85
21-23,25-31	5	10	15	35	55	75
24-Toth-a	6	12	18	39	62	85

NOTE: ***Manning** a-20, 27-30. Photo back-c F.C. #316, 2-12, 20, 21.*

REX DEXTER OF MARS (See Mystery Men Comics)
Fox Features Syndicate: Fall, 1940 (68 pgs.)

	GD	VG	FN	VF	VF/NM	NM-
1-Rex Dexter, Patty O'Day, & Zanzibar (Tuska-a) app.; Briefer-c/a	194	388	582	1242	2121	3000

REX HART (Formerly Blaze Carson; Whip Wilson #9 on)
Timely/Marvel Comics (USA): No. 6, Aug, 1949 - No. 8, Feb, 1950 (All photo-c)

	GD	VG	FN	VF	VF/NM	NM-
6-Rex Hart & his horse Warrior begin; Black Rider app; Captain Tootsie by Beck	26	52	78	152	249	345
7,8: 18 pg. Thriller in each. 8-Blaze the Wonder Collie app. in text	18	36	54	103	162	220

REX MORGAN, M.D. (Also see Harvey Comics Library)
Argo Publ.: Dec, 1955 - No. 3, Apr?, 1956

	GD	VG	FN	VF	VF/NM	NM-
1-r/Rex Morgan daily newspaper strips & daily panel-r of "These Women" by D'Alessio & "Timeout" by Jeff Keate	14	28	42	76	108	140
2,3	10	20	30	54	72	90

REX MUNDI (Latin for "King of the World")
Image Comics: No. 0, Aug, 2002 - No. 18, Apr, 2006 ($2.95/$2.99)

0-18-Arvid Nelson-s. 0-13-Eric Johnson-a. 14,15-Jim DiBartolo-a. 18-Ramos-c 3.00
Vol. 1: The Guardian of the Temple TPB (1/04, $14.95) r/#0-5 15.00
Book 1: The Guardian of the Temple TPB (Dark Horse, 11/06, $16.95) r/#0-5 & Brother Matthew web comic; Dysart intro. 17.00
Vol. 2: The River Underground TPB (4/05, $14.95) r/#6-11 15.00
Book 2: The River Underground (Dark Horse, 2006, $16.95) r/#6-11 17.00
Vol. 3: The Lost Kings TPB (Dark Horse, 9/06, $16.95) r/#12-17 17.00
Book Four: Crowd and Sword TPB (Dark Horse, 12/07, $16.95) r/#18 plus V2 #1-5 and story from Dark Horse Book of Monsters 17.00

REX MUNDI (Volume 2)
Dark Horse Comics: July, 2006 - No. 19, Aug, 2009 ($2.99)

1-19-Arvid Nelson-s. 1-JH Williams-c. 16-Chen-c. 18-Linsner-c 3.00
Book Five: The Valley at the End of the World TPB (11/08, $17.95) r/#6-12 18.00

REX THE WONDER DOG (See The Adventures of...)

RHUBARB, THE MILLIONAIRE CAT
Dell Publishing Co.: No. 423, Sept-Oct, 1952 - No. 563, June, 1954

	GD	VG	FN	VF	VF/NM	NM-
Four Color 423 (#1)	6	12	18	39	62	85
Four Color 466(5/53),563	5	10	15	34	55	75

RIB
Dilemma Productions: Oct, 1995 - April, 1996 ($1.95, B&W)

Ashcan, 1 3.00

RIB
Bookmark Productions: 1996 ($2.95, B&W)

1-Sakai-c; Andrew Ford-s/a 3.00

RIB
Caliber Comics: May, 1997 - No. 5, 1998 ($2.95, B&W)

1-5: 1-"Beginnings" pts. 1 & 2 3.00

RIBIT! (Red Sonja imitation)
Comico: Jan, 1989 - No. 4, April?, 1989 ($1.95, limited series)

1-4: Frank Thorne-c/a/scripts 3.00

RIBTICKLER (Also see Fox Giants)
Fox Feature Synd./Green Publ. (1957)/Norlen (1959): 1945, No. 2, 1946, No. 3, Jul-Aug, 1946 - No. 9, Jul-Aug, 1947; 1957; 1959

	GD	VG	FN	VF	VF/NM	NM-
1-Funny animal	15	30	45	90	140	190
2-(1946)	10	20	30	54	72	90
3-9: 3,5,7-Cosmo Cat app.	9	18	27	47	61	75
3,7,8 (Green Publ.-1957), 3,7,8 (Norlen Mag.-1959)	3	6	9	16	23	30

RICHARD DRAGON
DC Comics: July, 2004 - No. 12, Jun, 2005 ($2.50)

1-12: 1-Dixon-s/McDaniel-a/c; Ben Turner app. 2,3-Nightwing app. 4-6,11,12-Lady Shiva 2.50

RICHARD DRAGON, KUNG-FU FIGHTER (See The Batman Chronicles #5, Brave & the Bold, & The Question)
National Periodical Publ./DC Comics: Apr-May, 1975 - No. 18, Nov-Dec, 1977

	GD	VG	FN	VF	VF/NM	NM-
1-Intro Richard Dragon, Ben Stanley & O-Sensei; 1st app. Barney Ling; adaptation of Jim Dennis novel "Dragon's Fists" begins, ends #4	3	6	9	14	19	24
2,3: 2-Intro Carolyn Woosan; Starlin/Weiss-c/a; bondage-c. 3-Kirby-a(p); Giordano bondage-c	2	4	6	8	11	14
4-8-Wood inks. 4-Carolyn Woosan dies. 5-1st app. Lady Shiva	2	3	4	6	8	10
9-13,15-18: 9-Ben Stanley becomes Ben Turner; intro Preying Mantis. 16-1st app. Prof Ojo. 18-1st app. Ben Turner as The Bronze Tiger	1	2	3	5	7	9
14-"Spirit of Bruce Lee"	3	6	9	14	19	24

NOTE: ***Buckler** a-14. c-15, 18. **Chua** c-13. **Estrada** a-9, 13-18. **Estrada/Abel** a-10-12. **Estrada/Wood** a-4-8. **Giordano** c-1, 3-11. **Weiss** a-2(partial) c-2i.*

RICHARD THE LION-HEARTED (See Ideal a Classical Comic)

RICHIE RICH (See Harvey Collectors Comics, Harvey Hits, Little Dot, Little Lotta, Little Sad Sack, Million Dollar Digest, Mutt & Jeff, Super Richie & 3-D Dolly; also Tastee-Freez Comics in the Promotional Comics section)

RICHIE RICH (...the Poor Little Rich Boy) (See Harvey Hits #3, 9)
Harvey Publ.: Nov, 1960 - #218, Oct, 1982; #219, Oct, 1986 - #254, Jan, 1991

	GD	VG	FN	VF	VF/NM	NM-
1-(See Little Dot #1 for 1st app.)	231	462	693	2021	4011	6000
2	70	140	210	595	1173	1750
3-5	46	92	138	368	709	1050
6-10: 8-Christmas-c	27	54	81	197	386	575
11-20	17	34	51	124	242	360
21-30	12	24	36	88	162	235
31-40	10	20	30	71	126	180
41-50: 42(2/66)-X-mas-c	8	16	24	58	97	135
51-55,57-60: 59-Buck, prototype of Dollar the Dog	6	12	18	41	66	90
56-1st app. Super Richie	7	14	21	49	80	110
61-64,66-80: 71-Nixon & Robert Kennedy caricatures; outer space-c	5	10	15	30	48	65
65-Buck the Dog (Dollar prototype) on cover	6	12	18	43	69	95
81-99	4	8	12	22	34	45
100(12/70)-1st app. Irona the robot maid	4	8	12	26	41	55
101-111,117-120	3	6	9	14	20	26
112-116: All 52 pg. Giants	3	6	9	17	25	32
121-140: 137-1st app. Mr. Cheepers and Professor Keenbean	2	4	6	9	13	16
141-160: 145-Infinity-c. 155-3rd app. The Money Monster	2	4	6	8	10	12
161-180	1	3	4	6	8	10
181-199	1	2	3	5	6	8
200	1	3	4	6	8	10
201-218: 210-Stone-Age Riches app	1	2	3	4	5	7

219-254: 237-Last original material 6.00
Harvey Comics Classics Vol. 2 TPB (Dark Horse Books, 10/07, $19.95) Reprints Richie Rich's early appearances in this title, Little Dot and Richie Rich Success Stories, mostly B&W with some color stories; history and interview with Ernie Colón 20.00

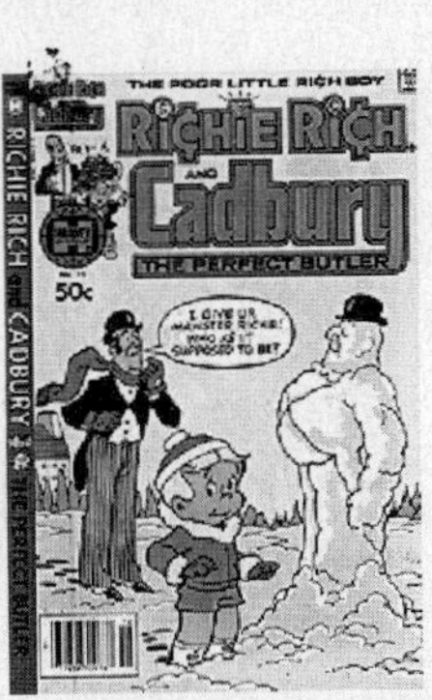

Richie Rich and Cadbury #16 © HARV

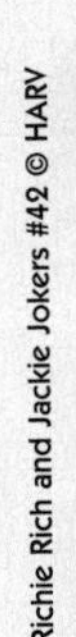
Richie Rich and Jackie Jokers #42 © HARV

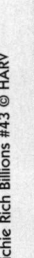

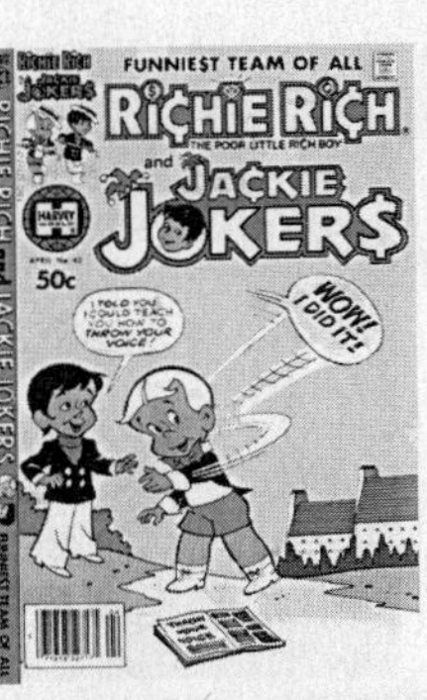

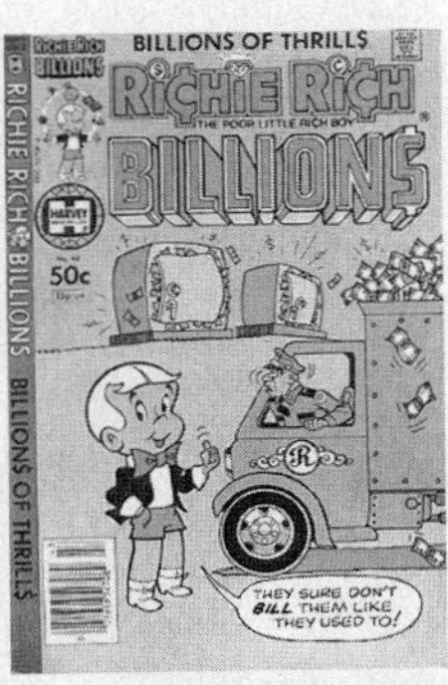

Richie Rich Billions #43 © HARV

RICHIE RICH
Harvey Comics: Mar, 1991 - No. 28, Nov, 1994 ($1.00, bi-monthly)

	GD 2.0	VG 4.0	FN 6.0	VF 8.0	VF/NM 9.0	NM- 9.2
1-28: Reprints best of Richie Rich						2.50
Giant Size 1-4 (10/91-10/93, $2.25, 68 pgs.)						3.00

RICHIE RICH ADVENTURE DIGEST MAGAZINE
Harvey Comics: 1992 - No. 7, Sept, 1994 ($1.25, quarterly, digest-size)

	GD 2.0	VG 4.0	FN 6.0	VF 8.0	VF/NM 9.0	NM- 9.2
1-7						4.00

RICHIE RICH AND...
Harvey Comics: Oct, 1987 - No. 11, May, 1990 ($1.00)

	GD 2.0	VG 4.0	FN 6.0	VF 8.0	VF/NM 9.0	NM- 9.2
1-Professor Keenbean						4.00
2-11: 2-Casper. 3-Dollar the Dog. 4-Cadbury. 5 Mayda Munny. 6-Irona. 7-Little Dot. 8-Professor Keenbean. 9-Little Audrey. 10-Mayda Munny. 11-Cadbury						3.00

RICHIE RICH AND BILLY BELLHOPS
Harvey Publications: Oct, 1977 (52 pgs., one-shot)

	GD 2.0	VG 4.0	FN 6.0	VF 8.0	VF/NM 9.0	NM- 9.2
1	2	4	6	9	12	15

RICHIE RICH AND CADBURY
Harvey Publ.: 10/77; #2, 9/78 - #23, 7/82; #24, 7/90 - #29, 1/91 (1-10: 52pgs.)

	GD 2.0	VG 4.0	FN 6.0	VF 8.0	VF/NM 9.0	NM- 9.2
1-(52 pg. Giant)	2	4	6	11	16	20
2-10-(52 pg. Giant)	2	4	6	8	10	12
11-23						6.00
24-29: 24-Begin $1.00-c						4.00

RICHIE RICH AND CASPER
Harvey Publications: Aug, 1974 - No. 45, Sept, 1982

	GD 2.0	VG 4.0	FN 6.0	VF 8.0	VF/NM 9.0	NM- 9.2
1	3	6	9	20	30	40
2-5	2	4	6	13	18	22
6-10: 10-Xmas-c	2	4	6	9	13	16
11-20	1	3	4	6	8	10
21-45: 22-Xmas-c						6.00

RICHIE RICH AND DOLLAR THE DOG (See Richie Rich #65)
Harvey Publications: Sept, 1977 - No. 24, Aug, 1982 (#1-10: 52 pgs.)

	GD 2.0	VG 4.0	FN 6.0	VF 8.0	VF/NM 9.0	NM- 9.2
1-(52 pg. Giant)	2	4	6	11	16	20
2-10-(52 pg. Giant)	2	4	6	8	10	12
11-24						6.00

RICHIE RICH AND DOT
Harvey Publications: Oct, 1974 (one-shot)

	GD 2.0	VG 4.0	FN 6.0	VF 8.0	VF/NM 9.0	NM- 9.2
1	3	6	9	16	22	28

RICHIE RICH AND GLORIA
Harvey Publications: Sept, 1977 - No. 25, Sept, 1982 (#1-11: 52 pgs.)

	GD 2.0	VG 4.0	FN 6.0	VF 8.0	VF/NM 9.0	NM- 9.2
1-(52 pg. Giant)	2	4	6	11	16	20
2-11-(52 pg. Giant)	2	4	6	8	10	12
12-25						6.00

RICHIE RICH AND HIS GIRLFRIENDS
Harvey Publications: April, 1979 - No. 16, Dec, 1982

	GD 2.0	VG 4.0	FN 6.0	VF 8.0	VF/NM 9.0	NM- 9.2
1-(52 pg. Giant)	2	4	6	9	13	16
2-(52 pg. Giant)	1	3	4	6	8	10
3-10	1	2	3	5	6	8
11-16						6.00

RICHIE RICH AND HIS MEAN COUSIN REGGIE
Harvey Publications: April, 1979 - No. 3, 1980 (50¢) (#1,2: 52 pgs.)

	GD 2.0	VG 4.0	FN 6.0	VF 8.0	VF/NM 9.0	NM- 9.2
1	2	4	6	9	13	16
2-3:	1	3	4	6	8	10

NOTE: *No. 4 was advertised, but never released.*

RICHIE RICH AND JACKIE JOKERS (Also see Jackie Jokers)
Harvey Publications: Nov, 1973 - No. 48, Dec, 1982

	GD 2.0	VG 4.0	FN 6.0	VF 8.0	VF/NM 9.0	NM- 9.2
1: 52 pg. Giant; contains material from unpublished Jackie Jokers #5	4	8	12	24	37	50
2,3-(52 pg. Giants). 2-R.R. & Jackie 1st meet	3	6	9	16	22	28
4,5	2	4	6	13	18	22
6-10	2	4	6	9	13	16
11-20,26: 11-1st app. Kool Katz. 26-Star Wars parody	1	3	4	6	8	10
21-25,27-40	1	2	3	4	5	7
41-48						6.00

RICHIE RICH AND PROFESSOR KEENBEAN
Harvey Comics: Sept, 1990 - No. 2, Nov, 1990 ($1.00)

	GD 2.0	VG 4.0	FN 6.0	VF 8.0	VF/NM 9.0	NM- 9.2
1,2						3.00

RICHIE RICH AND THE NEW KIDS ON THE BLOCK
Harvey Publications: Feb, 1991 - No. 3, June, 1991 ($1.25, bi-monthly)

	GD 2.0	VG 4.0	FN 6.0	VF 8.0	VF/NM 9.0	NM- 9.2
1-3: 1,2-New Richie Rich stories						3.00

RICHIE RICH AND TIMMY TIME
Harvey Publications: Sept, 1977 (50¢, 52 pgs, one-shot)

	GD 2.0	VG 4.0	FN 6.0	VF 8.0	VF/NM 9.0	NM- 9.2
1	2	4	6	9	12	15

RICHIE RICH BANK BOOK
Harvey Publications: Oct, 1972 - No. 59, Sept, 1982

	GD 2.0	VG 4.0	FN 6.0	VF 8.0	VF/NM 9.0	NM- 9.2
1	5	10	15	30	48	65
2-5: 2-2nd app. The Money Monster	3	6	9	16	23	30
6-10	2	4	6	11	16	20
11-20: 18-Super Richie app.	2	4	6	8	10	12
21-30	1	2	3	5	7	9
31-40	1	2	3	4	5	7
41-59						6.00

RICHIE RICH BEST OF THE YEARS
Harvey Publications: Oct, 1977 - No. 6, June, 1980 (128 pgs., digest-size)

	GD 2.0	VG 4.0	FN 6.0	VF 8.0	VF/NM 9.0	NM- 9.2
1(10/77)-Reprints	2	4	6	9	12	15
2-6(11/79-6/80, 95¢). #2(10/78)-Rep.. #3(6/79, 75¢)	1	2	3	5	7	9

RICHIE RICH BIG BOOK
Harvey Publications: Nov, 1992 - No. 2, May, 1993 ($1.50, 52 pgs.)

	GD 2.0	VG 4.0	FN 6.0	VF 8.0	VF/NM 9.0	NM- 9.2
1,2						3.00

RICHIE RICH BIG BUCKS
Harvey Publications: Apr, 1991 - No. 8, July, 1992 ($1.00, bi-monthly)

	GD 2.0	VG 4.0	FN 6.0	VF 8.0	VF/NM 9.0	NM- 9.2
1-8						3.00

RICHIE RICH BILLIONS
Harvey Publications: Oct, 1974 - No. 48, Oct, 1982 (#1-33: 52 pgs.)

	GD 2.0	VG 4.0	FN 6.0	VF 8.0	VF/NM 9.0	NM- 9.2
1	4	8	12	22	34	45
2-5: 2-Christmas issue	3	6	9	14	20	25
6-10	2	4	6	10	14	18
11-20	2	4	6	8	10	12
21-33	1	2	3	5	6	8
34-48: 35-Onion app.						6.00

RICHIE RICH CASH
Harvey Publications: Sept, 1974 - No. 47, Aug, 1982

	GD 2.0	VG 4.0	FN 6.0	VF 8.0	VF/NM 9.0	NM- 9.2
1-1st app. Dr. N-R-Gee	3	6	9	20	30	40
2-5	2	4	6	13	18	22
6-10	2	4	6	9	13	16
11-20	1	3	4	6	8	10
21-30	1	2	3	4	5	7
31-47: 33-Dr. Blemish app.						6.00

RICHIE RICH CASH MONEY
Harvey Comics: May, 1992 - No. 2, Aug, 1992 ($1.25)

	GD 2.0	VG 4.0	FN 6.0	VF 8.0	VF/NM 9.0	NM- 9.2
1,2						3.00

RICHIE RICH, CASPER AND WENDY - NATIONAL LEAGUE
Harvey Comics: June, 1976 (50¢)

	GD 2.0	VG 4.0	FN 6.0	VF 8.0	VF/NM 9.0	NM- 9.2
1-Newsstand version of the baseball giveaway	2	4	6	13	18	22

RICHIE RICH COLLECTORS COMICS (See Harvey Collectors Comics)

RICHIE RICH DIAMONDS
Harvey Publications: Aug, 1972 - No. 59, Aug, 1982 (#1, 23-45: 52 pgs.)

	GD 2.0	VG 4.0	FN 6.0	VF 8.0	VF/NM 9.0	NM- 9.2
1-(52 pg. Giant)	5	10	15	32	51	70
2-5	3	6	9	16	23	30
6-10	2	4	6	11	16	20
11-22	2	4	6	8	10	12
23-30-(52 pg. Giants)	2	4	6	8	11	14
31-45: 39-r/Origin Little Dot	1	2	3	5	7	9
46-50	1	2	3	4	5	7
51-59						6.00

RICHIE RICH DIGEST
Harvey Publications: Oct, 1986 - No. 42, Oct, 1994 ($1.25/$1.75, digest-size)

	GD 2.0	VG 4.0	FN 6.0	VF 8.0	VF/NM 9.0	NM- 9.2
1	1	3	4	6	8	10
2-10						6.00
11-20						5.00
21-42						4.00

RICHIE RICH DIGEST STORIES (...Magazine #?-on)
Harvey Publications: Oct, 1977 - No., 17, Oct, 1982 (75¢/95¢, digest-size)

	GD 2.0	VG 4.0	FN 6.0	VF 8.0	VF/NM 9.0	NM- 9.2
1-Reprints	2	4	6	9	12	15

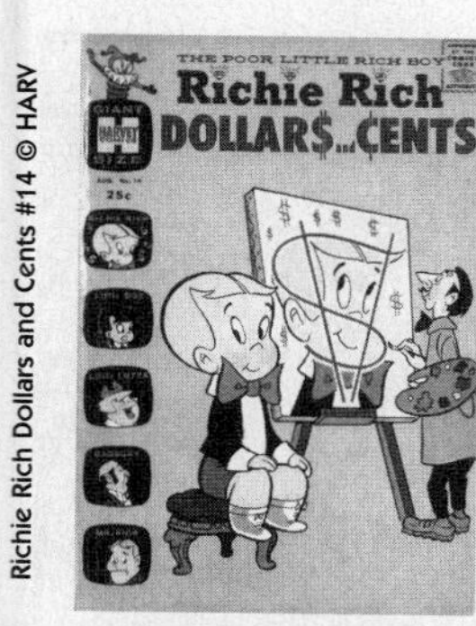

Richie Rich Dollars and Cents #14 © HARV

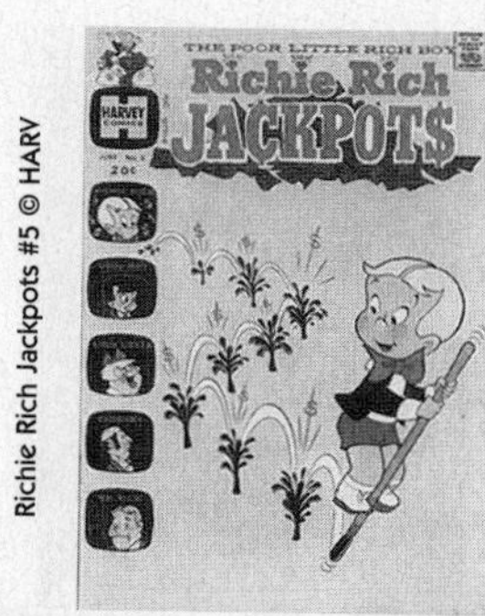

Richie Rich Jackpots #5 © HARV

Richie Rich Success Stories #7 © HARV

	GD 2.0	VG 4.0	FN 6.0	VF 8.0	VF/NM 9.0	NM- 9.2
2-10: Reprints	1	2	3	5	7	9
11-17: Reprints						6.00

RICHIE RICH DIGEST WINNERS
Harvey Publications: Dec, 1977 - No. 16, Sept, 1982 (75¢/95¢, 132 pgs., digest-size)

	GD 2.0	VG 4.0	FN 6.0	VF 8.0	VF/NM 9.0	NM- 9.2
1	2	4	6	9	12	15
2-5	1	2	3	5	7	9
6-16						6.00

RICHIE RICH DOLLARS & CENTS
Harvey Publications: Aug, 1963 - No. 109, Aug, 1982 (#1-43: 68 pgs.; 44-60, 71-94: 52 pgs.)

	GD 2.0	VG 4.0	FN 6.0	VF 8.0	VF/NM 9.0	NM- 9.2
1: (#1-64 are all reprint issues)	18	36	54	126	246	365
2	10	20	30	71	126	180
3-5: 5-r/1st app. of R.R. from Little Dot #1	9	18	27	63	107	150
6-10	7	14	21	47	76	105
11-20	5	10	15	30	48	65
21-30: 25-r/1st app. Nurse Jenny (Little Lotta #62)	4	8	12	22	34	45
31-43: 43-Last 68 pg. issue	3	6	9	18	27	35
44-60: All 52 pgs.	3	6	9	14	19	25
61-71	1	3	4	6	8	10
72-94: All 52 pgs.	2	4	6	8	10	12
95-99,101-109						6.00
100-Anniversary issue	1	2	3	5	7	9

RICHIE RICH FORTUNES
Harvey Publications: Sept, 1971 - No. 63, July, 1982 (#1-15: 52 pgs.)

	GD 2.0	VG 4.0	FN 6.0	VF 8.0	VF/NM 9.0	NM- 9.2
1	6	12	18	39	62	85
2-5	3	6	9	20	30	40
6-10	2	4	6	13	18	22
11-15: 11-r/1st app. The Onion	2	4	6	9	12	15
16-30	1	2	3	5	7	9
31-40	1	2	3	4	5	7
41-63: 62-Onion app.						6.00

RICHIE RICH GEMS
Harvey Publications: Sept, 1974 - No. 43, Sept, 1982

	GD 2.0	VG 4.0	FN 6.0	VF 8.0	VF/NM 9.0	NM- 9.2
1	3	6	9	20	30	40
2-5	2	4	6	13	18	22
6-10	2	4	6	9	13	16
11-20	1	3	4	6	8	10
21-30	1	2	3	4	5	7
31-43: 36-Dr. Blemish, Onion app. 38-1st app. Stone-Age Riches						6.00

RICHIE RICH GOLD AND SILVER
Harvey Publications: Sept, 1975 - No. 42, Oct, 1982 (#1-27: 52 pgs.)

	GD 2.0	VG 4.0	FN 6.0	VF 8.0	VF/NM 9.0	NM- 9.2
1	3	6	9	18	27	35
2-5	2	4	6	11	16	20
6-10	2	4	6	8	11	14
11-27	1	2	3	5	7	9
28-42: 34-Stone-Age Riches app.						6.00

RICHIE RICH GOLD NUGGETS DIGEST
Harvey Publications: Dec., 1990 - No. 4, June, 1991 ($1.75, digest-size)

	GD 2.0	VG 4.0	FN 6.0	VF 8.0	VF/NM 9.0	NM- 9.2
1-4						3.00

RICHIE RICH HOLIDAY DIGEST MAGAZINE (...Digest #4)
Harvey Publications: Jan, 1980 - #3, Jan, 1982; #4, 3/88; #5, 2/89 (annual)

	GD 2.0	VG 4.0	FN 6.0	VF 8.0	VF/NM 9.0	NM- 9.2
1-X-Mas-c	1	3	4	6	8	10
2-5: 2,3: All X-Mas-c. 4-(3/88, $1.25), 5-(2/89, $1.75)	1	2	3	4	5	7

RICHIE RICH INVENTIONS
Harvey Publications: Oct, 1977 - No. 26, Oct, 1982 (#1-11: 52 pgs.)

	GD 2.0	VG 4.0	FN 6.0	VF 8.0	VF/NM 9.0	NM- 9.2
1	2	4	6	11	16	20
2-5	2	4	6	8	10	12
6-11	1	2	3	5	6	8
12-26						6.00

RICHIE RICH JACKPOTS
Harvey Publications: Oct, 1972 - No. 58, Aug, 1982 (#41-43: 52 pgs.)

	GD 2.0	VG 4.0	FN 6.0	VF 8.0	VF/NM 9.0	NM- 9.2
1-Debut of Cousin Jackpots	5	10	15	30	48	65
2-5	3	6	9	16	23	30
6-10	2	4	6	11	16	20
11-15,17-20	2	4	6	8	10	12
16-Super Richie app.	2	4	6	9	12	15
21-30	1	2	3	5	7	9
31-40,44-50: 37-Caricatures of Frank Sinatra, Dean Martin, Sammy Davis, Jr. 45-Dr. Blemish app.	1	2	3	4	5	7
41-43 (52 pgs.)	1	3	4	6	8	10
51-58						6.00

RICHIE RICH MILLION DOLLAR DIGEST (...Magazine #?-on)(See Million Dollar Digest)
Harvey Publications: Oct, 1980 - No. 10, Oct, 1982 ($1.50)

	GD 2.0	VG 4.0	FN 6.0	VF 8.0	VF/NM 9.0	NM- 9.2
1	1	3	4	6	8	10
2-10						6.00

RICHIE RICH MILLIONS
Harvey Publ.: 9/61; #2, 9/62 - #113, 10/82 (#1-48: 68 pgs.; 49-64, 85-97: 52 pgs.)

	GD 2.0	VG 4.0	FN 6.0	VF 8.0	VF/NM 9.0	NM- 9.2
1: (#1-3 are all reprint issues)	21	42	63	148	287	425
2	11	22	33	79	140	200
3-5: All other giants are new & reprints. 5-1st 15 pg. Richie Rich story	9	18	27	65	113	160
6-10	8	16	24	58	97	135
11-20	6	12	18	41	66	90
21-30	4	8	12	28	44	60
31-48: 31-1st app. The Onion. 48-Last 68 pg. Giant	3	6	9	20	30	40
49-64: 52 pg. Giants	3	6	9	14	20	25
65-67,69-73,75-84	2	4	6	8	10	12
68-1st Super Richie-c (11/74)	2	4	6	13	18	22
74-1st app. Mr. Woody; Super Richie app.	2	4	6	8	11	14
85-97: 52 pg. Giants	2	4	6	8	11	14
98,99	1	2	3	4	5	7
100	1	2	3	5	7	9
101-113						6.00

RICHIE RICH MONEY WORLD
Harvey Publications: Sept, 1972 - No. 59, Sept, 1982

	GD 2.0	VG 4.0	FN 6.0	VF 8.0	VF/NM 9.0	NM- 9.2
1-(52 pg. Giant)-1st app. Mayda Munny	6	12	18	37	59	80
2-Super Richie app.	3	6	9	18	27	35
3-5	3	6	9	16	23	30
6-10: 9,10-Richie Rich mistakenly named Little Lotta on covers	2	4	6	11	16	20
11-20: 16,20-Dr. N-R-Gee	2	4	6	8	10	12
21-30	1	2	3	5	7	9
31-50	1	2	3	4	5	7
51-59						6.00
Digest 1 (2/91, $1.75)						5.00
2-8 (12/93, $1.75)						3.00

RICHIE RICH PROFITS
Harvey Publications: Oct, 1974 - No. 47, Sept, 1982

	GD 2.0	VG 4.0	FN 6.0	VF 8.0	VF/NM 9.0	NM- 9.2
1	3	6	9	20	30	40
2-5	2	4	6	13	18	22
6-10: 10-Origin of Dr. N-R-Gee	2	4	6	9	13	16
11-20: 15-Christmas-c	1	3	4	6	8	10
21-30	1	2	3	4	5	7
31-47						6.00

RICHIE RICH RELICS
Harvey Comics: Jan, 1988 - No.4, Feb, 1989 (75¢/$1.00, reprints)

	GD 2.0	VG 4.0	FN 6.0	VF 8.0	VF/NM 9.0	NM- 9.2
1-4						3.00

RICHIE RICH RICHES
Harvey Publications: July, 1972 - No. 59, Aug, 1982 (#1, 2, 41-45: 52 pgs.)

	GD 2.0	VG 4.0	FN 6.0	VF 8.0	VF/NM 9.0	NM- 9.2
1-(52 pg. Giant)-1st app. The Money Monster	6	12	18	37	59	80
2-(52 pg. Giant)	3	6	9	20	30	40
3-5	3	6	9	16	23	30
6-10: 7-1st app. Aunt Novo	2	4	6	11	16	20
11-20: 17-Super Richie app. (3/75)	2	4	6	8	10	12
21-40	1	2	3	5	6	8
41-45: 52 pg. Giants	1	3	4	6	8	10
46-59: 56-Dr. Blemish app.						6.00

RICHIE RICH SUCCESS STORIES
Harvey Publications: Nov, 1964 - No. 105, Sept, 1982 (#1-38: 68 pgs., 39-55, 67-90: 52 pgs.)

	GD 2.0	VG 4.0	FN 6.0	VF 8.0	VF/NM 9.0	NM- 9.2
1	17	34	51	119	230	340
2	10	20	30	67	116	165
3-5	9	18	27	60	100	140
6-10	6	12	18	41	66	90
11-20	5	10	15	34	55	75
21-30: 27-1st Penny Van Dough (8/69)	4	8	12	24	37	50
31-38: 38-Last 68 pg. Giant	3	6	9	20	30	40
39-55-(52 pgs.): 44-Super Richie app.	3	6	9	14	20	25
56-66	2	4	6	8	10	12
67-90: 52 pgs.	2	4	6	8	11	14

Richie Rich Vacation Digest #1 © HARV

Rifleman #9 © DELL

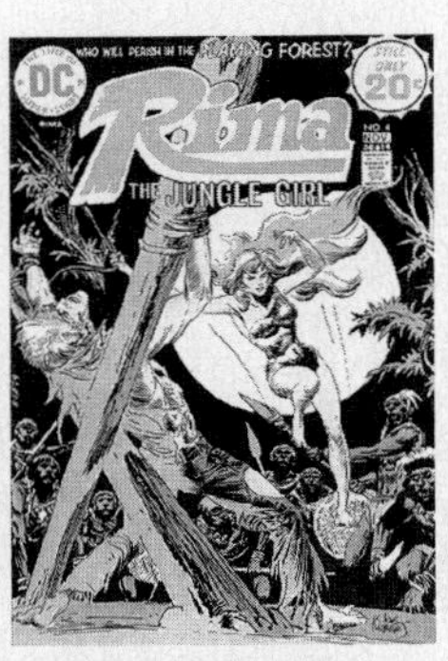

Rima, The Jungle Girl #4 © DC

	GD 2.0	VG 4.0	FN 6.0	VF 8.0	VF/NM 9.0	NM- 9.2
91-99,101-105: 91-Onion app. 101-Dr. Blemish app.						6.00
100	1	2	3	5	7	9

RICHIE RICH SUMMER BONANZA
Harvey Comics: Oct, 1991 ($1.95, one-shot, 68 pgs.)

	GD 2.0	VG 4.0	FN 6.0	VF 8.0	VF/NM 9.0	NM- 9.2
1-Richie Rich, Little Dot, Little Lotta						3.00

RICHIE RICH TREASURE CHEST DIGEST (...Magazine #3)
Harvey Publications: Apr, 1982 - No. 3, Aug, 1982 (95¢, Digest Mag.)
(#4 advertised but not publ.)

	GD 2.0	VG 4.0	FN 6.0	VF 8.0	VF/NM 9.0	NM- 9.2
1	1	2	3	5	7	9
2,3	1	2	3	4	5	7

RICHIE RICH VACATION DIGEST
Harvey Comics: Oct, 1991; Oct, 1992; Oct, 1993 ($1.75, digest-size)

	GD 2.0	VG 4.0	FN 6.0	VF 8.0	VF/NM 9.0	NM- 9.2
1-(10/91), 1-(10/92), 1-(10/93)						4.00

RICHIE RICH VACATIONS DIGEST
Harvey Publ.: 11/77; No. 2, 10/78 - No. 7, 10/81; No. 8, 8/82; No. 9, 10/82 (Digest, 132 pgs.)

	GD 2.0	VG 4.0	FN 6.0	VF 8.0	VF/NM 9.0	NM- 9.2
1-Reprints	2	4	6	9	12	15
2-6	1	2	3	5	7	9
7-9						6.00

RICHIE RICH VAULT OF MYSTERY
Harvey Publications: Nov, 1974 - No. 47, Sept, 1982

	GD 2.0	VG 4.0	FN 6.0	VF 8.0	VF/NM 9.0	NM- 9.2
1	3	6	9	20	30	40
2-5: 5-The Condor app.	2	4	6	13	18	22
6-10	2	4	6	9	13	16
11-20	1	3	4	6	8	10
21-30	1	2	3	4	5	7
31-47						6.00

RICHIE RICH ZILLIONZ
Harvey Publ.: Oct, 1976 - No. 33, Sept, 1982 (#1-4: 68 pgs.; #5-18: 52 pgs.)

	GD 2.0	VG 4.0	FN 6.0	VF 8.0	VF/NM 9.0	NM- 9.2
1	3	6	9	18	27	35
2-4: 4-Last 68 pg. Giant	2	4	6	11	16	20
5-10	2	4	6	8	10	12
11-18: 18-Last 52 pg. Giant	1	2	3	5	6	8
19-33						6.00

RICKY
Standard Comics (Visual Editions): No. 5, Sept, 1953

	GD 2.0	VG 4.0	FN 6.0	VF 8.0	VF/NM 9.0	NM- 9.2
5-Teenage humor	6	12	18	28	34	40

RICKY NELSON (TV)(See Sweethearts V2#42)
Dell Publishing Co.: No. 956, Dec, 1958 - No. 1192, June, 1961 (All photo-c)

	GD 2.0	VG 4.0	FN 6.0	VF 8.0	VF/NM 9.0	NM- 9.2
Four Color 956,998	17	34	51	119	230	340
Four Color 1115,1192: 1192-Manning-a	14	28	42	97	181	265

RIDE, THE (Also see Gun Candy flip-book)
Image Comics: June, 2004 - No. 2, July, 2004 ($2.95, B&W, anthology)

	GD 2.0	VG 4.0	FN 6.0	VF 8.0	VF/NM 9.0	NM- 9.2
1,2: Hughes-c/Wagner-s. 1-Hamner & Stelfreeze-a. 2-Jeanty & Pearson-a						3.00
... Die Valkyrie 1-3 (6/07 - No. 3, 2/08, $2.99) Stelfreeze-a/Wagner-s/Pearson-c						3.00
... Foreign Parts 1 (1/05, $2.95) Dixon-s/Haynes-a; Marz-s/Brunner-a; Pearson-c						3.00
... Halloween Special: The Key to Survival (10/07, $3.50) Tomm Coker-s/a						3.50
... Savannah 1 (4/07, $4.99) s/a by students of Savannah College of Art						5.00
... 2 For the Road 1 (10/04, $2.95) Dixon-s/Hamner & Gregory-a/Johnson-c						3.00
Vol. 1 TPB (2005, $9.99) r/#1,2, Foreign Parts, 2 For the Road; Chaykin intro.						10.00
Vol. 2 TPB (2005, $15.99) r/Gun Candy #1,2 & Die Valkyrie #1-3; sketch pages						16.00

RIDER, THE (Frontier Trail #6; also see Blazing Sixguns I.W. Reprint #10, 11)
Ajax/Farrell Publ. (Four Star Comic Corp.): Mar, 1957 - No. 5, 1958

	GD 2.0	VG 4.0	FN 6.0	VF 8.0	VF/NM 9.0	NM- 9.2
1-Swift Arrow, Lone Rider begin	13	26	39	72	101	130
2-5	8	16	24	42	54	65

RIDERS OF THE PURPLE SAGE (See Zane Grey & Four Color #372)

RIFLEMAN, THE (TV)
Dell Publ. Co./Gold Key No. 13 on: No. 1009, 7-9/59 - No. 12, 7-9/62; No. 13, 11/62 - No. 20, 10/64

	GD 2.0	VG 4.0	FN 6.0	VF 8.0	VF/NM 9.0	NM- 9.2
Four Color 1009 (#1)	21	42	63	148	287	425
2 (1-3/60)	11	22	33	78	139	200
3-Toth-a (4 pgs.); variant edition has back-c with "Something Special" comic strip	11	22	33	78	139	200
4-10: 6-Toth-a (4 pgs.)	10	20	30	70	123	175
11-20	8	16	24	54	90	125

NOTE: ***Warren Tufts** a-2-9. All have Chuck Connors & Johnny Crawford photo-c. Photo back c-13-15.*

RIFTWAR
Marvel Comics: July, 2009 - No. 5, Dec, 2009 ($3.99, limited series)

	GD 2.0	VG 4.0	FN 6.0	VF 8.0	VF/NM 9.0	NM- 9.2
1-5-Adaptation of Raymond E. Feist novel; Glass-s/Stegman-a						4.00

RIMA, THE JUNGLE GIRL
National Periodical Publications: Apr-May, 1974 - No. 7, Apr-May, 1975

	GD 2.0	VG 4.0	FN 6.0	VF 8.0	VF/NM 9.0	NM- 9.2
1-Origin, part 1 (#1-5: 20¢; 6,7: 25¢)	2	4	6	11	16	20
2-7: 2-4-Origin, parts 2-4. 7-Origin & only app. Space Marshal	2	3	4	6	8	10

NOTE: ***Kubert** c-1-7. **Nino** a-1-7. **Redondo** a-1-7.*

RING OF BRIGHT WATER (See Movie Classics)

RING OF THE NIBELUNG, THE
DC Comics: 1989 - No. 4, 1990 ($4.95, squarebound, 52 pgs., mature readers)

	GD 2.0	VG 4.0	FN 6.0	VF 8.0	VF/NM 9.0	NM- 9.2
1-4: Adapts Wagner cycle of operas, Gil Kane-c/a						5.00

RING OF THE NIBELUNG, THE
Dark Horse Comics: Feb, 2000 - Sept, 2001 ($2.95/$2.99/$5.99, limited series)

	GD 2.0	VG 4.0	FN 6.0	VF 8.0	VF/NM 9.0	NM- 9.2
Vol. 1 (The Rhinegold) 1-4: Adapts Wagner; P. Craig Russell-s/a						3.00
Vol. 2,3: Vol. 2 (The Valkyrie) 1-3: 1-(8/00). Vol. 3 (Siegfried) 1-3: 1-(12/00)						3.00
Vol. 4 (The Twilight of the Gods) 1-3: 1-(6/01)						3.00
4-(9/01, $5.99, 64 pgs.) Conclusion with sketch pages						6.00

RINGO KID, THE (2nd Series)
Marvel Comics Group: Jan, 1970 - No. 23, Nov, 1973; No. 24, Nov, 1975 - No. 30, Nov, 1976

	GD 2.0	VG 4.0	FN 6.0	VF 8.0	VF/NM 9.0	NM- 9.2
1-Williamson-a r-from #10, 1956.	3	6	9	17	25	32
2-11: 2-Severin-c. 11-Last 15¢ issue	2	4	6	10	14	18
12 (52 pg. Giant)	3	6	9	14	20	26
13-20: 13-Wildey-r. 20-Williamson-r/#1	2	4	6	8	11	14
21-30	2	3	4	6	8	10
27,28-(30¢-c variant, limited distribution)(5,7/76)	3	6	9	20	30	40

RINGO KID WESTERN, THE (1st Series) (See Wild Western & Western Trails)
Atlas Comics (HPC)/Marvel Comics: Aug, 1954 - No. 21, Sept, 1957

	GD 2.0	VG 4.0	FN 6.0	VF 8.0	VF/NM 9.0	NM- 9.2
1-Origin; The Ringo Kid begins	30	60	90	177	289	400
2-Black Rider app.; origin/1st app. Ringo's Horse Arab	15	30	45	90	140	190
3-5	12	24	36	69	97	125
6-8-Severin-a(3) each	13	26	39	74	105	135
9,11,12,14-21: 12-Orlando-a (4 pgs.)	10	20	30	56	76	95
10,13-Williamson-a (4 pgs.)	11	22	33	60	83	105

NOTE: ***Berg** a-8. **Maneely** a-1-5, 15, 16(text illos only), 17(4), 18, 20, 21; c-1-6, 8, 13, 15-18, 20. **J. Severin** c-10, 11. **Sinnott** a-1. **Wildey** a-16-18.*

RIN TIN TIN (See March of Comics #163,180,195)

RIN TIN TIN (TV) (...& Rusty #21 on; see Western Roundup under Dell Giants)
Dell Publishing Co./Gold Key: Nov, 1952 - No. 38, May-July, 1961; Nov, 1963 (All Photo-c)

	GD 2.0	VG 4.0	FN 6.0	VF 8.0	VF/NM 9.0	NM- 9.2
Four Color 434 (#1)	14	28	42	97	181	265
Four Color 476,523	8	16	24	56	93	130
4(3-5/54)-10	7	14	21	45	73	100
11-17,19,20	6	12	18	43	69	95
18(4-5/57) 1st app. of Rusty and the Cavalry of Fort Apache; photo-c	8	16	24	54	90	125
21-38: 36-Toth-a (4 pgs.)	5	10	15	34	55	75
... & Rusty 1 (11/63-Gold Key)	6	12	18	37	59	80

RIO (Also see Eclipse Monthly)
Comico: June, 1987 ($8.95, 64 pgs.)

	GD 2.0	VG 4.0	FN 6.0	VF 8.0	VF/NM 9.0	NM- 9.2
1-Wildey-c/a						9.00

RIO AT BAY
Dark Horse Comics: July, 1992 - No. 2, Aug, 1992 ($2.95, limited series)

	GD 2.0	VG 4.0	FN 6.0	VF 8.0	VF/NM 9.0	NM- 9.2
1,2-Wildey-c/a						3.00

RIO BRAVO (Movie) (See 4-Color #1018)
Dell Publishing Co.: June, 1959

	GD 2.0	VG 4.0	FN 6.0	VF 8.0	VF/NM 9.0	NM- 9.2
Four Color 1018-Toth-a; John Wayne, Dean Martin, & Ricky Nelson photo-c.	22	44	66	155	300	445

RIO CONCHOS (See Movie Comics)

RIOT (Satire)
Atlas Comics (ACI No. 1-5/WPI No. 6): Apr, 1954 - No. 3, Aug, 1954; No. 4, Feb, 1956 - No. 6, June, 1956

	GD 2.0	VG 4.0	FN 6.0	VF 8.0	VF/NM 9.0	NM- 9.2
1-Russ Heath-a	32	64	96	192	314	435
2-Li'l Abner satire by Post	23	46	69	136	223	310
3-Last precode (8/54)	20	40	60	120	195	270
4-Infinity-c; Marilyn Monroe "7 Year Itch" movie satire; Mad Rip-off ads	26	52	78	154	252	350

Rip Hunter Time Master #25 © DC

Ripley's Believe It or Not #1 © HARV

Rising Stars #14 © JMS & TCOW

GD 2.0 | VG 4.0 | FN 6.0 | VF 8.0 | VF/NM 9.0 | NM- 9.2

5-Marilyn Monroe, John Wayne parody; part photo-c
26 52 78 156 256 355
6-Lorna of the Jungle satire by Everett; Dennis the Menace satire-c/story; part photo-c 20 40 60 120 195 270
NOTE: *Berg a-3. **Burgos** c-1, 2. **Colan** a-1. **Everett** a-4, 6. **Heath** a-1. **Maneely** a-1, 2, 4-6; c-3, 4, 6. **Post** a-1-4. **Reinman** a-2. **Severin** a-4-6.*

RIOT GEAR
Triumphant Comics: Sept, 1993 - No. 11, July, 1994 ($2.50, serially numbered)
1-11: 1-2nd app. Riot Gear. 2-1st app. Rabin. 3,4-Triumphant Unleashed x-over. 3-1st app. Surzar. 4-Death of Captain Tich 2.50
Violent Past 1,2: 1-(2/94, $2.50) 2.50

R.I.P.
TSR, Inc.: 1990 - No. 8, 1991 ($2.95, 44 pgs.)
1-8-Based on TSR game 3.00

RIPCLAW (See Cyberforce)
Image Comics (Top Cow Prod.): Apr, 1995 - No. 3, June, 1995 (Limited series)
1/2-Gold, 1/2-San Diego ed., 1/2-Chicago ed. 1 3 4 6 8 10
1-3: Brandon Peterson-a(p) 3.00
Special 1 (10/95, $2.50) 2.50

RIPCLAW
Image Comics (Top Cow Prod.): V2#1, Dec, 1995 - No. 6, June, 1996 ($2.50)
V2#1-6: 5-Medieval Spawn/Witchblade Preview 2.50
...: Pilot Season 1 (2007, $2.99) Jason Aaron-s/Jorge Lucas-a/Tony Moore-c 3.00

RIPCORD (TV)
Dell Publishing Co.: Mar-May, 1962
Four Color 1294 7 14 21 47 76 105

R.I.P.D.
Dark Horse Comics: Oct, 1999 - No. 4, Jan, 2000 ($2.95, limited series)
1-4 3.00
TPB (2003, $12.95) r/#1-4 13.00

RIP HUNTER TIME MASTER (See Showcase #20, 21, 25, 26 & Time Masters)
National Periodical Publications: Mar-Apr, 1961 - No. 29, Nov-Dec, 1965
1-(3-4/61) 50 100 150 425 838 1250
2 26 52 78 190 363 535
3-5: 5-Last 10¢ issue 16 32 48 115 220 325
6,7-Toth-a in each 11 22 33 80 145 210
8-15 9 18 27 63 107 150
16-20: 20-Hitler c/s 7 14 21 49 80 110
21-29: 29-Gil Kane-c 6 12 18 43 69 95

RIP IN TIME (Also see Teenage Mutant Ninja Turtles #5-7)
Fantagor Press: Aug, 1986 - No.5, 1987 ($1.50, B&W)
1-5: Corben-c/a in all 3.00

RIP KIRBY (Also see Harvey Comics Hits #57, & Street Comix)
David McKay Publications: 1948
Feature Books 51,54: Raymond-c; 51-Origin 35 70 105 208 339 470

RIPLEY'S BELIEVE IT OR NOT! (See Ace Comics, All-American Comics, Mystery Comics Digest #1, 4, 7, 10, 13, 16, 19, 22, 25)

RIPLEY'S BELIEVE IT OR NOT!
Harvey Publications: Sept, 1953 - No. 4, March, 1954
1-Powell-a 14 28 42 76 108 140
2-4 10 20 30 54 72 90

RIPLEY'S BELIEVE IT OR NOT! (Continuation of Ripleys'...True Ghost Stories & Ripley's...True War Stories)
Gold Key: No. 4, April, 1967 - No. 94, Feb, 1980
4-Photo-c; McWilliams-a 4 8 12 24 37 50
5-Subtitled "True War Stories"; Evans-a; 1st Jeff Jones-a in comics? (2 pgs.) 4 8 12 24 37 50
6-10: 6-McWilliams-a. 10-Evans-a(2) 3 6 9 20 30 40
11-20: 15-Evans-a 3 6 9 16 23 30
21-30 2 4 6 13 18 22
31-38,40-60 2 4 6 9 13 16
39-Crandall-a 2 4 6 10 14 18
61-73 1 3 4 6 8 10
74,77-83-(52 pgs.) 2 4 6 9 13 16
75,76,84-94 1 2 3 5 6 8
Story Digest Mag. 1(6/70)-4-3/4x6-1/2", 148pp. 5 10 15 34 55 75
NOTE: ***Evanish** art by **Luiz Dominguez** #22-25, 27, 30, 31, 40. **Jeff Jones** a-5(2 pgs.). **McWilliams** a-65, 66, 70, 89. **Orlando** a-8. **Sparling** c-68. Reprints-74, 77-84, 87 (part); 91, 93 (all). **Williamson, Wood** a-80r/#1.*

RIPLEY'S BELIEVE IT OR NOT!
Dark Horse Comics: May, 2002 - No. 4 ($2.99, B&W, limited series)
1-3-Nord-c/a. 1-Stories of Amelia Earhart & D.B. Cooper 3.00

RIPLEY'S BELIEVE IT OR NOT! TRUE GHOST STORIES (Along with Ripley's...True War Stories, the three issues together precede the 1967 series that starts its numbering with #4) (Also see Dan Curtis)
Gold Key: June, 1965 - No. 2, Oct, 1966
1-Williamson, Wood & Evans-a; photo-c 8 16 24 52 86 120
2-Orlando, McWilliams-a; photo-c 4 8 12 28 44 60
Mini-Comic 1(1976-3-1/4x6-1/2") 2 4 6 8 11 14
11186(1977)-Golden Press; ($1.95, 224 pgs.)-All-r 4 8 12 24 37 50
11401(3/79)-Golden Press; ($1.00, 96 pgs.)-All-r 3 6 9 15 21 26

RIPLEY'S BELIEVE IT OR NOT! TRUE WAR STORIES (Along with Ripley's...True Ghost Stories, the three issues together precede the 1967 series that starts its numbering with #4)
Gold Key: Nov, 1965 (Aug, 1965 in indicia)
1-No Williamson-a 4 8 12 28 44 60

RIPLEY'S BELIEVE IT OR NOT! TRUE WEIRD
Ripley Enterprises: June, 1966 - No. 2, Aug, 1966 (B&W Magazine)
1,2-Comic stories & text 3 6 9 18 27 35

RISE OF APOCALYPSE
Marvel Comics: Oct, 1996 - No. 4, Jan, 1997 ($1.95, limited series)
1-4: Adam Pollina-c/a 2.50

RISING STARS
Image Comics (Top Cow): Mar, 1999 - No. 24, Mar, 2005 ($2.50/$2.99)
Preview-(3/99, $5.00) Straczynski-s 6.00
0-(6/00, $2.50) Gary Frank-a/c 2.50
1/2-(8/01, $2.95) Anderson-c; art & sketch pages by Zanier 3.00
1-Four covers; Keu Cha-c/a 1 2 3 5 7 9
1-($10.00) Gold Editions-four covers 10.00
1-($50.00) Holofoil-c 50.00
2-7: 5-7-Zanier & Lashley-a(p) 1 2 3 5 7 9
8-23: 8-13-Zanier & Lashley-a(p). 14-Immonen-a. 15-Flip book B&W preview of Universe. 15-23-Brent Anderson-a 3.00
24-($3.99) Series finale; Anderson-a/c 4.00
Born In Fire TPB (11/00, $19.95) r/#1-8; foreword by Neil Gaiman 20.00
Power TPB (2002, $19.95) r/#9-16 20.00
Prelude-(10/00, $2.95) Cha-a/Lashley-c 3.00
...: Visitations (2002, $8.99) r/#0, 1/2, Preview; new Anderson-c; cover gallery 9.00
Vol. 3: Fire and Ash TPB (2005, $19.99) r/#17-24; design pages & cover gallery 20.00
Vol. 4 TPB (2006, $19.99) r/Rising Stars Bright #1-3 and Voices of the Dead #1-6 20.00
Vol. 5 TPB (2007, $16.99) r/Rising Stars: Untouchable #1-5 and ...: Visitations 17.00
Wizard #0-(3/99) Wizard supplement; Straczynski-s 2.50
Wizard #1/2 10.00

RISING STARS BRIGHT
Image Comics (Top Cow): Mar, 2003 - No. 3, May, 2003 ($2.99, limited series)
1-3-Avery-s/Jurgens & Gorder-a/Beck-c 3.00

RISING STARS: UNTOUCHABLE
Image Comics (Top Cow): Mar, 2006 - No. 5, July, 2006 ($2.99, limited series)
1-5-Avery-s/Anderson-a 3.00

RISING STARS: VOICES OF THE DEAD
Image Comics (Top Cow): June, 2005 - No. 6, Dec, 2005 ($2.99, limited series)
1-6-Avery-s/Staz Johnson-a 3.00

RIVERDALE HIGH (Archie's... #7,8)
Archie Comics: Aug, 1990 - No. 8, Oct, 1991 ($1.00, bi-monthly)
1 4.00
2-8 3.00

RIVER FEUD (See Zane Grey & Four Color #484)

RIVETS
Dell Publishing Co.: No. 518, Nov, 1953
Four Color 518 4 8 12 24 37 50

RIVETS (A dog)
Argo Publ.: Jan, 1956 - No. 3, May, 1956
1-Reprints Sunday & daily newspaper strips 6 12 18 31 38 45
2,3 5 10 15 22 26 30

ROACHMILL

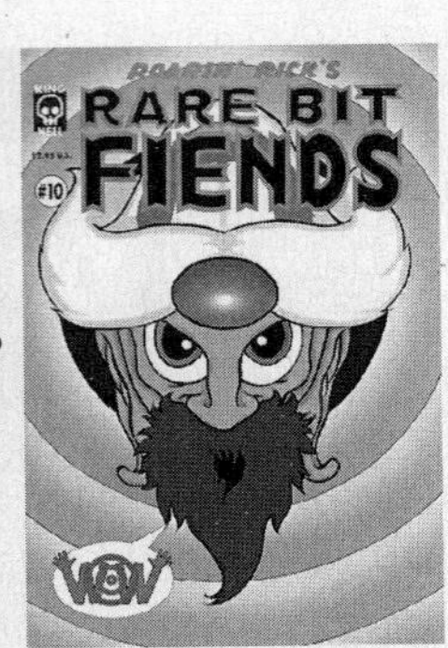

Roarin' Rick's Rare Bit Fiends #10 © King Hell

Robin #175 © DC

Robin Hood Tales #12 © DC

	GD 2.0	VG 4.0	FN 6.0	VF 8.0	VF/NM 9.0	NM- 9.2

Blackthorne Publ.: Dec, 1986 - No. 6, Oct, 1987 ($1.75, B&W)
1-6 2.50

ROACHMILL
Dark Horse Comics: May, 1988 - No. 10, Dec, 1990 ($1.75, B&W)
1-10: 10-Contains trading cards 2.50

ROAD RUNNER (See Beep Beep, the...)

ROAD TO PERDITION (Inspired the 2002 Tom Hanks/Paul Newman movie)
(Also see On the Road to Perdition)
DC Comics/Paradox Press: 1998, 2002 ($13.95, B&W paperback graphic novel)
nn-(1st printing) Max Allan Collins-s/Richard Piers Rayner-a 30.00
2nd & 3rd printings (2002, $13.95) 14.00
Movie photo cover edition (2002) 14.00

ROADTRIP
Oni Press: Aug, 2000 ($2.95, B&W, one-shot)
1-Reprints Judd Winick's back-up stories from Oni Double Feature #9,10 3.00

ROADWAYS
Cult Press: May, 1994 ($2.75, B&W, limited series)
1 2.75

ROARIN' RICK'S RARE BIT FIENDS
King Hell Press: July, 1994 - No. 21, Aug, 1996 ($2.95, B&W, mature)
1-21: Rick Veitch-c/a/scripts in all. 20-(5/96). 21-(8/96)-Reads Subtleman #1 on cover 3.00
Rabid Eye: The Dream Art of Rick Veitch ($14.95, B&W, TPB)-r/#1-8 & the appendix from #12 15.00
Pocket Universe (6/96, $14.95, B&W, TPB)-Reprints 15.00

ROBERT E. HOWARD'S CONAN THE BARBARIAN
Marvel Comics: 1983 ($2.50, 68 pgs., Baxter paper)
1-r/Savage Tales #2,3 by Smith, c-r/Conan #21 by Smith. 4.00

ROBERT LOUIS STEVENSON'S KIDNAPPED (See Kidnapped)

ROBIN (See Aurora, Birds of Prey, Detective Comics #38, New Teen Titans, Robin II, Robin III, Robin 3000, Star Spangled Comics #65, Teen Titans & Young Justice)

ROBIN (See Batman #457)
DC Comics: Jan, 1991 - No. 5, May, 1991 ($1.00, limited series)
1-Free poster by N. Adams; Bolland-c on all 4.00
1-2nd & 3rd printings (without poster) 2.50
2-5 3.00
2-2nd printing 2.50
Annual 1,2 (1992-93, $2.50, 68 pgs.): 1-Grant/Wagner scripts; Sam Kieth-c. 2-Intro Razorsharp; Jim Balent-c(p) 3.00

ROBIN (See Detective #668) (Also see Red Robin)
DC Comics: Nov, 1993 - No. 183, Apr, 2009 ($1.50/$1.95/$1.99/$2.25/$2.50/$2.99)
1-($2.95)-Collector's edition w/foil embossed-c; 1st app. Robin's car, The Redbird; Azrael as Batman app. 4.00
1-Newsstand ed. 2.50
0,2-49,51-66-Regular editions: 3-5-The Spoiler app. 6-The Huntress-c/story cont'd from Showcase '94 #5. 7-Knightquest: The Conclusion w/new Batman (Azrael) vs. Bruce Wayne. 8-KnightsEnd Pt. 5. 9-KnightsEnd Aftermath; Batman-c & app. 10-(9/94)-Zero Hour. 0-(10/94). 11-(11/94). 25-Green Arrow-c/app. 26-Batman app. 27-Contagion Pt. 3; Catwoman-c/app; Penguin & Azrael app. 28-Contagion Pt. 11. 29-Penguin app. 31-Wildcat-c/app. 32-Legacy Pt. 3. 33-Legacy Pt. 7. 35-Final Night. 46-Genesis. 52,53-Cataclysm pt. 7, conclusion. 55-Green Arrow app. 62-64-Flash-c/app. 2.50
14 ($2.50)-Embossed-c; Troika Pt. 4 3.00
50-($2.95)-Lady Shiva & King Snake app. 3.00
67-74,76-78: 67-72-No Man's Land 2.50
75-($2.95) 3.00
79-97: 79-Begin $2.25-c; Green Arrow app. 86-Pander Bros.-a 2.50
98,99-Bruce Wayne: Murderer x-over pt. 6, 11 2.50
100-($3.50) Last Dixon-s 3.50
101-147: 101-Young Justice x-over. 106-Kevin Lau-c. 121,122-Willingham-s/Mays-a. 125-Tim Drake quits. 126-Spoiler becomes the new Robin. 129-131-War Games. 132-Robin moves to Bludhaven, Batgirl app. 138-Begin $2.50-c. 139-McDaniel-a begins. 146-147-Teen Titans app. 2.50
148-174: 148-One Year Later; new costume. 150-Begin $2.99-c. 152,153-Boomerang app. 168,169-Resurrection of Ra's al Ghul x-over. 174 Spoiler unmasked 3.00
175-183: 175,176-Batman R.I.P. x-over. 180-Robin vs. Red Robin 3.00
#1,000,000 (11/98) 853rd Century x-over 2.50
Annual 3-5: 3-(1994, $2.95)-Elseworlds story. 4-(1995, $2.95)-Year One story. 5-(1996, $2.95)-Legends of the Dead Earth story 3.00
Annual 6 (1997, $3.95)-Pulp Heroes story. 4.00
Annual 7 (12/07, $3.99)-Pearson-c/a; prelude to Resurrection of Ra's al Ghul x-over 4.00
.../Argent 1 (2/98, $1.95) Argent (Teen Titans) app. 2.50
.../Batgirl: Fresh Blood TPB (2005, $12.99) r/#132,133 & Batgirl #58,59 13.00
...: Days of Fire and Madness (2006, $12.99, TPB) r/#140-145 13.00
...Eighty-Page Giant 1 (9/00, $5.95) Chuck Dixon-s/Diego Barreto-a 6.00
...: Flying Solo (2000, $12.95, TPB) r/#1-6, Showcase '94 #5,6 13.00
...Plus 1 (12/96, $2.95) Impulse-c/app.; Waid-s 3.00
...Plus 2 (12/97, $2.95) Fang (Scare Tactics) app. 3.00
...: Search For a Hero (2009, $19.99, TPB) r/#175-183; cover gallery 20.00
.../Spoiler Special 1 (8/08, $3.99) Follows Spoiler's return in Robin #174; Dixon-s 4.00
...: Teenage Wasteland (2007, $17.99, TPB) r/#154-162 18.00
...: The Big Leagues (2008, $12.99, TPB) r/#163-167 13.00
...: Unmasked (2004, $12.95, TPB) r/#121-125; Pearson-c 13.00
...: Violent Tendencies (2008, $17.99, TPB) r/#170-174 & Robin/Spoiler Special 1 18.00
...: Wanted (2007, $12.99, TPB) r/#148-153 13.00

ROBIN: A HERO REBORN
DC Comics: 1991 ($4.95, squarebound, trade paperback)
nn-r/Batman #455-457 & Robin #1-5; Bolland-c 5.00

ROBIN HOOD (See The Advs. of..., Brave and the Bold, Four Color #413, 669, King Classics, Movie Comics & Power Record Comics)

ROBIN HOOD (...& His Merry Men, The Illustrated Story of...) (See Classic Comics #7 & Classics Giveaways, 12/44)

ROBIN HOOD (Disney)
Dell Publishing Co.: No. 413, Aug, 1952; No. 669, Dec, 1955

	GD	VG	FN	VF	VF/NM	NM-
Four Color 413-(1st Disney movie Four Color book)(8/52)-Photo-c	9	18	27	65	113	160
Four Color 669 (12/55)-Reprints #413 plus photo-c	6	12	18	37	59	80

ROBIN HOOD (Adventures of... #7, 8)
Magazine Enterprises (Sussex Pub. Co.): No. 52, Nov, 1955 - No. 6, Jun, 1957

	GD	VG	FN	VF	VF/NM	NM-
52 (#1)-Origin Robin Hood & Sir Gallant of the Round Table	15	30	45	85	130	175
53 (#2), 3-6: 6-Richard Greene photo-c (TV)	12	24	36	67	94	120
I.W. Reprint #1,2,9: 1-r/#3. 2-r/#4. 9-r/#52 (1963)	2	4	6	9	13	16
Super Reprint #10,15: 10-r/#53. 15-r/#5	2	4	6	9	13	16

NOTE: *Bolle a-in all; c-52.* ***Powell*** *a-6.*

ROBIN HOOD (Not Disney)
Dell Publishing Co.: May-July, 1963 (one-shot)

	GD	VG	FN	VF	VF/NM	NM-
1	3	6	9	16	23	30

ROBIN HOOD (Disney) (Also see Best of Walt Disney)
Western Publishing Co.: 1973 ($1.50, 8-1/2x11", 52 pgs., cardboard-c)

	GD	VG	FN	VF	VF/NM	NM-
96151- "Robin Hood", based on movie, 96152- "The Mystery of Sherwood Forest", 96153- "In King Richard's Service", 96154- "The Wizard's Ring" each....	3	6	9	16	22	28

ROBIN HOOD
Eclipse Comics: July, 1991 - No. 3, Dec, 1991 ($2.50, limited series)
1-3: Timothy Truman layouts 2.50

ROBIN HOOD AND HIS MERRY MEN (Formerly Danger & Adventure)
Charlton Comics: No. 28, Apr, 1956 - No. 38, Aug, 1958

	GD	VG	FN	VF	VF/NM	NM-
28	10	20	30	54	72	90
29-37	8	16	24	42	54	65
38-Ditko-a (5 pgs.); Rocke-c	14	28	42	76	108	140

ROBIN HOOD TALES (Published by National Periodical #7 on)
Quality Comics Group (Comic Magazines): Feb, 1956 - No. 6, Nov-Dec, 1956

	GD	VG	FN	VF	VF/NM	NM-
1-All have Baker/Cuidera-c	32	64	96	188	307	425
2-6-Matt Baker-a	30	60	90	177	289	400

ROBIN HOOD TALES (Cont'd from Quality series)(See Brave & the Bold #5)
National Periodical Publ.: No. 7, Jan-Feb, 1957 - No. 14, Mar-Apr, 1958

	GD	VG	FN	VF	VF/NM	NM-
7-All have Andru/Esposito-c	36	72	108	211	343	475
8-14	30	60	90	177	289	400

ROBINSON CRUSOE (See King Classics & Power Record Comics)
Dell Publishing Co.: Nov-Jan, 1963-64

	GD	VG	FN	VF	VF/NM	NM-
1	3	6	9	15	21	26

ROBIN II (The Joker's Wild)
DC Comics: Oct, 1991 - No. 4, Dec, 1991 ($1.50, mini-series)
1-(Direct sales, $1.50)-With 4 diff.-c; same hologram on each 3.00
1-(Newsstand, $1.00)-No hologram; 1 version 2.50
1-Collector's set ($10.00)-Contains all 5 versions bagged with hologram trading card inside

Robin: Year One #4 © DC

Robocop (2010 series) #2 © Orion Pict.

Robotech #0 © Harmony Gold USA

GD 2.0 VG 4.0 FN 6.0 VF 8.0 VF/NM 9.0 NM- 9.2

2-(Direct sales, $1.50)-With 3 different-c 12.00
2-4-(Newsstand, $1.00)-1 version of each 2.50
2-Collector's set ($8.00)-Contains all 4 versions bagged with hologram trading card inside 2.50 9.00
3-(Direct sale, $1.50)-With 2 different-c 2.50
3-Collector's set ($6.00)-Contains all 3 versions bagged with hologram trading card inside 7.00
4-(Direct sales, $1.50)-Only one version 2.50
4-Collector's set ($4.00)-Contains both versions bagged with Bat-Signal hologram trading card 5.00
Multi-pack (All four issues w/hologram sticker) 8.00
Deluxe Complete Set ($30.00)-Contains all 14 versions of #1-4 plus a new hologram trading card; numbered & limited to 25,000; comes with slipcase & 2 acid free backing boards 35.00

ROBIN III: CRY OF THE HUNTRESS
DC Comics: Dec, 1992 - No. 6, Mar, 1993 (Limited series)
1-6 ($2.50, collector's ed.)-Polybagged w/movement enhanced-c plus mini-poster of newsstand-c by Zeck 3.00
1-6 ($1.25, newsstand ed.): All have Zeck-c 2.50

ROBIN 3000
DC Comics (Elseworlds): 1992 - No. 2, 1992 ($4.95, mini-series, 52 pgs.)
1,2-Foil logo; Russell-c/a 5.00

ROBIN: YEAR ONE
DC Comics: 2000 - No. 4, 2001 ($4.95, square-bound, limited series)
1-4: Earliest days of Robin's career; Javier Pulido-c/a. 2,4-Two-Face app. 5.00
TPB (2002, 2008, $14.95/$14.99, 2 printings) r/#1-4 15.00

ROBOCOP
Marvel Comics: Oct, 1987 ($2.00, B&W, magazine, one-shot)
1-Movie adaptation 4.00

ROBOCOP (Also see Dark Horse Comics)
Marvel Comics: Mar, 1990 - No. 23, Jan, 1992 ($1.50)
1-Based on movie 3.00
2-23 2.50
nn (7/90, $4.95, 52 pgs.)-r/B&W magazine in color; adapts 1st movie 5.00

ROBOCOP
Dynamite Entertainment: 2010 - Present ($3.50)
1-3-Follows the events of the first film; Neves-a 3.50

ROBOCOP (FRANK MILLER'S...) (Also see Promotional Comics section for FCBD Ed.)
Avatar Press: July, 2003 - No. 9, Jan, 2006 ($3.50/$3.99, limited series)
1-9-Frank Miller-s/Juan Ryp-a. 1-Three covers by Miller, Ryp, and Barrows. 2-Two covers 4.00

ROBOCOP: MORTAL COILS
Dark Horse Comics: Sept, 1993 - No. 4, Dec, 1993 ($2.50, limited series)
1-4: 1,2-Cago painted-c 2.50

ROBOCOP: PRIME SUSPECT
Dark Horse Comics: Oct, 1992 - No. 4, Jan, 1993 ($2.50, limited series)
1-4: 1,3-Nelson painted-c. 2,4-Bolton painted-c 2.50

ROBOCOP: ROULETTE
Dark Horse Comics: Dec, 1993 - No. 4, 1994 ($2.50, limited series)
1-4: 1,3-Nelson painted-c. 2,4-Bolton painted-c 2.50

ROBOCOP 2
Marvel Comics: Aug, 1990 ($2.25, B&W, magazine, 68 pgs.)
1-Adapts movie sequel 2.50

ROBOCOP 2
Marvel Comics: Aug, 1990; Late Aug, 1990 - #3, Late Sept, 1990 ($1.00, limited series)
nn-(8/90, $4.95, 68 pgs., color)-Same contents as B&W magazine 5.00
1: #1-3 reprint no number issue 3.00
2,3: 2-Guice-c(i) 2.50

ROBOCOP 3
Dark Horse Comics: July, 1993 - No. 3, Nov, 1993 ($2.50, limited series)
1-3: Nelson painted-c; Nguyen-a(p) 2.50

ROBOCOP VERSUS THE TERMINATOR
Dark Horse Comics: Sept, 1992 - No. 4, 1992 (Dec.) ($2.50, limited series)
1-4: Miller scripts & Simonson-c/a in all 3.00
1-Platinum Edition 6.00

GD 2.0 VG 4.0 FN 6.0 VF 8.0 VF/NM 9.0 NM- 9.2

NOTE: *All contain a different Robocop cardboard cut-out stand-up.*

ROBO DOJO
DC Comics (WildStorm): Apr, 2002 - No. 6, Sept, 2002 ($2.95, limited series)
1-6-Wolfman-s 3.00

ROBO-HUNTER (Also see Sam Slade...)
Eagle Comics: Apr, 1984 - No. 5, 1984 ($1.00)
1-5-2000 A.D. 2.50

R.O.B.O.T. BATTALION 2050
Eclipse Comics: Mar, 1988 ($2.00, B&W, one-shot)
1 2.50

ROBOT COMICS
Renegade Press: No. 0, June, 1987 ($2.00, B&W, one-shot)
0-Bob Burden story & art 2.50

ROBOTECH
Antarctic Press: Mar, 1997 - No. 11, Nov, 1998 ($2.95)
1-11, Annual 1 (4/98, $2.95) 3.00
...Class Reunion (12/98, $3.95, B&W) 4.00
...Escape (5/98, $2.95, B&W), ...Final Fire (12/98, $2.95, B&W) 3.00

ROBOTECH
DC Comics (WildStorm): No. 0, Feb, 2003 - No. 6, Jul, 2003 ($2.50/$2.95, limited series)
0-Tommy Yune-s; art by Jim Lee, Garza, Bermejo and others; pin-up pages by various 2.50
1-6 ($2.95)-Long Vo-a 3.00
...: From the Stars (2003, $9.95, digest-size) r/#0-6 & Sourcebook 10.00
... Sourcebook (3/03, $2.95) pin-ups and info on characters and mecha; art by various 3.00

ROBOTECH: COVERT-OPS
Antarctic Press: Aug, 1998 - No. 2, Sept, 1998 ($2.95, B&W, limited series)
1,2-Gregory Lane-s/a 3.00

ROBOTECH DEFENDERS
DC Comics: Mar, 1985 - No. 2, Apr, 1985 (Mini-series)
1,2 3.00

ROBOTECH IN 3-D (TV)
Comico: Aug, 1987 ($2.50)
1-Steacy painted-c 4.00

ROBOTECH: INVASION
DC Comics (WildStorm): Feb, 2004 - No. 5, July, 2004 ($2.95, limited series)
1-5-Faerber & Yune-s/Miyazawa & Dogan-a 3.00

ROBOTECH: LOVE AND WAR
DC Comics (WildStorm): Aug, 2003 - No. 6, Jan, 2004 ($2.95, limited series)
1-6-Long Vo & Charles Park-a/Faerber & Yune-s. 2-Variant-c by Warren 3.00

ROBOTECH MASTERS (TV)
Comico: July, 1985 - No. 23, Apr, 1988 ($1.50)
1-23 3.00

ROBOTECH: PRELUDE TO THE SHADOW CHRONICLES
DC Comics (WildStorm): Dec, 2005 - No. 5, Mar, 2006 ($3.50, limited series)
1-5-Yune-s/Dogan & Udon Studios-a 3.50

ROBOTECH: SENTINELS - RUBICON
Antarctic Press: July, 1998 ($2.95, B&W)
1 3.00

ROBOTECH SPECIAL
Comico: May, 1988 ($2.50, one-shot, 44 pgs.)
1-Steacy wraparound-c; partial photo-c 4.00

ROBOTECH THE GRAPHIC NOVEL
Comico: Aug, 1986 ($5.95, 8-1/2x11", 52 pgs.)
1-Origin SDF-1; intro T.R. Edwards, Steacy-c/a; 2nd printing also exists (12/86) 7.00

ROBOTECH: THE MACROSS SAGA (TV)(Formerly Macross)
Comico: No. 2, Feb, 1985 - No. 36, Feb, 1989 ($1.50)
2-10 4.00
11-36: 12,17-Ken Steacy painted-c. 26-Begin $1.75-c. 35,36-($1.95) 3.00
Volume 1-4 TPB (WildStorm, 2003, $14.95, 5-3/4" x 8-1/4")1-Reprints #2-6 & Macross #1. 2- r/#7-12. 3-r/#13-18. 4-r/#19-24 15.00

ROBOTECH: THE NEW GENERATION
Comico: July, 1985 - No. 25, July, 1988

Rocket Comics #2 © HILL

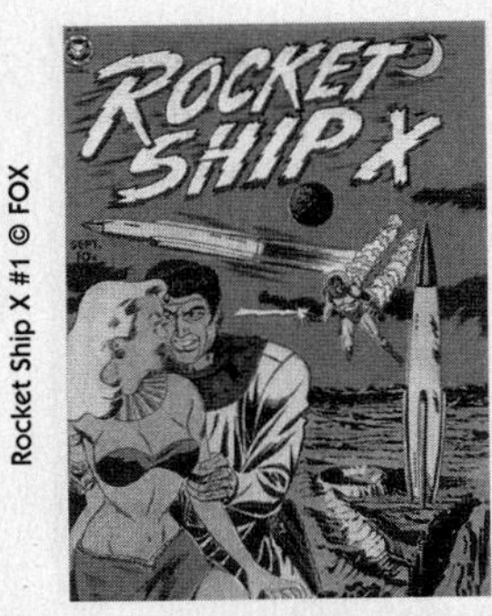

Rocket Ship X #1 © FOX

Rock n' Roll Comics #37 © Revo.

	GD 2.0	VG 4.0	FN 6.0	VF 8.0	VF/NM 9.0	NM- 9.2

1-25 3.00

ROBOTECH: VERMILION
Antarctic Press: Mar, 1997 - No. 4, ($2.95, B&W, limited series)
1-4 3.00

ROBOTECH: WINGS OF GIBRALTAR
Antarctic Press: Aug, 1998 - No. 2, Sept, 1998 ($2.95, B&W, limited series)
1,2-Lee Duhig-s/a 3.00

ROBOTIX
Marvel Comics: Feb, 1986 (75¢, one-shot)
1-Based on toy 3.00

ROBOTMEN OF THE LOST PLANET (Also see Space Thrillers)
Avon Periodicals: 1952 (Also see Strange Worlds #19)
1-McCann-a (3 pgs.); Fawcette-a 116 232 348 742 1271 1800

ROB ROY
Dell Publishing Co.: 1954 (Disney-Movie)
Four Color 544-Manning-a, photo-c 7 14 21 50 83 115

ROCK, THE (WWF Wrestling)
Chaos! Comics: June, 2001 ($2.99, one-shot)
1-Photo-c; Grant-s/Neves-a 3.00

ROCK & ROLL HIGH SCHOOL
Roger Corman's Cosmic Comics: Oct, 1995 ($2.50)
1-Bob Fingerman scripts 2.50

ROCK AND ROLLO (Formerly TV Teens)
Charlton Comics: V2#14, Oct, 1957 - No. 19, Sept, 1958
V2#14-19 6 12 18 31 38 45

ROCK COMICS
Landgraphic Publ.: Jul/Aug, 1979 ($1.25, tabloid size, 28 pgs.)
1-N. Adams-c; Thor(not Marvel's) story by Adams 3 6 9 14 19 24

ROCKET COMICS
Hillman Periodicals: Mar, 1940 - No. 3, May, 1940
1-Rocket Riley, Red Roberts the Electro Man (origin), The Phantom Ranger, The Steel Shark, The Defender, Buzzard Barnes and his Sky Devils, Lefty Larson, & The Defender, the Man with a Thousand Faces begin (1st app. of each); all have Rocket Riley-c 258 516 774 1651 2826 4000
2,3 126 252 378 806 1378 1950

ROCKETEER, THE (See Eclipse Graphic Album Series, Pacific Presents & Starslayer)

ROCKETEER ADVENTURE MAGAZINE, THE
Comico/Dark Horse Comics No. 3: July, 1988 ($2.00); No. 2, July, 1989 ($2.75); No. 3, Jan, 1995 ($2.95)
1-(7/88, $2.00)-Dave Stevens-c/a in all; Kaluta back-up-a; 1st app. Jonas (character based on The Shadow) 1 2 3 5 7 9
2-(7/89, $2.75)-Stevens/Dorman painted-c 6.00
3-(1/95, $2.95)-Includes pinups by Stevens, Gulacy, Plunkett, & Mignola 3.50
Volume 2-(9/96, $9.95, magazine size TPB)-Reprints #1-3 10.00

ROCKETEER SPECIAL EDITION, THE
Eclipse Comics: Nov, 1984 ($1.50, Baxter paper)(Chapter 5 of Rocketeer serial)
1-Stevens-c/a; Kaluta back-c; pin-ups inside 2 4 6 8 10 12
NOTE: *Originally intended to be published in Pacific Presents.*

ROCKETEER, THE: THE COMPLETE ADVENTURES
IDW Publishing: Oct, 2009 ($29.99/$75.00, hardcover)
HC-Reprints of Dave Stevens' Rocketeer stories in Starslayer #1-3, Pacific Presents #1,2, Rocketeer Special Edition and Rocketeer Adventure Magazine #1-3; all re-colored 30.00
... Deluxe Edition ($75.00, 8"x12" slipcased HC) larger size reprints of HC content plus 100 bonus pages of sketch art, layouts, design work; intro. by Thomas Jane 110.00
... Deluxe Edition 2nd printing ($75.00, oversized slipcased HC) 75.00

ROCKETEER, THE: THE OFFICIAL MOVIE ADAPTATION
W. D. Publications (Disney): 1991
nn-($5.95, 68 pgs.)-Squarebound deluxe edition 6.00
nn-($2.95, 68 pgs.)-Stapled regular edition 3.00
3-D Comic Book (1991, $7.98, 52 pgs.) 8.00

ROCKET KELLY (See The Bouncer, Green Mask #10); becomes Li'l Pan #6)
Fox Feature Syndicate: 1944; Fall, 1945 - No. 5, Oct-Nov, 1946
nn (1944), 1 (Fall, 1945) 35 70 105 208 339 470
2-The Puppeteer app. (costumed hero) 24 48 72 140 230 320
3-5: 5-(#5 on cover, #4 inside) 21 42 63 126 206 285

ROCKETMAN (Strange Fantasy #2 on) (See Hello Pal & Scoop Comics)
Ajax/Farrell Publications: June, 1952 (Strange Stories of the Future)
1-Rocketman & Cosmo 40 80 120 243 404 565

ROCKET RACCOON (Also see Incredible Hulk #271)
Marvel Comics: May, 1985 - No. 4, Aug, 1985 (color, limited series)
1-4: Mignola-a 2.50

ROCKET SHIP X
Fox Features Syndicate: September, 1951; 1952
1 62 124 186 394 677 960
1952 (nn, nd, no publ.)-Edited 1951-c (exist?) 39 78 117 231 378 525

ROCKET TO ADVENTURE LAND (See Pixie Puzzle...)

ROCKET TO THE MOON
Avon Periodicals: 1951
nn-Orlando-c/a; adapts Otis Adelbert Kline's "Maza of the Moon" 116 232 348 742 1271 1800

ROCK FANTASY COMICS
Rock Fantasy Comics: Dec, 1989 - No. 16?, 1991 ($2.25/$3.00, B&W)(No cover price)
1-Pink Floyd part 1 5.00
1-2nd printing ($3.00-c) 3.00
2,3: 2-Rolling Stones #1. 3-Led Zeppelin #1 4.00
2,3: 2nd printings ($3.00-c, 1/90 & 2/90) 3.00
4-Stevie Nicks Not published
5-Monstrosities of Rock #1; photo back-c 4.00
5-2nd printing ($3.00, 3/90 indicia, 2/90-c) 3.00
6-9,11-15,17,18: 6-Guns n' Roses #1 (1st & 2nd printings, 3/90)-Begin $3.00-c. 7-Sex Pistols #1. 8-Alice Cooper; not published. 9-Van Halen #1; photo back-c. 11-Jimi Hendrix #1; wraparound-c 3.00
10-Kiss #1; photo back-c 2 4 6 8 10 12
16-($5.00, 68 pgs.)-The Great Gig in the Sky(Floyd) 5.00

ROCK HAPPENING (See Bunny and Harvey Pop Comics:...)

ROCK N' ROLL COMICS
DC Comics: Dec./Jan 1956 (ashcan)
nn-Ashcan comic, not distributed to newsstands, only for in house use (no known sales)

ROCK N' ROLL COMICS
Revolutionary Comics: Jun, 1989 - No. 65 ($1.50/$1.95/$2.50, B&W/col. #15 on)
1-Guns N' Roses 1 2 3 5 6 8
1-2nd thru 7th printings. 7th printing (full color w/new-c/a) 2.50
2-Metallica 1 3 4 6 8 10
2-2nd thru 6th printings (6th in color) 2.50
3-Bon Jovi (no reprints) 1 2 3 5 6 8
4-8,10-65: 4-Motley Crue(2nd printing only, 1st destroyed). 5-Def Leppard (2 printings). 6-Rolling Stones(4 printings). 7-The Who (3 printings). 8-Skid Row; not published. 10-Warrant/Whitesnake(2 printings; 1st has 2 diff.-c). 11-Aerosmith (2 printings?). 12-New Kids on the Block(2 printings). 12-3rd printing; rewritten & titled NKOTB Hate Book. 13-Led Zeppelin. 14-Sex Pistols. 15-Poison; 1st color issue. 16-Van Halen. 17-Madonna. 18-Alice Cooper. 19-Public Enemy/2 Live Crew. 20-Queensryche/Tesla. 21-Prince? 22-AC/DC; begin $2.50-c. 23-Living Colour. 26-Michael Jackson. 29-Ozzy. 45,46-Grateful Dead. 49-Rush. 50,51-Bob Dylan. 56-David Bowie 5.00
9-Kiss 2 4 6 8 10 12
9-2nd & 3rd printings 2.50
NOTE: *Most issues were reprinted except #3. Later reprints are in color. #8 was not released.*

ROCKO'S MODERN LIFE (TV)
Marvel Comics: June, 1994 - No. 7, Dec, 1994 ($1.95) (Nickelodeon cartoon)
1-7 2.50

ROCKY AND HIS FIENDISH FRIENDS (TV)(Bullwinkle)
Gold Key: Oct, 1962 - No. 5, Sept, 1963 (Jay Ward)
1 (25¢, 80 pgs.) 15 30 45 104 197 290
2,3 (25¢, 80 pgs.) 11 22 33 74 132 190
4,5 (Regular size, 12¢) 8 16 24 54 90 125

ROCKY AND HIS FRIENDS (See Kite Fun Book & March of Comics #216 in the Promotional Comics section)

ROCKY AND HIS FRIENDS (TV)
Dell Publishing Co.: No. 1128, 8-10/60 - No.1311,1962 (Jay Ward)
Four Color #1128 (#1) (8-10/60) 29 58 87 212 406 600
Four Color #1152 (12-2/61), 1166, 1208, 1275, 1311('62) 18 36 54 126 246 365

Rocky Lane Western #8 © FAW

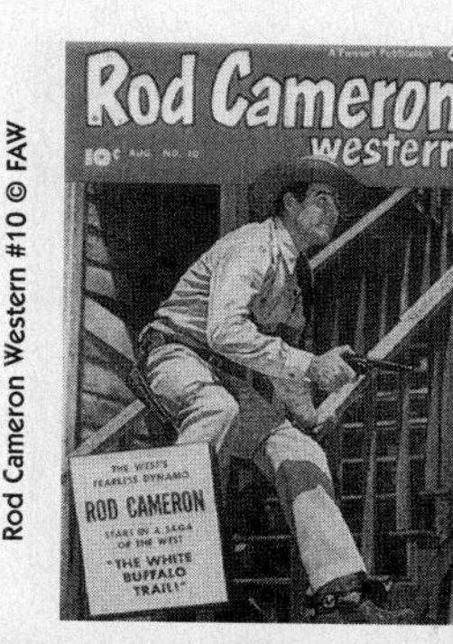

Rod Cameron Western #10 © FAW

Rom #2 © Parker Brothers

GD 2.0 | VG 4.0 | FN 6.0 | VF 8.0 | VF/NM 9.0 | NM- 9.2

GD 2.0 | VG 4.0 | FN 6.0 | VF 8.0 | VF/NM 9.0 | NM- 9.2

ROCKY HORROR PICTURE SHOW THE COMIC BOOK, THE
Caliber Press: Jul, 1990 - No. 3, Jan, 1991 ($2.95, mini-series, 52 pgs.)
1-3: 1-Adapts cult film plus photos, etc., 1-2nd printing 3.00
...Collection ($4.95) 5.00

ROCKY JONES SPACE RANGER (See Space Adventures #15-18)

ROCKY JORDEN PRIVATE EYE (See Private Eye)

ROCKY LANE WESTERN (Allan Rocky Lane starred in Republic movies & TV for a short time as Allan Lane, Red Ryder & Rocky Lane) (See Black Jack Fawcett Movie Comics, Motion Picture Comics & Six-Gun Heroes)
Fawcett Publications/Charlton No. 56 on: May, 1949 - No. 87, Nov, 1959
1 (36 pgs.)-Rocky, his stallion Black Jack, & Slim Pickens begin; photo-c begin, end #57; photo back-c 70 140 210 441 746 1050
2 (36 pgs.)-Last photo back-c 29 58 87 169 272 375
3-5 (52 pgs.): 4-Captain Tootsie by Beck 20 40 60 120 193 265
6,10 (36 pgs.): 10-Complete western novelette "Badman's Reward" 15 30 45 85 130 175
7-9 (52 pgs.) 15 30 45 94 147 200
11-13,15-17,19,20 (52 pgs.): 15-Black Jack's Hitching Post begins, ends #25. 20-Last Slim Pickens 14 28 42 78 112 145
14,18 (36 pgs.) 12 24 36 67 94 120
21,23,24 (52 pgs.): 21-Dee Dickens begins, ends #55,57,65-68 12 24 36 67 94 120
22,25-28,30 (36 pgs. begin) 11 22 33 62 86 110
29-Classic complete novel "The Land of Missing Men" with hidden land of ancient temple ruins (r-in #65) 15 30 45 85 130 175
31-40 11 22 33 60 83 105
41-54 10 20 30 54 72 90
55-Last Fawcett issue (1/54) 11 22 33 60 83 105
56-1st Charlton issue (2/54)-Photo-c 15 30 45 94 147 200
57,60-Photo-c 11 22 33 62 86 110
58,59,61-64,66-78,80-86: 59-61-Young Falcon app. 64-Slim Pickens app. 66-68: Reprints #30,31,32 9 18 27 52 69 85
65-r/#29, "The Land of Missing Men" 10 20 30 58 79 100
79-Giant Edition (68 pgs.) 11 22 33 67 90 115
87-Last issue 11 22 33 60 83 105
NOTE: *Complete novels in #10, 14, 18, 22, 25, 30-32, 36, 38, 39, 49. Captain Tootsie in #4, 12, 20. Big Bow and Little Arrow in #11, 28, 63. Black Jack's Hitching Post in #15-25, 64, 73.*

ROCKY LANE WESTERN
AC Comics: 1989 ($2.50, B&W, one-shot?)
1-Photo-c; Giordano reprints 4.00
Annual 1 (1991, $2.95, B&W, 44 pgs.)-photo front/back & inside-c; reprints 4.00

ROD CAMERON WESTERN (Movie star)
Fawcett Publications: Feb, 1950 - No. 20, Apr, 1953
1-Rod Cameron, his horse War Paint, & Sam The Sheriff begin; photo front/back-c begin 38 76 114 226 363 500
2 18 36 54 105 165 225
3-Novel length story "The Mystery of the Seven Cities of Cibola" 15 30 45 94 147 200
4-10: 9-Last photo back-c 14 28 42 82 121 160
11-19 13 26 39 72 101 130
20-Last issue & photo-c 14 28 42 76 108 140
NOTE: *Novel length stories in No. 1-8, 12-14.*

RODEO RYAN (See A-1 Comics #8)

ROGAN GOSH
DC Comics (Vertigo): 1994 ($6.95, one-shot)
nn-Peter Milligan scripts 7.00

ROGER DODGER (Also in Exciting Comics #57 on)
Standard Comics: No. 5, Aug, 1952
5-Teen-age 6 12 18 28 34 40

ROGER RABBIT (Also see Marvel Graphic Novel)
Disney Comics: June, 1990 - No. 18, Nov, 1991 ($1.50)
1-18-All new stories 3.00
In 3-D 1 (1992, $2.50)-Sold at Wal-Mart?; w/glasses 4.00

ROGER RABBIT'S TOONTOWN
Disney Comics: Aug, 1991 - No. 5, Dec, 1991 ($1.50)
1-5 2.50

ROGER ZELAZNY'S AMBER: THE GUNS OF AVALON
DC Comics: 1996 - No. 3, 1996 ($6.95, limited series)
1-3: Based on novel 7.00

ROG 2000
Pacific Comics: June, 1982 ($2.95, 44 pgs., B&W, one-shot, magazine)
nn-Byrne-c/a (r) 2 4 6 8 10 12
2nd printing (7/82) 1 2 3 4 5 7

ROG 2000
Fantagraphics Books: 1987 - No. 2, 1987 ($2.00, limited series)
1,2-Byrne-r 3.00

ROGUE (From X-Men)
Marvel Comics: Jan, 1995 - No. 4, Apr, 1995 ($2.95, limited series)
1-4: 1-Gold foil logo 4.00
TPB-($12.95) r/#1-4 13.00

ROGUE (Volume 2)
Marvel Comics: Sept, 2001 - No. 4, Dec, 2001 ($2.50, limited series)
1-4-Julie Bell painted-c/Lopresti-a; Rogue's early days with X-Men 2.50

ROGUE (From X-Men)
Marvel Comics: Sept, 2004 - No. 12, Aug, 2005 ($2.99)
1-12: 1-Richards-a. 4-Gambit app. 11-Sunfire dies, Rogue absorbs his powers 3.00
...: Going Rogue TPB (2005, $14.99) r/#1-6 15.00
...: Forget-Me-Not TPB (2006, $14.99) r/#7-12 15.00

ROGUE ANGEL: TELLER OF TALL TALES (Based on the Alex Archer novels)
IDW Publishing: Feb, 2008 - No. 5, Jun, 2008 ($3.99)
1-5-Annja Creed adventures; Barbara-Kesel-s/Renae De Liz-a 4.00

ROGUES GALLERY
DC Comics: 1996 ($3.50, one-shot)
1-Pinups of DC villains by various artists 3.50

ROGUES, THE (VILLAINS) (See The Flash)
DC Comics: Feb, 1998 ($1.95, one-shot)
1-Augustyn-s/Pearson-c 2.50

ROKKIN
DC Comics (WildStorm): Sept, 2006 - No. 6, Feb, 2007 ($2.99, limited series)
1-6-Hartnell-s/Bradshaw-a 3.00

ROLLING STONES: VOODOO LOUNGE
Marvel Comics: 1995 ($6.95, Prestige format, one-shot)
nn-Dave McKean-script/design/art 7.00

ROLY POLY COMIC BOOK
Green Publishing Co.: 1945 - No. 15, 1946 (MLJ reprints)
1-Red Rube & Steel Sterling begin; Sahle-c 31 62 93 182 296 410
6-The Blue Circle & The Steel Fist app. 20 40 60 114 182 250
10-Origin Red Rube retold; Steel Sterling story (Zip #41) 27 54 81 158 259 360
11,12: The Black Hood app. in both 19 38 57 112 179 245
14-Classic decapitation-c; the Black Hood app. 45 90 135 284 480 675
15-The Blue Circle & The Steel Fist app.; cover exact swipe from Fox Blue Beetle #1 32 64 96 188 307 425

ROM (Based on the Parker Brothers toy)
Marvel Comics Group: Dec, 1979 - No. 75, Feb, 1986
1-Origin/1st app. 2 4 6 13 18 22
2-16,19-23,28-30: 5-Dr. Strange. 13-Saga of the Space Knights begins. 19-X-Men cameo. 23-Powerman & Iron Fist app. 1 2 3 5 6 8
17,18-X-Men app. 2 4 6 9 12 15
24-27: 24-F.F. cameo; Skrulls, Nova & The New Champions app. 25-Double size. 26,27-Galactus app. 1 2 3 5 7 9
31-49,51-60: 31,32-Brotherhood of Evil Mutants app. 32-X-Men cameo. 34,35-Sub-Mariner app. 41,42-Dr. Strange app. 56,57-Alpha Flight app. 58,59-Ant-Man app. 6.00
50-Skrulls app. (52 pgs.) Pin-ups by Konkle, Austin 1 2 3 4 5 7
61-74: 65-West Coast Avengers & Beta Ray Bill app. 65,66-X-Men app. 6.00
75-Last issue 2 4 6 8 10 12
Annual 1-4: (1982-85, 52 pgs.) 6.00
NOTE: ***Austin** c-3i, 18i, 61i. **Byrne** a-74i; c-56, 57, 74. **Ditko** a-59-75p, Annual 4. **Golden** c-7-12, 19. **Guice** a-61i; c-55, 58, 60p, 70p. **Layton** a-59i, 72i; c-15, 59i, 69. **Miller** c-2p?, 3p, 17p, 18p. **Russell** a(i)-64, 65, 67, 69, 71, 75; c-64, 65i, 66, 71i, 75. **Severin** c-41p. **Sienkiewicz** a-53i; c-46, 47, 52-54, 68, 71p, Annual 2. **Simonson** c-18. **P. Smith** c-59p. **Starlin** c-67. **Zeck** c-50.*

ROMANCE (See True Stories of...)

ROMANCE AND CONFESSION STORIES (See Giant Comics Edition)
St. John Publishing Co.: No date (1949) (25¢, 100 pgs.)

Romantic Adventures #32 © ACG

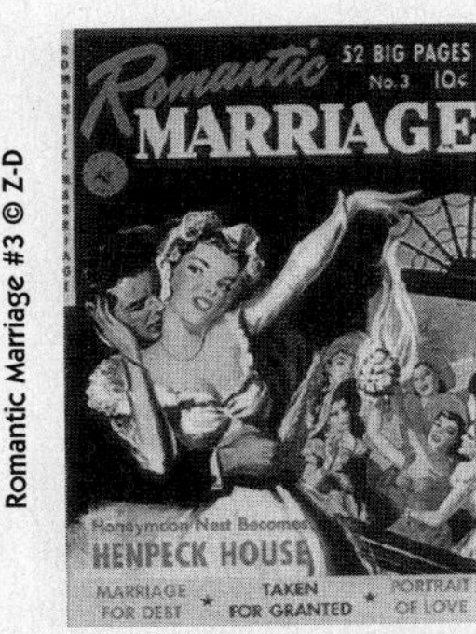

Romantic Marriage #3 © Z-D

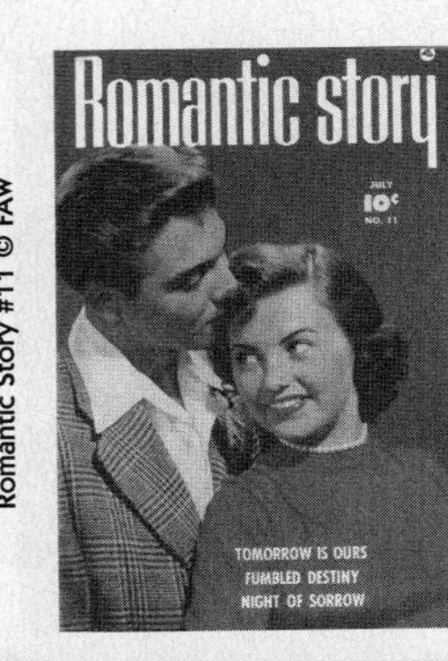

Romantic Story #11 © FAW

	GD 2.0	VG 4.0	FN 6.0	VF 8.0	VF/NM 9.0	NM- 9.2
1-Baker-c/a; remaindered St. John love comics	47	94	141	296	498	700

ROMANCE DIARY
Marvel Comics (CDS)(CLDS): Dec, 1949 - No. 2, Mar, 1950

	GD 2.0	VG 4.0	FN 6.0	VF 8.0	VF/NM 9.0	NM- 9.2
1,2	15	30	45	86	133	180

ROMANCE OF FLYING, THE
David McKay Publications: 1942

	GD 2.0	VG 4.0	FN 6.0	VF 8.0	VF/NM 9.0	NM- 9.2
Feature Books 33 (nn)-WW II photos	15	30	45	86	133	180

ROMANCES OF MOLLY MANTON (See Molly Manton)

ROMANCES OF NURSE HELEN GRANT, THE
Atlas Comics (VPI): Aug, 1957

	GD 2.0	VG 4.0	FN 6.0	VF 8.0	VF/NM 9.0	NM- 9.2
1	9	18	27	47	61	75

ROMANCES OF THE WEST (Becomes Romantic Affairs #3?)
Marvel Comics (SPC): Nov, 1949 - No. 2, Mar, 1950 (52 pgs.)

	GD 2.0	VG 4.0	FN 6.0	VF 8.0	VF/NM 9.0	NM- 9.2
1-Movie photo-c of Yvonne DeCarlo & Howard Duff (Calamity Jane & Sam Bass)	23	46	69	136	223	310
2-Photo-c	15	30	45	85	130	175

ROMANCE STORIES OF TRUE LOVE (Formerly True Love Problems & Advice Illustrated)
Harvey Publications: No. 45, 5/57 - No. 50, 3/58; No. 51, 9/58 - No. 52, 11/58

	GD 2.0	VG 4.0	FN 6.0	VF 8.0	VF/NM 9.0	NM- 9.2
45-51: 45,46,48-50-Powell-a	6	12	18	31	38	45
52-Matt Baker-a	9	18	27	47	61	75

ROMANCE TALES (Formerly Western Winners #6?)
Marvel Comics (CDS): No. 7, Oct, 1949 - No. 9, April, 1950 (7-9: photo-c)

	GD 2.0	VG 4.0	FN 6.0	VF 8.0	VF/NM 9.0	NM- 9.2
7	14	28	42	82	121	160
8,9: 8-Everett-a	10	20	30	56	76	95

ROMANCE TRAIL
National Periodical Publications: July-Aug, 1949 - No. 6, May-June, 1950
(All photo-c & 52 pgs.)

	GD 2.0	VG 4.0	FN 6.0	VF 8.0	VF/NM 9.0	NM- 9.2
1-Kinstler, Toth-a; Jimmy Wakely photo-c	57	114	171	359	605	850
2-Kinstler-a; Jim Bannon photo-c	32	64	96	186	298	410
3-Tex Williams photo-c; Kinstler, Toth-a	33	66	99	196	316	435
4-Jim Bannon as Red Ryder photo-c; Toth-a	25	50	75	145	233	320
5,6: Photo-c on both. 5-Kinstler-a	22	44	66	131	211	290

ROMAN HOLIDAYS, THE (TV)
Gold Key: Feb, 1973 - No. 4, Nov, 1973 (Hanna-Barbera)

	GD 2.0	VG 4.0	FN 6.0	VF 8.0	VF/NM 9.0	NM- 9.2
1	4	8	12	28	44	60
2-4	3	6	9	18	27	35

ROMANTIC ADVENTURES (My... #49-67, covers only)
American Comics Group (B&I Publ. Co.): Mar-Apr, 1949 - No. 67, July, 1956 (Becomes My... #68 on)

	GD 2.0	VG 4.0	FN 6.0	VF 8.0	VF/NM 9.0	NM- 9.2
1	18	36	54	107	169	230
2	11	22	33	64	90	115
3-10	9	18	27	52	69	85
11-20 (4/52)	8	16	24	44	57	70
21-45,51,52: 52-Last Pre-code (2/55)	8	16	24	40	50	60
46-49-3-D effect-c/stories (TrueVision)	13	26	39	74	105	135
50-Classic cover/story "Love of A Lunatic"	12	24	36	67	94	120
53-67	7	14	21	37	46	55

NOTE: *#1-23, 52 pgs.* ***Shelly*** *a-40. Whitney c/art in many issues.*

ROMANTIC AFFAIRS (Formerly Molly Manton's Romances #2 and/or Romances of the West #2 and/or Our Love #2?)
Marvel Comics (SPC): No. 3, Mar, 1950

	GD 2.0	VG 4.0	FN 6.0	VF 8.0	VF/NM 9.0	NM- 9.2
3-Photo-c from Molly Manton's Romances #2	10	20	30	56	76	95

ROMANTIC CONFESSIONS
Hillman Periodicals: Oct, 1949 - V3#1, Apr-May, 1953

	GD 2.0	VG 4.0	FN 6.0	VF 8.0	VF/NM 9.0	NM- 9.2
V1#1-McWilliams-a	17	34	51	98	154	210
2-Briefer-a; negligee panels	11	22	33	60	83	105
3-12	9	18	27	52	69	85
V2#1,2,4-8,10-12: 2-McWilliams-a	9	18	27	47	61	75
3-Krigstein-a	10	20	30	54	72	90
9-One pg. Frazetta ad	9	18	27	47	61	75
V3#1	8	16	24	44	57	70

ROMANTIC HEARTS
Story Comics/Master/Merit Pubs.: Mar, 1951 - No. 10, Oct, 1952; July, 1953 - No. 12, July, 1955

	GD 2.0	VG 4.0	FN 6.0	VF 8.0	VF/NM 9.0	NM- 9.2
1(3/51) (1st Series)	14	28	42	82	121	160
2	9	18	27	50	65	80
3-10: Cameron-a	8	16	24	44	57	70
1(7/53) (2nd Series)-Some say #11 on-c	10	20	30	54	72	90
2	8	16	24	42	54	65
3-12	7	14	21	37	46	55

ROMANTIC LOVE
Avon Periodicals/Realistic (No #14-19): 9-10/49 - #3, 1-2/50; #4, 2-3/51 - #13, 10/52; #20, 3-4/54 - #23, 9-10/54

	GD 2.0	VG 4.0	FN 6.0	VF 8.0	VF/NM 9.0	NM- 9.2
1-c-/Avon paperback #252	30	60	90	177	289	400
2-5: 3-c-/paperback Novel Library #12. 4-c-/paperback Diversey Prize Novel #5. 5-c-/paperback Novel Library #34	19	38	57	109	172	235
6- "Thrill Crazy" marijuana story; c-/Avon paperback #207; Kinstler-a	25	50	75	150	245	340
7,8: 8-Astarita-a(2)	18	36	54	105	165	225
9-12: 9-c-/paperback Novel Library #41; Kinstler-a. 10-c-/Avon paperback #212. 11-c-/paperback Novel Library #17; Kinstler-a. 12-c-/paperback Novel Library #13	19	38	57	109	172	235
13,21-23: 22,23-Kinstler-c	18	36	54	103	162	220
20-Kinstler-c/a	18	36	54	105	165	225
nn(1-3/53)(Realistic-r)	12	24	36	67	94	120

NOTE: ***Astarita*** *a-7, 10, 11, 21. Painted c-1-3, 5, 7-11, 13. Photo c-4, 6.*

ROMANTIC LOVE
Quality Comics Group: 1963-1964

	GD 2.0	VG 4.0	FN 6.0	VF 8.0	VF/NM 9.0	NM- 9.2
I.W. Reprint #2,3,8,11: 2-r/Romantic Love #2	2	4	6	9	12	15

ROMANTIC MARRIAGE (Cinderella Love #25 on)
Ziff-Davis/St. John No. 18 on (#1-8: 52 pgs.): #1-3 (1950, no months); #4, 5-6/51 - #17, 9/52; #18, 9/53 - #24, 9/54

	GD 2.0	VG 4.0	FN 6.0	VF 8.0	VF/NM 9.0	NM- 9.2
1-Photo-c; Cary Grant/Betsy Drake photo back-c.	21	42	63	124	202	280
2-Painted-c; Anderson-a (also #15)	15	30	45	84	127	170
3-9: 3,4,8,9-Painted-c; 5-7-Photo-c	14	28	42	80	115	150
10-Unusual format; front-c is a painted-c; back-c is a photo-c complete with logo, price, etc.	20	40	60	117	189	260
11-17 13-Photo-c. 15-Signed story by Anderson. 17-(9/52)-Last Z-D issue	13	26	39	74	105	135
18-22,24: 20-Photo-c	13	26	39	74	105	135
23-Baker-c; all stories are reprinted from #15	15	30	45	83	124	165

ROMANTIC PICTURE NOVELETTES
Magazine Enterprises: 1946

	GD 2.0	VG 4.0	FN 6.0	VF 8.0	VF/NM 9.0	NM- 9.2
1-Mary Worth-r; Creig Flessel-c	16	32	48	94	147	200

ROMANTIC SECRETS (Becomes Time For Love)
Fawcett/Charlton Comics No. 5 (10/55) on: Sept, 1949 - No. 39, 4/53; No. 5, 10/55 - No. 52, 11/64 (#1-39: photo-c)

	GD 2.0	VG 4.0	FN 6.0	VF 8.0	VF/NM 9.0	NM- 9.2
1-(52 pg. issues begin, end #?)	17	34	51	98	154	210
2,3	11	22	33	60	83	105
4,9-Evans-a	11	22	33	64	90	115
5-8,10(9/50)	9	18	27	50	65	80
11-23	8	16	24	44	57	70
24-Evans-a	9	18	27	50	65	80
25-39('53)	8	16	24	42	54	65
5 (Charlton, 2nd Series)(10/55, formerly Negro Romances #4)	10	20	30	56	76	95
6-10	8	16	24	44	57	70
11-20	4	8	12	22	34	45
21-35	3	6	9	19	29	38
36-52('64)	3	6	9	16	23	30

NOTE: ***Bailey*** *a-20.* ***Powell*** *a(1st series)-5, 7, 10, 12, 16, 17, 20, 26, 29, 33, 34, 36, 37.* ***Sekowsky*** *a-26.* ***Swayze*** *a(1st series)-16, 18, 19, 23, 26-28, 31, 32, 39.*

ROMANTIC STORY (Cowboy Love #28 on)
Fawcett/Charlton Comics No. 23 on: 11/49 - #22, Sum, 1953; #23, 5/54 - #27, 12/54; #28, 8/55 - #130, 11/73

	GD 2.0	VG 4.0	FN 6.0	VF 8.0	VF/NM 9.0	NM- 9.2
1-Photo-c begin, end #24; 52 pgs. begins	18	36	54	103	162	220
2	11	22	33	62	86	110
3-5	10	20	30	54	72	90
6-14	9	18	27	50	65	80
15-Evans-a	10	20	30	54	72	90
16-22(Sum, '53; last Fawcett issue). 21-Toth-a?	8	16	24	42	54	65
23-39: 26,29-Wood swipes	7	14	21	37	46	55
40-(100 pgs.)	11	22	33	64	90	115
41-50	3	6	9	21	32	42
51-80: 57-Hypo needle story	3	6	9	16	23	30
81-99	2	4	6	10	14	18
100	2	4	6	13	28	22

Ronin #4 © Frank Miller

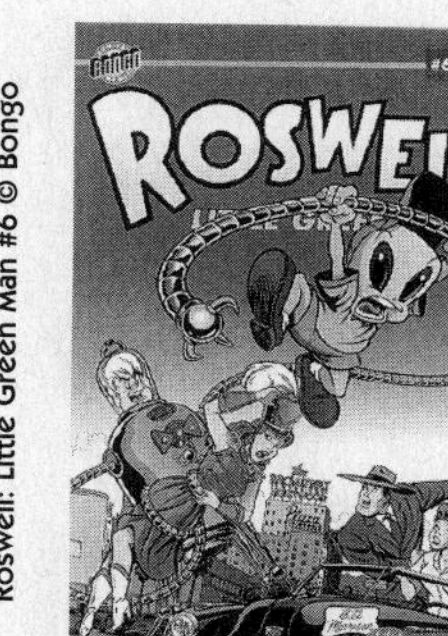

Roswell: Little Green Man #6 © Bongo

Roy Rogers Comics #26 © DELL

	GD 2.0	VG 4.0	FN 6.0	VF 8.0	VF/NM 9.0	NM- 9.2
101-130: 120-Bobby Sherman pin-up	2	4	6	9	12	15

NOTE: *Jim Aparo a-94. Powell a-7, 8, 16, 20, 30. Marcus Swayze a-2, 12, 20, 32.*

ROMANTIC THRILLS (See Fox Giants)

ROMANTIC WESTERN
Fawcett Publications: Winter, 1949 - No. 3, June, 1950 (All Photo-c)

	GD	VG	FN	VF	VF/NM	NM-
1	22	44	66	128	209	290
2-(Spr/50)-Williamson, McWilliams-a	20	40	60	114	182	250
3	15	30	45	85	130	175

ROMEO TUBBS (...That Lovable Teenager; formerly My Secret Life)
Fox Feature Syndicate/Green Publ. Co. No. 27: No. 26, 5/50 - No. 28, 7/50; No. 1, 1950; No. 27, 12/52

	GD	VG	FN	VF	VF/NM	NM-
26-Teen-age	11	22	33	64	90	115
28 (7/50)	10	20	30	58	79	100
27 (12/52)-Contains Pedro on inside; Wood-a (exist?)	15	30	45	84	127	170

RONALD McDONALD (TV)
Charlton Press (King Features Synd.): Sept, 1970 - No. 4, March, 1971

	GD	VG	FN	VF	VF/NM	NM-
1	8	16	24	56	93	130
2-4	5	10	15	32	51	70
V2#1,3-Special reprint for McDonald systems; "Not for resale" on cover	6	12	18	39	62	85

RONIN
DC Comics: July, 1983 - No. 6, Aug, 1984 ($2.50, limited series, 52 pgs.)

	GD	VG	FN	VF	VF/NM	NM-
1-5-Frank Miller-c/a/scripts in all	2	3	4	6	8	10
6-Scarcer; has fold-out poster.	2	4	6	8	10	12
Trade paperback (1987, $12.95)-Reprints #1-6						13.00

RONNA
Knight Press: Apr, 1997 ($2.95, B&W, one-shot)

1-Beau Smith-s 3.00

ROOK (See Eerie Magazine & Warren Presents: The Rook)
Warren Publications: Oct, 1979 - No. 14, April, 1982 (B&W magazine)

	GD	VG	FN	VF	VF/NM	NM-
1-Nino-a/Corben-c; with 8 pg. color insert	3	6	9	16	23	30
2-4,6,7: 2-Voltar by Alcala begins. 3,4-Toth-a	2	4	6	9	13	16
5,8-14: 11-Zorro-s. 12-14-Eagle by Severin	2	4	6	9	13	16

ROOK
Harris Comics: No. 0, Jun, 1995 - No. 4, 1995 ($2.95)

0-4: 0-short stories (3) w/preview. 4-Brereton-c. 3.00

ROOKIE COP (Formerly Crime and Justice?)
Charlton Comics: No. 27, Nov, 1955 - No. 33, Aug, 1957

	GD	VG	FN	VF	VF/NM	NM-
27	9	18	27	47	61	75
28-33	6	12	18	31	38	45

ROOM 222 (TV)
Dell Publishing Co.: Jan, 1970; No. 2, May, 1970 - No. 4, Jan, 1971

	GD	VG	FN	VF	VF/NM	NM-
1	5	10	15	34	55	75
2-4: 2,4-Photo-c. 3-Marijuana story. 4 r/#1	4	8	12	22	34	45

ROOTIE KAZOOTIE (TV)(See 3-D-ell)
Dell Publishing Co.: No. 415, Aug, 1952 - No. 6, Oct-Dec, 1954

	GD	VG	FN	VF	VF/NM	NM-
Four Color 415 (#1)	9	18	27	65	113	160
Four Color 459,502(#2,3), 4(4-6/54)-6	7	14	21	47	76	105

ROOTS OF THE SWAMP THING
DC Comics: July, 1986 - No.5, Nov, 1986 ($2.00, Baxter paper, 52 pgs.)

1-5: r/Swamp Thing #1-10 by Wrightson & House of Mystery-r. 1-new Wrightson-c (2-5 reprinted covers). 4.00

ROSE (See Bone)
Cartoon Books: Nov, 2000 - No. 3, Feb, 2002 ($5.95, lim. series, square-bound)

1-3-Prequel to Bone; Jeff Smith-s/Charles Vess painted-a/c 6.00
HC (2001, $29.95) r/#1-3; new Vess cover painting 30.00
SC (2002, $19.95) r/#1-3; new Vess cover painting 20.00
1-($6.00)-Blood & Glory Edition 6.00

ROSE AND THORN
DC Comics: Feb, 2004 - No. 6, July, 2004 ($2.95, limited series)

1-6-Simone-s/Melo-a/Hughes-c 3.00

ROSWELL: LITTLE GREEN MAN (See Simpsons Comics #19-22)
Bongo Comics: 1996 - No. 6 ($2.95, quarterly)

1-6 3.50
...Walks Among Us ('97, $12.95, TPB) r/ #1-3 & Simpsons flip books 13.00

ROUND TABLE OF AMERICA: PERSONALITY CRISIS (See Big Bang Comics)
Image Comics: Aug, 2005 ($3.50, one-shot)

1-Carlos Rodriguez-a/Pedro Angosto-s 3.50

ROUNDUP (...Western Crime Stories)
D. S. Publishing Co.: July-Aug, 1948 - No. 5, Mar-Apr, 1949 (All 52 pgs.)

	GD	VG	FN	VF	VF/NM	NM-
1-Kiefer-a	18	36	54	107	169	230
2-5: 2-Marijuana drug mention story	14	28	42	82	121	160

ROUTE 666
CrossGeneration Comics: July, 2002 - No. 22, Jun, 2004 ($2.95)

1-22-Bedard-s/Moline-a in most. 5-Richards-a. 15-McCrea-a 3.00
...: Highway to Horror (4/03, $15.95, TPB) r/#1-6 16.00
Vol. 2: Three-Ring Circus (2003, $15.95) r/#7-12 16.00

ROYAL ROY
Marvel Comics (Star Comics): May, 1985 - No.6, Mar, 1986 (Children's book)

1-6 4.00

ROY CAMPANELLA, BASEBALL HERO
Fawcett Publications: 1950 (Brooklyn Dodgers)

	GD	VG	FN	VF	VF/NM	NM-
nn-Photo-c; life story	59	118	177	375	643	910

ROY ROGERS (See March of Comics #17, 35, 47, 62, 68, 73, 77, 86, 91, 100, 105, 116, 121, 131, 136, 146, 151, 161, 167, 176, 191, 206, 221, 236, 250)

ROY ROGERS AND TRIGGER
Gold Key: Apr, 1967

	GD	VG	FN	VF	VF/NM	NM-
1-Photo-c; reprints	4	8	12	28	44	60

ROY ROGERS ANNUAL
Wilson Publ. Co., Toronto/Dell: 1947 ("Giant Edition" on-c)(132 pgs., 50¢)

nn-Less than 5 known copies. Front and back cover art are from Roy Rogers #2. Stories reprinted from Roy Rogers #2, Four Color #137 and Four Color #153. (A copy in VG/FN was sold in 1986 for $400, in 1996 for $1200 & in 2000 for $1500; a FN+ sold for $1,650; a GD sold for $448 in 2008 and a FN sold for $717 in 2009.)

ROY ROGERS COMICS (See Western Roundup under Dell Giants)
Dell Publishing Co.: No. 38, 4/44 - No. 177, 12/47 (#38-166: 52 pgs.)

	GD	VG	FN	VF	VF/NM	NM-
Four Color 38 (1944)-49 pg. story; photo front/back-c on all 4-Color issues (1st western comic with photo-c)	160	320	480	1400	2700	4000
Four Color 63 (1945)-Color photos on all four-c	40	80	120	312	581	850
Four Color 86,95 (1945)	29	58	87	217	401	585
Four Color 109 (1946)	22	44	66	163	302	440
Four Color 117,124,137,144	18	36	54	130	240	350
Four Color 153,160,166: 166-48 pg. story	16	32	48	116	216	315
Four Color 177 (36 pgs.)-32 pg. story	15	30	45	111	206	300
HC (Dark Horse Books, 8/08, $49.95) r/Four Color #38,63,86,95,109; Roy Rogers Jr intro.						50.00

ROY ROGERS COMICS (...& Trigger #92(8/55)-on)(Roy starred in Republic movies, radio & TV) (Singing cowboy) (Also see Dale Evans, It Really Happened #8, Queen of the West Dale Evans, & Roy Rogers' Trigger)
Dell Publishing Co.: Jan, 1948 - No. 145, Sept-Oct, 1961 (#1-19: 36 pgs.)

	GD	VG	FN	VF	VF/NM	NM-
1-Roy, his horse Trigger, & Chuck Wagon Charley's Tales begin; photo-c begin, end #145	65	130	195	553	1052	1550
2	24	48	72	172	319	465
3-5	17	34	51	120	223	325
6-10	14	28	42	103	184	265
11-19: 19-Chuck Wagon Charley's Tales ends	12	24	36	86	153	220
20 (52 pgs.)-Trigger feature begins, ends #46	12	24	36	87	156	225
21-30 (52 pgs.)	10	20	30	71	126	180
31-46 (52 pgs.): 37-X-Mas-c	9	18	27	60	100	140
47-56 (36 pgs.): 47-Chuck Wagon Charley's Tales returns, ends #133. 49-X-mas-c. 55-Last photo back-c	7	14	21	47	76	105
57 (52 pgs.)-Heroin drug propaganda story	7	14	21	49	80	110
58-70 (52 pgs.): 58-Heroin drug use/dealing story. 61-X-Mas-c	7	14	21	47	76	105
71-80 (52 pgs.): 73-X-Mas-c	6	12	18	41	66	90
81-91 (36 pgs. #81-on): 85-X-Mas-c	6	12	18	39	62	85
92-99,101-110,112-118: 92-Title changed to Roy Rogers and Trigger (8/55)	6	12	18	37	59	80
100-Trigger feature returns, ends #131	6	12	18	43	69	95
111,119-124-Toth-a	7	14	21	45	73	100
125-131: 125-Toth-a (1 pg.)	5	10	15	35	55	75
132-144-Manning-a. 132-1st Dale Evans-sty by Russ Manning. 138,144-Dale Evans featured	6	12	18	39	62	85

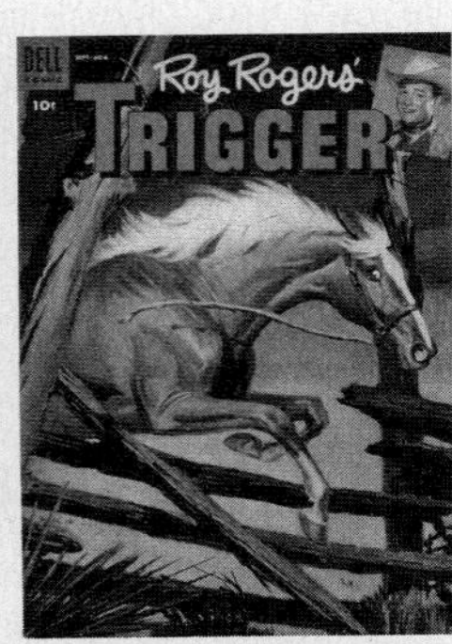

Roy Rogers' Trigger #14 © DELL

Runaways V2 #28 © MAR

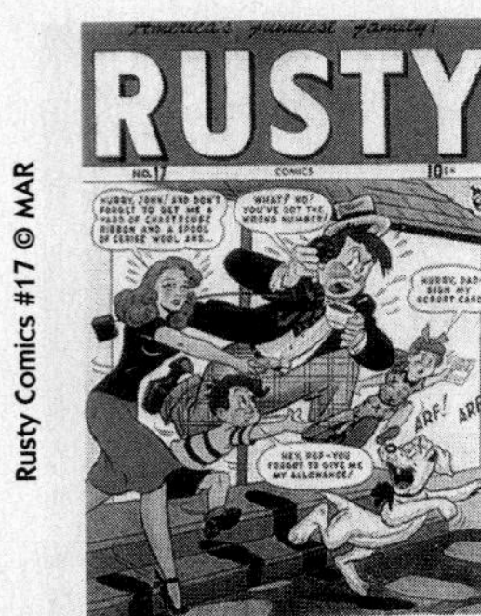

Rusty Comics #17 © MAR

	GD 2.0	VG 4.0	FN 6.0	VF 8.0	VF/NM 9.0	NM- 9.2
145-Last issue	7	14	21	47	76	105

NOTE: *Buscema a-74-108(2 stories each). **Manning** a-123, 124, 132-144. **Marsh** a-110. Photo back-c No. 1-9, 11-35, 38-55.*

ROY ROGERS' TRIGGER
Dell Publishing Co.: No. 329, May, 1951 - No. 17, June-Aug, 1955

	GD	VG	FN	VF	VF/NM	NM-
Four Color 329 (#1)-Painted-c	14	28	42	103	184	265
2 (9-11/51)-Photo-c	11	22	33	77	136	195
3-5: 3-Painted-c begin, end #17, most by S. Savitt	6	12	18	43	69	95
6-17: Title merges with Roy Rogers after #17	5	10	15	35	55	75

ROY ROGERS WESTERN CLASSICS
AC Comics: 1989 -No. 4 ($2.95/$3.95, 44pgs.) (24 pgs. color, 16 pgs. B&W)

1-4: 1-Dale Evans-r by Manning, Trigger-r by Buscema; photo covers & interior photos by Roy & Dale. 2-Buscema-r (3); photo-c & B&W photos inside. 3-Dale Evans-r by Manning; Trigger-r by Buscema plus other Buscema-r; photo-c — 4.00

RUDOLPH, THE RED-NOSED REINDEER
National Per. Publ.: 1950 - No. 13, Winter, 1962-63 (Issues are not numbered)

	GD	VG	FN	VF	VF/NM	NM-
1950 issue (#1); Grossman-c/a in all	21	42	63	124	202	280
1951-53 issues (3 total)	14	28	42	76	108	140
1954/55, 55/56, 56/57	12	24	36	67	94	120
1957/58, 58/59, 59/60, 60/61, 61/62	7	14	21	47	76	105
1962/63 (rare)(84 pgs.)(shows "Annual" in indicia)	11	22	33	74	132	190

NOTE: *13 total issues published. Has games & puzzles also.*

RUDOLPH, THE RED-NOSED REINDEER (Also see Limited Collectors' Edition C-20, C-24, C-33, C-42, C-50; and All-New Collectors' Edition C-53 & C-60)
National Per. Publ.: Christmas 1972 (Treasury-size)

	GD	VG	FN	VF	VF/NM	NM-
nn-Precursor to Limited Collectors' Edition title (scarce) (implied to be Lim. Coll .Ed. C-20)	20	40	60	142	276	410

RUFF AND REDDY (TV)
Dell Publ. Co.: No. 937, 9/58 - No. 12, 1-3/62 (Hanna-Barbera)(#9 on: 15¢)

	GD	VG	FN	VF	VF/NM	NM-
Four Color 937(#1)(1st Hanna-Barbera comic book)	12	24	36	82	149	215
Four Color 981,1038	8	16	24	52	86	120
4(1-3/60)-12: 8-Last 10¢ issue	7	14	21	45	73	100

RUGGED ACTION (Strange Stories of Suspense #5 on)
Atlas Comics (CSI): Dec, 1954 - No. 4, June, 1955

	GD	VG	FN	VF	VF/NM	NM-
1-Brodsky-c	14	28	42	76	108	140
2-4: 2-Last precode (2/55)	10	20	30	54	72	90

NOTE: ***Ayers** a-2, 3. **Maneely** c-2, 3. **Severin** a-2.*

RUINS
Marvel Comics (Alterniverse): July, 1995 - No. 2, Sept, 1995 ($5.00, painted, limited series)

1,2: Phil Sheldon from Marvels; Warren Ellis scripts; acetate-c — 5.00
Reprint (2009, $4.99) r/#1,2; cover gallery — 5.00

RULAH JUNGLE GODDESS (Formerly Zoot; I Loved #28 on) (Also see All Top Comics & Terrors of the Jungle)
Fox Features Syndicate: No. 17, Aug, 1948 - No. 27, June, 1949

	GD	VG	FN	VF	VF/NM	NM-
17	107	214	321	680	1165	1650
18-Classic girl-fight interior splash	71	142	213	454	777	1100
19,20	68	136	204	435	743	1050
21-Used in **SOTI**, pg. 388,389	69	138	207	442	759	1075
22-Used in **SOTI**, pg. 22,23	69	138	207	442	759	1075
23-27	53	106	159	334	567	800

NOTE: ***Kamen** c-17-19, 21, 22.*

RUNAWAY, THE (See Movie Classics)

RUNAWAYS
Marvel Comics: July, 2003 - No. 18, Nov, 2004 ($2.95/$2.25/$2.99)

1-($2.95) Vaughan-s/Alphona-a/Jo Chen-c — 3.00
2-9-($2.50) — 2.50
10-18-($2.99) 11,12-Miyazawa-a; Cloak and Dagger app. 16-The mole revealed — 3.00
Hardcover (2005, $34.99) oversized r/#1-18; proposal & sketch pages; Vaughan intro. — 35.00
Marvel Age Runaways Vol. 1: Pride and Joy (2004, $7.99, digest size) r/#1-6 — 8.00
...Vol. 2: Teenage Wasteland (2004, $7.99, digest size) r/#7-12 — 8.00
...Vol. 3: The Good Die Young (2004, $7.99, digest size) r/#13-18 — 8.00

RUNAWAYS (Also see X-Men/Runaways 2006 FCBD Edition in the Promotional Section)
Marvel Comics: Apr, 2005 - No. 30, Aug, 2008 ($2.99)

1-24: 1-6-Vaughan-s/Alphona-a/Jo Chen-c. 7,8-Miyazawa-a/Bachalo-c. 11-Spider-Man app. 12-New Avengers app. 18-Gert killed — 3.00
25-30-Joss Whedon-s/Michael Ryan-a. 25-Punisher app. — 3.00
...: Dead End Kids HC (2008, $19.99) r/#25-30 — 20.00
... Saga (2007, $3.99) re-caps the 2 series thru #24; 4 new pages w/Ramos-a; Ramos-c — 4.00
Hardcover (2006, $24.99) oversized r/#1-12 & X-Men/Runaways; script & sketch pages — 25.00
Hardcover Vol. 3 (2007, $24.99) oversized r/#13-24; sketch pages — 25.00
...Vol. 4: True Believers (2006, $7.99, digest size) r/#1-6 — 8.00
...Vol. 5: Escape To New York (2006, $7.99, digest size) r/#7-12 — 8.00
...Vol. 6: Parental Guidance (2006, $7.99, digest size) r/#13-18 — 8.00

RUNAWAYS (3rd series)
Marvel Comics: Oct, 2008 - No. 14, Nov, 2009 ($2.99/$3.99)

1-9,11-14: 1-6-Terry Moore-s/Humberto Ramos-a/c. 7-9-Miyazawa-a — 3.00
10-($3.99) Wolverine & the X-Men app.; Yost & Asmus-s; Pichelli & Rios-a; Lafuente-c — 4.00

RUN BABY RUN
Logos International: 1974 (39¢, Christian religious)

	GD	VG	FN	VF	VF/NM	NM-
nn-By Tony Tallarico from Nicky Cruz's book	2	4	6	9	12	15

RUN, BUDDY, RUN (TV)
Gold Key: June, 1967 (Photo-c)

	GD	VG	FN	VF	VF/NM	NM-
1 (10204-706)	3	6	9	18	27	35

RUNE (See Curse of Rune, Sludge & all other Ultraverse titles for previews)
Malibu Comics (Ultraverse): 1994 - No. 9, Apr, 1995 ($1.95)

	GD	VG	FN	VF	VF/NM	NM-
0-Obtained by sending coupons from 11 comics; came w/Solution #0, poster, temporary tattoo, card	1	2	3	5	6	8

1,2,4-9: 1-Barry Windsor-Smith-c/a/stories begin, ends #6. 5-1st app. of Gemini. 6-Prime & Mantra app. — 2.50
1-(1/94)-"Ashcan" edition flip book w/Wrath #1 — 2.50
1-Ultra 5000 Limited silver foil edition — 4.00
3-(3/94, $3.50, 68 pgs.)-Flip book w/Ultraverse Premiere #1 — 3.50
Giant Size 1 ($2.50, 44 pgs.)-B.Smith story & art. — 2.50

RUNE (2nd Series)(Formerly Curse of Rune)(See Ultraverse Unlimited #1)
Malibu Comics (Ultraverse): Infinity, Sept, 1995 - V2#7, Apr, 1996 ($1.50)

Infinity, V2#1-7: Infinity-Black September tie-in; black-c & painted-c exist. 1,3-7-Marvel's Adam Warlock app; regular & painted-c exist. 2-Flip book w/ "Phoenix Resurrection" Pt. 6 — 2.50
...Vs. Venom 1 (12/95, $3.95) — 4.00

RUNE: HEARTS OF DARKNESS
Malibu Comics (Ultraverse): Sept, 1996 - No. 3, Nov, 1996 ($1.50, lim. series)

1-3: Moench scripts & Kyle Hotz-c/a; flip books w/6 pg. Rune story by the Pander Bros. — 2.50

RUNE/SILVER SURFER
Marvel Comics/Malibu Comics (Ultraverse): Apr, 1995 ($5.95/$2.95, one-shot)

1 ($5.95, direct market)-BWS-c — 6.00
1 ($2.95, newstand)-BWS-c — 3.00
1-Collector's limited edition — 6.00

RUSE (Also see Archard's Agents)
CrossGeneration Comics: Nov, 2001 - No. 26, Jan, 2004 ($2.95)

1-Waid-s/Guice & Perkins-a — 5.00
2-26: 6-Jeff Johnson-a. 11,15-Paul Ryan-a. 12-Last Waid-s — 3.00
Enter the Detective Vol. 1 TPB (2002, $15.95) r/#1-6; Guice-c — 16.00
...: The Silent Partner Vol. 2 (3/03, $15.95, TPB) r/#7-12 — 16.00
...: Criminal Intent Vol. 3 ('03, $15.95, TPB) r/#13-18 — 16.00
Traveler 1,2 ($9.95): Digest-size editions of the TPBs — 10.00

RUSH CITY
DC Comics: Sept, 2006 - No. 6, May, 2007 ($2.99, limited series)

1-6: 1-Dixon-s/Green-a/Jock-c. 2,3-Black Canary app. — 3.00

RUSTLERS, THE (See Zane Grey Four Color 532)

RUSTY, BOY DETECTIVE
Good Comics/Lev Gleason: Mar-April, 1955 - No. 5, Nov, 1955

	GD	VG	FN	VF	VF/NM	NM-
1-Bob Wood, Carl Hubbell-a begins	9	18	27	47	61	75
2-5	6	12	18	31	38	45

RUSTY COMICS (Formerly Kid Movie Comics; Rusty and Her Family #21, 22; The Kelleys #23 on; see Millie The Model)
Marvel Comics (HPC): No. 12, Apr, 1947 - No. 22, Sept, 1949

	GD	VG	FN	VF	VF/NM	NM-
12-Mitzi app.	21	42	63	124	202	280
13	14	28	42	78	112	145
14-Wolverton's Powerhouse Pepper (4 pgs.) plus Kurtzman's "Hey Look"	22	44	66	130	213	295
15-17-Kurtzman's "Hey Look"	16	32	48	94	147	200
18,19	13	26	39	72	101	130
20-Kurtzman-a (5 pgs.)	17	34	51	98	154	210
21,22-Kurtzman-a (17 & 22 pgs.)	21	42	63	126	206	285

RUSTY DUGAN (See Holyoke One-Shot #2)

Saari #1 © P.L. Publ.

Sabrina #100 © AP

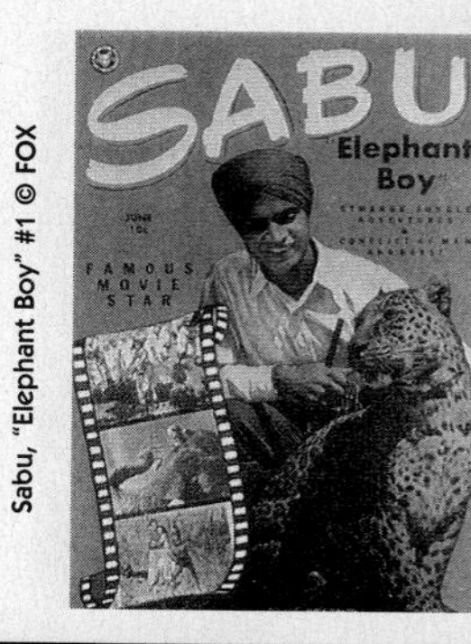

Sabu, "Elephant Boy" #1 © FOX

	GD 2.0	VG 4.0	FN 6.0	VF 8.0	VF/NM 9.0	NM- 9.2

RUSTY RILEY
Dell Publishing Co.: No. 418, Aug, 1952 - No. 554, April, 1954 (Frank Godwin strip reprints)

Four Color 418 (...a Boy, a Horse, and a Dog #1)	5	10	15	32	51	70
Four Color 451(2/53), 486 ('53), 554	4	8	12	26	41	50

RUULE
Beckett Comics: Dec, 2003 - No. 5, Apr, 2004 ($2.99)

1-5-David Mack-c/Mike Hawthorne-a 3.00

RUULE: KISS & TELL
Beckett Comics: Jun, 2004 - No. 8 ($1.99)

1-8: 1-Amano-s/c; Rousseau-a. 4-Maleev-c 2.00
TPB (2005, $19.99) r/#1-8 20.00

SAARI ("The Jungle Goddess")
P. L. Publishing Co.: November, 1951

1	45	90	135	284	480	675

SABAN POWERHOUSE (TV)
Acclaim Books: 1997 ($4.50, digest size)

1,2-Power Rangers, BeetleBorgs, and others 4.50

SABAN PRESENTS POWER RANGERS TURBO VS. BEETLEBORGS METALLIX (TV)
Acclaim Books: 1997 ($4.50, digest size, one-shot)

nn 4.50

SABAN'S MIGHTY MORPHIN POWER RANGERS
Hamilton Comics: Dec, 1994 - No. 6, May, 1995 ($1.95, limited series)

1-6: 1-w/bound-in Power Ranger Barcode Card 2.50

SABAN'S MIGHTY MORPHIN POWER RANGERS (TV)
Marvel Comics: 1995 - No. 8, 1996 ($1.75)

1-8 2.50

SABLE (Formerly Jon Sable, Freelance; also see Mike Grell's...)
First Comics: Mar, 1988 - No. 27, May, 1990 ($1.75/$1.95)

1-27: 10-Begin $1.95-c 2.50

SABLE & FORTUNE (Also see Silver Sable and the Wild Pack)
Marvel Comics: Mar, 2006 - No. 4, June, 2006 ($2.99, limited series)

1-4-John Burns-a/Brendan Cahill-s 3.00

SABRE (See Eclipse Graphic Album Series)
Eclipse Comics: Aug, 1982 - No. 14, Aug, 1985 (Baxter paper #4 on)

1-14: 1-Sabre & Morrigan Tales begin. 4-6-Incredible Seven origin 2.50

SABRETOOTH (See Iron Fist, Power Man, X-Factor #10 & X-Men)
Marvel Comics: Aug, 1993 - No. 4, Nov, 1993 ($2.95, lim. series, coated paper)

1-4: 1-Die-cut-c. 3-Wolverine app. 4.00
...Special 1 "In the Red Zone" (1995, $4.95) Chromium wraparound-c 6.00
V2 #1 (1/98, $5.95, one-shot) Wildchild app. 6.00
Trade paperback (12/94, $12.95) r/#1-4 13.00

SABRETOOTH
Marvel Comics: Dec, 2004 - No. 4, Feb, 2005 ($2.99, limited series)

1-4-Sears-a. 3,4-Wendigo app. 3.00
...: Open Season TPB (2005, $9.99) r/#1-4 10.00

SABRETOOTH AND MYSTIQUE (See Mystique and Sabretooth)

SABRETOOTH CLASSIC
Marvel Comics: May, 1994 - No. 15, July, 1995 ($1.50)

1-15: 1-3-r/Power Man & Iron Fist #66,78,84. 4-r/Spec. S-M #116. 9-Uncanny X-Men #212, 10-r/Uncanny X-Men #213. 11-r/ Daredevil #238. 12-r/Classic X-Men #10 3.00

SABRETOOTH: MARY SHELLEY OVERDRIVE
Marvel Comics: Aug, 2002 - No. 4, Nov, 2002 ($2.99, limited series)

1-4-Jolley-s; Harris-c 3.00

SABRINA (Volume 2) (Based on animated series)
Archie Publications: Jan, 2000 - No. 104, Sept, 2009 ($1.79/$1.99/$2.19/$2.25/$2.50)

1-Teen-age Witch magically reverted to 12 years old 4.00
2-10: 4-Begin $1.99-c 3.00
11-104: 38-Sabrina aged back to 16 years old. 39-Begin $2.19-c. 58-Manga-style begins; Tania Del Rio-a. 67-Josie and the Pussycats app. 101-Young Salem; begin $2.50-c 2.50

SABRINA'S CHRISTMAS MAGIC (See Archie Giant Series Magazine #196, 207, 220, 231, 243, 455, 467, 479, 491, 503, 515)

SABRINA'S HALLOWEEN SPOOOKTACULAR
Archie Publications: 1993 - 1995 ($2.00, 52 pgs.)

1-Neon orange ink-c; bound-in poster	1	2	3	5	6	8
2,3-Titled "Sabrina's Holiday Spectacular"						5.00

SABRINA, THE TEEN-AGE WITCH (TV)(See Archie Giant Series, Archie's Madhouse 22, Archie's TV..., Chilling Advs. In Sorcery, Little Archie #59)
Archie Publications: April, 1971 - No. 77, Jan, 1983 (52 pg.Giants No. 1-17)

1-52 pgs. begin, end #17	14	28	42	100	188	275
2-Archie's group x-over	8	16	24	58	97	135
3-5: 3,4-Archie's Group x-over	6	12	18	41	66	90
6-10	5	10	15	34	55	75
11-17(2/74)	4	8	12	26	41	55
18-30	3	6	9	19	29	38
31-40(8/77)	3	6	9	14	20	26
41-60(6/80)	2	4	6	10	14	18
61-70	2	4	6	8	11	14
71-76-low print run	2	4	6	11	16	20
77-Last issue; low print run	3	6	9	14	20	26

SABRINA, THE TEEN-AGE WITCH
Archie Publications: 1996 ($1.50, 32 pgs., one-shot)

1-Updated origin 5.00

SABRINA, THE TEEN-AGE WITCH (Continues in Sabrina, Vol. 2)
Archie Publications: May, 1997 - No. 32, Dec, 1999 ($1.50/$1.75/$1.79)

1-Photo-c with Melissa Joan Hart	1	2	3	5	6	8
2-10: 9-Begin $1.75-c						5.00
11-20						4.00
21-32: 24-Begin $1.79-c. 28-Sonic the Hedgehog-c/app.						3.00

SABU, "ELEPHANT BOY" (Movie; formerly My Secret Story)
Fox Features Syndicate: No. 30, June, 1950 - No. 2, Aug, 1950

30(#1)-Wood-a; photo-c from movie	26	52	78	154	252	350
2-Photo-c from movie; Kamen-a	19	38	57	111	176	240

SACHS & VIOLENS
Marvel Comics (Epic Comics): Nov, 1993 - No. 4, July, 1994 ($2.25, limited series, mature)

1-($2.75)-Embossed-c w/bound-in trading card 2.75
1-($3.50)-Platinum edition (1 for each 10 ordered) 4.00
2-4: Perez-c/a; bound-in trading card: 2-(5/94) 2.50
TPB (DC, 2006, $14.99) r/series; intro. by Peter David; creator bios. 15.00

SACRAMENTS, THE
Catechetical Guild Educational Society: Oct, 1955 (35¢)

30304	6	12	18	28	34	40

SACRED AND THE PROFANE, THE (See Eclipse Graphic Album Series #9 & Epic Illustrated #20)

SADDLE JUSTICE (Happy Houlihans #1,2) (Saddle Romances #9 on)
E. C. Comics: No. 3, Spring, 1948 - No. 8, Sept-Oct, 1949

3-The 1st E.C. by Bill Gaines to break away from M. C. Gaines' old Educational Comics format. Craig, Feldstein, H. C. Kiefer, & Stan Asch-a; mentioned in Love and Death	52	104	156	328	552	775
4-1st Graham Ingels-a for E.C.	45	90	135	284	480	675
5-8-Ingels-a in all	41	82	123	256	428	600

NOTE: *Craig and Feldstein art in most issues. Canadian reprints known; see Table of Contents.* ***Craig*** *c-3, 4.* ***Ingels*** *c-5-8. #4 contains a biography of* ***Craig.***

SADDLE ROMANCES (Saddle Justice #3-8; Weird Science #12 on)
E. C. Comics: No. 9, Nov-Dec, 1949 - No. 11, Mar-Apr, 1950

9,11: 9-Ingels-c/a. 11-Ingels-a; Feldstein-c	46	92	138	290	488	685
10-Wally Wood's 1st work at E. C.; Ingels-a; Feldstein-c	47	94	141	296	498	700

NOTE: *Canadian reprints known; see Table of Contents.* ***Wood/Harrison*** *a-10, 11.*

SADHU
Virgin Comics: July, 2006 - No. 8, June, 2007 ($2.99)

1-8: 1,2-Gotham Chopra-s/Jeevan Kang-a 3.00
...: The Silent Ones (8/07 - No. 5, 2/08, $2.99) 1-5 3.00
...: Wheel of Destiny (4/08 - No. 5, $2.99) 1,2 3.00

SADIE SACK (See Harvey Hits #93)

SAD SACK AND THE SARGE
Harvey Publications: Sept, 1957 - No. 155, June, 1982

1	13	26	39	93	172	250
2	8	16	24	52	86	120
3-10	6	12	18	41	66	90
11-20	5	10	15	32	51	70
21-30	3	6	9	20	30	40

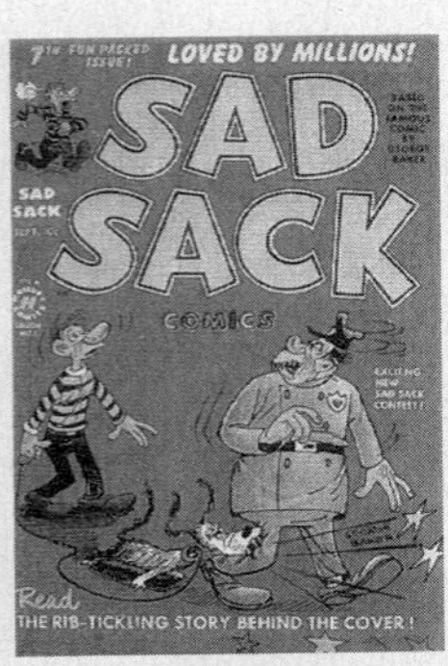

Sad Sack Comics #7 © HARV

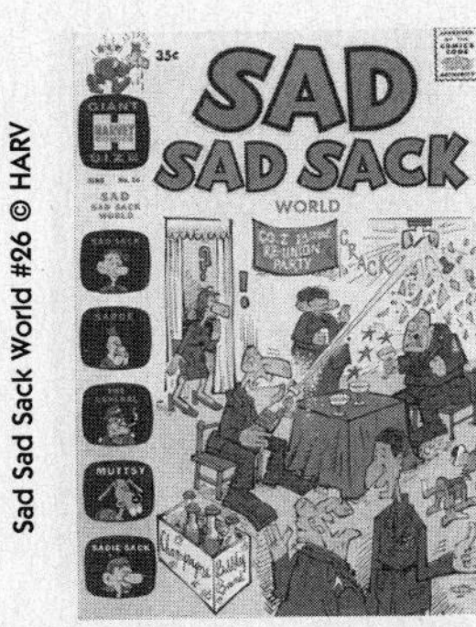

Sad Sad Sack World #26 © HARV

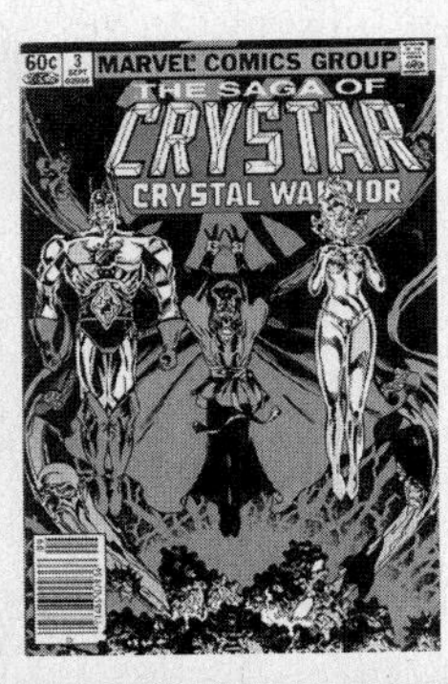

Saga of Crystar, Crystal Warrior #3 © MAR

	GD 2.0	VG 4.0	FN 6.0	VF 8.0	VF/NM 9.0	NM- 9.2
31-50	3	6	9	14	20	25
51-70	2	4	6	9	13	16
71-90,97-99	1	3	4	6	8	10
91-96: All 52 pg. Giants	2	4	6	9	13	16
100	2	4	6	8	10	12
101-120	1	2	3	4	5	7
121-155						5.00

SAD SACK COMICS (See Harvey Collector's Comics #16, Little Sad Sack, Tastee Freez Comics #4 & True Comics #55)
Harvey Publications/Lorne-Harvey Publications (Recollections) #288 On: Sept, 1949 - No. 287, Oct, 1982; No. 288, 1992 - No. 291, 1993

	GD 2.0	VG 4.0	FN 6.0	VF 8.0	VF/NM 9.0	NM- 9.2
1-Infinity-c; Little Dot begins (1st app.); civilian issues begin, end #21; based on comic strip	72	144	216	612	1206	1800
2-Flying Fool by Powell	27	54	81	197	386	575
3	16	32	48	115	220	325
4-10	12	24	36	85	155	225
11-21	8	16	24	58	97	135
22-("Back In The Army Again" on covers #22-36); "The Specialist" story about Sad Sack's return to Army	10	20	30	67	116	165
23-30	6	12	18	37	59	80
31-50	4	8	12	28	44	60
51-80,100: 62-"The Specialist" reprinted	3	6	9	20	30	40
81-99	3	6	9	16	23	30
101-140	3	6	9	14	19	24
141-170,200	2	4	6	11	16	20
171-199	2	4	6	9	13	16
201-207: 207-Last 12¢ issue	2	4	6	8	11	14
208-222	1	2	3	5	6	8
223-228 (25¢ Giants, 52 pgs.)	2	4	6	8	11	14
229-250	1	3	4	6	8	10
251-285						6.00
286,287-Limited distribution	1	2	3	5	7	9
288,289 ($2.75, 1992): 289-50th anniversary issue						6.00
290,291 ($1.00, 1993, B&W)						3.00
3-D 1 (1/54, 25¢)-Came with 2 pairs of glasses; titled "Harvey 3-D Hits"	16	32	48	112	214	315
...At Home for the Holidays 1 (1993, no-c price)-Publ. by Lorne-Harvey' X-Mas issue						4.00

NOTE: *The Sad Sack Comics comic book was a spin-off from a Sunday Newspaper strip launched through John Wheeler's Bell Syndicate. The previous Sunday page and the first 21 comics depicted the Sad Sack in civvies. Unpopularity caused the Sunday page to be discontinued in the early '50s. Meanwhile Sad Sack returned to the Army, by popular demand, in issue No. 22, remaining there ever since. Incidentally, relatively few of the first 21 issues were ever collected and remain scarce due to this.*

SAD SACK FUN AROUND THE WORLD
Harvey Publications: 1974 (no month)

	GD 2.0	VG 4.0	FN 6.0	VF 8.0	VF/NM 9.0	NM- 9.2
1-About Great Britain	2	4	6	11	16	20

SAD SACK GOES HOME
Harvey Publications: 1951 (16 pgs. in color, no cover price)

	GD 2.0	VG 4.0	FN 6.0	VF 8.0	VF/NM 9.0	NM- 9.2
nn-By George Baker	5	10	15	34	55	75

SAD SACK LAUGH SPECIAL
Harvey Publications: Winter, 1958-59 - No. 93, Feb, 1977 (#1-9: 84 pgs.; #10-60: 68 pgs.; #61-76: 52 pgs.)

	GD 2.0	VG 4.0	FN 6.0	VF 8.0	VF/NM 9.0	NM- 9.2
1-Giant 25¢ issues begin	10	20	30	71	126	180
2	6	12	18	41	66	90
3-10	5	10	15	32	51	70
11-30	4	8	12	26	41	55
31-60: 31-Hi-Fi Tweeter app. 60-Last 68 pg. Giant	3	6	9	16	23	30
61-76-(All 52 pg. issues)	2	4	6	10	14	18
77-93	1	2	3	5	6	8

SAD SACK NAVY, GOBS 'N' GALS
Harvey Publications: Aug, 1972 - No. 8, Oct, 1973

	GD 2.0	VG 4.0	FN 6.0	VF 8.0	VF/NM 9.0	NM- 9.2
1: 52 pg. Giant	3	6	9	16	23	30
2-8	2	4	6	9	12	15

SAD SACK'S ARMY LIFE (See Harvey Hits #8, 17, 22, 28, 32, 39, 43, 47, 51, 55, 58, 61, 64, 67, 70)

SAD SACK'S ARMY LIFE (...Parade #1-57, ...Today #58 on)
Harvey Publications: Oct, 1963 - No. 60, Nov, 1975; No. 61, May, 1976

	GD 2.0	VG 4.0	FN 6.0	VF 8.0	VF/NM 9.0	NM- 9.2
1-(68 pg. issues begin)	8	16	24	52	86	120
2-10	4	8	12	28	44	60
11-20	3	6	9	20	30	40
21-34: Last 68 pg. issue	3	6	9	16	23	30
35-51: All 52 pgs.	2	4	6	10	14	18
52-61	1	3	4	6	8	10

SAD SACK'S FUNNY FRIENDS (See Harvey Hits #75)
Harvey Publications: Dec, 1955 - No. 75, Oct, 1969

	GD 2.0	VG 4.0	FN 6.0	VF 8.0	VF/NM 9.0	NM- 9.2
1	10	20	30	71	126	180
2-10	6	12	18	41	66	90
11-20	4	8	12	24	37	50
21-30	3	6	9	18	27	35
31-50	3	6	9	14	20	25
51-75	2	4	6	9	13	16

SAD SACK'S MUTTSY (See Harvey Hits #74, 77, 80, 82, 84, 87, 89, 92, 96, 99, 102, 105, 108, 111, 113, 115, 117, 119, 121)

SAD SACK USA (...Vacation #8)
Harvey Publications: Nov, 1972 - No. 7, Nov, 1973; No. 8, Oct, 1974

	GD 2.0	VG 4.0	FN 6.0	VF 8.0	VF/NM 9.0	NM- 9.2
1	3	6	9	14	20	25
2-8	2	4	6	8	10	12

SAD SACK WITH SARGE & SADIE
Harvey Publications: Sept, 1972 - No. 8, Nov, 1973

	GD 2.0	VG 4.0	FN 6.0	VF 8.0	VF/NM 9.0	NM- 9.2
1-(52 pg. Giant)	3	6	9	14	20	25
2-8	2	4	6	8	10	12

SAD SAD SACK WORLD
Harvey Publ.: Oct, 1964 - No. 46, Dec, 1973 (#1-31: 68 pgs.; #32-38: 52 pgs.)

	GD 2.0	VG 4.0	FN 6.0	VF 8.0	VF/NM 9.0	NM- 9.2
1	7	14	21	49	80	110
2-10	4	8	12	26	41	55
11-20	3	6	9	20	30	40
21-31: 31-Last 68 pg. issue	3	6	9	16	23	30
32-39-(All 52 pgs)	2	4	6	10	14	18
40-46	1	3	4	6	8	10

SAFEST PLACE IN THE WORLD, THE
Dark Horse Comics: 1993 ($2.50, one-shot)

	GD 2.0	VG 4.0	FN 6.0	VF 8.0	VF/NM 9.0	NM- 9.2
1-Steve Ditko-c/a/scripts						2.50

SAFETY-BELT MAN
Sirius Entertainment: June, 1994 - No. 6, 1995 ($2.50, B&W)

	GD 2.0	VG 4.0	FN 6.0	VF 8.0	VF/NM 9.0	NM- 9.2
1-6: 1-Horan-s/Dark One-a/Sprouse-c. 2,3-Warren-c. 4-Linsner back-up story. 5,6-Crilley-a						3.00

SAFETY-BELT MAN ALL HELL
Sirius Entertainment: June, 1996 - No. 6, Mar, 1997 ($2.95, color)

	GD 2.0	VG 4.0	FN 6.0	VF 8.0	VF/NM 9.0	NM- 9.2
1-6-Horan-s/Fillbach Bros.-a						3.00

SAGA OF BIG RED, THE
Omaha World-Herald: Sept, 1976 ($1.25) (In color)

	GD 2.0	VG 4.0	FN 6.0	VF 8.0	VF/NM 9.0	NM- 9.2
nn-by Win Mumma; story of the Nebraska Cornhuskers (sports)						6.00

SAGA OF CRYSTAR, CRYSTAL WARRIOR, THE
Marvel Comics: May, 1983 - No. 11, Feb, 1985 (Remco toy tie-in)

	GD 2.0	VG 4.0	FN 6.0	VF 8.0	VF/NM 9.0	NM- 9.2
1,6: 1-(Baxter paper). 6-Nightcrawler app; Golden-c						4.00
2-5,7-11: 3-Dr. Strange app. 3-11-Golden-c (painted-4,5). 11-Alpha Flight app.						3.00

SAGA OF RA'S AL GHUL, THE
DC Comics: Jan, 1988 - No. 4, Apr, 1988 ($2.50, limited series)

	GD 2.0	VG 4.0	FN 6.0	VF 8.0	VF/NM 9.0	NM- 9.2
1-4-r/N. Adams Batman						6.00

SAGA OF SABAN'S MIGHTY MORPHIN POWER RANGERS (Also see Saban's Mighty Morphin Power Rangers)
Hamilton Comics: 1995 - No. 4, 1995 ($1.95, limited series)

	GD 2.0	VG 4.0	FN 6.0	VF 8.0	VF/NM 9.0	NM- 9.2
1-4						2.50

SAGA OF SEVEN SUNS, THE : VEILED ALLIANCES
DC Comics (WildStorm): 2004 ($24.95, hardcover graphic novel with dustjacket)

	GD 2.0	VG 4.0	FN 6.0	VF 8.0	VF/NM 9.0	NM- 9.2
HC-Kevin J. Anderson-s/Robert Teranishi-a						25.00
SC-(2004, $17.95)						18.00

SAGA OF THE ORIGINAL HUMAN TORCH
Marvel Comics: Apr, 1990 - No. 4, July, 1990 ($1.50, limited series)

	GD 2.0	VG 4.0	FN 6.0	VF 8.0	VF/NM 9.0	NM- 9.2
1-4: 1-Origin; Buckler-c/a(p). 3-Hitler-c						2.50

SAGA OF THE SUB-MARINER, THE
Marvel Comics: Nov, 1988 - No. 12, Oct, 1989 ($1.25/$1.50 #5 on, maxi-series)

	GD 2.0	VG 4.0	FN 6.0	VF 8.0	VF/NM 9.0	NM- 9.2
1-12: 9-Original X-Men app.						3.00

SAGA OF THE SWAMP THING, THE (See Swamp Thing)

SAILOR MOON (Manga)
Mixx Entertainment Inc.: 1998 - Present ($2.95)

	GD 2.0	VG 4.0	FN 6.0	VF 8.0	VF/NM 9.0	NM- 9.2
1	2	4	6	10	14	18

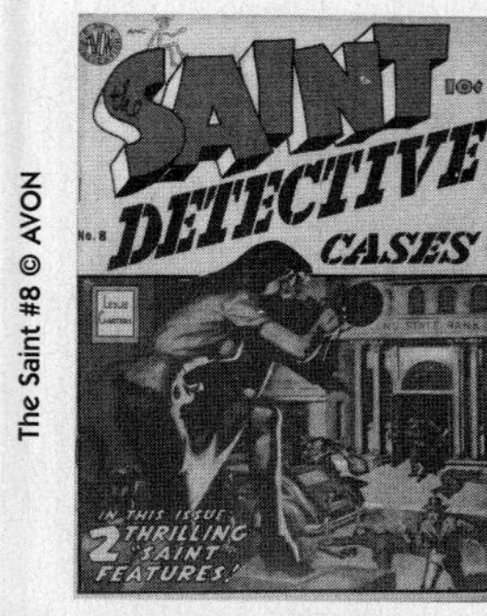

The Saint #8 © AVON

Salvation Run #4 © DC

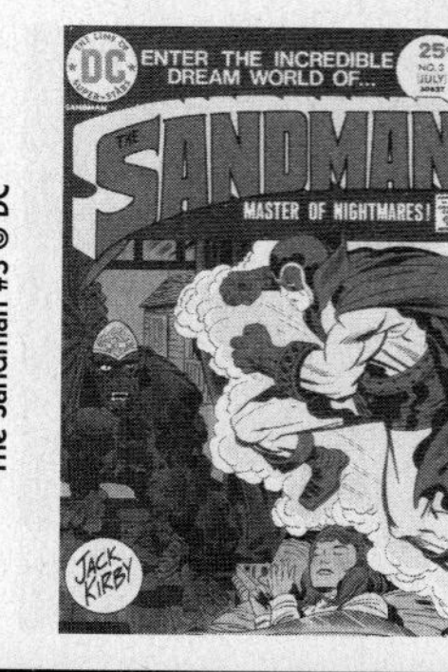

The Sandman #3 © DC

GD VG FN VF VF/NM NM-
2.0 4.0 6.0 8.0 9.0 9.2

1-(San Diego edition) 2 4 6 11 16 20
2-5 2 4 6 8 10 12
6-25 5.00
26-35 3.00
... Rini's Moon Stick 1 15.00

SAILOR ON THE SEA OF FATE (See First Comics Graphic Novel #11)

SAILOR SWEENEY (Navy Action #1-11, 15 on)
Atlas Comics (CDS): No. 12, July, 1956 - No. 14, Nov, 1956
12-14: 12-Shores-a. 13,14-Severin-c 9 18 27 52 69 85

SAINT, THE (Also see Movie Comics(DC) #2 & Silver Streak #18)
Avon Periodicals: Aug, 1947 - No. 12, Mar, 1952
1-Kamen bondage-c/a 86 172 258 546 936 1325
2 41 82 123 250 418 585
3-5: 4-Lingerie panels 37 74 111 222 361 500
6-Miss Fury app. by Tarpe Mills (14 pgs.) 50 100 150 315 533 750
7-c-/Avon paperback #118 29 58 87 172 281 390
8,9(12/50): Saint strip-r in #8-12; 9-Kinstler-c 26 52 78 154 252 350
10-Wood-a, 1 pg; c-/Avon paperback #289 26 52 78 154 252 350
11 20 40 60 117 189 260
12-c-/Avon paperback #123 22 44 66 128 209 290
NOTE: *Lucky Dale, Girl Detective in #1,2,4,6.* ***Hollingsworth*** *a-4, 6. Painted-c 7, 8, 10-12.*

SAINT ANGEL
Image Comics: Mar, 2000 - No. 4, Mar, 2001 ($2.95/$3.95)
0-Altstaetter & Napton-s/Altstaetter-a 3.00
1-4-($3.95) Flip book w/Deity. 1-(6/00). 2-(10/00) 4.00

ST. GEORGE
Marvel Comics (Epic Comics): June, 1988 - No.8, Oct, 1989 ($1.25,/$1.50)
1-8: Sienkiewicz-c. 3-begin $1.50-c 2.50

SAINT GERMAINE
Caliber Comics: 1997 - No. 8, 1998 ($2.95)
1-8: 1,5-Alternate covers 3.00

ST. SWITHIN'S DAY
Trident Comics: Apr, 1990 ($2.50, one-shot)
1-Grant Morrison scripts 3.00

ST. SWITHIN'S DAY
Oni Press: Mar, 1998 ($2.95, B&W, one-shot)
1-Grant Morrison-s/Paul Grist-a 3.00

SALOMÉ (See Night Music #6)

SALVATION RUN
DC Comics: Jan, 2008 - No. 7, Jul, 2008 ($2.99, limited series)
1-7-DC villains banished to an alien planet; Willingham-s/Chen-a/c. 1-Var-c by Corroney 3.00

SAM AND MAX, FREELANCE POLICE SPECIAL
Fishwrap Prod./Comico: 1987 ($1.75, B&W); Jan, 1989 ($2.75, 44 pgs.)
1 ($1.75, B&W, Fishwrap) 3.00
2 ($2.75, color, Comico) 2.75

SAM AND TWITCH (See Spawn and Case Files:...)
Image Comics (Todd McFarlane Prod.): Aug, 1999 - No. 26, Feb, 2004 ($2.50)
1-26: 1-19-Bendis-s. 1-14-Medina-a. 15-19-Maleev-a. 20-24-McFarlane-s/Maleev-a 2.50
Book One: Udaku (2000, $21.95, TPB) B&W reprint of #1-8 22.00
...: The Brian Michael Bendis Collection Vol. 1 (2/06, $24.95) r/#1-9 in color; sketch pages 25.00
...: The Brian Michael Bendis Collection Vol. 2 (6/07, $24.95) r/#10-19; cover gallery 25.00

SAM HILL PRIVATE EYE
Close-Up (Archie): 1950 - No. 7, 1951
1 16 32 48 92 144 195
2 10 20 30 56 76 95
3-7 10 20 30 54 72 90

SAMSON (1st Series) (Captain Aero #7 on; see Big 3 Comics)
Fox Features Syndicate: Fall, 1940 - No. 6, Sept, 1941 (See Fantastic Comics)
1-Samson begins, ends #6; Powell-a, signed 'Rensie;' Wing Turner by Tuska app; Fine-c?
219 438 657 1402 2401 3400
2-Dr. Fung by Powell; Fine-c? 80 160 240 508 874 1240
3-Navy Jones app.; Joe Simon-c 60 120 180 381 653 925
4-Yarko the Great, Master Magician begins 53 106 159 334 567 800
5,6: 6-Origin The Topper 43 86 129 271 461 650

SAMSON (2nd Series) (Formerly Fantastic Comics #10, 11)
Ajax/Farrell Publications (Four Star): No. 12, April, 1955 - No. 14, Aug, 1955
12-Wonder Boy 30 60 90 177 289 400
13,14: 13-Wonder Boy, Rocket Man 26 52 78 154 252 350

SAMSON (See Mighty Samson)

SAMSON & DELILAH (See A Spectacular Feature Magazine)

SAMUEL BRONSTON'S CIRCUS WORLD (See Circus World under Movie Classics)

SAMURAI (Also see Eclipse Graphic Album Series #14)
Aircel Publications: 1985 - No. 23, 1987 ($1.70, B&W)
1, 14-16-Dale Keown-a 3.00
1-(reprinted),2-12,17-23: 2 (reprinted issue exists) 2.50
13-Dale Keown's 1st published artwork (1987) 5.00

SAMURAI
Warp Graphics: May, 1997 ($2.95, B&W)
1 3.00

SAMURAI CAT
Marvel Comics (Epic Comics): June, 1991 - No. 3, Sept, 1991 ($2.25, limited series)
1-3: 3-Darth Vader-c/story parody 2.50

SAMURAI: HEAVEN & EARTH
Dark Horse Comics: Dec, 2004 - No. 5, Dec, 2005 ($2.99)
1-5-Luke Ross-a/Ron Marz-s 3.00
TPB (4/06, $14.95) r/#1-5; sketch pages and cover and pin-up gallery 15.00

SAMURAI: HEAVEN & EARTH (Volume 2)
Dark Horse Comics: Nov, 2006 - No. 5, June, 2007 ($2.99)
1-5-Luke Ross-a/Ron Marz-s 3.00
TPB (10/07, $14.95) r/#1-5; sketch pages and cover and pin-up gallery 15.00

SAMURAI JACK SPECIAL (TV)
DC Comics: Sept, 2002 ($3.95, one-shot)
1-Adaptation of pilot episode with origin story; Tartakovsky-s 4.00

SAMURAI: LEGEND
Marvel Comics (Soleil): 2008 - No. 4, 2009 ($5.99)
1-4-Genet-a/DiGiorgio-s; English version of French comic; preview of other titles 6.00

SAMUREE
Continuity Comics: May, 1987 - No. 9, Jan, 1991
1-9 3.00

SAMUREE
Continuity Comics: V2#1, May, 1993 - V2#4, Jan,1994 ($2.50)
V2#1-4-Embossed-c: 2,4-Adams plot, Nebres-i. 3-Nino-c(i) 2.50

SAMUREE
Acclaim Comics (Windjammer): Oct, 1995 - No. 2, Nov,1995 ($2.50, lim. series)
1,2 2.50

SAN DIEGO COMIC CON COMICS
Dark Horse Comics: 1992 - No.4, 1995 (B&W, promo comic for the San Diego Comic Con)
1-(1992)-Includes various characters published from Dark Horse including Concrete, The Mask, RoboCop and others; 1st app. of Sprint from John Byrne's Next Men; art by Quesada, Byrne, Rude, Burden, Moebius & others; pin-ups by Rude, Dorkin, Allred & others; Chadwick-c 1 2 3 5 7 9
2-(1993)-Intro of Legend imprint; 1st app. of John Byrne's Danger Unlimited, Mike Mignola's Hellboy, Art Adams' Monkeyman & O'Brien; contains stories featuring Concrete, Sin City, Martha Washington & others; Grendel, Madman, & Big Guy pin-ups; Don Martin-c.
2 4 6 8 10 12
3-(1994)-Contains stories featuring Barb Wire, The Mask, The Dirty Pair, & Grendel by Matt Wagner; contains pin-ups of Ghost, Predator & Rascals In Paradise; The Mask-c. 6.00
4-(1995)-Contains Sin City story by Miller (3pg.), Star Wars, The Mask, Tarzan, Foot Soldiers; Sin City & Star Wars flip-c 6.00

SANDMAN, THE (1st Series) (Also see Adventure Comics #40, New York World's Fair & World's Finest #3)
National Periodical Publ.: Winter, 1974; No. 2, Apr-May, 1975 - No. 6, Dec-Jan, 1975-76
1-1st app. Bronze Age Sandman by Simon & Kirby (last S&K collaboration)
7 14 21 45 73 100
2-6: 6-Kirby/Wood-c/a 4 8 12 22 34 45
The Sandman By Joe Simon & Jack Kirby HC (2009, $39.99, d.j.) r/Sandman app. from World's Finest #6,7, Adventure Comics #72-102 and Sandman #1; Morrow intro. 40.00
NOTE: ***Kirby*** *a-1p, 4-6p; c-1-5, 6p.*

SANDMAN (2nd Series) (See Books of Magic, Vertigo Jam & Vertigo Preview)
DC Comics (Vertigo imprint #47 on): Jan, 1989 - No. 75, Mar, 1996 ($1.50-$2.50, mature)

Sandman #59 © DC

Sandman Presents: The Furies SC © DC

Sandman: The Dream Hunters #1 © DC

GD 2.0 VG 4.0 FN 6.0 VF 8.0 VF/NM 9.0 NM- 9.2

1 ($2.00, 52 pgs.)-1st app. Modern Age Sandman (Morpheus); Neil Gaiman scripts begin; Sam Kieth-a(p) in #1-5; Wesley Dodds (G.A. Sandman) cameo. 4 8 12 24 37 50
2-Cain & Abel app. (from HOM & HOS) 3 6 9 14 19 24
3-5: 3-John Constantine app. 2 4 6 10 14 18
6,7 2 4 6 8 11 14
8-Death-c/story (1st app.)-Regular ed. has Jeanette Kahn publishorial & American Cancer Society ad w/no indicia on inside front-c 3 6 9 16 22 28
8-Limited ed. (600+ copies?); has Karen Berger editorial and next issue teaser on inside covers (has indicia) 5 10 15 34 55 75
9-14: 10-Has explaination about #8 mixup; has bound-in Shocker movie poster.
14-(52 pgs.)-Bound-in Nightbreed fold-out 2 4 6 8 10 12
15-20: 16-Photo-c. 17,18-Kelley Jones-a. 19-Vess-a 1 2 3 5 6 8
18-Error version w/1st 3 panels on pg. 1 in blue ink 3 6 9 20 30 40
19-Error version w/pages 18 & 20 facing each other 3 6 9 18 27 35
21,23-27: Seasons of Mist storyline. 22-World Without End preview. 24-Kelley Jones/Russell-a 6.00
22-1st Daniel (Later becomes new Sandman) 2 4 6 8 10 12
28-30 5.00
31-49,51-74: 36-(52 pgs.). 41,44-48-Metallic ink on-c. 48-Cerebus appears as a doll. 54-Re-intro Prez; Death app.; Belushi, Nixon & Wildcat cameos. 57-Metallic ink on c. 65-w/bound-in trading card. 69-Death of Sandman. 70-73-Zulli-a. 74-Jon J. Muth-a. 4.00
50-($2.95, 52 pgs.)-Black-c w/metallic ink by McKean; Russell-a; McFarlane pin-up 5.00
50-($2.95)-Signed & limited (5,000) Treasury Edition with sketch of Neil Gaiman 1 2 3 5 6 8
50-Platinum 20.00
75-($3.95)-Vess-a. 5.00
Special 1 (1991, $3.50, 68 pgs.)-Glow-in-the-dark-c 5.00
Absolute Sandman Special Edition #1 (2006, 50¢) sampling from HC; recolored r/#1 2.50
Absolute Sandman Volume One (2006, $99.00, slipcased hardcover) recolored r/#1-20; Gaiman's original proposal; script and pencils from #19; character sketch gallery 100.00
Absolute Sandman Volume Two (2007, $99.00, slipcased hardcover) recolored r/#21-39; r/A Gallery of Dreams one-shot; bonus stories, scripts and pencil art 100.00
Absolute Sandman Volume Three (2008, $99.00, slipcased hardcover) recolored r/#40-56; & Special #1; bonus galleries, scripts and pencil art; Jill Thompson intro. 100.00
Absolute Sandman Volume Four (2008, $99.00, slipcased hardcover) recolored r/#57-75; scripts & sketch pages for #57 & 75; gallery of Dreaming memorabilia; Berger intro. 100.00
...: A Gallery of Dreams ($2.95)-Intro by N. Gaiman 3.00
...: Preludes & Nocturnes ($29.95, HC)-r/#1-8. 30.00
...: The Doll's House (1990, $29.95, HC)-r/#8-16. 30.00
...: Dream Country ($29.95, HC)-r/#17-20. 30.00
...: Season of Mists ($29.95, Leatherbound HC)-r/#21-28. 50.00
...: A Game of You ($29.95, HC)-r/32-37, ...: Fables and Reflections ($29.95, HC)-r/Vertigo Preview #1, Sandman Special #1, #29-31, #38-40 & #50. ...: Brief Lives ($29.95, HC)-r/#41-49. ...: World's End ($29.95, HC)-r/#51-56 30.00
...: The Kindly Ones (1996, $34.95, HC)-r/#57-69 & Vertigo Jam #1 35.00
...: The Wake ($29.95, HC)-r/#70-75. 30.00

NOTE: *A new set of hardcover printings with new covers was introduced in 1998-99. Multiple printings exist of softcover collections.* ***Bachalo*** *a-12;* ***Kelley Jones*** *a-17, 18, 22, 23, 26, 27.* ***Vess*** *a-19, 75.*

SANDMAN: ENDLESS NIGHTS
DC Comics (Vertigo): 2003 ($24.95, hardcover, with dust jacket)

HC-Neil Gaiman stories of Morpheus and the Endless illustrated by Fabry, Manara, Prado, Quitely, Russell, Sienkiewicz, and Storey; McKean-c 25.00
...Special (11/03, $2.95) Previews hardcover; Dream story w/Prado-a; McKean-c 3.00
SC (2004, $17.95) 18.00

SANDMAN MIDNIGHT THEATRE
DC Comics (Vertigo): Sept, 1995 ($6.95, squarebound, one-shot)

nn-Modern Age Sandman (Morpheus) meets G.A. Sandman; Gaiman & Wagner story; McKean-c; Kristiansen-a 7.00

SANDMAN MYSTERY THEATRE (Also see Sandman (2nd Series) #1)
DC Comics (Vertigo): Apr, 1993 - No. 70, Feb, 1999 ($1.95/$2.25/$2.50)

1-G.A. Sandman advs. begin; Matt Wagner scripts begin 4.50
2-49: 5-Neon ink logo. 29-32-Hourman app. 38-Ted Knight (G.A. Starman) app. 42-Jim Corrigan (Spectre) app. 45-48-Blackhawk app. 2.50
50-($3.50, 48 pgs.) w/bonus story of S.A. Sandman, Torres-a 3.50
51-70 2.50
Annual 1 (10/94, $3.95, 68 pgs.)-Alex Ross, Bolton & others-a 5.00
...: Dr. Death and the Night of the Butcher (2007, $19.99) r/#21-28 20.00
...: The Face and the Brute (2004, $19.95) r/#5-12 20.00
...: The Hourman and The Python (2008, $19.99) r/#29-36 20.00
...: The Mist and The Phantom of the Fair (2009, $19.99) r/#37-44 20.00
...: The Scorpion (2006, $12.99) r/#17-20 13.00

GD 2.0 VG 4.0 FN 6.0 VF 8.0 VF/NM 9.0 NM- 9.2

...: The Tarantula (1995, $14.95) r/#1-4 15.00
...: The Vamp (2005, $12.99) r/#13-16 13.00

SANDMAN MYSTERY THEATRE (2nd Series)
DC Comics (Vertigo): Feb, 2007 - No. 5, Jun, 2007 ($2.99, limited series)

1-5-Wesley Dodds and Dian in 1997; Rieber-s/Nguyen-a 3.00

SANDMAN PRESENTS...
DC Comics (Vertigo)

Taller Tales TPB (2003, $19.95) r/S.P: The Thessaliad #1-4; Merv Pumpkinhead, Agent...; The Dreaming #55; S.P. Everything You Always...; new McKean-c; intro by Willingham 20.00

SANDMAN PRESENTS: BAST
DC Comics (Vertigo): Mar, 2003 - No. 3, May, 2003 ($2.95, limited series)

1-3-Kiernan-s/Bennett-a/McKean-c 3.00

SANDMAN PRESENTS: DEADBOY DETECTIVES (See Sandman #21-28)
DC Comics (Vertigo): Aug, 2001 - No. 4, Nov, 2001 ($2.50, limited series)

1-4:Talbot-a/McKean-c/Brubaker-s 2.50
TPB (2008, $12.99) r/#1-4 13.00

SANDMAN PRESENTS: EVERYTHING YOU ALWAYS WANTED TO KNOW ABOUT DREAMS...BUT WERE AFRAID TO ASK
DC Comics (Vertigo): Jul, 2001 ($3.95, one-shot)

1-Short stories by Willingham; art by various; McKean-c 4.00

SANDMAN PRESENTS: LOVE STREET
DC Comics (Vertigo): Jul, 1999 - No. 3, Sept, 1999 ($2.95, limited series)

1-3: Teenage Hellblazer in 1968 London; Zulli-a 3.00

SANDMAN PRESENTS: LUCIFER
DC Comics (Vertigo): Mar, 1999 - No. 3, May, 1999 ($2.95, limited series)

1-3: Scott Hampton painted-c/a 3.00

SANDMAN PRESENTS: PETREFAX
DC Comics (Vertigo): Mar, 2000 - No. 4, Jun, 2000 ($2.95, limited series)

1-4-Carey-s/Leialoha-a 3.00

SANDMAN PRESENTS: THE CORINTHIAN
DC Comics (Vertigo): Dec, 2001 - No. 3, Feb, 2002 ($2.95, limited series)

1-3-Macan-s/Zezelj-a/McKean-c 3.00

SANDMAN PRESENTS, THE: THE FURIES
DC Comics (Vertigo): 2002 ($24.95, one-shot)

Hardcover-Mike Carey-s/John Bolton-painted art; Lyta Hall's reunion with Daniel 30.00
Softcover-(2003, $17.95) 18.00

SANDMAN PRESENTS, THE: THESSALY: WITCH FOR HIRE
DC Comics (Vertigo): Apr, 2004 - No. 4, July, 2004 ($2.95, limited series)

1-4-Willingham-s/McManus-a/McPherson-c 3.00
TPB-(2005, $12.99) r/#1-4 13.00

SANDMAN PRESENTS, THE: THE THESSALIAD
DC Comics (Vertigo): Mar, 2002 - No. 4, Jun, 2002 ($2.95, limited series)

1-4-Willingham-s/McManus-a/McKean-c 3.00

SANDMAN, THE: THE DREAM HUNTERS
DC Comics (Vertigo): Oct, 1999 ($29.95/$19.95, one-shot graphic novel)

Hardcover-Neil Gaiman-s/Yoshitaka Amano-painted art 30.00
Softcover-(2000, $19.95) new Amano-c 20.00

SANDMAN, THE: THE DREAM HUNTERS
DC Comics (Vertigo): Jan, 2009 - No. 4, Apr, 2009 ($2.99, limited series)

1-4-Adaptation of the Gaiman/Amano GN by P. Craig Russell-s/a; 2 covers on each 3.00
HC (2009, $24.99) afterwords by Gaiman, Russell, Berger; cover gallery & sketch art 25.00

SANDS OF THE SOUTH PACIFIC
Toby Press: Jan, 1953

1 20 40 60 115 182 255

SANTA AND HIS REINDEER (See March of Comics #166)

SANTA AND THE ANGEL (See Dell Junior Treasury #7)
Dell Publishing Co.: Dec, 1949 (Combined w/Santa at the Zoo) (Gollub-a condensed from FC#128)

Four Color 259 5 10 15 34 55 75

SANTA AT THE ZOO (See Santa And The Angel)

SANTA CLAUS AROUND THE WORLD (See March of Comics #241 in Promotional Comics section)

SANTA CLAUS CONQUERS THE MARTIANS (See Movie Classics)

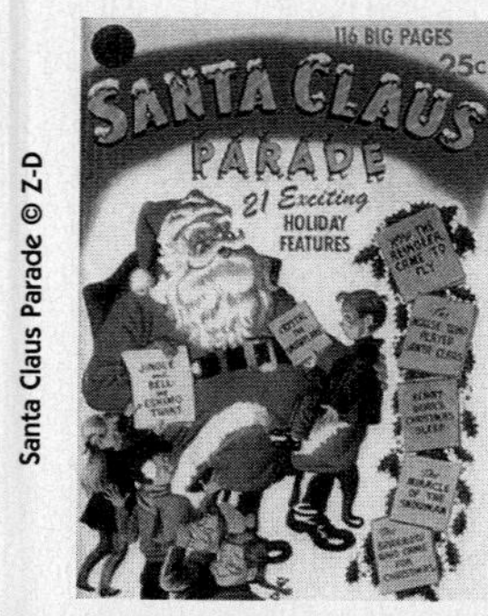

Santa Claus Parade © Z-D

Sarge Snorkel #3 © CC

Savage Dragon #139 © Erik Larsen

	GD 2.0	VG 4.0	FN 6.0	VF 8.0	VF/NM 9.0	NM- 9.2

SANTA CLAUS FUNNIES (Also see Dell Giants)
Dell Publishing Co.: Dec?, 1942 - No. 1274, Dec, 1961

	GD	VG	FN	VF	VF/NM	NM-
nn(#1)(1942)-Kelly-a	35	70	105	270	515	760
2(12/43)-Kelly-a	23	46	69	166	321	475
Four Color 61(1944)-Kelly-a	23	46	69	163	314	465
Four Color 91(1945)-Kelly-a	17	34	51	119	230	340
Four Color 128('46),175('47)-Kelly-a	14	28	42	100	188	275
Four Color 205,254-Kelly-a	13	26	39	90	165	240
Four Color 302,361,525,607,666,756,867	7	14	21	45	73	100
Four Color 958,1063,1154,1274	6	12	18	41	66	90

NOTE: *Most issues contain only one Kelly story.*

SANTA CLAUS PARADE
Ziff-Davis (Approved Comics)/St. John Publishing Co.: 1951; No. 2, Dec, 1952; No. 3, Jan, 1955 (25¢)

	GD	VG	FN	VF	VF/NM	NM-
nn(1951-Ziff-Davis)-116 pgs. (Xmas Special 1,2)	29	58	87	172	281	390
2(12/52-Ziff-Davis)-100 pgs.; Dave Berg-a	22	44	66	128	209	290
V1#3(1/55-St. John)-100 pgs.; reprints-c/#1	19	38	57	111	176	240

SANTA CLAUS' WORKSHOP (See March of Comics #50,168 in Promotional Comics section)
SANTA IS COMING (See March of Comics #197 in Promotional Comics section)
SANTA IS HERE (See March of Comics #49 in Promotional Comics section)
SANTA'S BUSY CORNER (See March of Comics #31 in Promotional Comics section)
SANTA'S CANDY KITCHEN (See March of Comics #14 in Promotional Comics section)
SANTA'S CHRISTMAS BOOK (See March of Comics #123 in Promotional Comics section)

SANTA'S CHRISTMAS COMICS
Standard Comics (Best Books): Dec, 1952 (100 pgs.)

	GD	VG	FN	VF	VF/NM	NM-
nn-Supermouse, Dizzy Duck, Happy Rabbit, etc.	18	36	54	105	165	225

SANTA'S CHRISTMAS LIST (See March of Comics #255 in Promotional Comics section)
SANTA'S HELPERS (See March of Comics #64, 106, 198 in Promotional Comics section)
SANTA'S LITTLE HELPERS (See March of Comics #270 in Promotional Comics section)
SANTA'S SHOW (See March of Comics #311 in Promotional Comics section)
SANTA'S SLEIGH (See March of Comics #298 in Promotional Comics section)
SANTA'S SURPRISE (See March of Comics #13 in Promotional Comics section)

SANTA'S TINKER TOTS
Charlton Comics: 1958

	GD	VG	FN	VF	VF/NM	NM-
1-Based on "The Tinker Tots Keep Christmas"	4	8	12	22	34	45

SANTA'S TOYLAND (See March of Comics #242 in Promotional Comics section)
SANTA'S TOYS (See March of Comics #12 in Promotional Comics section)
SANTA'S VISIT (See March of Comics #283 in Promotional Comics section)

SANTA THE BARBARIAN
Maximum Press: Dec, 1996 ($2.99, one-shot)

1-Fraga/Mhan-s/a 3.00

SANTIAGO (Movie)
Dell Publishing Co.: Sept, 1956 (Alan Ladd photo-c)

	GD	VG	FN	VF	VF/NM	NM-
Four Color 723-Kinstler-a	9	18	27	63	107	150

SARGE SNORKEL (Beetle Bailey)
Charlton Comics: Oct, 1973 - No. 17, Dec, 1976

	GD	VG	FN	VF	VF/NM	NM-
1	2	4	6	11	16	20
2-10	2	4	6	8	10	12
11-17	1	2	3	5	7	9

SARGE STEEL (Becomes Secret Agent #9 on; also see Judomaster)
Charlton Comics: Dec, 1964 - No. 8, Mar-Apr, 1966 (All 12¢ issues)

	GD	VG	FN	VF	VF/NM	NM-
1-Origin & 1st app.	4	8	12	24	37	50
2-5,7,8	3	6	9	16	23	30
6-2nd app. Judomaster	3	6	9	20	30	40

SATAN'S SIX
Topps Comics (Kirbyverse): Apr, 1993 - No. 4, July, 1993 ($2.95, lim. series)

1-4: 1-Polybagged w/Kirbychrome trading card; Kirby/McFarlane-c plus 8 pgs. Kirby-a(p); has coupon for Kirbychrome ed. of Secret City Saga #0. 2-4-Polybagged w/3 cards. 4-Teenagents preview 3.00

NOTE: ***Ditko** a-1. **Miller** a-1.*

SATAN'S SIX: HELLSPAWN
Topps Comics (Kirbyverse): June, 1994 - No. 3, July, 1994 ($2.50, limited series)

1-3: 1-(6/94)-Indicia incorrectly shows "Vol 1 #2". 2-(6/94) 2.50

SAURIANS: UNNATURAL SELECTION (See Sigil)
CrossGeneration Comics: Feb, 2002 - No. 2, Mar, 2002 ($2.95, limited series)

1,2-Waid-s/DiVito-a 3.00

SAVAGE
Image Comics (Shadowline): Oct, 2008 - No. 4, Jan, 2009 ($3.50, limited series)

1-4-Mayhew-c/a; Niles and Frank-s 3.50

SAVAGE COMBAT TALES
Atlas/Seaboard Publ.: Feb, 1975 - No. 3, July, 1975

	GD	VG	FN	VF	VF/NM	NM-
1,3: 1-Sgt. Stryker's Death Squad begins (origin); Goodwin-s	2	3	4	6	8	10
2-Toth-a; only app. War Hawk; Goodwin-s	2	4	6	8	10	12

NOTE: ***Buckler** c-3. **McWilliams** a-1-3; c-1. **Sparling** a-1, 3.*

SAVAGE DRAGON, THE (See Megaton #3 & 4)
Image Comics (Highbrow Entertainment): July, 1992 - No. 3, Dec, 1992 ($1.95, lim. series)

1-Erik Larsen-c/a/scripts & bound-in poster in all; 4 cover color variations w/4 different posters; 1st Highbrow Entertainment title 4.00
2-Intro SuperPatriot-c/story (10/92) 3.00
3-Contains coupon for Image Comics #0 3.00
3-With coupon missing 2.50
...Vs. Savage Megaton Man 1 (3/93, $1.95)-Larsen & Simpson-c/a. 3.00
TPB-('93, $9.95) r/#1-3 10.00

SAVAGE DRAGON, THE
Image Comics (Highbrow Entertainment): June, 1993 - Present ($1.95/$2.50/$2.99/$3.50)

1-Erik Larsen-c/a/scripts 4.00
2-30: 2-(Wondercon Exclusive): 2-($2.95, 52 pgs.)-Teenage Mutant Ninja Turtles-c/story; flip book features Vanguard #0 (See Megaton for 1st app.). 3-7: Erik Larsen-c/a/scripts. 3-Mighty Man back-up story w/Austin-a(i). 4-Flip book w/Ricochet. 5-Mighty Man flip-c & back-up plus poster. 6-Jae Lee poster. 7-Vanguard poster. 8-Deadly Duo poster by Larsen. 13A (10/94)-Jim Lee-c/a; 1st app. Max Cash (Condition Red). 13B (6/95)-Larsen story. 15-Dragon poster by Larsen. 22-TMNT-c/a; Bisley pin-up. 27-"Wondercon Exclusive" new-c. 28-Maxx-c/app. 29-Wildstar-c/app. 30-Spawn app. 3.00
25 ($3.95)-variant-c exists. 4.00
31-49,51-71: 31-God vs. The Devil; alternate version exists w/o expletives (has "God Is Good" inside Image logo) 33-Birth of Dragon/Rapture's baby. 34,35-Hellboy-c/app. 51-Origin of She-Dragon. 70-Ann Stevens killed 2.50
50-($5.95, 100 pgs.) Kaboom and Mighty Man app.; Matsuda-back-c; pin-ups by McFarlane, Simonson, Capullo and others 6.00
72-74: 72-Begin $2.95-c 3.00
75-($5.95) 6.00
76-99,101-106,108-114,116-124,126-127,129-131,133-136,138: 76-New direction starts. 83,84-Madman-c/app. 84-Atomics app. 97-Dragon returns home; Mighty Man app. 134-Bomb Queen app. 3.00
100-($8.95) Larsen-s/a; inked by various incl. Sienkiewicz, Timm, Austin, Simonson, Royer; plus pin-ups by Timm, Silvestri, Miller, Cho, Art Adams, Pacheco 9.00
107-($3.95) Firebreather, Invincible, Major Damage-c/app.; flip book w/Major Damage 4.00
115-($7.95, 100 pgs.) Wraparound-c; Freak Force app.; Larsen & Englert-a 8.00
125-($4.99, 64 pgs.) new story, The Fly, & various Mr. Glum reprints 5.00
128-Wesley and the villains from Wanted app.; J.G. Jones-c 4.00
132-($6.99, 80 pgs.) new story with Larsen-a; back-up story with Fosco-a 7.00
137-(8/08) Madman and Amazing Joy Buzzards-c/app. 3.00
137-(8/08) Variant cover with Barack Obama endorsed by Savage Dragon; yellow bkgrd 10.00
137-(8/08) 2nd printing of variant cover with Barack Obama and red background 3.00
137-3rd & 4th printings: 3rd-Blue background. 4th-Purple background 3.00
139-149,151-158: 139-Start $3.50-c; Invincible app. 140,141-Witchblade & Spawn app. 145-Obama-c/app. 148-Also a FCBD edition.155-Dragon War begins 3.50
150-($5.99, 100 pgs.) back up r/Daredevil's origin from Daredevil #18 (1943) 6.00
#0-(7/06, $1.95) reprints origin story from 2005 Image Comics Hardcover 2.50
...Archives Vol. 1 (12/06, $19.99) B&W rep. 1st mini-series #1-3 & #1-21 20.00
...Archives Vol. 2 (2007, $19.99) B&W rep. #22-50; roster pages of Dragon's fellow cops 20.00
...Companion (7/02, $2.95) guide to issues #1-100, character backgrounds 3.00
...Endgame (2/04, $15.95, TPB) r/#47-52 16.00
The Fallen (11/97, $12.95, TPB) r/#7-11, ...Possessed (9/98, $12.95, TPB) r/#12-16, ...Revenge (1998, $12.95, TPB) r/#17-21 13.00
...Gang War (4/00, $16.95, TPB) r/#22-26 17.00
.../Hellboy (10/02, $5.95) r/#34 & #35; Mignola-c 6.00
...Team-Ups (10/98, $19.95, TPB) r/team-ups 20.00
...: Terminated HC (2/03, $28.95) r/#34-40 & #1/2 29.00
...: This Savage World HC (2002, $24.95) r/#76-81; intro. by Larsen 25.00
...: This Savage World SC (2003, $15.95) r/#76-81; intro. by Larsen 16.00
...: Worlds at War SC (2004, $16.95) r/#41-46; intro. by Larsen; sketch pages 17.00

SAVAGE DRAGON ARCHIVES (Also see Dragon Archives, The)

Savage She-Hulk #1 © MAR

Savage Tales #4 © MAR

Scalped #16 © Aaron & Milosevic

GD 2.0 | VG 4.0 | FN 6.0 | VF 8.0 | VF/NM 9.0 | NM- 9.2

SAVAGE DRAGONBERT: FULL FRONTAL NERDITY
Image Comics: Oct, 2002 ($5.95, B&W, one-shot)

1-Reprints of the Savage Dragon/Dilbert spoof strips 6.00

SAVAGE DRAGON/DESTROYER DUCK, THE
Image Comics/ Highbrow Entertainment: Nov, 1996 ($3.95, one-shot)

1 4.00

SAVAGE DRAGON: GOD WAR
Image Comics: July, 2004 - No. 4, Oct, 2005 ($2.95, limited series)

1-4-Kirkman-s/Englert-a 3.00

SAVAGE DRAGON/MARSHALL LAW
Image Comics: July, 1997 - No. 2, Aug, 1997 ($2.95, B&W, limited series)

1,2-Pat Mills-s, Kevin O'Neill-a 3.00

SAVAGE DRAGON: SEX & VIOLENCE
Image Comics: Aug, 1997 - No. 2, Sept, 1997 ($2.50, limited series)

1,2-T&M Bierbaum-s, Mays, Lupka, Adam Hughes-a 3.00

SAVAGE DRAGON/TEENAGE MUTANT NINJA TURTLES CROSSOVER
Mirage Studios: Sept, 1993 ($2.75, one-shot)

1-Erik Larsen-c(i) only 3.00

SAVAGE DRAGON: THE RED HORIZON
Image Comics/ Highbrow Entertainment: Feb, 1997 - No. 3 ($2.50, lim. series)

1-3 3.00

SAVAGE FISTS OF KUNG FU
Marvel Comics Group: 1975 (Marvel Treasury)

1-Iron Fist, Shang Chi, Sons of Tiger; Adams, Starlin-a 3 6 9 18 27 35

SAVAGE HULK, THE (Also see Incredible Hulk)
Marvel Comics: Jan, 1996 ($6.95, one-shot)

1-Bisley-c; David, Lobdell, Wagner, Loeb, Gibbons, Messner-Loebs scripts; McKone, Kieth, Ramos & Sale-a. 7.00

SAVAGE RAIDS OF GERONIMO (See Geronimo #4)

SAVAGE RANGE (See Luke Short, Four Color 807)

SAVAGE RED SONJA: QUEEN OF THE FROZEN WASTES
Dynamite Entertainment: 2006 - No. 4, 2006 ($3.50, limited series)

1-4: 1-Three covers by Cho, Texeira & Homs; Cho & Murray-s/Homs-a 3.50
TPB (2007, $14.99) r/series; cover gallery and sketch pages 15.00

SAVAGE RETURN OF DRACULA
Marvel Comics: 1992 ($2.00, 52 pgs.)

1-r/Tomb of Dracula #1,2 by Gene Colan 3.00

SAVAGE SHE-HULK, THE (See The Avengers, Marvel Graphic Novel #18 & The Sensational She-Hulk)
Marvel Comics Group: Feb, 1980 - No. 25, Feb, 1982

1-Origin & 1st app. She-Hulk 2 4 6 8 10 12
2-5,25: 25-(52 pgs.) 6.00
6-24: 6-She-Hulk vs. Iron Man. 8-Vs. Man-Thing 5.00
NOTE: *Austin a-25i; c-23i-25i.* ***J. Buscema*** *a-1p; c-1, 2p.* ***Golden*** *c-8-11.*

SAVAGE SHE-HULK (Titled All New Savage She Hulk for #3,4)
Marvel Comics: Jun, 2009 - No. 4, Sept, 2009 ($3.99, limited series)

1-4-Lyra, daughter of the Hulk; She-Hulk & Dark Avengers app. 2-Campbell-c 4.00

SAVAGE SWORD OF CONAN (The... #41 on; ...The Barbarian #175 on)
Marvel Comics Group: Aug, 1974 - No. 235, July, 1995 ($1.00/$1.25/$2.25, B&W magazine, mature)

1-Smith-r; J. Buscema/N. Adams/Krenkel-a; origin Blackmark by Gil Kane (part 1, ends #3); Blackmark's 1st app. in magazine form-r/from paperback) & Red Sonja (3rd app.) 10 20 30 71 126 180
2-Neal Adams-c; Chaykin/N. Adams-a 6 12 18 37 59 80
3-Severin/B. Smith-a; N. Adams-a 4 8 12 28 44 60
4-Neal Adams/Kane-a(r) 4 8 12 22 34 45
5-10: 5-Jeff Jones frontispiece (r) 3 6 9 18 27 35
11-20 2 4 6 13 18 22
21-30 2 4 6 10 14 18
31-50: 34-3 pg. preview of Conan newspaper strip. 35-Cover similar to Savage Tales #1. 45-Red Sonja returns; begin $1.25-c 2 4 6 8 11 14
51-99: 63-Toth frontispiece. 65-Kane-a w/Chaykin/Miller/Simonson/Sherman finishes. 70-Article on movie. 83-Red Sonja-r by Neal Adams from #1 1 2 3 5 7 9
100 1 3 4 6 8 10
101-176: 163-Begin $2.25-c. 169-King Kull story. 171-Soloman Kane by Williamson (i). 172-Red Sonja story 6.00
177-199: 179,187,192-Red Sonja app. 190-193-4 part King Kull story. 196-King Kull story 5.00
200-220: 200-New Buscema-a; Robert E. Howard app. with Conan in story. 202-King Kull story. 204-60th anniversary (1932-92). 211-Rafael Kayanan's 1st Conan-a. 214-Sequel to Red Nails by Howard 6.00
221-230 1 2 3 5 7 9
231-234 2 4 6 9 12 15
235-Last issue 3 6 9 16 22 28
Special 1(1975, B&W)-B. Smith-r/Conan #10,13 3 6 9 17 25 32
Volume 1 TPB (Dark Horse Books, 12/07, $17.95, B&W) r/#1-10 and selected stories from Savage Tales #1-5 with covers 18.00
Volume 2 TPB (Dark Horse Books, 3/08, $17.95, B&W) r/#11-24 18.00
Volume 3 TPB (Dark Horse Books, 5/08, $19.95, B&W) r/#25-36 and selected pin-ups 20.00
Volume 4 TPB (Dark Horse Books, 9/08, $19.95, B&W) r/#37-48 and selected pin-ups 20.00
Volume 5 TPB (Dark Horse Books, 2/09, $19.95, B&W) r/#49-60 and selected pin-ups 20.00
NOTE: ***N. Adams*** *a-14p, 60, 83p(r).* ***Alcala*** *a-2 ,4, 7, 12, 15-20, 23, 24, 28, 59, 67, 69, 75, 76i, 80i, 82i, 83i, 89, 180i, 184i, 187i, 189i, 216p.* ***Austin*** *a-78i.* ***Boris*** *painted c-1, 4, 5, 7, 9, 10, 12, 15.* ***Brunner*** *a-30; c-8, 30.* ***Buscema*** *a-1-5, 7, 10-12, 15-24, 26-28, 31, 32, 36-43, 45, 47-58p, 60-67p, 70, 71-74p, 76-81p, 87-96p, 98, 99-101p, 190-204p; painted c-40.* ***Chaykin*** *c-31.* ***Chiodo*** *painted c-71, 76, 79, 81, 84, 85, 178.* ***Conrad*** *c-215, 217.* ***Corben*** *a-4, 16, 29.* ***Finlay*** *a-16.* ***Golden*** *a-98, 101; c-98, 101, 105, 106, 117, 124, 150.* ***Kaluta*** *a-11, 18; c-3, 91, 93.* ***Gil Kane*** *a-2, 3, 8, 13r, 29, 47, 64, 65, 67, 85p, 86p.* ***Rafael Kayanan*** *a-211-213, 215, 217.* ***Krenkel*** *a-9, 11, 14, 16, 24.* ***Morrow*** *a-7.* ***Nebres*** *a-93i, 101i, 107, 114.* ***Newton*** *a-6.* ***Nino*** *c/a-6.* ***Redondo*** *painted c-48-50, 52, 56, 57, 85i, 90, 96i.* ***Marie & John Severin*** *a-Special 1.* ***Simonson*** *a-7, 8, 12, 15-17.* ***Barry Smith*** *a-7, 16, 24, 82r, Special 1r.* ***Starlin*** *c-26.* ***Toth*** *a-64.* ***Williamson*** *a(i)-162, 171, 186. No. 8 , 10 & 16 contain a Robert E. Howard Conan adaptation.*

SAVAGE TALES (...Featuring Conan #4 on)(Magazine)
Marvel Comics Group: May, 1971; No. 2, 10/73; No. 3, 2/74 - No. 12, Summer, 1975 (B&W)

1-Origin/1st app. The Man-Thing by Morrow; Conan the Barbarian by Barry Smith (1st Conan x-over outside his own title); Femizons by Romita-r/in #3; Ka-Zar story by Buscema 17 34 51 119 230 340
2-B. Smith, Brunner, Morrow, Williamson-a; Wrightson King Kull reprint/ Creatures on the Loose #10 6 12 18 41 66 90
3-B. Smith, Brunner, Steranko, Williamson-a 5 10 15 32 51 70
4,5-N. Adams-c; last Conan (Smith-r/#4) plus Kane/N. Adams-a. 5-Brak the Barbarian begins, ends #8 4 8 12 28 44 60
6-Ka-Zar begins; Williamson-r; N. Adams-c 3 6 9 20 30 40
7-N. Adams-i 3 6 9 16 22 28
8,9,11: 8-Shanna, the She-Devil app. thru #10; Williamson-r 3 6 9 14 20 26
10-Neal Adams-a(i), Williamson-r 3 6 9 16 22 28
...Featuring Ka-Zar Annual 1 (Summer, '75, B&W)(#12 on inside)-Ka-Zar origin by Gil Kane; B. Smith-r/Astonishing Tales 3 6 9 17 25 32
NOTE: ***Boris*** *c-7, 10.* ***Buscema*** *a-5r, 6p, 8p; c-2.* ***Colan*** *a-1p.* ***Fabian*** *c-8.* ***Golden*** *a-1, 4; c-1.* ***Heath*** *a-10p, 11p.* ***Kaluta*** *c-9.* ***Maneely*** *r-2, 4(The Crusader in both).* ***Morrow*** *a-1, 2, Annual 1.* ***Reese*** *a-2.* ***Severin*** *a-1-7.* ***Starlin*** *a-5. Robert E. Howard adaptations-1-4.*

SAVAGE TALES
Marvel Comics Group: Nov, 1985 - No. 8, Dec, 1986 ($1.50, B&W, magazine, mature)

1-1st app. The Nam; Golden, Morrow-a 6.00
2-8: 2,7-Morrow-a. 4-2nd Nam story; Golden-a 4.00

SAVAGE TALES
Dynamite Entertainment: 2007 - Present ($4.99)

1-10: 1-Anthology; Red Sonja app.; three covers 5.00

SAVANT GARDE (Also see WildC.A.T.S...)
Image Comics/WildStorm Productions: Mar, 1997 - No. 7, Sept, 1997 ($2.50)

1-7 2.50

SAVED BY THE BELL (TV)
Harvey Comics: Mar, 1992 - No. 5, May, 1993 ($1.25, limited series)

1-5, Holiday Special (3/92), Special 1 (9/92, $1.50)-photo-c, Summer Break 1 (10/92) 2.50

SAW: REBIRTH (Based on 2004 movie Saw)
IDW Publ.: Oct, 2005 ($3.99, one-shot)

1-Guedes-a 4.00

SCALPED
DC Comics (Vertigo): Mar, 2007 - Present ($2.99, limited series)

1-34: 1-Aaron-s/Guera-a/Jock-c. 12-Leon-a 3.00
...: Casino Blood TPB (2008, $14.99) r/#6-11; intro. by Garth Ennis 15.00
...: Dead Mothers TPB (2008, $17.99) r/#12-18 18.00
...: High Lonesome TPB (2009, $14.99) r/#25-29; intro. by Jason Starr 15.00
...: Indian Country TPB (2007, $9.99) r/#1-5; intro. by Brian K. Vaughan 10.00
...: The Gravel in Your Guts (2009, $14.99) r/#19-24; intro. by Ed Brubaker 15.00

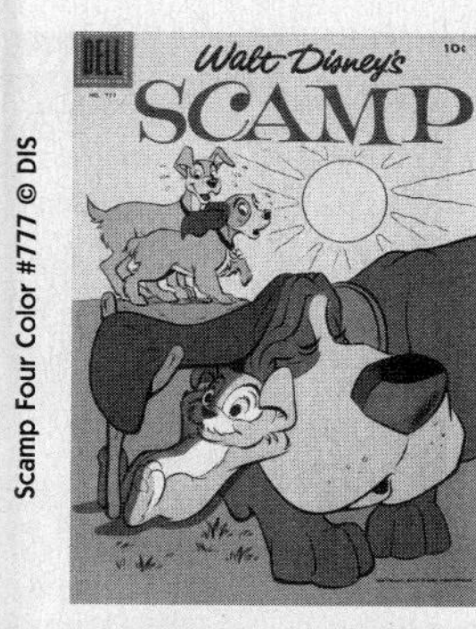

Scamp Four Color #777 © DIS

Scary Tales #25 © CC

Science Comics #2 © FOX

SCAMP (Walt Disney)(See Walt Disney's Comics & Stories #204)
Dell Publ. Co./Gold Key: No. 703, 5/56 - No. 1204, 8-10/61; 11/67 - No. 45, 1/79

	GD 2.0	VG 4.0	FN 6.0	VF 8.0	VF/NM 9.0	NM- 9.2
Four Color 703(#1)	8	16	24	58	97	135
Four Color 777,806('57),833	6	12	18	43	69	95
5(3-5/58)-10(6-8/59)	5	10	15	34	55	75
11-16(12-2/60-61), Four Color 1204(1961)	4	8	12	28	44	60
1(12/67-Gold Key)-Reprints begin	4	8	12	26	41	55
2(3/69)-10	2	4	6	13	18	22
11-20	2	4	6	8	11	14
21-45	1	2	3	4	5	7

NOTE: *New stories-#20(in part), 22-25, 27, 29-31, 34, 36-40, 42-45. New covers-#11, 12, 14, 15, 17-25, 27, 29-31, 34, 36-38.*

SCARAB
DC Comics (Vertigo): Nov, 1993 - No. 8, June, 1994 ($1.95, limited series)

1-8-Glenn Fabry painted-c: 1-Silver ink-c. 2-Phantom Stranger app. 2.50

SCARECROW OF ROMNEY MARSH, THE (See W. Disney Showcase #53)
Gold Key: April, 1964 - No. 3, Oct, 1965 (Disney TV Show)

	GD 2.0	VG 4.0	FN 6.0	VF 8.0	VF/NM 9.0	NM- 9.2
10112-404 (#1)	5	10	15	30	48	65
2,3	3	6	9	21	32	42

SCARECROW (VILLAINS) (See Batman)
DC Comics: Feb, 1998 ($1.95, one-shot)

1-Fegredo-a/Milligan-s/Pearson-c 2.50

SCARE TACTICS
DC Comics: Dec, 1996 - No. 12, Mar, 1998 ($2.25)

1-12: 1-1st app. 2.50

SCAR FACE (See The Crusaders)

SCARFACE: SCARRED FOR LIFE (Based on the 1983 movie)
IDW Publishing: Dec, 2006 - No. 5, Apr, 2007 ($3.99, limited series)

1-5-Tony Montana survives his shooting; Layman-s/Crosland-a 4.00
Scarface: Devil in Disguise (7/07 - No. 4, 10/07, $3.99) Alberto Dose-a 4.00

SCARLET O'NEIL (See Harvey Comics Hits #59 & Invisible...)

SCARLET SPIDER
Marvel Comics: Nov, 1995 - No. 2, Jan, 1996 ($1.95, limited series)

1,2: Replaces Spider-Man 2.50

SCARLET SPIDER UNLIMITED
Marvel Comics: Nov, 1995 ($3.95, one-shot)

1-Replaces Spider-Man Unlimited 4.00

SCARLET WITCH (See Avengers #16, Vision &... & X-Men #4)
Marvel Comics: Jan, 1994 - No. 4, Apr, 1994 ($1.75, limited series)

1-4 2.50

SCARY GODMOTHER (Hardcover story books)
Sirius: 1997 - Present ($19.95, HC with dust jackets, one-shots)

Volume 1 (9/97) Jill Thompson-s/a; first app. of Scary Godmother 20.00
Vol. 2 - The Revenge of Jimmy (9/98, $19.95) 20.00
Vol. 3 - The Mystery Date (10/99, $19.95) 20.00
Vol. 4 - The Boo Flu (9/02, $19.95) 20.00

SCARY GODMOTHER
Sirius: 2001 - No. 6, 2002 ($2.95, B&W, limited series)

1-6-Jill Thompson-s/a 3.00
...: Activity Book (12/00, $2.95, B&W) Jill Thompson-s/a 3.00
...: Bloody Valentine Special (2/98, $3.95, B&W) Jill Thompson-s/a; pin-ups by Ross, Mignola, Russell 4.00
...: Ghoul's Out For Summer (2002,$14.95, B&W) r/#1-6 15.00
...: Holiday Spooktakular (11/98, $2.95, B&W) Jill Thompson-s/a; pin-ups by Brereton, LaBan, Dorkin, Fingerman 3.00

SCARY GODMOTHER: WILD ABOUT HARRY
Sirius: 2000 - No. 3 ($2.95, B&W, limited series)

1-3-Jill Thompson-s/a 3.00
TPB (2001, $9.95) r/series 10.00

SCARY TALES
Charlton Comics: 8/75 - #9, 1/77; #10, 9/77 - #20, 6/79; #21, 8/80 - #46, 10/84

	GD 2.0	VG 4.0	FN 6.0	VF 8.0	VF/NM 9.0	NM- 9.2
1-Origin/1st app. Countess Von Bludd, not in #2	3	6	9	18	27	35
2,4,6,9,10: 4,9-Sutton-c/a. 4-Man-Thing copy	2	4	6	8	11	14
3-Sutton painted-c; Ditko-a	2	4	6	10	14	18
5,11-Ditko-c/a.	2	4	6	13	18	22
7,8-Ditko-a	2	4	6	9	13	16
12,15,16,19,21,39-Ditko-a	2	4	6	8	11	14
13,17,20	2	3	4	6	8	10
14,18,30,32-Ditko-c/a	2	4	6	10	14	18
22-29,33-37,39,40: 37,38,40-New-a. 39-All Ditko reprints and cover	1	2	3	5	7	9
31,38: 31-Newton-c/a. 38-Mr. Jigsaw app.	1	2	3	5	7	9
41-45-New-a. 41-Ditko-a(3). 42-45-(Low print)	2	3	4	6	8	10
46-Reprints (Low print)	2	4	6	9	13	16
1(Modern Comics reprint, 1977)						4.00

NOTE: ***Adkins** a-31i; c-31i. **Ditko** a-3, 5, 7, 8(2), 11, 12, 14-16r, 18(3)r, 19r, 21r, 30r, 32, 39r, 41(3); c-5, 11, 14, 18, 30, 32. **Newton** a-31p; c-31p. **Powell** a-18r. **Staton** a-1(2 pgs.), 4, 20r; c-1, 20. **Sutton** a-4, 9; c-4, 9. **Zeck** a-9.*

SCATTERBRAIN
Dark Horse Comics: Jun, 1998 - No. 4, Sept, 1998 ($2.95, limited series)

1-4-Humor anthology by Aragonés, Dorkin, Stevens and others 3.00

SCAVENGERS
Quality Comics: Feb, 1988 - No. 14, 1989 ($1.25/$1.50)

1-14: 9-13-Guice-c 2.50

SCAVENGERS
Triumphant Comics: 1993(nd, July) - No. 11, May, 1994 ($2.50, serially numbered)

1-9,0,10,11: 5,6-Triumphant Unleashed x-over. 9-(3/94). 0-Retail ed. (3/94, $2.50, 36 pgs.). 0-Giveaway edition (3/94, 20 pgs.). 0-Coupon redemption edition. 10-(4/94) 2.50

SCENE OF THE CRIME (Also see Vertigo: Winter's Edge #2)
DC Comics (Vertigo): May, 1999 - No. 4, Aug, 1999 ($2.50, limited series)

1-4-Brubaker-s/Lark-a 2.50
...: A Little Piece of Goodnight TPB ('00, $12.95) r/#1-4; Winter's Edge #2 13.00

SCHOOL DAY ROMANCES (...of Teen-Agers #4; Popular Teen-Agers #5 on)
Star Publications: Nov-Dec, 1949 - No. 4, May-June, 1950 (Teenage)

	GD 2.0	VG 4.0	FN 6.0	VF 8.0	VF/NM 9.0	NM- 9.2
1-Toni Gayle (later Toni Gay), Ginger Snapp, Midge Martin & Eve Adams begin	28	56	84	162	261	360
2,3: 3-Jane Powell photo on-c & true life story	20	40	60	117	186	255
4-Ronald Reagan photo on-c; L.B. Cole-c	31	62	93	181	291	400

NOTE: *All have **L. B. Cole** covers.*

SCHWINN BICYCLE BOOK (...Bike Thrills, 1959)
Schwinn Bicycle Co.: 1949; 1952; 1959 (10¢)

	GD 2.0	VG 4.0	FN 6.0	VF 8.0	VF/NM 9.0	NM- 9.2
1949	6	12	18	28	34	40
1952-Believe It or Not facts; comic format; 36 pgs.	5	10	14	20	24	28
1959	3	6	8	11	13	15

SCIENCE COMICS (1st Series)
Fox Features Syndicate: Feb, 1940 - No. 8, Sept, 1940

	GD 2.0	VG 4.0	FN 6.0	VF 8.0	VF/NM 9.0	NM- 9.2
1-Origin Dynamo (1st app., called Electro in #1), The Eagle (1st app.), & Navy Jones; Marga, The Panther Woman (1st app.), Cosmic Carson & Perisphere Payne, Dr. Doom begin; bondage/hypo-c; Electro-c	423	846	1269	3088	5444	7800
2-Classic Lou Fine Dynamo-c	232	464	696	1485	2543	3600
3-Classic Lou Fine Dynamo-c	187	374	561	1197	2049	2900
4-Kirby-a; Cosmic Carson-c by Joe Simon	168	336	504	1075	1838	2600
5-8: 5,8-Eagle-c. 6,7-Dynamo-c	100	200	300	635	1093	1550

NOTE: *Cosmic Carson by **Tuska**-#1-3; by **Kirby**-#4. **Lou Fine** c-1-3 only.*

SCIENCE COMICS (2nd Series)
Humor Publications (Ace Magazines?): Jan, 1946 - No. 5, 1946

	GD 2.0	VG 4.0	FN 6.0	VF 8.0	VF/NM 9.0	NM- 9.2
1-Palais-c/a in #1-3; A-Bomb-c	19	38	57	111	176	240
2	11	22	33	64	90	115
3-Feldstein-a (6 pgs.)	16	32	48	92	144	195
4,5: 4-Palais-c	9	18	27	52	69	85

SCIENCE COMICS
Ziff-Davis Publ. Co.: May, 1947 (8 pgs. in color)

	GD 2.0	VG 4.0	FN 6.0	VF 8.0	VF/NM 9.0	NM- 9.2
nn-Could be ordered by mail for 10¢; like the nn Amazing Adventures (1950) & Boy Cowboy (1950); used to test the market	39	78	117	240	395	550

SCIENCE COMICS (True Science Illustrated)
Export Publication Ent., Toronto, Canada: Mar, 1951 (Distr. in U.S. by Kable News Co.)

	GD 2.0	VG 4.0	FN 6.0	VF 8.0	VF/NM 9.0	NM- 9.2
1-Science Adventure stories plus some true science features; man on moon story	13	26	39	72	101	130

SCIENCE FICTION SPACE ADVENTURES (See Space Adventures)

SCION (Also see CrossGen Chronicles)
CrossGeneration Comics: July, 2000 - No. 43, Apr, 2004 ($2.95)

1-43: 1-Marz-s/Cheung-a 3.00
...: Conflict of Conscience Vol. 1 TPB (5/01, $19.95) r/#1-7; Adam Hughes-c 20.00

Scooby-Doo #119 © H-B

Scoop Comics #8 © CHES

Scream #1 © Skywald

	GD 2.0	VG 4.0	FN 6.0	VF 8.0	VF/NM 9.0	NM- 9.2
...: Blood For Blood Vol. 2 TPB (2002, $19.95) r/#8-14 & CrossGen Chronicles #2						20.00
...: Divided Loyalties Vol. 3 TPB (2002, $15.95) r/#15-21						16.00
...: Sanctuary Vol. 4 TPB (2003, $15.95) r/#22-27						16.00
Vol. 5: The Far Kingdom (2003, $15.95) r/#28-33						16.00
Vol. 6: The Royal Wedding (2004, $15.95) r/#34-39						16.00
Traveler Vol. 1-3 ($9.95) Digest-sized reprints of TPBs						10.00

SCI-SPY
DC Comics (Vertigo): Apr, 2002 - No. 6, Sept, 2002 ($2.50, limited series)

	GD	VG	FN	VF	VF/NM	NM-
1-6-Moench-s/Gulacy-c/a						2.50

SCI-TECH
DC Comics (WildStorm): Sept, 1999 - No. 4, Dec, 1999 ($2.50, limited series)

	GD	VG	FN	VF	VF/NM	NM-
1-4-Benes-a/Choi & Peterson-s						2.50

SCOOBY DOO (TV)(...Where are you? #1-16,26; ...Mystery Comics #17-25, 27 on)
(See March Of Comics #356, 368, 382, 391 in the Promotional Comics section)
Gold Key: Mar, 1970 - No. 30, Feb, 1975 (Hanna-Barbera)

	GD	VG	FN	VF	VF/NM	NM-
1	13	26	39	95	178	260
2-5	8	16	24	52	86	120
6-10	7	14	21	45	73	100
11-20: 11-Tufts-a	6	12	18	37	59	80
21-30	4	8	12	28	44	60

SCOOBY DOO (TV)
Charlton Comics: Apr, 1975 - No. 11, Dec, 1976 (Hanna-Barbera)

	GD	VG	FN	VF	VF/NM	NM-
1	6	12	18	41	66	90
2-5	4	8	12	26	41	55
6-11	4	8	12	22	34	45
nn-(1976, digest, 68 pgs., B&W)	4	8	12	24	37	50

SCOOBY-DOO (TV)(Newsstand sales only) (See Dynamutt & Laff-A-Lympics)
Marvel Comics Group: Oct, 1977 - No. 9, Feb, 1979 (Hanna-Barbera)

	GD	VG	FN	VF	VF/NM	NM-
1,6-9: 1-Dyno-Mutt begins	3	6	9	18	27	35
1-(35¢-c variant, limited distribution)(10/77)	8	16	24	54	90	125
2-5	3	6	9	16	22	28

SCOOBY-DOO (TV)
Harvey Comics: Sept, 1992 - No. 3, May, 1993 ($1.25)

	GD	VG	FN	VF	VF/NM	NM-
V2#1,2	1	2	3	4	5	7
Big Book 1,2 (11/92, 4/93, $1.95, 52 pgs.)	1	2	3	5	7	9
Giant Size 1,2 (10/92, 3/93, $2.25, 68 pgs.)	1	2	3	5	7	9

SCOOBY DOO (TV)
Archie Comics: Oct, 1995 -No. 21, June, 1997 ($1.50)

	GD	VG	FN	VF	VF/NM	NM-
1	1	2	3	5	6	8
2-21: 12-Cover by Scooby Doo creative designer Iwao Takamoto						5.00

SCOOBY DOO (TV)
DC Comics: Aug, 1997 - Present ($1.75/$1.95/$1.99/$2.25/$2.50)

	GD	VG	FN	VF	VF/NM	NM-
1						6.00
2-10: 5-Begin-$1.95-c						4.00
11-45: 14-Begin $1.99-c						2.50
46-89,91-152: 63-Begin $2.25-c. 75-With 2 Garbage Pail Kids stickers. 100-Wray-c						2.50
90-($2.95) Bonus stories						3.00
...Spooky Spectacular 1 (10/99, $3.95) Comic Convention story						4.00
...Spooky Spectacular 2000 (10/00, $3.95)						4.00
...Spooky Summer Special 2001 (8/01, $3.95) Staton-a						4.00
...Super Scarefest (8/02, $3.95) r/#20,25,30-32						4.00
Vol. 1: You Meddling Kids (2003, $6.95, digest-size) r/#1-5						7.00
Vol. 2: Ruh-Roh! (2003, $6.95, digest-size) r/#6-10						7.00
Vol. 3: All Wrapped Up! (2005, $6.95, digest-size) r/#11-15						7.00
Vol. 4: The Big Squeeze! (2005, $6.95, digest-size) r/#16-20						7.00
Vol. 5: Surf's Up! (2006, $6.99, digest-size) r/#21-25						7.00
Vol. 5: Space Fright! (2006, $6.99, digest-size) r/#26-30						7.00

SCOOP COMICS (Becomes Yankee Comics #4-7, a digest sized cartoon book; then after #8 it becomes Snap #9)
Harry 'A' Chesler (Holyoke): November, 1941 - No. 3, Mar, 1943; No. 8, 1944

	GD	VG	FN	VF	VF/NM	NM-
1-Intro. Rocketman & Rocketgirl & begins; origin The Master Key & begins; Dan Hastings begins; Charles Sultan-c/a	155	310	465	992	1696	2400
2-Rocket Boy begins; injury to eye story (reprinted in Spotlight #3); classic-c	168	336	504	1075	1838	2600
3-Injury to eye story-r from #2; Rocket Boy	74	128	222	470	810	1150
8-Formerly Yankee Comics; becomes Snap	45	90	135	284	480	675

SCOOTER (See Swing With...)

SCOOTER COMICS
Rucker Publ. Ltd. (Canadian): Apr, 1946

	GD	VG	FN	VF	VF/NM	NM-
1-Teen-age/funny animal	11	22	33	60	83	105

SCOOTER GIRL
Oni Press: May, 2003 - No. 6, Feb, 2004 ($2.99, B&W, limited series)

	GD	VG	FN	VF	VF/NM	NM-
1-6-Chynna Clugston-Major-s/a						3.00
TPB (5/04, $14.95, digest size) r/series; sketch pages						15.00

SCORPION
Atlas/Seaboard Publ.: Feb, 1975 - No. 3, July, 1975

	GD	VG	FN	VF	VF/NM	NM-
1-Intro.; bondage-c by Chaykin	2	4	6	10	14	18
2-Chaykin-a w/Wrightson, Kaluta, Simonson assists(p)	2	4	6	10	14	18
3-Jim Craig-c/a	2	4	6	8	11	14

NOTE: ***Chaykin** a-1, 2; c-1. **Colon** c-2. **Craig** c/a-3.*

SCORPION KING, THE (Movie)
Dark Horse Comics: March, 2002 - No. 2, Apr, 2002 ($2.99, limited series)

	GD	VG	FN	VF	VF/NM	NM-
1,2-Photo-c of the Rock; Richards-a						3.00

SCORPIO ROSE
Eclipse Comics: Jan, 1983 - No. 2, Oct, 1983 ($1.25, Baxter paper)

	GD	VG	FN	VF	VF/NM	NM-
1,2: Dr. Orient back-up story begins. 2-origin.						4.00

SCOTLAND YARD (Inspector Farnsworth of)(Texas Rangers in Action #5 on?)
Charlton Comics Group: June, 1955 - No. 4, Mar, 1956

	GD	VG	FN	VF	VF/NM	NM-
1-Tothish-a	14	28	42	80	115	150
2-4: 2-Tothish-a	10	20	30	54	72	90

SCOURGE OF THE GODS
Marvel Comics (Soleil): 2009 - No. 3, 2009 ($5.99, limited series)

	GD	VG	FN	VF	VF/NM	NM-
1-3-Mangin-s/Gajic-a; English version of French comic						6.00
...: The Fall 1-3 (2009 - No. 3, 2009)						6.00

SCOUT (See Eclipse Graphic Album #16, New America & Swords of Texas)
(Becomes Scout: War Shaman)
Eclipse Comics: Dec, 1985 - No. 24, Oct, 1987($1.75/$1.25, Baxter paper)

	GD	VG	FN	VF	VF/NM	NM-
1-15,17,18,20-24: 19-Airboy preview. 10-Bissette-a. 11-Monday, the Eliminator begins. 15-Swords of Texas						2.50
16,19: 16-Scout 3-D Special ($2.50), 16-Scout 2-D Limited Edition, 19-contains flexidisk ($2.50)						3.00
...Handbook 1 (8/87, $1.75, B&W)						2.50
Mount Fire (1989, $14.95, TPB) r/#8-14						15.00

SCOUT: WAR SHAMAN (Formerly Scout)
Eclipse Comics: Mar, 1988 - No. 16, Dec, 1989 ($1.95)

	GD	VG	FN	VF	VF/NM	NM-
1-16						2.50

SCRATCH
DC Comics: Aug, 2004 - No. 5, Dec, 2004 ($2.50, limited series)

	GD	VG	FN	VF	VF/NM	NM-
1-5-Sam Kieth-s/a/c; Batman app.						2.50

SCREAM (...Comics) (Andy Comics #20 on)
Humor Publications/Current Books(Ace Magazines): Autumn, 1944 - No. 19, Apr, 1948

	GD	VG	FN	VF	VF/NM	NM-
1-Teenage humor	16	32	48	92	144	195
2	10	20	30	56	76	95
3-16: 11-Racist humor (Indians). 16-Intro. Lily-Belle	9	18	27	47	61	75
17,19	8	16	24	42	54	65
18-Hypo needle story	9	18	27	47	61	75

SCREAM (Magazine)
Skywald Publ. Corp.: Aug, 1973 - No. 11, Feb, 1975 (68 pgs., B&W) (Painted-c on all)

	GD	VG	FN	VF	VF/NM	NM-
1-Nosferatu-c/1st app. (series thru #11); Morrow-a. Cthulhu/Necronomicon-s	7	14	21	49	80	110
2,3: 2-(10/73) Lady Satan 1st app. & series begins; Edgar Allan Poe adaptations begin (thru #11); Phantom of the Opera-s. 3-(12/73) Origin Lady Satan	5	10	15	32	51	70
4-1st Cannibal Werewolf and 1st Lunatic Mummy	4	8	12	28	44	60
5,7,8: 5,7-Frankenstein app. 8-Buckler-a; Werewolf-s; Slither-Slime Man-s	4	8	12	28	44	60
6, 9,10: 6-(6/74) Saga of The Victims/ I Am Horror, classic GGA Hewetson series begins (thru #11); Frankenstein 2073-s. 9-Severed head-c; Marcos-a. 9,10-Werewolf-s. 10-Dracula-c/s	5	10	15	30	48	65
11- (1975 Winter Special) "Mr. Poe and the Raven" story	5	10	15	32	51	70

NOTE: ***Buckler** a-8. **Hewetson** s-1-11. **Marcos** a-9. **Miralles** c-2. **Morrow** a-1. **Poe** s-2-11. **Segrelles** a-7; c-1.*

SCREEN CARTOONS
DC Comics: Dec, 1944 (cover only ashcan)

Scribbly #1 © DC

Sea Devils #16 © DC

Sea Hunt #4 © ZIV TV

GD VG FN VF VF/NM NM-
2.0 4.0 6.0 8.0 9.0 9.2

nn-Ashcan comic, not distributed to newsstands, only for in house use. Covers were produced, but not the rest of the book. A copy sold in 2006 for $400 and in 2008 for $500.

SCREEN COMICS
DC Comics: Dec, 1944 (cover only ashcan)
nn-Ashcan comic, not distributed to newsstands, only for in house use. Covers were produced, but not the rest of the book. A copy sold in 2006 for $400 and in 2008 for $500.

SCREEN FABLES
DC Comics: Dec, 1944 (cover only ashcan)
nn-Ashcan comic, not distributed to newsstands, only for in house use. Covers were produced, but not the rest of the book. A copy sold in 2006 for $400 and in 2008 for $500.

SCREEN FUNNIES
DC Comics: Dec, 1944 (cover only ashcan)
nn-Ashcan comic, not distributed to newsstands, only for in house use. Covers were produced, but not the rest of the book. A copy sold in 2006 for $400 and in 2008 for $500.

SCREEN GEMS
DC Comics: Dec, 1944 (cover only ashcan)
nn-Ashcan comic, not distributed to newsstands, only for in house use. Covers were produced, but not the rest of the book. A copy sold in 2006 for $400 and in 2008 for $500.

SCREWBALL SQUIRREL
Dark Horse Comics: July, 1995 - No. 3, Sept, 1995 ($2.50, limited series)
1-3: Characters created by Tex Avery 2.50

SCRIBBLY (See All-American Comics, Buzzy, The Funnies, Leave It To Binky & Popular Comics)
National Periodical Publ.: 8-9/48 - No. 13, 8-9/50; No. 14, 10-11/51 - No. 15, 12-1/51-52
1-Sheldon Mayer-c/a in all; 52 pgs. begin 90 180 270 567 959 1350
2 57 114 171 359 605 850
3-5 47 94 141 291 483 675
6-10 37 74 111 220 353 485
11-15: 13-Last 52 pgs. 32 64 96 188 302 415

SCUD: TALES FROM THE VENDING MACHINE
Fireman Press: 1998 - No. 5 ($2.50, B&W)
1-5: 1-Kaniuga-a. 2-Ruben Martinez-a 2.50

SCUD: THE DISPOSABLE ASSASSIN
Fireman Press: Feb, 1994 - No. 20, 1997 ($2.95, B&W)
Image Comics: No. 21, Feb, 2008 - No. 24, May, 2008 ($3.50, B&W)
1 6.00
1-2nd printing in color 2.50
2,3 4.00
4-20 3.00
21-24: 21-(2/08, $3.50) Ashley Wood-c. 22-Mahfood-c 3.50
Heavy 3PO ($12.95, TPB) r/#1-4 13.00
Programmed For Damage ($14.95, TPB) r/#5-9 15.00
Solid Gold Bomb ($17.95, TPB) r/#10-15 18.00

SEA DEVILS (See Limited Collectors' Edition #39,45, & Showcase #27-29)
National Periodical Publications: Sept-Oct, 1961 - No. 35, May-June, 1967
1-(9-10/61) 56 112 168 476 938 1400
2-Last 10¢ issue 30 60 90 221 428 635
3-Begin 12¢ issues thru #35 19 38 57 139 270 400
4,5 17 34 51 122 236 350
6-10 12 24 36 85 155 225
11,12,14-20 9 18 27 63 107 150
13-Kubert, Colan-a; Joe Kubert app. in story 9 18 27 64 110 155
21-35: 22-Intro. International Sea Devils; origin & 1st app. Capt. X & Man Fish 7 14 21 47 76 105
NOTE: ***Heath** a-Showcase 27-29, 1-10; c-Showcase 27-29, 1-10, 14-16. **Moldoff** a-16i.*

SEA DEVILS (See Tangent Comics/ Sea Devils)

SEADRAGON (Also see the Epsilion Wave)
Elite Comics: May, 1986 - No. 8, 1987 ($1.75)
1-8: 1-1st & 2nd printings exist 2.50

SEAGUY
DC Comics (Vertigo): July, 2004 - No. 3, Sept, 2004 ($2.95, limited series)
1-3-Grant Morrison-s/Cameron Stewart-a/c 3.00
TPB (2005, $9.95) r/#1-3 10.00

SEAGUY: THE SLAVES OF MICKEY EYE
DC Comics (Vertigo): Jun, 2009 - No. 3, Aug, 2009 ($3.99, limited series)
1-3-Grant Morrison-s/Cameron Stewart-a/c 4.00

SEA HOUND, THE (Captain Silver's Log Of The...)
Avon Periodicals: 1945 (no month) - No. 2, Sept-Oct, 1945
nn (#1)-29 pg. novel length sty-"The Esmeralda's Treasure"
18 36 54 105 165 225
2 13 26 39 74 105 135

SEA HOUND, THE (Radio)
Capt. Silver Syndicate: No. 3, July, 1949 - No. 4, Sept, 1949
3,4 10 20 30 54 72 90

SEA HUNT (TV)
Dell Publishing Co.: No. 928, 8/58 - No. 1041, 10-12/59; No. 4, 1-3/60 - No. 13, 4-6/62 (All have Lloyd Bridges photo-c)
Four Color 928(#1) 11 22 33 78 139 200
Four Color 994(#2), 4-13: Manning-a #4-6,8-11,13 8 16 24 54 90 125
Four Color 1041(#3)-Toth-a 8 16 24 54 90 125

SEA OF RED
Image Comics: Mar, 2005 - No. 13, Nov, 2006 ($2.95/$2.99/$3.50)
1-12-Vampirates at sea; Remender & Dwyer-s/Dwyer & Sam-a 3.00
13-($3.50) 3.50
Vol. 1: No Grave But The Sea (9/05, $8.95) r/#1-4 9.00
Vol. 2: No Quarter (2006, $11.99) r/#5-8 12.00
Vol. 3: The Deadlights (2006, $14.99) r/#9-13 15.00

SEAQUEST (TV)
Nemesis Comics: Mar, 1994 ($2.25)
1-Has 2 diff-c stocks (slick & cardboard); Alcala-i 2.50

SEARCH FOR LOVE
American Comics Group: Feb-Mar, 1950 - No. 2, Apr-May, 1950 (52 pgs.)
1 12 24 36 69 97 125
2 9 18 27 47 61 75

SEARCHERS, THE (Movie)
Dell Publishing Co.: No. 709, 1956
Four Color 709-John Wayne photo-c 22 44 66 157 304 450

SEARCHERS, THE
Caliber Comics: 1996 - No. 4, 1996 ($2.95, B&W)
1-4 3.00

SEARCHERS, THE : APOSTLE OF MERCY
Caliber Comics: 1997 - No. 2, 1997 ($2.95/$3.95, B&W)
1-($2.95) 3.00
2-($3.95) 4.00

SEARS (See Merry Christmas From...)

SEASON'S GREETINGS
Hallmark (King Features): 1935 (6-1/4x5-1/4", 24 pgs. in color)
nn-Cover features Mickey Mouse, Popeye, Jiggs & Skippy. "The Night Before Christmas" told one panel per page, each panel by a famous artist featuring their character. Art by Alex Raymond, Gottfredson, Swinnerton, Segar, Chic Young, Milt Gross, Sullivan (Messmer), Herriman, McManus, Percy Crosby & others (22 artists in all)
Estimated value... 950.00

SEBASTIAN O
DC Comics (Vertigo): May, 1993 - No. 3, July, 1993 ($1.95, limited series)
1-3-Grant Morrison scripts; Steve Yeowell-a 2.50
TPB (2004, $9.95) r/#1-3; intro. chronology by Morrison 10.00

SECOND LIFE OF DOCTOR MIRAGE, THE (See Shadowman #16)
Valiant: Nov, 1993 - No. 18, May, 1995 ($2.50)
1-18: 1-With bound-in poster. 5-Shadowman x-over. 7-Bound-in trading card 2.50
1-Gold ink logo edition; no price on-c 3.00

SECRET AGENT (Formerly Sarge Steel)
Charlton Comics: V2#9, Oct, 1966; V2#10, Oct, 1967
V2#9-Sarge Steel part-r begins 3 6 9 17 25 32
10-Tiffany Sinn, CIA app. (from Career Girl Romances #39); Aparo-a
3 6 9 14 19 24

SECRET AGENT (TV) (See Four Color #1231)
Gold Key: Nov, 1966; No. 2, Jan, 1968
1-Photo-c 8 16 24 58 97 135
2-Photo-c 6 12 18 41 66 90

SECRET AGENT X-9 (See Flash Gordon #4 by King)
David McKay Publ.: 1934 (Book 1: 84 pgs.; Book 2: 124 pgs.) (8x7-1/2")

Secret Hearts #135 © DC

Secret Invasion #3 © MAR

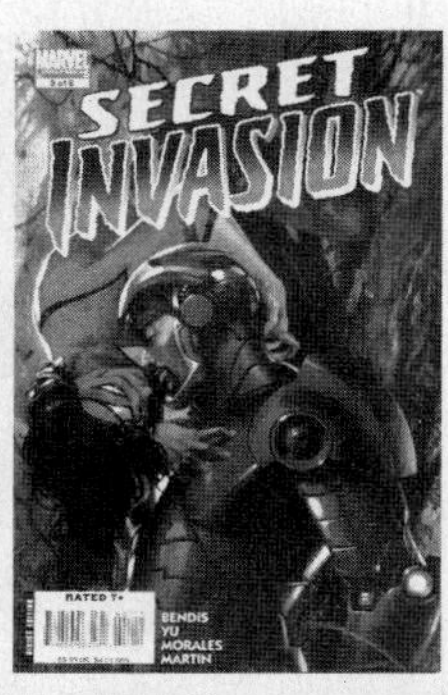

Secret Loves #1 © QUA

	GD 2.0	VG 4.0	FN 6.0	VF 8.0	VF/NM 9.0	NM- 9.2

Book 1-Contains reprints of the first 13 weeks of the strip by Alex Raymond; complete except for 2 dailies 43 86 129 271 461 650

Book 2-Contains reprints immediately following contents of Book 1, for 20 weeks by Alex Raymond; complete except for two dailies. Note: Raymond mis-dated the last five strips from 6/34, and while the dating sequence is confusing, the continuity is correct 39 78 117 234 385 535

SECRET AGENT X-9 (See Magic Comics)
Dell Publishing Co.: Dec, 1937 (Not by Raymond)

Feature Books 8 47 94 141 296 498 700

SECRET AGENT Z-2 (See Holyoke One-Shot No. 7)

SECRET CITY SAGA (See Jack Kirby's Secret City Saga)

SECRET DEFENDERS (Also see The Defenders & Fantastic Four #374)
Marvel Comics: Mar, 1993 - No. 25, Mar, 1995 ($1.75/$1.95)

1-($2.50)-Red foil stamped-c; Dr. Strange, Nomad, Wolverine, Spider Woman & Darkhawk begin 3.00
2-11,13-24: 9-New team w/Silver Surfer, Thunderstrike, Dr. Strange & War Machine. 13-Thanos replaces Dr. Strange as leader; leads into Cosmic Powers limited series; 14-Dr. Druid. 15-Bound in card sheet. 18-Giant Man & Iron Fist app. 2.50
12,25: 12-($2.50)-Prismatic foil-c. 25 ($2.50, 52 pgs.) 2.75

SECRET DIARY OF EERIE ADVENTURES
Avon Periodicals: 1953 (25¢ giant, 100 pgs., one-shot)

nn-(Rare)-Kubert-a; Hollingsworth-c; Sid Check back-c 213 426 639 1363 2332 3300

SECRET FILES & ORIGINS GUIDE TO THE DC UNIVERSE
DC Comics: Mar, 2000; Feb, 2002 ($6.95/$4.95)

2000 (3/00, $6.95)-Overview of DC characters; profile pages by various 7.00
2001-2002 (2/02, $4.95) Olivetti-c 5.00

SECRET FILES PRESIDENT LUTHOR
DC Comics: Mar, 2001 ($4.95, one-shot)

1-Short stories & profile pages by various; Harris-c 5.00

SECRET HEARTS
National Periodical Publications (Beverly)(Arleigh No. 50-113):
9-10/49 - No. 6, 7-8/50; No. 7, 12-1/51-52 - No. 153, 7/71

	GD	VG	FN	VF	VF/NM	NM-
1-Kinstler-a; photo-c begin, end #6	55	110	165	352	601	850
2-Toth-a (1 pg.); Kinstler-a	30	60	90	177	289	400
3,6 (1950)	26	52	78	154	252	350
4,5-Toth-a	26	52	78	156	256	355
7(12-1/51-52) (Rare)	40	80	120	246	411	575
8-10 (1952)	20	40	60	114	182	250
11-20	15	30	45	88	137	185
21-26: 26-Last precode (2-3/55)	14	28	42	80	115	150
27-40	7	14	21	47	76	105
41-50	5	10	15	34	55	75
51-60	5	10	15	30	48	65
61-75,100: 75-Last 10¢ issue	4	8	12	28	44	60
76-99,101-109	4	8	12	22	34	45
110- "Reach for Happiness" serial begins, ends #138	4	8	12	24	37	50
111-119,121-126	3	6	9	17	25	32
120,134-Neal Adams-c	4	8	12	24	37	50
127 (4/68)-Beatles cameo	4	8	12	24	37	50
128-133,135-142: 141,142- "20 Miles to Heartbreak", Chapter 2 & 3 (see Young Love for Chapters 1 & 4); Toth, Colletta-a	3	6	9	16	23	30
143-148,150-152: 144-Morrow-a	3	6	9	14	19	24
149,153: 149-Toth-a. 153-Kirby-i	3	6	9	15	21	26

SECRET HISTORY OF THE AUTHORITY: HAWKSMOOR
DC Comics (WildStorm): May, 2008 - No. 6, Oct, 2008 ($2.99, limited series)

1-6-Costa-s/Staples-a/Hamner-c 3.00
TPB (2009, $19.99) r/#1-6 20.00

SECRET INVASION (Also see Mighty Avengers, New Avengers, and Skrulls!)
Marvel Comics: June, 2008 - No. 8 ($3.99, limited series)

1-Skrull invasion; Bendis-s/Yu-a/Dell'Otto-c 4.00
1-Variant cover with blank area for sketches 4.00
1-McNiven variant-c 12.00
1-Yu variant-c 30.00
1-2nd printing with old Avengers variant-c by Yu 4.00
1 Director's Cut (2008, $4.99) r/#1 with script; concept and promo art; cover gallery 5.00
2-8-Dell'Otto-c. 8-Wasp killed 4.00
2-4-McNiven variant-c. 2-Avengers. 3-Nick Fury. 4-Tony Stark, Spider-Woman, Black Widow 6.00
2-8-Yu variant-c. 2-Hawkeye & Mockingbird. 3-Spider-Woman. 4-Nick Fury 10.00
5-Rubi variant-c 5.00
6-Cho Spider-Woman variant-c 8.00
...:Aftermath: Beta Ray Bill - The Green of Eden (6/09, $3.99) Brereton-a 4.00
...: Chronicles 1,2 (4/09,6/09, $5.99) reprints from New Avengers & Illuminati issues 6.00
... Dark Reign (2/09, $3.99) villain meeting after #8; previews new series; Maleev-a/c 4.00
... Dark Reign (2/09, $3.99) Variant Green Goblin cover by Bryan Hitch 8.00
... Requiem (2009, $3.99) Hank Pym becomes The Wasp; r/TTA #44 & Avengers #215 4.00
... Saga (2008, giveaway) history of the Skrulls told through reprint panels and text 2.25
...: The Infiltration TPB (2008, $19.99) r/FF #2; New Avengers #31,32,38,39; New Avengers: Illuminati #1,5; Mighty Avengers #7; and Avengers: The Initiative Annual #1 20.00
...: War of Kings (2/09, $3.99) Black Bolt and the Inhumans; Pelletier & Dazo-a 4.00
...: Who Do You Trust? (8/08, $3.99) short tie-in stories by various; Jimenez-c 4.00

SECRET INVASION: AMAZING SPIDER-MAN
Marvel Comics: Oct, 2008 - No. 3, Dec, 2008 ($2.99, limited series)

1-3-Jackpot battles a Super-Skrull; Santucci-a. 2-Menace app. 3.00

SECRET INVASION: FANTASTIC FOUR
Marvel Comics: July, 2008 - No. 3, Sept, 2008 ($2.99, limited series)

1-3-Skrulls and Lyja invade; Kitson-a/Davis-c 3.00
1-Variant Skrull cover by McKone 5.00

SECRET INVASION: FRONT LINE
Marvel Comics: Sept, 2008 - No. 5, Jan, 2009 ($2.99, limited series)

1-5-Ben Urich covering the Skrull invasion; Reed-s/Castiello-a 3.00

SECRET INVASION: INHUMANS
Marvel Comics: Oct, 2008 - No. 4, Jan, 2009 ($2.99, limited series)

1-4-Raney-a/Sejic-c/Pokasky-s; search for Black Bolt 3.00

SECRET INVASION: RUNAWAYS/YOUNG AVENGERS (Follows Runaways #30)
Marvel Comics: Aug, 2008 - No. 3, Nov, 2008 ($2.99, limited series)

1-3-Miyazawa-a/Ryan-c 3.00

SECRET INVASION: THOR
Marvel Comics: Oct, 2008 - No. 3, Dec, 2008 ($2.99, limited series)

1-3-Fraction-s/Braithwaite-a; Skrulls invade Asgard; Beta Ray Bill app. 3.00
1-2nd printing with Beta Ray Bill cover 3.00

SECRET INVASION: X-MEN
Marvel Comics: Oct, 2008 - No. 4, Jan, 2009 ($2.99, limited series)

1-4-Carey-s/Nord-a/Dodson-c; Skrulls invade San Francisco 3.00
1-2nd printing with variant Nord-c 3.00

SECRET ISLAND OF OZ, THE (See First Comics Graphic Novel)

SECRET LOVE (See Fox Giants & Sinister House of...)

SECRET LOVE
Ajax-Farrell/Four Star Comic Corp. No. 2 on: 12/55 - No. 3, 8/56; 4/57 - No. 5, 2/58; No. 6, 6/58

	GD	VG	FN	VF	VF/NM	NM-
1(12/55-Ajax, 1st series)	10	20	30	56	76	95
2,3	7	14	21	37	46	55
1(4/57-Ajax, 2nd series)	9	18	27	47	61	75
2-6: 5-Bakerish-a	7	14	21	35	43	50

SECRET LOVES
Comic Magazines/Quality Comics Group: Nov, 1949 - No. 6, Sept, 1950

	GD	VG	FN	VF	VF/NM	NM-
1-Ward-c	25	50	75	147	241	335
2-Ward-c	21	42	63	122	199	275
3-Crandall-a	14	28	42	82	121	160
4,6	12	24	36	67	94	120
5-Suggestive art "Boom Town Babe"; photo-c	14	28	42	82	121	160

SECRET LOVE STORIES (See Fox Giants)

SECRET MISSIONS (Admiral Zacharia's...)
St. John Publishing Co.: February, 1950

1-Joe Kubert-c; stories of U.S. foreign agents 20 40 60 114 182 250

SECRET MYSTERIES (Formerly Crime Mysteries & Crime Smashers)
Ribage/Merit Publications No. 17 on: No. 16, Nov, 1954 - No. 19, July, 1955

	GD	VG	FN	VF	VF/NM	NM-
16-Horror, Palais-a; Myron Fass-c	28	56	84	165	270	375
17-19-Horror. 17-Fass-c; mis-dated 3/54?	20	40	60	117	189	260

SECRET ORIGINS (1st Series) (See 80 Page Giant #8)
National Periodical Publications: Aug-Oct, 1961 (Annual) (Reprints)

1-Origin Adam Strange (Showcase #17), Green Lantern (Green Lantern #1), Challengers

Secret Origins (3rd series) #14 © DC

Secret Six (2009 series) #3 © DC

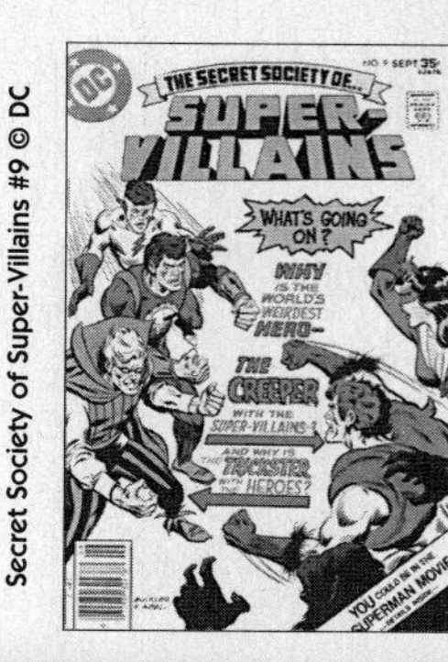

Secret Society of Super-Villains #9 © DC

	GD 2.0	VG 4.0	FN 6.0	VF 8.0	VF/NM 9.0	NM- 9.2

(partial-r/Showcase #6, 6 pgs. Kirby-a), J'onn J'onzz (Det. #225), The Flash (Showcase #4), Green Arrow (1 pg. text), Superman-Batman team (World's Finest #94), Wonder Woman (Wonder Woman #105) 46 92 138 368 709 1050
Replica Edition (1998, $4.95) r/entire book and house ads 5.00
Even More Secret Origins (2003, $6.95) reprints origins of Hawkman, Eclipso, Kid Flash, Blackhawks, Green Lantern's oath, and Jimmy Olsen-Robin team in 80 pg. Giant style 7.00

SECRET ORIGINS (2nd Series)
National Periodical Publications: Feb-Mar, 1973 - No. 6, Jan-Feb, 1974; No. 7, Oct-Nov, 1974 (All 20¢ issues) (All origin reprints)

1-Superman(r/1 pg. origin/Action #1, 1st time since G.A.), Batman(Detective #33), Ghost(Flash #88), The Flash(Showcase #4) 5 10 15 30 48 65
2-7: 2-Green Lantern & The Atom(Showcase #22 & 34), Supergirl(Action #252). 3-Wonder Woman (W.W. #1), Wildcat (Sensation #1). 4-Vigilante (Action #42) by Meskin, Kid Eternity(Hit #25). 5-The Spectre by Baily (More Fun #52,53). 6-Blackhawk(Military #1) & Legion of Super-Heroes(Superboy #147). 7-Robin (Detective #38), Aquaman (More Fun #73) 3 6 9 18 27 35
NOTE: *Infantino a-1. Kane a-2. Kubert a-1.*

SECRET ORIGINS (3rd Series)
DC Comics: 4/86 - No. 50, 8/90 (All origins)(52 pgs. #6 on)(#27 on: $1.50)

1-Origin Superman 6.00
2-6: 2-Blue Beetle. 3-Shazam. 4-Firestorm. 5-Crimson Avenger. 6-Halo/G.A. Batman 3.00
7-9,11,12,14-20,22-26: 7-Green Lantern (Guy Gardner)/G.A. Sandman. 8-Shadow Lass/Doll Man. 9-G.A. Flash/Skyman.11-G.A. Hawkman/Power Girl. 12-Challengers of Unknown/ G.A. Fury (2nd modern app.). 14-Suicide Squad; Legends spin-off. 15-Spectre/Deadman. 16-G.A. Hourman/Warlord. 17-Adam Strange story by Carmine Infantino; Dr. Occult. 18-G.A. Gr. Lantern/The Creeper. 19-Uncle Sam/The Guardian. 20-Batgirl/G.A. Dr. Mid-Nite. 22-Manhunters. 23-Floronic Man/Guardians of the Universe. 24-Blue Devil/Dr. Fate. 25-LSH/Atom. 26-Black Lightning/Miss America 2.50
10-Phantom Stranger w/Alan Moore scripts; Legends spin-off 2.50
13-Origin Nightwing; Johnny Thunder app. 2.50
21-Jonah Hex/Black Condor 2.50
27-30,36-38,40-49: 27-Zatara/Zatanna. 28-Midnight/Nightshade. 29-Power of the Atom/Mr. America; new 3 pg. Red Tornado story by Mayer (last app. of Scribbly, 8/88). 30-Plastic Man/Elongated Man. 36-Poison Ivy by Neil Gaiman & Mark Buckingham/Green Lantern. 37-Legion Of Substitute Heroes/Doctor Light. 38-Green Arrow/Speedy; Grell scripts. 40-All Ape issue. 41-Rogues Gallery of Flash. 42-Phantom Girl/GrimGhost. 43-Original Hawk & Dove/Cave Carson/Chris KL-99. 44-Batman app.; story based on Det. #40. 45-Blackhawk/ El Diablo. 46-JLA/LSH/New Titans. 47-LSH. 48-Ambush Bug/Stanley & His Monster/Rex the Wonder Dog/Trigger Twins. 49-Newsboy Legion/Silent Knight/Bouncing Boy 2.50
31-35,39: 31-JSA. 32-JLA. 33-35-JLI. 39-Animal Man-c/story continued in Animal Man #10; Grant Morrison scripts; Batman app. 3.00
50-($3.95, 100 pgs.)-Batman & Robin in text, Flash of Two Worlds, Johnny Thunder, Dolphin, Black Canary & Space Museum 5.00
Annual 1 (8/87)-Capt. Comet/Doom Patrol 3.00
Annual 2 ('88, $2.00)-Origin Flash II & Flash III 3.00
Annual 3 ('89, $2.95, 84 pgs.)-Teen Titans; 1st app. new Flamebird who replaces original Bat-Girl 3.00
Special 1 (10/89, $2.00)-Batman villains: Penguin, Riddler, & Two-Face; Bolland-c; Sam Kieth-a; Neil Gaiman scripts(2) 3.00
NOTE: ***Art Adams** a-33i(part). **M. Anderson** 8, 19, 21, 25i; c-19(part). **Aparo** c/a-10. **Bissette** c-23. **Bolland** c-7. **Byrne** c/a-Annual 1. **Colan** c/a-5p. **Forte** a-37. **Giffen** a-18p, 44p, 48. **Infantino** a-17, 50p. **Kaluta** c-39. **Gil Kane** a-2, 28; c-2p. **Kirby** c-19(part). **Erik Larsen** a-13. **Mayer** a-29. **Morrow** a-21. **Orlando** a-10. **Perez** a-50i, Annual 3i; c- Annual 3. **Rogers** a-6p. **Russell** a-27i. **Simonson** c-22. **Staton** a-36, 50p. **Steacy** a-35. **Tuska** a-4p, 9p.*

SECRET ORIGINS 80 PAGE GIANT (Young Justice)
DC Comics: Dec, 1998 ($4.95, one-shot)

1-Origin-s of Young Justice members; Ramos-a (Impulse) 5.00

SECRET ORIGINS FEATURING THE JLA
DC Comics: 1999 ($14.95, TPB)

1-Reprints recent origin-s of JLA members; Cassaday-c 15.00

SECRET ORIGINS OF SUPER-HEROES (See DC Special Series #10, 19)

SECRET ORIGINS OF SUPER-VILLAINS 80 PAGE GIANT
DC Comics: Dec, 1999 ($4.95, one-shot)

1-Origin-s of Sinestro, Amazo and others; Gibbons-c 5.00

SECRET ORIGINS OF THE WORLD'S GREATEST SUPER-HEROES
DC Comics: 1989 ($4.95, 148 pgs.)

nn-Reprints Superman, JLA origins; new Batman origin-s; Bolland-c 1 2 3 4 5 7

SECRET ROMANCE
Charlton Comics: Oct, 1968 - No. 41, Nov, 1976; No. 42, Mar, 1979 - No. 48, Feb, 1980

1-Begin 12¢ issues, ends #? 3 6 9 16 23 30
2-10: 9-Reese-a 2 4 6 10 14 18
11-16,18,19,21-30 2 4 6 8 11 14
17,20: 17-Susan Dey poster. 20-David Cassidy pin-up 2 4 6 10 14 18
31-48 2 3 4 6 8 10
NOTE: *Beyond the Stars app.-No. 9, 11, 12, 14.*

SECRET ROMANCES (Exciting Love Stories)
Superior Publications Ltd.: Apr, 1951 - No. 27, July, 1955

1 15 30 45 88 137 185
2 11 22 33 62 86 110
3-10 9 18 27 50 65 80
11-13,15-18,20-27 8 16 24 42 54 65
14,19-Lingerie panels 8 16 24 47 61 70

SECRET SERVICE (See Kent Blake of the...)

SECRET SIX (See Action Comics Weekly)
National Periodical Publications: Apr-May, 1968 - No. 7, Apr-May, 1969 (12¢)

1-Origin/1st app. 6 12 18 41 66 90
2-7 4 8 12 22 34 45

SECRET SIX (See Tangent Comics/ Secret Six)

SECRET SIX (See Villains United)
DC Comics: Jul, 2006 - No. 6, Jan, 2007 ($2.99, limited series)

1-6-Gail Simone-s/Brad Walker-a. 4-Doom Patrol app. 3.00
...: Six Degrees of Devastation TPB (2007, $14.99) r/#1-6 15.00

SECRET SIX
DC Comics: Nov, 2008 - Present ($2.99)

1-17: 1-Gail Simone-s/Nicola Scott-a. 2-Batman app. 8-Rodriguez-a. 11-13-Wonder Woman & Artemis app. 16-Black Alice app. 17-Blackest Night 3.00
...: Unhinged TPB (2009, $14.99) r/#1-7; intro. by Paul Cornell 15.00

SECRET SKULL
IDW Publ.: Aug, 2004 - No. 4, Nov, 2004 ($3.99)

1-4-Steve Niles-s/Chuck BB-a 4.00

SECRET SOCIETY OF SUPER-VILLAINS
National Per. Publ./DC Comics: May-June, 1976 - No. 15, June-July, 1978

1-Origin; JLA cameo & Capt. Cold app. 3 6 9 14 19 24
2-5,15: 2-Re-intro/origin Capt. Comet; Green Lantern x-over. 5-Green Lantern, Hawkman x-over; Darkseid app. 15-G.A. Atom, Dr. Midnite, & JSA app. 2 4 6 8 11 14
6-14: 9,10-Creeper x-over. 11-Capt. Comet; Orlando-i 2 3 4 6 8 10

SECRET SOCIETY OF SUPER-VILLAINS SPECIAL (See DC Special Series #6)

SECRETS OF HAUNTED HOUSE
National Periodical Publications/DC Comics: 4-5/75 - #5, 12-1/75-76; #6, 6-7/77 - #14, 10-11/78; #15, 8/79 - #46, 3/82

1 5 10 15 34 55 75
2-4 3 6 9 18 27 35
5-Wrightson-c 4 8 12 22 34 45
6-14 2 4 6 10 14 18
15-30 2 4 6 8 10 12
31,44: 31-(12/80) Mr. E series begins (1st app.), ends #41. 44-Wrightson-c 2 4 6 8 11 14
32-(1/81) Origin of Mr. E 2 4 6 8 10 12
33-43,45,46: 34,35-Frankenstein Monster app. 1 2 3 5 6 8
NOTE: ***Aparo** c-7. **Aragones** a-1. **B. Bailey** a-8. **Bissette** a-46. **Buckler** c-32-40p. **Ditko** a-9, 12, 41, 45. **Golden** a-10. **Howard** a-13i. **Kaluta** c-8, 10, 11, 14, 16, 29. **Kubert** c-41, 42. **Sheldon Mayer** a-43p. **McWilliams** a-35. **Nasser** a-24. **Newton** a-30p. **Nino** a-1, 13, 19. **Orlando** c-13, 30, 43, 45i. **N. Redondo** a-4, 5, 29. **Rogers** c-26. **Spiegle** a-31-41. **Wrightson** c-5, 44.*

SECRETS OF HAUNTED HOUSE SPECIAL (See DC Special Series #12)

SECRETS OF LIFE (Movie)
Dell Publishing Co.: 1956 (Disney)

Four Color 749-Photo-c 5 10 15 32 51 70

SECRETS OF LOVE (See Popular Teen-Agers...)

SECRETS OF LOVE AND MARRIAGE
Charlton Comics: V2#1, Aug, 1956 - V2#25, June, 1961

V2#1 4 8 12 26 41 55
V2#2-6 3 6 9 18 27 35
V2#7-9-(All 68 pgs.) 4 8 12 28 44 60
10-25 3 6 9 16 22 28

SECRETS OF MAGIC (See Wisco)

SECRETS OF SINISTER HOUSE (Sinister House of Secret Love #1-4)

Secrets of the Legion of Super-Heroes #2 © DC

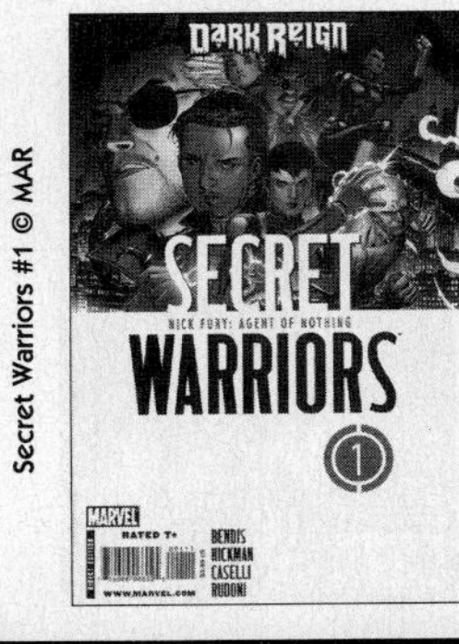

Secret Warriors #1 © MAR

Sensational She-Hulk #12 © MAR

	GD 2.0	VG 4.0	FN 6.0	VF 8.0	VF/NM 9.0	NM- 9.2

National Periodical Publ.: No. 5, June-July, 1972 - No. 18, June-July, 1974

	GD	VG	FN	VF	VF/NM	NM-
5-(52 pgs.).	6	12	18	39	62	85
6-9: 7-Redondo-a	4	8	12	22	34	45
10-Neal Adams-a(i)	4	8	12	24	37	50
11-18: 15-Redondo-a. 17-Barry-a; early Chaykin 1 pg. strip	3	6	9	16	22	28

NOTE: ***Alcala** a-6, 13, 14. **Glanzman** a-7. **Kaluta** c-6, 7. **Nino** a-8, 11-13. Ambrose Bierce adapt.-#14.*

SECRETS OF THE LEGION OF SUPER-HEROES
DC Comics: Jan, 1981 - No. 3, Mar, 1981 (Limited series)

	GD	VG	FN	VF	VF/NM	NM-
1-3: 1-Origin of the Legion. 2-Retells origins of Brainiac 5, Shrinking Violet, Sun-Boy, Bouncing Boy, Ultra-Boy, Matter-Eater Lad, Mon-El, Karate Kid & Dream Girl						4.00

SECRETS OF TRUE LOVE
St. John Publishing Co.: Feb, 1958

	GD	VG	FN	VF	VF/NM	NM-
1	7	14	21	37	46	55

SECRETS OF YOUNG BRIDES
Charlton Comics: No. 5, Sept, 1957 - No. 44, Oct, 1964; July, 1975 - No. 9, Nov, 1976

	GD	VG	FN	VF	VF/NM	NM-
5	4	8	12	28	44	60
6-10: 8-Negligee panel	3	6	9	20	30	40
11-20	3	6	9	18	27	35
21-30: Last 10¢ issue?	3	6	9	16	23	30
31-44(10/64)	2	4	6	11	16	20
1-(2nd series) (7/75)	2	4	6	13	18	22
2-9	2	4	6	8	10	12

SECRET SQUIRREL (TV)(See Kite Fun Book)
Gold Key: Oct, 1966 (12¢) (Hanna-Barbera)

	GD	VG	FN	VF	VF/NM	NM-
1-1st Secret Squirrel and Morocco Mole, Squiddly Diddly, Winsome Witch	10	20	30	73	129	185

SECRET STORY ROMANCES (Becomes True Tales of Love)
Atlas Comics (TCI): Nov, 1953 - No. 21, Mar, 1956

	GD	VG	FN	VF	VF/NM	NM-
1-Everett-a; Jay Scott Pike-c	15	30	45	90	140	190
2	10	20	30	56	76	95
3-11: 11-Last pre-code (2/55)	9	18	27	50	65	80
12-21	8	16	24	44	57	70

NOTE: ***Colletta** a-10, 14, 15, 17, 21; c-10, 14, 17.*

SECRET VOICE, THE (See Great American Comics Presents...)

SECRET WAR
Marvel Comics: Apr, 2004 - No. 5, Dec, 2005 ($3.99, limited series)

	GD	VG	FN	VF	VF/NM	NM-
1-Bendis-s/Dell'Otto painted-a/c;						5.00
1-2nd printing with gold logo on white cover and full-color Spider-Man						4.00
1-3rd printing with white cover and B&W sketched Spider-Man						4.00
2-5: 2-Wolverine-c. 3-Capt. America-c. 4-Black Widow-c. 5-Daredevil-c						4.00
2-2nd printing with white cover and B&W sketched Wolverine						4.00
...: From the Files of Nick Fury (2005, $3.99) Fury's journal entries; profiles of characters						4.00
HC (2005, $29.99, dust jacket) r/#1-5 & ...From the Files of Nick Fury; additional art						30.00
SC (2006, $24.99) r/#1-5 & ...From the Files of Nick Fury; additional art						25.00

SECRET WARRIORS (Also see 2009 Dark Reign titles)
Marvel Comics: Apr, 2009 - Present ($3.99)

	GD	VG	FN	VF	VF/NM	NM-
1-Bendis & Hickman-s/Caselli-a/Cheung-c; Nick Fury app.; Hydra dossier; sketch pages						4.00
2-13-($2.99) 8-Dark Avengers app.						3.00

SECRET WARS II (Also see Marvel Super Heroes...)
Marvel Comics Group: July, 1985 - No. 9, Mar, 1986 (Maxi-series)

	GD	VG	FN	VF	VF/NM	NM-
1,9: 9-(52 pgs.) X-Men app., Spider-Man app.						4.00
2-8: 2,8-X-Men app. 5-1st app. Boom Boom. 5,8-Spider-Man app.						3.00

SECRET WEAPONS
Valiant: Sept, 1993 - No. 21, May, 1995 ($2.25)

	GD	VG	FN	VF	VF/NM	NM-
1-10,12-21: 3-Reese-a(i). 5-Ninjak app. 9-Bound-in trading card. 12-Bloodshot app.						2.50
11-(Sept. on envelope, Aug on-c, $2.50)-Enclosed in manilla envelope; Bloodshot app; intro new team.						2.50

SECTAURS
Marvel Comics: June, 1985 - No. 8, Sept, 1986 (75¢) (Based on Coleco Toys)

	GD	VG	FN	VF	VF/NM	NM-
1-8, 1-Giveaway; same-c with "Coleco 1985 Toy Fair Collectors' Edition"						3.00

SECTION ZERO
Image Comics (Gorilla): June, 2000 - No. 3, Sept, 2000 ($2.50)

	GD	VG	FN	VF	VF/NM	NM-
1-3-Kesel-s/Grummett-a						2.50

SEDUCTION OF THE INNOCENT (Also see New York State Joint Legislative Committee to Study...)
Rinehart & Co., Inc., N. Y.: 1953, 1954 (400 pgs.) (Hardback, $4.00)(Written by Fredric Wertham, M.D.)(Also printed in Canada by Clarke, Irwin & Co. Ltd.)

	GD	VG	FN	VF	VF/NM	NM-
(1st Version)-with bibliographical note intact (pages 399 & 400)(several copies got out before the comic publishers forced the removal of this page)	150	300	450	650	775	900
Dust jacket only	36	72	108	211	343	475
(1st Version)-without bibliographical note	79	158	237	340	408	475
Dust jacket only	18	36	54	105	165	225
(2nd Version)-Published in England by Rinehart, 1954, 399 pgs. has bibliographical page; "Second print" listed on inside flap of the dust jacket; publication page has no "R" colophon; unlike 1st version	15	30	45	83	124	165
1972 r-/of 2nd version; 400 pgs. w/bibliography page; Kennikat Press	4	8	12	28	44	60

NOTE: *Material from this book appeared in the November, 1953 (Vol.70, pp50-53,214) issue of the **Ladies' Home Journal** under the title "What Parents Don't Know About Comic Books". With the release of this book, Dr. Wertham reveals seven years of research attempting to link juvenile delinquency to comic books. Many illustrations showing excessive violence, sex, sadism, and torture are shown. This book was used at the Kefauver Senate hearings which led to the Comics Code Authority. Because of the influence this book had on the comic industry and the collector's interest in it, we feel this listing is justified. Modern printings exist in limited editions. Also see **Parade of Pleasure**.*

SEDUCTION OF THE INNOCENT! (Also see Halloween Horror)
Eclipse Comics: Nov, 1985 - 3-D#2, Apr, 1986 ($1.75)

	GD	VG	FN	VF	VF/NM	NM-
1-6: Double listed under cover title from #7 on						3.00
3-D 1 (10/85, $2.25, 36 pgs.)-contains unpublished Advs. Into Darkness #15 (pre-code); Dave Stevens-c						4.00
2-D 1 (100 copy limited signed & #ed edition)(B&W)	1	2	3	5	6	8
3-D 2 (4/86)-Baker, Toth, Wrightson-c						5.00
2-D 2 (100 copy limited signed & #ed edition)(B&W)	1	2	3	5	7	9

NOTE: ***Anderson** r-2, 3. **Crandall** c/a(r)-1. **Meskin** c/a(r)-3, 3-D 1. **Moreira** r-2. **Toth** a-1-6r; c-4r. **Tuska** r-6.*

SEEKER
Sky Comics: Apr, 1994 ($2.50, one-shot)

	GD	VG	FN	VF	VF/NM	NM-
1						2.50

SEEKERS INTO THE MYSTERY
DC Comics (Vertigo): Jan, 1996 - No. 15, Apr, 1997 ($2.50)

	GD	VG	FN	VF	VF/NM	NM-
1-14: J.M. DeMatteis scripts in all. 1-4-Glenn Barr-a. 5,10-Muth-c/a. 6-9-Zulli-c/a. 11-14-Bolton-c; Jill Thompson-a						2.50
15-($2.95)-Muth-c/a						3.00

SEEKER 3000 (See Marvel Premiere #41)
Marvel Comics: Jun, 1998 - No. 4, Sept, 1998 ($2.99/$2.50, limited series)

	GD	VG	FN	VF	VF/NM	NM-
1-($2.99)-Set 25 years after 1st app.; wraparound-c						3.00
2-4-($2.50)						2.50
...Premiere 1 (6/98, $1.50) Reprints 1st app. from Marvel Premiere #41; wraparound-c						2.50

SELECT DETECTIVE (Exciting New Mystery Cases)
D. S. Publishing Co.: Aug-Sept, 1948 - No. 3, Dec-Jan, 1948-49

	GD	VG	FN	VF	VF/NM	NM-
1-Matt Baker-a	29	58	87	172	281	390
2-Baker, McWilliams-a	20	40	60	114	182	250
3	15	30	45	90	140	190

SEMPER FI (Tales of the Marine Corp)
Marvel Comics: Dec, 1988- No.9, Aug, 1989 (75¢)

	GD	VG	FN	VF	VF/NM	NM-
1-9: Severin-c/a						2.50

SENSATIONAL POLICE CASES (Becomes Captain Steve Savage, 2nd Series)
Avon Periodicals: 1952; No. 2, 1954 - No. 4, July-Aug, 1954

	GD	VG	FN	VF	VF/NM	NM-
nn-(1952, 25¢, 100 pgs.)-Kubert-a?; Check, Larsen, Lawrence & McCann-a; Kinstler-c	39	78	117	240	395	550
2-4: 2-Kirbyish-a (3-4/54). 4-Reprint/Saint #5	15	30	45	86	133	180
I.W. Reprint #5-(1963?, nd)-Reprints Prison Break #5(1952-Realistic); Infantino-a	3	6	9	16	23	30

SENSATIONAL SHE-HULK, THE (She-Hulk #21-23) (See Savage She-Hulk)
Marvel Comics: V2#1, 5/89 - No. 60, Feb, 1994 ($1.50/$1.75, deluxe format)

	GD	VG	FN	VF	VF/NM	NM-
V2#1-Byrne-c/a(p)/scripts begin, end #8						3.00
2,3,5-8: 3-Spider-Man app.						2.50
4,14-17,21-23: 4-Reintro G.A. Blonde Phantom. 14-17-Howard the Duck app. 21-23-Return of the Blonde Phantom. 22-All Winners Squad app.						2.50
9-13,18-20,24-49,51-60: 25-Thor app. 26-Excalibur app.; Guice-c. 29-Wolverine app. (3 pgs.). 30-Hobgoblin-c & cameo. 31-Byrne-c/a/scripts begin again. 35-Last $1.50-c. 37-Wolverine/Punisher/Spidey-c, but no app. 39-Thing app. 56-War Zone app.; Hulk cameo. 57-Vs. Hulk-c/story. 58-Electro-c/story. 59-Jack O'Lantern app.						2.50
50-($2.95, 52 pgs.)-Embossed green foil-c; Byrne app.; last Byrne-c/a; Austin, Chaykin, Simonson-a; Miller-a(2 pgs.)						3.00

NOTE: ***Dale Keown** a(p)-13, 15-22.*

SENSATIONAL SHE-HULK IN CEREMONY, THE

Sensational Spider-Man (2006 series) #38 © MAR

Sensation Comics #12 © DC

Serenity #2 © Universal Studios

	GD	VG	FN	VF	VF/NM	NM-
	2.0	4.0	6.0	8.0	9.0	9.2

Marvel Comics: 1989 - No. 2, 1989 ($3.95, squarebound, 52 pgs.)

nn-Part 1, nn-Part 2 4.00

SENSATIONAL SPIDER-MAN
Marvel Comics: Apr, 1989 ($5.95, squarebound, 80 pgs.)

1-r/Amazing Spider-Man Annual #14,15 by Miller & Annual #8 by Kirby & Ditko 6.00

SENSATIONAL SPIDER-MAN, THE
Marvel Comics: Jan, 1996 - No. 33, Nov, 1998 ($1.95/$1.99)

0 ($4.95)-Lenticular-c; Jurgens-a/scripts 5.00
1 5.00
1-($2.95) variant-c; polybagged w/cassette 1 2 3 5 6 8
2-5: 2-Kaine & Rhino app. 3-Giant-Man app. 4.00
6-18: 9-Onslaught tie-in; revealed that Peter & Mary Jane's unborn baby is a girl. 11-Revelations. 13-15-Ka-Zar app. 14,15-Hulk app. 3.00
19-24: Living Pharoah app. 22,23-Dr. Strange app. 2.50
25-($2.99) Spiderhunt pt. 1; Normie Osborne kidnapped 4.00
25-Variant-c 1 2 3 5 6 8
26-33: 26-Nauck-a. 27-Double-c with "The Sensational Hornet #1"; Vulture app. 28-Hornet vs. Vulture. 29,30-Black Cat-c/app. 33-Last issue; Gathering of Five concludes 2.50
#(-1) Flashback(7/97) Dezago-s/Wieringo-a 3.00
'96 Annual ($2.95) 3.00

SENSATIONAL SPIDER-MAN, THE (Previously Marvel Knights Spider-Man #1-22)
Marvel Comics: No. 23, Apr, 2006 - No. 41, Dec, 2007 ($2.99)

23-40: 23-25-Aguirre-Sacasa-s/Medina-a. 23-Wraparound-c. 24,34,37-Black Cat app. 26-New costume. 28-Unmasked; Dr. Octopus app.; Crain-a. 35-Black costume resumes 3.00
41-($3.99) One More Day pt. 3; Straczynski-s/Quesada-a/c 4.00
... Annual 1 (2007, $3.99) Flashbacks of Peter & MJ's relationship; Larroca-a/Fraction-s 4.00
... Feral HC (2006, $19.99, dustjacket) r/#23-27; sketch pages 20.00
Civil War: Peter Parker, Spider-Man TPB (2007, $17.99) r/#28-34; Crain cover concepts 18.00

SENSATION COMICS (Sensation Mystery #110 on)
National Per. Publ./All-American: Jan, 1942 - No. 109, May-June, 1952

1-Origin Mr. Terrific(1st app.), Wildcat(1st app.), The Gay Ghost, & Little Boy Blue; Wonder Woman (cont'd from All Star #8), The Black Pirate begin; intro. Justice & Fair Play Club 2850 5700 8550 21,090 40,545 60,000

1-Reprint, Oversize 13-1/2x10". WARNING: This comic is an exact duplicate reprint of the original except for its size. DC published it in 1974 with a second cover titling it as a Famous First Edition. There have been many reported cases of the outer cover being removed and the interior sold as the original edition. The reprint with the new outer cover removed is practically worthless. See Famous First Edition for value.

2-Etta Candy begins 470 940 1410 3431 6066 8700
3-W. Woman gets secretary's job 297 594 891 1900 3250 4600
4-1st app. Stretch Skinner in Wildcat 203 406 609 1289 2220 3150
5-Intro. Justin, Black Pirate's son 161 322 483 1030 1765 2500
6-Origin/1st app. Wonder Woman's magic lasso 165 330 495 1048 1799 2550
7-10 118 236 354 749 1287 1825
11,12,14-20 100 200 300 635 1093 1550
13-Hitler, Tojo, Mussolini-c (as bowling pins) 155 310 465 992 1696 2400
21-30 81 162 243 518 884 1250
31-33 60 120 180 381 658 935
34-Sargon, the Sorcerer begins (10/44), ends #36; begins again #52 64 128 192 406 696 985
35-40: 38-X-Mas-c 57 114 171 362 619 875
41-50: 43-The Whip app. 54 108 162 343 584 825
51-60: 51-Last Black Pirate. 56,57-Sargon by Kubert 53 106 159 334 567 800
61-67,69-80: 63-Last Mr. Terrific. 66-Wildcat by Kubert 45 90 135 284 480 675
68-Origin & 1st app. Huntress (8/47) 52 104 156 328 552 775
81-Used in **SOTI**, pg. 33,34; Krigstein-a 50 100 150 315 533 750
82-93: 83-Last Sargon. 86-The Atom app. 90-Last Wildcat. 91-Streak begins by Alex Toth. 92-Toth-a (2 pgs.) 45 90 135 284 480 675
94-1st all girl issue 65 130 195 416 708 1000
95-99,101-106: 95-Unmasking of Wonder Woman-c/story. 99-1st app. Astra, Girl of the Future, ends #106. 103-Robot-c. 105-Last 52 pgs. 106-Wonder Woman ends 58 116 174 371 636 900
100-(11-12/50) 68 136 204 435 743 1050
107-(Scarce, 1-2/52)-1st mystery issue; Johnny Peril by Toth(p), 8 pgs. & begins; continues from Danger Trail #5 (3-4/51)(see Comic Cavalcade #15 for 1st app.) 71 142 213 454 777 1100
108-(Scarce)-Johnny Peril by Toth(p) 60 120 180 381 658 935
109-(Scarce)-Johnny Peril by Toth(p) 71 142 213 454 777 1100

NOTE: ***Krigstein** a-(Wildcat)-81, 83, 84. **Moldoff** Black Pirate-1-25; Black Pirate not in 34-36, 43-48. **Oskner** c(i)-89-91, 94-106. Wonder Woman by **H. G. Peter**, all issues except #8, 17-19, 21; c-4-7, 9-18, 20-88, 92, 93. **Toth** a-91, 98; c-107. Wonder Woman c-1-106.*

SENSATION COMICS (Also see All Star Comics 1999 crossover titles)
DC Comics: May, 1999 ($1.99, one-shot)

1-Golden Age Wonder Woman and Hawkgirl; Robinson-s 2.50

SENSATION MYSTERY (Formerly Sensation Comics #1-109)
National Periodical Publ.: No. 110, July-Aug, 1952 - No. 116, July-Aug, 1953

110-Johnny Peril continues 47 94 141 296 498 700
111-116-Johnny Peril in all. 116-M. Anderson-a 47 94 141 296 498 700

NOTE: ***M. Anderson** c-110. **Colan** a-114p. **Giunta** a-112. **G. Kane** c(p)-108, 109, 111-115.*

SENSUOUS STREAKER
Marvel Publ.: 1974 (B&W magazine, 68pgs.)

1 4 8 12 24 37 50

SENTENCES: THE LIFE OF M.F. GRIMM
DC Comics (Vertigo): 2007 ($19.99, B&W graphic novel)

HC-Autobiography of Percy Carey (M.F. Grimm); Ronald Wimberly-a 20.00
SC (2008, $14.99) 15.00

SENTINEL
Marvel Comics: June, 2003 - No. 12, April, 2004 ($2.99/$2.50)

1-Sean McKeever-s/Udon Studios-a 3.00
2-12 3.00
Marvel Age Sentinel Vol. 1: Salvage (2004, $7.99, digest size) r/#1-6 8.00
Vol. 2: No Hero (2004, $7.99, digest size) r/#7-12; sketch pages 8.00

SENTINEL (2nd series)
Marvel Comics: Jan, 2006 - No. 5, May, 2006 ($2.99, limited series)

1-5-Sean McKeever-s/Joe Vriens-a 3.00
Vol. 3: Past Imperfect (2006, $7.99, digest size) r/#1-5 8.00

SENTINELS OF JUSTICE, THE (See Americomics & Captain Paragon &...)

SENTINEL SQUAD O*N*E
Marvel Comics: Mar, 2006 - No. 5, July, 2006 ($2.99, limited series)

1-5-Lopresti-a/Layman-s 3.00
Decimation: Sentinel Squad O*N*E (2006, $13.99, TPB) r/series; sketch pg. by Caliafore 14.00

SENTRY (Also see New Avengers)
Marvel Comics: Sept, 2000 - No. 5, Jan, 2001 ($2.99, limited series)

1-5-Paul Jenkins-s/Jae Lee-a. 3-Spider-Man-c/app. 4-X-Men, FF app. 3.00
.../Fantastic Four (2/01, $2.99) Continues story from #5; Winslade-a 3.00
.../Hulk (2/01, $2.99) Sienkiewicz-c/a 3.00
.../Spider-Man (2/01, $2.99) back story of the Sentry; Leonardi-a 3.00
.../The Void (2/01, $2.99) Conclusion of story; Jae Lee-a 3.00
.../X-Men (2/01, $2.99) Sentry and Archangel; Texeira-a 3.00
TPB (10/01, $24.95) r/#1-5 & all one-shots; Stan Lee interview 25.00
TPB (2nd edition, 2005, $24.99) 25.00

SENTRY (Follows return in New Avengers #10)
Marvel Comics: Nov, 2005 - No. 8, Jun, 2006 ($2.99, limited series)

1-8-Paul Jenkins-s/John Romita Jr.-a. 1-New Avengers app. 3-Hulk app. 3.00
1-(Rough Cut) (12/05, $3.99) Romita sketch art and Jenkins script; cover sketches 4.00
...: Reborn TPB (2006, $21.99) r/#1-8 22.00

SENTRY SPECIAL
Innovation Publishing: 1991 ($2.75, one-shot)(Hero Alliance spin-off)

1-Lost in Space preview (3 pgs.) 2.75

SERAPHIM
Innovation Publishing: May, 1990 ($2.50, mature readers)

1 2.50

SERENITY (Based on 2005 movie Serenity and 2003 TV series Firefly)
Dark Horse Comics: July, 2005 - No. 3, Sept, 2005 ($2.99, limited series)

1-3: Whedon & Matthews-s/Conrad-a. Three covers for each issue by various 4.00
...: Those Left Behind HC (11/07, $19.95, dustjacket) r/series; intro. by Nathan Fillion; pre-production art for the movie; Hughes-c 20.00
...: Those Left Behind TPB (1/06, $9.95) r/series; intro. by Nathan Fillion; Hughes-c 10.00

SERENITY BETTER DAYS (Firefly)
Dark Horse Comics: Mar, 2008 - No. 3, May, 2008 ($2.99, limited series)

1-3: Whedon & Matthews-s/Conrad-a; Adam Hughes-c 3.00

SERGEANT BARNEY BARKER (Becomes G. I. Tales #4 on)
Atlas Comics (MCI): Aug, 1956 - No. 3, Dec, 1956

1-Severin-c/a(4) 18 36 54 105 165 225
2,3: 2-Severin-c/a(4). 3-Severin-c/a(5) 14 28 42 76 108 140

SERGEANT BILKO (Phil Silvers Starring as...) (TV)

Sgt. Fury #146 © MAR

Sgt. Rock #352 © DC

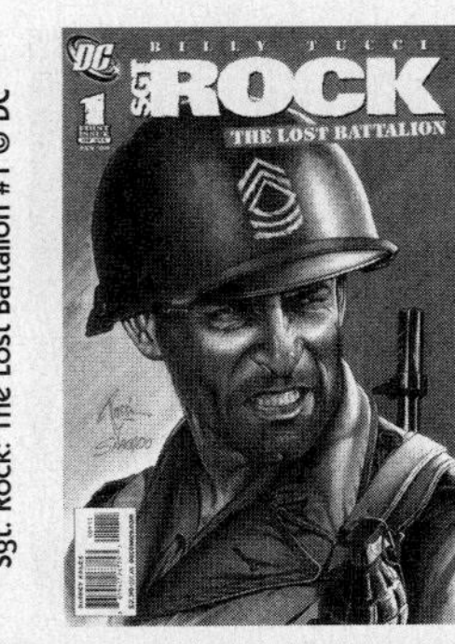

Sgt. Rock: The Lost Battalion #1 © DC

National Periodical Publications: May-June, 1957 - No. 18, Mar-Apr, 1960

	GD 2.0	VG 4.0	FN 6.0	VF 8.0	VF/NM 9.0	NM- 9.2
1-All have Bob Oskner-c	60	120	180	378	639	900
2	32	64	96	190	305	420
3-5	27	54	81	158	254	350
6-18: 11,12,15,17-Photo-c	22	44	66	127	204	280

SGT. BILKO'S PVT. DOBERMAN (TV)
National Periodical Publications: June-July, 1958 - No. 11, Feb-Mar, 1960

	GD 2.0	VG 4.0	FN 6.0	VF 8.0	VF/NM 9.0	NM- 9.2
1-Bob Oskner c-1-4,7,11	25	50	75	185	343	500
2	14	28	42	102	181	260
3-5: 5-Photo-c	10	20	30	71	126	180
6-11: 6,9-Photo-c	8	16	24	52	86	120

SGT. DICK CARTER OF THE U.S. BORDER PATROL (See Holyoke One-Shot)

SGT. FURY (& His Howling Commandos)(See Fury & Special Marvel Edition)
Marvel Comics Group (BPC earlier issues): May, 1963 - No. 167, Dec, 1981

	GD 2.0	VG 4.0	FN 6.0	VF 8.0	VF/NM 9.0	NM- 9.2
1-1st app. Sgt. Nick Fury (becomes agent of Shield in Strange Tales #135); Kirby/Ayers-c/a; 1st Dum-Dum Dugan & the Howlers	212	424	636	1855	3678	5500
2-Kirby-a	50	100	150	413	807	1200
3-5: 3-Reed Richards x-over. 4-Death of Junior Juniper. 5-1st Baron Strucker app.; Kirby-a	25	50	75	183	354	525
6-10: 8-Baron Zemo, 1st Percival Pinkerton app. 9-Hitler-c & app. 10-1st app. Capt. Savage (the Skipper)(9/64)	14	28	42	102	194	285
11,12,14-20: 14-1st Blitz Squad. 18-Death of Pamela Hawley	9	18	27	63	107	150
13-Captain America & Bucky app.(12/64); 2nd solo Capt. America x-over outside The Avengers; Kirby-a	39	78	117	297	574	850
13-2nd printing (1994)	2	4	6	8	10	12
21-24,26,28-30	6	12	18	41	66	90
25,27: 25-Red Skull app. 27-1st app. Eric Koenig; origin Fury's eye patch	6	12	18	43	69	95
31-33,35-50: 35-Eric Koenig joins Howlers. 43-Bob Hope, Glen Miller app. 44-Flashback on Howlers' 1st mission	4	8	12	24	37	50
34-Origin Howling Commandos	4	8	12	26	41	55
51-60	3	6	9	21	32	42
61-67: 64-Capt. Savage & Raiders x-over; peace symbol-c. 67-Last 12¢ issue; flag-c	3	6	9	17	25	32
68-80: 76-Fury's Father app. in WWI story	3	6	9	16	22	28
81-91: 91-Last 15¢ issue	2	4	6	13	18	22
92-(52 pgs.)	3	6	9	16	22	28
93-99: 98-Deadly Dozen x-over	2	4	6	11	16	20
100-Capt. America, Fantastic 4 cameos; Stan Lee, Martin Goodman & others app.	3	6	9	16	22	28
101-120: 101-Origin retold	2	4	6	9	13	16
121-130: 121-123-r/#19-21	2	4	6	8	10	12
131-167: 167-Reprints (from 1963)	2	3	4	6	8	10
133,134-(30¢-c variants, limited dist.)(5,7/76)	3	6	9	16	22	28
141,142-(35¢-c variants, limited dist.)(7,9/77)	4	8	12	22	34	45
Annual 1(1965, 25¢, 72 pgs.)-r/#4,5 & new-a	14	28	42	100	188	275
Special 2(1966)	6	12	18	43	69	95
Special 3(1967) All new material	4	8	12	28	44	60
Special 4(1968)	3	6	9	20	30	40
Special 5-7(1969-11/71)	3	6	9	16	23	30

NOTE: ***Ayers** a-8, Annual 1. **Ditko** a-15i. **Gil Kane** c-37, 96. **Kirby** a-1-7, 13p, 167p(r). Special 5; c-1-8, 10-20, 25, 167p. **Severin** a-44-46, 48, 162, 164; inks-49-79, Special 4, 6; c-4i, 5, 6, 44, 46, 110, 149i, 155i, 162-166. **Sutton** a-57p. Reprints in #80, 82, 85, 87, 89, 91, 93, 95, 99, 101, 103, 105, 107, 109, 111, 121-123, 145-155, 167.*

SGT. FURY AND HIS HOWLING COMMANDOS
Marvel Comics: July, 2009 ($3.99, one-shot)

1-John Paul Leon-a/c; WWII tale set in 1942; Baron Strucker app. 4.00

SGT. FURY AND HIS HOWLING DEFENDERS (See The Defenders #147)

SERGEANT PRESTON OF THE YUKON (TV)
Dell Publishing Co.: No. 344, Aug, 1951 - No. 29, Nov-Jan, 1958-59

	GD 2.0	VG 4.0	FN 6.0	VF 8.0	VF/NM 9.0	NM- 9.2
Four Color 344(#1)-Sergeant Preston & his dog Yukon King begin; painted-c begin, end #18	11	22	33	80	145	210
Four Color 373,397,419('52)	8	16	24	52	86	120
5(11-1/52-53)-10(2-4/54): 6-Bondage-c.	6	12	18	41	66	90
11,12,14-17	6	12	18	37	59	80
13-Origin Sgt. Preston	6	12	18	41	66	90
18-Origin Yukon King; last painted-c	6	12	18	41	66	90
19-29: All photo-c	7	14	21	49	80	110

SGT. ROCK (Formerly Our Army at War; see Brave & the Bold #52 & Showcase #45)
National Periodical Publications/DC Comics: No. 302, Mar, 1977 - No. 422, July, 1988

	GD 2.0	VG 4.0	FN 6.0	VF 8.0	VF/NM 9.0	NM- 9.2
302	4	8	12	26	41	55
303-310	3	6	9	14	20	26
311-320: 318-Reprints	2	4	6	10	14	18
321-350	2	4	6	8	10	12
329-Whitman variant (scarce)	3	6	9	14	19	24
351-399,401-421: 412-Mlle Marie & Haunted Tank	1	2	3	5	6	8
400-(6/85) Anniversary issue	2	4	6	8	10	12
422-1st Joe, Adam, Andy Kubert-a team; last issue	2	4	6	9	12	15
Annual 2-4: 2(1982)-Formerly Sgt. Rock's Prize Battle Tales #1. 3(1983). 4(1984)	2	4	6	8	10	12

NOTE: ***Estrada** a-322, 327, 331, 336, 337, 341, 342i. **Glanzman** a-384, 421. **Kubert** a-302, 303, 305r, 306, 328, 351, 356, 368, 373, 422; c-317, 318r, 319-323, 325-333-on, Annual 2, 3. **Severin** a-347. **Spiegle** a-382, Annual 2, 3. **Thorne** a-384. **Toth** a-385r. **Wildey** a-307, 311, 313, 314.*

SGT. ROCK: BETWEEN HELL AND A HARD PLACE
DC Comics (Vertigo): 2003 ($24.95, hardcover one-shot)

HC-Joe Kubert-a/c; Brian Azzarello-s 25.00
SC (2004, $17.95) 18.00

SGT. ROCK'S COMBAT TALES
DC Comics: 2005 ($9.99, digest)

Vol. 1-Reprints early app. in Our Army at War, G.I. Combat, Star Spangled War Stories 10.00

SGT. ROCK SPECIAL (Sgt. Rock #14 on; see DC Special Series #3)
DC Comics: Oct, 1988 - No. 21, Feb, 1992; No. 1, 1992; No. 2, 1994
($2.00, quarterly/monthly, 52 pgs)

	GD 2.0	VG 4.0	FN 6.0	VF 8.0	VF/NM 9.0	NM- 9.2
1-Reprint begin	2	4	6	8	11	14
2-21: All-r; 5-r/early Sgt. Rock/Our Army at War #81. 7-Tomahawk-r by Thorne. 9-Enemy Ace-r by Kubert. 10-All Rock issue. 11-r/1st Haunted Tank story. 12-All Kubert issue; begins monthly. 13-Dinosaur story by Heath(r). 14-Enemy Ace-r (22 pgs.) by Adams/Kubert. 15-Enemy Ace (22 pgs.) by Kubert. 16-Iron Major-c/story. 16,17-Enemy Ace-r. 19-r/Batman/Sgt. Rock team-up/B&B #108 by Aparo	1	2	3	5	6	8

1 (1992, $2.95, 68 pgs.)-Simonson-c; unpubbed Kubert-a; Glanzman, Russell, Pratt, & Wagner-a 6.00
2 (1994, $2.95) Brereton painted-c 4.00

NOTE: ***Neal Adams** r-1, 8, 14p. **Chaykin** a-2; r-3, 9(2pgs.); c-3. **Drucker** r-6. **Glanzman** r-20. **Golden** a-1. **Heath** a-2; r-5, 9-13, 16, 19, 21. **Krigstein** r-4, 8. **Kubert** r-1-17, 20, 21; c-1p, 2, 8, 14-21. **Miller** r-6p. **Severin** r-3, 6, 10. **Simonson** r-2, 4; c-4. **Thorne** r-7. **Toth** r-2, 8, 11. **Wood** r-4.*

SGT. ROCK SPECTACULAR (See DC Special Series #13)

SGT. ROCK'S PRIZE BATTLE TALES (Becomes Sgt. Rock Annual #2 on; see DC Special Series #18 & 80 Page Giant #7)
National Periodical Publications: Winter, 1964 (Giant - 80 pgs., one-shot)

	GD 2.0	VG 4.0	FN 6.0	VF 8.0	VF/NM 9.0	NM- 9.2
1-Kubert, Heath-r; new Kubert-c	32	64	96	245	473	700

... Replica Edition (2000, $5.95) Reprints entire issue 6.00

SGT. ROCK: THE LOST BATTALION
DC Comics: Jan, 2009 - No. 6, Jun, 2009 ($2.99, limited series)

1-6-Billy Tucci-s/a. 1-Tucci & Sparacio-c 3.00
HC (2009, $24.99, d.j.) r/#1-6; production art; cover art gallery 25.00

SGT. ROCK: THE PROPHECY
DC Comics: Mar, 2006 - No. 6, Aug, 2006 ($2.99, limited series)

1-6-Joe Kubert-s/a/c. 1-Variant covers by Andy and Adam Kubert 3.00
TPB (2007, $17.99) r/#1-6 18.00

SGT. STRYKER'S DEATH SQUAD (See Savage Combat Tales)

SERGIO ARAGONÉS' ACTIONS SPEAK
Dark Horse Comics: Jan, 2001 - No. 6, Jun, 2001 ($2.99, B&W, limited series)

1-6-Aragonés-c/a; wordless one-page cartoons 3.00

SERGIO ARAGONÉS' BLAIR WHICH?
Dark Horse Comics: Dec, 1999 ($2.95, B&W, one-shot)

nn-Aragonés-c/a; Evanier-s. Parody of "Blair Witch Project" movie 3.00

SERGIO ARAGONÉS' BOOGEYMAN
Dark Horse Comics: June, 1998 - No. 4, Sept, 1998 ($2.95, B&W, lim. series)

1-4-Aragonés-c/a 3.00

SERGIO ARAGONÉS DESTROYS DC
DC Comics: June, 1996 ($3.50, one-shot)

1-DC Superhero parody book; Aragonés-c/a; Evanier scripts 3.50

SERGIO ARAGONÉS' DIA DE LOS MUERTOS
Dark Horse Comics: Oct, 1998 ($2.95, one-shot)

1-Aragonés-c/a; Evanier scripts 3.00

SERGIO ARAGONÉS' GROO & RUFFERTO

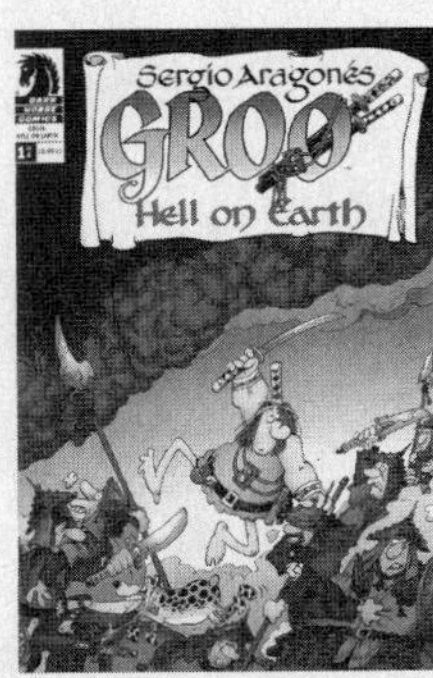

Sergio Aragonés' Groo: Hell n Earth #1 © Sergio Aragonés

Seven Soldiers: Zatanna #1 © DC

Shade, the Changing Man #57 © DC

	GD	VG	FN	VF	VF/NM	NM-
	2.0	4.0	6.0	8.0	9.0	9.2

Dark Horse Comics: Dec, 1998 - No. 4, Mar, 1999 ($2.95, lim. series)

1-3-Aragonés-c/a 3.00

SERGIO ARAGONÉS' GROO: DEATH AND TAXES
Dark Horse Comics: Dec, 2001 - No. 4, Apr, 2002 ($2.99, lim. series)

1-4-Aragonés-c/a; Evanier-s 3.00

SERGIO ARAGONÉS' GROO: HELL ON EARTH
Dark Horse Comics: Nov, 2007 - No. 4, Apr, 2008 ($2.99, lim. series)

1-4-Aragonés-c/a; Evanier-s 3.00

SERGIO ARAGONÉS' GROO: MIGHTIER THAN THE SWORD
Dark Horse Comics: Jan, 2000 - No. 4, Apr, 2000 ($2.95, lim. series)

1-4-Aragonés-c/a; Evanier-s 3.00

SERGIO ARAGONÉS' GROO: THE HOGS OF HORDER
Dark Horse Comics: Oct, 2009 - No. 4, Apr, 2010 ($3.99, lim. series)

1-4-Aragonés-c/a; Evanier-s 4.00

SERGIO ARAGONÉS' GROO THE WANDERER (See Groo...)

SERGIO ARAGONÉS' GROO: 25TH ANNIVERSARY SPECIAL
Dark Horse Comics: Aug, 2007 ($5.99, one-shot)

nn-Aragonés-c/a; Evanier scripts; wraparound cover 6.00

SERGIO ARAGONÉS' LOUDER THAN WORDS
Dark Horse Comics: July, 1997 - No. 6, Dec, 1997 ($2.95, B&W, limited series)

1-6-Aragonés-c/a 3.00

SERGIO ARAGONÉS MASSACRES MARVEL
Marvel Comics: June, 1996 ($3.50, one-shot)

1-Marvel Superhero parody book; Aragonés-c/a; Evanier scripts 3.50

SERGIO ARAGONÉS STOMPS STAR WARS
Marvel Comics: Jan, 2000 ($2.95, one-shot)

1-Star Wars parody; Aragonés-c/a; Evanier scripts 3.00

SEVEN
Intrinsic Comics: July, 2007 ($3.00)

1-Jim Shooter-s/Paul Creddick-a 3.00

SEVEN BLOCK
Marvel Comics (Epic Comics): 1990 ($4.50, one-shot, 52 pgs.)

1-Dixon-s/Zaffino-a 4.50
nn-(IDW Publ., 2004, $5.99) reprints #1 6.00

SEVEN BROTHERS (John Woo's...)
Virgin Comics: Oct, 2006 - No. 5, Feb, 2007 ($2.99)

1-5-Garth Ennis-s/Jeevan Kang-a. 1-Two covers by Amano & Horn. 2-Kang var-c 3.00
TPB (6/07, $14.99) r/#1-5; cover gallery, deleted scenes and concept art 15.00
Volume 2 (9/07 - No. 5, 2/08) 1-Edison George-a. 4,5-David Mack-c 3.00

SEVEN DEAD MEN (See Complete Mystery #1)

SEVEN DWARFS (Also see Snow White)
Dell Publishing Co.: No. 227, 1949 (Disney-Movie)

	GD	VG	FN	VF	VF/NM	NM-
Four Color 227	9	18	27	65	113	160

SEVEN MILES A SECOND
DC Comics (Vertigo Verité): 1996 ($7.95, one-shot)

nn-Wojnarowicz-s/Romberg-a 8.00

SEVEN SAMUROID, THE (See Image Graphic Novel)

SEVEN SEAS COMICS
Universal Phoenix Features/Leader No. 6: Apr, 1946 - No. 6, 1947(no month)

	GD	VG	FN	VF	VF/NM	NM-
1-South Sea Girl by Matt Baker, Capt. Cutlass begin; Tugboat Tessie by Baker app.	90	180	270	576	988	1400
2-Swashbuckler-c	68	136	204	432	746	1060
3,5,6: 3-Six pg. Feldstein-a	67	134	201	425	730	1035
4-Classic Baker-c	87	174	261	553	952	1350

NOTE: *Baker a-1-6; c-3-6.*

SEVEN SOLDIERS OF VICTORY (Book-ends for seven related mini-series)
DC Comics: No. 0, Apr, 2005; No. 1; Dec, 2006 ($2.95/$3.99)

0-Grant Morrison-s/J.H. Williams-a 3.00
1-($3.99) Series conclusion; Grant Morrison-s/J.H. Williams-a 4.00
... Volume One (2006, $14.99) r/#0, Shining Knight #1,2; Zatanna #1,2; Guardian #1,2; and Klarion the Witch Boy #1; intro. by Morrison; character design sketches 15.00
... Volume Two (2006, $14.99) r/Shining Knight #3,4; Zatanna #3; Guardian #3,4; and Klarion the Witch Boy #2,3 15.00
... Volume Three ('06, $14.99) r/Zatanna #4; Mister Miracle #1,2; Bulleteer #1,2; Frankenstein #1 and Klarion the Witch Boy #4; 15.00
... Volume Four ('07, $14.99) r/Mister Miracle #3,4; Bulleteer #3,4; Frankenstein #2-4 and Seven Soldiers of Victory #1; script pages 15.00

SEVEN SOLDIERS: BULLETEER
DC Comics: Jan, 2006 - No. 4, May, 2006 ($2.99, limited series)

1-4-Grant Morrison-s/Yanick Paquette-a/c 3.00

SEVEN SOLDIERS: FRANKENSTEIN
DC Comics: Jan, 2006 - No. 4, May, 2006 ($2.99, limited series)

1-4-Grant Morrison-s/Doug Mahnke-a/c 3.00

SEVEN SOLDIERS: GUARDIAN
DC Comics: May, 2005 - No. 4, Nov, 2005 ($2.99, limited series)

1-4-Grant Morrison-s/Cameron Stewart-a; Newsboy Army app. 3.00

SEVEN SOLDIERS: KLARION THE WITCH BOY
DC Comics: June, 2005 - No. 4, Dec, 2005 ($2.99, limited series)

1-4-Grant Morrison-s/Frazer Irving-a 3.00

SEVEN SOLDIERS: MISTER MIRACLE
DC Comics: Nov, 2005 - No. 4, May, 2006 ($2.99, limited series)

1-4: 1-Grant Morrison-s/Pasqual Ferry-a/c. 3,4-Freddie Williams II-a/c 3.00

SEVEN SOLDIERS: SHINING KNIGHT
DC Comics: May, 2005 - No. 4, Oct, 2005 ($2.99, limited series)

1-4-Grant Morrison-s/Simone Bianchi-a 3.00

SEVEN SOLDIERS: ZATANNA
DC Comics: June, 2005 - No. 4, Dec, 2005 ($2.99, limited series)

1-4-Grant Morrison-s/Ryan Sook-a 3.00

1776 (See Charlton Classic Library)

7TH VOYAGE OF SINBAD, THE (Movie)
Dell Publishing Co.: Sept, 1958 (photo-c)

	GD	VG	FN	VF	VF/NM	NM-
Four Color 944-Buscema-a	12	24	36	85	155	225

77 SUNSET STRIP (TV)
Dell Publ. Co./Gold Key: No. 1066, Jan-Mar, 1960 - No. 2, Feb, 1963 (All photo-c)

	GD	VG	FN	VF	VF/NM	NM-
Four Color 1066-Toth-a	10	20	30	71	126	180
Four Color 1106,1159-Toth-a	8	16	24	58	97	135
Four Color 1211,1263,1291, 01-742-209(7-9/62)-Manning-a in all	8	16	24	54	90	125
1,2: Manning-a. 1(11/62-G.K.)	8	16	24	54	90	125

77TH BENGAL LANCERS, THE (TV)
Dell Publishing Co.: May, 1957

	GD	VG	FN	VF	VF/NM	NM-
Four Color 791-Photo-c	7	14	21	47	76	105

SEYMOUR, MY SON (See More Seymour)
Archie Publications (Radio Comics): Sept, 1963

	GD	VG	FN	VF	VF/NM	NM-
1-DeCarlo-a?	3	6	9	20	30	40

SHADE, THE (See Starman)
DC Comics: Apr, 1997 - No. 4, July, 1997 ($2.25, limited series)

1-4-Robinson-s/Harris-c: 1-Gene Ha-a. 2-Williams/Gray-a 3-Blevins-a. 4-Zulli-a 3.00

SHADE, THE CHANGING MAN (See Cancelled Comic Cavalcade)
National Per. Publ./DC Comics: June-July, 1977 - No. 8, Aug-Sept, 1978

	GD	VG	FN	VF	VF/NM	NM-
1-1st app. Shade; Ditko-c/a in all	2	4	6	10	14	18
2-8	2	3	4	6	8	10

SHADE, THE CHANGING MAN (2nd series) (Also see Suicide Squad #16)
DC Comics (Vertigo imprint #33 on): July, 1990 - No. 70, Apr, 1996 ($1.50-$2.25, mature)

1-($2.50, 52 pgs.)-Peter Milligan scripts in all 4.00
2-41,45-49,51-59: 6-Preview of World Without End. 17-Begin $1.75-c. 33-Metallic ink on-c. 41-Begin $1.95-c 2.50
42-44-John Constantine app. 3.00
50-($2.95, 52 pgs.) 3.50
60-70: 60-begin $2.25-c 2.50
...: Edge of Vision TPB (2009, $19.99) r/#7-13 20.00
...: The American Scream TPB (2003, 2009, $17.95/$17.99) r/#1-6 18.00

NOTE: *Bachalo a-1-9, 11-13, 15-21, 23-26, 33-39, 42-45, 47, 49, 50; c-30, 33-41.*

SHADO: SONG OF THE DRAGON (See Green Arrow #63-66)
DC Comics: 1992 - No. 4, 1992 ($4.95, limited series, 52 pgs.)

Book One - Four: Grell scripts; Morrow-a(i) 5.00

Shadow Comics V2 #12 © Condé Nast

Shadowhawk #13 © Image

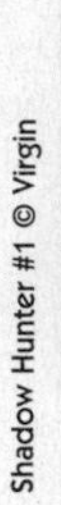

Shadow Hunter #1 © Virgin

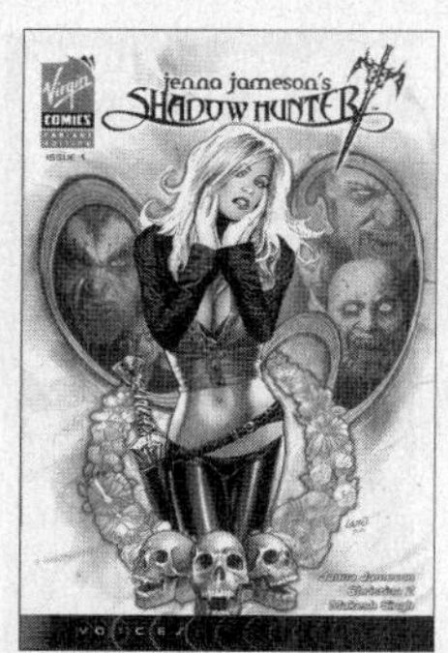

	GD 2.0	VG 4.0	FN 6.0	VF 8.0	VF/NM 9.0	NM- 9.2

SHADOW, THE (See Batman #253, 259 & Marvel Graphic Novel #35)

SHADOW, THE (Pulp, radio)
Archie Comics (Radio Comics): Aug, 1964 - No. 8, Sept, 1965 (All 12¢)

1-Jerrry Siegel scripts in all; Shadow-c. 8 16 24 56 93 130
2-8: 2-App. in super-hero costume on-c only; Reinman-a(backup). 3-Superhero begins; Reinman-a (book-length novel). 3,4,6,7-The Fly 1 pg. strips. 4-8-Reinman-a. 5-8-Siegel scripts. 7-Shield app. 5 10 15 32 51 70

SHADOW, THE
National Periodical Publications: Oct-Nov, 1973 - No. 12, Aug-Sept, 1975

1-Kaluta-a begins 6 12 18 39 62 85
2 3 6 9 20 30 40
3-Kaluta/Wrightson-a 4 8 12 22 34 45
4,6-Kaluta-a ends. 4-Chaykin, Wrightson part-i 3 6 9 18 27 35
5,7-12: 11-The Avenger (pulp character) x-over 2 4 6 11 16 20
NOTE: ***Craig** a-10. **Cruz** a-10-12. **Kaluta** a-1, 2, 3p, 4, 6; c-1-4, 6, 10-12. **Kubert** c-9. **Robbins** a-5, 7-9; c-5, 7, 8.*

SHADOW, THE
DC Comics: May, 1986 - No. 4, Aug, 1986 (limited series)

1-4: Howard Chaykin art in all 3.00
Blood & Judgement ($12.95)-r/1-4 13.00

SHADOW, THE
DC Comics: Aug, 1987 - No. 19, Jan, 1989 ($1.50)

1-19: Andrew Helfer scripts in all. 3.00
Annual 1,2 (12/87, '88,)-2-The Shadow dies; origin retold (story inspired by the movie "Citizen Kane"). 4.00
NOTE: ***Kyle Baker** a-7i, 8-19, Annual 2. **Chaykin** c-Annual 1. **Helfer** scripts in all. **Orlando** a-Annual 1. **Rogers** c/a-7. **Sienkiewicz** c/a-1-6.*

SHADOW, THE (Movie)
Dark Horse Comics: June, 1994 - No. 2, July, 1994 ($2.50, limited series)

1,2-Adaptation from Universal Pictures film 3.00
NOTE: ***Kaluta** c/a-1, 2.*

SHADOW AND DOC SAVAGE, THE
Dark Horse Comics: July, 1995 - No. 2, Aug, 1995 ($2.95, limited series)

1,2 3.50

SHADOW AND THE MYSTERIOUS 3, THE
Dark Horse Comics: Sept, 1994 ($2.95, one-shot)

1-Kaluta co-scripts. 3.00
NOTE: ***Stevens** c-1.*

SHADOW CABINET (See Heroes)
DC Comics (Milestone): Jan, 1994 - No. 17, Oct, 1995 ($1.75/$2.50)

0,1-17: 0-($2.50, 52 pgs.)-Silver ink-c; Simonson-c. 1-Byrne-c 2.50

SHADOW COMICS (Pulp, radio)
Street & Smith Publications: Mar, 1940 - V9#5, Aug-Sept, 1949
NOTE: *The Shadow first appeared on radio in 1929 and was featured in pulps beginning in April, 1931, written by Walter Gibson. The early covers of this series were reprinted from the pulp covers.*

V1#1-Shadow, Doc Savage, Bill Barnes, Nick Carter (radio), Frank Merriwell, Iron Munro, the Astonishing Man begin 461 922 1383 3319 5810 8600
2-The Avenger begins, ends #6; Capt. Fury only app. 210 420 630 1334 2292 3250
3(nn-5/40)-Norgil the Magician app.; cover is exact swipe of Shadow pulp from 1/33 148 296 444 947 1624 2300
4,5: 4-The Three Musketeers begins, ends #8. 5-Doc Savage ends 110 220 330 704 1202 1700
6,8,9: 9-Norgil the Magician app. 94 188 282 597 1024 1450
7-Origin/1st app. The Hooded Wasp & Wasplet (11/40); series ends V3#8; Hooded Wasp/Wasplet app. on-c thru #9 98 196 294 622 1074 1525
10-Origin The Iron Ghost, ends #11; The Dead End Kids begins, ends #14 94 188 282 597 1024 1450
11-Origin Hooded Wasp & Wasplet retold 94 188 282 597 1024 1450
12-Dead End Kids app. 87 174 261 553 952 1350
V2#1(11/41, Vol.II#2 in indicia) Dead End Kids -s 84 168 252 538 919 1300
2-(Rare, Vol.II#3 in indicia) Giant ant-c 161 322 483 1030 1765 2500
3-Origin & 1st app. Supersnipe (3/42); series begins; Little Nemo story (Vol.II#4 in indicia) 137 274 411 870 1498 2125
4,5: 4,8-Little Nemo story 73 146 219 464 800 1135
6-9: 6-Blackstone the Magician story 70 140 210 445 765 1085
10,12: 10-Supersnipe app.' Skull-c 68 136 204 432 746 1060
11-Classic Devil Kyoti World War 2 sunburst-c 79 158 237 502 864 1225
V3#1,2,5,7-12: 10-Doc Savage begins, not in V5#5, V6#10-12, V8#4 67 134 201 426 731 1035
3-1st Monstrodamus-c/sty 74 148 222 470 810 1150
4-2nd Monstrodamus; classic-c of giant salamander getting shot in the head 77 154 231 493 847 1200
6-Classic underwater-c 81 162 243 518 884 1250
V4#1-12 47 94 141 296 503 710
V5#1-12 42 84 126 265 445 625
V6#1-11: 9-Intro. Shadow, Jr. (12/46) 39 78 117 240 395 550
12-Powell-c/a; atom bomb panels 42 84 126 265 445 625
V7#1,2,5,7-9,12: 2,5-Shadow, Jr. app.; Powell-a 39 78 117 240 395 550
3,6,11-Powell-c/a 43 86 129 271 461 650
4-Powell-c/a; Atom bomb panels 45 90 135 284 480 675
10(1/48)-Flying Saucer-c/story (2nd of this theme; see The Spirit 9/28/47); Powell-c/a 57 114 171 362 624 885
V8#1-12-Powell-a. 8-Powell Spider-c/a 43 86 129 271 461 650
V9#1,5-Powell-a 42 84 126 265 445 625
2-4-Powell-c/a 43 86 129 271 461 650
NOTE: ***Binder** c-V3#1. **Powell** art in most issues beginning V6#12. Painted c-1-6.*

SHADOWDRAGON
DC Comics: 1995 ($3.50, annual)

Annual 1-Year One story 3.50

SHADOW EMPIRES: FAITH CONQUERS
Dark Horse Comics: Aug, 1994 - No. 4, Nov, 1994 ($2.95, limited series)

1-4 3.00

SHADOWHAWK (See Images of Shadowhawk, New Shadowhawk, Shadowhawk II, Shadowhawk III & Youngblood #2)
Image Comics (Shadowline Ink): Aug, 1992 - No. 4, Mar, 1993; No. 12, Aug, 1994 - No. 18, May, 1995 ($1.95/$2.50)

1-($2.50)-Embossed silver foil stamped-c; Valentino/Liefeld-c; Valentino-c/a/scripts in all; has coupon for Image #0; 1st Shadowline Ink title 4.00
1-With coupon missing 2.00
1-($1.95)-Newsstand version w/o foil stamp 2.50
2-13,0,1418: 2-Shadowhawk poster w/McFarlane-i; brief Spawn app.; wraparound-c w/silver ink highlights. 3-($2.50)-Glow-in-the-dark-c. 4-Savage Dragon-c/story; Valentino/Larsen-c. 5-11-(See Shadowhawk II and III). 12-Cont'd from Shadowhawk III; pull-out poster by Texeira.13-w/ShadowBone poster; WildC.A.T.s app. 0 (10/94)-Liefeld c/a/story; ShadowBart poster. 14-(10/94, $2.50)-The Others app. 16-Supreme app. 17-Spawn app.; story cont'd from Badrock & Co. #6. 18-Shadowhawk dies; Savage Dragon & Brigade app. 2.50
Special 1(12/94, $3.50, 52 pgs.)-Silver Age Shadowhawk flip book 3.50
Gallery (4/94, $1.95) 2.50
Out of the Shadows ($19.95)-r/Youngblood #2, Shadowhawk #1-4, Image Zero #0, Operation: Urban Storm (Never published) 20.00
.../Vampirella (2/95, $4.95)-Pt.2 of x-over (See Vampirella/Shadowhawk for Pt. 1) 5.00
NOTE: *Shadowhawk was originally a four issue limited series. The story continued in Shadowhawk II, Shadowhawk III & then became Shadowhawk again with issue #12.*

SHADOWHAWK II (Follows Shadowhawk #4)
Image Comics (Shadowline Ink): V2#1, May, 1993 - V2#3, Aug, 1993 ($3.50/$1.95/$2.95, limited series)

V2#1 ($3.50)-Cont'd from Shadowhawk #4; die-cut mirricard-c 3.50
2 ($1.95)-Foil embossed logo; reveals identity; gold-c variant exists 2.50
3 ($2.95)-Pop-up-c w/Pact ashcan insert 3.00

SHADOWHAWK III (Follows Shadowhawk II #3)
Image Comics (Shadowline Ink): V3#1, Nov, 1993 - V3#4, Mar, 1994 ($1.95, limited series);

V3#1-4: 1-Cont'd from Shadowhawk II; intro Valentine; gold foil & red foil stamped-c variations. 2-(52 pgs.)-Shadowhawk contracts HIV virus; U.S. Male by M. Anderson (p) in free 16 pg.insert. 4-Continues in Shadowhawk #12 2.50

SHADOWHAWK (Volume 2) (Also see New Man #4)
Image Comics: May, 2005 - Present ($2.99/$3.50)

1-4-Eddie Collins as Shadowhawk; Rodríguez-a; Valentino-co-plotter 3.00
5-15-($3.50) 5-Cover swipe of Superman Vs. Spider-Man treasury edition 3.50
...One Shot #1 (7/06, $1.99) r/Return of Shadowhawk 2.50
Return of Shadowhawk (12/04, $2.99) Valentino-s/a/c; Eddie Collins origin retold 3.00

SHADOWHAWKS OF LEGEND
Image Comics (Shadowline Ink): Nov, 1995 ($4.95, one-shot)

nn-Stories of past Shadowhawks by Kurt Busiek, Beau Smith & Alan Moore 5.00

SHADOW, THE: HELL'S HEAT WAVE (Movie, pulp, radio)
Dark Horse Comics: Apr, 1995 - No. 3, June, 1995 ($2.95, limited series)

1-3: Kaluta story 3.00

SHADOW HUNTER (Jenna Jameson's...)
Virgin Comics: No. 0, Dec, 2007 - Present ($2.99)

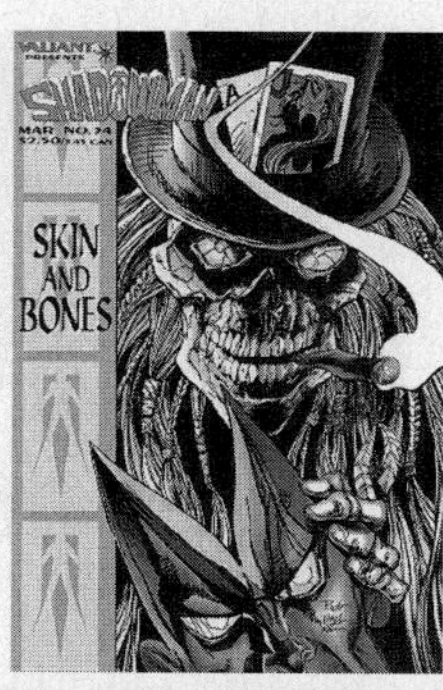

Shadowman #34 © Voyager Comm.

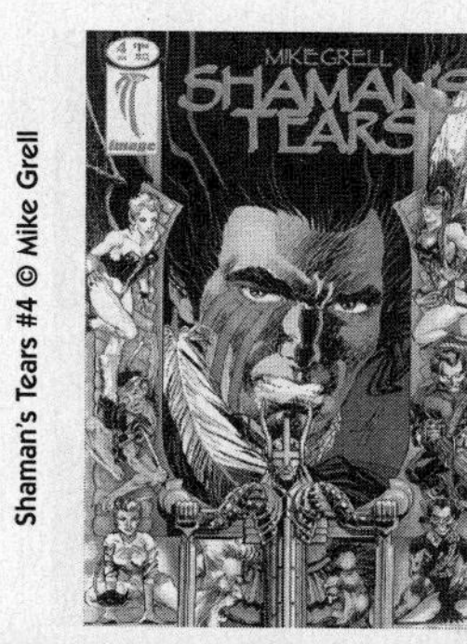

Shaman's Tears #4 © Mike Grell

Shanna, the She-Devil #3 © MAR

GD VG FN VF VF/NM NM-
2.0 4.0 6.0 8.0 9.0 9.2

0-Preview issue; creator interviews; gallery of covers for upcoming issues; Greg Horn-c 3.00
1-3: 1-Two covers by Horn & Land; Jameson & Christina Z-s/Singh-a. 2-Three covers 3.00

SHADOWHUNT SPECIAL
Image Comics (Extreme Studios): Apr, 1996 ($2.50)
1-Retells origin of past Shadowhawks; Valentino script; Chapel app. 2.50

SHADOW, THE: IN THE COILS OF THE LEVIATHAN (Movie, pulp, radio)
Dark Horse Comics: Oct, 1993 - No. 4, Apr, 1994 ($2.95, limited series)
1-4-Kaluta-c & co-scripter 3.00
Trade paperback (10/94, $13.95)-r/1-4 14.00

SHADOWLINE SAGA: CRITICAL MASS, A
Marvel Comics (Epic): Jan, 1990 - No. 7, July, 1990 ($4.95, lim. series, 68 pgs)
1-6: Dr. Zero, Powerline, St. George 5.00
7 ($5.95, 84 pgs.)-Morrow-a, Williamson-c(i) 6.00

SHADOWMAN (See X-O Manowar #4)
Valiant/Acclaim Comics (Valiant): May, 1992 - No. 43, Dec, 1995 ($2.50)
1-Partial origin 5.00
2-5: 3-1st app. Sousa the Soul Eater 4.00
6-43: 8-1st app. Master Darque. 16-1st app. Dr. Mirage (8/93). 15-Minor Turok app. 17,18-Archer & Armstrong x-over. 19-Aerosmith-c/story. 23-Dr. Mirage x-over. 24-(4/94). 25-Bound-in trading card. 29-Chaos Effect. 43-Shadowman jumps to his death 2.50
0-($2.50, 4/94)-Regular edition 2.50
0-($3.50)-Wraparound chromium-c edition 3.50
0-Gold 15.00
Yearbook 1 (12/94, $3.95) 4.00

SHADOWMAN (Volume 2)
Acclaim Comics (Valiant Heroes): Mar, 1997 - No. 20 ($2.50, mature)
1-20: 1-1st app. Zero; Garth Ennis scripts begin, end #4. 2-Zero becomes new Shadowman. 4-Origin; Jack Boniface (original Shadowman) rises from the grave. 5-Jamie Delano scripts begin. 9-Copycat-c 2.50
1-Variant painted cover 2.50
#0 Gold 5.00

SHADOWMAN (Volume 3)
Acclaim Comics: July, 1999 - No. 5, Nov, 1999 ($3.95/$2.50)
1-($3.95)-Abnett & Lanning-s/Broome & Benjamin-a 4.00
2-5-($2.50): 3,4-Flip book with Unity 2000 2.50

SHADOWMASTERS
Marvel Comics: Oct, 1989 - No.4, Jan, 1990 ($3.95, squarebound, 52 pgs.)
1-4: Heath-a(i). 1-Jim Lee-c; story cont'd from Punisher 4.00

SHADOW OF THE BATMAN
DC Comics: Dec, 1985 - No. 5, Apr, 1986 ($1.75, limited series)
1-Detective-r (all have wraparound-c) 1 2 3 5 6 8
2,3,5: 3-Penguin-c & cameo. 5-Clayface app. 6.00
4-Joker-c/story 1 2 3 4 5 7
NOTE: *Austin a(new)-2i, 3i; r-2-4i.* ***Rogers*** *a(new)-1, 2p, 3p, 4, 5; r-1-5p; c-1-5.* ***Simonson*** *a-1r.*

SHADOW OF THE TORTURER, THE
Innovation: July, 1991 - No. 3, 1992 ($2.50, limited series)
1-3: Based on Pocket Books novel 2.50

SHADOW ON THE TRAIL (See Zane Grey & Four Color #604)

SHADOWPACT (See Day of Vengeance)
DC Comics: Jul, 2006 - No. 25, Jul, 2008 ($2.99)
1-25: 1-Bill Willingham-s; Detective Chimp, Ragman, Blue Devil, Nightshade, Enchantress and Nightmaster app. 1-Superman app. 13-Zauriel app.; S. Hampton-a 3.00
...: Cursed TPB (2007, $14.99) r/#4,9-13 15.00
...: Darkness and Light TPB (2008, $14.99) r/#14-19 15.00
...: The Burning Age TPB (2008, $17.99) r/#20-25 18.00
...: The Pentacle Plot TPB (2007, $14.99) r/#1-3,5-8 15.00

SHADOW PLAY (Tales of the Supernatural)
Whitman Publications: June, 1982
1-Painted-c 1 2 3 5 6 8

SHADOWPLAY
IDW Publ.: Sept, 2005 - No. 4, Dec, 2005 ($3.99)
1-4-Benson-s/Templesmith-a; Christina Z-s/Wood-a; 2 covers by Templesmith & Wood 4.00
TPB (3/06, $17.99) r/series; flip book format 18.00

SHADOW REAVERS
Black Bull Ent.: Oct, 2001 - No. 5, Mar, 2002 ($2.99)
1-5-Nelson-a; two covers for each issue 3.00

GD VG FN VF VF/NM NM-
2.0 4.0 6.0 8.0 9.0 9.2

Limited Preview Edition (5/01, no cover price) 2.50

SHADOW RIDERS
Marvel Comics UK, Ltd.: June, 1993 - No. 4, Sept, 1993 ($1.75, limited series)
1-($2.50)-Embossed-c; Cable-c/story 2.75
2-4-Cable app. 2-Ghost Rider app. 2.50

SHADOWS
Image Comics: Feb, 2003 - No. 4, Nov, 2003 ($2.95)
1-4-Jade Dodge-s/Matt Camp-a/c 3.00

SHADOWS & LIGHT
Marvel Comics: Feb, 1998 - No. 3, July, 1998 ($2.99, B&W, quarterly)
1-3: 1-B&W anthology of Marvel characters; Black Widow art by Gene Ha, Hulk by Wrightson, Iron Man by Ditko & Daredevil by Stelfreeze; Stelfreeze painted-c. 2-Weeks, Sharp, Starlin, Thompson-a. 3-Buscema, Grindberg, Giffen, Layton-a 3.00

SHADOW'S FALL
DC Comics (Vertigo): Nov, 1994 - No. 6, Apr, 1995 ($2.95, limited series)
1-6: Van Fleet-c/a in all. 3.00

SHADOWS FROM BEYOND (Formerly Unusual Tales)
Charlton Comics: V2#50, October, 1966
V2#50-Ditko-c 4 8 12 22 34 45

SHADOW STATE
Broadway Comics: Dec, 1995 - No. 5, Apr, 1996 ($2.50)
1-5: 1,2-Fatale back-up story; Cockrum-a(p) 2.50
Preview Edition 1,2 (10-11/95, $2.50, B&W) 2.50

SHADOW STRIKES!, THE (Pulp, radio)
DC Comics: Sept, 1989 - No.31, May, 1992 ($1.75)
1-4,7-31: 31-Mignola-c 2.50
5,6-Doc Savage x-over 4.00
Annual 1 (1989, $3.50, 68 pgs.)-Spiegle a; Kaluta-c 3.50

SHADOW WAR OF HAWKMAN
DC Comics: May, 1985 - No. 4, Aug, 1985 (limited series)
1-4 2.50

SHAGGY DOG & THE ABSENT-MINDED PROFESSOR (See Four Color #1199, Movie Comics & Walt Disney Showcase #46)(Disney-Movie)
Dell Publ. Co.: No. 985, May, 1959
Four Color 985 7 14 21 50 83 115

SHALOMAN (Jewish-themed stories and history)
Al Wiesner/ Mark 1 Comics: 1989 - Present (B&W)
V1#1-Al Wiesner-s/a in all 4.50
2-9 2.50
V2 #1(The New Adventures)-4,6-10, V3 (The Legend of...) #1-12 2.75
V2 #5 (Color)-Shows Vol 2, No. 4 in indicia 3.00
V4 (The Saga of ...) #1(2004), 2-8: 8-Chanukah & The Holocaust 2.75
...: The Sequel (2009) 2.75
The Saga of Shaloman (20th Anniversary Edition) TPB (10/08, $15.99) r/V4 #1-8 16.00

SHAMAN'S TEARS (Also see Maggie the Cat)
Image Comics (Creative Fire Studio): 5/93 - No. 2, 8/93; No. 3, 11/94 - No. 0, 1/96 ($2.50/$1.95)
0-2: 0-(DEC-c, 1/96)-Last Issue. 1-(5/93)-Embossed red foil-c; Grell-c/a & scripts in all. 2-Cover unfolds into poster (8/93-c, 7/93 inside) 2.50
3-12: 3-Begin $1.95-c. 5-Re-intro Jon Sable. 12-Re-intro Maggie the Cat (1 pg.) 2.50

SHANG-CHI: MASTER OF KUNG-FU ("Master of Kung Fu" on cover for #1&2)
Marvel Comics: Nov, 2002 - No. 6, Apr, 2003 ($2.99, limited series)
1-6-Moench-s/Gulacy-c/a 3.00
...One-Shot 1 (11/09, $3.99, B&W) Deadpool app. 4.00
... Vol. 1: The Hellfire Apocalypse TPB (2003, $14.99) r/#1-6 15.00

SHANGRI-LA
Image Comics: Jan, 2004 ($7.95, B&W, square-bound graphic novel)
1-Marc Bryant-s/Shepherd Hendrix-a 8.00

SHANNA, THE SHE-DEVIL (See Savage Tales #8)
Marvel Comics Group: Dec, 1972 - No. 5, Aug, 1973 (All are 20¢ issues)
1-1st app. Shanna; Steranko-c; Tuska-a(p) 4 8 12 22 34 45
2-Steranko-c; heroin drug story 3 6 9 18 27 35
3-5 2 4 6 11 16 20

SHANNA, THE SHE-DEVIL
Marvel Comics: Apr, 2005 - No. 7, Oct, 2005 ($3.50, limited series)

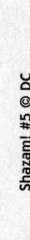

Shaolin Cowboy #1 © Geof Darrow

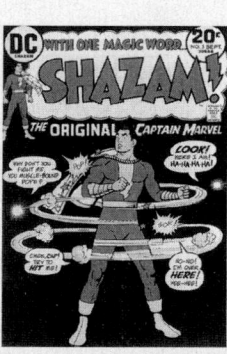

Shazam! #5 © DC

She-Hulk (2nd series) #15 © MAR

	GD 2.0	VG 4.0	FN 6.0	VF 8.0	VF/NM 9.0	NM- 9.2

1-7-Reintro of Shanna; Frank Cho-s/a/c in all 3.50
HC (2005, $24.99, dust jacket) r/#1-7 25.00
SC (2006, $16.99) r/#1-7 17.00

SHANNA, THE SHE-DEVIL: SURVIVAL OF THE FITTEST
Marvel Comics: Oct, 2007 - No. 4, Jan, 2008 ($2.99, limited series)

1-4-Khari Evans-a/c; Gray & Palmiotti-s 3.00
SC (2008, $10.99) r/#1-4 11.00

SHAOLIN COWBOY
Burlyman Entertainment: Dec, 2004 - Present ($3.50)

1-7-Geof Darrow-s/a. 3-Moebius-c 3.50

SHARK FIGHTERS, THE (Movie)
Dell Publishing Co.: Jan, 1957

Four Color 762-Buscema-a; photo-c 7 14 21 50 83 115

SHARK-MAN
Thrill House/Image Comics: Jul, 2006; Jul, 2007; Jan, 2008 - No. 3, Jun, 2008 ($3.99/$3.50)

1,2: 1-(Thrill House, 7/06, $3.99)-Steve Pugh-s/a. 2-(Image Comics, 7/07) 4.00
1-3: 1-(Image, 1/08, $3.50) reprints Thrill House #1 3.50

SHARKY
Image Comics: Feb, 1998 - No. 4, 1998 ($2.50, bi-monthly)

1-4: 1-Mask app.; Elliot-s/a. Horley painted-c. 3-Three covers by Horley, Bisley, & Horley/Elliot. 4-Two covers (swipe of Avengers #4 and wraparound) 2.50
1-($2.95) "$1,000,000" variant 3.00
2-($2.50) Savage Dragon variant-c 2.50

SHARP COMICS (Slightly large size)
H. C. Blackerby: Winter, 1945-46 - V1#2, Spring, 1946 (52 pgs.)

V1#1-Origin Dick Royce Planetarian 40 80 120 246 411 575
2-Origin The Pioneer; Michael Morgan, Dick Royce, Sir Gallagher, Planetarian, Steve Hagen, Weeny and Pop app. 36 72 108 211 343 475

SHARPY FOX (See Comic Capers & Funny Frolics)
I. W. Enterprises/Super Comics: 1958; 1963

1,2-I.W. Reprint (1958): 2-r/Kiddie Kapers #1 2 4 6 8 10 12
14-Super Reprint (1963) 2 4 6 8 10 12

SHATTER (See Jon Sable #25-30)
First Comics: June, 1985; Dec, 1985 - No. 14, Apr, 1988. ($1.75, Baxter paper/deluxe paper)

1 (6/85)-1st computer generated-a in a comic book (1st printing) 3.00
1-(2nd print.); 1(12/85)-14: computer generated-a & lettering in all 2.50
Special 1 (1988) 2.50

SHATTERED IMAGE
Image Comics (WildStorm Productions): Aug, 1996 - No. 4, Dec, 1996 ($2.50, lim. series)

1-4: 1st Image company-wide x-over; Kurt Busiek scripts in all. 1-Tony Daniel-c/a(p). 2-Alex Ross-c/swipe (Kingdom Come) by Ryan Benjamin & Travis Charest 2.50

SHAUN OF THE DEAD (Movie)
IDW Publishing: June, 2005 - No. 4, Sept, 2005 ($3.99, limited series)

1-4-Adaptation of 2004 movie; Zach Howard-a 4.00
TPB (12/05, $17.99) r/series; sketch pages and cover gallery 18.00

SHAZAM (See Billy Batson and the Magic of Shazam!, Giant Comics to Color, Limited Collectors' Edition, Power Of Shazam! and Trials of Shazam!)

SHAZAM! (TV)(See World's Finest #253 for story from unpublished #36)
National Periodical Publ./DC Comics: Feb, 1973 - No. 35, May-June, 1978

1-1st revival of original Captain Marvel since G.A. (origin retold), by C.C. Beck; Mary Marvel & Captain Marvel Jr. app.; Superman-c 6 12 18 39 62 85
2-5: 2-Infinity photo-c.; re-intro Mr. Mind & Tawny. 3-Capt. Marvel-r. (10/46). 4-Origin retold; Capt. Marvel-r. (1949). 5-Capt. Marvel Jr. origin retold; Capt. Marvel-r. (1948, 7 pgs.) 3 6 9 16 23 30
6,7,9-11: 6-photo-c; Capt. Marvel-r (1950, 6 pgs.). 9-Mr. Mind app. 10-Last C.C. Beck issue. 11-Schaffenberger-a begins. 3 6 9 14 19 24
8 (100 pgs.) 8-r/Capt. Marvel Jr. by Raboy; origin/C.M. #80; origin Mary Marvel/C.M.A. #18; origin Mr. Tawny/C.M.A. #79 6 12 18 39 62 85
12-17-(All 100 pgs.). 15-vs. Lex Luthor & Mr. Mind 5 10 15 30 48 65
18-24,26-30: 21-24-All reprints. 26-Sivana app. (10/76). 27-Kid Eternity teams up w/Capt. Marvel. 28-1st S.A. app. of Black Adam. 30-1st DC app. 3 Lt. Marvels 2 4 6 10 14 18
25-1st app. Isis 2 4 6 13 18 22
31-35: 31-1st DC app. Minuteman. 34-Origin Capt. Nazi & Capt. Marvel Jr. retold 2 4 6 13 18 22
...: The Greatest Stories Ever Told TPB (2008, $24.99) reprints; Alex Ross-c 25.00

NOTE: *Reprints in #1-8, 10, 12-17, 21-24.* ***Beck*** *a-1-10, 12-17r, 21-24r; c-1, 3-9.* ***Nasser*** *c-35p.* ***Newton*** *a-35p.* ***Raboy*** *a-5r, 8r, 17r.* ***Schaffenberger*** *a-11, 14-20, 25, 26, 27p, 28, 29-31p, 33i, 35i; c-20, 22, 23, 25, 26i, 27i, 28-33.*

SHAZAM! AND THE SHAZAM FAMILY! ANNUAL
DC Comics: 2002 ($5.95, squarebound, one-shot)

1-Reprints Golden Age stories including 1st Mary Marvel and 1st Black Adam 6.00

SHAZAM!: POWER OF HOPE
DC Comics: Nov, 2000 ($9.95, treasury size, one-shot)

nn-Painted art by Alex Ross; story by Alex Ross and Paul Dini 10.00

SHAZAM!: THE MONSTER SOCIETY OF EVIL
DC Comics: 2007 - No. 4, 2007 ($5.99, square-bound, limited series)

1-4: Jeff Smith-s/a/c in all. 1-Retelling of origin. 2-Mary Marvel & Dr. Sivana app. 6.00
HC (2007, $29.99, over-sized with dust jacket that unfolds to a poster) r/#1-4; Alex Ross intro.; Smith afterword; sketch pages, script pages and production notes 30.00
SC (2009, $19.99) r/#1-4; Alex Ross intro. 20.00

SHAZAM: THE NEW BEGINNING
DC Comics: Apr, 1987 - No. 4, July, 1987 (Legends spin-off) (Limited series)

1-4: 1-New origin & 1st modern app. Captain Marvel; Marvel Family cameo. 2-4-Sivana & Black Adam app. 3.00

SHEA THEATRE COMICS
Shea Theatre: No date (1940's) (32 pgs.)

nn-Contains Rocket Comics; MLJ cover in one color 10 20 30 56 76 95

SHE-BAT (See Murcielaga, She-Bat & Valeria the She-Bat)

SHE-DRAGON (See Savage Dragon #117)
Image Comics: July, 2006 ($5.99, one-shot)

nn- She-Dragon in Dimension-X; origin retold; Franchesco-a/Larsen-s; sketch pages 6.00

SHEENA (Movie)
Marvel Comics: Dec, 1984 - No. 2, Feb, 1985 (limited series)

1,2-r/Marvel Comics Super Special #34; Tanya Roberts movie 4.00

SHEENA, QUEEN OF THE JUNGLE (See Jerry Iger's Classic..., Jumbo Comics, & 3-D Sheena)
Fiction House Magazines: Spr, 1942; No. 2, Wint, 1942-43; No. 3, Spr, 1943; No. 4, Fall, 1948; No. 5, Sum, 1949; No. 6, Spr, 1950; No. 7-10, 1950(nd); No. 11, Spr, 1951 - No. 18, Wint, 1952-53 (#1-3: 68 pgs.; #4-7: 52 pgs.)

1-Sheena begins 274 548 822 1740 2995 4250
2 (Winter, 1942-43) 118 236 354 749 1287 1825
3 (Spring, 1943) 84 168 252 538 919 1300
4,5 (Fall, 1948, Sum, 1949): 4-New logo; cover swipe from Jumbo #20 52 104 156 322 549 775
6,7 (Spring, 1950, 1950) 44 88 132 276 468 660
8-10(1950 - Win/50, 36 pgs.) 40 80 120 246 411 575
11-18: 15-Cover swipe from Jumbo #43. 18-Used in **POP**, pg. 98 35 70 105 208 339 470
I.W. Reprint #9-r/#18; c-r/White Princess #3 4 8 12 28 44 60

NOTE: ***Baker*** *c-5-10?* ***Whitman*** *c-11-18(most).*

SHEENA, QUEEN OF THE JUNGLE
Devil's Due Publishing: Mar, 2007 - Present (99¢/$3.50)

1-5: 1-Rodi-s/Merhoff-a; 5 covers 3.50
... 99¢ Special (3/07) Revival of the character; Rodi-s/Cummings-a; sketch pages; history 2.25
...: Dark Rising (10/08 - Present) 1-3 3.50
... Trail of the Mapinguari (4/08, $5.50) Two covers 5.50

SHEENA 3-D SPECIAL (Also see Blackthorne 3-D Series #1)
Eclipse Comics: Jan, 1985 ($2.00)

1-Dave Stevens-c 5.00

SHE-HULK (Also see The Savage She-Hulk & The Sensational She-Hulk)
Marvel Comics: May, 2004 - No. 12, Apr, 2005 ($2.99)

1-4-Bobillo-a/Slott-s/Granov-c. 1-Avengers app. 4-Spider-Man-c/app. 3.00
5-12: Mayhew-c. 9-12-Pelletier-a. 10-Origin of Titania 3.00
Vol. 1: Single Green Female TPB (2004, $14.99) r/#1-6 15.00
Vol. 2: Superhuman Law TPB (2005, $14.99) r/#7-12 15.00

SHE-HULK (2nd series)
Marvel Comics: Dec, 2005 - No. 38, Apr, 2009 ($2.99)

1,2,4-7,9-24: 1-Bobillo-a/Slott-s/Horn-c. 1-New Avengers app. 2-Hawkeye-c/app. 9-Jen marries John Jameson. 12-Thanos app. 16-Wolverine app. 3.00
3-($3.99) 100th She-Hulk issue; new story w/art by various incl. Bobillo, Conner, Mayhew & Powell; r/Savage She-Hulk #1 and r/Sensational She-Hulk #1 4.00
8-Civil War 15.00

Sherlock Holmes #1 © Savage Tales

Shi: Masquerade #1 © Tucci

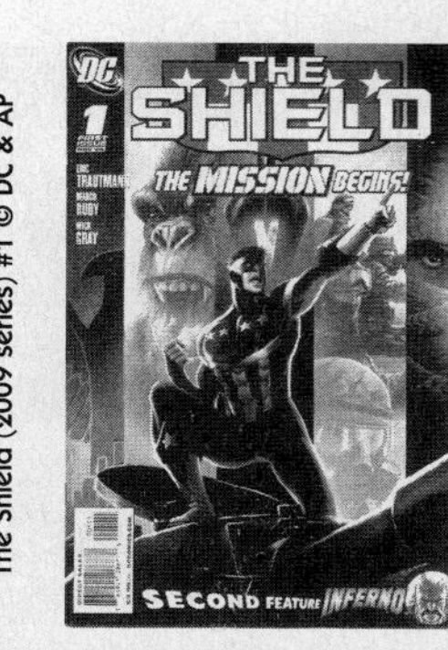

The Shield (2009 series) #1 © DC & AP

GD VG FN VF VF/NM NM-
2.0 4.0 6.0 8.0 9.0 9.2

GD VG FN VF VF/NM NM-
2.0 4.0 6.0 8.0 9.0 9.2

8-2nd printing with variant Bobillo-c 3.00
25-($3.99) Intro. the Behemoth; Juggernaut cameo; Handbook bio pages of She-Hulk 4.00
26-37: 27-Iron Man app. 30-Hercules app. 31-X-Factor app. 32,33-Secret Invasion 3.00
38-($3.99) Thundra, Valkyrie and Invisible Woman app. 4.00
...: Cosmic Collision 1 (2/09, $3.99) Lady Liberators app.; David-s/Asrar-a/Sejic-c 4.00
Vol. 3: Time Trials (2006, $14.99) r/#1-5; Bobillo sketch page 15.00
Vol. 4: Laws of Attraction (2007, $19.99) r/#6-12; Paul Smith sketch page 20.00
Vol. 5: Planet Without a Hulk (2007, $19.99) r/#14-21; Slott's original series pitch 20.00
...: Jaded HC (2008, $19.99) r/#22-27; cover gallery 20.00

SHERIFF BOB DIXON'S CHUCK WAGON (TV) (See Wild Bill Hickok #22)
Avon Periodicals: Nov, 1950

1-Kinstler-c/a(3) 14 28 42 76 108 140

SHERIFF OF TOMBSTONE
Charlton Comics: Nov, 1958 - No. 17, Sept, 1961

V1#1-Giordano-c; Severin-a 6 12 18 41 66 90
2 4 8 12 22 34 45
3-10 3 6 9 17 25 32
11-17 3 6 9 14 20 25

SHERLOCK HOLMES (See Marvel Preview, New Adventures of..., & Spectacular Stories)

SHERLOCK HOLMES (All New Baffling Adventures of...)(Young Eagle #3 on?)
Charlton Comics: Oct, 1955 - No. 2, Mar, 1956

1-Dr. Neff, Ghost Breaker app. 40 80 120 243 402 560
2 35 70 105 208 339 470

SHERLOCK HOLMES (Also see The Joker)
National Periodical Publications: Sept-Oct, 1975

1-Cruz-a; Simonson-c 3 6 9 16 23 30

SHERLOCK HOLMES
Dynamite Entertainment: 2009 - No. 5, 2009 ($3.50, limited series)

1-5-Cassaday-c/Moore & Reppion-s/Aaron Campbell-a 3.50

SHERRY THE SHOWGIRL (Showgirls #4)
Atlas Comics: July, 1956 - No. 3, Dec, 1956; No. 5, Apr, 1957 - No. 7, Aug, 1957

1-Dan DeCarlo-c/a in all 18 36 54 107 169 230
2 13 26 39 74 105 135
3,5-7 11 22 33 64 90 115

SHE'S JOSIE (See Josie)

SHEVA'S WAR
DC Comics (Helix): Oct, 1998 - No. 5, Feb, 1999 ($2.95, mini-series)

1-5-Christopher Moeller-s/painted-a/c 3.00

SHI (one-shots and TPBs)
Crusade Comics

...: Akai (2001, $2.99)-Intro. Victoria Cross; Tucci-a/c; J.C. Vaughn-s 3.00
...: Akai Victoria Cross Ed. ($5.95, edition of 2000) variant Tucci-c 6.00
...: C.G.I. (2001, $4.99) preview of unpublished series 5.00
.../ Cyblade: The Battle for the Independents (9/95, $2.95) Tucci-c; Hellboy, Bone app. 3.00
.../ Cyblade: The Battle for the Independents (9/95, $2.95) Silvestri variant-c . 3.00
.../ Daredevil: Honor Thy Mother (1/97, $2.95) Flip book 3.00
...: Judgment Night (200, $3.99) Wolverine app.; Battlebook card and pages; Tucci-a 4.00
...: Kaidan (10/96, $2.95) Two covers; Tucci-c; Jae Lee wraparound-c 3.00
...: Masquerade (3/98, $3.50) Painted art by Lago, Texeira, and others 3.50
...: Nightstalkers (9/97, $3.50) Painted art by Val Mayerik 3.50
...: Rekishi (1/97, $2.95) Character bios and story summaries of Shi: The Way of the Warrior told in Detective Joe Labianca's point of view; Christopher Golden script; Tucci-c; J.G. Jones-a; flip book w/Shi: East Wind Rain preview 3.00
...: The Art of War Tourbook (1998, $4.95) Blank cover for sketches; early Tucci-a inside 5.00
.../ Vampirella (10/97, $2.95) Ellis-s/Lau-a 3.00
... Vs. Tomoe (8/96, $3.95) Tucci-a/scripts; wraparound foil-c 4.00
... Vs. Tomoe (6/96, $5.00. B&W)-Preview Ed.; sold at San Diego Comic Con 5.00
The Definitive Shi Vol. 1 (2006-2007, $24.99, TPB) B&W r/Way of the Warrior, Tomoe, Rekishi, and Senryaku series; cover gallery with sketches; Tucci & Sparacio-c 25.00

SHI: BLACK, WHITE AND RED
Crusade Comics: Mar, 1998 - No. 2, May, 1998 ($2.95, B&W&Red, mini-series)

1,2-J.G. Jones-painted art 3.00
...- Year of the Dragon Collected Edition (2000, $5.95) r/#1&2 6.00

SHIDIMA
Image Comics: Jan, 2001 - No. 7, Nov, 2002 ($2.95, limited series)

1-7-Prequel to Warlands 3.00
#0-(10/01, $2.25) Short story and sketch pages 2.50

SHI: EAST WIND RAIN
Crusade Comics: Nov, 1997 - No. 2, Feb, 1998 ($3.50, limited series)

1,2-Shi at WW2 Pearl Harbor 3.50

S.H.I.E.L.D. (Nick Fury & His Agents of...) (Also see Nick Fury)
Marvel Comics Group: Feb, 1973 - No. 5, Oct, 1973 (All 20¢ issues)

1-All contain reprint stories from Strange Tales #146-155; new Steranko-c
3 6 9 14 19 24
2-New Steranko flag-c 2 4 6 10 14 18
3-5: 3-Kirby/Steranko-c(r). 4-Steranko-c(r) 2 4 6 8 10 12

NOTE: ***Buscema** a-3p(r). **Kirby** layouts 1-5; c-3 (w/**Steranko**). **Steranko** a-3r, 4r(2).*

SHIELD, THE (Becomes Shield-Steel Sterling #3; #1 titled Lancelot Strong; also see Advs. of the Fly, Double Life of Private Strong, Fly Man, Mighty Comics, The Mighty Crusaders, The Original... & Pep Comics #1)
Archie Enterprises, Inc.: June, 1983 - No. 2, Aug, 1983

1,2: Steel Sterling app. 2-Kanigher-s 4.00
America's 1st Patriotic Comic Book Hero, The Shield (2002, $12.95, TPB) r/Pep Comics #1-5, Shield-Wizard Comics #1; foreward by Robert M. Overstreet 13.00

SHIELD, THE (Archie Ent. character) (Continued from The Red Circle)
DC Comics: Nov, 2009 - Present ($3.99)

1-5: 1-Magog app.; Inferno back-up feature; Green Arrow app. 2,3-Grodd app. 4.00

SHIELD, THE: SPOTLIGHT (TV)
IDW Publishing: Jan, 2004 - No. 5, May, 2004 ($3.99)

1-5-Jeff Marriote-s/Jean Diaz-a/Tommy Lee Edwards-c 4.00
TPB (7/04, $19.99) r/#1-5; Michael Chiklis photo-c 20.00

SHIELD-STEEL STERLING (Formerly The Shield)
Archie Enterprises, Inc.: No. 3, Dec, 1983 (Becomes Steel Sterling No. 4)

3-Nino-a; Steel Sterling by Kanigher & Barreto 3.00

SHIELD WIZARD COMICS (Also see Pep Comics & Top-Notch Comics)
MLJ Magazines: Summer, 1940 - No. 13, Spring, 1944

1-(V1#5 on inside)-Origin The Shield by Irving Novick & The Wizard by Ed Ashe, Jr; Flag-c
503 1006 1509 3672 6486 9300
2-(Winter/40)-Origin The Shield retold; Wizard's sidekick, Roy the Super Boy begins (see Top-Notch #8 for 1st app.) 265 530 795 1694 2897 4100
3,4 165 330 495 1048 1799 2550
5-Dusty, the Boy Detective begins; Nazi bondage-c 142 284 426 909 1555 2200
6,7: 6-Roy the Super Boy app. 7-Shield dons new costume (Summer, 1942); S & K-c?
135 270 405 864 1482 2100
8-Nazi bondage-c; Hitler photo on-c 145 290 435 921 1586 2250
9-Japanese WWII bondage-c 97 194 291 621 1061 1500
10-Nazi swastica-c 100 200 300 635 1093 1550
11,12 92 184 276 584 1005 1425
13-Japanese WWII bondage/torture-c (scarce) 107 214 321 680 1165 1650

NOTE: ***Bob Montana** c-13. **Novick** c-1,3-6,8-11. **Harry Sahle** c-12.*

SHI: FAN EDITIONS
Crusade Comics: 1997

1-3-Two covers polybagged in FAN #19-21 3.00
1-3-Gold editions 4.00

SHI: HEAVEN AND EARTH
Crusade Comics: June, 1997 - No. 4, Apr, 1998 ($2.95)

1-4 3.00
4-($4.95) Pencil-c variant 5.00
Rising Sun Edition-signed by Tucci in FanClub Starter Pack 4.00
"Tora No Shi" variant-c 3.00

SHI: JU-NEN
Dark Horse Comics: July, 2004 - No. 4, May, 2005 ($2.99, mini-series)

1-4-Tucci-a/Tucci & Vaughn-s; origin retold 3.00
TPB (2/06, $12.95) r/#1-4; Tucci and Sparacio-c 13.00

SHINING KNIGHT (See Adventure Comics #66)

SHINOBI (Based on Sega video game)
Dark Horse Comics: Aug, 2002 ($2.99, one-shot)

1-Medina-a/c 3.00

SHIP AHOY
Spotlight Publishers: Nov, 1944 (52 pgs.)

1-L. B. Cole-c 19 38 57 109 172 235

SHIP OF FOOLS
Image Comics: Aug, 1997 - No. 3 ($2.95, B&W)

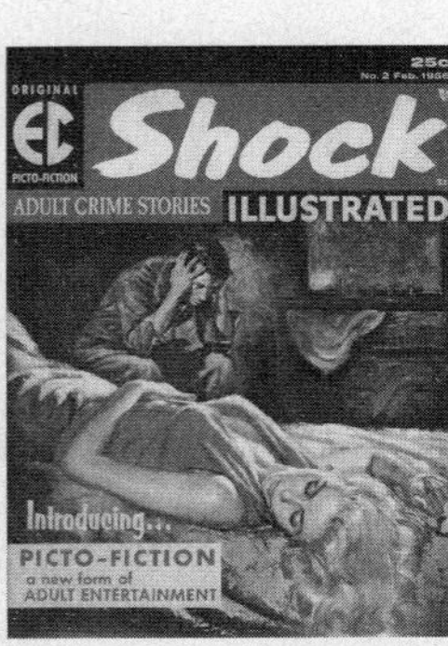

Shock Illustrated #2 © WMG

Shocking Mystery Cases #53 © STAR

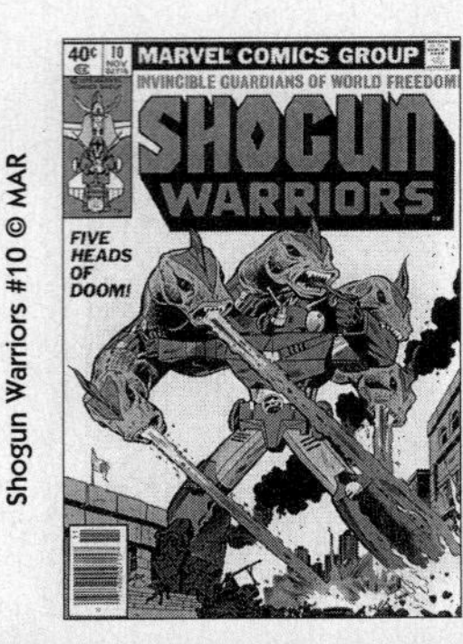

Shogun Warriors #10 © MAR

GD VG FN VF VF/NM NM-
2.0 4.0 6.0 8.0 9.0 9.2

GD VG FN VF VF/NM NM-
2.0 4.0 6.0 8.0 9.0 9.2

0-3-Glass-s/Oeming-a 3.00

SHI: POISONED PARADISE
Avatar Press: July, 2002 - No. 2, Aug, 2002 ($3.50, limited series)
1,2-Vaughn and Tucci-s/Waller-a; 1-Four covers 3.50

SHIPWRECKED! (Disney-Movie)
Disney Comics: 1990 ($5.95, graphic novel, 68 pgs.)
nn-adaptation; Spiegle-a 6.00

SHI: SEMPO
Avatar Press: Aug, 2003 - No. 2, ($3.50, B&W, limited series)
1,2-Vaughn and Tucci-s/Alves-a; 1-Four covers 3.50

SHI: SENRYAKU
Crusade Comics: Aug, 1995 - No. 3, Nov, 1995 ($2.95, limited series)
1-3: 1-Tucci-c; Quesada, Darrow, Sim, Lee, Smith-a. 2-Tucci-c; Silvestri, Balent, Perez, Mack-a. 3-Jusko-c; Hughes, Ramos, Bell, Moore-a 3.00
1-variant-c (no logo) 4.00
Hardcover ($24.95)-r/#1-3; Frazetta-c. 25.00
Trade Paperback ($13.95)-r/#1-3; Frazetta-c. 14.00

SHI: THE ILLUSTRATED WARRIOR
Crusade Comics: 2002 - No. 7, 2003 ($2.99, B&W)
1-7-Story text with Tucci full page art 3.00

SHI: THE SERIES
Crusade Comics: Aug, 1997 - No. 13 ($2.95, color #1-10, B&W #11)
1-10 3.00
11-13: 11-B&W. 12-Color; Lau-a 3.00
#0 Convention Edition 5.00

SHI: THE WAY OF THE WARRIOR
Crusade Comics: Mar, 1994 - No. 12, Apr, 1997 ($2.50/$2.95)
1/2 4.00
1 2 4 6 8 10 12
1-Commemorative ed., B&W, new-c; given out at 1994 San Diego Comic Con 2 4 6 10 14 18
1-Fan appreciation edition -r/#1 2.50
1-Fan appreciation edition (variant) 6.00
1- 10th Anniversary Edition (2004, $2.99) 3.00
2 5.00
2-Commemorative edition (3,000) 2 4 6 9 13 16
2-Fan appreciation edition -r/#2 2.50
3 4.00
4-7: 4-Silvestri poster. 7-Tomoe app. 2.50
5,6: 5-Silvestri variant-c. 6-Tomoe #1 variant-c 3.00
5-Gold edition 12.00
6,8-12: 6-Fan appreciation edition 2.50
8-Combo Gold edition 6.00
8-Signed Edition-(5000) 3.00
Trade paperback (1995, $12.95)-r/#1-4 13.00
Trade paperback (1995, $14.95)-r/#1-4 revised; Julie Bell-c 15.00

SHI: YEAR OF THE DRAGON
Crusade Comics: 2000 - No. 3, 2000 ($2.99, limited series)
1-3: 1-Two covers; Tucci-a/c; flashback to teen-aged Ana 3.00

SHMOO (See Al Capp's... & Washable Jones &...)

SHOCK (Magazine)
Stanley Publ.: May, 1969 - V3#4, Sept, 1971 (B&W reprints from horror comics, including some pre-code) (No V2#1,3)
V1#1-Cover-r/Weird Tales of the Future #7 by Bernard Baily; r/Weird Chills #1 7 14 21 49 80 110
2-Wolverton-r/Weird Mysteries 5; r-Weird Mysteries #7 used in **SOTI**; cover reprints cover to Weird Chills #1 6 12 18 37 59 80
3,5,6 4 8 12 26 41 55
4-Harrison/Williamson-r/Forbid. Worlds #6 4 8 12 28 44 60
V2#2(5/70), V1#8(7/70), V2#4(9/70)-6(1/71), V3#1-4: V2#4-Cover swipe from Weird Mysteries #6 4 8 12 24 37 50
NOTE: *Disbrow r-V2#4; Bondage c-V1#4, V2#6, V3#1.*

SHOCK DETECTIVE CASES (Formerly Crime Fighting Detective)
(Becomes Spook Detective Cases No. 22)
Star Publications: No. 20, Sept, 1952 - No. 21, Nov, 1952
20,21-L.B. Cole-c; based on true crime cases 23 46 69 136 223 310
NOTE: *Palais a-20. No. 21-Fox-r.*

SHOCK ILLUSTRATED (...Adult Crime Stories; Magazine format)
E. C. Comics: Sept-Oct, 1955 - No. 3, Spring, 1956 (Adult Entertainment on-c #1,2)(All 25¢)
1-All by Kamen; drugs, prostitution, wife swapping 18 36 54 105 165 225
2-Williamson-a redrawn from Crime SuspenStories #13 plus Ingels, Crandall, Evans & part Torres-i; painted-c 18 36 54 105 165 235
3-Only 100 known copies bound & given away at E.C. office; Crandall, Evans-a; painted-c; shows May, 1956 on-c 116 232 348 742 1271 1800

SHOCKING MYSTERY CASES (Formerly Thrilling Crime Cases)
Star Publications: No. 50, Sept, 1952 - No. 60, Oct, 1954 (All crime reprints?)
50-Disbrow "Frankenstein" story 42 84 126 265 445 625
51-Disbrow-a 27 54 81 158 259 360
52-60: 56-Drug use story 25 50 75 147 241 335
NOTE: *L. B. Cole covers on all; a-60(2 pgs.). Hollingsworth a-52. Morisi a-55.*

SHOCKING TALES DIGEST MAGAZINE
Harvey Publications: Oct, 1981 (95¢)
1-1957-58-r; Powell, Kirby, Nostrand-a 2 4 6 9 13 16

SHOCK ROCKETS
Image Comics (Gorilla): Apr, 2000 - No. 6, Oct, 2000 ($2.50)
1-6-Busiek-s/Immonen & Grawbadger-a. 6-Flip book w/Superstar preview 2.50
...: We Have Ignition TPB (Dark Horse, 8/04, $14.95, 6" x 9") r/#1-6 15.00

SHOCK SUSPENSTORIES (Also see EC Archives • Shock SuspenStories)
E. C. Comics: Feb-Mar, 1952 - No. 18, Dec-Jan, 1954-55
1-Classic Feldstein electrocution-c 84 168 252 672 1074 1475
2 46 92 138 368 584 800
3,4: 4-Used in **SOTI**, pg. 387,388 34 68 102 272 436 600
5-Hanging-c 41 82 123 328 527 725
6-Classic hooded vigilante bondage-c 56 112 168 448 712 975
7-Classic face melting-c 54 108 162 432 691 950
8-Williamson-a 33 66 99 264 425 585
9-11: 9-Injury to eye panel. 10-Junkie story 29 58 87 232 366 500
12- "The Monkey" classic junkie cover/story; anti-drug propaganda issue 37 74 111 296 473 650
13-Frazetta's only solo story for E.C., 7 pgs. 40 80 120 320 510 700
14-Used in Senate Investigation hearings 24 48 72 192 306 420
15-Used in 1954 Reader's Digest article, "For the Kiddies to Read" 21 42 63 168 272 375
16-18: 16- "Red Dupe" editorial; rape story 20 40 60 160 255 350
NOTE: *Ray Bradbury adaptations-1, 7, 9. Craig a-11; c-11. Crandall a-9-13, 15-18. Davis a-1-5. Evans a-7, 8, 14-18; c-16-18. Feldstein c-1, 7-9, 12. Ingels a-1, 2, 6. Kamen a-in all; c-10, 13, 15. Krigstein a-14, 18. Orlando a-1, 3-7, 9, 10, 12, 16, 17. Wood a-2-15; c-2-6, 14.*

SHOCK SUSPENSTORIES (Also see EC Archives • Shock SuspenStories)
Russ Cochran/Gemstone Publishing: Sept, 1992 - No. 18, Dec, 1996 ($1.50/$2.00/$2.50, quarterly)
1-18: 1-3: Reprints with original-c. 17-r/HOF #17 2.50

SHOGUN WARRIORS
Marvel Comics Group: Feb, 1979 - No. 20, Sept, 1980 (Based on Mattel toys of the classic Japanese animation characters) (1-3: 35¢; 4-19: 40¢; 20: 50¢)
1-Raydeen, Combatra, & Dangard Ace begin; Trimpe-a 2 4 6 9 12 15
2-20: 2-Lord Maurkon & Elementals of Evil app.; Rok-Korr app. 6-Shogun vs. Shogun. 7,8-Cerberus. 9-Starchild. 11-Austin-c. 12-Simonson-c. 14-16-Doctor Demonicus. 17-Juggernaut. 19,20-FF x-over 2 3 4 6 8 10

SHOOK UP (Magazine) (Satire)
Dodsworth Publ. Co.: Nov, 1958
V1#1 4 8 12 28 44 60

SHORT RIBS
Dell Publishing Co.: No. 1333, Apr - June, 1962
Four Color 1333 5 10 15 34 55 75

SHORTSTOP SQUAD (Baseball)
Ultimate Sports Ent. Inc.: 1999 ($3.95, one-shot)
1-Ripken Jr., Larkin, Jeter, Rodriguez app.; Edwards-c/a 4.00

SHORT STORY COMICS (See Hello Pal,...)

SHORTY SHINER (The Five-Foot Fighter in the Ten Gallon Hat)
Dandy Magazine (Charles Biro): June, 1956 - No. 3, Oct, 1956
1 7 14 21 37 46 55
2,3 5 10 15 24 30 35

SHOTGUN SLADE (TV)

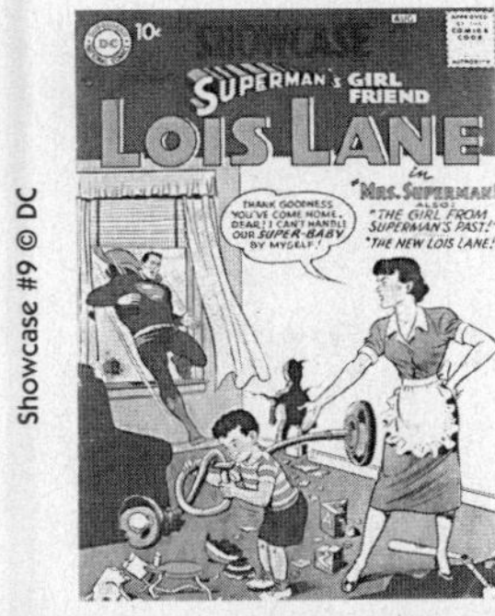

Showcase #9 © DC

Showcase #46 © DC

Showcase '95 #1 © DC

Dell Publishing Co.: No. 1111, July-Sept, 1960

	GD 2.0	VG 4.0	FN 6.0	VF 8.0	VF/NM 9.0	NM- 9.2
Four Color 1111-Photo-c	6	12	18	41	66	90

SHOWCASE (See Cancelled Comic Cavalcade & New Talent...)
National Per. Publ./DC Comics: 3-4/56 - No. 93, 9/70; No. 94, 8-9/77 - No. 104, 9/78

	GD 2.0	VG 4.0	FN 6.0	VF 8.0	VF/NM 9.0	NM- 9.2
1-Fire Fighters; w/Fireman Farrell	277	554	831	2424	4812	7200
2-Kings of the Wild; Kubert-a (animal stories)	84	168	252	714	1407	2100
3-The Frogmen by Russ Heath; Heath greytone-c (early DC example, 7-8/56)	88	176	264	748	1474	2200
4-Origin/1st app. The Flash (1st DC Silver Age hero, Sept-Oct, 1956); Kanigher-s; Infantino & Kubert-c/a; 1st app. Iris West and The Turtle; r/in Secret Origins #1 ('61 & '73); Flash shown reading G.A. Flash Comics #13; back-up story w/Broome-s/Infantino & Kubert-a	1600	3200	4800	17,000	35,500	54,000
5-Manhunters; Meskin-a	82	164	246	697	1374	2050
6-Origin/1st app. Challengers of the Unknown by Kirby, partly r/in Secret Origins #1 & Challengers #64,65 (1st S.A. hero team & 1st original concept S.A. series)(1-2/57)	303	606	909	2727	5464	8200
7-Challengers of the Unknown by Kirby (2nd app.) reprinted in Challengers of the Unknown #75	154	308	462	1348	2674	4000
8-The Flash (5-6/57, 2nd app.); origin & 1st app. Captain Cold	840	1680	2520	7600	13,050	18,500
9-Lois Lane (Pre-#1, 7-8/57) (1st Showcase character to win own series) Superman app. on-c	660	1320	1980	5280	9640	14,000
10-Lois Lane; Jor-El cameo; Superman app. on-c	242	484	726	2118	4209	6300
11-Challengers of the Unknown by Kirby (3rd)	146	292	438	1255	2453	3650
12-Challengers of the Unknown by Kirby (4th)	146	292	438	1255	2453	3650
13-The Flash (3rd app.); origin Mr. Element	311	622	933	2800	5600	8400
14-The Flash (4th app.); origin Dr. Alchemy, former Mr. Element (rare in NM)	337	674	1011	3033	6067	9100
15-Space Ranger (7-8/58, 1st app.)	154	308	462	1348	2674	4000
16-Space Ranger (9-10/58, 2nd app.)	76	152	228	646	1273	1900
17-(11-12/58)-Adventures on Other Worlds; origin/1st app. Adam Strange by Gardner Fox & Mike Sekowsky	192	384	576	1680	3340	5000
18-Adventures on Other Worlds (2nd A. Strange)	96	192	288	816	1608	2400
19-Adam Strange; 1st Adam Strange logo	104	208	312	884	1742	2600
20-Rip Hunter; origin & 1st app. (5-6/59); Moreira-a	84	168	252	714	1407	2100
21-Rip Hunter (7-8/59, 2nd app.); Sekowsky-c/a	46	92	138	368	709	1050
22-Origin & 1st app. Silver Age Green Lantern by Gil Kane and John Broome (9-10/59); reprinted in Secret Origins #2	460	920	1380	4140	8320	12,500
23-Green Lantern (11-12/59, 2nd app.); nuclear explosion-c	148	296	444	1258	2479	3700
24-Green Lantern (1-2/60, 3rd app.)	148	296	444	1258	2479	3700
25,26-Rip Hunter by Kubert. 25-Grey tone-c	39	78	117	297	574	850
27-Sea Devils (7-8/60, 1st app.); Heath-c/a	76	152	228	646	1273	1900
28-Sea Devils (9-10/60, 2nd app.); Heath-c/a	40	80	120	314	607	900
29-Sea Devils; Heath-c/a; grey tone c-27-29	43	86	129	344	672	1000
30-Origin Silver Age Aquaman (1-2/61) (see Adventure #260 for 1st S.A. origin)	78	156	234	663	1307	1950
31,32-Aquaman	40	80	120	321	623	925
33-Aquaman	40	80	120	321	623	925
34-Origin & 1st app. Silver Age Atom by Gil Kane & Murphy Anderson (9-10/61); reprinted in Secret Origins #2	118	236	354	1003	1977	2950
35-The Atom by Gil Kane (2nd); last 10¢ issue	55	110	165	468	922	1375
36-The Atom by Gil Kane (1-2/62, 3rd app.)	45	90	135	360	693	1025
37-Metal Men (3-4/62, 1st app.)	58	116	174	493	972	1450
38-Metal Men (5-6/62, 2nd app.)	35	70	105	270	515	760
39-Metal Men (7-8/62, 3rd app.)	27	54	81	194	377	560
40-Metal Men (9-10/62, 4th app.)	24	48	72	175	338	500
41,42-Tommy Tomorrow (parts 1 & 2). 42-Origin	15	30	45	107	204	300
43-Dr. No (James Bond); Nodel-a; originally published as British Classics Illustrated #158A & as #6 in a European Detective series, all with diff. painted-c. This Showcase #43 version is actually censored, deleting all racial skin color and dialogue thought to be racially demeaning (1st DC S.A. movie adaptation)(based on Ian Fleming novel & movie)	46	92	138	368	709	1050
44-Tommy Tomorrow	11	22	33	78	139	200
45-Sgt. Rock (7-8/63); pre-dates B&B #52; origin retold; Heath-c	35	70	105	271	523	775
46,47-Tommy Tomorrow	10	20	30	70	123	175
48,49-Cave Carson (3rd tryout series; see B&B)	9	18	27	61	103	145
50,51-I Spy (Danger Trail-r by Infantino), King Farady story (#50 has new 4 pg. story)	8	16	24	54	90	125
52-Cave Carson	8	16	24	56	93	130
53,54-G.I. Joe (11-12/64, 1-2/65); Heath-a	11	22	33	78	139	200
55-Dr. Fate & Hourman (3-4/65); origin of each in text; 1st solo app. G.A. Green Lantern in Silver Age (pre-dates Gr. Lantern #40); 1st S.A. app. Solomon Grundy	23	46	69	172	331	490
56-Dr. Fate & Hourman	14	28	42	102	194	285
57-Enemy Ace by Kubert (7-8/65, 4th app. after Our Army at War #155)	21	42	63	148	287	425
58-Enemy Ace by Kubert (5th app.)	17	34	51	122	236	350
59-Teen Titans (11-12/65, 3rd app.)	16	32	48	115	220	325
60-1st S. A. app. The Spectre; Anderson-a (1-2/66); origin in text	27	54	81	195	380	565
61-The Spectre by Anderson (2nd app.)	14	28	42	100	188	275
62-Origin & 1st app. Inferior Five (5-6/66)	9	18	27	65	113	160
63,65-Inferior Five. 63-Hulk parody. 65-X-Men parody (11-12/66)	6	12	18	43	69	95
64-The Spectre by Anderson (5th app.)	14	28	42	97	181	265
66,67-B'wana Beast	6	12	18	37	59	80
68-Maniaks (1st app., spoof of The Monkees)	6	12	18	39	62	85
69,71-Maniaks. 71-Woody Allen-c/app.	6	12	18	37	59	80
70-Binky (9-10/67)-Tryout issue; 1950's Leave It To Binky reprints with art changes	6	12	18	43	69	95
72-Top Gun (Johnny Thunder-r)-Toth-a	5	10	15	34	55	75
73-Origin/1st app. Creeper; Ditko-c/a (3-4/68)	12	24	36	85	155	225
74-Intro/1st app. Anthro; Post-c/a (5/68)	8	16	24	58	97	135
75-Origin/1st app. Hawk & the Dove; Ditko-c/a	11	22	33	78	139	200
76-1st app. Bat Lash (8/68)	8	16	24	54	90	125
77-1st app. Angel & The Ape (9/68)	7	14	21	49	80	110
78-1st app. Jonny Double (11/68)	5	10	15	32	51	70
79-1st app. Dolphin (12/68); Aqualad origin-r	6	12	18	43	69	95
80-1st S.A. app. Phantom Stranger (1/69); Neal Adams-c	10	20	30	70	123	175
81-Windy & Willy; r/Many Loves of Dobie Gillis #26 with art changes	6	12	18	37	59	80
82-1st app. Nightmaster (5/69) by Grandenetti & Giordano; Kubert-c	7	14	21	49	80	110
83,84-Nightmaster by Wrightson w/Jones/Kaluta ink assist in each; Kubert-c. 83-Last 12¢ issue 84-Origin retold; begin 15¢	7	14	21	49	80	110
85-87-Firehair; Kubert-a	3	6	9	16	23	30
88-90-Jason's Quest: 90-Manhunter 2070 app.	3	6	9	14	20	25
91-93-Manhunter 2070: 92-Origin. 93-(9/70) Last 15¢ issue	3	6	9	14	20	25
94-Intro/origin new Doom Patrol & Robotman(8-9/77)	2	4	6	11	16	20
95,96-The Doom Patrol. 95-Origin Celsius	2	3	4	6	8	10
97-99-Power Girl; origin-97,98; JSA cameos	2	3	4	6	8	10
100-(52 pgs.)-Most Showcase characters featured	2	4	6	10	14	18
101-103-Hawkman; Adam Strange x-over	2	3	4	6	8	10
104-(52 pgs.)-O.S.S. Spies at War	2	3	4	6	8	10

NOTE: ***Anderson** a-22-24i, 34-36i, 55, 56, 60, 61, 64, 101-103i; c-50i, 51i, 55, 56, 60, 61, 64. **Aparo** c-94-96. **Boring** c-10. **Estrada** a-104. **Fraden** c(p)-30, 31, 33. **Heath** c-3, 27-29. **Infantino** c/a(p)-4, 8, 13, 14; c-50p, 51p. **Gil Kane** a-22-24p, 34-36p; c-17-19, 22-24p(w/**Giella**), 31. **Kane/Anderson** c-34-36. **Kirby** c-11, 12. **Kirby/Stein** c-6, 7. **Kubert** a-2, 4i, 25, 26, 45, 53, 54, 72; c-25, 26, 53, 54, 57, 58, 82-87, 101-104; c-2, 4i. **Moreira** c-5. **Orlando** a-62p, 63p, 97i; c-62, 63, 97i. **Sekowsky** a-65p. **Sparling** a-78. **Staton** a-94, 95-99p, 100; c-97-100p.*

SHOWCASE '93
DC Comics: Jan, 1993 - No. 12, Dec, 1993 ($1.95, limited series, 52 pgs.)

1-12: 1-Begin 4 part Catwoman story & 6 part Blue Devil story; begin Cyborg story; Art Adams/Austin-c. 3-Flash by Charest (p). 6-Azrael in Bat-costume (2 pgs.). 7,8-Knightfall parts 13 & 14. 6-10-Deathstroke app. (6,10-cameo). 9,10-Austin-i. 10-Azrael as Batman in new costume app.; Gulacy-c. 11-Perez-c. 12-Creeper app.; Alan Grant scripts 3.00

NOTE: ***Chaykin** c-9. **Fabry** c-8. **Giffen** a-12. **Golden** c-3. **Zeck** c-6.*

SHOWCASE '94
DC Comics: Jan, 1994 - No. 12, Dec, 1994 ($1.95, limited series, 52 pgs.)

1-12: 1,2-Joker & Gunfire stories. 1-New Gods. 4-Riddler story. 5-Huntress-c/story w/app. new Batman. 6-Huntress-c/story w/app. Robin; Atom story. 7-Penguin story by Peter David, P. Craig Russell, & Michael T. Gilbert; Penguin-c by Jae Lee. 8,9-Scarface origin story by Alan Grant, John Wagner,& Teddy Kristiansen; Prelude to Zero Hour. 10-Zero Hour tie-in story. 11-Man-Bat. 3.00

NOTE: ***Alan Grant** scripts-3, 4. **Kelley Jones** c-12. **Mignola** c-3. **Nebres** a(i)-2. **Quesada** c-10. **Russell** a-7p. **Simonson** c-5.*

SHOWCASE '95
DC Comics: Jan, 1995 - No. 12, Dec, 1995 ($2.50/$2.95, limited series)

1-4-Supergirl story. 3-Eradicator-c.; The Question story. 4-Thorn c/story 3.00
5-12: 5-Thorn-c/story; begin $2.95-c. 8-Spectre story. 12-The Shade story by James Robinson & Wade Von Grawbadger; Maitresse story by Claremont & Alan Davis 3.00

SHOWCASE '96
DC Comics: Jan, 1996 - No. 12, Dec, 1996 ($2.95, limited series)

Showcase Presents Blackhawk V1 © DC

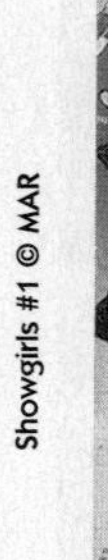
Showgirls #1 © MAR

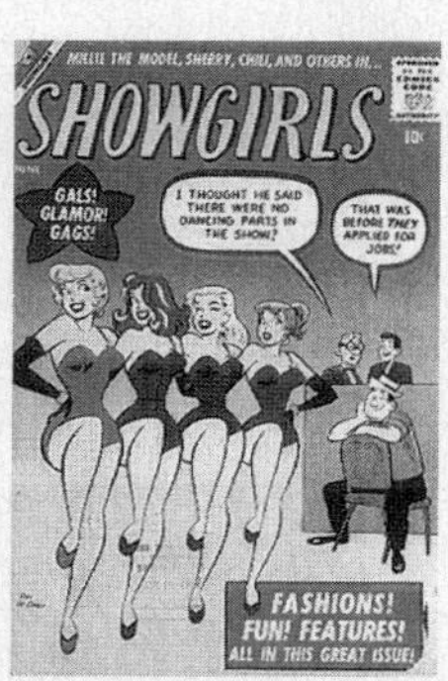

Shrek #1 © Dreamworks

1-12: 1-Steve Geppi cameo. 3-Black Canary & Lois Lane-c/story; Deadman story by Jamie Delano & Wade Von Grawbadger, Gary Frank-c. 4-Firebrand & Guardian-c/story; The Shade & Dr. Fate "Times Past" story by James Robinson & Matt Smith begins, ends #5. 6-Superboy-c/app.; Atom app.; Capt. Marvel (Mary Marvel)-c/app. 8-Supergirl by David & Dodson. 11-Scare Tactics app. 11,12-Legion of Super-Heroes vs. Brainiac. 12-Jesse Quick app. 3.00

SHOWCASE PRESENTS... (B&W archive reprints of DC Silver Age stories)
DC Comics: 2005 - Present ($9.99/$16.99, B&W, over 500 pgs., squarebound)

Adam Strange Vol. 1 (2007, $16.99) r/Showcase #17-19 & Mystery in Space #53-84 17.00
Ambush Bug (2009, $16.99) r/first app. in DC Comics Presents #52 other early app. 17.00
Aquaman Vol. 1 (2007, $16.99) r/Aquaman #1-6 & other early app. 17.00
Aquaman Vol. 2 (2008, $16.99) r/Aquaman #7-23 & other early app. 17.00
Aquaman Vol. 3 (2009, $16.99) r/Aquaman #24-39 & other early app. 17.00
The Atom Vol. 1 (2007, $16.99) r/Showcase #34-36 & The Atom #1-17 17.00
The Atom Vol. 2 (2008, $16.99) r/The Atom #18-38 17.00
Batgirl Vol. 1 (2007, $16.99) r/early apps. from Detective #359 (1967) thru 1975 17.00
Bat Lash Vol. 1 (2009, $9.99) r/#1-7, Showcase #76, DC Special Series #16, and Jonah Hex #49,51,52 10.00
Batman Vol. 1 (2006, $16.99) r/"new look" from Detective #327-342, Batman #164-174 17.00
Batman Vol. 2 (2007, $16.99) r/"new look" from Detective #343-358, Batman #175-188 17.00
Batman Vol. 3 (2008, $16.99) r/"new look" from Detective #359-375, Batman #189, 190-192,194-197,199-202 17.00
Batman and the Outsiders Vol. 1 (2007, $16.99) r/#1-19, Annual #1; Brave and the Bold #200; and New Teen Titans #37 17.00
Blackhawk Vol. 1 (2008, $16.99) r/#108-127 17.00
Booster Gold Vol. 1 (2008, $16.99) r/#1-25 & Action Comics #594 17.00
The Brave and the Bold Batman Team-ups Vol. 1 (2007, $16.99) r/#59,64,67-71,74-87 17.00
The Brave and the Bold Batman Team-ups Vol. 2 (2007, $16.99) r/#88-108 17.00
The Brave and the Bold Batman Team-ups Vol. 3 (2008, $16.99) r/#109-134 17.00
Challengers of the Unknown Vol. 1 (2006, $16.99) r/#1-17 & Showcase #6,7,11,12 17.00
Challengers of the Unknown Vol. 2 (2008, $16.99) r/#18-37 17.00
DC Comics Presents: The Superman Team-ups Vol. 1 (2009, $17.99) r/#1-26 18.00
The Doom Patrol Vol. 1 (2009, $16.99) r/#86-101 and My Greatest Adventure #80-85 17.00
The Elongated Man Vol. 1 ('06, $16.99) r/early apps. in Flash & Detective ('60-'68) 17.00
Eclipso Vol. 1 (2009, $9.99) r/stories from House of Secrets #61-80 10.00
Enemy Ace Vol. 1 (2008, $16.99) r/Our Army at War #151 & other early app. 17.00
The Flash Vol. 1 (2007, $16.99) r/Flash Comics #104 (last G.A. issue), Showcase #4,8,13,14 & The Flash #105-119 17.00
The Flash Vol. 2 (2008, $16.99) r/The Flash #120-140 17.00
The Flash Vol. 3 (2009, $16.99) r/The Flash #141-161 17.00
The Great Disaster Featuring The Atomic Knights and Hercules Vol. 1 (2007, $16.99) 17.00
Green Arrow Vol. 1 (2006, $16.99) r/Adventure #250-269, Brave and the Bold #50,71,85; Justice League of America #4; World's Finest #95-134,136,138,140 17.00
Green Lantern Vol. 1 (2005, $9.99) r/Showcase #22-24 & Green Lantern #1-17 10.00
Green Lantern Vol. 2 (2007, $16.99) r/Green Lantern #18-38 17.00
Green Lantern Vol. 3 (2008, $16.99) r/Green Lantern #39-59 17.00
Haunted Tank Vol. 1 ('06, $16.99) r/G.I. Combat #87-119, Brave & The Bold #52 and Our Army at War #155; Russ Heath-c 17.00
Haunted Tank Vol. 2 ('08, $16.99) r/G.I. Combat #120-156 17.00
Hawkman Vol. 1 ('07, $16.99) r/Brave&Bold #34-36,42-44, Mystery in Space #87-90, Hawkman #1-11, and The Atom #7 17.00
Hawkman Vol. 2 ('08, $16.99) r/Brave&Bold #70, Hawkman #12-27, The Atom #31, & The Atom and Hawkman #39-45 17.00
The House of Mystery Vol. 1 ('06, $16.99) r/House of Mystery #174-194 ('68-'71) 17.00
The House of Mystery Vol. 2 ('07, $16.99) r/House of Mystery #195-211 ('71-'73) 17.00
The House of Mystery Vol. 3 ('09, $16.99) r/House of Mystery #212-226 ('73-'74) 17.00
The House of Secrets Vol. 1 ('08, $16.99) r/House of Secrets #81-98 ('69-'72) 17.00
The House of Secrets Vol. 2 ('09, $17.99) r/House of Secrets #99-119 ('72-'74) 18.00
Jonah Hex Vol. 1 (2005, $16.99) r/All Star Western #10-12, Weird Western Tales #13,14, 16-33; plus the complete adventures of Outlaw from All Star Western #2-8 17.00
Justice League of America Vol. 1 ('05, $16.99) r/Brave & the Bold #28-30, J.L. of A. #1-16 and Mystery in Space #75 17.00
Justice League of America Vol. 2 ('07, $16.99) r/Justice League of America #17-36 17.00
Justice League of America Vol. 3 ('07, $16.99) r/Justice League of America #37-60 17.00
Justice League of America Vol. 4 ('09, $16.99) r/Justice League of America #61-83 17.00
Legion of Super-Heroes Vol. 1 ('07, $16.99) r/Adventure #247 & early app. thru 1964 17.00
Legion of Super-Heroes Vol. 2 ('08, $16.99) r/app. in Adventure & Superboy 1964-66 17.00
Legion of Super-Heroes Vol. 3 ('09, $16.99) r/Adventure #349-368 & S.P. Jimmy Olsen #106 17.00
Martian Manhunter Vol. 1 (2007, $16.99) r/Detective #225-304 & Batman #78 (prototype) 17.00
Martian Manhunter Vol. 2 ('09, $16.99) r/Detective #305-326 & House of Myst. #143-173 17.00
Metal Men Vol. 1 (2007, $16.99) r/#1-16; Brave & Bold #55, Showcase #37-40 17.00
Metamorpho Vol. 1 ('05, $16.99) r/Brave&Bold #57,58,66,68; Metamorpho #1-17;JLA #42 17.00
Phantom Stranger Vol. 1 (2006, $16.99) r/#1-21 (2nd series) & Showcase #80 17.00
Phantom Stranger Vol. 2 (2008, $16.99) r/#22-41 and various 1970-1978 appearances 17.00
Robin The Boy Wonder Vol. 1 (2007, $16.99) r/back-ups from Batman, Detective, WF 17.00
Secrets of Sinister House ('10, $17.99) r/#5-18 and Sinister House of Secret Love #1-4 18.00
Sgt. Rock Vol. 1 ('07, $16.99) r/G.I. Combat #68, Our Army at War #81-117 17.00
Sgt. Rock Vol. 2 ('08, $16.99) r/Our Army at War #118-148 17.00
Shazam! Vol. 1 ('06, $16.99) r/#1-33 17.00
Strange Adventures Vol. 1 ('08, $16.99) r/#54-73 17.00
Supergirl Vol. 1 ('07, $16.99) r/prototype from Superman #123 (8/58); 1st app. Action #252 (5/59) and early appearances thru Nov. 1961 17.00
Supergirl Vol. 2 ('08, $16.99) r/appearances in Action Comics #283-321 (1961-1965) 17.00
Superman Vol. 1 ('05, $9.99) r/Action #241-257 & Superman #122-134 (1958-59) 10.00
Superman Vol. 2 ('06, $16.99) r/Action #258-275 & Superman #134-145 (1959-61) 17.00
Superman Vol. 3 ('07, $16.99) r/Action #279-292 & Superman #146-156 & Annual #3,4 17.00
Superman Vol. 4 ('08, $16.99) r/Action #293-309 & Superman #157-166 (1962-64) 17.00
Superman Family Vol. 1 ('06, $16.99) Superman's Pal, Jimmy Olsen #1-22; Showcase #9 and Superman #22 17.00
Superman Family Vol. 2 ('08, $16.99) Superman's Pal, Jimmy Olsen #23-34; Showcase #10 and Superman's Girl Friend, Lois Lane #1-7 17.00
Superman Family Vol. 3 ('09, $16.99) Superman's Pal, Jimmy Olsen #35-44 and Superman's Girl Friend, Lois Lane #8-16 17.00
Teen Titans Vol. 1 ('06, $16.99) r/#1-18; Brave & the Bold #54,60; Showcase #59 17.00
Teen Titans Vol. 2 ('07, $16.99) r/#19-37, World's Finest #205 and Brave & Bold #83,94 17.00
The Unknown Soldier Vol. 1 ('06, $16.99) r/Star Spangled War Stories #158-188 17.00
The War That Time Forgot Vol. 1 ('07, $16.99) r/S.S.W.S. #90,92,94-125,127,128 17.00
Warlord Vol. 1 ('09, $16.99) r/#1-28 and debut in 1st Issue Special #1 17.00
Wonder Woman Vol. 1 ('07, $16.99) r/#98-117 17.00
Wonder Woman Vol. 2 ('08, $16.99) r/#118-137 17.00
World's Finest Vol. 1 ('07, $16.99) r/#71-111 & Superman #76 17.00
World's Finest Vol. 2 ('08, $16.99) r/#112-145 17.00

SHOWGIRLS (Formerly Sherry the Showgirl #3)
Atlas Comics (MPC No. 2): No. 4, 2/57; June, 1957 - No. 2, Aug, 1957

4-(2/57) Dan DeCarlo-c/a begins 11 22 33 64 90 115
1-(6/57) Millie, Sherry, Chili, Pearl & Hazel begin 14 28 42 76 108 140
2 11 22 33 60 83 105

SHREK (Movie)
Dark Horse Comics: Sept, 2003 - No. 3, Dec, 2003 ($2.99, limited series)

1-3-Takes place after 1st movie; Evanier-s/Bachs-a; CGI cover 3.00

SHROUD, THE (See Super-Villain Team-Up #5)
Marvel Comics: Mar, 1994 - No. 4, June, 1994 ($1.75, mini-series)

1-4: 1,2,4-Spider-Man & Scorpion app. 2.50

SHROUD OF MYSTERY
Whitman Publications: June, 1982

1 1 2 3 4 5 7

SHRUGGED
Aspen MLT, Inc.: No. 0, June, 2006 - No. 8, Feb, 2009 ($2.50/$2.99)

0-($2.50) Turner & Mastromauro-s/Gunnell-a; intro. story and character profiles 2.50
1-8-($2.99) 1-Six covers. 2-Three covers 3.00
... : Beginnings (5/06, $1.99) Prequel intro. to Ange and Dev; Gunnell-a; development art 2.50

SHUT UP AND DIE
Image Comics/Halloween: 1998 - No. 3, 1998 ($2.95,B&W, bi-monthly)

1-3: Hudnall-s 3.00

SICK (Sick Special #131) (Magazine) (Satire)
Feature Publ./Headline Publ./Crestwood Publ. Co./Hewfred Publ./ Pyramid Comm./Charlton Publ. No. 109 (4/76) on: Aug, 1960 - No. 134, Fall, 1980

V1#1-Jack Paar photo on-c; Torres-a; Untouchables-s; Ben Hur movie photo-s 16 32 48 112 214 315
2-Torres-a; Elvis app.; Lenny Bruce app. 10 20 30 71 126 180
3-5-Torres-a in all. 3-Khruschev-c; Hitler-s. 4-Newhart-s; Castro-s; John Wayne. 5-JFK/Castro-c; Elvis pin-up; Hitler. 9 18 27 63 107 150
6-Photo-s of Ricky Nelson & Marilyn Monroe; JFK 9 18 27 65 113 160

V2#1,2,4-8 (#7,8,10-14): 1-(#7) Hitler-s; Brando photo-s. 2-(#8) Dick Clark-s. 4-(#10) Untouchables-c; Candid Camera-s. 5-(#11) Nixon-c; Lone Ranger-s; JFK-s. 6-(#12) Beatnik-c/s. 8-(#14) Liz Taylor pin-up, JFK-s; Dobie Gillis-s; Sinatra & Dean Martin photo-s 8 16 24 58 97 135
3-(#9) Marilyn Monroe/JFK-c; Kingston Trio-s 9 18 27 63 107 150

V3#1-7(#15-21): 1-(#15) JFK app.; Liz Tayor/Richard Burton-s. 2-(#16) Ben Casey/ Frankenstein-c/s; Hitler photo-s. 5-(#19) Nixon back-c/s; Sinatra photo-s. 6-(#20) 1st Huckleberry Fink-c 5 10 15 34 55 75
8-(#22) Cassius Clay vs. Liston-s; 1st Civil War Blackouts-/Pvt. Bo Reargard w/ Jack Davis-a 6 12 18 39 62 85

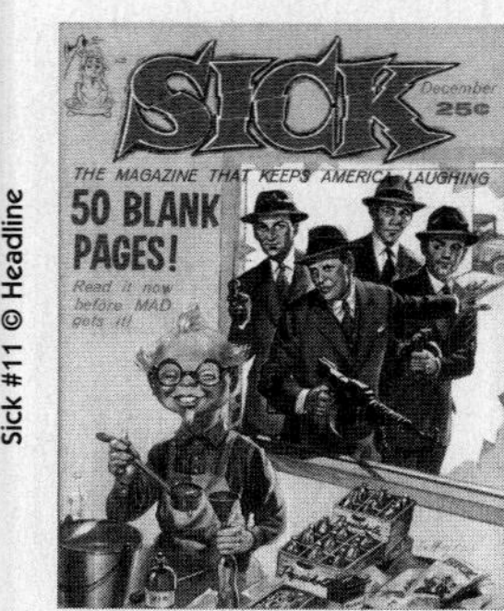

Sick #11 © Headline

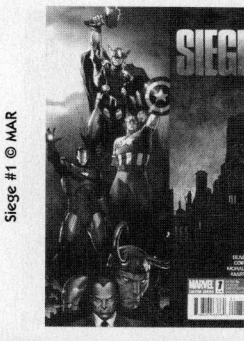

Siege #1 © MAR

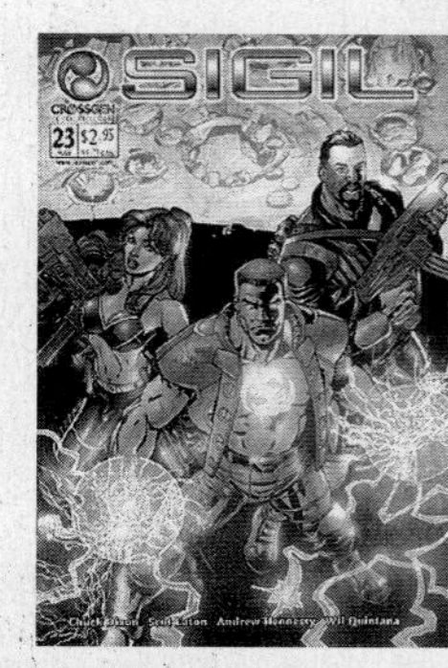

Sigil #23 © CRO

GD VG FN VF VF/NM NM-
2.0 4.0 6.0 8.0 9.0 9.2

V4#1-5 (#23-27): Civil War Blackouts-/Pvt. Bo Reargard w/ Jack Davis-a in all. 1-(#23) Smokey Bear-c; Tarzan-s. 2-(#24) Goldwater & Paar-s; Castro-s. 3-(#25) Frankenstein-c; Cleopatra/Liz Taylor-s; Steve Reeves photo-s. 4-(#26) James Bond-s; Hitler-s. 5-(#27) Taylor/Burton pin-up; Sinatra, Martin, Andress, Ekberg photo-s 4 8 12 28 44 60
28,31,36,39: 31-Pink Panther movie photo-s; Burke's Law-s. 39-Westerns; Elizabeth Montgomery photo-s; Beat mag-s 4 8 12 24 37 50
29,34,37,38: 29-Beatles-c by Jack Davis. 34-Two pg. Beatles-s & photo pin-up. 37-Playboy parody issue. 38-Addams Family-s 4 8 12 28 44 60
30,32,35,40: 30-Beatles photo pin-up; James Bond photo-s. 32-Ian Fleming-s; LBJ-s; Tarzan-s. 35-Beatles cameo; Three Stooges parody. 40-Tarzan-s; Crosby/Hope-s; Beatles parody 5 10 15 30 48 65
33-Ringo Starr photo-c & spoof on "A Hard Day's Night"; inside-c has Beatles photos 6 12 18 41 66 90
41,50,51,53,54,60: 41-Sports Illustrated parody-c/s. 50-Mod issue; flip-c w/1967 calendar w/Bob Taylor-a. 51-Get Smart-s. 53-Beatles cameo; nudity panels. 54-Monkees-c. 60-TV Daniel Boone-s 3 6 9 20 30 40
42-Fighting American-c revised from Simon/Kirby-c; "Good girl" art by Sparling; profile on Bob Powell; superhero parodies 6 12 18 37 59 80
43-49,52,55-59: 43-Sneaker set begins by Sparling. 45-Has #44 on-c & #45 on inside; TV Westerns-s; Beatles cameo. 46-Hell's Angels-s; NY Mets-s. 47-UFO/Space-c. 49-Men's Adventure mag. parody issue; nudity. 52-LBJ-s. 55-Underground culture special. 56-Alfred E. Neuman-c; inventors issue. 58-Hippie issue-c/s. 59-Hippie-s 3 6 9 17 25 32
61-64,66-69,71,73,75-80: 63-Tiny Tim-c & poster; Monkees-s. 64-Flip-c. 66-Flip-c; Mod Squad-s. 69-Beatles cameo; Peter Sellers photo-s. 71-Flip-c; Clint Eastwood-s. 76-Nixon-s; Marcus Welby-s. 78-Ma Barker-s; Courtship of Eddie's Father-s; Abbie Hoffman-s 3 6 9 16 22 28
65,70,74: 65-Cassius Clay/Brando/J. Wayne-c; Johnny Carson-s. 70-(9/69) John & Yoko-c, 1/2 pg. story. 74-Clay, Agnew, Namath & others as superheroes-c/s; Easy Rider-s; Ghost and Mrs. Muir-s 3 6 9 17 25 32
72-(84 pgs.) Xmas issue w/2 pg. slick color poster; Tarzan-s; 2 pg. Superman & superheroes-s 4 8 12 22 34 45
81-85,87-95,98,99: 81-(2/71) Woody Allen photo-s. 85 Monster Mag. parody-s; Nixon-s w/Ringo & John cameo. 88-Klute photo-s; Nixon paper dolls page. 92-Lily Tomlin; Archie Bunker pin-up. 93-Woody Allen 2 4 6 13 18 22
86,96,97,100: 86-John & Yoko, Tiny Tim-c; Love Story movie photo-s. 96-Kung Fu-c; Mummy-s, Dracula & Frankenstein app. 97-Superman-s; 1974 Calendar; Charlie Brown & Snoopy pin-up. 100-Serpico-s; Cosell-s; Jacques Cousteau-s 3 6 9 14 19 24
101-103,105-114,116,119,120: 101-Three Musketeers-s; Dick Tracy-s. 102-Young Frankenstein-s. 103-Kojak-s; Evel Knievel-s. 105-Towering Inferno-s; Peanuts/Snoopy-s. 106-Cher-c/s. 10 7-Jaws-c/s. 108-Pink Panther-c/s; Archie-s. 109-Adam & Eve-s(nudity). 110-Welcome Back Kotter-s. 111-Sonny & Cher-s. 112-King Kong-c/s. 120-Star Trek-s 2 4 6 9 13 16
104,115,117,118: 104-Muhammad Ali-c/s. 115-Charlie's Angels-s. 117-Bionic Woman & Six Million $ Man-c/s; Cher D'Flower begins by Sparling (nudity). 118-Star Wars-s; Popeye-s 2 4 6 11 16 20
121-125,128-130: 122-Darth Vader-s. 123-Jaws II-s. 128-Superman-c/movie parody. 130-Alien movie-s 2 4 6 10 14 18
126,127: 126-(68 pgs.) Battlestar Galactica-c/s; Star Wars-s; Wonder Woman-s. 127-Mork & Mindy-s; Lord of the Rings-s 2 4 6 13 18 22
131-(1980 Special) Star Wars/Star Trek/Flash Gordon wraparound-c/s; Superman parody; Battlestar Galactica-s 3 6 9 14 19 24
132,133: 132-1980 Election-c/s; Apocalypse Now-s. 133-Star Trek-s; Chips-s; Superheroes page 2 4 6 13 18 22
134 (scarce)(68 pg. Giant)-Star Wars-c; Alien-s; WKRP-s; Mork & Mindy-s; Taxi-s; MASH-s 4 8 12 21 30 40
Annual 1- Birthday Annual (1966)-3 pg. Huckleberry Fink fold out 4 8 12 23 34 50
Annual 2- 7th Annual Yearbook (1967)-Davis-c, 2 pg. glossy poster insert 4 8 12 23 34 50
Annual 3 (1968) "Big Sick Laff-in" on-c (84 pgs.)-w/psychedelic posters; Frankenstein poster 3 6 9 18 27 35
Annual 1969 "Great Big Fat Annual Sick", 1969 "9th Year Annual Sick", 1970, 1971 3 6 9 17 25 32
Annual 12,13-(1972,1973, 84 pgs.) 13-Monster-c 3 6 9 17 25 32
Annual 14,15-(1974,1975, 84 pgs.) 14-Hitler photo-s 3 6 9 17 25 32
Annual 2-4 (1980) 2 4 6 9 13 16
Special 1 (1980) Buck Rogers-c/s; MASH-s 3 6 9 14 19 24
Special 2 (1980) Wraparound Star Wars:Empire Strikes Back-c; Charlie's Angels/Farrah-s; Rocky-s; plus reprints 3 6 9 14 19 24
Yearbook 15(1975, 84 pgs.) Paul Revere-c 3 6 9 16 23 30
NOTE: ***Davis*** *a-42, 87; c-22, 23, 25, 29, 31, 32.* ***Powell*** *a-7, 31, 57.* ***Simon*** *a-1-3, 10, 41, 42, 87, 99; c-1, 47, 57, 59, 69, 91, 95-97, 99, 100, 102, 107, 112.* ***Torres*** *a-1-3, 29, 31, 47, 49.* ***Tuska*** *a-14, 41-43. Civil War Blackouts-23, 24. #42 has biography of Bob Powell.*

GD VG FN VF VF/NM NM-
2.0 4.0 6.0 8.0 9.0 9.2

SIDEKICK (Paul Jenkins'...)
Image Comics (Desperado): June, 2006 - No. 5, May, 2007 ($3.50, limited series)
1-5-Paul Jenkins-s/Chris Moreno-a 3.50
... Super Summer Sidekick Spectacular 1 (7/07, $2.99) 3.00
... Super Summer Sidekick Spectacular 2 (9/07, $3.50) 3.50

SIDEKICKS
Fanboy Ent., Inc.: Jun, 2000 - No. 3, Apr, 2001 ($2.75, B&W, lim. series)
1-3-J.Torres-s/Takesi Miyazawa-a. 3-Variant-c by Wieringo 2.75
...: Super Fun Summer Special (Oni Press, 7/03, $2.99) art by various incl. Wieringo 3.00
...: The Substitute (Oni Press, 7/02, $2.95) 3.00
...: The Transfer Student TPB (Oni Press, 6/02, $8.95, 9" x 6") r/#1-3 9.00
...: The Transfer Student TPB 2nd Ed. (10/03, $11.95, 9" x 6") r/#1-3; The Substitute 12.00

SIDESHOW
Avon Periodicals: 1949 (one-shot)
1-(Rare)-Similar to Bachelor's Diary 41 82 123 256 428 600

SIEGE
Marvel Comics: Mar, 2010 - No. 4 ($3.99, limited series)
1-3-Asgard is invaded; Bendis-s/Coipel-a 4.00
1-3-Variant covers by Dell'Otto 10.00
...: Storming Asgard - Heroes & Villains (3/10, $3.99) Dossiers on participants; Land-c 4.00
...: The Cabal (2/10, $3.99) series prelude; Bendis-s/Lark-a; covers by Finch & Davis 4.00

SIEGE: EMBEDDED
Marvel Comics: Mar, 2010 - No. 4 ($3.99, limited series)
1-3-Reed-s/Samnee-a/Granov-c; Ben Urich & Volstagg cover the invasion 4.00

SIEGEL AND SHUSTER: DATELINE 1930s
Eclipse Comics: Nov, 1984 - No. 2, Sept, 1985 ($1.50/$1.75, Baxter paper #1)
1,2: 1-Unpublished samples of strips from the '30s; includes 'Interplanetary Police'; Shuster-c. 2 ($1.75, B&W)-unpublished strips; Shuster-c 2.50

SIGIL (Also see CrossGen Chronicles)
CrossGeneration Comics: Jul, 2000 - No. 43, Jan, 2004 ($2.95)
1-43: 1-Barbara Kesel-s/Ben & Ray Lai-a. 12-Waid-s begin. 21-Chuck Dixon-s begin 3.00
...: Mark of Power TPB (5/01, $19.95) r/#1-7; Moeller painted-c 20.00
...: The Marked Man Vol. 2 TPB (2002, $19.95) r/#8-14 20.00
...: The Lizard God Vol. 3 TPB (2002, $15.95) r/#15-20 16.00
Vol. 4: Hostage Planet (4/03, $15.95) r/#21-26 16.00
Vol. 5: Death Match (2003, $15.95) r/#27-32 16.00

SIGMA
Image Comics (WildStorm): March, 1996 - No. 3, June, 1996 ($2.50, limited series)
1-3: 1-"Fire From Heaven" prelude #2; Coker-a. 2-"Fire From Heaven" pt. 6. 3-"Fire From Heaven" pt. 14. 2.50

SILENT DRAGON
DC Comics (WildStorm): Sept, 2005 - No. 6, Feb, 2006 ($2.99, limited series)
1-6-Tokyo 2066 A.D.; Leinil Yu-a/c; Andy Diggle-s 3.00
TPB (2006, $19.99) r/series; sketch page 20.00

SILENT HILL: DEAD/ALIVE
IDW Publishing: Dec, 2005 - No. 5, Apr, 2006 ($3.99, limited series)
1-5-Stakal-a/Ciencin-s. 1-Four covers. 2-5-Two covers 4.00

SILENT HILL: DYING INSIDE
IDW Publishing: Feb, 2004 - No. 5, June, 2004 ($3.99, limited series)
1-5-Based on the Konami computer game. 1-Templesmith-a; Ashley Wood-c 4.00
...: Paint It Black (2/05, $7.49) Ciencin-s/Thomas-a 7.50
...: The Grinning Man 5/05, $7.49) Ciencin-s/Stakal-a 7.50
TPB (8/04, $19.99) r/#1-5; Ashley Wood-c 20.00

SILENT HILL: SINNER'S REWARD
IDW Publishing: Feb, 2008 - No. 4, Apr, 2008 ($3.99, limited series)
1-4-Waltz-s/Stamb-a 4.00

SILENT INVASION, THE
Rengade Press: Apr, 1986 - No.12, Mar, 1988 ($1.70/$2.00, B&W)
1-12-UFO sightings of the '50's 3.00
Book 1- reprints ($7.95) 8.00

SILENT MOBIUS
Viz Select Comics: 1991 - No. 5, 1992 ($4.95, color, squarebound, 44 pgs.)
1-5: Japanese stories translated to English 5.00

Silly Tunes #6 © MAR

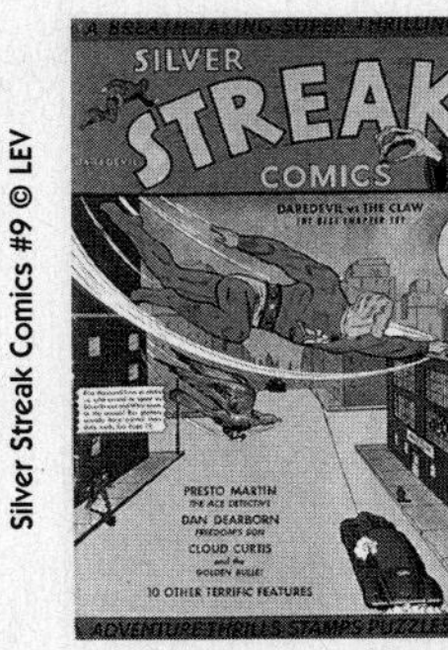

Silver Streak Comics #9 © LEV

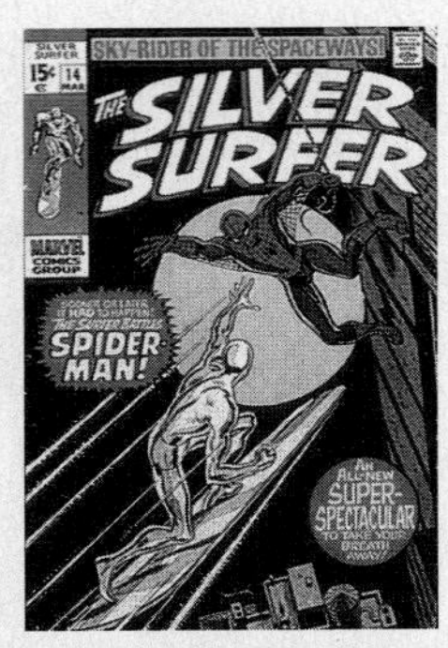

Silver Surfer #14 © MAR

	GD	VG	FN	VF	VF/NM	NM-
	2.0	4.0	6.0	8.0	9.0	9.2

GD VG FN VF VF/NM NM- 2.0 4.0 6.0 8.0 9.0 9.2

SILENT SCREAMERS (Based on the Aztech Toys figures)
Image Comics: Oct, 2000 ($4.95)

Nosferatu Issue - Alex Ross front & back-c 5.00

SILENT WAR
Marvel Comics: Mar, 2007 - No. 6, Aug, 2007 ($2.99, limited series)

1-6-Inhumans, Black Bolt and Fantastic Four app.; Hine-s/Irving-a/Watson-c 3.00
TPB (2007, $14.99) r/series 15.00

SILKE
Dark Horse Comics: Jan, 2001 - No. 4, Sept, 2001 ($2.95)

1-4-Tony Daniel-s/a 3.00

SILKEN GHOST
CrossGen Comics: June, 2003 - No. 5, Oct, 2003 ($2.95, limited series)

1-5-Dixon-s/Rosado-a 3.00
Traveler Vol. 1 (2003, $9.95) digest-sized reprint #1-5 10.00

SILLY PILLY (See Frank Luther's...)

SILLY SYMPHONIES (See Dell Giants)

SILLY TUNES
Timely Comics: Fall, 1945 - No. 7, June, 1947

	GD	VG	FN	VF	VF/NM	NM-
1-Silly Seal, Ziggy Pig begin	22	44	66	128	209	290
2-(2/46)	14	28	42	78	112	145
3-7: 6-New logo	11	22	33	64	90	115

SILVER (See Lone Ranger's Famous Horse...)

SILVER AGE
DC Comics: July, 2000 ($3.95, limited series)

1-Waid-s/Dodson-a; "Silver Age" style x-over; JLA & villains switch bodies 4.00
...: Challengers of the Unknown ($2.50) Joe Kubert-c; vs. Chronos 2.50
...: Dial H For Hero ($2.50) Jim Mooney-c; vs. Martian Manhunter 2.50
...: Doom Patrol ($2.50) Ramona Fradon-c/Peyer-s 2.50
...: Flash ($2.50) Carmine Infantino-c; Kid Flash and Elongated Man app. 2.50
...: Green Lantern ($2.50) Gil Kane-c/Busiek-s/Anderson-a; vs. Sinestro 2.50
...: Justice League of America ($2.50) Ty Templeton-c 2.50
...: Showcase ($2.50) Dick Giordano-c/a; Batgirl, Adam Strange app. 2.50
... Secret Files ($4.95) Intro. Agamemno; short stories & profile pages 5.00
...: Teen Titans ($2.50) Nick Cardy-c; vs. Penguin, Mr. Element, Black Manta 2.50
...: The Brave and the Bold ($2.50) Jim Aparo-c; Batman & Metal Men 2.50
... 80-Page Giant ($5.95) Conclusion of x-over; "lost" Silver Age stories 6.00

SILVERBACK
Comico: 1989 - No. 3, 1990 ($2.50, color, limited series, mature readers)

1-3: Character from Grendel: Matt Wagner-a 3.00

SILVERBLADE
DC Comics: Sept, 1987 - No. 12, Sept, 1988

1-12: Colan-c/a in all 2.50

SILVERHAWKS
Star Comics/Marvel Comics #6: Aug, 1987 - No. 6, June, 1988 ($1.00)

1-6 3.00

SILVERHEELS
Pacific Comics: Dec, 1983 - No. 3, May, 1984 ($1.50)

1-3 2.50

SILVER KID WESTERN
Key/Stanmor Publications: Oct, 1954 - No. 5, July, 1955

	GD	VG	FN	VF	VF/NM	NM-
1	10	20	30	54	72	90
2	6	12	18	31	38	45
3-5	6	12	18	28	34	40
I.W. Reprint #1,2-Severin-c: 1-r/#? 2-r/#1	2	4	6	8	11	14

SILVER SABLE AND THE WILD PACK (See Amazing Spider-Man #265 and Sable & Fortune)
Marvel Comics: June, 1992 - No. 35, Apr, 1995 ($1.25/$1.50

1-($2.00)-Embossed & foil stamped-c; Spider-Man app. 3.00
2-35: 4,5-Dr. Doom-c/story. 6,7-Deathlok-c/story. 9-Origin Silver Sable. 10-Punisher-c/s. 15-Capt. America-c/s. 16,17-Intruders app. 18,19-Venom-c/s. 19-Siege of Darkness x-over. 23-Daredevil (in new costume) & Deadpool app. 24-Bound-in card sheet. Li'l Sylvie backup story. 25-($2.00, 52 pgs.)-Li'l Sylvie backup story 2.50

SILVER STAR (Also see Jack Kirby's...)
Pacific Comics: Feb, 1983 - No. 6, Jan, 1984 ($1.00)

1-6: 1-1st app. Last of the Viking Heroes. 1-5-Kirby-c/a. 2-Ditko-a 5.00
...: Graphite Edition TPB (TwoMorrows Publ., 3/06, $19.95) r/series in B&W including Kirby's original pencils; sketch pages; original screenplay 20.00
Jack Kirby's Silver Star, Volume 1 HC (Image Comics, 2007, $34.99) r/series in color; sketch pages; original screenplay 35.00

SILVER STREAK COMICS (Crime Does Not Pay #22 on)
Your Guide Publs. No. 1-7/New Friday Publs. No. 8-17/Comic House Publ./ Newsbook Publ.: Dec, 1939 - No. 21, May, 1942; No. 23, 1946; No # 22 (Silver logo-#1-5)

	GD	VG	FN	VF	VF/NM	NM-
1-(Scarce)-Intro The Claw by Cole (r-/in Daredevil #21), Red Reeves, Boy Magician, & Captain Fearless; The Wasp, Mister Midnight begin; Spirit Man app. Silver metallic-c begin, end #5; Claw c-1,2,6-8	1075	2150	3225	7600	13,300	19,000
2-The Claw by Cole; Simon-c/a	389	778	1167	2723	4762	6800
3-1st app. & origin Silver Streak (2nd with lightning speed); Dickie Dean the Boy Inventor, Lance Hale, Ace Powers, Bill Wayne, & The Planet Patrol begin	331	662	993	2317	4059	5800
4-Sky Wolf begins; Silver Streak by Jack Cole (new costume); 1st app. Jackie, Lance Hale's sidekick	168	336	504	1075	1838	2600
5-Jack Cole c/a(2)	194	388	582	1242	2121	3000
6-(Scarce, 9/40)-Origin & 1st app. Daredevil who is mute (blue & yellow costume) by Jack Binder; The Claw returns; classic Cole Claw-c	1333	2666	4000	10,000	18,000	26,000
7-Titled "Claw vs. Daredevil" (regains voice & new costume-blue & red) by Jack Cole & three other Cole stories (38 pgs.) 2nd app. Daredevil, but 1st in new costume and 1st Daredevil-c by Cole. Classic battle issue; origin of Whiz, Silver Streak's falcon	741	1482	2223	5409	9555	13,700
8-Claw vs. Daredevil by Cole; last Cole Silver Streak; Cole Daredevil-c	337	674	1011	2359	4130	5900
9-Claw vs. Daredevil by Cole; Silver Streak-c by Bob Wood	260	412	618	1318	2259	3200
10-Origin & 1st app. Captain Battle (5/41); Claw vs. Daredevil by Cole;Silver Streak/Robot-c	171	342	513	1086	1868	2650
11-Intro. Mercury by Bob Wood, Silver Streak's sidekick; conclusion Claw vs. Daredevil by Rico; in 'Presto Martin,' 2nd pg., newspaper says 'Roussos does it again'	119	238	357	762	1306	1850
12-14: 12-Daredevil-c by Rico.13-Origin Thun-Dohr	86	172	258	546	936	1325
15, 17-Last Daredevil issue.	81	162	243	518	884	1250
16-Hitler-c	100	200	300	635	1093	1550
18-The Saint begins (2/42, 1st app.) by Leslie Charteris (see Movie Comics #2 by DC); The Saint-c	67	134	201	426	731	1035
19-21(1942): 20,21 have Wolverton's Scoop Scuttle. 21-Hitler app. in strip on cover	48	96	144	302	514	725
23(1946(An Atomic Comic)-Reprints; bondage-c	52	104	156	328	552	775
nn(2/46)(Newsbook Publ.)-R-/S.S. story from #4-7 plus 2 Captain Fearless stories, all in color; bondage/torture-c (scarce)	58	116	174	371	636	900

NOTE: ***Binder** c-3, 4, 13-15, 17. **Jack Cole** a-(Daredevil)-#6,8-10, (Dickie Dean)-#3-10, (Pirate Prince)-#7, (Silver Streak)-#4-8, nn; c-5 (Silver Streak), 6 (Claw), 7, 8 (Daredevil). **Everett** Red Reed begins #20. **Guardineer** a-#8-13. **Don Rico** a-11-17 (Daredevil); c-11, 12, 16. **Simon** a-3 (Silver Streak). **Bob Wood** a-9 (Silver Streak); c-9, 10. Captain Battle c-11, 13-15, 17. Claw c-#1, 2, 6-8. Daredevil c-7, 8, 12. Dickie Dean c-19. Ned of the Navy c-20 (war). The Saint c-18. Silver Streak c-5, 9, 10, 16, 23.*

SILVER STREAK COMICS (Homage with Golden Age size and Golden Age art styles)
Image Comics: No. 24, Dec, 2009 ($3.99, one-shot)

24-New Daredevil, Claw, Silver Streak & Captain Battle stories; Larsen, Grist, Gilbert-a 4.00

SILVER SURFER (See Fantastic Four, Fantasy Masterpieces V2#1, Fireside Book Series, Marvel Graphic Novel, Marvel Presents #8, Marvel's Greatest Comics & Tales To Astonish #92)

SILVER SURFER, THE (Also see Essential Silver Surfer)
Marvel Comics Group: Aug, 1968 - No. 18, Sept, 1970; June, 1982

	GD	VG	FN	VF	VF/NM	NM-
1-More detailed origin by John Buscema (p); The Watcher back-up stories begin (origin), end #7; (No. 1-7: 25¢, 68 pgs.)	50	100	150	400	775	1150
2	21	42	63	148	287	425
3-1st app. Mephisto	18	36	54	129	252	375
4-Lower distribution; Thor & Loki app.	41	82	123	328	639	950
5-7-Last giant size. 5-The Stranger app.; Fantastic Four app. 6-Brunner inks. 7-(8/69)-Early cameo Frankenstein's monster (see X-Men #40)	13	26	39	93	172	250
8-10: 8-18-(15¢ issues)	10	20	30	73	129	185
11-13,15-18: 15-Silver Surfer vs. Human Torch; Fantastic Four app. 17-Nick Fury app. 18-Vs. The Inhumans; Kirby-c/a	10	20	30	67	116	165
14-Spider-Man x-over	14	28	42	101	191	280

... Omnibus Vol. 1 Hardcover (2007, $74.99, dustjacket) r/#1-18 re-colored with original letter pages, Fantastic Four Annual #5 & Not Brand Echh #13; Lee and Buscema bios 75.00

	GD	VG	FN	VF	VF/NM	NM-
V2#1 (6/82, 52 pgs.)-Byrne-c/a	2	4	6	8	10	12

NOTE: ***Adkins** a-8-15i. **Brunner** a-6i. **J. Buscema** a-1-17p. **Colan** a-1-3p. **Reinman** a-1-4i. #1-14 were reprinted in Fantasy Masterpieces V2#1-14.*

SILVER SURFER (Volume 3) (See Marvel Graphic Novel #38)
Marvel Comics Group: V3#1, July, 1987 - No. 146, Nov, 1998

	GD	VG	FN	VF	VF/NM	NM-
1-Double size ($1.25)	1	2	3	5	7	9

2-17: 15-Ron Lim-c/a begins (9/88) 4.00

Silver Surfer: In Thy Name #1 © MAR

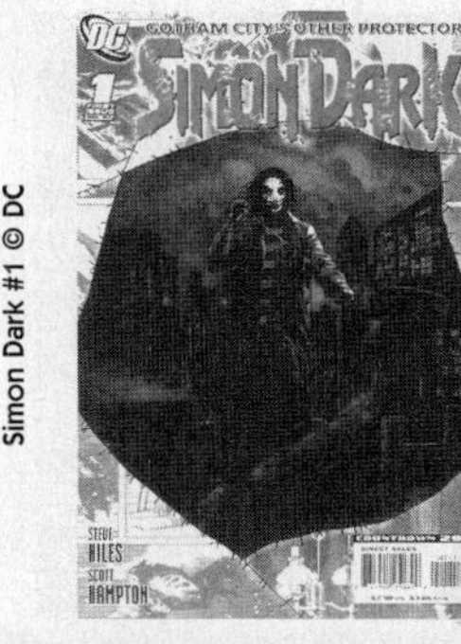

Simon Dark #1 © DC

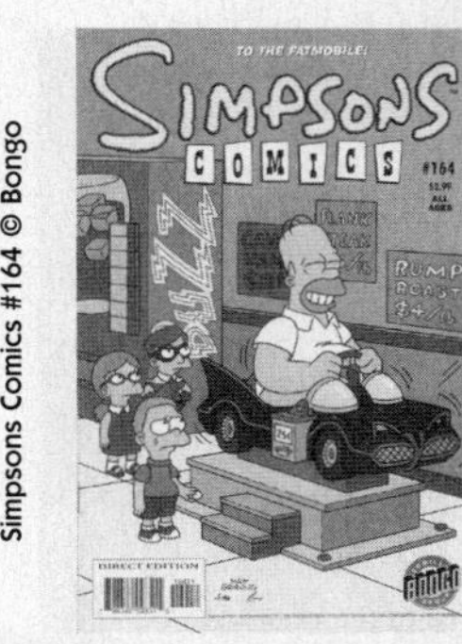

Simpsons Comics #164 © Bongo

	GD	VG	FN	VF	VF/NM	NM-
	2.0	4.0	6.0	8.0	9.0	9.2

18-33,39-43: 25,31 ($1.50, 52 pgs.). 25-Skrulls app. 32,39-No Ron Lim-c/a. 39-Alan Grant scripts 3.00
34-Thanos returns (cameo); Starlin scripts begin 5.00
35-38: 35-1st full Thanos app. in Silver Surfer (3/90); reintro Drax the Destroyer on last pg. (cameo). 36-Recaps history of Thanos; Capt. Marvel & Warlock app. in recap. 37-1st full app. Drax the Destroyer; Drax-c. 38-Silver Surfer battles Thanos 6.00
44,45,49-Thanos stories (c-44,45) 4.00
46-48: 46-Return of Adam Warlock (2/91); re-intro Gamora & Pip the Troll. 47-Warlock battles Drax. 48-Last Starlin scripts (also #50) 4.00
50-($1.50, 52 pgs.)-Embossed & silver foil-c; Silver Surfer has brief battle w/Thanos; story cont'd in Infinity Gauntlet #1 1 2 3 4 5 7
50-2nd & 3rd printings 2.50
51-59: 51-53: Infinity Gauntlet x-over . 54-57: Infinity Gauntlet x-overs. 54-Rhino app. 55,56-Thanos-c & app. 57-Thanos-c & cameo. 58,59-Infinity Gauntlet x-overs; 58-Lim-c only. 59-Thanos battles Silver Surfer-c/story; Thanos joins 3.00
60-74,76-99,101-124,126-139: 63-Capt. Marvel app. 67-69-Infinity War x-overs. 76-78-Jack of Hearts-c/s. 83-85-Infinity Crusade x-over; 83,84-Thanos cameo. 85-Storm, Wonder Man x-over. 86-Thor-c/s. 87-Dr. Strange & Warlock app. 88-Thanos-c/s. 82 (52 pgs.). 95-FF app. 96-Hulk & FF app. 97-Terrax & Nova app. 101-Bound in card sheet. 106-Doc Doom app. 121-Quasar & Beta Ray Bill app. 123-w/card insert; begin Garney-a. 126-Dr. Strange-c/app. 128-Spider-Man & Daredevil-c/app. 138-Thing-c 2.50
75-($2.50, 52 pgs.)-Embossed foil-c; Lim-c/a 3.00
100 ($2.25, 52 pgs.)-Wraparound-c 2.50
100 ($3.95, 52 pgs.)-Enhanced-c 4.00
125 ($2.95)-Wraparound-c; Vs. Hulk-c/app. 3.00
140-146: 140-142,144,145-Muth-c/a. 143,146-Cowan-a. 146-Last issue 2.50
#(-1) Flashback (7/97) 2.50
Annual 1 (1988, $1.75)-Evolutionary War app.; 1st Ron Lim-a on Silver Surfer (20 pg. back-up story & pin-ups) 5.00
Annual 2-7 ('89-'94, 68 pgs.): 2-Atlantis Attacks. 4-3 pg. origin story; Silver Surfer battles Guardians of the Galaxy. 5-Return of the Defenders, part 3; Lim-c/a (3 pgs. of pin-ups only). 6-Polybagged w/trading card; 1st app. Legacy; card is by Lim/Austin 3.00
Annual '97 ($2.99), .../Thor Annual '98 ($2.99) 3.00
Ashcan (1995, 75¢) reprints part of V1#3; Lim-c 2.50
...Dangerous Artifacts-(1996, $3.95)-Ron Marz scripts; Galactus-c/app. 4.00
Graphic Novel (1988, HC, $14.95) Judgment Day; Lee-s/Buscema-a 15.00
The Enslavers Graphic Novel (1990, $16.95) 17.00
Homecoming Graphic Novel (1991, $12.95, softcover) Starlin-s 15.00
Inner Demons TPB (4/98, $3.50)r/#123,125,126 3.50
...: Rebirth of Thanos TPB (2006, $24.99) r/#34-38, Thanos Quest #1,2; Logan's Run #6 25.00
...: The First Coming of Galactus nn (11/92, $5.95, 68 pgs.)-Reprints Fantastic Four #48-50 with new Lim-c 6.00
Wizard 1/2 2 4 6 9 12 15
NOTE: ***Austin*** *c(i)-7, 8, 71, 73, 74, 76, 79.* ***Cowan*** *a-143,146.* ***Cully Hamner*** *a-83p.* ***Ron Lim*** *a(p)-15-31, 33-38, 40-55, (56, 57-part-p), 60-65, 73-82, Annual 2, 4; c(p)-15-31, 32-38, 40-84, 86-92, Annual 2, 4-6.* ***Muth*** *c/a-140-142,144,145.* ***M. Rogers*** *a-1-10, 12, 19, 21; c-1-9, 11, 12, 21.*

SILVER SURFER (Volume 4)
Marvel Comics: Sept, 2003 - No. 14, Dec, 2004 ($2.25/$2.99)
1-6: 1-Milx-a; Jusko-c. 2-Jae Lee-c 2.50
7-14-($2.99) 3.00
...Vol. 1: Communion (2004, $14.99) r/#1-6 15.00

SILVER SURFER, THE
Marvel Comics (Epic): Dec, 1988 - No. 2, Jan, 1989 ($1.00, lim. series)
1,2: By Stan Lee scripts & Moebius-c/a 4.00
HC (1988, $19.95, dust jacket) r/#1,2; "Making Of" text section and sketch pages 30.00
...: Parable ('98, $5.99) r/#1&2 6.00

SILVER SURFER: IN THY NAME
Marvel Comics: Jan, 2008 - No. 4, Apr, 2008 ($2.99, limited series)
1-4-Spurrier-s/Huat-a. 1-Turner-c. 2-Dell'Otto-c. 3-Paul Pope-c. 4-Galactus app. 3.00

SILVER SURFER: LOFTIER THAN MORTALS
Marvel Comics: Oct, 1999 - No. 2, Oct, 1999 ($2.50, limited series)
1,2-Remix of Fantastic Four #57-60; Velluto-a 2.50

SILVER SURFER: REQUIEM
Marvel Comics: July, 2007 - No. 4, Oct, 2007 ($3.99, limited series)
1-4-Straczynski-s/Ribic-a. 1-Origin retold; Fantastic Four app. 4.00
HC (2007, $19.99) r/#1-4, Ribic cover sketches 20.00

SILVER SURFER/SUPERMAN
Marvel Comics: 1996 ($5.95,one-shot)
1-Perez-s/Lim-c/a(p) 6.00

SILVER SURFER VS. DRACULA
Marvel Comics: Feb, 1994 ($1.75, one-shot)
1-r/Tomb of Dracula #50; Everett Vampire-r/Venus #19; Howard the Duck back-up by Brunner; Lim-c(p) 2.50

SILVER SURFER/WARLOCK: RESURRECTION
Marvel Comics: Mar, 1993 - No. 4, June, 1993 ($2.50, limited series)
1-4: Starlin-c/a & scripts 2.50

SILVER SURFER/WEAPON ZERO
Marvel Comics: Apr, 1997 ($2.95, one-shot)
1-"Devil's Reign" pt. 8 3.00

SILVERTIP (Max Brand)
Dell Publishing Co.: No. 491, Aug, 1953 - No. 898, May, 1958
Four Color 491 (#1); all painted-c 8 16 24 52 86 120
Four Color 572,608,637,667,731,789,898-Kinstler-a 5 10 15 30 48 65
Four Color 835 5 10 15 30 48 65

SIMON DARK
DC Comics: Dec, 2007 - No. 18, May, 2009 ($2.99)
1-Intro. Simon Dark; Steve Niles-s/Scott Hampton-a/c 4.00
1-Second printing with full face variant cover 3.00
2-18 3.00
...: Ashes TPB (2009, $17.99) r/#7-12 18.00
...: The Game of Life TPB (2009, $17.99) r/#13-18 18.00
...: What Simon Does TPB (2008, $14.99) r/#1-6 15.00

SIMPSONS COMICS (See Bartman, Futurama, Itchy & Scratchy & Radioactive Man)
Bongo Comics Group: 1993 - Present ($1.95/$2.50/$2.99)
1-($2.25)-FF#1-c swipe; pull-out poster; flip book 1 2 3 5 6 8
2-5: 2-Patty & Selma flip-c/sty. 3-Krusty, Agent of K.L.O.W.N. flip-c/story. 4-Infinity-c; flip-c of Busman #1; w/trading card. 5-Wraparound-c w/trading card 5.00
6-40: All Flip books. 6-w/Chief Wiggum's "Crime Comics". 7-w/"McBain Comics". 8-w/"Edna, Queen of the Congo". 9-w/"Barney Gumble". 10-w/"Apu". 11-w/"Homer". 12-w/"White Knuckled War Stories". 13-w/"Jimbo Jones' Wedgie Comics". 14-w/"Grampa". 15-w/"Itchy & Scratchy". 16-w/"Bongo Grab Bag". 17-w/"Headlight Comics". 18-w/"Milhouse". 19,20-w/"Roswell". 21,22-w/"Roswell". 23-w/"Hellfire Comics". 24-w/"Lil' Homey". 36-39-Flip book w/Radioactive Man 4.00
41-49,51-99: 43-Flip book w/Poochie. 52-Dini-s. 77-Dixon-s. 85-Begin $2.99-c 3.00
50-($5.95) Wraparound-c; 80 pgs.; square-bound 1 2 3 4 5 7
100-($6.99) 100 pgs.; square-bound; clip issue of past highlights 7.00
101-164: 102-Barks Ducks homage. 117-Hank Scorpio app. 122-Archie spoof. 132-Movie poster enclosed. 132-133-Two-parter. 144-Flying Hellfish flashback. 150-w/Poster. 163-Aragonés-s/a 3.00
... A Go-Go (1999, $11.95)-r/#32-35; ...Big Bonanza (1998, $11.95)-r/#28-31, ...Extravaganza (1994, $10.00)-r/#1-4; infinity-c, ...On Parade (1998, $11.95)-r/#24-27, ...Simpsorama (1996, $10.95)-r/#11-14 12.00
Simpsons Classics 1-23 (2004-Present, $3.99, magazine-size, quarterly) reprints 4.00
Simpsons Comics Barn Burner ('04, $14.95) r/#57-61,63 15.00
Simpsons Comics Beach Blanket Bongo ('07, $14.95) r/#71-75,77 15.00
Simpsons Comics Belly Buster ('04, $14.95) r/#49,51,53-56 15.00
Simpsons Comics Hit the Road! ('08, $15.95) r/#85,86,88,89,90 16.00
Simpsons Comics Jam-Packed Jamboree ('06, $14.95) r/#64-69 15.00
Simpsons Comics Madness ('03, $14.95) r/#43-48 15.00
Simpsons Comics Royale ('01, $14.95) r/various Bongo issues 15.00
Simpsons Comics Treasure Trove 1-4 ('08-'09, $3.99, 6" x 8") r/various Bongo issues 4.00
Simpsons Summer Shindig ('07-'09, $4.99) 1-3-Anthology. 1-Batman/Ripken insert 5.00
Simpsons Winter Wing Ding ('06-'09, $4.99) 1-4-Holiday anthology. 1-Dini-s 5.00

SIMPSONS COMICS AND STORIES
Welsh Publishing Group: 1993 ($2.95, one-shot)
1-(Direct Sale)-Polybagged w/Bartman poster 6.00
1-(Newsstand Edition)-Without poster 4.00

SIMPSONS COMICS PRESENTS BART SIMPSON
Bongo Comics Group: 2000 - Present ($2.50/$2.99, quarterly)
1-52: 7-9-Dan DeCarlo-layouts. 13-Begin $2.99-c. 17,37-Bartman app. 50-Aragonés-s/a 3.00
The Big Book of Bart Simpson TPB (2002, $12.95) r/#1-4 13.00
The Big Bad Book of Bart Simpson TPB (2003, $12.95) r/#5-8 13.00
The Big Bratty Book of Bart Simpson TPB (2004, $12.95) r/#9-12 13.00
The Big Beefy Book of Bart Simpson TPB (2005, $13.95) r/#13-16 14.00
The Big Bouncy Book of Bart Simpson TPB (2006, $13.95) r/#17-20 14.00
The Big Beastly Book of Bart Simpson TPB (2007, $14.95) r/#21-24 15.00
The Big Brilliant Book of Bart Simpson TPB (2008, $14.95) r/#25-28 15.00

SIMPSONS FUTURAMA CROSSOVER CRISIS II (TV) (Also see Futurama/Simpsons Infinitely Secret Crossover Crisis)

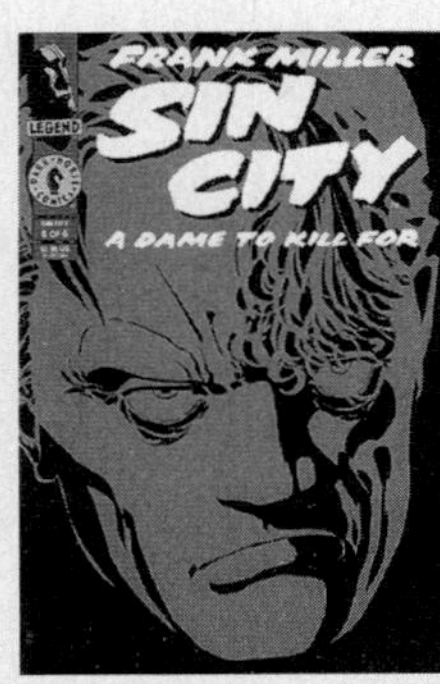

Sin City: A Dame to Kill For #6 © Frank Miller

Single Series #26 © UFS

Siren: Shapes #3 © J. Torres

GD VG FN VF VF/NM NM-
2.0 4.0 6.0 8.0 9.0 9.2

GD VG FN VF VF/NM NM-
2.0 4.0 6.0 8.0 9.0 9.2

Bongo Comics: 2005 - No. 2, 2005 ($3.00, limited series)
1,2-The Professor brings the Simpsons' Springfield crew to the 31st century 3.00

SIMPSONS SUPER SPECTACULAR (TV)
Bongo Comics: 2006 - Present ($2.99)
1-10: 2-Bartman, Stretch Dude and The Cupcake Kid team up; back-up story Brereton-a. 5-Ramona Fradon-a on Metamorpho spoof. 8-Spirit spoof. 9,10-Radioactive Man app. 3.00

SINBAD, JR (TV Cartoon)
Dell Publishing Co.: Sept-Nov, 1965 - No. 3, May, 1966
1 4 8 12 24 37 50
2,3 3 6 9 18 27 35

SIN CITY (See Dark Horse Presents, A Decade of Dark Horse, & San Diego Comic Con Comics #2,4)
Dark Horse Comics (Legend)
TPB ($15.00) Reprints early DHP stories 15.00
Booze, Broads & Bullets TPB ($15.00) 15.00

SIN CITY (FRANK MILLER'S...) (Reissued TPBs to coincide with the April 2005 movie)
Dark Horse Books: Feb, 2005 ($17.00/$19.00, 6" x 9" format with new Miller covers)
Volume 1: The Hard Goodbye ($17.00) reprints stories from Dark Horse Presents #51-62 and DHP Fifth Anniv. Special; covers and publicity pieces 17.00
Volume 2: A Dame to Kill For ($17.00) r/Sin City: A Dame to Kill For #1-6 17.00
Volume 3: The Big Fat Kill ($17.00) r/Sin City: The Big Fat Kill #1-5; pin-up gallery 17.00
Volume 4: That Yellow Bastard ($19.00) r/Sin City: That Yellow Bastard #1-6; pin-up gallery by Mike Allred, Kyle Baker, Jeff Smith and Bruce Timm; cover gallery 19.00
Volume 5: Family Values ($12.00) r/Sin City: Family Values GN 12.00
Volume 6: Booze, Broads & Bullets ($15.00) r/Sin City: The Babe Wore Red and Other Stories; Silent Night; story from A Decade of Dark Horse; Lost Lonely & Lethal; Sex & Violence; and Just Another Saturday Night 15.00
Volume 7: Hell and Back ($28.00) r/Sin City: Hell and Back #1-9; pin-up gallery 28.00

SIN CITY: A DAME TO KILL FOR
Dark Horse Comics (Legend): Nov, 1993 - No. 6, May, 1994 ($2.95, B&W, limited series)
1-6: Frank Miller-c/a & story in all. 1-1st app. Dwight. 6.00
Limited Edition Hardcover 85.00
Hardcover 25.00
TPB ($15.00) 15.00

SIN CITY: FAMILY VALUES
Dark Horse Comics (Legend): Oct, 1997 ($10.00, B&W, squarebound, one-shot)
nn-Miller-c/a & story 10.00
Limited Edition Hardcover 75.00

SIN CITY: HELL AND BACK
Dark Horse (Maverick): Jul, 1999 - No. 9 ($2.95/$4.95, B&W, limited series)
1-8-Miller-c/a & story. 7-Color 4.00
9-($4.95) 6.00

SIN CITY: JUST ANOTHER SATURDAY NIGHT
Dark Horse Comics (Legend): Aug, 1997 (Wizard 1/2 offer, B&W, one-shot)
1/2-Miller-c/a & story 1 2 3 5 6 8
nn (10/98, $2.50) r/#1/2 2.50

SIN CITY: LOST, LONELY & LETHAL
Dark Horse Comics (Legend): Dec, 1996 ($2.95, B&W and blue, one-shot)
nn-Miller-c/s/a; w/pin-ups 5.00

SIN CITY: SEX AND VIOLENCE
Dark Horse Comics (Legend): Mar, 1997 ($2.95, B&W and blue, one-shot)
nn-Miller-c/a & story 5.00

SIN CITY: SILENT NIGHT
Dark Horse Comics (Legend): Dec, 1995 ($2.95, B&W, one-shot)
1-Miller-c/a & story; Marv app. 5.00

SIN CITY: THAT YELLOW BASTARD (Second Ed. TPB listed under Sin City (Frank Miller's...)
Dark Horse Comics (Legend): Feb, 1996 - No. 6, July, 1996 ($2.95/$3.50, B&W and yellow, limited series)
1-5: Miller-c/a & story in all. 1-1st app. Hartigan. 5.00
6-($3.50) Error & corrected 5.00
Limited Edition Hardcover 25.00
TPB ($15.00) 15.00

SIN CITY: THE BABE WORE RED AND OTHER STORIES
Dark Horse Comics (Legend): Nov, 1994 ($2.95, B&W and red, one-shot)
1-r/serial run in Previews as well as other stories; Miller-c/a & scripts; Dwight app. 4.00

SIN CITY: THE BIG FAT KILL (Second Edition TPB listed under Sin City (Frank Miller's...)
Dark Horse Comics (Legend): Nov, 1994 - No. 5, Mar, 1995 ($2.95, B&W, limited series)
1-5-Miller story & art in all; Dwight app. 5.00
Hardcover 25.00
TPB ($15.00) 15.00

SIN CITY: THE FRANK MILLER LIBRARY
Dark Horse Books: Set 1, Nov, 2005; Set 2, Mar, 2006 ($150, slipcased hardcover, 8" x 12")
Set 1 - Individual hardcovers for Volume 1: The Hard Goodbye, Volume 2: A Dame to Kill For, Volume 3: The Big Fat Kill, Volume 4: That Yellow Bastard; new red foil stamped covers; slipcase box is black with red foil graphics 150.00
Set 2 - Individual hardcovers for Volume 5: Family Values, Volume 6: Booze, Broads & Bullets, Volume 7: Hell and Back, new red foil stamped covers; The Art of Sin City red hardcover; slipcase box is black with red foil graphics 150.00

SINDBAD (See Capt. Sindbad under Movie Comics, and Fantastic Voyages of Sindbad)

SINGING GUNS (See Fawcett Movie Comics)

SINGLE SERIES (Comics on Parade #30 on)(Also see John Hix...)
United Features Syndicate: 1938 - No. 28, 1942 (All 68 pgs.)
Note: See Individual Alphabetical Listings for prices
1-Captain and the Kids (#1)
2-Broncho Bill (1939) (#1)
3-Ella Cinders (1939)
4-Li'l Abner (1939) (#1)
5-Fritzi Ritz (#1)
6-Jim Hardy by Dick Moores (#1)
7-Frankie Doodle
8-Peter Pat (On sale 7/14/39)
9-Strange As It Seems
10-Little Mary Mixup
11-Mr. and Mrs. Beans
12-Joe Jinks
13-Looy Dot Dope
14-Billy Make Believe
15-How It Began (1939)
16-Illustrated Gags (1940)-Has ad for Captain and the Kids #1 reprint listed below
17-Danny Dingle
18-Li'l Abner (#2 on-c)
19-Broncho Bill (#2 on-c)
20-Tarzan by Hal Foster
21-Ella Cinders (#2 on-c; on sale 3/19/40)
22-Iron Vic
23-Tailspin Tommy by Hal Forrest (#1)
24-Alice in Wonderland (#1)
25-Abbie and Slats
26-Little Mary Mixup (#2 on-c, 1940)
27-Jim Hardy by Dick Moores (1942)
28-Ella Cinders & Abbie and Slats (1942)
1-Captain and the Kids (1939 reprint)-2nd Edition
1-Fritzi Ritz (1939 reprint)-2nd ed.

NOTE: *Some issues given away at the 1939-40 New York World's Fair (#6).*

SINGULARITY 7
IDW Publ.: July, 2004 - No. 4, Oct, 2004 ($3.99, limited series)
1-4-Templesmith-s/a 4.00

SINISTER HOUSE OF SECRET LOVE, THE (Becomes Secrets of Sinister House No. 5 on)
National Periodical Publ.: Oct-Nov, 1971 - No. 4, Apr-May, 1972
1 (all 52 pgs.) 17 34 51 122 236 350
2,4: 2-Jeff Jones-c 9 18 27 63 107 150
3-Toth-a; greytone-c 9 18 27 65 113 160

SINS OF YOUTH... (Also see Young Justice: Sins of Youth)
DC Comics: May 2000 ($4.95/$2.50, limited crossover series)
Secret Files 1 ($4.95) Short stories and profile pages; Nauck-c 5.00
...Aquaboy/Lagoon Man; Batboy and Robin; JLA Jr.; Kid Flash/Impulse; Starwoman and the JSA, Superman, Jr./Superboy, Sr.; The Secret/ Deadboy, Wonder Girls ($2.50-c) Old and young heroes switch ages 2.50

SIR APROPOS OF NOTHING
IDW Publishing: Nov, 2009 - Present ($3.99)
1-3-Peter David-s/Robin Riggs-a; two covers on each. 2-Kaluta-c 4.00

SIR CHARLES BARKLEY AND THE REFEREE MURDERS
Hamilton Comics: 1993 ($9.95, 8-1/2" x 11", 52 pgs.)
nn-Photo-c; Sports fantasy comic book fiction (uses real names of NBA superstars). Script by Alan Dean Foster, art by Joe Staton. Comes with bound-in sheet of 35 gummed "Moods of Charles Barkley" stamps. Photo/story on Barkley 2 4 6 8 10 12
Special Edition of 100 copies for charity signed on an affixed book plate by Barkley, Foster & Staton 150.00
Ashcan edition given away to dealers, distributors & promoters (low distribution). Four pages in color, balance of story in b&w 2 4 6 8 10 12

SIR EDWARD GREY, WITCHFINDER: IN THE SERVICE OF ANGELS (From Hellboy)
Dark Horse Comics: July, 2009 - No. 5, Nov, 2009 ($2.99, limited series)
1-5-Mignola-s/c; Stenbeck-a 3.00

SIREN (Also see Eliminator & Ultraforce)
Malibu Comics (Ultraverse): Sept, 1995 - No. 3, Dec, 1995 ($1.50)

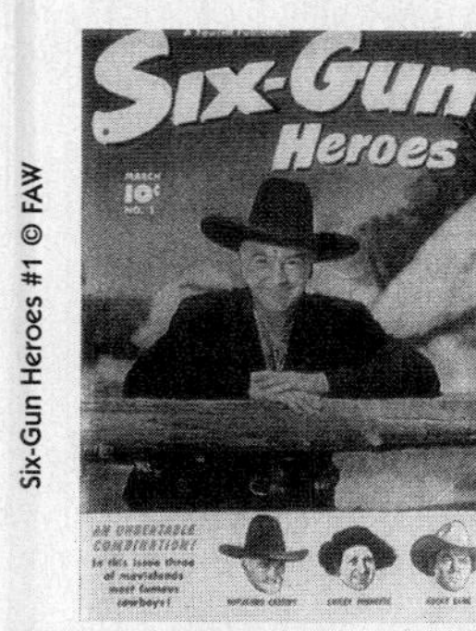

Six-Gun Heroes #1 © FAW

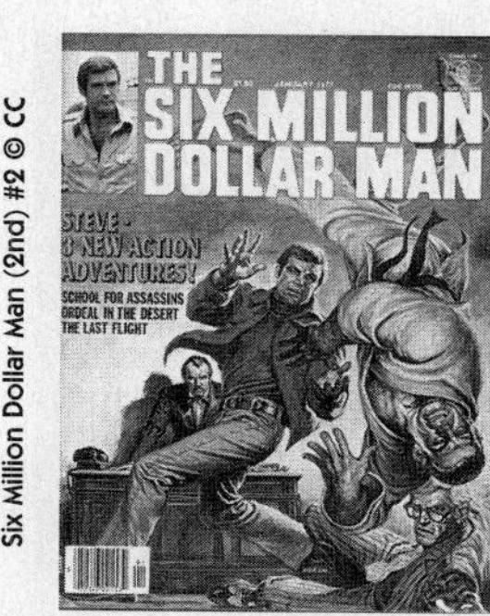

Six Million Dollar Man (2nd) #2 © CC

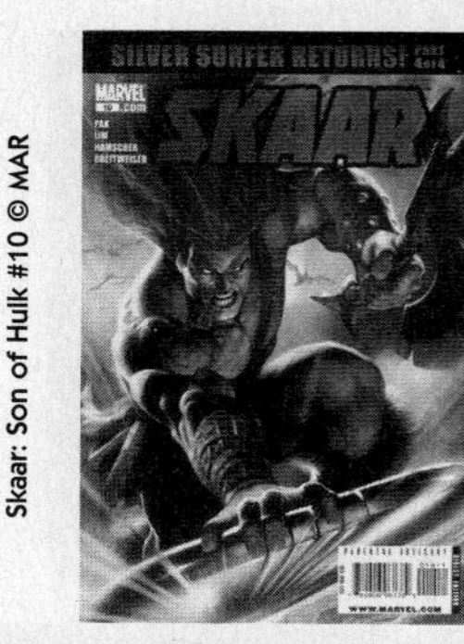

Skaar: Son of Hulk #10 © MAR

	GD 2.0	VG 4.0	FN 6.0	VF 8.0	VF/NM 9.0	NM- 9.2

Infinity, 1-3: Infinity-Black-c & painted-c exists. 1-Regular-c & painted-c; War Machine app.
2-Flip book w/Phoenix Resurrection Pt. 3 — 2.50
Special 1-(2/96, $1.95, 28 pgs.)-Origin Siren; Marvel Comic's Juggernaut-c/app. — 2.50

SIREN: SHAPES
Image Comics: May, 1998 - No. 3, Nov, 1998 ($2.95, B&W, limited series)
1-3-J. Torres -s — 3.00

SIR LANCELOT (TV)
Dell Publishing Co.: No. 606, Dec, 1954 - No. 775, Mar, 1957

	GD	VG	FN	VF	VF/NM	NM-
Four Color 606 (not TV)	7	14	21	49	80	110
Four Color 775(...and Brian)-Buscema-a; photo-c	9	18	27	65	113	160

SIR WALTER RALEIGH (Movie)
Dell Publishing Co.: May, 1955 (Based on movie "The Virgin Queen")

	GD	VG	FN	VF	VF/NM	NM-
Four Color 644-Photo-c	7	14	21	45	73	100

SISTERHOOD OF STEEL (See Eclipse Graphic Adventure Novel #13)
Marvel Comics (Epic Comics): Dec, 1984 -No. 8, Feb, 1986 ($1.50, Baxter paper, mature)
1-8 — 3.00

SIX
Image Comics: Aug, 2004 ($5.95, B&W)
1-Oeming-s/c; Beavers-a — 6.00

6 BLACK HORSES (See Movie Classics)

SIX FROM SIRIUS
Marvel Comics (Epic Comics): July, 1984 - No. 4, Oct, 1984 ($1.50, limited series, mature)
1-4: Moench scripts; Gulacy-c/a in all — 2.50

SIX FROM SIRIUS II
Marvel Comics (Epic Comics): Feb, 1986 - No. 4, May, 1986 ($1.50, limited series, mature)
1-4: Moench scripts; Gulacy-c/a in all — 2.50

SIX-GUN HEROES
Fawcett Publications: March, 1950 - No. 23, Nov, 1953 (Photo-c #1-23)

	GD	VG	FN	VF	VF/NM	NM-
1-Rocky Lane, Hopalong Cassidy, Smiley Burnette begin (same date as Smiley Burnette #1)	40	80	120	235	380	525
2	20	40	60	115	183	250
3-5: 5-Lash LaRue begins	15	30	45	85	130	175
6-15	13	26	39	74	105	135
16-22: 17-Last Smiley Burnette. 18-Monte Hale begins	11	22	33	62	86	110
23-Last Fawcett issue	12	24	36	67	94	120

NOTE: *Hopalong Cassidy photo c-1-3. Monte Hale photo c-18. Rocky Lane photo c-4, 5, 7, 9, 11, 13, 15, 17, 20, 21, 23. Lash LaRue photo c-6, 8, 10, 12, 14, 16, 19, 22.*

SIX-GUN HEROES (Cont'd from Fawcett; Gunmasters #84 on) (See Blue Bird)
Charlton Comics: No. 24, Jan, 1954 - No. 83, Mar-Apr, 1965 (All Vol. 4)

	GD	VG	FN	VF	VF/NM	NM-
24-Lash LaRue, Hopalong Cassidy, Rocky Lane & Tex Ritter begin; photo-c	15	30	45	94	147	200
25	10	20	30	58	79	100
26-30: 26-Rod Cameron story. 28-Tom Mix begins?	9	18	27	52	69	85
31-40: 38-40-Jingles & Wild Bill Hickok (TV)	8	16	24	44	57	70
41-46,48,50: 41-43-Wild Bill Hickok (TV)	8	16	24	42	54	65
47-Williamson-a, 2 pgs; Torres-a	8	16	24	44	57	70
49-Williamson-a (5 pgs.)	9	18	27	52	69	85
51-56,58-60: 58-Gunmaster app.	3	6	9	20	30	40
57-Origin & 1st app. Gunmaster	4	8	12	26	41	55
61,63-70	3	6	9	16	23	30
62-Origin Gunmaster	3	6	9	20	30	40
71-75,77,78,80-83	2	4	6	13	18	22
76,79: 76-Gunmaster begins. 79-1st app. & origin of Bullet, the Gun-Boy	3	6	9	14	19	24

SIXGUN RANCH (See Luke Short & Four Color #580)

SIX-GUN WESTERN
Atlas Comics (CDS): Jan, 1957 - No. 4, July, 1957

	GD	VG	FN	VF	VF/NM	NM-
1-Crandall-a; two Williamson text illos	18	36	54	105	165	225
2,3-Williamson-a in both	14	28	42	80	115	150
4-Woodbridge-a	10	20	30	58	79	100

NOTE: ***Ayers** a-2, 3. **Maneely** a-1; c-2, 3. **Orlando** a-2. **Pakula** a-2. **Powell** a-3. **Romita** a-1, 4. **Severin** c-1, 4. **Shores** a-2.*

SIX MILLION DOLLAR MAN, THE (TV)
Charlton Comics: 6/76 - No. 4, 12/76; No. 5, 10/77; No. 6, 2/78 - No. 9, 6/78

	GD	VG	FN	VF	VF/NM	NM-
1-Staton-c/a; Lee Majors photo on-c	3	6	9	16	22	28
2-9: 2-Neal Adams-c; Staton-a	2	4	6	11	16	20

SIX MILLION DOLLAR MAN, THE (TV)(Magazine)
Charlton Comics: July, 1976 - No. 7, Nov, 1977 (B&W)

	GD	VG	FN	VF	VF/NM	NM-
1-Neal Adams-c/a	3	6	9	20	30	40
2-Neal Adams-c	3	6	9	16	22	28
3-N. Adams part inks; Chaykin-a	2	4	6	13	18	22
4-7	2	4	6	10	14	18

SIX STRING SAMURAI
Awesome-Hyperwerks: Sept, 1998 ($2.95)
1-Stinsman & Fraga-a — 3.00

67 SECONDS
Marvel Comics (Epic Comics): 1992 ($15.95, 54 pgs., graphic novel)

	GD	VG	FN	VF	VF/NM	NM-
nn-James Robinson scripts; Steve Yeowell-c/a	2	4	6	11	14	18

SKAAR: SON OF HULK (Title continues in Son of Hulk #13)(Also see World War Hulk x-over)
Marvel Comics: Aug, 2008 - No. 12, Aug, 2009 ($2.99)
1-Garney-a/Pak-s; 2 covers by Pagulayan and Julie Bell; origin — 4.00
1-Second printing - 2 covers by Garney and Hulk movie image — 3.00
1-Third printing - Garney sketch variant-c — 3.00
2-12: 2-6-Back-up story with Guice-a. 7-12-Silver Surfer app. — 3.00
Planet Skaar Prologue 1 (7/09, $3.99) Panosian-a; Fantastic Four & She-Hulk app. — 4.00
... Presents - Savage World of Sakaar (11/08, $3.99) Pak-s/art by various; Garney-c — 4.00

SKATEMAN
Pacific Comics: Nov, 1983 (Baxter paper, one-shot)
1-Adams-c/a — 4.00

SKELETON HAND (...In Secrets of the Supernatural)
American Comics Gr. (B&M Dist. Co.): Sept-Oct, 1952 - No. 6, Jul-Aug, 1953

	GD	VG	FN	VF	VF/NM	NM-
1	45	90	135	284	480	675
2	33	66	99	194	317	440
3-6	26	52	78	152	249	345

SKELETON KEY
Amaze Ink: July, 1995 - No. 30, Jan, 1998 ($1.25/$1.50/$1.75, B&W)
1-30 — 3.00
Special #1 (2/98, $4.95) Unpublished short stories — 5.00
Sugar Kat Special (10/98, $2.95) Halloween stories — 3.00
Beyond The Threshold TPB (6/96. $11.95)-r/#1-6 — 12.00
Cats and Dogs TPB ($12.95)-r/#25-30 — 13.00
The Celestial Calendar TPB ($19.95)-r/#7-18 — 20.00
Telling Tales TPB ($12.95)-r/#19-24 — 13.00

SKELETON KEY (Volume 2)
Amaze Ink: 1999 - No. 4, 1999 ($2.95, B&W)
1-4-Andrew Watson-s/a — 3.00

SKELETON WARRIORS
Marvel Comics: Apr, 1995 - No. 4, July, 1995 ($1.50)
1-4: Based on animated series. — 2.50

SKIN GRAFT: THE ADVENTURES OF A TATTOOED MAN
DC Comics (Vertigo): July, 1993 - No. 4, Oct, 1993 ($2.50, lim. series, mature)
1-4 — 2.50

SKINWALKER
Oni Press: May, 2002 - No. 4, Sept, 2002 ($2.95, limited series)
1-4-Hurtt & Dela Cruz-a; Talon-c — 3.00
1-(5/05) Free Comic Book Day Edition — 2.50

SKI PARTY (See Movie Classics)

SKREEMER
DC Comics: May, 1989 - No. 6, Oct, 1989 ($2.00, limited series, mature)
1-6: Contains graphic violence; Milligan-s — 2.50
TPB (2002, $19.95) r/#1-6 — 20.00

SKRULL KILL KREW
Marvel Comics: Sept, 1995 - No. 5, Dec, 1995 ($2.95, limited series)
1-5: Grant Morrison & Mark Millar scripts; Steve Yeowell-a. 2,3-Cap America app. — 3.00
TPB (2006, $16.99) r/#1-5 — 17.00

SKRULL KILL KREW
Marvel Comics: Jun, 2009 - No. 5, Dec, 2009 ($3.99, limited series)
1-5-Felber-s/Robinson-a — 4.00

SKRULLS! (Tie-in to Secret Invasion crossover)
Marvel Comics: 2008 ($4.99, one-shot)

Sky Doll Vol. 1 © MC & Barbucci & Canepa

Slam-Bang Comics #5 © FAW

Sleeper #1 © WSP

GD 2.0 | VG 4.0 | FN 6.0 | VF 8.0 | VF/NM 9.0 | NM- 9.2

GD 2.0 | VG 4.0 | FN 6.0 | VF 8.0 | VF/NM 9.0 | NM- 9.2

1-Skrull history, profiles of Skrulls, their allies & foes; checklist of appearances; Horn-c 5.00

SKRULLS VS. POWER PACK (Tie-in to Secret Invasion crossover)
Marvel Comics: Sept, 2008 - No. 4 ($2.99, limited series)
1-4-Van Lente-s/Hamscher-a; Franklin Richards app. 3.00

SKUL, THE
Virtual Comics (Byron Preiss Multimedia): Oct, 1996 - No. 3, Dec, 1996 ($2.50, lim. series)
1-3: Ron Lim & Jimmy Palmiotti-a 2.50

SKULL & BONES
DC Comics: 1992 - No. 3, 1992 ($4.95, limited series, 52 pgs.)
Book 1-3: 1-1st app. 5.00

SKULL, THE SLAYER
Marvel Comics Group: Aug, 1975 - No. 8, Nov, 1976 (20¢/25¢)
1-Origin & 1st app.; Gil Kane-c 2 4 6 9 13 16
2-8: 2-Gil Kane-c. 5,6-(Regular 25¢-c). 8-Kirby-c 2 3 4 6 8 10
5,6-(30¢-c variants, limited distribution)(5,7/76) 3 6 9 18 27 35

SKY BLAZERS (CBS Radio)
Hawley Publications: Sept, 1940 - No. 2, Nov, 1940
1-Sky Pirates, Ace Archer, Flying Aces begin 60 120 180 381 653 925
2-WWII aerial battle-c 39 78 117 231 378 525

SKY DOLL
Marvel Comics (Soleil): 2008 - No. 3, 2008 ($5.99)
1-3-Barbucci & Canepa-s/a; English version of French comic; preview of other titles 6.00
...: Doll's Factory 1,2 (2009 - No. 2, 2009, $5.99) Barbucci & Canepa-s/a 6.00

SKYE RUNNER
DC Comics (WildStorm): June, 2006 - No. 6, Mar, 2007 ($2.99)
1-6: 1-Three covers; Warner-s/Garza-a. 2-Three covers, incl. Campbell 3.00

SKYMAN (See Big Shot Comics & Sparky Watts)
Columbia Comics Gr.: Fall?, 1941 - No. 2, Fall?, 1942; No. 3, 1948 - No. 4, 1948
1-Origin Skyman, The Face, Sparky Watts app.; Whitney-c/a; 3rd story-r from Big Shot #1; Whitney c-1-4 124 248 372 787 1356 1925
2 (1942)-Yankee Doodle 59 118 177 375 643 910
3,4 (1948) 39 78 117 240 395 550

SKYPILOT
Ziff-Davis Publ. Co.: No. 10, 1950(nd) - No. 11, Apr-May, 1951
10,11-Frank Borth-a; Saunders painted-c 15 30 45 83 124 165

SKY RANGER (See Johnny Law...)

SKYROCKET
Harry 'A' Chesler: 1944
nn-Alias the Dragon, Dr. Vampire, Skyrocket & The Desperado app.; WWII Japan zero-c 32 64 96 188 307 425

SKY SHERIFF (Breeze Lawson...) (Also see Exposed & Outlaws)
D. S. Publishing Co.: Summer, 1948
1-Edmond Good-c/a 14 28 42 76 108 140

SKY WOLF (Also see Airboy)
Eclipse Comics: Mar, 1988 - No. 3, Oct, 1988 ($1.25/$1.50/$1.95, lim. series)
1-3 2.50

SLAINE, THE BERSERKER (Slaine the King #21 on)
Quality: July, 1987 - No. 28, 1989 ($1.25/$1.50)
1-28 2.50

SLAINE, THE HORNED GOD
Fleetway: 1998 - No. 3 ($6.99)
1-3-Reprints series from 2000 A.D.; Bisley-a 7.00

SLAM BANG COMICS (Western Desperado #8)
Fawcett Publications: Mar, 1940 - No. 7, Sept, 1940 (Combined with Master Comics #7)
1-Diamond Jack, Mark Swift & The Time Retarder, Lee Granger, Jungle King begin & continue in Master 206 412 618 1318 2259 3200
2 84 168 252 538 919 1300
3-Classic-c 161 322 483 1030 1765 2500
4-7: 6-Intro Zoro, the Mystery Man (also in #7) 65 130 195 416 708 1000
Ashcan (1940) Not distributed to newsstands, only for in house use. A copy sold in 2006 for $4,500.

SLAPSTICK
Marvel Comics: Nov, 1992 - No. 4, Feb, 1993 ($1.25, limited series)
1-4: Fry/Austin-c/a. 4-Ghost Rider, D.D., F.F. app. 2.50

SLAPSTICK COMICS
Comic Magazines Distributors: nd (1946?) (36 pgs.)
nn-Firetop feature; Post-a(2) 25 50 75 147 241 335

SLASH-D DOUBLECROSS
St. John Publishing Co.: 1950 (Pocket-size, 132 pgs.)
nn-Western comics 21 42 63 122 199 275

SLAUGHTERMAN
Comico: Feb, 1983 - No. 2, 1983 ($1.50, B&W)
1,2 3.00

SLAVE GIRL COMICS (See Malu... & White Princess of the Jungle #2)
Avon Periodicals/Eternity Comics (1989): Feb, 1949 - No. 2, Apr, 1949 (52 pgs.); Mar, 1989 (B&W, 44 pgs)
1-Larsen-c/a 100 200 300 635 1093 1550
2-Larsen-a 71 142 213 454 777 1100
1-(3/89, $2.25, B&W, 44 pgs.)-r/#1 3.00

SLEDGE HAMMER (TV)
Marvel Comics: Feb, 1988 - No. 2, Mar,1988 ($1.00, limited series)
1,2 3.00

SLEEPER
DC Comics (WildStorm): Mar, 2003 - No. 12, Mar, 2004 ($2.95)
1-12-Brubaker-s/Phillips-c/a. 3-Back-up preview of The Authority: High Stakes pt. 2 3.00
...: All False Moves TPB (2004, $17.95) r/#7-12 18.00
...: Out in the Cold TPB (2004, $17.95) r/#1-6 18.00

SLEEPER: SEASON TWO
DC Comics (WildStorm): Aug, 2004 - No. 12, July, 2005 ($2.95/$2.99)
1-12-Brubaker-s/Phillips-c/a. 3.00
TPB (2009, $24.99) r/#1-12 25.00
...: A Crooked Line TPB (2005, $17.99) r/#1-6 18.00
...: The Long Way Home TPB (2005, $14.99) r/#7-12 15.00

SLEEPING BEAUTY (See Dell Giants & Movie Comics)
Dell Publishing Co.: No. 973, May, 1959 - No. 984, June, 1959 (Disney)
Four Color 973 (...and the Prince) 11 22 33 74 132 190
Four Color 984 (...Fairy Godmother's) 9 18 27 61 103 145

SLEEPWALKER
Marvel Comics: June, 1991 - No. 33, Feb, 1994 ($1.00/$1.25)
1-1st app. Sleepwalker 3.00
2-33: 4-Williamson-i. 5-Spider-Man-c/stor. 7-Infinity Gauntlet x-over. 8-Vs. Deathlok-c/story. 11-Ghost Rider-c/story. 12-Quesada-c/a(p) 14-Intro Spectra. 15-F.F.-c/story. 17-Darkhawk & Spider-Man x-over. 18-Infinity War x-over; Quesada/Williamson-c. 21,22-Hobgoblin app. 19-($2.00)-Die-cut Sleepwalker mask-c 2.50
25-($2.95, 52 pgs.)-Holo-grafx foil-c; origin 3.00
Holiday Special 1 (1/93, $2.00, 52 pgs.)-Quesada-c(p) 2.50

SLEEPWALKING
Hall of Heroes: Jan, 1996 ($2.50, B&W)
1-Kelley Jones-c 2.50

SLEEPY HOLLOW (Movie Adaption)
DC Comics (Vertigo): 2000 ($7.95, one-shot)
1-Kelley Jones-a/Seagle-s 8.00

SLEEZE BROTHERS, THE
Marvel Comics (Epic Comics): Aug, 1989 - No. 6, Jan, 1990 ($1.75, mature)
1-6: 4-6 (9/89 - 11/89 indicia dates) 2.50
nn-(1991, $3.95, 52 pgs.) 4.00

SLICK CHICK COMICS
Leader Enterprises: 1947(nd) - No. 3, 1947(nd)
1-Teenage humor 14 28 42 76 108 140
2,3 10 20 30 54 72 90

SLIDERS (TV)
Acclaim Comics (Armada): June, 1996 - No. 2, July, 1996 ($2.50, lim. series)
1,2: D.G. Chichester scripts; Dick Giordano-a. 2.50

SLIDERS: DARKEST HOUR (TV)
Acclaim Comics (Armada): Oct, 1996 - No. 3, Dec, 1996 ($2.50, limited series)
1-3 2.50

SLIDERS SPECIAL
Acclaim Comics (Armada): Nov, 1996 - No 3, Mar, 1997 ($3.95, limited series)

Smallville #1 © DC

Smash Comics #31 © QUA

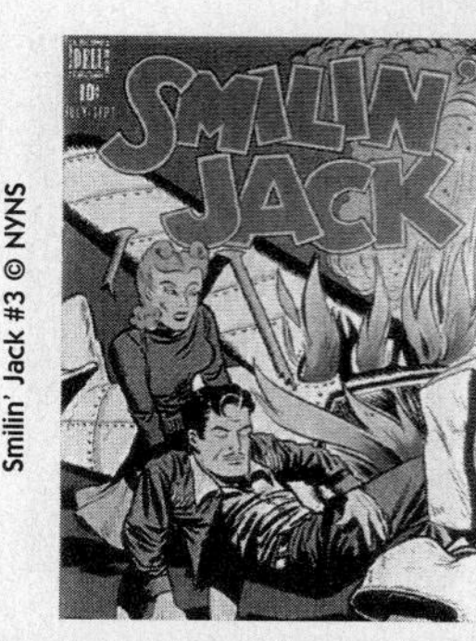

Smilin' Jack #3 © NYNS

GD 2.0 | VG 4.0 | FN 6.0 | VF 8.0 | VF/NM 9.0 | NM- 9.2

1-3: 1-Narcotica-Jerry O'Connell-s. 2-Blood and Splendor. 3-Deadly Secrets 4.00

SLIDERS: ULTIMATUM (TV)
Acclaim Comics (Armada): Sept, 1996 - No. 2, Sept, 1996 ($2.50, lim. series)

1,2 2.50

SLIMER! (TV cartoon) (Also see the Real Ghostbusters)
Now Comics: 1989 - No. 19, Feb?, 1991 ($1.75)

1-19: Based on animated cartoon 3.00

SLIM MORGAN (See Wisco)

SLINGERS (See Spider-Man: Identity Crisis issues)
Marvel Comics: Dec, 1998 - No. 12, Nov, 1999 ($2.99/$1.99)

0-(Wizard #88 supplement) Prelude story 2.50
1-($2.99) Four editions w/different covers for each hero, 16 pages common to all, the other pages from each hero's perspective 3.00
2-12: 2-Two-c. 12-Saltares-a 2.50

SLITHISS ATTACKS! (Also see Very Weird Tales)
Oceanspray Comics Group: Dec, 2001 – No. 4, Aug, 1984 ($3.00/$4.00)

1-($3.00) Origin and 1st app. of the monster Slithiss; 1st app. Overconfident Man 15.00
2-($4.00) 2nd app. Overconfident Man; "Chris Lamo" Newport, OR murder parody 12.00
3-($3.00) Rutland Vermont Halloween x-over; 3rd app. Overconfident Man 12.00
4-($3.00) 4th app. Overconfident Man 10.00
Special Edition 1($20.00) reprints #1-2 without letter column 20.00
Special Edition 1($20.00) second printing 20.00

NOTE: *Created in prevention classes taught by Jon McClure at the Oceanspray Family Center in Newport, OR and paid for by the Housing Authority of Lincoln County, all books are b&w with color covers. Bob Overstreet and other comics' professionals wrote letters of encouragement that were published in issues #2-4. Issues #1-2 penciled and inked by various artists; #3-4 penciled by James Gilmer. All comics feature characters created by students, signed and numbered by Jon McClure. Issue #1 had a 200 issue print run, while issues #2-4 have print runs of 100 each. Special Edition #1 had a print run of 26 issues, while the second printing had a 10 issue print run. Ties in with live action movie Face Eater released in 2007 and card game FaceEater to be released in 2010.*

SLUDGE
Malibu Comics (Ultraverse): Oct, 1993 - No. 12, Dec, 1994 ($2.50/$1.95)

1-($2.50, 48 pgs.)-Intro/1st app. Sludge; Rune flip-c/story Pt. 1 (1st app., 3 pgs.) by Barry Smith; The Night Man app. (3 pg. preview); The Mighty Magnor 1 pg strip begins by Aragonés (cont. in other titles) 3.00
1-Ultra 5000 Limited silver foil 4.00
2-11: 3-Break-Thru x-over. 4-2 pg. Mantra origin. 8-Bloodstorm app. 2.50
12 ($3.50)-Ultraverse Premiere #8 flip book; Alex Ross poster 3.50
...:Red Xmas (12/94, $2.50, 44 pgs.) 2.50

SLUGGER (Little Wise Guys Starring...)(Also see Daredevil Comics)
Lev Gleason Publications: April, 1956

1-Biro-c 7 14 21 35 43 50

SMALL GODS
Image Comics: Jun, 2004 - No. 12, Nov, 2005 ($2.95/$2.99, B&W)

1-12-Rand-s/Ferreyna-a 3.00
... Special #1 (6/05, $2.95) flip cover 3.00
Vol. 1: Killing Grin (1/05, $9.95, TPB) r/#1-4; sketch pages, cover gallery & script page 10.00

SMALLVILLE (Based on TV series)
DC Comics: May, 2003 - No. 11 ($3.50/$3.95, bi-monthly)

1-6-Photo-c. 1-Plunkett-a; interviews with cast; season 1 episode guide begins 3.50
7-11-($3.95) 7-Chloe Chronicles begin; season 2 episode guide begins 4.00
Vol. 1 TPB (2004, $9.95) r/#1-4 & Smallville: The Comic; photo-c 10.00

SMALLVILLE: THE COMIC (Based on TV series)
DC Comics: Nov, 2002 ($3.95, 64 pages, one-shot)

1-Photo-c; art by Martinez and Leon; interviews with cast; season 2 preview 4.00

SMASH COMICS (Becomes Lady Luck #86 on)
Quality Comics Group: Aug, 1939 - No. 85, Oct, 1949

1-Origin Hugh Hazard & His Iron Man, Bozo the Robot, Espionage, Starring Black X by Eisner, & Hooded Justice (Invisible Justice #2 on); Chic Carter & Wings Wendall begin; 1st Robot on the cover of a comic book (Bozo) 320 640 960 2240 3920 5600
2-The Lone Star Rider app; Invisible Hood gains power of invisibility; bondage/torture-c 134 268 402 851 1463 2075
3-Captain Cook & Eisner's John Law begin 68 136 204 432 746 1060
4,5: 4-Flash Fulton begins 65 130 195 416 708 1000
6-12: 12-One pg. Fine-a 58 116 174 371 636 900
13-Magno begins (8/40); last Eisner issue; The Ray app. in full page ad; The Purple Trio begins 59 118 177 375 643 910
14-Intro. The Ray (9/40) by Lou Fine & others 297 594 891 1990 3445 4900
15,16: 16-The Scarlet Seal begins 124 248 372 787 1356 1925
17-Wun Cloo becomes plastic super-hero by Jack Cole (9-months before Plastic Man) 129 258 387 826 1413 2000
18-Midnight by Jack Cole begins (origin & 1st app., 1/41) 165 330 495 1048 1799 2550
19-22: Last Ray by Fine; The Jester begins-#22 87 174 261 553 952 1350
23,24: 24-The Sword app.; last Chic Carter; Wings Wendall dons new costume #24,25 67 134 201 426 731 1035
25-Origin/1st app. Wildfire; Rookie Rankin begins 75 150 225 476 821 1165
26-30: 28-Midnight-c begin, end #85 64 128 192 406 696 985
31,32,34: The Ray by Rudy Palais; also #33 54 108 162 346 591 835
33-Origin The Marksman 62 124 186 394 680 965
35-37 49 98 147 309 522 735
38-The Yankee Eagle begins; last Midnight by Jack Cole; classic-c by Cole 98 196 294 622 1074 1525
39,40-Last Ray issue 50 100 150 315 533 750
41,44-50 40 80 120 246 411 575
42-Lady Luck begins by Klaus Nordling 132 264 396 838 1444 2050
43-Lady Luck-c (1st & only in Smash) 68 136 204 435 743 1050
51-60 30 60 90 177 289 400
61-70 23 46 69 136 223 310
71-85: 79-Midnight battles the Men from Mars-c/s 21 42 63 122 199 275

NOTE: ***Al Bryant** c-54, 63-68. **Cole** a-17-38, 68, 69, 72, 73, 78, 80, 83, 85; c-38, 60-62, 69-84. **Crandall** a-(Ray)-23-29, 35-38; c-36, 39, 40, 42-44, 46. **Fine** a(Ray)-14, 15, 16(w/**Tuska**), 17-22. **Fox** c-24-35. **Fuje** Ray-30. **Gil Fox** a-6-7, 9, 11-13. **Guardineer** a-(The Marksman)-39-?, 49, 52. **Gustavson** a-4-7, 9, 11-13 (The Jester)-22-46; (Magno)-13-21; (Midnight)-39(Cole inks), 49, 52, 63-65. **Kotzky** a-(Espionage)-33-38; c-45, 47-53. **Nordling** a-49, 52, 63-65. **Powell** a-11, 12, (Abdul the Arab)-13-24.Black X c-2, 6, 9, 11, 13, 16. Bozo the Robot c-1, 3, 5, 8, 10, 12, 14, 18, 20, 22, 24, 26. Midnight c-28-85. The Ray c-15, 17, 19, 21, 23, 25, 27. Wings Wendall c-4, 7.*

SMASH COMICS (Also see All Star Comics 1999 crossover titles)
DC Comics: May, 1999 ($1.99, one-shot)

1-Golden Age Doctor Mid-nite and Hourman 2.50

SMASH HIT SPORTS COMICS
Essankay Publications: V2#1, Jan, 1949

V2#1-L.B. Cole-c/a 28 56 84 165 270 375

SMAX (Also see Top Ten)
America's Best Comics: Oct, 2003 - No. 5, May, 2004 ($2.95, limited series)

1-5-Alan Moore-s/Zander Cannon-a 3.00
... Collected Edition (2004, $19.95, HC with dustjacket) r/#1-5 20.00
... Collected Edition SC (2005, $12.99) r/#1-5 13.00

SMILE COMICS (Also see Gay Comics, Tickle, & Whee)
Modern Store Publ.: 1955 (52 pgs.; 5x7-1/4") (7¢)

1 6 12 18 31 38 45

SMILEY BURNETTE WESTERN (Also see Patches #8 & Six-Gun Heroes)
Fawcett Publ.: March, 1950 - No. 4, Oct, 1950 (All photo front & back-c)

1-Red Eagle begins 33 66 99 192 309 425
2-4 21 42 63 125 200 275

SMILEY (THE PSYCHOTIC BUTTON) (See Evil Ernie)
Chaos! Comics: July, 1998 - Present ($2.95, one-shots)

1-Ivan Reis-a 3.00
... Holiday Special (1/99), ...'s Spring Break (4/99), ...Wrestling Special (5/99) 3.00

SMILIN' JACK (See Famous Feature Stories and Popular Comics) (Also see Super Book of Comics #1&2 and Super-Book of Comics #7&19 in the Promotional Comics section)
Dell Publishing Co.: No. 5, 1940 - No. 8, Oct-Dec, 1949

Four Color 5 71 142 213 454 777 1100
Four Color 10 (1940) 61 122 183 387 664 940
Large Feature Comic 12,14,25 (1941) 58 116 174 371 636 900
Four Color 4 (1942) 38 76 114 287 556 825
Four Color 14 (1943) 30 60 90 218 422 625
Four Color 36,58 (1943-44) 22 44 66 155 300 445
Four Color 80 (1945) 14 28 42 100 188 275
Four Color 149 (1947) 10 20 30 70 123 175
1 (1-3/48) 10 20 30 71 126 180
2 6 12 18 41 66 90
3-8 (10-12/49) 5 10 15 32 51 70

SMILING SPOOK SPUNKY (See Spunky)

SMITTY (See Popular Comics, Super Book #2, 4 & Super Comics)
Dell Publishing Co.: No. 11, 1940 - No. 7, Aug-Oct, 1949; No. 909, Apr, 1958

Four Color 11 (1940) 45 90 135 284 480 675
Large Feature Comic 26 (1941) 36 72 108 216 351 485
Four Color 6 (1942) 21 42 63 149 290 430
Four Color 32 (1943) 15 30 45 104 197 290

Snagglepuss #4 © H-B

Snow White and the Seven Dwarfs © DIS

Sojourn #6 © CRO

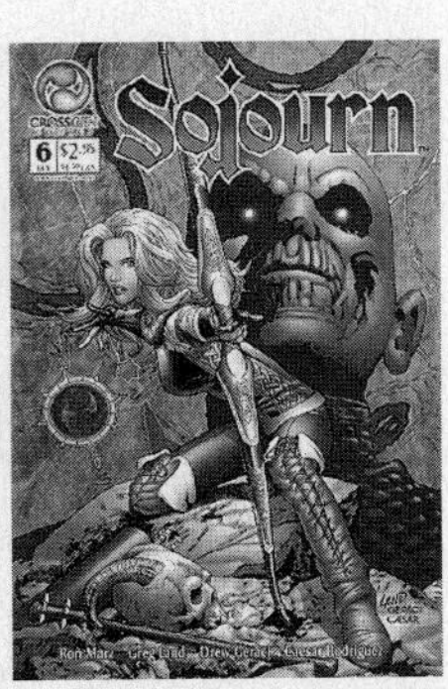

	GD 2.0	VG 4.0	FN 6.0	VF 8.0	VF/NM 9.0	NM- 9.2
Four Color 65 (1945)	12	24	36	86	158	230
Four Color 99 (1946)	10	20	30	73	129	185
Four Color 138 (1947)	9	18	27	64	110	155
1 (2-4/48)	9	18	27	63	107	150
2-(5-7/48)	5	10	15	32	51	70
3,4: 3-(8-10/48), 4-(11-1/48-49)	4	8	12	28	44	60
5-7, Four Color 909 (4/58)	4	8	12	24	37	50
SMOKEY BEAR (TV) (See March Of Comics #234, 362, 372, 383, 407)						
Gold Key: Feb, 1970 - No. 13, Mar, 1973						
1	3	6	9	19	29	38
2-5	2	4	6	10	14	18
6-13	2	4	6	8	10	12
SMOKEY STOVER (See Popular Comics, Super Book #5,17,29 & Super Comics)						
Dell Publishing Co.: No. 7, 1942 - No. 827, Aug, 1957						
Four Color 7 (1942)-Reprints	27	54	81	194	377	560
Four Color 35 (1943)	16	32	48	113	217	320
Four Color 64 (1944)	13	26	39	90	165	240
Four Color 229 (1949)	6	12	18	41	66	90
Four Color 730,827	5	10	15	32	51	70
SMOKEY THE BEAR (See Forest Fire for 1st app.)						
Dell Publ. Co.: No. 653, 10/55 - No. 1214, 8/61 (See March of Comics #234)						
Four Color 653 (#1)	10	20	30	71	126	180
Four Color 708,754,818,932	6	12	18	41	66	90
Four Color 1016,1119,1214	4	8	12	28	44	60
SMOKY (See Movie Classics)						
SMURFS (TV)						
Marvel Comics: 1982 (Dec) - No. 3, 1983						
1-3	2	4	6	9	12	15
...Treasury Edition 1 (64 pgs.)-r/#1-3	3	6	9	18	27	35
SNAFU (Magazine)						
Atlas Comics (RCM): Nov, 1955 - V2#2, Mar, 1956 (B&W)						
V1#1-Heath/Severin-a; Everett, Maneely-a	15	30	45	83	124	165
V2#1,2-Severin-a	11	22	33	62	86	110
SNAGGLEPUSS (TV)(See Hanna-Barbera Band Wagon, Quick Draw McGraw #5 & Spotlight #4)						
Gold Key: Oct, 1962 - No. 4, Sept, 1963 (Hanna-Barbera)						
1	8	16	24	58	97	135
2-4	6	12	18	43	69	95
SNAKE EYES (G.I. Joe)						
Devil's Due Publ.: Aug, 2005 - No. 6, Jan, 2006 ($2.95)						
1-6-Santalucia-a						3.00
...: Declassified TPB (4/06, $18.95) r/series; source guide						19.00
SNAKE PLISSKEN CHRONICLES, (John Carpenter's...)						
Hurricane Entertainment: June, 2003 - No. 4 ($2.99)						
Preview Issue (8/02, no cover price) B&W preview; John Carpenter interview						2.50
1-4: 1-Three covers; Rodriguez-a						3.00
SNAKES AND LADDERS						
Eddie Campbell Comics: 2001 ($5.95, B&W, one-shot)						
nn-Alan Moore-s/Eddie Campbell-a						6.00
SNAKES ON A PLANE (Adaptation of the 2006 movie)						
Virgin Comics: Oct, 2006 - No. 2, Nov, 2006 ($2.99, limited series)						
1,2: 1-Dixon-s/Purcell-a. JG Jones and photo-c. 2-Klebs, Jr.-a; Moore & photo-c						3.00
SNAKE WOMAN (Shekhar Kapur's...)						
Virgin Comics: July, 2006 - Present ($2.99)						
1-10: 1-6-Michael Gaydos-a/Zeb Wells-s. 1-Two covers by Gaydos & Singh						3.00
#0 (5/07, 99¢) origin of the Snake Goddess; background info; Gaydos-a/c						2.25
... Curse of the 68 (3/08 - No. 4, 5/08, $2.99) 1-4: 1-Ingale-a. 2-Manu-a						3.00
... Tale of the Snake Charmer 1-6 (6/07-12/07, $2.99) Vivek Shinde-a						3.00
... Vol. 1 TPB (6/07, $14.99) r/#1-5; Gaydos sketch pages; creator commentary						15.00
... Vol. 2 TPB (9/07, $14.99) r/#6-10; Cebulski intro.						15.00
SNAP (Formerly Scoop #8; becomes Jest #10,11 & Komik Pages #10)						
Harry 'A' Chesler: No. 9, 1944						
9-Manhunter, The Voice; WWII gag-c	26	52	78	154	252	350
SNAPPY COMICS						
Cima Publ. Co. (Prize Publ.): 1945						

	GD 2.0	VG 4.0	FN 6.0	VF 8.0	VF/NM 9.0	NM- 9.2
1-Airmale app.; 9 pg. Sorcerer's Apprentice adapt; Kiefer-a	33	66	99	194	317	440
SNARKY PARKER (See Life With...)						
SNIFFY THE PUP						
Standard Publ. (Animated Cartoons): No. 5, Nov, 1949 - No. 18, Sept, 1953						
5-Two Frazetta text illos	10	20	30	58	79	100
6-10	7	14	21	35	43	50
11-18	6	12	18	28	34	40
SNOOPER AND BLABBER DETECTIVES (TV) (See Whitman Comic Books)						
Gold Key: Nov, 1962 - No. 3, May, 1963 (Hanna-Barbera)						
1	7	14	21	49	80	110
2,3	6	12	18	37	59	80
SNOW WHITE (See Christmas With... (in Promotional Comics section), Mickey Mouse Magazine, Movie Comics & Seven Dwarfs)						
Dell Publishing Co.: No. 49, July, 1944 - No. 382, Mar, 1952 (Disney-Movie)						
Four Color 49 (...& the Seven Dwarfs)	50	100	150	400	775	1150
Four Color 382 (1952)-origin; partial reprint of Four Color 49	9	18	27	65	113	160
SNOW WHITE						
Marvel Comics: Jan, 1995 ($1.95, one-shot)						
1-r/1937 Sunday newspaper pages						2.50
SNOW WHITE AND THE SEVEN DWARFS						
Whitman Publications: April, 1982 (60¢)						
nn-r/Four Color 49	1	2	3	5	6	8
SNOW WHITE AND THE SEVEN DWARFS GOLDEN ANNIVERSARY						
Gladstone: Fall, 1987 ($2.95, magazine size, 52 pgs.)						
1-Contains poster	2	4	6	8	11	14
SOAP OPERA LOVE						
Charlton Comics: Feb, 1983 - No. 3, June, 1983						
1-3-Low print run	3	6	9	18	27	35
SOAP OPERA ROMANCES						
Charlton Comics: July, 1982 - No. 5, March, 1983						
1-5-Nurse Betsy Crane-r; low print run	3	6	9	18	27	35
SOCK MONKEY						
Dark Horse Comics: Sept, 1998 - No. 2, Oct, 1998 ($2.95/$2.99, B&W)						
1,2-Tony Millionaire-s/a						4.00
Vol. 2 -(Tony Millionaire's Sock Monkey) July, 1999 - No. 2, Aug, 1999						
1,2						3.00
Vol. 3 -(Tony Millionaire's Sock Monkey) Nov, 2000 - No. 2, Dec, 2000						
1,2						3.00
Vol. 4 -(Tony Millionaire's Sock Monkey) May, 2003 - No. 2, Aug, 2003						
1,2						3.00
...The Inches Incident (Sept, 2006 - No. 4, Apr, 2007) 1-4-Tony Millionaire-s/a						3.00
SOJOURN						
White Cliffs Publ. Co.: Sept, 1977 - No. 2, 1978 ($1.50, B&W & color, tabloid size)						
1,2: 1-Tor by Kubert, Eagle by Severin, E. V. Race, Private Investigator by Doug Wildey, T. C. Mars by Aragonés begin plus other strips	2	4	6	8	10	12
NOTE: Most copies came folded. Unfolded copies are worth 50% more.						
SOJOURN						
CrossGeneration Comics: July, 2001 - No. 34, May, 2004 ($2.95)						
Prequel -Ron Marz-s/Greg Land-c/a; preview pages						3.00
1-Ron Marz-s/Greg Land-c/a in most						6.00
2,3						5.00
4-24: 7-Immonen-a. 12-Brigman-a. 17-Lopresti-a. 21-Luke Ross-a						3.25
25-34: 25-$1.00-c. 34-Cariello-a						3.00
...: From the Ashes TPB (2001, $19.95) r/#1-6; Land painted-c						20.00
...: The Dragon's Tale TPB (2002, $15.95) r/#7-12; Jusko painted-c						16.00
...: The Warrior's Tale TPB (2003, $15.95) r/#13-18						16.00
Vol. 4: The Thief's Tale (2003, $15.95) r/#19-24						16.00
Vol. 5: The Sorcerer's Tale (Checker Book Publ.,2007, $17.95) r/#25-30						18.00
Vol. 6: The Berzerker's Tale (Checker Book Publ.,2007, $17.95) r/#31-34, Prequel						18.00
Traveler Vol.1,2 ($9.95) digest-sized reprints of TPBs						10.00
SOLAR (...Man of the Atom) (Also see Doctor Solar)						
Valiant/Acclaim Comics (Valiant): Sept, 1991 - No. 60, Apr, 1996 ($1.75-$2.50, 44 pgs.)						
1-Layton-a(i) on Solar; Barry Windsor-Smith-c/a	1	3	4	6	8	10
2-9: 2-Layton-a(i) on Solar, B. Smith-a. 3-1st app. Harada (11/91). 7-vs. X-O Armor						6.00

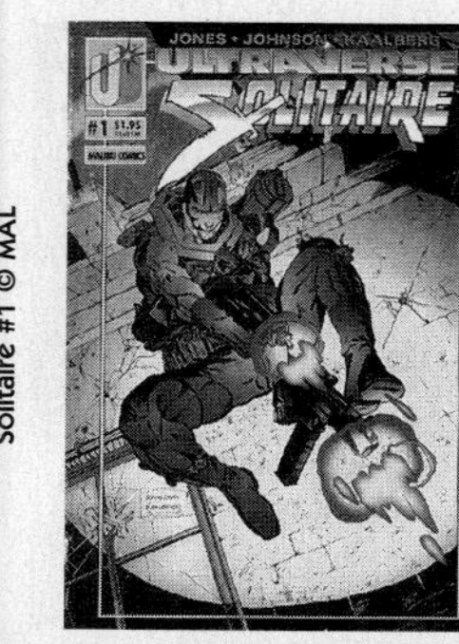

Solitaire #1 © MAL

Solomon Grundy #1 © DC

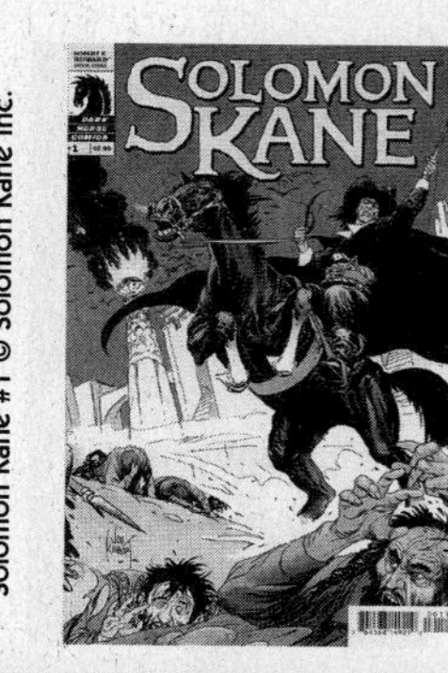

Solomon Kane #1 © Solomon Kane Inc.

	GD	VG	FN	VF	VF/NM	NM-
	2.0	4.0	6.0	8.0	9.0	9.2

10-(6/92, $3.95)-1st app. Eternal Warrior (6 pgs.); black embossed-c; origin & 1st app. Geoff McHenry (Geomancer) 1 3 4 6 8 11
10-($3.95)-2nd printing 4.00
11-15: 11-1st full app. Eternal Warrior. 12,13-Unity x-overs. 14-1st app. Fred Bender (becomes Dr. Eclipse). 15-2nd Dr. Eclipse 3.00
16-60: 17-X-O Manowar app. 23-Solar splits. 29-1st Valiant Vision book. 33-Valiant Vision; bound-in trading card. 38-Chaos Effect Epsilion Pt.1. 46-52-Dan Jurgens-a(p)/scripts w/Giordano-i. 53,54-Jurgens scripts only. 60-Giffen scripts; Jeff Johnson-a(p) 2.50
0-($9.95, trade paperback)-r/Alpha and Omega origin story; polybagged w/poster 10.00
...:Second Death (1994, $9.95)-r/issues #1-4. 10.00

NOTE: *#1-10 all have free 8 pg. insert "Alpha and Omega" which is a 10 chapter Solar origin story. All 10 centerfolds can pieced together to show climax of story.* ***Ditko*** *a-11p, 14p.* ***Giordano*** *a-46, 47, 48, 49, 50, 51, 52i.* ***Johnson*** *a-60p.* ***Jurgens*** *a-46, 47, 48, 49, 50 , 51, 52p.* ***Layton*** *a-1-3i; c-2i, 11i, 17i, 25i.* ***Miller*** *c-12.* ***Quesada*** *c-17p, 20-23p, 29p.* ***Simonson*** *c-13.* ***B. Smith*** *a-1-10; c-1, 3, 5, 7, 19i.* ***Thibert*** *c-22i, 23i.*

SOLAR LORD
Image Comics: Mar, 1999 - No. 7, Sept, 1999 ($2.50)
1-7-Khoo Fuk Lung-s/a 2.50

SOLARMAN (See Pendulum Ill. Originals)
Marvel Comics: Jan, 1989 - No. 2, May, 1990 ($1.00, limited series)
1,2 2.50

SOLAR, MAN OF THE ATOM (Man of the Atom on cover)
Acclaim Comics (Valiant Heroes): Vol. 2, May, 1997 ($3.95, one-shot, 46 pgs) (1st Valiant Heroes Special Event)
Vol. 2-Reintro Solar; Ninjak cameo; Warren Ellis scripts; Darick Robertson-a 4.00

SOLAR, MAN OF THE ATOM: HELL ON EARTH
Acclaim Comics (Valiant Heroes): Jan, 1998 - No. 4 ($2.50, limited series)
1-4-Priest-s/ Zircher-a(p) 2.50

SOLAR, MAN OF THE ATOM: REVELATIONS
Acclaim Comics (Valiant Heroes): Nov, 1997 ($3.95, one-shot, 46 pgs.)
1-Krueger-s/ Zircher-a(p) 4.00

SOLDIER & MARINE COMICS (Fightin' Army #16 on)
Charlton Comics (Toby Press of Conn. V1#11): No. 11, Dec, 1954 - No. 15, Aug, 1955; V2#9, Dec, 1956
V1#11 (12/54)-Bob Powell-a 9 18 27 50 65 80
V1#12(2/55)-15: 12-Photo-c. 14-Photo-c; Colan-a 6 12 18 31 38 45
V2#9(Formerly Never Again; Jerry Drummer V2#10 on) 6 12 18 28 34 40

SOLDIER COMICS
Fawcett Publications: Jan, 1952 - No. 11, Sept, 1953
1 14 28 42 76 108 140
2 8 16 24 44 57 70
3-5 8 16 24 42 54 65
6-11: 8-Illo. in **POP** 8 16 24 40 50 60

SOLDIERS OF FORTUNE
American Comics Group (Creston Publ. Corp.): Mar-Apr, 1951 - No. 13, Feb-Mar, 1953
1-Capt. Crossbones by Shelly, Ace Carter, Lance Larson begin 23 46 69 136 223 310
2 14 28 42 81 118 155
3-10: 6-Bondage-c 12 24 36 69 97 125
11-13 (War format) 9 18 27 47 61 75

NOTE: ***Shelly*** *a-1-3, 5.* ***Whitney*** *a-6, 8-11, 13; c-1-3, 5, 6.*

SOLDIERS OF FREEDOM
Americomics: 1987 - No. 2, 1987 ($1.75)
1,2 3.00

SOLDIER X (Continued from Cable)
Marvel Comics: Sept, 2002 - No. 12, Aug, 2003 ($2.99/$2.25)
1,10,11,12-($2.99) 1-Kordey-a/Macan-s. 10-Bollers-s/Ranson-a 3.00
2-9-($2.25) 2.50

SOLITAIRE (Also See Prime V2#6-8)
Malibu Comics (Ultraverse): Nov, 1993 - No. 12, Dec, 1994 ($1.95)
1-($2.50)-Collector's edition bagged w/playing card 3.00
1-12: 1-Regular edition w/o playing card. 2,4-Break-Thru x-over. 3-2 pg. origin The Night Man. 4-Gatefold-c. 5-Two pg. origin the Strangers 2.50

SOLO
Marvel Comics: Sept, 1994 - No. 4, Dec, 1994 ($1.75, limited series)
1-4: Spider-Man app. 2.50

SOLO (Movie)
Dark Horse Comics: July, 1996 - No. 2, Aug, 1996 ($2.50, limited series)
1,2: Adaptation of film; photo-c 2.50

SOLO (Anthology showcasing individual artists)
DC Comics: Dec, 2004 - No. 12, Oct, 2006 ($4.95/$4.99)
1-11: 1-Tim Sale-a; stories by Sale and various. 2-Richard Corben-a; stories by Corben and Arcudi. 3-Paul Pope. 4-Howard Chaykin. 5-Darwyn Cooke. 6-Jordi Bernet. 7-Michael Allred; Teen Titans & Doom Patrol app. 8-Teddy Kristiansen. 9-Scott Hampton. 10-Damion Scott. 11-Sergio Aragonés. 12-Brendan McCarthy 5.00

SOLO AVENGERS (Becomes Avenger Spotlight #21 on)
Marvel Comics: Dec, 1987 - No. 20, July, 1989 (75¢/$1.00)
1-Jim Lee-a on back-up story 3.00
2-20: 11-Intro Bobcat 2.50

SOLOMON AND SHEBA (Movie)
Dell Publishing Co.: No. 1070, Jan-Mar, 1960
Four Color 1070-Sekowsky-a; photo-c 8 16 24 58 97 135

SOLOMON GRUNDY
DC Comics: May, 2009 - No. 7, Nov, 2009 ($2.99)
1-7-Scott Kolins-s/a. 2-Bizarro app. 7-Blackest Night prelude 3.00

SOLOMON KANE (Based on the Robert E. Howard character. Also see Blackthorne 3-D Series #60 & Marvel Premiere)
Marvel Comics: Sept, 1985 - No. 6, July, 1986 (Limited series)
1-6: 1-Double size. 3-6-Williamson-a(i) 3.00

SOLOMON KANE
Dark Horse Comics: Sept, 2008 - No. 5, Feb, 2009 ($2.99)
1-5: 1-Two covers by Cassaday and Joe Kubert; Guevara-a 3.00
...: Death's Black Riders 1,2 (1/10 - No. 4, $3.50) 3.50

SOLUS
CG Entertainment, Inc.: Apr, 2003 - No. 8, Jan, 2004 ($2.95)
1-8: 1-4,6,7-George Pérez-a/c; Barbara Kesel-s. 5-Ryan-a. 8-Kirk-a 3.00
Vol. 1: Genesis (1/04, $15.95) r/#1-6 16.00

SOLUTION, THE
Malibu Comics (Ultraverse): Sept, 1993 - No. 17, Feb, 1995 ($1.95)
1,3-15: 1-Intro Meathook, Deathdance, Black Tiger, Tech. 4-Break-Thru x-over; gatefold-c. 5-2 pg. origin The Strangers. 11-Brereton-c 2.50
1-($2.50)-Newsstand ed. polybagged w/trading card 2.50
1-Ultra 5000 Limited silver foil 4.00
0-Obtained w/Rune #0 by sending coupons from 11 comics 3.00
2-($2.50, 48 pgs.)-Rune flip-c/story by B. Smith; The Mighty Magnor 1 pg. strip by Aragonés 2.50
16 ($3.50)-Flip-c Ultraverse Premiere #10 3.50
17 ($2.50) 2.50

SOMERSET HOLMES (See Eclipse Graphic Novel Series)
Pacific Comics/ Eclipse Comics No. 5, 6: Sept, 1983 - No. 6, Dec, 1984 ($1.50, Baxter paper)
1-6: 1-Brent Anderson-c/a. Cliff Hanger by Williamson in all 3.00

SONG OF THE SOUTH (See Brer Rabbit)

SONIC & KNUCKLES
Archie Comics: Aug, 1995 ($2.00)
1 6.00

SONIC DISRUPTORS
DC Comics: Dec, 1987 - No. 7, July, 1988 ($1.75, unfinished limited series)
1-7 3.00

SONIC'S FRIENDLY NEMESIS KNUCKLES
Archie Publications: July, 1996 - No. 3, Sept, 1996 ($1.50, limited series)
1-3 4.00

SONIC SUPER SPECIAL
Archie Publications: 1997 - Present ($2.00/$2.25/$2.29, 48 pgs)
1-3 4.00
4-6,8-15: 10-Sabrina-c/app. 15-Sin City spoof 3.00
7-(w/Image) Spawn, Maxx, Savage Dragon-c/app.; Valentino-a 3.00

SONIC THE HEDGEHOG (TV, video game)
Archie Comics: No. 0, Feb, 1993 - No. 3, May, 1993 ($1.25, mini-series)
0(2/93),1: Shaw-a(p) & covers on all 3 6 9 16 22 28
2,3 2 4 6 10 14 18

Sonic Universe #1 © Sega

Soulfire: Shadow Magic #4 © Aspen MLT

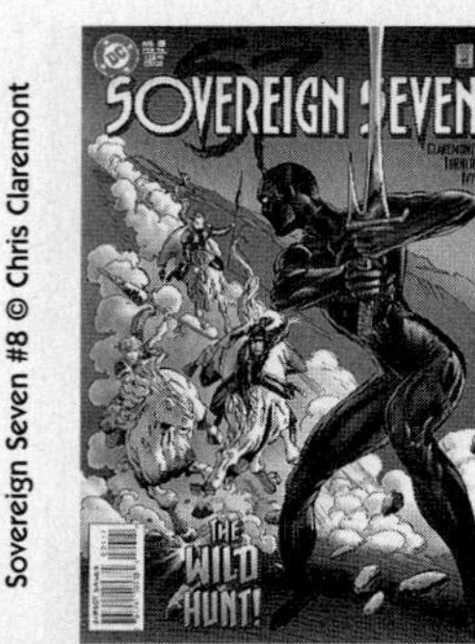

Sovereign Seven #8 © Chris Claremont

	GD 2.0	VG 4.0	FN 6.0	VF 8.0	VF/NM 9.0	NM- 9.2
Beginnings TPB (2003, $10.95) r/#0-3						11.00
...: The Beginning TPB (2006, $10.95) r/#0-3						11.00

SONIC THE HEDGEHOG (TV, video game) (Also see Promotional Comics section for Free Comic Book Day edition)
Archie Comics: July, 1993 - Present ($1.25-$2.99)

	GD	VG	FN	VF	VF/NM	NM-
1	3	6	9	18	27	35
2,3	2	4	6	13	18	22
4-10: 8-Neon ink-c.	2	4	6	10	14	18
11-20	2	4	6	9	12	15
21-30 ($1.50): 25-Silver ink-c	1	3	4	6	8	10
31-50	1	2	3	4	5	7
51-93						3.50
94-212: 117-Begin $2.19-c. 152-Begin $2.25-c. 157-Shadow app. 198-Begin $2.50						2.50
213-Begin $2.99-c						3.00
Triple Trouble Special (10/95, $2.00, 48 pgs.)						4.50

SONIC UNIVERSE (Sonic the Hedgehog)
Archie Publications: Apr, 2009 - Present ($2.50/$2.99)

1-15 2.50
16-Begin $2.99-c 3.00

SONIC VS. KNUCKLES "BATTLE ROYAL" SPECIAL
Archie Publications: 1997 ($2.00, one-shot)

1 4.00

SONIC X (Sonic the Hedgehog)
Archie Publications: Nov, 2005 - No. 40, Feb, 2009 ($2.25)

1-40: 1-Sam Speed app. 2.25

SON OF AMBUSH BUG (See Ambush Bug)
DC Comics: July, 1986 - No. 6, Dec, 1986 (75¢)

1-6: Giffen-c/a in all. 5-Bissette-a. 2.50

SON OF BLACK BEAUTY (Also see Black Beauty)
Dell Publishing Co.: No. 510, Oct, 1953 - No. 566, June, 1954

	GD	VG	FN	VF	VF/NM	NM-
Four Color 510, 566	4	8	12	26	41	55

SON OF FLUBBER (See Movie Comics)

SON OF HULK (Continues from Skaar: Son of Hulk #12) (See Realm of Kings)
Marvel Comics: No. 13, Sept, 2009 - No. 17, Jan, 2010 ($2.99)

13-17: 13,15-17-Galactus app. 3.00

SON OF M (Also see House of M series)
Marvel Comics: Feb, 2006 - No. 6, July, 2006 ($2.99, limited series)

1-6: 1-Powerless Quicksilver; Martinez-a. 2-Quicksilver regains powers; Inhumans app. 3.00
Decimation: Son of M (2006, $13.99, TPB) r/series; Martinez sketch pages 14.00

SON OF MUTANT WORLD
Fantagor Press: 1990 - No. 5, 1990? ($2.00, bi-monthly)

1-5: 1-3: Corben-c/a. 4,5 ($1.75, B&W) 3.00

SON OF ORIGINS OF MARVEL COMICS (See Fireside Book Series)

SON OF SATAN (Also see Ghost Rider #1 & Marvel Spotlight #12)
Marvel Comics Group: Dec, 1975 - No. 8, Feb, 1977 (25¢)

	GD	VG	FN	VF	VF/NM	NM-
1-Mooney-a; Kane-c(p), Starlin splash(p)	3	6	9	18	27	35
2,6-8: 2-Origin The Possessor. 8-Heath-a	2	4	6	10	14	18
3-5-(Regular 25¢ editions)(4-8/76): 5-Russell-p	2	4	6	10	14	18
3-5-(30¢-c variants, limited distribution)	4	8	12	20	30	40

SON OF SINBAD (Also see Abbott & Costello & Daring Adventures)
St. John Publishing Co.: Feb, 1950

	GD	VG	FN	VF	VF/NM	NM-
1-Kubert-c/a	39	78	117	240	395	550

SON OF SUPERMAN (Elseworlds)
DC Comics: 1999 ($14.95, prestige format, one-shot)

nn-Chaykin & Tischman-s/Williams III & Gray-a 15.00

SON OF TOMAHAWK (See Tomahawk)

SON OF VULCAN (Formerly Mysteries of Unexplored Worlds #1-48; Thunderbolt V3#51 on)
Charlton Comics: V2#49, Nov, 1965 - V2#50, Jan, 1966

	GD	VG	FN	VF	VF/NM	NM-
V2#49,50: 50-Roy Thomas scripts (1st pro work)	3	6	9	17	25	32

SONS OF KATIE ELDER (See Movie Classics)

SORCERY (See Chilling Adventures in... & Red Circle...)

SORORITY SECRETS
Toby Press: July, 1954

	GD	VG	FN	VF	VF/NM	NM-
1	10	20	30	54	72	90

SOULFIRE (MICHAEL TURNER PRESENTS:...)
Aspen MLT, Inc.: No. 0, 2004 - No. 10, Jul, 2009 ($2.50/$2.99)

0-($2.50) Turner-a/c; Loeb-s; intro. to characters & development sketches 2.50
1-($2.99) Two covers 3.00
1-Diamond Previews Exclusive 5.00
2-9: 2,3-Two covers. 4-Four covers 3.00
10-($3.99) Benitez-a 4.00
...: The Collected Edition Vol. 1 (5/05, $6.99) r/#1,2; cover gallery 7.00
Hardcover Volume 1 (12/05, $24.99) r/#0-5 & preview from Wizard Mag.; Johns intro. 25.00

SOULFIRE (MICHAEL TURNER PRESENTS:...) (Volume 2)
Aspen MLT, Inc.: No. 0, Oct, 2009 - Present ($2.50/$2.99)

0-($2.50) Marcus To-a 2.50
1,2-($2.99) 1-Five covers 3.00

SOULFIRE: CHAOS REIGN
Aspen MLT, Inc.: No. 0, June, 2006 - No. 3, Jan, 2007 ($2.50/$2.99)

0-($2.50) Three covers; Marcus To-a; J.T. Krul-s 2.50
1-3-($2.99) 1-Three covers 3.00
...: Beginnings (7/06, $1.99) Marcus To-a; J.T. Krul-s 2.25
...: Beginnings 1 (7/07, $1.99) Francisco Herrera-a; J.T. Krul-s 2.25

SOULFIRE: DYING OF THE LIGHT
Aspen MLT, Inc.: No. 0, 2004 - No. 5, Feb, 2006 ($2.50/$2.99)

0-($2.50) Three covers; Gunnell-a; Krul-s; back-story to the Soulfire universe 2.50
1-5-($2.99) 1-Five covers 3.00
... Vol. 1 TPB (2007, $14.99) r/#0-5; Gunnell sketch pages, cover gallery 15.00

SOULFIRE: NEW WORLD ORDER
Aspen MLT, Inc.: No. 0, Jul, 2007; May, 2009 - No. 5, Dec, 2009 ($2.50/$2.99)

0 (7/07, $2.50) Two covers; Herrera-a/Krul-s 2.50
1-5-($2.99) 1-Four covers 3.00

SOULFIRE: SHADOW MAGIC
Aspen MLT, Inc.: No. 0, Nov, 2008 - No. 5, May, 2009 ($2.50/$2.99)

0-($2.50) Two covers; Sana Takeda-a 2.50
1-5-($2.99) 1-Two covers 3.00

SOUL SAGA
Image Comics (Top Cow): Feb, 2000 - No. 5, Apr, 2001 ($2.50)

1-5: 1-Madureira-c; Platt & Batt-a 2.50

SOULSEARCHERS AND COMPANY
Claypool Comics: June, 1995 - No. 82, Jan, 2007 ($2.50, B&W)

1-10: Peter David scripts 5.00
11-25 3.00
26-82 2.50

SOULWIND
Image Comics: Mar, 1997 - No. 8 ($2.95, B&W, limited series)

1-8: 5-"The Day I Tried To Live" pt. 1 3.00
Book Five; The August Ones (Oni Press, 3/01, $8.50) 8.50
...The Kid From Planet Earth (1997, $9.95, TPB) 10.00
...The Kid From Planet Earth (Oni Press, 1/00, $8.50, TPB) 8.50
...The Day I Tried to Live (Oni Press, 4/00, $8.50, TPB) 8.50
The Complete Soulwind TPB ($29.95, 11/03, 8" x 5 1/2") r/Oni Books #1-5 30.00

SOUPY SALES COMIC BOOK (TV)(The Official...)
Archie Publications: 1965

	GD	VG	FN	VF	VF/NM	NM-
1	9	18	27	60	100	140

SOUTHERN KNIGHTS, THE (See Crusaders #1)
Guild Publ/Fictioneer Books: No. 2, 1983 - No. 41, 1993 (B&W)

	GD	VG	FN	VF	VF/NM	NM-
2-Magazine size	1	2	3	5	6	8
3-35, 37-41						3.00
36-($3.50-c)						3.50
Dread Halloween Special 1, Primer Special 1 (Spring, 1989, $2.25)						2.50
Graphic Novels #1-4						4.00

SOVEREIGN SEVEN (Also see Showcase '95 #12)
DC Comics: July, 1995 - No. 36, July, 1998 ($1.95) (1st creator-owned mainstream DC comic)

1-1st app. Sovereign Seven (Reflex, Indigo, Cascade, Finale, Cruiser, Network & Rampart); 1st app. Maitresse; Darkseid app.; Chris Claremont-s & Dwayne Turner-c/a begins 3.00
1-Gold 8.00
1-Platinum 40.00
2-25: 2-Wolverine cameo. 4-Neil Gaiman cameo. 5,8-Batman app. 7-Ramirez cameo

Space Adventures V3 #29 © CC

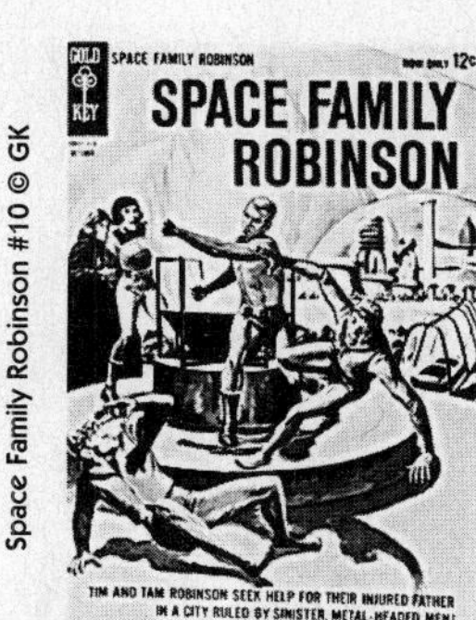

Space Family Robinson #10 © GK

Spaceman #1 © MAR

	GD 2.0	VG 4.0	FN 6.0	VF 8.0	VF/NM 9.0	NM- 9.2

(from the movie Highlander). 9-Humphrey Bogart cameo from Casablanca. 10-Impulse app; Manoli Wetherell & Neal Conan cameo from Uncanny X-Men #226. 11-Robin app. 16-Final Night. 24-Superman app. 25-Power Girl app. 2.50
26-36: 26-Begin $2.25-c. 28-Impulse-c/app. 2.50
Annual 1 (1995, $3.95)-Year One story; Big Barda & Lobo app.; Jeff Johnson-c/a 4.00
Annual 2 (1996, $2.95)-Legends of the Dead Earth; Leonardi-c/a 3.50
...Plus 1(2/97, $2.95)-Legion-c/app. 3.50
TPB-($12.95) r/#1-5, Annual #1 & Showcase '95 #12 13.00

SPACE: ABOVE AND BEYOND (TV)
Topps Comics: Jan, 1996 - No. 3, Mar, 1996 ($2.95, limited series)
1-3: Adaptation of pilot episode; Steacy-c. 3.00

SPACE: ABOVE AND BEYOND--THE GAUNTLET (TV)
Topps Comics: May, 1996 -No. 2, June, 1996 ($2.95, limited series)
1,2 3.00

SPACE ACE (Also see Manhunt!)
Magazine Enterprises: No. 5, 1952
5(A-1 #61)-Guardineer-a 54 108 162 343 584 825

SPACE ACE: DEFENDER OF THE UNIVERSE (Based on the Don Bluth video game)
CrossGen Comics: Oct, 2003 - No. 6 ($2.95, limited series)
1,2-Kirkman-s/Borges-a 3.00

SPACE ACTION
Ace Magazines (Junior Books): June, 1952 - No. 3, Oct, 1952
1-Cameron-a in all (1 story) 75 150 225 476 818 1160
2,3 53 106 159 334 567 800

SPACE ADVENTURES (War At Sea #22 on)
Capitol Stories/Charlton Comics: 7/52 - No. 21, 8/56; No. 23, 5/58 - No. 59, 11/64; V3#60, 10/67; V1#2, 7/68 - V1#8, 7/69; No. 9, 5/78 - No. 13, 3/79
1 53 106 159 334 567 800
2 27 54 81 158 259 360
3-5: 4,6-Flying saucer-c/stories 22 44 66 128 209 290
6-9: 7-Sex change story "Transformation". 8-Robot-c. 9-A-Bomb panel
20 40 60 117 189 260
10,11-Ditko-c/a. 10-Robot-c. 11-Two Ditko stories 52 104 156 328 557 785
12-Ditko-c (classic) 71 142 213 454 777 1100
13-(Fox-r, 10-11/54); Blue Beetle-c/story 16 32 48 92 144 195
14,15,17,18: 14-Blue Beetle-c/story; Fox-r (12-1/54-55, last pre-code).
15,17,18-Rocky Jones-c/s.(TV); 15-Part photo-c 20 40 60 117 189 260
16-Krigstein-a; Rocky Jones-c/story (TV) 22 44 66 128 209 290
19 15 30 45 86 133 180
20-Reprints Fawcett's "Destination Moon" 26 52 78 152 249 345
21-(8/56) (no #22)(Becomes War At Sea) 15 30 45 86 133 180
23-(5/58; formerly Nyoka, The Jungle Girl)-Reprints Fawcett's "Destination Moon"
22 44 66 132 216 300
24,25,31,32-Ditko-a. 24-Severin-a(signed "LePoer") 20 40 60 117 189 260
26,27-Ditko-a(4) each. 26,28-Flying saucer-c 21 42 63 124 202 280
28-30 11 22 33 62 86 110
33-Origin/1st app. Capt. Atom by Ditko (3/60) 50 100 150 315 533 750
34-40,42-All Captain Atom by Ditko 21 42 63 124 202 280
41,43,45-59: 45-Mercury Man app. 5 10 15 32 51 70
44-1st app. Mercury Man 5 10 15 34 55 75
V3#60(#1, 10/67)-Origin & 1st app. Paul Mann & The Saucers From the Future
5 10 15 32 51 70
2,5,6,8 (1968-69)-Ditko-a: 2-Aparo-c/a 3 6 9 20 30 40
3,4,7: 4-Aparo-c/a 3 6 9 16 23 30
9-13(1978-79)-Capt. Atom-r/Space Adventures by Ditko; 9-Reprints origin/1st app. Capt. Atom from #33 6.00
NOTE: *Aparo a-V3#60. c-V3#8.* ***Ditko*** *c-12, 31-42.* ***Giordano*** *c-3, 4, 7-9, 18p.* ***Krigstein*** *c-15.* ***Shuster*** *a-11. Issues 13 & 14 have Blue Beetle logos; #15-18 have Rocky Jones logos.*

SPACE ARK
Americomics (AC Comics)/ Apple Comics #3 on: June, 1985 - No. 5, Sept, 1987 ($1.75)
1-5: Funny animal (#1,2-color; #3-5-B&W) 2.50

SPACE BUSTERS
Ziff-Davis Publ. Co.: Spring, 1952 - No. 2, Fall, 1952
1-Krigstein-a(3); Painted-c by Norman Saunders 80 160 240 508 874 1240
2-Kinstler-a(2 pgs.); Saunders painted-c 61 122 183 387 664 940
NOTE: ***Anderson*** *a-2. Bondage c-2.*

SPACE CADET (See Tom Corbett,...)

SPACE CIRCUS
Dark Horse Comics: July, 2000 - No. 4, Oct, 2000 ($2.95, limited series)
1-4-Aragonés-a/Evanier-s 3.00

SPACE COMICS (Formerly Funny Tunes)
Avon Periodicals: No. 4, Mar-Apr, 1954 - No. 5, May-June, 1954
4,5-Space Mouse, Peter Rabbit, Super Pup (formerly Spotty the Pup), & Merry Mouse continue from Funny Tunes 8 16 24 40 50 60
I.W. Reprint #8 (nd)-Space Mouse-r 2 4 6 8 10 12

SPACED
Anthony Smith Publ. #1,2/Unbridled Ambition/Eclipse Comics #10 on: 1982 - No. 13, 1988 ($1.25/$1.50, B&W, quarterly)
1-($1.25-c) 3.00
2-13, Special Edition (1983, Mimeo) 2.50

SPACE DETECTIVE
Avon Periodicals: July, 1951 - No. 4, July, 1952
1-Rod Hathway, Space Detective begins, ends #4; Wood-c/a(3)-23 pgs.; "Opium Smugglers of Venus" drug story; Lucky Dale-r/Saint #4 113 226 339 718 1234 1750
2-Tales from the Shadow Squad story; Wood/Orlando-c; Wood inside layouts; "Slave Ship of Saturn" story 87 174 261 553 952 1350
3,4: 3-Kinstler-c. 4-Kinstlerish-a by McCann 42 84 123 267 451 635
I.W. Reprint #1(Reprints #2), 8(Reprints cover #1 & part Famous Funnies #191)
4 8 12 22 34 45
I.W. Reprint #9-Exist? 4 8 12 22 34 45

SPACE EXPLORER (See March of Comics #202)

SPACE FAMILY ROBINSON (TV)(...Lost in Space #15-37, ...Lost in Space On Space Station One #38 on)(See Gold Key Champion)
Gold Key: Dec, 1962 - No. 36, Oct, 1969; No. 37, 10/73 - No. 54, 11/78; No. 55, 3/81 - No. 59, 5/82 (All painted covers)
1-(Low distribution); Spiegle-a in all 21 42 63 148 287 425
2(3/63)-Family becomes lost in space 11 22 33 80 145 210
3-5 8 16 24 54 90 125
6-10: 6-Captain Venture back-up stories begin 6 12 18 43 69 95
11-20: 14-(10/65). 15-Title change (1/66) 5 10 15 30 48 65
21-36: 28-Last 12¢ issue. 36-Captain Venture ends 4 8 12 23 36 45
37-48: 37-Origin retold 2 4 6 10 14 18
49-59: Reprints #49,50,55-59 2 4 6 8 10 12
NOTE: *The TV show first aired on 9/15/65. Title changed after TV show debuted.*

SPACE FAMILY ROBINSON (See March of Comics #320, 328, 352, 404, 414)

SPACE GHOST (TV) (Also see Golden Comics Digest #2 & Hanna-Barbera Super TV Heroes #3-7)
Gold Key: March, 1967 (Hanna-Barbera) (TV debut was 9/10/66)
1 (10199-703)-Spiegle-a 29 58 87 212 406 600

SPACE GHOST (TV cartoon)
Comico: Mar, 1987 ($3.50, deluxe format, one-shot) (Hanna-Barbera)
1-Steve Rude-c/a 1 2 3 5 6 8

SPACE GHOST (TV cartoon)
DC Comics: Jan, 2005 - No. 6, June, 2005 ($2.95/$2.99, limited series)
1-6-Alex Ross-c/Ariel Olivetti-a/Joe Kelly-s; origin of Space Ghost 3.00
TPB (2005, $14.99) r/series; cover gallery 15.00

SPACE GIANTS, THE (TV cartoon)
FBN Publications: 1979 ($1.00, B&W, one-shots)
1-Based on Japanese TV series 2 4 6 9 12 15

SPACEHAWK
Dark Horse Comics: 1989 - No. 3, 1990 ($2.00, B&W)
1-3-Wolverton-c/a(r) plus new stories by others. 4.00

SPACE JAM
DC Comics: 1996 ($5.95, one-shot, movie adaption)
1-Wraparound photo cover of Michael Jordan 1 2 3 5 6 8

SPACE KAT-ETS (...in 3-D)
Power Publishing Co.: Dec, 1953 (25¢, came w/glasses)
1 30 60 90 177 289 400

SPACEKNIGHTS
Marvel Comics: Oct, 2000 - No. 5, Feb, 2001 ($2.99, limited series)
1-5-Starlin-s/Batista-a 3.00

SPACEMAN (Speed Carter...)
Atlas Comics (CnPC): Sept, 1953 - No. 6, July, 1954
1-Grey tone-c 69 138 207 442 759 1075

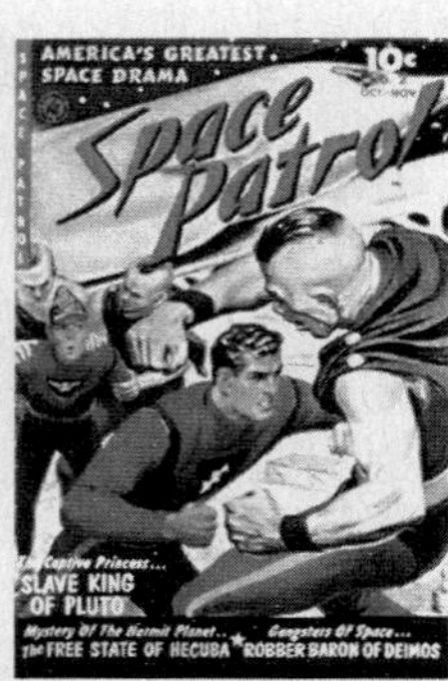

Space Patrol #2 © Z-D

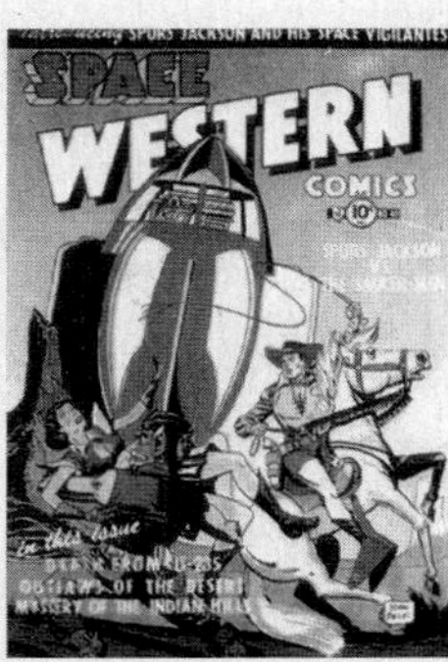

Space Western Comics #40 © CC

Sparkler Comics #62 © UFS

	GD 2.0	VG 4.0	FN 6.0	VF 8.0	VF/NM 9.0	NM- 9.2
2	43	86	129	271	461	650
3-6: 4-A-Bomb explosion-c	39	78	117	240	395	550

NOTE: *Everett c-1, 3. Heath a-1. Maneely a-1(3), 2(4), 3(3), 4-6; c-5, 6. Romita a-1. Sekowsky c-4. Sekowsky/Abel a-4(3). Tuska a-5(3).*

SPACE MAN
Dell Publ. Co.: No. 1253, 1-3/62 - No. 8, 3-5/64; No. 9, 7/72 - No. 10, 10/72

	GD	VG	FN	VF	VF/NM	NM-
Four Color 1253 (#1)(1-3/62)(15¢-c)	7	14	21	49	80	110
2,3: 2-(15¢-c). 3-(12¢-c)	4	8	12	28	44	60
4-8-(12¢-c)	4	8	12	22	34	45
9,10-(15¢-c): 9-Reprints #1253. 10-Reprints #2	2	4	6	9	12	15

SPACEMAN (From the Atomics)
Oni Press: July, 2002 ($2.95, one-shot)

	GD	VG	FN	VF	VF/NM	NM-
1-Mike Allred-s/a; Lawrence Marvit additional art						3.00

SPACE MOUSE (Also see Funny Tunes & Space Comics)
Avon Periodicals: April, 1953 - No. 5, Apr-May, 1954

	GD	VG	FN	VF	VF/NM	NM-
1	10	20	30	54	72	90
2	7	14	21	35	43	50
3-5	6	12	18	28	34	40

SPACE MOUSE (Walter Lantz...#1; see Comic Album #17)
Dell Publishing Co./Gold Key: No. 1132, Aug-Oct, 1960 - No. 5, Nov, 1963 (Walter Lantz)

	GD	VG	FN	VF	VF/NM	NM-
Four Color 1132,1244, 1(11/62)(G.K.)	4	8	12	28	44	60
2-5	4	8	12	24	37	50

SPACE MYSTERIES
I.W. Enterprises: 1964 (Reprints)

	GD	VG	FN	VF	VF/NM	NM-
1-r/Journey Into Unknown Worlds #4 w/new-c	3	6	9	16	22	28
8,9: 9-r/Planet Comics #73	3	6	9	16	22	28

SPACE: 1999 (TV) (Also see Power Record Comics)
Charlton Comics: Nov, 1975 - No. 7, Nov, 1976

	GD	VG	FN	VF	VF/NM	NM-
1-Origin Moonbase Alpha; Staton-c/a	3	6	9	16	22	28
2,7: 2-Staton-a	2	4	6	11	15	20
3-6: All Byrne-a; c-3,5,6	3	6	9	16	22	28
nn (Charlton Press, digest, 100 pgs., B&W, no cover price) new stories & art	4	8	12	26	41	55

SPACE: 1999 (TV)(Magazine)
Charlton Comics: Nov, 1975 - No. 8, Nov, 1976 (B&W) (#7 shows #6 inside)

	GD	VG	FN	VF	VF/NM	NM-
1-Origin Moonbase Alpha; Morrow-c/a	3	6	9	16	22	28
2-8: 2,3-Morrow-c/a. 4-6-Morrow-c. 5,8-Morrow-a	2	4	6	11	16	20

SPACE PATROL (TV)
Ziff-Davis Publishing Co. (Approved Comics): Summer, 1952 - No. 2, Oct-Nov, 1952 (Painted-c by Norman Saunders)

	GD	VG	FN	VF	VF/NM	NM-
1-Krigstein-a	90	180	270	576	988	1400
2-Krigstein-a(3)	65	130	195	416	708	1000

SPACE PIRATES (See Archie Giant Series #533)

SPACE RANGER (See Mystery in Space #92, Showcase #15 & Tales of the Unexpected)

SPACE SQUADRON (In the Days of the Rockets)(Becomes Space Worlds #6)
Marvel/Atlas Comics (ACI): June, 1951 - No. 5, Feb, 1952

	GD	VG	FN	VF	VF/NM	NM-
1-Space team; Brodsky c-1,5	68	136	204	432	746	1060
2: Tuska c-2-4	54	108	162	346	591	835
3-5: 3-Capt. Jet Dixon by Tuska(3). 4-Weird advs. begin	47	94	141	296	498	700

SPACE THRILLERS
Avon Periodicals: 1954 (25¢ Giant)

	GD	VG	FN	VF	VF/NM	NM-
nn-(Scarce)-Robotmen of the Lost Planet; contains 3 rebound comics of The Saint & Strange Worlds. Contents could vary	121	242	363	768	1322	1875

SPACE TRIP TO THE MOON (See Space Adventures #23)

SPACE USAGI
Mirage Studios: June, 1992 - No. 3, 1992 ($2.00, B&W, mini-series)
V2#1, Nov, 1993 - V2#3, Jan, 1994 ($2.75)

	GD	VG	FN	VF	VF/NM	NM-
1-3: Stan Sakai-c/a/scripts, V2#1-3						3.00

SPACE USAGI
Dark Horse Comics: Jan, 1996 - No. 3, Mar, 1996 ($2.95, B&W, limited series)

	GD	VG	FN	VF	VF/NM	NM-
1-3: Stan Sakai-c/a/scripts						3.00

SPACE WAR (Fightin' Five #28 on)
Charlton Comics: Oct, 1959 - No. 27, Mar, 1964; No. 28, Mar, 1978 - No. 34, 3/79

	GD	VG	FN	VF	VF/NM	NM-
V1#1-Giordano-c begin, end #3	13	26	39	90	165	240
2,3	8	16	24	52	86	120
4-6,8,10-Ditko-c/a	13	26	39	90	165	240
7,9,11-15 (3/62): Last 10¢ issue	6	12	18	39	62	85
16 (6/52)-27 (3/64): 18,19-Robot-c	5	10	15	32	51	70
28 (3/78),29-31,33,34-Ditko-c/a(r): 30-Staton, Sutton/Wood-a. 31-Ditko-c/a(3); same-c as Strange Suspense Stories #2 (1968); atom blast-c	1	3	4	6	8	10
32-r/Charlton Premiere V2#2; Sutton-a						5.00

SPACE WESTERN (Formerly Cowboy Western Comics; becomes Cowboy Western Comics #46 on)
Charlton Comics (Capitol Stories): No. 40, Oct, 1952 - No. 45, Aug, 1953

	GD	VG	FN	VF	VF/NM	NM-
40-Intro Spurs Jackson & His Space Vigilantes; flying saucer story	55	110	165	352	601	850
41,43-45: 41-Flying saucer-c. 45-Hitler app.	41	82	123	256	428	600
42-Atom bomb explosion-c	43	86	129	271	456	640

SPACE WORLDS (Formerly Space Squadron #1-5)
Atlas Comics (Male): No. 6, April, 1952

	GD	VG	FN	VF	VF/NM	NM-
6-Sol Brodsky-c	43	86	129	271	461	650

SPAGHETTI WESTERN
Oni Press: June, 2004 ($11.95, digest-size, widescreen, sepia & white)

	GD	VG	FN	VF	VF/NM	NM-
nn-Scott Morse-s/a; outer wraparound-c						12.00

SPANKY & ALFALFA & THE LITTLE RASCALS (See The Little Rascals)

SPANNER'S GALAXY
DC Comics: Dec, 1984 - No. 6, May, 1985 (limited series)

	GD	VG	FN	VF	VF/NM	NM-
1-6: Mandrake-c/a in all.						2.50

SPARKIE, RADIO PIXIE (Radio)(Becomes Big Jon & Sparkie #4)
Ziff-Davis Publ. Co.: Winter, 1951 - No. 3, July-Aug, 1952 (Painted-c)(Sparkie #2,3; #1?)

	GD	VG	FN	VF	VF/NM	NM-
1-Based on children's radio program	27	54	81	158	259	360
2,3: 3-Big Jon and Sparkie on-c only	18	36	54	105	165	225

SPARKLE COMICS
United Features Synd.: Oct-Nov, 1948 - No. 33, Dec-Jan, 1953-54

	GD	VG	FN	VF	VF/NM	NM-
1-Li'l Abner, Nancy, Captain & the Kids, Ella Cinders (#1-3: 52 pgs.)	15	30	45	83	124	165
2	9	18	27	50	65	80
3-10	8	16	24	40	50	60
11-20	7	14	21	35	43	50
21-32	6	12	18	28	34	40
33-(2-3/54) 2 pgs. early Peanuts by Schulz	10	20	30	54	72	90

SPARKLE PLENTY (See Harvey Comics Library #2 & Dick Tracy)

SPARKLER COMICS (1st series)
United Feature Comic Group: July, 1940 - No. 2, 1940

	GD	VG	FN	VF	VF/NM	NM-
1-Jim Hardy	40	80	120	235	380	525
2-Frankie Doodle	29	58	87	169	272	375

SPARKLER COMICS (2nd series)(Nancy & Sluggo #121 on)(Cover title becomes Nancy and Sluggo #101? on)
United Features Syndicate: July, 1941 - No. 120, Jan, 1955

	GD	VG	FN	VF	VF/NM	NM-
1-Origin 1st app. Sparkman; Tarzan (by Hogarth in all issues), Captain & the Kids, Ella Cinders, Danny Dingle, Dynamite Dunn, Nancy, Abbie & Slats, Broncho Bill, Frankie Doodle, begin; Spark Man c-1-9,11,12; Hap Hopper c-10,13	230	460	690	1449	2450	3450
2	76	152	228	479	807	1135
3,4	57	114	171	359	610	860
5-9: 9-Spark Man's new costume	54	108	162	338	562	785
10-Spark Man's secret ID revealed	54	108	162	338	562	785
11,12-Spark Man war-c. 12-Spark Man's new costume (color change)	41	82	123	256	428	600
13-Hap Hopper war-c	40	80	120	244	397	550
14-Tarzan-c by Hogarth	52	104	156	322	536	750
15,17: 15-Capt & Kids-c. 17-Nancy & Sluggo-c	35	70	105	203	327	450
16,18-Spark Man war-c	41	82	123	250	413	575
19-1st Race Riley and the Commandos-c/s	40	80	120	244	397	550
20-Nancy war-c	35	70	105	203	327	450
21,25,28,31,34,37,39-Tarzan-c by Hogarth	44	88	132	273	454	635
22-24,26,27,29,30: 22-Race Riley & the Commandos strips begin, ends #44	30	60	90	174	280	385
32,33,35,36,38,40	18	36	54	105	165	225
41,43,45,46,48,49	14	28	42	80	115	150
42,44,47,50-Tarzan-c (42,47,50 by Hogarth)	27	54	81	160	258	355

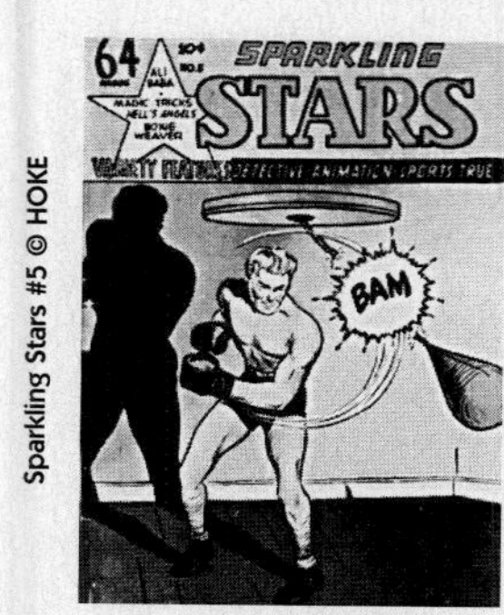

Sparkling Stars #5 © HOKE

Spawn #169 © TMP

Spawn: The Dark Ages #10 © TMP

	GD	VG	FN	VF	VF/NM	NM-
	2.0	4.0	6.0	8.0	9.0	9.2
51,52,54-70: 57-Li'l Abner begins (not in #58); Fearless Fosdick app. in #58	14	28	42	76	108	140
53-Tarzan-c by Hogarth	23	46	69	135	218	300
71-80	10	20	30	54	72	90
81,82,84-86: 86 Last Tarzan; lingerie panels	9	18	27	47	61	75
83-Tarzan-c; Li'l Abner ends	13	26	39	74	105	135
87-96,98-99	8	16	24	44	57	70
97-Origin Casey Ruggles by Warren Tufts	13	26	39	72	101	130
100	9	18	27	50	65	80
101-107,109-112,114-119	7	14	21	37	46	55
108,113-Toth-a	9	18	27	50	65	80
120-(10-11/54) 2 pgs. early Peanuts by Schulz	9	18	27	50	65	80

SPARKLING LOVE
Avon Periodicals/Realistic (1953): June, 1950; 1953

1(Avon)-Kubert-a; photo-c	23	46	69	136	223	310
nn(1953)-Reprint; Kubert-a	10	20	30	56	76	95

SPARKLING STARS
Holyoke Publishing Co.: June, 1944 - No. 33, March, 1948

1-Hell's Angels, FBI, Boxie Weaver, Petey & Pop, & Ali Baba begin	20	40	60	114	182	250
2-Speed Spaulding story	12	24	36	69	97	125
3-Actual FBI case photos & war photos	10	20	30	54	72	90
4-10: 7-X-Mas-c	9	18	27	50	65	80
11-19: 13-Origin/1st app. Jungo the Man-Beast-c/s	8	16	24	44	57	70
20-Intro Fangs the Wolf Boy	9	18	27	50	65	80
21-33: 29-Bondage-c. 31-Sid Greene-a	8	16	24	42	54	65

SPARK MAN (See Sparkler Comics)
Frances M. McQueeny: 1945 (36 pgs., one-shot)

1-Origin Spark Man r/Sparkler #1-3; female torture story; cover redrawn from Sparkler #1	32	64	96	186	298	410

SPARKS (William Katt Presents...)
Catastrophic Comics: June, 2008 - Present ($2.99)

1,2: 1-Folino-s/Ringuet-a; origin of Sparks 3.00

SPARKY WATTS (Also see Big Shot Comics & Columbia Comics)
Columbia Comic Corp.: Nov?, 1942 - No. 10, 1949

1(1942)-Skyman & The Face app; Hitler-c	77	154	231	493	847	1200
2(1943)	29	58	87	172	281	390
3(1944)	21	42	63	122	199	275
4(1944)-Origin	18	36	54	105	165	225
5(1947)-Skyman app.; Boody Rogers-c/a	15	30	45	88	137	185
6,7,9,10: 6(1947),10(1949)	11	22	33	60	83	105
8(1948)-Surrealistic-c	14	28	42	76	108	140

NOTE: *Boody Rogers c-1-8.*

SPARTACUS (Movie)
Dell Publishing Co.: No. 1139, Nov, 1960 (Kirk Douglas photo-c)

Four Color 1139-Buscema-a	12	24	36	85	155	225

SPARTACUS (Television series)
Devil's Due Publishing: Oct, 2009 - Present ($3.99)

1,2: 1-DeKnight-s. 2-Palmiotti-s 4.00

SPARTAN: WARRIOR SPIRIT (Also see WildC.A.T.S: Covert Action Teams)
Image Comics (WildStorm Productions): July, 1995 - No. 4, Nov, 1995 ($2.50, lim. series)

1-4: Kurt Busiek scripts; Mike McKone-c/a 2.50

SPAWN (Also see Curse of the Spawn and Sam & Twitch)
Image Comics (Todd McFarlane Prods.): May, 1992 - Present ($1.95/$2.50/$2.99)

1-1st app. Spawn; McFarlane-c/a begins; McFarlane/Steacy-c; 1st Todd McFarlane Productions title.	1	3	4	6	8	10
1-Black & white edition	2	4	6	11	16	20
2,3: 2-1st app. Violator; McFarlane/Steacy-c	1	2	3	5	7	9
4-Contains coupon for Image Comics #0	1	2	3	5	7	9
4-With coupon missing						3.00
4-Newsstand edition w/o poster or coupon						3.00
5-Cerebus cameo (1 pg.) as stuffed animal; Spawn mobile poster #1						6.00
6-8,10: 7-Spawn Mobile poster #2. 8-Alan Moore scripts; Miller poster. 10-Cerebus app.; Dave Sim scripts; 1 pg. cameo app. by Superman						4.00
9-Neil Gaiman scripts; Jim Lee poster; 1st Angela.						6.00
11-17,19,20,22-30: 11-Miller script; Darrow poster. 12-Bloodwulf poster by Liefeld. 14,15-Violator app. 16,17-Grant Morrison scripts; Capullo-c/a(p). 23,24-McFarlane-a/stories. 25-(10/94). 19-(10/94). 20-(11/94)						3.00

GD VG FN VF VF/NM NM-
2.0 4.0 6.0 8.0 9.0 9.2

18-Grant Morrison script, Capullo-c/a(p); low distr.	1	2	3	5	7	9
21-low distribution	1	2	3	5	7	9
31-49: 31-1st app. The Redeemer; new costume (brief). 32-1st full app. new costume. 38-40,42,44,46,48-Tony Daniel-c/a(p). 38-1st app. Cy-Gor. 40,41-Cy-Gor & Curse app.						4.00
50-($3.95, 48 pgs.)						3.00
51-66: 52-Savage Dragon app. 56-w/ Darkchylde preview. 57-Cy-Gor-c/app. 64-Polybagged w/McFarlane Toys catalog. 65-Photo-c of movie Spawn and McFarlane						3.00
67-97: 81-Billy Kincaid returns. 97-Angela-c/app.						2.50
98,99,101-149-($2.50): 98,99-Angela app.						2.50
100-($4.95) Angela dies; 6 covers by McFarlane, Ross, Miller, Capullo, Wood, Mignola						5.00
150-($4.95) 4 covers by McFarlane, Capullo, Tan, Jim Lee						5.00
151-184: 151-($2.95) Wraparound-c by Tan. 167-Clown app. 179-Mayhew-a						3.00
185-196: 185-McFarlane & Holguin-s/Portacio-a begins. 193-Sam & Twitch app.						3.00
Annual 1-Blood & Shadows ('99, $4.95) Ashley Wood-c/a; Jenkins-s						5.00
...: Armegeddon Complete Collection TPB ('07, $29.95) r/#150-163						30.00
...: Armegeddon, Part 1 TPB (10/06, $14.99) r/#150-155						15.00
...: Armegeddon, Part 2 TPB (2/07, $15.95) r/#156-164						16.00
...Bible-(8/96, $1.95)-Character bios						4.00
Book 1 TPB($9.95) r/#1-5; Book 2-r/#6-9,11; Book 3 -r/#12-15, Book 4- r/#16-20; Book 5-r/#21-25; Book 6- r/#26-30; Book 7-r/#31-34; Book 8-r/#35-38; Book 9-r/#39-42; Book 10-r/#43-47						11.00
Book 11 TPB ($10.95) r/#48-50; Book 12-r/#51-54						11.00
... Collection Vol. 1 (10/05, $19.95) r/#1-8,11,12; intro. by Frank Miller						20.00
... Collection Vol. 2 HC (7/07, $49.95) r/#13-33						50.00
... Collection Vol. 2 SC (9/06, $29.95) r/#13-33						30.00
... Collection Vol. 3 (3/07, $29.95) r/#34-54						30.00
... Collection Vol. 4 (9/07, $29.95) r/#55-75						30.00
... Collection Vol. 5 ('08, $29.95) r/#76-95						30.00
... Collection Vol. 6 (8/08, $29.95) r/#96-116; cover gallery						30.00
... Godslayer Vol. 1 (9/06, $6.99) Anacleto-c/a; Holguin-s; sketch pages						7.00
...: Neonoir TPB (11/08, $14.95) r/#170-175						15.00
...: New Flesh TPB ('07, $14.95) r/#166-169						15.00
...Simony (5/04, $7.95) English translation of French Spawn story; Briclot-a						8.00

NOTE: ***Capullo** a-16p-18p; c-16p-18p. **Daniel** a-38-40, 42, 44, 46. **McFarlane** a-1-15; c-1-15p. **Thibert** a-16i(part). Posters come with issues 1, 4, 7-9, 11, 12. #25 was released before #19 & 20.*

SPAWN-BATMAN (Also see Batman/Spawn: War Devil under Batman: One-Shots)
Image Comics (Todd McFarlane Productions): 1994 ($3.95, one-shot)

1-Miller scripts; McFarlane-c/a 6.00

SPAWN: BLOOD FEUD
Image Comics (Todd McFarlane Prods.): June, 1995 - No. 4, Sept, 1995 ($2.25, lim. series)

1-4-Alan Moore scripts, Tony Daniel-a 3.50

SPAWN FAN EDITION
Image Comics (Todd McFarlane Productions): Aug, 1996 - No. 3, Oct, 1996 (Giveaway, 12 pgs.) (Polybagged w/Overstreet's FAN)

1-3: Beau Smith scripts; Brad Gorby-a(p). 1-1st app. Nordik, the Norse Hellspawn. 2-1st app. McFallon. 3-1st app. Mercy	1	2	3	5	6	8
1-3-(Gold): All retailer incentives						16.00
1-3-Variant-c	1	2	3	5	6	8
2-(Platinum)-Retailer incentive						25.00

SPAWN GODSLAYER
Image Comics (Todd McFarlane Prods.): May, 2007 - No. 8, Apr, 2008 ($2.99)

1-8: 1-Holguin-s/Tan-a/Anacleto-c 3.00

SPAWN: THE DARK AGES
Image Comics (Todd McFarlane Productions): Mar, 1999 - No. 28, Oct, 2001 ($2.50)

1-Fabry-c; Holguin-s/Sharp-a; variant-c by McFarlane 2.50
2-28 2.50

SPAWN THE IMPALER
Image Comics (Todd McFarlane Prods.): Oct, 1996 - No. 3, Dec, 1996 ($2.95, limited series)

1-3-Mike Grell scripts, painted-a 3.00

SPAWN: THE UNDEAD
Image Comics (Todd McFarlane Prod.): Jun, 1999 - No. 9, Feb, 2000 ($1.95/$2.25)

1-9-Dwayne Turner-c/a; Jenkins-s. 7-9-($2.25-c) 2.50
TPB (6/08, $24.99) r/#1-9 25.00

SPAWN/WILDC.A.T.S
Image Comics (WildStorm): Jan, 1996 - No. 4, Apr, 1996 ($2.50, lim. series)

1-4: Alan Moore scripts in all. 3.00

SPECIAL AGENT (Steve Saunders...)(Also see True Comics #68)
Parents' Magazine Institute (Commended Comics No. 2): Dec, 1947 - No. 8, Sept, 1949 (Based on true FBI cases)

Special Edition Comics #1 © FAW

Spectacular Feature #11 © FOX

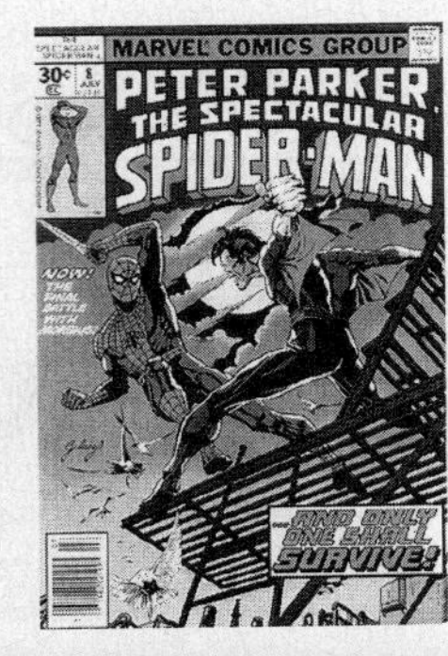

Spectacular Spider-Man #8 © MAR

	GD 2.0	VG 4.0	FN 6.0	VF 8.0	VF/NM 9.0	NM- 9.2
1-J. Edgar Hoover photo on-c	12	24	36	67	94	120
2	8	16	24	40	50	60
3-8	7	14	21	35	43	50

SPECIAL COLLECTORS' EDITION (See Savage Fists of Kung-Fu)

SPECIAL COMICS (Becomes Hangman #2 on)
MLJ Magazines: Winter, 1941-42

1-Origin The Boy Buddies (Shield & Wizard x-over); death of The Comet retold (see Pep #17); origin The Hangman retold; Hangman-c 300 600 900 2070 3635 5200

SPECIAL EDITION (See Gorgo and Reptisaurus)

SPECIAL EDITION COMICS
Fawcett Publications: 1940 (August) (68 pgs., one-shot)

1-1st book devoted entirely to Captain Marvel; C.C. Beck-c/a; only app. of Captain Marvel with belt buckle; Capt. Marvel appears with button-down flap; 1st story (came out before Captain Marvel #1) 757 1514 2271 5526 9763 14,000

NOTE: *Prices vary widely on this book. Since this book is all Captain Marvel stories, it is actually a pre-Captain Marvel #1. There is speculation that this book almost became **Captain Marvel** #1. After **Special Edition** was published, there was an editor change at Fawcett. The new editor commissioned Kirby to do a nn **Captain Marvel** book early in 1941. This book was followed by a 2nd book several months later. This 2nd book was advertised as a #3 (making Special Edition the #1, & the nn issue the #2). However, the 2nd book did come out as a #2.*

SPECIAL EDITION: SPIDER-MAN VS. THE HULK (See listing under The Amazing Spider-Man)

SPECIAL EDITION X-MEN
Marvel Comics Group: Feb, 1983 ($2.00, one-shot, Baxter paper)

1-r/Giant-Size X-Men #1 plus one new story 2 4 6 8 10 12

SPECIAL FORCES
Image Comics: Oct, 2007 - No. 4, Mar, 2009 ($2.99)

1-4-Iraq war combat; Kyle Baker-s/a/c 3.00

SPECIAL MARVEL EDITION (Master of Kung Fu #17 on)
Marvel Comics Group: Jan, 1971 - No. 16, Feb, 1974 (#1-3: 25¢, 68 pgs.; #4: 52 pgs.; #5-16: 20¢, regular ed.)

1-Thor-r by Kirby; 68 pgs. 3 6 9 20 30 40
2-4: Thor-r by Kirby; 2,3-68 pg. Giant. 4-(52 pgs.) 2 4 6 13 18 22
5-14: Sgt. Fury-r; 11-r/Sgt. Fury #13 (Capt. America) 2 4 6 8 10 12
15-Master of Kung Fu (Shang-Chi) begins (1st app., 12/73); Starlin-a; origin/1st app. Nayland Smith & Dr. Petrie 13 26 39 93 172 250
16-1st app. Midnight; Starlin-a (2nd Shang-Chi) 7 14 21 45 73 100
NOTE: *Kirby c-10-14.*

SPECIAL MISSIONS (See G.I. Joe...)

SPECIAL WAR SERIES (Attack V4#3 on?)
Charlton Comics: Aug, 1965 - No. 4, Nov, 1965

V4#1-D-Day (also see D-Day listing) 4 8 12 23 36 48
2-Attack! 3 6 9 16 22 28
3-War & Attack (also see War & Attack) 2 4 6 13 18 22
4-Judomaster (intro/1st app.; see Sarge Steel) 7 14 21 50 83 115

SPECIES (Movie)
Dark Horse Comics: June, 1995 - No. 4, Sept, 1995 ($2.50, limited series)

1-4: Adaptation of film 3.00

SPECIES: HUMAN RACE (Movie)
Dark Horse Comics: Nov, 1996 - No. 4, Feb, 1997 ($2.95, limited series)

1-4 3.00

SPECTACULAR ADVENTURES (See Adventures)

SPECTACULAR FEATURE MAGAZINE, A (Formerly My Confessions)
(Spectacular Features Magazine #12)
Fox Feature Syndicate: No. 11, April, 1950

11 (#1)-Samson and Delilah 27 54 81 160 263 365

SPECTACULAR FEATURES MAGAZINE (Formerly A Spectacular Feature Magazine)
Fox Feature Syndicate: No. 12, June, 1950 - No. 3, Aug, 1950

12 (#2)-Iwo Jima; photo flag-c 27 54 81 158 259 360
3-True Crime Cases From Police Files 22 44 66 128 209 290

SPECTACULAR SCARLET SPIDER
Marvel Comics: Nov, 1995 - No. 2, Dec, 1995 ($1.95, limited series)

1,2: Replaces Spectacular Spider-Man 2.50

SPECTACULAR SPIDER-MAN, THE (See Marvel Special Edition and Marvel Treasury Edition)

SPECTACULAR SPIDER-MAN, THE (Magazine)
Marvel Comics Group: July, 1968 - No. 2, Nov, 1968 (35¢)

1-(B&W)-Romita/Mooney 52 pg. story plus updated origin story with Everett-a(i) 12 24 36 83 152 220
1-Variation w/single c-price of 40¢ 12 24 36 83 152 220
2-(Color)-Green Goblin-c & 58 pg. story; Romita painted-c (story reprinted in King Size Spider-Man #9); Romita/Mooney-a 10 20 30 71 126 180

SPECTACULAR SPIDER-MAN, THE (Peter Parker...#54-132, 134)
Marvel Comics Group: Dec, 1976 - No. 263, Nov, 1998

1-Origin recap in text; return of Tarantula 6 12 18 41 66 90
2-Kraven the Hunter app. 3 6 9 18 27 35
3-5: 3-Intro Lightmaster. 4-Vulture app. 3 6 9 14 20 25
6-8-Morbius app.; 6-r/Marvel Team-Up #3 w/Morbius 3 6 9 16 22 28
7,8-(35¢-c variants, limited distribution)(6,7/77) 5 10 15 34 55 75
9-20: 9,10-White Tiger app. 11-Last 30¢-c. 17,18-Angel & Iceman app. (from Champions); Ghost Rider cameo. 18-Gil Kane-c 2 4 6 8 11 14
9-11-(35¢-c variants, limited distribution)(8-10/77) 3 6 9 20 30 40
21,24-26: 21-Scorpion app. 26-Daredevil app. 2 3 4 6 8 10
22,23-Moon Knight app. 2 4 6 8 10 12
27-Miller's 1st art on Daredevil (2/79); also see Captain America #235 5 10 15 32 51 70
28-Miller Daredevil (p) 4 8 12 26 41 55
29-55,57,59: 33-Origin Iguana. 38-Morbius app. 1 2 3 4 5 7
56-2nd app. Jack O'Lantern (Macendale) & 1st Spidey/Jack O'Lantern battle (7/81) 1 2 3 5 6 8
58-Byrne-a(p) 1 2 3 5 6 8
60-Double size; origin retold with new facts revealed 1 2 3 5 6 8
61-63,65-68,71-74: 65-Kraven the Hunter app. 6.00
64-1st app. Cloak & Dagger (3/82) 2 4 6 10 14 18
69,70-Cloak & Dagger app. 1 2 3 5 7 9
75-Double size 1 2 3 4 5 7
76-80: 78,79-Punisher cameo 6.00
81,82-Punisher, Cloak & Dagger app. 1 2 3 5 6 8
83-Origin Punisher retold (10/83) 2 4 6 8 10 12
84,86-89,91-99: 94-96-Cloak & Dagger app. 98-Intro The Spot 6.00
85-Hobgoblin (Ned Leeds) app. (12/83); gains powers of original Green Goblin (see Amazing Spider-Man #238) 2 4 6 8 10 12
90-Spider-Man's new black costume, last panel (ties w/Amazing Spider-Man #252 & Marvel Team-Up #141 for 1st app.) 2 3 4 6 8 10
100-(3/85)-Double size 1 2 3 4 5 7
101-115,117,118,120-129: 107-110-Death of Jean DeWolff. 111-Secret Wars II tie-in. 128-Black Cat new costume 5.00
116,119-Sabretooth-c/story 2 3 4 6 8 10
130-132: 130-Hobgoblin app. 131-Six part Kraven tie-in. 132-Kraven tie-in 2 3 4 6 8 10
133-140: 138-1st full app. Tombstone (origin #139). 140-Punisher cameo 5.00
141-143-Punisher app. 1 2 3 4 5 7
144-146,148-157: 151-Tombstone returns 4.00
147-1st brief app. new Hobgoblin (Macendale), 1 page; continued in Web of Spider-Man #48 2 4 6 8 11 14
158-Spider-Man gets new powers (1st Cosmic Spidey, cont'd in Web of Spider-Man #59) 1 2 3 5 6 8
159-Cosmic Spider-Man app. 1 2 3 4 5 7
160-170: 161-163-Hobgoblin app. 168-170-Avengers x-over. 169-1st app. The Outlaws 3.00
171-188,190-199: 180,181,183,184-Green Goblin app. 197-199-Original X-Men-c/story 3.00
189-($2.95, 52 pgs.)-Silver hologram on-c; battles Green Goblin; origin Spidey retold; Vess poster w/Spidey & Hobgoblin 4.00
189-(2nd printing)-Gold hologram on-c 3.00
195-(Deluxe ed.)-Polybagged w/"Dirt" magazine #2 & Beastie Boys/Smithereens music cassette 4.00
200-($2.95)-Holo-grafx foil-c; Green Goblin-c/story 4.00
201-219,221,222,224,226-228,230-247: 212-w/card sheet. 203-Maximum Carnage x-over. 204-Begin 4 part death of Tombstone story. 207,208-The Shroud-c/story. 208-Siege of Darkness x-over (#207 is a tie-in). 209-Black Cat back-up. 215,216-Scorpion app. 217-Power & Responsibility Pt. 4. 231-Return of Kaine; Spider-Man corpse discovered. 232-New Doc Octopus app. 233-Carnage-c/app. 235-Dragon Man cameo. 236-Dragon Man-c/app; Lizard app.; Peter Parker regains powers. 238,239-Lizard app. 239-w/card insert. 240-Revelations storyline begins. 241-Flashback 2.50
213-Collectors ed. polybagged w/16 pg. preview & animation cel; foil-c; 1st meeting Spidey & Typhoid Mary 3.00
213-Version polybagged w/Gamepro #7; no-c date, price 2.50
217,219 ($2.95)-Deluxe edition foil-c: flip book 3.00
220 ($2.25, 52 pgs.)-Flip book, Mary Jane reveals pregnancy 3.00
223,229: ($2.50) 229-Spidey quits 3.00
223,225: ($2.95)-223-Die Cut-c. 225-Newsstand ed. 3.00
225,229: ($3.95) 225-Direct Market Holodisk-c (Green Goblin). 229-Acetate-c,

Spectacular Spider-Man Annual #14 © MAR

The Spectre #3 © DC

Speed Comics #43 © HARV

GD 2.0 VG 4.0 FN 6.0 VF 8.0 VF/NM 9.0 NM- 9.2

Spidey quits
240-Variant-c 3.00
248,249,251-254,256: 249-Return of Norman Osborn 256-1st app. Prodigy 2.50
250-($3.25) Double gatefold-c 3.25
255-($2.99) Spiderhunt pt. 4 3.00
257-262: 257-Double cover with "Spectacular Prodigy #1"; battles Jack O'Lantern. 258-Spidey is cleared. 259,260-Green Goblin & Hobgoblin app. 262-Byrne-s 2.50
263-Final issue; Byrne-c; Aunt May returns 4.00
#(-1) Flashback (7/97) 2.50
Annual 1 (1979)-Doc Octopus-c & 46 pg. story 2 4 6 8 10 12
Annual 2 (1980)-Origin/1st app. Rapier 1 2 3 4 5 7
Annual 3-5: ('81-'83) 3-Last Man-Wolf 4.00
Annual 6-14: 8 ('88,$ 1.75)-Evolutionary War x-over; Daydreamer returns Gwen Stacy "clone" back to real self (not Gwen Stacy). 9 ('89, $2.00, 68 pgs.)-Atlantis Attacks. 10 ('90, $2.00, 68 pgs.)-McFarlane-a. 11 ('91, $2.00, 68 pgs.)-Iron Man app. 12 ('92, $2.25, 68 pgs.)-Venom solo story cont'd from Amazing Spider-Man Annual #26. 13 ('93, $2.95, 68 pgs.)-Polybagged w/trading card; John Romita, Sr. back-up-a 3.00
Special 1 (1995, $3.95)-Flip book 4.00

NOTE: ***Austin*** *c-21i, Annual 11i.* ***Buckler*** *a-103, 107-111, 116, 117, 119, 122, Annual 1, Annual 10; c-103, 107-111, 113, 116-119, 122, Annual 1.* ***Buscema*** *a-121.* ***Byrne*** *c(p)-17, 43, 58, 101, 102.* ***Giffen*** *a-120p.* ***Hembeck*** *c/a-86p.* ***Larsen*** *c-Annual 11p.* ***Miller*** *c-46p, 48p, 50, 51p, 52p, 54p, 55, 56p, 57, 60.* ***Mooney*** *a-7i, 11i, 21p, 23p, 25p, 26p, 29-34p, 36p, 37p, 39i, 41, 42i, 49p, 50i, 51i, 53p, 54-57i, 59-66i, 68i, 71i, 73-79i, 81-83i, 85i, 87-99i, 102i, 125p, Annual 1i, 2p.* ***Nasser*** *c-37p.* ***Perez*** *c-10.* ***Simonson*** *c-54i.* ***Zeck*** *a-22, 118, 131, 132; c-131, 132.*

SPECTACULAR SPIDER-MAN (2nd series)
Marvel Comics: Sept, 2003 - No. 27, June, 2005 ($2.25/$2.99)

1-Jenkins-s/Ramos-a/c; Venom-c/app. 3.00
2-26: 2-5-Venom app. 6-9-Dr. Octopus app. 11-13-The Lizard app. 14-Rivera painted-a. 15,16-Capt. America app. 17,18-Ramos-a. 20-Spider-Man gets organic webshooters 21,22-Caldwell-a. 23-26-Sarah & Gabriel app.; Land-c 2.25
27-($2.99) Last issue; Uncle Ben app. in flashback; Buckingham-a 3.00
... Vol. 1: The Hunger TPB (2003, $11.99) r/#1-5 12.00
... Vol. 2: Countdown TPB (2004, $11.99) r/#6-10 12.00
... Vol. 3: Here There Be Monsters TPB (2004, $9.99) r/#11-14 10.00
... Vol. 4: Disassembled TPB (2004, $14.99) r/#15-20 15.00
... Vol. 5: Sins Remembered (2005, $9.99) r/#23-26 10.00
... Vol. 6: The Final Curtain (2005, $14.99) r/#21,22,27 & Peter Parker: Spider-Man #39-41 15.00

SPECTACULAR STORIES MAGAZINE (Formerly A Star Presentation)
Fox Feature Syndicate (Hero Books): No. 4, July, 1950; No. 3, Sept, 1950

4-Sherlock Holmes (true crime stories) 36 72 108 214 347 480
3-The St. Valentine's Day Massacre (true crime) 24 48 72 140 230 320

SPECTRE, THE (1st Series) (See Adventure Comics #431-440, More Fun & Showcase)
National Periodical Publ.: Nov-Dec, 1967 - No. 10, May-June, 1969 (All 12¢)

1-(11-12/67)-Anderson-c/a 14 28 42 100 188 275
2-5-Neal Adams-c/a; 3-Wildcat x-over 9 18 27 65 113 160
6-8,10: 6-8-Anderson inks. 7-Hourman app. 7 14 21 49 80 110
9-Wrightson-a 8 16 24 52 86 120

SPECTRE, THE (2nd Series) (See Saga of the Swamp Thing #58, Showcase '95 #8 & Wrath of the...)
DC Comics: Apr, 1987 - No. 31, Oct, 1989 ($1.00, new format)

1-Colan-a begins 4.00
2-32: 9-Nudity panels. 10-Batman cameo. 10,11-Millennium tie-ins 3.00
Annual 1 (1988, $2.00)-Deadman app. 3.00

NOTE: ***Art Adams*** *c-Annual 1.* ***Colan*** *a-1-6.* ***Kaluta*** *c-1-3.* ***Mignola*** *c-7-9.* ***Morrow*** *a-9-15.* ***Sears*** *c/a-22.* ***Vess*** *c-13-15.*

SPECTRE, THE (3rd Series) (Also see Brave and the Bold #72, 75, 116, 180, 199 & Showcase '95 #8)
DC Comics: Dec, 1992 - No. 62, Feb, 1998 ($1.75/$1.95/$2.25/$2.50)

1-($1.95)-Glow-in-the-dark-c; Mandrake-a begins 5.00
2,3 3.00
4-7,9-12,14-20: 10-Kaluta-c. 11-Hildebrandt painted-c. 16-Aparo/K. Jones-a. 19-Snyder III-c. 20-Sienkiewicz-c 2.50
8,13-($2.50)-Glow-in-the-dark-c 3.00
21-62: 22-(9/94)-Superman-c & app. 23-(11/94). 43-Kent Williams-c. 44-Kaluta-c. 47-Final Night x-over. 49-Begin Bolton-c. 51-Batman-c/app. 52-Gianni-c. 54-Corben-c. 60-Harris-c 2.50
#0 (10/94) Released between #22 & #23 2.50
Annual 1 (1995, $3.95)-Year One story 4.00

NOTE: ***Bisley*** *c-27.* ***Fabry*** *c-2.* ***Kelley Jones*** *c-31.* ***Vess*** *c-5.*

SPECTRE, THE (4th Series) (Hal Jordan; also see Day of Judgment #5 and Legends of the DC Universe #33-36)
DC Comics: Mar, 2001 - No. 27, May, 2003 ($2.50/$2.75)

1-DeMatteis-s/Ryan Sook-c/a 3.00
2-27: 3,4-Superman & Batman-c/app. 5-Two-Face-c/app. 20-Begin $2.75-c. 21-Sinestro returns. 24-JLA app. 2.75

SPECTRE, THE (See Crisis Aftermath: The Spectre)

SPEEDBALL (See Amazing Spider-Man Annual #12, Marvel Super-Heroes & The New Warriors)
Marvel Comics: Sept, 1988(10/88-inside) - No. 11, July, 1989 (75¢)

1-11: Ditko/Guice a-1-4, c-1; Ditko a-1-10; c-1-11p 2.25

SPEED BUGGY (TV)(Also see Fun-In #12, 15)
Charlton Comics: July, 1975 - No. 9, Nov, 1976 (Hanna-Barbera)

1 3 6 9 16 22 28
2-9 2 4 6 10 14 18

SPEED CARTER SPACEMAN (See Spaceman)

SPEED COMICS (New Speed)(Also see Double Up)
Brookwood Publ./Speed Publ./Harvey Publications No. 14 on:
10/39 - #11, 8/40; #12, 3/41 - #44, 1-2/47 (#14-16: pocket size, 100 pgs.)

1-Origin & 1st app. Shock Gibson; Ted Parrish, the Man with 1000 Faces begins; Powell-a; becomes Champion #2 on?; has earliest? full page panel in comics 343 686 1029 2400 4200 6000
2-Powell-a 118 236 354 749 1287 1825
3 67 134 201 426 731 1035
4,5: 4-Powell-a? 5-Dinosaur-c 54 108 162 346 591 835
6-11: 7-Mars Mason begins, ends #11 50 100 150 315 533 750
12 (3/41; shows #11 in indicia)-The Wasp begins; Major Colt app. (Capt. Colt #12) 53 106 159 334 567 800
13-Intro. Captain Freedom & Young Defenders; Girl Commandos, Pat Parker (costumed heroine), War Nurse begins; Major Colt app. 60 120 180 381 653 925
14-16 (100 pg. pocket size, 1941): 14-2nd Harvey comic (See Pocket); Shock Gibson dons new costume. 15-Pat Parker dons costume, last in costume #23; no Girl Commandos 84 168 252 538 919 1300
17-Black Cat begins (4/42, early app.; see Pocket #1); origin Black Cat-r/Pocket #1; not in #40,41; S&K-c 82 164 246 528 902 1275
18-20-S&K-c 68 136 204 435 743 1050
21-Hitler, Tojo-c; Kirby-c 97 194 291 621 1061 1500
22-Kirby-c 68 136 204 435 743 1050
23-Origin Girl Commandos; Kirby-c 68 136 204 435 743 1050
24-Pat Parker team-up with Girl Commandos; Hitler, Tojo, & Mussolini-c 81 162 243 518 884 1250
25-30: 26-Flag-c 52 104 156 328 552 775
31-Schomburg Hitler & Tojo-c 90 180 270 576 988 1400
32-36-Schomburg-c 54 108 162 346 591 835
37,39-42, 44 41 82 123 256 428 600
38-Iwo-Jima Flag-c 43 86 129 271 461 650
43-Robot-c 45 90 135 284 480 675

NOTE: ***Al Avison*** *c-14-16, 30, 43.* ***Briefer*** *a-6, 7.* ***Jon Henri*** *(Kirbyesque) c-17-20.* ***Kubert*** *a-37, 38, 42-44.* ***Kirby/Caseneuve*** *c-21-23.* ***Cecelia Munson*** *a-7-11(Mars Mason).* ***Palais*** *c-37, 39-42.* ***Powell*** *a-1, 2, 4-7, 28, 31, 44.* ***Schomburg*** *c-31-36.* ***Tuska*** *a-3, 6, 7. Bondage c-18, 35. Captain Freedom c-16-24, 25(part), 26-44(w/Black Cat #27, 29, 31, 32-40). Shock Gibson c-1-15.*

SPEED DEMON (Also see Marvel Versus DC #3 & DC Versus Marvel #4)
Marvel Comics (Amalgam): Apr, 1996 ($1.95, one-shot)

1 2.50

SPEED DEMONS (Formerly Frank Merriwell at Yale #1-4?; Submarine Attack #11 on)
Charlton Comics: No. 5, Feb, 1957 - No. 10, 1958

5-10 7 14 21 35 43 50

SPEED FORCE (See The Flash 2nd Series #143-Cobalt Blue)
DC Comics: Nov, 1997 ($3.95, one-shot)

1-Flash & Kid Flash vs. Cobalt Blue; Waid-s/Aparo & Sienkiewicz-a; Flash family stories and pin-ups by various 4.00

SPEED RACER (Also see The New Adventures of...)
Now Comics: July, 1987 - No. 38, Nov, 1990 ($1.75)

1-38, 1-2nd printing 2.50
Special 1 (1988, $2.00) 2.50
Special 2 (1988, $3.50) 3.50

SPEED RACER (Also see Racer X)
DC Comics (WildStorm): Oct, 1999 - No. 3, Dec, 1999 ($2.50, limited series)

1-3-Tommy Yune-s/a; origin of Racer X; debut of the Mach 5 2.50
...: Born To Race (2000, $9.95, TPB) r/series & conceptual art 10.00
...: The Original Manga Vol. 1 ('00, $9.95, TPB) r/1950s B&W manga 10.00

SPEED RACER: CHRONICLES OF THE RACER
IDW Publishing: 2007 - No. 4, Apr, 2008 ($3.99)

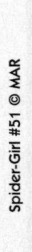

Spellbound #10 © MAR

Spider-Girl #51 © MAR

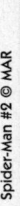

Spider-Man #2 © MAR

	GD	VG	FN	VF	VF/NM	NM-
	2.0	4.0	6.0	8.0	9.0	9.2

1-4-Multiple covers for each 4.00

SPEED RACER FEATURING NINJA HIGH SCHOOL
Now Comics: Aug, 1993 - No. 2, 1993 ($2.50, mini-series)

1,2: 1-Polybagged w/card. 2-Exists? 2.50

SPEED RACER: RETURN OF THE GRX
Now Comics: Mar, 1994 - No. 2, Apr, 1994 ($1.95, limited series)

1,2 2.50

SPEED SMITH-THE HOT ROD KING (Also see Hot Rod King)
Ziff-Davis Publishing Co.: Spring, 1952

	GD	VG	FN	VF	VF/NM	NM-
1-Saunders painted-c	23	46	69	136	223	310

SPEEDY GONZALES
Dell Publishing Co.: No. 1084, Mar, 1960

	GD	VG	FN	VF	VF/NM	NM-
Four Color 1084	5	10	15	34	55	75

SPEEDY RABBIT (See Television Puppet Show)
Realistic/I. W. Enterprises/Super Comics: nd (1953); 1963

	GD	VG	FN	VF	VF/NM	NM-
nn (1953)-Realistic Reprint?	2	4	6	9	13	16
I.W. Reprint #1 (2 versions w/diff. c/stories exist)-Peter Cottontail #?						
Super Reprint #14(1963)	2	4	6	8	10	12

SPELLBINDERS
Quality: Dec, 1986 - No. 12, Jan, 1988 ($1.25)

1-12: Nemesis the Warlock, Amadeus Wolf 2.50

SPELLBINDERS
Marvel Comics: May, 2005 - No. 6, Oct, 2005 ($2.99, limited series)

1-6-Carey-s/Perkins-a 3.00
...: Signs and Wonders TPB (2006, $7.99, digest) r/#1-6 8.00

SPELLBOUND (See The Crusaders)

SPELLBOUND (Tales to Hold You... #1, Stories to Hold You...)
Atlas Comics (ACI 1-15/Male 16-23/BPC 24-34): Mar, 1952 - #23, June, 1954; #24, Oct, 1955 - #34, June, 1957

	GD	VG	FN	VF	VF/NM	NM-
1-Horror/weird stories in all	71	142	213	454	777	1100
2-Edgar A. Poe app.	40	80	120	234	397	560
3-5: 3-Whitney-a; cannibalism story	35	70	105	208	339	470
6-Krigstein-a	35	70	105	208	339	470
7-10: 8-Ayers-a	30	60	90	177	289	400
11-16,18-20: 14-Ed Win-a	25	50	75	150	245	340
17-Krigstein-a	26	52	78	152	249	345
21-23: 23-Last precode (6/54)	21	42	63	122	199	275
24-28,30,31,34: 25-Orlando-a	20	40	60	114	182	250
29-Ditko-a (4 pgs.)	21	42	63	122	199	275
32,33-Torres-a	20	40	60	114	182	250

NOTE: ***Brodsky** a-5; c-1, 5-7, 10, 11, 13, 15, 25-27, 32. **Colan** a-17. **Everett** a-2, 5, 7, 10, 16, 28, 31; c-2, 8, 9, 14, 17-19, 28, 30. **Forgione/Abel** a-29. **Forte/Fox** a-16. **Al Hartley** a-2. **Heath** a-2, 4, 8, 9, 12, 14, 16; c-3, 4, 12, 16, 20, 21. **Infantino** a-15. **Keller** a-5. **Kida** a-2, 14. **Maneely** a-7, 14, 27; c-24, 29, 31. **Mooney** a-5, 13, 18. **Mac Pakula** a-22, 32. **Post** a-8. **Powell** a-19, 20, 32. **Robinson** a-1. **Romita** a-24, 26, 27. **R.Q. Sale** a-29. **Sekowsky** a-5. **Severin** c-29. **Sinnott** a-8, 16, 17.*

SPELLBOUND
Marvel Comics: Jan, 1988 - Apr, 1988 ($1.50, bi-weekly, Baxter paper)

1-5 2.50
6 ($2.25, 52 pgs.) 2.50

SPELLJAMMER (Also see TSR Worlds Comics Annual)
DC Comics: Sept, 1990 - No. 15, Nov, 1991 ($1.75)

1-15: Based on TSR game. 11-Heck-a. 2.50

SPENCER SPOOK (Formerly Giggle Comics)
American Comics Group: No. 100, Mar-Apr, 1955 - No. 101, May-June, 1955

	GD	VG	FN	VF	VF/NM	NM-
100,101	7	14	21	37	46	55

SPIDER, THE
Eclipse Books: 1991 - Book 3, 1991 ($4.95, 52 pgs., limited series)

Book 1-3-Truman-c/a 5.00

SPIDER-BOY (Also see Marvel Versus DC #3)
Marvel Comics (Amalgam): Apr, 1996 ($1.95)

1-Mike Wieringo-c/a; Karl Kesel story; 1st app. of Bizarnage, Insect Queen, Challengers of the Fantastic, Sue Storm: Agent of S.H.I.E.L. D., & King Lizard 2.50

SPIDER-BOY TEAM-UP
Marvel Comics (Amalgam): June, 1997 ($1.95, one-shot)

1-Karl Kesel & Roger Stern-s/Jo Ladronn-a(p) 2.50

SPIDER-GIRL (See What If... #105)
Marvel Comics: Oct, 1998 - No. 100, Sept, 2006 ($1.99/$2.25/$2.99)

	GD	VG	FN	VF	VF/NM	NM-
0-($2.99)-r/1st app. Peter Parker's daughter from What If #105; previews regular series, Avengers-Next and J2	1	2	3	4	5	7
1-DeFalco-s/Olliffe & Williamson-s	1	2	3	4	5	7

2-Two covers 4.00
3-16,18-20: 3-Fantastic Five-c/app. 10,11-Spider-Girl time-travels to meet teenaged Spider-Man 2.50
17-($2.99) Peter Parker suits up 3.00
21-24,26-49,51-59: 21-Begin $2.25-c. 31-Avengers app. 2.50
25-($2.99) Spider-Girl vs. the Savage Six 3.00
50-($3.50) 3.50
59-99-($2.99) 59-Avengers app.; Ben Parker born. 75-May in Black costume. 82-84-Venom bonds with Normie Osborn. 93-Venom-c. 95-Tony Stark app. 3.00
100-($3.99) Last issue; story plus Rogues Gallery, profile pages; r/#27,53 4.00
1999 Annual ($3.99) 4.00
Wizard #1/2 (1999) 3.00
... A Fresh Start (1/99,$5.99, TPB) r/#1&2 6.00
... Presents The Buzz and Darkdevil (2007, $7.99, digest) r/mini-series 8.00
TPB (10/01, $19.95) r/#0-8; new Olliffe-c 20.00
Marvel Age Spider-Girl Vol. 1: Legacy (2004, $7.99, digest size) r/#0-5 8.00
Marvel Age Spider-Girl Vol. 2: Like Father, Like Daughter (2004, $7.99, digest) r/#6-11 8.00
Spider-Girl Vol. 3: Avenging Allies (2005, $7.99, digest) r/#12-16 & 1999 Annual 8.00
Spider-Girl Vol. 4: Turning Point (2005, $7.99, digest) r/#17-21 & #1/2 8.00
Spider-Girl Vol. 5: Endgame (2006, $7.99, digest) r/#22-27 8.00
Spider-Girl Vol. 6: Too Many Spiders! (2006, $7.99, digest) r/#28-33 8.00
Spider-Girl Vol. 7: Betrayed (2006, $7.99, digest) r/#34-38 & #51 8.00
Spider-Girl Vol. 8: Duty Calls (2007, $7.99, digest) r/#39-44 8.00
Spider-Girl Vol. 9: Secret Lives (2007, $7.99, digest) r/#45-50 8.00

SPIDER-MAN (See Amazing..., Friendly Neighborhood..., Giant-Size..., Marvel Age..., Marvel Knights..., Marvel Tales, Marvel Team-Up, Spectacular..., Spidey Super Stories, Ultimate Marvel Team-Up, Ultimate..., Venom, & Web Of...)

SPIDER-MAN (Peter Parker Spider-Man on cover but not indicia #75-on)
Marvel Comics: Aug, 1990 - No. 98, Nov, 1998 ($1.75/$1.95/ $1.99)

	GD	VG	FN	VF	VF/NM	NM-
1-Silver edition, direct sale only (unbagged)	1	2	3	5	6	8

1-Silver bagged edition; direct sale, no price on comic, but $2.00 on plastic bag (125,000 print run) 20.00
1-Regular edition w/Spidey face in UPC area (unbagged); green-c 6.00
1-Regular bagged edition w/Spidey face in UPC area; green cover (125,000) 12.00
1-Newsstand bagged w/UPC code 8.00
1-Gold edition, 2nd printing (unbagged) with Spider-Man in box (400,000-450,000) 5.00
1-Gold 2nd printing w/UPC code; (less than 10,000 print run) intended for Wal-Mart; much scarcer than originally believed 120.00
1-Platinum ed. mailed to retailers only (10,000 print run); has new McFarlane-a & editorial material instead of ads; stiff-c, no cover price 130.00
2-26: 2-McFarlane-c/a/scripts continue. 6,7-Ghost Rider & Hobgoblin app. 8-Wolverine cameo; Wolverine storyline begins. 12-Wolverine storyline ends. 13-Spidey's black costume returns; Morbius app. 14-Morbius app. 15-Erik Larsen-c/a; Beast c/s. 16-X-Force-c/story w/Liefeld assists; continues in X-Force #4; reads sideways; last McFarlane issue. 17-Thanos-c/story; Leonardi/Williamson-c/a. 13,14-Spidey in black costume. 18-Ghost Rider-c/story. 18-23-Sinister Six storyline w/Erik Larsen-c/a/scripts. 19-Hulk & Hobgoblin-c & app. 20-22-Deathlok app. 22,23-Ghost Rider, Hulk, Hobgoblin app. 23-Wrap-around gatefold-c. 24-Infinity War x-over w/Demogoblin & Hobgoblin-c/story. 24-Demogoblin dons new costume & battles Hobgoblin-c/story. 26-($3.50, 52 pgs.)-Silver hologram on-c w/gatefold poster by Ron Lim; Spidey retells his origin. 4.00
26-2nd printing; gold hologram on-c 3.50
27-45: 32-34-Punisher-c/story. 37-Maximum Carnage x-over. 39,40-Electro-c/s (cameo #38). 41-43-Iron Fist-c/stories w/Jae Lee-c/a. 42-Intro Platoon. 44-Hobgoblin app. 3.00
46-49,51-53, 55, 56,58-74,76-81: 46-Begin $1.95-c; bound-in card sheet. 51-Power & Responsibility Pt. 3. 52,53-Venom app. 60-Kaine revealed. 61-Origin Kaine. 65-Mysterio app. 66-Kaine-c/app.; Peter Parker app. 67-Carnage-c/app. 68,69-Hobgoblin-c/app. 72-Onslaught x-over; Spidey vs. Sentinels. 74-Daredevil-c/app. 77-80-Morbius-c/app. 2.50
46-($2.95)-Polybagged; silver ink-c w/16 pg. preview of cartoon series & animation style print; bound-in trading card sheet 3.00
50-($2.50)-Newsstand edition 2.50
50-($3.95)-Collectors edition w/holographic-c 4.00
51-($2.95)-Deluxe edition foil-c; flip book 3.00
54-($2.75, 52 pgs.)-Flip book 2.75
57-($2.50) 2.50
57-($2.95)-Die cut-c 3.00
65-($2.95)-Variant-c; polybagged w/cassette 3.00
75-($2.95)-Wraparound-c; Green Goblin returns; death of Ben Reilly (who was the clone) 4.00
82-97: 84-Juggernaut app. 91-Double cover with "Dusk #1"; battles the Shocker.

Spider-Man #92 © MAR

Spider-Man: Election Day HC © MAR

Spider-Man/Black Cat: The Evil That Men Do #1 © MAR

GD 2.0 | VG 4.0 | FN 6.0 | VF 8.0 | VF/NM 9.0 | NM- 9.2

93-Ghost Rider app.
98-Double cover; final issue 2.50
#(-1) Flashback (7/97) 3.00
Annual '97 ($2.99), '98 ($2.99)-Devil Dinosaur-c/app. 2.50
3.00

NOTE: *Erik Larsen c/a-15, 18-23. M. Rogers/Keith Williams c/a-27, 28.*

SPIDER-MAN (one-shots, hardcovers and TPBs)

...& Arana Special: The Hunter Revealed (5/06, $3.99) Del Rio-s; art by Del Rio & various 3.00
...and Batman ('95, $5.95) DeMatteis-s; Joker, Carnage app. 6.00
...and Daredevil ('84, $2.00) 1-r/Spectacular Spider-Man #26-28 by Miller 3.00
...and The Human Torch in...Bahia de Los Muertos! 1 (5/09, $3.99) Beland-s/Juan Doe-a; Diablo app.; printed in two versions (English and Spanish language) 4.00
...: Back in Black HC (2007, $34.99, dustjacket) oversized r/Amaz. S-M #539-543, Friendly Neighborhood S-M #17-23 & Annual #1; cover pencils and sketch pages 35.00
...: Back in Black SC (2008, $24.99) same contents as HC 25.00
...: Back in Black Handbook (2007, $3.99) Official Handbook format; Lopresti-c 4.00
...: Birth of Venom TPB (2007, $29.99) r/Secret Wars #8, AS-M #252-259,298-300,315-317, AS-M Annual #25, Fantastic Four #274 and Web of Spider-Man #1 30.00
...: Brand New Day HC (2008, $24.99, dustjacket) r/Amaz. S-M #546-551, Spider-Man: Swing Shift and story from Venom Super-Special 25.00
...: Carnage nn (6/93, $6.95, TPB)-r/Amazing S-M #344,345,359-363; spot varnish-c 7.00
.../Daredevil (10/02, $2.99) Vatche Mavlian-c/a; Brett Matthews-s 3.00
...: Dead Man's Hand 1 (4/97, $2.99) 3.00
...: Death of the Stacys HC (2007, $19.99, dustjacket) r/Amazing Spider-Man #88-92 and #121,122; intro. by Gerry Conway; afterword by Romita; cover gallery incl. reprints 20.00
.../Dr. Strange: "The Way to Dusty Death" nn (1992, $6.95, 68 pgs.) 7.00
...: Election Day HC (2009, $29.99) r/#584-588; includes Barack Obama app from #583 30.00
.../Elektra '98-($2.99) vs. The Silencer 3.00
... Family (2005, $4.99, 100 pgs.) new story and reprints; Spider-Ham app. 5.00
... Fear Itself (3/09, $3.99) Spider-Man and Man-Thing; Stuart Moore-s/Joe Suitor-a 4.00
... Fear Itself Graphic Novel (2/92, $12.95) 18.00
Giant-Sized Spider-Man (12/98, $3.99) r/team-ups 4.00
Holiday Special 1995 ($2.95) 3.00
...: Hot Shots nn (1/96, $2.95) fold out posters by various, inc. Vess and Ross 3.00
Identity Crisis (9/98, $19.95, TPB) 20.00
...: Kraven's Last Hunt HC (2006, $19.99) r/Amaz. S-M #293,294; Web of S-M #31,32 and Spect. S-M #131-132; intro. by DeMatteis; Zeck-a; cover pencils and interior pencils 20.00
...: Legacy of Evil 1 (6/96, $3.95) Kurt Busiek script & Mark Texeira-c/a 4.00
...Legends Vol. 1: Todd McFarlane ('03, $19.95, TPB)-r/Amaz. S-M #298-305 20.00
...Legends Vol. 2: Todd McFarlane ('03, $19.99, TPB)-r/Amaz. S-M #306-314, & Spec. Spider-Man Annual #10 20.00
...Legends Vol. 3: Todd McFarlane ('04, $24.99, TPB)-r/Amaz. S-M #315-323,325,328 25.00
...Legends Vol. 4: Spider-Man & Wolverine ('03, $13.95, TPB) r/Spider-Man & Wolverine #1-4 and Spider-Man/Daredevil #1 14.00
.../Marrow (2/01, $2.99) Garza-a 3.00
.../Mary Jane: ... You Just Hit the Jackpot TPB (2009, $24.99) early apps. & key stories 25.00
...: One More Day HC (2008. $24.99, dustjacket) r/Amaz. S-M #544-545, Friendly N.S-M #24, Sensational S-M #41 and Marvel Spotlight: Spider-Man-One More Day 25.00
..., Peter Parker: Back in Black HC (2007, $34.99) oversized r/Sensational Spider-Man #35-40 & Annual #1, Spider-Man Family #1,2; Marvel Spotlight: Spider-Man and Spider-Man Back in Black Handbook; cover sketches 35.00
..., Punisher, Sabretooth: Designer Genes (1993, $8.95) 9.00
...Return of the Goblin TPB (See Peter Parker: Spider-Man)
...Revelations ('97, $14.99, TPB) r/end of Clone Saga plus 14 new pages by Romita Jr. 15.00
...: Saga of the Sandman TPB (2007, $19.99) r/1st app. Amazing S-M #4 and other app. 20.00
...: Son of the Goblin (2004, $15.99, TPB) r/AS-M#136-137,312 & Spec. S-M #189,200 16.00
... Special: Black and Blue and Read All Over 1 (11/06, $3.99) new story and r/ASM #12 4.00
Special Edition 1 (12/92-c, 11/92 inside)-The Trial of Venom; ordered thru mail with $5.00 donation or more to UNICEF; embossed metallic ink; came bagged w/bound-in poster; Daredevil app. 1 3 4 6 8 10
Super Special (7/95, $3.95)-Planet of the Symbiotes 4.00
The Best of Spider-Man Vol. 2 (2003, $29.99, HC with dust jacket) r/AS-M V2 #37-45, Peter Parker: S-M #44-47, and S-M's Tangled Web #10,11; Pearson-c 30.00
The Best of Spider-Man Vol. 3 (2004, $29.99, HC with d.j.) r/AS-M V2 #46-58, 500 30.00
The Best of Spider-Man Vol. 4 (2005, $29.99, HC with d.j.) r/#501-514; sketch pages 30.00
The Best of Spider-Man Vol. 5 (2006, $29.99, HC with d.j.) r/#515-524; sketch pages 30.00
The Complete Frank Miller Spider-Man (2002, $29.95, HC) r/Miller-s/a 30.00
The Death of Captain Stacy ($3.50) r/AS-M#88-90 3.50
The Death of Gwen Stacy ($14.95) r/AS-M#96-98,121,122 15.00
...: The Movie ($12.95) adaptation by Stan Lee-s/Alan Davis-a; plus r/Ultimate Spider-Man #8, Peter Parker #35, Tangled Web #10; photo-c 13.00
...: The Official Movie Adaptation ($5.95) Stan Lee-s/Alan Davis-a 6.00
...: The Other HC (2006, $29.99, dust jacket) r/Amazing S-M #525-528, Friendly Neighborhood S-M #1-4 and Marvel Knights S-M #19-22; gallery of variant covers 30.00
...: The Other SC (2006, $24.99) r/crossover; gallery of variant covers 25.00
...: The Other Sketchbook (2005, $2.99) sketch page preview of 2005-6 x-over 3.00
Torment TPB (5/01$15.95) r/#1-5, Spec. S-M #10 16.00
... Vs. Doctor Octopus ($17.95) reprints early battles; Sean Chen-c 18.00
... Vs. Punisher (7/00, $2.99) Michael Lopez-c/a 3.00
...Vs. Silver Sable (2006, $15.99, TPB)-r/Amazing Spider-Man #265,279-281 & Peter Parker, The Spectacular Spider-Man #128,129 16.00
...Vs. The Black Cat (2005, $14.99, TPB)-r/Amaz. S-M #194,195,204,205,226,227 15.00
...Vs. Venom (1990, $8.95, TPB)-r/Amaz. S-M #300,315-317 w/new McFarlane-c 9.00
...Visionaries (10/01, $19.95, TPB)-r/Amaz. S-M #298-305; McFarlane-a 20.00
...Visionaries: John Romita (8/01, $19.95, TPB)-r/Amaz. S-M #39-42, 50,68,69,108,109; new Romita-c 20.00
...Visionaries: Kurt Busiek (2006, $19.99, TPB)-r/Untold Tales of Spider-Man #1-8 20.00
...Visionaries: Roger Stern (2007, $24.99, TPB)-r/Amazing Spider-Man #206 & Spectacular Spider-Man #43-52,54; Stern interview 25.00
Wizard 1/2 ($10.00) Leonardi-a; Green Goblin app. 10.00

SPIDER-MAN ADVENTURES
Marvel Comics: Dec, 1994 - No. 15, Mar, 1996 ($1.50)

1-15 ($1.50)-Based on animated series 2.50
1-($2.95)-Foil embossed-c 3.00

SPIDER-MAN AND HIS AMAZING FRIENDS (See Marvel Action Universe)
Marvel Comics Group: Dec, 1981 (one-shot)

1-Adapted from NBC TV cartoon show; Green Goblin-c/story; 1st Spidey, Firestar, Iceman team-up; Spiegle-p 5.00

SPIDER-MAN AND POWER PACK
Marvel Comics: Jan, 2007 - No. 4, Apr, 2007 ($2.99, limited series)

1-4-Sumerak-s/Gurihiru-a; Sandman app. 3,4-Venom app. 3.00
...: Big City Heroes (2007, $6.99, digest) r/#1-4 7.00

SPIDER-MAN AND THE FANTASTIC FOUR
Marvel Comics: Jun, 2007 - No. 4, Sept, 2007 ($2.99, limited series)

1-4-Mike Wieringo-a/c; Jeff Parker-s. 1,4-Impossible Man app. 3.00
...: Silver Rage TPB (2007, $10.99) r/#1-4; series outline and cover sketches 11.00

SPIDER-MAN AND THE SECRET WARS
Marvel Comics: Feb, 2010 - No. 4, May, 2010 ($2.99, limited series)

1-4-Tobin-s/Scherberger-a. 3-Black costume app. 3.00

SPIDER-MAN AND THE INCREDIBLE HULK (See listing under Amazing...)

SPIDER-MAN AND THE UNCANNY X-MEN
Marvel Comics: Mar, 1996 ($16.95, trade paperback)

nn-r/Uncanny X-Men #27, Uncanny X-men #35, Amazing Spider-Man #92, Marvel Team-Up Annual #1, Marvel Team-Up #150, & Spectacular Spider-Man #197-199 17.00

SPIDER-MAN & WOLVERINE (See Spider-Man Legends Vol. 4 for TPB reprint)
Marvel Comics: Aug, 2003 - No. 4, Nov, 2003 ($2.99, limited series)

1-4-Matthews-s/Mavlian-a 3.00

SPIDER-MAN AND X-FACTOR
Marvel Comics: May, 1994 - No. 3, July, 1994 ($1.95, limited series)

1-3 2.50

SPIDER-MAN /BADROCK
Maximum Press: Mar, 1997 ($2.99, mini-series)

1A, 1B(#2)-Jurgens-s 3.00

SPIDER-MAN/BLACK CAT: THE EVIL THAT MEN DO (Also see Marvel Must Haves)
Marvel Comics: Aug, 2002 - No. 6, Mar, 2006 ($2.99, limited series)

1-6-Kevin Smith-s/Terry Dodson-c/a 3.00
HC (2006, $19.99, dust jacket) r/#1-6; script to #6 with sketches 20.00

SPIDER-MAN: BLUE
Marvel Comics: July, 2002 - No. 6, Apr, 2003 ($3.50, limited series)

1-6: Jeph Loeb-s/Tim Sale-a/c; flashback to early MJ and Gwen Stacy 3.50
HC (2003, $21.99, with dust jacket) over-sized r/#1-6; intro. by John Romita 22.00
SC (2004, $14.99) r/#1-6; cover gallery 15.00

SPIDER-MAN: BRAND NEW DAY (See Amazing Spider-Man Vol. 2)

SPIDER-MAN: BREAKOUT (See New Avengers #1)
Marvel Comics: June, 2005 - No. 5, Oct, 2005 ($2.99, limited series)

1-5-Bedard-s/Garcia-a. 1-U-Foes app. 5-New Avengers app. 3.00
TPB (2006, $13.99) r/#1-5 14.00

SPIDER-MAN: CHAPTER ONE
Marvel Comics: Dec, 1998 - No. 12, Oct, 1999 ($2.50, limited series)

1-Retelling/updating of origin; John Byrne-s/c/a 2.50

Spider-Man Family #8 © MAR

Spider-Man Loves Mary Jane #16 © MAR

Spider-Man Megazine #4 © MAR

GD 2.0 | VG 4.0 | FN 6.0 | VF 8.0 | VF/NM 9.0 | NM- 9.2

1-($6.95) DF Edition w/variant-c by Jae Lee 7.00
2-11: 2-Two covers (one is swipe of ASM #1); Fantastic Four app. 9-Daredevil. 11-Giant-Man-c/app. 2.50
12-($3.50) Battles the Sandman 3.50
0-(5/99) Origins of Vulture, Lizard and Sandman 2.50

SPIDER-MAN CLASSICS
Marvel Comics: Apr, 1993 - No. 16, July, 1994 ($1.25)
1-14,16: 1-r/Amaz. Fantasy #15 & Strange Tales #115. 2-16-r/Amaz. Spider-Man #1-15. 6-Austin-c(i) 2.50
15-($2.95)-Polybagged w/16 pg. insert & animation style print; r/Amazing Spider-Man #14 (1st Green Goblin) 3.00

SPIDER-MAN COLLECTOR'S PREVIEW
Marvel Comics: Dec, 1994 ($1.50, 100 pgs., one-shot)
1-wraparound-c; no comics 3.00

SPIDER-MAN COMICS MAGAZINE
Marvel Comics Group: Jan, 1987 - No. 13, 1988 ($1.50, digest-size)
1-13-Reprints 6.00

SPIDER-MAN: DEATH AND DESTINY
Marvel Comics: Aug, 2000 - No. 3, Oct, 2000 ($2.99, limited series)
1-3-Aftermath of the death of Capt. Stacy 3.00

SPIDER-MAN/ DOCTOR OCTOPUS: OUT OF REACH
Marvel Comics: Jan, 2004 - No. 5, May, 2004 ($2.99, limited series)
1-5: 1-Keron Grant-a/Colin Mitchell-s 3.00
Marvel Age... TPB (2004, $5.99, digest size) r/#1-5 6.00

SPIDER-MAN/ DOCTOR OCTOPUS: YEAR ONE
Marvel Comics: Aug, 2004 - No. 5, Dec, 2004 ($2.99, limited series)
1-5-Kaare Andrews-a/Zeb Wells-s 3.00

SPIDER-MAN FAIRY TALES
Marvel Comics: July, 2007 - No. 4, Oct, 2007 ($2.99, limited series)
1-4: 1-Cebulski-s/Tercio-a. 2-Henrichon-a. 3-Kobayashi-a. 4-Dragotta-p/Allred-i 3.00
TPB (2007, $10.99) r/#1-4 11.00

SPIDER-MAN FAMILY (Also see Amazing Spider-Man Family)
Marvel Comics: Apr, 2007 - No. 9, Aug, 2008 ($4.99, anthology)
1-9-New tales and reprints. 1-Black costume, Sandman, Black Cat app. 4-Agents of Atlas app., Kirk-a; Puppet Master by Eliopoulos. 8-Iron Man app. 9-Hulk app. 5.00
... Featuring Spider-Clan 1 (1/07, $4.99) new Spider-Clan story; reprints w/Spider-Man 2099 and Amazing Spider-Man #252 (black costume) 5.00
... Featuring Spider-Man's Amazing Friends 1 (10/06, $4.99) new story with Iceman and Firestar; Mini Marvels w/Giarrusso-a; reprints w/Spider-Man 2099 5.00
...: Back In Black (2007, $7.99, digest) r/new content from #1-3 8.00
...: Untold Team-Ups (2008, $9.99, digest) r/new content from #4-6 10.00

SPIDER-MAN: FRIENDS AND ENEMIES
Marvel Comics: Jan, 1995 - No. 4, Apr, 1995 ($1.95, limited series)
1-4-Darkhawk, Nova & Speedball app. 2.50

SPIDER-MAN: FUNERAL FOR AN OCTOPUS
Marvel Comics: Mar, 1995 - No. 3, May, 1995 ($1.50, limited series)
1-3 2.50

SPIDER-MAN/ GEN 13
Marvel Comics: Nov, 1996 ($4.95, one-shot)
nn-Peter David-s/Stuart Immonen-a 5.00

SPIDER-MAN: GET KRAVEN
Marvel Comics: Aug, 2002 - No. 6, Jan, 2003 ($2.99/$2.25, limited series)
1-($2.99) McCrea-a/Quesada-c; back-up story w/Rio-a 3.00
2-6-($2.25) 2-Sub-Mariner app. 2.50

SPIDER-MAN: HOBGOBLIN LIVES
Marvel Comics: Jan, 1997 - No. 3, Mar, 1997 ($2.50, limited series)
1-3-Wraparound-c 2.50
TPB (1/98, $14.99) r/#1-3 plus timeline 15.00

SPIDER-MAN: HOUSE OF M (Also see House of M and related x-overs)
Marvel Comics: Aug, 2005 - No. 5, Dec, 2005 ($2.99, limited series)
1-5-Waid & Peyer-s/Larroca-a; rich and famous Peter Parker in mutant-ruled world 3.00
House of M: Spider-Man TPB (2006, $13.99) r/series 14.00

SPIDER-MAN/ HUMAN TORCH
Marvel Comics: Mar, 2005 - No. 5, July, 2005 ($2.99, limited series)

GD 2.0 | VG 4.0 | FN 6.0 | VF 8.0 | VF/NM 9.0 | NM- 9.2

1-5-Ty Templeton-a/Dan Slott-s; team-ups from early days to the present 3.00
...: I'm With Stupid (2006, $7.99, digest) r/#1-5 8.00

SPIDER-MAN: INDIA
Marvel Comics: Jan, 2005 - No. 4, Apr, 2005 ($2.99, limited series)
1-4-Pavitr Prabhakar gains spider powers; Kang-a/Seetharaman-s 3.00

SPIDER-MAN: LEGEND OF THE SPIDER-CLAN (See Marvel Mangaverse for TPB)
Marvel Comics: Dec, 2002 - No. 5, Apr, 2003 ($2.25, limited series)
1-5-Marvel Mangaverse Spider-Man; Kaare Andrews-s/Skottie Young-c/a 2.50

SPIDER-MAN: LIFELINE
Marvel Comics: Apr, 2001 - No. 3, June, 2001 ($2.99, limited series)
1-3-Nicieza-s/Rude-c/a; The Lizard app. 3.00

SPIDER-MAN LOVES MARY JANE (Also see Mary Jane limited series)
Marvel Comics: Feb, 2006 - No. 20, Sept, 2007 ($2.99)
1-20-Mary Jane & Peter in high school; McKeever-s/Miyazawa-a/c. 5-Gwen Stacy app. 16-18,20-Firestar app. 17-Felecia Hardy app. 3.00
... Vol. 1: Super Crush (2006, $7.99, digest) r/#1-5; cover concepts page 8.00
... Vol. 2: The New Girl (2006, $7.99, digest) r/#6-10; sketch pages 8.00
... Vol. 3: My Secret Life (2007, $7.99, digest) r/#11-15; sketch pages 8.00
... Vol. 4: Still Friends (2007, $7.99, digest) r/#16-20 8.00
Hardcover Vol. 1 (2007, $24.99) oversized reprints of #1-5, Mary Jane #1-4 and Mary Jane: Homecoming #1-4; series proposals, sketch pages and covers; coloring process 25.00
Hardcover Vol. 2 (2008, $39.99) oversized reprints of #6-20, sketch & layout pages 40.00

SPIDER-MAN LOVES MARY JANE SEASON 2
Marvel Comics: Oct, 2008 - No. 5, Feb, 2009 ($2.99, limited series)
1-5-Terry Moore-s/c; Craig Rousseau-a 3.00
1-Variant-c by Alphona 8.00

SPIDER-MAN: MADE MEN
Marvel Comics: Aug, 1998 ($5.99, one-shot)
1-Spider-Man & Daredevil vs. Kingpin 6.00

SPIDER-MAN MAGAZINE
Marvel Comics: 1994 - No. 3, 1994 ($1.95, magazine)
1-3: 1-Contains 4 S-M promo cards & 4 X-Men Ultra Fleer cards; Spider-Man story by Romita, Sr.; X-Men story; puzzles & games. 2-Doc Octopus & X-Men stories 3.00

SPIDER-MAN: MAXIMUM CLONAGE
Marvel Comics: 1995 ($4.95)
Alpha #1-Acetate-c, Omega #1-Chromium-c. 5.00

SPIDER-MAN MEGAZINE
Marvel Comics: Oct, 1994 - No. 6, Mar, 1995 ($2.95, 100 pgs.)
1-6: 1-r/ASM #16,224,225, Marvel Team-Up #1 3.00

SPIDER-MAN NOIR
Marvel Comics: Dec, 2008 - No. 4, May, 2009 ($3.99, limited series)
1-4-Pulp-style Spider-Man in 1933; DiGiandomenico-a; covers by Zircher & Calero 4.00
...: Eyes Without a Face 1-4 (2/10 - No. 4, 5/10) DiGiandomenico-a; Zircher & Calero-c 4.00

SPIDER-MAN: POWER OF TERROR
Marvel Comics: Jan, 1995 - No. 4, Apr, 1995 ($1.95, limited series)
1-4-Silvermane & Deathlok app. 2.50

SPIDER-MAN/PUNISHER: FAMILY PLOT
Marvel Comics: Feb, 1996 - No. 2, Mar, 1996 ($2.95, limited series)
1,2 3.00

SPIDER-MAN: QUALITY OF LIFE
Marvel Comics: Jul, 2002 - No. 4, Oct, 2002 ($2.99, limited series)
1-4-All CGI art by Scott Sava; Rucka-s; Lizard app. 3.00
TPB (2002, $12.99) r/#1-4; a "Making of..." section detailing the CGI process 13.00

SPIDER-MAN: REDEMPTION
Marvel Comics: Sept, 1996 - No. 4, Dec, 1996 ($1.50, limited series)
1-4: DeMatteis scripts; Zeck-a 2.50

SPIDER-MAN/ RED SONJA
Marvel Comics: Oct, 2007 - No. 5, Feb, 2008 ($2.99, limited series)
1-5-Rubi-a/Oeming-s/Turner-c; Venom & Kulan Gath app. 3.00
HC (2008, $19.99, dustjacket) r/#1-5 and Marvel Team-Up #79; sketch pages 20.00

SPIDER-MAN: REIGN
Marvel Comics: Feb, 2007 - No. 4, May, 2007 ($3.99, limited series)
1-Kaare Andrews-s/a; red costume on cover 4.00
1-Variant cover with black costume 10.00

Spider-Man 1602 #1 © MAR

Spider-Man 2099 #23 © MAR

Spider-Man: With Great Power... #2 © MAR

GD 2.0 | VG 4.0 | FN 6.0 | VF 8.0 | VF/NM 9.0 | NM- 9.2

GD 2.0 | VG 4.0 | FN 6.0 | VF 8.0 | VF/NM 9.0 | NM- 9.2

2-4 4.00
HC (2007, $19.99, dustjacket) r/#1-4; sketch pages and cover variant gallery 20.00
HC 2nd printing (2007, $19.99, dustjacket) with variant black cover 20.00
SC (2008, $14.99) r/#1-4; sketch pages and cover variant gallery 15.00

SPIDER-MAN: REVENGE OF THE GREEN GOBLIN
Marvel Comics: Oct, 2000 - No. 3, Dec, 2000 ($2.99, limited series)
1-3-Frenz & Olliffe-a; continues in AS-M #25 & PP:S-M #25 3.00

SPIDER-MAN SAGA
Marvel Comics: Nov, 1991 - No. 4, Feb, 1992 ($2.95, limited series)
1-4: Gives history of Spider-Man: text & illustrations 3.00

SPIDER-MAN 1602
Marvel Comics: Dec, 2009 - No. 5, Apr, 2010 ($3.99, limited series)
1-5- Peter Parquagh from Marvel 1602; Parker-s/Rosanas-a 4.00

SPIDER-MAN: SWEET CHARITY
Marvel Comics: Aug, 2002 ($4.95, one-shot)
1-The Scorpion-c/app.; Campbell-c/Zimmerman-s/Robertson-a 5.00

SPIDER-MAN'S TANGLED WEB (Titled **"Tangled Web"** in indicia for #1-4)
Marvel Comics: Jun, 2001 - No. 22, Mar, 2003 ($2.99)
1-3: "The Thousand" on-c; Ennis-s/McCrea-a/Fabry-c 4.00
4-"Severance Package" on-c; Rucka-s/Risso-a; Kingpin-c/app. 5.00
5,6-Flowers for Rhino; Milligan-s/Fegredo-a 3.00
7-10,12,15-20,22: 7-9-Gentlemen's Agreement; Bruce Jones-s/Lee Weeks-a. 10-Andrews-s/a. 12-Fegredo-a. 15-Paul Pope-s/a. 18-Ted McKeever-s/a. 19-Mahfood-a. 20-Haspiel-a 3.00
11,13,21-($3.50) 11-Darwyn Cooke-s/a. 13-Phillips-a. 21-Christmas-s by Cooke & Bone 3.50
14-Azzarello & Scott Levy (WWE's Raven)-s about Crusher Hogan 4.00
TPB (10/01, $15.95) r/#1-6 16.00
Volume 2 TPB (4/02, $14.95) r/#7-11 15.00
Volume 3 TPB (2002, $15.99) r/#12-17; Jason Pearson-c 16.00
Volume 4 TPB (2003, $15.99) r/#18-22; Frank Cho-c 16.00

SPIDER-MAN TEAM-UP
Marvel Comics: Dec, 1995 - No. 7, June, 1996 ($2.95)
1-7: 1-w/ X-Men. 2-w/Silver Surfer. 3-w/Fantastic Four. 4-w/Avengers. 5-Gambit & Howard the Duck-c/app. 7-Thunderbolts-c/app. 3.00
... Special 1 (5/05, $2.99) Fantastic Four app.; Todd Dezago-s/Shane Davis-a 3.00

SPIDER-MAN: THE ARACHNIS PROJECT
Marvel Comics: Aug, 1994 - No. 6, Jan, 1995 ($1.75, limited series)
1-6-Venom, Styx, Stone & Jury app. 2.50

SPIDER-MAN: THE CLONE JOURNAL
Marvel Comics: Mar, 1995 ($2.95, one-shot)
1 3.00

SPIDER-MAN: THE CLONE SAGA
Marvel Comics: Nov, 2009 - No. 6, Apr, 2010 ($3.99, limited series)
1-6-Retelling of the saga with different ending; DeFalco & Mackie-s/Nauck-a 4.00

SPIDER-MAN: THE FINAL ADVENTURE
Marvel Comics: Nov, 1995 - No. 4, Feb, 1996 ($2.95, limited series)
1-4: 1-Nicieza scripts; foil-c 3.00

SPIDER-MAN: THE JACKAL FILES
Marvel Comics: Aug, 1995 ($1.95, one-shot)
1 2.50

SPIDER-MAN: THE LOST YEARS
Marvel Comics: Aug, 1995-No. 3, Oct, 1995; No. 0, 1996 ($2.95/$3.95,lim. series)
0-(1/96, $3.95)-Reprints. 4.00
1-3-DeMatteis scripts, Romita, Jr.-c/a 3.00
NOTE: ***Romita** c-0i. **Romita, Jr.** a-0r, 1-3p. c-0-3p. **Sharp** a-0r.*

SPIDER-MAN: THE MANGA
Marvel Comics: Dec, 1997 - No. 31, June, 1999 ($3.99/$2.99, B&W, bi-weekly)
1-($3.99)-English translation of Japanese Spider-Man 4.00
2-31-($2.99) 3.00

SPIDER-MAN: THE MUTANT AGENDA
Marvel Comics: No. 0, Feb, 1994; No. 1, Mar, 1994 - No. 3, May, 1994 ($1.75, limited series)
0-(2/94, $1.25, 52 pgs.)-Crosses over w/newspaper strip; has empty pages to paste in newspaper strips; gives origin of Spidey 2.50
1-3: Beast & Hobgoblin app. 1-X-Men app. 2.50

SPIDER-MAN: THE MYSTERIO MANIFESTO (Listed as "Spider-Man and Mysterio" in indicia)
Marvel Comics: Jan, 2001 - No. 3, Mar, 2001 ($2.99, limited series)
1-3-Daredevil-c/app.; Weeks & McLeod-a 3.00

SPIDER-MAN: THE PARKER YEARS
Marvel Comics: Nov, 1995 ($2.50, one-shot)
1 2.50

SPIDER-MAN 2: THE MOVIE
Marvel Comics: Aug, 2004 ($3.50/$12.99, one-shot)
1-($3.50) Movie adaptation; Johnson, Lim & Olliffe-a 3.50
TPB-($12.99) Movie adaptation; r/Amazing Spider-Man #50, Ultimate Spider-Man #14,15 13.00

SPIDER-MAN 2099 (See Amazing Spider-Man #365)
Marvel Comics: Nov, 1992 - No. 46, Aug, 1996 ($1.25/$1.50/$1.95)
1-(stiff-c)-Red foil stamped-c; begins origin of Miguel O'Hara (Spider-Man 2099); Leonardi/Williamson-c/a begins 3.00
1-2nd printing, 2-24,26-40: 2-Origin continued, ends #3. 4-Doom 2099 app. 13-Extra 16 pg. insert on Midnight Sons. 19-Bound-in trading cards. 35-Variant-c. 36-Two-c; Jae Lee-a. 37,38-Two-c 2.50
25-($2.25, 52 pgs.)-Newsstand edition 2.50
25-($2.95, 52 pgs.)-Deluxe edition w/embossed foil-c 3.00
41-46: 46-The Vulture app; Mike McKone-a(p) 3.00
Annual 1 (1994, $2.95, 68 pgs.) 3.00
Special 1 (1995, $3.95) 4.00
NOTE: ***Chaykin** c-37. **Ron Lim** a(p)-18; c(p)-13, 16, 18. **Kelley Jones** c/a-9. **Leonardi/Williamson** a-1-8, 10-13, 15-17, 19, 20, 22-25; c-1-13, 15, 17-19, 20, 22-25, 35.*

SPIDER-MAN 2099 MEETS SPIDER-MAN
Marvel Comics: 1995 ($5.95, one-shot)
nn-Peter David script; Leonardi/Williamson-c/a. 6.00

SPIDER-MAN UNIVERSE
Marvel Comics: Mar, 2000 - No. 7, Oct, 2000 ($4.95/$3.99, reprints)
1-5-Reprints recent issues from the various Spider-Man titles 5.00
6,7-($3.99) 4.00

SPIDER-MAN UNLIMITED
Marvel Comics: May, 1993 - No. 22, Nov, 1998 ($3.95, quarterly, 68 pgs.)
1-Begin Maximum Carnage storyline, ends; Carnage-c/story 5.00
2-12: 2-Venom & Carnage-c/story; Lim-c/a(p) in #2-6. 10-Vulture app. 4.00
13-22: 13-Begin $2.99-c; Scorpion-c/app. 15-Daniel-c; Puma-c/app. 19-Lizard-c/app. 20-Hannibal King and Lilith app. 21,22-Deodato-a 3.00

SPIDER-MAN UNLIMITED (Based on the TV animated series)
Marvel Comics: Dec, 1999 - No. 5, Apr, 2000 ($2.99/$1.99)
1-($2.99) Venom and Carnage app. 3.00
2-5: 2-($1.99) Green Goblin app. 2.50

SPIDER-MAN UNLIMITED (3rd series)
Marvel Comics: Mar, 2004 - No. 15, July, 2006 ($2.99)
1-16: 1-Short stories by various incl. Miyazawa & Chen-a. 2-Mays-a. 6-Allred-c. 14-Finch-c/a; Black Cat app. 3.00

SPIDER-MAN UNMASKED
Marvel Comics: Nov, 1996 ($5.95, one-shot)
nn-Art w/text 6.00

SPIDER-MAN: VENOM AGENDA
Marvel Comics: Jan, 1998 ($2.99, one-shot)
1-Hama-s/Lyle-c/a 3.00

SPIDER-MAN VS. DRACULA
Marvel Comics: Jan, 1994 ($1.75, 52 pgs., one-shot)
1-r/Giant-Size Spider-Man #1 plus new Matt Fox-a 2.50

SPIDER-MAN VS. WOLVERINE
Marvel Comics Group: Feb, 1987; V2#1, 1990 (68 pgs.)
1-Williamson-c/a(i); intro Charlemagne; death of Ned Leeds (old Hobgoblin)
2 4 6 12 16 20
V2#1 (1990, $4.95)-Reprints #1 (2/87) 5.00

SPIDER-MAN: WEB OF DOOM
Marvel Comics: Aug, 1994 - No. 3, Oct, 1994 ($1.75, limited series)
1-3 2.50

SPIDER-MAN: WITH GREAT POWER...
Marvel Comics: Mar, 2008 - No. 5, Sept, 2008 ($3.99, limited series)
1-5-Origin and early days re-told; Lapham-s/Harris-a/c 4.00

SPIDER-MAN: YEAR IN REVIEW

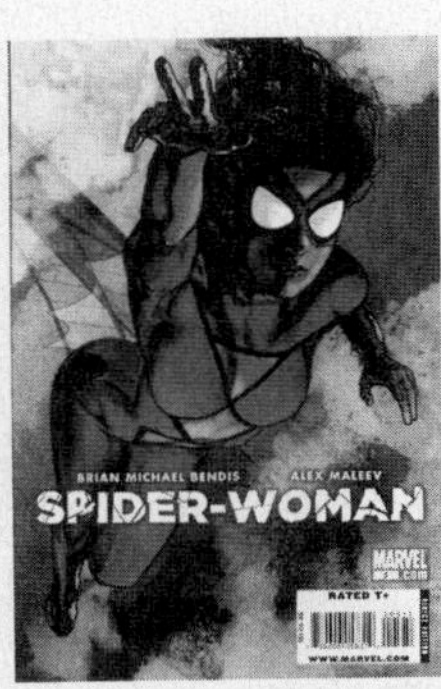
Spider-Woman (2009 series) #5 © MAR

Spin Angels #2 © MC Prods.

The Spirit #17 © Will Eisner

	GD 2.0	VG 4.0	FN 6.0	VF 8.0	VF/NM 9.0	NM- 9.2
Marvel Comics: Feb, 2000 ($2.99)						
1-Text recaps of 1999 issues						3.00
SPIDER REIGN OF THE VAMPIRE KING, THE (Also see The Spider)						
Eclipse Books: 1992 - No. 3, 1992 ($4.95, limited series, coated stock, 52 pgs.)						
Book One - Three: Truman scripts & painted-c						5.00
SPIDER'S WEB, THE (See G-8 and His Battle Aces)						
SPIDER-WOMAN (Also see The Avengers #240, Marvel Spotlight #32, Marvel Super Heroes Secret Wars #7, Marvel Two-In-One #29 and New Avengers)						
Marvel Comics Group: April, 1978 - No. 50, June, 1983 (New logo #47 on)						
1-New complete origin & mask added	2	4	6	11	16	20
2-5,7-18: 2-Excalibur app. 3,11,12-Brother Grimm app. 13,15-The Shroud-c/s. 16-Sienkiewicz-c	1	2	3	4	5	7
6,19,20,28,29,32: 6-Morgan LeFay app. 6,19,32-Werewolf by Night-c/s. 20,28,29-Spider-Man app. 32-Universal Monsters photo/Miller-c	1	2	3	5	6	8
21-27,30,31,33-36						6.00
37,38-X-Men x-over: 37-1st app. Siryn of X-Force; origin retold	2	4	6	8	10	12
39-49: 46-Kingpin app. 49-Tigra-c/story						5.00
50-(52 pgs.)-Death of Spider-Woman; photo-c	2	4	6	9	13	16
NOTE: ***Austin** a-37i. **Byrne** c-26p. **Infantino** a-1-19. **Layton** c-19. **Miller** c-32p.*						
SPIDER-WOMAN						
Marvel Comics: Nov, 1993 - No. 4, Feb, 1994 ($1.75, mini-series)						
V2#1-4: 1,2-Origin; U.S. Agent app.						2.50
SPIDER-WOMAN						
Marvel Comics: July, 1999 - No. 18, Dec, 2000 ($2.99/$1.99/$2.25)						
1-($2.99) Byrne-s/Sears-a						3.00
2-18: 2-11-($1.99). 2-Two covers. 12-Begin $2.25-c. 15-Capt. America-c/app.						2.50
SPIDER-WOMAN (Printed version of the motion comic for computers)						
Marvel Comics: Nov, 2009 - No. 7, May, 2010 ($3.99/$2.99)						
1-($3.99) Bendis-s/Maleev-a; covers by Maleev & Alex Ross; Jessica joins S.W.O.R.D.						4.00
2-6-($2.99) 2-4-Madame Hydra app. 6-Thunderbolts app.						3.00
7-($3.99) New Avengers app.						4.00
SPIDER-WOMAN: ORIGIN (Also see New Avengers)						
Marvel Comics: Feb, 2006 - No. 5, June, 2006 ($2.99, limited series)						
1-5-Bendis & Reed-s/Jonathan & Joshua Luna-a/c						3.00
1-Variant cover by Olivier Coipel						3.00
HC (2006, $19.99) r/series						20.00
SC (2007, $13.99) r/series						14.00
SPIDEY SUPER STORIES (Spider-Man) (Also see Fireside Books)						
Marvel/Children's TV Workshop: Oct, 1974 - No. 57, Mar, 1982 (35¢, no ads)						
1-Origin (stories simplified for younger readers)	5	10	15	30	48	65
2-Kraven	3	6	9	18	27	35
3-10,15: 6-Iceman. 15-Storm-c/sty	3	6	9	14	20	26
11-14,16-20: 19,20-Kirby-c	3	6	9	14	19	24
21-30: 24-Kirby-c	2	4	6	13	18	22
31-53: 31-Moondragon-c/app.; Dr. Doom app. 33-Hulk. 34-Sub-Mariner. 38-F.F. 39-Thanos-c/story. 44-Vision. 45-Silver Surfer & Dr. Doom app.	2	4	6	11	16	20
54-57: 56-Battles Jack O'Lantern-c/sty (exactly one year after 1st app. in Machine Man #19)	3	6	9	14	20	26
SPIKE AND TYKE (See M.G.M.'s...)						
SPIKE... (Also see Buffy the Vampire Slayer and related titles)						
IDW Publ.: Aug, 2005; Jan, 2006; Apr, 2006 ($7.49, squarebound, one-shots)						
...: Lost & Found (4/06, $7.49) Scott Tipton-s/Fernando Goni-a						8.00
...: Old Times (8/05, $7.49) Peter David-s/Fernando Goni-a; Cecily/Halfrek app.						8.00
...: Old Wounds (1/06, $7.49) Tipton-s/Goni-a; flashback to Black Dahlia murder case						8.00
TPB (7/06, $19.99) r/one-shots						20.00
SPIKE: AFTER THE FALL (Also see Angel: After the Fall) (Follows the last Angel TV episode)						
IDW Publ.: July, 2008 - No. 4, Oct, 2008 ($3.99, limited series)						
1-4-Lynch-s/Urru-a; multiple covers on each						4.00
SPIKE: ASYLUM (Buffy the Vampire Slayer)						
IDW Publ.: Sept, 2006 - No. 5, Jan, 2007 ($3.99, limited series)						
1-5-Lynch-s/Urru-a; multiple covers on each						4.00
SPIKE: SHADOW PUPPETS (Buffy the Vampire Slayer)						
IDW Publ.: June, 2007 - No. 4, Sept, 2007 ($3.99, limited series)						
1-4-Lynch-s/Urru-a; multiple covers on each						4.00
SPIKE VS. DRACULA (Buffy the Vampire Slayer)						
IDW Publ.: Feb, 2006 - No. 5, Mar, 2006 ($3.99, limited series)						
1-5: 1-Peter David-s/Joe Corroney-a; Dru and Bela Lugosi app.						4.00
SPIN & MARTY (TV) (Walt Disney's)(See Walt Disney Showcase #32)						
Dell Publishing Co. (Mickey Mouse Club): No. 714, June, 1956 - No. 1082, Mar-May, 1960 (All photo-c)						
Four Color 714 (#1)	12	24	36	85	155	225
Four Color 767,808 (#2,3)	9	18	27	63	107	150
Four Color 826 (#4)-Annette Funicello photo-c	21	42	63	148	287	425
5(3-5/58) - 9(6-8/59)	8	16	24	52	86	120
Four Color 1026,1082	8	16	24	52	86	120
SPIN ANGELS						
Marvel Comics (Soleil): 2009 - No. 4, 2009 ($5.99)						
1-4-English version of French comics; Jean-Luc Sala-s/Pierre-Mony Chan-a						6.00
SPINE-TINGLING TALES (Doctor Spektor Presents...)						
Gold Key: May, 1975 - No. 4, Jan, 1976 (All 25¢ issues)						
1-1st Tragg-r/Mystery Comics Digest #3	2	4	6	9	13	16
2-4: 2-Origin Ra-Ka-Tep-r/Mystery Comics Digest #1; Dr. Spektor #12. 3-All Durak-r issue; 4-Baron Tibor's 1st app.-r/Mystery Comics Digest #4; painted-c	1	2	3	5	7	9
SPINWORLD						
Amaze Ink (Slave Labor Graphics): July, 1997 - No. 4, Jan, 1998 ($2.95/$3.95, B&W, mini-series)						
1-3-Brent Anderson-a(p)						3.00
4-($3.95)						4.00
SPIRAL PATH, THE						
Eclipse Comics: July, 1986 - No. 2 ($1.75, Baxter paper, limited series)						
1,2						2.50
SPIRAL ZONE						
DC Comics: Feb, 1988 - No. 4, May, 1988 ($1.00, mini-series)						
1-4-Based on Tonka toys						2.50
SPIRIT, THE (Newspaper comics - see Promotional Comics section)						
SPIRIT, THE (1st Series)(Also see Police Comics #11 and The Best of the Spirit TPB)						
Quality Comics Group (Vital): 1944 - No. 22, Aug, 1950						
nn(#1)- "Wanted Dead or Alive"	107	214	321	680	1165	1650
nn(#2)- "Crime Doesn't Pay"	50	100	150	315	533	750
nn(#3)- "Murder Runs Wild"	41	82	123	258	434	610
4,5: 4-Flatfoot Burns begins, ends #22. 5-Wertham app.	36	72	108	211	343	475
6-10	30	60	90	177	289	400
11-Crandall-c	28	56	84	165	270	375
12-17-Eisner-c. 19-Honeybun app.	39	78	117	231	378	525
18-21-Strip-r by Eisner; Eisner-c	43	86	129	271	461	650
22-Used by N.Y. Legis. Comm; classic Eisner-c	103	206	309	659	1130	1600
Super Reprint #11-r/Quality Spirit #19 by Eisner	3	6	9	18	27	35
Super Reprint #12-r/Spirit #17 by Fine; Sol Brodsky-c	3	6	9	18	27	35
SPIRIT, THE (2nd Series)						
Fiction House Magazines: Spring, 1952 - No. 5, 1954						
1-Not Eisner	42	84	126	265	445	625
2-Eisner-c/a(2)	41	82	123	258	434	610
3-Eisner/Grandenetti-c	38	76	114	226	368	510
4-Eisner/Grandenetti-c; Eisner-a	39	78	117	231	378	525
5-Eisner-c/a(4)	41	82	123	251	418	585
SPIRIT, THE						
Harvey Publications: Oct, 1966 - No. 2, Mar, 1967 (Giant Size, 25¢, 68 pgs.)						
1-Eisner-r plus 9 new pgs.(origin Denny Colt, Take 3, plus 2 filler pgs.) (#3 was advertised, but never published)	9	18	27	63	107	150
2-Eisner-r plus 9 new pgs.(origin of the Octopus)	8	16	24	52	86	120
SPIRIT, THE (Underground)						
Kitchen Sink Enterprises (Krupp Comics): Jan, 1973 - No. 2, Sept, 1973 (Black & White)						
1-New Eisner-c & 4 pgs. new Eisner-a plus-r (titled Crime Convention)	4	8	12	22	34	45
2-New Eisner-c & 4 pgs. new Eisner-a plus-r (titled Meets P'Gell)	4	8	12	24	37	50
SPIRIT, THE (Magazine)						
Warren Publ. Co./Krupp Comic Works No. 17 on: 4/74 - No. 16, 10/76; No. 17, Winter, 1977 - No. 41, 6/83 (B&W w/color) (#6-14,16 are squarebound)						

The Spirit (2007 series) #15 © Will Eisner

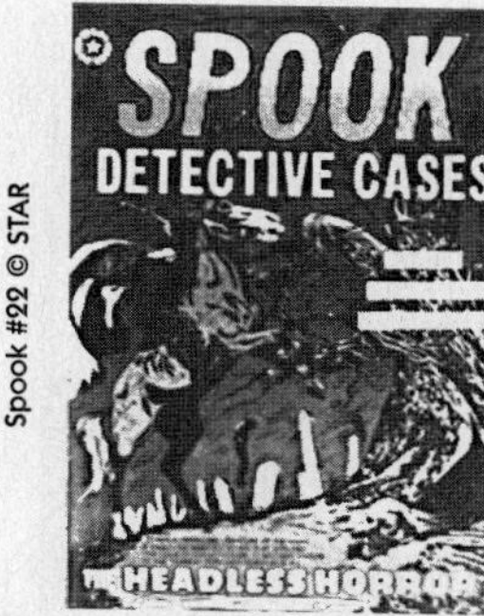

Spook #22 © STAR

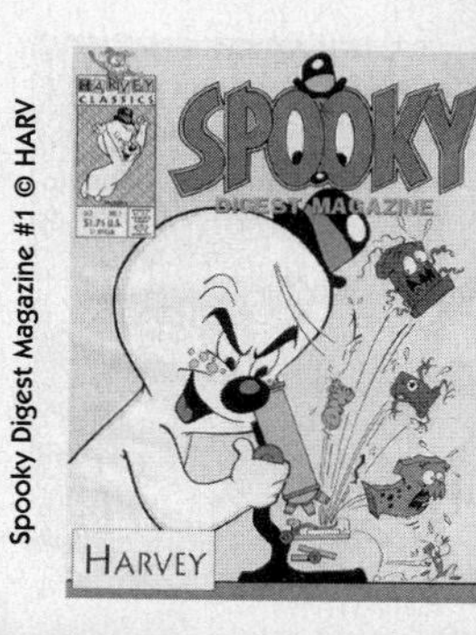

Spooky Digest Magazine #1 © HARV

	GD 2.0	VG 4.0	FN 6.0	VF 8.0	VF/NM 9.0	NM- 9.2
1-Eisner-r begin; 8 pg. color insert	7	14	21	45	73	100
2-5: 2-Powder Pouf-s; UFO-s. 4-Silk Satin-s	4	8	12	26	41	55
6-9,11-15: 7-All Ebony issue. 8-Female Foes issue. 8,12-Sand Seref-s. 9-P'Gell & Octopus-s. 12-X-Mas issue	4	8	12	24	37	50
10-Giant Summer Special ($1.50)-Origin	4	8	12	26	41	55
16-Giant Summer Special ($1.50)-Olga Bustle-c/s	4	8	12	24	37	50
17,18(8/78): 17-Lady Luck-r	3	6	9	16	23	30
19-21-New Eisner-a. 20,21-Wood-r (#21-r/A DP on the Moon by Wood). 20-Outer Space-r	3	6	9	16	23	30
22-41: 22,23-Wood-r (#22-r/Mission the Moon by Wood). 28-r/last story (10/5/52). 30-(7/81)-Special Spirit Jam issue w/Caniff, Corben, Bolland, Byrne, Miller, Kurtzman, Rogers, Sienkiewicz-a & 40 others. 36-Begin Spirit Section-r; r/1st story (6/2/40) in color; new Eisner-c/a(18 pgs.)($2.95). 37-r/2nd story in color plus 18 pgs. new Eisner-a. 38-41: r/3rd - 6th stories in color. 41-Lady Luck Mr. Mystic in color	3	6	9	14	20	25
Special 1(1975)-All Eisner-a (mail only, 1500 printed, full color)	11	22	33	78	139	200

NOTE: *Covers pencilled/inked by* **Eisner** *only #1-9,12-16; painted by Eisner & Ken Kelly #10 & 11; painted by Eisner #17-up; one color story reprinted in #1-10.* **Austin** *a-30i.* **Byrne** *a-30p.* **Miller** *a-30p.*

SPIRIT, THE
Kitchen Sink Enterprises: Oct, 1983 - No. 87, Jan, 1992 ($2.00, Baxter paper)

1-60: 1-Origin-r/12/23/45 Spirit Section. 2-r/ 1/20/46-2/10/46. 3-r/2/17/46-3/10/46. 4-r/3/17/46-4/7/46. 11-Last color issue. 54-r/section 2/19/50 — 4.00
61-87: 85-87-Reprint the Outer Space Spirit stories by Wood. 86-r/A DP on the Moon by Wood from 1952 — 4.00

SPIRIT, THE (Also see Batman/The Spirit in Batman one-shots)
DC Comics: Feb, 2007 - Present ($2.99)

1-32: 1-6,8-12-Darwyn Cooke-s/a/c. 2-P'Gell app. 3-Origin re-told. 7-Short stories by Baker, Bernet, Palmiotti, Simonson & Sprouse; Cooke-c. 13-Short stories by various — 3.00
... Book One HC (2007, $24.99, die-cut dust jacket) r/#1-6 and Batman/The Spirit — 25.00
... Book One SC (2007, $19.99) r/#1-6 and Batman/The Spirit — 20.00
... Book Two HC (2008, $24.99, die-cut dust jacket) r/#7-13 — 25.00
... Book Two SC (2009, $19.99) r/#7-13 — 20.00
... Book Three SC (2009, $19.99) r/#14-20 — 20.00
... Book Four SC (2009, $19.99) r/#21-25 — 20.00
... Book Five SC (2009, $19.99) r/#26-32 — 20.00
... Femme Fatales TPB (2008, $19.99) r/1940s stories focusing on the Spirit's female adversaries like Silk Satin, P'gell, Powder Pouf and Silken Floss; Michael Uslan intro. — 20.00
... Special 1 (2008, $2.99) r/stories from '47, '49, '50 newspaper strips; the Octopus app. — 3.00

SPIRIT JAM
Kitchen Sink Press: Aug, 1998 ($5.95, B&W, oversized, square-bound)

nn-Reprints Spirit (Magazine) #30 by Eisner & 50 others; and "Cerebus Vs. The Spirit" from Cerebus Jam #1 — 6.00

SPIRIT, THE: THE NEW ADVENTURES
Kitchen Sink Press: 1997 - No. 8, Nov, 1998 ($3.50, anthology)

1-Moore-s/Gibbons-c/a — 4.00
2-8: 2-Gaiman-s/Eisner-c. 3-Moore-s/Bolland-c/Moebius back-c. 4-Allred-s/a; Busiek-s/Anderson-a. 5-Chadwick-s/c/a(p); Nyberg-i. 6-S.Hampton & Mandrake-a — 3.50
Will Eisner's The Spirit Archives Volume 27 (Dark Horse, 2009, $49.95) r/#1-8 — 50.00

SPIRIT: THE ORIGIN YEARS
Kitchen Sink Press: May, 1992 - No. 10, Dec, 1993 ($2.95, B&W)

1-10: 1-r/sections 6/2/40(origin)-6/23/40 (all 1940s) — 3.00

SPIRITMAN (Also see Three Comics)
No publisher listed: No date (1944) (10¢)
(Triangle Sales Co. ad on back cover)

	GD	VG	FN	VF	VF/NM	NM-
1-Three 16pg. Spirit sections bound together, (1944, 10¢, 52 pgs.)	21	42	63	122	199	275
2-Two Spirit sections (3/26/44, 4/2/44) bound together; by Lou Fine	19	38	57	111	176	240

SPIRIT OF THE BORDER (See Zane Grey & Four Color #197)

SPIRIT OF THE TAO
Image Comics (Top Cow): Jun, 1998 - No. 15, May, 2000 ($2.50)

Preview — 5.00
1-14: 1-D-Tron-s/Tan & D-Tron-a — 2.50
15-($4.95) — 5.00

SPIRIT WORLD (Magazine)
National Periodical Publications: Fall, 1971 (B&W)

	GD	VG	FN	VF	VF/NM	NM-
1-New Kirby-a; Neal Adams-c; poster inside	7	14	21	47	76	105

(1/2 price without poster)

SPITFIRE (Female undercover agent)
Malverne Herald (Elliot)(J. R. Mahon): No. 132, 1944 (Aug) - No. 133, 1945

	GD	VG	FN	VF	VF/NM	NM-
132,133: Both have Classics Gift Box ads on b/c with checklist to #20. 132-British spitfire WWII-c. 133-Female agent/Nazi WWII-c	25	50	75	147	241	335

SPITFIRE AND THE TROUBLESHOOTERS
Marvel Comics: Oct, 1986 - No. 9, June, 1987 (Codename: Spitfire #10 on)

1-3,5-9 — 2.50
4-McFarlane-a — 3.00

SPITFIRE COMICS (Also see Double Up)
Harvey Publications: Aug, 1941 - No. 2, Oct, 1941 (Pocket size; 100 pgs.)

	GD	VG	FN	VF	VF/NM	NM-
1-Origin The Clown, The Fly-Man, The Spitfire & The Magician From Bagdad; British spitfire, Nazi bomber WWII-c	76	152	228	486	831	1175
2-(Rare) Fly-Man-c	69	138	207	442	759	1075

SPLITTING IMAGE
Image Comics: Mar, 1993 - No. 2, 1993 ($1.95)

1,2-Simpson-c/a; parody comic — 2.50

SPOOF
Marvel Comics Group: Oct, 1970; No. 2, Nov, 1972 - No. 5, May, 1973

	GD	VG	FN	VF	VF/NM	NM-
1-Infinity-c; Dark Shadows-c & parody	4	8	12	22	34	45
2-5: 2-All in the Family. 3-Beatles, Osmond's, Jackson 5, David Cassidy, Nixon & Agnew-c. 5-Rod Serling, Woody Allen, Ted Kennedy-c	3	6	9	16	23	30

SPOOK (Formerly Shock Detective Cases)
Star Publications: No. 22, Jan, 1953 - No. 30, Oct, 1954

	GD	VG	FN	VF	VF/NM	NM-
22-Sgt. Spook-r; acid in face story; hanging-c	39	78	117	240	395	550
23,25,27: 25-Jungle Lil-r. 27-Two Sgt. Spook-r	28	56	84	168	274	380
24-Used in **SOTI**, pgs. 182,183-r/Inside Crime #2; Transvestism story	29	58	87	172	281	390
26,28-30: 26-Disbrow-a. 28,29-Rulah app. 29-Jo-Jo app. 30-Disbrow-c/a(2); only Star-c	28	56	84	168	274	380

NOTE: **L. B. Cole** *covers-all issues except #30; a-28(1 pg.).* **Disbrow** *a-26(2), 28, 29(2), 30(2); No. 30 r/Blue Bolt Weird Tales #114.*

SPOOK COMICS
Baily Publications/Star: 1946

	GD	VG	FN	VF	VF/NM	NM-
1-Mr. Lucifer story	30	60	90	177	289	400

SPOOKY (The Tuff Little Ghost; see Casper The Friendly Ghost)
Harvey Publications: 11/55 - 139, 11/73; No. 140, 7/74 - No. 155, 3/77; No. 156, 12/77 - No. 158, 4/78; No. 159, 9/78; No. 160, 10/79; No. 161, 9/80

	GD	VG	FN	VF	VF/NM	NM-
1-Nightmare begins (see Casper #19)	43	86	129	344	672	1000
2	20	40	60	146	283	420
3-10(1956-57)	12	24	36	85	155	225
11-20(1957-58)	8	16	24	52	86	120
21-40(1958-59)	6	12	18	37	59	80
41-60	4	8	12	28	44	60
61-80,100	3	6	9	20	30	40
81-99	3	6	9	17	25	32
101-120	2	4	6	11	16	20
121-126,133-140	2	4	6	8	11	14
127-132: All 52 pg. Giants	2	4	6	11	16	20
141-161	1	2	3	5	7	9

SPOOKY
Harvey Comics: Nov, 1991 - No. 4, Sept, 1992 ($1.00/$1.25)

1 — 4.00
2-4: 3-Begin $1.25-c — 3.00
...Digest 1-3 (10/92, 6/93, 10/93, $1.75, 100 pgs.)-Casper, Wendy, etc. — 4.00

SPOOKY HAUNTED HOUSE
Harvey Publications: Oct, 1972 - No. 15, Feb, 1975

	GD	VG	FN	VF	VF/NM	NM-
1	3	6	9	18	27	35
2-5	2	4	6	10	14	18
6-10	2	4	6	8	10	12
11-15	1	2	3	5	7	9

SPOOKY MYSTERIES
Your Guide Publ. Co.: No date (1946) (10¢)

	GD	VG	FN	VF	VF/NM	NM-
1-Mr. Spooky, Super Snooper, Pinky, Girl Detective app.	19	38	57	112	179	245

SPOOKY SPOOKTOWN
Harvey Publ.: 9/61; No. 2, 9/62 - No. 52, 12/73; No. 53, 10/74 - No. 66, 12/76

	GD	VG	FN	VF	VF/NM	NM-
1-Casper, Spooky; 68 pgs. begin	16	32	48	112	214	315

Sports Stars #1 © MAR

Spyboy #1 © DH

Spy Smasher #5 © QUA

	GD 2.0	VG 4.0	FN 6.0	VF 8.0	VF/NM 9.0	NM- 9.2
2	9	18	27	63	107	150
3-5	7	14	21	45	73	100
6-10	5	10	15	34	55	75
11-20	4	8	12	24	37	50
21-39: 39-Last 68 pg. issue	3	6	9	20	30	40
40-45: All 52 pgs.	2	4	6	11	16	20
46-66: 61-Hot Stuff/Spooky team-up story	1	2	3	5	7	9

SPORT COMICS (Becomes True Sport Picture Stories #5 on)
Street & Smith Publications: Oct, 1940 (No mo.) - No. 4, Nov, 1941

	GD 2.0	VG 4.0	FN 6.0	VF 8.0	VF/NM 9.0	NM- 9.2
1-Life story of Lou Gehrig	54	108	162	340	588	835
2	31	62	93	182	296	410
3,4	26	52	78	154	252	350

SPORT LIBRARY (See Charlton Sport Library)

SPORTS ACTION (Formerly Sport Stars)
Marvel/Atlas Comics (ACI No. 2,3/SAI No. 4-14): No. 2, Feb, 1950 - No. 14, Sept, 1952

	GD 2.0	VG 4.0	FN 6.0	VF 8.0	VF/NM 9.0	NM- 9.2
2-Powell painted-c; George Gipp life story	43	86	129	269	455	640
1-(nd,no price, no publ., 52pgs, #1 on-c; has same-c as #2; blank inside-c (giveaway?)	22	44	66	132	216	300
3-Everett-a	24	48	72	142	234	325
4-11,14: Weiss-a	22	44	66	128	209	290
12,13: 12-Everett-c. 13-Krigstein-a	23	46	69	136	223	310

NOTE: *Title may have changed after No. 3, to Crime Must Lose No. 4 on, due to publisher change.* ***Sol Brodsky*** *c-4-7, 13, 14.* ***Maneely*** *c-3, 8-11.*

SPORT STARS
Parents' Magazine Institute (Sport Stars): Feb-Mar, 1946 - No. 4, Aug-Sept, 1946 (Half comic, half photo magazine)

	GD 2.0	VG 4.0	FN 6.0	VF 8.0	VF/NM 9.0	NM- 9.2
1- "How Tarzan Got That Way" story of Johnny Weissmuller	40	80	120	243	402	560
2-Baseball greats	26	52	78	154	252	350
3,4	23	46	69	136	223	310

SPORT STARS (Becomes Sports Action #2 on)
Marvel Comics (ACI): Nov, 1949 (52 pgs.)

	GD 2.0	VG 4.0	FN 6.0	VF 8.0	VF/NM 9.0	NM- 9.2
1-Knute Rockne; painted-c	45	90	135	284	480	675

SPORT THRILLS (Formerly Dick Cole; becomes Jungle Thrills #16)
Star Publications: No. 11, Nov, 1950 - No. 15, Nov, 1951

	GD 2.0	VG 4.0	FN 6.0	VF 8.0	VF/NM 9.0	NM- 9.2
11-Dick Cole begins; Ted Williams & Ty Cobb life stories	28	56	84	164	265	365
12-Joe DiMaggio, Phil Rizzuto stories & photos on-c; L.B. Cole-c/a	23	46	69	133	214	295
13-15-All L. B. Cole-c. 13-Jackie Robinson, Pee Wee Reese stories & photo on-c. 14-Johnny Weissmuler life story	24	48	72	133	214	295
Accepted Reprint #11 (#15 on-c, nd); L.B. Cole-c	10	20	30	54	72	90
Accepted Reprint #12 (nd); L.B. Cole-c; Joe DiMaggio & Phil Rizzuto life stories-r/#12	10	20	30	54	72	90

SPOTLIGHT (TV) (newsstand sales only)
Marvel Comics Group: Sept, 1978 - No. 4, Mar, 1979 (Hanna-Barbera)

	GD 2.0	VG 4.0	FN 6.0	VF 8.0	VF/NM 9.0	NM- 9.2
1-Huckleberry Hound, Yogi Bear; Shaw-a	3	6	9	20	30	40
2,4: 2-Quick Draw McGraw, Augie Doggie, Snooper & Blabber. 4-Magilla Gorilla, Snagglepuss	3	6	9	18	23	30
3-The Jetsons; Yakky Doodle	3	6	9	20	30	40

SPOTLIGHT COMICS
Country Press Inc.: Sept, 1940

nn-Ashcan, not distributed to newsstands, only for in house use. A NM copy sold in 2009 for $1015.

SPOTLIGHT COMICS (Becomes Red Seal Comics #14 on?)
Harry 'A' Chesler (Our Army, Inc.): Nov, 1944, No. 2, Jan, 1945 - No. 3, 1945

	GD 2.0	VG 4.0	FN 6.0	VF 8.0	VF/NM 9.0	NM- 9.2
1-The Black Dwarf (cont'd in Red Seal?), The Veiled Avenger, & Barry Kuda begin; Tuska-c	89	178	267	565	970	1375
2	56	112	168	356	608	860
3-Injury to eye story (reprinted from Scoop #3)	58	116	174	371	636	900

SPOTTY THE PUP (Becomes Super Pup #4, see Television Puppet Show)
Avon Periodicals/Realistic Comics: No. 2, Oct-Nov, 1953 - No. 3, Dec-Jan, 1953-54 (Also see Funny Tunes)

	GD 2.0	VG 4.0	FN 6.0	VF 8.0	VF/NM 9.0	NM- 9.2
2,3	7	14	21	35	43	50
nn (1953, Realistic-r)	4	7	9	14	16	18

SPUNKY (...Junior Cowboy)(...Comics #2 on)
Standard Comics: April, 1949 - No. 7, Nov, 1951

	GD 2.0	VG 4.0	FN 6.0	VF 8.0	VF/NM 9.0	NM- 9.2
1-Text illos by Frazetta	11	22	33	62	86	110
2-Text illos by Frazetta	9	18	27	47	61	75
3-7	6	12	18	31	38	45

SPUNKY THE SMILING SPOOK
Ajax/Farrell (World Famous Comics/Four Star Comic Corp.): Aug, 1957 - No. 4, May, 1958

	GD 2.0	VG 4.0	FN 6.0	VF 8.0	VF/NM 9.0	NM- 9.2
1-Reprints from Frisky Fables	10	20	30	54	72	90
2-4	6	12	18	31	38	45

SPY AND COUNTERSPY (Becomes Spy Hunters #3 on)
American Comics Group: Aug-Sept, 1949 - No. 2, Oct-Nov, 1949 (52 pgs.)

	GD 2.0	VG 4.0	FN 6.0	VF 8.0	VF/NM 9.0	NM- 9.2
1-Origin, 1st app. Jonathan Kent, Counterspy	27	54	81	158	259	360
2	17	34	51	98	154	210

SPYBOY
Dark Horse Comics: Oct, 1999 - No. 17, May, 2001 ($2.50/$2.95/$2.99)

	GD 2.0	VG 4.0	FN 6.0	VF 8.0	VF/NM 9.0	NM- 9.2
1-17: 1-6-Peter David-s/Pop Mhan-a. 7,8-Meglia-a. 9-17-Mhan-a						3.00
13.1-13.3 (4/03-8/03, $2.99), 13.2,13.3-Mhan-a						3.00
... Special (5/02, $4.99) David-s/Mhan-a						5.00

SPYBOY: FINAL EXAM
Dark Horse Comics: May, 2004 - No. 4, Aug, 2004 ($2.99, limited series)

	GD 2.0	VG 4.0	FN 6.0	VF 8.0	VF/NM 9.0	NM- 9.2
1-4-Peter David-s/Pop Mhan-a/c						3.00
TPB (2005, $12.95) r/series						13.00

SPYBOY/ YOUNG JUSTICE
Dark Horse Comics: Feb, 2002 - No. 3, Apr, 2002 ($2.99, limited series)

	GD 2.0	VG 4.0	FN 6.0	VF 8.0	VF/NM 9.0	NM- 9.2
1-3: 1-Peter David-s/Todd Nauck-a/Pop Mhan-c. 2-Mhan-a						3.00

SPY CASES (Formerly The Kellys)
Marvel/Atlas Comics (Hercules Publ.): No. 26, Sept, 1950 - No. 19, Oct, 1953

	GD 2.0	VG 4.0	FN 6.0	VF 8.0	VF/NM 9.0	NM- 9.2
26 (#1)	23	46	69	136	223	310
27(#2),28(#3, 2/51): 27-Everett-a; bondage-c	14	28	42	80	115	150
4(4/51) - 7,9,10	12	24	36	69	97	125
8-A-Bomb-c/story	14	28	42	80	115	150
11-19: 10-14-War format	10	20	30	56	76	95

NOTE: ***Sol Brodsky*** *c-1-5, 8, 9, 11-14, 17, 18.* ***Maneely*** *a-8; c-7, 10.* ***Tuska*** *a-7.*

SPY FIGHTERS
Marvel/Atlas Comics (CSI): March, 1951 - No. 15, July, 1953
(Cases from official records)

	GD 2.0	VG 4.0	FN 6.0	VF 8.0	VF/NM 9.0	NM- 9.2
1-Clark Mason begins; Tuska-a; Brodsky-c	25	50	75	147	241	335
2-Tuska-a	14	28	42	81	118	155
3-13: 3-5-Brodsky-c. 7-Heath-c	14	28	42	76	108	140
14,15-Pakula-a(3), Ed Win-a. 15-Brodsky-c	14	28	42	78	112	145

SPY-HUNTERS (Formerly Spy & Counterspy)
American Comics Group: No. 3, Dec-Jan, 1949-50 - No. 24, June-July, 1953 (#3-14: 52 pgs.)

	GD 2.0	VG 4.0	FN 6.0	VF 8.0	VF/NM 9.0	NM- 9.2
3-Jonathan Kent continues, ends #10	23	46	69	136	223	310
4-10: 4,8,10-Starr-a	14	28	42	80	115	150
11-15,17-22,24: 18-War-c begin. 21-War-c/stories begin	10	20	30	56	76	95
16-Williamson-a (9 pgs.)	15	30	45	88	137	185
23-Graphic torture, injury to eye panel	20	40	60	114	182	250

NOTE: ***Drucker*** *a-12.* ***Whitney*** *a-many issues; c-7, 8, 10-12, 15, 16.*

SPYMAN (Top Secret Adventures on cover)
Harvey Publications (Illustrated Humor): Sept, 1966 - No. 3, Feb, 1967 (12¢)

	GD 2.0	VG 4.0	FN 6.0	VF 8.0	VF/NM 9.0	NM- 9.2
1-Origin and 1st app. of Spyman. Steranko-a(p)-1st pro work; 1 pg. Neal Adams ad; Tuska-c/a, Crandall-a(i)	7	14	21	45	73	100
2-Simon-c; Steranko-a(p)	4	8	12	28	44	60
3-Simon-c	4	8	12	26	41	55

SPY SMASHER (See Mighty Midget, Whiz & Xmas Comics) (Also see Crime Smasher)
Fawcett Publications: Fall, 1941 - No. 11, Feb, 1943

	GD 2.0	VG 4.0	FN 6.0	VF 8.0	VF/NM 9.0	NM- 9.2
1-Spy Smasher begins; silver metallic-c	331	662	993	2317	4059	5800
2-Raboy-c	152	304	456	965	1658	2350
3,4: 3-Bondage-c. 4-Irvin Steinberg-c	102	204	306	648	1112	1575
5-7: Raboy-a; 6-Raboy-c/a. 7-Part photo-c (movie)	87	174	261	553	952	1350
8,11: War-c	73	146	219	467	796	1125
9-Hitler, Tojo, Mussolini-c.	107	214	321	680	1165	1650
10-Hitler-c	97	194	291	621	1061	1500

SPY THRILLERS (Police Badge No. 479 #5)
Atlas Comics (PrPI): Nov, 1954 - No. 4, May, 1955

	GD 2.0	VG 4.0	FN 6.0	VF 8.0	VF/NM 9.0	NM- 9.2
1-Brodsky c-1,2	21	42	63	122	199	275
2-Last precode (1/55)	14	28	42	78	112	145
3,4	11	22	33	62	86	110

SQUADRON SUPREME (Also see Marvel Graphic Novel - ...: Death of a Universe)

Squadron Supreme (2008 series) #8 © MAR

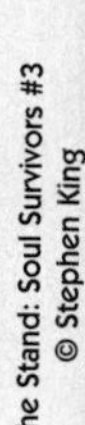

The Stand: Soul Survivors #3 © Stephen King

Star Comics V2 #1 © CHES

	GD 2.0	VG 4.0	FN 6.0	VF 8.0	VF/NM 9.0	NM- 9.2

Marvel Comics Group: Aug, 1985 - No. 12, Aug, 1986 (Maxi-series)
1-Double size 3.00
2-12 2.50
TPB ($24.99) r/#1-12; Alex Ross painted-c; printing inks contain some of the cremated remains of late writer Mark Gruenwald 25.00
TPB-2nd printing ($24.99): Inks contain no ashes 25.00
...Death of a Universe TPB (2006, $24.99) r/Marvel Graphic Novel, Thor #280, Avengers #5,6; Avengers/Squadron Supreme Annual and Squadron Supreme: New World Order 25.00

SQUADRON SUPREME (Also see Supreme Power)
Marvel Comics: May, 2006 - No. 7, Nov, 2006 ($2.99)
1-7-Straczynski-s/Frank-a/c 3.00
Saga of Squadron Supreme (2006, $3.99) summary of Supreme Power #1-18; plus Hyperion and Nighthawk limited series; wraparound-c; preview of Squadron Supreme #1 4.00
... Vol. 1: The Pre-War Years (2006, $20.99, dustjacket) r/#1-5 & Saga of S.S. 21.00

SQUADRON SUPREME
Marvel Comics: Sept, 2008 - No. 12, Aug, 2009 ($2.99)
1-12: 1-Set 5 years after Ultimate Power; Nick Fury app.; Chaykin-s/Turini-a/Land-c 3.00

SQUADRON SUPREME: HYPERION VS. NIGHTHAWK
Marvel Comics: Mar, 2007 - No. 4, June, 2007 ($2.99, limited series)
1-4-Hyperion and Nighthawk in Darfur; Gulacy-a/c; Guggenheim-s 3.00
TPB (2007, $10.99) r/#1-4 11.00

SQUADRON SUPREME: NEW WORLD ORDER
Marvel Comics: Sept, 1998 ($5.99, one-shot)
1-Wraparound-c; Kaminski-s 6.00

SQUALOR
First Comics: Dec, 1989 - Aug, 1990 ($2.75, limited series)
1-4: Sutton-a 2.75

SQUEE (Also see JohnnyThe Homicidal Maniac)
Slave Labor Graphics: Apr, 1997 - No. 4, May, 1998 ($2.95, B&W)
1-4: Jhonen Vasquez-s/a in all 3.00

SQUEEKS (Also see Boy Comics)
Lev Gleason Publications: Oct, 1953 - No. 5, June, 1954

	GD	VG	FN	VF	VF/NM	NM-
1-Funny animal; Biro-c; Crimebuster's pet monkey "Squeeks" begins	10	20	30	54	72	90
2-Biro-c	6	12	18	31	38	45
3-5: 3-Biro-c	6	12	18	28	34	40

S.R. BISSETTE'S SPIDERBABY COMIX
SpiderBaby Grafix: Aug, 1996 - No. 2 ($3.95, B&W, magazine size)
Preview-(8/96, $3.95)-Graphic violence & nudity; Laurel & Hardy app. 4.00
1,2 4.00

S.R. BISSETTE'S TYRANT
SpiderBaby Grafix: Sept, 1994 - No. 4 ($2.95, B&W)
1-4 4.00

STAINLESS STEEL RAT
Eagle Comics: Oct, 1985 - No. 6, Mar, 1986 (Limited series)
1 (52 pgs.; $2.25-c) 3.00
2-6 ($1.50) 2.50

STALKER (Also see All Star Comics 1999 and crossover issues)
National Periodical Publications: June-July, 1975 - No. 4, Dec-Jan, 1975-76

	GD	VG	FN	VF	VF/NM	NM-
1-Origin & 1st app; Ditko/Wood-c/a	2	4	6	9	13	16
2-4-Ditko/Wood-c/a	2	3	4	6	8	10

STALKERS
Marvel Comics (Epic Comics): Apr, 1990 - No. 12, Mar, 1991 ($1.50)
1-12: 1-Chadwick-c 2.50

STAMP COMICS (Stamps... on-c; Thrilling Adventures In...#8)
Youthful Magazines/Stamp Comics, Inc.: Oct, 1951 - No. 7, Oct, 1952

	GD	VG	FN	VF	VF/NM	NM-
1-(15¢) ('Stamps' on indicia No. 1-3,5,7)	27	54	81	156	251	345
2	15	30	45	86	133	180
3-6: 3,4-Kiefer, Wildey-a	14	28	42	81	118	155
7-Roy Krenkel (4 pgs.)	17	34	51	98	154	210

NOTE: *Promotes stamp collecting; gives stories behind various commemorative stamps. No. 2, 10¢ printed over 15¢ c-price.* ***Kiefer*** *a-1-7.* ***Kirkel*** *a-1-6.* ***Napoli*** *a-2-7.* ***Palais*** *a-2-4, 7.*

STAND, THE ... (Based on the Stephen King novel)
Marvel Comics: 2008 - Present ($3.99, limited series)
...: American Nightmares 1-5 (5/09 - No. 5, 10/09, $3.99) Aguirre-Sacasa-s/Perkins-a 4.00
...: Captain Trips 1-5 (12/08 - No. 5, 3/09, $3.99) Aguirre-Sacasa-s/Perkins-a 4.00
...: Soul Survivors 1-5 (12/09 - No. 5, 5/09, $3.99) Aguirre-Sacasa-s/Perkins-a 4.00

STAN LEE MEETS...
Marvel Comics: Nov, 2006 - Jan, 2007 ($3.99, series of one-shots)
Doctor Doom 1 (12/06) Lee-s/Larroca-a/c; Loeb-s/McGuinness-a; r/Fantastic Four #87 4.00
Doctor Strange 1 (11/06) Lee-s/Davis-a/c; Bendis-s/Bagley-a; r/Marvel Premiere #3 4.00
Silver Surfer 1 (1/07) Lee-s/Wieringo-a/c; Jenkins-s/Buckingham-a; r/S.S. #14 4.00
Spider-Man 1 (11/06) Lee-s/Coipel-a/c; Whedon-s/Gaydos-a; Hembeck-s/a; r/AS-M #87 4.00
The Thing 1 (12/06) Lee-s/Weeks-a/c; Thomas-s/Kolins-a; r/FF #79; FF #51 cover swipe 4.00
HC (2007, $24.99, dustjacket) r/one-shots; interviews and features 25.00

STANLEY & HIS MONSTER (Formerly The Fox & the Crow)
National Periodical Publ.: No. 109, Apr-May, 1968 - No. 112, Oct-Nov, 1968

	GD	VG	FN	VF	VF/NM	NM-
109-112	4	8	12	22	34	45

STANLEY & HIS MONSTER
DC Comics: Feb, 1993 - No. 4, May, 1993 ($1.50, limited series)
1-4 2.50

STAN SHAW'S BEAUTY & THE BEAST
Dark Horse Comics: Nov, 1993 ($4.95, one-shot)
1 5.00

STAR
Image Comics (Highbrow Entertainment): June, 1995 - No. 4, Oct, 1995 ($2.50, lim. series)
1-4 2.50

STARBLAST
Marvel Comics: Jan, 1994 - No. 4, Apr, 1994 ($1.75, limited series)
1-4: 1-($2.00, 52 pgs.)-Nova, Quasar, Black Bolt; painted-c 2.50

STAR BLAZERS
Comico: Apr, 1987 - No. 4, July, 1987 ($1.75, limited series)
1-4 3.00

STAR BLAZERS
Comico: 1989 ($1.95/$2.50, limited series)
1-5- Steacy wraparound painted-c on all 3.00

STAR BLAZERS (The Magazine of Space Battleship Yamato)
Argo Press: No. 0, Aug, 1995 - No. 3, Dec, 1995 ($2.95)
0-3 3.00

STAR BRAND
Marvel Comics (New Universe): Oct, 1986 - No. 19, May, 1989 (75¢/$1.25)
1-15: 14-begin $1.25-c 2.50
16-19-Byrne story & art; low print run 4.00
Annual 1 (10/87) 2.50
... Classic Vol. 1 TPB (2006, $19.99) r/#1-7 20.00

STARCHILD
Tailspin Press: 1992 - No. 12($2.25/$2.50, B&W)
1,2-('92),0(4/93),3-12: 0-Illos by Chadwick, Eisner, Sim, M. Wagner. 3-(7/93). 4-(11/93). 6-(2/94) 3.00

STARCHILD: MYTHOPOLIS
Image Comics: No. 0, July, 1997 - No. 4, Apr, 1998 ($2.95, B&W, limited series)
0-4-James Owen-s/a 3.00

STAR COMICS
Ultem Publ. (Harry 'A' Chesler)/Centaur Publications: Feb, 1937 - V2#7 (No. 23), Aug, 1939 (#1-6: large size)

	GD	VG	FN	VF	VF/NM	NM-
V1#1-Dan Hastings (s/f) begins	219	438	657	1402	2401	3400
2	97	194	291	621	1061	1500
3-Classic Black Americana cover (rare)	181	362	543	1158	1979	2800
4-6 (#6, 9/37): 4,5-Little Nemo-c/stories	81	162	243	518	884	1250
7-9: 8-Severed head centerspread; Impy & Little Nemo by Winsor McCay Jr, Popeye app. by Bob Wood; Mickey Mouse & Popeye app. as toys in Santa's bag on-c; X-Mas-c	73	146	219	467	796	1125
10 (1st Centaur; 3/38)-Impy by Winsor McCay Jr; Don Marlow by Guardineer begins	92	184	276	584	1005	1425
11-1st Jack Cole comic-a, 1 pg. (4/38)	69	138	207	442	759	1075
12-15: 12-Riders of the Golden West begins; Little Nemo app. 15-Speed Silvers by Gustavson & The Last Pirate by Burgos begins	56	112	168	356	611	865
16 (12/38)-The Phantom Rider & his horse Thunder begins, ends V2#6	58	116	174	371	636	900

V2#1(#17, 2/39)-Phantom Rider-c (only non-funny-c)

S.T.A.R. Corps #5 © DC

Starman #17 © DC

Starman (2nd series) #81 © DC

62 124 186 394 680 965

2-7(#18-23): 2-Diana Deane by Tarpe Mills app. 3-Drama of Hollywood by Mills begins. 7-Jungle Queen app. 50 100 150 315 533 750

NOTE: *Biro c-6, 9, 10.* ***Burgos** a-15, 16, V2#1-7.* ***Ken Ernst** a-10, 12, 14.* ***Filchock** c-15, 18, 22.* ***Gill Fox** c-14, 19.* ***Guardineer** a-6, 8-14.* ***Gustavson** a-13-16, V2#1-7.* ***Winsor McCay** c-4, 5.* ***Tarpe Mills** a-15, V2#1-7.* ***Schwab** c-20, 23.* ***Bob Wood** a-10, 12, 13; c-7, 8.*

STAR COMICS MAGAZINE
Marvel Comics (Star Comics): Dec, 1986 - No. 13, 1988 ($1.50, digest-size)

1,9-Spider-Man-c/s 2 4 6 8 11 14
2-8-Heathcliff, Ewoks, Top Dog, Madballs-r in #1-13 1 2 3 5 7 9
10-13 2 4 6 8 10 12

S.T.A.R. CORPS
DC Comics: Nov, 1993 - No. 6, Apr, 1994 ($1.50, limited series)

1-6: 1,2-Austin-c(i). 1-Superman app. 2.50

STARCRAFT (Based on the video game)
DC Comics (WildStorm): July, 2009 - No. 7, Jan, 2010 ($2.99)

1-7-Furman-s; two covers on each 3.00

STAR CROSSED
DC Comics (Helix): June, 1997 - No. 3, Aug, 1997 ($2.50, limited series)

1-3-Matt Howarth-s/a 2.50

STARDUST (See Neil Gaiman and Charles Vess' Stardust)

STARDUST KID, THE
Image Comics/Boom! Studios #4-on: May, 2005 - Present ($3.50)

1-4-J.M. DeMatteis-s/Mike Ploog-a 3.50

STAR FEATURE COMICS
I. W. Enterprises: 1963

Reprint #9-Stunt-Man Stetson-r/Feat. Comics #141 2 4 6 10 13 16

STARFIRE (Not the Teen Titans character)
National Periodical Publ./DC Comics: Aug-Sept, 1976 - No. 8, Oct-Nov, 1977

1-Origin (CCA stamp fell off cover art; so it was approved by code) 2 4 6 8 11 14
2-8 1 2 3 5 6 8

STAR HUNTERS (See DC Super Stars #16)
National Periodical Publ./DC Comics: Oct-Nov, 1977 - No. 7, Oct-Nov, 1978

1,7: 1-Newton-a(p). 7-44 pgs. 2 4 6 8 10 12
2-6 1 2 3 4 5 7

NOTE: ***Buckler** a-4-7p; c-1-7p.* ***Layton** a-1-5i; c-1-6i.* ***Nasser** a-3p.* ***Sutton** a-6i.*

STARJAMMERS (See X-Men Spotlight on Starjammers)

STARJAMMERS (Also see Uncanny X-Men)
Marvel Comics: Oct, 1995 - No. 4, Jan, 1996 ($2.95, limited series)

1-4: Foil-c; Ellis scripts 3.00

STARJAMMERS
Marvel Comics: Sept, 2004 - No. 6, Jan, 2005 ($2.99, limited series)

1-6-Kevin J. Anderson-s. 1-Garza-a. 2-6-Lucas-a 3.00

STARK TERROR
Stanley Publications: Dec, 1970 - No. 5, Aug, 1971 (B&W, magazine, 52 pgs.) (1950s Horror reprints, including pre-code)

1-Bondage, torture-c 7 14 21 45 73 100
2-4 (Gillmor/Aragon-r) 4 8 12 26 41 55
5 (ACG-r) 4 8 12 22 34 45

STARLET O'HARA IN HOLLYWOOD (Teen-age) (Also see Cookie)
Standard Comics: Dec, 1948 - No. 4, Sept, 1949

1-Owen Fitzgerald-a in all 26 52 78 152 249 345
2 15 30 45 85 130 175
3,4 14 28 42 76 108 140

STAR-LORD THE SPECIAL EDITION (Also see Marvel Comics Super Special #10, Marvel Premiere & Preview & Marvel Spotlight V2#6,7)
Marvel Comics Group: Feb, 1982 (one-shot, direct sales) (1st Baxter paper comic)

1-Byrne/Austin-a; Austin-c; 8 pgs. of new-a by Golden (p); Dr. Who story by Dave Gibbons; 1st deluxe format comic 6.00

STARLORD
Marvel Comics: Dec, 1996 - No. 3, Feb, 1997 ($2.50, limited series)

1-3-Timothy Zahn-s 2.50

STARLORD MEGAZINE
Marvel Comics: Nov, 1996 ($2.95, one-shot)

GD VG FN VF VF/NM NM-
2.0 4.0 6.0 8.0 9.0 9.2

1-Reprints w/preview of new series 3.00

STARMAN (1st Series) (Also see Justice League & War of the Gods)
DC Comics: Oct, 1988 - No. 45, Apr, 1992 ($1.00)

1-25,29-45: 1-Origin. 4-Intro The Power Elite. 9,10,34-Batman app. 14-Superman app. 17-Power Girl app. 38-War of the Gods x-over. 42-45-Eclipso-c/stories 2.50
26-1st app. David Knight (G.A.Starman's son). 5.00
27,28: 27-Starman (David Knight) app. 28-Starman disguised as Superman; leads into Superman #50 4.00

STARMAN (2nd Series) (Also see The Golden Age, Showcase 95 #12, Showcase 96 #4,5)
DC Comics : No. 0, Oct, 1994 - No. 80, Aug, 2001; No. 81, Mar, 2010 ($1.95/$2.25/$2.50)

0,1: 0-James Robinson scripts, Tony Harris-c/a(p) & Wade Von Grawbadger-a(i) begins; Sins of the Father storyline begins, ends #3; 1st app. new Starman (Jack Knight); reintro of the G.A. Mist & G.A. Shade; 1st app. Nash; David Knight dies 1 2 3 4 5 7
2-7: 2-Reintro Charity from Forbidden Tales of Dark Mansion. 3-Reintro/2nd app. "Blue" Starman (1st app. in 1st Issue Special #12); Will Payton app. (both cameos). 5-David Knight app. 6-The Shade "Times Past" story; Kristiansen-a. 7-The Black Pirate cameo 5.00
8-17: 8-Begin $2.25-c. 10-1st app. new Mist (Nash). 11-JSA "Times Past" story; Matt Smith-a. 12-16-Sins of the Child. 17-The Black Pirate app. 4.00
18-37: 18-G.A. Starman "Times Past" story; Watkiss-a. 19-David Knight app. 20-23-G.A. Sandman app. 24-26-Demon Quest; all 3 covers make-up triptych. 33-36-Batman-c/app. 37-David Knight and deceased JSA members app. 3.00
38-49,51-56: 38-Nash vs. Justice League Europe. 39,40-Crossover w/ Power of Shazam! #35,36; Bulletman app. 42-Demon-c/app. 43-JLA-c/app. 44-Phantom Lady-c/app. 46-Gene Ha-a. 51-Jor-El app. 52,53-Adam Strange-c/app. 2.50
50-($3.95) Gold foil logo on-c; Star Boy (LSH) app. 4.00
57-79: 57-62-Painted covers by Harris and Alex Ross. 72-Death of Ted Knight 2.50
80-($3.95) Final issue; cover by Harris & Robinson 4.00
81-(3/10, $2.99) Blackest Night one-shot; The Shade vs. David Knight; Harris-c 3.00
#1,000,000 (11/98) 853rd Century x-over; Snejbjerg-a 2.50
Annual 1 (1996, $3.50)-Legends of the Dead Earth story; Prince Gavyn & G.A. Starman stories; J.H. Williams III, Bret Blevins, Craig Hamilton-c/a(p) 4.00
Annual 2 (1997, $3.95)-Pulp Heroes story; 4.00
...80 Page Giant (1/99, $4.95) Harris-c 5.00
...Secret Files 1 (4/98, $4.95)-Origin stories and profile pages 5.00
...The Mist (6/98, $1.95) Girlfrenzy; Mary Marvel app. 2.50
A Starry Knight-($17.95, TPB) r/#47-53 18.00
Grand Guingnol-(2004, $19.95, TPB)-r/#61-73 20.00
Infernal Devices-($17.95, TPB) r/#29-35,37,38 18.00
Night and Day-($14.95, TPB)-r/#7-10,12-16 15.00
Sins of the Father-($12.95, TPB)-r/#0-5 13.00
Sons of the Father-($14.99, TPB)-r/#75-80 15.00
Stars My Destination-(2003, $14.95, TPB)-r/#55-60 15.00
Times Past-($17.95, TPB)-r/stories of other Starmen 18.00
The Starman Omnibus Vol. One (2008, $49.99, HC with dj) r/#0,1-16; Robinson intro. 50.00
The Starman Omnibus Vol. Two (2009, $49.99, HC with dj) r/#17-29, Annual #1, Showcase '95 #12, Showcase '96 #4,5; Harris intro.; merchandise gallery 50.00
The Starman Omnibus Vol. Three (2009, $49.99, HC with dj) r/#30-38, Annual #2, Starman Secret Files #1 and The Shade #1-4 50.00
The Starman Omnibus Vol. Four (2010, $49.99, HC with dj) r/#39-46, 80 Page Giant #1, Power of Shazam! #35,36; Starman: The Mist #1 and Batman/Hellboy/Starman #1,2 50.00

STARMASTERS
Marvel Comics: Dec, 1995 - No. 3, Feb, 1996 ($1.95, limited series)

1-3-Continues in Cosmic Powers Unlimited #4 2.50

STAR PRESENTATION, A (Formerly My Secret Romance #1,2; Spectacular Stories #4 on) (Also see This Is Suspense)
Fox Features Syndicate (Hero Books): No. 3, May, 1950

3-Dr. Jekyll & Mr. Hyde by Wood & Harrison (reprinted in Startling Terror Tales #10); "The Repulsing Dwarf" by Wood; Wood-c 57 114 171 362 619 875

STAR QUEST COMIX (Warren Presents... on cover)
Warren Publications: Oct, 1978 ($1.50, B&W magazine, 84 pgs., square-bound)

1-Corben, Maroto, Neary-a; Ken Kelly-c; Star Wars 2 4 6 9 12 15

STAR RAIDERS (See DC Graphic Novel #1)

STAR RANGER (Cowboy Comics #13 on)
Chesler Publ./Centaur Publ.: Feb, 1937 - No. 12, May, 1938 (Large size: No. 1-6)

1-(1st Western comic)-Ace & Deuce, Air Plunder; Creig Flessel-a 219 438 657 1402 2401 3400
2 94 188 282 597 1024 1450
3-6 81 162 243 518 884 1250
7-9: 8(12/37)-Christmas-c; Air Patrol, Gold coast app.; Guardineer centerfold

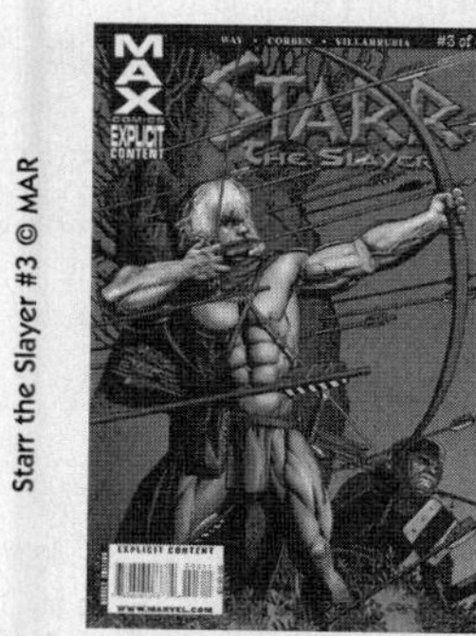

Starr the Slayer #3 © MAR

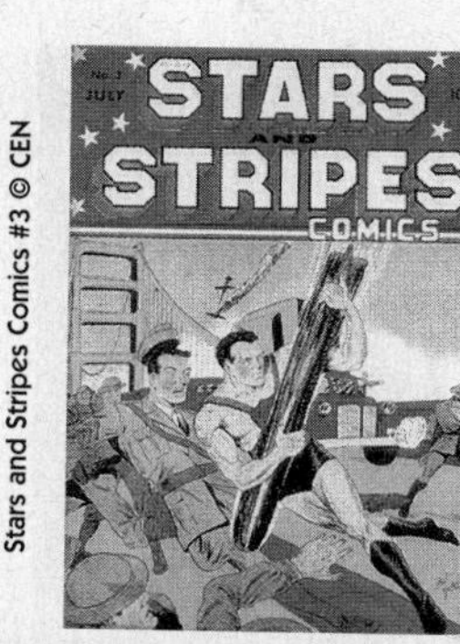

Stars and Stripes Comics #3 © CEN

Star Spangled Comics #83 © DC

GD VG FN VF VF/NM NM-
2.0 4.0 6.0 8.0 9.0 9.2

58 116 174 371 636 900
V2#10 (1st Centaur; 3/38) 90 180 270 576 988 1400
11,12 66 132 198 419 722 1025

NOTE: *J. Cole a-10, 12; c-12.* ***Ken Ernst*** *a-11.* ***Gill Fox*** *a-8(illo), 9, 10.* ***Guardineer*** *a-1, 3, 6, 7, 8(illos), 9, 10, 12.* ***Gustavson*** *a-8-10, 12.* ***Fred Schwab*** *c-2-11.* ***Bob Wood*** *a-8-10.*

STAR RANGER FUNNIES (Formerly Cowboy Comics)
Centaur Publications: V1#15, Oct, 1938 - V2#5, Oct, 1939

V1#15-Lyin Lou, Ermine, Wild West Junior, The Law of Caribou County by Eisner, Cowboy Jake, The Plugged Dummy, Spurs by Gustavson, Red Coat, Two Buckaroos & Trouble Hunters begin 97 194 291 621 1061 1500
V2#1 (1/39) 73 146 219 467 796 1125
2-5: 2-Night Hawk by Gustavson. 4-Kit Carson app. 60 120 180 381 653 925

NOTE: ***Jack Cole*** *a-V2#1, 3; c-V2#1.* ***Filchock*** *c-V2#2, 3.* ***Guardineer*** *a-V2#3.* ***Gustavson*** *a-V2#2.* ***Pinajian*** *c/a-V2#5.*

STAR REACH (Mature content)
Star Reach Publ.: Apr, 1974 - No. 18, Oct, 1979 (B&W, #12-15 w/color)

1-(75¢, 52 pgs.) Art by Starlin, Simonson. Chaykin-c/a; origin Death. Cody Starbuck-sty 3 6 9 16 23 30
1-2nd, 3th, and 4th printings ($1.00-$1.50-c) 6.00
2-11: 2-Adams, Giordano-a; 1st Stephanie Starr-c/s. 3-1st Linda Lovecraft. 4-1st Sherlock Duck. 5-1st Gideon Faust by Chaykin. 6-Elric-c. 7-BWS-c. 9-14-Sacred & Profane-c/s by Steacy. 11-Samurai 2 4 6 8 10 12
2-2nd printing 4.00
12-15 (44 pgs.): 12-Zelazny-s. Nasser-a, Brunner-c 2 4 6 9 12 15
16-18-Magazine size: 17-Poe's Raven-c/s 2 4 6 9 12 15

NOTE: ***Adams*** *c-2.* ***Bonivert*** *a-17.* ***Brunner*** *a-3,5; c-3,10,12.* ***Chaykin*** *a-1,4,5; c-1(1st ed),4,5; back-c-1(2nd,3rd,4th ed).* ***Gene Day*** *a-6,8,9,11,15.* ***Friedrich*** *s-2,3,8,10.* ***Gasbarri*** *a-7.* ***Gilbert*** *a-9,12.* ***Giordano*** *a-2.* ***Gould*** *a-6.* ***Hirota/Mukaide*** *s/a-7.* ***Jones*** *c-6.* ***Konz*** *a-17.* ***Leialoha*** *a-3,4,6-i, 13,15; c-13,15.* ***Lyda*** *a-6,12-15.* ***Marrs*** *a-2-5,7,10,14,15,16,18; c-18; back-c-2.* ***Mukaide*** *a-18.* ***Nasser*** *a-12.* ***Nino*** *a-6;* ***Russell*** *a-8,10; c-8.* ***Dave Sim*** *s-7; lettering-9.* ***Simonson*** *a-1.* ***Skeates*** *a-1,2.* ***Starlin*** *a-1(x2), 2(x2); back-c-1(1st ed); c-1(2nd,3rd,4th ed).* ***Barry Smith*** *c-7.* ***Staton*** *a-5,6,7.* ***Steacy*** *a-8-14; c-9,11,14,16.* ***Vosburg*** *a-2-5,7,10.* ***Workman*** *a-2-5,8. Nudity panels in most. Wraparound-c: 3-5,7-11,13-16,18.*

STAR REACH CLASSICS
Eclipse Comics: Mar, 1984 - No. 6, Aug, 1984 ($1.50, Baxter paper)

1-6: 1-Neal Adams-r/Star Reach #1; Sim & Starlin-a 3.00

STARR FLAGG, UNDERCOVER GIRL (See Undercover...)

STARRIORS
Marvel Comics: Aug, 1984 - Feb, 1985 (Limited series) (Based on Tomy toys)

1-4 3.00

STARR THE SLAYER
Marvel Comics (MAX): Nov, 2009 - No. 4, Feb, 2010 ($3.99, limited series)

1-4- Richard Corben-c/a; Daniel Way-s 4.00

STARS AND S.T.R.I.P.E. (Also see JSA)
DC Comics: July, 1999 - No. 14, Sept, 2000 ($2.95/$2.50)

0-($2.95) Moder and Weston-a; Starman app. 3.00
1-Johns and Robinson-s/Moder-a; origin new Star Spangled Kid 2.50
2-14: 4-Marvel Family app. 9-Seven Soldiers of Victory-c/app. 2.50
JSA Presents: Stars and S.T.R.I.P.E. Vol. 1 TPB (2007, $17.99) r/#1-8; Johns intro. 18.00
JSA Presents: Stars and S.T.R.I.P.E. Vol. 2 TPB (2008, $17.99) r/#0,9-14 18.00

STARS AND STRIPES COMICS
Centaur Publications: No. 2, May, 1941 - No. 6, Dec, 1941

2(#1)-The Shark, The Iron Skull, A-Man, The Amazing Man, Mighty Man, Minimidget begin; The Voice & Dash Dartwell, the Human Meteor, Reef Kinkaid app.; Gustavson Flag-c 223 446 669 1416 2433 3450
3-Origin Dr. Synthe; The Black Panther app. 123 246 369 787 1344 1900
4-Origin/1st app. The Stars and Stripes; injury to eye-c 103 206 309 659 1130 1600
5(#5 on cover & inside) 71 142 213 454 777 1100
5(#6)-(#5 on cover, #6 on inside) 71 142 213 454 777 1100

NOTE: ***Gustavson*** *c/a-3.* ***Myron Strauss*** *c-4, 5(#5), 5(#6).*

STAR SEED (Formerly Powers That Be)
Broadway Comics: No. 7, 1996 - No. 9 ($2.95)

7-9 3.00

STARSHIP TROOPERS
Dark Horse Comics: 1997 - No. 2, 1997 ($2.95, limited series)

1,2-Movie adaption 3.00

STARSHIP TROOPERS: BRUTE CREATIONS
Dark Horse Comics: 1997 ($2.95, one-shot)

1 3.00

STARSHIP TROOPERS: DOMINANT SPECIES
Dark Horse Comics: Aug, 1998 - No. 4, Nov, 1998 ($2.95, limited series)

1-4-Strnad-s/Bolton-c 3.00

STARSHIP TROOPERS: INSECT TOUCH
Dark Horse Comics: 1997 - No. 3, 1997 ($2.95, limited series)

1-3 3.00

STAR SLAMMERS (See Marvel Graphic Novel #6)
Malibu Comics (Bravura): May, 1994 - No. 4, Aug, 1994 ($2.50, unfinished limited series)

1-4: W. Simonson-a/stories; contain Bravura stamps 2.50

STAR SLAMMERS SPECIAL
Dark Horse Comics (Legend): June, 1996 ($2.95, one-shot)

nn-Simonson-c/a/scripts; concludes Bravura limited series. 3.00

STARSLAYER
Pacific Comics/First Comics No. 7 on: Feb, 1982 - No. 6, Apr, 1983; No. 7, Aug, 1983 - No. 34, Nov, 1985

1-Origin & 1st app.; excessive blood & gore; 1 pg. Rocketeer brief app. which continues in #2 5.00
2-Origin/1st full app. the Rocketeer (4/82) by Dave Stevens (Chapter 1 of Rocketeer saga; see Pacific Presents #1,2) 1 2 3 5 6 8
3-Chapter 2 of Rocketeer saga by Stevens 6.00
4,6,7: 7-Grell-a ends 3.00
5-2nd app. Groo the Wanderer by Aragones 1 2 3 4 5 7
8-34: 10-1st app. Grimjack (11/83, ends #17). 18-Starslayer meets Grimjack. 20-The Black Flame begins (9/84, 1st app.), ends #33. 27-Book length Black Flame story 2.50

NOTE: ***Grell*** *a-1-7; c-1-8.* ***Stevens*** *back c-2, 3.* ***Sutton*** *a-17p, 20-22p, 24-27p, 29-33p.*

STARSLAYER (The Director's Cut)
Acclaim Comics (Windjammer): June, 1994 - No. 8, Dec, 1995 ($2.50)

1-8: Mike Grell-c/a/scripts 2.50

STAR SPANGLED COMICS (Star Spangled War Stories #131 on)
National Periodical Publications: Oct, 1941 - No. 130, July, 1952

1-Origin/1st app. Tarantula; Captain X of the R.A.F., Star Spangled Kid (see Action #40), Armstrong of the Army begin; Robot-c 492 984 1476 3592 6346 9100
2 161 322 483 1030 1765 2500
3-5 102 204 306 648 1112 1575
6-Last Armstrong/Army; Penniless Palmer begins 62 124 186 394 680 965
7-(4/42)-Origin/1st app. The Guardian by S&K, & Robotman (by Paul Cassidy & created by Siegel);The Newsboy Legion (1st app.), Robotman & TNT begin; last Captain X 676 1352 2028 4935 8718 12,500
8-Origin TNT & Dan the Dyna-Mite 232 464 696 1485 2543 3600
9,10 165 330 495 1048 1799 2550
11-17 121 242 363 768 1322 1875
18-Origin Star Spangled Kid 150 300 450 953 1639 2325
19-Last Tarantula 121 242 363 768 1322 1875
20-Liberty Belle begins (5/43) 135 270 405 864 1482 2100
21-29-Last S&K issue; 23-Last TNT. 25-Robotman by Jimmy Thompson begins. 29-Intro Robbie the Robotdog 103 206 309 659 1130 1600
30-40: 31-S&K-c 60 120 180 381 653 925
41-51: 41,49-Kirby-c. 51-Robot-c by Kirby 54 108 162 343 584 825
52-64: 53 by S&K. 64-Last Newsboy Legion & The Guardian 48 96 144 302 514 725
65-Robin begins with c/app. (2/47); Batman cameo in 1 panel; Robin-c begins, end #95 171 342 513 1086 1868 2650
66-Batman cameo in Robin story 82 164 246 528 902 1275
67,68,70-80: 68-Last Liberty Belle? 72-Burnley Robin-c 67 134 201 426 731 1035
69-Origin/1st app. Tomahawk by F. Ray; atom bomb story & splash (6/47); black-c (rare in high grade) 145 290 435 921 1586 2250
81-Origin Merry, Girl of 1000 Gimmicks in Star Spangled Kid story 57 114 171 362 624 885
82,85: 82-Last Robotman? 85-Last Star Spangled Kid? 52 104 156 323 549 775
83-Tomahawk enters the lost valley, a land of dinosaurs; Capt. Compass begins, ends #130 52 104 156 325 555 785
84,87 (Rare): 87-Batman cameo in Robin 84 168 252 538 919 1300
86-Batman cameo in Robin story 58 116 174 371 636 900
88(1/49)-94: Batman-c/stories in all. 91-Federal Men begin, end #93. 94-Manhunters Around the World begin, end #121 60 120 180 381 653 925
95-Batman story; last Robin-c 54 108 162 340 575 810
96,98-Batman cameo in Robin stories. 96-1st Tomahawk-c (also #97-121)

Star Spangled Comics #129 © DC

Star Spangled War Stories #13 © DC

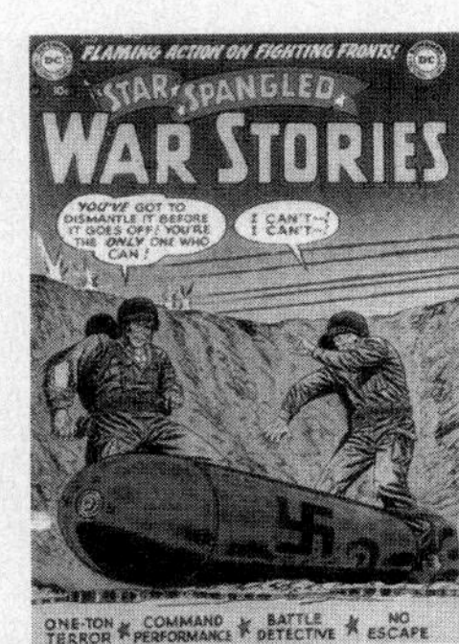

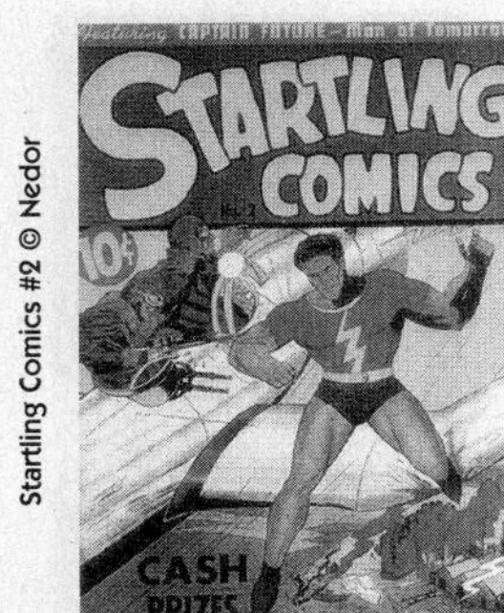

Startling Comics #2 © Nedor

	GD 2.0	VG 4.0	FN 6.0	VF 8.0	VF/NM 9.0	NM- 9.2
	39	78	117	240	395	550
97,99	34	68	102	204	332	460
100 (1/50)-Pre-Bat-Hound tryout in Robin story (pre-dates Batman #92).	40	80	120	246	411	575
101-109,118,119,121: 121-Last Tomahawk-c	32	64	96	190	310	430
110,111,120-Batman cameo in Robin stories. 120-Last 52 pg. issue	34	68	102	199	325	450
112-Batman & Robin story	36	72	108	214	347	480
113-Frazetta-a (10 pgs.)	41	82	123	256	428	600
114-Retells Robin's origin (3/51); Batman & Robin story	43	86	129	271	461	650
115,117-Batman app. in Robin stories	35	70	105	208	339	470
116-Flag-c	35	70	105	208	339	470
122-(11/51)-Ghost Breaker-c/stories begin (origin/1st app.), ends #130 (Ghost Breaker covers #122-130)	43	86	129	271	461	650
123-126,128,129	31	62	93	182	296	410
127-Batman app.	33	66	99	194	317	440
130-Batman cameo in Robin story	35	70	105	208	339	470

NOTE: *Most all issues after #29 signed by Simon & Kirby are not by them.* ***Bill Ely*** *c-122-130.* ***Mortimer*** *c-65-74(most), 76-95(most).* ***Fred Ray*** *c-96-106, 109, 110, 112, 113, 115-120.* ***S&K*** *c-7-31, 33, 34, 36, 37, 39, 40, 48, 49, 50-54, 56-58.* ***Hal Sherman*** *c-1-6.* ***Dick Sprang*** *c-75.*

STAR SPANGLED COMICS (Also see All Star Comics 1999 crossover titles)
DC Comics: May, 1999 ($1.99, one-shot)

1-Golden Age Sandman and the Star Spangled Kid 2.50

STAR SPANGLED KID (See Action #40, Leading Comics & Star Spangled Comics)

STAR SPANGLED WAR STORIES
DC Comics: Aug/Sept 1952

nn - Ashcan comic, not distributed to newsstands, only for in-house use. Cover art is Western Comics #28 with interior being Western Comics #13 (no known sales)

STAR SPANGLED WAR STORIES (Formerly Star Spangled Comics #1-130; Becomes The Unknown Soldier #205 on) (See Showcase)
National Periodical Publications: No. 131, 8/52 - No. 133, 10/52; No. 3, 11/52 - No. 204, 2-3/77

	GD 2.0	VG 4.0	FN 6.0	VF 8.0	VF/NM 9.0	NM- 9.2
131(#1)	135	270	405	864	1482	2100
132	81	162	243	518	884	1250
133-Used in **POP**, pg. 94	68	136	204	435	743	1050
3-6: 4-Devil Dog Dugan app. 6-Evans-a	50	100	150	315	533	750
7-10	29	58	87	212	406	600
11-20	24	48	72	175	338	500
21-30: 30-Last precode (2/55)	21	42	63	148	287	425
31-33,35-40	16	32	48	115	220	325
34-Krigstein-a	16	32	48	117	226	335
41-44,46-50: 50-1st S.A. issue	15	30	45	107	204	300
45-1st DC grey tone war-c (5/56)	34	68	102	262	506	750
51,52,54-63,65,66, 68-83	13	26	39	93	172	250
53-"Rock Sergeant," 3rd Sgt. Rock prototype; inspired "P.I. & The Sand Fleas" in G.I. Combat #56 (1/57)	22	44	66	157	304	450
64-Pre-Sgt. Rock Easy Co. story (12/57)	16	32	48	115	220	325
67-Two Easy Co. stories without Sgt. Rock	16	32	48	117	226	335
84-Origin Mlle. Marie	22	44	66	157	304	450
85-89-Mlle. Marie in all	15	30	45	107	204	300
90-1st app. "War That Time Forgot" series; dinosaur issue-c/story (4-5/60) (also see Weird War Tales #94 & #99)	48	96	144	384	742	1100
91,93-No dinosaur stories	15	30	45	107	204	300
92-2nd dinosaur-c/s	22	44	66	157	304	450
94 (12/60)- "Ghost Ace" story; Baron Von Richter as The Enemy Ace (predates Our Army at War #151)	26	52	78	190	370	550
95-99: Dinosaur-c/s	18	36	54	129	252	375
100-Dinosaur-c/story.	20	40	60	146	283	420
101-115: All dinosaur issues	15	30	45	107	204	300
116-125,127-133,135-137-Last dinosaur story; Heath Birdman-#129,131	13	26	39	93	172	250
126-No dinosaur story	11	22	33	78	139	200
134-Dinosaur story; Neal Adams-a	15	30	45	107	204	300
138-New Enemy Ace-c/stories begin by Joe Kubert (4-5/68), end #150 (also see Our Army at War #151 and Showcase #57)	15	30	45	110	210	310
139-Origin Enemy Ace (7/68)	11	22	33	80	145	210
140-143,145: 145-Last 12¢ issue (6-7/69)	9	18	27	60	100	140
144-Neal Adams/Kubert-a	9	18	27	65	113	160
146-Enemy Ace-c/app.	7	14	21	45	73	100
147,148-New Enemy Ace stories	8	16	24	52	86	120
149,150-Last new Enemy Ace by Kubert. Viking Prince by Kubert	7	14	21	49	80	110
151-1st solo app. Unknown Soldier (6-7/70); Enemy Ace-r begin (from Our Army at War, Showcase & SSWS); end #161	17	34	51	124	242	360
152-Reprints 2nd Enemy Ace app.	6	12	18	39	62	85
153,155-Enemy Ace reprints; early Unknown Soldier stories	5	10	15	34	55	75
154-Origin Unknown Soldier	13	26	39	93	172	250
156-1st Battle Album; Unknown Soldier story; Kubert-c/a	5	10	15	30	48	65
157-Sgt. Rock x-over in Unknown Soldier story.	4	8	12	28	44	60
158-163-(52 pgs.): New Unknown Soldier stories; Kubert-c/a. 161-Last Enemy Ace-r	4	8	12	24	37	50
164-183,200: 181-183-Enemy Ace vs. Balloon Buster serial app; Frank Thorne-a. 200-Enemy Ace back-up	3	6	9	14	20	26
184-199,201-204	2	4	6	11	16	20

NOTE: ***Anderson*** *a-28.* ***Chaykin*** *a-167.* ***Drucker*** *a-59, 61, 64, 66, 67, 73-84.* ***Estrada*** *a-149.* ***John Giunta*** *a-72.* ***Glanzman*** *a-167, 171, 172, 174.* ***Heath*** *a-42,122, 132, 133; c-67, 122, 132-134.* ***Kaluta*** *a-197i; c-167.* ***G. Kane*** *a-169.* ***Kubert*** *a-6-163(most later issues), 200.* ***Maurer*** *a-160, 165.* ***Severin*** *a-65, 162.* ***S&K*** *c-7-31, 33, 34, 37, 40.* ***Simonson*** *a-170, 172, 174, 180.* ***Sutton*** *a-168.* ***Thorne*** *a-183.* ***Toth*** *a-164.* ***Wildey*** *a-161. Suicide Squad in 110, 116-118, 120, 121, 127.*

STARSTREAM (Adventures in Science Fiction)(See Questar illustrated)
Whitman/Western Publishing Co.: 1976 (79¢, 68 pgs, cardboard-c)

	GD 2.0	VG 4.0	FN 6.0	VF 8.0	VF/NM 9.0	NM- 9.2
1-4: 1-Bolle-a. 2-4-McWilliams & Bolle-a	2	4	6	10	14	18

STARSTRUCK
Marvel Comics (Epic Comics): Feb, 1985 - No. 6, Feb, 1986 ($1.50, mature)

1-6: Kaluta-a 3.00

STARSTRUCK
Dark Horse Comics: Aug, 1990 - No. 4, Nov?, 1990 ($2.95, B&W, 52pgs.)

1-3: Kaluta-r/Epic series plus new-c/a in all 3.00
4 (68 pgs.)-contains 2 trading cards 3.00
Reprint 1-6 (IDW, 8/09 - No. 6, Feb, 2010, $3.99) newly colored; Galactic Girl Guides 4.00

STAR STUDDED
Cambridge House/Superior Publishers: 1945 (25¢, 132 pgs.); 1945 (196 pgs.)

	GD 2.0	VG 4.0	FN 6.0	VF 8.0	VF/NM 9.0	NM- 9.2
nn-Captain Combat by Giunta, Ghost Woman, Commandette, & Red Rogue app.; Infantino-a	34	68	102	199	325	450
nn-The Cadet, Edison Bell, Hoot Gibson, Jungle Lil (196 pgs.); copies vary; Blue Beetle in some	28	56	84	165	270	375

STARTLING COMICS
Better Publications (Nedor): June, 1940 - No. 53, Sept, 1948

	GD 2.0	VG 4.0	FN 6.0	VF 8.0	VF/NM 9.0	NM- 9.2
1-Origin Captain Future-Man Of Tomorrow, Mystico (By Sansone), The Wonder Man; The Masked Rider & his horse Pinto begins; Masked Rider formerly in pulps; drug use story	284	568	852	1818	3109	4400
2 -Don Davis, Espionage Ace begins	100	200	300	635	1093	1550
3	84	168	252	538	919	1300
4	60	120	180	381	653	925
5-9	52	104	156	322	549	775
10-The Fighting Yank begins (9/41, origin/1st app.)	400	800	1200	2800	4900	7000
11-2nd app. Fighting Yank	123	246	369	787	1344	1900
12-Hitler, Hirohito, Mussolini-c	123	246	369	787	1344	1900
13-15	65	130	195	416	708	1000
16-Origin The Four Comrades; not in #32,35	66	132	198	419	722	1025
17-Last Masked Rider & Mystico	50	100	150	315	533	750
18-Pyroman begins (12/42, origin)(also see America's Best Comics #3 for 1st app., 11/42)	102	204	306	648	1112	1575
19	50	100	150	315	533	750
20,21: 20-The Oracle begins (3/43); not in issues 26,28,33,34. 21-Origin The Ape, Oracle's enemy	52	104	156	328	557	785
22-34: 34-Origin The Scarab & only app.	51	102	153	318	539	760
35-Hypodermic syringe attacks Fighting Yank in drug story	52	104	156	328	557	785
36-43: 36-Last Four Comrades. 38-Bondage/torture-c. 40-Last Capt. Future & Oracle. 41-Front Page Peggy begins; A-Bomb-c. 43-Last Pyroman	45	90	135	284	480	675
44,45: 44-Lance Lewis, Space Detective begins; Ingels-c; sci/fi-c begin. 45-Tygra begins (intro/origin, 5/47); Ingels-c/a (splash pg. & inside f/c B&W ad)	71	142	213	454	777	1100
46-Classic Ingels-c; Ingels-a	115	230	345	730	1253	1775
47,48,50-53: 50,51-Sea-Eagle app.	66	132	198	419	722	1025
49-Classic Schomburg Robot-c; last Fighting Yank	443	886	1329	3234	5717	8200

NOTE: ***Ingels*** *a-44, 45; c-44, 45, 46(wash).* ***Schomburg*** *(****Xela****) c-21-43; 47-53 (airbrush).* ***Tuska*** *c-45? Bondage c-16, 21, 37, 46-49. Captain Future c-1-9, 13, 14. Fighting Yank c-10-12, 15-17, 21, 22, 24, 26, 28, 30, 32, 34, 36, 38, 40, 42. Pyroman c-18-20, 23, 25, 27, 29, 31, 33, 35, 37, 39, 41, 43.*

Startling Terror Tales #9 © STAR

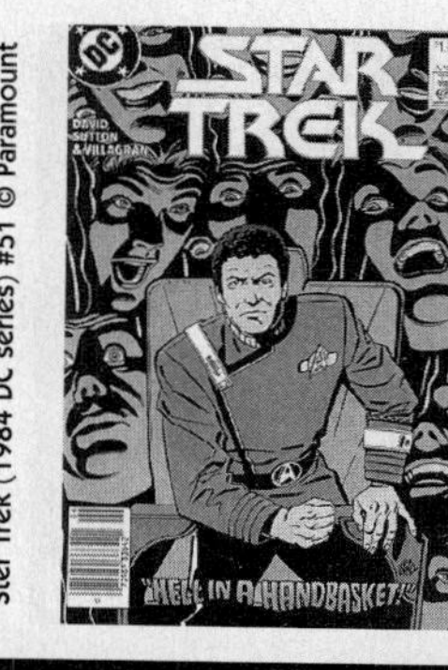

Ster Trek (1984 DC series) #51 © Paramount

Star Trek: Countdown #1 © Paramount

GD VG FN VF VF/NM NM-
2.0 4.0 6.0 8.0 9.0 9.2

GD VG FN VF VF/NM NM-
2.0 4.0 6.0 8.0 9.0 9.2

STARTLING STORIES: BANNER
Marvel Comics: July, 2001 - No. 4, Oct, 2001 ($2.99, limited series)
1-4-Hulk story by Azzarello; Corben-c/a 3.00
TPB (11/01, $12.95) r/1-4 13.00

STARTLING STORIES: FANTASTIC FOUR - UNSTABLE MOLECULES (See Fantastic Four - ...)

STARTLING STORIES: THE MEGALOMANIACAL SPIDER-MAN
Marvel Comics: Jun, 2002 ($2.99, one-shot)
1-Spider-Man spoof; Peter Bagge-s/a 3.00

STARTLING STORIES: THE THING
Marvel Comics: 2003 ($3.50, one-shot)
1-Zimmerman-s/Kramer-a; Inhumans and the Hulk app. 3.50

STARTLING STORIES: THE THING - NIGHT FALLS ON YANCY STREET
Marvel Comics: Jun, 2003 - No. 4, Sept, 2003 ($3.50, limited series)
1-4-Dorkin-s/Haspiel-a. 2,3-Frightful Four app. 3.50

STARTLING TERROR TALES
Star Publications: No. 10, May, 1952 - No. 14, Feb, 1953; No. 4, Apr, 1953 - No. 11, 1954
10-(1st Series)-Wood/Harrison-a (r/A Star Presentation #3) Disbrow/Cole-c; becomes 4 different titles after #10; becomes Confessions of Love #11 on, The Horrors #11 on, Terrifying Tales #11 on, Terrors of the Jungle #11 on & continues w/Startling Terror #11
76 152 228 486 831 1175
11-(8/52)-L. B. Cole Spider-c; r-Fox's "A Feature Presentation" #5 (blue-c)
168 336 504 1075 1838 2600
11-Black-c (variant; believed to be a pressrun change) (Unique)
174 348 522 1114 1907 2700
12,14 33 66 99 194 317 440
13-Jo-Jo-r; Disbrow-a 34 68 102 204 332 460
4-9,11(1953-54) (2nd Series): 11-New logo 29 58 87 172 281 390
10-Disbrow-a 35 70 105 208 339 470
NOTE: *L. B. Cole covers-all issues. Palais a-V2#8r, V2#11r.*

STAR TREK (TV) (See Dan Curtis Giveaways, Dynabrite Comics & Power Record Comics)
Gold Key: 7/67; No. 2, 6/68; No. 3, 12/68; No. 4, 6/69 - No. 61, 3/79
1-Photo-c begin, end #9; photo back-c is on all copies, no variant exists with an ad on the back-c 50 100 150 413 807 1200
2-Regular version has an ad on back-c 22 44 66 157 304 450
2 (rare variation w/photo back-c) 31 62 93 240 463 685
3-5-All have back-c ads 15 30 45 104 197 290
3 (rare variation w/photo back-c) 23 46 69 166 321 475
6-9 11 22 33 80 145 210
10-20 6 12 18 43 69 95
21-30 6 12 18 37 59 80
31-40 4 8 12 28 44 60
41-61: 52-Drug propaganda story 4 8 12 22 34 45
...the Enterprise Logs nn (8/76)-Golden Press, ($1.95, 224 pgs.)-r/#1-8 plus 7 pgs. by McWilliams (#11185)-Photo-c 6 12 18 39 62 85
...the Enterprise Logs Vol. 2 ('76)-r/#9-17 (#11187)-Photo-c
5 10 15 34 55 75
...the Enterprise Logs Vol. 3 ('77)-r/#18-26 (#11188); McWilliams-a (4 pgs.)-Photo-c
5 10 15 34 55 75
Star Trek Vol. 4 (Winter '77)-Reprints #27,28,30-34,36,38 (#11189) plus 3 pgs. new art 5 10 15 34 55 75
... : The Key Collection (Checker Book Publ. Group, 2004, $22.95) r/#1-8 23.00
... : The Key Collection Volume 2 (Checker, 2004, $22.95) r/#9-16 23.00
... : The Key Collection Volume 3 (Checker, 2005, $22.95) r/#17-24 23.00
... : The Key Collection Volume 4 (Checker, 2005, $22.95) r/#25-33 23.00
... : The Key Collection Volume 5 (Checker, 2006, $22.95) r/#34,36,38,39,40-43 23.00
NOTE: *McWilliams a-38, 40-44, 46-61. #29 reprints #1; #35 reprints #4; #37 reprints #5; #45 reprints #7. The tabloids all have photo covers and blank inside covers. Painted covers #10-44, 46-59.*

STAR TREK
Marvel Comics Group: April, 1980 - No. 18, Feb, 1982
1: 1-3-r/Marvel Super Special; movie adapt. 2 4 6 9 12 15
2-16: 5-Miller-c 1 2 3 5 6 8
17-Low print run 2 4 6 8 10 12
18-Last issue; low print run 2 4 6 10 14 18
NOTE: *Austin c-18i. Buscema a-13. Gil Kane a-15. Nasser c/a-7. Simonson c-17.*

STAR TREK (Also see Who's Who In Star Trek)
DC Comics: Feb, 1984 - No. 56, Nov, 1988 (75¢, Mando paper)
1-Sutton-a(p) begins 1 3 4 6 8 10
2-5 6.00
6-10: 7-Origin Saavik 5.00
11-20: 19-Walter Koenig story 4.00
21-32 3.50
33-($1.25, 52 pgs.)-20th anniversary issue 4.00
34-49: 37-Painted-c 3.00
50-($1.50, 52 pgs.) 4.00
51-56, Annual 1-3: 1(1985). 2(1986). 3(1988, $1.50) 3.00
...: To Boldly Go TPB (Titan Books, 7/05, $19.95) r/#1-6; Koenig foreward; cast interviews 20.00
...: The Trial of James T. Kirk TPB (Titan Books, 6/06, $19.95) r/#7-12; cast interviews 20.00
...: The Return of the Worthy TPB (Titan Books, 12/06, $19.95) r/#13-18; cast interviews 20.00
NOTE: *Morrow a-28, 35, 36, 56. Orlando c-8i. Perez c-1-3. Spiegle a-19. Starlin c-24, 25. Sutton a-1-6p, 8-18p, 20-27p, 29p, 31-34p, 39-52p, 55p; c-4-6p, 8-22p, 46p.*

STAR TREK
DC Comics: Oct, 1989 - No. 80, Jan, 1996 ($1.50/$1.75/$1.95/$2.50)
1-Capt. Kirk and crew 6.00
2,3 4.00
4-23,25-30: 10-12-The Trial of James T. Kirk. 21-Begin $1.75-c 3.00
24-($2.95, 68 pgs.)-40 pg. epic w/pin-ups 3.50
31-49,51-60 2.50
50-($3.50, 68 pgs.)-Painted-c 3.50
61-74,76-80 2.50
75 ($3.95) 4.00
Annual 1-6('90-'95, 68 pgs.): 1-Morrow-a. 3-Painted-c 4.00
Special 1-3 ('9-'95, 68 pgs.)-1-Sutton-a. 4.00
...: The Ashes of Eden (1995, $14.95, 100 pgs.)-Shatner story 15.00
...Generations (1994, $3.95, 68 pgs.)-Movie adaptation 4.00
...Generations (1994, $5.95, 68 pgs.)-Squarebound 6.00

STAR TREK...(TV)
DC Comics (WildStorm): one-shots
All of Me (4/00, $5.95, prestige format) Lopresti-a 6.00
Enemy Unseen TPB (2001, $17.95) r/Perchance to Dream, Embrace the Wolf, The Killing Shadows; Struzan-c 18.00
Enter the Wolves (2001, $5.95) Crispin & Weinstein-s; Mota-a/c 6.00
New Frontier - Double Time (11/00, $5.95)-Captain Calhoun's USS Excalibur; Peter David-s; Stelfreeze-c 6.00
Other Realities TPB (2001, $14.95) r/All of Me, New Frontier - Double Time, and DS9-N-Vector; Van Fleet-c 15.00
Special (2001, $6.95) Stories from all 4 series by various; Van Fleet-c 7.00

STAR TREK...
IDW Publishing: one-shots
...: Captain's Log: Sulu (1/10, $3.99) Manfredi-a 4.00

STAR TREK: ALIEN SPOTLIGHT
IDW Publishing: Sept, 2007 - Feb, 2008 ($3.99, series of one-shots)
... Andorians (11/07) Storrie-s/O'Grady-a; Counselor Troi app.; two art & one photo-c 4.00
... Borg (1/08) Harris-s/Murphy-a; Janeway & Next Gen crew app.; two art & one photo-c 4.00
... Cardassians (12/09) Padilla-a; Garak & Kira app. 4.00
... The Gorn (9/07) Messina-a; Chekov app.; two art & one photo-c 4.00
... Orions (12/07) Casagrande-a; Capt. Pike app.; two art & one photo-c 4.00
... Q (8/09) Casagrande-a; takes place after Star Trek 8 movie; two art & one photo-c 4.00
... Romulans (2/08) John Byrne-s/a; Kirk era; two art & one photo-c 4.00
... Romulans (5/09) Wagner Reis-a; David Williams-c 4.00
... Tribbles (3/09) Hawthorne-a; first encounter with Klingons; one art & one photo-c 4.00
... Vulcans (10/07) Spock's early Enterprise days with Capt. Pike; two art & one photo-c 4.00

STAR TREK: ASSIGNMENT EARTH
IDW Publishing: May, 2008 - No. 5, Sept, 2008 ($3.99, limited series)
1-5-Further adventures of Gary Seven and Roberta; John Byrne-s/a/c. 5-Nixon app. 4.00

STAR TREK: COUNTDOWN (Prequel to the 2009 movie)
IDW Publishing: Jan, 2009 - No. 4, Apr, 2009 ($3.99, limited series)
1-4: 1-Ambassador Spock on Romulus; intro. Nero; Messina-a 4.00

STAR TREK: CREW
IDW Publishing: Mar, 2009 - No. 5, Jul, 2009 ($3.99, limited series)
1-5: John Byrne-s/a; Captain Pike era 4.00

STAR TREK: DEBT OF HONOR
DC Comics: 1992 ($24.95/$14.95, graphic novel)
Hardcover ($24.95) Claremont-s/Hughes-a(p) 25.00
Softcover ($14.95) 15.00

STAR TREK: DEEP SPACE NINE (TV)
Malibu Comics: Aug, 1993 - No. 32, Jan, 1996 ($2.50)
1-Direct Sale Edition w/line drawn-c 4.00
1-Newsstand Edition with photo-c 3.00
0-(1/95, $2.95)-Terok Nor 3.00

Star Trek: Deep Space Nine #14 © Paramount

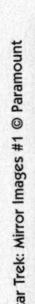

Star Trek: Mirror Images #1 © Paramount

Star Trek: The Next Generation #21 © Paramount

GD 2.0 | VG 4.0 | FN 6.0 | VF 8.0 | VF/NM 9.0 | NM- 9.2

2-30: 2-Polybagged w/trading card. 9-4 pg. prelude to Hearts & Minds 2.50
31-($3.95) 4.00
32-($3.50) 3.50
Annual 1 (1/95, $3.95, 68 pgs.) 4.00
Special 1 (1995, $3.50) 3.50
Ultimate Annual 1 (12/95, $5.95) 6.00
...:Lightstorm (12/94, $3.50) 3.50

STAR TREK: DEEP SPACE NINE (TV)
Marvel Comics (Paramount Comics): Nov, 1996 - No. 15, Mar, 1998 ($1.95/$1.99)
1-15: 12,13-"Telepathy War" pt. 2,3 2.50

STAR TREK: DEEP SPACE NINE: FOOL'S GOLD
IDW Publishing: Dec, 2009 - Present ($3.99)
1,2-Mantovani-a 4.00

STAR TREK: DEEP SPACE NINE -- N-VECTOR (TV)
DC Comics (WildStorm): Aug, 2000 - No. 4, Nov, 2000 ($2.50, limited series)
1-4-Cypress-a 2.50

STAR TREK DEEP SPACE NINE-THE CELEBRITY SERIES
Malibu Comics: May, 1995 ($2.95)
1-Blood and Honor; Mark Lenard script 3.00
1-Rules of Diplomacy; Aron Eisenberg script 3.00

STAR TREK: DEEP SPACE NINE HEARTS AND MINDS
Malibu Comics: June, 1994 - No. 4, Sept, 1994 ($2.50, limited series)
1-4 2.50
1-Holographic-c 4.00

STAR TREK: DEEP SPACE NINE, THE MAQUIS
Malibu Comics: Feb, 1995 - No. 3, Apr, 1995 ($2.50, limited series)
1-3-Newsstand-c, 1-Photo-c 2.50

STAR TREK: DEEP SPACE NINE/THE NEXT GENERATION
Malibu Comics: Oct, 1994 - No. 2, Nov, 1994 ($2.50, limited series)
1,2: Parts 2 & 4 of x-over with Star Trek: TNG/DS9 from DC Comics 2.50

STAR TREK: DEEP SPACE NINE WORF SPECIAL
Malibu Comics: Dec, 1995 ($3.95, one-shot)
1-Includes pinups 4.00

STAR TREK: DIVIDED WE FALL
DC Comics (WildStorm): July, 2001 - No. 4, Oct, 2001 ($2.95, limited series)
1-4: Ordover & Mack-s; Lenara Kahn, Verad and Odan app. 3.00

STAR TREK EARLY VOYAGES(TV)
Marvel Comics (Paramount Comics): Feb, 1997 - No. 17, Jun, 1998 ($2.95/$1.95/$1.99)
1-($2.95) 3.00
2-17 2.50

STAR TREK: ENTERPRISE EXPERIMENT
IDW Publishing: Apr, 2008 - No. 5, Aug, 2008 ($3.99, limited series)
1-5-Year Four story; D.C. Fontana & Derek Chester-s; Purcell-a 4.00

STAR TREK: FIRST CONTACT (Movie)
Marvel Comics (Paramount Comics): Nov, 1996 ($5.95, one-shot)
nn-Movie adaption 6.00

STAR TREK: KLINGONS: BLOOD WILL TELL
IDW Publishing: Apr, 2007 - No. 5 ($3.99, limited series)
1-5-Star Trek TOS episodes from the Klingon viewpoint; Messina-a. 2-Tribbles 4.00
1-($4.99) Klingon Language Variant; comic with Kliingon text; English script 5.00

STAR TREK: MIRROR IMAGES
IDW Publishing: June, 2008 - No. 5, Nov, 2008 ($3.99, limited series)
1-5-Further adventures in the Mirror Universe. 3-Mirror-Picard app. 4.00

STAR TREK: MIRROR MIRROR
Marvel Comics (Paramount Comics): Feb, 1997 ($3.95, one-shot)
1-DeFalco-s 4.00

STAR TREK: MISSION'S END
IDW Publishing: Mar, 2009 - No. 5, July, 2009 ($3.99, limited series)
1-5-Kirk, Spock, Bones crew, their last mission on the pre-movie Enterprise 4.00

STAR TREK MOVIE SPECIAL
DC Comics: 1984 (June) - No. 2, 1987 ($1.50); No. 1, 1989 ($2.00, 52 pgs)
nn-(#1)-Adapts Star Trek III; Sutton-p (68 pgs.) 3.00
2-Adapts Star Trek IV; Sutton-a; Chaykin-c. (68 pgs.) 3.00

GD 2.0 | VG 4.0 | FN 6.0 | VF 8.0 | VF/NM 9.0 | NM- 9.2

1 (1989)-Adapts Star Trek V; painted-c 3.00

STAR TREK: NERO
IDW Publishing: Aug, 2009 - No. 4, Nov, 2009 ($3.99, limited series)
1-4-Nero's ship after the attack on the Kelvin to the arrival of Spock 4.00

STAR TREK: NEW FRONTIER
IDW Publishing: Mar, 2008 - No. 5, July, 2008 ($3.99, limited series)
1-5-Capt. Calhoun & Adm. Shelby app.; Peter David-s 4.00

STAR TREK: OPERATION ASSIMILATION
Marvel Comics (Paramount Comics): Dec, 1996 ($2.95, one-shot)
1 3.00

STAR TREK: ROMULANS SCHISMS
IDW Publishing: Sept, 2009 - No. 3, Nov, 2009 ($3.99, limited series)
1-3-John Byrne-s/a/c 4.00

STAR TREK: ROMULANS THE HOLLOW CROWN
IDW Publishing: Sept, 2008 - No. 2, Oct, 2008 ($3.99, limited series)
1,2-John Byrne-s/a/c 4.00

STAR TREK VI: THE UNDISCOVERED COUNTRY (Movie)
DC Comics: 1992
1-($2.95, regular edition, 68 pgs.)-Adaptation of film 3.00
nn-($5.95, prestige edition)-Has photos of movie not included in regular edition; painted-c by Palmer; photo back-c 6.00

STAR TREK: SPOCK: REFLECTIONS
IDW Publishing: July, 2009 - No. 4, Oct, 2009 ($3.99, limited series)
1-4-Flashbacks of Spock's childhood and career; Messina & Manfredi-a 4.00

STAR TREK: STARFLEET ACADEMY
Marvel Comics (Paramount Comics): Dec, 1996 - No. 19, Jun, 1998 ($1.95/$1.99)
1-19: Begin new series. 12-"Telepathy War" pt. 1. 18-English & Klingon editions 2.50

STAR TREK: TELEPATHY WAR
Marvel Comics (Paramount Comics): Nov, 1997 ($2.99, 48 pgs., one-shot)
1-"Telepathy War" x-over pt. 6 3.00

STAR TREK - THE MODALA IMPERATIVE
DC Comics: Late July, 1991 - No. 4, Late Sept, 1991 ($1.75, limited series)
1-4 2.50
TPB ($19.95) r/series and ST:TNG - The Modala Imperative 20.00

STAR TREK: THE NEXT GENERATION (TV)
DC Comics: Feb, 1988 - No. 6, July, 1988 (limited series)
1 ($1.50, 52 pgs.)-Sienkiewicz painted-c 6.00
2-6 ($1.00) 4.00

STAR TREK: THE NEXT GENERATION (TV)
DC Comics: Oct, 1989 -No. 80, 1995 ($1.50/$1.75/$1.95)
1-Capt. Picard and crew from TV show 1 2 3 5 7 9
2,3 5.00
4-10 4.00
11-23,25-49,51-60 3.00
24,50: 24-($2.50, 52 pgs.). 50-($3.50, 68 pgs.)-Painted-c 5.00
61-74,76-80 2.50
75-($3.95, 50 pgs.) 4.00
Annual 1-6 ('90-'95, 68 pgs.) 4.00
Special 1 -3('93-'95, 68 pgs.)-1-Contains 3 stories 4.00
...The Series Finale (1994, $3.95, 68 pgs.) 4.00

STAR TREK: THE NEXT GENERATION (TV)
DC Comics (WildStorm): one-shots
Embrace the Wolf (6/00, $5.95, prestige format) Golden & Sniegoski-s 6.00
Forgiveness (2001, $24.95, HC) David Brin-s/Scott Hampton painted-a; dust jacket-c 30.00
Forgiveness (2002, $17.95, SC) 18.00
The Gorn Crisis (1/01, $29.95, HC) Kordey painted-a/dust jacket-c 30.00
The Gorn Crisis (1/01, $17.95, SC) Kordey painted-a 18.00

STAR TREK: THE NEXT GENERATION/DEEP SPACE NINE (TV)
DC Comics: Dec, 1994 - No. 2, Jan, 1995 ($2.50, limited series)
1,2-Parts 1 & 3 of x-over with Star Trek: DS9/TNG from Malibu Comics 2.50

STAR TREK: THE NEXT GENERATION: GHOSTS
IDW Publishing: Nov, 2009 - No. 5, Mar, 2010 ($3.99)
1-5-Cannon-s/Aranda-a 4.00

STAR TREK: THE NEXT GENERATION - ILL WIND

Star Trek: The Wrath of Khan #2 © Paramount

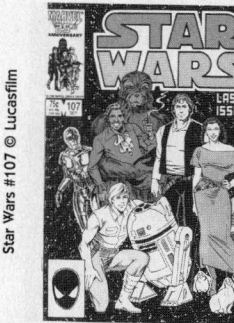

Star Wars #107 © Lucasfilm

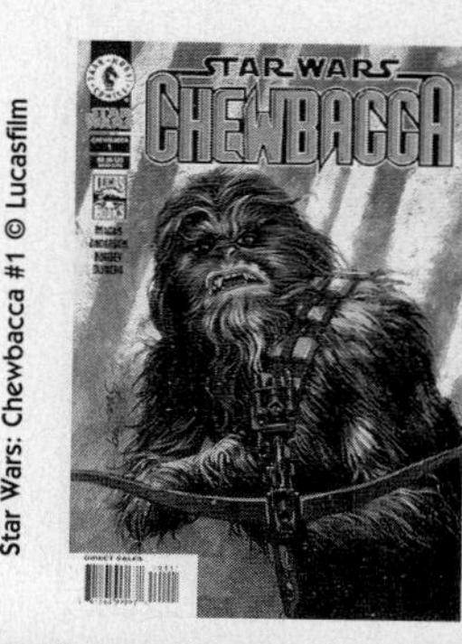

Star Wars: Chewbacca #1 © Lucasfilm

GD 2.0 | VG 4.0 | FN 6.0 | VF 8.0 | VF/NM 9.0 | NM- 9.2

DC Comics: Nov, 1995 - No. 4, Feb, 1996 ($2.50, limited series)
1-4: Hugh Fleming painted-c on all 2.50

STAR TREK: THE NEXT GENERATION: INTELLIGENCE GATHERING
IDW Publishing: Jan, 2008 - No. 5, May, 2008 ($3.99)
1-5-Messina-a/Scott & David Tipton-s; two covers on each 4.00

STAR TREK: THE NEXT GENERATION - PERCHANCE TO DREAM
DC Comics/WildStorm: Feb, 2000 - No. 4, May, 2000 ($2.50, limited series)
1-4-Bradstreet-c 2.50

STAR TREK: THE NEXT GENERATION - RIKER
Marvel Comics (Paramount Comics): July, 1998 ($3.50, one-shot)
1-Riker joins the Maquis 3.50

STAR TREK: THE NEXT GENERATION - SHADOWHEART
DC Comics: Dec, 1994 - No. 4, Mar, 1995 ($1.95, limited series)
1-4 2.50

STAR TREK: THE NEXT GENERATION - THE KILLING SHADOWS
DC Comics/WildStorm: Nov, 2000 - No. 4, Feb, 2001 ($2.50, limited series)
1-4-Scott Ciencin-s; Sela app. 2.50

STAR TREK: THE NEXT GENERATION: THE LAST GENERATION
IDW Publishing: Nov, 2008 - No. 5, Mar, 2009 ($3.99, limited series)
1-5-Purcell-a; alternate timeline with Klingon war; Sulu app. 4.00

STAR TREK: THE NEXT GENERATION - THE MODALA IMPERATIVE
DC Comics: Early Sept, 1991 - No. 4, Late Oct, 1991 ($1.75, limited series)
1-4 2.50

STAR TREK: THE NEXT GENERATION: THE SPACE BETWEEN
IDW Publishing: Jan, 2007 - No. 6, June, 2007 ($3.99)
1-6-Single issue stories from various seasons; photo & art covers 4.00

STAR TREK: THE WRATH OF KHAN
IDW Publishing: Jun, 2009 - No. 3, Jul, 2009 ($3.99, limited series)
1-3-Movie adaptation; Chee Yang Ong-a 4.00

STAR TREK UNLIMITED
Marvel Comics (Paramount Comics): Nov, 1996 - No. 10, July, 1998 ($2.95/$2.99)
1,2-Stories from original series and Next Generation 4.00
3-10: 3-Begin $2.99-c. 6-"Telepathy War" pt. 4. 7-Q & Trelane swap Kirk & Picard 3.50

STAR TREK UNTOLD VOYAGES
Marvel Comics (Paramount Comics): May, 1998 - No. 5, July, 1998 ($2.50)
1-5-Kirk's crew after the 1st movie 2.50

STAR TREK: VOYAGER
Marvel Comics (Paramount Comics): Nov, 1996 - No. 15, Mar, 1998 ($1.95/$1.99)
1-15: 13-"Telepathy War" pt. 5. 14-Seven of Nine joins crew 3.00

STAR TREK: VOYAGER
DC Comics/WildStorm: one-shots and trade paperbacks
- Elite Force (7/00, $5.95) The Borg app.; Abnett & Lanning-s 6.00
... Encounters With the Unknown TPB (2001, $19.95) reprints 20.00
- False Colors (1/00, $5.95) Photo-c and Jim Lee-c; Jeff Moy-a 6.00

STAR TREK: VOYAGER-- THE PLANET KILLER
DC Comics/WildStorm: Mar, 2001 - No. 3, May, 2001 ($2.95, limited series)
1-3-Voyager vs. the Planet Killer from the ST:TOS episode; Teranishi-a 3.00

STAR TREK: VOYAGER SPLASHDOWN
Marvel Comics (Paramount Comics): Apr, 1998 - No. 4, July, 1998 ($2.50, limited series)
1-4-Voyager crashes on a water planet 3.00

STAR TREK/ X-MEN
Marvel Comics (Paramount Comics): Dec, 1996 ($4.99, one-shot)
1-Kirk's crew & X-Men; art by Silvestri, Tan, Winn & Finch; Lobdell-s 5.00

STAR TREK/ X-MEN: 2ND CONTACT
Marvel Comics (Paramount Comics): May, 1998 ($4.99, 64 pgs., one-shot)
1-Next Gen. crew & X-Men battle Kang, Sentinels & Borg following First Contact movie 5.00
1-Painted wraparound variant cover 5.00

STAR TREK: YEAR FOUR (Also see Star Trek: Enterprise Experiment)
IDW Publishing: July, 2007 - No. 5, Nov, 2007 ($3.99, limited series)
1-5: 1-Original series crew; Tischman-s/Conley-a; three covers on each 4.00

STAR WARS (Movie) (See Classic..., Contemporary Motivators, Dark Horse Comics, The Droids, The Ewoks, Marvel Movie Showcase, Marvel Special Ed.)

GD 2.0 | VG 4.0 | FN 6.0 | VF 8.0 | VF/NM 9.0 | NM- 9.2

Marvel Comics Group: July, 1977 - No. 107, Sept, 1986
1-(Regular 30¢ edition)-Price in square w/UPC code; #1-6 adapt first movie; first issue on sale before movie debuted 6 12 18 39 62 95
1-(35¢-c; limited distribution - 1500 copies?)- Price in square w/UPC code (Prices vary widely on this book. In 2005 a CGC certified 9.4 sold for $6,500, a CGC certified 9.2 sold for $3,403, and a CGC certified 6.0 sold for $610) 100 200 300 850 1675 2500

NOTE: *The rare 35¢ edition has the cover price in a square box, and the UPC box in the lower left hand corner has the UPC code lines running through it.*

2-4-(30¢ issues). 4-Battle with Darth Vader 4 8 12 22 34 45
2-4-(35¢ with UPC code; not reprints) 9 18 27 63 107 150
5,6: 5-Begin 35¢-c on all editions. 6-Stevens-a(i). 3 6 9 14 20 25
7-20 2 4 6 8 11 14
21-70: 39-44-The Empire Strikes Back-r by Al Williamson in all. 50-Giant. 68-Reintro Boba Fett. 2 3 4 6 8 10
71-80 2 4 6 8 10 12
81-90: 81-Boba Fett app. 2 4 6 8 11 14
91,93-99: 98-Williamson-a. 2 4 6 10 14 18
92,100-106: 92,100-($1.00, 52 pgs.). 3 6 9 14 19 24
107(low dist.); Portacio-a(i) 6 12 18 37 59 80
1-9: Reprints; has "reprint" in upper lefthand corner of cover or on inside or price and number inside a diamond with no date or UPC on cover; 30¢ and 35¢ issues published 4.00
Annual 1 (12/79, 52 pgs.)-Simonson-c 2 4 6 8 10 12
Annual 2 (11/82, 52 pgs.), 3(12/83, 52 pgs.) 1 3 4 6 8 10
... A Long Time Ago...Vol. 1 TPB (Dark Horse Comics, 6/02, $29.95) r/#1-14 30.00
... A Long Time Ago...Vol. 2 TPB (Dark Horse Comics, 7/02, $29.95) r/#15-28 30.00
... A Long Time Ago...Vol. 3 TPB (Dark Horse Comics, 11/02, $29.95) r/#39-53 30.00
... A Long Time Ago...Vol. 4 TPB (Dark Horse Comics, 1/03, $29.95) r/#54-67 & Ann. 2 30.00
... A Long Time Ago...Vol. 5 TPB (Dark Horse Comics, 3/03, $29.95) r/#68-81 & Ann. 3 30.00
... A Long Time Ago...Vol. 6 TPB (Dark Horse Comics, 5/03, $29.95) r/#82-93 30.00
... A Long Time Ago...Vol. 7 TPB (Dark Horse Comics, 6/03, $29.95) r/#96-107 30.00

***Austin** a-11-15i, 21i, 38; c-12-15i, 21i. **Byrne** c-13p. **Chaykin** a-1-10p; c-1. **Golden** c/a-38. **Miller** c-47p; pin-up-43. **Nebres** c/a-Annual 2i. **Portacio** a-107i. **Sienkiewicz** c-92i, 98. **Simonson** a-16p, 49p, 51-63p, 65p, 66p; c-16, 49-51, 52p, 53-62, Annual 1. **Steacy** painted a-105i, 106i; c-105. **Williamson** a-39-44p, 50p, 98; c-39, 40, 41-44p. Painted c-81, 87, 92, 95, 98, 100, 105.*

STAR WARS (Monthly series) (Becomes Star Wars Republic #46-on)
Dark Horse Comics: Dec, 1998 - No. 45, Aug, 2005 ($2.50/$2.95/$2.99)
1-12: 1-6-Prelude To Rebellion; Strnad-s. 4-Brereton-c. 7-12-Outlander 3.00
5,6 (Holochrome-c variants) 6.00
13, 17-18-($2.95): 13-18-Emissaries to Malastare; Truman-s 3.00
14-16-($2.50) Schultz-c 3.00
19-45: 19-22-Twilight; Duursema-a. 23-26-Infinity's End. 42-45-Rite of Passage 3.00
#0 Another Universe.com Ed.($10.00) r/serialized pages from Pizzazz Magazine; new Dorman painted-c 10.00
... A Valentine Story (2/03, $3.50) Leia & Han Solo on Hoth; Winick-s/Chadwick-a/c 3.50
...: Rite of Passage (2004, $12.95) r/#42-45 13.00
...: The Stark Hyperspace War (903, $12.95) r/#36-39 13.00

STAR WARS: A NEW HOPE- THE SPECIAL EDITION
Dark Horse Comics: Jan, 1997 - No. 4, Apr, 1997 ($2.95, limited series)
1-4-Dorman-c 4.00

STAR WARS: BOBA FETT
Dark Horse Comics: Dec, 1995 - No. 3 ($3.95) (Originally intended as a one-shot)
1-Kennedy-c/a 6.00
2,3 5.00
Death, Lies, & Treachery TPB (1/98, $12.95) r/#1-3 13.00
... - Agent of Doom (11/00, $2.99) Ostrander-s/Cam Kennedy-a 3.00
... - Overkill (3/06, $2.99) Hughes-c/Andrews-s/Velasco-a 3.00
Twin Engines of Destruction (1/97, $2.95) 3.00

STAR WARS: BOBA FETT: ENEMY OF THE EMPIRE
Dark Horse Comics: Jan, 1999 - No. 4, Apr, 1999 ($2.95, limited series)
1-4-Recalls 1st meeting of Fett and Vader 3.00

STAR WARS: CHEWBACCA
Dark Horse Comics: Jan, 2000 - No. 4, Apr, 2000 ($2.95, limited series)
1-4-Macan-s/art by various incl. Anderson, Kordey, Gibbons; Phillips-c 3.00

STAR WARS: CLONE WARS ADVENTURES
Dark Horse Comics: 2004 - Present ($6.95, digest-sized)
1-9-Short stories inspired by Clone Wars animated series 7.00

STAR WARS: CRIMSON EMPIRE
Dark Horse Comics: Dec, 1997 - No. 6, May, 1998 ($2.95, limited series)

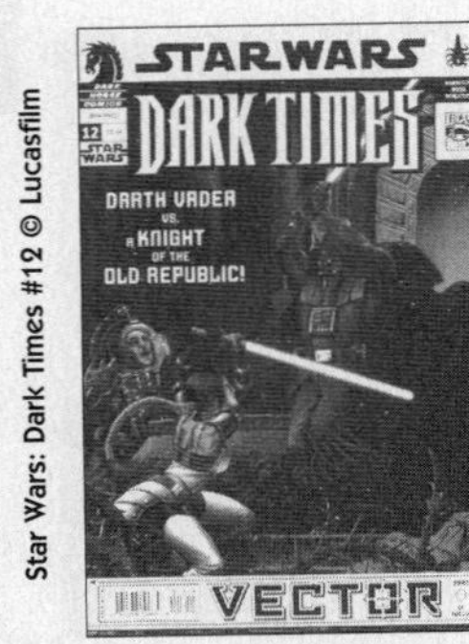

Star Wars: Dark Times #12 © Lucasfilm

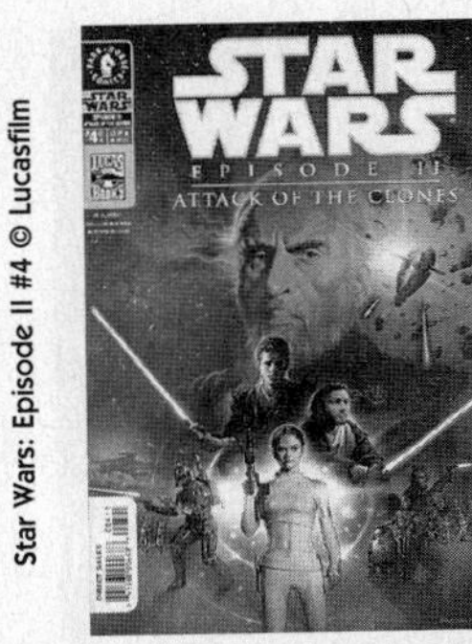

Star Wars: Episode II #4 © Lucasfilm

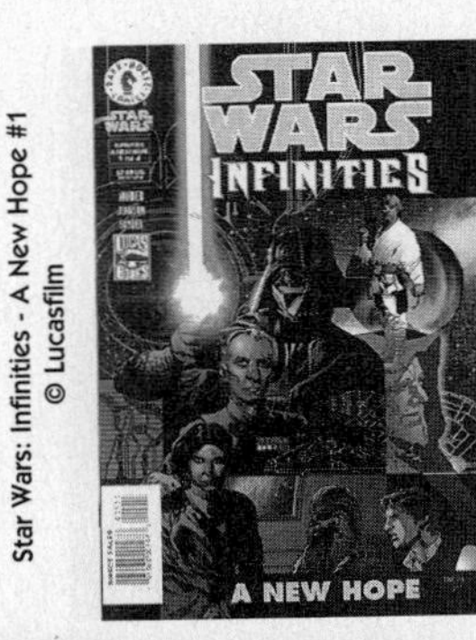

Star Wars: Infinities - A New Hope #1 © Lucasfilm

	GD 2.0	VG 4.0	FN 6.0	VF 8.0	VF/NM 9.0	NM- 9.2
1-Richardson-s/Gulacy-a	1	2	3	4	5	7
2-6						5.00

STAR WARS: CRIMSON EMPIRE II: COUNCIL OF BLOOD
Dark Horse Comics: Nov, 1998 - No. 6, Apr, 1999 ($2.95, limited series)

1-6-Richardson & Stradley-s/Gulacy-a 3.00

STAR WARS: DARK EMPIRE
Dark Horse Comics: Dec, 1991 - No. 6, Oct, 1992 ($2.95, limited series)

	GD 2.0	VG 4.0	FN 6.0	VF 8.0	VF/NM 9.0	NM- 9.2
Preview-(99¢)						3.00
1-All have Dorman painted-c	1	2	3	5	7	9
1-3-2nd printing						4.00
2-Low print run	2	4	6	8	10	12
3						6.00
4-6						4.00
Gold Embossed Set (#1-6)-With gold embossed foil logo (price is for set)						90.00
Platinum Embossed Set (#1-6)						120.00
Trade paperback (4/93, 16.95)						17.00
Dark Empire 1 - TPB 3rd printing (2003, $16.95)						17.00
Ltd. Ed. Hardcover ($99.95) Signed & numbered						100.00

STAR WARS: DARK EMPIRE II
Dark Horse Comics: Dec, 1994 - No. 6, May, 1995 ($2.95, limited series)

1-Dave Dorman painted-c 5.00
2-6: Dorman-c in all. 4.00
Platinum Embossed Set (#1-6) 35.00
Trade paperback ($17.95) 18.00
TPB Second Edition (9/06, $19.95) r/#1-6 and Star Wars: Empire's End #1,2 20.00

STAR WARS: DARK FORCE RISING
Dark Horse Comics: May, 1997 - No. 6, Oct, 1997 ($2.95, limited series)

1-6 4.00
TPB (2/98, $17.95) r/#1-6 18.00

STAR WARS: DARK TIMES (Continued from Star Wars Republic #84)(Continues in Star Wars: Rebellion #15)
Dark Horse Comics: Oct, 2006 - Present ($2.99)

1-15-Nineteen years before Episode IV; Doug Wheatley-a. 11-Celeste Morne awakens
13-15-Blue Harvest 3.00
#0-(7/09, $2.99) Prologue to Blue Harvest 3.00
... Volume 1: The Path To Nowhere (1/08, $17.95, TPB) r/#1-5 18.00

STAR WARS: DARTH MAUL
Dark Horse Comics: Sept, 2000 - No. 4, Dec, 2000 ($2.95, limited series)

1-4-Photo-c and Struzan painted-c; takes place 6 months before Ep. 1 3.00

STAR WARS: DROIDS (See Dark Horse Comics #17-19)
Dark Horse Comics: Apr, 1994 - #6, Sept, 1994; V2#1, Apr, 1995 - V2#8, Dec, 1995 ($2.50, limited series)

1-($2.95)-Embossed-c 4.00
2-6 , Special 1 (1/95, $2.50), V2#1-8 3.00
Star Wars Omnibus: Droids One TPB (6/08, $24.95) r/#1-6, Special 1, V2#1-8, Star Wars: The Protocol Offensive and "Artoo's Day Out" story from Star Wars Galaxy Magazine #1 25.00

STAR WARS: EMPIRE
Dark Horse Comics: Sept, 2002 - No. 40, Feb, 2006 ($2.99)

1-40: 1-Benjamin-a; takes place weeks before SW: A New Hope. 7,28-Boba Fett-c. 14-Vader after the destruction of the Death Star. 15-Death of Biggs; Wheatley-a 3.00
... Volume 1 (2003, $12.95, TPB) r/#1-4 13.00
... Volume 2 (2004, $17.95, TPB) r/#8-12,15 18.00
... Volume 3: The Imperial Perspective (2004, $17.95, TPB) r/#13,14,16-19 18.00
... Volume 4: The Heart of the Rebellion (2005, $17.95, TPB) r/#5,6,20-22 & Star Wars: A Valentine Story 18.00
... Volume 5 (2006, $14.95, TPB) r/#23-27 18.00
... Volume 6: In the Shadows of Their Fathers (10/06, $17.95, TPB) r/#29-34 18.00
... Volume 7: The Wrong Side of the War (1/07, $17.95, TPB) r/#34-40 18.00

STAR WARS: EMPIRE'S END
Dark Horse Comics: Oct, 1995 - No. 2, Nov, 1995 ($2.95, limited series)

1,2-Dorman-c 3.00

STAR WARS: EPISODE 1 THE PHANTOM MENACE
Dark Horse Comics: May, 1999 - No. 4 ($2.95, movie adaptation)

1-4-Regular and photo-c; Damaggio & Williamson-a 3.00
TPB ($12.95) r/#1-4 13.00
...Anakin Skywalker-Photo-c & Bradstreet-c, ...Obi-Wan Kenobi-Photo-c & Egeland-c, ...Queen Amidala-Photo-c & Bradstreet-c, ...Qui-Gon Jinn-Photo-c & Bradstreet-c 3.00
Gold foil covers; Wizard 1/2 10.00

STAR WARS: EPISODE II - ATTACK OF THE CLONES
Dark Horse Comics: Apr, 2002 - No. 4, May, 2002 ($3.99, movie adaptation)

1-4-Regular and photo-c; Duursema-a 4.00
TPB ($17.95) r/#1-4; Struzan-c 18.00

STAR WARS: EPISODE III - REVENGE OF THE SITH
Dark Horse Comics: May, 2005 - No. 4, May, 2005 ($2.99, movie adaptation)

1-4-Wheatley-a/Dorman-c 3.00
TPB ($12.95) r/#1-4; Dorman-c 13.00

STAR WARS: GENERAL GRIEVOUS
Dark Horse Comics: Mar, 2005 - No. 4, June, 2005 ($2.99, limited series)

1-4-Leonardi-a/Dixon-s 3.00
TPB (2005, $12.95) r/#1-4 13.00

STAR WARS HANDBOOK
Dark Horse Comics: July, 1998 - Present ($2.95, one-shots)

...X-Wing Rogue Squadron (7/98)-Guidebook to characters and spacecraft 3.00
...Crimson Empire (7/99) Dorman-c 3.00
...Dark Empire (3/00) Dorman-c 3.00

STAR WARS: HEIR TO THE EMPIRE
Dark Horse Comics: Oct, 1995 - No.6, Apr, 1996 ($2.95, limited series)

1-6: Adaptation of Zahn novel 3.00

STAR WARS: INFINITIES - A NEW HOPE
Dark Horse Comics: May, 2001 - No. 4, Oct, 2001 ($2.99, limited series)

1-4: "What If..." the Death Star wasn't destroyed in Episode 4 3.00
TPB (2002, $12.95) r/ #1-4 13.00

STAR WARS: INFINITIES - THE EMPIRE STRIKES BACK
Dark Horse Comics: July, 2002 - No. 4, Oct, 2002 ($2.99, limited series)

1-4: "What If..." Luke died on the ice planet Hoth; Bachalo-c 3.00
TPB (2/03, $12.95) r/ #1-4 13.00

STAR WARS: INFINITIES - RETURN OF THE JEDI
Dark Horse Comics: Nov, 2003 - No. 4, Mar, 2004 ($2.99, limited series)

1-4:"What If..." ; Benjamin-a 3.00

STAR WARS: INVASION
Dark Horse Comics: July, 2009 - Present ($2.99)

1-5-Jo Chen-c 3.00
#0-(10/09, $3.50) Dorman-c; Han Solo and Chewbacca app. 3.50

STAR WARS: JABBA THE HUTT
Dark Horse Comics: Apr, 1995 ($2.50, one-shots)

nn, ...The Betrayal, ...The Dynasty Trap, ...The Hunger of Princess Nampi 3.00

STAR WARS: JANGO FETT - OPEN SEASONS
Dark Horse Comics: Apr, 2002 - No. 4, July, 2002 ($2.99, limited series)

1-4: 1-Bachs & Fernandez-a 3.00

STAR WARS: JEDI
Dark Horse Comics: Feb, 2003 - Jun, 2004 ($4.99, one-shots)

... - Aayla Secura (8/03) Ostrander-s/Duursema-a 5.00
... - Count Dooku (11/03) Duursema-a 5.00
... - Mace Windu (2/03) Duursema-a 5.00
... - Shaak Ti (5/03) Ostrander-s/Duursema-a 5.00
... - Yoda (6/04) Barlow-s/Hoon-a 5.00

STAR WARS: JEDI ACADEMY - LEVIATHAN
Dark Horse Comics: Oct, 1998 - No. 4, Jan, 1999 ($2.95, limited series)

1-4: 1-Lago-c. 2-4-Chadwick-c 3.00

STAR WARS: JEDI COUNCIL: ACTS OF WAR
Dark Horse Comics: Jun, 2000 - No. 4, Sept, 2000 ($2.95, limited series)

1-4-Stradley-s; set one year before Episode 1 3.00

STAR WARS: JEDI QUEST
Dark Horse Comics: Sept, 2001 - No. 4, Dec, 2001 ($2.99, limited series)

1-4-Anakin's Jedi training; Windham-s/Mhan-a 3.00

STAR WARS: JEDI VS. SITH
Dark Horse Comics: Apr, 2001 - No. 6, Sept, 2001 ($2.99, limited series)

1-6: Macan-s/Bachs-a/Robinson-c 3.00

STAR WARS: KNIGHTS OF THE OLD REPUBLIC
Dark Horse Comics: Jan, 2006 - Present ($2.99)

1-49-Takes place 3,964 years before Episode IV. 1-6-Brian Ching-a/Travis Charest-c 3.00

Star Wars: Legacy #7 © Lucasfilm

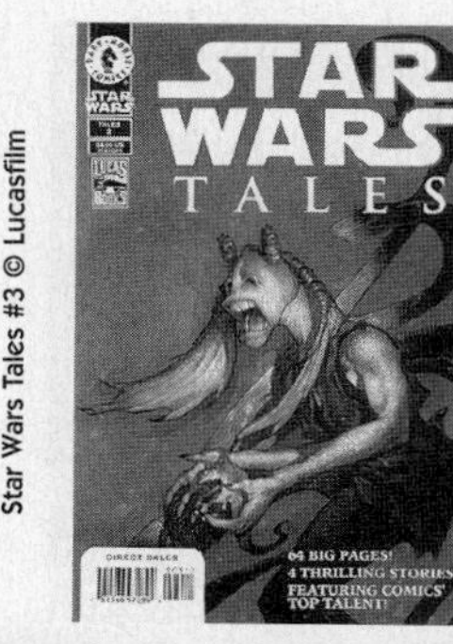

Star Wars Tales #3 © Lucasfilm

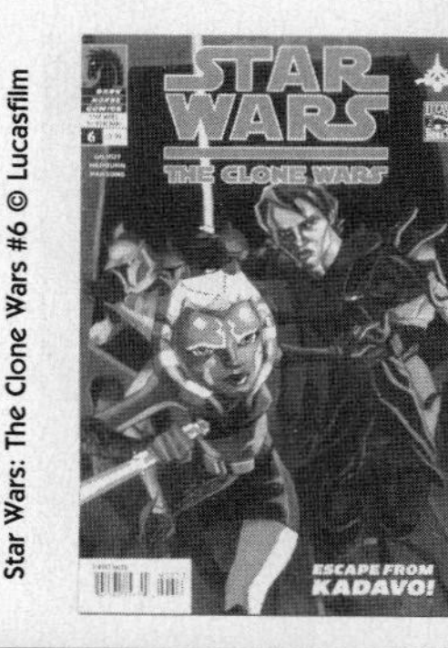

Star Wars: The Clone Wars #6 © Lucasfilm

	GD 2.0	VG 4.0	FN 6.0	VF 8.0	VF/NM 9.0	NM- 9.2

... Handbook (11/07, $2.99) profiles of characters, ships, locales 3.00
.../Rebellion #0 (3/06, 25¢) flip book preview of both series 2.50
... Vol. 1 Commencement TPB (11/06, $18.95) r/#0-6 19.00
... Vol. 2 Flashpoint TPB (5/07, $18.95) r/#17-12 19.00
... Vol. 3 Days of Fear, Nights of Anger TPB (1/08, $18.95) r/#13-18 19.00

STAR WARS: LEGACY
Dark Horse Comics: No. 0, June, 2006 - Present ($2.99)

0-(25¢) Dossier of characters, settings, ships and weapons; Duursema-c 2.50
0 1/2-(1/08, $2.99) Updated dossier of characters, settings, ships, and history 3.00
1-44: 1-Takes place 130 years after Episode IV; Hughes-c/Duursema-a. 4-Duursema-c 7,39-Luke Skywalker on-c. 16-Obi-Wan Kenobi app. 3.00
...: Broken Vol. 1 TPB (4/07, $17.95) r/#1-3,5,6 18.00

STAR WARS: MARA JADE
Dark Horse Comics: Aug, 1998 - No. 6, Jan, 1999 ($2.95, limited series)

1-6-Ezquerra-a 3.00

STAR WARS: OBSESSION (Clone Wars)
Dark Horse Comics: Nov, 2004 - No. 5, Apr, 2005 ($2.99, limited series)

1-5-Blackman-s/Ching-a/c; Anakin & Obi-Wan 5 months before Episode III 3.00
...: Clone Wars Vol. 7 (2005, $17.95) r/#1-5 and 2005 Free Comic Book Day edition 18.00

STAR WARS: PURGE
Dark Horse Comics: Dec, 2005 ($2.99, one-shot)

nn-Vader vs. remaining Jedi one month after Episode III; Hughes-c/Wheatley-a 5.00
... - Seconds To Die (11/09, $3.50) Vader app.; Charest-c/Ostrander-s 3.50

STAR WARS: QUI-GON & OBI-WAN - LAST STAND ON ORD MANTELL
Dark Horse Comics: Dec, 2000 - No. 3, Mar, 2001 ($2.99, limited series)

1-3: 1-Three covers (photo, Tony Daniel, Bachs) Windham-s 3.00

STAR WARS: QUI-GON & OBI-WAN - THE AURORIENT EXPRESS
Dark Horse Comics: Feb, 2002 - No. 2, Mar, 2002 ($2.99, limited series)

1,2-Six years prior to Phantom Menace; Marangon-a 3.00

STAR WARS: REBELLION (Also see Star Wars: Knights of the Old Republic flip book)
Dark Horse Comics: Apr, 2006 - Present ($2.99)

1-16-Takes place 9 months after Episode IV; Luke Skywalker app. 1-Badeaux-a/c 3.00
Vol. 1 TPB (2/07, $14.95) r/#0 (flip book) & #1-5 15.00

STAR WARS: REPUBLIC (Formerly Star Wars monthly series)
Dark Horse Comics: No. 46, Sept, 2002 - No. 83, Feb, 2006 ($2.99)

46-83-Events of the Clone Wars 3.00
...: Clone Wars Vol. 1 (2003, $14.95) r/#46-50 15.00
...: Clone Wars Vol. 2 (2003, $14.95) r/#51-53 & Star Wars: Jedi - Shaak Ti 15.00
...: Clone Wars Vol. 3 (2004, $14.95) r/#55-59 15.00
...: Clone Wars Vol. 4 (2004, $16.95) r/#54, 63 & Star Wars: Jedi - Aayla Secura & Dooku 17.00
...: Clone Wars Vol. 5 (2004, $17.95) r/#60-62, 64 & Star Wars: Jedi - Yoda 17.00
...: Clone Wars Vol. 6 (2005, $17.95) r/#65-71 18.00
(Clone Wars Vol. 7 - see Star Wars: Obsession)
...: Clone Wars Vol. 8 (2006, $17.95) r/#72-78 18.00
...: Clone Wars Vol. 9 (2006, $17.95) r/#79-83 & Star Wars: Purge 18.00
...: Honor and Duty TPB (5/06, $12.95) r/#46-48,78 13.00

STAR WARS: RETURN OF THE JEDI (Movie)
Marvel Comics Group: Oct, 1983 - No. 4, Jan, 1984 (limited series)

	GD	VG	FN	VF	VF/NM	NM-
1-4-Williamson-p in all; r/Marvel Super Special #27	1	3	4	6	8	10
Oversized issue (1983, $2.95, 10-3/4x8-1/4", 68 pgs., cardboard-c)-r/#1-4	2	4	6	10	13	16

STAR WARS: RIVER OF CHAOS
Dark Horse Comics: June, 1995 - No. 4, Sept, 1995 ($2.95, limited series)

1-4: Louise Simonson scripts 3.00

STAR WARS: SHADOWS OF THE EMPIRE
Dark Horse Comics: May, 1996 - No. 6, Oct, 1996 ($2.95, limited series)

1-6: Story details events between The Empire Strikes Back & Return of the Jedi; Russell-a(i). 3.00

STAR WARS: SHADOWS OF THE EMPIRE - EVOLUTION
Dark Horse Comics: Feb, 1998 - No. 5, June, 1998 ($2.95, limited series)

1-5: Perry-s/Fegredo-c. 3.00

STAR WARS: SHADOW STALKER
Dark Horse Comics: Sept, 1997 ($2.95, one-shot)

nn-Windham-a. 3.00

STAR WARS: SPLINTER OF THE MIND'S EYE
Dark Horse Comics: Dec, 1995 - No. 4, June, 1996 ($2.50, limited series)

1-4: Adaption of Alan Dean Foster novel 3.00

STAR WARS: STARFIGHTER
Dark Horse Comics: Jan, 2002 - No. 3, March, 2002 ($2.99, limited series)

1-3-Williams & Gray-c 3.00

STAR WARS: TAG & BINK ARE DEAD
Dark Horse Comics: Oct, 2001 - No. 2, Nov, 2001($2.99, limited series)

1,2-Rubio-s 3.00
Star Wars: Tag & Bink Were Here TPB (11/06, $14.95) r/both SW: Tag & Bink series 15.00

STAR WARS: TAG & BINK II
Dark Horse Comics: Mar, 2006 - No. 2, Apr, 2006($2.99, limited series)

1-Tag & Bink invade Return of the Jedi; Rubio-s. 2-T&B as Jedi younglings during Ep II 3.00

STAR WARS TALES
Dark Horse Comics: Sept, 1999 - No. 24, Jun, 2005 ($4.95/$5.95/$5.99, anthology)

1-4-Short stories by various 5.00
5-24 ($5.95/$5.99-c) Art and photo-c on each 6.00
Volume 1-6 ($19.95) 1-(1/02) r/#1-4. 2-('02) r/#5-8. 3-(1/03) r/#9-12. 4-(1/04) r/#13-16 5-(1/05) r/#17-20; introduction pages from #1-20. 6-(1/06) r/#21-24 20.00

STAR WARS: TALES - A JEDI'S WEAPON (See Promotional Comics section)

STAR WARS: TALES FROM MOS EISLEY
Dark Horse Comics: Mar, 1996 ($2.95, one-shot)

nn-Bret Blevins-a. 3.00

STAR WARS: TALES OF THE JEDI (See Dark Horse Comics #7)
Dark Horse Comics: Oct, 1993 - No. 5, Feb, 1994 ($2.50, limited series)

1-5: All have Dave Dorman painted-c. 3-r/Dark Horse Comics #7-9 w/new coloring & some panels redrawn 3.00
1-5-Gold foil embossed logo; limited # printed-7500 (set) 50.00
Star Wars Omnibus: Tales of the Jedi Volume One TPB (11/07, $24.95) r/#1-5, ... - The Golden Age of the Sith #0-5 and ... - The Fall of the Sith Empire #1-5 25.00

STAR WARS: TALES OF THE JEDI-DARK LORDS OF THE SITH
Dark Horse Comics: Oct, 1994 - No. 6, Mar, 1995 ($2.50, limited series)

1-6: 1-Polybagged w/trading card 3.00

STAR WARS: TALES OF THE JEDI-REDEMPTION
Dark Horse Comics: July, 1998 - No. 5, Nov, 1998 ($2.95, limited series)

1-5: 1-Kevin J. Anderson-s/Kordey-c 3.00

STAR WARS: TALES OF THE JEDI-THE FALL OF THE SITH EMPIRE
Dark Horse Comics: June, 1997 - No. 5, Oct, 1997 ($2.95, limited series)

1-5 3.00

STAR WARS: TALES OF THE JEDI-THE FREEDON NADD UPRISING
Dark Horse Comics: Aug, 1994 - No. 2, Nov, 1994 ($2.50, limited series)

1,2 3.00

STAR WARS: TALES OF THE JEDI-THE GOLDEN AGE OF THE SITH
Dark Horse Comics: July, 1996 - No. 5, Feb, 1997 (99¢/$2.95, limited series)

0-(99¢)-Anderson-s 3.00
1-5-Anderson-s 3.00

STAR WARS: TALES OF THE JEDI-THE SITH WAR
Dark Horse Comics: Aug, 1995 - No. 6, Jan, 1996 ($2.50, limited series)

1-6: Anderson scripts 3.00

STAR WARS: THE BOUNTY HUNTERS
Dark Horse Comics: July, 1999 - Oct, 1999 ($2.95, one-shots)

...Aurra Sing (7/99), ...Kenix Kil (10/99), ...Scoundrel's Wages (8/99) Lando Calrissian app. 3.00

STAR WARS: THE CLONE WARS (Based on the Cartoon Network series)
Dark Horse Comics: Sept, 2008 - Present ($2.99)

1-12: 1-6-Gilroy-s/Hepburn-a/Filoni-c 3.00

STAR WARS: THE FORCE UNLEASHED (Based on the LucasArts video game)
Dark Horse Comics: Aug, 2008 ($15.95, one-shot graphic novel)

GN-Intro. Starkiller, Vader's apprentice; takes place 2 years before Battle of Yavin 16.00

STAR WARS: THE JABBA TAPE
Dark Horse Comics: Dec, 1998 ($2.95, one-shot)

nn-Wagner-s/Plunkett-a 3.00

STAR WARS: THE LAST COMMAND
Dark Horse Comics: Nov, 1997 - No. 6, July, 1998 ($2.95, limited series)

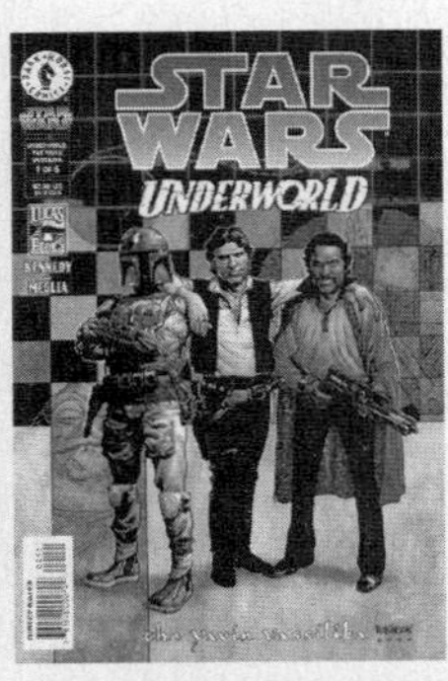

Star Wars: Underworld #1 © Lucasfilm

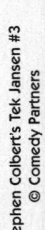

Stephen Colbert's Tek Jansen #3 © Comedy Partners

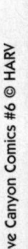

Steve Canyon Comics #6 © HARV

	GD	VG	FN	VF	VF/NM	NM-
	2.0	4.0	6.0	8.0	9.0	9.2

1-6:Based on the Timothy Zaun novel 4.00

STAR WARS: THE PROTOCOL OFFENSIVE
Dark Horse Comics: Sept, 1997 ($4.95, one-shot)
nn-Anthony Daniels & Ryder Windham-s 5.00

STAR WARS: UNDERWORLD - THE YAVIN VASSILIKA
Dark Horse Comics: Dec, 2000 - No. 5, June, 2001 ($2.99, limited series)
1-5-(Photo and Robinson covers) 3.00

STAR WARS: UNION
Dark Horse Comics: Nov, 1999 - No. 4, Feb, 2000 ($2.95, limited series)
1-4-Wedding of Luke and Mara Jade; Teranishi-a/Stackpole-s 3.00

STAR WARS: VADER'S QUEST
Dark Horse Comics: Feb, 1999 - No. 4, May, 1999 ($2.95, limited series)
1-4-Follows destruction of 1st Death Star; Gibbons-a 3.00

STAR WARS: VISIONARIES
Dark Horse Comics: Apr, 2005 ($17.95, TPB)
nn-Short stories from the concept artists for Revenge of the Sith movie 18.00

STAR WARS: X-WING ROGUE SQUADRON (Star Wars: X-Wing Rogue Squadron-The Phantom Affair #5-8 appears on cover only)
Dark Horse Comics: July, 1995 - No. 35, Nov, 1998 ($2.95)
1/2 8.00
1-24,26-35: 1-4-Baron scripts. 5-20-Stackpole scripts 3.00
25-($3.95) 4.00
The Phantom Affair TPB ($12.95) r/#5-8 13.00

STAR WARS: X-WING ROGUE SQUADRON: ROGUE LEADER
Dark Horse Comics: Sept, 2005 - No. 3, Nov, 2005 ($2.99)
1-3-Takes place one week after the Batttle of Endor 3.00

S.T.A.T.
Majestic Entertainment: Dec, 1993 ($2.25)
1 2.50

STATIC (Also see Eclipse Monthly)
Charlton Comics: No, 11, Oct, 1985 - No. 12, Dec, 1985
11,12-Ditko-c/a; low print run 6.00

STATIC (See Heroes)
DC Comics (Milestone): June, 1993 - No. 45, Mar, 1997 ($1.50/$1.75/$2.50)
1-($2.95)-Collector's Edition; polybagged w/poster & trading card & backing board (direct sales only) 4.00
1-Platinum Edition with red background cover 5.00
1-24,26-45: 2-Origin. 8-Shadow War; Simonson silver ink-c. 14-($2.50, 52 pgs.)-Worlds Collide Pt. 14. 27-Kent Williams-c 2.50
25 ($3.95) 4.00
...: Trial by Fire (2000, $9.95) r/#1-4; Leon-c 10.00

STATIC SHOCK!: REBIRTH OF THE COOL (TV)
DC Comics: Jan, 2001 - No. 4, Sept, 2001 ($2.50, limited series)
1-4: McDuffie-s/Leon-c/a 2.50

STATIC-X
Chaos! Comics: Aug, 2002 ($5.99)
1-Polybagged with music CD; metal band as super-heroes; Pulido-s 6.00

STEAMPUNK
DC/WildStorm (Cliffhanger): Apr, 2000 - No. 12, Aug, 2002 ($2.50/$3.50)
Catechism (1/00) Prologue -Kelly-s/Bachalo-a 2.50
1-4,6-11: 4-Four covers by Bachalo, Madureira, Ramos, Campbell 2.50
5,12-($3.50) 3.50
...: Drama Obscura ('03, $14.95) r/#6-12 15.00
...: Manimatron ('01, $14.95) r/#1-5, Catechism, Idiosincratica 15.00

STEED AND MRS. PEEL (TV)(Also see The Avengers)
Eclipse Books/ ACME Press: 1990 - No. 3, 1991 ($4.95, limited series)
Books One - Three: Grant Morrison scripts 5.00

STEEL (Also see JLA)
DC Comics: Feb, 1994 - No. 52, July, 1998 ($1.50/$1.95/$2.50)
1-8,0,9-52: 1-From Reign of the Supermen storyline. 6,7-Worlds Collide Pt. 5 &12. 8-(9/94). 0-(10/94). 9-(11/94). 46-Superboy-c/app. 50-Millennium Giants x-over 2.50
Annual 1 (1994, $2.95)-Elseworlds story 3.00
Annual 2 (1995, $3.95)-Year One story 4.00
...Forging of a Hero TPB (1997, $19.95) r/ early app. 20.00

STEEL: THE OFFICIAL COMIC ADAPTION OF THE WARNER BROS. MOTION PICTURE
DC Comics: 1997 ($4.95, Prestige format, one-shot)
nn-Movie adaption; Bogdanove & Giordano-a 5.00

STEELGRIP STARKEY
Marvel Comics (Epic Comics): June, 1986 - No. 6, July, 1987 ($1.50, limited series, Baxter paper)
1-6 2.50

STEEL STERLING (Formerly Shield-Steel Sterling; see Blue Ribbon, Jackpot, Mighty Comics, Mighty Crusaders, Roly Poly & Zip Comics)
Archie Enterprises, Inc.: No. 4, Jan, 1984 - No. 7, July, 1984
4-7: 4-6-Kanigher-s; Barreto-a. 5,6-Infantino-a. 6-McWilliams-a 4.00

STEEL, THE INDESTRUCTIBLE MAN (See All-Star Squadron #8 and J.L. of A. Annual #2)
DC Comics: Mar, 1978 - No. 5, Oct-Nov, 1978

	GD	VG	FN	VF	VF/NM	NM-
1	2	4	6	8	10	12
2-5: 5-44 pgs.	1	2	3	4	5	7

STEELTOWN ROCKERS
Marvel Comics: Apr, 1987 - No. 6, Sept, 1990 ($1.00, limited series)
1-6: Small town teens form rock band 2.50

STEPHEN COLBERT'S TEK JANSEN (From the animated shorts on The Colbert Report)
Oni Press: July, 2007 - No. 5, Jan, 2009 ($3.99, limited series)
1-Chantier-a/Layman & Peyer-s; back-up story by Massey-s/Rodriguez-a; Chantier-c 4.00
1-Variant-c by John Cassaday 6.00
1-Second printing with flip book of Cassaday & Chantier covers 4.00
2-5: 2-(6/08) Flip book with covers by Rodriguez & Wagner. 3-Flip-c by Darwyn Cooke 4.00

STEVE AUSTIN (See Stone Cold Steve Austin)

STEVE CANYON (See Harvey Comics Hits #52)
Dell Publishing Co.: No. 519, 11/53 - No. No. 1033, 9/59 (All Milton Caniff-a except #519, 939, 1033)

	GD	VG	FN	VF	VF/NM	NM-
Four Color 519 (1, '53)	8	16	24	56	93	130
Four Color 578 (8/54), 641 (7/55), 737 (10/56), 804 (5/57), 939 (10/58), 1033 (9/59) (photo-c)	5	10	15	34	55	75

STEVE CANYON
Grosset & Dunlap: 1959 (6-3/4x9", 96 pgs., B&W, no text, hardcover)

	GD	VG	FN	VF	VF/NM	NM-
100100-Reprints 2 stories from strip (1953, 1957)	6	12	18	31	38	45
100100 (softcover edition)	5	10	15	24	30	35

STEVE CANYON COMICS
Harvey Publ.: Feb, 1948 - No. 6, Dec, 1948 (Strip reprints, No. 4,5: 52pgs.)

	GD	VG	FN	VF	VF/NM	NM-
1-Origin; has biography of Milton Caniff; Powell-a, 2 pgs.; Caniff-a	20	40	60	117	186	255
2-Caniff, Powell-a in #2-6	14	28	42	80	115	150
3-6: 6-Intro Madame Lynx-c/story	14	28	42	76	108	140

STEVE CANYON IN 3-D
Kitchen Sink Press: June, 1986 ($2.25, one-shot)
1-Contains unpublished story from 1954 5.00

STEVE DITKO'S STRANGE AVENGING TALES
Fantagraphics Books: Feb, 1997 ($2.95, B&W)
1-Ditko-c/s/a 3.00

STEVE DONOVAN, WESTERN MARSHAL (TV)
Dell Publishing Co.: No. 675, Feb, 1956 - No. 880, Feb, 1958 (All photo-c)

	GD	VG	FN	VF	VF/NM	NM-
Four Color 675-Kinstler-a	8	16	24	52	86	120
Four Color 768-Kinstler-a	6	12	18	43	69	95
Four Color 880	5	10	15	30	48	65

STEVE ROPER
Famous Funnies: Apr, 1948 - No. 5, Dec, 1948

	GD	VG	FN	VF	VF/NM	NM-
1-Contains 1944 daily newspaper-r	12	24	36	69	97	125
2	9	18	27	47	61	75
3-5	8	16	24	40	50	60

STEVE SAUNDERS SPECIAL AGENT (See Special Agent)

STEVE SAVAGE (See Captain...)

STEVE ZODIAC & THE FIRE BALL XL-5 (TV)
Gold Key: Jan, 1964

	GD	VG	FN	VF	VF/NM	NM-
10108-401 (#1)	8	16	24	52	86	120

STEVIE (Mazie's boy friend)(Also see Flat-Top, Mazie & Mortie)

Stone #2 © Haberlin & Portacio

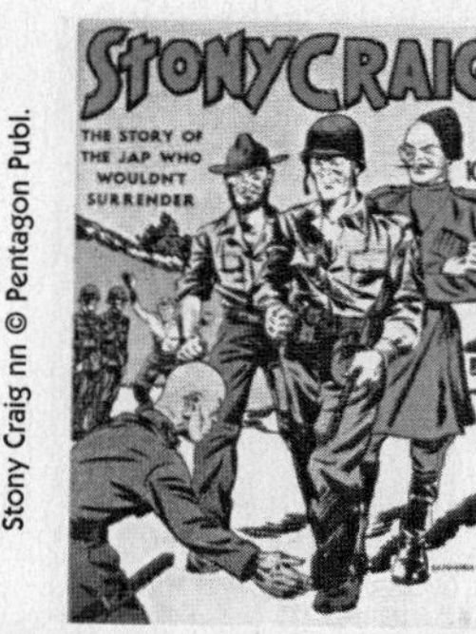

Stony Craig nn © Pentagon Publ.

Stormwatch #44 © WSP

GD 2.0 | VG 4.0 | FN 6.0 | VF 8.0 | VF/NM 9.0 | NM- 9.2

Mazie (Magazine Publ.): Nov, 1952 - No. 6, Apr, 1954
1-Teenage humor; Stevie, Mortie & Mazie begin 8 16 24 44 57 70
2-6 6 12 18 28 34 40

STEVIE MAZIE'S BOY FRIEND (See Harvey Hits #5)

STEWART THE RAT (See Eclipse Graphic Album Series)

ST. GEORGE (See listing under Saint...)

STIG'S INFERNO
Vortex/Eclipse: 1985 - No. 7, Mar, 1987 ($1.95, B&W)
1-7 ($1.95) 2.50
Graphic Album (1988, $6.95, B&W, 100 pgs.) 7.00

STING OF THE GREEN HORNET (See The Green Hornet)
Now Comics: June, 1992 - No. 4, 1992 ($2.50, limited series)
1-4: Butler-c/a 2.50
1-4 ($2.75)-Collectors Ed.; polybagged w/poster 3.00

STOKER'S DRACULA (Reprints unfinished Dracula story from 1974-75 with new ending)
Marvel Comics: 2004 - No. 4, May, 2005 ($3.99, B&W)
1-4: 1-Reprints from Dracula Lives! #5-8; Roy Thomas-s/Dick Giordano-a. 2-R/#10,11 & Legion of Monsters #1. 3,4-New story/artwork to finish story. 4-Giordano afterword 4.00
HC (2005, $24.99) r/#1-4; foreward by Thomas; Giordano afterword; bonus art & covers 25.00

STONE
Avalon Studios: Aug, 1998 - No. 4, Apr, 1999 ($2.50, limited series)
1-4-Portacio-a/Haberlin-s 2.50
1-Alternate-c 5.00
2-($14.95) DF Stonechrome Edition 15.00

STONE (Volume 2)
Avalon Studios: Aug, 1999 - No. 4, May, 2000 ($2.50)
1-4-Portacio-a/Haberlin-s 2.50
1-Chrome-c 5.00

STONE COLD STEVE AUSTIN (WWF Wrestling)
Chaos! Comics: Oct, 1999 - No. 4, Feb, 2000 ($2.95)
1-4-Reg. & photo-c; Steven Grant-s 3.00
1-Premium Ed. ($10.00) 10.00
Preview ($5.00) 5.00

STONE PROTECTORS
Harvey Pubications: May, 1994 - No. 3, Sept, 1994
nn (1993, giveaway)(limited distribution, scarce) 6.00
1-3-Ace Novelty action figures 4.00

STONEY BURKE (TV)
Dell Publishing Co.: June-Aug, 1963 - No. 2, Sept-Nov, 1963
1,2-Jack Lord photo-c on both 3 6 9 17 25 32

STONY CRAIG
Pentagon Publishing Co.: 1946 (No #)
nn-Reprints Bell Syndicate's "Sgt. Stony Craig" newspaper strips 8 16 24 40 50 60

STORIES BY FAMOUS AUTHORS ILLUSTRATED (Fast Fiction #1-5)
Seaboard Publ./Famous Authors Ill.: No. 6, Aug, 1950 - No. 13, Mar, 1951
1-Scarlet Pimpernel-Baroness Orczy 28 56 84 164 265 365
2-Capt. Blood-Raphael Sabatini 27 54 81 158 254 350
3-She, by Haggard 31 62 93 181 291 400
4-The 39 Steps-John Buchan 18 36 54 107 169 230
5-Beau Geste-P. C. Wren 18 36 54 107 169 230
NOTE: *The above five issues are exact reprints of Fast Fiction #1-5 except for the title change and new Kiefer covers on #1 and 2. Kiefer c(r)-3-5. The above 5 issues were released before Famous Authors #6.*
6-Macbeth, by Shakespeare; Kiefer art (8/50); used in **SOTI**, pg. 22,143; Kiefer-c; 36 pgs. 25 50 75 147 236 325
7-The Window; Kiefer-c/a; 52 pgs. 18 36 54 107 169 230
8-Hamlet, by Shakespeare; Kiefer-c/a; 36 pgs. 22 44 66 129 207 285
9,10: 9-Nicholas Nickleby, by Dickens; G. Schrotter-a; 52 pgs. 10-Romeo & Juliet, by Shakespeare; Kiefer-c/a; 36 pgs. 18 36 54 107 169 230
11-13: 11-Ben-Hur; Schrotter-a; 52 pgs. 12-La Svengali; Schrotter-a; 36 pgs. 13-Scaramouche; Kiefer-c/a; 36 pgs. 18 36 54 103 162 220
NOTE: *Artwork was prepared/advertised for #14, The Red Badge Of Courage. Gilberton bought out Famous Authors, Ltd. and used that story as C.I. #98. Famous Authors, Ltd. then published the Classics Junior series. The Famous Authors titles were published as part of the regular Classics Ill. Series in Brazil starting in 1952.*

STORIES FROM THE TWILIGHT ZONE
Skylark Pub: Mar, 1979, 68pgs. (B&W comic digest, 5-1/4x7-5/8")

GD 2.0 | VG 4.0 | FN 6.0 | VF 8.0 | VF/NM 9.0 | NM- 9.2

15405-2: Pfevfer-a, 56 pgs, new comics 3 6 9 18 27 35

STORIES OF ROMANCE (Formerly Meet Miss Bliss)
Atlas Comics (LMC): No. 5, Mar, 1956 - No. 13, Aug, 1957
5-Baker-a? 10 20 30 58 79 100
6-10,12,13 8 16 24 40 50 60
11-Baker, Romita-a; Colletta-c/a 10 20 30 54 72 90
NOTE: ***Ann Brewster** a-13. **Colletta** a-9(2), 11; c-5, 11.*

STORM
Marvel Comics: Feb, 1996 - No. 4, May, 1996 ($2.95, limited series)
1-4-Foil-c; Dodson-a(p); Ellis-s: 2-4-Callisto app. 3.50

STORM
Marvel Comics: Apr, 2006 - No. 6, Sept, 2006 ($2.99, limited series)
1-6: Ororo and T'Challa meet as teens; Eric Jerome Dickey-s 3.00
HC (2007, $19.99, dustjacket) r/#1-6 20.00
SC (2008, $14.99) r/#1-6 15.00

STORMBREAKER: THE SAGA OF BETA RAY BILL (Also see Thor)
Marvel Comics: Mar, 2005 - No. 6, Aug, 2005 ($2.99, limited series)
1-6-Oeming & Berman-s/DiVito-a; Galactus app. 6-Spider-Man app. 3.00
TPB (2006, $16.99) r/#1-6 17.00

STORMING PARADISE
DC Comics (WildStorm): Sept, 2008 - No. 6, Aug, 2009 ($2.99, limited series)
1-6-WW2 invasion of Japan; Dixon-s/Guice-a/c 3.00
TPB (2009, $19.99) r/#1-6 20.00

STORM SHADOW (G.I. Joe character)
Devil's Due Publishing: May, 2007 - No. 7, Nov, 2007 ($3.50)
1-7-Larry Hama-s 3.50

STORMWATCH (Also see The Authority)
Image Comics (WildStorm Prod.): May, 1993 - No. 50, Jul, 1997 ($1.95/$2.50)
1-8,0,9-36: 1-Intro StormWatch (Battalion, Diva, Winter, Fuji, & Hellstrike); 1st app. Weatherman; Jim Lee-c & part scripts; Lee plots in all. 1-Gold edition.1-3-Includes coupon for limited edition StormWatch trading card #00 by Lee. 3-1st brief app. Backlash. 0-($2.50)-Polybagged w/card; 1st full app. Backlash. 9-(4/94, $2.50)-Intro Defile. 10-(6/94),11,12-Both (8/94). 13,14-(9/94). 15-(10/94). 21-Reads #1 on-c. 22-Direct Market; Wildstorm Rising Pt. 9, bound-in card. 23-Spartan joins team. 25-(6/94, June 1995 on-c, $2.50). 35-Fire From Heaven Pt. 5. 36-Fire From Heaven Pt. 12 2.50
10-Alternate Portacio-c, see Deathblow #5 2.50
22-($1.95)-Newsstand, Wildstorm Rising Pt. 9 2.50
37-(7/96, $3.50, 38 pgs.)-Weatherman forms new team; 1st app. Jenny Sparks, Jack Hawksmoor & Rose Tattoo; Warren Ellis scripts begin; Justice League #1-c/swipe 3.50
38-49: 44-Three covers. 2.50
50-($4.50) 4.50
Special 1 ,2(1/94, 5/95, $3.50, 52 pgs.) 3.50
Sourcebook 1 (1/94, $2.50) 2.50
Forces of Nature ('99, $14.95, TPB) r/V1 #37-42 15.00
Lightning Strikes ('00, $14.95, TPB) r/V1 #43-47 15.00

STORMWATCH (Also see The Authority)
Image Comics (WildStorm): Oct, 1997 - No. 11, Sept, 1998 ($2.50)
1-Ellis-s/Jimenez-a(p); two covers by Bennett 2.50
1-($3.50)-Voyager Pack bagged w/Gen 13 preview 3.50
2-4: 4-1st app. Midnighter and Apollo 2.50
5-11: 7,8-Freefall app. 9-Gen13 & DV8 app. 2.50
A Finer World ('99, $14.95, TPB) r/V2 #4-9 15.00
Change or Die ('99, $14.95, TPB) r/V1 #48-50 & V2 #1-3 15.00
Final Orbit ('01, $9.95, TPB) r/V2 #10,11 & WildC.A.T.S./Aliens; Hitch-c 10.00

STORMWATCHER
Eclipse Comics (Acme Press): Apr, 1989 - No. 4, Dec, 1989 ($2.00, B&W)
1-4 2.50

STORMWATCH: P.H.D. (Post Human Division)
DC Comics (WildStorm): Jan, 2007 - No. 24, Jan, 2010 ($2.99)
1-24: 1-Two covers by Mahnke & Hairsine; Gage-s/Mahnke-a. 2-Var-c by Dell'Otto 3.00
...: Armageddon 1 (2/08, $2.99) Gage-s/Fernández-a/McKone-c 3.00
TPB (2007, $17.99) r/#1-4,6,7 & story from Worldstorm #1 18.00
... Book Two TPB (2008, $17.99) r/#5,8-12; sketch pages and concept art 18.00
... Book Three TPB (2009, $17.99) r/#13-19 18.00

STORMWATCH: TEAM ACHILLES
DC Comics (WildStorm): Sept, 2002 - No. 23, Aug, 2004 ($2.95)
1-8: 1-Two covers by Portacio; Portacio-a/Wright-s. 5,6-The Authority app. 3.00

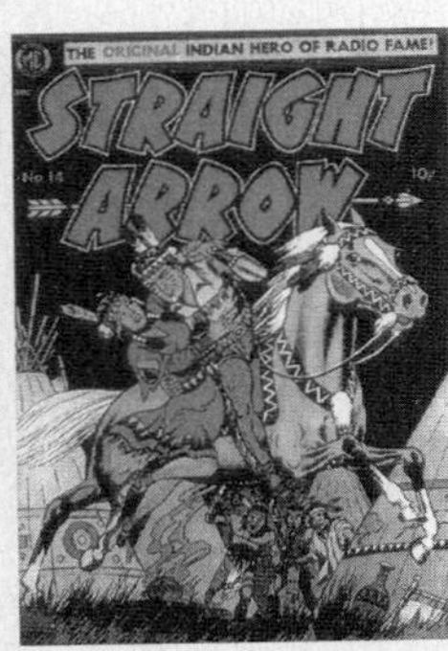

Straight Arrow #14 © ME

The Stranded #1 © Virgin Comics

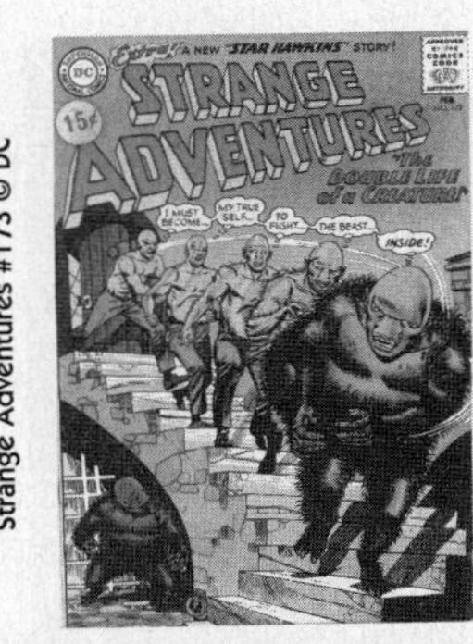

Strange Adventures #173 © DC

GD 2.0 | VG 4.0 | FN 6.0 | VF 8.0 | VF/NM 9.0 | NM- 9.2

GD 2.0 | VG 4.0 | FN 6.0 | VF 8.0 | VF/NM 9.0 | NM- 9.2

9-23: 9-Back-up preview of The Authority: High Stakes pt. 1 — 3.00
TPB (2003, $14.95) r/Wizard Preview and #1-6; Portacio art pages — 15.00
Book 2 (2004, $14.95) r/#7-11 & short story from Eye of the Storm Annual — 15.00

STORMY (Disney) (Movie)
Dell Publishing Co.: No. 537, Feb, 1954
Four Color 537 (...the Thoroughbred)-on top 2/3 of each page; Pluto story on bottom 1/3 — 5 10 15 30 48 65

STORY OF JESUS (See Classics Illustrated Special Issue)

STORY OF MANKIND, THE (Movie)
Dell Publishing Co.: No. 851, Jan, 1958
Four Color 851-Vincent Price/Hedy Lamarr photo-c — 7 14 21 47 76 105

STORY OF MARTHA WAYNE, THE
Argo Publ.: April, 1956
1-Newspaper strip-r — 6 12 18 29 36 42

STORY OF RUTH, THE
Dell Publishing Co.: No. 1144, Nov-Jan, 1961 (Movie)
Four Color 1144-Photo-c — 8 16 24 58 97 135

STORY OF THE COMMANDOS, THE (Combined Operations)
Long Island Independent: 1943 (15¢, B&W, 68 pgs.) (Distr. by Gilberton)
nn-All text (no comics); photos & illustrations; ad for Classic Comics on back cover (Rare) — 32 64 96 188 307 425

STORY OF THE GLOOMY BUNNY, THE (See March of Comics #9)

STRAIGHT ARROW (Radio)(See Best of the West & Great Western)
Magazine Enterprises: Feb-Mar, 1950 - No. 55, Mar, 1956 (All 36 pgs.)
1-Straight Arrow (alias Steve Adams) & his palomino Fury begin; 1st mention of Sundown Valley & the Secret Cave — 46 92 138 290 488 685
2-Red Hawk begins (1st app?) by Powell (origin), ends #55 — 23 46 69 136 223 310
3-Frazetta-c — 31 62 93 182 296 410
4,5: 4-Secret Cave-c — 21 42 63 122 199 275
6-10 — 17 34 51 100 158 215
11-Classic story "The Valley of Time", with an ancient civilization made of gold — 22 44 66 128 209 290
12-19 — 14 28 42 82 121 160
20-Origin Straight Arrow's Shield — 16 32 48 92 144 195
21-Origin Fury — 19 38 57 109 172 235
22-Frazetta-c — 25 50 75 147 241 335
23,25-30: 25-Secret Cave-c. 28-Red Hawk meets The Vikings — 11 22 33 62 86 110
24-Classic story "The Dragons of Doom!" with prehistoric pteradactyls — 14 28 42 82 121 160
31-38: 36-Red Hawk drug story by Powell — 10 20 30 54 72 90
39-Classic story "The Canyon Beast", with a dinosaur egg hatching a Tyranosaurus Rex — 14 28 42 76 108 140
40-Classic story "Secret of The Spanish Specters", with Conquistadors' lost treasure — 11 22 33 64 90 115
41,42,44-54: 45-Secret Cave-c — 9 18 27 50 65 80
43-Intro & 1st app. Blaze, S. Arrow's Warrior dog — 10 20 30 58 79 100
55-Last issue — 11 22 33 62 86 110
NOTE: ***Fred Meagher** a 1-55; c-1, 2, 4-21, 23-55. **Powell** a 2-55. **Whitney** a-1. Many issues advertise the radio premiums associated with Straight Arrow.*

STRAIGHT ARROW'S FURY (Also see A-1 Comics)
Magazine Enterprises: No. 119, 1954 (one-shot)
A-1 119-Origin; Fred Meagher-c/a — 15 30 45 85 130 175

STRANDED
Virgin Comics: Dec, 2007 - No. 5, June, 2008 ($2.99)
1-5-Carey-s/Kotian-a. 1-Silvestri-c. 2-5-Moeller-c — 3.00

STRANGE (Tales You'll Never Forget)
Ajax-Farrell Publ. (Four Star Comic Corp.): March, 1957 - No. 6, May, 1958
1 — 21 42 63 122 199 275
2-Censored r/Haunted Thrills — 13 26 39 74 105 135
3-6 — 10 20 30 56 76 95

STRANGE (Dr. Strange)
Marvel Comics (Marvel Knghts): Nov, 2004 - No. 6, July, 2005 ($3.50)
1-6-Straczynski & Barnes-s/Peterson-a; Dr. Strange's origin retold — 3.50
...: Beginnings and Endings TPB (2006, $17.99) r/#1-6 — 18.00

STRANGE (Dr. Strange)
Marvel Comics: Jan, 2010 - No. 4, Apr, 2010 ($3.99, limited series)
1-4-Waid-s/Rios-a/Coker-c — 4.00

STRANGE ADVENTURES
DC Comics: July/Aug 1950
nn - Ashcan comic, not distributed to newsstands, only for in-house use. Cover art is All Star Comics #47 with interior being Detective Comics #140. A second example has the interior of Detective Comics #146. A third example has an unidentified issue of Detective Comics as the interior. This is the only ashcan with multiple interiors. A FN+ copy sold for $1,000 in 2007.

STRANGE ADVENTURES
National Periodical Publ.: Aug-Sept, 1950 - No. 244, Oct-Nov, 1973 (No. 1-12: 52 pgs.)
1-Adaptation of "Destination Moon"; preview of movie w/photo-c from movie (also see Fawcett Movie Comic #2); adapt. of Edmond Hamilton's "Chris KL-99" in #1-3; Darwin Jones begins — 227 454 681 1986 3943 5900
2 — 102 204 306 867 1709 2550
3,4 — 71 142 213 604 1190 1775
5-8,10: 7-Origin Kris KL-99 — 61 122 183 519 1022 1525
9-(6/51)-Origin/1st app. Captain Comet (c/story) — 142 284 426 1207 2379 3550
11-20: 12,13,17,18-Toth-a. 14-Robot-c — 40 80 120 320 623 925
21-30: 28-Atomic explosion panel. 30-Robot-c — 33 66 99 254 495 735
31,34-38 — 31 62 93 236 456 675
32,33-Krigstein-a — 31 62 93 239 462 685
39-Ill. in **SOTI** "Treating police contemptuously" (top right) — 35 70 105 271 523 775
40-49-Last Capt. Comet; not in 45,47,48 — 30 60 90 228 439 650
50-53-Last precode issue (2/55) — 22 44 66 157 304 450
54-70 — 17 34 51 119 230 340
71-99 — 14 28 42 97 181 265
100 — 15 30 45 104 197 290
101-110: 104-Space Museum begins by Sekowsky — 11 22 33 78 139 200
111-116,118,119: 114-Star Hawkins begins, ends #185; Heath-a in Wood E.C. style — 11 22 33 74 132 190
117-(6/60)-Origin/1st app. Atomic Knights. — 47 94 141 376 726 1075
120-2nd app. Atomic Knights — 22 44 66 157 304 450
121,122,125,127,128,130,131,133,134: 134-Last 10¢ issue — 10 20 30 67 116 165
123,126-3rd & 4th app. Atomic Knights — 13 26 39 93 172 250
124-Intro/origin Faceless Creature — 10 20 30 73 129 185
129,132,135,138,141,147-Atomic Knights app. — 10 20 30 73 129 185
136,137,139,140,143,145,146,148,149,151,152,154,155,157-159: 159-Star Rovers app.; Gil Kane/Anderson-a. — 8 16 24 52 86 120
142-2nd app. Faceless Creature — 9 18 27 60 100 140
144-Only Atomic Knights-c (by M. Anderson) — 11 22 33 78 139 200
150,153,156,160: Atomic Knights in each. 153-(6/63)-3rd app. Faceless Creature; atomic explosion-c. 160-Last Atomic Knights — 8 16 24 58 97 135
161-179: 161-Last Space Museum. 163-Star Rovers app. 170-Infinity-c. 177-Intro/origin Immortal Man — 6 12 18 43 69 95
180-Origin/1st app. Animal Man — 16 32 48 113 217 320
181-183,185-189: 187-Intro/origin The Enchantress — 6 12 18 37 59 80
184-2nd app. Animal Man by Gil Kane — 10 20 30 73 129 185
190-1st app. Animal Man in costume — 13 26 39 90 165 240
191-194,196-200,202-204 — 5 10 15 32 51 70
195-1st full app. Animal Man — 7 14 21 50 83 115
201-Last Animal Man; 2nd full app. — 6 12 18 41 66 90
205-(10/67)-Intro/origin Deadman by Infantino & begin series, ends #216 — 14 28 42 97 181 265
206-Neal Adams-a begins — 11 22 33 74 132 190
207-210 — 10 20 30 67 116 165
211-216: 211-Space Museum-r. 216-(1-2/69)-Deadman story finally concludes in Brave & the Bold #86 (10-11/69); secret message panel by Neal Adams (pg. 13); tribute to Steranko — 9 18 27 60 100 140
217-r/origin & 1st app. Adam Strange from Showcase #17, begin-r; Atomic Knights-r begin — 3 6 9 16 22 28
218-221,223-225: 218-Last 12¢ issue. 225-Last 15¢ issue — 3 6 9 14 19 24
222-New Adam Strange story; Kane/Anderson-a — 3 6 9 20 30 40
226,227,230-236-(68-52 pgs.): 226, 227-New Adam Strange text story w/illos by Anderson (8,6 pgs.) 231-Last Atomic Knights-r. 235-JLA-c/s — 3 6 9 14 19 24
228,229 (68 pgs.) — 3 6 9 16 23 30
237-243 — 2 4 6 9 13 16
244-Last issue — 2 4 6 10 14 18
NOTE: ***Neal Adams** a-206-216; c-207-218, 228, 235. **Anderson** a-8-52, 94, 96, 99, 115, 117, 119-163, 217r, 218r, 222, 223-225r, 226, 229r, 242i(r); c-18, 19, 21, 23, 24, 27, 30, 32-44(most); c/r-157i, 190i, 217-224, 228-231, 233, 235-239, 241-243. **Ditko** a-188, 189. **Drucker** a-42, 43, 45. **Elias** a-212. **Finlay** a-2, 3, 6, 7, 210r, 229r.*

Strange Adventures (2009 series) #2 © DC

Strange Fantasy #5 © AJAX

Strange Mysteries #12 © SUPR

GD 2.0 | VG 4.0 | FN 6.0 | VF 8.0 | VF/NM 9.0 | NM- 9.2

Giunta a-237r. Heath a-116. Infantino a-10-101, 106-151, 154, 157-163, 180, 190, 218-221r, 223-244p(r); c-50; c(r)-190p, 197, 199-211, 218-221, 223-244. Kaluta c-238, 240. Gil Kane a-8-116, 124, 125, 130, 138, 146-157, 173-186, 204r, 222r, 227-231r; c(p)-11-17, 25, 154, 157. Kubert a-55(2 pgs.), 226; c-219, 220, 225-227, 232, 234. Moreira c-26, 28, 29, 71. Morrow c-230. Mortimer c-8. Powell a-4. Sekowsky a-71p, 97-162p, 217p(r), 218p(r); c-206, 217-219r. Simon & Kirby a-2r (2 pgs) Sparling a-201. Toth a-8, 12, 13, 17-19. Wood a-154i. Atomic Knights in #117, 120, 123, 126, 129, 132, 135, 138, 141, 144, 147, 150, 153, 156, 160. Atomic Knights reprints by Anderson in 217-221, 223-231. Chris KL99 in 1-3, 5, 7, 9, 11, 15. Capt. Comet covers-9-14, 17-19, 24, 26, 27, 32-44.

STRANGE ADVENTURES
DC Comics (Vertigo): Nov, 1999 - No. 4, Feb, 2000 ($2.50, limited series)
1-4: 1-Bolland-c; art by Bolland, Gibbons, Quitely 2.50

STRANGE ADVENTURES
DC Comics: May, 2009 - No. 8, Dec, 2009 ($3.99, limited series)
1-8: 1-Starlin-s in all; Adam Strange, Capt. Comet, Bizarro & Prince Gavyn app. 4.00

STRANGE AS IT SEEMS (See Famous Funnies-A Carnival of Comics, Feature Funnies #1, The John Hix Scrap Book & Peanuts)

STRANGE AS IT SEEMS
United Features Syndicate: 1939
Single Series 9, 1, 2 34 68 102 199 325 450

STRANGE ATTRACTORS
RetroGraphix: 1993 - No. 15, Feb, 1997 ($2.50, B&W)
1-15: 1-(5/93), 2-(8/93), 3-(11/93), 4-(2/94) 2.50
Volume One-($14.95, trade paperback)-r/#1-7 15.00

STRANGE ATTRACTORS: MOON FEVER
Caliber Comics: Feb, 1997 - No. 3, June, 1997 ($2.95, B&W, mini-series)
1-3 3.00

STRANGE COMBAT TALES
Marvel Comics (Epic Comics): Oct, 1993 - No. 4, Jan, 1994 ($2.50, limited series)
1-4 2.50

STRANGE CONFESSIONS
Ziff-Davis Publ. Co.: Jan-Mar (Spring on-c), 1952 - No. 4, Fall, 1952 (All have photo-c)
1(Scarce)-Kinstler-a 53 106 159 334 567 800
2(Scarce, 7-8/52) 38 76 114 226 368 510
3(Scarce, 9-10/52)-#3 on-c, #2 on inside; Reformatory girl story; photo-c 37 74 111 222 361 500
4(Scarce) 35 70 105 208 339 470

STRANGE DAYS
Eclipse Comics: Oct, 1984 - No. 3, Apr, 1985 ($1.75, Baxter paper)
1-3: Freakwave, Johnny Nemo, & Paradax from Vanguard Illustrated; nudity, violence & strong language 2.50

STRANGE DAYS (Movie)
Marvel Comics: Dec, 1995 ($5.95, squarebound, one-shot)
1-Adaptation of film 6.00

STRANGE FANTASY (Eerie Tales of Suspense!)(Formerly Rocketman #1)
Ajax-Farrell: Aug, 1952 - No. 14, Oct-Nov, 1954
2(#1, 8/52)-Jungle Princess story; Kamenish-a; reprinted from Ellery Queen #1 47 94 141 296 498 700
2(10/52)-No Black Cat or Rulah; Bakerish, Kamenish-a; hypo/meathook-c 42 84 126 265 445 625
3-Rulah story, called Pulah 39 78 117 240 395 550
4-Rocket Man app. (2/53) 38 76 114 226 368 510
5,6,8,10,12,14 27 54 81 160 263 365
7-Madam Satan/Slave story 38 76 114 226 368 510
9(w/Black Cat), 9(w/Boy's Ranch; S&K-a), 9(w/War)(A rebinding of Harvey interiors; not publ. by Ajax) 34 68 102 199 325 450
9-Regular issue; Steve Ditko's 3rd published work (tied with Captain 3D) 46 92 138 290 488 685
11-Jungle story 35 70 105 208 339 470
13-Bondage-c; Rulah (Kolah) story 35 70 105 208 339 470

STRANGE GALAXY
Eerie Publications: V1#8, Feb, 1971 - No. 11, Aug, 1971 (B&W, magazine)
V1#8-Reprints-c/Fantastic V19#3 (2/70) (a pulp) 4 8 12 22 34 45
9-11 3 6 9 18 27 35

STRANGE GIRL
Image Comics: June, 2005 - No. 18, Sept, 2007 ($2.95/$2.99/$3.50)
1-12: 1-Rick Remender-s/Eric Nguyen-a 3.00
13-18-($3.50) 3.50
... Vol. 1: Girl Afraid TPB (2005, $12.99) r/#1-4; sketch pages and pin-ups 13.00

STRANGE JOURNEY
America's Best (Steinway Publ.) (Ajax/Farrell): Sept, 1957 - No. 4, Jun, 1958 (Farrell reprints)
1 20 40 60 114 182 250
2-4: 2-Flying saucer-c. 3-Titanic-c 15 30 45 83 124 165

STRANGE LOVE (See Fox Giants)

STRANGE MYSTERIES
Superior/Dynamic Publications: Sept, 1951 - No. 21, Jan, 1955
1-Kamenish-a & horror stories begin 66 132 198 419 722 1025
2 38 76 114 226 368 510
3-5 35 70 105 208 339 470
6-8 31 62 93 182 296 410
9-Bondage 3-D effect-c 37 74 111 222 361 500
10-Used in **SOTI**, pg. 181 28 56 84 165 270 375
11-18 23 46 69 136 223 310
19-r/Journey Into Fear #1; cover is a splash from one story; Baker-r(2) 24 48 72 142 234 325
20,21-Reprints; 20-r/#1 with new-c 18 36 54 105 165 225

STRANGE MYSTERIES
I. W. Enterprises/Super Comics: 1963 - 1964
I.W. Reprint #9; Rulah-r/Spook #28; Disbrow-a 3 6 9 20 30 40
Super Reprint #10-12,15-17(1963-64): 10,11-r/Strange #2,1. 12-r/Tales of Horror #5 (3/53) less-c. 15-r/Dark Mysteries #23. 16-r/The Dead Who Walk. 17-r/Dark Mysteries #22 3 6 9 20 30 40
Super Reprint #18-r/Witchcraft #1; Kubert-a 3 6 9 20 30 40

STRANGE PLANETS
I. W. Enterprises/Super Comics: 1958; 1963-64
I.W. Reprint #1(nd)-Reprints E. C. Incredible S/F #30 plus-c/Strange Worlds #3 6 12 18 39 62 85
I.W. Reprint #9-Orlando/Wood-r/Strange Worlds #4; cover-r from Flying Saucers #1 7 14 21 49 80 110
Super Reprint #10-Wood-r (22 pg.) from Space Detective #1; cover-r/Attack on Planet Mars 7 14 21 49 80 110
Super Reprint #11-Wood-r (25 pg.) from An Earthman on Venus 8 16 24 54 90 125
Super Reprint #12-Orlando-r/Rocket to the Moon 7 14 21 49 80 110
Super Reprint #15-Reprints Journey Into Unknown Worlds #8; Heath, Colan-r 4 8 12 28 44 60
Super Reprint #16-Reprints Avon's Strange Worlds #6; Kinstler, Check-a 5 10 15 30 48 65
Super Reprint #18-r/Great Exploits #1 (Daring Adventures #6); Space Busters, Explorer Joe, The Son of Robin Hood; Krigstein-a 4 8 12 24 37 50

STRANGERS
Image Comics: Mar, 2003 - No. 6, Sept, 2003 ($2.95)
1-6-Randy & Jean-Marc Lofficier-s; two covers. 2-Nexus back-up story 3.00

STRANGERS, THE
Malibu Comics (Ultraverse): June, 1993 - No. 24, May, 1995 ($1.95/$2.50)
1-4,6-12,14-20: 1-1st app. The Strangers; has coupon for Ultraverse Premiere #0; 1st app. the Night Man (not in costume). 2-Polybagged w/trading card. 7-Break-Thru x-over. 8-2 pg. origin Solution. 12-Silver foil logo; wraparound-c. 17-Rafferty app. 2.50
1-With coupon missing 2.50
1-Full cover holographic edition, 1st of kind w/Hardcase #1 & Prime #1 6.00
1-Ultra 5000 limited silver foil 4.00
4-($2.50)-Newsstand edition bagged w/card 2.50
5-($2.50, 52 pgs.)-Rune flip-c/story by B. Smith (3 pgs.); The Mighty Magnor 1 pg. strip by Aragones; 3-pg. Night Man preview 2.50
13-($3.50, 68 pgs.)-Mantra app.; flip book w/Ultraverse Premiere #4 3.50
21-24 ($2.50) 2.50
...:The Pilgrim Conundrum Saga (1/95, $3.95, 68pgs.) 4.00

STRANGERS IN PARADISE
Antarctic Press: Nov, 1993 - No. 3, Feb, 1994 ($2.75, B&W, limited series)
1 5 10 15 30 48 65
1-2nd/3rd prints 1 2 3 5 6 8
2 (2300 printed) 4 8 12 22 34 45
3 3 6 9 16 23 30
Trade paperback (Antarctic Press, $6.95)-Red -c (5000 print run) 10.00
Trade paperback (Abstract Studios, $6.95)-Red-c (2000 print run) 15.00
Trade paperback (Abstract Studios, $6.95, 1st-4th printing)-Blue- 7.00

Strangers in Paradise (2nd series) #4 © Terry Moore

Strange Stories of Suspense #9 © MAR

Strange Tales #15 © MAR

	GD 2.0	VG 4.0	FN 6.0	VF 8.0	VF/NM 9.0	NM- 9.2
Hardcover ('98, $29.95) includes first draft pages						30.00
Gold Reprint Series ($2.75) 1-3-r/#1-3						2.75

STRANGERS IN PARADISE
Abstract Studios: Sept, 1994 - No. 14, July, 1996 ($2.75, B&W)

	GD 2.0	VG 4.0	FN 6.0	VF 8.0	VF/NM 9.0	NM- 9.2
1	2	4	6	9	13	16
1,3- 2nd printings						4.00
2,3: 2-Color dream sequence	1	2	3	5	6	8
4-10						4.00
4-6-2nd printings						2.75
11-14: 14-The Letters of Molly & Poo						3.00
Gold Reprint Series ($2.75) 1-13-r/#1-13						2.75
I Dream Of You ($16.95, TPB) r/#1-9						17.00
It's a Good Life ($8.95, TPB) r/#10-13						9.00

STRANGERS IN PARADISE (Volume Three)
Homage Comics #1-8/Abstract Studios #9-on: Oct, 1996 - No. 90, May, 2007 ($2.75-$2.99, color #1-5, B&W #6-on)

	GD 2.0	VG 4.0	FN 6.0	VF 8.0	VF/NM 9.0	NM- 9.2
1-Terry Moore-c/s/a in all; dream seq. by Jim Lee-a						4.00
1-Jim Lee variant-c	1	2	3	6	7	8
2-5						3.50
6-16: 6-Return to B&W. 13-15-High school flashback. 16-Xena Warrior Princess parody; two covers						3.00
17-89: 33-Color issue. 46-Molly Lane. 49-Molly & Poo. 86-David dies						3.00
90-Last issue; 3 covers of Katchoo, Francine and David forming a triptych						3.00
...Lyrics and Poems (2/99)						2.75
...Source Book (2003, $2.95) Background on characters & story arcs, checklists						3.00
Brave New World ('02, $8.95, TPB) r/#44,45,47,48						9.00
Child of Rage ($15.95, TPB) r/#31-38						16.00
David's Story (6/04, $8.95, TPB) r/#61-63						9.00
Ever After ('07, $15.95, TPB) r/#83-90						16.00
Flower to Flame ('03, $15.95, TPB) r/#55-60						16.00
Heart in Hand ('03, $12.95, TPB) r/#50-54						13.00
High School ('98, $8.95, TPB) r/#13-16						9.00
Immortal Enemies ('98, $14.95, TPB) r/#6-12						15.00
Love & Lies (2006, $14.95, TPB)r/#77-82						15.00
Love Me Tender ($12.95, TPB) r/#1-5 in B&W w/ color Lee seq.						13.00
Molly & Poo (2005, $8.95, TPB)r/#46,49,73						9.00
My Other Life ($14.95, TPB) r/#25-30						15.00
Pocket Book 1-5 ($17.95, 5 1/2" x 8", TPB) 1-r/Vol.1 & 2. 2-r/#1-17 in B&W. 3-r/#18-24,26-32,34-38. 4-r/#41-45,47,48,50-60. 5-r/#46,49,61-76						18.00
Sanctuary ($15.95, TPB) r/#17-24						16.00
Tattoo ($14.95, TPB) r/#70-76; sketch pages and fan tattoo photos						15.00
Tomorrow Now (11/04, $14.95, TPB) r/#64-69						15.00
Tropic of Desire ($12.95, TPB) r/#39-43						13.00
The Complete... : Volume 3 Part 1 HC ($49.95) r/#1-12						50.00
The Complete... : Volume 3 Part 2 HC ($49.95) r/#13-15,17-25						50.00
The Complete... : Volume 3 Part 3 HC ('01, $49.95) r/#26-38						50.00
The Complete... : Volume 3 Part 4 HC ('02, $39.95) r/#39-46,49						40.00
The Complete... : Volume 3 Part 5 HC ('03, $49.95) r/#47,48,50-57						50.00
The Complete... : Volume 3 Part 6 HC ('04, $49.95) r/#58-69						50.00
The Complete... : Volume 3 Part 7 HC ('06, $49.95) r/#70-80						50.00

STRANGE SPORTS STORIES (See Brave & the Bold #45-49, DC Special, and DC Super Stars #10)
National Periodical Publications: Sept-Oct, 1973 - No. 6, July-Aug, 1974

	GD 2.0	VG 4.0	FN 6.0	VF 8.0	VF/NM 9.0	NM- 9.2
1	3	6	9	16	23	30
2-6: 2-Swan/Anderson-a	2	4	6	9	13	16

STRANGE STORIES FROM ANOTHER WORLD (Unknown World #1)
Fawcett Publications: No. 2, Aug, 1952 - No. 5, Feb, 1953

	GD 2.0	VG 4.0	FN 6.0	VF 8.0	VF/NM 9.0	NM- 9.2
2-Saunders painted-c	50	100	150	315	533	750
3-5-Saunders painted-c	39	78	117	240	395	550

STRANGE STORIES OF SUSPENSE (Rugged Action #1-4)
Atlas Comics (CSI): No. 5, Oct, 1955 - No. 16, Aug, 1957

	GD 2.0	VG 4.0	FN 6.0	VF 8.0	VF/NM 9.0	NM- 9.2
5(#1)	40	80	120	246	411	575
6,9	25	50	75	150	245	340
7-E. C. swipe cover/Vault of Horror #32	26	52	78	154	252	350
8-Morrow/Williamson-a; Pakula-a	27	54	81	160	263	365
10-Crandall, Torres, Meskin-a	26	52	78	154	252	350
11-13: 12-Torres, Pakula-a. 13-E.C. art swipes	21	42	63	126	206	285
14-16: 14-Williamson/Mayo-a. 15-Krigstein-a. 16-Fox, Powell-a	23	46	69	136	223	310

NOTE: ***Everett** a-6, 7, 13; c-8, 9, 11-14. **Forte** a-12, 16. **Heath** a-5. **Maneely** c-5. **Morisi** a-11. **Morrow** a-13. **Powell** a-8. **Sale** a-11. **Severin** c-7. **Wildey** a-14.*

STRANGE STORY (Also see Front Page)
Harvey Publications: June-July, 1946 (52 pgs.)

	GD 2.0	VG 4.0	FN 6.0	VF 8.0	VF/NM 9.0	NM- 9.2
1-The Man in Black Called Fate by Powell	32	64	96	188	307	425

STRANGE SUSPENSE STORIES (Lawbreakers Suspense Stories #10-15; This Is Suspense #23-26; Captain Atom V1#78 on)
Fawcett Publications/Charlton Comics No. 16 on: 6/52 - No. 5, 2/53; No. 16, 1/54 - No. 22, 11/54; No. 27, 10/55 - No. 77, 10/65; V3#1, 10/67 - V1#9, 9/69

	GD 2.0	VG 4.0	FN 6.0	VF 8.0	VF/NM 9.0	NM- 9.2
1-(Fawcett)-Powell, Sekowsky-a	82	164	246	528	902	1275
2-George Evans horror story	48	96	144	302	514	725
3-5 (2/53)-George Evans horror stories	40	80	120	246	411	575
16(1-2/54)-Formerly Lawbreakers S.S.	29	58	87	172	281	390
17,21: 21-Shuster-a	23	46	69	136	223	310
18-E.C. swipe/HOF 7; Ditko-c/a(2)	39	78	117	240	395	550
19-Ditko electric chair-c; Ditko-a	53	106	159	334	567	800
20-Ditko-c/a(2)	39	78	117	240	395	550
22(11/54)-Ditko-c, Shuster-a; last pre-code issue; becomes This Is Suspense	36	72	108	211	343	475
27(10/55)-(Formerly This Is Suspense #26)	15	30	45	86	133	180
28-30,38	12	24	36	69	97	125
31-33,35,37,40-Ditko-c/a(2-3 each)	21	42	63	126	206	285
34-Story of ruthless business man, Wm. B. Gaines; Ditko-c/a	47	94	141	296	498	700
36-(15¢, 68 pgs.); Ditko-a(4)	26	52	78	154	252	350
39,41,52,53-Ditko-a	19	38	57	111	176	240
42-44,46,49,54-60	6	12	18	39	62	85
45,47,48,50,51-Ditko-c/a	14	28	42	97	181	265
61-74	5	10	15	30	48	65
75(6/65)-Reprints origin/1st app. Captain Atom by Ditko from Space Advs. #33; r/Severin-a/Space Advs. #24 (75-77: 12¢ issues)	11	22	33	80	145	210
76,77-Captain Atom-r by Ditko/Space Advs.	6	12	18	43	69	95
V3#1(10/67): 12¢ issues begin	3	6	9	20	30	40
V1#2-Ditko-c/a; atom bomb-c	3	6	9	20	30	40
V1#3-9: 3-8-All 12¢ issues. 9-15¢ issue	2	4	6	13	18	22

NOTE: ***Alascia** a-19. **Aparo** a-60, V3#1, 2, 4; c-V1#4, 8, 9. **Baily** a-1-3; c-2, 5. **Evans** c-3, 4. **Giordano** c-16, 17p, 24p, 25p. **Montes/Bache** c-66. **Powell** a-4. **Shuster** a-19, 21. **Marcus Swayze** a-27.*

STRANGE TALES (...Featuring Warlock #178-181; Doctor Strange #169 on)
Atlas (CCPC #1-67/ZPC #68-79/VPI #80-85)/Marvel #86(7/61) on:
June, 1951 - No. 168, May, 1968; No. 169, Sept, 1973 - No. 188, Nov, 1976

	GD 2.0	VG 4.0	FN 6.0	VF 8.0	VF/NM 9.0	NM- 9.2
1-Horror/weird stories begin	303	606	909	2121	3711	5300
2	107	214	321	680	1165	1650
3,5: 3-Atom bomb panels	81	162	243	518	884	1250
4-Cosmic eyeball story "The Evil Eye"	84	168	252	538	919	1300
6-9: 6-Heath-c/a. 7-Colan-a	57	114	171	362	624	885
10-Krigstein-a	60	120	180	381	653	925
11-14,16-20	42	84	126	265	445	625
15-Krigstein-a	42	84	126	266	451	635
21,23-27,29-34: 27-Atom bomb panels. 33-Davis-a. 34-Last pre-code issue (2/55)	37	74	111	222	361	500
22-Krigstein, Forte/Fox-a	38	76	114	226	368	510
28-Jack Katz story used in Senate Investigation report, pgs. 7 & 169	39	78	117	230	375	520
35-41,43,44: 37-Vampire story by Colan	21	42	63	148	287	425
42,45,59,61-Krigstein-a; #61 (2/58)	21	42	63	151	293	435
46-57,60: 51-(10/56) 1st S.A. issue. 53,56-Crandall-a. 60-(8/57)	19	38	57	139	270	400
58,64-Williamson-a in each, with Mayo-#58	20	40	60	142	276	410
62,63,65,66: 62-Torres-a. 66-Crandall-a	19	38	57	135	263	390
67-Prototype ish. (Quicksilver)	21	42	63	148	287	425
68,71,72,74,77,80: Ditko/Kirby-a in #67-80	19	38	57	139	270	400
69,70,73,75,76,78,79: 69-Prototype ish. (Prof. X). 70-Prototype ish. (Giant Man). 73-Prototype ish. (Ant-Man). 75-Prototype ish. (Iron Man). 76-Prototype ish. (Human Torch). 78-Prototype ish. (Ant-Man). 79-Prototype ish. (Dr. Strange) (12/60)	23	46	69	166	321	475
81-83,85-88,90,91-Ditko/Kirby-a in all: 86-Robot-c. 90-(11/61)-Atom bomb blast panel	18	36	54	129	252	375
84-Prototype ish. (Magneto)(5/61); has powers like Magneto of X-Men, but two years earlier; Ditko/Kirby-a	22	44	66	157	304	450
89-1st app. Fin Fang Foom (10/61) by Kirby	46	92	138	368	709	1050
92-Prototype ish. (Ancient One & Ant-Man); last 10¢ issue	19	38	57	139	270	400
93,95,96,98-100: Kirby-a	17	34	51	122	236	350
94-Creature similar to The Thing; Kirby-a	19	38	57	139	270	400

97-1st app. Aunt May & Uncle Ben by Ditko (6/62), before Amazing Fantasy #15;

Strange Tales #153 © MAR

Strange Tales (2009 series) #3 © MAR

Strange Worlds #2 © MAR

	GD 2.0	VG 4.0	FN 6.0	VF 8.0	VF/NM 9.0	NM- 9.2
(see Tales Of Suspense #7); Kirby-a	38	76	114	288	557	825
101-Human Torch begins by Kirby (10/62); origin recap Fantastic Four & Human Torch; Human Torch-c begin	112	224	336	952	1876	2800
102-1st app. Wizard; robot-c	40	80	120	320	623	925
103-105: 104-1st app. Trapster. 105-2nd Wizard	34	68	102	262	506	750
106,108,109: 106-Fantastic Four guests (3/63)	26	52	78	190	370	550
107-(4/63)-Human Torch/Sub-Mariner battle; 4th S.A. Sub-Mariner app. & 1st x-over outside of Fantastic Four	36	72	108	280	540	800
110-(7/63)-Intro Doctor Strange, Ancient One & Wong by Ditko	140	280	420	1190	2345	3500
111-2nd Dr. Strange	36	72	108	280	540	800
112,113	18	36	54	129	252	375
114-Acrobat disguised as Captain America, 1st app. since the G.A.; intro. & 1st app. Victoria Bentley; 3rd Dr. Strange app. & begin series (11/63)	40	80	120	314	607	900
115-Origin Dr. Strange; Human Torch vs. Sandman (Spidey villain; 2nd app. & brief origin); early Spider-Man x-over, 12/63	48	96	144	384	742	1100
116-(1/64)-Human Torch battles The Thing; 1st Thing x-over	16	32	48	115	220	325
117,118,120: 120-1st Iceman x-over (from X-Men)	13	26	39	93	172	250
119-Spider-Man x-over (2 panel cameo)	15	30	45	104	197	290
121,122,124,126-134: Thing/Torch team-up in 121-134. 126-Intro Clea. 128-Quicksilver & Scarlet Witch app. (1/65). 130-The Beatles cameo. 134-Last Human Torch; The Watcher-c/story; Wood-a(i)	10	20	30	73	129	185
123-1st app. The Beetle (see Amazing Spider-Man #21 for next app.); 1st Thor x-over (8/64); Loki app.	12	24	36	85	155	225
125-Torch & Thing battle Sub-Mariner (10/64)	13	26	39	90	165	240
135-Col. (formerly Sgt.) Nick Fury becomes Nick Fury Agent of Shield (origin/1st app.) by Kirby (8/65); series begins	18	36	54	129	252	375
136-140: 138-Intro Eternity	8	16	24	52	86	120
141-147,149: 145-Begins alternating-c features w/Nick Fury (odd #'s) & Dr. Strange (even #'s). 146-Last Ditko Dr. Strange who is in consecutive stories since #113; only full Ditko Dr. Strange-c this title. 147-Dr. Strange (by Everett #147-152) continues thru #168, then Dr. Strange #169	6	12	18	41	66	90
148-Origin Ancient One	8	16	24	54	90	125
150(11/66)-John Buscema's 1st work at Marvel	7	14	21	45	73	100
151-Kirby/Steranko-c/a; 1st Marvel work by Steranko	9	18	27	65	113	160
152,153-Kirby/Steranko-a	7	14	21	49	80	110
154-158-Steranko-a/script	7	14	21	49	80	110
159-Origin Nick Fury retold; Intro Val; Captain America-c/story; Steranko-a	8	16	24	54	90	125
160-162-Steranko-a/scripts; Capt. America app.	7	14	21	49	80	110
163-166,168-Steranko-a(p). 168-Last Nick Fury (gets own book next month) & last Dr. Strange who also gets own book	7	14	21	47	76	105
167-Steranko pen/script; classic flag-c	8	16	24	54	90	125
169-1st app. Brother Voodoo(origin in #169,170) & begin series, ends #173.	3	6	9	16	23	30
170-174: 174-Origin Golem	2	4	6	11	16	20
175-177: 177-Brunner-c	2	4	6	10	14	18
178-(2/75)-Warlock by Starlin begins; origin Warlock & Him retold; 1st app. Magus; Starlin-c/a/scripts in #178-181 (all before Warlock #9)	3	6	9	20	30	40
179-181-All Warlock. 179-Intro/1st app. Pip the Troll. 180-Intro Gamora. 181-(8/75)-Warlock story continued in Warlock #9	3	6	9	16	23	30
182-188: 185,186-(Regular 25¢ editions)	1	2	3	5	6	8
185,186-(30¢-c variants, limited distribution)(5,7/76)	2	4	6	11	16	20
Annual 1(1962)-Reprints from Strange Tales #73,76,78, Tales of Suspense #7,9, Tales to Astonish #1,6,7, & Journey Into Mystery #53,55,59; (1st Marvel annual?)	50	100	150	413	807	1200
Annual 2(7/63)-Reprints from Strange Tales #67, Strange Worlds (Atlas) #1-3, World of Fantasy #16; new Human Torch vs. Spider-Man story by Kirby/Ditko (1st Spidey x-over; 4th app.); Kirby-c	80	160	240	680	1340	2000

NOTE: ***Briefer*** *a-17.* ***Burgos*** *a-123p.* ***J. Buscema*** *a-174p.* ***Colan*** *a-7, 11, 20, 37, 53, 169-173p, 188p.* ***Davis*** *c-71.* ***Ditko*** *a-46, 50, 67-122, 123-125p, 126-146, 175r, 182-188r; c-51, 93, 115, 121, 146.* ***Everett*** *a-4, 21, 40-42, 73, 147-152, 164i; c-8, 10, 11, 13, 15, 24, 45, 49-54, 56, 58, 60, 61, 63, 148, 150, 152, 158i.* ***Forte*** *a-27, 43, 50, 53, 54, 60.* ***Heath*** *a-2, 6; c-6, 18-20.* ***Kamen*** *a-45.* ***G. Kane*** *c-170-173, 182p.* ***Kirby*** *Human Torch-101-105, 108, 109, 114, 120; Nick Fury-135p, 141-143p; (Layouts)-135-153; other* ***Kirby*** *a-67-100p; c-68-70, 72-74, 76-92, 94, 95, 101-114, 116-123, 125-130, 132-135, 136p, 138-145, 147, 149, 151p.* ***Kirby/Ayers*** *c-101-106, 108-110.* ***Kirby/Ditko*** *a-80, 88, 121; c-75, 93, 97, 100, 139.* ***Lawrence*** *a-29.* ***Leiber/ Fox*** *a-110-113.* ***Maneely*** *a-3, 7, 37, 42; c-33, 40.* ***Moldoff*** *a-20.* ***Mooney*** *a-174i.* ***Morisi*** *a-53, 56.* ***Morrow*** *a-54.* ***Orlando*** *a-41, 44, 46, 49, 52.* ***Powell*** *a-42, 44, 49, 54, 130-134p; c-131p.* ***Reinman*** *a-11, 50, 74, 88, 91, 95, 104, 106, 112i, 124-127i.* ***Robinson*** *a-17.* ***Romita*** *c-169.* ***Roussos*** *c-201i.* ***R.Q. Sale*** *a-56; c-16.* ***Sekowski*** *a-3, 11.* ***Severin*** *a(i)-136-138; c-137.* ***Starlin*** *a-178, 179, 180p, 181p; c-178-180, 181p.* ***Steranko*** *a-151-161, 162-168p; c-151i, 153, 155, 157, 159, 161, 163, 165, 167.* ***Torres*** *a-53, 62.* ***Tuska*** *a-14, 166p.* ***Whitney*** *a-149.* ***Wildey*** *a-42, 56.* ***Woodbridge*** *a-59. Fantastic Four cameos #101-134. Jack Katz app.-26.*

STRANGE TALES
Marvel Comics Group: Apr, 1987 - No. 19, Oct, 1988

	GD 2.0	VG 4.0	FN 6.0	VF 8.0	VF/NM 9.0	NM- 9.2
V2#1-19						2.50

STRANGE TALES
Marvel Comics: Nov, 1994 ($6.95, one-shot)

	GD 2.0	VG 4.0	FN 6.0	VF 8.0	VF/NM 9.0	NM- 9.2
V3#1-acetate-c						7.00

STRANGE TALES (Anthology; continues stories from Man-Thing #8 and Werewolf By Night #6)
Marvel Comics: Sept, 1998 - No. 2, Oct, 1998 ($4.99)

	GD 2.0	VG 4.0	FN 6.0	VF 8.0	VF/NM 9.0	NM- 9.2
1,2: 1-Silver Surfer app. 2-Two covers						5.00

STRANGE TALES (Humor anthology)
Marvel Comics: Nov, 2009 - No. 3, Jan, 2010 ($4.99, limited series)

	GD 2.0	VG 4.0	FN 6.0	VF 8.0	VF/NM 9.0	NM- 9.2
1-3: 1-Paul Pope, Kochalka, Bagge and others-s/a. 2-Bagge-c/a. 3-Sakai-c/a						5.00

STRANGE TALES: DARK CORNERS
Marvel Comics: May, 1998 ($3.99, one-shot)

	GD 2.0	VG 4.0	FN 6.0	VF 8.0	VF/NM 9.0	NM- 9.2
1-Anthology; stories by Baron & Maleev, McGregor & Dringenberg, DeMatteis & Badger; Estes painted-c						4.00

STRANGE TALES OF THE UNUSUAL
Atlas Comics (ACI No. 1-4/WPI No. 5-11): Dec, 1955 - No. 11, Aug, 1957

	GD 2.0	VG 4.0	FN 6.0	VF 8.0	VF/NM 9.0	NM- 9.2
1-Powell-a	45	90	135	284	480	675
2	29	58	87	170	278	385
3-Williamson-a (4 pgs.)	30	60	90	177	289	400
4,6,8,11	21	42	63	126	206	285
5-Crandall, Ditko-a	26	52	78	152	249	345
7,9: 7-Kirby, Orlando-a. 9-Krigstein-a	23	46	69	136	223	310
10-Torres, Morrow-a	21	42	63	126	206	285

NOTE: ***Baily*** *a-6.* ***Brodsky*** *c-2-4.* ***Everett*** *a-2, 6; c-6, 9, 11.* ***Heck*** *a-1.* ***Maneely*** *c-1.* ***Orlando*** *a-7.* ***Pakula*** *a-10.* ***Romita*** *a-1.* ***R.Q. Sale*** *a-3.* ***Wildey*** *a-3.*

STRANGE TERRORS
St. John Publishing Co.: June, 1952 - No. 7, Mar, 1953

	GD 2.0	VG 4.0	FN 6.0	VF 8.0	VF/NM 9.0	NM- 9.2
1-Bondage-c; Zombies spelled Zoombies on-c; Fine-*esque* -a	58	116	174	371	636	900
2	36	72	108	211	343	475
3-Kubert-a; painted-c	41	82	123	256	428	600
4-Kubert-a (reprinted in Mystery Tales #18); Ekgren painted-c; Fine-*esque* -a; Jerry Iger caricature	53	106	159	334	567	800
5-Kubert-a; painted-c	41	82	123	256	428	600
6-Giant (25¢, 100 pgs.)(1/53); bondage-c	53	106	159	334	567	800
7-Giant (25¢, 100 pgs.); Kubert-c/a	54	108	162	346	591	835

NOTE: ***Cameron*** *a-6, 7.* ***Morisi*** *a-6.*

STRANGE WORLD OF YOUR DREAMS
Prize Publications: Aug, 1952 - No. 4, Jan-Feb, 1953

	GD 2.0	VG 4.0	FN 6.0	VF 8.0	VF/NM 9.0	NM- 9.2
1-Simon & Kirby-a	64	128	192	406	696	985
2,3-Simon & Kirby-c/a. 2-Meskin-a	50	100	150	315	533	750
4-S&K-c; Meskin-a	41	82	123	256	428	600

STRANGE WORLDS (#18 continued from Avon's Eerie #1-17)
Avon Periodicals: 11/50 - No. 9, 11/52; No. 18, 10-11/54 - No. 22, 9-10/55 (No #11-17)

	GD 2.0	VG 4.0	FN 6.0	VF 8.0	VF/NM 9.0	NM- 9.2
1-Kenton of the Star Patrol by Kubert (r/Eerie #1 from 1947); Crom the Barbarian by John Giunta	139	278	417	883	1517	2150
2-Wood-a; Crom the Barbarian by Giunta; Dara of the Vikings app.; used in **SOTI**, pg. 112; injury to eye panel	126	252	378	806	1378	1950
3-Wood/Orlando-a (Kenton), Wood/Williamson/Frazetta/Krenkel/Orlando-a (7 pgs.); Malu Slave Girl Princess app.; Kinstler-c	239	478	717	1530	2615	3700
4-Wood-c/a (Kenton); Orlando-a; origin The Enchanted Daggar; Sultan-a; classic cover	135	270	405	864	1482	2100
5-Orlando/Wood-a (Kenton); Wood-c	74	148	222	470	810	1150
6-Kinstler-a(2); Orlando/Wood-c; Check-a	47	94	141	296	498	700
7-Fawcette & Becker/Alascia-a	41	82	123	248	417	585
8-Kubert, Kinstler, Hollingsworth & Lazarus-a; Lazarus Robot-c	41	82	123	248	417	585
9-Kinstler, Fawcette, Alascia-a	39	78	117	236	388	540
18-(Formerly Eerie #17)-Reprints "Attack on Planet Mars" by Kubert	32	64	96	188	307	425
19-r/Avon's "Robotmen of the Lost Planet"; last pre-code issue; Robot-c	32	64	96	188	307	425
20-War-c/story; Wood-c(r)/U.S. Paratroops #1	10	20	30	56	76	95
21,22-War-c/stories. 22-New logo	9	18	27	47	61	75
I.W. Reprint #5-Kinstler-a(r)/Avon's #9	4	8	12	24	37	50

STRANGE WORLDS
Marvel Comics (MPI No. 1,2/Male No. 3,5): Dec, 1958 - No. 5, Aug, 1959

Street Fighter #1 © Capcom

Street Sharks #2 © Street Wise

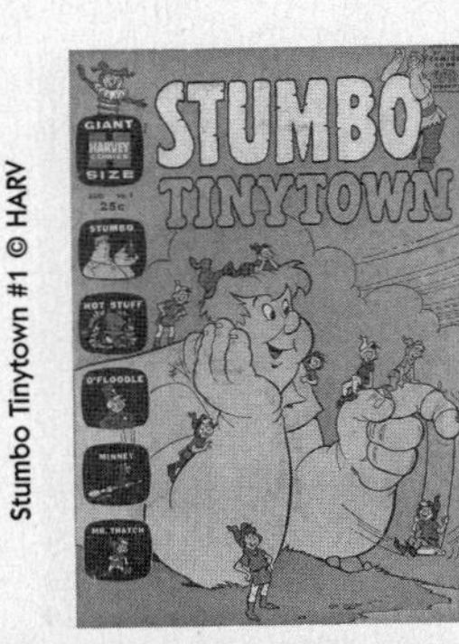

Stumbo Tinytown #1 © HARV

GD 2.0 | VG 4.0 | FN 6.0 | VF 8.0 | VF/NM 9.0 | NM- 9.2

1-Kirby & Ditko-a; flying saucer issue 89 178 267 565 970 1375
2-Ditko-c/a 50 100 150 315 533 750
3-Kirby-a(2) 41 82 123 256 428 600
4-Williamson-a 40 80 120 246 411 575
5-Ditko-a 37 74 111 218 354 490
NOTE: *Buscema a-3, 4. Ditko a-1-5; c-2.. Heck a-2. Kirby a-1, 3. Kirby/Brodsky c-1, 3-5.*

STRAWBERRY SHORTCAKE
Marvel Comics (Star Comics): Jun, 1985 - No. 6, Feb, 1986 (Children's comic)
1-6: Howie Post-a 2 3 4 6 8 10

STRAY
DC Comics (Homage Comics): 2001 ($5.95, prestige format, one-shot)
1-Pollina-c/a; Lobdell & Palmiotti-s 6.00

STRAY BULLETS (Also see Promotional Comics section for Free Comic Book Day edition)
El Capitan Books: 1995 - Present ($2.95/$3.50, B&W, mature readers)
1-David Lapham-c/a/scripts 2 4 6 8 10 12
2,3 6.00
4-8 3.50
9-21,31,32-($2.95) 3.00
22-30,33-40-($3.50) 22-Includes preview to Murder Me Dead 3.50
Innocence of Nihilism Volume 1 HC ($29.95, hardcover) r/#1-7 30.00
Somewhere Out West Volume 2 HC ($34.95, hardcover) r/#8-14 35.00
Other People Volume 3 HC ($34.95, hardcover) r/#15-22 35.00
Volume 1-3 TPB ($11.95, softcover) 1-r/#1-4. 2-r/#5-8. 3-r/ #9-12 12.00
Volume 4-7 TPB ($14.95) 4- r/#13-16. 5- r/#17-20. 6- r/#21-24. 7-r/#25-28 15.00
NOTE: *Multiple printings of most issues exist & are worth cover price.*

STRAY TOASTERS
Marvel Comics (Epic Comics): Jan, 1988 - No. 4, April, 1989 ($3.50, squarebound, limited series)
1-4: Sienkiewicz-c/a/scripts 3.50

STREET COMIX
Street Enterprises/King Features: 1973 (50¢, B&W, 36 pgs.)(20,000 print run)
1-Rip Kirby 2 4 6 8 11 14
2-Flash Gordon 2 4 6 10 14 18

STREETFIGHTER
Ocean Comics: Aug, 1986 - No. 4, Spr, 1987 ($1.75, limited series)
1-4: 2-Origin begins 3.00

STREET FIGHTER
Malibu Comics: Sept, 1993 - No. 3, Nov, 1993 ($2.95)
1-3: 3-Includes poster; Ferret x-over 3.00

STREET FIGHTER
Image Comics: Sept, 2003 - No. 14, Feb, 2005 ($2.95)
1-Back-up story w/Madureira-a; covers by Madureira and Tsang 3.00
2-6,8-14: 2-Two covers by Campbell and Warren; back-up story w/Warren-a 3.00
7-($4.50) Larocca-c 4.50
... Vol. 1 (3/04, $9.99, digest-size) r/main stories from #1-6 10.00

STREET FIGHTER: THE BATTLE FOR SHADALOO
DC Comics/CAP Co. Ltd.: 1995 ($3.95, one-shot)
1-Polybagged w/trading card & Tattoo 4.00

STREET FIGHTER II
Tokuma Comics (Viz): Apr, 1994 - No. 8, Nov, 1994 ($2.95, limited series)
1-8 3.00

STREET FIGHTER II
UDON Comics: No. 0, Oct, 2005 - Present ($1.99/$3.95/$2.95)
0-(10/05, $1.99) prelude to series; Alvin Lee-a 2.50
1-($3.95) Two covers by Alvin Lee & Ed McGuinness 4.00
2-5-($2.95) 3.00

STREET FIGHTER LEGENDS
UDON Comics: Aug, 2006 - Present ($3.95)
1-Spotlight on Sakura; two covers 4.00

STREETS
DC Comics: 1993 - No. 3, 1993 ($4.95, limited series, 52 pgs.)
Book 1-3-Estes painted-c 5.00

STREET SHARKS
Archie Publications: Jan, 1996 - No. 3, Mar, 1996 ($1.50, limited series)
1-3 2.50

STREET SHARKS
Archie Publications: May, 1996 - No. 6 ($1.50, published 8 times a year)
1-6 2.50

STRICTLY PRIVATE (You're in the Army Now)
Eastern Color Printing Co.: July, 1942 (#1 on sale 6/15/42)
1,2: Private Peter Plink. 2-Says 128 pgs. on-c 23 46 69 136 223 310

STRIKE!
Eclipse Comics: Aug, 1987 - No. 6, Jan, 1988 ($1.75)
1-6, ...Vs. Sgt. Strike Special 1 (5/88, $1.95) 2.50

STRIKEBACK! (The Hunt For Nikita)
Malibu Comics (Bravura): Oct, 1994 - No. 3, Jan, 1995 ($2.95, unfinished limited series)
1-3: Jonathon Peterson script, Kevin Maguire-c/a 3.00
1-Gold foil embossed-c 5.00

STRIKEBACK!
Image Comics (WildStorm Productions): Jan, 1996 - No. 5, May, 1996 ($2.50, limited series)
1-5: Reprints original Bravura series w/additional story & art by Kevin Maguire & Jonathon Peterson; new Maguire-c in all. 4,5-New story & art 2.50

STRIKEFORCE: AMERICA
Comico: Dec, 1995 ($2.95)
V2#1-Polybagged w/gaming card; S. Clark-a(p) 3.00

STRIKEFORCE: MORITURI
Marvel Comics Group: Dec, 1986 - No. 31, July, 1989
1-31: 14-Williamson-i. 13-Double size. 25-Heath-c 2.50

STRIKEFORCE MORITURI: ELECTRIC UNDERTOW
Marvel Comics: Dec, 1989 - No. 5, Mar, 1990 ($3.95, 52 pgs., limited series)
1-5 Squarebound 4.00

STRONG GUY REBORN (See X-Factor)
Marvel Comics: Sept, 1997 ($2.99, one-shot)
1-Dezago-s/Andy Smith, Art Thibert-a 3.00

STRONG MAN (Also see Complimentary Comics & Power of...)
Magazine Enterprises: Mar-Apr, 1955 - No. 4, Sept-Oct, 1955
1(A-1 #130)-Powell-c/a 23 46 69 136 223 310
2-4: (A-1 #132,134,139)-Powell-a. 2-Powell-c 18 36 54 105 165 225

STRONTIUM DOG
Eagle Comics: Dec, 1985 - No. 4, Mar, 1986 ($1.25, limited series)
1-4, Special 1: 4-Moore script. Special 1 (1986)-Moore script 2.50

STRYFE'S STRIKE FILE
Marvel Comics: Jan, 1993 ($1.75, one-shot, no ads)
1-Stroman, Capullo, Andy Kubert, Brandon Peterson-a; silver metallic ink-c; X-Men tie-in to X-Cutioner's Song 3.00
1-Gold metallic ink 2nd printing 2.50

STRYKEFORCE
Image Comics (Top Cow): May, 2004 - No. 5, Oct, 2004 ($2.99)
1-5-Faerber-s/Kirkham-a. 4,5-Preview of HumanKind 3.00
Vol. 1 TPB (2005, $16.99) r/#1-5 & Codename: Strykeforce #0-3; sketch pages 17.00

STUMBO THE GIANT (See Harvey Hits #49,54,57,60,63,66,69,72,78,88 & Hot Stuff #2)

STUMBO TINYTOWN
Harvey Publications: Oct, 1963 - No. 13, Nov, 1966 (All 25¢ giants)
1-Stumbo, Hot Stuff & others begin 15 30 45 104 197 290
2 9 18 27 61 103 145
3-5 7 14 21 45 73 100
6-13 6 12 18 37 59 80

STUNT DAWGS
Harvey Comics: Mar, 1993 ($1.25, one-shot)
1 2.50

STUNTMAN COMICS (Also see Thrills Of Tomorrow)
Harvey Publ.: Apr-May, 1946 - No. 2, June-July, 1946; No. 3, Oct-Nov, 1946
1-Origin Stuntman by S&K reprinted in Black Cat #9; S&K-c 116 232 348 742 1271 1800
2-S&K-c/a; The Duke of Broadway story 68 136 204 435 743 1050
3-Small size (5-1/2x8-1/2"; B&W; 32 pgs.); distributed to mail subscribers only; S&K-a; Kid Adonis by S&K reprinted in Green Hornet #37 94 188 282 597 1024 1450

Submarine Attack #41 © CC

Sub-Mariner Comics #32 © MAR

Sugar and Spike #6 © DC

	GD 2.0	VG 4.0	FN 6.0	VF 8.0	VF/NM 9.0	NM- 9.2

(Also see All-New #15, Boy Explorers #2, Flash Gordon #5 & Thrills of Tomorrow)

STUPID COMICS (Also see 40 oz. Collected)
Oni Press/Image Comics: July, 2000; Sept, 2002 - Present ($2.95, B&W)

1-(Oni Press, 7/00) Jim Mahfood 1 page satire strips reprinted from JAVA magazine 3.00
1-3-(Image Comics, 9/02; 10/03) Jim Mahfood 1 page and 2 page satire strips 3.00
TPB (4/06, $12.99) r/#1(Oni) and #1-3(Image); Phoenix New Times strips 13.00

STUPID HEROES
Mirage Studios: Sept, 1993 - No. 3, Dec, 1994 ($2.75, unfinished limited series)

1-3-Laird-c/a & scripts; 2 trading cards bound in 2.75

STUPID, STUPID RAT TAILS (See Bone)
Cartoon Books: Dec, 1999 - No. 3, Feb, 2000 ($2.95, limited series)

1-3-Jeff Smith-a/Tom Sniegoski-s 3.00

SUBHUMAN
Dark Horse Comics: Nov, 1998 - No. 4, Feb, 1999 ($2.95, limited series)

1-4-Mark Schultz-c 3.00

SUBMARINE ATTACK (Formerly Speed Demons)
Charlton Comics: No. 11, May, 1958 - No. 54, Feb-Mar, 1966

	GD	VG	FN	VF	VF/NM	NM-
11	4	8	12	26	41	55
12-20	3	6	9	19	29	38
21-30	3	6	9	17	25	32
31-54	3	6	9	14	20	26

NOTE: *Glanzman c/a-25. Montes/Bache a-38, 40, 41.*

SUB-MARINER (See All-Select, All-Winners, Blonde Phantom, Daring, The Defenders, Fantastic Four #4, Human Torch, The Invaders, Iron Man &..., Marvel Mystery, Marvel Spotlight #27, Men's Adventures, Motion Picture Funnies Weekly, Namora, Namor, The..., Prince Namor, The Sub-Mariner, Saga Of The..., Tales to Astonish #70 & 2nd series, USA & Young Men)

SUB-MARINER, THE (2nd Series)(Sub-Mariner #31 on)
Marvel Comics Group: May, 1968 - No. 72, Sept, 1974 (No. 43: 52 pgs.)

	GD	VG	FN	VF	VF/NM	NM-
1-Origin Sub-Mariner; story continued from Iron Man & Sub-Mariner #1	19	38	57	139	270	400
2-Triton app.	9	18	27	65	113	160
3-5: 5-1st Tiger Shark (9/68)	7	14	21	49	80	110
6,7,9,10: 6-Tiger Shark-c & 2nd app., cont'd from #5. 7-Photo-c. (1968). 9-1st app. Serpent Crown (origin in #10 & 12)	5	10	15	34	55	75
8-Sub-Mariner vs. Thing	9	18	27	65	113	160
8-2nd printing (1994)	2	4	6	8	10	12
11-13,15: 15-Last 12¢ issue	4	8	12	28	44	60
14-Sub-Mariner vs. G.A. Human Torch; death of Toro (1st modern app. & only app. Toro, 6/69)	6	12	18	41	66	90
16-20: 19-1st Sting Ray (11/69); Stan Lee, Romita, Heck, Thomas, Everett & Kirby cameos. 20-Dr. Doom app.	3	6	9	20	30	40
21,23-33,37-39,41,42: 25-Origin Atlantis. 30-Capt. Marvel x-over. 37-Death of Lady Dorma. 38-Origin retold. 42-Last 15¢ issue.	3	6	9	16	23	30
22,40: 22-Dr. Strange x-over. 40-Spider-Man x-over	3	6	9	17	25	32
34-Prelude (w/#35) to 1st Defenders story; Hulk & Silver Surfer x-over	8	16	24	56	93	130
35-Namor/Hulk/Silver Surfer team-up to battle The Avengers-c/story (3/71); hints at teaming up again	6	12	18	43	69	95
36-Wrightson-a(i)	3	6	9	20	30	40
43-King Size Special (52 pgs.)	3	6	9	20	30	40
44,45-Sub-Mariner vs. Human Torch	3	6	9	18	27	35
46-49,56,62,64-72: 47,48-Dr. Doom app. 49-Cosmic Cube story. 62-1st Tales of Atlantis, ends #66. 64-Hitler cameo. 67-New costume; F.F. x-over. 69-Spider-Man x-over (6 panels)	2	4	6	9	13	16
50-1st app. Nita, Namor's niece (later Namorita in New Warriors)	2	4	6	11	16	20
51-55,57,58,60,61,63-Everett issues: 61-Last artwork by Everett; 1st 4 pgs. completed by Mortimer; pgs. 5-20 by Mooney	2	4	6	10	14	18
59-1st battle with Thor; Everett-a	3	6	9	20	30	40
Special 1 (1/71)-r/Tales to Astonish #70-73	3	6	9	20	30	40
Special 2 (1/72)-(52 pgs.)-r/T.T.A. #74-76; Everett-a	3	6	9	16	23	30

NOTE: *Bolle a-67i. Buscema a(p)-1-8, 20, 24. Colan a(p)-10, 11, 40, 43, 46-49, Special 1, 2; c(p)-10, 11, 40. Craig a-17i, 19-23i. Everett a-45r, 50-55, 57, 58, 59-61(plot), 63(plot); c-47, 48i, 55, 57-59i, 61, Spec. 2. G. Kane c(p)-42-52, 58, 66, 70, 71. Mooney a-24i, 25i, 32-35i, 39i, 42i, 44i, 45i, 60i, 61i, 65p, 66p, 68i. Severin c/a-38i. Starlin c-59p. Tuska a-41p, 42p, 69-71p. Wrightson a-36i. #53, 54-r/stories Sub-Mariner Comics #41 & 39.*

SUB-MARINER (The Initiative, follows Civil War series)
Marvel Comics: Aug, 2007 - No. 6, Jan, 2008 ($2.99, limited series)

1-6: 1-Turner-c/Briones-a/Cherniss & Johnson-s; Iron Man app. 3-Yu-c; Venom app. 3.00
...: Revolution TPB (208, $14.99) r/#1-6 15.00

SUB-MARINER COMICS (1st Series) (The Sub-Mariner #1, 2, 33-42)(Official True Crime Cases #24 on; Amazing Mysteries #32 on; Best Love #33 on)
Timely/Marvel Comics (TCI 1-7/SePI 8/MPI 9-32/Atlas Comics (CCC 33-42)): Spring, 1941 - No. 23, Sum, 1947; No. 24, Wint, 1947 - No. 31, 4/49; No. 32, 7/49; No. 33, 4/54 - No. 42, 10/55

	GD	VG	FN	VF	VF/NM	NM-
1-The Sub-Mariner by Everett & The Angel begin	3050	6100	9150	23,000	43,500	64,000
2-Everett-a	568	1136	1704	4146	6823	10,500
3-Churchill assassination-c; 40 pg. S-M story	514	1028	1542	3752	6626	9500
4-Everett-a, 40 pgs.; 1 pg. Wolverton-a	389	778	1167	2723	4762	6800
5-Gabrielle/Klein-c	300	600	900	2070	3635	5200
6-10: 9-Wolverton-a, 3 pgs.; flag-c	300	600	900	1920	3310	4700
11-Classic Schomburg-c	300	600	900	1950	3375	4800
12-15	213	426	639	1363	2332	3300
16-20	174	348	522	1114	1907	2700
21-Last Angel; Everett-a	126	252	378	806	1378	1950
22-Young Allies app.	126	252	378	806	1378	1950
23-The Human Torch, Namora x-over (Sum/47); 2nd app. Namora after Marvel Mystery #82	152	304	456	965	1658	2350
24-Namora x-over (3rd app.)	127	254	381	807	1391	1975
25-The Blonde Phantom begins (Spr/48), ends No. 31; Kurtzman-a; Namora x-over; last quarterly issue	145	290	435	921	1586	2250
26-28: 28-Namora cover; Everett-a	126	252	378	806	1378	1950
29-31 (4/49): 29-The Human Torch app. 31-Capt. America app.	126	252	378	806	1378	1950
32 (7/49, Scarce)-Origin Sub-Mariner	226	452	678	1446	2473	3500
33 (4/54)-Origin Sub-Mariner; The Human Torch app.; Namora x-over in Sub-Mariner #33-42	110	220	330	704	1202	1700
34,35-Human Torch in each	89	178	267	565	970	1375
36,37,39-41: 36,39-41-Namora app.	87	174	261	553	952	1350
38-Origin Sub-Mariner's wings; Namora app.; last pre-code (2/55)	94	188	282	597	1024	1450
42-Last issue	97	194	291	621	1061	1500

NOTE: *Angel by Gustavson-#1, 8. Brodsky c-34-36, 42. Everett a-1-4, 22-24, 26-42; c-32, 33, 40. Maneely a-38; c-37, 39-41. Rico c-27-31. Schomburg c-1-4, 6, 8-18, 20. Sekowsky c-24. 25, 26(w/Rico). Shores c-21-23, 38. Bondage c-13, 22, 24, 25, 34.*

SUB-MARINER COMICS 70th ANNIVERARY SPECIAL
Marvel Comics: June, 2009 ($3.99, one-shot)

1-New WWII story, Breitweiser-a; Williamson-a; r/debut app. from Marvel Comics #1 4.00

SUB-MARINER: THE DEPTHS
Marvel Comics: Nov, 2008 - No. 5, May, 2009 ($3.99, limited series)

1-5-Peter Milligan-s/Esad Ribic-a/c 4.00

SUBSPECIES
Eternity Comics: May, 1991 - No. 4, Aug, 1991 ($2.50, limited series)

1-4: New stories based on horror movie 2.50

SUBTLE VIOLENTS
CFD Productions: 1991 ($2.50, B&W, mature)

	GD	VG	FN	VF	VF/NM	NM-
1-Linsner-c & story	1	3	4	8	10	12
San Diego Limited Edition	4	8	12	24	37	50

SUE & SALLY SMITH (Formerly My Secret Life)
Charlton Comics: V2#48, Nov, 1962 - No. 54, Nov, 1963 (Flying Nurses)

	GD	VG	FN	VF	VF/NM	NM-
V2#48	3	6	9	17	25	32
49-54	2	4	6	13	18	22

SUGAR & SPIKE (Also see The Best of DC & DC Silver Age Classics)
National Periodical Publications: Apr-May, 1956 - No. 98, Oct-Nov, 1971

	GD	VG	FN	VF	VF/NM	NM-
1 (Scarce)	309	618	927	2163	3782	5400
2	119	238	357	762	1306	1850
3-5: 3-Letter column begins	74	148	222	470	810	1150
6-10	45	90	135	284	480	675
11-20	37	74	111	222	361	500
21-29: 26-Christmas-c	26	52	78	154	252	350
30-Scribbly & Scribbly, Jr. x-over	27	54	81	158	259	360
31-40	20	40	60	117	189	260
41-60	9	18	27	63	107	150
61-80: 69-1st app. Tornado-Tot-c/story. 72-Origin & 1st app. Bernie the Brain	7	14	21	50	83	115
81-84,86-95: 84-Bernie the Brain apps. as Superman in 1 panel (9/69)	6	12	18	39	62	85
85 (68 pgs.)-r/#72	6	12	18	43	69	95
96 (68 pgs.)	7	14	21	47	76	105
97,98 (52 pgs.)	6	12	18	43	69	95

Sugarshock #1 © Joss Whedon

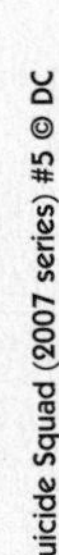
Suicide Squad (2007 series) #5 © DC

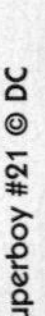
Superboy #21 © DC

GD 2.0 | VG 4.0 | FN 6.0 | VF 8.0 | VF/NM 9.0 | NM- 9.2

No. 1 Replica Edition (2002, $2.95) reprint of #1 3.00
NOTE: *All written and drawn by **Sheldon Mayer**. Issues with Paper Doll pages cut or missing are common.*

SUGAR BOWL COMICS (Teen-age)
Famous Funnies: May, 1948 - No. 5, Jan, 1949

1-Toth-c/a 15 30 45 83 124 165
2,4,5 9 18 27 50 65 80
3-Toth-a 10 20 30 56 76 95

SUGARFOOT (TV)
Dell Publishing Co.: No. 907, May, 1958 - No. 1209, Oct-Dec, 1961

Four Color 907 (#1)-Toth-a, photo-c 12 24 36 82 149 215
Four Color 992 (5-7/59), Toth-a, photo-c 11 22 33 76 136 195
Four Color 1059 (11-1/60), 1098 (5-7/60), 1147 (11-1/61), 1209-all photo-c. 1059,1098,1147-all have variant edition, back-c comic strip 8 16 24 58 97 135

SUGARSHOCK (Also see MySpace Dark Horse Presents)
Dark Horse Comics: Oct, 2009 ($3.50, one-shot)

1-Joss Whedon-s/Fabio Moon-a/c; story from online comic; Moon sketch pgs. 3.50

SUICIDE SQUAD (See Brave & the Bold and Doom Patrol & Suicide Squad Spec., Legends #3 & note under Star Spangled War stories)
DC Comics: May, 1987 - No. 66, June, 1992; No. 67, Mar, 2010 (Direct sales only #32 on)

1-66: 9-Millennium x-over. 10-Batman-c/story. 13-JLI app. (Batman). 16-Re-intro Shade The Changing Man. 23-1st Oracle. 27-34,36,37-Snyder-a. 40-43-"The Phoenix Gambit" Batman storyline. 40-Free Batman/Suicide Squad poster 2.50
67-(3/10, $2.99) Blackest Night one-shot; Fiddler rises as a Black Lantern; Califiore-a 3.00
Annual 1 (1988, $1.50)-Manhunter x-over 2.50
NOTE: ***Chaykin** c-1.*

SUICIDE SQUAD (2nd series)
DC Comics: Nov, 2001 - No. 12, Oct, 2002 ($2.50)

1-12-Giffen-s/Medina-a; Sgt. Rock app. 4-Heath-a. 10-J. Severin-a. 12-JSA app. 2.50

SUICIDE SQUAD (3rd series)
DC Comics: Nov, 2007 - No. 8, Jun, 2008 ($2.99, limited series)

1-8-Ostrander-s/Pina-a/Snyder III-c 3.00
...: From the Ashes TPB (2008, $19.99) r/#1-8 20.00

SUMMER FUN (See Dell Giants)

SUMMER FUN (Formerly Li'l Genius; Holiday Surprise #55)
Charlton Comics: No. 54, Oct, 1966 (Giant)

54 4 8 12 22 34 45

SUMMER FUN (Walt Disney's...)
Disney Comics: Summer, 1991 ($2.95, annual, 68 pgs.)

1-D. Duck, M. Mouse, Brer Rabbit, Chip 'n' Dale & Pluto, Li'l Bad Wolf, Super Goof, Scamp stories 4.00

SUMMER LOVE (Formerly Brides in Love?)
Charlton Comics: V2#46, Oct, 1965; V2#47, Oct, 1966; V2#48, Nov, 1968

V2#46-Beatles-c & 8 pg. story 13 26 39 93 172 250
47-(68 pgs.) Beatles-c & 12 pg. story 10 20 30 73 129 185
48 3 6 9 16 22 28

SUMMER MAGIC (See Movie Comics)

SUNDANCE (See Hotel Deparee...)

SUNDANCE KID (Also see Blazing Six-Guns)
Skywald Publications: June, 1971 - No. 3, Sept, 1971 (52 pgs.)(Pre-code reprints & new-s)

1-Durango Kid; Two Kirby Bullseye-r 3 6 9 16 22 28
2,3: 2-Swift Arrow, Durango Kid, Bullseye by S&K; Meskin plus 1 pg. origin. 3-Durango Kid, Billy the Kid, Red Hawk-r 2 4 6 11 16 20

SUNDAY PIX (Christian religious)
David C. Cook Pub/USA Weekly Newsprint Color Comics: V1#1, Mar,1949 - V16#26, July 19, 1964 (7x10", 12 pgs., mail subscription only)

V1#1 8 16 24 42 54 65
V1#2-up 6 12 18 27 33 38
V2#1-52 (1950) 5 10 15 23 28 32
V3-V6 (1951-1953) 4 9 13 18 22 26
V7-V11#1-7,23-52 (1954-1959) 2 4 6 13 18 22
V11#8-22 (2/22-5/31/59) H.G. Wells First Men in the Moon serial 3 6 9 14 19 24
V12#1-19,21-52; V13-V15#1,2,9-52; V16#1-26(7/19/64) 2 4 6 10 14 18
V12#20 (5/15/60) 2 page interview with Peanuts' Charles Schulz 4 8 12 24 37 50
V15#3-8 (2/24/63) John Glenn, Christian astronaut 3 6 9 16 23 30

SUN DEVILS
DC Comics: July, 1984 - No. 12, June, 1985 ($1.25, maxi series)

1-12: 6-Death of Sun Devil 2.50

SUNDIATA: A LEGEND OF AFRICA
NBM Publishing Inc.: 2002 ($15.95, hardcover with dustjacket)

nn-Will Eisner-s/a; adaptation of an African folk tale 16.00

SUN FUN KOMIKS
Sun Publications: 1939 (15¢, B&W & red)

1-Satire on comics (rare) 103 206 309 659 1130 1600

SUNFIRE & BIG HERO SIX (See Alpha Flight)
Marvel Comics: Sept, 1998 - No. 3, Nov, 1998 ($2.50, limited series)

1-3-Lobdell-s 2.50

SUN GIRL (See The Human Torch & Marvel Mystery Comics #88)
Marvel Comics (CCC): Aug, 1948 - No. 3, Dec, 1948

1-Sun Girl begins; Miss America app. 174 348 522 1114 1907 2700
2,3: 2-The Blonde Phantom begins 118 236 354 749 1287 1825

SUNNY, AMERICA'S SWEETHEART (Formerly Cosmo Cat #1-10)
Fox Features Syndicate: No. 11, Dec, 1947 - No. 14, June, 1948

11-Feldstein-c/a 119 238 357 762 1306 1850
12-14-Feldstein-c/a; 13,14-Lingerie panels. 13-L.B. Cole-a 87 174 261 553 952 1350
I.W. Reprint #8-Feldstein-a; r/Fox issue 10 20 30 73 129 185

SUN-RUNNERS (Also see Tales of the...)
Pacific Comics/Eclipse Comics/Amazing Comics: 2/84 - No. 3, 5/84; No. 4, 11/84 - No. 7, 1986 (Baxter paper)

1-7: P. Smith-a in #2-4 2.50
Christmas Special 1 (1987, $1.95)-By Amazing 2.50

SUNSET CARSON (Also see Cowboy Western)
Charlton Comics: Feb, 1951 - No. 4, 1951 (No month) (Photo-c on each)

1-Photo/retouched-c (Scarce, all issues) 70 140 210 441 746 1050
2-Kit Carson story; adapts "Kansas Raiders" w/Brian Donlevy, Audie Murphy & Margaret Chapman 52 104 156 322 536 750
3,4 40 80 120 244 397 550

SUNSET PASS (See Zane Grey & 4-Color #230)

SUPER ANIMALS PRESENTS PIDGY & THE MAGIC GLASSES
Star Publications: Dec, 1953 (25¢, came w/glasses)

1-(3-D Comics)-L. B. Cole-c 40 80 120 246 411 575

SUPER BAD JAMES DYNOMITE
5-D Comics: Dec, 2005 - No. 5, Feb, 2007 ($3.99)

1-5-Created by the Wayans brothers 4.00

SUPERBOY
DC Comics: Jan, 1942

nn-Ashcan comic, not distributed to newsstands, only for in house use. Covers were produced, but not the rest of the book. A CGC certified 9.2 copy sold in 2003 for $6,600.

SUPERBOY (See Adventure, Aurora, DC Comics Presents, DC 100 Page Super Spectacular #15, DC Super Stars, 80 Page Giant #10, More Fun Comics, The New Advs. of... & Superman Family #191, Young Justice)

SUPERBOY (1st Series)(...& the Legion of Super-Heroes with #231)
(Becomes The Legion of Super-Heroes No. 259 on)
National Periodical Publ./DC Comics: Mar-Apr, 1949 - No. 258, Dec, 1979 (#1-16: 52 pgs.)

1-Superman cover; intro in More Fun #101 (1-2/45) 838 1676 2514 6117 10,809 15,500
2-Used in **SOTI**, pg. 35-36,226 236 472 708 1499 2575 3650
3 181 362 543 1158 1979 2800
4,5: 5-1st pre-Supergirl tryout (c/story, 11-12/49) 124 248 372 787 1356 1925
6-9: 8-1st Superbaby 108 216 324 686 1181 1675
10-1st app. Lana Lang 118 236 354 749 1287 1825
11-15: 2nd Lana Lang app.; 1st Lana cover 81 162 243 518 884 1250
16-20: 20-2nd Jor-El cover 56 112 168 356 608 860
21-26,28-30: 21-Lana Lang app. 46 92 138 290 488 685
27-Low distribution 47 94 141 296 503 710
31-38: 38-Last pre-code issue (1/55) 39 78 117 240 395 550
39-48,50 (7/56) 36 72 108 216 351 485
49 (6/56)-1st app. Metallo (Jor-El's robot) 39 78 117 231 378 525
51-60: 52-1st S.A. issue. 56-Krypto-c 27 54 81 160 263 365
61-67 22 44 66 132 216 300

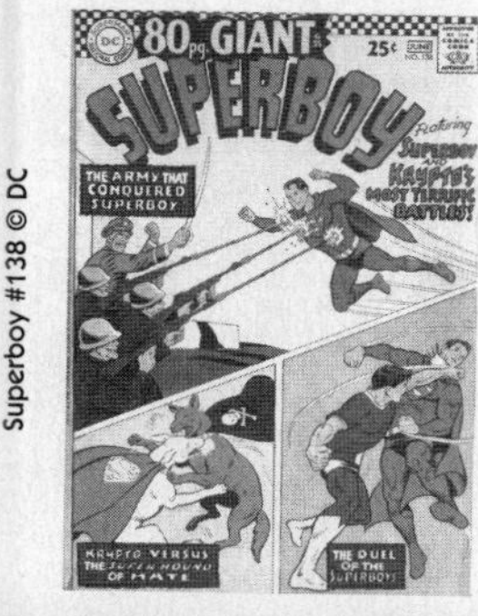

Superboy #138 © DC

Superboy #215 © DC

Superboy (3rd series) #18 © DC

GD VG FN VF VF/NM NM-
2.0 4.0 6.0 8.0 9.0 9.2

68-Origin/1st app. original Bizarro (10-11/58) 63 126 189 403 689 975
69-77,79: 76-1st Supermonkey 20 40 60 114 182 250
78-Origin Mr. Mxyzptlk & Superboy's costume 26 52 78 154 252 350
80-1st meeting Superboy/Supergirl (4/60) 24 48 72 142 234 325
81,83-85,87,88: 83-Origin/1st app. Kryptonite Kid 12 24 36 85 155 225
82-1st Bizarro Krypto 12 24 36 88 162 235
86-(1/61)-4th Legion app; Intro Pete Ross 19 38 57 139 270 400
89-(6/61)-1st app. Mon -El; 2nd Phantom Zone 26 52 78 190 370 550
90-92: 90-Pete Ross learns Superboy's I.D. 92-Last 10¢ issue
12 24 36 82 149 215
93-10th Legion app.(12/61); Chameleon Boy app. 12 24 36 85 155 225
94-97,99: 94-1st app. Superboy Revenge Squad 10 20 30 73 129 185
98-(7/62) Legion app; origin & 1st app. Ultra Boy; Pete Ross joins Legion
13 26 39 91 168 245
100-(10/62)-Ultra Boy app; 1st app. Phantom Zone villains, Dr. Xadu & Erndine. 2 pg. map of Krypton; origin Superboy retold; r-cover of Superman #1
19 38 57 133 259 385
101-120: 104-Origin Phantom Zone. 115-Atomic bomb-c. 117-Legion app.
9 18 27 63 107 150
121-128: 124-(10/65)-1st app. Insect Queen (Lana Lang). 125-Legion cameo. 126-Origin Krypto the Super Dog retold with new facts 8 16 24 56 93 130
129-(80-pg. Giant G-22)-Reprints origin Mon-El 9 18 27 65 113 160
130-137,139,140: 131-Legion statues cameo in Dog Legionnaires story. 132-1st app. Supremo. 133-Superboy meets Robin 7 14 21 47 76 105
138 (80-pg. Giant G-35) 8 16 24 52 86 120
141-146,148-155,157: 145-Superboy's parents regain their youth. 148-Legion app. 157-Last 12¢ issue 6 12 18 39 62 85
147(6/68)-Giant G-47; 1st origin of L.S.H. (Saturn Girl, Lightning Lad, Cosmic Boy); origin Legion of Super-Pets-r/Adv. #293 7 14 21 47 76 105
147 Replica Edition (2003, $6.95) reprints entire issue; cover recreation by Ordway 7.00
156,165,174 (Giants G-59,71,83): 165-r/1st app. Krypto the Superdog from Adventure Comics #210 6 12 18 37 59 80
158-164,166-171,175: 171-1st app. Aquaboy 3 6 9 18 27 35
172,173,176-Legion app.: 172-1st app. & origin Yango (The Super Ape). 176-Partial photo-c; last 15¢ issue 3 6 9 19 29 38
177-184,186,187 (All 52 pgs.): 182-All new origin of the classic World's Finest team (Superman & Batman) as teenagers (2/72, 22pgs). 184-Origin Dial H for Hero-r
3 6 9 20 30 40
185-Also listed as DC 100 Pg. Super Spectacular #12; Legion-c/story; Teen Titans, Kid Eternity(r/Hit #46), Star Spangled Kid-r(S.S. #55)
(see DC 100 Pg. Super Spectacular #12 for price)
188-190,192,194,196: 188-Origin Karkan. 196-Last Superboy solo story
2 4 6 13 18 22
191,193,195: 191-Origin Sunboy retold; Legion app. 193-Chameleon Boy & Shrinking Violet get new costumes. 195-1st app. Erg-1/Wildfire; Phantom Girl gets new costume
3 6 9 14 19 24
197-Legion series begins; Lightning Lad's new costume
3 6 9 20 30 40
198,199: 198-Element Lad & Princess Projectra get new costumes
3 6 9 14 20 26
200-Bouncing Boy & Duo Damsel marry; J'onn J'onzz cameo
3 6 9 16 23 30
201,204,206,207,209: 201-Re-intro Erg-1 as Wildfire. 204-Supergirl resigns from Legion. 206-Ferro Lad & Invisible Kid app. 209-Karate Kid gets new costume
2 4 6 11 16 20
202,205-(100 pgs.): 202-Light Lass gets new costume; Mike Grell's 1st comic work-i (5-6/74)
5 10 15 30 48 65
203-Invisible Kid killed by Validus 3 6 9 16 22 28
208,210: 208-(68 pgs.). 208-Legion of Super-Villains app. 210-Origin Karate Kid
3 6 9 14 20 26
211-220: 212-Matter-Eater Lad resigns. 216-1st app. Tyroc, who joins the Legion in #218
2 4 6 9 13 16
221-230,246-249: 226-Intro. Dawnstar. 228-Death of Chemical King
2 4 6 8 10 12
231-245: (Giants). 240-Origin Dawnstar. 242-(52 pgs.). 243-Legion of Substitute Heroes app. 243-245-(44 pgs.). 2 4 6 9 13 16
244,245-(Whitman variants; low print run, no issue# shown on cover)
3 6 9 14 20 26
246-248-(Whitman variants; low ...) 2 4 6 11 16 20
250-258: 253-Intro Blok. 257-Return of Bouncing Boy & Duo Damsel by Ditko
2 3 4 6 8 10
251-258-(Whitman variants; low print run) 2 4 6 10 14 18
Annual 1 (Sum/64, 84 pgs.)-Origin Krypto-r 17 34 51 119 230 340
Spectacular 1 (1980, Giant)-1st comic distributed only through comic stores; mostly-r

GD VG FN VF VF/NM NM-
2.0 4.0 6.0 8.0 9.0 9.2

2 4 6 8 10 12
...: The Greatest Team-Up Stories Ever Told TPB (2010, $19.99) r/team-ups with Robin, Supergirl, young versions of Aquaman, Green Arrow, Bruce Wayne; Davis-c 20.00

*NOTE: **Neal Adams** c-143, 145, 146, 148-155, 157-161, 163, 164, 166-168, 172, 173, 175, 176, 178. **M. Anderson** a-178,179, 245i. **Ditko** a-257p. **Grell** a-202i, 203-219, 220-224p, 235p; c-207-232, 235, 236p, 237, 239p, 240p, 243p, 246, 258. **Nasser** a(p)-222, 225, 226, 230, 231, 233, 236. **Simonson** a-237p. **Starlin** a(p)-239, 250, 251; c-238. **Staton** a-227p, 243-249p, 252-258p; c-247-251p. **Swan/Moldoff** c-109. **Tuska** a-172, 173, 176, 183, 235p. **Wood** inks-153-155, 157-161. Legion app.-172, 173, 176, 177, 183, 184, 188, 190, 191, 193, 195, 197-258.*

SUPERBOY (TV)(2nd Series)(The Adventures of...#19 on)
DC Comics: Feb, 1990 - No. 22, Dec, 1991 ($1.00/$1.25)

1-22: Mooney-a(p) in 1-8,18-20; 1-Photo-c from TV show. 8-Bizarro-c/story; Arthur Adams-a(i). 9-12,14-17-Swan-p 3.00
...Special 1 (1992, $1.75) Swan-a 3.00

SUPERBOY (3rd Series)
DC Comics: Feb, 1994 - No. 100, Jul, 2002 ($1.50/$1.95/$1.99/$2.25)

1-Metropolis Kid from Reign of the Supermen 4.00
2-8,0,9-24,26-76: 6,7-Worlds Collide Pts. 3 & 8. 8-(9/94)-Zero Hour x-over. 0-(10/94). 9-(11/94)-King Shark app. 21-Legion app. 28-Supergirl-c/app. 33-Final Night. 38-41-"Meltdown". 45-Legion-c/app. 47-Green Lantern-c/app. 50-Last Boy on Earth begins. 60-Crosses Hypertime. 68-Demon-c/app. 2.50
25-($2.95)-New Gods & Female Furies app.; w/pin-ups 3.50
77-99: 77-Begin $2.25-c. 79-Superboy's powers return. 80,81-Titans app. 83-New costume. 85-Batgirl app. 90,91-Our Worlds at War x-over 2.50
100-($3.50) Sienkiewicz-c; Grummett & McCrea-a; Superman cameo 3.50
#1,000,000 (11/98) 853rd Century x-over 2.50
Annual 1 (1994, $2.95, 68 pgs.)-Elseworlds story, Pt. 2 of The Super Seven (see Adventures Of Superman Annual #6) 3.00
Annual 2 (1995, $3.95)-Year One story 4.00
Annual 3 (1996, $2.95)-Legends of the Dead Earth 3.00
Annual 4 (1997, $3.95)-Pulp Heroes story 4.00
...Plus 1 (Jan, 1997, $2.95) w/Capt. Marvel Jr. 3.00
...Plus 2 (Fall, 1997, $2.95) w/Slither (Scare Tactics) 3.00
.../Risk Double-Shot 1 (Feb, 1998, $1.95) w/Risk (Teen Titans) 2.50

SUPERBOY & THE RAVERS
DC Comics: Sept, 1996 - No. 19, March, 1998 ($1.95)

1-19: 4-Adam Strange app. 7-Impulse-c/app. 9-Superman-c/app. 2.50

SUPERBOY COMICS
DC Comics: Jan. 1942

nn - Ashcan comic, not distributed to newsstands, only for in-house use. Cover art is Detective Comics #57 with interior being Action Comics #38. A CGC certified 9.2 copy sold for $6,600 in 2003 and for $15,750 in 2008.

SUPERBOY/ROBIN: WORLD'S FINEST THREE
DC Comics: 1996 - No. 2, 1996 ($4.95, squarebound, limited series)

1,2: Superboy & Robin vs. Metallo & Poison Ivy; Karl Kesel & Chuck Dixon scripts; Tom Grummett-c(p)/a(p) 5.00

SUPERBOY'S LEGION (Elseworlds)
DC Comics: 2001 - No. 2, 2001 ($5.95, squarebound, limited series)

1,2-31st century Superboy forms Legion; Farmer-s/i; Davis-a(p)/c 6.00

SUPER BRAT (Li'l Genius #5 on)
Toby Press: Jan, 1954 - No. 4, July, 1954

1 8 16 24 42 54 65
2-4: 4-Li'l Teevy by Mel Lazarus 5 10 15 24 30 35
I.W. Reprint #1,2,3,7,8('58): 1-r/#1 2 4 6 8 10 12
I.W. (Super) Reprint #10('63) 2 4 6 8 10 12

SUPERCAR (TV)
Gold Key: Nov, 1962 - No. 4, Aug, 1963 (All painted-c)

1 15 30 45 105 190 275
2,3 8 16 24 58 97 135
4-Last issue 9 18 27 63 107 150

SUPER CAT (Formerly Frisky Animals; also see Animal Crackers)
Star Publications #56-58/Ajax/Farrell Publ. (Four Star Comic Corp.):
No. 56, Nov, 1953 - No. 58, May, 1954; Aug, 1957 - No. 4, May, 1958

56-58-L.B. Cole-c on all 19 38 57 112 179 245
1(1957-Ajax)- "The Adventures of..." c-only 10 20 30 54 72 90
2-4 7 14 21 35 43 50

SUPER CIRCUS (TV)
Cross Publishing Co.: Jan, 1951 - No. 5, Sept, 1951 (Mary Hartline)

1-(52 pgs.)-Cast photos on-c 15 30 45 85 130 175

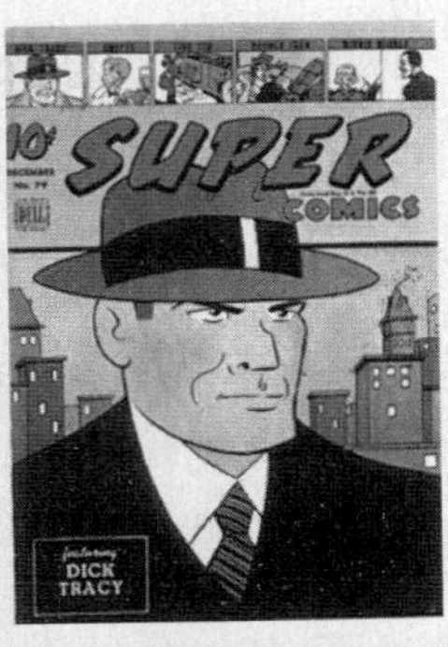

Super Comics #79 © DELL

Super Friends (2008 series) #23 © DC

Supergirl #4 © DC

	GD 2.0	VG 4.0	FN 6.0	VF 8.0	VF/NM 9.0	NM- 9.2
2-Cast photos on-c	10	20	30	58	79	100
3-5	9	18	27	50	65	80

SUPER CIRCUS (TV)
Dell Publ. Co.: No. 542, Mar, 1954 - No. 694, Mar, 1956 (Mary Hartline)

	GD 2.0	VG 4.0	FN 6.0	VF 8.0	VF/NM 9.0	NM- 9.2
Four Color 542: Mary Hartline photo-c	7	14	21	47	76	105
Four Color 592,694: Mary Hartline photo-c	6	12	18	43	69	95

SUPER COMICS
Dell Publishing Co.: May, 1938 - No. 121, Feb-Mar, 1949

	GD 2.0	VG 4.0	FN 6.0	VF 8.0	VF/NM 9.0	NM- 9.2
1-Terry & The Pirates, The Gumps, Dick Tracy, Little Orphan Annie, Little Joe, Gasoline Alley, Smilin' Jack, Smokey Stover, Smitty, Tiny Tim, Moon Mullins, Harold Teen, Winnie Winkle begin	292	584	876	1679	2590	3500
2	106	212	318	610	943	1275
3	94	188	282	541	833	1125
4,5: 4-Dick Tracy-c; also #8-10,17,26(part),31	73	146	219	420	648	875
6-10	58	116	174	334	517	700
11-20: 20-Smilin' Jack-c (also #29,32)	46	92	138	265	408	550
21-29: 21-Magic Morro begins (origin & 1st app., 2/40). 22,27-Ken Ernst-c (also #25?); Magic Morro c-22,25,27,34	35	70	105	203	327	450
30- "Sea Hawk" movie adaptation-c/story with Errol Flynn	36	72	108	212	341	470
31-40: 34-Ken Ernst-c	29	58	87	169	272	375
41-50: 41-Intro Lightning Jim. 43-Terry & The Pirates ends	24	48	72	143	229	315
51-60	19	38	57	109	172	235
61-70: 62-Flag-c. 65-Brenda Starr-r begin? 67-X-Mas-c	17	34	51	98	154	210
71-80	14	28	42	80	115	150
81-99	13	26	39	74	105	135
100	14	28	42	78	112	145
101-115-Last Dick Tracy (moves to own title)	10	20	30	56	76	95
116-121: 116,118-All Smokey Stover. 117-All Gasoline Alley. 119-121-Terry & The Pirates app. in all	9	18	27	50	65	80

SUPER COPS, THE
Red Circle Productions (Archie): July, 1974 (one-shot)

	GD 2.0	VG 4.0	FN 6.0	VF 8.0	VF/NM 9.0	NM- 9.2
1-Morrow-c/a; art by Pino, Hack, Thorne	2	4	6	8	10	12

SUPER COPS
Now Comics: Sept, 1990 - No. 4, Dec?, 1990 ($1.75)

	GD 2.0	VG 4.0	FN 6.0	VF 8.0	VF/NM 9.0	NM- 9.2
1-($2.75, 52 pgs.)-Dave Dorman painted-c (both printings)						2.75
2-4						2.50

SUPER CRACKED (See Cracked)

SUPER DC GIANT (25-50¢, all 68-52 pg. Giants)
National Per. Publ.: No. 13, 9-10/70 - No. 26, 7-8/71; V3#27, Summer, 1976 (No #1-12)

	GD 2.0	VG 4.0	FN 6.0	VF 8.0	VF/NM 9.0	NM- 9.2
S-13-Binky	11	22	33	76	136	195
S-14-Top Guns of the West; Kubert-c; Trigger Twins, Johnny Thunder, Wyoming Kid-r; Moreira-r (9-10/70)	5	10	15	34	55	75
S-15-Western Comics; Kubert-c; Pow Wow Smith, Vigilante, Buffalo Bill-r; new Gil Kane-a (9-10/70)	5	10	15	34	55	75
S-16-Best of the Brave & the Bold; Batman-r & Metamorpho origin-r from Brave & the Bold; Spectre pin-up.	4	8	12	26	41	55
S-17-Love 1970 (scarce)	25	50	75	183	354	525
S-18-Three Mouseketeers; Dizzy Dog, Doodles Duck, Bo Bunny-r; Sheldon Mayer-a	9	18	27	64	110	155
S-19-Jerry Lewis; Neal Adams pin-up	10	20	30	68	119	170
S-20-House of Mystery; N. Adams-c; Kirby-r(3)	7	14	21	47	76	105
S-21-Love 1971 (scarce)	30	60	90	220	428	635
S-22-Top Guns of the West; Kubert-c	4	8	12	24	37	50
S-23-The Unexpected	4	8	12	28	44	60
S-24-Supergirl	4	8	12	24	37	50
S-25-Challengers of the Unknown; all Kirby/Wood-r	4	8	12	22	34	45
S-26-Aquaman (1971)-r/S.A. Aquaman origin story from Showcase #30	4	8	12	22	34	45
27-Strange Flying Saucers Adventures (Sum, 1976)	3	6	9	18	27	35

NOTE: ***Sid Greene*** *r-27p(2),* ***Heath*** *r-27.* ***G. Kane*** *a-14r(2), 15, 27r(p).* ***Kubert*** *r-16.*

SUPER-DOOPER COMICS
Able Mfg. Co./Harvey: 1946 - No. 7, May, 1946; No. 8, 1946 (10¢, 32 pgs., paper-c)

	GD 2.0	VG 4.0	FN 6.0	VF 8.0	VF/NM 9.0	NM- 9.2
1-The Clock, Gangbuster app.	21	42	63	122	199	275
2	14	28	42	80	115	150
3,4,6	13	26	39	72	101	130
5-Capt. Freedom	14	28	42	80	115	150
7,8-Shock Gibson. 7-Where's Theres A Will by Ed Wheelan, Steve Case Crime Rover, Penny & Ullysses Jr. 8-Sam Hill app.	14	28	42	80	115	150

SUPER DUCK COMICS (The Cockeyed Wonder) (See Jolly Jingles)
MLJ Mag. No. 1-4(9/45)/Close-Up No. 5 on (Archie): Fall, 1944 - No. 94, Dec, 1960 (Also see Laugh #24)(#1-5 are quarterly)

	GD 2.0	VG 4.0	FN 6.0	VF 8.0	VF/NM 9.0	NM- 9.2
1-Origin; Hitler & Hirohito-c	71	142	213	454	777	1100
2-Bill Vigoda-c	28	56	84	165	270	375
3-5: 4-20-Al Fagaly-c (most)	19	38	57	111	176	240
6-10	15	30	45	83	124	165
11-20(6/48)	11	22	33	62	86	110
21,23-40 (10/51)	10	20	30	54	72	90
22-Used in **SOTI**, pg. 35,307,308	11	22	33	62	86	110
41-60 (2/55)	8	16	24	44	57	70
61-94	7	14	21	35	43	50

SUPER DUPER (Formerly Pocket Comics #1-4?)
Harvey Publications: No. 5, 1941 - No. 11, 1941

	GD 2.0	VG 4.0	FN 6.0	VF 8.0	VF/NM 9.0	NM- 9.2
5-Captain Freedom & Shock Gibson app.	32	64	96	188	307	425
8,11	20	40	60	114	182	250

SUPER DUPER COMICS (Formerly Latest Comics?)
F. E. Howard Publ.: No. 3, May-June, 1947

	GD 2.0	VG 4.0	FN 6.0	VF 8.0	VF/NM 9.0	NM- 9.2
3-1st app. Mr. Monster	20	40	60	114	182	250

SUPER FRIENDS (TV) (Also see Best of DC & Limited Collectors' Edition)
National Periodical Publications/DC Comics: Nov, 1976 - No. 47, Aug, 1981 (#14 is 44 pgs.)

	GD 2.0	VG 4.0	FN 6.0	VF 8.0	VF/NM 9.0	NM- 9.2
1-Superman, Batman, Robin, Wonder Woman, Aquaman, Atom, Wendy, Marvin & Wonder Dog begin (1st Super Friends)	5	10	15	32	51	70
2-Penquin-c/sty	3	6	9	16	23	30
3-5	3	6	9	14	20	26
6-10,14: 7-1st app. Wonder Twins & The Seraph. 8-1st app. Jack O'Lantern. 9-1st app. Icemaiden. 14-Origin Wonder Twins	2	4	6	13	18	22
11-13,15-30: 13-1st app. Dr. Mist. 25-1st app. Fire as Green Fury. 28-Bizarro app.	2	4	6	9	13	16
13-16,20-23,25,32-(Whitman variants; low print run, no issue# on cover)	2	4	6	11	16	20
31,47: 31-Black Orchid app. 47-Origin Fire & Green Fury	2	4	6	10	14	18
32-46: 36,43-Plastic Man app.	2	4	6	8	11	14
TBP (2001, $14.95) r/#1,6-9,14,21,27 & Limited Collectors' Edition C-41; Alex Ross-c						15.00
...: Truth, Justice and Peace TPB (2003, $14.95) r/#10,12,13,25,28,29,31,36,37						15.00

NOTE: ***Estrada*** *a-1p, 2p.* ***Orlando*** *a-1p.* ***Staton*** *a-43, 45.*

SUPER FRIENDS (All ages stories with puzzles and games)(Based on Mattel toy line)
DC Comics: May, 2008 - Present ($2.25)

	GD 2.0	VG 4.0	FN 6.0	VF 8.0	VF/NM 9.0	NM- 9.2
1-23-Superman, Batman, Wonder Woman, Aquaman, Flash & Green Lantern						2.50
...: Calling All Super Friends TPB (2009, $12.99) r/#8-14; puzzles and games						13.00
...: For Justice TPB (2009, $12.99) r/#1-7; puzzles and games						13.00

SUPER FUN
Gillmor Magazines: Jan, 1956 (By A.W. Nugent)

	GD 2.0	VG 4.0	FN 6.0	VF 8.0	VF/NM 9.0	NM- 9.2
1-Comics, puzzles, cut-outs by A.W. Nugent	7	14	21	35	43	50

SUPER FUNNIES (...Western Funnies #3,4)
Superior Comics Publishers Ltd. (Canada): Dec, 1953 - No. 4, Sept, 1954

	GD 2.0	VG 4.0	FN 6.0	VF 8.0	VF/NM 9.0	NM- 9.2
1-(3-D, 10¢)-...Presents Dopey Duck; make your own 3-D glasses cut-out inside front-c; did not come w/glasses	35	70	105	208	339	470
2-Horror & crime satire	14	28	42	82	121	160
3-Phantom Ranger-c/s; Geronimo, Billy the Kid app.	10	20	30	54	72	90
4-Phantom Ranger-c/story	10	20	30	54	72	90

SUPERGIRL
DC Comics: Feb. 1944

nn - Ashcan comic, not distributed to newsstands, only for in-house use. Cover art is Boy Commandos #1 with interior being Action Comics #80. A copy sold for $15,750 in 2008.

SUPERGIRL (See Action, Adventure #281, Brave & the Bold, Crisis on Infinite Earths #7, Daring New Advs. of..., Super DC Giant, Superman Family, & Super-Team Family)

SUPERGIRL
National Periodical Publ.: Nov, 1972 - No. 9, Dec-Jan, 1973-74; No. 10, Sept-Oct, 1974 (1st solo title)(20¢)

	GD 2.0	VG 4.0	FN 6.0	VF 8.0	VF/NM 9.0	NM- 9.2
1-Zatanna back-up stories begin, end #5	7	14	21	47	76	105
2-4,6,7,9	4	8	12	24	37	50
5,8,10: 5-Zatanna origin-r. 8-JLA x-over; Batman cameo. 10-Prez	4	8	12	26	41	55

NOTE: *Zatanna in #1-5, 7(Guest); Prez app. in #10. #1-10 are 20¢ issues.*

SUPERGIRL (Formerly Daring New Adventures of...)

Supergirl (2005 series) #35 © DC

Supergirl: Cosmic Adventures in the 8th Grade #4 © DC

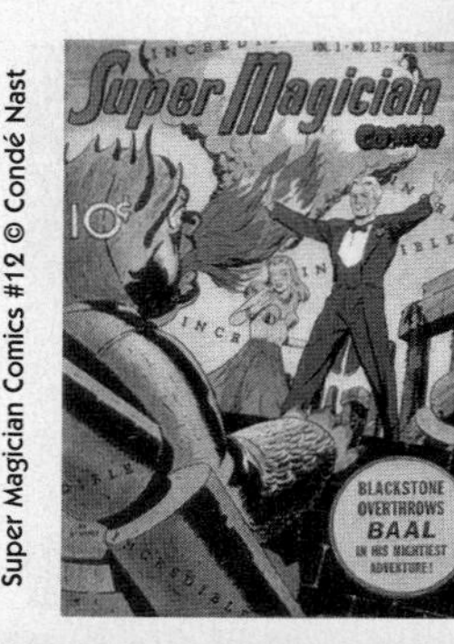

Super Magician Comics #12 © Condé Nast

	GD 2.0	VG 4.0	FN 6.0	VF 8.0	VF/NM 9.0	NM- 9.2

DC Comics: No. 14, Dec, 1983 - No. 23, Sept, 1984

14-23: 16-Ambush Bug app. 20-JLA & New Teen Titans app. 3.00

...Movie Special (1985)-Adapts movie; Morrow-a; photo back-c 4.00

SUPERGIRL
DC Comics: Feb, 1994 - No. 4, May, 1994 ($1.50, limited series)

1-4: Guice-a(i) 3.00

SUPERGIRL (See Showcase '96 #8)
DC Comics: Sept, 1996 - No. 80, May, 2003 ($1.95/$1.99/$2.25/$2.50)

1-Peter David scripts & Gary Frank-c/a 1 2 3 5 6 8

1-2nd printing 3.00

2,4-9: 4-Gorilla Grodd-c/app. 6-Superman-c/app. 9-Last Frank-a 4.00

3-Final Night, Gorilla Grodd app. 5.00

10-19: 14-Genesis x-over. 16-Power Girl app. 3.50

20-35: 20-Millennium Giants x-over; Superman app. 23-Steel-c/app. 24-Resurrection Man x-over. 25-Comet ID revealed; begin $1.99-c 3.00

36-46: 36,37-Young Justice x-over 2.50

47-49,51-74: 47-Begin $2.25-c. 51-Adopts costume from animated series. 54-Green Lantern app. 59-61-Our Worlds at War x-over. 62-Two-Face-c/app. 66,67-Demon-c/app. 68-74-Mary Marvel app. 70-Nauck-a. 73-Begin $2.50-c 2.50

50-($3.95) Supergirl's final battle with the Carnivore 4.00

75-80: 75-Re-intro. Kara Zor-El; cover swipe of Action Comics #252 by Haynes; Benes-a. 78-Spectre app. 80-Last issue; Romita-c 2.50

#1,000,000 (11/98) 853rd Century x-over 3.00

Annual 1 (1996, $2.95)-Legends of the Dead Earth 3.00

Annual 2 (1997, $3.95)-Pulp Heroes; LSH app.; Chiodo-c 4.00

...: Many Happy Returns TPB (2003, $14.95) r/#75-80; intro. by Peter David 15.00

...Plus (2/97, $2.95) Capt.(Mary) Marvel-c/app.; David-s/Frank-a 3.00

.../Prysm Double-Shot 1 (Feb, 1998, $1.95) w/Prysm (Teen Titans) 2.50

...: Wings (2001, $5.95) Elseworlds; DeMatteis-s/Tolagson-a 6.00

TPB-('98, $14.95) r/Showcase '96 #8 & Supergirl #1-9 15.00

SUPERGIRL (See Superman/Batman #8 & #19)
DC Comics: No. 0, Oct, 2005 - Present ($2.99)

0-Reprints Superman/Batman #19 with white variant of that cover 3.00

1-Loeb-s/Churchill-a; two covers by Churchill & Turner; Power Girl app. 5.00

1-2nd printing with B&W sketch variant of Turner-c 3.00

1-3rd printing with variant-c homage to Action Comics #252 by Churchill 3.00

2-4: 2-Teen Titans app. 3-Outsiders app.; covers by Turner & Churchill 3.00

5-($3.99) Supergirl vs. Supergirl; Churchill & Turner-c 4.00

6-49: 6-9-One Year Later; Power Girl app. 11-Intro. Powerboy. 12-Terra debut; Conner-a 20-Amazons Attack x-over. 21,22-Karate Kid app. 28-31-Resurrection Man app. 35,36-New Krypton x-over; Argo City story re-told; Superwoman app. 35-Ross-c. 36-Zor-El dies 3.00

50-($4.99) Lana Lang Insect Queen app.; Superwoman returns; back-up story co-written by Helen Slater with Chiang-a; Turner-c 5.00

50-Variant cover by Middleton 6.00

Annual 1 (11/09, $3.99) Origin of Superwoman 4.00

...: Beyond Good and Evil TPB (2008, $17.99) r/#23-27 and Action Comics #850 18.00

...: Candor TPB (2007, $14.99) r/#6-9; and pages from JSA Classified #2, Superman #223, Superman/Batman #27 and JLA #122,123 15.00

...: Identity TPB (2007, $19.99) r/#10-16 and story from DCU Infinite Holiday Special 20.00

...: Power TPB (2006, $14.99) r/#1-5 and Superman/Batman #19; variant-c gallery 15.00

...: Way of the World TPB (2009, $17.99) r/#28-33 18.00

...: Who is Superwoman TPB (2009, $17.99) r/#34,37-42 18.00

SUPERGIRL AND THE LEGION OF SUPER-HEROES (Continues from Legion of Super-Heroes #15, Apr, 2006)(Continues as Legion of Super-Heroes #37)
DC Comics: No. 16, May, 2006 - No. 36, Jan, 2008 ($2.99)

16-Supergirl appears in the 31st century 4.00

16-2nd printing 3.00

17-36: 23-Mon-El cameo. 24,25-Mon-El returns 3.00

...: Adult Education TPB (2007, $14.99) r/#20-25 & LSH #6,9,13-15 15.00

...: Dominator War TPB (2007, $14.99) r/#26-30 15.00

...: Strange Visitor From Another Century TPB (2006, $14.99) r/#16-19 & LSH #11,12,15 15.00

...: The Quest For Cosmic Boy TPB (2008, $14.99) r/#31-36 15.00

SUPERGIRL: COSMIC ADVENTURES IN THE 8TH GRADE (Cartoony all-ages title)
DC Comics: Feb, 2008 - No. 6, Jul, 2009 ($2.50, limited series)

1-6: 1-Supergirl lands on Earth; Eric Jones-a. 5,6-Comet & Streaky app. 2.50

TPB (2009, $12.99) r/#1-6; sketch art 13.00

SUPERGIRL/LEX LUTHOR SPECIAL (Supergirl and Team Luthor on-c)
DC Comics: 1993 ($2.50, 68 pgs., one-shot)

1-Pin-ups by Byrne & Thibert 2.50

SUPER GOOF (Walt Disney) (See Dynabrite & The Phantom Blot)

	GD 2.0	VG 4.0	FN 6.0	VF 8.0	VF/NM 9.0	NM- 9.2

Gold Key No. 1-57/Whitman No. 58 on: Oct, 1965 - No. 74, July, 1984

1 4 8 12 28 44 60

2-5 3 6 9 16 23 30

6-10 3 6 9 14 19 24

11-20 2 4 6 8 11 14

21-30 1 3 4 6 8 10

31-50 1 2 3 4 5 7

51-57 6.00

58,59 (Whitman) 1 2 3 5 6 8

60(8/80), 62(11/80) 3-pack only (scarce) 4 8 12 24 37 50

61(9-10/80) 3-pack only (rare) 4 8 12 26 41 55

63-66('81) 1 2 3 5 6 8

63 (1/81, 40¢-c) Cover price error variant (scarce) 2 4 6 10 14 18

67-69: 67(2/82), 68(2-3/82), 69(3/82) 6.00

70-74 (#90180 on-c; pre-pack, nd, nd code): 70(5/83), 71(8/83), 72(5/84), 73(6/84), 74(7/84) 3 6 9 16 22 28

NOTE: *Reprints in #16, 24, 28, 29, 37, 38, 43, 45, 46, 54(1/2), 56-58, 65(1/2), 72(r-#2).*

SUPER GREEN BERET (Tod Holton...)
Lightning Comics (Milson Publ. Co.): Apr, 1967 - No. 2, Jun, 1967

1-(25¢, 68 pgs) 5 10 15 32 51 70

2-(25¢, 68 pgs) 4 8 12 22 34 45

SUPER HEROES (See Giant-Size... & Marvel...)

SUPER HEROES
Dell Publishing Co.: Jan, 1967 - No. 4, June, 1967

1-Origin & 1st app. Fab 4 4 8 12 24 37 50

2-4 3 6 9 17 25 32

SUPER-HEROES BATTLE SUPER-GORILLAS (See DC Special #16)
National Periodical Publications: Winter, 1976 (52 pgs., all reprints, one-shot)

1-Superman, Batman, Flash stories; Infantino-a(p) 2 4 6 11 16 20

SUPER HEROES VERSUS SUPER VILLAINS
Archie Publications (Radio Comics): July, 1966 (no month given)(68 pgs.)

1-Flyman, Black Hood, Web, Shield-r; Reinman-a 6 12 18 41 66 90

SUPERHERO WOMEN, THE - FEATURING THE FABULOUS FEMALES OF MARVEL COMICS (See Fireside Book Series)

SUPERICHIE (Formerly Super Richie)
Harvey Publications: No. 5, Oct, 1976 - No. 18, Jan, 1979 (52 pgs. giants)

5-Origin/1st app. new costumes for Rippy & Crashman 2 4 6 9 13 16

6-18 2 4 6 8 10 12

SUPERIOR STORIES
Nesbit Publishers, Inc.: May-June, 1955 - No. 4, Nov-Dec, 1955

1-The Invisible Man by H.G. Wells 23 46 69 136 223 310

2-4: 2-The Pirate of the Gulf by J.H. Ingrahams. 3-Wreck of the Grosvenor by William Clark Russell. 4-The Texas Rangers by O'Henry 11 22 33 62 86 110

NOTE: ***Morisi*** *c/a in all. Kiwanis stories in #3 & 4. #4 has photo of Gene Autry on-c.*

SUPER MAGIC (Super Magician Comics #2 on)
Street & Smith Publications: May, 1941

V1#1-Blackstone the Magician-c/story; origin/1st app. Rex King (Black Fury); Charles Sultan-c; Blackstone-c begin 168 336 504 1075 1838 2600

SUPER MAGICIAN COMICS (Super Magic #1)
Street & Smith Publications: No. 2, Sept, 1941 - V5#8, Feb-Mar, 1947

V1#2-Blackstone the Magician continues; Rex King, Man of Adventure app. 64 128 192 406 696 985

3-Tao-Anwar, Boy Magician begins 41 82 123 249 417 585

4-7,9-12: 4-Origin Transo. 11-Supersnipe app. 39 78 117 232 381 530

8-Abbott & Costello story (1st app?, 11/42) 40 80 120 242 401 560

V2#1-The Shadow app. 41 82 123 249 417 585

2-12: 5-Origin Tigerman. 8-Red Dragon begins 21 42 63 122 199 275

V3#1-12: 5-Origin Mr. Twilight 21 42 63 122 199 275

V4#1-12: 5-KKK-c/sty. 11-Nigel Elliman Ace of Magic begins (3/46) 17 34 51 98 154 210

V5#1-6 17 34 51 98 154 210

7,8-Red Dragon by Edd Cartier-c/a 39 78 117 232 381 530

NOTE: ***Jack Binder*** *c-1-14(most). Red Dragon c-V5#7, 8.*

SUPERMAN (See Action Comics, Advs. of..., All-New Coll. Ed., All-Star Comics, Best of DC, Brave & the Bold, Cosmic Odyssey, DC Comics Presents, Heroes Against Hunger, JLA, The Kents, Krypton Chronicles, Limited Coll. Ed., Man of Steel, Phantom Zone, Power Record Comics, Special Edition, Steel, Super Friends, Superman: The Man of Steel, Superman: The Man of Tomorrow, Taylor's Christmas Tabloid, Three-Dimension Advs., World Of Krypton, World Of Metropolis, World Of Smallville & World's Finest)

Superman #24 © DC

Superman #124 © DC

Superman #232 © DC

GD 2.0 | VG 4.0 | FN 6.0 | VF 8.0 | VF/NM 9.0 | NM- 9.2

SUPERMAN (Becomes Adventures of...#424 on)
National Periodical Publ./DC Comics: Summer, 1939 - No. 423, Sept, 1986
(#1-5 are quarterly)

1(nn)-1st four Action stories reprinted; origin Superman by Siegel & Shuster; has a new 2 pg. origin plus 4 pgs. omitted in Action story; see The Comics Magazine #1 & More Fun #14-17 for Superman prototype app.; cover r/splash page from Action #10; 1st pin-up Superman on back-c - 1st pin-up in comics 30,000 60,000 90,000 225,000 362,500 500,000

1-Reprint, Oversize 13-1/2x10". **WARNING**: This comic is an exact duplicate reprint of the original except for its size. DC published it in 1978 with a second cover titling it as a Famous First Edition. There have been many reported cases of the outer cover being removed and the interior sold as the original edition. The reprint with the new outer cover removed is practically worthless. See Famous First Edition for value.

2-All daily strip-r; full pg. ad for N.Y. World's Fair 2000 4000 6000 15,000 25,000 35,000
3-2nd story-r from Action #5; 3rd story-r from Action #6
1150 2300 3450 8625 14,312 20,000
4-2nd mention of Daily Planet (Spr/40); also see Action #23; 2nd & 3rd app. Luthor (red-headed; also see Action #23) 703 1406 2109 5132 9066 13,000
5-4th Luthor app. (grey hair) 568 1136 1704 4146 7323 10,500
6,7: 6-1st splash pg. in a Superman comic. 7-1st Perry White? (11-12/40)
383 766 1149 2681 4691 6700
8-10: 10-5th app. Luthor (1st bald Luthor, 5-6/41) 349 698 1047 2443 4272 6100
11-13,15: 13-Jimmy Olsen & Luthor app. 290 580 870 1856 3178 4500
14-Patriotic Shield-c classic by Fred Ray 459 918 1377 3350 5925 8500
16,18-20: 16-1st Lois Lane-c this title (5-6/42); 2nd Lois-c after Action #29
239 478 717 1530 2615 3700
17-Hitler, Hirohito-c 343 686 1029 2400 4200 6000
21,22,25: 25-Clark Kent's only military service; Fred Ray's only super-hero story
161 322 483 1030 1765 2500
23-Classic periscope-c 194 388 582 1242 2121 3000
24-Classic Jack Burnley flag-c 290 580 870 1856 3178 4500
26-Classic war-c 258 516 774 1651 2826 4000
27-29: 27,29-Lois Lane-c. 28-Lois Lane Girl Reporter series begins, ends #40,42 142 284 426 909 1555 2200
28-Overseas edition for Armed Forces; same as reg. #28
142 284 426 909 1555 2200
30-Origin & 1st app. Mr. Mxyztplk (9-10/44)(pronounced "Mix-it-plk") in comic books; name later became Mxyzptlk ("Mix-yez-pit-l-ick"); the character was inspired by a combination of the name of Al Capp's Joe Blyfstyk (the little man with the black cloud over his head) & the devilish antics of Bugs Bunny; he 1st app. in newspapers 3/7/44; Superman flies for the first time 271 542 813 1734 2967 4200
31-40: 33-(3-4/45)-3rd app. Mxyztplk. 35,36-Lois Lane-c. 38-Atomic bomb story (1-2/46); delayed because of gov't censorship; Superman shown reading Batman #32 on cover. 40-Mxyztplk-c 119 238 357 762 1306 1850
41-50: 42-Lois Lane-c. 45-Lois Lane as Superwoman (see Action #60 for 1st app.). 46-(5-6/47)-1st app. Superboy this title? 48-1st time Superman travels thru time
97 194 291 621 1061 1500
51,52: 51-Lois Lane-c 82 164 246 528 902 1275
53-Third telling of Superman origin; 10th anniversary issue ('48); classic origin-c by Boring
300 600 900 2010 3505 5000
54,56-60: 57-Lois Lane as Superwoman-c. 58-Intro Tiny Trix
82 164 246 528 902 1275
55-Used in **SOTI**, pg. 33 84 168 252 538 919 1300
61-Origin Superman retold; origin Green Kryptonite (1st Kryptonite story); Superman returns to Krypton for 1st time & sees his parents for 1st time since infancy, discovers he's not an Earth man 155 310 465 992 1696 2400
62-70: 62-Orson Welles-c/story. 65-1st Krypton Foes: Mala, Kizo, & U-Ban. 66-2nd Superbaby story. 67-Perry Como-c/story. 68-1st Luthor-c this title (see Action Comics)
81 162 243 518 884 1250
71-75: 74-2nd Luthor-c this title. 75-Some have #74 on-c
77 154 231 493 847 1200
76-Batman x-over; Superman & Batman learn each other's I.D. for the 1st time (5-6/52) (also see World's Finest #71) 232 464 696 1485 2543 3600
77-81: 78-Last 52 pg. issue. 81-Used in **POP**, pg. 88
71 142 213 454 777 1100
82-87,89,90: 89-1st Curt Swan-c in title 65 130 195 416 708 1000
88-Prankster, Toyman & Luthor team-up 69 138 207 442 759 1075
91-95: 95-Last precode issue (2/55) 57 114 171 362 619 875
96-99: 96-Mr. Mxyztplk-c/story 52 104 156 324 550 775
100 (9-10/55)-Shows cover to #1 on-c 226 452 678 1146 2473 3500
101-105,107-110: 109-1st S.A. issue 48 96 144 302 514 725
106 (7/56)-Retells origin 50 100 150 315 533 750
111-120 43 86 129 271 461 650
121,122,124-127,129: 127-Origin/1st app. Titano. 129-Intro/origin Lori Lemaris, The Mermaid
39 78 117 240 395 550
123-Pre-Supergirl tryout-c/story (8/58). 53 106 159 334 567 800
128-(4/59)-Red Kryptonite used. Bruce Wayne x-over who protects Superman's i.d. (3rd story)
40 80 120 246 411 575
130-(7/59)-2nd app, Krypto, the Superdog with Superman (see Sup.'s Pal Jimmy Olsen #29) (all other previous app. w/Superboy) 41 82 123 256 428 600
131-139: 135-2nd Lori Lemaris app. 139-Lori Lemaris app.;
32 64 96 188 307 425
140-1st Blue Kryptonite & Bizarro Supergirl; origin Bizarro Jr. #1
33 66 99 194 317 440
141-145,148: 142-2nd Batman x-over 27 54 81 158 259 360
146-(7/61)-Superman's life story; back-up hints at Earth II. Classic-c
37 74 111 222 361 500
147(8/61)-7th Legion app; 1st app. Legion of Super-Villains; 1st app. Adult Legion; swipes-c to Adv. #247 34 68 102 199 325 450
149(11/61)-8th Legion app. (cameo); "The Death of Superman" imaginary story; last 10¢ issue 31 62 93 186 303 420
150,151,153,154,157,159,160: 157-Gold Kryptonite used (see Adv. #299); Mon -El app.; Lightning Lad cameo (11/62) 13 26 39 90 165 240
152,155,156,158,162: 152(4/62)-15th Legion app. 155-(8/62)-Legion app; Lightning Man & Cosmic Man, & Adult Legion app. 156,162-Legion app. 158-1st app. Flamebird & Nightwing & Nor-Kan of Kandor (12/62) 13 26 39 93 172 250
161-1st told death of Ma and Pa Kent 13 26 39 93 172 250
161-2nd printing (1987, $1.25)-New DC logo; sold thru So Much Fun Toy Stores (cover title: Superman Classic) 4.00
163-166,168-180: 166-XMas-c. 168-All Luthor issue; JFK tribute/memorial. 169-Bizarro Invasion of Earth-c/story; last Sally Selwyn. 170-Pres. Kennedy story is finally published after delay from #168 due to assassination. 172,173-Legion cameos. 174-Super-Mxyzptlk; Bizarro app. 11 22 33 74 132 190
167-New origin Brainiac, text reference of Brainiac 5 descending from adopted human son Brainiac II; intro Tharla (later Luthor's wife) 13 26 39 90 165 240
181,182,184-186,188-192,194-196,198,200: 181-1st 2465 story/series. 182-1st S.A. app. of The Toyman (1/66). 189-Origin/destruction of Krypton II.
9 18 27 63 107 150
183 (Giant G-18) 11 22 33 80 145 210
187,193,197 (Giants G-23,G-31,G-36) 10 20 30 67 116 165
199-1st Superman/Flash race (8/67): also see Flash #175 & World's Finest #198,199 (r-in Limited Coll. Ed. C-48) 29 58 87 212 406 600
201,203-206,208-211,213-216: 213-Brainiac-5 app. 216-Last 12¢ issue
6 12 18 39 62 85
202 (80-pg. Giant G-42)-All Bizarro issue 7 14 21 47 76 105
207,212,217 (Giants G-48,G-54,G-60): 207-30th anniversary Superman (6/68)
7 14 21 47 76 105
218-221,223-226,228-231 5 10 15 32 51 70
222,239(Giants, G-66,G-84) 6 12 18 43 69 95
227,232(Giants, G-72,G-78)-All Krypton issues 6 12 18 43 69 95
233-2nd app. Morgan Edge; Clark Kent switches from newspaper reporter to TV newscaster; all Kryptonite on earth destroyed; classic Neal Adams-c
9 18 27 63 107 150
234-238 5 10 15 32 51 70
240-Kaluta-a; last 15¢ issue 4 8 12 26 41 55
241-244 (All 52 pgs.): 241-New Wonder Woman app. 243-G.A.-r/#38
4 8 12 28 44 60
245-Also listed as DC 100 Pg. Super Spectacular #7; Air Wave, Kid Eternity, Hawkman-r; Atom-r/Atom #3 9 18 27 65 113 160
246-248,250,251,253 (All 52 pgs.): 246-G.A.-r/#40. 248-World of Krypton story. 251-G.A.-r/#45. 253-Finlay-a, 2 pgs., G.A.-r/#1 4 8 12 28 44 60
249,254-Neal Adams-a. 249-(52 pgs.); 1st app. Terra-Man (Swan-a) & origin-s by Dick Dillin (p) & Neal Adams (inks) 6 12 18 39 62 85
252-Also listed as DC 100 Pg. Super Spectacular #13; Ray(r/Smash #17), Black Condor, (r/Crack #18), Hawkman(r/Flash #24); Starman-r/Adv. #67; Dr. Fate & Spectre-r/More Fun #57; N. Adams-c (see DC 100 Pg. Super Spectacular #13 for price)
255-271,273-277,279-283: 263-Photo-c. 264-1st app. Steve Lombard. 276-Intro Capt. Thunder. 279-Batman, Batgirl app. 282-Luthor battlesuit 3 6 9 14 19 24
272,278,284-All 100 pgs. G.A.-r in all. 272-r/2nd app. Mr. Mxyztplk from Action #80
5 10 15 32 51 70
285-299: 289-Partial photo-c. 292-Origin Lex Luthor retold
2 4 6 9 13 16
300-(6/76) Superman in the year 2001 3 6 9 20 30 40
301-350: 301,320-Solomon Grundy app. 323-Intro. Atomic Skull. 327-329-(44 pgs.). 327-Kobra app. 330-More facts revealed about I.D. 331,332-1st/2nd app. Master Jailer. 335-Mxyzptlk marries Ms. Bgbznz. 336-Rose & Thorn app. 338-(8/79) 40th Anniv. issue; the bottled city of Kandor enlarged. 344-Frankenstein & Dracula app.
1 2 3 5 6 8
321-323,325-327,329-332,335-345,348,350 (Whitman variants; low print run; no issue # on cover) 2 4 6 9 13 16

Superman (2nd series) #50 © DC

Superman (2nd series) #207 © DC

Superman #681 © DC

GD 2.0 | VG 4.0 | FN 6.0 | VF 8.0 | VF/NM 9.0 | NM- 9.2

351-399: 353-Brief origin. 354,355,357-Superman 2020 stories (354-Debut of Superman III). 356-World of Krypton story (also #360,367,375). 366-Fan letter by Todd McFarlane. 372-Superman 2021 story. 376-Free 16 pg. preview Daring New Advs. of Supergirl. 377-Free 16 pg. preview Masters of the Universe 6.00
400 (10/84, $1.50, 68 pgs.)-Many top artists featured; Chaykin painted cover, Miller back-c; Steranko-s/a (10 pages) 1 2 3 4 5 7
401-422: 405-Super-Batman story. 408-Nuclear Holocaust-c/story. 411-Special Julius Schwartz tribute issue. 414,415-Crisis x-over. 422-Horror-c 5.00
409-(7/85) Variant-c with Superman/Superhombre logo (no reported sales)
423-Alan Moore scripts; Curt Swan-a/George Pérez-a(i); "Whatever Happened to the Man of Tomorrow?" story, cont'd in Action #583 2 4 6 8 10 12
Annual 1(10/60, 84 pgs.)-Reprints 1st Supergirl story/Action #252; r/Lois Lane #1; Krypto-r (1st Silver Age DC annual) 84 168 252 714 1407 2100
Annual 2(Win, 1960-61)-Super-villain issue; Brainiac, Titano, Metallo, Bizarro origin-r 38 76 114 294 567 840
Annual 3(Sum, 1961)-Strange Lives of Superman 25 50 75 183 354 525
Annual 4(Win, 1961-62)-11th Legion app; 1st Legion origins (text & pictures); advs. in time, space & on alien worlds 21 42 63 153 297 440
Annual 5(Sum, 1962)-All Krypton issue 17 34 51 124 242 360
Annual 6(Win, 1962-63)-Legion-r/Adv. #247 16 32 48 112 214 315
Annual 7(Sum, 1963)-Silver Anniversary Issue; origin-r/Superman-Batman team/Adv. #275; cover gallery of famous issues 12 24 36 88 162 235
Annual 8(Win, 1963-64)-All origins issue 11 22 33 80 145 210
Annual 9(8/64)-Was advertised but came out as 80 Page Giant #1 instead
Annual 9(1983)-Toth/Austin-a 1 2 3 4 5 7
Annuals 10-13: 10(1984, $1.25)-M. Anderson inks. 11(1985)-Moore scripts. 12(1986)-Bolland-c. 13-(1/08, $3.99) Camelot Falls finale 5.00
Special 1-3('83-'85): 1-G. Kane-c/a; contains German-r 5.00
The Amazing World of Superman "Official Metropolis Edition" (1973, $2.00, treasury-size)-Origin retold; Wood-r(i) from Superboy #153,161; poster incl. (half price if poster missing) 4 8 12 28 44 60
11195 (2/79, $1.95, 224 pgs.)-Golden Press 4 8 12 24 37 50

NOTE: ***N. Adams*** *a-249i, 254p; c-204-206, 210, 212-215, 219, 231i, 233-237, 240-243, 249-252, 254, 263, 307, 308, 313, 314, 317.* ***Adkins*** *a-323i.* ***Austin*** *c-368i.* ***Wayne Boring*** *art-late 1940's to early 1960's.* ***Buckler*** *a(p)-352, 363, 364, 369; c(p)-324-327, 356, 363, 368, 369, 373, 376, 378.* ***Burnley*** *a-252r; c-19-25, 30, 33, 34, 35p, 38p, 39p, 45p.* ***Fine*** *a-252r.* ***Kaluta*** *a-400.* ***Gil Kane*** *a-272r, 367, 372, 375, Special 2; c-374p, 375p, 377, 381, 382, 384-390, 392, Annual 9, Special 2.* ***Joe Kubert*** *c-216.* ***Morrow*** *a-238.* ***Mortimer*** *a-250r.* ***Perez*** *c-364p.* ***Fred Ray*** *a-25; c-6, 8-18.* ***Starlin*** *c-355.* ***Staton*** *a-354i, 355i.* ***Swan/Moldoff*** *c-149.* ***Williamson*** *a(i)-408-410, 412-416; c-408i, 409i.* ***Wrightson*** *a-400, 416.*

SUPERMAN (2nd Series) (Title continues numbering from Adventures of Superman #649)
DC Comics: Jan, 1987 - No. 226, Apr, 2006; No. 650, May, 2006 - Present (75¢-$2.99)

0-(10/94) Zero Hour; released between #93 & #94 2.50
1-Byrne-c/a begins; intro new Metallo 5.00
2-8,10: 3-Legends x-over; Darkseid-c & app. 7-Origin/1st app. Rampage. 8-Legion app. 3.00
9-Joker-c 4.50
11-15,17-20,22-49,51,52,54-56,58-67: 11-1st new Mr. Mxyzptlk. 12-Lori Lemaris revived. 13-1st app. new Toyman. 13,14-Millennium x-over. 20-Doom Patrol app.; Supergirl cameo. 31-Mr. Mxyzptlk app. 37-Newsboy Legion app. 41-Lobo app. 44-Batman storyline, part 1. 45-Free extra 8 pgs. 54-Newsboy Legion story. 63-Aquaman x-over. 67-Last $1.00-c 2.50
16,21: 16-1st app. new Supergirl (4/88). 21-Supergirl-c/story; 1st app. Matrix who becomes new Supergirl 4.00
50-($1.50, 52 pgs.)-Clark Kent proposes to Lois 5.00
50-2nd printing 2.50
53-Clark reveals i.d. to Lois (Cont'd from Action #662) 3.00
53-2nd printing 2.50
57-($1.75, 52 pgs.) 3.00
68-72: 65,66,68-Deathstroke-c/stories. 70-Superman & Robin team-up 2.50
73-Doomsday cameo 5.00
74-Doomsday Pt. 2 (Cont'd from Justice League #69); Superman battles Doomsday 6.00
73,74-2nd printings 2.50
75-($2.50)-Collector's Ed.; Doomsday Pt. 6; Superman dies; polybagged w/poster of funeral, obituary from Daily Planet, postage stamp & armband premiums (direct sales only) 2 4 6 10 14 18
75-Direct sales copy (no upc code, 1st print) 1 2 3 5 6 8
75-Direct sales copy (no upc code, 2nd-4th prints) 2.50
75-Newsstand copy w/upc code 1 2 3 5 6 8
75-Platinum Edition; given away to retailers 60.00
76,77-Funeral For a Friend parts 4 & 8 3.00
78-($1.95)-Collector's Edition with die-cut outer-c & mini poster; Doomsday cameo 3.00
78-($1.50)-Newsstand Edition w/poster and different-c; Doomsday-c & cameo 2.50
79-81,83-89: 83-Funeral for a Friend epilogue; new Batman (Azrael) cameo. 87,88-Bizarro-c/story 2.50
82-($3.50)-Collector's Edition w/all chromium-c; real Superman revealed; Green Lantern x-over from G.L. #46; no ads 6.00
82-($2.00, 44 pgs.)-Regular Edition w/different-c 2.50

GD 2.0 | VG 4.0 | FN 6.0 | VF 8.0 | VF/NM 9.0 | NM- 9.2

90-99: 93-(9/94)-Zero Hour. 94-(11/94). 95-Atom app. 96-Brainiac returns 2.50
100-Death of Clark Kent foil-c 4.00
100-Newsstand 3.00
101-122: 101-Begin $1.95-c; Black Adam app. 105-Green Lantern app. 110-Plastic Man-c/app. 114-Brainiac app; Dwyer-c. 115-Lois leaves Metropolis. 116-(10/96)-1st app. Teen Titans by Jurgens & Perez in 8 pg. preview. 117-Final Night. 118-Wonder Woman app. 119-Legion app. 122-New powers 2.50
123-Collector's Edition w/glow in the dark-c, new costume 6.00
123-Standard ed., new costume 4.00
124-149: 128-Cyborg-c/app. 131-Birth of Lena Luthor. 132-Superman Red/Superman Blue. 134-Millennium Giants. 136,137-Superman 2999. 139-Starlin-a. 140-Grindberg-a 2.50
150-($2.95) Standard Ed.; Brainiac 2.0 app.; Jurgens-s 3.00
150-($3.95) Collector's Ed. w/holo-foil enhanced variant-c 4.00
151-158: 151-Loeb-s begins; Daily Planet reopens 2.50
159-174: 159-$2.25-c begin. 161-Joker-c/app. 162-Aquaman-c/app. 163-Young Justice app. 165-JLA app.; Ramos; Madureira, Liefeld, A. Adams, Wieringo, Churchill-a. 166-Collector's and reg. editions. 167-Return to Krypton. 168-Batman-c/app.(cont'd in Detective #756). 171-173-Our Worlds at War. 173-Sienkiewicz-a (2 pgs.). 174-Adopts black & red "S" logo 2.50
175-($3.50) Joker: Last Laugh x-over; Doomsday-c/app. 3.50
176-189,191-199: 176,180-Churchill-a. 180-Dracula app. 181-Bizarro-c/app. 184-Return to Krypton II. 189-Van Fleet-c. 192,193,195,197-199-New Supergirl app. 2.50
190-($2.25) Regular edition 2.50
190-($3.95) Double-Feature Issue; included reprint of Superman: The 10¢ Adventure 4.00
200-($3.50) Gene Ha-c/art by various; preview art by Yu & Bermejo 3.50
201-Mr Majestic-c/app.; cover swipe of Action #1 2.50
202,203-Godfall parts 3,6; Turner-c; Caldwell-a(p). 203-Jim Lee sketch pages 2.50
204-Jim Lee-c/a begins; Azzarello-s 3.00
204-Diamond Retailer Summit edition with sketch cover 125.00
205-214: 205-Two covers by Jim Lee and Michael Turner. 208-JLA app. 211-Battles Wonder Woman 2.50
215-($2.99) Conclusion to Azzarello/Lee arc 3.00
216-218,220-226: 216-Captain Marvel app. 221-Bizarro & Zoom app. 226-Earth-2 Superman story; Chaykin,Sale, Benes, Ordway-a 2.50
219-Omac/Sacrifice pt. 1; JLA app. 3.00
219-2nd printing with red background variant-c 2.50
(Title continues numbering from Adventures of Superman #649)
650-(5/06) One Year Later; Clark powerless after Infinite Crisis 3.00
651-665,667-669,671-674.676-680: 652-Begin $2.99-c. 654-658,662-664,667-Pacheco-a. 665-Origin of Jimmy Olsen. 671-673-Insect Queen. 676-680-Ross-c 3.00
666, 670,675-($3.99) 666-Simonson-a. 670-The Third Kryptonian. 675-Ross-c 4.00
681-696: 681-683-New Krypton x-over; Ross-c. 685-Mon-El freed from Phantom Zone. 694-Mon-El new costume 3.00
#1,000,000 (11/98) 853rd Century x-over; Gene Ha-c 2.50
Annual 1,2: 1 (1987)-No Byrne-a. 2 (1988)-Byrne-a; Newsboy Legion; Guardian returns 4.00
Annual 3-6 ('91-'94 68 pgs.): 1-Armageddon 2001 x-over; Batman app.; Austin-c(i) & part inks. 4-Eclipso app. 6-Elseworlds sty 3.00
Annual 3-2nd & 3rd printings; 3rd has silver ink 2.50
Annual 7 (1995, $3.95, 69 pgs.)-Year One story 4.00
Annual 8 (1996, $2.95)-Legends of the Dead Earth story 3.00
Annual 9 (1997, $3.95)-Pulp Heroes story 4.00
Annual 10 (1998, $2.95)-Ghosts; Wrightson-c 3.00
Annual 11 (1999, $2.95)-JLApe; Art Adams-c 3.00
Annual 12 (2000, $3.50)-Planet DC 3.50
Annual 13 (1/08, $3.99) Finale of Camelot Falls 4.00
Annual 14 (10/09, $3.99) Origin of Mon-El re-told; Pina-a/Guedes-c 4.00
...: 80 Page Giant (2/99, $4.95) Jurgens-c 5.00
...: 80 Page Giant 2 (6/99, $4.95) Harris-c 5.00
...: 80 Page Giant 3 (11/00, $5.95) Nowlan-c; art by various 6.00
Special 1 (1992, $3.50, 68 pgs.)-Simonson-c/a 5.00

SUPERMAN (Hardcovers and Trade Paperbacks)
... and the Legion of Super-Heroes HC (2008, $24.99) r/Action Comics #858-863, covers and variants; intro. by Giffen; Gary Frank design sketch pages 25.00
... and the Legion of Super-Heroes SC (2009, $14.99) same contents as HC 15.00
...: Back in Action TPB (2007, $14.99) r/Action Comics #841-843 and DC Comics Presents #4,17,24; commentary by Busiek 15.00
.../Batman: Saga of the Super Sons TPB (2007, $19.99) r/Super Sons stories from '70s World's Finest #215,216,221,222,224,228,230,231,233,242,263 & Elseworlds 80-Page Giant 20.00
...: Brainiac HC (2009, $19.99, dustjacket) r/Action Comics #866-870 & Superman: New Krypton Special #1 20.00
...: Camelot Falls HC (2007, $19.99, dustjacket) r/Superman #654-658 20.00
...: Camelot Falls SC (2008, $12.99) r/Superman #654-658 13.00
...: Camelot Falls Vol. 2 HC (2008, $19.99, dj) r/Superman #662-664,667 & Ann. #13 20.00
...: Camelot Falls Vol. 2 The Weight of the World SC (2008, $12.99) r/Superman #662-664,667

Superman In the Fifties TPB © DC

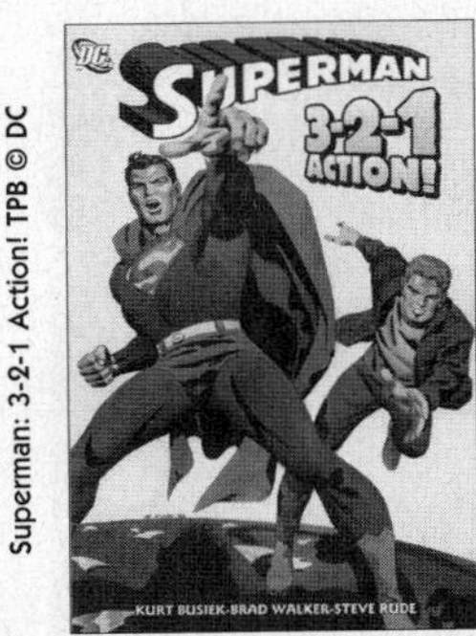

Superman: 3-2-1 Action! TPB © DC

Superman Vs. Brainiac TPB © DC

GD VG FN VF VF/NM NM-
2.0 4.0 6.0 8.0 9.0 9.2

& Ann. #13 13.00
...: Chronicles Vol. 1 ('06, $14.99, TPB) r/early Superman app. in Action Comics #1-13, New York World's Fair 1939 and Superman #1 15.00
...: Chronicles Vol. 2 ('07, $14.99, TPB) r/early Superman app. in Action Comics #14-20 and Superman #2,3 15.00
...: Chronicles Vol. 3 ('07, $14.99, TPB) r/early Superman app. in Action Comics #21-25, Superman #3,4 and New York World's Fair 1940 15.00
...: Chronicles Vol. 4 ('08, $14.99, TPB) r/early Superman app. in Action Comics #26-31, Superman #6,7 15.00
...: Chronicles Vol. 5 ('08, $14.99, TPB) r/early Superman app. in Action Comics #32-36, Superman #8,9 and World's Best Comics #1 15.00
...: Chronicles Vol. 6 ('09, $14.99, TPB) r/early Superman app. in Action Comics #37-40, Superman #10,11 and World's Finest Comics #2,3 15.00
...: Chronicles Vol. 7 ('09, $14.99, TPB) r/early Superman app. in Action Comics #41-43, Superman #12,13 and World's Finest Comics #4 15.00
...: Critical Condition ('03, $14.95, TPB) r/2000 Kryptonite poisoning storyline 15.00
.../ Doomsday: The Collection Edition (2006, $19.99) r/Superman/Doomsday: Hunter/Prey #1-3, Doomsday Ann. #1, Superman: The Doomsday Wars #1-3, Advs. of Superman #594 and Superman #175; intro. by Dan Jurgens 20.00
...: Daily Planet (2006, $19.99, TPB)-Reprints stories of Daily Planet staff 20.00
...: Emperor Joker TPB (2007, $14.99) reprints 2000 x-over from Superman titles 15.00
...: Endgame (2000, $14.95, TPB)-Reprints Y2K and Brainiac story line 15.00
...: Ending Battle (2009, $14.99, TPB) r/crossover of Superman titles from 2002 15.00
...: Eradication! The Origin of the Eradicator (1996, $12.95, TPB) 13.00
...: Escape From Bizarro World HC (2008, $24.99, dustjacket) r/Action #855-857; early apps. in Superman #140, DC Comics Presents #71 and Man of Steel #5; Vaughan intro. 25.00
...: Escape From Bizarro World SC (2009, $14.99) same contents as hardcover 15.00
...: Exile (1998, $14.95, TPB)-Reprints space exile following execution of Kryptonian criminals; 1st Eradicator 15.00
...: For Tomorrow Volume 1 HC (2005, $24.99, dustjacket) r/#204-209; intro by Azzarello; new cover and sketch section by Lee 25.00
...: For Tomorrow Volume 1 SC (2005, $14.99) r/#204-209; foil-stamped S emblem-c 15.00
...: For Tomorrow Volume 2 HC (2005, $24.99, dustjacket) r/#210-215; afterword and sketch section by Lee; new Lee-c with foil-stamped S emblem 25.00
...: For Tomorrow Volume 2 SC (2005, $14.99) r/#210-215; foil-stamped S emblem-c 15.00
...: Godfall HC (2004, $19.95, dustjacket) r/Action #812-813, Advs. of Superman #625-626, Superman #202-203; Caldwell sketch pages; Turner cover gallery; new Turner-c 20.00
...: Godfall SC (2004, $9.99) r/Action #812-813, Advs. of Superman #625-626, Superman #202-203; Caldwell sketch pages; Turner cover gallery; new Turner-c 10.00
...: Infinite Crisis TPB (2006, $12.99) r/Infinite Crisis #5, I.C. Secret Files and Origins 2006, Action Comics #836, Superman #226 and Advs. of Superman #649 13.00
... In the Forties ('05, $19.99, TPB) Intro. by Bob Hughes 20.00
... In the Fifties ('02, $19.95, TPB) Intro. by Mark Waid 20.00
... In the Sixties ('01, $19.95, TPB) Intro. by Mark Waid 20.00
... In the Seventies ('00, $19.95, TPB) Intro. by Christopher Reeve 20.00
... In the Eighties ('06, $19.99, TPB) Intro. by Jerry Ordway 20.00
... In the Name of Gog ('05, $17.99, TPB) r/Action Comics #820-825 18.00
... Kryptonite HC ('08, $24.99) r/Superman Confidential #1-5,11; Darwyn Cooke intro. 25.00
...: Last Son HC (2008, $19.99) r/Action Comics #844-846,851 and Annual #11; sketch pages and variant covers; Marc McClure intro. 20.00
... Mon-El HC ('10, $24.99) r/Superman #684-690, Action #874 & Annual #1, Superman: Secret Files 2009 #1 25.00
... : New Krypton Vol. 1 HC ('09, $24.99, d.j.) r/Superman #681, Action #871 & one-shots 25.00
... : New Krypton Vol. 2 HC ('09, $24.99, d.j.) r/Superman #682,683, Action #872,873 & Supergirl #35,36; gallery of covers and variants 25.00
... No Limits ('00, $14.95, TPB) Reprints early 2000 stories 15.00
...: Our Worlds at War Book 1 ('02, $19.95, TPB) r/1st half of x-over 20.00
...: Our Worlds at War Book 2 ('02, $19.95, TPB) r/2nd half of x-over 20.00
...: Our Worlds at War - The Complete Collection ('06, $24.99, TPB) r/entire x-over 25.00
...: Past and Future (2008, $19.99, TPB) r/time travel stories 1947-1983 18.00
...: President Lex TPB (2003, $17.95) r/Luthor's run for the White House; Harris-c 18.00
...: Redemption TPB (2007, $12.99) r/Superman #659,666 & Action Comics #848,849 13.00
...: Return to Krypton (2004, $17.95, TPB) r/2001-2002 x-over 18.00
...: Sacrifice (2005, $14.99, TPB) prelude x-over to Infinite Crisis; r/Superman #218-220, Advs. of Superman #642,643; Action #829, Wonder Woman #219,220 15.00
...: Shadows Linger (2008, $14.99, TPB) r/Superman #671-675 15.00
... : Strange Attractors (2006, $14.99, TPB) r/Action Comics #827,828,830-835 15.00
... : Tales From the Phantom Zone ('09, $19.99, TPB) r/Phantom Zone stories 1961-68 20.00
...: That Healing Touch TPB (2005, $14.99) r/Advs. of Superman #633-638 & Superman Secret Files 2004 15.00
...: The Adventures of Nightwing and Flamebird TPB (2009, $19.99)-reprints appearances in Superman Family #173,183-194 20.00
The Bottle City of Kandor TPB (2007, $14.99)-Reprints 1st app. in Action #242 and other stories; Nightwing and Flamebird app. 15.00

GD VG FN VF VF/NM NM-
2.0 4.0 6.0 8.0 9.0 9.2

The Coming of Atlas HC (2009, $19.99, dustjacket)-r/Superman #677-680 & Atlas' debut from First Issue Special #1 (1975); intro by James Robinson 20.00
The Death of Clark Kent (1997, $19.95, TPB)-Reprints Man of Steel #43 (1 page), Superman #99 (1 page),#100-102, Action #709 (1 page), #710,711, Advs. of Superman #523-525, Superman:The Man of Tomorrow #1 20.00
The Death of Superman (1993, $4.95, TPB)-Reprints Man of Steel #17-19, Superman #73-75, Advs. of Superman #496,497, Action #683,684, & Justice League #69 1 2 3 5 6 8
The Death of Superman, 2nd & 3rd printings 5.00
The Death of Superman Platinum Edition 15.00
...: The Greatest Stories Ever Told ('04, $19.95, TPB) Ross-c, Uslan intro. 20.00
...: The Greatest Stories Ever Told Vol. 2 ('06, $19.99, TPB) Ross-c, Greenberger intro. 20.00
...: The Journey ('06, $14.99, TPB) r/Action Comics #831 & Superman #217,221-225 15.00
...: The Man of Steel Vol. 2 ('03, $19.95, TPB) r/Superman #1-3, Action #584-586, Advs. of Superman #424-426 & Who's Who Update '87 20.00
...: The Man of Steel Vol. 3 ('04, $19.95, TPB) r/Superman #4-6, Action #587-589, Advs. of Superman #427-429; intro. by Ordway; new Ordway-c 20.00
...: The Man of Steel Vol. 4 ('05, $19.99, TPB) r/Superman #7,8; Action #590,591; Advs. of Superman #430,431; Legion of Super-Heroes #37,38; new Ordway-c 20.00
...: The Man of Steel Vol. 5 ('06, $19.99, TPB) r/Superman #9-11, Action #592-593, Advs. of Superman #432-435; intro. by Mike Carlin; new Ordway-c 20.00
...: The Man of Steel Vol. 6 ('08, $19.99, TPB) r/Superman #12 & Ann. #1, Action #594-595 & Ann. #1, Advs. of Superman Ann.#1; Booster Gold #23; new Ordway-c 20.00
The Third Kryptonian ('08, $14.99, TPB) r/Action #847, Superman #668-670 & Ann. #13 15.00
The Trial of Superman ('97, $14.95, TPB) reprints story arc 15.00
The World of Krypton ('08, $14.99, TPB) r/World of Krypton Vol. 2 #1-4 and various tales of Krypton and its history; Kupperberg intro. 15.00
The Wrath of Gog ('05, $14.99, TPB) reprints Action Comics #812-819 15.00
...: They Saved Luthor's Brain ('00, $14.95) r/ "death" and return of Luthor 15.00
...: 3-2-1 Action! ('08, $14.99) Jimmy Olsen super-powered stories; Steve Rude-c 15.00
...: 'Til Death Do Us Part ('01, $17.95) reprints; Mahnke-c 18.00
...: Time and Time Again (1994, $7.50, TPB)-Reprints 8.00
...: Transformed ('98, $12.95, TPB) r/post Final Night powerless Superman to Electric Superman 13.00
...: Unconventional Warfare (2005, $14.95, TPB) r/Adventures of Superman #625-632 and pages from Superman Secret Files 2004 15.00
...: Up, Up and Away! (2006, $14.99, TPB) r/Superman #650-653 and Action #837-840 15.00
... Vs. Brainiac (2008, $19.99, TPB) reprints 1st meeting in Action #242 and other duels 20.00
... Vs. Lex Luthor (2006, $19.99, TPB) reprints 1st meeting in Action #23 and 11 other classic duels 1940-2001 20.00
... Vs. The Flash (2005, $19.99, TPB) reprints their races from Superman #199, Flash #175, World's Finest #198, DC Comics Presents #1&2, Advs. of Superman #463 & DC First: Flash/Superman; new Alex Ross-c 20.00
... Vs. The Revenge Squad (1999, $12.95, TPB) 13.00
...: Whatever Happened to the Man of Tomorrow? TPB (1/97, $5.99) r/Superman #423 & Action Comics #583, intro. by Paul Kupperberg 6.00
...: Whatever Happened to the Man of Tomorrow? Deluxe Edition HC (2009, $24.99, d.j.) r/Superman #423, Action #583, DC Comics Presents #85, Superman Ann #11 25.00

*NOTE: **Austin** a(i)-1-3. **Byrne** a-1-16p, 17, 19-21p, 22; c-1-17, 20-22; scripts-1-22. **Guice** c/a-64. **Kirby** c-37p. **Joe Quesada** c-Annual 4. **Russell** c/a-23i. **Simonson** c-69i. #19-21 2nd printings sold in multi-packs.*

SUPERMAN (one-shots)
Daily News Magazine Presents DC Comics' Superman nn-(1987, 8 pgs.)-Supplement to New York Daily News; Perez-c/a 5.00
...: A Nation Divided (1999, $4.95)-Elseworlds Civil War story 5.00
... & Savage Dragon: Chicago (2002, $5.95) Larsen-a; Ross-c 6.00
... & Savage Dragon: Metropolis (11/99, $4.95) Bogdanove-a 5.00
...: At Earth's End (1995, $4.95)-Elseworlds story 5.00
...: Blood of My Ancestors (2003, $6.95)-Gil Kane & John Buscema-a 7.00
...: Distant Fires (1998, $5.95)-Elseworlds; Chaykin-s 6.00
...: Emperor Joker (10/00, $3.50)-Follows Action #769 3.50
...: End of the Century (2/00, $24.95, HC)-Immonen-s/a 25.00
...: End of the Century (2003, $17.95, SC)-Immonen-s/a 18.00
... For Earth (1991, $4.95, 52 pgs, printed on recycled paper)-Ordway wraparound-c 5.00
...IV Movie Special (1987, $2.00)-Movie adaptation; Heck-a 3.00
...Gallery, The 1 (1993, $2.95)-Poster-a 3.00
..., Inc. (1999, $6.95)-Elseworlds Clark as a sports hero; Garcia-Lopez-a 7.00
...: Infinite City HC (2005, $24.99, dustjacket) Mike Kennedy-s/Carlos Meglia-a 25.00
...: Infinite City SC (2006, $17.99) Mike Kennedy-s/Carlos Meglia-a 18.00
...: Kal (1995, $5.95)-Elseworlds story 6.00
...: Lex 2000 (1/01, $3.50)-Election night for the Luthor Presidency 3.50
...: Monster (1999, $5.95)-Elseworlds story; Anthony Williams-a 6.00
... Movie Special-(9/83)-Adaptation of Superman III; other versions exist with store logos on bottom 1/3 of-c 4.00
...: New Krypton Special 1-(12/08, $3.99) Funeral of Pa Kent; newly enlarged Kandor 4.00

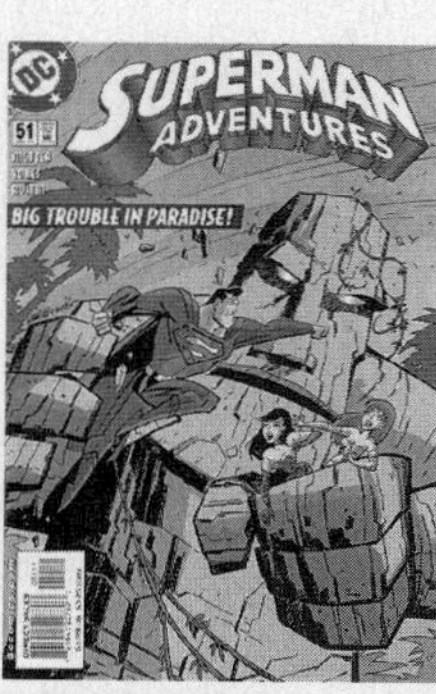

Superman Adventures #51 © DC

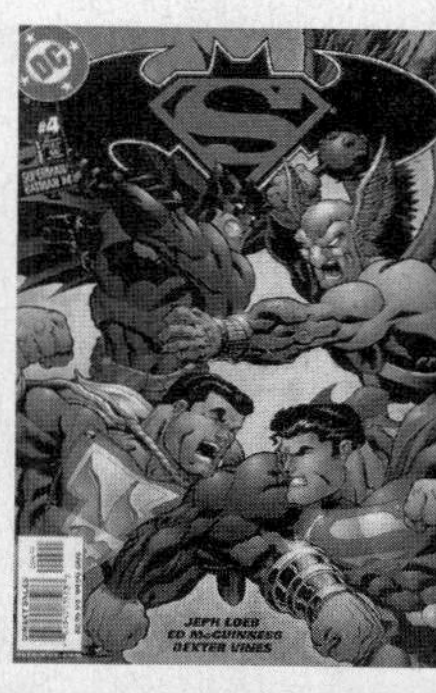

Superman/Batman #4 © DC

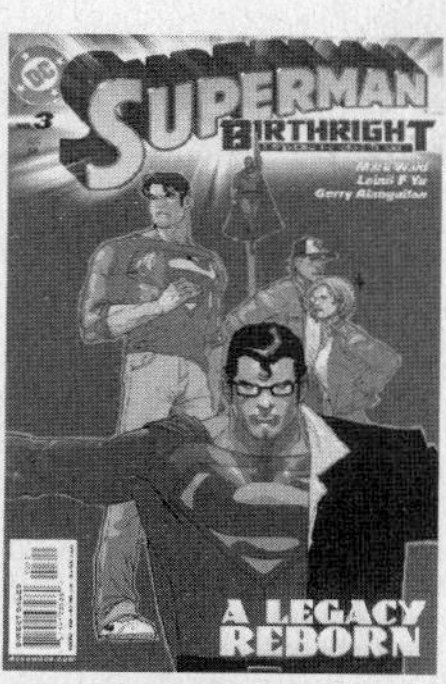

Superman: Birthright #3 © DC

GD VG FN VF VF/NM NM-
2.0 4.0 6.0 8.0 9.0 9.2

...: Our Worlds at War Secret Files 1-(8/01, $5.95)-Stories & profile pages 6.00
... Plus 1(2/97, $2.95)-Legion of Super-Heroes-c/app. 3.00
...'s Metropolis-(1996, $5.95, prestige format)-Elseworlds; McKeever-c/a 6.00
...: Speeding Bullets-(1993, $4.95, 52 pgs.)-Elseworlds 5.00
.../Spider-Man-(1995, $3.95)-r/DC and Marvel Presents... 4.00
... 10-Cent Adventure 1 (3/02, 10¢) McDaniel-a; intro. Cir-El Supergirl 2.25
...: The Earth Stealers 1-(1988, $2.95, 52 pgs, prestige format) Byrne script; painted-c 4.00
...: The Earth Stealers 1-2nd printing 3.00
...: The Legacy of Superman #1 (3/93, $2.50, 68 pgs.)-Art Adams-c; Simonson-a 4.00
...: The Last God of Krypton ('99,$4.95) Hildebrandt Bros.-a/Simonson-s 5.00
...: The Odyssey ('99, $4.95) Clark Kent's post-Smallville journey 5.00
...: 3-D (12/98, $3.95)-with glasses 4.00
.../Thundercats (1/04, $5.95) Winick-s/Garza-a; two covers by Garza & McGuinness 6.00
.../Through the Ages (2006, $3.99) r/Action #1, Superman ('87) #7; origins and pin-ups 4.00
.../Toyman-(1996, $1.95) 2.50
...: True Brit (2004, $24.95, HC w/dust jacket) Elseworlds; Kal-El's rocket lands in England; co-written by John Cleese and Kim Howard Johnson; John Byrne-a 25.00
...: True Brit (2005, $17.99, TPB) Elseworlds; Kal-El's rocket lands in England 18.00
...: Under A Yellow Sun (1994, $5.95, 68 pgs.)-A Novel by Clark Kent; embossed-c 6.00
... Vs. Darkseid: Apokolips Now! 1 (3/03, $2.95) McKone-a; Kara (Supergirl #75) app. 3.00
...: War of the Worlds (1999, $5.95)-Battles Martians 6.00
...: Where is thy Sting? (2001, $6.95)-McCormack-Sharp-c/a 7.00
...: Y2K (2/00, $4.95)-1st Brainiac 13 app.; Guice-c/a 5.00

SUPERMAN ADVENTURES, THE (Based on animated series)
DC Comics: Oct, 1996 - No. 66, Apr, 2002 ($1.75/$1.95/$1.99)

1-Rick Burchett-c/a begins; Paul Dini script; Lex Luthor app.; silver ink, wraparound-c 3.00
2-20,22: 2-McCloud scripts begin; Metallo-c/app. 3-Brainiac-c/app. 6-Mxyzptlk-c/app. 2.50
21-($3.95) 1st animated Supergirl 5.00
23-66: 23-Begin $1.99-c; Livewire app. 25-Batgirl-c/app. 28-Manley-a. 54-Retells Superman #233 "Kryptonite Nevermore" 58-Ross-c 2.25
Annual 1 (1997, $3.95)-Zatanna and Bruce Wayne app. 4.00
Special 1 (2/98, $2.95) Superman vs. Lobo 3.00
TPB (1998, $7.95) r/#1-6 8.00
... Vol 1: Up, Up and Away (2004, $6.95, digest) r/#16,19,22-24; Amancio-a 7.00
... Vol 2: The Never-Ending Battle (2004, $6.95) r/#25-29 7.00
... Vol 3: Last Son of Krypton (2006, $6.99) r/#30-34 7.00
... Vol 4: The Man of Steel (2006, $6.99) r/#35-39 7.00

SUPERMAN ALIENS 2: GOD WAR (Also see Superman Vs. Aliens)
DC Comics/Dark Horse Comics: May, 2002 - No. 4, Nov, 2002 ($2.99, limited series)

1-4-Bogdanove & Nowlan-a; Darkseid & New Gods app. 3.00
TPB (6/03, $12.95) r/#1-4 13.00

SUPERMAN & BATMAN: GENERATIONS (Elseworlds)
DC Comics: 1999 - No. 4, 1999 ($4.95, limited series)

1-4-Superman & Batman team-up from 1939 to the future; Byrne-c/s/a 5.00
TPB (2000, $14.95) r/series 15.00

SUPERMAN & BATMAN: GENERATIONS II (Elseworlds)
DC Comics: 2001 - No. 4, 2001 ($5.95, limited series)

1-4-Superman, Batman & others team-up from 1942-future; Byrne-c/s/a 6.00
TPB (2003, $19.95) r/series 20.00

SUPERMAN & BATMAN: GENERATIONS III (Elseworlds)
DC Comics: Mar, 2003 - No. 12, Feb, 2004 ($2.95, limited series)

1-12-Superman & Batman through the centuries; Byrne-c/s/a 3.00

SUPERMAN & BATMAN VS. ALIENS AND PREDATOR
DC Comics: 2007 - No. 2, 2007 ($5.99, squarebound, limited series)

1,2-Schultz-s/Olivetti-a 6.00
TPB (2007, $12.99) r/#1,2; pencil breakdown pages 13.00

SUPERMAN AND BATMAN VS. VAMPIRES AND WEREWOLVES
DC Comics: Early Dec, 2008 - No. 6, Late Feb, 2009 ($2.99, limited series)

1-6-Van Hook-s/Mandrake-a/c. 1-Wonder Woman app. 5-Demon-c/app. 3.00
TPB (2009, $14.99) r/#1-6; intro. by John Landis 15.00

SUPERMAN & BATMAN: WORLD'S FUNNEST (Elseworlds)
DC Comics: 2000 ($6.95, square-bound, one-shot)

nn-Mr. Mxyzptlk and Bat-Mite destroy each DC Universe; Dorkin-s; art by various incl. Ross, Timm, Miller, Allred, Moldoff, Gibbons, Cho, Jimenez 7.00

SUPERMAN & BUGS BUNNY
DC Comics: Jul, 2000 - No. 4, Oct, 2000 ($2.50, limited series)

1-4-JLA & Looney Tunes characters meet 2.50

SUPERMAN/BATMAN

GD VG FN VF VF/NM NM-
2.0 4.0 6.0 8.0 9.0 9.2

DC Comics: Oct, 2003 - Present ($2.95/$2.99)

1-Two covers (Superman or Batman in foreground) Loeb-s/McGuinness-a; Metallo app. 5.00
1-2nd printing (Batman cover) 3.00
1-3rd printing; new McGuinness cover 3.00
1-Diamond/Alliance Retailer Summit Edition-variant cover 100.00
2-6: 2,5-Future Superman app. 6-Luthor in battlesuit 3.00
7-Pat Lee-c/a; Superboy & Robin app. 3.00
8-Michael Turner-c/a; intro. new Kara Zor-El 5.00
8-Second printing with sketch cover 3.00
8-Third printing with new Turner cover 3.00
9-13-Michael Turner-c/a; Wonder Woman app. 10,13-Variant-c by Jim Lee 3.00
14-25: 14-18-Pacheco-a; Lightning Lord, Saturn Queen & Cosmic King app. 19-Supergirl app.; leads into Supergirl #1. 21-25-Bizarro app. 25-Superman & Batman covers; 2nd printing with white bkgrd cover 3.00
26-($3.99) Sam Loeb tribute issue; 2 covers by Turner; story & art by 26 various; back-up by Loeb & Sale 5.00
27-49: 27-Flashback to Earth-2 Power Girl & Huntress; Maguire-a. 34-36-Metal Men app. 3.00
50-($3.99) Thomas Wayne meets Jor-El; Justice League app. 4.00
51-68: 51,52-Mr. Mxyzptlk app. 66,67-Blackest Night; Man-Bat and Bizarro app. 3.00
Annual #1 (12/06, $3.99) Re-imaging of 1st meeting from World's Finest #71 4.00
Annual #2 (5/08, $3.99) Kolins-a; re-imaging of Superman as Supernova story 4.00
Annual #3 (3/09, $3.99) Composite Superman-c by Wrightson; Batista-a 4.00
...Absolute Power HC (2005, $19.99) r/#14-18 20.00
...Absolute Power SC (2006, $12.99) r/#14-18 13.00
...Enemies Among Us SC (2009, $12.99) r/#28-33 13.00
...Public Enemies HC (2004, $19.95) r/#1-6 & Secret Files 2003; sketch art pages 20.00
...Public Enemies SC (2005, $12.99) r/#1-6 & Secret Files 2003; sketch art pages 13.00
...Public Enemies SC (2009, $14.99) r/#1-6 & Secret Files 2003; sketch art pages 15.00
...Secret Files 2003 (11/03, $4.95) Reis-a; pin-ups by various; Loeb/Sale short-s 5.00
... : Supergirl HC (2004, $19.95) r/#8-13; intro by Loeb, cover gallery, sketch pages 20.00
... : Supergirl SC (2005, $12.99) r/#8-13; intro by Loeb, cover gallery, sketch pages 13.00
... : The Search For Kryptonite HC (2008, $19.99) r/#44-49; Davis sketch pages 20.00
... : The Search For Kryptonite SC (2009, $12.99) r/#44-49; Davis sketch pages 13.00
... : Torment HC (2008, $19.99) r/#37-42; cover gallery, Nguyen sketch pages 20.00
... : Vengeance HC (2006, $19.99) r/#20-25; sketch pages 20.00
... : Vengeance SC (2008, $12.99) r/#20-25; sketch pages 13.00

SUPERMAN/BATMAN: ALTERNATE HISTORIES
DC Comics: 1996 ($14.95, trade paperback)

nn-Reprints Detective Comics Annual #7, Action Comics Annual #6, Steel Annual #1, Legends of the Dark Knight Annual #4 15.00

SUPERMAN: BIRTHRIGHT
DC Comics: Sept, 2003 - No. 12, Sept, 2004 ($2.95, limited series)

1-12-Waid-s/Leinil Yu-a; retelling of origin and early Superman years 3.00
HC (2004, $29.95, dustjacket) r/series; cover gallery; Waid proposal with Yu concept art 30.00
SC (2005, $19.99) r/series; cover gallery; Waid proposal with Yu concept art 20.00

SUPERMAN COMICS
DC Comics: 1939

nn - Ashcan comic, not distributed to newsstands, only for in-house use. Cover art is Action Comics #7 with interior being Action Comics #8. A CGC certified 9.0 copy sold for $37,375 in 2005 and for $90,000 in 2007.

SUPERMAN CONFIDENTIAL (See Superman Hardcovers and TPBs listings for reprint)
DC Comics: Jan, 2007 - No. 14, Jun, 2008 ($2.99)

1-14: 1-5,9-Darwyn Cooke-s/Tim Sale-a/c; origin of Kryptonite re-told. 8-10-New Gods and Darkside app. 3.00
...: Kryptonite TPB (2009, $14.99) r/#1-5,11; intro. by Darwyn Cooke; Tim Sale sketch-a 15.00

SUPERMAN: DAY OF DOOM
DC Comics: Jan, 2003 - No. 4, Feb, 2003 ($2.95, weekly limited series)

1-4-Jurgens-s/Jurgens & Sienkiewicz-a 3.00
TPB (2003, $9.95) r/#1-4 10.00

SUPERMAN/DOOMSDAY: HUNTER/PREY
DC Comics: 1994 - No. 3, 1994 ($4.95, limited series, 52 pgs.)

1-3 5.00

SUPERMAN FAMILY, THE (Formerly Superman's Pal Jimmy Olsen)
National Per. Publ./DC Comics: No. 164, Apr-May, 1974 - No. 222, Sept, 1982

164-(100 pgs.) Jimmy Olsen, Supergirl, Lois Lane begin 5 10 15 30 48 65
165-169 (100 pgs.) 3 6 9 19 29 38
170-176 (68 pgs.) 3 6 9 14 19 24
177-190 (52 pgs.): 177-181-52 pgs. 182-Marshall Rogers-a; $1.00 issues begin;

Superman Family #171 © DC

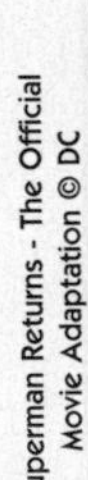

Superman Returns - The Official Movie Adaptation © DC

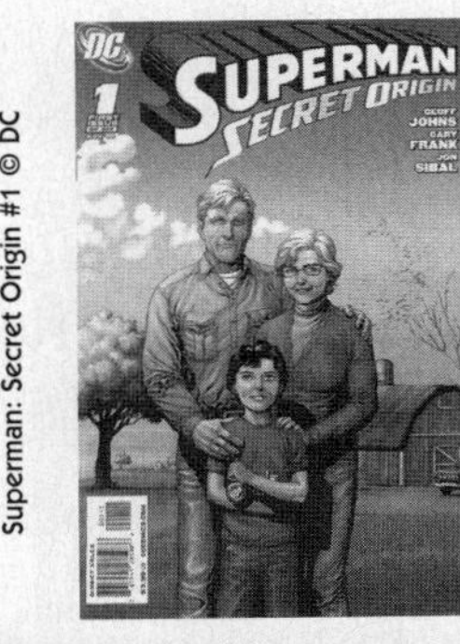

Superman: Secret Origin #1 © DC

	GD 2.0	VG 4.0	FN 6.0	VF 8.0	VF/NM 9.0	NM- 9.2
Krypto begins, ends #192. 183-Nightwing-Flamebird begins, ends #194. 189-Brainiac 5, Mon -El app.	2	4	6	9	13	16
191-193,195-199: 191-Superboy begins, ends #198	2	3	4	6	8	10
194,200: 194-Rogers-a. 200-Book length sty	2	4	6	8	10	12
201-210,212-222	1	2	3	5	6	8
211-Earth II Batman & Catwoman marry	2	4	6	8	10	12

NOTE: ***N. Adams*** *c-182-185.* ***Anderson*** *a-186i.* ***Buckler*** *c(p)-190, 191, 209, 210, 215, 217, 220.* ***Jones*** *a-191-193.* ***Gil Kane*** *c(p)-221, 222.* ***Mortimer*** *a(p)-191-193, 199, 201-222.* ***Orlando*** *a(i)-186, 187.* ***Rogers*** *a-182, 194.* ***Staton*** *a-191-194, 196p.* ***Tuska*** *a(p)-203, 207-209.*

SUPERMAN/FANTASTIC FOUR
DC Comics/Marvel Comics: 1999 ($9.95, tabloid size, one-shot)

1-Battle Galactus and the Cyborg; wraparound-c by Alex Ross and Dan Jurgens; Jurgens-s/a; Thibert-a 10.00

SUPERMAN FOR ALL SEASONS
DC Comics: 1998 - No, 4, 1998 ($4.95, limited series, prestige format)

1-Loeb-s/Sale-a/c; Superman's first year in Metropolis 6.00
2-4 5.00
Hardcover (1999, $24.95) r/#1-4 25.00

SUPERMAN FOR EARTH (See Superman one-shots)

SUPERMAN FOREVER
DC Comics: Jun, 1998 ($5.95, one-shot)

1-($5.95)-Collector's Edition with a 7-image lenticular-c by Alex Ross; Superman returns to normal; s/a by various 7.00
1-($4.95) Standard Edition with single image Ross-c 5.00

SUPERMAN/GEN13
DC Comics (WildStorm): Jun, 2000 - No. 3, Aug, 2000 ($2.50, limited series)

1-3-Hughes-s/ Bermejo-a; Campbell variant-c for each 2.50
TPB (2001, $9.95) new Bermejo-c; cover gallery 10.00

SUPERMAN: KING OF THE WORLD
DC Comics: June, 1999 ($3.95/$4.95, one-shot)

1-($3.95) Regular Ed. 4.00
1-($4.95) Collectors' Ed. with gold foil enhanced-c 5.00

SUPERMAN: LAST SON OF EARTH
DC Comics: 2000 - No. 2, 2000 ($5.95, limited series, prestige format)

1,2-Elseworlds; baby Clark rockets to Krypton; Gerber-s/Wheatley-a 6.00

SUPERMAN: LAST STAND ON KRYPTON
DC Comics: 2003 ($6.95, one-shot, prestige format)

1-Sequel to Superman: Last Son of Earth; Gerber-s/Wheatley-a 7.00

SUPERMAN: LOIS LANE (Girlfrenzy)
DC Comics: Jun, 1998 ($1.95, one shot)

1-Connor & Palmiotti-a 2.50

SUPERMAN/MADMAN HULLABALOO!
Dark Horse Comics: June, 1997 - No. 3, Aug, 1997 ($2.95, limited series)

1-3-Mike Allred-c/s/a 3.00
TPB (1997, $8.95) 9.00

SUPERMAN: METROPOLIS
DC Comics: Apr, 2003 - No. 12, Mar, 2004 ($2.95, limited series)

1-12-Focus on Jimmy Olsen; Austen-s. 1-6-Zezelj-a. 7-12-Kristiansen-a. 8,9-Creeper app. 3.00

SUPERMAN METROPOLIS SECRET FILES
DC Comics: Jun, 2000 ($4.95, one shot)

1-Short stories, pin-ups and profile pages; Hitch and Neary-c 5.00

SUPERMAN: PEACE ON EARTH
DC Comics: Jan, 1999 ($9.95, Treasury-sized, one-shot)

1-Alex Ross painted-c/a; Paul Dini-s 12.00

SUPERMAN: RED SON
DC Comics: 2003 - No. 3, 2003 ($5.95, limited series, prestige format)

1-Elseworlds; Superman's rocket lands in Russia; Mark Millar-s/Dave Johnson-c/a 10.00
2,3 6.00
TPB (2004, $17.95) r/#1-3; intro. by Tom DeSanto; sketch pages 18.00
... - The Deluxe Edition HC (2009, $24.99, d.j.) r/#1-3; sketch art by various 25.00

SUPERMAN RED/ SUPERMAN BLUE
DC Comics: Feb, 1998 ($4.95, one shot)

1-Polybagged w/3-D glasses and reprint of Superman 3-D (1955); Jurgens-plot/3-D cover; script and art by various 5.00
1-($3.95)-Standard Ed.; comic only, non 3-D cover 4.00

SUPERMAN RETURNS... (2006 movie)
DC Comics: Aug, 2006 ($3.99, movie tie-in stories by Singer, Dougherty and Harris)

Prequel 1 - Krypton to Earth; Olivetti-a/Hughes-c; retells Jor-El's story 6.00
Prequel 2 - Ma Kent; Kerschl-a/Hughes-c; Ma Kent during Clark childhood and absence 4.00
Prequel 3 - Lex Luthor; Leonardi-a/Hughes-c; Luthor's 5 years in prison 4.00
Prequel 4 - Lois Lane; Dias-a/Hughes-c; Lois during Superman's absence 4.00
The Movie and Other Tales of the Man of Steel (2006, $12.99, TPB) adaptation; origin from Amazing World of Superman; Action #810, Superman #185; Advs. of Superman #575 13.00
The Official Movie Adaptation (2006, $6.99) Pasko-s/Haley-a; photo-c 7.00
...: The Prequels TPB (2006, $12.99) r/the 4 prequels 13.00

SUPERMAN: SAVE THE PLANET
DC Comics: Oct, 1998 ($2.95, one-shot)

1-($2.95) Regular Ed.; Luthor buys the Daily Planet 3.00
1-($3.95) Collector's Ed. with acetate cover 4.00

SUPERMAN SCRAPBOOK (Has blank pages; contains no comics)

SUPERMAN: SECRET FILES
DC Comics: Jan, 1998; May 1999 ($4.95)

1,2: 1-Retold origin story, "lost" pages & pin-ups 5.00
... & Origins 2004 (8/04) pin-ups by Lee, Turner and others 5.00
... & Origins 2005 (1/06) short stories and pin-ups by various 5.00
... 2009 (10/09, $4.99) short stories and pin-ups about New Krypton x-over 5.00

SUPERMAN: SECRET IDENTITY
DC Comics: 2004 - No. 4, 2004 ($5.95, squarebound, limited series)

1-4-Busiek-s/Immonen-a/c 6.00

SUPERMAN: SECRET ORIGIN
DC Comics: Nov, 2009 - No. 6 ($3.99, limited series)

1-4-Geoff Johns-s/Gary Frank-a/c; origin mythos re-told. 2-Legion app. 4.00
1-4-Variant covers by Frank 6.00

SUPERMAN'S GIRLFRIEND LOIS LANE (See Action Comics #1, 80 Page Giant #3, 14, Lois Lane, Showcase #9, 10, Superman #28 & Superman Family)

SUPERMAN'S GIRLFRIEND LOIS LANE (See Showcase #9,10)
National Periodical Publ.: Mar-Apr, 1958 - No. 136, Jan-Feb, 1974; No. 137, Sept-Oct, 1974

	GD 2.0	VG 4.0	FN 6.0	VF 8.0	VF/NM 9.0	NM- 9.2
1-(3-4/58)	326	652	978	2934	5867	8800
2	84	168	252	714	1407	2100
3	54	108	162	459	905	1350
4,5	43	86	129	344	672	1000
6,7	35	70	105	266	513	760
8-10: 9-Pat Boone-c/story	30	60	90	220	428	635
11-13,15-19: 12-(10/59)-Aquaman app. 17-(5/60) 2nd app. Brainiac.	19	38	57	133	259	385
14-Supergirl x-over; Batman app. on-c only	19	38	57	139	270	400
20-Supergirl-c/sty	19	38	57	133	259	390
21-28: 23-1st app. Lena Thorul, Lex Luthor's sister; 1st Lois as Elastic Lass. 27-Bizarro-c/story	14	28	42	102	194	285
29-Aquaman, Batman, Green Arrow cover app. and cameo; last 10¢ issue	15	30	45	107	204	300
30-32,34-46,48,49	9	18	27	65	113	160
33(5/62)-Mon -El app.	10	20	30	68	119	170
47-Legion app.	10	20	30	68	119	170
50(7/64)-Triplicate Girl, Phantom Girl & Shrinking Violet app.	10	20	30	68	119	170
51-55,57-67,69: 59-Jor -El app.; Batman back-up sty	7	14	21	49	80	110
56-Saturn Girl app.	7	14	21	50	83	115
68-(Giant G-26)	9	18	27	60	100	140
70-Penguin & Catwoman app. (1st S.A. Catwoman, 11/66; also see Detective #369 for 3rd app.); Batman & Robin cameo	24	48	72	175	338	500
71-Batman & Robin cameo (3 panels); Catwoman story cont'd from #70 (2nd app.); see Detective #369 for 3rd app	14	28	42	101	191	280
72,73,75,76,78	6	12	18	39	62	85
74-1st Bizarro Flash (5/67); JLA cameo	6	12	18	41	66	90
77-(Giant G-39)	7	14	21	50	83	115
79-Neal Adams-c or c(i) begin, end #95,108	6	12	18	41	66	90
80-85,87,88,90-92: 92-Last 12¢ issue	5	10	15	30	48	65
86,95 (Giants G-51,G-63)-Both have Neal Adams-c	6	12	18	43	69	95
89,93: 89-Batman x-over; all N. Adams-c. 93-Wonder Woman-c/story	5	10	15	32	51	70
94,96-99,101-103,107-110	4	8	12	24	37	50
100	4	8	12	26	41	55
104-(Giant G-75)	6	12	18	39	62	85
105-Origin/1st app. The Rose & the Thorn.	6	12	18	39	62	85

Superman's Girlfriend Lois Lane #71 © DC

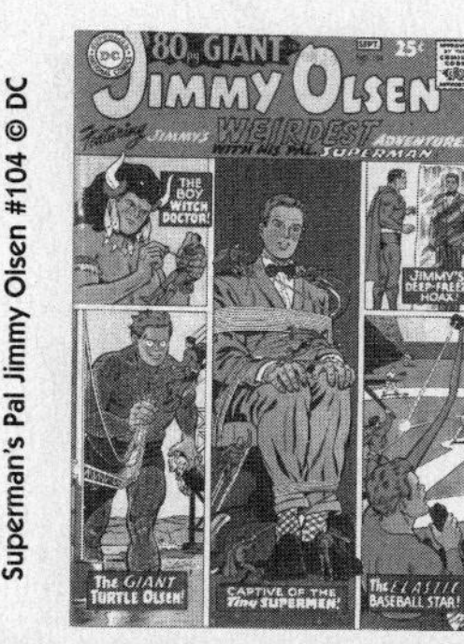

Superman's Pal Jimmy Olsen #104 © DC

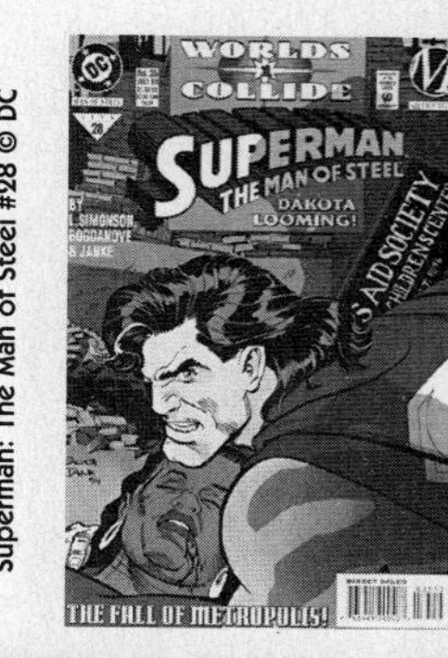

Superman: The Man of Steel #28 © DC

	GD 2.0	VG 4.0	FN 6.0	VF 8.0	VF/NM 9.0	NM- 9.2
106-"Black Like Me" story; Lois changes her skin color to black	7	14	21	49	80	110
111-Justice League-c/s; Morrow-a; last 15¢ issue	4	8	12	26	41	55
112,114-123 (52 pgs.): 122-G.A. Lois Lane-r/Superman #30. 123-G.A. Batman-r/Batman #35 (w/Catwoman)	4	8	12	24	37	50
113-(Giant G-87) Kubert-a (previously unpublished G.A. story)(scarce in NM)	6	12	18	43	69	95
124-135: 130-Last Rose & the Thorn. 132-New Zatanna story	3	6	9	16	23	30
136,137: 136-Wonder Woman x-over	3	6	9	18	27	35
Annual 1(Sum, 1962)-r/L. Lane #12; Aquaman app.	20	40	60	146	283	420
Annual 2(Sum, 1963)	14	28	42	101	191	280

NOTE: *Buckler a-117-121p.* ***Curt Swan or Kurt Schaffenberger*** *a-1-81(most); c(p)-1-15.*

SUPERMAN/SHAZAM: FIRST THUNDER
DC Comics: Nov, 2005 - No. 4, Feb, 2006 ($3.50, limited series)

1-4-Retells first meeting; Winick-s/Middleton-a. Dr. Sivana app. 3.50

SUPERMAN: SILVER BANSHEE
DC Comics: Dec, 1998 - No. 2, Jan, 1999 ($2.25, mini-series)

1,2-Brereton-s/c; Chin-a 2.50

SUPERMAN'S NEMESIS: LEX LUTHOR
DC Comics: Mar, 1999 - No. 4, Jun, 1999 ($2.50, mini-series)

1-4-Semeiks-a 2.50

SUPERMAN'S PAL JIMMY OLSEN (Superman Family #164 on)
(See Action Comics #6 for 1st app. & 80 Page Giant)
National Periodical Publ.: Sept-Oct, 1954 - No. 163, Feb-Mar, 1974 (Fourth World #133-148)

	GD 2.0	VG 4.0	FN 6.0	VF 8.0	VF/NM 9.0	NM- 9.2
1	520	1040	1560	4680	8840	13,000
2	140	280	420	1190	2345	3500
3-Last pre-code issue	80	160	240	680	1340	2000
4,5	52	104	156	442	871	1300
6-10	40	80	120	305	590	875
11-20: 15-1st S.A. issue	27	54	81	197	386	575
21-28,30	17	34	51	124	242	360
29-(6/58) 1st app. Krypto with Superman	19	38	57	133	259	385
31-Origin & 1st app. Elastic Lad (Jimmy Olsen)	16	32	48	113	217	320
32-40: 33-One pg. biography of Jack Larson (TV Jimmy Olsen). 36-Intro Lucy Lane. 37-2nd app. Elastic Lad & 1st cover app.	13	26	39	90	165	240
41-50: 41-1st J.O. Robot. 48-Intro/origin Superman Emergency Squad	10	20	30	73	129	185
51-56: 56-Last 10¢ issue	9	18	27	60	100	140
57-62,64-70: 57-Olsen marries Supergirl. 62-Mon-El & Elastic Lad app. but not as Legionnaires. 70-Element Boy (Lad) app.	7	14	21	45	73	100
63(9/62)-Legion of Super-Villains app.	7	14	21	47	76	105
71,74,75,78,80-84,86,89,90: 86-Jimmy Olsen Robot becomes Congorilla	6	12	18	37	59	80
72,73,76,77,79,85,87,88: 72(10/63)-Legion app; Elastic Lad (Olsen) joins. 73-Ultra Boy app. 76,85-Legion app. 76-Legion app. 77-Olsen with Colossal Boy's powers & costume; origin Titano retold. 79-(9/64)-Titled The Red-headed Beatle of 1000 B.C. 85-Legion app. 87-Legion of Super-Villains app. 88-Star Boy app.	6	12	18	39	62	85
91-94,96-98	5	10	15	30	48	65
95 (Giant G-25)	7	14	21	47	76	105
99-Olsen w/powers & costumes of Lightning Lad, Sun Boy & Element Lad	5	10	15	32	51	70
100-Legion cameo	5	10	15	34	55	75
101-103,105-112,114-120: 106-Legion app. 110-Infinity-c. 117-Batman & Legion cameo. 120-Last 12¢ issue	4	8	12	24	37	50
104 (Giant G-38)	6	12	18	39	62	85
113,122,131,140 (Giants G-50,G-62,G-74,G-86)	5	10	15	34	55	75
121,123-130,132	4	8	12	22	34	45
133-(10/70)-Jack Kirby story & art begins; re-intro Newsboy Legion; 1st app. Morgan Edge	6	12	18	41	66	90
134-1st app. Darkseid (1 panel, 12/70)	7	14	21	47	76	105
135-2nd app. Darkseid (1 pg. cameo; see New Gods & Forever People); G.A. Guardian app.	5	10	15	30	48	65
136-139: 136-Origin new Guardian. 138-Partial photo-c. 139-Last 15¢ issue	4	8	12	24	37	50
141-150: (25¢,52 pgs.). 141-Photo-c; Newsboy Legion-r by S&K begin; full pg. self-portrait of Jack Kirby; Don Rickles cameo. 149,150-G.A. Plastic Man-r in both; 150-Newsboy Legion app.	4	8	12	22	34	45
151-163	3	6	9	16	23	30

... Special 1 (12/08, $4.99) New Krypton tie-in; The Guardian and Dubbilex app. 5.00
... Special 2 (10/09, $4.99) New Krypton tie-in; Mon-El app.; Chang-a 5.00
Superman: The Amazing Transformations of Jimmy Olsen TPB (2007, $14.99) reprints Olsen's transformations into Wolf-Man, Elastic Lad, Turtle Boy and others; new Bolland-c 15.00

NOTE: *Issues #141-148 contain* ***Simon & Kirby*** *Newsboy Legion reprints from Star Spangled #7, 8, 9, 10, 11, 12, 13, 14 in that order.* ***N. Adams*** *c-109-112, 115, 117, 118, 120, 121, 132, 134-136, 147, 148.* ***Kirby*** *a-133-139p, 141-148p; c-133, 137, 139, 142, 145p.* ***Kirby/N. Adams*** *c-137, 138, 141-144, 146.* ***Curt Swan*** *c-1-14(most)., 140.*

SUPERMAN SPECTACULAR (Also see DC Special Series #5)
DC Comics: 1982 (Magazine size, 52 pgs., square binding)

	GD	VG	FN	VF	VF/NM	NM-
1-Saga of Superman Red/ Superman Blue; Luthor and Terra-Man app.; Gonzales & Colletta-a	1	3	4	6	8	10

SUPERMAN: STRENGTH
DC Comics: 2005 - No. 3, 2005 ($5.95, limited series)

1-3: Alex Ross-c/Scott McCloud-s/Aluir Amancio-a 6.00

SUPERMAN / SUPERGIRL: MAELSTROM
DC Comics: Early Jan, 2009 - No. 5, Mar, 2009 ($2.99, limited series)

1-5: Palmiotti & Gray-s/Noto-c/a; Darkseid app. 3.00
TPB (2009, $12.99) r/#1-5 13.00

SUPERMAN / SUPERHOMBRE
DC Comics: Apr, 1945

nn - Ashcan comic, not distributed to newsstands, only for in-house use (no known sales)

SUPERMAN / TARZAN: SONS OF THE JUNGLE
Dark Horse Comics: Oct, 2001 - No. 3, May, 2002 ($2.99, limited series)

1-3-Elseworlds; Kal-El lands in the jungle; Dixon-s/Meglia-a/Ramos-c 3.00

SUPERMAN: THE DARK SIDE
DC Comics: 1998 - No. 3, 1998 ($4.95, squarebound, mini-series)

1-3: Elseworlds; Kal-El lands on Apokolips 5.00

SUPERMAN: THE DOOMSDAY WARS
DC Comics: 1998 - No. 3, 1999 ($4.95, squarebound, mini-series)

1-3: Superman & JLA vs. Doomsday; Jurgens-s/a(p) 5.00

SUPERMAN: THE KANSAS SIGHTING
DC Comics: 2003 - No. 2, 2003 ($6.95, squarebound, mini-series)

1,2-DeMatteis-s/Tolagson-a 7.00

SUPERMAN: THE MAN OF STEEL (Also see Man of Steel, The)
DC Comics: July, 1991 - No. 134, Mar, 2003 ($1.00/$1.25/$1.50/$1.95/$2.25)

	GD	VG	FN	VF	VF/NM	NM-
0-(10/94) Zero Hour; released between #37 & #38						2.50
1-($1.75, 52 pgs.)-Painted-c						5.00
2-16: 3-War of the Gods x-over. 5-Reads sideways. 10-Last $1.00-c. 14-Superman & Robin team-up						3.00
17-1st brief app. Doomsday	1	2	3	4	5	7
17,18: 17-2nd printing. 18-2nd & 3rd printings						2.50
18-1st full app. Doomsday	1	2	3	5	7	9
19-Doomsday battle issue (c/story)						6.00
20-22: 20,21-Funeral for a Friend. 22-($1.95)-Collector's Edition w/die-cut outer-c & bound-in poster; Steel-c/story						2.50
22-($1.50)-Newsstand Ed. w/poster & different-c						2.50
23-49,51-99: 30-Regular edition. 32-Bizarro-c/story. 35,36-Worlds Collide Pt. 1 & 10. 37-(9/94)-Zero Hour x-over. 38-(11/94). 48-Aquaman app. 54-Spectre-c/app; Lex Luthor app. 56-Mxyzptlk-c/app. 57-G.A. Flash app. 58-Supergirl app. 59-Parasite-c/app.; Steel app. 60-Reintro Bottled City of Kandor. 62-Final Night. 64-New Gods app. 67-New powers. 75-"Death" of Mxyzptlk. 78,79-Millennium Giants. 80-Golden Age style. 92-JLA app. 98-Metal Men app.						2.50
30-($2.50)-Collector's Edition; polybagged with Superman & Lobo vinyl clings that stick to wraparound-c; Lobo-c/story						3.00
50 ($2.95)-The Trial of Superman						4.00
100-($2.99) New Fortress of Solitude revealed						3.00
100-($3.99) Special edition with fold out cardboard-c						4.00
101,102-101-Batman app.						2.50
103-133: 103-Begin $2.25. 105-Batman-c/app. 111-Return to Krypton. 115-117-Our Worlds at War. 117-Maxima killed. 121-Royal Flush Gang app. 128-Return to Krypton II.						2.50
134-($2.75) Last issue; Steel app.; Bogdanove-c						2.75
#1,000,000 (11/98) 853rd Century x-over; Gene Ha-c						2.50
Annual 1-5 ('92-'96,68 pgs.): 1-Eclipso app.; Joe Quesada-c(p). 2-Intro Edge. 3 -Elseworlds; Mignola-c; Batman app. 4-Year One story. 5-Legends of the Dead Earth story						3.00
Annual 6 (1997, $3.95)-Pulp Heroes story						4.00
...Gallery (1995, $3.50) Pin-ups by various						3.50

SUPERMAN: THE MAN OF TOMORROW
DC Comics: 1995 - No. 15, Fall, 1999 ($1.95, quarterly)

1-15: 1-Lex Luthor app. 3-Lex Luthor-c/app; Joker app. 4-Shazam! app. 5-Wedding of Lex Luthor. 10-Maxima-c/app. 13-JLA-c/app. 2.50

Superman: World of New Krypton #4 © DC

Supermouse #15 © STD

Supernatural Law #33 © Batton Lash

GD 2.0 | VG 4.0 | FN 6.0 | VF 8.0 | VF/NM 9.0 | NM- 9.2

GD 2.0 | VG 4.0 | FN 6.0 | VF 8.0 | VF/NM 9.0 | NM- 9.2

#1,000,000 (11/98) 853rd Century x-over; Gene Ha-c 2.50

SUPERMAN: THE SECRET YEARS
DC Comics: Feb, 1985 - No. 4, May, 1985 (limited series)

1-4-Miller-c on all 3.00

SUPERMAN: THE WEDDING ALBUM
DC Comics: Dec, 1996 ($4.95, 96 pgs, one-shot)

1-Standard Edition-Story & art by past and present Superman creators; gatefold back-c. Byrne-c 5.00
1-Collector's Edition-Embossed cardstock variant-c w/ metallic silver ink and matte and gloss varnishes 5.00
Retailer Rep. Program Edition (#'d to 250, signed by Bob Rozakis on back-c) 50.00
TPB ('97, $14.95) r/Wedding and honeymoon stories 15.00

SUPERMAN 3-D (See Three-Dimension Adventures)

SUPERMAN-TIM (See Promotional Comics section)

SUPERMAN VILLAINS SECRET FILES
DC Comics: Jun, 1998 ($4.95, one shot)

1-Origin stories, "lost" pages & pin-ups 5.00

SUPERMAN VS. ALIENS (Also see Superman Aliens 2: God War)
DC Comics/Dark Horse Comics: July, 1995 - No. 3, Sept, 1995 ($4.95, limited series)

1-3: Jurgens/Nowlan-a 5.00

SUPERMAN VS. MUHAMMAD ALI (See All-New Collectors' Edition C-56)

SUPERMAN VS. PREDATOR
DC Comics/Dark Horse Comics: 2000 - No. 3, 2000 ($4.95, limited series)

1-3-Micheline-s/Maleev-a 5.00
TPB (2001, $14.95) r/series 15.00

SUPERMAN VS. THE AMAZING SPIDER-MAN (Also see Marvel Treasury Edition No. 28)
National Periodical Publications/Marvel Comics Group: 1976
($2.00, Treasury sized, 100 pgs.)

1-Superman and Spider-Man battle Lex Luthor and Dr. Octopus; Andru/Giordano-a; 1st Marvel/DC x-over. 8 16 24 54 90 125
1-2nd printing; 5000 numbered copies signed by Stan Lee & Carmine Infantino on front cover & sold through mail 13 26 39 95 178 260
nn-(1995, $5.95)-r/#1 6.00

SUPERMAN VS. THE TERMINATOR: DEATH TO THE FUTURE
Dark Horse/DC Comics: Dec, 1999 - No. 4, Mar, 2000 ($2.95, limited series)

1-4-Grant-s/Pugh-a/c: Steel and Supergirl app. 3.00

SUPERMAN/WONDER WOMAN: WHOM GODS DESTROY
DC Comics: 1997 ($4.95, prestige format, limited series)

1-4-Elseworlds; Claremont-s 5.00

SUPERMAN WORKBOOK
National Periodical Publ./Juvenile Group Foundation: 1945 (B&W, reprints, 68 pgs)

nn-Cover-r/Superman #14 174 348 522 1114 1907 2700

SUPERMAN: WORLD OF NEW KRYPTON
DC Comics: May, 2009 - No. 12,Apr, 2010 ($2.99, limited series)

1-12: Robinson & Rucka-s/Woods-a; Frank-c and variant for each. 4-Green Lantern app. 3.00

SUPER MARIO BROS. (Also see Adventures of the..., Blip, Gameboy, and Nintendo Comics System)
Valiant Comics: 1990 - No. 5?, 1991 ($1.95, slick-c) V2#1, 1991 - No. 5, 1991

1-Wildman-a 4.00
2-5, V2#1-5-($1.50) 3.00
Special Edition 1 (1990, $1.95)-Wildman-a 3.00

SUPER MARKET COMICS
Fawcett Publications: No date (1950s)

nn - Ashcan comic, not distributed to newsstands, only for in-house use (no known sales)

SUPER MARKET VARIETIES
Fawcett Publications: No date (1950s)

nn - Ashcan comic, not distributed to newsstands, only for in-house use (no known sales)

SUPERMEN OF AMERICA
DC Comics: Mar, 1999 ($3.95/$4.95, one-shot)

1-($3.95) Regular Ed.; Immonen-s/art by various 4.00
1-($4.95) Collectors' Ed. with membership kit 5.00

SUPERMEN OF AMERICA (Mini-series)
DC Comics: Mar, 2000 - No. 6, Aug, 2000 ($2.50)

1-6-Nicieza-s/Braithwaite-a 2.50

SUPERMOUSE (...the Big Cheese; see Coo Coo Comics)
Standard Comics/Pines No. 35 on (Literary Ent.): Dec, 1948 - No. 34, Sept, 1955; No. 35, Apr, 1956 - No. 45, Fall, 1958

1-Frazetta text illos (3) 28 56 84 165 270 375
2-Frazetta text illos 15 30 45 84 127 170
3,5,6-Text illos by Frazetta in all 13 26 39 74 105 135
4-Two pg. text illos by Frazetta 14 28 42 78 112 145
7-10 9 18 27 47 61 75
11-20: 13-Racist humor (Indians) 7 14 21 37 46 55
21-45 6 12 18 31 38 45
1-Summer Holiday issue (Summer, 1957, 25¢, 100 pgs.)-Pines 14 28 42 80 115 150
2-Giant Summer issue (Summer, 1958, 25¢, 100 pgs.)-Pines; has games, puzzles & stories 10 20 30 58 79 100

SUPER-MYSTERY COMICS
Ace Magazines (Periodical House): July, 1940 - V8#6, July, 1949

V1#1-Magno, the Magnetic Man & Vulcan begins (1st app.); Q-13, Corp. Flint, & Sky Smith begin 309 618 927 2163 3782 5400
2 102 204 306 648 1112 1575
3-The Black Spider begins (1st app.) 81 162 243 518 884 1250
4-Origin Davy 57 114 171 362 619 875
5-Intro. The Clown & begin series (12/40) 60 120 180 381 658 935
6(2/41) 52 104 156 324 550 775
V2#1(4/41)-Origin Buckskin 50 100 150 315 533 750
2-6(2/42): 6-Vulcan begins again 47 94 141 298 504 710
V3#1(4/42),2: 1-Black Ace begins 42 84 126 265 445 625
3-Intro. The Lancer; Dr. Nemesis & The Sword begin; Kurtzman-c/a(2) (Mr. Risk & Paul Revere Jr.); Robot-c 53 106 159 334 567 800
4-Kurtzman-c/a; classic-c 87 174 261 553 952 1350
5-Kurtzman-a(2); L.B. Cole-a; Mr. Risk app. 51 102 153 318 539 760
6(10/43)-Mr. Risk app.; Kurtzman's Paul Revere Jr.; L.B. Cole-a 51 102 153 318 539 760
V4#1(1/44)-L.B. Cole-a 45 90 135 284 480 675
2-6(4/45): 2,5,6-Mr. Risk app. 32 64 96 188 307 425
V5#1(7/45)-6 32 64 96 188 307 425
V6#1,2,4,5,6: 4-Last Magno. Mr. Risk app. in #2,4-6. 6-New logo 26 52 78 154 252 350
3-Torture c-story 36 72 108 211 343 475
V7#1-6, V8#1-4,6 24 48 72 142 234 325
V8#5-Meskin, Tuska, Sid Greene-a 23 46 69 136 223 310

NOTE: ***Sid Greene** a-V7#4. **Mooney** c-V1#5, 6, V2#1-6. **Palais** a-V5#3, 4; c-V4#6-V5#4, V6#2, V8#4. Bondage c-V2#5, 6, V3#2, 5. Magno c-V1#1-V3#6, V4#2-V5#5, V6#2. The Sword c-V4#1, 6(w/Magno).*

SUPERNATURAL: BEGINNING'S END (Based on the CW television series)
DC Comics (WildStorm): Mar, 2010 - No. 6 ($2.99, limited series)

1-Prequel to the series; Dabb & Loflin-s/Olmos-a. 1-Olmos and photo-c 3.00

SUPERNATURAL FREAK MACHINE: A CAL MCDONALD MYSTERY
IDW Publishing: Mar, 2005 - No. 3 ($3.99)

1-3-Steve Niles-s/Kelley Jones-a 4.00

SUPERNATURAL LAW (Formerly Wolff & Byrd, Counselors of the Macabre)
Exhibit A Press: No. 24, Oct, 1999 - Present ($2.50/$2.95/$3.50, B&W)

24-35-Batton Lash-s/a. 29-Marie Severin-c. 33-Cerebus spoof 2.50
36-40-($2.95). 37-Frank Cho pin-up and story panels 3.00
(#41) ...First Amendment Issue (2005, $3.50) anti-censorship story; CBLDF info 3.50
(#42) With a Silver Bullet (2006, $3.50) new stories and pin-ups 3.50
(#43) At the Box Office (2006, $3.50) new stories and pin-ups 3.50
(#44) Wolff & Byrd: The Movie (2007, $3.50) new stories and pin-ups 3.50
45-($3.50) Toxic Avenger and Lloyd Kaufman app. 3.50
#1 (2005, $2.95) r/Wolff & Byrd with redrawn and re-toned art; relettered 3.00

SUPERNATURAL LAW SECRETARY MAVIS
Exhibit A Press: 2001 - Present ($2.95/$3.50, B&W)

1-3: 3-DeCarlo-c 3.00
4,5-($3.50) Jaime Hernandez-c 3.50

SUPERNATURAL: ORIGINS (Based on the CW television series)
DC Comics (WildStorm): July, 2007 - No. 6, Dec, 2007 ($2.99, limited series)

1-6: 1-Bradstreet-c; Johnson-s/Smith-a; back-up w/Johns-s/Hester-a 3.00
TPB (2008, $14.99) r/#1-6; sketch pages 15.00

SUPERNATURAL: RISING SON (Based on the CW television series)
DC Comics (WildStorm): Jun, 2008 - No. 6, Nov, 2008 ($2.99, limited series)

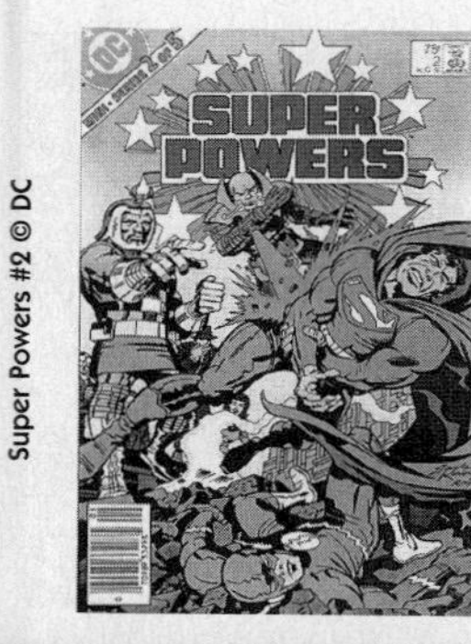

Super Powers #2 © DC

Super Soldiers #5 © MAR

Super-Villain Team-Up #2 © MAR

	GD 2.0	VG 4.0	FN 6.0	VF 8.0	VF/NM 9.0	NM- 9.2
1-6-Johnson & Dessertine-s/Olmos-a. 1-Oliver-c						3.00
1-Variant-c by Nguyen						6.00
TPB (2009, $14.99) r/#1-6						15.00

SUPERNATURALS
Marvel Comics: Dec, 1998 - No. 4, Dec, 1998 ($3.99, weekly limited series)

	GD 2.0	VG 4.0	FN 6.0	VF 8.0	VF/NM 9.0	NM- 9.2
1-4-Pulido-s/Balent-c; bound-in Halloween masks						4.00
1-4-With bound-in Ghost Rider mask (1 in 10)						4.00

SUPERNATURAL THRILLERS
Marvel Comics Group: Dec, 1972 - No. 6, Nov, 1973; No. 7, Jun, 1974 - No. 15, Oct, 1975

	GD 2.0	VG 4.0	FN 6.0	VF 8.0	VF/NM 9.0	NM- 9.2
1-It!; Sturgeon adap. (see Astonishing Tales #21)	3	6	9	20	30	40
2-4,6: 2-The Invisible Man; H.G. Wells adapt. 3-The Valley of the Worm; R.E. Howard adapt. 4-Dr. Jekyll & Mr. Hyde; R.L. Stevenson adapt.. 6-The Headless Horseman; last 20¢ issue	3	6	9	14	20	25
5-1st app. The Living Mummy	7	14	21	45	73	100
7-15: 7-The Living Mummy begins	3	6	9	18	27	35

NOTE: ***Brunner*** *c-11.* ***Buckler*** *a-5p.* ***Ditko*** *a-8r, 9r.* ***G. Kane*** *a-3p; c-3, 9p, 15p.* ***Mayerik*** *a-2p, 7, 8, 9p, 10p, 11.* ***McWilliams*** *a-14i.* ***Mortimer*** *a-4.* ***Steranko*** *c-1, 2.* ***Sutton*** *a-15.* ***Tuska*** *a-6p.*

SUPERPATRIOT (Also see Freak Force & Savage Dragon #2)
Image Comics (Highbrow Entertainment): July, 1993 - No. 4, Dec, 1993 ($1.95, lim. series)

	GD 2.0	VG 4.0	FN 6.0	VF 8.0	VF/NM 9.0	NM- 9.2
1-4: Dave Johnson-c/a; Larsen scripts; Giffen plots						2.50

SUPERPATRIOT: AMERICA'S FIGHTING FORCE
Image Comics: July, 2002 - No. 4, Oct, 2002 ($2.95, limited series)

	GD 2.0	VG 4.0	FN 6.0	VF 8.0	VF/NM 9.0	NM- 9.2
1-4-Cory Walker-a/c; Savage Dragon app.						3.00

SUPERPATRIOT: LIBERTY & JUSTICE
Image Comics (Highbrow Entertainment): July, 1995 - No. 4, Oct, 1995 ($2.50, lim. series)

	GD 2.0	VG 4.0	FN 6.0	VF 8.0	VF/NM 9.0	NM- 9.2
1-4: Dave Johnson-c/a. 1-1st app. Liberty & Justice						2.50
TPB (2002, $12.95) r/#1-4; new cover by Dave Johnson; sketch pages						13.00

SUPERPATRIOT: WAR ON TERROR
Image Comics: July, 2004 - No. 4, May, 2007 ($2.95/$2.99, limited series)

	GD 2.0	VG 4.0	FN 6.0	VF 8.0	VF/NM 9.0	NM- 9.2
1-4-Kirkman-s/Su-a						3.00

SUPER POWERS (1st Series)
DC Comics: July, 1984 - No. 5, Nov, 1984

	GD 2.0	VG 4.0	FN 6.0	VF 8.0	VF/NM 9.0	NM- 9.2
1-5: 1-Joker/Penguin-c/story; Batman app.; all Kirby-c. 5-Kirby c/a						5.00

SUPER POWERS (2nd Series)
DC Comics: Sept, 1985 - No. 6, Feb, 1986

	GD 2.0	VG 4.0	FN 6.0	VF 8.0	VF/NM 9.0	NM- 9.2
1-6: Kirby-c/a; Capt. Marvel & Firestorm join; Batman cameo; Darkseid storyline in all. 4-Batman cameo. 5,6-Batman app.						5.00

SUPER POWERS (3rd Series)
DC Comics: Sept, 1986 - No. 4, Dec, 1986

	GD 2.0	VG 4.0	FN 6.0	VF 8.0	VF/NM 9.0	NM- 9.2
1-4: 1-Cyborg joins; 1st app. Samurai from Super Friends TV show. 1-4-Batman cameos; Darkseid storyline in #1-4						4.00

SUPER PUP (Formerly Spotty The Pup) (See Space Comics)
Avon Periodicals: No. 4, Mar-Apr, 1954 - No. 5, 1954

	GD 2.0	VG 4.0	FN 6.0	VF 8.0	VF/NM 9.0	NM- 9.2
4,5: 4-Atom bomb-c. 5-Robot-c	6	12	18	31	38	45

SUPER RABBIT (See All Surprise, Animated Movie Tunes, Comedy Comics, Comic Capers, Ideal Comics, It's A Duck's Life, Movie Tunes & Wisco)
Timely Comics (CmPl): Fall, 1944 - No. 14, Nov, 1948

	GD 2.0	VG 4.0	FN 6.0	VF 8.0	VF/NM 9.0	NM- 9.2
1-Hitler & Hirohito-c; war effort paper recycling PSA by S&K; Ziggy Pig & Silly Seal begin	110	220	330	704	1202	1700
2	39	78	117	240	395	550
3-5	26	52	78	154	252	350
6-Origin	28	56	84	165	270	375
7-10: 9-Infinity-c	17	34	51	100	158	215
11-Kurtzman's "Hey Look"	18	35	54	105	165	225
12-14	17	34	51	100	158	215
I.W. Reprint #1,2('58),7,10('63): 1-r/#13. 2-r/#10.	2	4	6	9	13	16

SUPER RICHIE (Superichie #5 on) (See Richie Rich Millions #68)
Harvey Publications: Sept, 1975 - No. 4, Mar, 1976 (All 52 pg. Giants)

	GD 2.0	VG 4.0	FN 6.0	VF 8.0	VF/NM 9.0	NM- 9.2
1	3	6	9	16	23	30
2-4	2	4	6	11	16	20

SUPER SLUGGERS (Baseball)
Ultimate Sports Ent. Inc.: 1999 ($3.95, one-shot)

	GD 2.0	VG 4.0	FN 6.0	VF 8.0	VF/NM 9.0	NM- 9.2
1-Bonds, Piazza, Caminiti, Griffey Jr. app.; Martinbrough-c/a						4.00

SUPERSNIPE COMICS (Formerly Army & Navy #1-5)
Street & Smith Publications: V1#6, Oct, 1942 - V5#1, Aug-Sept, 1949
(See Shadow Comics V2#3)

	GD 2.0	VG 4.0	FN 6.0	VF 8.0	VF/NM 9.0	NM- 9.2
V1#6-Rex King - Man of Adventure (costumed hero, see Super Magic/Magician) by Jack Binder begins; Supersnipe by George Marcoux continues from Army & Navy #5; Bill Ward-a	113	226	339	712	1206	1700
7,10-12: 10,11-Little Nemo app.	53	106	159	330	553	775
8-Hitler, Tojo, Mussolini in Hell with Devil-c	110	220	330	704	1202	1700
9-Doc Savage x-over in Supersnipe; Hitler-c	116	232	348	742	1271	1800
V2 #1: Both V2#1(2/44) & V2#2(4/44) have V2#1 on outside-c; Huck Finn by Clare Dwiggins begins, ends V3#5 (rare)	77	154	231	481	816	1150
V2#2 (4/44) has V2#1 on outside-c; classic shark-c	45	90	135	279	465	650
3-12	39	78	117	230	370	510
V3#1-12: 8-Bobby Crusoe by Dwiggins begins, ends V3#12. 9-X-Mas-c	32	64	96	186	298	410
V4#1-12, V5#1: V4#10-X-Mas-c	23	46	69	133	214	295

NOTE: ***George Marcoux*** *c-V1#6-V3#4. Doc Savage app. in some issues.*

SUPER SOLDIER (See Marvel Versus DC #3)
DC Comics (Amalgam): Apr, 1996 ($1.95, one-shot)

	GD 2.0	VG 4.0	FN 6.0	VF 8.0	VF/NM 9.0	NM- 9.2
1-Mark Waid script & Dave Gibbons-c/a.						2.50

SUPER SOLDIER: MAN OF WAR
DC Comics (Amalgam): June, 1997 ($1.95, one-shot)

	GD 2.0	VG 4.0	FN 6.0	VF 8.0	VF/NM 9.0	NM- 9.2
1-Waid & Gibbons-s/Gibbons & Palmiotti-c/a.						2.50

SUPER SOLDIERS
Marvel Comics UK: Apr, 1993 - No. 8, Nov, 1993 ($1.75)

	GD 2.0	VG 4.0	FN 6.0	VF 8.0	VF/NM 9.0	NM- 9.2
1-($2.50)-Embossed silver foil logo						2.50
2-8: 5-Capt. America app. 6-Origin; Nick Fury app.; neon ink-c						2.50

SUPERSPOOK (Formerly Frisky Animals on Parade)
Ajax/Farrell Publications: No. 4, June, 1958

	GD 2.0	VG 4.0	FN 6.0	VF 8.0	VF/NM 9.0	NM- 9.2
4	8	16	24	44	57	70

SUPER SPY (See Wham Comics)
Centaur Publications: Oct, 1940 - No. 2, Nov, 1940 (Reprints)

	GD 2.0	VG 4.0	FN 6.0	VF 8.0	VF/NM 9.0	NM- 9.2
1-Origin The Sparkler	90	180	270	563	932	1300
2-The Inner Circle, Dean Denton, Tim Blain, The Drew Ghost, The Night Hawk by Gustavson, & S.S. Swanson by Glanz app.	54	108	162	338	562	785

SUPERSTAR: AS SEEN ON TV
Image Comics (Gorilla): 2001 ($5.95)

	GD 2.0	VG 4.0	FN 6.0	VF 8.0	VF/NM 9.0	NM- 9.2
1-Busiek-s/Immonen-a						6.00

SUPER STAR HOLIDAY SPECIAL (See DC Special Series #21)

SUPER-TEAM FAMILY
National Periodical Publ./DC Comics: Oct-Nov, 1975 - No. 15, Mar-Apr, 1978

	GD 2.0	VG 4.0	FN 6.0	VF 8.0	VF/NM 9.0	NM- 9.2
1-Reprints by Neal Adams & Kane/Wood; 68 pgs. begin, ends #4. New Gods app.	3	6	9	16	22	28
2,3: New stories	2	4	6	13	18	22
4-7: Reprints. 4-G.A. JSA-r & Superman/Batman/Robin-r from World's Finest. 5-52 pgs. begin	2	4	6	9	13	16
8-14: 8-10-New Challengers of the Unknown stories. 9-Kirby-a. 11-14: New stories	2	4	6	13	18	22
15-New Gods app. New stories	3	6	9	14	19	24

NOTE: ***Neal Adams*** *r-1-3.* ***Brunner*** *c-3.* ***Buckler*** *c-8p.* ***Tuska*** *a-7r.* ***Wood*** *a-1i(r), 3.*

SUPER TV HEROES (See Hanna-Barbera...)

SUPER-VILLAIN CLASSICS
Marvel Comics Group: May, 1983

	GD 2.0	VG 4.0	FN 6.0	VF 8.0	VF/NM 9.0	NM- 9.2
1-Galactus -The Origin; Kirby-a						6.00

SUPER-VILLAIN TEAM-UP (See Fantastic Four #6 & Giant-Size...)
Marvel Comics Group: 8/75 - No. 14, 10/77; No. 15, 11/78; No. 16, 5/79; No. 17, 6/80

	GD 2.0	VG 4.0	FN 6.0	VF 8.0	VF/NM 9.0	NM- 9.2
1-Giant-Size Super-Villain Team-Up #2; Sub-Mariner & Dr. Doom begin, end #10	4	8	12	26	41	55
2-5: 5-1st app. The Shroud	2	4	6	11	16	20
5-(30¢-c variant, limited distribution)(4/76)	4	8	12	22	34	45
6,7-(25¢ editions) 6-(6/76)-F.F., Shroud app. 7-Origin Shroud	2	4	6	8	10	12
6,7-(30¢-c, limited distribution)(6,8/76)	3	6	9	20	30	40
8-17: 9-Avengers app. 11-15-Dr. Doom & Red Skull app.	2	4	6	8	10	12
12-14-(35¢-c variants, limited distribution)(6,8,10/77)	4	8	12	24	37	50

NOTE: ***Buckler*** *c-4p, 5p, 7p.* ***Buscema*** *c-1.* ***Byrne/Austin*** *c-14.* ***Evans*** *a-1p, 3p.* ***Everett*** *a-1p.* ***Giffen*** *a-8p, 13p; c-13p.* ***Kane*** *c-2p, 9p.* ***Mooney*** *a-4i.* ***Starlin*** *c-6.* ***Tuska*** *r-1p, 15p.* ***Wood*** *r-15p.*

SUPER-VILLAIN TEAM-UP/ MODOK'S 11
Marvel Comics: Sept, 2007 - No. 5, Jan, 2008 ($2.99, limited series)

	GD 2.0	VG 4.0	FN 6.0	VF 8.0	VF/NM 9.0	NM- 9.2
1-5: 1-MODOK's origin re-told; Portela-a/Powell-c; Purple Man & Mentallo app.						3.00

Super Zombies #4 © DFI

Supreme #41 © Awesome

Suspense Comics #6 © Continental

GD 2.0 | VG 4.0 | FN 6.0 | VF 8.0 | VF/NM 9.0 | NM- 9.2

...TPB (2008, $13.99) r/#1-5 14.00

SUPER WESTERN COMICS (Also see Buffalo Bill)
Youthful Magazines: Aug, 1950 (One shot)

1-Buffalo Bill begins; Wyatt Earp, Calamity Jane & Sam Slade app; Powell-c/a
14 28 42 82 121 160

SUPER WESTERN FUNNIES (See Super Funnies)

SUPERWOMAN
DC Comics: Jan 1942

nn - Ashcan comic, not distributed to newsstands, only for in-house use. Cover art is More Fun Comics #73 with interior being Action Comics #38 (no known sales)

SUPERWORLD COMICS
Hugo Gernsback (Komos Publ.): Apr, 1940 - No. 3, Aug, 1940 (68 pgs.)

1-Origin & 1st app. Hip Knox, Super Hypnotist; Mitey Powers & Buzz Allen, the Invisible Avenger, Little Nemo begin; cover by Frank R. Paul (all have sci/fi-c) (Scarce) 757 1514 2271 5526 9763 14,000
2-Marvo 1-2 Go+, the Super Boy of the Year 2680 (1st app.); Paul-c (Scarce)
423 846 1269 3067 5384 7700
3 (Scarce) 343 686 1029 2400 4200 6000

SUPER ZOMBIES
Dynamite Entertainment: 2009 - No. 5, 2009 ($3.50)

1-5- Mel Rubi-a; Guggenheim & Gonzales-s; two covers for each by Rubi & Neves 3.50

SUPREME (Becomes ...The New Adventures #43-48)(See Youngblood #3)
(Also see Bloodwulf Special, Legend of Supreme, & Trencher #3)
Image Comics (Extreme Studios)/ Awesome Entertainment #49 on:
V2#1, Nov, 1992 - V2#42, Sept, 1996; V3#49 - No. 56, Feb, 1998

V2#1-Liefeld-a(i) & scripts; embossed foil logo 4.00
1-Gold Edition 6.00
2-(3/93)-Liefeld co-plots & inks; 1st app. Grizlock 3.00
3-42: 3-Intro Bloodstrike; 1st app. Khrome. 5-1st app. Thor. 6-1st brief app. The Starguard. 7-1st full app. The Starguard. 10-Black and White Pt 1 (1st app.) by Art Thibert (2 pgs. ea. installment). 25-(5/94)-Platt-c. 11-Coupon #4 for Extreme Prejudice #0; Black and White Pt. 7 by Thibert. 12-(4/94)-Platt-c. 13,14-(6/94). 15 (7/94). 16 (7/94)-Stormwatch app. 18-Kid Supreme Sneak Preview; Pitt app.19,20-Polybagged w/trading card. 20-1st app. Woden & Loki (as a dog); Overtkill app. 21-1st app. Loki (in true form). 21-23-Poly-bagged trading card. 32-Lady Supreme cameo. 33-Origin & 1st full app. of Lady Supreme (Probe from the Starguard); Babewatch! tie-in. 37-Intro Loki; Fraga-c. 40-Retells Supreme's past advs. 41-Alan Moore scripts begin; Supreme revised; intro The Supremacy; Jerry Ordway-c (Joe Bennett variant-c exists). 42-New origin w/Rick Veitch-a; intro Radar, The Hound Supreme & The League of Infinity 3.00
28-Variant-c by Quesada & Palmiotti 3.00
(#43-48-**See Supreme: The New Adventures**)
V3#49,51: 49-Begin $2.99-c 3.00
50-($3.95)-Double sized, 2 covers, pin-up gallery 4.00
52a,52b-($3.50) 3.50
53-56: 53-Sprouse-a begins. 56-McGuinness-c 3.00
Annual 1-(1995, $2.95) 3.00
...: Supreme Sacrifice (3/06, $3.99) Flip book with Suprema; Kirkman-s/Malin-a 4.00
...: The Return TPB (Checker Book Publ., 2003, $24.95) r/#53-56 & Supreme; The Return #1-6; Ross-c; additional sketch pages by Ross 25.00
...: The Story of the Year TPB (Checker Book Publ., 2002, $26.95) r/#41-52; Ross-c 27.00
NOTE: ***Rob Liefeld** a(i)-1, 2; co-plots-2-4; scripts-1, 5, 6. **Ordway** c-41. **Platt** c-12, 25. **Thibert** c(i)-7-9.*

SUPREME: GLORY DAYS
Image Comics (Extreme Studios): Oct, 1994 - No. 2, Dec, 1994 ($2.95/$2.50, limited series)

1,2: 2-Diehard, Roman, Superpatriot, & Glory app. 3.00

SUPREME POWER (Also see Squadron Supreme 2006 series)
Marvel Comics (MAX): Oct, 2003 - No. 18, Oct, 2005 ($2.99)

1-($2.99) Straczynski-s/Frank-a; Frank-c 3.00
1-($4.99) Special Edition with variant Quesada-c; includes r/early Squadron Supreme apps. 5.00
2-18: 4-Intro. Nighthawk. 6-The Blur debuts. 10-Princess Zarda returns. 17-Hyperion revealed as alien. 18-Continues in mini-series 3.00
Vol. 1: Contact TPB (2004, $14.99) r/#1-6 15.00
Vol. 2: Powers & Principalities TPB (2004, $14.99) r/#7-12 15.00
Vol. 3: High Command TPB (2005, $14.99) r/#13-18 15.00
Vol. 1 HC (2005, $29.99, 7 1/2" x 11" with dustjacket) r/#1-12; Avengers #85 & 86, Straczynski intro., Frank cover sketches and character design pages 30.00
Vol. 2 HC (2006, $29.99, 7 1/2" x 11" with dustjacket) r/#13-18; ...: Hyperion #1-5; character design pages 30.00

SUPREME POWER: HYPERION
Marvel Comics (MAX): Nov, 2005 - No. 5, Mar, 2006 ($2.99, limited series)

1-5: 1-Straczynski-s/Jurgens-a/Dodson-c 3.00
TPB (2006, $14.99) r/#1-5 15.00

SUPREME POWER: NIGHTHAWK
Marvel Comics (MAX): Nov, 2005 - No. 6, Apr, 2006 ($2.99, limited series)

1-6-Daniel Way-s/Steve Dillon-a; origin of Whiteface 3.00
TPB (2006, $16.99) r/#1-6; cover concept art 17.00

SUPREME: THE NEW ADVENTURES (Formerly Supreme)
Maximum Press: V3#43, Oct, 1996 - V3#48, May, 1997 ($2.50)

V3#43-48: 43-Alan Moore scripts begin; Joe Bennett-a; Rick Veitch-a (8 pgs.); Dan Jurgens-a (1 pg.); intro Citadel Supreme & Suprematons; 1st Allied Supermen of America 3.00

SUPREME: THE RETURN
Awesome Entertainment: May, 1999 - No. 6, June, 2000 ($2.99)

1-6: Alan Moore-s. 1,2-Sprouse & Gordon-a/c. 2,4-Liefeld-c. 6-Kirby app. 3.00

SURE-FIRE COMICS (Lightning Comics #4 on)
Ace Magazines: June, 1940 - No. 4, Oct, 1940 (Two No. 3's)

V1#1-Origin Flash Lightning & begins; X-The Phantom Fed, Ace McCoy, Buck Steele, Marvo the Magician, The Raven, Whiz Wilson (Time Traveler) begin (all 1st app.); Flash Lightning c-1-4 181 362 543 1158 1979 2800
2 82 164 246 528 902 1275
3(9/40), 3(#4)(10/40)-nn on-c, #3 on inside 60 120 180 381 653 925

SURF 'N' WHEELS
Charlton Comics: Nov, 1969 - No. 6, Sept, 1970

1 3 6 9 20 30 40
2-6 3 6 9 14 19 24

SURGE
Eclipse Comics: July, 1984 - No. 4, Jan, 1985 ($1.50, lim. series, Baxter paper)

1-4 Ties into DNAgents series 2.50

SURPRISE ADVENTURES (Formerly Tormented)
Sterling Comic Group: No. 3, Mar, 1955 - No. 5, July, 1955

3-5: 3,5-Sekowsky-a 9 18 27 47 61 75

SUSIE Q. SMITH
Dell Publishing Co.: No. 323, Mar, 1951 - No. 553, Apr, 1954

Four Color 323 (#1) 5 10 15 32 51 70
Four Color 377, 453 (2/53), 553 4 8 12 26 41 55

SUSPENSE (Radio/TV issues #1-11; Real Life Tales of... #1-4) (Amazing Detective Cases #3 on?)
Marvel/Atlas Comics (CnPC No. 1-10/BFP No. 11-29): Dec, 1949 - No. 29, Apr, 1953 (#1-8, 17-23: 52 pgs.)

1-Powell-a; Peter Lorre, Sidney Greenstreet photo-c from Hammett's "The Verdict"
59 118 177 375 643 910
2-Crime stories; Dennis O'Keefe & Gale Storm photo-c from Universal movie "Abandoned" 35 70 105 208 339 470
3-Change to horror 41 82 123 250 418 585
4,7-10: 7-Dracula-sty 32 64 96 188 307 425
5-Krigstein, Tuska, Everett-a 34 68 102 199 325 450
6-Tuska, Everett, Morisi-a 33 66 99 194 317 440
11-13,15-17,19,20 25 50 75 150 245 340
14-Clasic Heath Hypo-c; A-Bomb panels 37 74 111 222 361 500
18,22-Krigstein-a 26 52 78 154 252 350
21,23,24,26-29: 24-Tuska-a 22 44 66 132 216 300
25-Electric chair-c/story 32 64 96 188 307 425
NOTE: ***Ayers** a-20. **Briefer** a-5, 7, 27. **Brodsky** c-4, 6-9, 11, 16, 17, 25. **Colan** a-8(2), 9. **Everett** a-5, 6(2), 19, 23, 28; c-21-23, 26. **Fuje** a-29. **Heath** a-5, 6, 8, 10, 12, 14; c-14, 19, 24. **Maneely** a-12, 23, 24, 28, 29; c-5, 6p, 10, 13, 15, 18. **Mooney** a-24, 28. **Morisi** a-6, 12. **Palais** a-10. **Rico** a-7-9. **Robinson** a-29. **Romita** a-20(2), 25. **Sekowsky** a-11, 13, 14. **Sinnott** a-23, 25. **Tuska** a-5, 6(2), 12; c-12. **Whitney** a-15, 16, 22. **Ed Win** a-27.*

SUSPENSE COMICS
Continental Magazines: Dec, 1943 - No. 12, Sept, 1946

1-The Grey Mask begins; bondage/torture-c; L. B. Cole-a (7 pgs.)
423 846 1269 2959 5180 7400
2-Intro. The Mask; Rico, Giunta, L. B. Cole-a (7 pgs.)
268 536 804 1702 2926 4150
3-L.B. Cole-a; classic Schomburg-c (Scarce) 4500 9000 13,500 27,000 36,000 45,000
4-6: 4-L. B. Cole-c begin 206 412 618 1318 2259 3200
7,9,10,12: 9-L.B. Cole eyeball-c 161 322 483 1030 1765 2500
8-Classic L. B. Cole spider-c 411 822 1233 2877 5039 7200
11-Classic Devil-c 309 618 927 2163 3782 5400
NOTE: ***L. B. Cole** c-4-12. **Fuje** a-8. **Larsen** a-11. **Palais** a-10, 11. Bondage c-1, 3, 4.*

SUSPENSE DETECTIVE
Fawcett Publications: June, 1952 - No. 5, Mar, 1953

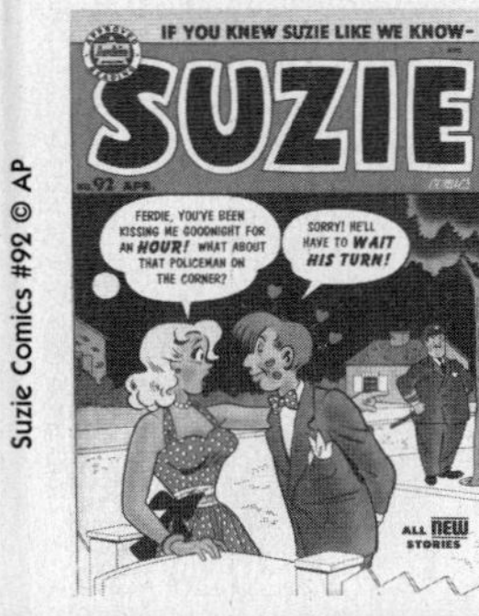

Suzie Comics #92 © AP

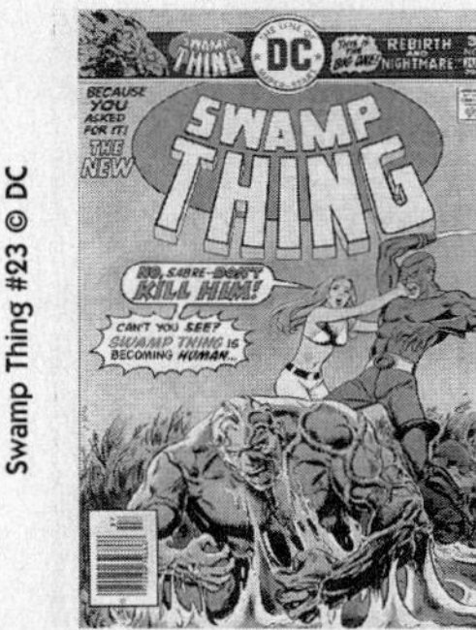

Swamp Thing #23 © DC

Sweethearts #119 © FAW

	GD	VG	FN	VF	VF/NM	NM-
	2.0	4.0	6.0	8.0	9.0	9.2

1-Evans-a (11 pgs); Baily-c/a 45 90 135 284 480 675
2-Evans-a (10 pgs.) 27 54 81 160 263 365
3-5 23 46 69 136 223 310
NOTE: **Baily** a-4, 5; c-1-3. **Sekowsky** a-2, 4, 5; c-5.

SUSPENSE STORIES (See Strange Suspense Stories)

SUSSEX VAMPIRE, THE (Sherlock Holmes)
Caliber Comics: 1996 ($2.95, 32 pgs., B&W, one-shot)
nn-Adapts Sir Arthur Conan Doyle's story; Warren Ellis scripts 3.00

SUZIE COMICS (Formerly Laugh Comix; see Laugh Comics, Liberty Comics #10, Pep Comics & Top-Notch Comics #28)
Close-Up No. 49,50/MLJ Mag./Archie No. 51 on: No. 49, Spring, 1945 - No. 100, Aug, 1954
49-Ginger begins 24 48 72 142 234 325
50-55: 54-Transvestism story. 55-Woggon-a 15 30 45 90 140 190
56-Katy Keene begins by Woggon 16 32 48 94 147 200
57-65 13 26 39 72 101 130
66-80 12 24 36 67 94 120
81-87,89-99 10 20 30 58 79 100
88,100: 88-Used in **POP**, pgs. 76,77; Bill Woggon draws himself in story.
100-Last Katy Keene 12 24 36 67 94 120
NOTE: **Al Fagaly** c-49-67. Katy Keene app. in 53-82, 85-100.

SWAMP FOX, THE (TV, Disney)(See Walt Disney Presents #2)
Dell Publishing Co.: No. 1179, Dec, 1960
Four Color 1179-Leslie Nielsen photo-c 8 16 24 56 93 130

SWAMP THING (See Brave & the Bold, Challengers of the Unknown #82, DC Comics Presents #8 & 85, DC Special Series #2, 14, 17, 20, House of Secrets #92, Limited Collectors' Edition C-59, & Roots of the...)

SWAMP THING
National Per. Publ./DC Comics: Oct-Nov, 1972 - No. 24, Aug-Sept, 1976
1-Wrightson-c/a begins; origin 16 32 48 115 220 325
2-1st brief app. Patchwork Man (1 panel) 8 16 24 56 93 130
3-1st full app. Patchwork Man (see House of Secrets #140)
6 12 18 43 69 95
4-6, 6 12 18 37 59 80
7-Batman-c/story 6 12 18 41 66 90
8-10: 10-Last Wrightson issue 5 10 15 32 51 70
11-20: 11-19-Redondo-a. 13-Origin retold (1 pg.) 3 6 9 18 27 35
21-24: 23,24-Swamp Thing reverts back to Dr. Holland. 23-New logo
3 6 9 18 27 35
Secret of the Swamp Thing (2005, $9.99, digest) r/#1-10 10.00
NOTE: **J. Jones** a-9i(assist). **Kaluta** a-9i. **Redondo** c-12-19, 21. **Wrightson** issues (#1-10) reprinted in DC Special Series #2, 14, 17, 20 & Roots of the Swamp Thing.

SWAMP THING (Saga Of The... #1-38,42-45) (See Essential Vertigo:...)
DC Comics (Vertigo imprint #129 on): May, 1982 - No. 171, Oct, 1996 (Direct sales #65 on)
1-Origin retold; Phantom Stranger series begins; ends #13; Yeates-c/a begins 6.00
2-15: 2-Photo-c from movie. 13-Last Yeates-a 4.00
16-19: Bissette-a. 5.00
20-1st Alan Moore issue 3 6 9 14 20 26
21-New origin 2 4 6 13 18 22
21 Special Editon (5/09, $1.00) reprint with "After Watchmen" cover frame 1.00
22,23,25: 25-John Constantine 1-panel cameo 2 4 6 9 12 15
24-JLA x-over; Last Yeates-c. 2 4 6 9 13 16
26-30 1 2 3 5 6 8
31-33,35,36: 33-r/1st app. from House of Secrets #92 6.00
34 1 2 3 5 7 9
37-1st app. John Constantine (Hellblazer) (6/85) 2 4 6 9 13 16
38-40: John Constantine app. 1 2 3 5 7 9
41-52,54-64: 44-Batman cameo. 44-51-John Constantine app. 46-Crisis x-over; Batman cameo. 49-Spectre app. 50-($1.25, 52 pgs.)-Deadman, Dr. Fate, Demon. 52-Arkham Asylum-c/story; Joker-c/cameo. 58-Spectre preview. 64-Last Moore issue 4.00
53-($1.25, 52 pgs.)-Arkham Asylum; Batman-c/story 5.00
65-83,85-99,101-124,126-149,151-153: 65-Direct sales only begins. 66-Batman & Arkham Asylum story. 70,76-John Constantine x-over; 76-X-over w/Hellblazer #9. 79-Superman-c/story. 85-Jonah Hex app. 102-Preview of World Without End. 116-Photo-c. 129-Metallic ink on-c. 140-Millar scripts begin, end #171 3.00
84-Sandman (Morpheus) cameo. 4.00
100,125,150: 100 ($2.50, 52 pgs.). 125-($2.95, 52 pgs.)-20th anniversary issue. 150 (52 pgs.)-Anniversary issue 3.00
154-171: 154-$2.25-c begins. 165-Curt Swan-a(p). 166,169,171-John Constantine & Phantom Stranger app. 168-Arcane returns 2.50
Annual 1,3-6('82-91): 1-Movie Adaptation; painted-c. 3-New format; Bolland-c. 4-Batman-c/story. 5-Batman cameo; re-intro Brother Power (Geek),1st app. since 1968 4.00
Annual 2 (1985)-Moore scripts; Bissette-a(p); Deadman, Spectre app. 7.00
Annual 7(1993, $3.95)-Children's Crusade 4.00
...A Murder of Crows (2001, $19.95)-r/#43-50; Moore-s 20.00
...: Earth To Earth (2002, $17.95)-r/#51-56; Batman app. 18.00
...: Infernal Triangles (2006, $19.99, TPB) r/#77-81 & Annual #3; cover gallery 20.00
...Love and Death (1990, $17.95)-r/#28-34 & Annual #2; Totleben painted-c 18.00
...: Regenesis (2004, $17.95, TPB) r/#65-70; Veitch-s 18.00
...: Reunion (2003, $19.95, TPB) r/#57-64; Moore-s 20.00
...: Roots (1998, $7.95) Jon J Muth-s/painted-a/c 8.00
Saga of the Swamp Thing ('87, '89)-r/#21-27 (1st & 2nd print) 13.00
...: Spontaneous Generation (2005, $19.99) r/#71-76 20.00
...: The Curse (2000, $19.95, TPB) r/#35-42; Bisley-c 20.00
NOTE: **Bissette** a(p)-16-19, 21-27, 29, 30, 34-36, 39-42, 44, 46, 50, 64; c-17i, 24-32p, 35-37p, 40p, 44p, 46-50p, 51-58, 61, 62, 63p. **Kaluta** c/a-74. **Spiegle** a-1-3, 6. **Sutton** a-98p. **Totleben** a(i)-10, 16-27, 29, 31, 34-40, 42, 44, 46, 48, 50, 53, 55i; c-25-32i, 33, 35-40i, 42i, 44i, 46-50i, 53, 55i, 59p, 64, 65, 68, 73, 76, 80, 82, 84, 89, 91-100, Annual 4, 5. **Vess** painted c-121, 129-139, Annual 7. **Williamson** 86i. **Wrightson** a-18i(r), 33r. John Constantine appears in #37-40, 44-51, 65-67, 70-77, 80-90, 99, 114, 115, 130, 134-138.

SWAMP THING
DC Comics (Vertigo): May, 2000 - No. 20, Dec, 2001 ($2.50)
1-3-Tefé Holland's return; Vaughan-s/Petersen-a; Hale painted-c. 3.00
4-20: 7-9-Bisley-c. 10-John Constantine-c/app. 10-12-Fabry-c. 13-15-Mack-c 18-Swamp Thing app. 2.50
Preview-16 pg. flip book w/Lucifer Preview 2.25

SWAMP THING
DC Comics (Vertigo): May, 2004 - No. 29, Sept, 2006 ($2.95/$2.99)
1-29: 1-Diggle-s/Breccia-a; Constantine app. 2-6-Sargon app. 7,8,20-Corben-c/a. 21-29-Eric Powell-c 3.00
...: Bad Seed (2004, $9.95) r/#1-6 10.00
...: Healing the Breach (2006, $17.99) r/#15-20 18.00
...: Love in Vain (2005, $14.99) r/#9-14 15.00

SWAT MALONE (America's Home Run King)
Swat Malone Enterprises: Sept, 1955
V1#1-Hy Fleishman-a 11 22 33 62 86 110

SWEATSHOP
DC Comics: Jun, 2003 - No. 6, Nov, 2003 ($2.95)
1-6-Peter Bagge-s/a; Destefano-a 3.00

SWEENEY (Formerly Buz Sawyer)
Standard Comics: No. 4, June, 1949 - No. 5, Sept, 1949
4,5: 5-Crane-a 9 18 27 47 61 75

SWEE'PEA (Also see Popeye #46)
Dell Publishing Co.: No. 219, Mar, 1949
Four Color 219 8 16 24 56 93 130

SWEET CHILDE
Advantage Graphics Press: 1995 - No. 2, 1995 ($2.95, B&W, mature)
1,2 3.00

SWEETHEART DIARY (Cynthia Doyle #66-on)
Fawcett Publications/Charlton Comics No. 32 on: Wint, 1949; #2, Spr, 1950; #3, 6/50 - #5, 10/50; #6, 1951(nd); #7, 9/51 - #14, 1/53; #32, 10/55; #33, 4/56 - #65, 8/62 (#1-14: photo-c)
1 19 38 57 111 176 240
2 12 24 36 67 94 120
3,4-Wood-a 15 30 45 85 130 175
5-10: 8-Bailey-a 10 20 30 54 72 90
11-14: 13-Swayze-a. 14-Last Fawcett issue 8 16 24 44 57 70
32 (10/55; 1st Charlton issue)(Formerly Cowboy Love #31)
9 18 27 50 65 80
33-40: 34-Swayze-a 7 14 21 35 43 50
41-(68 pgs.) 7 14 21 37 46 55
42-60 3 6 9 20 30 40
61-65 3 6 9 18 27 35

SWEETHEARTS (Formerly Captain Midnight)
Fawcett Publications/Charlton No. 122 on: #68, 10/48 - #121, 5/53; #122, 3/54; V2#23, 5/54 - #137, 12/73
68-Photo-c begin 17 34 51 98 154 210
69,70 11 22 33 60 83 105
71-80 9 18 27 50 65 80
81-84,86-93,95-99,105 8 16 24 44 57 70
85,94,103,110,117-George Evans-a 9 18 27 52 69 85
100 9 18 27 50 65 80
101,107-Powell-a 9 18 27 47 61 75

Sweet Sixteen #6 © PMI

Sweet Tooth #1 © Jeff Lemire

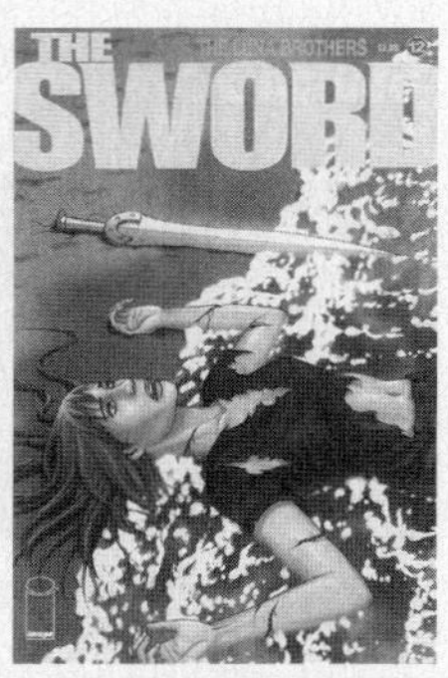
The Sword #12 © Luna Brothers

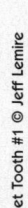

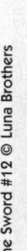

	GD 2.0	VG 4.0	FN 6.0	VF 8.0	VF/NM 9.0	NM- 9.2
102,104,106,108,109,112-116,118	8	16	24	42	54	65
111-1 pg. Ronald Reagan biography	10	20	30	54	72	90
119-Marilyn Monroe & Richard Widmark photo-c (1/54?); also appears in story; part Wood-a	60	120	180	381	653	925
120-Atom Bomb story	11	22	33	64	90	115
121-Liz Taylor/Fernanado Lamas photo-c	30	60	90	177	289	400
122-(1st Charlton? 3/54)-Marijuana story	12	24	36	69	97	125
V2#23 (5/54)-28: 28-Last precode issue (2/55)	8	16	24	40	50	60
29-39,41,43-45,47-50	4	8	12	24	37	50
40-Photo-c; Tommy Sands story	4	8	12	26	41	55
42-Ricky Nelson photo-c/story	8	16	24	56	93	130
46-Jimmy Rodgers photo-c/story	4	8	12	26	41	55
51-60	3	6	9	20	30	40
61-80,100	3	6	9	18	27	35
81-99	3	6	9	17	25	32
101-110	2	4	6	13	18	22
111-120,122-124,126-137	2	4	6	10	14	18
121,125-David Cassidy pin-ups	2	4	6	13	18	22

NOTE: *Photo c-68-121(Fawcett), 40, 42, 46(Charlton).* **Swayze** *a(Fawcett)-70-118(most).*

SWEETHEART SCANDALS (See Fox Giants)

SWEETIE PIE
Dell Publishing Co.: No. 1185, May-July, 1961 - No. 1241, Nov-Jan, 1961/62

	GD	VG	FN	VF	VF/NM	NM-
Four Color 1185 (#1)	5	10	15	30	48	65
Four Color 1241	4	8	12	24	37	50

SWEETIE PIE
Ajax-Farrell/Pines (Literary Ent.): Dec, 1955 - No. 15, Fall, 1957

	GD	VG	FN	VF	VF/NM	NM-
1-By Nadine Seltzer	10	20	30	54	72	90
2 (5/56; last Ajax?)	7	14	21	35	43	50
3-15	6	12	18	28	34	40

SWEET LOVE
Home Comics (Harvey): Sept, 1949 - No. 5, May, 1950 (All photo-c)

	GD	VG	FN	VF	VF/NM	NM-
1	10	20	30	58	79	100
2	7	14	21	37	46	55
3,4: 3-Powell-a	6	12	18	31	38	45
5-Kamen, Powell-a	9	18	27	47	61	75

SWEET ROMANCE
Charlton Comics: Oct, 1968

	GD	VG	FN	VF	VF/NM	NM-
1	3	6	9	14	20	25

SWEET SIXTEEN (...Comics and Stories for Girls)
Parents' Magazine Institute: Aug-Sept, 1946 - No. 13, Jan, 1948 (All have movie stars photos on covers)

	GD	VG	FN	VF	VF/NM	NM-
1-Van Johnson's life story; Dorothy Dare, Queen of Hollywood Stunt Artists begins (in all issues); part photo-c	22	44	66	128	209	290
2-Jane Powell, Roddy McDowall "Holiday in Mexico" photo on-c; Alan Ladd story	15	30	45	86	133	180
3,5,6,8-11: 5-Ann Francis photo on-c; Gregory Peck story. 6-Dick Haymes story. 8-Shirley Jones photo on-c. 10-Jean Simmons photo on-c; James Stewart story	12	24	36	69	97	125
4-Elizabeth Taylor photo on-c	26	52	78	154	252	350
7-Ronald Reagan's life story	22	44	66	128	209	290
12-Bob Cummings, Vic Damone story	13	26	39	74	105	135
13-Robert Mitchum's life story	14	28	42	76	108	140

SWEET XVI
Marvel Comics: May, 1991 - No. 5, Sept, 1991 ($1.00)

1-5: Barbara Slate story & art 3.00

SWEET TOOTH
DC Comics (Vertigo): Nov, 2009 - Present ($1.00/$2.99)

1-($1.00) Jeff Lemire-s/a 3.00
2-6-($2.99) 3.00

SWIFT ARROW (Also see Lone Rider & The Rider)
Ajax/Farrell Publications: Feb-Mar, 1954 - No. 5, Oct-Nov, 1954; Apr, 1957 - No. 3, Sept, 1957

	GD	VG	FN	VF	VF/NM	NM-
1(1954) (1st Series)	16	32	48	92	144	195
2	10	20	30	56	76	95
3-5: 5-Lone Rider story	9	18	27	50	65	80
1 (2nd Series) (Swift Arrow's Gunfighters #4)	9	18	27	50	65	80
2,3: 2-Lone Rider begins	8	16	24	40	50	60

SWIFT ARROW'S GUNFIGHTERS (Formerly Swift Arrow)
Ajax/Farrell Publ. (Four Star Comic Corp.): No. 4, Nov, 1957

	GD	VG	FN	VF	VF/NM	NM-
4	8	16	24	40	50	60

SWING WITH SCOOTER
National Periodical Publ.: June-July, 1966 - No. 35, Aug-Sept, 1971; No. 36, Oct-Nov, 1972

	GD	VG	FN	VF	VF/NM	NM-
1	9	18	27	60	100	140
2,6-10: 9-Alfred E. Newman swipe in last panel	5	10	15	32	51	70
3-5: 3-Batman cameo on-c. 4-Batman cameo inside. 5-JLA cameo	5	10	15	34	55	75
11-13,15-19: 18-Wildcat of JSA 1pg. text. 19-Last 12¢-c	3	6	9	20	30	40
14-Alfred E. Neuman cameo	3	6	9	21	32	42
20 (68 pgs.)	5	10	15	30	48	65
21-23,25-31	3	6	9	17	25	32
24-Frankenstein-c.	3	6	9	20	30	40
32-34 (68 pgs.). 32-Batman cameo. 33-Interview with David Cassidy. 34-Interview with Rick Ely (The Rebels)	4	8	12	28	44	60
35-(52 pgs.). 1 pg. app. Clark Kent and 4 full pgs. of Superman	7	14	21	49	80	110
36-Bat-signal refererence to Batman	3	6	9	20	30	40

NOTE: **Aragonés** *a-13 (1pg.), 18(1pg.), 30(2pgs.)* **Orlando** *a-1-11; c-1-11, 13. #20, 33, 34: 68 pgs.; #35: 52 pgs.*

SWISS FAMILY ROBINSON (Walt Disney's..; see King Classics & Movie Comics)
Dell Publishing Co.: No. 1156, Dec, 1960

	GD	VG	FN	VF	VF/NM	NM-
Four Color 1156-Movie-photo-c	7	14	21	49	80	110

S.W.O.R.D. (Sentient World Observation and Response Department)
Marvel Comics: Jan, 2010 - No. 5, May, 2010 ($3.99/$2.99)

1-($3.99) Cassaday-c/Gillen-s/Sanders-a; Commander Brand & Henry Gyrich app. 4.00
2-5-($2.99): 2,3-Cassaday-c. 4,5-Del Mundo-c 3.00

SWORD, THE
Image Comics: Oct, 2007 - No. 24 ($2.99)

1-Luna Brothers-s/a 4.00
1-(2nd printing) 3.00
2-22: 12-Zakros killed 3.00
..., Vol. 1: Fire (TPB, 2008, $14.99) r/#1-6 15.00
..., Vol. 2: Water (TPB, 2008, $14.99) r/#7-12 15.00

SWORD & THE DRAGON, THE
Dell Publishing Co.: No. 1118, June, 1960

	GD	VG	FN	VF	VF/NM	NM-
Four Color 1118-Movie, photo-c	7	14	21	50	83	115

SWORD & THE ROSE, THE (Disney)
Dell Publishing Co.: No. 505, Oct, 1953 - No. 682, Feb, 1956

	GD	VG	FN	VF	VF/NM	NM-
Four Color 505-Movie, photo-c	8	16	24	56	93	130
Four Color 682-When Knighthood Was in Flower-Movie, reprint of #505; Renamed the Sword & the Rose for the novel; photo-c	7	14	21	47	76	105

SWORD IN THE STONE, THE (See March of Comics #258 & Movie Comics & Wart and the Wizard)

SWORD OF DAMOCLES
Image Comics (WildStorm Productions): Mar, 1996 - No. 2, Apr, 1996 ($2.50, limited series)

1,2: Warren Ellis scripts. 1-Prelude to "Fire From Heaven" x-over; 1st app. Sword 2.50

SWORD OF DRACULA
Image Comics: Oct, 2003 - No. 6, Sept, 2004 ($2.95, B&W, limited series)

1-6-Tony Harris-c. 1,2-Greg Scott-a 3.00
TPB (IDW, 2/05, $14.99) r/series 15.00

SWORD OF RED SONJA: DOOM OF THE GODS
Dynamite Entertainment: 2007 - No. 4, 2007 ($3.50, limited series)

1-4-Lui Antonio-a; multiple covers on each 3.50

SWORD OF SORCERY
National Periodical Publications: Feb-Mar, 1973 - No. 5, Nov-Dec, 1973 (20¢)

	GD	VG	FN	VF	VF/NM	NM-
1-Leiber Fafhrd & The Grey Mouser; Chaykin/Neal Adams (Crusty Bunkers) art; Kaluta-c	3	6	9	14	20	25
2,3: 2-Wrightson-c(i); Adams-a(i). 3-Wrightson-i(5 pgs.)	2	4	6	8	11	14
4,5: 5-Starlin-a(p); Conan cameo	2	3	4	6	8	10

NOTE: **Chaykin** *a-1-4p; c-2p, 3-5.* **Kaluta** *a-3i.* **Simonson** *a-3i, 4i, 5p; c-5.*

SWORD OF THE ATOM
DC Comics: Sept, 1983 - No. 4, Dec, 1983 (Limited series)

1-4: Gil Kane-c/a in all 3.00
Special 1-3('84, '85, '88): 1,2-Kane-c/a each 3.00
TPB (2007, $19.99) r/#1-4 and Special #1-3 20.00

SWORDS OF TEXAS (See Scout #15)

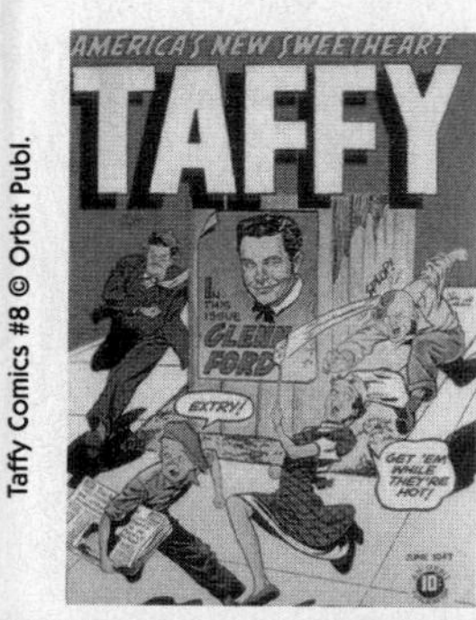

Taffy Comics #8 © Orbit Publ.

Tales Calculated To Drive You Bats #2 © AP

Tales From the Crypt #41 © WMG

	GD 2.0	VG 4.0	FN 6.0	VF 8.0	VF/NM 9.0	NM- 9.2

Eclipse Comics: Oct, 1987 - No. 4, Jan, 1988 ($1.75, color, Baxter paper)
1-4: Scout app. 2.50

SWORDS OF THE SWASHBUCKLERS (See Marvel Graphic Novel)
Marvel Comics (Epic Comics): May, 1985 - No. 12, Jun, 1987 ($1.50; mature)
1-12-Butch Guice-c/a (Cont'd from Marvel G.N.) 2.50

SWORN TO PROTECT
Marvel Comics: Sept, 1995 ($1.95) (Based on card game)
nn-Overpower Game Guide; Jubilee story 2.50

SYN
Dark Horse Comics: Aug, 2003 - No. 5, Feb, 2004 ($2.99, limited series)
1-5-Giffen-s/Titus-a 3.00

SYPHONS
Now Comics: V2#1, May, 1994 - V2#3, 1994 ($2.50, limited series)
V2#1-3: 1-Stardancer, Knightfire, Raze & Brigade begin 2.50
TPB (9/04, $15.95) B&W reprints #1-3; intro. by Tony Caputo 16.00

SYSTEM, THE
DC Comics (Vertigo Verite): May, 1996 - No. 3, July, 1996 ($2.95, lim. series)
1-3: Kuper-c/a 3.00
TPB (1997, $12.95) r/#1-3 13.00

TAFFY COMICS
Rural Home/Orbit Publ.: Mar-Apr, 1945 - No. 12, 1948
1-L.B. Cole-c; origin & 1st app. of Wiggles The Wonderworm plus 7 chapter WWII funny animal adventures 60 120 180 381 653 925
2-L.B. Cole-c with funny animal Hitler; Wiggles-c/stories in #1-4 37 74 111 222 361 500
3,4,6-12: 6-Perry Como-c/story. 7-Duke Ellington, 2 pgs. 8-Glenn Ford-c/story. 9-Lon McCallister part photo-c & story. 10-Mort Leav-c. 11-Mickey Rooney-c/story 15 30 45 83 124 165
5-L.B. Cole-c; Van Johnson-c/story 21 42 63 124 202 280

TAILGUNNER JO
DC Comics: Sept, 1988 - No. 6, Jan, 1989 ($1.25)
1-6 2.50

TAILS
Archie Publications: Dec, 1995 - No. 3, Feb, 1996 ($1.50, limited series)
1-3: Based on Sonic, the Hedgehog video game 4.00

TAILS OF THE PET AVENGERS (Also see Lockjaw and the Pet Avengers)
Marvel Comics: Apr, 2010 ($3.99, one-shot)
1-Lockjaw, Frog Thor, Zabu, Lockheed and Redwing in short solo stories by various 4.00

TAILSPIN
Spotlight Publishers: November, 1944
nn-Firebird app.; L.B. Cole-c 28 56 84 165 270 375

TAILSPIN TOMMY (Also see Popular Comics)
United Features Syndicate/Service Publ. Co.: 1940; 1946
Single Series 23(1940) 39 78 117 240 395 550
Best Seller (nd, 1946)-Service Publ. Co. 15 30 45 86 133 180

TAKE A CHANCE (C.E. Murphy's...)
Dabel Brothers Prods.: Dec, 2008 - No. 5, Apr, 2009 ($3.99)
1-4-C.E. Murphy-s/Ardian Syaf-a/c 4.00

TAKION
DC Comics: June, 1996 - No. 7, Dec, 1996 ($1.75)
1-7: Lopresti-c/a(p). 1-Origin; Green Lantern app. 6-Final Night x-over 2.50

TALENT SHOWCASE (See New Talent Showcase)

TALE OF ONE BAD RAT, THE
Dark Horse Comics: Oct, 1994 - No. 4, Jan, 1995 ($2.95, limited series)
1-4: Bryan Talbot-c/a/scripts 3.00
HC ($69.95, signed and numbered) R/#1-4 70.00

TALES CALCULATED TO DRIVE YOU BATS
Archie Publications: Nov, 1961 - No. 7, Nov, 1962; 1966 (Satire)
1-Only 10¢ issue; has cut-out Werewolf mask (price includes mask) 13 26 39 90 165 240
2-Begin 12¢ issues 8 16 24 52 86 120
3-6: 3-UFO cover 6 12 18 41 66 90
7-Storyline change 6 12 18 39 62 85
1(1966, 25¢, 44 pg. Giant)-r/#1; UFO cover 6 12 18 39 62 85

TALES CALCULATED TO DRIVE YOU MAD
E.C. Publications: Summer, 1997 - No. 8, Winter, 1999 ($3.99/$4.99, satire)
1-6-Full color reprints of Mad: 1-(#1-3), 2-(#4-6), 3-(#7-9), 4-(#10-12) 5-(#13-15), 6-(#16-18) 5.00
7,8-($4.99-c): 7-(#19-21), 8-(#22,23) 5.00

TALES FROM RIVERDALE DIGEST
Archie Publ.: June, 2005 - Present ($2.39/$2.49/$2.69, digest-size)
1-38: 1-Sabrina and Josie & the Pussycats app. 11-Begin $2.49-c. 34-Begin $2.69 2.69

TALES FROM THE AGE OF APOCALYPSE
Marvel Comics: 1996 ($5.95, prestige format, one-shots)
1, ...: Sinister Bloodlines (1997, $5.95) 6.00

TALES FROM THE BOG
Aberration Press: Nov, 1995 - No. 7, Nov, 1997 ($2.95/$3.95, B&W)
1-7 4.00
Alternate #1 (Director's Cut) (1998, $2.95) 3.00

TALES FROM THE BULLY PULPIT
Image Comics: Aug, 2004 ($6.95, square-bound)
1-Teddy Roosevelt and Edison's ghost with a time machine; Cereno-s/MacDonald-a 7.00

TALES FROM THE CLERKS (See Jay and Silent Bob, Clerks and Oni Double Feature)
Graphitti Designs, Inc.: 2006 ($29.95, TPB)
nn-Reprints all the Kevin Smith Clerks and Jay and Silent Bob stories; new Clerks II story with Mahfood-a; cover gallery, sketch pages, Mallrats credits covers; Smith intro. 30.00

TALES FROM THE CRYPT (Formerly The Crypt Of Terror; see Three Dimensional...) (Also see EC Archives • Tales From the Crypt)
E.C. Comics: No. 20, Oct-Nov, 1950 - No. 46, Feb-Mar, 1955
20-See Crime Patrol #15 for 1st Crypt Keeper 117 234 351 936 1493 2050
21-Kurtzman-r/Haunt of Fear #15(#1) 97 194 291 776 1238 1700
22-Moon Girl costume at costume party, one panel 77 154 231 616 983 1350
23-25: 24-E. A. Poe adaptation 60 120 180 480 765 1050
26-30: 26-Wood's 2nd EC-c 47 94 141 376 601 825
31-Williamson-a(1st at E.C.); B&W and color illos. in **POP**; Kamen draws himself, Gaines & Feldstein; Ingels, Craig & Davis draw themselves in his story 48 96 144 384 612 840
32,35-39: 38-Censored-c 42 84 126 336 538 740
33-Origin The Crypt Keeper 65 130 195 520 830 1140
34-Used in **POP**, pg. 83; lingerie panels 43 86 129 344 552 760
40-Used in Senate hearings & in Hartford Cournat anti-comics editorials-1954 43 86 129 344 547 750
41-45: 45-2 pgs. showing E.C. staff 41 82 123 328 539 720
46-Low distribution; pre-advertised cover for unpublished 4th horror title "Crypt of Terror" used on this book 49 98 147 392 621 850

NOTE: ***Ray Bradbury*** *adaptations-34, 36.* ***Craig*** *a-20, 22-24; c-20.* ***Crandall*** *a-38, 44.* ***Davis*** *a-24-46; c-29-46.* ***Elder*** *a-37, 38.* ***Evans*** *a-32-34, 36, 40, 41, 43, 46.* ***Feldstein*** *a-20-23; c-21-25, 28. Ingels a-in all.* ***Kamen*** *a-20, 22, 25, 27-31, 33-36, 39, 41-45.* ***Krigstein*** *a-40, 42, 45.* ***Kurtzman*** *a-21.* ***Orlando*** *a-27-30, 35, 37, 39, 41-45.* ***Wood*** *a-21, 24, 25; c-26, 27. Canadian reprints known; see Table of Contents.*

TALES FROM THE CRYPT (Magazine)
Eerie Publications: No. 10, July, 1968 (35¢, B&W)
10-Contains Farrell reprints from 1950s 5 10 15 32 51 70

TALES FROM THE CRYPT
Gladstone Publishing: July, 1990 - No. 6, May, 1991 ($1.95/$2.00, 68 pgs.)
1-r/TFTC #33 & Crime S.S. #17; Davis-c(r) 3.00
2-6: 2,3,5,6-Davis-c(r). 4-Begin $2.00-c; Craig-c(r) 3.00

TALES FROM THE CRYPT
Extra-Large Comics (Russ Cochran)/Gemstone Publishing: Jul, 1991 - No. 6 ($3.95, 10 1/4 x13 1/4", 68 pgs.)
1-Davis-c(r); Craig back-c(r); E.C. reprints 4.00
2-6 ($2.00, comic sized) 3.00

TALES FROM THE CRYPT
Russ Cochran: Sept, 1991 - No. 7, July, 1992 ($2.00, 64 pgs.)
1-7 3.00

TALES FROM THE CRYPT (Also see EC Archives • Tales From the Crypt)
Russ Cochran/Gemstone: Sept, 1992 - No. 30, Dec, 1999 ($1.50, quarterly)
1-4-r/Crypt of Terror #17-19, TFTC #20 w/original-c 3.00
5-30: 5-15 ($2.00)-r/TFTC #21-23 w/original-c. 16-30 ($2.50) 3.00
Annual 1-6('93-'99) 1-r/#1-5. 2- r/#6-10. 3- r/#11-15. 4- r/#16-20. 5-r/#21-25. 6- r/#26-30 14.00

TALES FROM THE CRYPT
Papercutz: July, 2007 - Present ($3.95)

Tales of Ghost Castle #1 © DC

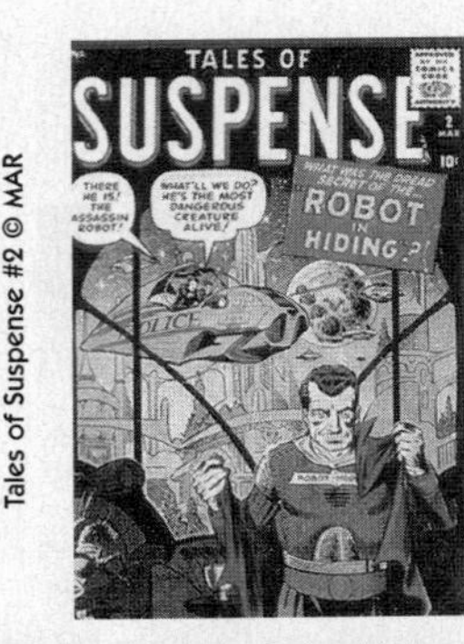

Tales of Suspense #2 © MAR

Tales of Suspense #46 © MAR

	GD 2.0	VG 4.0	FN 6.0	VF 8.0	VF/NM 9.0	NM- 9.2
1-6: 1-New stories in the same vein as the originals; Cryptkeeper app. Kyle Baker-c						4.00

TALES FROM THE GREAT BOOK
Famous Funnies: Feb, 1955 - No. 4, Jan, 1956 (Religious themes)

	GD	VG	FN	VF	VF/NM	NM-
1-Story of Samson; John Lehti-a in all	9	18	27	50	65	80
2-4: 2-Joshua. 3-Joash the Boy King. 4-David	7	14	21	35	43	50

TALES FROM THE HEART OF AFRICA (The Temporary Natives)
Marvel Comics (Epic Comics): Aug, 1990 ($3.95, 52 pgs.)

1 — 4.00

TALES FROM THE TOMB (Also see Dell Giants)
Dell Publishing Co.: Oct, 1962 (25¢ giant)

	GD	VG	FN	VF	VF/NM	NM-
1(02-810-210)-All stories written by John Stanley	15	30	45	104	197	290

TALES FROM THE TOMB (Magazine)
Eerie Publications: V1#6, July, 1969 - V7#3, 1975 (52 pgs.)

	GD	VG	FN	VF	VF/NM	NM-
V1#6	7	14	21	49	80	110
V1#7,8	6	12	18	39	62	85
V2#1-6: 4-LSD story-r/Weird V3#5. 6-Rulah-r	5	10	15	32	51	70
V3#1-Rulah-r	5	10	15	32	51	70
2-6('71),V4#1-5('72),V5#1-6('73),V6#1-6('74),V7#1-3('75)	4	8	12	28	44	60

TALES OF ASGARD
Marvel Comics Group: Oct, 1968 (25¢, 68 pgs.); Feb, 1984 ($1.25, 52 pgs.)

	GD	VG	FN	VF	VF/NM	NM-
1-Reprints Tales of Asgard (Thor) back-up stories from Journey into Mystery #97-106; new Kirby-c; Kirby-a	5	10	15	34	55	75
V2#1 (2/84)-Thor-r; Simonson-c						5.00

TALES OF ARMY OF DARKNESS
Dynamite Entertainment: 2006 ($5.95, one-shot)

1-Short stories by Kuhoric, Kirkman, Bradshaw, Sablik, Ottley, Acs, O'Hare and others — 6.00

TALES OF EVIL
Atlas/Seaboard Publ.: Feb, 1975 - No. 3, July, 1975 (All 25¢ issues)

	GD	VG	FN	VF	VF/NM	NM-
1-3: 1-Werewolf w/Sekowsky-a. 2-Intro. The Bog Beast; Sparling-a. 3-Origin The Man-Monster; Buckler-a(p)	2	4	6	8	10	12

NOTE: *Grandenetti a-1, 2. Lieber c-1. Sekowsky a-1. Sutton a-2. Thorne c-2.*

TALES OF GHOST CASTLE
National Periodical Publications: May-June, 1975 - No. 3, Sept-Oct, 1975 (All 25¢ issues)

	GD	VG	FN	VF	VF/NM	NM-
1-Redondo-a; 1st app. Lucien the Librarian from Sandman (1989 series)	3	6	9	16	23	30
2,3: 2-Nino-a. 3-Redondo-a.	2	4	6	9	13	16

TALES OF G.I. JOE
Marvel Comics: Jan, 1988 - No. 15, Mar, 1989

	GD	VG	FN	VF	VF/NM	NM-
1 ($2.25, 52 pgs.)						3.00
2-15 ($1.50): 1-15-r/G.I. Joe #1-15						2.50

TALES OF HORROR
Toby Press/Minoan Publ. Corp.: June, 1952 - No. 13, Oct, 1954

	GD	VG	FN	VF	VF/NM	NM-
1	39	78	117	240	395	575
2-Torture scenes	32	64	96	188	307	425
3-13: 9-11-Reprints Purple Claw #1-3	22	44	66	130	213	295
12-Myron Fass-c/a; torture scenes	23	46	69	136	223	310

NOTE: *Andru a-5. Baily a-5. Myron Fass a-2, 3, 12; c-1-3, 12. Hollingsworth a-2. Sparling a-6, 9; c-9.*

TALES OF JUSTICE
Atlas Comics(MjMC No. 53-66/Male No. 67): No. 53, May, 1955 - No. 67, Aug, 1957

	GD	VG	FN	VF	VF/NM	NM-
53	15	30	45	83	124	165
54-57: 54-Powell-a	11	22	33	60	83	105
58,59-Krigstein-a	12	24	36	67	94	120
60-63,65: 60-Powell-a	10	20	30	54	72	90
64,66,67: 64,67-Crandall-a. 66-Torres, Orlando-a	10	20	30	56	76	95

NOTE: *Everett a-53, 60. Orlando a-65, 66. Severin a-64; c-58, 60, 65. Wildey a-64, 67.*

TALES OF LEONARDO BLIND SIGHT (See Tales of the TMNT Vol. 2 #5)
Mirage Publishing: June, 2006 - No. 4, Sept, 2006 ($3.25, B&W, limited series)

1-4-Jim Lawson-s/a — 3.25

TALES OF SUSPENSE (Becomes Captain America #100 on)
Atlas (WPI No. 1,2/Male No. 3-12/VPI No. 13-18)/Marvel No. 19 on:
Jan, 1959 - No. 99, Mar, 1968

	GD 2.0	VG 4.0	FN 6.0	VF 8.0	VF/NM 9.0	NM- 9.2
1-Williamson-a (5 pgs.); Heck-c; #1-4 have sci/fi-c	154	308	462	1348	2674	4000
2,3: 2-Robot-c. 3-Flying saucer-c/story	54	108	162	459	905	1350
4-Williamson-a (4 pgs.); Kirby/Everett-c/a	43	86	129	344	672	1000
5-Kirby monster-c begin	39	78	117	297	574	850
6,8,10	34	68	102	262	506	750
7-Prototype ish. (Lava Man); 1 panel app. Aunt May (see Str. Tales #97)	37	74	111	283	547	810
9-Prototype ish. (Iron Man)	38	76	114	292	564	835
11,12,15,17-19: 12-Crandall-a.	28	56	84	204	395	585
13-Elektro-c/story	29	58	87	212	406	600
14-Intro/1st app. Colossus-c/sty	38	76	114	288	557	825
16-1st Metallo-c/story (4/61, Iron Man prototype)	33	66	99	254	490	725
20-Colossus-c/story (2nd app.)	30	60	90	218	422	625
21-25: 25-Last 10¢ issue	24	48	72	175	338	500
26,27,29,30,33,34,36-38: 33-(9/62)-Hulk 1st x-over cameo (picture on wall)	23	46	69	166	321	475
28-Prototype ish. (Stone Men)	23	46	69	170	328	485
31-Prototype ish. (Dr. Doom)	25	50	75	183	354	525
32-Prototype ish. (Dr. Strange)(8/62)-Sazzik The Sorcerer app.; "The Man and the Beehive" story, 1 month before TTA #35 (2nd Antman), came out after "The Man in the Ant Hill" in TTA #27 (1/62) (1st Antman)-Characters from both stories were tested to see which got best fan response	34	68	102	262	506	750
35-Prototype issue (The Watcher)	25	50	75	183	354	525
39 (3/63)-Origin/1st app. Iron Man & begin series; 1st Iron Man story has Kirby layouts	750	1500	2250	6750	13,375	20,000
40-2nd app. Iron Man (in new armor)	173	346	519	1514	3007	4500
41-3rd app. Iron Man; Dr. Strange (villain) app.	100	200	300	850	1675	2500
42-45: 45-Intro. & 1st app. Happy & Pepper	64	128	192	544	1072	1600
46,47: 46-1st app. Crimson Dynamo	50	100	150	413	807	1200
48-New Iron Man armor by Ditko	56	112	168	476	938	1400
49-1st X-Men x-over (same date as X-Men #3, 1/64); also 1st Avengers x-over (w/o Captain America); 1st Tales of the Watcher back-up story & begins (2nd app. Watcher; see F.F. #13)	72	144	216	612	1206	1800
50-1st app. Mandarin	36	72	108	280	540	800
51-1st Scarecrow	27	54	81	197	386	575
52-1st app. The Black Widow (4/64)	40	80	120	314	607	900
53-Origin The Watcher; 2nd Black Widow app.	27	54	81	197	386	575
54-56: 56-1st app. Unicorn	19	38	57	139	270	400
57-Origin/1st app. Hawkeye (9/64)	40	80	120	306	591	875
58-Captain America battles Iron Man (10/64)-Classic-c; 2nd Kraven app. (Cap's 1st app. in this title)	40	80	120	320	623	925
59-Iron Man plus Captain America double feature begins (11/64); 1st S.A. Captain America solo story; intro Jarvis, Avenger's butler; classic-c	40	80	120	320	623	925
60-2nd app. Hawkeye (#64 is 3rd app.)	23	46	69	166	321	475
61,62,64: 62-Origin Mandarin (2/65)	14	28	42	100	188	275
63-1st Silver Age origin Captain America (3/65)	30	60	90	218	422	625
65-G.A. Red Skull in WWII stories(also in #66);-1st Silver-Age Red Skull (5/65).	23	46	69	166	321	475
66-Origin Red Skull	17	34	51	122	236	350
67-70: 69-1st app. Titanium Man. 70-Begin alternating-c features w/Capt. America (even #'s) & Iron Man (odd #'s)	9	18	27	65	113	160
71-78: 75-1st app. Agent 13 later named Sharon Carter; intro Batroc. 78-Col. Nick Fury app.	7	14	21	49	80	110
79-Begin 3 part Iron Man Sub-Mariner battle story; Sub-Mariner-c & cameo; 1st app. Cosmic Cube; 1st modern Red Skull	9	18	27	60	100	140
80-Iron Man battles Sub-Mariner story cont'd in Tales to Astonish #82; classic Red Skull-c	9	18	27	60	100	140
81-98: 82-Intro the Adaptoid by Kirby (also in #83,84). 88-Mole Man app. in Iron Man story. 92-1st Nick Fury x-over (cameo, as Agent of S.H.I.E.L.D., 8/67). 94-Intro Modok. 95-Capt. America's i.d. revealed. 97-1st Whiplash. 98-1st brief app. new Zemo (son?); #99 is 1st full app.	7	14	21	45	73	100
99-Captain America story cont'd in Captain America #100; Iron Man story cont'd in Iron Man & Sub-Mariner #1	8	16	24	56	93	130

Onmibus (See Iron Man Omnibus for reprints of #39-83)

NOTE: *Abel a-73-81i(as Gary Michaels), J. Buscema a-1; c-3. Colan a-39, 73-99p; c(p)-73, 75, 77, 79, 81, 83, 85-87, 89, 91, 93, 95, 97, 99. Crandall a-12. Davis a-38. Ditko a-1-15, 17-44, 46, 47-49p; c-2, 10i, 13i, 23i. Kirby/Ditko a-7; c-10, 13, 22, 28, 34. Everett a-8. Forte a-5, 9. Giacoia a-82. Heath a-2, 10. Gil Kane a-88p, 89-91; c-88, 89-91p. Kirby a(p)-2-4, 6-35, 40, 41, 43, 59-75, 77-86, 92-99; layouts-69-75, 77; c(p)4-28(most), 29-56, 58-72, 74, 76, 78, 80, 82, 84, 86, 92, 94, 96, 98. Leiber/Fox a-42, 43, 45, 51. Reinman a-26, 44i, 49i, 52i, 53i. Tuska a-58, 70-74. Wood c/a-71i.*

TALES OF SUSPENSE
Marvel Comics: V2#1, Jan, 1995 ($6.95, one-shot)

V2#1-James Robinson script; acetate-c. — 7.00

TALES OF SUSPENSE: CAPTAIN AMERICA & IRON MAN #1 COMMEMORATIVE EDITION
Marvel Comics: 2004 ($3.99, one-shot)

nn-Reprints Captain America (2004) #1 and Iron Man (2004) #1 — 4.00

TALES OF SWORD & SORCERY (See Dagar)

Tales of the LSH #335 © DC

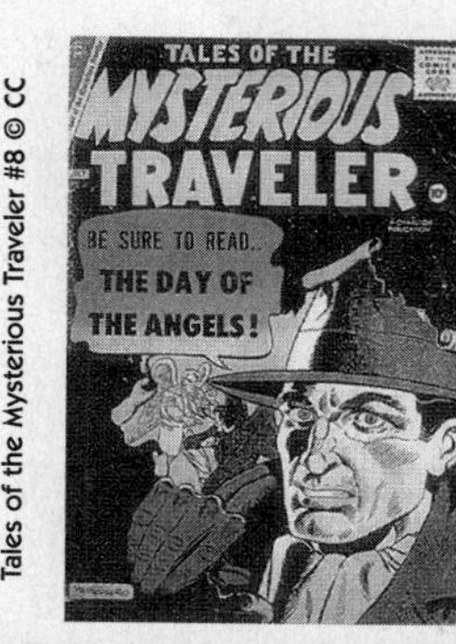

Tales of the Mysterious Traveler #8 © CC

Tales of the Sinestro Corps: Ion #1 © DC

	GD 2.0	VG 4.0	FN 6.0	VF 8.0	VF/NM 9.0	NM- 9.2

TALES OF TELLOS (See Tellos)
Image Comics: Oct, 2004 - No. 3, ($3.50, anthology)

	GD	VG	FN	VF	VF/NM	NM-
1-3: 1-Dezago-s; art by Yates & Rousseau; Wieringo-c. 3-Porter-a						3.50

TALES OF TERROR
Toby Press Publications: 1952 (no month)

	GD	VG	FN	VF	VF/NM	NM-
1-Fawcette-c; Ravielli-a	26	52	78	154	252	350

NOTE: *This title was cancelled due to similarity to the E.C. title.*

TALES OF TERROR (See Movie Classics)

TALES OF TERROR (Magazine)
Eerie Publications: Summer, 1964

	GD	VG	FN	VF	VF/NM	NM-
1	6	12	18	39	62	85

TALES OF TERROR
Eclipse Comics: July, 1985 - No. 13, July, 1987 ($2.00, Baxter paper, mature)

	GD	VG	FN	VF	VF/NM	NM-
1-13: 5-1st Lee Weeks-a. 7-Sam Kieth-a. 10-Snyder-a. 12-Vampire story						3.00

TALES OF TERROR (IDW's...)
IDW Publishing: Sept, 2004 ($16.99, hardcover)

	GD	VG	FN	VF	VF/NM	NM-
1-Anthology of short graphic stories and text stories; incl. 30 Days of Night						17.00

TALES OF TERROR ANNUAL
E.C. Comics: 1951 - No. 3, 1953 (25¢, 132 pgs., 16 stories each)

	GD	VG	FN	VF	VF/NM	NM-
nn(1951)(Scarce)-Feldstein infinity-c	800	1600	2400	6400	-	-
2(1952)-Feldstein-c	258	516	774	1651	2826	4000
3(1953)-Feldstein bondage/torture-c	206	412	618	1318	2259	3200

NOTE: *No. 1 contains three horror and one science fiction comic which came out in 1950. No. 2 contains a horror, crime, and science fiction book which generally had cover dates in 1951, and No. 3 had horror, crime, and shock books that generally appeared in 1952. All E.C. annuals contain four complete books that did not sell on the stands which were rebound in the annual format, minus the covers, and sold from the E.C. office and on the stands in key cities. The contents of each annual may vary in the same year. Crypt Keeper, Vault Keeper, Old Witch app. on all-c.*

TALES OF TERROR ILLUSTRATED (See Terror Illustrated)

TALES OF TEXAS JOHN SLAUGHTER (See Walt Disney Presents, 4-Color #997)

TALES OF THE BEANWORLD
Beanworld Press/Eclipse Comics: Feb, 1985 - No. 19, 1991; No. 20, 1993 - No. 21, 1993 ($1.50/$2.00, B&W)

	GD	VG	FN	VF	VF/NM	NM-
1-21						3.00

TALES OF THE BIZARRO WORLD
DC Comics: 2000 ($14.95, TPB)

	GD	VG	FN	VF	VF/NM	NM-
nn-Reprints early Bizarro stories; new Jaime Hernandez-c						15.00

TALES OF THE DARKNESS
Image Comics (Top Cow): Apr, 1998 - No. 4, Dec, 1998 ($2.95)

	GD	VG	FN	VF	VF/NM	NM-
1-4: 1,2-Portacio-c/a(p). 3,4-Lansing & Nocon-a(p)						3.00
1-American Entertainment Ed.						3.00
#1/2 (1/01, $2.95)						3.00

TALES OF THE DRAGON GUARD (English version of French comic title)
Marvel Comics (Soleil): Apr, 2010 - No. 3 ($5.99, limited series)

	GD	VG	FN	VF	VF/NM	NM-
1-Ange-s/Varanda-a						6.00

TALES OF THE GREEN BERET
Dell Publishing Co.: Jan, 1967 - No. 5, Oct, 1969

	GD	VG	FN	VF	VF/NM	NM-
1-Glanzman-a in 1-4 & 5r	4	8	12	20	30	40
2-5: 5-Reprints #1	3	6	9	16	23	30

TALES OF THE GREEN HORNET
Now Comics: Sept, 1990 - No. 2, 1990; V2#1, Jan, 1992 - No.4, Apr, 1992; V3#1, Sept, 1992 - No. 3, Nov, 1992

	GD	VG	FN	VF	VF/NM	NM-
1,2						2.50
V2#1-4 ($1.95)						2.50
V3#1 ($2.75)-Polybagged w/hologram trading card						3.00
V3#2,3 ($2.50)						2.50

TALES OF THE GREEN LANTERN CORPS (See Green Lantern #107)
DC Comics: May, 1981 - No. 3, July, 1981 (Limited series)

	GD	VG	FN	VF	VF/NM	NM-
1-3: 1-Origin of G.L. & the Guardians, Annual 1 (1/85)-Gil Kane-c/a						3.50
TPB (2009, $19.99) r/#1-3 & stories from G.L. #148-151-154,161,162,164-167 ('82-'83)						20.00
Volume 2 TPB (2010, $19.99) r/Annual #1 and stories from G.L. ('83-'85)						20.00

TALES OF THE INVISIBLE SCARLET O'NEIL (See Harvey Comics Hits #59)

TALES OF THE KILLERS (Magazine)
World Famous Periodicals: V1#10, Dec, 1970 - V1#11, Feb, 1971 (B&W, 52 pg)

	GD	VG	FN	VF	VF/NM	NM-
V1#10-One pg. Frazetta; r/Crime Does Not Pay	5	10	15	30	48	65
11-similar-c to Crime Does Not Pay #47; contains r/Crime Does Not Pay	4	8	12	26	41	55

TALES OF THE LEGION (Formerly Legion of Super-Heroes)
DC Comics: No. 314, Aug, 1984 - No. 354, Dec, 1987

	GD	VG	FN	VF	VF/NM	NM-
314-354: 326-r-begin						2.50
Annual 4,5 (1986, 1987)-Formerly LSH Annual						3.50

TALES OF THE MARINES (Formerly Devil-Dog Dugan #1-3)
Atlas Comics (OPI): No. 4, Feb, 1957 (Marines At War #5 on)

	GD	VG	FN	VF	VF/NM	NM-
4-Powell-a; Severin-c	10	20	30	56	76	95

TALES OF THE MARVELS
Marvel Comics: 1995/1996 (all acetate, painted-c)

	GD	VG	FN	VF	VF/NM	NM-
...Blockbuster 1 (1995, $5.95, one-shot), ...Inner Demons 1 (1996, $5.95, one shot), ...Wonder Years 1,2 (1995, $4.95, limited series)						6.00

TALES OF THE MARVEL UNIVERSE
Marvel Comics: Feb, 1997 ($2.95, one-shot)

	GD	VG	FN	VF	VF/NM	NM-
1-Anthology; wraparound-c; Thunderbolts, Ka-Zar app.						3.00

TALES OF THE MYSTERIOUS TRAVELER (See Mysterious...)
Charlton Comics: Aug, 1956 - No. 13, June, 1959; V2#14, Oct, 1985 - No. 15, Dec, 1985

	GD	VG	FN	VF	VF/NM	NM-
1-No Ditko-a; Giordano/Alascia-c	50	100	150	315	533	750
2-Ditko-a(1)	41	82	123	256	428	600
3-Ditko-c/a(1)	42	84	126	265	445	625
4-7-Ditko-c/a(3-4 stories each)	48	96	144	302	514	725
8,9-Ditko-a(1-3 each). 8-Rocke-c	41	82	123	250	418	585
10,11-Ditko-c/a(3-4 each)	44	88	132	277	469	660
12	18	36	54	105	165	225
13-Baker-a (r?)	19	38	57	111	176	240
V2#14,15 (1985)-Ditko-c/a-low print run	2	3	4	6	8	10

TALES OF THE NEW GODS
DC Comics: 2008 ($19.99, TPB)

	GD	VG	FN	VF	VF/NM	NM-
SC-Reprints from Jack Kirby's Fourth World, Orion and Mister Miracle Special						20.00

TALES OF THE NEW TEEN TITANS
DC Comics: June, 1982 - No. 4, Sept, 1982 (Limited series)

	GD	VG	FN	VF	VF/NM	NM-
1-4						4.00

TALES OF THE PONY EXPRESS (TV)
Dell Publishing Co.: No. 829, Aug, 1957 - No. 942, Oct, 1958

	GD	VG	FN	VF	VF/NM	NM-
Four Color 829 (#1)--Painted-c	5	10	15	30	48	65
Four Color 942-Title -Pony Express	5	10	15	30	48	65

TALES OF THE REALM
CrossGen Comics/MVCreations #4-on: Oct, 2003 - No. 5, May, 2004 ($2.95, limited series)

	GD	VG	FN	VF	VF/NM	NM-
1-5-Robert Kirkman-s/Matt Tyree-a						3.00
Volume 1 HC (8/04, $39.95, dust jacket) r/#1-5; sketch pages and concept art						40.00

TALES OF THE SINESTRO CORPS (See Green Lantern and Green Lantern Corps x-over)
DC Comics: Nov, 2007 - Jan, 2008 ($2.99/$3.99, one-shots)

	GD	VG	FN	VF	VF/NM	NM-
...: Cyborg-Superman (12/07, $2.99) Burnett-s/Blaine-a/VanSciver-c; JLA app.						3.00
...: Ion (1/08, $2.99) Marz-s/Lacombe-a/Benes-c; Sodam Yat app.						3.00
...: Parallax (11/07, $2.99) Marz-s/Melo-a; Kyle Rayner vs. Parallax						3.00
...: Superman-Prime (12/07, $3.99) Johns-s/VanSciver-c; origin re-told w/Ordway-a						4.00

TALES OF THE TEENAGE MUTANT NINJA TURTLES (See Teenage Mutant...)
Mirage Studios: May, 1987 - No. 7, Aug (Apr-c), 1989 (B&W, $1.50)

	GD	VG	FN	VF	VF/NM	NM-
1-7: 2-Title merges w/Teenage Mutant Ninja...						2.50

TALES OF THE TEEN TITANS (Formerly The New Teen Titans)
DC Comics: No. 41, Apr, 1984 - No. 91, July, 1988 (75¢)

	GD	VG	FN	VF	VF/NM	NM-
41,45-49: 46-Aqualad & Aquagirl join						3.00
42-44: The Judas Contract part 1-3 with Deathstroke the Terminator in all; concludes in Annual #3. 44-Dick Grayson becomes Nightwing (3rd to be Nightwing) & joins Titans; Jericho (Deathstroke's son) joins; origin Deathstroke						3.50
50,53-55: 50-Double size; app. Betty Kane (Bat-Girl) out of costume. 53-1st full app. Azrael; Deathstroke cameo. 54,55-Deathstroke-c/stories						3.50
51,52,56-91: 52-1st brief app. Azrael (not same as newer character). 56-Intro Jinx. 57-Neutron app. 59-r/DC Comics Presents #26. 60-91-r/New Teen Titans Baxter series. 68-B. Smith-c. 70-Origin Kole						2.50
Annual 3(1984, $1.25)-Part 4 of The Judas Contract; Deathstroke-c/story; Death of Terra; indicia says Teen Titans Annual; previous annuals listed as New Teen Titans Annual #1,2						4.00
Annual 4-(1986, $1.25)						2.50

TALES OF THE TEXAS RANGERS (See Jace Pearson...)

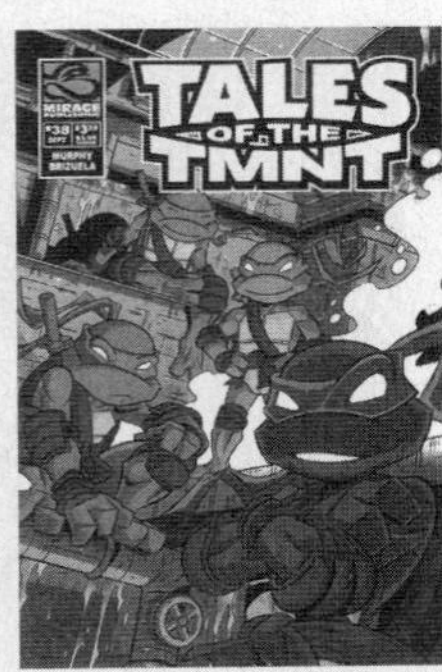

Tales of the TMNT #38 © MS

Tales of the Unexpected #4 © DC

Tales To Astonish #74 © MAR

TALES OF THE THING (Fantastic Four)
Marvel Comics: May, 2005 - No. 3, July, 2005 ($2.50, limited series)

	GD 2.0	VG 4.0	FN 6.0	VF 8.0	VF/NM 9.0	NM- 9.2
1-3-Dr. Strange app; Randy Green-c						2.50

TALES OF THE TMNT (Also see Teenage Mutant Ninja Turtles)
Mirage Studios: Jan, 2004 - Present ($2.95/$3.25, B&W)

	GD 2.0	VG 4.0	FN 6.0	VF 8.0	VF/NM 9.0	NM- 9.2
1-7: 1-Brizuela-a						3.00
8-67: 8-Begin $3.25-c. 47-Origin of the Super Turtles						3.25

TALES OF THE UNEXPECTED (Becomes The Unexpected #105 on)(See Adventure #75, Super DC Giant)
National Periodical Publications: Feb-Mar, 1956 - No. 104, Dec-Jan, 1967-68

	GD 2.0	VG 4.0	FN 6.0	VF 8.0	VF/NM 9.0	NM- 9.2
1	104	208	312	884	1742	2600
2	43	86	129	344	672	1000
3-5	32	64	96	245	473	700
6-10: 6-1st Silver Age issue	26	52	78	190	370	550
11,14,19,20	18	36	54	129	252	375
12,13,16,18,21-24: All have Kirby-a. 16-Characters named 'Thor' (with a magic hammer) and Loki by Kirby (8/57, characters do not look like Marvel's Thor & Loki)	22	44	66	157	304	450
15,17-Grey tone-c; Kirby-a	24	48	72	175	338	500
25-30	16	32	48	115	220	325
31-39	14	28	42	100	188	275
40-Space Ranger begins (8/59, 3rd ap.), ends #82	104	208	312	884	1742	2600
41,42-Space Ranger stories	39	78	117	297	574	850
43-1st Space Ranger-c this title; grey tone-c	68	136	204	578	1139	1700
44-46	27	54	81	197	386	575
47-50	22	44	66	161	311	460
51-60: 54-Dinosaur-c/story	18	36	54	129	252	375
61-67: 67-Last 10¢ issue	15	30	45	107	204	300
68-82: 82-Last Space Ranger	10	20	30	70	123	175
83-90,92-99	6	12	18	43	69	95
91,100: 91-1st Automan (also in #94,97)	7	14	21	45	73	100
101-104	6	12	18	39	62	85

NOTE: ***Neal Adams*** *c-104.* ***Anderson*** *a-50.* ***Brown*** *a-50-82(Space Ranger); c-19, 40, & many Space Ranger-c.* ***Cameron*** *a-24, 27, 29; c-24.* ***Heath*** *a-49.* ***Bob Kane*** *a-24, 48.* ***Kirby*** *a-12, 13, 15-18, 21-24; c-13, 18, 22.* ***Meskin*** *a-15, 18, 26, 27, 35, 66.* ***Moreira*** *a-16, 20, 29, 38, 44, 62, 71; c-38.* ***Roussos*** *c-10.* ***Wildey*** *a-31.*

TALES OF THE UNEXPECTED (See Crisis Aftermath: The Spectre)
DC Comics: Dec, 2006 - No. 8, Jul, 2007 ($3.99, limited series)

	GD 2.0	VG 4.0	FN 6.0	VF 8.0	VF/NM 9.0	NM- 9.2
1-8-The Spectre, Lapham-s/Battle-a; Dr. 13, Azzarello-s/Chiang-a. 4-Wrightson-c						4.00
1-Variant Spectre cover by Neal Adams						5.00
The Spectre: Tales of the Unexpected TPB (2007, $14.99) r/#4-8						15.00

TALES OF THE VAMPIRES (Also see Buffy the Vampire Slayer and related titles)
Dark Horse Comics: 2003 - No. 5, Apr, 2004 ($2.99, limited series)

	GD 2.0	VG 4.0	FN 6.0	VF 8.0	VF/NM 9.0	NM- 9.2
1-Short stories by Joss Whedon and others. 1-Totleben-c. 3-Powell-c. 4-Edlund-c						3.00
TPB (11/04, $15.95) r/#1-5; afterword by Marv Wolfman						16.00

TALES OF THE WEST (See 3-D...)

TALES OF THE WITCHBLADE
Image Comics (Top Cow Productions): Nov, 1996 - No. 9 ($2.95)

	GD 2.0	VG 4.0	FN 6.0	VF 8.0	VF/NM 9.0	NM- 9.2
1/2	1	2	3	5	7	9
1/2 Gold						15.00
1-Daniel-c/a(p)	1	3	4	6	8	10
1-Variant-c by Turner	2	4	6	9	12	15
1-Platinum Edition						30.00
2,3						6.00
4-6: 6-Green-c						5.00
7-9: 9-Lara Croft-c						3.00
7-Variant-c by Turner	1	2	3	5	6	8
Witchblade: Distinctions (4/01, $14.95, TPB) r/#1-6; Green-c						15.00

TALES OF THE WITCHBLADE COLLECTED EDITION
Image Comics (Top Cow): May, 1998 - No. 2 ($4.95/$5.95, square-bound)

	GD 2.0	VG 4.0	FN 6.0	VF 8.0	VF/NM 9.0	NM- 9.2
1,2: 1-r/#1,2. 2-($5.95) r/#3,4						6.00

TALES OF THE WIZARD OF OZ (See Wizard of OZ, 4-Color #1308)

TALES OF THE ZOMBIE (Magazine)
Marvel Comics Group: Aug, 1973 - No. 10, Mar, 1975 (75¢, B&W)

	GD 2.0	VG 4.0	FN 6.0	VF 8.0	VF/NM 9.0	NM- 9.2
V1#1-Reprint/Menace #5; origin	5	10	15	32	51	70
2,3: 2-Everett biog. & memorial	4	8	12	26	41	55
V2#1(#4)-Photos & text of James Bond movie "Live & Let Die"	3	6	9	21	32	42
5-10: 8-Kaluta-a	3	6	9	19	29	38
Annual 1(Summer,'75)(#11)-B&W; Everett, Buscema-a	3	6	9	21	32	42

NOTE: Brother Voodoo app. 2, 5, 6, 10. ***Alcala*** *a-7-9.* ***Boris*** *c-1-4.* ***Colan*** *a-2r, 6.* ***Heath*** *a-5r.* ***Reese*** *a-2.* ***Tuska*** *a-2r.*

TALES OF THUNDER
Deluxe Comics: Mar, 1985

	GD 2.0	VG 4.0	FN 6.0	VF 8.0	VF/NM 9.0	NM- 9.2
1-Dynamo, Iron Maiden, Menthor app.; Giffen-a						2.50

TALES OF VOODOO
Eerie Publications: V1#11, Nov, 1968 - V7#6, Nov, 1974 (Magazine)

	GD 2.0	VG 4.0	FN 6.0	VF 8.0	VF/NM 9.0	NM- 9.2
V1#11	7	14	21	45	73	100
V2#1(3/69)-V2#4(9/69)	5	10	15	30	48	65
V3#1-6('70): 4- "Claws of the Cat" redrawn from Climax #1	4	8	12	24	37	50
V4#1-6('71), V5#1-7('72), V6#1-6('73), V7#1-6('74)	4	8	12	24	37	50
Annual 1	4	8	12	26	41	55

NOTE: *Bondage-c-V1#10, V2#4, V3#4.*

TALES OF WELLS FARGO (TV)(See Western Roundup under Dell Giants)
Dell Publishing Co.: No. 876, Feb, 1958 - No. 1215, Oct-Dec, 1961

	GD 2.0	VG 4.0	FN 6.0	VF 8.0	VF/NM 9.0	NM- 9.2
Four Color 876 (#1)-Photo-c	9	18	27	60	100	140
Four Color 968 (2/59), 1023, 1075 (3/60), 1113 (7-9/60)-All photo-c. 1075,1113-Both have variant edition, back-c comic strip	8	16	24	56	93	130
Four Color 1167 (3-5/61), 1215-Photo-c	8	16	24	52	86	120

TALESPIN (Also see Cartoon Tales & Disney's Talespin Limited Series)
Disney Comics: June, 1991 - No. 7, Dec, 1991 ($1.50)

	GD 2.0	VG 4.0	FN 6.0	VF 8.0	VF/NM 9.0	NM- 9.2
1-7						2.50

TALES TO ASTONISH (Becomes The Incredible Hulk #102 on)
Atlas (MAP No. 1/ZPC No. 2-14/VPI No. 15-21/Marvel No. 22 on: Jan, 1959 - No. 101, Mar, 1968

	GD 2.0	VG 4.0	FN 6.0	VF 8.0	VF/NM 9.0	NM- 9.2
1-Jack Davis-a; monster-c.	154	308	462	1348	2674	4000
2-Ditko flying saucer-c (Martians); #2-4 have sci/fi-c.	60	120	180	510	1005	1500
3,4	43	86	129	344	672	1000
5-Prototype issue (Stone Men); Williamson-a (4 pgs.); Kirby monster-c begin	46	92	138	368	709	1050
6-Prototype issue (Stone Men)	36	72	108	280	540	800
7-Prototype issue (Toad Men)	36	72	108	280	540	800
8-10	33	66	99	257	496	735
11-14,17-20: 13-Swipes story from Menace #8	28	56	84	204	395	585
15-Prototype issue (Electro)	33	66	99	254	490	725
16-Prototype issue (Stone Men)	30	60	90	218	422	625
21-(7/61)-Hulk prototype	30	60	90	218	422	625
22-26,28-34: 32-Sandman prototype	23	46	69	166	321	475
27-1st Ant-Man app. (1/62); last 10¢ issue (see Strange Tales #73,78 & Tales of Suspense #32)	480	960	1440	4320	8660	13,000
35-(9/62)-2nd app. Ant-Man, 1st in costume; begin series & Ant-Man-c	173	346	519	1514	3007	4500
36-3rd app. Ant-Man	76	152	228	646	1273	1900
37-40: 38-1st app. Egghead	46	92	138	368	709	1050
41-43	38	76	114	288	557	825
44-Origin & 1st app. The Wasp (6/63)	50	100	150	400	775	1150
45-48: 48-Origin & 1st app. The Porcupine.	24	48	72	175	338	500
49-Ant-Man becomes Giant Man (11/63)	30	60	90	218	422	625
50,51,53-56,58: 50-Origin/1st app. Human Top (alias Whirlwind). 58-Origin Colossus	16	32	48	115	220	325
52-Origin/1st app. Black Knight (2/64)	19	38	57	139	270	400
57-Early Spider-Man app. (7/64)	35	70	105	271	523	775
59-Giant Man vs. Hulk feature story (9/64); Hulk's 1st app. this title	31	62	93	236	456	675
60-Giant Man & Hulk double feature begins	23	46	69	166	321	475
61-69: 61-All Ditko issue; 1st mailbag. 62-1st app./origin The Leader; new Wasp costume; Hulk pin-up page missing from many copies. 63-Origin Leader; 65-New Giant Man costume. 68-New Human Top costume. 69-Last Giant Man	12	24	36	85	155	225
70-Sub-Mariner & Incredible Hulk begins (8/65)	13	26	39	95	178	260
71-81: 72-Begin alternating-c features w/Sub-Mariner (even #'s) & Hulk (odd #'s). 79-Hulk vs. Hercules-c/story. 81-1st app. Boomerang	7	14	21	45	73	100
82-Iron Man battles Sub-Mariner (1st Iron Man x-over outside The Avengers & TOS); story cont'd from Tales of Suspense #80	8	16	24	52	86	120
83-91,94-99: 90-1st app. The Abomination. 97-X-Men cameo (brief)	6	12	18	41	66	90
92-1st Silver Surfer x-over (outside of Fantastic Four, 6/67); 1 panel cameo only	7	14	21	50	83	115
93-Hulk battles Silver Surfer-c/story (1st full x-over)	16	32	48	115	220	325

Tales Too Terrible to Tell #1 © NEC

Tangent Comics/The Joker #1 © DC

Tank Girl #4 © Deadline

GD 2.0 · VG 4.0 · FN 6.0 · VF 8.0 · VF/NM 9.0 · NM- 9.2

100-Hulk battles Sub-Mariner full-length story 8 16 24 52 86 120
101-Hulk story cont'd in Incredible Hulk #102; Sub-Mariner story continued in Iron Man & Sub-Mariner #1 8 16 24 56 93 130

NOTE: ***Ayers*** *c(i)-9-12, 16, 18, 19.* ***Berg*** *a-1.* ***Burgos*** *a-62-64p.* ***Buscema*** *a-85-87p.* ***Colan*** *a(p)-70-76, 78-82, 84, 85, 101; c(p)-71-76, 78, 80, 82, 84, 86, 88, 90.* ***Ditko*** *a-1, 3-48, 50i, 60-67p; c-2, 7i, 8i, 14i, 17i.* ***Everett*** *a-78, 79i, 80-84, 85-90i, 94i, 95, 96; c(i)-79-81, 83, 86, 88.* ***Forte*** *a-6.* ***Kane*** *a-76, 88-91; c-89, 91.* ***Kirby*** *a(p)-1, 5-34-40, 44, 49-51, 68-70, 82, 83; layouts-71-84; c(p)-1, 3-48, 50-70, 72, 73, 75, 77, 78, 79, 81, 85, 90.* ***Kirby/Ditko*** *a-7, 8, 12, 13, 50; c-7, 8, 10, 13.* ***Leiber/Fox*** *a-47, 48, 50, 51.* ***Powell*** *a-65-69p, 73, 74.* ***Reinman*** *a-6, 36, 45, 46, 54i, 56-60i.*

TALES TO ASTONISH (2nd Series)
Marvel Comics Group: Dec, 1979 - No. 14, Jan, 1981

V1#1-Reprints Sub-Mariner #1 by Buscema 2 3 4 6 8 10
2-14: Reprints Sub-Mariner #2-14 6.00

TALES TO ASTONISH
Marvel Comics: V3#1, Oct, 1994 ($6.95, one-shot)

V3#1-Peter David scripts; acetate, painted-c 7.00

TALES TO HOLD YOU SPELLBOUND (See Spellbound)

TALES TO OFFEND
Dark Horse Comics: July, 1997 ($2.95, one-shot)

1-Frank Miller-s/a, EC-style cover 3.50

TALES TOO TERRIBLE TO TELL (Becomes Terrology #10, 11)
New England Comics: Wint, 1989-90 - No. 11, Nov-Dec.1993 ($2.95/$3.50, B&W with card-stock covers)

1-($2.95) Reprints of non-EC pre-code horror; EC-style cover by Bissette 4.00
1-($3.50, 5-6/93) Second printing with alternate cover not by Bissette 4.00
2-8-($3.50) Story reprints, history of the pre-code titles and creators; cover galleries (B&W) inside & on back-c (color) 4.00
9-11-($2.95) 10,11-"Terrology" on cover 4.00

TALEWEAVER
DC Comics (WildStorm): Nov, 2001 - No. 6, Apr, 2002 ($3.50, limited series)

1-6-Philip Tan-a/Leonard Banaag-s. 2-Variant-c by Anacleto 3.50

TALKING KOMICS
Belda Record & Publ. Co.: 1947 (20 pgs, slick-c)

Each comic contained a record that followed the story - much like the Golden Record sets. Known titles: Chirpy Cricket, Lonesome Octopus, Sleepy Santa, Grumpy Shark, Flying Turtle, Happy Grasshopper
with records... 3 6 9 18 27 35

TALLY-HO COMICS
Swappers Quarterly (Baily Publ. Co.): Dec, 1944

nn-Frazetta's 1st work as Giunta's assistant; Man in Black horror story; violence; Giunta-c 47 94 141 296 498 700

TALULLAH (See Comic Books Series I)

TAMMY, TELL ME TRUE
Dell Publishing Co.: No. 1233, 1961

Four Color 1233-Movie 6 12 18 43 69 95

TANGENT COMICS
.../ THE ATOM, DC Comics: Dec, 1997 ($2.95, one-shot)
1-Dan Jurgens-s/Jurgens & Paul Ryan-a 3.00
.../ THE BATMAN, DC Comics: Sept, 1998 ($1.95, one-shot)
1-Dan Jurgens-s/Klaus Janson-a 3.00
.../ DOOM PATROL, DC Comics: Dec, 1997 ($2.95, one-shot)
1- Dan Jurgens-s/Sean Chen & Kevin Conrad-a 3.00
.../ THE FLASH, DC Comics: Dec, 1997 ($2.95, one-shot)
1-Todd Dezago-s/Gary Frank & Cam Smith-a 3.00
.../ GREEN LANTERN, DC Comics: Dec, '97 ($2.95, one-shot)
1-James Robinson-s/J.H. Williams III & Mick Gray-a 3.00
.../ JLA, DC Comics: Sept, 1998 ($1.95, one-shot)
1-Dan Jurgens-s/Banks & Rapmund-a 3.00
.../ THE JOKER, DC Comics: Dec, 1997 ($2.95, one-shot)
1-Karl Kesel-s/Matt Haley & Tom Simmons-a 3.00
.../ THE JOKER'S WILD, DC Comics: Sept, 1998 ($1.95, one-shot)
1-Kesel & Simmons-s/Phillips & Rodriguez-a 2.25
.../ METAL MEN, DC Comics: Dec, 1997 ($2.95, one-shot)
1-Ron Marz-s/Mike McKone & Mark McKenna-a 3.00
.../ NIGHTWING, DC Comics: Dec, 1997 ($2.95, one-shot)
1-John Ostrander-s/Jan Duursema-a 3.00
.../ NIGHTWING: NIGHTFORCE, DC Comics: Sept, 1998 ($1.95, one-shot)
1-John Ostrander-s/Jan Duursema-a 2.50
.../ POWERGIRL, DC Comics: Sept, 1998 ($1.95, one-shot)
1-Marz-s/Abell & Vines-a 2.50
.../ SEA DEVILS, DC Comics: Dec, 1997 ($2.95, one-shot)
1-Kurt Busiek-s/Vince Giarrano & Tom Palmer-a 3.00
.../ SECRET SIX, DC Comics: Dec, 1997 ($2.95, one-shot)
1-Chuck Dixon-s/Tom Grummett & Lary Stucker-a 3.00
.../ THE SUPERMAN, DC Comics: Sept, 1998 ($1.95, one-shot)
1-Millar-s/Guice-a 3.00
.../ TALES OF THE GREEN LANTERN, DC Comics: Sept, 1998 ($1.95, one-shot)
1-Story & art by various 3.00
.../ THE TRIALS OF THE FLASH, DC Comics: Sept, 1998 ($1.95, one-shot)
1-Dezago-s/Pelletier & Lanning-a 2.50
.../ WONDER WOMAN DC Comics: Sept, 1998 ($1.95, one-shot),
1-Peter David-s/Unzueta & Mendoza-a 3.00
... Volume One TPB (2007, $19.99) r/The Atom, Metal Men, Green Lantern, The Flash, Sea Devils one-shots; intro and new cover by Jurgens 20.00
... Volume Two TPB (2008, $19.99) r/Batman, Doom Patrol, Joker, Nightwing and Secret Six one-shots; new cover by Jurgens 20.00
... Volume Three TPB (2008, $19.99) r/The Superman, Wonder Woman, Nightwing: Nightforce, The Joker's Wild, The Trials of the Flash, Tales of the Green Lantern, Powergirl, and JLA one-shots; new cover by Jurgens 20.00

TANGENT: SUPERMAN'S REIGN
DC Comics: May, 2008 - No. 12, Apr, 2009 ($2.99, limited series)

1-12-Jurgens-s; Flash & Green Lantern app.; back-up histories of Tangent heroes 3.00
Volume 1 TPB (2009, $19.99) r/#1-6 & Justice League of America #16 20.00
Volume 2 TPB (2009, $19.99) r/#7-12 20.00

TANGLED WEB (See Spider-Man's Tangled Web)

TANK GIRL
Dark Horse Comics: May, 1991 - No. 4, Aug, 1991 ($2.25, B&W, mini-series)

1-Contains Dark Horse trading cards 6.00
2-4 4.00
...: Dark Nuggets (Image Comics, 12/09, $3.99) Martin-s/Dayglo-a 4.00

TANK GIRL: APOCALYPSE
DC Comics: Nov, 1995 - No. 4, Feb, 1996 ($2.25, limited series)

1-4 3.00

TANK GIRL: MOVIE ADAPTATION
DC Comics: 1995 ($5.95, 68 pgs., one-shot)

nn-Peter Milligan scripts 6.00

TANK GIRL: THE GIFTING
IDW Publishing: May, 2007 - No. 4, Aug, 2007 ($3.99)

1-4: 1-Ashley Wood-a/c; Alan Martin-s; 3 covers 4.00

TANK GIRL: THE ODYSSEY
DC Comics: May, 1995 - No.4, Oct, 1995 ($2.25, limited series)

1-4: Peter Milligan scripts; Hewlett-a 3.00

TANK GIRL 2
Dark Horse Comics: June, 1993 - No. 4, Sept, 1993 ($2.50, lim. series, mature)

1-4: Jamie Hewlett & Alan Martin-s/a 3.00
TPB (2/95, $17.95) r/#1-4 18.00

TAPPAN'S BURRO (See Zane Grey & 4-Color #449)

TAPPING THE VEIN (Clive Barker's...)
Eclipse Comics: 1989 - No. 5, 1992 ($6.95, squarebound, mature, 68 pgs.)

Book 1-5: 1-Russell-a, Bolton-c. 2-Bolton-a. 4-Die-cut-c 7.00
TPB (2002, $24.95, Checker Book Publ. Group) r/#1-5 25.00

TARANTULA (See Weird Suspense)

TARGET: AIRBOY
Eclipse Comics: Mar, 1988 ($1.95)

1 2.50

TARGET COMICS (...Western Romances #106 on)
Funnies, Inc./Novelty Publications/Star Publ.: Feb, 1940 - V10#3 (#105), Aug-Sept, 1949

V1#1-Origin & 1st app. Manowar, The White Streak by Burgos, & Bulls-Eye Bill by Everett; City Editor (ends #5), High Grass Twins by Jack Cole (ends #4), T-Men by Joe Simon (ends #9), Rip Rory (ends #4), Fantastic Feature Films by Tarpe Mills (ends #39), &

Target Comics V3 #2 © NOVP

Tarzan #10 © ERB

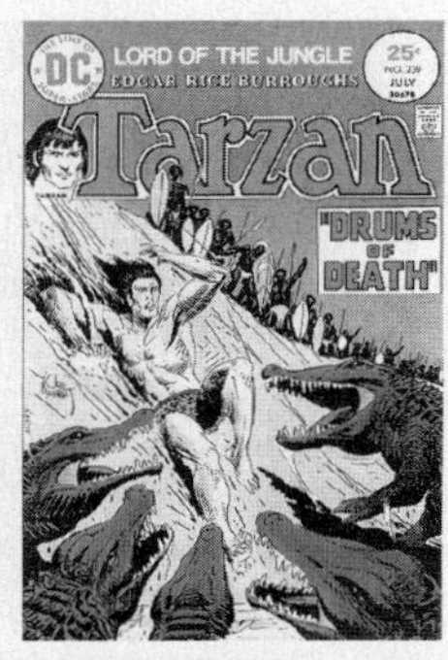

Tarzan #239 © ERB

GD VG FN VF VF/NM NM-
2.0 4.0 6.0 8.0 9.0 9.2

Calling 2-R (ends #14) begin; marijuana use story
500 1000 1500 3650 6450 9250
2-Everett-c/a 253 506 759 1607 2766 3925
3,4-Everett, Jack Cole-a 152 304 456 965 1658 2350
5-Origin The White Streak in text; Space Hawk by Wolverton begins (6/40)
(see Blue Bolt & Circus) 429 858 1287 3132 5516 7900
6-The Chameleon by Everett begins (7/40, 1st app.); White Streak origin cont'd. in text; early mention of comic collecting in letter column; 1st letter column in comics? (7/40)
216 432 648 1372 2361 3350
7-Wolverton Spacehawk-c/story (Scarce) 757 1514 2271 5526 9763 14,000
8-Classic sci-fi cover 187 374 561 1197 2049 2900
9,12: 12-(1/41) 142 284 426 909 1555 2200
10-Intro/1st app. The Target (11/40); Simon-c; Spacehawk-s; text piece by Wolverton
239 478 717 1530 2615 3700
11-Origin The Target & The Targeteers 179 358 537 1137 1956 2775
V2#1-Target by Bob Wood; Uncle Sam flag-c 87 174 261 553 952 1350
2-Ten part Treasure Island serial begins; Harold Delay-a; reprinted in Catholic Comics
V3#1-10 (see Key Comics #5) 77 154 231 493 847 1200
3-5: 4-Kit Carter, The Cadet begins 61 122 183 387 664 940
6-9: Red Seal with White Streak in #6-10 58 116 174 371 636 900
10-Classic-c 102 204 306 648 1112 1575
11,12: 12-10-part Last of the Mohicans serial begins; Delay-a
57 114 171 362 619 875
V3#1-3,5-7,9,10: 10-Last Wolverton issue 54 108 162 346 591 835
4-V for Victory-c 60 120 180 381 653 925
8-Hitler, Tojo, Flag-c; 6-part Gulliver Travels serial begins; Delay-a.
77 154 231 493 847 1200
11,12 18 36 54 105 165 225
V4#1-4,7-12: 8-X-Mas-c 14 28 42 76 108 140
5-Classic Statue of Liberty-c 15 30 45 85 130 175
6-Targetoons by Wolverton 15 30 45 85 130 175
V5#1-8 12 24 36 67 94 120
V6#1-4,6-10 11 22 33 64 90 115
5-Tojo-c 16 32 48 94 147 200
V7#1-12 10 20 30 58 79 100
V8#1,3-5,8,9,11,12 10 20 30 56 76 95
2,6,7-Krigstein-a 11 22 33 62 86 110
10-L.B. Cole-c 34 68 102 199 325 450
V9#1,4,6,8,10-L.B. Cole-c 32 64 96 192 314 435
2,3,5,7,9,11, V10#1 10 20 30 56 76 95
12-Classic L.B. Cole-c 37 74 111 222 361 500
V10#2,3-L.B. Cole-c 31 62 93 186 303 420

NOTE: ***Certa** c-V8#9, 11, 12, V9#5, 9, 11, V10#1. **Jack Cole** a-1-8. **Everett** a-1-9; c(signed Blake)-1, 2. **Al Fago** c-V6#8. **Sid Greene** c-V2#9, 12, V3#3. **Walter Johnson** c-V5#6, V6#4. **Tarpe Mills** a-1-4, 6, 8, 11, V3#1. **Rico** a-V7#4, 10, V8#5, 6, V9#3; c-V7#6, 8, 10, V8#2, 4, 6, 7. **Simon** a-1, 2. **Bob Wood** c-V2#2, 3, 5, 6.*

TARGET: THE CORRUPTORS (TV)
Dell Publishing Co.: No. 1306, Mar-May, 1962 - No. 3, Oct-Dec, 1962
(All have photo-c)

Four Color 1306(#1), #2,3 6 12 18 37 59 80

TARGET WESTERN ROMANCES (Formerly Target Comics; becomes Flaming Western Romances #3)
Star Publications: No. 106, Oct-Nov, 1949 - No. 107, Dec-Jan, 1949-50

106(#1)-Silhouette nudity panel; L.B. Cole-c 35 70 105 203 327 450
107(#2)-L.B. Cole-c; lingerie panels 29 58 87 169 272 375

TARGITT
Atlas/Seaboard Publ.: March, 1975 - No. 3, July, 1975

1-3: 1-Origin; Nostrand-a in all. 2-1st in costume. 3-Becomes Man-Stalker
2 3 4 6 8 10

TARZAN (See Aurora, Comics on Parade, Crackajack, DC 100-Page Super Spec., Edgar Rice Burroughs'..., Famous Feature Stories #1, Golden Comics Digest #4, 9, Jeep Comics #1-29, Jungle Tales of..., Limited Collectors' Edition, Popular, Sparkler, Sport Stars #1, Tip Top & Top Comics)

TARZAN
Dell Publishing Co./United Features Synd.: No. 5, 1939 - No. 161, Aug, 1947

Large Feature Comic 5('39)-(Scarce)-By Hal Foster; reprints 1st dailies from 1929
174 348 522 1114 1907 2700
Single Series 20('40)-By Hal Foster 119 238 357 762 1306 1850
Four Color 134(2/47)-Marsh-c/a 52 104 156 442 871 1300
Four Color 161(8/47)-Marsh-c/a 48 96 144 384 742 1100

TARZAN (...of the Apes #138 on)
Dell Publishing Co./Gold Key No. 132 on: 1-2/48 - No. 131, 7-8/62; No. 132, 11/62 - No. 206, 2/72

1-Jesse Marsh-a begins 96 192 288 816 1608 2400
2 43 86 129 344 672 1000
3-5 31 62 93 239 462 685
6-10: 6-1st Tantor the Elephant. 7-1st Valley of the Monsters
26 52 78 190 370 550
11-15: 11-Two Against the Jungle begins, ends #24. 13-Lex Barker photo-c begin
21 42 63 153 297 440
16-20 17 34 51 124 242 360
21-24,26-30 15 30 45 104 197 290
25-1st "Brothers of the Spear" episode; series ends #156,160,161,196-206
16 32 48 115 220 325
31-40 11 22 33 80 145 210
41-54: Last Barker photo-c 9 18 27 65 113 160
55-60: 56-Eight pg. Boy story 8 16 24 58 97 135
61,62,64-70 7 14 21 49 80 110
63-Two Tarzan stories, 1 by Manning 7 14 21 50 83 115
71-79 6 12 18 43 69 95
80-99: 80-Gordon Scott photo-c begin 6 12 18 39 62 85
100 6 12 18 43 69 95
101-109 6 12 18 37 59 80
110 (Scarce)-Last photo-c 6 12 18 43 69 95
111-120 5 10 15 34 55 75
121-131: Last Dell issue 5 10 15 32 51 70
132-1st Gold Key issue 5 10 15 34 55 75
133-138,140-154 4 8 12 26 41 55
139-(12/63)-1st app. Korak (Boy); leaves Tarzan & gets own book (1/64)
7 14 21 45 73 100
155-Origin Tarzan 5 10 15 32 51 70
156-161: 157-Banlu, Dog of the Arande begins, ends #159, 195. 169-Leopard Girl app.
4 8 12 22 34 45
162,165,168,171 (TV)-Ron Ely photo covers 4 8 12 23 36 48
163,164,166,167,169,170: 169-Leopard Girl app. 3 6 9 21 32 42
172-199,201-206: 178-Tarzan origin-r/#155; Leopard Girl app., also in #179, 190-193
3 6 9 19 29 38
200 4 8 12 22 34 45
Story Digest 1-(6/70, G.K., 148pp.)(scarce) 7 14 21 49 80 110

NOTE: *#162, 165, 168, 171 are TV issues. #1-153 all have **Marsh** art on Tarzan. #154-161, 163, 164, 166, 167, 172-177 all have **Manning** art on Tarzan. #178, 202 have **Manning** Tarzan reprints. No "Brothers of the Spear" in #1-24, 157-159, 162-195. #39-126, 128-156 all have **Russ Manning** art on "Brothers of the Spear". #196-201, 203-205 all have **Manning** B.O.T.S. reprints; #25-38, 127 all have Jesse **Marsh** art on B.O.T.S. #206 has a Marsh B.O.T.S. reprint. **Gollub** c-8-12. **Marsh** c-1-7. **Doug Wildey** a-162, 179-187. Many issues have front and back photo covers.*

TARZAN (Continuation of Gold Key series)
National Periodical Publications: No. 207, Apr, 1972 - No. 258, Feb, 1977

207-Origin Tarzan by Joe Kubert, part 1; John Carter begins (origin); 52 pg. issues
thru #209 5 10 15 34 55 75
208,209-(52 pgs.): 208-210-Parts 2-4 of origin. 209-Last John Carter
3 6 9 19 29 38
210-220: 210-Kubert-a. 211-Hogarth, Kubert-a. 212-214: Adaptations from "Jungle Tales of Tarzan". 213-Beyond the Farthest Star begins, ends #218. 215-218,224,225-All by Kubert. 215-part Foster-r. 219-223: Adapts "The Return of Tarzan" by Kubert
3 6 9 14 19 24
221-229: 221-223-Continues adaptation of "The Return of Tarzan". 226-Manning-a
2 4 6 10 14 18
230-DC 100 Page Super Spectacular; Kubert, Kaluta-a(p); Korak begins, ends #234; Carson of Venus app. 4 8 12 24 37 50
231-235-New Kubert-a.: 231-234-(All 100 pgs.)-Adapts "Tarzan and the Lion Man"; Rex, the Wonder Dog r-#232, 233. 235-(100 pgs.)-Last Kubert issue.
4 8 12 23 36 48
236,237,239-258: 240-243 adapts "Tarzan & the Castaways". 250-256 adapts "Tarzan the Untamed." 252,253-r/#213 2 4 6 8 10 12
238-(68 pgs.) 2 4 6 13 18 22
Comic Digest 1-(Fall, 1972, 50¢, 164 pgs.)(DC)-Digest size; Kubert-c; Manning-a
4 8 12 26 41 55
Edgar Rice Burroughs' Tarzan The Joe Kubert Years - Volume One HC (Dark Horse Books, 10/05, $49.95, dust jacket) recolored r/#207-214; intro. by Joe Kubert 50.00
Edgar Rice Burroughs' Tarzan The Joe Kubert Years - Volume Two HC (Dark Horse Books, 2/06, $49.95, dust jacket) recolored r/#215-224; intro. by Joe Kubert 50.00
Edgar Rice Burroughs' Tarzan The Joe Kubert Years - Volume Three HC (Dark Horse Books, 6/06, $49.95, dust jacket) recolored r/#225,227-235; Kubert intro. and sketch pages 50.00

NOTE: ***Anderson** a-207, 209, 217, 218. **Chaykin** a-216. **Finlay** a(r)-212. **Foster** strip-r #207-209, 211, 212, 221. **Heath** a-230i. **G. Kane** a(r)-232p, 233p. **Kubert** a-207-225, 227-235, 257r, 258r; c-207-249, 253. **Lopez** a-250-255p; c-250p, 251, 252, 254. **Manning** strip-r 230-235, 238. **Morrow** a-208. **Nino** a-231-234. **Sparling** a-230, 231. **Starr** a-233r.*

TARZAN (Lord of the Jungle)

Team America #11 © MAR

Team Titans #11 © DC

Team Youngblood #14 © Liefeld

	GD 2.0	VG 4.0	FN 6.0	VF 8.0	VF/NM 9.0	NM- 9.2

Marvel Comics Group: June, 1977 - No. 29, Oct, 1979

1-New adaptions of Burroughs stories; Buscema-a 2 4 6 8 10 12
1-(35¢-c variant, limited distribution)(6/77) 4 8 12 24 37 50
2-29: 2-Origin by John Buscema. 9-Young Tarzan. 12-14-Jungle Tales of Tarzan. 25-29-New stories 6.00
2-5-(35¢-c variants, limited distribution)(7-10/77) 3 6 9 16 23 30
Annual 1-3: 1-(1977). 2-(1978). 3-(1979) 1 2 3 4 5 7

NOTE: *N. Adams c-11i, 12i.* ***Alcala*** *a-9i, 10i; c-8i, 9i.* ***Buckler*** *c-25-27p, Annual 3p.* ***John Buscema*** *a-1-3, 4-18p, Annual 1; c-1-7, 8p, 9p, 10, 11p, 12p, 13, 14-19p, 21p, 22, 23p, 24p, 28p, Annual 1.* ***Mooney*** *a-22i.* ***Nebres*** *a-22i.* ***Russell*** *a-29i.*

TARZAN
Dark Horse Comics: July, 1996 - No. 20, Mar, 1998 ($2.95)

1-20: 1-6-Suydam-c 3.00

TARZAN / CARSON OF VENUS
Dark Horse Comics: May, 1998 - No. 4, Aug, 1998 ($2.95, limited series)

1-4-Darko Macan-s/Igor Korday-a 3.00

TARZAN FAMILY, THE (Formerly Korak, Son of Tarzan)
National Periodical Publications: No. 60, Nov-Dec, 1975 - No. 66, Nov-Dec, 1976

60-62-(68 pgs.): 60-Korak begins; Kaluta-r 2 4 6 10 14 18
63-66 (52 pgs.) 2 4 6 8 11 14

NOTE: *Carson of Venus-r 60-65. New John Carter-62-64, 65r, 66r. New Korak-60-66. Pellucidar feature-66. Foster strip r-60(9/4/32-10/16/32), 62(6/29/32-7/31/32), 63(10/11/31-12/13/31).* ***Kaluta*** *Carson of Venus-60-65.* ***Kubert*** *a-61, 64; c-60-64.* ***Manning*** *strip-r 60-62, 64.* ***Morrow*** *a-66r.*

TARZAN/JOHN CARTER: WARLORDS OF MARS
Dark Horse Comics: Jan, 1996 - No. 4, June, 1996 ($2.50, limited series)

1-4: Bruce Jones scripts in all. 1,2,4-Bret Blevins-c/a. 2-(4/96)-Indicia reads #3 3.00

TARZAN KING OF THE JUNGLE (See Dell Giant #37, 51)

TARZAN, LORD OF THE JUNGLE
Gold Key: Sept, 1965 (Giant) (25¢, soft paper-c)

1-Marsh-r 8 16 24 56 93 130

TARZAN: LOVE, LIES AND THE LOST CITY (See Tarzan the Warrior)
Malibu Comics: Aug. 10, 1992 - No. 3, Sept, 1992 ($2.50, limited series)

1-($3.95, 68 pgs.)-Flip book format; Simonson & Wagner scripts 4.00
2,3-No Simonson or Wagner scripts 3.00

TARZAN MARCH OF COMICS (See March of Comics #82, 98, 114, 125, 144, 155, 172, 185, 204, 223, 240, 252, 262, 272, 286, 300, 332, 342, 354, 366)

TARZAN OF THE APES
Metropolitan Newspaper Service: 1934? (Hardcover, 4x12", 68 pgs.)

1-Strip reprints 25 50 75 147 241 335

TARZAN OF THE APES
Marvel Comics Group: July, 1984 - No. 2, Aug, 1984 (Movie adaptation)

1,2: Origin-r/Marvel Super Spec. 4.00

TARZAN'S JUNGLE ANNUAL (See Dell Giants)

TARZAN'S JUNGLE WORLD (See Dell Giant #25)

TARZAN: THE BECKONING
Malibu Comics: 1992 - No. 7, 1993 ($2.50, limited series)

1-7 3.00

TARZAN: THE LOST ADVENTURE (See Edgar Rice Burroughs' ...)

TARZAN-THE RIVERS OF BLOOD
Dark Horse Comics: Nov, 1999 - No. 8 ($2.95, limited series)

1-4: Korday-c/a 3.00

TARZAN THE SAVAGE HEART
Dark Horse Comics: Apr, 1999 - No. 4, July, 1999 ($2.95, limited series)

1-4: Grell-c/a 3.00

TARZAN THE WARRIOR (Also see Tarzan: Love, Lies and the Lost City)
Malibu Comics: Mar, 19, 1992 - No. 5, 1992 ($2.50, limited series)

1-5: 1-Bisley painted pack-c (flip book format-c) 3.00
1-2nd printing w/o flip-c by Bisley 2.50

TARZAN VS. PREDATOR AT THE EARTH'S CORE
Dark Horse Comics: Jan, 1996 - No. 4, June, 1996 ($2.50, limited series)

1-4: Lee Weeks-c/a; Walt Simonson scripts 3.00

TASKMASTER
Marvel Comics: Apr, 2002 - No. 4, July, 2002 ($2.99, limited series)

1-4-Udon Studio-s/a. 1-Iron Man app. 3.00

TASMANIAN DEVIL & HIS TASTY FRIENDS
Gold Key: Nov, 1962 (12¢)

1-Bugs Bunny, Elmer Fudd, Sylvester, Yosemite Sam, Road Runner & Wile E. Coyote x-over 14 28 42 97 181 265

TATTERED BANNERS
DC Comics (Vertigo): Nov, 1998 - No. 4, Feb, 1999 ($2.95, limited series)

1-4-Grant & Giffen-s/McMahon-a 3.00

TEAM AMERICA (See Captain America #269)
Marvel Comics Group: June, 1982 - No. 12, May, 1983

1-12:1-Origin; Ideal Toy motorcycle characters. 9-Iron Man app. 11-Ghost Rider app. 12-Double size 2.50

NOTE: *There are 16 pg. variants known for most issues, possibly all. The only ad is on the inside front cover.*

TEAM HELIX
Marvel Comics: Jan, 1993 - No. 4, Apr, 1993 ($1.75, limited series)

1-4: Teen Super Group. 1,2-Wolverine app. 2.50

TEAM ONE: STORMWATCH (Also see StormWatch)
Image Comics (WildStorm Productions): June, 1995 - No. 2, Aug, 1995 ($2.50, lim. series)

1,2: Steven T. Seagle scripts 2.50

TEAM ONE: WILDC.A.T.S (Also see WildC.A.T.S)
Image Comics (WildStorm Productions): July, 1995 - No. 2, Aug, 1995 ($2.50, lim. series)

1,2: James Robinson scripts 2.50

TEAM 7
Image Comics (WildStorm): Oct, 1994 - No.4, Feb, 1995 ($2.50, limited series)

1-4: Dixon scripts in all, 1-Portacio variant-c 2.50

TEAM 7-DEAD RECKONING
Image Comics (WildStorm): Jan, 1996 - No. 4, Apr, 1996 ($2.50, limited series)

1-4: Dixon scripts in all 2.50

TEAM 7-OBJECTIVE HELL
Image Comics (WildStorm): May, 1995 - No. 3, July, 1995 ($1.95/$2.50, limited series)

1-($1.95)-Newstand; Dixon scripts in all; Barry Smith-c 2.50
1-3: 1-($2.50)-Direct Market; Barry Smith-c, bound-in card 2.50

TEAM SUPERMAN
DC Comics: July, 1999 ($2.95, one-shot)

1-Jeanty-a/Stelfreeze-c 3.00
...Secret Files 1 (5/98, $4.95)Origin-s and pin-ups of Superboy, Supergirl and Steel 5.00

TEAM TITANS (See Deathstroke & New Titans Annual #7)
DC Comics: Sept, 1992 - No. 24, Sept, 1994 ($1.75/$1.95)

1-Five different #1s exist w/origins in 1st half & the same 2nd story in each: Kilowat, Mirage, Nightrider w/Netzer/Perez-a, Redwing, & Terra w/part Perez-p; Total Chaos Pt. 3 3.00
2-24: 2-Total Chaos Pt 6. 11-Metallik app. 24-Zero Hour x-over 2.50
Annual 1,2 ('93, '94, $3.50, 68 pgs.): 2-Elseworlds tory 3.50

TEAM X/TEAM 7
Marvel Comics: Nov, 1996 ($4.95, one-shot)

1 5.00

TEAM X 2000
Marvel Comics: Feb, 1999 ($3.50, one-shot)

1-Kevin Lau-a; Bishop vs. Shi'ar Empire 3.50

TEAM YANKEE
First Comics: Jan, 1989 - No. 6, Feb, 1989 ($1.95, weekly limited series)

1-6 2.50

TEAM YOUNGBLOOD (Also see Youngblood)
Image Comics (Extreme Studios): Sept, 1993 - No. 22, Sept, 1995 ($1.95/$2.50)

1-22: 1-9-Liefeld scripts in all: 1,2,4-6,8-Thibert-c(i). 1-1st app. Dutch & Masada. 3-Spawn cameo. 5-1st app. Lynx. 7,8-Coupons 1 & 4 for Extreme Prejudice #0; Black and White Pt. 4 & 8 by Thibert. 8-Coupon #4 for E. P. #0. 9-Liefeld wraparound-c &(p)/a(p) on Pt. I. 16,17-Bagged w/trading card. 21-Angela & Glory-app. 2.50

TEAM ZERO
DC Comics (WildStorm Productions): Feb, 2006 - No. 6, Jul, 2006 ($2.99, limited series)

1-6-Dixon-s/Mahnke-a 3.00
TPB (2008, $17.99) r/#1-6 18.00

TECH JACKET
Image Comics: Nov, 2002 - No. 6, Apr, 2003 ($2.95)

1-6-Kirkman-s/Su-a 3.00
Vol. 1: Lost and Found TPB (7/03, $12.95, 7-3/4" x 5-1/4") B&W r/#1-6; Valentino intro. 13.00

Teenage Hotrodders #14 © CC

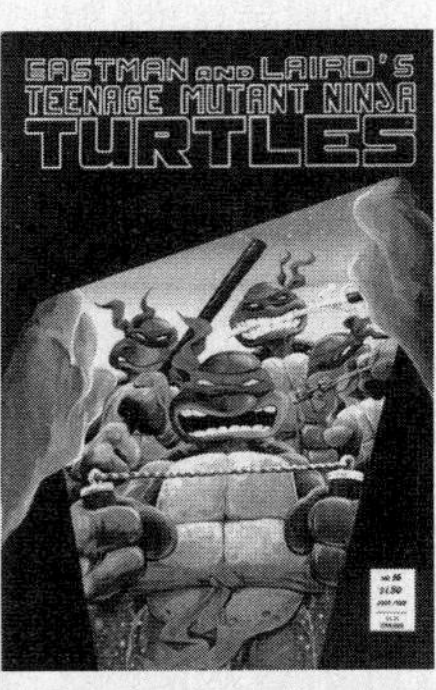

Teenage Mutant Ninja Turtles #16 © MS

Teenage Mutant Ninja Turtles V4 #1 © MS

	GD 2.0	VG 4.0	FN 6.0	VF 8.0	VF/NM 9.0	NM- 9.2

TEDDY ROOSEVELT & HIS ROUGH RIDERS (See Real Heroes #1)
Avon Periodicals: 1950

	GD 2.0	VG 4.0	FN 6.0	VF 8.0	VF/NM 9.0	NM- 9.2
1-Kinstler-c; Palais-a; Flag-c	18	36	54	105	165	225

TEDDY ROOSEVELT ROUGH RIDER (See Battlefield #22 & Classics Illustrated Special Issue)

TED MCKEEVER'S METROPOL (See Transit)
Marvel Comics (Epic Comics): Mar, 1991 - No. 12, Mar, 1992 ($2.95, limited series)

	GD 2.0	VG 4.0	FN 6.0	VF 8.0	VF/NM 9.0	NM- 9.2
V1#1-12: Ted McKeever-c/a/scripts						3.50

TED MCKEEVER'S METROPOL A.D.
Marvel Comics (Epic Comics): Oct, 1992 - No. 3, Dec, 1992 ($3.50, limited series)

	GD 2.0	VG 4.0	FN 6.0	VF 8.0	VF/NM 9.0	NM- 9.2
V2#1-3: Ted McKeever-c/a/scripts						3.50

TEENA
Magazine Enterprises/Standard Comics No. 20 on: No. 11, 1948 - No. 15, 1948; No. 20, Aug, 1949 - No. 22, Oct, 1950

	GD 2.0	VG 4.0	FN 6.0	VF 8.0	VF/NM 9.0	NM- 9.2
A-1 #11-Teen-age; Ogden Whitney-c	10	20	30	54	72	90
A-1 #12, 15	9	18	27	47	61	75
20-22 (Standard)	7	14	21	35	43	50

TEEN-AGE BRIDES (True Bride's Experiences #8 on)
Harvey/Home Comics: Aug, 1953 - No. 7, Aug, 1954

	GD 2.0	VG 4.0	FN 6.0	VF 8.0	VF/NM 9.0	NM- 9.2
1-Powell-a	11	22	33	62	86	110
2-Powell-a	8	16	24	44	57	70
3-7: 3,6-Powell-a	8	16	24	40	50	60

TEEN-AGE CONFESSIONS (See Teen Confessions)

TEEN-AGE CONFIDENTIAL CONFESSIONS
Charlton Comics: July, 1960 - No. 22, 1964

	GD 2.0	VG 4.0	FN 6.0	VF 8.0	VF/NM 9.0	NM- 9.2
1	4	8	12	24	37	50
2-10	3	6	9	16	23	30
11-22	2	4	6	13	18	22

TEEN-AGE DIARY SECRETS (Formerly Blue Ribbon Comics; becomes Diary Secrets #10 on)
St. John Publishing Co.: No. 4, 9/49; nn (#5), 9/49 - No. 7, 11/49; No. 8, 2/50; No. 9, 8/50

	GD 2.0	VG 4.0	FN 6.0	VF 8.0	VF/NM 9.0	NM- 9.2
4(9/49)-Oversized; part mag., part comic	34	68	102	199	325	450
nn(#5)(no indicia)-Oversized, all comics; contains sty "I Gave Boys the Green Light."	32	64	96	188	307	425
6,8: (Reg. size) -Photo-c; Baker-a(2-3) in each	34	68	102	199	325	450
7,9-Digest size (Pocket Comics); Baker-a(5); both have same contents; diff.-c	39	78	117	240	395	550

TEEN-AGE DOPE SLAVES (See Harvey Comics Library #1)

TEENAGE HOTRODDERS (Top Eliminator #25 on; see Blue Bird)
Charlton Comics: Apr, 1963 - No. 24, July, 1967

	GD 2.0	VG 4.0	FN 6.0	VF 8.0	VF/NM 9.0	NM- 9.2
1	6	12	18	37	59	80
2-10	3	6	9	20	30	40
11-24	3	6	9	17	25	32

TEEN-AGE LOVE (See Fox Giants)

TEEN-AGE LOVE (Formerly Intimate)
Charlton Comics: V2#4, July, 1958 - No. 96, Dec, 1973

	GD 2.0	VG 4.0	FN 6.0	VF 8.0	VF/NM 9.0	NM- 9.2
V2#4	4	8	12	28	44	60
5-9	3	6	9	20	30	40
10(9/59)-20	3	6	9	17	25	32
21-35	3	6	9	16	22	28
36-70	2	4	6	13	18	22
71-96: 61&62-Jonnie Love begins (origin). 80,84,88-David Cassidy pin-ups. 83-Bobby Sherman pin-up. 89-Danny Bonaduce pin-up	2	4	6	10	14	18

TEENAGE MUTANT NINJA TURTLES (Also see Anything Goes, Donatello, First Comics Graphic Novel, Gobbledygook, Grimjack #26, Leonardo, Michaelangelo, Raphael & Tales Of The...)
Mirage Studios: 1984 - No. 62, Aug, 1993 ($1.50/$1.75, B&W; all 44-52 pgs.)

	GD 2.0	VG 4.0	FN 6.0	VF 8.0	VF/NM 9.0	NM- 9.2
1-1st printing (3000 copies)-Origin and 1st app. of the Turtles and Splinter. Only printing to have ad for Gobbledygook #1 & 2; Shredder app. (#1-4: 7-1/2x11") (Prices vary widely on this book. In 2005 a CGC certified 9.4 sold for $8,300, a CGC certified 9.2 sold for $2,850, and a CGC certified 6.0 sold for $1,300. In 2009, a CGC 9.6 sold for $11,500)						
1-2nd printing (6/84)(15,000 copies)	3	6	9	14	19	24
1-3rd printing (2/85)(36,000 copies)	2	4	6	8	11	14
1-4th printing, new-c (50,000 copies)						5.00
1-5th printing, new-c (8/88-c, 11/88 inside)						4.00
1-Counterfeit. **Note**: Most counterfeit copies have a half inch wide white streak or scratch marks across the center of back cover. Black part of cover is a bluish black instead of a deep black. Inside paper is very white & inside cover is bright white (no value)						
2-1st printing (1984; 15,000 copies)	10	20	30	70	123	175
2-2nd printing	2	4	6	8	10	12
2-3rd printing; new Corben-c/a (2/85)						5.00
2-Counterfeit with glossy cover stock (no value).						
3-1st printing (1985, 44 pgs.)	8	16	24	52	86	120
3-Variant, 500 copies, given away in NYC. Has 'Laird's Photo' in white rather than light blue	10	20	30	71	126	180
3-2nd printing; contains new back-up story						5.00
4-1st printing (1985, 44 pgs.)	5	10	15	34	55	75
4,5-2nd printing (5/87, 11/87)						3.00
5-Fugitoid begins, ends #7; 1st full color-c (1985)	3	6	9	20	30	40
6-1st printing (1986)	3	6	9	14	20	25
6-2nd printing (4/88-c, 5/88 inside)						3.00
7-4 pg. Eastman/Corben color insert; 1st color TMNT (1986, $1.75-c); Bade Biker back-up story	2	4	6	9	12	15
7-2nd printing (1/89) w/o color insert						3.00
8-Cerebus-c/story with Dave Sim-a (1986)	2	4	6	8	10	12
9,10: 9 (9/86)-Rip In Time by Corben	1	2	3	5	6	8
11-15						5.00
16-18: 18-Mark Bode'-a						4.00
18-2nd printing ($2.25, color, 44 pgs.)-New-c						3.00
19-34: 19-Begin $1.75-c. 24-26-Veitch-c/a.						3.00
32-2nd printing ($2.75, 52 pgs., full color)						3.00
35-49,51: 35-Begin $2.00-c.						3.00
50-Features pin-ups by Larsen, McFarlane, Simonson, etc.						4.00
52-62: 52-Begin $2.25-c						3.00
nn (1990, $5.95, B&W)-Movie adaptation						6.00
Book 1,2($1.50, B&W): 2-Corben-c						3.00
...Christmas Special 1 (12/90, $1.75, B&W, 52 pgs.)-Cover title: Michaelangelo Christmas Special; r/Michaelangelo one-shot plus new Raphael story						3.00
... Color Special (11/09, $3.25) full color reprint of #1						3.25
...Special (The Maltese Turtle) nn (1/93, $2.95, color, 44 pgs.)						3.00
...Special: "Times" Pipeline nn (9/92, $2.95, color, 44 pgs.)-Mark Bode-c/a						3.00
Hardcover ($100)-r/#1-10 plus one-shots w/dust jackets - limited to 1000 w/letter of authenticity						100.00
Softcover ($40)-r/#1-10						40.00

TEENAGE MUTANT NINJA TURTLES
Mirage Studios: V2#1, Oct, 1993 - V2#13, Oct, 1995 ($2.75)

	GD 2.0	VG 4.0	FN 6.0	VF 8.0	VF/NM 9.0	NM- 9.2
V2#1-13: 1-Wraparound-c						3.00

TEENAGE MUTANT NINJA TURTLES
Image Comics (Highbrow Ent.): June, 1996 - No. 23, Oct, 1999 ($1.95-$2.95)

	GD 2.0	VG 4.0	FN 6.0	VF 8.0	VF/NM 9.0	NM- 9.2
1-23: 1-8: Eric Larsen-c(i) on all. 10-Savage Dragon-c/app.						3.00

TEENAGE MUTANT NINJA TURTLES
Mirage Publishing: V4#1, Dec, 2001 - No. 28 ($2.95, B&W)

	GD 2.0	VG 4.0	FN 6.0	VF 8.0	VF/NM 9.0	NM- 9.2
V4#1-9,11-28-Laird-s/a(i)/Lawson-a(p).						3.00
10-($3.95) Splinter dies						4.00

TEENAGE MUTANT NINJA TURTLES
Dreamwave Productions: June 2003 - No. 7 ($2.95, color)

	GD 2.0	VG 4.0	FN 6.0	VF 8.0	VF/NM 9.0	NM- 9.2
1-7-Animated style; Peter David-s/Lesean-a						3.00
Vol. 1 TPB (2003, $9.95) r/#1-4; cover gallery and sketch pages						10.00

TEENAGE MUTANT NINJA TURTLES (Adventures)
Archie Publications: Jan, 1996 - No. 3, Mar, 1996 ($1.50, limited series)

	GD 2.0	VG 4.0	FN 6.0	VF 8.0	VF/NM 9.0	NM- 9.2
1-3						2.50

TEENAGE MUTANT NINJA TURTLES ADVENTURES (TV)
Archie Comics: 8/88 - No. 3, 12/88; 3/89 - No. 72, Oct, 1995 ($1.00/$1.25/$1.50/$1.75)

	GD 2.0	VG 4.0	FN 6.0	VF 8.0	VF/NM 9.0	NM- 9.2
1-Adapts TV cartoon; not by Eastman/Laird						4.00
2,3 (Mini-series), 1 (2nd on-going series), 1-2nd printing						2.50
2-18,20-30: 5-Begins original stories not based on TV. 14-Simpson-a(p). 22-Colan-c/a						3.00
2-11: 2nd printings						2.50
19-1st Mighty Mutanimals (also in #20, 51-54)	1	2	3	5	6	8
31-49						4.50
50-Poster by Eastman/Laird	1	2	3	5	7	9
51-54: Mighty Mutanimals	2	4	6	8	10	12
55-60	1	2	3	4	5	7
61-70: 62-w/poster	2	3	4	6	8	10
71	2	4	6	8	10	12
72- Last issue	2	4	6	9	13	16
nn (1990, $2.50)-Movie adaptation						2.50
nn (Spring, 1991, $2.50, 68 pgs.)-(Meet Archie)						2.50
nn (Sum, 1991, $2.50, 68 pgs.)-(Movie II)-Adapts movie sequel						2.50
...Meet the Conservation Corps 1 (1992, $2.50, 68 pgs.)						2.50

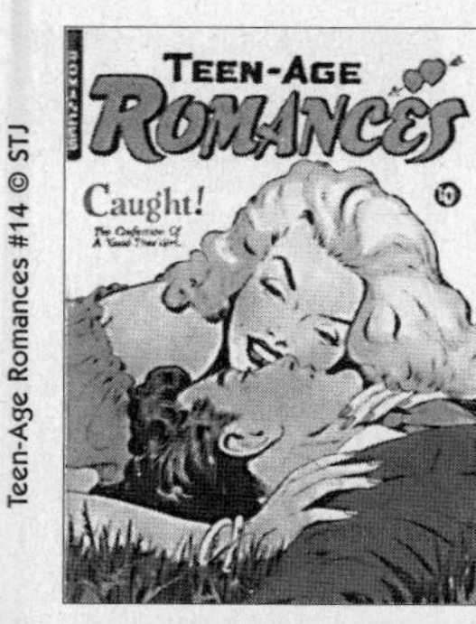

Teen-Age Romances #14 © STJ

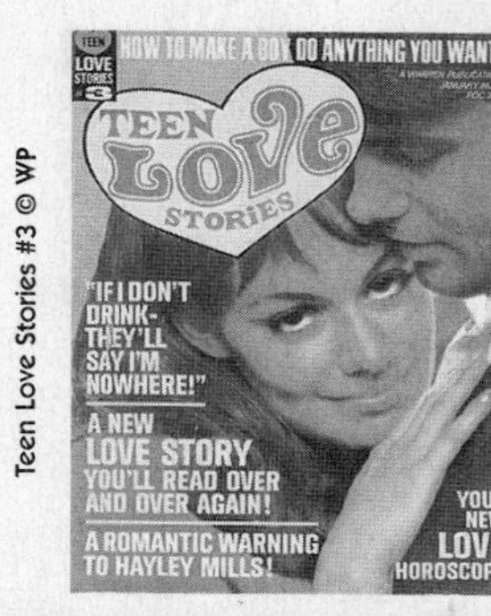

Teen Love Stories #3 © WP

Teen Titans #1 © DC

	GD 2.0	VG 4.0	FN 6.0	VF 8.0	VF/NM 9.0	NM- 9.2
...III The Movie: The Turtles are Back...In Time (1993, $2.50, 68 pgs.)						2.50
Special 1,4,5 (Sum/92, Spr/93, Sum/93, 68 pgs.)-1-Bill Wray-c						2.50
Giant Size Special 6 (Fall/93, $1.95, 52 pgs.)						2.50
Special 7-10 (Win/93-Fall//94, 52 pgs.): 9-Jeff Smith-c						2.50

NOTE: *There are 2nd printings of #1-11 w/B&W inside covers. Originals are color.*

TEENAGE MUTANT NINJA TURTLES CLASSICS DIGEST (TV)
Archie Comics: Aug, 1993 - No. 8, Mar, 1995? ($1.75)

	GD	VG	FN	VF	VF/NM	NM-
1-8: Reprints TMNT Advs.						4.00

TEENAGE MUTANT NINJA TURTLES/FLAMING CARROT CROSSOVER
Mirage Publishing: Nov, 1993 - No. 4, Feb, 1994 ($2.75, limited series)

	GD	VG	FN	VF	VF/NM	NM-
1-4: Bob Burden story						3.00

TEENAGE MUTANT NINJA TURTLES PRESENTS: APRIL O'NEIL
Archie Comics: Mar, 1993 - No. 3, June, 1993 ($1.25, limited series)

	GD	VG	FN	VF	VF/NM	NM-
1-3						3.00

TEENAGE MUTANT NINJA TURTLES PRESENTS: DONATELLO AND LEATHERHEAD
Archie Comics: July, 1993 - No. 3, Sept, 1993 ($1.25, limited series)

	GD	VG	FN	VF	VF/NM	NM-
1-3						3.00

TEENAGE MUTANT NINJA TURTLES PRESENTS: MERDUDE
Archie Comics: Oct, 1993 - No. 3, Dec, 1993 ($1.25, limited series)

	GD	VG	FN	VF	VF/NM	NM-
1-3-See Mighty Mutanimals #7 for 1st app. Merdude						3.00

TEENAGE MUTANT NINJA TURTLES/SAVAGE DRAGON CROSSOVER
Mirage Studios: Aug, 1995 ($2.75, one-shot)

	GD	VG	FN	VF	VF/NM	NM-
1						3.00

TEEN-AGE ROMANCE (Formerly My Own Romance)
Marvel Comics (ZPC): No. 77, Sept, 1960 - No. 86, Mar, 1962

	GD	VG	FN	VF	VF/NM	NM-
77-83	4	8	12	26	41	55
84-86-Kirby-c. 84-Kirby-a(2 pgs.). 85,86-(3 pgs.)	5	10	15	32	51	70

TEEN-AGE ROMANCES
St. John Publ. Co. (Approved Comics): Jan, 1949 - No. 45, Dec, 1955 (#3,7,10-18,21 are 1/2 inch taller than other issues)

	GD	VG	FN	VF	VF/NM	NM-
1-Baker-c/a(1)	52	104	156	328	552	775
2,3: 2-Baker-c/a. 3-Baker-c/a(3)	37	74	111	222	361	500
4,5,7,8-Photo-c; Baker-a(2-3) each	27	54	81	160	263	365
6-Photo-c; part magazine; Baker-a (10/49)	29	58	87	170	278	385
9-Baker-c/a; Kubert-a	36	72	108	216	351	485
10-12,20-Baker-c/a(2-3) each	30	60	90	177	289	400
13-19,21,22-Complete issues by Baker	36	72	108	216	351	485
23-25-Baker-c/a(2-3) each	29	58	87	170	278	385
26,27,33,34,36-40,42: Baker-c/a. 33,40-Signed story by Estrada. 38-Suggestive-c. 42-r/Cinderella Love #9; Last pre-code (3/55)	21	42	63	122	199	275
28-30-No Baker-a	12	24	36	67	94	120
31,32-Baker-c. 31-Estrada-s	18	36	54	105	165	225
35-Baker-c/a (16 pgs.)	21	42	63	126	206	285
41-Baker-c; Infantino-a(r); all stories are Ziff-Davis-r	18	36	54	105	165	225
43-45-Baker-c/a	21	42	63	122	199	275

TEEN-AGE TALK
I.W. Enterprises: 1964

	GD	VG	FN	VF	VF/NM	NM-
Reprint #1	2	4	6	10	14	18
Reprint #5,8,9: 5-r/Hector #? 9-Punch Comics #?; L.B. Cole-c reprint from School Day Romances #1	2	4	6	9	13	16

TEEN-AGE TEMPTATIONS (Going Steady #10 on)(See True Love Pictorial)
St. John Publishing Co.: Oct, 1952 - No. 9, Aug, 1954

	GD	VG	FN	VF	VF/NM	NM-
1-Baker-c/a; has story "Reform School Girl" by Estrada	65	130	195	416	708	1000
2,4-Baker-c	28	56	84	165	270	375
3,5-7,9-Baker-c/a	36	72	108	211	343	475
8-Teenagers smoke reefer; Baker-c/a	39	78	117	240	395	550

NOTE: *Estrada a-1, 3-5.*

TEEN BEAM (Formerly Teen Beat #1)
National Periodical Publications: No. 2, Jan-Feb, 1968

	GD	VG	FN	VF	VF/NM	NM-
2-Superman cameo; Herman's Hermits, Yardbirds, Simon & Garfunkel, Lovin Spoonful, Young Rascals app.; Orlando, Drucker-a(r); Monkees photo-c;	15	30	45	107	204	300

TEEN BEAT (Becomes Teen Beam #2)
National Periodical Publications: Nov-Dec, 1967

	GD	VG	FN	VF	VF/NM	NM-
1-Photos & text only; Monkees photo-c; Beatles, Herman's Hermits, Animals, Supremes, Byrds app.	16	32	48	115	220	325

TEEN COMICS (Formerly All Teen; Journey Into Unknown Worlds #36 on)
Marvel Comics (WFP): No. 21, Apr, 1947 - No. 35, May, 1950

	GD	VG	FN	VF	VF/NM	NM-
21-Kurtzman's "Hey Look"; Patsy Walker, Cindy (1st app.?), Georgie, Margie app.; Syd Shores-a begins, end #23	17	34	51	98	154	210
22,23,25,27,29,31-35: 22-(6/47)-Becomes Hedy Devine #22 (8/47) on?	14	28	42	81	118	155
24,26,28,30-Kurtzman's "Hey Look"	15	30	45	83	124	165

TEEN CONFESSIONS
Charlton Comics: Aug, 1959 - No. 97, Nov, 1976

	GD	VG	FN	VF	VF/NM	NM-
1	8	16	24	52	86	120
2	4	8	12	28	44	60
3-10	4	8	12	22	34	45
11-30	3	6	9	18	27	35
31-Beatles-c	11	22	33	78	139	200
32-36,38-55	3	6	9	15	21	26
37 (1/66)-Beatles Fan Club story; Beatles-c	11	22	33	78	139	200
56-58,60-97: 77-Partridge Family poster. 89,90-Newton-c	2	4	6	10	14	18
59-Kaluta's 1st pro work? (12/69)	3	6	9	19	29	38

TEENIE WEENIES, THE (America's Favorite Kiddie Comic)
Ziff-Davis Publishing Co.: No. 10, 1950 - No. 11, Apr-May, 1951 (Newspaper reprints)

	GD	VG	FN	VF	VF/NM	NM-
10,11-Painted-c	19	38	57	112	179	245

TEEN-IN (Tippy Teen)
Tower Comics: Summer, 1968 - No. 4, Fall, 1969

	GD	VG	FN	VF	VF/NM	NM-
nn(#1, Summer, 1968)(25¢) Has 3 full pg. B&W photos of Sonny & Cher, Donovan and Herman's Hermits; interviews and photos of Eric Clapton, Jim Morrison and others	10	20	30	68	119	170
nn(#2, Spring, 1969),3,4	6	12	18	41	66	90

TEEN LIFE (Formerly Young Life)
New Age/Quality Comics Group: No. 3, Winter, 1945 - No. 5, Fall, 1945 (Teenage magazine)

	GD	VG	FN	VF	VF/NM	NM-
3-June Allyson photo on-c & story	14	28	42	76	108	140
4-Duke Ellington photo on-c & story	11	22	33	64	90	115
5-Van Johnson, Woody Herman & Jackie Robinson articles; Van Johnson & Woody Herman photos on-c	14	28	42	78	112	145

TEEN LOVE STORIES (Magazine)
Warren Publ. Co.: Sept, 1969 - No. 3, Jan, 1970 (68 pgs., photo covers, B&W)

	GD	VG	FN	VF	VF/NM	NM-
1-Photos & articles plus 36-42 pgs. new comic stories in all; Frazetta-a	7	14	21	49	80	110
2,3: 2-Anti-marijuana story	5	10	15	32	51	70

TEEN ROMANCES
Super Comics: 1964

	GD	VG	FN	VF	VF/NM	NM-
10,11,15-17-Reprints	2	4	6	8	11	14

TEEN SECRET DIARY (Nurse Betsy Crane #12 on)
Charlton Comics: Oct, 1959 - No. 11, June, 1961; No. 1, 1972

	GD	VG	FN	VF	VF/NM	NM-
1	5	10	15	32	51	70
2	3	6	9	21	32	42
3-11	3	6	9	18	27	35
1 (1972)(exist?)	3	6	9	15	21	26

TEEN TALK (See Teen)

TEEN TITANS (See Brave & the Bold #54,60, DC Super-Stars #1, Marvel & DC Present, New Teen Titans, New Titans, Official...Index and Showcase #59)
National Periodical Publications/DC Comics: 1-2/66 - No. 43, 1-2/73; No. 44, 11/76 - No. 53, 2/78

	GD	VG	FN	VF	VF/NM	NM-
1-(1-2/66)-Titans join Peace Corps; Batman, Flash, Aquaman, Wonder Woman cameos	32	64	96	245	473	700
2	15	30	45	107	204	300
3-5: 4-Speedy app.	10	20	30	70	123	175
6-10: 6-Doom Patrol app.; Beast Boy x-over; readers polled on him joining Titans	8	16	24	54	90	125
11-18: 11-Speedy app. 13-X-Mas-c	7	14	21	45	73	100
19-Wood-i; Speedy begins as regular	7	14	21	47	76	105
20-22: All Neal Adams-a. 21-Hawk & Dove app.; last 12¢ issue. 22-Origin Wonder Girl	9	18	27	60	100	140
23-Wonder Girl dons new costume	5	10	15	34	55	75
24-31: 25-Flash, Aquaman, Batman, Green Arrow, Green Lantern, Superman, & Hawk & Dove guests; 1st app. Lilith who joins T.T. West in #50. 29-Hawk & Dove & Ocean Master app. 30-Aquagirl app. 31-Hawk & Dove app.; last 15¢ issue	5	10	15	30	48	65

Teen Titans (2003 series) #4 © DC

Teen Titans Go! #8 © DC

Tell It To The Marines #6 © TOBY

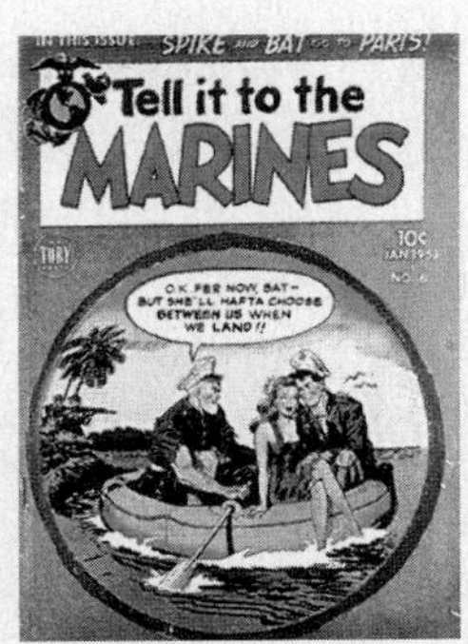

	GD	VG	FN	VF	VF/NM	NM-
	2.0	4.0	6.0	8.0	9.0	9.2

32-34,40-43 3 6 9 19 29 38
35-39-(52 pgs.): 36,37-Superboy-r. 38-Green Arrow/Speedy-r; Aquaman/Aqualad story. 39-Hawk & Dove-r. 4 8 12 22 34 45
44-(11/76) Dr. Light app.; Mal becomes the Guardian 3 6 9 14 19 24
45,47,49,51,52 2 4 6 13 18 22
46,48: 46-Joker's daughter begins (see Batman Family). 48-Intro Bumblebee; Joker's daughter becomes Harlequin 3 6 9 16 23 30
50-1st revival original Bat-Girl; intro. Teen Titans West 3 6 9 17 25 32
53-Origin retold 3 6 9 14 20 26
... Lost Annual 1 (3/08, $4.99) Sixties-era story by Bob Haney; Jay Stephens & Mike Allred-a; President Kennedy app.; Nick Cardy-c and sketch pages 5.00
NOTE: *Aparo a-36. Buckler c-46-53. Cardy c-1-16. Kane a(p)-19, 22-24, 39r. Tuska a(p)-31, 36, 38, 39. DC Super-Stars #1 (3/76) was released before #44.*

TEEN TITANS (Also see Titans Beat in the Promotional Comics section)
DC Comics: Oct, 1996 - No. 24, Sept, 1998 ($1.95)
1-Dan Jurgens-c/a(p)/scripts & George Pérez-c/a(i) begin; Atom forms new team (Risk, Argent, Prysm, & Joto); 1st app. Loren Jupiter & Omen; no indicia. 1-3-Origin. 4.00
2-24: 4,5-Robin, Nightwing, Supergirl, Capt. Marvel Jr. app. 12-"Then and Now" begins w/original Teen Titans-c/app. 15-Death of Joto. 17-Capt. Marvel Jr. and Fringe join. 19-Millennium Giants x-over. 23,24-Superman app. 3.00
Annual 1 (1997, $3.95)-Pulp Heroes story 4.00

TEEN TITANS (Also see Titans/Young Justice: Graduation Day)
DC Comics: Sept, 2003 - Present ($2.50/$2.99/$3.99)
1-McKone-c/a;Johns-s 4.00
1-Variant-c by Michael Turner 5.00
1-2nd and 3rd printings 2.50
2-Deathstroke app. 5.00
2-2nd printing 2.50
3-15: 4-Impulse becomes Kid Flash. 5-Raven returns. 6-JLA app. 2.50
16-33: 16-Titans go to 31st Century; Legion and Fatal Five app. 17-19-Future Titans app. 21-23-Dr. Light. 24,25-Outsiders #24,25 x-over. 27,28-Liefeld-a. 32,33-Infinite Crisis 2.50
34-49,51-71: 34-One Year Later begins; two covers by Daniel and Benes. 36-Begin $2.99-c. 40-Jericho returns. 42-Kid Devil origin; Snejbjerg-a. 43-Titans East. 48,49-Amazons Attack x-over; Supergirl app. 51-54-Future Titans app. 3.00
50-($3.99) Art by Pérez (4 pgs.), McKone (6 pgs.), Nauck and Green; future Titans app. 4.00
72-79: 72-Begin $3.99-c; Ravager back-up features. 77,78-Blackest Night 4.00
Annual 1 (4/06, $4.99) Infinite Crisis x-over; Benes-c 5.00
Annual 2009 (6/09, $4.99) Deathtrap x-over prelude; McKeever-s 5.00
... And Outsiders Secret Files and Origins 2005 (10/05, $4.99) Daniel-c 5.00
.../Legion Special (11/04, $3.50) (cont'd from #16) Reis-a; leads into 2005 Legion of Super-Heroes series; LSH preview by Waid & Kitson 3.50
#1/2 (Wizard mail offer) origin of Ravager; Reis-a 8.00
.../Outsiders Secret Files 2003 (12/03, $5.95) Reis & Jimenez-a; pin-ups by various 6.00
...: A Kid's Game TPB (2004, $9.95) r/#1-7; Turner-c from #1; McKone sketch pages 10.00
...: Beast Boys and Girls TPB (2005, $9.99) r/#13-15 and Beast Boy #1-4 10.00
...: Changing of the Guard TPB (2009, $14.99) r/#62-69 15.00
...: Deathtrap TPB (2009, $14.99) r/#70, Annual #1, Titans #12,13, Vigilante #4-6 15.00
...: Family Lost TPB (2004, $9.95) r/#8-12 & #1/2 10.00
...: Life and Death TPB (2006, $14.99) r/#29-33 and pages from Infinite Crisis x-over 15.00
...: On the Clock TPB (2008, $14.99) r/#55-61 15.00
.../ Outsiders: The Death and Return of Donna Troy (2006, $14.99) r/Titans/Young Justice: Graduation Day #1-3, Teen Titans/Outsiders Secret Files 2003 and DC Special: The Return of Donna Troy #1-4; cover gallery 15.00
.../ Outsiders: The Insiders (2006, $14.99) r/Teen Titans/ #24-26 & Outsiders #24,25,28 15.00
... Spotlight: Cyborg TPB (2009, $19.99) r/DC Special: Cyborg #1-6 20.00
... Spotlight: Raven TPB (2008, $14.99) r/DC Special: Raven #1-5 15.00
...: The Future is Now (2005, $9.99) r/#15-23 & Teen Titans/Legion Special 10.00
...: Titans Around the World TPB (2007, $14.99) r/#34-41 15.00
...: Titans of Tomorrow TPB (2008, $14.99) r/#50-54 15.00

TEEN TITANS GO! (Based on Cartoon Network series) (Also see Free Comic Book Day Edition in the Promotional Comics section)
DC Comics: Jan, 2004 - No. 55, Jul, 2008 ($2.25)
1-12,14-55: 1,2-Nauck-a/Bullock-c/J. Torres-s. 8-Mad Mod app. 14-Speedy-c. 28-Doom Patrol app. 31-Nightwing app. 36-Wonder Girl. 38-Mad Mod app.; Clugston-a 2.25
13-($2.95) Bonus pages with Shazam! reprint 3.00
Jam Packed Action (2005, $7.99, digest) adaptations of two TV episodes 8.00
... Vol 1: Truth, Justice, Pizza! (2004, $6.95, digest-size) r/#1-5 7.00
... Vol 2: Heroes on Patrol (2005, $6.99, digest-size) r/#6-10 7.00
... Vol 3: Bring It On! (2005, $6.99, digest-size) r/#11-15 7.00
... Vol 4: Ready For Action! (2006, $6.99, digest-size) r/#16-20 7.00
... Vol 5: On The Move! (2006, $6.99, digest-size) r/#21-25 7.00
... Titans Together TPB (2007, $12.99) r/#26-32 13.00

TEEN TITANS SPOTLIGHT
DC Comics: Aug, 1986 - No. 21, Apr, 1988
1-21: 7-Guice's 1st work at DC. 14-Nightwing; Batman app. 15-Austin-c(i). 18,19-Millennium x-over. 21-($1.00-c)-Original Teen Titans; Spiegle-a 3.00
*Note: **Guice** a-7p, 8p; c-7,8. **Orlando** c/a-11p. **Perez** c-1, 17i, 19. **Sienkiewicz** c-10*

TEEN TITANS YEAR ONE
DC Comics: Mar, 2008 - No. 6, Aug, 2008 ($2.99, limited series)
1-6-The original five form a team; Wolfram-s/Kerschl-a 3.00
TPB (2008, $14.99) r/#1-6; bonus pin-up 15.00

TEEPEE TIM (...Heap Funny Indian Boy)(Formerly Ha Ha Comics)
American Comics Group: No. 100, Feb-Mar, 1955 - No. 102, June-July, 1955
100-102 6 12 18 31 38 45

TEGRA JUNGLE EMPRESS (Zegra Jungle Empress #2 on)
Fox Features Syndicate: August, 1948
1-Blue Beetle, Rocket Kelly app.; used in **SOTI**, pg. 31 63 126 189 403 689 975

TEK JANSEN (See Stephen Colbert's...)

TEKNO COMIX HANDBOOK
Tekno Comix: May, 1996 ($3.95, one-shot)
1-Guide to the Tekno Universe 4.00

TEKNOPHAGE (See Neil Gaiman's...)

TEKNOPHAGE VERSUS ZEERUS
BIG Entertainment: July, 1996 ($3.25, one-shot)
1-Paul Jenkins script 3.25

TEKWORLD (William Shatner's... on-c only)
Epic Comics (Marvel): Sept, 1992 - Aug, 1994 ($1.75)
1-Based on Shatner's novel, TekWar, set in L.A. in the year 2120 3.00
2-24 2.50

TELEVISION (See TV)

TELEVISION COMICS (Early TV comic)
Standard Comics (Animated Cartoons): No. 5, Feb, 1950 - No. 8, Nov, 1950
5-1st app. Willy Nilly 10 20 30 54 72 90
6-8: #6 on inside has #2 on cover 8 16 24 42 54 65

TELEVISION PUPPET SHOW (Early TV comic) (See Spotty the Pup)
Avon Periodicals: 1950 - No. 2, Nov, 1950
1-1st app. Speedy Rabbit, Spotty The Pup 19 38 57 111 176 240
2 14 28 42 80 115 150

TELEVISION TEENS MOPSY (See TV Teens)

TELL IT TO THE MARINES
Toby Press Publications: Mar, 1952 - No. 15, July, 1955
1-Lover O'Leary and His Liberty Belles (with pin-ups), ends #6; Spike & Bat begin, end #6 19 38 57 111 176 240
2-Madame Cobra-c/story 12 24 36 67 94 120
3-5 10 20 30 54 72 90
6-12,14,15: 7-9,14,15-Photo-c 8 16 24 42 54 65
13-John Wayne photo-c 15 30 45 83 124 165
I.W. Reprint #9-r/#1 above 2 4 6 8 10 12
Super Reprint #16(1964)-r/#4 above 2 4 6 8 10 12

TELLOS
Image Comics: May, 1999 - No. 10, Nov, 2000 ($2.50)
1-Dezago-s/Wieringo-a 3.00
1-Variant-c ($7.95) 8.00
2-10: 4-Four covers 2.50
...: Maiden Voyage (3/01, $5.95) Didier Crispeels-a/c 6.00
...: Sons & Moons (2002, $5.95) Nick Cardy-c 6.00
...: The Last Heist (2001, $5.95) Rousseau-a/c 6.00
Prelude ($5.00, AnotherUniverse.com) 5.00
Prologue ($3.95, Dynamic Forces) 4.00
...Collected Edition 1 (12/99, $8.95) r/#1-3 9.00
... Colossal, Vol. 1 TPB (2008, $17.99) r/#1-10, Prelude, Prologue, Scatterjack-s from Section Zero #1, cover gallery, Wieringo sketch pages; Dezago afterword 18.00
...: Kindred Spirits (2/01, $17.95) r/#6-10, Section Zero #1 (Scatterjack-s) 18.00
...: Reluctant Heroes (2/01, $17.95) r/#1-5, Prelude, Prologue; sketchbook 18.00

TEMPEST (See Aquaman, 3rd Series)
DC Comics: Nov, 1996 - No. 4, Feb, 1997 ($1.75, limited series)

Tempest #2 © DC

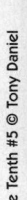

The Tenth #5 © Tony Daniel

Terminator: Revolution #1 © Studio Canal

1-4: Formerly Aqualad; Phil Jimenez-c/a/scripts in all 2.50

TEMPUS FUGITIVE
DC Comics: 1990 - No. 4, 1991 ($4.95, squarebound, 52 pgs.)

Book 1,2: Ken Steacy painted-c/a & scripts 6.00
Book 3,4-($5.95-c) 6.00
TPB (Dark Horse Comics, 1/97, $17.95) 18.00

TEN COMMANDMENTS (See Moses & the... and Classics Illustrated Special)

TENDER LOVE STORIES
Skywald Publ. Corp.: Feb, 1971 - No. 4, July, 1971 (Pre-code reprints and new stories)

1 (All 25¢, 52 pgs.) 4 8 12 24 37 50
2-4 3 6 9 19 29 38

TENDER ROMANCE (Ideal Romance #3 on)
Key Publications (Gilmour Magazines): Dec, 1953 - No. 2, Feb, 1954

1-Headlight & lingerie panels; B. Baily-c 18 36 54 107 169 230
2-Bernard Baily-c 11 22 33 64 90 115

TENSE SUSPENSE
Fago Publications: Dec, 1958 - No. 2, Feb, 1959

1 10 20 30 54 72 90
2 8 16 24 40 50 60

TEN STORY LOVE (Formerly a pulp magazine with same title)
Ace Periodicals: V29#3, June-July, 1951 - V36#5(#209), Sept, 1956 (#3-6: 52 pgs.)

V29#3(#177)-Part comic, part text; painted-c 15 30 45 84 127 170
4-6(1/52) 10 20 30 54 72 90
V30#1(3/52)-6(1/53) 9 18 27 52 69 85
V31#1(2/53),V32#2(4/53)-6(12/53) 9 18 27 50 65 80
V33#1(1/54)-3(5#54, #195), V34#4(7/54, #196)-6(10/54, #198)
9 18 27 47 61 75
V35#1(12/54, #199)-3(4/55, #201)-Last precode 8 16 24 44 57 70
V35#4-6(9/55, #201-204), V36#1(11/55, #205)-3, 5(9/56, #209)
8 16 24 42 54 65
V36#4-L.B. Cole-a 10 20 30 56 76 95

TENTH, THE
Image Comics: Jan, 1997 - No. 4, June, 1997 ($2.50, limited series)

1-4-Tony Daniel-c/a, Beau Smith-s 5.00
Abuse of Humanity TPB ($10.95) r/#1-4 11.00
Abuse of Humanity TPB (10/98, $11.95) r/#1-4 & 0(8/97) 12.00

TENTH, THE
Image Comics: Sept, 1997 - No. 14, Jan, 1999 ($2.50)

0-(8/97, $5.00) American Ent. Ed. 6.00
1-Tony Daniel-c/a, Beau Smith-s 6.00
2-9: 3,7-Variant-c 4.00
10-14 3.00
...Configuration (8/98) Re-cap and pin-ups 2.50
...Collected Edition 1 ('98, $4.95, square-bound) r/#1,2 5.00
...Special (4/00, $2.95) r/#0 and Wizard #1/2 3.00
Wizard #1/2-Daniel-s/Steve Scott-a 10.00

TENTH, THE (Volume 3) (The Black Embrace)
Image Comics: Mar, 1999 - No. 4, June, 1999 ($2.95)

1-4-Daniel-c/a 3.00
TPB (1/00, $12.95) r/#1-4 13.00

TENTH, THE (Volume 4) (Evil's Child)
Image Comics: Sept, 1999 - No. 4, Mar, 2000 ($2.95, limited series)

1-4-Daniel-c/a 3.00

TENTH, THE (Darkk Dawn)
Image Comics: July, 2005 ($4.99, one-shot)

1-Kirkham-a/Bonny-s 5.00

TENTH, THE : RESURRECTED
Dark Horse Comics: July, 2001 - No. 4, Feb, 2002 ($2.99, limited series)

1-4: 1-Two covers; Daniel-s/c; Romano-a 3.00

10th MUSE
Image Comics (TidalWave Studios): Nov, 2000 - No. 9, Jan, 2002 ($2.95)

1-Character based on wrestling's Rena Mero; regular & photo covers 3.00
2-9: 2-Photo and 2 Lashley covers; flip book Dollz preview. 5-Savage Dragon app.; 2 covers by Lashley and Larsen. 6-Tellos x-over 3.00

TEN WHO DARED (Disney)
Dell Publishing Co.: No. 1178, Dec, 1960

Four Color 1178-Movie, painted-c; cast member photo on back-c
7 14 21 49 80 110

TERMINAL CITY
DC Comics (Vertigo): July, 1996 - No. 9, Mar, 1997 ($2.50, limited series)

1-9: Dean Motter scripts, 7,8-Matt Wagner-c 2.50
TPB ('97, $19.95) r/series 20.00

TERMINAL CITY: AERIAL GRAFFITI
DC Comics (Vertigo): Nov, 1997 - No. 5, Mar, 1998 ($2.50, limited series)

1-5: Dean Motter-s/Lark-a/Chiarello-c 2.50

TERMINATOR, THE (See Robocop vs. ... & Rust #12 for 1st app.)
Now Comics: Sept, 1988 - No. 17, 1989 ($1.75, Baxter paper)

1-Based on movie 1 3 4 6 8 10
2-5 6.00
6-17: 12-($2.95, 52 pgs.)-Intro. John Connor 3.00
Trade paperback (1989, $9.95) 10.00

TERMINATOR, THE
Dark Horse Comics: Aug, 1990 - No. 4, Nov, 1990 ($2.50, limited series)

1-Set 39 years later than the movie 4.00
2-4 3.00

TERMINATOR, THE
Dark Horse Comics: 1998 - No. 4, Dec, 1998 ($2.95, limited series)

1-4-Alan Grant-s/Steve Pugh-a/c 3.00
...Special (1998, $2.95) Darrow-c/Grant-s 3.00

TERMINATOR, THE: ALL MY FUTURES PAST
Now Comics: V3#1, Aug, 1990 - V3#2, Sept, 1990 ($1.75, limited series)

V3#1,2 3.00

TERMINATOR, THE: ENDGAME
Dark Horse Comics: Sept, 1992 - No. 3, Nov, 1992 ($2.50, limited series)

1-3: Guice-a(p); painted-c 3.00

TERMINATOR, THE: HUNTERS AND KILLERS
Dark Horse Comics: Mar, 1992 - No. 3, May, 1992 ($2.50, limited series)

1-3 3.00

TERMINATOR, THE: ONE SHOT
Dark Horse Comics: July, 1991 ($5.95, 56 pgs.)

nn-Matt Wagner-a; contains stiff pop-up inside 6.00

TERMINATOR: REVOLUTION (Follows Terminator 2: Infinity series)
Dynamite Entertainment: 2008 - No. 5, 2009 ($3.50, limited series)

1-5-Furman-s/Antonio-a. 1-3-Two covers 3.50

TERMINATOR: SALVATION MOVIE PREQUEL
IDW Publishing: Jan, 2009 - No. 4, Apr, 2009 ($3.99, limited series)

1-4: Alan Robinson-a/Dara Naraghi-s 4.00
0-Salvation Movie Preview (4/09) Mariotte-s/Figueroa-a 4.00

TERMINATOR, THE: SECONDARY OBJECTIVES
Dark Horse Comics: July, 1991 - No. 4, Oct, 1991 ($2.50, limited series)

1-4: Gulacy-c/a(p) in all 3.00

TERMINATOR, THE: THE BURNING EARTH
Now Comics: V2#1, Mar, 1990 - V2#5, July, 1990 ($1.75, limited series)

V2#1: Alex Ross painted art (1st published work) 2 4 6 9 12 15
2-5: Ross-c/a in all 1 3 4 6 8 10
Trade paperback (1990, $9.95)-Reprints V2#1-5 12.00
Trade paperback (ibooks, 2003, $17.95)-Digitally remastered reprint 18.00

TERMINATOR, THE: THE DARK YEARS
Dark Horse Comics: Aug, 1999 - No. 4, Dec, 1999 ($2.95, limited series)

1-4-Alan Grant-s/Mel Rubi-a; Jae Lee-c 3.00

TERMINATOR: THE ENEMY FROM WITHIN, THE
Dark Horse Comics: Nov, 1991 - No. 4, Feb, 1992 ($2.50, limited series)

1-4: All have Simon Bisley painted-c 3.00

TERMINATOR 2: CYBERNETIC DAWN
Malibu: Nov, 1995 - No.4, Feb, 1996; No. 0. Apr, 1996 ($2.50, lim. series)

0 (4/96, $2.95)-Erskine-c/a; flip book w/Terminator 2: Nuclear Twilight 3.00
1-4: Continuation of film. 3.00

TERMINATOR 2: INFINITY
Dynamite Entertainment: 2007 - No. 7 ($3.50)

Terra #1 © DC

Terrors of the Jungle #10 © STAR

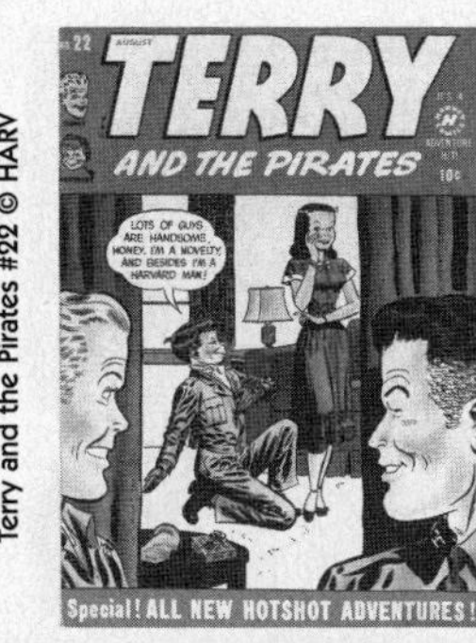

Terry and the Pirates #22 © HARV

	GD	VG	FN	VF	VF/NM	NM-
	2.0	4.0	6.0	8.0	9.0	9.2

1-7: 1-Furman-s/Raynor-a; 3 covers. 6,7-Painkiller Jane x-over 3.50

TERMINATOR 2: JUDGEMENT DAY
Marvel Comics: Early Sept, 1991 - No. 3, Early Oct, 1991 ($1.00, lim. series)

1-3: Based on movie sequel; 1-3-Same as nn issues 3.00
nn (1991, $4.95, squarebound, 68 pgs.)-Photo-c 5.00
nn (1991, $2.25, B&W, magazine, 68 pgs.) 3.00

TERMINATOR 2: NUCLEAR TWILIGHT
Malibu: Nov, 1995 - No.4, Feb, 1996; No. 0, Apr, 1996 ($2.50, lim. series)

0 (4/96, $2.95)-Erskine-c/a; flip book w/Terminator 2: Cybernetic Dawn 3.00
1-4:Continuation of film. 3.00

TERMINATOR 3: RISE OF THE MACHINES (... BEFORE THE RISE on cover)
Beckett Comics: July, 2003 - No. 6, Jan, 2004 ($5.95, limited series)

1-6: 1,2-Leads into movie; 2 covers on each. 3-6-Movie adaptation 6.00

TERRA (See Supergirl {2005 series} #12)
DC Comics: Jan, 2009 - No. 4, Feb, 2009 ($2.99, limited series)

1-4-Conner-a/c. 1,2,4-Power Girl app. 2-4-Geo-Force app. 3.00
TPB (2009, $14.99) r/#1-4 & Supergirl #12 15.00

TERRAFORMERS
Wonder Color Comics: April, 1987 - No. 2, 1987 ($1.95, limited series)

1,2-Kelley Jones-a 2.50

TERRANAUTS
Fantasy General Comics: Aug, 1986 - No. 2, 1986 ($1.75, limited series)

1,2 2.50

TERRA OBSCURA (See Tom Strong)
America's Best Comics: Aug, 2003 - No. 6, Feb, 2004 ($2.95)

1-6-Alan Moore & Peter Hogan-s/Paquette-a 3.00
TPB (2004, $14.95) r/#1-6 15.00

TERRA OBSCURA VOLUME 2 (See Tom Strong)
America's Best Comics: Oct, 2004 - No. 6, May, 2005 ($2.95)

1-6-Alan Moore & Peter Hogan-s/Paquette-a; Tom Strange app. 3.00
TPB (2005, $14.99) r/#1-6 15.00

TERRARISTS
Marvel Comics (Epic): Nov, 1993 - No. 4, Feb, 1994 ($2.50, limited series)

1-4-Bound-in trading cards in all 2.50

TERRIFIC COMICS (Also see Suspense Comics)
Continental Magazines: Jan, 1944 - No. 6, Nov, 1944

	GD	VG	FN	VF	VF/NM	NM-
1-Kid Terrific; opium story	320	640	960	2240	3920	5600
2-1st app. The Boomerang by L.B. Cole & Ed Wheelan's "Comics" McCormick, called the world's #1 comic book fan begins	229	458	687	1454	2502	3550
3-Diana becomes Boomerang's costumed aide; L.B. Cole-c	229	458	687	1454	2502	3550
4-Classic war-c (Scarce)	417	834	1251	2919	5110	7300
5-The Reckoner begins; Boomerang & Diana by L.B. Cole; Classic Schomburg bondage & hooded vigilante-c (Scarce)	900	1800	2700	5400	9700	14,000
6-L.B. Cole-c/a	206	412	618	1318	2259	3200

NOTE: ***L.B. Cole** a-1, 2(2), 3-6. **Fuje** a-5, 6. **Rico** a-2; c-1. **Schomburg** c-2, 5.*

TERRIFIC COMICS (Formerly Horrific; Wonder Boy #17 on)
Mystery Publ.(Comic Media)/(Ajax/Farrell): No. 14, Dec, 1954; No. 16, Mar, 1955 (No #15)

	GD	VG	FN	VF	VF/NM	NM-
14-Art swipe/Advs. into the Unknown #37; injury-to-eye-c; pg. 2, panel 5 swiped from Phantom Stranger #4; surrealistic Palais-a; Human Cross story; classic-c	68	136	204	435	743	1050
16-Wonder Boy-c/story (last pre-code)	27	54	81	160	263	365

TERRIFYING TALES (Formerly Startling Terror Tales #10)
Star Publications: No. 11, Jan, 1953 - No. 15, Apr, 1954

	GD	VG	FN	VF	VF/NM	NM-
11-Used in **POP**, pgs. 99,100; all Jo-Jo-r	49	98	147	309	522	735
12-Reprints Jo-Jo #19 entirely; L.B. Cole splash	47	94	141	296	503	710
13-All Rulah-r; classic devil-c	53	106	159	334	567	800
14-All Rulah reprints	44	88	132	277	469	660
15-Rulah, Zago-r; used in **SOTI**-r/Rulah #22	44	88	132	277	469	660

NOTE: *All issues have **L.B. Cole** covers; bondage covers-No. 12-14.*

TERROR ILLUSTRATED (Adult Tales of...)
E.C. Comics: Nov-Dec, 1955 - No. 2, Spring (April on-c), 1956 (Magazine, 25¢)

	GD	VG	FN	VF	VF/NM	NM-
1-Adult Entertainment on-c	21	42	63	122	199	275
2-Charles Sultan-a	15	30	45	88	137	185

NOTE: ***Craig, Evans, Ingels, Orlando** art in each. **Crandall** c-1, 2.*

TERROR INC. (See A Shadowline Saga #3)
Marvel Comics: July, 1992 - No. 13, July, 1993 ($1.75)

1-8,11-13: 6,7-Punisher-c/story. 13-Ghost Rider app. 2.50
9,10-Wolverine-c/story 3.00

TERROR INC.
Marvel Comics (MAX): Oct, 2007 - No. 5, Apr, 2008 ($3.99, limited series)

1-5: 1-Lapham-s/Zircher-a; origin of Mr. Terror retold 4.00

TERROR INC. - APOCALYPSE SOON
Marvel Comics (MAX): July, 2009 - No. 4, Sept, 2009 ($3.99, limited series)

1-4: 1-Lapham-s/Turnbull-a 4.00

TERRORS OF DRACULA (Magazine)
Modern Day Periodical/Eerie Publ.: Vol. 1 #3, May, 1979 - Vol. 3 #2, Sept, 1981 (B&W)

	GD	VG	FN	VF	VF/NM	NM-
Vol. 1 #3 (5/79, 1st issue)	4	8	12	26	41	55
#4(8/79), #5(11/79)	3	6	9	20	30	40
Vol. 2 #1-3: 1-(2/80). 2-(5/80). 3-(8/80)	3	6	9	17	25	32
Vol. 3 #1 (5/81), #2 (9/81)	3	6	9	19	29	38

TERRORS OF THE JUNGLE (Formerly Jungle Thrills)
Star Publications: No. 17, 5/52 - No. 21, 2/53; No. 4, 4/53 - No. 10, 9/54

	GD	VG	FN	VF	VF/NM	NM-
17-Reprints Rulah #21, used in **SOTI**; L.B. Cole bondage-c	47	94	141	296	498	700
18-Jo-Jo-r	36	72	108	214	347	480
19,20(1952)-Jo-Jo-r; Disbrow-a	34	68	102	199	325	450
21-Jungle Jo, Tangi-r; used in **POP**, pg. 100 & color illos.	37	74	111	222	361	500
4-10: All Disbrow-a. 5-Jo-Jo-r. 8-Rulah, Jo-Jo-r. 9-Jo-Jo-r; Disbrow-a; Tangi by Orlando10-Rulah-r	37	74	111	222	361	500

NOTE: ***L.B. Cole** c-all; bondage c-17, 19, 21, 5, 7.*

TERROR TALES (See Beware Terror Tales)

TERROR TALES (Magazine)
Eerie Publications: V1#7, 1969 - V6#6, Dec, 1974; V7#1, Apr, 1976 - V10, 1979? (V1-V6: 52 pgs.; V7 on: 68 pgs.)

	GD	VG	FN	VF	VF/NM	NM-
V1#7	7	14	21	47	76	105
V1#8-11('69): 9-Bondage-c	5	10	15	30	48	65
V2#1-6('70), V3#1-6('71), V4#1-7('72), V5#1-6('73), V6#1-6('74), V7#1,4('76) (no V7#2), V8#1-3('77)	4	8	12	26	41	55
V7#3-(7/76) LSD story-r/Weird V3#5	4	8	12	26	41	55
V9#2-4, V10#1(1/79)	4	8	12	28	44	60

TERROR TITANS
DC Comics: Dec, 2008 - No. 6, May, 2009 ($2.99, limited series)

1-6: 1-Ravager and Clock King at the Dark Side Club; Bennett-a. 3-Static app. 3.00
TPB (2009, $17.99) r/#1-6 18.00

TERRY AND THE PIRATES (See Famous Feature Stories, Merry Christmas From Sears Toyland, Popular Comics, Super Book #3,5,9,16,28, & Super Comics)

TERRY AND THE PIRATES
Dell Publishing Co.: 1939 - 1953 (By Milton Caniff)

	GD	VG	FN	VF	VF/NM	NM-
Large Feature Comic 2(1939)	87	174	261	553	952	1350
Large Feature Comic 6(1938)-r/1936 dailies	71	142	213	454	777	1100
Four Color 9(1940)	67	134	201	426	731	1035
Large Feature Comic 27('41), 6('42)	57	114	171	362	624	885
Four Color 44('43)	34	68	102	260	500	740
Four Color 101('45)	21	42	63	151	293	435
Family Album(1942)	20	40	60	114	182	250

TERRY AND THE PIRATES (Formerly Boy Explorers; Long John Silver & the Pirates #30 on) (Daily strip-r) (Two #26's)
Harvey Publications/Charlton No. 26-28: No. 3, 4/47 - No. 26, 4/51; No. 26, 6/55 - No. 28, 10/55

	GD	VG	FN	VF	VF/NM	NM-
3(#1)-Boy Explorers by S&K; Terry & the Pirates begin by Caniff; 1st app. The Dragon Lady	39	78	117	231	378	525
4-S&K Boy Explorers	22	44	66	132	216	300
5-11: 11-Man in Black app. by Powell	13	26	39	72	101	130
12-20: 16-Girl threatened with red hot poker	10	20	30	56	76	95
21-26(4/51)-Last Caniff issue & last pre-code issue	10	20	30	54	72	90
26-28('55)(Formerly This Is Suspense)-No Caniff-a	9	18	27	47	61	75

NOTE: ***Powell** a (Tommy Tween)-5-10, 12, 14; 15-17(1/2 to 2 pgs. each).*

TERRY BEARS COMICS (TerryToons, The... #4)
St. John Publishing Co.: June, 1952 - No. 3, Mar, 1953

	GD	VG	FN	VF	VF/NM	NM-
1-By Paul Terry	10	20	30	54	72	90
2,3	7	14	21	35	43	50

Terry-Toons Comics #50 © Paul Terry

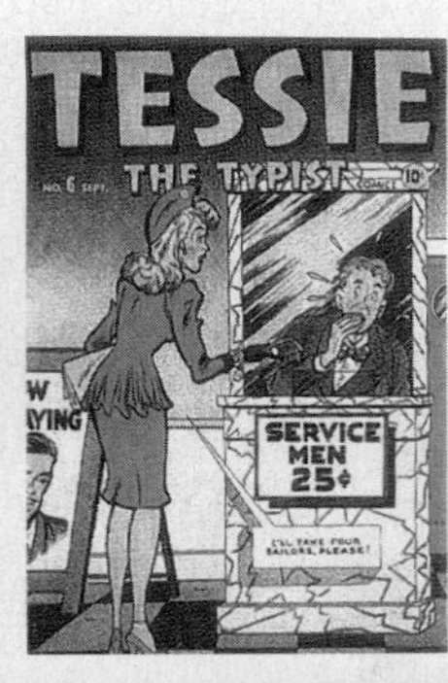

Tessie the Typist #6 © MAR

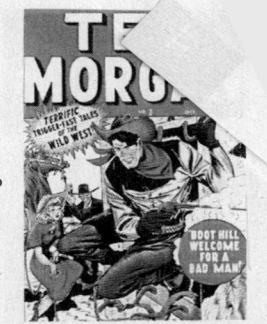

Tex Morgan #2 © MAR

GD VG FN VF VF/NM NM-
2.0 4.0 6.0 8.0 9.0 9.2

TERRY-TOONS ALBUM (See Giant Comics Edition)

TERRY-TOONS COMICS (1st Series) (Becomes Paul Terry's Comics #85 on; later issues titled "Paul Terry's...")
Timely/Marvel No. 1-59 (8/47)(Becomes Best Western No. 58 on?, Marvel)/ St. John No. 60 (9/47) on: Oct, 1942 - No. 86, May, 1951

1 (Scarce)-Features characters that 1st app. on movie screen; Gandy Goose & Sourpuss begin; war-c; Gandy Goose c-1-37 200 400 600 1280 2190 3100
2 68 136 204 435 743 1050
3-5 48 96 144 302 514 725
6,8-10: 9,10-World War II gag-c 37 74 111 222 361 500
7-Hitler, Hirohito, Mussolini-c 68 136 204 435 743 1050
11-20 24 48 72 142 234 325
21-37 18 36 54 103 162 220
38-Mighty Mouse begins (1st app., 11/45); Mighty Mouse-c begin, end #86; Gandy, Sourpuss welcome Mighty Mouse on-c 168 336 504 1075 1838 2600
39-2nd app. Mighty Mouse 53 106 159 334 567 800
40-49: 43-Infinity-c 28 56 84 165 270 375
50-1st app. Heckle & Jeckle (11/46) 45 90 135 284 480 675
51-60: 55-Infinity-c. 60-(9/47)-Atomic explosion panel; 1st St. John issue 16 32 48 94 147 200
61-86: 85,86-Same book as Paul Terry's Comics #85,86 with only a title change; published at same time? 14 28 42 82 121 160

TERRY-TOONS COMICS (2nd Series)
St. John Publishing Co./Pines: June, 1952 - No. 9, Nov, 1953; 1957; 1958

1-Gandy Goose & Sourpuss begin by Paul Terry 18 36 54 105 165 225
2 10 20 30 56 76 95
3-9 9 18 27 52 69 85
Giant Summer Fun Book 101,102-(Sum, 1957, Sum, 1958, 25¢, Pines)(TV) CBS Television Presents...; Tom Terrific, Mighty Mouse, Heckle & Jeckle Gandy Goose app. 14 28 42 80 115 150

TERRYTOONS, THE TERRY BEARS (Formerly Terry Bears Comics)
Pines Comics: No. 4, Summer, 1958 (CBS Television Presents...)

4 7 14 21 35 43 50

TESSIE THE TYPIST (Tiny Tessie #24; see Comedy Comics, Gay Comics & Joker Comics)
Timely/Marvel Comics (20CC): Summer, 1944 - No. 23, Aug, 1949

1-Doc Rockblock & others by Wolverton 77 154 231 493 847 1200
2-Wolverton's Powerhouse Pepper 40 80 120 246 411 575
3-(3/45)-No Wolverton 18 36 54 107 169 230
4,5,7,8-Wolverton-a. 4-(Fall/45) 31 62 93 186 303 420
6-Kurtzman's "Hey Look", 2 pgs. Wolverton-a 31 62 93 186 303 420
9-Wolverton's Powerhouse Pepper (8 pgs.) & 1 pg. Kurtzman's "Hey Look" 34 68 102 204 332 460
10-Wolverton's Powerhouse Pepper (4 pgs.) 32 64 96 188 307 425
11-Wolverton's Powerhouse Pepper (8 pgs.) 34 68 102 204 332 460
12-Wolverton's Powerhouse Pepper (4 pgs.) & 1 pg. Kurtzman's "Hey Look" 32 64 96 188 307 425
13-Wolverton's Powerhouse Pepper (4 pgs.) 32 64 96 188 307 425
14,15: 14-Wolverton's Dr. Whackyhack (1 pg.); 1-1/2 pgs. Kurtzman's "Hey Look". 15-Kurtzman's "Hey Look" (3 pgs.) & 3 pgs. Giggles 'n' Grins 23 46 69 136 223 310
16-18-Kurtzman's "Hey Look" (?, 2 & 1 pg.) 18 36 54 103 162 220
19-Annie Oakley story (8 pgs.) 14 28 42 80 115 150
20-23: 20-Anti-Wertham editorial (2/49) 14 28 42 76 108 140
NOTE: *Lana app.-21. Millie The Model app.-13, 15, 17, 21. Rusty app.-10, 11, 13, 15, 17.*

TESTAMENT
DC Comics (Vertigo): Feb, 2006 - No. 22, Mar, 2008 ($2.99)

1-22: 1-5-Rushkoff-s/Sharp-a. 6,7-Gross & Erskine-a 3.00
...: Akedah TPB (2006, $9.99) r/#1-5; Rushkoff intro. 10.00
...: Babel TPB (2007, $12.99) r/#11-16 13.00
...: Exodus TPB (2008, $14.99) r/#17-22 15.00
...: West of Eden TPB (2007, $12.99) r/#6-10; Rushkoff commentary 13.00

TEXAN, THE (Fightin' Marines #15 on; Fightin' Texan #16 on)
St. John Publishing Co.: Aug, 1948 - No. 15, Oct, 1951

1-Buckskin Belle 16 32 48 94 147 200
2 10 20 30 58 79 100
3,10: 10-Oversized issue 10 20 30 54 72 90
4,5,7,15-Baker-c/a 20 40 60 117 189 260
6,9-Baker-c 15 30 45 85 130 175
8,11,13,14-Baker-c/a(2-3) each 21 42 63 126 206 285
12-All Matt Baker-c/a; Peyote story 28 56 84 165 270 375
NOTE: ***Matt Baker** c-4-9, 11-15. **Larsen** a-4-6, 8-10, 15. **Tuska** a-1, 2, 7-9.*

GD VG FN VF VF/NM NM-
2.0 4.0 6.0 8.0 9.0 9.2

TEXAN, THE (TV)
Dell Publishing Co.: No. 1027, Sept-Nov, 1959 - No. 1096, May-July, 1960

Four Color 1027 (#1)-Photo-c 8 16 24 56 93 130
Four Color 1096-Rory Calhoun photo-c 8 16 24 52 86 120

TEXAS CHAINSAW MASSACRE
DC Comics (WildStorm): Jan, 2007 - No. 6, Jun, 2007 ($2.99, limited series)

1-6: 1-Two covers by Bermejo & Bradstreet; Abnett & Lanning-s 3.00
...: About a Boy #1 (9/07, $2.99) Abnett & Lanning-s/Gomez-a/Robertson-c 3.00
...: Book Two TPB (2009, $14.99) r/one shots & New Line Cinema's Tales of Horror story 15.00
...: By Himself #1 (10/07, $2.99) Abnett & Lanning-s/Craig-a/Robertson-c 3.00
...: Cut! #1 (8/07, $2.99) Pfeiffer-s/Raffaele-a/Robertson-c 3.00
...: Raising Cain 1-3 (7/08 - No. 3, 9/08, $3.50) Bruce Jones-s/Chris Gugliotti-a 3.50

TEXAS JOHN SLAUGHTER (See Walt Disney Presents, 4-Color #997, 1181 & #2)

TEXAS KID (See Two-Gun Western, Wild Western)
Marvel/Atlas Comics (LMC): Jan, 1951 - No. 10, July, 1952

1-Origin; Texas Kid (alias Lance Temple) & his horse Thunder begin; Tuska-a 23 46 69 136 223 310
2 13 26 39 74 105 135
3-10 10 20 30 56 76 95
NOTE: ***Maneely** a-1-4; c-1, 3, 5-10.*

TEXAS RANGERS, THE (See Jace Pearson of... and Superior Stories #4)

TEXAS RANGERS IN ACTION (Formerly Captain Gallant or Scotland Yard?)
Charlton Comics: No. 5, Jul, 1956 - No. 79, Aug, 1970 (See Blue Bird Comics)

5 8 16 24 44 57 70
6,7,9,10 6 12 18 28 34 40
8-Ditko-a (signed) 10 20 30 54 72 90
11-(68 pg. Giant) Williamson-a (5&8 pgs.); Torres/Williamson-a (5 pgs.) 10 20 30 54 72 90
12,14-20: 12-(68 pg. Giant) 5 10 15 23 28 32
13-Williamson-a (5 pgs); Torres, Morisi-a 8 16 24 42 54 65
21-30 3 6 9 16 22 28
31-59: 32-Both 10¢-c & 15¢-c exist 2 4 6 13 18 22
60-Riley's Rangers begin 3 6 9 14 19 24
61-65,68-70 2 4 6 8 11 14
66,67: 66-1st app. The Man Called Loco. 67-Origin 2 4 6 9 13 16
71-79: 77-(4/70) Ditko-c & a (8 pgs.) 1 3 4 6 8 10
76 (Modern Comics-r, 1977) 4.00

TEXAS SLIM (See A-1 Comics)

TEX DAWSON, GUN-SLINGER (Gunslinger #2 on)
Marvel Comics Group: Jan, 1973 (20¢)(Also see Western Kid, 1st series)

1-Steranko-c; Williamson-r (4 pgs.); Tex Dawson-r by Romita(3) from 1955; Tuska-r 3 6 9 16 23 30

TEX FARNUM (See Wisco)

TEX FARRELL (...Pride of the Wild West)
D. S. Publishing Co.: Mar-Apr, 1948

1-Tex Farrell & his horse Lightning; Shelly-c 15 30 45 88 137 185

TEX GRANGER (Formerly Calling All Boys; see True Comics)
Parents' Magazine Inst./Commended: No. 18, Jun, 1948 - No. 24, Sept, 1949

18-Tex Granger & his horse Bullet begin 12 24 36 67 94 120
19 10 20 30 54 72 90
20-24: 22-Wild Bill Hickok story. 23-Vs. Billy the Kid; Tim Holt app. 8 16 24 44 57 70

TEX MORGAN (See Blaze Carson and Wild Western)
Marvel Comics (CCC): Aug, 1948 - No. 9, Feb, 1950

1-Tex Morgan, his horse Lightning & sidekick Lobo begin 28 56 84 165 270 375
2 18 36 54 105 165 225
3-6: 3,4-Arizona Annie app. 14 28 42 76 108 140
7-9: All photo-c. 7-Captain Tootsie by Beck. 8-18 pg. story "The Terror of Rimrock Valley"; Diablo app. 18 36 54 105 165 225
NOTE: *Tex Taylor app.-6, 7, 9. **Brodsky** c-6. **Syd Shores** c-2, 5.*

TEX RITTER WESTERN (Movie star; singing cowboy; see Six-Gun Heroes and Western Hero)
Fawcett No. 1-20 (1/54)/Charlton No. 21 on: Oct, 1950 - No. 46, May, 1959 (Photo-c: 1-21)

1-Tex Ritter, his stallion White Flash & dog Fury begin; photo front/back-c begin 53 106 159 334 567 800
2 27 54 81 158 254 350
3-5: 5-Last photo back-c 20 40 60 115 183 250
6-10 15 30 45 88 137 185

Tex Taylor #1 © MAR

The Thing! #7 © CC

The Thing #24 © MAR

	GD 2.0	VG 4.0	FN 6.0	VF 8.0	VF/NM 9.0	NM- 9.2
11-19	12	24	36	69	97	125
20-Last Fawcett issue (1/54)	13	26	39	74	105	135
21-1st Charlton issue; photo-c (3/54)	15	30	45	88	137	185
22-B&W photo back-c begin, end #32	11	22	33	60	83	105
23-30: 23-25-Young Falcon app.	10	20	30	56	76	95
31-38,40-45	9	18	27	50	65	80
39-Williamson-a; Whitman-c (1/58)	10	20	30	56	76	95
46-Last issue	10	20	30	54	72	90

TEX TAYLOR (...The Fighting Cowboy on-c #1, 2)(See Blaze Carson, Kid Colt, Tex Morgan, Wild West, Wild Western, & Wisco)
Marvel Comics (HPC): Sept, 1948 - No. 9, March, 1950

	GD 2.0	VG 4.0	FN 6.0	VF 8.0	VF/NM 9.0	NM- 9.2
1-Tex Taylor & his horse Fury begin	29	58	87	170	278	385
2	15	30	45	88	137	185
3	14	28	42	82	121	160
4-6: All photo-c. 4-Anti-Wertham editorial. 5,6-Blaze Carson app.	15	30	45	92	144	195
7-9: 7-Photo-c;18 pg. Movie-Length Thriller "Trapped in Time's Lost Land!" with sabretoothed tigers, dinosaurs; Diablo app. 8-Photo-c; 18 pg. Movie-Length Thriller "The Mystery of Devil-Tree Plateau!" with dwarf horses, dwarf people & a lost miniature Inca type village; Diablo app. 9-Photo-c; 18 pg. Movie-Length Thriller "Guns Along the Border!" Captain Tootsie by Schreiber; Nimo the Mountain Lion app.	19	38	57	109	172	235

NOTE: *Syd Shores c-1-3.*

THANE OF BAGARTH (Also see Hercules, 1967 series)
Charlton Comics: No. 24, Oct, 1985 - No. 25, Dec, 1985

	GD 2.0	VG 4.0	FN 6.0	VF 8.0	VF/NM 9.0	NM- 9.2
24,25-Low print run						6.00

THANOS
Marvel Comics: Dec, 2003 - No. 12, Sept, 2004 ($2.99)

	GD 2.0	VG 4.0	FN 6.0	VF 8.0	VF/NM 9.0	NM- 9.2
1-12: 1-6-Starlin-s/a(p)/Milgrom-i; Galactus app. 7-12-Giffen-s/Lim-a						3.00
Vol. 4: Epiphany TPB (2004, $14.99) r/#1-6						15.00
Vol. 5: Samaritan TPB (2004, $14.99) r/#7-12						15.00

THANOS QUEST, THE (See Capt. Marvel #25, Infinity Gauntlet, Iron Man #55, Logan's Run, Marvel Feature #12, Marvel Universe: The End, Silver Surfer #34 & Warlock #9)
Marvel Comics: 1990 - No. 2, 1990 ($4.95, squarebound, 52 pgs.)

	GD 2.0	VG 4.0	FN 6.0	VF 8.0	VF/NM 9.0	NM- 9.2
1,2-Both have Starlin scripts & covers (both printings)	1	2	3	4	5	7
1-(3/2000, $3.99) r/material from #1&2						4.00

THAT DARN CAT (See Movie Comics & Walt Disney Showcase #19)

THAT'S MY POP! GOES NUTS FOR FAIR
Bystander Press: 1939 (76 pgs., B&W)

	GD 2.0	VG 4.0	FN 6.0	VF 8.0	VF/NM 9.0	NM- 9.2
nn-by Milt Gross	30	60	90	177	289	400

THAT WILKIN BOY (Meet Bingo...)
Archie Publications: Jan, 1969 - No. 52, Oct, 1982

	GD 2.0	VG 4.0	FN 6.0	VF 8.0	VF/NM 9.0	NM- 9.2
1-1st app. Bingo's Band, Samantha & Tough Teddy	4	8	12	28	44	60
2-5	3	6	9	16	23	30
6-11	2	4	6	13	18	22
12-26-Giants. 12-No # on-c	3	6	9	14	20	26
27-40(1/77)	2	4	6	8	10	12
41-49	1	2	3	4	5	7
50-52 (low print)	2	4	6	8	10	12

THB
Horse Press: Oct, 1994 - Present ($5.50/$2.50/$2.95, B&W)

	GD 2.0	VG 4.0	FN 6.0	VF 8.0	VF/NM 9.0	NM- 9.2
1 ($5.50) Paul Pope-s/a in all	1	2	3	5	6	8
1 (2nd Printing)-r/#1 w/new material						3.00
2 ($2.50)						5.00
3-5						4.00
69 (1995, no price, low distribution, 12 pgs.)-story reprinted in #1 (2nd Printing)						3.00
Giant THB-($4.95)						5.00
Giant THB 1 V2-(2003, $6.95)						7.00
...M3/THB: Mars' Mightiest Mek #1 (2000, $3.95)						4.00
...6A: Mek-Power #1, 6B: Mek-Power #2, 6C: Mek-Power #3 (2000, $3.95)						4.00
... 6D: Mek-Power #4 (2002, $4.95)						5.00

T.H.E. CAT (TV)
Dell Publishing Co.: Mar, 1967 - No. 4, Oct, 1967 (All have photo-c)

	GD 2.0	VG 4.0	FN 6.0	VF 8.0	VF/NM 9.0	NM- 9.2
1	4	8	12	22	34	45
2-4	3	6	9	17	25	32

THERE'S A NEW WORLD COMING
Spire Christian Comics/Fleming H. Revell Co.: 1973 (35/49¢)

	GD 2.0	VG 4.0	FN 6.0	VF 8.0	VF/NM 9.0	NM- 9.2
nn	2	4	6	8	11	14

THEY ALL KISSED THE BRIDE (See Cinema Comics Herald)

THIEF OF BAGHDAD
Dell Publishing Co.: No. 1229, Oct-Dec, 1961 (one-shot)

	GD 2.0	VG 4.0	FN 6.0	VF 8.0	VF/NM 9.0	NM- 9.2
Four Color 1229-Movie, Crandall/Evans-a, photo-c	7	14	21	45	73	100

THIMK (Magazine) (Satire)
Counterpoint: May, 1958 - No. 6, May, 1959

	GD 2.0	VG 4.0	FN 6.0	VF 8.0	VF/NM 9.0	NM- 9.2
1	10	20	30	58	79	100
2-6	8	16	24	40	50	60

THING!, THE (Blue Beetle #18 on)
Song Hits No. 1,2/Capitol Stories/Charlton: Feb, 1952 - No. 17, Nov, 1954

	GD 2.0	VG 4.0	FN 6.0	VF 8.0	VF/NM 9.0	NM- 9.2
1-Weird/horror stories in all; shrunken head-c	90	180	270	576	988	1400
2,3	58	116	174	371	636	900
4-6,8,10: 5-Severed head-c; headlights	53	106	159	334	567	800
7-Injury to eye-c & inside panel	71	142	213	454	777	1100
9-Used in **SOTI**, pg. 388 & illo "Stomping on the face is a form of brutality which modern children learn early"	82	164	246	528	902	1275
11-Necronomicon story; Hansel & Gretel parody; Injury-to-eye panel; Check-a	65	130	195	416	708	1000
12-1st published Ditko-c; "Cinderella" parody; lingerie panels. Ditko-a	90	180	270	576	988	1400
13,15-Ditko-c/a(3 & 5)	90	180	270	576	988	1400
14-Extreme violence/torture; Rumpelstiltskin story; Ditko-c/a(4)	92	184	276	584	1005	1425
16-Injury to eye panel	34	68	102	199	325	450
17-Ditko-c; classic parody "Through the Looking Glass"; Powell-r/Beware Terror Tales #1 & recolored	81	162	243	518	884	1250

NOTE: *Excessive violence, severed heads, injury to eye are common No. 5 on.* ***Al Fago*** *c-4.* ***Forgione*** *c-1i, 2, 6, 8, 9. All* ***Ditko*** *issues #14, 15.* ***Giordano*** *a-6.*

THING, THE (See Fantastic Four, Marvel Fanfare, Marvel Feature #11,12, Marvel Two-In-One and Startling Stories:...- Night Falls on Yancy Street)
Marvel Comics Group: July, 1983 - No. 36, June, 1986

	GD 2.0	VG 4.0	FN 6.0	VF 8.0	VF/NM 9.0	NM- 9.2
1-Life story of Ben Grimm; Byrne scripts begin						4.00
2-36: 5-Spider-Man, She-Hulk app.						3.00

NOTE: ***Byrne*** *a-2i, 7; c-1, 7, 36i; scripts-1-13, 19-22.* ***Sienkiewicz*** *c-13i.*

THING, THE (Fantastic Four)
Marvel Comics: Jan, 2006 - No. 8 ($2.99)

	GD 2.0	VG 4.0	FN 6.0	VF 8.0	VF/NM 9.0	NM- 9.2
1-8: 1-DiVito-a/Slott-s. 4-Lockjaw app. 6-Spider-Man app. 8-Super-Hero poker game						3.00
...: Idol of Millions TPB (2006, $20.99) r/#1-8; Divito sketch page						21.00

THING & SHE-HULK: THE LONG NIGHT (Fantastic Four)
Marvel Comics: May, 2002 ($2.99, one-shot)

	GD 2.0	VG 4.0	FN 6.0	VF 8.0	VF/NM 9.0	NM- 9.2
1-Hitch-c/a(pg. 1-25); Reis-a(pg. 26-39); Dezago-s						3.00

THING, THE (From Another World)
Dark Horse Comics: 1991 - No. 2, 1992 ($2.95, mini-series, stiff-c)

	GD 2.0	VG 4.0	FN 6.0	VF 8.0	VF/NM 9.0	NM- 9.2
1,2-Based on Universal movie; painted-c/a						3.00

THING, THE: FREAKSHOW (Fantastic Four)
Marvel Comics: Aug, 2002 - No. 4, Nov, 2002 ($2.99, limited series)

	GD 2.0	VG 4.0	FN 6.0	VF 8.0	VF/NM 9.0	NM- 9.2
1-4-Geoff Johns-s/Scott Kolins-a						3.00
TPB (2005, $17.99) r/#1-4 & Thing & She-Hulk: The Long Night one-shot						18.00

THING FROM ANOTHER WORLD: CLIMATE OF FEAR, THE
Dark Horse Comics: July, 1992 - No. 4, Dec, 1992 ($2.50, mini-series)

	GD 2.0	VG 4.0	FN 6.0	VF 8.0	VF/NM 9.0	NM- 9.2
1-4: Painted-c						3.00

THING FROM ANOTHER WORLD: ETERNAL VOWS
Dark Horse Comics: Dec, 1993 - No. 4, 1994 ($2.50, mini-series)

	GD 2.0	VG 4.0	FN 6.0	VF 8.0	VF/NM 9.0	NM- 9.2
1-4-Gulacy-c/a						3.00

THIRD WORLD WAR
Fleetway Publ. (Quality): 1990 - No. 6, 1991 ($2.50, thick-c, mature)

	GD 2.0	VG 4.0	FN 6.0	VF 8.0	VF/NM 9.0	NM- 9.2
1-6						2.50

THIRTEEN (...Going on 18)
Dell Publishing Co.: 11-1/61-62 - No. 25, 12/67; No. 26, 7/69 - No. 29, 1/71

	GD 2.0	VG 4.0	FN 6.0	VF 8.0	VF/NM 9.0	NM- 9.2
1	6	12	18	41	66	90
2-10	5	10	15	30	48	65
11-25	4	8	12	24	37	50
26-29-r	3	6	9	18	27	35

NOTE: ***John Stanley*** *script-No. 3-29; art?*

13: ASSASSIN
TSR, Inc.: 1990 - No. 8, 1991 ($2.95, 44 pgs.)

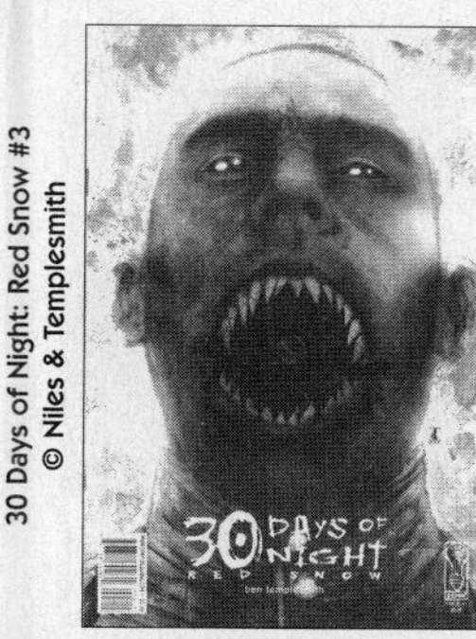

30 Days of Night: Red Snow #3 © Niles & Templesmith

This Magazine is Haunted #14 © FAW

Thor #342 © MAR

GD VG FN VF VF/NM NM-
2.0 4.0 6.0 8.0 9.0 9.2

1-8: Agent 13; Alcala-a(i); Springer back-up-a 3.00

13th SON, THE
Dark Horse Comics: Nov, 2005 - No. 4, Feb, 2006 ($2.99, limited series)

1-4-Kelley Jones-s/a/c 3.00

30 DAYS OF NIGHT
Idea + Design Works: June, 2002 - No. 3, Oct, 2002 ($3.99, limited series)

1-Vampires in Alaska; Steve Niles-s/Ben Templesmith-a/Ashley Wood-c 30.00
1-2nd printing 10.00
2 12.00
3 6.00
Annual 2004 (1/04, $4.99) Niles-s/art by Templesmith and others 5.00
Annual 2005 (12/05, $7.49) Niles-s/art by Nat Jones 7.50
... 5th Anniversary (10/07 - No. 3, $2.99) reprints original series 3.00
... Sourcebook (10/07, $7.49) Illustrated guide to the 30 Days world 7.50
... Three Tales TPB (7/06, $19.99) r/Annual 2005, ...: Dead Space #1-3, and short story from Tales of Terror (IDW's...) 20.00
TPB (2003, $17.99) r/#1-3, foreward by Clive Barker; script for #1 18.00
The Complete 30 Days of Night (2004, $75.00, oversized hardcover with slipcase) r/#1-3; prequel; script pages for #1-3; original cover and promotional materials 75.00

30 DAYS OF NIGHT: BEYOND BARROW
IDW Publishing: Sept, 2007 - No. 3, Dec, 2007 ($3.99, limited series)

1-3-Niles-s/Sienkiewicz-a/c 4.00

30 DAYS OF NIGHT: BLOODSUCKER TALES
IDW Publishing: Oct, 2004 - No. 8, May, 2005 ($3.99, limited series)

1-8-Niles-s/Chamberlain-a; Fraction-s/Templesmith-a/c 4.00
HC (8/05, $49.99) r/#1-8; cover gallery 50.00
SC (8/05, $24.99) r/#1-8; cover gallery 25.00

30 DAYS OF NIGHT: DEAD SPACE
IDW Publishing: Jan, 2006 - No. 3, Mar, 2006 ($3.99, limited series)

1-3-Niles and Wickline-s/Milx-a/c 4.00

30 DAYS OF NIGHT: EBEN & STELLA
IDW Publishing: May, 2007 - No. 3, July, 2007 ($3.99, limited series)

1-3-Niles and DeConnick-s/Randall-a/c 4.00

30 DAYS OF NIGHT: RED SNOW
IDW Publishing: Aug, 2007 - No. 3, Oct, 2007 ($3.99, limited series)

1-3-Ben Templesmith-s/a/c 4.00

30 DAYS OF NIGHT: RETURN TO BARROW
IDW Publishing: Mar, 2004 - No. 6, Aug, 2004 ($3.99, limited series)

1-6-Steve Niles-s/Ben Templesmith-a/c 4.00
TPB (2004, $19.99) r/#1-6; cover gallery 20.00

30 DAYS OF NIGHT: SPREADING THE DISEASE
IDW Publishing: Dec, 2006 - No. 5, Apr, 2007 ($3.99, limited series)

1-5: 1-Wickline-s/Sanchez-a. 3-5-Sandoval-a 4.00

30 DAYS OF NIGHT: 30 DAYS 'TIL DEATH
IDW Publishing: Dec, 2008 - No. 4, Mar, 2009 ($3.99, limited series)

1-4-David Lapham-s/a; covers by Lapham and Templesmith 4.00

THIRTY SECONDS OVER TOKYO (See American Library)

THIS IS SUSPENSE! (Formerly Strange Suspense Stories; Strange Suspense Stories #27 on)
Charlton Comics: No. 23, Feb, 1955 - No. 26, Aug, 1955

23-Wood-a(r)/A Star Presentation #3 "Dr. Jekyll & Mr. Hyde"; last pre-code issue
24 48 72 140 230 320
24-Censored Fawcett-r; Evans-a (r/Suspense Detective #1)
14 28 42 80 115 150
25,26: 26-Marcus Swayze-a 10 20 30 56 76 95

THIS IS THE PAYOFF (See Pay-Off)

THIS IS WAR
Standard Comics: No. 5, July, 1952 - No. 9, May, 1953

5-Toth-a 14 28 42 76 108 140
6,9-Toth-a 11 22 33 60 83 105
7,8: 8-Ross Andru-c 8 16 24 44 57 70

THIS IS YOUR LIFE, DONALD DUCK (See Donald Duck..., Four Color #1109)

THIS MAGAZINE IS CRAZY (Crazy #? on)
Charlton Publ. (Humor Magazines): V3#2, July, 1957 - V4#8, Feb, 1959 (25¢, magazine, 68 pgs.)

V3#2-V4#7: V4#5-Russian Sputnik-c parody 10 20 30 54 72 90
V4#8-Davis-a (8 pgs.) 10 20 30 58 79 100

THIS MAGAZINE IS HAUNTED (Danger and Adventure #22 on)
Fawcett Publications/Charlton No. 15(2/54) on: Oct, 1951 - No. 14, 12/53; No. 15, 2/54 - V3#21, Nov, 1954

1-Evans-a; Dr. Death as host begins 65 130 195 416 708 1000
2,5-Evans-a 44 88 132 277 469 660
3,4: 3-Vampire-c/story 35 70 105 208 339 470
6-9,11,12,14 26 52 78 154 252 350
10-Severed head-c 43 86 129 271 461 650
13-Severed head-c/story 42 84 126 265 445 625
15,20: 15-Dick Giordano-c. 20-Cover is swiped from panel in The Thing #16
21 42 63 126 206 285
16,19-Ditko-c. 19-Injury-to-eye panel; story-r/#1 40 80 120 246 411 575
17-Ditko-c/a(4); blood drainage story 47 94 141 296 498 700
18-Ditko-c/a(1 story); E.C. swipe/Haunt of Fear #5; injury-to-eye panel; reprints "Caretaker of the Dead" from Beware Terror Tales & recolored
41 82 123 258 434 610
21-Ditko-c, Evans-r/This Magazine Is Haunted #1 38 76 114 224 367 510

NOTE: ***Baily** a-1, 3, 4, 21r/#1. **Moldoff** c/a-1-13. **Powell** a-3-5, 11, 12, 17. **Shuster** a-18-20. Issues 19-21 have reprints which have been recolored from This Magazine is Haunted #1.*

THIS MAGAZINE IS HAUNTED (2nd Series) (Formerly Zaza the Mystic; Outer Space #17 on)
Charlton Comics: V2#12, July, 1957 - V2#16, May, 1958

V2#12-14-Ditko-c/a in all 39 78 117 240 395 550
15-No Ditko-c/a 13 26 39 74 105 135
16-Ditko-a(4). 27 54 81 158 259 360

THIS MAGAZINE IS WILD (See Wild)

THIS WAS YOUR LIFE (Religious)
Jack T. Chick Publ.: 1964 (3 1/2 x 5 1/2", 40 pgs., B&W and red)

nn, Another version (5x2 3/4", 26 pgs.) 2 4 6 10 14 18

THOR (See Avengers #1, Giant-Size..., Marvel Collectors Item Classics, Marvel Graphic Novel #33, Marvel Preview, Marvel Spectacular, Marvel Treasury Edition, Special Marvel Edition & Tales of Asgard)

THOR (Journey Into Mystery #1-125, 503-on)(The Mighty Thor #413-490)
Marvel Comics Group: No. 126, Mar, 1966 - No. 502, Sept, 1996

126-Thor continues (#125-130 Thor vs. Hercules) 23 46 69 166 321 475
127-130: 127-1st app. Pluto 10 20 30 73 129 185
131-133,135-140: 132-1st app. Ego. 136- Intro. Sif 9 18 27 63 107 150
134-Intro High Evolutionary 9 18 27 65 113 160
141-150: 146-Inhumans begin (early app.), end #151 (see Fantastic Four #45 for 1st app.). 146,147-Origin The Inhumans. 148,149-Origin Black Bolt in each. 149-Origin Medusa, Crystal, Maximus, Gorgon, Karnak 8 16 24 52 86 120
151-157,159,160: 159-Origin Dr. Blake (Thor) concl. 7 14 21 45 73 100
158-Origin-r/#83; origin Dr. Blake 9 18 27 63 107 150
161,167,170-179: 179-Last Kirby issue 5 10 15 34 55 75
162,168,169-Origin Galactus; Kirby-a 6 12 18 43 69 95
163,164-2nd & 3th brief app. Warlock (Him) 5 10 15 34 55 75
165-1st full app. Warlock (Him) (6/69, see Fantastic Four #67); last 12¢ issue; Kirby-a
8 16 24 52 86 120
166-2nd full app. Warlock (Him); battles Thor 7 14 21 45 73 100
180,181-Neal Adams-a 6 12 18 39 62 85
182-192: 192-Last 15¢ issue 4 8 12 24 37 50
193-(25¢, 52 pgs.); Silver Surfer x-over 9 18 27 65 113 160
194-199 3 6 9 20 30 40
200 4 8 12 24 37 50
201-206,208-224 2 4 6 11 16 20
207-Rutland, Vermont Halloween x-over 3 6 9 14 19 24
225-Intro. Firelord 3 6 9 17 25 32
226-245: 226-Galactus app. 2 4 6 9 12 15
246-250-(Regular 25¢ editions)(4-8/76) 2 4 6 9 12 15
246-250-(30¢-c variants, limited distribution) 4 8 12 22 34 45
251-280: 271-Iron Man x-over. 274-Death of Balder the Brave
1 2 3 5 7 9
260-264-(35¢-c variants, limited distribution)(6-10/77) 4 8 12 22 34 45
281-299: 294-Origin Asgard & Odin 1 2 3 4 5 7
300-(12/80)-End of Asgard; origin of Odin & The Destroyer
2 3 4 6 8 10
301-336,338-373,375-381,383: 316-Iron Man x-over. 332,333-Dracula app. 340-Donald Blake returns as Thor. 341-Clark Kent & Lois Lane cameo. 373-X-Factor tie-in 4.00
337-Simonson-c/a begins, ends #382; Beta Ray Bill becomes new Thor
2 4 6 8 10 12
374-Mutant Massacre; X-Factor app. 5.00
382-($1.25)-Anniversary issue; last Simonson-a 5.00

Thor #478 © MAR

Thor V2 #20 © MAR

Thor (2009 series) #11 © MAR

GD 2.0 | VG 4.0 | FN 6.0 | VF 8.0 | VF/NM 9.0 | NM- 9.2

384-Intro. new Thor 5.00
385-399,401-410,413-428: 385-Hulk x-over. 391-Spider-Man x-over; 1st Eric Masterson. 395-Intro Earth Force. 408-Eric Masterson becomes Thor. 427,428-Excalibur x-over 3.00
400,411: 400-($1.75, 68 pgs.)-Origin Loki. 411-Intro New Warriors (appears in costume in last panel); Juggernaut-c/story 5.00
412-1st full app. New Warriors (Marvel Boy, Kid Nova, Namorita, Night Thrasher, Firestar & Speedball) 6.00
429-431,434-443: 429,430-Ghost Rider x-over. 434-Capt. America x-over. 437-Thor vs. Quasar; Hercules app.;Tales of Asgard back-up stories begin. 443-Dr. Strange & Silver Surfer x-over; last $1.00-c 2.50
432,433: 432-(52 pgs.)-Thor's 300th app. (vs. Loki); reprints origin & 1st app. from Journey into Mystery #83. 433-Intro new Thor 3.00
444-449,451-473: 448-Spider-Man-c/story. 455,456-Dr. Strange back-up. 457-Old Thor returns (3 pgs.). 459-Intro Thunderstrike. 460-Starlin scripts begin. 465-Super Skrull app. 466-Drax app. 469,470-Infinity Watch x-over. 472-Intro the Godlings 2.50
450-($2.50, 68 pgs.)-Flip-book format; r/story JIM #87 (1st Loki) plus-c plus a gallery of past-c; gatefold-c 3.00
474,476-481,483-499: 474-Begin $1.50-c; bound-in trading cards. 459-Intro Thunderstrike, 460-Starlin scripts begin. 472-Intro the Godlings. 490-The Absorbing Man app. 491-Warren Ellis scripts begins, ends #494; Deodato-c/a begins. 492-Reintro The Enchantress; Beta Ray Bill dies. 495-Wm. Messner-Loebs scripts begin; Isherwood-c/a. 2.50
475 ($2.00, 52 pgs.)-Regular edition 2.50
475 ($2.50, 52 pgs.)-Collectors edition w/foil embossed-c 3.00
482 ($2.95, 84 pgs.)-400th issue 3.00
500 ($2.50)-Double-size; wraparound-c; Deodato-c/a; Dr. Strange app. 5.00
501-Reintro Red Norvell 3.00
502-Onslaught tie-in; Red Norvell, Jane Foster & Hela app. 4.00
600-up (See Thor 2007 series)
Special 2(9/66)-(See Journey Into Mystery for 1st annual)

	GD	VG	FN	VF	VF/NM	NM-
	9	18	27	63	107	150
Special 2 (2nd printing, 1994)	2	4	6	8	10	12
King Size Special 3(1/71)	4	8	12	22	34	45
Special 4(12/71)-r/Thor #131,132 & JIM #113	3	6	9	18	27	35

Annual 5,6: 5(11/76). 6(10/77)-Guardians of the Galaxy app.

	GD	VG	FN	VF	VF/NM	NM-
	2	4	6	9	13	16
Annual 7,8: 7(1978). 8(1979)-Thor vs. Zeus-c/story	1	3	4	6	8	10

Annual 9-12: 9('81). 10('82). 11('83). 12('84) 6.00
Annual 13-19('85-'94, 68 pgs.):14-Atlantis Attacks. 16-3 pg. origin; Guardians of the Galaxy x-over.18-Polybagged w/card 3.00
...Alone Against the Celestials nn (6/92, $5.95)-r/Thor #387-389 6.00
...Legends Vol. 2: Walter Simonson Book 2 TPB (2003, $24.99) r/#349-355,357-359 25.00
...Legends Vol. 3: Walter Simonson Book 3 TPB (2004, $24.99) r/#360-369 25.00
...: The Eternals Saga TPB (2006, $24.99) r/#283-291 & Annual #7; profile pages 25.00
...: The Eternals Saga Vol. 2 TPB ('07, $24.99) r/#292-301; Thomas & Gruenwald essays 25.00
... Visionaries: Mike Deodato Jr. TPB (2004, $19.99) r/#491-494,498-500 20.00
... Visionaries: Walter Simonson (Vol. 1) TPB (5/01, $24.95) r/#337-348 25.00
... Visionaries: Walter Simonson Vol. 4 TPB (2007, $24.99) r/#371-373 & Balder the Brave #1-4 25.00
... Visionaries: Walter Simonson Vol. 5 TPB (2008, $24.95) r/#375-382 25.00
...: Worldengine (8/96, $9.95)-r/#491-494; Deodato-c/a; story & new intermission by Warren Ellis 10.00

NOTE: ***Neal Adams*** *a-180,181; c-179-181.* ***Austin*** *a-342i, 346i; c-312i.* ***Buscema*** *a(p)-178, 182-213, 215-226, 231-238, 241-253, 254r, 256-259, 272-278, 283-285, 370, Annual 6, 8, 11i; c(p)-175, 182-196, 198-200, 202-204, 206, 211, 212, 215, 219, 221, 226, 256, 259, 261, 262, 272-278, 283, 289, 370, Annual 6.* ***Everett*** *a(i)-143, 170-175; c(i)-171, 172, 174, 176, 241.* ***Gil Kane*** *a-318p; c(p)-201, 205, 207-210, 216, 220, 222, 223, 231, 233-240, 242, 243, 318.* ***Kirby*** *a(p)-126-177, 179, 194r, 254r; c(p)-126-169, 171-174, 176-178, 249-253, 255, 257, 258, Annual 5, Special 2-4.* ***Mooney*** *a(i)-201, 204, 214-216, 218, 322i, 324i, 325i, 327i.* ***Sienkiewicz*** *c-332, 333, 335.* ***Simonson*** *a-260-271p, 337-354, 357-367, 380, Annual 7p; c-260, 263-271, 337-355, 357-369, 371, 373-382, Annual 7.* ***Starlin*** *c-213.*

THOR (Volume 2)
Marvel Comics: July, 1998 - No. 85, Dec, 2004 ($2.99/$1.99/$2.25)

1-($2.99)-Follows Heroes Return; Jurgens-s/Romita Jr. & Janson-a; wraparound-c; battles the Destroyer 5.00

	GD	VG	FN	VF	VF/NM	NM-
1-Variant-c	1	2	3	5	6	8

1-Rough Cut-($2.99) Features original script and pencil pages 3.00
1-Sketch cover 20.00
2-($1.99) Two covers; Avengers app. 3.00
3-11,13-23: 3-Assumes Jake Olson ID. 4-Namor-c/app. 8-Spider-Man-c/app. 14-Iron Man c/app. 17-Juggernaut-c 2.50
12-($2.99) Wraparound-c; Hercules appears 3.00
12-($10.00) Variant-c by Jusko 10.00
24,26-31,33,34: 24-Begin $2.25-c. 26-Mignola-c/Larsen-a. 29-Andy Kubert-a. 30-Maximum Security x-over; Beta Ray Bill-c/app. 33-Intro. Thor Girl 2.50
25-($2.99) Regular edition 3.00
25-($3.99) Gold foil enhanced cover 4.00

GD 2.0 | VG 4.0 | FN 6.0 | VF 8.0 | VF/NM 9.0 | NM- 9.2

32-($3.50, 100 pgs.) new story plus reprints w/Kirby-a; Simonson-a 3.50
35-($2.99) Thor battles The Gladiator; Andy Kubert-a 3.00
36-49,51-61: 37-Starlin-a. 38,39-BWS-c. 38-42-Immonen-a. 40-Odin killed. 41-Orbik-c. 44-'Nuff Said silent issue. 51-Spider-Man app. 57-Art by various. 58-Davis-a; x-over with Iron Man #64. 60-Brereton-c 2.50
50-($4.95) Raney-c/a; back-ups w/Nuckols-a & Armenta-s/Bennett-a 5.00
62-84: 62-Begin $2.99-c. 64-Loki-c/app. 80-Oeming-s begins; Avengers app. 3.00
85-Last issue; Thor dies; Oeming-s/DiVito-a/Epting-c 3.00
...1999 Annual ($3.50) Jurgens-s/a(p) 3.50
...2000 Annual ($3.50) Jurgens-s/Ordway-a(p); back-up stories 3.50
...2001 Annual ($3.50) Jurgens-s/Grummett-a(p); Lightle-c 3.50
...Across All Worlds (9/01, $19.95, TPB) r/#28-35 20.00
Avengers Disassembled: Thor TPB (2004, $16.99) r/#80-85; afterword by Oeming 17.00
...Resurrection ($5.99, TPB) r/#1,2 6.00
...: The Dark Gods (7/00, $15.95, TPB) r/#9-13 16.00
...Vol. 1: The Death of Odin (7/02, $12.99, TPB) r/#39-44 13.00
...Vol. 2: Lord of Asgard (9/02, $15.99, TPB) r/#45-50 16.00
...Vol. 3: Gods on Earth (2003, $21.99, TPB) r/#51-58, Avengers #63, Iron Man #64, Marvel Double-Shot #1; Beck-c 22.00
...Vol. 4: Spiral (2003, $19.99, TPB) r/#59-67; Brereton-c 20.00
...Vol. 5: The Reigning (2004, $17.99, TPB) r/#68-74 18.00
...Vol. 6: Gods and Men (2004, $13.99, TPB) r/#75-79 14.00

THOR (Also see Fantastic Four #538)(Resumes original numbering with #600)
Marvel Comics: Sept, 2007 - No. 12, Mar, 2009; No. 600, Apr, 2009 - Present ($2.99/$3.99)

1-Straczynski-s/Coipel-a/c 4.00
1-Variant-c by Michael Turner 5.00
1-Zombie variant-c by Suydam 5.00
1-Non-zombie variant-c by Suydam 5.00
2-12: 2-Two covers by Dell'Otto and Coipel. 3-Iron Man app.; McGuinness var-c. 4-Bermejo var-c. 5-Campbell var-c. 6-Art Adams var-c. 7,8-Djurdjevic-a/c; Coipel var-c 3.00
2-Second printing with wraparound-c 3.00

(After #12 [Mar, 2009] numbering reverted back to original Journey Into Mystery/Thor numbering with #600, Apr, 2009)

600 (4/09, $4.99) Two wraparound-c by Coipel & Djurdjevic; Coipel, Djurdjevic & Aja-a; r/Tales of Asgard from Journey Into Mystery #106,107,112,113,115; Kirby-a 5.00
601-603-($3.99) Djurdjevic-a. 602-Sif returns 4.00
604-607-($2.99) Tan-a. 607-Siege x-over 3.00
Annual 1 (11/09, $3.99) Suayan, Grindberg, Gaudiano-a; Djurdjevic-c 4.00
...: Ages of Thunder (6/08, $3.99) Fraction-s/Zircher-a/Djurdjevic-c 4.00
... & Hercules: Encyclopædia Mythologica (2009, $4.99) profile pages of the Pantheons 5.00
... Giant-Size Finale 1 (1/01, $3.99) Dr. Doom app.; r/origin from JIM #83 4.00
... God-Size Special (2/09, $3.99) story of Skurge the Executioner re-told; art by Brereton, Braithwaite, Allred and Sepulveda; plus reprint of Thor #362 (1985) 4.00
...: Man of War (1/09, $3.99) Fraction-s/Mann & Zircher-a/Djurdjevic-c 4.00
...: Reign of Blood (8/08, $3.99) Fraction-s/Evans & Zircher-a/Djurdjevic-c 4.00
...: The Trial of Thor (12/08, $3.99) Milligan-s/Nord-c/a 4.00
...: Truth of History (12/08, $3.99) Thor and crew in ancient Egypt; Alan Davis-s/a/c 4.00
... By J. Michael Straczynski Vol. 1 HC (2008, $19.99) r/#1-6; variant cover gallery 20.00

THOR: BLOOD OATH
Marvel Comics: Nov, 2005 - No. 6, Feb, 2006 ($2.99, limited series)

1-6-Oeming-s/Kolins-a/c 3.00
HC (2006, $19.99, dust jacket) r/series; afterword by Oeming 20.00
SC (2006, $14.99) r/series; afterword by Oeming 15.00

THOR CORPS
Marvel Comics: Sept, 1993 - No. 4, Jan, 1994 ($1.75, limited series)

1-4: 1-Invaders cameo. 2-Invaders app. 3-Spider-Man 2099, Rawhide Kid, Two-Gun Kid & Kid Colt app. 4-Painted-c 2.50

THOR: GODSTORM
Marvel Comics: Nov, 2001 - No. 3, Jan, 2002 ($3.50, limited series)

1-3-Steve Rude-c/a; Busiek-s; Avengers app. 3.50

THORION OF THE NEW ASGODS
Marvel Comics (Amalgam): June, 1997 ($1.95, one-shot)

1-Keith Giffen-s/John Romita Jr.-c/a 2.50

THOR: SON OF ASGARD
Marvel Comics: May, 2004 - No. 12, Mar, 2005 ($2.99, limited series)

1-12: Teenaged Thor, Sif, and Balder; Tocchini-a. 1-6-Granov-c. 7-12-Jo Chen-c 3.00
... Vol. 1: The Warriors Teen (2004, $7.99, digest) r/#1-6 8.00
... Vol. 2: Worthy (2005, $7.99, digest) r/#7-12 8.00

THOR: TALES OF ASGARD BY STAN LEE & JACK KIRBY
Marvel Comics: 2009 - No. 6, 2009 ($3.99, limited series)

Thrax #1 © Invisible College

3-D Batman 1953 © DC

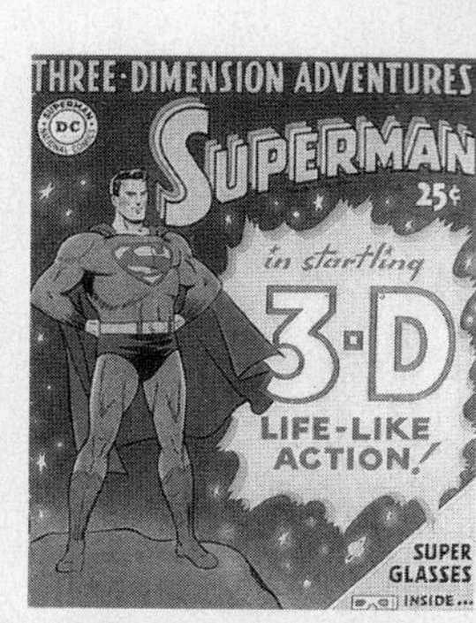

Three-Dimension Adventures © DC

	GD 2.0	VG 4.0	FN 6.0	VF 8.0	VF/NM 9.0	NM- 9.2

1-6-Reprints back-up stories from Journey Into Mystery #97-120; new covers by Coipel 4.00

THOR: THE LEGEND
Marvel Comics: Sept, 1996 ($3.95, one-shot)

nn-Tribute issue 4.00

THOR: VIKINGS
Marvel Comics (MAX): Sept, 2003 - No. 5, Jan, 2004 ($3.50, limited series)

1-5-Garth Ennis-s/Glenn Fabry-a/c 3.50
TPB (2004, $13.99) r/series 14.00

THOSE MAGNIFICENT MEN IN THEIR FLYING MACHINES (See Movie Comics)

THRAX
Event Comics: Nov, 1996 ($2.95, one-shot)

1 3.00

THREE CABALLEROS (Walt Disney's...)
Dell Publishing Co.: No. 71, 1945

Four Color 71-by Walt Kelly, c/a 62 124 186 527 1039 1550

THREE CHIPMUNKS, THE (TV) (Also see Alvin)
Dell Publishing Co.: No. 1042, Oct-Dec, 1959

Four Color 1042 (#1)-(Alvin, Simon & Theodore) 8 16 24 52 86 120

THREE COMICS (Also see Spiritman)
The Penny King Co.: 1944 (10¢, 52 pgs.) (2 different covers exist)

1,3,4-Lady Luck, Mr. Mystic, The Spirit app. (3 Spirit sections bound together); Lou Fine-a
26 52 78 154 252 350

NOTE: *No. 1 contains Spirit Sections 4/9/44 - 4/23/44, and No. 4 is also from 4/44.*

3-D (NOTE: The prices of all the 3-D comics listed include glasses. Deduct 40-50 percent if glasses are missing, and reduce slightly if glasses are loose.)

3-D ACTION
Atlas Comics (ACI): Jan, 1954 (Oversized, 15¢)(2 pairs of glasses included)

1-Battle Brady; Sol Brodsky-c 39 78 117 231 378 525

3-D ADVENTURE COMICS
Stats, Etc.: Aug, 1986 (one shot)

1-Promo material 4.00

3-D ALIEN TERROR
Eclipse Comics: June, 1986 ($2.50)

1-Old Witch, Crypt-Keeper, Vault Keeper cameo; Morrow, John Pound-a, Yeates-c 6.00
...in 2-D: 100 copies signed, numbered(B&W) 1 3 4 8 10 12

3-D ANIMAL FUN (See Animal Fun)

THREE DAYS IN EUROPE
Oni Press: Nov, 2002 - No. 5, Apr, 2003 ($2.95, B&W, limited series)

1-5-Johnston-s/Hawthorne-a 3.00
TPB (11/03, $14.95, digest-sized) r/#1-5 15.00

3-D BATMAN (Also see Batman 3-D)
National Periodical Publications: 1953 (Reprinted in 1966)

1953-(25¢)-Reprints Batman #42 & 48 (Penguin-c/story); Tommy Tomorrow story; came with pair of 3-D Bat glasses 103 206 309 659 1130 1600
1966-Reprints 1953 issue; new cover by Infantino/Anderson; has inside-c photos of Batman & Robin from TV show (50¢) 22 44 66 157 304 450

3-D CIRCUS
Fiction House Magazines (Real Adventures Publ.): 1953 (25¢, w/glasses)

1 32 64 96 188 307 425

3-D COMICS (See Mighty Mouse, Tor and Western Fighters)

3-D DOLLY
Harvey Publications: December, 1953 (25¢, came with 2 pairs of glasses)

1-Richie Rich story redrawn from his 1st app. in Little Dot #1; shows cover in 3-D on inside
47 94 141 296 498 700

3-D-ELL
Dell Publishing Co.: No. 1, 1953; No. 3, 1953 (3-D comics) (25¢, came w/glasses)

1-Rootie Kazootie (#2 does not exist) 34 68 102 199 325 450
3-Flukey Luke 32 64 96 188 307 425

3-D EXOTIC BEAUTIES
The 3-D Zone: Nov, 1990 ($2.95, 28 pgs.)

1-L.B. Cole-c 1 2 3 5 7 9

3-D FEATURES PRESENTS JET PUP
Dimensions Publications: Oct-Dec (Winter on-c), 1953 (25¢, came w/glasses)

1-Irving Spector-a(2) 34 68 102 199 325 450

3-D FUNNY MOVIES
Comic Media: 1953 (25¢, came w/glasses)

1-Bugsey Bear & Paddy Pelican 34 68 102 199 325 450

THREE-DIMENSION ADVENTURES (Superman)
National Periodical Publications: 1953 (25¢, large size, came w/glasses)

nn-Origin Superman (new art) 103 206 309 659 1130 1600

THREE DIMENSIONAL ALIEN WORLDS (See Alien Worlds)
Pacific Comics: July, 1984 (1st Ray Zone 3-D book)(one-shot)

1-Bolton-a(p); Stevens-a(i); Art Adams 1st published-a(p) 6.00

THREE DIMENSIONAL DNAGENTS (See New DNAgents)

THREE DIMENSIONAL E. C. CLASSICS (Three Dimensional Tales From the Crypt No. 2)
E. C. Comics: Spring, 1954 (Prices include glasses; came with 2 pair)

1-Stories by Wood (Mad #3), Krigstein (W.S. #7), Evans (F.C. #13), & Ingels (CSS #5); Kurtzman-c (rare in high grade due to unstable paper)
94 188 282 597 1024 1450

NOTE: *Stories redrawn to 3-D format. Original stories not necessarily by artists listed. CSS: Crime SuspenStories; F.C.: Frontline Combat; W.S.: Weird Science.*

THREE DIMENSIONAL TALES FROM THE CRYPT (Formerly Three Dimensional E. C. Classics)(Cover title: ...From the Crypt of Terror)
E. C. Comics: No. 2, Spring, 1954 (Prices include glasses; came with 2 pair)

2-Davis (TFTC #25), Elder (VOH #14), Craig (TFTC #24), & Orlando (TFTC #22) stories; Feldstein-c (rare in high grade) 92 184 276 584 1005 1425

NOTE: *Stories redrawn to 3-D format. Original stories not necessarily by artists listed. TFTC: Tales From the Crypt; VOH: Vault of Horror.*

3-D LOVE
Steriographic Publ. (Mikeross Publ.): Dec, 1953 (25¢, came w/glasses)

1 34 68 102 199 325 450

3-D NOODNICK (See Noodnick)

3-D ROMANCE
Steriographic Publ. (Mikeross Publ.): Jan, 1954 (25¢, came w/glasses)

1 34 68 102 199 325 450

3-D SHEENA, JUNGLE QUEEN (Also see Sheena 3-D)
Fiction House Magazines: 1953 (25¢, came w/glasses)

1-Maurice Whitman-c 68 136 204 432 746 1060

3-D SUBSTANCE
The 3-D Zone: July, 1990 ($2.95, 28 pgs.)

1-Ditko-c/a(r) 5.00

3-D TALES OF THE WEST
Atlas Comics (CPS): Jan, 1954 (Oversized) (15¢, came with 2 pair of glasses)

1 (3-D)-Sol Brodsky-c 39 78 117 231 378 525

3-D THREE STOOGES (Also see Three Stooges)
Eclipse Comics: Sept, 1986 - No. 2, Nov, 1986; No. 3, Oct, 1987; No. 4, 1989 ($2.50)

1-4: 3-Maurer-r. 4-r-/"Three Missing Links" 5.00
1-3 (2-D) 5.00

3-D WHACK (See Whack)

3-D ZONE, THE
The 3-D Zone (Renegade Press)/Ray Zone: Feb, 1987 - No. 20, 1989 ($2.50)

1,3,4,7-9,11,12,14,15,17,19,20: 1-r/A Star Presentation. 3-Picture Scope Jungle Advs. 4-Electric Fear. 7-Hollywood 3-D Jayne Mansfield photo-c. 8-High Seas 3-D, 9-Redmask-r. 11-Danse Macabre; Matt Fox c/a(r). 12-3-D Presidents. 14-Tyranostar. 15-3-Dementia Comics; Kurtzman-c, Kubert, Maurer-a. 17-Thrilling Love. 19-Cracked Classics. 20-Commander Battle and His Atomic Submarine 1 2 3 5 6 8
2,5,6,10,13,16,18: 2-Wolverton-r. 5-Krazy Kat-r. 6-Ratfink. 10-Jet 3-D; Powell & Williamson-r. 13-Flash Gordon. 16-Space Vixens; Dave Stevens-c/a. 18-Spacehawk; Wolverton-r
1 2 3 5 7 9

NOTE: ***Davis** r-19. **Ditko** r-19. **Elder** r-19. **Everett** r-19. **Feldstein** r-17. **Frazetta** r-17. **Heath** r-19. **Kamen** r-17. **Severin** r-19. **Ward** r-17,19. **Wolverton** r-2,18,19. **Wood** r-1,17. Photo c-12*

3 GEEKS, THE (Also see Geeksville)
3 Finger Prints: 1996 - No. 11, Jun, 1999 (B&W)

1,2 -Rich Koslowski-s/a in all 1 2 3 5 6 8
1-(2nd printing) 2.50
3-7, 9-11 2.50
8-(48 pgs.) 4.00
10-Variant-c 3.50
...48 Page Super-Sized Summer Spectacular (7/04, $4.95) 5.00

3 Geeks: Slab Madness! #1 © Rich Koslowski

300 #2 © Frank Miller

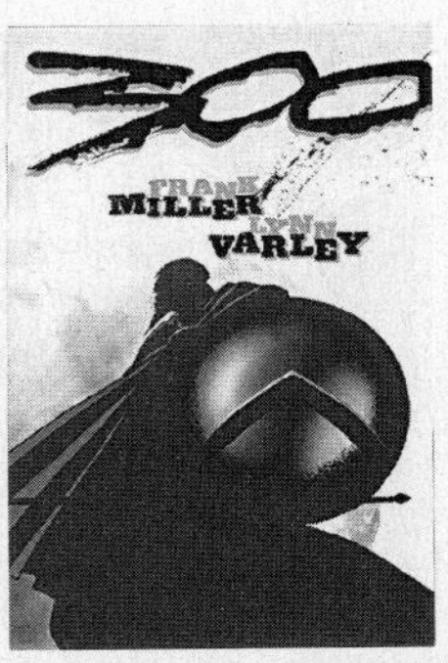

Thrilling Comics #7 © BP

GD 2.0 | VG 4.0 | FN 6.0 | VF 8.0 | VF/NM 9.0 | NM- 9.2

...Full Circle (7/03, $4.95) Origin story of the 3 Geeks; "Buck Rodinski" app. 5.00
How to Pick Up Girls If You're a Comic Book Geek (color)(7/97) 4.00
When the Hammer Falls TPB (2001, $14.95) r/#8-11 15.00

3 GEEKS: SLAB MADNESS!
3 Finger Prints: Sept, 2008 - No. 3, Mar, 2009 ($2.99, B&W, limited series)
1-3-Rich Koslowski-s/a; intro. The Cee-Gee-Cee 3.00

300 (Adapted for 2007 movie)
Dark Horse Comics: May, 1998 - No. 5, Sept, 1998 ($2.95/$3.95, limited series)
1-Frank Miller-s/c/a; Spartans vs. Persians war 15.00
1-Second printing 5.00
2-4 8.00
5-($3.95-c) 12.00
HC ($30.00) -oversized reprint of series 30.00

3 LITTLE KITTENS
BroadSword Comics: Aug, 2002 - No. 3, Dec, 2002 ($2.95, limited series)
1-3-Jim Balent-s/a; two covers 3.00

3 LITTLE PIGS (Disney)(...and the Wonderful Magic Lamp)
Dell Publishing Co.: No. 218, Mar, 1949
Four Color 218 (#1) 10 20 30 71 126 180

3 LITTLE PIGS, THE (See Walt Disney Showcase #15 & 21)
Gold Key: May, 1964; No. 2, Sept, 1968 (Walt Disney)
1-Reprints Four Color #218 3 6 9 20 30 40
2 3 6 9 15 21 26

THREE MOUSEKETEERS, THE (1st Series)(See Funny Stuff #1)
National Per. Publ.: 3-4/56 - No. 24, 9-10/59; No. 25, 8-9/60 - No. 26, 10-12/60
1 16 32 48 113 217 320
2 9 18 27 65 113 160
3-5,7,9,10 7 14 21 49 80 110
6,8-Grey tone-c 9 18 27 60 100 140
11-26: 24-Cover says 11/59, inside says 9-10/59 6 12 18 43 69 95
NOTE: *Rube Grossman a-1-26. Sheldon Mayer a-1-8; c-1-7.*

THREE MOUSEKETEERS, THE (2nd Series) (See Super DC Giant)
National Periodical Publications: May-June, 1970 - No. 7, May-June, 1971 (#5-7: 68 pgs.)
1-Mayer-r in all 5 10 15 34 55 75
2-4: 4-Doodles Duck begins (1st app.) 4 8 12 22 34 45
5-7:(68 pgs.). 5-Dodo & the Frog, Bo Bunny begin 5 10 15 32 51 70

THREE MUSKETEERS, THE (Also see Disney's The Three Musketeers)
Gemstone Publishing: 2004 ($3.95, squarebound, one-shot)
nn-Adaptation of the 2004 DVD movie; Petrossi-c/a 4.00

THREE NURSES (Confidential Diary #12-17; Career Girl Romances #24 on)
Charlton Comics: V3#18, May, 1963 - V3#23, Mar, 1964
V3#18-23 3 6 9 18 27 35

THREE RASCALS
I. W. Enterprises: 1958; 1963
I.W. Reprint #1,2,10: 1-(Says Super Comics on inside)-(M.E.'s Clubhouse Rascals) DeCarlo-a. #2-(1958). 10-(1963)-r/#1 2 4 6 8 10 12

THREE RING COMICS
Spotlight Publishers: March, 1945
1-Funny animal 16 32 48 92 144 195

THREE RING COMICS (Also see Captain Wizard & Meteor Comics)
Century Publications: April, 1946
1-Prankster-c; Captain Wizard, Impossible Man, Race Wilkins, King O'Leary, & Dr. Mercy app. 35 70 105 208 339 470

THREE ROCKETEERS (See Blast-Off)

THREE STOOGES (See Comic Album #18, Top Comics, The Little Stooges, March of Comics #232, 248, 268, 280, 292, 304, 316, 336, 373, Movie Classics & Comics & 3-D Three Stooges)

THREE STOOGES
Jubilee No. 1/St. John No. 1 (9/53) on: Feb, 1949 - No. 2, May, 1949; Sept, 1953 - No. 7, Oct, 1954
1-(Scarce, 1949)-Kubert-a; infinity-c 116 232 348 742 1271 1800
2-(Scarce)-Kubert, Maurer-a 81 162 243 518 884 1250
1(9/53)-Hollywood Stunt Girl by Kubert (7 pgs.) 68 136 204 432 746 1060
2(3-D, 10/53, 25¢)-Came w/glasses; Stunt Girl story by Kubert 48 96 144 302 514 725
3(3-D, 10/53, 25¢)-Came w/glasses; has 3-D-c 45 90 135 284 480 675

GD 2.0 | VG 4.0 | FN 6.0 | VF 8.0 | VF/NM 9.0 | NM- 9.2

4(3/54)-7(10/54): 4-1st app. Li'l Stooge? 39 78 117 240 395 550
NOTE: *All issues have **Kubert-Maurer** art & **Maurer** covers. 6, 7-Partial photo-c.*

THREE STOOGES
Dell Publishing Co./Gold Key No. 10 (10/62) on: No. 1043, Oct-Dec, 1959 - No. 55, June, 1972
Four Color 1043 (#1) 23 46 69 168 324 480
Four Color 1078,1127,1170,1187 12 24 36 86 158 230
6(9-11/61) - 10: 6-Professor Putter begins; ends #16 10 20 30 68 119 170
11-14,16,18-20 8 16 24 56 93 130
15-Go Around the World in a Daze (movie scenes) 9 18 27 60 100 140
17-The Little Monsters begin (5/64)(1st app.?) 9 18 27 60 100 140
21,23-30 7 14 21 45 73 100
22-Movie scenes from "The Outlaws Is Coming" 7 14 21 49 80 110
31-55 5 10 15 34 55 75
NOTE: *All Four Colors, 6-50, 52-55 have photo-c.*

THREE STOOGES IN 3-D, THE
Eternity Comics: 1991 ($3.95, high quality paper, w/glasses)
1-Reprints Three Stooges by Gold Key; photo-c 5.00

THREE STRIKES
Oni Press: Apr, 2003 - No. 5, Oct, 2003 ($2.99, B&W, limited series)
1-5-Brian Hurtt-a/DeFilippis & Weir-s 3.00
TPB (3/04, $14.95, digest-size) r/#1-5; Ed Brubaker intro. 15.00

3 WORLDS OF GULLIVER
Dell Publishing Co.: No. 1158, July, 1961 (2 issues exist with diff. covers)
Four Color 1158-Movie, photo-c 7 14 21 45 73 100

THRILL COMICS (See Flash Comics, Fawcett)

THRILLER
DC Comics: Nov, 1983 - No. 12, Nov, 1984 ($1.25, Baxter paper)
1-12: 1-Intro Seven Seconds; Von Eeden-c/a begins. 2-Origin. 5,6-Elvis satire 2.50

THRILLING ADVENTURES IN STAMPS COMICS (Formerly Stamp Comics)
Stamp Comics, Inc. (Very Rare): V1#8, Jan, 1953 (25¢, 100 pgs.)
V1#8-Harrison, Wildey, Kiefer, Napoli-a 75 150 225 476 818 1160

THRILLING ADVENTURE STORIES (See Tigerman)
Atlas/Seaboard Publ.: Feb, 1975 - No. 2, Aug, 1975 (B&W, 68 pgs.)
1-Tigerman, Kromag the Killer begin; Heath, Thorne-a; Doc Savage movie photos of Ron Ely 3 6 9 16 22 28
2-Heath, Toth, Severin, Simonson-a; Adams-c 3 6 9 20 30 40

THRILLING COMICS
Better Publ./Nedor/Standard Comics: Feb, 1940 - No. 80, April, 1951
1-Origin & 1st app. Dr. Strange (37 pgs.), ends #?; Nickie Norton of the Secret Service begins 300 600 900 2010 3505 5000
2-The Rio Kid, The Woman in Red, Pinocchio begins 132 264 396 838 1444 2050
3-The Ghost & Lone Eagle begin 86 172 258 546 936 1325
4-6,8-10 (11/40): 5-Dr. Strange changed to Doc Strange. 10-1st WWII-c (Nazi) 66 132 198 419 722 1025
7-Classic-c 90 180 270 576 988 1400
11-18,20 58 116 174 371 636 900
19-Origin & 1st app. The American Crusader (8/41), ends #39,41 65 130 195 416 708 1000
21-30: 24-Intro. Mike, Doc Strange's sidekick (1/42). 27-Robot-c. 29-Last Rio Kid 52 104 156 328 557 785
31-40: 36-Commando Cubs begin (7/43, 1st app.) 47 94 141 296 498 700
41-Classic Hitler & Mussolin WWII-c 129 258 387 826 1413 2000
42,43,45-51: 45-Hitler pict. on-c. 51(12/45)-Last WWII-c (Japanese) 40 80 120 246 411 575
44-Hitler WWII-c 119 238 357 762 1306 1850
52-Classic Schomburg hooded bondage-c; the Ghost ends 61 122 183 390 670 950
53,54: 53-The Phantom Detective begins. The Cavalier app. in both; no Commando Cubs in either 39 78 117 240 395 550
55-The Lone Eagle ends 38 76 114 228 369 510
56 (10/46)-Princess Pantha begins (not on-c), 1st app. 48 96 144 302 514 725
57-Doc Strange-c; 2nd Princess Pantha 42 84 126 265 445 625
58-66: All Princess Pantha jungle-c, w/Doc Strange #59, his last-c. 61-Ingels-a; The Lone Eagle app. 65-Last Phantom Detective & Commando Cubs. 66-Frazetta text illo 40 80 120 246 411 575

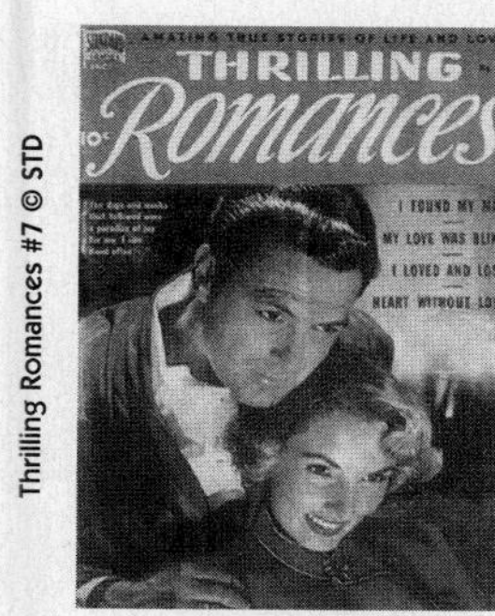

Thrilling Romances #7 © STD

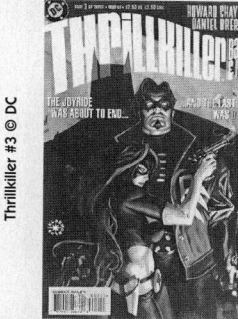

Thrillkiller #3 © DC

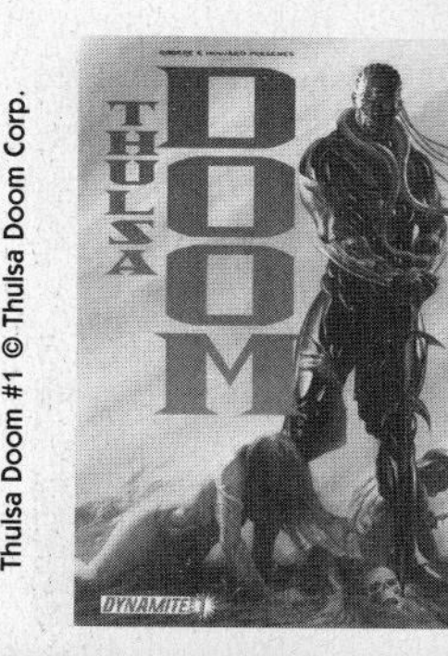

Thulsa Doom #1 © Thulsa Doom Corp.

	GD 2.0	VG 4.0	FN 6.0	VF 8.0	VF/NM 9.0	NM- 9.2

67,70,71-Last jungle-c; Frazetta-a(5-7 pgs.) in each 47 94 141 296 498 700
68,69-Frazetta-a(2), 8 & 6 pgs.; 9 & 7 pgs. 50 100 150 315 533 750
72,73: 72-Buck Ranger, Cowboy Detective c/stys begin (western theme), end #80;
Frazetta-a(5-7 ps.) in each 43 86 129 271 461 650
74-Last Princess Pantha; Tara app. 34 68 102 205 335 465
75-78: 75-All western format begins 14 28 42 81 118 155
79-Krigstein-a 15 30 45 83 124 165
80-Severin & Elder, Celardo, Moreira-a 15 30 45 83 124 165
NOTE: *Bondage c-5, 9, 13, 20, 22, 27-30, 38, 41, 52, 54, 70.* ***Kinstler*** *a-45.* ***Leo Morey*** *a-7.* ***Schomburg*** *(sometimes signed as* ***Xela****) c-7, 9-19, 36-80 (airbrush 62-71).* ***Tuska*** *a-62, 63. Woman in Red not in #19, 23, 31-33, 39-45. No. 45 exists as a Canadian reprint but numbered #48. No. 72 exists as a Canadian reprint with no* ***Frazetta*** *story. American Crusader c-20-24. Buck Ranger c-72-80. Commando Cubs c-37, 39, 41, 43, 45, 47, 49, 51. Doc Strange c-1-19, 25-36, 38, 40, 42, 44, 46, 48, 50, 52-57, 59. Princess Pantha c-58, 60-71.*

THRILLING COMICS (Also see All Star Comics 1999 crossover titles)
DC Comics: May, 1999 ($1.99, one-shot)
1-Golden Age Hawkman and Wildcat; Russ Heath-a 2.50

THRILLING CRIME CASES (Formerly 4Most; becomes Shocking Mystery Cases #50 on)
Star Publications: No. 41, June-July, 1950 - No. 49, July, 1952
41 28 56 84 165 270 375
42-45: 42-L. B. Cole-c/a (1); Chameleon story (Fox-r)
25 50 75 147 241 335
46-48: 47-Used in **POP**, pg. 84 24 48 72 142 234 325
49-(7/52)-Classic L. B. Cole-c 45 90 135 284 480 675
NOTE: ***L. B. Cole*** *c-all; a-43p, 45p, 46p, 49(2 pgs.).* ***Disbrow*** *a-48.* ***Hollingsworth*** *a-48.*

THRILLING ROMANCES
Standard Comics: No. 5, Dec, 1949 - No. 26, June, 1954
5 15 30 45 84 127 170
6,8 10 20 30 56 76 95
7-Severin/Elder-a (7 pgs.) 12 24 36 67 94 120
9,10-Severin/Elder-a; photo-c 11 22 33 62 86 110
11,14-21,26: 14-Gene Tierney & Danny Kaye photo-c from movie "On the Riviera".
15-Tony Martin/Janet Leigh photo-c 9 18 27 52 69 85
12-Wood-a (2 pgs.); Tyrone Power/ Susan Hayward photo-c
12 24 36 69 97 125
13-Severin-a 10 20 30 56 76 95
22-25-Toth-a 11 22 33 62 86 110
NOTE: *All photo-c.* ***Celardo*** *a-9, 16.* ***Colletta*** *a-23, 24(2).* ***Toth*** *text illos-19.* ***Tuska*** *a-9.*

THRILLING SCIENCE TALES
AC Comics: 1989 - No. 2 ($3.50, 2/3 color, 52 pgs.)
1,2: 1-r/Bob Colt #6(saucer); Frazetta, Guardineer (Space Ace), Wood, Krenkel, Orlando, Williamson-r; Kaluta-c. 2-Capt. Video-r by Evans, Capt. Science-r by Wood, Star Pirate-r by Whitman & Mysta of the Moon-r by Moreira 4.00

THRILLING TRUE STORY OF THE BASEBALL...
Fawcett Publications: 1952 (Photo-c, each)
...Giants-photo-c; has Willie Mays rookie photo-biography; Willie Mays, Eddie Stanky & others photos on-c 68 136 204 432 746 1060
...Yankees-photo-c; Yogi Berra, Joe DiMaggio, Mickey Mantle & others photos on-c
66 132 198 419 722 1025

THRILLING WONDER TALES
AC Comics : 1991 ($2.95, B&W)
1-Includes a Bob Powell Thun'da story 3.00

THRILLKILLER
DC Comics : Jan, 1997 - No. 3, Mar, 1997($2.50, limited series)
1-3-Elseworlds Robin & Batgirl; Chaykin-s/Brereton-c/a 3.00
...'62 ('98, $4.95, one-shot) Sequel; Chaykin-s/Brereton-c/a 5.00
TPB-(See Batman: Thrillkiller)

THRILLOGY
Pacific Comics: Jan, 1984 (One-shot, color)
1-Conrad-c/a 3.00

THRILL-O-RAMA
Harvey Publications (Fun Films): Oct, 1965 - No. 3, Dec, 1966
1-Fate (Man in Black) by Powell app.; Doug Wildey-a(2); Simon-c
5 10 15 34 55 75
2-Pirana begins (see Phantom #46); Williamson 2 pgs.; Fate (Man in Black)
app.; Tuska/Simon-c 4 8 12 22 34 45
3-Fate (Man in Black) app.; Sparling-c 3 6 9 19 29 38

THRILLS OF TOMORROW (Formerly Tomb of Terror)
Harvey Publications: No. 17, Oct, 1954 - No. 20, April, 1955
17-Powell-a (horror); r/Witches Tales #7 15 30 45 88 137 185
18-Powell-a (horror); r/Tomb of Terror #1 14 28 42 82 121 160
19,20-Stuntman-c/stories by S&K (r/from Stuntman #1 & 2); 19 has origin &
is last pre-code (2/55) 31 62 93 182 296 410
NOTE: ***Kirby*** *c-19, 20.* ***Palais*** *a-17.* ***Simon*** *c-18?*

THROBBING LOVE (See Fox Giants)

THROUGH GATES OF SPLENDOR
Spire Christian Comics (Flemming H. Revell Co.): 1973, 1974 (36 pages) (39-49 cents)
nn-1973 Edition 2 4 6 9 12 15
nn-1974 Edition 1 3 4 6 8 10

THULSA DOOM (Robert E. Howard character)
Dynamite Entertainment: 2009 - No. 4, 2009 ($3.50, limited series)
1-4-Alex Ross-c/Lui Antonio-a 3.00

THUMPER (Disney)
Dell Publishing Co.: No, 19, 1942 - No. 243, Sept, 1949
Four Color 19-Walt Disney's...Meets the Seven Dwarfs; reprinted in Silly Symphonies
46 92 138 368 709 1050
Four Color 243-...Follows His Nose 11 22 33 78 139 200

THUN'DA (...King of the Congo)
Magazine Enterprises: 1952 - No. 6, 1953
1(A-1 #47)-Origin; Frazetta c/a; only comic done entirely by Frazetta; all Thun'da stories, no Cave Girl 152 304 456 965 1658 2350
2(A-1 #56)-Powell-c/a begins, ends #6; Intro/1st app. Cave Girl in filler strip (also app. in 3-6)
23 46 69 136 223 310
3(A-1 #73), 4(A-1 #78) 17 34 51 98 154 210
5(A-1 #83), 6(A-1 #86) 15 30 45 94 147 200

THUN'DA TALES (See Frank Frazetta's...)

THUNDER AGENTS (See Dynamo, Noman & Tales Of Thunder)
Tower Comics: 11/65 - No. 17, 12/67; No. 18, 9/68, No. 19, 11/68, No. 20, 11/69 (No. 1-16: 68 pgs.; No. 17 on: 52 pgs.)(All are 25¢)
1-Origin & 1st app. Dynamo, Noman, Menthor, & The Thunder Squad; 1st app.
The Iron Maiden 18 36 54 129 252 375
2-Death of Egghead; A-bomb blast panel 10 20 30 70 123 175
3-5: 4-Guy Gilbert becomes Lightning who joins Thunder Squad; Iron Maiden app.
8 16 24 54 90 125
6-10: 7-Death of Menthor. 8-Origin & 1st app. The Raven
6 12 18 43 69 95
11-15: 13-Undersea Agent app.; no Raven story 6 12 18 39 62 85
16-19 6 12 18 37 59 80
20-Special Collectors Edition; all reprints 4 8 12 26 41 55
...Archives Vol. 1 (DC Comics, 2003, $49.95, HC) r/#1-4, restored and recolored 50.00
...Archives Vol. 2 (DC Comics, 2003, $49.95, HC) r/#5-7, Dynamo #1 50.00
...Archives Vol. 3 (DC Comics, 2003, $49.95, HC) r/#8-10, Dynamo #2 50.00
...Archives Vol. 4 (DC Comics, 2004, $49.95, HC) r/#11, Noman #1,2 & Dynamo #3 50.00
NOTE: ***Crandall*** *a-1, 4p, 5p, 18, 20r; c-18.* ***Ditko*** *a-6, 7p, 12p, 13?, 14p, 16, 18.* ***Giunta*** *a-6.* ***Kane*** *a-1, 5p, 6p?, 14, 16p; c-14, 15.* ***Reinman*** *a-13.* ***Sekowsky*** *a-6.* ***Tuska*** *a-1p, 7, 8, 10, 13-17, 19.* ***Whitney*** *a-9p, 10, 13, 15, 17, 18; c-17.* ***Wood*** *a-1-11, 15(w/****Ditko****-12, 18), (inks-#9, 13, 14, 16, 17), 19i, 20r; c-1-8, 9i, 10-13(#10 w/****Williamson****(p)), 16.*

T.H.U.N.D.E.R. AGENTS (See Blue Ribbon Comics, Hall of Fame Featuring the..., JCP Features & Wally Wood's...)
JC Comics (Archie Publications): May, 1983 - No. 2, Jan, 1984
1,2: 1-New Manna/Blyberg-c/a. 2-Blyberg-c 6.00

THUNDER BIRDS (See Cinema Comics Herald)

THUNDERBOLT (See The Atomic...)

THUNDERBOLT (Peter Cannon...; see Crisis on Infinite Earths & Peter...)
Charlton Comics: Jan, 1966; No. 51, Mar-Apr, 1966 - No. 60, Nov, 1967
1-Origin & 1st app. Thunderbolt 4 8 12 28 44 60
51-(Formerly Son of Vulcan #50) 3 6 9 20 30 40
52-59: 54-Sentinels begin. 59-Last Thunderbolt & Sentinels (back-up story)
3 6 9 14 19 24
60-Prankster app. 3 6 9 15 21 26
57,58 ('77)-Modern Comics-r 4.00
NOTE: ***Aparo*** *a-60.* ***Morisi*** *a-1, 51-56, 58; c-1, 51-56, 58, 59.*

THUNDERBOLT JAXON (Revival of 1940s British comics character)
DC Comics (WildStorm): Apr, 2006 - No. 5, Sept, 2006 ($2.99, limited series)
1-5-Dave Gibbons-s/John Higgins-a 3.00
TPB (2007, $19.99) r/#1-5; intro. by Gibbons; cover gallery 20.00

THUNDERBOLTS (Also see New Thunderbolts and Incredible Hulk #449)

Thunderbolts #126 © MAR

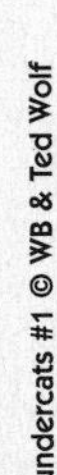

Thundercats #1 © WB & Ted Wolf

The Tick #10 © Ben Edlund

Marvel Comics: Apr, 1997 - No. 81, Sept, 2003; No. 100, May, 2006 - Present ($1.95-$2.99)

1-($2.99)-Busiek-s/Bagley-c/a 1 2 3 5 7 9
1-2nd printing; new cover colors 2.50
2-4: 2-Two covers. 4-Intro. Jolt 6.00
5-11: 9-Avengers app. 3.50
12-($2.99)-Avengers and Fantastic Four-c/app. 4.00
13-24: 14-Thunderbolts return to Earth. 21-Hawkeye app. 2.50
25-($2.99) Wraparound-c 3.00
26-38: 26-Manco-a 2.50
39-($2.99) 100 Page Monster; Iron Man reprints 3.00
40-49: 40-Begin $2.25-c; Sandman-c/app. 44-Avengers app. 47-Captain Marvel app. 49-Zircher-a 2.50
50-($2.99) Last Bagley-a; Captain America becomes leader 3.00
51-74,76,77,80,81: 51,52-Zircher-a; Dr. Doom app. 80,81-Spider-Man app. 2.50
75-($3.50) Hawkeye leaves the team; Garcia-a 3.50
78,79-($2.99-c) Velasco-a begins 3.00
(See New Thunderbolts for #82-99)
100 (5/06, $3.99) resumes from New Thunderbolts #18; back-up origin stories 4.00
101-109: 103-105-Civil War x-over 3.00
110-New team begins including Bullseye, Venom and Norman Osborn; Ellis-s/Deodato-a 5.00
111-136,138-141: 111-121-Ellis-s/Deodato-a. 112-Stan Lee cameo. 123-125-Secret Invasion x-over. 128-Dark Reign begins. 130,131-X-over with Deadpool #8,9. 141-Siege 3.00
137-(12/09, $3.99) Iron Fist and Luke Cage app. 4.00
Annual '97 ($2.99)-Wraparound-c 3.00
Annual 2000 ($3.50) Breyfogle-a 3.50
...: Breaking Point (1/08, $2.99, one-shot) Gage-s/Denham-a/Djurdjevic-c 3.00
... By Warren Ellis Vol. 1 HC (2007, $24.99, dustjacket) r/#150-154, ...: Desperate Measures and stories from Civil War: Choosing Sides and The Initiative 25.00
... By Warren Ellis Vol. 1: Faith in Monsters SC (2008, $19.99) same contents as HC 20.00
Civil War: Thunderbolts TPB (2007, $13.99) r/#101-105 14.00
...: Desperate Measures (9/07, $2.99, one-shot) Jenkins-s/Steve Lieber-a 3.00
...: Distant Rumblings (#-1) (7/97, $1.95) Busiek-s 5.00
First Strikes (1997, $4.99,TPB) r/#1,2 5.00
...: Guardian Protocols (2007, $10.99) r/#106-109 11.00
...: International Incident (4/08, $2.99, one-shot) Gage-s/Oliver-a/Djurdjevic-c 3.00
...: Life Sentences (7/01, $3.50) Adlard-a 3.50
...: Marvel's Most Wanted TPB ('98, $16.99) r/origin stories of original Masters of Evil 17.00
...: Reason in Madness (7/08, $2.99, one-shot) Gage-s/Oliver-a/Djurdjevic-c 3.00
Wizard #0 (bagged with Wizard #89) 2.50

THUNDERBOLTS PRESENTS: ZEMO - BORN BETTER
Marvel Comics: Apr, 2007 - No. 4, July, 2007 ($2.99, limited series)

1-4-History of Baron Zemo; Nicieza-s/Grummett-a/c 3.00
TPB (2007, $10.99) r/#1-4 11.00

THUNDERBUNNY (See Blue Ribbon Comics #13, Charlton Bullseye & Pep Comics #393)
Red Circle Comics: Jan, 1984 (Direct sale only)
WaRP Graphics: Second series No. 1, 1985 - No. 6, 1985
Apple Comics: No. 7, 1986 - No. 12, 1987

1-Humor/parody; origin Thunderbunny; 2 page pin-up by Anderson 5.00
(2nd series) 1,2-Magazine size 3.00
3-12-Comic size 2.50

THUNDERCATS (TV)
Marvel Comics (Star Comics)/Marvel #22 on: Dec, 1985 - No. 24, June, 1988 (75¢)

1-Mooney-c/a begins 2 4 6 8 11 14
2-20: 2-(65¢ & 75¢ cover exists). 12-Begin $1.00-c. 18-20-Williamson-i 1 2 3 5 7 9
21-24: 23-Williamson-c(i) 1 3 4 6 8 10

THUNDERCATS (TV)
DC Comics (WildStorm): No. 0, Oct, 2002 - No. 5, Feb, 2003 ($2.50/$2.95, limited series)

0-($2.50) J. Scott Campbell-c/a 3.00
1-5-($2.95) 1-McGuinness-a/c; variant cover by Art Adams; rebirth of Mumm-Ra 3.00
.../ Battle of the Planets (7/03, $4.95) Kaare Andrews-s/a; 2 covers by Campbell & Ross 5.00
...: Origins-Heroes & Villains (2/04, $3.50) short stories by various 3.50
...Reclaiming Thundera TPB (2003, $12.95) r/#0-5 13.00
... Sourcebook (1/03, $2.95) pin-ups and info on characters; art by various; A. Adams-c 3.00

THUNDERCATS: DOGS OF WAR
DC Comics (WildStorm): Aug, 2003 - No. 5, Dec, 2003 ($2.95, limited series)

1-5: 1-Two covers by Booth & Pearson; Booth-a/Layman-s. 2-4-Two covers 3.00
TPB (2004, $14.95) r/#1-5 15.00

THUNDERCATS: ENEMY'S PRIDE
DC Comics (WildStorm): Aug, 2004 - No. 5 ($2.95, limited series)

1-5-Vriens-a/Layman-s 3.00
TPB (2005, $14.99) r/#1-5 15.00

THUNDERCATS: HAMMERHAND'S REVENGE
DC Comics (WildStorm): Dec, 2003 - No. 5, Apr, 2004 ($2.95, limited series)

1-5-Avery-s/D'Anda-a. 2-Variant-c by Warren 3.00
TPB (2004, $14.95) r/#1-5 15.00

THUNDERCATS: THE RETURN
DC Comics (WildStorm): Apr, 2003 - No. 5, Aug, 2003 ($2.95, limited series)

1-5: 1-Two covers by Benes & Cassaday; Gilmore-s 3.00
TPB (2004, $12.95) r/series 13.00

THUNDER MOUNTAIN (See Zane Grey, Four Color #246)

THUNDERSTRIKE (See Thor #459)
Marvel Comics: June, 1993 - No. 24, July, 1995 ($1.25)

1-($2.95, 52 pgs.)-Holo-grafx lightning patterned foil-c; Bloodaxe returns 3.00
2-24: 2-Juggernaut-c/s. 4-Capt. America app. 4-6-Spider-Man app. 8-bound-in trading card sheet. 18-Bloodaxe app. 24-Death of Thunderstrike 2.50
Marvel Double Feature...Thunderstrike/Code Blue #13 ($2.50)-Same as Thunderstrike #13 w/Code Blue flip book 2.50

TICK, THE (Also see The Chroma-Tick)
New England Comics Press: Jun, 1988 - No. 12, May, 1993 ($1.75/$1.95/$2.25; B&W, over-sized)

Special Edition 1-1st comic book app. serially numbered & limited to 5,000 copies 5 10 15 34 55 75
Special Edition 1-(5/96, $5.95)-Double-c; foil-c; serially numbered (5,001 thru 14,000) & limited to 9,000 copies 6.00
Special Edition 2-Serially numbered and limited to 3000 copies 5 10 15 30 48 65
Special Edition 2-(8/96, $5.95)-Double-c; foil-c; serially numbered (5,001 thru 14,000) & limited to 9,000 copies 1 3 5 6 8
1-Regular Edition 1st printing; reprints Special Ed. 1 w/minor changes 4 8 12 24 37 50
1-2nd printing 6.00
1-3rd-5th printing 3.00
2-Reprints Special Ed. 2 w/minor changes 2 4 6 13 18 22
2-8-All reprints 3.00
3-5 ($1.95): 4-1st app. Paul the Samurai 1 3 4 6 8 10
6,8 ($2.25) 5.00
7-1st app. Man-Eating Cow 6.00
8-Variant with no logo, price, issue number or company logos. 2 4 6 10 14 18
9-12 ($2.75) 4.00
12-Special Edition; card-stock, virgin foil-c; numbered edition 2 4 6 13 18 22
Pseudo-Tick #13 (11/00, $3.50) Continues story from #12 (1993) 4.00
Promo Sampler-(1990)-Tick-c/story 1 2 3 5 6 8

TICK, THE (One shots)

... Big Back to School Special 1-(10/98, $3.50, B&W) Tick & Arthur undercover in H.S. 3.50
... Big Cruise Ship Vacation Special 1-(9/00, $3.50, B&W) 3.50
... Big Father's Day Special 1-(6/00, $3.50, B&W) 3.50
... Big Halloween Special 1-(10/99, $3.50, B&W) 3.50
... Big Halloween Special 2000 (10/00, $3.50) 3.50
... Big Halloween Special 2001 (9/01, $3.95) 4.00
... Big Mother's Day Special 1-(4/00, $3.50, B&W) 3.50
... Big Red-N-Green Christmas Spectacle 1-(12/01, $3.95) 4.00
... Big Romantic Adventure 1-(2/98, $2.95, B&W) Candy box-c with candy map on back 3.50
... Big Summer Annual 1-(7/99, $3.50, B&W) Chainsaw Vigilante vs. Barry 3.50
... Big Summer Fun Special 1-(8/98, $3.50, B&W) Tick and Arthur at summer camp 3.50
... Big Tax Time Terror 1-(4/00, $3.50, B&W) 3.50
... Big Year 2000 Spectacle 1-(3/00, $3.50, B&W) 3.50
... Incredible Internet Comic 1-(7/01, $3.95, color) r/New England Comics website story 4.00
Introducing the Tick 1-(4/02, $3.95, color) summary of Tick's life and adventures 4.00
The Tick's Back #0 -(8/97, $2.95, B&W) 3.00
The Tick's Comic Con Extravaganza -(6/07, $3.95, color) Wang-c 4.00
The Tick's 20th Anniversary Special Edition #1 (5/07, $5.95) short stories by various; history of the character; creator profiles; 2 covers by Suydam & Bisley 6.00

--MASSIVE SUMMER DOUBLE SPECTACLE
1,2-(7,8/00, $3.50, B&W) 3.50

TICK & ARTIE
1-(6/02, $3.50, color) prints strips from Internet comic 3.50
2-(10/02, $3.95) 4.00

Tick Tock Tales #3 © ME

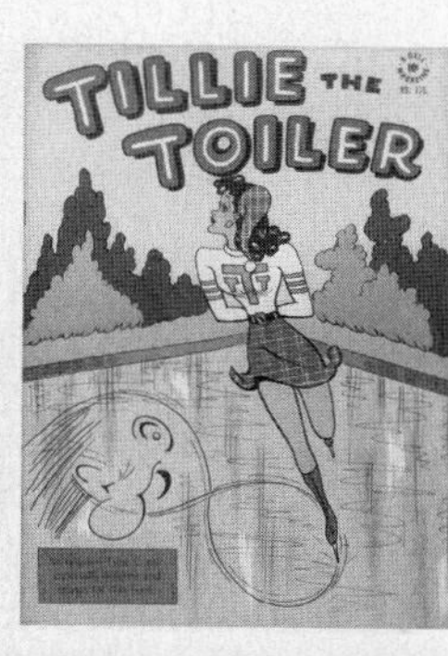

Tillie the Toiler Four Color #176 © DELL

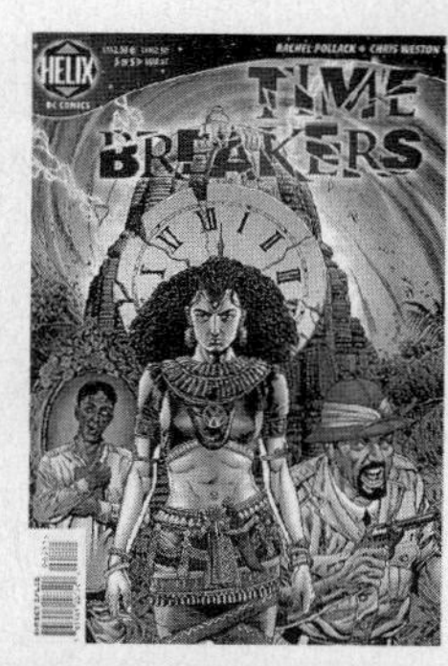

Time Breakers #3 © Pollack & Weston

GD 2.0 | VG 4.0 | FN 6.0 | VF 8.0 | VF/NM 9.0 | NM- 9.2

TICK AND ARTHUR, THE
New England Comics: Feb, 1999 - No. 6 ($3.50, B&W)
1-6-Sean Wang-s/a 3.50

TICK BIG BLUE DESTINY, THE
New England Comics: Oct, 1997 - No. 9 ($2.95)
1-4: 1-"Keen" Ed. 2-Two covers 3.50
1-($4.95) "Wicked Keen" Ed. w/die cut-c 5.00
5-($3.50) 3.50
6-Luny Bin Trilogy Preview #0 (7/98, $1.50) 3.50
7-9: 7-Luny Bin Trilogy begins 3.50

TICK BIG BLUE YULE LOG SPECIAL, THE
New England Comics: Dec, 1997; 1999 ($2.95, B&W)
1-"Jolly" and "Traditional" covers; flip book w/"Arthur Teaches the Tick About Hanukkah" 3.50
...1999 ($3.50) 3.50
Tick Big Yule Log Special 2001-(12/00, $3.50, B&W) 3.50

TICK, THE : CIRCUS MAXIMUS
New England Comics: Mar, 2000 - No. 4, Jun, 2000 ($3.50, B&W)
1-4-Encyclopedia of characters from Tick comics 3.50
Giant No. 1 (8/03, $14.95) r/#1-4, Redux 15.00
Redux No. 1 (4/01, $3.50) 3.50

TICK, THE - COLOR
New England Comics: Jan, 2001 - Present ($3.95)
1-6: 1-Marc Sandroni-a 4.00

TICK, THE : DAYS OF DRAMA
New England Comics: July, 2005 - No. 6, June, 2006 ($4.95/$3.95, limited series)
1-($4.95) Dave Garcia-a; has a mini-comic attached to cover 5.00
2-6-($3.95) 4.00

TICK, THE - HEROES OF THE CITY
New England Comics: Feb, 1999 - Present ($3.50, B&W)
1-6-Short stories by various 3.50

TICK KARMA TORNADO (The...)
New England Comics Press: Oct, 1993 - No. 9, Mar, 1995 ($2.75, B&W)
1-($3.25) 4.00
2-9: 2-$2.75-c begins 3.50

TICK NEW SERIES (The...)
New England Comics: Dec, 2009 - Present ($4.95)
1,2 5.00

TICK'S BIG XMAS TRILOGY, THE
New England Comics: Dec, 2002 - No. 3, Dec, 2002 ($3.95, limited series)
1-3 4.00

TICK'S GOLDEN AGE COMIC, THE
New England Comics: May, 2002 - No. 3, Feb, 2003 ($4.95, Golden Age size)
1-3-Facsimile 1940s-style Tick issue; 2 covers 5.00
Giant Edition TPB (9/03, $12.95) r/#1-3 13.00

TICK'S GIANT CIRCUS OF THE MIGHTY, THE
New England Comics: Summer, 1992 - No. 3, Fall, 1993 ($2.75, B&W, magazine size)
1-(A-O). 2-(P-Z). 3-1993 Update 4.00

TICKLE COMICS (Also see Gay, Smile, & Whee Comics)
Modern Store Publ.: 1955 (7¢, 5x7-1/4", 52 pgs)
1 6 12 18 28 34 40

TICK TOCK TALES
Magazine Enterprises: Jan, 1946 - V3#33, Jan-Feb, 1951
1-Koko & Kola begin 15 30 45 90 140 190
2 10 20 30 56 76 95
3-10 9 18 27 52 69 85
11-33: 19-Flag-c. 23-Muggsy Mouse, The Pixies & Tom-Tom the Jungle Boy app.
24-X-mas-c. 25-The Pixies & Tom-Tom app. 9 18 27 47 61 75

TIGER (Also see Comics Reading Libraries in the Promotional Comics section)
Charlton Press (King Features): Mar, 1970 - No. 6, Jan, 1971 (15¢)
1 3 6 9 14 19 24
2-6 2 4 6 8 11 14

TIGER BOY (See Unearthly Spectaculars)

TIGER GIRL
Gold Key: Sept, 1968 (15¢)
1(10227-809)-Sparling-c/a; Jerry Siegel scripts; advertising on back-c
4 8 12 26 41 55
1-Variant edition with pin-up on back cover 5 10 15 34 55 75

TIGERMAN (Also see Thrilling Adventure Stories)
Seaboard Periodicals (Atlas): Apr, 1975 - No. 3, Sept, 1975 (All 25¢ issues)
1-3: 1-Origin; Colan-c. 2,3-Ditko-p in each 2 4 6 8 11 14

TIGER WALKS, A (See Movie Comics)

TIGRA (The Avengers)
Marvel Comics: May, 2002 - No. 4, Aug, 2002 ($2.99, limited series)
1-4-Christina Z-s/Deodato-c/a 3.00

TIGRESS, THE
Hero Graphics: Aug, 1992 - No. 6?, June, 1993 ($3.95/$2.95/$3.95, B&W)
1,6: 1-Tigress vs. Flare. 6-44 pgs. 4.00
2-5: 2-$2.95-c begins 3.00

TILLIE THE TOILER (See Comic Monthly)
Dell Publishing Co.: No. 15, 1941 - No. 237, July, 1949
Four Color 15(1941) 45 90 135 284 480 675
Large Feature Comic 30(1941) 34 68 102 199 325 450
Four Color 8(1942) 23 46 69 163 314 465
Four Color 22(1943) 17 34 51 119 230 340
Four Color 55(1944), 89(1945) 13 26 39 91 168 245
Four Color 106('45),132('46): 132-New stories begin 10 20 30 68 119 170
Four Color 150,176,184 9 18 27 63 107 150
Four Color 195,213,237 7 14 21 50 83 115

TIMBER WOLF (See Action Comics #372, & Legion of Super-Heroes)
DC Comics: Nov, 1992 - No. 5, Mar, 1993 ($1.25, limited series)
1-5 2.50

TIME BANDITS
Marvel Comics Group: Feb, 1982 (one-shot, Giant)
1-Movie adaptation 4.00

TIME BEAVERS (See First Comics Graphic Novel #2)

TIME BREAKERS
DC Comics (Helix): Jan, 1997 - No. 5, May, 1997 ($2.25, limited series)
1-5-Pollack-s 2.50

TIMECOP (Movie)
Dark Horse Comics: Sept, 1994 - No. 2, Nov, 1994 ($2.50, limited series)
1,2-Adaptation of film 2.50

TIME FOR LOVE (Formerly Romantic Secrets)
Charlton Comics: V2#53, Oct, 1966; Oct, 1967 - No. 47, May, 1976
V2#53(10/66) Herman-s Hermits app. 3 6 9 20 30 40
1-(10/67) 4 8 12 22 34 45
2-(12/67) -10 3 6 9 15 21 26
11,12,14-20 2 4 6 11 16 20
13-(11/69) Ditko-a (7 pgs.) 3 6 9 16 23 30
21-29: 28-Shirley Jones poster. 29-Bobby Sherman pin-up
2 4 6 9 13 16
30-(10/72)-David Cassidy full page poster 3 6 9 17 25 32
31-47: 31-Bobby Sherman pin-up 2 4 6 8 11 14

TIMELESS TOPIX (See Topix)

TIMELY PRESENTS: ALL WINNERS
Marvel Comics: Dec, 1999 ($3.99)
1-Reprints All Winners Comics #19 (Fall 1946); new Lago-c 4.00

TIMELY PRESENTS: HUMAN TORCH
Marvel Comics: Feb, 1999 ($3.99)
1-Reprints Human Torch Comics #5 (Fall 1941); new Lago-c 4.00

TIME MACHINE, THE
Dell Publishing Co.: No. 1085, Mar, 1960 (H.G. Wells)
Four Color 1085-Movie, Alex Toth-a; Rod Taylor photo-c
14 28 42 97 181 265

TIME MASTERS
DC Comics: Feb, 1990 - No. 8, Sept, 1990 ($1.75, mini-series)
1-8: New Rip Hunter series. 5-Cave Carson, Viking Prince app. 6-Dr. Fate app. 2.50
TPB (2008, $19.99) r/#1-8 and Secret Origins #43; intro. by Geoff Johns 20.00

TIMESLIP COLLECTION

Tim Holt #38 © ME

Tim Tyler Cowboy #13 © KFS

Tiny Titans #2 © DC

GD 2.0 | VG 4.0 | FN 6.0 | VF 8.0 | VF/NM 9.0 | NM- 9.2

GD 2.0 | VG 4.0 | FN 6.0 | VF 8.0 | VF/NM 9.0 | NM- 9.2

Marvel Comics: Nov, 1998 ($2.99, one-shot)
1-Pin-ups reprinted from Marvel Vision magazine 3.00

TIMESLIP SPECIAL (The Coming of the Avengers)
Marvel Comics: Oct, 1998 ($5.99, one-shot)
1-Alternate world Avengers vs. Odin 6.00

TIMESTORM 2009/2099
Marvel Comics: June, 2009 - No. 4, Oct, 2009 ($3.99, limited series)
1-4-Punisher 2099 transports Spider-Man to 2099; Wolverine app.; Battle-a 4.00
...: Spider-Man One Shot (8/09, $3.99) Reed-s/Craig-a/Renaud-c 4.00
...: X-Men One Shot (8/09, $3.99) Reed-s/Irving-a/Renaud-c 4.00

TIME TO RUN (Based on 1973 Billy Graham movie)
Spire Christian Comics (Fleming H. Revell Co.): 1975 (39¢)
nn-By Al Hartley 2 4 6 8 11 14

TIME TUNNEL, THE (TV)
Gold Key: Feb, 1967 - No. 2, July, 1967 (12¢)
1-Photo back-c on both issues 7 14 21 47 76 105
2 5 10 15 34 55 75

TIME TWISTERS
Quality Comics: Sept, 1987 - No. 21, 1989 ($1.25/$1.50)
1-21: Alan Moore scripts in 1-4, 6-9, 14 (2 pg.). 14-Bolland-a (2 pg.). 15,16-Guice-c 2.50

TIME 2: THE EPIPHANY (See First Comics Graphic Novel #9)

TIMEWALKER (Also see Archer & Armstrong)
Valiant: Jan, 1994 - No. 15, Oct, 1995 ($2.50)
1-15,0(3/96): 2-"JAN" on-c, February, 1995 in indicia. 2.50
Yearbook 1 (5/95, $2.95) 3.00

TIME WARP (See The Unexpected #210)
DC Comics, Inc.: Oct-Nov, 1979 - No. 5, June-July, 1980 ($1.00, 68 pgs.)
1 2 4 6 10 14 18
2-5 2 4 6 8 10 12
NOTE: *Aparo a-1. Buckler a-1p. Chaykin a-2. Ditko a-1-4. Kaluta c-1-5. G. Kane a-2. Nasser a-4. Newton a-1-5p. Orlando a-2. Sutton a-1-3.*

TIME WARRIORS: THE BEGINNING
Fantasy General Comics: 1986 (Aug) - No. 2, 1986? ($1.50)
1,2-Alpha Track/Skellon Empire 2.50

TIM HOLT (Movie star) (Becomes Red Mask #42 on; also see Crack Western #72, & Great Western)
Magazine Enterprises: 1948 - No. 41, April-May, 1954 (All 36 pgs.)
1-(A-1 #14)-Line drawn-c w/Tim Holt photo on-c; Tim Holt, His horse Lightning & sidekick Chito begin 57 114 171 359 605 850
2-(A-1 #17)(9-10/48)-Photo-c begin, end #18 31 62 93 181 291 400
3-(A-1 #19)-Photo back-c 23 46 69 135 218 300
4(1-2/49),5: 5-Photo front/back-c 17 34 51 98 154 210
6-(5/49)-1st app. The Calico Kid (alias Rex Fury), his horse Ebony & Sidekick Sing-Song (begin series); photo back-c 28 56 84 162 261 360
7-10: 7-Calico Kid by Ayers. 8-Calico Kid by Guardineer (r-in/Great Western #10). 9-Map of Tim's Home Range 16 32 48 88 137 185
11-The Calico Kid becomes The Ghost Rider (origin & 1st app.) by Dick Ayers (r-in/Great Western I.W. #8); his horse Spectre & sidekick Sing-Song begin series 44 88 132 273 454 635
12-16,18-Last photo-c 14 28 42 80 115 150
17-Frazetta Ghost Rider-c 40 80 120 238 387 535
19,22,24: 19-Last Tim Holt-c; Bolle line-drawn-c begin; Tim Holt photo on covers #19-28, 30-41. 22-interior photo-c 12 24 36 69 97 125
20-Tim Holt becomes Redmask (origin); begin series; Redmask-c #20-on 16 32 48 94 147 200
21-Frazetta Ghost Rider/Redmask-c 37 74 111 220 353 485
23-Frazetta Redmask-c 29 58 87 169 272 375
25-1st app. Black Phantom 20 40 60 115 183 250
26-30: 28-Wild Bill Hickok, Bat Masterson team up with Redmask. 29-B&W photo-c 11 22 33 62 86 110
31-33-Ghost Rider ends 10 20 30 58 79 100
34-Tales of the Ghost Rider begins (horror)-Classic "The Flower Women" & "Hard Boiled Harry!" 14 28 42 82 121 160
35-Last Tales of the Ghost Rider 11 22 33 62 86 110
36-The Ghost Rider returns, ends #41; liquid hallucinogenic drug story 13 26 39 74 105 135
37-Ghost Rider classic "To Touch Is to Die!", about Inca treasure 13 26 39 74 105 135
38-The Black Phantom begins (not in #39); classic Ghost Rider "The Phantom Guns of Feather Gap!" 13 26 39 74 105 135
39-41: All 3-D effect c/stories 14 28 42 81 118 155
NOTE: *Dick Ayers a-7, 9-41. Bolle a-1-41; c-19, 20, 22, 24-28, 30-41.*

TIM McCOY (Formerly Zoo Funnies; Pictorial Love Stories #22 on)
Charlton Comics: No. 16, Oct, 1948 - No. 21, Aug, 1949 (Western Movie Stories)
16-John Wayne, Montgomery Clift app. in "Red River"; photo back-c 40 80 120 244 397 550
17-21: 17-Allan "Rocky" Lane guest stars. 18-Rod Cameron guest stars. 19-Whip Wilson, Andy Clyde guest star; Jesse James story. 20-Jimmy Wakely guest stars. 21-Johnny Mack Brown guest stars 33 66 99 196 316 435

TIMMY
Dell Publishing Co.: No. 715, Aug, 1956 - No. 1022, Aug-Oct, 1959
Four Color 715 (#1) 5 10 15 30 48 65
Four Color 823 (8/57), 923 (8/58), 1022 4 8 12 26 41 55

TIMMY THE TIMID GHOST (Formerly Win-A-Prize?; see Blue Bird)
Charlton Comics: No. 3, 2/56 - No. 44, 10/64; No. 45, 9/66; 10/67 - No. 23, 7/71; V4#24, 9/85 - No. 26, 1/86
3(1956) (1st Series) 12 24 36 69 97 125
4,5 8 16 24 42 54 65
6-10 3 6 9 20 30 40
11,12(4/58,10/58)-(100 pgs.) 6 12 18 43 69 95
13-20 3 6 9 18 27 35
21-45(1966) 3 6 9 14 19 24
1(10/67, 2nd series) 3 6 9 16 22 28
2-10 2 4 6 10 14 18
11-23: 23 (7/71) 1 3 4 8 10 12
24-26 (1985-86): Fago-r (low print run) 6.00

TIM TYLER (See Harvey Comics Hits #54)

TIM TYLER (Also see Comics Reading Libraries in the Promotional Comics section)
Better Publications: 1942
1 15 30 45 85 130 175

TIM TYLER COWBOY
Standard Comics (King Features Synd.): No. 11, Nov, 1948 - No. 18, 1950
11-By Lyman Young 9 18 27 50 65 80
12-18: 13-15-Full length western adventures 7 14 21 35 43 50

TINKER BELL (Disney, TV)(See Walt Disney Showcase #37)
Dell Publishing Co.: No. 896, Mar, 1958 - No. 982, Apr-June, 1959
Four Color 896 (#1)-The Adventures of... 8 16 24 56 93 130
Four Color 982-The New Advs. of... 8 16 24 52 86 120

TINY FOLKS FUNNIES
Dell Publishing Co.: No. 60, 1944
Four Color 60 15 30 45 104 197 290

TINY TESSIE (Tessie #1-23; Real Experiences #25)
Marvel Comics (20CC): No. 24, Oct, 1949 (52 pgs.)
24 13 26 39 72 101 130

TINY TIM (Also see Super Comics)
Dell Publishing Co.: No. 4, 1941 - No. 235, July, 1949
Large Feature Comic 4('41) 40 80 120 246 411 575
Four Color 20(1941) 37 74 111 218 354 490
Four Color 42(1943) 16 32 48 112 214 315
Four Color 235 6 12 18 37 59 80

TINY TITANS (Teen Titans)(See Promotional Comics section for Free Comic Book Day edition)
DC Comics: Apr, 2008 - Present ($2.25/$2.50)
1-24-All ages stories of Teen Titans in Elementary school; Baltazar & Franco-s/a 2.50
...: Adventures in Awesomeness TPB (2009, $12.99) r/#7-12; pin-ups 13.00
...: Welcome To The Treehouse TPB (2009, $12.99) r/#1-6; pin-ups 13.00
...: Sidekickin' It TPB (2010, $12.99) r/#13-18; pin-ups 13.00

TINY TOT COMICS
E. C. Comics: Mar, 1946 - No. 10, Nov-Dec, 1947 (For younger readers)
1(nn)-52 pg. issues begin, end #4 39 78 117 240 395 550
2 (5/46) 22 44 66 130 213 295
3-10: 10-Christmas-c 20 40 60 120 195 270

TINY TOT FUNNIES (Formerly Family Funnies; becomes Junior Funnies)
Harvey Publ. (King Features Synd.): No. 9, June, 1951
9-Flash Gordon, Mandrake, Dagwood, Daisy, etc. 8 16 24 42 54 65

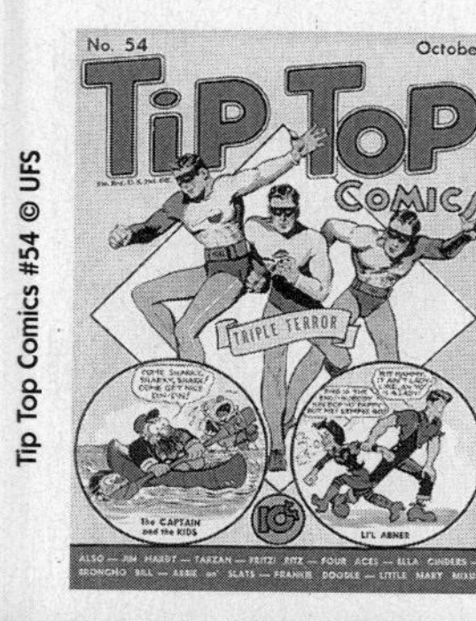

Tip Top Comics #54 © UFS

Titans (2008 series) #16 © DC

T-Man #6 © QUA

TINY TOTS COMICS
Dell Publishing Co.: 1943 (Not reprints)

	GD 2.0	VG 4.0	FN 6.0	VF 8.0	VF/NM 9.0	NM- 9.2
1-Kelly-a(2); fairy tales	39	78	117	240	395	550

TIPPY & CAP STUBBS (See Popular Comics)
Dell Publishing Co.: No. 210, Jan, 1949 - No. 242, Aug, 1949

	GD 2.0	VG 4.0	FN 6.0	VF 8.0	VF/NM 9.0	NM- 9.2
Four Color 210 (#1)	5	10	15	32	51	70
Four Color 242	4	8	12	26	41	55

TIPPY'S FRIENDS GO-GO & ANIMAL
Tower Comics: July, 1966 - No. 15, Oct, 1969 (25¢)

	GD 2.0	VG 4.0	FN 6.0	VF 8.0	VF/NM 9.0	NM- 9.2
1	9	18	27	65	113	160
2-5,7,9-15: 12-15 titled "Tippy's Friend Go-Go"	6	12	18	37	59	80
6-The Monkees photo-c	9	18	27	60	100	140
8-Beatles app. on front/back-c	11	22	33	74	132	190

TIPPY TEEN (See Vicki)
Tower Comics: Nov, 1965 - No. 25, Oct, 1969 (25¢)

	GD 2.0	VG 4.0	FN 6.0	VF 8.0	VF/NM 9.0	NM- 9.2
1	11	22	33	74	132	190
2-4,6-10	6	12	18	43	69	95
5-1 pg. Beatles pin-up	7	14	21	47	76	105
11-20: 16-Twiggy photo-c	6	12	18	41	66	90
21-25	6	12	18	37	59	80
Special Collectors' Editions nn-(1969, 25¢)	6	12	18	41	66	90

TIPPY TERRY
Super/I. W. Enterprises: 1963

	GD 2.0	VG 4.0	FN 6.0	VF 8.0	VF/NM 9.0	NM- 9.2
Super Reprint #14('63)-r/Little Groucho #1	2	4	6	8	10	12
I.W. Reprint #1 (nd)-r/Little Groucho #1	2	4	6	8	10	12

TIP TOP COMICS
United Features #1-188/St. John #189-210/Dell Publishing Co. #211 on:
4/36 - No. 210, 1957; No. 211, 11-1/57-58 - No. 225, 5-7/61

	GD 2.0	VG 4.0	FN 6.0	VF 8.0	VF/NM 9.0	NM- 9.2
1-Tarzan by Hal Foster, Li'l Abner, Broncho Bill, Fritzi Ritz, Ella Cinders, Capt. & The Kids begin; strip-r (1st comic book app. of each)	958	1916	2874	5461	8581	11,700
2	229	458	687	1305	2053	2800
3-Tarzan-c	204	408	612	1163	1832	2500
4	119	238	357	678	1064	1450
5-8,10: 7-Photo & biography of Edgar Rice Burroughs. 8-Christmas-c	83	166	249	473	749	1025
9-Tarzan-c	104	208	312	593	947	1300
11,13,16,18-Tarzan-c: 11-Has Tarzan pin-up	79	158	237	450	713	975
12,14,15,17,19,20: 20-Christmas-c	60	120	180	342	539	735
21,24,27,30-(10/38)-Tarzan-c	63	126	189	359	567	775
22,23,25,26,28,29	43	86	129	245	383	520
31,35,38,40	37	74	111	215	345	475
32,36-Tarzan-c: 32-1st published Jack Davis-a (cartoon). 36-Kurtzman panel (1st published comic work)	53	106	159	334	567	800
33,34,37,39-Tarzan-c	50	100	150	310	518	725
41-Reprints 1st Tarzan Sunday; Tarzan-c	53	106	159	334	567	800
42,44,46,48,49	31	62	93	181	291	400
43,45,47,50,52-Tarzan-c. 43-Mort Walker panel	40	80	120	240	390	540
51,53	30	60	90	174	280	385
54-Origin Mirror Man & Triple Terror, also featured on cover	38	76	114	222	356	490
55,56,58: Last Tarzan by Foster	25	50	75	147	236	325
57,59-62-Tarzan by Hogarth	32	64	96	186	298	410
63-80: 65,67-70,72-74,77,78-No Tarzan	15	30	45	88	137	185
81-90	14	28	42	80	115	150
91-99	13	26	39	72	101	130
100	14	28	42	76	108	140
101-140: 110-Gordo story. 111-Li'l Abner app. 118, 132-No Tarzan. 137-Sadie Hawkins Day story	10	20	30	54	72	90
141-170: 145,151-Gordo stories. 157-Last Li'l Abner; lingerie panels	8	16	24	44	57	70
171-188-Tarzan reprints by B. Lubbers in all. 173-Peanuts by Schulz begins; no Peanuts in #174-183	9	18	27	47	61	75
189-225-Peanuts (8 pgs.) in most	8	16	24	40	50	60
Bound Volumes (Very Rare) sold at 1939 World's Fair; bound by publisher in pictorial comic boards (also see Comics on Parade)						
Bound issues 1-12	309	618	927	2163	3782	5400
Bound issues 13-24	174	348	522	1114	1907	2700
Bound issues 25-36	155	310	465	992	1696	2400

NOTE: *Tarzan by **Foster**-#1-40, 44-50; by **Rex Maxon**-#41-43; by **Burne Hogarth**-#57, 59, 62.*

TIP TOPPER COMICS
United Features Syndicate: Oct-Nov, 1949 - No. 28, 1954

	GD 2.0	VG 4.0	FN 6.0	VF 8.0	VF/NM 9.0	NM- 9.2
1-Li'l Abner, Abbie & Slats	12	24	36	67	94	120
2	8	16	24	44	57	70
3-5: 5-Fearless Fosdick app.	8	16	24	40	50	60
6-10: 6-Fearless Fosdick app.	7	14	21	37	46	55
11-16	6	12	18	31	38	45
17(6-7/52) (2nd app. of Peanuts by Schulz in comics?) (see United Comics #22 for 5-6/52 app.)	11	22	33	62	86	110
18-26: 18-24,26-Early Peanuts (2 pgs.). 25-Early Peanuts (3 pgs.) 26-Twin Earths	10	20	30	56	76	95
27,28-Twin Earths	8	16	24	40	50	60

NOTE: *Many lingerie panels in Fritzi Ritz stories.*

TITAN A.E.
Dark Horse Comics: May, 2000 - No. 3, July, 2000 ($2.95, limited series)

	GD 2.0	VG 4.0	FN 6.0	VF 8.0	VF/NM 9.0	NM- 9.2
1-3-Movie prequel; Al Rio-a						3.00

TITANS (Also see Teen Titans, New Teen Titans and New Titans)
DC Comics: Mar, 1999 - No. 50, Apr, 2003 ($2.50/$2.75)

	GD 2.0	VG 4.0	FN 6.0	VF 8.0	VF/NM 9.0	NM- 9.2
1-Titans re-form; Grayson-s; 2 covers						3.00
2-11,13-24,26-50: 2-Superman-c/app. 9,10,21,22-Deathstroke app. 24-Titans from "Kingdom Come" app. 32-36-Asamiya-c. 44-Begin $2.75-c						2.75
12-($3.50, 48 pages)						3.50
25-($3.95) Titans from "Kingdom Come" app.; Wolfman & Faerber-s; art by Pérez, Cardy, Grumment, Jimenez, Dodson, Pelletier						4.00
Annual 1 ('00, $3.50) Planet DC; intro Bushido						3.50
... East Special 1 (1/08, $3.99) Winick-s/Churchill-a; continues in Titans #1 (2008)						4.00
...Secret Files 1,2 (3/99, 10/00; $4.95) Profile pages & short stories						5.00

TITANS (Also see Teen Titans)
DC Comics: Jun, 2008 - Present ($3.50/$2.99)

	GD 2.0	VG 4.0	FN 6.0	VF 8.0	VF/NM 9.0	NM- 9.2
1-Titans re-form again; Winick-s/Churchill-a; covers by Churchill & Van Sciver						3.50
2-20: 2-4-($2.99) Trigon returns. 6-10-Jericho app.						3.00
...: Lockdown TPB (2009, $14.99) r/#7-11						15.00
...: Old Friends HC (2008, $24.99) r/#1-6 & Titans East Special						25.00

TITANS/ LEGION OF SUPER-HEROES: UNIVERSE ABLAZE
DC Comics: 2000 - No. 4, 2000 ($4.95, prestige format, limited series)

	GD 2.0	VG 4.0	FN 6.0	VF 8.0	VF/NM 9.0	NM- 9.2
1-4-Jurgens-s/a; P. Jimenez-a; teams battle Universo						5.00

TITAN SPECIAL
Dark Horse Comics: June, 1994 ($3.95, one-shot)

	GD 2.0	VG 4.0	FN 6.0	VF 8.0	VF/NM 9.0	NM- 9.2
1-($3.95, 52 pgs.)						4.00

TITANS: SCISSORS, PAPER, STONE
DC Comics: 1997 ($4.95, one-shot)

	GD 2.0	VG 4.0	FN 6.0	VF 8.0	VF/NM 9.0	NM- 9.2
1-Manga style Elseworlds; Adam Warren-s/a(p)						5.00

TITANS SELL-OUT SPECIAL
DC Comics: Nov, 1992 ($3.50, 52 pgs., one-shot)

	GD 2.0	VG 4.0	FN 6.0	VF 8.0	VF/NM 9.0	NM- 9.2
1-Fold-out Nightwing poster; 1st Teeny Titans						3.50

TITANS/ YOUNG JUSTICE: GRADUATION DAY
DC Comics: Early July, 2003 - No. 3, Aug, 2003 ($2.50, limited series)

	GD 2.0	VG 4.0	FN 6.0	VF 8.0	VF/NM 9.0	NM- 9.2
1,2-Winick-s/Garza-a; leads into Teen Titans and The Outsiders series. 2-Lilith dies						2.50
3-Death of Donna Troy (Wonder Girl)						2.50
TPB (2003, $6.95) r/#1-3; plus previews of Teen Titans and The Outsiders series						7.00

T-MAN (Also see Police Comics #103)
Quality Comics Group: Sept, 1951 - No. 38, Dec, 1956

	GD 2.0	VG 4.0	FN 6.0	VF 8.0	VF/NM 9.0	NM- 9.2
1-Pete Trask, T-Man begins; Jack Cole-a	40	80	120	246	411	575
2-Crandall-c	22	44	66	128	209	290
3,7,8: All Crandall-c	20	40	60	118	192	265
4,5-Crandall-c/a each	21	42	63	124	202	280
6-"The Man Who Could Be Hitler" c/story; Crandall-c.	24	48	72	140	230	320
9,10-Crandall-c	18	36	54	105	165	225
11-Used in **POP**, pg. 95 & color illo.	15	30	45	84	127	170
12,13,15-19,21,22-26: 21- "The Return of Mussolini" c/story. 23-H-Bomb panel. 24-Last pre-code issue (4/55). 25-Not Crandall-a	13	26	39	74	105	135
14-Hitler-c	18	36	54	105	165	225
20-H-Bomb explosion-c/story	15	30	45	90	140	190
27-33,35-38	12	24	36	69	97	125
34-Hitler-c	15	30	45	88	137	185

NOTE: *Anti-communist stories common. **Crandall** c-2-10p. **Cuidera** c(i)-1-38. Bondage c-15.*

TMNT... (Also see Teenage Mutant Ninja Turtles and related titles)
Mirage Publishing: March 2007 ($3.25/$4.95, B&W, one-shots)

Tomahawk #114 © DC

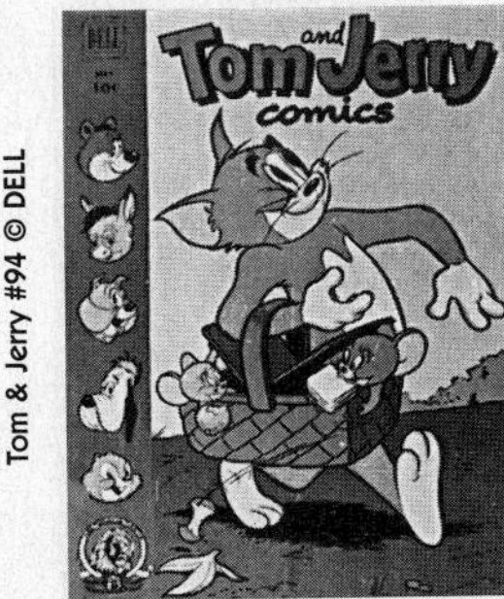

Tom & Jerry #94 © DELL

Tomb of Dracula #1 © MAR

	GD 2.0	VG 4.0	FN 6.0	VF 8.0	VF/NM 9.0	NM- 9.2
...: Raphael Movie Prequel 1; ...: Michelangelo Movie Prequel 2; ...: Donatello Movie Prequel 3; ...: April Movie Prequel 4; ...: Leonardo Movie Prequel 5; back-story for movie						3.25
...: The Official Movie Adaptation ($4.95) adapts 2007 movie; Munroe-c						5.00

TMNT MUTANT UNIVERSE SOURCEBOOK
Archie Comics: 1992 - No. 3, 1992? ($1.95, 52 pgs.)(Lists characters from A-Z)

	GD	VG	FN	VF	VF/NM	NM-
1-3: 3-New characters; fold-out poster						2.50

TNT COMICS
Charles Publishing Co.: Feb, 1946 (36 pgs.)

	GD	VG	FN	VF	VF/NM	NM-
1-Yellowjacket app.	31	62	93	182	296	410

TOBY TYLER (Disney, see Movie Comics)
Dell Publishing Co.: No. 1092, Apr-June, 1960

	GD	VG	FN	VF	VF/NM	NM-
Four Color 1092-Movie, photo-c	6	12	18	43	69	95

TODAY'S BRIDES
Ajax/Farrell Publishing Co.: Nov, 1955; No. 2, Feb, 1956; No. 3, Sept, 1956; No. 4, Nov, 1956

	GD	VG	FN	VF	VF/NM	NM-
1	9	18	27	47	61	75
2-4	6	12	18	31	38	45

TODAY'S ROMANCE
Standard Comics: No. 5, March, 1952 - No. 8, Sept, 1952 (All photo-c?)

	GD	VG	FN	VF	VF/NM	NM-
5-Photo-c	10	20	30	58	79	100
6-Photo-c; Toth-a	11	22	33	60	83	105
7,8	9	18	27	47	61	75

TOE TAGS FEATURING GEORGE A. ROMARO
DC Comics: Dec, 2004 - No. 6, May, 2005 ($2.95/$2.99)

	GD	VG	FN	VF	VF/NM	NM-
1-6-Zombie story by George Romaro; Wrightson-c/Castillo-a						3.00

TOKA (Jungle King)
Dell Publishing Co.: Aug-Oct, 1964 - No. 10, Jan, 1967 (Painted-c #1,2)

	GD	VG	FN	VF	VF/NM	NM-
1	5	10	15	30	48	65
2	3	6	9	18	27	35
3-10	3	6	9	16	22	28

TOKYO STORM WARNING (See Red/Tokyo Storm Warning for TPB)
DC Comics (Cliffhanger): Aug, 2003 - No. 3, Dec, 2003 ($2.95, limited series)

	GD	VG	FN	VF	VF/NM	NM-
1-3-Warren Ellis-s/James Raiz-a						3.00

TOMAHAWK (Son of... on-c of #131-140; see Star Spangled Comics #69 & World's Finest Comics #65)
National Periodical Publications: Sept-Oct, 1950 - No. 140, May-June, 1972

	GD	VG	FN	VF	VF/NM	NM-
1-Tomahawk & boy sidekick Dan Hunter begin by Fred Ray	174	348	522	1114	1907	2700
2-Frazetta/Williamson-a (4 pgs.)	66	132	198	419	722	1025
3-5	41	82	123	256	428	600
6-10: 7-Last 52 pg. issue	35	70	105	208	339	470
11-20	24	48	72	140	230	320
21-27,30: 30-Last precode (2/55)	21	42	63	124	202	280
28-1st app. Lord Shilling (arch-foe)	22	44	66	128	209	290
29-Frazetta-r/Jimmy Wakely #3 (3 pgs.)	26	52	78	154	252	350
31-40	18	36	54	105	165	225
41-50	10	20	30	71	126	180
51-56,58-60	9	18	27	63	107	150
57-Frazetta-r/Jimmy Wakely #6 (3 pgs.)	10	20	30	73	129	185
61-77: 77-Last 10¢ issue	8	16	24	58	97	135
78-85: 81-1st app. Miss Liberty. 83-Origin Tomahawk's Rangers	7	14	21	49	80	110
86-99: 96-Origin/1st app. The Hood, alias Lady Shilling	6	12	18	37	59	80
100	6	12	18	39	62	85
101-110: 107-Origin/1st app. Thunder-Man	4	8	12	28	44	60
111-115,120,122: 122-Last 12¢ issue	4	8	12	26	41	55
116-1st Neal Adams cover	6	12	18	43	69	95
117-119,121,123-130-Neal Adams-c	5	10	15	30	48	65
131-Frazetta-r/Jimmy Wakely #7 (3 pgs.); origin Firehair retold	3	6	9	21	32	42
132-135: 135-Last 15¢ issue	3	6	9	16	23	30
136-138,140 (52 pg. Giants)	3	6	9	19	29	38
139-Frazetta-r/Star Spangled #113	3	6	9	21	32	42

NOTE: *Fred Ray c-1, 2, 8, 11, 30, 34, 35, 40-43, 45, 46, 82. Firehair by **Kubert**-131-134, 136. **Maurer** a-138. **Severin** a-135. **Starr** a-5. **Thorne** a-137, 140.*

TOM AND JERRY (See Comic Album #4, 8, 12, Dell Giant #21, Dell Giants, Golden Comics Digest #1, 5, 8, 13, 15, 18, 22, 25, 28, 35, Kite fun Book & March of Comics #21, 46, 61, 70, 88, 103, 119, 128, 145, 154, 173, 190, 207, 224, 281, 295, 305, 321,333, 345, 361, 365, 388, 400, 444, 451, 463, 480)

TOM AND JERRY (...Comics, early issues) (M.G.M.)
(Formerly Our Gang No. 1-59) (See Dell Giants for annuals)
Dell Publishing Co./Gold Key No. 213-327/Whitman No. 328 on: No. 193, 6/48; No. 60, 7/49 - No. 212, 7-9/62; No. 213, 11/62 - No. 291, 2/75; No. 292, 3/77 - No. 342, 5/82 - No. 344, 6/84

	GD	VG	FN	VF	VF/NM	NM-
Four Color 193 (#1)-Titled "M.G.M. Presents..."	22	44	66	157	304	450
60-Barney Bear, Benny Burro cont. from Our Gang; Droopy begins	11	22	33	80	145	210
61	10	20	30	67	116	165
62-70: 66-X-Mas-c	8	16	24	56	93	130
71-80: 77,90-X-Mas-c. 79-Spike & Tyke begin	7	14	21	45	73	100
81-99	6	12	18	41	66	90
100	6	12	18	43	69	95
101-120	5	10	15	34	55	75
121-140: 126-X-Mas-c	5	10	15	30	48	65
141-160	4	8	12	26	41	55
161-200	4	8	12	24	37	50
201-212(7-9/62)(Last Dell issue)	4	8	12	22	34	45
213,214-(84 pgs.)-Titled "...Funhouse"	6	12	18	41	66	90
215-240: 215-Titled "...Funhouse"	3	6	9	17	25	32
241-270	2	4	6	11	16	20
271-300: 286- "Tom & Jerry"	2	4	6	8	11	14
301-327 (Gold Key)	1	3	4	6	8	10
328,329 (Whitman)	2	4	6	8	11	14
330(8/80),331(10/80), 332-(3-pack only)	3	6	9	20	30	40
333-341: 339(2/82), 340(2-3/82), 341(4/82)	2	4	6	8	10	12
342-344 (All #90058, no date, date code, 3-pack): 342(6/83), 343(8/83), 344(6/84)	3	6	9	14	19	24
Mouse From T.R.A.P. 1(7/66)-Giant, G. K.	5	10	15	30	48	65
Summer Fun 1(7/67, 68 pgs.)(Gold Key)-Reprints Barks' Droopy from Summer Fun #1	5	10	15	30	48	65

NOTE: *#60-87, 98-121, 268, 277, 289, 302 are 52 pgs.. Reprints-#225, 241, 245, 247, 252, 254, 266, 268, 270, 292-327, 329-342, 344.*

TOM & JERRY
Harvey Comics: Sept, 1991 - No. 18, Aug, 1994 ($1.25)

	GD	VG	FN	VF	VF/NM	NM-
1-18: 1-Tom & Jerry, Barney Bear-r by Carl Barks						3.00
50th Anniversary Special 1 (10/91, $2.50, 68 pgs.)-Benny the Lonesome Burro-r by Barks (story/a)/Our Gang #9						4.00

TOMB OF DARKNESS (Formerly Beware)
Marvel Comics Group: No. 9, July, 1974 - No. 23, Nov, 1976

	GD	VG	FN	VF	VF/NM	NM-
9	3	6	9	16	23	30
10-23: 11,16,18-21-Kirby-a. 15,19-Ditko-r. 17-Woodbridge-r/Astonishing #62; Powell-r. 20-Everett Venus-r/Venus #19. 22-r/Tales To Astonish #27; 1st Hank Pym. 23-Everett-r	2	4	6	10	14	18
20,21-(30¢-c variants, limited distribution)(5,7/76)	4	8	12	24	37	50

TOMB OF DRACULA (See Giant-Size Dracula, Dracula Lives, Nightstalkers, Power Record Comics & Requiem for Dracula)
Marvel Comics Group: Apr, 1972 - No. 70, Aug, 1979

	GD	VG	FN	VF	VF/NM	NM-
1-1st app. Dracula & Frank Drake; Colan-p in all; Neal Adams-c	15	30	45	107	204	300
2	8	16	24	52	86	120
3-6: 3-Intro. Dr. Rachel Van Helsing & Inspector Chelm. 6-Neal Adams-c	6	12	18	43	69	95
7-9	6	12	18	37	59	80
10-1st app. Blade the Vampire Slayer (who app. in 1998 and 2002 movies)	18	36	54	129	252	375
11,14-16,20:	4	8	12	28	44	60
12-2nd app. Blade; Brunner-c(p)	8	16	24	54	90	125
13-Origin Blade	9	18	27	65	113	160
17,19: 17-Blade bitten by Dracula. 19-Blade discovers he is immune to vampire's bite. 1st mention of Blade having vampire blood in him	6	12	18	39	62	85
18-Two-part x-over cont'd in Werewolf by Night #15	5	10	15	34	55	75
21,24-Blade app.	4	8	12	28	44	60
22,23,26,27,29	3	6	9	18	27	35
25-1st app. & origin Hannibal King	4	8	12	24	37	50
25-2nd printing (1994)	2	4	6	8	10	12
28-Blade app. on-c & inside as an illusion	4	8	12	24	37	50
30,41,42-45-Blade app. 45-Intro. Deacon Frost, the vampire who bit Blade's mother	4	8	12	22	34	45
31-40	3	6	9	16	23	30
43-45-(30¢-c variants, limited distribution)	6	12	18	41	66	90
46,47-(Regular 25¢ editions)(4-8/76)	2	4	6	13	18	22

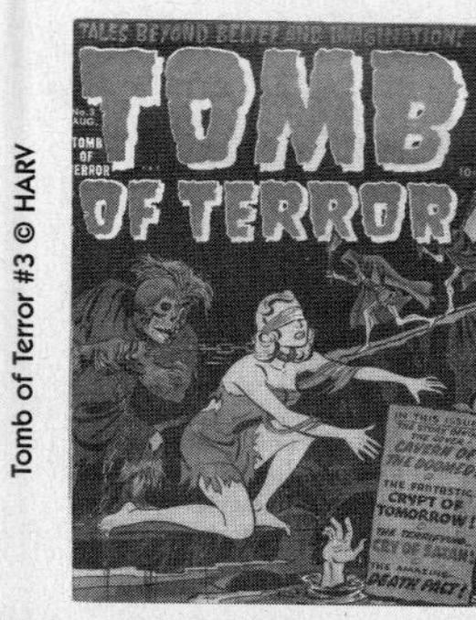

Tomb of Terror #3 © HARV

Tom Corbett, Space Cadet Four Color #400 © DELL

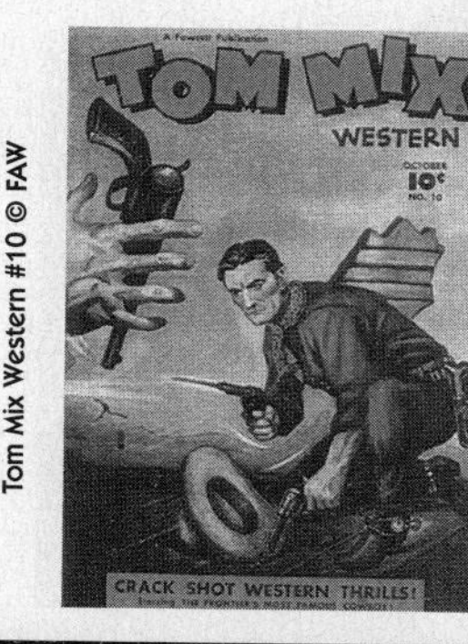

Tom Mix Western #10 © FAW

	GD 2.0	VG 4.0	FN 6.0	VF 8.0	VF/NM 9.0	NM- 9.2
46,47-(30¢-c variants, limited distribution)	4	8	12	22	34	45
48,49,51-57,59,60: 57,59,60-(30¢-c)	2	4	6	13	18	22
50-Silver Surfer app.	4	8	12	22	34	45
57,59,60-(35¢-c variants)(6-9/77)	4	8	12	24	37	50
58-All Blade issue (Regular 30¢ edition)	4	8	12	26	41	55
58-(35¢-c variant)(7/77)	7	14	21	49	80	110
61-69	2	4	6	13	18	22
70-Double size	4	8	12	22	34	45

NOTE: ***N. Adams** c-1, 6. **Colan** a-1-70p; c(p)-8, 38-42, 44-56, 58-70. **Wrightson** c-43.*

TOMB OF DRACULA, THE (Magazine)
Marvel Comics Group: Oct, 1979 - No. 6, Aug, 1980 (B&W)

	GD	VG	FN	VF	VF/NM	NM-
1,3: 1-Colan-a; features on movies "Dracula" and "Love at First Bite" w/photos. 3-Good girl cover-a; Miller-a (2 pg. sketch)	2	4	6	11	16	20
2,6: 2-Ditko-a (36 pgs.); Nosferatu movie feature. 6-Lilith story w/Sienkiewicz-a	2	4	6	8	11	14
4,5: Stephen King interview	2	4	6	13	18	22

NOTE: ***Buscema** a-4p, 5p. **Chaykin** c-5, 6. **Colan** a(p)-1, 3-6. **Miller** a-3. **Romita** a-2p.*

TOMB OF DRACULA
Marvel Comics (Epic Comics): 1991 - No. 4, 1992 ($4.95, 52 pgs., squarebound, mini-series)

	GD	VG	FN	VF	VF/NM	NM-
Book 1-4: Colan/Williamson-a; Colan painted-c						5.00

TOMB OF DRACULA
Marvel Comics: Dec, 2004 - No. 4, Mar, 2005 ($2.99, limited series)

	GD	VG	FN	VF	VF/NM	NM-
1-4-Blade app.; Tolagson-a/Sienkiewicz-c						3.00

TOMB OF LEGEIA (See Movie Classics)

TOMB OF TERROR (Thrills of Tomorrow #17 on)
Harvey Publications: June, 1952 - No. 16, July, 1954

	GD	VG	FN	VF	VF/NM	NM-
1	45	90	135	284	480	675
2	29	58	87	172	281	390
3-Bondage-c; atomic disaster story	30	60	90	177	289	400
4-12: 4-Heart ripped out. 8-12-Nostrand-a	28	56	84	165	270	375
13-Special S/F issue	39	78	117	231	378	525
14-Classic S/F-c; Check-a	55	110	165	352	601	850
15-S/F issue; c-shows face exploding	110	220	330	704	1202	1700
16-Special S/F issue; Nostrand-a	36	72	108	211	343	475

NOTE: ***Edd Cartier** a-13? **Elias** c-2, 5-16. **Kremer** a-1, 7; c-1. **Nostrand** a-8-12, 15r 16. **Palais** a-2, 3, 5-7. **Powell** a-1, 3, 5, 9-16. **Sparling** a-12, 13, 15.*

TOMB RAIDER (one-shots)
Image Comics (Top Cow Prod.)

	GD	VG	FN	VF	VF/NM	NM-
...: Arabian Nights (8/04, $5.99) Avery-s/Tan-a/c						6.00
... Cover Gallery 2006 (4/06, $2.99) artist galleries and series gallery; pin-ups						3.00
.../The Darkness Special 1 (2001, TopCowStore.com)-Wohl-s/Tan-a						3.00
Epiphany 1 (8/03, $4.99)-Jurgens-s/Banks-a/Haley-c; preview of Witchblade Animated						5.00
Takeover 1 (1/04, $2.99)-Benefiel-a/Daniel-c						3.00
... Vs. The Wolf-Men: Monster War 2005 (7/05, $2.99) 2nd part of Monster War x-over						3.00
.../Witchblade/Magdalena/Vampirella #1 (8/05, $2.99, B&W) three covers; Chin-a						3.00

TOMB RAIDER: JOURNEYS
Image Comics (Top Cow Prod.): Jan, 2002 - No. 12, May, 2003 ($2.50/$2.99)

	GD	VG	FN	VF	VF/NM	NM-
1-12: 1-Avery-s/Drew Johnson-a. 1-Two covers by Johnson & Hughes						3.00

TOMB RAIDER: THE GREATEST TREASURE OF ALL
Image Comics (Top Cow Prod.): 2002; Oct, 2005 ($6.99)

	GD	VG	FN	VF	VF/NM	NM-
Prelude (2002, 16 pgs., no cover price) Jusko-c/a						3.00
1-(10/05, $6.99) Jusko-a/Jurgens-s; sketch pages, reference photos, art in progress						7.00

TOMB RAIDER: THE SERIES (Also see Witchblade/Tomb Raider)(Also see Promotional Comics section for Free Comic Book Day edition)
Image Comics (Top Cow Prod.): Dec, 1999 - No. 50, Mar, 2005 ($2.50/$2.99)

	GD	VG	FN	VF	VF/NM	NM-
1-Jurgens-s/Park-a; 3 covers by Park, Finch, Turner						4.00
2-24,26-29,31-50: 21-Black-c w/foil. 31-Mhan-a. 37-Flip book preview of Stryke Force						3.00
25-Michael Turner-c/a; Witchblade app.; Endgame x-over with Witchblade #60 & Evo #1						3.00
30-($4.99) Tony Daniel-a						5.00
#0 (6/01, $2.50) Avery-s/Ching-a/c						2.50
#1/2 (10/01, $2.95) Early days of Lara Croft; Jurgens-s/Lopez-a						3.00
...: Chasing Shangri-La (2002, $12.95, TPB) r/#11-15						13.00
... Gallery (12/00, $2.95) Pin-ups & previous covers by various						3.00
... Magazine (6/01, $4.95) Hughes-c; r/#1,2; Jurgens interview						5.00
...: Mystic Artifacts (2001, $14.95, TPB) r/#5-10						15.00
...: Saga of the Medusa Mask (9/00, $9.95, TPB) r/#1-4; new Park-c						10.00
... Vol. 1 Compendium (11/06, $59.99) r/#1-50; variant covers and pin-up art						60.00

TOMB RAIDER/WITCHBLADE SPECIAL (Also see Witchblade/Tomb Raider)
Top Cow Prod.: Dec, 1997 (mail-in offer, one-shot)

	GD	VG	FN	VF	VF/NM	NM-
1-Turner-s/a(p); green background cover	1	3	4	6	8	10
1-Variant-c with orange sun background	1	3	4	6	8	10
1-Variant-c with black sides	1	3	4	6	8	10
1-Revisited (12/98, $2.95) reprints #1, Turner-c						3.00
...: Trouble Seekers TPB (2002, $7.95) rep. T.R./W & W/T.R. & W/T.R. 1/2; new Turner-c						8.00

TOMBSTONE TERRITORY
Dell Publishing Co.: No. 1123, Aug, 1960

	GD	VG	FN	VF	VF/NM	NM-
Four Color 1123	8	16	24	56	93	130

TOM CAT (Formerly Bo; Atom The Cat #9 on)
Charlton Comics: No. 4, Apr, 1956 - No. 8, July, 1957

	GD	VG	FN	VF	VF/NM	NM-
4-Al Fago-c/a	8	16	24	44	57	70
5-8	6	12	18	31	38	45

TOM CORBETT, SPACE CADET (TV)
Dell Publishing Co.: No. 378, Jan-Feb, 1952 - No. 11, Sept-Nov, 1954 (All painted covers)

	GD	VG	FN	VF	VF/NM	NM-
Four Color 378 (#1)-McWilliams-a	16	32	48	115	220	325
Four Color 400,421-McWilliams-a	10	20	30	70	123	175
4(11-1/53) - 11	8	16	24	54	90	125

TOM CORBETT SPACE CADET (See March of Comics #102)

TOM CORBETT SPACE CADET (TV)
Prize Publications: V2#1, May-June, 1955 - V2#3, Sept-Oct, 1955

	GD	VG	FN	VF	VF/NM	NM-
V2#1-Robot-c	32	64	96	188	307	425
2,3-Meskin-c	24	48	72	140	230	320

TOM, DICK & HARRIET (See Gold Key Spotlight)

TOM LANDRY AND THE DALLAS COWBOYS
Spire Christian Comics/Fleming H. Revell Co.: 1973 (35/49¢)

	GD	VG	FN	VF	VF/NM	NM-
nn-35¢ edition	2	4	6	13	18	22
nn-49¢ edition	2	4	6	9	12	15

TOM MIX WESTERN (Movie, radio star) (Also see The Comics, Crackajack Funnies, Master Comics, 100 Pages Of Comics, Popular Comics, Real Western Hero, Six Gun Heroes, Western Hero & XMas Comics)
Fawcett Publications: Jan, 1948 - No. 61, May, 1953 (1-17: 52 pgs.)

	GD	VG	FN	VF	VF/NM	NM-
1 (Photo-c, 52 pgs.)-Tom Mix & his horse Tony begin; Tumbleweed Jr. begins, ends #52,54,55	67	134	201	422	711	1000
2 (Photo-c)	33	66	99	192	309	425
3-5 (Painted/photo-c): 5-Billy the Kid & Oscar app.	23	46	69	135	218	300
6-8: 6,7 (Painted/photo-c). 8-Kinstler tempera-c	20	40	60	115	183	250
9,10 (Paint/photo-c) 9-Used in **SOTI**, pgs. 323-325	19	38	57	112	176	240
11-Kinstler oil-c	15	30	45	94	147	200
12 (Painted/photo-c)	15	30	45	86	133	180
13-17 (Painted-c, 52 pgs.)	15	30	45	86	133	180
18,22 (Painted-c, 36 pgs.)	14	28	42	81	118	155
19 (Photo-c, 52 pgs.)	15	30	45	83	124	165
20,21,23 (Painted-c, 52 pgs.)	14	28	42	81	118	155
24,25,27-29 (52 pgs.): 24-Photo-c begin, end #61. 29-Slim Pickens app.	13	26	39	72	101	130
26,30 (36 pgs.)	12	24	36	67	94	120
31-33,35-37,39,40,42 (52 pgs.): 39-Red Eagle app.	11	22	33	64	90	115
34,38 (36 pgs. begin)	11	22	33	60	83	105
41,43-60: 57-(9/52)-Dope smuggling story	9	18	27	47	61	75
61-Last issue	10	20	30	56	76	95

NOTE: *Photo-c from 1930s Tom Mix movies (he died in 1940). Many issues contain ads for Tom Mix, Rocky Lane, Space Patrol and other premiums. Captain Tootsie by **C.C. Beck** in #6-11, 20.*

TOM MIX WESTERN
AC Comics: 1988 - No. 2, 1989? ($2.95, B&W w/16 pgs. color, 44 pgs.)

	GD	VG	FN	VF	VF/NM	NM-
1-Tom Mix-r/Master #124,128,131,102 plus Billy the Kid-r by Severin; photo front/back/inside-c						3.50
2-($2.50, B&W)-Gabby Hayes-r; photo covers						3.00
...Holiday Album 1 (1990, $3.50, B&W, one-shot, 44 pgs.)-Contains photos & 1950s Tom Mix-r; photo inside-c						4.00

TOMMY OF THE BIG TOP (Thrilling Circus Adventures)
King Features Synd./Standard Comics: No. 10, Sep, 1948 - No. 12, Mar, 1949

	GD	VG	FN	VF	VF/NM	NM-
10-By John Lehti	9	18	27	50	65	80
11,12	6	12	18	31	38	45

TOMMYSAURUS REX
Image Comics: Aug, 2004 ($11.95, B&W, graphic novel)

	GD	VG	FN	VF	VF/NM	NM-
Vol. 1 - Doug TenNapel-s/a						12.00

TOMMY TOMORROW (See Action Comics #127, Real Fact #6, Showcase #41,42,44,46,47 & World's Finest #102)

Tomorrow Stories #1 © ABC

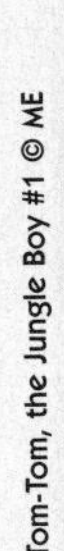
Tom-Tom, the Jungle Boy #1 © ME

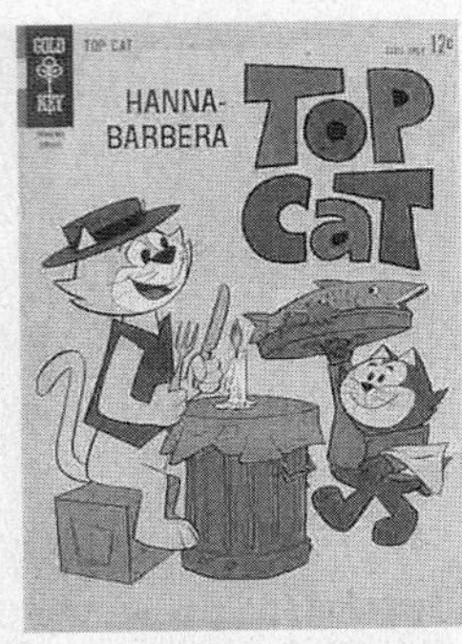

Top Cat #9 © H-B

GD 2.0 | VG 4.0 | FN 6.0 | VF 8.0 | VF/NM 9.0 | NM- 9.2

TOMOE (Also see Shi: The Way Of the Warrior #6)
Crusade Comics: July, 1995 - No. 3, June, 1996($2.95)
0-3: 2-B&W Dogs o' War preview. 3-B&W Demon Gun preview 3.00
0 (3/96, $2.95)-variant-c. 3.00
0-Commemorative edition (5,000) 2 4 6 8 10 12
1-Commemorative edition (5,000) 2 4 6 9 12 15
1-($2.95)-FAN Appreciation edition 3.00
TPB (1997, $14.95) r/#0-3 15.00

TOMOE: UNFORGETTABLE FIRE
Crusade Comics: June, 1997 ($2.95, one-shot)
1-Prequel to Shi: The Series 3.00

TOMOE-WITCHBLADE/FIRE SERMON
Crusade Comics: Sept, 1996 ($3.95, one-shot)
1-Tucci-c 5.00
1-($9.95)-Avalon Ed. w/gold foil-c 10.00

TOMOE-WITCHBLADE/MANGA SHI PREVIEW EDITION
Crusade Comics: July, 1996 ($5.00, B&W)
nn-San Diego Preview Edition 5.00

TOMORROW KNIGHTS
Marvel Comics (Epic Comics): June, 1990 - No. 6, Mar, 1991 ($1.50)
1-6: 1-($1.95, 52 pgs.) 2.50

TOMORROW STORIES
America's Best Comics: Oct, 1999 - No. 12, Aug, 2002 ($3.50/$2.95)
1-Two covers by Ross and Nowlan; Moore-s 3.50
2-12-($2.95) 3.00
... Special (1/06, $6.99) Nowlan-c; Moore-s; Greyshirt tribute to Will Eisner 7.00
... Special 2 (5/06, $6.99) Gene Ha-c; Moore-s; Promethea app. 7.00
Book 1 Hardcover (2002, $24.95) r/#1-6 25.00
Book 1 TPB (2003, $17.95) r/#1-6 18.00
Book 2 Hardcover (2004, $24.95) r/#7-12 25.00
Book 2 TPB (2005, $17.99) r/#7-12 18.00

TOM SAWYER (See Adventures of... & Famous Stories)

TOM SKINNER-UP FROM HARLEM (See Up From Harlem)

TOM STRONG (Also see Many Worlds of Tesla Strong)
America's Best Comics: June, 1999 - No. 36, May, 2006 ($3.50/$2.95/$2.99)
1-Two covers by Ross and Sprouse; Moore-s/Sprouse-a 4.00
1-Special Edition (9/09, $1.00) reprint with "After Watchmen" cover frame 1.00
2-36: 4-Art Adams-a (8 pgs.) 13-Fawcett homage w/art by Sprouse, Baker, Heath 20-Origin of Tom Stone. 22-Ordway-a. 31,32-Moorcock-s 3.00
...: Book One HC ('00, $24.95) r/#1-7, cover gallery and sketchbook 25.00
...: Book One TPB ('01, $14.95) r/#1-7, cover gallery and sketchbook 15.00
...: Book Two HC ('02, $24.95) r/#8-14, sketchbook 25.00
...: Book Two TPB ('03, $14.95) r/#8-14, sketchbook 15.00
...: Book Three HC ('04, $24.95) r/#15-19, sketchbook 25.00
...: Book Three TPB ('04, $17.95) r/#15-19, sketchbook 18.00
...: Book Four HC ('04, $24.95) r/#20-25, sketch pages 25.00
...: Book Four TPB ('05, $17.99) r/#20-25, sketch pages 18.00
...: Book Five HC ('05, $24.99) r/#26-30, sketch pages 25.00
...: Book Five TPB ('06, $17.99) r/#26-30, sketch pages 18.00
...: Book Six HC ('06, $24.99) r/#31-36 25.00
...: Book Six TPB ('08, $17.99) r/#31-36 18.00
...: The Deluxe Edition Book One (2009, $39.99, d.j.) r/#1-12; Moore intro.; sketch-a 40.00

TOM STRONG'S TERRIFIC TALES
America's Best Comics: Jan, 2002 - No. 12 ($3.50/$2.95)
1-Short stories; Moore-s; art by Adams, Rivoche, Hernandez, Weiss 3.50
2-12-($2.95) 2-Adams, Ordway, Weiss-a; Adams-c. 4-Rivoche-a. 5-Pearson, Aragonés-a 11-Timm-a 3.00
...: Book One HC ('04, $24.95) r/#1-6, cover gallery and sketch pages 25.00
...: Book One SC ('05, $17.99) r/#1-6, cover gallery and sketch pages 18.00
...: Book Two HC ('05, $24.95) r/#7-12, covers 25.00

TOM TERRIFIC! (TV)(See Mighty Mouse Fun Club Magazine #1)
Pines Comics (Paul Terry): Summer, 1957 - No. 6, Fall, 1958
(See Terry Toons Giant Summer Fun Book)
1-1st app.?; CBS Television Presents... 22 44 66 127 204 280
2-6-(scarce) 16 32 48 92 144 195

TOM THUMB
Dell Publishing Co.: No. 972, Jan, 1959
Four Color 972-Movie, George Pal 8 16 24 58 97 135

TOM-TOM, THE JUNGLE BOY (See A-1 Comics & Tick Tock Tales)
Magazine Enterprises: 1947 - No. 3, 1947; Nov, 1957 - No. 3, Mar, 1958
1-Funny animal 11 22 33 64 90 115
2,3(1947): 3-Christmas issue 9 18 27 47 61 75
Tom-Tom & Itchi the Monk 1(11/57) - 3(3/58) 5 10 15 24 30 35
I.W. Reprint No. 1,2,8,10: 1,2,8-r/Koko & Kola #? 2 4 6 8 10 12

TONGUE LASH
Dark Horse Comics: Aug, 1996 - No. 2, Sept, 1996 ($2.95, lim. series, mature)
1,2: Taylor-c/a 3.00

TONGUE LASH II
Dark Horse Comics: Feb, 1999 - No. 2, Mar, 1999 ($2.95, lim. series, mature)
1,2: Taylor-c/a 3.00

TONKA (Disney)
Dell Publishing Co.: No. 966, Jan, 1959
Four Color 966-Movie (Starring Sal Mineo)-photo-c 8 16 24 58 97 135

TONTO (See The Lone Ranger's Companion...)

TONY TRENT (The Face #1,2)
Big Shot/Columbia Comics Group: No. 3, 1948 - No. 4, 1949
3,4: 3-The Face app. by Mart Bailey 18 36 54 105 165 225

TOODLES, THE (The Toodle Twins with #1)
Ziff-Davis (Approved Comics)/Argo: No. 10, July-Aug, 1951; Mar, 1956 (Newspaper-r)
10-Painted-c, some newspaper-r by The Baers 12 24 36 67 94 120
...Twins 1(Argo, 3/56)-Reprints by The Baers 8 16 24 42 54 65

TOO MUCH COFFEE MAN
Adhesive Comics: July, 1993 - No. 10, Dec, 2000 ($2.50, B&W)
1-Shannon Wheeler story & art 2 4 6 9 12 15
2,3 1 2 3 5 7 9
4,5 6.00
6-10 3.00
Full Color Special-nn($2.95),2-(7/97, $3.95) 4.00

TOO MUCH COFFEE MAN SPECIAL
Dark Horse Comics: July, 1997 ($2.95, B&W)
nn-Reprints Dark Horse Presents #92-95 3.00

TOO MUCH HOPELESS SAVAGES
Oni Press: June, 2003 - No. 4, Apr, 2004 ($2.99, B&W, limited series)
1-4-Van Meter-s/Norrie-a 3.00
TPB (8/04, $11.95, digest-size) r/series 12.00

TOOTS AND CASPER
Dell Publishing Co.: No. 5, 1942
Large Feature Comic 5 20 40 60 114 182 250

TOP ADVENTURE COMICS
I. W. Enterprises: 1964 (Reprints)
1-r/High Adv. (Explorer Joe #2); Krigstein-r 2 4 6 11 16 20
2-Black Dwarf-r/Red Seal #22; Kinstler-c 2 4 6 13 18 22

TOP CAT (TV) (Hanna-Barbera)(See Kite Fun Book)
Dell Publishing Co./Gold Key No. 4 on: 12-2/61-62 - No. 3, 6-8/62; No. 4, 10/62 - No. 31, 9/70
1 (TV show debuted 9/27/61) 14 28 42 97 181 265
2-Augie Doggie back-ups in #1-4 8 16 24 54 90 125
3-5: 3-Last 15¢ issue. 4-Begin 12¢ issues; Yakky Doodle app. in 1 pg. strip. 5-Touché Turtle app. 6 12 18 43 69 95
6-10 5 10 15 32 51 70
11-20 4 8 12 24 37 50
21-31-Reprints 3 6 9 19 29 38

TOP CAT (TV) (Hanna-Barbera)(See TV Stars #4)
Charlton Comics: Nov, 1970 - No. 20, Nov, 1973
1 6 12 18 37 59 80
2-10 3 6 9 20 30 40
11-20 3 6 9 17 25 32
NOTE: *#8 (1/72) went on sale late in 1972 between #14 and #15 with the 1/73 issues.*

TOP COMICS
K. K. Publications/Gold Key: July, 1967 (All reprints)
nn-The Gnome-Mobile (Disney-movie) 2 4 6 13 18 22
1-Beagle Boys (#7), Beep Beep the Road Runner (#5), Bugs Bunny, Chip 'n' Dale, Daffy

Top Comics #3 © H-B

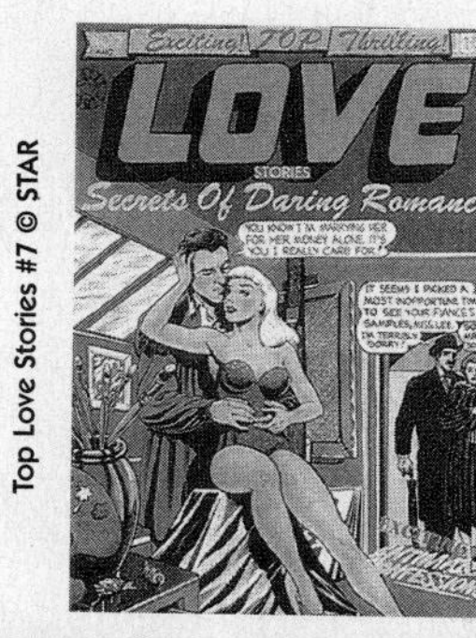

Top Love Stories #7 © STAR

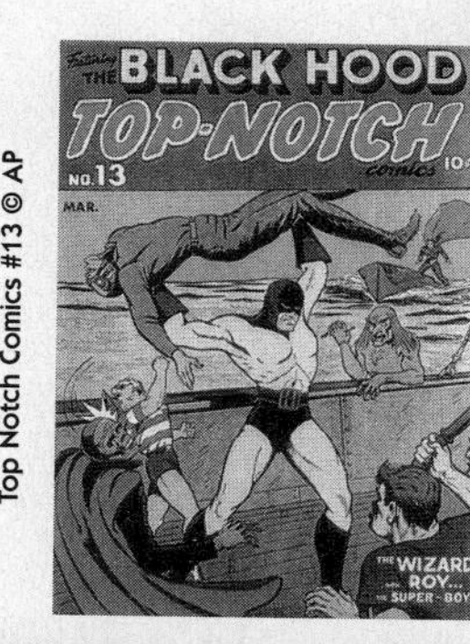

Top Notch Comics #13 © AP

	GD 2.0	VG 4.0	FN 6.0	VF 8.0	VF/NM 9.0	NM- 9.2
Duck (#50), Flipper, Huey, Dewey & Louie, Junior Woodchucks, Lassie, The Little Monsters (#71), Moby Duck, Porky Pig (has Gold Key label - says Top Comics on inside), Scamp, Super Goof, Tom & Jerry, Top Cat (#21), Tweety & Sylvester (#7), Walt Disney C&S (#322), Woody Woodpecker known issues; each character given own book	2	4	6	9	13	16
1-Donald Duck (not Barks), Mickey Mouse	2	4	6	13	18	22
1-Flintstones	4	8	12	22	34	45
1-Huckleberry Hound, Yogi Bear (#30)	3	6	9	14	19	24
1-The Jetsons	5	10	15	30	48	65
1-Tarzan of the Apes (#169)	3	6	9	16	22	28
1-Three Stooges (#35)	3	6	9	18	27	35
1-Uncle Scrooge (#70)	3	6	9	16	23	30
1-Zorro (r/G.K. Zorro #7 w/Toth-a; says 2nd printing)	3	6	9	14	19	24
2-Bugs Bunny, Daffy Duck, Mickey Mouse (#114), Porky Pig, Super Goof, Tom & Jerry, Tweety & Sylvester, Walt Disney's C&S (r/#325), Woody Woodpecker	2	4	6	9	12	15
2-Donald Duck (not Barks), Three Stooges, Uncle Scrooge (#71)-Barks-c, Yogi Bear (#30), Zorro (r/#8; Toth-a)	2	4	6	11	16	20
2-Snow White & 7 Dwarfs(6/67)(1944-r)	2	4	6	10	14	18
3-Donald Duck	2	4	6	11	16	20
3-Uncle Scrooge (#72)	2	4	6	13	18	22
3,4-The Flintstones	4	8	12	22	34	45
3,4: 3-Mickey Mouse (r/#115), Tom & Jerry, Woody Woodpecker, Yogi Bear. 4-Mickey Mouse, Woody Woodpecker	2	4	6	9	12	15

NOTE: *Each book in this series is identical to its counterpart except for cover, and came out at same time. The number in parentheses is the original issue it contains.*

TOP COW (Company one-shots)
Image Comics (Top Cow Productions)

	GD 2.0	VG 4.0	FN 6.0	VF 8.0	VF/NM 9.0	NM- 9.2
... Book of Revelations (7/03, $3.99)-Pin-ups and info; art by various; Gossett-c						4.00
... Convention Sketchbook 2004 (4/04, $3.00, B&W) art by various						3.00
... Preview Book 2005 (3/05, 99¢) Preview pages of Tomb Raider, Darkness, Rising Stars						2.50
... Productions, Inc./Ballistic Studios Swimsuit Special (5/95, $2.95)						3.00
...'s Best of: Dave Finch Vol. 1 TPB (8/06, $19.99) r/issues of Cybrforce, Aphrodite IX, Ascension and The Darkness; art & cover gallery						20.00
...'s Best of: Michael Turner Vol. 1 TPB (12/05, $24.99) r/Witchblade #1,10,12,18,19,25 & Witchblade/Tomb Raider chapters 1&3; Tomb Raider #25; art & cover gallery						25.00
... Secrets: Special Winter Lingerie Edition 1 (1/96, $2.95) Pin-ups						3.00
... 2001 Preview (no cover price) Preview pages of Tomb Raider; Jusko-a; flip cover & pages of Inferno						2.50

TOP COW CLASSICS IN BLACK AND WHITE
Image Comics (Top Cow): Feb, 2000 - Present ($2.95, B&W reprints)

	GD 2.0	VG 4.0	FN 6.0	VF 8.0	VF/NM 9.0	NM- 9.2
...: Aphrodite IX #1(9/00) B&W reprint						3.00
...: Ascension #1(4/00) B&W reprint plus time-line of series						3.00
...: Battle of the Planets #1(1/03) B&W reprint plus script and cover gallery						3.00
...: Darkness #1(3/00) B&W reprint plus time-line of series						3.00
...: Fathom #1(5/00) B&W reprint						3.00
...: Magdalena #1(10/02) B&W reprint plus time-line of series						3.00
...: Midnight Nation #1(9/00) B&W preview						3.00
...: Rising Stars #1(7/00) B&W reprint plus cover gallery						3.00
...: Tomb Raider #1(12/00) B&W reprint plus back-story						3.00
...: Witchblade #1(2/00) B&W reprint plus back-story						3.00
...: Witchblade #25(5/01) B&W reprint plus interview with Wohl & Haberlin						3.00

TOP DETECTIVE COMICS
I. W. Enterprises: 1964 (Reprints)

	GD 2.0	VG 4.0	FN 6.0	VF 8.0	VF/NM 9.0	NM- 9.2
9-r/Young King Cole #14; Dr. Drew (not Grandenetti)	2	4	6	10	14	18

TOP DOG (See Star Comics Magazine, 75¢)
Star Comics (Marvel): Apr, 1985 - No. 14, June, 1987 (Children's book)

	GD 2.0	VG 4.0	FN 6.0	VF 8.0	VF/NM 9.0	NM- 9.2
1-14: 10-Peter Parker & J. Jonah Jameson cameo						4.00

TOP ELIMINATOR (Teenage Hotrodders #1-24; Drag 'n' Wheels #30 on)
Charlton Comics: No. 25, Sept, 1967 - No. 29, July, 1968

	GD 2.0	VG 4.0	FN 6.0	VF 8.0	VF/NM 9.0	NM- 9.2
25-29	3	6	9	16	22	28

TOP FLIGHT COMICS: Four Star Publ.: 1947 (Advertised, not published)

TOP FLIGHT COMICS
St. John Publishing Co.: July, 1949

	GD 2.0	VG 4.0	FN 6.0	VF 8.0	VF/NM 9.0	NM- 9.2
1(7/49, St. John)-Hector the Inspector; funny animal	9	18	27	52	69	85

TOP GUN (See Luke Short, 4-Color #927 & Showcase #72)

TOP GUNS OF THE WEST (See Super DC Giant)

TOPIX (...Comics) (Timeless Topix-early issues) (Also see Men of Battle, Men of Courage & Treasure Chest)(V1-V5#1,V7 on-paper-c)
Catechetical Guild Educational Society: 11/42 - V10#15, 1/28/52 (Weekly - later issues)

	GD 2.0	VG 4.0	FN 6.0	VF 8.0	VF/NM 9.0	NM- 9.2
V1#1(8 pgs.,8x11")	24	48	72	140	230	320
2,3(8 pgs.,8x11")	14	28	42	80	115	150
4-8(16 pgs.,8x11")	11	22	33	64	90	115
V2#1-10(16 pgs.,8x11"): V2#8-Pope Pius XII	10	20	30	56	76	95
V3#1-10(16 pgs.,8x11"): V3#1-(9/44)	10	20	30	54	72	90
V4#1-10: V4#1-(9/45)	9	18	27	47	61	75
V5#1(10/46,52 pgs.,2(11/46),no #3),4(1/47)-9(6/47),10(7/47), no #13,4(10/47), 14(11/47),15(12/47)	8	16	24	40	50	60
11(8/47),12(9/47)-Life of Christ editions	10	20	30	54	72	90
V6#4(1/48),5(2/48),7(3/48),8(4/48),9(5/48),10(6/48),11(7/48)-14 (no #1-3,6)	7	14	21	35	43	50
V7#1(9/1/48)-20(6/15/49), 36 pgs.	6	12	18	29	36	42
V8#1(9/19/49)-3,5-11,13-30(5/15/50)	6	12	18	28	34	40
4-Dagwood Splits the Atom(10/10/49)-Magazine format	8	16	24	42	54	65
12-Ingels-a	10	20	30	54	72	90
V9#1(9/25/50)-11,13-30(5/14/51)	6	12	18	27	33	38
12-Special 36 pg. Xmas issue, text illos format	6	12	18	28	34	40
V10#1(10/1/51)-15: 14-Hollingsworth-a	6	12	18	27	33	38

TOP JUNGLE COMICS
I. W. Enterprises: 1964 (Reprint)

	GD 2.0	VG 4.0	FN 6.0	VF 8.0	VF/NM 9.0	NM- 9.2
1(nd)-Reprints White Princess of the Jungle #3, minus cover; Kintsler-a	3	6	9	16	23	30

TOP LOVE STORIES (Formerly Gasoline Alley #2)
Star Publications: No. 3, 5/51 - No. 19, 3/54

	GD 2.0	VG 4.0	FN 6.0	VF 8.0	VF/NM 9.0	NM- 9.2
3(#1)	22	44	66	129	207	285
4,5,7-9: 8-Wood story	18	36	54	105	165	225
6-Wood-a	23	46	69	135	218	300
10-16,18,19-Disbrow-a	18	36	54	105	165	225
17-Wood art (Fox-r)	19	38	57	112	176	240

NOTE: *All have* **L. B. Cole** *covers.*

TOP-NOTCH COMICS (...Laugh #28-45; Laugh Comix #46 on)
MLJ Magazines: Dec, 1939 - No. 45, June, 1944

	GD 2.0	VG 4.0	FN 6.0	VF 8.0	VF/NM 9.0	NM- 9.2
1-Origin/1st app. The Wizard; Kardak the Mystic Magician, Swift of the Secret Service (ends #3), Air Patrol, The Westpointer, Manhunters (by J. Cole), Mystic (ends #2) & Scott Rand (ends #3) begin; Wizard covers begin, end #8	514	1028	1542	3750	6625	9500
2-(1/40)-Dick Storm (ends #8), Stacy Knight M.D. (ends #4) begin; Jack Cole-a; 1st app. Nazis swastika on-c	242	484	726	1537	2644	3750
3-Bob Phantom, Scott Rand on Mars begin; J. Cole-a	171	342	513	1086	1868	2650
4-Origin/1st app. Streak Chandler on Mars; Moore of the Mounted only app.; J. Cole-a	150	300	450	953	1639	2325
5-Flag-c; origin/1st app. Galahad; Shanghai Sheridan begins (ends #8); Shield cameo; Novick-a; classic-c	168	336	504	1075	1838	2600
6-Meskin-a	110	220	330	704	1202	1700
7-The Shield x-over in Wizard; The Wizard dons new costume	142	284	426	909	1555	2200
8-Origin/1st app. The Firefly & Roy, the Super Boy (9/40, 2nd costumed boy hero after Robin?; also see Toro in Human Torch #1 (Fall/40)	153	306	459	972	1674	2375
9-Origin & 1st app. The Black Hood; 1st Black Hood-c & logo (10/40); Fran Frazier begins (Scarce)	622	1244	1866	4541	8021	11,500
10-2nd app. Black Hood	206	412	618	1318	2259	3200
11-3rd Black Hood	134	268	402	851	1463	2075
12-15	110	220	330	704	1202	1700
16-18,20	95	190	285	603	1039	1475
19-Classic bondage-c	103	206	309	659	1130	1600
21-30: 23-26-Roy app. 24-No Wizard. 25-Last Bob Phantom. 27-Last Firefly. 28-Suzie, Pokey Oakey begin. 29-Last Kardak	67	134	201	426	731	1035
31-44: 33-Dotty & Ditto by Woggon begins (2/43, 1st app.). 44-Black Hood series ends	42	84	126	265	445	625
45-Last issue	46	92	138	290	488	685

NOTE: ***J. Binder*** *a-1-3.* ***Meskin*** *a-2, 3, 6, 15.* ***Bob Montana*** *a-30; c-28-31.* ***Harry Sahle*** *c-42-45.* ***Woggon*** *a-33-40, 42. Bondage c-17, 19. Black Hood also appeared on radio in 1944.Black Hood app. on c-9-34, 41-44. Roy the Super Boy app. on c-8, 9, 11-27. The Wizard app. on c-1-8, 11-13, 15-22, 24, 25, 27. Pokey Oakey app. on c-28-43. Suzie app. on c-44-on.*

TOPPER & NEIL (TV)
Dell Publishing Co.: No. 859, Nov, 1957

	GD 2.0	VG 4.0	FN 6.0	VF 8.0	VF/NM 9.0	NM- 9.2
Four Color 859	5	10	15	30	48	65

Top Secrets #7 © S&S

Top 10 Season Two #1 © ABC

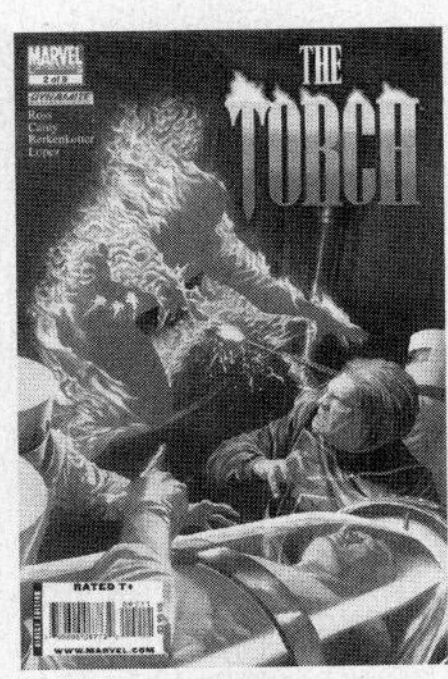

The Torch #2 © MAR

TOPPS COMICS: Four Star Publications: 1947 (Advertised, not published)

TOPS
July, 1949 - No. 2, Sept, 1949 (25¢, 10-1/4x13-1/4", 68 pgs.)
Tops Magazine, Inc. (Lev Gleason): (Large size-magazine format; for the adult reader)

	GD 2.0	VG 4.0	FN 6.0	VF 8.0	VF/NM 9.0	NM- 9.2
1 (Rare)-Story by Dashiell Hammett; Crandall/Lubbers, Tuska, Dan Barry, Fuje-a; Biro painted-c	129	258	387	826	1413	2000
2 (Rare)-Crandall/Lubbers, Biro, Kida, Fuje, Guardineer-a	123	246	369	787	1344	1900

TOPS COMICS
Consolidated Book Publishers: 1944 (10¢, 132 pgs.)

	GD 2.0	VG 4.0	FN 6.0	VF 8.0	VF/NM 9.0	NM- 9.2
2000-(Color-c, inside in red shade & some in full color)-Ace Kelly by Rick Yager, Black Orchid, Don on the Farm, Dinky Dinkerton (Rare)	26	52	78	152	249	345

NOTE: *This book is printed in such a way that when the staple is removed, the strips on the left side of the book correspond with the same strips on the right side. Therefore, if strips are removed from the book, each strip can be folded into a complete comic section of its own.*

TOPS COMICS (See Tops in Humor)
Consolidated Book (Lev Gleason): 1944 (7-1/4x5", 32 pgs.)

	GD 2.0	VG 4.0	FN 6.0	VF 8.0	VF/NM 9.0	NM- 9.2
2001-The Jack of Spades (costumed hero)	16	32	48	92	144	195
2002-Rip Raider	10	20	30	56	76	95
2003-Red Birch (gag cartoons)	5	10	15	22	26	30
2004-Gag cartoons	16	32	48	92	144	195

TOP SECRET
Hillman Publ.: Jan, 1952

	GD 2.0	VG 4.0	FN 6.0	VF 8.0	VF/NM 9.0	NM- 9.2
1	20	40	60	114	182	250

TOP SECRET ADVENTURES (See Spyman)

TOP SECRETS (...of the F.B.I.)
Street & Smith Publications: Nov, 1947 - No. 10, July-Aug, 1949

	GD 2.0	VG 4.0	FN 6.0	VF 8.0	VF/NM 9.0	NM- 9.2
1-Powell-c/a	36	72	108	211	343	475
2-Powell-c/a	25	50	75	147	241	335
3-6,8,10-Powell-a	22	44	66	132	216	300
9-Powell-c/a	23	46	69	136	223	310
7-Used in **SOTI**, pg. 90 & illo. "How to hurt people"; used by N.Y. Legis. Comm.; Powell-c/a	34	68	102	206	336	465

NOTE: ***Powell** c-1-3, 5-10.*

TOPS IN ADVENTURE
Ziff-Davis Publishing Co.: Fall, 1952 (25¢, 132 pgs.)

	GD 2.0	VG 4.0	FN 6.0	VF 8.0	VF/NM 9.0	NM- 9.2
1-Crusader from Mars, The Hawk, Football Thrills, He-Man; Powell-a; painted-c	47	94	141	296	498	700

TOPS IN HUMOR (See Tops Comics?)
Consolidated Book Publ. (Lev Gleason)/Wise Publs.: 1944 (7-1/4x5", #2 digest size)

	GD 2.0	VG 4.0	FN 6.0	VF 8.0	VF/NM 9.0	NM- 9.2
2001(#1)-Origin The Jack of Spades, Ace Kelly by Rick Yager, Black Orchid (female crime fighter) app.	16	32	48	92	144	195
2-Wise Publs.; WWII serviceman humor	11	22	33	64	90	115

TOP SPOT COMICS
Top Spot Publ. Co.: 1945

	GD 2.0	VG 4.0	FN 6.0	VF 8.0	VF/NM 9.0	NM- 9.2
1-The Menace, Duke of Darkness app.	35	70	105	208	339	470

TOPSY-TURVY (Teenage)
R. B. Leffingwell Publ.: Apr, 1945

	GD 2.0	VG 4.0	FN 6.0	VF 8.0	VF/NM 9.0	NM- 9.2
1-1st app. Cookie	14	28	42	80	115	150

TOP TEN
America's Best Comics: Sept, 1999 - No. 12, Oct, 2001 ($3.50/$2.95)

	GD 2.0	VG 4.0	FN 6.0	VF 8.0	VF/NM 9.0	NM- 9.2
1-Two covers by Ross and Ha/Cannon; Alan Moore-s/Gene Ha-a						3.50
2-11-($2.95)						3.00
12-($3.50)						3.50
Hardcover ('00, $24.95) Dust jacket with Gene Ha-a; r/#1-7						25.00
Softcover ('00, $14.95) new Gene Ha-c; r/#1-7						15.00
Book 2 HC ('02, $24.95) Dust jacket with Gene Ha-a; r/#8-12						25.00
Book 2 SC ('03, $14.95) new Gene Ha-c; r/#8-12						15.00
...: The Forty-Niners HC (2005, $24.99, dust jacket) prequel set in 1949; Moore-s/Ha-a						25.00

TOP TEN: BEYOND THE FARTHEST PRECINCT
America's Best Comics: Oct, 2005 - No. 5, Feb, 2006 ($2.99, limited series)

	GD 2.0	VG 4.0	FN 6.0	VF 8.0	VF/NM 9.0	NM- 9.2
1-5-Jerry Ordway-a/Paul DiFilippo-s						3.00
TPB (2006, $14.99) r/series; cover sketch pages						15.00

TOP TEN SEASON TWO
America's Best Comics: Dec, 2008 - No. 4, Mar, 2009 ($2.99, limited series)

	GD 2.0	VG 4.0	FN 6.0	VF 8.0	VF/NM 9.0	NM- 9.2
1-4-Cannon-s/Ha-a						3.00
... Special (5/09, $2.99) Cannon-s/Daxiong-a/Ha-c						3.00

TOR (Prehistoric Life on Earth) (Formerly One Million Years Ago)
St. John Publ. Co.: No. 2, Oct, 1953; No. 3, May, 1954 - No. 5, Oct, 1954

	GD 2.0	VG 4.0	FN 6.0	VF 8.0	VF/NM 9.0	NM- 9.2
3-D 2(10/53)-Kubert-c/a	14	28	42	76	108	140
3-D 2(10/53)-Oversized, otherwise same contents	12	24	36	67	94	120
3-D 2(11/53)-Kubert-c/a; has 3-D cover	12	24	36	67	94	120
3-5-Kubert-c/a: 3-Danny Dreams by Toth; Kubert 1 pg. story (w/self portrait)	14	28	42	76	108	140

NOTE: *The two October 3-D's have same contents and **Powell** art; the October & November issues are titled 3-D Comics. All 3-D issues are 25¢ and came with 3-D glasses.*

TOR (See Sojourn)
National Periodical Publications: May-June, 1975 - No. 6, Mar-Apr, 1976

	GD 2.0	VG 4.0	FN 6.0	VF 8.0	VF/NM 9.0	NM- 9.2
1-New origin by Kubert	2	4	6	8	10	12
2-6: 2-Origin-r/St. John #1						6.00

NOTE: ***Kubert** a-1, 2-6r; c-1-6. **Toth** a(p)-3r.*

TOR (3-D)
Eclipse Comics: July, 1986 - No. 2, Aug, 1987 ($2.50)

	GD 2.0	VG 4.0	FN 6.0	VF 8.0	VF/NM 9.0	NM- 9.2
1,2: 1-r/One Million Years Ago. 2-r/Tor 3-D #2						5.00
...2-D: 1,2-Limited signed & numbered editions	1	2	3	4	5	7

TOR
Marvel Comics (Epic Comics/Heavy Hitters): June, 1993 - No. 4, 1993 ($5.95, lim. series)

	GD 2.0	VG 4.0	FN 6.0	VF 8.0	VF/NM 9.0	NM- 9.2
1-4: Joe Kubert-c/a/scripts						6.00

TOR (Joe Kubert's...)
DC Comics: Jul, 2008 - No. 6, Dec, 2008 ($2.99, limited series)

	GD 2.0	VG 4.0	FN 6.0	VF 8.0	VF/NM 9.0	NM- 9.2
1-6-New story; Joe Kubert-c/a/scripts						3.00
Tor: A Prehistoric Odyssey HC (2009, $24.99, DJ) r/#1-6; Roy Thomas intro.; sketch-a						25.00

TOR BY JOE KUBERT
DC Comics: 2001 - 2003 ($49.95, hardcovers with dust jacket)

	GD 2.0	VG 4.0	FN 6.0	VF 8.0	VF/NM 9.0	NM- 9.2
Volume 1 (2001) r/One Million Years Ago #1 & 3-D Comics #1&2 in flat color; script pages, sketch pages, proposals for TV and newspapers strips; intro. by Roy Thomas						50.00
Volume 2 (2002) r/Tor (St. John) #3-5; Danny Dreams; portfolio section						50.00
Volume 3 (2003) r/Tor (DC '75) #1; (Marvel '93) #1-4; portfolio section						50.00

TORCH, THE
Marvel Comics (with Dynamite Ent.): Nov, 2009 - No. 8 ($3.99, limited series)

	GD 2.0	VG 4.0	FN 6.0	VF 8.0	VF/NM 9.0	NM- 9.2
1-6-Golden Age Human Torch; Alex Ross-c on all; Berkenkotter-a						4.00

TORCH OF LIBERTY SPECIAL
Dark Horse Comics (Legend): Jan, 1995 ($2.50, one-shot)

	GD 2.0	VG 4.0	FN 6.0	VF 8.0	VF/NM 9.0	NM- 9.2
1-Byrne scripts						2.50

TORCHY (...Blonde Bombshell) (See Dollman, Military, & Modern)
Quality Comics Group: Nov, 1949 - No. 6, Sept, 1950

	GD 2.0	VG 4.0	FN 6.0	VF 8.0	VF/NM 9.0	NM- 9.2
1-Bill Ward-c, Gil Fox-a	161	322	483	1030	1765	2500
2,3-Fox-c/a	68	136	204	432	746	1060
4-Fox-c/a(3), Ward-a (9 pgs.)	86	172	258	546	936	1325
5,6-Ward-c/a, 9 pgs; Fox-a(3) each	100	200	300	635	1093	1550
Super Reprint #16(1964)-r/#4 with new-c	10	20	30	60	93	125

TO RIVERDALE AND BACK AGAIN (Archie Comics Presents...)
Archie Comics: 1990 ($2.50, 68 pgs.)

	GD 2.0	VG 4.0	FN 6.0	VF 8.0	VF/NM 9.0	NM- 9.2
nn-Byrne-c, Colan-a(p); adapts NBC TV movie						5.00

TORMENTED, THE (Becomes Surprise Adventures #3 on)
Sterling Comics: July, 1954 - No. 2, Sept, 1954

	GD 2.0	VG 4.0	FN 6.0	VF 8.0	VF/NM 9.0	NM- 9.2
1,2: Weird/Horror stories	26	52	78	154	252	350

TORNADO TOM (See Mighty Midget Comics)

TORSO (See Jinx: Torso)

TOTAL ECLIPSE
Eclipse Comics: May, 1988 - No. 5, Apr, 1989 ($3.95, 52 pgs., deluxe size)

	GD 2.0	VG 4.0	FN 6.0	VF 8.0	VF/NM 9.0	NM- 9.2
Book 1-5: 3-Intro/1st app. new Black Terror. 4-Many copies have upside down pages and are mis-cut						4.00

TOTAL ECLIPSE
Image Comics: July, 1998 (one-shot)

	GD 2.0	VG 4.0	FN 6.0	VF 8.0	VF/NM 9.0	NM- 9.2
1-McFarlane-c; Eclipse Comics character pin-ups by Image artists						2.50

TOTAL ECLIPSE: THE SERAPHIM OBJECTIVE
Eclipse Comics: Nov, 1988 ($1.95, one-shot, Baxter paper)

	GD 2.0	VG 4.0	FN 6.0	VF 8.0	VF/NM 9.0	NM- 9.2
1-Airboy, Valkyrie, The Heap app.						3.00

TOTAL JUSTICE
DC Comics: Oct, 1996 - No. 3, Nov, 1996 ($2.25, bi-weekly limited series) (Based on toyline)

Total Eclipse #3 © ECL

Toy Story: Mysterious Stranger #1 © DIS/Pixar

Transformers #33 © Hasbro

	GD 2.0	VG 4.0	FN 6.0	VF 8.0	VF/NM 9.0	NM- 9.2

1-3 2.50

TOTAL RECALL (Movie)
DC Comics: 1990 ($2.95, 68 pgs., movie adaptation, one-shot)
1-Arnold Schwarzenegger photo-c 3.00

TOTAL WAR (M.A.R.S. Patrol #3 on)
Gold Key: July, 1965 - No. 2, Oct, 1965 (Painted-c)

	GD	VG	FN	VF	VF/NM	NM-
1-Wood-a in both issues	7	14	21	45	73	100
2	5	10	15	34	55	75

TOTEMS (Vertigo V2K)
DC Comics (Vertigo): Feb, 2000 ($5.95, one-shot)
1-Swamp Thing, Animal Man, Zatanna, Shade app.; Fegredo-c 6.00

TO THE HEART OF THE STORM
Kitchen Sink Press: 1991 (B&W, graphic novel)
Softcover-Will Eisner-s/a/c 15.00
Hardcover ($24.95) 25.00
TPB-(DC Comics, 9/00, $14.95) reprints 1991 edition 15.00

TO THE LAST MAN (See Zane Grey Four Color #616)

TOUCH OF SILVER, A
Image Comics: Jan, 1997 - No. 6, Nov, 1997 ($2.95, B&W, bi-monthly)
1-6-Valentino-s/a; photo-c: 5-color pgs. w/Round Table 3.00
TPB ($12.95) r/#1-6 13.00

TOUGH KID SQUAD COMICS
Timely Comics (TCI): Mar, 1942
1-(Scarce)-Origin & 1st app.The Human Top & The Tough Kid Squad; The Flying Flame app.
865 1730 2595 6315 11,158 16,000

TOWER OF SHADOWS (Creatures on the Loose #10 on)
Marvel Comics Group: Sept, 1969 - No. 9, Jan, 1971

	GD	VG	FN	VF	VF/NM	NM-
1-Romita-c, classic Steranko-a; Craig-a(p)	8	16	24	56	93	130
2,3: 2-Neal Adams-a. 3-Barry Smith, Tuska-a	5	10	15	30	48	65
4,6: 4-Marie Severin-c. 6-Wood-a	4	8	12	26	41	55
5-B. Smith-a(p), Wood-a; Wood draws himself (1st pg., 1st panel)	4	8	12	28	44	60
7-9: 7-B. Smith-a(p), Wood-a. 8-Wood-a; Wrightson-c. 9-Wrightson-c; Roy Thomas app.	5	10	15	30	48	65
Special 1(12/71, 52 pgs.)-Neal Adams-a; Romita-c	4	8	12	26	41	55

*NOTE: **J. Buscema** a-1p, 2p, Special 1r. **Colan** a-3p, 6p, Special 1. **J. Craig** a(r)-1p. **Ditko** a-6, 8, 9r, Special 1. **Everett** a-9(i)r; c-5i. **Kirby** a-9(p)r. **Severin** c-5p, 6. **Steranko** a-1p. **Tuska** a-3. **Wood** a-5-8. Issues 1-9 contain new stories with some pre-Marvel age reprints in 6-9. **H. P. Lovecraft** adaptation-9.*

TOXIC AVENGER (Movie)
Marvel Comics: Apr, 1991 - No. 11, Feb, 1992 ($1.50)
1-11: Based on movie character. 3,10-Photo-c 2.50

TOXIC CRUSADERS (TV)
Marvel Comics: May, 1992 - No. 8, Dec, 1992 ($1.25)
1-8: 1-3,8-Sam Kieth-c; based on USA Network cartoon 2.50

TOXIC GUMBO
DC Comics (Vertigo): 1998 ($5.95, one-shot, mature)
1-McKeever-a/Lydia Lunch-s 6.00

TOXIN (Son of Carnage)
Marvel Comics: June, 2005 - No. 6, Nov, 2005 ($2.99, limited series)
1-6-Milligan-s/Robertson-a; Spider-Man app. 3.00
...: The Devil You Know TPB (2006, $17.99) r/#1-6 18.00

TOYBOY
Continuity Comics: Oct, 1986 - No. 7, Mar, 1989 ($2.00, Baxter paper)
1-7 3.00
*NOTE: **N. Adams** a-1; c-1, 2,5. **Golden** a-7p; c-6,7. **Nebres** a(i)-1,2.*

TOYLAND COMICS
Fiction House Magazines: Jan, 1947 - No. 2, Mar, 1947; No. 3, July, 1947

	GD	VG	FN	VF	VF/NM	NM-
1-Wizard of the Moon begins	30	60	90	177	289	400
2,3-Bob Lubbers-c. 3-Tuska-a	17	34	51	100	158	215

*NOTE: All above contain strips by **Al Walker**.*

TOY STORY (Disney/Pixar movies)
BOOM! Entertainment (BOOM! KIDS): No. 0, Nov, 2009 - Present ($2.99)
0,1-Three covers 3.00

TOY STORY: MYSTERIOUS STRANGER (Disney/Pixar movies)
BOOM! Entertainment (BOOM! KIDS): May, 2009 - No. 4, July, 2009 ($2.99)
1-4-Jolley-s/Moreno-a. 1-Three covers. 2-4-Two covers 3.00

TOY TOWN COMICS
Toytown/Orbit Publ./B. Antin/Swapper Quarterly: 1945 - No. 7, May, 1947

	GD	VG	FN	VF	VF/NM	NM-
1-Mertie Mouse; L. B. Cole-c/a; funny animal	39	78	117	240	395	550
2-L. B. Cole-a	22	44	66	132	216	300
3-7-L. B. Cole-a. 5-Wiggles the Wonderworm-c	20	40	60	114	182	250

TRACKER
Image Comics (Top Cow): Nov, 2009 - Present ($2.99/$3.99)
1,2-Lincoln-s/Tsai-a. 1-Two covers 3.00
3-($3.99) 4.00

TRAGG AND THE SKY GODS (See Gold Key Spotlight, Mystery Comics Digest #3,9 & Spine Tingling Tales)
Gold Key/Whitman No. 9: June, 1975 - No. 8, Feb, 1977; No. 9, May, 1982 (Painted-c #3-8)

	GD	VG	FN	VF	VF/NM	NM-
1-Origin	3	6	9	14	19	24
2-8: 4-Sabre-Fang app. 8-Ostellon app.	2	4	6	8	11	14
9-(Whitman, 5/82) r/#1	1	2	3	5	7	9

*NOTE: **Santos** a-1, 2, 9r; c-3-7. **Spiegel** a-3-8.*

TRAIL BLAZERS (Red Dragon #5 on)
Street & Smith Publications: 1941; No. 2, Apr, 1942 - No. 4, Oct, 1942
(True stories of American heroes)

	GD	VG	FN	VF	VF/NM	NM-
1-Life story of Jack Dempsey & Wright Brothers	35	70	105	208	339	470
2-Brooklyn Dodgers-c/story; Ben Franklin story	22	44	66	128	209	290
3,4: 3-Fred Allen, Red Barber, Yankees stories	20	40	60	115	183	250

TRAIL COLT (Also see Extra Comics, Manhunt! & Undercover Girl)
Magazine Enterprises: 1949 - No. 2, 1949

	GD	VG	FN	VF	VF/NM	NM-
nn(A-1 #24)-7 pg. Frazetta-a r-in Manhunt #13; Undercover Girl app.; The Red Fox by L. B. Cole; Ingels-c; Whitney-a (Scarce)	39	78	117	240	395	550
2(A-1 #26)-Undercover Girl; Ingels-c; L. B. Cole-a (6 pgs.)	31	62	93	182	296	410

TRANSFORMERS, THE (TV)(See G.I. Joe and...)
Marvel Comics Group: Sept, 1984 - No. 80, July, 1991 (75¢/$1.00)

	GD	VG	FN	VF	VF/NM	NM-
1-Based on Hasbro Toys	3	6	9	16	23	30
2-5: 2-Golden-c. 3-(1/85) Spider-Man (black costume)-c/app. 4-Texeira-c; brief app. of Dinobots	2	4	6	10	14	18
6-10: 6-1st Josie Beller. 8-Dinobots 1st full app. 9-Circuit Breaker 1st full app. 10-Intro Constructicons	2	4	6	8	10	12
11-49: 11-1st app. Jetfire. 14-Jetfire becomes an Autobot; 1st app. of Grapple, Hoist, Smokescreen, Skids, and Tracks. 17-1st app. of Blaster, Powerglide, Cosmos, Seaspray, Warpath, Beachcomber, Preceptor, Straxus, Kickback, Bombshell, Shrapnel, Dirge, and Ramjet. 19-1st Omega Supreme. 21-1st app. of Aerialbots; 1st Slingshot; Circuit Breaker app. 22-Retells origin of Circuit Breaker, 1st Stunticons. 23-Battle at Statue of Liberty. 24-1st app. Protectobots, Combaticons; Optimus Prime killed. 25-1st Predacons. 26-Intro The Mechanic, Prime's Funeral. 27-1st Trypticon app.; Grimlock named new Autobot leader. 28-The Mechanic app. 29-Intro Scraplets, 1st app. of Triple Changers	1	2	3	4	5	7
50-60: 53-Jim Lee-c. 54-Intro Micromasters. 60-Brief 1st app. of Primus	2	3	4	6	8	10
61-70: 61-Origin of Cybertron and the Transformers, Unicron app.; app. of Primus, creator of the Transformers. 62-66 Matrix Quest 5-part series. 67-Jim Lee-c	2	4	6	9	13	16
71-77: 75-($1.50, 52 pgs.) (Low print run)	3	6	9	17	25	32
78,79 (Low print run)	4	8	12	22	34	45
80-Last issue	4	8	12	26	41	55

*NOTE: Second and third printings of most early issues (1-9?) exist and are worth less than originals. Was originally planned as a four issue mini-series. **Wrightson** a-64i(4 pgs.).*

TRANSFORMERS
IDW Publishing: No. 0, Oct, 2005 (99¢, one-shot)
0-Prelude to Transformers: Infiltration series; Furman-s/Su-a; 4 covers 2.50

TRANSFORMERS
IDW Publishing: Nov, 2009 - Present ($3.99)
1-3: Multple covers on each 4.00
...: Continuum (11/09, $3.99) Plot synopses of recent Transformers storylines 4.00

TRANSFORMERS: ALL HAIL MEGATRON
IDW Publishing: Jul, 2008 - No. 16, Oct, 2009 ($3.99, limited series)
1-16: 1-8,10-12-McCarthy-s/Guidi-a; 2 covers 4.00

TRANSFORMERS: ALLIANCE (Prequel to 2009 Transformers 2 movie)
IDW Publishing: Dec, 2008 - No. 4, Mar, 2009 ($3.99, limited series)
1-4-Milne-a; 2 covers 4.00

Transformers: Alliance #1 © Hasbro

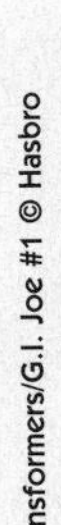
Transformers/G.I. Joe #1 © Hasbro

Transformers: Spotlight Jazz © Hasbro

	GD 2.0	VG 4.0	FN 6.0	VF 8.0	VF/NM 9.0	NM- 9.2

TRANSFORMERS ANIMATED: THE ARRIVAL
IDW Publishing: Sept, 2008 - No. 5, Dec, 2008 ($3.99, limited series)

1-5-Brizuela-a; 2 covers 4.00

TRANSFORMERS ARMADA (Continues as Transformers Energon with #19)
(Also see Promotional Comics section for FCBD Ed.)
Dreamwave Productions: July, 2002 - No. 18, Dec, 2003 ($2.95)

1-Sarracini-s/Raiz-a; wraparound gatefold-c 3.00
2-18 3.00
Vol. 1 TPB (2003, $13.95) r/#1-5 14.00
Vol. 2 TPB (2003, $15.95) r/#6-11 16.00

TRANSFORMERS ARMADA: MORE THAN MEETS THE EYE
Dreamwave Productions: Mar, 2004 - No. 3, May, 2004 ($4.95, limited series)

1-3-Pin-ups with tech info; art by Pat Lee & various 5.00

TRANSFORMERS, BEAST WARS: THE ASCENDING
IDW Publishing: Aug, 2007 - No. 4, Nov, 2007 ($3.99, limited series)

1-4-Furman-s/Figueroa-a; mulitple covers on all 4.00

TRANSFORMERS, BEAST WARS: THE GATHERING
IDW Publishing: Feb, 2006 - No. 4, May, 2006 ($2.99, limited series)

1-4-Furman-s/Figueroa-a; mulitple covers on all 3.00
TPB (8/06, $17.99) r/series; sketch pages & gallery of covers and variants 18.00

TRANSFORMERS: BUMBLEBEE
IDW Publishing: Dec, 2009 - Present ($3.99, limited series)

1,2: Zander Cannon-s; mulitple covers on all 4.00

TRANSFORMERS COMICS MAGAZINE (Digest)
Marvel Comics: Jan, 1987 - No. 10, July, 1988

	GD	VG	FN	VF	VF/NM	NM-
1,2-Spider-Man-c/s	2	4	6	9	12	15
3-10	2	4	6	8	10	12

TRANSFORMERS: DEFIANCE (Prequel to 2009 Transformers 2 movie)
IDW Publishing: Jan, 2009 - No. 4, Apr, 2009 ($3.99, limited series)

1-4-Mowry-s; 2 covers 4.00

TRANSFORMERS: DEVASTATION
IDW Publishing: Sept, 2007 - No. 6, Feb, 2008 ($3.99, limited series)

1-6-Furman-s/Su-a; multiple covers on all 4.00

TRANSFORMERS ENERGON (Continued from Transformers Armada #18)
Dreamwave Productions: No. 19, Jan, 2004 - No. 30, Dec, 2004 ($2.95)

19-30-Furman-s 3.00

TRANSFORMERS: ESCALATION
IDW Publishing: Nov, 2006 - No. 6, Apr, 2007 ($3.99, limited series)

1-6-Furman-s/Su-a; multiple covers 4.00

TRANSFORMERS: EVOLUTIONS - HEARTS OF STEEL
IDW Publishing: June, 2006 - No. 4, Sept, 2006 ($2.99, limited series)

1-4-Bumblebee meets John Henry in 1880s railroad times 3.00

TRANSFORMERS: GENERATION 1
Dreamwave Productions: Apr, 2002 - No. 6, Oct, 2002 ($2.95)

Preview- 6 pg. story; robot sketch pages; Pat Lee-a 2.00
1-Pat Lee-a; 2 wraparound covers by Lee 4.00
2-6: 2-Optimus Prime reactivated; 2 covers by Pat Lee 3.00
...Vol. 1 HC (2003, $49.95) r/#1-6; black hardcover with red foil lettering and art 50.00
...Vol. 1 TPB (2002, $17.95) r/#1-6 plus six page preview; 8 pg. preview of future issues 18.00

TRANSFORMERS: GENERATION 1 (Volume 2)
Dreamwave Productions: Apr, 2003 - No. 6, Sept, 2003 ($2.95)

1-6: 1-Pat Lee-a; 2 wraparound gatefold covers by Lee 3.00
1-($5.95) Chrome wraparound variant-c 6.00
...Vol. 2 TPB (IDW Publ., 3/06, $19.99) r/#1-6 plus cover gallery 20.00

TRANSFORMERS: GENERATION 1 (Volume 3)
Dreamwave Productions: No. 0, Dec, 2003 - Present ($2.95)

0-10: 0-Pat Lee-a. 1-Figueroa-a; wrapaound-c 3.00

TRANSFORMERS: GENERATION 2
Marvel Comics: Nov, 1993 - No. 12, Oct, 1994 ($1.75)

	GD	VG	FN	VF	VF/NM	NM-
1-($2.95, 68 pgs.)-Collector's ed. w/bi-fold metallic-c	1	3	4	6	8	10
1-11: 1-Newsstand edition (68 pgs.). 2-G.I. Joe app., Snake-Eyes, Scarlett, Cobra Commander app. 5-Red Alert killed, Optimus Prime gives Grimlock leadership of Autobots. 6-G.I. Joe app.	1	2	3	4	5	7
12-($2.25, 52 pgs.)	1	3	4	6	8	10

TRANSFORMERS: GENERATIONS
IDW Publishing: Mar, 2006 - No. 12, Mar, 2007 ($1.99/$2.49/$3.99)

1,2: 1-R/Transformers #7 (1985); preview of Transformers, Beast Wars. 2-R/#13 2.50
3-10-($2.49) 3-R/Transformers #14 (1986). 4-6-Reprint #16-18. 7-R/#24 2.50
11,12-($3.99) 4.00
Volume 1 (12/06, $19.99) r/#1-6; cover gallery 20.00

TRANSFORMERS/G.I. JOE
Dreamwave Productions: Aug, 2003 - No. 6, Mar, 2004 ($2.95/$5.25)

1-Art & gatefold wraparound-c by Jae Lee; Ney Rieber-s; variant-c by Pat Lee 3.00
1-($5.95) Holofoil wraparound-c by Norton 6.00
2-6-Jae Lee-a/c 3.00
TPB (8/04, $17.95) r/#1-6; cover gallery and sketch pages 18.00

TRANSFORMERS/G.I. JOE: DIVIDED FRONT
Dreamwave Productions: Oct, 2004 ($2.95)

1-Art & gatefold wraparound-c by Pat Lee 3.00

TRANSFORMERS: HEADMASTERS
Marvel Comics Group: July, 1987 - No. 4, Jan, 1988 ($1.00, limited series)

1-Springer, Akin, Garvey-a 5.00
2-4-Springer-c on all 4.00

TRANSFORMERS: INFILTRATION
IDW Publishing: Jan, 2006 - No. 6, June, 2006 ($2.99, limited series)

1-6-Furman-s/Su-a; multiple covers on all 3.00
... Cover Gallery (8/06, $5.99) 6.00

TRANSFORMERS: LAST STAND OF THE WRECKERS
IDW Publishing: Jan, 2010 - Present ($3.99, limited series)

1-Nick Roche-s/a; two covers 4.00

TRANSFORMERS: MAXIMUM DINOBOTS
IDW Publishing: Dec, 2008 - No. 5, Apr, 2009 ($3.99, limited series)

1-5-Furman-s/Roche-a; 2 covers for each 4.00

TRANSFORMERS: MEGATRON ORIGIN
IDW Publishing: May, 2007 - No. 4, Sept, 2008 ($3.99, limited series)

1-4-Alex Milne-a; 2 covers 4.00

TRANSFORMERS: MICROMASTERS
Dreamwave Productions: June, 2004 - No. 4 ($2.95, limited series)

1-4-Ruffolo-a; Pat Lee-c 3.00

TRANSFORMERS: MORE THAN MEETS THE EYE
Dreamwave Productions: Apr, 2003 - No. 8, Nov, 2003 ($5.25)

1-8-Pin-ups with tech info on Autobots and Decepticons; art by Pat Lee & various 5.25
Vol. 1,2 (2004, $24.95, TPB) 1-r/#1-4. 2-r/#5-8 25.00

TRANSFORMERS: MOVIE ADAPTATION (For the 2007 live action movie)
IDW Publishing: June, 2007 - No. 4, June, 2007 ($3.99, weekly limited series)

1-4: Wraparound covers on each; Milne-a 4.00

TRANSFORMERS: MOVIE PREQUEL (For the 2007 live action movie)
IDW Publishing: Feb, 2007 - No. 4, May, 2007 ($3.99, limited series)

1-4: 1-Origin of the Transformers on Cybertron; multiple covers on each 4.00
Special (6/08, $3.99) 2 covers 4.00
TPB (6/07, $19.99) r/series; gallery of covers and variants 20.00

TRANSFORMERS: REVENGE OF THE FALLEN OFFICIAL MOVIE ADAPTATION
(For the 2009 live action movie sequel)
IDW Publishing: May, 2009 - No. 4, June, 2009 ($3.99, weekly limited series)

1-4: Furman-s; 2 covers on each 4.00

TRANSFORMERS: SAGA OF THE ALLSPARK (From the 2007 live action movie)
IDW Publishing: Jul, 2008 - No. 4, Oct, 2008 ($3.99, limited series)

1-4-Launch of the Allspark into outer space; Furman-s/Roche-c 4.00

TRANSFORMERS: SPOTLIGHT
IDW Publishing: Sept, 2006 - Present ($3.99, multiple covers on each)

... Arcee (2/08); ... Blaster (1/08); ... Blurr (11/08); ... Cliffjumper (6/09); ... Cyclonus (6/08); ...Doubledealer (8/08); ...Drift (4/09); ...Grimlock (3/08); ...Hardhead (7/08); Hot Rod (11/06); ... Jazz (3/09); ... Kup (4/07); ... Metroplex (7/09); ... Mirage (3/08); ... Nightbeat (10/06); ... Ramjet (11/07); ... Shockwave (9/06); ... Sideswipe (9/08); ... Sixshot (12/06); ... Soundwave (3/07); ... Ultra Magnus (1/07) 4.00
... Optimus Prime: 3-D (11/08, $5.99, with glasses) Furman-s/Figueroa-a 6.00

TRANSFORMERS: STORMBRINGER
IDW Publishing: Jul, 2006 - No. 4, Oct, 2006 ($2.99, limited series)

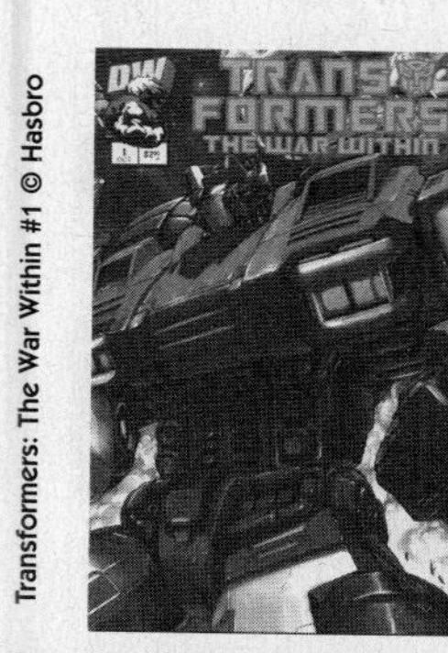

Transformers: The War Within #1 © Hasbro

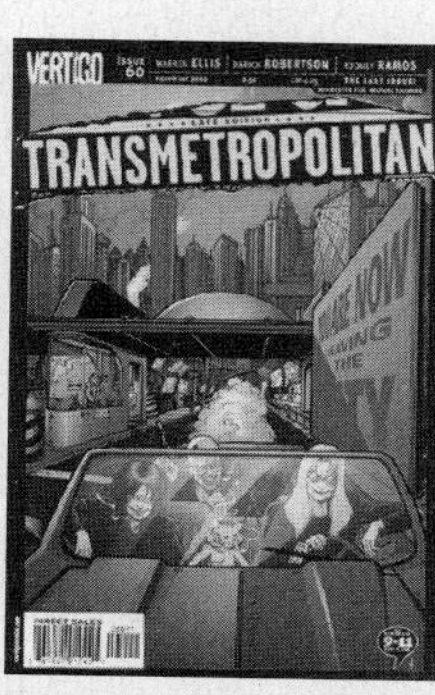

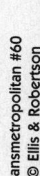

Transmetropolitan #60 © Ellis & Robertson

Treasure Chest V14 #18 © G. Pflaum

GD 2.0 VG 4.0 FN 6.0 VF 8.0 VF/NM 9.0 NM- 9.2

1-4-Furman-s/Figueroa-a; multiple covers on all 3.00
TPB (2/07, $17.99) r/series; cover gallery and sketch pages 18.00

TRANSFORMERS SUMMER SPECIAL
Dreamwave Productions: May, 2004 ($4.95)
1-Pat Lee-a; Figueroa-a 5.00

TRANSFORMERS: TALES OF THE FALLEN
IDW Publishing: Aug, 2009 - Present ($3.99, limited series)
1-4: 2,4-Furman-s mulitple covers on all 4.00

TRANSFORMERS: TARGET 2006
IDW Publishing: Apr, 2007 - No. 5, Aug, 2007 ($3.99, limited series)
1-5-Reprints from 1980s series; multiple covers on all 4.00

TRANSFORMERS: THE ANIMATED MOVIE
IDW Publishing: Oct, 2006 - No. 4, Jan, 2007 ($3.99, limited series)
1-4-Adapts animated movie; Don Figueroa-a 4.00

TRANSFORMERS, THE MOVIE
Marvel Comics Group: Dec, 1986 - No. 3, Feb, 1987 (75¢, limited series)
1-3-Adapts animated movie 4.00

TRANSFORMERS: THE REIGN OF STARSCREAM
IDW Publishing: Apr, 2008 - No. 5, Aug, 2008 ($3.99, limited series)
1-5-Continuation of the 2007 movie; Milne-a; multiple covers 4.00

TRANSFORMERS: THE WAR WITHIN
Dreamwave Productions: Oct, 2002 - No. 6, Mar, 2003 ($2.95)
1-6-Furman-s/Figueroa-a. 1-Wraparound gatefold-c 3.00
TPB (2003, $15.95) r/#1-6; plus cover gallery 16.00

TRANSFORMERS UNIVERSE
Marvel Comics Group: Dec, 1986 - No. 4, Mar, 1987 ($1.25, limited series)
1-4-A guide to all characters 6.00
TPB-r/#1-4 15.00

TRANSFORMERS WAR WITHIN: THE AGE OF WRATH
Dreamwave Productions: Sept, 2004 - No. 6 ($2.95, limited series)
1-3-Furman-s/Ng-a 3.00

TRANSFORMERS WAR WITHIN: THE DARK AGES
Dreamwave Productions: Oct, 2003 - No. 6 ($2.95)
1-6: 1-Furman-s/Wildman-a; two covers by Pat Lee & Figueroa 3.00
TPB (2004, $17.95) r/#1-6; plus cover gallery and design sketches 18.00

TRANSIT
Vortex Publ.: March, 1987 - No. 5, Nov, 1987 (B&W)
1-5-Ted McKeever-s/a 1 2 3 5 6 8

TRANSMETROPOLITAN
DC Comics (Helix/Vertigo): Sept, 1997 - No. 60, Nov, 2002 ($2.50)
1-Warren Ellis-s/Darick Robertson-a(p) 2 4 6 8 10 12
1-Special Edition (5/09, $1.00) r/#1 with "After Watchmen" cover frame 1.00
2,3 1 2 3 4 5 7
4-8 4.00
9-60: 15-Jae Lee-c. 25-27-Jim Lee-c. 37-39-Bradstreet-c 2.50
Back on the Street ('97, $7.95) r/#1-3 8.00
Back on the Street ('09, $14.99) r/#1-6; intro. by Garth Ennis 15.00
Dirge ('03, $14.95) r/#43-48 15.00
Filth of the City ('01, $5.95) Spider's columns with pin-up art by various 6.00
Gouge Away ('02/'09, $14.95/$14.99) r/#31-36 15.00
I Hate It Here ('00, $5.95) Spider's columns with pin-up art by various 6.00
Lonely City ('01/'09, $14.95/$14.99) r/#25-30; intro. by Patrick Stewart 15.00
Lust For Life ('98, $14.95) r/#4-12 15.00
Lust For Life ('09, $14.99) r/#7-12 15.00
One More Time ('04, $14.95) r/#55-60 15.00
Spider's Thrash ('02, $14.95) r/#37-42; intro. by Darren Aronofsky 15.00
Tales of Human Waste ('04, $9.95) r/Filth of the City, I Hate It Here & story from Vertigo Winter's Edge 2 10.00
The Cure ('03, $14.95) r/#49-54 15.00
The New Scum ('00, $12.95) r/#19-24 & Vertigo: Winter's Edge #3 13.00
The New Scum ('09, $14.99) r/#19-24 & Vertigo: Winter's Edge #3 15.00
Year of the Bastard ('99, $12.95)('09, $12.99) r/#13-18 13.00

TRANSMUTATION OF IKE GARUDA, THE
Marvel Comics (Epic Comics): July, 1991 - No. 2, 1991 ($3.95, 52 pgs.)
1,2 4.00

TRAPMAN
Phantom Comics: June, 1994 - No. 2, 1994? ($2.95, quarterly, unfinished limited series)
1,2 3.00

TRAPPED!
Periodical House Magazines (Ace): Oct, 1954 - No. 4, April, 1955
1 (All reprints) 10 20 30 54 72 90
2-4: 4-r/Men Against Crime #4 in its entirety 7 14 21 35 43 50
NOTE: *Colan a-1, 4. **Sekowsky** a-1.*

TRASH
Trash Publ. Co.: Mar, 1978 - No. 4, Oct, 1978 (B&W, magazine, 52 pgs.)
1,2: 1-Star Wars parody. 2-UFO-c 2 4 6 10 14 18
3-Parodies of KISS, the Beatles, and monsters 3 6 9 14 19 24
4-(84 pgs.)-Parodies of Happy Days, Rocky movies 3 6 9 14 20 26

TRAVELS OF JAIMIE McPHEETERS, THE (TV)
Gold Key: Dec, 1963
1-Kurt Russell photo on-c plus photo back-c 4 8 12 26 41 55

TREASURE CHEST (Catholic Guild; also see Topix)
George A. Pflaum: 3/12/46 - V27#8, July, 1972 (Educational comics)
(Not published during Summer)
V1#1 27 54 81 158 259 360
2-6 (5/21/46): 5-Dr. Styx app. by Baily 14 28 42 80 115 150
V2#1-20 (9/3/46-5/27/47) 11 22 33 60 83 105
V3#1-5,7-20 (1st slick cover) 10 20 30 54 72 90
V3#6-Jules Verne's "Voyage to the Moon" 11 22 33 64 90 115
V4#1-20 (9/9/48-5/31/49) 9 18 27 47 61 75
V5#1-20 (9/6/49-5/31/50) 8 16 24 44 57 70
V6#1-20 (9/14/50-5/31/51) 8 16 24 42 54 65
V7#1-20 (9/13/51-6/5/52) 8 16 24 40 50 60
V8#1-20 (9/11/52-6/4/53) 7 14 21 37 46 55
V9#1-20 ('53-'54), V10#1-20 ('54-'55) 7 14 21 35 43 50
V11('55-'56), V12('56-'57) 6 12 18 29 36 42
V13#1,3-5,7,9-V17#1 ('57-'63) 6 12 18 27 33 38
V13#2,6,8-Ingels-a 6 12 18 41 66 90
V17#2- "This Godless Communism" series begins(not in odd #'d issues); cover shows hammer & sickle over Statue of Liberty; 8 pg. Crandall-a of family life under communism 18 36 54 126 246 365
V17#3,5,7,9,11,13,15,17,19 3 6 9 16 23 30
V17#4,6,14- "This Godless Communism" stories 14 28 42 100 188 275
V17#8-Shows red octopus encompassing Earth, firing squad; 8 pgs. Crandall-a 16 32 48 112 214 315
V17#10- "This Godless Communism" - how Stalin came to power, part I; Crandall-a 15 30 45 107 204 300
V17#12-Stalin in WWII, forced labor, death by exhaustion; Crandall-a 15 30 45 107 204 300
V17#16-Kruschev takes over; de-Stalinization 15 30 45 107 204 300
V17#18-Kruschev's control; murder of revolters, brainwash, space race by Crandall 15 30 45 107 204 300
V17#20-End of series; Kruschev-people are puppets, firing squads hammer & sickle over Statue of Liberty, snake around communist manifesto by Crandall 17 34 51 119 230 340
V18#1-20, V19#11-20, V20#1-20(1964-65): V18#11-Crandall draws himself & 13 other artists on cover 3 6 9 16 22 28
V18#5- "What About Red China?" - describes how communists took over China 8 16 24 58 97 135
V19#1-10- "Red Victim" anti-communist series in all 8 16 24 58 97 135
V21-V25(1965-70)-(two V24#5's 11/7/68 & 11/21/68) (no V24#6) 3 6 9 14 19 24
V26, V27#1-8 (V26,27-68 pgs.) 3 6 9 16 22 28
Summer Edition V1#1-6('66), V2#1-6('67) 3 6 9 16 23 30
NOTE: ***Anderson** a-V18#13. **Borth** a-V7#10-19 (serial), V8#8-17 (serial), V9#1-10 (serial), V13#2, 6, 11, V14-V25 (except V22#1-3, 11-13), Summer Ed. V1#3-6. **Crandall** a-V16#7, 9, 12, 14, 16-18, 20; V17#1, 2, 4-6, 10, 12, 14, 16-18, 20; V18#1, 2, 3(2 pg.), 7, 9-20; V19#4, 11, 13, 16, 19, 20; V20#1, 2, 4, 6, 8-10, 12, 14-16, 18, 20; V21#1-5, 8-11, 13, 16-18; V22#3, 7, 9-11, 14; V23#3, 6, 9, 16, 18; V24#7, 8, 10, 13, 16; V25#8, 16; V27#1-7r, 8r(2 pg.), Summer Ed. V1#3-5, V2#3; c-V16#7, V18#2(part), 7, 11, V19#4, 19, 20, V20#15, V21#5, 9, V22#3, 7, 9, 11, V23#9, 16, V24#13, 16, V25#8, Summer Ed. V1#2 (back c-V1#2-5). **Powell** a-V10#11. V19#11, 15, V10#13, V13#6, 8 all have wraparound covers.*

TREASURE CHEST OF THE WORLD'S BEST COMICS
Superior, Toronto, Canada: 1945 (500 pgs., hard-c)
Contains Blue Beetle, Captain Combat, John Wayne, Dynamic Man, Nemo, Li'l Abner; contents can vary - represents random binding of extra books; Captain America on-c 90 180 270 576 988 1400

Treehouse of Horror #9 © Bongo

Trenchcoat Brigade #3 © DC

Trinity #3 © DC

	GD 2.0	VG 4.0	FN 6.0	VF 8.0	VF/NM 9.0	NM- 9.2

TREASURE COMICS
Prize Publications? (no publisher listed): No date (1943) (50¢, 324 pgs., cardboard-c)

1-(Rare)-Contains rebound Prize Comics #7-11 from 1942 (blank inside-c)	252	504	756	1613	2757	3900

TREASURE COMICS
Prize Publ. (American Boys' Comics): June-July, 1945 - No. 12, Fall, 1947

1-Paul Bunyan & Marco Polo begin; Highwayman & Carrot Topp only app.; Kiefer-a	48	96	144	302	514	725
2-Arabian Knight, Gorilla King, Dr. Styx begin	28	56	84	168	274	380
3,4,9,12: 9-Kiefer-a	23	46	69	136	223	310
5-Marco Polo-c; Krigstein-a	28	56	84	168	274	380
6,11-Krigstein-a; 11-Krigstein-c	27	54	81	160	263	365
7,8-Frazetta-a (5 pgs. each). 7-Capt. Kidd Jr. app.	41	82	123	256	428	600
10-Simon & Kirby-c/a	36	72	108	216	351	485

NOTE: *Barry a-9-11; c-12.* ***Kiefer*** *a-3, 5, 7; c-2, 6, 7.* ***Roussos*** *a-11.*

TREASURE ISLAND (See Classics Illustrated #64, Doc Savage Comics #1, King Classics, Movie Classics & Movie Comics)
Dell Publishing Co.: No. 624, Apr, 1955 (Disney)

Four Color 624-Movie, photo-c	8	16	24	54	90	125

TREASURY OF COMICS
St. John Publishing Co.: 1947; No. 2, July, 1947 - No. 4, Sept, 1947; No. 5, Jan, 1948

nn(#1)-Abbie an' Slats (nn on-c, #1 on inside)	14	28	42	80	115	150
2-Jim Hardy Comics; featuring Windy & Paddles	11	22	33	62	86	110
3-Bill Bumlin	10	20	30	54	72	90
4-Abbie an' Slats	11	22	33	62	86	110
5-Jim Hardy Comics #1	11	22	33	62	86	110

TREASURY OF COMICS
St. John Publishing Co.: Mar, 1948 - No. 5, 1948 (Reg. size); 1948-1950 (Over 500 pgs., $1.00)

1	19	38	57	111	176	240
2(#2 on-c, #1 on inside)	12	24	36	67	94	120
3-5	10	20	30	56	76	95
1-(1948, 500 pgs., hard-c)-Abbie & Slats, Abbott & Costello, Casper, Little Annie Rooney, Little Audrey, Jim Hardy, Ella Cinders (16 books bound together) (Rare)	123	246	369	787	1344	1900
1(1949, 500 pgs.)-Same format as above	110	220	330	704	1202	1700
1(1950, 500 pgs.)-Same format as above; different-c; (also see Little Audrey Yearbook) (Rare)	110	220	330	704	1202	1700

TREASURY OF DOGS, A (See Dell Giants)

TREASURY OF HORSES, A (See Dell Giants)

TREEHOUSE OF HORROR (Bart Simpson's...)
Bongo Comics: 1995 - Present ($2.95/$2.50/$3.50/$4.50/$4.99, annual)

1-(1995, $2.95)-Groening-c; Allred, Robinson & Smith stories	3.50
2-(1996, $2.50)-Stories by Dini & Bagge; infinity-c by Groening	3.00
3-(1997, $2.50)-Dorkin-s/Groening-c	3.00
4-(1998, $2.50)-Lash & Dixon-s/Groening-c	3.00
5-(1999, $3.50)-Thompson-s; Shaw & Aragonés-s/a; TenNapel-s/a	3.50
6-(2000, $4.50)-Mahfood-s/a; DeCarlo-a; Morse-s/a; Kuper-s/a	4.50
7-(2001, $4.50)-Hamill-s/Morrison-a; Ennis-s/McCrea-a; Sakai-s/a; Nixey-s/a; Brereton back-c	4.50
8-(2002, $3.50)-Templeton, Shaw, Barta, Simone, Thompson-s/a	3.50
9-(2003, $4.99)-Lord of the Rings-Brereton-a; Dini, Naifeh, Millidge, Boothby, Noto-s/a	5.00
10-(2004, $4.99)-Monsters of Rock w/Alice Cooper, Gene Simmons, Rob Zombie and Pat Boone; art by Rodriguez, Morrison, Morse, Templeton	5.00
11-(2005, $4.99)-EC style w/art by John Severin, Angelo Torres & Al Williamson and flip book with Dracula by Wolfman/Colan and Squish Thing by Wein/Wrightson	5.00
12-(2006, $4.99)-Terry Moore, Kyle Baker, Eric Powell-s/a	5.00
13-(2007, $4.99)-Oswalt, Posehn, Lennon-s; Guerra, Austin, Barta, Rodriguez-a	5.00
14-(2008, $4.99)-s/a by Niles & Fabry; Boothby & Matsumoto; Gilbert Hernandez	5.00
15-(2009, $4.99)-s/a by Jeffrey Brown, Tim Hensley, Ben Jones and others	5.00

TREKKER (See Dark Horse Presents #6)
Dark Horse Comics: May, 1987 - No. 6, Mar,1988 ($1.50, B&W)

1-6: Sci/Fi stories	2.50
Color Special 1 (1989, $2.95, 52 pgs.)	3.00
Collection ($5.95, B&W)	6.00
Special 1 (6/99, $2.95, color)	3.00

TRENCHCOAT BRIGADE, THE
DC Comics (Vertigo): Mar, 1999 - No. 4, Jun, 1999 ($2.50, limited series)

1-4: Hellblazer, Phantom Stranger, Mister E, Dr. Occult app.	2.50

	GD 2.0	VG 4.0	FN 6.0	VF 8.0	VF/NM 9.0	NM- 9.2

TRENCHER (See Blackball Comics)
Image Comics: May, 1993 - No. 4, Oct, 1993 ($1.95, unfinished limited series)

1-4: Keith Giffen-c/a/scripts. 3-Supreme-c/story	2.50

TRIALS OF SHAZAM!
DC Comics: Oct, 2006 - No. 12, May, 2008 ($2.99)

1-12: 1-8-Winick-s/Porter-a. 9-11-Cascioli-a. 10-Shadowpact app. 12-JLA app.	3.00
... Volume 1 TPB (2007, $14.99) r/#1-6 and story from DCU Brave New World #1	15.00
... Volume 2 TPB (2008, $14.99) r/#7-12	15.00

TRIB COMIC BOOK, THE
Winnipeg Tribune: Sept. 24, 1977 - Vol. 4, #36, 1980 (8-1/2"x11", 24 pgs., weekly) (155 total issues)

V1# 1-Color pages (Sunday strips)-Spiderman, Asterix, Disney's Scamp, Wizard of Id, Doonesbury, Inside Woody Allen, Mary Worth, & others (similar to Spirit sections)	2	4	6	10	14	18
V1#2-15, V2#1-52, V3#1-52, V4#1-33	1	3	4	6	8	10
V4#34-36 (not distributed)	2	4	6	11	16	20

NOTE: *All issues have Spider-Man. Later issues contain Star Trek and Star Wars. 20 strips in ea. The first newspaper to put Sunday pages into a comic book format.*

TRIBE (See WildC.A.T.S #4)
Image Comics/Axis Comics No. 2 on: Apr, 1993; No. 2, Sept, 1993 - No. 3, 1994 ($2.50/$1.95)

1-By Johnson & Stroman; gold foil & embossed on black-c	2.50
1-($2.50)-Ivory Edition; gold foil & embossed on white-c; available only through the creators	2.50
2,3: 2-1st Axis Comics issue. 3-Savage Dragon app.	2.50

TRIBUTE TO STEVEN HUGHES, A
Chaos! Comics: Sept, 2000 ($6.95)

1-Lady Death & Evil Ernie pin-ups by various artists; testimonials	7.00

TRICK 'R TREAT
DC Comics (WildStorm): 2009 ($19.95,SC)

nn-Short Halloween-themed story anthology; Andreyko-s; art by Huddleston & others	20.00

TRIGGER (See Roy Rogers'...)

TRIGGER
DC Comics (Vertigo): Feb, 2005 - No. 8, Sept, 2005 ($2.95/$2.99)

1-8-Jason Hall-s/John Watkiss-a/c	3.00

TRIGGER TWINS
National Periodical Publications: Mar-Apr, 1973 (20¢, one-shot)

1-Trigger Twins & Pow Wow Smith-r/All-Star Western #94,103 & Western Comics #81; Infantino-r(p)	2	4	6	13	18	22

TRINITY (See DC Universe: Trinity)

TRINITY
DC Comics: Aug, 2008 - No. 52, July, 2009 ($2.99, weekly series)

1-52-Superman, Batman & Wonder Woman star; Busiek-s/Bagley-a. 52-Wraparound-c	3.00
Vol. 1 TPB (2009, $29.99) r/#1-17	30.00
Vol. 2 TPB (2009, $29.99) r/#18-35	30.00
Vol. 3 TPB (2009, $29.99) r/#36-52	30.00

TRINITY ANGELS
Acclaim Comics (Valiant Heroes): July, 1997 - No. 12, June, 1998 ($2.50)

1-12-Maguire-s/a(p):4-Copycat-c	3.00

TRINITY: BLOOD ON THE SANDS
Image Comics (Top Cow): July, 2009 ($2.99, one-shot)

1-Witchblade, The Darkness and Angelus in the 14th century Arabian desert	3.00

TRIPLE GIANT COMICS (See Archie All-Star Specials under Archie Comics)

TRIPLE THREAT
Special Action/Holyoke/Gerona Publ.: Winter, 1945

1-Duke of Darkness, King O'Leary	32	64	96	188	307	425

TRIPLE-X
Dark Horse Comics: Dec, 1994 - No. 7, June, 1995 ($3.95, B&W, limited series)

1-7	4.00

TRIUMPH (Also see JLA #28-30, Justice League Task Force & Zero Hour)
DC Comics: June, 1995 - No. 4, Sept, 1995 ($1.75, limited series)

1-4: 3-Hourman, JLA app.	2.50

TRIUMPHANT UNLEASHED
Triumphant Comics: No. 0, Nov, 1993 - No. 1, Nov, 1993 ($2.50, lim. series)

Trojan War #3 © MAR

True Believers #5 © MAR

True Comics #14 © PMI

GD 2.0 | VG 4.0 | FN 6.0 | VF 8.0 | VF/NM 9.0 | NM- 9.2

0-Serially numbered, 0-Red logo, 0-White logo (no cover price; giveaway), 1-Cover is negative & reverse of #0-c 2.50

TROJAN WAR (Adaptation of Trojan war histories from ancient Greek and Roman sources)
Marvel Comics: July, 2009 - No. 5, Nov, 2009 ($3.99, limited series)
1-5-Roy Thomas-s/Miguel Sepulveda-a/Dennis Calero-c 4.00

TROLL (Also see Brigade)
Image Comics (Extreme Studios): Dec, 1993 ($2.50, one-shot, 44 pgs.)
1-1st app. Troll; Liefeld scripts; Matsuda-c/a(p) 2.50
Halloween Special (1994, $2.95)-Maxx app. 3.00
...Once A Hero (8/94, $2.50) 2.50

TROLLORDS
Tru Studios/Comico V2#1 on: 2/86 - No. 15, 1988; V2#1, 11/88 - V2#4, 1989 (1-15: $1.50, B&W)
1-15: 1-Both printings. 6-Christmas issue; silver logo 2.50
V2#1-4 ($1.75, color, Comico) 2.50
Special 1 ($1.75, 2/87, color)-Jerry's Big Fun Bk. 2.50

TROLLORDS
Apple Comics: July, 1989 - No. 6, 1990 ($2.25, B&W, limited series)
1-6: 1-"The Big Batman Movie Parody" 2.50

TROLL PATROL
Harvey Comics: Jan, 1993 ($1.95, 52 pgs.)
1 2.50

TROLL II (Also see Brigade)
Image Comics (Extreme Studios): July, 1994 ($3.95, one-shot)
1 4.00

TRON (Based on the video game and film)
Slave Labor Graphics: Apr, 2006 - Present ($3.50/$3.95)
1-4: 1-DeMartinis-a/Walker & Jones-s 3.50
5,6-($3.95) 4.00

TROUBLE
Marvel Comics (Epic): Sept, 2003 - No. 5, Jan, 2004 ($2.99, limited series)
1-5-Photo-c; Richard and Ben meet Mary and May; Millar-s/Dodson-a 3.00
1-2nd printing with variant Frank Cho-c 5.00

TROUBLED SOULS
Fleetway: 1990 ($9.95, trade paperback)
nn-Garth Ennis scripts & John McCrea painted-c/a. 10.00

TROUBLEMAKERS
Acclaim Comics (Valiant Heroes): Apr, 1997 - No. 19, June, 1998 ($2.50)
1-19: Fabian Nicieza scripts in all. 1-1st app. XL, Rebound & Blur; 2 covers. 8-Copycat-c. 12-Shooting of Parker 2.50

TROUBLE SHOOTERS, THE (TV)
Dell Publishing Co.: No. 1108, Jun-Aug, 1960
Four Color 1108-Keenan Wynn photo-c 5 10 15 34 55 75

TROUBLE WITH GIRLS, THE
Malibu Comics (Eternity Comics) #7-14/Comico V2#1-4/Eternity V2#5 on: 8/87 - #14, 1988; V2#1, 2/89 - V2#23, 1991? ($1.95, B&W/color)
1-14 ($1.95, B&W, Eternity)-Gerard Jones scripts & Tim Hamilton-c/a in all. 2.50
V2#1-23-Jones scripts, Hamilton-c/a. 2.50
Annual 1 (1988, $2.95) 3.00
Christmas Special 1 (12/91, $2.95, B&W, Eternity)-Jones scripts, Hamilton-c/a 3.00
Graphic Novel 1,2 (7/88, B&W)-r/#1-3 & #4-6 8.00

TROUBLE WITH GIRLS, THE: NIGHT OF THE LIZARD
Marvel Comics (Epic Comics/Heavy Hitters): 1993 - No. 4, 1993 ($2.50/$1.95, lim. series)
1-Embossed-c; Gerard Jones scripts & Bret Blevins-c/a in all 2.50
2-4: 2-Begin $1.95-c. 2.50

TROUT
Oni Press: Oct, 2001 - No. 2, Feb, 2002 ($2.95, B&W, limited series)
1,2-Troy Nixey-s/a 3.00

TRUE ADVENTURES (Formerly True Western)(Men's Adventures #4 on)
Marvel Comics (CCC): No. 3, May, 1950 (52 pgs.)
3-Powell, Sekowsky-a; Brodsky-c 17 34 51 98 154 210

TRUE ANIMAL PICTURE STORIES
True Comics Press: Winter, 1947 - No. 2, Spring-Summer, 1947
1,2 10 20 30 56 76 95

TRUE AVIATION PICTURE STORIES (Becomes Aviation Adventures & Model Building #16 on)
Parents' Mag. Institute: 1942; No. 2, Jan-Feb, 1943 - No. 15, Sept-Oct, 1946
1-(#1 & 2 titled ...Aviation Comics Digest)(not digest size) 15 30 45 85 130 175
2 10 20 30 56 76 95
3-14: 3-10-Plane photos on-c. 11,13-Photo-c 9 18 27 50 65 80
15-(Titled "True Aviation Adventures & Model Building") 9 18 27 47 61 75

TRUE BELIEVERS
Marvel Comics: Sept, 2008 - No. 5, Jan, 2009 ($2.99, limited series)
1-5-Cary Bates-s/Paul Gulacy-a. 1,2-Reed Richards app. 3-Luke Cage app. 3.00

TRUE BRIDE'S EXPERIENCES (Formerly Teen-Age Brides)
(True Bride-To-Be Romances No. 17 on)
True Love (Harvey Publications): No. 8, Oct, 1954 - No. 16, Feb, 1956
8-"I Married a Farmer" 9 18 27 50 65 80
9,10: 10-Last pre-code (2/55) 7 14 21 37 46 55
11-15 6 12 18 31 38 45
16-Last issue 7 14 21 37 46 55
NOTE: *Powell a-8-10, 12, 13.*

TRUE BRIDE-TO-BE ROMANCES (Formerly True Bride's Experiences)
Home Comics/True Love (Harvey): No. 17, Apr, 1956 - No. 30, Nov, 1958
17-S&K-c, Powell-a 10 20 30 56 76 95
18-20,22,25-28,30 6 12 18 31 38 45
21,23,24,29-Powell-a. 29-Baker-a (1 pg.) 7 14 21 35 43 50

TRUE COMICS (Also see Outstanding American War Heroes)
True Comics/Parents' Magazine Press: April, 1941 - No. 84, Aug, 1950
1-Marathon run story; life story Winston Churchill 31 62 93 182 296 410
2-Red Cross story; Everett-a 15 30 45 85 130 175
3-Baseball Hall of Fame story; Chiang Kai-Shek-c/s 17 34 51 100 158 215
4,5: 4-Story of American flag "Old Glory". 5-Life story of Joe Louis 14 28 42 80 115 150
6-Baseball World Series story 15 30 45 90 140 190
7-10: 7-Buffalo Bill story. 10,11-Teddy Roosevelt 11 22 33 62 86 110
11-14,16,18-20: 11-Thomas Edison, Douglas MacArthur stories. 13-Harry Houdini story. 14-Charlie McCarthy story. 18-Story of America begins, ends #26. 19-Eisenhower-c/s 10 20 30 54 72 90
15-Flag-c; Bob Feller story 10 20 30 58 79 100
17-Brooklyn Dodgers story 11 22 33 64 90 115
21-30: 24-Marco Polo story. 28-Origin of Uncle Sam. 29-Beethoven story. 30-Cooper Brothers baseball story 9 18 27 47 61 75
31-Red Grange "Galloping Ghost" story 8 16 24 40 50 60
32-46: 33-Origin/1st app. Steve Saunders, Special Agent of the FBI, series begins. 35-Mark Twain story. 38-General Bradley-c/s. 39-FDR story. 44-Truman story. 46-George Gershwin story 7 14 21 37 46 55
47-Atomic bomb issue (c/story, 3/46) 10 20 30 56 76 95
48-54,56-65: 49-1st app. Secret Warriors. 53-Bobby Riggs story. 58-Jim Jeffries (boxer) story; Harry Houdini story. 59-Bob Hope story; pirates-c/s. 60-Speedway Speed Demon-c/story. 7 14 21 35 43 50
55-(12/46)-1st app. Sad Sack by Baker (1/2 pg.) 9 18 27 47 61 75
66-Will Rogers-c/story 7 14 21 37 46 55
67-1st oversized issue (12/47); Steve Saunders, Special Agent begins 8 16 24 42 54 65
68-70,74-77,79: 68-70,74-77-Features Steve Sanders True FBI advs. 68-Oversized; Admiral Byrd-c/s. 69-Jack Benny story. 74-Amos 'n' Andy story 6 12 18 31 38 45
71-Joe DiMaggio-c/story. 9 18 27 47 61 75
72-Jackie Robinson story; True FBI advs. 8 16 24 40 50 60
73-Walt Disney's life story 9 18 27 47 61 75
78-Stan Musial-c/story; True FBI advs. 8 16 24 40 50 60
80-84 (Scarce)-All distr. to subscribers through mail only; paper-c. 80-Rocket trip to the moon story. 81-Red Grange story. 84-Wyatt Earp app. (1st app. in comics?); Rube Marquard story 18 36 54 103 162 220
(Prices vary widely on issues 80-84)
NOTE: *Bob Kane a-7. Palais a-80. Powell c/a-80. #80-84 have soft covers and combined with Tex Granger, Jack Armstrong, and Calling All Kids. #68-78 featured true FBI adventures.*

TRUE COMICS AND ADVENTURE STORIES
Parents' Magazine Institute: 1965 (Giant) (25¢)
1,2: 1-Fighting Hero of Viet Nam; LBJ on-c 3 6 9 18 27 35

TRUE COMPLETE MYSTERY (Formerly Complete Mystery)
Marvel Comics (PrPl): No. 5, Apr, 1949 - No. 8, Oct, 1949

True Crime Comics #4 © Magazine Village

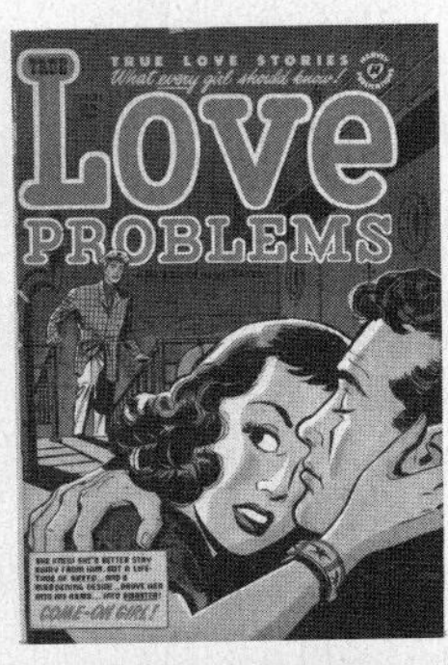

True Love Problems #25 © HARV

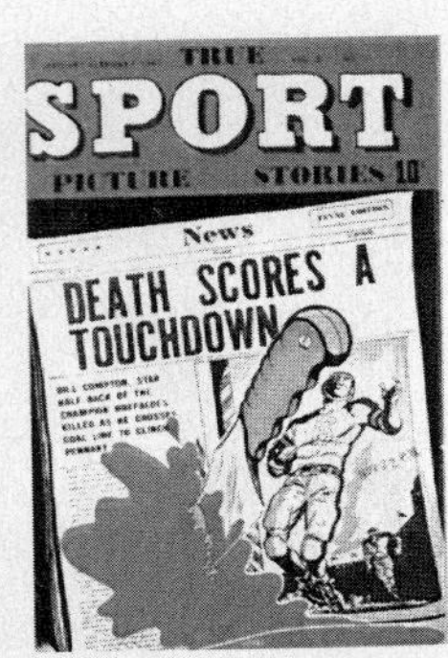

True Sport Picture Stories V3 #11 © S&S

	GD 2.0	VG 4.0	FN 6.0	VF 8.0	VF/NM 9.0	NM- 9.2
5	26	52	78	152	249	345
6-8: 6-8-Photo-c	20	40	60	114	182	250

TRUE CONFIDENCES
Fawcett Publications: 1949 (Fall) - No. 4, June, 1950 (All photo-c)

	GD 2.0	VG 4.0	FN 6.0	VF 8.0	VF/NM 9.0	NM- 9.2
1-Has ad for Fawcett Love Adventures #1, but publ. as Love Memoirs #1 as Marvel published the title first; Swayze-a	18	36	54	103	162	220
2-4: 3-Swayze-a. 4-Powell-a	11	22	33	64	90	115

TRUE CRIME CASES (...From Official Police Files)
St. John Publishing Co.: 1944 (25¢, 100 pg. Giant)

	GD 2.0	VG 4.0	FN 6.0	VF 8.0	VF/NM 9.0	NM- 9.2
nn-Matt Baker-c	47	94	141	296	498	700

TRUE CRIME COMICS (Also see Complete Book of...)
Magazine Village: No. 2, May, 1947; No. 3, July-Aug, 1948 - No. 6, June-July, 1949; V2#1, Aug-Sept, 1949 (52 pgs.)

	GD 2.0	VG 4.0	FN 6.0	VF 8.0	VF/NM 9.0	NM- 9.2
2-Jack Cole-c/a; used in **SOTI**, pgs. 81,82 plus illo. "A sample of the injury-to-eye motif" & illo. "Dragging living people to death"; used in **POP**, pg. 105; "Murder, Morphine and Me" classic drug propaganda story used by N.Y. Legis. Comm.	161	322	483	1030	1765	2500
3-Classic Cole-c/a; drug story with hypo, opium den & with drawing addict	116	232	348	742	1271	1800
4-Jack Cole-c/a; c-taken from a story panel in #3 (r-(2) **SOTI** & **POP** stories/#2?)	98	196	294	622	1074	1525
5-Jack Cole-c, Marijuana racket story (Canadian ed. w/cover similar to #3 exists w/out drug story)	66	132	198	419	722	1025
6-Not a reprint, original story (Canadian ed. reprints #4 w/different coloring on-c)	53	106	159	334	567	800
V2#1-Used in **SOTI**, pgs. 81,82 & illo. "Dragging living people to death"; Toth, Wood (3 pgs.), Roussos-a; Cole-r from #2	90	180	270	576	988	1400

NOTE: *V2#1 was reprinted in Canada as V2#9 (12/49); same-c & contents minus Wood-a.*

TRUE FAITH
Fleetway: 1990 ($9.95, graphic novel)

	GD 2.0	VG 4.0	FN 6.0	VF 8.0	VF/NM 9.0	NM- 9.2
nn-Garth Ennis scripts	2	4	6	12	16	20
Reprinted by DC/Vertigo ('97, $12.95)						13.00

TRUE GHOST STORIES (See Ripley's...)

TRUE LIFE ROMANCES (...Romance on cover)
Ajax/Farrell Publications: Dec, 1955 - No. 3, Aug, 1956

	GD 2.0	VG 4.0	FN 6.0	VF 8.0	VF/NM 9.0	NM- 9.2
1	10	20	30	58	79	100
2	8	16	24	40	50	60
3-Disbrow-a	8	16	24	44	57	70

TRUE LIFE SECRETS
Romantic Love Stories/Charlton: Mar-April, 1951 - No. 28, Sept, 1955; No. 29, Jan, 1956

	GD 2.0	VG 4.0	FN 6.0	VF 8.0	VF/NM 9.0	NM- 9.2
1-Photo-c begin, end #3?	14	28	42	82	121	160
2	9	18	27	50	65	80
3-11,13-19:	8	16	24	42	54	65
12-"I Was An Escort Girl" story	9	18	27	50	65	80
20-29: 25-Last precode (3/55)	7	14	21	37	46	55

TRUE LIFE TALES (Formerly Mitzi's Romances #8?)
Marvel Comics (CCC): No. 8, Oct, 1949 - No. 2, Jan, 1950 (52 pgs.)

	GD 2.0	VG 4.0	FN 6.0	VF 8.0	VF/NM 9.0	NM- 9.2
8(#1, 10/49), 2-Both have photo-c	11	22	33	64	90	115

TRUE LOVE
Eclipse Comics: Jan, 1986 - No. 2, Jan, 1986 ($2.00, Baxter paper)

	GD 2.0	VG 4.0	FN 6.0	VF 8.0	VF/NM 9.0	NM- 9.2
1,2-Love stories reprinted from pre-code Standard Comics; Toth-a(p) in both; 1-Dave Stevens-c. 2-Mayo-a						3.00

TRUE LOVE CONFESSIONS
Premier Magazines: May, 1954 - No. 11, Jan, 1956

	GD 2.0	VG 4.0	FN 6.0	VF 8.0	VF/NM 9.0	NM- 9.2
1-Marijuana story	14	28	42	80	115	150
2	9	18	27	47	61	75
3-11	8	16	24	42	54	65

TRUE LOVE PICTORIAL
St. John Publishing Co.: Dec, 1952 - No. 11, Aug, 1954

	GD 2.0	VG 4.0	FN 6.0	VF 8.0	VF/NM 9.0	NM- 9.2
1-Only photo-c	20	40	60	114	182	250
2-Baker-c/a	28	56	84	165	270	375
3-5(All 25¢, 100 pgs.): 4-Signed story by Estrada. 5-(4/53)-Formerly Teen-Age Temptations; Kubert-a in #3; Baker-c/a in #3-5	42	84	126	265	445	625
6,7: Baker-c/a; signed stories by Estrada	26	52	78	154	252	350
8,10,11-Baker-c/a	26	52	78	154	252	350
9-Baker-c	21	42	63	122	199	275

TRUE LOVE PROBLEMS AND ADVICE ILLUSTRATED (Becomes Romance Stories of True Love No. 45 on)
McCombs/Harvey Publ./Home Comics: June, 1949 - No. 6, Apr, 1950; No. 7, Jan, 1951 - No. 44, Mar, 1957

	GD 2.0	VG 4.0	FN 6.0	VF 8.0	VF/NM 9.0	NM- 9.2
V1#1	15	30	45	86	133	180
2-Elias-c	10	20	30	54	72	90
3-10: 3,4,7-9-Elias-c	8	16	24	42	54	65
11-13,15-23,25-31: 31-Last pre-code (1/55)	7	14	21	35	43	50
14,24-Rape scene	7	14	21	37	46	55
32-37,39-44	6	12	18	29	36	42
38-S&K-c	9	18	27	52	69	85

NOTE: ***Powell** a-1, 2, 7-14, 17-25, 28, 29, 33, 40, 41. #3 has True Love... on inside.*

TRUE MOVIE AND TELEVISION (Part teenage magazine)
Toby Press: Aug, 1950 - No. 3, Nov, 1950; No. 4, Mar, 1951 (52 pgs.)(1-3: 10¢)

	GD 2.0	VG 4.0	FN 6.0	VF 8.0	VF/NM 9.0	NM- 9.2
1-Elizabeth Taylor photo-c; Gene Autry, Shirley Temple app.	57	114	171	362	619	875
2-(9/50)-Janet Leigh/Liz Taylor/Ava Gardner & others photo-c; Frazetta John Wayne illo from J.Wayne Adv. Comics #2 (4/50)	41	82	123	256	428	600
3-June Allyson photo-c; Montgomery Cliff, Esther Williams, Andrews Sisters app; Li'l Abner featured; Sadie Hawkins' Day	31	62	93	182	296	410
4-Jane Powell photo-c (15¢)	20	40	60	114	182	250

NOTE: *16 pgs. in color, rest movie material in black & white.*

TRUE SECRETS (Formerly Our Love?)
Marvel (IPS)/Atlas Comics (MPI) #4 on: No. 3, Mar, 1950; No. 4, Feb, 1951 - No. 40, Sept, 1956

	GD 2.0	VG 4.0	FN 6.0	VF 8.0	VF/NM 9.0	NM- 9.2
3 (52 pgs.)(IPS one-shot)	15	30	45	84	127	170
4,5,7-10	10	20	30	56	76	95
6,22-Everett-a	12	24	36	67	94	120
11-20	9	18	27	52	69	85
21,23-28: 24-Colletta-c. 28-Last pre-code (2/55)	9	18	27	47	61	75
29-40: 34,36-Colletta-a	8	16	24	42	54	65

TRUE SPORT PICTURE STORIES (Formerly Sport Comics)
Street & Smith Publications: V1#5, Feb, 1942 - V5#2, July-Aug, 1949

	GD 2.0	VG 4.0	FN 6.0	VF 8.0	VF/NM 9.0	NM- 9.2
V1#5-Joe DiMaggio-c/story	37	74	111	218	354	490
6-12 (1942-43): 12-Jack Dempsey story	21	42	63	122	199	275
V2#1-12 (1943-45): 7-Stan Musial-c/story; photo story of the New York Yankees	20	40	60	115	185	255
V3#1-12 (1946-47): 7-Joe DiMaggio, Stan Musial, Bob Feller & others back from the armed service story. 8-Billy Conn vs. Joe Louis-c/story	19	38	57	111	176	240
V4#1-12 (1948-49), V5#1,2	18	36	54	105	165	225

NOTE: ***Powell** a-V3#10, V4#1-4, 6-8, 10-12; V5#1, 2; c-V3#10-12, V4#2-7, 9-12. **Ravielli** c-V5#2.*

TRUE STORIES OF ROMANCE
Fawcett Publications: Jan, 1950 - No. 3, May, 1950 (All photo-c)

	GD 2.0	VG 4.0	FN 6.0	VF 8.0	VF/NM 9.0	NM- 9.2
1	14	28	42	80	115	150
2,3: 3-Marcus Swayze-a	10	20	30	58	79	100

TRUE STORY OF JESSE JAMES, THE (See Jesse James, Four Color 757)

TRUE SWEETHEART SECRETS
Fawcett Publs.: 5/50; No. 2, 7/50; No. 3, 1951(nd); No. 4, 9/51 - No. 11, 1/53 (All photo-c)

	GD 2.0	VG 4.0	FN 6.0	VF 8.0	VF/NM 9.0	NM- 9.2
1-Photo-c; Debbie Reynolds?	15	30	45	88	137	185
2-Wood-a (11 pgs.)	18	36	54	105	165	225
3-11: 4,5-Powell-a. 8-Marcus Swayze-a. 11-Evans-a	11	22	33	64	90	115

TRUE TALES OF LOVE (Formerly Secret Story Romances)
Atlas Comics (TCI): No. 22, April, 1956 - No. 31, Sept, 1957

	GD 2.0	VG 4.0	FN 6.0	VF 8.0	VF/NM 9.0	NM- 9.2
22	10	20	30	56	76	95
23-24,26-31-Colletta-a in most:	8	16	24	42	54	65
25-Everett-a; Colletta-a	9	18	27	47	61	75

TRUE TALES OF ROMANCE
Fawcett Publications: No. 4, June, 1950

	GD 2.0	VG 4.0	FN 6.0	VF 8.0	VF/NM 9.0	NM- 9.2
4-Photo-c	10	20	30	54	72	90

TRUE 3-D
Harvey Publications: Dec, 1953 - No. 2, Feb, 1954 (25¢)(Both came with 2 pair of glasses)

	GD 2.0	VG 4.0	FN 6.0	VF 8.0	VF/NM 9.0	NM- 9.2
1-Nostrand, Powell-a	5	10	15	35	55	75
2-Powell-a	6	12	18	37	59	80

NOTE: *Many copies of #1 surfaced in 1984.*

TRUE-TO-LIFE ROMANCES (Formerly Guns Against Gangsters)
Star Publ.: #8, 11-12/49; #9, 1-2/50; #3, 4/50 - #5, 9/50; #6, 1/51 - #23, 10/54

	GD 2.0	VG 4.0	FN 6.0	VF 8.0	VF/NM 9.0	NM- 9.2
8(#1, 1949)	24	48	72	140	230	320

True War Experiences #2 © HARV

Tuffy #8 © STD

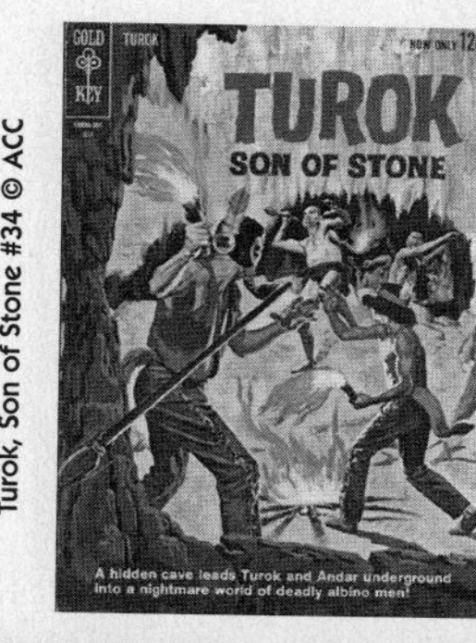

Turok, Son of Stone #34 © ACC

	GD 2.0	VG 4.0	FN 6.0	VF 8.0	VF/NM 9.0	NM- 9.2
9(#2),4-10	17	34	51	100	158	215
3-Janet Leigh/Glenn Ford photo on-c plus true life story of each	19	38	57	109	172	235
11,22,23	15	30	45	86	133	180
12-14,17-21-Disbrow-a	16	32	48	94	147	200
15,16-Wood & Disbrow-a in each	19	38	57	109	172	235

NOTE: *Kamen a-13. Kamen/Feldstein a-14. All have L.B. Cole covers.*

TRUE WAR EXPERIENCES
Harvey Publications: Aug, 1952 - No. 4, Dec, 1952

	GD	VG	FN	VF	VF/NM	NM-
1	8	16	24	56	93	130
2-4	5	10	15	32	51	70

TRUE WAR ROMANCES (Becomes Exotic Romances #22 on)
Quality Comics Group: Sept, 1952 - No. 21, June, 1955

	GD	VG	FN	VF	VF/NM	NM-
1-Photo-c	14	28	42	80	115	150
2-(10/52)	9	18	27	47	61	75
3-10: 3-(12/52). 9-Whitney-a	8	16	24	42	54	65
11-21: 20-Last precode (4/55). 14-Whitney-a	7	14	21	37	46	55

TRUE WAR STORIES (See Ripley's...)

TRUE WESTERN (True Adventures #3)
Marvel Comics (MMC): Dec, 1949 - No. 2, March, 1950

	GD	VG	FN	VF	VF/NM	NM-
1-Photo-c; Billy The Kid story	16	32	48	94	147	200
2-Alan Ladd photo-c	19	38	57	112	179	245

TRUMP
HMH Publishing Co.: Jan, 1957 - No. 2, Mar, 1957 (50¢, magazine)

	GD	VG	FN	VF	VF/NM	NM-
1-Harvey Kurtzman satire	25	50	75	150	245	340
2-Harvey Kurtzman satire	20	40	60	117	189	260

NOTE: *Davis, Elder, Heath, Jaffee art-#1,2; Wood a-1. Article by Mel Brooks in #2.*

TRUMPETS WEST (See Luke Short, Four Color #875)

TRUTH ABOUT CRIME (See Fox Giants)

TRUTH ABOUT MOTHER GOOSE (See Mother Goose, Four Color #862)

TRUTH BEHIND THE TRIAL OF CARDINAL MINDSZENTY, THE (See Cardinal Mindszenty in the Promotional Comics section))

TRUTHFUL LOVE (Formerly Youthful Love)
Youthful Magazines: No. 2, July, 1950

	GD	VG	FN	VF	VF/NM	NM-
2-Ingrid Bergman's true life story	12	24	36	67	94	120

TRUTH RED, WHITE & BLACK
Marvel Comics: Jan, 2003 - No. 6 ($3.50, limited series)

1-Kyle Baker-a/Robert Morales-s; the testing of Captain America's super-soldier serum 3.50
2-7: 3-Isaiah Bradley 1st dons the Captain America costume 3.50
TPB (2004, $17.99) r/series 18.00

TRY-OUT WINNER BOOK
Marvel Comics: Mar, 1988

1-Spider-Man vs. Doc Octopus 5.00

TSR WORLD (...Annual on cover only)
DC Comics: 1990 ($3.95, 84 pgs.)

1-Advanced D&D, ForgottenRealms, Dragonlance & 1st app. Spelljammer 4.00

TSUNAMI GIRL
Image Comics: 1999 - No. 3, 1999 ($2.95)

1-3-Sorayama-c/Paniccia-s/a 3.00

TUBBY (See Marge's...)

TUFF GHOSTS STARRING SPOOKY
Harvey Publications: July, 1962 - No. 39, Nov, 1970; No. 40, Sept, 1971 - No. 43, Oct, 1972

	GD	VG	FN	VF	VF/NM	NM-
1-12¢ issues begin	11	22	33	80	145	210
2-5	7	14	21	45	73	100
6-10	5	10	15	32	51	70
11-20	4	8	12	24	37	50
21-30: 29-Hot Stuff/Spooky team-up story	3	6	9	16	23	30
31-39,43	2	4	6	13	18	22
40-42: 52 pg. Giants	3	6	9	14	20	25

TUFFY
Standard Comics: No. 5, July, 1949 - No. 9, Oct, 1950

	GD	VG	FN	VF	VF/NM	NM-
5-All by Sid Hoff	7	14	21	35	43	50
6-9	5	10	15	23	28	32

TUFFY TURTLE
I. W. Enterprises: No date

	GD	VG	FN	VF	VF/NM	NM-
1-Reprint	2	4	6	8	11	14

TUG & BUSTER
Art & Soul Comics: Nov, 1995 - No. 7, Feb, 1998 ($2.95, B&W, bi-monthly)

1-7: Marc Hempel-c/a/scripts 3.00
1-(Image Comics, 8/98, $2.95, B&W) 3.00

TUROK
Acclaim Comics: Mar, 1998 - No. 4, Jun, 1998 ($2.50)

1-4-Nicieza-s/Kayanan-a 2.50
..., Child of Blood 1 (1/98, $3.95) Nicieza-s/Kayanan-a 4.00
... Evolution 1 (8/02, $2.50) Nicieza-s/Kayanan-a 2.50
..., Redpath 1 (10/97, $3.95) Nicieza-s/Kayanan-a 4.00
... / Shadowman 1 (2/99, $3.95) Priest-s/Broome & Jimenez-a 4.00
...: Spring Break in the Lost Land 1 (7/97, $3.95) Nicieza-s/Kayanan-a 4.00
...: Tales of the Lost Land 1 (4/98, $3.95) 4.00
...: The Empty Souls 1 (4/97, $3.95) Nicieza-s/Kayanan-a; variant-c 4.00

TUROK, DINOSAUR HUNTER (See Magnus Robot Fighter #12 & Archer & Armstrong #2)
Valiant/Acclaim Comics: June, 1993 - No. 47, Aug, 1996 ($2.50)

1-($3.50)-Chromium & foil-c 3.50
1-Gold foil-c variant 5.00
0, 2-47: 4-Andar app. 5-Death of Andar. 7-9-Truman/Glanzman-a. 11-Bound-in trading card. 16-Chaos Effect 2.50
Yearbook 1 (1994, $3.95, 52 pgs.) 4.00

TUROK, SON OF STONE (See Dan Curtis, Golden Comics Digest #31 & March of Comics #378, 399, 408)
Dell Publ. Co. #1-29(9/62)/Gold Key #30(12/62)-85(7/73)/Gold Key or Whitman #86(9/73)-125(1/80)/Whitman #126(3/81) on: No. 596, 12/54 - No. 29, 9/62; No. 30, 12/62 - No. 91, 7/74; No. 92, 9/74 - No. 125, 1/80; No. 126, 3/81 - No. 130, 4/82

	GD	VG	FN	VF	VF/NM	NM-
Four Color 596 (12/54)(#1)-1st app./origin Turok & Andar; dinosaur-c. Created by Matthew H. Murphy; written by Alberto Giolitti	50	100	150	425	838	1250
Four Color 656 (10/55)(#2)-1st mention of Lanok	30	60	90	228	439	650
3(3-5/56)-5: 3-Cave men	21	42	63	148	287	425
6-10: 8-Dinosaur of the deep; Turok enters Lost Valley; series begins. 9-Paul S. Newman-s (most issues thru end)	15	30	45	107	204	300
11-20: 17-Prehistoric Pygmies	12	24	36	85	155	225
21-29	9	18	27	63	107	150
30-1st Gold Key. 30-33-Painted back-c.	9	18	27	64	110	155
31-Drug use story	9	18	27	63	107	150
32-40	7	14	21	50	83	115
41-50	6	12	18	41	66	90
51-57,59,60	6	12	18	37	59	80
58-Flying Saucer c/story	6	12	18	39	62	85
61-70: 62-12¢ & 15¢ covers. 63,68-Line drawn-c	5	10	15	30	48	65
71-84: 84-Origin & 1st app. Hutec	4	8	12	26	41	55
85-99: 93-r-c/#19 w/changes. 94-r-c/#28 w/changes. 97-r-c/#31 w/changes. 98-r/#58 w/o spaceship & spacemen on-c. 99-r-c/#52 w/changes.	3	6	9	21	32	42
100	4	8	12	26	41	55
101-129: 114,115-(52 pgs.). 129(2/82)	4	8	12	22	34	45
130(4/82)-Last issue	6	12	18	37	59	80
Giant 1(30031-611) (11/66)-Slick-c; r/#10-12 & 16 plus cover to #11	11	22	33	74	132	190
Giant 1-Same as above but with paper-c	11	22	33	80	145	210

NOTE: *Most painted-c; line-drawn #63 & 130. **Alberto Gioletti** a-24-27, 30-119, 123; painted-c No. 30-129. **Sparling** a-117, 120-130. Reprints-#36, 54, 57, 75, 112, 114(1/3), 115(1/3), 118, 121, 125, 127(1/3), 128, 129(1/3), 130(1/3), Giant 1. Cover r-93, 94, 97-99, 126(all different from original covers.*

TUROK THE HUNTED
Valiant/Acclaim Comics: Mar, 1995 - No. 2, Apr, 1995 ($2.50, limited series)

1,2-Mike Deodato-a(p); price omitted on #1 2.50

TUROK THE HUNTED
Acclaim Comics (Valiant): Feb, 1996 - No. 2, Mar, 1996 ($2.50, limited series)

1,2-Mike Grell story 2.50

TUROK, TIMEWALKER
Acclaim Comics (Valiant): Aug, 1997 - No. 2, Sept, 1997 ($2.50, limited series)

1,2-Nicieza story 2.50

TUROK 2 (Magazine)
Acclaim Comics: Oct, 1998 ($4.99, magazine size)

...Seeds of Evil-Nicieza-s/Broome & Benjamin-a; origin back-up story 5.00
#2 Adon's Curse -Mack painted-c/Broome & Benjamin-a; origin pt. 2 5.00

TUROK 3: SHADOW OF OBLIVION

TV Casper and Company #2 © HARV

The Twelve #4 © MAR

Twilight Man #4 © First Publ.

	GD	VG	FN	VF	VF/NM	NM-
	2.0	4.0	6.0	8.0	9.0	9.2

GD VG FN VF VF/NM NM- 2.0 4.0 6.0 8.0 9.0 9.2

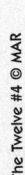

Acclaim Comics: Sept, 2000 ($4.95, one-shot)
1-Includes pin-up gallery 5.00

TURTLE SOUP
Mirage Studios: Sept, 1987 ($2.00, 76 pgs., B&W, one-shot)
1-Featuring Teenage Mutant Ninja Turtles 5.00

TURTLE SOUP
Mirage Studios: Nov, 1991 - No. 4, 1992 ($2.50, limited series, coated paper)
1-4: Features the Teenage Mutant Ninja Turtles 2.50

TV CASPER & COMPANY
Harvey Publications: Aug, 1963 - No. 46, April, 1974 (25¢ Giants)

	GD	VG	FN	VF	VF/NM	NM-
1- 68 pg. Giants begin; Casper, Little Audrey, Baby Huey, Herman & Catnip, Buzzy the Crow begin	11	22	33	80	145	210
2-5	6	12	18	43	69	95
6-10	5	10	15	30	48	65
11-20	4	8	12	24	37	50
21-31: 31-Last 68 pg. issue	3	6	9	18	27	35
32-46: All 52 pgs.	3	6	9	16	23	30

NOTE: *Many issues contain reprints.*

TV FUNDAY FUNNIES (See Famous TV...)

TV FUNNIES (See New Funnies)

TV FUNTIME (See Little Audrey)

TV LAUGHOUT (See Archie's...)

TV SCREEN CARTOONS (Formerly Real Screen)
National Periodical Publ.: No. 129, July-Aug, 1959 - No. 138, Jan-Feb, 1961

	GD	VG	FN	VF	VF/NM	NM-
129-138 (Scarce)	6	12	18	43	69	95

TV STARS (TV) (Newsstand sales only)
Marvel Comics Group: Aug, 1978 - No. 4, Feb, 1979 (Hanna-Barbera)

	GD	VG	FN	VF	VF/NM	NM-
1-Great Grape Ape app.	3	6	9	18	27	35
2,4: 4-Top Cat app.	3	6	9	16	22	28
3-Toth-c/a; Dave Stevens inks	3	6	9	17	25	32

TV TEENS (Formerly Ozzie & Babs; Rock and Rollo #14 on)
Charlton Comics: V1#14, Feb, 1954 - V2#13, July, 1956

	GD	VG	FN	VF	VF/NM	NM-
V1#14 (#1)-Ozzie & Babs	10	20	30	54	72	90
15 (#2)	6	12	18	33	41	48
V2#3(6/54) - 6-Don Winslow	6	12	18	31	38	45
7-13-Mopsy. 8(7/55). 9-Paper dolls	6	12	18	29	36	42

TWEETY AND SYLVESTER (1st Series) (TV) (Also see Looney Tunes and Merrie Melodies)
Dell Publishing Co.: No. 406, June, 1952 - No. 37, June-Aug, 1962

	GD	VG	FN	VF	VF/NM	NM-
Four Color 406 (#1)	10	20	30	71	126	180
Four Color 489,524	6	12	18	41	66	90
4 (3-5/54) - 20	5	10	15	32	51	70
21-37	4	8	12	28	44	60

(See March of Comics #421, 433, 445, 457, 469, 481)

TWEETY AND SYLVESTER (2nd Series)(See Kite Fun Book)
Gold Key No. 1-102/Whitman No. 103 on: Nov, 1963; No. 2, Nov, 1965 - No. 121, June, 1984

	GD	VG	FN	VF	VF/NM	NM-
1	4	8	12	28	44	60
2-10	3	6	9	18	27	35
11-30	2	4	6	13	18	22
31-50	2	4	6	9	12	15
51-70	1	3	4	6	8	10
71-102	1	2	3	5	6	8
103,104 (Whitman)	1	3	4	6	8	10
105(9/80),106(10/80),107(12/80) 3-pack only	3	6	9	20	30	40
108-116: 113(2/82),114(2-3/82),115(3/82),116(4/82)	2	4	6	8	10	12
117-121 (All # 90094 on-c; nd, nd code): 117(6/83). 118(7/83). 119(2/84)-r(1/3). 120(5/84). 121(6/84)	3	6	9	14	19	24
Digest nn (Charlton/Xerox Pub., 1974) (low print run)	3	6	9	16	23	30
Mini Comic No. 1(1976, 3-1/4x6-1/2")	1	3	4	6	8	10

TWELVE, THE (Golden Age Timely heroes)
Marvel Comics: No. 0; 2008; No. 1, Mar, 2008 - No. 12 ($2.99, limited series)
0-Rockman, Laughing Mask & Phantom Reporter intro. stories (1940s); series preview 3.00
1/2 (2008, $3.99) r/early app. of Fiery Mask, Mister E and Rockman; Weston-c 4.00
1-8-Straczynski-a/Weston-a; Timely heroes re-surface in the present 3.00

12 O'CLOCK HIGH (TV)
Dell Publishing Co.: Jan-Mar, 1965 - No. 2, Apr-June, 1965 (Photo-c)

	GD	VG	FN	VF	VF/NM	NM-
1- Sinnott-a	6	12	18	39	62	85
2	5	10	15	30	48	65

2099 A.D.
Marvel Comics: May, 1995 ($3.95, one-shot)
1-Acetate-c by Quesada & Palmiotti 4.00

2099 APOCALYPSE
Marvel Comics: Dec, 1995 ($4.95, one-shot)
1-Chromium wraparound-c; Ellis script 5.00

2099 GENESIS
Marvel Comics: Jan, 1996 ($4.95, one-shot)
1-Chromium wraparound-c; Ellis script 5.00

2099 MANIFEST DESTINY
Marvel Comics: Mar, 1998 ($5.99, one-shot)
1-Origin of Fantastic Four 2099; intro Moon Knight 2099 6.00

2099 UNLIMITED
Marvel Comics: Sept, 1993 - No. 10, 1996 ($3.95, 68 pgs.)
1-10: 1-1st app. Hulk 2099 & begins. 1-3-Spider-Man 2099 app. 9-Joe Kubert-c; Len Wein & Nancy Collins scripts 4.00

2099 WORLD OF DOOM SPECIAL
Marvel Comics: May, 1995 ($2.25, one-shot)
1-Doom's "Contract w/America" 2.50

2099 WORLD OF TOMORROW
Marvel Comics: Sept, 1996 - No. 8, Apr, 1997 ($2.50) (Replaces 2099 titles)
1-8: 1-Wraparound-c. 2-w/bound-in card. 4,5-Phalanx 2.50

21
Image Comics (Top Cow Productions): Feb, 1996 - No. 3, Apr, 1996 ($2.50)
1-3: Len Wein scripts 2.50
1-Variant-c 2.50

21 DOWN
DC Comics (WildStorm): Nov, 2002 - No. 12, Nov, 2003 ($2.95)
1-12: 1-Palmiotti & Gray-s/Saiz-a/Jusko-c 3.00
...: The Conduit (2003, $19.95, TPB) r/#1-7; intro. by Garth Ennis 20.00

24 (Based on TV series)
IDW Publishing: July, 2004 - Present ($6.99/$7.49, square-bound, one-shots)
...: Midnight Sun (7/05, $7.49) J.C. Vaughn & Mark Haynes-s; Renato Guedes-a 7.50
...: One Shot (7/04, $6.99)-Jack Bauer's first day on the job at CTU; Vaughn & Haynes-s; Guedes-a 7.00
...: Stories (1/05, $7.49) Manny Clark-a; Vaughn & Haynes-s 7.50

24: NIGHTFALL (Based on TV series)
IDW Publishing: Nov, 2006 - No. 6 ($3.99, limited series)
1-5-Two years before Season One; Vaughn & Haynes-s; Diaz-a; two covers 4.00

28 DAYS LATER (Based on the 2002 movie)
Boom! Studios: July, 2009 - Present ($3.99)
1-8-Covers by Bradstreet and Phillips 4.00

2020 VISIONS
DC Comics (Vertigo): May, 1997 - No. 12, Apr, 1998 ($2.25, limited series)
1-12-Delano-s: 1-3-Quitely-a. 4-"la tormenta"-Pleece-a 2.50

20,000 LEAGUES UNDER THE SEA (Movie)(See King Classics, Movie Comics & Power Record Comics)
Dell Publishing Co.: No. 614, Feb, 1955 (Disney)

	GD	VG	FN	VF	VF/NM	NM-
Four Color 614-Movie, painted-c	8	16	24	58	97	135

TWICE TOLD TALES (See Movie Classics)

TWILIGHT
DC Comics: 1990 - No. 3, 1991 ($4.95, 52 pgs, lim. series, squarebound, mature)
1-3: Tommy Tomorrow app; Chaykin scripts, Garcia-Lopez-c/a 5.00

TWILIGHT EXPERIMENT
DC Comics (WildStorm): Apr, 2004 - No. 6, Sept, 2005 ($2.95, limited series)
1-6-Gray & Palmiotti-s/Santacruz-a 3.00

TWILIGHT MAN
First Publishing: June, 1989 - No. 4, Sept, 1989 ($2.75, limited series)
1-4 2.75

TWILIGHT ZONE, THE (TV) (See Dan Curtis & Stories From...)

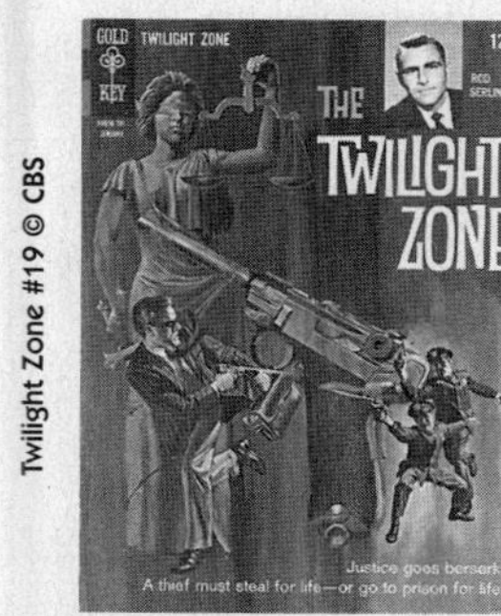

Twilight Zone #19 © CBS

Two-Face: Year One #1 © DC

Two-Gun Kid #75 © MAR

Dell Publishing Co./Gold Key/Whitman No. 92: No. 1173, 3-5/61 - No. 91, 4/79; No. 92, 5/82

	GD 2.0	VG 4.0	FN 6.0	VF 8.0	VF/NM 9.0	NM- 9.2
Four Color 1173 (#1)-Crandall-c/a	21	42	63	148	287	425
Four Color 1288-Crandall/Evans-c/a	12	24	36	85	155	225
01-860-207 (5-7/62-Dell, 15¢)	9	18	27	63	107	150
12-860-210 on-c; 01-860-210 on inside(8-10/62-Dell)-Evans-c/a (3 stories)						
	9	18	27	63	107	150
1(11/62-Gold Key)-Crandall/Frazetta-a (10 & 11 pgs.); Evans-a						
	13	26	39	93	172	250
2	8	16	24	58	97	135
3-11: 3(11 pgs.),4(10 pgs.),9-Toth-a	6	12	18	43	69	95
12-15: 12-Williamson-a. 13,15-Crandall-a. 14-Orlando/Crandall/Torres-a						
	5	10	15	35	55	75
16-20	4	8	12	26	41	55
21-25: 21-Crandall-a(r). 25-Evans/Crandall-a(r); Toth-r/#4; last 12¢ issue						
	3	6	9	20	30	40
26,27: 26-Flying Saucer-c/story; Crandall, Evans-a(r). 27-Evans-r(2)						
	3	6	9	19	29	38
28-32: 32-Evans-a(r)	3	6	9	17	25	32
33-51: 43-Celardo-a. 51-Williamson-a	2	4	6	13	18	22
52-70	2	4	6	10	14	18
71-82,86-91: 71-Reprint	2	4	6	8	11	14
83-(52 pgs.)	3	6	9	14	20	25
84-(52 pgs.) Frank Miller's 1st comic book work	5	10	15	30	48	65
85-Frank Miller-a (2nd)	3	6	9	17	25	32
92-(Whitman, 5/82) Last issue; r/#1.	2	4	6	9	13	16
Mini Comic #1(1976, 3-1/4x6-1/2")	2	4	6	8	10	12

NOTE: ***Bolle*** *a-13(w/**McWilliams**), 50, 55, 57, 59, 77, 78, 80, 83, 84.* ***McWilliams*** *a-59, 78, 80, 82, 84.* ***Miller*** *a-84, 85.* ***Orlando*** *a-15, 19, 20, 22, 23.* ***Sekowsky*** *a-3.* ***Simonson*** *a-50, 54, 55, 83r.* ***Weiss*** *a-39, 79r(#39). (See Mystery Comics Digest 3, 6, 9, 12, 15, 18, 21, 24). Reprints-26(1/3), 71, 73, 79, 83, 84, 86, 92. Painted c-1-91.*

TWILIGHT ZONE, THE (TV)
Now Comics: Nov, 1990 ($2.95); Oct, 1991; V2#1, Nov, 1991 - No. 11, Oct, 1992 ($1.95); V3#1, 1993 - No. 4, 1993 ($2.50)

	GD 2.0	VG 4.0	FN 6.0	VF 8.0	VF/NM 9.0	NM- 9.2
1-(11/90, $2.95, 52 pgs.)-Direct sale edition; Neal Adams-a, Sienkiewicz-c; Harlan Ellison scripts						3.00
1-(11/90, $1.75)-Newsstand ed. w/N. Adams-c						2.50
1-Prestige Format (10/91, $4.95)-Reprints above with extra Harlan Ellison short story						5.00
1-Collector's Edition (10/91, $2.50)-Non-code approved and polybagged; reprints 11/90 issue; gold logo, 1-Reprint ($2.50)-r/direct sale 11/90 version, 1-Reprint ($2.50)-r/newsstand 11/90 version each...						2.50
V2#1-Direct sale & newsstand ed. w/different-c						2.50
V2#2-8,10-11						2.50
V2#9-($2.95)-3-D Special; polybagged w/glasses & hologram on-c						3.00
V2#9-($4.95)-Prestige Edition; contains 2 extra stories & a different hologram on-c; polybagged w/glasses						5.00
V3#1-4, Anniversary Special 1 (1992, $2.50)						2.50
Annual 1 (4/93, $2.50)-No ads						2.50
...Science Fiction Special (3/93, $3.50)						3.50

TWINKLE COMICS
Spotlight Publishers: May, 1945

	GD 2.0	VG 4.0	FN 6.0	VF 8.0	VF/NM 9.0	NM- 9.2
1	24	48	72	140	230	320

TWIST, THE
Dell Publishing Co.: July-Sept, 1962

	GD 2.0	VG 4.0	FN 6.0	VF 8.0	VF/NM 9.0	NM- 9.2
01-864-209-Painted-c	4	8	12	24	37	50

TWISTED TALES (See Eclipse Graphic Album Series #15)
Pacific Comics/Independent Comics Group (Eclipse) #9,10: 11/82 - No. 8, 5/84; No. 9, 11/84; No. 10, 12/84 (Baxter paper)

	GD 2.0	VG 4.0	FN 6.0	VF 8.0	VF/NM 9.0	NM- 9.2
1-9: 1-B. Jones/Corben-c; Alcala-a; nudity/violence in al. 2-Wrightson-c; Ploog-a						4.00
10-Wrightson painted art; Morrow-a						6.00

NOTE: ***Bolton*** *painted c-4, 6, 7; a-7.* ***Conrad*** *a-1, 3, 5; c-1i, 3, 5.* ***Guice*** *a-8.* ***Wildey*** *a-3.*

TWO BIT THE WACKY WOODPECKER (See Wacky...)
Toby Press: 1951 - No. 3, May, 1953

	GD 2.0	VG 4.0	FN 6.0	VF 8.0	VF/NM 9.0	NM- 9.2
1	10	20	30	54	72	90
2,3	6	12	18	31	38	45

TWO FACE: YEAR ONE
DC Comics: 2008 - No. 2, 2008 ($5.99, squarebound, limited series)

	GD 2.0	VG 4.0	FN 6.0	VF 8.0	VF/NM 9.0	NM- 9.2
1,2-Origin re-told; Sable-s/Saiz & Haun-a						6.00

TWO-FISTED TALES (Formerly Haunt of Fear #15-17)
(Also see EC Archives • Two-Fisted Tales)
E. C. Comics: No. 18, Nov-Dec, 1950 - No. 41, Feb-Mar, 1955

	GD 2.0	VG 4.0	FN 6.0	VF 8.0	VF/NM 9.0	NM- 9.2
18(#1)-Kurtzman-c	91	182	273	728	1164	1600
19-Kurtzman-c	67	134	201	536	856	1175
20-Kurtzman-c	43	86	129	344	552	760
21,22-Kurtzman-c	35	70	105	280	450	620
23-25-Kurtzman-c	27	54	81	216	348	480
26-29,31-Kurtzman-c. 31-Civil War issue	20	40	60	160	255	350
30-Classic Davis-c	22	44	66	176	281	385
32-35: 33- "Atom Bomb" by Wood. 35-Civil War issue						
	20	40	60	160	255	350
36-41	16	32	48	128	266	275
Two-Fisted Annual (1952, 25¢, 132 pgs.)	103	206	309	773	1187	1600
Two-Fisted Annual (1953, 25¢, 132 pgs.)	77	154	231	578	889	1200

NOTE: ***Berg*** *a-29.* ***Colan*** *a-39p.* ***Craig*** *a-18, 19, 32.* ***Crandall*** *a-35, 36.* ***Davis*** *a-20-36, 40; c-30, 34, 35, 41, Annual 2.* ***Evans*** *a-34, 40, 41; c-40.* ***Feldstein*** *a-18.* ***Krigstein*** *a-41.* ***Kubert*** *a-32, 33.* ***Kurtzman*** *a-18-25; c-18-29, 31, Annual 1.* ***Severin*** *a-26, 28, 29, 31, 34-41 (No. 37-39 are all-**Severin** issues); c-36-39.* ***Severin/Elder*** *a-19-29, 31, 33, 36.* ***Wood*** *a-18-28, 30-35, 41; c-32, 33. Special issues: #26 (ChanJin Reservoir), 31 (Civil War), 35 (Civil War). Canadian reprints known; see Table of Contents. #25-Davis biog. #27-Wood biog. #28-Kurtzman biog.*

TWO-FISTED TALES
Russ Cochran/Gemstone Publishing: Oct, 1992 - No. 24, May, 1998 ($1.50/$2.00/$2.50)

	GD 2.0	VG 4.0	FN 6.0	VF 8.0	VF/NM 9.0	NM- 9.2
1-24: 1-4r/Two-Fisted Tales #18-21 w/original-c						2.50

TWO-GUN KID (Also see All Western Winners, Best Western, Black Rider, Blaze Carson, Kid Colt, Western Winners, Wild West, & Wild Western)
Marvel/Atlas (MCI No. 1-10/HPC No. 11-59/Marvel No. 60 on): 3/48(No mo.) - No. 10, 11/49; No. 11, 12/53 - No. 59, 4/61; No. 60, 11/62 - No. 92, 3/68; No. 93, 7/70 - No. 136, 4/77

	GD 2.0	VG 4.0	FN 6.0	VF 8.0	VF/NM 9.0	NM- 9.2
1-Two-Gun Kid & his horse Cyclone begin; The Sheriff begins						
	110	220	330	704	1202	1700
2	45	90	135	284	480	675
3,4: 3-Annie Oakley app.	37	74	111	218	354	490
5-Pre-Black Rider app. (Wint. 48/49); Anti-Wertham editorial (1st?)						
	39	78	117	231	378	525
6-10(11/49): 8-Blaze Carson app. 9-Black Rider app.						
	28	56	84	165	270	375
11(12/53)-Black Rider app.; 1st to have Atlas globe on-c; explains how Kid Colt became an outlaw	22	44	66	132	216	300
12-Black Rider app.	21	42	63	124	202	280
13-20: 14-Opium story	17	34	51	98	154	210
21-24,26-29	15	30	45	90	140	190
25,30: 25-Williamson-a (5 pgs.). 30-Williamson/Torres-a (4 pgs.)						
	15	30	45	94	147	200
31-33,35,37-40	9	18	27	60	100	140
34-Crandall-a	9	18	27	61	103	145
36,41,42,48-Origin in all	9	18	27	61	103	145
43,44,47	7	14	21	49	80	110
45,46-Davis-a	8	16	24	52	86	120
49,50,52,53-Severin-a(2/3) in each	7	14	21	45	73	100
51-Williamson-a (5 pgs.)	8	16	24	52	86	120
54,55,57,59-Severin-a(3) in each. 59-Kirby-a; last 10¢ issue (4/61)						
	7	14	21	45	73	100
56	6	12	18	41	66	90
58,60-New origin. 58-Kirby/Ayers-c/a "The Monster of Hidden Valley" cover/story (Kirby monster-c)	8	16	24	52	86	120
60-Edition w/handwritten issue number on cover	9	18	27	61	103	145
61,62-Kirby-a	6	12	18	41	66	90
63-74: 64-Intro. Boom-Boom	5	10	15	30	48	65
75-77-Kirby-a	5	10	15	34	55	75
78-89	4	8	12	22	34	45
90,95-Kirby-a	4	8	12	24	37	50
91,92: 92-Last new story; last 12¢ issue	3	6	9	20	30	40
93,94,96-99	3	6	9	14	19	24
100-Last 15¢-c	3	6	9	14	20	26
101-Origin retold/#58; Kirby-a	3	6	9	14	20	26
102-120-reprints	2	4	6	8	11	14
121-136-reprints. 129-131-(Regular 25¢ editions)	2	4	6	8	11	14
129-131-(30¢-c variants, limited distribution)(4-8/76)	4	8	12	26	41	55

NOTE: ***Ayers*** *a-13, 26, 27.* ***Davis*** *c-45-47.* ***Drucker*** *a-23.* ***Everett*** *a-82, 91.* ***Fuje*** *a-13.* ***Heath*** *a-3(2), 4(3), 5(2), 7; c-13, 21, 23, 53.* ***Keller*** *a-16, 19, 28.* ***Kirby*** *a-54, 55, 57-62, 75-77, 90, 95, 101, 119, 120, 129; c-10, 52, 54-65, 67-72, 74-76, 116.* ***Maneely*** *a-20; c-11, 12, 16, 19, 20, 25-28, 30, 35, 49.* ***Powell*** *a-38, 102, 104.* ***Severin*** *a-9, 29, 51, 55, 57, 99r(3); c-9, 51.* ***Shores*** *c-1-8, 11.* ***Trimpe*** *c-99.* ***Tuska*** *a-11, 12.* ***Whitney*** *a-87, 89-91, 98-113, 124, 129; c-87, 89, 91, 113.* ***Wildey*** *a-21.* ***Williamson*** *a-110r. Kid Colt in #13, 14, 16-21.*

TWO GUN KID: SUNSET RIDERS
Marvel Comics: Nov, 1995 - No. 2, Dec, 1995 ($6.95, squarebound, lim. series)

	GD 2.0	VG 4.0	FN 6.0	VF 8.0	VF/NM 9.0	NM- 9.2
1,2: Fabian Nicieza scripts in all. 1-Painted-c.						7.00

TWO GUN WESTERN (1st Series) (Formerly Casey Crime Photographer #1-4? or My Love #1-4?)

2001, A Space Odyssey #9 © MAR

Ultimate Avengers #1 © MAR

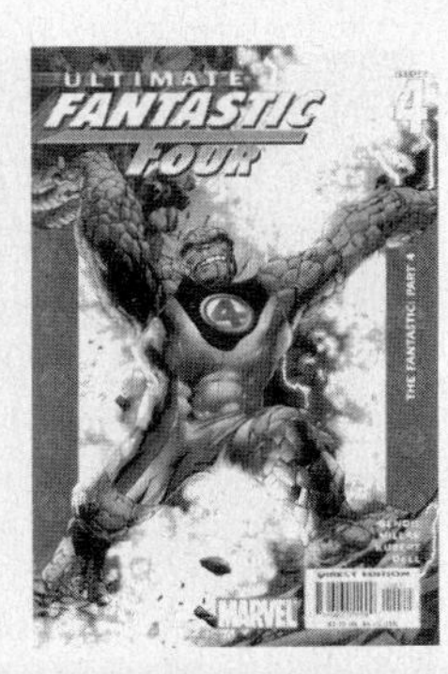

Ultimate Fantastic Four #4 © MAR

Marvel/Atlas Comics (MPC): No. 5, Nov, 1950 - No. 14, June, 1952
5-The Apache Kid (Intro & origin) & his horse Nightwind begin by Buscema
26 52 78 152 249 345
6-10: 8-Kid Colt, The Texas Kid & his horse Thunder begin?
19 38 57 111 176 240
11-14: 13-Black Rider app. 14 28 42 80 115 150
NOTE: *Maneely a-6, 7, 9; c-6, 11-13. Morrow a-9. Romita a-8. Wildey a-8.*

2-GUN WESTERN (2nd Series) (Formerly Billy Buckskin #1-3; Two-Gun Western #5 on)
Atlas Comics (MgPC): No. 4, May, 1956
4-Colan, Ditko, Severin, Sinnott-a; Maneely-c 15 30 45 88 137 185

TWO-GUN WESTERN (Formerly 2-Gun Western)
Atlas Comics (MgPC): No. 5, July, 1956 - No. 12, Sept, 1957
5-Return of the Gun-Hawk-c/story; Black Rider app. 15 30 45 85 130 175
6,7 12 24 36 67 94 120
8,10,12-Crandall-a 13 26 39 72 101 130
9,11-Williamson-a in both (5 pgs. each) 14 28 42 76 108 140
NOTE: *Ayers a-9. Colan a-5. Everett c-12. Forgione a-5, 6. Kirby a-12. Maneely a-6, 8, 12; c-5, 6, 8, 11. Morrow a-9, 10. Powell a-7, 11. Severin c-10. Sinnott a-5. Wildey a-9.*

TWO MINUTE WARNING
Ultimate Sports Ent.: 2000 - No. 2 ($3.95, cardstock covers)
1,2-NFL players & Teddy Roosevelt battle evil 4.00

TWO MOUSEKETEERS, THE (See 4-Color #475, 603, 642 under M.G.M.'s...;

TWO ON A GUILLOTINE (See Movie Classics)

TWO-STEP
DC Comics (Cliffhanger): Dec, 2003 - No. 3, Jul, 2004 ($2.95, limited series)
1-3-Warren Ellis-s/Amanda Conner-a 3.00

2000 A.D. MONTHLY/PRESENTS (Showcase #25 on)
Eagle Comics/Quality Comics No. 5 on: 4/85 - #6, 9/85; 4/86 - #54, 1991 ($1.25-$1.50, Mando paper)
1-6,1-25:1-4 r/British series featuring Judge Dredd; Alan Moore scripts begin.
1-25 ($1.25)-Reprints from British 2000 AD 2.50
26,27/28, 29/30, 31-54: 27/28, 29/30,31-Guice-c 2.50

2001, A SPACE ODYSSEY (Movie) (See adaptation in Treasury edition)
Marvel Comics Group: Dec, 1976 - No. 10, Sept, 1977 (30¢)
1-Kirby-c/a in all 3 6 9 14 19 24
2-7,9,10 2 4 6 8 10 12
7,9,10-(35¢-c variants, limited distribution)(6-9/77) 3 6 9 16 23 30
8-Origin/1st app. Machine Man (called Mr. Machine) 3 6 9 14 19 24
8-(35¢-c variant, limited distribution)(6,8/77) 4 8 12 28 44 60
...Treasury 1 ('76, 84 pgs.)-All new Kirby-a 3 6 9 16 22 28

2001 NIGHTS
Viz Premiere Comics: 1990 - No. 10, 1991 ($3.75, B&W, lim. series, mature readers, 84 pgs.)
1-10: Japanese sci-fi. 1-Wraparound-c 4.25

2010 (Movie)
Marvel Comics Group: Apr, 1985 - No. 2, May, 1985
1,2-r/Marvel Super Special movie adaptation. 2.50

TYPHOID (Also see Daredevil)
Marvel Comics: Nov, 1995 - No. 4, Feb, 1996 ($3.95, squarebound, lim. series)
1-4: Van Fleet-c/a 4.00

UFO & ALIEN COMIX
Warren Publishing Co.: Jan, 1978 (B&W magazine, 84 pgs., one-shot)
nn-Toth-a, J. Severin-a(r); Pie-s 2 4 6 10 14 18

UFO & OUTER SPACE (Formerly UFO Flying Saucers)
Gold Key: No. 14, June, 1978 - No. 25, Feb, 1980 (All painted covers)
14-Reprints UFO Flying Saucers #3 1 3 4 6 8 10
15,16-Reprints 1 3 4 6 8 10
17-25: 17-20-New material. 23-McWilliams-a. 24-(3 pg.-r). 25-Reprints UFO Flying Saucers #2 w/cover 1 3 4 6 8 10

UFO ENCOUNTERS
Western Publishing Co.: May, 1978 ($1.95, 228 pgs.)
11192-Reprints UFO Flying Saucers 4 8 12 24 37 50
11404-Vol.1 (128 pgs.)-See UFO Mysteries for Vol.2 3 6 9 20 30 40

UFO FLYING SAUCERS (UFO & Outer Space #14 on)
Gold Key: Oct, 1968 - No. 13, Jan, 1977 (No. 2 on, 36 pgs.)
1(30035-810) (68 pgs.) 4 8 12 28 44 60
2(11/70), 3(11/72), 4(11/74) 3 6 9 14 19 24
5(2/75)-13: Bolle-a #4 on 2 4 6 9 13 16

UFO MYSTERIES
Western Publishing Co.: 1978 ($1.00, reprints, 96 pgs.)
11400-(Vol.2)-Cont'd from UFO Encounters, pgs. 129-224
3 6 9 20 30 40

ULTIMAN GIANT ANNUAL (See Big Bang Comics)
Image Comics: Nov, 2001 ($4.95, B&W, one-shot)
1-Homage to DC 1960's annuals 5.00

ULTIMATE... (Collects 4-issue alternate titles from X-Men Age of Apocalypse crossovers)
Marvel Comics: May, 1995 ($8.95, trade paperbacks, gold foil covers)
Amazing X-Men, Astonishing X-Men, Factor-X, Gambit & the X-Ternals, Generation Next, X-Calibre, X-Man 9.00
Weapon X 10.00

ULTIMATE ADVENTURES
Marvel Comics: Nov, 2002 - No. 6, Dec, 2003 ($2.25)
1-6: 1-Intro. Hawk-Owl; Zimmerman-s/Fegredo-a. 3-Ultimates app. 2.50
One Tin Soldier TPB (2005, $12.99) r/#1-6 13.00

ULTIMATE ANNUALS
Marvel Comics: 2006; 2007 ($13.99, SC)
Vol. 1 (2006, $13.99) r/Ult. FF Ann. #1, Ult. X-Men Ann. #1, Ult S-M #1, Ultimates Ann #1 14.00
Vol. 2 (2007, $13.99) r/Ult. FF Ann. #2, Ult. X-Men Ann. #2, Ult S-M #2, Ultimates Ann #2 14.00

ULTIMATE ARMOR WARS (Follows Ultimatum x-over)
Marvel Comics: Nov, 2009 - No. 4, Apr, 2010 ($3.99, limited series)
1-4-Warren Ellis-s/Steve Kurth-a/Brandon Peterson-c. 1-Variant-c by Kurth 4.00

ULTIMATE AVENGERS (Follows Ultimatum x-over)
Marvel Comics: Oct, 2009 - Present ($3.99)
1-5-Mark Millar-s/Carlos Pacheco-a/c. 1-Variant-c by Yu 4.00

ULTIMATE CAPTAIN AMERICA
Marvel Comics: Dec, 2008 ($3.99, one-shot)
Annual 1 (12/08, $3.99) Origin of the Black Panther; Djurdjevic-a 4.00

ULTIMATE CIVIL WAR: SPIDER-HAM (See Civil War and related titles)
Marvel Comics: March, 2007 ($2.99, one-shot)
1-Spoof of Civil War series featuring Spider-Ham; art by various incl. Olivetti, Severin 3.00

ULTIMATE DAREDEVIL AND ELEKTRA
Marvel Comics: Jan, 2003 - No. 4, Mar, 2003 ($2.25, limited series)
1-4-Rucka-s/Larroca-c/a; 1st meeting of Elektra and Matt Murdock 2.50
... Vol.1 TPB (2003, $11.99) r/#1-4, Daredevil Vol. 2 #9; Larroca sketch pages 12.00

ULTIMATE ELEKTRA
Marvel Comics: Oct, 2004 - No. 5, Feb, 2005 ($2.25, limited series)
1-5-Carey-s/Larroca-c/a. 2-Bullseye app. 2.50
... : Devil's Due TPB (2005, $11.99) r/#1-5 12.00

ULTIMATE ENEMY (Follows Ultimatum x-over)
Marvel Comics: Mar, 2010 - Present ($3.99)
1,2-Bendis-s/Sandoval-a 1-Covers by McGuinness and Pearson 4.00

ULTIMATE EXTINCTION (See Ultimate Nightmare and Ultimate Secret limited series)
Marvel Comics: Mar, 2006 - No. 5, July, 2006 ($2.99, limited series)
1-5-The coming of Gah Lak Tus; Ellis-s/Peterson-a 3.00
TPB (2006, $12.99) r/#1-5 13.00

ULTIMATE FANTASTIC FOUR (Continues in Ultimatum mini-series)
Marvel Comics: Feb, 2004 - No. 60, Apr, 2009 ($2.25/$2.50/$2.99)
1-Bendis & Millar-s/Adam Kubert-a/Hitch-c 5.00
2-20: 2-Adam Kubert-a/c; intro. Moleman 7-Ellis-s/Immonen-a begin; Dr. Doom app. 13-18-Kubert-a. 19,20-Jae Lee-a. 20-Begin $2.50-c 3.00
21-Marvel Zombies; begin Greg Land-c/a; Mark Millar-s; variant-c by Land 4.00
22-29,33-59: 24-26-Namor app. 28-President Thor. 33-38-Ferry-a. 42-46-Silver Surfer 3.00
30-32-Marvel Zombies; Millar-s/Land-a; Dr. Doom app. 4.00
30-32-Zombie variant-c by Suydam 5.00
50-White variant-c by Kirkham 5.00
60-($3.99) Ultimatum crossover; Kirkham-a 4.00
Annual 1 (10/05, $3.99) The Inhumans app.; Jae Lee-a/Mark Millar-s/Greg Land-c 4.00
Annual 2 (10/06, $3.99) Mole Man app.; Immonen & Irving-a/Carey-s 4.00
.../Ult. X-Men Annual 1 (11/08, $3.99) Continued from Ult. X-Men/Ult. F.F. Annual #1 4.00
.../X-Men 1 (3/06, $2.99) Carey-s/Ferry-a; continued from Ult. X-Men/Fantastic Four #1 3.00
... Vol. 1: The Fantastic (2004, $12.99, TPB) r/#1-6; cover gallery 13.00

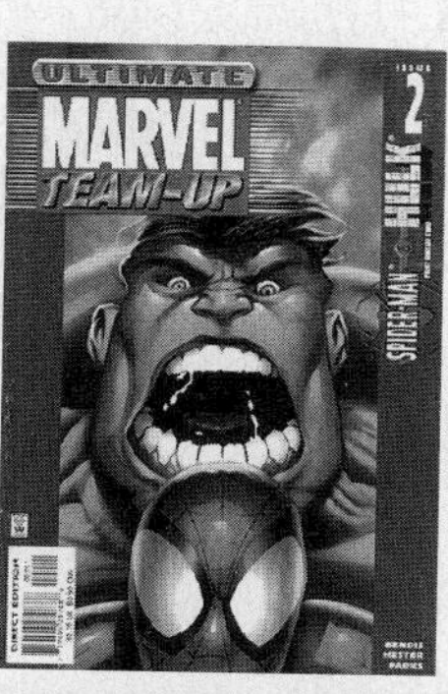

Ultimate Marvel Team-Up #2 © MAR

Ultimate Origins #1 © MAR

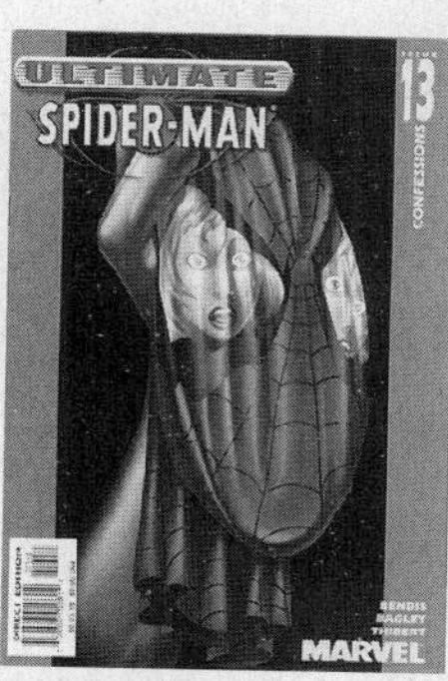

Ultimate Spider-Man #13 © MAR

... Vol. 2: Doom (2004, $12.99, TPB) r/#7-12 13.00
... Vol. 3: N-Zone (2005, $12.99, TPB) r/#13-18 13.00
... Vol. 4: Inhuman (2005, $12.99, TPB) r/#19,20 & Annual #1 13.00
... Vol. 5: Crossover (2006, $12.99, TPB) r/#21-26 13.00
... Vol. 6: Frightful (2006, $14.99, TPB) r/#27-32; gallery of cover sketches & variants 15.00
... Vol. 7: God War (2007, $16.99, TPB) r/#33-38 17.00
... Vol. 8: Devils (2007, $12.99, TPB) r/#39-41 & Annual #2 13.00
... Vol. 9: Silver Surfer (2007, $13.99, TPB) r/#42-46 14.00
Volume 1 HC (2005, $29.99, 7x11", dust jacket) r/#1-12; introduction, proposals and scripts by Millar and Bendis; character design pages by Hitch 30.00
Volume 2 HC (2006, $29.99, 7x11", dust jacket) r/#13-20; Jae Lee sketch page 30.00
Volume 3 HC (2007, $29.99, 7x11", dust jacket) r/#21-32; Greg Land sketch pages 30.00
Volume 4 HC (2007, $29.99, 7x11", dust jacket) r/#33-41, Annual #2, Ultimate FF/X-Men and Ultimate X-Men/FF; character design pages 30.00
Volume 5 HC (2008, $34.99, 7x11", dust jacket) r/#42-53 35.00

ULTIMATE GALACTUS TRILOGY
Marvel Comics: 2007 ($34.99, hardcover, dustjacket)
HC-Oversized reprint of Ultimate Nightmare #1-5, Ultimate Secret #1-4, Ultimate Vision #0, and Ultimate Extinction #1-5; sketch pages and cover galery 35.00

ULTIMATE HULK
Marvel Comics: Dec, 2008 ($3.99, one-shot)
Annual 1 (12/08, $3.99) Zarda battles Hulk; McGuinness & Djurdjevic-a/Loeb-s 4.00

ULTIMATE HUMAN
Marvel Comics: Mar, 2008 - No. 4, Jun, 2008 ($2.99, limited series)
1-4-Iron Man vs. The Hulk; The Leader app.; Ellis-s/Nord-a 3.00
HC (2008, $19.99) r/#1-4 20.00

ULTIMATE IRON MAN
Marvel Comics: May, 2005 - No. 5, Feb, 2006 ($2.99, limited series)
1-Origin of Iron Man; Orson Scott Card-s/Andy Kubert-a; two covers 3.00
1-2nd & 3rd printings; each with B&W variant-c 3.00
2-5-Kubert-c 3.00
Volume 1 HC (2006, $19.99, dust jacket) r/#1-5; rough cut of script for #1, cover sketches 20.00
Volume 1 SC (2006, $14.99) r/#1-5; rough cut of script for #1, cover sketches 15.00

ULTIMATE IRON MAN II
Marvel Comics: Feb, 2008 - No. 5, July, 2008 ($2.99, limited series)
1-5-Early days of the Iron Man prototype; Orson Scott Card-s/Pasqual Ferry-a/c 3.00

ULTIMATE MARVEL FLIP MAGAZINE
Marvel Comics: July, 2005 - No. 26, Aug, 2007 ($3.99/$4.99)
1-11-Reprints Ultimate Fantastic Four and Ultimate X-Men in flip format 4.00
12-26-($4.99) 5.00

ULTIMATE MARVEL MAGAZINE
Marvel Comics: Feb, 2001 - No. 11, 2002 ($3.99, magazine size)
1-11: Reprints of recent stories from the Ultimate titles plus Marvel news and features. 1-Reprints Ultimate Spider-Man #1&2. 11-Lord of the Rings-c 4.00

ULTIMATE MARVEL SAMPLER
Marvel Comics: 2007 (no cover price, limited series)
1-Previews of 2008 Ultimate Marvel story arcs; Finch-c 3.00

ULTIMATE MARVEL TEAM-UP (Spider-Man Team-up)
Marvel Comics: Apr, 2001 - No. 16, July, 2002 ($2.99/$2.25)
1-Spider-Man & Wolverine; Bendis-s in all; Matt Wagner-a/c 5.00
2,3-Hulk; Hester-a 3.50
4,5,9-16: 4,5-Iron Man; Allred-a. 9-Fantastic Four; Mahfood-a. 10-Man-Thing; Totleben-a. 11-X-Men; Clugston-Major-a. 12,13-Dr. Strange; McKeever-a.14-Black Widow; Terry Moore-a. 15,16-Shang-Chi; Mays-a 3.00
6-8-Punisher; Sienkiewicz-a. 7,8-Daredevil app. 4.00
TPB (11/01, $14.95) r/#1-5 15.00
... Ultimate Collection TPB ('06, $29.99) r/#1-16 & Ult. Spider-Man Spec.; sketch pages 30.00
HC (8/02, $39.99) r/#1-16 & Ult. Spider-Man Special; Bendis afterword 30.00
...: Vol. 2 TPB (2003, $11.99) r/#9-13; Mahfood-c 12.00
...: Vol. 3 TPB (2003, $12.99) r/#14-16 & Ultimate Spider-Man Super Special; Moore-c 13.00

ULTIMATE NEW ULTIMATES (Follows Ultimatum x-over)
Marvel Comics: May, 2010 - Present ($3.99)
1-Jeph Loeb-s/Frank Cho-a; 6-page wraparound-c by Cho; Defenders app. 4.00
1-Villains variant-c by Yu 8.00

ULTIMATE NIGHTMARE (Leads into Ultimate Secret limited series)
Marvel Comics: Oct, 2004 - No. 5, Feb, 2005 ($2.25, limited series)
1-5: Ellis-s; Ultimates, X-Men, Nick Fury app. 1,2,4,5-Hairsine-a/c. 3-Epting-a 2.50

GD VG FN VF VF/NM NM-
2.0 4.0 6.0 8.0 9.0 9.2

Ultimate Galactus Book 1: Nightmare TPB (2005, $12.99) r/Ultimate Nightmare #1-5 13.00

ULTIMATE ORIGINS
Marvel Comics: Aug, 2008 - No. 5, Dec, 2008 ($2.99, limited series)
1-5-Bendis-s/Guice-a. 1-Nick Fury origin in the 1940s. 2-Capt. America origin 3.00

ULTIMATE POWER
Marvel Comics: Dec, 2006 - No. 9, Feb, 2008 ($2.99, limited series)
1-9: 1-Ultimate FF meets the Squadron Supreme; Bendis-s; Land-a/c. 2-Spider-Man, X-Men and the Ultimates app. 6-Doom app. 3.00
1-Variant sketch-c 5.00
1-Director's Cut (2007, $3.99) r/#1 and B&W pencil and ink pages; covers to #2,3 4.00
HC (2008, $34.99) oversized r/series; profile pages; B&W sketch art 35.00

ULTIMATES, THE (Avengers of the Ultimate line)
Marvel Comics: Mar, 2002 - No. 13, Apr, 2004 ($2.25)
1-Intro. Capt. America; Millar-s/Hitch-a & wraparound-c 6.00
2-Intro. Giant-Man and the Wasp 4.00
3-12: 3-1st Capt. America in new costume. 4-Intro. Thor. 5-Ultimates vs. The Hulk. 8-Intro. Hawkeye 3.00
13-($3.50) 3.50
... Saga (2007, $3.99) Re-caps 1st 2 Ultimates series; new framing art by Charest; prelude to Ultimates 3 series; Brooks-c 4.00
... Volume 1 HC (2004, $29.99) oversized r/series; commentary pages with Millar & Hitch; cover gallery and character design pages; intro. by Joss Whedon 30.00
... Volume 1: Super-Human TPB (8/02, $12.99) r/#1-6 13.00
... Volume 2: Homeland Security TPB (2004, $17.99) r/#7-13 18.00

ULTIMATES 2
Marvel Comics: Feb, 2005 - No. 13, Feb, 2007 ($2.99/$3.99)
1-Millar-s/Hitch-a; Giant-Man becomes Ant-Man 3.00
2-11: 6-Intro. The Defenders. 7-Hawkeye shot. 8-Intro The Liberators 3.00
12,13-($3.99) Wraparound-c; X-Men, Fantastic Four, Spider-Man app. 4.00
13-Variant white cover featuring The Wasp 40.00
Annual 1 (10/05, $3.99) Millar-s/Dillon-a/Hitch-c; Defenders app. 4.00
Annual 2 (10/06, $3.99) Deodato-a; flashback to WWII with Sook-a; Falcon app. 4.00
HC (2007, $34.99) oversized r/series; commentary pages with Millar & Hitch; cover gallery, sketch and script pages; intro. by Jonathan Ross 35.00
... Volume 1: Gods & Monsters TPB (2005, $15.99) r/#1-6 16.00
... Volume 2: Grand Theft America TPB (2007, $19.99) r/#7-13; cover gallery w/sketches 20.00

ULTIMATES 3
Marvel Comics: Feb, 2008 - No. 5, Nov, 2008 ($2.99)
1-Loeb-s/Madureira-a; two gatefold wraparound covers by Madureira; Scarlet Witch shot 3.00
1,2-Second printings: 1-Wraparound cover by Madureira. 2-Madureira-c 3.00
2-5: 2-Spider-Man app. 3-Wolverine app. 5-Two gatefold wraparound-c (Heroes & Ultron) 3.00
2-Variant Thor cover by Turner 8.00
3-Variant Scarlet Witch cover by Cho 8.00
4-Variant Valkyrie cover by Finch 4.00

ULTIMATE SECRET (See Ultimate Nightmare limited series)
Marvel Comics: May, 2005 - No. 4, Dec, 2005 ($2.99, limited series)
1-4-Ellis-s; Captain Marvel app. 1,2-McNiven-a. 2,3-Ultimates & FF app. 3.00
Ultimate Galactus Book 2: Secret TPB (2006, $12.99) r/#1-4 13.00

ULTIMATE SECRETS
Marvel Comics: 2008 ($3.99, one-shot)
1-Handbook-styled profiles of secondary teams and characters from Ultimate universe 4.00

ULTIMATE SIX (Reprinted in Ultimate Spider-Man Vol. 5 hardcover)
Marvel Comics: Nov, 2003 - No. 7, June, 2004 ($2.25) (See Ultimate Spider-Man for TPB)
1-The Ultimates & Spider-Man team-up; Bendis-s/Quesada & Hairsine-a; Cassaday-c 5.00
2-7-Hairsine-a; Cassaday-c 2.50

ULTIMATE SPIDER-MAN
Marvel Comics: Oct, 2000 - No. 133, June, 2009 ($2.99/$2.25/$2.99/$3.99)
1-Bendis-s/Bagley & Thibert-a; cardstock-c; introduces revised origin and cast separate from regular Spider-continuity 6 12 18 41 66 90
1-Variant white-c (Retailer incentive) 9 18 27 60 100 140
1-DF Edition 4 8 12 28 44 60
1-Free Comic Book Day giveaway & Kay Bee Toys variant - (See Promotional Comics section)
2-Cover with Spider-Man on car 3 6 9 18 27 35
2-Cover with Spider-Man swinging past building 3 6 9 18 27 35
3,4: 4-Uncle Ben killed 3 6 9 16 23 30
5-7: 6,7-Green Goblin app. 3 6 9 18 27 35
8-13: 13-Reveals secret to MJ 1 2 3 5 7 9
14-21: 14-Intro. Gwen Stacy & Dr. Octopus 5.00

Ultimate Spider-Man (2009 series) #1 © MAR

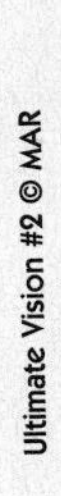

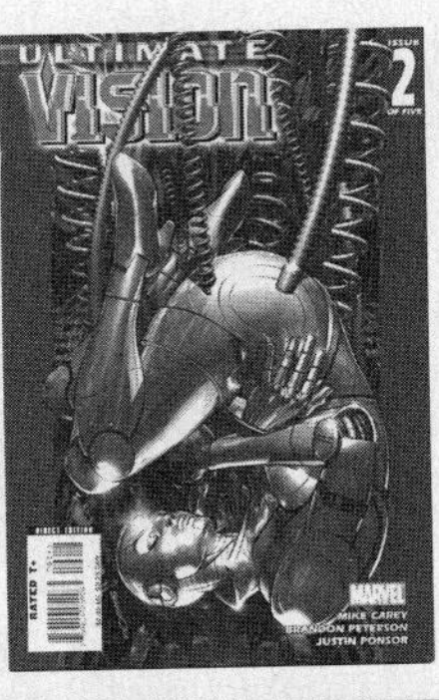

Ultimate Vision #2 © MAR

Ultimate X-Men #100 © MAR

GD VG FN VF VF/NM NM-
2.0 4.0 6.0 8.0 9.0 9.2

22-($3.50) Green Goblin returns 3.50
23-32 2.50
33-1st Ultimate Venom-c; intro. Eddie Brock 3.00
34-38-Ultimate Venom 2.50
39-49,51-59: 39-Nick Fury app. 43,44-X-Men app. 46-Prelude to Ultimate Six; Sandman app. 51-53-Elektra app. 54-59-Doctor Octopus app. 2.50
50-($2.99) Intro. Black Cat 3.00
60-Intro. Ultimate Carnage on cover 3.00
61-Intro Ben Reilly; Punisher app. 2.50
62-Gwen Stacy killed by Carnage 3.00
63-92: 63,64-Carnage app. 66,67-Wolverine app. 68,69-Johnny Storm app. 78-Begin $2.50-c. 79-Debut Moon Knight. 81-85-Black Cat app. 90-Vulture app. 91-94-Deadpool 2.50
93-99: 93-Begin $2.99-c. 95-Morbius & Blade app. 97-99-Clone Saga 3.00
100-($3.99) Wraparound-c; Clone Saga; re-cap of previous issues 4.00
101-103-Clone Saga continues; Fantastic Four app. 102-Spider-Woman origin 3.00
104-($3.99) Clone Saga concludes; Fantastic Four and Dr. Octopus app. 4.00
105-132: 106-110-Daredevil app. 111-Last Bagley art; Immonen-a (6 pgs.) 112-Immonen-a; Norman Osborn app. 118-Liz Allen ignites. 123,128-Venom app. 129-132-Ultimatum 3.00
133-($3.99) Ultimatum crossover; Spider-Woman app. 4.00
Annual 1 (10/05, $3.99) Kitty Pryde app.; Bendis-s/Brooks-a/Bagley-c 4.00
Annual 2 (10/06, $3.99) Punisher, Moon Knight and Daredevil app.; Bendis-s/Brooks-a 4.00
Annual 3 (12/08, $3.99) Mysterio app.; Bendis-s/Lafuente-a 4.00
Collected Edition (1/01, $3.99) r/#1-3 4.00
...Special (7/02, $3.50) art by Bagley and various incl. Romita,Sr., Brereton, Cho, Mack, Sienkiewicz, Phillips, Pearson, Oeming, Mahfood, Russell 3.50
Ultimate Spider-Man 100 Project (2007, $10.00, SC, charity book for the HERO Initiative) collection of 100 variant covers by Romita Sr. & Jr., Cho, Bagley, Quesada and more 10.00
...: Venom HC (2007, $19.99) r/#33-39 20.00
...(Vol. 1): Power and Responsibility TPB (4/01, $14.95) r/#1-7 15.00
...(Vol. 2): Learning Curve TPB (12/01, $14.95) r/#8-13 15.00
...(Vol. 3): Double Trouble TPB (6/02, $17.95) r/#14-21 18.00
Vol. 4: Legacy TPB (2002, $14.99) r/#22-27 15.00
Vol. 5: Public Scrutiny TPB (2003, $11.99) r/#28-32 12.00
Vol. 6: Venom TPB (2003, $15.99) r/#33-39 16.00
Vol. 7: Irresponsible TPB (2003, $12.99) r/#40-45 13.00
Vol. 8: Cats & Kings TPB (2004, $17.99) r/#47-53 18.00
Vol. 9: Ultimate Six TPB (2004, $17.99) r/#46 & Ultimate Six #1-7 18.00
Vol. 10: Hollywood TPB (2004, $12.99) r/#54-59 13.00
Vol. 11: Carnage TPB (2004, $12.99) r/#60-65 13.00
Vol. 12: Superstars TPB (2005, $12.99) r/#66-71 13.00
Vol. 13: Hobgoblin TPB (2005, $15.99) r/#72-78 16.00
Vol. 14: Warriors TPB (2005, $17.99) r/#79-85 18.00
Vol. 15: Silver Sable TPB (2006, $15.99) r/#86-90 & Annual #1 16.00
Vol. 16: Deadpool TPB (2006, $19.99) r/#91-96 & Annual #2 20.00
Vol. 17: Clone Saga TPB (2007, $24.99) r/#97-105 25.00
Vol. 18: Ultimate Knights TPB (2007, $13.99) r/#106-111 14.00
Vol. 19: Death of a Goblin TPB (2008, $14.99) r/#112-117 18.00
Hardcover (3/02, $34.95, 7x11", dust jacket) r/#1-13 & Amazing Fantasy #15; sketch pages and Bill Jemas' initial plot and character outlines 35.00
Volume 2 HC (2003, $29.99, 7x11", dust jacket) r/#14-27; pin-ups & sketch pages 30.00
Volume 3 HC (2003, $29.99, 7x11", dust jacket) r/#28-39 & #1/2; script pages 30.00
Volume 4 HC (2004, $29.99, 7x11", dust jacket) r/#40-45, 47-53; sketch pages 30.00
Volume 5 HC (2004, $29.99, 7x11", dust jacket) r/#46,54-59, Ultimate Six #1-7 30.00
Volume 6 HC (2005, $29.99, 7x11", dust jacket) r/#60-71; sketch page 30.00
Volume 7 HC (2006, $29.99, 7x11", dust jacket) r/#72-85; sketch & profile pages 30.00
Volume 8 HC (2007, $29.99, 7x11", dust jacket) r/#86-96 & Annual #1&2; sketch page 30.00
Volume 9 HC (2008, $39.99, 7x11", dust jacket) r/#97-111; sketch pages 40.00
Volume 10 HC (2009, $39.99, 7x11", dust jacket) r/#112-122; sketch pages 40.00
Wizard #1/2 1 3 4 6 8 10

ULTIMATE SPIDER-MAN (Follows Ultimatum x-over)
Marvel Comics: Oct, 2009 - Present ($3.99)

1-7: 1-Bendis-s/Lafuente-a/c; new Mysterio. 1-Variant-c by Djurdjevic. 7-Miyazawa-a 4.00

ULTIMATE TALES FLIP MAGAZINE
Marvel Comics: July, 2005 - No. 26, Aug, 2007 ($3.99/$4.99)

1-11-Each reprints 2 issues of Ultimate Spider-Man in flip format 4.00
12-26-($4.99) 5.00

ULTIMATE VISION
Marvel Comics: No. 0, Jan, 2007 - No. 5, Jan, 2008 ($2.99, limited series)

0-Reprints back-up serial from Ultimate Extinction and related series; pin-ups 3.00
1-5: 1-(2/07) Carey-s/Peterson-a/c 3.00
TPB (2007, $14.99) r/#0-5; design pages and cover gallery 15.00

ULTIMATE WAR
Marvel Comics: Feb, 2003 - No. 4, Apr, 2003 ($2.25, limited series)

1-4-Millar-s/Bachalo-c/a; The Ultimates vs. Ultimate X-Men 2.50
Ultimate X-Men Vol. 5: Ultimate War TPB (2003, $10.99) r/#1-4 11.00

ULTIMATE WOLVERINE VS. HULK
Marvel Comics: Feb, 2006 - No. 6, July, 2009 ($2.99, limited series)

1,2-Leinil Yu-a/c; Damon Lindelof-s. 2-(4/06) 3.00
1,2-(2009) New printings 3.00
3-6: 3-(5/09) Intro. She-Hulk. 4-Origin She-Hulk 3.00

ULTIMATE X (Follows Ultimatum x-over)
Marvel Comics: Apr, 2010 - Present ($3.99)

1,2: 1-Jeph Loeb-s/Art Adams-a; two covers by Adams 4.00

ULTIMATE X-MEN (Also see Promotional Comics section for FCBD Ed.)
Marvel Comics: Feb, 2001 - No. 100, Apr, 2009 ($2.99/$2.25/$2.50)

1-Millar-s/Adam Kubert & Thibert-a; cardstock-c; introduces revised origin and cast separate from regular X-Men continuity 3 6 9 14 20 25
1-DF Edition 30.00
1-DF Sketch Cover Edition 45.00
2 2 4 6 11 16 20
3-6 2 4 6 8 11 14
7-10 6.00
11-24,26-33: 13-Intro. Gambit. 18,19-Bachalo-a. 23,24-Andrews-a 3.00
25-($3.50) leads into the Ultimate War mini-series; Kubert-a 3.50
34-Spider-Man-c/app.; Bendis-s begin; Finch-a 4.00
35-74: 35-Spider-Man app. 36,37-Daredevil-c/app. 40-Intro. Angel. 42-Intro. Dazzler. 44-Beast dies. 46-Intro. Mr. Sinister. 50-53-Kubert-a; Gambit app. 54-57,59-63-Immonen-a. 60-Begin $2.50-c. 61-Variant Coipel-c. 66-Kirkman-s begin. 69-Begin $2.99-c 3.00
61-Retailer Edition with variant Coipel B&W sketch-c 10.00
75-($3.99) Turner-c; intro. Cable; back-up story with Emma Frost's students 4.00
76-99: 76-Intro. Bishop. 91-Fantastic Four app. 92-96-Phoenix app. 96-Spider-Man app. 99-Ultimatum x-over 3.00
100-($3.99) Ultimatum x-over; Brooks-a 4.00
Annual 1 (10/05, $3.99) Vaughan-s/Raney-a; Gambit & Rogue in Vegas 4.00
Annual 2 (10/06, $3.99) Kirkman-s/Larroca-a; Nightcrawler & Dazzler 4.00
.../Fantastic Four 1 (2/06, $2.99) Carey-s/Ferry-a; concluded in Ult. Fantastic Four/X-Men 3.00
.../Ult. Fantastic Four Ann. 1 (11/08, $3.99) Continues in Ult. F.F./Ult. X-Men Annual #1 4.00
.../Fantastic Four TPB (2006, $12.99) reprints Ult X-Men/Ult. FF x-over and Official Handbook of the Ultimate Marvel Universe #1-2 13.00
... Ultimate Collection Vol. 1 (2006, $24.99) r/#1-12 & #1/2; unused Bendis script for #1 25.00
... Ultimate Collection Vol. 2 (2007, $24.99) r/#13-25; Kubert cover sketch pages 25.00
...: (Vol. 1) The Tomorrow People TPB (7/01, $14.95) r/#1-6 15.00
...: (Vol. 2) Return to Weapon X TPB (4/02, $14.95) r/#7-12 15.00
Vol. 3: World Tour TPB (2002, $17.99) r/#13-20 18.00
Vol. 4: Hellfire and Brimstone TPB (2003, $12.99) r/#21-25 13.00
Vol. 5 (See Ultimate War)
Vol. 6: Return of the King TPB (2003, $16.99) r/#26-33 17.00
Vol. 7: Blockbuster TPB (2004, $12.99) r/#34-39 13.00
Vol. 8: New Mutants TPB (2004, $12.99) r/#40-45 13.00
Vol. 9: The Tempest TPB (2004, $10.99) r/#46-49 11.00
Vol. 10: Cry Wolf TPB (2005, $8.99) r/#50-53 9.00
Vol. 11: The Most Dangerous Game TPB (2005, $9.99) r/#54-57 10.00
Vol. 12: Hard Lessons TPB (2005, $12.99) r/#58-60 & Annual #1 13.00
Vol. 13: Magnetic North TPB (2006, $12.99) r/#61-65 13.00
Vol. 14: Phoenix? TPB (2006, $14.99) r/#66-71 15.00
Vol. 15: Magical TPB (2007, $11.99) r/#72-74 & Annual #2 12.00
Vol. 16: Cable TPB (2007, $14.99) r/#75-80; sketch pages 15.00
Vol. 17: Sentinels TPB (2008, $17.99) r/#81-88 18.00
Volume 1 HC (8/02, $34.99, 7x11", dust jacket) r/#1-12 & Giant-Size X-Men #1; sketch pages and Millar and Bendis' initial plot and character outlines 35.00
Volume 2 HC (2003, $29.99, 7x11", dust jacket) r/#13-25; script for #20 30.00
Volume 3 HC (2003, $29.99, 7x11", dust jacket) r/#26-33 & Utimate War #1-4 30.00
Volume 4 HC (2005, $29.99, 7x11", dust jacket) r/#34-45 30.00
Volume 5 HC (2006, $29.99, 7x11", dust jacket) r/#46-57; Vaughan intro.; sketch pages 30.00
Volume 6 HC (2006, $29.99, 7x11", dust jacket) r/#58-65, Annual #1 & Wizard #1/2 30.00
Volume 7 HC (2007, $29.99, 7x11", dust jacket) r/#66-74, Annual #2 30.00
Wizard #1/2 2 4 6 9 12 15

ULTIMATUM
Marvel Comics: Jan, 2009 - No. 5, July, 2009 ($3.99, limited series)

1-5-Loeb-s/Finch-a; cover by Finch & ; Ultimate heroes vs. Magneto 4.00
1-5-Variant covers by McGuinness 8.00
5-Double gatefold variant-c by Finch 4.00
March on Ultimatum Saga ('08, giveaway) text and art panel history of Ultimate universe 2.25

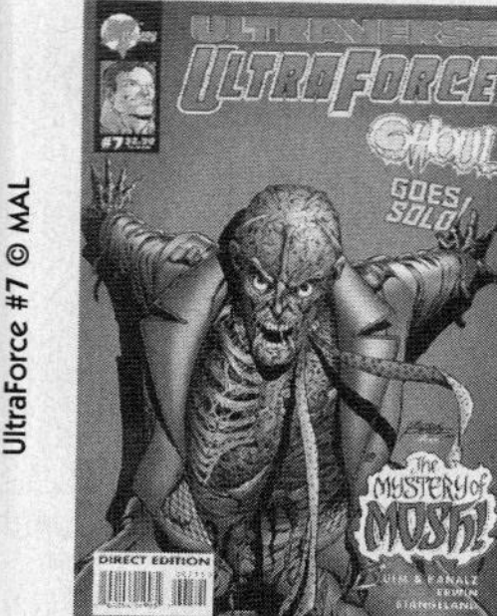

UltraForce #7 © MAL

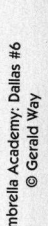

Umbrella Academy: Dallas #6 © Gerald Way

Uncanny Tales #2 © MAR

	GD 2.0	VG 4.0	FN 6.0	VF 8.0	VF/NM 9.0	NM- 9.2

...: Fantastic Four Requiem 1 (9/09,$3.99) Pokaski-s/Atkins-a; Dr. Strange app. 4.00
...: Spider-Man Requiem 1,2 (8/09, 9/09,$3.99) Bendis-s/Bagley & Immonen-a 4.00
...: X-Men Requiem 1 (9/09,$3.99) Coleite-s/Oliver-a/Brooks-c 4.00
NOTE: *Numerous variant covers and 2nd & 3rd printings exist.*

ULTRA
Image Comics: Aug, 2004 - No. 8, Mar, 2005 ($2.95, limited series)

1-8: 1-Intro. Ultra/Pearl Penalosa; Luna Brothers-s/a 3.00
Vol. 1: Seven Days TPB (4/05, $17.95) r/#1-8; sketch pages 18.00

ULTRAFORCE (1st Series) (Also see Avengers/Ultraforce #1)
Malibu Comics (Ultraverse): Aug, 1994 - No. 10, Aug, 1995 ($1.95/$2.50)

0 (9/94, $2.50)-Perez-c/a. 2.50
1-($2.50, 44 pgs.)-Bound-in trading card; team consisting of Prime, Prototype, Hardcase, Pixx, Ghoul, Contrary & Topaz; Gerard Jones scripts begin, ends #6; Perez-c/a begins. 2.50
1-Ultra 5000 Limited Silver Foil Edition 4.00
1-Holographic-c, no price 6.00
2-5: Perez-c/a in all. 2 (10/94, $1.95)-Prime quits, Strangers cameo. 3-Origin of Topaz; Prime rejoins. 5-Pixx dies. 2.50
2 ($2.50)-Florescent logo; limited edition stamp on-c 3.00
6-10: 6-Begin $2.50-c, Perez-c/a. 7-Ghoul story, Steve Erwin-a. 8-Marvel's Black Knight enters the Ultraverse (last seen in Avengers #375); Perez-c/a. 9,10-Black Knight app.; Perez-c. 10-Leads into Ultraforce/Avengers Prelude 2.50
Malibu "Ashcan ": Ultraforce #0A (6/94) 2.50
.../Avengers Prelude 1 (8/95, $2.50)-Perez-c. 2.50
.../Avengers 1 (8/95, $3.95)-Warren Ellis script; Perez-c/a; foil-c 4.00

ULTRAFORCE (2nd Series)(Also see Black September)
Malibu Comics (Ultraverse): Infinity, Sept, 1995 - V2#15, Dec, 1996 ($1.50)

Infinity, V2#1-15: Infinity-Team consists of Marvel's Black Knight, Ghoul, Topaz, Prime & redesigned Prototype; Warren Ellis scripts begin, ends #3; variant-c exists. 1-1st app.Cromwell, Lament & Wreckage. 2-Contains free encore presentation of Ultraforce #1; flip book "Phoenix Resurrection" Pt. 7. 7-Darick Robertson, Jeff Johnson & others-a. 8,9-Intro. Future Ultraforce (Prime, Hellblade, Angel of Destruction, Painkiller & Whipslash); Gary Erskine-c/a. 9-Foxfire app. 10-Len Wein scripts & Deodato Studios-c/a begin. 10-Lament back-up story. 11-Ghoul back-up story by Pander Bros. 12-Ultraforce vs. Maxis (cont'd in Ultraverse Unlimited #2); Exiles & Iron Clad app. 13-Prime leaves; Hardcase returns 2.50
Infinity (2000 signed) 4.00
.../Spider-Man ($3.95)-Marv Wolfman script; Green Goblin app; 2 covers exist. 4.00

ULTRAGIRL
Marvel Comics: Nov, 1996 - No. 3 Mar, 1997($1.50, limited series)

1-3: 1-1st app. 2.50

ULTRA KLUTZ
Onward Comics: 1981; 6/86 - #27, 1/89, #28, 4/90 - #31, 1990? ($1.50/$1.75/$2.00, B&W)

1 (1981)-Re-released after 2nd #1 2.50
1-30: 1-(6/86). 27-Photo back-c 2.50
31-($2.95, 52 pgs.) 3.00

ULTRAMAN
Nemesis Comics: Mar, 1994 - No. 4, Sept, 1994 ($1.75/$1.95)

1-($2.25)-Collector's edition; foil-c; special 3/4 wraparound-c 3.00
1-($1.75)-Newsstand edition 2.50
2-4: 3-$1.95-c begins 2.50
#(-1) (3/93) 2.50

ULTRAMAN TIGA
Dark Horse Comics: Aug, 2003 - No. 10, June, 2004 ($3.99)

1-10-Khoo Fuk Lung-a/Tony Wong-s 4.00

ULTRAVERSE DOUBLE FEATURE
Malibu Comics (Ultraverse): Jan, 1995 ($3.95, one-shot, 68 pgs.)

1-Flip-c featuring Prime & Solitaire. 4.00

ULTRAVERSE ORIGINS
Malibu Comics (Ultraverse): Jan, 1994 (99¢, one-shot)

1-Gatefold-c; 2 pg. origins all characters 2.50
1-Newsstand edition; different-c, no gatefold 2.50

ULTRAVERSE PREMIERE
Malibu Comics (Ultraverse): 1994 (one-shot)

0-Ordered thru mail w/coupons 5.00

ULTRAVERSE UNLIMITED
Malibu Comics (Ultraverse): June, 1996; No. 2, Sept, 1996 ($2.50)

1,2: 1-Adam Warlock returns to the Marvel Universe; Rune-c/app. 2-Black Knight, Reaper & Sierra Blaze return to the Marvel Universe 2.50

ULTRAVERSE YEAR ONE
Malibu Comics (Ultraverse): 1994 ($4.95, one-shot)

nn-In-depth synopsis of the first year's titles & stories. 5.00

ULTRAVERSE YEAR TWO
Malibu Comics (Ultraverse): Aug, 1995 ($4.95, one-shot)

nn-In-depth synopsis of second year's titles & stories 5.00

ULTRAVERSE YEAR ZERO: THE DEATH OF THE SQUAD
Malibu Comics (Ultraverse): Apr, 1995 - No. 4, July, 1995 ($2.95, lim. series)

1-4: 3-Codename: Firearm back-up story. 3.00

UMBRELLA ACADEMY: APOCALYPSE SUITE (See FCBD edition in Promotional Section)
Dark Horse Comics: Sept, 2007 - No. 6, Feb, 2008 ($2.99, limited series)

1-Origin of the Umbrella Aademy; Gerald Way-s/Gabriel Bá-a/James Jean-c 5.00
1-White variant-c by Bá 15.00
1-Variant-c by Gerald Way 10.00
1-2nd printing with variant-c by Bá 3.00
2-6 3.00
Vol.1: Apocalypse Suite TPB (7/08, $17.95) r/#1-6, FCBD story and web shorts; design art; Grant Morrison intro.; cover gallery 18.00

UMBRELLA ACADEMY: DALLAS
Dark Horse Comics: Nov, 2008 - No. 6, May, 2009 ($2.99, limited series)

1-6-Gerald Way-s/Gabriel Bá-a/c 3.00
1-Wraparound variant-c by Jim Lee 5.00

UNBIRTHDAY PARTY WITH ALICE IN WONDERLAND (See Alice In Wonderland, Four Color #341)

UNBOUND
Image Comics (Desperado): Jan, 1998 ($2.95, B&W)

1-Pruett-s/Peters-a 3.00

UNCANNY ORIGINS
Marvel Comics: Sept, 1996 - No. 14, Oct, 1997 (99¢)

1-14: 1-Cyclops. 2-Quicksilver. 3-Archangel. 4-Firelord. 5-Hulk. 6-Beast. 7-Venom. 8-Nightcrawler. 9-Storm. 10-Black Cat. 11-Black Knight. 12-Dr. Strange. 13-Daredevil. 14-Iron Fist 2.50

UNCANNY TALES
Atlas Comics (PrPI/PPI): June, 1952 - No. 56, Sept, 1957

	GD 2.0	VG 4.0	FN 6.0	VF 8.0	VF/NM 9.0	NM- 9.2
1-Heath-a; horror/weird stories begin	90	180	270	576	988	1400
2	48	96	144	302	514	725
3-5	42	84	126	265	445	625
6-Wolvertonish-a by Matt Fox	43	86	129	271	461	650
7-10: 8-Atom bomb story; Tothish-a (by Sekowsky?). 9-Crandall-a	39	78	117	231	378	525
11-20: 17-Atom bomb panels; anti-communist story; Hitler story. 19-Krenkel-a. 20-Robert Q. Sale-c	29	58	87	170	278	385
21-25,27: 25-Nostrand-a?	25	50	75	150	245	340
26-Spider-Man prototype c/story	36	72	108	211	343	475
28-Last precode issue (1/55); Kubert-a; #1-28 contain 2-3 sci/fi stories each	26	52	78	154	252	350
29-41,43-49,51	19	38	57	109	172	235
42,54,56-Krigstein-a	19	38	57	112	179	245
50,53,55-Torres-a	19	38	57	109	172	235
52-Oldest Iron Man prototype (2/57)	28	56	84	165	270	375

NOTE: ***Andru** a-15, 27. **Ayers** a-14, 22, 28, 37. **Bailey** a-51. **Briefer** a-19, 20. **Brodsky** c-1, 3, 4, 6, 8, 12-16, 19. **Brodsky/Everett** c-9. **Cameron** a-47. **Colan** a-11, 16, 17, 49, 52. **Drucker** a-37, 42, 45. **Everett** a-2, 9, 12, 32, 36, 39, 48; c-7, 11, 17, 39, 41, 50, 52, 53. **Fass** a-9, 10, 15, 24. **Forte** a-18, 27, 33-35, 52, 53. **Heath** a-13, 14; c-5, 10, 18. **Keller** a-3. **Lawrence** a-14, 17, 19, 23, 27, 28, 35. **Maneely** a-4, 8, 10, 16, 29, 35; c-2, 22, 26, 33, 38. **Moldoff** a-23. **Morisi** a-48, 52. **Morrow** a-46, 51. **Orlando** a-49, 50, 53. **Powell** a-12, 18, 34, 36, 38, 43, 50, 56. **Robinson** a-3, 13. **Reinman** a-12, 36. **Romita** a-10. **Roussos** a-8. **Sale** a-34, 47, 53; c-20. **Sekowsky** a-25. **Sinnott** a-14, 15, 38, 52. **Torres** a-53. **Tothish**-a by **Andru**-27. **Wildey** a-22, 48.*

UNCANNY TALES
Marvel Comics Group: Dec, 1973 - No. 12, Oct, 1975

	GD 2.0	VG 4.0	FN 6.0	VF 8.0	VF/NM 9.0	NM- 9.2
1-Crandall-r/Uncanny Tales #9('50s)	3	6	9	18	27	35
2-12: 7,12-Kirby-a	2	4	6	11	16	20

NOTE: ***Ditko** reprints-#4, 6-8, 10-12.*

UNCANNY X-MEN, THE (See **X-Men, The**, 1st series, #142-on)

UNCANNY X-MEN AND THE NEW TEEN TITANS (See Marvel and DC Present...)

UNCENSORED MOUSE, THE
Eternity Comics: Apr, 1989 - No. 2, Apr, 1989 ($1.95, B&W)(Came sealed in plastic bag) (Both contain racial stereotyping & violence)

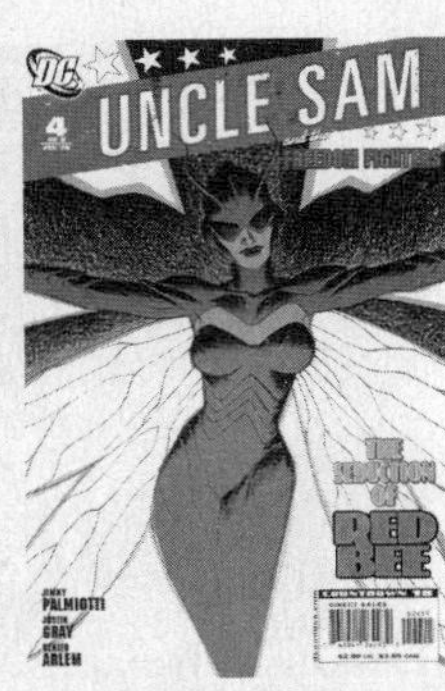

Uncle Sam and the Freedom Fighters #4 © DC

Uncle Sam Quarterly #1 © QUA

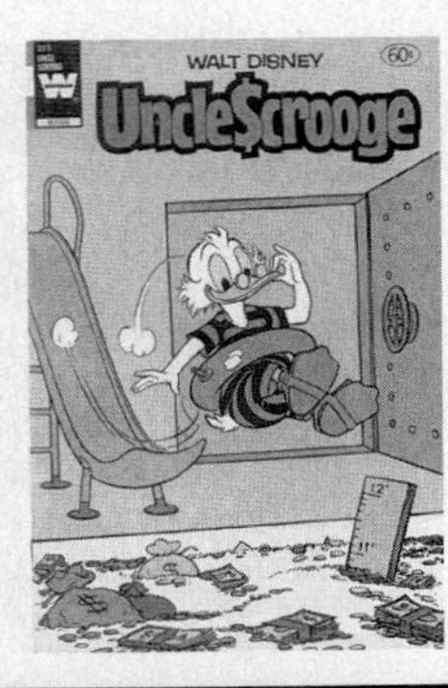

Uncle Scrooge #203 © DIS

GD 2.0 | VG 4.0 | FN 6.0 | VF 8.0 | VF/NM 9.0 | NM- 9.2

1,2-Early Gottfredson strip-r in each 2 4 6 11 16 20
NOTE: *Both issues contain unauthorized reprints. Series was cancelled.* **Win Smith** *r-1, 2.*

UNCLE CHARLIE'S FABLES
Lev Gleason Publ.: Jan, 1952 - No. 5, Sept, 1952 (All have Biro painted-c)
1-Norman Maurer-a; has Biro's picture 15 30 45 88 137 185
2-Fuje-a; Biro photo 10 20 30 54 72 90
3-5 9 18 27 47 61 75

UNCLE DONALD & HIS NEPHEWS DUDE RANCH (See Dell Giant #52)

UNCLE DONALD & HIS NEPHEWS FAMILY FUN (See Dell Giant #38)

UNCLE JOE'S FUNNIES
Centaur Publications: 1938 (B&W)
1-Games, puzzles & magic tricks, some interior art; Bill Everett-c
61 122 183 390 670 950

UNCLE MILTY (TV)
Victoria Publications/True Cross: Dec, 1950 - No. 4, July, 1951 (52 pgs.)(Early TV comic)
1-Milton Berle photo on-c of #1,2 54 108 162 343 584 825
2 35 70 105 208 339 470
3,4 29 58 87 172 281 390

UNCLE REMUS & HIS TALES OF BRER RABBIT (See Brer Rabbit, 4-Color #129, 208, 693)

UNCLE SAM
DC Comics (Vertigo): 1997 - No. 2, 1997 ($4.95, limited series)
1,2-Alex Ross painted c/a. Story by Ross and Steve Darnell 5.00
Hardcover (1998, $17.95) 18.00
Softcover (2000, $9.95) 10.00

UNCLE SAM AND THE FREEDOM FIGHTERS
DC Comics: Sept, 2006 - No. 8, Apr, 2007 ($2.99, limited series)
1-8-Acuña-a/c; Gray & Palmiotti-s. 3-Intro. Black Condor 3.00
TPB (2007, $14.99) r/#1-8 and story from DCU Brave New World #1 15.00

UNCLE SAM AND THE FREEDOM FIGHTERS
DC Comics: Nov, 2007 - No. 8, Jun, 2008 ($2.99, limited series)
1-8-Gray & Palmiotti-s/Arlem-a/Johnson-c 3.00
...: Brave New World TPB (2008, $14.99) r/#1-8 15.00

UNCLE SAM QUARTERLY (Blackhawk #9 on)(See Freedom Fighters)
Quality Comics Group: Autumn, 1941 - No. 8, Fall, 1943 (see National Comics)
1-Origin Uncle Sam; Fine/Eisner-c, chapter headings, 2 pgs. by Eisner; (2 versions: dark cover, no price; light cover with price sticker); Jack Cole-a
377 754 1131 2639 4620 6600
2-Cameos by The Ray, Black Condor, Quicksilver, The Red Bee, Alias the Spider, Hercules & Neon the Unknown; Eisner, Fine-c/a 132 264 396 838 1444 2050
3-Tuska-c/a; Eisner-a(2) 97 194 291 621 1061 1500
4 87 174 261 553 952 1350
5,7-Hitler, Mussolini & Tojo-c 113 226 339 718 1234 1750
6,8 67 134 201 426 731 1035
NOTE: **Kotzky** *(or* **Tuska***) a-3-8.*

UNCLE SCROOGE (Disney) (Becomes Walt Disney's... #210 on) (See Cartoon Tales, Dell Giants #33, 55, Disney Comic Album, Donald and Scrooge, Dynabrite, Four Color #178, Gladstone Comic Album, Walt Disney's Comics & Stories #98, Walt Disney's ...)
Dell #1-39/Gold Key #40-173/Whitman #174-209: No. 386, 3/52 - No. 39, 8-10/62; No. 40, 12/62 - No. 209, 7/84
Four Color 386(#1)-in "Only a Poor Old Man" by Carl Barks; r-in Uncle Scrooge & Donald Duck #1('65) & The Best of Walt Disney Comics ('74). The 2nd cover app. of Uncle Scrooge (see Dell Giant Vacation Parade #2 (7/51) for 1st-c) 177 354 531 1549 3075 4600
1-(1986)-Reprints F.C. #386; given away with lithograph "Dam Disaster at Money Lake" & as a subscription offer giveaway to Gladstone subscribers
3 6 9 15 20 24
Four Color 456(#2)-in "Back to the Klondike" by Carl Barks; r-in Best of U.S. & D.D. #1('66) & Gladstone C.A. #4 92 184 276 782 1541 2300
Four Color 495(#3)-r-in #105 62 124 186 527 1039 1550
4(12-2/53-54)-r-in Gladstone Comic Album #11 46 92 138 368 709 1050
5-r-in Gladstone Special #2 & Walt Disney Digest #1
40 80 120 306 591 875
6-r-in U.S. #106,165,233 & Best of U.S. & D.D. #1('66)
33 66 99 254 490 725
7-The Seven Cities of Cibola by Barks; r-in #217 & Best of D.D. & U.S. #2 ('67)
30 60 90 228 439 650
8-10: 8-r-in #111,222. 9-r-in #104,214. 10-r-in #67 26 52 78 190 370 550
11-20: 11-r-in #237. 17-r-in #215. 19-r-in Gladstone C.A. #1. 20-r-in #213
22 44 66 157 304 450

GD 2.0 | VG 4.0 | FN 6.0 | VF 8.0 | VF/NM 9.0 | NM- 9.2

21-30: 24-X-Mas-c. 26-r-in #211 17 34 51 124 242 360
31-35,37-40: 34-r-in #228. 40-X-Mas-c 14 28 42 102 194 285
36-1st app. Magica De Spell; Number one dime 1st identified by name
16 32 48 116 223 330
41-60: 48-Magica De Spell-c/story (3/64). 49-Sci/fi-c. 51-Beagle Boys-c/story (8/64) 12 24 36 86 158 230
61-63,65,66,68-71:71-Last Barks issue w/original story (#71-he only storyboarded the script)
11 22 33 78 139 200
64-(7/66) Barks Vietnam War story "Treasure of Marco Polo" banned for reprints by Disney from 1977-1989 because of its Third World revolutionary war theme. It later appeared in the hardcover Carl Barks Library set (4/89) and Walt Disney's Uncle Scrooge Adventures #42 (1/97) 16 32 48 115 220 325
67,72,73: 67,72,73-Barks-r 10 20 30 71 126 180
74-84: 74-Barks-r(1pg.). 75-81,83-Not by Barks. 82,84-Barks-r begin
8 16 24 52 86 120
85-100 7 14 21 45 73 100
101-110 6 12 18 37 59 80
111-120 4 8 12 28 44 60
121-141,143-152,154-157 4 8 12 22 34 45
142-Reprints Four Color #456 with-c 4 8 12 23 36 48
153,158,162-164,166,168-170,178,180: No Barks 3 6 9 16 22 28
159-160,165,167 3 6 9 16 23 30
161(r/#14), 171(r/#11), 177(r/#16),183(r/#6)-Barks-r 3 6 9 16 23 30
172(1/80),173(2/80)-Gold Key. Barks-a 3 6 9 18 27 35
174(3/80),175(4/80),176(5/80)-Whitman. Barks-a 4 8 12 23 36 48
177(6/80),178(7/80) 4 8 12 24 37 50
179(9/80)(r/#9)-(Very low distribution) 36 72 108 277 531 785
180(11/80),181(12/80, r/4-Color #495), pre-pack? 6 12 18 37 59 80
182-195: 182-(50¢-c). 184,185,187,188-Barks-a. 182,186,191-194-No Barks. 189(r/#5), 190(r/#4), 195(r/4-Color #386) 3 6 9 16 23 30
182(1/81, 40¢-c) Cover price error variant 4 8 12 23 36 48
196(4/82),197(5/82): 196(r/#13) 3 6 9 18 27 35
198-209 (All #90038 on-c; pre-pack; no date or date code): 198(4/83), 199(5/83), 200(6/83), 201(6/83), 202(7/83), 203(7/83), 204(8/83), 205(8/83), 206(4/84), 207(5/83), 208(6/84), 209(7/84). 198-202,204-206: No Barks. 203(r/#12), 207(r/#93,92), 208(r/U.S. #18), 209(r/U.S. #21)-Barks-r 3 6 9 20 30 40
Uncle Scrooge & Money(G.K.)-Barks-r/from WDC&S #130 (3/67)
5 10 15 34 55 75
Mini Comic #1(1976)(3-1/4x6-1/2")-r/U.S. #115; Barks-c
2 4 6 8 10 12
NOTE: **Barks** *c-Four Color 386, 456, 495, #4-37, 39, 40, 43-71.*

UNCLE SCROOGE (See Walt Disney's Uncle Scrooge for previous issues)
Boom Entertainment (BOOM! Kids): No. 384, Oct, 2009 - Present ($2.99)
384-389: 384-Magica de Spell app.; 2 covers 3.00

UNCLE SCROOGE & DONALD DUCK
Gold Key: June, 1965 (25¢, paper cover)
1-Reprint of Four Color #386(#1) & lead story from Four Color #29
8 16 24 54 90 125

UNCLE SCROOGE COMICS DIGEST
Gladstone Publishing: Dec, 1986 - No. 5, Aug, 1987 ($1.25, Digest-size)
1,3 1 2 3 5 6 8
2,4 6.00
5 (low print run) 1 2 3 5 7 9

UNCLE SCROOGE GOES TO DISNEYLAND (See Dell Giants)
Gladstone Publishing Ltd.: Aug, 1985 ($2.50)
1-Reprints Dell Giant w/new-c by Mel Crawford, based on old cover
2 4 6 8 10 12
...Comics Digest 1 ($1.50, digest size) 2 4 6 8 11 14

UNCLE SCROOGE IN COLOR
Gladstone Publishing: 1987 ($29.95, Hardcover, 9-1/4"X12-1/4", 96 pgs.)
nn-Reprints "Christmas on Bear Mountain" from Four Color 178 by Barks; Uncle Scrooge's Christmas Carol (published as Donald Duck & the Christmas Carol, A Little Golden Book), reproduced from the original art as adapted by Norman McGary from pencils by Barks; and Uncle Scrooge the Lemonade King, reproduced from the original art, plus Barks' original pencils 4 8 12 24 37 50
nn-Slipcase edition of 750, signed by Barks, issued at $79.95 300.00

UNCLE SCROOGE THE LEMONADE KING
Whitman Publishing Co.: 1960 (A Top Top Tales Book, 6-3/8"x7-5/8", 32 pgs.)
2465-Storybook pencilled by Carl Barks, finished art adapted by Norman McGary
36 72 108 277 531 785

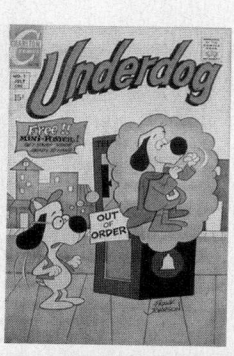

Underdog #1 © Leonardo TTV

Underworld Story nn © AVON

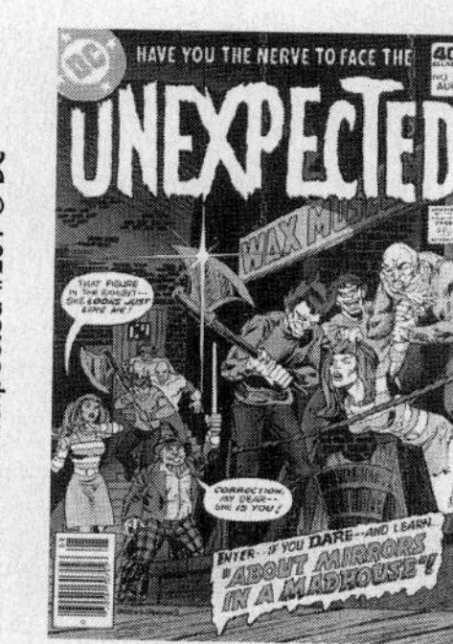

The Unexpected #201 © DC

GD 2.0 | VG 4.0 | FN 6.0 | VF 8.0 | VF/NM 9.0 | NM- 9.2

UNCLE WIGGILY (See March of Comics #19) (Also see Animal Comics)
Dell Publishing Co.: No. 179, Dec, 1947 - No. 543, Mar, 1954

Four Color 179 (#1)-Walt Kelly-c 15 30 45 104 197 290
Four Color 221 (3/49)-Part Kelly-c 9 18 27 63 107 150
Four Color 276 (5/50), 320 (#1, 3/51) 8 16 24 52 86 120
Four Color 349 (9-10/51), 391 (4-5/52) 6 12 18 43 69 95
Four Color 428 (10/52), 503 (10/53), 543 5 10 15 34 55 75

UNDEAD, THE
Chaos! Comics (Black Label): Feb, 2002 ($4.99, B&W)

1-Pulido-s/Denham-a 5.00

UNDERCOVER GIRL (Starr Flagg) (See Extra Comics, Manhunt! & Trail Colt)
Magazine Enterprises: No. 5, 1952 - No. 7, 1954

5(#1)(A-1 #62)-Fallon of the F.B.I. in all 37 74 111 218 349 480
6(A-1 #98), 7(A-1 #118)-All have Starr Flagg 35 70 105 203 327 450
NOTE: *Powell c-6, 7. Whitney a-5-7.*

UNDERDOG (TV)(See Kite Fun Book, March of Comics #426, 438, 467, 479)
Charlton Comics/Gold Key: July, 1970 - No. 10, Jan, 1972; Mar, 1975 - No. 23, Feb, 1979

1 (1st series, Charlton)-1st app. Underdog 9 18 27 65 113 160
2-10 6 12 18 37 59 80
1 (2nd series, Gold Key) 7 14 21 45 73 100
2-10 4 8 12 24 37 50
11-20: 13-1st app. Shack of Solitude 3 6 9 19 29 38
21-23 3 6 9 20 30 40

UNDERDOG
Spotlight Comics: 1987 - No. 3?, 1987 ($1.50)

1-3 4.00

UNDERDOG (Volume 2)
Harvey Comics: Nov, 1993 - No. 5, July, 1994 ($2.25)

1-5 4.00
Summer Special (10/93, $2.25, 68 pgs.) 4.00

UNDERSEA AGENT
Tower Comics: Jan, 1966 - No. 6, Mar, 1967 (25¢, 68 pgs.)

1-Davy Jones, Undersea Agent begins 9 18 27 60 100 140
2-6: 2-Jones gains magnetic powers. 5-Origin & 1st app. of Merman.
6-Kane/Wood-c(r) 6 12 18 39 62 85
NOTE: *Gil Kane a-3-6; c-4, 5. Moldoff a-2i.*

UNDERSEA FIGHTING COMMANDOS (See Fighting Undersea...)
I.W. Enterprises: 1964

I.W. Reprint #1,2('64): 1-r/#? 2-r/#1; Severin-c 2 4 6 9 13 16

UNDERTAKER (World Wrestling Federation)
Chaos! Comics: Feb, 1999 - No. 10, Jan, 2000 ($2.50/$2.95)

Preview (2/99) 2.50
1-10: Reg. and photo covers for each. 1-(4/99) 3.00
1-($6.95) DF Ed.; Brereton painted-c 7.00
...Halloween Special (10/99, $2.95) Reg. & photo-c 3.00
Wizard #0 2.50

UNDERWATER CITY, THE
Dell Publishing Co.: No. 1328, 1961

Four Color 1328-Movie, Evans-a 7 14 21 47 76 105

UNDERWORLD (...True Crime Stories)
D. S. Publishing Co.: Feb-Mar, 1948 - No. 9, June-July, 1949 (52 pgs.)

1-Moldoff (Shelly)-c; excessive violence 46 92 138 290 488 685
2-Moldoff (Shelly)-c; Ma Barker story used in **SOTI**, pg. 95; female electrocution panel;
lingerie art 42 84 126 265 445 625
3-McWilliams-c/a; extreme violence, mutilation 39 78 117 270 395 550
4-Used in Love and Death by Legman; Ingels-a 34 68 102 204 332 460
5-Ingels-a 24 48 72 140 230 320
6-9: 8-Ravielli-a. 9-R.Q. Sale-a 20 40 60 114 182 250

UNDERWORLD
DC Comics: Dec, 1987 - No. 4, Mar, 1988 ($1.00, limited series, mature)

1-4 2.50

UNDERWORLD (Movie)
IDW Publishing: Sept, 2003; Dec, 2005 ($6.99)

1-Movie adaptation; photo-c 7.00
... Evolution (12/05, $7.49) adaptation of movie sequel; Vazquez-a 7.50
TPB (7/04, $19.99) r/#1 and Underworld:Red in Tooth and Claw #1-3 20.00

UNDERWORLD
Marvel Comics: Apr, 2006 - No. 5, Aug, 2006 ($2.99, limited series)

1-5: Staz Johnson-a. 2-Spider-Man app. 3,4-Punisher app. 3.00

UNDERWORLD CRIME
Fawcett Publications: June, 1952 - No. 9, Oct, 1953

1 34 68 102 199 325 450
2 21 42 63 122 199 275
3-6,8,9 (8,9-exist?) 19 38 57 112 179 245
7-(6/53)-Bondage/torture-c 48 96 144 302 514 725

UNDERWORLD: RED IN TOOTH AND CLAW (Movie)
IDW Publishing: Feb, 2004 - No. 3, Apr, 2004 ($3.99, limited series)

1-3-The early days of the Vampire and Lycan war; Postic & Marinkovich-a 4.00

UNDERWORLD: RISE OF THE LYCANS (Movie)
IDW Publishing: Nov, 2008 - No. 2, Nov, 2008 ($3.99, limited series)

1,2-Grevioux-s/Huerta-a 4.00

UNDERWORLD STORY, THE (Movie)
Avon Periodicals: 1950

nn-(Scarce)-Ravielli-c 29 58 87 172 281 390

UNDERWORLD UNLEASHED
DC Comics: Nov, 1995 - No. 3, Jan, 1996 ($2.95, limited series)

1-3: Mark Waid scripts & Howard Porter-c/a(p) 3.50
...: Abyss: Hell's Sentinel 1-($2.95)-Alan Scott, Phantom Stranger, Zatanna app. 3.00
...: Apokolips-Dark Uprising 1 ($1.95) 2.50
...: Batman-Devil's Asylum 1-($2.95)-Batman app. 3.00
...: Patterns of Fear-($2.95) 3.00
TPB (1998, $17.95) r/#1-3 & Abyss-Hell's Sentinel 18.00

UNEARTHLY SPECTACULARS
Harvey Publications: Oct, 1965 - No. 3, Mar, 1967

1-(12¢)-Tiger Boy; Simon-c 4 8 12 26 41 55
2-(25¢ giants)-Jack Q. Frost, Tiger Boy & Three Rocketeers app.; Williamson, Wood, Kane-a;
r-1 story/Thrill-O-Rama #2 5 10 15 30 48 65
3-(25¢ giants)-Jack Q. Frost app.; Williamson/Crandall-a; r-from Alarming Advs. #1,1962
5 10 15 30 48 65
NOTE: *Crandall a-3r. G. Kane a-2. Orlando a-3. Simon, Sparling, Wood c-2. Simon/Kirby a-3r. Torres a-1?. Wildey a-1(3). Williamson a-2, 3r. Wood a-2(2).*

UNEXPECTED, THE (Formerly Tales of the...)
National Per. Publ./DC Comics: No. 105, Feb-Mar, 1968 - No. 222, May, 1982

105-Begin 12¢ cover price 7 14 21 45 73 100
106-113: 113-Last 12¢ issue (6-7/69) 5 10 15 30 48 65
114,115,117,118,120-125 4 8 12 22 34 45
116 (36 pgs.)-Wrightson-a? 4 8 12 23 36 48
119-Wrightson-a, 8pgs.(36 pgs.) 5 10 15 32 51 70
126,127,129-136-(52 pgs.) 4 8 12 22 34 45
128(52 pgs.)-Wrightson-a 5 10 15 32 51 70
137-156 3 6 9 14 20 25
157-162-(100 pgs.) 4 8 12 28 44 60
163-188: 187,188-(44 pgs.) 2 4 6 10 14 18
189,190,192-195 ($1.00, 68 pgs.): 189 on are combined with House of Secrets
& The Witching Hour 2 4 6 11 16 20
191-Rogers-a(p) ($1.00, 68 pgs.) 2 4 6 13 18 22
196-222: 200-Return of Johnny Peril by Tuska. 205-213-Johnny Peril app.
210-Time Warp story. 222-Giffen-a 2 3 4 6 8 10
NOTE: *Neal Adams c-110, 112-115, 118, 121, 124. J. Craig a-195. Ditko a-189, 221p, 222p; c-222. Drucker a-107r, 132r. Giffen a-219, 222. Kaluta c-203, 212. Kirby a-127r, 162. Kubert c-204, 214-216, 219-221. Mayer a-217p, 220, 221p. Moldoff a-136r. Moreira a-133. Mortimer a-212p. Newton a-204p. Orlando a-202; c-191. Perez a-217p. Redondo a-155, 166, 195. Reese a-145. Sparling a-107, 205-209p, 212p. Spiegle a-217. Starlin c-198. Toth a-126r, 127r. Tuska a-127, 132, 134, 136, 139, 152, 180, 200p. Wildey a-128r, 193. Wood a-122i, 133i, 137i, 138i. Wrightson a-161r(2 pgs.). Johnny Peril in #106-114, 116, 117, 200, 205-213.*

UNEXPECTED ANNUAL, THE (See DC Special Series #4)

UNHOLY UNION
Image Comics (Top Cow): July, 2007 ($3.99, one-shot)

1-Witchblade & The Darkness meet Hulk, Ghost Rider & Doctor Strange; Silvestri-c 4.00

UNIDENTIFIED FLYING ODDBALL (See Walt Disney Showcase #52)

UNION
Image Comics (WildStorm Productions): June, 1993 - No. 0, July, 1994 ($1.95, lim. series)

0-(7/94, $2.50) 2.50
0-Alternate Portacio-c (See Deathblow #5) 5.00
1-($2.50)-Embossed foil-c; Texeira-c/a in all 2.50
1-($1.95)-Newsstand edition w/o foil-c 2.50

United Comics #1 © UFS

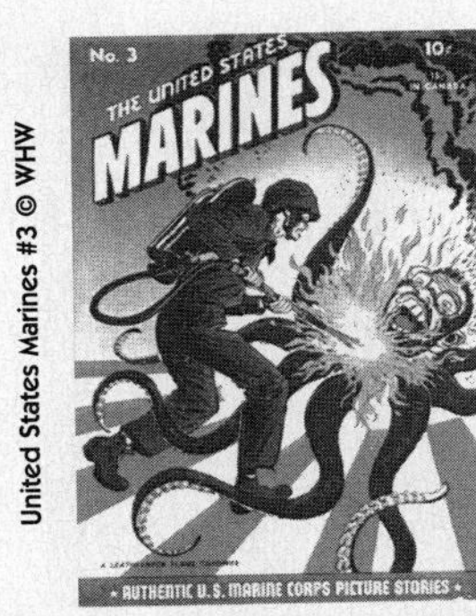

United States Marines #3 © WHW

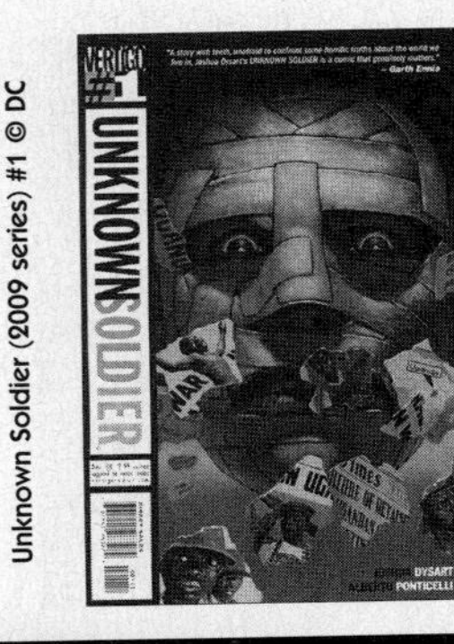

Unknown Soldier (2009 series) #1 © DC

GD 2.0 | VG 4.0 | FN 6.0 | VF 8.0 | VF/NM 9.0 | NM- 9.2

2-4: 4-(7/94) 2.50

UNION
Image Comics (WildStorm Prod.): Feb, 1995 - No. 9, Dec, 1995 ($2.50)
1-3,5-9: 3-Savage Dragon app. 6-Fairchild from Gen 13 app. 2.50
4-($1.95, Newsstand)-WildStorm Rising Pt. 3 2.50
4-($2.50, Direct Market)-WildStorm Rising Pt. 3, bound-in card 2.50

UNION: FINAL VENGEANCE
Image Comics (WildStorm Productions): Oct, 1997 ($2.50)
1-Golden-c/Heisler-s 2.50

UNION JACK
Marvel Comics: Dec, 1998 - No. 3, Feb, 1999 ($2.99, limited series)
1-3-Raab-s/Cassaday-s/a 3.00

UNION JACK
Marvel Comics: Nov, 2006 - No. 4, Feb, 2007 ($2.99, limited series)
1-4-Gage-s/Perkins-c/a 3.00
...: London Falling TPB (2007, $10.99) r/#1-4; Perkins sketch page 11.00

UNITED COMICS (Formerly Fritzi Ritz #7; has Fritzi Ritz logo)
United Features Syndicate: Aug, 1940; No. 8, 1950 - No. 26, Jan-Feb, 1953
1(68 pgs.)-Fritzi Ritz & Phil Fumble 23 46 69 136 223 310
8-Fritzi Ritz, Abbie & Slats 8 16 24 44 57 70
9-21: 20-Strange As It Seems; Russell Patterson Cheesecake-a
8 16 24 40 50 60
22-(5-6/52) 2 pgs. early Peanuts by Schulz (1st in comics?)
13 26 39 72 101 130
23-26: 23-(7-8/52). 24-(9-10/52). 25-(11-12/52). 26-(1-2/53). All have 2 pgs. early Peanuts by Schulz 10 20 30 56 76 95
NOTE: *Abbie & Slats reprinted from Tip Top.*

UNITED NATIONS, THE (See Classics Illustrated Special Issue)

UNITED STATES AIR FORCE PRESENTS: THE HIDDEN CREW
U.S. Air Force: 1964 (36 pgs.)
nn-Schaffenberger-a 2 4 6 10 14 18

UNITED STATES FIGHTING AIR FORCE (Also see U.S. Fighting Air Force)
Superior Comics Ltd.: Sept, 1952 - No. 29, Oct, 1956
1 13 26 39 72 101 130
2 8 16 24 42 54 65
3-10 7 14 21 37 46 55
11-29 7 14 21 35 43 50

UNITED STATES MARINES
William H. Wise/Life's Romances Publ. Co./Magazine Ent. #5-8/Toby Press #7-11: 1943 - No. 4, 1944; No. 5, 1952 - No. 8, 1952; No. 7 - No. 11, 1953
nn-Mart Bailey-c/a; Marines in the Pacific theater 20 40 60 117 189 260
2-Bailey-a; Tojo classic-c 53 106 159 334 567 800
3-Tojo-c 47 94 141 296 498 700
4-WWII photos; Tony DiPreta-a 14 28 42 78 112 145
5(A-1 #55)-Bailey-a, 6(A-1 #60), 7(A-1 #68), 8(A-1 #72)
10 20 30 58 79 100
7-11 (Toby) 9 18 27 50 65 80
NOTE: *Powell a-5-7.*

UNITY
Valiant: No. 0, Aug, 1992 - No. 1, 1992 (Free comics w/limited dist., 20 pgs.)
0 (Blue)-Prequel to Unity x-overs in all Valiant titles; B. Smith-c/a. (Free to everyone that bought all 8 titles that month.) 2.50
0 (Red)-Same as above, but w/red logo (5,000). 3.00
1-Epilogue to Unity x-overs; B. Smith-c/a. (1 copy available for every 8 Valiant books ordered by dealers.) 2.50
1 (Gold), 1-(Platinum)-Promotional copy. 6.00
... : The Lost Chapter 1 (Yearbook) (2/95, $3.95)-"1994" in indicia 4.00

UNITY 2000 (See preludes in Shadowman #3,4 flipbooks)
Acclaim Comics: Nov, 1999 - No. 3, Jan, 2000 ($2.50, unfinished limited series planned for 6 issues)
Preview -B&W plot preview and cover art; paper cover 2.50
1-3-Starlin-a/Shooter-s 2.50

UNIVERSAL MONSTERS
Dark Horse Comics: 1993 ($4.95/$5.95, 52 pgs.)(All adapt original movies)
Creature From the Black Lagoon nn-($4.95)-Art Adams/Austin-c/a, Dracula nn-($4.95), Frankenstein nn-($3.95)-Painted-c/a, The Mummy nn-($4.95)-Painted-c
1 2 3 4 5 7

...: Cavalcade of Horror TPB (1/06, $19.95) r/one-shots; Eric Powell intro. & cover 20.00

UNIVERSAL PRESENTS DRACULA-THE MUMMY& OTHER STORIES
Dell Publishing Co.: Sept-Nov, 1963 (one-shot, 84 pgs.) (Also see Dell Giants)
02-530-311-r/Dracula 12-231-212, The Mummy 12-437-211 & part of Ghost Stories No. 1
17 34 51 119 230 340

UNIVERSAL SOLDIER (Movie)
Now Comics: Sept, 1992 - No. 3, Nov, 1992 (Limited series, polybagged, mature)
1-3 ($2.50, Direct Sales) 1-Movie adapatation; hologram on-c (all direct sales editions have painted-c) 2.50
1-3 ($1.95, Newsstand)-Rewritten & redrawn code approved version; all newsstand editions have photo-c 2.50

UNIVERSAL WAR ONE
Marvel Comics (Soleil): 2008 - No. 3, 2008 ($5.99, limited series)
1-3-Denis Bajram-s/a; English version of French comic. 1-Bajram interview 6.00
...: Revelations 1-3 (2009 - No. 3, 2009, $5.99) Bajram-s/a 6.00

UNIVERSE
Image Comics (Top Cow): Sept, 2001 - No. 8, July, 2002 ($2.50)
1-7-Jenkins-s 2.50
8-($4.95) extra short-s by Jenkins; pin-up pages 5.00

UNIVERSE X (See Earth X)
Marvel Comics: Sept, 2000 - No. 12, Sept, 2001 ($3.99/$3.50, limited series)
0-Ross-c/Braithwaite-a/Ross & Krueger-s 4.00
1-12: 5-Funeral of Captain America 3.50
... Beasts (6/00, $3.99) Yeates-a/Ross-c 4.00
... Cap (Capt. America) (2/01, $3.99) Yeates & Totleben-a/Ross-c; Cap dies 4.00
... 4 (Fantastic 4) (10/00, $3.99) Brent Anderson-a/Ross-c 4.00
... Iron Men (9/01, $3.99) Anderson-a/Ross-c; leads into #12 4.00
... Omnibus (6/01, $3.99) Ross B&W sketchbook and character bios 4.00
Sketchbook- Wizard supplement; B&W character sketches and bios 2.50
...Spidey (1/01, $3.99) Romita Sr. flashback-a/Guice-a/Ross-c 4.00
...X (11/01, $3.99) Series conclusion; Braithwaith-a/Ross wraparound-c 4.00
Volume 1 TPB (1/02, $24.95) r/#0-7 & Spidey, 4, & Cap; new Ross-c 25.00
Volume 2 TPB (6/02, $24.95) r/#8-12 &X, Beasts, Iron Men and Omnibus 25.00

UNKNOWN, THE
BOOM! Studios: May, 2009 - No. 4, Aug, 2009 ($3.99)
1-4-Mark Waid-s/Minck Oosterveer-a; two covers on each 4.00
...: The Devil Made Flesh 1-4 (9/09 - No. 4, 12/09, $3.99) Waid-s/Oosterveer-a 4.00

UNKNOWN MAN, THE (Movie)
Avon Periodicals: 1951
nn-Kinstler-c 28 56 84 165 270 375

UNKNOWN SOLDIER (Formerly Star-Spangled War Stories)
National Periodical Publications/DC Comics: No. 205, Apr-May, 1977 - No. 268, Oct, 1982 (See Our Army at War #168 for 1st app.)
205 3 6 9 16 23 30
206-210,220,221,251: 220,221 (44pgs.). 251-Enemy Ace begins
2 4 6 13 18 22
211-218,222-247,250,252-264 2 4 6 10 14 18
219-Miller-a (44 pgs.) 3 6 9 16 22 28
248,249,265-267: 248,249-Origin. 265-267-Enemy Ace vs. Balloon Buster.
2 4 6 10 14 18
268-Death of Unknown Soldier 3 6 9 18 27 35
NOTE: ***Chaykin** a-234. **Evans** a-265-267; c-235. **Kubert** c-Most. **Miller** a-219p. **Severin** a-251-253, 260, 261, 265-267. **Simonson** a-254-256. **Spiegle** a-258, 259, 262-264.*

UNKNOWN SOLDIER, THE (Also see Brave &the Bold #146)
DC Comics: Winter, 1988-'89 - No. 12, Dec, 1989 ($1.50, maxi-series, mature)
1-12: 8-Begin $1.75-c 4.00

UNKNOWN SOLDIER
DC Comics (Vertigo): Apr, 1997 - No 4, July, 1997 ($2.50, mini-series)
1-Ennis-s/Plunkett-a/Bradstreet-c in all 6.00
2-4 4.00
TPB (1998, $12.95) r/#1-4 13.00

UNKNOWN SOLDIER
DC Comics (Vertigo): Dec, 2008 - Present ($2.99)
1-16-Dysart-s/Ponticelli-a; intro. Lwanga Moses. 1-Two covers by Kordey and Corben 3.00
...: Haunted House TPB (2009, $9.99) r/#1-6; glossary 10.00

UNKNOWN WORLD (Strange Stories From Another World #2 on)
Fawcett Publications: June, 1952

Unknown Worlds #49 © ACG

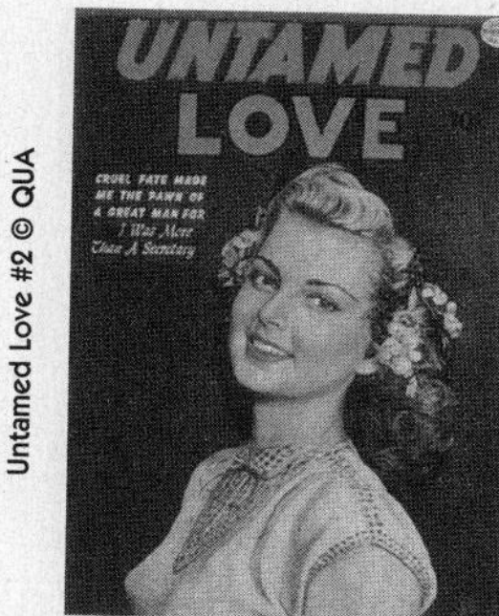

Untamed Love #2 © QUA

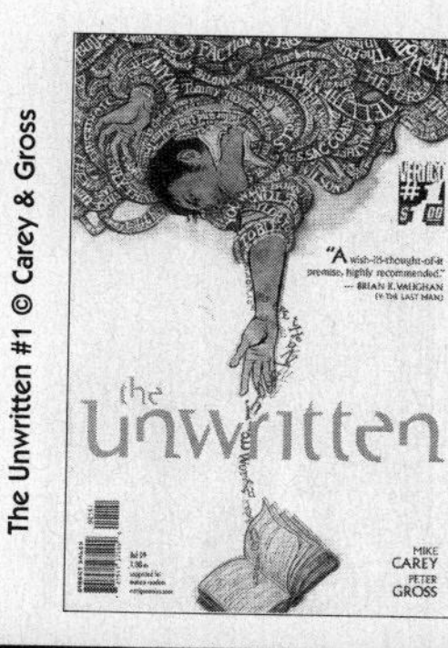

The Unwritten #1 © Carey & Gross

GD VG FN VF VF/NM NM-
2.0 4.0 6.0 8.0 9.0 9.2

1-Norman Saunders painted-c 45 90 135 284 480 675

UNKNOWN WORLDS (See Journey Into...)

UNKNOWN WORLDS
American Comics Group/Best Synd. Features: Aug, 1960 - No. 57, Aug, 1967

1-Schaffenberger-c 19 38 57 133 259 385
2-Dinosaur-c/story 11 22 33 78 139 200
3-5 9 18 27 65 113 160
6-11: 9-Dinosaur-c/story. 11-Last 10¢ issue 8 16 24 54 90 125
12-19: 12-Begin 12¢ issues?; ends #57 6 12 18 43 69 95
20-Herbie cameo (12-1/62-63) 7 14 21 45 73 100
21-35: 31-Herbie one pagers thru #39 5 10 15 32 51 70
36- "The People vs. Hendricks" by Craig; most popular ACG story ever
5 10 15 34 55 75
37-46 4 8 12 28 44 60
47-Williamson-a r-from Adventures Into the Unknown #96, 3 pgs.; Craig-a
5 10 15 30 48 65
48-57: 53-Frankenstein app. 4 8 12 26 41 55
NOTE: ***Ditko** a-49, 50p, 54. **Forte** a-3, 6, 11. **Landau** a-56(2). **Reinman** a-3, 9, 13, 20, 22, 23, 36, 38, 54. **Whitney** c/a-most issues. John Force, Magic Agent app.-35, 36, 48, 50, 52, 54, 56.*

UNKNOWN WORLDS OF FRANK BRUNNER
Eclipse Comics: Aug, 1985 - No. 2, Aug, 1985 ($1.75)

1,2-B&W-r in color 3.50

UNKNOWN WORLDS OF SCIENCE FICTION
Marvel Comics: Jan, 1975 - No. 6, Nov, 1975; 1976 ($1.00, B&W Magazine)

1-Williamson/Krenkel/Torres/Frazetta-r/Witzend #1, Neal Adams-r/Phase 1; Brunner & Kaluta-r; Freas/Romita-c 3 6 9 16 22 28
2-6: 5-Kaluta text illos 3 6 9 14 19 24
Special 1(1976,100 pgs.)-Newton painted-c 3 6 9 16 22 28
NOTE: ***Brunner** a-2; c-4, 6. **Buscema** a-Special 1p. **Chaykin** a-5. **Colan** a(p)-1, 3, 5, 6. **Corben** a-4. **Kaluta** a-2, Special 1(ext illos); c-2. **Morrow** a-3, 5. **Nino** a-3, 6, Special 1. **Perez** a-2, 3. Ray Bradbury interview in #1.*

UNLIMITED ACCESS (Also see Marvel Vs. DC))
Marvel Comics: Dec, 1997 - No. 4, Mar, 1998 ($2.99/$1.99, limited series)

1-Spider-Man, Wonder Woman, Green Lantern & Hulk app. 3.50
2,3-($1.99): 2-X-Men, Legion of Super-Heroes app. 3-Original Avengers vs. original Justice League 2.50
4-($2.99) Amalgam Legion vs. Darkseid & Magneto 3.00

UN-MEN, THE
DC Comics (Vertigo): Oct, 2007 - No. 13, Oct, 2008 ($2.99)

1-13-Whalen-s/Hawthorne-a/Hanuka-c 3.00
...: Children of Paradox TPB (2008, $19.99) r/#6-13 20.00
...: Get Your Freak On! TPB (2008, $9.99) r/#1-5; cover gallery 10.00

UNSANE (Formerly Mighty Bear #13, 14? or The Outlaws #10-14?)(Satire)
Star Publications: No. 15, June, 1954

15-Disbrow-a(2); L. B. Cole-c 34 68 102 199 325 450

UNSEEN, THE
Visual Editions/Standard Comics: No. 5, 1952 - No. 15, July, 1954

5-Horror stories in all; Toth-a 41 82 123 258 434 610
6,7,9,10-Jack Katz-a 30 60 90 177 289 400
8,11,13,14 23 46 69 136 223 310
12,15-Toth-a. 12-Tuska-a 30 60 90 177 289 400
NOTE: ***Nick Cardy** c-12. **Fawcette** a-13, 14. **Sekowsky** a-7, 8(2), 10, 13, 15.*

UNTAMED
Marvel Comics (Epic Comics/Heavy Hitters): June, 1993 - No. 3, Aug, 1993 ($1.95, lim. series)

1-($2.50)-Embossed-c 2.75
2,3 2.50

UNTAMED LOVE (Also see Frank Frazetta's Untamed Love)
Quality Comics Group (Comic Magazines): Jan, 1950 - No. 5, Sept, 1950

1-Ward-c, Gustavson-a 26 52 78 152 249 345
2,4: 2-5-Photo-c 16 32 48 94 147 200
3,5-Gustavson-a 17 34 51 100 158 215

UNTOLD LEGEND OF CAPTAIN MARVEL, THE
Marvel Comics: Apr, 1997 - No. 3, June, 1997 ($2.50, limited series)

1-3 2.50

UNTOLD LEGEND OF THE BATMAN, THE (Also see Promotional section)
DC Comics: July, 1980 - No. 3, Sept, 1980 (Limited series)

1-Origin; Joker-c; Byrne's 1st work at DC 6.00
2,3 4.50
NOTE: ***Aparo** a-1i, 2, 3. **Byrne** a-1p.*

GD VG FN VF VF/NM NM-
2.0 4.0 6.0 8.0 9.0 9.2

UNTOLD ORIGIN OF THE FEMFORCE, THE (Also see Femforce)
AC Comics: 1989 ($4.95, 68 pgs.)

1-Origin Femforce; Bill Black-a(i) & scripts 6.00

UNTOLD TALES OF CHASTITY
Chaos! Comics: Nov, 2000 ($2.95, one-shot)

1-Origin; Steven Grant-s/Peter Vale-c/a 3.00
1-Premium Edition with glow in the dark cover 13.00

UNTOLD TALES OF LADY DEATH
Chaos! Comics: Nov, 2000 ($2.95, one-shot)

1-Origin of Lady Death; Cremator app.; Kaminski-s 3.00
1-Premium Edition with glow in the dark cover by Steven Hughes 13.00

UNTOLD TALES OF PURGATORI
Chaos! Comics: Nov, 2000 ($2.95, one-shot)

1-Purgatori in 57 B.C.; Rio-a/Grant-s 3.00
1-Premium Edition with glow in the dark cover 13.00

UNTOLD TALES OF SPIDER-MAN (Also see Amazing Fantasy #16-18)
Marvel Comics: Sept, 1995 - No. 25, Sept, 1997 (99¢)

1-Kurt Busiek scripts begin; Pat Olliffe-c/a in all (except #9). 3.00
2-22, -1(7/97), 23-25: 2-1st app. Batwing. 4-1st app. The Spacemen (Gantry, Orbit, Satellite & Vacuum). 8-1st app. The Headsman; The Enforcers (The Big Man, Montana, The Ox & Fancy Dan) app. 9-Ron Frenz-a. 10-1st app. Commanda. 16-Reintro Mary Jane Watson. 21-X-Men-c/app. 25-Green Goblin 2.50
...'96-(1996, $1.95, 46 pgs.)-Kurt Busiek scripts; Mike Allred-c/a; Kurt Busiek & Pat Olliffe app. in back-up story; contains pin-ups 2.50
...'97-(1997, $1.95)-Wraparound-c 2.50
...: Strange Encounters ('98, $5.99) Dr. Strange app. 6.00

UNTOLD TALES OF THE NEW UNIVERSE (Based on Marvel's 1986 New Universe titles)
Marvel Comics: May, 2006 ($2.99, series of one-shots)

...: D. P. 7 - Takes place between issues #4 & 5 of D. P. 7 series; Bright-a/Cebulski-s 3.00
...: Justice - Peter David-s/Carmine Di Giandomenico-a 3.00
...: Nightmask - Takes place between issues #4 & 5 of Nightmask series; The Gnome app. 3.00
...: Psi-Force - Tony Bedard-s/Russ Braun-a 3.00
...: Star Brand - Romita & Romita Jr.-c/Pulido-a 3.00
TPB (2006, $15.99) r/one-shots & stories from Amaz. Fantasy #18,19 & New Avengers #16 16.00

UNTOUCHABLES, THE (TV)
Dell Publishing Co.: No. 1237, 10-12/61 - No. 4, 8-10/62 (All have Robert Stack photo-c)

Four Color 1237(#1) 19 38 57 135 263 390
Four Color 1286 14 28 42 97 181 265
01-879-207, 12-879-210(01879-210 on inside) 9 18 27 63 107 150

UNTOUCHABLES
Caliber Comics: Aug, 1997 - No. 4 ($2.95, B&W)

1-4: 1-Pruett-s; variant covers by Kaluta & Showman 3.00

UNUSUAL TALES (Blue Beetle & Shadows From Beyond #50 on)
Charlton Comics: Nov, 1955 - No. 49, Mar-Apr, 1965

1 30 60 90 177 289 400
2 15 30 45 90 140 190
3-5 14 28 42 76 108 140
6-Ditko-c only 16 32 48 94 147 200
7,8-Ditko-c/a. 8-Robot-c 28 56 84 165 270 375
9-Ditko-c/a (20 pgs.) 31 62 93 182 296 410
10-Ditko-c/a(4) 32 64 96 188 307 425
11-(3/58, 68 pgs.)-Ditko-a(4) 31 62 93 182 296 410
12,14-Ditko-a 19 38 57 111 176 240
13,16-20 7 14 21 45 73 100
15-Ditko-c/a 24 48 72 140 230 320
21,24,28 6 12 18 37 59 80
22,23,25-27,29-Ditko-a 10 20 30 68 119 170
30-49 4 8 12 28 44 60
NOTE: ***Colan** a-11. **Ditko** c-22, 23, 25-27, 31(part).*

UNWRITTEN, THE
DC Comics (Vertigo): July, 2009 - Present ($1.00/$2.99)

1-($1.00) Intro. Tommy Taylor; Mike Carey-s/Peter Gross-a; two covers (white & black) 3.00
2-9-($2.99) 3.00
...: Tommy Taylor and the Bogus Identity TPB (2010, $9.99) r/#1-5; sketch art; prose 10.00

UP FROM HARLEM (Tom Skinner...)
Spire Christian Comics (Fleming H. Revell Co.): 1973 (35/49¢)

nn 2 4 6 8 11 14

USA Comics 70th Anniversary Special #1 © MAR

Usagi Yojimbo #108 © Stan Sakai

U.S. War Machine V2 #1 © MAR

	GD	VG	FN	VF	VF/NM	NM-
	2.0	4.0	6.0	8.0	9.0	9.2

UP-TO-DATE COMICS
King Features Syndicate: No date (1938) (36 pgs.; B&W cover) (10¢)
nn-Popeye & Henry cover; The Phantom, Jungle Jim & Flash Gordon by Raymond, The Katzenjammer Kids, Curley Harper & others. Note: Variations in content exist. 25 50 75 147 241 335

UP YOUR NOSE AND OUT YOUR EAR (Satire)
Klevart Enterprises: Apr, 1972 - No. 2, June, 1972 (52 pgs., magazine)
V1#1,2 2 4 6 11 16 20

URTH 4 (Also see Earth 4)
Continuity Comics: May, 1989 - No. 4, Dec, 1990 ($2.00, deluxe format)
1-4: Ms. Mystic characters. 2-Neal Adams-c(i) 3.00

URZA-MISHRA WAR ON THE WORLD OF MAGIC THE GATHERING
Acclaim Comics (Armada): 1996 - No. 2, 1996 ($5.95, limited series)
1,2 6.00

U.S. (See Uncle Sam)

USA COMICS
Timely Comics (USA): Aug, 1941 - No. 17, Fall, 1945
1-Origin Major Liberty (called Mr. Liberty #1), Rockman by Wolverton; 1st app. The Whizzer by Avison; The Defender with sidekick Rusty & Jack Frost begin; The Young Avenger only app.; S&K-c plus 1 pg. art 1140 2280 3420 8400 15,200 20,000
2-Origin Captain Terror & The Vagabond; last Wolverton Rockman; Hitler-c 400 800 1200 2800 4900 7000
3-No Whizzer 300 600 900 2070 3635 5200
4-Last Rockman, Major Liberty, Defender, Jack Frost, & Capt. Terror; Corporal Dix app. 297 594 891 1900 3250 4600
5-Origin American Avenger & Roko the Amazing; The Blue Blade, The Black Widow & Victory Boys, Gypo the Gypsy Giant & Hills of Horror only app.; Sergeant Dix begins; no Whizzer; Hitler, Mussolini & Tojo-c 290 580 870 1856 3178 4500
6-Captain America (ends #17), The Destroyer, Jap Buster Johnson, Jeep Jones begin; Terror Squad only app. 377 754 1131 2639 4620 6600
7-Captain Daring, Disk-Eyes the Detective by Wolverton app.; origin & only app. Marvel Boy (3/43); Secret Stamp begins; no Whizzer, Sergeant Dix; classic Schomburg-c 411 822 1233 2877 5039 7200
8,10: 10-The Thunderbird only app. 300 600 900 1950 3375 4800
9-Last Secret Stamp; Hitler-c; classic-c 300 600 900 2070 3635 5200
11,12: 11-No Jeep Jones 206 412 618 1318 2259 3200
13-17: 13-No Whizzer; Jeep Jones ends. 15-No Destroyer; Jap Buster Johnson ends 145 290 435 921 1586 2250
NOTE: ***Brodsky** c-14. **Gabrielle** c-4. **Schomburg** c-6, 7, 10, 12, 13, 15-17. **Shores** a-1, 4; c-9, 11. **Ed Win** a-4. Cover features: 1-The Defender; 2, 3-Captain Terror; 4-Major Liberty; 5-Victory Boys; 6-17-Captain America & Bucky.*

USA COMICS 70TH ANNIVERSARY SPECIAL
Marvel Comics: Sept, 2009 ($3.99, one-shot)
1-New story of The Destroyer; Arcudi-s/Ellis-a; r/All Winners #3; two covers 4.00

U.S. AGENT (See Jeff Jordan...)

U.S. AGENT (See Captain America #354)
Marvel Comics: June, 1993 - No. 4, Sept, 1993 ($1.75, limited series)
1-4 2.50

U.S. AGENT
Marvel Comics: Aug, 2001 - No. 3, Oct, 2001 ($2.99, limited series)
1-3: Ordway-s/a(p)/c. 2,3-Captain America app. 3.00

USAGI YOJIMBO (See Albedo, Doomsday Squad #3 & Space Usagi)
Fantagraphics Books: July, 1987 - No. 38 ($2.00/$2.25, B&W)
1 1 2 3 5 7 9
1,8,10-2nd printings 2.50
2-9 4.00
10,11: 10-Leonardo app. (TMNT). 11-Aragonés-a 6.00
12-29 3.00
30-38: 30-Begin $2.25-c 3.00
Color Special 1 (11/89, $2.95, 68 pgs.)-new & r 3.50
Color Special 2 (10/91, $3.50) 3.50
Color Special #3 (10/92, $3.50)-Jeff Smith's Bone promo on inside-c 3.50
Summer Special 1 (1986, B&W, $2.75)-r/early Albedo issues 3.00

USAGI YOJIMBO
Mirage Studios: V2#1, Mar, 1993 - No. 16, 1994 ($2.75)
V2#1-16: 1-Teenage Mutant Ninja Turtles app. 3.00

USAGI YOJIMBO
Dark Horse Comics: V3#1, Apr, 1996 - Present ($2.95/$2.99/$3.50, B&W)
V3#1-99,101-116: Stan Sakai-c/a 3.00
100-(1/07, $3.50) Stan Sakai roast by various incl. Aragonés, Wagner, Miller, Geary 3.50
117-125-($3.50) 3.50
Color Special #4 (7/97, $2.95) "Green Persimmon" 3.00
Daisho TPB ('98, $14.95) r/Mirage series #7-14 15.00
Demon Mask TPB ('01, $15.95) 16.00
Glimpses of Death TPB (7/06, $15.95) r/#76-82 16.00
Grasscutter TPB ('99, $16.95) r/#13-22 17.00
Gray Shadows TPB ('00, $14.95) r/#23-30 15.00
Seasons TPB ('99, $14.95) r/#7-12 15.00
Shades of Death TPB ('97, $14.95) r/Mirage series #1-6 15.00
The Brink of Life and Death TPB ('98, $14.95) r/Mirage series #13,15,16 & Dark Horse series #1-6 15.00
The Shrouded Moon TPB (1/03, $15.95) r/#46-52 16.00

U.S. AIR FORCE COMICS (Army Attack #38 on)
Charlton Comics: Oct, 1958 - No. 37, Mar-Apr, 1965
1 6 12 18 43 69 95
2 4 8 12 23 36 48
3-10 3 6 9 20 30 40
11-20 3 6 9 18 27 35
21-37 3 6 9 16 22 28
NOTE: ***Glanzman** c/a-9, 10, 12. **Montes/Bache** a-33.*

USA IS READY
Dell Publishing Co.: 1941 (68 pgs., one-shot)
1-War propaganda 40 80 120 246 411 575

U.S. BORDER PATROL COMICS (Sgt. Dick Carter of the...) (See Holyoke One Shot)

USER
DC Comics (Vertigo): 2001 - No. 3, 2001 ($5.95, limited series)
1-3-Devin Grayson-s; Sean Phillips & John Bolton-a 6.00

U.S. FIGHTING AIR FORCE (Also see United States Fighting Air Force)
I. W. Enterprises: No date (1960s?)
1,9(nd): 1-r/United States Fighting...#?. 9-r/#1 2 4 6 8 11 14

U.S. FIGHTING MEN
Super Comics: 1963 - 1964 (Reprints)
10-r/With the U.S. Paratroops #4(Avon) 2 4 6 9 13 16
11,12,15-18: 11-r/Monty Hall #10. 12,16,17,18-r/U.S. Fighting Air Force #10,3,?&? 15-r/Man Comics #11 2 4 6 9 13 16

U.S. JONES (Also see Wonderworld Comics #28)
Fox Features Syndicate: Nov, 1941 - No. 2, Jan, 1942
1-U.S. Jones & The Topper begin; Nazi-c 126 252 378 806 1378 1950
2-Nazi-c 84 168 252 538 919 1300

U.S. MARINES
Charlton Comics: Fall, 1964 (12¢, one-shot)
1-1st app. Capt. Dude; Glanzman-a 3 6 9 21 32 42

U.S. MARINES IN ACTION
Avon Periodicals: Aug, 1952 - No. 3, Dec, 1952
1-Louis Ravielli-c/a 10 20 30 54 72 90
2,3: 3-Kinstler-c 8 16 24 40 50 60

U.S. 1
Marvel Comics Group: May, 1983 - No. 12, Oct, 1984 (7,8: painted-c)
1-12: 2-Sienkiewicz-c. 3-12-Michael Golden-c 2.50

U.S. PARATROOPS (See With the...)

U.S. PARATROOPS
I. W. Enterprises: 1964?
1,8: 1-r/With the U.S. Paratroops #1; Wood-c. 8-r/With the U.S. Paratroops #6; Kinstler-c 2 4 6 9 13 16

U.S. TANK COMMANDOS
Avon Periodicals: June, 1952 - No. 4, Mar, 1953
1-Kinstler-c 11 22 33 60 83 105
2-4: Kinstler-c 8 16 24 44 57 70
I.W. Reprint #1,8: 1-r/#1. 8-r/#3 2 4 6 9 13 16
NOTE: ***Kinstler** a-I.W. #1; c-1-4, I.W. #1, 8.*

U.S. WAR MACHINE (Also see Iron Man and War Machine)
Marvel Comics (MAX): Nov, 2001 - No. 12, Jan, 2002 ($1.50, B&W, weekly limited series)
1-12-Chuck Austen-s/a/c 2.50

Valley of the Dinosaurs #1 © H-B

Valor #8 © DC

Vampirella #22 © WP

GD VG FN VF VF/NM NM-
2.0 4.0 6.0 8.0 9.0 9.2

TPB (12/01, $14.95) r/#1-12 15.00

U.S. WAR MACHINE 2.0
Marvel Comics (MAX): Sept, 2003 - No. 3, Sept, 2003 ($2.99, weekly, limited series)
1-3-Austen-s/Christian Moore-CGI art 3.00

"V" (TV)
DC Comics: Feb, 1985 - No. 18, July, 1986
1-Based on TV movie & series (Sci/Fi) 3.00
2-18: 17,18-Denys Cowan-c/a 2.50

VACATION COMICS (Also see A-1 Comics)
Magazine Enterprises: No. 16, 1948 (one-shot)
A-1 16-The Pixies, Tom Tom, Flying Fredd & Koko & Kola 6 12 18 31 38 45

VACATION DIGEST
Harvey Comics: Sept, 1987 ($1.25, digest size)
1 1 2 3 5 6 8

VACATION IN DISNEYLAND (Also see Dell Giants)
Dell Publishing Co./Gold Key (1965): Aug-Oct, 1959; May, 1965 (Walt Disney)
Four Color 1025-Barks-a 16 32 48 112 214 315
1(30024-508)(G.K., 5/65, 25¢)-r/Dell Giant #30 & cover to #1 ('58); celebrates Disneyland's 10th anniversary 5 10 15 35 55 75

VACATION PARADE (See Dell Giants)

VALERIA THE SHE BAT
Continuity Comics: May, 1993 - No. 5, Nov, 1993
1-Premium; acetate-c; N. Adams-a/scripts; given as gift to retailers 1 2 3 5 6 8
5 (11/93)-Embossed-c; N. Adams-a/scripts 3.00
NOTE: *Due to lack of continuity, #2-4 do not exist.*

VALERIA THE SHE BAT
Acclaim Comics (Windjammer): Sept, 1995 - No.2, Oct, 1995 ($2.50, limited series)
1,2 2.50

VALKYRIE (See Airboy)
Eclipse Comics: May,1987 - No. 3, July, 1987 ($1.75, limited series)
1-3: 2-Holly becomes new Black Angel 2.50

VALKYRIE
Marvel Comics: Jan, 1997 ($2.95, one-shot)
1-w/pin-ups 3.00

VALKYRIE!
Eclipse Comics: July, 1988 - No. 3, Sept, 1988 ($1.95, limited series)
1-3 2.50

VALLEY OF THE DINOSAURS (TV)
Charlton Comics: Apr, 1975 - No. 11, Dec, 1976 (Hanna-Barbara)
1-W. Howard-i 3 6 9 14 19 24
2,4-11: 2-W. Howard-i 2 4 6 8 11 14
3-Byrne text illos (early work, 7/75) 2 4 6 10 14 18

VALLEY OF THE DINOSAURS (Volume 2)
Harvey Comics: Oct, 1993 ($1.50, giant-sized)
1-Reprints 5.00

VALLEY OF GWANGI (See Movie Classics)

VALOR
E. C. Comics: Mar-Apr, 1955 - No. 5, Nov-Dec, 1955
1-Williamson/Torres-a; Wood-c/a 28 56 84 224 355 485
2-Williamson-c/a; Wood-a 21 42 63 168 272 375
3,4: 3-Williamson, Crandall-a. 4-Wood-c 16 32 48 128 207 285
5-Wood-c/a; Williamson/Evans-a 15 30 45 120 190 260
NOTE: ***Crandall** a-3, 4. **Ingels** a-1, 2, 4, 5. **Krigstein** a-1-5. **Orlando** a-3, 4; c-3. **Wood** a-1, 2, 5; c-1, 4, 5.*

VALOR
Gemstone Publishing: Oct, 1998 - No. 5, Feb, 1999 ($2.50)
1-5-Reprints 2.50

VALOR (Also see Legion of Super-Heroes & Legionnaires)
DC Comics: Nov, 1992 - No. 23, Sept, 1994 ($1.25/$1.50)
1-22: 1-Eclipso The Darkness Within aftermath. 2-Vs. Supergirl. 4-Vs. Lobo. 12-Lobo cameo. 14-Legionnaires, JLA app. 17-Austin-c(i); death of Valor. 18-22-Build-up to Zero Hour 2.50
23-Zero Hour tie-in 3.00

VALOR THUNDERSTAR AND HIS FIREFLIES

GD VG FN VF VF/NM NM-
2.0 4.0 6.0 8.0 9.0 9.2

Now Comics: Dec, 1986 ($1.50)
1-Ordway-c(p) 2.50

VAMPI (Vampirella's...)
Harris Publications (Anarchy Studios): Aug, 2000 - No. 25, Feb, 2003 ($2.95/$2.99)
Limited Edition Preview Book (5/00) Preview pages & sketchbook 3.00
1-(8/00, $2.95) Lau-a(p)/Conway-s 3.00
1-Platinum Edition 20.00
2-25: 17-Barberi-a 3.00
2-25-Deluxe Edition variants ($9.95): 4-Finch-c. 5-Wieringo-c. 6-Cha-c 10.00
...Digital 1 (11/01, $2.95) CGI art; Haberlin-s 3.00
...Digital Preview (Anarchy Studios, 7/01, $2.95) preview of CGI art 3.00
Switchblade Kiss HC (2001, $24.95) r/#1-6 25.00
Vicious Preview Ed. (Apr, 2003, $1.99) Flip book w/ Xin: Journey of the Monkey King Preview Ed. 2.50
Wizard #1/2 (mail order, $9.95) includes sketch pages 10.00

VAMPIRE BITES
Brainstorm Comics: May, 1995 - No. 2, Sept, 1996 ($2.95, B&W)
1,2:1-Color pin-up 3.00

VAMPIRE LESTAT, THE
Innovation Publishing: Jan, 1990 - No. 12, 1991 ($2.50, painted limited series)
1-Adapts novel; Bolton painted-c on all 2 4 6 10 14 18
1-2nd printing (has UPC code, 1st prints don't) 3.00
1-3rd & 4th printings 2.50
2-1st printing 1 2 3 5 6 8
2-2nd & 3rd printings 2.50
3-5 5.00
3-6,9-2nd printings 2.50
6-12 3.00

VAMPIRELLA (Magazine)(See Warren Presents)
Warren Publishing Co./Harris Publications #113: Sept, 1969 - No. 112, Feb, 1983; No. 113, Jan, 1988? (B&W)
1-Intro. Vampirella in original costume & wings; Frazetta-c/intro. page; Adams-a; Crandall-a 40 80 120 314 607 900
2-1st app. Vampirella's cousin Evily-c/s; 1st/only app. Draculina, Vampirella's blonde twin sister 15 30 45 104 197 290
3 (Low distribution) 36 72 108 280 540 800
4,6 11 22 33 79 142 205
5,7,9: 5,7-Frazetta-c. 9-Barry Smith-a; Boris/Wood-c 11 22 33 80 145 210
8-Vampirella begins by Tom Sutton as serious strip (early issues-gag line) 12 24 36 83 152 220
10-No Vampi story; Brunner, Adams, Wood-a 7 14 21 50 83 115
11-Origin & 1st app. Pendragon; Frazetta-c 8 16 24 56 93 130
12-Vampi by Gonzales begins 8 16 24 56 93 130
13-15: 14-1st Maroto-a; Ploog-a 8 16 24 56 93 130
16,22,25: 16-1st full Dracula-c/app. 22-Color insert preview of Maroto's Dracula. 25-Vampi on cocaine-s 8 16 24 52 86 120
17,18,20,21,23,24: 17-Tomb of the Gods begins by Maroto, ends #22. 18-22-Dracula-s 7 14 21 50 83 115
19 (1973 Annual) Creation of Vampi text bio 9 18 27 60 100 140
26,28,34,35,39,40: All have 8 pg. color inserts. 28-Board game inside covers. 34,35-1st Fleur the Witch Woman. 39,40-Color Dracula-s. 40-Wrightson bio 6 12 18 37 59 80
27 (1974 Annual) New color Vampi-s; mostly-r 6 12 18 41 66 90
29,38,45: 38-2nd Vampi as Cleopatra/Blood Red Queen of Hearts; 1st Mayo-a. 6 12 18 37 59 80
30-32: 30-Intro. Pantha; Corben-a(color). 31-Origin Luana, the Beast Girl. 32-Jones-a 6 12 18 37 59 80
33-Wrightson-a; Pantha ends 6 12 18 37 59 80
36,37: 36-1st Vampi as Cleopatra/Blood Red Queen of Hearts; issue has 8 pg. color insert. 37-(1975 Annual) 6 12 18 39 62 85
41-44,47,48: 41-Dracula-s 5 10 15 32 51 70
46-(10/75) Origin-r from Annual 1 5 10 15 34 55 75
49-1st Blind Priestess; The Blood Red Queen of Hearts storyline begins; Poe-s 5 10 15 32 51 70
50-Spirit cameo by Eisner; 40 pg. Vampi-s; Pantha & Fleur app.; Jones-a 5 10 15 32 51 70
51-53,56,57,59-62,65,66,68,75,79,80,82-86,88,89: 60-62,65,66-The Blood Red Queen of Hearts app. 60-1st Blind Priestess-c 4 8 12 24 37 50
54,55,63,81,87: 54-Vampi-s (42 pgs.); 8 pg. color Corben-a. 55-All Gonzales-a(r). 63-10 pgs. Wrightson-a 4 8 12 24 37 50
58,70,72: 58-(92 pgs.) 70-Rook app. 4 8 12 28 44 60

Vampirella #113 © WP

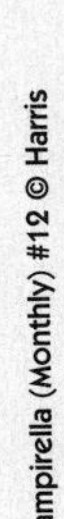
Vampirella (Monthly) #12 © Harris

Vampirella Lives #2 © Harris

GD VG FN VF VF/NM NM-
2.0 4.0 6.0 8.0 9.0 9.2

64,73: 64-(100 pg. Giant) All Mayo-a; 70 pg. Vampi-s. 73-69 pg. Vampi-s; Mayo-a 5 10 15 30 48 65
67,69,71,74,76-78-All Barbara Leigh photo-c 4 8 12 28 44 60
90-99: 90-Toth-a. 91-All-r; Gonzales-a. 93-Cassandra St. Knight begins, ends #103; new Pantha series begins, ends #108 4 8 12 24 37 50
100 (96 pg. r-special)-Origin reprinted from Ann. 1; mostly reprints; Vampirella appears topless in new 21 pg. story 8 16 24 56 93 130
101-104,106,107: All lower print run. 101,102-The Blood Red Queen of Hearts app. 107-All Maroto reprint-a issue 6 12 18 41 66 90
105,108-110: 108-Torpedo series by Toth begins; Vampi nudity splash page. 110-(100 pg. Summer Spectacular) 6 12 18 41 66 90
111,112: Low print run. 111-Giant Collector's Edition ($2.50) 112-(84 pgs.) last Warren issue 8 16 24 52 86 120
113 (1988)-1st Harris Issue; very low print run 26 52 78 190 363 535
Annual 1(1972)-New definitive origin of Vampirella by Gonzales; reprints by Neal Adams (from #1), Wood (from #9) 25 50 75 183 354 525
Special 1 (1977) Softcover (color, large-square bound)-Only available thru mail order 15 30 45 107 204 300
Special 1 (1977) Hardcover (color, large-square bound)-Only available through mail order (scarce)(500 produced, signed & #'d) 32 64 96 245 473 700
#1 1969 Commemorative Edition (2001, $4.95) reprints entire #1 5.00
...Crimson Chronicles Vol. 1 (2004, $19.95, TPB) reprints stories from #1-10 20.00
...Crimson Chronicles Vol. 2 (2005, $19.95, TPB) reprints stories from #11-18 20.00
...Crimson Chronicles Vol. 3 (2005, $19.95, TPB) reprints stories from #19-28 20.00
...Crimson Chronicles Vol. 4 (2006, $19.95, TPB) reprints stories from #29-41 20.00

NOTE: ***Ackerman*** *s-1-3.* ***Neal Adams*** *a-1, 10p, 19p(r/#10), 44(1 pg.), Annual 1.* ***Alcala*** *a-78, 90, 93i.* ***Bodé/Todd*** *c-3.* ***Bodé/Jones*** *c-4.* ***Boris/Wood*** *c-9.* ***Brunner*** *a-10, 12(1 pg.).* ***Corben*** *a-30, 31, 33, 36, 54; c-30, 31, 33, 54.* ***Crandall*** *a-1, 19(r/#1).* ***Frazetta*** *c-1, 5, 7, 11, 31.* ***Heath*** *a-58, 61, 67, 76-78, 83.* ***Infantino*** *a-57-62.* ***Jones*** *a-5, 9, 12, 27, 32 (color), 33(2 pg.), 34, 50i, 83r.* ***Ken Kelly*** *c-6, 38, 39, 40(back-c), 46, 70, 95.* ***Nebres*** *a-84, 88-90, 92-96.* ***Nino*** *a-59i, 61i, 67, 76, 85, 90.* ***Ploog*** *a-14.* ***Barry Smith*** *a-9.* ***Starlin*** *a-78.* ***Sutton*** *a-1-5, 7-11, Annual 1.* ***Toth*** *a-90i, 108, 110.* ***Wood*** *a-9, 10, 12, 19(r/#12), 27r, Annual 1; c-9(partial).* ***Wrightson*** *a-33(w/****Jones****), 40(Bio cameo) 63r. All reprint issues-19, 74, 83, 91, 105, 107, 109, 111. Annuals from 1973 on are included in regular numbering. Later annuals are same format as regular issues. Color inserts (8 pgs.) in 22, 25-28, 30-35, 39, 40, 45, 46, 49, 54, 55, 67, 72. 16 pg color insert in #36.*

VAMPIRELLA (Also see Cain/… & Vengeance of…)
Harris Publications: Nov, 1992 - No. 5, Nov, 1993 ($2.95)

0-Bagged 5.00
0-Gold 3 6 9 16 23 30
1-Jim Balent inks in #1-3; Adam Hughes c-1-3 2 4 6 11 16 20
1-2nd printing 5.00
1-(11/97) Commemorative Edition 3.00
2 2 4 6 9 12 15
3-5: 4-Snyder III-c. 5-Brereton painted-c 1 2 3 5 6 8
Trade paperback nn (10/93, $5.95)-r/#1-4; Jusko-c 1 2 3 4 5 7

NOTE: *Issues 1-5 contain certificates for free* ***Dave Stevens*** *Vampirella poster.*

VAMPIRELLA (THE NEW MONTHLY)
Harris Publications: Nov, 1997 - No. 26, Apr, 2000 ($2.95)

1-3-"Ascending Evil" -Morrison & Millar-s/Conner & Palmiotti-a. 1-Three covers by Quesada/Palmiotti, Conner, and Conner/Palmiotti 3.00
1-3-($9.95) Jae Lee variant covers 10.00
1-($24.95) Platinum Ed.w/Quesada-c 25.00
4-6-"Holy War"-Small & Stull-a, 4-Linsner variant-c 3.00
7-9-"Queen's Gambit"-Shi app. 7-Two covers. 8-Pantha-c/app. 3.00
7-($9.95) Conner variant-c 10.00
10-12-"Hell on Earth"; Small-a/Coney-s. 12-New costume 3.00
10-Jae Lee variant-c 1 3 4 6 8 10
13-15-"World's End" Zircher-p; Pantha back-up, Texeira-a 3.00
16,17: 16-Pantha-c;Texeira-a; Vampi back-up story. 17-(Pantha #2) 3.00
18-20-"Rebirth": Jae Lee-c on all. 18-Loeb-s/Sale-a. 19-Alan Davis-a. 20-Bruce Timm-a 3.00
18-20-($9.95) Variant covers: 18-Sale. 19-Davis. 20-Timm 12.00
21-26: 21,22-Dangerous Games; Small-a. 23-Lady Death-c/app.; Cleavenger-a. 24,25-Lau-a. 26-Lady Death & Pantha-c/app.; Cleavenger-a. 3.00
0-(1/99) also variant-c with Pantha #0; same contents 3.00
TPB ($7.50) r/#1-3 "Ascending Evil" 8.00
Ascending Evil Ashcan (8/97, $1.00) 2.50
...: Grant Morrison/Mark Millar Collection TPB (2006, $24.95) r/#1-6; interviews 25.00
Hell on Earth Ashcan (7/98, $1.00) 2.50
... Presents: Tales of Pantha TPB (2006, $19.95) r/stories from #13-17 & one-shots 20.00
The End Ashcan (3/00, $6.00) 6.00
...30th Anniversary Celebration Preview (7/99) B&W preview of #18-20 10.00

VAMPIRELLA
Harris Publications: June, 2001 - No. 22, Aug, 2003 ($2.95/$2.99)

1-Four covers (Mayhew w/foil logo, Campbell, Anacleto, Jae Lee) Mayhew-a; Mark Millar-s 3.00

GD VG FN VF VF/NM NM-
2.0 4.0 6.0 8.0 9.0 9.2

2-22: 2-Two covers (Mayhew & Chiodo). 3-Timm var-c. 4-Horn var-c. 7-10-Dawn Brown-a; Pantha back-up w/Texeira-a. 15-22-Conner-c 3.00
Giant-Size Ashcan (5/01, $5.95) B&W preview art and Mayhew interview 6.00
...: Halloween Trick & Treat (10/04, $4.95) stories & art by various; three covers 5.00
... : Nowheresville Preview Edition (3/01, $2.95)- previews Mayhew art and photo models 3.00
...Nowheresville TPB (1/02, $12.95) r/#1-3 with cover gallery 13.00
... Summer Special #1 (2005, $5.95) Batman Begins photo-c and 2 variant-c 6.00
...: 2006 Halloween Special (2006, $2.95) Conner-c; Hester-s/Segovia-a; 4 covers 3.00

VAMPIRELLA & PANTHA SHOWCASE
Harris Publications: Jan, 1997 ($1.50, one-shot)

1-Millar-s/Texeira-c/a; flip book w/"Blood Lust"; Robinson-s/Jusko-c/a 3.00

VAMPIRELLA & THE BLOOD RED QUEEN OF HEARTS
Harris Publications: Sept, 1996 ($9.95, 96 pgs., B&W, squarebound, one-shot)

nn-r/Vampirella #49,60-62,65,66,101,102; John Bolton-c; Michael Bair back-c 1 3 4 6 8 10

VAMPIRELLA: BLOODLUST
Harris Publications: July, 1997 - No. 2, Aug, 1997 ($4.95, limited series)

1,2-Robinson-s/Jusko-painted c/a 5.00

VAMPIRELLA CLASSIC
Harris Publications: Feb, 1995 - No. 5, Nov, 1995 ($2.95, limited series)

1-5: Reprints Archie Goodwin stories. 3.00

VAMPIRELLA COMICS MAGAZINE
Harris Publications: Oct, 2003 - Present ($3.95/$9.95, magazine-sized)

1-9-($3.95) 1-Texiera-c; b&w and color stories, Alan Moore interview; reviews. 2-KISS interview. 4-Chiodo-c. 6-Brereton-c 4.00
1-9-($9.95) 1-Three covers (Model Photo cover, Palmiotti-c, Wheatley Frankenstein-c) 10.00

VAMPIRELLA: CROSSOVER GALLERY
Harris Publications: Sept, 1997 ($2.95, one-shot)

1-Wraparound-c by Campbell, pinups by Jae Lee, Mack, Allred, Art Adams, Quesada & Palmiotti and others 3.00

VAMPIRELLA: DEATH & DESTRUCTION
Harris Publications: July, 1996 - No. 3, Sept, 1996 ($2.95, limited series)

1-3: Amanda Conner-a(p) in all. 1-Tucci-c. 2-Hughes-c. 3-Jusko-c 3.00
1-($9.95)-Limited Edition; Beachum-c 10.00

VAMPIRELLA/DRACULA & PANTHA SHOWCASE
Harris Publications: Aug, 1997 ($1.50, one-shot)

1-Ellis, Robinson, and Moore-s; flip book w/"Pantha" 3.00

VAMPIRELLA/DRACULA: THE CENTENNIAL
Harris Publications: Oct, 1997 ($5.95, one-shot)

1-Ellis, Robinson, and Moore-s; Beachum, Frank/Smith, and Mack/Mays-a Bolton-painted-c 6.00

VAMPIRELLA: INTIMATE VISIONS
Harris Publications: 2006 ($3.95, one-shots)

..., Amanda Conner 1 - r/Vampirella Monthly #1 with commentary; interview; 2 covers 4.00
..., Joe Jusko 1 - r/Vampirella; Blood Lust #1 with commentary; interview; 2 covers 4.00

VAMPIRELLA: JULIE STRAIN SPECIAL
Harris Publications: Sept, 2000 ($3.95, one-shot)

1-Photo-c w/yellow background; interview and photo gallery 4.00
1-Limited Edition ($9.95); cover photo w/black background 10.00

VAMPIRELLA/LADY DEATH (Also see Lady Death/Vampirella)
Harris Publications: Feb, 1999 ($3.50, one-shot)

1-Small-a/Nelson painted-c 3.50
1-Valentine Edition ($9.95); pencil-c by Small 10.00

VAMPIRELLA: LEGENDARY TALES
Harris Publications: May, 2000 - No. 2, June, 2000 ($2.95, B&W)

1,2-Reprints from magazine; Cleavenger painted-c 3.00
1,2-($9.95) Variant painted-c by Mike Mayhew 10.00

VAMPIRELLA LIVES
Harris Publications: Dec, 1996 - No. 3, Feb, 1997 ($3.50/$2.95, limited series)

1-Die cut-c; Quesada & Palmiotti-c, Ellis-s/Conner-a 3.50
1-Deluxe Ed.-photo-c 3.50
2,3-($2.95)-Two editions (1 photo-c): 3-J. Scott Campbell-c 3.00

VAMPIRELLA: MORNING IN AMERICA
Harris Publications/Dark Horse Comics: 1991 - No. 4, 1992 ($3.95, B&W, lim. series, 52 pgs.)

Vampirella/Witchblade #1 © Harris & TCOW

Vampire Tales #9 © MAR

Vamps: Pumpkin Time #3 © Lee & Simpson

	GD 2.0	VG 4.0	FN 6.0	VF 8.0	VF/NM 9.0	NM- 9.2

1,2-All have Kaluta painted-c 1 2 3 5 6 8
3,4 1 3 4 6 8 10

VAMPIRELLA OF DRAKULON
Harris Publications: Jan, 1996 - No. 5, Sept, 1996 ($2.95)
0-5: All reprints. 0-Jim Silke-c. 3-Polybagged w/card. 4-Texeira-c 3.00

VAMPIRELLA/PAINKILLER JANE
Harris Publications: May, 1998 ($3.50, one-shot)
1-Waid & Augustyn-s/Leonardi & Palmiotti-a 3.50
1-($9.95) Variant-c 10.00

VAMPIRELLA PIN-UP SPECIAL
Harris Publications: Oct, 1995 ($2.95, one-shot)
1-Hughes-c, pin-ups by various 5.00
1-Variant-c 5.00

VAMPIRELLA QUARTERLY
Harris Publications: Spring, 2007 - Present ($4.95/$4.99, quarterly)
Spring, 2007 - Summer 2008-New stories and re-colored reprints; five or six covers 5.00

VAMPIRELLA: RETRO
Harris Publications: Mar, 1998 - No. 3, May, 1998 ($2.50, B&W, limited series)
1-3: Reprints; Silke painted covers 3.00

VAMPIRELLA: REVELATIONS
Harris Publications: No. 0, Oct, 2005 - No. 3, Feb, 2006 ($2.99, limited series)
0-3-Vampirella's origin retold, Lilith app.; Carey-s/Lilly-a; two covers on each 4.00
... Book 1 TPB (2006, $12.95) r/series; Carey interview, script for #1, Lilly sketch pages 13.00

VAMPIRELLA: SAD WINGS OF DESTINY
Harris Publications: Sept, 1996 ($3.95, one-shot)
1-Jusko-c 4.00

VAMPIRELLA: SECOND COMING
Harris Publications: 2009 - No. 4 ($1.99, limited series)
1-4: 1-Hester-s/Sampere-a; multiple covers on each. 3,4-Rio-a 2.00

VAMPIRELLA/SHADOWHAWK: CREATURES OF THE NIGHT (Also see Shadowhawk)
Harris Publications: 1995 ($4.95, one-shot)
1 5.00

VAMPIRELLA/SHI (See Shi/Vampirella)
Harris Publications: Oct, 1997 ($2.95, one-shot)
1-Ellis-s 3.00
1-Chromium-c 6.00

VAMPIRELLA: SILVER ANNIVERSARY COLLECTION
Harris Publications: Jan, 1997 - No. 4 Apr, 1997 ($2.50, limited series)
1-4: Two editions: Bad Girl by Beachum, Good Girl by Silke 3.00

VAMPIRELLA'S SUMMER NIGHTS
Harris Publications: 1992 (one-shot)
1-Art Adams infinity cover; centerfold by Stelfreeze 3 7 10 19 27 35

VAMPIRELLA STRIKES
Harris Publications: Sept, 1995 - No. 8, Dec, 1996 ($2.95, limited series)
1-8: 1-Photo-c. 2-Deodato-c; polybagged w/card. 5-Eudaemon-c/app; wraparound-c; alternate-c exists. 6-(6/96)-Mark Millar script; Texeira-c; alternate-c exists. 7-Flip book 3.00
1-Newsstand Edition; diff. photo-c., 1-Limited Ed.; diff. photo-c 3.00
Annual 1-(12/96, $2.95) Delano-s; two covers 3.00

VAMPIRELLA: 25TH ANNIVERSARY SPECIAL
Harris Publications: Oct, 1996 ($5.95, squarebound, one-shot)
nn-Reintro The Blood Red Queen of Hearts; James Robinson, Grant Morrison & Warren Ellis scripts; Mark Texeira, Michael Bair & Amanda Conner-a(p); Frank Frazetta-c 6.00
nn-($6.95)-Silver Edition 7.00

VAMPIRELLA VS. HEMORRHAGE
Harris Publications: Apr, 1997($3.50)
1 3.50

VAMPIRELLA VS. PANTHA
Harris Publications: Mar, 1997 ($3.50)
1-Two covers; Millar-s/Texeira-c/a 3.50

VAMPIRELLA/WETWORKS (See Wetworks/Vampirella)
Harris Publications: June, 1997 ($2.95, one-shot)
1 3.00
1-($9.95) Alternate Edition; cardstock-c 10.00

VAMPIRELLA/WITCHBLADE
Harris Publications: 2003; Oct, 2004; Oct, 2005 ($2.99, one-shots)
1-Brian Wood-s/Steve Pugh-a; 3 covers by Texeira, Conner and Pugh 3.00
...: The Feast (10/05, $2.99) Joyce Chin-a; covers by Chin, Conner, Rodriguez 3.00
...: Union of the Damned (10/04, $2.99, one-shot) Sharp-a; three covers 3.00
Trilogy TPB (2006, $12.95) r/one-shots; art gallery and gallery of multiple covers 13.00

VAMPIRE'S CHRISTMAS, THE (Also see Dark Ivory)
Image Comics: Oct, 2003 ($5.95, over-sized graphic novel)
nn-Linsner-s/a; Dubisch-painted-a 6.00

VAMPIRE TALES
Marvel Comics Group: Aug, 1973 - No. 11, June, 1975 (75¢, B&W, magazine)
1-Morbius, the Living Vampire begins by Pablo Marcos (1st solo Morbius series & 5th Morbius app.) 7 14 21 49 80 110
2-Intro. Satana; Steranko-r 5 10 15 32 57 70
3,5,6: 3-Satana app. 5-Origin Morbius. 6-1st Lilith app. in this title (see Giant-Size Chillers #1 for debut) 4 8 12 28 44 60
4,7 4 8 12 22 34 45
8-1st solo Blade story (see Tomb of Dracula) 5 10 15 32 51 70
9-Blade app. 4 8 12 28 44 60
10,11 4 8 12 22 34 45
Annual 1(10/75)-Heath-r/#9 4 8 12 22 34 45
NOTE: ***Alcala*** *a-6, 8, 9i.* ***Boris*** *c-4, 6.* ***Chaykin*** *a-7.* ***Everett*** *a-1r.* ***Gulacy*** *a-7p.* ***Heath*** *a-9.* ***Infantino*** *a-3r.* ***Gil Kane*** *a-4, 5r.*

VAMPIRE VERSES, THE
CFD Productions: Aug, 1995 - No. 4, 1995 ($2.95, B&W, mature)
1-4 3.00

VAMPI VICIOUS
Harris Publications (Anarchy Studios): Aug, 2003 - No. 3, Nov, 2003 ($2.99)
1-3: 1-McKeever-s/Dogan-a; 3 covers by Dogan, Lau & Noto. 3-Kau-a 3.00

VAMPI VICIOUS CIRCLE
Harris Publications (Anarchy Studios): Jun, 2004 - No. 3, Sept, 2004 ($2.99/$9.95)
1-3: B. Clay Moore-s 3.00
1-3-($9.95) Limited Edition w/variant-c. 1-Noto-c. 2-Norton-c. 3-Lucas-c 10.00

VAMPI VICIOUS RAMPAGE
Harris Publications (Anarchy Studios): Feb, 2005 - No. 2, Apr, 2005 ($2.99)
1,2: Raab-s/Lau-a; two covers on each 3.00

VAMPI VS. XIN
Harris Publications (Anarchy Studios): Oct, 2004 - No. 2, Jan, 2005 ($2.99)
1,2-Faerber-s/Lau-a; two covers 3.00

VAMPS
DC Comics (Vertigo): Aug, 1994 - No. 6, Jan, 1995 ($1.95, lim. series, mature)
1-6-Bolland-c 3.00
Trade paperback ($9.95)-r/#1-6 10.00

VAMPS: HOLLYWOOD & VEIN
DC Comics (Vertigo): Feb, 1996 - No. 6, July, 1996 ($2.25, lim. series, mature)
1-6: Winslade-c 2.50

VAMPS: PUMPKIN TIME
DC Comics (Vertigo): Dec, 1998 - No. 3, Feb, 1999 ($2.50, lim. series, mature)
1-3: Quitely-c 2.50

VANGUARD (...Outpost: Earth) (See Megaton)
Megaton Comics: 1987 ($1.50)
1-Erik Larsen-c(p) 3.00

VANGUARD (See Savage Dragon #2)
Image Comics (Highbrow Entertainment): Oct, 1993 - No. 6, 1994 ($1.95)
1-6: 1-Wraparound gatefold-c; Erik Larsen back-up-a; Supreme x-over. 3-(12/93)-Indicia says December 1994. 4-Berzerker back-up. 5-Angel Medina-a(p) 3.00

VANGUARD (See Savage Dragon #2)
Image Comics: Aug, 1996 - No. 4, Feb, 1997 ($2.95, B&W, limited series)
1-4 3.00

VANGUARD: ETHEREAL WARRIORS
Image Comics: Aug, 2000 ($5.95, B&W)
1-Fosco & Larsen-a 6.00

VANGUARD ILLUSTRATED
Pacific Comics: Nov, 1983 - No. 11, Oct, 1984 (Baxter paper)(Direct sales only)

Vault of Horror #35 © WMG

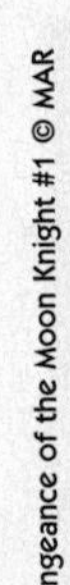

Vengeance of the Moon Knight #1 © MAR

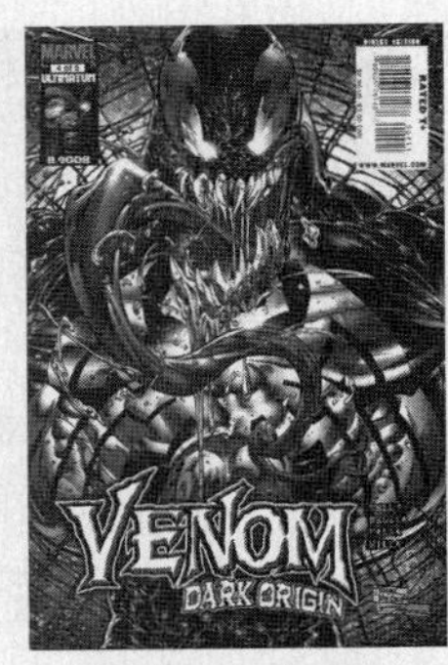

Venom: Dark Origin #4 © MAR

	GD 2.0	VG 4.0	FN 6.0	VF 8.0	VF/NM 9.0	NM- 9.2

1-6,8-11: 1,7-Nudity scenes. 2-1st app. Stargrazers (see Legends of the Stargrazers; Dave Stevens-c 3.00
7-1st app. Mr. Monster (r-in Mr. Monster #1) 5.00
NOTE: ***Evans** a-7. **Kaluta** c-5, 7p. **Perez** a-6; c-6. **Rude** a-1-4; c-4. **Williamson** c-3.*

VANGUARD: STRANGE VISITORS
Image Comics: Oct, 1996 - No.4, Feb, 1997 ($2.95, B&W, limited series)

1-4: 3-Supreme-c/app. 3.00

VAN HELSING: FROM BENEATH THE RUE MORGUE (Based on the 2004 movie)
Dark Horse Comics: Apr, 2004 ($2.99, one-shot)

1-Hugh Jackman photo-c; Dysart-s/Alexander-a 3.00

VANITY (See Pacific Presents #3)
Pacific Comics: Jun, 1984 - No. 2, Aug, 1984 ($1.50, direct sales)

1,2: Origin 2.50

VARIETY COMICS (The Spice of Comics)
Rural Home Publ./Croyden Publ. Co.: 1944 - No. 2, 1945; No. 3, 1946

	GD	VG	FN	VF	VF/NM	NM-
1-Origin Captain Valiant	21	42	63	122	199	275
2-Captain Valiant	14	28	42	80	115	150
3(1946-Croyden)-Captain Valiant	12	24	36	69	97	125

VARIETY COMICS (See Fox Giants)

VARSITY
Parents' Magazine Institute: 1945

	GD	VG	FN	VF	VF/NM	NM-
1	8	16	24	44	57	70

VAULT OF EVIL
Marvel Comics Group: Feb, 1973 - No. 23, Nov, 1975

	GD	VG	FN	VF	VF/NM	NM-
1 (1950s reprints begin)	3	6	9	17	25	32
2-23: 3,4-Brunner-c. 11-Kirby-a	2	4	6	11	16	20

NOTE: ***Ditko** a-14r, 15r, 20-22r. **Drucker** a-10r(Mystic #52), 13r(Uncanny Tales #42). **Everett** a-11r(Menace #2), 13r(Menace #4); c-10. **Heath** a-5r. **Gil Kane** c-1, 6. **Kirby** a-11. **Krigstein** a-20r(Uncanny Tales #54). **Reinman** r-1. **Tuska** a-6r.*

VAULT OF HORROR (Formerly War Against Crime #1-11) (Also see EC Archives)
E. C. Comics: No. 12, Apr-May, 1950 - No. 40, Dec-Jan, 1954-55

	GD	VG	FN	VF	VF/NM	NM-
12 (Scarce)-ties w/Crypt Of Terror as 1st horror comic	486	972	1458	3888	6194	8500
13-Morphine story	101	202	303	808	1292	1775
14	89	178	267	712	1131	1550
15- "Terror in the Swamp" is same story w/minor changes as "The Thing in the Swamp" from Haunt of Fear #15	77	154	231	616	983	1350
16	59	118	177	472	749	1025
17-Classic werewolf-c	67	134	201	536	856	1175
18,19	47	94	141	376	601	825
20-25: 22-Frankenstein-c & adaptation. 23-Used in **POP**, pg. 84; Davis-a(2); Ingels bio. 24-Craig bio.	39	78	117	312	499	685
26-B&W & color illos in **POP**	39	78	117	312	499	685
27-36: 30-Dismemberment-c. 31-Ray Bradbury biog. 32-Censored-c. 35-X-Mas-c. 36- "Pipe Dream" classic opium addict story by Krigstein; "Twin Bill" cited in articles by T.E. Murphy, Wertham	33	66	99	264	420	575
37-1st app. Drusilla, a Vampirella look alike; Williamson-a	33	66	99	264	425	585
38-39: 39-Bondage-c	31	62	93	248	399	550
40-Low distribution	39	78	117	312	499	685

NOTE: ***Craig** art in all but No. 13 & 33; c-12-40. **Crandall** a-33, 34, 39. **Davis** a-17-38. **Evans** a-27, 28, 30, 32, 33. **Feldstein** a-12-16. **Ingels** a-13-20, 22-40. **Kamen** a-15-22, 25, 29, 35. **Krigstein** a-36, 38-40. **Kurtzman** a-12, 13. **Orlando** a-24, 31, 40. **Wood** a-12-14. #22, 29 & 31 have Ray Bradbury adaptations. #16 & 17 have H. P. Lovecraft adaptations.*

VAULT OF HORROR, THE
Gladstone Publ.: Aug, 1990 - No. 6, June, 1991 ($1.95, 68 pgs.)(#4 on: $2.00)

1-Craig-c(r); all contain EC reprints 4.00
2-6: 2,4-6-Craig-c(r). 3-Ingels-c(r) 3.00

VAULT OF HORROR
Russ Cochran/Gemstone Publishing: Sept, 1991 - No. 5, May, 1992 ($2.00); Oct, 1992 - No. 29, Oct, 1999 ($1.50/$2.00/$2.50)

1-29: E.C reprints. 1-4r/VOH #12-15 w/original-c 4.00

V...-COMICS (Morse code for "V" - 3 dots, 1 dash)
Fox Features Syndicate: Jan, 1942 - No. 2, Mar-Apr, 1942

	GD	VG	FN	VF	VF/NM	NM-
1-Origin V-Man & the Boys; The Banshee & The Black Fury, The Queen of Evil, & V-Agents begin; Nazi-c	129	258	387	826	1413	2000
2-Nazi bondage/torture-c	90	180	270	576	988	1400

VECTOR
Now Comics: 1986 - No. 4, 1986? ($1.50, 1st color comic by Now Comics)

1-4: Computer-generated art 2.50

VEILS
DC Comics (Vertigo): 1999 ($24.95, one-shot)

Hardcover-($24.95) Painted art and photography; McGreal-s 25.00
Softcover ($14.95) 15.00

VELOCITY (Also see Cyberforce)
Image Comics (Top Cow Productions): Nov, 1995 - No. 3, Jan, 1996 ($2.50, limited series)

1-3: Kurt Busiek scripts in all. 2-Savage Dragon-c/app. 3.00
...: Pilot Season 1 (10/07, $2.99) Casey-s/Maguire-a 3.00

VENGEANCE OF THE MOON KNIGHT
Marvel Comics: Nov, 2009 - Present ($3.99)

1-6: 1-Hurwitz-s/Opeña-a; covers by Yu, Ross and Finch; back-up r/Moon Knight #1 ('80) 2-Sentry app. 5-Spider-Man app. 4.00

VENGEANCE OF VAMPIRELLA (Becomes Vampirella: Death & Destruction)
Harris Comics: Apr, 1994 - No. 25, Apr, 1996 ($2.95)

1-($3.50)-Quesada/Palmiotti "bloodfoil" wraparound cover 6.00
1-2nd printing; blue foil-c 3.00
1-Gold 18.00
2-8: 8-Polybagged w/trading card 4.00
9-25: 10-w/coupon for Hyde -25 poster. 11,19-Polybagged w/ trading card. 25-Quesada & Palmiotti red foil-c 3.00
...: Bloodshed (1995, $6.95) 7.00

VENGEANCE OF VAMPIRELLA: THE MYSTERY WALK
Harris Comics: Nov, 1995 ($2.95, one-shot)

0 3.00

VENGEANCE SQUAD
Charlton Comics: July, 1975 - No. 6, May, 1976 (#1-3 are 25¢ issues)

	GD	VG	FN	VF	VF/NM	NM-
1-Mike Mauser, Private Eye begins by Staton	2	4	6	8	11	14
2-6: Morisi-a in all	1	2	3	5	6	8
5,6 (Modern Comics-r, 1977)						4.00

VENOM
Marvel Comics: June, 2003 - No. 18, Nov, 2004 ($2.25)

1-7-Herrera-a/Way-s. 6,7-Wolverine app. 2.50
8-18-($2.99): 8-10-Wolverine-c/app.; Kieth-c. 11-Fantastic Four app. 3.00
... Vol. 1: Shiver (2004, $13.99, TPB) r/#1-5 14.00
... Vol. 2: Run (2004, $19.99, TPB) r/#6-13 20.00
... Vol. 3: Twist (2004, $13.99, TPB) r/#14-18 14.00

VENOM: Marvel Comics (Also see Amazing Spider-Man #298-300)

... ALONG CAME A SPIDER, 1/96 - No. 4, 4/96 ($2.95)-Spider-Man & Carnage app. 3.00
... CARNAGE UNLEASHED, 4/95 - No. 4, 7/95 ($2.95) 3.00
... DARK ORIGIN, 10/08 - No. 5, 2/09 ($2.99) 1-5-Medina-a 3.00
... DEATHTRAP: THE VAULT, 3/93 ($6.95) r/Avengers: Deathtrap: The Vault 7.00
... FUNERAL PYRE, 8/93- No. 3, 10/93 ($2.95)-#1-Holo-grafx foil-c; Punisher app. in all 3.00

VENOM: LETHAL PROTECTOR
Marvel Comics: Feb, 1993 - No. 6, July, 1993 ($2.95, limited series)

1-Red holo-grafx foil-c; Bagley-c/a in all 5.00
1-Gold variant sold to retailers 15.00

	GD	VG	FN	VF	VF/NM	NM-
1-Black-c (at least 58 copies have been authenticated by CGC since 2000)	9	18	27	63	107	150

NOTE: Counterfeit copies of the black-c exist and are valueless
2-6: Spider-Man app. in all 3.00

... LICENSE TO KILL,6/97 - No. 3, 8/97 ($1.95) 2.50
... NIGHTS OF VENGEANCE, 8/94 - No. 4, 11/94 ($2.95), #1-Red foil-c 3.00
... ON TRIAL, 3/97 - No. 3, 5/97 ($1.95) 2.50
... SEED OF DARKNESS, 7/97 ($1.95) #(-1) Flashback 2.50
... SEPARATION ANXIETY,12/94- No. 4, 3/95 ($2.95) #1-Embossed-c 3.00
... SIGN OF THE BOSS,3/97 - No. 2, 10/97 ($1.99) 2.50
... SINNER TAKES ALL, 8/95 - No. 5, 10/95 ($2.95) 3.00
... SUPER SPECIAL, 8/95($3.95) #1-Flip book 4.00
... THE ENEMY WITHIN, 2/94 - No. 3, 4/94 ($2.95)-Demogoblin & Morbius app.
1-Glow-in-the-dark-c 3.00
... THE FINALE, 11/97 - No. 3, 1/98 ($1.99) 2.50

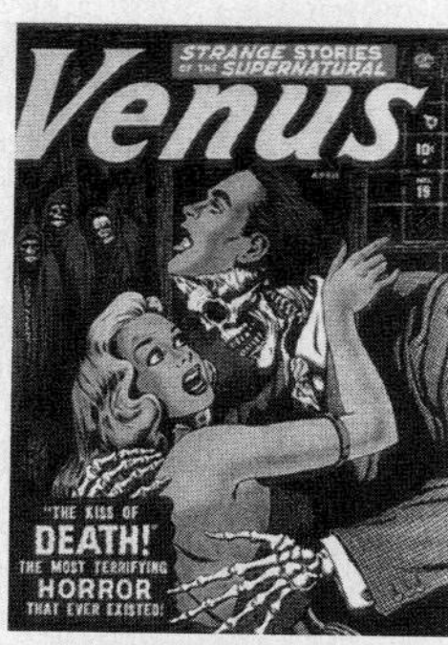

Venus #19 © MAR

Veronica #13 © AP

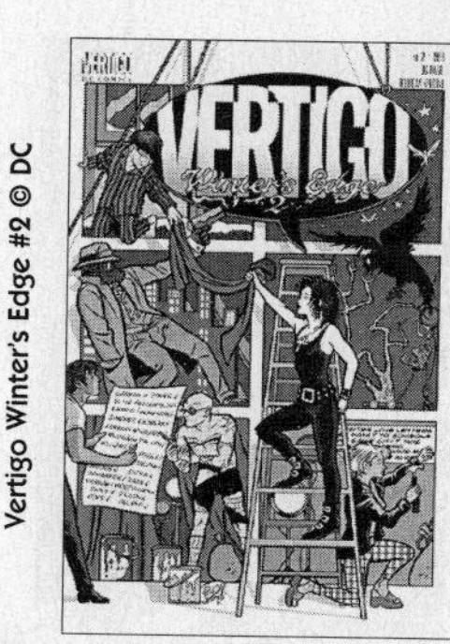

Vertigo Winter's Edge #2 © DC

GD VG FN VF VF/NM NM-
2.0 4.0 6.0 8.0 9.0 9.2

... THE HUNGER, 8/96- No. 4, 11/96 ($1.95) 2.50
... THE HUNTED, 5/96-No. 3, 7/96 ($2.95) 3.00
... THE MACE, 5/94 - No. 3, 7/94 ($2.95)-#1-Embossed-c 3.00
... THE MADNESS, 11/93- No. 3, 1/94 ($2.95)-Kelley Jones-c/a(p).
1-Embossed-c; Juggernaut app. 3.00
... TOOTH AND CLAW, 12/96 - No. 3, 2/97 ($1.95)-Wolverine-c/app. 2.50
... VS. CARNAGE, 9/04 - No. 4, 12/04 ($2.99)-Milligan-s/Crain-a; Spider-Man app. 3.00
TPB (2004, $9.99) r/#1-4 10.00

VENTURE
AC Comics (Americomics): Aug, 1986 - No. 3, 1986? ($1.75)
1-3: 1-3-Bolt. 1-Astron. 2-Femforce. 3-Fazers 2.50

VENTURE
Image Comics: Jan, 2003 - No. 4, Sept, 2003 ($2.95)
1-4-Faerber-s/Igle-a 3.00

VENUS (See Agents of Atlas, Marvel Spotlight #2 & Weird Wonder Tales)
Marvel/Atlas Comics (CMC 1-9/LCC 10-19): Aug, 1948 - No. 19, Apr, 1952 (Also see Marvel Mystery #91)
1-Venus & Hedy Devine begin; 1st app. Venus; Kurtzman's "Hey Look"
155 310 465 992 1696 2400
2 84 168 252 538 919 1300
3,5 61 122 183 387 664 940
4-Kurtzman's "Hey Look" 61 122 183 390 670 950
6-9: 6-Loki app. 7,8-Painted-c. 9-Begin 52 pgs.; book-length feature "Whom the Gods Destroy!"
53 106 159 334 567 800
10-S/F-horror issues begin (7/50) 76 152 228 486 831 1175
11-S/F end of the world (11/50) 87 174 261 553 952 1350
12-Colan-a 50 100 150 315 533 750
13-16-Venus by Everett, 2-3 stories each; covers-#13,15,16; 14-Everett part cover (Venus).
86 172 258 546 936 1325
17-19-Classic Everett horror & skull covers; Venus app. 17-Bondage-c (scarce)
161 322 483 1030 1765 2500

NOTE: ***Berg*** *s/f story-13.* ***Everett*** *c-13, 14(part; Venus only), 15-19.* ***Heath*** *s/f story-11.* ***Maneely*** *s/f story 10(3pg.), 16.* ***Morisi*** *a-19.* ***Syd Shores*** *c-6.*

VERI BEST SURE FIRE COMICS
Holyoke Publishing Co.: No date (circa 1945) (Reprints Holyoke one-shots)
1-Captain Aero, Alias X, Miss Victory, Commandos of the Devil Dogs, Red Cross, Hammerhead Hawley, Capt. Aero's Sky Scouts, Flagman app.; same-c as Veri Best Sure Shot #1 39 78 117 231 378 525

VERI BEST SURE SHOT COMICS
Holyoke Publishing Co.: No date (circa 1945) (Reprints Holyoke one-shots)
1-Capt. Aero, Miss Victory by Quinlan, Alias X, The Red Cross, Flagman, Commandos of the Devil Dogs, Hammerhead Hawley, Capt. Aero's Sky Scouts; same-c as Veri Best Sure Fire #1 39 78 117 231 378 525

VERMILLION
DC Comics (Helix): Oct, 1996 - No. 12, Sept, 1997 ($2.25/$2.50)
1-12: 1-4: Lucius Shepard scripts. 4,12-Kaluta-c 2.50

VERONICA (Also see Archie's Girls, Betty &...)
Archie Comics: Apr, 1989 - Present
1-(75¢-c) 7.00
2-10: 2-(75¢-c) 4.50
11-38 3.50
39-Love Showdown pt. 4, Cheryl Blossom 5.50
40-70: 34-Neon ink-c 3.00
71-199: 134-Begin $2.19-c. 152,155-Cheryl Blossom app. 163-Begin $2.25-c 2.50

VERONICA'S PASSPORT DIGEST MAGAZINE (Becomes Veronica's Digest Magazine #3 on)
Archie Comics: Nov, 1992 - No. 6 ($1.50/$1.79, digest size)
1 5.00
2-6 3.00

VERONICA'S SUMMER SPECIAL (See Archie Giant Series Magazine #615, 625)

VERTICAL
DC Comics (Vertigo): 2003 ($4.95, 3-1/4" wide pages, one-shot)
1-Seagle-s/Allred & Bond-a; odd format 1/2 width pages with some 20" long spreads 5.00

VERTIGO DOUBLE SHOT
DC Comics (Vertigo): 2008 ($2.99)
1-Reprints House of Mystery (2008) #1 and Young Liars #1 in flip-book format 3.00

VERTIGO: FIRST CUT

GD VG FN VF VF/NM NM-
2.0 4.0 6.0 8.0 9.0 9.2

DC Comics (Vertigo): 2008 ($4.99, TPB)
TPB-Reprints first issues of DMZ, Army@Love, Jack of Fables, Exterminators, Scalped, Crossing Midnight, and Loveless; preview of Air 5.00

VERTIGO: FIRST OFFENSES
DC Comics (Vertigo): 2005 ($4.99, TPB)
TPB-Reprints first issues of The Invisibles, Preacher, Fables, Sandman Mystery Theater, and Lucifer 5.00

VERTIGO: FIRST TASTE
DC Comics (Vertigo): 2005 ($4.99, TPB)
TPB-Reprints first issues of Y: The Last Man, 100 Bullets, Transmetropolitan, Books of Magick: Life During Wartime, Death: The High Cost of Living, and Saga of the Swamp Thing #21 (Alan Moore's first story on that title) 5.00

VERTIGO GALLERY, THE: DREAMS AND NIGHTMARES
DC Comics (Vertigo): 1995 ($3.50, one-shot)
1-Pin-ups of Vertigo characters by Sienkiewicz, Toth, Van Fleet & others; McKean-c 4.00

VERTIGO JAM
DC Comics (Vertigo): Aug, 1993 ($3.95, one-shot, 68 pgs.)(Painted-c by Fabry)
1-Sandman by Neil Gaiman, Hellblazer, Animal Man, Doom Patrol, Swamp Thing, Kid Eternity & Shade the Changing Man 5.00

VERTIGO POP! BANGKOK
DC Comics (Vertigo): July, 2003 - No. 4, Oct, 2003 ($2.95, limited series)
1-4-Camuncoli-c/a; Jonathan Vankin-s 3.00

VERTIGO POP! LONDON
DC Comics (Vertigo): Jan, 2003 - No. 4, Apr, 2003 ($2.95, limited series)
1-4-Philip Bond-c/a; Peter Milligan-s 3.00

VERTIGO POP! TOKYO
DC Comics (Vertigo): Sept, 2002 - No. 4, Dec, 2002 ($2.95, limited series)
1-4-Seth Fisher-c/a; Jonathan Vankin-s 3.00
Tokyo Days, Bangkok Nights TPB (2009, $19.99) r/#1-4 & Vertogo Pop! Bangkok #1-4 20.00

VERTIGO PREVIEW
DC Comics (Vertigo): 1992 (75¢, one-shot, 36 pgs.)
1-Vertigo previews; Sandman story by Neil Gaiman 2.50

VERTIGO RAVE
DC Comics (Vertigo): Fall, 1994 (99¢, one-shot)
1-Vertigo previews 2.50

VERTIGO SECRET FILES
DC Comics (Vertigo): Aug, 2000 ($4.95)
...: Hellblazer 1 (8/00, $4.95) Background info and story summaries 5.00
...: Swamp Thing 1 (11/00, $4.95) Backstories and origins; Hale-c 5.00

VERTIGO VERITE: THE UNSEEN HAND
DC Comics (Vertigo): Sept, 1996 - No. 4, Dec, 1996 ($2.50, limited series)
1-4: Terry LaBan scripts in all 2.50

VERTIGO VISIONS
DC Comics (Vertigo): June, 1993 - Present (one-shots)
Dr. Occult 1 (7/94, $3.95) 4.00
Dr. Thirteen 1 (9/98, $5.95) Howarth-s 6.00
Prez 1 (7/95, $3.95) 4.00
The Geek 1 (6/93, $3.95) 4.00
The Eaters ($4.95, 1995)-Milligan story. 5.00
The Phantom Stranger 1 (10/93, $3.50) 3.50
Tomahawk 1 (7/98, $4.95) Pollack-s 5.00

VERTIGO WINTER'S EDGE
DC Comics (Vertigo): 1998, 1999 ($7.95/$6.95, square-bound, annual)
1-Winter stories by Vertigo creators; Desire story by Gaiman/Bolton; Bolland wraparound-c 8.00
2,3-($6.95)-Winter stories: 2-Allred-c. 3-Bond-c; Desire by Gaiman/Zulli 7.00

VERTIGO X ANNIVERSARY PREVIEW
DC Comics (Vertigo): 2003 (99¢, one-shot, 48 pgs.)
1-Previews of upcoming titles and interviews; Endless Nights, Shade, The Originals 2.25

VERY BEST OF DENNIS THE MENACE, THE
Fawcett Publ.: July, 1979 - No. 2, Apr, 1980 (95¢/$1.00, digest-size, 132 pgs.)
1,2-Reprints 2 4 6 8 10 12

VERY BEST OF DENNIS THE MENACE, THE
Marvel Comics Group: Apr, 1982 - No. 3, Aug, 1982 ($1.25, digest-size)

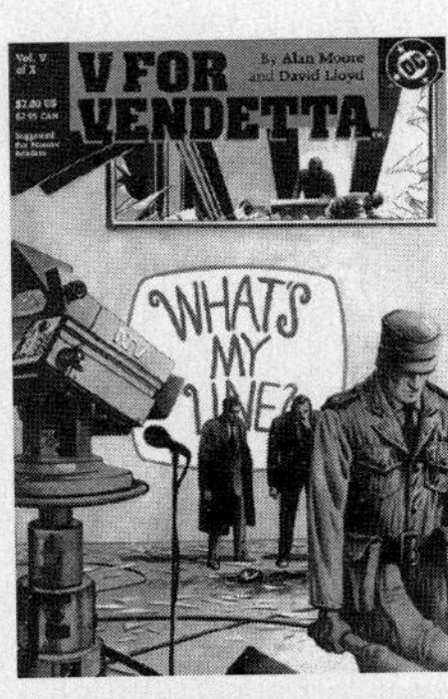

V For Vendetta #5 © DC

Victorian Undead #1 © WSP

Vigilante (2009 series) #8 © DC

	GD 2.0	VG 4.0	FN 6.0	VF 8.0	VF/NM 9.0	NM- 9.2
1-3: Reprints	2	3	4	6	8	10
1,2-Mistakenly printed with DC logo on cover	2	4	6	9	12	15

NOTE: ***Hank Ketcham** c-all. A few thousand of #1 & 2 were printed with DC emblem.*

VERY VICKY
Meet Danny Ocean: 1993? - No. 8, 1995 ($2.50, B&W)
1-8, ...: Calling All Hillbillies (1995, $2.50) 2.50

VERY WEIRD TALES (Also see Slithiss Attacks!)
Oceanspray Comics Group: Aug, 2002 - No. 2, Oct, 2002 ($4.00)
1-Mutant revenge, methamphetamine, corporate greed horror stories 8.00
2-Weird fantasy and horror stories 4.00
NOTE: *Created in prevention classes taught by Jon McClure at the Oceanspray Family Center in Newport, Oregon, and paid for by the Housing Authority of Lincoln County. All books are b&w with color covers. Issues #1-2 penciled and inked by various artists. All comics feature characters created by students and are signed and numbered by Jon McClure. Issues #1-2 have print runs of 100 each.*

VEXT
DC Comics: Mar, 1999 - No. 6, Aug, 1999 ($2.50, limited series)
1-6-Giffen-s. 1-Superman app. 2.50

V FOR VENDETTA
DC Comics: Sept, 1988 - No. 10, May, 1989 ($2.00, maxi-series)

	GD	VG	FN	VF	VF/NM	NM-
1-Alan Moore scripts in all; David Lloyd-a	1	2	3	4	5	7

2-10 5.00
HC (1990) Limited edition 60.00
HC (2005, $29.99, dustjacket) r/series; foreward by Lloyd; promo art and sketches 30.00
Trade paperback (1990, $14.95) 15.00

VIC BRIDGES FAZERS SKETCHBOOK AND FACT FILE
AC Comics: Nov, 1986 ($1.75)
1 3.00

VICE
Image Comics (Top Cow): Nov, 2005 - No. 5 ($2.99)
1-5-Coleite-s/Kirkham-a. 1-Three covers 3.00
1-Code Red Edition; variant Benitez-c 3.00

VIC FLINT(Crime Buster...)(See Authentic Police Cases #10-14 & Fugitives From Justice #2)
St. John Publ. Co.: Aug, 1948 - No. 5, Apr, 1949 (Newspaper reprints; NEA Service)

	GD	VG	FN	VF	VF/NM	NM-
1	14	28	42	76	108	140
2	10	20	30	54	72	90
3-5	9	18	27	47	61	75

VIC FLINT (Crime Buster...)
Argo Publ.: Feb, 1956 - No. 2, May, 1956 (Newspaper reprints)

	GD	VG	FN	VF	VF/NM	NM-
1,2	9	18	27	47	61	75

VIC JORDAN (Also see Big Shot Comics #32)
Civil Service Publ.: April, 1945

	GD	VG	FN	VF	VF/NM	NM-
1-1944 daily newspaper-r	14	28	42	76	108	140

VICKI (Humor)
Atlas/Seaboard Publ.: Feb, 1975 - No. 4, Aug, 1975 (No. 1,2: 68 pgs.)

	GD	VG	FN	VF	VF/NM	NM-
1,2-(68 pgs.)-Reprints Tippy Teen; Good Girl art	4	8	12	26	41	55
3,4 (Low print)	4	8	12	28	44	60

VICKI VALENTINE (...Summer Special #1)
Renegade Press: July, 1985 - No. 4, July, 1986 ($1.70, B&W)
1-4: Woggon, Rausch-a; all have paper dolls. 2-Christmas issue 3.00

VICKY
Ace Magazine: Oct, 1948 - No. 5, June, 1949

	GD	VG	FN	VF	VF/NM	NM-
nn(10/48)-Teenage humor	8	16	24	40	50	60
4(12/48), nn(2/49), 4(4/49), 5(6/49): 5-Dotty app.	7	14	21	35	43	50

VICTORIAN UNDEAD
DC Comics (WildStorm): Jan, 2010 - Present ($2.99)
1-3-Sherlock Holmes vs. Zombies; Edginton-s/Fabbri-a. 1-Two covers (Moore, Coleby) 3.00

VIC TORRY & HIS FLYING SAUCER (Also see Mr. Monster's...#5)
Fawcett Publications: 1950 (one-shot)

	GD	VG	FN	VF	VF/NM	NM-
nn-Book-length saucer story by Powell; photo/painted-c	69	138	207	442	759	1075

VICTORY
Topps Comics: June, 1994 ($2.50, unfinished limited series)
1-Kurt Busiek script; Giffen-c/a; Rob Liefeld variant-c exists 2.50

VICTORY
Image Comics: May, 2003 - No. 4, Feb, 2004 ($2.95, limited series)
1-4: 1-Two covers; Francisco-a. 4-Two covers 3.00

VICTORY (Volume 2)
Image Comics: Aug, 2004 - No. 4, Jan, 2005 ($2.95, limited series)
1-4: 1-Three covers; Francisco-a 3.00

VICTORY COMICS
Hillman Periodicals: Aug, 1941 - No. 4, Dec, 1941 (#1 by Funnies, Inc.)

	GD	VG	FN	VF	VF/NM	NM-
1-The Conqueror by Bill Everett, The Crusader, & Bomber Burns begin; Conqueror's origin in text; Everett-c	300	600	900	1980	3440	4900
2-Everett-c/a	129	258	387	826	1413	2000
3,4	84	168	252	538	919	1300

VIC VERITY MAGAZINE
Vic Verity Publ: 1945; No. 2, Jan?, 1947 - No. 7, Sept, 1946 (A comic book)

	GD	VG	FN	VF	VF/NM	NM-
1-C. C. Beck-c/a	24	48	72	142	234	325
2-Beck-c	15	30	45	85	130	175
3-7: 6-Beck-a. 7-Beck-c	14	28	42	80	115	150

VIDEO JACK
Marvel Comics (Epic Comics): Nov, 1987 - No. 6, Nov, 1988 ($1.25)
1-5 2.50
6-Neal Adams, Keith Giffen, Wrightson, others-a 4.00

VIETNAM JOURNAL
Apple Comics: Nov, 1987 - No. 16, Apr, 1991 ($1.75/$1.95, B&W)
1-16: Don Lomax-c/a/scripts in all, 1-2nd print 3.00
...: Indian Country Vol. 1 (1990, $12.95)-r/#1-4 plus one new story 13.00

VIETNAM JOURNAL: VALLEY OF DEATH
Apple Comics: June, 1994 - No. 2, Aug, 1994 ($2.75, B&W, limited series)
1,2: By Don Lomax 4.00

VIGILANTE, THE (Also see New Teen Titans #23 & Annual V2#2)
DC Comics: Oct, 1983 - No. 50, Feb, 1988 ($1.25, Baxter paper)
1-Origin 3.00
2-16,19-49: 3-Cyborg app. 4-1st app. The Exterminator; Newton-a(p). 6,7-Origin. 20,21-Nightwing app. 35-Origin Mad Bomber. 47-Batman-c/s 2.50
17,18-Alan Moore scripts 4.00
50-Ken Steacy painted-c 3.00
Annual nn, 2 ('85, '86) 2.50

VIGILANTE
DC Comics: Nov, 2005 - No. 6, Apr, 2006 ($2.99, limited series)
1-6-Bruce Jones-s. 1,2,4-6-Ben Oliver-a 3.00

VIGILANTE
DC Comics: Feb, 2009 - No. 12, Jan, 2010 ($2.99)
1-12: 1-Wolfman-s/Leonardi-a. 3-Nightwing app. 5-X-over with Titans and Teen Titans 3.00

VIGILANTE: CITY LIGHTS, PRAIRIE JUSTICE (Also see Action Comics #42, Justice League of America #78, Leading Comics & World's Finest #244)
DC Comics: Nov, 1995 - No. 4, Feb, 1996 ($2.50, limited series)
1-4: James Robinson scripts/Tony Salmons-a/Mark Chiarello-c 2.50
TPB (2009, $19.99) r/#1-4 20.00

VIGILANTES, THE
Dell Publishing Co.: No. 839, Sept, 1957

	GD	VG	FN	VF	VF/NM	NM-
Four Color 839-Movie	7	14	21	47	76	105

VIGILANTE 8: SECOND OFFENSE
Chaos! Comics: Dec, 1999 ($2.95, one-shot)
1-Based on video game 3.00

VIKING
Image Comics: Apr, 2009 - Present ($2.99)
1-4-Ivan Brandon-s/Nic Klein-a 3.00

VIKINGS, THE (Movie)
Dell Publishing Co.: No. 910, May, 1958

	GD	VG	FN	VF	VF/NM	NM-
Four Color 910-Buscema-a, Kirk Douglas photo-c	8	16	24	54	90	125

VILLAINS AND VIGILANTES
Eclipse Comics: Dec, 1986 - No. 4, May, 1987 ($1.50/$1.75, limited series, Baxter paper)
1-4: Based on role-playing game. 2-4 ($1.75-c) 2.50

VILLAINS UNITED (Leads into Infinite Crisis)
DC Comics: July, 2005 - No. 6, Dec, 2005 ($2.95/$2.50, limited series)
1-6-Simone-s/JG Jones-c. 1-The Secret Six and the "Society" form 3.00
...: Infinite Crisis Special 1 (6/06, $4.99) Simone-s/Eaglesham-a 5.00

Vinyl Underground #6 © Spencer & Gane

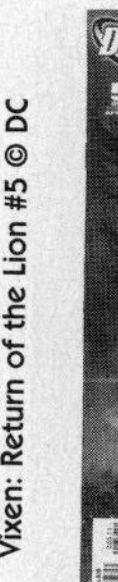

Vixen: Return of the Lion #5 © DC

Voodoo #7 © AJAX

GD 2.0 | VG 4.0 | FN 6.0 | VF 8.0 | VF/NM 9.0 | NM- 9.2

TPB (2005, $12.99) r/#1-6; background info on villains 13.00

VILLAINY OF DOCTOR DOOM, THE
Marvel Comics: 1999 ($17.95, TPB)

nn-Reprints early battle with the Fantastic Four 18.00

VIMANARAMA
DC Comics (Vertigo): Apr, 2005 - No. 3, June, 2005 ($2.95, limited series)

1-3-Grant Morrison-s/Philip Bond-a 3.00
TPB (2005, $12.99) r/#1-3 13.00

VINTAGE MAGNUS (...Robot Fighter)
Valiant: Jan, 1992 - No. 4, Apr, 1992 ($2.25, limited series)

1-4: 1-Layton-c; r/origin from Magnus R.F. #22 2.50

VINYL UNDERGROUND
DC Comics (Vertigo): Dec, 2007 - No. 12, Nov, 2008 ($2.99)

1-12: 1-Spencer-s/Gane & Stewart-a/Phillips-c 3.00
...: Pretty Dead Things TPB ('08, $17.99) r/#6-12 18.00
...: Watching the Detectives TPB ('08, $9.99) r/#1-5; David Laphan intro. 10.00

VIOLATOR (Also see Spawn #2)
Image Comics (Todd McFarlane Prods.): May, 1994 - No. 3, Aug, 1994 ($1.95, lim. series)

1-Alan Moore scripts in all 5.00
2,3: Bart Sears-c(p)/a(p) 4.00

VIOLATOR VS. BADROCK
Image Comics (Extreme Studios): May, 1995 - No. 4, Aug, 1995 ($2.50, limited series)

1-4: Alan Moore scripts in all. 1-1st app Celestine; variant-c (3?) 2.50

VIOLENT MESSIAHS (...: Lamenting Pain on cover for #9-12, numbered as #1-4)
Image Comics: June, 2000 - No. 12 ($2.95)

1-Two covers by Travis Smith and Medina 4.00
1-Tower Records variant edition 5.00
2-8: 5-Flip book sketchbook 3.00
9-12-Lamenting Pain; 2 covers on each 3.00
...: Genesis (12/01, $5.95) r/'97 B&W issue, Wizard 1/2 prologue 6.00
...: The Book of Job TPB (7/02, $24.95) r/#1-8; Foreward by Gossett 25.00

VIP (TV)
TV Comics: 2000 ($2.95, unfinished series)

1-Based on the Pamela Lee (Anderson) TV show; photo-c 3.00

VIPER (TV)
DC Comics: Aug, 1994 - No. 4, Nov, 1994 ($1.95, limited series)

1-4-Adaptation of television show 2.50

VIRGINIAN, THE (TV)
Gold Key: June, 1963

1(10060-306)-Part photo-c of James Drury plus photo back-c
4 8 12 28 44 60

VIRTUA FIGHTER (Video Game)
Marvel Comics: Aug, 1995 (2.95, one-shot)

1-Sega Saturn game 3.00

VIRUS
Dark Horse Comics: 1993 - No. 4, 1993 ($2.50, limited series)

1-4: Ploog-c 2.50

VISION, THE
Marvel Comics: Nov, 1994 - No. 4, Feb, 1995 ($1.75, limited series)

1-4 2.50

VISION, THE (AVENGERS ICONS: ...)
Marvel Comics: Oct, 2002 - No. 4, Jan, 2003 ($2.99, limited series)

1-4-Geoff Johns-s/Ivan Reis-a 3.00
...: Yesterday and Tomorrow TPB (2005, $14.99) r/#1-4 & Avengers #57 (1st app.) 15.00

VISION AND THE SCARLET WITCH, THE (See Marvel Fanfare)
Marvel Comics Group: Nov, 1982 - No. 4, Feb, 1983 (Limited series)

1-4: 2-Nuklo & Future Man app. 3.00

VISION AND THE SCARLET WITCH, THE
Marvel Comics Group: Oct, 1985 - No. 12, Sept, 1986 (Maxi-series)

V2#1-12: 1-Origin; 1st app. in Avengers #57. 2-West Coast Avengers x-over 2.50

VISIONS
Vision Publications: 1979 - No. 5, 1983 (B&W, fanzine)

1-Flaming Carrot begins(1st app?); N. Adams-c 5 10 15 32 51 70

GD 2.0 | VG 4.0 | FN 6.0 | VF 8.0 | VF/NM 9.0 | NM- 9.2

2-N. Adams, Rogers-a; Gulacy back-c; signed & numbered to 2000
4 8 12 28 44 60
3-Williamson-c(p); Steranko back-c 3 6 9 20 30 40
4-Flaming Carrot-c & info. 3 6 9 20 30 40
5-1 pg. Flaming Carrot 3 6 9 14 20 25

NOTE: ***Eisner** a-4. **Miller** a-4. **Starlin** a-3. **Williamson** a-5. After #4, Visions became an annual publication of The Atlanta Fantasy Fair.*

VISITOR, THE
Valiant/Acclaim Comics (Valiant): Apr, 1995 - No. 13, Nov, 1995 ($2.50)

1-13: 8-Harbinger revealed. 13-Visitor revealed to be Sting from Harbinger 2.50

VISITOR VS. THE VALIANT UNIVERSE, THE
Valiant: Feb, 1995 - No. 2, Mar, 1995 ($2.95, limited series)

1,2 3.00

VIX
Image Comics: Jun, 2008 ($3.50)

1-Hosely-s/Humphreys-a 3.50

VIXEN: RETURN OF THE LION (From Justice League of America)
DC Comics: Dec, 2008 - No. 5, Apr, 2009 ($2.99, limited series)

1-5-G. Willow Wilson-s/Cafu-a; Justice League app. 3.00
TPB (2009, $17.99) r/#1-5 18.00

VOGUE (Also see Youngblood)
Image Comics (Extreme Studios): Oct, 1995 - No.3, Jan, 1996 ($2.50, limited series)

1-3: 1-Liefeld-c, 1-Variant-c 2.50

VOID INDIGO (Also see Marvel Graphic Novel)
Marvel Comics (Epic Comics): 11/84 - No. 2, 3/85 ($1.50, direct sales, unfinished series, mature)

1,2: Cont'd from Marvel G.N.; graphic sex & violence 2.50

VOLCANIC REVOLVER
Oni Press: Dec, 1998 - No. 3, Mar, 1999 ($2.95, B&W, limited series)

1-3: Scott Morse-s/a 3.00
TPB (12/99, $9.95, digest size) r/#1-3 and Oni Double Feature #7 prologue 10.00

VOLTRON (TV)
Modern Publishing: 1985 - No. 3, 1985 (75¢, limited series)

1-3: Ayers-a in all 5.00

VOLTRON: A LEGEND FORGED (TV)
Devils Due Publishing: Jul, 2008 - No. 5, Apr, 2009 ($3.50)

1-5-Blaylock-s/Bear-a; 4 covers 3.50

VOLTRON: DEFENDER OF THE UNIVERSE (TV)
Image Comics: No. 0, May, 2003 - No. 5, Sept, 2003 ($2.50)

0-Jolley-s/Brooks-a; character pin-ups with background info 2.50
1-5-($2.95) 1-Three covers by Norton, Brooks and Andrews; Norton-a 3.00
...: Revelations TPB (2004, $11.95, digest-sized) r/#1-5; cover gallery 12.00

VOLTRON: DEFENDER OF THE UNIVERSE (TV)
Image Comics: Jan, 2004 - No. 11, Dec, 2004 ($2.95)

1-11: 1-Jolley-s; wraparound-c 3.00

VOODA (Jungle Princess) (Formerly Voodoo) (See Crown Comics)
Ajax-Farrell (Four Star Publications): No. 20, April, 1955 - No. 22, Aug, 1955

20-Baker-c/a (r/Seven Seas #6) 39 78 117 240 395 550
21,22-Baker-a plus Kamen/Baker story, Kimbo Boy of Jungle, & Baker-c(p) in all.
22-Censored Jo-Jo-r (name Powaa) 36 72 108 211 343 475

NOTE: *#20-22 each contain one heavily censored-r of South Sea Girl by **Baker** from Seven Seas Comics with name changed to Vooda. #20-r/Seven Seas #6; #21-r/#4; #22-r/#3.*

VOODOO (Weird Fantastic Tales) (Vooda #20 on)
Ajax-Farrell (Four Star Publ.): May, 1952 - No. 19, Jan-Feb, 1955

1-South Sea Girl-r by Baker 60 120 180 381 653 925
2-Rulah story-r plus South Sea Girl from Seven Seas #2 by Baker (name changed from Alani to El'nee) 49 98 147 309 522 735
3-Bakerish-a; man stabbed in face 40 80 120 246 411 575
4,8-Baker-r. 8-Severed head panels 40 80 120 246 411 575
5-7,9,10: 5-Nazi death camp story (flaying alive). 6-Severed head panels
36 72 108 211 343 475
11-18: 14-Zombies take over America. 15-Opium drug story-r/Ellery Queen #3. 16-Post nuclear world story.17-Electric chair panels
31 62 93 182 296 410
19-Bondage-c; Baker-r(2)/Seven Seas #5 w/minor changes & #1, heavily modified; last pre-code; contents & covers change to jungle theme

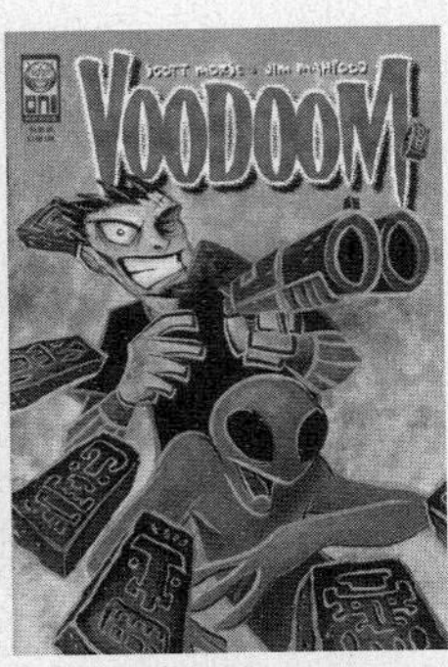

Voodoom #1 © Morse & Mahfood

Wagon Train #9 © DELL

Walking Dead #60 © R. Kirkman

	GD 2.0	VG 4.0	FN 6.0	VF 8.0	VF/NM 9.0	NM- 9.2
	39	78	117	231	378	525
Annual 1(1952, 25¢, 100 pgs.)-Baker-a (scarce)	129	258	387	826	1413	2000

VOODOO
Image Comics (WildStorm): Nov, 1997 - No. 4, Mar, 1998 ($2.50, lim. series)

	GD	VG	FN	VF	VF/NM	NM-
1-4:Alan Moore-s in all; Hughes-c. 2-4-Rio-a						2.50
1-Platinum Ed						10.00
Dancing on the Dark TPB ('99, $9.95) r/#1-4						10.00
...-Zealot: Skin Trade (8/95, $4.95)						5.00

VOODOO (See Tales of...)

VOODOO CHILD (Weston Cage & Nicolas Cage's...)
Virgin Comics: July, 2007 - No. 6, Dec, 2007 ($2.99)

	GD	VG	FN	VF	VF/NM	NM-
1-6: 1-Mike Carey-s/Dean Hyrapiet-a; covers by Hyrapiet & Templesmith						3.00
Vol. 1 TPB (1/08, $14.99) r/#1-6; variant covers; intro by Weston Cage & Nicolas Cage						15.00

VOODOOM
Oni Press: June, 2000 ($4.95, B&W)

	GD	VG	FN	VF	VF/NM	NM-
1-Scott Morse-s/Jim Mahfood-a						5.00

VORTEX
Vortex Publs.: Nov, 1982 - No. 15, 1988 (No month) ($1.50/$1.75, B&W)

	GD	VG	FN	VF	VF/NM	NM-
1 ($1.95)-Peter Hsu-a; Ken Steacy-c; nudity	1	2	3	5	7	9
2,12: 2-1st app. Mister X (on-c only). 12-Sam Kieth-a						6.00
3-11,13-15						3.00

VORTEX
Comico: 1991 - No. 2? ($2.50, limited series)

	GD	VG	FN	VF	VF/NM	NM-
1,2: Heroes from The Elementals						2.50

VOYAGE TO THE BOTTOM OF THE SEA (Movie, TV)
Dell Publishing Co./Gold Key: No. 1230, Sept-Nov, 1961; Dec, 1964 - #16, Apr, 1970 (Painted-c)

	GD	VG	FN	VF	VF/NM	NM-
Four Color 1230 (1961)	10	20	30	71	126	180
10133-412(#1, 12/64)(Gold Key)	8	16	24	52	86	120
2(7/65) - 5: Photo back-c, 1-5	5	10	15	34	55	75
6-14	4	8	12	28	44	60
15,16-Reprints	3	6	9	18	27	35

VOYAGE TO THE DEEP
Dell Publishing Co.: Sept-Nov, 1962 - No. 4, Nov-Jan, 1964 (Painted-c)

	GD	VG	FN	VF	VF/NM	NM-
1	5	10	15	34	55	75
2-4	4	8	12	24	37	50

WACKO
Ideal Publ. Corp.: Sept, 1980 - No. 3, Oct, 1981 (84 pgs., B&W, magazine)

	GD	VG	FN	VF	VF/NM	NM-
1-3	2	4	6	8	11	14

WACKY ADVENTURES OF CRACKY (Also see Gold Key Spotlight)
Gold Key: Dec, 1972 - No. 12, Sept, 1975

	GD	VG	FN	VF	VF/NM	NM-
1	3	6	9	14	20	26
2	2	4	6	10	14	18
3-12	2	4	6	8	10	12

(See March of Comics #405, 424, 436, 448)

WACKY DUCK (...Comics #3-6; formerly Dopey Duck; Justice Comics #7 on) (See Film Funnies)
Marvel Comics (NPP): No. 3, Fall, 1946 - No. 6, Summer, 1947; Aug, 1948 - No. 2, Oct, 1948

	GD	VG	FN	VF	VF/NM	NM-
3	23	46	69	136	223	310
4-Infinity-c	20	40	60	120	195	270
5,6(1947)-Becomes Justice comics	18	36	54	105	165	225
1(1948)	18	36	54	103	165	220
2(1948)	14	28	42	81	118	155
I.W. Reprint #1,2,7('58): 1-r/Wacky Duck #6	2	4	6	9	13	16
Super Reprint #10(I.W. on-c, Super-inside)	2	4	6	9	13	16

WACKY QUACKY (See Wisco)

WACKY RACES (TV)
Gold Key: Aug, 1969 - No. 7, Apr, 1972 (Hanna-Barbera)

	GD	VG	FN	VF	VF/NM	NM-
1	5	10	15	34	55	75
2-7	4	8	12	22	34	45

WACKY SQUIRREL (Also see Dark Horse Presents)
Dark Horse Comics: Oct, 1987 - No. 4, 1988 ($1.75, B&W)

	GD	VG	FN	VF	VF/NM	NM-
1-4: 4-Superman parody						2.50
Halloween Adventure Special 1 (1987, $2.00)						2.50
Summer Fun Special 1 (1988, $2.00)						2.50

WACKY WITCH (Also see Gold Key Spotlight)
Gold Key: March, 1971 - No. 21, Dec, 1975

	GD	VG	FN	VF	VF/NM	NM-
1	4	8	12	24	37	50
2	3	6	9	14	20	26
3-10	2	4	6	10	14	18
11-21	2	4	6	8	10	12

(See March of Comics #374, 398, 410, 422, 434, 446, 458, 470, 482)

WACKY WOODPECKER (See Two Bit the...)
I. W. Enterprises/Super Comics: 1958; 1963

	GD	VG	FN	VF	VF/NM	NM-
I.W. Reprint #1,2,7 (nd-reprints Two Bit...): 7-r/Two-Bit, the Wacky Woodpecker #1.	2	4	6	8	11	14
Super Reprint #10('63): 10-r/Two-Bit, The Wacky Woodpecker #?	2	4	6	8	11	14

WAGON TRAIN (1st Series) (TV) (See Western Roundup under Dell Giants)
Dell Publishing Co.: No. 895, Mar, 1958 - No. 13, Apr-June, 1962 (All photo-c)

	GD	VG	FN	VF	VF/NM	NM-
Four Color 895 (#1)	10	20	30	71	126	180
Four Color 971(#2),1019(#3)	7	14	21	45	73	100
4(1-3/60),6-13	6	12	18	39	62	85
5-Toth-a	6	12	18	43	69	95

WAGON TRAIN (2nd Series)(TV)
Gold Key: Jan, 1964 - No. 4, Oct, 1964 (All front & back photo-c)

	GD	VG	FN	VF	VF/NM	NM-
1-Tufts-a in all	5	10	15	32	51	70
2-4	4	8	12	24	37	50

WAITING PLACE, THE
Slave Labor Graphics: Apr, 1997 - No. 6, Sept, 1997 ($2.95)

	GD	VG	FN	VF	VF/NM	NM-
1-6-Sean McKeever-s						3.00
Vol. 2 - 1(11/99), 2-11						3.00
12-($4.95)						5.00

WAITING ROOM WILLIE (See Sad Case of...)

WAKE THE DEAD
IDW Publ.: Sept, 2003 - No. 5, Mar, 2004 ($3.99, limited series)

	GD	VG	FN	VF	VF/NM	NM-
1-5-Steve Niles-s/Chee-a						4.00
TPB (6/04, $19.99) r/series; intro. by Michael Dougherty; embossed die cut cover						20.00

WALK IN (Dave Stewart's ...)
Virgin Comics: Dec, 2006 - No. 6, May, 2007 ($2.99)

	GD	VG	FN	VF	VF/NM	NM-
1-6: 1-5-Parker-s/Padlekar-a. 6-Parker-a						3.00

WALKING DEAD, THE
Image Comics: Oct, 2003 - Present ($2.95/$2.99, B&W)

	GD	VG	FN	VF	VF/NM	NM-
1-Robert Kirkman-s in all/Tony Moore-a						40.00
1 Special Edition (5/08, $3.99) r/#1; Kirkman afterword; original script and proposal						4.00
2						15.00
3-10: 3-6-Tony Moore-a. 7-Charlie Adlard-a begins						5.00
11-70: 61-Preview of Chew						3.00
... Book 1 HC (2006, $29.99) r/#1-12; sketch pages, cover gallery; Kirkman afterword						30.00
... Book 2 HC (2006, $29.99) r/#13-24; sketch pages, cover gallery						30.00
... Book 3 HC (2007, $29.99) r/#25-36; sketch pages, cover gallery						30.00
...Vol. 1: Days Gone Bye (5/04, $9.95, TPB) r/#1-4						10.00
...Vol. 2: Miles Behind Us (10/04, $12.95, TPB) r/#7-12						13.00
...Vol. 3: Safety Behind Bars (2005, $12.95, TPB) r/#13-18						13.00
...Vol. 4: The Heart's Desire (2005, $12.99, TPB) r/#19-24						13.00
...Vol. 5: The Best Defense (2006, $12.99, TPB) r/#25-30						13.00
...Vol. 6: This Sorrowful Life (2007, $12.99, TPB) r/#31-36						13.00
...Vol. 7: The Calm Before (2007, $12.99, TPB) r/#37-42						13.00

WALL•E (Based on the Disney/Pixar movie)
BOOM! Studios: No. 0, Nov, 2009 - Present ($2.99)

	GD	VG	FN	VF	VF/NM	NM-
0-3: Prequel; J. Torres-s						3.00

WALLY (Teen-age)
Gold Key: Dec, 1962 - No. 4, Sept, 1963

	GD	VG	FN	VF	VF/NM	NM-
1	3	6	9	21	32	42
2-4	3	6	9	17	25	32

WALLY THE WIZARD
Marvel Comics (Star Comics): Apr, 1985 - No. 12, Mar, 1986 (Children's comic)

	GD	VG	FN	VF	VF/NM	NM-
1-12: Bob Bolling a-1,3; c-1,9,11,12						5.00
1-Variant with "Star Chase" game on last page and inside back-c						9.00

WALLY WOOD'S T.H.U.N.D.E.R. AGENTS (See Thunder Agents)
Deluxe Comics: Nov, 1984 - No. 5, Oct, 1986 ($2.00, 52 pgs.)

Walt Disney Comics Digest #15 © DIS

Walt Disney Christmas Parade #1 © DIS

Walt Disney's Comics and Stories #57 © DIS

GD 2.0 | VG 4.0 | FN 6.0 | VF 8.0 | VF/NM 9.0 | NM- 9.2

1-5: 5-Jerry Ordway-c/a in Wood style 6.00

NOTE: ***Anderson** a-2i, 3i. **Buckler** a-4. **Ditko** a-3, 4. **Giffen** a-1p-4p. **Perez** a-1p, 2, 4; c-1-4.*

WALT DISNEY CHRISTMAS PARADE (Also see Christmas Parade)
Whitman Publ. Co. (Golden Press): Wint, 1977 ($1.95, cardboard-c, 224 pgs.)

11191-Barks-r/Christmas in Disneyland #1, Dell Christmas Parade #9 & Dell Giant #53 4 8 12 26 41 55

WALT DISNEY COMICS DIGEST
Gold Key: June, 1968 - No. 57, Feb, 1976 (50¢, digest size)

1-Reprints Uncle Scrooge #5; 192 pgs. 7 14 21 50 83 115
2-4-Barks-r 5 10 15 34 55 75
5-Daisy Duck by Barks (8 pgs.); last published story by Barks (art only) plus 21 pg. Scrooge-r by Barks 8 16 24 52 86 120
6-13-All Barks-r 4 8 12 22 34 45
14,15 3 6 9 16 23 30
16-Reprints Donald Duck #26 by Barks 3 6 9 21 32 42
17-20-Barks-r 3 6 9 18 27 35
21-31,33,35-37-Barks-r; 24-Toth Zorro 3 6 9 16 23 30
32,41,45,47-49 2 4 6 11 16 20
34,38,39: 34-Reprints 4-Color #318. 38-Reprints Christmas in Disneyland #1. 39-Two Barks-r/WDC&S #272, 4-Color #1073 plus Toth Zorro-r 3 6 9 16 23 30
40-Mickey Mouse-r by Gottfredson 2 4 6 13 18 22
42,43-Barks-r 2 4 6 13 18 22
44-(Has Gold Key emblem, 50¢)-Reprints 1st story of 4-Color #29,256,275,282 5 10 15 32 51 70
44-Republished in 1976 by Whitman; not identical to original; a bit smaller, blank back-c, 69¢ 3 6 9 16 23 30
46,50,52-Barks-r. 52-Barks-r/WDC&S #161,132 2 4 6 11 16 20
51-Reprints 4-Color #71 3 6 9 16 23 30
53-55: 53-Reprints Dell Giant #30. 54-Reprints Donald Duck Beach Party #2. 55-Reprints Dell Giant #49 2 4 6 10 14 18
56-r/Uncle Scrooge #32 (Barks) 2 4 6 13 18 22
57-r/Mickey Mouse Almanac('57) & two Barks stories 2 4 6 11 16 20

NOTE: *Toth a-52r. #1-10, 196 pgs.; #11-41, 164 pgs.; #42 on, 132 pgs. Old issues were being reprinted & distributed by Whitman in 1976.*

WALT DISNEY GIANT (Disney)
Bruce Hamilton Co. (Gladstone): Sept, 1995 - No. 7, Sept, 1996 ($2.25, bi-monthly, 48 pgs.)

1-7: 1-Scrooge McDuck in the Yukon; Rosa-c/a/scripts plus r/F.C. #218. 2-Uncle Scrooge-r by Barks plus 17 pg. text story. 3-Donald the Mighty Duck; Rosa-c; Barks & Rosa-r. 4-Mickey and Goofy; new-a (story actually stars Goofy. Mickey Mouse by Caesar Ferioli; Donald Duck by Giorgio Cavazzano (1st in U.S.). 6-Uncle Scrooge & the Jr. Woodchucks; new-a and Barks-r. 7-Uncle Scrooge-r by Barks plus new-a 3.00

NOTE: *Series was initially solicited as Uncle Walt's Collectory. Issue #8 was advertised, but later cancelled.*

WALT DISNEY PAINT BOOK SERIES
Whitman Publ. Co.: No dates; circa 1975 (Beware! Has 1930s copyright dates) (79¢-c, 52 pgs. B&W, treasury-sized) (Coloring books, text stories & comics-r)

#2052 (Whitman #886-r) Mickey Mouse & Donald Duck Gag Book 3 6 9 21 32 42
#2053 (Whitman #677-r) 3 6 9 21 32 42
#2054 (Whitman #670-r) Donald-c 4 8 12 23 36 48
#2055 (Whitman #627-r) Mickey-c 3 6 9 21 32 42
#2056 (Whitman #660-r) Buckey Bug-c 3 6 9 19 29 38
#2057 (Whitman #887-r) Mickey & Donald-c 3 6 9 21 32 42

WALT DISNEY PRESENTS (TV)(Disney)
Dell Publishing Co.: No. 997, 6-8/59 - No. 6, 12-2/1960-61; No. 1181, 4-5/61 (All photo-c)

Four Color 997 (#1) 7 14 21 49 80 110
2(12-2/60)-The Swamp Fox(origin), Elfego Baca, Texas John Slaughter (Disney TV show) begin 5 10 15 32 51 70
3-6: 5-Swamp Fox by Warren Tufts 5 10 15 30 48 65
Four Color 1181-Texas John Slaughter 7 14 21 47 76 105

WALT DISNEY'S CHRISTMAS PARADE (Also see Christmas Parade)
Gladstone: Winter, 1988; No. 2, Winter, 1989 ($2.95, 100 pgs.)

1-Barks-r/painted-c 2 4 6 8 10 12
2-Barks-r 1 2 3 5 7 9

WALT DISNEY'S CHRISTMAS PARADE
Gemstone Publishing: Dec, 2003; 2004, 2005, 2006,2008 ($8.95/$9.50, prestige format)

1-4: 1-Reprints and 3 new European holiday stories. 2-All reprints. 3-Reprints and 2 new stories, 4-Reprints and 5 new stories 9.00
5-($9.50) R/Uncle Scrooge #47 and European stories 9.50

WALT DISNEY'S COMICS AND STORIES (Cont. of Mickey Mouse Magazine) (#1-30 contain Donald Duck newspaper reprints) (Titled "Comics And Stories" #264 to #?; titled "Walt Disney's Comics And Stories" #511 on)
Dell Publishing Co./Gold Key #264-473/Whitman #474-510/Gladstone #511-547/ Disney Comics #548-585/Gladstone #586-633/Gemstone Publishing #634-698/ Boom! Kids #699-on: 10/40 - #263, 8/62; #264, 10/62 - #510, 7/84; #511, 10/86 - #633, 2/99; #634, 7/03 - #698, 11/08; #699, 10/09 - Present

NOTE: The whole number can always be found at the bottom of the title page in the lower left-hand or right hand panel.

1(V1#1-c; V2#1-indicia)-Donald Duck strip-r by Al Taliaferro & Gottfredson's Mickey Mouse begin 2200 4400 6600 15,400 27,700 40,000
2 838 1676 2514 6117 10,809 15,500
3 360 720 1080 2520 4410 6300
4-X-Mas-c; 1st Huey, Dewey & Louie-c this title (See Mickey Mouse Magazine V4#2 for 1st-c ever) 277 554 831 1759 3030 4300
4-Special promotional, complimentary issue; cover same except one corner was blanked out & boxed in to identify the giveaway (not a paste-over). This special pressing was probably sent out to former subscribers to Mickey Mouse Mag. whose subscriptions had expired. (Very rare-5 known copies) 389 778 1167 2723 4762 6800
5-Goofy-c 226 452 678 1446 2473 3500
6-10: 8-Only Clarabelle Cow-c. 9-Taliaferro-c (1st) 187 374 561 1197 2049 2900
11-14: 11-Huey, Dewey & Louie-c/app. 142 284 426 909 1555 2200
15-17: 15-The 3 Little Kittens (17 pgs.). 16-The 3 Little Pigs (29 pgs.); X-Mas-c. 17-The Ugly Duckling (4 pgs.) 123 246 369 787 1344 1900
18-21 110 220 330 704 1202 1700
22-30: 22-Flag-c. 24-The Flying Gauchito (1st original comic book story done for WDC&S). 27-Jose Carioca by Carl Buettner (2nd original story in WDC&S) 92 184 276 584 1005 1425
31-New Donald Duck stories by Carl Barks begin (See F.C. #9 for 1st Barks Donald Duck) 389 778 1167 2723 4762 6800
32-Barks-a 226 452 678 1446 2473 3500
33-Barks-a; infinity-c 158 316 474 1003 1727 2450
34-Gremlins by Walt Kelly begin, end #41; Barks-a 123 246 369 787 1344 1900
35,36-Barks-a 116 232 348 742 1271 1800
37-Donald Duck by Jack Hannah 68 134 204 435 743 1050
38-40-Barks-a. 39-X-Mas-c. 40,41-Gremlins by Kelly 77 154 231 493 847 1200
41-50-Barks-a. 43-Seven Dwarfs-c app. (4/44). 45-50-Nazis in Gottfredson's Mickey Mouse Stories 65 130 195 416 708 1000
51-60-Barks-a. 51-X-Mas-c. 52-Li'l Bad Wolf begins, ends #203 (not in #55). 58-Kelly flag-c 33 66 99 254 490 725
61-70: Barks-a. 61-Dumbo story. 63,64-Pinocchio stories. 63-Cover swipe from New Funnies #94. 64-X-Mas-c. 65-Pluto story. 66-Infinity-c. 67,68-Mickey Mouse Sunday-r by Bill Wright 30 60 90 218 422 625
71-80: Barks-a. 75-77-Brer Rabbit stories, no Mickey Mouse. 76-X-Mas-c 24 48 72 175 338 500
81-87,89,90: Barks-a. 82-Goofy-c. 82-84-Bongo stories. 86-90-Goofy & Agnes app. 89-Chip 'n' Dale story 20 40 60 146 283 420
88-1st app. Gladstone Gander by Barks (1/48) 24 48 72 176 343 510
91-97,99: Barks-a. 95-1st WDC&S Barks-c. 96-No Mickey Mouse; Little Toot begins, ends #97. 99-X-Mas-c 19 38 57 133 259 385
98-1st Uncle Scrooge app. in WDC&S (11/48) 31 62 93 236 456 675
100-(1/49)-Barks-a 22 44 66 157 304 450
101-110-Barks-a. 107-Taliaferro-c; Donald acquires super powers 16 32 48 115 220 325
111,114,117-All Barks-a 14 28 42 100 188 275
112-Drug (ether) issue (Donald Duck) 14 28 42 97 181 265
113,115,116,118-123: No Barks. 116-Dumbo x-over. 121-Grandma Duck begins, ends #168; not in #135,142,146,155 10 20 30 73 129 185
124,126-130-All Barks-a. 124-X-Mas-c 12 24 36 85 155 225
125-1st app. Junior Woodchucks (2/51); Barks-a 16 32 48 115 220 325
131,133,135-137,139-All Barks-a 11 22 33 80 145 210
132-Barks-a(2) (D. Duck & Grandma Duck) 12 24 36 83 152 220
134-Intro. & 1st app. The Beagle Boys (11/51) 19 38 57 135 263 390
138-Classic Scrooge money story 16 32 48 112 214 315
140-(5/52)-1st app. Gyro Gearloose by Barks; 2nd Barks Uncle Scrooge-c; 3rd Uncle Scrooge cover app. 19 38 57 135 263 390
141-150-All Barks-a. 143-Little Hiawatha begins, ends #151,159 10 20 30 67 116 165
151-170-All Barks-a 9 18 27 60 100 140
171-199-All Barks-a 8 16 24 54 90 125
200 8 16 24 58 97 135
201-240: All Barks-a. 204-Chip 'n' Dale & Scamp begin 7 14 21 47 76 105
241-283: Barks-a. 241-Dumbo x-over. 247-Gyro Gearloose begins, ends #274.

Walt Disney's Comics and Stories #521 © DIS

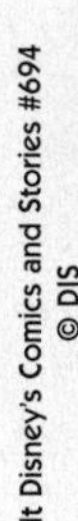

Walt Disney's Comics and Stories #694 © DIS

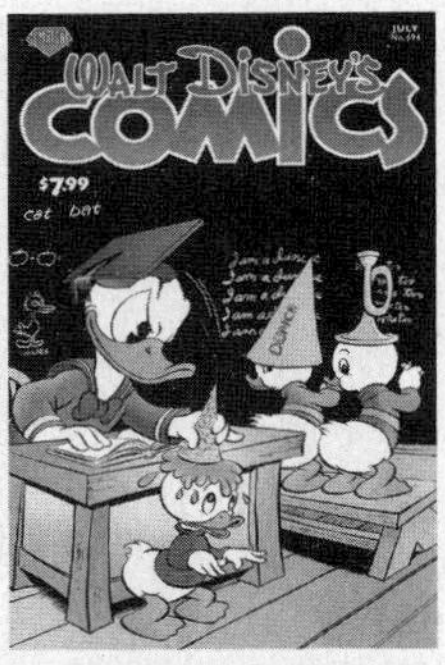

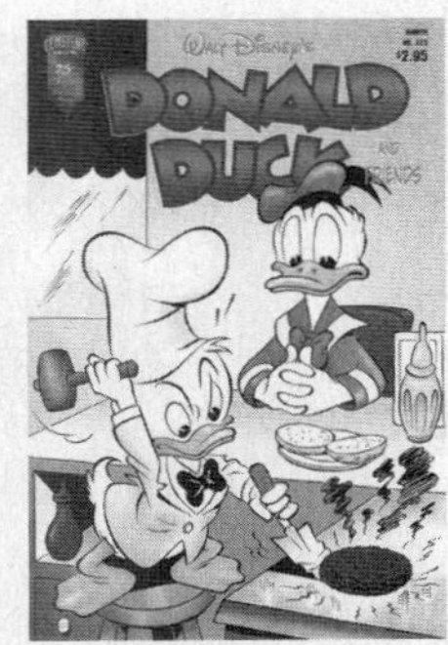

Walt Disney's Donald Duck and Friends #325 © DIS

	GD 2.0	VG 4.0	FN 6.0	VF 8.0	VF/NM 9.0	NM- 9.2
256-Ludwig Von Drake begins, ends #274	6	12	18	41	66	90
284,285,287,290,295,296,309-311-Not by Barks	3	6	9	20	30	40
286,288,291-294,297,298,308-All Barks stories; 293-Grandma Duck's Farm Friends. 297-Gyro Gearloose. 298-Daisy Duck's Diary-r	4	8	12	24	37	50
289-Annette-c & back-c & story; Barks-s	4	8	12	28	44	60
299-307-All contain early Barks-r (#43-117). 305-Gyro Gearloose	4	8	12	26	41	55
312-Last Barks issue with original story	4	8	12	26	41	55
313-315,317-327,329-334,336-341	3	6	9	16	22	28
316-Last issue published during life of Walt Disney	3	6	9	16	22	28
328,335,342-350-Barks-r	3	6	9	16	22	28
351-360-With posters inside; Barks reprints (2 versions of each with & without posters)	4	8	12	26	41	55
351-360-Without posters...	3	6	9	14	19	24
361-400-Barks-r	3	6	9	14	20	26
401-429-Barks-r	3	6	9	14	19	24
430,433,437,438,441,444,445,466-No Barks	2	4	6	8	11	14
431,432,434-436,439,440,442,443-Barks-r	2	4	6	10	14	18
446-465,467-473-Barks-r	2	4	6	9	13	16
474(3/80),475-478 (Whitman)	3	6	9	14	19	24
479(8/80),481(10/80)-484(1/81) pre-pack only	5	10	15	30	48	65
480 (8-12/80)-(Very low distribution)	10	20	30	70	123	175
484 (1/81, 40¢-c) Cover price error variant (scarce)	5	10	15	34	55	75
485-499: 494-r/WDC&S #98	2	4	6	11	16	20
500-510 (All #90011 on-c; pre-packs): 500(4/83), 501(5/83), 502&503(7/83), 504-506(all 8/83), 507(4/84), 508(5/84), 509(6/84), 510(7/84). 506-No Barks	2	4	6	13	18	22
511-Donald Duck by Daan Jippes (1st in U.S.; in all through #518); Gyro Gearloose Barks-r begins (in most through #547); Wuzzles by Disney Studio (1st by Gladstone)	3	6	9	17	25	32
512,513	2	4	6	10	14	18
514-516,520	2	4	6	8	10	12
517-519,521,522,525,527,529,530,532-546: 518-Infinity-c. 522-r/1st app. Huey, Dewey & Louie from D. Duck Sunday. 535-546-Barks-r. 537-1st Donald Duck by William Van Horn in WDC&S. 541-545-52 pgs. 546,547-68 pgs. 546-Kelly-r. 547-Rosa-a						6.00
523,524,526,528,531,547: Rosa-s/a in all. 523-1st Rosa 10 pager	2	4	6	9	12	15
548-($1.50, 6/90)-1st Disney issue; new-a; no M. Mouse	1	2	3	4	5	7
549,551-570,572,573,577-579,581,584 ($1.50): 549-Barks-r begin, ends #585, not in #555, 556, & 564. 551-r/1 story from F.C. #29. 556,578-r/Mickey Mouse Cheerios Premium by Dick Moores. 562,563,568-570, 572, 581-Gottfredson strip-r. 570-Valentine issue; has Mickey/Minnie centerfold. 584-Taliaferro strip-r						4.00
550 ($2.25, 52 pgs.)-Donald Duck by Barks; previously printed only in The Netherlands (1st time in U.S.); r/Chip 'n Dale & Scamp from #204						5.00
571-($2.95, 68 pgs)-r/Donald Duck's Atom Bomb by Barks from 1947 Cheerios premium						6.00
574-576,580,582,583 ($2.95, 68 pgs.): 574-r/1st Pinocchio Sunday strip (1939-40). 575-Gottfredson-r, Pinocchio-r/WDC&S #64. 580-r/Donald Duck's 1st app. from Silly Symphony strip 12/16/34 by Taliaferro; Gottfredson strip-r begin; not in #584 & 600. 582,583-r/Mickey Mouse on Sky Island from WDC&S #1,2						5.00
585 ($2.50, 52 pgs.)-r/#140; Barks-r/WDC&S #140						5.00
586,587: 586-Gladstone issues begin again; begin $1.50-c; Gottfredson-r begins (not in #600). 587-Donald Duck by William Van Horn begins						4.00
588-597: 588,591-599-Donald Duck by William Van Horn						3.00
598,599 ($1.95, 36 pgs.): 598-r/1st drawings of Mickey Mouse by Ub Iwerks						3.00
600 ($2.95, 48 pgs.)-L.B. Cole-c(r)/WDC&S #1; Barks-r/WDC&S #32 plus Rosa, Jippes, Van Horn-r and new Rosa centerspread						4.00
601-611 ($5.95, 64 pgs., squarebound, bi-monthly): 601-Barks-c, r/Mickey Mouse V1#1, Rosa-a/scripts. 602-Rosa-c. 604-Taliaferro strip-r/1st Silly Symphony Sundays from 1932. 604,605-Jippes-a. 605-Walt Kelly-c; Gottfredson "Mickey Mouse Outwits the Phantom Blot" r/F.C. #16						6.00
612-633 ($6.95): 633-(2/99) Last Gladstone issue						7.00
634-675: 634-(7/03) First Gemstone issue; William Van Horn-c. 666-Mickey's Inferno						7.00
676-681: 676-Begin $7.50-c. 677-Bucky Bug's 75th Anniversary						7.50
682-698-($7.99)						8.00
699-704: 699-(9/09, $2.99) First BOOM! Kids issue. 700-Back-up story w/Van Horn-a						3.00

NOTE: *(#1-38, 68 pgs.; #39-42, 60 pgs.; #43-57, 61-134, 143-168, 446, 447, 52 pgs.; #58-60, 135-142, 169-540, 36 pgs.)*

NOTE: ***Barks*** *art in all issues #31 on, except where noted; c-95, 96, 104, 108, 109, 130-172, 174-178, 183, 198-200, 204, 206-209, 212-216, 218, 220, 226, 228-233, 235-238, 240-243, 247, 250, 253, 256, 260, 261, 276-283, 288-292, 295-298, 301, 303, 304, 306, 307, 309, 310, 313-316, 319, 321, 322, 324, 326, 328, 329, 331, 332, 334, 341, 342, 350, 351, 527r, 530r, 540(never before published), 546r, 557-586r(most), 596p, 601p.* ***Kelly*** *a-24p, 34-41, 43; r-522-524, 546, 547, 582, 583; covers(most)-34-118, 531r, 537r, 541r-543r, 562r, 571r, 605r. Walt Disney's Comics & Stories featured Mickey Mouse serials which were in practically every issue from #1 through #394 and #511 to date. The titles of the serials, along with the issues they are in, are listed in previous editions of this price guide.* ***Floyd Gottfredson*** *Mickey Mouse serials in issues #1-14, 18-66, 69-74, 78-100, 128, 562, 563, 568-572, 582, 583, 586-599 , 601-603 , 605-present , plus "Service with a Smile" in #13; "Mickey Mouse in a Warplant" (3 pgs.), and "Pluto Catches a Nazi Spy" (4 pgs.) in #62; "Mystery Next Door", #93; "Sunken Treasure", #94; "Aunt Marissa", #95 (r in #575); "Gangland", #98 (r in #562); "Thanksgiving Dinner", #99 (r in #567); and "The Talking Dog", #100 (r in #563); "Morty's Escapade," #128. "The Brave Little Tailor", #580; "Introducing Mickey Mouse Movies ", #581; Circus Roustabout, #585; "Rumplewatt the Giant", #604. Mickey Mouse by* ***Paul Murry*** *#152-547 except 155-57 (****Dick Moore****), 327-29 (****Tony Strobl****), 348-50 (****Jack Manning****), 533 (****Bill Wright****).* ***Don Rosa*** *story/a-523, 524, 526, 528, 531, 547, 601-present.* ***Al Taliaferro*** *Silly Symphonies in #5-"Three Little Pigs"; #13-"Birds of a Feather"; #14-"The Boarding School Mystery"; #15-"Cookieland" and "Three Little Kittens"; #16-"The Practical Pig"; #17-"The Ugly Duckling"; "The Wise Little Hen" in #580; and "Ambrose the Robber Kitten"; #19-"Penguin Isle"; and "Bucky Bug" in #20-23, 25, 26, 28 (one continuous story from 1932-34; first 2 pgs. not Taliaferro).* ***Gottfredson*** *strip r-562, 563, 568-572, 581, 585, 586, 590.* ***Taliaferro*** *strip r-584, 580.* ***Van Horn*** *a-537, 545, 561, 574, 587, 588, 591-present.*

WALT DISNEY'S COMICS DIGEST
Gladstone: Dec, 1986 - No. 7, Sept, 1987

	GD 2.0	VG 4.0	FN 6.0	VF 8.0	VF/NM 9.0	NM- 9.2
1	1	2	3	5	6	8
2-7						6.00

WALT DISNEY'S COMICS PENNY PINCHER
Gladstone: May, 1997 - No. 4, Aug, 1997 (99¢, limited series)

	GD 2.0	VG 4.0	FN 6.0	VF 8.0	VF/NM 9.0	NM- 9.2
1-4						2.50

WALT DISNEY'S DONALD AND MICKEY (Formerly Walt Disney's Mickey and Donald)
Gladstone (Bruce Hamilton Co.): No. 19, Sept, 1993 - No. 30, 1995 ($1.50, 36 & 68 pgs.)

	GD 2.0	VG 4.0	FN 6.0	VF 8.0	VF/NM 9.0	NM- 9.2
19,21-24,26-30: New & reprints. 19,21,23,24-Barks-r. 19,26-Murry-r. 22-Barks "Omelet" story r/WDC&S #146. 27-Mickey Mouse story by Caesar Ferioli (1st U.S work). 29-Rosa-c; Mickey Mouse story actually starring Goofy (does not include Mickey except on title page.)						4.00
20,25-($2.95, 68 pgs.): 20-Barks, Gottfredson-r						5.00

NOTE: *Donald Duck stories were all reprints.*

WALT DISNEY'S DONALD DUCK ADVENTURES (D.D. Adv. #1-3)
Gladstone: 11/87-No. 20, 4/90 (1st Series); No. 21,8/93-No. 48, 2/98(3rd Series)

	GD 2.0	VG 4.0	FN 6.0	VF 8.0	VF/NM 9.0	NM- 9.2
1	1	2	3	4	5	7
2-r/F.C. #308						3.00
3,4,6,7,9-11,13,15-18: 3-r/F.C. #223. 4-r/F.C. #62. 9-r/F.C. #159, "Ghost of the Grotto". 11-r/F.C. #159, "Adventure Down Under." 16-r/F.C. #291; Rosa-c. 18-r/FC #318; Rosa-c						3.00
5,8-Don Rosa-c/a						5.00
12($1.50, 52pgs)-Rosa-c/a w/Barks poster						6.00
14-r/F.C. #29, "Mummy's Ring"						4.00
19($1.95, 68 pgs.)-Barks-r/F.C. #199 (1 pg.)						3.00
20($1.95, 68 pgs.)-Barks-r/F.C. #189 & cover-r; William Van Horn-a						3.00
21,22: 21-r/D.D. #46. 22-r/F.C. #282						3.00
23-25,27,29,31,32-($1.50, 36 pgs.): 21,23,29-Rosa-c. 23-Intro/1st app. Andold Wild Duck by Marco Rota. 24-Van Horn-a. 27-1st Pat Block-a, "Mystery of Widow's Gap." 31,32-Block-c						2.50
26,28($2.95, 68 pgs.): 26-Barks-r/F.C. #108, "Terror of the River". 28-Barks-r/F.C. #199, "Sheriff of Bullet Valley"						4.00
30($2.95, 68 pgs.)-r/F.C. #367, Barks' "Christmas for Shacktown"						4.00
33($1.95, 68 pgs.)-r/F.C. #408, Barks' "The Golden Helmet;"Van Horn-c						3.00
34-43: 34-Resume $1.50-c. 34,35,37-Block-a/scripts. 38-Van Horn-c/a						2.50
44-48-($1.95-c)						2.50

NOTE: ***Barks*** *a-1-22r, 26r, 28r, 33r, 36r; c-3r, 8r, 10r, 14r, 20r.* ***Block*** *a-27, 30, 34, 35, 37; c-27, 30-32, 34, 35, 37; c-27, 30, 31, 32, 34, 35, 37.* ***Rosa*** *a-5, 8, 12, 43; c-13, 16, 18, 21, 23, 43.*

WALT DISNEY'S DONALD DUCK ADVENTURES (2nd Series)
Disney Comics: June, 1990 - No. 38, July, 1993 ($1.50)

	GD 2.0	VG 4.0	FN 6.0	VF 8.0	VF/NM 9.0	NM- 9.2
1-Rosa-a & scripts						5.00
2-21,23,25,27-33,35,36,38: 2-Barks-r/WDC&S #35; William Van Horn-a begins, ends #20. 9-Barks-r/F.C. #178. 9,11,14,17-No Van Horn-a. 11-Mad #1 cover parody. 14-Barks-r. 17-Barks-r. 21-r/FC #203 by Barks. 29-r/MOC #20 by Barks						3.00
22,24,26,34,37: 22-Rosa-a (10 pgs.) & scripts. 24-Rosa-a & scripts. 26-r/March of Comics #41 by Barks. 34-Rosa-c/a. 37-Rosa-a; Barks-r						4.00

NOTE: ***Barks*** *r-2, 4, 9(F.C. #178), 14(D.D. #45), 17, 21, 26, 27, 29 , 35, 36(D.D #60)-38.* ***Taliaferro*** *a-34r, 36r.*

WALT DISNEY'S DONALD DUCK ADVENTURES (Take-Along Comic)
Gemstone Publishing: July, 2003 - No. 21, Nov, 2006 ($7.95, 5" x 7-1/2")

	GD 2.0	VG 4.0	FN 6.0	VF 8.0	VF/NM 9.0	NM- 9.2
1-21-Mickey Mouse & Uncle Scrooge app. 9-Christmas-c						8.00
... , The Barks/Rosa Collection Vol. 2 (3/08, $8.99) reprints Donald Duck's Atom Bomb, Super Snooper & The Trouble With Dimes by Barks; The Duck Who Fell to Earth, Super Snooper Strikes Again & The Money Pit by Rosa						9.00
... , The Barks/Rosa Collection Vol. 3 (9/08, $8.99) r/FC #408 "The Golden Helmet" by Barks & DDA #43 "The Lost Charts of Columbus" by Rosa; cover gallery and bonus art						9.00

WALT DISNEY'S DONALD DUCK AND FRIENDS (Continues as Donald Duck and Friends)
Gemstone Publishing: No. 308, Oct, 2003 - No. 346, Dec, 2006 ($2.95)

	GD 2.0	VG 4.0	FN 6.0	VF 8.0	VF/NM 9.0	NM- 9.2
308-346: 308-Numbering resumes from Gladstone Donald Duck series; Halloween-c. 332-Halloween-c; r/#26 by Carl Barks						3.00

WALT DISNEY'S DONALD DUCK AND MICKEY MOUSE (Formerly Walt Disney's Donald

Walt Disney's Mickey and Donald #12 © DIS

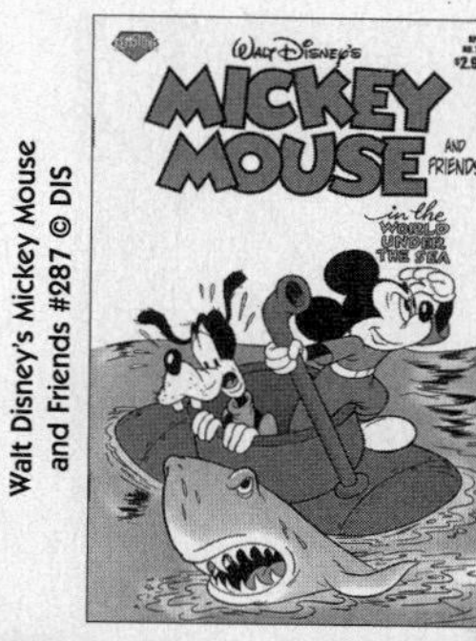

Walt Disney's Mickey Mouse and Friends #287 © DIS

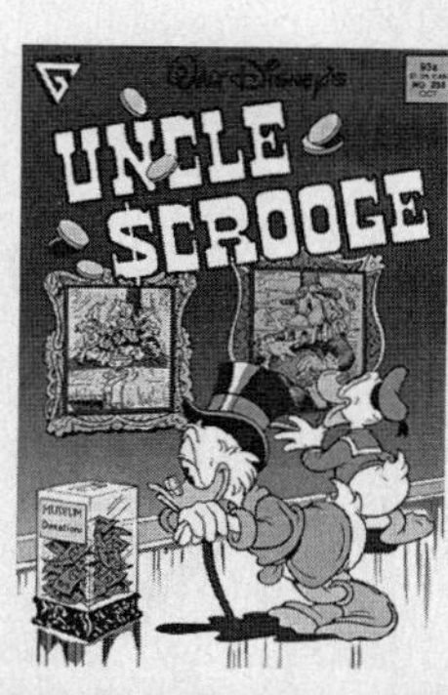

Walt Disney's Uncle Scrooge #238 © DIS

	GD 2.0	VG 4.0	FN 6.0	VF 8.0	VF/NM 9.0	NM- 9.2

and Mickey)
Gladstone (Bruce Hamilton Company): Sept, 1995 - No. 7, Sept, 1996 ($1.50, 32 pgs.)

Issue	GD	VG	FN	VF	VF/NM	NM-
1-7: 1-Barks-r and new Mickey Mouse stories in all. 5,6-Mickey Mouse stories by Caesar Ferioli. 7-New Donald Duck and Mickey Mouse x-over story; Barks-r/WDC&S #51						2.50

NOTE: *Issue #8 was advertised, but cancelled.*

WALT DISNEY'S DONALD DUCK AND UNCLE SCROOGE
Gemstone Publishing: Nov, 2005 ($6.95, square-bound one-shot)

Issue	GD	VG	FN	VF	VF/NM	NM-
nn-New story by John Lustig and Pat Block and r/Uncle Scrooge #59						7.00

WALT DISNEY'S DONALD DUCK FAMILY
Gemstone Publishing: Jun, 2008 ($8.99, square-bound)

Issue	GD	VG	FN	VF	VF/NM	NM-
... The Daan Jippes Collection Vol. 1 - R/Barks-s re-drawn by Jippes for Dutch comics						9.00

WALT DISNEY'S DONALD DUCK IN THE CASE OF THE MISSING MUMMY
Gemstone Publishing: Oct, 2007 ($8.99, square-bound one-shot)

Issue	GD	VG	FN	VF	VF/NM	NM-
nn-New story by Shelley and Pat Block and r/Donald Duck FC #29						9.00

WALT DISNEY SHOWCASE
Gold Key: Oct, 1970 - No. 54, Jan, 1980 (No. 44-48: 68pgs., 49-54: 52pgs.)

Issue	GD	VG	FN	VF	VF/NM	NM-
1-Boatniks (Movie)-Photo-c	3	6	9	18	27	35
2-Moby Duck	3	6	9	14	19	24
3,4,7: 3-Bongo & Lumpjaw-r. 4,7-Pluto-r	2	4	6	10	14	18
5-$1,000,000 Duck (Movie)-Photo-c	3	6	9	16	22	28
6-Bedknobs & Broomsticks (Movie)	3	6	9	16	22	28
8-Daisy & Donald	2	4	6	11	16	20
9- 101 Dalmatians (cartoon feat.); r/F.C. #1183	3	6	9	17	25	32
10-Napoleon & Samantha (Movie)-Photo-c	3	6	9	17	22	28
11-Moby Duck-r	2	4	6	10	14	18
12-Dumbo-r/Four Color #668	2	4	6	11	16	20
13-Pluto-r	2	4	6	10	14	18
14-World's Greatest Athlete (Movie)-Photo-c	3	6	9	16	22	28
15- 3 Little Pigs-r	2	4	6	11	16	20
16-Aristocats (cartoon feature); r/Aristocats #1	3	6	9	16	22	28
17-Mary Poppins; r/M.P. #10136-501-Photo-c	3	6	9	16	22	28
18-Gyro Gearloose; Barks-r/F.C. #1047,1184	3	6	9	18	27	35
19-That Darn Cat; r/That Darn Cat #10171-602-Hayley Mills photo-c	3	6	9	16	22	28
20,23-Pluto-r	2	4	6	11	16	20
21-Li'l Bad Wolf & The Three Little Pigs	2	4	6	10	14	18
22-Unbirthday Party with Alice in Wonderland; r/Four Color #341	3	6	9	14	19	24
24-26: 24-Herbie Rides Again (Movie); sequel to "The Love Bug"; photo-c. 25-Old Yeller (Movie); r/F.C. #869; Photo-c. 26-Lt. Robin Crusoe USN (Movie); r/Lt. Robin Crusoe USN #10191-601; photo-c	2	4	6	11	16	20
27-Island at the Top of the World (Movie)-Photo-c	3	6	9	14	19	24
28-Brer Rabbit, Bucky Bug-r/WDC&S #58	2	4	6	11	16	20
29-Escape to Witch Mountain (Movie)-Photo-c	3	6	9	14	19	24
30-Magica De Spell; Barks-r/Uncle Scrooge #36 & WDC&S #258	3	6	9	21	32	42
31-Bambi (cartoon feature); r/Four Color #186	2	4	6	13	18	22
32-Spin & Marty-r/F.C. #1026; Mickey Mouse Club (TV)-Photo-c	3	6	9	14	19	24
33-40: 33-Pluto-r/F.C. #1143. 34-Paul Revere's Ride with Johnny Tremain (TV); r/F.C. #822. 35-Goofy-r/F.C. #952. 36-Peter Pan-r/F.C. #442. 37-Tinker Bell & Jiminy Cricket-r/F.C. #982,989. 38,39-Mickey & the Sleuth, Parts 1 & 2. 40-The Rescuers (cartoon feature)	2	4	6	9	13	16
41-Herbie Goes to Monte Carlo (Movie); sequel to "Herbie Rides Again"; photo-c	2	4	6	10	14	18
42-Mickey & the Sleuth	2	4	6	9	13	16
43-Pete's Dragon (Movie)-Photo-c	2	4	6	13	18	22
44-Return From Witch Mountain (new) & In Search of the Castaways-r (Movies)-Photo-c; 68 pg. giants begin	3	6	9	14	19	24
45-The Jungle Book (Movie); r/#30033-803	3	6	9	17	25	32
46-48: 46-The Cat From Outer Space (Movie)(new), & The Shaggy Dog (Movie)-r/F.C. #985; photo-c. 47-Mickey Mouse Surprise Party-r. 48-The Wonderful Advs. of Pinocchio-r/F.C. #1203; last 68 pg. issue	2	4	6	10	14	18
49-54: 49-North Avenue Irregulars (Movie); Zorro-r/Zorro #11; 52 pgs. begin; photo-c. 50-Bedknobs & Broomsticks-r/#6; Mooncussers-r/World of Adv. #1; photo-c. 51-101 Dalmatians-r. 52-Unidentified Flying Oddball (Movie); r/Picnic Party #8; photo-c. 53-The Scarecrow-r (TV). 54-The Black Hole (Movie)-Photo-c (predates Black Hole #1)	2	4	6	9	13	16

WALT DISNEY'S MAGAZINE (TV)(Formerly Walt Disney's Mickey Mouse Club Magazine) (50¢, bi-monthly)
Western Publishing Co.: V2#4, June, 1957 - V4#6, Oct, 1959

Issue	GD	VG	FN	VF	VF/NM	NM-
V2#4-Stories & articles on the Mouseketeers, Zorro, & Goofy and other Disney characters & people	7	14	21	45	73	100
V2#5, V2#6(10/57)	6	12	18	41	66	90
V3#1(12/57), V3#3-5	6	12	18	37	59	80
V3#2-Annette Funicello photo-c	11	22	33	77	136	195
V3#6(10/58)-TV Zorro photo-c	8	16	24	52	86	120
V4#1(12/58) - V4#2-4,6(10/59)	6	12	18	37	59	80
V4#5-Annette Funicello photo-c, w/ 2-photo articles	11	22	33	77	136	195

NOTE: *V2#4-V3#6 were 11-1/2x8-1/2", 48 pgs.; V4#1 on were 10x8", 52 pgs. (Peak circulation of 400,000).*

WALT DISNEY'S MERRY CHRISTMAS (See Dell Giant #39)

WALT DISNEY'S MICKEY AND DONALD (M & D #1,2)(Becomes Walt Disney's Donald & Mickey #19 on)
Gladstone: Mar, 1988 - No. 18, May, 1990 (95¢)

Issue	GD	VG	FN	VF	VF/NM	NM-
1-Don Rosa-a; r/1949 Firestone giveaway						6.00
2-8: 3-Infinity-c. 4-8-Barks-r						3.00
9-15: 9-r/1948 Firestone giveaway; X-Mas-c						3.00
16($1.50, 52 pgs.)-r/FC #157						5.00
17-(68 pgs.) Barks M.M.-r/FC #79 plus Barks D.D.-r; Rosa-a; x-mas-c						6.00
18($1.95, 68 pgs.)-Gottfredson-r/WDC&S #13,72-74; Kelly-c(r); Barks-r						5.00

NOTE: ***Barks** reprints in 1-15, 17, 18. **Kelly** c-13r, 14 (r/Walt Disney's C&S #58), 18r.*

WALT DISNEY'S MICKEY MOUSE ADVENTURES (Take-Along Comic)
Gemstone Publishing: Aug, 2004 - No. 12 ($7.95, 5" x 7-1/2")

Issue	GD	VG	FN	VF	VF/NM	NM-
1-12-Goofy, Donald Duck & Uncle Scrooge app.						8.00

WALT DISNEY'S MICKEY MOUSE AND BLOTMAN IN BLOTMAN RETURNS
Gemstone Publishing: Dec, 2006 ($5.99, squarebound, one-shot)

Issue	GD	VG	FN	VF	VF/NM	NM-
nn-Wraparound-c by Noel Van Horn; Super Goof back-up story						6.00

WALT DISNEY'S MICKEY MOUSE AND FRIENDS (See Mickey Mouse and Friends for #296)
Gemstone Publishing: No. 257, Oct, 2003 - No. 295, Dec, 2006 ($2.95)

Issue	GD	VG	FN	VF	VF/NM	NM-
257-295: 257-Numbering resumes from Gladstone Mickey Mouse series; Halloween-c. 285-Return of the Phantom Blot						3.00

WALT DISNEY'S MICKEY MOUSE CLUB MAGAZINE (TV)(Becomes Walt Disney's Magazine)
Western Publishing Co.: Winter, 1956 - V2#3, Apr, 1957 (11-1/2x8-1/2", quarterly, 48 pgs.)

Issue	GD	VG	FN	VF	VF/NM	NM-
V1#1	14	28	42	98	184	270
2-4	8	16	24	58	97	135
V2#1,2	7	14	21	47	76	105
3-Annette photo-c	13	26	39	90	165	240
Annual(1956)-Two different issues; ($1.50-Whitman); 120 pgs., cardboard covers, 11-3/4x8-3/4"; reprints	14	28	42	98	184	270
Annual(1957)-Same as above	12	24	36	83	152	220

WALT DISNEY'S MICKEY MOUSE MEETS BLOTMAN
Gemstone Publishing: Aug, 2005 ($5.99, squarebound, one-shot)

Issue	GD	VG	FN	VF	VF/NM	NM-
nn-Wraparound-c by Noel Van Horn; Super Goof back-up story						6.00

WALT DISNEY'S PINOCCHIO SPECIAL
Gladstone: Spring, 1990 ($1.00)

Issue	GD	VG	FN	VF	VF/NM	NM-
1-50th anniversary edition; Kelly-r/F.C. #92						3.00

WALT DISNEY'S SPRING FEVER
Gemstone Publishing: Apr, 2007; Apr, 2008 ($9.50, squarebound)

Issue	GD	VG	FN	VF	VF/NM	NM-
1,2: 1-New stories and reprints incl. "Mystery of the Swamp" by Carl Barks						9.50

WALT DISNEY'S THE ADVENTUROUS UNCLE SCROOGE MCDUCK
Gladstone: Jan, 1998 - No. 2, Mar, 1998 ($1.95)

Issue	GD	VG	FN	VF	VF/NM	NM-
1,2: 1-Barks-a(r). 2-Rosa-a(r)						2.50

WALT DISNEY'S THE JUNGLE BOOK
W.D. Publications (Disney Comics): 1990 ($5.95, graphic novel, 68 pgs.)

Issue	GD	VG	FN	VF	VF/NM	NM-
nn-Movie adaptation; movie rereleased in 1990						6.00
nn-($2.95, 68 pgs.)-Comic edition; wraparound-c						3.00

WALT DISNEY'S UNCLE SCROOGE (Formerly Uncle Scrooge #1-209)
Gladstone #210-242/Disney Comics #243-280/Gladstone #281-318/Gemstone #319 on: No. 210, 10/86 - No. 242, 4/90; No. 243, 6/90 - No. 318, 2/99; No. 319, 7/03 - No. 383, 11/08

Issue	GD	VG	FN	VF	VF/NM	NM-
210-1st Gladstone issue; r/WDC&S #134 (1st Beagle Boys)	2	4	6	9	13	16
211-218: 216-New story ("Go Slowly Sands of Time") plotted and partly scripted by Barks. 217-r/U.S. #7, "Seven Cities of Cibola"	2	4	6	9	12	15
219-"Son Of The Sun" by Rosa (his 1st pro work)	3	6	9	14	20	25
220-Don Rosa-a/scripts	1	2	3	5	6	8
221-223,225,228-234,236-240						4.00
224,226,227,235: 224-Rosa-c/a. 226,227-Rosa-a. 235-Rosa-a/scripts						5.00
241-($1.95, 68 pgs.)-Rosa finishes over Barks-r						6.00

Walt Disney's Uncle Scrooge #366 © DIS

Wambi, Jungle Boy #7 © FH

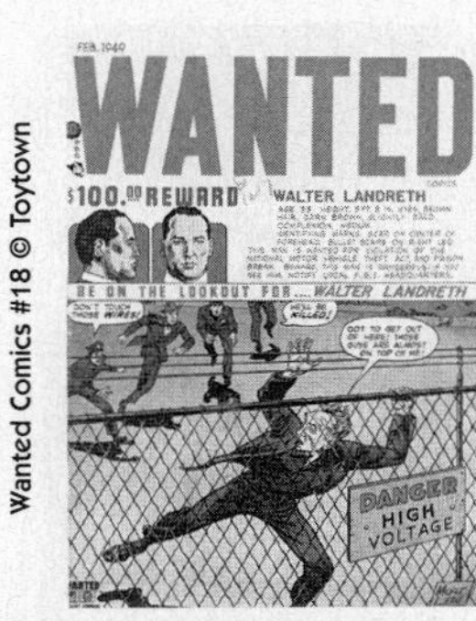

Wanted Comics #18 © Toytown

	GD	VG	FN	VF	VF/NM	NM-
	2.0	4.0	6.0	8.0	9.0	9.2
242-($1.95, 68 pgs.)-Barks-r; Rosa-a(1 pg.)						6.00
243-249,251-260,264-275,277-280,282-284-($1.50): 243-1st by Disney Comics. 274-All Barks issue. 275-Contains centerspread by Rosa. 279-All Barks issue; Rosa-c. 283-r/WDC&S #98						3.00
250-($2.25, 52 pgs.)-Barks-r; wraparound-c						4.00
261-263,276-Don Rosa-c/a						5.00
281-Gladstone issues start again; Rosa-c						6.00
285-The Life and Times of Scrooge McDuck Pt. 1; Rosa-c/a/scripts	1	3	4	6	8	10
286-293: The Life and Times of Scrooge McDuck Pt. 2-8; Rosa-c/a/scripts. 293-($1.95, 36 pgs.)-The Life and Times of Scrooge McDuck Pt. 9						6.00
294-299, 301-308-($1.50, 32 pgs.): 294-296-The Life and Times of Scrooge McDuck Pt. 10-12. 297-The Life and Times of Uncle Scrooge Pt. 0; Rosa-c/a/scripts						3.00
300-($2.25, 48 pgs.)-Rosa-c; Barks-r/WDC&S #104 and U.S. #216; r/U.S. #220; includes new centerfold.						4.00
309-($6.95) Low print run						15.00
310-($6.95) Low print run						30.00
311-320-($6.95) 318-(2/99) Last Gladstone issue. 319-(7/03) First Gemstone issue; The Dutchman's Secret by Don Rosa						10.00
321-360						7.00
361-366: 361-Begin $7.50-c						7.50
367-383-($7.99)						8.00
... Adventures, The Barks/Rosa Collection Vol. 1 (Gemstone, 7/07, $8.50) reprints Pygmy Indians appearances in U.S. #18 by Barks and WDC&S #633 by Rosa						8.50
Walt Disney's The Life and Times of Scrooge McDuck by Don Rosa TPB (Gemstone, 2005, $16.99) Reprints #285-296, with foreword, commentaries & sketch pages by Rosa						17.00
Walt Disney's The Life and Times of Scrooge McDuck Companion by Don Rosa TPB (Gemstone, 2006, $16.99) additional chapters, with foreword & commentaries						17.00

NOTE: ***Barks** r-210-218, 220-223, 224(2pg.), 225-234, 236-242, 245, 246, 250-253, 255, 256, 258, 261(2 pg.), 265, 267, 268, 270(2), 272-284, 299-present; c(r)-210, 212, 221, 228, 229, 232, 233, 284. scripts-287, 293. **Rosa** a-219, 220, 224, 226, 227, 235, 261-263, 268, 275-277, 285-289; c-219, 224, 231, 261-263, 276, 278-281, 285-296; scripts-219, 220, 224, 235, 261-263, 268, 276, 285-296.*

WALT DISNEY'S UNCLE SCROOGE ADVENTURES (U. Scrooge Advs. #1-3)
Gladstone Publishing: Nov, 1987 - No. 21, May, 1990; No. 22, Sept, 1993 - No. 54, Feb, 1998

	GD	VG	FN	VF	VF/NM	NM-
1-Barks-r begin, ends #26	1	2	3	5	6	8
2-4						4.00
5,9,14: 5-Rosa-c/a; no Barks-r. 9,14-Rosa-a						5.00
6-8,10-13,15-19: 10-r/U.S. #18(all Barks)						3.00
20,21 ($1.95, 68 pgs.) 20-Rosa-c/a. 21-Rosa-a						5.00
22 ($1.50)-Rosa-c; r/U.S. #26						5.00
23-($2.95, 68 pgs.)-Vs. The Phantom Blot-r/P.B. #3; Barks-r						4.00
24-26,29,31,32,34-36: 24,25,29,31,32-Rosa-c. 25-r/U.S. #21						2.50
27-Guardians of the Lost Library - Rosa-c/a/story; origin of Junior Woodchuck Guidebook						3.00
28-($2.95, 68 pgs.)-r/U.S. #13 w/restored missing panels						4.00
30-($2.95, 68 pgs.)-r/U.S. #12; Rosa-c						4.00
33-($2.95, 64 pgs.)-New Barks story						3.00
37-54						2.50

NOTE: ***Barks** r-1-4, 6-8, 10-13, 15-21, 23, 22, 24; c(r)-15, 16, 17, 21. **Rosa** a-5, 9, 14, 20, 21, 27, 51; c-5, 13, 14, 17(finishes), 20, 22, 24, 25, 27, 28, 51; scripts-5, 9, 14, 27.*

WALT DISNEY'S UNCLE SCROOGE AND DONALD DUCK
Gladstone: Jan, 1998 - No. 2, Mar, 1998 ($1.95)

	GD	VG	FN	VF	VF/NM	NM-
1,2: 1-Rosa-a(r)						2.50

WALT DISNEY'S UNCLE SCROOGE ADVENTURES IN COLOR
Gladstone Publ.: Dec, 1995 - Present ($8.95/$9.95, squarebound, 56 issue limited series) (Polybagged w/card) (Series chronologically reprints all the stories written & drawn by Carl Barks)

	GD	VG	FN	VF	VF/NM	NM-
1-56: 1-(12/95)-r/FC #386. 15-(12/96)-r/US #15. 16-(12/96)-r/US #16. 18-(1/97)-r/US #18						10.00

WALT DISNEY'S VACATION PARADE
Gemstone Publishing: 2004 - Present ($8.95/$9.95, squarebound, annual)

	GD	VG	FN	VF	VF/NM	NM-
1-3: 1-Reprints stories from Dell Giant Comics Vacation Parade 1 (July 1950)						9.00
4,5-($9.95): 4-(5/07). 5-(7/08)						10.00

WALT DISNEY'S WHEATIES PREMIUMS (See Wheaties in the Promotional section)

WALT DISNEY'S WORLD OF THE DRAGONLORDS
Gemstone Publishing: 2005 ($12.99, squarebound, graphic novel)

	GD	VG	FN	VF	VF/NM	NM-
SC-Uncle Scrooge, Donald & nephews app.; Byron Erickson-s/Giorgio Cavazzano-a						13.00

WALT DISNEY TREASURES - DISNEY COMICS: 75 YEARS OF INNOVATION
Gemstone Publishing: 2006 ($12.99, TPB)

	GD	VG	FN	VF	VF/NM	NM-
SC-Reprints from 1930-2004, including debut of Mickey Mouse newspaper strip						13.00

WALT DISNEY TREASURES - UNCLE SCROOGE: A LITTLE SOMETHING SPECIAL
Gemstone Publishing: 2008 ($16.99, TPB)

	GD	VG	FN	VF	VF/NM	NM-
SC-Uncle Scrooge classics from 1954-2006, including "The Seven Cities of Cibola"						17.00

WALTER LANTZ ANDY PANDA (Also see Andy Panda)
Gold Key: Aug, 1973 - No. 23, Jan, 1978 (Walter Lantz)

	GD	VG	FN	VF	VF/NM	NM-
1-Reprints	3	6	9	14	19	24
2-10-All reprints	2	4	6	9	12	15
11-23: 15,17-19,22-Reprints	1	2	3	5	7	9

WALT KELLY'S...
Eclipse Comics: Dec, 1987; Apr, 1988 ($1.75/$2.50, Baxter paper)

	GD	VG	FN	VF	VF/NM	NM-
...Christmas Classics 1 (12/87)-Kelly-r/Peter Wheat & Santa Claus Funnies, ...Springtime Tales 1 (4/88, $2.50)-Kelly-r						2.50

WALTONS, THE (See Kite Fun Book)

WALT SCOTT (See Little People)

WALT SCOTT'S CHRISTMAS STORIES (See Christmas Stories, 4-Color #959, 1062)

WAMBI, JUNGLE BOY (See Jungle Comics)
Fiction House Magazines: Spr, 1942; No. 2, Win, 1942-43; No. 3, Spr, 1943; No. 4, Fall, 1948; No. 5, Sum, 1949; No. 6, Spr, 1950; No. 7-10, 1950(nd); No. 11, Spr, 1951 - No. 18, Win, 1952-53 (#1-3: 68 pgs.)

	GD	VG	FN	VF	VF/NM	NM-
1-Wambi, the Jungle Boy begins	94	188	282	597	1024	1450
2 (1942)-Kiefer-c	50	100	150	315	533	750
3 (1943)-Kiefer-c/a	39	78	117	240	395	550
4 (1948)-Origin in text	26	52	78	154	252	350
5 (Fall, 1949, 36 pgs.)-Kiefer-c/a	23	46	69	136	223	310
6-10: 7-(52 pgs.)-New logo	19	38	57	112	179	245
11-18	15	30	45	83	124	165
I.W. Reprint #8('64)-r/#12 with new-c	3	6	9	14	20	25

NOTE: ***Alex Blum** c-8. **Kiefer** c-1-5. **Whitman** c-11-18.*

WANDERERS (See Adventure Comics #375, 376)
DC Comics: June, 1988 - No. 13, Apr, 1989 ($1.25) (Legion of Super-Heroes spin off)

	GD	VG	FN	VF	VF/NM	NM-
1-13: 1,2-Steacy-c. 3-Legion app.						2.50

WANDERING STAR
Pen & Ink Comics/Sirius Entertainment No. 12 on: 1993 - No. 21, Mar, 1997 ($2.50/$2.75, B&W)

	GD	VG	FN	VF	VF/NM	NM-
1-1st printing; Teri Sue Wood c/a/scripts in all	1	2	3	5	6	8
1-2nd and 3rd printings						2.75
2-1st printing.						4.00
2-21: 2-2nd printing. 12-(1/96)-1st Sirius issue						2.75
Trade paperback ($11.95)-r/1-7; 1st printing of 1000, signed and #'d						18.00
Trade paperback-2nd printing, 2000 signed						15.00
TPB Volume 2,3 (11/98, 12/98, $14.95) 2-r/#8-14, 3-r/#15-21						15.00

WANTED
Image Comics (Top Cow): Dec, 2003 - No. 6, Feb, 2004 ($2.99)

	GD	VG	FN	VF	VF/NM	NM-
1-Three covers; Mark Millar-s/J.G. Jones-a; intro Wesley Gibson						3.00
1-4-Death Row Edition; r/#1-4 with extra sketch pages and deleted panels						3.00
2-6: 2-Cameos of DC villains. 6-Giordano-a in flashback scenes						3.00
...Dossier (5/04, $2.99) Pin-ups and character info; art by Jones, Romita Jr. & others						3.00
... Movie Edition Vol. 1 TPB (2008, $19.99) r/#1-6 & Dossier; movie photo-c; sketch pages & cover gallery; interviews with movie cast and director						20.00
HC (2005, $29.99) r/#1-6 & Dossier; intro by Vaughan, sketch pages & cover gallery						30.00

WANTED COMICS
Toytown Publications/Patches/Orbit Publ.: No. 9, Sept-Oct, 1947 - No. 53, April, 1953 (#9-33: 52 pgs.)

	GD	VG	FN	VF	VF/NM	NM-
9-True crime cases; radio's Mr. D. A. app.	25	50	75	147	241	335
10,11: 10-Giunta-a; radio's Mr. D. A. app.	15	30	45	88	137	185
12-Used in **SOTI**, pg. 277	17	34	51	98	154	210
13-Heroin drug propaganda story	15	30	45	86	133	180
14-Marijuana drug mention story (2 pgs.)	15	30	45	83	124	165
15-17,19,20	13	26	39	74	105	135
18-Marijuana story, "Satan's Cigarettes"; r-in #45 & retitled	25	50	75	147	241	335
21,22: 21-Krigstein-a. 22-Extreme violence	14	28	42	76	108	140
23,25-34,36-38,40-44,46-48,53	11	22	33	62	86	110
24-Krigstein-a; "The Dope King", marijuana mention story	15	30	45	84	127	170
35-Used in **SOTI**, pg. 160	14	28	42	82	121	160
39-Drug propaganda story "The Horror Weed"	18	36	54	103	162	220
45-Marijuana story from #18	13	26	39	74	105	135
49-Has unstable pink-c that fades easily; rare in mint condition						

Wanted, The World's Most Dangerous Villains #8 © DC

War Battles #7 © HARV

War Comics #2 © DELL

	GD 2.0	VG 4.0	FN 6.0	VF 8.0	VF/NM 9.0	NM- 9.2
	13	26	39	74	105	135
50-Has unstable pink-c like #49; surrealist-c by Buscema; horror stories	14	28	42	80	115	150
51- "Holiday of Horror" junkie story; drug-c	15	30	45	85	130	175
52-Classic "Cult of Killers" opium use story	15	30	45	84	127	170

NOTE: *Buscema c-50, 51. Lawrence and Leav c/a most issues. Syd Shores c/a-48; c-37. Issues 9-46 have wanted criminals with their descriptions & drawn picture on cover.*

WANTED: DEAD OR ALIVE (TV)
Dell Publishing Co.: No. 1102, May-July, 1960 - No. 1164, Mar-May, 1961

	GD	VG	FN	VF	VF/NM	NM-
Four Color 1102 (#1)-Steve McQueen photo-c	12	24	36	85	155	225
Four Color 1164-Steve McQueen photo-c	9	18	27	63	107	150

WANTED, THE WORLD'S MOST DANGEROUS VILLAINS (See DC Special)
National Periodical Publ.: July-Aug, 1972 - No. 9, Aug-Sept, 1973 (All reprints & 20¢ issues)

	GD	VG	FN	VF	VF/NM	NM-
1-Batman, Green Lantern (story r-from G.L. #1), & Green Arrow	3	6	9	20	30	40
2-Batman/Joker/Penguin-c/story r-from Batman #25; plus Flash story (r-from Flash #121)	3	6	9	16	23	30
3-9: 3-Dr. Fate(r/More Fun #65), Hawkman(r/Flash #100), & Vigilante(r/Action #69). 4-Green Lantern(r/All-American #61) & Kid Eternity(r/Kid Eternity #15). 5-Dollman/Green Lantern. 6-Burnley Starman; Wildcat/Sargon. 7-Johnny Quick(r/More Fun #76), Hawkman(r/Flash #90), Hourman by Baily(r/Adv. #72). 8-Dr. Fate/Flash(r/Flash #114). 9-S&K Sandman/Superman	3	6	9	14	19	24

NOTE: *B. Bailey a-7r. Infantino a-2r. Kane r-1, 5. Kubert r-3i, 6, 7. Meskin r-3, 7. Reinman r-4, 6.*

WAR (See Fightin' Marines #122)
Charlton Comics: Jul, 1975 - No. 9, Nov, 1976; No. 10, Sept, 1978 - No. 47, 1984

	GD	VG	FN	VF	VF/NM	NM-
1-Boyette painted-c	2	4	6	11	16	20
2-10: 3-Sutton painted-c	1	3	4	6	8	10
11-20	1	2	3	4	5	7
21-40						6.00
41,42,44-47 (lower print run): 47-Reprints	1	2	3	4	5	7
43 (2/84) (lower print run) Ditko-a (7 pgs.)	2	3	4	6	8	10
7,9 (Modern Comics-r, 1977)						4.00

WAR, THE (See The Draft & The Pitt)
Marvel Comics: 1989 - No. 4, 1990 ($3.50, squarebound, 52 pgs.)

	GD	VG	FN	VF	VF/NM	NM-
1-4: Characters from New Universe						3.50

WAR ACTION (Korean War)
Atlas Comics (CPS): April, 1952 - No. 14, June, 1953

	GD	VG	FN	VF	VF/NM	NM-
1	20	40	60	114	182	250
2-Hartley-a	12	24	36	69	97	125
3-10,14: 7-Pakula-a. 14-Colan-a	10	20	30	54	72	90
11-13-Krigstein-a. 11-Romita-a	10	20	30	58	79	100

NOTE: *Berg c-11. Brodsky a-2; c-1-4. Heath a-1; c-7, 14. Keller a-6. Maneely a-1; c-12. Sale a-7. Tuska a-2, 8.*

WAR ADVENTURES
Atlas Comics (HPC): Jan, 1952 - No. 13, Feb, 1953

	GD	VG	FN	VF	VF/NM	NM-
1-Tuska-a	18	36	54	107	169	230
2	11	22	33	62	86	110
3-7,9-13: 3-Pakula-a. 7-Maneely-c. 9-Romita-a	10	20	30	54	72	90
8-Krigstein-a	10	20	30	58	79	100

NOTE: *Brodsky c-1-3, 6, 8, 11, 12. Heath a-2, 5, 7, 10; c-4, 5, 9, 13. Reinman a-13. Robinson a-3; c-10.*

WAR ADVENTURES ON THE BATTLEFIELD (See Battlefield)

WAR AGAINST CRIME! (Becomes Vault of Horror #12 on)
E. C. Comics: Spring, 1948 - No. 11, Feb-Mar, 1950

	GD	VG	FN	VF	VF/NM	NM-
1-Real Stories From Police Records on-c #1-9	77	154	231	493	847	1200
2,3	45	90	135	284	480	675
4-9	41	82	123	256	428	600
10-1st Vault Keeper app. & 1st Vault of Horror	223	446	669	1784	2842	3900
11-2nd Vault Keeper app.; 1st EC horror-c	143	286	429	1144	1822	2500

NOTE: *All have Johnny Craig covers. Feldstein a-4, 7-9. Harrison/Wood a-11. Ingels a-1, 2, 8. Palais a-8. Changes to horror with #10.*

WAR AGAINST CRIME
Gemstone Publishing: Apr, 2000 - No. 11, Feb, 2001 ($2.50)

	GD	VG	FN	VF	VF/NM	NM-
1-11: E.C. reprints						2.50

WAR AND ATTACK (Also see Special War Series #3)
Charlton Comics: Fall, 1964; V2#54, June, 1966 - V2#63, Dec, 1967

	GD	VG	FN	VF	VF/NM	NM-
1-Wood-a (25 pgs.)	5	10	15	30	48	65
V2#54(6/66)-#63 (Formerly Fightin' Air Force)	3	6	9	16	22	28

NOTE: *Montes/Bache a-55, 56, 60, 63.*

WAR AT SEA (Formerly Space Adventures)
Charlton Comics: No. 22, Nov, 1957 - No. 42, June, 1961

	GD 2.0	VG 4.0	FN 6.0	VF 8.0	VF/NM 9.0	NM- 9.2
22	7	14	21	37	46	55
23-30	6	12	18	27	33	38
31-42	3	6	9	17	25	32

WAR BATTLES
Harvey Publications: Feb, 1952 - No. 9, Dec, 1953

	GD	VG	FN	VF	VF/NM	NM-
1-Powell-a; Elias-c	9	18	27	63	107	150
2-Powell-a	5	10	15	34	55	75
3-5,7-9: 3,7-Powell-a. 5-Flamethrower cover	5	10	15	32	51	70
6-Nostrand-a	6	12	18	39	62	85

WAR BIRDS
Fiction House Magazines: 1952(nd) - No. 3, Winter, 1952-53

	GD	VG	FN	VF	VF/NM	NM-
1	16	32	48	94	147	200
2,3	11	22	33	62	86	110

WARBLADE: ENDANGERED SPECIES (Also see WildC.A.T.S: Covert Action Teams)
Image Comics (WildStorm Productions): Jan, 1995 - No. 4, Apr, 1995 ($2.50, limited series)

	GD	VG	FN	VF	VF/NM	NM-
1-4: 1-Gatefold wraparound-c						2.50

WAR COMBAT (Becomes Combat Casey #6 on)
Atlas Comics (LBI No. 1/SAI No. 2-5): March, 1952 - No. 5, Nov, 1952

	GD	VG	FN	VF	VF/NM	NM-
1	16	32	48	94	147	200
2	10	20	30	58	79	100
3-5	9	18	27	52	69	85

NOTE: *Berg a-2, 4, 5. Brodsky c-1, 2, 4, 5. Henkel a-5. Maneely a-1, 4; c-3. Reinman a-2.*

WAR COMICS (War Stories #5 on)(See Key Ring Comics)
Dell Publishing Co.: May, 1940 (No month given) - No. 4, Sept, 1941

	GD	VG	FN	VF	VF/NM	NM-
1-Sikandur the Robot Master, Sky Hawk, Scoop Mason, War Correspondent begin; McWilliams-c; 1st war comic	58	116	174	371	636	900
2-Origin Greg Gilday (5/41)	34	68	102	199	325	450
3-Joan becomes Greg Gilday's aide	23	46	69	136	223	310
4-Origin Night Devils	24	48	72	140	230	320

WAR COMICS
Marvel/Atlas (USA No. 1-41/JPI No. 42-49): Dec, 1950 - No. 49, Sept, 1957

	GD	VG	FN	VF	VF/NM	NM-
1	26	52	78	154	252	350
2	15	30	45	85	130	175
3-10	13	26	39	74	105	135
11-Flame thrower w/burning bodies on-c	15	30	45	88	137	185
12-20: 16-Romita-a	11	22	33	62	86	110
21,23-32: 26-Valley Forge story. 32-Last pre-code issue (2/55)	10	20	30	54	72	90
22-Krigstein-a	10	20	30	58	79	100
33-37,39-42,44,45,47,48: 40-Romita-a	10	20	30	54	72	90
38-Kubert/Moskowitz-a	10	20	30	58	79	100
43,49-Torres-a. 43-Severin/Elder E.C. swipe from Two-Fisted Tales #31	10	20	30	58	79	100
46-Crandall-a	10	20	30	58	79	100

NOTE: *Ayers a-17. Berg a-13. Colan a-4, 36, 48, 49; c-17. Drucker a-37, 43, 48. Everett a-17. Heath a-6-9, 16, 19, 25, 36; c-11, 16, 19, 23, 25, 26, 29-32, 36. G. Kane a-19. Lawrence a-36. Maneely a-7, 9, 13, 14, 20, 23; c-6, 27, 37. Orlando a-42, 48. Pakula a-26, 40. Ravielli a-27. Reinman a-11, 16, 26. Robinson a-15; c-13. Severin a-26, 27; c-48. Shores a-13. Sinnott a-37.*

WAR DANCER (Also see Charlemagne, Doctor Chaos #2 & Warriors of Plasm)
Defiant: Feb, 1994 - No. 6, July, 1994 ($2.50)

	GD	VG	FN	VF	VF/NM	NM-
1-3,5,6: 1-Intro War Dancer; Weiss-c/a begins. 1-3-Weiss-a(p). 6-Pre-Schism issue						2.50
4-($3.25, 52 pgs.)-Charlemagne app.						3.25

WAR DOGS OF THE U.S. ARMY
Avon Periodicals: 1952

	GD	VG	FN	VF	VF/NM	NM-
1-Kinstler-c/a	15	30	45	83	124	165

WARFRONT
Harvey Publications: 9/51 - #35, 11/58; #36, 10/65; #39, 2/67

	GD	VG	FN	VF	VF/NM	NM-
1-Korean War	10	20	30	70	123	175
2	6	12	18	39	62	85
3-10	5	10	15	32	51	70
11,12,14,16-20	4	8	12	28	44	60
13,15,22-Nostrand-a	6	12	18	39	62	85
21,23-27,31-33,35	4	8	12	28	44	60
28-30,34-Kirby-c	6	12	18	41	66	90
36-(12/66)-Dynamite Joe begins, ends #39; Williamson-a	5	10	15	32	51	70
37-Wood-a (17 pgs.)	5	10	15	32	51	70
38,39-Wood-a, 2-3 pgs.; Lone Tiger app.	4	8	12	28	44	60

NOTE: *Powell a-1-6, 9-11, 14, 17, 20, 23, 25-28, 30, 31, 34, 36. Powell/Nostrand a-12, 13, 15. Simon c-36?, 38.*

War Heroes #7 © DELL

Warlands: Dark Tide Rising #3 © DW

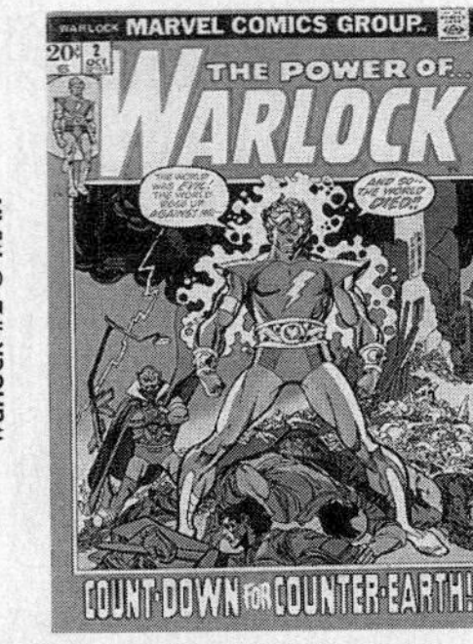

Warlock #2 © MAR

WAR FURY
Comic Media/Harwell (Allen Hardy Assoc.): Sept, 1952 - No. 4, Mar, 1953

	GD 2.0	VG 4.0	FN 6.0	VF 8.0	VF/NM 9.0	NM- 9.2
1-Heck-c/a in all; Palais-a; bullet hole in forehead-c; all issues are very violent; soldier using flame thrower on enemy	34	68	102	199	325	450
2-4: 4-Morisi-a	18	36	54	105	165	225

WAR GODS OF THE DEEP (See Movie Classics)

WARHAWKS
TSR, Inc.: 1990 - No. 10, 1991 ($2.95, 44 pgs.)

	GD 2.0	VG 4.0	FN 6.0	VF 8.0	VF/NM 9.0	NM- 9.2
1-10-Based on TSR game, Spiegle a-1-6						3.00

WARHEADS
Marvel Comics UK: June, 1992 - No. 14, Aug, 1993 ($1.75)

	GD 2.0	VG 4.0	FN 6.0	VF 8.0	VF/NM 9.0	NM- 9.2
1-Wolverine-c/story; indicia says #2 by mistake						3.00
2-14: 2-Nick Fury app. 3-Iron Man-c/story. 4,5-X-Force. 5-Liger vs. Cable. 6,7-Death's Head II app. (#6 is cameo)						2.50

WAR HEROES (See Marine War Heroes)

WAR HEROES
Dell Publishing Co.: 7-9/42 (no month); No. 2, 10-12/42 - No. 10, 10-12/44 (Quarterly)

	GD 2.0	VG 4.0	FN 6.0	VF 8.0	VF/NM 9.0	NM- 9.2
1-General Douglas MacArthur-c	26	52	78	154	252	350
2-James Doolittle and other officers-c	15	30	45	85	130	175
3,5: 3-Pro-Russian back-c	13	26	39	74	105	135
4-Disney's Gremlins app.	18	36	54	107	169	230
6-10: 6-Tothish-a by Discount	10	20	30	56	76	95

NOTE: *No. 1 was to be released in July, but was delayed. Painted c-4, 6-9.*

WAR HEROES
Ace Magazines: May, 1952 - No. 8, Apr, 1953

	GD 2.0	VG 4.0	FN 6.0	VF 8.0	VF/NM 9.0	NM- 9.2
1	11	22	33	62	86	110
2-Lou Cameron-a	8	16	24	42	54	65
3-8: 6,7-Cameron-a	7	14	21	37	46	55

WAR HEROES (Also see Blue Bird Comics)
Charlton Comics: Feb, 1963 - No. 27, Nov, 1967

	GD 2.0	VG 4.0	FN 6.0	VF 8.0	VF/NM 9.0	NM- 9.2
1,2: 2-John F. Kennedy story	4	8	12	24	37	50
3-10	3	6	9	17	25	32
11-26	3	6	9	14	19	24
27-1st Devils Brigade by Glanzman	3	6	9	17	25	32

NOTE: ***Montes/Bache** a-3-7, 21, 25, 27; c-3-7.*

WAR HEROES
Image Comics: July, 2008 - No. 6 ($2.99, limited series)

	GD 2.0	VG 4.0	FN 6.0	VF 8.0	VF/NM 9.0	NM- 9.2
1-3-Soldiers given super powers; Mark Millar-s/Tony Harris-a/c; four covers						3.00

WAR IS HELL
Marvel Comics Group: Jan, 1973 - No. 15, Oct, 1975

	GD 2.0	VG 4.0	FN 6.0	VF 8.0	VF/NM 9.0	NM- 9.2
1-Williamson-a(r), 5 pgs.; Ayers-a	3	6	9	16	23	30
2-8-Reprints. 6-(11/73). 7-(6/74). 7,8-Kirby-a	2	4	6	9	13	16
9-Intro Death	5	10	15	30	48	65
10-15-Death app.	3	6	9	16	23	30

NOTE: ***Bolle** a-3r. **Powell** a-1. **Woodbridge** a-1. Sgt. Fury reprints-7, 8.*

WAR IS HELL: THE FIRST FLIGHT OF THE PHANTOM EAGLE
Marvel Comics (MAX): May, 2008 - No. 5, Sept, 2008 ($3.99, limited series)

	GD 2.0	VG 4.0	FN 6.0	VF 8.0	VF/NM 9.0	NM- 9.2
1-5-World War I fighter pilots; Ennis-s/Chaykin-a/Cassaday-c						4.00

WARLANDS
Image Comics: Aug, 1999 - No. 12, Feb, 2001 ($2.50)

	GD 2.0	VG 4.0	FN 6.0	VF 8.0	VF/NM 9.0	NM- 9.2
1-9,11,12-Pat Lee-a(p)/Adrian Tsang-s						2.50
10-($2.95) Flip book w/Shidima preview						3.00
... Chronicles 1,2 (2/00, 7/00; $7.95) 1-r/#1-3. 2-r/#4-6						8.00
...Darklyte TPB (8/01, $14.95) r/#0,1/2,1-6 w/cover gallery; new Lee-c						15.00
...Epilogue: Three Stories (3/01, $5.95) includes r/Wizard #1/2 & AE #0						6.00
Another Universe #0						3.00
Wizard #1/2						5.00

WARLANDS: THE AGE OF ICE (Volume 2)
Image Comics: July, 2001 - No. 9, Nov, 2002 ($2.95)

	GD 2.0	VG 4.0	FN 6.0	VF 8.0	VF/NM 9.0	NM- 9.2
#0-(2/02, $2.25)						2.50
#1/2 (4/02, $2.25)						2.50
1-9: 2-Flip book preview of Banished Knights						3.00
TPB (2003, $15.95) r/#1-9						16.00

WARLANDS: DARK TIDE RISING (Volume 3)
Image Comics: Dec, 2002 - No. 6, May, 2003 ($2.95)

	GD 2.0	VG 4.0	FN 6.0	VF 8.0	VF/NM 9.0	NM- 9.2
1-6: 1-Wraparound gatefold-c						3.00

WARLOCK (The Power of...)(Also see Avengers Annual #7, Fantastic Four #66, 67, Incredible Hulk #178, Infinity Crusade, Infinity Gauntlet, Infinity War, Marvel Premiere #1, Marvel Two-In-One Annual #2, Silver Surfer V3#46, Strange Tales #178-181 & Thor #165)
Marvel Comics Group: Aug, 1972 - No. 8, Oct, 1973; No. 9, Oct, 1975 - No. 15, Nov, 1976

	GD 2.0	VG 4.0	FN 6.0	VF 8.0	VF/NM 9.0	NM- 9.2
1-Origin by Kane	8	16	24	52	86	120
2,3	4	8	12	26	41	55
4-8: 4-Death of Eddie Roberts	3	6	9	17	25	32
9-Starlin's 2nd Thanos saga begins, ends #15; new costume Warlock; Thanos cameo only; story cont'd from Strange Tales #178-181; Starlin-c/a in #9-15	4	8	12	24	37	50
10-Origin Thanos & Gamora; recaps events from Capt. Marvel #25-34. Thanos vs.The Magus-c/story	4	8	12	26	41	55
11-Thanos app.; Warlock dies	3	6	9	19	29	38
12-14: (Regular 25¢ edition) 14-Origin Star Thief; last 25¢ issue	3	6	9	16	23	30
12-14-(30¢-c, limited distribution)	4	8	12	28	44	60
15-Thanos-c/story	3	6	9	17	25	32

NOTE: ***Buscema** a-2p; c-8p. **G. Kane** a-1p, 3-5p; c-1p, 2, 3, 4p, 5p, 7p. **Starlin** a-9-14p, 15; c-9, 10, 11p, 12p, 13-15. **Sutton** a-1-8i.*

WARLOCK (...Special Edition on-c)
Marvel Comics Group: Dec, 1982 - No. 6, May, 1983 ($2.00, slick paper, 52 pgs.)

	GD 2.0	VG 4.0	FN 6.0	VF 8.0	VF/NM 9.0	NM- 9.2
1-Warlock-r/Strange Tales #178-180.						4.00
2-6: 2-r/Str. Tales #180,181 & Warlock #9. 3-r/Warlock #10-12(Thanos origin recap). 4-r/Warlock #12-15. 5-r/Warlock #15, Marvel Team-Up #55 & Avengers Ann. #7. 6-r/2nd half Avengers Annual #7 & Marvel Two-in-One Annual #2						4.00
Special Edition #1(12/83)						4.00

NOTE: ***Byrne** a-5r. **Starlin** a-1-6r; c-1-6(new). Direct sale only.*

WARLOCK
Marvel Comics: V2#1, May, 1992 - No. 6, Oct, 1992 ($2.50, limited series)

	GD 2.0	VG 4.0	FN 6.0	VF 8.0	VF/NM 9.0	NM- 9.2
V2#1-6: 1-Reprints 1982 reprint series w/Thanos						2.50

WARLOCK
Marvel Comics: Nov, 1998 - No. 4, Feb, 1999 ($2.99, limited series)

	GD 2.0	VG 4.0	FN 6.0	VF 8.0	VF/NM 9.0	NM- 9.2
1-4-Warlock vs. Drax						3.00

WARLOCK (M-Tech)
Marvel Comics: Oct, 1999 - No. 9, June, 2000 ($1.99/$2.50)

	GD 2.0	VG 4.0	FN 6.0	VF 8.0	VF/NM 9.0	NM- 9.2
1-5: 1-Quesada-c. 2-Two covers						2.50
6-9: 6-Begin $2.50-c. 8-Avengers app.						2.50

WARLOCK
Marvel Comics: Nov, 2004 - No. 4, Feb, 2005 ($2.99, limited series)

	GD 2.0	VG 4.0	FN 6.0	VF 8.0	VF/NM 9.0	NM- 9.2
1-4-Adlard-a/Williams-c						3.00

WARLOCK AND THE INFINITY WATCH (Also see Infinity Gauntlet)
Marvel Comics: Feb, 1992 - No. 42, July, 1995 ($1.75) (Sequel to Infinity Gauntlet)

	GD 2.0	VG 4.0	FN 6.0	VF 8.0	VF/NM 9.0	NM- 9.2
1-Starlin-scripts begin; brief origin recap; sequel to Infinity Gauntlet						3.00
2,3: 2-Reintro Moondragon						2.50
4-24,26: 7-Reintro The Magus; Moondragon app.; Thanos cameo on last 2 pgs. 8,9-Thanos battles Gamora-c/story. 8-Magus & Moondragon app. 10-Thanos-c/story; Magus app. 13-Hulk x-over. 21-Drax vs. Thor						2.50
25-($2.95, 52 pgs.)-Die-cut & embossed double-c; Thor & Thanos app.						3.00
28-42: 28-$1.95-c begins; bound-in card sheet						2.50

NOTE: ***Austin** c/a-1-4i, 7i. **Leonardi** a(p)-3, 4. **Medina** c/a(p)-1, 2, 5; 6, 9, 10, 14, 15, 20. **Williams** a(i)-8, 12, 13, 16-19.*

WARLOCK CHRONICLES
Marvel Comics: June, 1993 - No. 8, Feb, 1994 ($2.00, limited series)

	GD 2.0	VG 4.0	FN 6.0	VF 8.0	VF/NM 9.0	NM- 9.2
1-($2.95)-Holo-grafx foil & embossed-c; origin retold; Starlin scripts begin; Keith Williams-a(i) in all						3.00
2-8: 3-Thanos & Mephisto-c/story. 4-Vs. Magus-c/s. 8-Contains free 16 pg. Razorline insert						2.50

WARLOCK 5
Aircel Pub.: 11/86 - No. 22, 5/89; V2#1, June, 1989 - V2#5, 1989 ($1.70, B&W)

	GD 2.0	VG 4.0	FN 6.0	VF 8.0	VF/NM 9.0	NM- 9.2
1-5,7-11-Gordon Derry-s/Denis Beauvais-a thru #11. 5-Green Cyborg on-c. 5-Misnumbered as #6 (no #6); Blue Girl on-c.						2.50
12-22-Barry Blair-s/a. 18-$1.95-c begins						3.00
V2#1-5 ($2.00, B&W)-All issues by Barry Blair						2.50
Compilation 1,2: 1-r/#1-5 (1988, $5.95); 2-r/#6-9						6.00

WARLORD (See 1st Issue Special #8) (B&W reprints in Showcase Presents: Warlord)
National Periodical Publications/DC Comics #123 on: 1-2/76; No.2, 3-4/76; No.3, 10-11/76 - No. 133, Win, 1988-89

	GD 2.0	VG 4.0	FN 6.0	VF 8.0	VF/NM 9.0	NM- 9.2
1-Story cont'd. from 1st Issue Special #8	3	6	9	20	30	40
2-Intro. Machiste	2	4	6	11	16	20

Warlord (2009 series) #2 © DC

War Machine (2009 series) #1 © MAR

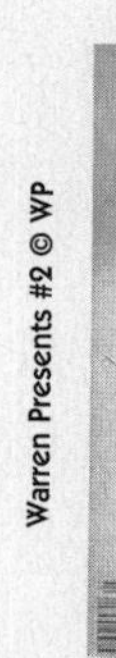
Warren Presents #2 © WP

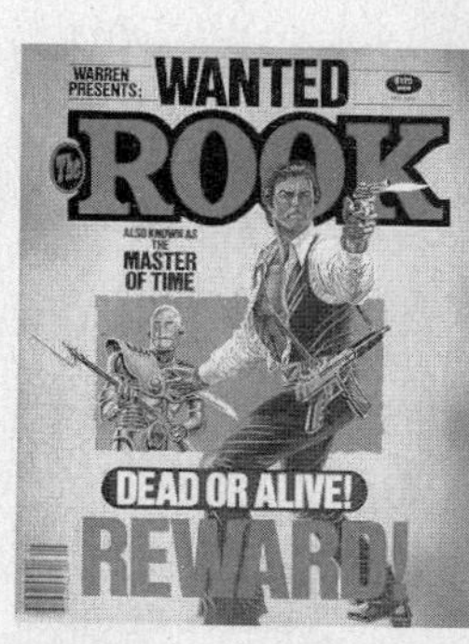

GD 2.0 | VG 4.0 | FN 6.0 | VF 8.0 | VF/NM 9.0 | NM- 9.2

3-5 2 4 6 8 10 12
6-10: 6-Intro Mariah. 7-Origin Machiste. 9-Dons new costume 1 2 3 5 6 8
11-20: 11-Origin-r. 12-Intro Aton. 15-Tara returns; Warlord has son 5.00
21-36,40,41: 27-New facts about origin. 28-1st app. Wizard World. 32-Intro Shakira. 40-Warlord gets new costume 4.00
22-Whitman variant edition 2 4 6 13 18 22
37-39: 37,38-Origin Omac by Starlin. 38-Intro Jennifer Morgan, Warlord's daughter. 39-Omac ends. 5.00
42-48: 42-47-Omac back-up series. 48-(52 pgs.)-1st app. Arak; contains free 14 pg. Arak Son of Thunder; Claw The Unconquered app. 4.00
49-62,64-99,101-132: 49-Claw The Unconquered app. 50-Death of Aton. 51-Reprints #1. 55-Arion Lord of Atlantis begins, ends #62. 91-Origin w/new facts. 114,115-Legends x-over. 125-Death of Tara. 131-1st DC work by Rob Liefeld (9/88) 3.00
63-The Barren Earth begins; free 16pg. Masters of the Universe preview 4.00
100-($1.25, 52 pgs.) 4.00
133-($1.50, 52 pgs.) 4.00
Annual 1-6 ('82-'87): 1-Grell-c,/a(p). 6-New Gods app. 4.00
The Savage Empire TPB (1991, $19.95) r/#1-10,12 & First Issue Special #8; Grell intro. 25.00
NOTE: *Grell a-1-15, 16-50p, 51r, 52p, 59p, Annual 1p; c-1-70, 100-104, 112, 116, 117, Annual 1, 5. Wayne Howard a-64i. Starlin a-37-39p.*

WARLORD
DC Comics: Jan, 1992 - No. 6, June, 1992 ($1.75, limited series)
1-6: Grell-c & scripts in all 2.50

WARLORD
DC Comics: Apr, 2006 - No. 10, Jan, 2007 ($2.99)
1-10: 1-Bruce Jones-s/Bart Sears-a. 10-Winslade-a 3.00

WARLORD
DC Comics: Jun, 2009 - Present ($2.99)
1-11: 1-Grell-s/Prado-a/Grell-c. 7-9,11-Grell-s/a/c. 10-Hardin-a 3.00

WARLORDS (See DC Graphic Novel #2)

WAR MACHINE (Also see Iron Man #281,282 & Marvel Comics Presents #152)
Marvel Comics: Apr, 1994 - No. 25, Apr, 1996 ($1.50)
"Ashcan" edition (nd, 75¢, B&W, 16 pgs.) 2.50
1-($2.00, 52 pgs.)-Newsstand edition; Cable app. 2.25
1-($2.95, 52 pgs.)-Collectors ed.; embossed foil-c 3.00
2-14, 16-25: 2-Bound-in trading card sheet; Cable app. 2,3-Deathlok app. 8-red logo 2.50
8-($2.95)-Polybagged w/16 pg. Marvel Action Hour preview & acetate print; yellow logo 3.00
15 ($2.50)-Flip book 2.50

WAR MACHINE (Also see Dark Reign and Secret Invasion crossovers)
Marvel Comics: Feb, 2009 - No. 12, Feb, 2010 ($2.99)
1-12: 1-5-Pak-s/Manco-a/c; cyborg Jim Rhodes. 10-12-Dark Reign 3.00
1-Variant Titanium Man cover by Deodato 6.00

WAR MAN
Marvel Comics (Epic Comics): Nov, 1993 - No. 2, Dec, 1993 ($2.50, lim. series)
1,2 2.50

WAR OF KINGS
Marvel Comics: May, 2009 - No. 6, Oct, 2009 ($3.99, limited series)
1-6-Pelletier-a/Abnett & Lanning-s; Inhumans vs. the Shi'Ar 4.00
... Saga (2009, giveaway) synopsies of stories involving Kree, Shi'Ar, Inhumans, etc. 2.25
...: Savage World of Skaar 1 (8/09, $3.99) Gorgon & Starbolt land on Sakaar 4.00
...: Who Will Rule? 1 (11/09, $3.99) Pelletier-a; profile pages 4.00

WAR OF KINGS: ASCENSION
Marvel Comics: June, 2009 - No. 4, Sept, 2009 ($3.99, limited series)
1-4-Alves-a/Abnett & Lanning-s; Darkhawk app. 4.00

WAR OF KINGS: DARKHAWK (Leads into War Of Kings: Ascension limited series)
Marvel Comics: Apr, 2009 - No. 2, May, 2009 ($3.99, limited series)
1,2-Cebulski-s/Tolibao & Dazo-a/Peterson-c; r/Darkhawk #1,2 (1991) origin 4.00

WAR OF KINGS: WARRIORS
Marvel Comics: Sept, 2009 - No. 2, Oct, 2009 ($3.99, limited series)
1,2-Prequel to x-over; Gage-s/Asrar & Magno-a 4.00

WAR OF THE GODS
DC Comics: Sept, 1991 - No. 4, Dec, 1991 ($1.75, limited series)
1-4: Perez layouts, scripts & covers. 1-Contains free mini posters (Robin, Deathstroke). 2-4-Direct sale versions include 4 pin-ups printed on cover stock plus different-c 2.50

WAR OF THE UNDEAD
IDW Publishing: Jan, 2007 - No. 3, Apr, 2007 ($3.99, limited series)
1-3-Bryan Johnson-s/Walter Flanagan-a 4.00

WAR OF THE WORLDS, THE
Caliber: 1996 - No. 5 ($2.95, B&W, 32 pgs.)(Based on H. G. Wells novel)
1-5: 1-Randy Zimmerman scripts begin 3.00

WARP
First Comics: Mar, 1983 - No. 19, Feb, 1985 ($1.00/$1.25, Mando paper)
1-Sargon-Mistress of War app.; Brunner-c/a thru #9 2.50
2-19: 2-Faceless Ones begin. 10-New Warp advs., & Outrider begin 2.50
Special 1-3: 1(7/83, 36 pgs.)-Origin Chaos-Prince of Madness; origin of Warp Universe begins, ends #3. 2(1/84)-Lord Cumulus vs. Sargon Mistress of War ($1.00). 3(6/84)-Chaos-Prince of Madness 2.50

WARPATH (Indians on the...)
Key Publications/Stanmor: Nov, 1954 - No. 3, Apr, 1955
1 11 22 33 62 86 110
2,3 8 16 24 40 50 60

WARPED
Empire Entertainment (Solson): Jun, 1990 - No. 2, Oct-Nov, 1990 (B&W mag)
1,2 2.50

WARP GRAPHICS ANNUAL
WaRP Graphics: Dec, 1985; 1988 ($2.50)
1-Elfquest, Blood of the Innocent, Thunderbunny & Myth Adventures 5.00
1 (1988) 4.00

WARREN PRESENTS
Warren Publications: Jan, 1979 - No. 14, Nov, 1981(B&W magazine)
1-Eerie, Creepy, & Vampirella-r; Ring of the Warlords; Merlin-s; Dax-s; Sanjulian-c 3 6 9 15 21 26
2-6(10/79): 2-The Rook. 3-Alien Invasions Comix. 4-Movie Aliens. 5-Dracula '79. 6-Strange Stories of Vampires Comix 2 4 6 9 13 16
8(10/80)-r/1st app. Pantha from Vamp. #30 2 4 6 11 16 20
9(11/80) Empire Encounters Comix 2 4 6 10 14 18
13(10/81),14(11/81):13-Sword and Sorcery Comix 3 6 9 14 19 24
(#7,10,11,12 may not exist, or may be a Special below)
Special-Alien Collectors Edition (1979) 3 6 9 14 19 24
Special-Close Encounters of the Third Kind (1978) 2 4 6 9 13 16
Special-Lord of the Rings (6/79) 3 6 9 19 29 38
Special-Meteor (1/80) 2 4 6 9 13 16
Special-Moonraker/James Bond (10/79) 2 4 6 9 13 16
Special-Star Wars (1977) 3 6 9 19 29 38

WAR REPORT
Ajax/Farrell Publications (Excellent Publ.): Sept, 1952 - No. 5, May, 1953
1 14 28 42 76 108 140
2-Flame thrower w/burning bodies on-c 14 28 42 80 115 150
3,5 8 16 24 44 57 70
4-Used in **POP**, pg. 94 9 18 27 50 65 80

WARRIOR (Wrestling star)
Ultimate Creations: May, 1996 - No. 4, 1997 ($2.95)
1-4: Warrior scripts; Callahan-c/a. 3-Wraparound-c. 4-Warrior #3 in indicia; pin-ups 3.00
1-Variant-c. 5.00
X-Mas (11/96, $3.50) listed as "No. 3" in indicia; pin-ups by various; Quesada-c 3.50

WARRIOR COMICS
H.C. Blackerby: 1945 (1930s DC reprints)
1-Wing Brady, The Iron Man, Mark Markon 21 42 63 126 206 285

WARRIOR OF WAVERLY STREET, THE
Dark Horse Comics: Nov, 1996 - No. 2, Dec, 1996 ($2.95, mini-series)
1,2-Darrow-c 3.00

WARRIORS
CFD Productions: 1993 (B&W, one-shot)
1-Linsner, Dark One-a 2 4 6 10 14 18

WARRIORS, THE : OFFICIAL MOVIE ADAPTATION (Based on the 1979 movie)
Dabel Brothers Publishing: Feb, 2009 - No. 5 ($3.99, limited series)
1,2: 1-Three covers plus wraparound photo-c; Dibari-a 4.00
...: Jailbreak 1 (7/09, $3.99) Apon & Herman-a 4.00

WARRIORS OF PLASM (Also see Plasm)
Defiant: Aug, 1993 - No. 13, Aug, 1995 ($2.95/$2.50)
1-4: Shooter-scripts; Lapham-c/a: 1-1st app. Glory. 4-Bound-in fold-out poster 3.00
5-7,10-13: 5-Begin $2.50-c. 13-Schism issue 2.50

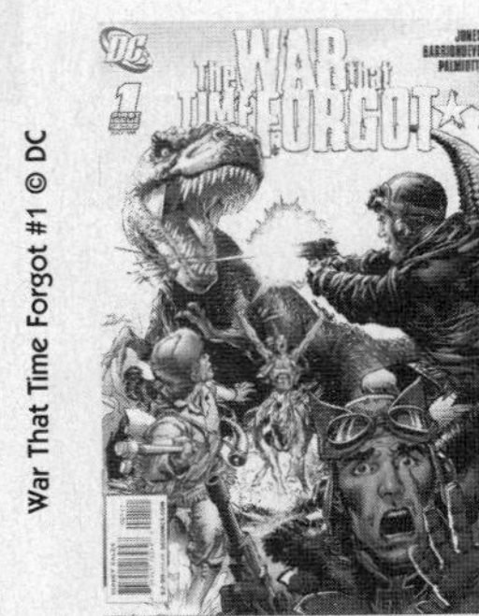

War That Time Forgot #1 © DC

Watchmen #1 © DC

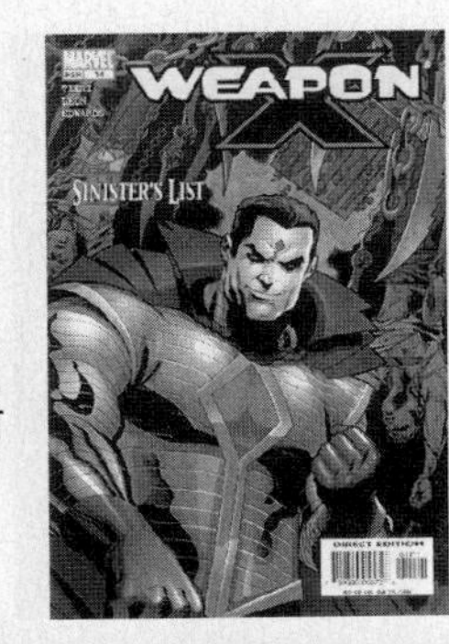

Weapon X #14 © MAR

	GD	VG	FN	VF	VF/NM	NM-
	2.0	4.0	6.0	8.0	9.0	9.2

8,9-($2.75, 44 pgs.) 2.75
The Collected Edition (2/94, $9.95)-r/Plasm #0, WOP #1-4 & Splatterball 10.00

WAR ROMANCES (See True...)

WAR SHIPS
Dell Publishing Co.: 1942 (36 pgs.)(Similar to Large Feature Comics)

	GD	VG	FN	VF	VF/NM	NM-
nn-Cover by McWilliams; contains photos & drawings of U.S. war ships	18	36	54	103	162	220

WAR STORIES (Formerly War Comics)
Dell Publ. Co.: No. 5, 1942(nd); No. 6, Aug-Oct, 1942 - No. 8, Feb-Apr, 1943

	GD	VG	FN	VF	VF/NM	NM-
5-Origin The Whistler	26	52	78	152	249	345
6-8: 6-8-Night Devils app. 8-Painted-c	20	40	60	114	182	250

WAR STORIES (Korea)
Ajax/Farrell Publications (Excellent Publ.): Sept, 1952 - No. 5, May, 1953

	GD	VG	FN	VF	VF/NM	NM-
1	13	26	39	72	101	130
2	8	16	24	42	54	65
3-5	8	16	24	40	50	60

WAR STORIES (See Star Spangled...)

WAR STORY
DC Comics (Vertigo): Nov, 2001 - Present ($4.95, series of World War II one-shots)

...: Archangel (4/03) Ennis-s/Erskine-a 5.00
...: Condors (3/03) Ennis-s/Ezquerra-a 5.00
...: D-Day Dodgers (12/01) Ennis-s/Higgins-a 5.00
...: J For Jenny (2/03) Ennis-s/Lloyd-a 5.00
...: Johann's Tiger (11/01) Ennis-s/Weston-a 5.00
...: Nightingale (2/02) Ennis-s/Lloyd-a 5.00
...: Screaming Eagles (1/02) Ennis-s/Gibbons-a 5.00
...: The Reivers (1/03) Ennis-s/Kennedy-a 5.00
Vol. 1 (2004, $19.95) r/Johann's Tiger, D-Day Dodgers, Screaming Eagles, Nightingale 20.00
Vol. 2 (2006, $19.99) r/J For Jenny, The Reivers, Condors, Archangel; Ennis afterword 20.00

WARSTRIKE
Malibu Comics (Ultraverse): May, 1994 - No. 7, Nov, 1995 ($1.95)

1-7: 1-Simonson-c 2.50
1-Ultra 5000 Limited silver foil 4.00
Giant Size 1 (12/94, 2.50, 44pgs.)-Prelude to Godwheel 2.50

WART AND THE WIZARD (See The Sword & the Stone under Movie Comics)
Gold Key: Feb, 1964 (Walt Disney)(Characters from Sword in the Stone movie)

	GD	VG	FN	VF	VF/NM	NM-
1 (10102-402)	4	8	12	28	44	60

WAR THAT TIME FORGOT, THE
DC Comics: Jul, 2008 - No. 12, Jun, 2009 ($2.99, limited series)

1-12: 1-Bruce Jones-s/Al Barrionuevo-a/Neal Adams-c; Enemy Ace app. 3.00
... Vol. 1 TPB (2009, $17.99) r/#1-6 18.00
... Vol. 2 TPB (2009, $17.99) r/#7-12 18.00

WARTIME ROMANCES
St. John Publishing Co.: July, 1951 - No. 18, Nov, 1953

	GD	VG	FN	VF	VF/NM	NM-
1-All Baker-c/a	43	86	129	271	461	650
2-All Baker-c/a	32	64	96	192	314	435
3,4-All Baker-c/a	31	62	93	182	296	410
5-8-Baker-c/a(2-3) each	29	58	87	170	278	385
9,11,12,16,18: Baker-c/a each. 9-Two signed stories by Estrada	23	46	69	136	223	310
10,13-15,17-Baker-c only	20	40	60	114	182	250

WAR VICTORY ADVENTURES (#1 titled War Victory Comics)
U.S. Treasury Dept./War Victory/Harvey Publ.: Sum, 1942 - No. 3, Wint, 1943-44 (5¢/10¢)

	GD	VG	FN	VF	VF/NM	NM-
1-(5¢)(Promotion of Savings Bonds)-Featuring America's greatest comic art by top syndicated cartoonists; Blondie, Joe Palooka, Green Hornet, Dick Tracy, Superman, Gumps, etc.; (36 pgs.); all profits were contributed to U.S.O. & Army/Navy relief funds	42	84	126	265	445	625
2-(10¢) Battle of Stalingrad story; Powell-a (8/43); flag & WWII Japanese-c	39	78	117	240	395	550
3-(10¢) Capt. Red Cross-c & text only; WWII Nazi-c; Powell-a	39	78	117	240	395	550

WAR WAGON, THE (See Movie Classics)

WAR WINGS
Charlton Comics: Oct, 1968

	GD	VG	FN	VF	VF/NM	NM-
1	3	6	9	14	20	26

WARWORLD!
Dark Horse Comics: Feb, 1989 ($1.75, B&W, one-shot)

1-Gary Davis sci/fi art in Moebius style 2.50

WASHABLE JONES AND THE SHMOO (Also see Al Capp's Shmoo)
Toby Press: June, 1953

	GD	VG	FN	VF	VF/NM	NM-
1- "Super-Shmoo"	19	38	57	109	172	235

WASH TUBBS (See The Comics, Crackajack Funnies)
Dell Publishing Co.: No. 11, 1942 - No. 53, 1944

	GD	VG	FN	VF	VF/NM	NM-
Four Color 11 (#1)	28	56	84	203	377	550
Four Color 28 (1943)	19	38	57	135	250	365
Four Color 53	14	28	42	102	181	260

WASTELAND
DC Comics: Dec, 1987 - No. 18, May, 1989 ($1.75-$2.00 #13 on, mature)

1-5(4/88), 5(5/88), 6(5/88)-18: 13,15-Orlando-a 2.50
NOTE: *Orlando a-12, 13, 15. Truman a-10; c-13.*

WATCHMEN
DC Comics: Sept, 1986 - No. 12, Oct, 1987 (maxi-series)

	GD	VG	FN	VF	VF/NM	NM-
1-Alan Moore scripts & Dave Gibbons-c/a in all	2	4	6	11	16	20
1-(2009, $1.50) Second printing						1.50
2-12	2	4	6	9	12	15

Hardcover Collection-Slip-cased-r/#1-12 w/new material; produced by Graphitti Designs 100.00
HC (2008, $39.99) recolored r/#1-12; design & promotional art; Moore & Gibbons intros 40.00
Trade paperback (1987, $14.95)-r/#1-12 25.00

WATER BIRDS AND THE OLYMPIC ELK (Disney)
Dell Publishing Co.: No. 700, Apr, 1956

	GD	VG	FN	VF	VF/NM	NM-
Four Color 700-Movie	5	10	15	34	55	75

WATERWORLD: CHILDREN OF LEVIATHAN
Acclaim Comics: Aug, 1997 - No. 4, Nov, 1997 ($2.50, mini-series)

1-4 2.50

WAY OF THE RAT
CrossGeneration Comics: Jun, 2002 - No. 24, June, 2004 ($2.95)

1-24: 1-Dixon-s/ Jeff Johnson-a. 5-Whigham-a. 9,14-Luke Ross-a 3.00
Free Comic Book Day Special (6/03) reprints #1 w/features, interviews, CrossGen info 2.25
...: The Walls of Zhumar Vol. 1 (1/03, $15.95) r/#1-6 16.00
Vol. 2: The Dragon's Wake (2003, $15.95) r/#7-12 16.00

WEAPON X
Marvel Comics: Apr, 1994 ($12.95, one-shot)

nn-r/Marvel Comics Presents #72-84 13.00

WEAPON X
Marvel Comics: Mar, 1995 - No. 4, June, 1995 ($1.95)

1-Age of Apocalypse 4.00
2-4 2.50

WEAPON X
Marvel Comics: Nov, 2002 - No. 28, Nov, 2004 ($2.25/$2.99)

1-7: 1-Sabretooth-c/app.; Tieri-s/Jeanty-a 2.50
8-28: 8-Begin $2.99-c. 14-Invaders app. 15-Chamber joins. 16-18,21-25-Wolverine app. 3.00
Vol. 1: The Draft TPB (2003, $21.99) r/#1-5, #1/2 & The Draft one-shots 22.00
Vol. 2: The Underground TPB (2003, $19.99) r/#6-13 20.00
Wizard #1/2 (2002) 5.00

WEAPON X: DAYS OF FUTURE NOW
Marvel Comics: Sept, 2005 - No. 5, Jan, 2006 ($2.99, limited series)

1-5-Tieri-s/Sears-a; Chamber, Sauron & Fantomex app. 3.00
TPB (2006, $13.99) r/#1-5 14.00

WEAPON X: FIRST CLASS
Marvel Comics: Jan, 2009 - No. 3, Mar, 2009 ($3.99, limited series)

1-3:1-Sabretooth-c/app. 2-Deadpool-c/app. 4.00

WEAPON X: THE DRAFT (Leads into 2002 Weapon X series)
Marvel Comics: Oct, 2002 ($2.25, one-shots)

...Kane 1- JH Williams-c/Raimondi-a 2.50
...Marrow 1- JH Williams-c/Badeaux-a 2.50
...Sauron 1- JH Williams-c/Kerschl-a; Emma Frost app. 2.50
...Wild Child 1- JH Williams-c/Van Sciver-a; Aurora (Alpha Flight) app. 2.50
...Zero 1- JH Williams-c/Plunkett-a; Wolverine app. 2.50

WEAPON ZERO
Image Comics (Top Cow Productions): No. T-4(#1), June, 1995 - No. T-0(#5), Dec, 1995 ($2.50, limited series)

The Web (2009 series) #1 © AP

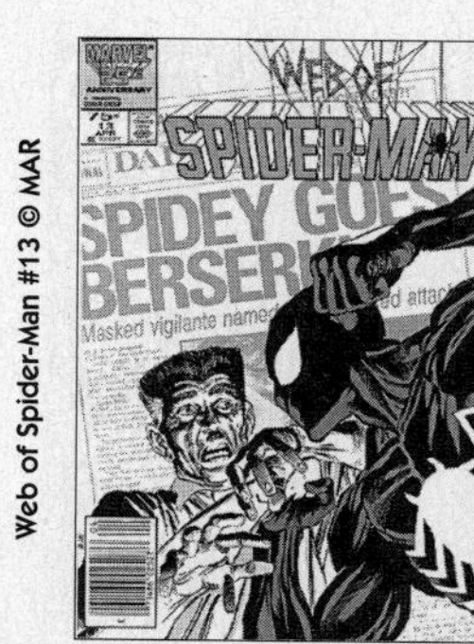

Web of Spider-Man #13 © MAR

Websprinners: Tales of Spider-Man #7 © MAR

	GD 2.0	VG 4.0	FN 6.0	VF 8.0	VF/NM 9.0	NM- 9.2

T-4(#1): Walt Simonson scripts in all. 5.00
T-3(#2) - T-1(#4) 4.00
T-0(#5) 3.00

WEAPON ZERO
Image Comics (Top Cow Productions): V2#1, Mar, 1996 - No. 15, Dec, 1997 ($2.50)
V2#1-Walt Simonson scripts. 3.00
2-14: 8-Begin Top Cow. 10-Devil's Reign 2.50
15-($3.50) Benitez-a 3.50

WEAPON ZERO/SILVER SURFER
Image Comics/Marvel Comics: Jan, 1997($2.95, one-shot)
1-Devil's Reign Pt. 1 3.00

WEASELGUY: ROAD TRIP
Image Comics: Sept, 1999 - No. 2 ($3.50, limited series)
1,2-Steve Buccellato-s/a 3.50
1-Variant-c by Bachalo 5.00

WEASELGUY/WITCHBLADE
Hyperwerks: July, 1998 ($2.95, one-shot)
1-Steve Buccellato-s/a; covers by Matsuda and Altstaetter 3.00

WEASEL PATROL SPECIAL, THE (Also see Fusion #17)
Eclipse Comics: Apr, 1989 ($2.00, B&W, one-shot)
1-Funny animal 2.50

WEAVEWORLD
Marvel Comics (Epic): Dec, 1991 - No. 3, 1992 ($4.95, lim. series, 68 pgs.)
1-3: Clive Barker adaptation 5.00

WEB, THE (Also see Mighty Comics & Mighty Crusaders)
DC Comics (Impact Comics): Sept, 1991 - No. 14, Oct, 1992 ($1.00)
1-14: 5-The Fly x-over 9-Trading card inside 2.50
Annual 1 (1992, $2.50, 68 pgs.)-With Trading card 3.00
NOTE: *Gil Kane c-5, 9, 10, 12-14. Bill Wray a(i)-1-9, 10(part).*

WEB, THE (Continued from The Red Circle)
DC Comics: Nov, 2009 - Present ($3.99)
1-5: 1-Roger Robinson-a; The Hangman back-up feature. 3-Batgirl app. 5-Caldwell-a 4.00

WEB OF EVIL
Comic Magazines/Quality Comics Group: Nov, 1952 - No. 21, Dec, 1954
1-Used in **SOTI**, pg. 388. Jack Cole-a; morphine use story
60 120 180 381 653 925
2-4,6,7: 2,3-Jack Cole-a. 4,6,7-Jack Cole-c/a 41 82 123 256 428 600
5-Electrocution-c/story; Jack Cole-c/a 48 96 144 302 514 725
8-11-Jack Cole-a 39 78 117 240 395 550
12,13,15,16,19-21 25 50 75 147 241 335
14-Part Crandall-c; Old Witch swipe 26 52 78 154 252 350
17-Opium drug propaganda story 26 52 78 152 249 345
18-Acid-in-face story 26 52 78 154 252 350
NOTE: *Jack Cole a(2 each)-2, 6, 8, 9. Cuidera c-1-21i. Ravielli a-13.*

WEB OF HORROR
Major Magazines: Dec, 1969 - No. 3, Apr, 1970 (Magazine)
1-Jeff Jones painted-c; Wrightson-a, Kaluta-a 8 16 24 58 97 135
2-Jones painted-c; Wrightson-a(2), Kaluta-a 7 14 21 50 83 115
3-Wrightson-c/a (1st published-c); Brunner, Kaluta, Bruce Jones-a
9 18 27 63 107 150

WEB OF MYSTERY
Ace Magazines (A. A. Wyn): Feb, 1951 - No. 29, Sept, 1955
1 55 110 165 352 601 850
2-Bakerish-a 32 64 96 188 307 425
3-10: 4-Colan-a 28 56 84 165 270 375
11-18,20-26: 12-John Chilly's 1st cover art. 13-Surrealistic-c. 20-r/The Beyond #1
24 48 72 142 234 325
19-Reprints Challenge of the Unknown #6 used in N.Y. Legislative Committee
24 48 72 142 234 325
27-Bakerish-a(r/The Beyond #2); last pre-code ish 22 44 66 128 209 290
28,29: 28-All-r 17 34 51 100 158 215
NOTE: *This series was to appear as "Creepy Stories", but title was changed before publication. Cameron a-6, 8, 11-13, 17-20, 22, 24, 25, 27; c-8, 13, 17. Palais a-28r. Sekowsky a-1-3, 7, 8, 11, 14, 21, 29. Tothish a-by Bill Discount #16. 29-all-r, 19-28-partial-r.*

WEB OF SCARLET SPIDER
Marvel Comics: Oct, 1995 - No. 4, Jan, 1996 ($1.95, limited series)
1-4: Replaces "Web of Spider-Man" 2.50

WEB OF SPIDER-MAN (Replaces Marvel Team-Up)
Marvel Comics Group: Apr, 1985 - No. 129, Sept, 1995
1-Painted-c (5th app. black costume?) 2 4 6 9 12 15
2,3 5.00
4-8: 7-Hulk x-over; Wolverine splash 4.00
9-13: 10-Dominic Fortune guest stars; painted-c 4.00
14-17,19-28: 19-Intro Humbug & Solo 3.00
18-1st app. Venom (behind the scenes, 9/86) 3.00
29-Wolverine, new Hobgoblin (Macendale) app. 1 2 3 5 6 8
30-Origin recap The Rose & Hobgoblin I (entire book is flashback story); Punisher & Wolverine cameo 4.00
31,32-Six part Kraven storyline begins 5.00
33-37,39-47,49: 36-1st app. Tombstone 3.00
38-Hobgoblin app.; begin $1.00-c 4.00
48-Origin Hobgoblin II(Demogoblin) cont'd from Spectacular Spider-Man #147; Kingpin app. 1 2 3 5 7 9
50-($1.50, 52 pgs.) 3.50
51-58 2.50
59-Cosmic Spidey cont'd from Spect. Spider-Man 3.50
60-89,91-99,101-106: 66,67-Green Goblin (Norman Osborn) app. as a super-hero. 69,70-Hulk x-over. 74-76-Austin-c(i). 76-Fantastic Four x-over. 78-Cloak & Dagger app. 81-Origin/1st app. Bloodshed. 84-Begin 6 part Rose & Hobgoblin II storyline; last $1.00-c. 86-Demon leaves Hobgoblin; 1st Demogoblin. 93-Gives brief history of Hobgoblin. 93,94-Hobgoblin (Macendale) Reborn-c/story, parts 1,2; MoonKnight app. 94-Venom cameo. 95-Begin 4 part x-over w/Spirits of Venom w/Ghost Rider/Blaze/Spidey vs. Venom & Demogoblin (cont'd in Ghost Rider/Blaze #5,6). 96-Spirits of Venom part 3; painted-c. 101,103-Maximum Carnage x-over. 103-Venom & Carnage app. 104-106-Nightwatch back-up stories 2.50
90-($2.95, 52 pgs.)-Polybagged w/silver hologram-c, gatefold poster showing Spider-Man & Spider-Man 2099 (Williamson-i) 3.50
90-2nd printing; gold hologram-c 3.00
100-($2.95, 52 pgs.)-Holo-grafx foil-c; intro new Spider-Armor 4.00
107-111: 107-Intro Sandstorm; Sand & Quicksand app. 2.50
112-116, 118, 119, 121-124, 126-128: 112-Begin $1.50-c; bound-in trading card sheet. 113-Regular Ed.; Gambit & Black Cat app. 118-1st solo clone story; Venom app. 2.50
113-($2.95)-Collector's ed. polybagged w/foil-c; 16 pg. preview of Spider-Man cartoon & animation cel 3.00
117-($1.50)-Flip book; Power & Responsibility Pt.1 2.50
117-($2.95)-Collector's edition; foil-c; flip book 3.00
119-($6.45)-Direct market edition; polybagged w/ Marvel Milestone Amazing Spider-Man #150 & coupon for Amazing Spider-Man #396, Spider-Man #53, & Spectacular Spider-Man #219. 7.00
120 ($2.25)-Flip book w/ preview of the Ultimate Spider-Man 2.50
125 ($3.95)-Holodisk-c; Gwen Stacy clone 4.00
125,129: 25 ($2.95)-Newsstand. 129-Last issue 3.00
Annual 1 (1985) 3.00
Annual 2 (1986)-New Mutants; Art Adams-a 1 2 3 5 6 8
Annual 3-10 ('87-'94, 68 pgs.): 4-Evolutionary War x-over. 5-Atlantis Attacks; Captain Universe by Ditko (p) & Silver Sable stories; F.F. app. 6-Punisher back-up plus Capt. Universe by Ditko; G. Kane-a. 7-Origins of Hobgoblin I, Hobgoblin II, Green Goblin I & II & Venom; Larsen/Austin-c. 9-Bagged w/card 3.00
Super Special 1 (1995, $3.95)-flip book 4.00
NOTE: *Art Adams a-Annual 2. Byrne c-3-6. Chaykin c-10. Mignola a-Annual 2. Vess c-1, 8, Annual 1, 2. Zeck a-6i, 31, 32; c-31, 32.*

WEB OF SPIDER-MAN (Anthology)
Marvel Comics: Dec, 2009 - Present ($3.99)
1-7: 1-Spider-Girl in all; Ben Reilly app. 2-6-Origins of villains retold. 7-Lizard app. 4.00

WEBSPINNERS: TALES OF SPIDER-MAN
Marvel Comics: Jan, 1999 - No. 18, Jun, 2000 ($2.99/$2.50)
1-DeMatteis-s/Zulli-a; back-up story w/Romita Sr. art 3.00
1-($6.95) DF Edition 7.00
2,3: 2-Two covers 2.50
4-11,13-18: 4,5-Giffen-a; Silver Surfer-c/app. 7-9-Kelly-s/Sears and Smith-a. 10,11-Jenkins-s/Sean Phillips-a 2.50
12-($3.50) J.G. Jones-c/a; Jenkins-s 3.50

WEDDING BELLS
Quality Comics Group: Feb, 1954 - No. 19, Nov, 1956
1-Whitney-a 15 30 45 90 140 190
2 10 20 30 58 79 100
3-9: 8-Last precode (4/55) 9 18 27 47 61 75
10-Ward-a (9 pgs.) 14 28 42 82 121 160
11-14,17 8 16 24 42 54 65

Wednesday Comics #1 © DC

Weird Comics #4 © FOX

Weird Horrors #7 © STJ

GD VG FN VF VF/NM NM-
2.0 4.0 6.0 8.0 9.0 9.2

GD VG FN VF VF/NM NM-
2.0 4.0 6.0 8.0 9.0 9.2

15-Baker-c 12 24 36 69 97 125
16-Baker-c/a 15 30 45 83 124 165
18,19-Baker-a each 11 22 33 62 86 110

WEDDING OF DRACULA
Marvel Comics: Jan, 1993 ($2.00, 52 pgs.)

1-Reprints Tomb of Dracula #30,45,46 2.50

WEDNESDAY COMICS (Newspaper-style, twice folded pages on 20" x 14" newsprint)
DC Comics: Sept, 2009 - No. 12, Nov, 2009 ($3.99, weekly limited series)

1-12-Superman, Batman, Kamandi, Hawkman, Deadman, Green Lantern, Flash, Teen Titans, Metamorpho, Adam Strange, Supergirl, Metal Men, Wonder Woman, The Demon with Catwoman, Sgt. Rock; s-a/ by various incl. Ryan Sook, Joe Kubert, Gaiman, Allred, Risso, Kyle Baker, Paul Pope, Conner, Simonson, Garcia-Lopez, Stelfreeze, Bermejo 4.00

WEEKENDER, THE (Illustrated...)
Rucker Pub. Co.: V1#1, Sept, 1945? - V1#4, Nov, 1945; V2#1, Jan, 1946 - V2#3, Aug, 1946 (52 pgs.)

V1#1-4: 1-Same-c as Zip Comics #45, inside-c and back-c blank; Steel Sterling, Senor Banana, Red Rube and Ginger. 2-Capt. Victory on-c. 3-Super hero-c; Mr. E, Dan Hastings, Sky Chief and the Echo. 4-Same-c as Punch Comics #10 (9/44); r/Hale the Magician (7 pgs.) & r/Mr. E (8 pgs.-Lou Fine? or Gustavson?) plus 3 humor strips & many B&W photos & r/newspaper articles plus cheesecake photos of Hollywood stars
17 34 51 98 154 210

V2#1-Same-c as Dynamic Comics #11; 36 pgs. comics, 16 in newspaper format with photos; partial Dynamic Comics reprints; 4 pgs. of cels from the Disney film Pinocchio; Little Nemo story by Winsor McCay, Jr.; Jack Cole-a 19 38 57 109 172 235

V2#2,3: 2-Same-c as Dynamic Comics #9 by Raboy; Dan Hastings (Tuska), Rocket Boy, The Echo, Lucky Coyne. 3-Humor-c by Boddington?; Dynamic Man, Ima Slooth, Master Key, Dynamic Boy, Captain Glory 17 34 51 98 154 210

WEIRD
Eerie Publications: V1#10, 1/66 - V8#6, 12/74; V9#1, 1/75 - V14#3, Nov, 1981 (Magazine) (V1-V8: 52 pgs.; V9 on: 68 pgs.)

V1#10(#1)-Intro. Morris the Caretaker of Weird (ends V2#10); Burgos-a
8 16 24 54 90 125
11,12 5 10 15 34 55 75
V2#1-4(10/67), V3#1(1/68), V2#6(4/68)-V2#7,9,10(12/68)
5 10 15 34 55 75
V2#8-r/Ditko's 1st story/Fantastic Fears #5 6 12 18 41 66 90
V3#1(2/69)-V3#4 5 10 15 30 48 65
V3#5(12/69)-Rulah reprint; "Rulah" changed to "Pulah", LSD story reprinted in Horror Tales V4#4, Tales From the Tomb V2#4, & 20 5 10 15 30 48 65
V4#1-6('70), V5#1-6('71), V6#1-7('72), V7#1-7('73), V8#1-3, V8#4(8/74), V8#4(10/74), (V8#5 does not exist), V8#6('74), V9#1-4(1/75-'76), V10#1-3('77), V11#1-4('78), V12#1(2/79)-V14#3(11/81) 5 10 15 30 48 65

NOTE: *There are two V8#4 issues (8/74 & 10/74). V9#4 (12/76) has a cover swipe from Horror Tales V5#1 (2/73). There are two V13#3 issues (6/80 & 9/80).*

WEIRD
DC Comics (Paradox Press): Sum, 1997 - Present ($2.99, B&W, magazine)

1-4: 4-Mike Tyson-c 3.00

WEIRD, THE
DC Comics: Apr, 1988 - No. 4, July, 1988 ($1.50, limited series)

1-4: Wrightson-c/a in all 4.00

WEIRD ADVENTURES
P. L. Publishing Co. (Canada): May-June, 1951 - No. 3, Sept-Oct, 1951

1- "The She-Wolf Killer" by Matt Baker (6 pgs.) 58 116 174 371 636 900
2-Bondage/hypodermic panel 45 90 135 284 480 675
3-Male bondage/torture-c; severed head story 40 80 120 246 411 575

WEIRD ADVENTURES
Ziff-Davis Publishing Co.: No. 10, July-Aug, 1951

10-Painted-c 39 78 117 240 395 550

WEIRD CHILLS
Key Publications: July, 1954 - No. 3, Nov, 1954

1-Wolverton-r/Weird Mysteries No. 4; blood transfusion-c by Baily
94 188 282 597 1024 1450
2-Extremely violent injury to eye-c by Baily; Hitler story
113 226 339 718 1234 1750
3-Bondage E.C. swipe-c by Baily 48 96 144 302 514 725

WEIRD COMICS
Fox Features Syndicate: Apr, 1940 - No. 20, Jan, 1942

1-The Birdman, Thor, God of Thunder (ends #5), The Sorceress of Zoom, Blast Bennett, Typhon, Voodoo Man, & Dr. Mortal begin; George Tuska bondage-c
476 952 1428 3475 6138 8800
2-Lou Fine-c 234 468 702 1486 2556 3625
3,4: 3-Simon-c. 4-Torture-c 123 246 369 787 1344 1900
5-Intro. Dart & sidekick Ace (8/40) (ends #20); bondage/hypo-c
127 254 381 807 1391 1975
6,7-Dynamite Thor app. in each. 6-Super hero covers begin
94 188 282 597 1024 1450
8-Dynamo, the Eagle (11/40, early app.; see Science #1) & sidekick Buddy & Marga, the Panther Woman begin 92 184 276 584 1005 1425
9,10: 10-Navy Jones app. 74 148 222 470 810 1150
11-19: 16-Flag-c. 17-Origin The Black Rider. 55 110 165 352 601 850
20-Origin The Rapier; Swoop Curtis app; Churchill & Hitler-c
81 162 243 518 884 1250

NOTE *Cover features: Sorceress of Zoom-4; Dr. Mortal-5; Dart & Ace-6-13, 15; Eagle-14, 16-20.*

WEIRD FANTASY (Formerly A Moon, A Girl, Romance; becomes Weird Science-Fantasy #23 on)
E. C. Comics: No. 13, May-June, 1950 - No. 22, Nov-Dec, 1953

13(#1) (1950) 200 400 600 1600 2550 3500
14-Necronomicon story; Cosmic Ray Bomb explosion-c/story by Feldstein; Feldstein & Gaines star 97 194 291 776 1238 1700
15,16: 16-Used in **SOTI**, pg. 144 66 132 198 528 839 1150
17 (1951) 54 108 162 432 691 950
6-10: 6-Robot-c 46 92 138 368 584 800
11-13 (1952): 11-Feldstein bio. 12-E.C. artists cameo; Orlando bio. 13-Anti-Wertham "Cosmic Correspondence" 37 74 111 296 473 650
14-Frazetta/Williamson(1st team-up at E.C.)/Krenkel-a (7 pgs.); Orlando draws E.C. staff
50 100 150 400 638 875
15-Williamson/Evans-a(3), 4,3,&7 pgs. 37 74 111 296 473 650
16-19-Williamson/Krenkel-a in all. 18-Williamson/Feldstein-c. 19-Williamson bio.
35 70 105 280 445 610
20-Frazetta/Williamson-a (7 pgs.) 39 78 117 312 494 675
21-Frazetta/Williamson-c & Williamson/Krenkel-a 51 102 153 408 654 900
22-Bradbury adaptation 28 56 84 224 355 485

NOTE: ***Ray Bradbury** adaptations-13, 17-20, 22. **Crandall** a-22. **Elder** a-17. **Feldstein** a-13(#1)-8; c-13(#1)-18 (#18 w/**Williamson**), 20. **Harrison/Wood** a-13. **Kamen** a-13(#1)-16, 18-22. **Krigstein** a-22. **Kurtzman** a-13(#1)-17(#5), 6. **Orlando** a-9-22 (2 stories in #16); c-19, 22. **Severin/Elder** a-18-21. **Wood** a-13(#1)-14, 17(2 stories ea. in #10-13). Ray Bradbury adaptations in #17-19, 22. Canadian reprints exist; see Table of Contents.*

WEIRD FANTASY
Russ Cochran/Gemstone Publ.: Oct, 1992 - No. 22, Jan, 1998 ($1.50/$2.00/$2.50)

1-22: 1,2: 1,2-r/Weird Fantasy #13,14; Feldstein-c. 3-5-r/Weird Fantasy #15-17 4.00

WEIRD HORRORS (Nightmare #10 on)
St. John Publishing Co.: June, 1952 - No. 9, Oct, 1953

1-Tuska-a 58 116 174 371 636 900
2,3: 3-Hashish story 37 74 111 222 361 500
4,5 33 66 99 194 317 440
6-Ekgren-c; atomic bomb story 53 106 159 334 567 800
7-Ekgren-c; Kubert, Cameron-a 54 108 162 343 584 825
8,9-Kubert-c/a 41 82 123 256 428 600

NOTE: ***Cameron** a-7, 9. **Finesque** a-1-5. **Forgione** a-6. **Morisi** a-3. Bondage c-8.*

WEIRD MYSTERIES
Gillmor Publications: Oct, 1952 - No. 12, Sept, 1954

1-Partial Wolverton-c swiped from splash page "Flight to the Future" in Weird Tales of the Future #2; "Eternity" has an Ingels swipe 100 200 300 635 1093 1550
2- "Robot Woman" by Wolverton; Bernard Baily-c reprinted in Mister Mystery #18; acid in face panel 129 258 387 826 1413 2000
3,6: Both have decapitation-c 65 130 195 416 708 1000
4- "The Man Who Never Smiled" (3 pgs.) by Wolverton; Classic B. Baily skull-c
129 258 387 826 1413 2000
5-Wolverton story "Swamp Monster" (6 pgs.). Classic exposed brain-c
156 312 465 992 1696 2400
7-Used in **SOTI**, illo "Indeed", illo "Sex and blood" 89 178 267 565 970 1375
8-Wolverton-c panel-r/#5; used in a '54 Readers Digest anti-comics article by T. E. Murphy entitled "For the Kiddies to Read" 60 120 180 381 653 925
9-Excessive violence, gore & torture 57 114 171 362 619 875
10-Silhouetted nudity panel 52 104 156 328 557 785
11,12: 12-r/Mr. Mystery #8(2), Weird Mysteries #3 & Weird Tales of the Future #6
49 98 147 309 522 735

NOTE: ***Baily** c-2-12. Anti-Wertham column in #5. #1-12 all have 'The Ghoul Teacher' (host).*

WEIRD MYSTERIES (Magazine)
Pastime Publications: Mar-Apr, 1959 (35¢, B&W, 68 pgs.)

1-Torres-a; E. C. swipe from Tales From the Crypt #46 by Tuska "The Ragman"
11 22 33 60 83 105

Weird Science-Fantasy 1953 Annual © WMG

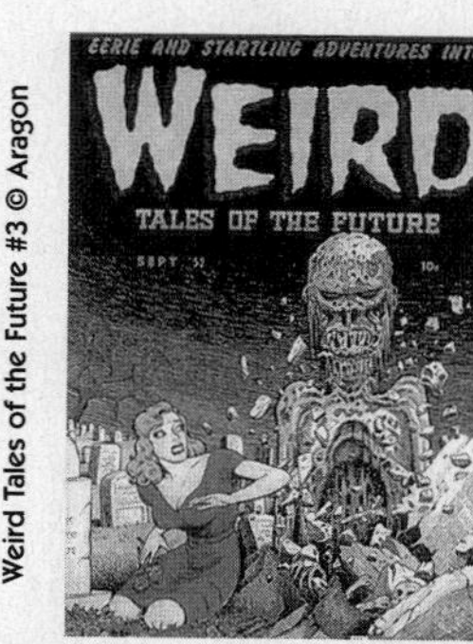

Weird Tales of the Future #3 © Aragon

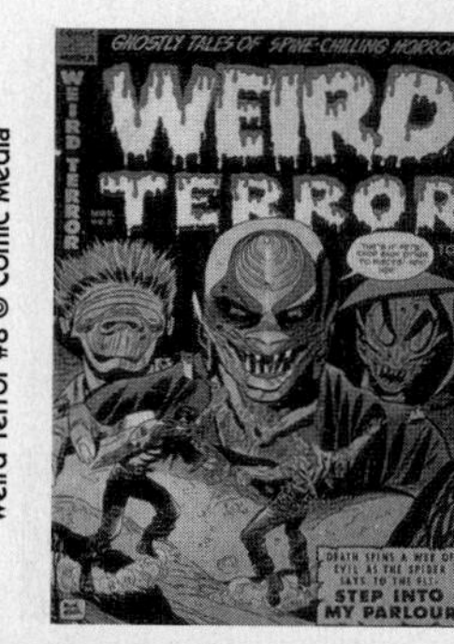

Weird Terror #8 © Comic Media

WEIRD MYSTERY TALES (See DC 100 Page Super Spectacular)

WEIRD MYSTERY TALES (See Cancelled Comic Cavalcade)
National Periodical Publications: July-Aug, 1972 - No. 24, Nov, 1975

	GD 2.0	VG 4.0	FN 6.0	VF 8.0	VF/NM 9.0	NM- 9.2
1-Kirby-a; Wrightson splash pg.	5	10	15	34	55	75
2-Titanic-c/s	3	6	9	20	30	40
3,21: 21-Wrightson-c	3	6	9	17	25	32
4-10	2	4	6	13	18	22
11-20,22-24	2	4	6	10	14	18

NOTE: *Alcala a-5, 10, 13, 14. **Aparo** c-4. **Bailey** a-8. **Bolle** a-8?. **Howard** a-4. **Kaluta** a-4, 24; c-1. **G. Kane** a-10. **Kirby** a-1, 2p, 3p. **Nino** a-5, 6, 9, 13, 16, 21. **Redondo** a-9, 17. **Sparling** c-6. **Starlin** a-3?, 4. **Wood** a-23.*

WEIRD ROMANCE (Seduction of the Innocent #9)
Eclipse Comics: Feb, 1988 ($2.00, B&W)

	GD 2.0	VG 4.0	FN 6.0	VF 8.0	VF/NM 9.0	NM- 9.2
1-Pre-code horror-r; Lou Cameron-r(2)						3.00

WEIRD SCIENCE (Formerly Saddle Romances) (Becomes Weird Science-Fantasy #23 on)
(Also see EC Archives • Weird Science)
E. C. Comics: No. 12, May-June, 1950 - No. 22, Nov-Dec, 1953

	GD 2.0	VG 4.0	FN 6.0	VF 8.0	VF/NM 9.0	NM- 9.2
12(#1) (1950)-"Lost in the Microcosm" classic-c/story by Kurtzman; "Dream of Doom" stars Gaines & E.C. artists	200	400	600	1600	2550	3500
13-Flying saucers over Washington-c/story, 2 years before supposed UFO sighting	94	188	282	752	1201	1650
14-Robot, End of the World-c/story by Feldstein	89	178	267	712	1131	1550
15-War of Worlds-c/story (1950)	81	162	243	648	1037	1425
5-Atomic explosion-c	61	122	183	488	782	1075
6-8,10	51	102	153	408	654	900
9-Wood's 1st EC-c	54	108	162	432	691	950
11-14 (1952) 11-Kamen bio. 12-Wood bio	37	74	111	296	473	650
15-18-Williamson/Krenkel-a in each; 15-Williamson-a. 17-Used in **POP**, pgs. 81,82. 18-Bill Gaines doll app. in story	39	78	117	312	499	685
19,20-Williamson/Frazetta-a (7 pgs. each). 19-Used in **SOTI**, illo "A young girl on her wedding night stabs her sleeping husband to death with a hatpin..." 19-Bradbury bio.	49	98	147	392	621	850
21-Williamson/Frazetta-a (6 pgs.); Wood draws E.C. staff; Gaines & Feldstein app. in story	49	98	147	392	621	850
22-Williamson/Frazetta/Krenkel-a (8 pgs.); Wood draws himself in his story (last pg. & panel)	49	98	147	392	621	850

NOTE: ***Elder** a-14, 19. **Evans** a-22. **Feldstein** a-12(#1)-8; c-12(#1)-8, 11. **Ingels** a-15. **Kamen** a-12(#1)-13, 15-18, 20, 21. **Kurtzman** a-12(#1)-7. **Orlando** a-10-22. **Wood** a-12(#1), 13(#2), 5-22 (#9, 10, 12, 13 all have 2 **Wood** stories); c-9, 10, 12-22. Canadian reprints exist; see Table of Contents. Ray Bradbury adaptations in #17-22.*

WEIRD SCIENCE
Gladstone Publishing: Sept, 1990 - No. 4, Mar, 1991 ($1.95/$2.00, 68 pgs.)

	GD 2.0	VG 4.0	FN 6.0	VF 8.0	VF/NM 9.0	NM- 9.2
1-4: Wood-c(r); all reprints in each						3.00

WEIRD SCIENCE (Also see EC Archives • Weird Science)
Russ Cochran/Gemstone Publishing: Sept, 1992 - No. 22, Dec, 1997 ($1.50/$2.00/$2.50)

	GD 2.0	VG 4.0	FN 6.0	VF 8.0	VF/NM 9.0	NM- 9.2
1-22: 1,2: r/Weird Science #12,13 w/original-c. ,4-r/#14,15. 5-7-w/original-c						3.00

WEIRD SCIENCE-FANTASY (Formerly Weird Science & Weird Fantasy)
(Becomes Incredible Science Fiction #30)
E. C. Comics: No. 23 Mar, 1954 - No. 29, May-June, 1955 (#23,24: 15¢)

	GD 2.0	VG 4.0	FN 6.0	VF 8.0	VF/NM 9.0	NM- 9.2
23-Williamson, Wood-a; Bradbury adaptation	36	72	108	288	457	625
24-Williamson & Wood-a; Harlan Ellison's 1st professional story, "Upheaval!", later adapted into a short story as "Mealtime", and then into a TV episode of Voyage to the Bottom of the Sea as "The Price of Doom"	36	72	108	288	457	625
25-Williamson-c; Williamson/Torres/Krenkel-a plus Wood-a; Bradbury adaptation; cover price back to 10¢	39	78	117	312	501	690
26-Flying Saucer Report; Wood, Crandall-a; A-bomb panels	37	74	111	296	473	650
27-Adam Link/I Robot series begins?	36	72	108	288	457	625
28-Williamson/Krenkel/Torres-a; Wood-a	37	74	111	296	468	640
29-Frazetta-c; Williamson/Krenkel & Wood-a; last pre-code issue; new logo	100	200	300	800	1275	1750

NOTE: ***Crandall** a-26, 27, 29. **Evans** a-26. **Feldstein** c-24, 26, 28. **Kamen** a-27, 28. **Krigstein** a-23-25. **Orlando** a-in all. **Wood** a-in all; c-23, 27. The cover to #29 was originally intended for Famous Funnies #217 (Buck Rogers), but was rejected for being "too violent."*

WEIRD SCIENCE-FANTASY
Russ Cochran/Gemstone Publishing: Nov, 1992 - No. 7, May , 1994 ($1.50/$2.00/$2.50)

	GD 2.0	VG 4.0	FN 6.0	VF 8.0	VF/NM 9.0	NM- 9.2
1-7: 1,2: r/Weird Science-Fantasy #23,24. 3-7 r/#25-29						3.00

WEIRD SCIENCE-FANTASY ANNUAL
E. C. Comics: 1952, 1953 (Sold thru the E. C. office & on the stands in some major cities) (25¢, 132 pgs.)

	GD 2.0	VG 4.0	FN 6.0	VF 8.0	VF/NM 9.0	NM- 9.2
1952-Feldstein-c	271	542	813	2033	3117	4200
1953-Feldstein-c	167	334	501	1253	1877	2500

NOTE: *The 1952 annual contains books cover-dated in 1951 & 1952, and the 1953 annual from 1952 & 1953. Contents of each annual may vary in same year.*

WEIRD SECRET ORIGINS
DC Comics: Oct, 2004 ($5.95, square-bound, one-shot)

	GD 2.0	VG 4.0	FN 6.0	VF 8.0	VF/NM 9.0	NM- 9.2
nn-Reprints origins of Dr. Fate, Spectre, Congorilla, Metamorpho, Animal Man & others						6.00

WEIRD SUSPENSE
Atlas/Seaboard Publ.: Feb, 1975 - No. 3, July, 1975

	GD 2.0	VG 4.0	FN 6.0	VF 8.0	VF/NM 9.0	NM- 9.2
1-3: 1-Tarantula begins. 3-Freidrich-s	2	4	6	8	10	12

NOTE: ***Boyette** a-1-3. **Buckler** c-1, 3.*

WEIRD SUSPENSE STORIES (Canadian reprints of Crime SuspenStories #1-3; see Table of Contents)

WEIRD TALES ILLUSTRATED
Millennium Publications: 1992 - No. 2, 1992 ($2.95, high quality paper)

	GD 2.0	VG 4.0	FN 6.0	VF 8.0	VF/NM 9.0	NM- 9.2
1,2-Bolton painted-c. 1-Adapts E.A. Poe & Harlan Ellison stories. 2-E.A. Poe & H.P. Lovecraft adaptations						3.50
1-($4.95, 52 pgs.)-Deluxe edition w/Tim Vigil-a not in regular #1; stiff-c; Bolton painted-c						5.00

WEIRD TALES OF THE FUTURE
S.P.M. Publ. No. 1-4/Aragon Publ. No. 5-8: Mar, 1952 - No. 8, July-Aug, 1953

	GD 2.0	VG 4.0	FN 6.0	VF 8.0	VF/NM 9.0	NM- 9.2
1-Andru-a(2); Wolverton partial-c	107	214	321	680	1165	1650
2,3-Wolverton-c/a(3) each. 2- "Jumpin Jupiter" satire by Wolverton begins, ends #5	148	296	444	947	1624	2300
4- "Jumpin Jupiter" satire, partial Wolverton-c	129	258	387	826	1413	2000
5-Wolverton-c/a(2); "Jumpin Jupiter" satire	148	296	444	947	1624	2300
6-Bernard Baily-c	55	110	165	352	601	850
7- "The Mind Movers" from the art to Wolverton's "Brain Bats of Venus" from Mr. Mystery #7 which was cut apart, pasted up, partially redrawn, and rewritten by Harry Kantor, the editor; Baily-c	129	258	387	826	1413	2000
8-Reprints Weird Mysteries #1(10/52) minus cover; gory cover showing heart ripped out, by B. Baily	84	168	252	538	919	1300

WEIRD TALES OF THE MACABRE (Magazine)
Atlas/Seaboard Publ.: Jan, 1975 - No. 2, Mar, 1975 (75¢, B&W)

	GD 2.0	VG 4.0	FN 6.0	VF 8.0	VF/NM 9.0	NM- 9.2
1-Jeff Jones painted-c; Boyette-a	3	6	9	20	30	40
2-Boris Vallejo painted-c; Severin-a	4	8	12	24	37	50

WEIRD TERROR (Also see Horrific)
Allen Hardy Associates (Comic Media): Sept, 1952 - No. 13, Sept, 1954

	GD 2.0	VG 4.0	FN 6.0	VF 8.0	VF/NM 9.0	NM- 9.2
1- "Portrait of Death", adapted from Lovecraft's "Pickman's Model"; lingerie panels, Hitler story	58	116	174	371	636	900
2,3: 2-Text on Marquis DeSade, Torture, Demonology, & St. Elmo's Fire. 3-Extreme violence, whipping, torture; article on sin eating, dowsing	48	96	144	302	514	725
4-Dismemberment, decapitation, article on human flesh for sale, Devil, whipping	48	96	144	302	514	725
5-Article on body snatching, mutilation; cannibalism story	42	84	126	265	445	625
6-Dismemberment, decapitation, man hit by lightning	45	90	135	284	480	675
7-Body burning in fireplace-c	45	90	135	284	480	675
8,11: 8-Decapitation story; Ambrose Bierce adapt. 11-End of the world story w/atomic blast panels; Tothish-a by Bill Discount	42	84	126	265	445	625
9,10,13: 13-Severed head panels	38	76	114	228	369	510
12-Discount-a	38	76	114	228	369	510

NOTE: ***Don Heck** a-most issues; c-1-13. **Landau** a-6. **Morisi** a-2-5, 7, 9, 12. **Palais** a-1, 5, 6, 8(2), 10, 12. **Powell** a-10. **Ravielli** a-11, 20.*

WEIRD THRILLERS
Ziff-Davis Publ. Co. (Approved Comics): Sept-Oct, 1951 - No. 5, Oct-Nov, 1952 (#2-5: painted-c)

	GD 2.0	VG 4.0	FN 6.0	VF 8.0	VF/NM 9.0	NM- 9.2
1-Rondo Hatton photo-c	89	178	267	565	970	1375
2-Toth, Anderson, Colan-a	62	124	186	394	680	965
3-Two Powell, Tuska-a; classic-c; Everett-a	87	174	261	553	952	1350
4-Kubert, Tuska-a	59	118	177	375	648	920
5-Powell-a	54	108	162	348	594	840

NOTE: ***M. Anderson** a-2, 3. **Roussos** a-4. #2, 3 reprinted in Nightmare #10 & 13; #4, 5 reprinted in Amazing Ghost Stories #16 & #15.*

WEIRD VAMPIRE TALES (Comic magazine)
Modern Day Periodical Pub.: V3 #1, Apr, 1979 - V5 #3, Mar, 1982 (B&W)

	GD 2.0	VG 4.0	FN 6.0	VF 8.0	VF/NM 9.0	NM- 9.2
V3 #1 (4/79) First issue, no V1 or V2	4	8	12	26	41	55
V3 #2-4	3	6	9	20	30	40
V4 #2 (4/80), V4 #3 (7/80) (no V4 #1)	3	6	9	18	27	35
V5 #1 (1/81), V5 #2 (two issues, 4/81 & 8/81)	3	6	9	18	27	35
V5 #3 (3/82) Last issue; low print	4	8	12	22	34	45

Weird War Tales #35 © DC

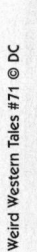

Weird Western Tales #71 © DC

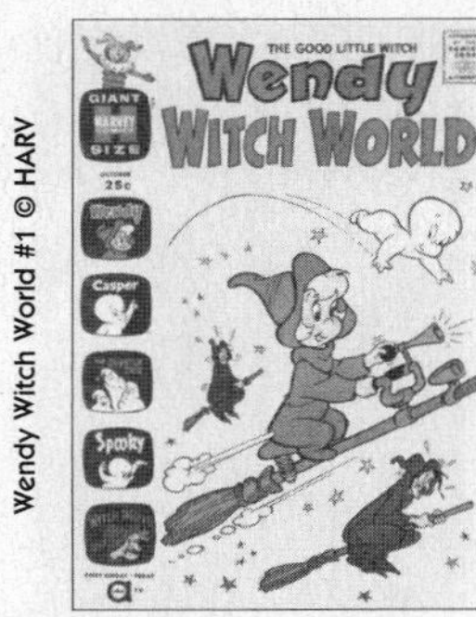

Wendy Witch World #1 © HARV

GD VG FN VF VF/NM NM-
2.0 4.0 6.0 8.0 9.0 9.2

WEIRD WAR TALES
National Periodical Publ./DC Comics: Sept-Oct, 1971 - No. 124, June, 1983 (#1-5: 52 pgs.)

1-Kubert-a in #1-4,7; c-1-7 23 46 69 166 321 475
2,3-Drucker-a: 2-Crandall-a. 3-Heath-a 10 20 30 73 129 185
4,5: 5-Toth-a; Heath-a 9 18 27 60 100 140
6,7,9,10: 6,10-Toth-a. 7-Heath-a 6 12 18 41 66 90
8-Neal Adams-c/a(i) 7 14 21 47 76 105
11-20 4 8 12 22 34 45
21-35 3 6 9 16 23 30
36-(68 pgs.)-Crandall & Kubert-r/#2; Heath-r/#3; Kubert-c
3 6 9 18 27 35
37-50: 38,39-Kubert-c 2 4 6 9 13 16
51-63: 58-Hitler-c/app. 60-Hindenburg-c/s 2 4 6 8 11 14
64-Frank Miller-a (1st DC work) 4 8 12 26 41 55
65-67,69-89,91,92: 89-Nazi Apes-c/s. 2 3 4 6 8 10
68-Frank Miller-a (2nd DC work) 3 6 9 18 27 35
90-Hitler app. 2 4 6 8 10 12
93-Intro/origin Creature Commandos 2 4 6 8 10 12
94-Return of War that Time Forgot; dinosaur-c/s 2 4 6 9 12 15
95,96,98,102-123: 98-Sphinx-c. 102-Creature Commandos battle Hitler. 110-Origin/1st app. Medusa. 123-1st app. Captain Spaceman 2 3 4 6 8 10
97,99,100,101,124: 99-War that Time Forgot. 100-Creature Commandos in War that Time Forgot. 101-Intro/origin G.I. Robot 2 4 6 8 10 12

NOTE: ***Chaykin** a-76, 82. **Ditko** a-95, 99, 104-106. **Evans** c-73, 74, 83, 85. **Kane** c-116, 118. **Kubert** c-55, 58, 60, 62, 72, 75-81, 87, 88, 90-96, 100, 103, 104, 106, 107. **Newton** a-122. **Starlin** c-89. **Sutton** a-91, 92, 103. **Creature Commandos** -93, 97, 100, 102, 105, 108-112, 114, 116-119, 121, 124. **G.I. Robot** - 101, 108, 111, 113, 116-118, 120, 122. **War That Time Forgot** - 94, 99, 100, 103, 106, 109, 120.*

WEIRD WAR TALES
DC Comics (Vertigo): June, 1997 - No. 4, Sept, 1997 ($2.50)

1-4-Anthology by various 3.00

WEIRD WAR TALES
DC Comics (Vertigo): April, 2000 ($4.95, one-shot)

1-Anthology by various; last Biukovic-a 5.00

WEIRD WESTERN TALES (Formerly All-Star Western)
National Per. Publ./DC Comics: No. 12, June-July, 1972 - No. 70, Aug, 1980

12-(52 pgs.)-3rd app. Jonah Hex; Bat Lash, Pow Wow Smith reprints; El Diablo by Neal Adams/Wrightson 13 26 39 93 172 250
13-Jonah Hex-c & 4th app.; Neal Adams-a 9 18 27 61 103 145
14-Toth-a 7 14 21 45 73 100
15-Adams-c/a; no Jonah Hex 4 8 12 28 44 60
16,17,19,20 4 8 12 28 44 60
18,29: 18-1st all Jonah Hex issue (7-8/73) & begins. 29-Origin Jonah Hex
6 12 18 41 66 90
21-28,30: Jonah Hex in all 4 8 12 22 34 45
31-38: Jonah Hex in all. 38-Last Jonah Hex 3 6 9 18 27 35
39-Origin/1st app. Scalphunter & begins 2 4 6 11 16 20
40-47,50-69: 64-Bat Lash-c/story 2 3 4 6 8 10
48,49: (44 pgs.)-1st & 2nd app. Cinnamon 2 4 6 8 10 12
70-Last issue 2 4 6 8 11 14

NOTE: ***Alcala** a-16, 17. **Evans** inks-39-48; c-39i, 40, 47. **G. Kane** a-15, 20. **Kubert** c-12, 33. **Starlin** c-44, 45. **Wildey** a-26. 48 & 49 are 44 pgs..*

WEIRD WESTERN TALES (Blackest Night crossover)
DC Comics: No. 71, March, 2010 ($2.99, one-shot)

71-Jonah Hex, Scalphunter, Super-Chief, Firehair and Bat Lash rise as Black Lanterns 3.00

WEIRD WESTERN TALES
DC Comics (Vertigo): Apr, 2001 - No. 4, Jul, 2001 ($2.50, limited series)

1-4-Anthology by various 2.50

WEIRD WONDER TALES
Marvel Comics Group: Dec, 1973 - No. 22, May, 1977

1-Wolverton-r/Mystic #6 (Eye of Doom) 3 6 9 18 27 35
2-10 2 4 6 13 18 22
11-22: 16-18-Venus-r by Everett from Venus #19,18 & 17. 19-22-r/Dr. Droom (re-named Dr. Druid) by Kirby. 22-New art by Byrne 2 4 6 11 16 20
15-17-(30¢-c variants, limited distribution)(4-8/76) 3 6 9 16 23 30

NOTE: *All 1950s & early 1960s reprints. **Check** r-1. **Colan** r-17. **Ditko** r-4, 5, 10-13, 19-21. **Drucker** r-12, 20. **Everett** r-3(Spellbound #16), 6(Astonishing #10), 9(Adv. Into Mystery #5). **Heath** a-13r. **Heck** a-1or, 14r. **Gil Kane** c-1, 2, 10. **Kirby** r-4, 6, 10, 11, 13, 15-22; c-17, 19, 20. **Krigstein** r-19. **Kubert** r-22. **Maneely** r-8. **Mooney** r-7p. **Powell** r-3, 7. **Torres** r-7. **Wildey** r-2, 7.*

WEIRD WORLDS (See Adventures Into...)

WEIRD WORLDS (Magazine)
Eerie Publications: V1#10(12/70), V2#1(2/71) - No. 4, Aug, 1971 (52 pgs.)

V1#10-Sci-fi/horror 5 10 15 30 48 65
V2#1-4 4 8 12 26 41 55

WEIRD WORLDS (Also see Ironwolf: Fires of the Revolution)
National Periodical Publications: Aug-Sept, 1972 - No. 9, Jan-Feb, 1974; No. 10, Oct-Nov, 1974 (All 20¢ issues)

1-Edgar Rice Burrough's John Carter Warlord of Mars & David Innes begin (1st DC app.); Kubert-c 3 6 9 14 20 25
2-4: 2-Infantino/Orlando-c. 3-Murphy Anderson-c. 4-Kaluta-a
2 4 6 9 13 16
5-7: .5-Kaluta-c. 7-Last John Carter. 2 4 6 8 10 12
8-10: 8-Iron Wolf begins by Chaykin (1st app.) 2 4 6 8 10 12

NOTE: ***Neal Adams** a-2i, 3i. John Carter by **Andersonin** #1-3. **Chaykin** c-7, 8. **Kaluta** a-4; c-4-6, 10. **Orlando** a-4i; c-2, 3, 4i. **Wrightson** a-2i, 4i.*

WELCOME BACK, KOTTER (TV) (See Limited Collectors' Edition #57 for unpublished #11)
National Periodical Publ./DC Comics: Nov, 1976 - No. 10, Mar-Apr, 1978

1-Sparling-a(p) 3 6 9 16 23 30
2-10: 3-Estrada-a 2 4 6 10 14 18

WELCOME SANTA (See March of Comics #63,183)

WELCOME TO HOLSOM
Gospel Publishing House: 2005 - Present (no cover price)

1-12-Craig Schutt-s/Steven Butler-a 2.50

WELCOME TO THE LITTLE SHOP OF HORRORS
Roger Corman's Cosmic Comics: May, 1995 -No. 3, July, 1995 ($2.50, limited series)

1-3 2.50

WELCOME TO TRANQUILITY
DC Comics (WildStorm): Feb, 2007 - No. 12, Jan, 2008 ($2.99)

1-12: 1-Simone-s/Googe-a; two covers by Googe and Campbell. 8-Pearson-a 3.00
...: Armageddon 1 (1/08, $2.99) Gage-s/Googe-a 3.00
... Book One TPB (2008, $19.99) r/#1-6 and variant cover gallery 20.00
... Book Two TPB (2008, $19.99) r/#7-12; sketch pages 20.00

WELLS FARGO (See Tales of...)

WENDY AND THE NEW KIDS ON THE BLOCK
Harvey Comics: Mar, 1991 - No. 3, July, 1991 ($1.25)

1-3 2.50

WENDY DIGEST
Harvey Comics: Oct, 1990 - No. 5, Mar, 1992 ($1.75, digest size)

1-5 4.00

WENDY PARKER COMICS
Atlas Comics (OMC): July, 1953 - No. 8, July, 1954

1 11 22 33 60 83 105
2 8 16 24 44 57 70
3-8 8 16 24 40 50 60

WENDY, THE GOOD LITTLE WITCH (TV)
Harvey Publ.: 8/60 - #82, 11/73; #83, 8/74 - #93, 4/76; #94, 9/90 - #97, 12/90

1-Wendy & Casper the Friendly Ghost begin 27 54 81 197 386 575
2 13 26 39 95 178 260
3-5 10 20 30 70 123 175
6-10 7 14 21 49 80 110
11-20 6 12 18 37 59 80
21-30 4 8 12 28 44 60
31-50 3 6 9 18 27 35
51-64,66-69 2 4 6 13 18 22
65 (2/71)-Wendy origin. 3 6 9 17 25 32
70-74: All 52 pg. Giants 3 6 9 16 23 30
75-93 2 4 6 9 13 16
94-97 (1990, $1.00-c): 94-Has #194 on-c 5.00
(See Casper the Friendly Ghost #20 & Harvey Hits #7, 16, 21, 23, 27, 30, 33)

WENDY THE GOOD LITTLE WITCH (2nd Series)
Harvey Comics: Apr, 1991 - No. 15, Aug, 1994 ($1.00/$1.25 #7-11/$1.50 #12-15)

1-15-Reprints Wendy & Casper stories. 12-Bunny app. 3.00

WENDY WITCH WORLD
Harvey Publications: 10/61; No. 2, 9/62 - No. 52, 12/73; No. 53, 9/74

1-(25¢, 68 pg. Giants begin) 14 28 42 97 181 265
2-5 8 16 24 52 86 120
6-10 6 12 18 37 59 80
11-20 4 8 12 28 44 60
21-30 4 8 12 22 34 45

Werewolf By Night V2 #1 © MAR

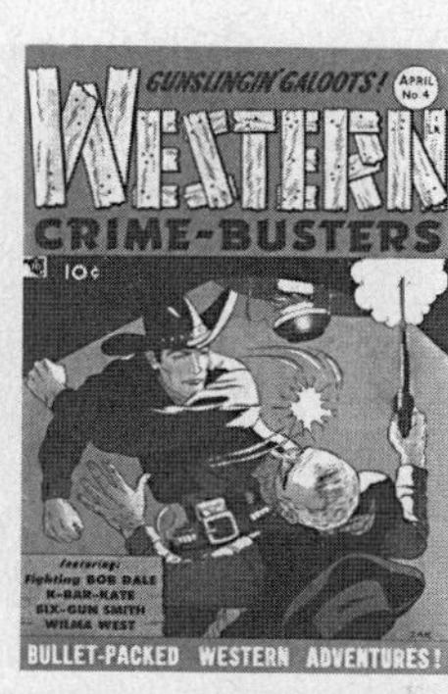

Western Crime-Busters #4 © TM

Western Fighters #1 © HILL

	GD 2.0	VG 4.0	FN 6.0	VF 8.0	VF/NM 9.0	NM- 9.2
31-39: 39-Last 68 pg. issue	3	6	9	17	25	32
40-45: 52 pg. issues	2	4	6	13	18	22
46-53	2	4	6	9	13	16

WEREWOLF (Super Hero) (Also see Dracula & Frankenstein)
Dell Publishing Co.: Dec, 1966 - No. 3, April, 1967

	GD 2.0	VG 4.0	FN 6.0	VF 8.0	VF/NM 9.0	NM- 9.2
1-1st app.	4	8	12	24	37	50
2,3	3	6	9	16	22	28

WEREWOLF BY NIGHT (See Giant-Size..., Marvel Spotlight #2-4 & Power Record Comics)
Marvel Comics Group: Sept, 1972 - No. 43, Mar, 1977

	GD 2.0	VG 4.0	FN 6.0	VF 8.0	VF/NM 9.0	NM- 9.2
1-Ploog-a cont'd. from Marvel Spotlight #4	13	26	39	90	165	240
2	7	14	21	45	73	100
3-5	5	10	15	32	51	70
6-10	4	8	12	24	37	50
11-14,16-20	3	6	9	18	27	35
15-New origin Werewolf; Dracula-c/story cont'd from Tomb of Dracula #18; classic Ploog-c	4	8	12	28	44	60
21-31	3	6	9	14	19	24
32-Origin & 1st app. Moon Knight (8/75)	10	20	30	73	129	185
33-2nd app. Moon Knight	6	12	18	39	62	85
34,36,38-43: 35-Starlin/Wrightson-c	2	4	6	13	18	22
37-Moon Knight app; part Wrightson-c	3	6	9	20	30	40
38,39-(30¢-c variants, limited distribution)(5,7/76)	4	8	12	22	34	45

NOTE: **Bolle** a-6i. **G. Kane** a-11p, 12p; c-21, 22, 24-30, 34p. **Mooney** a-7i. **Ploog** 1-4p, 5, 6p, 7p, 13-16p; c-5-8, 13-16. **Reinman** a-8i. **Sutton** a(i)-9, 11, 16, 35.

WEREWOLF BY NIGHT (Vol. 2, continues in Strange Tales #1 (9/98))
Marvel Comics Group: Feb, 1998 - No. 6, July, 1998 ($2.99)

	GD 2.0	VG 4.0	FN 6.0	VF 8.0	VF/NM 9.0	NM- 9.2
1-6-Manco-a: 2-Two covers. 6-Ghost Rider-c/app.						3.00

WEREWOLVES & VAMPIRES (Magazine)
Charlton Comics: 1962 (One Shot)

	GD 2.0	VG 4.0	FN 6.0	VF 8.0	VF/NM 9.0	NM- 9.2
1	9	18	27	63	107	150

WEREWOLVES ON THE MOON: VERSUS VAMPIRES
Dark Horse Comics: June, 2009 - No. 3 ($3.50, limited series)

	GD 2.0	VG 4.0	FN 6.0	VF 8.0	VF/NM 9.0	NM- 9.2
1,2-Dave Land-s & Fillbach Brothers-s/a						3.50

WEST COAST AVENGERS
Marvel Comics Group: Sept, 1984 - No. 4, Dec, 1984 (lim. series, Mando paper)

	GD 2.0	VG 4.0	FN 6.0	VF 8.0	VF/NM 9.0	NM- 9.2
1-Origin & 1st app. W.C. Avengers (Hawkeye, Iron Man, Mockingbird & Tigra)						4.00
2-4						3.00

WEST COAST AVENGERS (Becomes Avengers West Coast #48 on)
Marvel Comics Group: Oct, 1985 - No. 47, Aug, 1989

	GD 2.0	VG 4.0	FN 6.0	VF 8.0	VF/NM 9.0	NM- 9.2
V2#1-41						3.00
42-47: 42-Byrne-a(p)/scripts begin. 46-Byrne-c; 1st app. Great Lakes Avengers						3.00
Annual 1-3 (1986-1988): 3-Evolutionary War app.						3.00
Annual 4 (1989, $2.00)-Atlantis Attacks; Byrne/Austin-a						3.00

WESTERN ACTION
I. W. Enterprises: No. 7, 1964

	GD 2.0	VG 4.0	FN 6.0	VF 8.0	VF/NM 9.0	NM- 9.2
7-Reprints Cow Puncher #? by Avon	2	4	6	8	11	14

WESTERN ACTION
Atlas/Seaboard Publ.: Feb, 1975

	GD 2.0	VG 4.0	FN 6.0	VF 8.0	VF/NM 9.0	NM- 9.2
1-Kid Cody by Wildey & The Comanche Kid stories; intro. The Renegade	2	4	6	8	10	12

WESTERN ACTION THRILLERS
Dell Publishers: Apr, 1937 (10¢, square binding; 100 pgs.)

	GD 2.0	VG 4.0	FN 6.0	VF 8.0	VF/NM 9.0	NM- 9.2
1-Buffalo Bill, The Texas Kid, Laramie Joe, Two-Gun Thompson, & Wild West Bill app.	84	168	252	538	919	1300

WESTERN ADVENTURES COMICS (Western Love Trails #7 on)
Ace Magazines: Oct, 1948 - No. 6, Aug, 1949

	GD 2.0	VG 4.0	FN 6.0	VF 8.0	VF/NM 9.0	NM- 9.2
nn(#1)-Sheriff Sal, The Cross-Draw Kid, Sam Bass begin	21	42	63	122	199	275
nn(#2)(12/48)	13	26	39	74	105	135
nn(#3)(2/49)-Used in **SOTI**, pgs. 30,31	14	28	42	76	108	140
4-6	11	22	33	62	86	110

WESTERN BANDITS
Avon Periodicals: 1952 (Painted-c)

	GD 2.0	VG 4.0	FN 6.0	VF 8.0	VF/NM 9.0	NM- 9.2
1-Butch Cassidy, The Daltons by Larsen; Kinstler-a; c-part-r/paperback Avon Western Novel #1	16	32	48	92	144	195

WESTERN BANDIT TRAILS (See Approved Comics)

St. John Publishing Co.: Jan, 1949 - No. 3, July, 1949

	GD 2.0	VG 4.0	FN 6.0	VF 8.0	VF/NM 9.0	NM- 9.2
1-Tuska-a; Baker-c; Blue Monk, Ventrilo app.	28	56	84	165	270	375
2-Baker-c	22	44	66	128	209	290
3-Baker-c/a; Tuska-a	26	52	78	154	252	350

WESTERN COMICS (See Super DC Giant #15)
National Per. Publ: Jan-Feb, 1948 - No. 85, Jan-Feb, 1961 (1-27: 52pgs.)

	GD 2.0	VG 4.0	FN 6.0	VF 8.0	VF/NM 9.0	NM- 9.2
1-Wyoming Kid & his horse Racer, The Vigilante in "Jesse James Rides Again" (Meskin-a), Cowboy Marshal, Rodeo Rick begin	77	154	231	481	816	1150
2	37	74	111	215	345	475
3,4-Last Vigilante	33	66	99	192	309	425
5-Nighthawk & his horse Nightwind begin (not in #6); Captain Tootsie by Beck	28	56	84	162	261	360
6,7,9,10	21	42	63	125	200	275
8-Origin Wyoming Kid; 2 pg. pin-ups of rodeo queens	35	70	105	203	327	450
11-20	18	36	54	103	162	220
21-40: 24-Starr-a. 27-Last 52 pgs. 28-Flag-c	14	28	42	82	121	160
41,42,44-49: 49-Last precode issue (2/55)	14	28	42	80	115	150
43-Pow Wow Smith begins, ends #85	14	28	42	81	118	155
50-60	12	24	36	67	94	120
61-85-Last Wyoming Kid. 77-Origin Matt Savage Trail Boss. 82-1st app. Fleetfoot, Pow Wow's girlfriend	10	20	30	56	76	95

NOTE: **G. Kane, Infantino** art in most. **Meskin** a-1-4. **Moreira** a-28-39. **Post** a-3-5.

WESTERN CRIME BUSTERS
Trojan Magazines: Sept, 1950 - No. 10, Mar-Apr, 1952

	GD 2.0	VG 4.0	FN 6.0	VF 8.0	VF/NM 9.0	NM- 9.2
1-Six-Gun Smith, Wilma West, K-Bar-Kate, & Fighting Bob Dale begin; headlight-a	36	72	108	216	351	485
2	19	38	57	111	176	240
3-5: 3-Myron Fass-c	18	36	54	105	165	225
6-Wood-a	32	64	96	188	307	425
7-Six-Gun Smith by Wood	32	64	96	188	307	425
8	18	36	54	105	165	225
9-Tex Gordon & Wilma West by Wood; Lariat Lucy app.	32	64	96	188	307	425
10-Wood-a	29	58	87	172	281	390

WESTERN CRIME CASES (Formerly Indian Warriors #7,8; becomes The Outlaws #10 on)
Star Publications: No. 9, Dec, 1951

	GD 2.0	VG 4.0	FN 6.0	VF 8.0	VF/NM 9.0	NM- 9.2
9-White Rider & Super Horse; L. B. Cole-c	21	42	63	122	199	275

WESTERNER, THE (Wild Bill Pecos)
"Wanted" Comic Group/Toytown/Patches: No. 14, June, 1948 - No. 41, Dec, 1951 (#14-31: 52 pgs.)

	GD 2.0	VG 4.0	FN 6.0	VF 8.0	VF/NM 9.0	NM- 9.2
14	15	30	45	85	130	175
15-17,19-21: 19-Meskin-a	9	18	27	52	69	85
18,22-25-Krigstein-a	11	22	33	60	83	105
26(4/50)-Origin & 1st app. Calamity Kate, series ends #32; Krigstein-a	14	28	42	78	112	145
27-Krigstein-a(2)	13	26	39	74	105	135
28-41: 33-Quest app. 37-Lobo, the Wolf Boy begins	8	16	24	40	50	60

NOTE: **Mort Lawrence** a-20-27, 29, 37, 39; c-19, 22-24, 26, 27. **Leav** c-14-18, 20, 31. **Syd Shores** a-39; c-34, 35, 37-41.

WESTERNER, THE
Super Comics: 1964

	GD 2.0	VG 4.0	FN 6.0	VF 8.0	VF/NM 9.0	NM- 9.2
Super Reprint 15-17: 15-r/Oklahoma Kid #? 16-r/Crack West. #65; Severin-c; Crandall-r. 17-r/Blazing Western #2; Severin-c	2	4	6	8	11	14

WESTERN FIGHTERS
Hillman Periodicals/Star Publ.: Apr-May, 1948 - V4#7, Mar-Apr, 1953 (#1-V3#2: 52 pgs.)

	GD 2.0	VG 4.0	FN 6.0	VF 8.0	VF/NM 9.0	NM- 9.2
V1#1-Simon & Kirby-c	36	72	108	216	351	485
2-Not Kirby-a	14	28	42	80	115	150
3-Fuje-c	12	24	36	67	94	120
4-Krigstein, Ingels, Fuje-a	13	26	39	74	105	135
5,6,8,9,12	10	20	30	54	72	90
7,10-Krigstein-a	11	22	33	62	86	110
11-Williamson/Frazetta-a	30	60	90	177	289	400
V2#1-Krigstein-a	11	22	33	62	86	110
2-12: 4-Berg-a	8	16	24	44	57	70
V3#1-11,V4#1,4-7	8	16	24	42	54	65
12,V4#2,3-Krigstein-a	11	22	33	62	86	110
3-D 1(12/53, 25¢, Star Publ.)-Came w/glasses; L. B. Cole-c	36	72	108	211	343	475

NOTE: **Kinstlerish** a-V2#6, 8, 9, 12; V3#2, 5-7, 11, 12; V4#1(plus cover). **McWilliams** a-11. **Powell** a-V2#2.

Western Hearts #7 © STD

Western Kid #3 © MAR

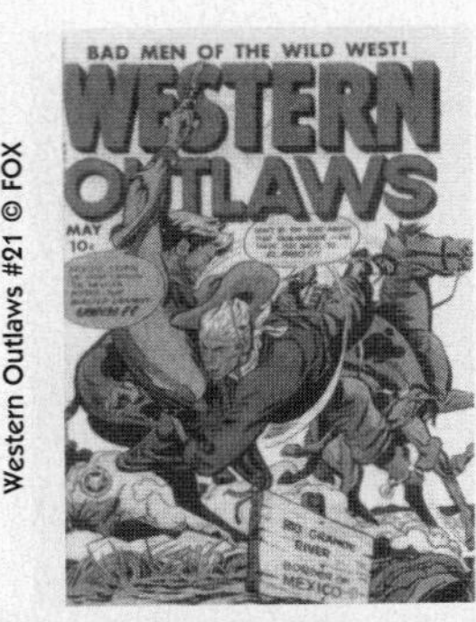

Western Outlaws #21 © FOX

	GD 2.0	VG 4.0	FN 6.0	VF 8.0	VF/NM 9.0	NM- 9.2

*Reinman a-1-12, V4#3. **Rowich** c-5, 6i. **Starr** a-5.*

WESTERN FRONTIER
P. L. Publishers: Apr-May, 1951 - No. 7, 1952

1	14	28	42	76	108	140
2	8	16	24	44	57	70
3-7	7	14	21	37	46	55

WESTERN GUNFIGHTERS (1st Series) (Apache Kid #11-19)
Atlas Comics (CPS): No. 20, June, 1956 - No. 27, Aug, 1957

20	13	26	39	74	105	135
21-Crandall-a	13	26	39	74	105	135
22-Wood & Powell-a	18	36	54	103	162	220
23,24: 23-Williamson-a. 24-Toth-a	13	26	39	74	105	135
25-27	10	20	30	54	72	90

*NOTE: **Berg** a-20. **Colan** a-20, 26, 27. **Crandall** a-21. **Heath** a-25. **Maneely** a-24, 25; c-22, 23, 25. **Morisi** a-24. **Morrow** a-26. **Pakula** a-23. **Severin** c-20, 27. **Torres** a-26. **Woodbridge** a-27.*

WESTERN GUNFIGHTERS (2nd Series)
Marvel Comics Group: Aug, 1970 - No. 33, Nov, 1975 (#1-6: 25¢, 68 pgs.)

1-Ghost Rider begins; Fort Rango, Renegades & Gunhawk app.	5	10	15	34	55	75
2,3,5,6: 2-Origin Nightwind (Apache Kid's horse)	3	6	9	19	29	38
4-Barry Smith-a	4	8	12	22	34	45
7-(52 pgs) Origin Ghost Rider retold	3	6	9	17	25	32
8-13: 10-Origin Black Rider. 12-Origin Matt Slade	2	4	6	13	18	22
14-Steranko-c	3	6	9	16	23	30
15-20	2	4	6	9	13	16
21-33	2	4	6	8	11	14

*NOTE: **Baker** r-2, 3. **Colan** r-2. **Drucker** r-3. **Everett** a-6i. **G. Kane** c-29, 31. **Kirby** a-1p(r), 5, 10-12; c-19, 21. **Kubert** r-2. **Maneely** r-2, 10. **Morrow** r-29. **Severin** c-10. **Shores** a-3, 4. **Barry Smith** a-4. **Steranko** c-14. **Sutton** a-1, 2i, 5, 4. **Torres** r-26('57). **Wildey** r-8, 9. **Williamson** r-2, 18. **Woodbridge** r-27('57). Renegades in #4, 5; Ghost Rider in #1-7.*

WESTERN HEARTS
Standard Comics: Dec, 1949 - No. 10, Mar, 1952 (All photo-c)

1-Severin-a; Whip Wilson & Reno Browne photo-c	23	46	69	136	223	310
2-Beverly Tyler & Jerome Courtland photo-c from movie "Palomino"; Williamson/Frazetta-a (2 pgs.)	23	46	69	136	223	310
3-Rex Allen photo-c	14	28	42	80	115	150
4-7,10: 4-Severin & Elder, Al Carreno-a. 5-Ray Milland & Hedy Lamarr photo-c from movie "Copper Canyon". 6-Fred MacMurray & Irene Dunn photo-c from movie "Never a Dull Moment". 7-Jock Mahoney photo-c. 10-Bill Williams & Jane Nigh photo-c	14	28	42	78	112	145
8-Randolph Scott & Janis Carter photo-c from "Santa Fe"; Severin & Elder-a	14	28	42	80	115	150
9-Whip Wilson & Reno Browne photo-c; Severin & Elder-a	15	30	45	83	124	165

WESTERN HERO (Wow Comics #1-69; Real Western Hero #70-75)
Fawcett Publications: No. 76, Mar, 1949 - No. 112, Mar, 1952

76(#1, 52 pgs.)-Tom Mix, Hopalong Cassidy, Monte Hale, Gabby Hayes, Young Falcon (ends #78,80), & Big Bow and Little Arrow (ends #102,105) begin; painted-c begin	20	40	60	115	183	250
77 (52 pgs.)	14	28	42	78	112	145
78,80-82 (52 pgs.): 81-Capt. Tootsie by Beck	13	26	39	74	105	135
79,83 (36 pgs.): 83-Last painted-c	11	22	33	64	90	115
84-86,88-90 (52 pgs.): 84-Photo-c begin, end #112. 86-Last Hopalong Cassidy	12	24	36	67	94	120
87,91,95,99 (36 pgs.): 87-Bill Boyd begins, ends #95	10	20	30	58	79	100
92-94,96-98,101 (52 pgs.): 96-Tex Ritter begins. 101-Red Eagle app.	11	22	33	62	86	110
100 (52 pgs.)	12	24	36	67	94	120
102-111: 102-Begin 36 pg. issues	10	20	30	58	79	100
112-Last issue	11	22	33	62	86	110

NOTE: 1/2 to 1 pg. Rocky Lane (Carnation) in 80-83, 86, 88, 97. Photo covers feature Hopalong Cassidy #84, 86, 89; Tom Mix #85, 87, 90, 92, 94, 97; Monte Hale #88, 91, 93, 95, 98, 100, 104, 107, 110; Tex Ritter #96, 99, 101, 105, 108, 111; Gabby Hayes #103.

WESTERN KID (1st Series)
Atlas Comics (CPC): Dec, 1954 - No. 17, Aug, 1957

1-Origin; The Western Kid (Tex Dawson), his stallion Whirlwind & dog Lightning begin	18	36	54	107	169	230
2 (2/55)-Last pre-code	11	22	33	62	86	110
3-8	10	20	30	54	72	90
9,10-Williamson-a in both (4 pgs. each)	10	20	30	56	76	95
11-17	8	16	24	44	57	70

*NOTE: **Ayers** a-6, 7. **Maneely** c-2-7, 10, 13-15. **Romita** a-1-17; c-1, 12. **Severin** c-16, 17.*

WESTERN KID, THE (2nd Series)
Marvel Comics Group: Dec, 1971 - No. 5, Aug, 1972 (All 20¢ issues)

1-Reprints; Romita-c/a(3)	3	6	9	17	25	32
2,4,5: 2-Romita-a; Severin-c. 4-Everett-r	2	4	6	11	16	20
3-Williamson-a	3	6	9	14	19	24

WESTERN KILLERS
Fox Features Syndicate: nn, July?, 1948; No. 60, Sept, 1948 - No. 64, May, 1949; No. 6, July, 1949

nn(#59?)(nd, F&J Trading Co.)-Range Busters; formerly Blue Beetle #57?	24	48	72	140	230	320
60 (#1, 9/48)-Extreme violence; lingerie panel	26	52	78	152	249	345
61-Jack Cole, Starr-a	21	42	63	122	199	275
62-64, 6 (#6-exist?)	19	38	57	111	176	240

WESTERN LIFE ROMANCES (My Friend Irma #3 on?)
Marvel Comics (IPP): Dec, 1949 - No. 2, Mar, 1950 (52 pgs.)

1-Whip Wilson & Reno Browne photo-c	20	40	60	114	182	250
2-Audie Murphy & Gale Storm photo-c	16	32	48	94	147	200

WESTERN LOVE
Prize Publ.: July-Aug, 1949 - No. 5, Mar-Apr, 1950 (All photo-c & 52 pgs.)

1-S&K-a; Randolph Scott photo-c from movie "Canadian Pacific" (see Prize Comics #76)	31	62	93	182	296	410
2,5-S&K-a: 2-Whip Wilson & Reno Browne photo-c. 5-Dale Robertson photo-c	23	46	69	136	223	310
3,4: 3-Pat Williams photo-c	15	30	45	85	130	175

*NOTE: **Meskin & Severin/Elder** a-2-5.*

WESTERN LOVE TRAILS (Formerly Western Adventures)
Ace Magazines (A. A. Wyn): No. 7, Nov, 1949 - No. 9, Mar, 1950

7	12	24	36	67	94	120
8,9	10	20	30	54	72	90

WESTERN MARSHAL (See Steve Donovan...)
Dell Publishing Co.: No. 534, 2-4/54 - No. 640, 7/55 (Based on Ernest Haycox's "Trailtown")

Four Color 534 (#1)-Kinstler-a	6	12	18	39	62	85
Four Color 591 (10/54), 613 (2/55), 640-All Kinstler-a	5	10	15	34	55	75

WESTERN OUTLAWS (Junior Comics #9-16; My Secret Life #22 on)
Fox Features Syndicate: No. 17, Sept, 1948 - No. 21, May, 1949

17-Kamen-a; Iger shop-a in all; 1 pg. "Death and the Devil Pills" r-in Ghostly Weird #122	32	64	96	188	307	425
18-21	19	38	57	111	176	240

WESTERN OUTLAWS
Atlas Comics (ACI No. 1-14/WPI No. 15-21): Feb, 1954 - No. 21, Aug, 1957

1-Heath, Powell-a; Maneely hanging-c	21	42	63	122	199	275
2	12	24	36	67	94	120
3-10: 7-Violent-a by R.Q. Sale	10	20	30	54	72	90
11,14-Williamson-a in both (6 pgs. each)	11	22	33	60	83	105
12,18,20,21: Severin covers	9	18	27	50	65	80
13,15: 13-Baker-a. 15-Torres-a	10	20	30	54	72	90
16-Williamson text illo	9	18	27	50	65	80
17,19-Crandall-a. 17-Williamson text illo	10	20	30	54	72	90

*NOTE: **Ayers** a-7, 10, 18, 20. **Bolle** a-21. **Colan** a-5, 10, 11, 17. **Drucker** a-11. **Everett** a-9, 10. **Heath** a-1; c-3, 4, 8, 16. **Kubert** a-9p. **Maneely** a-13, 16, 17, 19; c-1, 5, 7, 9, 10, 12, 13. **Morisi** a-18. **Powell** a-3, 16. **Romita** a-7, 13. **Severin** a-8, 16, 19; c-17, 18, 20, 21. **Tuska** a-6, 15.*

WESTERN OUTLAWS & SHERIFFS (Formerly Best Western)
Marvel/Atlas Comics (IPC): No. 60, Dec, 1949 - No. 73, June, 1952

60 (52 pgs.)	21	42	63	122	199	275
61-65: 61-Photo-c	16	32	48	94	147	200
66-Story contains 5 hangings	16	32	48	94	147	200
68-72	14	28	42	76	108	140
67-Cannibalism story	16	32	48	94	147	200
73-Black Rider story; Everett-c	15	30	45	83	124	165

*NOTE: **Maneely** a-62, 67; c-62, 69-73. **Robinson** a-68. **Sinnott** a-70. **Tuska** a-69-71.*

WESTERN PICTURE STORIES (1st Western comic)
Comics Magazine Company: Feb, 1937 - No. 4, June, 1937

1-Will Eisner-a	194	388	582	1242	2121	3000
2-Will Eisner-a	100	200	300	635	1093	1550
3,4: 3-Eisner-a. 4-Caveman Cowboy story	84	168	252	538	919	1300

WESTERN PICTURE STORIES (See Giant Comics Edition #6, 11)

WESTERN ROMANCES (See Target...)

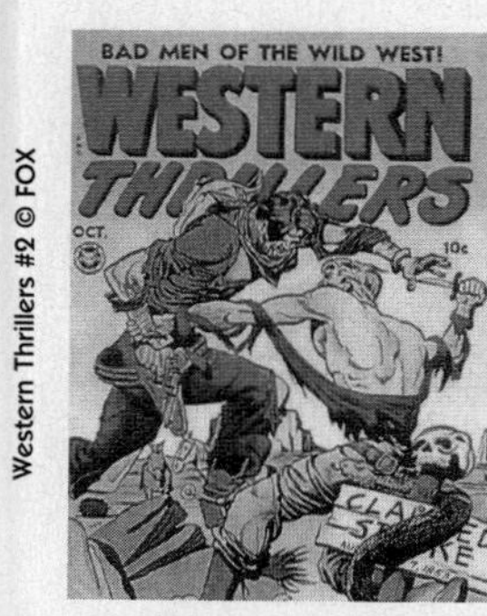

Western Thrillers #2 © FOX

Wetworks (2006 series) #15 © WSP

What If? #24 © MAR

GD 2.0 | VG 4.0 | FN 6.0 | VF 8.0 | VF/NM 9.0 | NM- 9.2

WESTERN ROUGH RIDERS
Gillmor Magazines No. 1,4 (Stanmor Publ.): Nov, 1954 - No. 4, May, 1955
1 9 18 27 47 61 75
2-4 7 14 21 35 43 50

WESTERN ROUNDUP (See Dell Giants & Fox Giants)

WESTERN SERENADE
DC Comics: May/June, 1949
nn - Ashcan comic, not distributed to newsstands, only for in-house use (no known sales)

WESTERN TALES (Formerly Witches...)
Harvey Publications: No. 31, Oct, 1955 - No. 33, July-Sept, 1956
31,32-All S&K-a; Davy Crockett app. in each 18 36 54 107 169 230
33-S&K-a; Jim Bowie app. 18 36 54 103 162 220
NOTE: *#32 & 33 contain Boy's Ranch reprints.* ***Kirby*** *c-31.*

WESTERN TALES OF BLACK RIDER (Formerly Black Rider; Gunsmoke Western #32 on)
Atlas Comics (CPS): No. 28, May, 1955 - No. 31, Nov, 1955
28 (#1): The Spider (a villain) dies 19 38 57 112 179 245
29-31 14 28 42 82 121 160
NOTE: ***Lawrence*** *a-30.* ***Maneely*** *c-28-30.* ***Severin*** *a-28.* ***Shores*** *c-31.*

WESTERN TEAM-UP
Marvel Comics Group: Nov, 1973 (20¢)
1-Origin & 1st app. The Dakota Kid; Rawhide Kid-r; Gunsmoke Kid-r by Jack Davis
4 8 12 22 34 45

WESTERN THRILLERS (My Past Confessions #7 on)
Fox Features Syndicate/M.S. Distr. No. 52: Aug, 1948 - No. 6, June, 1949; No. 52, 1954?
1- "Velvet Rose" (Kamenish-a); "Two-Gun Sal", "Striker Sisters" (all women outlaws issue); Brodsky-c 48 96 144 302 514 725
2 24 48 72 140 230 320
3-6: 4,5-Bakerish-a; 5-Butch Cassidy app. 19 38 57 111 176 240
52-(Reprint, M.S. Dist.)-1954? No date given (becomes My Love Secret #53)
9 18 27 47 61 75

WESTERN THRILLERS (Cowboy Action #5 on)
Atlas Comics (ACI): Nov, 1954 - No. 4, Feb, 1955 (All-r/Western Outlaws & Sheriffs)
1 5 30 45 88 137 185
2-4 10 20 30 54 72 90
NOTE: ***Heath*** *c-3.* ***Maneely*** *a-1; c-2.* ***Powell*** *a-4.* ***Robinson*** *a-4.* ***Romita*** *c-4.* ***Tuska*** *a-2.*

WESTERN TRAILS (Ringo Kid Starring in...)
Atlas Comics (SAI): May, 1957 - No. 2, July, 1957
1-Ringo Kid app.; Severin-c 14 28 42 76 108 140
2-Severin-c 9 18 27 50 65 80
NOTE: ***Bolle*** *a-1, 2.* ***Maneely*** *a-1, 2.* ***Severin*** *c-1, 2.*

WESTERN TRUE CRIME (Becomes My Confessions)
Fox Features Syndicate: No. 15, Aug, 1948 - No. 6, June, 1949
15(#1)-Kamen-a; formerly Zoot #14 (5/48)? 32 64 96 188 307 425
16(#2)-Kamenish-a; headlight panels, violence 23 46 69 136 223 310
3-Kamen-a 25 50 75 147 241 335
4-6: 4-Johnny Craig-a 15 30 45 90 140 190

WESTERN WINNERS (Formerly All-Western Winners; becomes Black Rider #8 on & Romance Tales #7 on?)
Marvel Comics (CDS): No. 5, June, 1949 - No. 7, Dec, 1949
5-Two-Gun Kid, Kid Colt, Black Rider; Shores-c 31 62 93 182 296 410
6-Two-Gun Kid, Black Rider, Heath Kid Colt story; Captain Tootsie by C.C. Beck
26 52 78 152 249 345
7-Randolph Scott Photo-c w/true stories about the West
26 52 78 152 249 345

WEST OF THE PECOS (See Zane Grey, 4-Color #222)

WESTWARD HO, THE WAGONS (Disney)
Dell Publishing Co.: No. 738, Sept, 1956 (Movie)
Four Color 738-Fess Parker photo-c 9 18 27 63 107 150

WE3
DC Comics (Vertigo): Oct, 2004 - No. 3, May, 2005 ($2.95, limited series)
1-3-Domestic animal cyborgs: Grant Morrison-s/Frank Quitely-a 3.00
TPB (2005, $12.99) r/series 13.00

WETWORKS (See WildC.A.T.S: Covert Action Teams #2)
Image Comics (WildStorm): June, 1994 - No. 43, Aug, 1998 ($1.95/$2.50)
1-"July" on-c; gatefold wraparound-c; Portacio/Williams-c/a 3.00
1-Chicago Comicon edition 6.00
1-(2/98, $4.95) "3-D Edition" w/glasses 5.00
2-4 2.50
2-Alternate Portacio-c, see Deathblow #5 6.00
5-7,9-24: 5-($2.50). 13-Portacio-c. 16,17-Fire From Heaven Pts. 4 & 11 2.50
8 ($1.95)-Newstand, Wildstorm Rising Pt. 7 2.25
8 ($2.50)-Direct Market, Wildstorm Rising Pt. 7 2.50
25-($3.95) 4.00
26-43: 32-Variant-c by Pat Lee & Charest. 39,40-Stormwatch app. 42-Gen 13 app. 2.50
Sourcebook 1 (10/94, $2.50)-Text & illustrations (no comics) 2.50
Voyager Pack (8/97, $3.50)- #32 w/Phantom Guard preview 3.50

WETWORKS
DC Comics (WildStorm): Nov, 2006 - No. 15, Jan, 2008 ($2.99)
1-15: 1-Carey-s/Portacio-a; two covers by Portacio and Van Sciver. 2-Golden var-c 3-Pearson var-c. 4-Powell var-c 3.00
...: Armageddon 1 (1/08, $2.99) Gage-s/Badeaux-a 3.00
... Book One (2007, $14.99) r/#1-5 and stories from Eye of the storm Annual and Coup D'Etat Afterword 15.00
... Book Two (2008, $14.99) r/#6-9,13-15 15.00

WETWORKS/VAMPIRELLA (See Vampirella/Wetworks)
Image Comics (WildStorm Productions): July, 1997 ($2.95, one-shot)
1-Gil Kane-c 3.00

WHACK (Satire)
St. John Publishing Co. (Jubilee Publ.): Oct, 1953 - No. 3, May, 1954
1-(3-D, 25¢)-Kubert-a; Maurer-c; came w/glasses 27 54 81 158 259 360
2,3-Kubert-a in each. 2-Bing Crosby on-c; Mighty Mouse & Steve Canyon parodies. 3-Li'l Orphan Annie parody; Maurer-c 15 30 45 84 127 170

WHACKY (See Wacky)

WHA...HUH?
Marvel Comics: 2005 ($3.99, one-shot)
1-Humor spoofs of Marvel characters; Mahfood-a/c; Bendis, Stan Lee and others-s 4.00

WHAM COMICS (See Super Spy)
Centaur Publications: Nov, 1940 - No. 2, Dec, 1940
1-The Sparkler, The Phantom Rider, Craig Carter and his Magic Ring, Detecto, Copper Slug, Speed Silvers by Gustavson, Speed Centaur & Jon Linton (s/f) begin
161 322 483 1030 1765 2500
2-Origin Blue Fire & Solarman; The Buzzard app. 103 206 309 659 1130 1600

WHAM-O GIANT COMICS
Wham-O Mfg. Co. : April, 1967 (98¢, newspaper size, one-shot)(Six issue subscription was advertised)
1-Radian & Goody Bumpkin by Wood; 1 pg. Stanley-a; Fine, Tufts-a; flying saucer reports; wraparound-c 9 18 27 63 107 150

WHAT IF? (1st Series) (What If? Featuring... #13 & #?-33) (Also see Hero Initiative)
Marvel Comics Group: Feb, 1977 - No. 47, Oct, 1984; June, 1988 (All 52 pgs.)
1-Brief origin Spider-Man, Fantastic Four 3 6 9 18 27 35
2-Origin The Hulk retold 2 4 6 9 13 16
3-5: 3-Avengers. 4-Invaders. 5-Capt. America 2 4 6 8 10 12
6-10,13,17: 7-Betty Brant as Spider-Girl. 8-Daredevil; Spidey parody. 9-Origins Venus, Marvel Boy, Human Robot, 3-D Man. 13-Conan app.; John Buscema-c/a(p). 17-Ghost Rider & Son of Satan app. 2 3 4 6 8 10
11,12,14-16: 11-Marvel Bullpen as F.F. 1 2 3 5 6 8
18-26,29: 18-Dr. Strange. 19-Spider-Man. 22-Origin Dr. Doom retold
1 2 3 4 5 7
27-X-Men app.; Miller-c 3 6 9 14 19 24
28-Daredevil by Miller; Ghost Rider app. 2 4 6 10 14 18
30-"What If...Spider-Man's Clone Had Lived?" 2 4 6 8 10 12
31-Begin $1.00-c; featuring Wolverine & the Hulk; X-Men app.; death of Hulk, Wolverine & Magneto 3 6 9 14 20 26
32-34,36-47: 32,36-Byrne-a. 34-Marvel crew each draw themselves. 37-Old X-Men & Silver Surfer app. 39-Thor battles Conan 5.00
35-What if Elektra had lived?; Miller/Austin-a. 2 3 4 6 8 10
Special 1 ($1.50, 6/88)-Iron Man, F.F., Thor app. 4.00
... Classic Vol. 1 TPB (2004, $24.99) r/#1-6; checklist 25.00
... Classic Vol. 2 TPB (2005, $24.99) r/#7-12 25.00
... Classic Vol. 3 TPB (2006, $24.99) r/#14,15,17-20 25.00
... Classic Vol. 4 TPB (2007, $24.99) r/#21-26; checklist of all What If? series/issues 25.00
NOTE: ***Austin*** *a-27p, 32i, 34, 35i; c-35i, 36i.* ***J. Buscema*** *a-13p, 15p; c-10, 13p, 23p.* ***Byrne*** *a-32i, 36; c-36p.* ***Colan*** *a-21p; c-17p, 18p, 21p.* ***Ditko*** *a-35, Special 1.* ***Golden*** *c-29, 40-42.* ***Guice*** *a-40p.* ***Gil Kane*** *a-3p, 24p; c(p)-2-4, 7, 8.* ***Kirby*** *a-11p; c-9p, 11p.* ***Layton*** *a-32i, 33i; c-30, 32p, 33i, 34.* ***Mignola*** *c-39i.* ***Miller*** *a-28p, 32i, 34(1), 35p; c-27, 28p.* ***Mooney*** *a-8i, 30i.* ***Perez*** *a-15p.* ***Robbins*** *a-4p.* ***Sienkiewicz*** *c-43-46.* ***Simonson*** *a-15p, 32i.* ***Starlin*** *a-32i.* ***Stevens*** *a-8, 16i(part).* ***Sutton*** *a-2i, 18p, 28.* ***Tuska*** *a-5p.* ***Weiss*** *a-37p.*

What If? Wolverine Enemy of the State #1 © MAR

What The--?! #7 © MAR

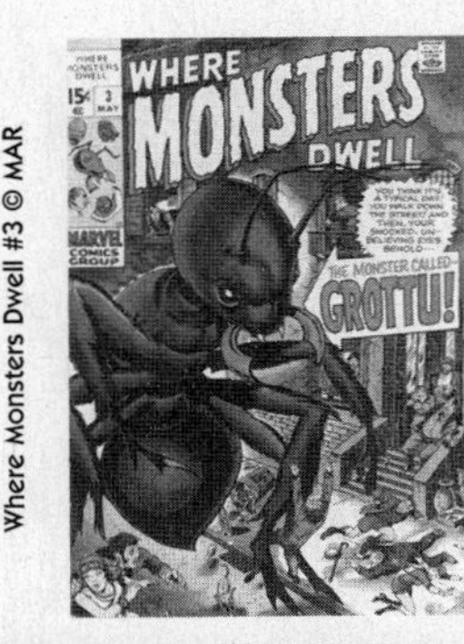

Where Monsters Dwell #3 © MAR

GD VG FN VF VF/NM NM-
2.0 4.0 6.0 8.0 9.0 9.2

WHAT IF...? (2nd Series)
Marvel Comics: V2#1, July, 1989 - No. 114, Nov, 1998 ($1.25/$1.50)
V2#1-...The Avengers Had Lost the Evol. War 4.00
2-5: 2-Daredevil, Punisher app. 3.00
6-X-Men app. 4.00
7-Wolverine app.; Liefeld-c/a(1st on Wolvie?) 5.00
8,10,11,13-15,17-30: 10-Punisher app. 11-Fantastic Four app.; McFarlane-c(i).13-Prof. X; Jim Lee-c. 14-Capt. Marvel; Lim/Austin-c.15-F.F.; Capullo-c/a(p). 17-Spider-Man/Kraven. 18-F.F. 19-Vision. 20,21-Spider-Man. 22-Silver Surfer by Lim/Austin-c/a 23-X-Men. 24-Wolverine; Punisher app. 25-(52 pgs.)-Wolverine app. 26-Punisher app. 27-Namor/F.F. 28,29-Capt. America. 29-Swipes cover to Avengers #4. 30-(52 pgs.)-F.F. 3.00
9,12-X-Men 3.50
16-Wolverine battles Conan; Red Sonja app.; X-Men cameo 4.00
31-50: 31-Cosmic Spider-Man & Venom app.; Hobgoblin cameo. 32,33-Phoenix; X-Men app. 35-Fantastic Five (w/Spidey). 36-Avengers vs. Guardians of the Galaxy. 37-Wolverine; Thibert-c(i). 38-Thor; Rogers-p(part). 40-Storm; X-Men app. 41-(52 pgs.)-Avengers vs. Galactus. 42-Spider-Man. 43-Wolverine. 44-Venom/Punisher. 45-Ghost Rider. 46-Cable. 47-Magneto. 49-Infinity Gauntlet w/Silver Surfer & Thanos. 50-(52 pgs.)-Foil embossed-c; "What If Hulk Had Killed Wolverine" 3.00
51-(7/93) "What If the Punisher Became Captain America" (see it happen in 2007's Punisher War Journal #6-10) 6.00
52-104: 52-Dr. Doom. 54-Death's Head. 57-Punisher as Shield. 58-"What if Punisher Had Killed Spider-Man" w/cover similar to Amazing S-M #129. 59-...Wolverine led Alpha Flight. 60-X-Men Wedding Album. 61-Bound-in card sheet. 61,86,88-Spider-Man. 74,77,81,84,85-X-Men. 76-Last app. Watcher in title. 78-Bisley-c. 80-Hulk. 87-Sabretooth. 89-Fantastic Four. 90-Cyclops & Havok. 91-The Hulk. 93-Wolverine. 94-Juggernaut. 95-Ghost Rider. 100-($2.99, double-sized) Gambit and Rogue, Fantastic Four 3.00
105-Spider-Girl (Peter Parker's daughter) debut; Sienkiewicz-a; (Betty Brant also app. as a Spider-Girl in What If? (1st series) #7) 2 4 6 12 16 20
106-114: 106-Gambit. 108-Avengers. 111-Wolverine. 114-Secret Wars 2.50
#(-1) Flashback (7/97) 3.00

WHAT IF...? (one-shots)
Marvel Comics: Feb, 2005 ($2.99)
... Aunt May Had Died Instead of Uncle Ben? - Brubaker-s/DiVito-a/Brase-c 3.00
... Dr. Doom Had Become The Thing? - Karl Kesel-s/Paul Smith-a/c 3.00
... General Ross Had Become The Hulk? - Peter David-s/Pat Olliffe-a/Gary Frank-c 3.00
... Jessica Jones Had Joined The Avengers? - Bendis-s/Gaydos-a/McNiven-c 3.00
... Karen Page Had Lived? - Bendis-s/Lark-a/c 3.00
... Magneto and Professor X Had Formed The X-Men Together? - Claremont-s/Raney-a 3.00
What If...: Why Not? TPB (2005, $16.99) r/one-shots 17.00

WHAT IF... (one-shots)
Marvel Comics: Feb, 2006 ($2.99)
... : Captain America - Fought in the Civil War?; Bedard-s/Di Giandomenico-a 3.00
... : Daredevil - The Devil Who Dares; Daredevil in feudal Japan; Veitch-s/Edwards-a 3.00
... : Fantastic Four - Were Cosmonauts?; Marshall Rogers-a/c; Mike Carey-s 3.00
... : Submariner - Grew Up on Land?; Pak-s/Lopez-a 3.00
... : Thor - Was the Herald of Galactus?; Kirkman-s/Oeming-a/c 3.00
... : Wolverine - In the Prohibition Era; Way-s/Proctor-a/Harris-c 3.00
What If: Mirror Mirror TPB (2006, $16.99) r/one-shots; design pages and Rogers sketches 17.00

WHAT IF ?... (one-shots altering recent Marvel "event" series)
Marvel Comics: Jan, 2007 - Feb, 2007 ($3.99)
... Avengers Disassembled; Parker-s/Lopresti-a/c 4.00
... Spider-Man The Other; Peter David-s/Khoi Pham-a; Venom app. 4.00
... Wolverine Enemy of the State; Robinson-s/DiGiandomenico-a/Alexander-c 4.00
... X-Men Age of Apocalypse; Remeder-s/Wilkins-a/Djurdjevic-c 4.00
... X-Men Deadly Genesis; Hine-s/Yardin-a/c 4.00
What If?: Event Horizon TPB (2007, $16.99) r/one-shots; design pages and cover sketches 17.00

WHAT IF ?... (one-shots altering recent Marvel "event" series)
Marvel Comics: Dec, 2007 - Feb, 2008 ($3.99)
... Annihilation; Nova, Iron Man and Captain America app. 4.00
... Civil War; 2 covers by Silvestri & Djurdjevic 4.00
... Planet Hulk; Pagulayan-c; Kirk, Sandoval & Hembeck-a 4.00
... Spider-Man vs. Wolverine; Romita Jr.-c; Henry-a; Nick Fury app. 4.00
... X-Men - Rise and Fall of the Shi'ar Empire; Coipel-c 4.00
What If?: Civil War TPB (2008, $16.99) r/one-shots; design pages and cover sketches 17.00

WHAT IF ?... (one-shots altering recent Marvel "event" series)
Marvel Comics: Feb, 2009 ($3.99) (Serialized back-up Runaways story in each issue)
... Fallen Son; if Iron Man had died instead of Capt. America; McGuinness-c 4.00
... House of M; if the Scarlet Witch had said "No more powers" instead; Cheung-c 4.00
... Newer Fantastic Four; team of Spider-Man, Hulk, Iron Man and Wolverine 4.00
... Secret Wars; if Doctor Doom had kept the Beyonder's power; origin re-told 4.00
... Spider-Man Back in Black; if Mary Jane had been shot instead of Aunt May 4.00

WHAT IF ?... (one-shots)
Marvel Comics: Feb, 2010 ($3.99)
... Astonishing X-Men; if Ord resurrected Jean Grey; Campbell-c 4.00
... Daredevil vs. Elektra; Kayanan-a; Klaus Janson-c swipe of Daredevil #168 4.00
... Secret Invasion; if the Skrulls succeeded; Yu-c 4.00
... Spider-Man: House of M; if Gwen Stacy survived the House of M; Dodson-c 4.00
... World War Hulk; if the heroes lost the war; Romita Jr.-c 4.00

'WHAT'S NEW? - THE COLLECTED ADVENTURES OF PHIL & DIXIE'
Palliard Press: Oct, 1991 - No. 2, 1991 ($5.95, mostly color, sq.-bound, 52 pgs.)
1,2-By Phil Foglio 6.00

WHAT THE- -?!
Marvel Comics: Aug, 1988 - No. 26, 1993 ($1.25/$1.50/$2.50, semi-annual #5 on)
1-All contain parodies 3.00
2-24: 3-X-Men parody; Todd McFarlane-a. 5-Punisher/Wolverine parody; Jim Lee-a. 6-Punisher, Wolverine, Alpha Flight. 9-Wolverine. 16-EC back-c parody. 17-Wolverine/Punisher parody. 18-Star Trek parody w/Wolverine. 19-Punisher, Wolverine, Ghost Rider. 21-Weapon X parody. 22-Punisher/Wolverine parody 2.50
25-Summer Special 1 (1993, $2.50)-X-Men parody 2.50
26-Fall Special ($2.50, 68 pgs.)-Spider-Ham 2099-c/story; origin Silver Surfer; Hulk & Doomsday parody; indicia reads "Winter Special." 2.50
NOTE: ***Austin*** *a-6i.* ***Byrne*** *a-2, 6, 10; c-2, 6-8, 10, 12, 13.* ***Golden*** *a-22.* ***Dale Keown*** *a-8p(8 pgs.).* ***McFarlane*** *a-3.* ***Rogers*** *c-15i, 16p.* ***Severin*** *a-2.* ***Staton*** *a-21p.* ***Williamson*** *a-2i.*

WHEE COMICS (Also see Gay, Smile & Tickle Comics)
Modern Store Publications: 1955 (7¢, 5x7-1/4", 52 pgs.)
1-Funny animal 6 12 18 28 34 40

WHEEDIES (See Panic #11 -EC Comics)

WHEELIE AND THE CHOPPER BUNCH (TV)
Charlton Comics: July, 1975 - No. 7, July, 1976 (Hanna-Barbera)
1-3: 1-Byrne text illo (see Nightmare for 1st art); Staton-a. 2-Byrne-a. 2,3-Mike Zeck text illos. 3-Staton-a; Byrne-c/a 3 6 9 16 23 30
4-7-Staton-a 2 4 6 12 16 20

WHEN KNIGHTHOOD WAS IN FLOWER (See The Sword & the Rose, 4-Color #505, 682)

WHEN SCHOOL IS OUT (See Wisco in Promotional Comics section)

WHERE CREATURES ROAM
Marvel Comics Group: July, 1970 - No. 8, Sept, 1971
1-Kirby/Ayers-c/a(r) 4 8 12 22 34 45
2-8: 2-5,7,8-Kirby-c/a(r). 6-Kirby-a(r) 3 6 9 17 25 32
NOTE: ***Ditko*** *r-1-6, 7.* ***Heck*** *r-2, 5. All contain pre super-hero reprints.*

WHERE IN THE WORLD IS CARMEN SANDIEGO (TV)
DC Comics: June, 1996 - No. 4, Dec, 1996 ($1.75)
1-4: Adaptation of TV show 2.50

WHERE MONSTERS DWELL
Marvel Comics Group: Jan, 1970 - No. 38, Oct, 1975
1-Kirby/Ditko-r; all contain pre super-hero-r 4 8 12 24 37 50
2-10: 4-Crandall-a(r) 3 6 9 18 27 35
11,13-20: 11-Last 15¢ issue. 18,20-Starlin-c 3 6 9 16 22 28
12-Giant issue (52 pgs.) 3 6 9 20 30 40
21-37: 21-Reprints 1st Fin Fang Foom app. 2 4 6 13 18 22
38-Williamson-r/World of Suspense #3 3 6 9 14 20 26
NOTE: ***Colan*** *r-12.* ***Ditko*** *a(r)-4, 6, 8, 10, 12, 17-19, 23-25, 37.* ***Kirby*** *r-1-3, 5-16, 18-27, 30-32, 34-36, 38; c-12?* ***Reinman*** *a-3r, 4r, 12r.* ***Severin*** *c-15.*

WHERE'S HUDDLES? (TV) (See Fun-In #9)
Gold Key: Jan, 1971 - No. 3, Dec, 1971 (Hanna-Barbera)
1 3 6 9 19 29 38
2,3: 3-r/most #1 2 4 6 11 16 20

WHIP WILSON (Movie star) (Formerly Rex Hart; Gunhawk #12 on; see Western Hearts, Western Life Romances, Western Love)
Marvel Comics: No. 9, April, 1950 - No. 11, Sept, 1950 (#9,10: 52 pgs.)
9-Photo-c; Whip Wilson & his horse Bullet begin; origin Bullet; issue #23 listed on splash page; cover changed to #9 51 102 153 316 526 735
10,11: Both have photo-c. 11-36 pgs. 29 58 87 169 272 375
I.W. Reprint #1(1964)-Kinstler-c; r-Marvel #11 3 6 9 16 22 28

WHIRLWIND COMICS (Also see Cyclone Comics)
Nita Publication: June, 1940 - No. 3, Sept, 1940
1-Origin & 1st app. Cyclone; Cyclone-c 232 464 696 1485 2543 3600
2,3: Cyclone-c 100 200 300 635 1093 1550

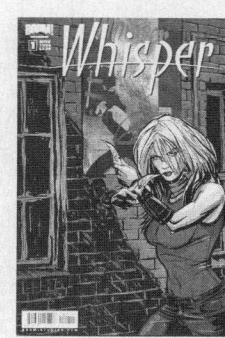

Whisper #1 © BOOM & Grant

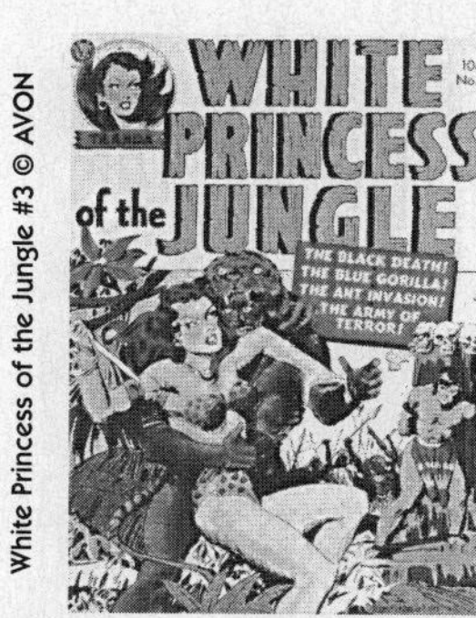

White Princess of the Jungle #3 © AVON

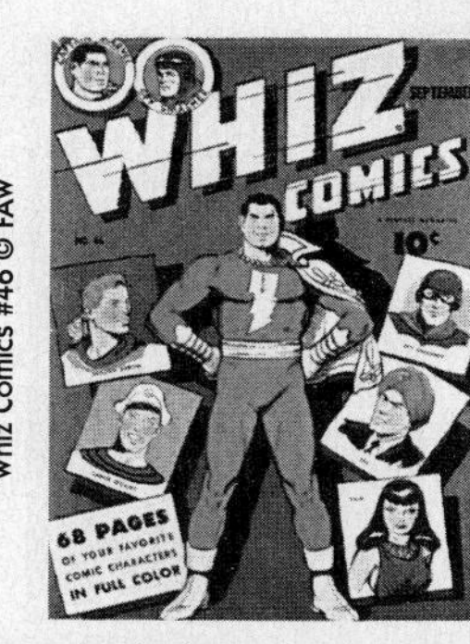

Whiz Comics #46 © FAW

	GD 2.0	VG 4.0	FN 6.0	VF 8.0	VF/NM 9.0	NM- 9.2

WHIRLYBIRDS (TV)
Dell Publishing Co.: No. 1124, Aug, 1960 - No. 1216, Oct-Dec, 1961

Four Color 1124 (#1)-Photo-c 8 16 24 56 93 130
Four Color 1216-Photo-c 8 16 24 52 86 120

WHISKEY DICKEL, INTERNATIONAL COWGIRL
Image Comics: Aug, 2003 ($12.95, softcover, B&W)

nn-Mark Ricketts-s/Mike Hawthorne-a; pin-up by various incl. Oeming, Thompson, Mack 13.00

WHISPER (Female Ninja)
Capital Comics: Dec, 1983 - No. 2, 1984 ($1.75, Baxter paper)

1,2: 1-Origin; Golden-c, Special (11/85, $2.50) 2.50

WHISPER (Vol. 2)
First Comics: Jun, 1986 - No. 37, June, 1990 ($1.25/$1.75/$1.95)

1-37 2.50

WHISPER
Boom! Studios: Nov, 2006 ($3.99)

1-Grant-s/Dzialowski-a 4.00

WHITE CHIEF OF THE PAWNEE INDIANS
Avon Periodicals: 1951

nn-Kit West app.; Kinstler-c 16 32 48 92 144 195

WHITE EAGLE INDIAN CHIEF (See Indian Chief)

WHITE FANG
Disney Comics: 1990 ($5.95, 68 pgs.)

nn-Graphic novel adapting new Disney movie 6.00

WHITE INDIAN
Magazine Enterprises: No. 11, July, 1953 - No. 15, 1954

11(A-1 94), 12(A-1 101), 13(A-1 104)-Frazetta-r(Dan Brand) in all from Durango Kid.
11-Powell-c 22 44 66 127 204 280
14(A-1 117), 15(A-1 135)-Check-a; Torres-a-#15 14 28 42 76 108 140

NOTE: *#11 contains reprints from Durango Kid #1-4; #12 from #5, 9, 10, 11; #13 from #7, 12, 13, 16. #14 & 15 contain all new stories.*

WHITEOUT (Also see Queen & Country)
Oni Press: July, 1998 - No. 4, Nov, 1998 ($2.95, B&W, limited series)

1-4: 1-Matt Wagner-c. 2-Mignola-c. 3-Gibbons-c 3.00
TPB (5/99, $10.95) r/#1-4; Miller-c 11.00

WHITEOUT: MELT
Oni Press: Sept, 1999 - No. 4, Feb, 2000 ($2.95, B&W, limited series)

1-4-Greg Rucka-s/Steve Lieber-a 3.00
Whiteout: Melt, The Definitive Edition TPB (9/07, $13.95) r/#1-4; Rucka afterword 14.00

WHITE PRINCESS OF THE JUNGLE (Also see Jungle Adventures & Top Jungle Comics)
Avon Periodicals: July, 1951 - No. 5, Nov, 1952

1-Origin of White Princess (Taanda) & Capt'n Courage (r); Kinstler-c
55 110 165 352 601 850
2-Reprints origin of Malu, Slave Girl Princess from Avon's Slave Girl Comics #1 w/Malu changed to Zora; Kinstler-c/a(2) 40 80 120 246 411 575
3-Origin Blue Gorilla; Kinstler-c/a 37 74 111 218 354 490
4-Jack Barnum, White Hunter app.; r/Sheena #9 32 64 96 188 307 425
5-Blue Gorilla by McCann?; Kinstler inside-c; Fawcette/Alascia-a(3)
34 68 102 199 325 450

WHITE RIDER AND SUPER HORSE (Formerly Humdinger V2#2; Indian Warriors #7 on; also see Blue Bolt #1, 4Most & Western Crime Cases)
Novelty-Star Publications/Accepted Publ.: No. 4, 9/50 - No. 6, 3/51

4-6-Adapts "The Last of the Mohicans". 4(#1)-(9/50)-Says #11 on inside
16 32 48 92 144 195
Accepted Reprint #5(r/#5),6 (nd); L.B. Cole-c 9 18 27 50 65 80

NOTE: *All have* **L. B. Cole** *covers.*

WHITE TIGER
Marvel Comics: Jan, 2007 - No. 6, Nov, 2007 ($2.99, limited series)

1-6: 1-David Mack-c; Pierce & Liebe-s/Briones-a; Spider-Man & Black Widow app. 3.00
...: A Hero's Compulsion SC (2007,$14.99) r/#1-6; re-cap art and profile page 15.00

WHITE WILDERNESS (Disney)
Dell Publishing Co.: No. 943, Oct, 1958

Four Color 943-Movie 6 12 18 43 69 95

WHITMAN COMIC BOOK, A
Whitman Publishing Co.: Sept., 1962 (136 pgs.; 7-3/4x5-3/4; hardcover) (B&W)

1-3,5,7: 1-Yogi Bear. 2-Huckleberry Hound. 3-Mr. Jinks and Pixie & Dixie. 5-Augie Doggie & Loopy de Loop. 7-Bugs Bunny-r from #47,51,53,54 & 55
7 14 21 45 73 100
4,6: 4-The Flintstones. 6-Snooper & Blabber Fearless Detectives/Quick Draw McGraw of the Wild West 7 14 21 49 80 110
8-Donald Duck-reprints most of WDC&S #209-213. Includes 5 Barks stories, 1 complete Mickey Mouse serial by Paul Murry & 1 Mickey Mouse serial missing the 1st episode
8 16 24 54 90 125

NOTE: *Hanna-Barbera #1-6(TV), reprints of British tabloid comics. Dell reprints-#7,8.*

WHIZ COMICS (Formerly Flash & Thrill Comics #1)(See 5 Cent Comics)
Fawcett Publications: No. 2, Feb, 1940 - No. 155, June, 1953

1-(nn on cover, #2 inside)-Origin & 1st newsstand app. Captain Marvel (formerly Captain Thunder) by C. C. Beck (created by Bill Parker), Spy Smasher, Golden Arrow, Ibis the Invincible, Dan Dare, Scoop Smith, Sivana, & Lance O'Casey begin
7000 14,000 21,000 40,000 67,500 95,000
(The only Mint copy sold in 1995 for $176,000 cash)

1-Reprint, oversize 13-1/2x10". **WARNING**: This comic is an exact duplicate reprint (except for dropping "Gangway for Captain Marvel" from-c) of the original except for its size. DC published it in 1974 with a second cover titling it as a Famous First Edition. There have been many reported cases of the outer cover being removed and the interior sold as the original edition. The reprint with the new outer cover removed is practically worthless. See Famous First Edition for value.

2-(3/40, nn on cover, #3 inside); cover to Flash #1 redrawn, pg. 12, panel 4; Spy Smasher reveals I.D. to Eve 465 930 1395 3395 5998 8600
3-(4/40, #3 on-c, #4 inside)-1st app. Beautia 331 662 993 2317 4059 5800
4-(5/40, #4 on cover, #5 inside)-Brief origin Capt. Marvel retold
297 594 891 1888 3244 4600
5-Captain Marvel wears button-down flap on splash page only
252 504 756 1613 2757 3900
6-10: 7-Dr. Voodoo begins (by Raboy-#9-22) 184 368 552 1168 2009 2850
11-14: 12-Capt. Marvel does not wear cape 126 252 378 806 1378 1950
15-Origin Sivana; Dr. Voodoo by Raboy 135 270 405 864 1482 2100
16-18-Spy Smasher battles Captain Marvel 129 258 307 826 1413 2000
19-Classic shark-c 103 206 309 659 1130 1600
20 89 178 267 565 970 1375
21-(9/41)-Origin & 1st cover app. Lt. Marvels, the 1st team in Fawcett comics. In this issue, Capt. Death similar to Ditko's later Dr. Strange 92 184 276 584 1005 1425
22-24: 23-Only Dr. Voodoo by Tuska 69 138 207 442 759 1075
25-(12/41)-Captain Nazi jumps from Master Comics #21 to take on Capt. Marvel solo after being beaten by Capt. Marvel/Bulletman team, causing the creation of Capt. Marvel Jr.; 1st app./origin of Capt. Marvel Jr. (part II of trilogy origin by CC. Beck & Mac Raboy); Captain Marvel sends Jr. back to Master #22 to aid Bulletman against Capt. Nazi; origin Old Shazam in text 568 1136 1704 4146 7323 10,500
26-30 60 120 180 381 653 925
31,32: 32-1st app. The Trolls; Hitler/Mussolini satire by Beck
53 106 159 334 567 800
33-Spy Smasher, Captain Marvel x-over on cover and inside
60 120 180 381 653 925
34,36-40: 37-The Trolls app. by Swayze 40 80 120 246 411 575
35-Captain Marvel & Spy Smasher-c 49 98 147 309 522 735
41-50: 43-Spy Smasher, Ibis, Golden Arrow x-over in Capt. Marvel. 44-Flag-c. 47-Origin recap (1 pg.) 36 72 108 214 347 480
51-60: 52-Capt. Marvel x-over in Ibis. 57-Spy Smasher, Golden Arrow, Ibis cameo
29 58 87 172 281 390
61-70 27 54 81 160 263 365
71,77-80 26 52 78 152 249 345
72-76-Two Captain Marvel stories in each; 76-Spy Smasher becomes Crime Smasher
26 52 78 154 252 350
81-99: 86-Captain Marvel battles Sivana Family; robot-c. 91-Infinity-c
26 52 78 152 249 345
100-(8/48)-Anniversary issue 29 58 87 172 281 390
101-106: 102-Commando Yank app. 106-Bulletman app.
25 50 75 147 241 335
107-149: 107-Capitol Building photo-c. 108-Brooklyn Bridge photo-c. 112-Photo-c. 139-Infinity-c. 140-Flag-c. 142-Used in **POP**, pg. 89
25 50 75 147 241 335
150-152-(Low dist.) 29 58 87 170 278 385
153-155-(Scarce):154,155-1st/2nd Dr. Death stories 39 78 117 231 378 525

NOTE: ***C.C. Beck*** *Captain Marvel-No. 25(part).* ***Krigstein*** *Golden Arrow-No. 75, 78, 91, 95, 96, 98-100.* ***Mac Raboy*** *Dr. Voodoo-No. 9-22. Captain Marvel-No. 25(part).* ***M.Swayze*** *a-37, 38, 59; c-38.* ***Schaffenberger*** *c-138-155(most).* ***Wolverton*** *1/2 pg. "Culture Corner"-No. 65-67, 68(2 1/2 pgs), 70-85, 87-96, 98-100, 102-109, 112-121, 123, 125, 126, 128-131, 133, 134, 136, 142, 143, 146.*

WHIZ KIDS (Also see Big Bang Comics)
Image Comics: Apr, 2003 ($4.95, B&W, one-shot)

1-Galahad, Cyclone, Thunder Girl and Moray app.; Jeff Austin-a 5.00

Whodunnit? #1 © ECL

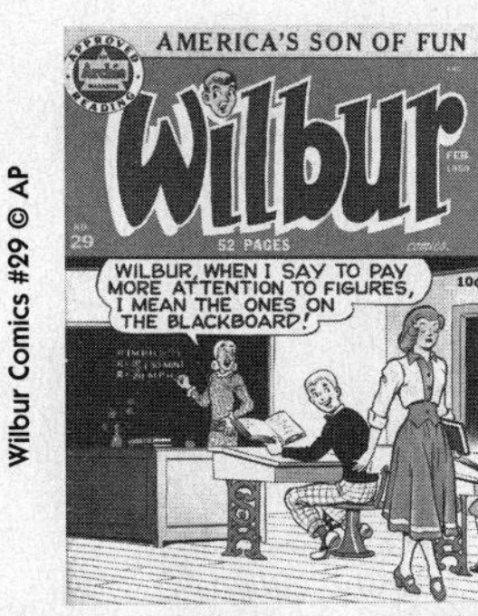

Wilbur Comics #29 © AP

Wild Bill Hickok #1 © AVON

	GD 2.0	VG 4.0	FN 6.0	VF 8.0	VF/NM 9.0	NM- 9.2

WHOA, NELLIE (Also see Love & Rockets)
Fantagraphics Books: July, 1996 - No. 3, Sept, 1996 ($2.95, B&W, lim. series)

1-3: Jamie Hernandez-c/a/scripts						3.00

WHODUNIT
D.S. Publishing Co.: Aug-Sept, 1948 - No. 3, Dec-Jan, 1948-49 (#1,2: 52 pgs.)

1-Baker-a (7 pgs.)	24	48	72	140	230	320
2,3-Detective mysteries	13	26	39	74	105	135

WHODUNNIT?
Eclipse Comics: June, 1986 - No. 3, Apr, 1987 ($2.00, limited series)

1-3: Spiegle-a. 2-Gulacy-c						2.50

WHO FRAMED ROGER RABBIT (See Marvel Graphic Novel)

WHO IS NEXT?
Standard Comics: No. 5, Jan, 1953

5-Toth, Sekowsky, Andru-a; crime stories	20	40	60	114	182	250

WHO IS THE CROOKED MAN?
Crusade: Sept, 1996 ($3.50, B&W, 40 pgs.)

1-Intro The Martyr, Scarlet 7 & Garrison						3.50

WHO'S MINDING THE MINT? (See Movie Classics)

WHO'S WHO IN STAR TREK
DC Comics: Mar, 1987 - #2, Apr, 1987 ($1.50, limited series)

1,2						6.00

NOTE: ***Byrne** a-1, 2. **Chaykin** c-1, 2. **Morrow** a-1, 2. **McFarlane** a-2. **Perez** a-1, 2. **Sutton** a-1, 2.*

WHO'S WHO IN THE LEGION OF SUPER-HEROES
DC Comics: Apr, 1987 - No. 7, Nov, 1988 ($1.25, limited series)

1-7						4.00

WHO'S WHO: THE DEFINITIVE DIRECTORY OF THE DC UNIVERSE
DC Comics: Mar, 1985 - No. 26, Apr, 1987 (Maxi-series, no ads)

1-DC heroes from A-Z						4.00
2-26: All have 1-2 pgs-a by most DC artists						4.00

NOTE: ***Art Adams** a-4, 11, 18, 20. **Anderson** a-1-5, 7-12, 14, 15, 19, 21, 23-25. **Aparo** a-2, 3, 9, 10, 12, 13, 14, 15, 17, 18, 21, 23. **Byrne** a-4, 7, 14, 16, 18i, 19, 22i, 24; c-22. **Cowan** a-3-5, 8, 10-13, 16-18, 22-25. **Ditko** a-19-22. **Evans** a-20. **Giffen** a-1, 3,-6, 8, 13, 15, 17, 18, 23. **Grell** a-6, 9, 14, 20, 23, 25, 26. **Infantino** a-1-10, 12, 15, 17-22, 24, 25. **Kaluta** a-14, 21. **Gil Kane** a-1-11, 13, 14, 16, 19, 21-23, 25. **Kirby** a-2-6, 8-18, 20, 22, 25. **Kubert** a-2, 3, 7-11, 19, 20, 25. **Erik Larsen** a-24. **McFarlane** a-10-12, 17, 19, 25, 26. **Morrow** a-4, 7, 25, 26. **Orlando** a-1, 4, 10, 11, 21i. **Perez** a-1-5, 8-19, 22-26; c-1-4, 13-18. **Rogers** a-1, 2, 5-7, 11, 12, 15, 24. **Starlin** a-13, 14, 16. **Stevens** a-4, 7, 18.*

WHO'S WHO UPDATE '87
DC Comics: Aug, 1987 - No. 5, Dec, 1987 ($1.25, limited series)

1-5: Contains art by most DC artists						3.00

NOTE: ***Giffen** a-1. **McFarlane** a-1-4; c-4. **Perez** a-1-4.*

WHO'S WHO UPDATE '88
DC Comics: Aug, 1988 - No. 4, Nov, 1988 ($1.25, limited series)

1-4: Contains art by most DC artists						3.00

NOTE: ***Giffen** a-1. **Erik Larsen** a-1.*

WICKED, THE
Avalon Studios: Dec, 1999 - No. 7, Aug, 2000 ($2.95)

Preview-(7/99, $5.00, B&W)						5.00
1-7-Anacleto-c/Martinez-a						3.00
...: Medusa's Tale (11/00, $3.95, one shot) story plus pin-up gallery						4.00
...: Vol. 1: Omnibus (2003, $19.95) r/#0-8; Drew-c						20.00

WILBUR COMICS (Teen-age) (Also see Laugh Comics, Laugh Comix, Liberty Comics #10 & Zip Comics)
MLJ Magazines/Archie Publ. No. 8, Spring, 1946 on: Sum', 1944 - No. 87, 11/59; No. 88, 9/63; No. 89, 10/64; No. 90, 10/65 (No. 1-46: 52 pgs.) (#1-11 are quarterly)

1	54	108	162	343	584	825
2(Fall, 1944)	30	60	90	177	289	400
3,4(Wint, '44-45; Spr, '45)	21	42	63	126	206	285
5-1st app. Katy Keene (Sum, '45) & begin series; Wilbur story same as Archie story in Archie #1 except Wilbur replaces Archie	107	214	321	680	1165	1650
6-10: 10-(Fall, 1946)	24	48	72	140	230	320
11-20	15	30	45	88	137	185
21-30: 30-(4/50)	11	22	33	64	90	115
31-50	9	18	27	52	69	85
51-70	8	16	24	44	57	70
71-90: 88-Last 10¢ issue (9/63)	4	8	12	26	41	55

NOTE: *Katy Keene in No. 5-56, 58-61, 63-69. **Al Fagaly** c-6-9, 12-24 at least. **Vigoda** c-2.*

WILD
Atlas Comics (IPC): Feb, 1954 - No. 5, Aug, 1954

1	26	52	78	154	252	350
2	16	32	48	94	147	200
3-5	15	30	45	85	130	175

NOTE: ***Berg** a-5; c-4. **Burgos** c-3. **Colan** a-4. **Everett** a-1-3. **Heath** a-2, 3, 5. **Maneely** a-1-3, 5; c-1, 5. **Post** a-2, 5. **Ed Win** a-1, 3.*

WILD! (This Magazine Is...) (Satire)
Dell Publishing Co.: Jan, 1968 - No. 3, 1968 (35¢, magazine, 52 pgs.)

1-3: Hogan's Heroes, The Rat Patrol & Mission Impossible TV spoofs	3	6	9	14	19	24

WILD ANIMALS
Pacific Comics: Dec, 1982 ($1.00, one-shot, direct sales)

1-Funny animal; Sergio Aragones-a; Shaw-c/a						4.00

WILD BILL ELLIOTT (Also see Western Roundup under Dell Giants)
Dell Publishing Co.: No. 278, 5/50 - No. 643, 7/55 (No #11,12) (All photo-c)

Four Color 278(#1, 52pgs.)-Titled "Bill Elliott"; Bill & his horse Stormy begin; photo front/back-c begin	12	24	36	86	158	230
2 (11/50), 3 (52 pgs.)	8	16	24	52	86	120
4-10(10-12/52)	6	12	18	41	66	90
Four Color 472(6/53),520(12/53)-Last photo back-c	5	10	15	34	55	75
13(4-6/54) - 17(4-6/55)	5	10	15	32	51	70
Four Color 643 (7/55)	5	10	15	30	48	65

WILD BILL HICKOK (Also see Blazing Sixguns)
Avon Periodicals: Sept-Oct, 1949 - No. 28, May-June, 1956

1-Ingels-c	23	46	69	136	223	310
2-Painted-c; Kit West app.	13	26	39	74	105	135
3-5-Painted-c (4-Cover by Howard Winfield)	10	20	30	54	72	90
6-10,12: 8-10-Painted-c. 12-Kinsler-c?	10	20	30	54	72	90
11,13,14-Kinstler-c/a (#11-c & inside-f/c art only)	10	20	30	58	79	100
15,17,18,20: 18-Kit West story. 20-Kit West by Larsen	9	18	27	47	61	75
16-Kamen-a; r-3 stories/King of the Badmen of Deadwood	9	18	27	50	65	80
19-Meskin-a	9	18	27	47	61	75
21-Reprints 2 stories/Chief Crazy Horse	8	16	24	44	57	70
22-McCann-a?; r/Sheriff Bob Dixon's...	8	16	24	44	57	70
23-27: 23-Kinstler-c. 24-27-Kinstler-c/a(r) (24,25-r?)	8	16	24	44	57	70
28-Kinstler-c/a (new); r-/Last of the Comanches	9	18	27	47	61	75
I.W. Reprint #1-r/#2; Kinstler-c	2	4	6	9	13	16
Super Reprint #10-12: 10-r/#18. 11-r/#?. 12-r/#8	2	4	6	9	13	16

NOTE: *#23, 25 contain numerous editing deletions in both art and script due to code. **Kinstler** c-6, 7, 11-14, 17, 18, 20-22, 24-28. **Howard Larsen** a-1, 2, 4, 5, 6(3), 7-9, 11, 12, 17, 18, 20-24, 26. **Meskin** a-7. **Reinman** a-6, 17.*

WILD BILL HICKOK AND JINGLES (TV)(Formerly Cowboy Western) (Also see Blue Bird)
Charlton Comics: No. 68, Aug, 1958 - No. 75, Dec, 1959

68,69-Williamson-a (all are 10¢ issues)	11	22	33	60	83	105
70-Two pgs. Williamson-a	8	16	24	42	54	65
71-75 (#76, exist?)	6	12	18	28	34	40

WILD BILL PECOS WESTERN (Also see The Westerner)
AC Comics: 1989 ($3.50, 1/2 color/1/2 B&W, 52 pgs.)

1-Syd Shores-c/a(r)/Westerner; photo back-c						4.00

WILD BOY OF THE CONGO (Also see Approved Comics)
Ziff-Davis No. 10-12,4-8/St. John No. 9,11 on: No. 10, 2-3/51 - No. 12, 8-9/51; No. 4, 10-11/51 - No. 9, 10/53; No. 11-#15,6/55 (No #10, 1953)

10(#1)(2-3/51)-Origin; bondage-c by Saunders (painted); used in **SOTI**, pg. 189; painted-c begin thru #9 (except #7)	23	46	69	136	223	310
11(4-5/51),12(8-9/51)-Norman Saunders painted-c	14	28	42	78	112	145
4(10-11/51)-Saunders painted bondage-c	14	28	42	78	112	145
5(Winter,'51)-Saunders painted-c	12	24	36	69	97	125
6,8,9(10/53): Painted-c. 6-Saunders-c	12	24	36	69	97	125
7(8-9/52)-Kinstler-a	14	28	42	78	112	145
11-13-Baker-c. 11-r/#7 w/new Baker-c; Kinstler-a (2 pgs.)	15	30	45	84	127	170
14(4/55)-Baker-c; r-#12('51)	15	30	45	84	127	170
15(6/55)	10	20	30	58	79	100

WILDCAT (See Sensation Comics #1)

WILDC.A.T.S ADVENTURES (TV cartoon)
Image Comics (WildStorm): Sept, 1994 - No. 10, June, 1995 ($1.95/$2.50)

1-10						2.50

WildC.A.T.S #10 © WSP

Wildcats V5 #13 © WSP

Wildcats Version 3.0 #1 © WSP

	GD 2.0	VG 4.0	FN 6.0	VF 8.0	VF/NM 9.0	NM- 9.2

Sourcebook 1 (1/95, $2.95) 3.00

WILDC.A.T.S: COVERT ACTION TEAMS (Also see Alan Moore's... for TPB reprints)
Image Comics (WildStorm Productions): Aug, 1992 - No. 4, Mar, 1993; No. 5, Nov, 1993 - No. 50, June, 1998 ($1.95/$2.50)

1-1st app; Jim Lee/Williams-c/a & Lee scripts begin; contains 2 trading cards (Two diff versions of cards inside); 1st WildStorm Productions title 4.50
1-All gold foil signed edition 12.00
1-All gold foil unsigned edition 8.00
1-Newsstand edition w/o cards 3.00
1-"3-D Special"(8/97, $4.95) w/3-D glasses; variant-c by Jim Lee. 5.00
2-($2.50)-Prism foil stamped-c; contains coupon for Image Comics #0 & 4 pg. preview to Portacio's Wetworks (back-up) 4.50
2-With coupon missing 2.25
2-Direct sale misprint w/o foil-c 3.00
2-Newsstand ed., no prism or coupon 2.50
3-Lee/Liefeld-c (1/93-c, 12/92 inside) 3.50
4-($2.50)-Polybagged w/Topps trading card; 1st app. Tribe by Johnson & Stroman; Youngblood cameo 3.50
4-Variant w/red card 6.00
5-7-Jim Lee/Williams-c/a; Lee script 3.00
8-X-Men's Jean Grey & Scott Summers cameo 4.00
9-12: 10-1st app. Huntsman & Soldier; Claremont scripts begin, ends #13. 11-1st app. Savant, Tapestry & Mr. Majestic. 3.00
11-Alternate Portacio-c, see Deathblow #5 5.00
13-19,21-24: 15-James Robinson scripts begin, ends #20. 15,16-Black Razor story. 21-Alan Moore scripts begin, end #34; intro Tao & Ladytron; new WildC.A.T.S team forms (Mr. Majestic, Savant, Condition Red (Max Cash), Tao & Ladytron). 22-Maguire-a 3.00
20-($2.50)-Direct Market, WildStorm Rising Pt. 2 w/bound-in card 3.00
20-($1.95)-Newsstand, WildStorm Rising Part 2 2.50
25-($4.95)-Alan Moore script; wraparound foil-c. 5.00
26-49: 29-(5/96)-Fire From Heaven Pt 7; reads Apr on-c. 30-(6/96)-Fire From Heaven Pt. 13; Spartan revealed to have transplanted personality of John Colt (from Team One: WildC.A.T.S). 31-(9/96)-Grifter rejoins team; Ladytron dies 2.50
40-($3.50)Voyager Pack bagged w/Divine Right preview 5.00
50-($3.50) Stories by Robinson/Lee, Choi & Peterson/Benes, and Moore/Charest; Charest sketchbook; Lee wraparound-c 4.00
50-Chromium cover 6.00
Annual 1 (2/98, $2.95) Robinson-s 3.00
Compendium (1993, $9.95)-r/#1-4; bagged w/#0 10.00
Sourcebook 1 (9/93, $2.50)-Foil embossed-c 2.50
Sourcebook 1-($1.95)-Newsstand ed. w/o foil embossed-c 2.50
Sourcebook 2 (11/94, $2.50)-wraparound-c 2.50
Special 1 (11/93, $3.50, 52 pgs.)-1st Travis Charest WildC.A.T.S-a 3.50
...A Gathering of Eagles (5/97, $9.95, TPB) r/#10-12 10.00
.../ Cyberforce: Killer Instinct TPB (2004, $14.95) r/#5-7 & Cyberforce V2 #1-3 15.00
...Gang War ('98, $16.95, TPB) r/#28-34 17.00
...Homecoming (8/98, $19.95, TPB) r/#21-27 20.00
James Robinson's Complete Wildc.a.t.s TPB (2009, $24.99) r/#15-20,50; Annual 1, WildStorm Rising #1, Team One Wildc.a.t.s #1,2; cover and pin-up gallery 25.00

WILDCATS
DC Comics (WildStorm): Mar, 1999 - No. 28, Dec, 2001 ($2.50)

1-Charest-a; six covers by Lee, Adams, Bisley, Campbell, Madureira and Ramos; Lobdell-s 3.00
1-($6.95) DF Edition; variant cover by Ramos 7.00
2-28: 2-Voodoo cover. 3-Bachalo variant-c. 5-Hitch-a/variant-c. 7-Meglia-a. 8-Phillips-a begins. 17-J.G. Jones-c. 18,19-Jim Lee-c. 20,21-Dillon-a 2.50
Annual 2000 (12/00, $3.50) Bermejo-a; Devil's Night x-over 3.50
...: Battery Park ('03, $17.95, TPB) r/#20-28; Phillips-c 18.00
... Ladytron (10/00, $5.95) Origin; Casey-s/Canete-a 6.00
... Mosaic (2/00, $3.95) Tuska-a (10 pg. back-up story) 4.00
...: Serial Boxes ('01, $14.95, TPB) r/#14-19; Phillips-c 15.00
...: Street Smart ('00, $24.95, HC) r/#1-6; Charest-c 25.00
...: Street Smart ('02, $14.95, SC) r/#1-6; Charest-c 15.00
...: Vicious Circles ('00, $14.95, TPB) r/#8-13; Phillips-c 15.00

WILDCATS (Volume 4)
DC Comics (WildStorm): Dec, 2006 ($2.99)

1-Grant Morrison-s/Jim Lee-a; Jim Lee-c 3.00
1-Variant-c by Todd McFarlane/Jim Lee 6.00
...: Armageddon 1 (2/08, $2.99) Gage-s/Caldwell-a 3.00

WILDCATS (Volume 5) (World's End on cover for #1,2)
DC Comics (WildStorm): Sept, 2008 - Present ($2.99)

1-19: 1-Christos Gage-s/Neil Googe-a. 5-Woods-a 3.00
...: Family Secrets TPB (2010, $17.99) r/#8-12 18.00
...: World's End TPB (2009, $17.99) r/#1-7 18.00

WILDC.A.T.S/ ALIENS
Image Comics/Dark Horse: Aug, 1998 ($4.95, one-shot)

	GD	VG	FN	VF	VF/NM	NM-
1-Ellis-s/Sprouse-a/c; Aliens invade Skywatch; Stormwatch app.; death of Winter; destruction of Skywatch	1	2	3	5	6	8
1-Variant-c by Gil Kane	1	3	4	6	8	10

WILDCATS: NEMESIS
DC Comics (WildStorm): Nov, 2005 - No. 9, July, 2006 ($2.99, limited series)

1-9: 1-Robbie Morrison-s/Talent Caldwell & Horacio Domingues-a/Caldwell-c 3.00
TPB (2006, $19.99) r/#1-9; cover gallery 20.00

WILDC.A.T.S: SAVANT GARDE FAN EDITION
Image Comics/WildStorm Productions: Feb, 1997 - No. 3, Apr, 1997 (Giveaway, 8 pgs.) (Polybagged w/Overstreet's FAN)

1-3: Barbara Kesel-s/Christian Uche-a(p) 3.00
1-3-(Gold): All retailer incentives 10.00

WILDC.A.T.S TRILOGY
Image Comics (WildStorm Productions): June, 1993 - No. 3, Dec, 1993 ($1.95, lim. series)

1-($2.50)-1st app. Gen 13 (Fairchild, Burnout, Grunge, Freefall) Multi-color foil-c; Jae Lee-c/a in all 5.00
1-($1.95)-Newsstand ed. w/o foil-c 2.50
2,3-($1.95)-Jae Lee-c/a 2.50

WILDCATS VERSION 3.0
DC Comics (WildStorm): Oct, 2002 - No. 24, Oct, 2004 ($2.95)

1-24: 1-Casey-s/Nguyen-a; two covers by Nguyen and Rian Hughes and Nguyen. 8-Back-up preview of The Authority: High Stakes pt. 3 3.00
...: Brand Building TPB (2003, $14.95) r/#1-6 15.00
...: Full Disclosure TPB (2004, $14.95) r/#7-12 15.00

WILDC.A.T.S/ X-MEN: THE GOLDEN AGE (See also X-Men/WildC.A.T.S.: The Dark Age)
Image Comics (WildStorm Productions): Feb, 1997 ($4.50, one-shot)

1-Lobdell-s/Charest-a; Two covers (Charest, Jim Lee) 5.00
1-"3-D" Edition ($6.50) w/glasses 7.00

WILDC.A.T.S/ X-MEN: THE MODERN AGE
Image Comics (WildStorm Productions): Aug, 1997 ($4.50, one-shot)

1-Robinson-s/Hughes-a; Two covers (Hughes, Paul Smith) 5.00
1-"3-D" Edition ($6.50) w/glasses 7.00

WILDC.A.T.S/ X-MEN: THE SILVER AGE
Image Comics (WildStorm Productions): June, 1997 ($4.50, one-shot)

1-Lobdell-s/Jim Lee-a; Two covers(Neal Adams, Jim Lee) 5.00
1-"3-D" Edition ($6.50) w/glasses 7.00

WILDCORE
Image Comics (WildStorm Prods.): Nov, 1997 - No. 10, Dec, 1998 ($2.50)

1-10: 1-Two covers (Booth/McWeeney, Charest) 2.50
1-($3.50)-Voyager Pack w/DV8 preview 3.50
1-Chromium-c 5.00

WILD DOG
DC Comics: Sept, 1987 - No. 4, Dec, 1987 (75¢, limited series)

1-4 2.50
Special 1 (1989, $2.50, 52 pgs.) 2.50

WILDERNESS TREK (See Zane Grey, Four Color 333)

WILDFIRE (See Zane Grey, FourColor 433)

WILDFLOWER
Sirius Entertainment/Neko Press: 1996 - Present (B&W)

1-5-('96, $2.50) Billy Martinez-s/a 2.50
... Beginnings TPB (Neko Press, 2003, $14.99) r/#1-5 15.00
... Dark Euphoria 1 (2004, $2.99) Kiethan Jones-a/c; Martinez-s 3.00
... Dark Euphoria 1,2 (2004, $3.99) w/alternate-c by Martinez 4.00
... Tribal Screams 1-4 (12/00 - 2/03, $2.99) 3.00
... Tribal Screams 1 ($4.99) w/alternate-c by Dark One 5.00
... Y2K (16 pgs, edition of 2000) each contains an original Martinez sketch 10.00

WILD FRONTIER (Cheyenne Kid #8 on)
Charlton Comics: Oct, 1955 - No. 7, Apr, 1957

	GD	VG	FN	VF	VF/NM	NM-
1-Davy Crockett	10	20	30	54	72	90
2-6-Davy Crockett in all	7	14	21	37	46	55
7-Origin & 1st app. Cheyenne Kid	9	18	27	47	61	75

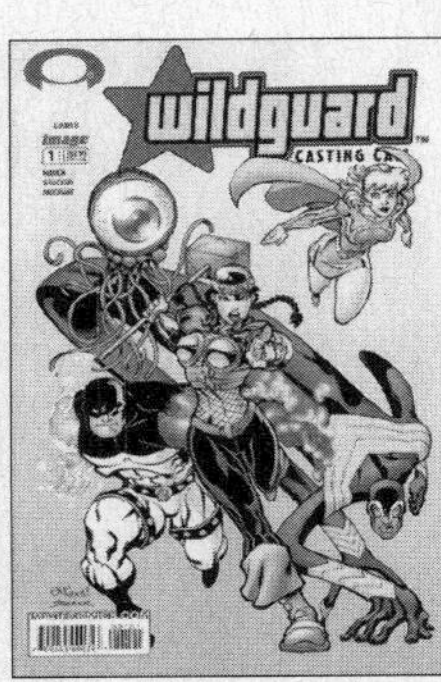

Wildguard: Casting Call #1 © Todd Nauck

Wildstorm Revelations #2 © WSP

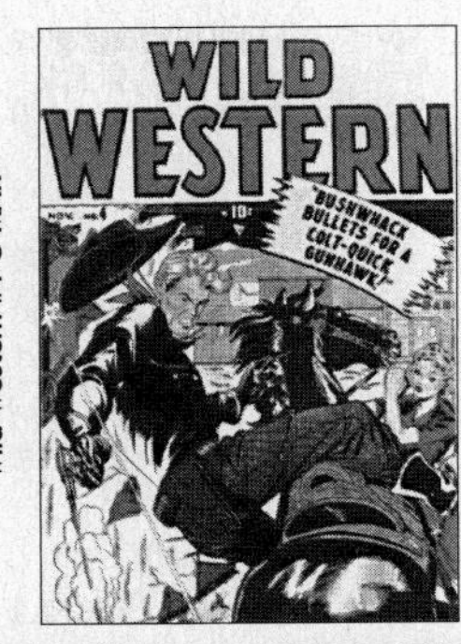

Wild Western #4 © MAR

GD VG FN VF VF/NM NM-
2.0 4.0 6.0 8.0 9.0 9.2

GD VG FN VF VF/NM NM-
2.0 4.0 6.0 8.0 9.0 9.2

WILD GIRL
DC Comics (WildStorm): Jan, 2005 - No. 6, Jun, 2005 ($2.95/$2.99)
1-6-Leah Moore & John Reppion-s/Shawn McManus-a/c 3.00

WILDGUARD: CASTING CALL
Image Comics: Sept, 2003 - No. 6, Feb, 2004 ($2.95)
1-6: 1-Nauck-s/a; two covers by Nauck and McGuinness. 2-Wieringo var-c. 6-Noto var-c 3.00
... Vol. 1: Casting Call (1/05, $17.95, TPB) r/#1-6; cover gallery; Todd Nauck bio 18.00
Wildguard: Fire Power 1 (12/04, $3.50) Nauck-a; two covers 3.50
Wildguard: Fool's Gold (7/05 - No. 2, 7/05, $3.50) 1,2-Todd Nauck-s/a 3.50
Wildguard: Insider (5/08 - No. 3, 7/08, $3.50) 1-3-Todd Nauck-s/a 3.50

WILDSIDERZ
DC Comics (WildStorm): No. 0, Aug, 2005 - No. 2, Jan, 2006 ($1.99/$3.50)
0-(8/05, $1.99) Series preview & character profiles; J. Scott Campbell-a 2.50
1,2: 1-(10/05, $3.50) J. Scott Campbell-s/a; Andy Hartnell-s 3.50

WILDSTAR (Also see The Dragon & The Savage Dragon)
Image Comics (Highbrow Entertainment): Sept, 1995 - No. 3, Jan, 1996 ($2.50, lim. series)
1-3: Al Gordon scripts; Jerry Ordway-c/a 2.50

WILDSTAR: SKY ZERO
Image Comics (Highbrow Entertainment): Mar, 1993 - No. 4, Nov, 1993 ($1.95, lim. series)
1-4: 1-($2.50)-Embossed-c w/silver ink; Ordway-c/a in all 2.50
1-($1.95)-Newsstand ed. w/silver ink-c, not embossed 2.50
1-Gold variant 6.00

WILD STARS
Collector's Edition/Little Rocket Productions: Summer, 1984 - Present (B&W)
Vol. 1 #1 (Summer 1984, $1.50) 5.00
Vol. 2 #1 (Winter 1988, $1.95) Foil-c; die-cut front & back-c 5.00
Vol. 3: #1-6-Brunner-c; Tierney-s. 1,2-Brewer-a. 3-6-Simons-a 3.00
7-($5.95) Simons-a 6.00
TPB (2004, $17.95) r/Vol. 1-3 18.00

WILDSTORM
Image Comics/DC Comics (WildStorm Publishing): 1994 - Present (one-shots, TPBs)
... After the Fall TPB (2009, $19.99) r/back-up stories from Wildcats V5 #1-11, The Authority V5 #1-11; Gen 13 V4 #21-28, and Stormwatch: PHD #13-20 20.00
...Annual 2000 (12/00, $3.50) Devil's Night x-over; Moy-a 3.50
...: Armageddon TPB (2008, $17.99) r/Armageddon one-shots in Midnighter, Welcome To Tranquility, Wetworks, Gen13, Stormwatch PHD, and Wildcats titles 18.00
...Chamber of Horrors (10/95, $3.50)-Bisley-c 3.50
...Fine Arts: Spotlight on Gen13 (2/08, $3.50) art and covers with commentary 3.50
...Fine Arts: Spotlight on Jim Lee (2/07, $3.50) art and covers by Lee with commentary 3.50
...Fine Arts: Spotlight on J. Scott Campbell (5/07, $3.50) art and covers with commentary 3.50
...Fine Arts: Spotlight on The Authority (1/08, $3.50) art and covers with commentary 3.50
...Fine Arts: Spotlight on WildCATs (3/08, $3.50) art and covers with commentary 3.50
...Fine Arts: The Gallery Collection (12/98, $19.95) Lee-c 20.00
...Halloween 1 (10/97, $2.50) Warner-c 2.50
...Rarities 1(12/94, $4.95, 52 pgs.)-r/Gen 13 1/2 & other stories 5.00
...Summer Special 1 (2001, $5.95) Short stories by various; Hughes-c 6.00
...Swimsuit Special 1 (12/94, $2.95), ...Swimsuit Special 2 (1995, $2.50) 3.00
...Swimsuit Special '97 #1 (7/97, $2.50) 2.50
...Thunderbook 1 (10/00, $6.95) Short stories by various incl. Hughes, Moy 7.00
...Ultimate Sports 1 (8/97, $2.50) 2.50
...Universe Sourcebook (5/95, $2.50) 2.50
...Universe 2008 Convention Exclusive ('08, no cover price) preview of World's End x-over 2.50

WILDSTORM!
Image Comics (WildStorm Publishing): Aug, 1995 - No. 4, Nov, 1995 ($2.50, B&W/color, anthology)
1-4: 1-Simonson-a 2.50

WILDSTORM REVELATIONS
DC Comics (WildStorm): Mar, 2008 - No. 6, May, 2008 ($2.99, limited series)
1-6-Beatty & Gage-s/Craig-a. 2-The Authority app. 3.00
TPB (2008, $17.99) r/#1-6; cover sketches 18.00

WILDSTORM RISING
Image Comics (WildStorm Publishing): May, 1995 - No.2, June, 1995 ($1.95/$2.50)
1-($2.50)-Direct Market, WildStorm Rising Pt. 1 w/bound-in card 2.50
1-($1.95)-Newstand, WildStorm Rising Pt. 1 2.50
2-($2.50)-Direct Market, WildStorm Rising Pt. 10 w/bound-in card; continues in WildC.A.T.S #21. 2.50
2-($1.95)-Newstand, WildStorm Rising Pt. 10 2.50
Trade paperback (1996, $19.95)-Collects x-over; B. Smith-c 20.00

WILDSTORM SPOTLIGHT
Image Comics (WildStorm Publishing): Feb, 1997 - No. 4 ($2.50)
1-4: 1-Alan Moore-s 2.50

WILDSTORM UNIVERSE '97
Image Comics (WildStorm Publishing): Dec, 1996 - No. 3 ($2.50, limited series)
1-3: 1-Wraparound-c. 3-Gary Frank-c 2.50

WILDTHING
Marvel Comics UK: Apr, 1993 - No. 7, Oct, 1993 ($1.75)
1-($2.50)-Embossed-c; Venom & Carnage cameo 2.50
2-7: 2-Spider-Man & Venom. 6-Mysterio app. 2.50

WILD THING (Wolverine's daughter in the M2 universe)
Marvel Comics: Oct, 1999 - No. 5, Feb, 2000 ($1.99)
1-5: 1-Lim-a in all. 2-Two covers 2.50
Wizard #0 supplement; battles the Hulk 2.50
Spider-Girl Presents Wild Thing. Crash Course (2007, $7.99, digest) r/#0-5 8.00

WILDTIMES
DC Comics (WildStorm Productions): Aug, 1999 ($2.50, one-shots)
...Deathblow #1 -set in 1899; Edwards-a; Jonah Hex app., ...DV8 #1 -set in 1944; Altieri-s/p; Sgt. Rock app., ...Gen13 #1 -set in 1969; Casey-s/Johnson-a; Teen Titans app., ...Grifter #1 -set in 1923; Paul Smith-a, ...Wetworks #1 -Waid-s/Lopresti-a; Superman app. 2.50
...WildC.A.T.s #0 -Wizard supplement; Charest-c 2.50

WILD WEST (Wild Western #3 on)
Marvel Comics (WFP): Spring, 1948 - No. 2, July, 1948
1-Two-Gun Kid, Arizona Annie, & Tex Taylor begin; Shores-c
34 68 102 199 325 450
2-Captain Tootsie by Beck; Shores-c 22 44 66 132 216 300

WILD WEST (Black Fury #1-57)
Charlton Comics: V2#58, Nov, 1966
V2#58 2 4 6 11 16 20

WILD WEST C.O.W.-BOYS OF MOO MESA (TV)
Archie Comics: Dec, 1992 - No. 3, Feb, 1993 (limited series)
V2#1, Mar, 1993 - No. 3, July, 1993 ($1.25)
1-3,V2#1-3 2.50

WILD WESTERN (Formerly Wild West #1,2)
Marvel/Atlas (WFP): No. 3, 9/48 - No. 57, 9/57 (3-11: 52 pgs, 12-on: 36 pgs)
3(#1)-Tex Morgan begins; Two-Gun Kid, Tex Taylor, & Arizona Annie continue from Wild West
27 54 81 158 259 360
4-Last Arizona Annie; Captain Tootsie by Beck; Kid Colt app.
20 40 60 114 182 250
5-2nd app. Black Rider (1/49); Blaze Carson, Captain Tootsie (by Beck) app.
23 46 69 136 223 310
6-8: 6-Blaze Carson app; anti-Wertham editorial 15 30 45 88 137 185
9-Photo-c; Black Rider begins, ends #19 19 38 57 109 172 235
10-Charles Starrett photo-c 22 44 66 128 209 290
11-(Last 52 pg. issue) 15 30 45 85 130 175
12-14,16-19: All Black Rider-c/stories. 12-14-The Prairie Kid & his horse Fury app.
15 30 45 83 124 165
15-Red Larabee, Gunhawk (origin), his horse Blaze, & Apache Kid begin, end #22; Black Rider-c/story 15 30 45 84 127 170
20-30: 20-Kid Colt-c begin. 24-Has 2 Kid Colt stories. 26-1st app. The Ringo Kid? (2/53); 4 pg. story. 30-Katz-a 12 24 36 69 97 125
31-40 10 20 30 54 72 90
41-47,49-51,53,57 9 18 27 47 61 75
48-Williamson/Torres-a (4 pgs); Drucker-a 10 20 30 56 76 95
52-Crandall-a 10 20 30 56 76 95
54,55-Williamson-a in both (5 & 4 pgs.), #54 with Mayo plus 2 text illos
10 20 30 56 76 95
56-Baker-a? 9 18 27 47 61 75

NOTE: *Annie Oakley in #46, 47. Apache Kid in #15-22, 39. Arizona Kid in #21, 23. Arrowhead in #34-39. Black Rider in #5, 9-19, 33-44. Fighting Texan in #17. Kid Colt in #4-6, 9-11, 20-47, 52, 54-56. Outlaw Kid in #43. Red Hawkins in #13, 14. Ringo Kid in #26, 39, 41, 43, 44, 46, 47, 50, 52-56. Tex Morgan in #3, 4, 6, 9, 11. Tex Taylor in #3-6, 9, 11. Texas Kid in #23-25. Two-Gun Kid in #3-6, 9, 11, 12, 33-39, 41. Wyatt Earp in #47.* ***Ayers*** *a-41, 42, 53, 54.* ***Berg*** *a-26; c-24.* ***Colan*** *a-49.* ***Forte*** *a-28, 30.* ***Al Hartley*** *a-16.* ***Heath*** *a-4, 5, 8; c-34, 44.* ***Keller*** *a-24, 26(2), 29-40, 44-46, 48, 52.* ***Maneely*** *a-10, 12, 15, 16, 28, 35, 38, 40-45; c-18-22, 33, 35, 36, 38-42, 45, 53, 54, 56, 57.* ***Morisi*** *a-23, 52.* ***Pakula*** *a-42, 52.* ***Powell*** *a-51.* ***Romita*** *a-24(2).* ***Severin*** *a-46, 47; c-48.* ***Shores*** *a-3, 5, 30, 31, 33, 35, 36, 38, 41; c-3-5.* ***Sinnott*** *a-34-39.* ***Wildey*** *a-43. Bondage c-19.*

WILD WESTERN ACTION (Also see The Bravados)
Skywald Publ. Corp.: Mar, 1971 - No. 3, June, 1971 (25¢, reprints, 52 pgs.)

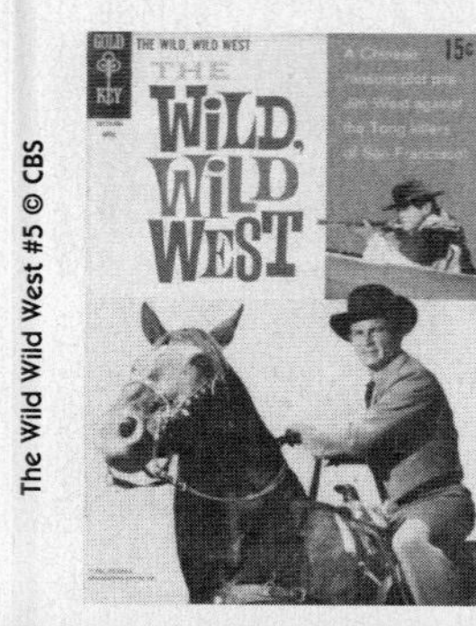

The Wild Wild West #5 © CBS

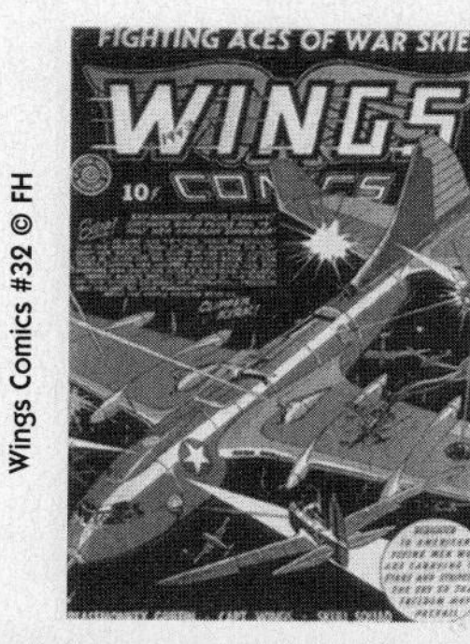

Wings Comics #32 © FH

Winnie-The-Pooh #8 © DIS

GD 2.0 | VG 4.0 | FN 6.0 | VF 8.0 | VF/NM 9.0 | NM- 9.2

1-Durango Kid, Straight Arrow-r; with all references to "Straight" in story relettered to "Swift"; Bravados begin; Shores-a (new) 3 6 9 14 20 26
2,3: 2-Billy Nevada, Durango Kid. 3-Red Mask, Durango Kid 2 4 6 10 14 18

WILD WESTERN ROUNDUP
Red Top/Decker Publications/I. W. Enterprises: Oct, 1957; 1960-'61
1(1957)-Kid Cowboy-r 5 10 15 22 26 30
I.W. Reprint #1('60-61)-r/#1 by Red Top 2 4 6 8 11 14

WILD WEST RODEO
Star Publications: 1953 (15¢)
1-A comic book coloring book with regular full color cover & B&W inside 8 16 24 44 57 70

WILD WILD WEST, THE (TV)
Gold Key: June, 1966 - No. 7, Oct, 1969 (All have Robert Conrad photo-c)
1-McWilliams-a 12 24 36 82 149 215
1-Variant edition with photo back-c (scarce) 13 26 39 90 165 240
2-Robert Conrad photo-c; McWilliams-a 9 18 27 60 100 140
2-Variant edition with Conrad photo back-c (scarce) 9 18 27 65 113 160
3-7 7 14 21 50 83 115
3-Variant edition with photo back-c (scarce) 9 18 27 60 110 140

WILD, WILD WEST, THE (TV)
Millennium Publications: Oct, 1990 - No. 4, Jan?, 1991 ($2.95, limited series)
1-4-Based on TV show 3.00

WILKIN BOY (See That...)

WILL EISNER READER
Kitchen Sink Press: 1991 ($9.95, B&W, 8 1/2" x 11", TPB)
nn-Reprints stories from Will Eisner's Quarterly; Eisner-s/a/c 10.00
nn-(DC Comics, 10/00, $9.95) 10.00

WILL EISNER'S JOHN LAW: ANGELS AND ASHES, DEVILS AND DUST
IDW Publ.: Apr, 2006 - No. 4 ($3.99, B&W, limited series)
1-New stories with Will Eisner's characters; Gary Chaloner-s/a 4.00

WILLIE COMICS (Formerly Ideal #1-4; Crime Cases #24 on; Li'l Willie #20 & 21) (See Gay Comics, Laugh, Millie The Model & Wisco)
Marvel Comics (MgPC): #5, Fall, 1946 - #19, 4/49; #22, 1/50 - #23, 5/50 (No #20 & 21)
5(#1)-George, Margie, Nellie the Nurse & Willie begin 23 46 69 136 223 310
6,8,9 14 28 42 83 124 165
7(1),10,11-Kurtzman's "Hey Look" 15 30 45 84 127 170
12,14-18,22,23 14 28 42 80 115 150
13,19-Kurtzman's "Hey Look" (#19-last by Kurtzman?) 14 28 42 81 118 155
NOTE: *Cindy app. in #17. Jeanie app. in #17. Little Lizzie app. in #22.*

WILLIE MAYS (See The Amazing...)

WILLIE THE PENGUIN
Standard Comics: Apr, 1951 - No. 6, Apr, 1952
1-Funny animal 9 18 27 47 61 75
2-6 6 12 18 28 34 40

WILLIE THE WISE-GUY (Also see Cartoon Kids)
Atlas Comics (NPP): Sept, 1957
1-Kida, Maneely-a 9 18 27 50 65 80

WILLOW
Marvel Comics: Aug, 1988 - No. 3, Oct, 1988 ($1.00)
1-3-R/Marvel Graphic Novel #36 (movie adaptation) 3.00

WILL ROGERS WESTERN (Formerly My Great Love #1-4; see Blazing & True Comics #66)
Fox Features Syndicate: No. 5, June, 1950 - No. 2, Aug, 1950
5(#1) 31 62 93 186 303 420
2: Photo-c 26 52 78 154 252 350

WILL TO POWER (Also see Comic's Greatest World)
Dark Horse Comics: June, 1994 - No. 12, Aug, 1994 ($1.00, weekly limited series, 20 pgs.)
1-12: 12-Vortex kills Titan. 2.50
NOTE: ***Mignola** c-10-12. **Sears** c-1-3.*

WILL-YUM!
Dell Publishing Co.: No. 676, Feb, 1956 - No. 902, May, 1958
Four Color 676 (#1), 765 (1/57), 902 4 8 12 26 41 55

WIN A PRIZE COMICS (Timmy The Timid Ghost #3 on?)
Charlton Comics: Feb, 1955 - No. 2, Apr, 1955
V1#1-S&K-a; Poe adapt; E.C. War swipe 67 134 201 426 731 1035
2-S&K-a 48 96 144 302 514 725

WINDY & WILLY (Also see Showcase #81)
National Periodical Publications: May-June, 1969 - No. 4, Nov-Dec, 1969
1- r/Dobie Gillis with some art changes begin 5 10 15 30 48 65
2-4 3 6 9 19 29 38

WINGS COMICS
Fiction House Mag.: 9/40 - No. 109, 9/49; No. 110, Wint, 1949-50; No. 111, Spring, 1950; No. 112, 1950(nd); No. 113 - No. 115, 1950(nd); No. 116, 1952(nd); No. 117, Fall, 1952 - No. 122, Wint, 1953-54; No. 123 - No. 124, 1954(nd)
1-Skull Squad, Clipper Kirk, Suicide Smith, Jane Martin, War Nurse, Phantom Falcons, Greasemonkey Griffin, Parachute Patrol & Powder Burns begin 271 542 813 1734 2967 4200
2 100 200 300 635 1093 1550
3-5 68 136 204 432 746 1060
6-10: 8-Indicia shows #7 (#8 on cover) 54 108 162 343 584 825
11-15 49 98 147 309 522 735
16-Origin & 1st app. Captain Wings & begin series 53 106 159 334 567 800
17-20 42 84 126 265 445 625
21-30 40 80 120 246 411 575
31-40 37 74 111 218 354 490
41-50 30 60 90 177 289 400
51-60: 60-Last Skull Squad 28 56 84 165 270 375
61-67: 66-Ghost Patrol begins (becomes Ghost Squadron #71 on), ends #112? 25 50 75 150 245 340
68,69: 68-Clipper Kirk becomes The Phantom Falcon-origin, Part 1; part 2 in #69 25 50 75 150 245 340
70-72: 70-1st app. The Phantom Falcon in costume, origin-Part 3; Capt. Wings battles Col. Kamikaze in all 24 48 72 144 237 330
73-99: 80-Phantom Falcon by Larsen. 99-King of the Congo begins? 24 48 72 144 237 330
100-(12/48) 25 50 75 150 245 340
101-124: 111-Last Jane Martin. 112-Flying Saucer-c/story (1950). 115-Used in **POP**, pg. 89 19 38 57 111 176 240
NOTE: *Bondage covers are common. Captain Wings battles Sky Hag-#75, 76; ...Mr. Atlantis-#85-92; ...Mr. Pupin(Red Agent)-#98-103. Capt. Wings by **Elias**-#52-64, 68, 69; by **Lubbers**-#29-32, 70-111; by **Renee**-#33-46. **Evans** a-85-106, 108-111(Jane Martin); text illos-72-84. **Larsen** a-52, 59, 64, 73-77. Jane Martin by **Fran Hopper**-#68-84; Suicide Smith by **John Celardo**-#72, 74, 76, 80-104; by **Hollingsworth**-#68-70, 105-109, 111; Ghost Squadron by **Astarita**-#67-79; by **Maurice Whitman**-#80-111. King of the Congo by **Moreira**-#99, 100. Skull Squad by **M. Baker**-#52-60; Clipper Kirk by **Baker**-#60, 61; by **Colan**-#53; by **Ingels**-(some issues?). Phantom Falcon by **Larsen**-#73-84. **Elias** c-58-72. **Fawcette** c-3-12, 16, 17, 19, 22-33. **Lubbers** c-74-109. **Tuska** a-5. **Whitman** c-110-124. **Zolnerwich** c-15, 21.*

WINGS OF THE EAGLES, THE
Dell Publishing Co.: No. 790, Apr, 1957 (10¢ & 15¢ editions exist)
Four Color 790-Movie; John Wayne photo-c; Toth-a 13 26 39 94 175 255

WINKY DINK (Adventures of...)
Pines Comics: No. 75, Mar, 1957 (one-shot)
75-Marv Levy-c/a 6 12 18 31 38 45

WINKY DINK (TV)
Dell Publishing Co.: No. 663, Nov, 1955
Four Color 663 (#1) 8 16 24 52 86 120

WINNIE-THE-POOH (Also see Dynabrite Comics)
Gold Key No. 1-17/Whitman No. 18 on: January, 1977 - No. 33, July, 1984 (Walt Disney) (Winnie-The-Pooh began as Edward Bear in 1926 by Milne)
1-New art 3 6 9 17 25 32
2-5: 5-New material 2 4 6 10 14 18
6-17: 12-up-New material 2 4 6 8 11 14
18,19(Whitman) 2 4 6 10 14 18
20,21('80) pre-pack only 4 8 12 24 37 50
22('80) (scarcer) pre-pack only 5 10 15 30 48 65
23-28: 27(2/82), 28(4/82) 2 4 6 11 16 20
29-33 (#90299 on-c, no date or date code; pre-pack): 29(4/82), 30(5/83), 31(8/83), 32(4/84), 33(7/84) 3 6 9 17 25 32

WINNIE WINKLE (See Popular Comics & Super Comics)
Dell Publishing Co.: 1941 - No. 7, Sept-Nov, 1949
Large Feature Comic 2 (1941) 28 56 84 165 270 375
Four Color 94 (1945) 12 24 36 85 155 225
Four Color 174 8 16 24 58 97 135
1(3-5/48)-Contains daily & Sunday newspaper-r from 1939-1941 8 16 24 52 86 120

Wise Little Hen nn © DIS

Witchblade #60 © TCOW

Witchblade Animated #1 © TCOW

	GD 2.0	VG 4.0	FN 6.0	VF 8.0	VF/NM 9.0	NM- 9.2
2 (6-8/48)	6	12	18	37	59	80
3-7	4	8	12	28	44	60

WINTER MEN, THE
DC Comics (WildStorm): Oct, 2005 - No. 5, Nov, 2006 ($2.99, limited series)

	GD	VG	FN	VF	VF/NM	NM-
1-5-Brett Lewis-s/John Paul Leon-a						3.00
... Winter Special (2/09, $3.99) Lewis-s/Leon-a						4.00
TPB (2010, $19.99) r/#1-5 & Winter Special; original proposal, development & sketch-a						20.00

WINTER SOLDIER: WINTER KILLS (See Captain America 2005 series)
Marvel Comics: Feb, 2007 ($3.99, one-shot)

	GD	VG	FN	VF	VF/NM	NM-
1-Flashback to Christmas Eve 1944; Toro & Sub-Mariner app.; Brubaker-s/Weeks-a						4.00

WINTERWORLD
Eclipse Comics: Sept, 1987 - No. 3, Mar, 1988 ($1.75, limited series)

	GD	VG	FN	VF	VF/NM	NM-
1-3						2.50

WISDOM
Marvel Comics (MAX): Jan, 2007 - No. 6, July, 2007 ($3.99, limited series)

	GD	VG	FN	VF	VF/NM	NM-
1-6: 1-Hairsine-a/c; Cornell-s. 3-6-Manuel Garcia-a						4.00
...: Rudiments of Wisdom TPB (2007, $21.99) r/#1-6; series pitch and sketch page						22.00

WISE GUYS (See Harvey...)

WISE LITTLE HEN, THE
David McKay Publ./Whitman: 1934 ,1935(48 pgs.); 1937 (Story book)

nn-(1934 edition w/dust jacket)(48 pgs. with color, 8-3/4x9-3/4") -Debut of Donald Duck (see Advs. of Mickey Mouse); Donald app. on cover with Wise Little Hen & Practical Pig; painted cover; same artist as the B&W's from Silly Symphony Cartoon, The Wise Little Hen (1934) (McKay)

	GD	VG	FN	VF	VF/NM	NM-
Book w/dust jacket	239	478	717	1530	2615	3700
Dust jacket only	55	110	165	352	601	850
nn-(1935 edition w/dust jacket), same as 1934 ed.	139	278	417	883	1517	2150
888 (1937)(9-1/2x13", 12 pgs.)(Whitman) Donald Duck app.	34	68	102	199	325	450

WISE SON: THE WHITE WOLF
DC Comics (Milestone): Nov, 1996 - No. 4, Feb, 1997 ($2.50, limited series)

	GD	VG	FN	VF	VF/NM	NM-
1-4: Ho Che Anderson-c/a						2.50

WIT AND WISDOM OF WATERGATE (Humor magazine)
Marvel Comics: 1973, 76 pgs., squarebound

	GD	VG	FN	VF	VF/NM	NM-
1-Low print run	4	8	12	28	44	60

WITCHBLADE (Also see Cyblade/Shi, Tales Of The..., & Top Cow Classics)
Image Comics (Top Cow Productions): Nov, 1995 - Present ($2.50/$2.99)

	GD	VG	FN	VF	VF/NM	NM-
0	1	2	3	5	6	8
1/2-Mike Turner/Marc Silvestri-c.	3	6	9	20	30	40
1/2 Gold Ed., 1/2 Chromium-c	3	6	9	20	30	40
1/2-(Vol. 2, 11/02, $2.99) Wohl-s/Ching-a/c						3.00
1-Mike Turner-a(p)	4	8	12	21	30	40
1,2-American Ent. Encore Ed.	1	2	3	4	5	7
2,3	2	4	6	11	16	20
4,5	2	4	6	9	13	16
6-9: 8-Wraparound-c. 9-Tony Daniel-a(p)	1	2	3	5	7	9
9-Sunset variant-c	2	4	6	8	10	12
9-DF variant-c	2	4	6	11	16	20
10-Flip book w/Darkness #0, 1st app. the Darkness	2	4	6	8	10	12
10-Variant-c	2	4	6	9	12	15
10-Gold logo	3	6	9	16	23	30
10-($3.95) Dynamic Forces alternate-c	1	2	3	5	6	8
11-15						5.00
16-19: 18,19-"Family Ties" Darkness x-over pt. 1,4						4.00
18-Face to face variant-c, 18-American Ent. Ed., 19-AE Gold Ed.	1	2	3	5	6	8
20-25: 24-Pearson, Green-a. 25-($2.95) Turner-a(p)						3.00
25 (Prism variant)						30.00
25 (Special)						15.00
26-39: 26-Green-a begins						2.50
27 (Variant)						10.00
40-49,51-53: 40-Begin Jenkins & Veitch-s/Keu Cha-a. 47-Zulli-c/a						2.50
40-Pittsburgh Convention Preview edition; B&W preview of #40						3.00
41-eWanted Chrome-c edition						5.00
49-Gold logo	1	2	3	5	6	8
50-($4.95) Darkness app.; Ching-a; B&W preview of Universe						5.00
54-59: 54-Black outer-c with gold foil logo; Wohl-s/Manapul-a						2.50
55-Variant Battle of the Planets Convention cover						3.00
60-74,76-91,93-99: 60-($2.99) Endgame x-over with Tomb Raider #25 & Evo #1. 64,65-Magdalena app. 71-Kirk-a. 77,81-85-Land-c. 80-Four covers. 87-Bachalo-a						3.00
75-($4.99) Manapul-a						5.00
92-($4.99) Origin of the Witchblade; art by various incl. Bachalo, Perez, Linsner, Cooke						5.00
100-($4.99) Five covers incl. Turner, Silvestri, Linsner; art by various; Jake dies						5.00
101-124,126-135: 103-Danielle Baptiste gets the Witchblade; Linsner variant-c. 116-124-Sejic-a. 126-128-War of the Witchblades. 134,135-Aphrodite IV app.						3.00
125-($3.99) War of the Witchblades begins; 3 covers; Sejic-a						4.00
... and Tomb Raider (4/05, $2.99) Jae Lee-c; art by Lee and Texiera						3.00
...: Animated (8/03, $2.99) Magdalena & Darkness app.; Dini-s/Bone, Bullock, Cooke-a/c						3.00
... Annual 2009 (4/09, $3.99) Basaldua-a						4.00
...: Art of the Witchblade (7/06, $2.99) pin-ups by various incl. Turner, Land, Linsner						3.00
...: Bearers of the Blade (7/06, $2.99) pin-up/profiles of bearers of the Witchblade						3.00
...: Blood Oath (8/04, $4.99) Sara teams with Phenix & Sibilla; Roux-a						5.00
...: Blood Relations TPB (2003, $12.99) r/#54-58						13.00
... Compendium Vol. 1 (2006, $59.99) r/#1-50; gallery of variant covers and art						60.00
... Compendium Vol. 2 (2007, $59.99) r/#51-100; gallery of variant covers and art						60.00
... Cover Gallery Vol. 1 (12/05, $2.99) intro. by Stan Lee						3.00
.../Darkchylde (7/00, $2.50) Green-s/a(p)						2.50
.../Dark Minds (6/04, $9.99) new story plus r/Dark Minds/Witchblade #1						10.00
.../Darkness: Family Ties Collected Edition (10/98, $9.95) r/#18,19 and Darkness #9,10						10.00
.../Darkness Special (12/99, $3.95) Green-c/a						4.00
...: Demon 1 (2003, $6.99) Mark Millar-s/Jae Lee-c/a						7.00
.../Devi (4/08, $3.99) Basaldua-a/Land-c; continues in Devi/Witchblade						4.00
...: Distinctions (See Tales of the Witchblade)						
.../Elektra (3/97, $2.95) Devil's Reign Pt. 6						3.00
... Gallery (11/00, $2.95) Profile pages and pin-ups by various; Turner-c						3.00
Infinity (5/99, $3.50) Lobdell-s/Pollina-c/a						3.50
.../Lady Death (11/01, $4.95) Manapul-c/a						5.00
...: Prevailing TPB (2000, $14.95) r/#20-25; new Turner-c						15.00
...: Revelations TPB (2000, $24.95) r/#9-17; new Turner-c						25.00
.../The Punisher (6/07, $3.99) Marz-s/Melo-a/Linsner-c						4.00
.../Tomb Raider #1/2 (7/00, $2.95) Covers by Turner and Cha						3.00
...: Vol. 1 TPB (1/08, $4.99) r/#80-85; Marz intro.; cover gallery						5.00
...: Vol. 2 TPB (2/08, $14.99) r/#86-92; cover gallery						15.00
...: Vol. 3 TPB (3/08, $14.99) r/#93-100; Edginton intro.; cover gallery						15.00
... vs. Frankenstein: Monster War 2005 (8/05, $2.99) pt. 3 of x-over						3.00
...: Witch Hunt Vol. 1 TPB (2/06, $14.99) r/#80-85; Marz intro.; Choi afterward; cover gallery						15.00
Wizard #500						10.00
.../Wolverine (6/04, $2.99) Basaldua-c/a; Claremont-s						3.00

WITCHBLADE/ALIENS/THE DARKNESS/PREDATOR
Dark Horse Comics/Top Cow Productions: Nov, 2000 ($2.99)

	GD	VG	FN	VF	VF/NM	NM-
1-3-Mel Rubi-a						3.00

WITCHBLADE COLLECTED EDITION
Image Comics (Top Cow Productions): July, 1996 - No. 8 ($4.95/$6.95, squarebound, limited series)

	GD	VG	FN	VF	VF/NM	NM-
1-7-($4.95): Two issues reprinted in each						5.00
8-($6.95) r/#15-17						7.00
...Slipcase (10/96, $10.95)-Packaged w/ Coll. Ed. #1-4						11.00

WITCHBLADE: DESTINY'S CHILD
Image Comics (Top Cow): Jun, 2000 - No. 3, Sept, 2000 ($2.95, lim. series)

	GD	VG	FN	VF	VF/NM	NM-
1-3: 1-Boller-a/Keu Cha-c						3.00

WITCHBLADE: MANGA (Takeru Manga)
Image Comics (Top Cow): Feb, 2007 - No. 12, Mar, 2008 ($2.99/$3.99)

	GD	VG	FN	VF	VF/NM	NM-
1-4-Colored reprints of Japanese Witchblade manga. 1-Three covers. 2-Two covers						3.00
5-12-($3.99)						4.00

WITCHBLADE: OBAKEMONO
Image Comics (Top Cow Productions): 2002 ($9.95, one-shot graphic novel)

	GD	VG	FN	VF	VF/NM	NM-
1-Fiona Avery-s/Billy Tan-a; forward by Straczynski						10.00

WITCHBLADE: SHADES OF GRAY
Dynamite Ent./Top Cow: 2007 - No. 4, 2007 ($3.50, lim. series)

	GD	VG	FN	VF	VF/NM	NM-
1,2: 1-Sara Pezzini meets Dorian Gray; Segovia-a; multiple covers						3.50

WITCHBLADE/ TOMB RAIDER SPECIAL (Also see Tomb Raider/...)
Image Comics (Top Cow Productions): Dec, 1998 ($2.95)

	GD	VG	FN	VF	VF/NM	NM-
1-Based on video game character; Turner-a(p)						3.00
1-Silvestri variant-c						5.00
1-Turner bikini variant-c						10.00
1-Prism-c						12.00
Wizard 1/2 -Turner-s						10.00

WITCHCRAFT (See Strange Mysteries, Super Reprint #18)

Witchcraft #2 © AVON

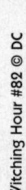

Witching Hour #82 © DC

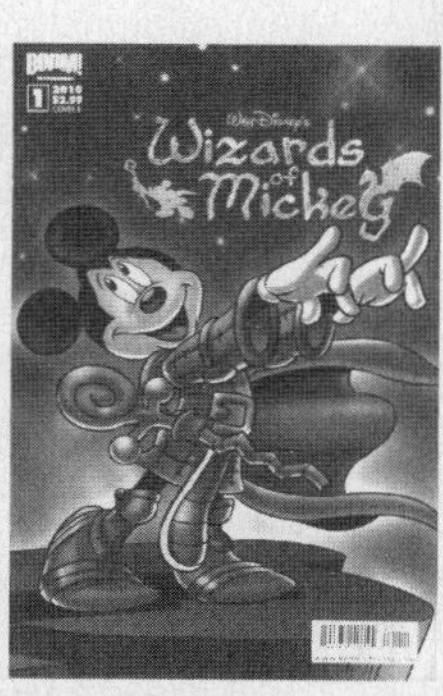

Wizards of Mickey #1 © DIS

	GD 2.0	VG 4.0	FN 6.0	VF 8.0	VF/NM 9.0	NM- 9.2

Avon Periodicals: Mar-Apr, 1952 - No. 6, Mar, 1953

1-Kubert-a; 1 pg. Check-a	73	146	219	467	796	1125
2-Kubert & Check-a; classic skull-c	52	104	156	323	549	775
3,6: 3-Lawrence-a; Kinstler inside-c	42	84	126	265	445	625
4-People cooked alive c/story	50	100	150	315	533	750
5-Kelly Freas painted-c	54	108	162	343	584	825

NOTE: *Hollingsworth a-4-6; c-4, 6.* ***McCann*** *a-3?*

WITCHCRAFT
DC Comics (Vertigo): June, 1994 - No. 3, Aug, 1994 ($2.95, limited series)

1-3: James Robinson scripts & Kaluta-c in all 4.00
1-Platinum Edition 8.00
Trade paperback-(1996, $14.95)-r/#1-3; Kaluta-c 15.00

WITCHCRAFT: LA TERREUR
DC Comics (Vertigo): Apr, 1998 - No. 3, Jun, 1998 ($2.50, limited series)

1-3: Robinson-s/Zulli & Locke-a; interlocking cover images 2.50

WITCHES
Marvel Comics: Aug, 2004 - No. 4, Sept, 2004 ($2.99, limited series)

1-4: 1,2-Deodato, Jr-a; Dr. Strange app. 3,4-Conrad-a 3.00
... Vol. 1: The Gathering (2004, $9.99) r/series 10.00

WITCHES TALES (Witches Western Tales #29,30)
Witches Tales/Harvey Publications: Jan, 1951 - No. 28, Dec, 1954 (date misprinted as 4/55)

1-Powell-a (1 pg.)	55	110	165	352	601	850
2-Eye injury panel	36	72	108	211	343	475
3-7,9,10	27	54	81	160	263	365
8-Eye injury panels	28	56	84	165	270	375
11-13,15,16: 12-Acid in face story	25	50	75	147	241	335
14,17-Powell/Nostrand-a. 17-Atomic disaster story	26	52	78	156	256	355
18-Nostrand-a; E.C. swipe/Shock S.S.	26	52	78	156	256	355
19-Nostrand-a; E.C. swipe/ "Glutton"; Devil-c	28	56	84	165	270	375
20-24-Nostrand-a. 21-E.C. swipe; rape story. 23-Wood E.C. swipes/Two-Fisted Tales #34	26	52	78	156	256	355
25-Nostrand-a; E.C. swipe/Mad Barber; decapitation-c	43	86	129	271	461	650
26-28: 27-r/#6 with diff.-c. 28-r/#8 with diff.-c	19	38	57	111	176	240

NOTE: ***Check*** *a-24.* ***Elias*** *c-8, 10, 16-27.* ***Kremer*** *a-18; c-25.* ***Nostrand*** *a-17-25; 14, 17(w/****Powell****).* ***Palais*** *a-1, 2, 4(2), 5(2), 7-9, 12, 14, 15, 17.* ***Powell*** *a-3-7, 10, 11, 19-27. Bondage-c 1, 3, 5, 6, 8, 9.*

WITCHES TALES (Magazine)
Eerie Publications: V1#7, July, 1969 - V7#1, Feb, 1975 (B&W, 52 pgs.)

V1#7(7/69)	7	14	21	45	73	100
V1#8(9/69), 9(11/69)	6	12	18	37	59	80
V2#1-6('70), V3#1-6('71)	5	10	15	30	48	65
V4#1-6('72), V5#1-6('73), V6#1-6('74), V7#1	4	8	12	26	41	55

NOTE: *Ajax/Farrell reprints in early issues.*

WITCHES' WESTERN TALES (Formerly Witches Tales)(Western Tales #31 on)
Harvey Publications: No. 29, Feb, 1955 - No. 30, Apr, 1955

29,30-Featuring Clay Duncan & Boys' Ranch; S&K-r/from Boys' Ranch including-c. 29-Last pre-code	18	36	54	107	169	230

WITCHFINDER, THE
Image Comics (Liar): Sept, 1999 - No. 3, Jan, 2000 ($2.95)

1-3-Romano-a/Sharon & Matthew Scott-plot 3.00

WITCH HUNTER
Malibu Comics (Ultraverse): Apr, 1996 ($2.50, one-shot)

1 2.50

WITCHING, THE
DC Comics (Vertigo): Aug, 2004 - No. 10, May, 2005 ($2.95/$2.99)

1-10-Vankin-s/Gallagher-a/McPherson-c. 1,2-Lucifer app. 3.00

WITCHING HOUR ("The ..." in later issues)
National Periodical Publ./DC Comics: Feb-Mar, 1969 - No. 85, Oct, 1978

1-Toth-a, plus Neal Adams-a (2 pgs.)	13	26	39	93	172	250
2,6: 6-Toth-a	7	14	21	47	76	105
3,5-Wrightson-a; Toth-p. 3-Last 12¢ issue	7	14	21	50	83	115
4,12-Toth-a	5	10	15	32	51	70
7-11-Adams-c; Toth-a in all. 8-Adams-a	6	12	18	41	66	90
13-Neal Adams-c/a, 2pgs.	6	12	18	43	69	95
14-Williamson/Garzon, Jones-a; N. Adams-c	7	14	21	45	73	100
15	3	6	9	18	27	35
16-21-(52 pg. Giants)	4	8	12	22	34	45
22-37,39,40	2	4	6	13	18	22
38-(100 pgs.)	5	10	15	32	51	70
41-60	2	4	6	9	13	16
61-83,85	2	4	6	8	10	12
84-(44 pgs.)	2	4	6	8	11	14

NOTE: *Combined with The Unexpected with #189.* ***Neal Adams*** *c-7-11, 13, 14.* ***Alcala*** *a-24, 27, 33, 41, 43.* ***Anderson*** *a-9, 38.* ***Cardy*** *c-4, 5.* ***Kaluta*** *a-7.* ***Kane*** *a-12p.* ***Morrow*** *a-10, 13, 15, 16.* ***Nino*** *a-31, 40, 45, 47.* ***Redondo*** *a-20, 23, 24, 34, 65; c-53.* ***Reese*** *a-23.* ***Sparling*** *a-1.* ***Toth*** *a-1, 3-12, 38r.* ***Tuska*** *a-11, 12.* ***Wood*** *a-15.*

WITCHING HOUR, THE
DC Comics (Vertigo): 1999 - No. 3, 2000 ($5.95, limited series)

1-3-Bachalo & Thibert-c/a; Loeb & Bachalo-s 6.00
Hardcover (2000, $29.95) r/#1-3; embossed cover 30.00
Softcover (2003, $19.95), (2009, $19.99) r/#1-3 20.00

WITHIN OUR REACH
Star Reach Productions: 1991 ($7.95, 84 pgs.)

nn-Spider-Man, Concrete by Chadwick, Gift of the Magi by Russell; X-mas stories; Chadwick-c; Spidey back-c 8.00

WITH THE MARINES ON THE BATTLEFRONTS OF THE WORLD
Toby Press: 1953 (no month) - No. 2, Mar, 1954 (Photo covers)

1-John Wayne story	29	58	87	172	281	390
2-Monty Hall in #1,2	10	20	30	56	76	95

WITH THE U.S. PARATROOPS BEHIND ENEMY LINES (Also see U.S. Paratroops...; #2-6 titled U.S. Paratroops...)
Avon Periodicals: 1951 - No. 6, Dec, 1952

1-Wood-c & inside f/c	17	34	51	98	154	210
2-Kinstler-c & inside f/c only	11	22	33	60	83	105
3-6: 6-Kinstler-c & inside f/c only	10	20	30	54	72	90

NOTE: ***Kinstler*** *c-2, 4-6.*

WITNESS, THE (Also see Amazing Mysteries, Captain America #71, Ideal #4, Marvel Mystery #92 & Mystic #7)
Marvel Comics (MjMe): Sept, 1948

1(Scarce)-Rico-c?	239	478	717	1530	2615	3700

WITTY COMICS
Irwin H. Rubin Publ./Chicago Nite Life News No. 2: 1945 - No. 2, 1945

1-The Pioneer, Junior Patrol; Japanese war-c	30	60	90	177	289	400
2-The Pioneer, Junior Patrol	15	30	45	86	133	180

WIZARD OF FOURTH STREET, THE
Dark Horse Comics: Dec, 1987 - No. 2, 1988 ($1.75, B&W, limited series)

1,2: Adapts novel by S/F author Simon Hawke 2.50

WIZARD OF OZ (See Classics Illustrated Jr. 535, Dell Jr. Treasury No. 5, First Comics Graphic Novel, Marvelous..., & Marvel Treasury of Oz)
Dell Publishing Co.: No. 1308, Mar-May, 1962 (TV)

Four Color 1308	11	22	33	78	139	200

WIZARDS OF MICKEY (Mickey Mouse)
BOOM! Studios: Jan, 2010 - Present ($2.99)

1,2-Ambrosio-s; 3 covers on each 3.00

WIZARD'S TALE, THE
Image Comics (Homage Comics): 1997 ($19.95, squarebound, one-shot)

nn-Kurt Busiek-s/David Wenzel-painted-a/c 20.00

WOLF & RED
Dark Horse Comics: Apr, 1995 - No. 3, June, 1995 ($2.50, limited series)

1-3: Characters created by Tex Avery 2.50

WOLFF & BYRD, COUNSELORS OF THE MACABRE (Becomes Supernatural Law with issue #24)
Exhibit A Press: May, 1994 - No. 23, Aug, 1999 ($2.50, B&W)

1-23-Batton Lash-s/a 2.50

WOLF GAL (See Al Capp's...)

WOLFMAN, THE (See Movie Classics)

WOLFPACK
Marvel Comics: Feb, 1988 ($7.95); Aug, 1988 - No. 12, July, 1989 (Lim. series)

1-1st app./origin (Marvel Graphic Novel #31) 8.00
1-12 2.50

WOLVERINE (See Alpha Flight, Daredevil #196, 249, Ghost Rider; Wolverine; Punisher, Havok &..., Incredible Hulk #180, Incredible Hulk &..., Kitty Pryde And..., Marvel Comics Presents, New Avengers, Power Pack, Punisher and..., Rampaging ..., Spider-Man vs... & X-Men #94)

WOLVERINE (See Incredible Hulk #180 for 1st app.)

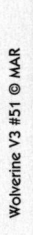

Wolverine V2 #124 © MAR

Wolverine V3 #51 © MAR

Wolverine V3 #82 © MAR

GD VG FN VF VF/NM NM-
2.0 4.0 6.0 8.0 9.0 9.2

Marvel Comics Group: Sept, 1982 - No. 4, Dec, 1982 (limited series)

1-Frank Miller-c/a(p) in all; Claremont-s 5 10 15 34 55 75
2-4 4 8 12 26 41 55
... By Claremont & Miller HC (2006, $19.99) r/#1-4 & Uncanny X-Men #172-173 20.00
TPB 1(7/87, $4.95)-Reprints #1-4 with new Miller-c 2 4 6 10 14 18
TPB nn (2nd printing, $9.95)-r/#1-4 2 4 6 8 10 12

WOLVERINE
Marvel Comics: Nov, 1988 - No. 189, June, 2003 ($1.50/$1.75/$1.95/$1.99/$2.25)

1 4 8 12 22 34 45
2 2 4 6 13 18 22
3-5: 4-BWS back-c 2 4 6 9 13 16
6-9: 6-McFarlane back-c. 7,8-Hulk app. 1 3 4 6 8 10
10-1st battle with Sabretooth (before Wolverine had his claws)
3 6 9 16 23 30
11-16: 11-New costume 1 2 3 5 6 8
17-20: 17-Byrne-c/a(p) begins, ends #23 1 2 3 4 5 7
21-30: 24,25,27-Jim Lee-c. 26-Begin $1.75-c 5.00
31-40,44,47 4.00
41-Sabretooth claims to be Wolverine's father; Cable cameo 6.00
41-Gold 2nd printing ($1.75) 2.50
42-Sabretooth, Cable & Nick Fury app.; Sabretooth proven not to be Wolverine's father
1 2 3 5 6 8
42-Gold ink 2nd printing ($1.75) 2.50
43-Sabretooth cameo (2 panels); saga ends 5.00
45,46-Sabretooth-c/stories 5.00
48-51: 48,49-Sabretooth app. 48-Begin 3 part Weapon X sequel. 50-(64 pgs.)-Die cut-c; Wolverine back to old yellow costume; Forge, Cyclops, Jubilee, Jean Grey & Nick Fury app. 51-Sabretooth-c & app. 4.00
52-74,76-80: 54-Shatterstar (from X-Force) app. 55-Gambit, Jubilee, Sunfire-c/story. 55-57,73-Gambit app. 57-Mariko Yashida dies (Late 7/92). 58,59-Terror, Inc. x-over. 60-64-Sabretooth storyline (60,62,64-c) 4.00
75-($3.95, 68 pgs.)-Wolverine hologram on-c 5.00
81-84,86: 81-bound-in card sheet 3.00
85-($2.50)-Newsstand edition 3.00
85-($3.50)-Collectors edition 5.00
87-90 ($1.95)-Deluxe edition 3.00
87-90 ($1.50)-Regular edition 2.50
91-99,101-114: 91-Return from "Age of Apocalypse," 93-Juggernaut app. 94-Gen X app. 101-104-Elektra app. 104-Origin of Onslaught. 105-Onslaught x-over. 110-Shaman-c/app. 114-Alternate-c 3.00
100 ($3.95)-Hologram-c; Wolverine loses humanity 1 2 3 5 7 9
100 ($2.95)-Regular-c. 4.00
115-124: 115- Operation Zero Tolerance 2.50
125-($2.99) Wraparound-c; Viper secret 3.00
125-($6.95) Jae Lee variant-c 7.00
126-144: 126,127-Sabretooth-c/app. 128-Sabretooth & Shadowcat app.; Platt-a. 129-Wendigo-c/app. 131-Initial printing contained lettering error. 133-Begin Larsen-s/ Matsuda-a. 138-Galactus-c/app. 139-Cable app.; Yu-a. 142,143-Alpha Flight app. 2.50
145-($2.99) 25th Anniversary issue; Hulk and Sabretooth app. 3.00
145-($3.99) Foil enhanced cover (also see Promotional section for Nabisco mail-in ed.) 5.00
146-149: 147-Apocalypse: The Twelve; Angel-c/app. 149-Nova-c/app. 2.50
150-($2.99) Steve Skroce-s/a 3.00
151-174,176-182,184-189: 151-Begin $2.25-c. 154,155-Liefeld-s/a. 156-Churchill-a. 159-Chen-a begins. 160-Sabretooth app. 163-Texeira-a(p). 167-BWS-c. 172,173-Alpha Flight app. 176-Colossus app. 185,186-Punisher app. 2.50
175,183-($3.50) 175-Sabretooth app. 3.50
#(-1) Flashback (7/97) Logan meets Col. Fury; Nord-a 2.50
Annual nn (1990, $4.50, squarebound, 52 pgs.)-The Jungle Adventure; Simonson scripts; Mignola-c/a 5.00
Annual 2 (12/90, $4.95, squarebound, 52 pgs.)-Bloodlust 5.00
Annual nn (#3, 8/91, $5.95, 68 pgs.)-Rahne of Terror; Cable & The New Mutants app.; Andy Kubert-c/a (2nd print exists) 6.00
Annual '95 (1995, $3.95) 4.00
Annual '96 (1996, $2.95)- Wraparound-c; Silver Samurai, Yukio, and Red Ronin app. 3.00
Annual '97 ($2.99) - Wraparound-c 3.00
Annual 1999, 2000 ($3.50) : 1999-Deadpool app. 3.50
Annual 2001 ($2.99) - Tieri-s; JH Williams-c 3.00
...Battles The Incredible Hulk nn (1989, $4.95, squarebound, 52 pg.) r/Incr. Hulk #180,181 5.00
Best of Wolverine Vol. 1 HC (2004, $29.99) oversized reprints of Hulk #181, mini-series #1-4, Capt. America Ann, #8, Uncanny X-Men #205 & Marvel Comics Presents #72-84 30.00
...Black Rio (11/98, $5.99)-Casey-s/Oscar Jimenez-a 6.00
...Blood Debt TPB (7/01, $12.95)-r/#150-153; Skroce-c 13.00
...Blood Hungry nn (1993, $6.95, 68 pgs.)-Kieth-r/Marvel Comics Presents #85-92 w/ new Kieth-c 7.00
...: Bloody Choices nn (1993, $7.95, 68 pgs.)-r/Graphic Novel; Nick Fury app. 8.00
... Cable Guts and Glory (10/99, $5.99) Platt-a 6.00
... Classic Vol. 1 TPB (2005, $12.99) r/#1-5 13.00
... Classic Vol. 2 TPB (2005, $12.99) r/#6-10 13.00
... Classic Vol. 3 TPB (2006, $14.99) r/#11-16; The Gehenna Stone Affair 15.00
... Classic Vol. 4 TPB (2006, $14.99) r/#17-23 15.00
... Classic Vol. 5 TPB (2007, $14.99) r/#24-30 15.00
.../Deadpool: Weapon X TPB (7/02, $21.99)-r/#162-166 & Deadpool #57-60 22.00
... Doombringer (11/97, $5.99)-Silver Samurai-c/app. 6.00
... Evilution (9/94, $5.95) 6.00
...: Global Jeopardy 1 (12/93, $2.95, one-shot)-Embossed-c; Sub-Mariner, Zabu, Ka-Zar, Shanna & Wolverine app.; produced in cooperation with World Wildlife Fund 3.00
...:Inner Fury nn (1992, $5.95, 52 pgs.)-Sienkiewicz-c/a 6.00
...: Judgment Night (2000, $3.99) Shi app.; Battlebook 4.00
...: Killing (9/93)-Kent Williams-a 6.00
...: Knight of Terra (1995, $6.95)-Ostrander script 7.00
... Legends Vol. 2: Meltdown (2003, $19.99) r/Havok & Wolverine: Meltdown #1-4 20.00
... Legends Vol. 3 (2003, $12.99) r/#181-186 13.00
... Legends Vol. 4,5: 4-(See Wolverine: Xisle). 5-(See Wolverine: Snikt!)
... Legends Vol. 6: Marc Silvestri Book 1 (2004, $19.99) r/#31-34, 41-42, 48-50 20.00
.../ Nick Fury: The Scorpio Connection Hardcover (1989, $16.95) 25.00
.../ Nick Fury: The Scorpio Connection Softcover(1990, $12.95) 15.00
...: Not Dead Yet (12/98, $14.95, TPB)-r/#119-122 15.00
...: Save The Tiger 1 (7/92, $2.95, 84 pgs.)-Reprints Wolverine stories from Marvel Comics Presents #1-10 w/new Kieth-c 3.00
...Scorpio Rising ($5.95, prestige format, one-shot) 6.00
.../Shi: Dark Night of Judgment (Crusade Comics, 2000, $2.99) Tucci-a 3.00
...Triumphs And Tragedies-(1995, $16.95, trade paperback)-r/Uncanny X-Men #109,172,173, Wolverine limited series #4, & Wolverine #41,42,75 17.00
...Typhoid's Kiss (6/94, $6.95)-r/Wolverine stories from Marvel Comics Presents #109-116 7.00
...Vs. Spider-Man 1 (3/95, $2.50) -r/Marvel Comics Presents #48-50 2.50
.../Witchblade 1 (3/97, $2.95) Devil's Reign Pt. 5 4.00
Wizard #1/2 (1997) Joe Phillips-a(p) 10.00

NOTE: ***Austin** c-3i. **Bolton** c(back)-5. **Buscema** a-1-16,25,27p; c-1-10. **Byrne** a-17-22p, 23; c-1(back), 17-22, 23p. **Colan** a-24. **Andy Kubert** c/a-51. **Jim Lee** c-24, 25, 27. **Silvestri** a(p)-31-43, 45, 46, 48-50, 52, 53, 55-57; c-31-42p, 43, 45p, 46p, 48, 49p, 50p, 52p, 53p, 55-57p. **Stroman** a-44p; c-60p. **Williamson** a-1i, 3-8i; c(i)-1, 3-6.*

WOLVERINE (Volume 3) (Titled Dark Wolverine from #75 on)
Marvel Comics: July, 2003 - Present ($2.25/$2.50/$2.99)

1-Rucka-s/Robertson-a 4.00
2-19: 6-Nightcrawler app. 13-16-Sabretooth app. 3.00
20-Millar-s/Romita, Jr.-a begin, Elektra app. 4.00
20-B&W variant-c 5.00
21-39: 21-Elektra-c/app. 23,24-Daredevil app. 26-28-Land-c. 29-Quesada-c; begin $2.50-c. 33-35-House of M. 36,37-Decimation. 36-Quesada-c. 39-Winter Soldier app. 3.00
40,43-48: 40-Begin $2.99-c; Winter Soldier app.; Texeira-a. 43-46-Civil War; Ramos-a. 45-Sub-Mariner app. 3.00
41,49-($3.99) 41-C.P. Smith-a/Stuart Moore-s 4.00
42-Civil War 5.00
50-($3.99) Sabretooth app.; Bianchi-a/c & Loeb-s begin; wraparound-c; McGuinness-a 4.00
50-($3.99) Variant Edition; uncolored art and cover; Bianchi pencil art page 4.00
51-55-(Regular and variant uncolored editions) Bianchi-a/Loeb-s; Sabretooth app. 3.00
55-EC-style variant-c by Greg Land 5.00
56-($3.99) Howard Chaykin-a/c 4.00
57-65: 57-61-Suydam Zombie-c; Chaykin-a. 62-65-Mystique app. 3.00
66-Old Man Logan begins; Millar-s/McNiven-a; McNiven wraparound-c 3.00
66-Variant-c by Michael Turner 5.00
66-Variant sketch-c by Michael Turner 20.00
66-2nd printing with McNiven variant-c of Logan and Hulk gang member 3.00
67-74: 67-72-Old Man Logan (concludes in Wolverine: Old Man Logan Giant-Sized Special). 67-Intro. Ashley, Spider-Man's granddaughter.72-Red Skull app. 73,74-Andy Kubert-a 3.00
75-($3.99) Dark Reign, Daken as Wolverine on Osborn's team; Camuncoli-a 4.00
76-83-Multiple covers for each: 76-Dark Reign; Yu-c. 82,83-Siege 3.00
Annual 1 (12/07, $3.99) Hurwitz-s/Frusin-a 4.00
Annual 2 (11/08, $3.99) Swierczynski-s/Deodato-a/c 4.00
...: Blood & Sorrow TPB (2007, $13.99) r/#41,49, stories from Giant-Size Wolverine #1 and X-Men Unlimited #12 14.00
...: Chop Shop 1 (1/09, $2.99) Benson-s/Boschi-a/Hanuka-c 3.00
Civil War: Wolverine TPB (2007, $17.99) r/#42-48; gallery of B&W cover inks 18.00
... Dangerous Games 1 (8/08, $3.99) Spurrier-s/Oliver-a; Remender-s/Opena-a 4.00
...Enemy of the State HC Vol. 1 (2005, $19.99) r/#20-25; Ennis intro.; variant covers 20.00
...Enemy of the State HC Vol. 2 (2005, $19.99) r/#26-32 20.00
...Enemy of the State SC Vol. 1 (2005, $14.99) r/#20-25; Ennis intro.; variant covers 15.00
...Enemy of the State SC Vol. 2 (2006, $16.99) r/#26-32 17.00

Wolverine: First Class #21 © MAR

Wolverine: Origins #16 © MAR

Wolverine: Xisle #1 © MAR

GD VG FN VF VF/NM NM-
2.0 4.0 6.0 8.0 9.0 9.2

...Enemy of the State - The Complete Edition (2006, $34.99) r/#20-32; Ennis intro.; sketch pages, variant covers and pin-up art 35.00
...: Evolution SC (2008, $14.99) r/#50-55 15.00
...: Flies to a Spider (2/09, $3.99) Bradstreet-c/Hurwitz-s/Opena-a 4.00
...: Killing Made Simple (10/08, $3.99) Yost-s/Turnbull-a 4.00
...: Mr. X (5/10, $3.99) Tieri-s/Diaz-a/Mattina-c 4.00
...: Old Man Logan Giant-Sized Special (11/09, $4.99) Continued from #72; cover gallery 5.00
...Origins & Endings HC (2006, $19.99) r/#36-40 20.00
...Origins & Endings SC (2006, $13.99) r/#36-40 14.00
...: Revolver (8/09, $3.99) Gischler-s/Pastoras-a 4.00
... Saga (2009, giveaway) history of the character in text and comic panels 2.50
...: Saudade (2008, $4.99) English adaptation of Wolverine story from French comic 5.00
...: Savage (4/10, $3.99) J. Scott Campbell-c; The Lizard app. 4.00
...Special: Firebreak (2/08, $3.99) Carey-s/Kolins-a; Lolos-a 4.00
...: Switchback 1 (3/09, $3.99) short stories; art by Pastoras & Doe 4.00
...: The Amazing Immortal Man & Other Bloody Tales (7/08, $3.99) Lapham short stories 4.00
...: The Anniversary (6/09, $3.99) Mariko flashback short stories; art by various 4.00
...: The Death of Wolverine HC (2008, $19.99) r/#56-61 20.00
...: Under the Boardwalk (2/10, $3.99) Coker-a 4.00
...Vol. 1: The Brotherhood (2003, $12.99) r/#1-6 13.00
...Vol. 2: Coyote Crossing (2004, $11.99) r/#7-11 12.00
... Weapon X Files (2009, $4.99) Handbook-style pages of Wolverine characters 5.00

WOLVERINE AND POWER PACK
Marvel Comics: Jan, 2009 - No. 4, Apr, 2009 ($2.99, limited series)
1-4-Sumerak-s. 1,2-GuriHiru-a. 1-Sauron app. 3-Meet Wolverine as a child; Koblish-a 3.00

WOLVERINE AND THE PUNISHER: DAMAGING EVIDENCE
Marvel Comics: Oct, 1993 - No. 3, Dec, 1993 ($2.00, limited series)
1-3: 2,3-Indicia says "The Punisher and Wolverine..." 3.00

WOLVERINE/CAPTAIN AMERICA
Marvel Comics: Apr, 2004 - No. 4, Apr, 2004 ($2.99, limited series)
1-4-Derenick-a/c 3.00

WOLVERINE: DAYS OF FUTURE PAST
Marvel Comics: Dec, 1997 - No. 3, Feb, 1998 ($2.50, limited series)
1-3: J.F. Moore-s/Bennett-a 2.50

WOLVERINE/DOOP (Also see X-Force and X-Statix)(Reprinted in X-Statix Vol. 2)
Marvel Comics: July, 2003 - No. 2, July, 2003 ($2.99, limited series)
1,2-Peter Milligan-s/Darwyn Cooke & J. Bone-a 3.00

WOLVERINE: FIRST CLASS
Marvel Comics: May, 2008 - No. 21, Jan, 2010 ($2.99)
1-21: 1-Wolverine and Kitty Pryde's first mission; DiVito-a. 2,9-Sabretooth app. 3.00

WOLVERINE/GAMBIT: VICTIMS
Marvel Comics: Sept, 1995 - No. 4, Dec, 1995 ($2.95, limited series)
1-4: Jeph Loeb scripts & Tim Sale-a; foil-c 4.00

WOLVERINE/HULK
Marvel Comics: Apr, 2002 - No. 4, July, 2002 ($3.50, limited series)
1-4-Sam Kieth-s/a/c 3.50
Wolverine Legends Vol. 1: Wolverine/Hulk (2003, $9.99, TPB) r/#1-4 10.00

WOLVERINE: MANIFEST DESTINY
Marvel Comics: Dec, 2008 - No. 4, Mar, 2009 ($2.99, limited series)
1-4-Aaron-s/Segovia-a 3.00

WOLVERINE: NETSUKE
Marvel Comics: Nov, 2002 - No. 4, Feb, 2003 ($3.99, limited series)
1-4-George Pratt-s/painted-a 4.00

WOLVERINE: NOIR (1930s Pulp-style)
Marvel Comics: Apr, 2009 - No. 4, Sept, 2009 ($3.99, limited series)
1-4-C.P. Smith-a/Stuart Moore; covers by Smith & Calero; alternate Logan as detective 4.00

WOLVERINE: ORIGINS
Marvel Comics: June, 2006 - Present ($2.99)
1-15: 1-Daniel Way-s/Steve Dillon-a/Quesada-c 3.00
1-10-Variant covers. 1-Turner. 2-Quesada & Hitch. 3-Bianchi. 4-Dell'Otto. 7-Deodato 4.00
16-($3.99) Captain America WW2 app.; preview of Wolverine #56; r/X-Men #268 4.00
16-Variant-c by McGuinness 4.00
17-24: 17-20-Capt. America & Bucky app. 21-24-Deadpool app.; Bianchi-c 3.00
25-($3.99) Deadpool app.; Bianchi-c; r/Deadpool's 1st app. in New Mutants #98 4.00
26-44: 26-Origin of Dakan; Way-s/Segovia-a/Land-c. 28-Hulk & Wendigo app. 3.00
Annual 1 (9/07, $3.99) Way-s/Andrews-a; flashback to 1932 4.00

GD VG FN VF VF/NM NM-
2.0 4.0 6.0 8.0 9.0 9.2

... Vol. 1 - Born in Blood HC (2006, $19.99, dustjacket) r/#1-5; variant covers 20.00
... Vol. 1 - Born in Blood SC (2007, $13.99) r/#1-5; variant covers 14.00
... Vol. 2 - Savior HC (2007, $19.99, dustjacket) r/#6-10; variant covers 20.00
... Vol. 2 - Savior SC (2007, $13.99) r/#6-10; variant covers 14.00
... Vol. 3 - Swift & Terrible HC (2007, $19.99, dustjacket) r/#11-15 20.00
... Vol. 3 - Swift & Terrible SC (2007, $13.99) r/#11-15 14.00
... Vol. 4 - Our War HC (2008, $19.99, dustjacket) r/#16-20 & Annual #1 20.00
... Vol. 4 - Our War SC (2008, $14.99) r/#16-20 & Annual #1 15.00

WOLVERINE/PUNISHER
Marvel Comics: May, 2004 - No. 5, Sept, 2004 ($2.99, limited series)
1-5: Milligan-s/Weeks-a 3.00
... Vol. 1 TPB (2004, $13.99) r/series 14.00

WOLVERINE/PUNISHER REVELATIONS (Marvel Knights)
Marvel Comics: Jun, 1999 - No. 4, Sept, 1999 ($2.95, limited series)
1-4: Pat Lee-a(p) 4.00
...: Revelation (4/00, $14.95, TPB) r/#1-4 15.00

WOLVERINE SAGA
Marvel Comics: Sept, 1989 - No. 4, Mid-Dec, 1989 ($3.95, lim. series, 52 pgs.)
1-Gives history; Liefeld/Austin-c (front & back) 5.00
2-4: 2-Romita, Jr./Austin-c. 4-Kaluta-c 5.00

WOLVERINE: SNIKT!
Marvel Comics: July, 2003 - No. 5, Nov, 2003 ($2.99, limited series)
1-5-Manga-style; Tsutomu Nihei-s/a 3.00
Wolverine Legends Vol. 5: Snikt! TPB (2003, $13.99) r/#1-5 14.00

WOLVERINE: SOULTAKER
Marvel Comics: May, 2005 - No. 5, Aug, 2005 ($2.99, limited series)
1-5-Yoshida-s/Nagasawa-a/Terada-c; Yukio app. 3.00
TPB (2005, $13.99) r/#1-5 14.00

WOLVERINE: THE END
Marvel Comics: Jan, 2004 - No. 6, Dec, 2004 ($2.99, limited series)
1-5-Jenkins-s/Castellini-a 3.00
1-Wizard World Texas variant-c 20.00
TPB (2005, $14.99) r/#1-5 15.00

WOLVERINE: THE ORIGIN
Marvel Comics: Nov, 2001 - No. 6, July, 2002 ($3.50, limited series)
1-Origin of Logan; Jenkins-s/Andy Kubert-a; Quesada-c 40.00
1-DF edition 60.00
2 15.00
3 9.00
4-6 5.00
HC (3/02, $34.95, 11" x 7-1/2") r/#1-6; dust jacket; sketch pages and treatments 35.00
HC (2006, $19.99) r/#1-6; dust jacket; sketch pages and treatments 20.00
SC (2002, $14.95) r/#1-6; afterwords by Jemas and Quesada 15.00

WOLVERINE WEAPON X
Marvel Comics: June, 2009 - Present ($3.99)
1-11: 1-5,11-Aaron-s/Garney-a. 1-Four covers. 2,3-Two covers. 10-CP Smith-a 4.00

WOLVERINE: XISLE
Marvel Comics: June, 2003 - No. 5, June, 2003 ($2.50, weekly limited series)
1-5-Bruce Jones-s/Jorge Lucas-a 2.50
Wolverine Legends Vol. 4 TPB (2003, $13.99) r/ #1-5 14.00

WOMEN IN LOVE (A Feature Presentation #5)
Fox Features Synd./Hero Books: Aug, 1949 - No. 4, Feb, 1950

	GD 2.0	VG 4.0	FN 6.0	VF 8.0	VF/NM 9.0	NM- 9.2
1	32	64	96	192	314	435
2-Kamen/Feldstein-c	27	54	81	160	263	365
3	19	38	57	111	176	240
4-Wood-a	21	42	63	126	206	285

WOMEN IN LOVE (Thrilling Romances for Adults)
Ziff-Davis Publishing Co.: Winter, 1952 (25¢, 100 pgs.)

	GD 2.0	VG 4.0	FN 6.0	VF 8.0	VF/NM 9.0	NM- 9.2
nn-(Scarce)-Kinstler-a; painted-c	55	110	165	352	601	850

WOMEN OF MARVEL
Marvel Comics: 2006, 2007 ($24.99, TPB)
SC-Reprints 1st apps. of Dazzler, Ms. Marvel, Shanna, The Cat plus notable stories of other female Marvel characters; Mayhew-c 25.00
Vol. 2 (2007) More stories of female Marvel characters; Mayhew-c; cover process art 25.00

WOMEN OUTLAWS (My Love Memories #9 on)(Also see Red Circle)
Fox Features Syndicate: July, 1948 - No. 8, Sept, 1949

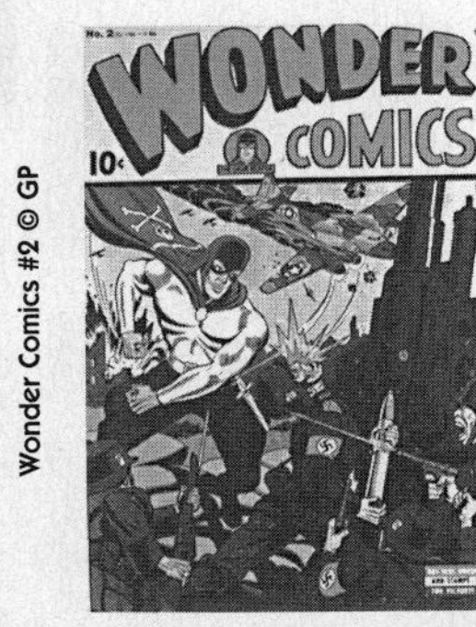

Wonder Comics #2 © GP

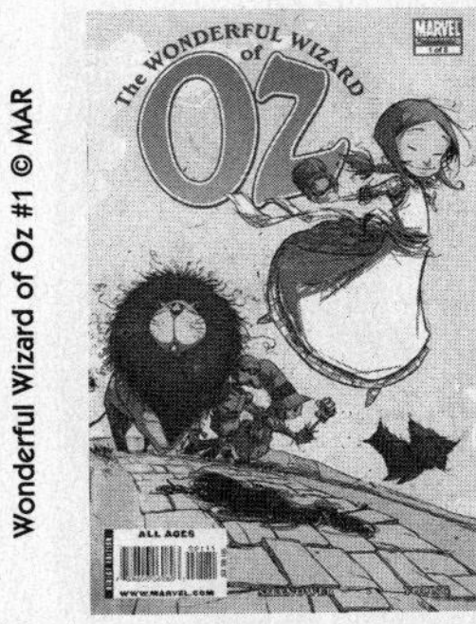

Wonderful Wizard of Oz #1 © MAR

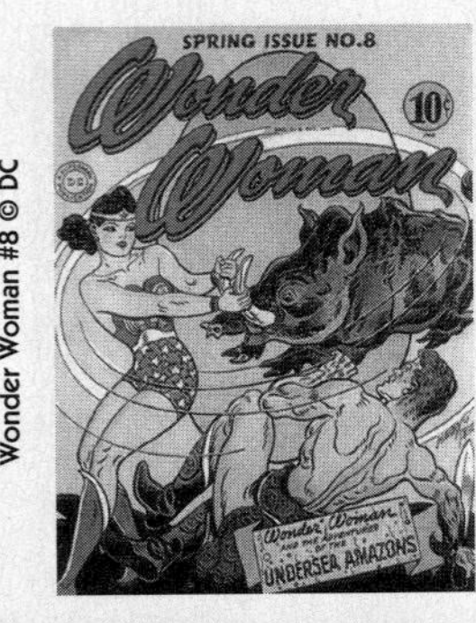

Wonder Woman #8 © DC

GD VG FN VF VF/NM NM-
2.0 4.0 6.0 8.0 9.0 9.2

GD VG FN VF VF/NM NM-
2.0 4.0 6.0 8.0 9.0 9.2

1-Used in **SOTI**, illo "Giving children an image of American womanhood"; negligee panels
79 158 237 502 864 1225
2,3: 3-Kamenish-a 59 118 177 375 643 910
4-8 47 94 141 296 498 700
nn(nd)-Contains Cody of the Pony Express; same cover as #7
31 62 93 182 296 410

WOMEN TO LOVE
Realistic: No date (1953)
nn-(Scarce)-Reprints Complete Romance #1; c-/Avon paperback #165
39 78 117 240 395 550

WONDER BOY (Formerly Terrific Comics) (See Blue Bolt, Bomber Comics & Samson)
Ajax/Farrell Publ.: No. 17, May, 1955 - No. 18, July, 1955 (Code approved)
17-Phantom Lady app. Bakerish-c/a 47 94 141 296 498 700
18-Phantom Lady app. 39 78 117 240 395 550
NOTE: *Phantom Lady not by Matt Baker.*

WONDER COMICS (Wonderworld #3 on)
Fox Features Syndicate: May, 1939 - No. 2, June, 1939 (68 pgs.)
1-(Scarce)-Wonder Man only app. by Will Eisner; Dr. Fung (by Powell), K-5 begins;
Bob Kane-a; Eisner-c 1425 2850 4275 10,700 19,100 27,500
2-(Scarce)-Yarko the Great, Master Magician (see Samson) by Eisner begins; 'Spark' Stevens by Bob Kane, Patty O'Day, Tex Mason app. Lou Fine's 1st-c; Fine-a (2 pgs.); Yarko-c (Wonder Man-c #1) 476 952 1428 3475 6138 8800

WONDER COMICS
Great/Nedor/Better Publications: May, 1944 - No. 20, Oct, 1948
1-The Grim Reaper & Spectro, the Mind Reader begin; Hitler/Hirohito bondage-c
206 412 618 1318 2259 3200
2-Origin The Grim Reaper; Super Sleuths begin, end #8,17
74 148 222 470 810 1150
3-5: 3-Indicia reads "Vol. 1, #2" 66 132 198 419 722 1025
6-10: 6-Flag-c. 8-Last Spectro. 9-Wonderman begins
53 106 159 334 567 800
11-14: 11-Dick Devens, King of Futuria begins, ends #14. 11,12-Ingels-c & splash pg. 14-Bondage-c 64 128 192 406 696 985
15-Tara begins (origin), ends #20 73 146 219 467 796 1125
16,18: 16-Spectro app.; last Grim Reaper. 18-The Silver Knight begins
64 128 192 406 696 985
17-Wonderman with Frazetta panels; Jill Trent with all Frazetta inks
65 130 195 416 708 1000
19-Frazetta panels 64 128 192 406 696 985
20-Most of Silver Knight by Frazetta 73 146 219 464 800 1135
NOTE: ***Ingels** c-11, 12. **Roussos** a-19. **Schomburg (Xela)** c-1-10; (airbrush)-13-20. Bondage c-12, 13, 15. Cover features: Grim Reaper #1-8; Wonder Man #9-15; Tara #16-20.*

WONDER DUCK (See Wisco)
Marvel Comics (CDS): Sept, 1949 - No. 3, Mar, 1950
1-Funny animal 17 34 51 98 154 210
2,3 12 24 36 69 97 125

WONDERFUL ADVENTURES OF PINOCCHIO, THE (See Movie Comics & Walt Disney Showcase #48)
Whitman Publishing Co.: April, 1982 (Walt Disney)
nn-(#3 Continuation of Movie Comics?); r/FC #92 6.00

WONDERFUL WIZARD OF OZ (Adaptation of the original 1900 L. Frank Baum book) (Also see the sequel Marvelous Land of Oz)
Marvel Comics: Feb, 2009 - No. 8, Sept, 2009 ($3.99, limited series)
1-8-Eric Shanower-a/Skottie Young-a/c 4.00
1-Variant Good Witch & Dorothy wraparound cover by J. Scott Campbell 8.00
1-Variant Scarecrow & Dorothy cover by Eric Shanower 10.00
... Sketchbook (2008, giveaway) Young character design sketches; Shanower intro. 2.25
HC (2009, $29.99, dustjacket) r/#1-8; Shanower intro.; cover gallery; sketch art 30.00

WONDERFUL WORLD FOR BOYS AND GIRLS
DC Comics: May, 1964
nn - Ashcan comic, not distributed to newsstands, only for in-house use (no known sales)

WONDERFUL WORLD OF DISNEY, THE (Walt Disney)
Whitman Publishing Co.: 1978 (Digest, 116 pgs.)
1-Barks-a (reprints) 3 6 9 16 23 30
2 (no date) 2 4 6 11 16 20

WONDERFUL WORLD OF THE BROTHERS GRIMM (See Movie Comics)

WONDER GIRL (Cassandra Sandsmark from Teen Titans)
DC Comics: Nov, 2007 - No. 6, Apr, 2008 ($2.99, limited series)
1-6-Torres-s/Greene-a; Hercules app. 2-6-Female Furies app. 5,6-Wonder Woman app. 3.00
Teen Titans Spotlight: Wonder Girl TPB (2008, $17.99) r/#1-6 18.00

WONDERLAND COMICS
Feature Publications/Prize: Summer, 1945 - No. 9, Feb-Mar, 1947
1-Alex in Wonderland begins; Howard Post-c 20 40 60 117 189 260
2-Howard Post-c/a(2) 13 26 39 72 101 130
3-9: 3,4-Post-c 10 20 30 58 79 100

WONDER MAN (See The Avengers #9, 151)
Marvel Comics Group: Mar, 1986 ($1.25, one-shot, 52 pgs.)
1 3.00

WONDER MAN
Marvel Comics Group: Sept, 1991 - No. 29, Jan, 1994 ($1.00)
1-29: 1-Free fold out poster by Johnson/Austin. 1-3-Johnson/Austin-c/a. 2-Avengers West Coast x-over. 4 Austin-c(i) 2.50
Annual 1 (1992, $2.25)-Immonen-a (10 pgs.) 3.00
Annual 2 (1993, $2.25)-Bagged w/trading card 2.50

WONDER MAN
Marvel Comics: Feb, 2007 - No. 5, June, 2007 ($2.99, limited series)
1-5: 1-Peter David-s/Andrew Currie-a; Beast app. 4-Nauck-a 3.00
...: My Fair Super Hero TPB (2007, $13.99) r/#1-5; Currie sketch page 14.00

WONDERS OF ALADDIN, THE
Dell Publishing Co.: No. 1255, Feb-Apr, 1962
Four Color 1255-Movie 6 12 18 43 69 95

WONDER WOMAN (See Adventure Comics #459, All-Star Comics, Brave & the Bold, DC Comics Presents, JLA, Justice League of America, Legend of..., Power Record Comics, Sensation Comics, Super Friends and World's Finest Comics #244)

WONDER WOMAN
DC Comics: Jan 1942
1-Ashcan comic, not distributed to newsstands, only for in-house use. Cover art is Sensation Comics #1 with interior being Sensation Comics #2. A CGC certified 8.5 copy sold for $17,250 in 2002.

WONDER WOMAN
National Periodical Publications/All-American Publ./DC Comics:
Summer, 1942 - No. 329, Feb, 1986
1-Origin Wonder Woman retold (more detailed than All Star #8); H. G. Peter-c/a begins
2600 5200 7800 19,500 35,750 52,000
1-Reprint, Oversize 13-1/2x10". **WARNING:** This comic is an exact reprint of the original except for its size. DC published it in 1974 with a second cover titling it as a Famous First Edition. There have been many reported cases of the outer cover being removed and the interior sold as the original edition. The reprint with the new outer cover removed is practically worthless. See Famous First Edition for value.
2-Origin/1st app. Mars; Duke of Deception app. 429 858 1287 3121 5511 7900
3 258 516 774 1651 2826 4000
4,5: 5-1st Dr. Psycho app. 200 400 600 1280 2190 3100
6-9: 6-1st Cheetah app. 153 306 459 972 1674 2375
10-Invasion from Saturn classic sci-fi-c/s 160 320 480 1016 1746 2475
11-20 116 232 348 742 1271 1800
21-30: 23-Story from Wonder Woman's childhood 95 190 285 603 1039 1475
31-33,35-40: 38-Last H.G. Peter-c 71 142 213 454 777 1100
34-Robot-c 74 148 222 470 810 1150
41-44,46-49: 49-Used in **SOTI**, pgs. 234,236; last 52 pg. issue
63 126 189 403 689 975
45-Origin retold 126 252 378 806 1378 1950
50-(44 pgs.)-Used in **POP**, pg. 97 65 130 195 416 708 1000
51-60: 60-New logo 54 108 162 343 584 825
61-72: 62-Origin of W.W. i.d. 64-Story about 3-D movies. 70-1st Angle Man app. 72-Last pre-code (2/55) 50 100 150 315 533 750
73-90: 80-Origin The Invisible Plane. 85-1st S.A. issue. 89-Flying saucer-c/story 45 90 135 284 480 675
91-94,96,97,99: 97-Last H. G. Peter-a 40 80 120 246 411 575
95-A-Bomb-c 41 82 123 256 428 600
98-New origin & new art team (Andru & Esposito) begin (5/58); origin W.W. id w/new facts
42 84 126 265 445 625
100-(8/58) 45 90 135 284 480 675
101-104,106,108-110 37 74 111 222 361 500
105-(Scarce, 4/59)-W. W.'s secret origin; W. W. appears as girl (no costume yet) (called Wonder Girl - see DC Super-Stars #1) 142 284 426 909 1555 2200
107-1st advs. of Wonder Girl; 1st Merboy; tells how Wonder Woman won her costume
43 86 129 271 461 650
111-120 30 60 90 177 289 400
121-126: 121-1st app. Wonder Woman Family. 122-1st app. Wonder Tot. 124-Wonder Woman

Wonder Woman #177 © DC

Wonder Woman (2nd series) #139 © DC

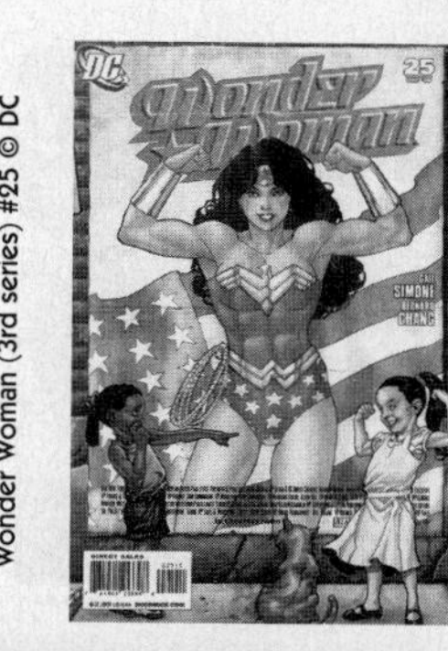

Wonder Woman (3rd series) #25 © DC

	GD 2.0	VG 4.0	FN 6.0	VF 8.0	VF/NM 9.0	NM- 9.2
Family app. 126-Last 10¢ issue	24	48	72	142	234	325
127-130: 128-Origin The Invisible Plane retold. 129-3rd app. Wonder Woman Family (#133 is 4th app.)	13	26	39	93	172	250
131-150: 132-Flying saucer-c	11	22	33	78	139	200
151-155,157,158,160-170 (1967): 151-Wonder Girl solo issue	9	18	27	60	100	140
156-(8/65)-Early mention of a comic book shop & comic collecting; mentions DCs selling for $100 a copy	9	18	27	63	107	150
159-Origin retold (1/66); 1st S.A. origin?	10	20	30	71	126	180
171-176	7	14	21	47	76	105
177-W. Woman/Supergirl battle	9	18	27	60	100	140
178-1st new Wonder Woman on-c only; appears in old costume w/powers inside	9	18	27	61	103	145
179-Classic-c; wears no costume to issue #203	8	16	24	58	97	135
180-195: 180-Death of Steve Trevor. 182-Last 12¢ issue. 195-Wood inks	5	10	15	34	55	75
196 (52 pgs.)-Origin-r/All Star #8 (6 out of 9 pgs.)	6	12	18	37	59	80
197,198 (52 pgs.)-Reprints	6	12	18	37	59	80
199-Jeff Jones painted-c; 52 pgs.	8	16	24	54	90	125
200 (5-6/72)-Jeff Jones-c; 52 pgs.	8	16	24	58	97	135
201,202-Catwoman app. 202-Fafhrd & The Grey Mouser debut.	4	8	12	24	37	50
203,205-210,212: 212-The Cavalier app.	3	6	9	18	27	35
204-Return to old costume; death of I Ching.	4	8	12	24	37	50
211,214-(100 pgs.)	7	14	21	50	83	115
213,215,216,218-220: 220-N. Adams assist	3	6	9	16	23	30
217: (68 pgs.)	3	6	9	20	30	40
221,222,224-227,229,230,233-236,238-240	2	4	6	10	14	18
223,228,231,232,237,241,248: 223-Steve Trevor revived as Steve Howard & learns W.W.'s I.D. 228-Both Wonder Women team up & new World War II stories begin, end #243. 231,232: JSA app. 237-Origin retold. 240-G.A. Flash app. 241-Intro Bouncer; Spectre app. 248-Steve Trevor Howard dies (44 pgs.)	2	4	6	11	16	20
242-246,252-266,269,270: 243-Both W. Women team-up again. 269-Last Wood a(i) for DC? (7/80)	2	3	4	6	8	10
247,249-251,271: 247,249 (44 pgs.). 249-Hawkgirl app. 250-Origin/1st app. Orana, the new Wonder Woman. 251-Orana dies. 271-Huntress & 3rd Life of Steve Trevor begin	2	4	6	8	10	12
250-252,255-262,264-(Whitman variants, low print run, no issue # on cover)	2	4	6	11	16	20
267,268-Re-intro Animal Man (5/80 & 6/80)	2	4	6	8	10	12
272-280,284-286,289,290,294-299,301-325						6.00
281-283: Joker-c/stories in Huntress back-ups	2	3	4	6	8	10
287,288,291-293: 287-New Teen Titans x-over. 288-New costume & logo. 291-293-Three part epic with Super-Heroines	1	2	3	4	5	7
300-($1.50, 76 pgs.)-Anniv. issue; Giffen-a; New Teen Titans, Bronze Age Sandman, JLA & G.A. Wonder Woman app.; 1st app. Lyta Trevor who becomes Fury in All-Star Squadron #25; G.A. Wonder Woman & Steve Trevor revealed as married	1	2	3	4	5	7
326-328	1	2	3	4	5	7
329 (Double size)-S.A. W.W. & Steve Trevor wed	2	4	6	9	13	16
...: Chronicles Vol. 1 TPB (2010, $17.99) reprints debut in All Star Comics #8, apps. in Sensation Comics #1-9 and Wonder Woman #1						18.00
Diana Prince: Wonder Woman Vol. 1 TPB (2008, $19.99) r/#178-183						20.00
Diana Prince: Wonder Woman Vol. 2 TPB (2008, $19.99) r/#185-189, Brave and the Bold #87, and Superman's Girl Friend, Lois Lane #93						20.00
Diana Prince: Wonder Woman Vol. 3 TPB ('08, $19.99) r/#190-198, World's Finest #204						20.00
Diana Prince: Wonder Woman Vol. 4 TPB ('09, $19.99) r/#199-204, Brave & Bold #105						20.00
...: The Greatest Stories Ever Told TPB (2007, $19.99) intro. by Lynda Carter; Ross-c						20.00

NOTE: ***Andru/Esposito** c-66-160(most). **Buckler** a-300. **Colan** a-288-305p; c-288-290p. **Giffen** a-300p. **Grell** c-217. **Kaluta** c-297. **Gil Kane** c-294p, 303-305, 307, 312, 314. **Miller** c-298p. **Morrow** c-233. **Nasser** a-232p; c-231p, 232p. **Bob Oskner** c(i)-39-65(most). **Perez** c-283p, 284p. **Spiegle** a-312. **Staton** a(p)-241, 271-287, 289, 290, 294-299; c(p)-241, 245, 246. Huntress back-up stories 271-287, 289, 290, 294-299, 301-321.*

WONDER WOMAN

DC Comics: Feb, 1987 - No. 226, Apr, 2006 (75¢/$1.00/$1.25/$1.95/$1.99/$2.25/$2.50)

	GD 2.0	VG 4.0	FN 6.0	VF 8.0	VF/NM 9.0	NM- 9.2
0-(10/94) Zero Hour; released between #90 & #91	2	3	4	6	8	10
1-New origin; Perez-c/a begins	1	2	3	5	6	8
2-5						6.00
6-20: 9-Origin Cheetah. 12,13-Millennium x-over. 18,26-Free 16 pg. story						4.50
21-49: 24-Last Perez-a; scripts continue thru #62						3.50
50-($1.50, 52 pgs.)-New Titans, Justice League						4.50
51-62: Perez scripts. 60-Vs. Lobo; last Perez-c. 62-Last $1.00-c						3.50
63-New direction & Bolland-c begin; Deathstroke story continued fromW. W. Special #1						4.50
64-84						3.00
85-1st Deodato-a; ends #100	3	5	7	10	12	14
86-88: 88-Superman-c & app.						6.00
89-97: 90-(9/94)-1st Artemis. 91-(11/94). 93-Hawkman app. 96-Joker-c						4.50
98,99						3.50
100 ($2.95, Newsstand)-Death of Artemis; Bolland-c ends.						4.50
100 ($3.95, Direct Market)-Death of Artemis; foil-c.						6.00
101-119, 121-125: 101-Begin $1.95-c; Byrne-c/a/scripts begin. 101-104-Darkseid app. 105-Phantom Stranger cameo. 106-108-Phantom Stranger & Demon app. 107,108-Arion app. 111-1st app. new Wonder Girl. 111,112-Vs. Doomsday. 112-Superman app. 113-Wonder Girl-c/app; Sugar & Spike app.						2.50
120 ($2.95)-Perez-c						3.00
126-149: 128-Hippolyta becomes new W.W. 130-133-Flash (Jay Garrick) & JSA app. 136-Diana returns to W.W. role; last Byrne issue. 137-Priest-s. 139-Luke-s/Paquette-a begin; Hughes-c thru #146						2.50
150-($2.95) Hughes-c/Clark-a; Zauriel app.						3.00
151-158-Hughes-c. 153-Superboy app.						2.50
159-163: 159-Begin $2.25-c. 160,161-Clayface app. 162,163-Aquaman app.						2.50
164-171: Phil Jimenez-s/a begin; Hughes-c; Batman app. 168,169-Pérez co-plot 169-Wraparound-c.170-Lois Lane-c/app.						2.50
172-Our Worlds at War; Hippolyta killed						3.00
173,174: 173-Our Worlds at War; Darkseid app. 174-Every DC heroine app.						2.50
175-($3.50) Joker: Last Laugh; JLA app.; Jim Lee-c						3.50
176-199: 177-Paradise Island returns. 179-Jimenez-c. 184,185-Hippolyta-c/app.; Hughes-c 186-Cheetah app. 189-Simonson-s/Ordway-a begin. 190-Diana's new look. 195-Rucka-s/Drew Johnson-a begin. 197-Flash-c/app. 198,199-Noto-c						2.50
200-($3.95) back-up stories in 1940s and 1960s styles; pin-ups by various						4.00
201-218,220-225: 203,204-Batman-c/app. 204-Matt Wagner-c. 212-JLA app. 214-Flash app. 215-Morales-a begins. 218-Begin $2.50-c. 220-Batman app.						2.75
219-Omac tie-in/Sacrifice pt. 4; Wonder Woman kills Max Lord; Superman app.						3.00
219-(2nd printing) Altered cover with red background						2.50
226-Last issue; flashbacks to meetings with Superman; Rucka-s/Richards-a						3.00
#1,000,000 (11/98) 853rd Century x-over; Deodato-c						3.00
Annual 1,2: 1 ('88, $1.50)-Art Adams-a. 2 ('89, $2.00, 68 pgs.)-All women artists issue; Perez-c(i)/a.						4.00
Annual 3 (1992, $2.50, 68 pgs.)-Quesada-c(p)						3.00
Annual 4 (1995, $3.50)-Year One						3.50
Annual 5 (1996, $2.95)-Legends of the Dead Earth story; Byrne scripts; Cockrum-a						3.00
Annual 6 (1997, $2.95)-Pulp Heroes						4.00
Annual 7,8 ('98,'99, $2.95)-7-Ghosts; Wrightson-c. 8-JLApe, A.Adams-c						3.00
...: Beauty and the Beasts TPB (2005, $19.95) r/#15-19 & Action Comics #600						20.00
...: Bitter Rivals TPB (2004, $13.95) r/#200-205; Jones-c						13.00
...: Challenge of the Gods TPB ('04, $19.95) r/#8-14; Pérez-s/a						20.00
...: Destiny Calling TPB (2006, $19.99) r/#20-24 & Annual #1; Pérez-c & pin-up gallery						20.00
...Donna Troy (6/98, $1.95) Girlfrenzy; Jimenez-a						2.50
...: Down To Earth TPB (2004, $14.95) r/#195-200; Greg Land-c						15.00
... 80-Page Giant 1 (2002, $4.95) reprints in format of 1960s' 80-Page Giants						5.00
...: Eyes of the Gorgon TPB ('05, $19.99) r/#206-213						20.00
Gallery (1996, $3.50)-Bolland-c; pin-ups by various						4.00
...: Gods and Mortals TPB ('04, $19.95) r/#1-7; Pérez-a						20.00
...: Gods of Gotham TPB ('01, $5.95) r/#164-167; Jimenez-s/a						6.00
...: Land of the Dead TPB ('06, $12.99) r/#214-217 & Flash #219						13.00
Lifelines TPB ('98, $9.95) r/#106-112; Byrne-c/a						10.00
...: Mission's End TPB ('06, $19.99) r/#218-226; cover gallery						20.00
...: Our Worlds at War (10/01, $2.95) History of the Amazons; Jae Lee-c						3.00
...: Paradise Found TPB ('03, $14.95) r/#171-177, Secret Files #3; Jimenez-s/a						15.00
...: Paradise Lost TPB ('02, $14.95) r/#164-170; Jimenez-s/a						15.00
Plus 1 (1/97, $2.95)-Jesse Quick-c/app.						3.00
Second Genesis TPB (1997, $9.95)-r/#101-105						10.00
Secret Files 1-3 (3/98, 7/99, 5/02; $4.95)						5.00
Special 1 (1992, $1.75, 52 pgs.)-Deathstroke-c/story continued in Wonder Woman #63						4.00
...: The Blue Amazon (2003, $6.95) Elseworlds; McKeever-a						7.00
The Challenge Of Artemis TPB (1996, $9.95)-r/#94-100; Deodato-c/a						10.00
...: The Once and Future Story (1998, $4.95) Trina Robbins-s/Doran & Guice-a						5.00

NOTE: ***Art Adams** a-Annual 1. **Byrne** c/a 101-107. **Bolton** a-Annual 1. **Deodato** a-85-100. **Perez** a-Annual 1; c-Annual 1(i). **Quesada** c(p)-Annual 3.*

WONDER WOMAN (Also see Amazons Attack mini-series)

DC Comics: Aug, 2006 - Present ($2.99)

	GD 2.0	VG 4.0	FN 6.0	VF 8.0	VF/NM 9.0	NM- 9.2
1-Donna Troy as Wonder Woman after Infinite Crisis; Heinberg-s/Dodson-a/c						3.00
1-Variant-c by Adam Kubert						4.00
2-40: 2-4-Giganta & Hercules app. 6-Jodi Picoult-s begins. 8-Hippolyta returns. 9-12-Amazons Attack tie-in; JLA app. 14-17-Simone-s/Dodson-a/c. 20-23-Stalker app. 26-33-Rise of the Olympian. 40-Power Girl app.						3.00
14-DC Nation Convention giveaway edition						6.00
... Annual 1 (11/07, $3.99) Story cont'd from #4; Heinberg-s/Dodson-a/c; back-up Frank-a						4.00
...: Ends of the Earth HC (2009, $24.99) r/#20-25						25.00

Wonderworld Comics #14 © FOX

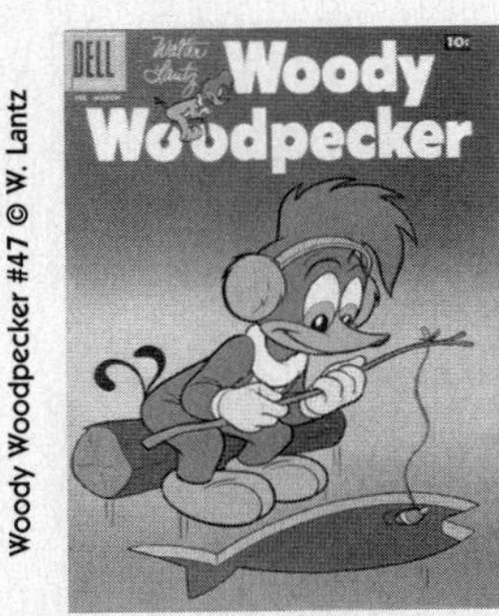

Woody Woodpecker #47 © W. Lantz

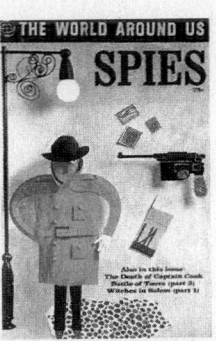

The World Around Us #35 © GIL

	GD 2.0	VG 4.0	FN 6.0	VF 8.0	VF/NM 9.0	NM- 9.2

...: Love and Murder HC (2007, $19.99) r/#6-10 20.00
...: Rise of the Olympian HC (2009, $24.99) r/#26-33 & pages from DC Universe #0 25.00
...: Rise of the Olympian SC (2009, $14.99) r/#26-33 & pages from DC Universe #0 15.00
...: The Circle HC (2008, $24.99) r/#14-19; Mercedes Lackey intro.;Dodson sketch pages 25.00
...: The Circle SC (2009, $14.99) r/#14-19; Mercedes Lackey intro.;Dodson sketch pages 15.00
...: Who is Wonder Woman? HC (2007, $19.99) r/#1-4 & Annual #1; Vaughan intro. 20.00
...: Who is Wonder Woman? SC (2009, $14.99) r/#1-4 & Annual #1; Vaughan intro. 15.00

WONDER WOMAN: AMAZONIA
DC Comics: 1997 ($7.95, Graphic Album format, one shot)
1-Elseworlds; Messner-Loebs-s/Winslade-a 8.00

WONDER WOMAN SPECTACULAR (See DC Special Series #9)

WONDER WOMAN: SPIRIT OF TRUTH
DC Comics: Nov, 2001 ($9.95, treasury size, one-shot)
nn-Painted art by Alex Ross; story by Alex Ross and Paul Dini 10.00

WONDER WOMAN: THE HIKETEIA
DC Comics: 2002 ($24.95, hardcover, one-shot)
nn-Wonder Woman battles Batman; Greg Rucka-s/J.G. Jones-a 25.00
Softcover (2003, $17.95) 18.00

WONDERWORLD COMICS (Formerly Wonder Comics)
Fox Features Syndicate: No. 3, July, 1939 - No. 33, Jan, 1942

	GD	VG	FN	VF	VF/NM	NM-
3-Intro The Flame by Fine; Dr. Fung (Powell-a), K-51 (Powell-a?), & Yarko the Great, Master Magician (Eisner-a) continues; Eisner/Fine-c	692	1384	2076	5052	8926	12,800
4-Lou Fine-c	326	652	978	2282	3991	5700
5,6,9,10: Lou Fine-c	187	374	561	1197	2049	2900
7-Classic Lou Fine-c	309	618	927	2163	3782	5400
8-Classic Lou Fine-c	284	568	852	1818	3109	4400
11-Origin The Flame	145	290	435	921	1586	2250
12-15:13-Dr. Fung ends; last Fine-c(p)	116	232	348	742	1271	1800
16-20	86	172	258	546	936	1325
21-Origin The Black Lion & Cub	79	158	237	502	864	1225
22-27: 22,25-Dr. Fung app.	61	123	183	290	670	950
28-Origin & 1st app. U.S. Jones (8/41); Lu-Nar, the Moon Man begins	84	168	252	538	919	1300
29,31,33	50	100	150	315	533	750
30-Intro & Origin Flame Girl	92	184	276	584	1005	1425
32-Hitler-c	81	162	243	518	884	1250

NOTE: *Spies at War by* **Eisner** *in #13, 17. Yarko by* **Eisner** *in #3-11.* **Eisner** *text illos-3.* **Lou Fine** *a-3-11; c-3-13, 15(i); text illos-4.* **Nordling** *a-4-14.* **Powell** *a-3-12.* **Tuska** *a-5-9. Bondage-c 14, 15, 28, 31, 32. Cover features: The Flame-#3, 5-31; U.S. Jones-#32, 33.*

WONDERWORLDS
Innovation Publishing: 1992 ($3.50, squarebound, 100 pgs.)
1-Rebound super-hero comics, contents may vary; Hero Alliance, Terraformers, etc. 3.50

WOODSY OWL (See March of Comics #395)
Gold Key: Nov, 1973 - No. 10, Feb, 1976 (Some Whitman printings exist)

	GD	VG	FN	VF	VF/NM	NM-
1	2	4	6	13	18	22
2-10	2	4	6	8	10	12

WOODY WOODPECKER (Walter Lantz... #73 on?)(See Dell Giants for annuals)
(Also see The Funnies, Jolly Jingles, Kite Fun Book, New Funnies)
Dell Publishing Co./Gold Key No. 73-187/Whitman No. 188 on:
No. 169, 10/47 - No. 72, 5-7/62; No. 73, 10/62 - No. 201, 3/84 (nn 192)

	GD	VG	FN	VF	VF/NM	NM-
Four Color 169(#1)-Drug turns Woody into a Mr. Hyde	17	34	51	119	230	340
Four Color 188	11	22	33	78	139	200
Four Color 202,232,249,264,288	8	16	24	58	97	135
Four Color 305,336,350	6	12	18	41	66	90
Four Color 364,374,390,405,416,431('52)	5	10	15	34	55	75
16 (12-1/52-53) - 30('55)	4	8	12	28	44	60
31-50	4	8	12	22	34	45
51-72 (Last Dell)	3	6	9	18	27	35
73-75 (Giants, 84 pgs., Gold Key)	5	10	15	32	51	70
76-80	3	6	9	16	22	28
81-103: 103-Last 12¢ issue	3	6	9	14	19	24
104-120	2	4	6	11	16	20
121-140	2	4	6	9	12	15
141-160	1	3	4	6	8	10
161-187	1	2	3	5	7	9
188,189 (Whitman)	2	4	6	9	13	16
190(9/80),191(11/80)-pre-pack only	4	8	12	22	34	45
(No #192)						
193-197: 196(2/82), 197(4/82)	2	4	6	11	16	20
198-201 (All #90062 on-c, no date or date code, pre-pack): 198(6/83), 199(7/83), 200(8/83), 201(3/84)	3	6	9	16	22	28
Christmas Parade 1(11/68-Giant)(G.K.)	4	8	12	26	41	55
Summer Fun 1(6/66-G.K.)(84 pgs.)	5	10	15	30	48	65
nn (1971, 60¢, 100 pgs. digest) B&W one page gags	3	6	9	17	25	32

NOTE: *15¢ Canadian editions of the 12¢ issues exist. Reprints-No. 92, 102, 103, 105, 106, 124, 125, 152, 153, 157, 162, 165, 194(1/3)-200(1/3).*

WOODY WOODPECKER (See Comic Album #5,9,13, Dell Giant #24, 40, 54, Dell Giants, The Funnies, Golden Comics Digest #1, 3, 5, 8, 15, 16, 20, 24, 32, 37, 44, March of Comics #16, 34, 85, 93, 109, 124, 139, 158, 177, 184, 203, 222, 239, 249, 261, 420, 454, 466, 478, New Funnies & Super Book #12, 24)

WOODY WOODPECKER
Harvey Comics: Sept, 1991 - No. 15, Aug, 1994 ($1.25)
1-15: 1-r/W.W. #53 2.50
50th Anniversary Special 1 (10/91, $2.50, 68 pgs.) 3.00

WOODY WOODPECKER AND FRIENDS
Harvey Comics: Dec, 1991 - No. 4, 1992 ($1.25)
1-4 2.50

WORD WARRIORS (Also see Quest for Dreams Lost)
Literacy Volunteers of Chicago: 1987 ($1.50, B&W)(Proceeds donated to help literacy)
1-Jon Sable by Grell, Ms. Tree, Streetwolf; Chaykin-c 3.00

WORLD AROUND US, THE (Illustrated Story of...)
Gilberton Publishers (Classics Illustrated): Sep, 1958 -No. 36, Oct, 1961 (25¢)

	GD	VG	FN	VF	VF/NM	NM-
1-Dogs; Evans-a	9	18	27	52	69	85
2-4: 2-Indians; Check-a. 3-Horses; L. B. Cole-c. 4-Railroads; L. B. Cole-a (5 pgs.)	9	18	27	47	61	75
5-Space; Ingels-a	10	20	30	56	76	95
6-The F.B.I.; Disbrow, Evans, Ingels-a	10	20	30	56	76	95
7-Pirates; Disbrow, Ingels, Kinstler-a	9	18	27	52	69	85
8-Flight; Evans, Ingels, Crandall-a	9	18	27	52	69	85
9-Army; Disbrow, Ingels, Orlando-a	9	18	27	47	61	75
10-13: 10-Navy; Disbrow, Kinstler-a. 11-Marine Corps. 12-Coast Guard; Ingels-a (9 pgs.). 13-Air Force; L.B. Cole-c	9	18	27	47	61	75
14-French Revolution; Crandall, Evans, Kinstler-a	10	20	30	56	76	95
15-Prehistoric Animals; Al Williamson-a, 6 & 10 pgs. plus Morrow-a	10	20	30	58	79	100
16-18: 16-Crusades; Kinstler-a. 17-Festivals; Evans, Crandall-a. 18-Great Scientists; Crandall, Evans, Torres, Williamson, Morrow-a	9	18	27	52	69	85
19-Jungle; Crandall, Williamson, Morrow-a	10	20	30	58	79	100
20-Communications; Crandall, Evans, Torres-a	10	20	30	56	76	95
21-American Presidents; Crandall/Evans, Morrow-a	10	20	30	56	76	95
22-Boating; Morrow-a	8	16	24	44	57	70
23-Great Explorers; Crandall, Evans-a	9	18	27	52	69	85
24-Ghosts; Morrow, Evans-a	10	20	30	56	76	95
25-Magic; Evans, Morrow-a	10	20	30	56	76	95
26-The Civil War	11	22	33	62	86	110
27-Mountains (High Advs.); Crandall/Evans, Morrow, Torres-a	9	18	27	52	69	85
28-Whaling; Crandall, Evans, Morrow, Torres, Wildey-a; L.B. Cole-c	9	18	27	52	69	85
29-Vikings; Crandall, Evans, Torres, Morrow-a	10	20	30	58	79	100
30-Undersea Adventure; Crandall/Evans, Kirby, Morrow, Torres-a	10	20	30	56	76	95
31-Hunting; Crandall/Evans, Ingels, Kinstler, Kirby-a	9	18	27	52	69	85
32,33: 32-For Gold & Glory; Morrow, Kirby, Crandall, Evans-a. 33-Famous Teens; Torres, Crandall, Evans-a	9	18	27	52	69	85
34-36: 34-Fishing; Crandall/Evans-a. 35-Spies; Kirby, Morrow?, Evans-a. 36-Fight for Life (Medicine); Kirby-a	9	18	27	52	69	85

NOTE: See Classics Illustrated Special Edition. Another *World Around Us* issue entitled *The Sea* had been prepared in 1962 but was never published in the U.S. It was published in the British/European *World Around Us* series. Those series then continued with seven additional WAU titles not in the U.S. series.

WORLD BELOW, THE
Dark Horse Comics: Mar, 1999 - No. 4, Jun, 1999 ($2.50, limited series)
1-4-Paul Chadwick-s/c/a 2.50
TPB (1/07, $12.95) r/#1-4; intro. by Chadwick; gallery of sketches and covers 13.00

WORLD BELOW, THE: DEEPER AND STRANGER
Dark Horse Comics: Dec, 1999 - No. 4, Mar, 2000 ($2.95, B&W)
1-4-Paul Chadwick-s/c/a 3.00

WORLD FAMOUS HEROES MAGAZINE
Comic Corp. of America (Centaur): Oct, 1941 - No. 4, Apr, 1942 (comic book)

World of Fantasy #3 © MAR

World of Warcraft #3 © Blizzard Ent.

Worlds Collide #1 © DC

	GD 2.0	VG 4.0	FN 6.0	VF 8.0	VF/NM 9.0	NM- 9.2

1-Gustavson-c; Lubbers, Glanzman-a; Davy Crockett, Paul Revere, Lewis & Clark, John Paul Jones stories; Flag-c 110 220 330 704 1202 1700
2-Lou Gehrig life story; Lubbers-a 47 94 141 296 498 700
3,4-Lubbers-a. 4-Wild Bill Hickok story; 2 pg. Marlene Dietrich story 43 86 129 271 461 650

WORLD FAMOUS STORIES
Croyden Publishers: 1945
1-Ali Baba, Hansel & Gretel, Rip Van Winkle, Mid-Summer Night's Dream 14 28 42 76 108 140

WORLD IS HIS PARISH, THE
George A. Pflaum: 1953 (15¢)
nn-The story of Pope Pius XII 6 12 18 29 36 42

WORLD OF ADVENTURE (Walt Disney's...)(TV)
Gold Key: Apr, 1963 - No. 3, Oct, 1963 (12¢)
1-Disney TV characters; Savage Sam, Johnny Shiloh, Capt. Nemo, The Mooncussers 3 6 9 21 32 42
2,3 3 6 9 15 21 26

WORLD OF ARCHIE, THE (See Archie Giant Series Mag. #148, 151, 156, 160, 165, 171, 177, 182, 188, 193, 200, 208, 213, 225, 232, 237, 244, 249, 456, 461, 468, 473, 480, 485, 492, 497, 504, 509, 516, 521, 532, 543, 554, 565, 574, 587, 599, 612, 627)

WORLD OF ARCHIE
Archie Comics: Aug, 1992 - No. 22 ($1.25/$1.50)
1 4.00
2-15: 9-Neon ink-c 3.00
16-22 2.50

WORLD OF FANTASY
Atlas Comics (CPC No. 1-15/ZPC No. 16-19): May, 1956 - No. 19, Aug, 1959
1 47 94 141 296 498 700
2-Williamson-a (4 pgs.) 31 62 93 182 296 410
3-Sid Check, Roussos-a 27 54 81 158 259 360
4-7 21 42 63 126 206 285
8-Matt Fox, Orlando, Berg-a 23 46 69 136 223 310
9-Krigstein-a 22 44 66 128 209 290
10-15: 10-Colan-a. 11-Torres-a 19 38 57 111 176 240
16-Williamson-a (4 pgs.); Ditko, Kirby-a 26 52 78 154 252 350
17-19-Ditko, Kirby-a 26 52 78 154 252 350
NOTE: ***Ayers** a-3. **B. Baily** a-4. **Berg** a-5, 6, 8. **Brodsky** c-3. **Check** a-3. **Ditko** a-17, 19. **Everett** a-2; c-4-7, 9, 12, 13. **Forte** a-4, 8. **Infantino** a-14. **Kirby** c-15, 17-19. **Krigstein** a-9. **Maneely** c-2, 14. **Mooney** a-14. **Morrow** a-7. **Orlando** a-8, 13, 14. **Pakula** a-9. **Powell** a-4, 6. **Reinman** a-8, 10. **R.Q. Sale** a-3, 7, 9, 10. **Severin** c-1.*

WORLD OF GIANT COMICS, THE (See Archie All-Star Specials under Archie Comics)

WORLD OF GINGER FOX, THE (Also see Ginger Fox)
Comico: Nov, 1986 ($6.95, 8 1/2 x 11", 68 pgs., mature)
Graphic Novel ($6.95) 7.00
Hardcover ($27.95) 28.00

WORLD OF JUGHEAD, THE (See Archie Giant Series Mag. #9, 14, 19, 24, 30, 136, 143, 149, 152, 157, 161, 166, 172, 178, 183, 189, 194, 202, 209, 215, 227, 233, 239, 245, 251, 457, 463, 469, 475, 481, 487, 493, 499, 505, 511, 517, 523, 531, 542, 553, 564, 577, 590, 602)

WORLD OF KRYPTON, THE (World of...#3) (See Superman #248)
DC Comics, Inc.: 7/79 - No. 3, 9/79; 12/87 - No. 4, 3/88 (Both are lim. series)
1-3 (1979, 40¢; 1st comic book mini-series): 1-Jor-El marries Lara. 3-Baby Superman sent to Earth; Krypton explodes; Mon-el app. 5.00
1-4 (75¢)-Byrne scripts; Byrne/Simonson-c 3.00

WORLD OF METROPOLIS, THE
DC Comics: Aug, 1988 - No. 4, July, 1988 ($1.00, limited series)
1-4: Byrne scripts 3.00

WORLD OF MYSTERY
Atlas Comics (GPI): June, 1956 - No. 7, July, 1957
1-Torres, Orlando-a; Powell-a? 47 94 141 296 498 700
2-Woodish-a 20 40 60 120 195 270
3-Torres, Davis, Ditko-a 24 48 72 140 230 320
4-Pakula, Powell-a 24 48 72 140 230 320
5,7: 5-Orlando-a 20 40 60 117 189 260
6-Williamson/Mayo-a (4 pgs.); Ditko-a; Colan-a; Crandall text illo 24 48 72 140 230 320
NOTE: ***Ayers** a-4. **Brodsky** c-2, 5, 6. **Colan** a-6, 7. **Everett** c-1, 3. **Pakula** a-4, 6. **Romita** a-2. **Severin** c-7.*

WORLD OF SMALLVILLE
DC Comics: Apr, 1988 - No. 4, July, 1988 (75¢, limited series)
1-4: Byrne scripts 3.00

WORLD OF SUSPENSE
Atlas News Co.: Apr, 1956 - No. 8, July, 1957
1 40 80 120 246 411 575
2-Ditko-a (4 pgs.) 24 48 72 140 230 320
3,7-Williamson-a in both (4 pgs.); #7-with Mayo 23 46 69 136 223 310
4-6,8 20 40 60 117 189 260
NOTE: ***Berg** a-6. **Cameron** a-2. **Ditko** a-2. **Drucker** a-1. **Everett** a-1, 5; c-6. **Heck** a-5. **Maneely** a-1; c-1-3. **Orlando** a-5. **Powell** a-6. **Reinman** a-4. **Roussos** a-6. **Shores** a-1.*

WORLD OF WARCRAFT (Based on the Blizzard Entertainment video game)
DC Comics (WildStorm): Jan, 2008 - No. 25, Jan, 2010 ($2.99)
1-Walt Simonson-s/Lullabi-a; cover by Samwise Didier 8.00
1-Variant cover by Jim Lee 12.00
1,2-Second printing with Jim Lee sketch cover 5.00
2-Two covers by Jim Lee and Samwise Didier 5.00
3-24: 3-14-Two covers on each 3.00
25-($3.99) Walt & Louise Simonson-s 4.00
... Special 1 (2/10, $3.99) Costa-s/Mhan-a/c 4.00
... Book One HC (2008, $19.99, dustjacket) r/#1-7; intro. by Chris Metzen of Blizzard 20.00
... Book One SC (2009, $14.99) r/#1-7; intro. by Chris Metzen of Blizzard 15.00
... Book Two HC (2009, $19.99, dustjacket) r/#8-14 20.00

WORLD OF WARCRAFT:ASHBRINGER
DC Comics (WildStorm): Nov, 2008 - No. 4, Feb, 2009 ($3.99)
1-4-Neilson-s/Lullabi & Washington-a; 2 covers by Robinson & Lullabi 4.00

WORLD OF WHEELS (Formerly Dragstrip Hotrodders)
Charlton Comics: No. 17, Oct, 1967 - No. 32, June, 1970
17-20-Features Ken King 3 6 9 18 27 35
21-32-Features Ken King 3 6 9 16 22 28
Modern Comics Reprint 23(1978) 5.00

WORLD OF WOOD
Eclipse Comics: 1986 - No. 4, 1987; No. 5, 2/89 ($1.75, limited series)
1-4:1-Dave Stevens-c. 2-Wood/Stevens-c 4.00
5 ($2.00, B&W)-r/Avon's Flying Saucers 5.00

WORLD'S BEST COMICS
DC Comics: Feb 1940
nn - Ashcan comic, not distributed to newsstands, only for in-house use. Cover art is Action Comics #29 with interior being Action Comics #24 (no known sales)

WORLD'S BEST COMICS (World's Finest Comics #2 on)
National Per. Publications (100 pgs.): Spring, 1941 (Cardboard-c)(DC's 6th annual format comic)
1-The Batman, Superman, Crimson Avenger, Johnny Thunder, The King, Young Dr. Davis, Zatara, Lando, Man of Magic, & Red, White & Blue begin; Superman, Batman & Robin covers begin (inside-c is blank); Fred Ray-c; 15¢ cover price 1475 2950 4425 10,400 17,700 25,000

WORLD'S BEST COMICS: GOLDEN AGE SAMPLER
DC Comics: 2003 (99¢, one-shot, samples from DC Archive editions)
1-Golden Age reprints from Superman #6, Batman #5, Sensation #11, Police #11 2.50

WORLD'S BEST COMICS: SILVER AGE SAMPLER
DC Comics: 2004 (99¢, one-shot, samples from DC Archive editions)
1-Silver Age reprints from Justice League #4, Adventure #247, Our Army at War #81 2.50

WORLDS BEYOND (Stories of Weird Adventure)(Worlds of Fear #2 on)
Fawcett Publications: Nov, 1951
1-Powell, Bailey-a; Moldoff-c 47 94 141 296 498 700

WORLDS COLLIDE
DC Comics: July, 1994 ($2.50, one-shot)
1-($2.50, 52 pgs.)-Milestone & Superman titles x-over 2.50
1-($3.95, 52 pgs.)-Polybagged w/vinyl clings 4.00

WORLD'S FAIR COMICS (See New York...)

WORLD'S FINEST (Also see Legends of The World's Finest)
DC Comics: 1990 - No. 3, 1990 ($3.95, squarebound, limited series, 52 pgs.)
1-3: Batman & Superman team-up against The Joker and Lex Luthor; Dave Gibbons scripts & Steve Rude-c/a. 2,3-Joker/Luthor painted-c by Steve Rude 5.00
TPB-(1992, $19.95) r/#1-3; Gibbons intro. 20.00
...: The Deluxe Edition HC (2008, $29.99) r/#1-3; Gibbons intro. from 1992; Gibbons story outline and sketches; Rude sketch pages and notes 30.00

WORLD'S FINEST
DC Comics: Dec, 2009 - No. 4, Mar, 2010 ($2.99, limited series)

World's Finest Comics #7 © DC

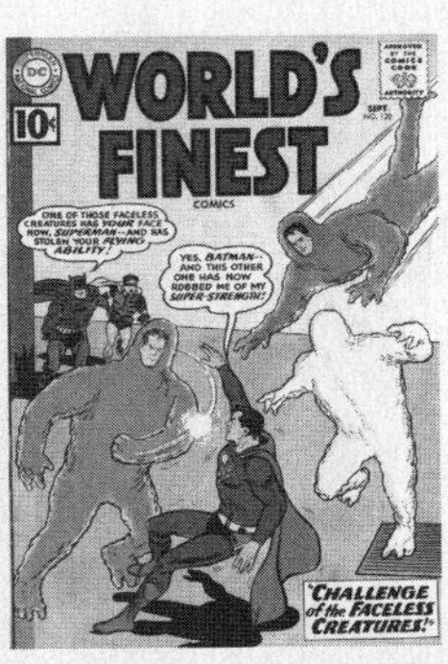

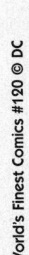

World's Finest Comics #120 © DC

World's Finest Comics #323 © DC

GD 2.0 | VG 4.0 | FN 6.0 | VF 8.0 | VF/NM 9.0 | NM- 9.2

1-4: Gates-s/two covers by Noto on each. 3-Supergirl/Batgirl team up. 4-Noto-a 3.00

WORLD'S FINEST COMICS (Formerly World's Best Comics #1)
National Periodical Publ./DC Comics: No. 2, Sum, 1941 - No. 323, Jan, 1986 (#1-17 have cardboard covers) (#2-9 have 100 pgs.)

2 (100 pgs.)-Superman, Batman & Robin covers continue from World's Best; (cover price 15¢ #2-70) 423 846 1269 3000 5250 7500
3-The Sandman begins; last Johnny Thunder; origin & 1st app. The Scarecrow 320 640 960 2240 3920 5600
4-Hop Harrigan app.; last Young Dr. Davis 245 490 735 1568 2684 3800
5-Intro. TNT & Dan the Dyna-Mite; last King & Crimson Avenger 245 490 735 1568 2684 3800
6-Star Spangled Kid begins (Sum/42); Aquaman app.; S&K Sandman with Sandy in new costume begins, ends #7 181 362 543 1158 1979 2800
7-Green Arrow begins (Fall/42); last Lando & Red, White & Blue; S&K art 181 362 543 1158 1979 2800
8-Boy Commandos begin (by Simon(p) #12); last The King; includes "Minute Man Answers the Call" promo 171 342 513 1086 1868 2650
9-Batman cameo in Star Spangled Kid; S&K-a; last 100 pg. issue; Hitler, Mussolini, Tojo-c 206 412 618 1318 2259 3200
10-S&K-a; 76 pg. issues begin 161 322 483 1030 1765 2500
11-17: 17-Last cardboard cover issue 135 270 405 864 1482 2100
18-20: 18-Paper covers begin; last Star Spangled Kid. 19-Joker story. 20-Last quarterly issue 129 258 387 826 1413 2000
21-30: 21-Begin bi-monthly. 30-Johnny Everyman app. 89 178 267 565 970 1375
31-40: 33-35-Tomahawk app. 35-Penguin app. 82 164 246 528 902 1275
41-50: 41-Boy Commandos end. 42-The Wyoming Kid begins (9-10/49), ends #63. 43-Full Steam Foley begins, ends #48. 48-Last square binding. 49-Tom Sparks, Boy Inventor begins; robot-c 66 132 198 419 722 1025
51-60: 51-Zatara ends. 54-Last 76 pg. issue. 59-Manhunters Around the World begins (7-8/52), ends #62 63 126 189 403 689 975
61-64: 61-Joker story. 63-Capt. Compass app. 61 122 183 390 670 950
65-Origin Superman; Tomahawk begins (7-8/53), ends #101 90 180 270 576 988 1400
66-70-(15¢ issues, scarce)-Last 15¢, 68pg. issue 65 130 195 416 708 1000
71-(10¢ issue, scarce)-Superman & Batman begin as team (7-8/54); were in separate stories until now; Superman & Batman exchange identities; 10¢ issues begin 142 284 426 909 1555 2200
72,73-(10¢ issue, scarce) 94 188 282 597 1024 1450
74-Last pre-code issue 66 132 198 419 722 1025
75-(1st code approved, 3-4/55) 65 130 195 416 708 1000
76-80: 77-Superman loses powers & Batman obtains them 52 104 156 322 549 775
81-90: 84-1st S.A. issue. 88-1st Joker/Luthor team-up. 89-2nd Batmen of All Nations (aka Club of Heroes). 90-Batwoman's 1st app. in World's Finest (10/57, 3rd app. anywhere) plus-c app. 28 56 84 204 395 585
91-93,95-99: 96-99-Kirby Green Arrow. 99-Robot-c 21 42 63 148 287 425
94-Origin Superman/Batman team retold 51 102 153 408 792 1175
100 (3/59) 34 68 102 262 506 750
101-110: 102-Tommy Tomorrow begins, ends #124 14 28 42 100 188 275
111-121: 111-1st app. The Clock King. 113-Intro. Miss Arrowette in Green Arrow; 1st Bat-Mite/Mr. Mxyzptlk team-up (11/60). 117-Batwoman-c. 121-Last 10¢ issue 12 24 36 83 152 220
122-128: 123-2nd Bat-Mite/Mr. Mxyzptlk team-up (2/62). 125-Aquaman begins (5/62), ends #139 (Aquaman #1 is dated 1-2/62) 10 20 30 67 116 165
129-Joker/Luthor team-up-c/story 11 22 33 79 139 200
130-142: 135-Last Dick Sprang story. 140-Last Green Arrow. 142-Origin The Composite Superman (villain); Legion app. 8 16 24 56 93 130
143-150: 143-1st Mailbag. 144-Clayface/Brainiac team-up; last Clayface until Action #443 7 14 21 47 76 105
151-153,155,157-160: 157-2nd Super Sons story; last app. Kathy Kane (Bat-Woman) until Batman Family #10; 1st Bat-Mite Jr. 6 12 18 39 62 85
154-1st Super Sons story; last Bat-Woman in costume until Batman Family #10. 6 12 18 43 69 95
156-1st Bizarro Batman; Joker-c/story 10 20 30 67 116 165
161,170 (80-Pg. Giants G-28,G-40) 7 14 21 45 73 100
162-165,167,168,171,172: 168,172-Adult Legion app. 5 10 15 32 51 70
166-Joker-c/story 6 12 18 37 59 80
169-3rd app. new Batgirl(9/67)(cover and 1 panel cameo); 3rd Bat-Mite/Mr. Mxyzptlk team-up 5 10 15 34 55 75
173-('68)-1st S.A. app. Two-Face as Batman becomes Two-Face in story 9 18 27 61 103 145
174-Adams-c 5 10 15 34 55 75
175,176-Neal Adams-c/a; both reprint J'onn J'onzz origin/Detective #225,226 6 12 18 37 59 80
177-Joker/Luthor team-up-c/story 5 10 15 34 55 75
178-(9/68) Intro. of Super Nova (revived in "52" weekly series); Adams-c 6 12 18 37 59 80
179-(80 Page Giant G-52) -Adams-c; r/#94 6 12 18 41 66 90
180,182,183,185,186: Adams-c on all. 182-Silent Knight-r/Brave & Bold #6. 185-Last 12¢ issue. 186-Johnny Quick-r 4 8 12 26 41 55
181,184,187: 187-Green Arrow origin-r by Kirby (Adv. #256) 4 8 12 24 37 50
188,197:(Giants G-64,G-76; 64 pages) 6 12 18 37 59 80
189-196: 190-193-Robin-r 3 6 9 20 30 40
198,199-3rd Superman/Flash race (see Flash #175 & Superman #199). 199-Adams-c 9 18 27 64 110 155
200-Adams-c 4 8 12 24 37 50
201-203: 203-Last 15¢ issue. 3 6 9 18 27 35
204,205-(52 pgs.) Adams-c: 204-Wonder Woman app. 205-Shining Knight-r (6 pgs.) by Frazetta/Adv. #153; Teen Titans x-over 3 6 9 20 30 40
206 (Giant G-88, 64 pgs.) 5 10 15 32 51 70
207,212-(52 pgs.) 3 6 9 20 30 40
208-211(25¢-c) Adams-c: 208-(52 pgs.) Origin Robotman-r/Det. #138. 209-211-(52 pgs.) 3 6 9 21 32 42
213,214,216-222,229: 217-Metamorpho begins, ends #220; Batman/Superman team-ups resume. 229-r/origin Superman-Batman team 2 4 6 11 16 20
215-(12/72-1/73) Intro. Batman Jr. & Superman Jr. (see Superman/Batman: Saga of the Super Sons TPB for all the Super Sons stories) 3 6 9 18 27 35
223-228-(100 pgs.). 223-N. Adams-r. 223-Deadman origin. 226-N. Adams, S&K, Toth-r; Manhunter part origin-r/Det. #225,226. 227-Deadman app. 5 10 15 30 48 65
230-(68 pgs.) 3 6 9 17 25 32
231-243,247,248: 242-Super Sons. 248-Last Vigilante 2 4 6 8 11 14
244-246-Adams-c: 244-$1.00, 84 pg. issues begin; Green Arrow, Black Canary, Wonder Woman, Vigilante begin; 246-Death of Stuff in Vigilante; origin Vigilante retold 3 6 9 14 19 24
249-252 (84 pgs.) Ditko-a: 249-The Creeper begins by Ditko, 84 pgs. 250-The Creeper origin retold by Ditko. 252-Last 84 pg. issue 2 4 6 13 18 22
253-257,259-265: 253-Capt. Marvel begins; 68 pgs. begin, end #265. 255-Last Creeper. 256-Hawkman begins. 257-Black Lightning begins. 263-Super Sons. 264-Clay Face app. 2 4 6 8 10 12
258-Adams-c 2 4 6 9 12 15
266-270,272-282-(52 pgs.). 267-Challengers of the Unknown app.; 3 Lt. Marvels return. 268-Capt. Marvel Jr. origin retold. 274-Zatanna begins. 279, 280-Capt. Marvel Jr. & Kid Eternity learn they are brothers 1 3 4 6 8 10
271-(52pgs.) Origin Superman/Batman team retold 2 4 6 8 10 12
283-299: 284-Legion app. 1 2 3 4 5 7
300-($1.25, 52pgs.)-Justice League of America, New Teen Titans & The Outsiders app.; Perez-a (4 pgs.) 1 2 3 5 6 8
301-322: 304-Origin Null and Void. 309,319-Free 16 pg. story in each (309-Flash Force 2000, 319-Mask preview) 4.00
323-Last issue 6.00

NOTE: ***Neal Adams*** *a-230ir; c-174-176, 178-180, 182, 183, 185, 186, 199-205, 208-211, 244-246, 258.* ***Austin*** *a-244-246i.* ***Burnley*** *a-8, 10; c-7-9, 11-14, 15p?, 16-18p, 20-31p.* ***Colan*** *a-274p, 297, 299.* ***Ditko*** *a-249-255.* ***Giffen*** *a-322; c-284p, 322.* ***G. Kane*** *a-38, 174r, 282, 283; c-281, 282, 289.* ***Kirby*** *a-187.* ***Kubert*** *Zatara-40-44.* ***Miller*** *c-285p.* ***Mooney*** *c-134.* ***Morrow*** *a-245-248.* ***Mortimer*** *c-16-21, 26-71.* ***Nasser*** *a(p)-244-246, 259, 260.* ***Newton*** *a-253-281p.* ***Orlando*** *a-224r.* ***Perez*** *a-300i; c-271, 276, 277p, 278p.* ***Fred Ray*** *c-1-5.* ***Fred Ray/Robinson*** *c-13-16.* ***Robinson*** *a-5, 6, 9-11, 13?, 14-16; c-6.* ***Rogers*** *a-259p.* ***Roussos*** *a-212r.* ***Simonson*** *c-291.* ***Spiegle*** *a-275-278, 284.* ***Staton*** *a-262p, 273p.* ***Swan/Moldoff*** *c-126.* ***Swan/Mortimer*** *c-79-82.* ***Toth*** *a-228r.* ***Tuska*** *a-230r, 250p, 252p, 254p, 257p, 283p, 284p, 308p. Boy Commandos by* ***Infantino*** *#39-41.*

WORLD'S FINEST COMICS DIGEST (See DC Special Series #23)

WORLD'S FINEST: OUR WORLDS AT WAR
DC Comics: Oct, 2001 ($2.95, one-shot)

1-Concludes the Our Worlds at War x-over; Jae Lee-c; art by various 3.00

WORLD'S GREATEST ATHLETE (See Walt Disney Showcase #14)

WORLD'S GREATEST SONGS
Atlas Comics (Male): Sept, 1954

1-(Scarce)-Heath & Harry Anderson-a; Eddie Fisher life story plus-c; gives lyrics to Frank Sinatra song "Young at Heart" 39 78 117 240 395 550

WORLD'S GREATEST STORIES
Jubilee Publications: Jan, 1949 - No. 2, May, 1949

1-Alice in Wonderland; Lewis Carroll adapt. 32 64 96 188 307 425
2-Pinocchio 30 60 90 177 289 400

WORLDS OF FEAR (Stories of Weird Adventure)(Formerly Worlds Beyond #1)

World War Hulk #1 © MAR

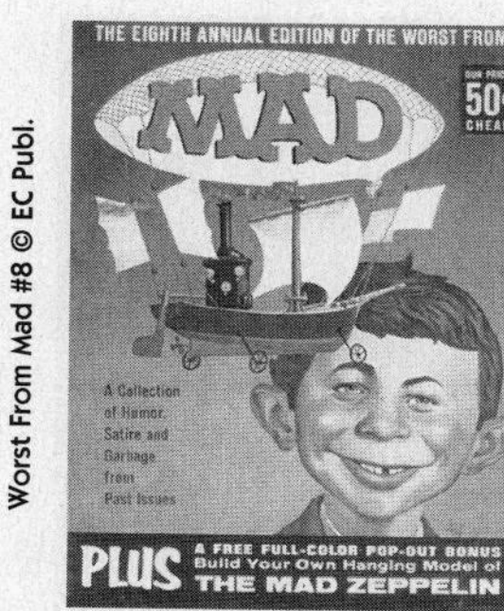

Worst From Mad #8 © EC Publ.

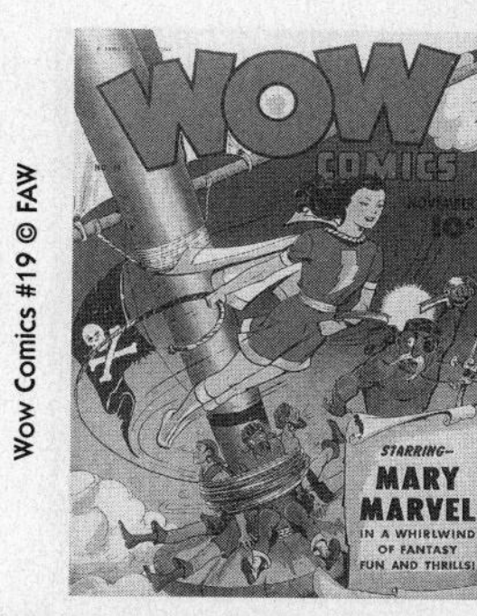

Wow Comics #19 © FAW

GD 2.0 | VG 4.0 | FN 6.0 | VF 8.0 | VF/NM 9.0 | NM- 9.2

Fawcett Publications: V1#2, Jan, 1952 - V2#10, June, 1953

V1#2 47 94 141 296 498 700
3-Evans-a 40 80 120 246 411 575
4-6(9/52) 38 76 114 226 368 510
V2#7-9 34 68 102 204 332 460
10-Saunders painted-c; man with no eyes surrounded by eyeballs-c plus eyes ripped out story 97 194 291 621 1061 1500

NOTE: *Moldoff c-2-8. Powell a-2, 4, 5. Sekowsky a-4, 5.*

WORLDSTORM
DC Comics (WildStorm): Nov, 2006 (Dec on cover) - Present ($2.99)

1,2-Previews and pin-ups for re-launched WildStorm titles.1-Art Adams-c 3.00

WORLDS UNKNOWN
Marvel Comics Group: May, 1973 - No. 8, Aug, 1974

1-r/from Astonishing #54; Torres, Reese-a 3 6 9 16 22 28
2-8 2 4 6 10 14 18

NOTE: *Adkins/Mooney a-5. Buscema c/a-4p. W. Howard c/a-3i. Kane a(p)-1,2; c(p)-5, 6, 8. Sutton a-2. Tuska a(p)-7, 8; c-7p. No. 7, 8 has Golden Voyage of Sinbad movie adaptation.*

WORLD WAR HULK (See Incredible Hulk #106)
Marvel Comics: Aug, 2007 - No. 5, Jan, 2008 ($3.99, limited series)

1-Hulk returns to Earth; Iron Man and Avengers app.; Romita Jr.-a/Pak-s/Finch-c 4.00
1-Variant cover by Romita Jr. 6.00
2-5: 2-Hulk battles The Avengers and FF; Finch-c. 3,4-Dr. Strange app. 5-Sentry app. 4.00
2-5-Variant cover by Romita Jr. 6.00
...: Aftersmash 1 (1/08, $3.99) Sandoval-a/Land-c; Hercules, Iron Man app. 4.00
...: Gamma Files (2007, $3.99) profile pages of Hulk characters 4.00
...Prologue: World Breaker 1 (7/07, one-shot) Rio, Weeks, Phillips, Miyazawa-a 4.00
TPB (2008, $19.99) r/#1-5 20.00

WORLD WAR HULK AFTERSMASH: DAMAGE CONTROL
Marvel Comics: Mar, 2008 - No. 3, May, 2008 ($2.99, limited series)

1-3-The clean-up; McDuffie-s. 2-Romita- Jr.-c. 3-Romita Sr.-c 3.00

WORLD WAR HULK AFTERSMASH: WARBOUND
Marvel Comics: Feb, 2008 - No. 5, Jun, 2008 ($2.99, limited series)

1-5-Kirk & Sandoval-a/Cheung-c 3.00

WORLD WAR HULK: FRONT LINE (See Incredible Hulk #106)
Marvel Comics: Aug, 2007 - No. 6, Dec, 2007 ($2.99, limited series)

1-6-Ben Urich & Sally Floyd report World War Hulk; Jenkins-s/Bachs-a 3.00
TPB (2008, $16.99) r/#1-5 & WWH Prologue: World Breaker 17.00

WORLD WAR HULK: GAMMA CORPS
Marvel Comics: Sept, 2007 - No. 4, Jan, 2008 ($2.99, limited series)

1-4-Tieri-s/Ferreira-a/Roux-c 3.00
TPB (2008, $10.99) r/#1-4 11.00

WORLD WAR HULK: X-MEN (See New Avengers: Illuminati and Incredible Hulk #92)
Marvel Comics: Aug, 2007 - No. 3, Oct, 2007 ($2.99, limited series)

1-3-Gage-s/DiVito-a/McGuinness-c; Hulk invades the Xavier Institute 3.00
TPB (2008, $24.99) r/#1-3, Avengers: The Initiative #4-5, Irredeemable Ant-Man #10, Iron Man #19-20, and Ghost Rider #12-13 25.00

WORLD WAR STORIES
Dell Publishing Co.: Apr-June, 1965 - No. 3, Dec, 1965

1-Glanzman-a in all 4 8 12 26 41 55
2,3 3 6 9 17 25 32

WORLD WAR II (See Classics Illustrated Special Issue)

WORLD WAR II: 1946
Antarctic Press: Oct, 1998 - No. 2 ($3.95, B&W)

1,2-Nomura-s/a 4.00

WORLD WAR III
Ace Periodicals: Mar, 1953 - No. 2, May, 1953

1-(Scarce)-Atomic bomb blast-c; Cameron-a 103 206 309 659 1130 1600
2-Used in **POP**, pg. 78 & B&W & color illos; Cameron-a 60 120 180 381 653 925

WORLDWATCH
Wild and Wooly Press: June, 2004 - No. 3, Dec, 2004 ($2.95)

1-3-Austen-s/Derenick-a. 1-B&W. 2,3-Color 3.00

WORLD WITHOUT END
DC Comics: 1990 - No. 6, 1991 ($2.50, limited series, mature, stiff-c)

1-6: Horror/fantasy; all painted-c/a 2.50

GD 2.0 | VG 4.0 | FN 6.0 | VF 8.0 | VF/NM 9.0 | NM- 9.2

WORLD WRESTLING FEDERATION BATTLEMANIA
Valiant: 1991 - No. 5?, 1991 ($2.50, magazine size, 68 pgs.)

1-5: 5-Includes 2 free pull-out posters 4.00

WORST FROM MAD, THE (Annual)
E. C. Comics: 1958 - No. 12, 1969 (Each annual cover is reprinted from the cover of the Mad issues being reprinted)(Value is 1/2 if bonus is missing)

nn(1958)-Bonus; record labels & travel stickers; 1st Mad annual; r/Mad #29-34 43 86 129 271 461 650
2(1959)-Bonus is small 33 1/3 rpm record entitled "Meet the Staff of Mad"; r/Mad #35-40 42 84 126 265 445 625
3(1960)-Has 20x30" campaign poster "Alfred E. Neuman for President"; r/Mad #41-46 17 34 51 122 236 350
4(1961)-Sunday comics section; r/Mad #47-54 16 32 48 116 223 330
5(1962)-Has 33-1/3 record; r/Mad #55-62 23 46 69 166 321 475
6(1963)-Has 33-1/3 record; r/Mad #63-70 23 46 69 166 321 475
7(1964)-Mad protest signs; r/Mad #71-76 10 20 30 73 129 185
8(1965)-Build a Mad Zeppelin 11 22 33 80 145 210
9(1966)-33-1/3 rpm record; Beatles on-c 16 32 48 113 217 320
10(1967)-Mad bumper sticker 7 14 21 47 76 105
11(1968)-Mad cover window stickers 6 12 18 43 69 95
12(1969)-Mad picture postcards; Orlando-a 6 12 18 43 69 95

NOTE: *Covers: Bob Clarke-#8. Mingo-#7, 9-12.*

WOTALIFE COMICS (Formerly Nutty Life #2; Phantom Lady #13 on)
Fox Features Syndicate/Norlen Mag.: No. 3, Aug-Sept, 1946 - No. 12, July, 1947; 1959

3-Cosmo Cat, Li'l Pan, others begin 11 22 33 60 83 105
4-12-Cosmo Cat, Li'l Pan in all 9 18 27 47 61 75
1(1959-Norlen)-Atomic Rabbit, Atomic Mouse; reprints cover to #6; reprints entire book? 8 16 24 40 50 60

WOTALIFE COMICS
Green Publications: 1957 - No. 5, 1957

1 7 14 21 35 43 50
2-5 5 10 15 22 26 30

WOW COMICS ("Wow, What A Magazine!" on cover of first issue)
Henle Publishing Co.: July, 1936 - No. 4, Nov, 1936 (52 pgs., magazine size)

1-Buck Jones in "The Phantom Rider" (1st app. in comics), Fu Manchu; Capt. Scott Dalton begins; Will Eisner-a (1st in comics); Baily-a(1); Briefer-c 300 600 900 1950 3375 4800
2-Ken Maynard, Fu Manchu, Popeye by Segar plus article on Popeye; Eisner-a 203 406 609 1289 2220 3150
3-Eisner-c/a(3); Popeye by Segar, Fu Manchu, Hiram Hick by Bob Kane, Space Limited app.; Jimmy Dempsey talks about Popeye's punch; Bob Ripley Believe it or Not begins; Briefer-a 190 380 570 1207 2079 2950
4-Flash Gordon by Raymond, Mandrake, Popeye by Segar, Tillie The Toiler, Fu Manchu, Hiram Hick by Bob Kane; Eisner-a(3); Briefer-c/a 237 474 711 1505 2590 3675

WOW COMICS (Real Western Hero #70 on)(See XMas Comics)
Fawcett Publ.: Winter, 1940-41; No. 2, Summer, 1941 - No. 69, Fall, 1948

nn(#1)-Origin Mr. Scarlet by S&K; Atom Blake, Boy Wizard, Jim Dolan, & Rick O'Shay begin; Diamond Jack, The White Rajah, & Shipwreck Roberts, only app.; 1st mention of Gotham City in comics; the cover was printed on unstable paper stock and is rarely found in fine or mint condition; blank inside-c; bondage-c by Beck 1350 2700 4050 10,400 18,700 27,000
2 (Scarce)-The Hunchback begins 290 580 870 1856 3178 4500
3 (Fall, 1941) 116 232 348 742 1271 1800
4-Origin & 1st app. Pinky 119 238 357 762 1306 1850
5 71 142 213 454 777 1100
6-Origin & 1st app. The Phantom Eagle (7/15/42); Commando Yank begins 71 142 213 454 777 1100
7,8,10: 10-Swayze-c/a on Mary Marvel 61 122 183 390 670 950
9 (1/6/43)-Capt. Marvel, Capt. Marvel Jr., Shazam app.; Scarlet & Pinky x-over; Mary Marvel-c/stories begin (cameo #9) 168 336 504 1075 1838 2600
11-17,19,20: 15-Flag-c 47 94 141 296 503 710
18-1st app. Uncle Marvel (10/43); infinity-c 49 98 147 309 522 735
21-30: 23-Robot-c. 28-Pinky x-over in Mary Marvel 31 62 93 182 296 410
31-40: 32-68-Phantom Eagle by Swayze 22 44 66 128 209 290
41-50 20 40 60 120 195 270
51-58: Last Mary Marvel 20 40 60 114 182 250
59-69: 59-Ozzie (teenage) begins. 62-Flying Saucer gag-c (1/48). 65-69-Tom Mix stories (cont'd in Real Western Hero) 18 36 54 105 165 225

NOTE: *Cover features: Mr. Scarlet-#1-5; Commando Yank-#6, 7, (w/Mr. Scarlet #8); Mary Marvel-#9-56, (w/Commando Yank-#46-50), (w/Mr. Scarlet & Commando Yank-#51), (w/Mr. Scarlet & Pinky #53), (w/Phantom*

WWE Heroes #1 © WWE

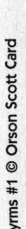

Wyrms #1 © Orson Scott Card

X-Babies #3 © MAR

GD 2.0	VG 4.0	FN 6.0	VF 8.0	VF/NM 9.0	NM- 9.2

Eagle #54, 56), (w/Commando Yank & Phantom Eagle #58); Ozzie-#59-69.

WRAITHBORN
DC Comics (WildStorm): Nov, 2005 - No. 6, July, 2006 ($2.99, limited series)

1-6-Marcia Chen & Joe Benitez-s/a 3.00
TPB (2007, $19.99) r/series; sketch pages and unused cover sketches 20.00

WRATH (Also see Prototype #4)
Malibu Comics: Jan, 1994 - No. 9, Nov, 1995 ($1.95)

1-9: 2-Mantra x-over. 3-Intro/1st app. Slayer. 4,5-Freex app. 8-Mantra & Warstrike app. 9-Prime app. 2.50
1-Ultra 5000 Limited silver foil 4.00
Giant Size 1 (2.50, 44 pgs.) 2.50

WRATH OF THE SPECTRE, THE
DC Comics: May, 1988 - No. 4, Aug, 1988 ($2.50, limited series)

1-3: Aparo-r/Adventure #431-440 5.00
4-Three scripts intended for Adventure #441-on, but not drawn by Aparo until 1988 6.00
TPB (2005, $19.99) r/series; Peter Sanderson intro. 20.00

WRECK OF GROSVENOR (See Superior Stories #3)

WRETCH, THE
Caliber: 1996 ($2.95, B&W)

1-Phillip Hester-a/scripts 3.00

WRETCH, THE
Amaze Ink: 1997 - No. 4, 1998 ($2.95, B&W)

1-4-Phillip Hester-a/scripts 3.00
... Vol. 1: Everyday Doomsday (4/03, $13.95) 14.00

WRINGLE WRANGLE (Disney)
Dell Publishing Co.: No. 821, July, 1957

Four Color 821-Based on movie "Westward Ho, the Wagons"; Marsh-a; Fess Parker photo-c 8 16 24 52 86 120

WULF THE BARBARIAN
Atlas/Seaboard Publ.: Feb, 1975 - No. 4, Sept, 1975

1,2: 1-Origin; Janson-a. 2-Intro. Berithe the Swordswoman; Janson-a w/Neal Adams, Wood, Reese-a assists 2 4 6 8 11 14
3,4: 3-Skeates-s. 4-Friedrich-s 2 3 4 6 8 10

WWE HEROES (WWE Wrestling)
Titan Comics: Apr, 2010 - Present ($3.99)

1-Two covers by Andy Smith and Liam Sharp 4.00

WYATT EARP
Atlas Comics/Marvel No. 23 on (IPC): Nov, 1955 - #29, June, 1960; #30, Oct, 1972 - #34, June, 1973

1 21 42 63 122 199 275
2-Williamson-a (4 pgs.) 14 28 42 76 108 140
3-6,8-11: 3-Black Bart app. 8-Wild Bill Hickok app. 11 22 33 60 83 105
7,12-Williamson-a, 4 pgs. ea.; #12 with Mayo 11 22 33 60 83 105
13-20: 17-1st app. Wyatt's deputy, Grizzly Grant 10 20 30 54 72 90
21-Davis-c 9 18 27 50 65 80
22-24,26-29: 22-Ringo Kid app. 23-Kid From Texas app. 29-Last 10¢ issue 8 16 24 42 54 65
25-Davis-a 8 16 24 44 57 70
30-Williamson-r (1972) 2 4 6 13 18 22
31-34-Reprints. 32-Torres-a(r) 2 4 6 9 13 16

NOTE: ***Ayers** a-8, 10(2), 17, 20(4), 26(5). **Berg** a-9. **Everett** c-6. **Kirby** c-25, 29. **Maneely** a-1; c-1-4, 8, 12, 17, 20. **Maurer** a-2(2), 3(4), 4(4), 8(4). **Severin** a-4, 9(4), 10; c-2, 9, 10, 14. **Wildey** a-5, 17, 24, 28.*

WYATT EARP (TV) (Hugh O'Brian Famous Marshal)
Dell Publishing Co.: No. 860, Nov, 1957 - No. 13, Dec-Feb, 1960-61 (Hugh O'Brian photo-c)

Four Color 860 (#1)-Manning-a 9 18 27 65 113 160
Four Color 890,921(6/58)-All Manning-a 7 14 21 49 80 110
4 (9-11/58) - 12-Manning-a. 4-Variant edition exists with back-c comic strip; Russ Manning-a. 5-Photo back-c 6 12 18 37 59 80
13-Toth-a 6 12 18 39 62 85

WYATT EARP FRONTIER MARSHAL (Formerly Range Busters) (Also see Blue Bird)
Charlton Comics: No. 12, Jan, 1956 - No. 72, Dec, 1967

12 9 18 27 47 61 75
13-19 6 12 18 31 38 45
20-(68 pgs.)-Williamson-a(4), 8,5,5,& 7 pgs. 10 20 30 54 72 90
21-(100 pgs.) Mastroserio, Maneely, Severin-a (signed LePoer) 5 10 15 32 51 70
22-30 3 6 9 16 23 30
31-50 2 4 6 12 16 20
51-72 (1967) 2 4 6 9 11 14

GD 2.0	VG 4.0	FN 6.0	VF 8.0	VF/NM 9.0	NM- 9.2

WYNONNA EARP
Image Comics (WildStorm Productions): Dec, 1996 - No. 5, Apr, 1997 ($2.50)

1-5-Smith-s/Chin-a 2.50

WYNONNA EARP: HOME ON THE STRANGE
IDW Publishing: Dec, 2003 - No. 3, Feb, 2004 ($3.99)

1-3-Smith-s/Ferreira-a 4.00

WYRMS
Marvel Comics (Dabel Brothers): Feb, 2007 - No. 6, Jan, 2008 ($2.99)

1-6-Orson Scott Card & Jake Black-s. 1-3-Batista-a 3.00
TPB (2008, $14.99) r/#1-6 15.00

X (Comics' Greatest World: X #1 only) (Also see Comics' Greatest World & Dark Horse Comics #8)
Dark Horse Comics: Feb, 1994 - No. 25, Apr, 1996 ($2.00/$2.50)

1-25: 3-Pit Bulls x-over. 8 -Ghost-c & app. 18-Miller-c.; Predator app. 19-22-Miller-c. 2.50
Hero Illustrated Special #1,2 (1994, $1.00, 20 pgs.) 2.50
One Shot to the Head (1994, $2.50, 36 pgs.)-Miller-c. 2.50

NOTE: ***Miller** c-18-22. **Quesada** c-6. **Russell** a-6.*

XANADU COLOR SPECIAL
Eclipse Comics: Dec, 1988 ($2.00, one-shot)

1-Continued from Thoughts & Images 2.50

XAVIER INSTITUTE ALUMNI YEARBOOK (See X-Men titles)
Marvel Comics: Dec, 1996 ($5.95, square-bound, one-shot)

1-Text w/art by various 6.00

X-BABIES
Marvel Comics: Dec, 2009 - No. 4, Mar, 2010 ($3.99, limited series)

1-4-Schigiel-s/Chabot-a; Skottie Young 4.00
...: Murderama (8/98, $2.95) J.J. Kirby-a 3.50
...: Reborn (1/00, $3.50) J.J. Kirby-a 3.50

X-CALIBRE
Marvel Comics: Mar, 1995 - No. 4, July, 1995 ($1.95, limited series)

1-4-Age of Apocalypse 2.50

XENA (TV)
Dynamite Entertainment: 2006 - 2007 ($3.50)

1-4-Three covers on each; Neves-a/Layman-s 3.50
Vol. 2 #1-4-(Dark Xena) Four covers; Salonga-a/Layman-s 3.50
Annual 1 (2007, $4.95) Three covers; Salonga-a/Champagne-s 5.00
... Vol. 2: Dark Xena TPB (2007, $14.99) r/Vol. 2 #1-4; variant cover gallery 15.00

XENA / ARMY OF DARKNESS: WHAT...AGAIN?!
Dynamite Entertainment: 2008 - No. 4, 2009 ($3.50, limited series)

1-4-Xena, Gabrielle, & Autolycus team up with Ash; Montenegro-a; two covers on each 3.50

XENA: WARRIOR PRINCESS (TV)
Topps Comics: Aug, 1997 - No. 0, Oct, 1997 ($2.95)

1-Two stories by various; J. Scott Campbell-c 1 3 4 6 8 10
1,2-Photo-c 1 3 4 6 8 10
2-Stevens-c 6.00
0-(10/97)-Lopresti-c, 0-(10/97)-Photo-c 1 2 3 5 6 8
...First Appearance Collection ('97, $9.95) r/Hercules the Legendary Journeys #3-5 and 5-page story from TV Guide 10.00

XENA: WARRIOR PRINCESS (TV)
Dark Horse Comics: Sept, 1999 - No. 14, Oct, 2000 ($2.95/$2.99)

1-14: 1-Mignola-c and photo-c. 2,3-Bradstreet-c & photo-c 3.00

XENA: WARRIOR PRINCESS AND THE ORIGINAL OLYMPICS (TV)
Topps Comics: Jun, 1998 - No. 3, Aug, 1998 ($2.95, limited series)

1-3-Regular and Photo-c; Lim-a/T&M Bierbaum-s 3.00

XENA: WARRIOR PRINCESS-BLOODLINES (TV)
Topps Comics: May, 1998 - No. 2, June, 1998 ($2.95, limited series)

1,2-Lopresti-s/c/a. 2-Reg. and photo-c 3.00
1-Bath photo-c, 1-American Ent. Ed. 4.00

XENA: WARRIOR PRINCESS / JOXER: WARRIOR PRINCE (TV)
Topps Comics: Nov, 1997 - No. 3, Jan, 1998 ($2.95, limited series)

1-3-Regular and Photo-c; Lim-a/T&M Bierbaum-s 3.00

Xena: Warrior Princess and the Original Olympics #1 © Studio USA

X-Factor (2006 series) #32 © MAR

X-Files #25 © 20th Century Fox

	GD 2.0	VG 4.0	FN 6.0	VF 8.0	VF/NM 9.0	NM- 9.2

XENA: WARRIOR PRINCESS-THE DRAGON'S TEETH (TV)
Topps Comics: Dec, 1997 - No. 3, Feb, 1998 ($2.95, limited series)
1-3-Regular and Photo-c; Teranishi-a/Thomas-s 3.00

XENA: WARRIOR PRINCESS-THE ORPHEUS TRILOGY (TV)
Topps Comics: Mar, 1998 - No. 3, May, 1998 ($2.95, limited series)
1-3-Regular and Photo-c; Teranishi-a/T&M Bierbaum-s 3.00

XENA: WARRIOR PRINCESS VS. CALLISTO (TV)
Topps Comics: Feb, 1998 - No. 3, Apr, 1998 ($2.95, limited series)
1-3-Regular and Photo-c; Morgan-a/Thomas-s 3.00

XENOBROOD
DC Comics: No. 0, Oct, 1994 - No. 6, Apr, 1995 ($1.50, limited series)
0-6: 0-Indicia says "Xenobroods" 2.50

XENON
Eclipse Comics: Dec, 1987 - No. 23, Nov. 1, 1988 ($1.50, B&W, bi-weekly)
1-23 2.50

XENOZOIC TALES (Also see Cadillacs & Dinosaurs, Death Rattle #8)
Kitchen Sink Press: Feb, 1986 - No. 14, Oct, 1996
1-Mark Schultz-s/a in all 1 3 4 6 8 10
1(2nd printing)(1/89) 3.00
2-14 5.00
Volume 1 ($14.95) r/#1-6 & Death Rattle #8 15.00
Volume 2 (5/03, $14.95, TPB) B&W r/#7-14; intro by Frank Cho 15.00

XENYA
Sanctuary Press: Apr, 1994 - No. 3 ($2.95)
1-3: 1-Hildebrandt-c; intro Xenya 3.00

XERO
DC Comics: May, 1997 - No. 12, Apr, 1998 ($1.75)
1-7 2.50
8-12 2.50

X-FACTOR (Also see The Avengers #263, Fantastic Four #286 and Mutant X)
Marvel Comics Group: Feb, 1986 - No. 149, Sept, 1998
1-($1.25, 52 pgs)-Story recaps 1st app. from Avengers #263; story cont'd from F.F. #286; return of original X-Men (now X-Factor); Guice/Layton-a; Baby Nathan app. (2nd after X-Men #201) 6.00
2-4 4.00
5-1st brief app. Apocalypse (2 pages) 5.00
6-1st full app. Apocalypse 2 4 6 8 10 12
7-10: 10-Sabretooth app. (11/86, 3 pgs.) cont'd in X-Men #212; 1st app. in an X-Men comic book 4.00
11-22: 13-Baby Nathan app. in flashback. 14-Cyclops vs. The Master Mold. 15-Intro wingless Angel 3.00
23-1st brief app. Archangel (2 pages) 1 2 3 4 5 7
24-1st full app. Archangel (now in Uncanny X-Men); Fall Of The Mutants begins; origin Apocalypse 1 2 3 5 7 9
25,26: Fall Of The Mutants; 26-New outfits 3.00
27-39,41-83,87-91,93-99,101: 35-Origin Cyclops. 38,50-(52 pgs.): 50-Liefeld/McFarlane-c. 51-53-Sabretooth app. 52-Liefeld-c(p). 54-Intro Crimson; Silvestri-c/a(p). 60-X-Tinction Agenda x-over; New Mutants (w/Cable) x-over in #60-62; Wolverine in #62. 60-Gold ink 2nd printing. 61,62-X-Tinction Agenda. 62-Jim Lee-c. 63-Portacio/Thibert-c/a(p) begins, ends #69. 65-68-Lee co-plots. 65-The Apocalypse Files begins, ends #68. 66,67-Baby Nathan app. 67-Inhumans app. 68-Baby Nathan is sent into future to save his life. 69,70-X-Men(w/Wolverine) x-over. 71-New team begins (Havok, Polaris, Strong Guy, Wolfsbane & Madrox); Stroman-c/a begins. 71-2nd printing ($1.25). 75-(52 pgs.). 77-Cannonball (of X-Force) app. 87-Quesada-c/a(p) in monthly comic begins,ends #92. 88-1st app. Random 2.50
40-Rob Liefield-c/a (4/89, 1st at Marvel?) 3.00
84-86 -Jae Lee a(p); 85,86-Jae Lee-c. Polybagged with trading card in each; X-Cutioner's Song x-overs. 3.00
92-($3.50, 68 pgs.)-Wraparound-c by Quesada w/Havok hologram on-c; begin X-Men 30th anniversary issues; Quesada-a. 5.00
92-2nd printing 2.50
100-($2.95, 52 pgs.)-Embossed foil-c; Multiple Man dies. 5.00
100-($1.75, 52 pgs.)-Regular edition 2.50
102-105,107: 102-bound-in card sheet 2.50
106-($2.00)-Newsstand edition 2.50
106-($2.95)-Collectors edition 3.00
108-124,126-148: 112-Return from Age of Apocalypse. 115-card insert. 119-123-Sabretooth app. 123-Hound app. 124-w/Onslaught Update. 126-Onslaught x-over; Beast vs. Dark Beast. 128-w/card insert; return of Multiple Man. 130-Assassination of Grayson Creed. 146,148-Moder-a 2.50
125-($2.95)-"Onslaught"; Post app.; return of Havok 4.00
149-Last issue 3.00
#(-1) Flashback (7/97) Matsuda-a 2.50
Annual 1-9: 1-(10/86-'94, 68 pgs.) 3-Evolutionary War x-over. 4-Atlantis Attacks; Byrne/Simonson-a;Byrne-c. 5-Fantastic Four, New Mutants x-over; Keown 2 pg. pin-up. 6-New Warriors app.; 5th app. X-Force cont'd from X-Men Annual #15. 7-1st Quesada-a(p) on X-Factor plus-c(p). 8-Bagged w/trading card. 9-Austin-a(i) 3.00
...Prisoner of Love (1990, $4.95, 52 pgs.)-Starlin scripts; Guice-a 5.00
... Visionaries: Peter David Vol. 1 TPB (2005, $15.99) r/#71-75 16.00
... Visionaries: Peter David Vol. 2 TPB (2007, $15.99) r/#76-78 & Incr. Hulk #390-392 16.00
... Visionaries: Peter David Vol. 3 TPB (2007, $15.99) r/#79-83 & Annual #7 16.00
NOTE: ***Art Adams*** *a-41p, 42p.* ***Buckler*** *a-50p.* ***Liefeld*** *a-40; c-40, 50i, 52p.* ***McFarlane*** *c-50i.* ***Mignola*** *c-70.* ***Brandon Peterson*** *a-78p(part).* ***Whilce Portacio*** *c/a(p)-63-69.* ***Quesada*** *a(p)-87-92, Annual 7. c(p)-78, 79, 82, Annual 7.* ***Simonson*** *c/a-10, 11, 13-15, 17-19, 21, 23-31, 33, 34, 36-39; c-12, 16.* ***Paul Smith*** *a-44-48; c-43.* ***Stroman*** *a(p)-71-75, 77, 78(part), 80, 81; c(p)-71-77, 80, 81, 84.* ***Zeck*** *c-2.*

X-FACTOR (Volume 2)
Marvel Comics: June, 2002 - No. 4, Oct, 2002 ($2.50)
1-4: Jensen-s/Ranson-a. 1-Phillips-c. 2,3-Edwards-c 2.50

X-FACTOR
Marvel Comics: Jan, 2006 - Present ($2.99)
1-24: 1-Peter David-s/Ryan Sook-a. 8,9-Civil War. 21-24-Endangered Species back-up 3.00
25-49: 25-27-Messiah Complex x-over; Finch-c. 26-2nd printing with new Eaton-c 3.00
50-(12/09, $3.99) Madrox in the future; DeLandro-a/Yardin-c 4.00
200-(2/10, $4.99) Resumes original series numbering; 3 covers; Fantastic Four app. 5.00
201-203-($2.99) 201,202-Dr. Doom and the Fantastic Four app. 3.00
... Special: Layla Miller (10/08, $3.99) David-s/DeLandro-a 4.00
...: The Quick and the Dead (7/08, $2.99) Raimondi-a; Quicksilver regains powers 3.00
...: The Longest Night HC (2006, $19.99, dust jacket) r/#1-6; sketch pages by Sook 20.00
...: The Longest Night SC (2007, $14.99) r/#1-6; sketch pages by Sook 15.00
...: Life and Death Matters HC (2007, $19.99, dust jacket) r/#7-12 20.00
...: Life and Death Matters SC (2007, $14.99) r/#7-12 15.00
...: The Many Lives of Madrox SC (2007, $14.99) r/#13-17 15.00
...: Heart of Ice HC (2007, $19.99, dust jacket) r/#18-24 20.00
...: Heart of Ice SC (2008, $17.99, dust jacket) r/#18-24 18.00

X-51 (Machine Man)
Marvel Comics: Sept, 1999 - No. 12, Jul, 2000 ($1.99/$2.50)
1-7: 1-Joe Bennett-a. 2-Two covers 2.50
8-12: 8-Begin $2.50-c 2.50
Wizard #0 2.50

X-FILES, THE (TV)
Topps Comics: Jan, 1995 - No. 41, July, 1998 ($2.50)
-2(9/96)-Black-c; r/X-Files Magazine #1&2 1 3 4 6 8 10
-1(9/96)-Silver-c; r/Hero Illustrated Giveaway 1 3 4 6 8 10
0-($3.95)-Adapts pilot episode 4.00
0-"Mulder" variant-c 1 2 3 5 6 8
0-"Scully" variant-c 1 2 3 5 6 8
1/2-W/certificate 3 6 9 14 20 25
1-New stories based on the TV show; direct market & newsstand editions; Miran Kim-c on all 3 6 9 16 23 30
2 2 4 6 10 14 18
3,4 1 2 3 5 6 8
5-10 4.00
11-41: 11-Begin $2.95-c. 21-W/bound-in card. 40,41-Reg. & photo-c 3.00
Annual 1,2 ($3.95) 4.00
Afterflight TPB ($5.95) Art by Thompson, Saviuk, Kim 6.00
Collection 1 TPB ($19.95)-r/#1-6. 20.00
Collection 2 TPB ($19.95)-r/#7-12, Annual #1. 20.00
...Fight the Future ('98, $5.95) Movie adaptation 6.00
Hero Illustrated Giveaway (3/95) 2 4 6 9 12 15
Special Edition 1-5 ($4.95)-r/#1-3, 4-6, 7-9, 10-12, 13, Annual 1 5.00
Star Wars Galaxy Magazine Giveaway (B&W) 1 3 4 6 8 10
Trade paperback ($19.95) 20.00
Volume 1 TPB (Checker Books, 2005, $19.95) r/#13-17, #0, Season One: Squeeze 20.00
Volume 2 TPB (Checker Books, 2005, $19.95) r/#18-24, #1/2, Comics Digest #1 20.00
Volume 3 TPB (Checker Books, 2006, $19.95) r/#23-26, Fire, Ice, Hero Ill. Giveaway 20.00

X-FILES, THE (TV)
DC Comics (WildStorm): No. 0, Sept, 2008 - No. 6, Jun, 2009 ($3.99/$3.50)
0-($3.99) Spotnitz-s/Denham-a; photo-c 4.00
1-6-($3.50) 1-Spotnitz-s/Denham-a; 2 covers. 4-Wolfman-s 3.50
TPB (2009, $19.99) r/#0-6 20.00

X-Force (2008) #9 © MAR

X-Man #50 © MAR

X-Men #14 © MAR

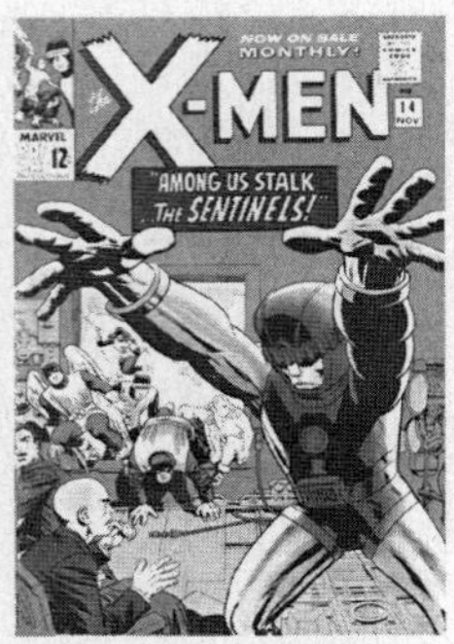

	GD	VG	FN	VF	VF/NM	NM-
	2.0	4.0	6.0	8.0	9.0	9.2

X-FILES COMICS DIGEST, THE
Topps Comics: Dec, 1995 - No. 3 ($3.50, quarterly, digest-size)

1-3: 1,2: New X-Files stories w/Ray Bradbury Comics-r 4.00
NOTE: *Adlard a-1, 2. Jack Davis a-2r. Russell a-1r.*

X-FILES, THE: GROUND ZERO (TV)
Topps Comics: Nov, 1997 - No. 4, March, 1998 ($2.95, limited series)

1-4-Adaptation of the Kevin J. Anderson novel 3.00

X-FILES, THE: SEASON ONE (TV)
Topps Comics: July, 1997 - July, 1998 ($4.95, adaptations of TV episodes)

1,2,Squeeze, Conduit, Ice, Space, Fire, Beyond the Sea, Shadows 5.00

X-FORCE (Becomes X-Statix) (Also see The New Mutants #100)
Marvel Comics: Aug, 1991 - No. 129, Aug, 2002 ($1.00-$2.25)

1-($1.50, 52 pgs.)-Polybagged with 1 of 5 diff. Marvel Universe trading cards inside (1 each); 6th app. of X-Force; Liefeld-c/a begins 4.00
1-1st printing with Cable trading card inside 5.00
1-2nd printing; metallic ink-c (no bag or card) 2.50
2-4: 2-Deadpool-c/story. 3-New Brotherhood of Evil Mutants app. 4-Spider-Man x-over; cont'd from Spider-Man #16; reads sideways 3.00
5-10: 6-Last $1.00-c. 7,9-Weapon X back-ups. 8-Intro The Wild Pack (Cable, Kane, Domino, Hammer, G.W. Bridge, & Grizzly); Liefeld-c/a (4); Mignola-a. 10-Weapon X full-length story (part 3). 11-1st Weapon Prime; Deadpool-c/story 3.00
11-15,19-24,26-33: 15-Cable leaves X-Force 2.50
16-18-Polybagged w/trading card in each; X-Cutioner's Song x-overs 3.00
25-($3.50, 52 pgs.)-Wraparound-c w/Cable hologram on-c; Cable returns 4.00
34-37,39-45: 34-bound-in card sheet 2.50
38,40-43: 38-($2.00)-Newsstand edition. 40-43 ($1.95)-Deluxe edition 2.50
38-($2.95)-Collectors edition (prismatic) 5.00
44-49,51-67: 44-Return from Age of Apocalypse. 45-Sabretooth app. 49-Sebastian Shaw app. 52-Blob app., Onslaught cameo. 55-Vs. S.H.I.E.L.D. 56-Deadpool app. 57-Mr. Sinister & X-Man-c/app. 57,58-Onslaught x-over. 59-W/card insert; return of Longshot. 60-Dr. Strange 2.50
50 ($3.95)-Gatefold wrap-around foil-c 4.00
50 ($3.95)-Liefeld variant-c 5.00
68-74: 68-Operation Zero Tolerance 2.50
75,100-($2.99): 75-Cannonball-c/app. 3.00
76-99,101,102: 81-Pollina poster. 95-Magneto-c. 102-Ellis-s/Portacio-a 2.50
103-115: 103-Begin $2.25-c; Portacio-a thru #106. 115-Death of old team 2.25
116-New team debuts; Allred-c/a; Milligan-s; no Comics Code stamp on-c 4.00
117-129: 117-Intro. Mr. Sensitive. 120-Wolverine-c/app. 123-'Nuff Said issue. 124-Darwyn Cooke-a/c. 128-Death of U-Go Girl. 129-Fegredo-a 2.50
#(-1) Flashback (7/97) story of John Proudstar; Pollina-a 2.50
Annual 1-3 ('92-'94, 68 pgs.)-1-1st Greg Capullo-a(p) on X-Force. 2-Polybagged w/trading card; intro X-Treme & Neurtap 3.00
...And Cable '95 (12/95, $3.95)-Impossible Man app. 4.00
...And Cable '96, ...'97 ('96, 7/97) -'96-Wraparound-c 3.00
...And Spider-Man: Sabotage nn (11/92, $6.95)-Reprints X-Force #3,4 & Spider-Man #16 7.00
.../ Champions '98 ($3.50) 3.50
Annual 99 ($3.50) 3.50
...: Famous, Mutant & Mortal HC (2003, $29.99) oversized r/#116-129; foreward by Milligan; gallery of covers and pin-ups; script for #123 30.00
...New Beginnings TPB (10/01, $14.95) r/#116-120 15.00
...Rough Cut ($2.99) Pencil pages and script for #102 3.00
...Youngblood (8/96, $4.95)-Platt-c 5.00
NOTE: *Capullo a(p)-15-25, Annual 1; c(p)-14-27. Rob Liefeld a-1-7, 9p; c-1-9, 11p; plots-1-12. Mignola a-8p.*

X-FORCE
Marvel Comics: Oct, 2004 - No. 6, Mar, 2005 ($2.99, limited series)

1-6-Liefeld-c/a; Nicieza-s. 5,6-Wolverine & The Thing app. 3.00
X-Force & Cable Vol. 1: The Legend Returns (2005, $14.99) r/#1-6 15.00

X-FORCE
Marvel Comics: Apr, 2008 - Present ($2.99)

1-Crain-a; Wolverine & X-23 app.; two covers (regular and bloody) by Crain on #1-5 4.00
2-21,23-25: 2,3-Bastion app. 4-6-Archangel app. 7-10-Choi-a. 9-11-Ghost Rider app. 3.00
22-($3.99) Necrosha x-over; Crain-a 4.00
...Annual 1 (2/10, $3.99) Kirkman-s/Pearson-a/c; Deadpool back-up w/Barberi-a 4.00
.../Cable: Messiah War 1 (5/09, $3.99) Choi-a; covers by Andrews and Choi 4.00
... Special: Ain't No Dog (8/08, $3.99) Huston-s/Palo-a; Dell'Edera-a; Hitch-c 4.00

X-FORCE MEGAZINE
Marvel Comics: Nov, 1996 ($3.95, one-shot)

1-Reprints 4.00

X-FORCE: SHATTERSTAR
Marvel Comics: Apr, 2005 - No. 4, July, 2005 ($2.99, limited series)

1-4-Liefeld-c/s; Michaels-a 3.00
TPB (2005, $15.99) r/#1-4 & New Mutants #99,100 16.00

X-INFERNUS
Marvel Comics: Feb, 2009 - No. 4, May, 2009 ($3.99, limited series)

1-4-Illyana Rasputin in Limbo; Cebulski-s/Camuncoli-a/Finch-c 4.00

XIN: JOURNEY OF THE MONKEY KING
Anarchy Studios: May, 2003 - No. 3, July, 2003 ($2.99)

Preview Edition (Apr, 2003, $1.99) Flip book w/ Vampi Vicious Preview Edition 2.50
1-3-Kevin Lau-a. 1-Three covers by Lau, Park and Nauck. 2-Three covers 3.00

XIN: LEGEND OF THE MONKEY KING
Anarchy Studios: Nov, 2002 - No. 3, Jan, 2003 ($2.99)

Preview Edition (Summer 2002, Diamond Dateline supplement) 2.50
1-3-Kevin Lau-a. 1-Two covers by Lau & Madureira. 2-Two covers by Lau & Oeming 3.00
TPB (10/03, $12.95) r/#1-3; cover gallery and sketch pages 13.00

X-MAN (Also see X-Men Omega & X-Men Prime)
Marvel Comics: Mar, 1995 - No. 75, May, 2001 ($1.95/$1.99/$2.25)

1-Age of Apocalypse 5.00
1-2nd print 2.50
2-4,25: 25-($2.99)-Wraparound-c 3.00
5-24, 26-28: 5-Post Age of Apocalypse stories begin. 5-7-Madelyne Pryor app. 10-Professor X app. 12-vs. Excalibur. 13-Marauders, Cable app. 14-Vs. Cable; Onslaught app. 15-17-Vs. Holocaust. 17-w/Onslaught Update. 18-Onslaught x-over; X-Force-c/app; Marauders app. 19-Onslaught x-over. 20-Abomination-c/app.; w/card insert. 23-Bishop app. 24-Spider-Man, Morbius-c/app. 27-Re-appearance of Aurora(Alpha Flight) 2.50
29-49,51-62: 29-Operation Zero Tolerance. 37,38-Spider-Man-c/app. 56-Spider-Man app. 2.50
50-($2.99) Crossover with Generation X #50 3.00
63-74: 63-Ellis & Grant-s/Olivetti-a begins. 64-Begin $2.25-c 2.50
75 ($2.99) Final issue; Alcatena-a 3.00
#(-1) Flashback (7/97) 2.50
...'96, ...'97-($2.95)-Wraparound-c; '96-Age of Apocalypse 3.00
...: All Saints' Day ('97, $5.99) Dodson-a 6.00
.../Hulk '98 ($2.99) Wraparound-c; Thanos app. 3.00

XMAS COMICS
Fawcett Publications: 12?/1941 - No. 2, 12?/1942; (50¢, 324 pgs.)
No. 7, 12?/1947 (25¢, 132 pgs.)(#3-6 do not exist)

	GD	VG	FN	VF	VF/NM	NM-
1-Contains Whiz #21, Capt. Marvel #3, Bulletman #2, Wow #3, & Master #18; front & back-c by Raboy. Not rebound, remaindered comics; printed at same time as originals	400	800	1200	2800	4900	7000
2-Capt. Marvel, Bulletman, Spy Smasher	168	336	504	1075	1838	2600
7-Funny animals (Hoppy, Billy the Kid & Oscar)	65	130	195	416	708	1000

XMAS COMICS
Fawcett Publications: No. 4, Dec, 1949 - No. 7, Dec, 1952 (50¢, 196 pgs.)

	GD	VG	FN	VF	VF/NM	NM-
4-Contains Whiz, Master, Tom Mix, Captain Marvel, Nyoka, Capt. Video, Bob Colt, Monte Hale, Hot Rod Comics, & Battle Stories. Not rebound, remaindered comics; printed at the same time as originals. Stocking on cover is made of green or red felt	71	142	213	454	777	1100
5-7-Same as above. 5- Red felt on-c. 7-Bill Boyd app.; stocking on cover is made of green felt (novelty cover)	55	110	165	352	601	850

X-MEN, THE (See Adventures of Cyclops and Phoenix, Amazing Adventures, Archangel, Brotherhood, Capt. America #172, Classic X-Men, Exiles, Further Adventures of Cyclops & Phoenix, Gambit, Giant-Size..., Heroes For Hope..., Kitty Pryde & Wolverine, Marvel & DC Present, Marvel Collector's Edition:..., Marvel Fanfare, Marvel Graphic Novel, Marvel Super Heroes, Marvel Team-Up, Marvel Triple Action, The Marvel X-Men Collection, New Mutants, Nightcrawler, Official Marvel Index To..., Rogue, Special Edition..., Ultimate..., Uncanny..., Wolverine, X-Factor, X-Force, X-Terminators)

X-MEN, THE (1st series)(Becomes Uncanny X-Men at #142)(The X-Men #1-93; X-Men #94-141) (The Uncanny X-Men on-c only #114-141)
Marvel Comics Group: Sept, 1963 - No. 66, Mar, 1970; No. 67, Dec, 1970 - No. 141, Jan, 1981

	GD	VG	FN	VF	VF/NM	NM-
1-Origin/1st app. X-Men (Angel, Beast, Cyclops, Iceman & Marvel Girl); 1st app. Magneto & Professor X	850	1700	2550	8000	17,000	26,000
2-1st app. The Vanisher	154	308	462	1348	2674	4000
3-1st app. The Blob (1/64)	92	184	276	782	1541	2300
4-1st Quicksilver & Scarlet Witch & Brotherhood of the Evil Mutants (3/64); 1st app. Toad; 2nd app. Magneto	94	188	282	799	1575	2350
5-Magneto & Evil Mutants-c/story	64	128	192	544	1072	1600
6,7: 6-Sub-Mariner app. 7-Magneto app.	51	102	153	434	855	1275
8,9,11: 8-1st Unus the Untouchable. 9-Early Avengers app. (1/65); 1st Lucifer. 11-1st app. The Stranger.	42	84	126	336	656	975
10-1st S.A. app. Ka-Zar & Zabu the sabertooth (3/65)	43	86	129	344	672	1000

X-Men #35 © MAR

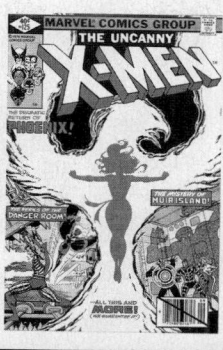

X-Men #125 © MAR

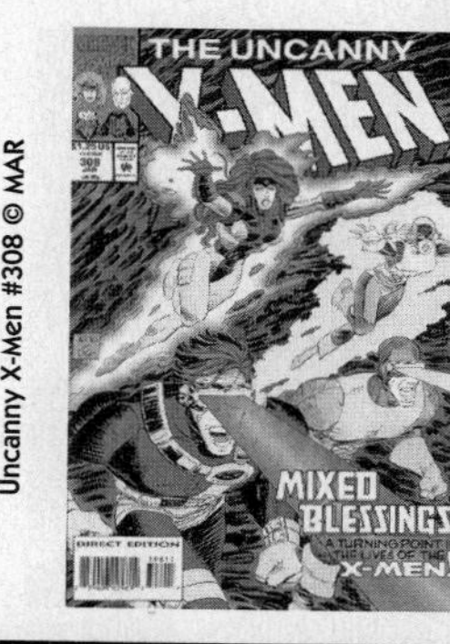

Uncanny X-Men #308 © MAR

	GD 2.0	VG 4.0	FN 6.0	VF 8.0	VF/NM 9.0	NM- 9.2
12-Origin Prof. X; Origin/1st app. Juggernaut	48	96	144	384	742	1100
13-Juggernaut and Human Torch app.	32	64	96	245	473	700
14,15: 14-1st app. Sentinels. 15-Origin Beast	33	66	99	254	490	725
16-20: 19-1st app. The Mimic (4/66)	19	38	57	139	270	400
21-27,29,30: 27-Re-enter The Mimic (r-in #75); Spider-Man cameo	14	28	42	100	188	275
28-1st app. The Banshee (1/67)(r-in #76)	19	38	57	139	270	400
28-2nd printing (1994)	2	4	6	8	10	12
31-34,36,37,39: 34-Adkins-c/a. 39-New costumes	11	22	33	80	145	210
35-Spider-Man x-over (8/67)(r-in #83); 1st app. Changeling	24	48	72	175	338	500
38,40: 38-Origins of the X-Men series begins, ends #57. 40-(1/68) 1st app. Frankenstein's monster at Marvel	12	24	36	83	152	220
41-49: 42-Death of Prof. X (Changeling disguised as). 44-1st S.A. app. G.A. Red Raven. 49-Steranko-c; 1st Polaris	10	20	30	73	129	185
50,51-Steranko-c/a	11	22	33	78	139	200
52	10	20	30	68	119	170
53-Barry Smith-c/a (his 1st comic book work)	11	22	33	78	139	200
54,55-B. Smith-c. 54-1st app. Alex Summers who later becomes Havok. 55-Summers discovers he has mutant powers	11	22	33	78	139	200
56,57,59-63,65-Neal Adams-a(p). 56-Intro Havok w/o costume. 60-1st Sauron. 65-Return of Professor X.	11	22	33	80	145	210
58-1st app. Havok in costume; N. Adams-a(p)	13	26	39	95	178	260
62,63-2nd printings (1994)	2	4	6	8	10	12
64-1st app. Sunfire	11	22	33	78	139	200
66-Last new story w/original X-Men; battles Hulk	12	24	36	85	155	225
67-70: 67-Reprints begin, end #93. 67-70: (52 pgs.)	9	18	27	60	100	140
71-93: 71-Last 15¢ issue. 72: (52 pgs.). 73-86-r/#25-38 w/new-c. 83-Spider-Man-c/story. 87-93-r/#39-45 with covers	8	16	24	52	86	120
94 (8/75)-New X-Men begin (see Giant-Size X-Men for 1st app.); Colossus, Nightcrawler, Thunderbird, Storm, Wolverine, & Banshee join; Angel, Marvel Girl & Iceman resign	70	140	210	550	875	1200
95-Death of Thunderbird	16	32	48	115	220	325
96,97	10	20	30	73	129	185
98,99-(Regular 25¢ edition)(4,6/76)	10	20	30	71	126	180
98,99-(30¢-c variants, limited distribution)	17	34	51	124	242	360
100-Old vs. New X-Men; part origin Phoenix; last 25¢ issue (8/76)	11	22	33	80	145	210
100-(30¢-c variant, limited distribution)	20	40	60	146	283	420
101-Phoenix origin concludes	12	24	36	88	162	235
102-104: 102-Origin Storm. 104-1st brief app. Starjammers; Magneto-c/story	8	16	24	56	93	130
105-107-(Regular 30¢ editions). 106-(8/77)Old vs. New X-Men. 107-1st full app. Starjammers; last 30¢ issue	8	16	24	52	86	120
105-107-(35¢-c variants, limited distribution)	13	26	39	90	165	240
108-Byrne-a begins (see Marvel Team-Up #53)	8	16	24	56	93	130
109-1st app. Weapon Alpha (becomes Vindicator)	8	16	24	52	86	120
110,111: 110-Phoenix joins	6	12	18	43	69	95
112-116	6	12	18	43	69	95
117-119: 117-Origin Professor X	6	12	18	37	59	80
120-1st app. Alpha Flight, story line begins (4/79); 1st app. Vindicator (formerly Weapon Alpha); last 35¢ issue	8	16	24	52	86	120
121-1st full Alpha Flight story	7	14	21	49	80	110
122-128: 123-Spider-Man x-over. 124-Colossus becomes Proletarian	5	10	15	32	51	70
129-Intro Kitty Pryde (1/80); last Banshee; Dark Phoenix saga begins; intro. Emma Frost (White Queen)	6	12	18	39	62	85
130-1st app. The Dazzler by Byrne (2/80)	5	10	15	34	55	75
131-135: 131-Dazzler app.; 1st White Queen-c. 133-Wolverine app. 134-Phoenix becomes Dark Phoenix	5	10	15	32	51	70
136,138: 138-Dazzler app.; Cyclops leaves	4	8	12	28	44	60
137-Giant; death of Phoenix	6	12	18	37	59	80
139-Alpha Flight app.; Kitty Pryde joins; new costume for Wolverine	5	10	15	32	51	70
140-Alpha Flight app.	5	10	15	32	51	70
141-Intro Future X-Men & The New Brotherhood of Evil Mutants; 1st app. Rachel (Phoenix II); Death of Franklin Richards	5	10	15	34	55	75

X-MEN: Titled THE UNCANNY X-MEN #142, Feb, 1981 - Present

	GD 2.0	VG 4.0	FN 6.0	VF 8.0	VF/NM 9.0	NM- 9.2
142-Rachel app.; deaths of alt. future Wolverine, Storm & Colossus	6	12	18	41	66	90
143-Last Byrne issue	5	10	15	32	51	70
144-150: 144-Man-Thing app. 145-Old X-Men app. 148-Spider-Woman, Dazzler app. 150-Double size	2	4	6	9	13	16
151-157,159-161,163,164: 161-Origin Magneto. 163-Origin Binary. 164-1st app. Binary as Carol Danvers	2	4	6	8	10	12
158-1st app. Rogue in X-Men (6/82, see Avengers Annual #10)	3	6	9	16	22	28
162-Wolverine solo story	2	4	6	10	14	18
165-Paul Smith-c/a begins, ends #175	2	4	6	8	11	14
166-170: 166-Double size; Paul Smith-a. 167-New Mutants app. (3/83); same date as New Mutants #1; 1st meeting w/X-Men; ties into N.M. #3,4; Starjammers app.; contains skin "Tattooz" decals. 168-1st brief app. Madelyne Pryor (last page) in X-Men (see Avengers Annual #10)	2	3	4	6	8	10
171-Rogue joins X-Men; Simonson-c/a	2	4	6	13	18	22
172-174: 172,173-Two part Wolverine solo story. 173-Two cover variations, blue & black. 174-Phoenix cameo	1	2	3	5	7	9
175-(52 pgs.)-Anniversary issue; Phoenix returns	2	4	6	8	10	12
176-185,187-192,194-199: 181-Sunfire app. 182-Rogue solo story. 184-1st app. Forge (8/84). 190,191-Spider-Man & Avengers x-over. 195-Power Pack x-over	1	2	3	5	6	8
186,193: 186-Double-size; Barry Smith/Austin-a. 193-Double size; 100th app. New X-Men; 1st app. Warpath in costume (see New Mutants #16)	1	2	3	5	7	9
200-(12/85, $1.25, 52 pgs.)	1	2	3	5	7	9
201-(1/86)-1st app. Cable? (as baby Nathan; see X-Factor #1); 1st Whilce Portacio-c/a(i) on X-Men (guest artist)	3	6	9	16	22	28
202-204,206-209: 204-Nightcrawler solo story; 2nd Portacio-a(i) on X-Men. 207-Wolverine/Phoenix story	1	2	3	5	6	8
205-Wolverine solo story by Barry Smith	2	4	6	9	13	16
210,211-Mutant Massacre begins	3	6	9	14	19	24
212,213-Wolverine vs. Sabretooth (Mutant Mass.)	3	6	9	16	22	28
214-221,223,224: 219-Havok joins (7/87); brief app. Sabretooth. 221-1st app. Mr. Sinister	1	2	3	4	5	7
222-Wolverine battles Sabretooth-c/story	3	6	9	14	20	26
225-242: 225-227: Fall Of The Mutants. 226-Double size. 240-Sabretooth app. 242-Double size, X-Factor app., Inferno tie-in	1	2	3	4	5	7
243,245-247: 245-Rob Liefeld-a(p)	1	2	3	4	5	7
244-1st app. Jubilee	3	6	9	16	23	30
248-1st Jim Lee art on X-Men (1989)	2	4	6	13	18	22
248-2nd printing (1992, $1.25)						3.00
249-252: 252-Lee-c	1	2	3	4	5	7
253-255: 253-All new X-Men begin. 254-Lee-c	1	2	3	4	5	7
256,257-Jim Lee-c/a begins	1	2	3	5	7	9
258-Wolverine solo story; Lee-c/a	1	2	3	5	7	9
259-Silvestri-c/a; no Lee-a	1	2	3	4	5	7
260-265-No Lee-a. 260,261,264-Lee-c	1	2	3	4	5	7
266-(8/90) 1st full app. Gambit (see Annual #14)-No Lee-a	4	8	12	22	34	45
267-Jim Lee-c/a resumes; 2nd full Gambit app.	2	4	6	9	13	16
268-Capt. America, Black Widow & Wolverine team-up; Lee-a	2	4	6	10	14	18
268,270: 268-2nd printing. 270-Gold 2nd printing						3.00
269,273-275: 269-Lee-a. 273-New Mutants (Cable) & X-Factor x-over; Golden, Byrne & Lee part pencils. 275-(52 pgs.)-Tri-fold-c by Jim Lee (p); Prof. X	1	2	3	4	5	7
270-X-Tinction Agenda begins	1	2	3	5	6	8
271,272-X-Tinction Agenda	1	2	3	5	6	8
275-Gold 2nd printing						2.50
276-280: 277-Last Lee-c/a. 280-X-Factor x-over						6.00
281-(10/91)-New team begins (Storm, Archangel, Colossus, Iceman & Marvel Girl); Whilce Portacio-c/a begins; Byrne scripts begin; wraparound-c (white logo)	1	2	3	4	5	7
281-2nd printing with red metallic ink logo w/o UPC box ($1.00-c); does not say 2nd printing inside						3.00
282-1st brief app. Bishop (cover & 1 page)	2	4	6	8	10	12
282-Gold ink 2nd printing ($1.00-c)						3.00
283-1st full app. Bishop (12/91)	2	4	6	8	10	12
284-299: 284-Last $1.00-c. 286,287-Lee plots. 287-Bishop joins team. 288-Lee/Portacio plots. 290-Last Portacio-c/a. 294-Peterson-a(p) begins (#292 is 1st Peterson-c). 294-296 ($1.50)-Bagged w/trading card in each; X-Cutioner's Song x-overs; Peterson/Austin-c/a on all						4.00
300-($3.95, 68 pgs.)-Holo-grafx foil-c; Magneto app.						6.00
301-303,305-309,311						3.00
303,307-Gold Edition	1	2	3	5	6	8
304-($3.95, 68 pgs.)-Wraparound-c with Magneto hologram on-c; 30th anniversary issue; Jae Lee-a (4 pgs.)						6.00
310-($1.95)-Bound-in trading card sheet						3.00
312-$1.50-c begins; bound-in card sheet; 1st Madureira						4.00
313-321						3.00

Uncanny X-Men #366 © MAR

Uncanny X-Men #500 © MAR

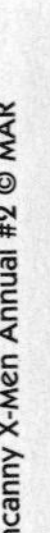
Uncanny X-Men Annual #2 © MAR

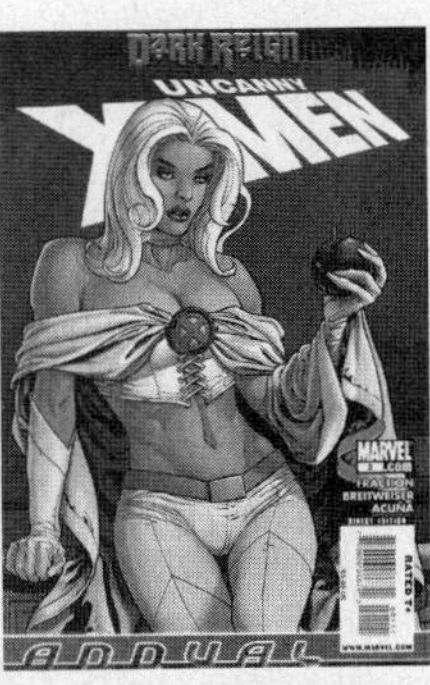

GD 2.0 | VG 4.0 | FN 6.0 | VF 8.0 | VF/NM 9.0 | NM- 9.2

316,317-($2.95)-Foil enhanced editions 4.00
318-321-($1.95)-Deluxe editions 3.00
322-Onslaught 5.00
323,324,326-346: 323-Return from Age of Apocalypse. 328-Sabretooth-c. 329,330-Dr. Strange app. 331-White Queen-c/app. 334-Juggernaut app.; w/Onslaught Update. 335-Onslaught, Avengers, Apocalypse, & X-Man app. 336-Onslaught. 338-Archangel's wings return to normal. 339-Havok vs. Cyclops; Spider-Man app. 341-Gladiator-c/app. 342-Deathbird cameo; two covers. 343,344-Phalanx 3.00
325-($3.95)-Anniverary issue; gatefold-c 5.00
342-Variant-c 1 3 4 6 8 10
347-349:347-Begin $1.99-c. 349-"Operation Zero Tolerance" 3.00
350-($3.99, 48 pgs.) Prismatic etched foil gatefold wraparound-c; Trial of Gambit; Seagle-s begin 1 2 3 5 6 8
351-359: 353-Bachalo-a begins. 354-Regular-c. 355-Alpha Flight-c/app. 356-Original X-Men-c 3.00
354-Dark Phoenix variant-c 5.00
360-($2.99) 35th Anniv. issue; Pacheco-c 3.00
360-($3.99) Etched Holo-foil enhanced-c 4.00
360-($6.95) DF Edition with Jae Lee variant-c 7.00
361-374: 361-Gambit returns; Skroce-a. 362-Hunt for Xavier pt. 1; Bachelo-a. 364-Yu-a. 366-Magneto-c. 369-Juggernaut-c 3.00
375-($2.99) Autopsy of Wolverine 4.00
376-379: 376,377-Apocalypse: The Twelve 3.00
380-($2.99) Polybagged with X-Men Revolution Genesis Edition preview 4.00
381,382,384-389,391-393: 381-Begin $2.25-c; Claremont-s. 387-Maximum Security 3.00
383-($2.99) 3.50
390-Colossus dies to cure the Legacy Virus 4.00
394-New look X-Men begins; Casey-s/Churchill-c/a 3.50
395-399-Poptopia. 398-Phillips & Wood-a 3.00
400-($3.50) Art by Ashley Wood, Eddie Campbell, Hamner, Phillips, Pulido and Matt Smith; wraparound-c by Wood 4.00
401-415: 401-'Nuff Said issue; Garney-a. 404,405,407-409,413-415-Phillips-a 3.00
416-421: 416-Asamiya-a begins. 421-Garney-a 3.00
422-($3.50) Alpha Flight app.; Garney-a 4.00
423-(25¢-c) Holy War pt. 1; Garney-a/Philip Tan-c 3.00
424-449,452-454: 425,426,429,430-Tan-a. 428-Birth of Nightcrawler. 437-Larroca-a begins. 444-New team, new costumes; Claremont-s/Davis-a begins. 448,449-Coipel-a 3.00
450,451,455-459-X-23 app.; Davis-a 3.00
460-471: 460-Begin $2.50-c; Raney-a. 462-465-House of M. 464-468-Bachalo-a 3.00
472-499: 472-Begin $2.99-c; Bachalo-a. 475-Wraparound-c. 492-494-Messiah Complex 3.00
500-($3.99) X-Men new HQ in San Francisco; Magneto app.; Land & Dodson-a; wraparound covers by Alex Ross and Greg Land 4.00
500-Classic X-Men Dynamic Forces variant-c by Ross 8.00
500-X-Men variant-c by Michael Turner 30.00
500-X-Women variant-c by Dodson 15.00
501-511,515-521,523: 501-Brubaker & Fraction-s/Land-a. 523-Second Coming 3.00
512-514,522-($3.99). 513,514-Utopia x-over. 522-Portacio-a 4.00
#(-1) Flashback (7/97) Ladronn-c/Hitch & Neary-a 3.00
Special 1(12/70)-Kirby-c/a; origin The Stranger 10 20 30 68 119 170
Special 2(11/71, 52 pgs.) 8 16 24 52 86 120
Annual 3(1979, 52 pgs.)-New story; Miller/Austin-c; Wolverine still in old yellow costume 4 8 12 28 44 60
Annual 4(1980, 52 pgs.)-Dr. Strange guest stars 2 4 6 10 14 18
Annual 5(1981, 52 pgs.) 2 3 4 6 8 10
Annual 6-8('82-'84 52 pgs.)-6-Dracula app. 1 2 3 4 5 7
Annual 9,10('85, '86)-9-New Mutants x-over cont'd from New Mutants Special Ed. #1; Art Adams-a. 10-Art Adams-a 2 4 6 8 10 12
Annual 11-13:('87-'89, 68 pgs.): 12-Evolutionary War; A.Adams-a(p). 13-Atlantis Attacks 4.00
Annual 14(1990, $2.00, 68 pgs.)-1st app. Gambit (minor app., 5 pgs.); Fantastic Four, New Mutants (Cable) & X-Factor x-over; Art Adams-c/a(p) 3 6 9 16 23 30
Annual 15 (1991, $2.00, 68 pgs.)-4 pg. origin; New Mutants x-over; 4 pg. Wolverine solo back-up story; 4th app. X-Force cont'd from New Warriors Annual #1 4.00
Annual 16-18 ('92-'94, 68 pgs.)-16-Jae Lee-c/a(p). 17-Bagged w/card 3.00
Annual '95-(11/95, $3.95)-Wraparound-c 4.00
Annual '96,'97-Wraparound-c 3.00
.../Fantastic Four Annual '98 ($2.99) Casey-s 3.00
Annual '99 ($3.50) Jubilee app. 3.50
Annual 2000 ($3.50) Cable app.; Ribic-a 3.50
Annual 2001 ($3.50, printed wide-ways) Ashley Wood-c/a; Casey-s 3.50
Annual (Vol. 2) #1 (8/06, $3.99) Storm & Black Panther wedding prelude 4.00
Annual (Vol. 2) #2 (3/09, $3.99) Dark Reign; flashback to Sub-Mariner/Emma Frost 4.00
....At The State Fair of Texas (1983, 36 pgs., one-shot); Supplement to the Dallas Times Herald 2 4 6 9 12 15

GD 2.0 | VG 4.0 | FN 6.0 | VF 8.0 | VF/NM 9.0 | NM- 9.2

...: The Dark Phoenix Saga TPB 1st printing (1984, $12.95) 40.00
...: The Dark Phoenix Saga TPB 2nd-5th printings 30.00
...: The Dark Phoenix Saga TPB 6th-10th printings 20.00
... Days of Future Past TPB (2004, $19.99) r/#138-143 & Annual #4 20.00
... Eve of Destruction TPB (2005, $14.99) r/#391-393 & X-Men #111-113; Churchill-c 15.00
...:Dream's End (2004, $17.99)-r/Death of Colossus story arc from Uncanny X-Men #388-390, Cable #87, Bishop #16 and X-Men #108,110; debut pages from Giant-Size X-Men #1 18.00
... From The Ashes TPB (1990, $14.95) r/#168-176 15.00
... Future History - The Messiah War Sourcebook (2009, $3.99) Cable's files on X-Men 4.00
...: God Loves, Man Kills ($6.95)-r/Marvel Graphic Novel #5 7.00
...: God Loves, Man Kills - Special Edition (2003, $4.99)-reprint with new Hughes-c 5.00
...: God Loves, Man Kills HC (2007, $19.99) reprint with Claremont & Anderson interviews; original artist Neal Adams' six sketch pages and interview 20.00
...: Hope (5/10, $2.99) Collects Cable and Hope back-ups; Dillon-a 3.00
House of M: Uncanny X-Men TPB (2006, $13.99) r/#462-465 and selections from Secrets Of The House of M one-shot 14.00
...In The Days of Future Past TPB (1989, $3.95, 52 pgs.) 4.00
...Old Soldiers TPB (2004, $19.99) r/#213,215 & Ann. #11; New Mutants Ann. #2&3 20.00
...Poptopia TPB (10/01, $15.95) r/#394-399 16.00
...: Rise & Fall of the Shi'Ar Empire HC (2007, $34.99, dustjacket) r/#475-486; bonus art 35.00
...: Rise & Fall of the Shi'Ar Empire SC (2008, $29.99) r/#475-486; bonus art 30.00
...: Sword of the Braddocks (5/09, $3.99) Psylocke vs. Slaymaster; Claremont-s 4.00
...: The Complete Onslaught Epic Book 1 TPB (2007, $29.99) r/X-Men #53-54, Uncanny X-Men #334-335, Fantastic Four #414-415, Avengers #400-401, Onslaught: X-Men, Cable #34 and Incredible Hulk #444 30.00
...: The Complete Onslaught Epic Book 2 TPB ('08, $29.99) r/Excalibur #100, Wolverine #104, X-Factor #125-126, Amazing Spider-Man #415, Green Goblin #12, Spider-Man #72, Punisher #11, X-Man #18 & X-Force #57 30.00
...: The Extremists TPB (2007, $13.99) r/#487-491 14.00
Uncanny X-Men Omnibus Vol. 1 HC (2006, $99.99, dust jacket) r/Giant-Size X-Men #1, (Uncanny) X-Men #94-131 & Annual #3; cover gallery, promo and sketch art 100.00
Vignettes TPB (9/01, $17.95) r/Claremont & Bolton Classic X-Men #1-13 18.00
Vignettes Vol. 2 TPB (2005, $17.99) r/Claremont & Bolton Classic X-Men #14-25 18.00
... Vol. 1: Hope TPB (2003, $12.99) r/#410-415; Harris-c 13.00
... Vol. 2: Dominant Species TPB (2003, $11.99) r/#416-420; Asamiya-c 12.00
... Vol. 3: Holy War TPB (2003, $17.99) r/#421-427 18.00
... Vol. 4: The Draco TPB (2004, $15.99) r/#428-434 16.00
... Vol. 5: She Lies with Angels TPB (2004, $11.99) r/#437-441 12.00
... Vol. 6: Bright New Mourning TPB (2004, $14.99) r/#435,436,442,443 & (New) X-Men #155,156; Larroca sketch covers 15.00
...Vs. Apocalypse Vol. 1: The Twelve TPB (2008, $29.99) r/#376-377, Cable #73-76, X-Men #96,97 and Wolverine #145-147 30.00
... - The New Age Vol. 1: The End of History (2004, $12.99) r/#444-449 13.00
... - The New Age Vol. 2: The Cruelest Cut (2005, $11.99) r/#450-454 12.00
... - The New Age Vol. 3: On Ice (2006, $15.99) r/#455-461 16.00
... - The New Age Vol. 4: End of Greys (2006, $14.99) r/#466-471 15.00
... - The New Age Vol. 5: First Foursaken (2006, $11.99) r/#472-474 & Annual #1 12.00

NOTE: **Art Adams** *a-Annual 9, 10p, 12p, 14p; c-218p.* **Neal Adams** *a-56-63p, 65p; c-56-63.* **Adkins** *a-34, 35p; c-31, 34, 35.* **Austin** *a-108i, 109i, 111-117i, 119-143i, 186i, 204i, 228i, 294-297i, Annual 3i, 7i, 9i, 13; c-109-111i, 114-122i, 123, 124-141i, 142, 143, 196i, 204i, 228i, 294-297i, Annual 3i.* **J. Buscema** *c-42, 43, 45.* **Buscema/Tuska** *a-45.* **Byrne** *a(p)-108, 109, 111-143, 273; c(p)-113-116, 127, 129, 131-141.* **Capullo** *c-14.* **Ditko** *r-86, 89-91, 93.* **Everett** *c-73.* **Golden** *a-273, Annual 7p.* **Guice** *a-216p, 217p.* **G. Kane** *c(p)-33, 74-76, 79, 80, 94, 95.* **Kirby** *a(p)-1-17 (#12-17, 67r-layouts); c(p)-1-17, 25, 30 (18, 26-parts).* **Layton** *a-105i; c-112i, 113i.* **Jim Lee** *a(p)-248, 256-258, 267-277; c(p)-252, 254, 256-261, 264, 267, 270, 275-277, 286.* **Perez** *a-Annual 3p; c(p)-112, 128, Annual 3.* **Peterson** *a(p)-294-300, 304(part); c(p)-294-299.* **Whilce Portacio** *a(p)-281-286, 289, 290; a(i)-267; c-281-285p, 289p, 290; c(i)-267.* **Romita, Jr.** *a-300; c-300.* **Roussos** *a-84i.* **Simonson** *a-171p; c-171, 217.* **B. Smith** *a-53, 186p, 198p, 205, 214; c-53-55, 186p, 198, 205, 212, 214, 216.* **Paul Smith** *a(p)-165-170, 172-175, 278; c-165-170, 172-175, 278.* **Sparling** *a-78p.* **Steranko** *a-50p, 51p; c-49-51.* **Sutton** *a-106i.* **Art Thibert** *a(i)-281-286; c(i)-281, 282, 284, 285.* **Toth** *a-12p, 67p(r).* **Tuska** *a-40-42i, 43-46p, 88i(r); c-39-41, 77p, 78p.* **Williamson** *a-202i, 203i, 211i; c-202i, 203i, 206i.* **Wood** *c-14i.*

UNCANNY X-MEN AND THE NEW TEEN TITANS (See Marvel and DC Present...)

UNCANNY X-MEN: FIRST CLASS
Marvel Comics: Sept, 2009 - Present ($2.99)

1-7: 1-The X-Men #94 (1975) team; Cruz-a; Inhumans app. 3.00
... Giant-Size Special (8/09, $3.99) short stories by various; Scottie Young-c 4.00

X-MEN (2nd Series)
Marvel Comics: Oct, 1991 - Present ($1.00-$2.99)

1 a-d (four different covers, $1.50, 52 pgs.)-Jim Lee-c/a begins, ends #11; new team begins (Cyclops, Beast, Wolverine, Gambit, Psylocke & Rogue); new Uncanny X-Men & Magneto app.; 4.00
1 e ($3.95)-Double gate-fold-c consisting of all four covers from 1a-d by Jim Lee; contains all pin-ups from #1a-d plus inside-c foldout poster; no ads; printed on coated stock 5.00
2-7: 4-Wolverine back to old yellow costume (same date as Wolverine #50); last $1.00-c. 5-Byrne scripts. 6-Sabretooth-c/story 5.00
8-10: 8-Gambit vs. Bishop-c/story; last Lee-a; Ghost Rider cameo cont'd in Ghost Rider #26.

X-Men #33 © MAR

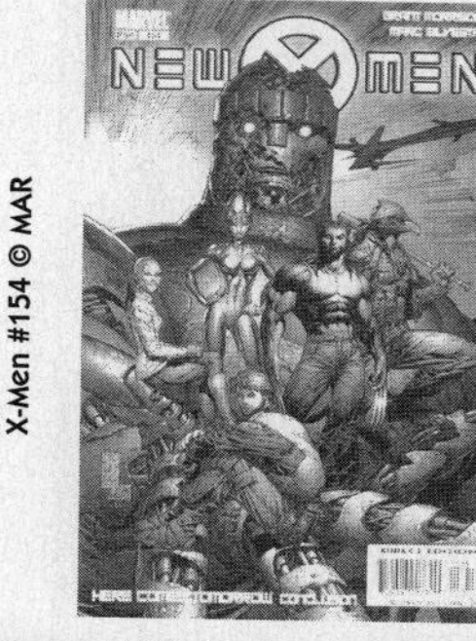
X-Men #154 © MAR

X-Men #200 © MAR

GD VG FN VF VF/NM NM-
2.0 4.0 6.0 8.0 9.0 9.2

9-Wolverine vs. Ghost Rider; cont'd/G.R. #26. 10-Return of Longshot 5.00
11-13,17-24,26-29,31: 12,13-Art Thibert-c/a. 28,29-Sabretooth app. 4.00
11-Silver ink 2nd printing; came with X-Men board game
2 4 6 9 12 15
14-16-($1.50)-Polybagged with trading card in each; X-Cutioner's Song x-overs; 14-Andy Kubert-c/a begins 4.00
25-($3.50, 52 pgs.)-Wraparound-c with Gambit hologram on-c; Professor X erases Magneto's mind 2 4 6 8 10 12
25-30th anniversary issue w/B&W-c with Magneto in color & Magneto hologram & no price on-c 2 4 6 9 12 15
25-Gold 30.00
30-($1.95)-Wedding issue w/bound-in trading card sheet 5.00
32-37: 32-Begin $1.50-c; bound-in card sheet. 33-Gambit & Sabretooth-c/story 3.00
36,37-($2.95)-Collectors editions (foil-c) 5.00
38-44,46-49,51-53, 55-65: 42,43- Paul Smith-a. 46,49,53-56-Onslaught app. 51-Waid scripts begin, end #56. 54-(Reg. edition)-Onslaught revealed as Professor X. 55,56-Onslaught x-over; Avengers, FF & Sentinels app. 56-Dr. Doom app. 57-Xavier taken into custody; Byrne-c/swipe (X-Men,1st Series #138). 59-Hercules-c/app. 61-Juggernaut-c/app. 62-Re-intro. Shang Chi; two covers. 63-Kingpin cameo. 64- Kingpin app. 3.00
45-($3.95)-Annual issue; gatefold-c 5.00
50-($2.95)-Vs. Onslaught, wraparound-c. 4.00
50-($3.95)-Vs. Onslaught, wraparound foil-c. 5.00
50-($2.95)-Variant gold-c. 3 6 9 20 30 40
50-($2.95)-Variant silver-c. 1 2 3 5 6 8
54-(Limited edition)-Embossed variant-c; Onslaught revealed as Professor X
3 6 9 16 23 30
66-69,71-74,76-79: 66-Operation Zero Tolerance. 76-Origin of Maggott 3.00
70-($2.99, 48 pgs.)-Joe Kelly-s begin, new members join 3.50
75-($2.99, 48 pgs.) vs. N'Garai; wraparound-c 3.50
80-($3.99) 35th Anniv. issue; holo-foil-c 5.00
80-($2.99) Regular-c 3.50
80-($6.95) Dynamic Forces Ed.; Quesada-c 7.00
81-93,95: 82-Hunt for Xavier pt. 2. 85-Davis-a. 86-Origin of Joseph. 87-Magneto War ends. 88-Juggernaut app. 3.00
94-($2.99) Contains preview of X-Men: Hidden Years 3.50
96-99: 96,97-Apocalypse: The Twelve 3.00
100-($2.99) Art Adams-c; begin Claremont-s/Yu-a 4.00
100-DF alternate-c 1 3 4 6 8 10
101-105,107,108,110-114: 101-Begin $2.25-c. 107-Maximum Security x-over; Bishop-c/app. 108-Moira MacTaggart dies; Senator Kelly shot. 111-Magneto-c. 112,113-Eve of Destruction 3.00
106-($2.99) X-Men battle Domina 3.50
109-($3.50, 100 pgs.) new and reprinted Christmas-themed stories 4.00
114-Title change to "New X-Men," Morrison-s/Quitely-c/a begins 4.00
115-Two covers (Quitely & BWS) 3.00
116-125,127-149: 116-Emma Frost joins. 117,118-Van Sciver-a. 121,122,135-Quitely-a. 127-Leon & Sienkiewicz-a. 128-Kordey-a. 132,139-141-Jimenez-a. 136-138-Quitely-a 142-Sabretooth app.; Bachalo-c/a thru #145. 146-Magneto returns; Jimenez-a 3.00
126-($3.25) Quitely-a; defeat of Cassanova 3.50
150-($3.50) Jean Grey dies again; last Jimenez-a 4.00
151-156: 151-154-Silvestri-c/a 3.00
157-169: 157-X-Men Reload begins 3.00
170-184: 171- Begin $2.50-c. 175,176-Crossover with Black Panther #8,9. 181-184-Apocalypse returns 3.00
185-199,201-229,231-234: 185-Begin $2.99-c. 188-190,192-194,197-199-Bachalo-a. 195,196,201-203-Ramos-a. 201-204-Endangered Species back-up. 205-207-Messiah Complex x-over. 208-Romita Jr.-a. 210-Starts X-Men: Legacy. 228,229-Acuña-a 3.00
200-($3.99) Two wraparound covers by Bachalo & Finch; Bachalo & Ramos-a 4.00
230-($3.99) Acuña-a; Rogue vs. Emplate 4.00
#(-1) Flashback (7/97); origin of Magneto 3.00
Annual 1-3 ('92-'94, $2.25-$2.95, 68 pgs.) 1-Lee-c & layouts; #2-Bagged w/card 4.00
Special '95 ($3.95) 4.00
... '96,...'97-Wraparound-c 3.00
.../ Dr. Doom '98 Annual ($2.99) Lopresti-a 3.00
... Annual '99 ($3.50) Adam Kubert-c 3.50
Annual 2000 ($3.50) Art Adams-c/Claremont-s/Eaton-a 3.50
...2001 Annual ($3.50) Morrison-s/Yu-a; issue printed sideways 3.50
...2007 Annual #1 (3/07, $3.99) Casey-s/Brooks-a; Cable and Mystique app. 4.00
...Legacy Annual 1 (11/09, $3.99) Acuña-a; Emplate returns 4.00
Animation Special Graphic Novel (12/90, $10.95) adapts animated series 11.00
Ashcan #1 (1994, 75¢) Introduces new team members 2.25
Ashcan (75¢ Ashcan Edition) (1994) 2.25
... Archives Sketchbook (12/00, $2.99) Early B&W character design sketches by various incl. Lee, Davis, Yu, Pacheco, BWS, Art Adams, Liefeld 3.00

GD VG FN VF VF/NM NM-
2.0 4.0 6.0 8.0 9.0 9.2

...: Bizarre Love Triangle TPB (2005, $9.99)-r/X-Men #171-174 10.00
.../ Black Panther TPB (2006, $11.99)-r/X-Men #175,176 & Black Panther (2005) #8,9 12.00
...: Blinded By the Light (2007, $14.99)-r/X-Men #200-204 15.00
...: Blood of Apocalypse (2006, $17.99)-r/X-Men #182-187 18.00
...: Day of the Atom (2005, $19.99)-r/X-Men #157-165 20.00
Decimation: X-Men - The Day After TPB (2006, $15.99) r/#177-181 & Decimation: House of M - The Day After 16.00
...: Declassified (10/00, $3.50) Profile pin-ups by various; Jae Lee-c 3.50
...: Endangered Species (8/07, $3.99) prologue to 17-part back-up series in X-Men titles 4.00
...: Endangered Species HC (2008, $24.99, d.j.) over-sized r/prologue and 17-part series 25.00
...: Fatal Attractions ('94, $17.95)-r/x-Factor #92, X-Force #25, Uncanny X-Men #304, X-Men #25, Wolverine #75, & Excalibur #71 18.00
...: Golgotha (2005, $12.99)-r/X-Men #166-170 13.00
... Millennial Visions (8/00, $3.99) Various artists interpret future X-Men 4.00
... Millennial Visions 2 (1/02, $3.50) Various artists interpret future X-Men 3.50
...: Mutant Genesis (2006, $19.99)-r/X-Men #1-7; sketch pages and extra art 20.00
New X-Men: E is for Extinction TPB (11/01, $12.95) r/#114-117 13.00
New X-Men: Imperial TPB (7/02, $19.99) r/#118-126; Quitely-c 20.00
New X-Men: New Worlds TPB (2002, $14.99) r/#127-133; Quitely-c 15.00
New X-Men: Riot at Xavier's TPB (2003, $11.99) r/#134-138; Quitely-c 12.00
New X-Men: Vol. 5: Assault on Weapon Plus TPB (2003, $14.99) r/#139-145 15.00
New X-Men: Vol. 6: Planet X TPB (2004, $12.99) r/#146-150 13.00
New X-Men: Vol. 7: Here Comes Tomorrow TPB (2004, $10.99) r/#151-154 11.00
New X-Men: Volume 1 HC (2002, $29.99) oversized r/#114-126 & 2001 Annual 30.00
New X-Men: Volume 2 HC (2003, $29.99) oversized r/#127-141; sketch & script pages 30.00
New X-Men: Volume 3 HC (2004, $29.99) oversized r/#142-154; sketch & script pages 30.00
New X-Men Omnibus HC (2006, $99.99) oversized r/#114-154 & Annual 2001; Morrison's original pitch; sketch & script pages; variant covers & promo art; Carey intro. 140.00
...: Odd Men Out (2008, $3.99) Two unpublished stories with Dave Cockrum-a 4.00
... Original Sin 1 (12/08, $3.99) Wolverine and Daken; Deodato & Eaton-a 4.00
... Origin: Colossus (7/08, $3.99) Yost-s/Hairsine-a; Piotr Rasputin before joining X-Men 4.00
...: Pixies and Demons Director's Cut (2008, $3.99) r/FCBD 2008 story with script 4.00
... Pizza Hut Mini-comics-(See Marvel Collector's Edition: X-Men in Promotional Comics section)
... Premium Edition #1 (1993)-Cover says "Toys 'R' Us Limited Edition X-Men" 2.25
...: Rarities (1995, $5.95)-Reprints 6.00
...: Return of Magik Must Have (2008, $3.99) r/X-Men Unlimited #14, New X-Men #37 and X-Men: Divided We Stand #2; Coipel-c 4.00
...: Road Trippin' ('99, $24.95, TPB) r/X-Men road trips 25.00
...: Supernovas ('07, $34.99, oversized HC w/d.j.) r/X-Men 188-199 & Annual #1 35.00
...: Supernovas ('08, $29.99, SC) r/X-Men 188-199 & Annual #1 30.00
...: The Coming of Bishop ('95, $12.95)-r/Uncanny X-Men #282-285, 287,288 13.00
...: The Magneto War (3/99, $2.99) Davis-a 3.00
...: The Rise of Apocalypse ('98, $16.99)-r/Rise Of Apocalypse #1-4, X-Factor #5,6 17.00
... Visionaries: Chris Claremont ('98, $24.95)-r/Claremont-s; art by Byrne, BWS, Jim Lee 25.00
... Visionaries: Jim Lee ('02, $29.99)-r/Jim Lee-a from various issues between Uncanny X-Men #248 & 286; r/Classic X-Men #39 and X-Men Annual #1 30.00
... Visionaries: Joe Madureira (7/00, $17.95)-r/Uncanny X-Men #325,326,329,330,341-343; new Madureira-c 18.00
... Vs. Hulk (3/09, $3.99) Claremont-s/Raapack-a; r/X-Men #66 4.00
...: Zero Tolerance ('00, $24.95, TPB) r/crossover series 25.00
NOTE: ***Jim Lee** a-1-11p; c-1-6p, 7, 8, 9p, 10, 11p. **Art Thibert** a-6-9i, 12, 13; c-6i, 12, 13.*

X-MEN ADVENTURES (TV)
Marvel Comics: Nov, 1992 - No. 15, Jan, 1994 ($1.25)(Based on animated series)

1-Wolverine, Cyclops, Jubilee, Rogue, Gambit 3.50
2-15: 3-Magneto-c/story. 6-Sabretooth-c/story. 7-Cable-c/story. 10-Archangel guest star. 11-Cable-c/story. 15-($1.75, 52 pgs.) 3.00

X-MEN ADVENTURES II (TV)
Marvel Comics: Feb, 1994 - No. 13, Feb, 1995 ($1.25/$1.50)(Based on 2nd TV season)

1-13: 4-Bound-in trading card sheet. 5-Alpha Flight app. 3.00
...Captive Hearts/Slave Island (TPB, $4.95)-r/X-Men Adventures #5-8 5.00
...The Irresistible Force, The Muir Island Saga (5.95, 10/94, TPB) r/X-Men Advs. #9-12 6.00

X-MEN ADVENTURES III (TV)(See Adventures of the X-Men)
Marvel Comics: Mar, 1995 - No. 13, Mar, 1996 ($1.50) (Based on 3rd TV season)

1-13 3.00

X-MEN: AGE OF APOCALYPSE
Marvel Comics: May, 2005 - No. 6, June, 2005 ($2.99, weekly limited series)

1-6-Bachalo-c/a; Yoshida-s; follows events in the "Age of Apocalypse" storyline 3.00
... One Shot (5/05, $3.99) prequel to series; Hitch wraparound-c; pin-ups by various 4.00
X-Men: The New Age of Apocalypse TPB (2005, $20.99) r/#1-6 & one-shot 21.00

X-MEN ALPHA
Marvel Comics: 1994 ($3.95, one-shot)

X-Men: Children of the Atom #4 © MAR

X-Men Forever (2nd series) #18 © MAR

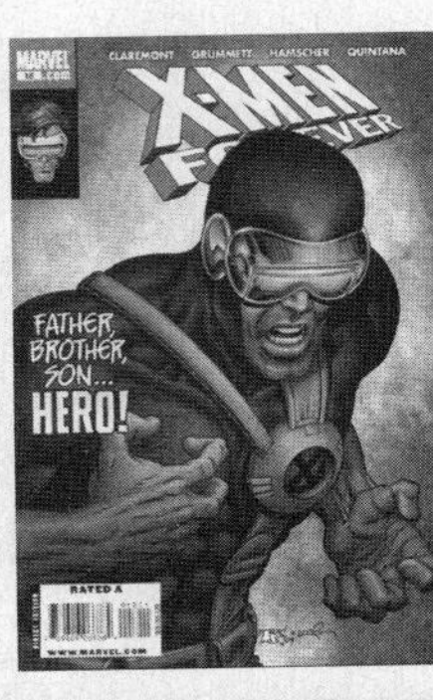

X-Men: Liberators #4 © MAR

	GD 2.0	VG 4.0	FN 6.0	VF 8.0	VF/NM 9.0	NM- 9.2
nn-Age of Apocalypse; wraparound chromium-c	1	2	3	5	6	8
nn ($49.95)-Gold logo						50.00

X-MEN/ALPHA FLIGHT
Marvel Comics Group: Dec, 1985 - No. 2, Dec, 1985 ($1.50, limited series)
1,2: 1-Intro The Berserkers; Paul Smith-a 5.00

X-MEN/ALPHA FLIGHT
Marvel Comics Group: May, 1998 - No. 2, June, 1998 ($2.99, limited series)
1,2-Flashback to early meeting; Raab-s/Cassaday-s/a 3.00

X-MEN AND POWER PACK
Marvel Comics: Dec, 2005 - No. 4, Mar, 2006 ($2.99, limited series)
1-4-Sumerak-s/Gurihiru-a. 1-Wolverine & Sabretooth app. 3.00
...: The Power of X (2006, $6.99, digest size) r/#1-4 7.00

X-MEN AND THE MICRONAUTS, THE
Marvel Comics Group: Jan, 1984 - No. 4, Apr, 1984 (Limited series)
1-4: Guice-c/a(p) in all 4.00

X-MEN: APOCALYPSE/DRACULA
Marvel Comics: Apr, 2006 - No. 4, July, 2006 ($2.99, limited series)
1-4-Tieri-s/Henry-a/Jae Lee-c 3.00
TPB (2006, $10.99) r/series; cover gallery 11.00

X-MEN ARCHIVES
Marvel Comics: Jan, 1995 - No. 4, Apr, 1995 ($2.25, limited series)
1-4: Reprints Legion stories from New Mutants. 4-Magneto app. 3.00

X-MEN ARCHIVES FEATURING CAPTAIN BRITAIN
Marvel Comics: July, 1995 - No. 7, 1996 ($2.95, limited series)
1-7: Reprints early Capt. Britain stories 3.00

X-MEN BLACK SUN (See Black Sun:...)

X-MEN BOOKS OF ASKANI
Marvel Comics: 1995 ($2.95, one-shot)
1-Painted pin-ups w/text 3.00

X-MEN: CHILDREN OF THE ATOM
Marvel Comics: Nov, 1999 - No. 6 ($2.99, limited series)
1-6-Casey-s; X-Men before issue #1. 1-3-Rude-c/a. 4-Paul Smith-a/Rude-c. 5,6-Essad Ribic-c/a 3.00
TPB (11/01, $16.95) r/series; sketch pages; Casey intro. 17.00

X-MEN CHRONICLES
Marvel Comics: Mar, 1995 - No. 2, June, 1995 ($3.95, limited series)
1,2: Age of Apocalypse x-over. 1-wraparound-c 5.00

X-MEN: CLANDESTINE
Marvel Comics: Oct, 1996 - No. 2, Nov, 1996 ($2.95, limited series, 48 pgs.)
1,2: Alan Davis-c(p)/a(p)/scripts & Mark Farmer-c(i)/a(i) in all; wraparound-c 3.00

X-MEN CLASSIC (Formerly Classic X-Men)
Marvel Comics: No. 46, Apr, 1990 - No. 110, Aug, 1995 ($1.25/$1.50)
46-110: Reprints from X-Men. 54-(52 pgs.). 57,60-63,65-Russell-c(i); 62-r/X-Men #158(Rogue). 66-r/#162(Wolverine). 69-Begins-r of Paul Smith issues (#165 on). 70,79,90,97(52 pgs.). 70-r/X-Men #166. 90-r/#186. 100-($1.50). 104-r/X-Men #200 3.00

X-MEN CLASSICS
Marvel Comics Group: Dec, 1983 - No. 3, Feb, 1984 ($2.00, Baxter paper)
1-3: X-Men-r by Neal Adams 6.00
NOTE: *Zeck c-1-3.*

X-MEN: COLOSSUS BLOODLIINE
Marvel Comics: Nov, 2005 - No. 5, Mar, 2006 ($2.99, limited series)
1-5-Colossus returns to Russia; David Hine-s/Jorge Lucas-a; Bachalo-c 3.00
TPB (2006, $13.99) r/#1-5 14.00

X-MEN: DEADLY GENESIS (See Uncanny X-Men #475)
Marvel Comics: Jan, 2006 - No. 6, July, 2006 ($3.99/$3.50, limited series)
1-($3.99) Silvestri-c swipe of Giant-Size X-Men #1; Hairsine-a/Brubaker-s 4.00
2-6-($3.50) 2-Silvestri-c; Banshee killed. 4-Intro Kid Vulcan 3.50
HC (2006, $24.99, dust jacket) r/#1-6 25.00
SC (2006, $19.99) r/#1-6 20.00

X-MEN: DIE BY THE SWORD
Marvel Comics: Dec, 2007 - No. 5, Feb, 2008 ($2.99, limited series)
1-5-Excalibur and The Exiles app.; Claremont-s/Santacruz-a 3.00
TPB (2008, $13.99) r/#1-5; handbook pages of Merlyn, Roma and Saturne 14.00

X-MEN: DIVIDED WE STAND
Marvel Comics: June, 2008 - No. 2, July, 2008 ($3.99, limited series)
1,2-Short stories by various; Peterson-c 4.00

X-MEN: EARTHFALL
Marvel Comics: Sept, 1996 ($2.95, one-shot)
1-r/Uncanny X-Men #232-234; wraparound-c 3.00

X-MEN: EMPEROR VULCAN
Marvel Comics: Nov, 2007 - No. 5, Mar, 2008 ($2.99, limited series)
1-5: 1-Starjammers app.; Yost-s/Diaz-a/Tan-c 3.00
TPB (2008, $13.99) r/#1-5 14.00

X-MEN: EVOLUTION (Based on the animated series)
Marvel Comics: Feb, 2002 - No. 9, Sept, 2002 ($2.25)
1-9: 1-8-Grayson-s/Udon-a. 9-Farber-s/J.J.Kirby-a 3.00
TPB (7/02, $8.99) r/#1-4 9.00
Vol. 2 TPB (2003, $11.99) r/#5-9; Asamiya-c 12.00

X-MEN FAIRY TALES
Marvel Comics: July, 2006 - No. 4, Oct, 2006 ($2.99, limited series)
1-4-Re-imagining of classic stories; Cebulski-s. 2-Baker-a. 3-Sienkiewicz-a. 4-Kobayashi-a 3.00
TPB (2006, $10.99) r/#1-4 11.00

X-MEN/ FANTASTIC FOUR
Marvel Comics: Feb, 2005 - No. 5, June, 2005 ($3.50, limited series)
1-5-Pat Lee-a/c; Yoshida-s; the Brood app. 3.50
HC (2005, $19.99, 7 1/2" x 11", dustjacket) oversized r/#1-5; cover gallery 20.00

X-MEN FIRST CLASS
Marvel Comics: Nov, 2006 - No. 8, Jun, 2007 ($2.99, limited series)
1-8-Xavier's first class of X-Men; Cruz-a/Parker-s. 5-Thor app. 7-Scarlet Witch app. 3.00
... Special 1 (7/07, $3.99) Nowlan-c; Nowlan, Paul Smith, Coover, Dragotta & Allred-a 4.00
... - Tomorrow's Brightest HC (2007, $24.99, d.j) r/#1-8; cover & character design art 25.00
... - Tomorrow's Brightest SC (2007, $19.99) r/#1-8; cover & character design art 20.00

X-MEN FIRST CLASS (2nd series)
Marvel Comics: Aug, 2007 - No. 16, Nov, 2008 ($2.99)
1-16: 1-Cruz-a/Parker-s; Fantastic Four app. 8-Man-Thing app. 10-Romita Jr.-c 3.00
... Giant-Size Special 1 (12/08, $3.99) 5 new short stories; Haspiel-a; r/X-Men #40 4.00
... - Mutant Mayhem TPB (2008, $13.99) r/#1-5 & X-Men First Class Special 14.00

X-MEN FIRST CLASS FINALS
Marvel Comics: Apr, 2009 - No. 4, July, 2009 ($3.99, limited series)
1-4-Cruz-a/Parker-s. 1-3-Coover-a 4.00

X-MEN FIRSTS
Marvel Comics: Feb, 1996 ($4.95, one-shot)
1-r/Avengers Annual #10, Uncanny X-Men #266, #221; Incredible Hulk #181 5.00

X-MEN FOREVER
Marvel Comics: Jan, 2001 - No. 6, June, 2001 ($3.50, limited series)
1-6-Jean Grey, Iceman, Mystique, Toad, Juggernaut app.; Maguire-a 3.50

X-MEN FOREVER
Marvel Comics: Aug, 2009 - Present ($3.99, limited series)
1-20: 1-Claremont-s/Grummett-a/c. 7-Nick Fury app. 4.00
... Alpha 1 (2009, $4.99) r/X-Men (1991) #1-3; 8 page preview of X-Men Forever #1 5.00

X-MEN: HELLFIRE CLUB
Marvel Comics: Jan, 2000 - No. 4, Apr, 2000 ($2.50, limited series)
1-4-Origin of the Hellfire Club 2.50

X-MEN: HIDDEN YEARS
Marvel Comics: Dec, 1999 - No. 22, Sept. 2001 ($3.50/$2.50)
1-New adventures from pre-#94 era; Byrne-s/a(p) 3.50
2-4,6-11,13-22-($2.50): 2-Two covers. 3-Ka-Zar app. 8,9-FF-c/app. 3.00
5-($2.75) 3.00
12-($3.50) Magneto-c/app. 3.50

X-MEN: KING BREAKER
Marvel Comics: Feb, 2009 - No. 4, May, 2009 ($3.99, limited series)
1-4-Emperor Vulcan and a Shi'ar invasion; Havok, Rachel Grey and Polaris app. 4.00

X-MEN: KITTY PRYDE - SHADOW & FLAME
Marvel Comics: Aug, 2005 - No. 5, Dec, 2005 ($2.99, limited series)
1-5-Akira Yoshida-s/Paul Smith-a/c; Kitty & Lockheed go to Japan 3.00
TPB (2006, $14.99) r/#1-5 15.00

X-MEN: LIBERATORS

X-Men Noir #1 © MAR

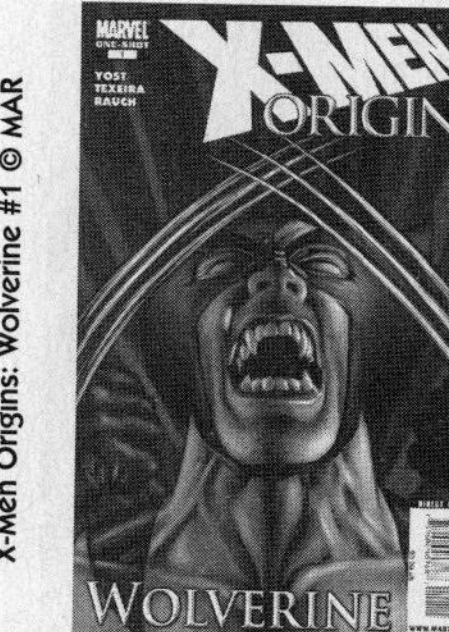

X-Men Origins: Wolverine #1 © MAR

X-Men: The 198 #1 © MAR

	GD	VG	FN	VF	VF/NM	NM-
	2.0	4.0	6.0	8.0	9.0	9.2

Marvel Comics: Nov, 1998 - No. 4, Feb, 1999 ($2.99, limited series)
1-4-Wolverine, Nightcrawler & Colossus; P. Jimenez 3.00

X-MEN LOST TALES
Marvel Comics: 1997 ($2.99)
1,2-r/Classic X-Men back-up stories 3.00

X-MEN: MAGNETO TESTAMENT
Marvel Comics: Nov, 2008 - No. 5, Mar, 2009 ($3.99, limited series)
1-5-Max Eisenhardt in 1930s Nazi-occupied Poland; Pak-s/DiGiandomenico-a. 5-Back-up story of artist Dina Babbitt with Neal Adams-a 4.00

X-MEN: MANIFEST DESTINY
Marvel Comics: Nov, 2008 - No. 5, Mar, 2009 ($3.99, limited series)
1-5-Short stories of X-Men re-location to San Francisco; s/a by various 4.00
... Nightcrawler 1 (5/09, $3.99) Molina & Syaf-a; Mephisto app. 4.00

X-MEN: MESSIAH COMPLEX
Marvel Comics: Dec, 2007 ($3.99)
1-Part 1 of x-over with X-Men, Uncanny X-Men, X-Factor and New X-Men; 2 covers 4.00
... - Mutant Files (2007, $3.99) Handbook pages of x-over participants; Kolins-c 4.00
HC (2008, $39.99, oversized) r/#1, Uncanny X-Men #492-494, X-Men #205-207, New X-Men #44-46 and X-Factor #25-27 40.00

X-MEN NOIR
Marvel Comics: Nov, 2008 - No. 4, May, 2009 ($3.99, limited series)
1-4-Pulp-style story set in 1930s NY; Van Lente-s/Calero-a 4.00
...: Mark of Cain (2/10 - No. 4, 5/10, $3.99) an Lente-s/Calero-a 4.00

X-MEN OMEGA
Marvel Comics: June, 1995 ($3.95, one-shot)
nn-Age of Apocalypse finale 1 3 4 6 8 10
nn-($49.95)-Gold edition 50.00

X-MEN: ORIGINS
Marvel Comics: Oct, 2008 - Present ($3.99, series of one-shots)
...: Beast (11/08) High school years; Carey-s; painted-a/c by Woodward 4.00
...: Cyclops (3/10) Magneto app.; Delperdang-a/Granov-c 4.00
...: Gambit (8/09) Mr. Sinister, Sabretooth and the Marauders app.; Yardin-a 4.00
...: Iceman (1/10) Noto-a 4.00
...: Jean Grey (10/08) Childhood & early X-days; McKeever-s; Mayhew painted-a/c 4.00
...: Sabretooth (4/09) Childhood and early meetings with Wolverine; Panosian-a/c 4.00
...: Wolverine (6/09) Pre-X-Men days and first meeting with Xavier; Texeira-a/c 4.00

X-MEN: PHOENIX
Marvel Comics: Dec, 1999 - No. 3, Mar, 2000 ($2.50, limited series)
1-3: 1-Apocalypse app. 3.00

X-MEN: PHOENIX - ENDSONG
Marvel Comics: Mar, 2005 - No. 5, June, 2005 ($2.99, limited series)
1-5-The Phoenix Force returns to Earth; Greg Land-c/a; Greg Pak-s 3.00
HC (2005, $19.99, dust jacket) r/#1-5; Land sketch pages 20.00
SC (2006, $14.99) 15.00

X-MEN: PHOENIX - LEGACY OF FIRE
Marvel Comics: July, 2003 - No. 3, Sep, 2003 ($2.99, limited series)
1-3-Manga-style; Ryan Kinnard-s/a/c; intro page art by Adam Warren 3.00

X-MEN: PHOENIX - WARSONG
Marvel Comics: Nov, 2006 - No. 5, Mar, 2007 ($2.99, limited series)
1-5-Tyler Kirkham-a/Greg Pak-s/Marc Silvestri-c 3.00
HC (2007, $19.99, dustjacket) r/#1-5; variant cover gallery and Handbook pages 20.00
SC (2007, $14.99) r/#1-5; variant cover gallery and Handbook pages 15.00

X-MEN: PIXIE STRIKES BACK
Marvel Comics: Apr, 2010 - No. 4 ($3.99, limited series)
1,2-Kathryn Immonen-s/Sara Pichelli-a/Stuart Immonen-c 4.00

X-MEN PRIME
Marvel Comics: July, 1995 ($4.95, one-shot)
nn-Post Age of Apocalyse begins 1 3 4 6 8 10

X-MEN RARITIES
Marvel Comics: 1995 ($5.95, one-shot)
nn-Reprints hard-to-find stories 6.00

X-MEN ROAD TO ONSLAUGHT
Marvel Comics: Oct, 1996 ($2.50, one-shot)
nn-Retells Onslaught Saga 3.00

	GD	VG	FN	VF	VF/NM	NM-
	2.0	4.0	6.0	8.0	9.0	9.2

X-MEN: RONIN
Marvel Comics: May, 2003 - No. 5, July, 2003 ($2.99, limited series)
1-5-Manga-style X-Men; Torres-s/Nakatsuka-a 3.00

X-MEN: SEARCH FOR CYCLOPS
Marvel Comics: Oct, 2000 - No. 4, Mar, 2001 ($2.99, limited series)
1-4-Two covers (Raney, Pollina); Raney-a 3.00

X-MEN: SECOND COMING
Marvel Comics: May, 2010 ($3.99)
1-Cable & Hope return to the present; Bastion app.; Finch-a; covers by Granov & Finch 4.00
...: Prepare (4/10, free) previews x-over; short story w/Immonen-a; cover sketch art 1.00

X-MEN / SPIDER-MAN ("X-Men and Spider-Man" on cover)
Marvel Comics: Jan, 2009 - No. 4, Apr, 2009 ($3.99, limited series)
1-4: 1-Team-up from pre-blue Beast days; Kraven app.; Gage-s/Alberti-a 4.00

X-MEN SPOTLIGHT ON... STARJAMMERS (Also see X-Men #104)
Marvel Comics: 1990 - No. 2, 1990 ($4.50, 52 pgs.)
1,2: Features Starjammers 4.50

X-MEN SURVIVAL GUIDE TO THE MANSION
Marvel Comics: Aug, 1993 ($6.95, spiralbound)
1 7.00

X-MEN: THE COMPLETE AGE OF APOCALYPSE EPIC
Marvel Comics: 2005 - Vol. 4, 2006 ($29.99, TPB)
Book 1-4: Chronological reprintings of the crossover 30.00

X-MEN: THE EARLY YEARS
Marvel Comics: May, 1994 - No. 17, Sept, 1995 ($1.50/$2.50)
1-16: r/X-Men #1-8 w/new-c 3.00
17-$2.50-c; r/X-Men #17,18 3.00

X-MEN: THE END
Marvel Comics: Oct, 2004 - No. 6, Feb, 2005 ($2.99, limited series)
1-6-Claremont-s/Chen-a/Land-c 3.00
... Book One: Dreamers and Demons TPB (2005, $14.99) r/#1-6 15.00

X-MEN: THE END - HEROES AND MARTYRS (Volume 2)
Marvel Comics: May, 2005 - No. 6, Oct, 2005 ($2.99, limited series)
1-6-Claremont-s/Chen-a/Land-c; continued from X-Men: The End 3.00
... Vol. 2 TPB (2006, $14.99) r/#1-6 15.00

X-MEN: THE END (MEN & X-MEN) (Volume 3)
Marvel Comics: Mar, 2006 - No. 6, Aug, 2006 ($2.99, limited series)
1-6-Claremont-s/Chen-a. 1-Land-c. 2-6-Gene Ha-c 3.00
... Vol. 3 TPB (2006, $14.99) r/#1-6 15.00

X-MEN: THE MANGA
Marvel Comics: Mar, 1998 - No. 26, June, 1999 ($2.99, B&W)
1-26-English version of Japanese X-Men comics: 23,24-Randy Green-c 3.00

X-MEN: THE MOVIE
Marvel Comics: Aug, 2000; Sept, 2000
Adaptation (9/00, $5.95) Macchio-s/Williams & Lanning-a 6.00
Adaptation TPB (9/00, $14.95) Movie adaptation and key reprints of main characters; four photo covers (movie X, Magneto, Rogue, Wolverine) 15.00
Prequel: Magneto (8/00, $5.95) Texeira & Palmiotti-a; art & photo covers 6.00
Prequel: Rogue (8/00, $5.95) Evans & Nikolakakis-a; art & photo covers 6.00
Prequel: Wolverine (8/00, $5.95) Waller & McKenna-a; art & photo covers 6.00
TPB X-Men: Beginnings (8/00, $14.95) reprints 3 prequels w/photo-c 15.00

X-MEN 2: THE MOVIE
Marvel Comics: 2003
Adaptation (6/03, $3.50) Movie adaptation; photo-c; Austen-s/Zircher-a 3.50
Adaptation TPB (2003, $12.99) Movie adaptation & r/Prequels Nightcrawler & Wolverine 13.00
Prequel: Nightcrawler (5/03, $3.50) Kerschl-a; photo cover 3.50
Prequel: Wolverine (5/03, $3.50) Mandrake-a; photo cover; Sabretooth app. 3.50

X-MEN: THE 198 (See House of M)
Marvel Comics: Mar, 2006 - No. 5, July, 2006 ($2.99, limited series)
1-5-Hine-s/Muniz-a 3.00
... Files (2006, $3.99) profiles of the 198 mutants who kept their powers after House of M 4.00
Decimation: The 198 (2006, $15.99, TPB) r/#1-5 & X-Men: The 198 Files 16.00

X-MEN: THE TIMES AND LIFE OF LUCAS BISHOP
Marvel Comics: Apr, 2009 - No. 3, June, 2009 ($3.99, limited series)
1-3-Swierczynski-s/Stroman-a. 1-Bishop's birth and childhood 4.00

X-Men 2099 #12 © MAR

X-Men: Worlds Apart #1 © MAR

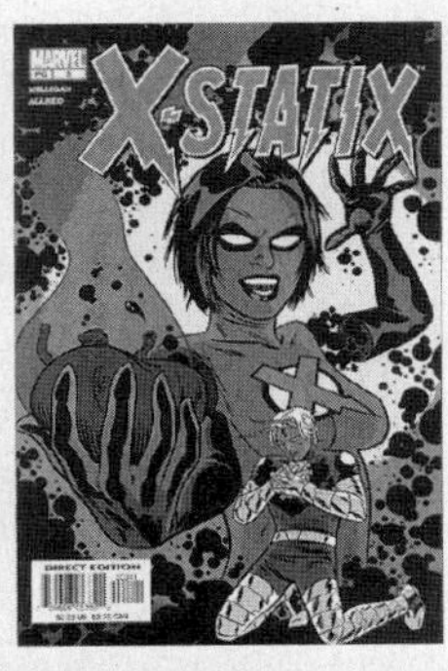

X-Statix #2 © MAR

GD VG FN VF VF/NM NM-
2.0 4.0 6.0 8.0 9.0 9.2

GD VG FN VF VF/NM NM-
2.0 4.0 6.0 8.0 9.0 9.2

X-MEN: THE ULTRA COLLECTION
Marvel Comics: Dec, 1994 - No. 5, Apr, 1995 ($2.95, limited series)

1-5: Pin-ups; no scripts 3.00

X-MEN: THE WEDDING ALBUM
Marvel Comics: 1994 ($2.95, magazine size, one-shot)

1-Wedding of Scott Summers & Jean Grey 3.00

X-MEN TRUE FRIENDS
Marvel Comics: Sept, 1999 - No. 3, Nov, 1999 ($2.99, limited series)

1-3-Claremont-s/Leonardi-a 3.00

X-MEN 2099 (Also see 2099: World of Tomorrow)
Marvel Comics: Oct, 1993 - No. 35, Aug, 1996 ($1.25/$1.50/$1.95)

1-($1.75)-Foil-c; Ron Lim/Adam Kubert-a begins 3.50
1-2nd printing ($1.75) 3.00
1-Gold edition (15,000 made); sold thru Diamond for $19.40 20.00
2-24,26-35: 3-Death of Tina; Lim-c/a(p) in #1-8. 8-Bound-in trading card sheet. 35-Nostromo (from X-Nation) app; storyline cont'd in 2099: World of Tomorrow 3.00
25-($2.50)-Double sized 3.50
Special 1 ($3.95) 4.00
...: Oasis ($5.95, one-shot) -Hildebrandt Bros.-c/a 6.00

X-MEN ULTRA III PREVIEW
Marvel Comics: 1995 ($2.95)

nn-Kubert-a 3.00

X-MEN UNIVERSE
Marvel Comics: Dec, 1999 - Present ($4.99/$3.99)

1-8-Reprints stories from recent X-Men titles 5.00
9-15-($3.99) 4.00

X-MEN UNIVERSE: PAST, PRESENT AND FUTURE
Marvel Comics: Feb, 1999 ($2.99, one-shot)

1-Previews 1999 X-Men events; background info 3.00

X-MEN UNLIMITED
Marvel Comics: 1993 - No. 50, Sept, 2003 ($3.95/$2.99, 68 pgs.)

1-Chris Bachalo-c/a; Quesada-a. 5.00
2-11: 2-Origin of Magneto script. 3-Sabretooth-c/story. 10-Dark Beast vs. Beast; Mark Waid script. 11-Magneto & Rogue 4.00
12-33: 12-Begin $2.99-c; Onslaught x-over; Juggernaut-c/app. 19-Caliafore-a. 20-Generation X app. 27-Origin Thunderbird. 29-Maximum Security x-over; Bishop-c/app. 30-Mahfood-a. 31-Stelfreeze-c/a. 32-Dazzler; Thompson-c/a 33-Kaluta-c 3.00
34-37,39,40-42-($3.50) 34-Von Eeden-a. 35-Finch, Conner, Maguire-a. 36-Chiodo-c/a; Larroca, Totleben-a. 39-Bachalo-c; Pearson-a. 41-Bachalo-c; X-Statix app. 3.50
38-($2.25) Kitty Pryde; Robertson-a 3.00
43-50-($2.50) 43-Sienkiewicz-c/a; Paul Smith-a. 45-Noto-c. 46-Bisley-a. 47-Warren-s/Mays-a. 48-Wolverine story w/Isanove painted-a 3.00
X-Men Legends Vol. 4: Hated and Feared TPB (2003, $19.99) r/stories by various 20.00
NOTE: *Bachalo c/a-1. Quesada a-1. Waid scripts-10*

X-MEN UNLIMITED
Marvel Comics: Apr, 2004 - No. 14, Jun, 2006 ($2.99)

1-14: 1-6-Pat Lee-c; short stories by various. 2-District X preview; Granov-a 3.00

X-MEN VS. AGENTS OF ATLAS
Marvel Comics: Dec, 2009 - No. 2, Jan, 2010 ($3.99, limited series)

1,2-Pagulayan-a. 1-McGuinness-c. 2-Granov-c 4.00

X-MEN VS. DRACULA
Marvel Comics: Dec, 1993 ($1.75)

1-r/X-Men Annual #6; Austin-c(i) 3.00

X-MEN VS. THE AVENGERS, THE
Marvel Comics Group: Apr, 1987 - No. 4, July, 1987 ($1.50, limited series, Baxter paper)

1 4.00
2-4 3.00

X-MEN VS. THE BROOD, THE
Marvel Comics Group: Sept, 1996 - No. 2, Oct, 1996 ($2.95, limited series)

1,2-Wraparound-c; Ostrander-s/Hitch-a(p) 3.00
TPB('97, $16.99) reprints X-Men/Brood: Day of Wrath #1,2 & Uncanny X-Men #232-234 17.00

X-MEN VISIONARIES
Marvel Comics: 1995,1996,2000 (trade paperbacks)

nn-($8.95) Reprints X-Men stories; Adam & Andy Kubert-a 9.00
...2: The Neal Adams Collection (1996) r/X-Men #56-63,65 30.00
...2: The Neal Adams Col. (2nd printing, 2000, $24.95) new Adams-c 25.00

X-MEN/WILDC.A.T.S.: THE DARK AGE (See also WildC.A.T.S./X-Men...)
Marvel Comics: 1998 ($4.50, one-shot)

1-Two covers (Broome & Golden); Ellis-s 4.50

X-MEN: WORLDS APART
Marvel Comics: Dec, 2008 - No. 4, Mar, 2009 ($3.99, limited series)

1-4-Storm and the Black Panther vs. the Shadow King. 1-Campbell-c 4.00

X-NATION 2099
Marvel Comics: Mar, 1996 - No. 6, Aug, 1996 ($1.95)

1-($3.95)-Humberto Ramos-a(p); wraparound, foil-c 4.00
2-6: 2,3-Ramos-a. 4-Exodus-c/app. 6-Reed Richards app 3.00

X NECROSIA
Marvel Comics: Dec, 2009 ($3.99)

1-Beginning of X-Force/X-Men/New Mutants x-over; Crain-a; Selene returns 4.00
...: The Gathering (2/10, $3.99) Wither, Blink, Senyaka. Mortis & Eliphas short stories 4.00

X-O MANOWAR (1st Series)
Valiant/Acclaim Comics (Valiant) No. 43 on: Feb, 1992 - No. 68, Sept, 1996 ($1.95/$2.25/$2.50, high quality)

0-(8/93, $3.50)-Wraparound embossed chromium-c by Quesada; Solar app.; origin Aric (X-O Manowar) 3.50
0-Gold variant 5.00
1-Intro/1st app. & partial origin of Aric (X-O Manowar); Barry Smith/Layton-a 1 2 3 5 6 8
2-4: 2-B. Smith/Layton-c. 3-Layton-c(i). 4-1st app. Shadowman 6.00
5-15: 5-B. Smith-c. 6-Begin $2.25-c; Ditko-a(p). 7,8-Unity x-overs. 7-Miller-c. 8-Simonson-c. 12-1st app. Randy Calder. 14,15-Turok-c/stories 3.00
15-Hot pink logo variant; came with Ultra Pro Rigid Comic Sleeves box; no price on cover 4.00
16-24,26-43: 20-Serial number contest insert. 27-29-Turok x-over. 28-Bound-in trading card. 30-1st app. new "good skin"; Solar app. 33-Chaos Effect Delta Pt. 3. 42-Shadowman app.; includes X-O Manowar Birthquake! Prequel 2.50
25-($3.50)-Has 16 pg. Armorines #0 bound-in w/origin 3.50
44-68: 44-Begin $2.50-c. 50-X, 50-O, 51, 52, 63-Bart Sears-c/a/scripts. 68-Revealed that Aric's past stories were premonitions of his future 2.50
...: Birth HC (2008, $24.95) recolored reprints #0-6; script and breakdowns for #0; cover gallery; new "The Rise of Lydia" story by Layton and Leeke 25.00
Trade paperback nn (1993, $9.95)-Polybagged with copy of X-O Database #1 inside 10.00
Yearbook 1 (4/95, $2.95) 3.00
NOTE: *Layton a-1i, 2i(part); c-1, 2i, 3i, 6i, 21i. Reese a-4i(part); c-26i.*

X-O MANOWAR (2nd Series)(Also see Iron Man/X-O Manowar: Heavy Metal)
Acclaim Comics (Valiant Heroes): V2#1, Oct, 1996 - No. 21, Jun, 1998 ($2.50)

V2#1-21: 1-Mark Waid & Brian Augustyn scripts begin; 1st app. Donavon Wylie; Rand Banion dies; painted variant-c exists. 2-Donavon Wylie becomes new X-O Manowar. 7-9-Augustyn-s. 10-Copycat-c 2.50

X-O MANOWAR FAN EDITION
Acclaim Comics (Valiant Heroes): Feb, 1997 (Overstreet's FAN giveaway)

1-Reintro the Armorines & the Hard Corps; 1st app. Citadel; Augustyn scripts; McKone-c/a 4.00

X-O MANOWAR/IRON MAN: IN HEAVY METAL (See Iron Man/X-O Manowar: Heavy Metal)
Acclaim Comics (Valiant Heroes): Sept, 1996 ($2.50, one-shot)
(1st Marvel/Valiant x-over)

1-Pt 1 of X-O Manowar/Iron Man x-over; Arnim Zola app.; Nicieza scripts; Andy Smith-a 2.50

XOMBI
DC Comics (Milestone): Jan, 1994 - No. 21, Feb, 1996 ($1.75/$2.50)

0-($1.95)-Shadow War x-over; Simonson silver ink varnish-c 2.50
1-21: 1-John Byrne-c 2.50
1-Platinum 8.00

X-PATROL
Marvel Comics (Amalgam): Apr, 1996 ($1.95, one-shot)

1-Cruz-a(p) 2.50

XSE
Marvel Comics: Nov, 1996 - No. 4, Feb, 1997 ($1.95, limited series)

1-4: 1-Bishop & Shard app. 2.50
1-Variant-c 3.00

X-STATIX
Marvel Comics: Sept, 2002 - No. 26, Oct, 2004 ($2.99/$2.25)

X-Treme X-Men #1 © MAR

X-23 #1 © MAR

Yellowjacket Comics #6 © F. Comunale

	GD 2.0	VG 4.0	FN 6.0	VF 8.0	VF/NM 9.0	NM- 9.2

1-($2.99)Allred-a/c; intro. Venus Dee Milo; back-up w/Cooke-a 3.00
2-9-($2.25) 4-Quitely-c. 5-Pope-c/a 2.50
10-26: 10-Begin $2.99-c; Bond-a; U-Go Girl flashback. 13,14-Spider-Man app. 21-25-Avengers app. 26-Team dies 3.00
... Vol. 1: Good Omens TPB (2003, $11.99) r/#1-5 12.00
... Vol. 2: Good Guys & Bad Guys TPB (2003, $15.99) r/#6-10 & Wolverine/Doop #1&2 16.00
... Vol. 3: Back From the Dead TPB (2004, $19.99) r/#11-18 20.00
... Vol. 4: X-Statix Vs. the Avengers TPB (2004, $19.99) r/#19-26; pin-ups 20.00

X-STATIX PRESENTS: DEAD GIRL
Marvel Comics: Mar, 2006 - No. 5, July, 2006 ($2.99, limited series)
1-5-Dr. Strange, Dead Girl, Miss America, Tike app. Milligan-s/Dragotta & Allred-a 3.00
TPB (2006, $13.99) r/series 14.00

X-TERMINATORS
Marvel Comics: Oct, 1988 - No. 4, Jan, 1989 ($1.00, limited series)
1-1st app.; X-Men/X-Factor tie-in; Williamson-i 3.00
2-4 2.50

X, THE MAN WITH THE X-RAY EYES (See Movie Comics)

X-TREME X-MEN (Also see Mekanix)
Marvel Comics: July, 2001 - No. 46, Jun, 2004 ($2.99/$3.50)
1-Claremont-s/Larroca-c/a 4.00
2-24: 2-Two covers (Larroca & Pacheco); Psylocke killed 3.00
25-35, 40-46: 25-30-God Loves, Man Kills II; Stryker app.; Kordey-a 3.00
36-39-($3.50) 3.50
Annual 2001 ($4.95) issue opens longways 5.00
... Vol. 1: Destiny TPB (2002, $19.95) r/#1-9 20.00
... Vol. 2: Invasion TPB (2003, $19.99) r/#10-18 20.00
... Vol. 3: Schism TPB (2003, $16.99) r/#19-23; X-Treme X-Posé #1&2 17.00
... Vol. 4: Mekanix TPB (2003, $16.99) r/Mekanix #1-6 17.00
... Vol. 5: God Loves Man Kills TPB (2003, $19.99) r/#25-30 20.00
... Vol. 6: Intifada TPB (2004, $16.99) r/#24,31-35 17.00
... Vol. 7: Storm the Arena TPB (2004, $16.99) r/#36-39 17.00
... Vol. 8: Prisoner of Fire TPB (2004, $19.99) r/#40-46 and Annual 2001 20.00

X-TREME X-MEN: SAVAGE LAND
Marvel Comics: Nov, 2001 - No. 4, Feb, 2002 ($2.99, limited series)
1-4-Claremont-s/Sharpe-c/a; Beast app. 3.00

X-TREME X-POSE
Marvel Comics: Jan, 2003 - No. 2, Feb, 2003 ($2.99, limited series)
1,2-Claremont-s/Ranson-a/Migliari-c 3.00

X-23 (See debut in NYX #3)(See NYX X-23 HC for reprint)
Marvel Comics: Mar, 2005 - No. 6, July, 2005 ($2.99, limited series)
1-Origin of the Wolverine clone girl; Tan-a 4.00
1-Variant Billy Tan-c with red background 5.00
2-6-Origin continues 3.00
2-Variant B&W sketch-c 5.00
One shot 1 (5/10, $3.99) Urasov-c/Lui-s; Wolverine & Jubilee app. 4.00
...: Innocence Lost TPB (2006, $15.99) r/#1-6 16.00

X-23: TARGET X
Marvel Comics: Feb, 2007 - No. 6, July, 2007 ($2.99, limited series)
1-6-Kyle & Yost-s/Choi & Oback-a. 6-Gallery of variant covers and sketches 3.00
TPB (2007, $15.99) r/#1-6; gallery of variant covers and sketches 16.00

X-UNIVERSE
Marvel Comics: May, 1995 - No. 2, June, 1995 ($3.50, limited series)
1,2: Age of Apocalypse 5.00

X-VENTURE (Super Heroes)
Victory Magazines Corp.: July, 1947 - No. 2, Nov, 1947
1-Atom Wizard, Mystery Shadow, Lester Trumble begin
110 220 330 704 1202 1700
2 54 108 162 346 591 835

XYR (See Eclipse Graphic Album Series #21)

YAK YAK
Dell Publishing Co.: No. 1186, May-July, 1961 - No. 1348, Apr-June, 1962
Four Color 1186 (#1)- Jack Davis-c/a; 2 versions, one minus 3 pgs.
8 16 24 58 97 135
Four Color 1348 (#2)-Davis c/a 8 16 24 52 86 120

YAKKY DOODLE & CHOPPER (TV) (See Dell Giant #44)
Gold Key: Dec, 1962 (Hanna-Barbera)
1 7 14 21 50 83 115

YANG (See House of Yang)
Charlton Comics: Nov, 1973 - No. 13, May, 1976; V14#15, Sept, 1985 - No. 17, Jan, 1986 (No V14#14, series resumes with #15)
1-Origin; Sattler-a begins; slavery-s 2 4 6 11 16 20
2-13(1976) 1 2 3 6 9 10
15-17(1986): 15-Reprints #1 (Low print run) 6.00
3,10,11(Modern Comics-r, 1977) 4.00

YANKEE COMICS
Harry 'A' Chesler: Sept, 1941 - No. 7, 1942?
1-Origin The Echo, The Enchanted Dagger, Yankee Doodle Jones, The Firebrand, & The Scarlet Sentry; Black Satan app.; Yankee Doodle Jones app. on all covers
187 374 561 1197 2049 2900
2-Origin Johnny Rebel; Major Victory app.; Barry Kuda begins
81 162 243 518 884 1250
3,4: 4-(3/42) 59 118 177 375 643 910
4 (nd, 1940s; 7-1/4x5", 68 pgs, distr. to the service)-Foxy Grandpa, Tom, Dick & Harry, Impy, Ace & Deuce, Dot & Dash, Ima Slooth by Jack Cole (Remington Morse publ.)
14 28 42 76 108 140
5-7 (nd; 10¢, 7-1/4x5", 68 pgs.)(Remington Morse publ.)-urges readers to send their copies to servicemen. 12 24 36 67 94 120

YANKEE DOODLE THE SPIRIT OF LIBERTY
Spire Publications: 1984 (no price, 36 pgs)
nn-Al Hartley-s/c/a 2 4 6 8 11 14

YANKS IN BATTLE
Quality Comics Group: Sept, 1956 - No. 4, Dec, 1956; 1963
1-Cuidera-c(i) 10 20 30 58 79 100
2-4: Cuidera-c(i) 8 16 24 40 50 60
I.W. Reprint #3(1963)-r/#?; exist? 2 4 6 9 12 15

YARDBIRDS, THE (G. I. Joe's Sidekicks)
Ziff-Davis Publishing Co.: Summer, 1952
1-By Bob Oskner 10 20 30 56 76 95

YARN MAN (See Megaton Man)
Kitchen Sink : Oct, 1989 ($2.00, B&W, one-shot)
1-Donald Simpson-c/a/scripts 2.50

YARNS OF YELLOWSTONE
World Color Press: 1972 (50¢, 36 pgs.)
nn-Illustrated by Bill Chapman 2 4 6 9 12 15

YEAH!
DC Comics (Homage): Oct, 1999 - No. 9, Jun, 2000 ($2.95)
1-Bagge-s/Hernandez-a 3.00
2-9: 2-Editorial page contains adult language 3.00

YELLOW CLAW (Also see Giant Size Master of Kung Fu)
Atlas Comics (MjMC): Oct, 1956 - No. 4, Apr, 1957
1-Origin by Joe Maneely 103 206 309 659 1130 1600
2-Kirby-a 84 168 252 538 919 1300
3,4-Kirby-a; 4-Kirby/Severin-a 81 162 243 518 884 1250
NOTE: *Everett c-3. Maneely c-1. Reinman a-2i, 3. Severin c-2, 4.*

YELLOWJACKET COMICS (Jack in the Box #11 on)(See TNT Comics)
E. Levy/Frank Comunale/Charlton: Sept, 1944 - No. 10, June, 1946
1-Intro & origin Yellowjacket; Diana, the Huntress begins; E.A. Poe's "The Black Cat" adaptation 66 132 198 419 722 1025
2-Yellowjacket-c begin, end #10 41 82 123 256 428 600
3,5 40 80 120 246 411 575
4-E.A. Poe's "Fall of the House Of Usher" adaptation; Palais-a
41 82 123 256 428 600
6 48 96 144 302 514 725
7-Classic skull-c; Toth-a (1 pg. gag feature) 97 194 291 621 1061 1500
8-10: 1,3,4,6-10-Have stories narrated by old witch in "Tales of Terror" (1st horror series?)
47 94 141 296 503 710

YELLOWSTONE KELLY (Movie)
Dell Publishing Co.: No. 1056, Nov-Jan, 1959/60
Four Color 1056-Clint Walker photo-c 6 12 18 37 59 80

YELLOW SUBMARINE (See Movie Comics)

YEAR ONE: BATMAN/RA'S AL GHUL
DC Comics: 2005 - No. 2, 2005 ($5.99, squarebound, limited series)

Yosemite Sam #34 © WB

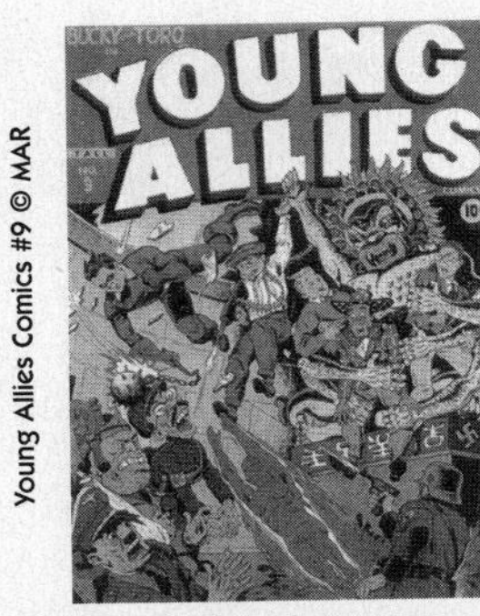

Young Allies Comics #9 © MAR

Youngblood #10 © Awesome Ent.

GD 2.0 VG 4.0 FN 6.0 VF 8.0 VF/NM 9.0 NM- 9.2

1-Devin Grayson-s/Paul Gulacy-a 6.00
TPB (2006, $9.99) r/#1,2 10.00

YEAR ONE: BATMAN SCARECROW
DC Comics: 2005 - No. 2, 2005 ($5.99, squarebound, limited series)

1-Scarecrow's origin; Bruce Jones-s/Sean Murphy-a 6.00

YIN FEI THE CHINESE NINJA
Leung's Publications: 1988 - No. 8, 1990 ($1.80/$2.00, 52 pgs.)

1-8 2.50

YOGI BEAR (See Dell Giant #41, Golden Comics Digest, Kite Fun Book, March of Comics #253, 265, 279, 291, 309, 319, 337, 344, Movie Comics under "Hey There It's..." & Whitman Comic Books)

YOGI BEAR (TV) (Hanna-Barbera) (See Four Color #990)
Dell Publishing Co./Gold Key No. 10 on: No. 1067, 12-2/59-60 - No. 9, 7-9/62; No. 10, 10/62 - No. 42, 10/70

Four Color 1067 (#1)-TV show debuted 1/30/61 10 20 30 71 126 180
Four Color 1104,1162 (5-7/61) 7 14 21 49 80 110
4(8-9/61) - 6(12-1/61-62) 6 12 18 37 59 80
Four Color 1271(11/61) 6 12 18 37 59 80
Four Color 1349(1/62)-Photo-c 8 16 24 58 97 135
7(2-3/62) - 9(7-9/62)-Last Dell 6 12 18 37 59 80
10(10/62-G.K.), 11(1/63)-titled "Yogi Bear Jellystone Jollies" (80 pgs.); 11-X-Mas-c
7 14 21 47 76 105
12(4/63), 14-20 5 10 15 30 48 65
13(7/63, 68 pgs.)-Surprise Party 7 14 21 47 76 105
21-30 3 6 9 20 30 40
31-42 3 6 9 17 25 32

YOGI BEAR (TV)
Charlton Comics: Nov, 1970 - No. 35, Jan, 1976 (Hanna-Barbera)

1 4 8 12 28 44 60
2-6,8-10 3 6 9 16 23 30
7-Summer Fun (Giant, 52 pgs.) 4 8 12 28 44 60
11-20 3 6 9 16 22 28
21-35: 28-31-partial-r 2 4 6 11 16 20
Digest (nn, 1972, 75¢-c, B&W, 100 pgs.) (scarce) 3 6 9 19 29 38

YOGI BEAR (TV)(See The Flintstones, 3rd series & Spotlight #1)
Marvel Comics Group: Nov, 1977 - No. 9, Mar, 1979 (Hanna-Barbera)

1,7-9: 1-Flintstones begin (Newsstand sales only) 3 6 9 16 23 30
2-6 2 4 6 11 16 20

YOGI BEAR (TV)
Harvey Comics: Sept, 1992 - No. 6, Mar, 1994 ($1.25/$1.50) (Hanna-Barbera)

V2#1-6 3.00
...Big Book V2#1,2 ($1.95, 52 pgs): 1-(11/92). 2-(3/93) 3.00
...Giant Size V2#1,2 ($2.25, 68 pgs.): 1-(10/92). 2-(4/93) 3.00

YOGI BEAR (TV)
Archie Publ.: May, 1997

1 3.00

YOGI BEAR'S EASTER PARADE (See The Funtastic World of Hanna-Barbera #2)

YOGI BERRA (Baseball hero)
Fawcett Publications: 1951 (Yankee catcher)

nn-Photo-c (scarce) 71 142 213 454 777 1100

YOSEMITE SAM (...& Bugs Bunny) (TV)
Gold Key/Whitman: Dec, 1970 - No. 81, Feb, 1984

1 4 8 12 28 44 60
2-10 3 6 9 16 22 28
11-20 2 4 6 10 14 18
21-30 2 4 6 8 11 14
31-50 1 3 4 6 8 10
51-65 (Gold Key) 1 2 3 5 6 8
66,67 (Whitman) 2 4 6 8 10 12
68(9/80), 69(10/80), 70(12/80) 3-pack only 3 6 9 18 27 35
71-78: 76(2/82), 77(3/82), 78(4/82) 2 4 6 8 11 14
79-81 (All #90263 on-c, no date or date code; 3-pack): 79(7/83). 80(8/83). 81(2/84)-(1/3-r)
2 4 6 13 18 22

(See March of Comics #363, 380, 392)

YOUNG ALLIES COMICS (All-Winners #21; see Kid Komics #2)
Timely Comics (USA 1-7/NPI 8,9/YAI 10-20): Sum, 1941 - No. 20, Oct, 1946

1-Origin/1st app. The Young Allies (Bucky, Toro, others); 1st meeting of Captain America & Human Torch; Red Skull-c & app.; S&K-c/splash; Hitler-c; Note: the cover was altered after its preview in Human Torch #5. Stalin was shown with Hitler but was removed due to Russia becoming an ally 1342 2684 4026 10,105 17,803 25,500
2-(Winter, 1941)-Captain America & Human Torch app.; Simon & Kirby-c
389 778 1167 2723 4762 6800
3-Fathertime, Captain America & Human Torch app.; Remember Pearl Harbor issue (Spring, 1942); Stan Lee scripts; Vs. Japenese-c/full-length story
300 600 900 1980 3440 4900
4-The Vagabond & Red Skull, Capt. America, Human Torch app. Classic Red Skull-c
423 846 1269 3088 5444 7800
5-Captain America & Human Torch app. 216 432 648 1372 2361 3350
6,7 153 306 459 972 1374 2375
8-Classic Schomburg WW2 bondage-c 168 336 504 1075 1838 2600
9-Hitler, Tojo, Mussolini-c. 200 400 600 1280 2190 3100
10-Classic Schomburg Hooded Villain bondage-c; origin Tommy Tyme & Clock of Ages; ends #19
168 336 504 1075 1838 2600
11-20: 12-Classic decapitation story 103 206 309 659 1130 1600

NOTE: ***Brodsky** c-15. **Gabrielle** a-3; c-3, 4. **S&K** c-1, 2. **Schomburg** c-5-13, 16-19. **Shores** c-20.*

YOUNG ALLIES 70TH ANNIVERSARY SPECIAL
Marvel Comics: Aug, 2009 ($3.99, one-shot)

1-Bucky & Young Allies app.; Stern-s/Rivera-a; Terry Vance rep. from Marvel Myst. #14 4.00

YOUNG ALL-STARS
DC Comics: June, 1987 - No. 31, Nov, 1989 ($1.00, deluxe format)

1-31: 1-1st app. Iron Munro & The Flying Fox. 8,9-Millennium tie-ins 2.50
Annual 1 (1988, $2.00) 2.50

YOUNG AVENGERS
Marvel Comics: Apr, 2005 - No. 12, Aug, 2006 ($2.99)

1-Intro. Iron Lad, Patriot, Hulkling, Asgardian; Heinberg-s/Cheung-a 5.00
1-Director's Cut (2005, $3.99) r/#1 plus character sketches; original script 4.00
2-12: 3-6-Kang app. 7-DiVito-a. 9-Skrulls app. 3.00
... Special 1 (2/06, $3.99) origins of the heroes; art by various incl. Neal Adams, Jae Lee, Bill Sienkiewicz, Gene Ha, Michael Gaydos and Pasqual Ferry 4.00
... Vol. 1: Sidekicks HC (2005, $19.99, dustjacket) r/#1-6; character design sketches 20.00
... Vol. 1: Sidekicks TPB (2006, $14.99) r/#1-6; character design sketches 15.00
... Vol. 2: Family Matters HC (2006, $22.99, dustjacket) r/#7-12 & YA Special #1 23.00
... Vol. 2: Family Matters SC (2007, $17.99) r/#7-12 & YA Special #1 18.00
HC (2008, $29.99, d.j.) oversized reprint of #1-12 and Special #1; script & sketch pages 30.00

YOUNG AVENGERS PRESENTS
Marvel Comics: Mar, 2008 - No. 6, Aug, 2008 ($2.99, limited series)

1-4: 1-Patriot; Bucky app. 2-Hulkling; Captain Marvel app. 3-Wiccan & Speed. 4-Vision. 5-Stature. 6-Hawkeye; Clint Barton app.; Alan Davis-a 3.00

YOUNGBLOOD (See Brigade #4, Megaton Explosion & Team Youngblood)
Image Comics (Extreme Studios): Apr, 1992 - No. 4, Feb, 1993 ($2.50, lim. series); No. 6, June, 1994 (No #5) - No. 10, Dec, 1994 ($1.95/$2.50)

1-Liefeld-c/a/scripts in all; flip book format with 2 trading cards; 1st Image/Extreme Studios title. 5.00
1,2-2nd printing 2.50
2-(JUN-c, July 1992 indicia)-1st app. Shadowhawk in solo back-up story; 2 trading cards inside; flip book format; 1st app. Prophet, Kirby, Berzerkers, Darkthorn 2.50
3,0,4,5: 3-(OCT-c, August 1992 indicia)-Contains 2 trading cards inside (flip book); 1st app. Supreme in back-up story; 1st app. Showdown. 0-(12/92, $1.95)-Contains 2 trading cards; 2 cover variations exist, green or beige logo; w/Image #0 coupon. 4-(2/93)-Glow-in-the-dark cover w/2 trading cards; 2nd app. Dale Keown's The Pitt; Bloodstrike app. 5-Flip book w/Brigade #4 2.50
6-($3.50, 52 pgs.)-Wraparound-c 3.50
7-10: 7, 8-Liefeld-c(p)/a(p)/story. 8,9-(9/94) 9-Valentino story & art 2.50
Battlezone 1 (May-c, 4/93 inside, $1.95)-Arsenal book; Liefeld-c(p) 2.50
Battlezone 2 (7/94, $2.95)-Wraparound-c 3.00
...Super Special (Winter '97, $2.99) Sprouse -a 3.00
Yearbook 1 (7/93, $2.50)-Fold out panel; 1st app. Tyrax & Kanan 2.50
Vol. 1 HC (2008, $34.99) oversized r/#1-5, recolored and remastered; sketch art and cover gallery; Mark Millar intro. 35.00
TPB (1996, $16.95)-r/Team Youngblood #8-10 & Youngblood #6-8,10 17.00

YOUNGBLOOD
Image Comics (Extreme Studios)/Maximum Press No. 14: V2#1, Sept, 1995 - No. 14, Dec, 1996 ($2.50)

V2#1-10,14: Roger Cruz-a in all. 4-Extreme Destroyer Pt. 4 w/gaming card. 5-Variant-c exists. 6-Angela & Glory. 7-Shadowhunt Pt. 3; Shadowhawk app. 8,10-Thor (from Supreme) app. 10-(7/96). 14-(12/96)-1st Maximum Press issue 2.50

YOUNGBLOOD (Volume 3)
Awesome/ Awesome-Hyperwerks #2: Feb, 1998 - No. 2, Aug, 1998 ($2.50)

Youngblood V4 #8 © Rob Liefeld

Young Liars #8 © David Lapham

Young Love #2 © PRIZE

	GD 2.0	VG 4.0	FN 6.0	VF 8.0	VF/NM 9.0	NM- 9.2
1-Alan Moore-s/Skroce & Stucker-a; 12 diff. covers						2.50
2-(8/98) Skroce & Liefeld covers						2.50
...Imperial 1 (Arcade Comics, 6/04, $2.99) Kirkman-sMychaels-a						3.00

YOUNGBLOOD (Volume 4)
Image Comics: Jan, 2008 - Present ($2.99/$3.99)

	GD	VG	FN	VF	VF/NM	NM-
1-7-Casey-s/Donovan-a; two covers by Donovan & Liefeld on each						3.00
8-Obama flip cover by Liefeld; Obama app. in story						3.00
9-($3.99) Obama flip cover by Liefeld; Free Agent rejoins; Obama app. in story						4.00

YOUNGBLOOD: STRIKEFILE
Image Comics (Extreme Studios): Apr, 1993 - No. 11, Feb, 1995 ($1.95/$2.50/$2.95)

	GD	VG	FN	VF	VF/NM	NM-
1-10: 1-($1.95)-Flip book w/Jae Lee-c/a & Liefeld-c/a in #1-3; 1st app. The Allies,Giger, & Glory. 3-Thibert-i asisst. 4-Liefeld-c(p); no Lee-a. 5-Liefeld-c(p). 8-Platt-c						3.00

NOTE: *Youngblood: Strikefile began as a four issue limited series.*

YOUNGBLOOD/X-FORCE
Image Comics (Extreme Studios): July, 1996 ($4.95, one-shot)

	GD	VG	FN	VF	VF/NM	NM-
1-Cruz-a(p); two covers exist						5.00

YOUNG BRIDES (True Love Secrets)
Feature/Prize Publ.: Sept-Oct, 1952 - No. 30, Nov-Dec, 1956 (Photo-c: 1-4)

	GD	VG	FN	VF	VF/NM	NM-
V1#1-Simon & Kirby-a	37	74	111	218	354	490
2-S&K-a	20	40	60	117	189	260
3-6-S&K-a	18	36	54	105	165	225
V2#1-7,10-12 (#7-18)-S&K-a	17	34	51	98	154	210
8,9-No S&K-a	9	18	27	52	69	85
V3#1-3(#19-21)-Last precode (3-4/55)	9	18	27	50	65	80
4,6(#22,24), V4#1,3(#25,27)	8	16	24	44	57	70
V3#5(#23)-Meskin-c	9	18	27	47	61	75
V4#2(#26)-All S&K issue	16	32	48	94	147	200
V4#4(#28)-S&K-a	14	28	42	80	115	150
V4#5,6(#29,30)	9	18	27	50	65	80

YOUNG DR. MASTERS (See The Adventures of Young Dr. Masters)

YOUNG DOCTORS, THE
Charlton Comics: Jan, 1963 - No. 6, Nov, 1963

	GD	VG	FN	VF	VF/NM	NM-
V1#1	3	6	9	21	32	42
2-6	3	6	9	14	19	24

YOUNG EAGLE
Fawcett Publications/Charlton: 12/50 - No. 10, 6/52; No. 3, 7/56 - No. 5, 4/57 (Photo-c: 1-10)

	GD	VG	FN	VF	VF/NM	NM-
1-Intro Young Eagle	18	36	54	103	162	220
2-Complete picture novelette "The Mystery of Thunder Canyon"	10	20	30	58	79	100
3-9	9	18	27	50	65	80
10-Origin Thunder, Young Eagle's Horse	8	16	24	44	57	70
3-5(Charlton)-Formerly Sherlock Holmes?	7	14	21	35	43	50

YOUNG GUNS SKETCHBOOK
Marvel Comics: Feb, 2005 ($3.99, one-shot)

	GD	VG	FN	VF	VF/NM	NM-
1-Sketch pages from 2005 Marvel projects by Coipel, Granov, McNiven, Land & others						4.00

YOUNG HEARTS
Marvel Comics (SPC): Nov, 1949 - No. 2, Feb, 1950

	GD	VG	FN	VF	VF/NM	NM-
1-Photo-c	15	30	45	84	127	170
2-Colleen Townsend photo-c from movie	10	20	30	58	79	100

YOUNG HEARTS IN LOVE
Super Comics: 1964

	GD	VG	FN	VF	VF/NM	NM-
17,18: 17-r/Young Love V5#6 (4-5/62)	2	4	6	9	13	16

YOUNG HEROES (Formerly Forbidden Worlds #34)
American Comics Group (Titan): No. 35, Feb-Mar, 1955 - No. 37, Jun-Jul, 1955

	GD	VG	FN	VF	VF/NM	NM-
35-37-Frontier Scout	10	20	30	54	72	90

YOUNG HEROES IN LOVE
DC Comics: June, 1997 - No. 17; #1,000,000, Nov, 1998 ($1.75/$1.95/$2.50)

	GD	VG	FN	VF	VF/NM	NM-
1-1st app. Young Heroes; Madan-a						3.00
2-17: 3-Superman-c/app. 7-Begin $1.95-c						2.50
#1,000,000 (11/98, $2.50) 853 Century x-over						2.50

YOUNG INDIANA JONES CHRONICLES, THE
Dark Horse Comics: Feb, 1992 - No. 12, Feb, 1993 ($2.50)

	GD	VG	FN	VF	VF/NM	NM-
1-12: Dan Barry scripts in all						2.50

NOTE: *Dan Barry a(p)-1, 2, 5, 6, 10; c-1-10.* ***Morrow*** *a-3, 4, 5p, 6p.* ***Springer*** *a-1i, 2i.*

YOUNG INDIANA JONES CHRONICLES, THE
Hollywood Comics (Disney): 1992 ($3.95, squarebound, 68 pgs.)

	GD	VG	FN	VF	VF/NM	NM-
1-3: 1-r/YIJC #1,2 by D. Horse. 2-r/#3,4. 3-r/#5,6						4.00

YOUNG JUSTICE (Also see Teen Titans and Titans/Young Justice)
DC Comics: Sept, 1998 - No. 55, May, 2003 ($2.50/$2.75)

	GD	VG	FN	VF	VF/NM	NM-
1-Robin, Superboy & Impulse team-up; David-s/Nauck-a						4.00
2,3: 3-Mxyzptlk app.						3.00
4-20: 4-Wonder Girl, Arrowette and the Secret join. 6-JLA app. 13-Supergirl x-over. 20-Sins of Youth aftermath						3.00
21-49: 25-Empress ID revealed. 28,29-Forever People app. 32-Empress origin. 35,36-Our Worlds at War x-over. 38-Joker: Last Laugh. 41-The Ray joins. 42-Spectre-c/app. 44,45-World Without YJ x-over pt. 1,5; Ramos-c. 48-Begin $2.75-c						2.75
50-($3.95) Wonder Twins,CM3 and other various DC teen heroes app.						4.00
51-55: 53,54-Darkseid app. 55-Last issue; leads into Titans/Young Justice mini-series						2.75
#1,000,000 (11/98) 853 Century x-over						2.50
...: A League of Their Own (2000, $14.95, TPB) r/#1-7, Secret Files #1						15.00
...: 80-Page Giant (5/99, $4.95) Ramos-c; stories and art by various						5.00
...: In No Man's Land (7/99, $3.95) McDaniel-c						4.00
...: Our Worlds at War (8/01, $2.95) Jae Lee-c; Linear Men app.						3.00
...: Secret Files (1/99, $4.95) Origin-s & pin-ups						5.00
...: The Secret (6/98, $1.95) Girlfrenzy; Nauck-a						2.50

YOUNG JUSTICE: SINS OF YOUTH (Also see Sins of Youth x-over issues and Sins of Youth: Secret Files)
DC Comics: May, 2000 - No. 2, May, 2000 ($3.95, limited series)

	GD	VG	FN	VF	VF/NM	NM-
1,2-Young Justice, JLA & JSA swap ages; David-s/Nauck-a						4.00
TPB (2000, $19.95) r/#1,2 & all x-over issues						20.00

YOUNG KING COLE (...Detective Tales)(Becomes Criminals on the Run)
Premium Group/Novelty Press: Fall, 1945 - V3#12, July, 1948

	GD	VG	FN	VF	VF/NM	NM-
V1#1-Toni Gayle begins	32	64	96	188	307	425
2	15	30	45	90	140	190
3-4	15	30	45	84	127	170
V2#1-7(8-9/46-7/47): 6,7-Certa-c	12	24	36	67	94	120
V3#1,3-6,8,9,12: 3-Certa-c. 5-McWilliams-c/a. 8,9-Harmon-c	11	22	33	64	90	115
2-L.B. Cole-a; Certa-c	15	30	45	90	140	190
7-L.B. Cole-c/a	20	40	60	120	195	270
10,11-L.B. Cole-c	18	36	54	105	165	225

YOUNG LAWYERS, THE (TV)
Dell Publishing Co.: Jan, 1971 - No. 2, Apr, 1971

	GD	VG	FN	VF	VF/NM	NM-
1	3	6	9	16	23	30
2	2	4	6	11	16	20

YOUNG LIARS (David Lapham's...)(See Vertigo Double Shot for reprint of #1)
DC Comics (Vertigo): May, 2008 - No. 18, Oct, 2009 ($2.99)

	GD	VG	FN	VF	VF/NM	NM-
1-18: 1-Intro. Sadie Dawkins; David Lapham-s/a/c in all						3.00
...: Daydream Believer TPB (2008, $9.99) r/#1-6; Gerald Way intro.						10.00
...: Maestro TPB (2009, $14.99) r/#7-12; Peter Milligan intro.						15.00
...: Rock Life TPB (2010, $14.99) r/#13-18; Brian Azzarello intro.						15.00

YOUNG LIFE (Teen Life #3 on)
New Age Publ./Quality Comics Group: Summer, 1945 - No. 2, Fall, 1945

	GD	VG	FN	VF	VF/NM	NM-
1-Skip Homeier, Louis Prima stories	15	30	45	90	140	190
2-Frank Sinatra photo on-c plus story	18	36	54	103	162	220

YOUNG LOVE (Sister title to Young Romance)
Prize(Feature)Publ.(Crestwood): 2-3/49 - No. 73, 12-1/56-57; V3#5, 2-3/60 - V7#1, 6-7/63

	GD	VG	FN	VF	VF/NM	NM-
V1#1-S&K-c/a(2)	50	100	150	315	533	750
2-Photo-c begin; S&K-a	27	54	81	158	259	360
3-S&K-a	20	40	60	114	182	250
4-6-Minor S&K-a	15	30	45	83	124	165
V2#1(#7)-S&K-a(2)	20	40	60	114	182	250
2-5(#8-11)-Minor S&K-a	14	28	42	78	112	145
6,8(#12,14)-S&K-c only. 14-S&K 1 pg. art	15	30	45	86	133	180
7,9-12(#13,15-18)-S&K-c/a	20	40	60	114	182	250
V3#1-4(#19-22)-S&K-c/a	18	36	54	107	169	230
5-7,9-12(#23-25,27-30)-Photo-c resume; S&K-a	15	30	45	88	137	185
8(#26)-No S&K-a	9	18	27	52	69	85
V4#1,6(#31,36)-S&K-a	15	30	45	83	124	165
2-5,7-12(#32-35,37-42)-Minor S&K-a	13	26	39	72	101	130
V5#1-12(#43-54), V6#1-9(#55-63)-Last precode; S&K-a in #1,2,4-6,8	9	18	27	50	65	80
V6#10-12(#64-66)	5	10	15	30	48	65
V7#1-7(#67-73)	4	8	12	26	41	55
V3#5(2-3/60),6(4-5/60)(Formerly All For Love)	4	8	12	24	37	50
V4#1(6-7/60)-6(4-5/61)	4	8	12	23	36	48

Young Men #27 © MAR

Young Romance Comics #7 © PRIZE

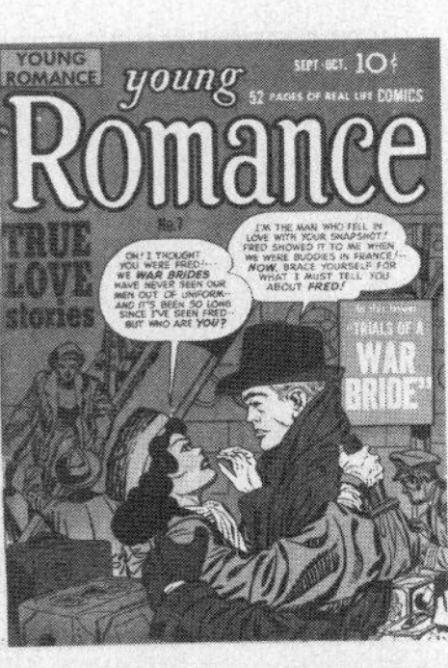

Ythaq: The Forsaken World #2 © MC Prods.

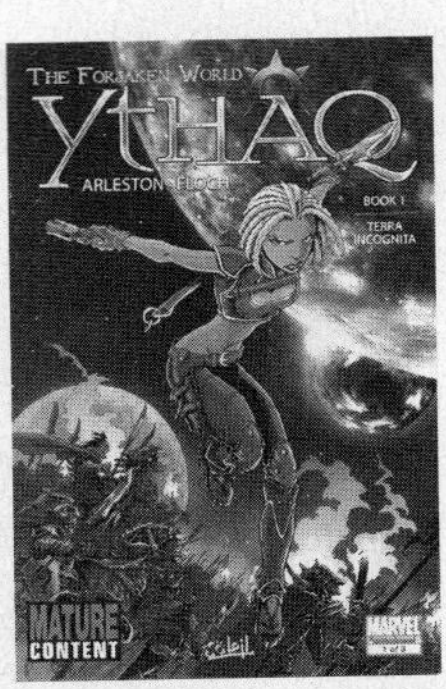

	GD 2.0	VG 4.0	FN 6.0	VF 8.0	VF/NM 9.0	NM- 9.2
V5#1(6-7/61)-6(4-5/62)	4	8	12	23	36	48
V6#1(6-7/62)-6(4-5/63), V7#1	4	8	12	22	34	45

NOTE: *Meskin a-14(2), 27, 42.* **Powell** *a-V4#6.* **Severin/Elder** *a-V1#3. S&K art not in #53, 57, 61, 63-65. Photo-c most V3#5-V5#11.*

YOUNG LOVE
National Periodical Publ.(Arleigh Publ. Corp #49-61)/DC Comics: #39, 9-10/63 - #120, Wint./75-76; #121, 10/76 - #126, 7/77

	GD	VG	FN	VF	VF/NM	NM-
39	6	12	18	39	62	85
40-50	4	8	12	28	44	60
51-68,70	4	8	12	26	41	55
69-(68 pg. Giant)(8-9/68)	6	12	18	43	69	95
71,72,74-77,80	3	6	9	20	30	40
73,78,79-Toth-a	3	6	9	21	32	42
81-99: 88-96-(52 pg. Giants)	3	6	9	19	29	38
100	3	6	9	20	30	40
101-106,115-120	3	6	9	16	23	30
107 (100 pgs.)	8	16	24	56	93	130
108-114 (100 pgs.)	7	14	21	50	83	115
121-126 (52 pgs.)	4	8	12	26	41	55

NOTE: **Bolle** *a-117.* **Colan** *a-107r.* **Nasser** *a-123, 124.* **Orlando** *a-122.* **Simonson** *c-125.* **Toth** *a-73, 78, 79, 122-125r.* **Wood** *a-109r(4 pgs.).*

YOUNG LOVER ROMANCES (Formerly & becomes Great Lover...)
Toby Press: No. 4, June, 1952 - No. 5, Aug, 1952

	GD	VG	FN	VF	VF/NM	NM-
4,5-Photo-c	9	18	27	50	65	80

YOUNG LOVERS (My Secret Life #19 on)(Formerly Brenda Starr?)
Charlton Comics: No. 16, July, 1956 - No. 18, May, 1957

	GD	VG	FN	VF	VF/NM	NM-
16,17('56): 16-Marcus Swayze-a	10	20	30	56	76	95
18-Elvis Presley picture-c, text story (biography)(Scarce)	63	126	189	403	689	975

YOUNG MARRIAGE
Fawcett Publications: June, 1950

	GD	VG	FN	VF	VF/NM	NM-
1-Powell-a; photo-c	13	26	39	74	105	135

YOUNG MEN (Formerly Cowboy Romances)(...on the Battlefield #12-20(4/53); ...In Action #21)
Marvel/Atlas Comics (IPC): No. 4, 6/50 - No. 11, 10/51; No. 12, 12/51 - No. 28, 6/54

	GD	VG	FN	VF	VF/NM	NM-
4-(52 pgs.)	20	40	60	114	182	250
5-11	14	28	42	80	115	150
12-23: 12-20-War format. 21-23-Hot Rod issues starring Flash Foster	14	28	42	76	108	140
24-(12/53)-Origin Captain America, Human Torch, & Sub-Mariner which are revived thru #28; Red Skull app.	300	600	900	2010	3505	5000
25-28: 25-Romita-c/a (see Men's Advs.). 27-Death of Golden Age Red Skull	129	258	387	826	1413	2000
25-2nd printing (1994)	2	4	6	8	10	12

NOTE: **Berg** *a-7, 14, 17, 18, 20; c-17?* **Brodsky** *c-4-9, 13, 14, 16, 17, 21-25.* **Burgos** *c-26-28.* **Colan** *a-14, 15, 20.* **Everett** *a-18-20.* **Heath** *a-13, 14.* **Maneely** *c-10-12, 15.* **Pakula** *a-14, 15.* **Robinson** *c-18. Captain America by* **Romita**-*#24?, 25, 26?, 27, 28. Human Torch by* **Burgos**-*#25, 27, 28. Sub-Mariner by* **Everett**-*#24-28.*

YOUNG REBELS, THE (TV)
Dell Publishing Co.: Jan, 1971

	GD	VG	FN	VF	VF/NM	NM-
1-Photo-c	3	6	9	14	19	24

YOUNG ROMANCE COMICS (The 1st romance comic)
Prize/Headline (Feature Publ.) (Crestwood): Sept-Oct, 1947 - V16#4, June-July, 1963 (#1-33: 52 pgs.)

	GD	VG	FN	VF	VF/NM	NM-
V1#1-S&K-c/a(2)	58	116	174	371	636	900
2-S&K-c/a(2-3)	36	72	108	211	343	475
3-6-S&K-c/a(2-3) each	32	64	96	188	307	425
V2#1-6(#7-12)-S&K-c/a(2-3) each	28	56	84	165	270	375
V3#1-3(#13-15): V3#1-Photo-c begin; S&K-a	19	38	57	109	172	235
4-12(#16-24)-Photo-c; S&K-a	19	38	57	109	172	235
V4#1-11(#25-35)-S&K-a	18	36	54	103	162	220
12(#36)-S&K, Toth-a	19	38	57	109	172	235
V5#1-12(#37-48), V6#4-12(#52-60)-S&K-a	18	36	54	103	162	220
V6#1-3(#49-51)-No S&K-a	10	20	30	56	76	95
V7#1-11(#61-71)-S&K-a in most	15	30	45	83	124	165
V7#12(#72), V8#1-3(#73-75)-Last precode (12-1/54-55)-No S&K-a	9	18	27	50	65	80
V8#4(#76, 4-5/55), 5(#77)-No S&K-a	8	16	24	44	57	70
V8#6-8(#78-80, 12-1/55-56)-S&K-a	13	26	39	72	101	130
V9#3,5,6(#81, 2-3/56, 83,84)-S&K-a	13	26	39	72	101	130
4, V10#1(#82,85)-All S&K-a	14	28	42	78	112	145
V10#2-6(#86-90, 10-11/57)-S&K-a	8	16	24	56	93	130
V11#1,2,5,6(#91,92,95,96)-S&K-a	8	16	24	56	93	130
3,4(#93,94), V12#2,4,5(#98,100,101)-No S&K	5	10	15	30	48	65
V12#1,3,6(#97,99,102)-S&K-a	8	16	24	56	93	130
V13#1(#103)-Powell-a; S&K's last-a for Crestwood	8	16	24	56	93	130
2,4-6(#104-108)	4	8	12	26	41	55
V13#3(#105, 4-5/60)-Elvis Presley-c app. only	8	16	24	54	90	125
V14#1-6, V15#1-6, V16#1-4(#109-124)	4	8	12	24	37	50

NOTE: **Meskin** *a-16, 24(2), 33, 47, 50.* **Robinson/Meskin** *a-6.* **Leonard Starr** *a-11. Photo c-13-32, 34-65. Issues 1-3 say "Designed for the More* **Adult** *Readers of* **Comics**" *on cover.*

YOUNG ROMANCE COMICS (Continued from Prize series)
National Periodical Publ.(Arleigh Publ. Corp. No. 127): No. 125, Aug-Sept, 1963 - No. 208, Nov-Dec, 1975

	GD	VG	FN	VF	VF/NM	NM-
125	7	14	21	50	83	115
126-140	5	10	15	30	48	65
141-153,156-162,165-169	4	8	12	22	34	45
154-Neal Adams-c	5	10	15	32	51	70
155-1st publ. Aragonés-s (no art)	5	10	15	30	48	65
163,164-Toth-a	4	8	12	26	41	55
170-172 (68 pg. Giants): 170-Michell from Young Love ends; Lily Martin, the Swinger begins	5	10	15	30	48	65
173-183 (52 pgs.)	4	8	12	23	36	48
184-196	3	6	9	17	25	32
197-204-(100 pgs.)	7	14	21	50	83	115
205-208	3	6	9	16	23	30

YOUNG X-MEN
Marvel Comics: May, 2008 - No. 12, May, 2009 ($2.99)

1-12: 1-Cyclops forms new team; Guggenheim-s/Paquette-a/Dodson-c. 11,12-Acuña-a 3.00

YOUR DREAMS (See Strange World of...)

YOUR UNITED STATES
Lloyd Jacquet Studios: 1946

	GD	VG	FN	VF	VF/NM	NM-
nn-Used in **SOTI**, pg. 309,310; Sid Greene-a	23	46	69	136	223	310

YOUTHFUL HEARTS (Daring Confessions #4 on)
Youthful Magazines: May, 1952 - No. 3, Sept, 1952

	GD	VG	FN	VF	VF/NM	NM-
1- "Monkey on Her Back" swipes E.C. drug story/Shock SuspenStories #12; Frankie Laine photo on-c; Doug Wildey-a in al	30	60	90	177	289	400
2,3: 2-Vic Damone photo on-c. 3-Johnny Raye photo on-c	20	40	60	114	182	250

YOUTHFUL LOVE (Truthful Love #2)
Youthful Magazines: May, 1950

	GD	VG	FN	VF	VF/NM	NM-
1	14	28	42	82	121	160

YOUTHFUL ROMANCES
Pix-Parade #1-14/Ribage #15 on: 8-9/49 - No. 5, 4/50; No. 6, 2/51; No. 7, 5/51 - #14, 10/52; #15, 1/53 - #18, 7/53; No. 5, 9/53 - No. 9, 8/54

	GD	VG	FN	VF	VF/NM	NM-
1-(1st series)-Titled Youthful Love-Romances	26	52	78	154	252	350
2-Walter Johnson c-1-4	16	32	48	94	147	200
3-5	14	28	42	82	121	160
6,7,9-14(10/52, Pix-Parade; becomes Daring Love #15). 10(1/52)-Mel Torme photo-c/story. 12-Tony Bennett photo-c, 8pg. story & text bio.13-Richard Hayes (singer) photo-c/story; Bob & Ray photo/text story.	14	28	42	76	108	140
8-Frank Sinatra photo/text story; Wood-c/a	20	40	60	114	182	250
15-18 (Ribage)-All have photos on-c. 15-Spike Jones photo-c/story. 16-Tony Bavaar photo-c	13	26	39	72	101	130
5(9/53, Ribage)-Les Paul & Mary Ford photo-c/story; Charlton Heston photo/text story	12	24	36	67	94	120
6-9: 6-Bobby Wayne (singer) photo-c/story; Debbie Reynolds photo/text story. 7(2/54)-Tony Martin photo-c/story; Cyd Charise photo/text story. 8(5/54)-Gordon McCrae photo-c/story. (8/54)-Ralph Flanagan (band leader) photo-c/story; Audrey Hepburn photo/text story	11	22	33	60	86	110

YTHAQ: NO ESCAPE
Marvel Comics (Soleil): 2009 - No. 3, 2009 ($5.99, limited series)

1-3-English language version of French comic; Arleston-s/Floch-a 6.00

YTHAQ: THE FORSAKEN WORLD
Marvel Comics (Soleil): 2008 - No. 3, 2009 ($5.99, limited series)

1-3-English language version of French comic; Arleston-s/Floch-a 6.00

Y: THE LAST MAN
DC Comics (Vertigo): Sept, 2002 - No. 60, Mar, 2008 ($2.95/$2.99)

	GD	VG	FN	VF	VF/NM	NM-
1-Intro. Yorick Brown; Vaughan-s/Guerra-a/J.G. Jones-c	2	4	6	8	10	12
2	1	2	3	5	6	8

Y: The Last Man #57 © Vaughan & Guerra

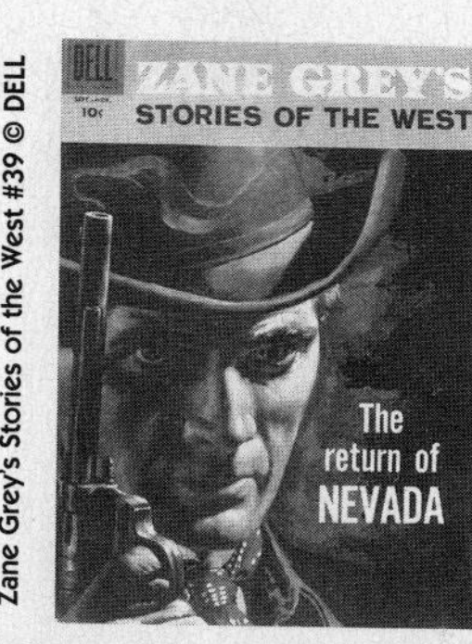
Zane Grey's Stories of the West #39 © DELL

Zero Killer #6 © Arvid Nelson

	GD 2.0	VG 4.0	FN 6.0	VF 8.0	VF/NM 9.0	NM- 9.2

3-5 6.00
6-59: 16,17-Chadwick-a. 21,22-Parlov-a. 32,39-41,48,53,54-Sudzuka-a. 3.00
60-($4.99) Final issue; sixty years in the future 5.00
... Double Feature Edition (2002, $5.95) r/#1,2 6.00
... Special Edition (2009, $1.00) r/#1, "After Watchmen" trade dress on cover 1.00
... - Cycles TPB (2003, $12.95) r/#6-10; sketch pages by Guerra 13.00
... - Girl on Girl TPB (2005, $12.99) r/#32-36 13.00
... - Kimono Dragons TPB (2006, $14.99) r/#43-48 15.00
... - Motherland TPB (2007, $14.99) r/#49-54 15.00
... - One Small Step TPB (2004, $12.95) r/#11-17 13.00
... - Paper Dolls TPB (2006, $14.99) r/#37-42 15.00
... - Ring of Truth TPB (2005, $14.99) r/#24-31 15.00
... - Safeword TPB (2004, $12.95) r/#18-23 13.00
... - Unmanned TPB (2002, $12.95) r/#1-5 13.00
... - Whys and Wherefores TPB (2008, $14.99) r/#55-60 15.00
... - The Deluxe Edition Book One HC (2008, $29.99, dustjacket) oversized r/#1-10; Guerra sketch pages 30.00
... - The Deluxe Edition Book Two HC (2009, $29.99, dustjacket) oversized r/#11-23; full script to #18 30.00

Y2K: THE COMIC
New England Comics Press: Oct, 1999 ($3.95, one-shot)

1-Y2K scenarios and survival tips 4.00

YUPPIES FROM HELL (Also see Son of...)
Marvel Comics: 1989 ($2.95, B&W, one-shot, direct sales, 52 pgs.)

1-Satire 3.00

ZAGO, JUNGLE PRINCE (My Story #5 on)
Fox Features Syndicate: Sept, 1948 - No. 4, Mar, 1949

	GD	VG	FN	VF	VF/NM	NM-
1-Blue Beetle app.; partial-r/Atomic #4 (Toni Luck)	62	124	186	394	677	960
2,3-Kamen-a	51	102	153	321	541	760
4-Baker-c	43	86	129	271	461	650

ZANE GREY'S STORIES OF THE WEST
Dell Publishing Co./Gold Key 11/64: No. 197, 9/48 - No. 996, 5-7/59; 11/64 (All painted-c)

	GD	VG	FN	VF	VF/NM	NM-
Four Color 197(#1)(9/48)	11	22	33	79	140	200
Four Color 222,230,236('49)	7	14	21	47	76	105
Four Color 246,255,270,301,314,333,346	5	10	15	32	51	70
Four Color 357,372,395,412,433,449,467,484	4	8	12	28	44	60
Four Color 511-Kinstler-a; Kubert-a	5	10	15	32	51	70
Four Color 532,555,583,604,616,632(5/55)	4	8	12	28	44	60
27(9-11/55) - 39(9-11/58)	4	8	12	28	44	60
Four Color 996(5-7/59)	4	8	12	28	44	60
10131-411-(11/64-G.K.)-Nevada; r/4-Color #996	3	6	9	20	30	40

ZANY (Magazine)(Satire)(See Frantic & Ratfink)
Candor Publ. Co.: Sept, 1958 - No. 4, May, 1959

	GD	VG	FN	VF	VF/NM	NM-
1-Bill Everett-c	12	24	36	69	97	125
2-4: 4-Everett-c	9	18	27	47	61	75

ZATANNA (See Adv. Comics #413, JLA #161, Supergirl #1, World's Finest Comics #274)
DC Comics: July, 1993 - No. 4, Oct, 1993 ($1.95, limited series)

1-4 2.50
...: Everyday Magic (2003, $5.95, one-shot) Dini-s/Mays-a/Bolland-c; Constantine app. 6.00
Special 1(1987, $2.00)-Gray Morrow-c/a 3.00

ZAZA, THE MYSTIC (Formerly Charlie Chan; This Magazine Is Haunted V2#12 on)
Charlton Comics: No. 10, Apr, 1956 - No. 11, Sept, 1956

	GD	VG	FN	VF	VF/NM	NM-
10,11	12	24	36	69	97	125

ZEALOT (Also see WildC.A.T.S: Covert Action Teams)
Image Comics: Aug, 1995 - No. 3, Nov, 1995 ($2.50, limited series)

1-3 2.50

ZEGRA JUNGLE EMPRESS (Formerly Tegra)(My Love Life #6 on)
Fox Features Syndicate: No. 2, Oct, 1948 - No. 5, April, 1949

	GD	VG	FN	VF	VF/NM	NM-
2	62	124	186	394	677	960
3-5	49	98	147	308	522	735

ZEN (Intergalactic Ninja)
Zen Comics Publishing: No. 0, Apr, 2003 - No. 4, Aug, 2003 ($2.95)

0-4-Bill Maus-a/Steve Stern-s. 0-Wraparound-c 3.00

ZEN INTERGALACTIC NINJA
No Publisher: 1987 -1993 ($1.75/$2.00, B&W)

	GD	VG	FN	VF	VF/NM	NM-
1	2	4	6	10	14	18
2-6: Copyright-Stern & Cote	1	3	4	6	8	10

V2#1-4-($2.00) 3.00
V3#1-5-($2.95) 3.00
... :Christmas Special 1 (1992, $2.95) 3.00
... :Earth Day Special 1 (1993, $2.95) 3.00

ZEN, INTERGALACTIC NINJA (mini-series)
Zen Comics/Archie Comics: Sept, 1992 - No. 3, 1992 ($1.25)(Formerly a B&W comic by Zen Comics)

1-3: 1-Origin Zen; contains mini-poster 3.00

ZEN INTERGALACTIC NINJA
Entity Comics: No. 0, June-July, 1993 - No. 3, 1994 ($2.95, B&W, limited series)

0-Gold foil stamped-c; photo-c of Zen model 3.00
1-3: Gold foil stamped-c; Bill Maus-c/a 3.00
0-(1993, $3.50, color)-Chromium-c by Jae Lee 3.50
...Sourcebook 1-(1993, $3.50) 3.50
...Sourcebook '94-(1994, $3.50) 3.50

ZEN INTERGALACTIC NINJA: APRIL FOOL'S SPECIAL
Parody Press: 1994 ($2.50, B&W)

1-w/flip story of Renn Intergalactic Chihuahua 3.00

ZEN INTERGALACTIC NINJA COLOR
Entity Comics: 1994 - No. 7, 1995 ($2.25)

1-($3.95)-Chromium die cut-c 4.00
1, 0-($2.25)-Newsstand; Jae Lee-c; r/...All New Color Special #0 3.00
2-($2.50)-Flip book 3.00
2-($3.50)-Flip book, polybagged w/chromium trading card 3.50
3-7 3.00
Summer Special (1994, $2.95) 3.00
Yearbook: Hazardous Duty 1 (1995) 3.00
Zen-isms 1 (1995, 2.95) 3.00
Ashcan-Tour of the Universe-(no price) w/flip cover 3.00

ZEN INTERGALACTIC NINJA COMMEMORATIVE EDITION
Zen Comics Publishing: 1997 ($5.95, color)

1-Stern-s/Cote-a 6.00

ZEN INTERGALACTIC NINJA MILESTONE
Entity Comics: 1994 - No. 3, 1994 ($2.95, limited series)

1-3: Gold foil logo; r/Defend the Earth 3.00

ZEN INTERGALATIC NINJA SPRING SPECTACULAR
Entity Comics: 1994 ($2.95, B&W, one-shot)

1-Gold foil logo 3.00

ZEN INTERGALACTIC NINJA STARQUEST
Entity Comics: 1994 - No. 6, 1995 ($2.95, B&W)

1-6: Gold foil logo 3.00

ZEN, INTERGALACTIC NINJA: THE HUNTED
Entity Comics: 1993 - No. 3, 1994 ($2.95, B&W, limited series)

1-3: Newsstand Edition; foil logo 3.00
1-($3.50)-Polybagged w/chromium card by Kieth; foil logo 3.50

ZERO GIRL
DC Comics (Homage): Feb, 2001 - No. 5, Jun, 2001 ($2.95, limited series)

1-5-Sam Kieth-s/a 3.00
TPB (2001, $14.95) r/#1-5; intro. by Alan Moore 15.00

ZERO GIRL: FULL CIRCLE
DC Comics (Homage): Jan, 2003 - No. 5, May, 2003 ($2.95, limited series)

1-5-Sam Kieth-s/a 3.00
TPB (2003, $17.95) r/#1-5 18.00

ZERO HOUR: CRISIS IN TIME (Also see Showcase '94 #8-10)
DC Comics: No. 4(#1), Sept, 1994 - No. 0(#5), Oct, 1994 ($1.50, limited series)

4(#1)-0(#5) 4.00
"Ashcan"-(1994, free, B&W, 8 pgs.) several versions exist 2.25
TPB ('94, $9.95) 10.00

ZERO KILLER
Dark Horse Comics: Jul, 2007 - No.6, Oct, 2009 ($2.99)

1-6-Arvid Nelson-s/Matt Camp-a 3.00

ZERO PATROL, THE
Continuity Comics: Nov, 1984 - No. 2 ($1.50); 1987 - No. 5, May, 1989 ($2.00)

1,2: Neal Adams-c/a; Megalith begins 4.00
1-5 (#1,2-reprints above, 1987) 3.00

Zip Comics #39 © MLJ

Zombie Proof #1 © J.C. Vaughn & Vincent Spencer

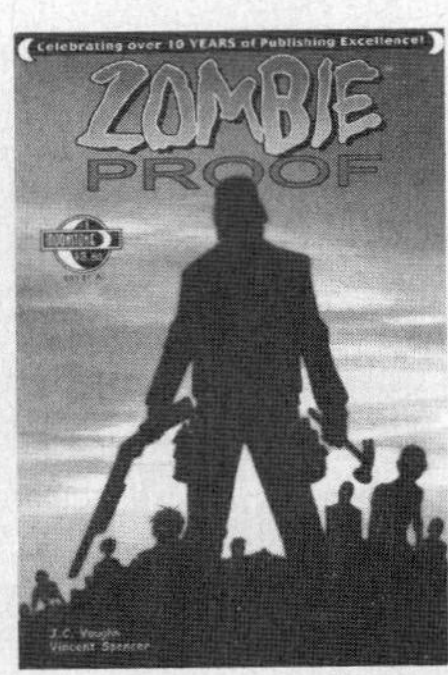

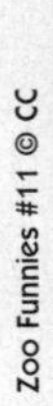
Zoo Funnies #11 © CC

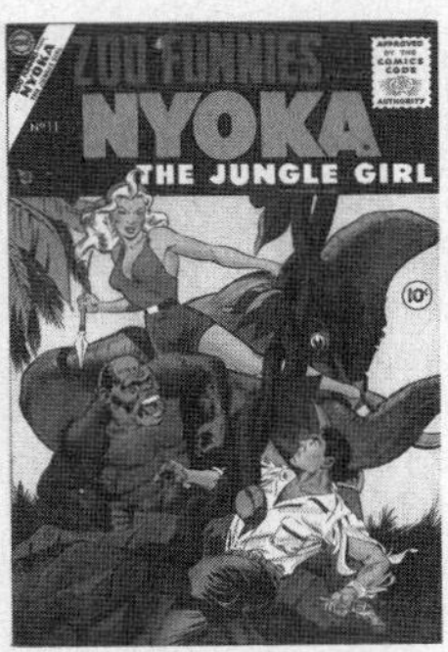

ZERO TOLERANCE
First Comics: Oct, 1990 - No. 4, Jan, 1991 ($2.25, limited series)

	GD 2.0	VG 4.0	FN 6.0	VF 8.0	VF/NM 9.0	NM- 9.2
1-4: Tim Vigil-c/a(p) (his 1st color limited series)						3.00

ZERO ZERO
Fantagraphics: Mar, 1995 -No. 27 ($3.95/$4.95, B&W, anthology, mature)

	GD 2.0	VG 4.0	FN 6.0	VF 8.0	VF/NM 9.0	NM- 9.2
1-7,9-15,17-25						5.00
8,16						6.00
26-($4.95) Bagge-c						5.00

ZIGGY PIG-SILLY SEAL COMICS (See Animal Fun, Animated Movie-Tunes, Comic Capers, Krazy Komics, Silly Tunes & Super Rabbit)
Timely Comics (CmPL): Fall, 1944 - No. 4, Summer, 1945; No. 5, Summer, 1946; No. 6, Sept, 1946

	GD 2.0	VG 4.0	FN 6.0	VF 8.0	VF/NM 9.0	NM- 9.2
1-Vs. the Japanese	29	54	87	170	278	385
2-(Spring, 1945)	15	30	45	85	130	175
3-5	14	28	42	81	118	155
6-Infinity-c	15	30	45	88	137	185
I.W. Reprint #1(1958)-r/Krazy Komics	2	4	6	9	13	16
I.W. Reprint #2,7,8	2	4	6	9	13	16

ZIP COMICS
MLJ Magazines: Feb, 1940 - No. 47, Summer, 1944 (#1-7?: 68 pgs.)

	GD 2.0	VG 4.0	FN 6.0	VF 8.0	VF/NM 9.0	NM- 9.2
1-Origin Kalathar the Giant Man, The Scarlet Avenger, & Steel Sterling; Mr. Satan (by Edd Ashe), Nevada Jones (masked hero) & Zambini, the Miracle Man, War Eagle, Captain Valor begins	459	918	1377	3350	5925	8500
2-Nevada Jones adds mask & horse Blaze	245	490	735	1568	2684	3800
3-Biro robot-c	203	406	609	1289	2220	3150
4,5-Biro WW2-c	161	322	483	1030	1765	2500
6-8-Biro-c	142	284	426	909	1555	2200
9-Last Kalathar & Mr. Satan; classic-c	160	320	480	1016	1746	2475
10-Inferno, the Flame Breather begins, ends #13	152	304	456	965	1658	2350
11,12: 11-Inferno without costume	110	220	330	704	1202	1700
13-Electrocution-c	127	254	381	807	1391	1975
14,16,19	103	206	309	659	1130	1600
15-Classic spider-c	139	278	417	883	1517	2150
17-Last Scarlet Avenger; women in bondage being cooked alive-c by Biro	132	264	396	838	1444	2050
18-Wilbur begins (9/41, 1st app.)	132	264	396	838	1444	2050
20-Origin & 1st app. Black Jack (11/41); Hitler-c	181	362	543	1158	1979	2800
21,23-26: 25-Last Nevada Jones. 26-Black Witch begins; last Captain Valor; "Remember Pearl Harbor!" cover caption	94	188	282	597	1024	1450
22-Classic-c	168	336	504	1075	1838	2600
27-Intro. Web (7/42) plus-c app.	187	374	561	1197	2049	2900
28-Origin Web	158	316	474	1003	1727	2450
29-The Hyena app. (scarce)	90	180	270	576	988	1400
30	62	124	186	394	677	960
31,33-38: 34-1st Applejack app. 35-Last Zambini, Black Jack. 38-Last Web issue	50	100	150	315	533	750
32-Classic skeleton Nazi WW2-c	90	180	270	576	988	1400
39-Red Rube begins (origin, 8/43)	50	100	150	315	533	750
40-46: 45-Wilbur ends	45	90	135	284	480	675
47-Last issue; scarce	47	94	141	296	498	700

NOTE: ***Biro** a-5, 9, 17; c-3-17. **Meskin** a-1-3, 5-7, 9, 10, 12, 13, 15, 16 at least. **Montana** c-29, 30, 32-35. **Novick** c-18-28, 31. **Sahle** c-37, 38, 40-46. Bondage c-8, 9, 33, 34. Cover features: Steel Sterling-1-43, 47; (w/Blackjack-20-27 & Web-27-35), 28-39; (w/Red Rube-40-43); Red Rube-44-47.*

ZIP-JET (Hero)
St. John Publishing Co.: Feb, 1953 - No. 2, Apr-May, 1953

	GD 2.0	VG 4.0	FN 6.0	VF 8.0	VF/NM 9.0	NM- 9.2
1-Rocketman-r from Punch Comics; #1-c from splash in Punch #10	77	154	231	493	847	1200
2	49	98	147	308	522	735

ZIPPY THE CHIMP (CBS TV Presents...)
Pines (Literary Ent.): No. 50, March, 1957; No. 51, Aug, 1957

	GD 2.0	VG 4.0	FN 6.0	VF 8.0	VF/NM 9.0	NM- 9.2
50,51	8	16	24	40	50	60

ZODY, THE MOD ROB
Gold Key: July, 1970

	GD 2.0	VG 4.0	FN 6.0	VF 8.0	VF/NM 9.0	NM- 9.2
1	3	6	9	16	23	30

ZOMBIE
Marvel Comics: Nov, 2006 - No. 4, Feb, 2007 ($3.99, limited series)

	GD 2.0	VG 4.0	FN 6.0	VF 8.0	VF/NM 9.0	NM- 9.2
1-4-Kyle Hotz-a/c; Mike Raicht-s						4.00
TPB (2007, $13.99) r/#1-4						14.00
...: Simon Garth (1/08 - No. 4, 4/08) Hotz-s/a/c						4.00

ZOMBIE KING
Image Comics: No. 0, June, 2005 ($2.95, B&W, one-shot)

	GD 2.0	VG 4.0	FN 6.0	VF 8.0	VF/NM 9.0	NM- 9.2
0-Frank Cho-s/a						5.00

ZOMBIE PROOF
Moonstone: 2007 - Present ($3.50)

	GD 2.0	VG 4.0	FN 6.0	VF 8.0	VF/NM 9.0	NM- 9.2
1-3: 1-J.C. Vaughn-s/Vincent Spencer-a; two covers by Spencer and Neil Vokes						3.50
1-Baltimore Comic-Con 2007 variant-c by Vokes (ltd. ed. of 500)						5.00
2-Big Apple 2008 Convention Edition; Tucci-c (ltd. ed. of 250)						5.00
3-Convention Edition; Beck-c (ltd. ed. of 100)						5.00

ZOMBIES!: ECLIPSE OF THE UNDEAD
IDW Publ.: Nov, 2006 - No. 4, Feb, 2007 ($3.99, limited series)

	GD 2.0	VG 4.0	FN 6.0	VF 8.0	VF/NM 9.0	NM- 9.2
1-4-Torres-s/Herrera-a; two covers						4.00

ZOMBIES!: FEAST
IDW Publ.: May, 2006 - No. 5, Oct, 2006 ($3.99, limited series)

	GD 2.0	VG 4.0	FN 6.0	VF 8.0	VF/NM 9.0	NM- 9.2
1-5: 1-Chris Bolton-a/Shane McCarthy-s. 3-Lorenzana-a						4.00

ZOMBIES!: HUNTERS
IDW Publ.: May, 2008 - Present ($3.99, limited series)

	GD 2.0	VG 4.0	FN 6.0	VF 8.0	VF/NM 9.0	NM- 9.2
1-Don Figueroa-a/c; Dara Naraghi-s						4.00

ZOMBIE TALES THE SERIES
BOOM! Studios: Apr, 2008 - No. 12, Mar, 2009 ($3.99)

	GD 2.0	VG 4.0	FN 6.0	VF 8.0	VF/NM 9.0	NM- 9.2
1-Niles-s; Lansdale-s/Barreto-a; two covers on each						4.00

ZOMBIE WORLD (one-shots)
Dark Horse Comics

	GD 2.0	VG 4.0	FN 6.0	VF 8.0	VF/NM 9.0	NM- 9.2
... :Eat Your Heart Out (4/98, $2.95) Kelley Jones-c/s/a						3.00
... :Home For The Holidays (12/97, $2.95)						3.00

ZOMBIE WORLD: CHAMPION OF THE WORMS
Dark Horse Comics: Sept, 1997 - No. 3, Nov, 1997 ($2.95, limited series)

	GD 2.0	VG 4.0	FN 6.0	VF 8.0	VF/NM 9.0	NM- 9.2
1-3-Mignola & McEown-c/s/a						3.00

ZOMBIE WORLD: DEAD END
Dark Horse Comics: Jan, 1998 - No. 2, Feb, 1998 ($2.95, limited series)

	GD 2.0	VG 4.0	FN 6.0	VF 8.0	VF/NM 9.0	NM- 9.2
1,2-Stephen Blue-c/s/a						3.00

ZOMBIE WORLD: TREE OF DEATH
Dark Horse Comics: Jun, 1999 - No. 4, Oct, 1999 ($2.95, limited series)

	GD 2.0	VG 4.0	FN 6.0	VF 8.0	VF/NM 9.0	NM- 9.2
1-4-Mills-s/Deadstock-a						3.00

ZOMBIE WORLD: WINTER'S DREGS
Dark Horse Comics: May, 1998 - No. 4, Aug, 1998 ($2.95, limited series)

	GD 2.0	VG 4.0	FN 6.0	VF 8.0	VF/NM 9.0	NM- 9.2
1-4-Fingerman-s/Edwards-a						3.00

ZONE (Also see Dark Horse Presents)
Dark Horse Comics: 1990 ($1.95, B&W)

	GD 2.0	VG 4.0	FN 6.0	VF 8.0	VF/NM 9.0	NM- 9.2
1-Character from Dark Horse Presents						2.50

ZONE CONTINUUM, THE
Caliber Press: 1994 ($2.95, B&W)

	GD 2.0	VG 4.0	FN 6.0	VF 8.0	VF/NM 9.0	NM- 9.2
1						3.00

ZOO ANIMALS
Star Publications: No. 8, 1954 (15¢, 36 pgs.)

	GD 2.0	VG 4.0	FN 6.0	VF 8.0	VF/NM 9.0	NM- 9.2
8-(B&W for coloring)	8	16	24	40	50	60

ZOO FUNNIES (Tim McCoy #16 on)
Charlton Comics/Children Comics Publ.: Nov, 1945 - No. 15, 1947

	GD 2.0	VG 4.0	FN 6.0	VF 8.0	VF/NM 9.0	NM- 9.2
101(#1)(11/45, 1st Charlton comic book)-Funny animal; Al Fago-c	21	42	63	122	199	275
2(12/45, 52 pgs.) Classic-c	15	30	45	83	124	165
3-5	11	22	33	62	86	110
6-15: 8-Diana the Huntress app.	9	18	27	52	69	85

ZOO FUNNIES (Becomes Nyoka, The Jungle Girl #14 on?)
Capitol Stories/Charlton Comics: July, 1953 - No. 13, Sept, 1955; Dec, 1984

	GD 2.0	VG 4.0	FN 6.0	VF 8.0	VF/NM 9.0	NM- 9.2
1-1st app.? Timothy The Ghost; Fago-c/a	11	22	33	64	90	115
2	8	16	24	42	54	65
3-7	7	14	21	37	46	55
8-13-Nyoka app.	9	18	27	52	69	85
1(1984) (Low print run)	1	2	3	4	5	7

ZOONIVERSE
Eclipse Comics: 8/86 - No. 6, 6/87 ($1.25/$1.75, limited series, Mando paper)

	GD 2.0	VG 4.0	FN 6.0	VF 8.0	VF/NM 9.0	NM- 9.2
1-6						2.50

Zoot #7 © FOX

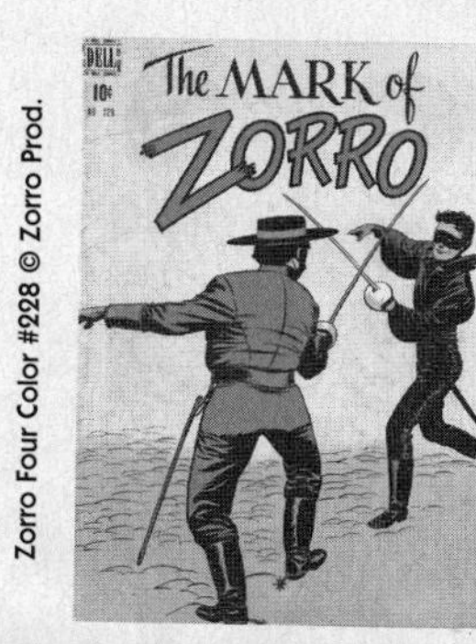

Zorro Four Color #228 © Zorro Prod.

Zorro (2008 series) #12 © Zorro Prods.

ZOO PARADE (TV)
Dell Publishing Co.: #662, 1955 (Marlin Perkins)

	GD 2.0	VG 4.0	FN 6.0	VF 8.0	VF/NM 9.0	NM- 9.2
Four Color 662	5	10	15	32	51	70

ZOOM COMICS
Carlton Publishing Co.: Dec, 1945 (one-shot)

	GD 2.0	VG 4.0	FN 6.0	VF 8.0	VF/NM 9.0	NM- 9.2
nn-Dr. Mercy, Satannas, from Red Band Comics; Capt. Milksop origin retold	39	78	117	240	395	550

ZOOT (Rulah Jungle Goddess #17 on)
Fox Features Syndicate: nd (1946) - No. 16, July, 1948 (Two #13s & 14s)

	GD 2.0	VG 4.0	FN 6.0	VF 8.0	VF/NM 9.0	NM- 9.2
nn-Funny animal only	21	42	63	122	199	275
2-The Jaguar app.	19	38	57	109	172	235
3(Fall, 1946) - 6-Funny animals & teen-age	12	24	36	69	77	125
7-(6/47)-Rulah, Jungle Goddess (origin/1st app.)	107	214	321	680	1165	1650
8-10	71	142	213	454	777	1100
11-Kamen bondage-c	74	148	222	470	810	1150
12-Injury-to-eye panels, torture scene	53	106	159	334	567	800
13(2/48)	53	106	159	334	567	800
14(3/48)-Used in **SOTI**, pg. 104, "One picture showing a girl nailed by her wrists to trees with blood flowing from the wounds, might be taken straight from an ill. ed. of the Marquis deSade"	68	136	204	435	743	1050
13(4/48),14(5/48)-Western True Crime #15 on?	53	106	159	334	567	800
15,16	53	106	159	334	567	800

ZORRO (Walt Disney with #882)(TV)(See Eclipse Graphic Album)
Dell Publishing Co.: May, 1949 - No. 15, Sept-Nov, 1961 (Photo-c 882 on)
(Zorro first appeared in a pulp story Aug 19, 1919)

	GD 2.0	VG 4.0	FN 6.0	VF 8.0	VF/NM 9.0	NM- 9.2
Four Color 228 (#1)	19	38	57	139	270	400
Four Color 425,617,732	11	22	33	80	145	210
Four Color 497,538,574-Kinstler-a	12	24	36	85	155	225
Four Color 882-Photo-c begin;1st TV Disney; Toth-a	14	28	42	102	194	285
Four Color 920,933,960,976-Toth-a in all	11	22	33	79	142	205
Four Color 1003('59)-Toth-a	11	22	33	79	142	205
Four Color 1037-Annette Funicello photo-c	14	28	42	97	181	265
8(12-2/59-60)	8	16	24	56	93	130
9-Toth-a	9	18	27	60	100	140
10,11,13-15-Last photo-c	8	16	24	54	90	125
12-Toth-a; last 10¢ issue	9	18	27	60	100	140

NOTE: ***Warren Tufts** a-4-Color 1037, 8, 9, 10, 13.*

ZORRO (Walt Disney)(TV)
Gold Key: Jan, 1966 - No. 9, Mar, 1968 (All photo-c)

	GD 2.0	VG 4.0	FN 6.0	VF 8.0	VF/NM 9.0	NM- 9.2
1-Toth-a	8	16	24	52	86	120
2,4,5,7-9-Toth-a. 5-r/F.C. #1003 by Toth	5	10	15	30	48	65
3,6-Tufts-a	4	8	12	28	44	60

NOTE: *#1-9 are reprinted from Dell issues. **Tufts** a-3, 4. #1-r/F.C. #882. #2-r/F.C. #960. #3-r/#12-c & #8 inside. #4-r/#9-c & insides. #6-r/#11(all); #7-r/#14-c. #8-r/F.C. #933 inside & back-c & #976-c. #9-r/F.C. #920.*

ZORRO (TV)
Marvel Comics: Dec, 1990 - No. 12, Nov, 1991 ($1.00)

	GD 2.0	VG 4.0	FN 6.0	VF 8.0	VF/NM 9.0	NM- 9.2
1-12: Based on TV show. 12-Toth-c						3.00

ZORRO (Also see Mask of Zorro)
Topps Comics: Nov, 1993 - No. 11, Nov, 1994 ($2.50/$2.95)

	GD 2.0	VG 4.0	FN 6.0	VF 8.0	VF/NM 9.0	NM- 9.2
0-(11/93, $1.00, 20 pgs.)-Painted-c; collector's ed.						2.50
1,4,6-9,11: 1-Miller-c. 4-Mike Grell-c. 6-Mignola-c. 7-Lady Rawhide-c by Gulacy. 8-Perez-c. 10-Julie Bell-c. 11-Lady Rawhide-c						3.00
2-Lady Rawhide-app. (not in costume)						5.00
3-1st app. Lady Rawhide in costume, 3-Lady Rawhide-c by Adam Hughes	1	2	3	5	6	8
5-Lady Rawhide app.						4.00
10-($2.95)-Lady Rawhide-c/app.						3.00
The Lady Wears Red (12/98, $12.95, TPB) r/#1-3						13.00
Zorro's Renegades (2/99, $14.95, TPB) r/#4-8						15.00

ZORRO
Dynamite Entertainment: 2008 - Present ($3.50)

	GD 2.0	VG 4.0	FN 6.0	VF 8.0	VF/NM 9.0	NM- 9.2
1-20: 1-Origin retold; Wagner-s; three covers. 2-20-Two covers on all						3.50

ZORRO MATANZAS
Dynamite Entertainment: 2010 - No. 4 ($3.99)

	GD 2.0	VG 4.0	FN 6.0	VF 8.0	VF/NM 9.0	NM- 9.2
1-3-Mayhew-a/McGregor-s						4.00

ZOT!
Eclipse Comics: 4/84 - No. 10, 7/85; No. 11, 1/87 - No. 36 7/91 ($1.50, Baxter-p)

	GD 2.0	VG 4.0	FN 6.0	VF 8.0	VF/NM 9.0	NM- 9.2
1						5.00
2,3						4.00
4-10: 4-Origin. 10-Last color issue						3.00
101/2 (6/86, 25¢, Not Available Comics) Ashcan; art by Feazell & Scott McCloud						4.00
11-14,15-35-($2.00-c) B&W issues						3.00
141/2 (Adventures of Zot! in Dimension 101/2)(7/87) Antisocialman app.						3.00
36-($2.95-c) B&W						5.00
... The Complete Black and White Collection TPB (2008, $24.95) r/#11-36 with commentary, interviews and bonus artwork						25.00

Z-2 COMICS (Secret Agent...)(See Holyoke One-Shot #7)

ZULU (See Movie Classics)

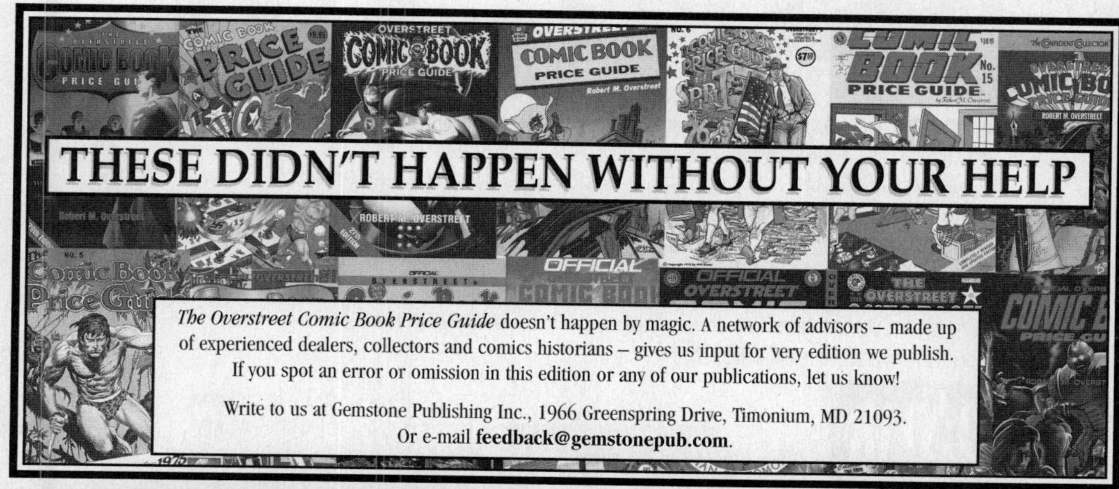

PayPal
VERIFIED

COMICS

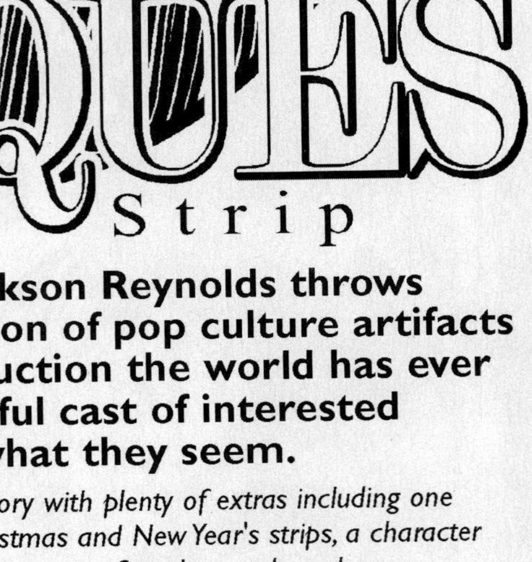

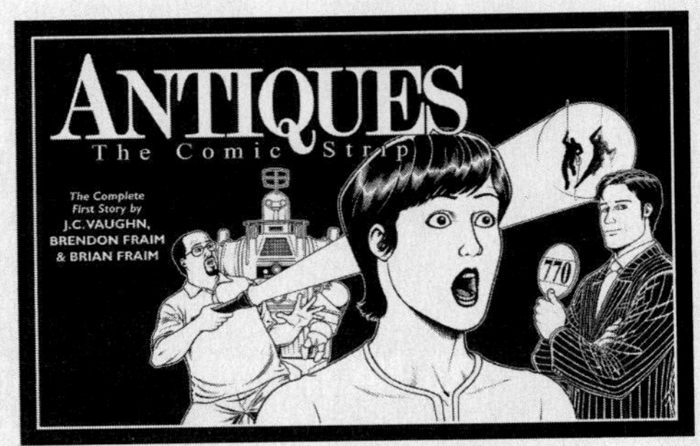
ANTIQUES
The Comic Strip
The Complete
First Story by
J.C. VAUGHN,
BRENDON FRAIM
& BRIAN FRAIM
770

BUSINESS CARD ADS

THE OVERSTREET COMIC BOOK PRICE GUIDE BUSINESS CARD ADS are a great way to advertise in the Guide! Simply send us your business card and we'll reduce it and run it as is. Have your ad seen by thousands of serious comic book collectors for an entire year! If you are a comic book or collectible dealer, retail establishment, mail-order house, etc., you can reach potential customers throughout the United States and around the world in our **BUSINESS CARDS ADS**!

For more information, contact our Advertising Dept.
Gemstone Publishing, Inc., 1966 Greenspring Dr., Timonium, MD 21093
or e-mail **feedback@gemstonepub.com**.

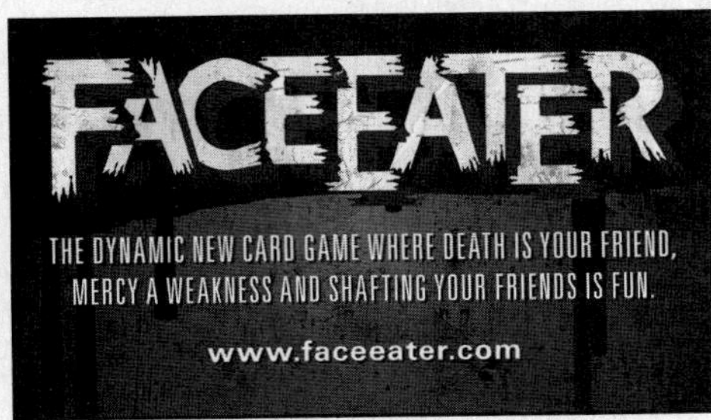

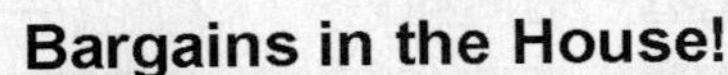

fanfare
SPORTS & ENTERTAINMENT, INC.
COMIC BOOKS • ORIGINAL ART • SPORTS CARDS
SCI-FI & FANTASY GAMES • USED CDs, DVDs & VIDEO GAMES
4415 S. WESTNEDGE AVE.
KALAMAZOO, MI 49008
www.fanfare-se.com
(269) 349-8866

COMICS TO ASTONISH
9400 SNOWDEN RIVER PKWY
COLUMBIA, MD 21045
MONDAY-SATURDAY 12-8PM
410-381-2732
WE SELL!
-COMICS OLD AND NEW!
-MAGIC THE GATHERING!
-WIZKIDS!
-NON SPORT CARDS!
-GRADED COMICS!
-STATUES!
-ACTION FIGURES!
-TPB'S!
-MANGA AND ANIME!
-DC DIRECT!
-COMIC SUPPLIES!
-ORIGINAL COMIC ART!
Check out our new website w/h tons of CGC books
CONTACT:
KEEGAN F. CONRAD
410-381-2732
COMICS2U@AOL.COM
WE BUY!
-ALL COMICS 30'S TO 80'S!
-ENTIRE COLLECTIONS!
-BRONZE TO GOLDEN AGE!
-GRADED BOOKS!
-ORIGINAL COMIC ART AND COVERS!
WE HAVE OVER 80,000 BACK ISSUES!
CHECK OUT OUR WEB COMIC AT:
WWW.FATGUYBLACKGUYBALDGUY.COM
WWW.COMICSTOASTONISH.COM
CRIS TANZ '06

BUSINESS CARD ADS

The Overstreet Comic Book Price Guide doesn't happen by magic. A network of advisors – made up of experienced dealers, collectors and comics historians – gives us input for very edition we publish. If you spot an error or omission in this edition or any of our publications, let us know!

Write to us at Gemstone Publishing Inc., 1966 Greenspring Drive, Timonium, MD 21093.
Or e-mail **feedback@gemstonepub.com**.

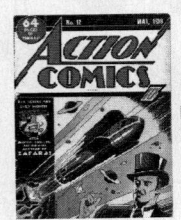

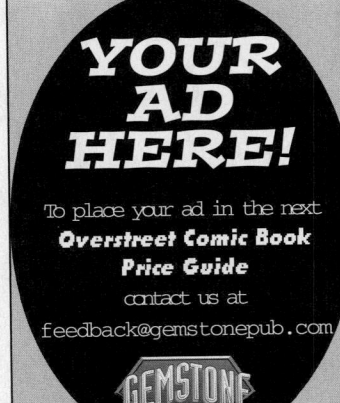

DIRECTORY LISTINGS

COLORADO

All C's Collectibles
1250 S. Abilene St.
Aurora, CO 80012
PH: (303) 751-6882
FAX: (303) 695-7827
ALLCS@comcast.net
www.AllCsCollectibles.com
(a-g,i,l-o,r-u,w,x,3-5)

RTS Unlimited, Inc.
P. O. Box 150412
Lakewood, CO 80215
PH: (303) 403-1840
FAX: (303) 403-1837
rtsunlimited@earthlink.net
www.RTSUnlimited.com
(a,b,c,e,f)

CONNECTICUT

Showcase New England
Dan Greenhalgh
67 Gail Drive
Northford, CT 06472
PH: (203) 484-4579
FAX: (203) 484-4837
comics@showcasene.com

Wonderland Comics
112 Main Street #15
Putnam, CT 06260
PH: (860) 963-1027
FAX: (860) 935-0000
WonderlandComics@aol.com
www.WonderlandComics.com
(a-j,l,r-x,1-5)

DELAWARE

The Comic Book Shop
1711 Marsh Rd.
Wilmington, DE 19810
PH: (302) 477-1119
comicshop@
thecomicbookshop.com
www.thecomicbookshop.com
(a-g,l,r,t,u,w,x,1-5)

FLORIDA

Pedigree Comics, Inc.
12541 Equine Lane
Wellington, FL 33414
PH: (877) 626-6427
FAX: (561) 422-1120
E-Mail: DougSchmell
@pedigreecomics.com
www.pedigreecomics.com

Samuel Frazer
11005 Lakeland Circle
Fort Myers, FL 33913
PH/FAX: (239) 768-0649
sfrazer457@aol.com
(a,b,o)

GregWhiteComics.com
P.O. Box 45-0003
Kissimmee, FL 34745
PH: (407) 870-0400
gwhite@gregwhitecomics.com
www.gregwhitecomics.com
(a-c,e,m,o,t)

Phil's Comic Shoppe
6512 West Atlantic Blvd.
Margate, FL 33063
PH: (954) 977-6947
philscomix@worldnet.att.net
http://stores.ebay.com/Phils-Comic-Shoppe
(b-f,m,w)

ZAP Boom Ka-Pow Comics & Games
7641 Pines Blvd.
Pembroke Pines, FL 33024
PH: (954) 962-3322
Mike@ZapBoomKa-Pow.com
www.ZapBoomKa-Pow.com
(b,d-i,k,q,r,t,u,w,x,z,3-5)

Collector's Comics
901 E. Prima Vista Blvd.
Port St. Lucie, FL 34952
PH/FAX: (772) 878-9229
collectorscomics@comcast.net
www.collectorscomics.net
(a-f,h,i,m,q,r,u-x,z,1,3-5)

CGC
P.O. Box 4738
Sarasota, FL 34230
PH: (877) NM-COMIC
FAX: (941) 360-2558
www.CGCcomics.com

David T. Alexander Collectibles
P.O. Box 273086
Tampa, FL 33618
PH: (813) 968-1805
FAX: (813) 264-6226
davidt@cultureandthrills.com
www.dtacollectibles.com
(a-c,e,l-o,r,s)

GEORGIA

Odin's Comics
937 Killian Hill Rd.
Lilburn, GA 30047
PH: (770) 923-0123
FAX: (770) 925-8200
odinscomics@aol.com
www.odinscomics.com
(a-i,r,t,u,w,x,1-5)

ILLINOIS

Yesterday
1143 W. Addison St.
Chicago, IL 60613
PH: (773) 248-8087
(a-c,e,f,l,n-p,r-t,x-z,1,3,4)

The Paper Escape
205 West First Street
Dixon, IL 61021
PH: (815) 284-7567
paperescape
@paperescape.com
www.paperescape.com
(b-d,f-j,p-r,t,u,w,z,1-4)

GEM Comics
125 W. First St.
Elmhurst, IL 60126
PH: (630) 833-8787
(b-j,r,t,u,w,x,5)

Dreamland Comics
105 W. Rockland Rd.
Libertyville, IL 60048
PH: (847) 680-0727
FAX: (847) 680-4495
info@dreamland-comics.com
www.dreamland-comics.com
(b-d,f-j,r,t,u,w,4,5)

Al N' Ann's Collectibles
3819 W. Main St.
McHenry, IL 60050
PH: (815) 344-9696
info@alnanns.com
www.alnanns.com
(c,d,f,g,i,r,u-x,2,4,5)

Reel Art
707 S. Harvey
Oak Park, IL 60304
PH: (708) 288-7378
cglaberson@reelart.biz
(a-c,e,g,h,j,l,n-p,r-t,v-x,2,4)

INDIANA

Comics Ina Flash
P.O. Box 3611
Evansville, IN 47735-3611
PH: (812) 401-6127
comicflash@aol.com
www.comicsinaflash.com

Books Comics and Things
2212 Maplecrest Rd.
Fort Wayne, IN 46815
PH: (260) 493-6116
bct@bctcomics.com
www.SuperHeroGameLand.com
(a-j,r,u,w,1,3-5)

Books Comics and Things
5936 W. Jefferson Blvd.
Fort Wayne, IN 46804
PH: (260) 755-2425
jscott@bctcomics.com
www.bctcomics.com
(a-k,r,u,w,1-5)

IOWA

Mayhem
2532 Lincoln Way
Ames, IA 50014
PH/FAX: (515) 292-3510
shop@mayhemcomics.com
www.mayhemcomics.com
(b-d,f-j,r,u,w,x,1-5)

Daydreams Comics
21 S. Dubuque St.
Iowa City, IA 52240
PH: (319) 354-6632
daydreamscomics@yahoo.com
www.daydreamscomics.com

KANSAS

B•Bop Comics South
5336 W. 95th Street
Prairie Village, KS 66207
PH: (913) 383-1777
(a-g,i,j,l,m,p-u,w,x,2-5)

Prairie Dog Comics
4800 W. Maple, Suite 122
Wichita, KS 67209
PH: (316) 942-3456
pdc@pdcomics.com
www.pdcomics.com
(a-y,1-5)

KENTUCKY

Comic Book World, Inc.
7130 Turfway Rd.
Florence, KY 41042
PH: (859) 371-9562
FAX: (859) 371-6925
comicbw@one.net
www.comicbookworld.com
(a-j,n-p,r,t,u,w,1-5)

Comic Book World, Inc.
6905 Shepherdsville Rd.
Louisville, KY 40219
PH: (502) 964-5500
FAX: (502) 964-5500
cbwdoug@bellsouth.net
www.comicbookworld.com
(a-j,n-p,r,u,w,x,4,5)

Leroy Harper
P.O. Box 212
West Paducah, KY 42086
PH: (270) 748-9364
LHCOMICS@hotmail.com

MARYLAND

E. Gerber
1720 Belmont Ave.; Suite C
Baltimore, MD 21244

Esquire Comics.com
Mark S. Zaid, ESQ.
P.O. Box 3422492
Bethesda, MD 20827
PH: (202) 498-0011
esquirecomics@aol.com
www.esquirecomics.com
(b-k,r,u,w,4,5)

Alternate Worlds
72 Cranbrook Road
Yorktowne Plaza
Cockeysville, MD 21030
PH: (410) 666-3290
altworldstore@att.net
(b-j,r,t,u,w,1-5)

Comics To Astonish Inc.
9400 Snowden River Pkwy.
Suite 112
Columbia, MD 21045
PH: (410) 381-2732
comics2u@aol.com
www.ComicsToAstonish.com
(a-k,m,r,t,u,w,z,2,3,5)

Greg Reece's Rare Comics
Frederick, MD
PH: (240) 575-8600
greg@gregreececomics.com
www.gregreececomics.com

Diamond Comic Distributors
1966 Greenspring Drive
Timonium, MD 21093
PH: (800) 45-COMIC

MASSACHUSETTS

Gary Dolgoff
116 Pleasant St.
Easthampton, MA 01027
PH: (413) 529-0326
FAX: (413) 529-9824
gary@garydolgoffcomics.com
www.garydolgoffcomics.com

That's Entertainment II
56 John Fitch Highway
Fitchburg, MA 01420
PH: (978) 342-8607
fitch@thatse.com
www.ThatsE.com
(a-z,1-5)

Jerry Weist
18 Edgemoor Rd.
Gloucester, MA 10930
PH: (978) 283-1419
jerryweist@comcast.net

Superworld Comics, Inc.
456 Main St., Suite F
Holden, MA 01520
PH: (508) 829-2259
LVanLiew@aol.com
www.Superworldcomics.com
(a-c,e,m)

Bill Cole Enterprises Inc.
P.O. Box 60
Randolph, MA 02368-0060
PH: (781) 986-2653
FAX: (781) 986-2656
sales@bcemylar.com
www.bcemylar.com

The Outer Limits
437 Moody St.
Waltham, MA 02453
PH: (781) 891-0444
askOuterLimits@aol.com
www.myspace.com/eouterlimits
(a-h,j,l-p,r-x,z,1-5)

That's Entertainment
244 Park Avenue (Rt. 9)
Worcester, MA 01609
PH: (508) 755-4207
ken@thatse.com
www.ThatsE.com
(a-z,1-5)

MICHIGAN

Motor City Comics
33228 W. 12 Mile Rd.
PMB 286
Farmington Hills, MI 48334
PH: (248) 426-8059
FAX: (248) 426-8064
sales@motorcitycomics.com
www.motorcitycomics.com
(a-c,l-o,r,v,w,x)

Tardy's Collector's Corner, Inc.
2009 Eastern Ave. S.E.
Grand Rapids, MI 49507
PH: (616) 247-7828
tccorner@iserv.net
www.tardys.com
(a-f,l,n,p,r,u,w)

Fanfare Sports & Entertainment, Inc.
4415 S. Westnedge Ave.
Kalamazoo, MI 49008
PH: (269) 349-8866
info.fanfare@charterinternet.com
www.fanfare-se.com
(a-k,m,r,t,u,w-z,1-5)

Harley Yee Comics
P.O. Box 51758
Livonia, MI 48151-5758
PH: (800) 731-1029
FAX: (734) 421-7928
HarleyComx@aol.com
www.HarleyYeeComics.com

Comics Archives Inc.
25650 Plymouth Road
Redford, MI 48239
PH: (313) 937-8860
FAX: (313) 937-9663
carchives@twmi.rr.com
www.ComicsArchives.com
(b-d,f,t,z)

MINNESOTA

Source Comics & Games
1601 West Larpenteur Ave.
Falcon Heights, MN 55113
PH: (651) 645-0386
FAX: (651) 644-0922
BobSource@aol.com
www.SourceCandG.com
(a-n,p-r,t,u,w-z,1-5)

Midway Book & Comic
1579 University Ave.
St. Paul, MN 55104
PH: (651) 644-7605
FAX: (651) 644-8786
(a-f,n-p)

Uncle Sven's Comic Shoppe
1838 St. Clair Ave.
St. Paul, MN 55105
PH: (651) 699-3409
svenscomics@aol.com

MISSISSIPPI

Action Island
579 Highway 51, Suite D
Ridgeland, MS 39157
PH: (601) 856-1789
actionisland@hotmail.com
www.actionisland.com
(a-f,q,s,u,w,x,3,4)

MISSOURI

The Comix Strip
821 Broadway, Suite D
POB 1931
Cape Girardeau, MO 63701
PH: (573) 335-9908
mobettercomics@hotmail.com
(a-f,l-s,u,w-z,1-5)

B•Bop Comics & Games Midtown
3940 Main Street
Kansas City, MO 64111
PH: (816) 753-2267 (BBOP)
(a-k,m,p-u,w,x,z,1-5)

B•Bop Comics & Games North
(formerly Comic Cavern)
6320 N.W. Barry Rd.
Kansas City, MO 64154
PH: (816) 746-4569
(a-j,l,p-u,w,x,z,1-5)

Comic Relief
2224 N. 3rd St.
St. Charles, MO 63301
PH: (636) 940-1244
comicbookrelief@aol.com
www.comicbookrelief.com
(a-d,f,r,t-x,5)

NEBRASKA

Robert Beerbohm Comic Art
P.O. Box 507
Fremont, NE 68026
PH: (402) 727-4071
Robert@BLBComics.com
www.BLBComics
(a,b,c,e,l-o,r)

NEVADA

Redbeard's Book Den
P.O. Box 217
Crystal Bay, NV 89402
PH: (775) 831-4848
FAX: (775) 831-4483
www.redbeardsbookden.com
(a,b,c,l,o,p)

Cosmic Comics!
3300 E. Tropicana
Suite G
Las Vegas, NV 89121
PH: (702) 451-6611
fudge-man@cox.net
http://stores.ebay.com/cosmic-comics-las-vegas
(a-d,f,j,5)

NEW HAMPSHIRE

Rare Books & Comics
James F. Payette
P.O. Box 750
Bethlehem, NH 03574
PH: (603) 869-2097
FAX: (603) 869-3475
JimPayette@msn.com
(a,b,c,e,n,o,p)

Jetpack Comics LLC
37 North Main Street
Rochester, NH 03867
PH: (603) 330-9636
info@jetpackcomics.com
(a-l,t,u,w,x,1-5)

NEW JERSEY

Neat Stuff Collectibles
Brian Schutzer
704 76th Street
North Bergen, NJ 07047
PH: 1-800-903-7246
neatstuffcollectibles@yahoo.com
www.NeatStuffCollectibles.com

Main St. Comics
74 N. Main St.
Milltown, NJ 08850
PH: (732) 828-7886
mscomics@aol.com
www.myspace.com/mscomics
(a-g,i,l,r,t,u,w,x,4)

J&S Comics
168 W. Sylvania Ave.
Neptune, NJ 07753
PH: (732) 988-5717
jandscomics@aol.com
www.jscomics.com

Fat Jack's Comicrypt
521 White Horse Pike
Oaklyn, NJ 08107
PH: (856) 858-3877
FAX: (215) 963-9361
fatjacks@comicrypt.com
www.fatjackscomicrypt.com
(b-g,j,l,r,u,w)

J&S Comics
Jim Walsh
98 Madison Avenue
Red Bank, NJ 07701
PH: (732) 988-5717
jandscomics@aol.com
www.jscomics.com

All-Star Auctions
Nadia Mannarino
122 West End Avenue
Ridgewood, NJ 07450
PH: (201) 652-1305
FAX: (501) 325-6504
nadia@allstarauctions.net
www.allstarauctions.net

JHV Associates
(By Appointment Only)
P. O. Box 317
Woodbury Heights, NJ 08097
PH: (856) 845-4010
FAX: (856) 845-3977
JHVassoc@hotmail.com
(a,b,n,s)

NEW MEXICO

Astro-Zombies
3100 Central Ave. SE
Albuquerque, NM 87106
PH: (505) 232-7800
info@astrozombies.com
www.astrozombies.com
(a-g,i,l,m,r,t,u,w,x,y,2-5)

NEW YORK

Silver Age Comics
22-55 31 St.
Astoria, NY 11105
PH: (718) 721-9691
PH: (800) 278-9691
FAX: (718) 728-9691
gus@silveragecomics.com
www.silveragecomics.com
(a-g,j-o,r,t,u,w,x,z,2-4)

Excellent Adventures Comics
110 Milton Ave. (Rt. #50)
Ballston Spa, NY 12020
PH/FAX: (518) 884-9498
jbelskis37@aol.com
www.myspace.com/EAComics
(a-f,m-p,r-x,1-4)

Pinocchio Collectibles
1814 McDonald Ave.
(off Ave. P)
Brooklyn, NY 11223
PH: (718) 645-2573
(b-d,f,i,t,w,x)

St. Mark's Comics
148 Montague St.
Brooklyn, NY 11201
PH: (718) 935-0911
FAX: (212) 477-1294
sales@stmarkscomics.com
(c-g,j,l,p-u,w,x,1-5)

HighGradeComics.com
17 Bethany Drive
Commack, NY 11725
PH: (631) 543-1917
FAX: (631) 864-1921
BobStorms@
HighGradeComics.com
www.HighGradeComics.com
(a,b,c,e)

Fantasy-Comics
P.O. Box 732
Goldens Bridge NY 10526
PH: (914) 301-5252
FAX: (914) 232-3027
buying@fantasy-comics.com
www.Fantasy-Comics.com

Comicollectors.net
Marnin Rosenberg
P.O. Box 2047
Great Neck, NY 11022
PH: (516) 466-8147
www.comiccollectors.net
www.collectorsassemble.com

The Comic Depot, LLC
(Stewarts Plaza)
2538 Route 9N
Greenfield Center, NY 12833
PH: (518) 893-2900
comicdep@comicdepotLLC.com
www.comicdepotLLC.com
(a-d,f-i,u,w,5)

Mahopac Cards & Comics
50 Miller Road
P.O. Box 444
Mahopac, NY 10541
PH: (845) 621-2699
FAX: (845) 621-6719
mahopaccards@aol.com
www.mahopaccards.com

Best Comics International
1300 Jericho Turnpike
New Hyde Park, NY 11040
PH: (516) 328-1900
TommyBest@aol.com
www.bestcomics.com
(a-d,f,r-t,w,3-5)

St. Mark's Comics
11 St. Mark's Pl.
New York, NY 10003
PH: (212) 598-9439
FAX: (212) 477-1294
sales@stmarkscomics.com
(a-g,j,l,o-x,z,1-5)

Metropolis Collectibles
873 Broadway
Suite 201
New York, NY 10003
PH: (800) 229-6387
FAX: (212) 260-4304
E-Mail: buying@
metropoliscomics.com
www.metropoliscomics.com

Midtown Comics
459 Lexington Ave.
(Corner of 45th Street)
New York, NY 10017
PH: (800) 411-3341
PH: (212) 302-8192
info@midtowncomics.com
www.midtowncomics.com

Midtown Comics
200 West 40th Street
(Corner of 7th Ave, 2nd floor)
New York, NY 10018
PH: (800) 411-3341
PH: (212) 302-8192
info@midtowncomics.com
www.midtowncomics.com

Bags Unlimited, Inc.
7 Canal St.
Rochester, NY 14608
PH: (800) 767-2247
FAX: (585) 328-8526
info@bagsunlimited.com
www.bagsunlimited.com

Four Color Comics
Rob Rogovin
P.O. Box 1399
Scarsdale, NY 10583
PH: (914) 722-4696
FAX: (914) 722-7657
keybooks@aol.com
www.fourcolorcomics.com

Fourth World Comics
33 Route 111
Smithtown, NY 11787
PH: (631) 366-4440
fourgle@aol.com
(b-k,q,r,t-x,z,1-5)

Quality Comix
1830 South Road
Wappingers Falls, NY 12590
PH: (800) 548-3314
info@QualityComix.com
www.QualityComix.com

NORTH DAKOTA

Barry's Collectors Corner
Grand Cities Mall
Grand Forks, ND 58201
PH: (701) 795-1386
UNDBKB@aol.com
(a-z,1-5)

OHIO

Queen City Comic and Card Company
6101 Montgomery Rd.
Cincinnati, OH 45213
PH: (513) 351-5674
QCComics@aol.com
www.QueenCityComics.com
(a-g,r-u,w,5)

Up Up & Away!
4016 Harrison Avenue
Cincinnati, OH 45211
PH: (513) 661-6300
FAX: (513) 661-6312
kendall@upupandawaycomics.com
www.upupandawaycomics.com
(a-j,m,u,w,2-5)

Bookery Discount Warehouse
13 W. Main St.
Fairborn, OH 45324
PH: (937) 879-3940
BookeryFan@aol.com
www.BookeryFantasy.com
(b,c,e,j,k,p,w,z,1-4)

Bookery Fantasy - Collectibles
18 W. Main St.
Fairborn, OH 45324
PH: (937) 878-0144
BookeryFan@aol.com
www.BookeryFantasy.com
(a-c,e,l-q,s)

Bookery Fantasy - Comics
16 W. Main St.
Fairborn, OH 45324
PH: (937) 879-1408
BookeryFan@aol.com
www.BookeryFantasy.com
(d-f,j,u,w,1-4)

Bookery Fantasy - Gaming
15 W. Main St.
Fairborn, OH 45324
PH: (937) 879-3940
BookeryFan@aol.com
www.BookeryFantasy.com
(g,h,i,5)

Queen City Comic and Card Company
6600 Dixie Highway
Fairfield, OH 45014
PH: (513) 860-5805
QCComics@aol.com
www.QueenCityComics.com
(b-f,r,t,w,5)

Comics and Friends
7850 Mentor Ave.
Mentor, OH 44060
PH: (440) 255-4242
joe@comicsandfriends.com
www.comicsandfriends.com
(a-f,j,l,m,r,u,w,x,1-5)

Parker's Records & Comics
1222 Suite C Rt. 28
Milford, OH 45150
PH/FAX: (513) 575-3665
dkparker39@fuse.net
www.parkersrc.com
(a-d,f-i,y)

OKLAHOMA

Mammoth Comics
4616 E. 11 St.
Tulsa, OK 74112
PH: (918) 836-9636
MammothComics@Gmail.com
www.MammothComics.com
(a-f)

Want List Comics
(Appointment Only)
P.O. Box 701932
Tulsa, OK 74170
PH: (918) 299-0440
E-Mail: wlc777@cox.net
(a,b,c,m,n,o,s,t,x,3)

Second Chance Books & Comics
3909 North MacArthur
Warr Acres, OK 73122
PH: (877) 706-READ
orders@
second-chance-books.com
www.second-chance-books.com
(b-f,h,j,p-r,w,x,z,1,3,4)

OREGON

Nostalgia Collectibles
527 Willamette Street
Eugene, OR 97401
PH: (541) 484-9202
darrell7g@comcast.net
(a-g,l,n-r,t,u,w,3-5)

Future Dreams
1847 East Burnside St.
Suite 116
Portland, OR 97214-1587
PH: (503) 231-8311
fdb@hevanet.com
(b-h,j,l,p-u,w,1-4)

PENNSYLVANIA

Beachead Comics
1601 W. Chew St.
Allentown, PA 18102
PH/FAX: (610) 437-6372
BeachCom@aol.com
www.beacheadcomics.com
(a-g,i-l,p-u,w,x,z,1,3,4)

Dreamscape Comics
302 W. Broad St.
Bethlehem, PA 18018
PH: (610) 867-1178
nyutko@ptd.net
www.DreamscapeComics.com
(b-j,l,n,p,q,t,u,w-z,1-5)

New Dimension Comics
Clearview Mall
101 Clearview Circle
Butler, PA 16001
PH: (724) 282-5283
butler@ndcomics.com
www.ndcomics.com
(a-l,n,o,r,t,u,w,x,1-5)

New Dimension Comics
Piazza Plaza
20550 Route 19 (Perry Hwy.)
Cranberry Township, PA
16066
PH: (724) 776-0433
cranberry@ndcomics.com
www.ndcomics.com
(a-l,n,o,r,t,u,w,x,1-5)

New Dimension Comics Megastore
516 Lawrence Ave.
Ellwood City, PA 16117
PH: (724) 758-2324
ec@ndcomics.com
www.ndcomics.com
(a-l,n,o,r,t,u,w,x,1-5)

Comic Collection
931 Bustleton Pike
Feasterville, PA 19053
PH: (215) 357-3322
comicdeity@aol.com
www.comicdeity.com
(a-n,q-z,1-5)

Comic Universe
446 MacDade Blvd.
Folsom, PA 19033
PH: (610) 461-7960
chessflink@yahoo.com
www.ComicUniverse.net
(a-g,j-m,p,r,t-x,z,1-5)

Fat Jack's Comicrypt
2006 Sansom St.
Philadelphia, PA 19103
PH: (215) 963-0788
FAX: (215) 963-9361
fatjacks@comicrypt.com
www.fatjackscomicrypt.com
(a-j,l,r,u,w,5)

Ontario Street Comics
2235 E. Ontario St.
Philadelphia, PA 19134
PH: (215) 288-7338
WFink27240@aol.com
(a-d,f-j,r,t,u,w,2,5)

Eide's Entertainment
1121 Penn Ave.
Pittsburgh, PA 15222
PH: (412) 261-0900
FAX: (412) 261-3102
eides@eides.com
www.eides.com
(a-g,i-z,1-5)

Dave's American Comics
Buying All 10¢ & 12¢
original priced comics
P.O. Box 8198
Radnor, PA 19087-8198
PH: (610) 275-8817 or
Hotline: (800) 938-0325
FAX: (714) 288-8992
davesamerican@earthlink.net
www.terryscomics.com
(a,b,d-h,m,n,q)

New Dimension Comics
Pittsburgh Century III Mall
3075 Clairton Rd. #940
West Mifflin, PA 15213
PH: (412) 655-8661
century3@ndcomics.com
www.ndcomics.com
(a-l,n,o,r,t,u,w,x,1-5)

Comics World
1002 Graham Ave.
Windber, PA 15963
PH: (814) 467-4116
FAX: (814) 467-4416
pcomicon@floodcity.net
www.pittsburghcomicon.com
(b-d,f,h,i,u,w,x,2,4,5)

Hake's Americana
P.O. Box 12001
York, PA 17402
PH: (866) 404-9800
www.hakes.com

TENNESSEE

Comics Universe
1869 Hwy 45 Bypass
Jackson, TN 38305
PH/FAX: (731) 664-9131
(a-f,m,p-r,u,w)

Dewayne's World - Comics & Games
459 E. Sullivan Street
Kingsport, TN 37660
PH: (423) 247-8997
dewayne@dewaynes-world.com
www.dewaynes-world.com
(a-d,f-i,r,u,w,4,5)

The Great Escape
1925 Broadway
Nashville, TN 37203
PH: (615) 327-0646
TGE@bellsouth.net
www.TheGreatEscapeOnline.com
(a-p,r-u,w-z,1-5)

TEXAS

Lone Star Comics
511 E. Abram St.
Arlington, TX 76010
PH: (817) 860-7827
FAX: (817) 860-2769
customerservice@
lonestarcomics.com
www.mycomicshop.com/
overstreet
(a-f,j,n,p,1-4)

Comic Heaven
P.O. Box 900
Big Sandy, TX 75755
PH: (903) 636-5555
www.comicheaven.net

Classics Incorporated
Matt Nelson
1440 Halsey Way, Suite #114
Carrollton, TX 75007
PH: (972) 980-8040
www.classicsincorporated.com
Spectre52@aol.com

Worldwide Comics
1440 Halsey Way, Suite #110
Carrollton, TX 75007
PH: (972) 345-2505
www.wwcomics.com
Spectre52@aol.com

Heritage Auction Galleries
3500 Maple Avenue
17th Floor
Dallas, TX 75219-3941
PH: (800) 872-6467
www.HA.com

Titan Comics
3701 W. Northwest Hwy #125
Dallas, TX 75220
PH: (214) 350-4420
FAX: (214) 956-0560
comix99999@aol.com
www.titancomics.com
(a-f,i,r,u)

Duncanville Bookstore
101 W. Camp Wisdom Rd.
Suite J
Duncanville, TX 75116
PH: (972) 298-7546
FAX: (972) 298-1777
AndyMac2570@aol.com
www.DuncanvilleBookstore.com
(a-f,l,n,p,r-u,w-y,3-5)

William Hughes' Vintage Collectables
P.O. Box 270244
Flower Mound, TX 75027
PH: (972) 539-9190
FAX: (972) 691-8837
Whughes199@yahoo.com
www.VintageCollectables.net

Bedrock City Comic Co.
6517 Westheimer
Houston, TX 77057
PH: (713) 780-0675
www.bedrockcity.com
(a-g,j-o,r-x,z,1-5)

Bedrock City Comic Co.
4683 FM1960 West
Houston, TX 77069
PH: (281) 444-9763
www.bedrockcity.com
(a-g,j-o,r-x,z,1-5)

Third Planet Sci-Fi Superstore
2718 SW Freeway
Houston, TX 77098
PH: (713) 528-1067
FAX: (832) 448-9146
Ben@Third-Planet.com
www.Third-Planet.com
(a-z,1-5)

Bedrock City Comic Co.
106 W. Bay Area Blvd.
Webster, TX 77598
PH: (281) 557-2748
www.bedrockcity.com
(a-g,j-o,r-x,z,1-5)

VIRGINIA

Trilogy Shop #2
700 E. Little Creek Rd.
Norfolk, VA 23518
PH: (757) 587-2540
FAX: (757) 587-5637
trilogy2@TrilogyComics.net
www.TrilogyComics.net
(d,f,h,j,5)

B & D Comic Shop
802 Elm Avenue SW
Roanoke, VA 24016
PH: (540) 342-6642
FAX: (540) 342-6694
bdcomics1@verizon.net
www.banddcomics.com
(c-f,r,w)

Trilogy Comics #1
5773 Princess Anne Rd.
Virginia Beach, VA 23462
PH: (757) 490-2205
FAX: (757) 671-7721
trilogy1@TrilogyComics.net
www.TrilogyComics.net
(a-j,n-p,r-u,w,x,3-5)

WASHINGTON

Fantasy Illustrated
(aka **Rocket Comics**)
P.O. Box 13443
Mill Creek, WA 98082
PH: (425) 750-4513
FAX: (425) 787-1353
rocketbat@msn.com
(a-c,n,o)

Dreamstrands Comics, Inc.
115 N. 85th St.
Seattle, WA 98103
PH: (206) 297-3737
delanor@dreamstrands.com
www.dreamstrands.com
(b-d,f,g,i,j,r,t,u,w,x,3-5)

Golden Age Collectables
1501 Pike Place Market
#401 Lower Level
Seattle, WA 98101
PH: (206) 622-9799
FAX: (206) 622-9595
GACollect@Gmail.com
www.GoldenAgeCollectables.com
(a-x,1-5)

WEST VIRGINIA

Comic World
1204 - 4th Avenue
Huntington, WV 25701
PH: (304) 522-3923
comicbooklady@aol.com
(a-f,l,r,t,u,w,5)

WISCONSIN

Nationwide Comics
Buying All 10¢ & 12¢
original priced comics
Janesville, WI 53545
Hotline: (800) 938-0325
PH: (608) 752-8128
FAX: (714) 288-8992
Bart@nationwidecomics.net
www.nationwidecomics.net
(a,b,d-h,m,n,q)

Capital City Comics
1910 Monroe St.
Madison, WI 53711
PH: (608) 251-8445

Jef Hinds Comics
PO Box 44803
Madison, WI 53744-4803
PH: (608) 277-8750
jhcomics@jhcomics.com
www.jhcomics.com
(a-c,e,m-o,s,w)

CANADA

ALBERTA

Another Dimension
424B - 10 St. NW
Calgary, Alberta T2N 1V9
PH: (403) 283-7078
FAX: (403) 283-7080
comics@
another-dimension.com
www.another-dimension.com
(a-f,j,l,m,q,r,u,w,x,z,1-4)

BRITISH COLUMBIA

Rare Golden Age Comics
Vancouver, BC
PH: (604) 220-9410
RareGoldenAge@hotmail.com
www.RareGoldenAge.com
(a-c,e,m-o,s)

MANITOBA

Doug Sulipa's Comic World
Box 21986
Steinbach, MB., R5G 1B5
PH: (204) 346-3674
FAX: (204) 346-1632
cworld@mts.net
www.dougcomicworld.com
(a-c,e,l,n,o,p,r,s,t,y,z,1,3,4)

Comics America
552 Academy Road
Winnipeg, MB, R3N 0E3
PH: (204) 489-0580
FAX: (204) 489-0589
comics_america@mts.net
www.comicsamerica.com

ONTARIO

Big B Comics
1045 Upper James St.
Hamilton, ONT. L9C 3A6
PH: (905) 318-9636
FAX: (905) 318-9055
walt@bigbcomics.com
www.bigbcomics.com
(a-d,f,g,j,u,w,x)

B.A.'s COMICS
426 Hamilton Road
London, ONT. N5Z 1R9
PH: (519) 439-9636
ba.lm@rogers.com
(a-f,l,n)

Pendragon Comics
3759 Lakeshore Boulevard West
Toronto, ONT M8W 1R1
PH: (416) 253-6974
pendragoncomics@rogers.com

QUEBEC

Heroes Comics
1116 Cure LaBelle
Laval, QC H7V 2V5
PH: (450) 686-9155
heroescomics@videotron.ca
(a-j,r,t-x,2-5)

AUSTRALIA

Fats Comics
462 Ipswich Rd.
Annerley
Brisbane Queensland 4103
PH: 07 3848 1974
fatscomics@optusnet.com.au
kingoil@hotmail.com
(a,b,d,e,g,j,k,n,p,s,t,u)

UNITED KINGDOM

2 Tone Comics
40 Market Street
Hebden Bridge,
West Yorkshire HX7 6AA
PH: +01422 845666
Amonkey21@aol.com
www.2ToneComics.com
(a-d,f,l,m,q,u)

INTERNET

ComicLink Auctions & Exchange
PH: (718) 246-0300
buysell@ComicLink.com
www.ComicLink.com

GLOSSARY

a - Story art; a(i) - Story art inks; a(p) - Story art pencils;
a(r) - Story art reprint.

ADULT MATERIAL - Contains story and/or art for "mature" readers. Re: sex, violence, strong language.

ADZINE - A magazine primarily devoted to the advertising of comic books and collectibles as its first publishing priority as opposed to written articles.

ALLENTOWN COLLECTION - A collection discovered in 1987-88 just outside Allentown, Pennsylvania. The Allentown collection consisted of 135 Golden Age comics, characterized by high grade and superior paper quality.

ANNUAL - (1) A book that is published yearly; (2) Can also refer to some square bound comics.

ARRIVAL DATE - The date written (often in pencil) or stamped on the cover of comics by either the local wholesaler, newsstand owner, or distributor. The date precedes the cover date by approximately 15 to 75 days, and may vary considerably from one locale to another or from one year to another.

ASHCAN - A publisher's in-house facsimile of a proposed new title. Most ashcans have black and white covers stapled to an existing coverless comic on the inside; other ashcans are totally black and white. In modern parlance, it can also refer to promotional or sold comics, often smaller than standard comic size and usually in black and white, released by publishers to advertise the forthcoming arrival of a new title or story.

ATOM AGE - Comics published from 1946-1956.

B&W - Black and white art.

BACK-UP FEATURE - A story or character that usually appears after the main feature in a comic book; often not featured on the cover.

BAD GIRL ART - A term popularized in the early '90s to describe an attitude as well as a style of art that portrays women in a sexual and often action-oriented way.

BAXTER PAPER - A high quality, heavy, white paper used in the printing of some comics.

BC - Abbreviation for Back Cover.

BI-MONTHLY - Published every two months.

BI-WEEKLY - Published every two weeks.

BONDAGE COVER - Usually denotes a female in bondage.

BOUND COPY - A comic that has been bound into a book. The process requires that the spine be trimmed and sometimes sewn into a book-like binding.

BRITISH ISSUE - A comic printed for distribution in Great Britain; these copies sometimes have the price listed in pence or pounds instead of cents or dollars.

BRITTLENESS - A severe condition of paper deterioration where paper loses its flexibility and thus chips and/or flakes easily.

BRONZE AGE - Comics published from 1970 to 1984.

BROWNING - (1) The aging of paper characterized by the ever-increasing level of oxidation characterized by darkening; (2) The level of paper deterioration one step more severe than tanning and one step before brittleness.

c - Cover art; c(i) - Cover inks; c(p) - Cover pencils; c(r) - Cover reprint.

CAMEO - The brief appearance of one character in the strip of another.

CANADIAN ISSUE - A comic printed for distribution in Canada; these copies sometimes have no advertising.

CCA - Abbreviation for Comics Code Authority.

CCA SEAL - An emblem that was placed on the cover of all CCA approved comics beginning in April-May, 1955.

CENTER CREASE - See Subscription Copy.

CENTERFOLD or CENTER SPREAD - The two folded pages in the center of a comic book at the terminal end of the staples.

CERTIFIED GRADING - A process provided by a professional grading service that certifies a given grade for a comic and seals the book in a protective Slab.

CF - Abbreviation for Centerfold.

CFO - Abbreviation for Centerfold Out.

CGC - Abbreviation for the certified comic book grading company, Comics Guaranty, LLC.

CIRCULATION COPY - See Subscription Copy.

CIRCULATION FOLD - See Subscription Fold.

CLASSIC COVER - A cover considered by collectors to be highly desirable because of its subject matter, artwork, historical importance, etc.

CLEANING - A process in which dirt and dust is removed.

COLOR TOUCH - A restoration process by which colored ink is used to hide color flecks, color flakes, and larger areas of missing color. Short for Color Touch-Up.

COLORIST - An artist who paints the color guides for comics. Many modern colorists use computer technology.

COMIC BOOK DEALER - (1) A seller of comic books; (2) One who makes a living buying and selling comic books.

COMIC BOOK REPAIR - When a tear, loose staple or centerfold has been mended without changing or adding to the original finish of the book. Repair may involve tape, glue or nylon gossamer, and is easily detected; it is considered a defect.

COMICS CODE AUTHORITY - A voluntary organization comprised of comic book publishers formed in 1954 to review (and possibly censor) comic books before they were printed and distributed. The emblem of the CCA is a white stamp in the upper right hand corner of comics dated after February 1955. The term "post-Code" refers to the time after this practice started, or approximately 1955 to the present.

COMPLETE RUN - All issues of a given title.

CON - A convention or public gathering of fans.

CONDITION - The state of preservation of a comic book, often inaccurately used interchangeably with Grade.

CONSERVATION - The European Confederation of Conservator-Restorers' Organizations (ECCO) in its professional guidelines, defines conservation as follows: "Conservation consists mainly of direct action carried out on cultural heritage with the aim of stabilizing condition and retarding further deterioration."

COPPER AGE - Comics published from 1984 to 1992.

COSMIC AEROPLANE COLLECTION - A collection from Salt Lake City, Utah discovered by Cosmic Aeroplane Books, characterized by the moderate to high grade copies of 1930s-40s comics with pencil check marks in the margins of inside pages. It is thought that these comics were kept by a commercial illustration school and the check marks were placed beside panels that instructors wanted students to draw.

COSTUMED HERO - A costumed crime fighter with "developed" human powers instead of super powers.

COUPON CUT or COUPON MISSING - A coupon has been neatly removed with scissors or razor blade from the interior or exterior of the comic as opposed to having been ripped out.

COVER GLOSS - The reflective quality of the cover inks.

COVER TRIMMED - Cover has been reduced in size by neatly cutting away rough or damaged edges.

COVERLESS - A comic with no cover attached. There is a niche demand for coverless comics, particularly in the case of hard-to-find key books otherwise impossible to locate intact.

C/P - Abbreviation for Cleaned and Pressed. See Cleaning.

CREASE - A fold which causes ink removal, usually resulting in a white line. See Reading Crease.

CROSSOVER - A story where one character appears prominently in the story of another character. See X-Over.

CVR - Abbreviation for Cover.

DEALER - See Comic Book Dealer.

DEACIDIFICATION - Several different processes that reduce acidity in paper.

DEBUT - The first time that a character appears anywhere.

DEFECT - Any fault or flaw that detracts from perfection.

DENVER COLLECTION - A collection consisting primarily of early 1940s high grade number one issues bought at auction in Pennsylvania by a Denver, Colorado dealer.

DIE-CUT COVER - A comic book cover with areas or edges precut by a printer to a special shape or to create a desired effect.

DISTRIBUTOR STRIPES - Color brushed or sprayed on the edges of comic book stacks by the distributor/wholesaler to code them for expedient exchange at the sales racks. Typical colors are red, orange, yellow, green, blue, and purple. Distributor stripes are not a defect.

DOUBLE - A duplicate copy of the same comic book.

DOUBLE COVER - When two covers are stapled to the comic interior instead of the usual one; the exterior cover often protects the interior cover from wear and damage. This is considered a desirable situation by some collectors and may increase collector value; this is not considered a defect.

DRUG PROPAGANDA STORY - A comic that makes an editorial stand about drug use.

DRUG USE STORY - A comic that shows the actual use of drugs: needle use, tripping, harmful effects, etc.

DRY CLEANING - A process in which dirt and dust is removed.

DUOTONE - Printed with black and one other color of ink. This process was common in comics printed in the 1930s.

DUST SHADOW - Darker, usually linear area at the edge of some comics stored in stacks. Some portion of the cover was not covered by the comic immediately above it and it was exposed to settling dust particles. Also see Oxidation Shadow and Sun Shadow.

EDGAR CHURCH COLLECTION - See Mile High Collection.

EMBOSSED COVER - A comic book cover with a pattern, shape or image pressed into the cover from the inside, creating a raised area.

ENCAPSULATION - Refers to the

process of sealing certified comics in a protective plastic enclosure. Also see Slabbing.

EYE APPEAL - A term which refers to the overall look of a comic book when held at approximately arm's length. A comic may have nice eye appeal yet still possess defects which reduce grade.

FANZINE - An amateur fan publication.

FC - Abbreviation for Front Cover.

FILE COPY - A high grade comic originating from the publisher's file; contrary to what some might believe, not all file copies are in Gem Mint condition. An arrival date on the cover of a comic does not indicate that it is a file copy, though a copyright date may.

FIRST APPEARANCE - See Debut.

FLASHBACK - When a previous story is recalled.

FOIL COVER - A comic book cover that has had a thin metallic foil hot stamped on it. Many of these "gimmick" covers date from the early '90s, and might include chromium, prism and hologram covers as well.

FOUR COLOR - Series of comics produced by Dell, characterized by hundreds of different features; named after the four color process of printing. See One Shot.

FOUR COLOR PROCESS - The process of printing with the three primary colors (red, yellow, and blue) plus black.

FUMETTI - Illustration system in which individual frames of a film are colored and used for individual panels to make a comic book story. The most famous example is DC's *Movie Comics* #1-6 from 1939.

GATEFOLD COVER - A double-width fold-out cover.

GENRE - Categories of comic book subject matter; e.g. Science Fiction, Super-Hero, Romance, Funny Animal, Teenage Humor, Crime, War, Western, Mystery, Horror, etc.

GIVEAWAY - Type of comic book intended to be given away as a premium or promotional device instead of being sold.

GLASSES ATTACHED - In 3-D comics, the special blue and red cellophane and cardboard glasses are still attached to the comic.

GLASSES DETACHED - In 3-D comics, the special blue and red cellophane and cardboard glasses are not still attached to the comic; obviously less desirable than Glasses Attached.

GOLDEN AGE - Comics published from 1938 (*Action Comics* #1) to 1945.

GOOD GIRL ART - Refers to a style of art, usually from the 1930s-50s, that portrays women in a sexually implicit way.

GREY-TONE COVER - A cover art style in which pencil or charcoal underlies the normal line drawing, used to enhance the effects of light and shadow, thus producing a richer quality. These covers, prized by most collectors, are sometimes referred to as Painted Covers but are not actually painted.

HC - Abbreviation for Hardcover.

HEADLIGHTS - Forward illumation devices installed on all automobiles and many other vehicles... OK, OK, it's a euphemism for a comic book cover prominently featuring a woman's breasts in a provocative way. Also see Bondage Cover for another collecting euphemism that has long since outlived its appropriateness in these politically correct times.

HOT STAMPING - The process of pressing foil, prism paper and/or inks on cover stock.

HRN - Abbreviation for Highest Reorder Number. This refers to a method used by collectors of Gilberton's *Classic Comics* and *Classics Illustrated* series to distinguish first editions from later printings.

ILLO - Abbreviation for Illustration.

IMPAINT - Another term for Color Touch.

INDICIA - Publishing and title information usually located at the bottom of the first page or the bottom of the inside front cover. In some pre-1938 comics and many modern comics, it is located on internal pages.

INFINITY COVER - Shows a scene that repeats itself to infinity.

INKER - Artist that does the inking.

INTRO - Same as Debut.

INVESTMENT GRADE COPY - (1) Comic of sufficiently high grade and demand to be viewed by collectors as instantly liquid should the need arise to sell; (2) A comic in VF or better condition; (3) A comic purchased primarily to realize a profit.

ISSUE NUMBER - The actual edition number of a given title.

ISH - Short for Issue.

JLA - Abbreviation for Justice League of America.

JSA - Abbreviation for Justice Society of America.

KEY, KEY BOOK or KEY ISSUE - An issue that contains a first appearance, origin, or other historically or artistically important feature considered especially desirable by collectors.

LAMONT LARSON - Pedigreed collection of high grade 1940s comics with the initials or name of its original owner, Lamont Larson.

LENTICULAR COVERS or "FLICKER" COVERS - A comic book cover overlayed with a ridged plastic sheet such that the special artwork underneath appears to move when the cover is tilted at different angles perpendicular to the ridges.

LETTER COL or LETTER COLUMN - A feature in a comic book that prints and sometimes responds to letters written by its readers.

LINE DRAWN COVER - A cover published in the traditional way where pencil sketches are overdrawn with india ink and then colored. See also Grey-Tone Cover, Photo Cover, and Painted Cover.

LOGO - The title of a strip or comic book as it appears on the cover or title page.

LSH - Abbreviation for Legion of Super-Heroes.

MAGIC LIGHTNING COLLECTION - A collection of high grade 1950s comics from the San Francisco area.

MARVEL CHIPPING - A bindery (trimming/cutting) defect that results in a series of chips and tears at the top, bottom, and right edges of the cover, caused when the cutting blade of an industrial paper trimmer becomes dull. It was dubbed Marvel Chipping because it can be found quite often on Marvel comics from the late '50s and early '60s but can also occur with any company's comic books from the late 1940s through the middle 1960s.

MILE HIGH COLLECTION - High grade collection of over 22,000 comics discovered in Denver, Colorado in 1977, originally owned by Mr. Edgar Church. Comics from this collection are now famous for extremely white pages, fresh smell, and beautiful cover ink reflectivity.

MODERN AGE - A catch-all term applied to comics published since 1992.

MYLAR™ - An inert, very hard, space-age plastic used to make high quality protective bags and sleeves for comic book storage. "Mylar" is a trademark of the DuPont Co.

ND - Abbreviation for No Date.

NN - Abbreviation for No Number.

NO DATE - When there is no date given on the cover or indicia page.

NO NUMBER - No issue number is given on the cover or indicia page; these are usually first issues or one-shots.

N.Y. LEGIS. COMM. - New York Legislative Committee to Study the Publication of Comics (1951).

ONE-SHOT - When only one issue is published of a title, or when a series is published where each issue is a different title (e.g. Dell's *Four Color Comics*).

ORIGIN - When the story of a character's creation is given.

OVER GUIDE - When a comic book is priced at a value over *Guide* list.

OXIDATION SHADOW - Darker, usually linear area at the edge of some comics stored in stacks. Some portion of the cover was not covered by the comic immediately above it, and it was exposed to the air. Also see Dust Shadow and Sun Shadow.

p - Art pencils.

PAINTED COVER - (1) Cover taken from an actual painting instead of a line drawing; (2) Inaccurate name for a grey-toned cover.

PANELOLOGIST - One who researches comic books and/or comic strips.

PANNAPICTAGRAPHIST - One possible term for someone who collects comic books; can you figure out why it hasn't exactly taken off in common parlance?

PAPER COVER - Comic book cover made from the same newsprint as the interior pages. These books are extremely rare in high grade.

PARADE OF PLEASURE - A book about the censorship of comics.

PB - Abbreviation for Paperback.

PEDIGREE - A book from a famous and usually high grade collection - e.g. Allentown, Lamont Larson, Edgar Church/Mile High, Denver, San Francisco, Cosmic Aeroplane, etc. Beware of non-pedigree collections being promoted as pedigree books; only outstanding high grade collections similar to those listed qualify.

PENCILER - Artist that does the pencils...you're figuring out some of these definitions without us by now, aren't you?

PERFECT BINDING - Pages are glued to the cover as opposed to being stapled to the cover, resulting in a flat binded side. Also known as Square Back or Square Bound.

PG - Abbreviation for Page.

PHOTO COVER - Comic book cover featuring a photographic image instead of a line drawing or painting.

PIECE REPLACEMENT - A process by which pieces are added to replace areas of missing paper.

PIONEER AGE - Comics published from the 1500s to 1828.

PLATINUM AGE - Comics published from 1883 to 1938.

POLYPROPALENE - A type of plastic used in the manufacture of comic book bags; now considered harmful to paper and not recommended for long term storage of comics.

POP - Abbreviation for the anti-comic book volume, *Parade of Pleasure*.

POST-CODE - Describes comics published after February 1955 and usually displaying the CCA stamp in the upper right-hand corner.

POUGHKEEPSIE - Refers to a large collection of Dell Comics file copies believed to have originated from the warehouse of Western Publishing in Poughkeepsie, NY.

PP - Abbreviation for Pages.

PRE-CODE - Describes comics published before the Comics Code Authority seal began appearing on covers in 1955.

PRE-HERO DC - A term used to describe *More Fun* #1-51 (pre-Spectre), *Adventure* #1-39 (pre-Sandman), and *Detective* #1-26 (pre-Batman). The term is actually inaccurate because technically there were "heroes" in the above books.

PRE-HERO MARVEL - A term used to describe *Strange Tales* #1-100 (pre-Human Torch), *Journey Into Mystery* #1-82 (pre-Thor), *Tales To Astonish* #1-35 (pre-Ant Man), and *Tales Of Suspense* #1-38 (pre-Iron Man).

PRESERVATION - Another term for Conservation.

PRESSING - A term used to describe a variety of processes or procedures, professional and amateur, under which an issue is pressed to eliminate wrinkles, bends, dimples and/or other perceived defects and thus improve its appearance. Some types of pressing involve disassembling the book and performing other work on it prior to its pressing and reassembly. Some methods are generally easily discerned by professionals and amateurs. Other types of pressing, however, can pose difficulty for even experienced professionals to detect. In all cases, readers are cautioned that unintended damage can occur in some instances. Related defects will diminish an issue's grade correspondingly rather than improve it.

PROVENANCE - When the owner of a book is known and is stated for the purpose of authenticating and documenting the history of the book. Example: A book from the Stan Lee or Forrest Ackerman collection would be an example of a value-adding provenance.

PULP - Cheaply produced magazine made from low grade newsprint. The term comes from the wood pulp that was used in the paper manufacturing process.

QUARTERLY - Published every three months (four times a year).

R - Abbreviation for Reprint.

RARE - 10-20 copies estimated to exist.

RAT CHEW - Damage caused by the gnawing of rats and mice.

RBCC - Abbreviation for Rockets Blast Comic Collector, one of the first and most prominent adzines instrumental in developing the early comic book market.

READING COPY - A comic that is in FAIR to GOOD condition and is often used for research; the condition has been sufficiently reduced to the point where general handling will not degrade it further.

READING CREASE - Book-length, vertical front cover crease at staples, caused by bending the cover over the staples. Square-bounds receive these creases just by opening the cover too far to the left.

REILLY, TOM - A large high grade collection of 1939-1945 comics with 5000+ books.

REINFORCEMENT - A process by which a weak or split page or cover is reinforced with adhesive and reinforcement paper.

REPRINT COMICS - In earlier decades, comic books that contained newspaper strip reprints; modern reprint comics usually contain stories originally featured in older comic books.

RESTORATION - Any attempt, whether professional or amateur, to enhance the appearance of an aging or damaged comic book using additive procedures. These procedures may include any or all of the following techniques: recoloring, adding missing paper, trimming, re-glossing, reinforcement, glue, etc. Amateur work can lower the value of a book, and even professional restoration has now gained a negative aura in the modern marketplace from some quarters. In all cases a restored book can never be worth the same as an unrestored book in the same condition. There is no consensus on the inclusion of pressing, non-aqueous cleaning, tape removal and in some cases staple replacement in this definition. Until such time as there is consensus, we encourage continued debate and interaction among all interested parties and reflection upon the standards in other hobbies and art forms.

REVIVAL - An issue that begins republishing a comic book character after a period of dormancy.

ROCKFORD - A high grade collection of 1940s comics with 2000+ books from Rockford, IL.

ROLLED SPINE - A condition where the left edge of a comic book curves toward the front or back; a defect caused by folding back each page as the comic was read.

ROUND BOUND - Standard saddle stitch binding typical of most comics.

RUN - A group of comics of one title where most or all of the issues are present. See Complete Run.

S&K - Abbreviation for the legendary creative team of Joe Simon and Jack Kirby, creators of Marvel Comics' Captain America.

SADDLE STITCH - The staple binding of magazines and comic books.

SAN FRANCISCO COLLECTION - (see Reilly, Tom)

SCARCE - 20-100 copies estimated to exist.

SEDUCTION OF THE INNOCENT - An inflammatory book written by Dr. Frederic Wertham and published in 1953; Wertham asserted that comics were responsible for rampant juvenile deliquency in American youth.

SET - (1) A complete run of a given title; (2) A grouping of comics for sale.

SEMI-MONTHLY - Published twice a month, but not necessarily Bi-Weekly.

SEWN SPINE - A comic with many

spine perforations where binders' thread held it into a bound volume. This is considered a defect.

SF - Abbreviation for Science Fiction (the other commonly used term, "sci-fi," is often considered derogatory or indicative of more "low-brow" rather than "literary" science fiction, i.e. "sci-fi television."

SILVER AGE - Comics published from 1956 to 1970.

SILVER PROOF - A black and white actual size print on thick glossy paper hand-painted by an artist to indicate colors to the engraver.

SLAB - Colloquial term for the plastic enclosure used by grading certification companies to seal in certified comics.

SLABBING - Colloquial term for the process of encapsulating certified comics in a plastic enclosure.

SOTI - Abbreviation for Seduction of the Innocent.

SPINE - The left-hand edge of the comic that has been folded and stapled.

SPINE ROLL - A condition where the left edge of the comic book curves toward the front or back, caused by folding back each page as the comic was read.

SPINE SPLIT SEALED - A process by which a spine split is sealed using an adhesive.

SPLASH PAGE - A Splash Panel that takes up the entire page.

SPLASH PANEL - (1) The first panel of a comic book story, usually larger than other panels and usually containing the title and credits of the story; (2) An oversized interior panel.

SQUARE BACK or SQUARE BOUND - See Perfect Binding.

STORE STAMP - Store name (and sometimes address and telephone number) stamped in ink via rubber stamp and stamp pad.

SUBSCRIPTION COPY - A comic sent through the mail directly from the publisher or publisher's agent. Most are folded in half, causing a subscription crease or fold running down the center of the comic from top to bottom; this is considered a defect.

SUBSCRIPTION CREASE - See Subscription Copy.

SUBSCRIPTION FOLD - See Subscription Copy. Differs from a Subscription Crease in that no ink is missing as a result of the fold.

SUN SHADOW - Darker, usually linear area at the edge of some comics stored in stacks. Some portion of the cover was not covered by the comic immediately above it, and it suffered prolonged exposure to light. A serious defect, unlike a Dust Shadow, which can sometimes be removed. Also see Oxidation Shadow.

SUPER-HERO - A costumed crime fighter with powers beyond those of mortal man.

SUPER-VILLAIN - A costumed criminal with powers beyond those of mortal man; the antithesis of Super-Hero.

SWIPE - A panel, sequence, or story obviously borrowed from previously published material.

TEAR SEALS - A process by which a tear is sealed using an adhesive.

TEXT ILLO. - A drawing or small panel in a text story that almost never has a dialogue balloon.

TEXT PAGE - A page with no panels or drawings.

TEXT STORY - A story with few if any illustrations commonly used as filler material during the first three decades of comics.

3-D COMIC - Comic art that is drawn and printed in two color layers, producing a 3-D effect when viewed through special glasses.

3-D EFFECT COMIC - Comic art that is drawn to appear as if in 3-D but isn't.

TITLE - The name of the comic book.

TITLE PAGE - First page of a story showing the title of the story and possibly the creative credits and indicia.

TRIMMED - (1) A bindery process which separates top, right, and bottom of pages and cuts comic books to the proper size; (2) A repair process in which defects along the edges of a comic book are removed with the use of scissors, razor blades, and/or paper cutters. Comic books which have been repaired in this fashion are considered defectives.

TTA - Abbreviation for *Tales to Astonish*.

UK - Abbreviation for British edition (United Kingdom).

UNDER GUIDE - When a comic book is priced at a value less than *Guide* list.

UPGRADE - To obtain another copy of the same comic book in a higher grade.

VARIANT COVER - A different cover image used on the same issue.

VERY RARE - 1 to 10 copies estimated to exist.

VICTORIAN AGE - Comics published from 1828 to 1883.

WANT LIST - A listing of comics needed by a collector, or a list of comics that a collector is interested in purchasing.

WAREHOUSE COPY - Originating from a publisher's warehouse; similar to file copy.

WHITE MOUNTAIN COLLECTION - A collection of high grade 1950s and 1960s comics which originated in New England.

X-OVER - Short for Crossover.

ZINE - Short for Fanzine.

FEATURE ARTICLE INDEX

Over the years, *The Overstreet Comic Book Price Guide* has grown into much more than a simple catalog of values. Almost since the very beginning, Bob has worked hard to make sure that the book reflects the latest information about the hobby, and this has resulted in some fascinating in-depth articles about aspects of the industry and the rich history of comics. Sadly, many of you may never have read a lot of these articles, or even knew they existed.

These two pages contain a comprehensive index to every feature article ever published in *The Overstreet Comic Book Price Guide*. From interviews with legendary creators to exhaustively researched retrospectives, it's all here. Enjoy this look back at the Overstreet legacy, and remember, many of these editions are still available through Gemstone and your local comic book dealer.

Note: The first three editions of *The Guide* had no feature articles, but from #4 on, a tradition was born that has carried through to the very volume. This index begins with the 4th edition and lists all articles published up to and including last year's 39th edition of *The Guide*.

AUTHOR (S)	TITLE	EDITION	PGS.
Adams, Weldon	Comics in the Schools - 1926: The Lost Comic Book History of the Lone Star State	#35 (2005)	1001-1006
Andrae, Thomas	The Enduring Magic of Disney Comics (written with Bruce Hamilton)	#17 (1987)	A-85-90
	Of Superman and Kids With Dreams: An Interview with Jerry Siegel and Joe Shuster	#18 (1988)	A-79-98
	Origins of the Dark Knight: A Conversation with Batman Artists (with Bob Kane and Jerry Robinson)	#19 (1989)	A-72-93
	Green Lantern's Light! A History by... (with Keif Fromm)	#23 (1993)	A-71-79
Bails, Jerry	Secrets Behind All-Star Comics (More Than You May Want to Know)	#04 (1974)	26-37
Barrington, Stephen	Supergirl: Back for Justice	#36 (2006)	1048-1051
Beck, C.C.	Mr. Mind and the Monster Society of Evil	#15 (1985)	A-89-93
Beerbohm, Robert L.	The American Comic Book: 1897-1932 The Beginning: The Platinum Age	#27 (1997)	1-15
	New Discoveries Beyond the Platinum Age (with Richard D. Olsen, Ph.D.)	#30 (2000)	226-234
	The Golden Age and Beyond: Origins of the Modern Comic Book (written with Richard D. Olsen, Ph.D.)	#30 (2000)	242-249
Blumberg, Arnold T.	Gotham Knights - A Conversation with Jerry Robinson	#27 (1997)	A-25-27
	The World of Tomorrow: How Comics of the Past Portrayed the 1990s	#28 (1998)	82-88
	Invasion of the Giant (and Not So Giant) Robots!	#28 (1998)	83-87
	One For All and All for One	#29 (1999)	107-112
	History with a Twist	#30 (2000)	18-22
	The Marketing of a Medium	#30 (2000)	195-198
	Why the Fantastic Four Made it to Forty	#31 (2001)	20-24
	Brownie Points	#31 (2001)	30-32
	Re-Creations in a Flash (Murphy Anderson profile)	#31 (2001)	39-40
	Superman: Patriotic Covers Through the Years	#32 (2002)	40-43
	Spidey Goes Hollywood	#32 (2002)	44-46
	Mutant Movie Stars: The "New" X-Men Storm the Silver Screen	#33 (2003)	854-856
	Through Waves and Flames: The Elemental Entrance of the Sub-Mariner	#33 (2003)	858-860
	Comic Book Ages: Start the Discussion (with J.C. Vaughn)	#33 (2003)	866-867
	Comic Book Ages: Defining Eras (with J.C. Vaughn)	#34 (2004)	948-951
	Going Green: The Best of the Hulk	#34 (2004)	956-959
Boatner, E. B.	Carl Barks: From Burbank to Calisota	#07 (1977)	A-37-57
	Good Lord! choke...gasp...It's EC!	#09 (1979)	A-43-76
	L. B. Cole: The Man Behind the Mask	#11 (1981)	A-55-72
Borock, Steve	Comic Book Certification: An Overview of Comic Guaranty, LLC.	#35 (2005)	1007-1011

AUTHOR (S)	TITLE	EDITION	PGS.
	An Insiders Look at CGC and Comic Book Certification	#36 (2006)	1044-1047
	CGC, The Art and Science of Comic Book Certification	#37 (2007)	1036-1039
	A CGC Primer: How Professional Comic Book Certification Works	#38 (2008)	1052-1055
Braden, Scott	Strange Adventures - A Conversation with Murphy Anderson	#27 (1997)	A-30-32
	Built to Last (with J.C. Vaughn)	#28 (1998)	89-102
Calhoun, Pat S.	Living on Borrowed Time! A Nostalgic Look at the Early Years of DC's Challengers of the Unknown (with Gary M. Carter)	#24 (1994)	A-157-164
	100 Years - A Century of Comics	#25 (1995)	A-107-123
Carter, Gary M.	DC Before Superman (written with Ken Lane Carter)	#13 (1983)	A-72-86
	The Silver Age... The Beginning: A Comparative Chronology of the First Sliver Age Comic Books	#20 (1990)	A-94-107
	Journey into the Unknown World of Atlas Fantasy (written with Pat S. Calhoun)	#22 (1992)	A-87-103
	Silver Sagas of the Scarlet Speedster: Whirlwind Adventures of the Fastest Man Alive! 1956-1960	#23 (1993)	A-80-86
CGC Grading Team	A CGC Primer: How Professional Comic Book Certification Works	#39 (2009)	1029-1032
Chesney, Landon	The Archives of the Comic Book Price Guide	#06 (1976)	44-45
Colabuono, Gary	Golden Age Ashcans - Comics' First Editions (with Mark Zaid)	#38 (2008)	1040-1045
DeFuccio, Jerry	An Interview with Will Eisner, Creator of the Spirit	#06 (1976)	31-37
	Norman Mingo and Alfred: The World's Greatest Facelift	#12 (1982)	A-45-57
	Charles Clarence Beck: The World's Second Mightiest Mortal	#15 (1985)	A-78-88
Dempsey, "Little" Jimmy	Great Old Radio Premiums	#13 (1983)	A-62-63
DeStefano, Brandon	Comics at the Movies: A Brief History of Comic Characters on the Big Screen	#39 (2009)	1033-1039
Disbrow, Jay	Confessions of a Former Comic Book Artist	#08 (1978)	A-31-38
Estrada, Jackie	Friends of Lulu Sound Off on Comics	#28 (1998)	79-81
Fulop, Scoot D.	Archie Comics Publications: The Mirth of a Legend	#21 (1991)	A-77-78
Hamilton, Bruce	The Mystery of the 12 Missing EC's	#25 (1995)	A-99-106
	Special Feature: Grading - The Next Revolution for Comic Books	#29 (1999)	17-21
Hancer, Kevin B.	Edgar Rice Burroughs and the Comics	#05 (1975)	33-38
Hessee, Tim	The Pop Hollinger Story: The First Comic Book Collector/Dealer	#12 (1982)	A-58-66
Huesman, Mark	Legiondary Adventures	#29 (1999)	101-106
Hughes, Rob	When the Bat Flew Alone!	#39 (2009)	1041-1054
Irons, Christopher	The Man Behind the Cover - L. B. Cole	#18 (1988)	A-77
Kronenberg, Michael	Indelible Shadows: The Spectacular Rise of Artist Jim Lee	#36 (2006)	1052-1055
	Patriot Act!!! (Captain America profile)	#37 (2007)	1024-1029
Leavitt, Craig	Katy Keene - The Overstreet Connection	#14 (1984)	A-67-78
Lee, Stan	Twenty-Five Years? I Don't Believe It!	#16 (1986)	A-82-84
Marek, Carl, et al.	Good Girl Art - An Introduction: Why it Was and What it Was (produced by the American Comic Book Co.)	#06 (1976)	38-43
	Esoteric Comics: The Ultimate Collection (produced by the American Comic Book Co. in Consultation with Scott Shaw)	#07 (1977)	A-30-35
	Women in Comics (in collaboration with Art Amsie)	#08 (1978)	A-54-75
	For Those Who Know How to Look	#09 (1979)	A-35-42
Miller, John Jackson	From "A Long Time Ago" To Today's Galaxy	#38 (2008)	1046-1051
Moore, Dale	Comic Book Charites: Lifelines of the Industry	#34 (2004)	964-966
Murray, Will	Marvel's Hammer: The Mighty Thor	#36 (2006)	1028-1039
	The Untold Origin of Daredevil	#37 (2007)	1030-1035
Novinskie, Charles S.	Sixty Years of Wonder Woman	#31 (2001)	26-29

AUTHOR (S)	TITLE	EDITION	
Olsen, Richard D. Ph.D.	The American Comic Book: 1897-1932	#26 (1996)	1-2
	The American Comic Book: 1933-Present The Modern Comic Book	#26 (1996)	10-11
	The Golden Age and Beyond: The Modern Comic Book (Revised)	#27 (1997)	23-24
	The Golden Age and Beyond: The Modern Comic Book (Revised)	#28 (1998)	211-211
Olshevsky, George	The Origin of Marvel Comics	#10 (1980)	A-46-73
Overstreet, Robert M.	Bob's Bizarre Tales	#30 (2000)	42-63
	And When The Vault Was Opened... (with Gary M. Carter)	#38 (2008)	1036-1039
Overstreet Staff	The Man Behind the Cover - Ron Dias	#17 (1987)	A-84
Rausch, Barbara A.	Katy WHO?...Never Heard of it...	#14 (1984)	A-52-56
Ray, Benn	A Brief History of Super-Teams: Top Ten Greatest Super-Teams	#29 (1999)	108-112
Robbins, Trina	Tarpe Mills - An Appreication	#08 (1978)	A-76
Saffel, Steve	Spider-Man: An Amazing Success Story	#22 (1992)	A-77-86
Schiff, Jack	Reminiscience of a Comic Book Editor (with Gene Reed)	#13 (1983)	A-64-70
Seals, John	Standing on the Shoulders of Giants: The HERO Initiative	#39 (2009)	1025-1027
Shooter, Jim	Marvel and Me	#16 (1986)	A-85-96
Taylor, Terry	Walt Disney's Snow White and the Seven Dwarfs - Fifty Years of Collectibles	#17 (1987)	A-101-111
Thomas, Harry B.	1941: Comic Books Go To War: Those fabulous comics of World War II (with Gary M. Carter)	#21 (1991)	A-79-98
Townsend, John Ph.D.	Three Uncanny Decades of X-Men	#24 (1994)	A-146-156
Vaughn, J.C.	Built to Last (with Scott Braden)	#28 (1998)	89-102
	The American Comic Book: 1897 - 1932 In the Beginning: The Platinum Age	#28 (1998)	201-203
	Avenues of Collecting: A Walk Through the Comic Book Neighborhood	#29 (1999)	91-94
	Just Another Justice League?	#29 (1999)	95-100
	EC, MAD and Beyond: Al Feldstein	#30 (2000)	24-28
	Flights to EC and Beyond with Al Williamson	#30 (2000)	36-39
	Extraordinary! (John K. Snyder III profile)	#31 (2001)	42-44
	Bendis! (Brian Michael Bendis profile)	#31 (2001)	46-48
	Archie at 60	#32 (2002)	47-49
	A Brief History of the Justice Society	#33 (2003)	850-852
	Variant Watch: Ultimate Spider-Man #1	#33 (2003)	862-863
	Comic Book Ages: Start the Discussion (with Arnold T. Blumberg)	#33 (2003)	866-867
	Comic Book Ages: Defining Eras (with Arnold T. Blumberg)	#34 (2004)	948-951
	70 Years and Still Quacking	#34 (2004)	952-955
	(Joe) Simon Says	#34 (2004)	960-963
	Enduring Duo: Wolfman & Perez (Teen Titans at 25, Crisis at 20)	#35 (2005)	993-995
	Little Lulu at 70 (and 60)	#35 (2005)	996-997
	Iron Man: Heavy Metal	#35 (2005)	998-1000
	Publisher Spotlight: Dark Horse Comics	#35 (2005)	1012-1013
	Wonder Woman: Revisited and Renewed	#36 (2006)	1041-1043
	The Semi-Secret Origins of The Overstreet Comic Book Price Guide (Bob Overstreet interview)	#37 (2007)	1016-1023
Ward, Bill	The Man Behind Torchy	#08 (1978)	A-40-53
Weist, Jerry	The Golden Age and Beyond: A Short History of Comic Book Fandom & Comic Book Collecting in America	#26 (1996)	652-667
Zaid, Mark	Golden Age Ashcans - Comics' First Editions (with Gary Colabuono)	#38 (2008)	1040-1045
Zone, Ray	Anaglyphs - A Survey of 3-D Comic Books	#11 (1981)	A-44-53

CGC Turns 10!

A Decade of Comic Book Certification Innovation

By the CGC Grading Team

As *The Overstreet Comic Book Price Guide* reaches its incredible anniversary of 40 years with this edition, CGC, too, has passed an important milestone: it has turned 10 years old!

Comic book collecting looks a lot different today than it did when we first started. Innovations have emerged from many different places...from publishers, through the internet and other new technologies, and from the vision of a great number of dedicated hobbyists. We'd like to think that CGC has also played a part in shaping the way that comic books are collected today. CGC pioneered independent grading for comic books, and later we introduced online registries and third-party signature witnessing. Let's look at CGC's certification process and how it's changed the landscape for collectors.

Forming CGC, Ten Years Ago

CGC opened in January of 2000 under the umbrella of the Certified Collectibles Group, which also includes the largest rare coin certification company in the world, Numismatic Guaranty Corporation (NGC), and the leading currency certification company, Paper Money Guaranty (PMG). To form CGC, the Collectibles Group sought out talented and ethical individuals to grade comic books. Experts needed necessary skills to verify a comic book's authenticity and to detect restoration that can affect its value. To identify these individuals, many of the most respected individuals in the hobby were consulted, and, based on their recommendations, a core grading team was selected.

Having aided in the selection of the grading team, the hobby's leaders were again called upon to develop a uniform grading standard. Everyone seemed to agree that the *Overstreet Guide* was the foundation of this standard, but there were a number of subjective interpretations of its published definitions. It was critical to understand how these guidelines were being applied to the everyday buying and selling of comics. To accomplish this, approximately 50 of the hobby's top experts took part in a grueling grading test. Their grades were averaged and an accurate grading standard reflecting the collective experience of the hobby's most prominent figures was thus developed. CGC now had the best standard and the best team to apply it.

The next step was to develop a tamper-evident holder for the long-term storage and display of certified comics. This proved to be a significant technical challenge. Exhaustive material tests were conducted to determine that they were archival safe. To create a true first line of defense in a prudent plan for storage, it was determined that the comic book should be sealed in a soft inner well, then sealed again inside a tamper evident hard plastic case with interlocking ridges to enable compact storage. The CGC certified grade appears on a label sealed inside the holder for an additional level of security.

The CGC Process

Every day, CGC's Receiving Department opens the newly arrived packages and immediately verifies that the number of books in each package matches the number shown on the invoice. Once this is done, a more detailed comparison is made to ensure that their invoice descriptions correspond to the actual comics. This information is entered into a computer, and the comics will henceforth be traceable at all stages of the grading process by their invoice number and their line number within that invoice. Each book is placed within protective Mylar that has affixed to it a label bearing the invoice and line item numbers, information which is duplicated on the label in a bar-coded inscription for quick reading by the computer. Before any grading is performed, each book is examined by a CGC Restoration Detection Expert. If any form of restoration work is detected, this information is entered into the computer so that it will be available to the grading team.

After being examined by a Restoration Detection Expert, a book then passes to a pre-grader. All CGC graders are prohibited from commercially buying and selling comic books – a firm policy at the Certified Collectibles Group that ensures we remain independent and impartial always. At this stage the comic books reside in barcoded Mylar sleeves, and have been separated from their original invoice. This step is taken to ensure that graders do not know whose books they are grading, as a further guarantee of their impartiality. The pre-grader begins the grading process by counting the book's pages and, for certain tier levels, entering into the computer any peculiarities or flaws that may affect a book's grade. Some examples of this would be "a tear on third page," "a corner crease – does not break color," "a 1/4" inch spine split," and so forth. He then enters this information, if necessary, into the

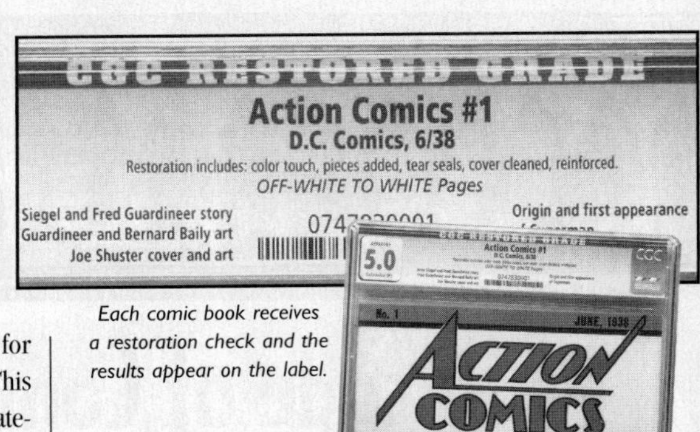

Each comic book receives a restoration check and the results appear on the label.

"Graders Notes" field and assigns his grading opinion.

When the next grader examines the comic, he is not able to see the first person's assigned grade, so as to not influence his own evaluation. After determining his own grade for the comic, he can then view the Graders Notes entered by the previous grader, and he may add to this commentary if he believes more remarks are in order. This same process is repeated as the comic passes to the Grading Finalizer. He makes a final restoration check before determining his own grade, at which time he then reviews the grades and notes entered by the previous graders. If all grades are in agreement or are very close, he will then assign the book's final grade. If there is disagreement among the graders, a discussion will ensue until a final determination is made and the book forwarded.

After each comic has been graded and the necessary numbers and text have been entered into their respective data fields, all the comics on a particular invoice are taken from the Grading Department into the Encapsulation Department. Here, appropriately color-coded labels are printed out bearing the appropriate descriptive text, including each book's grade and identification number. This last item is extremely important, as it serves to make each certified comic unique and is also an important deterrent to counterfeiting CGC's valued product. All of the above information is duplicated in a bar code, which appears underneath the written text on the comic's label.

The newly-printed labels are stacked in the same sequence as the comics to be encapsulated with them, ensuring that each book and its label match one another. The comic is now ready to be fitted inside an archival-quality interior well, which is then sealed within a transparent capsule, along with the book's color-coded label. This is accomplished through a combination of compression and ultrasonic vibration.

After encapsulation, all comics are returned briefly to the Grading Department for a quality control inspection. Here, they are examined to make certain that their labels are correct for both the grade and its accompanying descriptive information. The quality control person also inspects each book and holder for the quality of its presentation. CGC is careful to make certain that the comics it certifies are not only accurately graded but attractively presented, as well.

The steps now completed, the result is a newly-encapsulated CGC comic, ready to be shipped to its proud owner.

CGC Innovations

Much of CGC certification consists of new processes conceived and implemented for the first time or brought to comics from other collectibles fields through other Certified Collectibles Group divisions. One of the great tools that certification has brought to the hobby is the CGC Census. The CGC Census is a detailed population report of all the comics certified by CGC, listing, for every issue, the total number of books in each grade. It is a fundamentally important tool for researching a book's relative rarity, and we provide this information for free on our website. Along with the *Guide*, this has become a basic tool for exploring the field of collectible comics, and ten years ago this information was simply not available in the highly precise format.

Another CGC innovation is the Comics Registry. The Registry is a tool (also free!) that allows collectors to post their collection of CGC-certified comics online. This gives collectors an opportunity to share their collection with other enthusiasts. And collectors can compete for annual awards for the highest-quality collections and the best-presented collections. The Registry plays a fundamental role in helping collectors to develop clear goals and to maintain their focus – two critical components of building a world class collection. It is also one of the most popular online resources that CGC has created...over 2,000 collectors participate and have listed over 150,000 comic books in their collections combined!

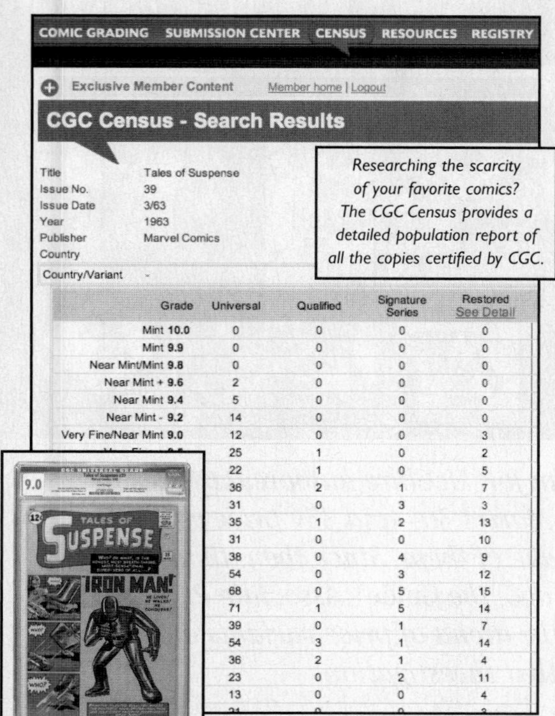

COMIC GRADING SUBMISSION CENTER CENSUS RESOURCES REGISTRY

Exclusive Member Content Member home | Logout

CGC Census - Search Results

Title: Tales of Suspense
Issue No.: 39
Issue Date: 3/63
Year: 1963
Publisher: Marvel Comics
Country:
Country/Variant: -

Grade	Universal	Qualified	Signature Series	Restored See Detail
Mint 10.0	0	0	0	0
Mint 9.9	0	0	0	0
Near Mint/Mint 9.8	0	0	0	0
Near Mint + 9.6	2	0	0	0
Near Mint 9.4	5	0	0	0
Near Mint - 9.2	14	0	0	0
Very Fine/Near Mint 9.0	12	0	0	3
	25	1	0	2
	22	1	0	5
	36	2	1	7
	31	0	3	3
	35	1	2	13
	31	0	0	10
	38	0	4	9
	54	0	3	12
	68	0	5	15
	71	1	5	14
	39	0	1	7
	54	3	1	14
	36	2	1	4
	23	0	2	11
	13	0	0	4

Researching the scarcity of your favorite comics? The CGC Census provides a detailed population report of all the copies certified by CGC.

CGC also pioneered independent, witnessed signature authentication in combination with our other certification services, the CGC Signature Series. Getting comic books signed by creators has been a part of our hobby since early fandom. But signature authentication is a tricky venture. Photographs and videotapes are fine methods, but are not foolproof. Certificates of Authenticity (COA), although accepted in our hobby, are definitely not foolproof either. Our yellow Signature Series label is used when a comic book has been signed or been sketched on by a creator in the presence of a CGC representative, assuring the signature's or sketch's authenticity. Only books that meet CGC's strict criteria for authenticity are eligible for the Signature Series label. In addition to the certified grade, the yellow label includes who signed it and when it was signed. If appropriate, a Signature Series label may state at which venue a book was signed.

A Signature Series encapsulation provides an assurance of authenticity for the signature. In this case, it's the perpetually protected prodigious penmanship of the legendary Stan Lee.

We even offer CGC Signature Series certification at onsite venues, which brings us to one final innovation from CGC: onsite grading. We perform our services at a select number of conventions throughout the year, providing unprecedented access and turnaround times for independent comic book certification. It is a serious undertaking to take our process on the road, and we're very proud that we have been able to bring our services to collectors' backyards in this way.

Comics continue to play a vital role in our popular culture and creative arts. In ten more years, on the occasion of the *Guide's* 50th anniversary and our 20th, we look forward to reporting more incredible news and innovations.

For more information on comic book certification and CGC's many services, please visit their website at www.CGCcomics.com

A History of Publisher Experimentation and

VARIANT COMIC BOOKS

by Jon Martin McClure

In 1997 and 1998, writer and historian Jon McClure authored articles in Comic Book Marketplace *detailing the Marvel 30¢ and 35¢ price variants. At first, many didn't know what to make of them. Since then, though, the market has spoken. More than a year ago, the* Guide's *Associate Publisher, J.C. Vaughn, asked McClure to revisit the arena of price variants on a broader scale. Here are the results of that investigation:*

Godzilla is a gigantic monster with a notoriously bad temper. Who knew that one day, his comic book progeny could cause more turmoil in the collecting world than a rampage through Tokyo?

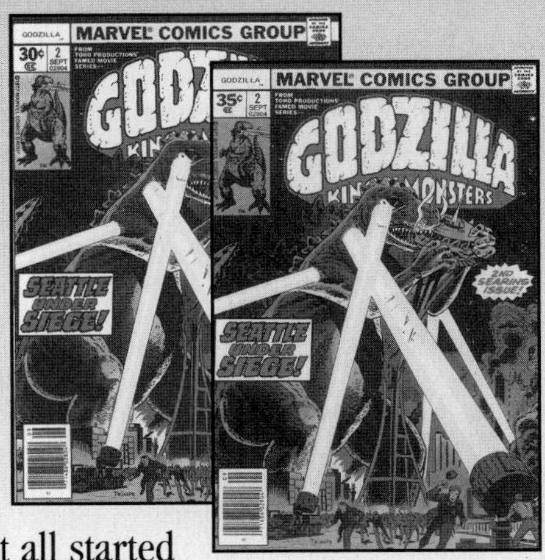

It all started with a 35¢ price copy of *Godzilla* #2.

The year was 1997, and I knew immediately there was something strange about it because I remember paying 30¢ at a Circle K for my copy in 1977. The book came from a long box of 1970s Marvels I picked up from a wholesaler, a little mid to high-grade inventory. Fortunately, having not yet processed the group into stock, I quickly found four more issues with the "wrong" price. Having previously sold two 35¢ variants of *Star Wars* #1, I realized there had to be many more variants out there, and before long I found some 30¢ Marvel variants as well. The time had finally come to call Bob Overstreet.

I dialed Gemstone's number in Baltimore and selected Bob's extension. In case you've never spoken with him, I'd describe Bob as a polite, genial southern gentleman. When his pleasant voice answered, "This is Bob," I introduced myself and told him I'd been planning on calling him for the past twenty years but had been waiting until I had something important to say. "Well, for God's sake, what is it?" he asked.

I told him I had discovered several hundred Marvel comics that nobody knows about. His response was immediate: "That's impossible! Marvel is the most heavily-researched comics company ever," he said.

I offered to have proof on his desk the next day. I asked him if I was right, then could I join the team, and he said, "Absolutely." When I called the next day he was genuinely surprised and I have been an Advisor to the *The Overstreet Comic Book Price Guide* ever since.

Bob wanted proof of more than the handful I could provide before listing them all. At the time, I had been reading Gemstone's *Comic Book Marketplace* magazine for several years. Edited by Gary Carter, it was the finest comics publication of its kind, and in my mind remains the best magazine ever published on the subject of comics. I initially disseminated the existence of Marvel cover price variants in *Comic Book Marketplace* #51(9/97) and #55(1/98), and in an update that appeared in #66(1/99).

Three years later all of the Marvel variants were listed in the *Guide*. Completists pursue one of everything, and demand for Direct versus Newsstand editions (or vice versa), and other types of variants, may soon justify individual listings. Because subjectivity is involved, and for the sake of clarity, I have included *second and later printings, Deluxe Editions, Direct Market Editions, U.S. Published Editions intended for foreign distribution, and many other types of variants,* in the variant definitions, and this history of variants covers books from approximately 1937-1994.

Some promotional variants are not included due to space, but many useful examples of such are, and additional Variants will inevitably surface. "Underground Comix" Variants exist that are not included, although the Variant definitions herein do not exclude such books from identical categorization. Jay Kennedy's 1982 Underground price guide has a prophetic Variant joke on its cover, and is necessary to identify Variants listed in Dan Fogel's 2006 Underground price guide.

Types of Variants

The best definition I know for a "Variant" comic book is (1) *any non-standard edition created for distribution with a unique purpose*, (2) *anything reprinted for distribution under the same title with some changes to the cover and/or contents*, and (3) *any non-standard edition created for distribution in an unplanned or imperfect way.* The primary characteristic of a variant is a *strong similarity* to the "regular" or standard edition.

Type 1 Variants: Cover Price Test Market Variants with regional or otherwise limited distribution, published simultaneously with standard or "regular" editions. Such variants exist because publishers want to test the market prior to raising prices. The indicia and all aspects of the book, *except for the cover price,* are identical to regular editions. Examples include Marvel 30 and 35¢ variants, and Archie 15¢ variants.

Archie's Girls Betty and Veronica #88 15¢ variant (April 1963)

Type 1a Variants: Cover Price Variants intended for foreign distribution with limited regional distribution, published simultaneously with standard or "regular" editions. The indicia and all aspects of the book, *except for the cover price and sometimes the company logo,* are identical to regular U.S. editions. One example is the Marvel Pence Price Variants, with the "Marvel All-Colour Comics" cover banners. Other examples include the Canadian Gold Key and Whitman cover price variants.

Type 1b Variants: Cover Price Reverse Variants with regional or otherwise limited distribution, published simultaneously with standard or "regular" editions. Reverse Variants exist because material is accidentally printed with a lower price than intended, a mistake not always sufficient for the publisher to destroy otherwise saleable goods. The indicia and all aspects of the book are identical to regular editions, regardless of whether it is intended for U.S. or foreign distribution, and the primary characteristic is that *there is another version with the same cover logo and markings and the correct cover price*. The Gold Key 30¢ and Whitman 40¢ price variants are perfect examples.

Type 1c Variants: Cover Variants with limited *or* standard distribution, published simultaneously with standard or "regular" editions. This type of Variant exists because publishers choose to experiment with the market without making widespread appearance changes to their logos or regular editions, or to capitalize on current popularity. The indicia and all aspects of the book are identical to regular editions *except for the front, inside, and/or back cover deviations, with variant covers sometimes noted inside*. If one book has two *different* covers, it may be impossible to identify a "regular" edition beyond "cover 1a, 1b," etc. DC's *Fury of Firestorm* #61 Superman logo variant is one example. A good multiple cover example is DC's *Batman: Legends of the Dark Knight* #1.

Type 2 Variants: After-market reprints with changes and/or omissions made. These Variants may be labeled "reprint" on the cover but most have minor cover changes without the "reprint" notation, such as a missing UPC code or a price increase. The indicia and all aspects of the book, except for the cover, is identical to regular editions, although sometimes the indicia reads, "This is a reprint of a previously published issue." Such Variants are published to capitalize on current popularity, and are sold in the same market and approximate time period as the originals. Marvel's voluminous versions of *Star Wars* #1 are good examples, as one or more of the characteristics listed will appear.

Type 2a Variants: After-market reprints identical to the original printing except with no later printing notation, and with only minor changes, such as new interior ads, published to capitalize on current popularity, and sold in the same market and same approximate time period as the originals. One example is Marvel's 1980s *G.I. Joe* reprints.

Type 2b Variants: After-market reprints identical to the original printing, including the original cover price, except for current ads. "Second Printing" is sometimes noted after the original indicia, although no copyright date may be present. Such variants are not sold in the same market as the originals and may promote a business partner. Marvel's 1994 *Amazing Adult Fantasy* #13, and DC's 1980s-1990s *Batman* reprints are examples.

Type 2c Variants: After-market reprints identical or nearly identical to the original printing, including the cover price, except for current ads on the back cover and inside covers, and with original ads labeled "facsimile." "Second Printing" is sometimes noted in the indicia but a current copyright date is often not present. Such Variants are not sold in the same market as the originals and may promote a business partner. One example is Marvel's 1994 reprint of *Young Men* #25.

Type 3 Variants: Licensed after-market reprints identical to the originals with a color cover, but with B&W interior pages and in a larger size, with original ads except for back cover ads promoting the series. The current copyright date, indicia and publisher's information is present. One example is Don Marin's "Remember When" reprints.

Type 3a Variants: Licensed after-market reprints promoting a business partner with a random mix of reprinted stories using a single cover with different contents. Back and inside covers and pages contain ads and games that reflect the business being promoted. Original stories appear to be unaltered and a current copyright date is present, but no information is provided regarding the original sources or publication dates. One good example is Harvey's *Astro Comics* giveaways that promote American Airlines.

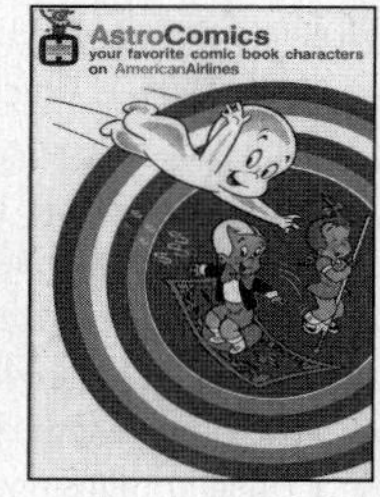

Type 3b Variants: Licensed after-market reprints promoting a business partner with changes and/or omissions made to the cover, sometimes with a back-up story replaced to fit the theme of the product, and/or with the centerfold replaced by an ad. The cover may include the name of the business partner, and such Variants are sometimes given away as premiums, with or without a cover price. Some books say "complimentary copy" on the cover. Specific issues may be reprinted but all issues may have the same issue number on the cover. The current copyright date appears in the indicia, and the back and/or inside covers and pages may contain ads from one or more sponsors. One good example is the many reprints of *Action Comics* #1.

Type 4 Variants: Second and later printings with the same cover price, a different cover price, or no cover price, and/or a later copyright date in the indicia, sometimes with a different cover and/or new house ads, articles, letters and/or other deviations such as cardstock covers, sold in the same market but in a different time period. Classics Illustrated comics' myriad editions is one example, and another is Spire Christian Comics' many printings.

Type 4a Variants: Second and later printings, usually but not always complimentary copies, that are educational and/or political in nature, altered for a specific purpose, that are otherwise identical to the standard or "regular" editions. Good examples include DC's WWII giveaways with simplified text for Navy servicemen, Gilberton's *Picture Parade* V1, #1 that exists as a "contents unknown" teacher's edition, and Twin Circle's communist propaganda reprint of the American Security Council's *Design for Survival*.

Type 5 Variants: Deluxe editions of standard editions published simultaneously to capitalize on current popularity with extra features such as signed and/or limited print runs, and including, but not limited to, enhanced and/or different covers and other deviations. One example is Marvel's many versions of *Spider-Man* #1.

Type 6 Variants: Direct Market Cover Variants published simultaneously with Newsstand Editions for the purpose of controlling distribution. This type of Variant exists because publishers offer a larger discount to retailers on a non-returnable basis, and except for cover deviations, is identical to Newsstand Editions. The indicia and all aspects of the books are identical *except for the covers*, and both are considered standard editions. One example is Marvel's early Direct Market Editions.

Type 6a Variants: Newsstand Cover Variants published simultaneously with Direct Editions with *only the U.S., Canadian, or U.K. price on the cover*, whereas Direct Editions have two prices, and sometimes all three prices. The indicia and all aspects of the books, *except for the cover price(s)*, are identical and all are considered standard editions. DC, Marvel, Warren, Whitman and other publishers produced single cover price variants during the 1980s.

Type 7 Variants: Cover Variants published simultaneously with standard editions sold concurrently by the same publisher. This type of variant exists because publishers seek to broaden their market. The indicia and all aspects of the book, *except for the cover logo*, and minor changes, such as a missing cover date, are identical to regular editions. One example is the Gold Key "Whitmans."

Type 7a Variants: Licensed Cover Variants published simultaneously with standard editions sold concurrently by a business partner. Such variants exist because publishers seek to broaden their market by allowing distribution to a market outside of their normal access. The indicia and all aspects of the book, *except for the cover logo*, and minor changes, such as a missing issue number or cover date, are identical to regular editions. One example is the DC "Whitmans."

Type 7b Variants: Cover Variants published before and/or after the standard or "regular" editions by the same publisher with a different cover logo, and sold in a different market. Such variants exist because publishers seek to increase their sales by pursuing distribution in a different market. The indicia and all aspects of the book, *except for the cover logo*, and minor changes such as a missing cover date and different ads, are identical to regular editions. Western Publishing's *Top Comics* series is a perfect example of such experimentation.

Type 8 Variants: After-market reprints released by the same publisher under a different company name with the same title, in a different time period than the originals, with a customized cover promoting the original issue with new ads. One example is Realistic Comics' *Cowpuncher* issue from 1953 that reprints issue #1 with an early 1950s recycled Avon painted paperback cover that advertises the stories inside.

Type 8a Variants: Licensed after-market reprints released by a different publisher in a different time period than the originals, that include minor cover changes and new ads, but which otherwise have the same contents. One example is Modern Promotions' Charlton reprints.

Type 8b Variants: Licensed after-market reprints released by a different publisher under the same title in a different time period than the originals, with new ads, using the same covers with *different* contents. One example is Accepted Publications' *Indian Warriors* issue with the cover to issue #7 but with the contents of #11 inside. Such variants are *not* legitimate representative copies.

Type 9 Variants: Unlicensed after-market reprints with the same title and issue number that are virtually identical. Such counterfeit copies are designed to pass for the scarce original books that have become pricy collector's items. One example is *Cerebus* #1.

Type 9a Variants: Unlicensed after-market reprints that have the same title, cover and issue number with only minor cover changes and new ads, but with different contents. One example is the I.W. reprint of *U.S. Paratroops Behind Enemy Lines* #1 with modified art on the cover. Such variants are *not* legitimate representative copies.

Type 9b Variants: Unlicensed after-market reprints with the same title and issue number as another book with the same title and issue number. Both have only minor cover changes, but both have *different* contents. The two I.W. issues of *Speedy Rabbit* #1 are perfect examples because no "regular" edition can be identified.

Type 10 Variants: Cover printing errors *known* to the publisher with a last minute correction and limited distribution, with almost all issues released as intended. The "Black Circle Variants" published by Marvel are superior examples.

Type 10a Variants: Cover printing errors *unknown* to the publisher, in limited distribution, with most issues released as originally intended. Missing information and/or incorrect colors are the common elements. One notorious example is *Fantastic Four* #110 featuring a green "Thing," with blue faces and pink uniforms on the others.

Type 10b Variants: Internal printing errors *unknown* to the publisher, in limited distribution, such as pages out of sequential order, a missing centerfold, zero to four cover staples, inverted and/or unintended contents, multiple covers, etc., with limited distribution. *Sandman* #9, with Karen Berger's commentary instead of Jeanette Kahn's editorial, and *Sandman* #18-19 with pages out of sequence, both serve as examples. Recalled books that contain "inappropriate" or adult content due to an editorial oversight also qualify.

Type 11 Variants: Contemporary "Ashcans," oversized, intended for limited distribution to dealers as a giveaway for promotion of products about to be released. Unlike their standard-size counterparts, such pre-release items are un-inked Black and White (B&W) versions of the standard or "regular" issue, without any extra features.

Type 11a Variants: Contemporary "Ashcans" in standard comic size or otherwise, intended for distribution and promotion of products just released or about to be released, whether sold or given away. Such Variants are often near-finished copies of the final edition, and often contain a few extras such as storyboards, concept sketches, commentary, and un-inked penciled covers and/or pages.

Type 12 Variants: Oversized after-market reprints usually with the original ads, released by the publisher or a licensed business partner, sometimes with an outer cardstock cover, with or without the promotion of other products. One example is DC's *Famous First Editions* series, and another is Modern Promotions' *Battlestar Galactica* Treasury that reprints *Marvel Comics Super Special #8.*

Type 12a Variants: Undersized after-market reprints, with new ads or no ads at all, usually without original backup stories, released by the publisher or a licensed business partner, with or without the promotion of other products. One example is the mini-reprint of *Amazing Spider-Man* #42, originally November 1966, attached to the cover of the February 1969 issue of *Esquire Magazine*; another example is DC's 1989 cereal premium mini-reprints of *Untold Legend of the Batman* #1-3. Because such variants are novelty items that are hard to read and often missing important aspects of the original issue, they are *not* legitimate representative copies.

Type 13 Variants: Published simultaneously with standard or "regular" editions, such Variants come with ad inserts bound on stiff cardstock, always four pages in length, that promote a business partner, but which *change the structure and size of the comic*. Staples are sometimes closer than normal, and the book is sometimes slightly taller, by up to 1/16 of an inch. Mark Jewelers created this unique variant, with ads designed to appeal to military personnel on government bases in the U.S. and overseas. Due to the binding process, high-grade copies better than VF/NM are hard to find.

Type 13a Variants: Published simultaneously with standard or "regular" editions, such Variants come with ads inserted on cardstock, regular paper or glossy paper, usually four pages in length regardless of dimensions, that promote a business partner and/or the publisher. One superior example is *Monsters on the Prowl* #13, which includes a bizarrely risque' lingerie page with women wearing teddies and a close-up of a woman in panties that reads, "Best things in life are free," and another is the mini-booklet printed on cardstock found in *Conan* #47 entitled "Mighty Marvel marches through your door," which promotes Marvel's comics and magazines and also contains paid ads.

Type 14 Variants: Published simultaneously with standard or "regular" editions, such books are *Variants* of Variants, and are otherwise identical to regular copies. The primary characteristic is that the book is intended as a variant edition, yet at least one Variant aspect is *unintentional*. One superior example is *Captain America* #212 with the Marvel Comics Group stripe at the top of the book an empty yellow line, that exists only as a 35¢ cover Test Market variant. Since this mutant book is both a Type 10a and a Type 1 Variant, it is therefore a rare Type 14 Double Variant.

Type 15 Variants: Phantom Variants rumored to exist that are scarcer than a Sasquatch interview. Such variants rarely surface, and are often wishful thinking, memory error, incorrect identification, or a fruitless hoax. One example is the Whitman version of *DC Comics Presents* #22, and another is *Yanks in Battle* #3. Such unconfirmed comics tend to lurk in the mist.

Related Items that Do Not a Variant Make

One of several categories not included in the variants list is *Reprints under a new title*. Marvel reprint titles from the 1970s sometimes have new character names as well as missing panels, the latter to reduce page counts for more ads.

Such reprints have an indicia that reads, "Originally presented as..." followed by the original title, but have new titles, and sometimes new covers with altered and/or missing panels, and thus do not qualify as Variants. Marvel's 1974 *Night Rider*, which reprints the 1967 *Ghost Rider* title with only a name change, allows for the introduction of the new "*Ghost Rider*" in 1972.

Power Records comics are good examples of incomplete and seriously mutilated reprint combinations that are actually new and unique products. Books never intended for distribution such as Golden Age ashcans, with only 1-5 copies printed for copyright purposes, do not qualify as variants, because they contain previously published comic covers with a new title, with random issues unrelated to the apparent theme of the book inside, and thus form a unique product. Books created from parts *after the fact*, such as extra comic book covers being attached to coverless comics regardless of title, subject matter, or publisher do not qualify. Because such oddities are combined without regard to anything besides turning a profit from what would otherwise be trash, they are not legitimate variants. Giving such mutant constructions a variant category would be creating a monster, because bogus homemade variants would inevitably surface. Equally ridiculous are the so-called "price sticker" variants, where a comic has an aftermarket sticker on the cover over the printed price; greed and deception do not a variant make.

Rebound comics comprise another closely related category outside of the variant definitions, because it is a new product with a new title. Rebound comics usually contain three to six issues that did not sell, typically but not always with their covers removed. Because stories sometimes begin or end on the inside front and back covers, some rebound comics contain incomplete stories and often have different contents. Some rebound comics contain an *unintentional* mix of comics, while others have an *intentional* mix of comics from various publishers, and have variant covers; a superior example is *Double Comics* from the early 1940s. Variants of rebound comics exist of both U.S. published and foreign published first printings. Regardless of completeness, graphic novels and rebounds do not qualify as variants. Polybagged comics are identical to standard editions except for trading cards and/or similar *unattached* extras found inside, and so are not included in the variant definitions.

Another category of interest is Foreign Published U.S. Reprints that were never intended for U.S. distribution, such as the "Philippine Marvel" books with different ads and missing cover prices. *Phantom Stranger* #35 is the only known "Philippine DC" example. Australian and South African reprints also exist but are not Variants. Hybrid Canadian published versions of U.S. books exist from the 1948-1954 era and contain stories from two or more comics, and keep the original title of one of the reprinted stories inside, but not necessarily for the same issue number. One example is the highly sought after *Weird SuspenStories* #1-3, which contain material from EC's *Crime SuspenStories,* an original product with a new title. Canadian Editions exist of many U.S. books that were published in the same or near same time period that contain the entire U.S. book along with new art and text, new and/or altered covers and different ads, and can be identified by the words "Canadian Edition" on the cover, in the indicia, or both. Other examples exist that are identical to U.S. editions except for the "Canadian Edition" notation in the indicia and different ads. Such Canadian Editions of U.S. comics exist from the late 1940s to mid 1950s because the distribution of U.S. comics into Canada was restricted or not allowed, with ads being one of the points of contention. Printing plates were sent to Canada to bypass the rules, pushing U.S. products into the market faster without having to cross the border, with reprints roughly 10 times scarcer than their U.S. counterparts. Titles normally released in the same time period sometimes had a lag time of one or more months, and sometimes contents accidentally got switched. Some Canadian Editions have lower page counts, with 52 page books cut to 36 pages, and many have inferior paper covers. Most publishers replaced U.S. ads with Canadian ones, and some just left inner covers blank. Many Marvel annuals from 1961-1965 exist as Canadian reprints with blank inside front and back covers. Although Sparta, Illinois is often mentioned, most modern comic books published for U.S. distribution in the 1980s originated in Canada from Ronald's Printing, later known as Quebecor Printing and then WorldColor Press, based in Montreal.

Readers in the United Kingdom had a difficult time experiencing the superhero Silver Age of DC and Marvel Comics, as distribution was sketchy for nearly three decades due to logistical problems such as books getting water damaged in transit. Prohibitive shipping costs and unsold returns thinned profits for an already marginal market. American companies had difficulty competing with popular U.K. comics that had dedicated followers of characters dating back to the 1930s, like Beano, Dandy, and other classics. 1950s publishers often printed separate foreign English Language editions for their market, mostly square-bound giants, in an avalanche of B&W anthology comics with mixed contents from U.S. publishers, and produced by various U.K. publishers including Arnold, Strato, L. Miller & Sons, John Spencer, Top Sellers, World, and others, which was the limited exposure to the Golden Age that U.K. readers received. Horror and Sci-Fi titles dominated the market throughout the 1950s and early 1960s, but some publishers also dared to dabble in Superhero comics. Prior to the resurgence of such characters as the Flash with the release of *Showcase* #4 (9-10/56), Golden Age comics were largely unknown to European readers beyond a few Batman and Superman reprints. According to Duncan McAlpine, "American comics books were not officially distributed in Great Britain until as late as the [beginning] of 1960..." (*The Comic Book Price Guide 1997-1998* by Duncan McAlpine, p. 715); in fact, *Detective Comics* #272(10/59) is the earliest known DC issue, followed closely by other issues the following month, such as *Action Comics* #258(11/59), which were stamped with the pence price in ink on the cover, often in an awkward place such as on a character's face or on a word balloon.

Beginning around 1960 and continuing successfully well into the 1980s, Alan Class emerged as the most prolific of the U.K. giant B&W anthology comics publishers.

From the early 1960s and beyond, Alan Class occasionally included a reprint of the Marvel superhero comics in his horror and sci-fi anthologies, with some reprints altered and/or shortened. In early 1966, the U.K. Market got their own editions of U.S. superhero comic reprints with these titles: *Fantastic* (Power Comics Publications) #1 (2/18/1967) through #89 (10/26/1968), featuring the *Avengers, Doctor Strange, Incredible Hulk, Iron Man*, and *Thor*; *Pow!* (Odhams Publications), #1(1/21/67) – 51, featuring *Spider-Man and Nick Fury*, and #52 (1/14/68) – 86 (9/7/68), featuring the *Fantastic Four*; *Smash* (Odhams Publications) #1 (2/5/66) through #162 (4/3/71), featuring the *Avengers, Daredevil, Incredible Hulk* and the *Fantastic Four*; *Terrific* (Power Comic Publications) #1 (4/15/67) through #43 (2/3/68), featuring the *Avengers, Doctor Strange, and Sub-Mariner*; and *Wham* (Odhams Publishing) #112 (8/6/66) through #187 (1/13/68), featuring the *Fantastic Four*. *Fantastic* and *Terrific* are magazine size, while *Pow! Smash*, and *Wham* are larger and very much like "Sunday Funnies" with rough edges.

In the early 1970s a slicker version of the British weeklies emerged as thin glossy-covered magazine-size comics that serialize 1970s Marvels into several parts with new splash pages and new covers by unidentified artists, reprinting stories from various Marvel titles in B&W with new titles. One good example is *Mighty World of Marvel* #1 (10/7/72) – 19 (2/10/73), which started over as *Spider-Man Comics Weekly* #1 (2/17/73), and then continued as *Super Spider-Man with the Super-Heroes* with #158 until changing to *Super Spider-Man and the Titans* with #199, which continued as *Super Spider-Man and Captain Britain* with #231 until changing to *Spider-Man Comic* with #311, which continued as *The Spectacular Spider-Man Weekly* with #334 until changing to *Spider-Man and Hulk Weekly* with #376, which continued as *Super Spider-Man TV Comic* with #450 until changing to *Spider-Man and his Amazing Friends* with #553, returning to the title *Spider-Man Comic* with #634 until changing to *Spidey Comic* with issue #652, and ending with issue #666 (12/14/85), a run that lasted over 13 years and which prevented a large number of U.S. published for foreign distribution variants of *Amazing Spider-Man* comics from ever being produced. Many Bronze Age books have no Pence price variants for the same reason. British weeklies remained strong sellers into the early 1980s until standard U.S. editions with multi-regional prices began to appear on Direct Market Editions cover dated October 1982. Such magazines featured Silver and Bronze Age reprints, some from Marvel's B&W magazines and some from the color comics, with letter columns and an "international" editorial response. Two volumes entitled *The Marvel Collection* were released with 10 random British weeklies rebound inside a new cardstock cover, and were sold in the U.S. with other "remaindered" books from 1976-1977 by B. Dalton and Waldenbooks stores, despite the fact that the books clearly state in the indicia, "Not to be sold in the U.S.A. or Canada."

Publishers of Variants:

Aardvark-Vanaheim

Cerebus #1 exists as a Type 9 Variant with a glossy inside cover instead of the flat appearance on the inside of the real first issue. A counterfeit of issue #2 is also rumored to exist.

Accepted Publications

Accepted Publications are undated reprints from 1955. No indicia contain the copyright dates, but by using identical ads published in some Marvel Comics from 1955, they were indeed dateable. Accepted Publications comics are Type 8b Variants with the same title and issue numbers but with mixed contents and covers, and are *not* legitimate representative copies. The following 13 titles and 25 issues exist, with the majority fairly easy to acquire: *Algie* (1953-1954) #1-3, *Animal Adventures* (1953-1954) #1-3, *Blue Bolt* (1949-1953) #103, *Dick Cole* (1948-1950) #6, nn, *4Most* (1941-1950) #38-40, *Frisky Animals* (1951-1953) *#53, Frisky Fables* (1945-1950) #43, *Holiday Comics* (1951-1952) #2, 4, *Indian Warriors* (1951) #8, nn, *Phil Rizzuto* (1951) nn, *Popular Teen-Agers* (1950-1954) #5-6, *Sport Thrills* (1950-1951) #12, nn, and *White Rider* (1950-1951) nn(2).

Algie has an alleged variant of issue #1 listed in the *Guide*, a so-called binding error with the contents to *Secret Mysteries* #19 inside. It is *not* a Variant, but rather a mutant product made from bits and pieces. We know this because Timor's *Algie* #1 was printed in December 1953, while the interior to Superior/Dynamic's *Strange Mysteries* #19 was printed in July 1955. There is also a *Holiday Comics* #2 Type 10a Cover Error Variant published by Star with no blue color on the cover. Issue numbers and contents of Accepted Reprints appear to be random. Most Accepted Publications reprints are of Star Publications comics, but Curtis, Fawcett, Novelty, and Timor books were also reprinted.

Archie Comic Publications

(see So Much Fun! Inc., and Spire Christian Comics)

Like most major publishers, Archie Publications occasionally allowed business partners to use their comics for special promotions. *Pep Comics* #118(11/56) is one example of a Type 3b Variant of a standard issue. Seven other books published in November 1956 were not giants or annuals, and may also exist as variants: *Archie Comics* #83, *Archie's Girls Betty and Veronica* #27, *Archie's Joke Book Magazine* #25, *Katy Keene* #31, *Li'l Jinx* #11, *Pat the Brat* #17, and *Wilbur* #69. Earlier and later examples may also exist.

From 1960 to 1961 nearly *all* of the major publishers were looking to raise the 10¢ cover price for regular comics, which had remained the same for over 26 years. Archie raised their price to 12¢ per copy in December 1961 with the exception of *Archie's Girls Betty and Veronica* #72(12/61) and *Archie's Madhouse* #16(12/61), both priced at 10¢. Books such as *Archie Comics* #124(12/61) listed "10¢ per copy" in the indicia yet had the new 12¢ cover price, an oversight not uncommon when major changes are afoot. Archie comics cover dated from 12/61 to 2/62 have a small price box format, with the exception of *Archie's Pal Jughead* #81(2/62), *Archie's Girls Betty and Veronica* #74(2/62), and *Laugh Comics* #131(2/62) which have large price boxes. The large price box format became universal with issues cover dated March 1962.

The first mention of an Archie cover price variant was in the 30th Annual Overstreet Guide, where a copy of *Archie's Jokebook* #66(10/62) with a 15¢ price is noted. Four years later collector/dealer Bill Alexander found a copy of *Laugh Comics* #144(3/63) with a 15¢ cover price, and he sent me a scan. I wondered if it was a Type 1a Canadian Variant like the 35¢ copies of *Archie Giant Series Magazine*, *Archie Pals 'n' Gals*, *Little Archie*, Archie annuals and other giants with regular 25¢ cover prices produced from the late 1950s through the mid 1960s, all of which note in their indicia, "25¢ per copy in the U.S., 35¢ in Canada." Archie 15¢ price variants were cover dated from March 1962 to April 1963, and their indicia lack a Canadian price.

Having verified examples from all titles but *Josie,* and from every month in this time period, it is likely that all books within this window exist. Such Type 1 Test Market Variants have contents that are identical to regular 12¢ cover price Archie comics of the era, and all read "12¢ per copy" in the indicia. Doug Sulipa has a massive inventory of Archie comics and found only two variants when he checked his stock. Doug is based in Canada and has many Type 1a Canadian price variants well represented from most major publishers from virtually every comics era (including hundreds of 35¢ cover price Archie Giants), proving conclusively that the 15¢ issues are *not* Canadian editions, and we estimate they are 100-200 times scarcer than their 12¢ counterparts. Bill Alexander spent over a year helping me pin down the range of 15¢ variants, which extends to an astounding fourteen months, probably the longest test market experiment in comic book history. We extend a special thanks to collector Steve Barghusen, who generously shared with us his Variant of *Pep Comics* #153(3/62).

The following list of 12 titles and 106 issues probably all exist as Type 1 Test Market 15¢ Cover Price Variants of 12¢ Archie comics, 3/62 to 4/63. As we go to print, 37 issues (over one third) are confirmed to exist, noted at the end of each title.

Adventures of the Fly #18-25 (3, 5, 7, 9-11/62, 2, 4/63), #21, 23; *Adventures of the Jaguar* #5-11 (3, 5, 7, 9-11/62, 2/63), #8-9, 11; *Archie Comics* #126-136 (3, 5-9, 11-12/62, 2-4/63), #128, 130, 134; *Archie's Girls Betty and Veronica* #75-88 (3-12/62, 1-4/63), #77, 82-84, 86, 88; *Archie's Joke Book Magazine* #61-69 (4, 6-10, 12/62, 2, 4/63), #63-64, 66; *Archie's Madhouse* #18-25(4, 6, 8-10, 12/62, 2, 4/63), #18-19, 21, 24; *Archie's Pal Jughead* #82-95 (3-12/62, 1-4/63), #88, 91-92; *Josie* #1 (2/63), *Laugh Comics* #132-145 (3-12/62, 1-4/63), #135, 141, 144; *Life with Archie* #13-19 (3, 5, 7, 9, 11/62, 1, 3/63), #15-16, 18; *Pep Comics* #153-161 (3-5, 7-8, 10-11/62, 1, 3/63), #153-154, 156, 158; and *Tales Calculated to Drive You Bats* #3-7 (3, 5, 7, 9, 11/62), #5-7.

The #1 key book in this amazing group of variants is *Archie's Madhouse* #22, featuring the first appearance of Sabrina the Teen-Age Witch, with issues #24 and #25 being her second and third appearances. The investment potential for a Variant copy of *Archie's Madhouse* #22 is enormous. The first and second appearances of Big Ethel in *Archie's Pal Jughead* #84 and #87 are noteworthy, as are Crickett O'Dell's first and second appearances in *Archie Comics* #133 and in *Archie's Pal Jughead* #95. *Archie's Girls Betty and Veronica* #75 is another key book with potential, valued highly for the infamous story of Betty and Veronica selling their souls to the Devil to win Archie's heart. *Josie* #1 is a scarce key with investment potential and her second appearance. Also noteworthy is *Pep Comics* #161, Josie's third appearance. *Archie's Madhouse* #18 is a minor key because of the format change to non-Archie characters. *Archie's Pals 'n' Gals* #23(Winter/62) is Josie's first appearance, but is not on the list because it is a giant.

I expect many collectors to feel an allure for finding five previously unknown Silver Age keys. At the same time *Amazing Fantasy* #15(8/62) was hitting the stands, Archie was engaged in an experiment that eluded detection for almost fifty years! Some Silver Age Archie comics have horror and sci-fi theme covers, and 41 of them are found in the test market period alone: *Adventures of the Fly* #18-19, 21-23, *Adventures of the Jaguar* #5, 7-11, *Archie Comics* #127, *Archie's Girls Betty and Veronica* #75, 77, 79-80, *Archie's Joke Book Magazine* #64, *Archie's Madhouse* #18-19, 21-22, 24-25, *Archie's Pal Jughead* #82, 85-86, 88, *Laugh Comics* #132-133, 136, 139, *Pep Comics* #153-158, and *Tales Calculated to Drive You Bats* #3-4, 6-7. These comics sell for an average of 50% more than surrounding issues. From 1958-1969, 121 regular and 21 giant-sized comics had sci-fi and horror covers. *Archie's Girls Betty and Veronica* #320(10/82) is the first appearance of Cheryl Blossom, which is cover-dated the same as *Jughead* #325(10/82), the second appearance of Cheryl Blossom, and which was released two weeks later; both books are Bronze Age key issues, both sell above *Guide* prices, and both exist as Type 1a Canadian Price Variants. Such Type 1a Variants exist of *all* Newsstand Editions

***Pep Comics** #153 (March 1962) is the earliest 15¢ variant from Archie Comic Publications.*

cover dated 9/82 to 4/97, and also exist of *all* Digests, cover dated 9/82 to 12/97. *Basically Strange* #1(12/82) exists as a Type 10b variant with pages out of sequence.

Catechetical Guild

The Catechetical Guild was a "cold war" publisher that released many sociopolitical titles without variants, but the following titles have several different types of variants confirmed, and all are quite rare: *Blood is the Harvest* (1950) exists as a B&W edition and an untrimmed edition. *Cardinal Mindszenty* (1949) exists as an untrimmed press proof and a preview copy. *Commandments* (1954) exists as a reprint from 1958 with a new cover. *If the Devil Would Talk* (1950) exists as a smaller B&W version, as well as a reprint from 1958 with altered art and text to appease church criticism of the original edition. *Is This Tomorrow?* (1947) exists as an advance B&W copy marked "confidential" with script and art edited out of the regular edition, while others exist with a 10¢ price on the cover, and still others with an empty circle instead of a price. *Labor is a Partner* (1949) exists as a confidential preview oversized B&W edition. *Red Iceberg* (1960) was reprinted 4 times with different back covers. While some of the Catechetical Guild variants are clearly identifiable using the lexicon of Types, some do not qualify as variants because they were not intended for distribution, and others are so unique that listing the individual qualities is more practical than creating new definitions.

Charlton Publications

(Also see King Features and Modern Promotions)

Blue Bird Comics (1959-1965) are Type 3b promotional reprints of Charlton comics, used to promote Blue Bird Shoes: funny animal, hot rod, humor, mystery, war and western titles exist, and issues published in the same year often share the same issue number on the cover, regardless of the book reprinted, with different shoe store names printed directly onto the covers, instead of stamped on like *Buster Brown Comics* (1945-1959). King Features published new books as educational tools, but a handful of King Features comics were Charlton reprints with activities replacing original ads. *Beetle Bailey* #67-68(2, 4/69), and #71-73(10-11/69, 1/70) exist as promotional freebies. *Charlton Classics Library* (1973) Vol. 10, #1, (title: *1776*), supposedly exists as a theater giveaway and a Newsstand Edition, but no theater variant has surfaced; perhaps Newsstand Editions were given away at the premiere, creating the rumor of a separate promotional edition. *Teen-Age Love* #22(9/61) exists as a Type 10a Variant with no cover price. At least one Type 10b Variant apparently exists with blank inside covers: *U.S. Air Force* #18(10/61). Some nn issues of *My Little Margie* and *Robin Hood and his Merry Men* also exist with blank inside covers, and others are likely to exist.

Texas Rangers in Action #32(3/62) exists as a Type 1 Test Market 15¢ cover price variant. All comic publishers considered raising prices in 1961, and by mid 1962 all standard comics cost between 12 and 15¢ each. The following 16 issues from March 1962 may exist as Type 1 Test Market price variants: *Brides in Love* #29, *Fightin' Air Force* #31, *Fightin' Army* #45, *High-School Confidential Diary* #11, *Hot Rods and Racing Cars* #56, *Konga* #5, *Li'l Genius* #37, *Love Diary* #20, *My Little Margie* #40, *Nurse Betsy Crane* #15, *Romantic Story* #59, *Six-Gun Heroes* #67, *Space War* #15, *Submarine Attack* #32, *Teen Confessions* #16, and *Timmy the Timid Ghost* #31. Earlier and later examples may exist. Type 1a Canadian Price Variants exist from for all books cover dated 2/83 to 8/84. Some Charlton comics with cover dates from at least 5/61 through 11/63 exist as Type 1a Pence cover price variants, as do some issues with cover dates from at least 10/73 through 5/76. 1957 saw some "test market" experimentation with funny animal, romance, and war titles, but these were regular editions stamped with a pence price. *Haunted* #62(7/82) exists as a Type 10b Variant with inverted contents.

Texas Rangers in Action *#32 (March 1962) is a Test Market 15¢ variant.*

Chick Publications

Chick Publications' *The Crusaders* series exist as Type 4 Variants. Over 200 different titles in over 100 languages of 24 page mini-comics with up to 40 printings of each, for a total of over half a billion in total circulation, make Chick Publications the most prolific comics publisher. Chick's black and white philosophy steps well beyond the darkest of Steve Ditko's harshest Ayn Rand-inspired Objectivist comic book stories, although Rand and Ditko are proponents of personal responsibility and not religion. Chick's hardcore Christian beliefs pound the reader with the message, "It's His way or the Hell way." Out of print examples in nice shape sell for $20 and up. They can be identified by the code on the back cover, with first printings having an "A," (note: some examples exist with a few other letters appearing before the "A"). The scarcest examples are: *Breakthrough, Don't Read this Book, Kiss India Goodbye, Kiss the Protestant Goodbye, Lost Continent, Losing that Old Zip, Missionaries are Fools, My Name in the Vatican, Operation Somebody Cares, Pssst! Isn't it Time, Secret of Prayer, Secret Weapon, This Book is Banned, Titanic, Wordless Gospel-New Guinea Version,* and *You are About to See.*

Classics Illustrated

(Also see Twin Circle)

Classics Illustrated is the ultimate comic book title when it comes to Variants, and the history of the entire series is explained in condensed format by Dan Malan in the *Overstreet Guide*, but is fully explained in his book, *The Complete Guide to Classic Collectibles, V1*. Over 10,000 English and foreign language editions exist, which often have different numbers and usually altered contents as well, disqualifying them as Variants. Many unique foreign titles exist that do not exist as U.S. editions. *Classics Illustrated* comics printed in Canada that were intended for U.S. distribution are *not* Variants. One example of this is issue #2 (HRN 89), *Ivanhoe,* which reads, "Printed in Canada" on the splash page but reads, "Printed in U.S.A." in the indicia and has an American ad with a New York address on the back cover. *Classics Illustrated* comics printed in Canada for Canadian distribution were not intended for U.S. distribution and are *not* Variants. A small number of Canadian editions have blank inside front and back covers, but more often than not, have text stories that replace U.S. ads, making such foreign editions desirable to Classics Illustrated completists regardless of variant definitions.

Classics Illustrated comics printed in the U.K. for British distribution are *not* variants. Some U.K. editions have pence cover prices only, while others have Australian and South African cover prices listed below the pence price. There are 71 known British editions of *Classics Illustrated* that have the same issue numbers as their U.S. counterparts, published by Thorpe and Porter from 1952-1962: #5-7, 10, 14-17, 22-23, 25, 29, 31-32, 37, 42, 46, 48-49, 53, 55, 57, 60, 62, 64, 68-69, 71-74, 77-80, 82, 84, 86, 88-91, 94, 96-101, 103-109, 111-115, 118-126, and 129. According to Duncan McAlpine, issues #95(5/52) *All Quiet on the Western Front,* and #110((8/53) *A Study in Scarlet*, had standard U.S. editions that were distributed in the UK by Thorpe and Porter, probably with U.K. cover prices, thus making them Type 1a Variants. Thorpe and Porter also published issues #95 and #110 with different titles for its own U.K. series, which are *not* Variants, and similar undocumented examples may also exist. Dan Malan's *The Complete Guide to Classic Collectibles, V2,* lists such foreign editions in detail.

Most issues of *Classics Illustrated* have several U.S. printings that are Type 4 Variants with regular and/or cardstock covers, new covers, and different prices. Some changes, deletions, and fluctuations are unique to *Classics Illustrated* comics, but most would fall under the Type 1c category, and many of those are original issues. *Classics Illustrated* reprints with Variant editions are *not* Type 14 Double Variants because they are *intentionally unique reprinted products without an unintentional variant component*. A Type 1c Variant of #5 (9/42), *Moby Dick*, is known to exist with the inside front cover house ad pushing free copies of #5 that were to be given away by variety stores to hype the sale of *Classics Illustrated* comics, and offers multiple titles at a savings from the Newsstand price. Although meant as a giveaway, some copies were apparently bound into books with regular editions. Raymond True owns the only unbound copy known to exist, and his input concerning this unique and historical Variant is appreciated. The regular edition has an essay contest that begins, "Dear Reader," and ends with, "Yours for Victory and Peace, The Editor." The regular edition is sometimes mistaken for the Variant edition; the winners of the essay contest were listed on the inside front cover of #10(4/43), *Robinson Crusoe*. Variant editions of *Classics Illustrated* comics also exist of #2, 8-10, 17-23, 26, 37, 42, 44, 46, 49-51, 54-55, 58, 61, 64, 95, 105, 152-153, and 160. The title *Classics Giveaways* has multiple Variants published from 1941 to 1969, including Type 3b Twin Circle giveaways from 1967-1968, and similar Variants exist of some *Classics Illustrated Jr.* Twin Circle editions are recognizable by the empty price box found on the covers, with stickers or ink prices sometimes later added. Five U.S. published issues were not reprinted, so the only issues *without* Variants are: *A Christmas Carol* #53(11/48), *The Cloister and the Hearth* #66(12/49), *The Black Tulip* #73(7/50), *Mr. Midshipman Easy* #74(8/50), and *In Freedom's Cause* #168(Winter/69). In 1989, the restaurant chain Long John Silver's published a Type 3b Variant of #64, *Treasure Island*.

Comics Magazine Company

Funny Picture Stories (1936), V2, #7 also exists as a Type 3b promotional giveaway.

Consolidated Magazines

Key Comics #5(1946) exists as a Type 1c Variant with a back cover ad for an unpublished comic book pre-marketed as *Masterpieces Illustrated*.

David McKay Publications

Feature Books began in 1937 with newspaper strip reprints; several early issues were advertised in #3-4(7-8/37) with different covers, making them Type 1c Variants.

DC Comics

(Also see Don Maris, and So Much Fun! Inc.)

New Book of Comics #1(1937) was thought to have been a giveaway until I found a variant in 1998, the cover of which was published in *Comic Book Marketplace* #66(1/99, page 61). It is the only copy known to have a cover price, and another notable difference is that the cover states "96 Pages Full Color." Some issues cover dated Summer 1940 and September 1940 exist as Type 1a 15¢ Canadian price variants and are extremely rare. Currently, four such books are confirmed to exist: *Action Comics* #28(9/40), *Batman* #2(Summer/40), *Detective Comics* #43(9/40), and *More Fun Comics* #59(9/40). Others likely to exist include *Adventure Comics* #54(9/40), *All-American Comics* #18(9/40), *All-Star Comics* #1(Summer/40), *Flash Comics* #10(9/40), *Mutt and Jeff Comics* #2(Summer/40), and *Superman* #5(Summer/40). Subsequent issues had both U.S. and Canadian prices on the covers. Six Type 4a Variant giveaways exist with simplified text, produced for U.S. Navy servicemen during World War II: *Action Comics* #80-81, 84(1-2, 5/45), *Detective Comics* #97(3/45), and *Superman* #33-34(3, 5/45). DC sometimes experimented with the market using format instead of price, with one extended "title" employing digest, giant, and treasury-sized comics in the Silver and Bronze Age, while veiling their numbering system so chief competitor Marvel would not benefit. For details, see my article in *Comic Book Marketplace* #69 (7/99) concerning "giant-size" books, such as the "lost" 80 page giant *Young Love* #69 (8-9/68), another experiment within an experiment.

Type 7a Whitman Variants exist of some titles cover dated March 1978 through August 1980 that were originally sold in bagged sets of three, some with 40¢ cover prices and others with an empty price box. The DC logo was replaced with a Whitman logo, with issue numbers and dates obscured or missing. *DC Comics Presents* is the only title that didn't have a Whitman logo over the DC logo, for obvious reasons. Although they are about 20 to 100 times scarcer than regular copies, the average scarcity is about 40 to 1. Whitman Variants of *Wonder Woman* sell faster than variants of a title like *Superboy*, but all are sought after and scarce in VF/NM or better condition, with issues cover dated 1/80 particularly difficult to find. *Action Comics* #506 (6/80), *The Brave and the Bold* #143 (9/78), *DC Comics Presents* #22 (6/80), *Justice League of America* #177-178 (4-5/80), and *Super Friends* #17 (12/78) are rumored to exist as variants. An anonymous scan of a Whitman *DC Comics Presents* #22 has surfaced but remains unconfirmed.

Superboy and the Legion of Super-Heroes #244 *(October 1978) with the Whitman cover logo.*

Two of the scarcest Type 7a Variants, *Sgt. Rock* #329 (6/79) and *Warlord* #22(6/79), were published in June 1979 and are war themed. Only *DC Comics Presents* #10(6/79) with a *Sgt. Rock* team-up seems to fit the "third issue" profile, but since it is not scarce, it may have been included in other Superman-themed Whitman bags as well. No variants are confirmed from 6/78, 3-4/79, 4/80 or 7/80. The following 15 titles and 164 issues that are cover dated from 3/78 to 8/80 are Type 7a Variants confirmed to exist: *Action Comics* #481(3/78), 482-483, 485-492, 495-499, 501-505, 507-508(6/80), *Batman* #306(12/78), 307-308, 311-320, 323-324, 326(8/80), *Brave and the Bold* #144(10/78), 145-147, 150-159, 165(8/80), *DC Comics Presents* #1(7-8/78), 2-4, 9-12, 14-16, 19, 21(5/80), *Flash* #268(12/78), 273-276, 278, 283, 286(6/80), *Green Lantern* #116(5/79), 117-119, 121(10/79), *Justice League of America* #158(9/78), 160-162, 166-169, 171-173, 176, 179, 181(8/80), *Legion of Super-Heroes* #261(3/80), 263-264, 266(8/80), *New Adventures of Superboy* #1(1/80), 2, 5-6, 8(8/80), *Sgt. Rock* #329(6/79), *Superboy and the Legion of Super-Heroes* #244(10/78), 245-248, 251-258(12/79), *Super Friends* #13(8/78), 14-16, 20-23, 25, 32(5/80), *Superman* #321(3/78), 322-323, 325-327, 329-332, 335-345, 348, 350(8/80), *Warlord* #22(6/79), and *Wonder Woman* #250 (12/78), 251-252, 255-264 (12/79).

The scarcest variants are *Sgt Rock* #329 (6/79), *Warlord* #22 (6/79), *Flash* #286 (6/80), *Justice League of America* #179 (6/80), *New Adventures of Superboy* #6 (6/80), *Legion of Super-Heroes* #264 (6/80), *Superman* #348 (6/80), *Action Comics* #508 (6/80), and *Super Friends* #32 (5/80), based on data from Byron Glass and Doug Sulipa. Two Type 7a Variant Whitman Treasury Editions exist: *All-New Collector's Edition* #C-56 (1978, *Superman versus Muhammad Ali*), and *Famous First Edition* #C-61 (1979, *Superman* #1, Summer/39). Type 1a Pence cover variants exist of 32 titles cover dated March 1978 to June 1980, so many issues have 3 versions. The earliest examples are *Action Comics* #480 (2/78), *Aquaman* #60 (2/78) and *Showcase* #97 (2/78), and the latest is *Brave and the Bold* #179 (10/81). Five scarce Type 1a Pence price variants are known to exist from the early Bronze Age: *Action Comics* #402 (7/71), *Adventure Comics* #408 (7/71), *Detective Comics* #413 (7/71), *Flash* #208 (8/71), and *Superman's Pal Jimmy Olsen* #139 (7/71). Chief competitor Marvel had been publishing Type 1a Variants for over a decade, beginning with issues cover dated July 1960, and DC was apparently experimenting with the U.K. market in 1971, albeit briefly, with books priced at 5 pence for 36 page comics and 7 1/2 pence for 52 page comics, compared to Marvel's prices of 6 pence and 8 pence each. Type 1a Pence price variants exist of DC comics cover dated 3/78 to 9/81. Type 1a Canadian single cover price variants exist of all Newsstand Editions and Digests from 10/82 to 9/88, but prior to this such variants do not exist because the U.S. and Canadian prices were the same. Non-variant Direct Market editions with U.K. and U.S. prices exist that are cover dated 10/81 to 9/82, and non-variant multi-regional Direct Market editions with Canadian, U.K. and U.S. prices exist with all books cover dated 10/82 on.

Superboy Spectacular #1 (1980) was the first comic distributed *only* through comic stores, and exists as a rare Type 1c Variant that was only available to book club members; a book club emblem sits in place of the issue number, date and price in the upper right hand corner. *Amethyst* #1-2 (5-6/83) both exist as Type 1 75¢ cover price variants of 60¢ issues, reportedly test marketed in Austin and Kansas City. *Warlord* #108 (8/86) has a Type 1c variant with a blue caption box that reads, "...And Morgan has nowhere left to run!" Type 1c

Justice League #3 (July 1987) with the Superman Comics cover logo.

variants of *Fury of Firestorm* #61(7/87) and *Justice League* #3(7/87) exist with a "Superman Comics" logo in place of the standard DC logo. Beginning in January 1981 and sporadically continuing to at least March 1983, DC published comics with 4 page slick ad inserts in some titles, and because the ad inserts were in *all* of the Newsstand and Direct Market editions, they are incomplete without the inserts and thus *not* variants; regular paper inserts exist outside of this time period that are also *not* variants. *Elson's Presents* contain three DC issues from 1/81 that were published simultaneously with their regular, single-issue counterparts without covers, and are *not* Variants, but form a new and unique product. Six 1977 Type 3b Pizza Hut variants exist of *Superman* #97 (5/55) and #113 (5/57), *Batman* #122-123 (3-4/59), and *Wonder Woman* #60 (7-8/53) and #62 (11-12/53). *Untold Legend of the Batman* #1-3 (7-9/80) exists as a 1989 set of Type 12a mini-variants. The following Type 10a cover variants are known to exist: *Batman* #307 (1/79) with issue number and month in a blue box; *Sandman* #1 (Winter/74) with a purple background; *Tarzan* #229 (3/74) with the DC logo and price in red, and *Wonder Woman* #66 (5/54) with a green eagle. *Sandman* #9 exists with a Karen Berger editorial instead of Jeanette Kahn's, and #18-19 exist with pages out of sequence: all three are Type 10b variants.

From the mid-1980s to the mid-1990s, many Type 2b promotional variants were sold in bagged three-packs, and some were giveaways. Almost all were *Batman* reprints with new ads. Some bagged sets contain issues of *DC Comics Presents* #55 (3/83) and *World's Finest Comics* #289 (3/83), sold in 3 packs with *Batman* #357 (3/83) at Walgreen's. Some *Batman* variants read, "Compliments of Mervyn's" on the cover, making them Type 3b Variants. Food, game, and toy companies ran ads that replace the originals, and reprints have up to six printings, all with various deviations such as UPC box messages, back cover ads, no month noted on the cover, single or multiple prices, etc. The earliest of such Variants confirmed to exist are *Batman* #352-353(10-11/82), 356-357, and 362 with no reprinting date indicated; the cover dates of other confirmed variant issues of *Batman* extend from 7/86 to 10/96 and include: #397-416, 421-425, 427, 430-432, 457, 489-495, 497, 500, 503-504, 506, 509-511, 515, 520, 523-524, 529-533, and 535.

Many Type 12 variants of classic issues exist, some of the best produced by DC, like the *Famous First Editions* series of oversized identical reprints within an outer cover. Numerous Type 3b Variants exist of *Action Comics* #1 (6/38): one is a 16 page version with a paper cover that reads "Reprint of the first Superman feature," in a box at the bottom of the cover, and an otherwise identical "Safeguard" giveaway also exists, both from 1976. A 1983 Nestle Quick Variant of *Action Comics* #1 exists with a 10¢ cover price; a 1987 edition exists with a 50¢ price in a black box; a 1988 edition exists with a 50¢ price in a white box, in both Direct and Newsstand Editions; a 1992 reprint exists with a \$1 price, as does a 10¢ version, both part of different "Death of Superman" collector's sets. A 1984 *Detective Comics* #27 (5/39) Variant exists as a 32 page issue from Nabisco/Oreo with a paper cover. *Detective Comics* #38 (4/40) and #359 (1/67, #350 on the cover) exist as mid 1980s Toys R Us Replica Edition Variants.

Dell

(Also see Gold Key/Whitman)

The earliest known Dell variant is *Large Feature Comic* #3 entitled *Heigh-Yo Silver! The Lone Ranger* (1938); regular copies have 10¢ covers, but this book exists as a Type 1a 15¢ Canadian cover price variant, as does *Large Feature Comic* #8(1938) entitled *Dick Tracy The Racket Buster.* Both examples are oversized with B&W pages inside a rough cardboard cover. Series One includes issues #1-6, 8-9 with 76 pages, while issues #7 and #10-30 have 52 pages each. Other *Large Feature Comics* Variants are likely to exist, especially of issues #4-7, but the entire series could exist as Type 1a Canadian price variants. Both #3 and #7 feature *The Lone Ranger*, and both are additionally referenced in the *Guide* as "Whitman" #710 and #715, but are text stories mixed with illustrations, unlike the Dick Tracy issue which contains newspaper strip reprints. *Donald Duck* nn (1938) exists as a Type 1a 15¢ Canadian price variant with B&W newspaper strips from 1936-1937, in comic book form inside a cardboard cover.

The 15¢ Canadian cover price variant of 1938's **Large Feature Comic** #3 Heigh-Yo Silver! The Lone Ranger.

In 1947, Dell published a giant issue intended for Canadian distribution only, with the title *Roy Rogers Annual,* with rebound U.S. issues, making it a new and unique product and *not* a Variant. From 1948-1951, due to a customs embargo, Canadian citizens were only able to buy issues that were separately published in Canada by Bell Features, Wilson, etc., without U.S. ads. Such Canadian editions are *not* variants and changed ads, covers, page counts and issue numbers, and are 10-50 times scarcer than U.S. editions. Canadian editions known to exist include *Bugs Bunny Christmas Parade* #1(11/50), *Christmas Parade* #1(11/49), and *Vacation Parade* #1(7/50). Such Canadian editions of 1949-1950 *Dell Giants* are *not* Variants, have page counts of 68 instead of 132 pages, and have 15¢ covers. Other non-variant Canadian editions that may exist include *Christmas Funnies* #2(11/51), *Christmas Parade* #2-3(1950, 1951), and *Vacation Parade* #2(7/51). Dell began publishing giant square-bound comics for U.S. distribution in 1949 with the title *Christmas Parade* #1 that has 132 pages; *Vacation Parade* #1(7/50) also has 132 pages. No Type 1a Canadian price Dell Giant variants have yet been confirmed from 1951 or from 1960-1961. One 35¢ Type 1 Test Market Canadian price variant known to exist as a *Dell Giant* is *Western Roundup* #1(6/52); the indicia reads, "25¢ per copy" without a Canadian price which Dell *always* included, and the price is at mid-cover instead of at the top of the book like standard editions, with the original price imperfectly obfuscated and barely perceivable. Bill Alexander discovered this variant while assisting me with Type 1a Variant research, and it is among the earliest Type 1 variants known to exist. Doug Sulipa believes he remembers selling a *Tarzan's Jungle Annual* #1(8/52) 35¢ Canadian price variant several years ago, so other examples are likely to exist in this time period. Type 1a 30¢ Canadian price variants of *Dell Giants* exist from mid 1953 to mid 1958. Type 1a 35¢ Canadian price variants exist from mid 1958 to 1959, the latter scarcer than the former. The largest *Dell Giant* is *Peter Pan Treasure Chest* #1(1/53) with 212 pages. Thereafter *Dell Giants* ranged between 100, 112, and 116 pages until September 1959, beginning again in the second series with *Tom and Jerry Picnic Time* #21(9/59) at 84 pages, and continuing until December 1961. Many of these giants have back covers with and without ads, with the "comic art back" variants bringing a premium of about 25-50%, and which after mid 1952 are Type 1a Canadian price variants. One scarce example, *Tom and Jerry's Back to School* (9/56), is a 100 page giant with an "Apple for the Teacher" cut-out on the back cover instead of the ad found on the back cover of the standard edition.

A 30¢ Canadian Price Variant for ***Dell Giant Pogo Parade*** *#1 (September 1953).*

Many, but not all, standard 10¢ cover Dell comics from 6/56 to 1-2/61 have Type 1a U.S. published 15¢ Canadian price variants, and the majority of those currently confirmed to exist are *Four Color* titles. Examples that are not *Four Color* issues include titles like *Huckleberry Hound, Looney Tunes,* and *Maverick*, just to name a few. Type 1a Pence price variants also exist from this time period, but instead of having only a higher price, both the original U.S. price and the Pence cover price usually appear on the covers, although some books with *only* the pence price exist. The earliest known Pence price variant of a *Four Color* issue is #1087 (4-6/60) featuring *Peter Gunn,* and the latest known example is #1236 which is undated, featuring *King of Kings;* about one third of the books in this time period are confirmed to exist, and most of them probably do exist. A Pence price variant of *Zorro* #14 (6-8/61) exists with three cover prices, with the 15¢ cover price repeated in Dell's "Canadian" style black circle; *The Lone Ranger* #139 (4/61) also exists in this unusual variant format, and other examples may also exist. Pence price variants were published sporadically, if not universally, with books cover dated from at least 4/60 to 8/61, and the handful of books with three cover prices provides a clue as to why Canadian Type 1a variants are missing from 1960-1961: Dell distributed standard U.S. 15¢ editions to Canada because Dells were the most expensive standard size comics on the market, and would not have sold with an even *higher* Canadian price, as they were overpriced for the era and poor sellers in the U.S., hence their scarcity. Some, but definitely not all, books cover dated from early to mid 1961 had two redundant 15¢ cover prices. *Dell Giant* #42(4/61), *Marge's Little Lulu & Tubby in Australia*, and #43(5/61), *Mighty Mouse in Outer Space*, are the only Giant Pence price variants known to exist, and both have Variant back covers with ads for Twinkles cereal.

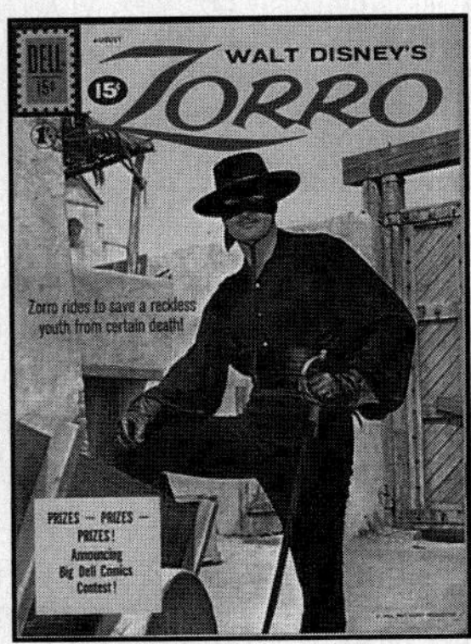

This Pence price variant of ***Zorro*** *#14 from 1961 has 3 prices on the cover.*

Mickey Mouse #33 exists with two copyright dates, 10-11/53 and 12-1/54. Some books have been reported to have 12¢ variant covers. *Four Color* #1057(12/59) featuring *Mickey Mouse* is confirmed to exist as a 12¢ cover variant, with a different back cover than the original printing, which is probably a mid-1960s reprint, because the only other known example is *Four Color* #1235 (3-5/65) featuring *Mister Magoo*, with a 12¢ cover and an indicia stating "second printing." All Dell comics from 5/61 to 7/62 have 15¢ cover prices, but as is often the case, the price change from 10¢ per copy was not entirely consistent. The earliest known standard edition that exists with a 15¢ price, with "February" printed on the cover, is *Looney Tunes* #232 (2/61), and the latest known standard edition with a 10¢ price, with "April" printed on the cover, is *Colt .45* #8 (2-4/61). Whether published monthly, bi-monthly, quarterly, or as a one-shot, all comics from 1961 with "May" on the cover and beyond have 15¢ covers, and this is true of books dated in the indicia from 3-5/61 on, and comics dated in the indicia through 7-9/62 also have 15¢ covers. Comics dated in the indicia 8-10/62 and 9-11/62 have 12¢ covers, even if "August" or "September" is printed on the cover. Some books cover dated from 1-4/61, and a few earlier examples going back into the 1950s, were produced with no cover price at all on U.S. and/or Canadian versions; such entire print runs with no¢ cover price are *not* Variants unless another version with a ¢ cover price exists, although some Pence Price Variants do exist of the same issues. Western ultimately split with Dell, partially over Dell's ill-conceived and unsuccessful price-hiking experiment to produce a higher quality of comic, beginning with issues cover dated 10/62, otherwise known as Gold Key comics.

Many Dells have Type 1c back cover variants, some with photos and others with comic art or gags, probably created for Canadian distribution without the U.S. ads. *Four Color* #710 (6/56) *Francis the Famous Talking Mule* is the earliest known example. A list of these is being compiled by Patrick K. Simpson and will see print in an update in a future article, but for now, other confirmed issues include: #915 (7/58), #1047 (11/59), #1165 (3-5/61), #1195 (4/61), #1215 (10-12/61), #1226 (9/61), #1244 (11-1/62), #1268 (11/61), #1299 (3/62), and #1354 (4-6/62), the last issue. Type 1c cover variants exist of comics outside of the *Four Color* title as well; *Bat Masterson* #2(5-7/60) and *Movie Classics*: *The Mummy* (9-11/62) both exist with different back covers. *Four Color* #847 (1/58) exists with two different front covers, as does #668 (12/55), which was reprinted in January 1958 with Timothy Mouse added to Dumbo's trunk. Some *Four Color* issue numbers were skipped and do not exist, as such books were released as individual titles. *Ensign O'Toole* #2(1964), *Espionage* #2 (8-10/64), *Gulliver's Travels* #2-3 (1966), and *War Heroes* #11 (3/45) still evade detection and probably do not exist. *The Lone Ranger* #37 (7/51) is both a Type 10a and 10b variant with the *Lone Ranger* shown in a red shirt on the cover and the interior of the book; because there is no *intentional* variant quality to the book, it is *not* a Type 14 Double Variant.

Don Maris' "Remember When" Publications

The 1975 "Remember When" series published by collector Don Maris reprinted classic Golden Age issues in B&W with color covers and higher quality paper than the similar Dynapubs reprints produced in 1974. Companies with material reprinted include DC, Fawcett, Hillman, Quality, Vital, and Your Guide. Only *Hit Comics* #1 (7/40) was reprinted by both publishers. Don Maris' reprints are exact replicas of the originals except the pages are B&W instead of color, with back cover ads promoting other reprints, and original ads otherwise included. Ten Type 3 variants exist, including: *Air Fighters Comics* #2 (11/41), *All Star Comics* #3 (Winter/40), *Blackhawk* #9 (Winter/44), *Hit Comics* #1 (7/40), *Plastic Man* #2 (2/44), *Police Comics* #1 (8/41), *Silver Streak Comics* #1 (12/39), 6 (9/40), *Uncle Sam Quarterly* #1 (Autumn/41), *Whiz Comics* #1 (2/40), and *Wow Comics* #1 (Winter/40-41).

Dynapubs

In 1970 Alan Light started publishing *The Buyer's Guide to Comics Fandom*. His "Flashback" *Nostalgia Incorporated* Series was introduced in 1973 and ran for 10 issues, featuring the following Type 3 variants: *Human Torch* #5a (Fall/41, #1), *Air Fighters Comics* #2 (11/42, #2), *All Star Comics* #3 (Winter/40, #3), *Whiz Comics* #1 (2/40, #4), *Police Comics* #1 (8/41, #5), *Silver Streak Comics* #1 (12/39, #6), *Blackhawk* #9 (Winter/44, #7), *Uncle Sam Quarterly* #1 (Autumn/41, #8), *Silver Streak Comics* #6 (9/40, #9), and *Wow Comics* #1 (Winter/40, #10). In 1974 and 1976, Alan Light published B&W Golden Age reprints with color covers. "Flashback" editions are complete reprints of the original issues numbered #1-38, except for back cover ads for other Dynapubs products. Reprinted publishers include DC, Fawcett, Lev Gleason, MLJ, Quality, Timely, and Your Guide. The following 38 Type 3 variants exist, with the "Flashback" issue number in parentheses after the original title, issue number and cover date: *All Select Comics* #1 (Fall/43, #14), *All Star Comics* #2 (Fall/40, #13), #4 (3-4/41, #6), *All Winners* #1 (Summer/41, #23), *America's Greatest Comics* #1 (5/41, #25), *Bulletman* #1 (Summer/41, #30), *Captain Marvel Adventures* #1 (3/41, #10), #2 (Summer/41, #15), #3 (Fall/41, #32), *Captain Marvel Jr.* #1 (11/42, #17), *Daredevil Battles Hitler* #1 (7/41, #1), *Doll Man Quarterly* #1 (Fall/41, #9), *Hit Comics* #1 (7/40, #31), *Human Torch* #2 (Fall/40, #21), *Marvel Mystery Comics* #4 (2/40, #26), *Master Comics* #21 (12/41, #18), #22 (1/42, #22), *Military Comics* #1 (8/41, #5), *Pep Comics* #1 (1/40, #7), #17 (7/41, #16), *Plastic Man* #1 (Summer/43, #11), *Special Comics* #1 (Winter/41-42, #4), *Special Edition Comics* #1 (8/40, #2), *Spy Smasher* #1 (Fall/41, #24), *Sub-Mariner Comics* #1 (Spring/41, #19), *U.S.A. Comics* #1 (8/41, #3), *New York World Fair Comics* 1939 (#12), 1940 (#20), and *Young Allies* #1 (Summer/41, #8). Six final "Flashback" issues appeared in 1976: *Captain Marvel Adventures* #7 (2/42, #35), *Captain Midnight* #1 (9/42, #37), *Flash Comics* #15 (3/41, #36), *Ibis the Invincible* #1 (1/42, #34), *Plastic Man* #2 (2/44, #33), and *World's Finest Comics* #8 (Winter/42, #38).

Eastern Color Printing Company

Toy Land Funnies (1934) and *Toy World Funnies* (1933) both exist as *Funnies on Parade* Type 3b cover variants that are promotional giveaways.

EC Comics

Crime SuspenStories #1 (10-11/50) exists as a variant with the number #15 inside that was stamped over. *Picture Stories from the Bible* (1942-1946), was published by All-American, Bible Pictures Ltd., DC, and EC, the latter in 1955-1956. Up to eight printings are known to exist of these Type 4a variants. *E.C. Classic Reprints,* published by East Coast Comix Company from May 1973 to 1976, lasted for 12 issues, with all but one under their original title: *The Crypt of Terror* #1 (5/73), the first in the series, is a new title that reprints *Tales from the Crypt* #46 (2/55), and which was the original title intended by William M. Gaines as a fourth EC Horror title, before Frederick Wertham's *Seduction of the Innocent* (1953, 1954) dealt EC a near-fatal blow. Eleven other issues are Type 8a Variants: *Crime SuspenStories* #25(11/54, #6), *Haunt of Fear* #12(4/52, #4), *Haunt of Fear* #23 (2/54, #10), *Shock SuspenStories* #2 (4-5/52, #12), *Shock SuspenStories* #6 (12-1/53, #8), *Shock SuspenStories* #12 (12-1/54, #3), *Two-Fisted Tales* #34 (7-8/54, #9), *Vault of Horror* #26 (8-9/52, #7), *Weird Fantasy* #13 (5-6/52, #5), *Weird Science* #12 (3-4/52, #11), and *Weird Science* #15 (9-10/52, #2). From 1985-1986, Russ Cochran published twelve *EC Classics*, some with a mix of stories and some true to the originals.

Eclipse Comics

Total Eclipse #4 (5/88) exists as a Type 10b variant with pages #7-14 upside down.

Fawcett Publications

Captain Marvel Adventures #62 (6/46) exists as a Type 1c back cover variant edition: one edition has a *Popular Mechanics* ad, and the other has an "Items for one dollar" ad. *Mighty Midget Comics* were Type 12a mini-reprint variants of Fawcett comics published by Samuel E. Lowe & Co., from 1942-1943. Such variants were glued to the covers of *Captain Marvel Adventures* #20-21 (1-2/43), and 23 (4/43). Although the series is known as *Mighty Midget Comics,* all of the issues were numbered #11, and titles include: *Bulletman*, *Captain Marvel*, *Captain Marvel Adventures, Captain Marvel Jr.*, *Golden Arrow*, *Ibis the Invincible*, and *Spy Smasher*. Covers and contents were sometimes mixed, and these books were also sold separately with other children's products. Type 1c variants exist with back cover ads that were not glued to the Newsstand Editions.

Fiction House Magazines

Planet Comics #52 (1/48) has a Type 10a cover error variant with no green ink.

Gilberton Company

Picture Parade (1953) V1, #1 exists as a Type 4a variant teacher's edition.

Gold Key/Whitman Comics

(Also see Dell)

Western Publishing began printing Dell Comics in the 1930s, and eventually published their own line of Gold Key comics beginning with books cover dated October 1962, including many original titles, and continued publishing titles from the most successful cartoon character licensee, Walt Disney Productions, as well as many popular Hanna-Barbera titles. Western changed the name of their comics line to Whitman comics in 1980. Currently over 7000 unique Gold Key/Whitman comics, digests, and treasuries are known to exist. *Golden Magazine* V1, #1 (2/64) began a long-running experiment as an educational children's monthly that featured activities, cartoons, and comics similar to the late 1960s "Gold Key Club," which allowed readers to interact with the publisher and create characters, much like DC's "Dial 'H' for Hero" series that appeared in *House of Mystery* and later in *Adventure Comics*. Most *Golden Magazine* issues had ads for Gold Key comics as well as *Golden Comics Digest* and *Walt Disney Comics Digest*. *Golden Magazine's* cover symbol, a parrot named Cracky, appeared in features called "Jokes by Cracky" and "The Cracker Barrel," beginning with the first issue. Featured on many painted covers, Cracky eventually launched Gold Key's *Wacky Adventures of Cracky* (1972). Some issues have 3 page glossy color sections of *Little Lulu* comics, including V6, #1 (1/69), V6, #4 (4/69), V6, #7-8 (7-8/69), and V7, #4 (4/70).

Whitman Comic Book (9/62) is an eight-issue hardcover comic series that was simultaneously published. Issues #1-6 are reprints of U.K. comics, with #7-8 being U.S. reprints. *The Flintstones at the N. Y. World's Fair* (1964) exists with both 25¢ and 29¢ cover prices, but are listed as J.W. Brooks and Warren Publishing for the latter version, despite being Hanna-Barbera characters otherwise exclusively published by Western during this time period. A treasury-sized Whitman edition of *Walt Disney's Jungle Book* (1/68) is the first Whitman version of a Gold Key book, with the standard size issue released later, cover dated March 1968, which is an early experiment with both format and cover logo. More than a dozen treasury-sized comic-book-story coloring books were published with a Whitman logo in the 1970s, featuring DC and Marvel characters in separate books, none of which are Variants. There are three digest-sized Whitman titles with fourteen Type 7 variants confirmed to exist: *Golden Comics Digest* #20 (11/71) - 48 (1/76); #32 - 33 (9, 11/73), 43 (5/75) - 46 (9-10/75), *Mystery Comics Digest* #1 (3/72) - 26 (10/75); #13 - 14 (9-10/73), 23 (5/75), and *Walt Disney's Comics Digest* #32 (12/71) - 57 (2/76); #43 - 44 (10, 12/73), 52-54 (4, 6, 8/75). *Walt Disney Paint Book* (1975) is a coloring book series that partially reprints 1930s comic magazines with the original dates.

One version of **Fantastic Voyage** #2 has a cover banner not found on the regular edition.

Some titles are known to have Type 1c variants: *Avengers* #1(11/68) exists as a standard edition with an ad on the back cover and has a photo back cover variant, *Fantastic Voyage* #2 (12/69) exists as a variant with a cover banner that reads "Civilian Miniaturized Defense Force," and *Movie Comics: Darby O'Gill and the Little People* (1/70) has a variant with a photo inside front and back cover, and a "Word about Leprechauns" story on the inside back cover. *Star Trek* #1 (10/67) is said to have a photo back cover variant, but this is the *only* version that exists and is *not* a variant. *Star Trek* #2(6/68) exists with an ad on the back cover and also as a scarcer photo back cover variant; both versions exist with 12 and 15¢ covers. *Star Trek* #3 (12/68) exists as a standard edition with an ad on the back cover and also as a scarcer photo back cover variant. *Tiger Girl* #1 (9/68) exists as a back cover variant with a pin-up instead of an ad. *Walt Disney's Comics and Stories* #351-360 (12/69-9/70) have standard 15¢ editions and also 25¢ Type 5 variant editions with a poster inside. From 1973 to 1975, Gold Key comics contained Mark Jewelers inserts in about 60% of the issues that were sold overseas in military bases in England, Italy, and elsewhere. Type 1a Gold Key Pence cover price variants are known to exist, with cover dates ranging from 5/73 to 11/75. Earlier and later examples may also exist.

Top Comics was an experiment dated July 1967 that featured reprinted comics in plastic bags of five for 59¢, and these reprints feature a new version of an old logo. *Uncle Scrooge: The Lemonade King* #2465(1960) is a small Disney children's book with Carl Barks art that says "Top Top Tales" and "Whitman" on the cover. *Quick Draw McGraw: Badmen Beware* #2469(1960), a Hanna-Barbera product, has the same cover symbol, a top that is remarkably similar to that of the *Top Comics* logo. Trademarks are often recycled and appear long after their prior usage, like Western's obscure 1992-1993 Gold Key *Golden Comics to Color* series. A total of twenty *Top Comics* without cover prices were sold in four different bagged sets of five each, and are Type 7b Variants. All *Top Comics* except for *Gnome Mobile* were reprints; the *Movie Comics* version of *Gnome Mobile* is dated October 1967, which makes the *Top Comics* issue the first printing. *Top Comics* was the prototype for Western's new plan of using their department store connections to sell bags of comics. With a distribution system in place, Whitman editions of Gold Key comics became a reality in late 1971.

Two versions of The Gnome Mobile in **Movie Comics** *and* **Top Comics**, *both released in 1967.*

Boris Karloff Tales of Mystery #80-86 (2, 4, 6, 8-11/78) are 48-page giants and probably do not exist as Whitman editions. *Walt Disney Showcase #48*(1/79) is confirmed to exist as a Whitman edition, the only giant-size issue of its kind. Whitman variants bring about 50% over *Guide* on average. Years of hard work and research by Patrick K. Simpson, Doug Sulipa, and others created a list that is close to completion. Previously unknown books still occasionally surface. Doug Sulipa estimates Whitman logo issues to be 20-50 times scarcer than Gold Keys. The following list of Type 7 cover logo variants contains 94 titles and 1,633 comics, or about 69% of them, for which Whitman variants have been confirmed to exist, with cover dates ranging from 11/71 to 4/80, with 2377 variant issues possible. All possibilities are listed, with confirmed variants listed after.

Adam 12 #1 (12/73) - 10 (2/76), #3 (5/74) - 6, 8-10; *Addams Family* #1 (10/74) - 3 (4/75), #1; *Adventures of Mighty Mouse* #166 (3/79) -172 (1/80), #166, 168-169, 171-172; *Adventures of Robin Hood* #1 (3/74) - 7 (1/75), #1-7; *Amazing Chan & the Chan Clan* #1 (5/73) -4 (2/74), #1-3 (11/73); *Aristokittens* #2 (4/72) - 9 (10/75), #2-9; *Baby Snoots* #6 (11/71) - 22 (11/75), #7 (2/72) –22; *Battle of the Planets* #1 (6/79) - 5 (2/80), #1-5; *Beagle Boys* #13 (7/72) - 47 (2/79), #13 (7/72) - 16, 18-24, 26-32, 34-39, 41-47; *Beagle Boys versus Uncle Scrooge* #1 (3/79) - 12 (2/80), #1-9, 11-12; *Beep Beep, the Roadrunner* #27 (12/71) - 88 (2/80), #27-33, 35, 37-40, 42-47, 51-55, 57-60, 63-68, 70-88; *Beetle Bailey* #120 (4/78) - 131 (4/80), #120-128, 130-131; *Boris Karloff Tales of Mystery* #38 (12/71) - 97 (2/80), #49 (8/73), 53-57, 59, 62-66, 69-71, 74-78, 87-88 (1/79); *Brothers of the Spear* #1 (6/72) - 17 (2/76), #9 (6/74) - 13, 15-17; *Buck Rogers* #2 (8/79) - 6 (2/80), #2-6; *Bugs Bunny* #139 (11/71) - 217 (2/80), #139-144, 146, 148, 150-152, 155-159, 164-170, 172-176, 178-179, 181-190, 194-217; *Bullwinkle* #3 (4/72) - 25 (2/80), #3-7, 9, 13-17, 20-22, 24-25; *Chip 'n' Dale* #13 (12/71) - 64 (1/80), #13-17, 20-24, 26-31, 33-38, 40-43, 45-64; *Christmas Parade* #9 (1/72), *Daffy Duck* #72 (11/71) - 127 (2/80), #72-77, 80-81, 83-84, 87, 89-91, 95-99, 101-104, 106-111, 115-123, 126-127; *Dagar* #1 (10/72) - 18 (12/76), #5 (10/73), 7-11, 13-15, 17-18; *Daisy and Donald* #1 (5/73) - 41 (11/79), #1-8, 11-14, 16-20, 22-27, 29, 31-41; *Dark Shadows* #11 (11/71) - 35 (2/76), #21 (8/73) –22, 25, 27-28, 30, 33-35; *Donald Duck* #140 (11/71) - 216 (2/80), #140-145, 148, 150-161, 164, 166-168, 172-178, 180-191, 193-213, 216; *Fat Albert* #1 (3/74) - 29 (2/79), #2 (6/74) - 3, 8-11, 13-15, 17-21, 24-29; *Flash Gordon* #19 (9/78) - 27 (1/80), #19-27; *Fun-In* #10 (1/72) - 15 (12/74), #10-11, 13-15; *Funky Phantom* #1 (3/72) - 13 (3/75), #1-4, 7, 10-12 (11/74); *Gold Key Champion* #1 (3/78) - 2 (5/78), *Gold Key Spotlight* #1 (5/76) - 11 (2/78), #1-2, 5-10 (10/77); *Grimm's Ghost Stories* #1 (1/72) - 54 (11/79), #11 (8/73), 15-22, 24-25, 28-29, 32-35, 37-42, 46-48 (11/78); *Hair*

Bear Bunch #1 (2/72) - 9 (2/74), #1-4, 6-8 (11/73); *Happy Days* #1 (3/79) - 6 (2/80), #1-4, 6; *Harlem Globetrotters* #1 (4/72) - 12 (1/75), #1-3, 5, 7, 9-11 (10/74); *H.R. Pufnstuf* #6 (1/72) - 8 (7/72), #6-8; *Huey Dewey and Louie Junior Woodchucks* #12 (1/72) - 61 (2/80), #12-16, 19, 21-23, 25-30, 33, 35-41, 43-48, 51-59, 61; *Inspector* #1 (7/74) - 19 (2/78), #2 (10/74) –3, 6-8, 10, 12, 14-17 (10/77); *Jungle Twins* #1 (4/72) - 17 (11/75), #7 (10/73), 9-13, 15, 17; *Korak, Son of Tarzan* #44 (11/71) - 45(1/72), *Krofft Supershow* #1 (4/78) - 6 (1/79), #1-6; *Lancelot Link, Secret Chimp* #3 (11/71) - 8 (2/73), #4 (2/72) –6 (8/72); *Lidsville* #1 (10/72) - 5 (10/73), #1, 3, 5; *Little Lulu* #207 (9/72) - 257 (1/80), #207, 210, 212-215, 217-222, 226, 229-231, 233-234, 237, 239-240, 245, 247-250, 253-254, 256-257; *Little Monsters* #15 (12/71) - 44 (2/78), #15-18, 22, 25-27, 30-32, 34, 39, 41-42; *Little Stooges* #1 (2/72) - 7 (3/74), #1, 5 (9/73); *Lone Ranger* #17 (11/72) - 28 (3/77), #18 (9/74) –20, 22-24, 26 (9/76); *Looney Tunes* #1 (4/75) - 30 (2/80), #3 (8/75), 5-6, 8-9, 12-16, 18, 21-27, 29-30; *Magnus Robot Fighter* #29 (11/71) - 46 (1/77), #35 (5/74) - 38, 40-45 (10/76); *Marge's Little Lulu* #202 (12/71) - 206 (8/72), #202, 204-206; *Mickey Mouse* #133 (12/71) - 204 (2/80), #133, 135-137, 140-141, 143-154, 157-161, 163-175, 177-178, 180-201, 204 (2/80); *Microbots* #1 (12/71), *Mighty Samson* #21 (8/72) - 31 (3/76), #24 (6/74) -27, 29-31; *Moby Duck* #12 (1/74) - 30 (2/78), #13 (4/74), 15-16, 19-24, 26, 28-29 (1/78); *Mod Wheels* #4 (11/71) - 19 (1/76), #14 (10/74), 16, 18-19; *Movie Comics: Lady and the Tramp* nn (3/72), nn; *New Terrytoons* #14 (11/71) - 54 (1/79), #15 (2/72) - 18, 20-23, 25-28, 33-34, 36, 38-39, 41, 43-46, 49, 52-54; *Occult Files of Dr. Spektor* #1 (4/73) - 24 (2/77), #4 (10/73), 7, 9-10, 12, 15, 17-18, 21-22; *O.G. Whiz* #4 (11/71) - 11(1/79), #5 (2/72) - 6, 8-11; *O'Malley and the Alley Cats* #3 (7/72) - 9 (1/74), #3-6, 8 (10/73); *Pink Panther* #4 (1/72) - 73 (2/80), #4-8, 10-11, 13-15, 18-22, 27, 29-31, 34-39, 41-48, 50-73; *Popeye* #139 (5/78) - 156 (3/80), #140 (7/78) –150, 152-155; *Porky Pig* #39 (12/71) - 93 (1/80), #39-44, 47, 49-51, 53-57, 61-65, 67-71, 73-81, 83-89, 91, 93; *Raggedy Ann and Andy* #1 (12/71) - 6(9/73), #1-3, 6; *Ripley's Believe It or Not* #30 (12/71) - 94 (2/80), #42 (8/73) - 43, 47-50, 52, 55-60, 64-65, 69-73, 84-85 (1/79); *Roman Holidays* #1 (2/73) - 4 (11/73), #2 (5/73) - 4; *Scamp* #7 (5/72) - 45 (1/79), #7-9, 12-13, 15-21, 24-38, 40-45; *Scooby Doo* #9 (12/71) - 30 (2/75), #9-13, 15, 17, 19-21, 24-29 (12/74); *Smokey Bear* #8 (12/71) - 13 (3/73), #8-11 (9/72); *Space Family Robinson* #37 (10/73) - 54 (12/77), #37, 39, 41, 43-47, 49, 52-53 (10/77); *Spine-Tingling Tales* #1 (5/75) - 4(1/76), #3(11/75) - 4; *Star Trek* #12 (11/71) - 61 (3/79), #20 (9/73), 23-27, 29, 31-36, 38-41, 45-48, 51-61; *Super Goof* #19 (11/71) -57 (2/80), #20 (2/72) –23, 26-33, 35-37, 39-40, 42-43, 45-57; *Tarzan* #205 (12/71) - 206 (2/72), *Three Stooges* #53 (12/71) - 55 (6/72), #53-55; *Tom and Jerry* #261 (12/71) - 327 (2/80), #261-267, 270, 272-273, 275, 280-287, 289, 292-300, 303-304, 308-314, 317-319, 322, 324-327; *Tragg and the Sky Gods* #1 (6/75) - 8 (2/77), #2 (9/75), 4, 6-7 (11/76); *Turok, Son of Stone* #76 (1/72) - 125 (1/80), #89 (3/74) - 95, 98-99, 101-102, 104-106, 110-111, 113, 116-117, 119 (1/79); *Tweety and Sylvester* #21 (12/71) - 102 (2/80), #21-26, 29, 31-33, 36-41, 47-55, 57-64, 66-74, 79-97, 99-102; *Twilight Zone* #40 (11/71) - 91 (4/79), #51 (8/73), 55-60, 62, 64-70, 72-73, 77-80, 85-88 (12/78); *UFO & Outer Space* #14 (6/78) - 25 (2/80), #14-19, 22-23 (10/79); *UFO Flying Saucers* #3 (11/72) - 13 (1/77), #4 (11/74) -5, 7-9, 11-12(11/76); *Uncle Scrooge* #96(12/71) - 173(2/80), #96-101, 104, 106-117, 120-125, 128-133, 135, 137-147, 150-170, 172-173; *Underdog* #1 (3/75) - 23 (2/79), #3 (9/75) –5, 7-9, 10-12, 14-15, 18-23; *Wacky Adventures of Cracky* #1 (12/72) - 12 (9/75), #2 (3/73), 4-5, 7-9 (12/74); *Wacky Races* #5 (11/71) - 7 (4/72), #6 (2/72) –7; *Wacky Witch* #5 (1/72) - 21 (12/75), #5-9, 10-17, 20 (10/75); *Walt Disney Showcase* #6 (1/72) - 54 (1/80), #6-10, 14, 16-18, 20-21, 23-26, 30-43, 48 (1/79); *Walt Disney's Comics and Stories* #374 (11/71) - 473 (2/80), #375(12/71), 379-381, 383, 395-396, 400, 402-404, 406-409, 411-412, 414, 418-419, 422-426, 428-435, 437-446, 450-451, 453, 455-473; *Walter Lantz' Andy Panda* #1 (8/73) - 23 (1/78), #1-2, 4-6, 9-14, 16, 18-21 (9/77); *Where's Huddles* #3 (12/71), #3; *Winnie the Pooh* #1 (1/77) - 17 (2/80), #2 (5/77) - 3, 5-15, 17; *Woodsy Owl* #1 (11/73) - 10 (2/76), #1, 3-5, 8, 10; *Woody Woodpecker* #120 (11/71) - 187 (2/80), #120-125, 128, 130-133, 135-139, 144-149, 151-152, 154-160, 163-164, 166-175, 177-182, 185-187; and *Yosemite Sam* #5 (12/71) - 65 (2/80), #5-9, 12-13, 15-18, 20-25, 29-34, 36-41, 43-48, 50, 52-63, 65.

About 90% of all 63 titles of Type 1a Gold Key Canadian price variants are confirmed to exist with cover dates ranging from April 1968 to August 1968 for 15¢ covers of 12¢ issues, from March 1972 to April 1973 for 20¢ covers of 15¢ issues, and from January to July 1984 for 75¢ covers of 60¢ issues; all books within these windows of time are likely to exist unless accidentally skipped. Eight issues exist that have an empty banner where the "16-Page Fun Catalog" on standard versions is advertised: *Boris Karloff Tales of Mystery* #58 (12/74), *Bullwinkle* #10 (1/74), *Jungle Twins* #12 (1/75), *Mickey Mouse* #146 (12/73), *Mod Wheels* #15 (1/75), *Ripley's Believe It or Not* #44 (12/73), *Scooby Doo* #22 (12/73), and *Uncle Scrooge* #109 (12/73). Delays in publishing sometimes contributed to numbering errors, and 8 books do not exist: *Buck Rogers* #10, *Daffy Duck* #132-133, *Daisy and Donald* #48, *Popeye* #160-161, *Porky Pig* #99, and *Woody Woodpecker* #192. The date "13/81" always follows 2/82 and only appears on ten books: *Bugs Bunny* #234, *Chip 'n' Dale* #76, *Daffy Duck* #140, *Donald Duck* #237, *Huey Dewey and Louie* #373, *Super Goof* #68, *Tom and Jerry* #340, *Tweety and Sylvester* #114, *Uncle Scrooge* #194, and *Walt Disney's Comics and Stories* #496.

Western was sometimes forced to honor contractual agreements at the midnight hour, which caused several monthly issues to be published at once, wreaking havoc with their dating and numbering system. In late 1981, Whitman briefly changed the cover logos to specify Direct Market copies, known today as "White logo" variants. "Beginning with comics printed in November, the direct sales copies of all Whitmans will be printed without the yellow underneath the corner trademark and number... [in order to prevent] ...conventionally distributed copies [from] being returned for credit, which was one of the reasons distribution had been spotty to comic shops over the past year..." (*Comic Reader* #196, page 7). The following 31 titles and 54 issues are Type 6 cover variants confirmed to exist: *Beep Beep, the Roadrunner* #100 (3/82), *Bugs Bunny* #237 (5/82), *Chip 'n' Dale* #75-77 (2/82, 13/81, 3/82), *Dagar the Invincible* #19 (4/82), *Daisy and Donald* #53 (2/82), *Doctor Solar, Man of the Atom* #30-31 (2-3/82), *Donald Duck* #236-240 (2/82, 13/81, 3-5/82), *Flash Gordon* #36-37 (2-3/82), *Grimm's Ghost Stories* #59 (5/82), *Little Lulu* #265 (3/82), *Looney Tunes* #42-43 (2, 4/82), *Mickey Mouse* #215-216 (2, 4/82), *Mighty Samson* #32 (4/82), *Movie Comics: Snow White* nn (4/82), *Movie Comics: Pinocchio* nn (4/82), *Occult Files of Doctor Spektor* #25 (5/82), *Pink Panther* #82-83 (3-4/82), *Popeye #166* (2/82), *Shadowplay* #1 (6/82), *Space Family Robinson* #59 (5/82), *Super Goof* #67 (2/82), *Tom and Jerry* #339 (2/82), *Tragg and the Sky Gods* #9 (5/82), *Tweety and Sylvester* #114 (13/81), 116 (4/82), *Uncle Scrooge* #193-197 (2/82, 13/81, 3-5/82), *Walt Disney's Comics and Stories* #495-499 (2/82, 13/81, 3-5/82), *Winnie the Pooh* #27 (2/82), and *Yosemite Sam* #76-78 (2-4/82).

A Type 10a variant of *Porky Pig* #67 (6/76) exists with a "White logo," a printing error produced before Direct Market editions existed. Whitman variants were published simultaneously with their Gold Key counterparts, and sometimes Gold Key issues were produced incorrectly, without the higher price they were supposed to receive. Some issues exist with three versions: a standard Gold Key edition, a standard Whitman edition, and a Variant Gold Key edition. Doug Sulipa has a solid inventory of the 30¢ cover variant Gold Key issues, which indicates they were designed for Canadian distribution, and are thus the only comics ever published for Canadian distribution with a *lower* cover price than their standard U.S. counterparts, albeit accidentally.

Eleven Type 7 Whitman 35¢ cover variants of Gold Key issues from December 1977 to March 1978 exist and are noted below with an asterisk. The following list of 38 titles and 59 comics are Type 1b 30¢ reverse variants of 35¢ Gold Key comics, cover dated December 1977 to March 1978, that are confirmed to exist: *Beagle Boys* #39-40 (12/77, 2/78), *Beep Beep, the Roadrunner* #69 (1/78), *Boris Karloff Tales of Mystery* #79 (12/77), *Bugs Bunny* #191-193 (12/77, 1-2/78), *Bullwinkle* #18-19 (12/77, 3/78), *Chip 'n' Dale* #50 (1/78*), *Daffy Duck* #112-113 (12/77, 2/78), *Daisy and Donald* #28 (1/78), *Donald Duck* #190-191 (12/77, 1/78), *Fat Albert* #22-23 (12/77, 2/78), *Gold Key Spotlight* #11 (2/78), *Huey Dewey and Louie Junior Woodchucks* #47-48 (12/77*, 2/78), *Inspector* #18-19 (12/77, 2/78), *Little Lulu* #243 (1/78), *Little Monsters* #43-44 (12/77, 2/78), *Looney Tunes* #17-18 (12/77, 2/78*), *Mickey Mouse* #178, 180 (12/77*, 2/78), *Moby Duck* #29-30 (1/78*, 3/78), *New Terrytoons* #48 (1/78), *Pink Panther* #49 (1/78), *Porky Pig* #79 (1/78), *Ripley's Believe It or Not* #76 (2/78), *Scamp* #39 (1/78), *Space Family Robinson* #54 (12/77), *Star Trek* #50 (1/78), *Super Goof* #45 (3/78*), *Tom and Jerry* #301, 303 (12/77, 2/78), *Turok, Son of Stone* #113 (1/78*), *Tweety and Sylvester* #76-78 (12/77, 1-2/78), *Twilight Zone* #82 (1/78), *Uncle Scrooge* #147-149 (12/77*, 1-2/78), *Underdog* #16-17 (12/77, 2/78), *Walt Disney Showcase* #42 (1/78*), *Walt Disney's Comics and Stories* #448-449 (1-2/78), *Walter Lantz' Andy Panda* #23 (1/78), *Winnie the Pooh* #5 (2/78*), *Woody Woodpecker* #163 (2/78), and *Yosemite Sam* #49-50 (12/77, 2/78*). Only three books on the list are cover dated March 1978: *Bullwinkle* #19, *Moby Duck* #30, and *Super Goof* #45, probably because Western realized they were repeating their mistake, and stopped production with the first three-pack of comics from the latest batch. Giant-sized issues were not produced for Canadian distribution, thus *Mickey Mouse* #179 (1/78) and *Tom and Jerry* #302 (1/78) do not exist as Type 1b variants.

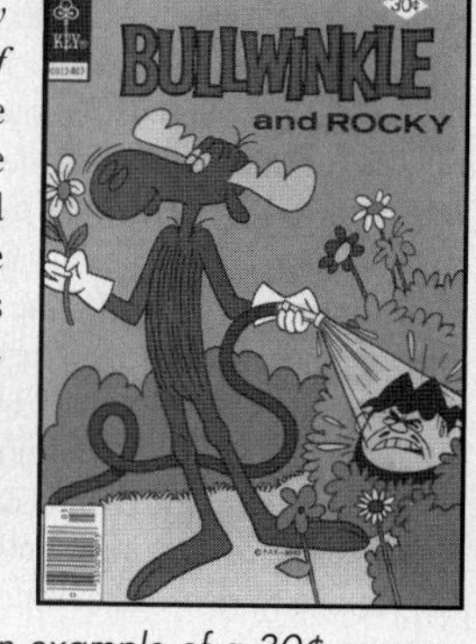

An example of a 30¢ reverse variant, ***Bullwinkle #19*** *(March 1978), which normally had a 35¢ price.*

The following nine comics are Type 1b 40¢ Whitman reverse variants of 50¢ Whitman comics, cover dated November 1980 to January 1981, that are confirmed to exist: *Bugs Bunny* #222-223 (11/80, 1/81), *Donald Duck* #225 (1/81), *Huey Dewey and Louie* #67 (1/81), *Little Lulu* #262 (1/81), *Pink Panther* #78 (1/81), *Super Goof* #63 (1/81), *Uncle Scrooge* #182 (1/81), and *Walt Disney's Comics and Stories* #484(1/81). Doug Sulipa has no copies of Whitman 40¢ cover variants in stock, and thus they were probably not intended for Canadian distribution. Few if any comics' publishers perfectly coordinate their price changes: *Jungle Twins* #10 has a 20¢ cover, and *Scooby Doo* #26 has a 25¢ cover, both cover dated July 1974. The lowest print runs are Type 1a Canadian 75¢ cover price variants.

Not all Whitman comics were sold in bags. In January 2001, at a flea market in Eugene, Oregon, I found a cardboard box of ten Whitman comics cover dated from 7/77 to 9/77, and a Warner Brothers box with ten Whitman comics cover dated from 7/77 to 8/77. Both boxes have painted covers with previously unknown Disney and Warner Brothers character art. At the time I was using dates of issue from *The Comic Reader* combined with patterns of advertising found on the inside front and back covers of 1980s Whitmans as a means of dating the 105 undated issues produced from May 1982 to July 1984. Disney historian Michael Naiman helped track down Wally Green, Whitman's former managing editor. When I spoke with him in 2001, I asked what he thought had killed Whitman, and he answered, "Because they went with lower print runs, the profit margin was less, and with reduced sales and a higher cost to print each issue, the profit margin wasn't there. They never took that into consideration." Wally summed it up well by saying, "They didn't know what the hell they were doing."

Green Publications

(Also see Norlen Magazines)

Green was the original name for a small publisher that reprinted original covers and contents in 1957. Both Green and their other company named Norlen, published only a handful of titles, books that are *not* legitimate representative copies of the originals. *Cosmo Cat* #2, for example, has the cover to #3. The Norlen issues read, "1959 Edition" on the covers and are otherwise identical. When I noticed the same titles and issue numbers, I decided to check the business addresses, which proved that they were the same outfit at the same address. *All Top Comics* has five variant #6 issues under different names, including Green (1957), Literary Entertainment (1958), Norlen (1959) with 2 Variants of #6, and Cornell [n.d.]. Existing variants include *All Top Comics #6 (5 Variants, four company names), Animal Crackers* #9 (Green and Norlen), *Cosmo Cat* #2-4 (Green and Norlen), *Ribtickler* #3, 7-8 (Green and Norlen), and *Wotalife* #1-5 (Green and Norlen), all of which are Type 8b variants.

Harvey Publications

Boy's Ranch #5-6 (6, 8/51) exist as Type 3b variants identical to the originals except for the Simon & Kirby centerfolds which are replaced with shoe store ads. *Richie Rich, Casper & Wendy National League* (1976) have Type 3b variants for a dozen different teams plus at least one with a Newsstand edition. *Weather-Bird Comics* (1957) are simultaneously published issues that were promotional giveaways for shoe stores, some of which contain key issues, such as *Hot Stuff, the Little Devil* #1(10/57) and *Harvey Hits* #3(11/57), the first book devoted to *Richie Rich*. Because the covers are all identical, they are Type 3a variants, at least as far as *Weather-Bird* is concerned, but they could also be considered Type 1c cover variants of Silver Age key issues; they are not rebound comics because there is only one set of staples and the covers are perfectly aligned with the interior books, with the only indicia inside that of the Harvey original issue given an alternate cover for promotional purposes. *Astro Comics* are Type 3a variants published in 1968 that contain assorted reprinted stories with the same cover. Post 1968 *Astro Comics* use the same cover, but with numbers or symbols on the covers that make them clearly identifiable, and thus they are *not* variants. Most if not all Type 1a 35¢ Canadian price variants exist of 25¢ Harvey Giants from 1959 to 3/74.

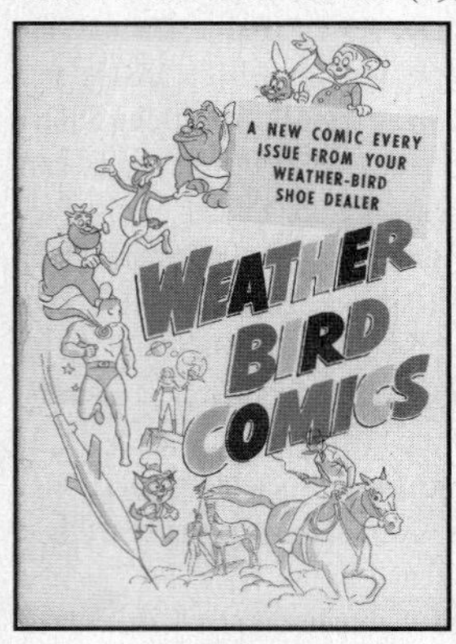

The promotional give-away ***Weather-Bird Comics*** *(1957) had identical covers with a variety of inside content.*

I.W. and Super Comics

I.W. Publications began in 1958 and was named after the company's owner, Israel Waldman. The company published comics in 1958, 1963 and 1964. As of 1963, the company used the name "Super Comics" and changed its cover logo to match. In place of the normal Comics Code Authority seal of approval, a little box reads, "A Top Quality Comic," which appeared on all 1958 I.W. reprints, while 1963-1964 issues have a "Super Comics" seal of quality. The 1958 books reprinted the original covers with minor changes. Covers were often used multiple times on the same title, and some books have contents that do not match the original cover, Type 9a variants. One title, *Pee-Wee Pixies* (1958, 1963) has three total issues (#1, 8, 10), with the same cover. Waldman was later involved with Skywald Publications in the early to mid-1970s, which reprinted old horror comic stories in B&W magazines, and some color comics as well. Many of the color comics contained new material, but some stories that appeared in Skywald's *Tender Love Stories* (1971) and other titles came from the I.W./Super Comics inventory.

Waldman's strategy was direct and effective: he would buy out printing plates and original art from defunct comics publishers, sometimes gaining possession of material from companies still in business, probably by accident. There is no legitimate reason for issues of *Plastic Man* or *The Spirit* to have been published by Super Comics in 1963-1964. Waldman allegedly dealt directly with Eastern Color to obtain material from defunct publishers who owed Eastern money. Waldman successfully avoided one risk that every other publisher had to endure: he accepted no returns (*Andru & Esposito*, 2006, p. 74). Unlike other I.W. issues, *My Secret Marriage* #9 (1958) notes in the indicia, "Reprinted by Eastern Color." The indicia of all I.W. books also read, "Reproduction in part or whole is prohibited," which is ironic because Waldman was able to obtain and reprint material from at least 27 companies, some without any legal right or permission, including Ace, Ajax, Avon, Cambridge House, Harry A. Chessler, Comic Media, E.C., Fiction House, Fox, Marvel, Merit, Nesbit, Novac, Prize, Quality, Realistic, Red Top, Spark, Standard, Stanley Morse, Star, St. John, Stanhall, Steinway, Superior, Toby, and Universal Phoenix Features. Only further research will ultimately provide the total number of publishers and details hidden in the contents of I.W./Super Comics.

Joe Simon describes Israel Waldman as cordial but "...all business. He took the comic books out of the envelope I shoved at him: *Bullseye, Foxhole, In Love, Police Trap*. He rifled through a few pages of each, [and] set them down next to [his] checkbook. I was disappointed that he hadn't read a story or two." Simon told Waldman, "We need to keep the copyrights." Normally this sort of deal would include legal documents and agreements, "...but Waldman didn't have the time or the inclination to mess around with such trifles." Waldman reportedly said, "So keep them. What do I need with copyrights?" (*The Comic Book Makers,* p. 165.) Al Hewetson, an editor and writer for Skywald Publications until its demise in 1975, claims he left Jim Warren's employment for the creative freedom Waldman embodied. Waldman ran Skywald with his son and Sol Brodsky, the latter having worked with him on I.W./Super Comics. "He once told me his philosophy of management," Hewetson quotes Waldman: "Surround yourself with extremely competent people, and leave them alone to do their job." Waldman was a savvy businessman and apparently also a nice person; Pablo Marcos recounts their first meeting and Waldman's kindness as the reason he kept working with Skywald when other publishers were paying him more money. (*Skywald Horror-Mood*, pp. 68, 182.)

No I.W. or Super Comics were cover dated because they were designed to have an indefinite shelf life. Waldman was the first publisher to sell comics in plastic bags, in groups of three. Waldman's bags were generic blanks, allowing retailers to set their own price. Major publishers like Charlton, D.C., Gold Key and others would later follow this practice, selling slightly discounted groups of two to five comics per bag, with company logos and best-selling characters prominently featured on the bags. Wholesaling bagged comics to discount retail and grocery stores put Waldman's products in a different category, that of toys and novelties. Keeping I.W./Super Comics under the radar was a cunning strategy that kept him out of the clutches of the Comics Code Authority, a problem that would have increased expenses, to say nothing of publishing delays and potential legal problems. Few books from the 1958 period qualify as Variants, with none yet identified in the 1963-1964 period, as most if not all issues have new covers and reprint random issues regardless of the issue number. Some material purchased by Waldman is unpublished material from failed comics companies. Professionals including Abel, Andru, Colletta, Esposito, Severin, Simon and others, created covers for the reprints and the unpublished stories, some of which are first printings, including issues of *Danger* (1963-1964), *Daring Adventures* (1958, 1963-1964), and *Fantastic Adventures* (1963-1964).

One Variant example is Avon's *U.S. Paratroops Behind Enemy Lines* #1 and the I.W. reprint of the same title. The covers are the same except for some minor changes to the I.W. version, but the contents are from a different issue than #1, making it a Type 9a Variant. Another terrific and unique example of an I.W. Variant is the title *Speedy Rabbit*, which has two first issues with different covers and contents, making them Type 9b Variants. A few books state "I.W." on the cover and "Super Comics" in the indicia. Consider *Human Fly* #1 (1958), a book with Blue Beetle and other reprints, where the Human Fly never makes an appearance! Waldman preferred turning a profit to fruitless perfectionism, unlike certain unnamed comics historians, some of whom have argued that the I.W. and Super Comics issue numbers are meaningless, but all of the books can be dated with the issue numbers. Issues that read #1-9 were published in 1958, and issues that read #10-11 were published in 1963. Books assigned #12 were published in both 1963 and 1964, and comparing ads from other comics of the time would probably determine the specific years. Waldman avoided the number #13, possibly to evade the karmic debt inherent in many horror comic stories of the day. Issues that read #14-18 were published in 1964. I.W. comics published 168 books in 1958, and 173 Super Comics were published in 1963-1964. About 25% are scarce and rarely for sale, while another 25% are elusive, and about 50% are easily acquired. The existence of *Yanks in Battle* #3 (1958) remains in doubt, but 117 titles and 341 I.W. and Super Comics are confirmed to exist, with the correct issue numbers listed here for the first time anywhere:

Algie (1964) #15, *Apache* (1958) #1, *Avenger* (1958) #9, *Battle Stories* (1963-1964) #10-12, 15-18, *Billy and Buggy Bear* (1958, 1963) #1, 7, 10, *Black Knight* (1963) #11, *Blazing Six-Guns* (1958, 1963-1964) #1, 8-12, 15-18, *Brain* (1958, 1963-1964) #1-4, 8-10, 14, 18, *Buccaneer* (1958, 1963) #1, 8, 12, *Buster Bear* (1958, 1963) #9-10, *Candy* (1963-1964) #12, 16-17, *Casper Cat* (1958,1964) #1, 7, 14, *Cosmo Cat* (1958) #1, *Cowboys'n' Injuns* (1958, 1963) #1, 7, 10, *Danger* (1963-1964) #10-12, 15-18, *Danger is our Business* (1958) #9, *Daring Adventures* (1958, 1963-1964) #8-12, 15-18, *Dogface Dooley* (1958, 1964) #1, 17, *Doll Man* (1963-1964) #11, 15, 17, *Dream of Love* (1958) #1-2, 8-9, *Dr. Fu Manchu* (1958) #1, *Dynamic Adventures* (1958) #8-9, *Dynamic Comics* (1958) #1, *Eerie* (1958) #1, 8-9, *Eerie Tales* (1963-1964) #10-12, 15, *Famous Funnies* (1964) #15, 17-18, *Fantastic Adventures* (1963-1964) #10-12, 15-18, *Fantastic Tales* (1958) #1, *Fighting Daniel Boone* (1958) #1, *Firehair* (1958) #8, *Foxhole* (1963-1964) #11-12, 15-18, *Frontier Romances* (1958) #1, 9, *Full of Fun* (1958) #8, *Great Action Comics* (1958) #1, 8-9, *Great Western* (1958) #1-2, 8-9, *Gunfighters* (1963-64) #10-12, 15-16, 18, *Hollywood Secrets of Romance* (1958) #9, *Human Fly* (1958, 1963) #1, 10, *Indian Braves* (1958) #1, *Indians of the Wild West* (1958) #9, *Intimate Confessions* (1958, 1963-1964) #9-10, 12, 18, *Jet Power* (1958) #1-2, *Jungle Adventures* (1963-1964) #10, 12, 15, 17-18,

The I.W. reprint of U.S. Paratroops has the distinctive IW logo in the upper left corner.

Jungle Comics (1958) #1, 9, *Ka'a'nga* (1958) #1, 8, *Kat Karson* (1958) #1, *Kiddie Kapers* (1963-1964) #10, 14-15, 17, *Kid Koko* (1958) #1-2, *Kit Carson* (1963) #10, *Krazy Krow* (1958) #1, 2, 7, *Leo the Lion* (1958) #1, *Little Eva* (1958, 1963-1964) #1-4, 6-10, 12, 14, 16, 18, *Little Spunky* (1958) #1, *Love and Marriage* (1958, 1963-1964) #2, 8, 11, 14-15, 17, *Malu in the Land of Adventure* (1958) #1, *Man o' Mars* (1958) #1, *Marmaduke Monk* (1958, 1963) #1, 14, *Marty Mouse* (1958) #1, *Master Detective* (1964) #17, *Meet Merton* (1958, 1963-1964) #9, 11, 18, *Mighty Atom and the Pixies* (1958) #1, *Muggsy Mouse* (1958, 1963) #1-2, 14, *Muggy-Doo, Boy Cat* (1963-1964) #12, 16, *My Secret Marriage* (1958) #9, *Mystery Tales* (1964) #16-18, *Pee-Wee Pixies* (1958, 1963) #1, 8, 10, *Pinky the Egghead* (1958, 1964) #1-2, 14, *Planet Comics* (1958) #1, 8-9, *Plastic Man* (1963-1964) #11, 16, 18, *Police Trap* (1963-1964) #11, 16-18, *Purple Claw* (1958) #8, *Realistic Romances* (1958) #1, 8-9, *Red Mask* (1958) #1-3, 8, *Robin Hood* (1958, 1963-1964) #1-2, 9-10, 15, *Romantic Love* (1958, 1963) #2-3, 8, 10-11, *Sensational Police Cases* (1958) #5, *Sharpy Fox* (1958, 1964) #1-2, 14, *Sheena, Queen of the Jungle* (1958) #9, *Silver Kid Western* (1958) #1-2, *Space Comics* (1958) #8, *Space Detective* (1958) #1, 8, *Space Mysteries* (1958) #1, 8-9, *Speedy Rabbit* (1958, 1964) #1(2 versions exist), 14, *Spirit* (1963-1964) #11-12, *Star Feature Comics* (1958) #9, *Strange Mysteries* (1958, 1963-1964) #9-12, 15-18, *Strange Planets* (1958, 1963-1964) #1, 9-12, 15-16, 18, *Strange Worlds* (1958) #5, *Sunny, America's Sweetheart (1958) #8, Super Brat* (1958, 1963) #1-3, 7-8, 10, *Super Rabbit* (1958, 1963) #1-2, 7, 10, *Teen Romances* (1958, 1964) #10-11, 15-17, *Teen-Age Talk* (1958) #1, 5, 8-9, *Tell It to the Marines* (1958, 1964) #1, 9, 16, *Three Rascals* (1958, 1963) #1-2, 10, *Tippy Terry* (1958, 1964) #1, 14, *Tom-Tom the Jungle Boy* (1958, 1963) #1-2, 8-10, *Top Adventure Comics* (1958) #1-2, *Top Detective Comics* (1958) #9, *Top Jungle Comics* (1958) #1-2, *Torchy* (1964) #16, *Tuffy Turtle* (1958) #1, *Undersea Commandos* (1958) #1-2, *U.S. Fighting Air Force* (1958) #1, 9, *U.S. Fighting Men* (1963-1964) #10-12, 15-18, *U.S. Paratroops* (1958) #1, 8, *U.S. Tank Commandos* (1958) #1, 8, *Wacky Duck* (1958, 1963) #1-2, 7, 10, *Wacky Woodpecker* (1958, 1963) #1-2, 7, 10, *Wambi* (1958) #8, *Western Action* (1958) #7, *Westerner* (1964) #15-17, *Whip Wilson* (1958) #1, *Wild Bill Hickok* (1958, 1963-1964) #1, 10-12, *Wild Western Roundup* (1958) #1, *Young Hearts in Love (*1964) #17-18, and *Ziggy Pig* (1958) #1-2, 7-8.

King Features

King Features were printed by Charlton Publications and published educational and promotional giveaways, some of which were original. *Beetle Bailey* #67-68(2, 4/69) exist as 1969 armed forces giveaways with "complimentary copy" printed on the covers, and *Flash Gordon* #1(9/66) exists as a 1968 army giveaway with "complimentary copy" printed on the cover; all three are Type 3b variants. *Flash Gordon* #9(10/67) exists as a Type 1a Pence variant, and other unknown variants are likely to exist. Phantom #29 (1968) is rumored to exist as a foreign edition, but there is no U.S. published counterpart.

MAD Magazine

Some Type 1a Canadian cover price variants exist from 1964 and from 1/78 to 1/79.

Marvel Comics

(Also see Charlton, Modern Promotions and So Much Fun! Inc.)

Marvel Comics #1 (10-11/39) has two versions, one with November stamped inside over the October date, and the scarcer version without the overprint. Two unnumbered 132 page B&W issues of *Marvel Mystery Comics* exist: one from 1942-1943 with the cover of #33 in color, with blank inside covers, that contains *Captain America Comics* #22 (1/43) and *Marvel Mystery Comics* #41 (3/43), and another from 1943-1944, also with the cover to #33 and with blank inside covers, that contains *Captain America* #18 (9/42) and *Marvel Mystery Comics* #33 (7/42). *Blue Bird Comics* (1947-1950) are promotional reprints by various shoe stores, 36 pages in length, including material from *Human Torch* and *Sub-Mariner Comics*, but are *not* legitimate representative copies. Four Type 3b variants were released in 1966 as *Golden Record Comic* books, sealed tight with a 33 1/3 rpm record, including *Amazing Spider-Man* #1 (3/63), *Avengers* #4 (3/64), *Fantastic Four* #1 (11/61), and *Journey into Mystery* #83 (8/62). Such variants are true to the originals except for missing numbers and prices on the covers, and with interior ads replaced by *Golden Record Comic* ads. The *Journey into Mystery* #83 variant has one original back-up story replaced with a Thor story, but is otherwise a solid reprint of the original. A Type 12a mini-reprint of *Amazing Spider-Man* #42 exists, originally cover dated November 1966, that was attached to the cover of February 1969's *Esquire Magazine*.

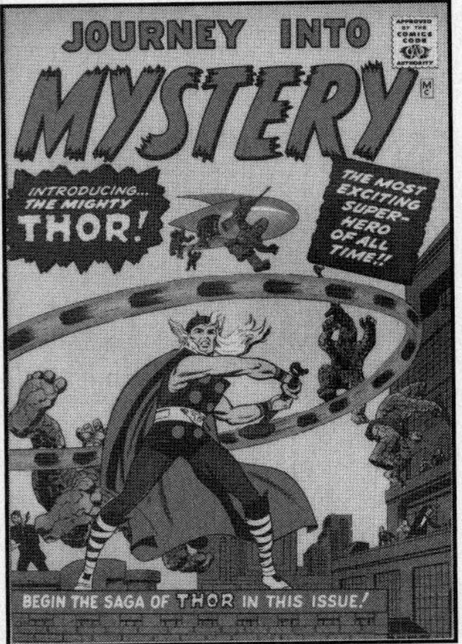

Golden Record Comic *reprint of* ***Journey Into Mystery*** *#83 has no price or issue number on the cover.*

Spectacular Spider-Man #1 (7/68) exists as a Type 1a Canadian price variant with a 40¢ price on the cover, instead of the standard dual-priced 35 and 40¢ U.S. and Canadian edition. Crazy #1(2/73) exists as a Type 1c variant with the word "bonus" where the 20¢ cover price should be, a reprint inserted into *Crazy* magazine #58(1/80), following the tradition of *Nostalgic MAD* inserts. *Warlock* #8(10/73) exists as a USC (United Service Club) Army ad insert Variant. *Fantastic*

Four #128 is *not* a variant and is the only Marvel comic ever published with a 4 page glossy centerfold of pin-ups, a unique one-shot experiment. *Outlaw Kid* #9(12/71) is *not* a variant either, but has printed on the spine the 25¢ price, "Outlaw Kid," and "Marvel Comics Group," as only 52 page giants had during this time period, when Marvel briefly tested 25¢ square-bound giants for several months in late 1971. One variation of such giants is the 52 page saddle-stitched format issues, or "round-bounds," that became an experiment within an experiment, and only four such issues exist: *Monsters on the Prowl* #13 (10/71), *My Love* #14 (11/71), *Mighty Marvel Western* #15 (12/71), and *Captain America Special* #2 (1/72). *Monsters on the Prowl* #13 also exists as a unique Type 13a Variant containing a four-page glossy National Diamond Sales insert with the last page an ad from California Gift House that includes a bizarrely risque' lingerie page with women wearing teddies and a close-up of a woman in panties that reads, "Best things in life are free." *Conan* #47(2/75) exists as a Type 13a Variant with a mini-booklet printed on cardstock inserted in *Conan* #47 entitled, "Mighty Marvel Marches Through Your Door," which promotes Marvel's comics and magazines and also contains paid ads. The scarcest Marvel round-bound in ¢ format is the 52 page giant *My Love* #14. *Conan the Barbarian* #11 (11/71), *Fantastic Four* #116 (11/71), and *Where Monsters Dwell* #12 (11/71) were incorrectly printed with 6 Pence British prices, when other 52 page giants were priced at 8 pence each, but they are *not* Variants because the entire print runs are thusly priced. *Amazing Spider-Man Annual* #14 (1980) and *X-Men Annual* #4(1980) were the only saddle-stitched issues to appear that year, and *Fantastic Four Annual* #15 is the last squarebound issue to appear that year, as many annuals were skipped in 1980. From 1981 on, Marvel annuals exist only as round-bounds.

Marvel published some Type 10 variants in January 1962 on the cusp of changing prices from 10 to 12¢ per copy, and at least one book was released with a ten¢ cover, *Linda Carter, Student Nurse* #3(1/62). Only three issues got stuck with last minute changes that were quickly rejected: these January 1962 "Black Circle Variants" include *Gunsmoke Western* #69, *Journey into Mystery* #76, and *Love Romances* #79. All three books have black ink in the price circle that imperfectly obfuscates the original 10¢ price, with a 12¢ price positioned next to it, but the vast majority of the run exists with only the 12¢ price. Most printing errors concerning a book's cover involve missing color(s) or information. The following Type 10a and 10b variants range from the Golden to the Modern Age, with classic issues and a few curious examples noted in detail: *Amazing Spider-Man* #85 (6/70), 96 (5/71), 114 (11/72), 149 (10/75), 188 (1/79), 342 (12/90), 375 (3/93), *Avengers* #146 (4/76), 170 (4/78), 178 (12/78), 375 (3/93), *Captain America Comics* #1 (3/41, no red), *Captain America* #103 (7/68, blue star on shield), 210 (6/77), *Conan* #88 (7/78), *Daredevil* #1 (4/64, faded costume), 132 (4/76), *Devil Dinosaur* #1 (4/78), *Doctor Strange* #21, 24 (2, 8/77), *Fantastic Four* #110 (5/71, a green "Thing"), 119 (2/72), *Howard the Duck* #6 (11/76), *Incredible Hulk* #190 (8/75), *Invaders* #38 (3/79), *Iron Man* #15, 19 (7, 11/69), *Marvel Premiere* #34 (2/77), *Marvel Spotlight* #1 (7/79, no #1 on the cover), #27 (4/76), *Marvel's Greatest Comics* #81 (1/79), *Sgt. Fury* #109 (4/73), *Spectacular Spider-Man* #23, 27 (10/78, 2/79), 160 (1/90), *Spider-Man Unlimited* #3 (11/93, production strip on top), *Tales of Suspense* #62 (2/65), *Thor* #281 (3/79), *Web of Spider-Man* #90 (7/92, no hologram), *Western Outlaws* #2 (4/54), and *What If?*#12 (12/78). *Amazing Spider-Man* #188, *Marvel's Greatest Comics* #81, and *Spectacular Spider-Man* #160 each have two moderately different Type 10a variants. A Type 10b variant exists of *Amazing Spider-Man* #5, with a green web-slinger on p. 13.

Marvel's 30¢ and 35¢ Cover price variants are now among the hottest of all Bronze Age comics. The 30¢ variants sell at 300% of the price of regular 25¢ editions at a minimum, and up to 1000% or higher in some cases. The scarcer 35¢ variants sell at 600% of the price of regular 30¢ editions at a minimum, and up to 2000% or higher in some cases. The scarce horror, war, and western reprint variants sell for a premium in any grade. Strangely enough, despite mentions in fanzines of the day, no one cared. *The Comic Reader* #128 (3/76), p. 5, reports that "...certain test areas of the country have been receiving 30¢ Marvels for a couple of months already...[the] Grand Rapids, Michigan area is one." *Marvel Review*, a fanzine from mid-1976, begins in issue #1 reviewing May 1976 Marvels, and issue #2 reviews June Marvels, showing covers in B&W, including *Inhumans* #5 and *Ka-Zar* #16, noted on p. 19 as: "...the first of the 30¢ books from Marvel." Both books were another experiment within an experiment, as all copies have 30¢ covers and are *not* variants. Collector/dealer Dan Cusimano publicized a letter from Sol Brodsky confirming that the *Star Wars* #1-4 variants were indeed experimental.

The following list of 181 books and 59 titles with cover dates ranging from April to August 1976 exist as Type 1 30¢ Cover Price Variants: *Adventures on the Planet of the Apes* #5-7 (4, 6, 8/76), *Amazing Adventures* #36-37 (5,7/76), *Amazing Spider-Man* #155-159 (4-8/76), *Astonishing Tales* #35-36 (5, 7/76), *Avengers* #146-150 (4-8/76), *Black Goliath* #2-4 (4, 6, 8/76), *Captain America* #196-200 (4-8/76), *Captain Marvel* #44-45 (5, 7/76), *Chamber of Chills* #22-23 (5, 7/76), *Champions* #5-7 (4, 6, 8/76), *Conan* #61-65 (4-8/76), *Daredevil* #132-136 (4-8/76), *Defenders* #34-38 (4-8/76), *Doctor Strange* #13-17 (4-8/76), *Eternals* #1-2 (7-8/76), *Fantastic Four* #169-173 (4-8/76), *Ghost Rider* #17-19 (4, 6, 8/76), *Howard the Duck* #3-4 (5, 7/76), *Incredible Hulk* #198-202 (4-8/76), *Inhumans* #4, 6 (4, 8/76), *Invaders* #6-7 (5, 7/76), *Iron Fist* #4-6 (4, 6, 8/76), *Iron Man* #85-89 (4-8/76), *Jungle Action* #21-22 (5, 7/76), *Ka-Zar* #15, 17(4, 8/76), *Kid Colt Outlaw* #205-209 (4-8/76), *Kull* #16 (8/76), *Marvel Adventures* #3-5 (4, 6, 8/76), *Marvel Chillers* #4-6 (4, 6, 8/76), *Marvel Double Feature* #15-17 (4, 6, 8/76), *Marvel Feature* #4-5(5, 7/76), *Marvel Premiere* #29-31 (4, 6, 8/76), *Marvel Presents* #4-6 (4, 6, 8/76), *Marvel's Greatest Comics* #63-64 (5, 7/76), *Marvel Spotlight* #27-29 (4, 6, 8/76), *Marvel Super Heroes* #57-58

(5, 7/76), *Marvel Tales* #66-70 (4-8/76), *Marvel Team-Up* #44-48 (4-8/76), *Marvel Triple Action* #29-30 (5, 7/76), *Marvel Two-in-One* #15-18 (5-8/76), *Master of Kung-Fu* #39-43 (4-8/76), *Mighty Marvel Western* #45 (6/76), *Omega* #2-3 (5, 7/76), *Powerman* #30-34 (4-8/76), *Rawhide Kid* #133-134 (5, 7/76), *Ringo Kid* #27-28 (5, 7/76), *Sgt. Fury* #133-134 (5, 7/76), *Skull* #5-6 (5, 7/76), *Son of Satan* #3-5 (4, 6, 8/76), *Strange Tales* #185-186 (5, 7/76), *Super-Villain Team-Up* #5-7 (4, 6, 8/76), *Thor* #246-250 (4-8/76), *Tomb of Darkness* #20-21 (5, 7/76), *Tomb of Dracula* #43-47 (4-8/76), *Two-Gun Kid* #129-131 (4, 6, 8/76), *Warlock* #12-14 (4, 6, 8/76), *Weird Wonder Tales* #15-17 (4, 6, 8/76), *Werewolf by Night* #38-39 (5, 7/76), and *X-Men* #98-100 (4, 6, 8/76).

The 10 rarest 30¢ price variants presented in order of scarcity, with approximately 6-12 copies known to exist of each in any grade, are *Weird Wonder Tales* #15, *Ringo Kid* #28, *Kid Colt* #209, 205-208, and *Two-Gun Kid* #131, 130, and 129. Other hard-to-find issues to find include *Chamber of Chills* #22-23, *Marvel Double Feature* #15-17, *Marvel Tales* #66, *Mighty Marvel Western* #45, *Rawhide Kid* #133-134, *Ringo Kid* #27, *Sgt. Fury* #133-134, *Tomb of Darkness* #20-21, *Weird Wonder Tales* #16-17, and *Werewolf by Night* #38-39. Western titles had low print runs, due to marginal sales and high returns. The most common 30-centers seem to be *Black Goliath* #2-4, *Defenders* #34-38, *Doctor Strange* #13-17, *Eternals* #1-2, *Howard the Duck* #3, *Kull* #16, *Marvel Presents* #4-6, *Omega* #2-3, and *Super-Villain Team-Up* #5. *X-Men* #98-100 are harder to find than *Amazing Spider-Man* #155-159, with #155 scarcer than #156-159, and *X-Men* #100 scarcer than #98-99. *Iron Man* #89 is the scarcest non-reprint superhero variant.

The following list of 184 books and 52 titles with cover dates ranging from June to October 1977 exist as Type 1 35¢ Cover Price Variants: *Amazing Spider-Man* #169-173 (6-10/77), *Avengers* #160-164 (6-10/77), *Black Panther* #4-5 (7, 9/77), *Captain America* #210-214 (6-10/77), *Captain Marvel* #51-52 (7, 9/77), *Champions* #14-15 (7, 9/77), *Conan* #75-79 (6-10/77), *Daredevil* #146-148 (6-7, 9/77), *Defenders* #48-52 (6-10/77), *Doctor Strange* #23-25 (6, 8, 10/77), *Eternals* #12-16 (6-10/77), *Fantastic Four* #183-187 (6-10/77), *Flintstones* #1 (10/77), *Ghost Rider* #24-26 (6, 8, 10/77), *Godzilla* #1-3 (8-10/77), *Howard the Duck* #13-17 (6-10/77), *Human Fly* #1-2 (9-10/77), *Incredible Hulk* #212-216 (6-10/77), *Inhumans* #11-12 (6, 8/77), *Invaders* #17-21 (6-10/77), *Iron Fist* #13-15 (6, 8-9/77), *Iron Man* #99-103 (6-10/77), *John Carter, Warlord of Mars* #1-5 (6-10/77), *Kid Colt Outlaw* #218-220 (6, 8, 10/77), *Kull* #21-23 (6, 8, 10/77), *Logan's Run* #6-7 (6-7/77), *Marvel Premiere* #36-38 (6, 8, 10/77), *Marvel Presents* #11-12 (6, 8/77), *Marvel's Greatest Comics* #71-73 (7, 9-10/77), *Marvel Super Action* #2-3 (7, 9/77), *Marvel Super Heroes* #65-66 (7, 9/77), *Marvel Tales* #80-84 (6-10/77), *Marvel Team-Up* #58-62 (6-10/77), *Marvel Triple Action* #36-37 (7, 9/77), *Marvel Two-in-One* #28-32 (6-10/77), *Master of Kung-Fu* #53-57 (6-10/77), *Ms. Marvel* #6-10 (6-10/77), *Nova* #10-14 (6-10/77), *Omega* #9-10 (7, 10/77), *Powerman* #44-47 (6-8, 10/77), *Rawhide Kid* #140-141 (7, 9/77), *Red Sonja* #4-5 (7, 9/77), *Scooby Doo* #1 (10/77), *Sgt. Fury* #141-142 (7, 9/77), *Spectacular Spider-Man* #7-11 (6-10/77), *Star Wars* #1-4 (7-10/77), *Super-Villain Team-Up* #12-14 (6, 8, 10/77), *Tarzan* #1-5 (6-10/77), *Tomb of Dracula* #57-60 (6-9/77), *2001: A Space Odyssey* #7-10 (6-9/77), *and X-Men* #105-107 (6, 8, 10/77).

The 10 rarest 35¢ price variants presented in order of scarcity, with approximately one to five copies known to exist in any grade, are *Kid Colt* #218 (with one known VG/F copy), *Flintstones* #1, *Scooby Doo* #1, *Kid Colt* #219-220, *Rawhide Kid* #140-141, *Sgt. Fury* #141-142, and *Marvel Super Action* #2. When I presented my findings at the Overstreet Advisors meeting in Baltimore in 1999 and explained that the Marvel price variants were eventually going to be the most valuable books published after 1964, I was considered insane and treated with mockery and derision by the majority of attendees. Eleven years later, as you hold the 40th annual edition of *The Overstreet Comic Book Price Guide* in your hands, the market has spoken: Marvel price variants sell for more money *in grade* than any other comics published in the last 45 years. In November 2009 a non-CGC copy of *Amazing Spider-Man* #169 (6/77) sold in apparent 2.0 good condition on eBay for $152.50, which is just over 10 times *Guide*; the same price spread would put a 9.2 copy at just over $2800, which is likely what the future holds, based on scarcity and demand. The most common 35¢ variant, *Star Wars* #1 (7/77), sold in 2007 for $10,500 in CGC 9.4, in 2008 for $12,025, and in 2009 in CGC 9.6 for $26,250. *Iron Fist* #14 (8/77) has outrun other Bronze Age keys and sits in second place, having sold in 2007 for $5,200 in CGC 9.4, in CGC 9.2 in 2008 for $4,100, and selling most recently in CGC 9.4 in 2009 for $6,100. The *Iron Fist* #14 variant is far scarcer than *Star Wars* #1 variant, with only 20 or so copies confirmed to exist compared to hundreds of copies. *Captain America* #212 (8/77) exists as a variant with an empty yellow line where the Marvel stripe should be, but *only* as a Type 1 35¢ cover price variant, and because this mutant issue is both a Type 1 and 10a variant, it is also a rare Type 14 Double Variant. *Marvel's Greatest Comics* #74 (11/77) Direct Market edition exists as a 30¢ mistake and is *not* a Type 1b reverse variant as some have suggested, because the *entire*

***Iron Fist** #14* *(August 1977) is the second most valued 35¢ variant trailing only* ***Star Wars** #1.*

run has a 30¢ cover price, whereas the entire run of Newsstand editions of *Marvel's Greatest Comics* #74 has the correct 35¢ cover price. *Marvel Super Special* #5 (1978) was withdrawn from U.S. distribution and exists only as a foreign edition in French, and thus is *not* a variant.

There are 7 different types of Direct Market Editions that change over time. Type A Direct Market editions have the price and issue number in a diamond, with a UPC barcode, and exist with or without the month in the diamond and are the scarcest, with only about 1 in 20 existing copies found in this format, used from 2-9/77. Type B Direct Market editions have the price and issue number in a diamond, with a blank UPC box and without a month in the diamond, with about 1 in 15 existing copies found in this format, used from 10/77 to 6/78. Type C Direct Market editions have the price and issue number in a diamond with a normal UPC box, with the month inside a white diamond in a black box. There is no "cc" next to the price, with about 1 in 15 existing copies found in this format, used from 8-9/78. Type D Direct Market editions have the price and issue number in a diamond and over a starburst, with a blank UPC box, and exist with or without the month in the diamond, with about 1 in 10 issues existing in this format, used from 10/78 to 2/79. Type E Direct Market editions have the price and issue number in a white flattened diamond within a black square with UPC barcode lines that have a diagonal slash through them and exist with or without the month in the diamond, with about 1 in 5 existing copies found in this format, used from 5/79 to 2/80. Type F Direct Market editions have a Spider-Man in the UPC box, used from 3/80 to 2/84, and Type G Direct Market editions have character images in the UPC box, sometimes featuring Spider-Man or the title character of the book, a methodology used from 3/84 to 6/93, and Types F and G are more common than their predecessors. *Captain America* #234 (6/79) is an exception; although it was intended to be a Type E Direct Market Edition, they forgot the flattened diamond and used the standard square box, making it different but *not* a Variant. The last use of the direct diamond on the cover was 9/82. All examples from 10/82 through 3/87 carried the Marvel "M" around the price. The words "Direct Edition" appear in the UPC box from 7/93 up on all issues. All issues dated 4/78 to 7/78 in the indicia had no month on the covers as an experiment to increase shelf life, as initially reported in *Comic Reader* #152(1/78), p. 2. From 1980-1985, Direct and Newsstand editions exist in equal quantities. From 1986-1990, the Direct Market editions are somewhat less common. From 1991-1996 Newsstand editions are 2-10 times scarcer than Direct Market editions. Note that Direct Market editions generally hit the stands two or more weeks before Newsstand editions, but were simultaneously published. Direct Market editions cover dated from 2/77 to 2/80 are considered Variants and had low distribution. Direct Market editions cover dated 3/80 and later are standard editions along as are their Newsstand edition counterparts.

What do the Tooth Fairy and standard-size "Marvel Whitmans" have in common? *They don't exist!* To be fair, there *are* Marvel Whitman comics, but it's an easy collection to complete, because only six of them exist, and all are treasury-size Type 7a variants: *Marvel Treasury Edition* #17-18 (1978, *Incredible Hulk and Amazing Spider-Man*), *Marvel Special Edition* #1-3 (1977-1978, *Star Wars*), and *Marvel Special Edition* #3 (V2, #1, 1978, *Close Encounters of the Third Kind*). So-called "Marvel Whitmans" are actually the first Direct Market editions beginning with issues cover dated 2/77 and ending with 5/79, before disappearing forever with issues cover dated 9/82. Some books were "skipped" between 2/77 and 5/79, specifically 1-3/78, 7/78, and 3-4/79. These gaps, the packaging of Direct Market editions and DC Whitmans in Whitman bags, and some conclusion jumping in the pages of *Comics' Buyer's Guide* ultimately led to the misconception and widespread use of the nickname "Marvel Whitmans."

Type 6 Variants exist because Marvel wanted to prevent dealers from returning Direct Market editions for higher newsstand credit, and were designed to be *obviously* different with their appearance, a large diamond in the upper left corner of the cover. The Direct Market was an evolution as certain as the cursed barcodes introduced in June 1976, and the large diamond was its clumsy initial introduction to a market that began to form in the late 1960s to mid 1970s through the efforts of people like Robert Beerbohm, Bud Plant, and Phil Seuling, primarily at conventions and local shops. Direct

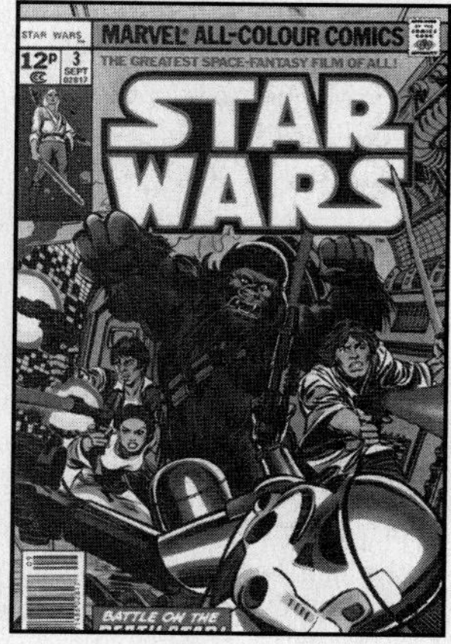

Star Wars *#3 (September 1977) can be found in the regular 30¢ edition, 30¢ with "Reprint" in box, 35¢ in diamond box, 35¢ diamond box with "Reprint" and 12 Pence with "Marvel All-Colour Comics" banner at top.*

Market editions of 1977 look more normal than the 1978-1979 "Starburst" Direct Market editions, with the latter's cover titles awkwardly repeated next to the Comics Code Authority stamp on the Marvel stripe. No Whitman publications *of any kind* have been published without the brand name on the cover, and no Whitman comics have *ever* had a cover date.

In order to exist, "Marvel Whitmans" would have to be a Variant *third version*. Comics in Whitman bags are identical to those sold as Direct Market Editions in the late 1970s *because they are the same books*. Whitman did not buy the rights to Marvel's books, but most early Direct Market editions were packaged in Whitman bags and distributed by Western Publishing, who did sometimes purchase the rights to other publisher's books. Publishers like Charlton, DC, and Marvel employed Western's bagged distribution service to market their books from 1967 and 1984. Archivist and comics author John Jackson Miller once wrote, "We're convinced: From 1977 to early 1979, any diamond-label copy was probably sold by Whitman. In fact, this printing wouldn't have existed *without* Whitman...[and] if Whitman wasn't always the sole purchaser of these...copies from 1977 to early 1979, it ordered the vast majority. We take as proof the gaps in printing, which we found when we constructed our own timeline...there are two major gaps in the Marvel "diamond-label" editions, both of which support the claim the Whitman drove the "diamond" market." (*Comics Buyer's Guide* #1609, October 2005, p. 40).

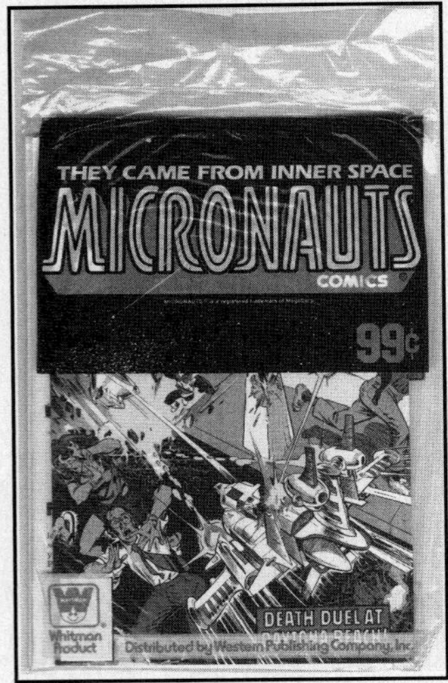

*These **Micronauts** issues were Marvel's Direct Market editions packaged in Whitman bags and distributed by Western Publishing.*

There are three gaps in printing for both the Marvel Direct Market editions and the DC Whitmans that were cover dated from 2/77 to 4/80. Marvel Direct editions are missing for the months of 1-3/78, 7/78, 3-4/79. The only gap that lines up is 3/79 to 4/79. DC Whitmans went missing for issues cover dated 6/78, 3-4/79, and 4/80. During the longest gap, that of January to March 1978, Western published Type 1b and Type 6 variants of Gold Key and Whitman comics, regardless of other licensee's books. Missing months and multiple gaps were par for the course with Western's bagged comics and always had been. Production occurred during windows of opportunity with a focus on priority.

The first gap in printing for Direct Market editions occurs from 1-3/78, otherwise known as the *Star Wars* explosion, when Marvel had amazing success printing and reprinting *Star Wars* comics. Overwhelmed with *Star Wars* reprints, Direct Market editions temporarily fell by the wayside, and only *Star Wars* #7-9(1-3/78) were produced during this unique gap. Western Publishing went on to reprint all three of the *Marvel Treasury Editions, with the Whitman logo*, maintaining the pattern of all Whitman books ever published, *because Western owned them*. The second gap in printing for Direct Market editions is 7/78. Western published Whitman variants of Gold Key comics during this month as well as DC Whitmans. DC Whitmans were skipped the previous month in June 1978 but Marvel's Direct Market editions did get printed. The third gap in printing for Direct Market editions occurs from 3-4/79, and Miller points out that this gap of two missing months is the same for Marvel Direct Market editions and DC Whitmans, adding, "That can't be a coincidence: Whitman must have been driving the printing for both. After that, the Marvel label changes in June from the fat diamond to the skinny one - and DC's Whitman output suddenly skyrockets." (*Comics Buyer's Guide* #1609, October 2005, page 40.) The delayed release of the *Superman* movie explains this pause. "Whitman, obviously in anticipation of the...Superman film, has begun a toy-store blitz of Superman merchandise, including plastic bagged DC Comics with the Whitman symbol." (*The Comic Reader* #157, 6/78, p. 5.) DC Whitmans were printed prior to the film delay, and the decision to wait before printing more delayed the Marvels. Doug Sulipa says he received Newsstand Editions during the printing gaps, proving that distribution continued without interruption, the gaps being one of many arguments used in support of the "Marvel Whitman" theory. Miller updated his opinion recently in the *Guide*, and it seems our opinions differ only on what to call them, as he says that "Marvel Whitmans" were designed differently to keep them "...from reentering the newsstand system as returns." (*The Overstreet Comic Book Price Guide* #38, 2008, p. 1048).

Clearly, the nickname "Marvel Whitman" is easier to say than "Direct Market edition," although I question the value of this convenience when considering its effect on the market, considering the acronym "DME" would be easily understood. Bagging comics made it affordable to painlessly introduce the first Direct Market Editions without resorting to expensive small print runs. Profit was the objective, which explains minor inconsistencies, such as comics that exist with UPC codes, some that exist without, and some with both versions, like *Star Wars* #11(5/78). "Western has signed an agreement with Marvel to distribute Marvel Comics in Western's plastic bag series which is apparently doing quite well. The two companies will not be mixed in the bags. We believe that those Marvels to appear in bags will have slightly different covers in that a diamond will cover the space that currently houses the cover date and Curtis company symbol. The cost of three 30¢ comics will be 79 cents." (*The Comic Reader* #140, February 1977, p. 10). Call them what you will, but they are what they are.

A variant of *Tower of Shadows* #5(5/70) exists as a Type 10b Variant with inverted contents. A Variant of *Amazing Spider-Man* #84(5/70) exists as an "All detergent" giveaway from 1983. *Ka-Zar the Savage* #12(3/82) exists as a Type 10b variant printed with a missing panel, with only 1600 known copies correctly printed, and also exists as a second printing, while *Ka-Zar the Savage* #29(12/83), a giant-size issue, was not intended as a newsstand edition but exists as one. *Dennis the Menace Comics Digest* #1(4/82) has a variant with the DC emblem on the cover, and the same is true of *The Very Best of Dennis the Menace* #1-2(4, 6/82). *Micronauts* #57(3/84), a giant-size issue, should not exist as a newsstand edition but does. *Moon Knight* #25(11/82), a giant-size issue, was intended to be a newsstand edition but does not exist as such. *Heathcliff* #1(4/85) exists as a Type 1c variant with a "Star Chase" game on the last page and on the inside back cover, and also as a Type 13 variant with a 4 page Mark Jewelers insert. *Planet Terry* #1(4/85) exists as a Type 1c variant with a "Star Chase" game on the last page and on the inside back cover, as does *Wally the Wizard* #1(4/85). *Classic X-Men* #36(6/89) exists as a variant newsstand edition with no UPC code. *Excalibur: The Sword is Drawn* #1 (4/92) exists as a Type 10a variant with no cover price and two later printings. *Venom: Lethal Protector* #1(2/93) exists with both gold and black cover Type 5 variant editions. Type 12a Shan-Lon mini-reprints exist from the early 1990s, including *Amazing Spider-Man* #1 (3/63) and *Captain America* #113 (5/69).

Type 1a pence price variants exist sporadically of titles cover dated July 1960 to November 1964 minus their cover dates, with no issues published at all from 12/64 to 8/65. Beginning with issues cover dated 9/65 and continuing through 11/67, the cover month is present. Early Pence price variants had the cover month removed due to shipping delays from the U.S., as books usually took at least one month to arrive overseas, and Marvel wanted to prolong their shelf life. There are no Pence price variants of issues cover dated 12/67 through 3/69. Marvel licensed their U.K. business partners to reprint material from different time periods, titles, and characters so as to avoid competing with themselves with Pence price variants outside of the breaks in production. Marvel resumed sporadic production of Pence price variants with books cover dated 4/69 through 3/74, published no books from 4/74 to 7/74, and continued production with books cover dated 8/74 through 9/80, with the cover altered to read "Marvel All-Colour Comics," in one form or another. Pence price variants in regular format continue with books cover dated 10/80 to 12/81, but issues cover dated 9/81 to 12/81 had the cover month deleted, another short-lived experiment to extend shelf life; issues cover dated 1/82 to 9/82 continue in regular format with the cover month restored. Marvel ceased production of Pence price variants at this point, when multi-regional prices first appeared on Direct Market editions cover dated 10/82. Canadian variants, with a single higher cover price, exist for all newsstand editions comics beginning with issues cover dated 10/82 and continuing through issues cover dated 8/86, with no variants of Direct Market editions during this time period; prior to this such variants do not exist, as the U.S. and Canadian prices were the same, with the only known exception being *Spectacular Spider-Man* #1(7/68). Oversized Pence Price Variants exist from at least 1974 to 1978, beginning with *Marvel Treasury Edition, Spectacular Spider-Man* #1 (1974) priced at 40 pence, and continuing sporadically through at least the *Star Wars* treasuries from 1978, and possibly through the 1981 issues as well.

In the 1982-1986 period about 10% of Marvel's print run was Canadian, with Newsstand and Direct Market editions split at about 50% each; because Newsstand editions have a far lower survival rate than Direct Market Editions, Canadian Newsstand editions may be as scarce or scarcer than Pence price variants, with both estimated to have original print runs equivalent to approximately 5% of U.S. print runs, but with an estimated survival rate of only 1-2%. Because almost all Pence price variants are still in the U.K., they appear quite rare in the U.S. Many Pence price variants are now uncommon even in Britain, because many large U.K. dealers, and many collectors, have been importing U.S. editions to the U.K. while avoiding pence issues that were considered inferior. Pence price variants exist of many Silver Age key issues, including historic gems such as *Amazing Fantasy* #15 (8/62), *Amazing Spider-Man* #1 (3/63), *Fantastic Four* #1 (11/61), *Incredible Hulk* #1 (5/62), and *Tales to Astonish* #27 (1/62). Not all books were published as Pence price variants, and some key issues were skipped, especially during the Bronze Age, including *Amazing Spider-Man* #129 (2/74), *Incredible Hulk* #181 (11/74), and *X-Men* #94 (8/75). Some highlights and key issues from the Bronze Age of Pence price variants confirmed to exist include: *Amazing Adventures* #11 (3/72), *Astonishing Tales* #25 (8/74), *Avengers* #93 (11/71), *Daredevil* #168 (1/81), *Ghost Rider* #1-2 (9-10/73), *Incredible Hulk* #141 (7/71), *Iron Man* #55 (2/73) and #128 (11/79), *Marvel Spotlight* #12 (10/73), *Son of Satan* #1 (12/75), *Sub-Mariner* #34-35 (2-3/71), *Tomb of Dracula #10* (7/73) and #12 (9/73), *Werewolf by Night* #32-33 (8-9/75), and *X-Men* #120 (4/79).

Daredevil *#168*
15p cover
(January 1981)
is a key issue from the Bronze Age of Pence price variants.

G.I. Joe, A Real American Hero, was so popular in the mid-1980s that it was heavily reprinted. Type 2a variant second printings known to exist include issues #2, 6-8, 10-12, 14, 17-19, 21, 23, 25-27, 29-30, 34, 36-38, 49, 51-53, 55, and 63-64. Third printings known to exist include #21 and #29, and others are likely to exist, although the only way to tell later printings from originals or one another is the different internal ads. From 1992 to 1994, Marvel Comics and JC Penney sold boxes of Type 2b variants known as "Vintage Pack Reprints," and since I bought a set in 1994 from a comic shop, it seems that distribution was not exclusive. The 1992 group consists of 20 comics, 19 of which are superhero reprints, including *Captain America* #384 (4/91), *Daredevil* #267, 273 (6, 11/89), *Darkhawk* #5 (7/91), *Fantastic Four* #351, 355 (4, 8/91), *Iron Man* #258 (7/90), *New Warriors* #10 (4/91), *Silver Surfer* #32-33 (12/89, 1/90), *Sleepwalker* #8 (1/92), *Spectacular Spider-Man* #145-146 (12/88, 1/99), *Uncanny X-Men* #268 (9/90), *Web of Spider-Man* #81, 83 (10, 12/91), *Wonderman* #2 (10/91), and *X-Men Classic* #47 (5/90). One *Marvel Masterworks* edition of the *Incredible Hulk* #1 (5/62) with a non-glossy newsprint cover and the word "facsimile" visible above the price was also included. The 1993 group consists of 20 comics, 10 of which are modern superhero reprints, including *Amazing Spider-Man* #330 (3/90), *Captain America* #241, 371 (1/80, 6/90), *Excalibur* #27 (8/90), *Ghost Rider* #10 (2/91), *Incredible Hulk* #330 (4/87), *Namor* #6 (11/03), *New Warriors* #3 (3/90), *What If* #4 (10/89), and *Uncanny X-Men* #245 (6/89). There are three *Marvel Masterworks* editions with darker grey covers than regular editions, and with newsprint covers instead of glossy: *Amazing Spider-Man* #1 (3/63), *Tales of Suspense* #39 (3/63), and *X-Men* #1 (9/63). Seven other classic reprints include *Avengers* #4 (3/64), *Fantastic Four* #51 (6/66), *Spectacular Spider-Man* #26-27 (1-2/79), *Thor* #312(10/81), and *X-Men* #60-61 (9-10/69). The 1994 group is the most historical, but not all issues were reprinted from the originals. According to the indicia, *Fantastic Four* #66 was printed from *Marvel's Greatest Comics* #49(5/74), *Sgt. Fury* #13 was printed from *Special Marvel Edition* #11(7/73), and *X-Men* #28 was printed from *X-Men* #76(6/72). All three sets have new ads except for one issue, *Young Men* #25, which has the word "facsimile" under the original ads inside, a Type 2c variant. The 15 issues are: *Amazing Adult Fantasy #13 (6/62), Amazing Spider-Man Special #5 (11/68), Avengers #88 (5/71), Captain America #109 (1/69), Fantastic Four #66-67 (9-10/67), Incredible Hulk #140 (6/71), Sgt. Fury #13 (12/64), Sub-Mariner #8 (12/68), Thor Special #2 (9/66), Tomb of Dracula #25 (10/74), X-Men #28, 62-63 (1/67, 11-12/69), and Young Men #25 (2/54).* Marvel Pressman issues are Type 12a variants created as a game promotion, with reprints of *Uncanny X-Men* #297, 303, 307 (2, 8, 12/93), and *X-Men* #11(8/92).

Modern Promotions

Modern Promotions began publishing comics in 1972 with treasury-sized editions of newspaper strip reprints featuring *Beetle Bailey*, *The Katzenjammer Kids* and *Mandrake the Magician*, followed in 1973 by *Flash Gordon, Henry*, and *Little Iodine*, all of which are scarce in any grade. In 1977 Modern produced its so-called Modern Comics line, an erratic series of mostly marginal quality Charlton reprints from the 1960s and 1970s, which were marketed in bagged sets of three. In 1978 Modern published *Battlestar Galactica*, a treasury edition reprinting *Marvel Comics Super Special* #8 (1978). In 1979 they erratically published two B&W horror magazines, *Terrors of Dracula* and *Weird Vampire Tales*, both of which ceased by March 1982, and which are related to the Eerie Publications B&W horror magazines of the 1960s and 1970s, rumored to contain some incomplete and/or altered reprints. In 1977 they produced a handful of Hanna-Barbera Big Little Books. In 1985 they published a three issue original comic called *Voltron*. The 1977 Modern Comics Charlton reprint series contains material from early 1967 to late 1976, but only *Judo Master* #1(#93, 2/67) has a new issue number.

The following 32 titles and 62 "Modern Comics" reprints are 1977 Type 8a variants:

Army War Heroes #36 (2/70), *Attack* #13 (9/73), *Beyond the Grave* #2 (10/75), *Billy the Kid* #109 (10/74), *Blue Beetle* #1, 3 (6, 10/67), *Captain Atom* #83-85, 87 (11/66, 1, 3, 8/67), *Cheyenne Kid* #87, 89 (11/71, 3/72), *Creepy Things* #2-4, 6 (10, 12/75, 2,6/76), *Doomsday +1* #5 (3/76), *Drag n' Wheels* #58 (3/73), *E-Man* #1-4, 9-10 (10, 12/73, 6, 8/74, 7, 9/75), *Fightin' Army* #108 (3/73), *Fightin' Marines* #120 (1/75), *Geronimo Jones* #7 (8/72), *Ghost Manor* #19 (7/74), *Ghostly Haunts* #40-41 (9, 11/74), *Haunted Love* #1 (4/73), *Hercules* #10-11 (4-5/67), *House of Yang* #1-2 (7, 10/75), *Judo Master* #1, 94, 96, 98 (2, 4, 8, 12/67), *Many Ghosts of Doctor Graves* #12, 25 (2/69, 4/71), *Midnight Tales* #12, 17 (4/75, 3/76), *Monster Hunters* #1-2 (8, 10/75), *Outlaws of the West* #64, 79 (5/67, 1/70), *Peacemaker* #1-2 (3, 5/67), *Scary Tales* #1 (8/75), *Texas Rangers* #76 (2/70), *Thunderbolt* #57-58 (5, 7/67), *Vengeance Squad* #5-6 (3, 5/76), *War* #7, 9 (7, 11/76), *World of Wheels* #23 (12/68), and *Yang* #3, 10-11 (7/74, 11/75, 1/76).

Norlen Magazines

(Also see Green Publications)

Norlen was another name for Green, a small publisher that reprinted original covers and contents in 1959. Both Green and their pseudonym Norlen published only a handful of titles, and did so in a way that the numbered issues, all Type 8b variants, are *not* legitimate representative copies. The Norlen issues read, "1959 Edition" on the covers.

Penny King Co.

Three Comics (1944) exists as a Type 1c variant with two different covers.

Quality Comics Group

Feature Comics #26(11/39) has four different Type 10a Cover Error variants that exist, including three with missing colors and one example with a blank back cover.

Realistic Comics

Avon published comics in 1953 with the "Realistic"

imprint, a logo they first used in 1951 with some of their paperbacks and on their own comics published from 1951-1952, such as the title *Intimate Confessions*. Realistic comics are Type 8 variant reprints that are "no number" one shots with painted covers recycled from Avon paperbacks. Covers differ only in that they advertise the stories inside. New titles are *not* variants but are unique, original products. Existing issues include: *Campus Romance*, *Cowpuncher*, *Flying Saucers* (with two pages of new Wallace Wood art), *Jesse James*, *Kit Carson and the Blackfeet Warrior*, *Romantic Love*, *Sparkling Love*, *Speedy Rabbit*, *Spotty the Pup*, and *Women to Love*.

Remington Morse Publications

Yankee Comics #4(3/42) – 7(1942) exist as Type 12a variants, and are 68 page miniature reprints distributed to servicemen during WWII, published between 1943-1945.

So Much Fun! Inc.

In 1987 Archie Comics, DC Comics, and Marvel Comics each allowed So Much Fun! Inc. toy stores to distribute reprints of a few of their books. All 12 issues are uncommon because print runs were limited to 5,000, and most copies are found in low grade. The word "classic" appears under the titles on the covers (except for the *Incredible Hulk*) and So Much Fun! Inc., appears in the UPC code box on all of the books. The Archie issues are: *Archie Comics* #282 (7/79) and *Betty and Veronica* #289 (1/80). The DC issues are: *Batman* #401 (11/86), *Justice League of America* #217(8/83), *Star Trek* #6 (7/84), *Superman* #161 (5/63), and *Superman: The Man of Steel* #1 (7/91). The Marvel issues are *Amazing Spider-Man* #292 (9/87), *Fantastic Four* #306 (9/87), *G. I. Joe, A Real American Hero* #63 (9/87), *Incredible Hulk* #335 (9/87), and *Uncanny X-Men* #221(9/87). Of such Type 3b variants, *Incredible Hulk* and *Amazing Spider-Man* generate the most interest.

The So Much Fun! Inc. reprint of ***Amazing Spider-Man*** *#292 (September 1987).*

Spire Christian Comics

Produced by the Fleming H. Revell company from 1972-1984, Spire was one of the most prolific of the religious publishers. Spire is the most collected of the religious comics, and most are found in low grade, so a Fine copy is desirable and Very Fine or better copies are relatively scarce, although a warehouse find in the summer of 2008 added some high-grade books to the marketplace. Earlier editions are more common than the later Barbour editions, which were published into the early 1990s. The 19 Archie titles are the most sought after, often selling for double *Guide*. The scarcest examples are *Archie's Circus* (1990), *Archie's Sports Scene* (1983), and *Christmas with Archie* (1973).

While some books were released only as first editions, most Spire comics exist as Type 4 variants. First editions and reprints have no issue numbers, but the books have copyright dates inside and the cover price can help to date them, beginning with 35¢ in 1972, and over time increasing to 69¢ by 1984. Second and later printings are easily identified from the copyright date and cover price. Of the non-Archie titles, the two most requested books that bring double *Guide* are *Hansi, The Girl Who Loved the Swastika* (1973), and *Hello, I'm Johnny Cash* (1976). The scarcest examples are *Barney Bear Family Fun* (1982), *Barney Bear Family Tree* (1982), *Barney Bear: The Swamp Gang* (1977), *Barney Bear Toyland* (1982), and *Yankee Doodle the Spirit of Liberty* (1984).

Star Publications

Startling Terror Tales #11(8/52) exists as a Type 10 variant edition with a black cover, theoretically due to a "pressrun change," while the standard edition has a blue cover.

Star Rider Productions

Star Rider and the Peace Machine #2(10/82) exists as a Type 10b variant with stories printed out of sequence.

Timely

Mystic Comics #4(8/40) has two versions, one with an August cover date sticker over the July date, and a Type 10a Variant, with the July date stamped over with "August" in silver ink. The *Adventures of Big Boy* (1956) is the longest running promotional comic; "East and West" variant copies exist, and other as yet undocumented variants also exist.

Twin Circle

(Also see Classics Illustrated)

In 1967, *Classics Illustrated* was sold to Patrick Frawley and his Catholic publication, *Twin Circle*. From 1968-1976, Twin Circle (the Catholic Newspaper) serialized *Classics Illustrated* comics and published Type 4 variants of Classics Illustrated books. A number of Twin Circle editions of *Classics Illustrated* exist, as well as a Type 4a variant reprint of the political comic book *Design for Survival* (1968).

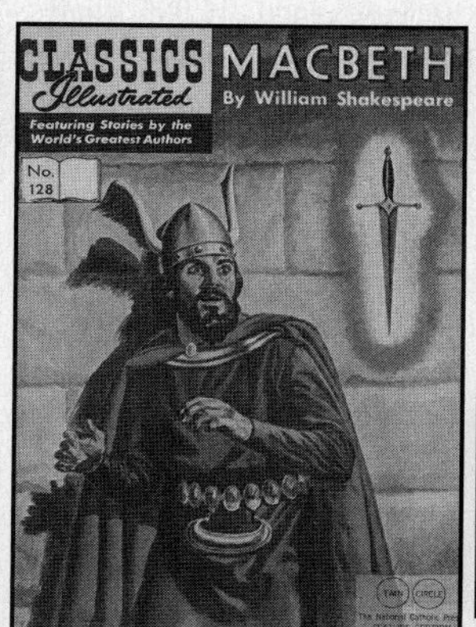

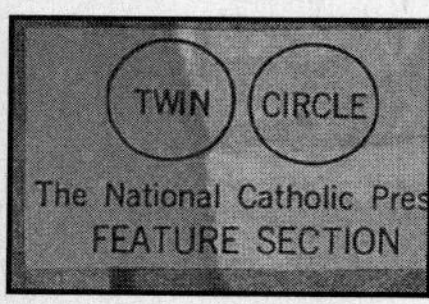

The Twin Circle reprint of ***Classics Illustrated*** *#128 has the red logo and no cover price.*

United Features Syndicate

Captain and the Kids #1(1938) exists as a Type 2 variant dated December 1939 that reads "Reprint" on the cover.

VALIANT

Most VALIANT (later "Valiant") variants were produced with limited print runs of 5,000 each, although some were produced with only 2,500 print runs. Additional examples may exist. Post-1994 Type 1c variants exist with no cover price that came in blister packs as promotional items that were internally identical to newsstand and direct market copies exist without cover prices. Three pre-1994 examples include: *Captain N: The Game Master* #1 (1990), *Legend of Zelda* #1 (1990), and an nn issue of *Super Mario Brothers* (1990).

Other Type 1c variant issues known to exist include: *Archer and Armstrong* #0 Gold (7/92) June inside, *Armorines* #0 (6/94) Gold and stand alone card stock cover, *Bloodshot* #0 (3/94) Gold and Type 14 double variant Platinum edition of 25 copies, *Chaos Effect Alpha* Gold (1994), *Chaos Effect Alpha* Red (1994) and *Chaos Effect Omega* Gold (1994) considered the scarcest Valiant comic; *Deathmate* #1 *(9/93)* Prologue Gold, #2 (9/93) Black Gold, #3 (10/93) Yellow Gold, #4 (10/93) Blue Gold, #5 (11/93) Red Gold, #6 (2/94) Epilogue Gold, *Eternal Warrior* #1 (8/92) Gold embossed and Gold flat, *Harbinger* #0(1/92) Pink; *HARDCorps* #1 (12/92) Gold, #5(4/93) Defense Fund 25,000 copies, *Magnus Robot Fighter* #21 (2/93) Gold, *Ninjak* #1 (2/94) Gold, *Predator Versus Magnus* #1 (10/92) Platinum, *PsiLords* #1(9/94) Gold, *Rai and the Future Force* #9 (5/93) Gold, *Second Life of Dr. Mirage* #1 (11/93) Gold, *Shadowman* #0 (4/94) Gold and non-chrome, *Solar* #10(6/92) second printing, *Turok* #1 (6/93) Gold, *Unity* #0 (8/92) Gold, Platinum, and Red (thought to be the scarcest early Valiant variant), *X-O Manowar* #0 (8/93) Gold, #1/2 (11/94) Gold *Wizard* giveaway, #15 (4/93) Pink Ultra-Pros Supplies giveaway.

The Gold edition of ***Archer & Armstrong*** *#0 has the gold logo at the upper left.*

Warren Publishing Co.

Type 1a Variants exist of *Creepy, Eerie*, and *Vampirella*, with many issues known from 3/77 to 3/83. *Vampirella* #113 (1988) exists as a Type 1a variant with a $4.95 cover price and the standard $3.95 price; both are Newsstand editions.

Western Publishing

(Also see Dell, Gold Key, and Whitman)

The promotional comic *Mutual of Omaha's Wild Kingdom* (1965), received a different front and back cover when reprinted by Western in 1966, a Type 4 variant.

Whitman

(Also see DC, Gold Key, and Marvel)

How we categorize books, and especially what we name them, has a tremendous impact upon value and desirability. Just as calling early Direct Market editions "Marvel Whitmans" may *increase* their value, calling any U.S. Published intended for foreign distribution cover price variants "reprints," or "foreign editions," instead of "Canadian Price Variants" or "Pence Price Variants," may *reduce* their value. CGC has improved its Type 1a variant description in recent years; variants once referred to as "U.K. Editions" are now referred to as "Country/Variant" books, but terms such as "Pence Price Variant" or "Canadian Price Variant" would be better still. Pence price variants often sell for half or less of regular U.S. editions, and this disparity of "value" increases dramatically with high-grade books and expensive key issues, when collectors are hesitant to drop serious money for the "wrong kind of copy." The lexicon of definitions provides a powerful tool for understanding what exists and the inherent differences between variant issues, but such definitions should never replace calling an item what it is: naming a book a "Type 6 Variant" instead of a "Direct Market edition" is one self-defeating example. The open market will always determine *true value*, indifferent to predictions or dealer bias, the latter sometimes influenced to knowingly identify a book incorrectly for financial gain.

Due to the broad scope and complexity of this article, it should be considered a work in progress. Please contact the *Guide* with proof of unknown material and contribute to the body of knowledge. Several excellent websites were referenced for the writing of this article, including www.bipcomics.com, www.comics.org, and www.stlcomics.com. The author offers his heartfelt thanks to everyone who helped in its development, including many people that space has prevented me from mentioning, including his loving wife for her support.

Collector and writer Jon McClure, an award-winning historian, is a longtime Advisor to The Overstreet Comic Book Price Guide. He recently released a feature length film, FaceEater (2007), with director Jarrod Perrott, and in 2010 will release the card game FaceEater that he created and illustrated, partnering with John Harris of a5, a marketing company based in Chicago. He is currently writing a book about comic history, a zombie comic book series, some short stories, and another screenplay, and lives with his wife Dyan, three cats and a dog in Durango, Colorado.

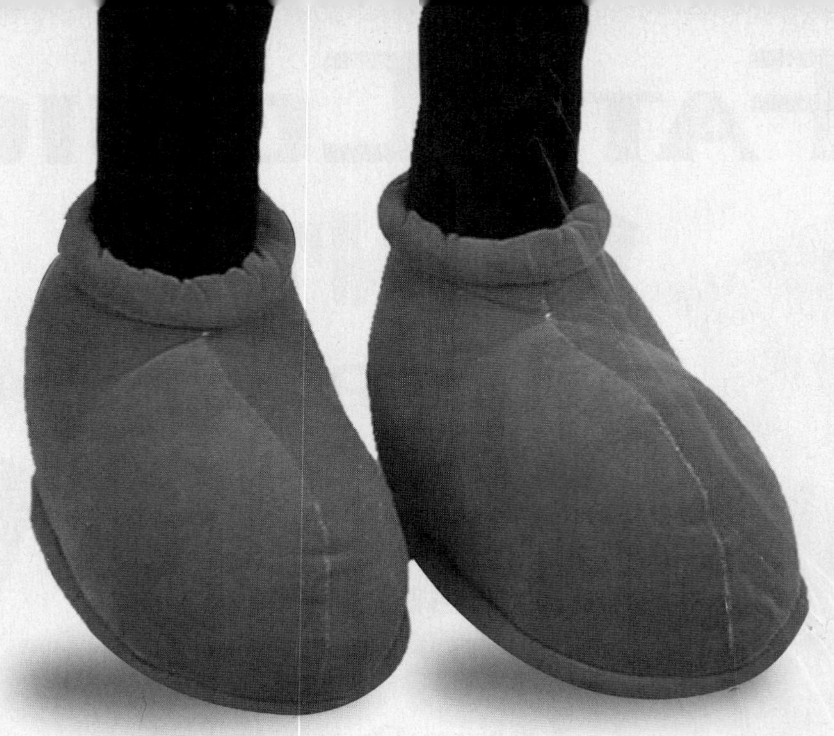

pop culture with character
GEPPI'S
entertainment
MUSEUM

H&V COMICS
OPEN
LOOKING FOR A
COMIC SHOP NEAR YOU?
COMIC SHOP LOCATOR SERVICE
COMICS
BLACK FRIDAY CONCERT
COMICS
comicshoplocator.com
888-COMIC-BOOK

CONAN #1: When Marvel Went Barbarian

By Charles S. Novinskie

Celebrating its 40th anniversary right alongside The Overstreet Comic Book Price Guide *is* Conan the Barbarian *#1, which debuted from Marvel Comics in 1970. A landmark comic in many ways, we asked Overstreet Advisor Charlie Novinskie for his thoughts on the subject.*

I was twelve years old when I picked up *Conan the Barbarian #1* at my local newsstand in Shamokin, Pennsylvania. That comic changed the way I looked at comics. It was different: it stood out from the other super-hero comics that were piled in front of me.

Years later, it's pretty clear that *Conan* #1 also changed comics as a whole, too.

The concept of licensed comics was propelled to the forefront, as was the genre of sword and sorcery.

Roy Thomas, former Editor-in-Chief and longtime *Conan the Barbarian* scribe, remembers discussing the possibility of adapting Conan at Marvel: "Stan Lee had no feel for what sword and sorcery was, but I had bought (though I hadn't read them) all the Conan paperbacks that had come out to date, largely because of the Frazetta covers."

Thomas wrote a memo to Martin Goodman stating that a sword and sorcery comic would contain some of the same qualities our super-hero comics did: a strong hero, beautiful women, monsters, and villains (in this case, sorcerers).

"I noticed in a new Conan paperback that L. Sprague de Camp listed the mailing address of the literary agent for the Howard estate, Glenn Lord," Thomas continued. "I contacted him offering $200 an issue, and he accepted, convinced I suppose by my argument that a six-figure comic book print run might increase the audience for Conan."

It was Thomas that suggested the title *Conan the Barbarian* because, though that phrase doesn't actually occur anywhere in Howard's stories, it was one the character was known by, and had *not* been the title of one of the paperbacks (though it had been the title of one of the Gnome Press hardcovers from the 1950s).

Conan #1 sold quite well, but each of the next half dozen issues dropped in sales. Thomas recalled Lee stepping in around the time of *Conan* #8.

"Stan 'suggested' that we have more humanoid foes for Conan on the covers than giant spiders, man-headed snakes, apes in armor, and women turning into tigers. With #8-9 and afterward, the sales picked up, and afterwards *Conan the Barbarian* was never in danger of cancellation for another 25 or so years."

It was this experiment in 1970 by Marvel Comics that changed the way publishers viewed licensed properties. The character Conan, in fact, became a mini licensing industry all its own as *Conan the Barbarian* spawned the very popular black & white magazine *The Savage Sword of Conan,* the sister title *King Conan* and, for a time, *Giant-Size Conan,* as well as a newspaper comic strip and comics about Kull, Solomon Kane, and other Robert E. Howard heroes.

A quick glance at the pages of *The Overstreet Comic Book Price Guide* shows that the Conan property continues to thrive in the comic market, all because of the *Conan the Barbarian #1* published by Marvel forty years ago.

"Sometimes those events seem as close in time to me as if they happened a couple of years ago, instead of four decades ago," Thomas said, "while at other times, they seem so distant in the mists of time that they truly might have occurred in the Hyborian Age itself!"

After a few years in decline, Dark Horse Comics successfully relaunched the comic book version of the character in 2004 with *Conan* #0. It was followed by a 50-issue series, then a new series entitled *Conan the Cimmerian,* also a number of one-shots and specials, and a series of books collecting the old Marvel Comics run.

Charles S. Novinskie is an Overstreet Advisor, comic historian, and a Hero Initiative board member.

NEW! FIRST TIME IN COMIC-BOOK FORM!

CONAN THE BARBARIAN

15¢

1

OCT

APPROVED BY THE COMICS CODE AUTHORITY

CONAN

THE BARBARIAN

MARVEL COMICS GROUP

TO THE DEATH!

THE COMING OF CONAN!

Television, Animation, & Adaptations

By Charles S. Novinskie

As we talked about Conan the Barbarian *#1 and other comics that saw release in 1970, the same year* The Overstreet Comic Book Price Guide *debuted, we noticed an interesting trend. Overstreet Advisor Charlie Novinksie checked them out for us.*

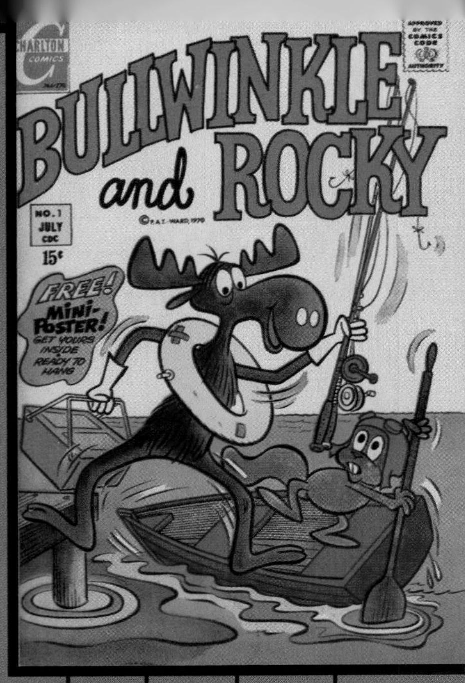

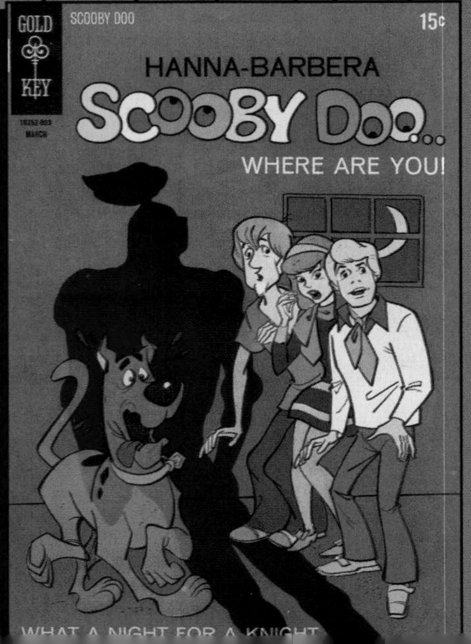

The fact that television dominated the country's consciousness in the seventies is evident by the number of comic books that appeared in 1970 based on television programming – especially animation! Unlike today's television market overburdened by an unimaginable number of cable outlets, 1970's television was basic and dominated by the major three networks – ABC, NBC, and CBS; and kids were tuning in in record numbers!

Two publishers, Charlton and Gold Key, fought it out for dominance over the television/animation comic market in an attempt to draw kids to comics. Gold Key published new titles based on television hits including *Scooby Doo, Yosemite Sam & Bugs Bunny*, and *Smokey Bear*, while Charlton contributed new #1 comics in the form of *Bullwinkle*, *Dudley Do-Right*, *The Flintstones*, *The Jetsons* (which had just ended at Gold Key), *Magilla Gorilla*, *Quick Draw McGraw*, *Top Cat*, *Underdog*, and *Yogi Bear*.

Television animation wasn't the only avenue pursued by comic publishers in 1970 as Dell jumped on board with comics based on live action shows like *Nanny and the*

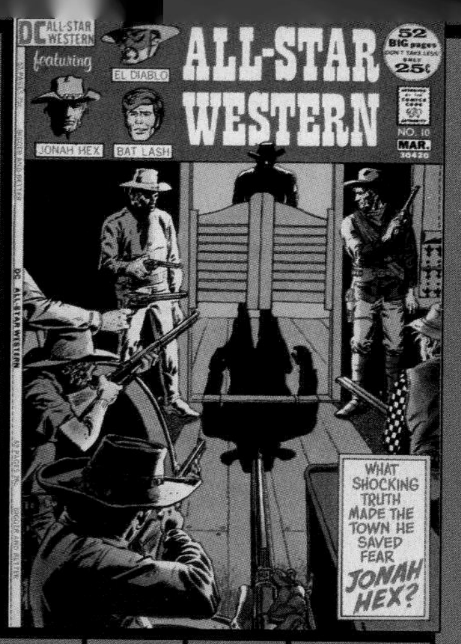

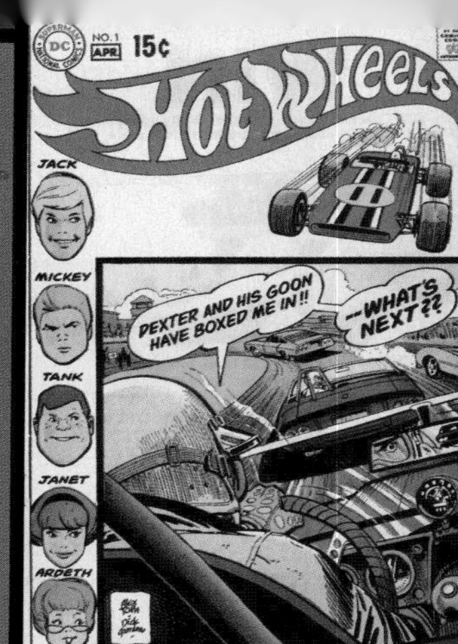

Professor, *The New People*, and *Room 222*.

Turning off the television, Marvel also took advantage of their library of materials repackaging their horror and monster stories in titles like *Amazing Adventures*, *Astonishing Tales*, *Fear*, *Where Creatures Roam*, and *Where Monsters Dwell*.

Westerns hung on with a few notable titles, *All Star Western* from DC is most notable for the first appearance of Jonah Hex in issue #10 while Marvel launched *The Ringo Kid* and *Western Gunfighters*.

Marvel also added reprints in a new *Ka-Zar* comic and published a six issue run of *Harvey*. Rounding out the #1 titles for 1970 was *Baby Snoots* by Gold Key, *Hot Wheels* by DC (most notable for artwork by Neal Adams and Alex Toth), and Marvel's attempt at a humor magazine, titled *Spoof*.

Two black and white horror mags also appeared in 1970: *Ghoul Tales* by Stanley Publishing, and *Nightmare* by Skywald. A black and white reprint of Sunday strips of *John Carter: House of Greystoke* rounded out the run of 1970 premieres.

Charlie Novinskie enjoys everything from the seventies (what he can remember of them anyway) and invites anyone that would like to reminisce to drop him an e-mail at: charlienovinskie@hotmail.com.

RECORD SETTERS

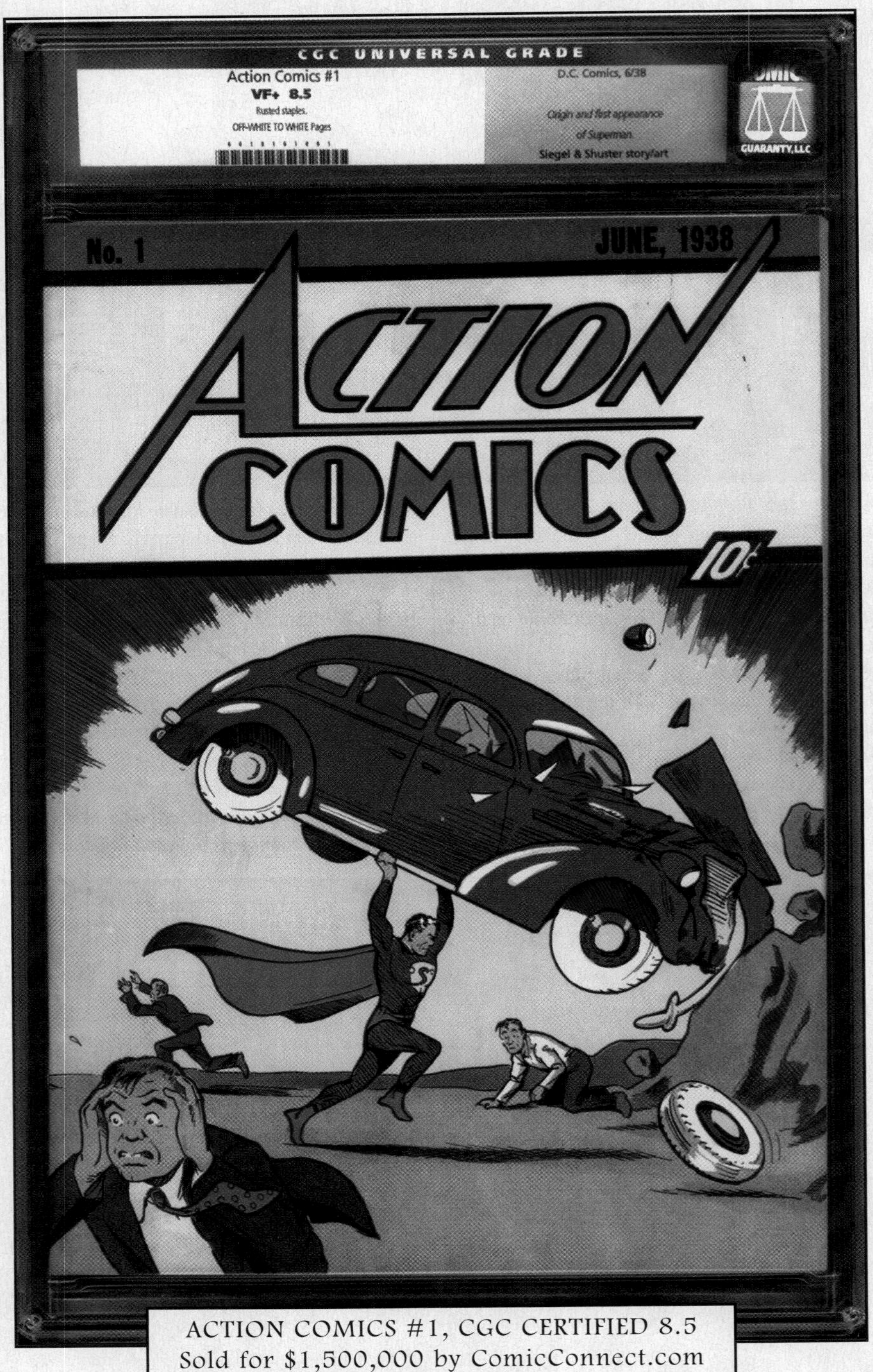

ACTION COMICS #1, CGC CERTIFIED 8.5
Sold for $1,500,000 by ComicConnect.com
on March 30, 2010. © DC

RECORD SETTERS

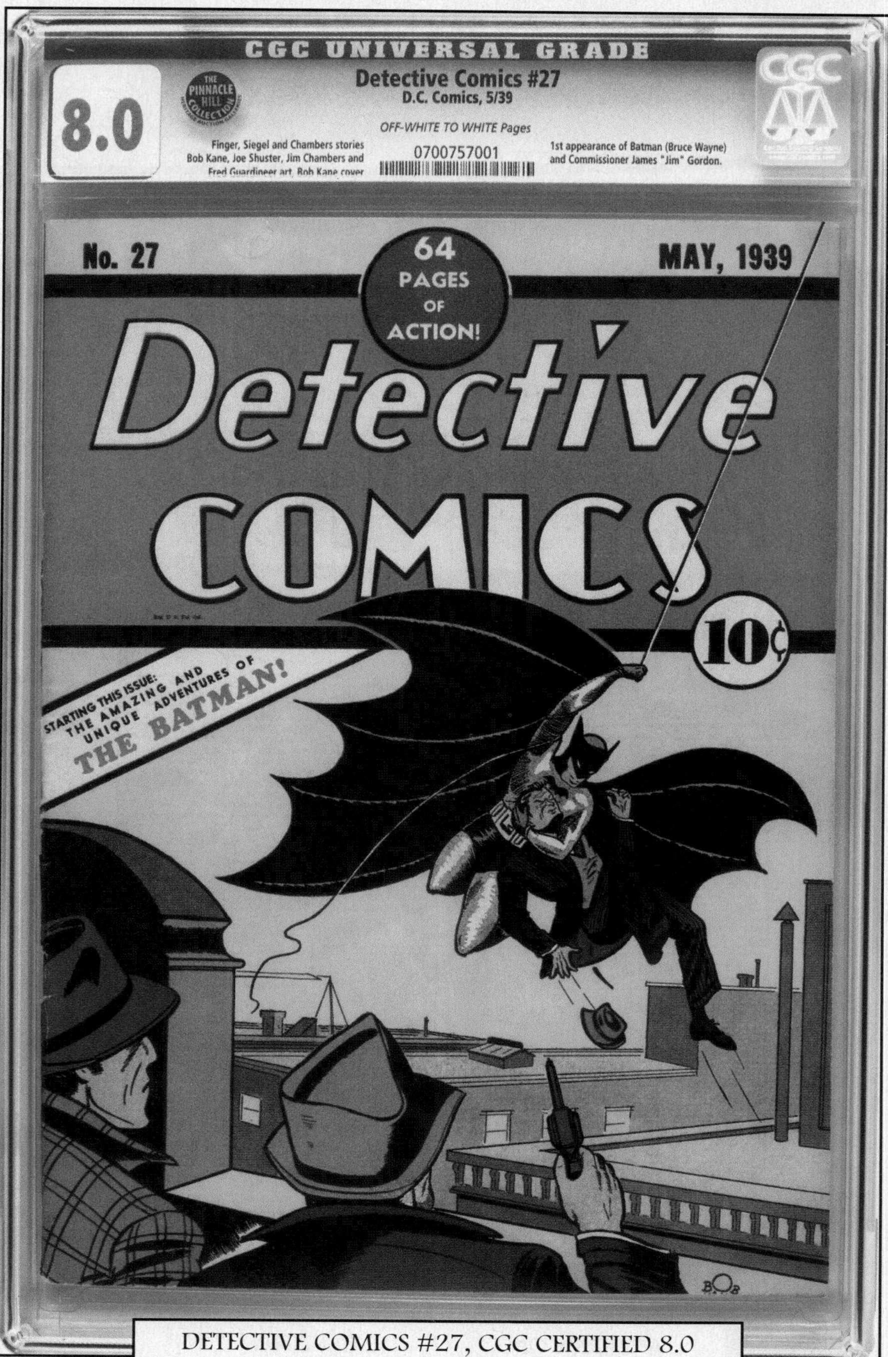

DETECTIVE COMICS #27, CGC CERTIFIED 8.0
Sold for $1,075,500 by Heritage Auction Galleries
on February 25, 2010. © DC

RECORD SETTERS

ACTION COMICS #1, CGC CERTIFIED 8.0
Sold for $1,000,000 by ComicConnect.com
on February 22, 2010. © DC

RECORD SETTERS

AMAZING FANTASY #15, CGC 9.2
Sold for $190,000 by Pedigree Comics
in February 2009. © MAR

SHOWCASE #4, CGC 9.6
Sold for $179,250 by Heritage
in May 2009. © DC

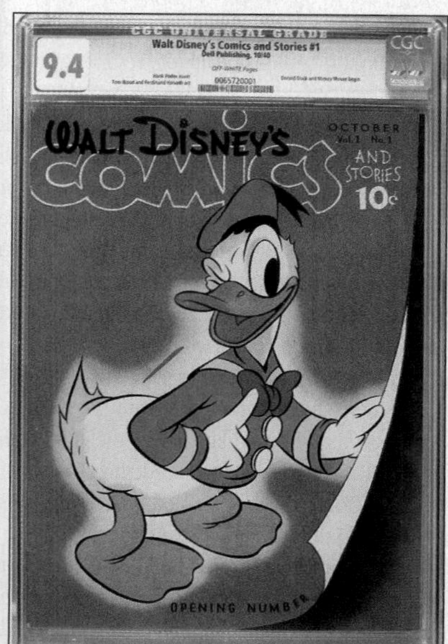

WALT DISNEY'S COMICS AND STORIES #4,
CGC 9.4
Sold for $116,512 by Heritage
in November 2008. © DIS

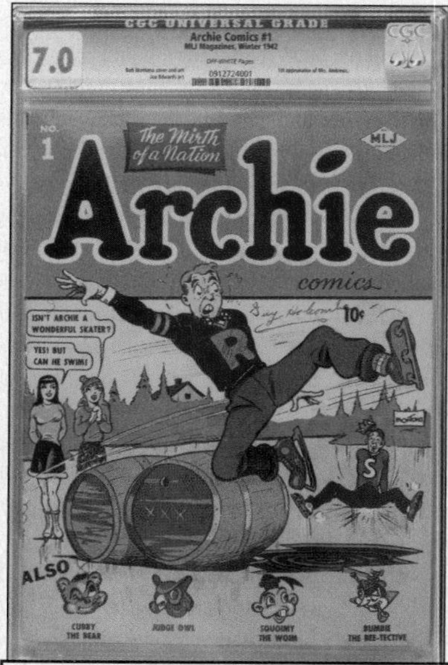

ARCHIE COMICS #1, CGC 7.0
Sold for $38,837 by Heritage
in August 2009. © AP

My Friend, Leonard Brown

By Richard D. Olson, Ph.D.

As we celebrate the 40th anniversary of this book, we asked noted historian and Overstreet Advisor Richard Olson to take a look back at his close friend Leonard Brown, one of the pioneering back-issue retailers.

Leonard Brown loved old comic books, especially the Disney books, and so did I. I guess that made it inevitable that we would finally meet as we both grew up in Long Beach, CA. 1959 marked the beginning of a true friendship that would last until his death to cancer in 2007. During those 48 years, I watched him change the face of the comic book hobby and business in Southern California.

He had already run a few ads selling comics before we met, but we soon became partners, had business cards printed indicating that we bought old comic books, and arranged for a friend to write a feature story on us in *The Long Beach Press-Telegram* describing how two young guys were operating a mail-order comic book business. Our efforts resulted in a great inventory – and in many customers. Collectors would also see our cards and call us, and were happy to pay up to $10.00 for special books they wanted. Probably the most famous collector in our area was Rick Durell, and we sold him many books.

Leonard was the first person I knew who stressed the importance of the book's condition. Even then, we charged a premium for books that looked like new, and our customers were happy to pay it.

Our most memorable time together occurred one hot summer night when we went to an older part of Los Angeles to meet a man who said he had three boxes of great old comics. Leonard rang the doorbell, the door opened, and a man about 6'2' and weighing 240 pounds was standing there stark naked with a half gallon bottle of wine in his hand. I will always remember him smiling and saying, "Won't you boys please come in?" I shook my head no, but Leonard pushed me through the door. We talked with him for a couple of hours until he finished his wine, and then bought his books. There were two boxes of early books like *Marvel Mystery Comics* #8-10, *All Winners Comics* #1, and *All Select Comics* #1, all in beautiful condition. The third box contained 10 mint copies of each of the first 23 issues of *MAD*.

Leonard began talking about opening a store. He realized we needed a place for people to come to sell us their books. By this time we were speculating on whether a comic would ever break the $100 barrier, and I didn't think the business had the kind of future I wanted. At this same time, he met Malcolm Willits, a noted Disney collector but also a movie memorabilia collector, and they decided to open the store while I opted out for graduate school.

Friday, March 5, 1965, was a champagne preview of Collectors Book Store by invitation only, with the store to open for business the following day. A dozen leading collectors, led by Rick Durell, were invited to attend. The store was at 1717 North Wilcox Avenue in Hollywood, very close to the famous intersection of Hollywood and Vine!

This was the first store in its own building dedicated to the sales of comic books, science fiction material, and movie memorabilia. They had to struggle to make a success of the store, but they made it because of their dedication and hard work. Malcolm drove all over the country on buying trips while Leonard made deals and sorted the material all night long to have it available for sale the next day. Leonard han-

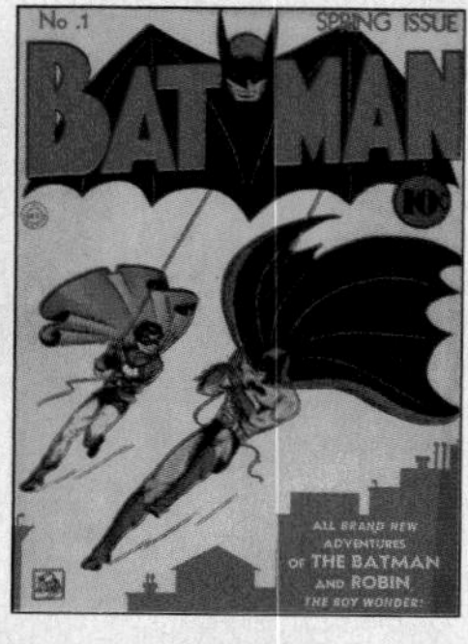

dled the comics and Malcolm operated the movie section. They both worked very long, hard hours to make it a success.

From the beginning, this was a store operated by collectors for collectors. If a stranger came in and said he wanted to invest in the first ten issues of Spider-Man, Leonard was likely to tell him that he didn't have any of those issues. But if a regular customer came in and wanted one of those same books, Leonard was likely to give him a reduced price, especially if he were young.

Publicity was the key to success. They loaded an old trunk with hundreds of great comics and then arranged to apparently buy it at an auction where the press just happened to be in attendance. Their good fortune and pictures of some of the books went out on the wire services and Collectors Bookstore began hearing from collectors all over America.

There were ups and downs, but eventually they were able to lease a giant bank building at 6763 Hollywood Blvd. I might note that they made good use of the vault and had it filled with great material. Once, when I returned home to visit my parents, I met Leonard at the store and we entered the vault and he suggested that I look at the Batman section. He had twelve copies of *Batman* #1 in beautiful shape. Another visit revealed two dozen perfect copies of the Donald Duck *March of Comics* #20 and #41 – and he said that they could have had more.

The store was now on firm financial ground and recognized as the greatest store of its type in the country. Just as importantly, they paved the way for other dedicated collectors to open stores.

My wife and I were on vacation at Niagara Falls when he called to tell me that he was dying from mesothelioma and asked if I could return for one last visit. It was an emotional reunion but we had a great week together, and it also gave me a chance to get to know his wonderful wife, Isis, better. While I was there, Malcolm was able to visit one afternoon and the three of us enjoyed a very special day together.

PERSPECTIVE ON HISTORY:

Stephen Fishler

By J.C. Vaughn

At the age of 6, Stephen Fishler discovered comics at Discount Books and Comics in Bensonhurst, Brooklyn. That discovery set him on the path that would lead him to being involved in the first and third million dollar comic book sales, though of course there were a few steps in between.

It started with weekly pilgrimages with his brother to Discount Books and Comics.

"The store's owner, Joe Yrbe, a walking encyclopedia of comic book history, was a concentration camp survivor who lost his entire family in the Holocaust and trusted no one. For some reason he took a liking to my brother and me, and week in and week out, he doled out that comic history, in little kid-sized, bite-sized pieces," Fishler said.

"By the age of 7, I could rattle off story title and characters for every Silver Age *Flash* issue below #200," he said. It wasn't long until he transformed from a new reader into a collector.

"I recall the exact moment I became an official comic book collector. It was 1974, but I remember as if it were yesterday. I was in Joe's comic store and asked him a question that had been rattling around in my 7-year old brain. 'Joe, why do you only have issues of Flash above issue 100? Why don't you have any of the issues below 100?' He then told me about an earlier title called *Flash Comics*, published in the 1940s (might as well have been the 1840s to a 7 year old) that starred Jay Garrick, the original Flash. I was bowled over. I was not sure about much in life but the one thing that I did know was that I was put on this earth in order to own every issue of *Flash Comics*. Indiana Jones had his Ark. I had *Flash Comics*. And yes, I still have my complete set of *Flash Comics*. #77 was the first issue of *Flash Comics* I ever bought and #35 was the last issue I needed to complete the run."

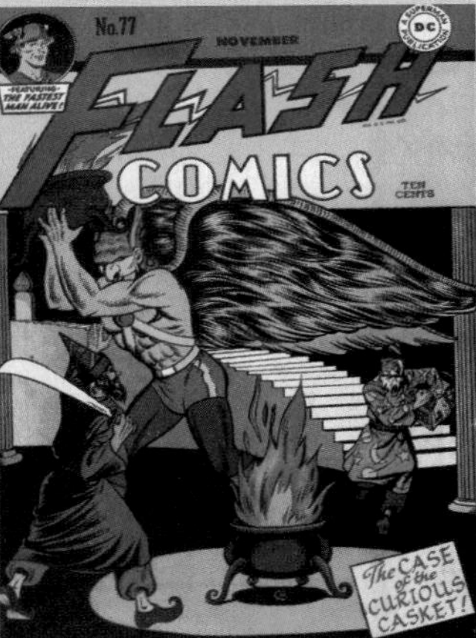

Attending early Creation and Seuling conventions, he was able to amass what he calls "a rather impressive collection of vintage comics" in a short period. This collection would eventually become the core of his inventory when he started Metropolis Collectibles in 1984, but he believes he was actually a dealer by the time he was eight.

One early impression carried by those who were in the business at the time was of a rather young Stephen Fishler showing up in a suit, with a briefcase, to buy and sell comics. What made him take the business seriously at a young age?

"I loved the thrill of the hunt. The acquisition of great comic books is something that I immensely enjoyed and I took it very seriously. Dealers were set up at shows in order to sell books and make money. And I was there to buy comics at levels that I felt were a good value. In countless cases, I would walk away with a dealer's entire inventory and that dealer would call it a very successful day. You could call it a win-win situation all around. Having said that, it was not really about making money, it was about enjoying and acquiring these relics of the past. It is an appreciation that I fear some collectors today do not take the time to enjoy," he said.

He said that dealing in comics has prevented him from ever holding an actual job.

"I can honestly say that comic dealing has prevented me from ever holding an actual job. I have never gone on a job interview. I have never had a resume. Simply stated, owning my own business put my fate squarely in my own hands, which is exactly as I liked it," he said.

The aspect of not having a "real job" hasn't prevented him from taking the business of comics seriously. In fact, he is frequently ready with observations about the business side of things, just as he is with points of comic book history.

"The publication of the first *Overstreet Guide* set in motion a course that slowly but surely established a solid foundation for comic books as a collectible commodity. Over the years, people have looked at vintage comic books as a source of steady price appreciation, which in turn has brought in consistent waves of buyers into the market year in and year out," he said.

10 Point Grading Scale

10.0	GM	Gem Mint
9.9	MT	Mint
9.8	NM/MT	Near Mint/Mint
9.6	NM+	Near Mint+
9.4	NM	Near Mint
9.2	NM-	Near Mint-
9.0	VF/NM	Very Fine/Near Mint
8.5	VF+	Very Fine+
8.0	VF	Very Fine
7.5	VF-	Very Fine-
7.0	FN/VF	Fine/Very Fine
6.5	FN+	Fine+
6.0	FN	Fine
5.5	FN-	Fine-
5.0	VG/FN	Very Good/Fine
4.5	VG+	Very Good+
4.0	VG	Very Good
3.5	VG-	Very Good-
3.0	GD/VG	Good/Very Good
2.5	GD+	Good+
2.0	GD	Good
1.8	GD-	Good-
1.5	FR/GD	Fair/Good
1.0	FR	Fair
0.5	PR	Poor

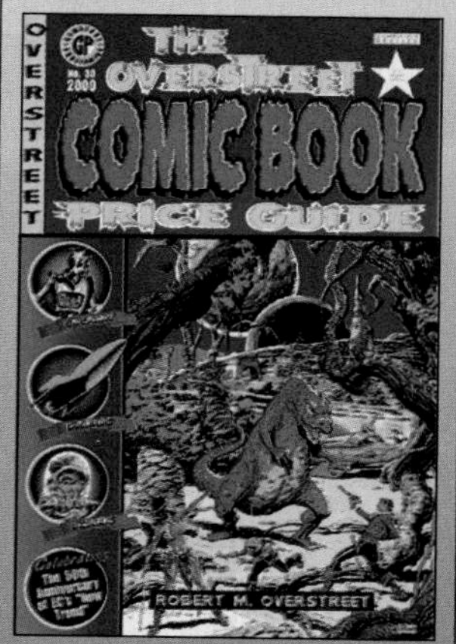

A little over a decade ago, he championed moving from the old, 100-point grading system to the 10-point system that has become commonly accepted. At that point Metropolis Collectibles had used a 42-point scale for many years, while the original edition of *The Overstreet Comic Book Grading Guide* used a 100-point system, which was difficult for many to understand.

Fishler promoted the 10-point system to *Guide* publisher and author Robert M. Overstreet, and then to others. Meetings were held with other Overstreet Advisors and eventually Comics Guaranty (CGC), which was then in its infancy.

"It would be difficult to imagine that the adoption of the 10-point system in *The Overstreet Comic Book Price Guide* #30 would have come about as it did without Stephen Fishler's drive," Overstreet said. "The acceptance of it has meant a lot to the marketplace."

Fishler believes that collectors' conversion to using the number grade without relying on the traditional nomenclature grades is a testament to this. Many would assert that this has aided in the sustained improvement of liquidity for rare, vintage, high-end comics.

Of course people said the Titanic was unsinkable and that housing prices never would come down. Fishler, though, said he sees the strong performance continuing.

"The supply of investment grade comic books will forever be limited. And to a reasonable extent, the demand will always be consistent and strong. Couple that with a genuine love of comic history that the average collector possesses, and the fact that you can't say that about every collectible category," he said.

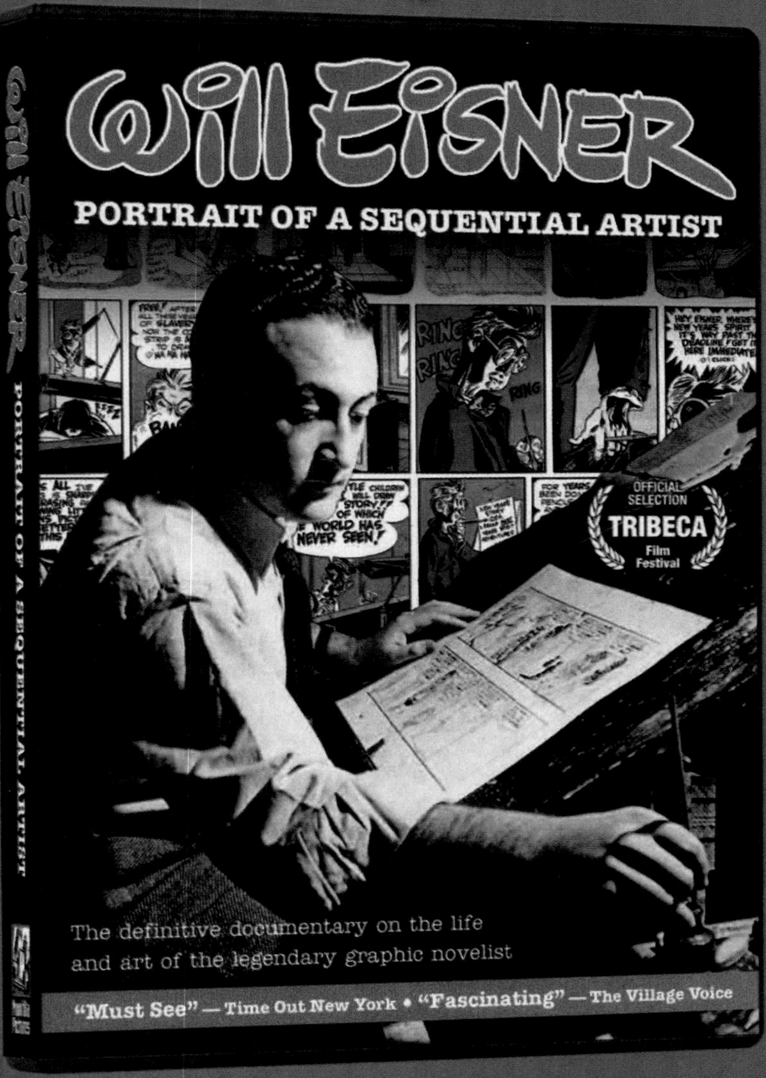

GEPPI'S ENTERTAINMENT MUSEUM PRESENTS

The OVERSTREET HALL OF FAME

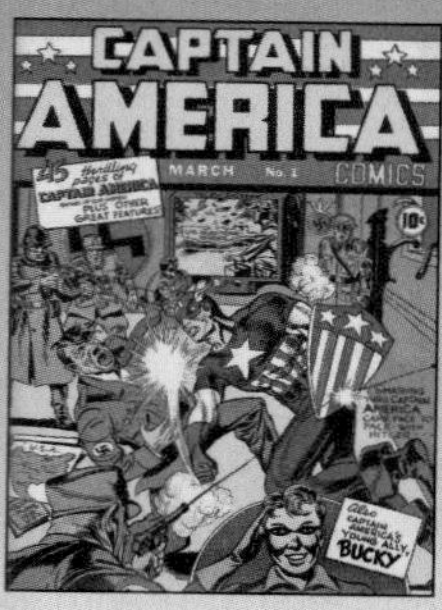

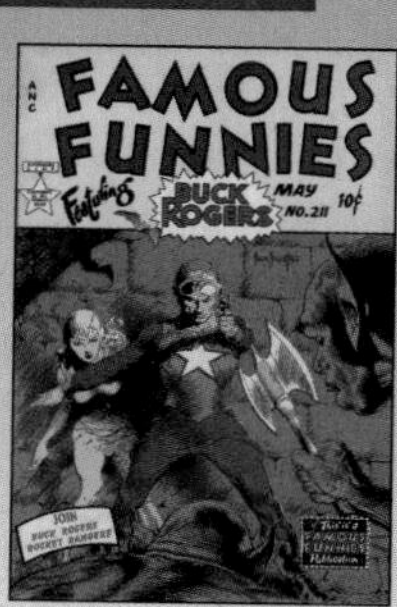

The Overstreet Hall of Fame was conceived to single out individuals who have made great contributions to the comic book arts. This includes writers, artists, editors, publishers and others who have plied their craft in insightful and meaningful ways.

While such evaluations are inherently subjective, they also serve to aid in reflecting upon those who shaped the experience of reading comic books over the years. This year's class of inductees begins on this next page. First, though, we offer a list of the previous inductees:

Class of 2006
Murphy Anderson
Jim Aparo
Jim Lee
Mac Raboy

Class of 2007
Dave Cockrum
Steve Ditko
Bruce Hamilton
Martin Nodell
George Pérez
Jim Shooter
Dave Stevens
Alex Toth
Michael Turner

Class of 2008
Carl Barks
Will Eisner
Al Feldstein
Harvey Kurtzman
Stan Lee
Marshall Rogers
John Romita, Sr.
John Romita, Jr.
Julius Schwartz
Mike Wieringo

Class of 2009
Neal Adams
Matt Baker
Chris Claremont
Palmer Cox
Bill Everett
Frank Frazetta
Neil Gaiman
William M. Gaines
Carmine Infantino
Jack Kirby
Joe Kubert
Paul Levitz
Russ Manning
Todd McFarlane
Don Rosa
John Severin
Joe Simon
Al Williamson

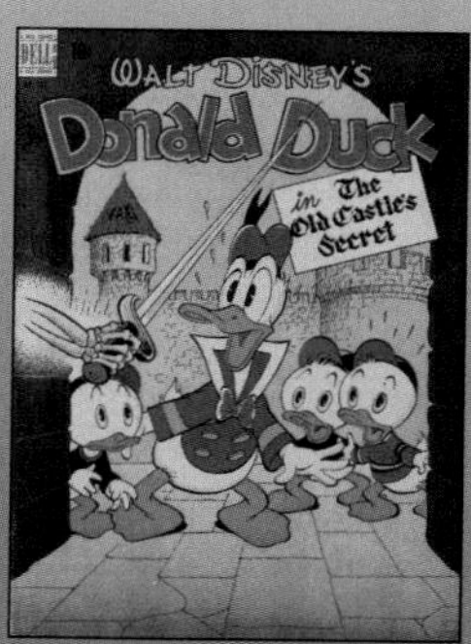

HALL OF FAME

Who knew that all those gutters could be so funny? Sergio Aragonés (1937-) never let panel borders get in the way of telling quick and delightful comic stories, and his margin cartoons ("marginals") in the pages of *MAD Magazine* not only raised doodling to a high art but packed the periodical with laughs in every conceivable corner. Thanks to the marginals and his "A *Mad* Look At..." features, Aragonés - often called "The World's Fastest Cartoonist" - has been a beloved fixture of the magazine since 1963. In 1982 he also introduced us to *Groo*, a lovable and seriously inept barbarian that has an insatiable love of cheese dip and an unerring knack for getting into, or causing, trouble. In all of his work, Aragonés' melodic, hyper-detailed style is instantly recognizable (as is his trademark moustache), and his joy in sharing humor with the world is evident in every line.

- Dr. Arnold T. Blumberg

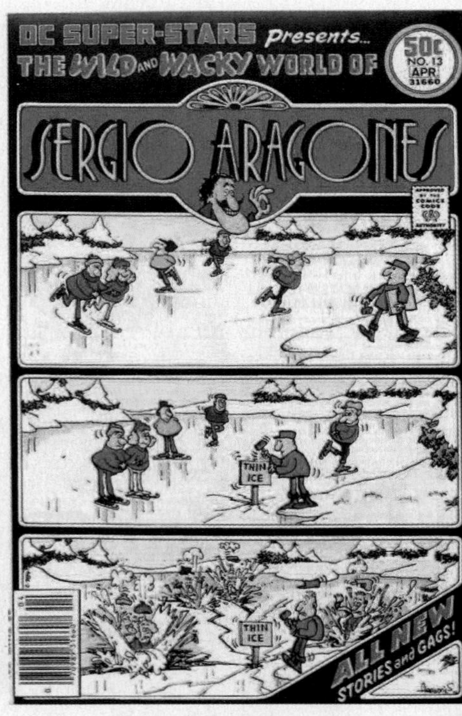

DC SUPER-STARS #13
March-April 1977. © DC

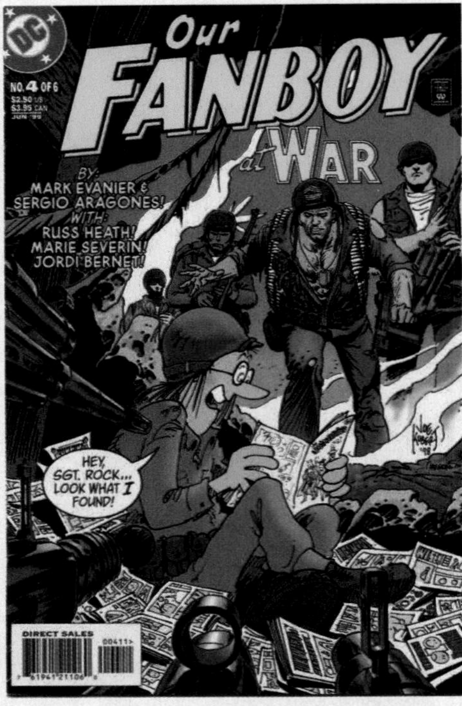

FANBOY #4
June 1999. © Horsefeathers, Inc. & DC

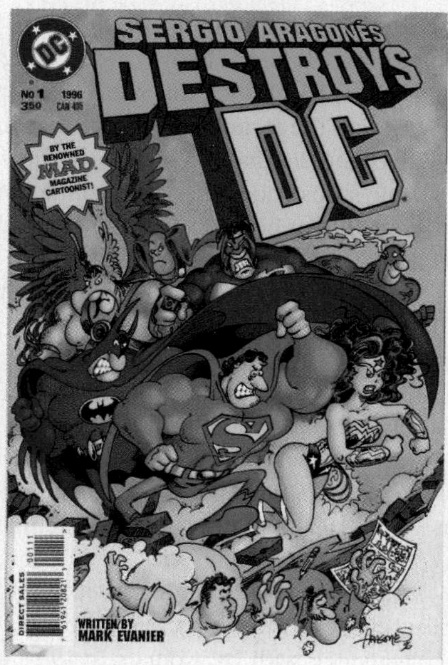

SERGIO ARAGONÉS DESTROYS DC #1
June 1996. © DC

SERGIO ARAGONÉS MASSACRES MARVEL #1
June 1996. © MAR

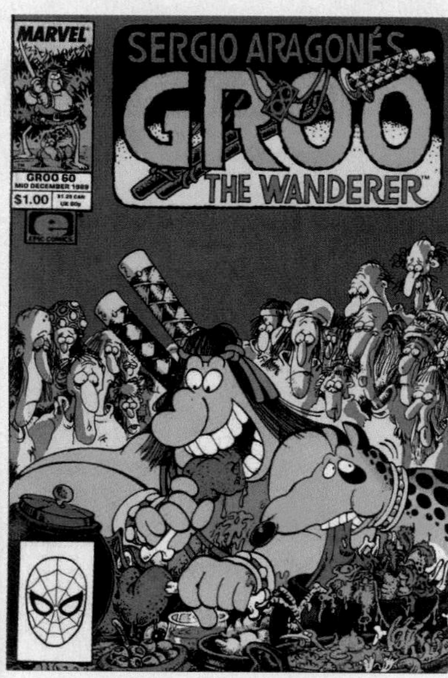

SERGIO ARAGONÉS
GROO THE WANDERER #60
December 1989. © Sergio Aragonés

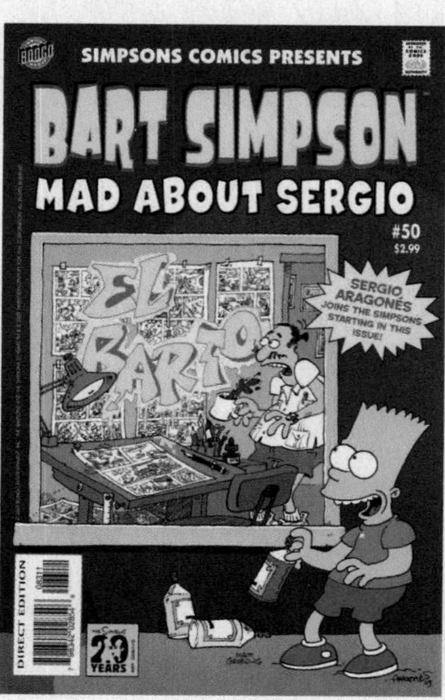

SIMPSON COMICS PRESENTS
BART SIMPSON COMICS #50
2009. © Bongo

ALL-AMERICAN COMICS #1
April 1939. © DC

Pioneer, publisher, promoter and advocate Maxwell Charles Gaines is known for creating the idea in 1933 of repackaging the Sunday newspaper comic strip into the format we recognize as modern comic books and distributing them to the newsstand. Comic strips had been collected into books since the 1800s, but he felt by folding a full tabloid page of eight or sixteen pages down twice to produce a 32-page or a 64-page comic magazine that it could be sold for 10¢, even during the Great Depression.

He tried first with *Funnies On Parade*, then with *Famous Funnies, A Carnival of Comics*, both done as promotional comics. *Famous Funnies*, Series 1, was the following step. The next issue, also #1, dated July, 1934 was distributed as the first newsstand comic magazine. The series lasted until 1955.

In 1938 Gaines (with Jack Liebowitz) started All-American Publications, which was a separate company co-marketed with DC Comics. In 1944, DC bought out Gaines, who then started a new line, Educational Comics (EC). He died in a boating accident in 1947.

-Robert M. Overstreet

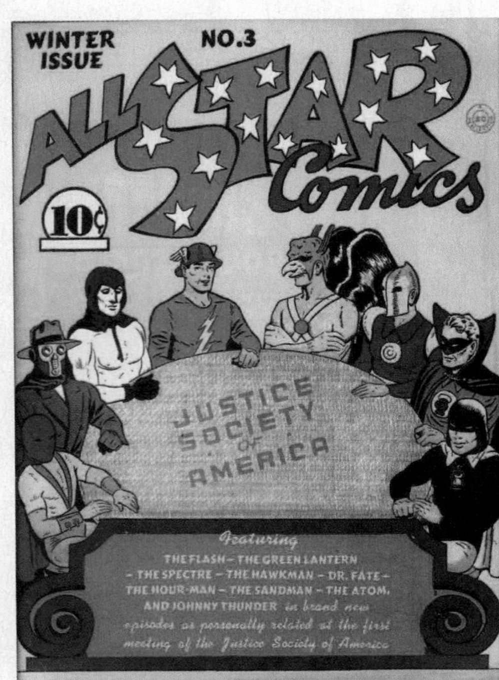

ALL STAR COMICS #3
Winter 1940. © DC

FAMOUS FUNNIES #1
July 1934. © EAS

FLASH COMICS #1
January 1940. © DC

FUNNIES ON PARADE
1933. © EAS

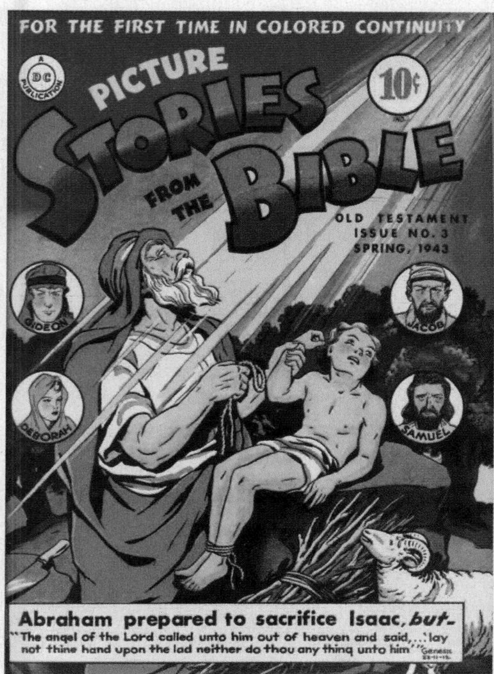

PICTURE STORIES FROM THE BIBLE #3
Spring 1943. © DC

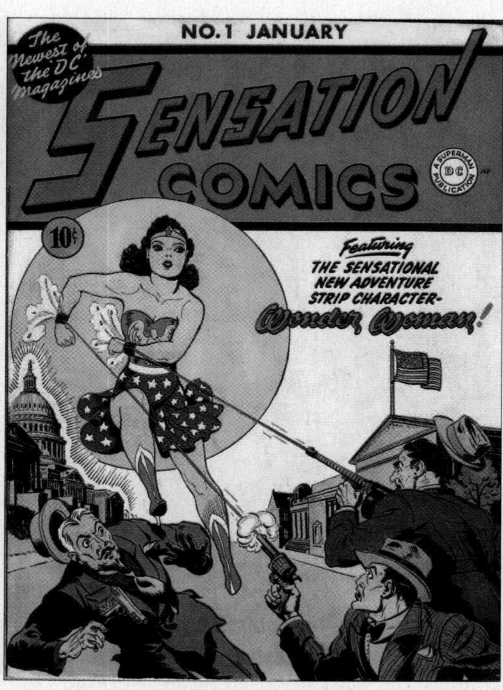

SENSATION COMICS #1
January 1942. © DC

Ask the average fan to name the greatest creators in the history of comics and the name Archie Goodwin will not leap to the minds of many, because so much of Archie's brilliant work was behind the scenes or flew under the mainstream radar. But ask the creators with whom he worked! Ask other all-time great writers, artists, editors and creators! Gather the elders, the best of the best and ask them! His name will be among the first mentioned. Archie Goodwin was an amazing writer with outstanding story sense, penetrating insight, a gift for dialogue, an effortless knack for character, a flair for drama and utter mastery of the art of delivering the payoff. His sheer creativity ranks with the best ever. He was an all-time great editor and teacher. He made everyone he worked with better. On top of that, Archie Goodwin was a fine, wonderful, noble and honorable soul, loved and respected by everyone because he deserved it. This industry may never see his like again. How sad. He is desperately missed.
- Jim Shooter

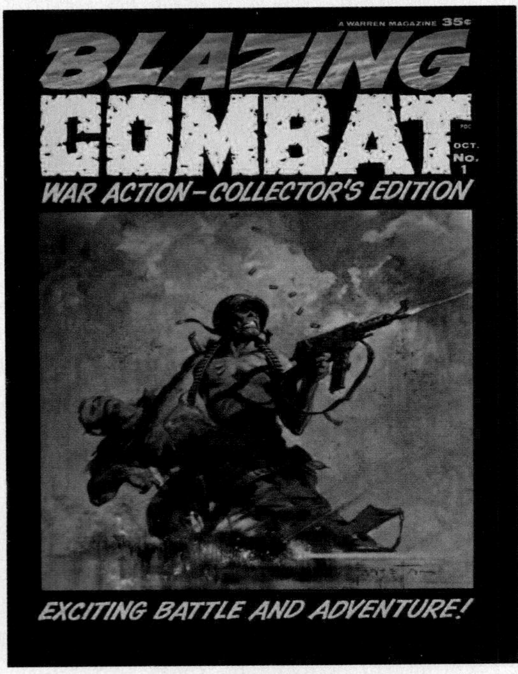

BLAZING COMBAT #1
October 1965. © WP

CREEPY #17
October 1967. © WP

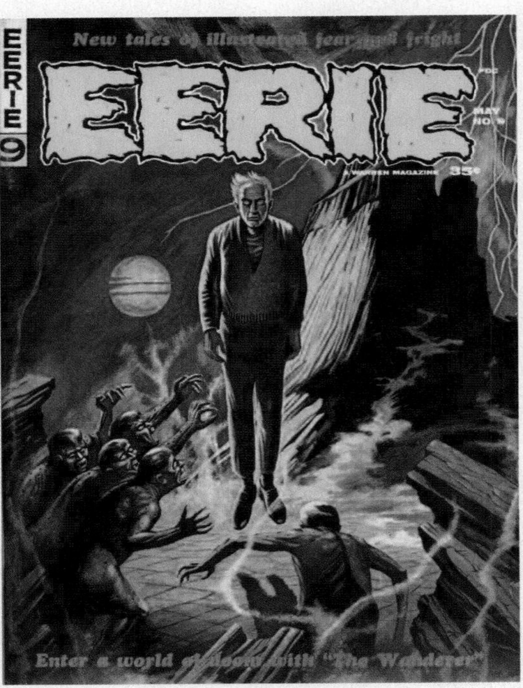

EERIE #9
May 1967. © WP

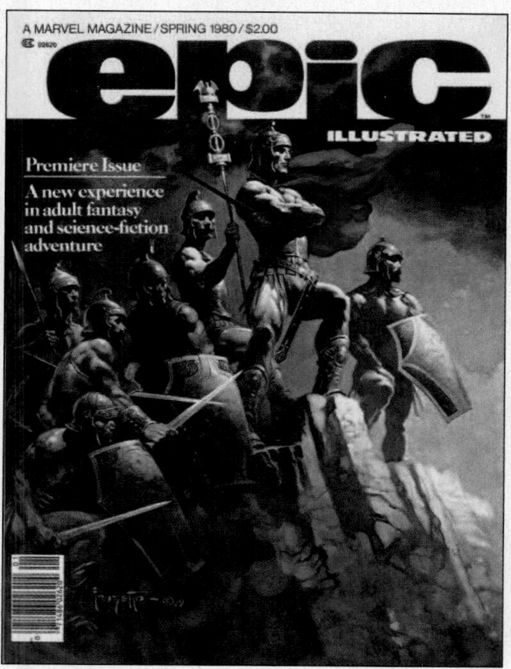

EPIC ILLUSTRATED #1
Spring 1980. © MAR

MANHUNTER #1
1984. © DC

STAR WARS HARDCOVER COLLECTION
Reprints of newspaper strips. 1991. © Lucasfilm

VAMPIRELLA #100
October 1981. © WP

HALL OF FAME

It's a daunting task to bring the world of dreams to vivid, waking life, but Winsor McCay (1867-1934) managed to do that for newspaper readers every week through his landmark artistic achievements, the ground-breaking strips *Dreams of a Rarebit Fiend* and *Little Nemo in Slumberland*. Chronicling the night-time adventures of a little boy as he navigated a wonderland of imagination from 1905-1927, McCay's *Nemo* was a powerful exploration of childlike discovery and lush, expressive art. As an animator, McCay was a pioneer that introduced the world to *Gertie the Dinosaur* in 1914 and employed vaudevillian techniques to blend live-action and animation long before Roger Rabbit was born. His work in comic strips and cartoons inspired the likes of Walt Disney, Bill Watterson, Maurice Sendak and many more. It is absolutely fair to say that without McCay, the world of comic characters as we know it would simply not exist.
- ATB

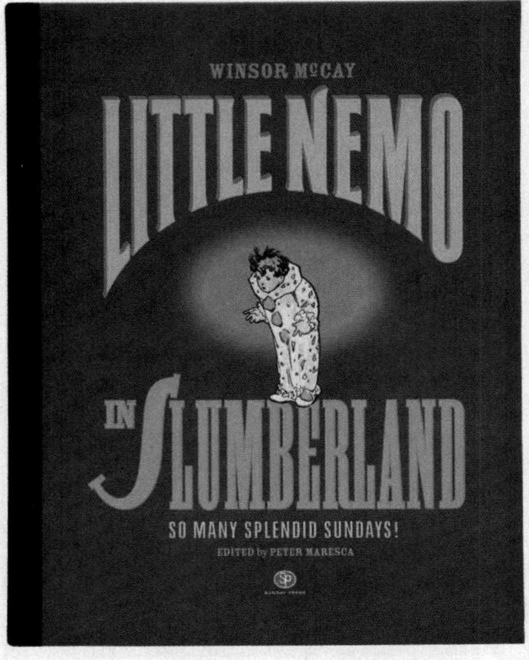

LITTLE NEMO IN SLUMBERLAND
SO MANY SPLENDID SUNDAYS!
2005. © Sunday Press

GERTIE THE DINOSAUR
Animation drawing. 1914.

DREAM OF THE RAREBIT FIEND
Newspaper strip panels. 1905. © NY Herald Tribune

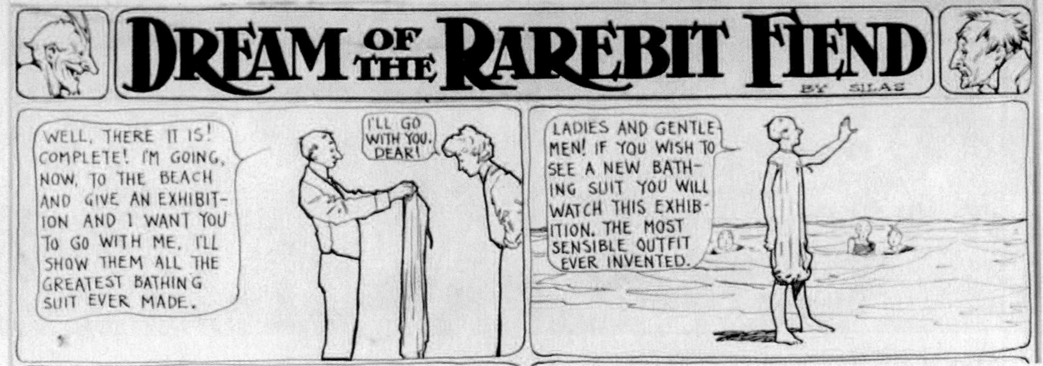

LITTLE NEMO IN SLUMBERLAND
Undated print and bisque statues from 1914.

LITTLE SAMMY SNEEZE
December 1905. © NY Herald Co.

Having worked for both Marvel and DC on titles like *Daredevil*, *Incredible Hulk*, *Batman: A Death in the Family* and *Gotham by Gaslight* (which launched DC's "Elseworlds" line), artist Mike Mignola (1962-) blended his love of Lovecraft-like horror and pulp/B-movie monster mashes, tinkering at his table like a latter-day Frankenstein until the bulky, huge-handed, nearly hornless, bright red paranormal crusader known as Hellboy leapt from the pages of Dark Horse Comics in 1994. Broadening his accomplishments to include scripting many of Hellboy's tales, Mignola's distinctive artistic style mixed Jack Kirby-like intensity with a darker layer of expressionistic shadow and shape. Mignola has also brought his artistic eye to Hollywood with conceptual work on Coppola's *Bram Stoker's Dracula* and the forthcoming *Lord of the Rings* prequel, *The Hobbit*. He also had the rare opportunity to help usher his own creation onto the silver screen via Guillermo del Toro's two *Hellboy* feature films.
- ATB

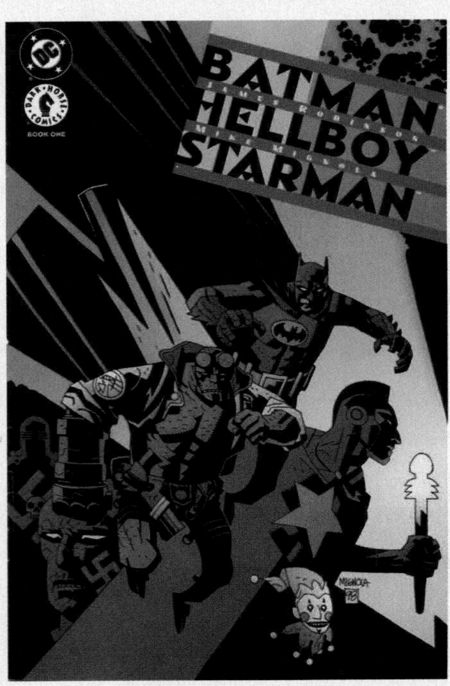

BATMAN/HELLBOY/STARMAN #1
January 1999. © DC, DH & Mike Mignola

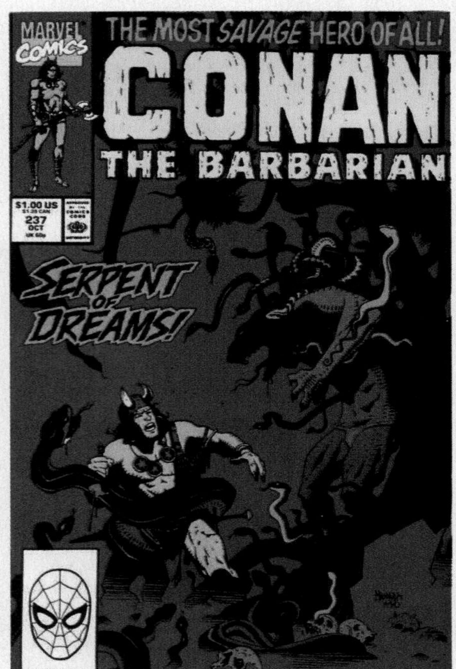

CONAN THE BARBARIAN #237
October 1990. © Conan Properites Inc.

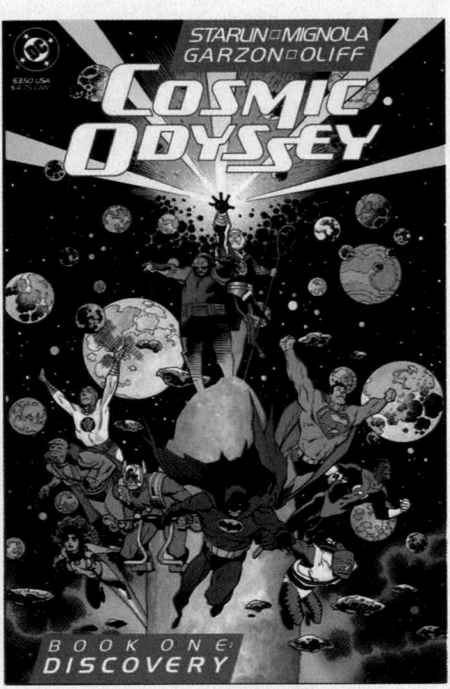

COSMIC ODYSSEY #1
1988. © DC

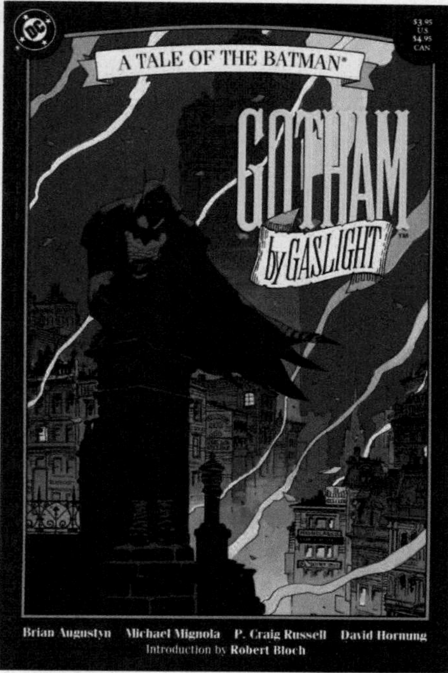

GOTHAM BY GASLIGHT #1
1989. © DC

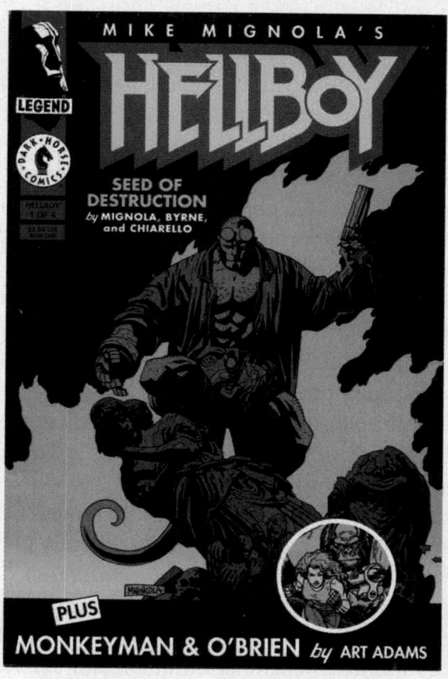

HELLBOY: SEED OF DESTRUCTION#1
March 1994. © Mike Mignola

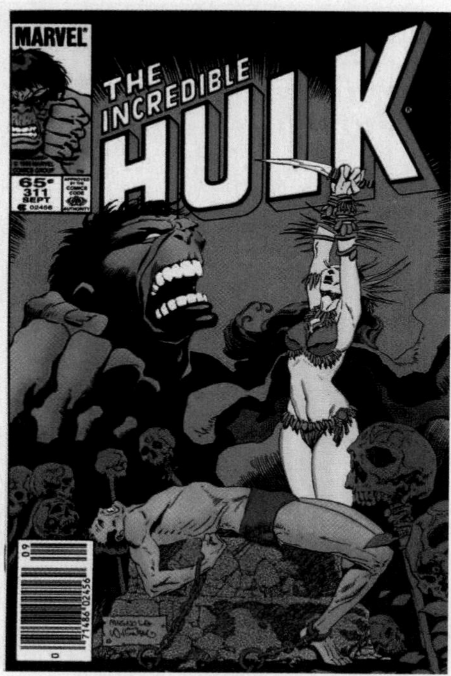

INCREDIBLE HULK #311
September 1985. © MAR

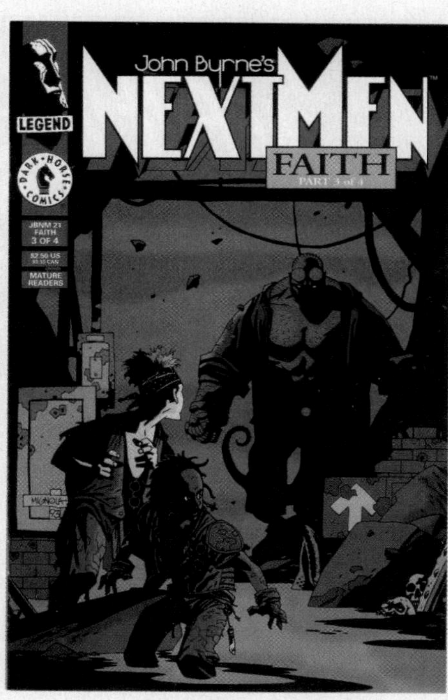

JOHN BYRNE'S NEXT MEN #21
December 1993. © John Byrne & Mike Mignola

After illustrating a few stories for Gold Key's *The Twilight Zone* and DC's *Weird War Tales* and *Unknown Soldier*, and following a story in Marvel's *John Carter: Warlord of Mars* #18, Frank Miller landed a two-part fill-in job on *Peter Parker, the Spectacular Spider-Man* #27-28, which guest-starred Daredevil, a character who he would define and which in return would define his early success.

Miller took over as regular artist on *Daredevil* #158. By the time Elektra was featured on the cover of *Daredevil* #168, he was writing it as well. With inker Klaus Janson, he turned it into one of Marvel's most popular titles.

He also illustrated the first *Wolverine* mini-series, unleashed *Ronin*, and then turned his attention to Bruce Wayne's future with *Batman: The Dark Knight Returns,* which became a perennial best seller in its collected edition. Subsequently he wrote another run on *Daredevil* and *Batman: Year One*, both with artist David Mazzuccheli, before turning creator-owned projects such as *Sin City* and *300*. He continues to create in both film and comics.
- J.C. Vaughn

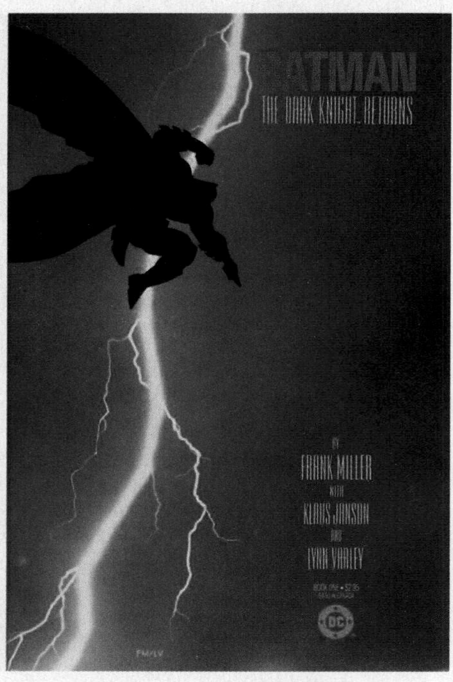

BATMAN THE DARK KNIGHT RETURNS #1
March 1986. © DC

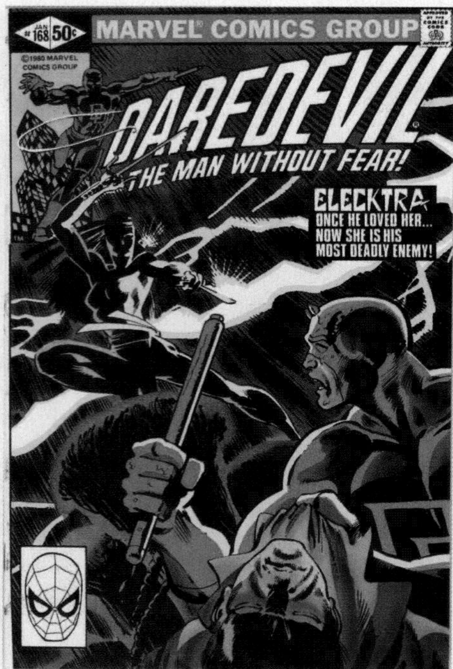

DAREDEVIL #169
January 1981. © MAR

RONIN #4
January 1984. © DC

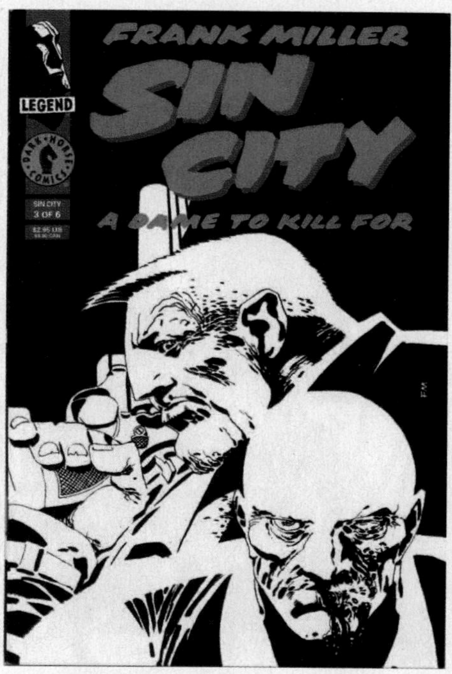

SIN CITY: A DAME TO KILL FOR #3
February 1994. © Frank Miller

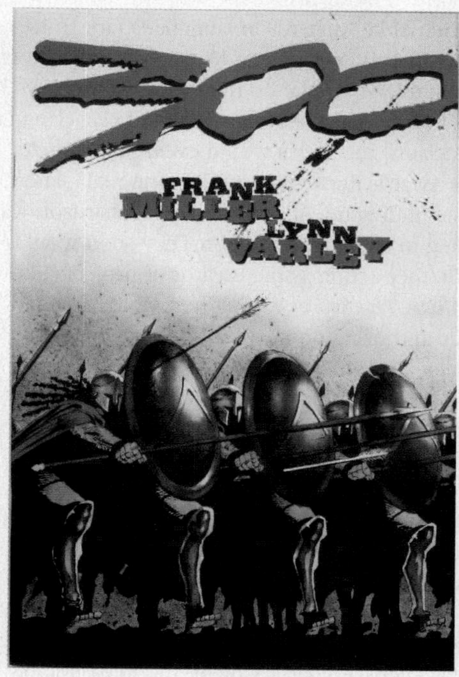

300 #1
May 1998. © Frank Miller

THE TWILIGHT ZONE #84
June 1978. © Cayuga Prods.

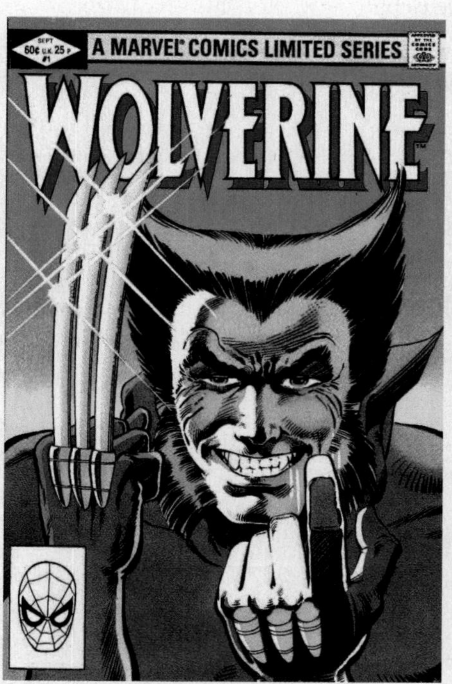

WOLVERINE #1
Mini-series. September 1982. © MAR

When Mike Richardson launched Dark Horse Comics in 1986 with *Dark Horse Presents* #1, very few could have predicted the events of the next 24 years. Even when *Concrete* #1 started garnering critical acclaim (the series would eventually win 26 Eisner Awards during its run), no one really knew what an independent powerhouse Richardson was building in Milwaukie, Oregon. They soon would.

Whether acting as the creator of projects like *The Mask*, *The Secret*, *Living with the Dead*, and *Cut*, co-authoring non-fiction books such as *Comics Between the Panels* and *Blast Off!*, developing comic book-inspired films, or championing the work of other creators, he said he founded the company with the goal of establishing an ideal atmosphere for creative professionals.

Over time, creators such as Frank Miller, Geoff Darrow, Dave Gibbons, Stan Sakai, Sergio Aragonés, Arthur Adams, Harlan Ellison, Matt Wagner, Mike Allred, Mike Mignola, Mike Baron, Steve Rude, Jim Shooter, and Dave Stevens, and licensed properties such as Aliens, Predator, Conan, and most notably Star Wars have made their home at Richardson's company with dazzling results.
- Steve Geppi

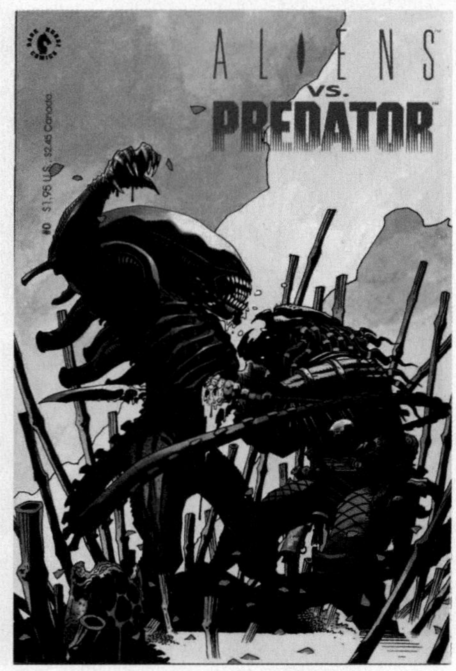

ALIENS VS. PREDATOR #0.
July 1990. © 20th Century Fox

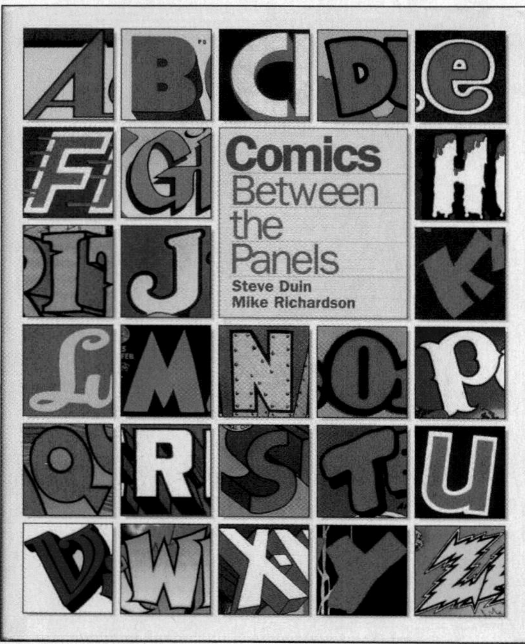

COMICS BETWEEN THE PANELS
1998. © Duin & Richardson

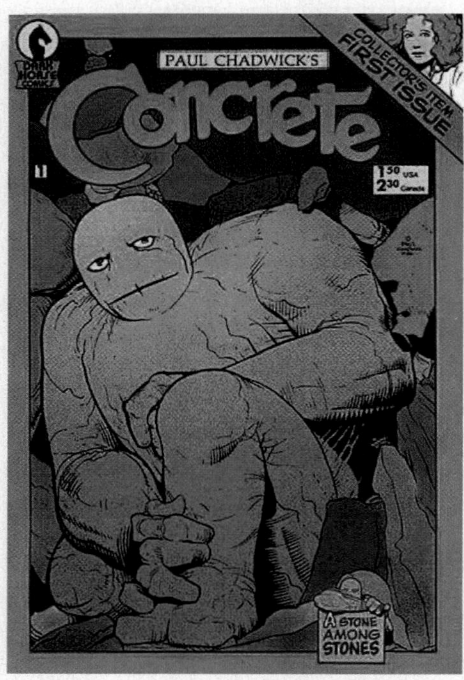

CONCRETE #1
March 1987. © Paul Chadwick

DARK HORSE PRESENTS #1
July 1986. © DH

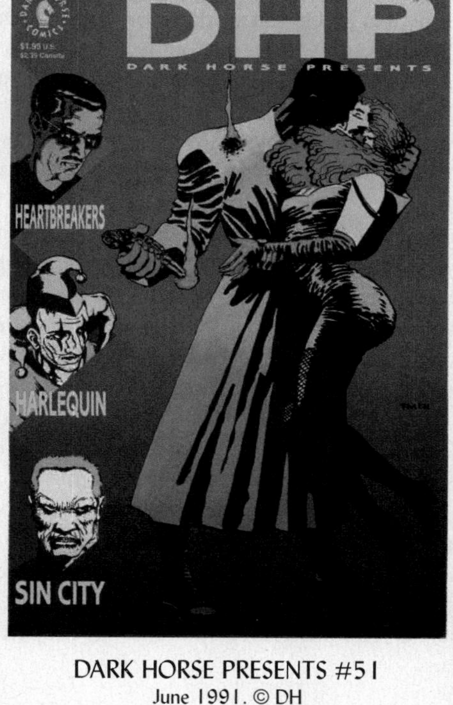

DARK HORSE PRESENTS #51
June 1991. © DH

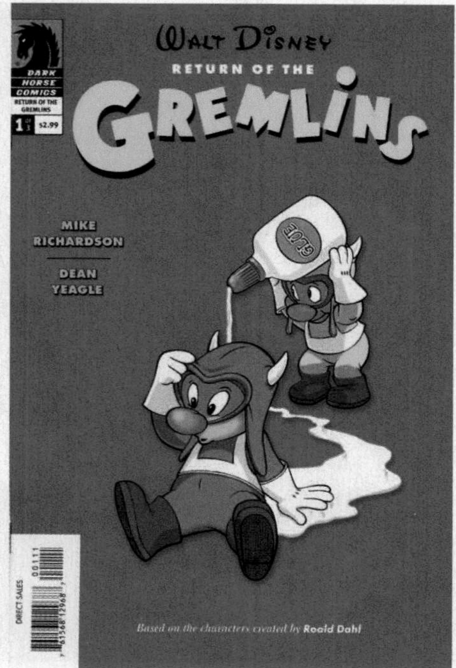

RETURN OF THE GREMLINS #1
March 2008. © DIS

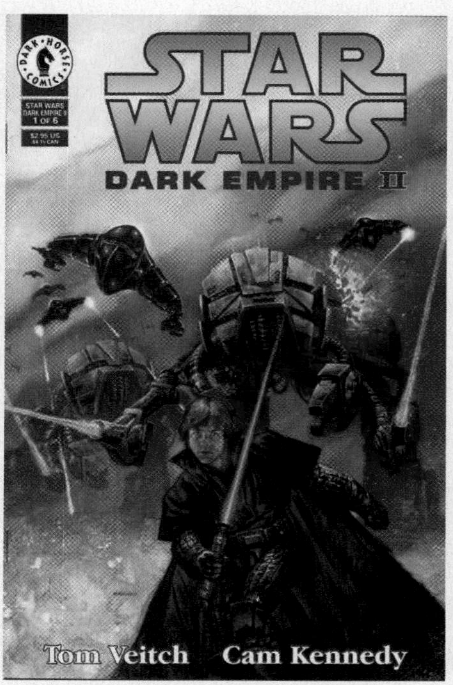

STAR WARS DARK EMPIRE II #1
December 1994. © Lucasfilm

Jerry Robinson was a Columbia University student when he met and began working for Batman creator Bob Kane in 1939. He started out working on backgrounds and lettering, teamed with Kane and writer Bill Finger. He quickly became the main inker for the character. When Kane and Finger discussed adding a sidekick for Batman while preparing for *Detective Comics* #38, Robinson suggested Robin, drawing inspiration from N.C. Wyeth's illustration of Robin Hood. In time for *Batman* #1, he (along with Finger) is unofficially credited with creating the Joker as well.

After working for Kane, then on staff at DC and illustrating comic books for others, Robinson had a highly successful career in newspaper comic strips and editorial cartooning. He served as President of the National Cartoonists Society and the Association of American Editorial Cartoonists, founded the Cartoonists & Writers Syndicate. He, along with Neal Adams and others, championed the cause of Superman creators Jerry Siegel and Joe Shuster receiving royalties for their creation.

In 1999, Robinson created the manga property Astra.

- JCV

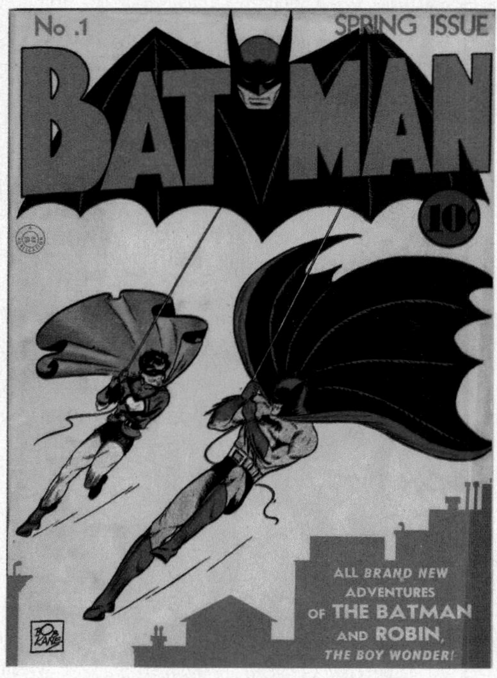

BATMAN #1
Spring 1940. © DC

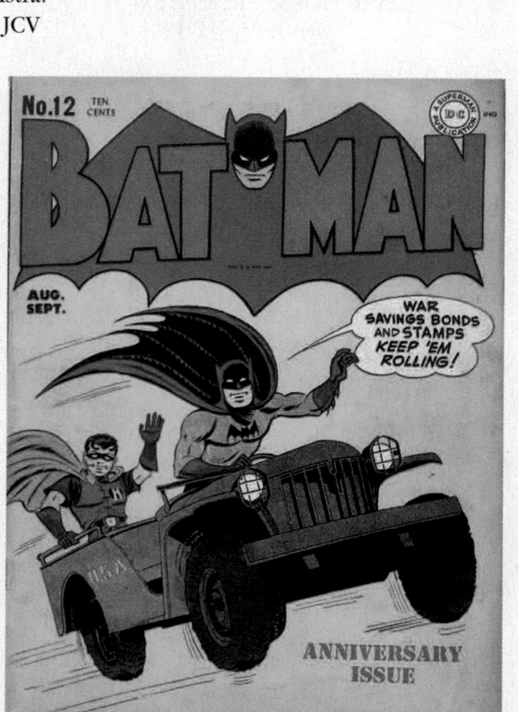

BATMAN #12
August-September 1942. © DC

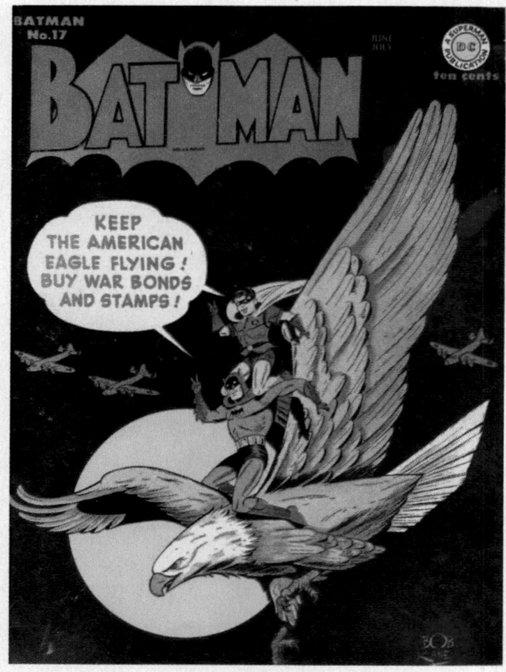

BATMAN #17
June-July 1943. © DC

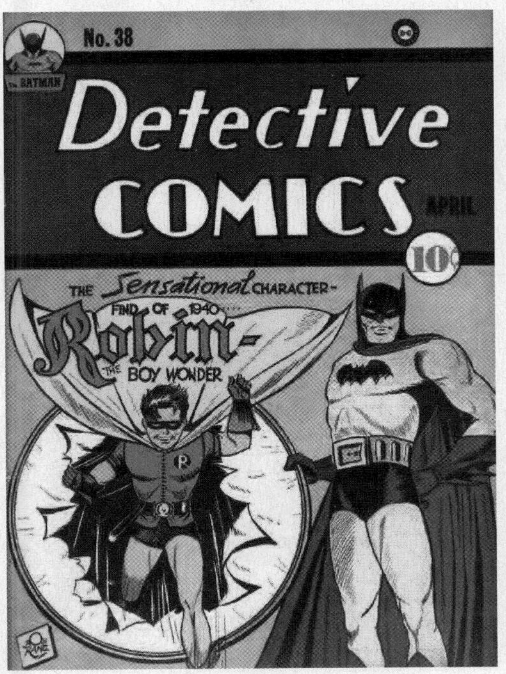

DETECTIVE COMICS #38
April 1940. © DC

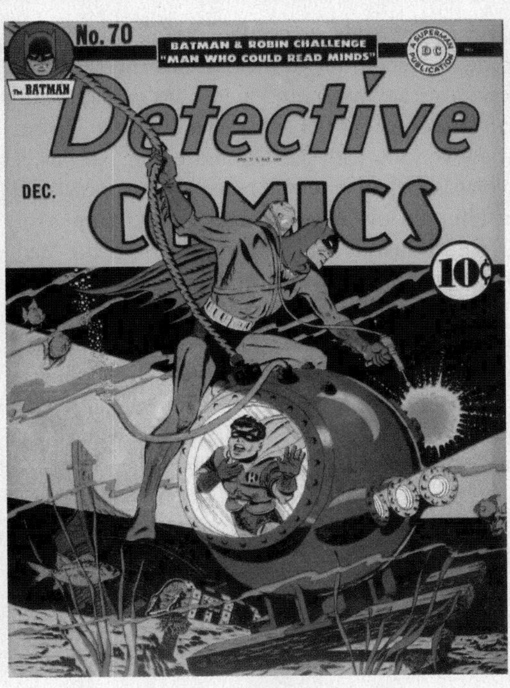

DETECTIVE COMICS #70
December 1942. © DC

DETECTIVE COMICS #76
June 1943. © DC

GREEN HORNET COMICS #29
March 1946. © HARV

By the time his greatest creation had become a worldwide sensation in the late '30s and early '40s, he was already beginning to lose his eyesight, but artist Joe Shuster (1914-1992) had vision to spare when working with partner and writer Jerry Siegel to craft the quintessential hero - Superman. Based on a mutual love of science fiction and pulp adventure shared by the Cleveland teens, the Man of Steel debuted in 1938 in *Action Comics* #1 (DC) with Shuster's hand shaping the dynamic look that would remain more or less intact for the next 70 years. Although marginalized by the industry in later years, Shuster eventually earned permanent credit for his role in Superman's creation thanks to a crusade spearheaded by the likes of industry star Neal Adams. Today every Superman comic and production still proclaims: "Superman created by Jerry Siegel and Joe Shuster." For a man that saw the future clearly even through fading sight, there is no better epitaph.
- ATB

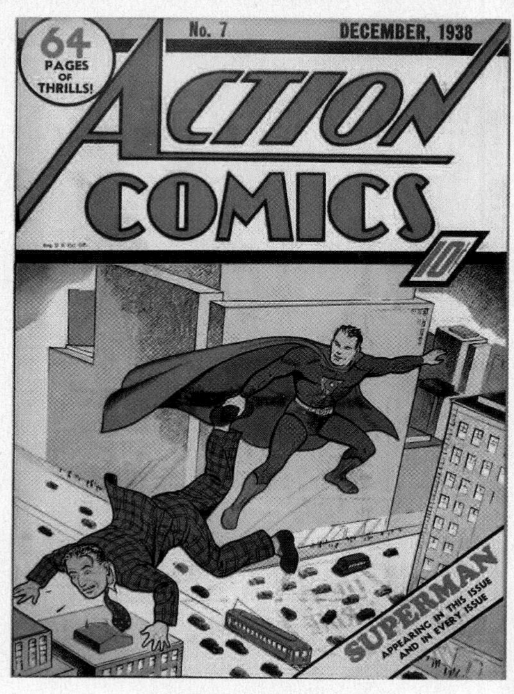

ACTION COMICS #7
December 1938. © DC

SUPERMAN NEWSPAPER PAGE
1941. © DC

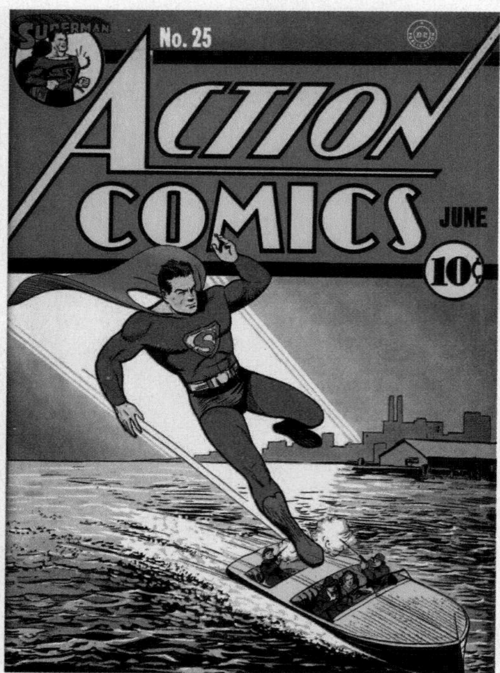

ACTION COMICS #25
June 1940. © DC

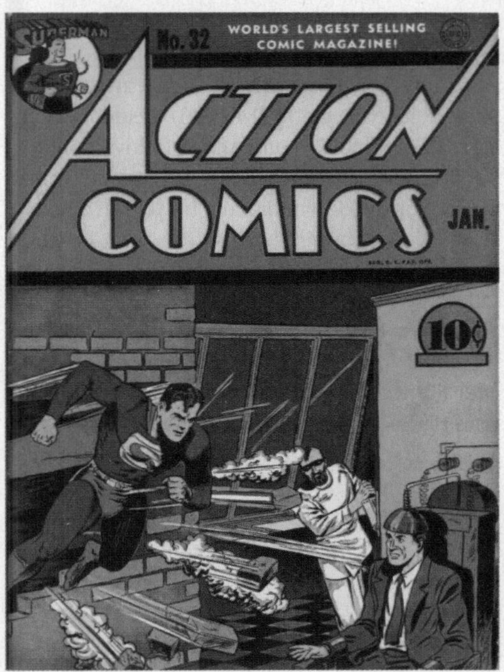

ACTION COMICS #32
January 1941. © DC

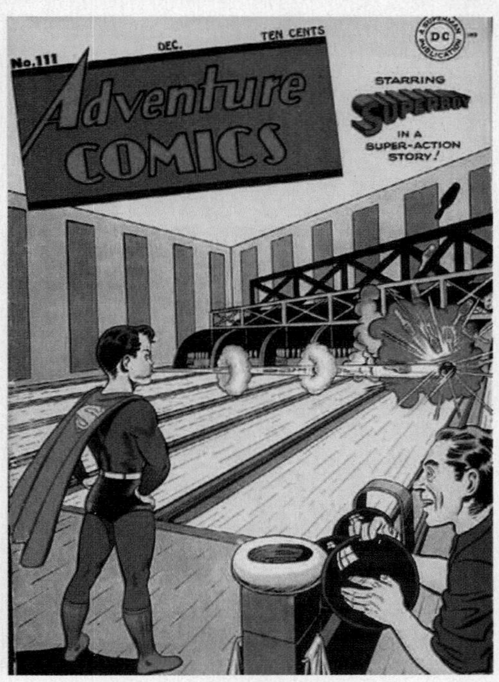

ADVENTURE COMICS #111
December 1946. © DC

SUPERMAN #1
Summer 1939. © DC

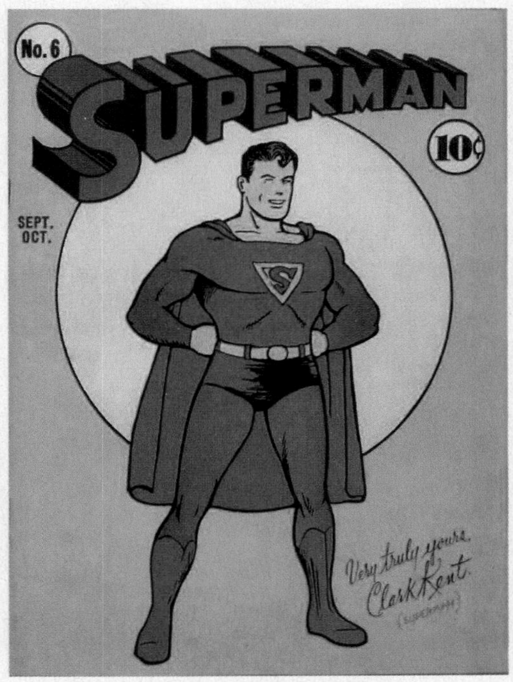

SUPERMAN #6
September-October 1940. © DC

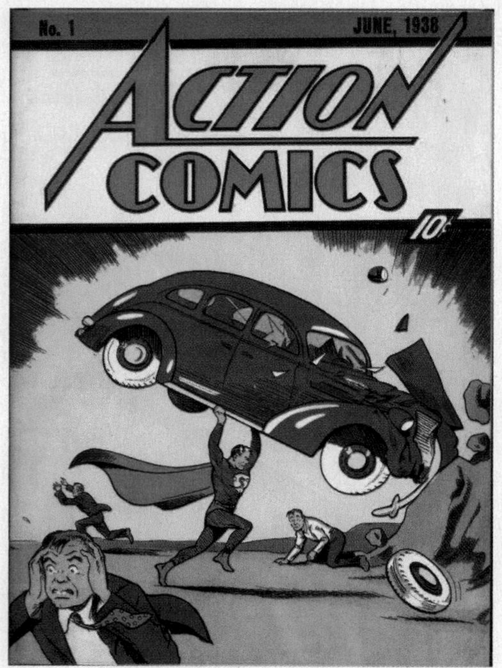

ACTION COMICS #1
June 1938. © DC

He was a Jewish kid from Cleveland with big dreams and a knack for writing high-flying adventure. Together with his friend, artist Joe Shuster, Jerry Siegel (1914-1996) created a character that would become the definitive comic book superhero for the next 70 years. Superman was a worldwide multimedia hit within a few years of his debut in *Action Comics* #1 in 1938, and although Siegel also created the creepy crusader known as the Spectre, it was the Man of Tomorrow that would cement Siegel's name in the annals of pop culture. Sadly, much of Siegel's later life was consumed more with legal battles than flights of fantasy as he (and later his family) fought to wrest control of his super-successful creations from DC. The ongoing courtroom saga has often obscured Siegel's accomplishments as one of the architects of the Golden Age and our modern mythology.
- ATB

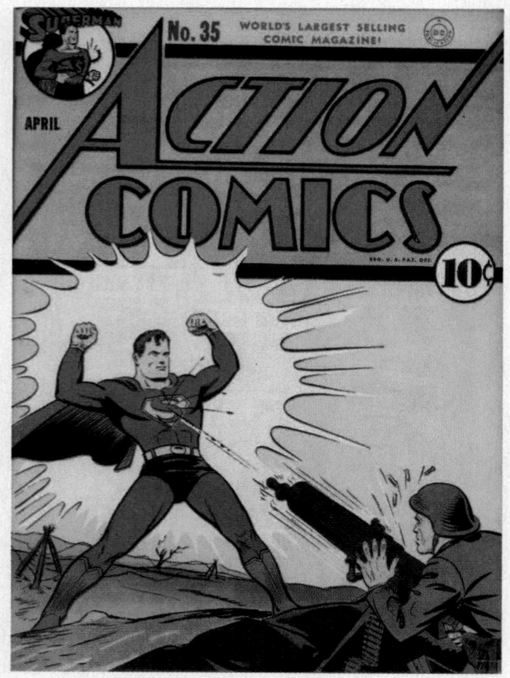

ACTION COMICS #35
April 1941. © DC

SUPERMAN NEWSPAPER PAGE
1941. © DC

ADVENTURE COMICS #340
January 1966. © DC

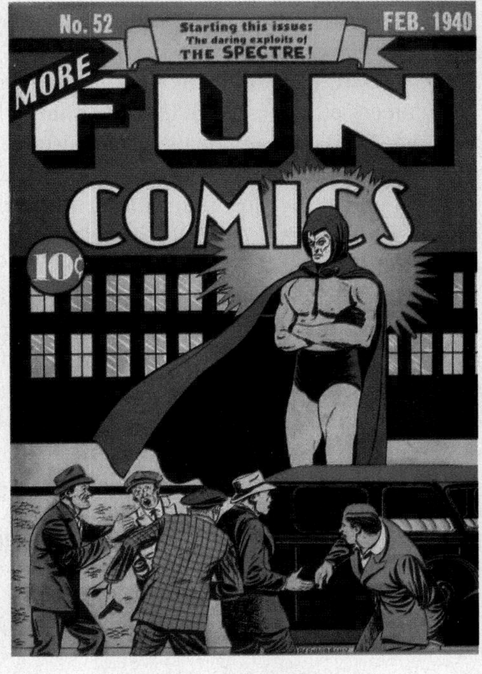

MORE FUN COMICS #52
February 1940. © DC

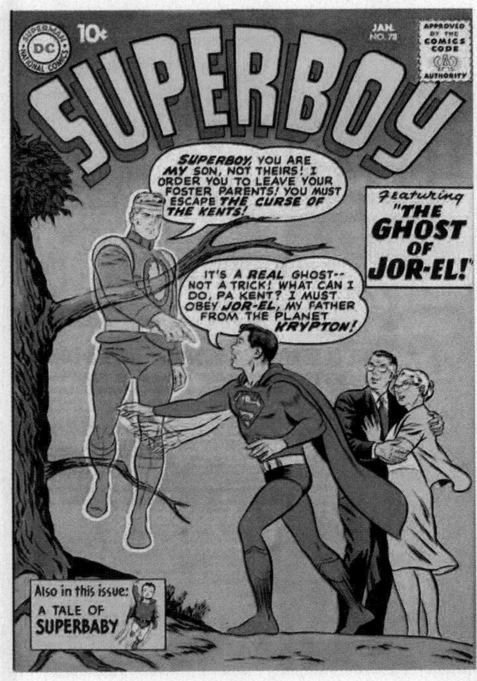

SUPERBOY #78
January 1960. © DC

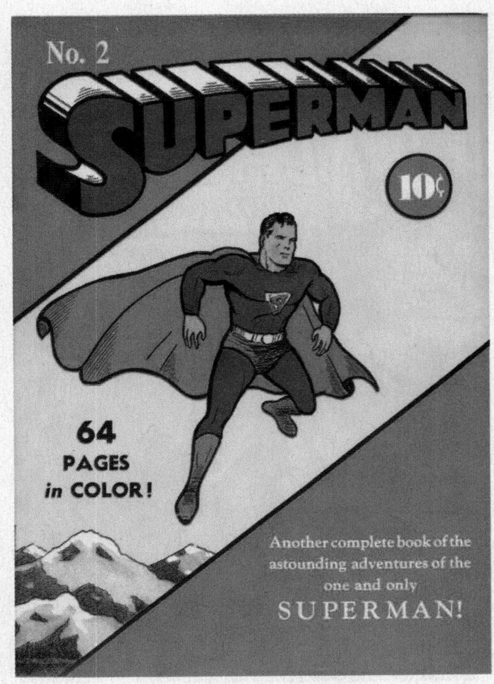

SUPERMAN #2
Fall 1939. © DC

His covers for Marvel's *Captain America*, *Incredible Hulk*, and *Nick Fury, Agent of S.H.I.E.L.D.* are some of the most iconic and innovative pieces of pop art from the 1960s. Jim Steranko (1938-) was, perhaps auspiciously, born the year the Golden Age began, but he is far more than just one of the most influential artists of the Marvel Age. His *Chandler: Red Tide* helped to define the very meaning of the term "graphic novel," his conceptual artwork for *Raiders of the Lost Ark* breathed life into Indiana Jones - the man whose name was synonymous with adventure - and his two-volume *The Steranko History of Comics* offered a unique insight into the development of the medium during the Golden Age. Today the award-winning Steranko stands as one of comicdom's living legends with awards and honors that serve as testament to his indelible contributions.
- ATB

CAPTAIN AMERICA #113
May 1969. © MAR

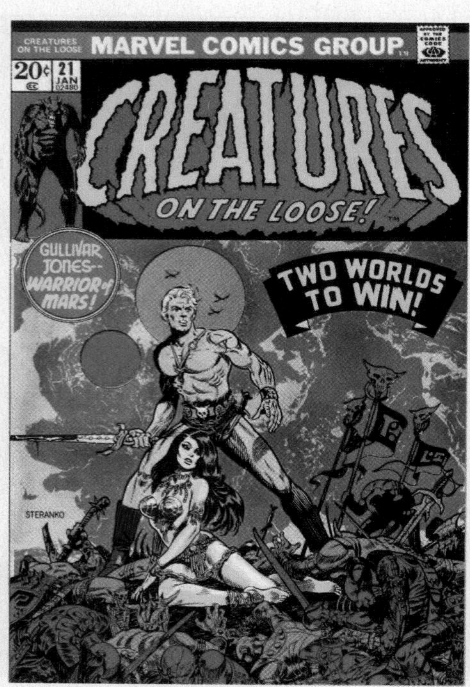

CREATURES ON THE LOOSE #21
January 1971. © MAR

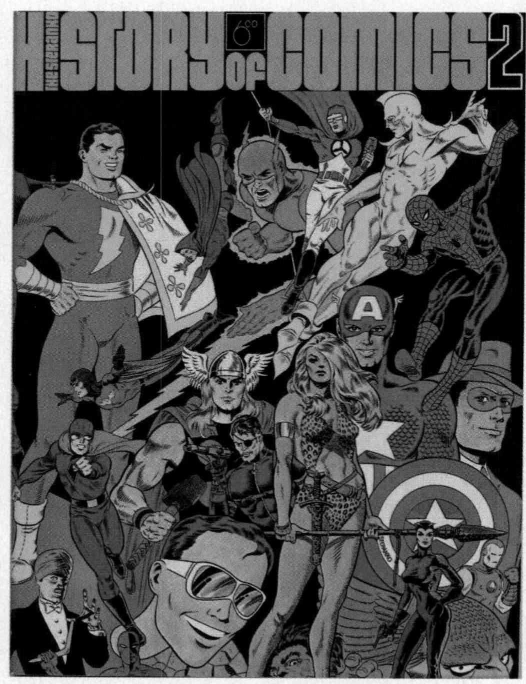

HISTORY OF COMICS VOL. 2
1970. © Jim Steranko

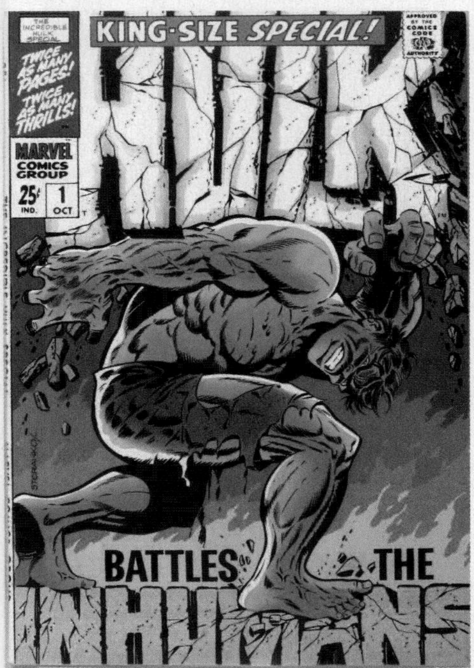

INCREDIBLE HULK ANNUAL #1
October 1968. © MAR

NICK FURY, AGENT OF S.H.I.E.L.D. #1
June 1968. © MAR

STRANGE TALES #167
April 1968. © MAR

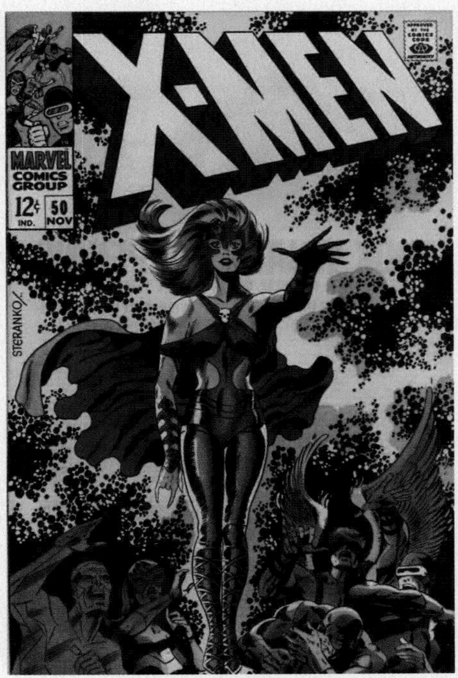

X-MEN #50
November 1968. © MAR

Wallace A. Wood landed his first comic work with Will Eisner as a back-up artist on The Spirit in 1948. He also began lettering for Fox Features Syndicate, then drew stories for their love and western titles. Over the next few years he worked for Avon, Better-Standard, EC, Fawcett, Fox, Kirby Publishing Co., Youthful Magazines and Ziff-Davis.

After trying multiple genres with EC, he soon found his niche in science fiction. His work on EC's *Weird Fantasy* and *Weird Science* followed covers on Avon's *Attack On Planet Mars*, *Flying Saucers*, *Earth Man on Venus*, *Space Detective* and *Strange Worlds*. No one could draw spaceship interior instrumentation and machinery like him.

He became the first Marvel Comics artist to get a cover blurb when Stan Lee touted Wood's arrival on *Daredevil* #5. In the years that followed, he continued to produce beautiful work for DC, Charlton, Gold Key, Harvey, Tower (where he launched the *T.H.U.N.D.E.R. Agents*), Warren and Atlas-Seaboard, as well as a number of self-published projects. Wood took his own life in 1981.

- RMO

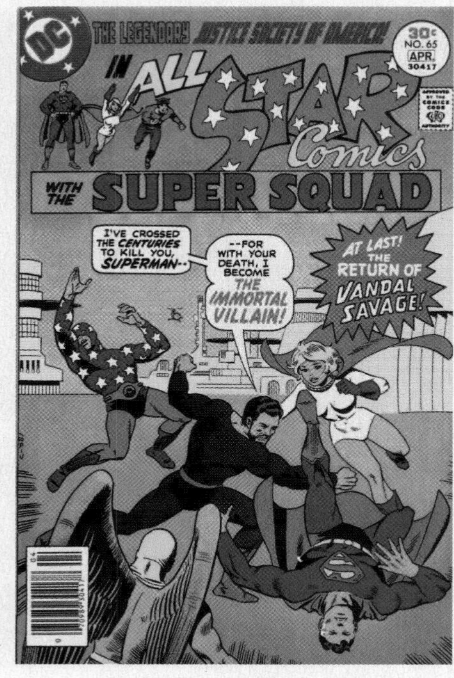

ALL-STAR COMICS #65
March-April 1977. © DC

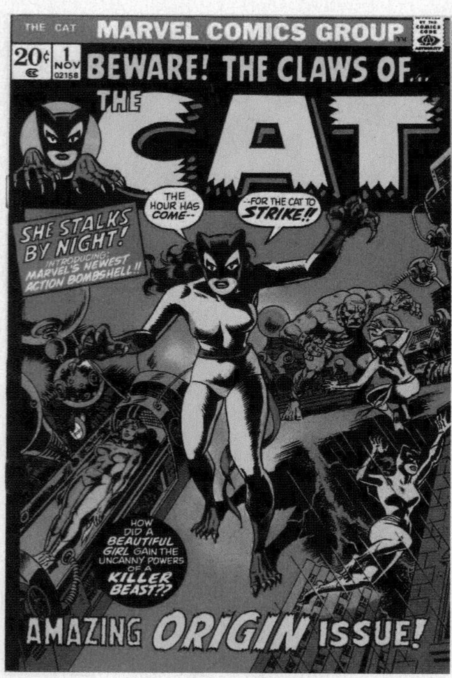

THE CAT #1
November 1972. © MAR

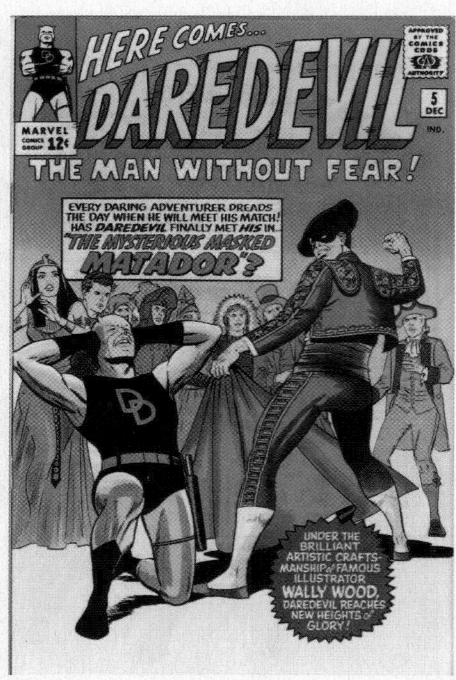

DAREDEVIL #5
December 1964. © MAR

HEROES, INC. PRESENTS CANNON
1969. © Wally Wood

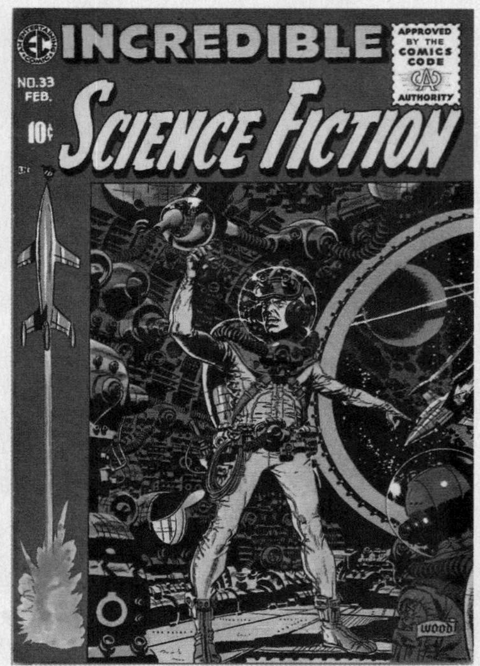

INCREDIBLE SCIENCE FICTION #33
January-February 1956. © WMG

SPIRIT NEWSPAPER SECTION #1
August 3, 1952. © Will Eisner Studios

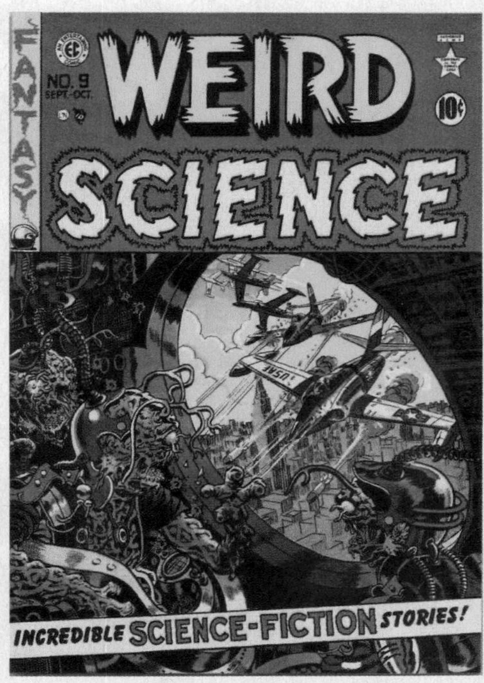

WEIRD SCIENCE #9
September-October 1951. © WMG

HOW COMICS ARE MADE

GIVEN THAT THIS GUIDE IS ALL ABOUT COMICS, WE THOUGHT ON OUR 40TH ANNIVERSARY WE SHOULD TAKE A LOOK AT HOW THEY COME TO BE. OUR FRIENDS AT DC COMICS WERE HAPPY TO OBLIGE WITH THIS LOOK AT THE ORIGINS OF A SUPERMAN STORY. THERE ARE MANY DIFFERENT APPROACHES, BUT THIS ONE STARTS WITH THE SCRIPT BY WRITER CHUCK DIXON, WHICH IS THEN SENT TO AN EDITOR FOR COMMENTS OR CHANGES.

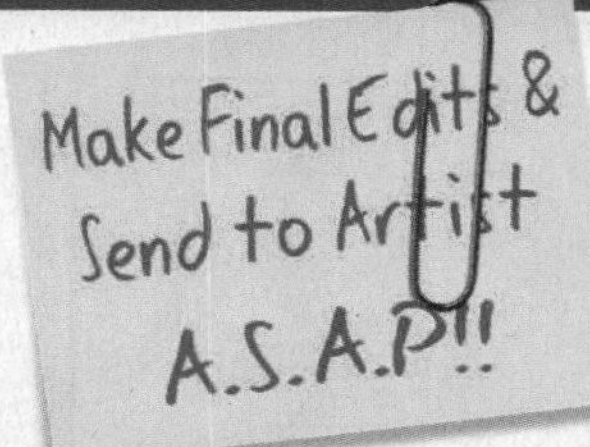
Make Final Edits &
Send to Artist
A.S.A.P!!

SUPERMAN Script

"CLOSE CALL"
Script: Chuck Dixon
Pencils: Renato Guedes
Inks: Marc Campos
Colors: Alex Sinclair & Mike Cavallaro
Lettering: Rob Leigh

PANEL ONE
LOIS LANE is speeding along a multi-lane bridge speaking on her cell phone as she tools along. She's in a convertible and we're looking down at her as she drives. On the front seat, we see an open laptop, notes and other reporter paraphernalia from the Daily Planet.

CAPTION: METROPOLIS.

LOIS: I'M TELLING YOU… ~~I THINK~~ I'VE UNCOVERED WHO'S BEHIND THESE RECENT ATTACKS!

PHONE: (ELECTRONIC, SMALL) SHOULDN'T YOU GO TO THE AUTHORITIES, LOIS?

BF

LOIS: AND MISS BREAKING THE BIGGEST STORY OF THE YEAR? NOT ON YOUR--

PANEL TWO
Closer shot - LOIS looks alarmed and grabs the wheel with both hands, dropping the cell phone.

stet: keep cell phone in hand

LOIS: (SMALL) ---LIFE?

PHONE: (ELECTRONIC, SMALL) LOIS?

LOIS: SOMETHING'S **WRONG** WITH THE BRAKES!

PANEL THREE
LOIS' convertible crashes through a guard rail and off the bridge. It sustains damage from going through the guard rail.

LOIS: NO!!!

PANEL FOUR
Our Big Money shot and the largest panel on the page. We're looking down at a dramatic angle as SUPERMAN catches the falling convertible. He's stopped the car from plunging into the river below. LOIS stares at him in stunned surprise. SUPERMAN is smiling. Below him we can see the long drop to the river. Add some river traffic for scale. Maybe have a tug pushing a barge.

Try Drawing from a few different angles

LOIS: SUPERMAN!

SUPERMAN: YOU REALLY SHOULD **THINK** ABOUT A HANDS-FREE CELL PHONE, LOIS.

CAPTION: (SMALL) CONTINUED IN ACTION COMICS!

Use comic logo

STAGE TWO: THE PENCIL ARTIST, IN THIS CASE THE VERY TALENTED RENATO GUEDES (***24: MIDNIGHT SUN***), ROUGHS OUT THE PAGES. SOMETIMES THIS IS DONE IN BLUE PENCIL, WHICH WILL NOT NORMALLY REPRODUCE.

STAGE THREE: ONCE THE PAGE IS FULLY DESIGNED AND APPROVED (AND ONCE ANY CORRECTIONS HAVE BEEN MADE), THE ARTIST THEN RENDERS IT AS A PENCIL ILLUSTRATION, DRAWING OVER OR ERASING THE BLUE PENCIL.

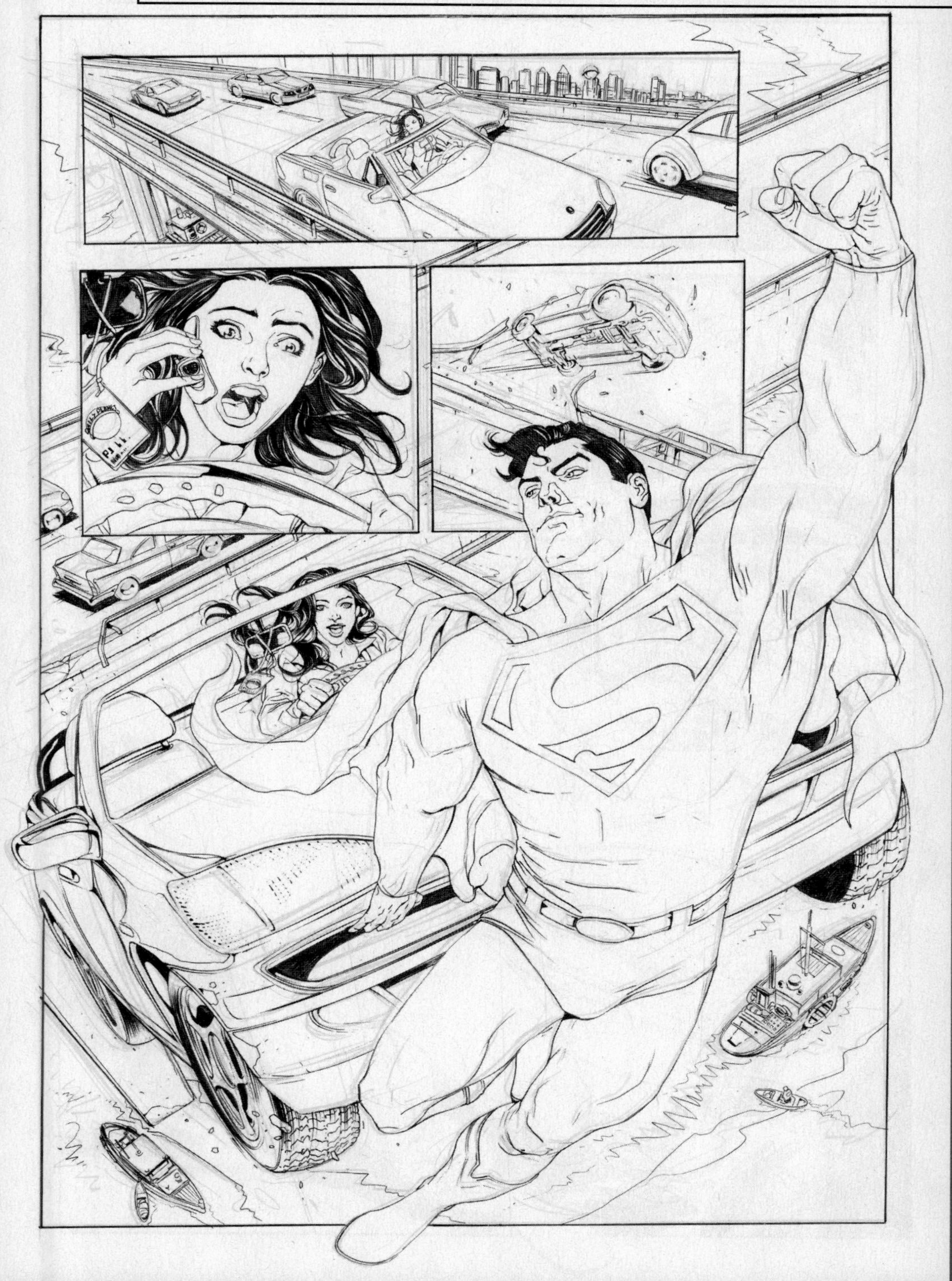

STAGE FOUR: ONE THE PENCIL STAGE IS FINISHED, THEN THE PAGE IS SENT TO THE INKER (IN THIS CASE MARC CAMPOS), WHO APPLIES THE INK TO CREATE THICKER LINES, ADD DEFINITION AND FILL IN THE BACKGROUNDS.

STAGE FIVE: NEXT COMES THE COLOR, IN THIS CASE BY ALEX SINCLAIR AND MIKE CAVALLARO. IN THE MODERN WORLD OF COMPUTER COLORING, THEY CAN USE A FULLER AND MORE VIBRANT RANGE THAN WAS POSSIBLE IN THE PAST.

STAGE SIX: FINALLY THE LETTERER (FOR THIS STORY, ROB LEIGH) APPLIES THE WORD BALLOONS, CAPTION BOXES, LOGOS AND TEXT. THE PAGE IS THEN ASSEMBLED WITH THE OTHERS THAT COMPRISE THE REST OF THE STORY!

METROPOLIS.
I'M TELLING YOU... I'VE UNCOVERED WHO'S BEHIND THESE RECENT ATTACKS!
SHOULDN'T YOU GO TO THE AUTHORITIES, LOIS?
AND MISS BREAKING THE BIGGEST STORY OF THE YEAR? NOT ON YOUR--
--LIFE?
LOIS?
SOMETHING'S WRONG WITH THE BRAKES!
NO!!
SUPERMAN!
YOU SHOULD REALLY THINK ABOUT A HANDS-FREE CELL PHONE, LOIS.
Continued in ACTION COMICS

MOONSTONE
CAPTAIN ACTION
CA
The legendary super hero is back in action!
Exciting new series starts Summer 2010
And don't miss the return of the original robots from space!
ZEROIDS
Get in on the Action at:
www.CaptainActionNow.com
moonstonebooks.com

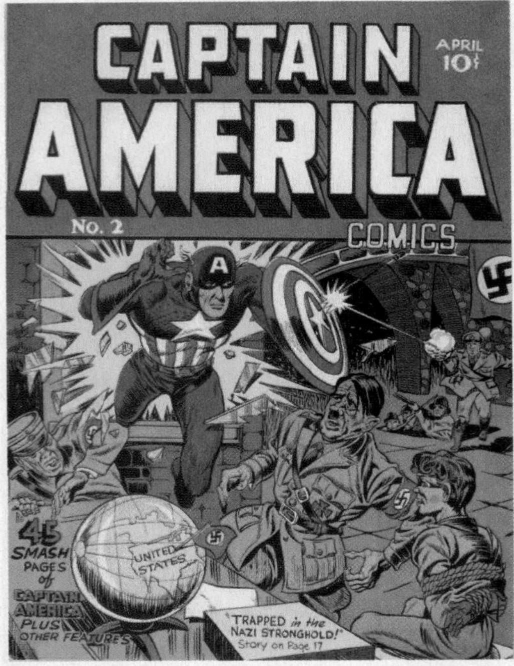

CAPTAIN AMERICA COMICS #2
April 1941. Joe Simon cover. © MAR

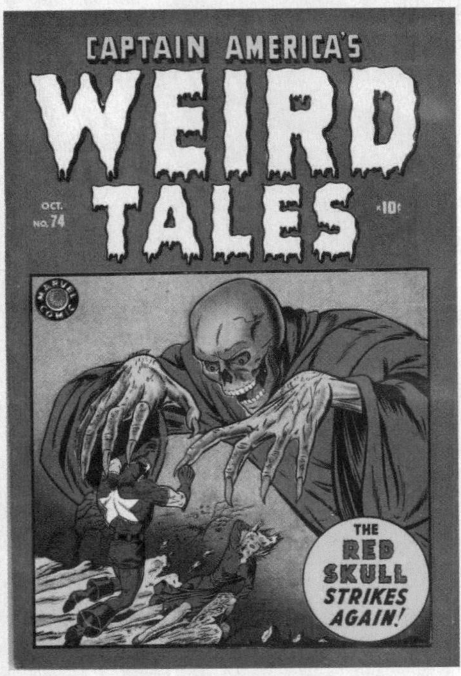

CAPTAIN AMERICA'S WEIRD TALES #74
October 1949. Martin Nodell cover. © MAR

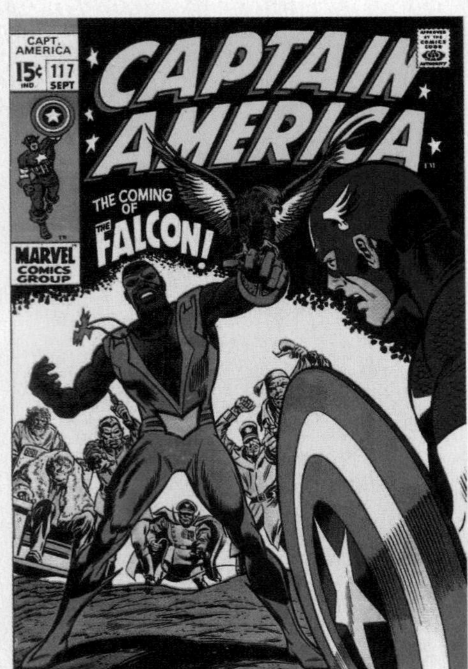

CAPTAIN AMERICA #117
September 1969. Debut of the Falcon. © MAR

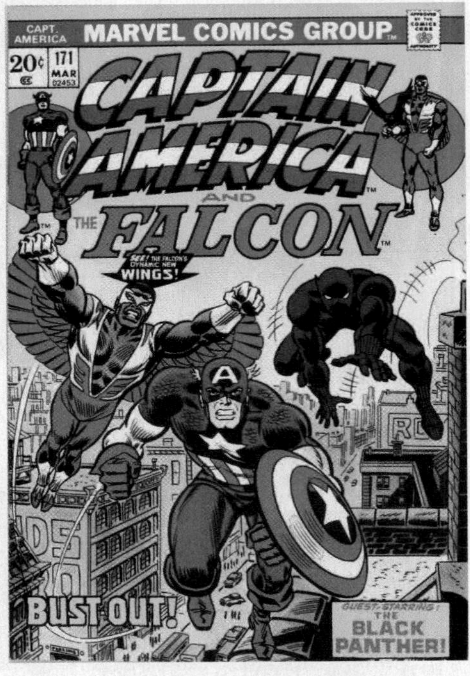

CAPTAIN AMERICA #171
March 1974. John Romita cover. © MAR

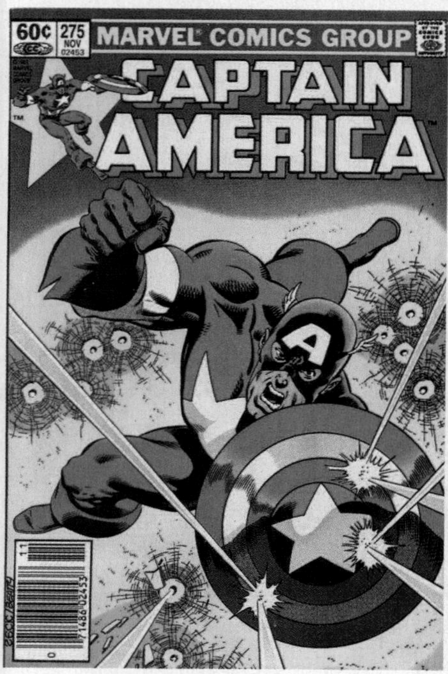

CAPTAIN AMERICA #275
November 1983. Mike Zeck cover. © MAR

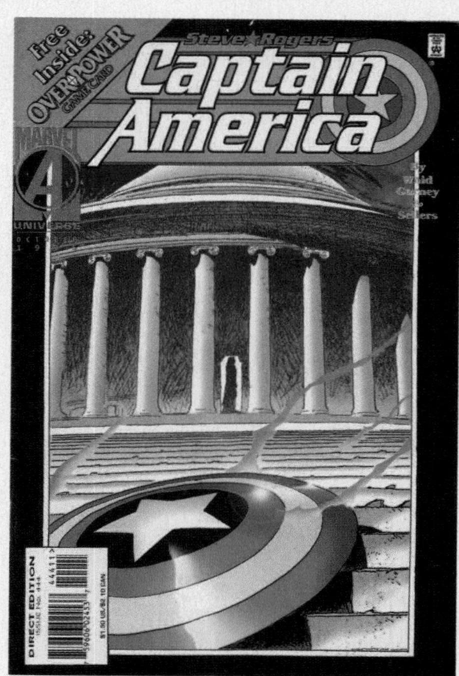

CAPTAIN AMERICA #444
October 1995. Ron Garney cover. © MAR

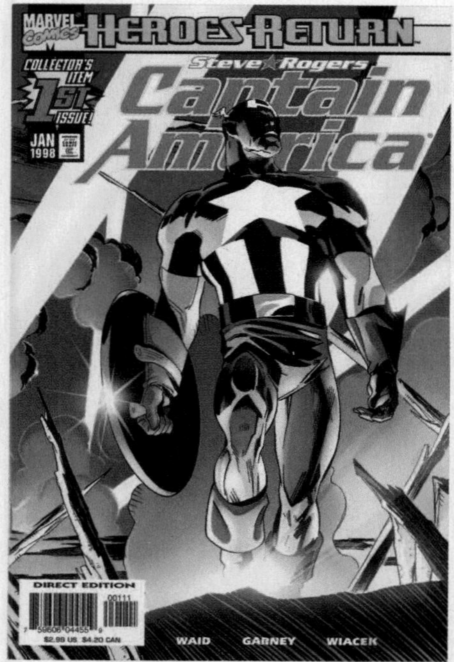

CAPTAIN AMERICA Vol. 3 #1
January 1998. Heroes Return. © MAR

CAPTAIN AMERICA Vol. 4 #6
December 2002. John Cassaday cover. © MAR

CONAN THE BARBARIAN #19
October 1972. Barry Windsor-Smith cover. © CPI

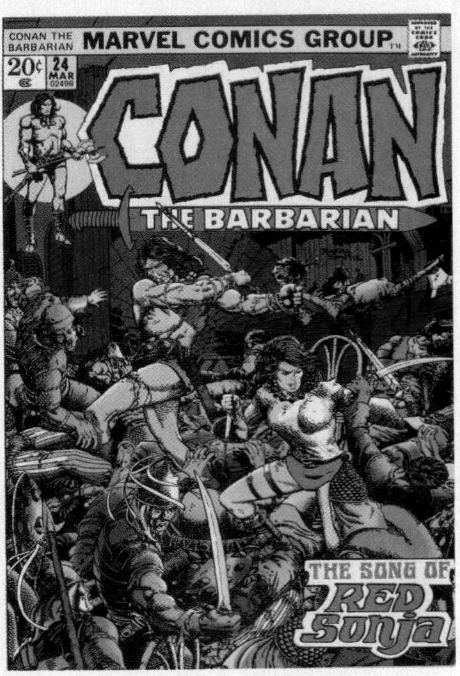

CONAN THE BARBARIAN #24
March 1973. First full Red Sonja app. © CPI

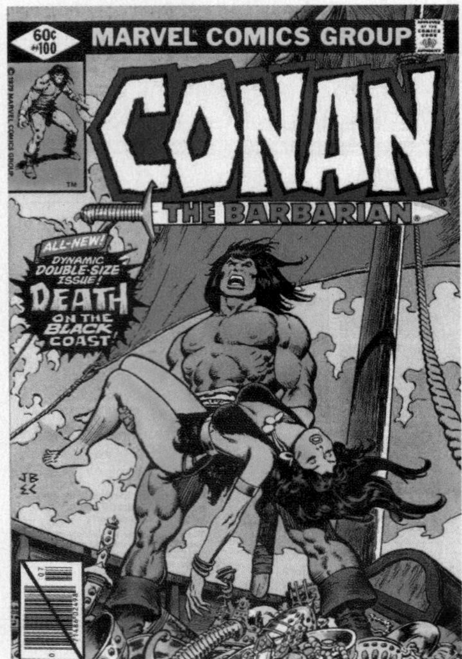

CONAN THE BARBARIAN #100
July 1979. John Buscema cover. © CPI

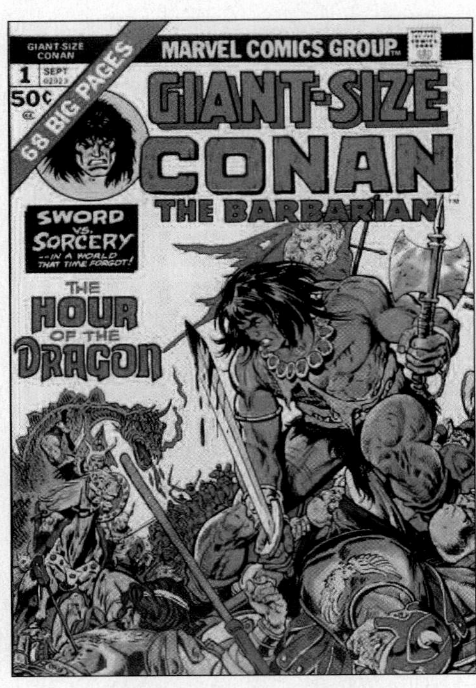

GIANT-SIZE CONAN #1
September 1974. Gil Kane cover. © CPI

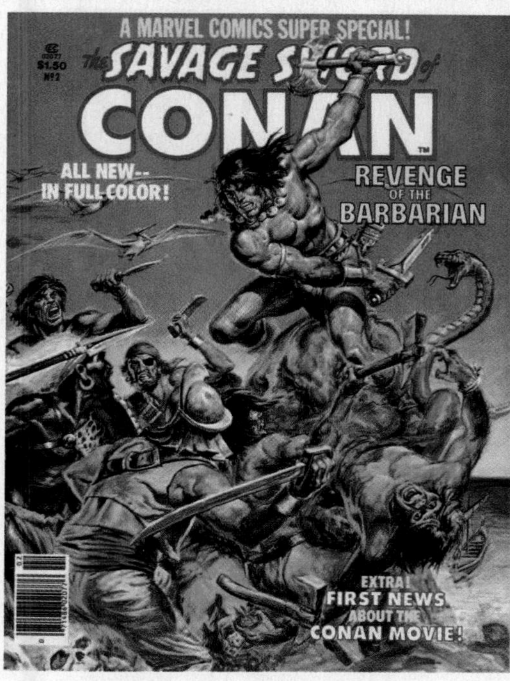

MARVEL COMICS SUPER SPECIAL #2
1977. Earl Norem cover. © CPI

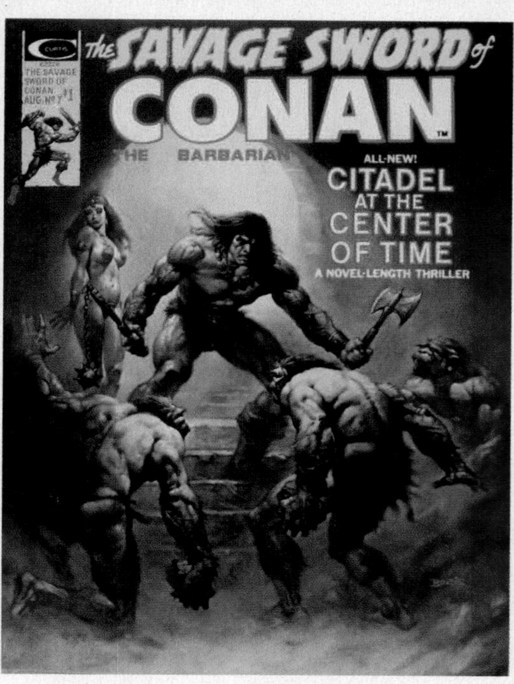

SAVAGE SWORD OF CONAN #7
August 1975. Boris Vallejo cover. © CPI

CONAN: THE LEGEND #0
November 2003. Cary Nord cover. © CPI

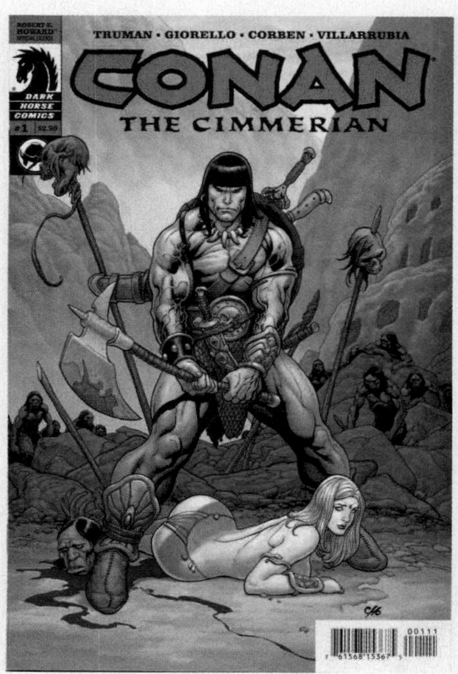

CONAN THE CIMMERIAN #1
July 2008. Frank Cho cover. © CPI

THUNDER AGENTS #1
Novenber 1965. Wally Wood cover. © John Carbonaro

THUNDER AGENTS #3
March 1966. Wally Wood cover. © John Carbonaro

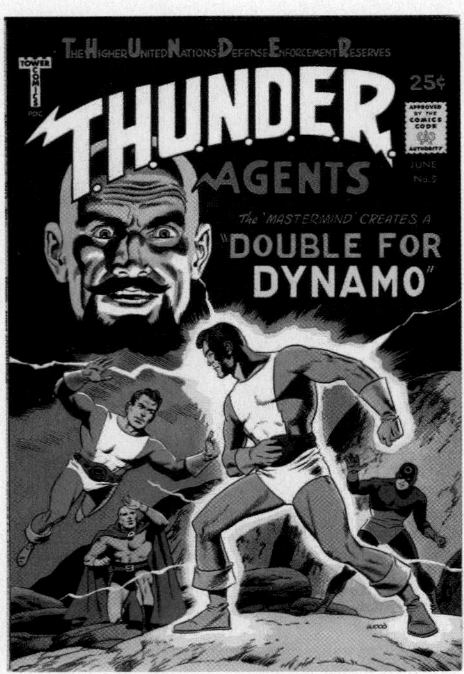

THUNDER AGENTS #5
June 1966. Wally Wood cover. © John Carbonaro

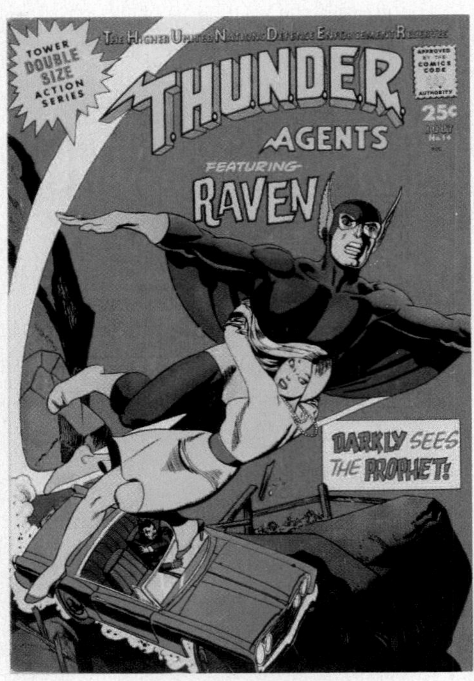

THUNDER AGENTS #14
July 1967. Gil Kane cover. © John Carbonaro

GALLERY

DYNAMO #2
October 1966. Wally Wood cover. © John Carbonaro

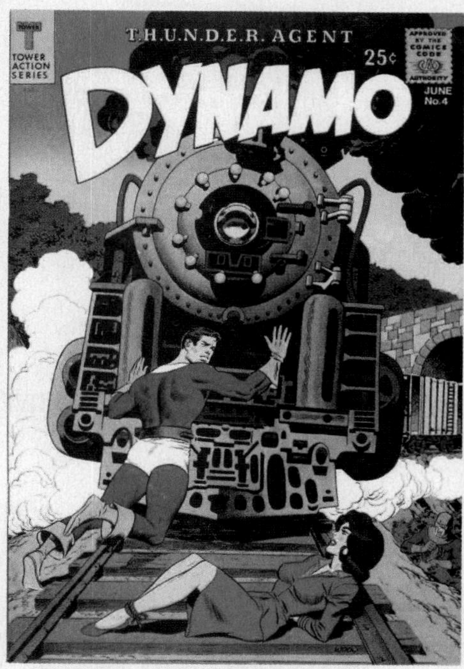

DYNAMO #4
June 1967. Wally Wood cover. © John Carbonaro

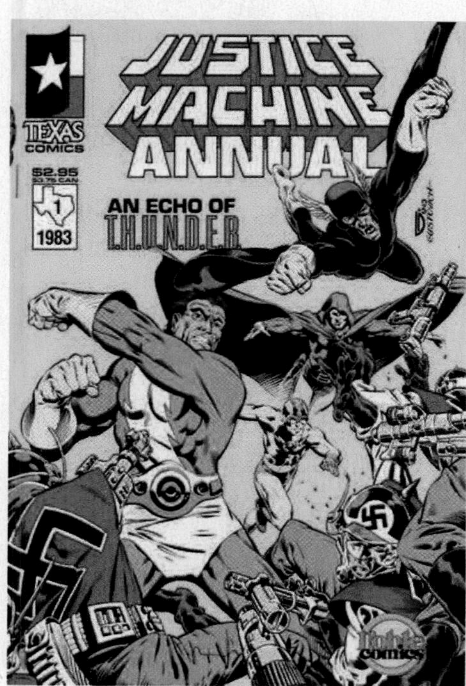

JUSTICE MACHINE ANNUAL #1
January 1984. © Michael Gustovich

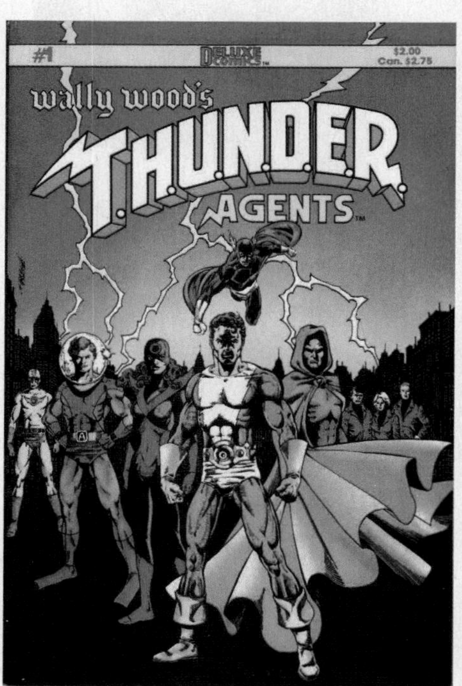

WALLY WOOD'S THUNDER AGENTS #1
November 1984. George Pérez cover. © Wally Wood

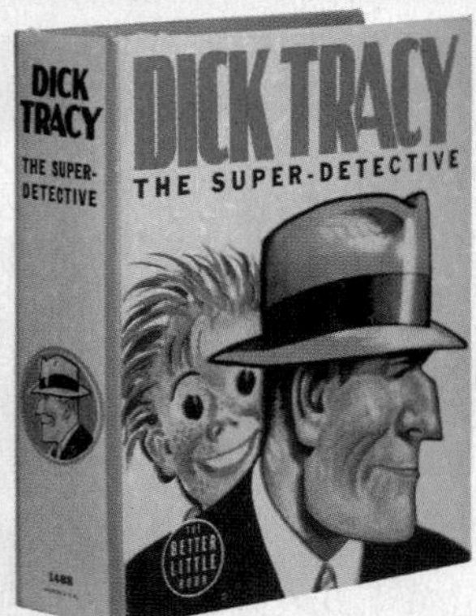

DICK TRACY THE SUPER-DETECTIVE
BLB #1488 - 1939. © NYNS

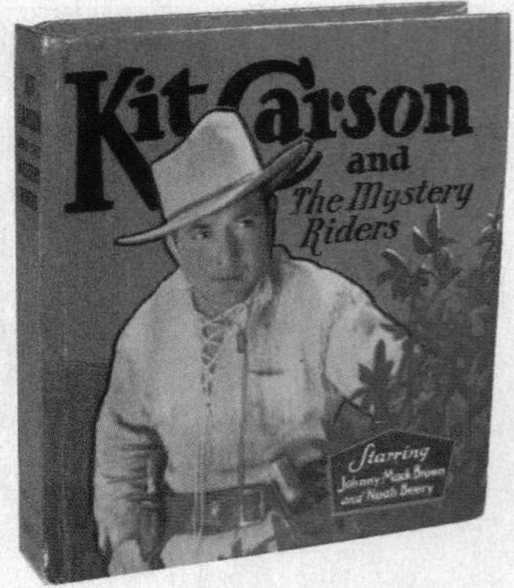

KIT CARSON
AND THE MYSTERY RIDERS
BLB #1105 - 1935. © Saalfield

THE LOST WORLD
JURASSIC PARK 2
Chronicle Books - 1997. © Universal

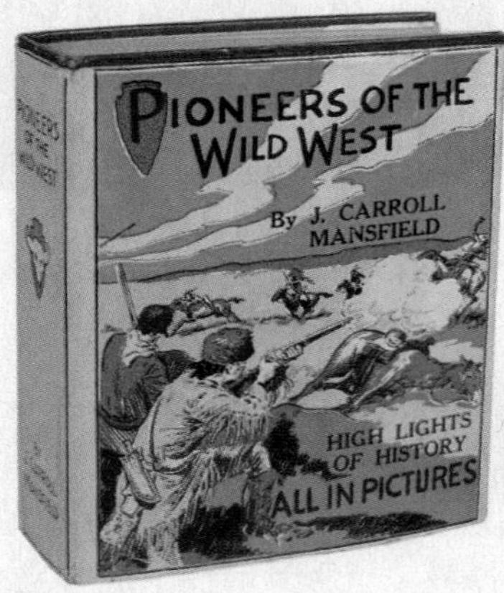

PIONEERS OF THE WILD WEST
1933. © World Syndicate

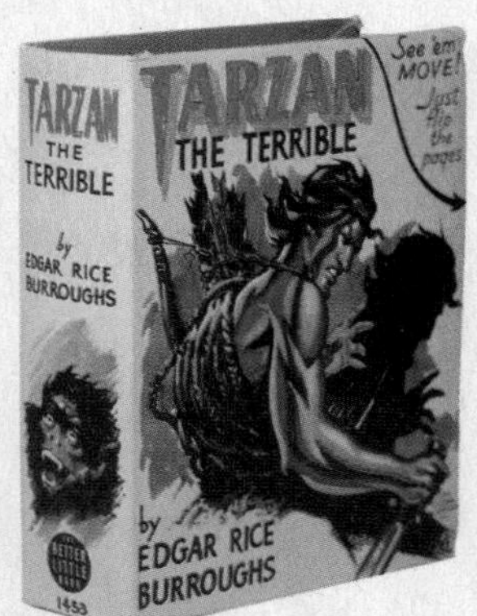

TARZAN THE TERRIBLE
BLB #1453 - 1942. © ERB

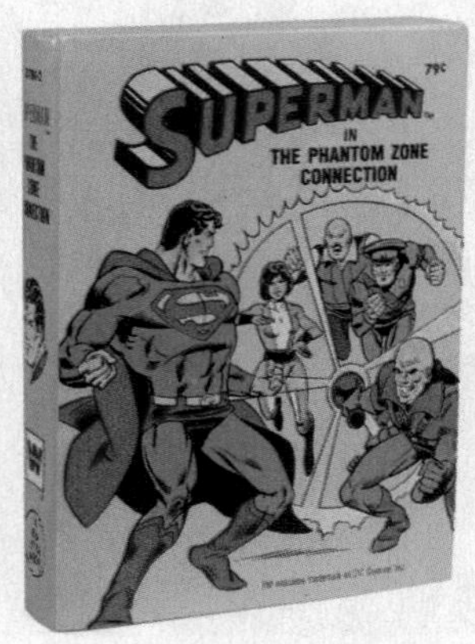

SUPERMAN IN THE
PHANTOM ZONE CONNECTION
BLB #5780-2 - 1980. © DC

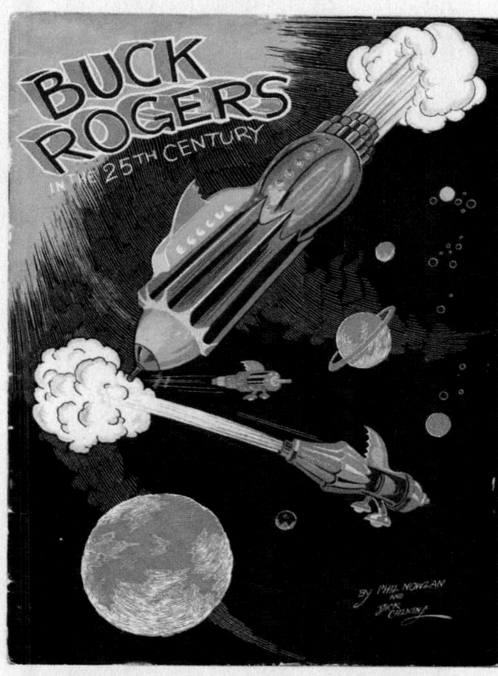

BUCK ROGERS IN THE 25TH CENTURY
1933. Kellogg's Corn Flakes giveaway #370A
© KING

EVEL KNIEVEL
1974. Marvel Comics and Ideal Toy giveaway
© Ideal Toy Corp.

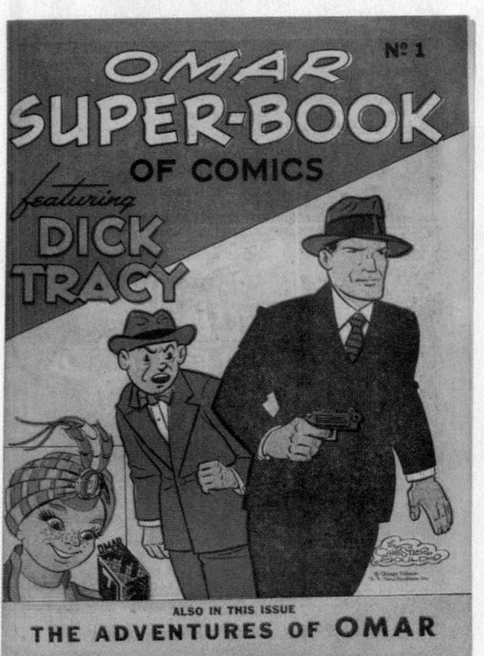

SUPER-BOOK OF COMICS #1
1944. Omar Bread premium. © NYNS

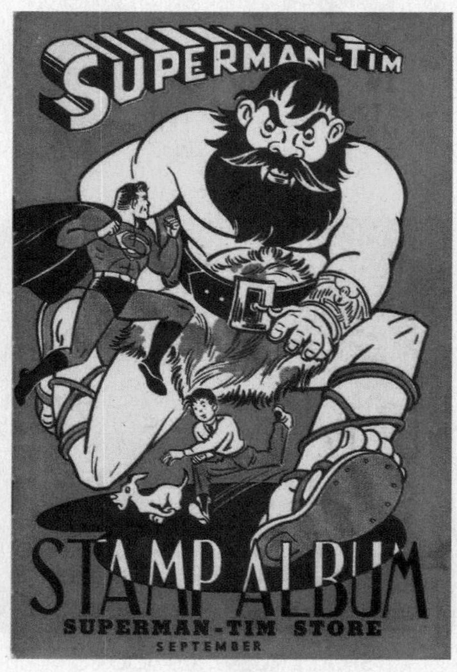

SUPERMAN-TIM nn
September 1948. © DC

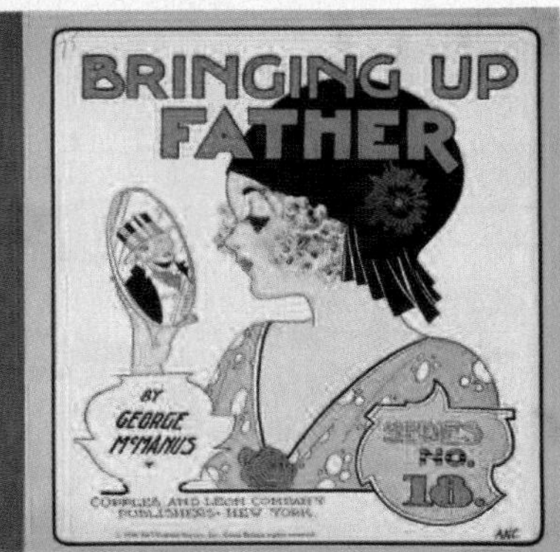

BRINGING UP FATHER #18
1930. © Cupples & Leon Co.

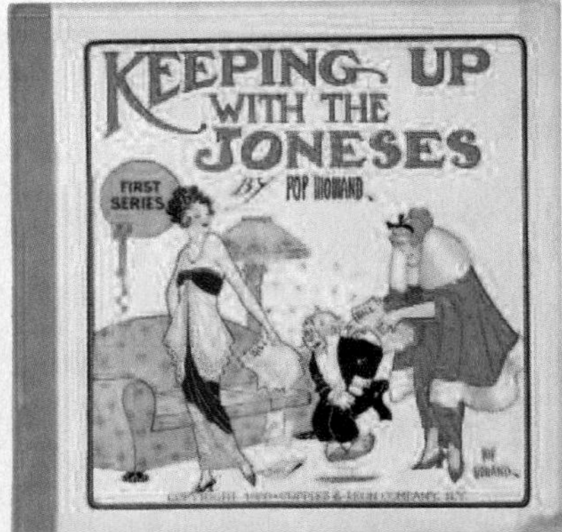

KEEPING UP WITH THE JONESES #1
1920. © Cupples & Leon Co.

HANS UND FRITZ
1917. © Saalfield

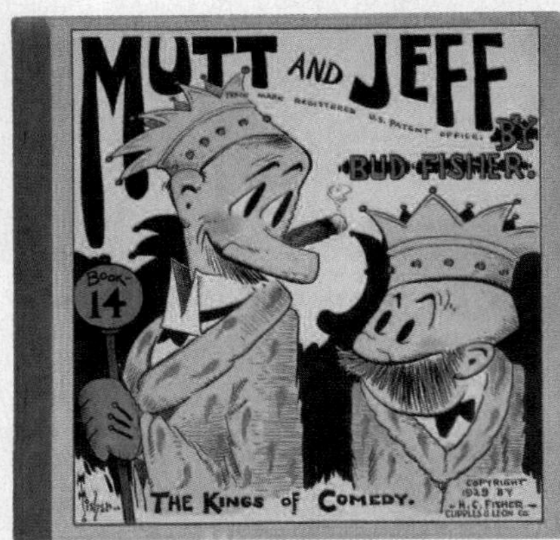

MUTT AND JEFF BOOK 14
1929. © Cupples & Leon Co.

SECRET AGENT X-9 BOOK 2
1934. © David McKay Publ.

WINNIE WINKLE #1
1930. © Cupples & Leon Co.

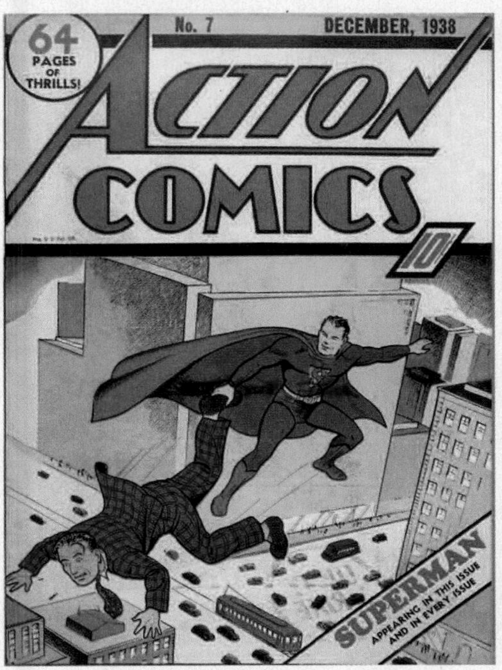

ACTION COMICS #7
December 1938. © DC

CLASSIC COMICS #7
December 1942. © GIL

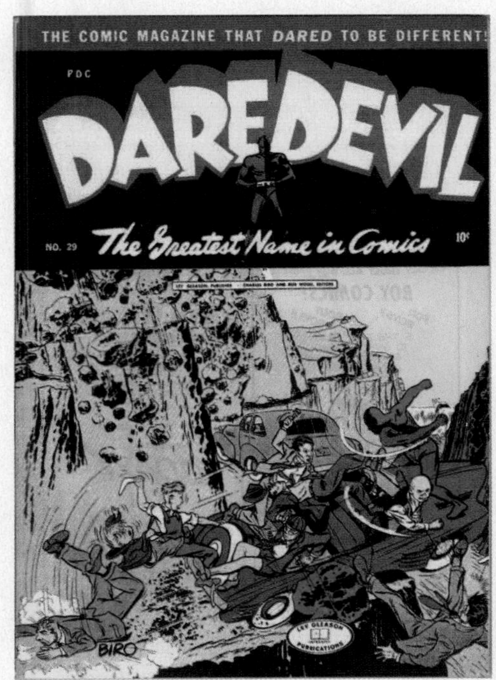

DAREDEVIL #29
March 1945. © LEV

HANGMAN COMICS #3
Summer 1942. © MLJ

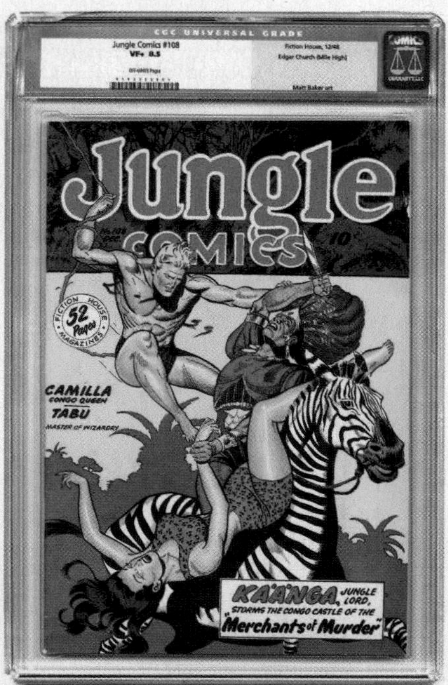

JUNGLE COMICS #108
Mile High copy. December 1948. © FH

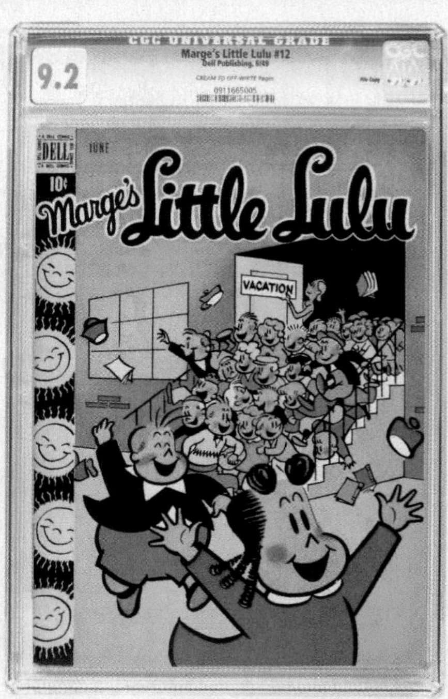

MARGE'S LITTLE LULU #12
June 1949. © M. Buell

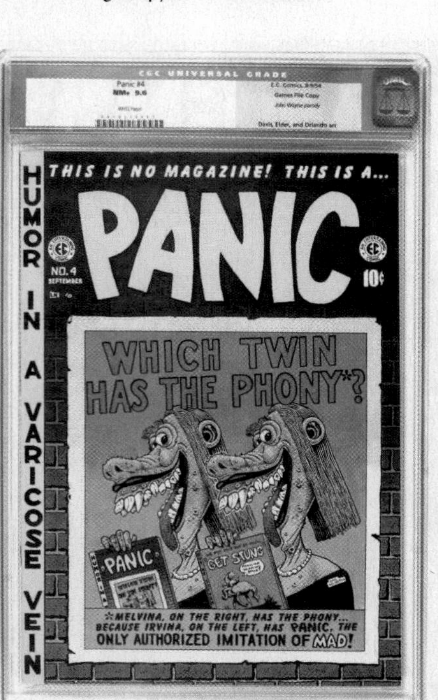

PANIC #4
August-September 1954. © WMG

POPULAR COMICS #61
March 1941. © DELL

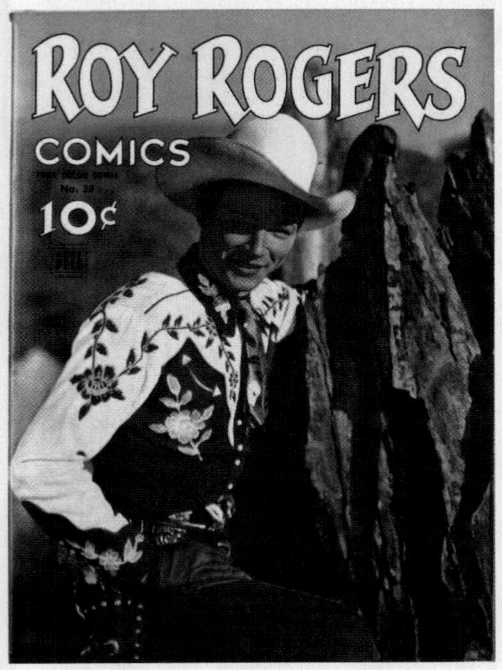

ROY ROGERS FOUR COLOR #38
April 1944. © Roy Rogers

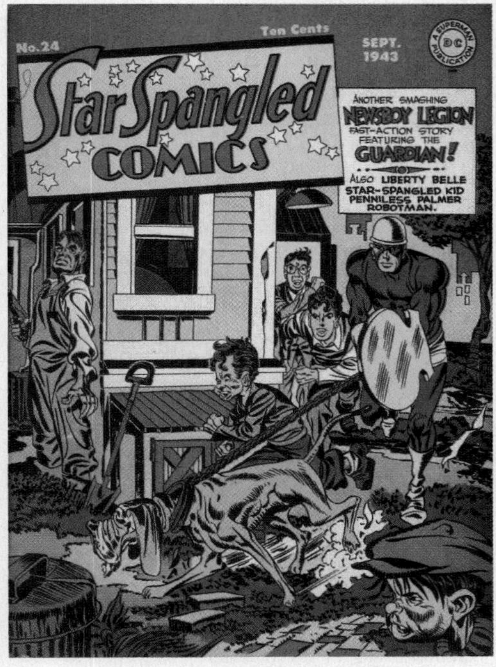

STAR SPANGLED COMICS #24
September 1943. © DC

TRUE LOVE PICTORIAL #6
October1953. © STJ

WHIZ COMICS #77
August 1946. © FAW

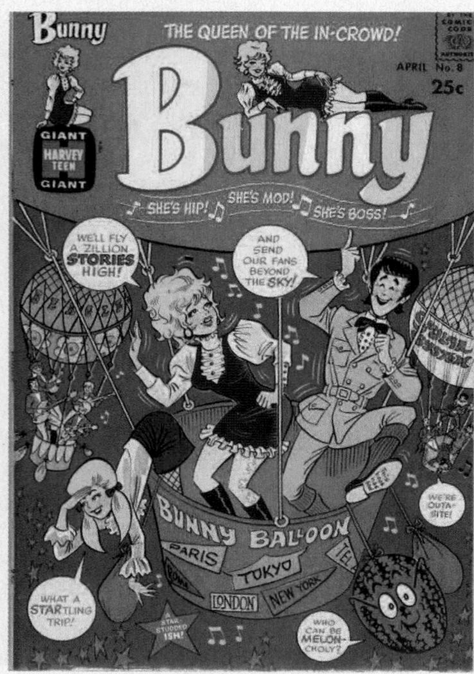

BUNNY #8
April 1969. © HARV

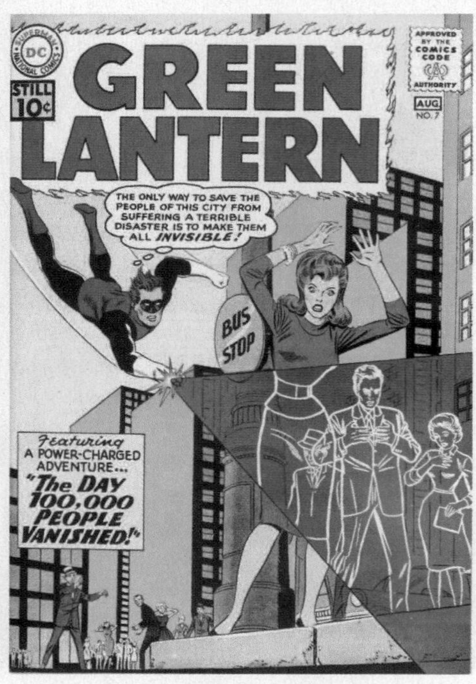

GREEN LANTERN #7
Debut of Sinestro. July-August 1961. © DC

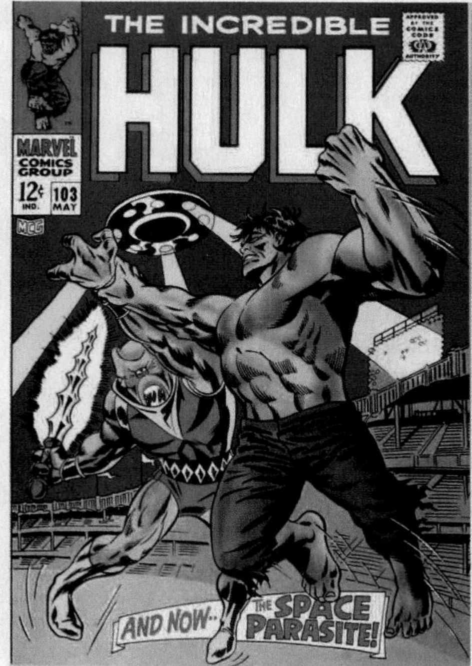

THE INCREDIBLE HULK #103
May 1968. © MAR

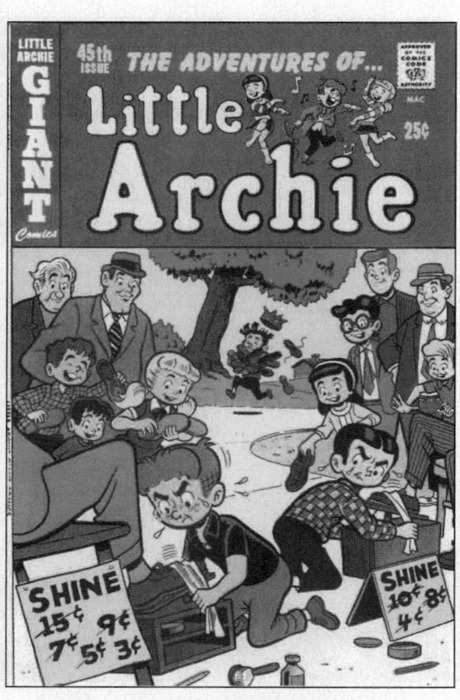

LITTLE ARCHIE #45
1967. © AP

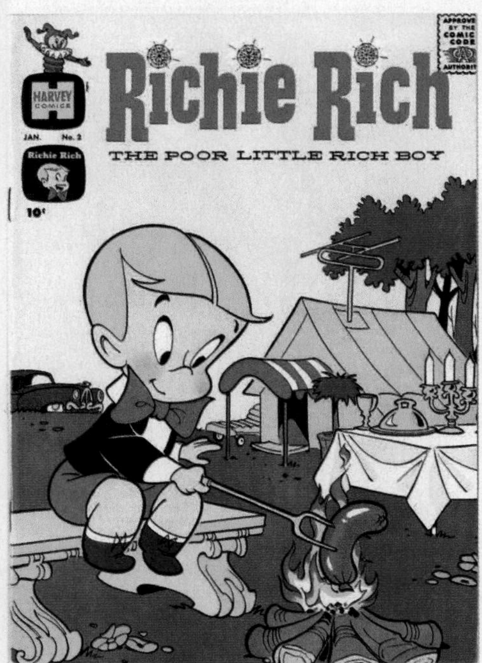

RICHIE RICH #2
January 1961. © HARV

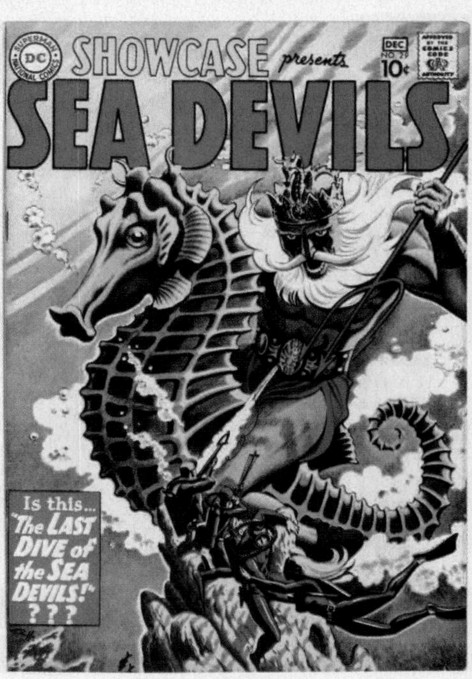

SHOWCASE #29
November-December 1960. © DC

TEEN TITANS #19
January-February 1969. © DC

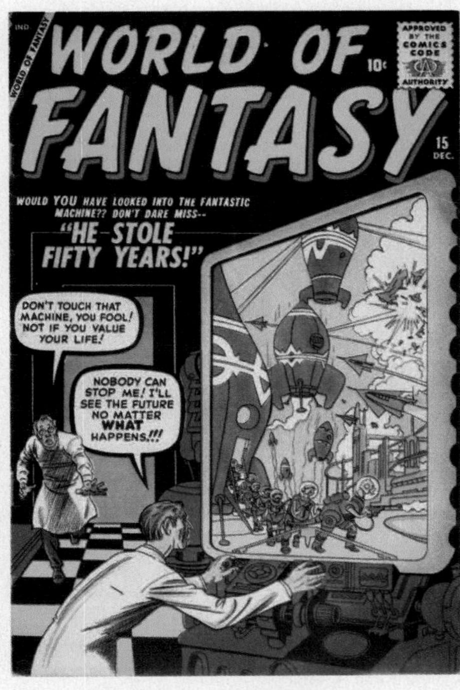

WORLD OF FANTASY #15
December 1958. © MAR

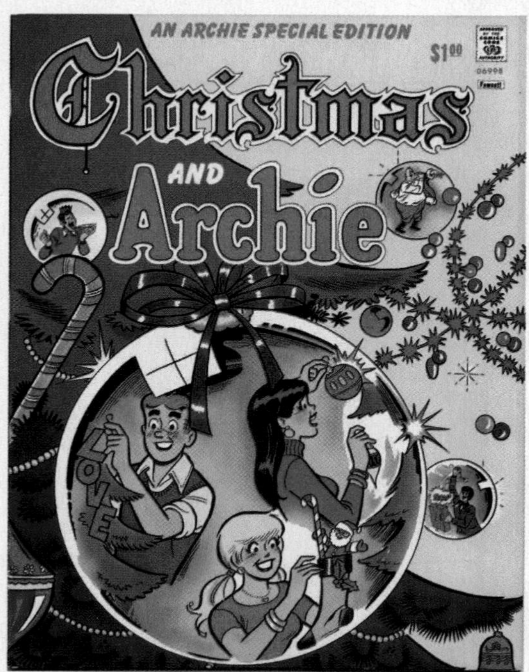

ARCHIE SPECIAL EDITION,
CHRISTMAS AND ARCHIE #1
January 1975. © AP

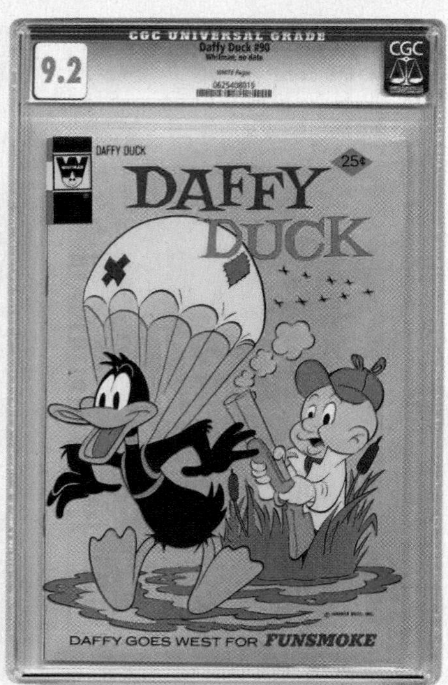

DAFFY DUCK #90
1974. © WB

DETECTIVE COMICS #447
May 1975. © DC

IRON MAN #66
February 1974. © MAR

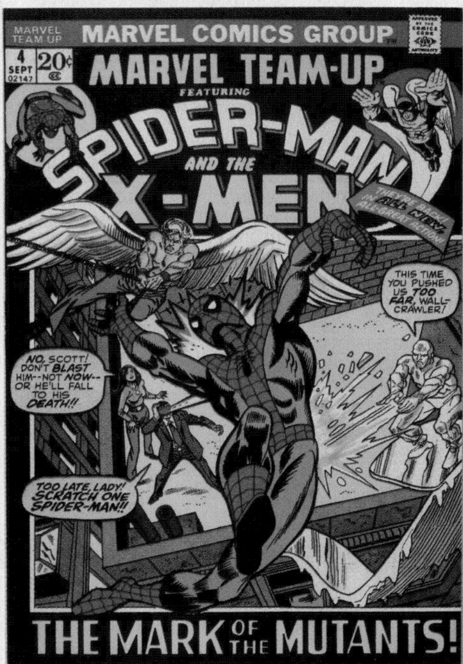

MARVEL TEAM-UP #4
September 1972. © MAR

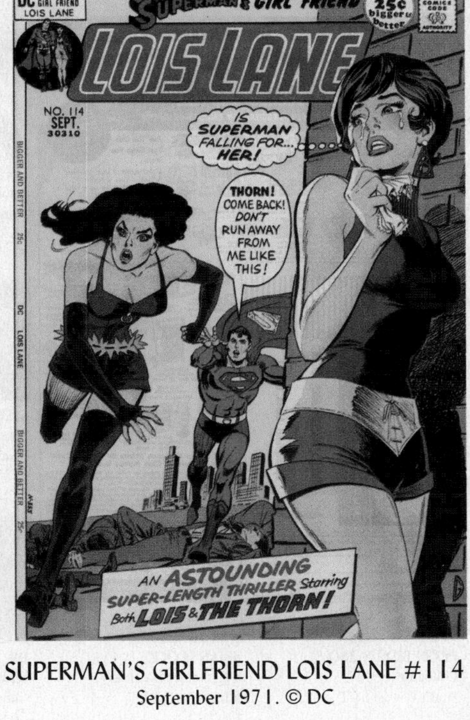

SUPERMAN'S GIRLFRIEND LOIS LANE #114
September 1971. © DC

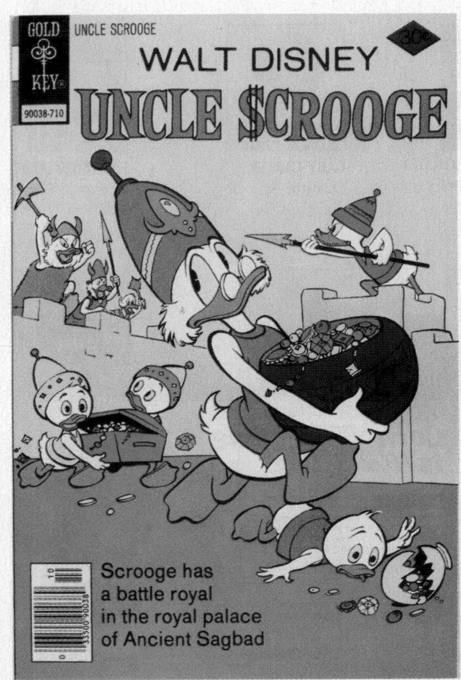

UNCLE SCROOGE #145
October 1977. © DIS

VAMPIRELLA #75
January 1979. © WP

OVERSTREET ADVISORS

WELDON ADAMS
Comics Historian
Fort Worth, TX

GRANT ADEY
Fats Comics
Brisbane, QLD,
Australia

DAVID T. ALEXANDER
David Alexander Comics
Tampa, FL

TYLER ALEXANDER
David Alexander Comics
Tampa, FL

LON ALLEN
Heritage Comics Auctions
Dallas, TX

DAVE ANDERSON
Want List Comics
Tulsa, OK

STEPHEN BARRINGTON
Flea Market Comics
Chickasaw, AL

LAUREN BECKER
Warp 9 Comics
Clawson, MI

ROBERT BEERBOHM
Robert Beerbohm
Comic Art
Fremont, NE

JON BERK
Collector
Hartford, CT

PETER BILELIS, ESQ.
Collector
South Windsor, CT

BRIAN BLOCK
WB Auction Services
Adamstown, PA

DR. ARNOLD T. BLUMBERG
Curator
Geppi's Entertainment
Museum

STEVE BOROCK
Heritage Comics Auctions
Dallas, TX

KEVIN BOYD
CGC Signature Series Director
Toronto, ONT Canada

MIKE BRODER
Tropic Comics
Fort Lauderdale, FL

MICHAEL BROWNING
Collector
Danville, WV

MICHAEL CARBONARO
Neatstuffcollectibles.com
Englewood, NJ

GARY CARTER
Collector
Coronado, CA

FRANK CWIKLIK
Metropolis Comics
New York, NY

JOHN CHRUSCINSKI
Tropic Comics
Lyndora, PA

GARY COLABUONO
Dealer/Collector
Arlington Heights, IL

BILL COLE
Bill Cole Enterprises, Inc.
Randolph, MA

TIM COLLINS
RTS Unlimited, Inc.
Lakewood, CO

ANDREW COOKE
Writer/Director
New York City, NY

JON B. COOKE
Editor - Comic Book
Artist Magazine
West Kingston, RI

JACK COPLEY
Coliseum of Comics
Florida

DAN CUSIMANO
Flying Donut Trading Co.
Reston, VA

PETER DIXON
Paradise Comics
Toronto, ONT
Canada

GARY DOLGOFF
Gary Dolgoff Comics
Easthampton, MA

OVERSTREET ADVISORS

WALTER DURAJLIJA
Big B Comics
Hamilton, ONT
Canada

KEN DYBER
Collector
Portland, OR

BRUCE ELLSWORTH
Fats Comics
Brisbane, QLD, Australia

CONRAD ESCHENBERG
Collector/Dealer
Cold Spring, NY

MICHAEL EURY
Author
Lake Oswego, OR

RICHARD EVANS
Bedrock City Comics
Houston, TX

D'ARCY FARRELL
Pendragon Comics
Toronto, ONT Canada

STEPHEN FISHLER
Metropolis Collectibles, Inc.
New York, NY

DAN FOGEL
Hippy Comix, Inc.
El Sobrante, CA

CHRIS FOSS
Heroes & Dragons
Columbia, SC

STEPHEN H. GENTNER
Golden Age Specialist
Portland, OR

STEVE GEPPI
Diamond Int. Galleries
Timonium, MD

MICHAEL GOLDMAN
Motor City Comics
Farmington Hills, MI

TOM GORDON III
ComicsPriceGuide.com
Hampstead, MD

JAMIE GRAHAM
Graham Crackers
Chicago, IL

DANIEL GREENHALGH
Showcase New England
Northford, CT

ERIC J. GROVES
Dealer/Collector
Oklahoma City, OK

JOHN HAINES
Dealer/Collector
Kirtland, OH

JIM HALPERIN
Heritage Comics
Auctions
Dallas, TX

MARK HASPEL
Primary Grader
Certified Guaranty Co.,
LLC

JOHN HAUSER
Dealer/Collector
New Berlin, WI

JEF HINDS
Jef Hinds Comics
Madison, WI

GREG HOLLAND
Collector
Alexander, AR

BILL HUGHES
Dealer/Collector
Flower Mound, TX

ROB HUGHES
Arch Angels
Manhattan Beach, CA

WILLIAM INSIGNARES
Demolition Comics
Tampa, FL

ED JASTER
Heritage Comics Auctions
Dallas, TX

BRIAN KETTERER
Collector
Philadelphia, PA

DENNIS KEUM
Fantasy Comics
Goldens Bridge, NY

PHIL LEVINE
Dealer/Collector
Three Bridges, NJ

OVERSTREET ADVISORS

PAUL LITCH
Modern Age Specialist
Certified Guaranty Co., LLC

LARRY LOWERY
Big Little Books Specialist
Danville, CA

JOE MANNARINO
All Star Auctions
Ridgewood, NJ

NADIA MANNARINO
All Star Auctions
Ridgewood, NJ

HARRY MATETSKY
Collector
Middletown, NJ

DAVE MATTEINI
Collector
New York, NY

JON McCLURE
Comics Historian, Writer
Durango, CO

TODD MCDEVITT
New Dimension Comics
Cranberry Township, PA

MIKE McKENZIE
Alternate Worlds
Cockeysville, MD

FRED McSURLEY
Dealer/Collector
Holland, Ohio

PETER MEROLO
Collector
Sedona, AZ

JOHN JACKSON MILLER
Comics Historian, Writer
Waupaca, WI

BRENT MOESHLIN
Quality Comix
Montgomery, AL

STEVE MORTENSEN
Colossus Comics
Santa Clara, CA

MICHAEL NAIMAN
Silver Age Specialist
Chapel Hill, NC

MARC NATHAN
Cards, Comics & Collectibles
Reisterstown, MD

JOSHUA NATHANSON
ComicLink
Brooklyn, NY

MATT NELSON
Classics Incorporated
Carrolltown, TX

JAMIE NEWBOLD
Southern California Comics
San Diego, CA

CHARLIE NOVINSKIE
Silver Age Specialist
Grand Junction, CO

RICHARD OLSON
Collector/Academician
Poplarville, MS

TERRY O'NEILL
Terry's Comics
Orange, CA

GEORGE PANTELA
GPAnalysis for Comics
Hampton, Victoria,
Australia

JIM PAYETTE
Golden Age Specialist
Bethlehem, NH

CHRIS PEDRIN
Pedrin Conservatory
Redwood City, CA

JOHN PETTY
Collector/Historian
Dallas, TX

JIM PITTS
Surf City Comix
Mountain View, CA

BILL PONSETI
Collector
Saucier, MS

RON PUSSELL
Redbeard's Book Den
Crystal Bay, NV

GREG REECE
Greg Reece's Rare Comics
Ijamsville, MD

OVERSTREET ADVISORS

STEPHEN RITTER
Collector
Beavercreek, OH

DAVE ROBIE
Big Little Books Specialist
Lancaster, PA

ROBERT ROGOVIN
Four Color Comics
Scarsdale, NY

MARNIN ROSENBERG
Collectors Assemble
Great Neck, NY

CHUCK ROZANSKI
Mile High Comics
Denver, CO

BARRY SANDOVAL
Heritage Comics Auctions
Dallas, TX

MATT SCHIFFMAN
Bronze Age Specialist
Bend, OR

DOUG SCHMELL
Pedigree Comics, Inc.
Wellington, FL

JOHN SNYDER
Collector
York, PA

MARK SQUIREK
Diamond Int. Galleries
Timonium, MD

TONY STARKS
Silver Age Specialist
Evansville, IN

WEST STEPHAN
Collector
Bradenton, FL

AL STOLTZ
Basement Comics
Havre de Grace, MD

KEN STRIBLING
Action Island
Jackson, MS

DOUG SULIPA
"Everything 1960-1996"
Manitoba, Canada

CHRIS SWARTZ
Collector
San Diego, CA

MAGGIE THOMPSON
Comics Buyer's Guide
Iola, WI

MICHAEL TIERNEY
The Comic Book Store
Little Rock, AR

TED VAN LIEW
Superworld Comics
Worcester, MA

JOE VERENEAULT
JHV Associates
Woodbury Heights, NJ

BOB WAYNE
DC Comics
New York City, NY

LON WEBB
Dark Adventure Comics
Norcross, GA

JERRY WEIST
Sotheby's
Gloucester, MA

RICK WHITELOCK
New Force Comics
Lynn Haven, FL

MIKE WILBUR
Diamond Int. Galleries
Timonium, MD

MARK WILSON
PGC Mint
Castle Rock, WA

ALEX WINTER
Hake's Americana
York, PA

HARLEY YEE
Dealer/Collector
Detroit, MI

MARK ZAID
EsquireComics.com
Bethesda, MD

VINCENT ZURZOLO, JR.
Metropolis Collectibles, Inc.
New York, NY

OVERSTREET PRICE GUIDE BACK ISSUES

The Overstreet® Comic Book Price Guide has held the record for being the longest running annual comic book publication. We are now celebrating our 40th anniversary, and the demand for the Overstreet® price guides is very strong. Collectors have created a legitimate market for them, and they continue to bring record prices each year. Collectors also have a record of comic book prices going back further than any other source in comic fandom. The prices listed below are for NM condition only, with GD-25% and FN-50% of the NM value. Canadian editions exist for a couple of the early issues. Abbreviations: SC-softcover, HC-hardcover, L-leather bound.

1970 — #1 White SC $1825.00

1970 — #1 Blue SC (2nd Printing) $1550.00

1972 — #2 SC $650.00; #2 HC $1100.00

1973 — #3 SC $325.00; #3 HC $950.00

1974 — #4 SC $165.00; #4 HC $475.00

1975 — #5 SC $155.00; #5 HC $260.00

1976 — #6 SC $105.00; #6 HC $155.00

1977 — #7 SC $155.00; #7 HC $230.00

1978 — #8 SC $130.00; #8 HC $180.00

1979 — #9 SC $130.00; #9 HC $180.00

1980 — #10 SC $140.00; #10 HC $190.00

1981 — #11 SC $85.00; #11 HC $115.00

1982

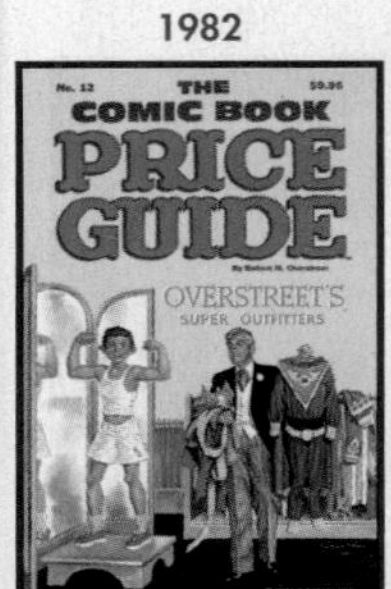

#12 SC $85.00
#12 HC $115.00

1983

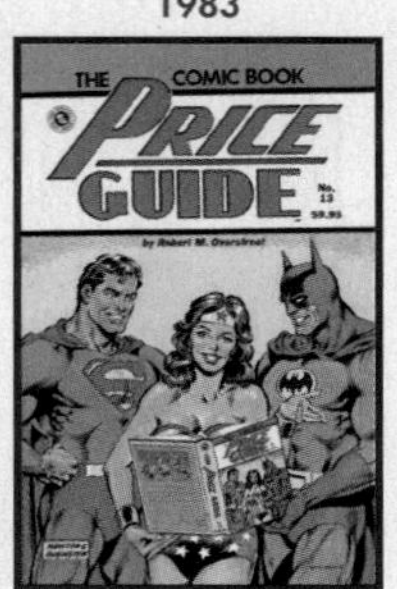

#13 SC $85.00
#13 HC $115.00

1984

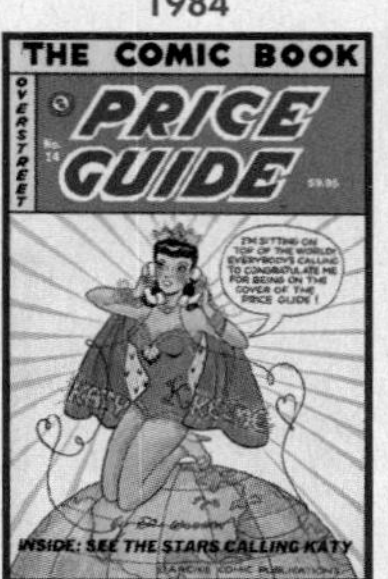

#14 SC $55.00
#14 HC $110.00
#14 L $170.00

1985

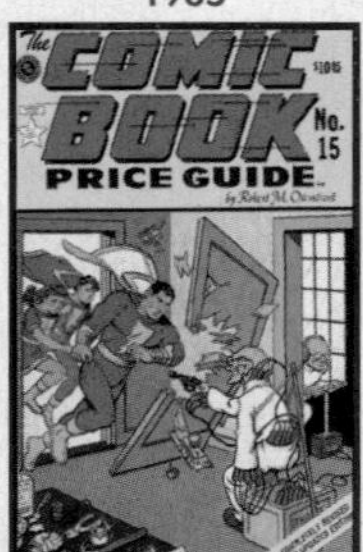

#15 SC $55.00
#15 HC $80.00
#15 L $160.00

1986

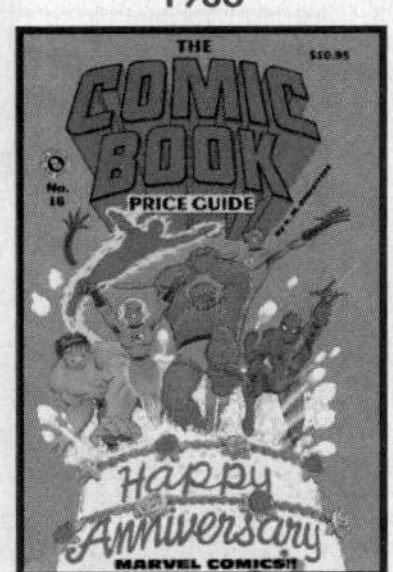

#16 SC $60.00
#16 HC $85.00
#16 L $170.00

1987

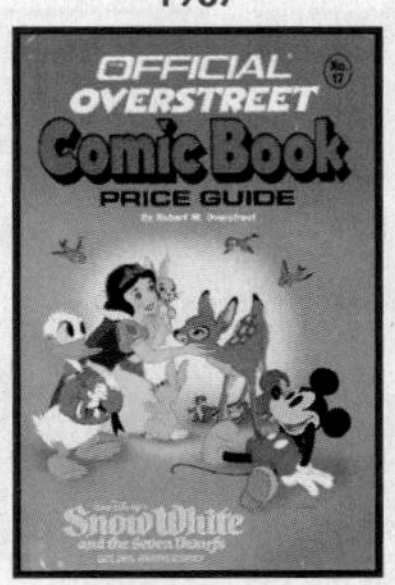

#17 SC $55.00
#17 HC $110.00
#17 L $160.00

1988

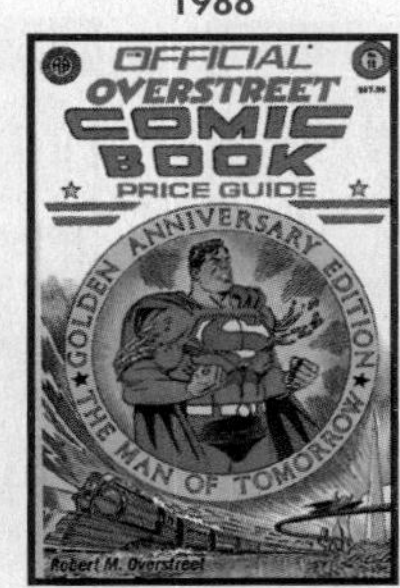

#18 SC $45.00
#18 HC $65.00
#18 L $160.00

1989

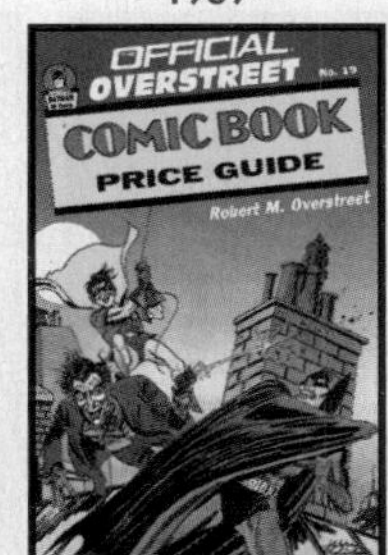

#19 SC $50.00
#19 HC $60.00
#19 L $170.00

1990

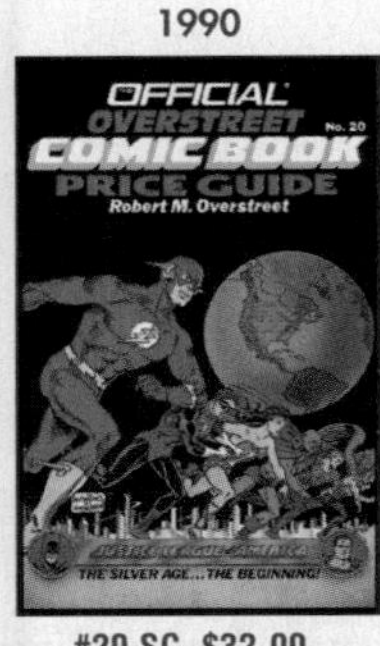

#20 SC $32.00
#20 HC $50.00
#20 L $135.00

1991

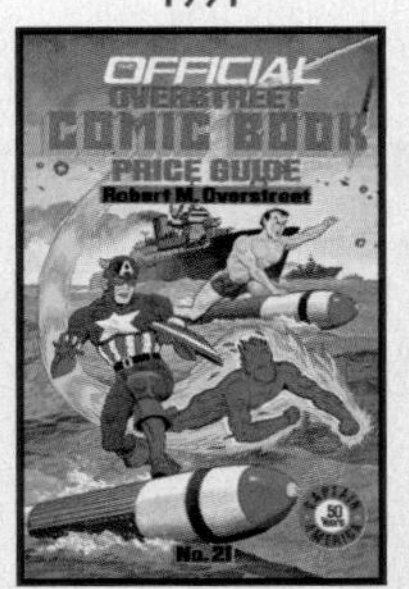

#21 SC $40.00
#21 HC $60.00
#21 L $145.00

1992

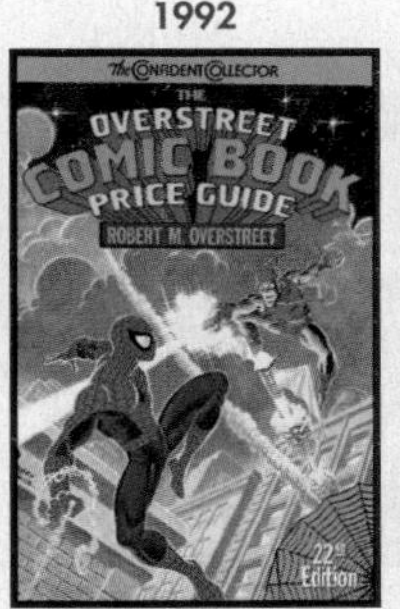

#22 SC $32.00
#22 HC $50.00

1993

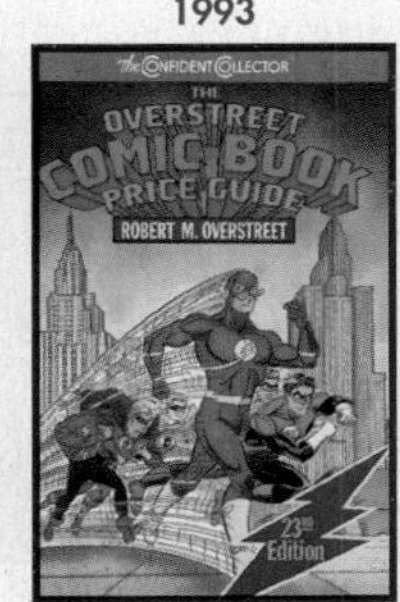

#23 SC $32.00
#23 HC $50.00

1994

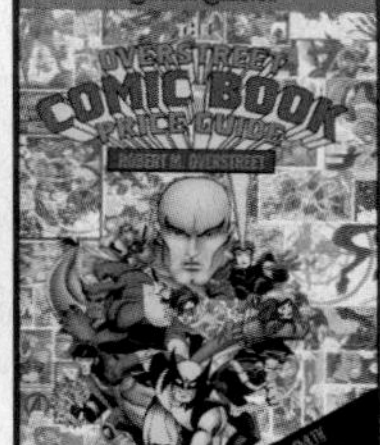

#24 SC $26.00
#24 HC $36.00

1995

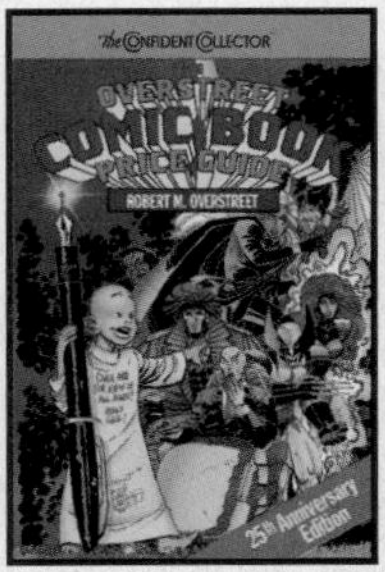

#25 SC $26.00
#25 HC $36.00
#25 L $110.00

1996

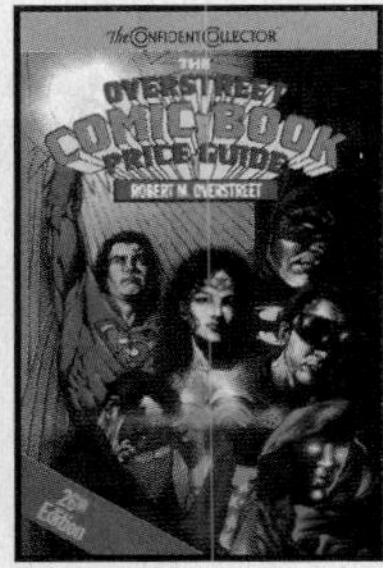

#26 SC $20.00
#26 HC $30.00
#26 L $100.00

1997

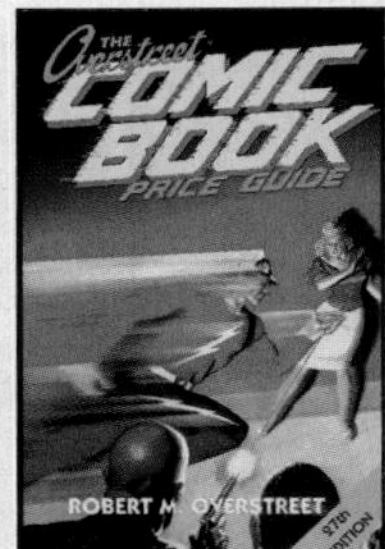

#27 SC $22.00
#27 HC $38.00
#27 L $125.00

1997

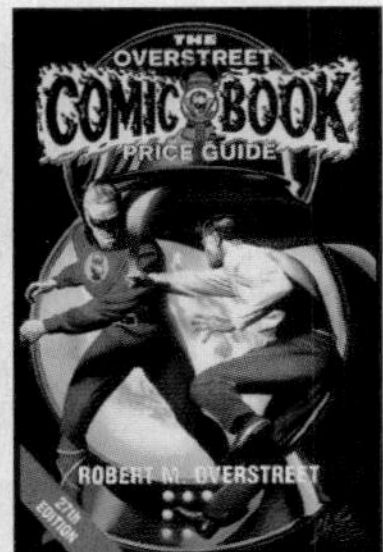

#27 SC $22.00
#27 HC $38.00
#27 L $125.00

1998

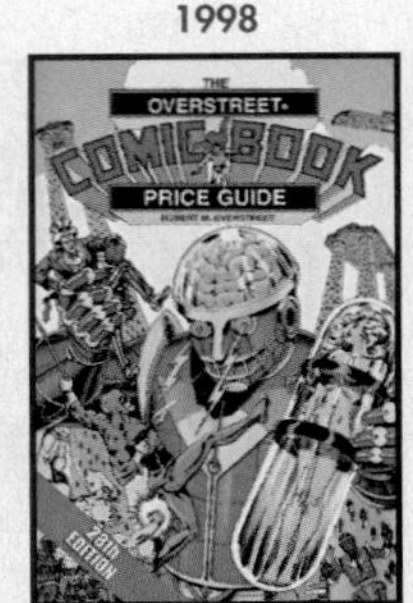

#28 SC $20.00
#28 HC $35.00

1998

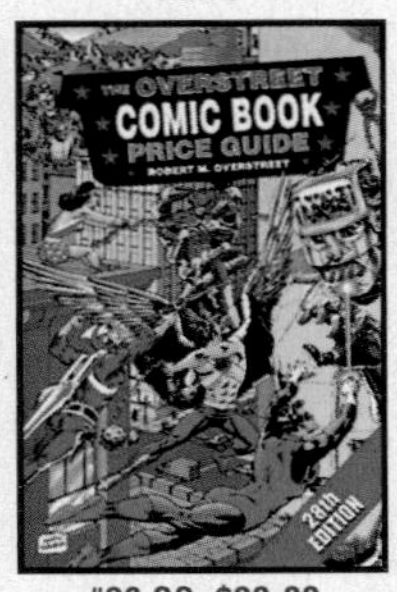

#28 SC $20.00
#28 HC $35.00

1999

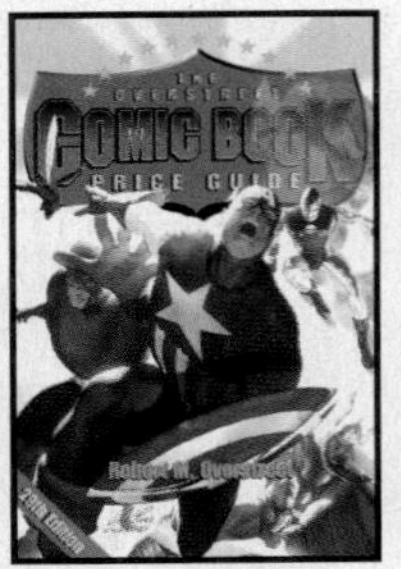

#29 SC $25.00
#29 HC $40.00

1999

#29 SC $20.00
#29 HC $37.00

2000

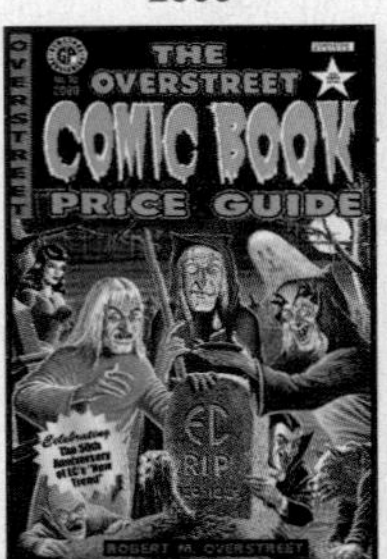

#30 SC $22.00
#30 HC $32.00

2000

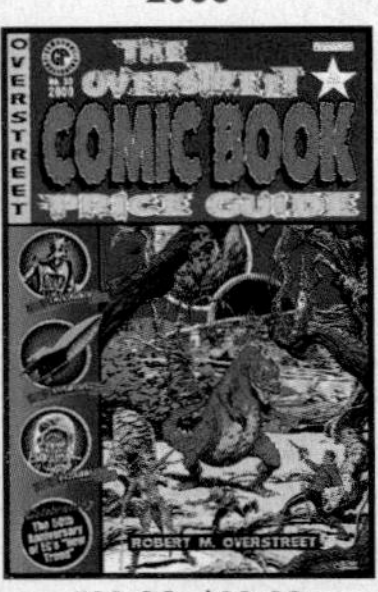

#30 SC $22.00
#30 HC $32.00

2001

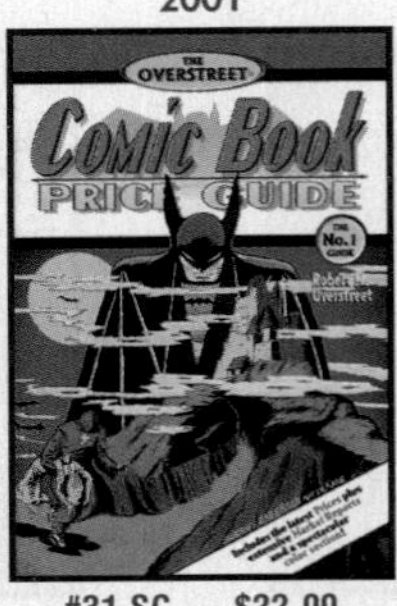

#31 SC $22.00
#31 HC $32.00

2001

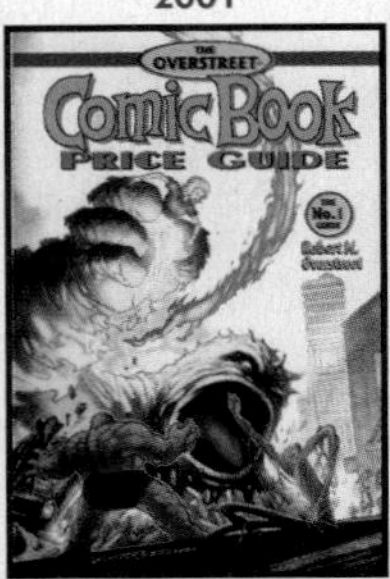

#31 SC $22.00
#31 HC $32.00

2001

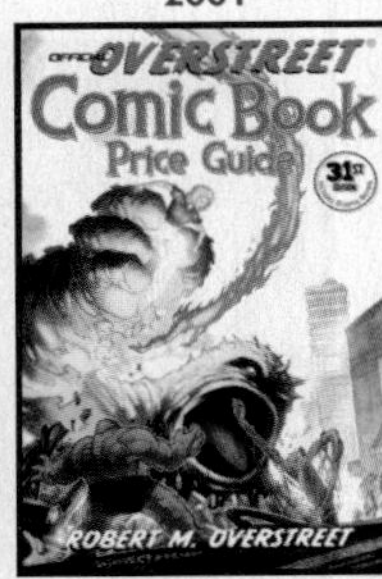

#31 Bookstore Ed.
SC only $22.00

2002

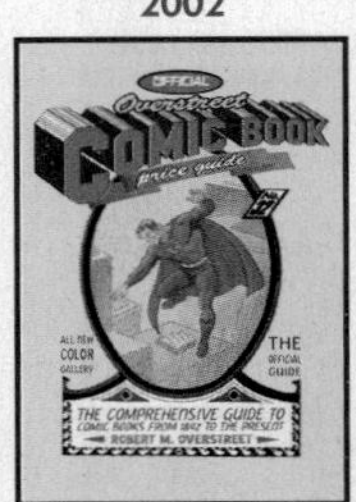

#32 SC $22.00
#32 HC $32.00

2002

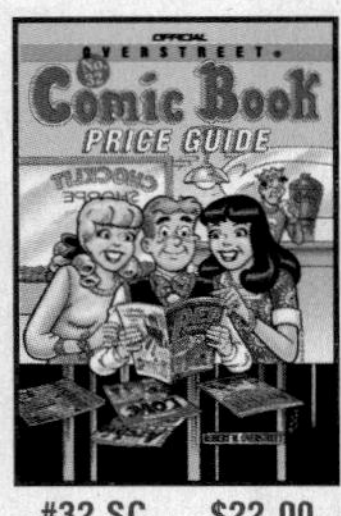

#32 SC $22.00
#32 HC $32.00

2002

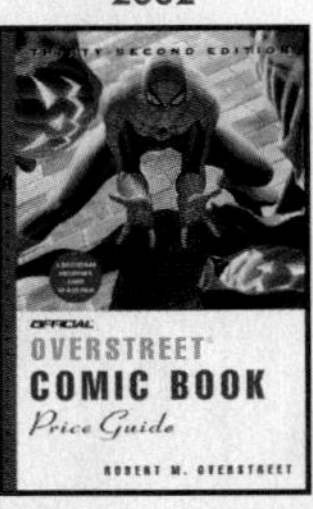

#32 Bookstore Ed.
SC only $22.00

2003

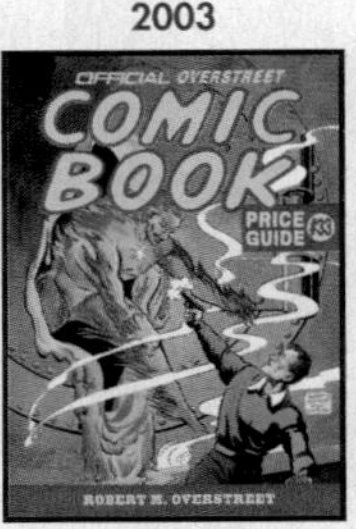

#33 SC $25.00
#33 HC $32.00

2003

#33 SC $25.00
#33 HC $32.00

2003

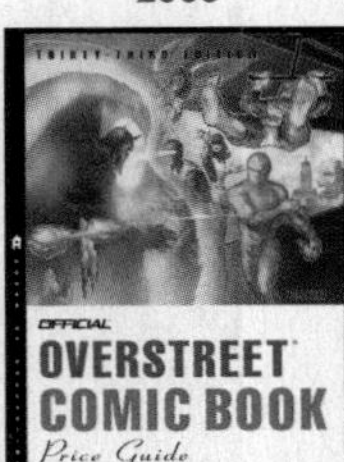

#33 Bookstore Ed.
SC only $25.00

2004

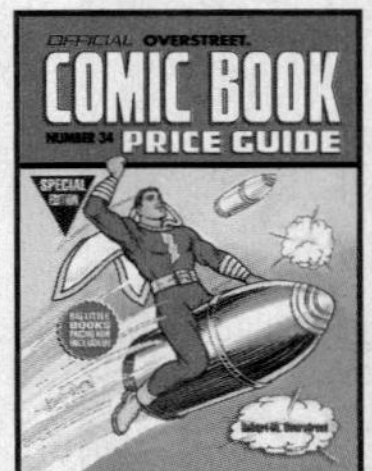

#34 SC $25.00
#34 HC $32.00

2004

#34 SC $25.00
#34 HC $32.00

2004

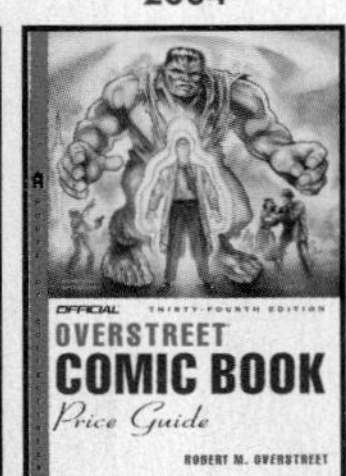

#34 Bookstore Ed.
SC only $25.00

2005

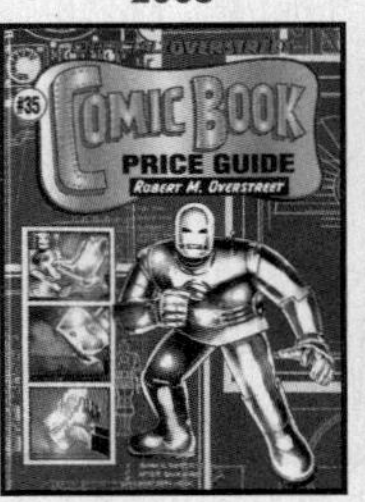

#35 SC $25.00
#35 HC $32.00

2005

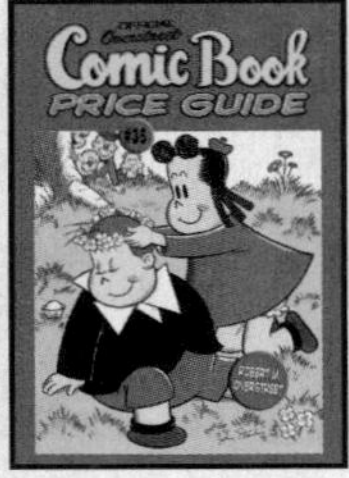

#35 SC $25.00
#35 HC $55.00

2005

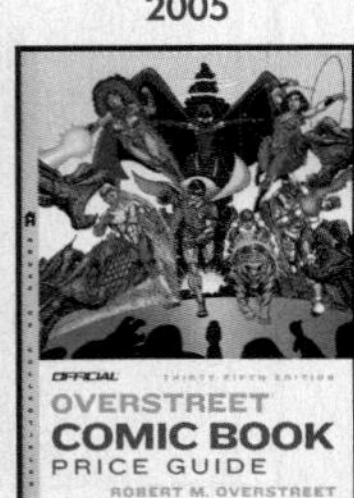

#35 Bookstore Ed.
SC only $25.00

2006

#36 SC $25.00
#36 HC $32.00

2006

#36 SC $25.00
#36 HC $32.00

2006

#36 Bookstore Ed.
SC only $25.00

2007

#37 SC $30.00
#37 HC $35.00

2007

#37 SC $30.00
#37 HC $35.00

2007

#37 Bookstore Ed.
SC only $30.00

2008

#38 SC $30.00
#38 HC $35.00

2008

#38 SC $30.00
#38 HC $35.00

2008

#38 Bookstore Ed.
SC only $30.00

2009

#39 SC $30.00
#39 HC $35.00

2009

#39 SC $30.00
#39 HC $35.00

2009

#39 Bookstore Ed.
SC only $30.00

#31 Workbook - 2001
$35.00

#32 Workbook - 2002
$35.00

#33 Workbook - 2003
$37.00

#34 Workbook - 2004
$37.00

#35 Workbook - 2005
$37.00

#36 Workbook - 2006
$37.00

#37 Workbook - 2007
$37.00

#38 Workbook - 2008
$37.00

ADVERTISERS' INDEX

A

B

C

D

E

F

G

H

I

J

L

M

N

P

Q

R

S

T

U

V

W

Y